ISBN 978-0-364-72397-5
PIBN 10780723

FB &c Ltd, Dalton House, 60 Windsor Avenue, London, SW19 2RR.
Company number 08720141. Registered in England and Wales.

For support please visit www.forgottenbooks.com

Vol. XI., No. 1. Office, 63 Bible House, N. Y. THURSDAY, JAN. 5, 1888. Annual Subscription, $1.50.

CONTENTS OF THIS NUMBER.

PORTRAITS AND LIVES OF REV. W. F. AND MRS. RE QUA, Faith Missionaries in the Indian Territory.
THE COMING GLORY. Dr. Talmage's Sermon Last Sunday Morning.
ANECDOTES RELATED AT RECENT EVANGELISTIC MEETINGS.
NOTES OF THE PROPHETIC CONFERENCE AT ADELAIDE, AUSTRALIA.
A Paralytic Healed—A Bishop Among the Chippewas—A Conflict Averted.
JESUS WALKING ON THE SEA. By Mrs. M. Baxter.
NOT BOUND YET. A New Sermon by C. H. Spurgeon.
Gems from New Books: A Yankee Marriage.
PORTRAIT AND LIFE OF THE LATE EX-SECRETARY MANNING.
PICTURE OF THE RUINS IN THE CALABRIAN EARTHQUAKE.
THE DISCOVERY IN THE OLD BUREAU. (With Illustration.)
THE FAMILY OF TRIPE COURT. A Serial Story (Continued.)
CALENDAR OF SCRIPTURE TEXTS FOR 1888.

The REV. W. F. and MRS. RE QUA—Faith Missionaries in the Indian Territory—Scenes in their Work.

Vol. XI., No. 1. Office, 63 Bible House, N. Y. THURSDAY, JAN. 5, 1888. Annual Subscription, $1.50.

CONTENTS OF THIS NUMBER.

PORTRAITS AND LIVES OF REV. W. F. AND MRS. RE QUA, Faith Missionaries in the Indian Territory.
THE COMING GLORY. Dr. Talmage's Sermon Last Sunday Morning.
ANECDOTES RELATED AT RECENT EVANGELISTIC MEETINGS.
NOTES OF THE PROPHETIC CONFERENCE AT ADELAIDE, AUSTRALIA.
A Paralytic Healed—A Bishop Among the Chippewas—A Conflict Averted.
JESUS WALKING ON THE SEA. By Mrs. M. Baxter.
NOT BOUND YET. A New Sermon by C. H. Spurgeon.
Gems from New Books: A Yankee Marriage.
PORTRAIT AND LIFE OF THE LATE EX-SECRETARY MANNING.
PICTURE OF THE RUINS IN THE CALABRIAN EARTHQUAKE.
THE DISCOVERY IN THE OLD BUREAU. (With Illustration.)
THE FAMILY OF TRIPE COURT. A Serial Story (Continued.)
CALENDAR OF SCRIPTURE TEXTS FOR 1888.

The REV. W. F. and MRS. RE QUA—Faith Missionaries in the Indian Territory—Scenes in their Work.

REV. W. F. RE QUA.

Faith Missionary In The Indian Territory.

The Principle of Mission Work—Mr. Re Qua's Enterprise—A Work for God—His Early Life—Settlement at Pavilion. N. Y.—Removal to Aurora, Ill.—Impressed with the Needs of the Indians—Convinced that He was Called to the Work—Decides to Go Out in Faith Alone—Mrs. Re Qua's Character—Her Early Development—Remarkable Impression of a Sermon—The Labor at McAlister—Work in Indian Homes—How their Faith has been Honored.

TO many readers of this journal, the devoted Evangelist and his gifted wife, whose portraits appear on this page, are very well known. Not a few of them have had personal communications with them, and Mr. and Mrs. Re Qua have frequently expressed their grateful appreciation of the kind gifts, and hearty encouragements which they have received since they commenced their arduous work from those who have read of it in these columns. To all such and to others who realize the grandeur of consecration and self sacrifice the portraits and illustrations published herewith will be welcome.

Unconverted persons are often puzzled by the lives of Christians, but nothing is so great

A Mystery

to them as missionary labor. That any man capable of earning a livelihood in a civilized country, and especially any man with refined tastes and the prospects of gaining distinction, should voluntarily abandon home and friends and civilization and go out into certain hardship and probable danger, simply to preach the gospel to the ignorant and degraded heathen, seems an act of lunacy. Yet hundreds of men and women have gone, and are still going, who are neither lunatics nor fanatics. They are Christians to whom the glorious Gospel of Christ is a grand reality, and they delight in sacrificing themselves, that they may carry it to those who sit in darkness and are perishing for lack of it. They are not deceived as to what they are doing; they know that their work can bring them neither fortune, nor fame, nor worldly advantage of any kind; but they count all that the world can give as nothing compared with the delight of working for Christ and proclaiming the life-giving message to dying men. "The love of Christ which constraineth" is the key to their lives. It is a motive principle, the power of which the world has never gauged and cannot understand. Its effects produce astonishment, sometimes contempt and ridicule, but it works yet, more mightily than any of those principles to which the world yields respect. It is this principle alone which explains the work to which Mr. and Mrs. Re Qua have consecrated their lives.

Our American Heathen

are as difficult a problem to the Church as they are to the Government. The Indians have suffered so much at the hands of the whites that they have, not unnaturally, conceived a prejudice against the white man's religion, as well as his civilization and his government. The efforts made to evangelize them have been for the greater part unsuccessful and have met with a resistance not so much active as sullen. Yet, where the Indian's heart has been reached, notably in cases where devoted and consecrated ladies have given themselves to the work, the results have been such as to assure us of the hopefulness of more extended effort. A solemn sense of the responsibility of every individual Christian for the benighted condition of the red men forced itself on Mr. Re Qua during his residence in Illinois, as it has on many Christian men in other States, and it grew at length so intolerable, that, cost what it would, he determined to give himself to the work of missionary labors among them. He believed that by going into their midst and living among them he could reach their hearts, and trusting in God alone for sustenance, he went, and is now laboring at his post. Such men are rare, for an undertaking of that kind needs courage and endurance and faith of the apostolic type. It will therefore be interesting to learn what manner of man he is.

W. F. Re Qua was born thirty-one years ago at Whitewater, Wis., where at that time his father, Rev. J. D. Re Qua, was stationed as minister, of the Methodist Episcopal Church. While an infant only seven months old he was deprived of a mother's care. She went to her grave in the first blush of motherhood, the prey of consumption. Kind relatives did what they could to supply her place to the helpless babe, for about two years, when his father married a second time. The stepmother, a pious and amiable lady, then undertook the care of him, and for six years most conscientiously and affectionately watched over his development. But again, this time at the age of nine years, he was bereaved; his stepmother fell asleep in Jesus, leaving the child without maternal care.

His Conversion

occurred in 1873, when he was seventeen years of age. With the ardor that has characterized his subsequent life he immediately looked around for Christian employment. His energy and devotedness were noticed by his own and his father's friends, and he was urged to give himself entirely to the Lord's work. It was some time before he could attain the assurance that he was called to the ministry; but the success which followed his labors, and the fact that God was making use of such efforts as his occupation permitted him to enter upon, for the salvation of souls, convinced him that it was his duty to give himself wholly to the work of preaching the gospel. He therefore entered on a course of preparatory study at Lima, N. Y. During his studies there he was led to unite himself with the Baptist denomination, and at the end of his course he entered the Baptist Theological Seminary at Rochester N. Y.

His First Charge

was at Pavilion N. Y., though prior to that, during his theological studies he had eagerly accepted numerous opportunities for preaching, and had been encouraged by many tokens of the Divine blessing. At Pavilion he labored earnestly, and with a success so marked that invitations to larger spheres were pressed upon him. Finally he was led to accept an invitation from Aurora Ill., to become pastor of the large and influential Park Place Baptist Church in that town. It was while laboring there, in a position which might well gratify the ambition of so young a man, that the call to missionary work among the Indians was manifest to him. It was not in Mr. Re Qua's nature to act the part of Jonah and close his ears to the call. Nevertheless, it must have required an effort to obey it. Rigid self-examination, a conscientious endeavor to discover the path of duty, and much earnest prayer for guidance brought him to decision, and he resigned his pastorate. His church at first refused to accept his resignation, but after a period of reconsideration Mr. Re Qua still believed that he was called to the Indian work, and the church accordingly submitted to his decision. A farewell meeting was held, in which the community outside the church joined in expressing esteem for him and recognition of his services. From Aurora he went direct to the Indian Territory where he has since then devoted himself indefatigably to his new duties.

MRS. W. F. RE QUA.

SOME three years ago a notice of a volume of poems in this journal attracted the attention of its readers to this gifted lady. Their singular grace and purity of diction, combined with their high spirituality, rendered the selections published, as we happen to know, very precious to some suffering Christians, and those who purchased the volume were still further benefited by its pages. To them the name of Harriet Warner Re Qua has a music all its own, and the fact that she has voluntarily gone into exile with her husband, to cheer and aid him in his work, braving the terrors of the inhospitable climate and enduring the hardships of frontier life, will enhance the high estimate previously formed of her character.

Mrs. Re Qua is a direct descendant of Elder John Leland, a famous Baptist preacher, originally of Vermont. For many generations back

Her Ancestors

on both sides were noted for their piety and their liberal support of Christian work. Her maternal grandfather especially, was known for the munificence with which he contributed to the cause of Christ. Any weak church, needing an edifice for worship, or struggling under a burden of debt, or unable to give its minister the remuneration of which he was worthy, found a friend in the good old man, who seemed to hold his property as a trust which he must administer for the public good.

In her girlhood Mrs. Re Qua attracted the notice of friends and teachers by her extraordinary talents. At the age of only nine years, verses of remarkable ability seemed to flow from her pen almost without effort, and she ornamented the dwelling of her parents and those of her friends with drawings and paintings which would have done credit to an artist of riper years.

The Consecration

of her talents and her whole being to Christ, came to her in early life. She was only thirteen years of age when the vanity of all wordly pursuits was revealed to her, and she gave herself and her future into the hands of Christ, to use them for His glory. She united with the church, and devoted herself, as she had opportunity, to Christian work. With a disposition naturally modest and retiring, she united a peculiar sensitiveness to the voice of duty, which, to her, was the voice of God. Many times in the course of her early Christian life, she occupied positions from which she would have shrunk had she listened to the dictates of natural feeling, but in each case she received such intimations of her call, that when the opportunity came, she would have deemed herself recreant to her duty had she neglected it.

One of the most remarkable of these came after her marriage. As she sat alone one evening meditating on the Word of God, a passage of Scripture was impressed upon her with peculiar distinctness. As she dwelt upon it, it appeared to open before her into a wide vista of teaching. She had never heard it used as a text, but it seemed to teem with spiritual lessons of deep and practical power. Almost unconsciously she arranged them in their several lines, and a sermon was formed in her mind. No idea of ever preaching that or any other sermon crossed her thought, but there the sermon was, as clearly defined as any clergyman might have it on entering his pulpit on a Sunday morning. She was aroused from her meditation by the arrival of her husband from a pastoral excursion. A singular fact was, that he was the bearer of an urgent request from a distant village, that she would deliver an evangelistic address there at an approaching meeting. "The preparations of the heart in man and the answer of the tongue is from the Lord," and Mrs. Re Qua could not but realize the fact, and wonder at the mysterious way in which it had been brought about in her case. It may be added that the delivery of the sermon was much blessed of God.

From that time forward Mrs. Re Qua was a valued and active fellow-laborer of her husband in his work, and God signally owned and blessed her efforts. When he felt himself called to the work among the Indians, she placed no obstacles in his way. If God had called him to hardship and self-sacrifice, she was ready to stand right loyally by his side and give him her sympathy and wifely support. It was in this spirit that she gave up the comforts, so dear to a refined and educated lady, and went out to make her home in a rough log cabin, through which wind and snow found ready access, but which by the spirit of consecration became more noble than a palace.

The following poem, written in the early days of the family settlement in the Indian Territory, shows the spirit in which she entered on her labor:

UNDER THE CLOUD;

Under the clouds to-day,
Blinded by mists of sin,
Too dense the vapors to let one ray
Of God's pure sunlight in;
Playing with pebbles and toys,
Gathering flowers by the way
Frail as the gossamer wreaths of frost
On the smiling brow of May;
Clinging to all with a fervent clasp,
The frail heart's surest stay,
Reeds that will shatter within grasp;
They will see it all some day,
Some day—
God grant that the light be not shut out
Till the fearful judgment day!

Sowing and watering tares,
Tending them day by day,
Burdened and saddened with cumbering cares
It were nobler to fling away.
Broidering garlands of flowers,
Roses and lilies fair,
Meet for the shrine in pleasure's bowers,
With *folly* to bind them there.
Beautiful—ah! but the *fearful cost*
The *gems* that are flung away,
And the mortgaged soul that may soon be lost,
They will see it all some day,
Some day—
God grant that the light be not shut out
Till the fearful judgment day.

Adorning with purple and gold
Forms that will sleep at last
At the feet of the earth-worm, enshrined with mold,
Thro' the march of centuries vast,
Gathering up chaff, as they go
To the Bar, with steadiest care,
As if—God have mercy!—they did not know.
The Judge of the earth was there,
Gathering up chaff and dropping the sheaves;
Bartering gold for clay;
For diamonds of truth choosing worthless leaves—
They will see it all some day,
Some day—
God grant that the light be not shut out
Till the fearful judgment day!

WORK IN THE INDIAN TERRITORY.

(*See Illustrations, first page.*)

IT has been with the utmost difficulty that information has been obtained from Mr. and Mrs. Re Qua as to their position and work in the Indian Territory. They believe that as they are working for God there, He will see that they do not lack support. From others, however, among them the Rev. Frances E. Townsley, pastor of the Fairfield Baptist Church, Nebraska, and M. Soniser, a teacher among the Choctaws, some graphic reports have been received. From Miss Townsley we learn that both Mr. and Mrs. Re Qua are fully occupied in the work they set out to do. Mrs. Re Qua visits in the Indian homes (*see Illustration*), teaches the children, counsels the mothers, who are eager to receive her help, and are deeply grateful to the white lady who will come into their home and talk to them of Jesus. Mr. Re Qua goes from place to place, occasionally getting a ride in a wagon, but generally doing his journeys of ten or twelve miles on foot. In the summer he preaches in the open air, under a covering of branches, while the Indians come from all quarters in their wagons to attend his service (*see Illustration*). Mr. Soniser is eloquent about the impression produced by the work on the Indians. They have grown, he says, to love the missionary and his wife, who have not clung to the line of railroad, but have come right into their midst to live, and are evidently poorer than themselves. They do not seem to regret the elegancies and comforts of their Illinois home, though now their only home is a poor cabin twelve feet by fourteen, by no means weatherproof.

A Work of Faith.

is the accurate definition of their labor. No society supports the missionaries; they look to God alone for support, and to Him alone their wants are made known. It is easy to see, however, that the hardships they bear so cheerfully are of no light character. It was very touching to read, a week or two ago, of their joy of receiving, from a kindly reader of this journal, a barrel of clothing, and reading between the lines, to infer that, but for its arrival, the winter would have found them poorly protected from its rigor. There is no need to make any appeal on their behalf. God, who knows their trials and their needs, and who has provided for them hitherto, is still able to supply all their wants. He has stewards in every city of this broad land, who count it an honor and a privilege to minister to the wants of His servants. "Whosoever," said the Master, "shall give you a cup of water to drink, in My name, *because ye belong to Christ*, verily I say unto you, he shall not lose his reward" (Mark 9: 41). Mr. and Mrs. Re Qua are safe in His hands, for of the many who love Him, and who delight to do His will, there are some who will take care that the self-denying work to which they have given themselves, does not fail for lack of funds. Our readers may be fully assured that any offering they may be able and willing to make, will be thankfully received by Rev. W. F. Re Qua, McAllister, Ind. Ter.

ANECDOTES RELATED AT RECENT EVANGELISTIC MEETINGS.

Drifting Down the Stream—The Rev. Mr. Graham said at a convention in Glasgow: "There is an old saying I used to hear in my youth—'There is no standing still in Zion,' and I think there is a great deal of truth in it. We are either going forward or falling back. I have seen a man rowing up a stream where there was a strong current. If he stopped rowing, or even slackened his speed, see what happened! He drifted slowly but surely down the stream. So it is in the Christian life. There is no standing still. Let a Christian who has been striving after God cease to strive or slacken his effort, and soon, like the man in the strong current, he is drifting down to untold dangers.

On Speaking Terms with Jesus—Mr. Gardiner relates: "A young Christian woman, while talking to her neighbor one day, earnestly asked her, 'Do you know Jesus?' 'Oh, yes!' was the reply. 'But do you know Him to speak to?' persisted the questioner. 'Well, no; not exactly.' Then the missionary let her see that it was not knowing Christ at all, unless she knew Him personally, as a Saviour and a Friend to whom she could go and speak, to whom she could tell her troubles and ask for advice. Too many people, unfortunately, are content with knowing Christ distantly, as the Saviour of the world; but as the ever present God, the helpful Friend they have never known Him."

Giving Up for Christ—The Rev. Mr. Figgis observed: "Sometimes when one is asked to give up all for Christ, it means the giving up of a pursuit or pleasure which is then life's happiness. Three or four years ago it fell to my lot to be the instrument in God's hands to point out to a Christian brother that such a sacrifice was necessary. But two or three weeks ago I met that same person again, and he was praising God and counting it all as gain, and rejoicing that he had been allowed to give up something for Christ. The Lord must have a full surrender if we are to consecrate ourselves to Him. In return, He gives us all that He has. He gives Himself. Where is the comparison? And with what fulness of joy and sweet contentment He fills us."

Conquering a Fit of Shivering—The Rev. Mr. Haslam related: "Years ago a friend came up to me, and, placing his hand upon my shoulder said, 'Are you willing to give up all to God, no matter what it be?' At this unexpected question quite a shiver and a trembling went through me. 'Ah,' he said, 'I see you are not prepared to do this; I am sorry I put the question; and he at once changed the subject. After he had left, I said, half-aloud, 'Lord, I am sure I can trust Thee. Why did I not say 'Yes?' I went to my own room, and there I gave myself up unreservedly to the Lord, but while I did so, again that shiver and trembling passed through me, but I knew it was only the old nature fighting against the Spirit, and I came off conqueror. After this I was very happy, and why should I not be? I was one of God's own children, and no one else has any right to be happy. Next day, I said, 'Lord, I am going out to walk, and if it is Thy will I should like to meet that friend to-day again, and I should like him to ask me the same question!' I went out and walked for an hour, and did not meet him, and was just about to enter my home when he came up to me. I do not know whether it was my countenance that was changed, or what it was, but he stepped up to me, and again placing his hand upon my shoulder, he said, 'Are you willing to give up all to the Lord, no matter what it be?' 'Yes,' I said, 'and thank Him, too.'"

The Fire that Falls from Heaven—Mr. Figgis said: "Never shall I forget a servant of the Lord, a most devoted Christian, who had been used of God in many countries, and, among others, had pointed an anxious Lord Chancellor to Christ. He came to our town of Brighton, and gathering the ministers together he said to them, 'I know that many of you are very careful about your ministry and very careful about your orthodoxy. But has the fire of God fallen upon you as it fell upon the sacrifices of Abel and Elijah, showing they were accepted by the Lord. Has the fire fallen upon you? If it has not, let us first look if we have prepared the sacrifice and put ourselves upon the altar, for until we have offered the sacrifice God cannot accept it.' It is through such people, dead to themselves but living in Christ, that God does His noblest and greatest work."

A Rash Captain's Folly.—Mr. Forbes Remarks: "During a great storm at Aberdeen a steamer was trying to make the harbor, across the mouth of which there extended a high bar. The tide was low, and although the waves were large there was very little water on the bar. When the steamer was sighted, the pilots at once put out, warning the captain to put back; but he was determined to enter the harbor that night. And on he drove the ship. On and on she came buried in foam, until she had almost reached the breakwater. On her deck could be seen the forms of the passengers and crew as they pleaded with the captain to put back. But he was obstinate; on he drove to destruction. The vessel grounded on the bar and was dashed to pieces, and scarcely one of the whole ship-full was saved. That captain, by his mad folly, destroyed not only himself, but also those who sailed with him. Many thus go headlong to spiritual destruction, and find out only when it is too late, that those were right who warned them of the danger ahead; let those persons who make light of the warnings of Christian men take heed before it is too late."

A Frozen Sparrow Revived.—Mr. Haslam also: said "A few years ago we had a very severe winter; everything seemed to be bitten by the severity of the frost, and, in many cases, the birds were frozen to death. One day, while passing along the road that leads to my home, I saw a little bird lying on the frozen ground. 'Ah,' I exclaimed, 'there is another of these poor little creatures fallen a victim to the cold,' and, as I stooped to lift it, it had just strength enough left to flutter into a hedge close by. I put out my hand and lifted the little creature, and it lay quite still, as if dead. But I kept breathing upon it until I was rewarded by a slight flutter in my hand. Still I breathed my warm breath upon it until vitality was quite restored, and I thought how glad the children would be, and how we should keep it warm, and how I should love and cherish the tiny creature until the cold weather was over, and it would sing to me a glad, happy song in return. But as life came back, it struggled to get free, but I held it firm, for I knew what was best for it. Still it continued to struggle, until, at last, it flew out of my reach. Foolish little bird, to free itself from one who wanted to cherish it, and to go away to be frozen to death in the next blizzard. That is just what God wants to do with you, whose spiritual life is almost frozen to death. He longs to have you in the hollow of His hand, where no harm can come near you."

THE COMING GLORY.

Dr. Talmage's Sermon Preached Last Sunday Morning, January 1, 1888.

"Eye hath not seen, nor ear heard, neither have entered into the heart of man, the things which God hath prepared for them that love Him." 1 Cor. 2: 9.

The Approaching Obsequies of the Nineteenth Century—The Splendors Beyond—The Paris of Antiquity—The Glories of Corinth—Its Citizens Incapable of Conceiving the Celestial Magnificence—Calculations of the Dimensions of the New Jerusalem—In What Heaven Surpasses Conception—I. Its Salubrity—The Rejuvenated Octogenarian—The Rehabilitated Invalid—II. Its Splendors—Marvellous Pageantry—Magnificent Buildings—III. Its Reunions—No Good-by—A Child's Thrilling Question—The Wonderful Introductions—IV. Its Explanations—V. Its Song—The Singers of the Age.

1888. How strange it looks, and how strange it sounds! Not only is the past year dead, but the century is dying. Only twelve more long breaths and the old giant will have expired. None of the past centuries will be present at the obsequies. Only the twentieth century will see the nineteenth buried. As all

The Years Are Hastening

past, and all our lives on earth will soon be ended, I propose to cheer myself, and cheer you, with the glories to come, which shall utterly eclipse all the glories past; for my text tells us that eye hath not seen, nor ear heard, anything like the advancing splendors.

The city of Corinth has been called *the Paris of antiquity*. Indeed, for splendor the world holds no such wonder to-day. It stood on an isthmus washed by two seas, the one sea bringing the commerce of Europe, the other sea bringing the commerce of Asia. From her wharves, in the construction of which whole kingdoms had been absorbed, war-galleys with three banks of oars pushed out and confounded the navy-yards of all the world. Huge-handed machinery, such as modern invention cannot equal, lifted ships from the sea on one side and transported them on trucks across the isthmus and sat them down in the sea on the other side.

The revenue officers of the city went down through the olive groves that lined the beach to collect a tariff from all nations. The mirth of all people sported in her Isthmian games, and the beauty of all lands sat in her theatres, walked her porticoes, and threw itself on the altar of her stupendous dissipations.

Column and Statue and Temple

bewildered the beholder. There were white marble fountains into which, from apertures at the side, there rushed waters everywhere known for health-giving qualities. Around these basins, twisted into wreaths of stone, there were all the beauties of sculpture and architecture; while standing, as if to guard the costly display, was a statue of Hercules of burnished Corinthian brass. Vases of terra-cotta adorned the cemeteries of the dead—vases so costly that Julius Cæsar was not satisfied until he had captured them for Rome. Armed officials, the Corintharii, paced up and down to see that no statue was defaced, no pedestal overthrown, no bas-relief touched. From the edge of the city a hill arose, with

Its Magnificent Burden

of columns, towers and temples (one thousand slaves waiting at one shrine), and a citadel so thoroughly impregnable that Gibraltar is a heap of sand compared with it. Amid all that strength and magnificence Corinth stood and defied the world.

Oh! it was not to rustics, who had never seen anything grand, that Paul uttered this text. They had heard the best music that had come from the best instruments in all the world; they had heard songs floating from morning porticoes and melting in evening groves; they had passed their whole lives among pictures and sculpture and architecture and Corinthian brass, which had been molded and shaped until there was no chariot wheel in which it had not sped, and no tower in which it had not glittered, and no gateway that it had not adorned. Ah, it was

A Bold Thing

for Paul to stand there amid all that, and say: "All this is nothing. These sounds that come from the temple of Neptune are not music compared with the harmonies of which I speak. These waters rushing in the basin of Pyrene are not pure. These statues of Bacchus and Mercury are not exquisite. Your citadel of Acrocorinthus is not strong compared with that which I offer to the poorest slave that puts down his burden at that brazen gate. You Corinthians think this is a splendid city; you think you have heard all sweet sounds, and seen all beautiful sights; but I tell you eye hath not seen nor ear heard, neither have entered into the heart of man the things which God hath prepared for them that love Him."

You see my text sets forth the idea that, however exalted our ideas of Heaven, they come far

Short of the Reality

Some wise men have been calculating how many furlongs long and wide is the new Jerusalem; and they have calculated how many inhabitants there are on the earth; how long the earth will probably stand; and then they come to this estimate: that after all the nations have been gathered to Heaven, there will be room for each soul—a room sixteen feet long and fifteen feet wide. It would not be large enough for me. I am glad to know that no human estimate is sufficient to take the dimensions. "Eye hath not seen, nor ear heard," nor arithmetics calculated.

I first remark that we can get no idea of

The Health of Heaven.

When you were a child, and you went out in the morning, how you bounded along the road or street—you had never felt sorrow or sickness. Perhaps later you felt a glow in your cheek, and a spring in your step, and an exuberance of spirits, and a clearness of eye, that made you thank God you were permitted to live. The nerves were harp-strings, and the sunlight was a doxology, and the rustling leaves were the rustling of the robes of a great crowd rising up to praise the Lord. You thought that you knew what it was to be well, but there is no perfect health on earth. The diseases of past generations came down to us. The airs that float now upon the earth are not like those which floated above Paradise. They are charged with impurities and distempers. The most elastic and robust health of earth, compared with that which those experience before whom the gates have been opened, is nothing but sickness and emaciation. Look at that soul standing before the throne. On earth she was

A Life-long Invalid.

See her step now, and hear her voice now. Catch, if you can, one breath of that celestial air. Health in all the pulses—health of vision; health of spirits; immortal health. No racking cough, no sharp pleurisies, no consuming fevers, no exhausting pains, no hospitals of wounded men. Health swinging in the air; health flowing in all the streams; health blooming on the banks. No headaches, no sideaches, no backaches. That child that died in the agonies of croup, hear her voice now ringing in the anthem! That old man that went bowed down with the infirmities of age, see him walk now with the step of an immortal athlete—forever young again! That night when the needle-woman fainted away in the garret, a wave of the heavenly air resuscitated her forever. For everlasting years to have neither ache nor pain nor weakness nor fatigue. "Eye hath not seen it, ear hath not heard it."

I remark, further, that we can, in this world, get no just idea of

The Splendors of Heaven.

John tries to describe them. He says "the twelve gates are twelve pearls," and that "the foundations of the wall are garnished with all manner of precious stones." As we stand looking through the telescope of St. John, we see a blaze of amethyst and pearl and emerald and sardonyx and chrysoprasus and sapphire, a mountain of light, a cataract of color, a sea of glass, and a city like the sun.

John bids us look again, and we see thrones, thrones of the prophets, thrones of the patriarchs, thrones of the angels, thrones of the apostles, thrones of the martyrs, throne of Jesus—throne of God. And we turn round to see the glory, and it is thrones! thrones! thrones!

John bids us look again, and we see the great procession of the redeemed passing; Jesus, on a white horse, leads the march, and al'

The Armies of Heaven

following on white horses. Infinite cavalcade passing, passing; empires pressing into line, ages following ages. Dispensation tramping on after dispensation. Glory in the track of glory. Europe, Asia, Africa, North and South America, pressing into lines. Islands of the seas shoulder to shoulder. Generations before the flood following generations after the flood, and as Jesus rises at the head of that great host, and waves His sword in signal of victory, all crowns are lifted, and all ensigns slung out, and all chimes rung, and all hallelujahs chanted, and some cry, "Glory to God most high!" and some, "Hosanna to the son of David!" and some, "Worthy is the Lamb that was slain"—till all exclamations of endearment and homage in the vocabulary of heaven are exhausted, and there comes up surge after surge of "Amen! Amen! and Amen!"

"Eye hath not seen it, ear hath not heard it." Skim from the summer waters the brightest sparkles, and you will get no idea of the sheen of the everlasting sea. Pile up the splendors of earthly cities, and they would not make a stepping-stone by which you might mount to the city of God. Every house is a palace. Every step is a triumph. Every covering of the head a coronation. Every meal is a banquet. Every stroke from the tower is a wedding-bell. Every day is a jubilee, every hour a rapture, and every moment an ecstacy. "Eye hath not seen it, ear hath not heard it."

I remark further, we can get no idea of

The Re-unions of Heaven.

If you have ever been across the seas and met a friend, or even an acquaintance, in some strange city, you remember how your blood thrilled, and how glad you were to see him. What will be our joy, after we have passed the seas of death, to meet in the bright city of the sun those from whom we have long been separated. After we have been away from our friends ten or fifteen years, and we come upon them, we see how differently they look. Their hair has turned, and wrinkles have come in their faces, and we say, "How you have changed!" But oh, when we stand before the throne, all cares gone from the face, all marks of sorrow disappeared, and feeling the joy of that blessed land, methinks we will say to each other, with an exultation we cannot now imagine, "How you have changed!"

In this world we only meet to part. It is good-by, good-by. Farewells floating in the air. We hear it at the rail-car window, and at the steamboat wharf—good-by. Children lisp it, and old age answers it. Sometimes we say it in a light way—"good-by," and sometimes with anguish in which the soul breaks down. Good-by! Ah! that is the word that ends the thanksgiving banquet; that is the word that comes in to close the Christmas chant. Good-by, good-by. But not so in heaven. Welcomes in the air, welcomes at the gates, welcomes at the house of many mansions—but

No Good-by.

That group is constantly being augmented. They are going up from our circles of earth to join it—little voices to join the anthem—little hands to take hold in the great home-circle—little feet to dance in the eternal glee—little crowns to be cast down before the feet of Jesus. Our friends are in two groups—a group this side of the river, and a group on the other side of the river. Now there goes one from this to that, and another from this to that, and soon we will all be gone over. How many of your oved ones have already entered upon that blessed place? If I should take paper and pencil, do you think I could put them all down? Ah, my friends, the waves of Jordan roar so hoarsely we cannot hear the joy on the other side when that group is augmented.

A little child's mother had died, and they comforted her. They said, "Your mother has gone to heaven, don't cry;" and the next day they went to the graveyard, and they laid the body of the mother down into the ground; and the little girl came up to the verge of the grave, and, looking at the body of her mother, said:

"Is This Heaven?"

Oh! we have no idea what heaven is. It is the grave here—it is darkness here—but there is merry-making yonder. Methinks when a soul arrives, some angel takes it around to show it the wonders of that blessed place. The usher-angel says to the newly arrived, "These are the martyrs that perished at Piedmont; these were torn to pieces at the Inquisition; this is the throne of the great Jehovah; this is Jesus." "*I am going to see Jesus,*" said a dying boy; "I am going to see Jesus." The missionary said, "You are sure you will see Him?" "Oh, yes; that's *what I want to go to heaven for.*" "But," said the missionary, "suppose Jesus should go away from heaven—what then?" "I should follow Him," said the dying boy. "But if Jesus went down to hell—what then?" The dying boy thought for a moment, and then said, "Where Jesus is there can be no hell!" Oh, to stand in His presence! That will be heaven! Oh, to put our hand in that Hand which was wounded for us on the Cross—to go around amid the groups of the redeemed, and shake hands with the prophets and apostles and martyrs, and with our own dear, beloved ones! That will be the great re-union: we cannot imagine it now!

Our Loved Ones

seem so far away. When we are in trouble and lonesome, they don't seem to come to us. We go on to the banks of the Jordan and call across to them, but they don't seem to hear. We say, "Is it well with the child? is it well with the loved ones?" and we listen to hear if any voice come back over the waters. None! none! Unbelief says, "They are dead, and they are annihilated," but, blessed be God! we have a Bible that tells us different. We open it and we find they are neither dead nor annihilated—that they never were so much alive as now—that they are only waiting for our coming, and that we shall join them on the other side of the river. Oh, glorous re-union, we cannot grasp it now! "Eye hath not seen, nor ear heard, neither have entered into the heart of man, the things which God hath prepared for them that love Him." Oh, what

A Place of Explanation

it will be! I see, every day, profound mysteries of providence. There is no question we ask oftener than Why? There are hundreds of graves in Greenwood and Laurel Hill that need to be explained. Hospitals for the blind and lame, asylums for the idiotic and insane, alms-houses for the destitute, and a world of pain and misfortune that demand more than human solution. Ah! God will clear it all up. In the light that pours from the throne, no dark mystery can live. Things now utterly inscrutable will be illumined as plainly as though the answer were written on the jasper wall, or sounded in the temple anthem. Bartimeus will thank God that he was blind; and Joseph that he was cast into the pit; and Daniel that he denned with the lions; and Paul that he was hump-backed; and David that he was driven from Jerusalem; and that invalid, that for twenty years he could not lift his head from the pillow; and that widow, that she had such hard work to earn bread for her children.

The Song

will be all the grander for earth's weeping eyes and aching heads and exhausted hands and scourged backs and martyred agonies. But we can get no idea of that anthem here. We appreciate the power of secular music, but do we appreciate the power of sacred song? There is nothing more inspiriting to me than a whole congregation lifted on the wave of holy melody. When we sing some of those

Dear Old Psalms

and tunes, they rouse all the memories of the past. Why, some of them were cradle songs in our father's house! They are all sparkling with the morning dew of a thousand Christian Sabbaths. They were sung by brothers and sisters gone now—by voices that were aged and broken in the music—voices none the less sweet because they did tremble and break.

When I hear these old songs sung, it seems as if all the old country meeting homes joined in the chorus, and city church and sailor's Bethel and Western cabins, until the whole continent lifts the Doxology, and the sceptres of eternity beat time in the music. Away then with your starveling tunes that chill the devotions of the sanctuary, and make the people sit silent when Jesus is marching on to victory. When generals come back from victorious wars, don't we cheer them and shout, "Huzza, huzza"? and when Jesus passes along in the conquest of the earth, shall we not have for Him one loud, ringing cheer?

"All hail the power of Jesus' name!
Let angels prostrate fall,
Bring forth the royal diadem,
And crown Him Lord of all."

But, my friends, if music on earth is so sweet, what will it be in heaven! They all know the tune there. All the best singers of all the ages will join it—choirs of white-robed children, choirs of patriarchs, choirs of apostles. Morning stars clapping their cymbals. Harpers with their harps. Great anthems of God roll on! roll on!—other empires joining the harmony till the thrones are all full, and the nations all saved. Anthem shall touch anthem, chorus join chorus, and all the sweet sounds of earth and heaven be poured into the ear of Christ. David of the harp will be there. Gabriel of the trumpet will be there. Germany, redeemed, will pour its deep, bass voice into the song, and Africa will add to the music with her matchless voices. I wish we could

Anticipate that Song.

I wish in our closing hymn to-day we might catch an echo that slips from the gates. Who knows but that when the heavenly door opens to-day to let some soul through, there may come forth the strain of the jubilant voices until we catch it? Oh, that as the song drops down from heaven, it might meet half way a song coming up from earth.

They rise for the Doxology, all the multitude of the blest! Let us rise with them; and so at this hour the joys of the Church on earth and the joys of the Church in heaven will mingle their chalices, and the dark apparel of our morning will seem to whiten into the spotless raiment of the skies. God grant that through the mercy of our Lord Jesus we may all get there!

[Dr. Talmage announced that next Sabbath he will begin a course of sermons to the women of America, with practical hints for men, the following subjects among others: "The Women Who Have to Fight the Battle of Life Alone;" "Marriage for Worldly Success Without Reference to Moral Character;" "Is Engagement as Binding as Marriage?" "Women Who Are Already Uncongenially Married;" "Influences Abroad for the Destruction of Women;" "Wifely Ambition Right and Wrong;" "What Kind of Men Women Should Avoid;" "Simplicity as Opposed to Affectation;" "Reformation in Dress;" "Plain Women;" "The Female Sceptic;" and "Christian Housewifery."]

THE LATE EX-SECRETARY MANNING.

(*See Portrait on page 12.*)

IN our last week's issue the critical condition of Mr. Daniel Manning was reported. The sad intelligence of his death is now recorded. He continued to sink slowly but surely, and on December 24 he died, calmly and peacefully, like a wearied man falling asleep. He was buried at Albany on December 27, the President and his Cabinet, with Governor Hill and a large number of distinguished men attending, as a mark of respect for the deceased statesman.

Mr. Manning's career was a typical one. At starting he seemed to have everything against him, and in any other country in the world would have been considered a very fortunate man if he had been able to save enough money out of his weekly earnings to support him in sickness and old age. Here, the genius, industry and perseverance he possessed enabled him to rise, until he held the proud position of second officer in the Cabinet, at the head of the department in which are conducted the vast financial concerns of the nation.

Mr. Manning was born in Albany, N. Y., August 16, 1831. He was therefore in his fifty-seventh year when he died. He was of English, Irish and Dutch extraction. His parents were so poor that they found it necessary to send him to work when he was only eleven years of age. He found employment as office boy in the establishment of the Albany *Atlas*, where he swept the office, ran errands, and was at the beck and call of every one on the premises. But the boy meant to rise, and he did his work faithfully. His evenings were given to study, and he soon learned to read and set type. In a few years he rose from grade to grade, until he was foreman of the composing room. The paper was merged into the *Argus*, and then Manning distinguished himself in a new line. He had taught himself short-hand, and obtained a place on the *Argus* staff of reporters. The same faithful, painstaking character distinguished him there, his reports of the State Senate proceedings being remarkably accurate.

He became, while engaged as a reporter, intimately acquainted with prominent politicians at Albany—an acquaintance which was maintained after he left the reporters' desk and became managing editor of the *Argus*. In 1873 he assumed sole charge of the *Argus*, and was elected President of the company, which position he held to within a year or two of his death. When the fight against the Tweed Ring was begun, Mr. Manning identified himself with Samuel J. Tilden, Charles O'Connor, and other anti-Ring Democrats. He became a fast and trusted friend of Mr. Tilden, and was a prominent member of the Democratic State Convention in 1874, at which Mr. Tilden was nominated for Governor. The Albany *Argus* was unflagging in its advocacy of all the measures of reform which were started and pushed forward by Governor Tilden. Mr. Manning had been a member of the Democratic State Committee since 1876. He was its Secretary in 1879 and 1880, and its Chairman from 1881 to 1883.

On the election of Mr. Cleveland to the Presidency, Mr. Manning, with whom he had been intimately associated in Albany, was made Secretary of the Treasury. He devoted himself to his duties with untiring assiduity, often laboring, long after the clerks had left, far into the night. His health began to suffer; less, however, from overwork than from the bad sanitary condition of the Treasury building, in which most of his hours were passed, and which still exists, in spite of the warnings and complaints sent to Congress on the subject. There he contracted the disease which has proved fatal to him. On March 23, 1886, he swooned in his office, and, from that time on, never recovered his health. He resigned and went to Europe for rest and change of scene, but gained little benefit. He returned on June 12 last, and made an effort to resume business. It was futile, however; he was soon prostrated, and went to his home in Albany to die.

A PARALYTIC HEALED.

THE following testimony, recently given, is published in *Thy Healer:** "It is little more than six weeks ago since I heard of Divine Healing. I had been very ill. For the last thirteen years I had never been well, but for the last three or four years I was increasingly ill through weakness of the nerves, and about six weeks ago I had *a stroke of paralysis*. I went as soon as possible after that to the sea-side, but came back none the better. I heard of Divine Healing. I said it was too good to be true. I went to see a lady, who, they said, had been healed by the Lord. She said it was not absolutely necessary for me to go Bethshan, for I could be healed where I was; but she advised me, notwithstanding, to go. 'You can get your *body* healed *here*,' she said, 'but if you want your *soul* benefited, go to Bethshan. As to your body, just give it to Jesus now.' For many years I had given Him my soul. She said, 'Come, kneel down, and I will pray with you.' I was past praying for myself, and could not. She said, 'Take Him now.' I answered, 'I will try.' 'Never mind trying, but take Him.' I said, 'I will give myself to Him as I go home in the car,' and I did so, and He healed me. And now since I have been to Bethshan it has been heaven upon earth."

A BISHOP AMONG THE CHIPPEWAS.

A VISITATION among the Indians in Minnesota, recently made by Assistant Bishop Gilbert, is described in the *Churchman*. He seems to be indebted largely to the Indian women for his means of locomotion, and he gives a graphic account of their services. He says: "A number of Indians from Leech Lake accompanied the party in their canoes, going to attend the Indian convocation which had been appointed at Red Lake. Many of the canoes were *manned* entirely by *women*. It was quite a sight to see the flotilla emerge suddenly on some lake and swarm over it, the olive-complexioned, dark-eyed women bending to the paddle, their long, black hair bound in two braids falling from their bonnetless heads, the look of eagerness in their eyes, and the sides of the canoes all in motion from the paddles, giving it the appearance, at a little distance, of a vast centipede, swiftly making its way over the waters. When they came to a portage they were as quick as the men to pick the canoe out of the water and, inverting it over the head, to carry it across the portage, though it weighed perhaps eighty pounds. Others came along packing a great load on their backs, and perhaps *on top of the highest part of the load a baby clinging*, both mother and baby equally at home. When night came camp was made, the men and women lighted their fires a little apart, but when the time came for family prayers before lying down, the men went over to the women's fire, and held *a joint service*. The Ojibway hymn rang out among the listening woods, and the prayers for pardon, peace and protection ascended toward the clear sky."

A CONFLICT AVERTED.

IN the interior of the great island of New Guinea, are many tribes who have never seen a white man and are wholly uncivilized. Mr. Savage, the well known missionary of New Guinea, reports his meeting with one of these tribes—the Tugeri. They are a predatory, wandering tribe, who approach the coast only when driven by necessity and then for the purpose of plunder. Their coming is greatly dreaded by the more peaceable natives, some of whom have been Christianized. Last year they attacked a village called Saibaia, but were driven off after a fierce conflict. Recently they returned in greater force, meaning to surprise the town, but their approach was discovered by their camp-fires, and the Saibaians armed themselves for defense. Mr. Savage urged the Christians to make signs of peace and to approach the hostile party without arms. The Tugeri received them with a show of friendship, both parties however, fearing treachery. Yet is was not long before they were mingling freely, shaking hands and exchanging presents. They separated without any trouble. Another meeting was urged by the missionary, which again resulted in a friendly conference. But the Tugeri were greatly alarmed at the sight of Mr. Savage, whom they had not seen before. He was feared more than the guns and hatchets of the Saibaians. At first he held out a piece of calico, but no one dared to come near. "After more than a quarter of an hour's coaxing," says Mr. Savage, "one plucked up courage enough to try the experiment of taking a piece of calico. He would come a little way, then stand perfectly still and look in blank bewilderment, as though he would say: 'Shall I, or shall I not?' At last, by several such stages, he came near enough to snatch the piece of calico from my hand, and retreated as fast as his legs would carry him." Before the interview closed the Tugeri all came up to touch the skin of the white man, and anything he asked for was gladly given him.

Subsequently the Tugeri withdrew, making many signs of friendship, and Mr. Savage believes that the way is now open for the carrying of the gospel to another tribe in New Guinea.

*A monthly magazine edited by Mrs. M. Baxter, containing original articles on Holiness and Divine Healing. Annual subscription 75 cents. May be had from the office of this journal, 63 Bible House, New York.

NOTES OF THE PROPHETIC CONFERENCE AT ADELAIDE, AUSTRALIA.

Pastor H. Husty spoke of the reasons for holding Second Advent Conferences. He said that it was unnecessary to give special prominence to this subject in the days of the Apostles, as it then occupied a leading position in all their teaching. Since then it had been sadly neglected, and by many professing Christians entirely rejected. We mourned over the corruptions that had crept into Christianity, as predicted by Christ and His Apostles, but rejoiced in the fact that the Lord Jesus was coming again, according to His promise, and coming to restore all things. We therefore not only loved the Lord, but loved His appearing, and felt it to be for our spiritual welfare to speak to one another about this great and glorious event. We met to strengthen and confirm each other's faith in the promise of the Lord's return, which was very necessary, as we were frequently brought into contact with those who treated the subject with indifference, if not contempt.

Another object we had in view in these conferences was to endeavor to remove any difficulties out of the way of those who sincerely desired to accept this truth, that they might rejoice with us in the glorious prospect that it opened up.

The subject introduced by *Pastor Finlayson* was, "The Cleansing of the Blood of Christ, and the Purifying Effect on the Hearts of Believers of the Hope of His Appearing." As God is a pure and holy God, freedom from sin is absolutely necessary in order to communion with Him; and as He can only take delight in His people when they are pure, He has made provision for this state of purification as well as cleansing.

Among the special effects produced by the "blessed hope" might be mentioned preparedness for service or for the Lord's Coming, which was widely different from preparedness for death. Again, the affections were purified by looking for the coming of the Lord Jesus, as they could not be by any other means. It then became not so much a question of what the world thinks of those who are looking for Christ's coming as what the Lord thinks of them. This "blessed hope" purifies Christians from the world, and separates them from it, so that they occupy a Nazarite position.

Pastor T. A. Fieldwick, gave an eloquent address on "Christ as Prophet, Priest and King." In dealing with the first part of his subject, he said that Christ is the author and subject of prophecy, and foretold His own death and resurrection, the destruction of Jerusalem, and other events. Secondly, Christ as a Priest is partly earthly, and is partly heavenly. He had to offer a sacrifice, and He offered Himself; and having finished the earthly part of His office He has, as our great High Priest, gone to appear in heaven for us.

Thirdly, as to the distinctive kingly office of Christ. He will make and administer the laws of His Kingdom, and these must be promptly and implicitly obeyed. Some have an idea that Christ is reigning as King now, but instead of such being the case, Satan is represented in Scripture as being the Prince of this world. Satan offered Christ the kingdoms of this world on certain conditions, but He would not accept them on the terms mentioned. He said: "My Kingdom is not of this world (or age)." He is gone to receive His Kingdom from His Father, and will return by-and-bye to take possession of it. Christ is never said to be King over His Church, which is to be united to Him and associated with Him in His Kingdom.

Christians are now being prepared, by the discipline they are passing through, to be with Christ, the governing body, during His Millennial reign. According to God's gracious promise we are constituted kings, but the kingdom, like the Church, is at present a mystery, which will not be revealed and established till the revelation of Christ from heaven. Christ is now waiting at His Father's side till He comes with His Bride, the Church, to set up His Kingdom; and that glorious event will be the Jubilee of Israel and of the world, as set forth in the ninety-eighth, ninety-ninth, one-hundredth and other prophetic Psalms.

Pastor A. E. Green gave a stirring address on "Our Lord's second coming a motive to earnest and Evangelistic effort;" and in introducing the subject, he said it is frequently asserted that believers in the Second Advent of Christ are not practical soul-winners. If this could be substantiated it would be a very serious charge, but while this might be true in a few instances, he considered the reverse was the case generally. To Israel of old was entrusted the important work of manifesting God to the world; but Israel, by rejecting Christ, had lost that position, and this task was now given to the Church. The Church is warned in Rom. 7 of the danger of neglecting her duty in testifying of Christ, and she has to bear witness both to the first and second coming of the Lord Jesus. The commission given to the Church was to "preach the Gospel to every creature," for the gathering of the Church out of the world; and Christ will not come again until the Bride is complete. He may come at any moment, and we must therefore strive to win souls by evangelistic effort to hasten His appearing. Our part in the first resurrection depends upon our testimony, as set forth in the parable of the ten virgins, five of whom had their lights burning, and were witnessing, in order to save. Our reward and position in the Millennium depends upon our faithfulness, as taught by the Apostle Paul in II Tim. 4:1–8; 1 Cor. 3. 8, 14, 15; and 1 Thess. 2:19. The apostles used the truth of Christ's second coming as a motive to zeal and earnestness in the work of evangelization, and believed that their reward depended upon the faithful discharge of their duty in this particular. The first preachers of the Gospel were firm believers in the return of their Lord according to His promise, and the most successful evangelists of the present day, such as Moody, Hudson Taylor, Pentecost, Muller, Guinness and Varley were all thorough and ardent premillennarians.

Pastor F. Boyling concluded with an interesting and very practical address on "The reason for the Lord's delay as stated by the Apostle Peter." The speaker quoted from the Apostle's Second Epistle (3:9), in which it is said that God is long-suffering, "not willing that any should perish, but that all should come to repentance." The Lord, he said, is swift to save, but slow to punish, and as instances of God's long-suffering and readiness to pardon the penitent he mentioned the preaching of Noah to the antediluvians and Jonah to the Ninevites. God's long-suffering is peculiar to Himself, and has never been ascribed to the heathen deities. In certain cases afflictions are used by God as a means of saving some; and as a striking proof of the Lord's long-suffering, Christ is now tarrying at the right hand of God that sinners may be saved and that all may come to repentance. Christ has waited long, but it is quite certain that He will not wait for ever.

The Conference was a successful one, both as regards the number that attended, and the addresses that were delivered. The portions of Scripture read, and the hymns that were sung, had a direct bearing upon the subject of the Lord's Advent; and probably the only regret, if any, was that such gatherings did not take place oftener.

JESUS WALKING ON THE SEA.

By Mrs. M. Baxter.

S. S. Lesson for January 15, Matthew 14 : 22-36; Golden Text, Matthew 14 : 27.

Ver. 22. Christ Breaks up the Assembly—An Urgent Need for Doing So. See John 6: 15—Danger of the Spiritual Kingdom Becoming Secular—The Disciples Dismissed First—Were in Sympathy with the Movement—Assured that Jesus would meet Them—Ver. 23. His Invariable Recourse in a Crisis—Solitary Meditation and Prayer—Ver. 24. A Common Experience on Inland Lakes Surrounded by Hills—Ver. 25. Between Three and Six A. M.—The Disciples nearer their Destination than they Knew. See John 6: 21—Ver. 26 and 27. Superstitious Alarm Allayed—A Tranquillizing Assurance for All Time—Ver. 28-31—Peter Always Unconscious of His Own Weakness—Ver. 32-36. Christ Accepting Worship—An Opportunity not Neglected

ALTHOUGH the time of quiet which Jesus had proposed for His disciples and Himself had been so quickly interrupted, yet He had not forgotten it; and, having provided for the multitude, "He constrained His disciples to get into a ship, and to go before Him unto the other side, while He sent the multitudes away." How came it that the multitudes could be prevailed on to depart, when, but a day or two before, they had followed Him on foot out of the cities? In the first instance, Jesus recognized His Father's will in the interruption, and submitted to it with joy. The people had needs which He was to satisfy. The whole multitude *now* knew Him as the Healer of the sick, and as the Great Provider, and they went away satisfied. Only God can judge when it is best for an evangelist to leave a place where a blessed work of God is going on. When *He* sends the multitudes away, they do not go away empty. When they were gone, Jesus returned to His

Habitual Communion

with His Father. To Him prayer was not a duty which was to occupy a certain hour of the day; it was His very life, and all He did or said was but the carrying out of the plans received in secret from His Father, the speaking out of the words which He had received from Him. If our work were more the result of our intercourse with God, there would be more done for eternity than there is. O, that we understood more, that every bit of spiritual work which we do is really done by God, and not by us. We really have spiritual gifts, but "all these worketh that one and the self-same Spirit." Let us not conceit ourselves that *we* are the doers, the workers: God works, and no man or no devil can hinder Him. But He lets us be intelligent, willing, co-operating sympathizing instruments in His hand. If, through our self-sufficiency, we reverse this order, and, in our conceptions, *we* are the workers, and God is the Helper, no wonder a great deal of the work comes to naught, and has to be undone.

Jesus was still busy with His Father, while the disciples were crossing the lake in their little ship. Jesus Himself had provided for their rest, and yet it seemed as though everything were against it. There was no rest, "for the wind was contrary," and their boat was tossing continually. How understand this? Again and again, when we have received from the Lord's hand a precious time of rest from work, that very time has been filled with sore temptations, family or business trials, or with some attack of sickness, and friends have been ready to say we were doing wrong not to be at work. But friends are not always, not even often, the true interpreters of God's thoughts. He wants us to learn how to take counsel with Him, and to give Him the credit of doing all things well. It is often when the pressure of work is less, that

God Teaches Us

more, not by happy feelings, and a sweet sense of nearness to Him in prayer, but by the tossings of inward or outward trial, and by His deliverance out of it. It was far on in the night; the darkness and the absence of Jesus made the storm seem all the more severe. But right through that darkness His eye of love was upon them, and, towards morning, He "went unto them, walking on the sea." Their first impulse was to look on His presence as an additional trial; they thought He was a spirit, "and they cried out for fear." Things had reached a climax, and He said, "Be of good cheer; it is I, be not afraid." "A word spoken in due season, how good is it." (Prov. 15 : 23). This was the word they needed, and yet there was a doubt in their hearts. It was contrary to natural law, and to all their past experience, for a man of solid flesh and blood to walk upon the water; and neither their own sight nor the voice of Jesus, fully convinced them that it was He. O, how often, in times of severe trial, in which all the experience of the past has been against us (for in this special form of trial, temptation or sickness we always *have* gone under), how impossible it seems that we should ever be raised! But

Where Is Jesus?

God has "set Him at His own right hand in the heavenly places, far above all principality and power and might and dominion, and every name that is named, not only in this [age], but also in that which is to come, and hath put *all* things in subjection under His feet." If all things are under *His* feet, and God "hath raised us up together, and made us sit together in heavenly places in Christ Jesus" (Eph. 1 : 20-22; 2 : 6), then that which is under His feet is under ours also. All praise be to Him! Perhaps a glimmer of this truth may have flashed into the mind of Peter when he said, "Lord, if it be Thou, bid me come unto Thee, on the water, And He said, Come." Here was sufficient warrant for Peter to venture.

But what a lesson for us! If Jesus is above and superior to it, He is altogether Master of the circumstances which try and toss us; then we have a right to come to Him with all these things under our feet, as they are under His. He reigns, and where He is, there shall also His servant be (John 12 : 26). He is greater than the trial; so can we be. God does not want us to be unreal; to call evil good, and good evil. He has never said that sickness, poverty, famine, death, are anything else than evils in themselves, but He wants us to see Him above them, and to hear Him say, "It is I, be not afraid." He would not have us think that the trial comes necessarily from Him. Satan was permitted to afflict Job, but he could do only just what God permitted, and no more. God wants us to see that wherever the trial comes from, He is at hand, close by, to deliver.

Peter came down out of the ship; it was

An Act of Faith,

and it pleased God. Had Jesus not said, "Come," it would have been unjustifiable presumption, but the word of Jesus made it obedience in Peter. To his great joy, he found that the waves which had been tossing him were now like solid ground under his feet. It was the presence of Jesus, the Maker of the world which suspended for a moment His own laws. Peter was doing impossibilities. There would be more of doing impossibilities in the lives of us all, if we took by faith more fully the place Jesus has given us with Him above circumstances; and if we looked at Him rather than the trials which toss and tire us. It was glorious for Peter to be thus walking on the water, which he had feared would drown him. He was drawing nearer Jesus when he saw the wind boisterous. In order to see it, he had looked off from Jesus, the wind's Master, and thus his conquering faith gave way, and he lived in the power of human experience again. Occupied with experience, it overcame him; faith gave way; he was afraid, and he began to sink. Yet one resource was left him, he cried, "Lord, save me." Instantly, the hand of power was stretched out; Jesus caught him, "and said unto him, O, thou of little faith, wherefore didst thou doubt?" It was a question with Peter, whether the wind or Jesus was to be most regarded. Reader, are you under some heavy trial, and it seems as though there were no way out? Some one whom you have trusted for years has proved untrue, and you have lost your confidence in him; you feel nothing can undo it; your heart is broken. Or, it may be that, in the work of God, some terrible inconsistency has crept in, the name of Christ has been brought into reproach; the thing is done, and nothing can undo it. It may be there is trial in your family; a dear son or daughter has been brought under the influence of an evil companion, some habit of sin has been formed, and your heart is broken; it seems as though prayer were unanswered. Perhaps it is something nearer still—husband or wife has caused untold suffering. Or it may be that in business some unexpected blow has fallen, and you are involved in difficulties which affect others, and you would rather be in a poorhouse than wrong anybody.

What is to be Done?

You cannot alter the circumstances, but you can walk with Jesus above them all. O, child of God, take courage; Jesus says, "Come," Jesus says, "It is I, be not afraid." What will happen? When you and Jesus walk upon the waves of trial together, and come together both into the ship, the wind will cease. In some way or other the Lord will lift the trial, or make it so blessed that it ceases to be a trial. "Then they that were in the ship came and worshipped Him, saying, 'Of a truth Thou art the Son of God.'" This was the first acknowledgment of Jesus as the Son of God, and it was the consequence of His miraculous power. How can blind, shortsighted men presume to say that the exercise of His divine power is not needed in this day when scepticism abounds!

Arrived in the land of Genesaret, the people heard of Jesus. Numbers of those who were healed and fed upon the mountain-side had had time to tell other sick and needy ones of all the helping which they had received. No sooner did they hear that He had landed than "they sent out into all that country round about, and brought unto Him all that were diseased, and besought Him that they might only touch the hem of His garment; and as many as touched were made perfectly whole."

The Touch Recognized Jesus.

A little boy of nine years old, son of one of the Gospel Union evangelists, was suffering from skin disease which covered his arms and chest. His father had been reading at family prayer about Naaman. It was Saturday night, and when the little boy had his bath, he said, "Mamma, I shall dip seven times in my bath and I am sure God will make me well." He did so; and sure enough, in a day or two the disease, which had been long upon him, was gone. The little boy had touched *Him*.

CHRISTIAN HERALD AND SIGNS OF OUR TIMES.

OFFICE, 63 BIBLE HOUSE, NEW YORK.

ENTERED AT THE POST-OFFICE AT NEW YORK, N. Y., AS SECOND-CLASS MATTER.

Published Weekly. Subscription price, $1.50 a year; $1 eight months; 75 cents six months; sent two months on trial for 25 cents; always payable in advance. Single copies for sale by, or can be ordered at all newsdealers.

Remittances by Mail should be by Post-office money order, bank cheques, or drafts or express money order, and should always be made payable to THE CHRISTIAN HERALD.

Receipts are not sent, the receipt of the paper by a subscriber is a sufficient proof that his remittance has been received. If the paper does not arrive promptly, please advise us, that we may see if the address is correctly entered.

Change of Address. Name of Post Office and State, of both old and new address, should always be given in case of removal.

CURRENT EVENTS.

A Hearty and Sincere New Year's Greeting is tendered to all its subscribers and readers, by THE CHRISTIAN HERALD, on this, its first visit to them in the year of our Lord 1888. Without pride or egotism, it counts with confidence on a cordial welcome. Never in its past history have its friends and subscribers been so unanimous as this year, in their assurances of approval and high appreciation. Down to the time of writing these words, although some thousands of letters from readers have been received, there has not been one among them containing words of condemnation or hostile criticism. When we consider that differences of opinion are inevitable, and that "offences must come," this singular unanimity is very remarkable, and it cannot but be regarded as an evidence that the readers are persons of a high type of Christian character, who, recognizing unity of spirit, are not offended by divergence in minor details. It is also gratifying, because it is an evidence that the blessing and guidance of God, which has been earnestly sought by the proprietors, managers, and editors constantly, throughout the past year, have been given. Many cases of conversion are reported as having followed the reading of the pages of the paper, and many ministers state that the aid they have derived from its teachings and suggestions has had the best results. For all this, thanks are due to the Supreme Source of all blessing. Profoundly conscious of that fact, clearly aware of its own weakness and deficiencies, and sensible that its large and rapidly increasing circulation involves more weighty responsibilities than ever, THE CHRISTIAN HERALD earnestly asks the prayers of all its readers during this new year. The editor especially desires to make this a personal request. God has given him the privilege of editing every number of the paper, without exception, that has been issued in America during the past ten years, and his experience has deepened his sense of dependence on Divine wisdom for the future. He therefore earnestly asks his readers, while accepting best wishes for their happiness and prosperity during the year on which we have entered, to remember THE CHRISTIAN HERALD in their prayers.

The Proceedings of the Fishery Commissioners, up to the time of their adjournment for the holidays, were kept secret, and various rumors more or less favorable to a settlement were circulated. The latest, which was published last week, has a basis of probability in it, and certain events in Canada, combined with an utterance of Sir Charles Tupper, lend confirmation to it. It is to the effect, that the English and Canadian commissioners have decided to agree to a proposal made by Mr. Bayard during the conference, to refer to arbitration the two main questions at issue, namely: First, whether Canada shall give our fishing vessels the commercial rights which we accord to their fishing vessels, and, secondly, whether the three-mile limit shall follow the indentations of the shore. Mr. Bayard is said to be confident that any arbitrators who might be chosen, would give the United States all the Government claims; but litigants who carry their cases to court usually have that confidence. If England and Canada consent to the arbitration, it may be inferred that they do not consider an adverse decision a foregone conclusion.

The Proposals Before the Senate, for the erection of Government buildings in various cities, indicate the ideas most likely to prevail in Congress as to the best method of reducing the surplus. It is proposed to erect thirty-six new buildings, and to raise the limit of expenditures in several others in course of erection. The amount of money these projects call for is $10,241,000. In three instances over a million dollars are asked for on account of a single building, and in one of those cases the city in which it is to be erected has only eighty thousand inhabitants. It is probable that some of these appropriations will be refused and others reduced, but if the spirit manifested in the projects prevails, these proposals and a River and Harbor bill constructed on the same lines will relieve Congress of the work of dealing with the surplus in any other way. It is evident already, that the gigantic surplus is having the effect predicted in directly inciting Congress to extravagant expenditure.

The Restriction of Immigration, which is the object of four separate bills now before Congress, was discussed on December 29, at Detroit Mich., by Senator Palmer, who is the author of one of the bills. He said that in his scheme the details are left, measurably, to the Secretary of State, who, if he finds one system not stringent enough, may adopt another. In a word, the bill is desired as an entering wedge for legislation which will be added as the exigencies of the times may demand. From the circular reports received from our consuls in Hungary, one can learn that men marry in Hungary upon an express stipulation that they go to America and earn enough money with which to return and support their families. This, it will be readily seen, is everything but conducive to the welfare of this country. Senator Palmer's bill has an advantage over the others in that it prohibits the landing of Mormons. The Senator thinks that existing laws are sufficient to regulate the German, Scandinavian and British immigration, but they do not enable us to exclude immigrants of other nationalities who are no more homogeneous than the Chinese.

The Defects and Mismanagement of the Navy, are so often and so justly the subject of comment, that justice demands an acknowledgment of its good qualities, when that is possible. An occasion of that kind now occurs. The gigantic derelict lumber raft, mentioned in these colums last week, constituted so serious a danger to commerce while drifting in the track of incoming steamers, that the Government telegraphed to the Brooklyn Navy-yard an order to the United States Steamer *Enterprise* to go in search of it. The *Enterprise* was expected to be in the yard for three weeks longer, and the Captain was acting as President of a Board of Inquiry in an important matter, so that some delay in obeying the order would have been excusable. Yet, to the credit of the captain and the navy-yard the *Enterprise* started on its quest *within two hours* of the receipt of the telegram, and succeeded in finding the fragments of the raft.

A Gigantic Strike on the Philadelphia and Reading Railroad was imminent all through last week. Some journals asserted that it would involve sixty-five thousand men in idleness, but that estimate was evidently too large, as no district of the Knights of Labor in Pennsylvania has so many members. The trouble arose at Port Richmond, where certain employees were ordered to move flour consigned to the Philadelphia Grain Elevator Company. The men refused, and were discharged, whereupon twelve hundred men struck. An appeal was taken to the executive committee of the Knights of Labor, who, after a heated discussion in which marked difference of opinion was manifested, ordered a general strike. On Tuesday, December 27, the difficulty was believed to have been arranged and the strike was declared off. But the next day it was resumed, the men claiming that the Company had not kept faith with them. On Thursday last, a convention of the employees was held and sat all night. A general strike was then ordered, which if obeyed, will paralyze freight business on the road.

Another Revolution is Threatened in Hawaii. A dispute has arisen as to the exercise of the King's veto. The Legislature has passed a resolution, "that it was the sense of the Assembly that the act of the King in vetoing two bills relating to the abolition of the office of Governor was unconstitutional," and a committee of thirteen from the Assembly and a committee of the Cabinet waited upon the King and notified him of the fact. A letter received in New York from a member of the Legislature says, "I am glad that we are all through with the day's excitement in the Legislature. We nearly all went armed, as it was reported that we were to be mobbed by the King's followers. Upon assembling, we found two more bills returned to us with the King's veto. They were the Liquor and Police bills, which had been passed by the Legislature. According to the new constitution, the King cannot veto any bill unless by and with the advice and consent of the Cabinet. His doing so would be an act of war against that body and the Legislature. I am so glad that the war-ships are here; without them we would have trouble." Other correspondence is to the same tenor, and King Kalakaua's fall appears to be generally expected in the Islands.

A Judicial Reduction of Irish Rentals is announced in the *Gazette*, the Government's official organ. On December 27, it published an order signed by Commissioners Lytton and Wrench, prescribing reductions of rents throughout practically the whole of Ireland, ranging from six to twenty-two per cent. The average being fourteen per cent., the aggregate reduction is estimated at $10,000,000. The reduction is permanent and applies to arrears since 1881. Such a concession, if it had been made a few years ago, would have been welcomed in Ireland with general gratitude; now, however, it is said to be received everywhere with indifference, except by the persons interested.

The Rumors of Approaching War in Europe continued to cause uneasiness throughout last week. The Russian press, which has assumed a bellicose attitude, has done more to increase the disquietude than even the concentration of troops on the Austrian frontier. This is due to the fact, that there is a rigid press censorship in Russia, and a journal publishing articles of which the Czar disapproved would be in danger of prompt suppression. There is, therefore, greater significance in Russia than elsewhere in the utterances of the leading journals. Among those that were published last week was an article, evidently inspired by the Government, which stated that a war between Russia and Austria would not necessarily involve Germany, and that the Russian Government has obtained the knowledge that the terms of the treaty of alliance leave Germany free not to interfere unless Austria is threatened with a collapse which would involve territorial losses. It also asserted that England would not interfere unless the integrity of Turkey were threatened. If Russia is convinced of these two facts, war is almost certain, as she would have little difficulty in vanquishing Austria alone. The Crimean War resulted from a similar impression; Russia ventured to a point from which she could not honorably retreat before learning the strength of the combination against her.

Contributions to the Fund for Supplying colored ministers in the South with this journal have been received, since our last acknowledgment, to the amount of twelve dollars. They are, from Bridgton, Me., $1; Chester, Mass., $1; Wyoming, Pa., $3; Lowell, Mass., $2; Franklin Park, N. J., $2; Camden, N. Y., $1; Sterling, Mass., $1; Bozeman, Mont., $1. These amounts will bring joy into the homes of twelve worthy ministers, who have been hoping and praying that they may have the paper another year. There are many others who are anxiously awaiting similar news.

The Late Mrs. John Jacob Astor Did Not forget, in her will, the causes she had supported during her life. The list of bequests published on Thursday last includes $25,000 to the Domestic and Foreign Mission Society of the Protestant Episcopal Church; $25,000 to the Woman's Hospital of the State of New York; $25,000 to St. Luke's Hospital; 25,000 to the Young Women's Christian Association; $25,000 to the Children's Aid Society, as a fund to be invested, and its interest used to send street waifs out West and settle them on farms; and a further sum of $10,000 to the same Society, for the support of Mrs. Astor's favorite school on the East side of New York.

An Excellent Example to Wealthy Men is set by ex-Gov. Alger, of Detroit, Mich. He has made Christmas of 1887 more joyous to many families by his munificence. He began his work on December 26, by fitting out five hundred newsboys, selected on account of their good conduct, with a suit of clothes and a warm shirt each. His next act was to supply one thousand of the most needy families in the city with a ton of coal; or, if they do not use coal stoves, a cord of hard wood; and, in addition, a barrel of flour. The families thus assisted are those who have been brought into a suffering condition through no fault of their own. In one case a wife and eight children had been deserted by a drunken husband, who left the city weeks ago. The family were on the point of starvation. In one house a cripple was vainly striving to keep a dependent family from want. The list presents an almost frightful array of cruel and base desertions, of sickness and disability, helpless old age, and deplorable want, but no more than a similar investigation would disclose in any large city in the land.

A Naive Suggestion by an Unemployed Country youth was made recently in New York. A Wall Street journal says that one of the most wealthy merchants in the city received a call, a day or two before Christmas, from a young man in search of employment. The applicant having presented his letter of introduction, sat waiting for the great man to open the conversation. The merchant, really desirous to forward the wishes of the youth, asked him what kind of position he would like. "Well," said the applicant, looking round at the somewhat luxurions office, "I think I should like just such a position as yours." The great man replied: "Yes; it is a very pleasant position, but it took me many years to get it." He might have added that those years were years of toil and trial. Young Christians are often distressed by doubts of their conversion, when they hear some experienced brother describe his joys. They forget that it is the result of long years of trial and suffering. (Rom. 5: 3-5.)

A Mysterious Subterranean Phenomenon is reported from Pennsylvania. A press despatch from Tusseyville, on December 28, states that the people have been alarmed by strange noises, which came from the ground between two mountains known as Thick Head and Sand Mountain, south of Tusseyville. All the previous week the noises were distinctly heard, like the distant rumbling of thunder. The most remarkable was observed by a person who was on Thick Head, when the rumbling began in Sand Mountain, just opposite. At first it was deep, but low, and increased in violence, until it became as the tumult of a mass of rocks rolling down a mountain side. The person who heard the sound says that it rolled down the mountain from top to bottom, increasing in volume and speed as it went down, and terminating in a loud crash at the bottom, but no movement was perceptible on the surface of the mountain. These and other mysterious phenomena, occurring in other lands, are premonitions of the approaching final convulsion, and Christ said that such warnings would be given. (Luke 21: 25.)

A Flying Leap Through the Air was Unexpectedly taken by a farmer at Bridgewater, N.Y., a few days ago. A large oak tree stood on a high bluff on his farm overlooking the Honsatonic. The heavy rains washed the soil away around it, and one day the top became too heavy for the roots to hold up, and it fell over away from the river. The farmer found it lying almost upon the ground, and, as coal is high, he determined to cut it up for his fireplace. He began at the top and lopped off some of the smaller limbs and brush. Then he mounted the trunk and cut away on a larger limb. He had just severed it when he was astonished to find himself flying through the air directly over the river. The tree, relieved of its weight, had sprung back into its original position, and, acting as a spring-board, had given him an ærial trip that might have been fatal. As it was, he fell into the icy waters of the Housatonic and escaped with a chill. The tree seems likely to stand and grow again, its roots being firm in the soil. So it is sometimes in our churches. A member seems to be utterly overthrown by worldly prosperity or by some sin, but if his root is in Christ, the loss of property or the removal of the burden of transgression is followed by restoration to his original position before God (Hos. 6: 1, 2.)

An Amusing History of an Immigrant's wanderings, is given by the New York *Times*. It states that on December 28 a German immigrant reached Monticello, N. Y., after having spent nearly three weeks in getting there from New York City, which is only a four hours' ride by railway from that place. When he landed from the German steamer he inquired his way to Monticello, and as his money was getting low, and the distance comparatively short to a vigorous young man, he resolved to make the journey on foot. After walking four days he found himself in Philadelphia. He was there two days before he could get his bearings. Then he walked back to New York, and from there to Middletown, where he was within twenty miles of his destination. He was directed to the right road, but after tramping about for a couple of days, he turned up in Matteawan, Dutchess County, on the east side of the Hudson. At Matteawan he was again turned toward Monticello, and two or three days of wandering brought him to Goshen. There he was put on the road to Monticello, and he finally reached that place. There are many Christians who could tell an analagous story of their spiritual experience, when they were trying to win salvation by their own exertions, instead of accepting Christ's finished work. (Rom. 10: 6-8.)

The Romantic Recovery of Sight by a Blind girl, was reported in the New York *Sun* on December 29. It states that a young lady, a distant relative of the late President Arthur, has for about a year been totally blind. She was of a highly nervous temperament, and after completing her education fell into a bad state of health. She went to Europe for rest and change of scene, and to some extent regained vigor. There she became engaged to a young Scotchman, a member of the largest publishing firm in Glasgow. She returned to America in the summer of 1886 and went South, to nurse her grandfather, who was in his last illness. After his death she became despondent, and was in that condition in August, when the Charleston earthquake occurred. The nervous shock it gave her had the strange effect of producing dimness of vision, and finally, total blindness. The most celebrated occulists and specialists in nervous disorders were consulted, but could do her no good. To her friends they said that she was doomed to lifelong blindness. The girl, learning this fact, sent a message to her Scotch lover, releasing him from the engagement. The manly young Scotchman came over by the next steamer, and went straight to her home. He told her that he would not consent to the engagement being broken. He declared that he loved her and would marry her, whether she remained blind or not. His conduct produced such a burst of joy in the girl's heart, that it seemed to transform her whole being. She became bright and cheerful, and regained her physical health rapidly. The most astonishing effect, however, was on her eyes. She began to perceive the difference between light and darkness, and gradually to discern conspicuous objects. She is now able to see as well as ever she could. The influenee of the soul over the body, which physicians cannot trace, but of which this and other cases give clear proof, is evidently mightier than we know. Its most blessed effects, however, are those produced on persons wandering in the darkness of sin and unbelief. With them, as with this girl, love is the agent. When they realize that God loves them, even in their dark state, they come to Him and receive light and life (II Tim. 1: 10).

BRIEF NOTES.

The English Baptist Union has appointed a deputation of ministers to wait on Mr. C. H. Spurgeon, to ask him to reconsider his withdrawal from the Union.

The Rev. B. Fay Mills has promised to conduct a series of Union Evangelistic services in Philadelphia, during this month.

The Swedish Evangelical Lutheran Mission of Chicago has dedicated its new building. The Rev. F. P. Goodwin, Professor D. C. Marquis, the Rev. F. A. Noble, and the Rev. Arthur Little took part in the exercises.

The services conducted by Messrs. Crossley and Hunter, in Toronto, have produced much good in the city. One church where they labored, reports an addition of more than one hundred persons for membership.

A Pittsburg pastor writes: "The Moody meetings in this city were a great success, estimated by the size of congregations, the apparent interest, and the numbers visiting the inquiry rooms. Of the inquirers a good many were members of churches who were living careless lives.

The Presbyterian ministers, of Pittsburgh, have adopted a resolution, declaring their disapprobation of Sunday newspapers. The resolution calls upon all lovers of law and order, and of a religious Sabbath, to withdraw their patronage from papers that publish Sunday editions.

The Rev. Dr. James Powell, Corresponding Secretary of the American Missionary Association, died at his home, in Brooklyn, of apoplexy, on December 27. On Sunday, December 25, his forty-fifth birthday, he delivered two addresses in Brooklyn—one in Dr. McLeod's church, and one to the children in Dr. Meredith's church.

When Dr. Munhall's evangelistic meetings closed in Toronto, seven hundred and three inquirers' cards were received, and of these, two hundred and fifteen asked for Methodist churches, one hundred and seventy-one for Presbyterian, one hundred and twenty-five for Episcopalian, ninety-three for Baptist, and thirty-two for Congregational.

Mrs. Wilder and her daughter are on their way back to India. Mrs. Wilder is the widow of the well-known missionary, and the mother of one of the young men who have been visiting the colleges in the interests of foreign missions. They go to the field where Mr. and Mrs. Wilder spent thirty years, and where the daughter was born. They are self-supporting missionaries.

The Evangelical Alliance, at its assembly in Washington, authorized the issue of a circular, suggesting that Christians of all evangelical denominations in each city, meet regularly for conference and to organize plans for city visitation. Such visitation to include a knowledge of the sick and deserving poor, the number and location of saloons and places of ill repute, and all the evil influences that affect the moral character of the community.

Mayor Howland, of Toronto, in a recent address in New York, describing the immunity of that city from the control of the saloons, ascribed it to two causes. First—a property qualification which shuts out from the ballot-box a class of citizens who are easily handled by the saloons; and secondly, that women who possess the necessary amount of property are allowed to vote.

The Citizens' Law and Order League, having for its specific work to secure obedience to the laws for the prevention of pauperism, insanity, and crime produced by the sale of intoxicating liquors, will hold its sixth annual meeting in the city of Philadelphia on the 21st and 22d days of February, 1888. All persons desiring information as to the purpose of the League or in relation to the national meeting, are requested to address the Secretary at 28 School Street, Boston, Mass.

NOT BOUND YET.

A New Sermon by Pastor C. H. Spurgeon.

"Wherein I suffer trouble as an evil doer, even unto bonds; but the word of God is not bound." II Tim 2: 9

The Grave turned from a Blind Alley into a Tunnel—Paul's Self Forgetfulness—Bound but Rejoicing in an Unbound Gospel—I. How the Gospel is Unbound—It can be Preached—Many Attempts to Bind it—Can Reach the Heart—A Conversion on Shipboard—A Soul Saved Through a Collision at Sea—An Infidel's Prayer Test—Can Comfort the Depressed—Will be Fulfilled—II. Why it is not Bound—A Hungering World—The Terrible Cry in the Bread Riots—John Bunyan's Answer—III. Can Work Apart from the Worker.

YOU will observe, if you read the verse which precedes, which indeed it would be wrong to dissever from the text, that the doctrine of the resurrection of our Lord Jesus Christ was the sheet-anchor of Paul's comfort, as it was the great substance of his preaching. "Remember that Jesus Christ of the seed of David, was raised from the dead according to my gospel: wherein I suffer trouble, as an evil doer, even unto bonds; but the word of God is not bound." Perhaps we do not give sufficient prominence to the doctrine of the resurrection of Jesus Christ from the dead. Possibly, also, for this reason, we do not fully grasp the idea of "the power of His resurrection." Our Lord's death was not the close of His career; He still passed onward. From the cross to the sepulchre was still forward. With weeping and mourning they laid Him in the tomb: surely that was the *finis* of His course. Ah, no! He passed into the grave, it is true; but He also passed through it. The grave had hitherto seemed a *cul-de-sac*, a blind alley, from which

There was no Exit

All the footsteps pointed to entrance, but none to return. It looked like a dread abyss swallowing all, and offering passage-way to none. See what our Lord Jesus has done! He has made a tunnel of it for all His redeemed to pass into the kingdom: we enter at the grave to emerge in the resurrection into eternal life. In this lies part of the power of His resurrection, that He has opened the kingdom of heaven to all believers. It looked like an iron door, or gate of death, but He has unhinged it, yea, He has taken it quite away. The grave was once "a charnel-house to fence the relics of lost innocence," but it is so no longer, the imprisoning stone is rolled away. By passing through death our Lord has made a thoroughfare for us. We take death and the grave in transit now; they do not hinder our advance to glory, and immortality, and eternal life. Our course is ever onward whatever may lie in the way.

In the strength of that truth, Paul, when he found himself in prison,

Expected to Come Out

of it; when he saw great difficulties in the way to heaven, he expected to go through those difficulties, and to come out with gain at the further end thereof. This helped to cheer him in his darkest moments. His brave heart thus spoke within him, and said, "What if I should be even dead and buried, I shall rise again; and if the gospel should seem dead and buried, yet it will rise again; and if the particular cause which I am advocating in Rome should seem dead and buried, yet it must come to life again. I take courage from the great truth, that the Lord Jesus Christ rose from the dead."

I like much this self-forgetting sentence of the apostle, "I suffer trouble, as an evil doer, even unto bonds; but the word of God is not bound." He is shut up in the gloomy dungeon at Rome. No hideous dens could be worse than Roman dungeons usually were. No prison is a desirable place, but a Roman prison was a very vestibule of death. Paul is not only in prison, but in bonds; his right arm is chained to the left hand of a soldier; he cannot do anything except under the inspection of his enforced companion, who, kindly as he may be disposed, cannot be so closely bound to him without causing him much discomfort. One would not like to be chained to the best man that ever lived, and much less to a rough Roman soldier. Paul is in bonds; as he writes, his fetters clank; but he makes light of it, and finds more than sufficient comfort in the reflection, "I suffer as an evil doer, even unto bonds; but the word of God is not bound."

I. First, then, in what sense is it true, that "the word of God is not bound?" That

The Word is not Bound

is, at this time, true in many senses; and first, it is not bound so that it cannot be preached. Paul could preach it even when in bonds, and he did preach it, so that the gospel was made known throughout Cæsar's palace, and there were saints in the imperial household. Many came to and fro into the Prætorian guard-room, and heard the word from the mouth of the apostle. You may be quite sure that he never neglected to make known the message of the gospel to all that visited him in his prison, so that the word of God was not bound even with respect to himself. And, dear friends, whatever saddens us at this hour, we rejoice that the word of God still finds a tongue and a voice wherewith to speak to the multitudes. Nineteen centuries after Paul, we have still an open Bible and a free pulpit. Blessed be God for this!

There have been a great many

Attempts to Bind the Word

of God, but yet it has not been bound. The preachers of the holy faith of Christ have been hunted to the death; they have "wandered about in sheep-skins and goat-skins, destitute, afflicted, tormented," but the word of God has not been bound. When Hamilton was burned in Scotland, there was such an impetus given to the gospel through his burning that the adversaries of the gospel were wont to say, "Let us burn no more martyrs in public, for the smoke of Hamilton's burning has made many eyes to smart until they were opened." So, no doubt, it always was. The word of God is not bound by the binding of the preachers.

"The word of God is not bound" so as to be no longer a living, working power among men. Sometimes the enemies of truth have thought that they had silenced the last witness, and then there has been an unexpected outburst, and the old faith has been to the front again. A desperate and subtle attempt is now being made, but it will be assuredly foiled through the wisdom of God. Yet, if it should come to this, that they should get rid of all the preachers of the gospel—of the men who would thunder out God's word like Boanerges, or speak it out in tender tones as Barnabas—if the last of the faithful testifiers were consigned to the tomb, God would be sure to raise up another generation to publish his truth, so that the word of God should not lack a spokesman in the midst of the earth. The devil's work is never done: one word from the Lord, and it is all undone in a trice.

Another sense must be remembered: the word of God is not bound so that it cannot reach the heart. You may have, perhaps, dear friend, some very obdurate relative about whose salvation you have very great concern. You have prayed long, and have used the means within your reach perseveringly; you have also used extraordinary means, and you have looked for an immediate result. But as yet the hard heart does not melt; as yet you see no tear of repentance, and hear no cry of faith. Do not give anybody up in despair: while God is almighty, have hope for the chief of sinners.

A Conversion On Ship Board.

Had we not, a little while ago, an instance of one whom we were praying for at a prayer-meeting, and *that night, while we were praying*, it was a moonlight night, and as he was walking the deck of the ship, the Lord met with him? When no tongue was able to reach him, the memory of what he had heard at home came over his soul, and he was humbled before God. I was telling, just a little while ago, at our prayer-meeting, a very singular instance of how, just lately, three or four sermons on Sunday evenings have been made most useful to a young friend. He was going away to Australia unconverted, and without God. He went on board to depart, and when the vessel steamed out of dock, it ran into another ship, and he was obliged to wait and spend almost a month here, whilst the vessel was being repaired. The Lord met with him on those Sunday nights, and he has gone now, leaving in his mother's heart the sweet persuasion that he has found his mother's God. The God of all grace has ways of getting at human hearts when to our thinking every avenue is fast closed.

But sometimes we are apt to think a case is more hopeless still, when in addition to natural depravity, and the absence of the means of grace, there springs up a scepticism, perhaps a downright derision, of the word of God, and of things sacred. One is apt to think then, "It is all over now; it is of no further use praying for such an one." I am not so sure that the case is any the worse for being openly declared.

Nothing is More Deadly

than absolute indifference; and sometimes, when a man begins to avow himself an infidel, it is only that his conscience is troubling him, and he is obliged to take some drug wherewith to stifle it; no drug is more handy for his use than avowed Infidelity. A profession of scepticism is often nothing more than the whistling of the boy as he goes through the churchyard, and is afraid of ghosts, and therefore "whistles hard to keep his courage up." They try to get rid of the thought of God, because of that ghost of conscience which makes cowards of them all. Even blasphemy and infidelity yield to the conquering touch of sovereign grace.

I knew a man who had lived a life of carelessness and indifference, with occasional outbursts of drunkenness and other vices. This man happened one day, on Peckham Rye, to hear a preacher say that if any man would ask anything of God, He would give it to him. The assertion was much too broad, and might have done harm; but this man accepted it as

A Test,

and resolved that he would ask, and thus would see if there was a God. On the Saturday morning of that week, when he was going early to his work, the thought came upon him, "Perhaps there is a God after all." He was ready to swoon as the possibility struck him, and there and then he offered the test petition, concerning a matter which concerned himself and his fellow-workmen. His prayer was granted in a remarkable manner, and he came then to be a believer in God. He is more than that now, and has found his way to be a believer in all that God has spoken, and has found peace through believing in Jesus Christ. It struck me as wonderful that this man, who never had any religious care at all before, should, on a sudden, be turned to serve the living God. The preacher on Peckham Rye never had a more unlikely hearer, and yet he succeeded with him. Oh, pray for them, pray for them, for though *you* cannot reach them, "the word of God is not bound."

Still further, it is not bound as to its power to comfort the soul. I have—perhaps you have in your measure—to deal with persons under conviction of sin, with others who are suffering through ill-health, or mental decline, with some who groan under Satanic temptation, and various forms of mental trial causing awful depression of spirits. We have spoken to certain of them many times, without being able to bring them light and comfort. We put the gospel very plainly to them, and try to place it in different lights, hoping that somehow or other they may see hope. Alas! we are often unable to touch the wound of their spirit. The captive is too closely shut up in prison for us to set him free. But here is a blessed truth: "The word of God is not bound." Perhaps we put too much of our own explanation with the Lord's own word; perhaps we have thought that clever illustrations were needful, and so have overlaid the truth with our poor imagination. When we have come to the end of our explanations and our illustrations, it may be that the word which is not bound will come in, and give liberty to the captives.

Thus I have given you several senses of the text. There is another one. The word of God is not bound in the sense that it cannot be fulfilled. I now allude principally to the

Promises and Prophecies

of God's word. If there is a promise of deliverance to you, and you cannot see the way in which you are to be delivered, you may not, therefore, doubt the promise, for that would dishonor the Lord who spake it. The word of God is not bound; the word of God will cleave its own way, and reach its own destination. Thou art come, perhaps, to thy last penny, but He hath said, "I will never leave thee, nor forsake thee." Thou hast come to thy last grain of strength, but He fainteth not, neither is He weary, and He hath said, "As thy days, so shall thy strength be." And so shall it be. Oh, that we could believe the promises of God! We do not half believe them, brethren.

There is yet one other sense. "The word of God is not bound," so that it cannot endure and prevail unto the end. I know there are those who think it dead, and therefore they are anxious to attend its funeral, and bury it out of sight, while the new theology shall dance on its grave. They call us poor old fogies for believing in the old gospel, and tell us to go home and order our coffins, and leave the world to these wiser men. They begin to crow as if their work of defeating us had been unquestionably done. We are out of date; we are dead; we are extinct! Perhaps so! Perhaps so! But we think they will be mistaken in their imagination, for the word of God is not defeated after all. Philosophy and heresy are in league, and they gather their armies in haste. The Lord shall make them as the sheaves of the threshing-floor. Wherefore, let us be of good comfort, brothers, and rest quite sure that, though we are beaten, the word of God is not beaten, and that though we are in a minority, and our preaching at a discount, it does not matter—"The word of God is not bound."

II. For a moment or two I have further to enquire, what are the reasons why the word of God is not bound? It is not bound, because it is the voice of the Almighty. If the gospel be indeed the gospel of God, and these truths be a revelation of God

Omnipotence is in Them.

Moreover, the Holy Ghost puts forth His power in connection with the Word of God, and as He is divine He is unconquerable. He comes as a rushing, mighty wind, and who can stay Him? He comes as fire, and who can stand before His flaming vehemence? If you wanted another reason less strong than these two, I should say, "How can it be bound while it is so needful to men?" There are certain things which if men want they will have. I have heard say that in the old Bread Riots, when men were actually starving for bread, no word had such a terribly threatening and alarming power about it as the word "Bread!" when shouted by a starving crowd. I have read a description by one who once heard this cry; he said he had been startled at night by a cry of "Fire!" but when he heard

The Cry of "Bread! Bread!"

from those that were hungry, it seemed to cut him like a sword. Whatever bread had been in his possession he must at once have handed it out. So it is with the gospel; when men are once aware of their need of it, there is no monopolizing it. None can make "a ring" or "a corner" over the commodity of heavenly truth.

It cannot be hid, because there are so many that want it. They are pining, these myriads of London, these myriads all over the world; and though they hardly know it, yet there is a cry coming up for ever from them for something which they can never find, except in Christ. You may set up altars, and put up your gimcrackeries, but they won't have them instead of the gospel. You may preach your speculations, and tell them "modern thought" has done away with the old gospel, but as soon as the Holy Spirit shows them their state by nature, and their future danger, they sweep all this rubbish away.

I have one thing else to tell you. The Word of God is not bound, because, when once it gets into men's hearts, it works such an enthusiasm in them that you cannot bind it. The converted man must talk to his work-mates about it. You may say, "It would be very irregular for you to hold a meeting; it would be out of all character for a mere workingman to stand up on the village green;" but he is very likely to do it. In our own land there was

No Binding the Word

of God, for those who knew it felt compelled to spread it. There is Master Bunyan; they have put him in prison, and his family is nearly starving, and they bring him up, and they say, "You shall go out of prison, John, if you won't preach. *Go home and tag your laces*, that is what you have to do, and leave the Gospel alone; what have you got to do with *that?*" But honest John answers, "I cannot help it. If you let me out of prison to-day, I will preach again to-morrow, by the help of God. I will lie here till the moss grows on my eyelids, but I will never promise to cease preaching the Gospel." The love of Christ is such that, when it once pours into a man's heart, it must run out at his lips in loving testimony.

III. Now I come to the close. One or two other facts run parallel to the text. Paul is bound, but the Word of God is not bound. Read it thus: the preacher has had a bad week, he is full of aches and pains, he feels ill: but the Word of God is not ill. We preach

A Healthy Gospel,

if we are unhealthy ourselves. In this let the invalid rejoice. Dear suffering worker, your work shall not suffer, for it is a sound Gospel which you preach, though you yourself are hampered by a poor, weak body! "What will become of the congregation when a certain minister dies?" Well, he will be dead, but the Word of God will not be dead. God buries His workmen, but His work goes on. One light goes out, but another torch flames forth. Star by star sinks beneath the horizon, but another star appears on the other side to make glad the night. The Word of God is not dead when the preacher is dead. "Oh, but the worker is so feeble!" The Word of God is not feeble. "But the worker feels so stupid." But the Word of God is not stupid. "But the worker is so unfit." But the Word of God is not unfit. You see it all comes to this: the preacher is bound, but the Word of God is not bound: the worker is feeble, but the Word of God is not feeble.

But you bitterly and truthfully lament that Christian men are nowadays very devoid of zeal. "All hearts are cold in every place;" the old fire burns low. But the Word of God is not cold, nor lukewarm, nor in any way losing its old fire. "Such and such a congregation is as frozen as the North Pole." Yes, but the word of God is not frozen: divine truth is not turned into an iceberg.

Do Not Fret Yourself

into despair as to the condition of the church, since the Lord liveth. "Yes," says one, "but I am disgusted with the cases I have lately met with of false brethren." Yes, but the word of God is not false. "But they walk so inconsistently." I know they do, but the word of God is not inconsistent. "But they say they have disproved the faith." Yes, they have disproved their own faith, but they have not disproved the word of God for all that. The word of God is not affected by the falsehood of men.

"Oh, but," says one, "it is an awful thing to think of the spiritual ruin of so many that are round about us, who hear the gospel, and yet after all wilfully refuse it, and die in their sins." Truly this is a grievous fact: they appear to be bound by their sins like beasts for the slaughter, but the word of God is not bound or injured. O sinners, you cannot overcome God's word! You have defeated its influence of love upon yourselves, but it is not defeated after all. I pray you, cease to fight against the Lord; for the word of God is not bound. However much you may try to bind it, you shall find that it has its liberty, and it will in the next world have liberty to accuse and to condemn if you will not give it liberty now to persuade and to save you. God bless you, dear friends, for Christ's sake! Amen.

[The prayers of the readers of this journal are requested for the blessing of God upon its Editors, and those whose sermons, articles or labors for Christ are printed in it; and that its circulation may be used by the Holy Spirit for the conversion of many sinners and the quickening of God's people. Dr. Talmage and Mr. Spurgeon especially request prayer every Sunday morning on behalf of their labors.]

GEMS FROM NEW BOOKS.

THE GEORGIA LADY'S MARRIAGE WITH A WOUNDED YANKEE.*

I HEARD a great many of the facts [about the marriage of the Yankee soldier to the daughter of the old and proud Georgia family] from old Aunt Fountain, one of the Tomlinson negroes, who for some reason or other was permitted to sell ginger cakes and persimmon beer under the wide-spreading china-trees in Rockville on public days and during court-week. I made no attempt to coax Aunt Fountain to tell me about Trunion [the Yankee bridegroom] for I knew it would be difficult for her *not* to talk about him. She waited awhile, evidently to pique my curiosity; but as I betrayed none, and even made an effort to talk about something else, she began:

"Well, Suh, you ax me 'bout Marse Fess Trunion. I know you bleege ter like dat man. He aint b'long ter we-all folks, no furder dan he my young Mistiss' ole man, but der ain' no finer white man dan him. No, suh, dee ain'. I tell you dat pintedly. I say dis about Marse Fess Trunion, ef he aint got de blood he got de breedin'. Ef he ain good ez de Tomlinsons, he lots better dan some folks what I know. I pick dat man up myse'f en I knows him mos' good ez if he wuz one er we-all."

"What do you mean when you say you picked him up?" I asked, unable to restrain my impatience.

"Well, suh, de fus time I see Marse Fess Trunion wuz turreckerly atter de Sherman army come 'long; dem wuz hot times, suh, cold ez de wedder wuz. Dee wuz in-about er million un um, look like ter me, en dey des ravage de face er de yeth. Dey tuck all de hosses, en all de cows, en all de chickens, yes suh, dey cert'n'y did. Man come 'long en 'low aunty, you free now,' en den he tuck all my ginger cakes w'at I been bakin' 'g'inst Chris'mus; en den I say, 'ef I wuz free ez you is, suh, I'd fling you down en take dem ginger-cakes 'way fum you.' Yes suh, I tole him dat, it make me mad fer to see de way dat man walk off wid my ginger-cakes, I got so mad suh, dat I foller 'long atter him little ways but dat ain' do no good, kaze he cum to whar dee wuz some yuther men, en dee 'vide up dem cakes till dee want no cake lef', den I struck 'cross de plantation en walked 'bout in de drizzlin' rain till I cool off."

"Well, suh, I ain' walk fur fo' it seems like I year some un talkin'. I stop I did en listen, en still I year um. I ain' see nobody, suh, but still I year um. I walk fus' dis away and den dat away, en den I walk 'roun' en 'roun', en den it pop in my min' 'bout the big gully. Well, suh, fo' I get dar I see hoss tracks, en dee led right up ter de brink I look in, I did, en down dar dee wuz a man en a hoss, yes suh; dee wuz bofe down dar. De man wuz layin' out flat on he back, en de hoss he wuz layin' sorter up en down de gulley en right on top er one er de man's legs, en eve'y time de hoss'd scramble en try

* From Free Joe and other Georgia Sketches, by Joel Chandler Harris, a volume full of sweetly pathetic incidents of the war and subsequent days; 236 pages, price $1.00. Published by *Charles Scribner's Sons*, 745 Broadway, New York.

The Late Mr. Daniel Manning. (*See page 5.*)

The Earthquake at Calabria—Searching for Bodies.

fer git up de man 'ud talk at him. Bimeby I crope up nigher de aidge, en wen de man see me he holler out, 'Hol' on aunty, don't you fall down yer!'

"I ax him, I say, 'Marster, is you hurted much?' Kaze time I look at him I know he ain de villyun wat made off wi' my ginger-cakes, den he 'low 'I speck I hurt purty bad, aunty, en de wuss on it is dat my hoss keep hurtin me mo'.

"Den I went in de big-house en tell Mistiss 'bout de man down dere in de gully, en how he done hurted so bad he he ain' kin walk. Den Mistiss, she draw herse'f up and ax w'at business dat man er any yuther man got on her plan'ation. I say 'yessum, dat so; but he done dar, en ef he stay dar he gwine die dar'.'

"Den my young mistiss—dat's Miss Lady, suh—she say dat dough she 'spize um all dez as bad az she kin, dat man mus' be brung away from dar, kase, she say, she don't keer how yuther folks go on, de Tomlinsons is *bleese to do like Christun people*. Yes, suh; she say dem very words. Den Mistiss, she 'low dat de man kin be brung up, en put in de corn-crib, but Miss Lady she say no, he mus be brung en put right dar in de big 'ouse in one er de up-sta'rs rooms, kase maybe some er dem State er Georgy boys mought be hurted up dar in de norf, en want some place fer to stay at.

"Well, suh, I went back out in de yard, en den I went 'cross ter de nigger-quarter, en I ain' got fur till *I year my ole man prayin'* in dar some'r's. I know 'im by he v'ice, suh, en he was prayin' des like it wuz camp-meetin' time. I hunt roun' fer 'im, suh, en bimeby I fin' 'im; den I tell him 'bout de man down dar in de gully, en my ole man put out atter one er de hosses, en he brung 'im back; en we hitch 'im up in de spring-waggin, en atter dat man we went. Yes, suh; we did dat. En' w'en we git dar, me en my ole man, we pick 'im up des like he wuz a baby. We cyard 'im home en put 'im up st'ars, en dar he stayed fer many's de day."

"Well, suh, dat man w'at I fin' out dar in de gully wuz Marse Fess Trunion. Yes, suh, de ve'y same man. Dee ain' no tellin' w'at dat po' creetur gone thoo wid. He had fever, he had pneumony, en he had dat broke leg. Our w'ite folks, dee des spized 'im kaze he bin wid Sherman army. Dee say he wuz Yankee; but I tell um, suh, dat if Yankee look dat away dee wuz cert'n'y mighty like we-all.

"By dat time, suh, de war wuz done done, en dee wuz tough times. Dee cert'n'y wuz, suh. De railroads wuz all broke up, en eve'y thing look like it gwine helter-skelter right straight ter ruin. I speck de Tomlinsons, proud ez de wuz, would er bin mightily pincht fer fin' bread en meat. But dee ain' never want fer it yit, suh. Kaze w'en me en my ole man git whar we can't move no furder, Mars Fess Trunion, he tuck holt er de place en he fetcht it right side up terrectly. He say ter me dat he gwine pay he board dat away, suh, but he ain' say it whar de Tomlinsons kin year 'im.

"Well, suh, dat w'ite man, he work en he scuffle; he hire niggers, en he turn um off; he plan, en he projict; en 'tain' so mighty long, suh, 'fo' he got eve'y thing gwine straight. How he done it, i'll never tell you suh; but do it he did. He put he own money in dar, suh, kaze dee wuz two times dat I knows un w'en he git money out'n de pos'-office, en I see 'im pay it out to de niggers, suh. En all dat time he look like he de happies' w'ite man on top er de grown', suh. T' want long, suh, 'fo' we all knowed dat Mars Fess wuz gwine marry Miss Lady."

THE EARTHQUAKE IN CALABRIA.

(*See Illustration.*)

NEWS has been received of another severe earthquake. The inhabitants of Calabria, in Italy, a region about equidistant from the volcanoes of Vesuvius and Etna, have long enjoyed an immunity from earthquakes, which have in past times been very frequent and disastrous in that locality. The destruction now reported would appear to indicate that, during the interval of quiet, nature's forces had been gathering for a mighty convulsion. Among the towns, which are partly destroyed by the visitation are Bisignano, in the province of Cosenza, and Rogliano and Gravina. There were two shocks which were felt all over Calabria. A panic of a most distressing character occurred amongst the population, 4,000 of whom were rendered homeless. After the first shock the whole of the inhabitants took refuge in the streets, and this prevented a greater disaster.

Happily there is no reason to believe that the destruction of life on this occasion is so great as it was in 1857, or even in 1835, when many thousands of the inhabitants perished. Two hundred soldiers rendered valuable aid by erecting barracks for the temporary accommodation of the homeless, while ample relief was sent by the Municipality of Rome and the Government to the sufferers, who were in a pitiable condition. Our readers will not fail to remember that earthquakes are one of the signs which antedate the coming of Christ, and every one that occurs sounds a note of warning to those who are saying, "Where is the promise of His coming?" (II Peter 3: 4-7.)

A DISCOVERY IN A BUREAU.

(*See Illustration on page 13.*)

"THERE is one thing in your house that excites my curiosity," said a gentleman who was spending a night with an old college friend, and sat talking with him after the other members of the family had retired.

"What is that?" asked Mr. Gifford, the host.

"I cannot understand why you have that common, worm-eaten old bureau among the handsome and elegant furniture in your library; you do not seem to have been bitten by the 'Early English craze,' and you cannot admire the bureau for its beauty, for it is as plain and ugly as it can be. Why do you keep it and give it the place of honor?"

"Ah! it does look out of place, does it not? Well, do you know, that old bureau is a precious heirloom: it has associations which I can never, forget, and I hope my sons never will. My father brought it with him when he came to America from Scotland, and he told me its story, which I have repeated to my boys. I'll tell it you, too, if you care to hear it."

"By all means. I am interested in old family legends."

"That bureau originally belonged to my great-grandfather, a worthy Presbyterian of the strictest type, a truly God-fearing man. He was agent, or steward, or some such thing to a Scotch nobleman, who, though a Godless rake himself, knew the value of a man of piety in the management of his estates. Very large sums of money passed through his hands in the course of a year, as he received all the rents on the estate, and paid for all repairs to the buildings and any new barns, etc., that might be erected. Every penny however was duly accounted for at the end of the year, and the balance handed over to the nobleman. The building account, which was always the largest, was settled annually also. The builder was not a man of my ancestor's selection, for he was a wicked, unscrupulous man, but he had done some underhand work

"OUT OF THE DEPTHS."

BY LILLA M. ALEXANDER.

[Fro]m the depths where billows overwhelmed me,
Tossed by the tempest and wave,
[Hel]pless and sinking with terror,
I cried to the Master to save.

Lord! save or I perish: around me,
[R]ise the billows, their crests gleaming white,
[An]d beyond lies a wide waste of waters,
Enshrouded in fast falling night."

Lord! carest Thou not that I perish?
I know that Thou carest, or why
[H]ands that cross there on Calvary's summit—
The cross where Thou camest to die."

[H]e hears me! and lo, at His coming,
The gloom and the darkness retreat;
[An]d the waves that in fury were raging,
Grow calm at the touch of His feet.

[An]d the blackness that shrouded the heavens,
Is rolled like a curtain away;
[F]or the smile of His face like the sunlight,
Turns night to the gladness of day.

[I] can smile at my fears and my terrors,
Now that He standeth so near—
[N]ow that the storm has abated,
And the sea lieth shining and clear.

I am safe for His arms are about me,
I am safe for He calls me His own;
Oh! I see that no mortal can fathom,
Oh! depths of compassion unknown.

[Y]et His eyes with a gentle reproving
Are fill'd as He turns them on me;
"Why did'st thou doubt, ah thou weak one?
Was I not caring for thee?"

"Why did'st thou fear 'mid the darkness?
Could'st thou not trust in My grace?
[F]or the heart that I count truly faithful,
Will trust tho' the clouds hide My face."

J. E. JEWETT, Publisher, 77 Bible House, New York Will furnish the above poem in leaflet form at twenty cents per hundred. A Sample Packet of 50 leaflets assorted (no two alike) will be sent post-paid for ten cents. Postage stamps taken.

THE GARDEN.—For the management of vegetable gardens and practical instructions concerning the culture of flowers—for hints and information concerning all kinds of seeds, planting and cultivating all vegetables and flowers, D. M. Ferry & Co.'s Seed Annual for 1888 will be found as complete as any work of a similar character ever issued. The variety and extraordinary range of the information given renders their Annual worthy the attention of every one interested in having luscious vegetables or beautiful flowers. D. M. Ferry & Co. make the growing and sale of Onion Seed a leading specialty, and give so much information on onion culture as to make their Annual of permanent value to all onion growers and gardeners. The Annual can be had for the asking. Address D. M. FERRY & Co., Detroit, Mich.

THE CHRISTIAN HERALD ALMANAC FOR 1888.

JANUARY.

1	S	Teach me Thy statutes. Ps. 119 : 26.
2	M	I am Thine, save me. Ps. 119 : 94.
3	Tu	O forsake me not utterly. Ps. 119 : 8.
4	W	I will instruct and teach thee. Ps. 32 : 8.
5	Th	Hear my prayer, O Lord. Ps. 102 : 1.
6	F	I have heard in a time accepted. II Cor. 6
7	S	Thy kingdom come. Matt. 6 : 10.
8	S	Behold, I come quickly. Rev. 22 : 12.
9	M	All nations shall serve Him. Ps. 72 : 11.
10	Tu	Give us this day our daily bread. Matt. 6.
11	W	Bread shall be given him. Isa. 33 : 16.
12	Th	Forgive us our sins. Luke 11 : 4.
13	F	Deliver us from evil. Luke 11 : 4.
14	S	Shall no evil happen to the just. Prov. 12.
15	S	Lead us not into temptation. Luke 11 : 4.
16	M	Let me not be ashamed. Ps. 119 : 116.
17	Tu	Hold Thou me up. Ps. 119 : 117.
18	W	His mercy endureth forever. Ps. 136 : 1.
19	Th	Before they call I will answer. Isa. 65.
20	F	My beloved is mine and I am His. Cant. 2
21	S	He giveth more grace. James 4 : 6.
22	S	The Lord is my portion. Lam. 3 : 24.
23	M	Let not your heart be troubled. John 14.
24	Tu	The Father Himself loveth you. John 16.
25	W	I will heal thee of thy wounds. Jer. 30.
26	Th	I will not leave you comfortless. John 14.
27	F	Thy blessing is upon Thy people. Ps. 3.
28	S	He that hath the Son hath Life. I John.
29	S	Now are we the sons of God. I John 3 : 2.
30	M	Peace be unto you. John 20 : 21.
31	Tu	I am married unto you, saith the Lord.

FEBRUARY.

1	W	I have waited for salvation. Gen. 49 : 18.
2	Th	I will settle you. Ezek. 36 : 11.
3	F	Bless the Lord, O my soul. Ps. 103 : 1.
4	S	I will trust, and not be afraid. Isa. 12 : 2.
5	S	The Lord will provide. Gen. 22 : 14.
6	M	Thou hast been my help. Ps. 27 : 9.
7	Tu	Thou hast visited me in the night. Ps. 17
8	W	He helped me. Ps. 116 : 6.
9	Th	Thou, Lord, hast made me glad. Ps. 92.
10	F	Thy mercy, O Lord, held me up. Ps. 94.
11	S	The Lord hath heard my supplication.
12	S	I sought the Lord and He heard me.
13	M	The Lord was my stay. II Sam. 22 : 19.
14	Tu	His fruit was sweet to my taste. Cant. 2.
15	W	His banner over me was love. Cant. 2 : 4.
16	Th	Our fellowship is with the Father.
17	F	God setteth the solitary in families.
18	S	Thy right hand hath holden me up.
19	S	Thy gentleness hath made me great.
20	M	Ye have known the Father. I John 2 : 13.
21	Tu	He knoweth them that trust in Him.
22	W	George Washington's Birthday.
23	Th	He knoweth the way I take. Job 23 : 10.
24	F	I know that I shall not be ashamed.
25	S	I know nothing by myself. I Cor. 4 : 4.
26	S	I know that I shall be justified. Job. 13.
27	M	I know that my Redeemer liveth. Job 19.
28	Tu	Thou canst do everything. Job 42 : 2.
29	W	But God knoweth your hearts. Luke 16.

MARCH.

1	Th	I know how to be abased. Phil. 4 : 12.
2	F	I know how to abound. Phil. 4 : 12.
3	S	He giveth power to the faint. Isa. 40 : 29.
4	S	He shall choose our inheritance. Ps. 47.
5	M	He shall direct thy paths. Prov. 3 : 6.
6	Tu	He is faithful that promised. Heb. 10:23.
7	W	He hath chosen us in Him. Eph. 1 : 4.
8	Th	He was bruised for our iniquities. Isa. 53
9	F	He led them by the right way. Ps. 107.
10	S	He will keep the feet of His saints.
11	S	He shall teach you all things. John 14.
12	M	He shall pluck my feet out. Ps. 25 : 15.
13	Tu	He will subdue our iniquities. Micah 7.
14	W	He first loved us. I John 4 : 19.
15	Th	He hath done all things well. Mark 7:37.
16	F	He delighteth in mercy. Micah 7 : 18.
17	S	He healeth the broken in heart. Ps. 147.
18	S	He hath chosen us in Him. Eph. 1 : 4.
19	M	He openeth, and no man shutteth.
20	Tu	Behold, He cometh with clouds. Rev. 1:7.
21	W	He hath dealt bountifully with me.
22	Th	My people shall never be ashamed.
23	F	Do all in the name of the Lord. Col. 3:17.
24	S	Called, and chosen, and faithful. Rev. 17.
25	S	I will remember their sin no more.
26	M	For I will restore health unto thee.
27	Tu	Ask what I shall give thee. I Kings 3 : 5.
28	W	The Lord shall judge His people. Heb. 10.
29	Th	Thou shalt see greater things. John 1:50.
30	F	Good Friday. Draw nigh to God.
31	S	Wait on the Lord and keep His way.

APRIL.

1	S	Easter Sunday. Take heed. Luke 8.
2	M	Follow thou Me. John 21 : 22.
3	Tu	The tree is known by his fruit. Matt. 12.
4	W	Let Thine hand help me. Ps. 119 : 173.
5	Th	Let not sin reign in your body. Rom. 6.
6	F	Sin shall not have dominion. Rom. 6:14.
7	S	Cleanse Thou me from secret faults.
8	S	Walk before Me. Gen. 17 : 1.
9	M	Be ye holy, for I am holy. I Peter 1 : 16.
10	Tu	Our sufficiency is of God. II Cor. 3 : 5.
11	W	Draw me, we will run after Thee. Cant. 1.
12	Th	Trust in Him at all times. Ps. 62 : 8.
13	F	Lord, increase our faith. Luke 17 : 5.
14	S	Call upon Me in the day of trouble.
15	S	O haste Thee to help me. Ps. 22 : 19.
16	M	I will help thee, saith the Lord. Isa. 41.
17	Tu	Seek ye Me, and ye shall live. Amos 5.
18	W	A threefold cord is not broken. Eccl. 4.
19	Th	Cast thy burden upon the Lord. Ps. 55.
20	F	He shall sustain thee. Ps. 55 : 22.
21	S	Lovest thou Me more than these?
22	S	As many as I love, I rebuke. Rev. 3 : 19.
23	M	I lay down My life for the sheep.
24	Tu	Continue ye in My love. John 15 : 9.
25	W	Be thou faithful unto death. Rev. 2 : 10.
26	Th	Because I live, ye shall live also. John 14.
27	F	Fear not; I am the first and the last.
28	S	Without Me ye can do nothing. John 15.
29	S	If any man serve Me, let him follow Me.
30	M	I have prayed for thee. Luke 22 : 32.

MAY.

1	Tu	My grace is sufficient for thee. II Cor. 12.
2	W	Every one that asketh receiveth. Matt. 7.
3	Th	Of thorns men do not gather figs.
4	F	Watch and pray. Matt. 26 : 41.
5	S	In your patience possess ye your souls.
6	S	It shall be told thee what thou must do.
7	M	But I have a few things against thee.
8	Tu	Faith is counted for righteousness.
9	W	And hope maketh not ashamed. Rom. 5.
10	Th	Love is the fulfilling of the law. Rom. 13.
11	F	I loveth the habitation of Thy house.
12	S	There is no fear in love. I John 4 : 18.
13	S	Blessed is the man whose hope the Lord is
14	M	By grace are ye saved through faith.
15	Tu	Looking for that blessed hope. Tit. 2:13.
16	W	The love of Christ constraineth us.
17	Th	We are saved by hope. Rom. 8 : 24.
18	F	Lord, I believe, help Thou mine unbelief.
19	S	The hope is laid up for us in heaven.
20	S	The just shall live by faith. Heb. 10 : 38.
21	M	Lovest thou Me. Jno. 21 : 17.
22	Tu	Rejoice in hope of the glory of God.
23	W	His great love wherewith He loved us.
24	Th	In the day of adversity consider. Eccl. 7.
25	F	I will be with him in trouble. Ps. 91 : 15.
26	S	He woundeth, His hands make whole.
27	S	For ye serve the Lord Christ. Col. 3 : 24.
28	M	Get wisdom; get understanding. Prov. 4.
29	Tu	Thou art a shield for me. Ps. 3 : 3.
30	W	Decoration Day. Yet shall he live.
31	Th	Christ Jesus is made unto us wisdom.

JUNE.

1	F	Abide in Me. John 15 : 4.
2	S	Where I am, there may ye be. John 14.
3	S	Be clothed with humility. I Peter 5 : 5.
4	M	He hath respect unto the lowly. Ps. 138.
5	Tu	Be at peace among yourselves. I Thes. 5.
6	W	And the Lord shall reward thee. Prov. 25.
7	Th	Quit you like men, be strong. I Cor. 16.
8	F	Thou wilt show me the path of life.
9	S	God requireth that which is past. Eccl. 3.
10	S	Now it is high time to awake. Rom. 13.
11	M	Oh that I were as in months past. Job 29.
12	Tu	Thou hast put gladness in my heart.
13	W	Ye shall have tribulation. John 16 : 33.
14	Th	We are the people of His pasture. Ps. 95.
15	F	They shall feed in the ways. Isa. 49 : 9.
16	S	I have led thee in right paths. Prov. 4.
17	S	The year of my redeemed is come. Isa. 63.
18	M	Ye were the servants of sin. Rom. 6 : 17.
19	Tu	The darkness is past. I John 2 : 8.
20	W	Ye have not believed God. Rom. 11 : 30.
21	Th	Through a glass, darkly. I Cor. 13 : 12.
22	F	My cup runneth over. Ps. 23 : 5.
23	S	His God doth teach him. Isa. 28 : 26.
24	S	We shall see Him as He is. I John 3 : 2.
25	M	All things are yours. I Cor. 3 : 22.
26	Tu	Whatsoever he doeth shall prosper. Ps. 1
27	W	By faith ye stand. II Cor. 1 : 24.
28	Th	In Thy presence is fulness of joy. Ps. 16.
29	F	For our heart shall rejoice in Him.
30	S	And your joy no man taketh from you.

JULY.

1	S	I will look unto the Lord. Micah 7 : 7.
2	M	What time I am afraid, I will trust.
3	Tu	He knoweth the way that I take. Job 23.
4	W	Independence Day. A strong nation.
5	Th	Hide not Thy face from Thy servant.
6	F	I will manifest Myself to him. John 14.
7	S	O Lord, remember me. Jer. 15 : 15.
8	S	My meditation of Him. Ps. 104 : 34.
9	M	Thou shalt not be forgotten of Me.
10	Tu	I wait for the Lord, my soul doth wait.
11	W	With my song will I praise Him. Ps. 28.
12	Th	I will yet praise Thee more and more.
13	F	O when wilt Thou come unto me?
14	S	He will come and save you. Isa. 35 : 4.
15	S	Joined unto the Lord. I Cor. 6 : 17.
16	M	If children, then heirs. Rom. 8 : 17.
17	Tu	My God will hear me. Micah 7 : 7.
18	W	Thy comforts delight my soul. Ps. 94:19.
19	Th	Ye have put off the old man. Col. 3 : 9.
20	F	The fruit of the Spirit is love, joy, peace.
21	S	Thou art no more a servant, but a son.
22	S	We are buried with Him. Rom. 6 : 4.
23	M	Ye are Christ's. I Cor. 3 : 24.
24	Tu	Our old man is crucified with Him.
25	W	I know whom I have believed. II Tim. 1.
26	Th	Let us consider one another. Heb. 10:24.
27	F	The Lord forsaketh not His saints.
28	S	The Lord hath His way. Nah. 1 : 3.
29	S	The Father Himself loveth you. John 16.
30	M	I go to prepare a place for you. John 14.
31	Tu	The coming of the Lord draweth nigh.

AUGUST.

1	W	My blessing upon thine offspring. Is. 44.
2	Th	Let your speech be alway with grace.
3	F	Come boldly unto the throne. Heb. 4:16.
4	S	By the grace of God I am what I am.
5	S	God giveth grace unto the humble.
6	M	I will strengthen thee. Isa. 41 : 10.
7	Tu	We may find grace to help in time of need
8	W	Grant me Thy law graciously. Ps. 119:29.
9	Th	Thou hast found grace in My sight.
10	F	God hath dealt graciously with me.
11	S	Ye have tasted that the Lord is gracious.
12	S	The people found grace in the wilderness.
13	M	Ye are not under law, but under grace.
14	Tu	Grace be with all that love our Lord
15	W	I loved thee with an everlasting love.
16	Th	I will never leave thee. Heb. 13 : 5.
17	F	I have refined thee. Isa. 48 : 10.
18	S	I have overcome the world. John 16 : 33.
19	S	I will deliver thee. Ps. 1 : 15.
20	M	Let the peace of God rule in your hearts.
21	Tu	I have chosen thee. Isa. 48 : 10.
22	W	A lamp for Mine anointed. Ps. 132 : 17.
23	Th	I will make darkness light before them.
24	F	I will divide him a portion with the great
25	S	With loving kindness have I drawn thee
26	S	I have laid help upon One that is mighty
27	M	A way in the wilderness. Isa. 43 : 19.
28	Tu	Should such a man as I flee. Neh. 6 : 11.
29	W	Wilt thou be unto me as the waters?
30	Th	I will receive you. II Cor. 6 : 17.
31	F	I have heard thee in a time accepted.

SEPTEMBER.

1	S	I will hearken unto you. Jer. 29 : 12.
2	S	I have yet many things to say unto you.
3	M	I will give thee a crown of life. Rev. 2:10.
4	Tu	I have seen the affliction of My people.
5	W	I will give you rest. Matt. 11 : 28.
6	Th	Lord, what wilt Thou have me to do?
7	F	Look unto Me, and be ye saved. Isa. 45.
8	S	Let not thine heart envy sinners. Prov. 23
9	S	I will hear; for I am gracious. Exod. 22.
10	M	Stand fast in the Lord. I Thess. 3 : 8.
11	Tu	I am the Lord, I change not. Mal. 3 : 6.
12	W	Should it be according to Thy mind?
13	Th	The will of the Lord be done. Acts 21:14.
14	F	Thou shalt not be forgotten of Me.
15	S	Who is sufficient for these things?
16	S	Hath God forgotten to be gracious.
17	M	God shall supply all your need. Phil. 4.
18	Tu	Is anything too hard for the Lord?
19	W	Nothing shall be impossible. Luke 1:37.
20	Th	Why go I mourning? Ps. 43 : 2.
21	F	Return unto thy rest, O my soul. Ps. 116.
22	S	I will not fail thee, nor forsake thee.
23	S	The Judge of all the earth. Gen. 18 : 25.
24	M	Wisdom is better than rubies. Prov. 8.
25	Tu	To obey is better than sacrifice. I Sam. 15
26	W	A poor man is better than a liar. Prov. 19
27	Th	Thy loving kindness is better than life.
28	F	The mediator of a better covenant.
29	S	How much better is Thy love than wine.
30	S	Open rebuke is better than secret love.

OCTOBER.

1	M	Sorrow is better than laughter. Eccl. 7:3.
2	Tu	A faithful man shall abound. Prov. 28.
3	W	It is the Spirit that quickeneth. John 6.
4	Th	He saveth us by the washing. Titus 3:5.
5	F	Ye are washed, ye are sanctified. I Cor. 6.
6	S	Peace through the blood. Col. 1 : 20.
7	S	I will pour out My Spirit unto you.
8	M	The Spirit helpeth our infirmities.
9	Tu	The Spirit of truth will guide you.
10	W	Thou shalt be like a spring of water.
11	Th	In the wilderness shall waters break out.
12	F	Access by one Spirit to the Father.
13	S	The Lord shall satisfy thy soul. Isa. 58.
14	S	I pour water upon him that is thirsty.
15	M	When I see the blood, I will pass over.
16	Tu	Grieve not the Holy Spirit of God. Eph. 4
17	W	Will the Lord be favorable no more?
18	Th	The Spirit and the bride say, Come.
19	F	Acquaint thyself with Him. Job 22 : 21.
20	S	Mercy and truth are met together.
21	S	Our God is merciful. Ps. 116 : 5.
22	M	He is our peace. Eph. 2 : 14.
23	Tu	Thou, Lord, art plenteous in mercy.
24	W	Mercy rejoiceth against judgment.
25	Th	Ye shall be led forth with peace. Isa. 55.
26	F	According to His mercy He saved us.
27	S	He will speak peace unto His people.
28	S	By mercy and truth iniquity is purged.
29	M	God is rich in mercy. Eph. 2 : 4.
30	Tu	As we have received mercy, we faint not.
31	W	I will betroth thee unto Me in mercies.

NOVEMBER.

1	Th	Thou hast magnified Thy mercy. Gen. 19
2	F	His mercy is on them that fear Him.
3	S	The Lord will bless His people. Ps. 29.
4	S	His mercies are great. II Sam. 24 : 14.
5	M	O satisfy us early with Thy mercy.
6	Tu	For a small moment have I forsaken thee.
7	W	But with great mercies will I gather thee
8	Th	The law is right. Prov. 8 : 28.
9	F	Ye are born again by the word of God.
10	S	The truth shall make you free. John 8.
11	S	In the way of righteousness is life.
12	M	My doctrine shall drop as the rain.
13	Tu	By the law is the knowledge of sin.
14	W	Hear, and your soul shall live. Isa. 55:3.
15	Th	Believe His prophets, so shall ye prosper
16	F	According to your faith be it unto you.
17	S	The just shall live by faith. Rom. 1 : 17.
18	S	We have access with confidence by faith.
19	M	I will trust in the covert of Thy wings.
20	Tu	Let Thy saints shout for joy. Ps. 132 : 9.
21	W	Fight the good fight of faith. I Tim. 6:12.
22	Th	Thanksgiving Day. What thou owest
23	F	I had fainted, unless I had believed.
24	S	We walk by faith, not by sight. II Cor. 5.
25	S	Be thou an example of the believers.
26	M	I live by the faith of the Son of God.
27	Tu	His mercy endureth for ever. Ps. 106 : 1.
28	W	His name is the Lord of hosts. Jer. 46:18.
29	Th	Every knee should bow. Phil. 2 : 10.
30	F	I will praise the name of God with a song

DECEMBER.

1	S	Thy name is as ointment. Cant. 1 : 3.
2	S	Lord, save me. Matt. 14 : 30.
3	M	The desire of our soul is to Thy name.
4	Tu	Blessed be Thy glorious name. Neh. 9:5.
5	W	His name shall endure for ever. Ps. 72.
6	Th	His name hath made this man strong.
7	F	He saved them for His name's sake.
8	S	They were baptized in the name of Jesus.
9	S	Lord, increase our faith. Luke 17 : 5.
10	M	Lead me in Thy truth, and teach me.
11	Tu	Help Thou mine unbelief. Mark 9 : 24.
12	W	Help us, O Lord our God. II Chron. 14.
13	Th	I am thy salvation. Ps. 35 : 3.
14	F	Rejoice the soul of Thy servant. Ps. 86:4.
15	S	Be not wroth very sore, O Lord. Isa. 64:9
16	S	Hide Thy face from my sins. Ps. 51 : 9.
17	M	In wrath remember mercy. Hab. 3 : 2.
18	Tu	Uphold me with Thy free Spirit. Ps. 51.
19	W	Let my heart be sound in Thy statutes.
20	Th	Leave me not, neither forsake me.
21	F	O keep my soul, and deliver me. Ps. 25.
22	S	O Lord, open Thou my lips. Ps. 51 : 15.
23	S	There is none other name. Acts 4 : 12.
24	M	Give me neither poverty nor riches.
25	Tu	Christmas Day. Thy kingdom come.
26	W	Lord, teach us to pray. Luke 11 : 1.
27	Th	Deliver me from oppression. Ps. 119:134.
28	F	Have respect unto the covenant. Ps. 74.
29	S	Look upon Mine affliction and My pain.
30	S	Hold Thou me up. Ps. 119 : 117.
31	M	Lord, make me to know mine end.

ECLIPSES.

In the year 1888 there will be five Eclipses, three of the Sun and two of the Moon, as follows:

I. A Total Eclipse of the Moon, January 28, visible in nearly all parts of the world.

II. A Partial Eclipse of the Sun, February 11, invisible in the United States.

III. A Partial Eclipse of the Sun, July 9, invisible in the United States.

IV. A Total Eclipse of the Moon, July 12, 23, visible in the United States.

V. A Partial Eclipse of the Sun, August 7, invisible in the United States.

MORNING STARS.

Mercury, until January 18, from March 3 to May 10, from July 9 to August 23, and from October 31 to December 28.
Venus, until July 11.
Mars, until January 5.
Jupiter, until February 24, and after December 8.
Saturn, from August 1 to November 11.
Uranus, until January 7, and after October 10.
Neptune, from May 20 to August 24.

EVENING STARS.

Mercury, from January 18 to March 3, and from May 10 to July 9, from August 23 to October 31, and after December 28.
Venus, after July 11.
Mars, after January 5.
Jupiter, from February 24 to December 8.
Saturn, until August 1, and after November 11.
Uranus, from January 7 to October 10.
Neptune, until May 20, and after August 24.

RATES OF POSTAGE.

Letters, prepaid by stamps, 2 cts. each oz. or fraction thereof to all parts of the United States and Canada. For *registering* letters 10 cts. additional. *Drop* or *local* letters, 1 ct. each oz. prepaid; 2 cts. in cities with carriers. Government *Postal Cards*, one cent each; if anything except address is pasted on a postal card, letter postage is charged. For 10 cts. additional, immediate delivery of any letter in places designated by the Department. *Second-class matter:* Postage on all *newspapers* and *periodicals* sent to any part of the United States to subscribers must be prepaid at the office of mailing. 1 cent each four ounces or part. *Fourth-class matter:* On all blank cards or envelopes, seeds, cuttings, bulbs, drawings, samples of merchandise, etc., the postage is 1 cent for each ounce.

nly touched it. Immediately, a broad red face ppeared at the peephole, and then bars and olts seemed to be drawn inside, a key turned he lock, and finally the great door swung back; lisclosing to view a paved courtyard, and a wilderness of redbrick walls towering so high as to hide the sky above.

On one side of the courtyard, close to the entrance, was the porter's lodge, and, on the other, a little building about the same size, where new patients were taken in on arrival, to have their admission orders verified and their bundles examined, so that no spirits, or eatables, or anything contrary to rules and regulations should pass into the building, etc. The Infirmary porter, a stout, red-faced personage in a blue uniform and brass buttons, came to the cab-door and regarded the new-comers with stern, official eyes.

"Have you the order?" he asked, in loud, resounding tones; his voice was quite a match for the Infirmary door-bell.

"Yes," said Tom.

"Able to walk?" he asked.

"No," replied Tom, glancing round at Bridget, who was leaning back in the cab, nervous and trembling, dismayed at the great strange place she had come to, and the sharp, stern tones of the porter. Yet she still had one little comfort at her heart, "Baby was going in with her!"

In less time than it takes to write it, a chair was brought out to the cab, and Bridget was carried on it into the office opposite the porter's lodge. Tom followed with the baby, and Jemmy Wiggles with his cab drove away.

The office was a small room with a bare stone floor, and nothing in it save a desk, and a fire burning sluggishly in the grate. A hard-featured woman in a dark gown and a close cap was here to receive Bridget. She went through her work, as laid down by the Board of Charities, with as quick despatch as possible. A friendly welcome to be given was not one of the things set down by those gentlemen in the rules. She was merely to be in her place when new patients arrived, to examine their bundles, and say which ward they were to be taken to. So she did not even pass a "Good-day" to Bridget, but took her bundle from Tom, and began overhauling it. The porter went to the desk and looked at the admission order, and entered some things in a book. And Bridget sat pale and nervous in the chair, while Tom, still holding the baby, stood by and talked to her in a low, troubled voice.

"There's visitin' days, ain't there Bridge?"

"Yes," nodded Bridget.

"The children, and me, and Mrs. Job 'll be able to come and see you," said Tom miserably. Then he turned to the hard-featured woman, and asked, "What days are the visitin' days, ma'm?"

The woman frowned on him. She had divined the state of the family: an unhappy wife, and child, and a drinking husband. Tom's face told the tale. "Sundays are the usual visiting days," she barked out, "but the Infirmary's closed to visitors for the present, by order of the Board, owing to the prevalence of small-pox, and won't be open again till further notice. There it is on the walls," nodding at a printed card on a nail; "you can read for yourself!"

Bridget heard the hard news; she would never see Poll or Sue! No friend, then, would be allowed in to see her, to tell her how the home was getting on! She would never get a friendly hand-clasp or hear a friendly voice!—all this rushed across her mind and chilled her. Yet there was ever that little comfort at her heart, "Baby was going in with her."

The bundle having been examined, and the proper entries made in the day-book by the porter, the hard-featured woman rang a bell that clanged in the distance, and roughly intimated to the husband and wife that the time had come to say "Good-bye," and that they had better be quick about it.

Tom kissed Bridget; he leant forward to give her the baby, but, before it reached the mother's outstretched arms, an arm clad in blue cloth and brass buttons thrust itself forward and placed a barrier between mother and child.

"There's no order for the child," said the stern, hard voice of the porter.

"It's not weaned," urged the mother faintly but quickly.

"What's its age?" inquired the porter.

"What's the little 'un's age, Bridge?" inquired Tom, with an anxious air, but Bridget seemed not to be able to speak. "Eleven months, just about, sir," he said, turning to the porter.

"Over age!" said the official, still making a barrier with his arm. "Children over nine months not admitted with their mothers. Read the rules!" nodding over his shoulder at another printed card on the wall.

"Sir! sir!" began Tom imploringly.

"The Board's rules, not mine!" said the porter, cutting him short. "You'll have to take the child back, sir!"

"Here's its things," said the hard-featured woman, handing to Tom the few tiny garments that she had cast from the mother's bundle; the poor little ragged nightgowns and shirts that Mrs. Job had been at such pains to wash yesterday night.

Tom looked at Bridget, expecting her to make some sign, to burst out in passionate entreaty and tears, and, if entreaty and tears did not avail to gain entrance for her little one, to refuse, with the determination of which he knew she was capable, to enter the Infirmary herself. But, to his astonishment, she did neither of these things; she only went very pale, and an anguished look passed over her face.

Surely, *not*—now that he was to take the baby home, he thought she would make that last appeal to *him* that he had been expecting in the cab. He knew with what despair she would think of the baby in *his* custody. But Bridget said not a word; she made no appeal.

"Victoria Ward," said the porter to the two Infirmary officers who appeared at the office door, in answer to the bell, to carry Bridget away. "Now, sir," to Tom, "time's up!"

Tom, hanging his head in misery, held the baby out for Bridget to kiss, and as he did so, almost as if it knew what was taking place, the baby made what I may call the *pitiful lip*—mothers know it well—that is, when the tiny infant lips, pressed closely together, are drawn down at the sides, and the whole little face works with tears that it seems trying to suppress. Mothers rush at their babies then and hug them up, and kiss them, and call them all the "darlings" and the "pet lambs" in the world.

Bridget saw the pitiful lip and felt the keen pain of other mothers, but she made no attempt to take her baby. She kissed it twice passionately, with her eyes closed—she dared not look at it—and then, with a smothered sob, covering her face with her shawl, she leant back in the chair, and Tom saw her borne away.

Half an hour later Bridget found herself lying in a vast, light, high place, as wide and as long, it seemed to her, as Tripe Court itself. There were windows as lofty, she imagined, as the side windows of St. Peter's Mission Church, running from end to end of the whitewashed walls on either side, and under the windows, rows of narrow beds, as white, they looked to Bridget, as the driven snow, each bed with a head upon its pillow, and at the foot a little red shawl, folded square, giving a bright patch of color to the long, regular lines of snowy counterpanes. There were miles, it seemed to Bridget, of bare boards, without a speck on them, and down the centre of this wholesome floor, in the wide spaces between the rows of beds, there were placed at intervals large, spotless, wooden tables, having, as their one ornament, in the centre, a mug or jug of simple, bright-colored flowers. There was a stove at either end, and the air was pleasantly warm, though the large ventilators in all the windows were open. On the walls hung large illuminated texts, and pictures in plain frames representing scenes in the life of our Saviour.

Two or three old women, in gray almshouse clothes and close caps and felt shoes, were passing to and fro, fetching and carrying; and, more noticeable still, flitting in and out amongst the snowy beds, were two young women in black gowns and linen bib aprons and white caps, whose stiff little edging of gauffered frills set off becomingly the fresh-complexioned faces underneath. These were "Sister Anne" and "Sister Mary," nurses; and the place where Bridget found herself was the Victoria Ward, the largest in the workhouse Infirmary.

Here were gathered together all sorts and conditions of women, and contrasts of every kind were to be found in close proximity to each other. Here in this bed was the brown, battered-faced old woman, accustomed to sell apples and oranges in the street, balancing a basket on her head, her lips, nose and mouth all widened out in straight lines, as if the weight of the basket had flattened her features generally. There in the next a young, fresh-faced girl, an actress, who had fallen from a height in one of the theatres and injured her spine; in the bed next to her a degraded-looking Frenchwoman, whose language and behavior at times shocked everybody: next to her a silvery-haired elderly woman, who had been once, before sickness broke her—oh, the sorrow of it!—a governess in a nobleman's family. She was there, with all her instincts fine and gentle still; and wonderful memories of old grand times in the past—of which she never spoke. The nurses and doctors knew, however, she was different from the rest, though she lay between the same coarse sheets, and ate the same food and fared exactly like the others. There was her voice to tell them, for one thing—no truer indication of breeding is there than the voice—and there were her long, refined hands, and that subtle something about the gently nurtured which asserts itself without effort of its own, no matter what its company or what its surroundings; in the prison, in the barrack-room, in the workhouse, detection is sure. Next to the governess a wrinkled old creature they called "Biddy," a match seller, who had spent half her life in prison for drunkenness. She was eighty now, and blind and light-headed; so she was here; and so on.

A strange, mixed crew, representing nearly every class, and full, as I have said, of striking contrast—the old and young, the lovely and the unlovely, the murmuring and unthankful and the patient and grateful (very few of the latter), and almost every other contrast save rich and poor; only one of those estates was represented here, and that largely; everybody was poor, but nobody was rich. Poverty was the common ground on which everybody met; poverty had mixed them up together in this way, regardless of social distinctions and natural preferences. However taciturn and reticent any one might be about themselves, the inquisitive and curious about them could be certain of this much, that one, at least, of their ailments was named poverty. Poverty here was an accepted fact, there was no blinking at it or hiding it, and though in this case it dwelt in such a large, beautiful, healthy building, it made its grim presence felt in the deep undertone of sadness and discontent which pervaded the atmosphere of the place.

(To be continued.)

for the nobleman of a bad kind, in one of that lord's escapades, and was therefore in favor. My ancestor had peremptory orders to give all building work into his hands, therefore, and he did so, paying the whole year's account on the day after Christmas-day.

"One year, however, the old gentleman was absent on that day. His eldest son had decided to come to America to try his fortune, and my ancestor wanted to go with him to the vessel to see the last of him. He did not return until three days afterward, for travelling was slow in those days. He arrived home late at night and went straight to bed. Whether the agitation of parting with his son had affected him, or the unaccustomed travelling, I do not know, but that night he had a fit of apoplexy, and the next morning he was dead.

"Now the extraordinary fact was discovered that there was a deficiency in his accounts amounting to about three thousand dollars. For over thirty years there had not been a penny wrong, yet now there was this large sum! His widow was sure it would be explained, but no clue to the mystery was found. People shook their heads over it, and were afraid the old gentleman had yielded to temptation in his last days. The builder especially was severe. He wanted his money, he said, and he supposed the old man had given it to his son to start him in America. That idea was so plausible that it was generally accepted, except by our family, who knew that he was incapable of dishonesty. The builder talked to the nobleman, and convinced him, and the end of it was that all the belongings of our family were sold to make good the deficiency. All except that old bureau, and a few other poor sticks of furniture. The family name was disgraced, but every member of it was convinced that vindication would come some day.

It did come, but not for several years, and the widow was dead then. The second son, my grandfather (the eldest was drowned on his voyage here), had a hard life. He clung to the old spot, because running away seemed like admitting the truth of the slander. He was a cabinet-maker, but work was dull; and one day when he had nothing to do, he determined to put the old bureau in good shape and sell it to help him pay his rent. He had scarcely begun his job, when in removing one of the shelves he released a spring, and a secret door in the back flew open. That surprised him. He had used the bureau for years, yet had never suspected that there was a door there. He looked in, hoping there might be money there, but there was nothing but a few papers. He took them out and examined them; then he uttered a loud shout of joy, which made his wife drop her work and rush to his side. The vindication so long expected was in his hand. A letter from the builder and a receipt for three thousand dollars showed that the old man, knowing that he would be away on the usual day of settlement, had paid the building account *before* starting on his journey; and the unscrupulous builder, counting on the receipt being lost, had concealed the fact. My grandfather was overcome with joy. The money was recovered, and that of course was welcome; but what he cared for most was the vindication of the family name. It was in that same old bureau yonder that the papers were found, and now you know why I treasure it."

The Discovery in the Old Bureau.

THE FAMILY OF TRIPE COURT.

By Brenda.

(*Continued from page 830.*)

A BITTER PARTING.

THE Infirmary, as I have said, lay quite a long distance off, altogether apart from the poorhouse, and in another parish. The way to it from Tripe Court was for many a mile through dingy streets and populous districts, with car-tracks intersecting the roads, and omnibuses innumerable, and heavy traffic of all kinds, and a din such as only citizens know, but towards the end—the last mile or two—of the journey, as one got nearer the Infirmary, the character of the road changed, and the air seemed to get purer and the atmosphere lighter. One found one's self in a quiet neighborhood, full of rows and rows of two-storied newly built houses.

The poorhouse Infirmary was a brand-new red-brick building, having been recently erected at a great cost, and the site chosen for it out here on account of its healthiness and the cheapness of the land. It was lofty and vast, built on four sides of a square, and with a broad piece of ground all round it laid out in turf.

The windows were large, running from end to end, tier upon tier, of this great building, each pane of glass shining and clean to let the genial sun in when it shone, and each window having its ventilator for the fresh air to enter by. The Infirmary stood upon ground that was one of those "only the other day fields," and fields there were still on two sides of it, for there was no other building beyond it. On spring days, wafts of serene country air seemed to enter at the doors and windows, and the patients could see real primroses and buttercups and dasies spangling the quiet grass.

As Bridget's hack drew up to the gates, the sun which had been trying for the last half-hour to penetrate the dull winter sky, suddenly shone out, lighting up the great angular red-brick pile, which towered so conspicuously above everything else.

On the road, after they had left Tripe Court far behind them, Tom, looking very miserable, turned to Bridget and expressed his sorrow for what had happened, protesting that it should never happen again, declaring he would "cut" the drink, and begging her forgiveness.

Bridget was too suffering to speak much, or, indeed, even to listen. She scarcely heeded his words: those promises had been made so often only to be broken, and she had not the least more faith that they would be kept now. Tom half expected that to-day, leaving home and the children, she would make one last appeal to him; he would have been better satisfied if she had, for not doing so showed him how far gone in despair was Bridget's heart. He remembered the time when she used to appeal to him, when she used to go down on her knees before him and weep, and beseech him to give up that which was ruining him, body and soul, and making a wreck of their happiness and home; but that was long ago—Tom did not care to count how many years. Bridget never did so now; tears and beseechings she had found all in vain, and she had learnt her sad lesson of having to work and to bear and to suffer in silence.

And yet another lesson: that one that has its fulfilment exemplified almost every day in our police-courts, when bleeding and bruised wives, egged on by relatives who think the limit of long-sufferance has been reached, come to take out a summons against their brutal husbands, but who are ready at the first sign of contrition—the first penitent word—"to make it all up," and to forgive and clasp the hand that dealt them the cruel blow overnight. Yes. Bridget has learnt the lesson of forgiving "until seventy times seven." She always forgave Tom, no matter how many times he transgressed in the week. And true to her old habit, she did so again to-day. Heedless of his other words, in the bewildering din of the streets, she heard his prayer for forgiveness, and, in token that he had it, she nodded her head and said. "All right, Tom."

The sun shone out, I have said, just as Jemmy Wiggles's cab drew up before the Infirmary gates, which were unlocked and opened by a man wearing a cap with "Gate-keeper" written on it, and who came out from a kind of sentry-box stationed just within. The cab, with its melancholy party, passed through into the enclosure up a broad roadway that led to the main entrance of the Infirmary—a huge prison-like door, with heavy nails in it, and a grated peep-hole. Jemmy Wiggles flung the reins on his horse's back and got down from his seat. He rang cautiously a formidable-looking bell at the side, and, when he had done so, he appeared quite startled, for it did not make the little tinkle-tankle of door-bells generally—it made a noise like a railway-bell, and went resounding and echoing all over the place, and yet he had

Entered according to Act of Congress in the year 1887, in the office of the Librarian of Congress at Washington.

Vol. XI., No. 2. Office, 63 Bible House, N. Y. THURSDAY, JANUARY 12, 1888. Annual Subscription, $1.50.

CONTENTS OF THIS NUMBER.

PICTURE OF THE EMPEROR OF GERMANY, HIS ELDEST SON, GRANDSON AND GREAT-GRANDSON with Sketches of their Lives.

THE WOMEN OF AMERICA. Dr. Talmage's Sermon Last Sunday Morning.

ANECDOTES RELATED AT RECENT EVANGELISTIC MEETINGS.

THE SEVENTY SEPTENNARIES.

CURRENT EVENTS: The Speaker's Committees—The Great Strike in Pennsylvania—A Significant Election in England etc.

A Fight for Life With a Bear—A God-Directed Shilling—A Missionary's Escape from a Chinese Mob—A Paralyzed Cripple's Testimony—An African King Mollified—A Chinese Gate Keeper.

SMALL-RAIN PREACHING. A New Sermon by C. H. Spurgeon.

PORTRAITS OF THE CROWN PRINCESS OF GERMANY, AND DR. MORELL MACKENZIE, with Picture of the Villa Zirio at San Remo.

HAZELTINE'S REMORSE. (With Illustration.)

THE FAMILY OF TRIPE COURT. (Continued.)

JESUS AND THE AFFLICTED. By Mrs. Baxter.

The Emperor of Germany, His Eldest Son, Grandson and Great-Grandson.

THE HOHENZOLLERNS.

THE group depicted on the first page is one that is sufficiently remarkable to arrest attention. It represents the four generations of the German Imperial family, in the line of succession to the Imperial throne. In the centre the aged Emperor, now more than ninety years old; on his right, his eldest son, the Crown Prince, whose character and achievements have endeared him to the whole German nation, and whose mysterious affliction, whether it be cancer of the throat, as is feared, or some less fatal malady, has called forth public sympathy in a most astonishing degree. On the Emperor's left is his grandson, Prince William, the next heir but one to the throne, and on his knees the babe, Prince Frederick, the son of Prince William and the great grandson of the Emperor. Truly a most remarkable group.

THE EMPEROR.

Remarkable Vicissitudes—A Memorable Meeting with his Mother—Her Queenly Virtues—Early Bravery—First Entry Into France—His Exile in 1848—Recall and Campaign in the Palatinate—Becomes Regent in 1858—Succeeds his Brother in 1861—Momentous Appointment of Bismarck—The Austro-Prussian War of 1866—The Franc German War of 1870—Emperor of Germany.

THE most prominent events in the career of the aged Emperor of Germany stand in sharp contrast with each other. In his long life of ninety years he has passed through vicissitudes of the most momentous character, not to himself only, but to Germany and all Europe. He was born on March 22, 1797, and is the second son of Frederick William III., King of Prussia, and the grand-nephew of Frederick the Great. The first authentic glimpse we have of him is one of gloom and sadness. Its date is in the late October, 1806, when he was little more than nine years old. A dull, dreary day was nearing its close when a beautiful and noble lady with a few attendants entered Schwedt, a small town on the banks of the Oder, in the province of Brandenburg. She was flying through Prussia to the Russian frontier. Her first business on her arrival at Schwedt was to seek out another party which had preceded her. It was composed of a tutor and two boys. She found them, and the two boys were wrapped in their mother's arms while she caressed them and wept over them. The lady was Queen Louise, the wife of Frederick William III., King of Prussia, and the younger of the two boys is now the aged Emperor of Germany. The battle of Jena had been fought a few days before that meeting at Schwedt, and it was the news that in that battle Napoleon had defeated her husband and the Prussian army which sent

The Fugitive Queen

with her two sons toward the frontier. "In the future," said the beautiful Queen, addressing her sons—"in the future, when your mother no longer lives, call this unhappy hour up in your memories. Shed tears over your mother's memory, as I now weep over the prostration of my country. But do not be satisfied with tears. Act; develop your powers. Be men, and strive for the name of soldiers and heroes." Not long afterward, Queen Louise died broken-hearted, but her words lived in the heart of her younger son. If her sight had been prophetic, even that hour, dark as it was, would have been illumined by a vision that would have consoled her. Could she have looked across an interval of sixty-four years, she would have seen the boy she was then caressing, a white-haired, stalwart soldier-king, returning in triumph to his capital with a Napoleon a captive in his train.

Queen Louise was no ordinary woman, and it is probable that her influence exercised no little power in the formation of her son's character. While still a mere girl, she had been brought from Mecklenburg, to become the wife of the Crown Prince of Prussia, and had been introduced into a court that was a perfect cesspool of debauchery. King Frederick William II., her husband's father, was an abandoned, vicious man, whose rule in court and state was directed by a bevy of mistresses, and whose life was made up of disgusting orgies. His example was followed by his nobles, and the whole court was vicious and corrupt. The young girl in the midst of this debauchery was preserved by God from contamination, and the home over which she presided was the one pure spot in the reeking court atmosphere of Berlin. In 1797 her husband succeeded to the throne on the death of his vicious father, and a new order of court life was inaugurated.

Those were troublous times, and the boy was early introduced to scenes of warfare and bloodshed. He was made an officer in his tenth year,

The Youngest Member of the Army,

as he is now the oldest. He gave proof of his intrepidity even at that early age, for at the battle of La Fère Champenoise he was intrusted with the conveyance of an order to the general in command of a division, and galloped with it through a hot fire of artillery, and won his first military decoration, that of St. George, by his bravery. After a short interval of six years, during which Prussia groaned under the heel of Napoleon I., the outbreak of war once more called the Prince to the field. With his father he crossed the Rhine in 1813, and for the first time set foot on French territory. With the downfall of Napoleon in 1815, his youthful military exploits ended.

His Exile

in 1848 is another remarkable epoch in the history of the Emperor. His father had then been dead eight years, and his brother Frederick William IV. was King of Prussia. The troubles of that time were as perplexing as those of the preceding time, but they were of a different character. The people of Prussia were agitated by the general discontent that passed through Europe like a subterranean convulsion, and they rose in insurrection. They demanded that the promise of Constitutional government, given to them by the late King, should now be kept, and Frederick William, strongly supported by his brother, the present Emperor, refused it. The people then took up arms, and on March 21, after a fight in the streets of Berlin, in which two hundred and sixteen men were killed fighting behind barricades, the King surrendered. He sent away his troops, banished his brother, who was unpopular with the people, and summoned a Constitutional Convention, which assembled in Berlin on May 22, 1848. A period of anarchy followed, in which arsenals were plundered and outrages of all kinds committed. On December 5 the Constitutional Convention was dissolved, and the King and his ministers framed a Constitution to suit themselves. The King immediately recalled his brother, and commissioned him to suppress the insurrection, which still flourished in Baden and the Palatinate. He proceeded with so much vigor, that in six weeks the King's authority was re-established throughout the country.

King of Prussia.

In 1858 the King was seized with mental illness, and, he having no children, William was made Regent. Three years later the King died, and on January 2, 1861, William succeeded him. The coronation took place on October 18.

The most momentous step William ever took, and one that has colored every event of his reign, and has changed the history of Europe, was taken the following year. He took Otto von Bismarck from a diplomatic post, and made him his chief adviser. Since that time Bismarck has been the virtual ruler of the country, and William has loyally supported, and, in a sense, obeyed him. The events of the past twenty years are fresh in the recollection of the public, and only require brief mention.

Emperor of Germany.

In June, 1866, war was declared against Austria, and after a short campaign, in which William I. and the royal princes took part, Austria was compelled to make a humiliating peace. This gave Prussia the position she had long craved, of head of the North German Confederation, comprising twenty-two States, containing a population of twenty-nine millions.

The terrible Franco-German War of 1870–71, in which Prussia and France joined in death grapple for the chief place in Europe, resulted in the complete humiliation of France, and also in the realization of Prince Bismarck's idea of a united Germany. On January 18, 1871, in the Hall of Mirrors, in the Palace of the French Kings at Versailles, King William of Prussia was proclaimed Emperor of Germany

THE CROWN PRINCE.

THE second figure, in the order of age, in the group pictured on the first page is the oldest son of the Emperor, the Crown Prince Frederick William Nicholas Charles. He was born at Potsdam on October 18, 1831, and is therefore now fifty-six years of age. While little more than a child he entered the military service, rose to the rank of general, and held numerous appointments. In 1866, when war broke out between Prussia and Austria, he had under his orders three army corps, besides the Guard Corps under Prince Augustus of Würtemberg. The Crown Prince led his army of 125,000 men from Silesia through the passes of the Sudetic Hills, an operation exposed to great difficulties, and to considerable danger. After a series of severe battles, he reached the field of Sadowa in the crisis of the battle, and decided the fortunes of the day. His march from Miletin to Koniggrätz, and his series of victories on entering Bohemia, established his reputation as an energetic commander.

In the war between Germany and France the Crown Prince bore a conspicuous part. The close of July, 1870, found him on the Rhine frontier, in command of the Third German Army, comprising in all about 200,000 men and 500 guns. To his part fell some of the most severe fighting of the campaign including the battles of Weissenburg and Woerth. His corps also played a most important part in the decisive day of Sedan. With his cousin Prince Frederick Charles, he sustained the terrific onslaught of MacMahon's forces, and conducted the difficult operation of crossing the River Meuse. He subsequently assisted in the investiture of the French capital, and remained in the vicinity of Paris until the conclusion of peace. On October 28, he was created a Field-Marshal of Prussia, and on November 8, a Russian Field-Marshal. In 1878, when the Emperor was wounded by the assassin Nobiling, the Crown Prince was appointed Regent till his father's recovery.

The Crown Prince is exceedingly popular in Germany—how popular was not known until last year, when rumors began to circulate that his life was in danger. The report that he was suffering from *cancer of the throat* produced the utmost concern throughout Germany, and keen anxiety manifested ever since in his state. Medical opinion is still divided as to the nature of the disease, and hopes are entertained by some of the physicians that the growth which has appeared in his throat may not be cancer, after all. The noble qualities which have distinguished his public career have been conspicuous in his sickness, and his physicians speak in terms of the highest admiration of his equanimity patience and cheerfulness.

The Prince married on January 25, 1858, Vi[illegible]toria Adelaide, Princess Royal of Great Brita[illegible] *whose portrait appears on page twenty-eight,* [illegible] whom he has seven children, three sons a[illegible] four daughters.

PRINCE WILLIAM.

The third member of the group on the [illegible] page is the eldest son of the Crown Prin[illegible]nd the Princess Victoria, Frederick William [illegible] Albert. He is nearly twenty-nine years [illegible], having been born January 27, 1859. It w[illegible] be difficult to imagine a greater contrast of po[illegible]sition and character than that existing [illegible]een him and his father. It is in part du[illegible] his training. Both the Emperor and Pri[illegible] Bismarck have repeateested their dissatisfaction with the Cnce, who is a man of peaceful tempersh a strong leaning toward constitutionment. The Emperor's belief in thight of kings, and Bismarck's high-hajestic policy, have never had the syf the heir to the throne. He is conder the domination of his wife, thPrincess, who is notoriously the ablestf Europe.

The Emperor arck perceive that when Frederick co throne, Germany will be ruled on th pattern, and the Emperor will be a stitutional sovereign like Queen Victo have never concealed their horrot state of government, and they hae Princess's life a burden to her in ce. Among other trials she had to u been the alienation of her eldeshe Emperor, under Prince Bismarck'sxercised his right to control and education of his grandson, who in tof nature will wear the crown of Gernce William has, in consequence, been abhor the constitutional principleother, with which his father has bed. The Emperor could not change views, but he has endeavored, and tent succeeded, in molding his grandacter on his own model. Prince Wkes England, and things English, and be a strong personal ruler like hiser.

The young man his position in the Bismarck party in, and there is no more intensely vidisan of that section, as opposed ncess's or English party, than he. Sleath of his father unhappily precededof his grandfather, and so he follow tieror on the throne, he is precisely thenan to answer any demand for increar liberty, as Rehoboam answered thf the ten tribes (1. Kings 12: 14), andent temper of the German people, th not be dissimilar.

Prince William altogether an enviable one. Thoughagnificent station, with the prospect g the most powerful ruler in Europeonally the prey of disease and deforndisease which affected his grand-uFrederick William IV., and which sflict in greater or less degree the He, in alternate generations, has man in his constitution. The technic the part affected is *otitis media*, wheen the tympanum and the base of thhe Prince is subject to abscesses which, at intervals, drain off the poisystem. Should a time come when accumulates and no abscess relieveimation of the brain will set in and heito insanity, or die a raving maniac. the Prince suffers from a deformitynd and arm are almost useless to hire withered, and it is only by a great e is able, at reviews to conceal its weapublic observation.

Prince Williamd in 1881 to Princess Victoria, of olstein-Augustenburg, a lady of wer, popular neither with court nor pe

PRINCE FREDERICK,

the great-grandsoperor, who, in the illustration on th, is depicted lying a babe in the emreat-grandfather, is too young to tory. But he is of more ous interny. The two lives whi stand betd the throne are both precarious, impossible that the successor of the r Emperor may be the babe he is nursing. In that case, Germany werned, during his minority, by a Rea terrific struggle would take placene two sections of the court as to . It is impossible to read of theselals and troubles, without thankfulpublican institutions save us from culties.

ANECDOTES RELATED AT RECENT EVANGELISTIC MEETINGS.

Trying to Buy Salvation.—The Rev. Mr. Hood at the Glasgow convention, said: "Many years ago I went to visit an old woman. I took her some cakes, and read the Bible and prayed with her. Why did I do this. Because, I am sorry to say, my heart was not right with God, and I knew it; so I tried to win His favor in this way, just as it were trying to pay for my salvation; but it would not do. I had to come and be reconciled to Him, through the death of His Son, and since then I have given myself up in full surrender to Him."

A Ruined Marquis' Gratitude.—The Rev. Mr. Graham said: "A marquis who, by an unforeseen event, had lost all his property, but who fully trusted God, on being made aware of his loss at once dropped on his knees and said, 'Oh God, I thank Thee that Thou hast done, not my will, but thine.' God's will in this case, even though it involved such a financial loss, was acceptable to His sincere follower. Some people talk of God's will being acceptable, as if it were acceptable to God, but not to them. That is puerile. When we say God's will is acceptable, we should mean acceptable to His servants, to Christians who accept His will, even when opposed to their own, joyfully."

The Latch on Our Side of the Door.—The Rev. W. Haslam observed: "When I was walking in one of the London streets a short time ago, a Paris pastor came forward and accosted me thus: 'Excuse me, but were you not in Paris some time ago?' I said 'Yes, I was,' and then he inquired, "Did you not in one of your addresses there say that *the latch was on our side of the door?*' 'Yes, I believe I did say so,' I replied. 'Well,' he answered, 'I always thought it was on the Lord's side, and I kept knocking and knocking and knocking, until you said those words, and what a joy came over me! I lifted the latch and let the Saviour in. Since then all has been changed, my church, my congregation, my work, and everything about me!' And the good pastor was changed too. Oh, dear friends, remember that the latch is on your own side of the door" (Revelation 3: 20.)

Father's Welcome Home—The Rev. Mr. Hood remarked: "At one period I had occasion to leave home for a considerable time, and when I returned my two girls had just come from school, and, hearing me speak in the hall, they came down-stairs to greet me. The elder came walking down coolly and calmly without the least emotion, and kept her eyes fixed upon my travelling bag all the time, while her look seemed to say, 'I wonder what father has brought for me?' Her younger sister came running down, breathless with haste, and throwing her arms around my neck, she could only say, while she clung to me, 'Father! father! father! I am *so* glad to have you home.' I need not tell you which of my two girls pleased me most. Ah! I think that is just what many of God's own children do. They come too frequently to see *what they can get* from Him. Oh, let us no longer draw nigh to Him in such a spirit, but rather let us be sending up one continual song of praise to Him who has promised to withhold no good thing from His loving children."

False Props Knocked Away.—An Evangelist said: "There was a man who was in the habit of attending my meetings, a respectable, intelligent workingman, and who possessed good reasoning faculties. I knew he was very anxious about his soul, but I did not speak to him on the subject, for I saw that the Holy Spirit was moving within him. Sometimes he would go into a great passion, but still I did not speak to him. One day he came to me, and said, 'If ever I had props before, they are all gone now.' 'Thank God,' I replied, 'and if ever you rested upon props, they were all of your own making; they never came from God.' 'Now,' he continued, 'I want to know how to come to Christ.' It was easy to deal with a man in that state of mind. 'Do you believe in the Word of God?' I asked. 'Yes, I think I do,' was the hesitating reply. 'And you believe in the Lord Jesus Christ?' 'Oh, yes, I believe in Him.' 'But,' I said, to test the man, 'how can you believe in Him whom you never have seen nor felt?' He answered: 'Just because God says it.' 'Very well,' I replied, 'All you have to do is to receive Christ who is now beside us, for, "As many as received Him, to them gave He power to become the sons of God." Then the man bowed his head a moment and prayed. Then raising it again, he said: 'Now I know that I am a son of God. It was all false propping before; but now I trust firmly on the Rock of Ages.' That man has since lived an active Christian life, and only last week he addressed a Gospel meeting."

Turned Out by an Infidel.—After Climbing up a dark staircase, a missionary entered the back room of the top floor of a large house, but its infidel inhabitant, with abusive language, quickly turned him out again. Nothing daunted, the missionary repeated his effort to gain admission. On one occasion, finding the door ajar, the missionary observed the man painting a scene for a neighboring theatre, expressed his admiration of the picture, and of the man's artistic skill, and thus gave the first blow to his opposition. He was drawn into conversation and pointed to Christ. But the man was found to be a socialist leader, and a writer for several low publications. The missionary at length agreed to his wish that he should read a socialist print, on the condition that the socialist should read the "Gospel of St. John." The proposition was on both sides carried out. The man's rudeness ceased. He had become a student of the Word of God, and the Holy Spirit having applied that word to his conscience, his sin of six-and-twenty years was quickly terminated in the presence of the missionary and his wife by a lawful entrance upon marriage bonds. The man's hearty avowal then was, "*I serve the Lord Christ, and must obey Him.*" He mingled with his former infidel companions, and successfully directed them to Jesus. They saw and wondered at the change, and the organized infidelity of that district received a check.

"In the Jungle."—A Careless Young Officer in India joined some friends in an expedition to shoot tigers in the jungle. He had a day's sport, but, in some way, toward evening he missed his companions and was left alone. He made every effort to find his way out, but all in vain. He fired off his ammunition in the hope of finding some guide, but without success. He then realized his perilous position, but determined to part with his life as dearly as possible. Night was fast approaching, so he sought safety from the wild animals in a tree. Before he climbed it, however, he thought he would pray for God's help, though it was years since he had ever knelt down for this purpose. The young man repeated the prayer learnt in early days, until he came to one sentence. "Forgive me all my sins, for Jesus Christ's sake." At that moment it pleased God by His spirit to recall to his memory, as it seemed to him, the long course of sins he had committed. It seemed all spread out before him as in a panorama. Whatever he had said or done amiss came back to him in such a way that it weighed like a mighty burden on his conscience. The perilous position in which he stood, the consciousness that he might that very night have to face a terrible death, together with the instruction of early days, was thus made the means of awakening him to the sense of his sin, and of leading him most truly to seek pardon from God. This one prayer he offered again and again, "Forgive me all my sins, for Jesus Christ's sake." Then he arose from his knees, and found it was quite dark. But some rays of light and comfort had entered his heart. But a few minutes had elapsed, and he heard the sound of a rifle. He answered it by a shout, which was heard by the friends who had come to seek for him. Thus was he saved from danger; but he returned to his tent a far different man, and eventually became a true Christian.

THE WOMEN OF AMERICA.

Women Who Fight The Battle of Life Alone.

Dr. Talmage's Sermon, Preached Last Sunday Morning, January 8, 1888.

"Every wise woman buildeth her house." Prov. 14 : 1.

Single Lives Better than Bad Marriages—Women who Support Husbands and Sons—A Union of Dove and Vulture—Celibacy a Necessity for Some—The Miseries they Escape—Girls Should Learn the Science of Self-Support—Why They Fail—Things They Can Do—Shoemaking Better than Slipper-Embroidering—The Unromantic and Commonplace to be Cultivated—Two Sad Sights—Learn to Provide Life's Indispensables—Women who Have Succeeded—The Daughter of the Regiment.

WOMAN a mere adjunct to man, an appendix to the masculine volume, an appendage, a sort of after-thought, something thrown in to make things even—that is the heresy entertained and implied by some men. This is evident to them: Woman's insignificance, as compared to man, is evident to them, because Adam was first created, and then Eve. They don't read the whole story, or they would find that the porpoise and the bear and the hawk were created before Adam, so that this argument, drawn from priority of creation, might prove that the sheep and the dog were greater than man. No. Woman was an independent creation, and was intended, if she chose, to live alone, to walk alone, act alone, think alone, and fight her battles alone. The Bible says it is not good for man to be alone, but never says it is not good for woman to be alone; and the simple fact is, that many women who are harnessed for life in the marriage relation would be a thousand-fold better off if they were alone.

Who are these men who, year after year, hang around hotels and engine-houses and theatre doors, and come in and out to bother busy clerks and merchants and mechanics, doing nothing, when there is plenty to do? They are

Men Supported by their Wives

and mothers. If the statistics of any of our cities could be taken on this subject, you would find that a vast multitude of women not only support themselves, but masculines. A great legion of men amount to nothing, and a woman, by marriage, manacled to one of these nonentities, needs condolence. A woman standing outside the marriage relation is several hundred thousand times better off than a woman badly married. Many a bride, instead of a wreath of orange blossoms, might more properly wear a bunch of nettles and nightshade, and, instead of the Wedding March, a more appropriate tune would be the Dead March in Saul, and, instead of a banquet of confectionery and ices, there might be more appropriately spread a table covered with apples of Sodom.

The Dove and the Vulture.

Many an attractive woman, of good sound sense in other things, has married one of these men to reform him. What was the result? Like when a dove, noticing that a vulture was rapacious and cruel, set about to reform it, and said, "I have a mild disposition, and I like peace, and was brought up in the quiet of a dove-cote, and I will bring the vulture to the same liking by marrying him." So, one day, after the vulture declared he would give up his carnivorous habits and cease longing for blood of flock and herd, at an altar of rock covered with moss and lichen, the twain were married, a bald-headed eagle officiating, the vulture saying, "With all my dominion of earth and sky, I thee endow, and promise to love and cherish till death do us part." But one day the dove in her fright, saw the vulture busy at a carcass, and cried, "Stop that! did you not promise me that you would quit your carnivorous and filthy habits if I married you?" "Yes," said the vulture, "but if you don't like my way, you can leave," and with one angry stroke of beak, and another fierce clutch of claw, the vulture left the dove eyeless and wingless and lifeless. And a flock of robins flying past, cried to each other and said, "See there! that comes from a dove's marrying a vulture to reform him."

Many a woman who has had the hand of a young inebriate offered, but declined it, or who was asked to chain her life to a man selfish, or of bad temper, and refused the shackles, will bless God throughout all eternity that she escaped that earthly Pandemonium.

Enforced Celibacy.

Besides all this, in our country about one million men were sacrificed in our Civil War, and that decreed a million women to celibacy. Besides that, since the war, several armies of men as large as the Federal and Confederate armies put together, have fallen under malt liquors and distilled spirits, so full of poisoned ingredients that the work was done more rapidly, and the victims fell while yet young. And if fifty thousand men are destroyed every year by strong drink before marriage, that makes in the twenty-three years since the war one million one hundred and fifty thousand men slain, and decrees one million one hundred and fifty thousand women to celibacy. Take, then, the fact that so many women are unhappy in their marriage, and the fact that the slaughter of two million one hundred and fifty thousand men, by war and rum combined, decides that at least that number of women shall be unaffianced for life, my text comes in with a cheer and a potency and appropriateness that I never saw in it before when it says, "Every wise woman buildeth her house;" that is, let woman be her own architect, lay out her own plans, be her own supervisor, achieve her own destiny.

In addressing these women who will have to fight the battle alone, I congratulate you on

Your Happy Escape.

Rejoice forever that you will not have to navigate the faults of the other sex, when you have faults enough of your own. Think of the bereavements you avoid, of the risks of unassimilated temper which you will not have to run, of the cares you will never have to carry, and of the opportunity of outside usefulness from which marital life would have partially debarred you, and that you are free to go and come as one who has the responsibilities of a household can seldom be. God has not given you a hard lot, as compared with your sisters. When young women shall make up their minds at the start that masculine companionship is not a necessity in order to happiness, and that there is a strong probability that they will have to fight the battle of life alone, they will be getting the timber ready for their own fortune, and their saw and axe and plane sharpened for its construction, since "Every wise woman buildeth her house."

As no boy ought to be brought up without learning some business at which he could earn a livelihood, so no girl ought to be brought up without learning

The Science of Self-Support.

The difficulty is that many a family goes sailing on the high tides of success, and the husband and father depends on his own health and acumen for the welfare of his household, but one day he gets his feet wet, and in three days pneumonia has closed his life, and the daughters are turned out on a cold world to earn bread, and there is nothing practical that they can do. The friends come in and hold consultation.

"Give music lessons," says an outsider. Yes, that is a useful calling, and if you have great genius for it, go on in that direction. But there are enough music teachers now starving to death in all our towns and cities, to occupy all the piano stools and sofas and chairs and front-door steps of the city. Besides that, the daughter has been playing only for amusement, and is only at the foot of the ladder, to the top of which a great multitude of masters on piano and harp and flute and organ have climbed.

"Put the bereft daughters as saleswomen in stores," says another adviser. But there they must compete with salesmen of long experience, or with men who have served an apprenticeship in commerce and who began as shop boys at ten years of age. Some kind-hearted dry-goods man, having known the father, now gone, says, "We are not in need of any more help just now, but send your daughters to my store, and I will do as well by them as possible." Very soon the question comes up, Why do not the female employees of that establishment get as much wages as the male employees? For the simple reason, in many cases, the females were suddenly flung by misfortune behind that counter, while the males have from the day they left the public school been learning the business.

How is this evil to be cured? Start clear back in the homestead and

Teach Your Daughters

that life is an earnest thing, and that there is a possibility, if not a strong probability, that they will have to fight the battle of life alone. Let every father and mother say to their daughters, "Now, what would you do for a livelihood if what I now own were swept away by financial disaster, or old age, or death should end my career?"

"Well, I could paint on pottery and do such decorative work." Yes, that is beautiful, and if you have genius for it go on in that direction. But there are enough busy at that now to make a line of hardware from here to the East River and across the bridge.

"Well, I could make recitations in public and earn my living as a dramatist; I could render *King Lear* or *Macbeth* till your hair would rise on end, or give you Sheridan's Ride or Dickens's Pickwick." Yes, that is a beautiful art, but ever and anon, as now, there is an epidemic of dramatization that makes hundreds of households nervous with the cries and shrieks and groans of young tragediennes dying in the fifth act, and the trouble is that while your friends would like to hear you, and really think that you could surpass Ristori and Charlotte Cushman and Fanny Kemble of the past, to say nothing of the present, you could not, in the way of living, in ten years earn ten cents.

My advice to all girls and all unmarried women, whether in affluent homes or in homes where most stringent economies are grinding, to learn to do some kind of work that the world must have while the world stands. I am glad to see a marvellous change for the better, and that women have found out that there are hundreds of practical

Things that a Woman can Do

for a living if she begins soon enough, and that men have been compelled to admit it. You and I can remember when the majority of occupations were thought inappropriate for women; but our Civil War came, and the hosts of men went forth from North and South; and to conduct the business of our cities during the patriotic absence, women were demanded by the tens of thousands to take the vacant places; and multitudes of women, who had been hitherto supported by fathers and brothers and sons, were compelled from that time to take care of themselves. From that time a mighty change took place favorable to female employment.

Among the occupations appropriate for woman I place the following, into many of which she has already entered, and all the others she will enter: *Stenography*, and you may find her at nearly all the reportorial stands in our educational, political and religious meetings. *Savings banks*, the work clean and honorable, and who so great a right to toil there, for a woman founded the first savings bank—Mrs. Priscilla Wakefield? *Copyists*, and there is hardly a professional man that does not need the service of her penmanship; and, as amanuensis, many of the greatest books of our day have been dictated for her writing. There they are as florists and confectioners and music teachers and book-keepers, for which they are specially

Qualified by Patience and Accuracy;

and *Wood-engraving*, in which the Cooper Institute has turned out so many qualified; and *Telegraphy*, for which she is specially prepared, as thousands of the telegraphic offices will testify. *Photography*, and in nearly all our establishments they may be found there at cheerful work. As *workers in ivory* and gutta percha and gum elastic and tortoise-shell and gilding, and in chemicals, in porcelain, in terra cotta. As *post-mistresses*, and the President is giving them appointments all over the land.

As *proof-readers, as translators*, as modellers, as designers, as draught-women, as lithographers, as teachers in schools and seminaries, for which they are especially endowed,

The First Teacher

of every child, by Divine arrangement, being a woman. As physicians, having graduated after a regular course of study from the female colleges of our large cities, where they get as scientific and thorough preparation as any doctors ever had, and go forth to a work which no one but women could so appropriately and delicately do. On the lecturing platform; for you know the brilliant success of Mrs. Livermore and Mrs. Hallowell and Mrs. Willard and Mrs. Lathrop. As physiological lecturers to their own sex, for which service there is a demand appalling and terrific. As preachers of the Gospel, and all the protests of ecclesiastical courts cannot hinder them, for they have a pathos and a power in their religious utterances that men can never reach. Witness all those who have heard their mother pray.

O, young women of America! as many of you will have to fight your own battles alone, do not wait until you are flung of disaster, and your father is dead, and all the resources of your family have been scattered; but now, while in a good house and environed by all prosperities, learn how to do some kind of

Work that the World Must Have

as long as the world stands. Turn your attention from the embroidery of fine slippers, of which there is a surplus, and make a useful shoe. Expend the time in which you adorn a cigar-case in learning how to make a good, honest loaf of bread. Turn your attention from the making of flimsy nothings to the manufacturing of important somethings.

Much of the time spent in young ladies' seminaries in studying what are called the "higher branches," might better be expended in teaching them something by which they could support themselves. If you are going to be teachers, or if you have so much assured wealth that you can always dwell in those high regions, trigonometry of course, metaphysics of course, Latin and Greek and German and French and Italian of course, and a hundred other things of course; but if you are not expecting to teach, and your wealth is not established beyond misfortune, after you have learned the ordinary branches, take hold of that kind of study that will pay in dollars and cents in case you are thrown on your own resources. Learn to do something better than anybody else. Buy Virginia Penny's book, entitled "The Employments of Women," and learn there are five hundred ways in which a woman may earn a living.

"No, no!" says some young woman, "I will not undertake anything so

Unromantic And Commonplace

as that. An excellent author writes that after he had, in a book, argued for efficiency in womanly work in order to success, and positive apprenticeship by way of preparation, a prominent chemist advertised that he would teach a class of women to become druggists and apothecaries if they would go through an apprenticeship as men do; and a printer advertised that he would take a class of women to learn the printer's trade if they would go through an apprenticeship as men do, and how many, according to the account of the authoress, do you suppose applied to become skilled in the druggist business and printing business? Not one!

"But," you ask, "what would my father and mother say if they saw I was doing such

Unfashionable Work?"

Throw the whole responsibility upon the pastor of the Brooklyn Tabernacle, who is constantly hearing of young women in all these cities, who, unqualified by their previous luxurious surroundings for the awful struggle of life into which they have been suddenly hurled, seemed to have nothing left them but a choice between starvation and damnation. There they go along the street seven o'clock in the wintry mornings, through the slush and storm, to the place where they shall earn only half enough for subsistence, the daughters of once prosperous merchants, lawyers, clergymen, artists, bankers and capitalists, who brought up their children under the infernal delusion that it was not high-toned for women to learn a profitable calling. Young women! take this affair in your own hand, and let there be an insurrection in all prosperous families of Brooklyn and New York and Christendom on the part of the daughters of this day, demanding knowledge in occupations and styles of business by which they may be their own defence and their own support if all fatherly and husbandly and brotherly hands forever fail them. I have seen

Two Sad Sights—

the one a woman in all the glory of her young life, stricken by disease, and in a week lifeless in a home of which she had been the pride. As her hands were folded over the still heart and her eyes closed for the last slumber, and she was taken out amid the lamentations of kindred and friends, I thought that was a sadness immeasurable. But I have seen something compared with which that scene was bright and songful. It was a young woman who had been all her days amid wealthy surroundings, by the visit of death and bankruptcy to the household turned out on a cold world without one lesson about how to get food or shelter, and into the awful whirlpool of city life, where strong ships have gone down, and for twenty years not one word has been heard from her. Vessels last week went out on the Atlantic Ocean looking for a shipwrecked craft that was left alone and forsaken on the sea a few weeks ago, with the idea of bringing it into port. But who shall ever bring again into the harbor of peace and hope and heaven that lost womanly immortal, driven in what tempest, aflame in what conflagration, sinking into what abyss? O God, help! O Christ, rescue!

My sisters, give not your time to learning fancy work which the world may dispense with in hard times, but connect your skill with

The Indispensables of Life.

The world will always want something to wear and something to eat, and shelter and fuel for the body, and knowledge for the mind, and religion for the soul. And all these things will continue to be the necessaries, and if you fasten your energies upon occupations and professions thus related, the world will be unable to do without you. Remember, that in proportion as you are skilful in anything, your rivalries become less. For unskilled toil, women by the million. But you may rise to where there are only a thousand; and still higher, till there are only a hundred; and still higher, till there are only ten; and still higher, in some particular department, till there is only a unit, and that yourself. For a while you may keep wages and a place through the kindly sympathies of an employer, but you will eventually get no more compensation than you can make yourself worth.

Let me say to all women who have already entered upon the battle of life, that the time is coming when woman shall not only get as much salary and wages as men get, but for certain styles of employment women will have higher salary and more wages, for the reason that for some styles of work they have more adaptation. But this

Justice Will Come to Woman,

not through any sentiment of gallantry, not because woman is physically weaker than man, and, therefore, ought to have more consideration shown her, but because through her finer natural taste and more grace of manner, and quicker perception, and more delicate touch, and more educated adroitness, she will, in certain callings, be to her employer worth ten per cent. more, or twenty per cent. more than the other sex. She will not get it by asking for it, but by earning it, and it shall be hers by lawful conquest.

Now, men of America, be fair, and

Give the Women a Chance.

Are you afraid that they will do some of your work, and hence harm your prosperities? Remember that there are scores of thousands of men doing women's work. Do not be afraid! God knows the end from the beginning, and He knows how many people this world can feed and shelter, and when it gets too full He will end the world, and, if need be, start another. God will halt the inventive faculty, which, by producing a machine that will do the work of ten or twenty or a hundred men and women, will leave that number of people without work. I hope that there will not be invented another sewing machine, or reaping machine, or corn-thresher, or any other new machine, for the next five hundred years. We want no more wooden hands and iron hands and steel hands and electric hands substituted for men and women, who would otherwise do the work and get the pay and earn the livelihood.

But God will arrange all, and all we have to do is to do our best and trust Him for the rest. Let me cheer all women fighting the battle of life alone, with the fact of thousands of

Women Who Have Won

the day. Mary Lyon, founder of Mount Holyoke Female Seminary, fought the battle alone; Adelaide Newton, the tract distributor, alone; Fidelia Fisk, the consecrated missionary, alone; Dorothea Dix, the angel of the insane asylums, alone; Caroline Herschel, the indispensable reinforcement of her brother, alone; Maria Takrzewska, the heroine of the Berlin hospital, alone; Helen Chalmers, patron of sewing-schools for the poor of Edinburgh, alone. And thousands and tens of thousands of women, of whose bravery and self-sacrifice and glory of character the world has made no record, but whose deeds are in the heavenly archives of martyrs who fought the battle alone, and, though unrecognized for the short thirty or fifty or eighty years of their earthly existence, shall through the quintillion ages of the higher world be pointed out with the admiring cry, "These are they who came out of great tribulation and had their robes washed and make white in the blood of the Lamb."

Let me also say, for the encouragement of all women fighting the battle of life alone, that their conflict will soon end. There is one word written over the faces of many of them, and that word is Despair. My sister, you need

Appeal to Christ,

who comforted the sisters of Bethany in their domestic trouble, and who in His last hours forgot all the pangs of His own hands and feet and heart, as He looked into the face of maternal anguish, and called a friend's attention to it, in substance saying, "John, I cannot take care of her any longer. Do for her as I would have done, if I had lived. Behold thy mother!" If, under the pressure of unrewarded and unappreciated work, your hair is whitening and the wrinkles come, rejoice that you are nearing the hour of escape from your very last fatigue, and may your departure be as pleasant as that of Isabella Graham, who closed her life with a smile and the word "Peace."

The daughter of a regiment in any army is all surrounded by bayonets of defence, and, in the battle, whoever falls, she is kept safe. And you are the daughter of the regiment commanded by the Lord of Hosts. After all, you are not fighting the battle of life alone. All heaven is on your side. You will be wise to appropriate to yourself the words of sacred rhythm:

One who has known in storms to sail
  I have on board;
Above the roaring of the gale
  I hear my Lord.

He holds me; when the billows smite
  I shall not fall.
If short, 'tis sharp; if long, 'tis light;
  He tempers all.

A GOD-DIRECTED SHILLING.

In a recently published autobiography of an earnest clergyman, not a famous one, but one who sincerely tried to do the will of the Master, and tread in His footsteps, the following incident is related: "On one occasion I had been visiting among some of my poorer parishioners, when suddenly I bethought me that I had not lately been to see one of the most regular attendants upon my ministry—a hard-working and God-fearing woman, Ann Davis by name. It was about 5 o'clock on Saturday afternoon; I was very tired, my dinner hour not far distant, and barely time sufficed me to return home punctually for the meal. 'I must go and see her on Monday,' I thought. 'I have not time to do so to-day.' Simultaneously, however, there arose in my mind a strange and unaccountable persuasion that I must pay her a visit, not only that day, but that very hour. In a few minutes, without in any way being able to explain why, I found myself standing at the door of my lowly friend's cottage, and knocked at once for admittance. After some slight delay, Ann Davis herself descended from the little chamber above, and I, already half repenting my mission in my anxiety not to be late, hastened to greet her thus: 'I can't stay this afternoon, Ann, for I am already late, but I had not been to see you for some little time, and I did not like to leave you so long without knowing how you and William were getting on.' Slipping a shilling into her hand, I was about to retrace my steps as quickly as I had come, when to my utter surprise poor Ann, unable to utter a single word, suddenly burst into tears. After she had somewhat composed herself, she related to me how her faith had been greatly tried that day, because her husband was at work away from home, and had failed to send her the expected post-office order which should provide for her and the children during the coming week. 'You see, sir,' she said, 'I have nothing in the house, and William had made me promise years ago that I would never go into debt, however much we were pressed. I was feeling low and dull about it, and had just gone up-stairs to beg the Lord to look in mercy upon us and send me something to feed the children with to-morrow, when you knocked at the door and gave me this shilling.' 'My God shall supply all your need,' involuntarily escaped my lips, and I then related to Ann how I had felt constrained to come and see her, though so pressed for time."

A CHINESE GATE-KEEPER'S APPLICATION.

A private letter from Mr. Price, of Tai-ku, contains news of a remarkable conversion, the first fruit of the Shanse mission. Its publication was secured by the editor of the *Missionary Herald*. Mr. Price says: "Last Sunday (August 28), after the Chinese service, a man came to me and said: 'I repent of my past false deeds and habits; I believe in Jesus, and desire to receive baptism.' You will know how rejoiced we all were when I tell you this is the first application of this kind in the history of the Shanse Mission, and that *we had been praying for this man for some time.* In the afternoon the man came to my room and gave a very interesting and satisfactory account of his conversion. Everything connected with his experience showed earnestness, sincerity, and faith in the Saviour. Later in the week Mr. Clapp talked with him, and was delighted with his manner, and convinced that he had really passed from death unto life.

"This man has been in and about our mission for nearly three years. He was brother Stimson's gatekeeper for a long time, and during that time daily received religious instruction. At one time Mr. Stimson thought he was under conviction, but he did not have the boldness to come out and bear the persecutions he knew he would meet in serving the Lord. His name is Lao Wang. He has a wife and four children, whom he is now seeking to lead to Christ. He is a man of personal influence, cordial and free in his manner, and wins friends wherever he lives. He has a pretty good knowledge of Scriptural truth, reads pretty well, and I doubt not God will use him to bring others to Himself. Others will turn unto the Lord, many of them, I confidently believe; but we shall never forget that the breaking away of the clouds, the first triumph of the gospel in this heathen city, was due to Lao Wang, who came out alone and confessed his Saviour, and thus became the first convert in the Shanse Mission."

A MISSIONARY'S ESCAPE.

The value of medical work, in connection with missions, was proved in China during the excitement produced by the tension between China and France in the Tonquin war. Among the most prominent missionaries was Dr. Wenyon, who had charge of the Fatshan Hospital. He went to Tonquin during the war to relieve the wounded soldiers. He says: "I had a body-guard of Chinese soldiers, who watched me as if I had been a child. If I went ashore from my boat to pluck a flower on the banks of the river, they were after me in a moment; and, when walking through native villages and towns, they marched before me, kicking the pigs and dogs out of the way, and shouting to the people to 'clear the road,' making such a disturbance that I often wished we could go out for our walks alone. One morning, in the interior of the province of Kwang-si, Mr. Anderson and I managed to slip ashore without the soldiers, and at length came to a large town, which we entered. We had not been long in the town before we wished we were safely out of it, or that we had the soldiers with us. The people crowded round us in a most menacing manner, and the cry, 'Kill the barbarian devils!' was heard on every hand. Struggling through the mob towards the river, a tradesman standing in the doorway of his shop caught sight of us, and at once called out, 'Dr. Wenyon.' 'What!' I said, 'do you know me!' 'I should think I do,' he replied. 'You cured my arm at the hospital in Fatshan. Come in, and have a cup of tea!' That simple episode acted like a spell, and changed at once the conduct of the mob from riot and ridicule to order and respect, and we got back safely."

A PARALYZED CRIPPLE'S TESTIMONY.

Mrs. M. Baxter has received the following narrative, which she publishes in her monthly magazine, *Thy Healer*,* from a lady who, four years ago, was brought to Bethshan in an apparently dying condition, but who was healed there, and is now still living and in good health.

"I was brought to Bethshan by a man who never expected to conduct me anywhere but in a hearse to the cemetery. I had suffered for seven years, for two of which I was in my bed in great agony. This leg (the right) was withered; this arm (the right) was paralysed, and I had an internal cancer as well—that is what they said at the London Hospital. I had a doctor at home; but as he did not do me much good, I tried another. I lived at Wanstead, and was one night carried to Plaistow from Canning Town to a doctor there. *I was taken by night, so as not to be seen.* They all said it was a hopeless case. I was a Christian, and knew Jesus, but never thought that Jesus would heal me. I never thought such a thing, and never heard of such a thing, until a dear man who had been to Bethshan said to me: 'Mrs. Clarke, don't you think the Lord will heal you?' 'No, no,' I said, 'God's will is for me to lie here.' After this my daughter was one day sitting by the side of my bed reading the Bible and THE CHRISTIAN HERALD. She turned to me and said: 'Mother, don't you think it is possible that the Lord can heal you?' 'Yes,' I answered, 'I know He can do it, for He can do all things.' There are a great many who think that, but they do not try Him. Then, when I was alone with God, I said: 'My Father, am I Thy child?' I seemed to hear His voice asking me; 'Daughter, what wilt thou that I should do unto thee?' I answered: 'That I might recover the use of my limbs. In a moment after that I slept, and never woke until the morning, and then I felt well. I called my husband. I said, 'I am well.' 'Nonsense,' he said. However, I felt I was healed, and I went on trusting the Lord. Then a friend wrote for me to Bethshan, and a lady came to see me on the next Saturday. She said: 'You have been in bed so long; do you think you can come to Bethshan? Remember, there are no doctors or nurses there?' However, I came on the next Wednesday. My husband sent for a man to bring me to Bethshan in an arm-chair in his cart. He brought me to Bethshan, and two men carried me in, and laid me on a chair bed. All the people looked at me. I looked, as they said afterward, a dying woman. Three days after I came here, there was a lady that came and wanted to see me. I told her what the Lord had done for me. She wondered. But I had been to the Great Physician."

* A monthly magazine edited by Mrs. M. Baxter, containing original articles on Holiness and Divine Healing. Annual subscription 75 cents. May be had from the office of this journal, 63 Bible House, New York.

AN AFRICAN KING MOLLIFIED.

The work in the West African field has recently passed through a crisis, which seemed at one time to threaten its existence. The danger and deliverance are described in a letter from Mr. and Mrs. Fay to the *Missionary Herald*. The two missionaries were visiting a village called Kuwa, when their camp was rudely broken up by messengers from the new king of Bihé. They were ordered to leave directly, and told that the village should be plundered and burned if they did not obey. For the sake of the villagers they did obey, and on reaching home received a letter from the king's quarters demanding "why the whites were running all over the country without permission," and ordering them to appear at the palace the next day. "We began to think," say the missionaries, "that we had caught a Tartar, so instead of taking fifteen pieces of cloth, which they had intended as a fitting present for a new king, Messrs. Fay and Sanders took twenty pieces and started for the palace. You may imagine their pleasure when they found the king a lank individual, apparently without much strength of will, and the Tartar element entirely due to a nephew of his. Against this fellow all the headmen are united, as he intends to control the king, and they want that duty themselves. This being the case, they were all ready to disagree with the king. The old man was therefore very meek, and only said he was glad to see the missionaries, and that their present was satisfactory. The headmen were loud in their protestations of friendship. Even Cisambu, who pulled up a fence-post to club Mr. Sanders the last time he was there, came to shake hands as friendly as possible. We hope now that we can keep on good terms with the chief."

A FIGHT WITH A BEAR.

A life and death struggle in a forest is described in a press despatch from Gazzan, Pa. It states that two city sportsmen arrived there two weeks ago, to hunt foxes and pheasants in the Clearfield woods. When they stated their intention they were warned by the native hunters that they would find bigger game than foxes in the woods and had better be prepared for bears. The city men, however, ridiculed the idea, and said they did not believe a bear had been seen in those woods for a quarter of a century. They accordingly set out early in the morning with their guns and kits. Late the same night they returned in a most deplorable condition. One of them had his arm broken, and both had their clothes torn to ribbons, and the flesh on various parts of their bodies severely lacerated. They stated that, after penetrating the wood to the distance of five miles, they separated to set traps, and that while one of them was so engaged he was startled by the appearance of a large she-bear. He fired at her, but the light cartridge in his gun irritated the beast without seriously harming her. Then ensued a desperate struggle, in which the hunter defended himself with his axe. He succeeded in disabling the bear, but in falling she fell upon him and broke his arm. His companion returned, and in trying to get his friend from under the bear, he aroused the beast from the insensibility which a blow of the axe had produced, and she attacked him. He received several dangerous wounds from her claws before he succeeded in killing her. The young men admitted that it would have been better for them, if they had given heed to the warning of the men who knew the woods. They had been too self-confident. The same fault often brings disaster on young people, especially those who set out to "see life" in our great cities. They are overcome of temptation and fall victims to the great enemy of souls (Prov. 28 : 26).

THE SEVENTY SEPTENNARIES.

By the Rev. John Storie, F. R. S. T.

Daniel 9: 20-27.

Daniel's Anxiety and Perplexity—He Had Studied Prophecy—Knew From Books That a Crisis was Approaching—Sought to Understand It—His Solicitude for His People—The Revelation of the Three Periods—I. Relate to the History of Israel—II. The Six Momentous Events to Occur in the Seventy Sevens—III. The Date of Their Commencement—IV. The Pause in the Continuity—Between the Sixty-ninth and Seventieth Septennary—Not Described Because Not Relating to the Jews—V. The Last Awful Septennary.

WHEN this revelation was made to Daniel, his mind was perplexed and anxious as to the future of his people. Questions are pressing on his mind, as a Jewish patriot and prophet, at once practical and prophetic. The seventy years of captivity now closing, are they to end the tribulation, the degradation and the exile of his people? Is the time come when his people are to be restored to their own land; God's covenant with them revived; and their city and temple rebuilt, to be the seat of the Messiah's throne and the glory of the whole earth? A future glad and grateful! Yet he knew that while the longing of his own heart, and that of a few of the faithful of his people, was toward the city of their fathers and the temple of their God, a second and a third generation had become rooted in Babylon, which was their birthplace. If their expatriation is now to end,

What Means Will God Employ

to hasten or constrain their return? Will He lead them back by the hand of a second Moses, or will the Messiah in glory head their returning bands? He knew that their captivity had not wrought that repentance which could sanctify them as the chosen of heaven; and how then could God fulfil to them His great promise; raise up from the house of David the promised King; and give to Him and to Israel the power and dominion now? He knew, too, that ere the kingdom of the Most High could be established on the earth, four great Gentile powers were to sway the world; that of these the Chaldean alone had fallen; and that three more—the last of them the basest and the worst, were yet to rise to trample and oppress it. What then—if the imposed captivity of seventy years is now to end—

What is in God's Future?

What for Israel? What for the nations? Is a second period to intervene of rebuke and trial, of rebellion and chastisement, ere His own people are ready for the Messiah and the nations ripe for judgment? And if so, what? And how long? Thus doubting, sad at heart, feeling his own sin and the sin of his people, in difficulty and in the dark, the prophet seeks light and guidance from his God; and in answer to that prayer he receives

The Marvellous Revelation

following, in respect to the future of his people, its crime and sorrows, the times of the Gentiles, the last persecution of Israel, and the final consummation: "Seventy sevens have been cut off upon Thy people and upon the Holy City, to consummate and end the transgression, and to seal up sins, and to cover iniquity, and to bring in everlasting righteousness, and to seal up vision and prophet, and to anoint a Holy of Holies. Know, therefore, and understand: from the going forth of the decree to restore and rebuild Jerusalem unto Messiah, the Prince shall be seven sevens and sixty and two sevens. The street shall be restored and built, and the wall (or fosse), but in the pressure of

Troublous Times.

And after the sixty and two sevens shall Messiah be cut off; and there is nought for Him. And the people of a prince—the coming one—shall destroy the city and the sanctuary and its end (or his end) shall be in the overflowing (that is of divine wrath); and unto the end is war, a decree of desolation, and He (that is, the Prince who shall come) shall confirm a covenant to the many, or the majority (that is of the Jewish people) for one seven; and in the middle of the seven he shall cause sacrifice and oblation to cease; and upon the wing (or over the summit) of abominations, shall come the desolator even until the consummation, and that which has been determined shall be poured upon the desolate."

I. Here we are to note that the entire prediction relates to the future of Israel and their city Jerusalem. Seventy sevens are determined upon *Thy people* and upon *Thy Holy City*. This is

The Key to the Prophecy

—and we are to observe, next, that the word rendered in our version weeks is in the Hebrew sevens, a simple numeral. When used by Daniel in a previous passage to express a week of time, it has added to it the word days: "In these days I was mourning three weeks, three sevens of days" (Daniel 10: 2). But at this time, not days but years are in the prophet's mind. "I, Daniel, understood by books the number of the *years* whereof the Word of the Lord came to Jeremiah, the prophet, that he would accomplish seventy years in the desolation of Jerusalem" (Daniel 9: 2). These years of the captivity are now ending: is the sin and chastisement of his people to terminate with them? No! The revelation now made to him declares; not yet; not at the end of this expiring seventy; not till the end of seven times seventy more. The words then are to be read, seventy septennaries, or four hundred and ninety years, have been cut off upon Thy people and the Holy City.

II. While these seven times seventy years are running their course,

The Six Greatest Events

in all time, the most awful in that conflict between heaven and hell, which is proceeding here, are to be decided. These are: *first*, to consummate transgression; that is, to fill up the permitted measure of sin and transgression; to concentrate and complete all that the powers of hell can put in force within the scope and limits of humanity; to bring to a final climax the supreme manifestation of all this in the rejection and crucifixion of the Son of God by Israel, in the final apostacy of the Gentile churches, and in the rise, dominion, incarnation and defiance of heaven by the man of sin. *Second*, to seal up sins, that is, to arrest, restrain and terminate the sins of men; to deliver the world from their presence and their curse: to bury them as in a tomb,

Secured by the Seal of Heaven;

and to shut up man's great enemy in the abyss, so that he may no longer darken the earth or tempt the nations. *Third*, to cover iniquity; that is, to so expiate iniquity by a great and adequate atonement, that it shall be hid from the sight of heaven. *Fourth*, to bring in everlasting righteousness; that is, to bring into this fallen world a righteousness, which is to put man in right normal relations with God, and to introduce that reign of covenant grace, during which His law shall be within the hearts of men, and His spirit poured upon all flesh. *Fifth*, to seal up vision and prophet, that is to lay them past, to store them amid the archives of heaven with the stamp and inscription as confirmed, authenticated, fulfilled. *Sixth*, to anoint a Holy of Holies, or, as the words may be literally rendered, a holiness of holinesses; that is, to consecrate with the unction from on high a hallowed city and a hallowed race, with a sanctuary that the Messiah is Himself to rear.

These are the six grand issues which these seventy times seven years are to bring to completion. They reach on in their course to the fulfilling of prophecy to the consummation, the regeneration, to the restitution of all things.

III. Of these seventy septennaries, or four hundred and ninety years,

The Commencing Date

is given: the going forth of the command to restore and rebuild Jerusalem. This then is the date we seek; the date of the going forth of the command to restore and to build the sacred city which which gave the Jews again renewed existence as a nation, and a centre and stronghold in their own land. Of this decree the date is known.

IV. It is now to be carefully noted, that these four hundred and ninety years do not proceed, in unbroken sequence to their close. They divide into

Three Periods.

There is first a period of seven septennaries, or forty-nine years; a second of sixty-two septennaries, or four hundred and thirty-four years; and then a final and severed period of one septennary, or seven years. The first period of forty-nine years probably covers the time of rebuilding the city and raising its walls. On this immediately follows the second period of four hundred and thirty-four years. These two together give an extended period of four hundred and eighty-three years. It begins with the going forth of the royal command, and ends with the greatest crime in the history of man. "And after the sixty and two weeks shall Messiah be cut off; and there shall be nothing for Him." This is the event that is to mark the end of that period; the closing event of that fateful time; the event that is to stamp a character indelible on this, the four hundred and eighty-third year from the date of that decree.

V. One septennary, the last, still remains. It does not immediately follow on the sixty-nine. It is held in reserve. There is

A Break in the Consecution

of the times; a long pause—a pause that has lasted now for more than eighteen centuries, when Messiah is rejected and cut off by Israel, his covenant with them is suspended, and the times of the Gentiles commence. It is the suspension foretold by Hosea (Hos. 3: 4-5). It is the commencement of the parenthetic dispensation revealed to Paul (Romans 11: 25). During these long centuries there has been an entire cessation of God's dealings with Israel as a covenant people; as to prophecy, its voice is almost entirely silent; the Gospel has been preached to the nations; the Jews scattered; the city and the sanctuary destroyed, and wars have desolated the land.

In the days of Titus this desolation began; through all these Gentile ages it has continued, and so frequent have been the captures of Jerusalem, by Roman and Persian and Saracen and Turk, that the ancient city, buried beneath successive layers of ruin, is now found from fifty to eighty feet below the level of the soil. But this parenthetic dispensation is now surely near its close. This awful week, the last septennary of time, is about to begin. The Anti-christ will arise in power; the Messiah will be seen in parousia in these terrestrial heavens, and the events described in the Book of Revelation will be consummated.

CHRISTIAN HERALD AND SIGNS OF OUR TIMES.

OFFICE, 63 BIBLE HOUSE, NEW YORK.

ENTERED AT THE POST-OFFICE AT NEW YORK, N. Y., AS SECOND-CLASS MATTER.

Published Weekly. Subscription price, $1.50 a year; $1 eight months; 75 cents six months; sent two months on trial for 25 cents; always payable in advance. Single copies for sale by, or can be ordered at, all newsdealers.

Remittances by Mail should be by Post-office money order, bank cheques, or drafts or express money order, and should always be made payable to THE CHRISTIAN HERALD.

[illegible] are not sent, the receipt of the paper by a subscriber is a sufficient proof that his remittance has been received. If the paper does not arrive promptly, please advise us, that we may see if the address is correctly entered.

Change of Address. Name of Post Office and State, of both old and new address, should always be given in case of removal.

CURRENT EVENTS.

The Treasury Statement Issued Last Week contains figures that should prompt patriotic Congressmen to an effort to reduce public burdens. Of the fifty-four millions applied to the reduction of the public debt during the past half year, nearly three millions was spent in premiums. That is to say, the Government paid that amount for the privilege of anticipating payments not due. Tax-payers who contributed to the surplus may wisely consider that fact. Their money has been used, not only to pay the public debt, but to pay the creditors of the Government a bonus to receive their money before the stipulated time. It is true, that the Government does not lose by the transaction in the end, because it saves the interest, but it is an anomalous condition of affairs, which cannot be continued without loss and inconvenience. The Revenue increased during the half year, over the corresponding period of 1886, by more than eleven millions, nearly one-half of which was in the Internal Revenue. The increase in pensions was eleven and a half millions.

The Admission of Four New States Besides Utah to the Union is pressed in Washington. They are the four Territories of Dakota, Montana, Washington and New Mexico. Of these, Dakota is fully qualified by population to become a State, but Montana, in 1880, had less than 40,000 inhabitants, and Washington had only about 75,000, but has been developing with considerable rapidity. New Mexico is believed at present to have no chance of admission, as it is stated that neither by the extent nor the character of its population is it prepared to become a State. The consideration that will weigh with Congress, however, will be the balancing of political parties, especially in the Senate and Electoral College.

The Speaker's Appointment of the Standing Committees of the House, as announced on Thursday last, has given rise to much discontent in his own party and among Republicans. Complaint is made that Mr. Carlisle has paid too much attention to the principle of seniority, and that, in many cases, a man has been reappointed, simply because he held the same position in a former Congress, though, while holding it, he demonstrated his unfitness for the position. It must, however, be remembered that no Speaker yet has ever succeeded in making up committees so as to give complete satisfaction. The strong pressure brought to bear on the Speaker, to change the Chairmanship of the Appropriation Committee, failed, and Mr. Randall is once more installed there. That appointment is one of the strongest evidences that compromise in the Democratic party is to prevail. Mr. Mills, of Texas, is made Chairman of the Ways and Means Committee, which is a disappointment to Mr. Cox, of New York, and his friends. The appointment of Mr. Bliss to the chairmanship of the Committee on Pensions causes no little surprise; but the most extraordinary selection is that of Mr. Clements, of Georgia, for the chair of the Committee on Civil Service Reform. The significance of this appointment appears, when it is remembered that Mr. Clements has gone conspicuously on record, as an advocate of the repeal of the law. He was the author of the minority report in the last Congress, in which he boldly declared that the law was "at variance with the genius and spirit of our institutions," and expressed his conviction that the offices and their emoluments should go to the dominant party. New York has gained two chairmen by the new distribution, though she has now no representative on the two committees of Ways and Means and Appropriations.

A Remarkable Speech by Senator Sherman was delivered on January 4 in the Senate, which, it may be presumed, will become very familiar as a campaign document next fall. It was devoted to an exhaustive examination of the principles enunciated by the President in his message. Mr. Sherman admitted the danger of the gigantic surplus, but joined issue directly with the President, on the question of the best way to deal with it. He censured the President for his refusal to approve the River and Harbor Bill and for his veto of the Dependent Pension Bill, which he characterized as withholding "from Union soldiers appropriations made for their relief." He also condemned the House for its failure to spend money on coast defences, the increase of the navy and the commercial marine, for postal communication with the South American States, and for "the encouragement and support of schools." Mr. Sherman's plan appears to be to apply the surplus to projects of general usefulness, rather than to reduce taxation and so prevent a surplus accumulating.

The Great Strike of Miners in Pennsylvania went into effect on January 3. Over thirty thousand men and boys quitted work. Those working for individual mine owners joined in the strike, though the employers in several cases agreed to pay the rate demanded. The men replied, however, that it was resolved to bring the Reading Company to terms, and that could only be done by united effort. It is thought, however, that if the strike is protracted the individual collieries will be able to resume work, as the men will not be likely, in the depth of winter, to be obstinate in a purely sympathetic strike. The Reading Company stated, at the close of last week, that in all thirty-eight thousand of their employees were on strike, twenty thousand miners and eighteen thousand railroad hands. That would imply that ten thousand of the striking miners belong to individual collieries. The magnitude of the strike astonishes the employers and the public. It was not expected that the men would stand together so firmly and obey the order to strike so promptly. The fact, however, imparts some encouragement in the prospect of intervention. Many large consumers of coal, especially the iron works, must suffer seriously by a coal famine, and some will have to shut down. This will throw other men out of employ, and it is hoped that the men thus idle and the employers being losers too, will bring influence to bear respectively on each side of the Reading trouble, and effect an arrangement.

The Governor of New York, in his Message to the Legislature last week, made two suggestions of more than local interest. The first was, to change the date of local elections from the fall to the spring of the year. The object of the change is obvious. When both local and national elections take place on the same day, there is an opportunity for deals and corrupt bargains that smart politicians know how to use. It is notorious that, in more than one important election, arrangements were made by which large blocks of votes were split up, the politicians who were anxious for the control of the city and careless about national affairs trading votes for the national candidates in exchange for votes for local candidates. If the elections take place on different dates it will not be so easy to arrange such bargains. Governor Hill's second suggestion relates to court administration, and springs out of the Jacob Sharp case. He proposes that the Court of Appeals shall have power to sustain a conviction, if satisfied of the guilt of the accused, although admitting that improper evidence was received at the first trial. At present, if the Court of Appeals holds that the Judge of the Court below erred in allowing certain evidence to be given, it must grant a new trial.

The Socialistic Remarks of Cardinal Manning, which caused so widespread a sensation when cabled to this country last week, appear to have given as great a shock in Europe as here. It is felt that the Cardinal has given direct encouragement to acts of lawlessness. In contending that natural right to food prevails over laws of property, he has endorsed the principles of the socialists, and has given the sanction of his position and influence to robbery and spoliation in all cases in which the thief can plead hunger. The starving people of London did not need such an incentive to violence, and it may lead many of them into trouble with the police. The Cardinal's remarks will not be a surprise, however, to students of prophecy, who will recognize in them a sign of the times. The Rev. M. Baxter, and other expositors of prophecy long ago expressed their belief that in the last years of this age the Romish Church will be the ally of socialism.

The Publication of the Forged Documents which imposed on the Czar, took place last week. They are letters purporting to have been written by Prince Ferdinand, of Bulgaria, to the Countess of Flanders and other persons, stating that he had promises of Germany's secret support, and that, but for that encouragement, he would not have accepted the Bulgarian throne. When these documents were shown to the Czar, they naturally irritated him against Germany, but in the recent interview between the Czar and Bismarck, the latter denied the truth of the statements, and Prince Ferdinand denounced the letters as forgeries. Though the publication has had a good effect on the situation, it has not checked the movement of Russian troops. Cable despatches state that the Black Sea fleet is being equipped for active service. Four gunboats have been sent to the Kilia arm of the Danube, and a numerous flotilla of vessels designed for river service is being concentrated at Odessa. The formidable extent of these preparations gives rise to the suspicion that the Czar contemplates a sudden descent upon Bulgaria, while making provision for defence against Austria.

An Election of a Member of Parliament at Winchester caused some excitement throughout England and Ireland on January 5. A Conservative is generally elected by that constituency, but strong efforts were made by the Liberals to gain the seat. Large sums of money were spent in printing, and eminent orators, English and Irish, made speeches in favor of the Gladstone candidate. He also had the support of the Temperance party, as his opponent was a brewer. In spite of these advantages, however, he was defeated by the Conservative, who had a larger majority than his predecessor scored in 1886. The event has caused gloom through the Liberal party. It is regarded as an indication that the popular reaction is not so general as was supposed.

The Pacific Assurances Interchanged on New Year's Day in Europe are being eagerly scanned, and their value appreciated. Among the more important is the statement that President Carnot of France instructed M. Herbette, the French Ambassador at Berlin, to assure Emperor William that while he remains at the head of the republic of France, no French Government will be permitted to adopt a warlike policy. A despatch from Vienna to the Cologne *Gazette* says that William also received a message from the Emperor of Austria in which this passage occurred: "God grant that the unsettled political situation may speedily be cleared, so that our peoples may be reassured and the blessings of peace preserved."

Contributions to the Fund for Supplying colored ministers in the South with this journal, were received last week to the amount of $45.70. They were from Philadelphia, Pa. $1.50; New Grand Chain, Ill. $1; Trenton, N. J. $1; Norwood, Minn. $1; New York, N. Y. $25; Centreville, Mass. $2; Marysville, Kan. $1; Sandusky, O. $4.95; Southport, N. Y. 75c; Seaward, Me. $4; New York, N. Y. $1; Nassau, Bahamas, 50c; Poughkeepsie, N. Y. $2. On behalf of the many ministers to whom these sums will be the means of blessing we most heartily thank the donors. We cherish the hope that the comparatively small sum now needed, to send the paper to every minister whose term has expired, will be received.

Especial Attention is Called to the Meeting of the New York Society for the Suppression of Vice, which is to be held in the Hall of the Young Men's Christian Association on Twenty-Third Street and Fourth Avenue, on Tuesday next, January 17, at eight o'clock. This will be a very important meeting, as the sneers and jibes of the secular press have been recently directed against the Society with renewed virulence, on account of the seizures of obscene pictures by Mr. Comstock. It may be hoped that Christian men will, by their presence, give the Society the encouragement it ought to have.

Dr. Talmage's Acceptance of a Military Appointment was announced last week. He was chosen to succeed the late Rev. Henry Ward Beecher as chaplain of the famous Thirteenth Regiment of Brooklyn. In the course of his letter of acceptance, Dr. Talmage said: "The honor would be appreciated by any one who has interest in good citizenship. I thank you for the high compliment, and accept the position. It calls me back to an office which I held twenty-five years ago in war times, when, as chaplain, I went out with a regiment from Philadelphia, and, for a time, gave up preaching and a pulpit, in that city, for preaching by a drum-head stand at the front, and mingled in the sad scenes of field and hospital service. So, I am glad that your call does not find me a novice for the position. I shall enter fully into all that pertains to the welfare of the regiment, and feel a joy in administering to men of all sects and denominations of religion, the boundary line between them so insignificant that I am at home anywhere."

An Indirect Reproof in Church and a Retort were overheard on January 1. In each of two adjoining pews of Grace Church, that morning, were a young lady and her friend. One of the young ladies was evidently not accustomed to attending the services of the Protestant Episcopal Communion, for she had no prayer-book, and made none of the responses nor changed her posture as her fellow worshippers did. This conduct stirred the anger of the lady in the next pew, who said to her friend, in a whisper clearly audible in the next pew: "Why do these people come to church to stare about and take no part in the service? It is scandalous." The lady thus reproved, who was not staring about, but had her head bowed reverentially, bridled up instantly and remarked to her escort that people who paid so much attention to others could not be taking a very heartfelt part in the service themselves. There is reason to fear that neither lady profited much by that service. The spirit of criticism, and the disposition to condemn those who differ from us, are violations of the apostolic injunction. (Rom 14: 4-7.)

The Mysterious Discovery of a Dead Æronaut is reported in a press despatch from Owensborough, Ky. A few days ago a large balloon was seen by the people of that town sailing overhead. Its shape could only just be made out, as it was so high above them. It was noticed, however, that it was descending, and some hours after its first appearance its downward course became more rapid. About nightfall it was so near the earth that its shape and general appearance could be discerned. The next day a party went in search of it in the direction where it was last seen. They found it in a swamp, ten miles south of Hamesville. They were horrified to find near the air-ship the emaciated remains of a man who had evidently been its solitary voyager. As there were no wounds or bruises on the body, it was evident that the man must have died before the balloon touched the ground, and his general appearance indicated that he had died from want of food and air. Who he was and where he came from could not be discovered. It is supposed that he lost control of the balloon, and it ascended to a great altitude, where human life could not be sustained. Many souls have been lost by an analogous course. Those who soar into metaphysical speculation, instead of devoting their minds to practical usefulness, are liable to lose themselves in their mental wanderings, and their faith perishes (1 Tim. 6: 3-5).

A Story of a Flag was Related to a Reporter of a Southern journal on January 3. The man who told it is a native of Nashville, Tenn., but during the past twenty years has been in business in New York. He spent the holidays in his native State, and was much interested, in going through it, by observing the various signs of improvement and development. He was especially gratified by the appearance of the thriving town of South Pittsburg, but he had one grave fault to find with it. The town did not show its patriotism. To one of the citizens he said: "You have not got a flag-pole in your whole town. The men down there in your shops don't know that there is such a thing as the Stars and Stripes, so far as you have shown them." "We've been too busy to pay much attention to decorations," interposed South Pittsburg's representative, looking around with evident pride at the business buildings that his town boasts. "Too busy!" said the visitor, "well I am not;" And stepping into a telegraph office he wired to New York for a one hundred dollar flag, and superintended the erection of a tall flag-pole in readiness for the arrival of the Stars and Stripes. There are many Christians whose lives resemble that town. They have been too busy making money to take their stand openly on the Lord's side. Christ demands of all His followers that they confess Him before men. (Luke. 12: 8.)

A Mutually Disappointed Bride and Bridegroom met at Castle Garden, New York, on Thursday last. When the steamship *Bolivia*, from Gibraltar, discharged her passengers, a young Italian girl, extremely bright and pretty, stepped ashore. She said she had come over to be married to Signor Pellegrino, a fellow-countryman, who was in business in Brooklyn. She had never seen him, but his aunt and her mother had arranged the match. Pellegrino and his aunt were on hand to meet the girl. The signor wore his every-day clothes, which, as his occupation is that of a cellar-digger, were not too clean. The aunt was a withered old woman of forbidding appearance. When the girl was introduced to the two, she refused to carry out her part of the arrangement. An appeal was made to the Italian Consul, when it was disclosed that Pellegrino had sent forty dollars to Italy for a wife, and the girl's mother had accepted the money, paying twenty-four dollars of it for her daughter's passage out. The girl is disappointed at not being married, and Pellegrino is disappointed because, having purchased her, she will not be his wife. He cannot be made to understand that his immoral bargain will not be recognized in the United States. It may be hoped that the poor girl will meet with Christian friends here, who can tell her of another purchase by One who so loved His bride that He purchased her, not with corruptible things, but with His precious blood. (Eph. 5: 25.)

Crawling Through Fire was the Way by which an engineer saved his life, on December 30, at Glendale, Pa. He is employed at the Glendale Iron Works, and, on that day, had to examine the interior of one of the large boilers there. He took with him a can of crude petroleum, which he placed in the boiler, near the open end, while he worked at the other end of the boiler. By some mysterious cause, the oil in the can was exploded, and caught fire. That end of the boiler was at once filled with the flames of the burning oil. The engineer crouched down in his end of the boiler, with his back to the flames, supposing that he could hold out against the heat and smoke of the fire until the oil was all consumed. The heat became so intense and the smoke so dense and suffocating, however, that he saw that he must either escape from the boiler at once, or meet with a terrible death. The only way was to crawl through the flame and smoke between him and the opening in the boiler. Holding his breath to avoid inhaling the flame, and covering his eyes to protect them from the fire, at last he reached open air, when he fell unconscious. Some[illegible] the only way to eternal life seems to be th[illegible] an ordeal as appalling. It is so in the [illegible] drunkards, morphia habitués, and vicious men, whose deprivation of indulgence involves awful suffering. Though they have a stronger inducement to make the effort than even this engineer, too often they do not realize its value, and shrink from the ordeal. (Matt. 18: 8, 9.)

BRIEF NOTES.

Mr. Philip Phillips, "the Singing Pilgrim," will hold meetings next week, January 16, 17, 18, in the Seventh Street Methodist Episcopal Church, New York.

Mr. Moody has promised to hold conventions in several cities of Iowa next month. Ottumwa, Burlington and Cedar Rapids are among the places named.

Major Whittle is commencing services this week at Fort Madison, Iowa. After the close of which he expects to go to Cedar Rapids and Marshalltown.

By the formation of Societies of Christian Endeavor from among the young people of localities in New England, a number of almost dead churches in rural districts have been revived, and have become stronger than ever.

Dr. John Hall, in a recent address, called attention to the fact that there are 100,000 inhabitants south of Fourteenth Street in New York City, and eleven churches less in the area than there were ten years ago.

Dr. L. W. Munhall and Prof. and Mrs. Towner are laboring at Baltimore, Md. The results of their labors in Ohio are becoming more apparent since their departure. Large as the blessing was seen to be while they were there, its full extent was not perceived as it now is.

Reports from Columbia, Mo., show that the work of the Rev. H. W. Brown and Mr. E. C. Avis was much blessed there. At Fayette, Mo., also large additions have been made to the churches of all denominations through God's blessing on the services.

The evangelistic services conducted by the pastor, Rev. Francis Edward Smiley, at the Wharton Street Presbyterian Church, Philadelphia, have resulted in a great blessing to the church. The church is now too large for its building, and arrangements are being made for the erection of a larger one.

Henry F. Williams, lately State Secretary of the Young Men's Christian Associations of Minnesota, and formerly State Secretary of Ohio, has been appointed by the International Committee, its secretary in the Railroad Department of its work, in place of Edwin D. Ingersoll, who is compelled by sickness to resign.

Two American missionaries, laboring in Japan, would be glad to receive back numbers of this journal, if any subscribers have them to spare. The Japanese are learning English, and the missionaries find that THE CHRISTIAN HERALD is much appreciated by them. They may be mailed to the Rev. H. Loomis, Yokohama, Japan; or to the Rev. Charles Ely, D.D., 5 Ysukiji, Tokio, Japan.

The town of Wakefield, Wis., has been burned to the ground as the result of the playfulness of a monkey. Having been given the freedom of a theatre by the proprietor, the monkey about midnight applied the oil of a kerosene lamp to his hair, and then setting fire to himself scattered the flames, the entire building becoming ignited in a few moments. Within an hour the business portion of the town was in ashes.

Evangelist B. Fay Mills will open a series of meetings in Philadelphia, on Sunday next. Ten churches have united in inviting him—two Methodist, one Baptist, one Episcopal, one German Reformed, one Evangelical Southern, one Congregational and three Presbyterian. From February 20 to March 13 he hopes to be in Providence, where two Congregational, two Methodist and two Baptist churches have joined in the invitation.

SMALL-RAIN PREACHING.

A New Sermon by Pastor C. H. Spurgeon.

"As the small rain upon the tender herb." Deuteronomy 32 : 2.

A Mighty Preacher—I. His Tender Sermon—Full of Doctrine—And Rebuke—Does not Black the Eyes to Improve the Sight—Declares God's Wrath—Jonathan Edwards Interrupted—Should be Done Tenderly—The Tenderness of Christ's Preaching—The Vigor of Man and the Affection of Woman Combined—A Model for Preachers—A Welcome Complaint—Difference between Irrigation and Inundation—II. A Penetrating Sermon—Hearers Needing Dictionaries more than Bibles—Ballooning in Theology—III. Results Expected—Means Adapted to the End—The Hit-or-Miss Preaching.

THIS is the language of the great prophet Moses: "My doctrine shall drop as the rain, my speech shall distil as the dew, as the small rain upon the tender herb, and as the showers upon the grass." We read of Moses that he was a prophet mighty in word and deed: he combined with his incomparable teaching an unequalled degree of marvellous miracle-working. He was equally great as a law-giver and as an administrator. This

Double Power

was found in no other prophet till our Lord Jesus Christ himself came. The other prophets were, many of them, mighty in deed, but not in word; And others mighty in word but not in deed. Samuel spoke mightily in the name of the Lord, but his miracles were few. Elijah was a great doer, but few of his words remain. The combination of the two was peculiar to Moses, and afterwards to him of whom Moses had said aforetime, "The Lord thy God will raise up unto thee a Prophet, from the midst of thee, of thy brethren, like unto me; unto Him ye shall hearken." Yet we perceive that this might of word, which dwelt in Moses, displayed itself frequently in a mild and gentle utterance: in the text, he declares that his doctrine should drop as rain, and distil as dew, and that it should be "as the small rain upon the tender herb." The highest power is consistent with the lowliest tenderness. He that is mightiest in word is mighty, not so much in thunder and earthquake and fire, as in a silent persuasiveness. God is often most present where there is least of apparent force; the still, small voice had God in it when it was written "The Lord was not in the wind."

I intend to make three observations upon my text. Moses says that his doctrine should be as the small rain upon the tender herb.

I. Our first observation is, Moses meant to be tender. Moses intended, in the sermon he was about to preach, to be exceedingly gentle.

He Would Water Minds

as tender herbs, and water them in the same fashion as the small rain does. He would not be a beating hail, nor even a down-pouring shower, but he would be "as the small rain upon the tender herb." And this is the more remarkable, because he was about to preach *a doctrinal sermon*. Does he not say, "My *doctrine* shall drop as the rain"? Time was when a doctrinal sermon seemed to be most appropriately preached with clenched fists. I trust we are learning better, and that we try now to let doctrine distil as rain, and drop as dew, "as the small rain upon the tender herb."

It is at certain turning-points of the road our duty to contend earnestly for the faith once delivered to the saints, but we are to recollect that our contentions are the contentions of love, and that it ill becomes the man who holds the truth of a loving Saviour to hold it in bitterness, or contend for it with rancor. *You will possibly think that I have been guilty* in this matter, but I cannot make such a confession to any large extent. I have felt no bitterness; and when I have spoken forcibly, I have yet restrained myself from harder things which I might truthfully have brought forth. Yet, I regret that I have been forced into controversy for which I have no taste, and in which I have no pleasure. I have been driven to it: I have never sought it. To spread the gospel I should choose the gentler method: it is only to defend it that I have to draw the sword. Fight for truth, yea, be willing to live or die for truth; but if you wish to spread it, you will do it best by letting it drop as rain, and distil as dew, gently and tenderly, "as the small rain upon the tender herb."

It is equally remarkable that this discourse was

A Sermon of Rebuke.

He rebuked the people, and rebuked them, too, with no small degree of sternness. Yet he felt that he had rebuked with the utmost meekness, and had still been as the soft dew and gentle rain. Ah, brethren! upbraiding must be done in tenderness. Rebukes given in an unkind spirit had better not be given at all. Wisdom does not learn her exercises among the athletes, but among calm scholars. *We do not black people's eyes to make them see*, nor bully them into peace, nor kick them into heaven. To strive, and cry, and lift up, and cause clamorous voices to be heard in the streets is not Christ's way. Not a syllable have we to say against zeal, even when it breaks over all bounds of propriety; but it is the zeal which we value, and not the outbursts by themselves. We question greatly whether too often physical force is not mistaken for spiritual power; and this is an error of a mischievous kind. Dear brethren, it is well to observe this: that, though it was a doctrinal discourse, it was tender; and though it was a rebuking discourse, with Moses for preacher, yet it was "as small rain upon the tender herb."

Yet once more, in this discourse, this swan's song, this final deliverance of the great judge in Israel, he was about to

Declare the Wrath

of God; for here we read words like these: "A fire is kindled in mine anger, and shall burn unto the lowest hell, and shall consume the earth with her increase, and set on fire the foundations of the mountains. I will heap mischiefs upon them; I will spend mine arrows upon them;" and so on. Never stronger, sterner language: but even this was made to drop as the small rain. And if ever there is a time when the sluices should be pulled up, and the floods of sympathy should flow, it is when we preach the wrath of God. I am certain that, to preach the wrath of God with a hard heart, and a cold lip, and a tearless eye, and an unfeeling spirit, is to harden men, and not to benefit them. If we preach these terrors of the Lord persuasively, we have hit the nail on the head, for what saith the apostle: "Knowing therefore the terror of the Lord, we persuade men?" Gently, as a nurse persuadeth a child, though in the background is the rod,

We Would Woo Men

to Jesus, till we win them. I remember one servant of God who could not help interrupting the great New England minister by crying out, "Mr. Edwards, Mr. Edwards, is He not a God of mercy after all?" I hope I should never, under any circumstances, give occasion for such a question. Though the Lord is a God of vengeance upon such as refuse His Son, and reject His grace, yet is He abundant in mercy, tenderness, and longsuffering, and delighteth not in the death of any, but that they should turn unto Him and live. Therefore let us give space for mercy to persuade while justice threatens.

Now, beloved friends, if Moses meant to be tender, how much more truly was Jesus tender! The representative of the law aimed at tenderness: how much more the incarnation of the gospel! He who came with ten broken commands to threaten men was tender: how much more He who comes with five wounds, founts of eternal pardon, to persuade men! How winning is the meek and lowly Lamb of God! The Sermon on the Mount, I have sometimes thought, was such as an inspired woman might fitly have preached, it is so full of heart, and so exceedingly pitiful. For the most part, throughout His ministry, though masculine to the last degree, yet there is a softness, a pathos of love; as if in the person of Christ we had both man and woman, as in the first Adam at the creation. Jesus is the head of the race, completely combining in His own person all the vigor of the man, and all the affection of the woman. Oh yes, our Lord's manner was gentleness itself.

Furthermore, His style of speech was compassionately considerate, even as the dew seems to consider the withered grass, and the small rain to adapt itself to the tender herb. In His teaching He evidently thought of the feeble, and suited Himself to those depressed by grief. You find

No Hard Words Thrown In

to make the speaker seem wise. There are difficulties about His doctrine inherent to the nature of truth, but they are never aggravated by His style. For the most part, in the early days of His preaching to the outside multitude, He gave them little more than moral truth, for that was all they were able to bear. It sometimes amuses me to see how certain "modern thought" men prove themselves to belong to the outside many, and not to the inner circle of disciples; for they take the Sermon on the Mount, and extol it as the summit of the doctrine of Jesus, whereas it was only His discourse to the multitude, and not such spiritual teaching as He gave to His apostles when alone. There were gleams and glintings of the divinely spiritual truth flashing out of the moral truth like flames from a fire; but for the most part He gave the crowd that which it could receive, and not that which would have been above their heads.

The Lord was very careful as to the manner of his teaching, and as to the matter of His teaching, too, even to His chosen. "I have yet many things to say unto you," said He, "but ye cannot bear them now." There was a gradual development in His teaching as He saw the minds of men were prepared to receive the truth which He should speak; from which method of wisdom and prudence let His disciples learn a lesson.

So we learn that Moses meant to be tender, and Jesus was tender. What else do we learn? Why, that all the servants of Jesus Christ ought to be tender: for, if Moses was so, much more should we be. I know there are many here who are preachers of the Gospel. Dear brethren, let us endeavor, with all our might, to be always considerate towards those whom we address. Let us think of them as tender herbs, for many are so in their weakness, sorrowfulness, irritability, and ignorance. I am persuaded that

We Fix Too High a Standard

when we preach, and assume that our people know a great deal more than they do. I am sure we need frequently to go over again the elements, the fundamentals, the simplest doctrines, of the gospel to our congregations; for, though there be some that are fathers, for whom we are grateful, yet it is true to-day, as it was in Paul's day, we have not many fathers; and we ought not to preach with an eye to the few fathers, but with an eye to the many children. We shall do well if the babes in grace are fed by us, and to do this our preaching must be "as the small rain upon the tender herb." We must try to the utmost of our ability to be very plain and simple, for many will not understand us even then. I was greatly

Pleased With a Complaint

brought against me the other day, to which I plead guilty, and I expect I shall plead guilty to it for many a day to come. Some one said, "Mr. Spurgeon gives us meat, but there's no gristle; he cuts out all the bone." They wanted a bit or two of hard bone, just to try their teeth on. Alas, many have broken more than a tooth over the novel teaching of "modern thought!" Now, I have never been particularly earnest, when feeding my flock, to seek out the poisonous pastures, just to see how much of injurious fodder they could bear without sickening. No; I have had regard to those who are not yet able to discern the differences in spiritual things, and therefore I have led them to those ancient pastures where the saints were content to feed in days gone by.

When I have been travelling, especially in southern France and Italy, I have come upon places where the river has burst its banks, and covered all the land with water: then, instead of blessing the fields, it has swept everything out of them, and buried them in mud, and killed the crops. There is *a great difference between irrigation and inundation;* and some preachers forget this. A sermon may sometimes act in that fashion to some of God's dear, tender ones; it may be a perfect deluge of doctrine, sweeping up by the roots those

Feeble Plants

not very deeply rooted in the faith. God's children cannot all of them receive a mass of doctrine all at once, but they have a fine appetite, and if you give them time, they will gradually appropriate, masticate, and inwardly digest all the truth of God, so that they will be nourished up thereby, and made to grow. Let every minister of Christ remember this, and patiently instruct his hearers as they are able to bear it.

And so, dear friends, I will say one thing more upon this point, which is, let every Christian remember this, for every Christian is to try and bring souls to Christ. We are all to be teachers of the Gospel, according to our ability; and the way to do it is to be "as the small rain upon the tender herb." Perhaps, dear friend, you say, "Well, I should be small rain, without any great effort, for I have not much in me." Just so; but yet that small rain has a way of its own, by which it makes up for being so small. How is that? say you. Why, by continuing to fall, day after day. Any gardener will tell you that with many hours of small rain, there is more done than with a drenching shower.

Constant Dropping Penetrates,

saturates and abides. Little deeds of kindness win love even more surely than one bounteous act. If you cannot say much of Gospel truth at a time, keep on saying a little, and saying it often. As you learn, teach; as you get, give; as you receive, distribute. Be as the small rain upon the tender herb. Be content to drop a word or two to-day, and another word or two to-morrow. Soon you may safely say twice as much, and in a week's time you may hold a long and distinctly religious conversation. It may soon happen that where the door was rudely shut in your face, you will become a welcome visitor, whereas had you forced your way in at first, you would have effectually destroyed all future opportunity. There is a great deal in speaking at the right moment. We may show our wisdom in *not* doing and in *not* saying, as much as in doing and saying. Time is a great ingredient in success. To speak out of season will show our zeal, but not always our sense. We are to be instant out of season as well as in season, but this does not involve incessant talking. I commend to everyone who would be a winner of souls by personal effort, the symbol, "as the small rain upon the tender herb."

II. The second head is, Moses hoped to be penetrating; "as the small rain upon the tender herb." Now, small rain is meant to enter the herb, so that it may drink in the nourishment and be truly refreshed. The rain is not to drench the herb, and it is not to flood it; it is to feed it, to revive it, to refresh it. This was

What Moses Aimed At.

Beloved, this is what all true preachers of Christ aim at. We long that the word which we speak may enter into the soul of man, may be taken up into the innermost nature and may produce its own divine result.

Why is it some people never seem to take in the word? I suppose, first, because some of it may be above their understanding. If you hear a sermon, and you do not know at all what the good man is about, how can it benefit you? If the preacher uses the high-class pulpit-language of the day, which is not English but a sort of English-Latin, produced rather by reading than by conversation with ordinary mortals; why then, the hearer usually loses his time and the preacher his labor. One said to me, "If I went to such and such a place I should not want my Bible, but I should need a dictionary, for otherwise I should not know what was meant." May that never be the case with us! When people cannot understand the meaning of our language, how can we expect that they can drink in the inner sense?

Ballooning in Theology

is all very fine, but it is of no use to poor souls down here below, who cannot hope to be allowed a place in the car. Many do not drink in the sacred word, because it seems to them too good to be true. This is limiting the goodness of God: God is so good that nothing can be too good to be looked for from Him. Many persons do not receive the gospel promise to the full, because they do not think it is true to them; anybody else may be blessed in that way, but they cannot think it probable that *they* shall be. Though the gospel is particularly directed to sinners, to such as "labor and are heavy-laden," and to such as need a Saviour, yet these good folks think, "Surely grace could never reach to *us*. Oh, how we lose our labor and fail to comfort men, because of the unbelief, which pretends to be the child of humility, but is really the off-spring of pride! The small rain does not get at the tender herb, because the herb shrinks from the silver drops which would cherish it.

III. I shall conclude with this third reflection, that Moses hoped to see results. You may, perhaps, say that you do not see this in the text. Will you kindly look again? "As the small rain upon the tender herb." Now, observe, in looking about among mankind, that whenever wise men expect any result from their labors, they always go to work in a manner suited and adapted to the end they have in view. If Moses means that his speech shall bless those he compares to tender herbs, he makes it like small rain. I see clearly that he seeks a result, for he adapts his means. There is a kind of trying to do good which I call

The "Hit-or-Miss" Style

of doing it. When a person wants to water plants, and they are tender herbs, if he looks for results he does not drench them: that would look as if he had no real object, but simply went through a piece of routine. Moses meant what he was doing. Finding the people to be comparable to tender herbs, he adapted his speech to them, and made it like the small rain. Now, what will be the result if we do the same? Why, brethren, when a man's discourse is like small rain to the tender herb, he sees the weak and perishing one *revive* and lift up his head. The herb was withering at first, it lay down as you see a newly planted thing do, faint and ready to die; but the small rain came, and it seemed to say, "Thank you," and it looked up, and lifted its head, and recovered from its swoon. You will see a reviving effect produced upon faint hearts and desponding minds. You will be a comforter, you will cheer away the fears of many, and make glad the timid and fearful. What a blessing it is when you see that result, for there is so much the more joy in the world, and God is so much the more glorified!

When you water tender herbs, and see them *grow*, you have a reward. It is delightful to

Watch the Development,

and increase of grace in those who are under our care. This has been an exceedingly sweet pleasure to me. I quote my own instance, because I have no doubt it is repeated in many of you. It has been a great delight to me to meet men serving God, and preaching the gospel gloriously, who were once young converts, and needed my fostering care. I know men, deacons of churches, fathers in Israel, that I recollect talking to twenty or twenty-five years ago, when they could not speak a word for Jesus, for they were not assured of their own salvation. I rejoice to see them leaders of the flock, whereas once they were poor, feeble lambs. I carried them in my bosom, and now they might almost carry me. I am glad enough to learn from them, and sit at their feet.

Once more, we water plants that we may see them bring forth fruit and become fit for use So shall we see those whom God blesses by our means become a joy to the Lord Himself, yielding fruits of holiness, patience and obedience, such as Jesus Christ delights in. Let us quit clouds and skies, and condescend to men of low estate. Let us come down from communing with the philosophers of culture, and the apostles of a new theology, to the ordinary people who live around us, and cannot comprehend these fine fictions. Let us come down to the streets and lanes, and do what we can for the poor, the fallen, the ignorant. Let us go with Jesus, in the gentleness and sweetness of His divine compassion, to the little children in years, and the babes in grace. So shall we be like Moses; so shall we be, better still, like the Lamb of God, to whose name be glory for ever and ever. Amen.

GEMS FROM NEW BOOKS.

THE DYING 'LONGSHOREMAN.*

I HEARD a brother minister tell a story of a poor, ignorant 'longshoreman, whom he visited on his dying-bed, and who was tormented by the thought of the grave, and of the fearful change which would pass upon his poor body. The minister quoted to him, "I will write upon him My new name," and, "His name shall be in their foreheads." A light came into his eyes. His harsh features were glorified. "I'm going, then," said he, "into the next world like a new-born baby; and God, He is my father; and He'll christen me with a new name; and He'll name me after Himself, just as if I'd never lived before; and neither saints nor devils will know anything of old John and his sins." And then, raising himself with the remnant of his fast failing strength and lifting his hands, he cried out, "O, but that's glorious! I thank my God!" Brethren, death has not been a curse if it has enabled you to say, "Therefore will I remember Thee."

So, then, the past is behind us. The dawn of the New-Year reddens the hill-tops. As we look back, let us remember God. How can we help it as we review this year, so crowded with His mercies? I had almost said, how can we remember anything else? We are wishing each other "A Happy New-Year." We have its happiness in our own hands. We have only to put our hand in God's and the thing is done.

The Single-Handed Struggle.

On a lonely road a man is wont to take up with whatever companion he can find; and if God set you to walk that lonely path of yours so that you might find and walk with Him, you know whether He did you a service or not. You know whether the days when you had no company but God were the most miserable days of your life. Sometimes in your travels you have found in the chance acquaintance of your solitary days a man so true and wise and helpful, that you have even changed your own route that you might journey farther in his company; and it would not be strange if, when you had come into days more fruitful in companionship and in kindly ministries of men to yourself, you should have said to the Divine Friend of your lonely hours, "Abide with me. If thy presence go not with me, carry me not up hence." In your retrospect of your lonely days, and of your single-handed struggle, as you are pleased to call it, the first prompting of your heart is to say, "I will remember Thee."

Arithmetic in Church.

A Scotch youth was telling his companion his experience in the study of arithmetic. Says he: "I plagued the master sore with wanting to understand everything before I could go on with my sums. Says he one day, 'My man, *if you will aye understand afore ye do as ye're tell't, ye'll never understand anything;* but if ye do the thing as I tell ye, ye'll be in the m'dst of it afore ye know ye're goin' into it.' I just thought I would try him. It was long division that I boglet most. Well, I went on, and I could do

* From "The Covenant of Peace." By Marvin R. Vincent, D.D. A series of discourses, dealing in a direct and practical fashion with "certain hard, painful and puzzling phases of Christian experience." It is full of precious consolation and encouragement for the tempted, the unsuccessful, the discouraged and the weary. 315 pages; price, $1.75. Published by *Anson D. F. Randolph & Company*, 38 West Twenty-third Street, New York.

THE CHRISTIAN HERALD AND SIGNS OF OUR TIMES. JAN. 12, 1888.

The Crown Princess of Germany.

The Villa Zirio of San Remo.

Sir Morell Mackenzie.

the thing well enough, and aye I thought the master was wrong, for I never knew the reason of all that beginning at the wrong end, and takin' down the substractin' and all that, you would hardly believe it, it was only this very day I was sitting in the kirk. It was a long psalm they were singing: long division came into my head again, and first one bit glimmering of light came in, and soon another and before the psalm was done I saw through the whole process of it. But, you see, if I had not done as I was told, and learned all about how it was done beforehand, I should have had nothing to go reasoning about, and would have found out nothing."

I think about the whole matter is contained in that little story. You will acquire divine knowledge in the same way as you acquire human knowledge, by the road of obedience. So many fail because they do not like to obey without knowing the reason why. They want God to deal with them as equals, not as inferiors. To follow this line of implicit obedience is to become children; and that, they think, is not dignified. But there is no other way so far as I know. Christ allows no other way, "Except ye become as little children ye cannot enter into the kingdom of God." *No man ever understands the Bible until he has honestly tried to live it.*

THE CROWN PRINCESS OF GERMANY.

(See Portrait.)

THE difficult position occupied by this beautiful and able lady is described in the sketch of her husband (on page 18). All who know her, even h r enemies, acknowledge her remarkable abilities and the majestic force of her character. A distinguished writer, who has had ample opportunities of forming an opinion, says she is clever, learned, and has diplomatic skill equal if not superior to Prince Bismarck himself, who is her great antagonist. In the contest between them she is entitled to our sympathy, for the principles which have brought her into conflict with the Chancellor and the Court are the principles of constitutional liberty and the recognition of popular rights.

The Crown Princess is the eldest daughter of the Queen of England. She was born November 21, 1840, and is now therefore in her forty-eighth year. Her education was conducted under the personal supervision of her father, Prince Albert, but she showed early in life a marked independence of character, and while following the lines of reading and study he marked out for her, made excursions on her own account into other fields of literature, which saved her from the narrowness of mind which characterized him. She is a most admirable wife and mother, and her husband's devotion to her is almost worship.

THE VILLA ZIRIO, SAN REMO.

THE CROWN PRINCE'S PRESENT RESIDENCE.

(See Illustration.)

THERE is no difference of opinion among the Crown Prince's physicians as to the importance of his breathing the mildest and most salubrious air, in his present condition. He has, therefore, on their advice, gone to San Remo, a town in the north of Italy, on the shores of the Mediterranean, where he occupies the Villa Zirio, formerly the residence of the Duke d'Aosta.

The Villa Zirio is truly a delightful residence. It is surrounded with palm and orange trees, and Oriental vegetation, and the place is illuminated and warmed by continued sunshine, while the health-giving breezes from the Mediterranean are wafted through its open windows. There with his devoted wife, his younger children, and about thirty attendants, the Prince is spending the winter.

SIR MORELL MACKENZIE, M. D.,

THE CROWN PRINCE'S PHYSICIAN.

(See Portrait).

THE responsibility of a physician was never more clearly perceived, than it is in the person of the distinguished specialist, whose portrait appears on this page. When the Crown Prince of Germany was first seized with the affection of the throat, the most eminent physicians in the Fatherland pronounced his malady cancer, and advised an operation, which would have destroyed his voice and might have killed him. They believed, however, that his life would have been saved to his country by the operation. If the operation was not performed, then they said he must surely die. The Crown Princess naturally shrank from subjecting her husband to treatment which must make him dumb for life, and might precipitate the calamity it was intended to avert. She therefore summoned Dr. Mackenzie, the English physician, and under his advice, the operation was not performed. The German doctors denounce both him and the Crown Princess, and declare that the only chance of prolonging the Crown Prince's life has been rejected. Still, Dr. Mackenzie remains calm and confident, and it remains to be seen whether the result will justify him or the German doctors.

Dr. Mackenzie is not so young as he looks. He was born in 1837, and is therefore, now fifty-one years of age. He received his professional education at the London Hospital Medical College, and afterwards studied in Paris and Vienna. As a student, he had a most brilliant and successful career. In 1863, he founded the Hospital for Diseases of the Throat, in London, and in the same year obtained the Jacksonian Prize from the Royal College of Surgeons, for an essay on Diseases of the Larynx. He was soon afterwards elected assistant-physician to the London Hospital, becoming in due course full physician, and was appointed Lecturer on Diseases of the Throat, an appointment which he still holds. Dr. Mackenzie visited this country in 1882. While in Washington, he was the guest of Dr. Carroll Morgan, of that city. In a recent interview, Dr. Morgan described Dr. Mackenzie as "cool, keen, intellectual and ambitious, of perfect self-possession and great skill.

HAZELTINE'S REMORSE.

(See Illustration on page 29).

IN the early morning hours of a winter's day a young man quitted the office of a daily journal, and, without staying to join in the conversation of his brother scribes, around the city editor's desk, hurried down stairs into the street. He could not restrain his impatience for his car to start, and when it reached the nearest point to his home, he swung himself off and ran as for his life. He stopped at a little frame house, in which an upper window was brilliantly lighted, and was admitted by an old woman, whose garb plainly told that she was a hired nurse.

"How is she now?" was his eager question.

"No better, Mr. Hazeltine," was the old woman's reply. "Just talk, talk, talk, all the time; furrin language mostly, and always as fast as her tongue can go."

The young man addressed as Mr. Hazeltine hurried up-stairs, and stood beside the bed of the sufferer. She was his wife, and as he looked down at the flushed face and beautiful disordered hair, a look of unutterable anguish passed across his face.

"Doctor said nothing more could be done," said the nurse, who had come in and stood beside the distracted husband. "He's coming in again in the morning, but, seems to me, she wont live to see him."

"I'll just go and get a wash, nurse," said Mr. Hazeltine, "and then I'll come and relieve you. I guess you are tired."

"No more than you be, sir; you must be most weared out, work and watch all the time; you'll kill yourself."

"Oh, don't mind me; I shall be all right if she lives."

He went into another room and tried, by the copious application of cold water, to refresh himself for his watch by the sufferer's bed. On his way back to the room, he stopped suddenly, and returned. Shutting the door he knelt down and prayed earnestly. It was more than three years since he had prayed, and now it seemed less like prayer than agonizing self-abasement—wrestling like Jacob's that anxious night by the brook Jabbok. How much he had to confess and deplore! Three years before that night he was a student, preparing for the work of the ministry. Full of hope and energy, a young man of great promise, from whom the professors of his college and his many friends expected great things, he had gone to a famous health resort for a brief rest and recuperation, before entering upon his life work. There he fell under the fascination of a beautiful woman, whose loveliness of form and feature dazzled him and infatuated him. His one passion was a love of music, and the lady was an accomplished musician. This riveted his chains, and when, joined with her musical talents, she showed much sparkling wit and brilliant conversational power, he became her slave. He exerted himself to win her favor, and succeeded. Without knowing anything of her antecedents, or any more of her personally than he had seen in a few brief weeks, he married her. It all seemed like a dream, so rapidly had his passion carried him along.

Hazeltine's Prayer in the Crisis of His Wife's Illness.

A few days convinced him that the work to which he had consecrated his life was no longer possible. His wife was not only irreligious, but a scoffer. Yet her personal charms held him captive, and, for her sake, he proved false to his God. He easily secured a position on a city newspaper, where his talents secured him a good income, and, giving up prayer and all religious observances, he abandoned himself blindly to a life of pleasure.

That was Hazeltine's past. It lay stretched before his mental gaze, in those chill morning hours, in all its hideous shame and wickedness. He loved his wife, ah, how dearly! Yet she was dying now, and he had never tried to win her to Christ. Nay, more; by his example he had confirmed her in her contempt for religion and her disbelief in its power. This agony was his punishment, and it was almost more than he could bear. He rose, at last, and with a blanched face went to the room in which his wife lay, hovering between life and death. The rapid, delirious talk had ceased when he entered, and the beautiful face lay still in exhaustion on the pillow. It was a sad scene; even the hired nurse was shedding tears. It seemed as if every breath must be the last.

"I am going to pray for her, nurse," said the young husband. "God alone can save her."

The old woman covered her face, and Hazeltine, taking one of his wife's hands in his own, knelt down and prayed earnestly that God would recall the fleeting spirit, that opportunity might yet be given for repentance and regeneration. Never, in his life, had his whole soul been so poured out in agonizing pleading, and when he rose, it was with a firm conviction that his prayer was answered. Almost before he had regained his feet, his wife opened her eyes and looked at him. For the first time in many days he saw there the light of recognition. The crisis was past.

Very tenderly and lovingly Hazeltine nursed his wife back to life. He told her of the prayer which preceded the change in her illness, and she was awed. He told her, too, as he had not done before, his own history, and of the terrible backsliding of his life. Whether it was harder for the backsliding husband or the irreligious wife to enter into life with God, it would not be easy to say. They both sought forgiveness, humbly and earnestly, and to all who so seek, it is not denied.

THE FAMILY OF TRIPE COURT.

By Brenda.

(Continued from page 14.)

CHARITY'S CHILDREN.

BRIDGET had never lived before in any place so grand and clean and healthy as the Infirmary, yet she heard more murmuring and saw more discontent there than she had ever done in Tripe Court. It was a new experience to her, as to many more under that roof, though there were some who had been there for years, and would never leave it until they were carried to the grave. She was no philosopher, only a poor hard-working woman, yet she was gifted with a woman's penetration, and perceived the truth that philosophers have always insisted upon, that human felicity does not depend so much on outward circumstances as on the disposition of the man or woman. There are some who bear their ills so cheerfully, and are so thankful for the mercies they have, that they are happier than others whose lot is almost without a cross. So it was in the Infirmary. It was not the greatest sufferers nor the most hopeless who repined most.

Content was found here and there, it is true, but they were isolated cases: discontent was the rule of this great almshouse hospital. Dire necessity had brought nearly everybody under its broad roof. They had fought against coming till the brokers at home had seized the bed underneath them, till the last crust had been eaten, till the last penny had been spent, till their last friend had deserted them, till, as in Bridget's case, they were unable to do another stroke of work; and though, in comparison to the home they had left, the Infirmary was almost a palace, and its food sumptuous to the starvation fare they had left behind them, there were few who would not have returned to that home if they could, with all its squalor and all its misery and all its starvation, just because it was *home*.

This Infirmary was a beautiful place; what could they want better as a residence? Why, some people wondered, could not they settle down, and accept it as home? Yes, but *places* do not make homes; homes are made up of loved, familiar presences; of little children's prattle and sweet caresses; of little hopes, little joys, little troubles, little disappointments, and all the greater vicissitudes of life, shared with and borne by hearts whose sympathies and interests are identical with our own. The people here found themselves in a palace of strangers, and therefore did not feel it to be a palace, much less a home, but rather a place of punishment, into which the hard treatment of an unkind world had at last forced them. And so the greater number of them lay with sore, rebellious hearts, murmuring against God's decrees and chastisements, and longing, oh, longing so! to be back in the little old, dirty, familiar spot, where the frosts used to bite them, and hunger pinch them; yet it was *home*.

Bridget Mite, laundress, was, like all the rest, unreconciled to the parish's magnificent hospitality, deeply lonely in its crowd, and feeling exactly as if she had come to a place of punishment. Parted from her baby—the most dreadful thing that could possibly happen to her, she thought—poor Bridget felt that the last drop in her most bitter cup had been added—sorrow could go no farther—and there was a despair at her heart when she was carried away, after parting with husband and child, that only God knew the depth of. She had reached the darkest point in all her dark life: on the ocean of her troubles the last little ray of light had gone out; she was left lonely amidst the waves, only the sound of their restless surging, in her ears, and no gleam in the east.

No, no gleam in the east yet; but sunrise was nearer at hand than it seemed possible it could be. It is always darkest before dawn, and over the waste of dreary waters God was leading her, by her very helplessness, into safe anchorage and transcendent light. It is often so in God's dealings with men and women, especially with those who are naturally strong and energetic, and independent in character, and who, finding the world going against them, try to fight it, and shape their own destiny, not discerning that their chastening is from God, and therefore never learning the lesson it designs to teach—

> ". . . . . The soul's surrendered choice,
> The settling of the will,
> Lying down gently on the Cross
> God's purpose to fulfil."

Not very often till they are divested of everything earthly, and they feel themselves crushed and ruined, and they are obliged to own themselves helpless and undone, will men and women give up the blind struggling and contending with the world, and yield themselves, still and submissive, into God's hands, there to be treated as it seems to Him best.

For the first few hours after her arrival in the Victoria Ward of the Infirmary, Bridget was in too much pain of body to think much. She was undressed at once and put into one of the snowy little beds. She was given a tumbler of milk to drink, of which she was glad, for she was feverish and thirsty. Then the doctor came and examined her injured limb, and after that she was conscious of having lotions and bandages applied by one of the fresh-complexioned nurses in white bib apron and cap. The jolting in Jemmy Wiggles's cab, and the movement of the journey generally, had increased the inflammation in Bridget's leg, and she lay with puckered brow and tightly closed eyes and mouth, trying to keep in the groans that now and then escaped her, when the sharp stabs of pain came, and made her wince.

She felt feverish and hot, and longed for a drink again—oh, that milk they had given her before, how delicious it was! so cold and refreshing to her parched lips! But she was suffering too much to ask for anything. It was all she could manage to do, to lie there quietly and stifle her groans; from a feeling of shyness she desired to make no noise. Bridget was a sensitive woman, and wished to avoid the attention of the strangers around her. She opened her eyes once, and saw they were all observing her from their pillows opposite. She closed her eyes again, now tighter than ever, and was conscious of a new, keen sensation, that of publicity, which is indeed veritable pain to some natures, to the sensitive and home-loving.

Presently dinner came; old women in poorhouse clothes brought it in on large trays—steaming boiled mutton to-day, for the majority, and potatoes and huge hunches of bread, and beer; for some, beef-tea and chicken, and barley-water. They carried a portion to each bedside in turn, and those who were able sat up and partook of it, wearing the little red shawl that lay folded at the foot of the counterpane. A nice little bedtable was supplied to each patient, and those of them who were too ill or too old to sit up, were fed with spoon or drinking-cup by the nurses. There was nothing lacking at this feast in quality, quantity and comfort—all were good; yet there was not general content. Sisters Anne and Mary sang grace, but few joined in it, few closed their eyes and said "Amen."

The world's spirit of rapacity and greed now showed itself. Certain of the women scanned their neighbors' plates, and angry voices were heard complaining that their own plates were not so full. "They'd have their food weighed;" "They'd complain to the Board;" or, "The beer was short measure—Mrs. Brown's there was up to the brim, *theirs* didn't touch it, though it was frothed;" or, "Why should Peggy Lee have chicken and they not? Doctors had ordered it? Then doctors favored her, and they'd complain to the Board;" and so on all about the ward. The complaints were made to, sometimes hurled at, the nurses, who took them for the most part patiently; they were so accustomed to hear the food grumbled at, and the relative quantities questioned, it seemed hardly worth while to take any notice.

Dinner was brought in turn to Bridget, but she could not eat anything; she drank the barley-water offered, and that was all. More hours passed, afternoon hours, in which most of the patients dozed—those of them who could. Some, like Bridget, were in too much pain to sleep; others, principally the very aged, seemed somehow unable to do so, though they were trying their best, and were weary enough, as was evidenced by their frequent yawns, ending in a kind of worn-out groan, that very old people indulge in when they are tired. The little women in gray clothes took chairs close to the stove, and soon their close-capped heads were nodding, first to one side and then to the other, in sound sleep. Sisters Anne and Mary wrote letters at the table; and so the afternoon passed.

Twilight came, the gas was lit, then everybody who had been sleeping woke up, and the same women who had clattered in with the dinner now clattered in with the tea on large trays. Mugs full to the brim of steaming tea, and plates of thick slices of bread-and-butter, were served out at each bedside, bed-tables were put across, red shawls put on again. There was less grumbling at this meal than at dinner, though the quality of the tea was denounced by some as "rubbishy trash. They'd have it out with the Board, see if they wouldn't!" and so on, in the old style of ungrateful murmuring at good provision. Bridget again ate nothing, but drank the tea to the last drop. Her hot, flushed face attracted the attention of the woman who brought it to her.

"Are you so hot?" she said, wonderingly, screwing up her little squinting eyes at her. "Do you feel bad?"

"Yes," nodded Bridget.

"Well, the doctor 'll be round again soon," said the woman, shuffling away in her felt shoes to somebody else.

More hours passed, during which the doctor did come again, and ordered fresh treatment for Bridget. The lotion was to be changed to one more soothing; the leg was to be dressed in a different way, and she was to have a draught that would quiet her nerves. At last a great bell rang somewhere in the building, an aggressive, hurry-scurry sort of bell. That was the signal for the gas being lowered, and all the attendants leaving the ward save one in poor-house garb, and Sister Mary, who were on duty yet for a few more hours. Then silence reigned, and night fell on the Victoria Ward, bringing to most of the strangely assorted company gathered there, night's blessed accompaniment, sleep.

Then the company dreamed: the battered-faced old apple-seller that she had made a good bargain with her oranges, which she had boiled to look worth twopence; the fresh-faced actress, that she was in the theatre, poising herself to take the dangerous leap which had resulted in fall and injury; the Frenchwoman, that she was in the gay, lighted streets of her capital again, revelling in the glare and the glitter and the falseness of its show. The silver-haired elderly woman, the ex-governess, lay with a smile on her lips—ah, poor lady! she was doubtless living over again, in her dreams, some of those old grand times in the past; she was back, perhaps, under the shade of the broad chestnuts in a nobleman's park, on a summer's afternoon, the birds singing overhead, and the deer feeding away there in the glades. Who would have guessed that those gentle white hands would one day lie on the coarse sheets of a poor-house! that that graceful girl would one day be taking her sleep beside a crazy old creature of the gutter, whose dreams were all of gin-palaces and adroit evasions of the police!—for "Biddy," the drunken old cigar-light seller, lay in the next bed.

Yes; the kind, soft angel, Sleep, passed swiftly through the ward, and touched most pillows, yet not all. She passed over some, amongst them Bridget's. No sleep came to hers. At the fall of night she grew to be in less pain: the doctor's orders had been carried out, the lotion and the draught soothed her, the flush left her cheek, and the stabs in her leg gradually ceased; but still she did not sleep. With the soothing of her bodily, her mental being awoke into activity, and the stabs came to mind and heart instead. She began thinking of them all at home, and when she did that, a thousand questions pressed on her brain to disturb and harass her. Had Tom got safe back with baby? and if so, how were they managing? Would Polly remember, she wondered, to put the shawl over the head of baby's cradle when they laid it down, to keep the draught out? Would anybody remember to stop up the great hole in the wainscotting that that big rat came out of the other day? Had she made it plain to Tom about the money, and those debts that were owing her? What food would they give baby? Would Poll have the sense to ask Mrs. Job—would they know how to soothe it if it cried?

Ah, her poor little precious, darling baby! She heard its cry in her ears; she felt it in her arms, pressed close up against her. Whenever she looked down through the silent night she saw its little pale face, and its little bright black eyes looking up at her out of the darkness. She thought of it as she saw it last, making "the pitiful lip." Then—there was no one to see her now, everybody was asleep, and darkness covered her—poor Bridget began crying softly to herself. But not everybody was asleep; some one else lay wakeful, too, on her bed, a woman next to her, on the left, who caught the sound of Bridget's sobs. She rose up on her elbow, and leant over towards Bridget's bed.

"Ma'am," she whispered low, "can I do anything for you?"

"No, thank you," sobbed Bridget, turning her head to see who had spoken. She could not make out much, just a very small face bent towards her in the darkness, and a little hump in the bed, as if the figure on it were very small.

"You feels a bit lonely and strange, ma'am?" whispered the neighbor. "The first night and all, away from home. You leave husband and children, perhaps?"

"Yes," sobbed Bridget, "and a baby not weaned, and I don't know how it'll get on to-night, or who'll take care of it time I'm away."

"Do you know them verses, ma'am," pursued her neighbor, "that begins 'There is an eye'?"

Bridget nodded "No."

"Well, then, I'd like to say them to you. There's a wonderful deal of comfort in 'em, I always think."

And the woman repeated in a low, husky voice the beautiful hymn beginning:

"There is an eye that never sleeps
Beneath the wing of night;
There is an ear that never shuts
When sink the beams of light.

"There is an arm that never tires
When human strength gives way;
There is a love that never fails
When earthly loves decay."

She paused after saying it. Bridget only sobbed, not having got much comfort out of the words. She was not a religious woman—she would have said she had no time for being that. The faith she once had, as a child, and as a woman before trouble overwhelmed her, seemed dead within her, and she had left off praying a long while ago.

"I," said the little woman softly to Bridget, "will wield that power for you to-night. I will pray that that eye, that arm, that love, may reach and be around your little baby to-night, and I'm just as *sure* that no harm will be allowed to happen to it, and that it will be taken care of, as I am that there is a God in heaven." Bridget was conscious the next minute of a kiss on her forehead. The little woman had shuffled with difficulty out of bed to give it to her. "There," she said, shuffling back again, "I should be scolded if I were caught, but I couldn't help it. I would have given anything—twenty pounds if I had had it—for somebody to have kissed me the first night I came in; I was like *you*, ma'am, fit to break my heart, and nobody spoke to me a kind word."

It was only a *stranger's* kiss! not like that of kith and kin—yet the touch of human lips was a comfort to poor Bridget. She dwelt on the thought, too, that some one was going to pray for her baby, though her faith in prayer and in Jesus, our great High-Priest and Intercessor, was so faint and cold. And by and by Bridget's sobs grew hushed, and at last she too fell asleep and dreamed.

(To be Continued.)

JESUS AND THE AFFLICTED.

By Mrs. M. Baxter.

S. S. Lesson for January 22. Matt. 15 : 21-31.
Golden Text, James 5 : 13.

Ver. 21. Jesus Goes into Phœnicia—On the Coast of the Mediterranean—Ver. 22. A Gentile Woman a Descendant of the Canaanites—Analagous to Our Indians—Her Knowledge Shows how Far Christ's Fame had Spread—Prayed for Mercy on Herself, Though the Affliction was on Her Daughter—Her Faith—Did not Doubt Christ's Power—Recognized His Messiahship—Demoniacal Possession Distressing—Men Possessed Now and Not Grievously Vexed—Ver. 23. Christ's Silence a Test of Faith—The Interposition of the Disciples—Sprang from their Own Discomfort—Vers. 24-27. The Importunity of the Woman, an Example—Proof Against Humiliation and Repulse—Ver. 28. Her Request Granted—Her Faith Honored—Vers. 30-31. The Effect of the Miracles—People Glorified God.

"MANY are the afflictions of the righteous: but the Lord delivereth him out of them all" (Ps. 34 : 19). Many speak of affliction as though it must necessarily mean sickness. But this is a wrong use of terms. To afflict is, "to visit with calamity, to grieve, to torment," and affliction means "calamity, sorrow, grief;" whereas sickness means the state of being sick, disease, illness, malady, nausea." The Word of God distinguishes between the two. Our blessed Lord led His disciples to expect and to endure afflictions. In the world ye shall have tribulations (John 16 : 33). "It is enough for the disciple that he be as his Master, and the servant as his Lord" (Matt. 10 : 25). Paul charged Timothy to "*endure* afflictions (II Tim. 4 : 5); and James says, "Take, my brethren, the prophets, for an example of suffering, affliction and of patience" (James 5 : 10). Yet the same blessed Saviour who thus taught His disciples to endure affliction, always took away sickness, and taught them to do the same. And the apostle James gives definite directions to the sick and the afflicted when he says, "Is any among you afflicted? let him pray. Is any merry? let him sing psalms. Is any sick among you? let him call for the elders of the church, and let them pray over him, anointing him with oil in the name of the Lord, and the prayer of faith shall save the sick, and the Lord shall raise him up; and if he have committed sins, they shall be forgiven him" (James 5 : 13-15). Thus we see that, while sickness is one kind of affliction, it is one for which

Jesus Has Provided A Remedy,

which it glorifies Him for us to accept. It was so habitual with Jesus to heal disease wherever He went that it was always expected of Him. Our last chapter closed with a great work of healing among those who touched the hem of His garment in the land of Gennesareth; "as many as touched were made perfectly whole." From thence, after a conversation with some delegates from the Scribes and Pharisees of Jerusalem, who had come down to Galilee, not to learn but to question the work of Jesus, He "departed into the coasts of Tyre and Sidon." It was no caprice which led Him there. He had a work to do, and He went there, as elsewhere, in obedience to His Father. Jesus and the needy one soon came in contact: a woman of Canaan came out of the same coasts, and cried unto Him, saying, "Have mercy on me, O Lord, Thou Son of David! my daughter is grievously vexed with a devil." Some people believe that this terrible scourge of possession with a devil existed only in our Lord's time. No one who has witnessed delirium tremens or morphia delirium, nor yet the insanity which comes from uncontrolled pride or selfishness, or unsubdued temper, can have any such idea. Those who have been thus possessed will always say, "I was under the power of the devil and could not help myself." Let anyone visit the cell of the murderer, or speak with the lost of either sex, when the Spirit of God begins to show them the reality of things, and you will hear their

Unanimous Testimony

to the actual power of Satan over their souls and their bodies. Jesus would never have added to His charge to His disciples for all time, "In My name shall they cast out devils" (Mark 16 : 17), if this world has no devils to cast out. The poor woman said, "Have mercy on *me*." The enemy cannot have power over one member of a family without the whole house being affected by it. Sometimes it may take the form of the most fearful depression; every condemnatory passage of Scripture is brought to the mind of the poor victim, and the face is only an index of the deep hoplessness and gloom which the enemy brings upon the soul. Sometimes it is an unclean spirit, and then hearts are broken with the shame and sin brought into the family. Sometimes it is a blaspheming spirit, and then the poor victim, even when trying to pray, is filled with wicked thoughts against God. Thank God, James tells us to resist the devil, and he will flee from us (James 4 : 7); he is a conquered foe. But there are some who are so under his power that they cannot resist him, and God will hear the prayers and respond to the faith of others for them.

When the poor woman thus prayed, Jesus "answered her not a word!" How unlike Him it seemed! But Jesus did

Nothing Without a Purpose.

While He had it in His heart to save the daughter, He would exercise the faith of the mother, and teach His disciples by it. Thousands of times blessings have been lost by God's children, and Jesus has lost an opportunity of glorifying Himself, because they have not had patience to wait out the fulfilment of His purposes. The disciples became impatient, and said, "Send her away; for she crieth after us." Perhaps they felt it would be more convenient to them and better for the cause of Christ, if her case were dealt with quickly. How often have we been under the same impression! When the eyes of many were on an abandoned drunkard or profligate, how we have sometimes wanted to hurry God into doing His work quickly for the credit of His cause! And when some more than usually bad case of cancer or lameness, or of advanced consumption, came for healing, how often have we heard one and another pray for instantaneous healing, as though God's cause would fail if it were not done just then. And perhaps the very eagerness to bring God into our narrow thoughts was that which hindered Him. He looked for faith, which would have rested the case with Him in quiet certainty. He found, instead, restlessness and anxiety, which manifested the very opposite to faith. Jesus answered, "I am not sent but unto the lost sheep of the house of Israel."

I am Not Sent.

Jesus did nothing without authority. He always *followed*, and never led His Father, although He could say, "I and My Father are One" (John 10 : 30). But the woman had a fixed conviction that Jesus *could* not in the end turn away from her plea, and she acted on it, and came "and worshipped Him saying, Lord, help me." True, *she* was not one of "the lost sheep of the House of Israel," but whatever *she* was, Jesus was still the great Physician, Jesus had brought the tidings that God "loved the world." He had told men that the Son of Man was not come "to destroy men's lives, but to save them." And so, in spite of present appearances, in spite of His own very words, she acted on what He had proved Himself to be—a Friend, a Physician, a Saviour, to all who came to Him. This was faith. The woman rested in what *He* was, not in what *she* was. From first to last, her claim upon Him was His own character, and that only. He was the Son of David, and, as such, she first besought Him; as such she claimed that He would help one who was outside the fold of Israel. But she was to meet with a stronger rebuff. "He answered and said, It is not meet to take the children's bread and to cast it to dogs." She had not shown herself a dog, and had she yielded to one bit of personal feeling, she might have felt deeply wounded. It was true the Jews did call the Gentiles "Gentile dogs," but it was unlike Jesus to speak thus. Yet no such thought seems to have occupied her mind. On the contrary, she said "Truth, Lord," thus taking the place of the dog which He had assigned her; "Truth, Lord; yet the dogs eat of the crumbs which fall from their master's table." She met every rebuff by faith in Him. And the heart of Jesus was glad; He loves to be trusted and His heart went out to the persistent mother when He said, "O woman, great is thy faith; be it unto thee even as thou wilt."

"Even as Thou Wilt."

This is the kind of "good measure, pressed down, and shaken together, and running over," that God loves to give in answer to prayer, where hearts are empty enough of self to bear it. "And her daughter was made whole from that very hour." Why are answers to prayers delayed? This is a question so often asked, so often badly answered, or not answered at all. In this case, it was to bring out the faith of the Syro Phœnician woman. When Daniel was fasting three full weeks, the answer to his prayer, which was started on its way as soon as he *began* to pray, was delayed all the time he continued to mourn and fast, exactly "one and twenty days," i. e., three full weeks (Dan. 10: 2, 12). Why? Because it is wrong to fast? certainly not, but because he had been taught (Dan. 9 : 23) that God heard at the begining of his prayer, and thus he should have learned to trust. God educates us in faith by everything which happens. If we are disappointed that the answer does not come at the time or in the way which we have pictured to ourselves it should come, do not let us therefore lose faith in God. Faith believes "that He *is*, and that He is a Rewarder of them that diligently seek Him" (Heb. 11 :6). If "He *is*" all that He says He is, we can afford to see things turn out contrary to our expectations; it will be an opportunity for Him to verify His own Word in His own way.

"Jesus departed from thence, and came nigh unto the sea of Galilee; and went up into a mountain, and sat down there." He loved the quiet and purity of mountains. "And great multitudes came unto Him, having with them those that were lame, blind, dumb, maimed, and many others, and cast them down at Jesus' feet." It was no easy thing to bring such up the mountain side. Many would needs be carried or brought on asses. But so sure were they of healing, that they would make any effort to get transported to where Jesus was; they must meet *Him*, this was the one necessity. There they lay all round Him, and He healed them, "insomuch that the multitude wondered, when they saw the dumb to speak, the maimed to be whole, the lame to walk and the blind to see; and they glorified the God of Israel." We need only to have *really* to do with Him, and our sick ones would be healed as certainly now as then. We thank Him for thousands who have been already blest in soul and healed in body by His hand alone.

AMEN.

I cannot say,
Beneath the pressure of life's care to-day,
I joy in these:
But I can say
That I had rather walk this rugged way,
If Him it please.

I cannot feel
That all is well when dark'ning clouds conceal
The shining sun:
But then I know
God lives and loves; and say, since it is so,
"Thy will be done."

I cannot speak
In happy tones; the tear-drops on my cheek
Show I am sad;
But I can speak
Of grace to suffer with submission meek,
Until made glad.

I do not see
Why God should e'en permit some things to be,
When He is love;
But I can see
Though often dimly, through the mystery,
His hand above.

I may not try
To keep the hot tears back; but hush that sigh,
"It might have been;"
And try to still
Each rising murmur, and to God's sweet will
Respond—AMEN.

—*F. G. Browning.*

J. E. Jewett, Publisher, 77 Bible House, New York will furnish the above poem in leaflet form at twenty cents per hundred. A *Sample Packet* of 50 leaflets assorted (no two alike), will be sent post-paid for ten cents. Postage stamps taken.

THE TALMUD.

What It Is and What it Knows about Jesus and his Followers. By Rev. Bernhard Pick, Ph.D. Ideal Edition, Small Pica type, cloth, *50c.*; postage 6c.

One of the most interesting and valuable of recent contributions to religious literature. It answers popular curiosity as to what the Talmud is, and gives to students information of transcendant value, not heretofore accessible.

"The Talmud is the slow growth of several centuries. It is a chaos of Jewish learning, wisdom and folly, a continent of rubbish with hidden pearls of true maxims and poetic fables."—Philip Schaff.

"Here, then, we find a prodigious mass of contradictory opinions, an infinite number of casuistical cases, a logic of scholastic theology, some recondite wisdom, and much rambling dotage: many puerile tales and oriental fancies; ethics and sophisms, reasonings and unreasonings, subtle solutions, and maxims and riddles."—Benjamin Disraeli.

"It has proved a grateful task to wander through the mazes of the Talmud and cull flowers yet sparkling with the very dew of Eden. Figures in shining garments haunt its recesses. Prayers of deep devotion, sublime confidence and noble benediction, echo in its ancient tongue. Sentiments of lofty courage, of high resolve, of infantile tenderness, of far-seeing prudence, fall from the lips of venerable sages. No less practicable would it be to stray with an opposite intention, and to extract venom, instead of honey, from the flowers that seem to spring up in self-sown profusion. Fierce, intolerant, vindictive hatred for mankind; idle subtlety; pride and self-conceit amounting to insanity; indelicacy pushed to a grossness that renders what it calls virtue more hateful than the vice of more modest people: all these strung together would give no more just an idea of the Talmud than would the chaplets of its lovelier flowers."—*Edinburgh Review.*

HISTORY of the JEWS.

The Jews Since the Destruction of Jerusalem. Brevier type, double leaded; cloth, *15c.*; postage 3c.

"A very interesting and valuable sketch, exceedingly well written, of the political condition, numerical strength, and employments of the Jewish people in the different countries, since their dispersion at the destruction of their National Capital."—*The Guardian*, Philadelphia.

"This monograph may be regarded as the fullest treatment of this subject in the briefest compass. We have found it fascinating reading, and share more and more as we proceed in the author's strong and just sympathy for this outcast and oppressed race."—*Christian Evangelist*, St. Louis.

Apocryphal LIFE OF JESUS.

By Rev. Bernhard Pick, Ph.D. Ideal Edition, Small Pica type, cl., *50c.*; post. 6c.

"Dr. Pick has done a good service in translating these extra-canonical narratives. They form a highly interesting addition to Christian literature, and the accompanying notes increase their value."—*Lutheran Observer*, Phila.

"These narratives are of decided value as a *foil* to set off the brightness, beauty, and simplicity of the Gospels. When one reads the infinite absurdities of which even good men have been guilty, when trying to supplement the silence of scriptures on the childhood and youth of our Lord: and compares, with such human attempts, the *inspired* narrative, these apocryphal Gospels become at once evidential in value."—*Presbyterian*, Wilmington, N. C.

The Literary Revolution Catalogue (84 pages) sent free on application. Alden's publications are *NOT* sold by *book-sellers*—no discounts allowed except as advertised. Books sent for *examination before payment*, satisfactory reference being given. (1bd277)

JOHN B. ALDEN, Publisher, NEW YORK:
293 Pearl St.; P. O. Box 1227. CHICAGO: Lakeside Building, Clark and Adams Sts.

SPECIAL NOTICE. *Any readers of the Christian Herald who wish to procure the above books published by Mr. J. B. Alden, can send their orders to me at the same price as above, and the books will be sent promptly and guaranteed to reach you safely.*

J. E. JEWETT, 77 Bible House, New York.

Vol. XI., No. 3. Office, 63 Bible House. N. Y. THURSDAY, JANUARY 19, 1888. Annual Subscription, $1.50.

CONTENTS OF THIS NUMBER.

PORTRAIT AND LIFE OF MR. JOHN J. HARWOOD, THE CHRISTIAN MAYOR OF MANCHESTER, ENGLAND.
WORLDLY MARRIAGES. Dr. Talmage's Sermon Last Sunday Morning.
ANECDOTES RELATED AT RECENT EVANGELISTIC MEETINGS.
DARK PROSPECTS FOR ENGLAND. By Rev. M. Baxter.
THE ECCLESIASTICAL COBBLER. By Dr. McGlynn.
CURRENT EVENTS: The New Cabinet Nominations—Projected Reform of National Banks—Attempt to Mediate in the Gigantic Strike in Pennsylvania—Mayor Hewitt on Gifts of Land to Churches and Charities—Another Earthquake in the South, etc.
THE SYMBOLIC CUP. A New Sermon by C. H. Spurgeon.
Gems from New Books: The Scottish Primer, etc.
PICTURE OF THE PAMPAS IN SOUTH AMERICA.
A Hotel Keeper's Complaint—A Prodigious Gas Bill—The Last Operation—The Troubles at Ponape—Tangled in Electric Wires.
A MOMENTOUS MEETING AT A GATE. (With Illustration)
THE FAMILY OF TRIPE COURT. (Continued.)
PETER CONFESSING CHRIST. By Mrs. M. Baxter.

MANCHESTER IN 1887 AS SEEN FROM THE RAILWAY.

MANCHESTER AS IT WAS IN THE YEAR 1728.

Mr. John James Harwood, the Christian Mayor of Manchester, England—Scene in Picadilly, Manchester.

JOHN JAMES HARWOOD.

THE CHRISTIAN IN MUNICIPAL HONOR.

Religion and Obscurity not Necessarily Allied—A Conspicuous Instance of Integrity in Honor—A Unique Distinction—A Third Term in Office—His Early Struggles and Savings—A Bank-book Consecrated—Twenty-five Years in Sunday-school Work—A Church Official's Testimony—The City he Governs—Its Antiquity—Religious History—Commercial Growth.

YOUNG men who are disposed to regard the profession of religion as a bar to success in life, often need encouragement in fighting their battle with the tempter, who would have them postpone confessing Christ, until they have secured all this world has to give. While it is true that the Christian man is not promised success in life, as a consequence of his discipleship, but is entitled to expect divine support under the trials of life, rather than immunity from them, there are to be found conspicuous instances of men "making the best of both worlds." It is well that such cases should not be overlooked, if only as an answer to the charge that real vital religion renders a man unfit for business life. One such case, remarkable above the average, both in high spirituality on the one side, and financial and honorable achievement on the other, has recently occupied public attention to a considerable extent in Great Britain. It may interest our readers to know something of the man and his life, and they will not forget that such success as he has had is more remarkable there than here, as the opportunities for rising in an old country are far less numerous than in a new one.

John James Harwood, whom his fellow-citizens have honored by electing him

Thrice Mayor of Manchester

is a man whose private life, when he was a working plasterer, was distinguished by his devotion to Christ and His cause, and who, in his exalted municipal position, has lost none of his sanctity by his elevation. It is no small distinction in a country, where birth and rank count for so much, to be chosen to fill the office of Mayor in the second city of the kingdom; but it is an almost unique honor to have filled it with so much capacity as to be invited a second, and now a third, time to rule the city. Rightly estimated, the honor conferred upon him entitles him to greater respect than does the grandest title which aristocrats inherit. And this has come to him while consistently living a Christian life and engaging in numerous spheres of Christian usefulness.

Mr. Harwood was born at Accrington in 1832, and, therefore, is now fifty-five years of age. About 1853 he entered the employ of a Mr. Ward, a plasterer and painter in Strangeways, Manchester. After four years' work he was appointed foreman, which position he held for four years more, when he was admitted as a partner into the firm. The partnership with Mr. Ward lasted just another term of four years, and then Mr. Harwood took the business entirely to himself, and, by his assiduous and painstaking attention and energy, soon made it one of the largest of its kind in Europe.

"Seest thou a man diligent in his business? He shall stand before kings; he shall not stand before mean men," is most applicable to the career of Mr. Harwood. Up to a recent date he might have been found at his place of business at six o'clock every morning. Many of the principal buildings in Manchester have been plastered and decorated by his firm, including all the large railway stations and the Exchange, around the dome of which is inscribed in bold characters the beautiful words, "A good name is rather to be chosen than great riches, and loving favor than silver and gold." Mr. Harwood might have adopted those words as

The Motto of his Life,

for his success has been achieved by hard and honest work, not by speculations of any kind. Nor has it been by sordid love of money as his chief good; more than once he has shown that he esteemed other things above lucre. When the present palatial Town Hall was built, he was offered the plastering and decorating, but as the English law forbids any member of a corporation to accept a municipal contract, he would, if he had taken it, have had to resign his seat in the Council; but though it involved the loss of a large and lucrative contract, he refused to do so, preferring the honor and opportunity of serving his fellow-townsmen to monetary gain.

Mr. Harwood's success in public life dates from 1866, when he was elected to a seat in the Town Council, which he retained with growing popularity until 1881, when he was appointed an alderman. An influential Manchester journal says: "Mr. Harwood has been, from the first, a most industrious member of the Council, and few men have exercised greater influence upon the municipal affairs of the city during a corresponding period of service." Another local journal remarks: "From the outset he has made his mark as a speaker in the Council. He is always well informed, speaks to the point, and has an impressive style of delivery. It was a matter of course that a man possessing this combination of debating power and capacity for hard work should take front rank." After such cordial testimonies as these, it is not surprising to learn that Mr. Harwood was

First Elected Mayor

in 1884. His first term of office added so materially to his high reputation, that when his successor died on the very eve of the Jubilee celebrations, Alderman Harwood was *recalled* to fill the vacant chair. And, at the expiration of his second term of office, the man whom, for his conspicuous merit and solid ability, his fellow-citizens delight to honor, received at the recent election the distinction of a *third* term of the chief magistracy. The *Methodist Evangelist* says: "We believe he is the first Methodist who has ever occupied the civic chair in that city. Seldom has there been an instance in which high character and sterling worth, utterly unsupported in the first instance by influence or wealth, have been so conspicuously triumphant. The crown of all this, in our estimation, is the fact that he has found the pearl of great price." Mr. Harwood enjoys equal

Honor in the Church

to which he belongs. He is a member of the New Connection Methodists, an evangelistic body of Christians. For many years he was greatly attached to the denominational interest at Bethesda Chapel, Pendleton. As soon as he was married, he and his wife, who was an industrious worker, began to put something away in the savings bank every week. At the end of two years a new church project was floated. Among those who laid their gifts upon the altar were the mayor and his wife, who *"presented their bank-book,* with the *whole* of their two years' savings, towards this project. Removing to another part of the town, Mr. Harwood joined Salem Chapel, Strangeways, where he has been, not simply "an outside buttress of the Methodist New Connection Church," but an inside pillar, and, in spite of his extensive business and municipal engagements, an active worker. He has been a Sunday-school teacher, superintendent, class-leader, local preacher, trustee and circuit steward for upwards of twenty-five years, and won universal esteem. As

A Preacher of the Gospel

he is much appreciated, having an earnest manner and a voice full of sympathy and sweetness. A number of illuminated addresses, which have been presented by various public bodies, adorn the walls of Mr. Harwood's house, but the one that will be of most interest, perhaps, to our readers was presented to him by his own church, in the year 1884, and reads as follows: "We, the Officers and Teachers of Salem Sunday-school, Strangeways, Manchester, beg respectfully to assure you of our gratification and joy, at your elevation to the Mayoralty of the City of Manchester, by the unanimous vote of the Council, a position for which your long and varied public services qualify you. Your connection with our school for *twenty-five years,* during twenty of which you have filled the honorable position of Superintendent, and the various benefactions and other acts of kindness which you have shown, entitle you to our esteem and gratitude, which we would hereby cordially express. The character you have always borne, for constant industry, thorough integrity, and Christian virtue, has been such as to afford a high example to the young, with whom you, as superintendent of the schools, have been brought in contact, and we trust that the force of that example will be long felt. We pray that God, who has guided you hitherto, may guide you still, and that, during your period of office, you may be enabled by Him to signally serve your generation, according to His Holy Will."

Another Testimony

is given by the superintendent appointed by the church council, to the oversight of the district in which Mr. Harwood lives and works. He notes with joy and gratitude, that social and municipal distinctions have not diminished his zeal, nor drawn him into habits inconsistent with his religious profession. He says: "In his public life, especially as Mayor of Manchester, the true Christian has shown forth distinctly. There is no parade of piety—he hates all parade—but there is an undertone in all his utterances which cannot be misunderstood. He is a man of deep religious feeling, which is heightened by an unusually *distinct faith in an over-ruling Providence*—a faith largely the outcome of experiences. Both he and his wife are

Exceedingly Kind to the Poor;

and their children are, in this respect, following in their steps. He is a man of strong convictions as to the duties of others, as well as his own, but he is full of kindness, and never turns his back upon a friend." Such a man is an honor to any community. He is a living proof that Christianity is adapted to the life of modern days, and that a man in serving God does not necessarily lose earthly honors and distinctions.

THE CITY OF MANCHESTER.

Cottonopolis, as this great centre of the cotton industry is sometimes called, is a city very familiar by name to citizens of the United States, with whom it has, for the last century, had extensive commercial transactions. The picture on the first page, below the portrait of Mayor Harwood, represents Piccadilly, the chief street of the city, as seen from Market Street, presenting on the right hand side a view of the Infirmary, an institution conducted with much kindliness and skill, and which, under God, has been found to be a real blessing, by thousands of the sons and daughters of suffering.

The history of Manchester goes back to a very early period of British story. The Romans certainly had a station there; and on the authority of an existing sepulchral monument found on the spot, it appears that

The Ancient City

was garrisoned by the first cohort of the Frisian auxiliaries attached to the 20th Legion, stationed at Chester. It must have been a place of some importance in Roman times. Many relics of Roman occupation have been found, especially in the localities which bear the significant names of *Castle* field and *Camp* field, of inscribed altars and other stones, coins and medals, of Consular and Imperial dates, a bronze statue, and many fragments of pottery, etc.

That the Saxons, in their turn, were induced, by the natural advantages of the site, to form a settlement here, would be sufficiently proved by its name of *Mameceaster* or *Mamecestre*—the shape which the name retains from the Domesday survey down to the fourteenth century.

In 1579, Sir Thomas West, with the concurrence of his son, sold the manor to John Lucye, a citizen of London, who held a mortgage of £3,000 ($15,000) upon it; and Lucye resold it for £3,500 to Nicholas Mosley, Esq., Alderman of London, in whose family it continued for about two centuries and a half, until, on the incorporation of the town, Sir Oswald Mosley, Bart., sold the manor to the Corporation.

Its Religious History

has been a troubled one. In the Church arrangements of the Presbyterians, Manchester was the first Classical division of the county of Lancaster. The Congregationalists rapidly gained strength in the town and neighboring districts. Warden Heyrick got up a petition to Parliament, signed by 8,500 persons, praying the exercise of its authority to put down all Anabaptists, Brownists, heretics, schismatics, and blasphemers, declaring "that toleration would be the putting of a sword into a madman's hand, a cup of poison into the hand of a child, a letting loose of madmen with firebrands in their hands, an appointing a City of Refuge, in men's consciences, for the devil to fly to, a laying of the stumbling-block before the blind, a proclaiming liberty to the wolves to come into Christ's fold to prey upon His lambs, a toleration of soul-murther (the greatest murther of all others), and for the establishing whereof damned souls in hell would accurse men on earth." The Committee of Sequestrations appointed by the Independents, dissolved the Presbyterian College, and turned the Warden and Fellows adrift on paltry pensions. Cromwell summoned representatives from the town to his Parliament.

Manchester's Status,

as a manufacturing city, dates from religious persecution. The Refugees from the Netherlands, fleeing from the Duke of Alva's persecution, settled there and established the commercial prominence of the city. During the sixteenth century Manchester seems to have made rapid and great progress in the extent of its population, manufactures and size; and then there seems to have been a long interval, until, in quite modern times, the place again began to progress "by leaps and bounds."

It was first *the importation of cotton* in the earlier part of the eighteenth century, and next, the invention of machinery in the latter part of the century, and, finally, the application of steam-power in the earlier years of the present century, which gradually left the woollen trade behind, and made Manchester the centre of the manufacture of cotton goods; and the extension of the cotton trade into foreign markets gave rise to that wonderfully rapid growth of the town which has, at length, made it, for enterprise and wealth, the second city of the Empire. The progress it has made, during the last hundred and fifty years, is shown in

The Contrasted Illustrations

on each side of the Mayor's portrait. It has lost its clear atmosphere and rural beauty, but the smoke that now floats from its tall chimneys tells the story of thriving industry and growing wealth. This is not the place to do more than make a note of some epochs in the history of the manufactures of the place—of Richard Arkwright's water-frame (patented in 1769), and James Hargreaves' spinning jenny (patented in 1770), and Arkwright's improved carding machine (in 1785), and Samuel Compton's mule jenny (about 1800); and the inventions and improvements which followed rapidly upon these, when the minds of ingenious men were once earnestly turned into this direction, cannot even be noted.

A very notable feature of the last twenty years is, that Manchester proper is no longer a manufacturing town. The mills have nearly all been transferred to the suburbs and to the neighboring towns and villages. Land is too valuable now in the town itself to be thus occupied. It is the centre of a vast manufacturing district, with more inhabitants to the square mile than in London; it is said that a circle of thirty mile radius, drawn round the City Hall, would include a population greater than the circle of London, of which St. Paul's Cathedral is the centre.

ANECDOTES RELATED AT RECENT EVANGELISTIC MEETINGS

A Merchant's Call to Evangelize.—Mr. Allanson, an evangelist, remarked: "On one occasion, when I was sitting quietly in my office, a gentleman came in and said, 'Sir, the Lord has lately laid this greatly on my heart,' and taking from his pocket a list of names of churches, he continued, 'You do not know much about churches, but I do, and have been for years a church-member, and regret to say that in too many of them the Gospel of salvation is not preached. Now go and preach the Gospel, and if you find, as perhaps you may, that the people will not listen to you in the churches in your own district, then,' he said, handing me the list, 'here are many in districts in which you are unknown, and in which, if you give yourself up to the Lord, you could do a glorious work for Him.' I took the list as a direct call from God, and began to do the work of evangelizing. And God did bless my work. Many hardened sinners were led to see their need of Christ, and received Him; and as for myself, I was filled to overflowing with my unspeakable joy."

A Kiss Returned For a Blow.—A Christian worker observes: "Before my conversion I was met by a man, who accosted me with the question, 'Do you know that the Lord can save you?' The whole-heartedness of the man struck me. He continued, 'Do you know that the Lord can not only save, but can also make you a good, pure, holy man?' I looked at him; then, raising my hand, I struck him on the face with my clenched fist. 'You are a fool,' I cried; 'do you know to whom you are speaking? Do you know that I am a confirmed drunkard, a man who has come from a drunkards' retreat, and that I have not changed my clothes for three days? Do you think that the Lord can save *me?* Man, you are a fool.' The next minute his arms were around me, and, clasping me tight, he whispered, 'Yes, sir, Jesus loves you!' He was but a poor workingman, and one whom, if I had met him under any other circumstances, I should have scorned. I was touched with his kindness. Tears filled my eyes as I accompanied him to a hall, where I was pointed to Christ, and where I gave myself to Him. I who had never done a good, unselfish action in my life stepped into the kingdom of God three-parts inebriated, simply resting on the text, John 3:16."

Quelling a Riot.—The Following Incident is related of the late Rev. Henry Barne: A mob threatened to disturb the peace of Tiverton, and the town authorities, having vainly endeavored to maintain order, sent up an urgent appeal to him, "Would he come down and disperse the crowd?" Mounting his horse, he was quickly on the outskirts of the fray. Seated high over the heads of the infuriated mob, he was master of the situation, and for a few minutes surveyed the scene unobserved. Then with his keen, far-seeing eye, which took in everything at a glance, he at once singled out the ring-leaders of the riot. Satisfied in his own mind as to their identity, and promptly resolved as to what he should do, he dismounted, flung his bridle to a bystander, and boldly going forward into the midst of the tumult, with his active, muscular frame, and powerful brawny chest, collared his men—one with either hand—and in spite of their resistance, so cowed them by his authoritative bearing, that he compelled them to walk down the street in this humiliating position, not halting a moment, until he had safely lodged them in the cells of the town jail; the fickle crowd meantime following behind, laughing and applauding, and evidently relishing the whole thing.

Sweet Memory of a Dead Child.—Captain Hatfield remarks: "Last Sunday, in a meeting at which I was asked to speak, I was told that there was a gentleman who sought an interview with me. I went down the passage, and there, at the door, a gentleman stepped forward and said, 'Captain Hatfield, I believe.' And then he went on to tell me that the last time I was speaking in that meeting his little girl was there, and that I had spoken to her, and the result was that she had found her Saviour. She went home full of the glad news and told it to her parents. 'Her mother and I,' said the gentleman, 'were hard and stern with her. We told her not to speak of such nonsense, for we did not believe in it at all. Still my child did not get disheartened. She said but little on the subject, but her life just shone for Jesus. Hers was but a short life, but a very peaceful and beautiful one. She has died, sir, but not in vain, for when her spirit went up to God, I determined to find out the source of my child's happiness. So I came here to-night to see the man who led her to Jesus. And,' said the bereaved father, with tears in his eyes, 'I, too, have found the Saviour to-night. My wife would not come with me, for she still says she does not believe in these things, but I hope she will soon change her mind as I have changed mine.'"

From a Preacher to an Apostate.—"At One of the fashionable spas in Germany," says the late Rev. H. Barne in his autobiography, "I met with a family of a gentleman, who was at that time an avowed sceptic. In former years he had been regarded as a zealous preacher of the gospel, but had abandoned the Church of his fathers, on account of certain theological doubts and difficulties which had arisen in his mind. Strange to relate, two years afterwards, when I had been appointed chaplain of the Taunton Union, and there became acquainted with an old man—one of its inmates—whom I found to be an earnest, humble and deeply taught Christian, I learned from him in one of my ministeral visits that he had been first brought to know the Saviour under the teaching of that very clergyman—then a sceptic—who had crossed my path during my sojourn abroad. Here was an instance of one who formerly had been the instrument of bringing another to the knowledge of the Truth, now an apostate. In the early period of his life to be made *the means* of converting a fellow sinner from the evil of his ways; that sinner to become a monument of grace, to the praise of God's glory; yet he himself, in the latter days of his career—it was to be feared—a castaway. It is an awful fact to realize that Judas was numbered among the twelve apostles, 'and obtained part of their ministry,' yet notwithstanding, he went out from them, because he was not one of them, falling 'by transgression, that he might go to his own place.'"

The Fatal Door.—The French Chevalier, Gerard de Kampis, was a very rich and a very proud man. Soon after the completion of his magnificent castle, he wished to have a house-warming, and accordingly all his great neighbors were invited to a great feast. At the conclusion of a sumptuous repast, his guests made speech after speech, in which the host was lauded, and told that he was the most fortunate man alive. As the Chevalier loved flattery, it may be imagined how proud and delighted he was. One among the guests, however, said nothing for a time. When each man had made his speech, he uttered the following singular observation upon the happiness of the host: "Sir Knight, in order that your felicity should be complete, you require but one thing; but this is a very important item." "And what thing is that?" demanded the Knight, opening wide his eyes. "One of your doors must be walled up," replied his guest. At this strange rejoinder, several of the guests began to laugh, and Gerard himself looked as much as to say, "This man has gone mad." Wishing, however, to have the clue to this enigma, he continued, "But which door do you mean?" "I mean that through which you will *one day be carried to your grave,*" replied the other. These words struck both guests and host, and made the latter reflect most seriously. The proud man remembered the vanity of all earthly things. He became completely altered, and made good uses of his riches in the service of man and for the glory of God.

WORLDLY MARRIAGES.

Dr. Talmage's Second Sermon to the Women of America, Preached last Sunday Morning, January 15, 1888.

"And there was a man in Maon whose possessions were in Carmel, and the man was very great, and he had three thousand sheep and a thousand goats." 1 Sam. 25 : 2.

An Oriental Sot—His Beautiful Wife—Why She may have Married Him—Madame Roland's Marriage and Death—The Requisites for a Woman's Happy Marriage—Good and Genial Character in her Husband—Godliness in the Mansion—Examples of Wealthy Christians—Godliness Tending to Prosperity—Permanent Worldly Success Generally in Christians' Hands—A Typical Sacrifice—Devilish Arts Triumphant—A Wife Becoming a Slave—Imprisoned in a Castle—Two Miserable Duchesses—The Foreign Ducal Visitor of Last Summer—His Character no Bar to Welcome—An Evil Woman can Stop—Marriage with a King—Cleopatra's Concealment—Her Conquest—A Greater Alliance.

MY text introduces us to a drunken bloat of large property. Before the day of safety deposits and Government bonds and national banks, people had their investment in flocks and herds, and this man, Nabal, of the text, had much of his possessions in live-stock. He came also of a distinguished family, and had glorious Caleb for an ancestor. But this descendant was a sneak, a churl,

A Sot and a Fool.

One instance to illustrate: It was a wool-raising country, and at the time of shearing a great feast was prepared for the shearers; and David and his warriors, who had in other days saved from destruction the threshing-floors of Nabal, sent to him, asking, in this time of plenty, for some bread for their starving men. And Nabal cried out: "Who is David?" As though an Englishman had said, "Who is Wellington?" or a German should say, "Who is Von Moltke?" or an American should say, "Who is Washington?" Nothing did Nabal give to the starving men, and that night the scoundrel lay dead drunk at home; and the Bible gives us a full length picture of him, sprawling and maudlin and helpless.

Now that was the man whom Abigail, the lovely and gracious and good woman, married—a tuberose planted beside a thistle, a palm-branch twined into a wreath of deadly nightshade. Surely that was not one of the matches made in heaven. We throw up our hands in horror at that wedding. How did she ever consent to link her destinies with such a creature. Well, she no doubt thought that it would be an honor to be associated with an aristocratic family; and no one can despise a great name. Beside this, wealth would come, and with it

Chains of Gold,

and mansions lighted by swinging lamps of aromatic oil, and resounding with the cheer of banqueters, seated at tables laden with wines from the richest vineyards, and fruits from ripest orchards, and nuts threshed from foreign woods, and meats smoking in platters of gold, set on by slaves in bright uniform.

Before she plighted her troth with this dissipated man, she sometimes said to herself: "How can I endure him? To be associated for life with such a debauchee I cannot and will not!" But then again she said to herself: "It is time I was married, and this is a cold world to depend on, and perhaps I might do worse, and may be I will make a sober man out of him, and marriage is a lottery, anyhow." And when, one day, this representative of a great house presented himself in a parenthesis of sobriety, and with an assumed geniality and gallantry of manner, and with promises of fidelity and kindness and self-abnegation, a June morning smiled on a March squall, and the great-souled woman surrendered her happiness to the keeping of this infamous son of fortune, whose possessions were in Carmel; "and the man was very great, and he had three thousand sheep, and a thousand goats."

Behold here a domestic tragedy repeated every hour of every day, all over Christendom—marriage for worldly success, without regard to character. So Marie Jeanne Philipon, the daughter of the humble engraver, became

The Famous Madame Roland

of history, the vivacious and brilliant girl, united with the cold, formal, monotonous man, because he came of an affluent family of Amiens, and had lordly blood in his veins. The day when, through political revolution, this patriotic woman was led to the scaffold, around which lay piles of human heads that had fallen from the axe, and she said to an aged man whom she had comforted as they ascended the scaffold, "Go first, that you may not witness my death," and then, undaunted, took her turn to die—that day was to her only the last act of a tragedy, of which her marriage day was the first.

Good and genial character in a man,

The Very First Requisite

for a woman's happy marriage. Mistake me not as depreciative of worldly prosperities. There is a religious cant that would seem to represent poverty as a virtue, and wealth as a crime. I can take you through a thousand mansions, where God is as much worshipped as He ever was in a cabin. The Gospel inculcates the virtues which tend toward wealth. In the millennium we will all dwell in palaces, and ride in chariots, and sit at sumptuous banquets, and sleep under rich embroideries, and live four or five hundred years, for, if according to the Bible, in those times a child shall die a hundred years old, the average of human life will be at least five centuries.

The whole tendency of sin is toward poverty, and the whole tendency of righteousness is toward wealth. Godliness is profitable for the life that now is, as well as for that which is to come. No inventory can be made of the picture-galleries consecrated to God, and of sculpture and of libraries, and pillared magnificence, and of parks and fountains and gardens in the ownership of good men and women. The two most lordly residences in which I was ever a guest, had morning and evening prayers, all the employees present, and all day long there was an air of cheerful piety in the conversation and behavior. Lord Radstock carried the Gospel to the Russian nobility. Lord Cavan and Lord Cairns spent their vacation in evangelistic services. Lord Congleton became missionary to Bagdad. And the Christ who was born in an Eastern caravansary has lived in a palace.

What Riches Can Do.

It is a grand thing to have plenty of money; and horses that don't compel you to take the dust of every lumbering and lazy vehicle; and books of history that give you a glimpse of all the past; and shelves of poetry to which you may go and ask Milton or Tennyson or Spencer or Tom Moore or Robert Burns to step down and spend an evening with you; and other shelves to which you may go while you feel disgusted with the shams of the world, and ask Thackeray to express your chagrin, or Charles Dickens to expose Pecksniffianism, or Thomas Carlyle to thunder your indignation; or the other shelves where the old Gospel writers stand ready to warn and cheer us, while they open doors into that City which is so bright the noonday sun is abolished.

There is no virtue in owning a horse that takes four minutes to go a mile, if you can own one that can go in a little over two minutes and a half; no virtue in running into the teeth of a northeast wind with thin apparel if you can afford furs;

No Virtue in Being Poor

when you can honestly be rich. There are names of men and women that I have only to mention, and they suggest not only wealth, but religion and generosity and philanthropy, such as Amos Lawrence, James Lenox, Peter Cooper, William E. Dodge, Lord Shaftesbury, Miss Catherine Wolfe and Mrs. Astor. A recent writer says, that of fifty leading business men in one of our Eastern cities, and of the fifty leading business men of one of our Western cities, three-fourths of them are Christians.

The fact is, that about all the brain and the business genius is on the side of religion. *Infidelity is incipient insanity.* All infidels are cranks. Many of them talk brightly, but you soon find that in their mental machinery there is a screw loose. When they are not lecturing against Christianity they are sitting in bar-rooms, squirting tobacco juice, and when they get mad swear till the place is sulphurous. They only talk to keep their courage up, and at best will feel like the infidel who begged to be buried with his Christian wife and daughter, and when asked why he wanted such burial, replied: "If there be a resurrection of the good, as some folks say there will be, my Christian wife and daughter will somehow get me up and take me along with them."

Men may pretend to despise religion, but they are rank hypocrites. The sea-captain was right when he came up to the village on the seacoast, and insisted on paying ten dollars to the church, although he did not attend himself. When asked his reason, he said that he had been in the habit of carrying cargoes of oysters and clams from that place, and he found, since that church was built, the people were more honest than they used to be, for before the church was built he often found the load, when he came to count it, a thousand clams short. Yes. Godliness is profitable for both worlds. Most of the great, honest,

Permanent Worldly Successes

are by those who reverence God and the Bible. But what I do say is that if a man have nothing but social position and financial resources, a woman who puts her happiness by marriage in his hand, re-enacts the folly of Abigail when she accepted disagreeable Nabal, "whose possessions were in Carmel; and the man was very great, and he had three thousand sheep, and a thousand goats."

If there be good moral character accompanied by affluent circumstances, I congratulate you. If not, let the morning lark fly clear of the Rocky Mountain eagle.

The Sacrifice of Woman

on the altar of social and financial expectation is cruel and stupendous. I sketch you a scene you have more than once witnessed. A comfortable home, with nothing more than ordinary surroundings; but an attractive daughter carefully and Christianly reared. From the outside world comes in a man with nothing but money, unless you count profanity and selfishness and fondness for champagne and general recklessness as a part of his possession. He has his coat collar turned up when there is no chill in the air, but because it gives him an air of abandon; and eyeglass, not because he is near-sighted, but because it gives a classical appearance; and with an attire somewhat loud, a cane thick enough to be the club of Hercules and clutched at the middle, his conversation interlarded with French phrases inaccurately pronounced, and a sweep of manner indicating that he was not born like most folks, but terrestrially landed. By

Arts Learned of the Devil

he insinuates himself into the affections of the daughter of that Christian home. All the kindred congratulate her on the almost supernatural prospects. Reports come in that the young man is fast in his habits, that he has broken several young hearts, and that he is mean and selfish and cruel. But all this is covered up with the fact that he has several houses in his own name, and has large deposits at the bank, and, more than all, has a father worth many hundred thousand dollars and very feeble in health, and may any day drop off, and this is the only son; and a round dollar held close to one's eye is large enough to shut out a great desert, and how much more will several bushels of dollars shut out!

The marriage day comes and goes. The wedding ring was costly enough, and the orange blossoms fragrant enough, and the benediction solemn enough, and the wedding march stirring enough. And the audience shed tears of sympathetic gladness, supposing that the craft containing the two has sailed off on a placid lake, although God knows that they are

Launched on a Dead Sea,

its waters brackish with tears, and ghastly with ghastly faces of despair, floating to the surface and then going down. There they are, the newly married pair in their new home. He turns out to be a tyrant. Her will is nothing, his will everything. Lavish of money for his own pleasure, he begrudges her the pennies he pinches out into her trembling palm. Instead of the kind words she left behind in her former home, now there are complaints and fault-findings. He is the master, and she the slave.

The worst villain on earth is the man who, having captured a woman from her father's house, and after the oath of the marriage altar has been pronounced, says, by his manner if not his words: "I have you now in my power. What can you do? My arm is stronger than yours. My voice is louder than yours. My fortune is greater than yours. My name is mightier than yours. Now crouch before me like a dog. Now crawl away from me like a reptile. You are nothing but a woman, anyhow. Down, you miserable wretch!" Can halls of mosaic, can long lines of Etruscan bronze, or statuary by Palmer and Powers and Crawford and Chantry and Canova, can galleries rich from the pencil of Bierstadt and Church and Kenset and Cole and Cropsey, could flutes played on by an Ole Bull, or pianos fingered by a Gottschalk, or solos warbled by a Sonntag, could wardrobes like that of a Marie Antoinette, could jewels like those of a Eugenie, make a wife in such a companionship happy?

Imprisoned in a Castle!

Her gold bracelets are the chains of a lifelong servitude. There is a sword over her every feast, not like that of Damocles staying suspended, but dropping through her lacerated heart. Her wardrobe is full of shrouds for deaths which she dies daily, and she is buried alive, though buried under gorgeous upholstery. There is one word that sounds under the arches, and rolls along the corridors, and weeps in the falling fountains, and echoes in the shutting of every door, and groans in every note of stringed and wind instrument: "Woe! Woe!" The oxen and sheep, in olden times, brought to a temple of Jupiter to be sacrificed, used to be covered with ribbons and flowers—ribbons on the horns and flowers on the neck. But the floral and ribboned decoration did not make the stab of the butcher's knife less deathful, and all the chandeliers you hang over such a woman, and all the robes with which you enwrap her, and all the ribbons with which you adorn her, and all the bewitching charms with which you embank her footsteps, are the ribbons and flowers of a horrible butchery,

As if to show how wretched a good woman may be in splendid surroundings, we have two recent illustrations,

Two Ducal Palaces

in Great Britain. They are the focus of the best things that are possible in art, in literature, in architecture, the accumulation of other estates, until their wealth is beyond calculation, and their grandeur beyond description. One of the castles has a cabinet set with gems that cost two million five hundred thousand dollars, and the walls of it bloom with Rembrandts and Claudes and Poussins and Guidos and Raphaels, and there are Southdown flocks in summer grazing on its lawns, and Arab steeds prancing at the doorways on the "first open day at the kennels." From the one castle the duchess has removed with her children, because she can no longer endure the orgies of her husband, the duke, and in the other castle the duchess remains, confronted by insults and abominations, in the presence of which I do not think God or decent society requires a good woman to remain.

Alas for those ducal country-seats! They on a large scale illustrate what on a smaller scale may be seen in many places, that without moral character in a husband, all the accessories of wealth are to a wife's soul tantalization and mockery. When Abigail finds Nabal, her husband, beastly drunk, as she comes home from interceding for his fortune and life, it was no alleviation that the old brute had possessions in Carmel, and "was very great, and had three thousand sheep, and one thousand goats," and he the worst goat among them. The animal in his nature seized the soul and ran off with it. Before things are right in this world

Genteel Villains

are to be expurgated. Instead of being welcomed into respectable society because of the amount of stars and garters and medals and estates they represent, they ought to be fumigated two or three years before they are allowed, without peril to themselves, to put their hand on the door-knob of a moral house. The time must come when a masculine estray will be as repugnant to good society as a feminine estray, and no coat of arms or family emblazonry or epaulet can pass a Lothario unchallenged among the sanctities of home life. By what law of God or common sense, is an Absalom better than a Delilah, a Don Juan better than a Messalina? The brush that paints the one black must paint the other black.

But what a spectacle it was when last summer much of "watering-place" society went wild with enthusiasm over an unclean foreign dignitary, whose name in both hemispheres is a synonym for profligacy, and princesses of American society from all parts of the land had him ride in their carriages and sit at their tables, though they knew him to be a portable lazaretto, a charnel house of moral putrefaction, his breath a typhoid, his foot that of a Satyr and his touch death. Here is an evil that men cannot stop, but women may.

Keep All Such Out

of your parlors, have no recognition for them in the street, and no more think of allying your life and destiny with theirs than "gales from Araby" would consent to pass the honeymoon with an Egyptian plague. All that money or social position a bad man brings to a woman in marriage is a splendid despair, a gilded horror, a brilliant agony, a prolonged death; and the longer the marital union lasts, the more evident will be the fact, that she might better never have been born. Yet you and I have been at brilliant weddings, where, before the feast was over, the bridegroom's tongue was thick, and his eye glassy, and his step a stagger, as he clicked glasses with jolly comrades, all going, with lightning express train, to the fatal crash over the embankment of a ruined life and a lost eternity.

Woman, join not your right hand with such a right hand. Accept from such an one no jewel for finger or ear, lest that sparkle of precious stone turn out to be the eye of a basilisk; and let not the ring come on the finger of your right hand, lest that ring turn out to be one link of a chain that shall bind you in never-ending captivity. In the name of God and heaven and home, in the name of all time and all eternity, I forbid the banns! Consent not to join one of the many regiments of women who have married for worldly success without regard to moral character.

If you are ambitious, O woman, for noble affiancing, why not

Marry a King?

And to that honor you are invited by the Monarch of heaven and earth, and this day a voice from the sky sounds forth: "As the bridegroom rejoiceth over the bride, so shall thy God rejoice over thee." Let Him put upon thee the ring of this royal marriage. Here is an honor worth reaching after. By repentance and faith you may come into a marriage with the Emperor of universal dominion, and you may be an Empress unto God forever, and reign with Him in palaces that the centuries cannot crumble, or cannonades demolish.

High, worldly marriage is not necessary for woman, or marriage of any kind, in order to your happiness. Celibacy has been honored by the best Being that ever lived and His greatest apostles—Christ and Paul. What higher honor could single life on earth have? But what you need, O woman, is to be affianced forever and forever, and the banns of that marriage I am this moment here and now ready to publish. Let the angels of heaven bend from their galleries of light to witness, while I pronounce you one—a loving God and a forgiven soul.

One of the most stirring passages in history with which I am acquainted, tells us how Cleopatra, the exiled Queen of Egypt, won the sympathies of Julius Cæsar, the conqueror, until he became the bridegroom, and she the bride. Driven from her throne, she sailed away on the Mediterranean Sea in a storm, and when the large ship anchored, she put out with one womanly friend in a small boat, until she arrived at Alexandria, where was Cæsar, the great general. Knowing that she would not be permitted to land or pass the guards on the way to Cæsar's palace, she laid upon the bottom of the boat some shawls and scarfs and richly dyed upholstery, and then lay down upon them, and her friend wrapped her in them, and she was admitted ashore in this wrapping of goods, which was announced as

A Present for Cæsar.

This bundle was permitted to pass the guards of the gates of the palace and was put down at the feet of the Roman general. When the bundle was unrolled, there rose before Cæsar one whose courage and beauty and brilliancy are the astonishment of the ages. This exiled queen of Egypt told the story of her sorrows, and he promised her that she should get back her throne in Egypt and take the throne of wifely dominion in his own heart. Afterward they made a triumphal tour in a barge that the pictures of many art galleries have called "Cleopatra's Barge," and that barge was covered with silken awning, and its deck was soft with luxuriant carpets, and the oars were silver-tipped, and the prow was gold mounted, and the air was redolent with the spicery of tropical gardens, and resonant with the music that made the night glad as the day.

You may rejoice, O woman, that you are not a Cleopatra, and that the One to whom you may be affianced had none of the sins of Cæsar, the conqueror. But it suggests to me how you, a soul exiled from happiness and peace, may find your way to the feet of the Conqueror of earth and sky. Though it may be a dark night of spiritual agitation in which you put out into the harbor of peace, you may sail, and when all the wrappings of fear, and doubt and sin shall be removed you will be found at the feet of Him who will put you on a throne to be acknowledged as His in the day when all the silver trumpets of the sky shall proclaim: "Behold the bridegroom cometh;" and in a barge of light you sail with Him the river whose source is the foot of the throne, and whose mouth is at the sea of glass mingled with fire.

THE LAST OPERATION.

AMONG the testimonies to Divine Healing published by Rev. A. B. Simpson in his *Word, Work and World* is the following: Mrs Stahl came to Berachah Home, New York, in October last, suffering from severe spinal trouble, which had been so painful, that years ago an operation was necessary. The relief was only slight. Fifteen times since then she had needed surgical treatment, which, though exceedingly painful, she gladly accepted, as it brought a temporary relief from the acute agony that made it necessary. Hearing through Rev. Mr. Haugh that the Lord had so marvellously healed him, she was brought to New York to hear more of the truth of Christ as a healer. On the previous Friday she was carried into the Tabernacle, and lay, during the service, on pillows in one of the pews. She accepted with a child's faith the teaching which was given, and in a few days she went up and down stairs a healed woman, rejoicing in God as her physical life. At the recent Convention she gave her testimony clearly, and all could see from her shining face that Christ had been revealed to her in spiritual as well as physical power.

DARK PROSPECTS FOR ENGLAND IN 1888, 1889 AND 1890.

By Rev. M. Baxter.

The Last Happy Christmas—Coming Difficulties and Reverses—Three Thrones of Mark—The Present Situation of Protestant Europe—The Edge of the Abyss—The Sixth Vial near its Termination—The Impending Social Revolutionary Earthquake—European War Inevitable—Loss of Ireland and India—Lord Salisbury's Warning.

CHRISTMAS DAY, 1887, on the eve of which these words are penned, will be the most happy, prosperous and auspicious anniversary of the Birth of Christ, that Britain will ever again witness, before the End of this Age in April, 1901. Each of the succeeding nine Christmases, until 1897, when Antichrist's three and a half years universal desolation begins, will find Britain increasingly overwhelmed by

Difficulties and Reverses

on all sides, like the victim in the historically famed torture-chamber, the walls of which were daily contracted by machinery, until the hapless prisoner within was crushed by their remorseless pressure.

Ruskin, in his 'Stones of Venice,' has well remarked: "Since the first dominion of men was asserted over the ocean, three thrones of mark, beyond all others, have been set upon its sands —*the thrones of Tyre Venice and England.* Of the first of these great Powers only the memory remains; of the second, there remains only the ruin; the third, inheriting their greatness, *may, if it forget their example, be led through prouder eminence to less pitied destruction.* The exaltation, the sin, and the punishment of Tyre, have been recorded for us in some of the most touching words ever uttered by the prophets of Israel. But we read them as a lovely song, and *close our ears to the sternness of their warning.*"

Prophetic students well know the blackness and depth of

The Abyss of Desolation

upon the edge of which all Christendom, and especially Protestant Christendom, now stands —for numerous expositors agree that the closing years of this 19th century, will most probably be the closing years of the present Gentile dispensation, introductory to the Millennial dispensation of 1,000 years—and that we are now living just before the termination of the Sixth Vial of Revelation 16, in this historical fulfilment, when the mystic *Euphrates* or Turkish Mohammedan empire is *drying up*, and consequently, the Jews are returning to Jerusalem in increased numbers, and "the three evil spirits" of Spiritualism, Revolutionary Democracy, and Mohammedan and Romanist fanatical conspiracy "are going forth from Dragon, Wildbeast, and False Prophet, to gather the nations to the *war of the Great Day* of God Almighty toward Armageddon. Then will follow the Seventh Vial during the few years preceding 1901, and there shall be a political and

Social Revolutionary Earthquake

throughout the world, "such as was not since men were upon the earth, so mighty an earthquake, and so great," and which will in fact be Daniel's final "Time of Trouble, such as was not since there was a nation even to that same time," predicted in his twelfth chapter, and which is the same as "the Great Tribulation such as was not since the beginning of the world, no, nor ever shall be" foretold by Christ in his eschatological discourse in Matthew 24, immediately to precede His future Advent in the clouds of heaven.

The astonishing circumstance is, that we are now enjoying so much peace and prosperity up to the *very latest year*, 1888, to which it is possible, according to prophecy, for European peace to be preserved unbroken. There is such a long series of Prophetic Events to be accomplished, before the End of this Age in Passover Week, April 1901, that the first event of the whole series, viz.,

Gigantic European Wars,

gradually changing twenty-three kingdoms into ten kingdoms, by 1891, cannot possibly begin later than 1889, the centenary of the French Revolution, and is in the highest degree likely to begin in 1888, because it is contrary to all precedent in History that twenty-three kingdoms could be changed into ten, in so short a space as two years, which is all the interval there would be from 1889 to 1891. Then Napoleon has afterwards to rise to reign over Syria, and make a covenant with the Jews on April 21, 1894. (Daniel 7. 24.)

Now as England, being inside Cæsar's Roman Empire countries, must be one of the Ten Confederated Kingdoms by 1891, and must be separated from Ireland, which does not belong to Cæsar's Roman Empire, by that time, therefore, we can only infer that England will be so disastrously involved in European wars between 1888 and 1891, that "its difficulty will be Ireland's opportunity," and when the whole of the British soldiers, including all available regulars, militia, reserve men, and volunteers, shall be imperatively needed elsewhere, Ireland, being entirely evacuated by British troops, will rise up, as in 1782, and demand another Grattan's Parliament, which will practically render it independent of England. A great

Rebellion in India,

issuing in its independence, likewise, will be the accompaniment or result of Ireland obtaining complete Home Rule. This was remarked by Lord Salisbury, at Derby, on December 19, 1887, who said that the loss of Ireland would be found to involve the loss of India. And the utter military unpreparedness of England to defend India, and at the same time to take part in a general European war, is strikingly shown by a noted statesman in the *Fortnightly Review* for November and December. That statesman shows that Germany has 5,000,000 of armed and trained soldiers; France and Austria each have 2,000,000 or 3,000,000; but Britain has not got more than 500.000. In

The Approaching European War

in 1888 or 1889. France is predicted by Daniel to defeat Germany and gain the Rhine as its boundary line. How will England be then able to resist 3,000,000 French soldiers, flushed with victory, and with loud cries of "A Londres," swooping down on London, and levying an indemnity of $500,000,000 or more, which they will certainly be disposed to do, if England is allied with the defeated Germany in that war—an alliance which at present seems more probable than an Anglo-French alliance.

If, on the other hand, England is allied with France in that war, it may escape invasion. But we cannot understand how England can lose the Highlands of Scotland above the Roman Wall by 1891 (if it is to do so, as some maintain, because the Highlands did not belong to Cæsar's Roman Empire any more than Ireland did), except it be the result of so great a catastrophe as a successful invasion of Britain.

London has been compared to Jerusalem in ancient times, as the great centre of Bible, tract and missionary influence, and its destiny may be similar to that of Jerusalem, which was captured by foreign invaders long before its final destruction.

The *Rev. Samuel Garratt*, in his "Midnight Cry," says, "When we see what God did to Jerusalem, how can we help asking ourselves, What will He do to London, where there is so much true Christianity, and at the same time so much impiety? Will London be made desolate? We have been stripped, by steam navigation, of that naval defence in which we once trusted to be to us instead of bulwarks and towers. No one who does not shut his eyes, doubts that there is the will, if there is the power, to deal the fatal blow. Are we better than Jerusalem? And if not, why should we not share her fate? Sure I am that unless God be with us, none of our plans will save us. Without God London may become a desolation."

Lord Salisbury forcibly referred, in his speech at Derby, on December 19, to the

Menacing War Clouds

in Europe, and the necessity of England being prepared for coming conflicts, and also to the ruin staring farmers in the face from the importation of cheap corn from foreign countries. He said: "In sad and sober truth, it is impossible that the vast European armaments, constantly growing, can continue to watch each other without creating some well-founded solicitude in those to whom the peace of Europe is a matter of the deepest interest. These great, heavy overcharged clouds, charged with the electricity of war, near each other, come closer and closer. Who is he who shall be bold enough to prophesy that at any given time the thunderclap shall not ensue? I say that the mere existence of these growing armaments is a constant and steady danger, and that he would be a bold man who would extend his prophecies to many years from this time. I believe that, more intensely than ever the rulers, all rulers, of Europe at this time are deeply anxious for peace. But there are great waves of popular sentiment sweeping over the nations of Europe, and no man knows what impulse they may give to the councils of the rulers whom they seem to obey, but whom they in reality govern. I wish to draw a moral for ourselves. In past times danger announced itself afar. If there was a prospect of war, there was a preliminary diplomatic trouble which gave ample opportunity for preparation, That state of things has passed away. If the thunderclap of war should ever break, *it would give you no warning*, and if by any untoward chance you should be involved in it, your fate will depend upon the preparation you have made in time of peace."

A HOTEL-KEEPER'S COMPLAINT.

AMONG the reminiscences called forth by the death of ex-Secretary Manning, whose portrait appeared in this journal two weeks ago, is an amusing incident related of his relations with the proprietor of the Arlington Hotel, in Washington, where Mr. Manning had a suite of rooms, before going to housekeeping.

The hotel-keeper, who is an Albany man by birth, and knew Mr. Manning well before the latter became Secretary of the Treasury, went one night, after twelve o'clock, to Mr. Manning's rooms, where the Secretary, with five clerks, was working hard at the Treasury documents. He knocked loudly at the door and was bidden enter.

"What do you want?" gruffly inquired the Secretary, annoyed at the intrusion.

"I want you to behave yourself," as gruffly replied the hotel man.

"Why, great Scott!" the Secretary retorted, evidently jumping at the conclusion that a fuss had been made in some other room, and that the landlord had mistaken the parties. "There is no noise here. What does this thing mean?"

"It means business," savagely replied the landlord. "I want these clerks to bundle up their papers and get out of here at once. It is after midnight, and here you are, working as if the safety of the republic demanded that you should kill yourself in this outrageous way. I have known you, man and boy, for over forty years, and I don't propose to become *particeps criminis* in your suicide, nor do I care to suffer the injury to my hotel which your death and funeral under such circumstances would entail upon it. I want you to behave yourself, or else you must seek other quarters!"

The genial Secretary laughed aloud at his landlord's earnestness, and directed the clerks to go home. Then the twain sat down, and the genial Secretary listened to the landlord's expostulation, and to a long lecture on the wickedness of overwork and violation of the rules of health. He promised reformation, but shortly thereafter went to house-keeping, and was removed from the restraining influences of the Arlington's proprietor.

Mr. Manning might have resented the landlord's expostulation as officious interference, had he not perceived that his conduct was prompted by genuine disinterested concern for him. It would be well if ungodly men were similarly discerning, when Christian friends, moved by fear of a far more terrible catastrophe, plead with them to give less attention to business and more to spiritual health. (Ezek. 2 : 7.)

THE ECCLESIASTICAL COBBLER.

IN an address delivered in New York on January 8, Dr. McGlynn, the excommunicated Roman Catholic priest, whose portrait and life appeared in this journal on February 3, 1887, gave utterance to some weighty warnings about the pope, whom be dubbed "The Ecclesiastical Cobbler." He said, that at the present time the pope's influence on American politics was mischievous. An alliance existed between one of his representatives here, and a political organization *to get votes through the confessional.* In the days of Tweed an arrangement had been made one Sunday evening, by which the Roman Catholic schools got money out of the State Treasury through a similar bargain. Finally he said, "*The more politics you take from Rome, the less religion you will get.* The pope's entrance into politics has been

The Curse of Every Nation.

"God forbid that the hated thing should be revived. The flatterers of the pope are making him an intolerable nuisance. Is it necessary for the office of Peter, that his successor to-day shall be the greatest enemy of his country, that the see of Peter should incur the hatred of the patriotic loving Italians, because the kingdom of the pope was the only obstacle to Italian unity?

"What," Dr. McGlynn asked, "has the pope to do with politics? A great many years ago—it is nineteen hundred years ago—there stood upon the earth a Man, who alone of all men dared to say of Himself, 'I am the way, and the truth, and the life.' The Son of God said, 'Learn of Me, because I am meek and humble of heart.' That man said, 'Blessed are the peacemakers, for they shall be called the children of God.' That man said, '*My kingdom is not of this world.*' When men would make Him king He fled to the mountains alone and spent the night in prayer. He was a man of sorrows, acquainted with grief. He refused to have any part and parcel in the mere temporal things of the world. The office (of the papacy) is salutary only in proportion as it is exercised in conformity with Him who would have no earthly kingdom, whose crown was a crown of thorns, who was to be exalted, not on the shoulders of men, but on the horrid, ignominious gibbet, where He proved His love for all His children."

Speaking of the character of the Apostle Peter, whose succes or the pope claims to be, Dr. McGlynn said: "You find nothing of that in him who is as great and as good as His Holiness Pope Leo XIII. We hear nothing of the incredible assertions of

The Last of the Popes

(pausing and smiling)—I should have said the latest of the Popes. Modern delusion, Pope worship, Pope deification, attributes to a poor old man, tottering on the brink of the grave, ignorant of the geography of most of the world, all the triumphs of the Church throughout the wide world. The first Pope did not arrogate to himself the appointment of other apostles. He permitted his colleagues to appoint one in the place of Judas. After three centuries, it was the policy of Constantine, the Emperor, to become a Christian. We Christians of to-day can see what a sad mistake it was, what a pitiful thing it was, that the Church of Christ was edged around by the temporal gifts of Constantine. From that dates the beginning of the corruption of the Church. The power which Constantine gave to the Church is the Imperial Purple. The privilege of wearing it came from Constantine or his successors. Emperors, kings and princes lavished wealth upon the Church, and it is a thousand pities that the Church accepted so perilous a gift."

Need of the Reformation.

He dwelt upon the corruption of morals "in both clergy and laity,' and attributed "the interminable confusion of the Middle Ages" to that corruption. He spoke of the Reformation. "It was this corruption which made necessary the Protestant Reformation. It is not," he said, "my business to defend the destruction of any of the good things that the Protestant Reformation destroyed. It actually took away precious doctrines and inestimable sacraments. But it could not be delayed much longer." The Papacy had become so corrupt that Alexander VI., of infamous memory, had his illegitimate children, Lucrezia and Cæsar Borgia, occupying his own palace. Cæsar Borgia was a swashbuckler, and by permission of 'his Holy Father, the Pope,' went up and down the State, slashing and killing. Lucrezia Borgia was another of the beautiful children of His Holiness Alexander VI. And at the time he ruled the Church, a flaxen haired little German boy was playing around the streets of Saxony, and his name was Martin Luther.

"It is not in the power of any Pope or council to create any new doctrine of faith. If it is new it is not a doctrine, and they convict themselves out of their own mouths. Did you see the rubbish in the newspapers, of the Pope sitting in his high chair, as an oracle of doctrine that we are bound to believe in. A man in this city actually dared, from a Catholic pulpit, to preach such rubbish as that! He said substantially that every word of the Holy Father was the utterance of the Holy Ghost. What nonsense! Will the world ever accept such rot as that? Does not that make the cheeks of you Catholics tingle and burn with shame? Let us not indulge in that brutal, fulsome, disgraceful flattery of a poor old bag of bones, seventy-eight years old, a poor, tottering, absent-minded old man, with one foot in the grave."

The significance of the foregoing observations consists in the fact that they were not made by a Protestant, but by a man who still avows himself a Roman Catholic, who was until last year a priest, and had held that office for about thirty years. He must therefore have had ample opportunity for learning the facts.

TROUBLES IN PONAPE.

THE report of bloodshed in Ponape, following the arrest of Mr. Doane, as described in these columns, has been confirmed by the publication, in the *Missionary Herald*, of extracts from the journal of Mr. Rand, one of the missionaries there. They recount the events which occurred while Mr. Doane was a prisoner on trial at Manila. It appears from them that the governor and other Spanish officials were really killed, as reported, though the missionaries endeavored to prevent the attack. It grew out of an attempt to arrest some natives who resisted, and, being aided by their friends, fell upon the Spaniards and killed them. Shortly afterward, a boat was on its way to the Spanish ship off the island, when a native fired into it. The fire was returned, and then the action became general. An attack was made on the governor's party, who took refuge in the fort. They held their ground till after midnight, when it was getting too hot for them, and they tried to flee to the ship, over the flats. A short distance from the shore they were all killed, the governor, doctor, secretary, captain of the soldiers, and many others. "As near as I can find out," says Mr. Rand," about ten Ponapeans and forty Spaniards were killed."

Mr. Rand further says, that he set out to go over to meet the chiefs, and then go on board the Spanish ship, but the missionary ladies, Miss Fletcher and Miss Palmer, with the Christian natives, were decidedly of opinion that it would be unwise. He therefore sent a letter to the chiefs, begging them not to allow their people to seize the ship, and sent a message also to the ship's captain. The captain, who had always seemed a different man from the late governor, answered that he would cease hostilities whenever the natives would do so, and he prepared a paper promising the same. He offered it to the chiefs, who also signed it. Thus peace was restored before the return of Mr. Doane from Manila on the same ship which brought the new Spanish governor. In closing his account, Mr. Rand expresses himself as pleased with the first appearance of this governor. He writes: "I went with Mr. Doane to Kenan, yesterday, to try and get the tribes to return the boat, cannon, and other Spanish property taken by them in the war. We finally succeeded as to boat, one cannon, etc.; the other cannon may be returned later."

TANGLED IN ELECTRIC WIRES

THE singular death of a horse, and the narrow escape of pedestrians, in a crowded thoroughfare of New York, is reported by the daily journals. On January 8, about nine o'clock in the evening, while a Fourth Avenue car was passing the corner of Fourteenth Street, one of the horses became entangled in a length of telephone wire, which had fallen from its fastenings on the roof of the German Savings Bank across the electric light wires. The horse received a severe electric shock and began to rear and prance about in a very lively manner. The driver stopped the car and endeavored to gain control of the frightened animal, but without avail. The more the horse jumped about, the more he became entangled in the wires. The passengers in the car became frightened, and left the car hurriedly. A large crowd collected, and the driver was assailed with all sorts of advice. After fifteen minutes' delay, an inspector and lineman of the Illuminating Company appeared on the scene, and cut the wires with which the horse was entangled. The animal staggered a few steps after being released, and then fell dead. During the stoppage of the traffic, several persons among the crowd that gathered, were about to lay hold of the wire to disentangle it from the affrighted animal, and were only restrained by those who knew the character of the wire. It looked so innocent and harmless that it was a natural thing to seize it, but if any one had done so, without having on the rubber gloves that the linemen wear, they would have been killed on the spot. It is not safe to regard everything as harmless that appears so, and that may be said of other things besides electric wires. Many a young man in our large cities, has been betrayed into calamity worse than death, by the lures spread by Satan and labelled harmless (Prov. 3:5.)

A PRODIGIOUS GAS BILL.

THE payment of the largest bill for gas ever delivered to a private consumer is reported in the *Missouri Republican*. It states that recently a lady called at the office of the gas company about the supply of gas in her house. The secretary referred to his ledger, but could not find any record of the account, though he traced back the entries of ten years. A workman was sent to examine the meter, and to remedy the defect complained of, and it was found that the meter was worn out. Certain marks upon it gave a clue to the date at which it had been put in the house, and in that way the mystery was solved. It was found that in transferring the accounts from one ledger to another, that particular meter had been overlooked. The consumer had been burning gas for ten years, without receiving any bill or any demand for payment. An explanation was made to him, and a bill for $780 presented as an estimate of the debt owing. The consumer, being an honorable man, did not take advantage of his legal rights, but promptly paid the bill. He might naturally have thought that, as bills were not presented at the regular intervals, he would never be called upon to pay for his gas. That is the mistake some persons make about their sinful lives. When no evil happens to them, and they continue to prosper while living in sin, they think either that there is no God, or that He is careless about it. They forget than an awful record is rolling up against them, with which they will be confronted in the end, unless, through faith in Christ, they obtain remission through His blood. (Ps. 50: 21.)

CHRISTIAN HERALD AND SIGNS OF OUR TIMES.

OFFICE; 63 BIBLE HOUSE, NEW YORK.

ENTERED AT THE POST-OFFICE AT NEW YORK, N. Y., AS SECOND-CLASS MATTER.

Published Weekly. Subscription price, $1.50 a year; $1 eight months; 75 cents six months; sent two months on trial for 25 cents; always payable in advance. Single copies for sale by, or can be ordered at, all newsdealers.

Remittances by Mail should be by Post-office money order, bank cheques, or drafts or express money order, and should always be made payable to THE CHRISTIAN HERALD.

Receipts are not sent, the receipt of the paper by a subscriber is a sufficient proof that his remittance has been received. If the paper does not arrive promptly, please advise us, that we may see if the address is correctly entered.

Change of Address. Name of Post Office and State, of both old and new address, should always be given in case of removal.

Some Subscribers are Concerned Because the date of the address labels on their copies of th s journal has not been changed. That inaccuracy has been unavoidable because renewals have come in larger numbers than it was possible to indicate by change of type. The work is progressing rapidly, and in a short time every label will be accurate. Each subscription has been duly credited in the office books, and each subscriber who has renewed may accept the receipt of his copy of the paper as a proof that his subscription has been duly received and entered to his credit.

CURRENT EVENTS.

The New Cabinet Nominations Were Not confirmed by the Senate last week. It was decided by the Committees to report favorably the nomination of Mr. Vilas to be Secretary of the Interior, and Mr. Dickinson to be Postmaster-General, but to report adversely Mr. Lamar's nomination to the Supreme Court bench. On the latter question the five Republican members of the Committee voted against the nomination, and the four Democratic members, Messrs. Pugh, Coke, Vest and George, in favor of it. Mr. Lamar has formally resigned his office as Secretary of the Interior, in order to relieve the Senate of embarrassment and to facilitate his successor in the Department. No special objection is likely to be made in the Senate to the Vilas and Dickinson nominations, and many Senators are disposed to vote upon them and get the calendar free before taking up the Lamar case, which Mr. Chandler, who is leading the opposition, has resolved to resist to the last. A letter, however, from Senator Stewart, of Nevada, promising to vote for confirmation, and stating his reasons for doing so, was published last week, and appears to indicate the probability of Mr. Lamar's nomination being confirmed eventually.

The Work of Making a Final Survey of the route for the Nicaragua Canal has been commenced. A lengthy letter, giving detailed reports of the expedition, was published last week. It states that the engineers have received a warm welcome at Greytown. They were met by Commissioners appointed by the Nicaraguan Government, and assured of cordial assistance and co-operation. Mr. Peary, who spoke for the Americans, thanked the commission for the reception accorded the party, and said he congratulated Nicaragua upon the nearness of the day when she would be mistress of the Bosphorus of the Western Hemisphere. Elaborate plans have been arranged for attaining the greatest accuracy in the surveys. The location of the route will be designated so minutely, with underground stations, the marking of trees and other natural objects, that there will be no difficulty in identifying any point at any future time. Weekly reports relative to provisions and instruments, progress of work, and of the efficiency of members of the party, will be made. On all hands the good-will of the Nicaraguans toward the expedition is evidenced both among government officials and the masses of the people. The people seem to vie with one another in endeavoring to assist the engineers, and frequently during the day, while running the line of survey through and about the town, the residents send them choice fruits and aid them in various ways.

The Reform of the National Banking System promised before Congress assembled, was introduced in the Senate on January 10 by Senator Voorhees. It is stated to be an embodiment of the suggestions made from time to time by Controller Trenholm. Among its most important provisions are those which forbid that the officers of a bank shall constitute a majority of the Board of Directors; require that the Directors shall take an oath to inform themselves as to the business and condition of the bank; forbid the organization of national banks, with branches; divide national banks into two classes—those with a capital of $250,000 and less, and those having more than that amount of capital; reduce the amount of bonds required to be deposited by the smaller banks from one-quarter to one-tenth of their capital; and that by the larger banks from $50,000 to $25,000; and give more elasticity to the present laws, which limit to one-tenth of the capital of the bank loans of money, providing at the same time a penalty for making loans contrary to law.

Churches and Charitable Institutions in New York are not likely to remember with gratitude the administration of the present Mayor. The Commissioners on Thursday last had under consideration the proposal to erect a new building for a church on land granted by the city more than twenty years ago, and a second application from a hospital to occupy a vacant city lot adjoining the hospital. "Not an inch of the city's land shall *ever* be given to any charitable institution," shouted the Mayor, "unless for adequate compensation." It was explained that at the hospital the city's poor often received free medical advice, and that the favor asked was not a great one. The Mayor, however, was obdurate and repeated his declaration that not an inch of land should ever be given to any religious or charitable institution. The public will add to the declaration the clause which the Mayor must have meant to add, but omitted—"while Mayor Hewitt has power to refuse it." Happily the term for which the Mayor was elected will have an end, and by none is its termination so eagerly anticipated as by some who voted and worked to elect him.

A Slight Earthquake in North Carolina occasioned widespread alarm in that State on Thursday last. A press despatch from Charlotte says: "Two slight shocks of earthquake were felt here this morning. The time of the first was 9:54 A. M., and the second was eight seconds later. Signal Officer Barry says the vibrations were from north to south. The shocks were greatest in the western portion of the city. A mirror was shaken off the mantel at P. E. Linnel's house. No other damage is reported. The people are excited, fearing another disaster like that of 1886. It was felt also at Raleigh, Wilmington and Savannah, Ga. At Charleston, S. C., the disturbance was also noticed by some persons, though it was so slight as not to be felt by the majority of the people. At Columbia, S. C., buildings were severely shaken, and doors, windows, crockery and glassware rattled in a lively manner. People sleeping were rudely awakened, and many rushed into the streets. The vibrations continued about ten seconds, and were accompanied by loud detonations."

An Effort to Mediate in the Gigantic Strike of the miners and employees of the Reading Railroad Company was made on January 11 by a committee of merchants. The committee was appointed at a meeting of Schuylkill County merchants to meet the Reading management and try to settle the differences between them and the miners, as the strike entailed great damage to all the manufacturing and commercial interests in the district. Mr. Corbin, the President of the road, listened attentively to the representations of the committee, and their appeals for arbitration. He remained firm, however. He said that while he heartily sympathized with the object of the committee, which was to end the strike, the position and duty of the Company were perfectly clear. He said there was nothing the Company could submit to arbitration. The subject of the railroad strike was closed; that strike was over. The men who left the service of the Company were discharged, and would, under no circumstances, be taken back. The leaders of the striking miners, he understood, would not be satisfied even if the question of wages should be conceded. They would demand that all the new men on the railroad should be discharged, and all the discharged men be taken back. This alone would make arbitration impossible. The mining industry at the close of last week was practically suspended. Signs of suffering among the families of the men are already making their appearance, and in other districts the rise in the price of coal is entailing much privation on the poor.

The Discovery of Another Plot to Assassinate the Czar is reported in the cable despatches. Arrangements had been made for a series of Court balls and festivities in St. Petersburg, to commence on the Russian New Year's day (January 13), and to continue for two weeks. The Czar and Czarina were to come from Gatschina to lead the gaiety. Orders, however, were given early in the week countermanding the invitations. The European correspondent of the New York *Herald* cables that the change was due to the arrest of a railroad official who was suspected of Nihilism. Among his papers was found proof that he had kept the Nihilists informed of the arrangements for the Czar's journeys to the Capital, and clues were also obtained to the conspirators in a daring plot to kill the Czar on the very night following the arrest. A large number of persons have been arrested in St. Petersburg for participation in the plot. Among those arrested were several officers of the army who had just arrived in St. Petersburg from the provinces. Private despatches from Warsaw say that the conspiracy had its centre in St. Petersburg, and that it was of unusual magnitude as regards both the number and the position of the persons implicated.

Hopeful Reports of the Condition of the Crown Prince of Germany were cabled last week. The Emperor, in speaking of him to a deputation, said that the news regarding the Crown Prince was excellent, and that the worst fears had passed away. The hope was now justified that the Prince would be able to return to Berlin in the spring. Count Rodolinskl the Crown Prince's Chamberlain, who on January 11 returned from San Remo, says that the Crown Prince's general health is better than it has been for years past.

The Removal of the Bodies of the Napoleons to a magnificent mausoleum in England, took place with imposing ceremonies on January 9. The Empress Eugenie was anxious that the remains of her husband, Napoleon III., and her son, should rest at Chiselhurst, near the mansion she has so long occupied, and where the Emperor died. The owner of all the surrounding land, however, has a prejudice against Frenchmen and Roman Catholics, and refused to sell her a plot of ground on which to erect the mausoleum she wished to rear over them. The Empress therefore bought land at Farnborough, thirty-two miles from London, where she has built the mausoleum, at a cost of half a million dollars. Large numbers of persons witnessed the removal of the bodies. A detachment of English soldiers bore the coffins to gun-carriages, on which they were taken to the railroad depot. Another detachment met the train at its journey's end, and in the same way the massive coffins were conveyed to their new resting-place.

Bishop Riley's Work in Mexico has on Several occasions elicited warm words of approval from the Rt. Rev. A. Cleveland Coxe, Bishop of Western New York, who thoroughly understands its character, and who has none of that tenderness toward Roman Catholicism which impels the Ritualistic clergy to look coldly on a movement distinctly aggressive on papal influence. His latest utterance, published a few days ago, is unqualified in its endorsement of the effort in which many of our readers have engaged. He said: "Some of our people, and *most heartily I am with them*, have resolved to aid, so far as they may, those suffering Christians in Mexico who exercise their undoubted right to regard themselves as the Reformed National Church of Mexico, and who feel that to forfeit this position would be to lose their claims upon Christendom, and also their hold upon the national conscience; to say nothing of the property which they have no right to hold if they become the mission of a foreign Church."

The Rev. Jacob Freshman's Work Among the Jews is making real progress. His annual report, issued last week, chronicles the baptism of six converted Jews, beside several others who, having begun the study of Christianity under his guidance, have removed to other cities, where they have been baptized. Several others who have given encouraging evidence of their faith, have so far held back from open confession, knowing that it will cost them discharge from employment, and ostracism by family and friends. Mr. Freshman's hands would be strengthened, in such cases, if he knew of Christian employers to whom he could send such men for temporary occupation, until they could find regular work by which they could support themselves. Mr. Freshman gratefully acknowledges the kindness of God, on whom he and his devoted wife depend for daily food. This has been given them during another year, and they have also received gifts for their work, which have reduced the mortgage on the Hebrew Christian church to $10,000. He has also been able to aid in establishing a similar work in Chicago. All who sympathize with him in his labor, can help him to maintain and extend it by sending contributions addressed Rev. Jacob Freshman, 17 St. Mark's Place, New York.

A Gift for the Crown Prince of Germany was sent from Saginaw, Mich., on January 11. An elderly German woman, belonging to the working class, entered the office of an express company, and presenting a package, asked the cost of sending it to San Remo, Italy. It was addressed to the Crown Prince, and the old woman said it was medicine which would cure Unser Fritz's throat. She was clearly in earnest, and was modest and sensible. The clerk told her that six dollars would cover the cost of transportation, and she paid the amount and departed. It was an affecting evidence of her devotion, for the six dollars must have made an appreciable inroad on her savings. We cannot but wish that a similar spirit of devotion to the Prince of Heaven was more prevalent among His subjects. They cannot benefit Him, but He has said that those who do good to His followers, because they are His, are counted to have done good to Him personally. (Matt. 25:40.)

A Distressing Exposure Occurred in a Brooklyn home recently. A German drug-clerk, aged twenty-nine, came to live there with his wife and child two years ago. He led an exemplary life, was devoted to his wife and little one, and being thoroughly acquainted with his business and very skillful, was prospering moderately. As he had the confidence of his employers, and was much respected by all who knew him, there was general surprise when he was brought to his home on January 7 by two detectives. He had asked, as a favor, that he might be taken there before going to prison, so that he might break the sad intelligence to his wife gently. He told her that five years ago he came to this country from Germany, and obtained employment in a wholesale drug-store in New York. He drifted into bad company and robbed his employers, covering up the crime with forgery. He was detected, tried and sentenced to five years' imprisonment. In the prison his medical knowledge and intelligence were appreciated, and he was placed in charge of the drugs in the hospital, and was found very useful. His position secured him many privileges, and he availed himself of his opportunities to escape. He went to Montreal, found employment and married. Later, he came back to New York and obtained the Brooklyn situation. But that day he had been recognized on the street, and must go back to prison to serve out the remainder of his sentence. It seems very sad that, having lived a blameless life since leaving prison, he should have to go back for that old offence, but everyone recognizes the justice of his doom. It is that principle which makes the atonement of Christ a necessity for salvation. The sinner against God, though he might repent and reform, could not be sure of forgiveness for past sins if the Saviour had not died to atone for them. (Rom. 3:25.)

A Singular Blunder Occurred at a Funeral at Hudson, O., on Jan. 7. A resident of that city, a Roman Catholic gentleman, died a few days before that date at Akron. And as it was determined to bury him at Hudson, an undertaker was appointed, and notified that the body would arrive by a certain train, which he was to meet. He made his arrangements, had a hearse in readiness, and when the train arrived took charge of a coffin that was on board, and removed it to the Roman Catholic church. It was not, however, the body which he was instructed to inter. That body did not reach the Akron depot in time to go by the train specified, but the corpse carried by the train was that of a Protestant lady who died in Akron, and was being conveyed to Macedonia, a station beyond Hudson. The funeral party was on the train, and did not discover until reaching Macedonia that the corpse was not on the train. They made inquiries, and learned that it had been taken off at Hudson. They immediately returned to that place, and found that the funeral service had been held in the Roman Catholic church, and the body was being lowered into the grave. Explanations were made, and the coffiu opened, when the claim of the friends of the deceased lady was clearly established. It is well for us that, though a mistake of that kind may happen as to the body, there can be no mistake as to the destination of the soul. We are assured that "the Lord knoweth them that are His." (II Tim. 2:19.)

A Camel Hunt in Broadway, New York, caused some excitement on January 10. Two men, one of whom has been an Arizona cowboy, were walking home about ten o'clock that evening, when they met, at Broadway and Twelfth Street, a crowd of excited persons running down-town. The cause of their fright was soon perceived. A big camel was tearing madly down the street in zigzag fashion, sometimes on the sidewalk and sometimes in the carriageway. The rolling gait of the beast seemed to demand as much room as three or four horses, and the people rushed in all directions to get out of its way. A cab containing two ladies was being driven up Broadway at the time, and the horse seeing the ungainly beast—evidently a novel experience to him—took fright and became unmanageable. It turned crosswise, bringing the cab directly in the camel's way, much to the alarm of the ladies. The camel went full tilt at the cab, nearly upsetting it. It checked his course, and the ex-cowboy, seizing the opportunity, ran forward, and grasping the camel by the nose, brought it to its knees. He held it there for some minutes, until a man came up with a halter in his hand, which he slipped over the camel's head. He said the camel belonged to a menagerie, and was being led across town, when it managed to slip its halter and run away. The scared people were astonished when they saw how easily the ex-cowboy tamed the beast which had terrified them. It is so with the great enemy of souls. The Bible teaches that he is overcome by those who, trusting in Christ, are bold enough to resist him. (James 4:7.)

A Lawyer's Broken Heart is Assigned as the cause of his death by the physician who attended him. The lawyer was a citizen of Minneapolis, Minn. He died on January 10, and in the certificate of death his physician states that in his opinion he had no physical ailment whatever, but died of a broken heart. He graduated from Amherst College with high honors in 1878 and a brilliant career was predicted for him. After practicing his profession in Minneapolis for a few years, he made a decided success and worked most assiduously. A few months ago, however, his eyes began to grow dim, and in spite of skilful treatment he became totally blind. His savings were soon spent, and he had to apply to his friends, who cheerfully supplied his wants. But the sense of disappointment and the consciousness of his own helplessness, with the knowledge that all his life he would be a burden upon others, preyed upon his mind, and though physically in perfect health, he began to fail slowly but surely. It seemed that he did not care to live. Three weeks ago he was seen to be sinking rapidly, and on Tuesday of last week he died. His temperament is said to have been morbidly sensitive, to which his sense of dependence was intolerable. Happily for the Christian who feels himself completely helpless, *his* sense of dependence on his Heavenly Father has a contrary effect. Though his heart is broken, too, he lives a newer, stronger, better life. (Gal. 2:20.)

BRIEF NOTES.

Mr. E. P. Telford commences meetings in the First Methodist Episcopal Church, Lynn, Mass., next Sunday. His three weeks' services in Dr. Knowles's church, in the same city, were very largely attended, and much good was accomplished.

A Canadian contemporary states that during a service in a certain church, recently, while the collection box was being passed around, a young man deposited a nickel therein, and detained the box while he took out four cents change. He afterward complained that one of the cents was counterfeit.

Mr. and Miss Parker, the evangelists from Mr. C. H. Spurgeon's church in London, have been holding meetings at Rahway, N. J. While they were at Salem, N. J., three services were held each day, and so much interest aroused, that revival meetings were continued by the pastors after the evangelists left.

Mr. Puttenham has been holding services at Port Hope, Canada, in connection with the Gospel Union, of which the Rev. M. Baxter is President. They were the means of stirring up the people to united effort for the winter's work. Four days' services have also been held by him at Orangeville, with much success.

Dr. J. M. Thoburn, of Calcutta, India, is holding special revival services in the Madison Avenue M. E. Church, New York. They commenced last Sunday, and continue two weeks. Service each day at three and eight o'clock. Dr. Thoburn's name is a power in the Methodist Church the world over, and many will gladly avail themselves of this opportunity of hearing him.

Dr. Alfred S. Patton, the well-known Baptist minister and journalist, died in Brooklyn, N. Y., on January 13. He was sixty-two years of age, an Englishman by birth, but had been in this country from childhood. He was Chaplain of the Massachusetts State Senate in 1862 and 1863. Exceedingly affable, genial and scholarly, he had hosts of friends and was much beloved.

Rev. E. P. Hammond is at San Diego, Cal., holding a series of meetings with most gratifying results. Three years ago San Diego had a population of 3,000; now there are 25,000. The seating capacity of the churches is only between 2,000 and 3,000. Open air meetings have, therefore, been a necessity. Efforts are now being made to secure a large tent in which the meetings may be held.

Fifty thousand dollars has been bequeathed by the late William Hilton, of Boston, to each of the following-named charities: The American Board, American Home Missionary Society, Massachusetts General Hospital, Phillips' Academy, Andover, Harvard, Amherst, and Williams—the sum to be used by these colleges for the education of needy students. Twenty-five thousand dollars each are also bequeathed to the American Missionary Associations and the Boston City Missionary Society. Ten thousand dollars each is also given to the Boston Young Women's Christian Association, the Home for Little Wanderers, and Abbot Academy.

THE SYMBOLIC CUP.

A New Sermon by Pastor C. H. Spurgeon.

"For this is My blood of the new testament, which is shed for many for the remission of sins." —Matt. 26 : 28.

Christ Antedating His Passion—The Lessons of the Symbolical Cup—I. The Importance of the Blood—Suggests Suffering—Tells of Love—Should be a Vivid Remembrance—Personal and Happy—To Continue till the End—II. Its Connection with the Covenant—A Remarkable Conversion of a Garroter—III. Its Connection with Remission—IV. Its Connection with Men—Shed for the Many, not the Few—An Argument with the Devil.

THE Lord Jesus Christ was then alive, sitting at the table, and yet, pointing to the cup filled with red wine, he said, "This is My blood, which is shed for many." This proves that He could not have intended that the wine was literally His blood. Surely it is no longer necessary to refute the gross and carnal dogma of transubstantiation, which is obviously absurd. Enjoying loving intercourse with His chosen disciples, He spake freely: His heart did not study accuracy so much as feeling; and so, in speech as in feeling, He antedated His great work of atonement, and spoke of it as done. To set forth the future intent of the blessed ordinance of the Lord's Supper, He must of necessity treat His death as an accomplished fact; and His complete absorption in His work made it easy and natural for Him to do so. He ignores moods and tenses; "His work is before Him."

Dear friends, I am going to preach to you again upon the corner-stone of the Gospel. How many times will this make, I wonder? The doctrine of Christ crucified is always with me. As the Roman sentinel in Pompeii stood to his post even when the city was destroyed, so do I stand to the truth of the atonement, though the Church is being buried beneath the boiling mud-showers of modern heresy. Everything else can wait, but this one truth must be proclaimed with a voice of thunder. Others may preach as they will, but as for this pulpit, it shall always resound with the substitution of Christ.

You have before you a cup filled with wine; which Jesus has just blessed, and presented to His disciples. As you look, hear Him speak of the cup as His blood; for thus He would teach us a solemn lesson.

I. Note, first, the importance of the precious blood of Christ. The vital importance of the great truth of the death of Christ as a vicarious sacrifice, is set before us in this cup, which is

The Memorial

of His blood shed for many. Blood represents suffering; but it goes further, and suggests suffering unto death. "The blood is the life thereof," and when blood is too copiously shed, death is suggested. Remember, that in the Sacred Supper you have the bread as a separate emblem of the body, and then the wine as a separate symbol of the blood: thus you have a clear picture of death, since the blood is separated from the flesh. "As often as ye eat this bread and drink this cup, ye do show the Lord's death."

Upon the death of Christ you are invited to fix your attention, and upon that only. In the suffering of our Lord unto death, we see the boundless stretch of His love. "Greater love hath no man than this, that he lay down his life for his friends." It means something more. We have called our Lord, in our hymn, "Giver of life for life," and that is what this cup means. He gave up His life that we might live. The pouring out of His blood has made our peace with God. Jehovah made the soul of His only-begotten an offering for sin, that the guilty might be cleared. That is what the cup means: it means the dead of Jesus in our stead.

Our blessed Saviour would have us hold His death in great reverence: it is to be our chief memory. Both the emblems of the Lord's Supper set forth the Saviour's death. This peculiarly Christian ordinance teaches nothing, if it does not teach this. Christ's death for men is the great doctrine of the Church. Leave out the Cross, and you have killed the religion of Jesus. Atonement by the blood of Jesus is not an arm of Christian truth; it is the heart of it. No teaching is healthy which throws the Cross into the background. The other day, when I was inquiring about the welfare of a certain congregation, my informant told me that there had been few additions to the church, although the minister was a man of ability and industry. Furthermore, he let me see the reason for failure, for he added. "I have attended there for several years, and during all that time I do not remember hearing a sermon upon the sacrifice of Christ. The atonement is not denied, but it is left out." If this be so, what is to become of our Churches? If the light of the atonement is put under a bushel, the darkness will be dense.

Beloved, the precious blood of Christ should be had by us in vivid remembrance. He would not have us know Him after the flesh, and forget the spiritual nature of His griefs; but yet He would have us know that He was in a real body when He bled, and that He died a real death, and became most truly fit for burial; and therefore, He symbolizes His blood, not by some airy fancy, or mystic sign, but by common wine in the cup.

The dear memorials of our Lord's blood-shedding are intended for

A Personal Remembrance.

Beloved, we *must* come into personal contact with the death of Christ. This is essential. We must each one say, "He loved me, and gave Himself for me." In His blood you must be personally washed; by His blood you must be personally reconciled to God; through His blood you must personally have access to God; and by His blood you must personally overcome the enemy of your souls.

Once more: our Saviour meant us to maintain the doctrine of His death, and the shedding of His blood for the remission of sins, even to the end of time, for He made it to be of perpetual remembrance. We drink this cup "until He come." If the Lord Jesus had foreseen with approbation the

Changes in Religious Thought

which would be brought about by growing "culture," He would surely have arranged a change of symbols to suit the change of doctrines. Would He not have warned us that, towards the end of the nineteenth century, men would become so "enlightened," that the faith of Christendom must of necessity, take a new departure, and therefore He had appointed a change of sacramental memorials? But He has not warned us of the coming of those eminently great and wise men, who have changed all things, and abolished the old-fashioned truths for which martyrs died. Brethren, I do not believe in the wisdom of these men, and their changes I abhor; but had there been any ground for such changes, the Lord's Supper would not have been made of perpetual obligation. The perpetuity of ordinances indicates a perpetuity of doctrine.

But hear the moderns talk: "The Apostles, the Fathers, the Puritans, they were excellent men, no doubt, but then, you see, they lived before the uprise of those wonderful scientific men, who have enlightened us so much." Let me repeat what I have said. If we had come to a new point as to believing, should we not have come to a new point as to the ordinances in which those beliefs are embodied? I think so. The evident intent of Christ in giving us settled ordinances, and especially in settling this one, which so clearly commemorates His blood-shedding, was, that we might know that the truth of His sacrifice is for ever fixed and settled, and must unchangeably remain

The Essence Of His Gospel.

Neither nineteen centuries nor nineteen thousand centuries can make the slightest difference in this truth, nor in the relative proportion of this truth to other truths, so long as this dispensation lasts. Until He comes a second time without a sin-offering unto salvation, the grand work of His first coming must be kept first and foremost in all our teaching, trusting and testifying. As in the Southern Hemisphere the Cross is the mariners' guide, so, under all skies, is the death of our Redeemer the pole star of our hope upon the sea of life. In life and in death we will glory in the Cross of Christ, and never be ashamed of it, be we where we may.

II. Secondly, note well the connection of the blood of Christ with the covenant. Read the text again: "This is My blood of the new testament." The translation would be better, "This is my blood of the covenant." What is this covenant?

The Covenant

is that which I read to you just now in Jeremiah 31, 33: "This shall be the covenant that I will make with the house of Israel; After those days, saith the Lord, I will put my law in their inward parts, and write it in their hearts; and will be their God, and they shall be my people." See also Jeremiah 32 : 40; "And I will make an everlasting covenant with them, that I will not turn away from them, to do them good; but I will put my fear in their hearts, that they shall not depart from me." Turn also to Ezekiel 11 : 19: "I will put a new spirit within you; and I will take the stony heart out of their flesh, and will give them an heart of flesh." Look in the same prophecy at 36 : 26: "A new heart also will I give you, and a new spirit will I put within you: and I will take away the stony heart out of your flesh, and I will give you an heart of flesh." What a Magna Charta is this! The old covenant saith, "Keep the law and live." The new covenant is, "Thou shalt live, and I will lead thee to keep my law, for I will write it on thine heart." Happy men, who know their standing under this covenant!

The chaplain of a jail, a dear friend of mine, once told me of a surprising case of conversion, in which a knowledge of the covenant of grace was the chief instrument of the Holy Spirit. My friend had under his charge a man most cunning and brutal. He was singularly repulsive, even in comparison with other convicts: He had been renowned for his daring, and for the utter absence of all feeling when committing acts of violence. I think he had been called

"The King of the Garroters."

The chaplain had spoken to him several times, but had not succeeded even in getting an answer. The man was sullenly set against all instruction. At last he expressed a desire for a certain book, but as it was not in the library, the chaplain pointed to the Bible, which was placed in his cell, and said, "Did you ever read *that* Book?" He gave no answer, but looked at the good man as if he would kill him. The question was kindly repeated, with the assurance that he would find it well worth reading. "Sir," said the convict, "you would not ask me such a question if you knew who I was. What have I to do with a Book of that sort?" He was told that his character was well known to the chaplain, and that, for this very reason, he recommended the Bible as a Book which would suit his case. "It would do me no good," he cried; "I am past all feeling." Doubling up his fist he struck the iron door of the cell, and said, "My heart is as hard as that iron; there is nothing in any book that will ever touch me."

"Well," said the chaplain, "You want a new heart. Did you ever read the covenant of grace?" To which the man answered, sullenly, by inquiring what he meant by such talk. His friend replied, "Listen to these words: 'A new heart, also, will I give you, and a new spirit will I put within you.'" The words struck the man with amazement, as well they might; he asked to have the passage found for him in the Bible. He read the words again and again; and when the chaplain came back to him next day, the wild beast was tamed. "Oh, sir," he said, "I never dreamed of such a promise! I never believed it possible that God would speak in such a way as that to men. If He gives me a new heart, it will be a miracle of mercy; and yet I think," he said, "He is going to work that miracle upon me, for the very hope of a new nature is beginning to touch me as I never was touched before." That man became gentle in manner, obedient to authority, and childlike in spirit. Though my friend has nothing left of the sanguine hopes he once entertained of converted criminals, he yet believes that in this case, no observer could have questioned the thorough nature of the work, and yet the only means was the doctrine of the covenant.

You will, perhaps, say to me, "Why did our translators use the word 'testament' in our Authorized Version?" They were hardly so wise as usual in this instance, for "covenant" is the better word of the two to set forth the original; but yet the idea of a testament is there also. The original may signify either or both. The word "settlement," which has dropped out of use, nowadays, was often employed by our forefathers, when they spoke of the everlasting arrangement of grace. The word settlement might take in both covenant and testament—there is a covenant of grace, but the covenant stipulation being fulfilled by our Lord Jesus, the arrangement becomes virtually a testament, through which, by the will of God, countless blessings are secured to the heirs of salvation. O my brethren, as God's covenanted ones, drink ye of the cup with joy, and renew your pledge with the Lord your God!

III. A third point comes up in the text very manifestly: The blood has an intimate

Connection With Remission.

The text says, "This is My blood of the new covenant, which is shed for many for the remission of sins." Jesus suffering, bleeding, dying, has procured for sinners the forgiveness of their sins. Of what sins? Of all sins of every sort and kind, however heinous, aggravated and multiplied. The blood of the covenant takes every sin away, be it what it may; there was never a sin believingly confessed and taken to Christ that ever baffled His power to cleanse it. This fountain has never been tried in vain. Murderers, thieves, liars, adulterers, and what not, have come to Jesus by penitence and faith, and their sins have been put away.

Of what nature is the remission? It is pardon, freely given, acting immediately, and abiding for ever, so that there is no fear of the guilt ever being again laid to the charge of the forgiven one. Through the precious blood our sins are blotted out, cast into the depths of the sea, and removed as far from us as the East is from the West. Our sins cease to be; they are made an end of; they cannot be found against us any more for ever.

How is it that the blood of Jesus effects this? The secret lies in the vicarious or substitutionary character of our Lord's suffering and death. Because He stood in our place, the justice of God is vindicated, and the threatening of the law is fulfilled. It is now just for God to pardon sin. Christ's bearing the penalty of human sin, instead of men, has made the moral government of God perfect in justice, has laid a basis for peace of conscience, and has rendered sin immeasurably hateful, though its punishment does not fall upon the believer.

And for what end is this remission of sins secured? We mistake, if we think that the pardon of sins is God's ultimatum. No, no; it is but a beginning, a means to

A Further Purpose.

He forgives our sins with the design of curing our sinfulness. We are pardoned that we may become holy. God forgives the sin, that He may purify the sinner. He aims at the death of thy sinfulness, that thou mayest henceforth love Him, and serve Him, and crucify the lusts which crucified thy Lord. The Lord aims at working in thee the likeness of His dear Son. Jesus hath saved thee by His self-sacrificing obedience to justice, that thou mayest yield thy whole soul to God, and be willing to die for the upholding of the kingdom of love and truth. The death of Christ for thee, pledges thee to be dead to sin, that by His resurrection from the dead thou mayest rise into newness of life, and so become like thy Lord. Pardon aims at this.

IV. I cannot forget to notice, in closing, the connection of the blood with men. We are told in the text that this blood is

Shed "for Many

for the remission of sins." In that large word "many" let us exceedingly rejoice. Christ's blood was not shed for the handful of apostles alone. There were but eleven of them who really partook of the blood symbolized by the cup. The Saviour does not say, "This is my blood which is shed for you, the favored eleven;" but "shed for many." Jesus did not die for the clergy alone. I recollect in Martin Luther's life that he saw, in one of the Romish churches, *a picture of the Pope*, and the cardinals, and bishops and priests and monks and friars, all on board a ship. They were all safe, every one of them. As for the laity, poor wretches, they were struggling in the sea, and many of them drowning. Only those were saved to whom the good men in the ship were so kind as to hand out a rope or a plank. This is not our Lord's teaching; His blood is shed "for many," and not for the few. He is not the Christ of a caste or a class, but the Christ of all conditions of men. His blood is shed for many sinners, that their sins may be remitted.

This blood is shed for many. A group of half-a-dozen converts makes us very glad, and so it should; but oh, to have half-a-dozen thousand at once! Why not? This blood is shed "for many." Let us cast the great net into the sea. You young men, preach the Gospel in the streets of this crowded city, for it is meant for many! You who go from door to door, do not think you can be too hopeful, since your Saviour's blood is shed for many, and Christ's "many" is a very great many. It is

Shed for All

who ever shall believe in Him—shed for thee, sinner, if thou wilt now trust Him. Only confess thy sin, and trust Christ, and be assured that Jesus died in thy place and stead.

This is no mystery. Bread and wine are ours by eating and drinking; Christ is ours by our receiving Him. The merit of His precious blood becomes ours by that simple, child-like faith, which accepts Jesus to be our all. We say, "Here it is; I believe in it; I take it; I accept it as my own." It is yours. No man can take from you that which you have eaten and drunk. Christ is yours for ever, if you receive Him into your heart. Whenever thou hast any doubt about whether Christ is thine, take Him over again. I like to begin again. Often I find the best way of going forward is to go back to my first faith in Jesus, and, as a sinner, renew my confidence in my Saviour. "Oh," says the devil, "thou art a preacher of the gospel, but thou dost not know it thyself." At one time I used to argue with the accuser; but he is not worth it, and it is by no means profitable to one's own heart.

We Cannot Convince the Devil.

It is better to refer him to our Lord. When he tells me I am not a saint, I answer, "Well, what am I, then?" "A sinner," says he. "Well, so are you!" "Ah!" saith he, "you will be lost." "No," say I, "that is why I shall not be lost, since Jesus Christ came into the world to save sinners, and I therefore trust in Him to save me." This is what Martin Luther calls cutting the devil's head off with his own sword.

You say, "If I take Christ to myself as a man takes a cup and drinks the contents, am I saved?" Yes, thou art. "How am I to know it?" Know it because God says so. "He that believeth in Him hath everlasting life." If I did not feel a pulse of that life (as I did not at first), I nevertheless would believe that I had it, simply on the strength of the divine assurance. Since my conversion, I have felt the pulsings of a life more strong and forcible than the life of the most vigorous youth that ever ran without weariness; but there are times when it is not so. Just now I feel the heavenly life joyously leaping within me; but when I do not feel it, I fall back on this: God has said, "He that believeth in Him hath everlasting life." God's words against all my feelings! I would sing with the children, "Nothing but the Blood of Jesus." Shut your eyes to all things but the Cross. Jesus died, and rose again and went to heaven, and all your hope must go with him! Come, my hearer, take Jesus by a distinct act of faith, this morning! May God the Holy Ghost constrain thee to do so, and then thou mayest go rejoicing! So be it, in the name of Jesus.

[The prayers of the readers of this journal are requested for the blessing of God upon its Editors, and those whose sermons, articles or labors for Christ are printed in it; and that its circulation may be used by the Holy Spirit for the conversion of many sinners and the quickening of God's people. Dr. Talmage and Mr. Spurgeon especially request prayer every Sunday morning on behalf of their labors.]

GEMS FROM NEW BOOKS.

THE SCOTTISH PRIMER.*

THOMAS GUTHRIE tells us that as soon as the children could put letters and syllables together in the elementary schools of Scotland, they were turned into the book of Proverbs; and he traces a great deal of the sagacity and strength of the Scottish character to this early training in that richest of all ethical and philosophical books. Says he: "Think of a child being put down to read such sentences as 'Tom has a dog,' 'The cat is here,' when he might be reading such words as 'God is love,' and 'Train up a child in the way he should go.'" Do not take the Bible away from children, but do not make it a task-book. Do not gather around the memories of childhood any evil recollections regarding your severity, in compelling them to commit to memory the sacred Word. Make it the joy and privilege of their lives; show them how it is the richest of luxuries to be able to know what God has said, and to be able to quote God's wishes in God's own words.

Unconscious Usefulness.

"But the lad knew not anything" (I Sam. 20: 39). A sentence of this kind leads us to think of the unconscious ministries of life. The "little lad" supposed that he was simply finding out arrows, which were shot by Jonathan. May we not be doing work of this kind, and supposing all the time that we are occupied only with frivolous engagements? As of a matter of fact, we know very little about the mystery of life. In running an errand, we may be carrying a gospel. In sitting in a sick-chamber, we may be connecting that room of dreariness and solitude with the very precincts of heaven itself. God sends us upon errands which look trivial; we suppose that we are almost wasting our time; we think that men of our abilities might be more profitably employed; let us be rebuked by the incident before us, for no man can really tell the issue of his simplest transactions.

An Ineffaceable Epitaph.

"For Jonathan's sake" (II Sam. 9: 1). Nothing could be done for Jonathan. He had passed away; but there is always the next best thing to be done. Blessed are they whose quick ingenuity is inspired to find out the next best thing. Who does not long to have his father and mother back again, at least for one whole summer day, that he might load them with proofs of gratitude and love? They had such a weary time of it; they were but poor; they never saw splendid cities or fine sights, or heard noble music, or looked upon things great, but from a distance; they were always in the field ploughing, in the market-place bartering, or in the sick-chamber suffering. To have them back one day, month, year—a whole round year! We should live in their delight and find heaven in their contentment. Yet see to it that this sentiment, so pure, like the dew of the morning, be critically examined. The value of

* From "The People's Bible." Vol. VII. Discourses by Rev. Joseph Parker, D. D. This volume comprises the chapters from I Samuel 18 to I Kings 13. Dr. Parker's terse annotations on the text are of great value in elucidating the meaning of passages often misunderstood, while his more extended comments are marked by his well-known originality and epigrammatic power. 362 pages; price $1.50. Published by *Funk & Wagnalls*, 18 Astor Place, New York.

A View on the South American Pampas.

it will be shown by what is done now to those who are alive. We cannot do the departed any good, for they have passed beyond the human touch; but we can do deeds to the poor, the ignorant, the out-of-the-way, the suffering, which will be a happy memorial to those we have lost. Take some poor child, open its way in life, and when you have done so, set up in your heart's memory a stone, bearing the inscription, "Sacred to the memory of a loving parent." So write the epitaph of the dead, and the writing shall never be obliterated.

THE PAMPAS OF SOUTH AMERICA.

(See Illustration.)

THE vast prairies of South America, to which the name of pampas is given, occupy an area of about a *million and a half square miles*. They are spread over the southern and western regions of the Argentine Republic and part of Patagonia, to the slopes of the Andes. This does not include the level lands of Peru, which from their resemblance in soil and general productions, are frequently called by the same name. The word is from the Quichua language, and means a valley or plain. It is believed by geologists, that at some time, inconceivably remote, the vast plain was the bed of the ocean. Enormous boulders bearing proofs of having once been under water, are found there, and under the soil which has accumulated in the course of centuries, gravel and sand are found like that at the ocean bottom. It is thought from a careful study of the geological formation, that there must have been a sudden and gigantic convulsion, raising the level of the pampas fully fourteen hundred feet, and a subsequent gradual rise of a hundred feet more, due in part to deposits of soil and the decay of vegetation.

The pampas, as we now know them, are mere prairie land, varying in fertility and the character of the soil. In their more sterile parts, only hard plants with long thorns grow, but as they near the slopes of the Cordilleras, groups of stunted bushes are found, and still nearer, the beautiful pampas grasses appear, while in some districts, as in the province of Buenos Ayres, there is luxuriant sod, which furnishes good food for stock. No trees are met with, except those that have been planted. Lakes or pools exist, but as they depend for their supply on the varying rainfall, they are frequently dried up.

Animals like the prairie dog, called on the pampas Biscacha, abound. They scratch and burrow in the soil, and are the abomination of the farmers on the borders. Travellers, too, have frequently experienced dangerous falls by their horses, after nightfall, stepping into these biscacha-holes. The armadillo, alpaca, puma and jaguar, with serpents, poisonous and harmless, in great abundance, roam over the vast plains. A kind of partridge, of large size, abounds, and is a favorite prey of the hunters, who pursue it on horseback. Large flocks of ostriches haunt the interior plains, and so heedless are they, and so unacquainted with the character of civilized life, that they have been known to continue feeding on the line of railroad which crosses the pampas to Tucuman, after the warning scream of the engine whistle has been given, until the train has passed over their mangled bodies.

The Gaucho is the human inhabitant, or the peasant of the pampas, particularly of the River Plata country. He generally calls himself a Spaniard, but in most cases the Indian blood predominates in his veins. He spends most of his life on horseback, the lasso, by his side.

Among them are some bad characters, whose treachery and cruelty render them dangerous; but, as a rule, when they have not been drinking they are not quarrelsome. The opening of the railroad has already begun to change the character of their life, as it has brought settlers from England, Ireland and other countries, who are making fortunes by raising sheep and cattle.

As the country is being opened up, opportunities are presented for Christian usefulness. There, as everywhere else in South America, the land lies in gross darkness. Those persons who profess any religion, avow themselves Roman Catholics, and with them the profession is but an empty form. How much good might be done by earnest, devoted work by native evangelists properly trained, no mind can estimate. This is one of the projects which Bishop Riley hopes to initiate through his work in Mexico. He has already sent through South America quantities of Christian tracts in Spanish, with portions of the Bible in the same tongue, and he is longing for the time when, from the Mexican Church, converts will go forth to follow these silent messengers with the Word of Life. The responsibility of the Christians of the United States for the enlightenment of the South American continent is becoming more generally realized, and it cannot take a more practical shape than by furnishing the money necessary to make Mexico what Bishop Riley longs to see it—the centre of Christian influence and work for all the Spanish-speaking people of South America.

A MOMENTOUS MEETING AT A GATE.

(See Illustration on Page 45.)

"YOU will have to get rid of that stableman of yours, father; he has been drinking again," said Tom Haldane, a stalwart young man, who with his wife and little son had come over from their own farm to spend an evening at the old homestead. Two younger brothers of the speaker, as tall and strong as he, and two beautiful sisters of some seventeen and twenty summers, made up the family group gathered around the hale old farmer and his gray-haired wife.

"Oh! I am very sorry for that," said Mr. Haldane. "Will has not touched a drop of liquor for six months. He must have had some special temptation; I must inquire about it."

"That is always your way, father," said Tom. "You will inquire, and listen to a pitiful story and promises of amendment, and end by forgiving him, and very likely giving him five dollars to make up the money he has squandered. You are a great deal too easy with your men."

"I know, my son, I know. Your brothers here tell me the same thing, and, I think, Jennie and Gracie agree with them. Still, I like the gospel rule, 'Till seventy times seven.' Will has good points in him, and if he does reform, as he is trying to do, he will make a good man. *A man is worth saving*."

"You will never save Will, father," said John Haldane, one of the brothers. "He is too far gone. Why, how many times has he promised before? How many times have you forgiven him already?"

"Not seventy times seven yet, my boy. Will has failed often, I know; still, I have not lost hope of him altogether. I knew a worse case than his come out right. But that was through a good woman's love."

"What case was that you knew, father?" asked Gracie, his younger daughter, a pretty, bright-eyed girl. "You never told us about it."

"Oh, it happened a long while ago. It was a case I knew across in the old country. It made a deep impression on me at the time, and I have never forgotten it."

"Let us hear it now," said Gracie.

"He Went Where He Could See the Gate of the Cottage."

"You think it is romantic because I spoke of love," said her father; "but it is altogether prosaic, plain matter of fact. Well, it is soon told. The hero of it was not much of a character—a simple, rustic young fellow, such as you young fellows call 'a regular Hayseed.' But Hayseed in this case was disposed to bad and crooked ways, and had a strong propensity to drink. He seemed to be always thirsty. He was a good farm hand, and could have had plenty of work, but he fell into idle and dissolute ways, until he was the black sheep of the parish. Everyone lost faith in him, after he had tried to reform several times and failed. Even the good, kind-hearted parson gave him up. He was considered hopeless by all who knew him, except one, and that was the girl he loved. She was only a blacksmith's daughter, but she was pretty, and as good as she was beautiful. She believed in him, and for her sake he made another effort. It was in the summer-time. Work was plenty, but Hayseed's thirst was intolerable. He stuck to water, however, but his fellow-workers only laughed, and said that would not last long. But his sweetheart held to him with that fidelity that good women sometimes show. Her father had forbidden him the house, but the girl would go out at sunset to the gate of the garden, and there give him a kiss and a helpful word. That gave him heart for another day's battle.

"The struggle went on in that way until Whitsuntide, and then young Hayseed broke down completely. It was a time of jollity in the village, and he could not resist. His unusual abstinence, I expect, gave his appetite increased potency. Anyhow, he was worse than he had ever been, got quarrelsome, engaged in a fight, and was locked up by the constable. He was sentenced to ten days in prison. That was a disgrace that had never happened to him before. When he came out, he had not the courage to hold up his head. He could not face the village after that, and he lay down under a hedge on an unfrequented road, to decide whether he should get a rope and hang himself or go to America. He inclined to the former, for he had lost faith in himself now.

"It was near sundown, and he had not made up his mind. Anyhow, he would have one more look at the cottage where lived the girl who had held to him last of all. 'God bless her for that,' he said. He had no hope that she would come to the gate to look for him, though she would know that he was out of jail; but, as he confessed, he had no right to expect her. He made his way, however, to a field from which he could see that dear gate that was hallowed to him by associations with her. He stood, leaning on a stick and looking a last good-by to it in the distance, when to his glad amazement he saw the trim little figure he knew so well, trip lightly down the garden, and, leaning over the gate look this way and that, and he knew for whom.

"You may be sure, it did not take him long to leap the old stile and go to her side. I cannot tell you what was said, but young Hayseed came away with eyes red with tears and a strong purpose in his heart. 'If God will help me, I will try again,' he said at parting. 'He will, you may be sure, and I will keep my word,' was the reply, softly but firmly spoken.

"Well, to make the story short, he took fresh heart that night, made his way to America, turned over a new leaf, and his bright-eyed sweetheart followed a year or two after, and married him. I believe they got along very well and prospered moderately."

"Ah!" said Gracie, as Mr. Haldane finished, 'she must have had great faith in him. I guess, she must have had a pretty hard time keeping him straight after they were married. He could not have made her a good husband."

"Ha, ha!" laughed Mr. Haldane. "I can't say about that. I know she made him a good wife. You must ask your mother about the other side."

"Yes, thank God," said Mrs. Haldane, "the best husband a woman ever had, and the best thing I ever did was to go to the gate that night."

THE FAMILY OF TRIPE COURT.

By Brenda.

(Continued from page 30.)

BRIDGET'S FRIENDS.

FOR several days after her admission into the Infirmary, Bridget Mite lay very ill. Fever and inflammation ran high, and it seemed at one time probable that she might have to lose her leg altogether. Impure air and poor, scant food had combined to make her general condition of health so bad that the wound seemed unable to heal; mortification was feared, in which case amputation of the limb would have been found necessary.

In the intervals of her sufferings, when she was able to look about her and to notice things, Bridget discovered that Mrs. Treeby's description of the Poor-house Infirmary was all true; a fine, big, airy place, it was, "and clean," and Bridget saw the [illegible] between it and her own place—yet still she was unreconciled to being there. She thought of the little close, dark room, smelling of rats and mice—"her pig-stye of a place," as Mrs. Treehy had unfeelingly called it, in Tripe Court—with ardent affection, and pined to be back; not because she preferred dirt to cleanliness, darkness to light, the smell of rats and mice to the smell of flowers and fresh air—oh no, no!—but because she pined for a sight of the home faces, for a sound of the home voices, for a touch of home hands. She inquired so often of the nurses "when they thought there'd be visitin' days again" that they grew tired of making the same answer, "When small-pox is better," and at last told her not to bother them with that question again.

The only person who tried to comfort her on the point, and did not mind answering her twenty times a day if she asked about it, was that little woman in the bed on her left, who had prayed for her and kissed her, the first night of her arrival in the Infirmary. During those days that Bridget lay so ill, this little woman, Mrs. Cherry, as she was called, seemed to Bridget to be keeping watch by her. In her moments of ease Mrs. Cherry rejoiced and thanked God for her; when in her greatest pain, Mrs. Cherry encouraged her; when the nurses spoke sharply to Bridget, Mrs. Cherry smoothed down their roughness with the balm of her own kind words, and every night Mrs. Cherry repeated aloud to Bridget that hymn—

"There is an eye that never sleeps,"

and every night prayed for her home and baby, so that Bridget got quite to lean on the little woman, and if anything had happened to remove her from her side, Bridget would have felt she had lost a friend. She had her suffering times, though, with the rest: there were days when poor little Mrs. Cherry was silent, and lay with her small face pinched and white on the pillow, and every one knew she had one of her "bad turns" on. Her complaints were a diseased hip-joint, paralysis of one arm, and poverty of course.

In the afternoon hours of one day at the end of the week, when most of the patients were dozing after dinner and the ward was very quiet, Bridget turned her hot face round towards Mrs. Cherry, and asked, "How long have I been in now? Can you remember when I came?"

"To be sure, ma'am," said Mrs. Cherry, "you came in Tuesday; this is Saturday; you've been in just four days."

"Only four days!" said Bridget wonderingly; "dear, dear, it seems like four months since I left'em all."

"Yes, ma'am, because you've been so bad and suffered such a deal, poor dear," said Mrs. Cherry soothingly, "the time do seem long at first."

"How long have *you* been in, ma'am?" inquired Bridget languidly.

"Seven years come next August," replied Mrs. Cherry, slowly; "I was five years in the old Infirmary before this new one was built, and I've been here two. Yes, seven years in August it'll be, and it's not likely I shall ever go out; yet there's a deal to be thankful for! I used."

she continued cheerfully, seeing that Bridget was somewhat easier, and thinking to distract her mind with a little pleasant talk—"I used to live in the Vale of Aylesbury, in Buckinghamshire. I kept a turnpike-gate there for many a year, along with my husband, and a rare pretty little place it was, on a fine white road, with lovely tall trees running along it both sides. We sold Banbury cakes and ginger-beer and candies.

"The only trouble we had was the *boys*. They used to come along our way after school, sometimes, and creep up to our bit of a window and tap, tap at the panes with their sticks a purpose to upset all the bottles of sweets and ginger-beer and things on the ledge. Oh! me and my husband used to get so wild; we used to run out with broom, or poker, or anythink we could catch up, and try to catch 'em. But the young rascals would dodge round the place, that wasn't much bigger than a sentry-box, as quick as cats, and keep us running round and round it at the try-to-catch game, till we were ready to drop! Oh! the boys *was* a plague. Bless their young hearts, how they used to laugh when the hardbake, and then the brandy-balls, and then the peppermint-sticks, and then the bulls'-eyes, and then the bottles of ginger-beer used to go *crash* on the brick floor inside. I can laugh now when I think of how *they* laughed, and the mad sort of scuffle and tumble and yelping there used to be when they saw the big stick or the poker coming round the corner at them! I wonder where them little lads are now," pondered Mrs. Cherry; "all grown men, of course—I dare say telling their children sometimes of the pranks they used to be up to at the turnpike-gate when they was boys."

"Had you ever any children, ma'am?" asked Bridget.

"Yes, four sons, and I buried 'em all same day as I buried my husband," said the little woman, impressively. "After we left the pike, we went into the oil and tallow-candle line in London, and one December night, when I was away on a visit, our house and shop caught fire, and my poor husband and four boys were all suffocated in their beds. There was all about it in the newspapers. It was the cause of this arm being paralyzed, and the commencement of all my illness. Well, people were very kind; they sent me money through the clergyman—quite a nice little sum it reached. My brother-in-law had it to invest, and somehow it got lost [Mrs. Cherry had forgiven the wrong long ago, so did not mention, what was the fact, that her brother-in-law had robbed her of the money], and after that I got into poverty, and at last had to come into the House. But there," she said again, with a bright look, and heartily, "I have so *much* to be thankful for. I can never go out, but in the summer-time from my bed here, when the window's open, I can lie and look at the daisies growing in the fields there, and it's so beautiful. Yes, God is *very* good to me, bless His holy Name."

Here was a lesson for the grumbling and discontented; this poor little woman, paralyzed and diseased, and never likely to be any better, doomed, probably, to lie on a poorhouse bed till the end of her days, praising and blessing God for the sight of a few field flowers! How true the words—

"Some murmur when their sky is clear,
And wholly bright to view,
If one small speck of dark appear
In their great heaven of blue:
And some with thankful love are filled
If but one streak of light,
One ray of God's good mercy gild
The darkness of their night."

Mrs. Cherry talked no more now. Bridget had closed her eyes, and her face was drawn again in pain.

Sunday came; church bells were heard ringing in the distance; the nurses came out in their clean white caps, there was better dinner fare, a pudding after the meat, and, to many, the lower-natured, greedy ones, this pudding made the whole point of Sunday. To those it did not much signify that visitors had been forbidden for the present; there was always the pudding to look forward to. To some, however, the point of Sunday was very different; it occurred at four o'clock in the afternoon for *them*. All the patients of the Roman Catholic faith were together in one ward; those in the Victoria Ward had professed themselves, on entering the Infirmary, as belonging to the Episcopal Church, such, at least, of those who claimed to be of any religion at all. And so, at four o'clock, the gas having been lit, and all made ready, one of the clergy from a neighboring church, who had acted as chaplain to the Infirmary, accompanied by four fresh-faced little boys in surplices, entered the ward and held a short service.

He began with some of the church prayers; then he prayed in his own language for the people he was amongst. This minister of consolation knew that he had "all sorts and conditions" before him, and he tried, as far as possible, to think of each one's need. He prayed for those dead in trespasses and sins, who rejected and denied Christ, that they might be converted and brought into the true fold at last; he prayed for the very aged and sick who were unable to pray for themselves; he prayed especially for the lonely ones—ah! he knew so well that *loneliness* was the fashion of this place—and for the broken-hearted and afflicted, that they might learn to find communion and consolation in Christ, who, Himself a Man of Sorrows, could feel for each one as no earthly friend could, since

"None ever knew such pain before,
Such infinite affliction,
None ever felt a grief like His
In that dread Crucifixion."

He prayed for those who had once held the faith and lost it, those who had once known Christ, and had fallen away in the hurry and turmoil and fever of life; and he prayed that these might be restored and uplifted, pleading the words, "I, if I be lifted up, will draw all men unto Me," and that the music of the Gospel might lead the despairing and weary ones home. Finally, he commended all those poor people for whom he had been praying, to the care and keeping of Him who was able "to save them to the uttermost," and present them "faultless before the presence of His glory, with exceeding joy." The prayer ended, the four fresh-faced little chorister-boys stood up, and, in full-throated, rich tones, sang the hymn, beginning:

"Hark, hark, my soul! angelic songs are swelling
O'er earth's green fields and ocean's wave-beat shore;
How sweet the truth those blessed strains are telling
Of that new life when sin shall be no more!"

There had been many in the ward, this afternoon, too sick or too careless to listen much to the prayers, but, at the sound of the boys' singing, every one's attention was arrested, every one lent due ear to *that*. The most suffering and the most careless, even the flippant Frenchwoman, listened. Poor Bridget turned her aching head round on the pillow and drank in the sounds. She had not heard anything like them for many a day, for she had long ago given up going to church. She had no *time* for it, she would say, in the week, and on Sundays, well, she was always too dead beat, too utterly done, to make the effort. Ah! poor Bridget; she was one of those brought before Christ in the chaplain's prayer, "who had once held the faith and lost it, who had once known Christ and had fallen away" in the hurry and tumult of her feverish life. As the hymn proceeded, her dark, anxious eyes filled with tears, and by the time the last line was sung—

"And heaven, the heart's true home, will come at last,"

they were falling in large drops down her cheek. She saw the chaplain afterwards go down the long line of beds opposite, and say and give something to each patient in turn. Then he came over to the other side of the ward, and did the same. In turn he came to Bridget's bedside and gave her a little card with the words illuminated on it, "Come unto Me, all ye that labor and are heavy laden, and I will give you rest.'

And the chaplain said, lowly bending over her, seeing her tears, and her poor, harassed, weary face, "Dear sister, tired and heavy laden, Christ has sent you this message to-day, '*Come*,' and He promises to give you *rest*. Cast yourself and your burden, whatever it be, at the foot of the Cross this day, in obedience to His message, and contemplate Him as your risen Saviour, and find all your rest in Him." Then he passed on to the next bed, and so on all down the ward, till he reached the door where he turned and pronounced the blessing, "The peace of God, which passeth all understanding, keep your hearts and minds through Christ Jesus." Then the chaplain and the little choir-boys disappeared, and the old women in gray, came running in with the tea-trays. At the sight of the food, many tucked their cards away hurriedly under their pillows; the Frenchwoman tore up hers into atoms, but Bridget kept hers clasped tight in her hands.

It happened this Sunday night that poor little Mrs. Cherry had one of "her bad turns" on. Since tea-time her chirruping, bright little voice had not been heard in the ward, and everybody saw that her face was the color of wax as it lay on the pillow. At night she was not able to say the usual hymn to Bridget, or to pray for her; it troubled her that she could not; she thought Bridget might be depending on it, for she had told Mrs. Cherry she never prayed herself now; she had *once* done it, oh! yes, when she was a child, and after she was grown up a while, but not of late years; she had lost her belief in prayer and she never had any time.

In the silence of this Sunday night any one watching beside Mrs. Cherry would have seen suddenly a bright look come over her pinched little face, as if a piece of good news had come to her. Was she hearing the choir-boys singing again in her dreams? No: Mrs. Cherry was not sleeping; she was awake; what caused her face to shine at that moment was a sound she caught in the stillness, close beside her, a voice saying in a feeble, stumbling sort of way, "Come unto Me, all ye that labor and are heavy laden, and I will give you rest." It was her poor friend the laundress, Bridget Mite, comforting herself with the words of the message that had been brought to her that afternoon.

As the days went on, the good, regular food, the light and pure air and cleanliness, and, above all, the quiet and bodily rest of her life in the Infirmary, told favorably upon Bridget, and she began gradually, but surely, to improve in health. She lost her severe pain, her leg commenced to heal, and she had an appetite for her food, though her enjoyment of it was ever marred by the thought of hungry faces and an empty larder at home.

With leisure to notice the cleanliness and order and airiness of the Infirmary as she lay on her bed in these recovering days, Bridget began to take herself to task for not keeping her place in Tripe Court better. She told herself she might have kept the floors better scrubbed; the Infirmary floors were only wooden, yet how beautiful they looked because they were so well scrubbed; and she might have put things tidier, and set the window open to let the air and light in to purify it sometimes. When she went back she would try to do all these things, and make the home a little nicer for "them all," meaning her husband and children, of whom she thought so often and with such affection.

Yet she no longer fretted as she had done in the first days of her entering the Infirmary. She seemed to have cast her burden somewhere, and Mrs. Cherry often heard her repeating again and again, in the still night watches, the message sent to her on that first Sunday afternoon in the Infirmary, "Come unto Me, all ye that labor and are heavy laden, and I will give you rest." Poor Bridget knew it not, but the "music of the Gospel" was leading her—Home.

(*To be Continued.*)

PETER CONFESSING CHRIST.

By Mrs. M. Baxter.

S. S. Lesson for January 29. Matt. 16: 13-28.
Golden Text, Matt. 10: 32.

Ver. 13. A Mountainous Region Called the Switzerland of Palestine—A Period of Teaching for the Disciples—The Crucial Question of Christianity—All Hangs Upon That—Ver. 14. All Give Him High Estimate—Ver. 15. A Personal Question—Ver. 16. A Double Aspect—Manward and Godward—Explicit and Unqualified—Ver. 17-20. The Source of Peter's Knowledge Stated—That Belief Always a Revelation—The Confession as a Foundation—Christ as a Builder—The Living Stones Used—Peter's Confession a Characteristic of all—The Keys Used at Pentecost—Vers. 21-23. A Painful Revelation—Why He Must Go—Peter as a Mouthpiece of Satan—Vers. 24-28. The Conditions of Discipleship—The Suffering and the Glory.

THE Pharisees and Sadducees, who were always at loggerheads with one another on points of doctrine, yet found a marvellous ground of unity in opposing the Son of God. They could not deny that He "went about doing good, and healing all that were oppressed of the devil" (Acts 10: 38), for the evidence of it was continually before their eyes. They could not deny that His charity in feeding the hungry was twice done on an enormous scale, and they knew, too, that His personal expenditure was very small, for He had "not where to lay His head," (Luke 9: 58); and must work a miracle in order to pay the taxes (Matt. 17: 24-27). Therefore, they must know that the multitude were fed by divine power and not by earthly munificence. Yet, in their insolent and sinful unbelief, they came and asked of Him a sign from heaven. What more could they want! Alas, how true were His words: "His people's heart is waxed gross, and their ears are dull of hearing, and their eyes have they closed; lest at any time they should see with their eyes, and hear with their ears, and should understand with their heart, and should be converted, and I should heal them." (Matt. 13: 15.) Jesus took occasion to say to His disciples, "Take heed, and beware of

The Leaven of the Pharisees,

and of the Sadducees." The carnally minded disciples lost time, as many of us do, by reasoning among themselves, instead of asking Jesus the meaning of what He said. They came to the conclusion: "It is because we have taken no bread." So much for the reasoning of even converted men! They were very far out in their calculations, but Jesus came to the rescue, and said unto them, "O ye of little faith, why reason ye among yourselves, because ye have brought no bread? Do ye not yet understand, neither remember the five loaves of the five thousand, and how many baskets ye took up? Neither the seven loaves of the four thousand, and how many baskets ye took up?" If the Pharisees were blind, O how doubly blind were the disciples! Was not the fact of these miracles sufficient guarantee that His disciples should not want for bread as long as they were with Him? Thus they understood that it was the doctrine and spirit of the Pharisees and Sadducees which He would have them avoid.

What was this doctrine and spirit? They did not keep their word, "They say, and do not." They expected of others what they would not do themselves. "They bind heavy burdens and grievous to be borne, and lay them on men's shoulders, but they themselves will not move them with one of their fingers." "All their works they do to be seen of men." They like to have people flatter them: "they love the uppermost rooms at feasts, and to be called of men, Rabbi, Rabbi." They, "for a pretence, make long prayers," while they have no real acquaintance with God (Matt. 23: 3-14). In fact, they are one great sham, all outside, and hollow like an empty eggshell. Jesus would have His disciples real, solid, true, substantial, in faith and practice. A religion which collapses with the removal of a favorite minister, with the pain of a little injustice, with the misunderstanding of a few friends, or with the call for a little self-denial, is only an outside thing—it is "the leaven of the Pharisees and of the Sadducees," and the sooner its owner knows the truth about himself, the better.

"When Jesus came into the courts of Cæsarea Philippi, He asked His disciples,

Whom Do Men Say

that I, the Son of Man, am?" And they said: "Some say that Thou art John the Baptist; some Elias: and others Jeremias, or one of the prophets." Yes; anything short of the true Messiah. Men would acknowledge Jesus then, as now, to be the best of men, but they would not have it that He was the Man, God's fellow (Zec. 13: 5), the Messiah, the mighty God" (Isa. 9: 6), who should come into the world. Men's hearts are just the same now as ever; man's belief in himself is such that he wants always to reject the idea of a God who is his superior, to whom he is responsible, who is greater and wiser than he; Almighty and Omniscient. Such a God at once makes man a sinner, if he does not humble himself and take the place of the creature; and the natural heart will bring up argument after argument to disprove the existence of such a God, and to repudiate the allegiance which is due to Him.

One feature of the present age, perhaps the worst of all the forms of opposition to Jesus which Satan has organized, is that of supreme and contemptuous indifference. A great deal of the agnosticism of the day is of this kind. It is not only "I don't know," but it is also, "I don't care to know anything about Jesus." just as with the Pharisees of old: "As for this fellow, we know not from whence He is" (John 9: 29). In the time of Jesus, the Pharisees said of Him: "He hath a devil and is mad;" "He deceiveth the people" (John 10:20; 7: 12); they called Him "a man gluttonous, and a winebibber, a friend of publicans and sinners" (Matt. 11: 19), and tried to prove that He was a blasphemer (Matt. 26: 65: 66). But all they said was powerless to undo the blessed witness for His Father which He bore so steadfastly. And all that man says now against Christ as a Saviour, a Sanctifier, a Healer, cannot stay the tide of glorious salvation, which is bearing on thousands and thousands of those who trust in Him. In opposition to this testimony of His enemies, the very evil spirits bore witness to Him (Mark 1: 24. (Luke 4: 41.) Pilate, who condemned Him to be crucified, was forced to acknowledge, "I find no fault in Him" (John 19: 6). The very centurion, who commanded the soldiers who crucified Him, cried out: "Truly, this Man was the Son of God" (Mark 15: 39). Such are the various witnesses as to who Jesus is!

"But Whom Say Ye

that I am?" This is the question for us. What witness are we bearing to Jesus? There are many who bear witness to the forgiveness of their sins, the cleanness of their heart, the sweetness of their experience, the earnestness of their work, the devotion of their zeal—but O how refreshing it is to hear those whose hearts are full of Jesus, tell out, not what *they* are, but what *He* is! Peter was the first to speak, "Thou art the Christ, the Son of the living God." He was not the first to acknowledge this on earth: the demons who had come out of many cried out, and said, "Thou art Christ the Son of God" (Luke 4: 41). And yet it was not from these demons that Peter had learned it. Jesus said to him, "Blessed art thou, Simon Bar-jona (i.e., son of Jona), for flesh and blood hath not revealed it unto thee, but my Father which is in heaven." Our witness of Jesus will be *only* just what God reveals to us: a stream cannot rise higher than its source. What, then,

Do We Say of Jesus?

In the family, do all the members see in us that Jesus is love and patience and forbearance? Does our life say of Jesus, "God is love"? Do all our actions speak of the "meekness and gentleness of Christ"? (2 Cor. 10: 1.) Do men hear from us the testimony, in times of difficulty, that "the Lord will provide," that "He careth for" us, that our Father which is in heaven knoweth that we have need of all these things? (Gen. 22: 14, margin; 1 Pet. 5: 7; Matt. 6: 32.) Or do they see us desponding, hear us grumbling, find us anxious, just as though all these things which are said of God were only a poem of the imagination? Do men see in us that sin does not have dominion over us, that God *has* delivered us from the kingdom of darkness, and that the besetting sins, which used to conquer us, are now under His dominion, and our very desires changed by His indwelling? Can we tell, and do our lives bear out our words, that Jesus is indeed a Deliverer? "Whom say ye that I am?" A Saviour? My Saviour? A Shepherd? My Shepherd? A Provider? My Provider? A Friend?

My Friend?

Jesus taught Peter that the very gates of hell should not prevail against His church, and that the power to bind and to loose (connected with united prayer, Matt. 18: 18-20) was committed to her. And it was from this time that Jesus began to open up to His disciples the truth, so unpalatable to them, and which they never fully received till after His resurrection, that He must be a suffering Messiah. A strange revolution has taken place in the minds of believers for some ages past, and converted men, as a rule, have been occupied almost exclusively with Christ as a suffering Messiah; and the coming of the Lord with His saints in glory, to reign on earth, is believed only by the few. Yet the first disciples saw nothing else, and in the Old Testament fully nine-tenths of the prophecies of Jesus concern His reign in glory, while only about one-tenth concern His sufferings. Peter, who was not yet filled with the Holy Ghost, and was, consequently, very full of himself, was inclined to presume upon the commendation which the Lord had just given him. Poor human nature, how little encouragement it can stand! Peter actually took upon himself to rebuke the Lord, and said

"Pity Thyself.

Lord, this shall not be unto thee (margin)." Pity Thyself! Jesus would not be Jesus if He did. There was no germ of self-pity in the Lord. No; He said, "If any man will come after *Me*; let him deny himself (not pity himself) and take up his cross and follow Me." Self pity is taking our own part, and being sorry for ourselves, and thinking how badly treated we are, and nursing up the sore instead of letting Jesus' compassion in, and letting Him heal the wounds and put the wrong things right. If Jesus had given way to self pity, He would have come right out of the plan of His Father, and our Redemption would not have been accomplished. Jesus spoke of the suggestion as Satan's, and said, moreover, "Whosoever will save his life (seek his own interests), shall lose it; and whosoever will lose his life for My sake, shall find it." Yes; if we die to ourselves in Christ, we find a better life, so wondrously free, above the fear of man, above the fear of evil, safe in the arms of Jesus. How much have we to learn! Peter, after confessing Jesus as the Son of God, yet savored the things that were of men, and not those of God!

WHY NOT TRUST JESUS?

"Life everlasting" He offers to thee—
Pardoning grace setting sin's captive free;
Love that is infinite, perfect, divine—
Such is the portion which now may be thine.
Why not! oh, why not trust Jesus?

"Peace, passing knowledge." He giveth His own;
Joy that thou otherwise never had'st known
Wilt thou not come? and, in coming, be blest,
Proving the sweetness of perfect heart-rest.
Why not! oh, why not trust Jesus?

Treasures unfathomed are hid in His store,
Drawing from which thou but findest still more:
Fear not to bathe in Love's ocean so wide,
'Neath the deep waves of that ne'er ebbing tide.
Why not! oh, why not trust Jesus?

"Fulness of blessing" there dwelleth in Him—
Fulness o'erflowing that fills to the brim:
"His is the Bounty"—but thine is the need;
Grace, only grace, can the poor sinner plead.
Why not! oh, why not trust Jesus?

"Marvellous love," passing all human thought,
Love which alone could these wonders have wrought—
Such is the love that is waiting for thee,
Tenderly whispering, "Come unto Me."

Perfect in loveliness, matchlessly fair,
Peerless in beauty, beyond all compare;
Christ the unchanging, Who loves to the end—
This MY Beloved, and this is MY Friend.
Why not! oh, why not trust Jesus?

—*Selected.*

J. E. JEWETT, Publisher, 77 Bible House, New York will furnish the above poem in leaflet form at twenty cents per hundred. *A Sample Packet* of 50 leaflets assorted (no two alike), will be sent post-paid for ten cents. Postage stamps taken.

MEXICO

Contributions in aid of Christian work in Mexico are most pressingly needed, and can be mailed to the address of

BISHOP H. C. RILEY,
Care of J. P. HEATH,
43 Bible House, New York.

UNIVERSITY PIANOS FROM $180 TO $1500. FINEST PIANOS IN THE WORLD. SOLD DIRECT TO FAMILIES, saving the enormous expenses of agents. Sent with beautiful cover, stool and book, for trial in your own home before you buy. Guaranteed six years. Send for catalogue to Marshal & Smith Piano Co., 235 E. 21st St., N. Y.

GRIND YOUR OWN Bone, Meal, Oyster Shells, Graham Flour & Corn in the **$5 HAND MILL** (F. Wilson's Patent.) 100 per cent. more made in keeping Poultry. Also POWER MILLS and FARM FEED MILLS. Circulars and testimonials sent on appl'c'n. WILSON BROS. Easton, Pa.

FOR GAS. **BAILEY'S** COMPOUND Light-Spreading Silver-Plated CORRUGATED GLASS **REFLECTORS!** A wonderful invention for *LIGHTING* Churches, Halls, &c. Handsome designs. Satisfaction guaranteed. Catalogue & price list free. BAILEY REFLECTOR CO., 113 Wood St., Pittsburgh, Pa. FOR OIL.

"**FLORIDA** FACTS" BOTH BRIGHT AND BLUE. Latest and best. Illustrated, candid book. Invaluable to intending settlers, tourists, or investors. 160 pages, 58 engravings and colored plates, 50 cents. O. M. CROSBY, author, 99 Franklin Street, New York.

OPIUM Morphine Habit Cured in 10 to 20 days. No pay till cured. Dr. J. Stephens, Lebanon, O.

DIAMOND DYES

COLOR EVERYTHING.

Unequalled for Silk, Wool, Cotton and all Fabrics and Fancy Goods. Brilliant, Durable and Economical. Any one can use them.

32 COLORS—10 CENTS EACH.

Remember, these are the only Pure, Harmless and Unadulterated Dyes.

Beware of other Dyes, because often Poisonous, Adulterated, Weak and Worthless.

We warrant these Dyes to color more goods, package for package, than any other Dyes ever made, and to give more brilliant and durable colors. Sample cards free.

THE DIAMOND PAINTS,
GOLD, SILVER, BRONZE and COPPER

For gilding Fancy Baskets, Frames, Lamps, Chandeliers, and for all kinds of ornamental work. Equal to any of the high-priced kinds, and only 10 cents a package. Also Artists' Black for Ebonizing.

Sold by Druggists everywhere. Send postal for Sample Card, directions for coloring Photos, doing fancy work, and making ink.

WELLS, RICHARDSON & CO., Burlington, Vt.

Gospel Hymns, No. 5

BY IRA D. SANKEY, JAMES McGRANAHAN AND GEO. C. STEBBINS.

NOW READY.

Will be used by Mr. MOODY at Louisville.

SIX YEARS HAVING ELAPSED SINCE GOSPEL Hymns No. 4 was issued, Christian workers throughout the land have felt the need of additional new songs, and to meet this demand GOSPEL HYMNS No. 5 has been prepared. Each piece in the book has been carefully tested by the authors, and only those retained that are especially adapted for use in devotional services.

Gospel Hymns No. 5

Contains a greater number of **new songs** than any of the preceding volumes, together with the best of the old favorites, and standard selections of unquestioned merit.

This collection contains 208 pages, of the same size and shape as other numbers of the series, but, while greatly increased in size, the prices are the same as for preceding single volumes, viz:

Price per 100, by Express, Charges not Prepaid.

Music Edition, Board Covers, ... $30.00
Word Edition, Paper Covers, ... 5.00
" **(Minion Type) Board Covers,** 10.00

If ordered by mail, add five cents per copy to Music and two cents to Word Edition.

Former editions of **GOSPEL HYMNS** are still published. No. 5 is not expected to supersede but supplement them.

Orders may be sent to either of the Publishers, or any book or music dealer.

PUBLISHED BY

BIGLOW & MAIN,	The JOHN CHURCH CO.
76 E. Ninth St., New York	74 W. 4th St., Cincinnati,
81 Randolph St., Chicago	19 E. 16th St., New York.

"*Demonology or Spiritualism,* Ancient and Modern."—"An effective weapon."—"A sword of fire."—"Only unanswerable work on the subject."—Startling disclosures.—History *facts* and data.—Scores saved already. Whole communities rescued. Every family, preacher and christian worker needs one. 310 pp. 12mo, cloth. Price reduced to $1. Sent by mail, postpaid, on receipt of price. Address **J. E. JEWETT,** 77 Bible House, New York.

WANTED AGENTS to sell the Child's Bible. We have sold to more than three-quarters of all the Protestant families in many towns. One woman who commenced last January has sold over 700 copies. For full particulars address **CASSELL & CO., LIMITED,** 40 Dearborn St., Chicago. 822 Broadway, New York.

AGENTS Send for E. B. TREAT'S ... of new books ... MOTHER ... and HEAV... and poetry ... authors ... elegantly ... $1 for ... Bible, $2.00. By mail. E. B. TREAT

HOUSE BUILT ... EVERY ... canvasser who takes a given num... grand, new book "Beau... full particulars and picture of house ... Dept., of the Co-Operative Building Pla... ...way, New York

Works by Dr. Geikie.

"The appearance of these books has marked an epoch in the study of the Bible. An amount of light and information which is as wonderful as it is gratifying."—*Central Baptist*, St. Louis.

THE HOLY LAND—Illustrated.

The Holy Land and the Bible. A Book of Scripture Illustrations gathered in Palestine. Beautifully printed from Small Pica type, with numerous fine illustrations and a map. In 2 vols., small quarto, elegantly bound in half Morocco, price $2.00; postage, 30c.: the same bound in one volume, cloth, $1.25; postage, 20c. *In press, ready soon; specimen pages and illustrations now ready, sent free.*

"In this fascinating work the author brings vividly before the reader, in graphic language, the prominent places in the Holy Land that are associated with Bible History. The work is of intense interest from beginning to end, and is crowded with information of the highest importance for the understanding of the Holy Scriptures of both the Old and the New Testament.

"I visited Palestine with the intention of gathering illustrations of the sacred writings from its hills and valleys, its rivers and lakes, its plains and uplands, its plants and animals, its skies, its soil, and, above all, from the pictures of ancient times still presented on every side in the daily life of its people. Nothing is more instructive or can be more charming, when reading Scripture, than the illumination of its texts from such sources, throwing light upon it's constantly-recurring Oriental imagery and local allusions, and revealing the exact meaning of words and phrases which otherwise could not be adequately understood. The land is, in fact, a natural commentary on the sacred writings."—*Author's Preface.*

HOURS with the BIBLE.

Hours with the Bible. In six vols., 12mo, Brevier type, leaded, illustrated. I. Creation to Patriarchs; II. Moses to Judges; III. Samson to Solomon; IV. Rehoboam to Hezekiah; V. Manasseh to Zedekiah; VI. Kalis to Malachi. Per vol., cloth, 45c.; half Morocco, 60c.; per set, cloth, $2.40; half Morocco, $3.30; postage 8c. per vol. *Now ready.*

"It is the best connected popular exposition of the Old Testament, and deserves its immense popularity."—REV. J. MAX HARK, Lancaster, Pa.

"'Hours with the Bible' fills a place which no commentary can occupy, as it brings to bear upon the Biblical record a vast amount of information—geographical, historical, scientific—not available in an ordinary commentary. The celebrated author's style is charming, and Mr. Alden has put out the work in a style equally charming."—*The Guardian*, Philadelphia, Pa.

"This author is one of the most reverent and conservative of our time, following the old paths faithfully, and yet never following them blindly. He does not fear to dissent from traditional views when the truth demands it, but he has no leanings toward liberal or novel theories. Taken altogether, we know no work of like design that can be commended with so little qualification. For the average *reader there is nothing that compares to it.*"—*Christian Evangelist*, St. Louis.

A BOOK for YOUNG MEN.

Entering on Life. A book for Young Men. By CUNNINGHAM GEIKIE, D.D. Ideal Edition, Long Primer type, fine cloth, price reduced from $1.00 to 40c.; post. 6c. *Ready.*

"When such a man as the wise and gentle Dean Alford recommends a book, all is said, and said as only a few can say it. Every parent, every teacher, every friend of the race, every believer in things of good repute, must echo his convictions, and join with him in bearing witness to the good sense, the exquisite fancy, the pathos, piety, and sound moral reasoning that illuminates every page. Dr. Geikie strikes the golden mean between the merely didactic and the merely literary, his style embracing the essentials of rare culture united with a happy and elevated orthodox train of thought."—*The Week*, Toronto.

A GREAT and NOBLE WORK.

Life and Words of Christ. By CUNNINGHAM GEIKIE, D.D. 16mo, 838 pages, Brevier type, cloth, 45c.; half Morocco, 60c.; postage 12c. *Now ready.*

"A great and noble work, rich in information, eloquent and scholarly in style, earnestly devout in feeling."—*Literary World.*

"A work of gigantic industry, and, what is the chief point, it breathes the spirit of true faith in Christ. I rejoice at such a magnificent creation, and wonder at the extent of reading it shows."—DR. DELITZSCH.

The Literary Revolution Catalogue (84 pages) sent free on application. ALDEN'S publications are *NOT* sold by *book-sellers*—no discounts allowed except as advertised. Books sent for *examination before payment*, satisfactory reference being given. (1bd297)

JOHN B. ALDEN, Publisher, NEW YORK:
393 Pearl St.; P. O. Box 1227. CHICAGO: Lakeside Building, Clark and Adams Sts.

SPECIAL NOTICE.—*Any readers of the Christian Herald who wish to procure the above books or any other publications of Mr. J. B. Alden, can send their orders to me at his published prices and the books will be sent promptly and guaranteed to reach you safely.* **J. E. JEWETT, 77 Bible House, New York.**

THE DINGEE & CONARD CO'S LEADING SPECIALTIES.

ROSES

ALL VARIETIES, SIZES AND PRICES
FINE EVER-BLOOMING PERPETUAL, CLIMBING AND MOSS ROSES.
NEW AND RARE FLOWER SEEDS.

HARDY PLANTS, New Moon Flower, Clematis, Spring Bulbs, JAPAN LILIES. New Chrysanthemums, and our Wonderful ORNAMENTAL VEGETABLES. *Everything sent* safely by mail or express *to all points.* We offer Choice NEW THINGS and STERLING NOVELTIES in all departments. Our NEW GUIDE, 110 pp., elegantly illustrated, describes over 1500 NEWEST and CHOICEST Varieties of ROSES, SEEDS, PLANTS and BULBS, and tells how to grow them. Free. If you wish to plant anything, send for it. 20 Years Established. *Over 60 Large Greenhouses.* THE DINGEE & CONARD CO. ROSE GROWERS, WEST GROVE, Chester Co., Pa.

Over 6,000,000 PEOPLE USE

FERRY'S SEEDS.

D. M. FERRY & CO. are admitted to be The LARGEST SEEDSMEN in the world. D. M. FERRY & Co's Illustrated, Descriptive and Priced SEED ANNUAL For 1888 Will be mailed FREE to ALL applicants, and to last season's customers without ordering it. Invaluable to all. Every one using Garden, Field or Flower Seeds should send for it. Address D. M. FERRY & CO., Detroit, Mich.

BURPEE'S SEEDS,

FARM ANNUAL FOR 1888

Will be sent FREE to all who write for it. It is a Handsome Book of 128 pp., with hundreds of illustrations, Colored Plates, and tells all about the BEST GARDEN, FARM, and FLOWER Bulbs, Plants, and Valuable New Books on Garden Topics. It describes Rare Novelties in VEGETABLES and FLOWERS, of real value, which cannot be obtained elsewhere. Send address on a postal for the most complete Catalogue published, to

W. ATLEE BURPEE & CO., PHILADELPHIA, PA.

Vol. XI., No. 4. Office, 63 Bible House, N. Y. THURSDAY, JANUARY 26, 1888. Annual Subscription, $1.50.

CONTENTS OF THIS NUMBER.

PORTRAIT AND LIFE OF THE RT. REV. ARTHUR CLEVELAND COXE, Bishop of Western New York, and Pictures of Mexican Buildings.
BROKEN PROMISES OF MARRIAGE. Dr. Talmage's Sermon Last Sunday Morning to the Women of America.
THE CHURCH OF JESUS IN MEXICO. By Bishop Alfred Lee.
TRUE READING OF THE SIGNS OF OUR TIMES. By Dr. Faussett.
A Tract Refused and Accepted—A Music-Teacher's Helplessness—A Good Samaritan Shoe-Black—A High Caste Convert—A Rescued Waif, etc.
A LITTLE SANCTUARY. A New Sermon by C. H. Spurgeon.
PICTURE OF LADY DUFFERIN'S TRAINED INDIAN NURSES.
MRS. LACY'S BROKEN ENGAGEMENT. (With Illustration.)
THE FAMILY OF TRIPE COURT. A Serial Story. (Continued.)
THE TRANSFIGURATION. By Mrs. M. Baxter.

THE EXECUTIVE MANSION OF MEXICO.

THE CATHEDRAL OF PUEBLA.

THE CHURCH OF THE REFORMATION IN MEXICO.

The Rt. Rev. Arthur Cleveland Coxe, Bishop of Western New York, the Advocate of Mexican Missions.

THE RT. REV. A. CLEVELAND COXE.

Bishop of Western New York.

His Spirit of Love and Toleration—Personal Life—Birth in 1818—Ordination in 1841—Work in Hartford—Removal to Baltimore in 1854—Elected Bishop of Texas in 1856—The Office Declined—Return to New York in 1863—The Recognition of the Universities—Elected Bishop of Western New York—Interest in Missions—Champions the Work in Mexico—His Perception of Insidious Designs—His appeal for Help.

IN a recently published answer to an appeal for direction in a painful dispute, the eminent bishop whose portrait appears on the first page, referred the appellant to the apostolic word (James 3: 18): "The fruit of righteousness is sown in peace of them that make peace." In doing so, Dr. Coxe furnished the key to his character and work. He has never cultivated the spirit of the disciples, who said (Mark 9: 38): "Master, we saw one casting out devils in thy name, and he followeth not us: and *we forbade him because he followeth not us.* But Jesus said, Forbid him not." Dr. Coxe has always been prompt to recognize the value of real earnest work for the salvation of souls and the promotion of Christ's cause on earth; and the fact that some who are engaged in such labor hold different views as to Church government and other details, from those held by him and the Church of which he is a pillar, does not deter him from wishing them God-speed and aiding them if they have need of help.

The Personal Life

of the Right Rev. Arthur Cleveland Coxe, D. D., LL. D., has been one of consecration and devotion to Christian labor throughout. He was born at Mendham, N. J., on May 10, 1818, and is, therefore, now nearly seventy years old. He comes of a family that has been prominent in Maryland for two hundred years. It is connected by marriage with that of the President of the United States, of whom the bishop is a cousin. He studied at the University of the City of New York, and in 1838, at the early age of twenty, he graduated with distinction.

A course of theological study at the General Theological Seminary followed his graduation from the university, and in 1841 he passed with honor, and was ordained on June 27 by Bishop B. T. Onderdonk, of New York. His first labors were at St. Ann's, Morrisania, N. Y., where he remained until Easter, 1842, when he removed to Hartford, Conn., where he became rector of St. John's. He remained there for eleven years, doing valuable and earnest work with remarkable success. In 1854, owing to personal circumstances, he felt it his duty to remove southward, and he accepted the rectory of Grace Church, Baltimore, Md. He had not been there more than two years when an effort was made to bring him into episcopal labor. He was elected Bishop of Texas. This honor, however, Dr. Coxe felt it his duty at that time to decline, and he continued his work in Baltimore for seven years longer. His talents and services, however, brought other recognitions, which were accepted. The degree of D. D. was conferred upon him by St. James's College, Hagerstown, Md., in 1856. To this Trinity College, Hartford, Conn., added the degree of S. T. D., and Kenyon College, Gambier, O., the degree of LL. D.

In 1863 Dr. Coxe returned to New York, as Rector of Calvary Church, but he had been there only two years when

A Second Call

to the office of Bishop came to him, and at this time it could not be disregarded. He was elected Assistant Bishop of Western New York, and was consecrated on January 4, 1865. Three years later, on the death of Bishop De Lancey, he took full charge of the diocese.

Bishop Coxe has taken a deep interest in the cause of foreign missions, and, in spite of his arduous episcopal labors, and the numerous works which have issued from his pen, he has found time to act on the Mission Boards of the Church, and to promote missionary enterprises. The Greek Mission especially, had his ardent co-operation. To such a man the work Bishop Riley is doing in Mexico, could not fail to commend itself. He stood by it manfully, and all the more valiantly, when he saw it menaced by enemies of various kinds. The opposition manifested itself in so many shapes and disguises, and pursued tactics so diverse, that it was difficult to understand the underlying general principle at work in each. Bishop Coxe, however, though he has never directly expressed his opinion, appears to have detected it. When he made his remarkable address lately, on Ultramontanism, before the Evangelical Alliance, exposing, in masterly style, the ways of the Jesuits, it was not difficult to understand his

Championship of the Church of Jesus

in Mexico against its enemies in Mexico, and in the United States, some of whom belong to the Protestant Episcopal Church, though in some cases they are affiliated in principle, and in other cases by family relationship with the Romish Church. Such a work as that Bishop Riley is doing, in enlightening the people of Mexico, necessarily excites the deepest and most virulent animosity in the Roman Catholic Church, because the priests perceive that it not only undermines their spiritual power over the people, but deprives them of the political power, that they have so long wielded to the unhappiness of the nation. While fighting against it directly, they saw that the most effective attack upon it would be a flank charge by any friends of their own in the Ritualistic party in the Church to which Bishop Riley belongs.

Two charges on Bishop Riley's attenuated ranks were made. Remarks from persons in high places began to be uttered, questioning the propriety of intrusion on ground already occupied by the ancient Church of Rome. Another and more subtle idea was then industriously circulated. It was urged that Christian work in Mexico ought to be a mission work from the Protestant Episcopal Church in the United States, and the Church in Mexico to be not national and independent, but governed and controlled by the Church here. This attack was the more dangerous because it imposed on persons who did not perceive its motive, through not understanding the prejudices and apprehensions of the Mexican people. With their dread of annexation by the United States, and their resolve to resist the first entry of the wedge, any Christian work stamped with the nationality of the United States would be misunderstood, and doomed at once. The priests in denouncing it as a foreign movement, could appeal to the patriotism of the people, with good prospects of success. They could thus divert public attention from its spiritual character, from questions of doctrine and practice to political questions, and to the insidious design which they would impute to it, of trying to undermine the political independence of the State. Dr. Riley understood the astute manœuvre and refused to become a party to it though he was not able to convince his Episcopal brethren of its true character. He lost the pecuniary support of the Church, and since then has carried on the work at his own charges with such aid as the Christian public has given him.

A Manful Appeal

on behalf of the work came from Bishop Coxe on December 11, 1887. In the course of it he said: "It has been well said, the moment you accept this work, you have the noblest mission, in point of fact, in which you have ever engaged. The Church of England and our own Church have long recognized the principle of this kind of mission, giving aid to National Churches to reform themselves; not reducing them to missions of other churches." Therefore Bishop Coxe earnestly appealed for voluntary support for them in their noble self-denial.

As many misleading statements are now being industriously circulated we publish herewith, at the request of Bishop Riley, a statement written some years ago by Bishop Alfred Lee, of Delaware, on his return to his diocese, after personally inspecting the work in Mexico.

THE CHURCH OF JESUS IN MEXICO.

ITS ORIGIN, HISTORY AND AIMS.

By the Late Rt. Rev. Alfred Lee, Bishop of Delaware.

The Dawn of Spiritual Light—The Circulation of the Word—Aguilar, the Pioneer—An Enlightenment Like Luther's—The First Congregation—His Early Death—The Call to Dr. Riley—A Post of Danger—The Romish Champion Transformed—The Work of Aguas—His Death—Dr. Riley Succeeds Him—The Character of the Church—What it May Accomplish.

SPIRITUAL light is now breaking upon Mexico, and within the last few years a movement has been in progress in that Republic, full of promise and hope. Viewed in its origin, nature and growth, and in connection with the country in which it appeared, it may be considered one of the remarkable movements of the age. It certainly has strong claims upon the attention and sympathy of the lovers of Scriptural truth and pure, primitive Christianity. Romanism, however deeply rooted in the sacred associations, early prejudices and social habits of the people, has no longer an undisputed field.

A New Communion

has arisen, presenting the faith of the Lord Jesus Christ in a widely different aspect, and from small beginnings has been rapidly spreading. Of the origin and history of this infant Church a brief outline will be now presented.

Of this plant, now growing so vigorously, it may be emphatically said, "The Seed was the Word of God." It sprang up from the bosom of the Papal Communion through the silent influence of the Holy Scriptures. When the attempt was made to seat the unfortunate Maximilian upon the throne of Mexico, advantage was taken of the new condition of things to introduce a considerable supply of copies of the Bible in the Spanish tongue. The book found readers. Some of the precious seed fell upon ground prepared by Divine grace for its reception. Among those thus enlightened was a presbyter named Manuel Aguilar. Upon him the reading of the volume produced like effects as upon Luther in the convent of Erfurth. He not only rejoiced in the discovery which was so precious to his own soul, but he longed to extend to others the blessings he had found. By him

The First Protestant Congregation,

for the worship of God in the Spanish tongue and the preaching of the gospel, was gathered in the city of Mexico. The thought of Aguilar was to establish a Reformed Catholic Church, evangelical in doctrine and assimilated in model and polity to the primitive apostolic pattern. He began with a little congregation of about fifty persons, which increased steadily under his assiduous labors. But his course was a brief one. His own exertions were exhausting; and persecution, none the less malignant if restrained from actual violence, was exceedingly harassing. Within two years he succumbed, pressing, in his last moments, the Bible to his heart. Among his papers was found the translation of a little volume, in which the right and duty of every man to search the Scriptures was powerfully argued. This was published by the Rev. H. C. Riley, and proved an effective ally to his work.

The attention of the bereaved flock was directed to a Presbyter of the Protestant Episcopal Church in the United States, of American parentage, but of Chilian birth and education, who was ministering in the Spanish tongue to an Episcopal congregation in the city of New York. In view of the admirable fitness of the Rev. Henry C. Riley for the work in Mexico, it is no presumption to recognize the hand of God in this call. It was a startling summons to Mr. Riley, urging him to leave his kindred and congregation for

A Post of Certain Danger

and uncertain results. After examining all the difficulties and perils involved, Mr. Riley decided to give himself to the work. Constrained by the love of Christ and zeal for the extension of His kingdom, he "counted not his life dear unto himself, and none of these things moved him." He went on his own responsibility, and mainly at his own charges.

Arriving in Mexico in 1869, he re-collected, as far as practicable, the scattered flock of Aguilar, teaching both publicly and from house to house. He labored not less effectively with his pen, circulating numbers of tracts explanatory of the great doctrines of the Gospel. He soon attracted public attention, and the jealous eyes of the dominant Church watched him with inquisitorial vigilance. A Catholic society, with a layman for president, was formed with the express object of counteracting his growing influence. But, in spite of opposition, Mr. Riley's hearers multiplied. He obtained from the Government one of the sequestrated conventual churches. San José de Gracia, and prepared to transfer thither his services. The rage of his enemies waxed hot. The Romish party, unable to crush him by violence, determined to employ argument. For this purpose they selected one of the most eminent and learned ecclesiastics of the capital,

Manuel Aguas,

a Dominican friar, and very popular as a preacher. He examined Mr. Riley's publications, with the intention of preparing a refutation. But the Lord led him by a way that he knew not. He was himself vanquished by the power of the truth. "There fell from his eyes as it had been scales." He discovered that he had been all his life in darkness, and that the work he had undertaken to oppose was of the Lord. He sought personal conference with Mr. Riley, and after painful conflict and deep searchings of heart, he joined himself to that which he had been wont to look upon as an odious sect. This open adhesion to the new doctrine was a shock to his former associates not unlike that occasioned by the conversion of Saul of Tarsus. The church of San José de Gracia was about to be occupied by the congregation under Dr. Riley's care. Loud and deep were the threats. What added fuel to the flame was the announcement that the preacher on that occasion would be none other than Manuel Aguas!

With apostolic boldness the converted friar ascended the pulpit, and before an immense audience proclaimed the gospel. The favoring hand of God averted the danger. Manuel Aguas concluded his sermon without interruption, and went forward with zeal and intrepidity in his new vocation. From that time he was united with Mr. Riley in the oversight of the church. He was elected its first bishop, and had every qualification for a leader. Trained in all the learning of the Romish school, and conversant with the system of eternal administration, he could speak intelligently upon all the points that came under discussion. Of unblemished character, as well as great intellectual powers, he commanded the respect of his bitterest enemies. Embracing the grand verities of the gospel with simple, childlike faith, and proclaiming them with fervor and eloquence, he attracted large numbers to hear the Word, and had the entire confidence and affection of the flock to whom he ministered. He seemed, indeed, precisely the man for the arduous and important charge for which he had been selected, "a chosen vessel of the Lord."

The anger and astonishment created among his old associates may be imagined, He was, of course,

Speedily Excommunicated,

but his enemies could not, as a former generation would have done, consign him to the tender mercies of the Inquisition. He was challenged to a public disputation. This he gladly accepted, and named as the question for discussion, "Is the Church of Rome guilty of idolatry?" Public expectation was intensely aroused, and on the day appointed thousands wended their way to San José. Great precautions were taken by the friends of Aguas for his safety. It was with difficulty that way was made for him through the dense masses to the platform. But when he arrived, his antagonist did not make his appearance. The Roman authorities had thought better of it, and concluded not to allow the discussion. Their selected theologian, who in good faith had been preparing himself, was sent to a distant place; Aguas was alone. He had the field to himself, and he did not fail to take advantage of the great opportunity. He boldly accused Rome of the sin of idolatry, and sustained the charge by convincing proofs. Strange things were brought to the ears of many of his auditors, and the shock given to the Roman system was a heavy one.

Aguas was busy with his pen as well as in his public ministry. In particular he replied to the sentence of excommunication in a tract, which, for forcible style, is worthy to be compared with "The Provincial Letters" of Pascal.

Through the labors of Aguas, Riley and some faithful helpers, the work prospered greatly, and extended from the capital to neighboring towns and villages. A simple liturgy was prepared, and proved a very efficient aid in diffusing the principles of the gospel and building up congregations. Bible-readers, men unversed in scholastic lore, but full of faith and zeal, carried the glad tidings from village to village, experiencing often the same treatment as the first heralds of the cross, but persevering and undismayed. In the city of Mexico

An Important Acquisition

was made in the purchase of another of the old conventual churches—San Francisco. This is a magnificent edifice, in which an audience of two thousand might be assembled, with a chapel adjacent capable of accommodating three hundred persons, situated on the principal street of the city. The church is only inferior to the cathedral in dimensions, and of a better style of architecture. It is every way suited to be a centre of mission work. Hitherto the chapel only has been used, but efforts are now made to put the church in repair, and great advantages are anticipated from its use in public worship.

The course of Aguas, like that of Aguilar, was soon terminated. In labors he was most abundant, preaching from twelve to fifteen sermons a week, in addition to manifold cares of oversight and pastoral duty. Under these exertions, as well as the harassing effects of persecution and calumny upon a sensitive spirit, his health gave way. In 1872 he rested from his labors.

From the beginning the ideal in the minds of the leaders of this movement was a church purified from Romish errors and corruptions, but retaining the primitive constitution of the Spanish Ante-Nicene Church. The hope was cherished at the outset of obtaining the adhesion of one of the Mexican bishops, and thus perpetuating the ministry in the order which they desired, but the way was not then opened. Afterwards, having elected Aguas as their future bishop, they looked forward to the day when he could be consecrated to his office. Disappointed in this earnest desire, they still waited patiently without resorting to any other mode of ordination. So far as possible the sacraments were administered by Dr. Riley and converted presbyters. It was a memorable day, February 24, 1875, when the first ordination in Mexico was held by a Protestant bishop. The full service of our Church in the Spanish tongue was used, the sermon being preached by the Rev. Dr. Riley.

As in the era of the Reformation, the revulsion from Rome is strong and decided. Papal corruption and oppression are to them

Fearful Realities.

Those who have given up friends and prospects of earthly advantage, and are hazarding their lives in the struggle for a pure faith, are not inclined to compromise with such an enemy. Two doctrines especially hold in their minds the same high position with which they were regarded by the champions of the Reformation—the Holy Scriptures, the standard of faith and practice, and the right of every man to read them under his responsibility to God; and justification by the merits of Jesus Christ, through faith alone.

The rapid increase of the "Church of Jesus," in Mexico, is fitted to awaken strong hopes for the future. It counts now (in 1875) over fifty congregations. Many of these are small, but others number from three to four hundred, and in some villages the larger part of the population is embraced. The reformation in morals is in such places very observable. It is safe to reckon that over six thousand souls are at this time under the influence of the Church. An evidence of the extent to which the work has spread, was furnished by the visit of delegations from remote congregations, some of whom have travelled many miles.

As in apostolic days, the converts are largely "the poor of this world rich in faith." The obloquy encountered, and the worldly sacrifices to be made, are great obstacles in the way of persons of high social position. It is "hard for the rich man to enter into the kingdom of God."

The Spirit of Persecution

is none the less bitter because its outward demonstrations are checked by law. There is no reason to doubt that the present Government is sincere in its desire to enforce the laws of toleration, and it succeeds in the capital as well as could be expected. But in remote districts its arm is comparatively weak, while an ignorant and fanatical populace is easily incited to violence. The "Church of Jesus," in Mexico, has had its martyrs and confessors. But the spirit of genuine Christianity is shown not only in willingness to suffer and die for Christ, but also in the return of good for evil and blessings for curses. There has been little complaint heard from the suffering Church. Indignities, revilings and outrages have been patiently borne, and, "with well-doing, they seek to put to silence the ignorance of foolish men." Like the early Christians, they are assailed by false and odious accusations.

While the evangelist is exposed to obvious dangers from fanatical bigotry, there is not the same risk for the native worker as for the foreigner. The missionary from abroad arouses national and political as well as religious prejudices. And herein is largely the hope and

Promise of the Movement

under consideration. It is of Mexican origin, and carried forward by native laborers. Peradventure God, in His Providence, is thus preparing the way for the extension of the pure gospel among the millions on this continent speaking the Spanish tongue. We know how inaccessible they have seemed to missionary enterprise. But let a Mexican Church be established, presenting the truth as it is in Jesus, and the light thus enkindled would extend its beams to the Antilles and the Continental Spanish American States. A great company of preachers would go forth, sister churches would spring up, and light-towers be kindled along the Atlantic and Pacific coasts. Nay, it is no extreme supposition that the radiance will extend across the ocean, and that from the countries to which Spain sent her fierce, armed propagandists in the sixteenth century, may be returned to her the much-needed influences of pure and apostolic Christianity.

Such hopes are not to be put aside as idle dreams, when we see what has already been done. A reformed Church, numbering more than fifty congregations, and celebrating its worship in grand temples in the very heart of the city of Mexico, has been gathered within the space of ten years, in the face of virulent prejudice and fanatical opposition. Surely such a work, opening such prospects, may well cheer the hearts and encourage the hopes of the lovers of truth and holiness.

To us the hearts and wishes of that which is in truth the Church of Christ, in Mexico, are now turned. We can engage with peculiar advantage in a grand and holy work. "A great door and effectual is opened unto us of the Lord." If it be added, "and there are many adversaries," this is no new experience in the history of Christ's religion.

ALFRED LEE.

BROKEN PROMISES OF MARRIAGE.

Dr. Talmage's Third Sermon

TO THE WOMEN OF AMERICA.

Preached last Sunday Morning, January 22, 1888.

"I have opened my mouth unto the Lord, and I cannot go back." Judges 11: 35.

Jephthah's Vow—An Unknown Sacrifice Promised—His Daughter's Appearance a Horror to Him—Doubts About her Fate—An Overmastering Consideration—Caution as to Promises—Painful Dilemmas—The Victims of Broken Promises—In Asylums and Cemeteries—The Sanctity of a Promise—Recognized in Business—Engagement as Binding as Marriage—Exceptions Rare—A Captain's Desertion of his Ship—Betrothal a Golden Gate—Queen Elizabeth's Amours—Other Noted Lovers—No Excuse for Blunders—Caution Indispensable for Women—Despicable Triflers of Both Sexes—Questions About Divorce—Only the Last Resort—Better Remedies—The Betrothed Engineer's Struggle on the Dykes.

GENERAL JEPHTHAH, the Commander-in-chief of the Israelitish forces, is buckling on the sword for the extermination of the pestiferous Ammonites, and looking up to the sky, he promises that if God will give him the victory, he will put to death and sacrifice as a burnt offering the first thing that comes out from the door of his homestead when he goes back. The hurrahing of triumph soon runs along the line of all the companies, regiments and divisions of Jephthah's army. A worse beaten enemy than those Ammonites never strewed any plain with their carcases. General Jephthah, fresh from his victory, is now on his way home. As he comes over the hills and through the valleys, the whole march for his men is a cheer, but for him

A Great Anxiety,

for he remembers his vow to slay and burn the first thing that comes forth from his house to greet him after his victory. Perhaps it may be the old watch-dog that shall first come out; and who could get heart to beat out the life of a faithful creature like that, as he comes fawning and barking and frisking, and putting up his paw against his master in merry welcome after long absence? No; it was not that which came forth to meet Jephthah. Perhaps it may be a young dove let out from its cage in the General's home, which, gaining its liberty, may seem to rejoice in public gladness and flutter on the shoulder of the familiar head of the household. But who could have the heart to slay such a winged innocent? No; it was not that which came forth to meet Jephthah. Or it may be some good neighbor that will rush out to greet him after having first been in to tell the family of the near approach of the General. But who could slay a neighbor who had come on the scene to rejoice over the reunited household? No; it was not that which came forth to meet Jephthah.

As he advances upon his home the door opens, and out of it comes one whose appearance under other circumstances would have been an indescribable joy, but under

The Pledge of a Sacrifice

becomes a horror which blanches his cheek and paralyzes his form and almost hurls him flat to the earth. His child, his only child, his daughter, comes skipping out to greet him, her step keeping time to a timbrel which she shakes and smites. Did ever a conqueror's cheer end in such a bitter groan?

All the glories of victorious war are blotted out from Jephthah's memory, and his banner is folded in grief, and his sword goes back into the scabbard with dolorous clang, and the muffled drum takes the place of the cymbals, and the "tremolo" the place of the trumpet, and he cries out: "Alas, my daughter, thou hast brought me very low, and thou art one of them that trouble me; for I have opened my mouth to the Lord, and I cannot go back." During two months, amid the mountains, without shelter the maidens who would have been at her wedding ranged with Jephthah's daughter up and down, bewailing her coming sacrifice.

Commentators and theologians are in dispute as to whether that girl was slain or not, and as to whether, if she were slain, it was right or wrong in Jephthah to be the executioner, a discussion into which I shall not be diverted from

The Overmastering Consideration

that we had better look out what we promise, better be cautious what engagement we make, better that in regard to all matters of betrothal and plighted vow we feel the responsibility, lest we have either to sacrifice the truth or sacrifice an immortal being, and we be led to cry out with the paroxysm of a Jephthah: "I have opened my mouth unto the Lord, and I cannot go back."

There is one ward in almost all the insane asylums, and a large region in almost every cemetery, that you need to visit. They are occupied by the men and women who are the

Victims of Broken Promises

of marriage. The women in those wards and in those mortuary receptacles are in the majority, because woman lives more in her affections than does man, and laceration of them, in her case, is more apt to be a dementia and a fatality. In some regions of this land the promise of marriage is considered to have no solemnity or binding force. It was only made in fun. They may change their mind. The engagement may stand until some one more attractive in person, or opulent in estate, appears on the scene; then the rings are returned, and the amatory letters, and all relationship ceases. And so there are ten thousand Jephthah's daughters sacrificed as burnt offerings. The whole subject needs to be taken out of the realm of comedy into tragedy, and men and women need to understand that, while there are exceptions to the rule, once having solemnly pledged to each other heart and hand, the forfeiture and abandonment of that pledge makes the transgressor in the sight of God a perjurer, and so the Day of Judgment will reveal it. The one has lied to the other; and all liars shall have their place in the lake that burneth with fire and brimstone. If a man or woman make

A Promise in the Business World,

is there any moral obligation to fulfil it? If a man sign a note for five hundred dollars, ought he to pay it? If a contract be signed involving the building of a house, or the furnishing of a bill of goods, ought they stand by that contract? "Oh, yes," always answered. Then I ask the further question: Is the heart, the happiness, the welfare, the temporal and eternal destiny of a man or woman worth as much as the house, worth five hundred dollars, worth anything? The realm of profligacy is filled with men and women as a result of the wrong answer to that question. The most aggravating, stupendous and God-defying lie is a lie in the shape of broken espousal.

But suppose a man changes his mind, ought he not back out? Not one in ten thousand.

What If I Change My Mind

about a promissory note, and decline to pay it, and suddenly put my property in such shape that you could not collect your note? How would you like that? That, you say, would be a fraud. So is the other a fraud, and punish it God will certainly, as you live, and just as certainly if you do not live. I have known men, betrothed to loving and good womanhood, resigning their engagement, and the victim went down in hasty consumption, while suddenly the recreant man would go up the aisle of a church in brilliant bridal party, and the two promised "I will," with a solemnity that seemed ensurance of a lifetime happiness. But the simple fact was, that was the first act of a Shakesperian play entitled "Taming the Shrew." He found out, when too late, that he had not married into the family of the "Graces," but into the family of the "Furies." To the day of his death, the murder of his first betrothal followed him.

The Bible extols one who "sweareth to his own hurt and changeth not. That is, when you make a promise, keep it at all hazards. There may be cases where deception has been used at the time of engagement, and extraordinary circumstances where the promise is not binding, but in nine hundred and ninety-nine cases out of a thousand, engagement is

As Binding as Marriage.

Robert Burns, with all his faults, well knew the force of a marital engagement. In obedience to some rustic idea, he standing on one side the brook Ayr, and Mary Campbell on the other, they bathed their hands in the water and then put them on the boards of a Bible, making their pledge of fidelity. On the cover of the Old Testament of that book, to this day in Robert Burns's handwriting may be found the words, "Lev: 19: 12. 'Ye shall not swear by my name falsely; I am the Lord.'" And on the cover of the New Testament in his own handwriting: "Mat. 5: 33: 'Thou shalt not forswear thyself, but shalt perform unto the Lord thine oaths.'"

Suppose a ship-captain offers his services to take a ship out to sea. After he gets a little way he comes alongside of a vessel with a more beautiful flag, and which has perhaps a richer cargo, and is bound for a more attractive port. Suppose he rings a bell for the engineer to slow up, and the screw stops. Now I see the captain being lowered over the side of the vessel into a small boat, and he crosses to the

Gayer and Wealthier Craft,

and climbs up the sides, and is seen walking the bridge of the other ship. I pick up his resigned speaking-trumpet and I shout through it: "Captain, what does this mean? Did you not promise to take this ship to Southampton, England?" "Yes," says the captain, "but I have changed my mind, and I have found I can do better, and I am going to take charge here. I shall send back to you all the letters I got while managing that ship, and everything I got from your ship, and it will be all right." You tell me that the worst fate for such a captain as that is too good for him. But it is just what a man or woman does who promises to take one through the voyage of life, across the ocean of existence, and then breaks the promise.

What American society needs to be taught is that betrothal is an act so solemn and tremendous that all men and women must stand back from it until they are sure it is right, and sure that it is best, and sure that no retreat will be desired. Before that promise of lifetime companionship, any amount of romance that you wish, any ardor of friendship, any coming and going. But

Espousal is a Gate,

a golden gate, which one should not pass, unless he or she expects never to return. Engagement is the porch of which marriage is the castle, and you have no right in the porch if you do not mean to pass into the castle. The trouble has always been that this whole subject of affiance has been relegated to the realm of frivolity and joke, and considered not worth a sermon, or even a serious paragraph. And so the massacre of human lives has gone on, and the devil has had it his own cruel way, and what is mightily needed is that pulpit and platform and printing-press all speak a word of unmistakable and thunderous protest on this subject of infinite importance.

We put clear out into thin poesy and light reading the marital engagements of Petrarch and his Laura, Dante and his Beatrice, Chaucer and his Philippa, Lorenzo de Medici and his Lucretia; Spencer and his Rosalind, Waller and his Saccharissa, not realizing that it was the style of their engagement that

Decided their Happiness

or wretchedness, their virtue or their profligacy. All the literary and military and religious glory of Queen Elizabeth's reign cannot blot out from one of the most conspicuous pages of history her infamous behavior towards Seymour and Philip and Melville and Leicester and others. All the ecclesiastical robes that Dean Swift ever rustled through consecrated places cannot hide from intelligent people of all ages the fact that by promises of marriage, which he never fulfilled, he broke the heart of Jane Waring after an engagement of seven years, and the heart of Stella after an engagment of fourteen years, and the poetic stanzas he dedicated to their excellences only make the more immortal his own perfidy.

"But suppose I should make a mistake," says some man or woman, "and I find it out after the engagement and before marriage?" My answer is, you have

No Excuse for a Mistake

on this subject. There are so many ways of finding out all about the character and preferences and dislikes and habits of a man or woman, that if you have not brain enough to form a right judgment in regard to him or her, you are not so fit a candidate for the matrimonial altar as you are for an idiot asylum. Notice what society your especial friend prefers, whether he is industrious or lazy, whether she is neat or slatternly, what books are read, what was the style of ancestry, noble or depraved; and if there be any unsolved mystery about the person under consideration, postpone all promise until the mystery is solved.

Jackson's Hollow, Brooklyn, was part of the city not built on for many years, and every time I crossed it I said to myself or to others, why is not this land built on? I found out afterward that the title to the land was in controversy, and no one wanted to build there until that question was decided. Afterward I understood the title was settled, and now buildings are going up all over it. Do not build your happiness for this world on a character, masculine or feminine, that has not a settled and undisputed title to honor and truth and sobriety and righteousness.

O woman, you have more need to pause before making such an important promise than man, because if you make a mistake it is worse for you. If a man blunder about promise of marriage or go on to an unfortunate marriage, he can spend his evenings away, and can go to the club or the Republican or Democratic headquarters, and absorb his mind in city or State or national elections, or smoke himself stupid or drink himself drunk. But there is no place of regular retreat for you, O woman, and you could not take narcotics or intoxicants and keep your respectability. Before you promise, pray and think and study and advise. There will never again in your earthly history be a time when you so much need God.

It seems to me that the world ought to cast out from business credits and from good neighborhood those who boast of the number of hearts they have won, as the Indian boasts of the number of scalps he has taken. If a man will lie to a woman and a woman will lie to a man about so important a matter as that of a lifetime's welfare, they will lie about a bill of goods and lie about finances and lie about anything. Society to-day is brim full of gallants and man-milliners and

Carpet Knights and Coquettes,

and those most God-forsaken of all wretches—flirts. And they go about drawing-rooms and the parlors of watering-places, simpering and bowing and scraping and whispering, and then return to the club-rooms, if they be men, or to their special gatherings, if they be women, to chatter and giggle over what was said to them in confidence. Condign punishment is apt to come upon them, and they get paid in their own coin. I could point you to a score whom society has let drop very hard, in return for their base traffic in human hearts.

And here my idea widens, and I have to say, not only to those who have made a mistake in solemn promise of marriage, but to those who have already at the altar been pronounced one when they are two, or in diversity of tastes and likes and dislikes are neither one nor two, but a dozen—make the best you can of an awful mistake. And here let me answer letters that come from every State of the American Union, and from across the sea, and are coming year after year from men and women who are terrifically allianced and tied together in a hard knot—a very hard knot. The letters run something like this: "What ought I to do? my husband is a drunkard." "My wife is a gad-about, and will not stay at home." "My companion is ignorant, and hates books, and I revel in them." "I like music, and a piano sets my husband crazy." "I am fond of social life, and my husband is a recluse." "I am trying to be good, and my life-long associate is very bad; what shall I do?" My answer is, there are certain good reasons for divorcement. The Bible recognizes them; but it must be

The Very Last Resort,

and only after all reasonable attempts at reclamation and adjustment have proved a dead failure. When such attempts fail, it is generally because of meddlesome outsiders; and women tell the wronged wife how she ought to stand on her rights, and men tell the wronged husband how he ought to stand on his rights. And let husband and wife, in an unhappy marriage relation, stand punctiliously on their rights, and there will be no readjustment, and only one thing will be sure to them, and that is a hell on earth.

If you are unhappily married, in most cases I advise you to make the best you can of an awfully bad bargain. Do not project your peculiarities more than is necessary. Perhaps you may have some faults of your own, which the other party in the marital alliance may have to suffer. You are in the same yoke. If you pull aside, the yoke will only twist your neck. Better pull ahead. The world is full of

People Who Made Mistakes

about many things, and among other things about betrothal and marriage, and yet have been tolerably happy and very useful in the strength of God, and by the grace promised in every time of need, if those who seek it conquer the disadvantageous circumstances. I am acquainted with lovely women, married to contemptible-men, and genial men yoked with termagants inspired of the devil. And yet, under these disadvantages my friends are useful and happy. God helps people in other kinds of martyrdom and to sing in the flame, and He will help you in your lifelong misfortune.

Remember the patience of Job. What a wife he had! At a time, when he was one great blotch of eruptions, and his property was destroyed by a tornado, and, more than all, bereavement had come and the poor man needed all wise counsel, she advises him to go to cursing and swearing. She wanted him to poultice his boils with blasphemy. But he lived right on through his

Marital Disadvantages,

recovered his health and his fortune, and raised a splendid family, and the closing paragraph of the Book of Job has such a jubilance that I wonder people do not oftener read it: "So the Lord blessed the latter end of Job more than his beginning."

Now, my badly married friend of either sex, if Job could stand it by the help of God, then

You Can Stand It

by the same divine reinforcement. You have other relations, O woman, beside the wifely relation. If you are a mother, train up your children for God and heaven. If you are a member of a church, help move on its enterprises. You can get so much of the grace of God in your heart, that all your home trials will seem insignificant. How little difference does it make what your unrighteous husband calls you, if God calls you His child, and you are an heiress of whole kingdoms beyond the sky?

Immerse yourself in some kind of outside usefulness, something that will enlist your prayers, your sympathies, your hand, your needle, your voice. Get your heart on fire with love to God and the disenthrallment of the human race, and the troubles of your home will be blotted out in the glory of your consecrated life. I cry out to you, O woman, as Paul exclaims in his letter to the Corinthians: "What knowest thou, O wife, whether thou shalt save thy husband?" And if you cannot save him, you can help in the grander, mightier enterprise of helping save the world. Out of the awful mistake of your marriage rise into the sublimest life of self-sacrifice for God and suffering humanity. Instead of settling down to mope over your domestic woes, enlist your energies for the world's redemption.

Some parts of Holland keep out the ocean only by dykes or walls of stout masonry.

The Dutch Engineer

having these dykes in charge was soon to be married to a maiden living in one of the villages, the existence of which depended on the strength of these dykes. And there was to be a great feast in one of the villages that approaching evening, in honor of the coming bridegroom. That day a great storm threatened the destruction of the dykes, and hence the destruction of thousands of lives in the villages sheltered by that stone wall. The ocean was in full wrath, beating against the dykes, and the tides and the terror were still rising. "Shall I go to the feast," says the engineer, "or shall I go and help my workmen take care of the dykes?" "Take care of the dykes," he said to himself, "I must and will." As he appeared on the wall, the men working there were exhausted, and shouted: "Here comes the engineer. Thank God! Thank God!"

The wall was giving way stone by stone, and the engineer had a rope fastened around his body, and some of the workmen had ropes fastened around their bodies, and were let down amid the wild surges that beat the wall. Everything was giving way. "More stones!" cried the men. "More mortar!" But the answer came: "There is no more!" "Then," cried the engineer, "take off your clothes and with them stop the holes in the wall." And so in the chill and darkness and surf it was done, and with the workmen's apparel the openings in the wall were partially filled. But still the tide rose, and still the ocean reared itself for more awful stroke and for the overwhelming of thousands of lives in the villages. "Now we have done all we can," said the engineer, "down on your knees, my men, and pray to God for help." And on the trembling and parting dykes they prayed till the wind changed and the sea subsided, and the villages below, which, knowing nothing of the peril, were full of romp and dance and hilarity, were gloriously saved.

What We Want

in this work of walling back the oceans of poverty and drunkenness and impurity and sin is the help of more womanly and manly hands. Oh how the tides come in! Atlantic surge of sorrow after Atlantic surge of sorrow, and the tempests of human hate and Satanic fury are in full cry. O, woman of many troubles, what are all the feasts of worldly delight, if they were offered you, compared with the opportunity of helping build and support barriers which sometimes seem giving way through man's treachery and the world's assault?

O Woman, to the Dykes!

Bring prayer, bring tears, bring cheering words! Help! Help! And having done all, kneel with us on the quaking wall until the God of the wind and the sea shall hush the one and silence the other. To the dykes! Sisters, mothers, wives, daughters, of America, to the dykes! The mightiest catholicon for all the wounds and wrongs of woman or man is complete absorption in the work to rescue others. Save some man, some woman, some child! In that effort you will forget or be helped to bear your own trials, and in a little while God will take you up out of your disturbed and harrowing conjugal relation of earth into a heaven all the happier because of preceding distress. When Queen Elizabeth of England was expiring it was arranged that the exact moment of her death should be signalled to the people by the dropping of a sapphire ring from a window into the hands of an officer, who carried it at the top of his speed to King James of Scotland. But your departure from the scene of your earthly woes, if you are ready to go, will not be the dropping of a sapphire to the ground, but the setting of a jewel in the King's coronet. Blessed be His glorious name forever!

THE TRUE READING OF THE SIGNS OF OUR TIMES.

By Rev. A. R. Faussett, D. D.*

The Newspaper in the Bible—Christ's Twofold Work—A Common Mistake—The Peculiarity of our Times—Similarity to those Before the First Advent—The Growing Unification of the World—Cheering Signs—The Double Epiphany—Two Rabbis at the Wailing-Place.

CECIL once said, "A Christian in a prison with his Bible can tell what is going on in the outer world." Brethren, the Word of God is our "light shining in a dark place" till the day dawn. The Emperor's chaplain challenged the stammerer, Notker, of St. Gall, in olden time: "You say God reveals Himself to His children. Can you tell me what God is now doing?" "Yes," was the reply; "what He is always doing—exalting the humble and debasing the proud." Yes, this is what God comes to do, especially at the Epiphany of the Glory of Him who is the great God and our Saviour. He comes for

A Twofold Work,

for the rapture of his saints, the lowly ones of the earth, who shall be exalted in transfigured bodies with Himself, and then in flaming fire to take vengeance on those who would not know God, nor obey the Gospel of our Lord Jesus Christ.

"But," says an objector, "does not our Lord command, 'Go ye, make disciples of all nations'?" Yes; but He did not say that the Gospel would *convert* all nations in the present age; God (according to Acts 15: 14) is "*taking out of* the Gentiles now a people for His Name." The gospel of the kingdom is to be preached in all the world, for a witness unto all nations (Matt. 24: 14); a witness such as that of Enoch and Noah to the men before the flood, so that the world is left without excuse if it neglects it.

But will the world have rejected it when Christ shall come? Let Himself answer. "When the Son of Man cometh shall He find faith on the earth?" (Luke 18: 8.) The state of the world at His coming He compares to that of men before the flood, and that of Sodom on the eve of its destruction. "They did eat, drank, married wives, were given in marriage, until Noah entered the ark, and the flood came and destroyed them all." (Luke 18: 27.) "They bought, sold, planted, builded, but the same day that Lot went out of Sodom it rained fire and brimstone, and destroyed them all; even thus shall it be in the day when the Son of man is revealed." How exactly herein the Lord photographs our bustling, self-seeking, intensely worldly age! The past ages, too, have been so.

The Peculiarity of Our Age,

as it was in Noah's times, is that the sons of God ally themselves, through the lust of the flesh and the lust of the eye, with the daughters of men; in other words, the Church is yielding itself to the world's fascinations, instead of being separate from it, and witnessing for God against its corruptions. So God will soon say, "My Spirit shall not always strive (or judge) in man." "He who now letteth (or restraineth) shall be taken out of the way." Yes, and the elect Church, alone faithful among the faithless, shall cease to "torment the dwellers upon earth" by their witness; for believers shall be "caught up" in transfigured bodies to "meet the Lord in the air." Then shall the full development of "lawlessness," which is yet "in mystery," take place.

The signs before and at our Lord's first Advent have their counterpart just before His second Advent. There were the

Three Schools of Thought

then, represented by the Pharisees, the Sadducees and the Herodians. These answer respectively to (1) the Formalists, who "in the last days (II Tim. 3: 5) have the form of godliness, but deny its power;" (2) the Rationalistic unbelievers; (3) the worldlings (Rev. 16: 14), whose god is self and the world. And these develop into the whole world and the ten kings under Antichrist, being gathered by these miracle-working demon spirits (Rev. 16: 14) to the war of that great day of God Almighty. So far from the present world age developing into universal peace before Christ comes, its issue is the reverse (Joel 3: 11–21): "Assemble yourselves, ye heathen, gather together multitudes, multitudes in the valley of decision. Beat your ploughshares into swords, and your pruning-hooks into spears." This is exactly the reverse of what (Isa. 2: 4) shall be after the Lord has come to reign on Zion, and over all nations; then "they shall beat their swords into ploughshares, and their spears into pruning hooks." So Joel, too, foretells that in "the day of the Lord," after His awful judgment with 'His mighty ones on the wicked multitudes gathered against Jerusalem, the new age shall see "Israel's God, Jehovah, dwelling in Zion." Then, and not till then, "nation shall not lift up sword against nation, neither shall they learn war any more."

A Significant Feature of Our Age

is the marvellous unification of the world, space and distance being almost annihilated by the railway, the electric telegraph, the telephone and the steamship. Separating hedges are being levelled down, so that the earth is being prepared to be one grand field for the manifestation of its coming King; but first, Antichrist will gather his hosts. Then Jehovah will say (Psa. 1). "Gather My saints unto Me." So Rome combined in one political unity the kingdoms of the then known world; God's providence thereby prepared His way for Christ's First Advent and the kingdom of grace on earth, just as they are now being unified for the speedily coming kingdom of glory.

But there must first come the awful conflict foretold in Joel 3. Zech. 13 and 14, and Rev. 19. Christ comes as the antitypical David, the man of war, first; then, as the antitypical Solomon, the prince of peace.

Signs Bright and Dark.

Thus the signs of the Lord's coming are already appearing, alike the dark and the bright ones. Of the latter is the increased interest taken in the Holy Land (Ps. 102: 13–17), as foretold: "Thou wilt arise and have mercy upon Zion, for the time to favor her, yea, the set time, is come; for thy servants take pleasure in her stones, and favor the dust thereof." Never since Jerusalem was first trodden down by the Gentiles has such interest been taken in identifying the sites and stones of Palestine. The Temple's foundation-stones, with their Phœnician marks of Hiram's stone-masons, the Moabite stone, and the Palestine Exploration Society's Ordnance map, are being carefully studied. The number of Jews in Palestine, according to the Bishop of Jerusalem, has risen in a few years from 15,000 to 42,000. The gathering together (Heb. 10: 25) of believers in brotherly conferences on the coming kingdom, and the increase of the knowledge of it, are the pledges foretold (Dan. 12 and Mal. 3) of our speedy "gathering together" "unto our manifested king." (II Thess. 2: 1.)

The Double Epiphany.

It may be objected: "If definite signs are given us, to precede the Lord's coming, such as the return of the Jews in unbelief (Zech. 12–14) unto their own land, and the Gospel witness unto all nations, how can the Lord's coming be as that of 'a thief in such a day and hour as men think not'? The only doctrine that can solve the difficulty is that which close search of Scripture reveals: The Lord's coming for His people is not simultaneous with His coming to take vengeance on the apostate world. He *first* comes *for* His people in the air: He next comes *with* His people, and His feet shall stand on the Mount of Olives. No special signs are needed by or given to His people; they are charged, "Watch ye, and pray always." He might have come, and may come at any hour, without sign for them. The special signs given refer to His subsequent descent to the earth. The signs given must precede the Lord's coming with His glorified saints to take vengeance on Antichrist and his world confederacy at Jerusalem; as to this coming, Zech. 14: 5 saith, "The Lord my God shall come, and all the saints with thee." (Ps. 1.) He could not come *with* His saints unless He had previously come *for* them. These are "the armies in heaven on white horses, and clothed in linen clean and white, the righteousness of the saints" (Rev. 19: 8, 14) who follow the Word of God, the King of kings, about to "smite the nations and rule them with a rod of iron." "But," say some, "the spiritual revivals and evangelistic missions now oppose the doctrine that our age is tending to apostacy." Thank God! These revivals are preparing an elect people out of the masses for His coming: but not so the world.

Two Rabbis met at the wailing-place, west of the Temple area, amidst the foundation-stones which testify of glories long past. One wore a look of inconsolable grief, the other of joy. "Why do you weep?" asked the joyful Rabbi. "I weep for the desolations of Zion. And why do you rejoice?" "I rejoice at Zion's coming consolations; for as surely as Jehovah fulfilled His threats of her desolation, so will He fulfil His promises of her glorious and eternal consolation." Let us, too, amidst the solemn signs on every side, lift up our heads, for our redemption draweth nigh—and what a glorious redemption!

* From his article in this month's *Prophetic News*; for sale, price six cents, at this office, 63 Bible House, New York.

A TRACT REFUSED AND ACCEPTED.

TALKING recently with a Christian worker, who in the war-time was a member of the Christian Commission, the editor of this journal heard an interesting reminiscence, which shows how acts of love and kindness may open the doors of an obdurate heart.

Our friend was at the front, and was distributing tracts among the soldiers. He offered one to a Scotchman, but was somewhat roughly bidden to put up those things. He for one had no use for them. He was reminded that death was very busy in that place, and that the tracts were prepared to help men in that trying hour. The Scotchman, however, said he knew all about religion, and had no respect for it, or its professors.

The Christian worker went his way, and a little later came upon a row of wounded men lying on the ground, some of them dying. He noticed that the ground on which they lay was rough, and in many places pebbles projected, which must be very painful to the backs of the sufferers. Laying down his bag of tracts, he collected some logs which had been felled, and rolled them to the place where the men lay. His object was to make a rude bed or two for the worst cases. By putting two logs near together and laying crosswise from one log to the other the staves of broken barrels, of which there were plenty around, he constructed two or three comparatively comfortable beds, with some elasticity in them. The men perceived his object, and voluntarily hunted up more logs and staves, until every wounded man had an extemporized bed. One of them, on being lifted from the ground to the bed, raised his uninjured arm, and throwing it around the neck of the Christian man, whose compassion was thus shown, drew his face down to him, and, rough soldier as he was, kissed him. "*I have a wife at home in Connecticut,*" he said, "*who will pray for you every night, when she knows what you have done for me.*"

Raising himself, the Christian man turned to take up his tracts, having done some hours of exhausting work in the hot sunshine. As he did so, he encountered the Scotchman who had rebuffed him in the morning. "He said, "I did not know you Christian Commission men did this kind of work. I thought it was all preaching and praying. There's some sense in this. Give me your hand; and I'll take your tract too, now."

Further talk with the Scotchman followed, and he admitted that he came of a pious family; and that his brother and sister were praying for him daily, to be preserved amid the perils of the battle-field and for his soul's salvation.

Before they parted, the two men knelt down together in the wood, and the Scotchman, with tears, was praying for forgiveness. Eventually he found peace and made public profession of his faith.

A MUSIC-TEACHER'S HELPLESSNESS.

IN this month's number of *Thy Healer*,* which is edited by Mrs. M. Baxter, is published the following testimony of a music-teacher who had the well-known premonitory symptoms of paralysis: "Last spring I began to lose the use of my arms, the left more particularly. They gradually got worse—my wrists being also very weak. As I get my living as a teacher of music, this caused me a great deal of anxiety, as, of course, I have to play the piano a great deal; but with my bad wrists I was quite powerless to do anything of the kind. The muscles of my left arm felt as if they were being drawn up, and it became quite useless. I went to a doctor, and he said I must give up playing entirely, for a time, which I did, but with no good result; so I came to Bethshan, and took the Lord for my Healer. After coming away, I really felt the Holy Spirit had come to me: I had such a happy feeling. On the following morning, although my wrists were still painful, I felt impelled to go to the piano and play. I did so, looking for the strength that Christ had promised me, and was able to play as well as ever. It seemed like one of the miracles of old, so suddenly were my wrists healed. Since then they continued getting stronger, and are quite well now. I am also getting bodily stronger, and am now able to get through a great deal more study and work without getting tired, and feel sure that I shall be quite strong in time. I feel that I cannot be thankful enough to God for healing me. He has been so good to me so many times before, but this seemed at first almost too good to be true. I would like you to read this in the Hall at Bethshan, and make use in any way of my testimony, so that God's power of healing may be spread abroad, and more may be brought to realize that He is the Healer of the body as well as of the soul."

A GOOD SAMARITAN SHOE-BLACK.

THE disposition prevalent in business circles, to subordinate every energy to the promotion of selfish interests, is not absolutely universal. Good men are found in all our cities, who will stretch out a helping hand to a brother fallen in life's struggle, and who do not treat their employees as "hands" to be paid the lowest market rate and no more, and to be discharged when they fall sick. It would be well for the Church and the world if every man who names the name of Christ could be counted among such kindly employers, as he would be, if he obeyed the apostolic injunction, "Bear ye one another's burdens, and so fulfil the law of Christ." (Gal. 6:2.) An example of the true Christian spirit, found where it might not be expected, is thus related in the New York *Commercial Advertiser*:

"A reporter called to a little bootblack near the City Hall to give him a shine yesterday. The little fellow came rather slowly for one of that lively guild, and planted his box down under the reporter's foot. Before he could get his brushes out, another larger boy ran up, and calmly pushing the little one aside, said, 'Here, you go sit down, Jimmy.' The reporter at once became indignant at what he took to be a piece of outrageous bullying, and sharply told the new-comer to clear out. 'Oh, dat's all right, boss,' was the reply; 'I'm only goin' to do it fur him. You see he's been sick in the hospital fur more'n a month, and can't do much work yet, so us boys all turn in and give him a lift when we can; savy?' 'Is that so, Jimmy,' asked the reporter, turning to the smaller boy. 'Yes, sir,' wearily replied the boy, and as he looked up, the pallid, pinched face could be discerned even through the grime that covered it; 'he does it fur me, if you'll let him.'

"'Certainly, go ahead;' and as the bootblack plied the brush, the reporter plied him with questions: 'You say all the boys help him in this way?' 'Yes, sir. When they ain't got no job themselves, and Jimmy gets one, they turns in and helps him, 'cause he aint very strong yet, ye see.' 'What percentage do you charge him on a job?' 'Hey!' queried the youngster; 'I don't know what you mean.' 'I mean what part of the money do you give Jimmy, and how much do you keep out of it?' 'You bet yer life I don't keep none; I aint no such sneak as that.' 'So you give it all to him, do you?' 'Yes, I do. All the boys give up what they gets on his jobs. I'd like to catch any feller sneaking it on a sick boy, I would.' The shine being completed, the reporter handed the urchin a quarter, saying, 'I guess you're a pretty good fellow, so you keep ten cents and give the rest to Jimmy there.' 'Can't do it, sir; it's his customer. Here, Jim.' He threw him the coin, and was off like a shot after a customer for himself, a veritable rough diamond."

* A monthly magazine edited by Mrs. M. Baxter, containing original articles on Holiness and Divine Healing. Annual subscription 75 cents. May be had from the office of this journal, 63 Bible House, New York.

A HIGH-CASTE CONVERT.

THE following incident is related in a letter, published in *The Mission Field*, from Rev. William W. Scudder, D. D., who is now laboring in the Arcot Mission in India. When he first went there, in December, 1884, he made the acquaintance of a young man of good abilities and high caste, but a heathen. Dr. Scudder says of him: "He is a young man of the Balgy caste, and connected with some of the most respectable families in Madanapalle. He came to this place from Cuddapah a number of years ago with his uncle, who is a pleader in the courts. He attended for a while the Government school, and obtain a good plain education. After a while he obtained a position in the civil dispensary as a compounder of medicines. When he first entered upon this situation he was brought under influences which made him a thorough atheist, and a bitter opposer of the Christian religion. He, however, came into daily contact with our Christians, and gradually his prejudices began to yield, and he listened with increasing interest to the claims of Christianity as set forth by them. The result was that his heart was drawn powerfully to the loving Saviour. Shortly after meeting with this change of heart he broke his caste, first secretly by eating in the house of one of our native Christians, and afterwards publicly by taking food openly in the house of a catechist. From that time he proclaimed his purpose to join the Christian religion. There was, of course, a good deal of stir and excitement among his own caste people. They used their utmost powers to dissuade him from bringing upon them the disgrace which would attend the baptism of one of their number. Great pressure was brought to bear upon him from various quarters to prevent him from joining us. I am happy to say that the young man withstood all these assaults; and in reply to all their efforts, expressed his determination never to give up his Saviour. He now preaches the Word daily in the public reading-room."

A RESCUED STREET WAIF.

IN the course of the work to which Dr. T. J. Barnardo has devoted his life—that of rescuing the homeless children of the London streets, he met with an interesting case, which he thus describes: "Her name is Esther, and she is nine years old. She was born in Golden Lane, and had never been out of London in her life: so that what wonder if the world meant to her only a dreary mass of dirty slums! She was always on the edge of hunger: she never had at one time, from her babyhood up, more than the ragged clothes she wore day by day. She had lost her mother 'ever so long ago,' as she put it. Esther's father was a casual laborer. After the death of his wife, who, by going out doing chores, had been the real bread-winner to the family, times became worse. The head of the family, never at any time possessed of much energy or force of character, obtained food for himself and his three children at home by selling the furniture piece by piece. Of course the end was not long in coming. Soon he was destitute and homeless, and for Esther there began a long series of wanderings through the common lodging-houses of London. At the time the application on behalf of Esther reached me, her father was a shoeblack earning casual pennies on the streets of Clerkenwell. He was one of those fathers who are no fathers, and whose paternal protection would have been of little avail against the nameless dangers to a young girl of a lodging-house life, to which their penury condemned them. The wolf at the door was overcoming their resistance; they had both been in the almshouse, and more than once poor Esther and her father had walked the streets all night. What could the future of a little girl under such circumstances be expected to turn out? To her, our Ilford home has, indeed, been an Ark of safety; and if Esther turns out well, as I hope and believe she will, she will owe it, under God, to the agency of our Cottage Homes. Alas! alas! there are thousands of girl waifs like little nine-year-old Esther still unrescued, whose cry is continually going up to God from out the darkest depths of our city slums. How long? Ah, it is for Christians everywhere, for the servants of the merciful Saviour of little children, alone to give an answer to that question."

A DYING MAN'S GRIP ON A KEY.

IN the course of an address to the Evangelical Alliance by the Rev. A. J. Gordon, D. D., of Boston, which is published in his *Watchword*, the following incident was related: "An eminent clergyman of England has described his visit to the death-bed of a wealthy parishioner. As he knelt by his side he twice requested him to give him his hand while he prayed, which he strangely declined to do. But as soon as the death gasp was over and the blankets were turned down, the reason was apparent. It was found that both hands were holding his safe-key in their death-grip, so that he had no hand of fellowship to extend to the minister praying for his soul. Where are the Church's hands to-day, when the greatest opportunity ever brought within the reach of any generation of Christians is just within her grasp? Is it possible that, with the memory of Him 'who though rich, for our sakes became poor,' ever before us, we should be found impotent to take hold of this opportunity, because we could not let go of our safe-keys?

"Here is a momentous question on which both the safety of the Church and her hold upon the masses largely depend. In this world as well as in the world to come, there is an impassable gulf between Dives and Lazarus. If the Church deliberately chooses the company of Dives, putting on purple and fine linen and faring sumptuously every day, she cannot keep with Lazarus. The attempt may be made to effect conciliation by tossing biscuits across the gulf. But this will not do. It is not money that is wanted so much as fellowship, to bring the disaffected masses into sympathy with the Church. If only the Church could once more stand forth, transfigured in its primitive ideal, it would be certain to repeat its primitive conquests. Let the ministers of our great metropolitan churches who enjoy munificent salaries begin the reform by becoming like the chief apostle, poor that they make many rich; and let the millionaire pew-holders follow their lead by parting their goods to such as have need, and see if the growing spirit of communism would not be speedily arrested, not by the counter-irritant of ridicule, but by the emollient of Christ-like example."

CHRISTIAN HERALD AND SIGNS OF OUR TIMES.

OFFICE, 63 BIBLE HOUSE, NEW YORK.

ENTERED AT THE POST-OFFICE AT NEW YORK, N. Y., AS SECOND-CLASS MATTER.

Published Weekly. Subscription price, $1.50 a year; $1 eight months; 75 cents six months; sent two months on trial for 25 cents; always payable in advance. Single copies for sale by, or can be ordered at, all newsdealers.

Remittances by Mail should be by Post-office money order, bank cheques, or drafts or express money order, and should always be made payable to THE CHRISTIAN HERALD.

Receipts are not sent, the receipt of the paper by a subscriber is a sufficient proof that his remittance has been received. If the paper does not arrive promptly, please advise us, that we may see if the address is correctly entered.

Change of Address. Name of Post Office and State, of both old and new address, should always be given in case of removal.

CURRENT EVENTS.

A Proposal to Distribute About Twenty million dollars among the States and Territories passed the Senate on January 18. It is a repayment of the direct tax collected from them under the act of August 5, 1861. Though it was at the time estimated to produce twenty millions, it yielded actually only $17,350,000, and it is believed that not more than that amount will be repaid. While the bill was under discussion, Senator Vance made a proposal, for which only sixteen Senators voted, to add to it a refund of the tax collected on raw cotton under the act of July 1, 1862. It is expected that this attempt will be renewed in the House with success. The raw cotton tax yielded, in round numbers, $68,000,000. If the proposal to add this to the direct tax bill should succeed, the measure would take over $85,000,000 out of the Treasury. Senator Quay, of Pennsylvania, voted in favor of the return of the raw cotton tax, and if it passes the House as an amendment, it is predicted that other Republicans and Northern Democrats in the Senate will vote for it. The bulk of it would go to the Southern States.

The Cabinet Nominations were All Confirmed by the Senate last week. Mr. Lamar's nomination to the Supreme Court bench was strenuously opposed to the last. Mr. Evarts, Mr. Edmunds and Mr. Ingalls were the most conspicuous speakers against confirmation. When Mr. Riddleberger, of Virginia, and Mr. Stewart, of Nevada, decided to vote against their party on the question, it was evident that further resistance was useless, and Mr. Stanford, of California, gave the one other Republican vote necessary for confirmation. Apart from those three Senators the vote was strictly on party lines. Mr. Vilas and Mr. Dickinson received confirmation without division. On January 18 Mr. Lamar was sworn in and took his seat on the bench.

The Fatal Effects of the Blizzard in the Northwest were not known until the middle of last week, owing to the wholesale destruction of the telegraph wires. It first made its appearance on the evening of January 11, and continued with few pauses until the morning of January 14. During that period *two hundred and thirty-five persons perished* with cold, and many more are missing, with but little chance of ever being found alive. A despatch from St. Paul says that an hour or two before the storm, the weather was warm and balmy, and people took advantage of it to go to town. A cloud gathered suddenly and swept across the sky, snow began to fall and the wind rose. The mercury fell to *thirty degrees below zero.* All the while the wind increased in fury, the snow fell thicker, and was hurled along by the wind. On the prairie an object forty feet distant could not be seen. A man's voice could not be heard six feet distant. The air was full of snow as fine as flour, and the roaring of the wind and the darkness caused by so much snow in the air made the scene the most dismal, drear and forsaken that man ever looked upon. Every railroad in Dakota, Minnesota and many Iowa, Nebraska and Wisconsin railroads were blocked. Children going home from school were overtaken by the storm and frozen to death. Men lost their way in going only a few blocks from their homes, were blinded by the storm, and fell helpless into drifts and perished. A party of seven farmers who started from St. Paul shortly before the blizzard came on never reached home, and four of them have been found frozen to death. A school-teacher near Stoloff, fearing two of her pupils might not reach home safely, accompanied them, and all three were overpowered by the intolerable cold and died. When found they were huddled close together, the teacher with her dress wrapped around the children. Many persons who escaped with their lives had their limbs frozen. No storm so severe has been experienced in twenty-four years.

Radical Changes in the Law Regulating capital punishment are under the consideration of the New York Legislature. It is proposed to abolish death by hanging, and substitute electricity as the fatal agent. The culprit is to be seated in a chair with metal plates at the head and feet, to which electric light wires are to be attached, and the current continued until the man is dead. It is also provided that instead of a year often elapsing, as at present, between sentence and execution, there shall not be more than eight weeks nor less than four, and that during that time only persons holding the written order of the court shall be permitted to visit the condemned criminal. Also that the body shall not be given to the family to be exhibited and interred with display, as is now done, but shall be given to a medical college for dissection, or buried in quicklime within the precincts of the jail. Another important provision is the exclusion of reporters from the execution, and a prohibition of newspapers publishing anything more than the bare announcement that sentence has been executed. The bill is the result of a Commission appointed by the Legislature, and is based on suggestions collected by the Commission from judges, sheriffs and physicians. From these classes the Commission received two hundred letters. Of these 80 were against a change, 87 favored electricity, 8 poisons, 5 the guillotine, and 4 the garrote.

The Opposition of the Mayor of New York to any grants of land to churches or charities, which was mentioned in these columns last week, is being defended by the Mayor's friends on the ground that it is the first duty of an official to protect the property of the city. The publication of the defence was made at an unpropitious time. On the same day an announcement appeared in the New York *Herald*, that one hundred and eighteen city lots had been granted by the Mayor and corporation to the Manhattan Elevated Railroad Company at the nominal rental of forty dollars each a year. Their market value is stated to be two hundred dollars a year each. It would appear that monopolies find more favor in the Mayor's eyes than churches and charities.

Renewed Efforts to Induce the Reading Company to submit to arbitration the differences between themselves and the striking railroad men and miners were made last week without avail. The suspension of many large enterprises and the increased burden of higher prices on the general public, appear inevitable. This will be felt most severely by the poor, who are unable to purchase their winter's coal in the fall, and who have, in a large number of cases, to buy it by the bag through the winter. They are now paying at the rate of *ten dollars a ton* for it, and the price must go still higher if the strike is not settled. The miners, it appears, were earning on an average, the men with the boys, $2.72 a day, and they struck rather than submit to a reduction. The dispute as to wages, however, is less difficult to arrange than that other question as to the employment of non-union men, which has been at the root of the majority of strikes in other trades. The union men contend that a man who enjoys the benefits of union influence on hours and wages ought to contribute to the support of the unions, and that when he does so he has the right to refuse to be associated with a man who does not accept this responsibility. The employer, on the other hand, claims the right to employ whom he chooses, and he naturally prefers the men who do not organize against him. This is the main question at issue and until it is definitely settled, the conflict between capital and labor must go on.

The Two Leaders of the Riots in Trafalgar Square, London, on November 13, were placed on trial last week. They were Mr. Cunninghame Graham, a Scotch member of Parliament and the socialist Burns. An attempt was made by the defence to raise the question of the right of public meeting in the Square, but the Judge took the view that if a public meeting was prohibited the attempt to hold it by the use of force was illegal. As there could be no question that the defendants had used force and had led the attack on the police—even their own witnesses being compelled to admit the fact—conviction was a necessity. They were sentenced to six weeks' imprisonment.

The German Reichstag was Occupied with the discussion of the new army bill last week. It passed the amendment relating to the period of service, the effect of which will be to enable men entering the active army before their twentieth year to leave the landwehr earlier. In the course of the sitting General von Schellendorf, the Minister of War, stated that the measure would give the army in time of war an addition of nearly seven hundred thousand trained men. The cost is estimated at between 80,000,000 and 100,000,000 marks. The statement of the Minister of War destroys the effect of the argument, which German journals have been so industriously pressing, that Germany's effective forces being small as compared with those of her neighbors, her influence is pacific.

A Favorable Report of the Condition of the Crown Prince of Germany was published on January 19 by the *Lancet*, the chief medical journal of Great Britain. It states that its news is authoritative, implying that it was furnished by the Crown Prince's physician, Sir Morel Mackenzie. It is to the effect that the Prince progresses so rapidly toward recovery that he looks forward to returning to Potsdam in the spring. German journals are, however, sceptical as to the cure, and state that in the best medical circles the opinion is still held that the Prince's days are numbered, the only opportunity of saving his life by an operation having been allowed to pass unused.

The British Government is Disturbed by a difficulty in Scotland similar to that which is at the root of the Irish trouble. Tenant farmers and the peasants complain that the land-owners are destroying small holdings to make room for large sheep farms and deer forests. As the families of the poor agriculturists increase, there is an increased demand for small farms, as the farm that supported a man and his wife and children does not yield enough for the support of the family when the sons grow up and have children of their own. Many farmers have subdivided their holdings to meet the difficulty, but that plan involves general poverty, and cannot be continued indefinitely. The land-owners recommend emigration, but there are cases in which that remedy cannot be applied. Just now many of the Scottish crofters are unable to pay their rent, and they not only resist dispossess proceedings, but are actually taking possession, by force, of vacant farms, for which they have no prospect of paying rent. The trouble is to be laid before Parliament when it meets.

Contributions to the Fund for Supplying colored ministers in the South with this journal have been received since our last acknowledgment to the amount of $30. They are from: Montclair, N. J., $5; Lone Star, Tex., $1; Jamestown, Mo., $2; Bridgton, Me. 50 cents; Providence, R. I., $1; Rock City, Ill., $1; from "A well wisher," $1; Brooklyn, N. Y., $1; Carluke, Ont., Can., 50 cents; Archer, Tex., $1; Lakeville, Cal., $4; Des Moines, Iowa, $1; Archer, Tex., $1; Jewett City, Conn., $1.50; Spring City, Ohio, $1; Allegheny City, Pa., $1.50; St. Joseph, Mo., $5; Monmouth, Me., $1. This sum gives us the pleasure of putting thirty more names on the list. We shall be sincerely glad, if sufficient money is received, to send the paper this year to every colored minister who has applied for it.

The Separation of Pastor C. H. Spurgeon from the Baptist Union appears to be final. On his return from his sojourn at Mentone, a deputation of ministers waited upon him to urge him to withdraw his resignation of membership. It is reported that concessions practically pledging the Union to a declaration of evangelical principles were made. The deputation, however, reported to the executive committee on January 18, that the efforts made to retain Mr. Spurgeon as a member of the Union had been futile. In spite of the observations made by the secular press, it is quite clear that Mr. Spurgeon's adherence to the principles and doctrines of the Baptist Church is as firm as ever.

The Objectionable Theatre Posters which shock decent people in all our great cities are being suppressed in Chicago. The Mayor of that city, on January 18, noticing some large colored posters on the walls, indicating in unmistakable manner the character of an opera company about to visit Chicago, notified the firm of bill posters who hung them, that he had revoked their license for putting up posters. It was also semi-officially announced that if the performance outlined on the bills was given, the theatre license will also be revoked. The firm promptly sent out a gang of men to cover the objectionable posters with white paper, and that being done, the Mayor permitted them to resume business. They have promised that hereafter all lithographs and show bills of theatrical companies shall pass inspection by the Chief of Police before being posted. The example of Mayor Roche deserves to be followed by the mayors of other cities.

A Curious Case of Conscience Money Restored to the Government occurred recently. A press despatch from Washington states that a few days ago a letter containing one dollar was received from Hillsboro, Kan., by the Postmaster-General. The writer of the letter said: "Enclosed find one dollar which belongs to the Government, and which I send you to pay back for what I have done wrong, as I used a three-cent stamp once on a letter which had been used once, and you find it thirty-three and one-half fold the amount out of which I cheated the Government, as I was a boy thirteen or fourteen years of age. I am sorry that I have to make such a report about me." Though the man makes abundant restitution, his letter clearly shows that he does not consider his character rehabilitated thereby. It may be hoped that if, as is probable, he is similarly concerned about his offences against God he may learn the efficacy of the Blood which not only brings pardon but cleansing. (1 John 1:7.)

A Somnambulist Walking Barefoot Through the snow startled the people of a New Jersey village on January 14. It was a bitter cold night, and the snow was deep on the ground. About midnight sleepers were aroused by loud knocks on their doors. Looking out, they saw a man clad in night garments only, bareheaded and without shoes, going from house to house, knocking on the door of each. He did not wait anywhere for admittance, but went straight on his way. He went to a farm-house at some distance, where, however, he did wait and piteously begged to be taken in. He said that he was given to walking in his sleep, and he had just awakened and found himself out in the snow, with no idea of how he came there. He was employed at a farm on the other side of the village, and must have risen in his sleep and walked a considerable distance before waking. His feet and hands were cut and bleeding, and he was almost frozen to death. The farmer warmed him, lent him some clothes, and accompanied him back to his home, where it was found that he had broken a window in making his exit. His injuries and his exposure have brought on a serious fit of illness, from which it is doubtful if he will recover. That neither the injuries nor the severe cold should have awakened the man earlier seems extraordinary, and shows how deep his sleep must have been. His case was typical of those which Christian workers often meet with, whom neither trouble nor warning seems able to awake to a sense of their position before God. As the apostle said, they have "the spirit of slumber, eyes that they should not see, and ears that they should not hear." (Rom. 11:8.)

A Lady's Complaint Against a Matrimonial agency came before the New York City Court on January 20. The lady stated that, being desirous of marrying, she applied to the agent in question, and, having paid five dollars as a registration fee, he undertook to provide her with a husband. She appeared to be fairly well educated, and had a considerable fortune. After waiting what appeared to her a reasonable time without result, she went again to the agent and paid him fifty dollars, stipulating, as she alleges, that if a husband should not be found for her within a specified time, the money should be returned. The agent introduced her to more than thirty gentlemen who wanted wives, but those who proposed to her were men whom she could not accept, and the others did not propose. The lady, therefore, applied to the agent for the return of her fifty dollars, and being refused, has brought suit for its recovery. All silly women who are tempted to respond to the advertisements of matrimonial agents should take warning by this case. If she had succeeded in buying marriage, she could not have bought love, without which marriage is a misery. (Sol. Song 8:7.) Anxious sinners desiring union with Christ are also sometimes deluded with the hope that the payment of money for His cause, either in life or by bequest, will promote it. They utterly misunderstand the offer of salvation; it is free, but it cannot be had without personal and entire consecration. (Acts 8:20, 21.)

The Recovery of a Long Lost Daughter is reported from Detroit, Mich. Twenty years ago a citizen of New York returned from the war, and made inquiries for his wife and child. He said he had received no word of them all the time of his service in the army, and though he had written to them, and the friends who might be supposed to know of them, he could learn nothing. They were comparatively strangers in the city, and in the disorganized state of public affairs they seemed to have completely dropped out of sight. After a long search, he learned that his wife had been killed in a railroad accident the very week after he had left her to go with the army. No one seemed to know what had become of his baby daughter after her mother's death. He had not the means to continue the search longer, and he settled in Minnesota and went into business. He did not succeed at first, but of late years he has managed to accumulate a fortune. He never abandoned the hope of recovering his daughter, though every year rendered the prospect darker. He kept up communication with friends in New York living near his old home, and a few days ago received word that letters had been received making inquiries about him from a girl living in domestic service in Michigan. He obtained her address, and went to Detroit without loss of time. When he saw her, her likeness to his dead wife convinced him immediately that his long lost daughter was found, and he took her to his home rejoicing. When sinners begin inquiring for their heavenly Father, He never fails to meet them and receive them with joy. (1 Chron. 28:9.)

A Curious Legal Decision was Handed down by the Court of Appeals, at Albany, N. Y., on January 17. The question submitted to the court was *whether a tomb is a dwelling*. It was the appeal of a convicted prisoner against the sentence of the court below. He had broken into a burial vault at Binghampton and examined a corpse interred there, in order to obtain evidence for a suit respecting the art of embalming. It was important for him to ascertain in what condition the body that had been embalmed then was. The family objected to the corpse being disturbed, but the man broke into the vault in spite of them, and made his examination. He was arrested for burglary, tried, convicted, and sentenced to a year's imprisonment. In appealing to the higher court, he contended that whatever his offence might be, it was not burglary, inasmuch as a tomb is not a dwelling. The court has agreed with him, and reversed his sentence. Those persons who pay more respect to the decisions of courts than to the dicta of the Bible should take note of this judgment. The court is right, but a dwelling is needed after death, and there is one provided, "eternal in the heavens," for all who, through Christ, have a title to it. (II Cor. 5:1.)

BRIEF NOTES.

Monday prayer-meetings for business men are now held in the Board of Trade rooms, Philadelphia.

Miss Grace Weiser has commenced a series of services in Harlem, in the Methodist church, at 109th Street and Madison Avenue, New York.

Rev. Thomas Harrison is this week conducting meetings every evening at Jane Street M. E. Church, New York, of which Rev. Stephen Merritt is pastor.

The late Mr. L. J. Curtis, the millionaire manufacturer, of Meriden, Conn., has left $750,000 to the Home for Aged Women and Orphans, which he built and maintained during his life.

Mrs. Warnes Huntly's meetings in and around Pittsburgh, Pa., continue to be much blessed. Some remarkable conversions have taken place, and a very successful temperance work has been inaugurated. Her address is Lawn Street, Soho, Pittsburgh, Pa.

The idiotic practical joker made another victim last week. Daniel J. Grady, of Brooklyn, N. Y., died from lockjaw, which resulted from a severe cut he received in falling backward, when a facetious acquaintance pulled away the chair on which he was about to sit.

President Timothy Dwight received on the 3d inst. a $20,000 gift for Yale University from Alexander Duncan, of London, who was graduated in 1825. Mr. Duncan states that he desires the money to be used in providing for the immediate necessities of the University.

The Pilgrim's Progress has been translated into Japanese. It is profusely illustrated by native artists, who have depicted Christian and Faithful with shaven heads and in Yokohama costume. The dungeon of Giant Despair is the wooden cage used for the confinement of Japanese criminals.

Ben Hogan has been working in Cincinnati. The *Times-Star*, of that city, describes his visit to the workhouse, where he addressed the prisoners. He drew his illustrations from the lives of noted cracksmen, pointing out the inevitable misery of a dishonest career, and inviting his hearers to Christ. The convicts listened with breathless interest, and were deeply moved. His services in Wesley Chapel each evening were densely crowded.

To-day is the day appointed for prayer for colleges. Prof. L. D. Wishard, of Princeton, and C. K. Ober, of Williams, the college secretaries of the Y. M. C. A., earnestly desire the special prayers of all Christians for their work. They have personally addressed over one hundred thousand college students in the United States and Canada since they entered that sphere of labor. The College Y. M. C. A. has now a branch in nearly three hundred colleges in the United States, Europe, Japan, China, etc. It has now over 11,000 students as members.

The campaign for local option in St. Louis, Mo., opened on January 16, with the issue of an appeal to vote against the sale of liquor. It was signed by clergymen, judges, bankers, lawyers and prominent business men. The signers say: "We ask the co-operation of every citizen, without regard to social, business, political or religious conditions or affiliations, and we pledge our earnest, honest efforts to prevent fanaticism, personal ambitions, political or religious prejudices from controlling or affecting the campaign."

A LITTLE SANCTUARY.

A New Sermon by Pastor C. H. Spurgeon.

"Therefore say, Thus saith the Lord God; Although I have cast them far off among the heathen, and although I have scattered them among the countries, yet will I be to them as a little sanctuary in the countries where they shall come." Ezek. 11: 16.

The Prosperous Scorning the Unfortunate—Comfort from God—I. Where God's People may Be—Under Chastisement—Where the Lord has Placed them—In Places of Discomfort—Of Spiritual Barrenness—Under Oppression—II. The Promise of a Little Sanctuary—A Place of Refuge A Place of Worship—A Place of Stillness—A Place of Mercy—Of Communion and Revelation—Why the Christian's Candles are Blown Out.

THE text begins with "therefore." There was a reason for God's speaking in this way. It is profitable to trace the why and the wherefore of the gracious words of the Lord. The way by which a promise comes usually shines with a trail of light. Upon reading the connection we observe that those who had been carried captive were insulted by those who tarried at Jerusalem. They spoke in a very cruel manner to those with whom they should have sympathized. How often do prosperous brothers look with scorn on the unfortunate! Many a time the cruel word of man has been the cause of a tender word from God. Because of the unkindness of these people, therefore God, in loving kindness, addressed in words of tender grace those whom they despised. As in our Saviour's days the opposition of the Pharisees acted upon the Saviour like a steel to the flint, and fetched bright sparks of truth out of Him, so the wickedness of man has often been the cause why the grace of God has been more fully revealed. This is some solace when under the severe

Chastisement of Human Tongues.

Personally, I am glad of this comfort. I would gladly be at peace with all men: I would not unnecessarily utter a word of provocation; but it is a world in which you cannot live at peace unless you are willing to be unfaithful to your conscience. Offences, therefore, will come. But why should we fret unduly under this trial when we perceive that out of opposition to the cause of God occasions arise for the grandest displays of God's love and power? If from the showers we gain our harvests, we will not mourn when the heavens gather blackness, and the rain pours down.

Now to proceed at once to our text, seeing that the occasion of it is a sufficient preface. Let us notice, first, *where God's people may be, and yet be God's people.* They may be by God's own hand "scattered among the countries, and cast far off among the heathen." And, secondly, *what God will be to them when they are in such circumstances.* "Yet will I be to them as a little sanctuary in the countries where they come."

I. First, then,

Where God's People May Be.

If you ask where they may be, the answer to the question is, first, they may be under chastisement. If you will remember, in the Book of Deuteronomy, God threatened Israel that if they, as a nation, sinned against Him, they should be scattered among the nations, and cast far off among the heathen. Many a time they so sinned. I need not recapitulate the story of their continued transgressions and multiplied backslidings. The Lord was slow to fulfil His utmost threatenings, but put forth His utmost patience, till there was no more room for long-suffering. At last the threatened chastisement fell upon them, and fierce nations carried them away in bonds to the far-off lands of their dread. They were not utterly destroyed: their being scattered among the people showed that they still existed. Though they were a people scattered and peeled, yet they were a people, even as at this day.

But, assuredly, the chosen seed came under chastisement. When, by the rivers of Babylon, they sat down and wept; yea, they wept when they remembered Zion, then were they under the Lord's heavy hand. The instructed among them knew that their being in exile was the fruit of the transgressions of their fathers, and the result of their own offences against God. And yet, though they were under chastisement, God loved them, and had a choice word for them, which I will by and by endeavor to explain to you; for the Lord said, "Although I have cast them far off among the heathen, yet will I be to them as a little sanctuary."

Beloved, you and I may lie under the rod of God, and we may smart sorely because of our iniquities, even as David did; and yet we may be the children of God towards whom He has thoughts of grace. We may be in great spiritual darkness, and may be

Compelled to Confess

that our own sins have procured this unto ourselves. And yet, for all that, the Lord may have sent the chastisement in love, and in nothing else but love; and He may intend by it, not our destruction, but the destruction of the flesh; not our rejection, but our refining; not our curse, but our cleansing. Let us take comfort, seeing that God has a word to say to His mourners and to His afflicted, and that word in the text is a "yet" which serves to show that there is a clear limit to his anger. He smites, but it is with an "although" and a "yet:" He scatters them to a distance, but He sends a promise after them, and says, "I will be to them as a little sanctuary."

But, secondly, wherever they are, whether they are under chastisement or not, they are where the Lord has put them. Read the text carefully: "Although *I* have cast them far off among the heathen, and although *I* have scattered them among the countries." The Lord's hand was in their banishment and dispersion: Jehovah Himself inflicted the chastisement for sin. You say to me, "Why, it was Nebuchadnezzar who carried them away: the Babylonians and the Chaldeans took them captive." Yes, I know it was so; but the Lord regards these as instruments in His hand, and He says, "I have done it." just as Job, when the Chaldeans and the Sabeans had swept away his property, and his children had been destroyed through the agency of Satan, yet said, "The Lord gave, and the Lord hath taken away." The Lord was as truly in the taking away as He was in the giving. It is

Well to Look Beyond

all second causes and instrumentalities. Do not get angry with those who are the nearer agents, but look to the First Cause. Do not get fretting about the Chaldeans and Sabeans. Let them alone, and Satan too. What have you to do with them? Your business is with God. See *His* hand, and bow before it. Say, "The Lord gave, and the Lord hath taken away." Come to that, for then you will be able to say, "Blessed be the name of the Lord."

Note, next, that the people of God may dwell in places of great discomfort. The Jews were not in those days like the English, who colonize and find a home in the Far West, or even dwell at ease beneath sultry skies. An ancient Hebrew out of his own country was a fish out of water: out of his proper element. The Jew tarried at home. "I dwell among mine own people," said a noble woman of that nation; and she did but speak the mind of a home-loving people who settled each one upon his own patch of ground, and sat down under his vine and fig-tree, none making him afraid. Their Lord had driven them into a foreign country, where everything was different from their ways—where all the customs of the people were strange and singular. They would be a marked and despised people, nobody would fraternize with them, but all would pass them by in scorn.

The Jews excited much prejudice, for, as their great adversary, the wicked Haman, said, "their laws were diverse from all people," and their customs had a peculiarity about them which kept them a distinct race. It must have been a great discomfort to God's people to dwell among idolaters, and to be forced to witness obscene rites and revolting practices. God's own favored ones in these days may be living where they are as much out of place as lambs among wolves, or

Doves Among Hawks.

Do not imagine that God makes a nest of down for all His eaglets. Why, they would never take to flying if He did not put thorns under them, and stir up their nest that they may take to their wings, and learn the heavenward flight to which they are predestinated! And so He often puts us where we are very uncomfortable. Some of God's servants feel this in a very peculiar manner, for their soul is among lions, and they dwell among those whose tongues are set on fire of hell.

The beloved of God may yet be in a place of great barrenness as to all spiritual good. "I have cast them far off among the heathen"—far off from my temple—far off from the place of my worship—far off from the shrine of my glory. "I have scattered them among the countries," where they will learn no good—where, on the contrary, they will see every abominable thing, and often feel like Lot, who was vexed with the filthy conversation of the people among whom he dwelt. We are not kept apart from the wicked by high walls, or guards of heavenly soldiery. Even our Lord did not pray that we should be taken out of the world. Grace builds neither monasteries nor nunneries. Our

Education for Eternity

may necessitate tribulation, and bereavement from visible comforts. To be weaned from all reliance on outward means may be for our good, that we may be driven in upon the Lord, and made to know that He is all in all.

Worse still, the Lord's chosen may be under oppression through surrounding ungodliness and sin. The captive Israelites found Babylonia and Chaldea to be a land of grievous oppression. They ridiculed them, and bade them sing them one of the songs of Zion. Even Daniel, in his high position under the Persian monarch, found that he was not without adversaries, who rested not till they had cast him into a den of lions. Those who were far away, whether in Babylonia or in Persia, found themselves the constant subjects of assault from the triumphant foe. Is it not still true of us, as well as of our Saviour, "Out of Egypt have I called my Son"? Expect still to meet with opposition and oppression while you are passing to the land where the seed shall possess the heritage.

But enough of that; I am making a very long story about the grievous routes through which we wend our way to the Celestial City. We climb on hands and knees up the Hill Difficulty; we tremblingly descend the steep of Humiliation. We feel our way through the tremendous pass of the Shadow of Death, and hasten through Vanity Fair, and walk warily across the Enchanted Ground. Not much of the way could one fall in love with. Are you in difficult places? Be not dismayed, for this way runs the road to glory. Sigh not for the dove's wing to hurry to your rest, but take the appointed path: the footsteps of your Lord are there.

II. So, now, I hasten at once into the sweet part of the subject, which consists of

What God will be to His People

when they get into these circumstances. "Yet will I be to them as a little sanctuary in the countries where they shall come." Brethren, the great sanctuary stood on Mount Zion, "beautiful for situation, the joy of the whole earth." That glorious place which Solomon had builded was the shrine to which the Hebrew turned his eye: he prayed with his window open toward Jerusalem. Alas! when the tribes were carried away captive, they could not carry the holy and beautiful house with them; neither could they set up its like within the brazen gates of the haughty city. "Now," says the Lord God in infinite condescension, "I will be a travelling temple to them. I will be as a little sanctuary to each one of them. They shall carry my temple about with them. Wherever they are, I will be, as it were, a holy place to them." In using the word "little," the gracious God would seem to say, "I will condescend to them, and I will be as they are. I will bow down to their littleness, and I will be to each little one of them a little sanctuary."

A sanctuary was

A Place of Refuge.

You know how Joab fled to the horns of the altar to escape from Solomon's armed men: he ran to the temple, hoping to find sanctuary there. In past ages, churches and abbeys and altars have been used as places of sanctuary to which men have fled when in danger of their lives. Take that sense, and couple it with the cities of refuge which were set up throughout all Israel, to which the man who killed another by misadventure might flee to hide himself from the manslayer. Now, beloved fellow-believer, wherever you are, wherever you dwell, God will be to you a constant place of refuge. You shall flee from sin to God in Christ Jesus.

O my hearer, make the Lord, which is my refuge, even the Most High, thy habitation, and then shalt thou know the truth of this text: "God is our refuge and strength, a very present help in trouble." Wherever thou art cast, God will be to thee a suitable refuge, a little haven for thy little boat: not little in the sense that He cannot well protect thee; not little in the sense that His word is a small truth, or a small comfort, or a small protection, but little in this respect—that it shall be near thee, accessible to thee, adapted to thee. It is as though the refuge were portable in all our wanderings, a protection to be carried and kept in hand in all weathers. Thou shalt carry it about with thee wherever thou art, this "little sanctuary." Thy God, and thy thoughts of thy God, and thy faith in thy God, shall be to thee a daily, perpetual, available refuge.

Next, a sanctuary signifies also

A Place of Worship.

It is a place where the divine presence is peculiarly manifested—a holy place. It usually means a place where God dwells, a place where God has promised to meet with His people, a place of acceptance, where prayers and praises and offerings come up with acceptance on His altar. Now, notice, God says to His people, when they are far away from the temple and Jerusalem, "I will be to them as a little sanctuary." When a man lives near to God, and abides in Him, he should shake off the folly of superstition, and talk no more of holy places. God Himself, His own presence, makes a place of worship. Whenever you go to sea, God in yo cabin shall be to you a little sanctuary. When you travel by railway, the carriage shall, through the Lord's presence, be a little sanctuary. God's presence, seen in a bit of moss, made in the desert for Mungo Park a little sanctuary. How often have the streets of London been to some of us as the golden pavements of the New Jerusalem, for God has been there! The Lord Himself is the temple of saints in heaven, and He is their temple on earth.

Now, go a little further. Our God is to us a place of stillness. The Holy of Holies was great for holiness, but not for space. There was this peculiarity about it, that it was the shrine of unbroken quiet. What repose one might enjoy who could dwell in the secret place of the Most High! How one sighs for stillness! Those who live in the wear and tear of this city life—and it is an

Awful Wear and Tear

—might well pay down untold gold to be still for a while. What would we not give for quiet, absolute quiet, when everything should be still, and the whirring wheels of care should cease to revolve for at least a little while? I sometimes propose to myself to wait upon God and be still. Alas! There is the bell! Who is this? Somebody that will chatter for a quarter of an hour about nothing! Well, that intruder has gone; let us pray. We are on our knees. What is this? A telegram! One is half frightened at the very sight of it: it is opened, and it calls you away to matters which are the reverse of quieting. Where is stillness to be had? The only prescription I can give is this promise: "I will be to them as a little sanctuary."

The sanctuary was a place of mercy. God was not there in power to destroy, nor in subtle wisdom to discover folly: He was there in mercy, waiting to forgive. Now, dear friends, God says, "I will be to them as a little sanctuary;" that is to say, an accessible throne of mercy, an accessible palace of mercy. When men have no mercy on you, go to God. When you have no mercy on yourself—and sometimes you have not—run away to God. Draw near to Him, and He will be to you as a little sanctuary.

Go a stage further. That sanctuary of which we read in the Old Testament was not only a place of great stillness, great mercy, and great condescension but it was a place of great holiness. "Holiness becometh thy house." This applied to the whole temple, but the inner shrine was called "sanctum sanctorum"—the Holy of Holies, for so the Hebrews make a superlative. It was the holiest place that could be. The world is an unholy place, and at times it is most grievously so. You mix up with people who defile you; how can you help it? Your daily business calls you to see and hear many things which are defiling. When these things are more than ordinarily glaring, you say to yourself, "Oh, for a lodge in some vast wilderness, that I might get away from the very sight of men!" I was with

A Mountain-Climbing Friend,

some time ago, and, being thirsty, I drank some water from a fountain by the roadside. When I held the cup to my companion, he refused it, saying, "I don't drink that." I said, "Why don't you drink it?" He answered, "I wait till I have climbed up into the mountains, where mortal men never pollute the streams, and then I drink. I like drinking of fountains at which none but birds sip: where the stream pours forth from God's hand, pure as crystal." Alas! I cannot climb with my Alpine friend as to material things; but what a blessed thing it is to get right away from man, and drink of the river of God, which is full of water, and know the joys of His own right hand, which are for evermore! What bliss to enter into the Holy of Holies! Now, you cannot do that by getting into a cell, or by shutting yourselves up in your room; but you can enter the most holy place by communion with God. Here is the promise; the text means this—"I will be to them as a little sanctuary—a little Holy of Holies

Lastly, God will be to us a place of communion and of revelation. In the holy place was the ark: God is to us the ark of the covenant. He has entered into covenant with man, towards us He has a throne of grace, and there He meets us, even in Christ Jesus, who is our propitiation. Within that ark there were three things: the rod of Aaron, that divine work of Christ which always buds; the pot of manna, the emblem and token of the living bread, whereon His people feed; and the tablets of the law unbroken, in all their splendor, whereby the saints are justified. O brethren, if you want anything, if you want everything, go to God for it! He will be to you as a little sanctuary; that is to say, He will bring to you everything which was inside that holy place.

If, at this time, you have lost many of the comforts of this life, and seem bereaved of friends, then find God in your "little sanctuary." Go home to your chamber with holy faith and humble love, and take Him to be your all in all, and He will be all in all to you. Pray after this fashion—"O Lord, so work in me by thy Spirit that I may find Thee in all things, and all things in Thee!" The Lord has

Ways of Weaning Us

from the visible and the tangible, and bringing us to live upon the invisible and the real, in order to prepare us for that next stage, that better life, that higher place, where we shall really deal with eternal things only. *God blows out our candles*, and makes us find our light in Him, to prepare us for that place in which they need no candle, for the glory of God is their light; and where, strange to tell, they have no temple, for the Lord God Almighty and the Lamb are the temple thereof. Oh, that God would gradually lift us up above all the outward, above all the visible, and bring us more and more into the inward and unseen! For Christ's sake, we ask it. Amen.

GEMS FROM NEW BOOKS.

TITLE AND WEALTH RENOUNCED.*

Andrienne Vignier subsequently visited us, and by her tender nursing of my beloved mother, and in other ways, proved a friend in trouble. Her history ought to be written in full—a brief outline must suffice.

An only child of Protestant parents, their castle and estate could not be inherited by her, but passed to the brother's son. He was a Roman Catholic, and from childhood was Andrienne's ardent lover. Owing to an accident when ten years old, Andrienne was taken to Italy for spinal treatment. There every effort was made to induce the child to abjure her Protestant notions. She described to me the endeavor to frighten her; after some brave refusal, she was told that evil spirits would come to her if she were not in the true Church, and phosphoric outlines were made to pass before her on the wall as she lay in bed. All in vain! then she was taken one evening into the chapel, to confess; refusing to do so (I only wish I could repeat her clever answers), she was locked up all night alone in the chapel. The morning found the brave child firmer than ever.

Years went on, till her coming of age was to decide the choice—to be a loved wife and a countess in the castle of her ancestors, or to earn her bread as a governess in a strange land. No dogma, no obstinacy, ruled her; in the strong, firm persuasion that Roman Catholic doctrines could not be proved by Holy Scripture, and that as they detract from the glory of Jesus Christ, and substitute the merits of Virgin and saints, this true follower of Christ counted all things but loss, and literally gave up lover, house and lands for His name's sake. It was soon after this that I met her in that singular way.

Once again, after the trial of loneliness, the count tried again. She was walking with her pupils, when an Italian greyhound ran caressingly to her. She knew then its master was not far distant. Two interviews followed, not only with herself, but her English friends; but when Jesus Christ is a reality in the heart, we must be more than conquerors.

Her later path was one of wonderful ministry; not only in England, but away in Naples, noble deeds could be told of her generous rescue of some in distress. Andrienne gave me a singular detail of her assisting two escaped nuns, and their revelations strongly confirmed her Protestant faith. I will not give particulars, as I did not write them then. Brave Andrienne! when the Son of Man comes in His glory, your name and your confession of faith shall be confessed by Him, and His smile will be your eternal compensation.

Victims of Liquor.

One Saturday evening, after ten o'clock, I was led to visit a dying man, with some nourishment for the night. Turning up a sad street of saloons, I was just in time to rescue one of my Sunday scholars, twelve years old. Her drunken mother was literally beating her head against the wall. "My poor child, why is this?" "Mother is beating me because I won't go in with her to drink." This explained the sad, weary look I often noticed on Sundays. I took her to sleep at her grandmother's. That led me to pass the door of a fine young husband in my night-class. There he stood, breaking every

* From the autobiography of Maria Vernon G. Havergal, edited by her sister, Mrs. J. Miriam Crane. This sister of the famous poetess lived a life of beautiful Christian love and usefulness, of which these journals and letters are the modest record. 336 pages; price $1.50. Published by *Anson D. F. Randolph & Co.*, 38 West Twenty-third Street, New York

A Class of Trained Native Nurses in India, Organised by Countess Dufferin.

dish and plate, and the pretty crockery lay in bits on the floor. The wife, with baby's forehead bleeding from its drunken father's blow, stood crying in the street. I saw her safely to her mother's, who herself knew what it was to take refuge in a pig-sty. No wonder I am a strong teetotaller, and nothing is so convincing as to be able to say, "See, I have tried it myself, and even when ordered brandy medically, I have just turned it out, and taken hot water and ginger."

THE COUNTESS DUFFERIN'S TRAINED NATIVE NURSES OF INDIA.

(*See Illustration*).

MENTION was made in these columns on December 22 (page 807) of a petition in a locket sent by a royal lady in India to Queen Victoria. The petition called the Queen's attention to the fact that thousands of women in India were suffering from diseases which might be cured by proper medical treatment, but owing to the ridiculous customs of the country the European physicians who attended their husbands, brothers, or sons were not permitted to attend them. The lady begged that the Queen would do something to remedy this evil. Happily, however, the appeal became known, and one noble lady —the Countess of Dufferin, wife of the Viceroy of India—took the matter into consideration and established training-schools for native ladies, who could visit the zenanas without difficulty. One of the most successful of the local organizations is in the central provinces. In order to give this class the necessary practical training, and at the same time afford help to the suffering women of the neighborhood, a separate ward is being erected near the Mayo Hospital through the liberality of the native gentlemen of the district, one of whom, Seth Castur Chand, Rai Bahadur, has promised 13,000 rupees ($6,500) towards the building expenses: and another, Rai Bahadur Mukund Balkrishna Buti, has offered to pay for the furnishing. *Our illustration, which is engraved from a photograph, shows the women already trained and now training* at Nagpur under Dr. Barter, who is seated in the centre of the group, with Kali Krishna Ghose on his right hand. That this class is attracting women of good caste, may be inferred from the fact that one of those who lately joined is a highly educated Brahmin lady, the head mistress of a girls' school, who has temporarily vacated her post in order to qualify as a nurse. It may be hoped that this institution will be the means not only of alleviating physical suffering, but will be blessed to the spiritual good of the women of India.

MRS. LACY'S ENGAGEMENT

(*See illustration on page 61.*)

"HOW restless you are, child," said a stately old lady, as her granddaughter, a girl of some eighteen summers, threw aside the book she was reading and went to the window, where she stood, eagerly looking out. "Your friend Harold will not be here a minute the earlier for your worry. You have tried embroidery, tried drawing, tried reading, and could not settle to anything. My poor girl, do try to get control over your nerves, or you will prepare a pile of troubles for yourself. You will wear yourself out before you reach half my age. Come and sit on this ottoman and tell me about Harold."

Mrs. Lacy could not have suggested a more absorbing topic. Edith ceased her nervous, restless movements, and poured into her grandmother's ear a glowing description of the young man whom she was beginning to look upon as a lover. He was coming to see her this morning, having found, as Edith was pleased to infer, that her few days' absence from home on a visit to her grandmother tried his patience.

"I think you said you were not actually engaged?" Mrs. Lacy asked.

"Oh, no!" said Edith, "not formally, you know; but I am sure he is fond of me, and I just dote upon him."

"Do not be in a hurry about the engagement, dear," said Mrs. Lacy. "Try to understand his character, before you promise to marry him. Young men are apt to appear at their best while they are lovers, and the light in your own eyes, too, casts a glamor over them. You cannot easily see them as they actually are."

"Oh! I know Harold through and through. He is just perfect," said the exaggerative girl.

"I am afraid that proves that you don't know him," Mrs. Lacy said, quietly. "Now be persuaded and make a calm study of his character. If he has faults—as who has not?—find them out before you are engaged. If you find them out afterward and discover that you cannot be happy with him, what would you do?"

"Break the engagement, I suppose, grandma!"

"And perhaps your own heart, too. It is an awful agonizing work sometimes, Edith. I speak from experience."

"Dear old Grandma! You do not mean to say that you had anything so romantic in your life? But why not? you were a young lady once, of course. How strange it seems! Had you many lovers? Were you beautiful? Let me see if I can imagine what you were like."

"You can do better than that, dear. Come up-stairs and I will show you my portrait painted when I was young."

They went to a room which the old lady rarely used in her latter days, and which Edith had never been in before. Mrs. Lacy threw back the shutters, and pointing to a recess said, "There, Edith, that was a good portrait of me as I was before I married. It was painted for a young man who never possessed either that or the original, happily for him and me too." It represented a young lady, tall and well formed, with a wealth of auburn hair. Her upraised hand, in which was a fan, was holding back a curtain, the deep rich color of which threw into strong relief the delicacy of her complexion.

"O Grandmamma, how beautiful!" Edith exclaimed. "And you were really like that? Now you must tell me about that broken engagement. Did you suffer, you poor dear?"

"I cannot bear to speak of it now without a shudder. He was my ideal of a husband at that time. Anyone of my girl friends would have accepted him gladly, and I think the knowledge that they liked him piqued me a little. We were members of the same church, and that satisfied my mother and father, who would not have consented to an engagement with any but a religious man. I thought, as you said just now, that he was perfect."

"And you never married him! How sad!" Edith interpolated.

"Yes, it was sad at the time, but I was very glad afterward. It was not until about three months after our engagement that I became conscious of a change in my feeling toward him. I put it from me then in horror, for I regarded an engagement as sacred as a marriage. But it wound itself around me like a deadly snake, until it was crushing my young life. I began to analyze my feeling, and I found that my repugnance — for it grew to that — came upon me after spending a few hours alone with him. When other persons were with us I did not feel it. But when we were alone, there was no subject that we talked of on which we felt alike. He had a hard, cold, worldly disposition, that showed itself in spite of him. He took a low, sordid view of everything. Even in religion he had been anxious to get his soul saved that he might escape perdition, and had no conception or aspiration after the life Christ's followers ought to live. He did not understand the truths Christ came to teach. His idea of religion was like a life insurance. Self-denial, self-sacrifice, disinterested effort for the good of others, seemed to him absurd and Quixotic. In short, he was selfish; and though he lavished gifts on me, it was only because he regarded me as part of himself."

"How dreadful!" exclaimed Edith; "and you did not suspect it before?"

Mrs. Lacy's Picture.

"No; he concealed it so well that no one suspected it, because he had the idea that charitable gifts were well laid out in purchasing public esteem. It was the principles of the man that disgusted me, and they were revealed when he talked confidentially with me."

"What did you do, dear Grandma?"

"I bore it for a month or two, trying, hoping, to believe that I was mistaken. Then, when that was useless, in the hope of leading him to higher, broader ground; when that failed, I gave myself to prayer. It seemed infamous in me to break my promise to him. Yet gradually a better spirit than that of pride in keeping a rash promise came to my aid, and I believe God sent it to me in answer to prayer. I saw that he, as well as I, would be made miserable by our union. We could never have any real union of heart, could never even converse in harmony, for our first principles were antagonistic. At last I resolved to tell him. It would be impossible for me to describe the agonizing struggles by which I reached that decision, for somehow I loved and pitied him, in spite of his faults and the disposition that I abhorred. Finally I told him, and after the first outburst of anger and sorrow, he admitted that he too had detected the uncongeniality between us. I was weak and foolish, he thought. Well, we had many anxious talks about it, and during that time my grief at seeing his suffering almost made me yield. But God gave me strength to do my duty, and He saved me from a marriage that would have been like a living death. In His strength I conquered. The engagement was broken. The gossips had a nine days' wonder, but all turned out well. Both he and I have been glad ever since that neither pain nor scandal scared me from doing what my conscience told me was right."

THE FAMILY OF TRIPE COURT.

By Brenda.

(Continued from page 30.)

TOM'S JOURNEY.

WHEN the great gates clanged behind him on leaving the Poor-house Infirmary that morning that Bridget entered it, Tom Mite felt as if he had seen his wife pass from him into another world; he felt as far separated from her as if the grave divided them. From the low, depressed condition to which drink had brought him, his mind took the gloomiest view of everything; and instead of regarding the Infirmary as a place where people went to get well, he looked upon it rather as a place expressly designed to kill them. And a great fear possessed him that he would never see Bridget again; that she would certainly die there, and he would never be able to show his penitence, and make up to her for the wrong he had done her.

He might have continued to hang about the Infirmary gates all day, but in his arms was the baby, the strongest link, it suddenly struck him, that he could have now with poor Bridget, and it might get cold if he lingered, and hungry if it wasn't fed; he must go home and tell Mrs. Job it wasn't admitted, and see about the other children too. That was what would please Bridget best if she could know. On reflection, Tom felt quite a comfort in having the baby, of whom he was sure Bridget was thinking every moment; it seemed to bring him nearer to her. Holding the thing in his arms that was so infinitely precious and dear to her and about whom she would be continually thinking, Tom took a peep at its little face—it was sleeping—drew the woollen wrap Mrs. Job had lent tighter around its little body, and then stepped out to begin the homeward journey.

He did not reckon how long a walk it would be when he began it; driving along in Jemmy Wiggles's cab, he had not taken much notice of anything, and had lost count of the distance altogether. It had been in reality a very long drive from Tripe Court to the Infirmary, but to Tom it had seemed to be quite a short one. For the first mile or two he found the way not difficult; it lay through a new district of neat little houses, and he traversed its long rows of streets with little Dinah asleep and cuddled up in his arms, meeting but very few people and pulled up by no obstacles at the crossings; there were no cabs and carts about; nothing from end to end of the long, quiet roads was to be seen save here and there a street vender with his barrow, crying cheap vegetables, or a man wheeling a tray of gray paper flags and windmills — little toys for the children.

It was later, when Tom Mite got into the more populated parts, that he discovered what poor legs he had now for walking, and what a poor nerve he had for the crossings. Before he had gone a quarter of the way homewards his legs began to shake and feel feeble under him, and he would stand trembling on the verge of the pavement for five minutes, sometimes, before he would trust himself to cross to the other side. And he felt the same nervous dread and shrinking in the crowds hurrying past him in the streets; he felt as if people were going to knock him down every second, and, if they brushed his shoulder ever so slightly, he trembled and felt overcome.

"It was all for the want of a *drink*," he supposed.

Conscience shouted in his ear:

"A thousand times No, Tom Mite! If it had not been for the *drinks*, you would never have felt as you do now; it's the *drinks* that have destroyed your nerve, and made you what you are—a poor, shaky, nerveless creature, afraid of your fellow-men, and not able to look a jaded cab-horse in the face!"

He plodded on, but became conscious now of a new difficulty—that of "passing the corners," as Mrs. Treeby had called it. He had found the jostling crowds and the crossings stiff difficulties enough, but they were nothing to this new one. The manner in which, after a time, Tom Mite took to passing these "corners," or, in other words liquor saloons, was like nothing I know of so much as a horse shying at a gate-post. He made a kind of swerve in his course, not turning his head, but his eyes, round in the direction of the saloons, whose great doors, as they swung backwards and forwards, emitted those peculiar intoxicating fumes, so repulsive and horrible to most, but so seductive and pleasant to the nostrils of drunkards.

Tom passed a good many rum-shops in this fashion of "shying." He thought of Bridget each time as he had seen her carried away that morning out of his sight, with her shawl covering her eyes and her bosom heaving. He thought of her meek "All right, Tom," in the cab, when he had prayed for her forgiveness. He thought of that smothered sob he had heard after she had kissed her baby. Yes, the thought of those things made Tom Mite pass a great many "corners." As he proceeded on his way his nervousness and exhaustion increased; this was natural, for he had walked many miles, and he had had nothing in the way of food. But he never "shied" at the bakeries; *hunger* was not what he felt.

At last somebody in the crowd really did push up against him, and as nearly as possible knock him down. He staggered, and his hat fell off, but he managed somehow to keep his feet. In picking up his hat, little Dinah, who had been sleeping heavily hitherto in his arms, was roused. She began crying lustily, and turning her little head about from side to side in the wrap that covered her. She was thoroughly awakened, and it was no good Tom's jogging her up and down, and trying to smother her up again to go to sleep. She wouldn't be hushed up, she wouldn't be quiet; she cried at the tip-top of her frail little voice, which could be very rasping and assertive when she wanted to be fed. And food was what the poor babe wanted; she had gone a good many hours without it, far beyond her usual time, and she was aware of it, and cried accordingly.

"Of course it's a *drink* that she wants," said Tom to himself, hurrying along, with the baby screaming and battling with her hands under the shawl. "Nobody can get along without drinks. We *both* want a drink, that's the fact of it." Then a feeling of shame smote him, as he compared the babe's innocent craving for the food God had provided for it, with his own unhallowed craving for that which had been his curse, and which had been the indirect means of depriving the babe of its natural food. This recalled him to his better self. At any rate, the baby should have *her* drink first; he had six poor coins in his pocket; it would pay for a drink for them both. But the baby first. So he stepped along, on the lookout anxiously for a dairy.

Not all the din of the cabs and carts and omnibuses and noise of the streets could drown the sound of little Dinah's crying. People began looking at Tom indignantly, as if he were ill-treating his child.

"What are you doing to that baby?" asked a policeman at one of the crossings, while Tom was standing tremblingly on the brink, as it were, afraid as usual of committing himself to the mighty stream of traffic which flowed between him and the opposite pavement.

"I'm a-doing nothing," answered Tom, grumpily, scowling at the policeman.

"Then what's it screaming for like that?" asked the policeman.

"It wants a *drink*," said Tom, "that's why."

"Just what *you've* been having, I guess," remarked the constable, as he condescendingly nipped Tom's coat-sleeve at the elbow, and piloted him safely across.

Tom came to a dairy at last; rather a nice one it was, with a golden cow in the window, and eggs, and two little shrub plants. The walls were all of clean blue and white tiles, and on the spotless wooden counter there stood big shining cans of milk, and beside them a row of glass tumblers. On Tom's entering the shop with his screaming baby, a smart little woman came out of the room at the back, leaving in her hurry the door open. And through it could be seen such a cosy little place, as clean as the shop, with a bright fire and a kettle singing on it, for it was getting towards tea-time, and the flickering of the fire-light showed up a table set for the meal, and, in a corner, a cradle with a child tucked comfortably up in it.

"Milk, sir?" asked the woman, with her eyes fixed on his noisy parcel. Tom nodded, and threw a penny down on the counter. The woman quickly ladled out a pennyworth of the sweet white fluid from one of the shining cans, and handed it to him in a tumbler. To her astonishment, Tom did not toss it off down his own throat, as she had expected. He put his foot on a chair, and sat the baby up, and proceeded to give the milk to the baby. The babe's mouth was wide open, crying, and of course the milk went into it at a good rate; it filled it in a second, and then began a gurgling and a spluttering and a choking, that surprised Tom and horrified the woman.

"Stop, man! Whatever can you be thinking of?" she almost screamed, running out from behind the counter. "Pat it on the back; it's *choking*, you stupid fellah!" Without waiting for Tom to do it, the woman snatched the baby out of his arms, and putting it over her own, thumped its little back with decision till it was somewhat recovered. Then—

"Whatever were you thinking of?" she asked again, looking up indignantly at Tom. "Is the child used to take milk out of a drinking glass?"

"No, of course it ain't," replied Tom; "its not weaned, so of course it feels a bit strange with its lips against a glass."

"Then whatever do *you* do going feeding it?" asked the woman severely, still patting its back while she held it over her arm. "What's its *mother* about away from it, I should like to know? She ought to be *ashamed* of herself!"

This was too much for Tom's feelings. He burst into tears, and said in a broken voice:

"Don't, don't!"

"Is its mother dead, then? Oh! I'm sorry, sir, pardon me," said the woman softly, and she turned the baby round and kissed it.

"No, not dead," explained Tom, when he could speak; "she's gone into the Poor-house Infirmary this morning; they wouldn't take the baby in—over age—and I was bringing it back."

"Poor little dear, it's hungry, then, of course," said the woman, with all her best feeling aroused. "I'll see if it'll take a drink out of my child's bottle. Come in, sir, and sit down," carrying the baby and leading the way into her snug little room. It was very kind of the milk-shop proprietress this, for Tom Mite, with his dirty boots and ragged clothes and drunken-looking face, was anything but an inviting subject for hospitality.

She sat down with Tom's baby on her lap before the fire, and tried feeding it through the long India-rubber tube attached to the bottle of milk she had got already prepared for her own child when it should wake. She had no difficulty in making it take the milk in this way; Tom's baby was so hungry it sucked it all up to the last drop, and seemed disinclined to give up the tube when it was gone.

"I believe it would take more," said the woman, "but I won't give it now, in case it should get stomach-ache. I have an old feeding-bottle," she continued, "with the tube in it and everything fit for use, that I'll give you for your baby, sir, and I'll put a drop of milk-and-water in it, ready for it when you get home."

Tom thanked her for her kindness, and with this good present in his hand, and a satisfied baby in his arms, he left the hospitable little milk-shop, and turned out into the streets again to continue his way home.

The afternoon was drawing in, foggy and bitterly cold; the lamps were being lit everywhere, and the rum-shops were just a blaze of gas, enticing men and women by crowds out of the cold, raw air to go in for warmth and drink. Tom passed two saloons, shying, of course, after he had left the milk-shop, but when he came to a *third*, he seemed perfectly unable to get himself past. He wavered, and stopped in the very middle of the pavement; then somebody pushed him, but the push did not make him move away after that. There was a street lamp near, exactly opposite the saloon, and he went and leant against the lamp-post in full view of his great temptation.

"You have some money in your pocket, Tom, just enough for a pint of beer," whispered the tempter's voice in his ear; "you have had nothing all day; you have fed the baby; who could blame you for taking now just a half-pint of ale to help you along? There was your promise to Bridget, never to touch drink again; yes, but she didn't believe you; she'll feel none the worse to-night if you break your promise; it was only what she expected you to do! And if you go in there, you will get warm and cheered up, and you can sit as long as you like if you just take a drop. There is nothing for you to go home to, except wretchedness, with Bridget away and everybody scowling at you for your treatment of her. In *there*, you'll get to feel quite jolly again. You had better go in, Tom; you had indeed."

Yet still Tom hesitated. He heard that sob of Bridget's again, he saw her great troubled eyes looking at him through the gathering darkness, he saw her overshadowing the baby in his arms each time he started to take it into the unholy atmosphere of that flaring gin-palace. He was thus being swayed backwards and forwards in his mind, propelled one minute towards those swinging doors, drawn back the next by a force as irresistible in power as the one urging him to sin, when suddenly, as he leant there with little Dinah in his arms under the street lamp, a young lady, warmly muffled up, stepped aside from the crowd, and offered him a letter.

"It's an invitation," said the lady, answering his inquiring look. "I've got a party to-night; a great many people are coming; there will be light and music and warmth, and plenty of *drink*. You'll find all about it in the invitation—the hour, the place, and everything. I hope I shall see you there."

And before Tom could say a word either of acceptance or refusal, the young lady hurried off, and he saw her disappear, where do you think?—into the rum-shop opposite!

Tom unfolded his letter, and read under the gas in large printed words, "Sir, pray come to a party to-night that I am giving at No. 10 Blank Street, at half-past seven precisely. Come early. Wives and children will be welcome. Warmth, lights, plum-cake, and drink in abundance. Your sincere friend, Maria Hill."

Tom read it and re-read it. Thought he: "I think I'll go. It 'ud be one way of passing the time. And Poll and Sue 'll like the cake, if I take them. Unless it's a hoax. I wonder if it's a hoax."

But something inclined Tom to think it was not a hoax. At any rate he would have a try for this party, and as it was at half-past seven precisely, and he had got to get to Tripe Court—yet some distance off—to fetch Poll and Sue, and find his way back to Blank Street after that, he had not any time to lose. He began walking out again, resolved to defer his drink till later. The invitation promised "drink in abundance;" would it be the right *sort* of drink, beer and rum? he wondered, as he sped on with his mind full of it.

"Yes," he thought it would; it looked so very nice and hopeful, the young lady having gone into that saloon.

(*To be Continued.*)

THE TRANSFIGURATION.

By Mrs. M. Baxter.

S. S. Lesson for February 5, Matt. 17:1–13 Golden Text, Luke. 9:35.

Ver. 1. Six Days After the Revelation of Christ's Death to His Disciples—On Mount Hermon—Three Representative Disciples—The Inner Circle—Ver. 2. A Revelation of His Heavenly Majesty—To Support them in the Approaching Ordeal—Ver. 3. Representatives of the Old Dispensation—The Lawgiver and the Prophet—Luke Says they Talked of His Approaching Death—The most Momentous Event of all Time—Ver. 4. Peter Prosaic and Practical—Ver. 5. The Divine Injunction—The Appointed Teacher for the World—Vers. 6–9. Christ's Gentle Reassurance—The Sight for all Workers—Jesus Only—Vers. 10–13. A Clear Statement Forgotten Afterward—John Baptist's Place Authoritatively Assigned.

OUR blessed Lord had been teaching Peter that, although he had been distinctly taught of God that Jesus was the Christ, yet he was still carnal in his conceptions, for he savored not the things that were of God but those that were of men. His instinct was rather to save Jesus from temporal suffering than to enter into the thought of God in man's redemption; and this sympathy, altogether on man's level, was distasteful to the Son of God. He came to teach and to exemplify a life in which self should be, not pitied, but denied; not considered, but ignored; He asked the question: What is a man profited, if he shall gain the whole world and lose his own soul? or what shall a man give in exchange for his soul?" The calculations of Jesus were all for eternity, He looked on every earthly thing in its bearing on the great hereafter, and He has made it our privilege to do the same. Jesus then opened before His disciples a glimpse of His kingdom of glory. "For the Son of man shall come in the glory of His Father, with His angels, and then He shall reward every man according to his works. Verily, I say unto you, There be some standing here, which shall not taste of death till they see the Son of man

Coming in His Kingdom."

In the humble carpenter of Nazareth they had learned to see Christ, the Son of the living God; but all their thoughts about the kingdom of God, notwithstanding the teaching of Jesus (chap. 13), were of a temporal reign, according to the prophecies of the Old Testament. It was difficult for them to take in that "the Kingdom of God is righteousness, and peace, and joy in the Holy Ghost." (Rom. 14:17.) But how should they see the Son of man coming in His kingdom? "After six days Jesus taketh Peter, James, and John his brother, and bringeth them up into an high mountain apart, and was transfigured before them: and His face did shine as the sun, and His raiment was white as the light. And, behold, there appeared unto them Moses and Elias talking with Him." It was Jesus, yet in wondrous glory; Man still, yet man illuminated with His glorious divinity. He was in His kingdom, but that kingdom did not consist of thrones and crowns, lands and armies; it was a kingdom of glorified men. The specimens which the disciples saw were Moses and Elias: the man of the law and the man of the prophecies; and both in glory, both conversing with Jesus. He reigns among His redeemed and glorified ones both on earth and in heaven; He has "His inheritance in the saints." (Eph. 1:18.) Moses and Elias did just what the disciples were so slow to do; "they spake of His decease which He should accomplish at Jerusalem." (Luke 9:31); they were ready to enter into the thoughts of God, and to see things from His standpoint; *they* savored the things which be of God, and not those that be of men. All through the economy of His grace, God has had

Death and Resurrection

in view. From the death of Abel, who, "being dead, yet speaketh" (Heb. 11:4), right on through the flood, the offering up of Isaac, the history of Joseph, God's dealing with Moses, etc., God has shown that it is not through what is good or advantageous in man that He works, but that it is through the death, and humiliation, and bringing to naught of the earthly, that He brings forth the heavenly. Abel preached through his death; The flood regenerated the earth through death and destruction; Joseph came through rejection, slavery, and false accusations to the place of power; Moses had to die to all "the wisdom of the Egyptians," and to be for forty years a simple shepherd, that he might be made God's instrument to deliver Israel! Thus also "the kingdom of Christ cometh not with observation," not through the greatness, the talent, the power, or the holiness of man, but through God coming in on the ruin and failure of man to build up a kingdom which is "not of this world." (John 18:36.)

It was only when Moses and Elias appeared that Peter said, "Lord, it is good for us to be here." He liked the company of these men, was in danger of esteeming Moses and Elias more than Jesus. "If Thou wilt," he said, "let us make here three tabernacles: one for Thee, and one for Moses, and one for Elias."

O, how Natural it is

for the human heart to wish to be always on the mountain, always in the glory, always in spiritual enjoyment, while the poor lost world around is going to perdition! Poor Peter! in this also, he savored not the things that be of God, but the things that be of men; in this, also he showed how self ruled him, and how carnal nature possessed him. Who can claim to have been delivered from himself and his carnal nature, who relishes more the company of God's saints than communion with God alone? The tender love of Jesus covered the glory with a cloud, a cloud which shut out the saints but revealed Jesus; and a voice came out of the cloud, which said, "This is My beloved Son, in whom I am well pleased;

Hear Ye Him,"

It is our life's vocation to hear Jesus, and to take into heart and will and affections what He says. By nature, we are not receptive; self is far more ready to teach than to learn; it is grace which makes men learners. Moses had to become a learner before he became a leader; Jesus in the temple heard and asked questions, and the apostle James exhorts us to be "swift to hear, slow to speak." (James 1:19.) What a rebuke this was to Peter, who had been, just six days before, taking Jesus Himself to task! O, if we were faithful in hearing Jesus, in listening for the answer, after we have asked His direction, how could we ever make a mistake; how could we fall under the power of a temptation; how miss the right word to speak, or the right time to be silent? The most powerful Christians are those who hear Jesus, and who give Him the opportunity of speaking to them, and so whatever they do is divinely done, and never has to be undone. I know that whatsoever God doeth it shall be forever: nothing can be put to it, nor anything taken from it. (Ecc. 3:14.) All which is done according to the counsel of God is really done by God Himself, who uses our members as instruments of righteousness. O, it is pitiable to think how much time we have lost, how many words we have spoken in vain, how many prayers have been like "beating the air," because we took the command, and did not wait first to "hear Him."

"When the disciples heard it, they fell on their face, and were sore afraid." How strange it is that we should ever be afraid or disheartened by a rebuke from God! Is it not a proof of His endearing love that He should educate His children? He teaches us that if we endure chastening (Greek, *education*), God dealeth with us as with sons, and that He educates us "for our profit, that we might be partakers of His holiness." (Heb. 12:7, 10.) Yet how many Christians are like pettish, unthinking children! they sulk and fret when God corrects them, as though He were their enemy!

"Jesus came and touched them, and said Arise, and be not afraid. And when they had lifted up their eyes, they saw no man but Jesus only." They were to *hear* no man and *see* no man but Jesus. Moses

"Endured, as Seeing Him

who is invisible" and thus, in every emergency, He turned quite naturally, and without hesitation, to God. Whether it was the need of a way through the sea, a failure in the bread supply, whether the want of water in the desert, whether a cure from the bite of serpents, or an attack of the Amalekites upon the people, his unvarying resource was God. Although he was "learned in all the wisdom of the Egyptians, and was mighty in words and in deeds," we never find him in a single instance relying on that learning, or on any national or acquired power, which he possessed. He lived, walked, governed, prayed, with his eye fixed on God. This is real faith. A more dependent man than Moses could not be conceived, as far as his relations to God were concerned; a more independent man in his relations to man would be hard to discover. Why, O why do we not always live enduring, "as seeing Him who is invisible"?

With "Jesus only" the disciples came down from the mount, the glory was gone; Jesus was, to sight and sense, the humble man they had always seen Him; yet they had received a revelation of Him which was hidden from the eyes of man. And Jesus forbid them to tell the vision to anyone, until He should be risen again from the dead. After His resurrection, He sent the Holy Ghost upon His disciples; then Peter and the rest were baptized into God, and buried by that baptism into death; self was then replaced by Christ, and they began to savor the things that be of God, and not the things that be of men. Had they, in their carnal state, become witness to the transfiguration of Christ, it would only have led people to attempt, in more desperate earnestness, what, again and again, they had already attempted—to make Jesus a king. (John 6:15.) The disciples, still occupied with the vision which they had seen, asked, "Why then say the scribes that Elias must first come? And Jesus answered and said unto them, Elias truly shall first come and restore all things. But I say unto you, that Elias is come already, and they know him not, but have done unto him whatsoever they listed. Likewise shall also the Son of man suffer of them." They understood his reference to John the Baptist, but they did not yet understand about the suffering Messiah.

From the glory of the mount of transfiguration, they came to the theatre of Satan's working. While Jesus was upon the mount with the three disciples, a distracted father had brought his son, with the terrible scourge of

Epilepsy,

to the eight disciples. Of that number was the traitor Judas and the unbelieving Thomas. No wonder that the father had brought the child in vain to such a company! Jesus said to the father, "Bring him hither to me." O, parents who have diseased or epileptic children, do not bring them to disciples to be cured, but take them straight to the great Healer; He alone can rebuke the devil, who throws them into fits, or oppresses them with disease; He has power over all sickness, and all infirmity, and He has a right to cure, because He has taken our infirmities and borne our sickness. Jesus rebuked the devil; and he departed out of Him; and the child was cured from that very hour. The disciples came to Jesus with a very natural and a very important question, "Why could not we cast him out?" He said, "Because of your unbelief." Only those are blest in healing who see God's side of the question, and estimate His power, willingness, according to His own word. He goes on to say: "If ye have faith as a grain of mustard seed, and shall say unto this mountain, remove hence to yonder place; and it shall remove, and *nothing shall be impossible to you.*" This is God's measure. Let us not depreciate it by our unbelief.

"GRIEVE NOT THE SPIRIT."

Oh! grieve Him not away!
That sacred Spirit, inward pleading;
Not always will He stay
If thou resist His holy leading.
He calls thee now,
To Jesus bow;
O soul, for thee the Lord hung bleeding!

A crown is on that brow,
For thee, O sinner, was that dear head wounded!
Canst thou not see it now,
That loving face with thorns surrounded?
Accursed for thee
Upon the tree,
The blessed One in whom all grace abounded!

He knocketh yet once more,
Where many a time, with dewy face and sighing
He's called to thee before,
Ah! what, O soul, was thy replying?
"Oh, go thy way!
Some far off day,
I'll listen to Thy tears, Thy groans, Thy dying."

A time will surely come,
When thou, O soul! thy Lord denying,
Shall meet Him in His home,
And see the throne, the angels lowly lying.
In that sad day
Thy Judge will say,
"Depart, accursed, thou heed'st not my dying."

Then grieve Him not away,
Once more those wounds, that dear side riven,
Are calling thee *to-day*.
Stay not, but seek—implore to be forgiven.
Now he will hear,
His spirit's near,
The angel waits to write thy name in heaven.

—*Selected.*

J. E. JEWETT, Publisher, 77 Bible House, New York will furnish the above poem in leaflet form at twenty cents per hundred. *A Sample Packet of 50 leaflets* assorted (no two alike), will be sent post-paid for ten cents. Postage stamps taken.

Entered according to Act of Congress in the year 1887, in the office of the Librarian of Congress at Washington.

Vol. XI., No. 5. Office, 63 Bible House, N. Y. THURSDAY, FEBRUARY 2, 1888. Annual Subscription, $1.50.

CONTENTS OF THIS NUMBER.

PORTRAIT AND LIFE OF REV. W. WYATT GILL, B. A., Missionary in New Guinea.
DOMINION OF FASHION. Dr. Talmage's Sermon Last Sunday Morning to the Women of America.
ANECDOTES RELATED AT RECENT EVANGELISTIC MEETINGS.
THE PROPHETS AND THE APOCALYPSE.
Mr. Re Qua's Work Among the Indians—Difficulties with African Patients—A Free Thinker's Vow—A Modern Naaman—The Bible for Parisian Catholics—A Singing Service on an Indian Veranda.
THE VICTIMS OF THE NORTHWESTERN BLIZZARD. (With Two Illustrations.)
THE SECRET OF POWER. A New Sermon by C. H. Spurgeon.
Gems from New Books: An Engineer's Vindication.
AGNES MENDON'S PICTURE. (With Illustration.)
THE FAMILY OF TRIPE COURT. (Continued.)
JESUS AND THE LITTLE ONES. By Mrs. M. Baxter.

THE REV. WYATT GILL, B. A., Missionary in the South Sea Islands—A TOWN IN NEW GUINEA.

REV. W. WYATT GILL, B. A.,

Missionary in the Pacific and New Guinea.

Born in 1828—Student Life—How He Joined the Mission Enterprise—Sets Sail for the Pacific in 1851—His Thirty-three Years' Work There—Translating the Bible—Extracts from His History of the Mission—Suspicious Natives—In Peril—A Critical Moment—Rubbing Noses—In the Midst of Irate Savages—A Chief's Pledge.

ONE of the grandest missionary enterprises of recent times is that in New Guinea and the adjacent islands, controlled and directed by the devoted missionary whose portrait appears on the first page. Some description of the work has already been given in these columns; we now, with the portrait of Mr. Gill and a picture of a New Guinea village, give further details of the mission.

William Wyatt Gill was born in December, 1828, at Bristol, England. He is, therefore, now in his sixtieth year. He was converted in early life under the ministry of the Rev. T. E. Thoresby; and soon afterward, feeling himself called to the ministry of the gospel, commenced preparatory training as a student of Highbury College. He was then nineteen years old. He applied himself to study with so much success that three years later, in 1850, he was able to pass the severe examination at the University of London, and graduated B. A. The perusal in early life of the history of the martyr Williams's missionary enterprises deeply interested him in the conversion of the heathen world. In 1851 he was introduced to the late Rev. A. Buzacott, who was about to return to the Pacific in the mission barque *John Williams*, with five recruits for the mission-field, and a warm friendship sprang up between them. Mr. Gill's interest in mission work was observed by the veteran with delight, and when at the last moment before starting one of the young missionaries was taken ill, Mr. Buzacott at once suggested to Mr. Gill that he apply for the vacant place. Mr. Gill offered himself, and was at once accepted by the directors of the London Missionary Society, and was solemnly set apart for the work at old Spafields Chapel, London. In fourteen days from the offer of service he was

Sailing for the Pacific.

For upwards of twenty years Mr. Gill labored on the island of Mangaia (peace), in the Hervey Group. So successful was he, and so remarkable a faculty for organization did he develop, that the society under whose auspices he worked perceived that he could aid them better by superintendence of the general work in the Pacific than by direct effort. He was therefore entrusted with the duty of selecting and assigning teachers, native and English, for mission work. In 1872 he was privileged to locate teachers for the first time on the mainland of New Guinea; Loyalty Island teachers in the neighborhood of the Fly River, and Raratongan teachers in the southeast peninsula of that vast island. He also found time to write and publish several works adapted to arouse the interest of the Christian public in the mission work in Oceanica. His first volume was entitled "Life in the Southern Isles." About the same time was published his "Myths and Songs of the South Pacific," with an introduction by the well-known Professor Max Müller.

In 1876 the devoted missionary imported a printing-press, which he set up at Raratonga, from which portions of the Bible and religious works, translated into the vernacular, issued in large numbers under his supervision.

Thirty-three Years' Labor

in the islands of the Pacific, by Mr. Gill, have been marvellously blessed of God, and he has now retired from active service in the field to devote himself to the task of translating and printing the entire Bible in the native language. He has also, in conjunction with his colleague, the Rev. James Chalmers, whose portrait and life appeared in this journal on September 1, 1887, written a history of the mission, entitled "Work and Adventure in New Guinea." This volume, which is full of matter of thrilling interest, records in simple, modest words, the trials, dangers and struggles of the work in which Mr. Gill has spent his life. We cannot give a better idea of that work than by selecting a few extracts from the book.

Hostility Disarmed.

In October, 1878, a visit was paid to the villages beyond Port Moresby. The vessel in which the three missionaries sailed anchored at that place, and they went ashore and proceeded up the country towards East Cape. "We did not see a strange native all the way," says Mr. Chalmers. "We had our hammocks made fast in the bush by the river-side, and rested until three P. M., when we started for the river Laroki, about seven miles off, in a southeast direction. After sunset we reached the point where the river was to be crossed, and there we meant to remain for the night. We had a bath, then supper, and evening prayers: after which we slung our hammocks to the trees, in which we rested well. Soon sleep came, and all seemed quiet.

"At three A. M. of October 26 we struck camp, and after morning prayers we began to cross the river, which was not over four feet in the deepest part. The moon was often hidden by dark clouds, so we had some difficulty in keeping to the path. We reached a deserted village about six, and after we had partaken of breakfast, we set off for the mountains. Armed natives soon appeared on the ridge shouting *Misi Lao, Misi Lao* (*See Illustration No.* 1). Ruatoka, our guide, called back, *Misi Lao* and all was right—spears were put away, and they came to meet us, escorting us to a kind of reception-room, where we all squatted, glad to get in the shade from the sun.

"After resting about two hours, we proceeded to the next village, five miles farther along the ridge. After walking some miles, we came unexpectedly on some natives. As soon as they saw us they rushed for their spears, and seemed determined to dispute our way. By a number of signs—touching our chins with our right hands, etc.—they understood we were not foes, so they soon became friendly. At the next village an old man lay outside on the platform of a house; he looking terribly frightened as we approached him, but as, instead of injuring him we gave him a present, he soon rallied and got us water to drink. After a short stay, we returned to where we thought of camping for the night, but for want of water we went on to the village we had visited in the forenoon."

In the spring of 1878 the work of

Exploring the South Coast

of New Guinea was commenced, the missionaries sailing from east to west in the little steamer *Ellangowan*, commanded by Captain Dudfield, and manned by an efficient native crew. Communication was held with some two hundred villages; one hundred and five were personally visited, and ninety for the first time by a white man, in parts hitherto unknown and amongst tribes supposed to be hostile. "I resolved," says Mr. Chalmers, "come what might, to travel unarmed, trusting to Him in whose work I was engaged, and feeling that no harm could come to me in His care.

"After visiting several villages, and finding that Inverary Bay was thickly populated, I went on board. The following morning many canoes came alongside, and on our getting up steam were much afraid. It was evident they wanted to show us that they had confidence in us, but it was difficult with the steam up, the snorting and general commotion on board being so great. We warned them on getting up anchor to clear off. Why should they? There was no sail, nor were we going to move. A commotion aft, canoes with crews clearing away to a very safe distance. One canoe hanging on is pulled under, a wild shout, a moment's silence, and then there is a loud roar of laughter, when they see canoe and paddles appear astern at some distance. Keeping on, we anchored outside of the Roux Islands, in a fine, safe harbor.

"We had some difficulty in getting a canoe to come alongside, and it was not until we had fastened a piece of red cloth to a stick and floated it astern that the first canoe would come near. Once alongside, we were soon fraternizing, and on seeing this other canoes came off, and trading for curios began. Asking the captain to keep on trading as long as possible, I resolved to go ashore, to see the chief of one of the villages. The tide was far out when our boat touched the beach. A crowd met us and in every hand was a club or spear. I went on to the bow, to spring ashore, but was

Warned Not to Land.

I told them I had come to see the chief, had a present for him, and must see him. An elderly woman came close up to the boat, saying, 'You must not land, but I will take the present, or,' pointing to a young man close by, 'he will take it for his father,' he being the chief's son. 'No; I must see the chief for myself,' I said; 'but the son I should also like to know, and will give him a present too.'

"Springing ashore, followed by the mate, a fine, daring fellow, not the least afraid of natives, I walked up the long beach to the village to the chief's house. The old man was seated on the platform in front of the house, and did not rise to receive us. I told him who I was, and the object of my coming. He heard me through, and treated the whole as stale news. I placed my present in front of him, and waited for some word of satisfaction, but none escaped the stern old chieftain. Presents of beads were handed to little children in arms, but indignantly returned.

"'Gould,' said I to the mate, 'I think we had better get away from here; keep eyes all around, and let us make quietly to the beach.' To the chief I said, 'Friend, I am going; you stay.' Lifting his eyebrows, he said, 'Go.' We were followed by the crowd, one man with a large round club walking behind me, and, as I considered, uncomfortably near. (*See Illustration No.* 2.) Had I that club in my hand, I thought, I should feel a little more comfortable. When on the beach, we saw the canoes had left the vessel, and were hurrying ashore; our boat was soon afloat, still we had some distance to go; I must have that club, or I fear that club will have me. I had a large piece of hoop-iron, such as is highly prized by the natives, in my satchel; taking it, I wheeled quickly round, presented it to the savage, whose eyes were dazzled as with a bar of gold. With my left hand I suddenly caught the club, and before he became conscious of what was done, I was heading the procession, armed as a savage, and much more comfortable. We got safely away, thank God."

Among Angry Savages.

"After visiting the Keakaro and Aroma districts, our journeyings were nearly brought to a sudden termination. When we got half-way between the point next to McFarlane Harbor and Mailu, where there is a boat entrance, we saw the boat, and waved to them to approach. They came near to the surf, but not near enough for us to get on board. I called out to them to proceed to the boat entrance at Mailu. Great numbers of natives were with us; we saw, in the distance, numbers more sitting on the beach, and armed. Some of those following us were armed. When within two miles of where the boat was to await us, we came upon a crowd of men and women; the former carried spears, clubs, or pieces of hard wood used in opening cocoa-nuts; the women had clubs. The teacher heard them discussing as to the best place for the attack; and, not knowing that he knew what they said, he heard much that left no doubt in our minds that murder was meant.

I carried a satchel, which had beads and hoop-iron in it; they tried to get it. I gave presents of beads; some were indignantly returned. I was in front, between two men with clubs, who kept telling me I was a bad man. I held their hands, and kept them so that they could not use their clubs. Two men, when near the village, came close up behind me with large wooden clubs, which were taken from them by two women, who ran off to the village. Things looked black, and each of us prayed in silence to Him who rules over the heathen. Soon a man came rushing along, seized the club, and took it from the man on my left, and threw it in the sea. He tried to do the same with the one on my right; but he was too light a man, and did not succeed. An old chief came hurriedly to meet us, calling out, 'Mine is the peace! What have these foreigners done, that you want to kill them?' He closed up to the teacher, and took him by the hand. Another chief walked close behind me. They began to talk loudly amongst themselves. Some were finding fault that we should have been allowed to get near the village, and others that there was yet time. Tho boat was anchored some distance off: we got her nearer; and, when ready to move off to the boat, I opened my satchel, gave hoop-iron to our friends the chiefs, and threw beads among the crowd. I shouted for Kapumaria, and a sturdy young fellow fought his way through the crowd. I gave him a piece of hoop-iron, and, with our friendly chiefs, he forced the crowd back, calling on us to be quick and follow. So into the water we got, the chiefs calling, 'Go quick; go quick!' We got on board (*See Illustration No. 3*); with poles and oars got the boat off, set sails, and away for Kerepunu. Before changing clothes, we thanked God our Father for His protection."

Minor Trials

which are merely alluded in the book were numerous, and they would have been hard to bear had not the missionaries been so full of love to Christ and to His work that they could overcome natural disgust. One of these unpleasantnesses was in the mode of salutation in fashion in good South Sea society. As in Polynesia, the natives of the villages on the shores of the Gulf of Papua instead of shaking hands *rub noses* when meeting, and it was not at all pleasant to the English missionaries when an affectionate chief met them, his face got up for the occasion, the paint still wet, or perhaps in mourning, and that only recently put on, and insisted on rubbing noses.

"During my stay at Delena," says the missionary, "one of those warlike

Incursions by Hostile Tribes,

so common in New Guinea, took place. My presence and influence happily brought about an early and satisfactory settlement of the dispute. I extract the following from my journal: 'Last night I slept lightly. Women and children crowd into camp, with all their belongings, and ask for protection. We are told to keep a good look-out—and that we shall. It is now daylight, so we do not care much. The fight has begun in the village. Some Loloans, running after Delena natives, rush up-hill: we warn them back, and they retire. There is a loud shout for us to go to the village and fight. I leave Bob with guns and cartridges to keep watch over camp. I have more confidence in the skirmish unarmed, and have no wish for the irate savages to think I have come to fight. I shout out *Maino* (a friend), and soon there is a hush in the terrible storm. I am allowed to walk through the village, disarm one or two, and, on my return to our friend Kone's end of the village, he whispers to me, 'There is Arua,' understanding him to mean the chief, or *vata tauna* (sorcerer). I take his weapons from him, link him on to me, and walk him up the hill. I speak kindly to him, show him the flag, and tell him we are *maino* (friends), and warn him that his people must on no account ascend the hill. All right, he will stop the fighting.

'I sit down to write this, when again they rush up for me, saying Kone was to be killed. Leaving Bob with arms in charge, I go down to the village, and without my hat. More canoes have arrived. What a crowd of painted fiends! I get surrounded and

No Way of Escape.

Sticks and spears rattle round. I get a knock on the head, and a piece of stick falls on my hand. Arua and Luma of Lolo assure me they will not ascend the hill, and we had better not interfere with them. 'Right friend; but you must stop, and on no account injure my friend Kone.' It would frighten them were we to go armed to the village; but then we dare not stay here twenty-four hours after. I can do more for the natives unarmed. I am glad I am able to mix with both parties; it shows they mean us no harm, and speaks well for the future. No one was killed, but several were wounded, and a few houses destroyed. They have made peace at last, and I have had a meeting in the village with all.'

A Chief's Promise.

One more incident only from the charming volume to which we are indebted, and our sketch of this important and perilous missionary work in New Guinea must close. Mr. Gill says: "After walking through Mama's village, we made for Moapa, which is in truth a perfect cluster of villages. The population is very dense. The mission house is finely situated, overlooking the villages. Crowds of pretty little girls crowded to have the privilege of touching our hands, and to beg for *kuku* (tobacco). At length we arrived at the Chief Koapena's house, which is a very substantial structure. This chief has been to Cooktown, and has seen a little of the ways of white people. He has passed his word that there shall be *no more killing of white men*. Roapena may be fifty years old, muscular and well proportioned. He has lately been bereaved of two wives, but three remain to solace this much-feared chief. He has numbers of children and grandchildren. He is a brave fellow."

ANECDOTES RELATED AT RECENT EVANGELISTIC MEETINGS.

A Reclaimed Drunkard Relates: "Two months after I had been saved, I was holding in my hand a large jar of whisky. All my old desire for drink came back to me with awful power. I hesitated, and was in doubt, but the thought that God says, 'Be thou clean,' came to me, and appealing to God for help, I poured the liquor out into the gutter. A little later in the day I was similarly tempted, through the mistaken kindness of a friend, but, through God's grace, I again conquered. I immediately went to the Lord, and said, 'Oh, Lord, I gave up myself wholly to Thee to keep me.' And next morning, at a prayer and testimony meeting, I could step out on the platform and say that the Lord had given me victory over my besetting sin."

An Unexpected Congratulation.—"In the pretty rural parish of Seend, where I much enjoyed the affection and sympathy of my friends, I had to encounter, at times, much reproach and opposition for the truth's sake. However, I felt then, as I still do, that the opposition of *some* is the best commendation a minister can have, and was content to let it be so. The offence of the Cross shall never cease, and most certainly it had not at the time of which I am speaking. During one of these little occasional storms, an excellent farmer and well-known local preacher among the particular Baptists, Mr. Harry Pocock by name, accosted me on the high road, and shaking me warmly by the hand exclaimed, 'Sir, I congratulate you! You've escaped the Woe.' 'The Woe, Mr. Pocock! What do you mean?' I inquired. 'Why, sir, the Woe. "Woe unto you when all men speak well of you!"' (Luke 6: 26.)

An Hotel Landlord Converted.—A Temperance speaker says: "There was a man, who, while passing through a town, was taken suddenly ill in the hotel at which he was staying. The landlord sent for the doctor, who, after examining the visitor, said that he had only a very short time to live. The landlady sent for a neighboing minister, who tried to point out to the dying man the way of life. 'My dear friend,' he said, 'I am sorry to see you so very far gone; you have but a short time to live.' 'Yes,' said the man, 'only three hours.' 'I hope you are safe in J·sus,' continued the minister. 'No,' replied the nan, faintly, 'I have not time now. It would take me many weeks, and I have only three hours!' But he was shown it did not need three hours, nor three minutes, that if he would only believe on the Lord Jesus Christ, he would be saved. The Holy Spirit graciously made the message effective, and the minister of the Gospel left the dying man trusting in Christ. When the patient was left alone, he called the landlord to pray with and help him to praise God for His great salvation. The landlord said he could not pray, but the invalid insisted, and, at length, the man knelt down, and Christ just saved him as He had done the sick man. Next day, when the minister called, the landlady met him and told him the sick man had passed away, but resting on Jesus he had received an abundant entrance, and that even in that short time between his conversion and death he had been instrumental in leading her husband to the Cross."

The Chiefs' Quarrel Ended.—**Mr. Thomas** Canning said: "There is a touching story of a North American Indian, who was a great chief. There was nothing among all his treasures that he loved so much as his little daughter. Another chief, a friend of the former, and a constant visitor, also loved the little girl, who looked upon these two, her father and his friend, as the only two beings in the whole world worth loving. But there came a time when the two chiefs quarrelled, and the little girl no longer saw her friend. She was not a strong child, and, shortly after the quarrel between the chiefs, she became seriously ill, and soon it was evident that she must die. One day, as her father bent over her, watching her fade away, she said to him, 'Father, I want you to be friends with ——' (naming the other chief). The father started back, passion depicted on every feature. He could not be friends with that man. But there lay his daughter dying, and it was her request, probably her last. He bowed his head, and said, hoarsely, 'Yes, I will.' The girl died, and at her grave there stood on the one side the grief-stricken father, tears streaming down his face, while, on the other, was the alien chief, also in tears; and they became firmer friends than ever, over the grave of her whom they both loved. So, over the dead body of Christ, the propitiation for our sins, God the Father extends His hand to the sinner, whom He thus reconciles to Himself forever."

How to Get Access to a Cellar in West London was the difficulty of a city missionary. He knew that within there resided a monster of crime, suffering and disease. The door had been bolted against that missionary month after month, so that he could not get admission. At length he determined to try the combined power of prayer and the sword of the Spirit. *Outside* the cellar door he stood, and *in a very loud voice* read an appropriate portion of the sacred Scriptures, and then knelt down on the stairs hard by, and poured out his soul in fervent supplications to the God of all grace, that He would be pleased to have mercy on the degraded young woman within. The missionary spoke so loudly, that she could not help hearing every word that fell from his lips. She burst open the door, and cried out, "I can't stand this any longer!" The missionary rushed gladly in, forced open the cellar window to ventilate the place, and then, with kind and tender words, declared the message of the Saviour's Cross. His instructions on this and on future occasions were the means of her conversion. The change in her case was astonishing. She entered one of the hospitals, where she was visited by other missionaries; and her health was restored. She afterwards entered service, where, as a virtuous and consistent Christian, she adorned her profession. Two years later, when she had become a tract distributor, the speaker had an opportunity of conversing with her. Her language was evidently that of a grateful, simple-hearted Christian. Others who knew her history came to the same conclusion, and believed that she was indeed "a brand plucked from the burning."

DOMINION OF FASHION.

Dr. Talmage's Fourth Sermon

TO THE WOMEN OF AMERICA.

Preached last Sunday Morning, January 29, 1888.

"The woman shall not wear that which pertaineth to a man, neither shall a man put on a woman's garment: for all that do so are abomination unto the Lord thy God." Deut. 22:5.

The Abomination of Bloomerism—The Fashion Plate an Index of Morals—Hybrids of both Sexes—Fashion not Wholly Mischievous—The Canonization of Bluntness—Fashion a False Standard—Stimulates Mammon Worship—Ruinous Rivalry—Leads to Flattery and Hypocricy—Lying About Pictures—Frozen Dignity—Leads to Unhappiness—Disease and Imbecility—A Worldling's Life and Death—End of a Woman of Fashion—Noble Contrasts—Queen Elizabeth of Castile at a Review.

GOD thought womanly attire of enough importance to have it discussed in the Bible. Paul the Apostle, by no means a sentimentalist, and accustomed to dwell on the great themes of God and the resurrection, writes about the arrangement of woman's hair and the style of her jewelry; and in my text, Moses, his ear yet filled with the thunder at Mount Sinai, declares that womanly attire must be in marked contrast with masculine attire, and infraction of that law excites the indignation of high heaven. Just in proportion as the morals of a country or an age are depressed is that law defied. Show me the fashion plates of any century from the time of the Deluge to this, and I will tell you the exact state of public morals.

Bloomerism

in this country years ago seemed about to break down this divine law, but there was enough of good in American society to beat back the indecency. Yet ever and anon we have imported from France, or perhaps invented on this side the sea a style that proposes as far as possible to make women dress like men; and thousands of young women catch the mode, until some one goes a little too far in imitation of masculinity, and the whole custom, by the good sense of American womanhood, is obliterated.

The costumes of the countries are different, and in the same country may change, but there is a divinely ordered dissimilarity which must be forever observed. Any divergence from this is administrative of vice and runs against the keen thrust of the text, which says: "The woman shall not wear that which pertaineth unto a man, neither shall a man put on a woman's garment, for all that do so are abomination unto the Lord thy God."

Many years ago a French authoress, signing herself George Sand, by her corrupt but brilliant writings depraved homes and libraries innumerable, and was a literary grandmother of all the present French and American authors, who have written things so much worse that they have made her putrefaction quite presentable. That French authoress put on masculine attire. She was consistent. Her writings and her behavior were perfectly accordant.

My text abhors masculine women and

Womanish Men.

What a sickening thing it is to see a man copying the speech, the walk, the manner of a woman. The trouble is that they do not imitate a sensible woman, but some female imbecile. And they simper, and they go with mincing step, and lisp, and scream at nothing, and take on a languishing look, and bang their hair, and are the nauseation of honest folks of both sexes. O man, be a man! You belong to quite a respectable sex. Do not try to cross over, and so become a hybrid; neither one nor the other, but a failure, half-way between. Alike repugnant are

Masculine Women.

They copy a man's stalking gait and go down the street with the stride of a walking-beam. They wish they could smoke cigarettes, and some of them do. They talk boisterously and try to sing bass. They do not laugh, they roar. They cannot quite manage the broad profanity of the sex they rival, but their conversation is often a half-swear; and if they said "O Lord" in earnest prayer as often as they say it in lightness they would be high up in sainthood. Withal there is an assumed rugosity of apparel, and they wear a man's hat, only changed by being in two or three places smashed in and a dead canary clinging to the general wreck, and a man's coat tucked in here and there according to an unaccountable æsthetics. O woman, stay a woman! You also belong to a very respectable sex. Do not try to cross over. If you do you will be a failure as a woman and only a nondescript of a man. We already have enough intellectual and moral bankrupts in our sex without your coming over to make worse the deficit.

My text also sanctions fashion. Indeed, it sets a fashion! There is a great deal of senseless

Cant About Fashion.

A woman or man who does not regard it is unfit for good neighborhood. The only question is what is right fashion and what is wrong fashion. Before I stop I want to show you that fashion has been one of the most potent of reformers and one of the vilest of usurpers. Sometimes it has been an angel from heaven, and at others it has been the mother of abominations. As the world grows better there will be as much fashion as now, but it will be a righteous fashion. In the future life white robes always have been and always will be in the fashion.

There is a great outcry against this submission to social custom, as though any consultation of the tastes and feelings of others were deplorable; but without it the world would have neither law, order, civilization nor common decency. There has been

A Canonization of Bluntness.

There are men and women who boast that they can tell you all they know and hear about you, especially if it be unpleasant. Some have mistaken rough behavior for frankness, when the two qualities do not belong to the same family. You have no right, with your eccentricities, to crash in upon the sensitiveness of others. There is no virtue in walking with hoofs over fine carpets. The most jagged rock is covered with blossoming moss. The storm that comes jarring down in thunder strews rainbow colors upon the sky and silvery drops on the orchard.

There are men who pride themselves on their *capacity to "stick" others*. They say, "I have brought him down; didn't I make him squirm!" Others pride themselves on their outlandish apparel. They boast of being out of the fashion. They wear a queer hat. They ride in an odd carriage. By dint of perpetual application they would persuade the world that they are perfectly indifferent to public opinion. They are more proud of being "out of fashion" than others are of being in. They are utterly and universally disagreeable. Their rough corners have never been worn off. They prefer a hedgehog to a lamb.

The accomplishments of life are in no wise productive of effeminacy or enervation. Good manners and a respect for the tastes of others are indispensable. The Good Book speaks favorably of those who are a "peculiar" people; but that does not sanction the behavior of queer people. There is no excuse, under any circumstances, for not being the lady or gentleman.

Rudeness is Sin.

We have no words too ardent to express our admiration for the refinements of society. There is no law, moral or divine, to forbid elegance of demeanor, or ornaments of gold, or gems for the person, artistic display in the dwelling, gracefulness of gait and bearing, polite salutation or honest compliments; and he who is shocked or offended by these had better, like the old Scythians, wear tiger-skins and take one wild leap back into midnight barbarism. As Christianity advances there will be better apparel, higher styles of architecture, more exquisite adornments, sweeter music, more correct behavior and more thorough ladies and gentlemen.

But there is another story to be told. Wrong fashion is to be charged with many of the worst evils of society, and its path has often been strewn with the bodies of the slain. It has set up

A False Standard

by which people are to be judged. Our common sense, as well as all the divine intimations on the subject, teach us that people ought to be esteemed according to their individual and moral attainments. The man who has the most nobility of soul should be first, and he who has the least of such qualities should stand last. No crest or shield or escutcheon can indicate one's moral peerage. Titles of Duke, Lord, Esquire, Earl, Viscount or Patrician ought not to raise one into the first rank. Some of the meanest men I have ever known had at the end of their name D. D., LL. D. and F. R. S. Truth, honor, charity, heroism, self-sacrifice, should win highest favor; but inordinate fashion says: "Count not a woman's virtues; count her adornments." "Look not at the contour of the head, but see the way she combs her hair." "Ask not what noble deeds have been accomplished by that man's hand; but is it white and soft?" Ask not what good sense is in her conversation, but "In what was she dressed?" Ask not whether there was hospitality and cheerfulness in the house, but "In what style do they live?"

As a consequence, some of the most ignorant and vicious men are at the top, and some of the most virtuous and intelligent at the bottom. During the last war we suddenly saw men hurled up into the highest social positions. Had they suddenly reformed from evil habits, or graduated in science, or achieved some good work for society? No: they simply had obtained a Government contract! This accounts for the utter chagrin which people feel at the treatment they receive when they lose their property. Hold up your head

Amid Financial Disaster

like a Christian! Fifty thousand subtracted from a good man leaves how much? Honor; truth; faith in God; triumphant hope; and a kingdom of ineffable glory, over which he is to reign forever and ever. If the owner of millions should lose a penny out of his pocket would he sit down on a curbstone and cry? And shall a man possessed of everlasting fortunes wear himself out with grief because he has lost worldly treasure? You have only lost that in which hundreds of wretched misers surpass you; and you have saved that which the Cæsars and the Pharaohs and the Alexanders could never afford. And yet society thinks differently, and you see the most intimate friendships broken up as the consequence of financial embarrassments.

Proclamation has gone forth: "Velvets must go up and plain apparel must come down," and the question is: "How does the coat fit?" not "Who wears it?" The power that bears the tides of excited population up and down our streets, and rocks the world of commerce, and thrills all nations, transatlantic and cisatlantic, is clothes. It decides the last offices of respect; and how long the dress shall be totally black; and when it may subside into spots of grief on silk, calico or gingham. Men die in good circumstances, but by reason of extravagant funeral expenses are wellnigh insolvent before they get buried.

Wrong fashion is productive of a most

Ruinous Rivalry.

The expenditure of many households is adjusted by what their neighbors have, not by what they themselves can afford to have; and the great anxiety is as to who shall have the finest house and the most costly equipage. The weapons used in the warfare of social life are not minie rifles, and Dahlgren guns, and Hotchkiss shells, but chairs and mirrors and vases and Gobelins and Axminsters. Many household establishments are like racing steamboat, propelled at the utmost strain and risk, and just coming to a terrific explosion. "Who cares," say they, "if we only come out ahead?" There is no one cause to-day of more financial embarrassment and of more dishonesties than this determination at all hazards to live as well as or better than other people. There are persons who will risk their eternity upon one pier mirror, or who will dash out the splendors of heaven to get another trinket.

There are scores of men in the dungeons of the penitentiary who risked honor, business, everything, in the effort to shine like others. Though the heavens fall they must be "in the fashion." The most famous frauds of the day have resulted from this feeling. It keeps hundreds of men struggling for their commercial existence. The trouble is that some are caught and incarcerated if their larceny be small. If it be great they escape and build their castle on the Rhine.

Again: Wrong fashion makes people unnatural and untrue. It is a factory from which has come forth more hollow and unmeaning

Flatteries and Hypocrisies

than the Lowell mills ever turned out shawls and garments. Fashion is the greatest of all liars. It has made society insincere. You know not what to believe. When people ask you to come, you do not know whether or not they want you to come. When they send their regards, you do not know whether it is an expression of their heart, or an external civility. We have learned to take almost everything at a discount. Word is sent, "Not at home," when they are only too lazy to dress themselves. They say: "The furnace has just gone out," when in truth they have had no fire in it all winter. They apologize for the unusual barrenness of their table, when they never live any better. They decry their most luxurious entertainments to win a shower of approval. They apologize for their appearance, as though it were unusual, when always at home they look just so. They would make you believe that some nice sketch on the wall was the work of a master-painter. "It was an heir-loom, and once hung on the walls of a castle; and a duke gave it to their grandfather." People who will not lie about anything else will lie about a picture. On a small income we must make the world believe that we are affluent, and our life becomes a cheat, a counterfeit and a sham.

Few people are really natural and unaffected When I say this I do not mean to slur cultured manners. It is right that we should have more admiration for the sculptured marble than for the unhewn block of the quarry. From many circles in life fashion has driven out vivacity.

A Frozen Dignity

instead floats about the room, and iceberg grinds against iceberg. You must not laugh outright; it is vulgar. You must smile. You must not dash rapidly across the room; you must glide. There is a round of bows and grins and flatteries, and oh's and ah's and simperings, and namby-pambyism—a world of which is not worth one good, round, honest peal of laughter. From such a hollow round the tortured guest retires at the close of the evening, and assures his host that he has enjoyed himself.

Thus social life has been contorted and deformed, until, in some mountain cabin, where rustics gather to the quilting or the apple-paring, there is more good cheer than in all the frescoed icehouses of the metropolis. We want in all the higher circles of society more warmth of heart and naturalness of behavior, and not so many refrigerators.

Again: Wrong fashion is

Incompatible with Happiness.

Those who depend for their comfort upon the admiration of others are subject to frequent disappointment. Somebody will criticise their appearance, or surpass them in brilliancy, or will receive more attention. Oh, the jealousy and detraction and heart-burnings of those who move in this bewildered maze! Poor butterflies! Bright wings do not always bring happiness. "She that liveth in pleasure is dead while she liveth." The revelations of high life that come to the challenge and the fight are only the occasional croppings out of disquietudes that are, underneath, like the stars of heaven for multitude, but like the demons of the pit for hate. The misery that will to-night in the cellar cuddle up in the straw is not so utter as the princely disquietude which stalks through splendid drawing-rooms, brooding over the slights and offences of luxurious life. The bitterness of life seems not so unfitting when drunk out of a pewter mug as when it pours from the chased lips of a golden chalice. In the sharp crack of the voluptuary's pistol, putting an end to his earthly misery, I hear the confirmation that in a hollow, fastidious life there is no peace.

Again: Devotion to wrong fashion is

Productive of Physical Disease,

mental imbecility and spiritual withering. Apparel insufficient to keep out the cold and the rain, or so fitted upon the person that the functions of life are restrained; late hours filled with excitement and feasting; free drafts of wine that make one not beastly intoxicated, but only fashionably drunk; and luxurious indolence—are the instruments by which this unreal life pushes its disciples into valetudinarianism and the grave. Along the walks of prosperous life death goes a-mowing—and such harvests as are reaped! Materia Medica has been exhausted to find curatives for these physiological devastations. Dropsies, cancers, consumptions, gout and almost every infirmity in all the realm of pathology have been the penalties paid. To counteract the damage, Pharmacy has gone forth with medicament, panacea, elixir, embrocation, salve and cataplasm.

To-night, with swollen feet upon cushioned ottoman, and groaning with aches innumerable, will be the votary of luxurious living, not half so happy as his groom or coal-heaver. Wrong fashion is the world's undertaker, and drives thousands of hearses to Greenwood and Laurel Hill and Mount Auburn.

But, worse than that, this folly is an

Intellectual Depletion.

This endless study of proprieties and etiquette, patterns and styles, is bedwarfing to the intellect. I never knew a woman or a man of extreme fashion that knew much. How belittling the study of the cut of a coat, or the tie of a cravat, or the wrinkle in a sleeve, or the color of a ribbon! How they are worried if something gets untied, or hangs awry, or is not nicely adjusted! With a mind capable of measuring the height and depth of great subjects; able to unravel mysteries, to walk through the universe, to soar up into the infinity of God's attributes—hovering perpetually over a new style of cloak! I have known men, reckless as to their character and regardless of interests momentous and eternal, exasperated by the shape of a vest-button.

Worse than all—this folly is not satisfied until it extirpates every moral sentiment and

Blasts the Soul.

A wardrobe is the rock upon which many a soul has been riven. The excitement of a luxurious life has been the vortex that has swallowed up more souls than the Maelstrom off Norway ever destroyed ships. What room for elevating themes in a heart filled with the trivial and unreal? Who can wonder that in this haste for sun-gilded baubles and winged thistle-down men and women should tumble into ruin? The travellers to destruction are not all clothed in rags. In the wild tumult of the Last Day—the mountains falling, the heavens flying, the thrones uprising, the universe assembling; amid the boom of the last great thunder-peal, and under the crackling of a burning world—what will become of the disciple of fashion?

The Worldling's Career.

But watch the career of one thoroughly artificial. Through inheritance, or, perhaps, his own skill, having obtained enough for purposes of display, he feels himself thoroughly established. He sits aloof from the common herd, and looks out of his window upon the poor man, and says: "Put that dirty wretch off my steps immediately!" On Sabbath days he finds the church, but mourns the fact that he must worship with so many of the inelegant, and says: "They are perfectly awful! That man that you put in my pew had a coat on his back that did not cost five dollars." He struts through life unsympathetic with trouble, and says: "I cannot be bothered." Is delighted with some doubtful story of Parisian life, but thinks there are some very indecent things in the Bible. Walks arm in arm with the successful man of the world, but does not know his own brother. Loves to be praised for his splendid house, and, when told that he looks younger, says: "Well, really, do you think so?"

But the brief strut of his life is about over. Up-stairs he dies. No angel wings hovering about him. No Gospel promises kindling up the darkness; but exquisite embroidery, elegant pictures, and a bust of Shakspeare on the mantel. The pulses stop. The minister comes in to read of the Resurrection, that day when the dead shall come up—both he that died on the floor and he that expired under princely upholstery. He is carried out to burial. Only a few mourners, but a great array of carriages. Not one common man at the funeral. No befriended orphan to weep a tear on his grave. No child of want pressing through the ranks of the weeping, saying: "He is the last friend I have."

What now? He was a great man. Shall not chariots of salvation come down to the other side of the Jordan and escort him up to the palace? Shall not the angels exclaim: "Turn out! A prince is coming." Will the bells chime? Will there be harpers with their harps, and trumpeters with their trumpets?

No! No! No! There will be a shudder, as though a calamity had happened. Standing on heaven's battlement, a watchman will see something shoot past, with fiery downfall, and shriek: "Wandering star—for whom is reserved the blackness of darkness!" But sadder yet is the

Closing of a Woman's Life

that has been worshipful of worldliness, all the wealth of a lifetime's opportunity wasted. What a tragedy! A woman on her dying pillow, thinking of what she might have done for God and humanity, and yet having done nothing! Compare her demise with that of a Harriet Newell, going down to peacefully die in the Isle of France, reviewing her lifetime sacrifices for the redemption of India; or the last hours of Elizabeth Hervey, having exchanged her bright New England home for a life at Bombay amid stolid heathenism, that she might illumine it, saying in her last moments: "If this is the dark valley, it has not a dark spot in it; all is light, light!" or the exit of Mrs. Lennox, falling under sudden disease at Smyrna, breathing out her soul with the last words, "Oh, how happy!" or the departure of Mrs. Sarah D. Comstock, spending her life for the salvation of Burmah, giving up her children that they might come home to America to be educated, and saying as she kissed them good-by, never to see them again, "O Jesus! I do this for Thee!" or the going of ten thousand good women, who in less resounding spheres have lived not for themselves, but for God and the alleviation of human suffering.

That was a brilliant scene when, in 1485, in the campaign for the capture of Ronda,

Queen Elizabeth of Castile,

on horseback, side by side with King Ferdinand, rode out to review the troops. As she, in bright armor, rode along the lines of the Spanish host, and waved her jewelled hand to the warriors, and ever and anon uttered words of cheer to the worn veterans who, far away from their homes, were risking their lives for the kingdom, it was a spectacle that illumines history. But more glorious will be the scene when that consecrated Christian woman, crowned in heaven, shall review the souls that on earth she clothed and fed and medicined and evangelized, and then introduced into the ranks celestial. As on the white horse of victory, side by side with the king, this queen unto God forever shall ride past the lines of those in whose salvation she bore a part, the scene will surpass anything ever witnessed on earth in the life of Joan of Arc, or Penelope, or Semiramis, or Aspasia, or Marianne, or Margaret of Anjou. Ride on, victor!

MR. RE QUA'S INDIAN WORK.

THE efforts being made by the Rev. W. F. and Mrs. Re Qua to spread the knowledge of Christ among the Indians in the Indian Territory are beginning to bear fruit. We learn that Mr. Re Qua has succeeded in making arrangements for the opening of three mission schools in the spring, and has found suitable persons willing to labor in them. The statements of simple unvarnished facts, which have come under the observation of these self-sacrificing workers, show how urgently such work as theirs is needed. The Indians appear utterly destitute of even rudimentary knowledge of morality. Whole families, in many cases of three generations, eat, live and sleep in a single room, and the most shocking condition of relations results. Mr. Re Qua spends the week in visiting among the cabins, and in many instances, especially among the sick, has been used of God for the enlightenment of dark souls. He gladly informs us that he will be able now to extend this work, as a kind friend in Philadelphia has sent him *a present of fifty dollars* to be spent in the purchase of a horse for these journeys. On a recent Sunday he succeeded, in spite of the severe weather, in gathering an audience of about forty persons in a cabin that could be reached conveniently by all. It had no windows, but sufficient light and more than sufficient of the cold, raw wind were admitted at the open door. In spite of the discomfort, there was more earnestness and desire for knowledge than the preacher often finds in churches luxuriously carpeted and comfortably warmed. The two brave missionaries with their little four-year-old daughter are enduring many privations, but they are cheerful and full of faith in God's loving care. Many of our readers have already contributed to their support as they thankfully acknowledge, and the good work still needs their aid. Their address is McAlister, Indian Territory.

DIFFICULTIES WITH AFRICAN PATIENTS.

THE excellent work of training medical missionaries carried on by Dr. Dowkontt is receiving much encouragement, but could be indefinitely extended if there were more funds for the work.*

The Doctor has recently received a letter from Dr. A. Sims, whose portrait and life appeared in this journal on July 14, 1887. Dr. Sims is now at Leopoldville, in the Congo Free State, Africa. He says: "I am living in a district where the gospel is only begun to be preached, and where the native system of charms is in full rigor, and consequently have only five or six patients a day. I visit from house to house, seeking out the sick, but most of them I cannot get to come, and some not more than once, if at all. No matter, at present, for I am also trying to bring *success by the other method*. I have translated the Gospel of John in the Bateke and Bayansi languages, and am busy preaching to them in their town. I don't despair of seeing plenty of patients in the end. Dr. Scholes, on the coast and Dr. Harrison, some miles higher up Stanley Pool, seem to be in the same unsuccessful state as I, for the same reasons.

"A missionary colleague who has a fair number of patients, because he has many inquirers at his stations, sends me his experience in dealing with them. He writes me: 'I have been having a very large number of patients here until the last few days, when two died of dropsy, which seems to have made them lose all faith in my medical skill. These people are peculiar. They do not take into consideration the large number of dropsical patients we have had come here lately (there has been quite an epidemic of Beri-Beri), and have been cured, but they only look at the two deaths, and they are frightened. This is largely due, no doubt, to the peculiar way in which they regard sickness, death and medicine. As you know, they believe *sickness and death are the work of malignant beings* operating through human beings, and medicine is that which will negative all malign influences; therefore they do not consider it matters which medicine they take, and are quite unwilling to describe symptoms; in fact, they regard your questions as quite irrelevant. When they get the medicine one must be careful to enjoin upon them to *drink* it, otherwise they will probably be contented with merely putting it by the bedside, and will have lost all faith in it if by the morning they are not quite well. Should the individual die, confidence evaporates at once.

"'The people are always expecting to discover some medicine or charm somewhere that will enable them to triumph over death and live forever. We tell them it is the Gospel they want, but the gospel is too intangible and abstract for many, and they don't care for it. Nevertheless the work here is not without signs of hopefulness. We have a few, I believe, real converts, and should have had more, I do not doubt, if only the people had been sufficiently taught.'"

* *Subscriptions will be gratefully received if sent to Geo. D. Dowkontt, M. D., 118 East 45 St., New York, N. Y.*

A FREE-THINKER'S VOW.

AN interesting case occurred recently in one of the McAll mission stations in Paris. A child was brought by its mother to the station to be baptized. The mother told a strange story of the means by which she was allowed to bring her daughter. She said that her husband was a determined atheist, who was very much exasperated when he heard that she and their little girl had been to the McAll mission. She pleaded with him, and begged that the little one might be baptized and have a religious education. The man refused with threats, and resisted all his wife's pleadings. Soon afterward the child fell ill and her life was despaired of. The father, who loved her dearly, was in a state of agonizing anxiety. At last he told the mother that if the child did not die she might bring her up as she wished. The girl did recover, and the infidel kept his vow. The mother brought her to the mission and publicly consecrated her to God.

Subscriptions for the support of the McAll missions in France, may be sent to Mrs. Marine J. Chase, 1622 Locust Street, Philadelphia, Penn., who is President of the American auxiliary.

A MODERN NAAMAN.

A REMARKABLE testimony is published by Miss Carrie F. Judd, of Buffalo, N. Y. It is that of Mrs. Burdge, who writes under date of December 1, 1887. She states that, after being several years an invalid, her physician, finding that she did not recover, but rather grew worse, suggested a consultation. An eminent professor in a medical college consulted with the physician. Mrs. Burdge was not informed of the result, but to her friends the two medical men said she was suffering from cancer. Shortly afterward the lady consulted another physician, who made no concealment of his diagnosis. He told her she had cancer, and advised an operation. This, however, she shrank from. She had an invalid friend, who came to visit her about this time, and, to Mrs. Burdge's astonishment, appeared to have quite recovered. She was still more amazed when her friend told her that God had healed her through faith and prayer. Mrs. Burdge was at that time in Cleveland, O., where meetings were being held by an evangelist, who declared the power and will of Christ to heal the body. She went to his meeting, expecting, she says, that he would just lay his hands on her and she would recover. Nothing of the kind of course took place. She was taught to look to God for healing, and to consecrate herself to Him, and to give to Him the strength and renewed life she was hoping to receive. It was some time before she could shake off the expectation that by some human instrumentality healing would come to her. Eventually the evangelist left her, telling her that it was a personal matter between her and God. Left to herself, and thoroughly convinced that God could and would heal her, she went to Him in prayer, and at length, solemnly pledged her future life, be it long or short, to His service. Healing came to her immediately, and she now declares herself strong and well, and has found herself equal to exertion in walking and working, beyond any she ever knew.

A BIBLE FOR PARISIAN CATHOLICS.

THE American *McAll Record* calls attention to a remarkable movement among the Roman Catholics of Paris. The atheistic tendencies of the dominant political party in France have scared the priests and bishops of that church, who fear that the country will lapse into infidelity. They have been moved to contend against it and have actually begun the campaign by arranging for a more extended circulation of the Bible, and have caused a better translation of it to be prepared. We may hope that they will build better than they know, and that the people will be led by their efforts, not only from infidelity, but into the truth as it is in Jesus. The following is the report:

It is an interesting fact that such a prominent secular newspaper as *Le Matin*, of Paris, hails as an event "of great social importance, of interest to humanity at large, and not alone to literature," the new translation of the Bible into modern French, by Henri Laserre, a well-known Romanist. This translation has received the *imprimatur* of the archbishopric of Paris, and the approval of Rome, and the book is spreading rapidly among Roman Catholic readers. They see in this replacing of the former imperfect and antiquated translation by one "flowing, readable, faithful and interesting" (to quote again from *Le Matin*), the means designed by God—not to correct the errors of their own faith; this, of course, they do not find necessary, but—to meet the atheistic propaganda now so actively carried on, and virtually fostered even by Government.

They see, as the editor of *Le Matin* points out, that it is by the Bible only that the Church can make headway against the demoralizing and materializing influence of the present recoil against religious teaching in the public schools. It is very possible that Romanists, embittered by the laws which have entirely withdrawn the education of the young men from the priests and monks whose business it formerly was, exaggerate the demoralizing tendencies of the present system; none the less is it true that in finding an antidote to this danger in the reading of the Bible, they are finding that which shall surely bring them into the true light.

A SINGING SERVICE ON A VERANDA

A LETTER from Miss Lathrop, who is in Allahabad, India, published in the *Missionary Link*, contains the following description of a visit by invitation to the women of a village in India:

Some little time ago, we were told that in a large village on the banks of the Jumna there were women and girls wishing to be taught. It was far away, and involved us in long walks through winding lanes and half-shoe deep in dirt. The appearance of everything was much better than we usually find in entering a village. Large brick houses, freshly whitened, with gardens and imposing gateways, and on the raised verandas groups of well dressed men leisurely smoking their hookas. A woman was watching for us at the entrance of a lane, and took us at first to a house where, on the veranda, soon gathered twenty or more girls wishing to form a school, and a crowd of women and babies were on the edge of the veranda. I had a low camp-stool with me, and was very glad to sit after the long walk, but women and children crowded so that I could scarcely get a breath. The morning was hot and close, and the position for a time not enviable. A teacher will go daily. Settling a few things for her future help, we read and talked and sang. Nothing else quiets a noisy group so soon, by arresting the attention of all, as a native air set to Christian words. I sat near a partly open door, and was conscious someone was standing inside; when a little at liberty, I turned and saw a sweet-faced young woman and a little girl. The woman was dressed in a clean white saree, and arms, neck, ears and nose were adorned with jewels. When I spoke first she was startled and retreated a few steps, but soon come back and I had a pleasant talk with her. A young brother of her husband came to me and said she was anxious to learn, but her husband being away, she dared not say so. I hope both she and the child may be allowed.

THE PROPHETS AND THE APOCALYPSE.

By Rev. N. West, D. D.*

The Millennium in the Old Testament—Progressive Development in Prophecy—Both Advents at First Appearing as One—Confused Ideas of the Kingdom—Daniel Perceives the Separation of the Advents—The Sky-Line Widening—The Seventy Weeks Revealed—The Interval Between the Sixty-ninth and Seventieth—Our Age—The Second Advent at the End of the Seventieth Week—The Colossus in the Grave Yard.

THERE is an idea very common throughout Christendom, not only among pre-millennialists, but also among post-millennialists, viz., that the doctrine of the "Millennium," or "The Thousand Years Kingdom," is found only in the New Testament, and only in one passage, and that, moreover, a very obscure passage, in a very obscure and symbolical book. And just because of this so popular and erroneous impression, I have thought it would be of service to many to show, in a general way, how utterly incorrect is this almost universal view of the matter, and how contrary it is to the clear teaching of the Old Testament itself. Believing, as I do, in the plenary verbal inspiration of the word of God, in the organic unity and genetic development of Old Testament prophecy, in the continuance of that development even under New Testament fulfilment, and yet more in the Apocalypse of John as the crown and consummation of all the Apocalypses given to the prophets, I felt confident that, somewhere in the Old Testament, I would find "the thousand years" of John not merely described as to their character, but defined as to their locality in history, by definite events marking the beginning or opening of those years, and marking also their end or close, and so add one more fresh proof to the truth of Augustine's maxim, and confirm forever the unchanging and unchangeable verity of God's words. And so I found it.

In order to get a clear conception of the fulfilment of Old Testament prophecy, you must *combine* the events which you now know to

Belong to Both Advents

of Messiah; in other words, you must remember that the *first* Advent of Messiah only brought a *partial* fulfilment of the prophetic word which yet awaits the *second* Advent in order to complete it, or secure its plenary accomplishment. Joel's prophecy as to the outpouring of the Spirit in the last days, and of the great and notable day of the Lord, with all its terrestrial and celestial phenomena, the final redemption of Israel, and the transfiguration of the Holy Land, was only incipiently and partly fulfilled to a few, an election out of Israel, at the first coming of Christ. But there is to be

A Grander Fulfilment

still in coming days, when, now that a second dispersion and sifting of Israel has occurred, since James spoke, there shall be fullness of the Gentiles "after this;" and finally, the fallen booth of David, or Israel's proper Kingdom, as the prophets picture it, will be re-erected with the fullness of I rael converted to God, and the glorious Millennial age heave into view. So is it with reference to Isaiah's Redeemer coming to Zion, and Hosea's Israel's abiding alone for many days, and Micah's halting daughter of Zion, to whom, at length, comes the "former dominion." Whatever occurred to Israel graciously, at the first coming of Christ, was only a preliminary fulfilment to be exhaustively completed for Israel, at His Second Coming. Such is the law of prophecy and the law of fulfilment, and it will save us from many an error, if only we are careful to remember it.

From first to last, the Kingdom of God, in its rise, progress, and consummation, i. e., the empire of sovereignty of God in the individual soul, in the world, the kingdom spiritually, and

The Kingdom Outwardly and Politically,

is the one grand theme of the Old Testament. And it comes by stages and forms and degrees of development, as I have intimated. To that one end, the realization of the Kingdom of God, was this planet, and the universe, created, even "all things." There is much confusion as to the idea of the "*kingdom.*" Some think of it in one way, some another, and some confound it, as Augustine did, with the church. The "*kingdom*" as predicted by the prophets is both inward and outward, both spiritual and material, both finite and infinite, both past, present and to come, both temporal and everlasting. As a polity to take the place of all earthly empires, it is impossible apart from nationality. Believing Israel, viewed as "the Church in the wilderness," was prior to the nation established in royalty in the Old Land. And so, in the days to come, Israel's nationality must be restored, before the kingdom as predicted in Daniel, Micah, Zechariah, Ezekiel and all the prophets can be restored to Israel.

The *Basileia*, or kingdom, means the sovereignty of God in history, providence and grace, and this is exercised in various ways. The Messianic kingdom has Christ as King, first spiritually, then politically in days to come, Israel always in the front. In this strict and proper sense, the difference between the church and the kingdom is the difference between a house and a state or empire. The church is the "House of God," the "House of Christ," as Paul tells us, while yet we are watching and waiting and expecting, to receive in its fullness of outward glory that very kingdom into which, spiritually, we have already been translated.

The events belonging to each advent are found in Isaiah and the pre-exile prophets, but

The Advents are not Separated,

save in one passage where the separation is implied. Isa. 24: 20-23. In the prophet Daniel, however, we find them sundered. The one end has become two. There is a coming of Messiah in humiliation, and to be "cut off" at a certain specified time. This you see in Dan. 9: 25. Then there is a coming of Messiah in the clouds of heaven, at the end of a long period following the first end. This you see in Dan. 7: 9, 22. Messiah comes at the beginning of the fourth prophetic empire. He comes also at its close. You have sailed up to your sky-line, and another one lies beyond it. You have reached the advent and find that it is parted into two advents with an intervening age, the age we ourselves are living in, the age when Israel is nationally cast away.

Look at the words of the revealing angel to Daniel, in the ninth chapter. He tells the prophet that the glorious Messianic Redemption foretold for Israel, as a nation, in pre-exile prophecy, will not come at the close of the seventy years of Babylonish Captivity, but that

Seventy Weeks

of years are measured off in God's counsel, and determined upon, for the continuance of Israel's distress, because of Israel's unreadiness to receive Messiah, and that only at the end of those weeks of years, will Israel's apostacy be finished, or restrained, and Israel's national sins covered up, and reconciliation for national iniquity be made, and abiding righteousness be brought in, and vision and prophet then become verified in history, and a new Sanctuary be consecrated to God. Read verse 24 of this 9th chapter. He explains still further. He tells the prophet that the Jews will reject their Messiah, at His first coming, i. e., at the close of the 69th week of years, or 483 years from the "going forth of the commandment" by Artaxerxes to restore and rebuild Jerusalem. He adds, still further, that because of this rejection, Israel will again be scattered, Jerusalem being destroyed by the Romans, and that down to the consummation, wars and desolations are decreed. This is just what Christ Himself repeated.

The angel then explains the 70th week, dividing it into two parts of three and a half years, or 1,260 days each, and concludes by telling the prophet that the "prince to come," the "desolator," who is the same as the "Little Horn," out of the fourth Empire, will, at last, be destroyed under the vials of the outpoured wrath of God. The 70th week follows the Great Interval which itself follows the 69th week, or Death of Messiah, or Destruction of Jerusalem, i. e., "it closes the Church—Historical period or Times of the Gentiles, i. e., the period of Israel's national rejection, and lies directly in front of the Second Coming of Messiah." You see precisely, then, that the Great

Interval of Our Age

or Dispensation, lies between the 69th and the 70th weeks of Daniel, and that, after the 70th week, the Kingdom comes to Israel, not before. The interval is that of Israel's National non-existence. It is the period during which the Colossus of Gentile power still stands unstruck by the Mountain Stone. It is the period of the Valley of Dry Bones, during which Israel remains nationally dead in the grave. What a picture we have, as prophecy goes on developing the ages and the ends, of the condition of Israel in the age between the First and Second Coming of Christ, in fact from the Captivity to the Final Redemption! It is that of a vast graveyard as Ezekiel saw it. It is that of a proud Colossus, as Daniel saw it. Combine the two visions. What we have is the Colossus of Gentile power standing like a monumental stone in the midst of Israel's graveyard, with a "*Hic jacet Israel*" on the breast of the Image, a picture of Israel's national fate down to the time when the prophetic word and the Spirit of God reanimate dead Israel into national restoration and religious life, the Coming again of the Redeemer to Zion. Never can the kingdom come in the shape foretold in prophecy, until that Gentile Colossus comes down, and those bleaching bones are requickened by the Spirit of life from God. Impossible that the Millennial Age should be the time of Israel's national death and burial in the grave!

It is at the close of the 70th week that glory comes, a week still future. That 70th week in the whole time covered by

The Seals, Trumpets, and Vials

of John's Apocalypse. The apostle goes to Daniel for his "three and a half" or time times and half a time, or 1,260 days or forty-two months. He takes Daniel 9: 26, 27 and elaborates it and connects it organically with chapters second and seventh and twelfth. And just as the seventieth week in Daniel is to put an end to Israel's apostacy, and bring with it the recovery of Israel, the destruction of Antichrist, the overthrow of the Colossus or beast, and the resurrection of the faithful dead, so is it with John. After this seventieth week, and only after this, comes the Millennial Age and Israel's glory in the kingdom. At Messiah's first coming He was cut off and there was "nothing to Him;" at His second coming His enemies are cut off and there is everything to Him, a Messianic kingdom crown and people, a visible sovereignty under the whole heaven, a kingdom wide as the world.

* From his address at the Believers' Meeting for Bible Study held at Niagara. All the addresses at the Conference have been revised and corrected by the speakers and published in a pamphlet of 193 pages; price 50 cents, by *A. G. Watson*. Willard Tract Depository, Toronto, Ont., Canada.

CHRISTIAN HERALD AND SIGNS OF OUR TIMES.

OFFICE, 63 BIBLE HOUSE, NEW YORK.

ENTERED AT THE POST-OFFICE AT NEW YORK, N. Y., AS SECOND-CLASS MATTER.

Published Weekly. Subscription price, $1.50 a year; $1 eight months; 75 cents six months; sent two months on trial for 25 cents; always payable in advance. Single copies for sale by, or can be ordered at, all newsdealers.

Remittances by Mail should be by Post-office money order, bank cheques, or drafts or express money order, and should always be made payable to THE CHRISTIAN HERALD.

Receipts are not sent, the receipt of the paper by a subscriber is a sufficient proof that his remittance has been received. If the paper does not arrive promptly, please advise us, that we may see if the address is correctly entered.

Change of Address. Name of Post Office and State, of both old and new address, should always be given in case of removal.

CURRENT EVENTS.

Uniform Postage Throughout the North American continent is now an accomplished fact. The convention with Canada, which was signed on January 25, completes the work which was partially done by the convention with Mexico. Not only can a letter be mailed for two cents to any part of the continent, but small parcels of merchandise can be sent through the mails without the heavy charges for consul's fees previously exacted. A great commercial advantage is thus gained. Under the former postal convention no provision was made for the interchange of merchandise through the mails. A cumbrous and costly system of assessing duties consequently existed which is now simplified, and arrangements are made by which the post office collects the duty when the parcel is delivered.

The International Arbitration Question is now under consideration in the Senate Committee on foreign affairs. On January 23 Senator Hoar presented the Massachusetts Memorial, praying Congress to move in the matter. Senator Hoar in presenting the memorial referred to the deputation of English members of Parliament, which came last fall to present the project of arbitration of international disputes to the President. He said it was a message fit for the one country to send and the other country to welcome. It may be hoped that Congress will deal with the subject, as a treaty of that character between this country and England would form a precedent which other nations might follow. Its direct advantages also would be valuable. In case of a difficulty arising between the two Governments, the fact of both disputants being already pledged to arbitration, the necessity of fulfilling this pledge, at least in the first instance, might often tide over safely the only perilous period in the controversy.

The Urgent Need of Electoral Reform and the abuses most prominent in our present system formed the subject of an important debate in the Hall of the Young Men's Christian Association of New York, on January 24. Mr. Allen Thorndike Rice, who had a somewhat unhappy experience as a Congressional candidate in 1886, gave an exhaustive address on the subject. He stated that he was informed when he became a candidate that it would be necessary to hire a number of "workers" at five dollars a head, there being in every district a considerable vote that could be secured only in that way. He declined to appoint and pay workers, and lost the election. He said that any project of ballot reform will be imperfect unless it covers two strategic points. First, the candidate's money must cease to be an essential factor; secondly, absolute secrecy of the ballot must be ensured. The printing and distribution of tickets, he contended, ought to be a public expense, and if tickets were printed containing the name of every candidate, leaving the voter to erase the names of those for whom he did not vote or mark those for whom he did vote, the end would be secured without party bias. Mr. Rice said that under our present system the expenses of a successful candidature in a metropolitan district were so excessive that no poor man, had he the talents of a Webster, may expect election to any high office in the gift of the people without mortgaging his official action in advance to the persons, companies or organizations that defray his expenses. This fact alone would in time tend to destroy a Republican Government, and to substitute the rule of commercial oligarchies and political conspiracies for the rule of the people.

The Invitation from Australia to the United States to take part in the forthcoming International Exhibition at Melbourne, was formally accepted last week by the passage in the House of a joint resolution. An appropriation for the purpose was also made. The international fair in the capital of Victoria will open on the first of August and continue six months. This is only one of several such undertakings contemplated and in part arranged. In April an exhibition is to be held in Barcelona, and this will doubtless attract more American interest on account of its distance. Still more important will be next year's centennial show in Paris; and for this an appropriation of $200,000 is proposed in a bill now pending in Congress. In all these enterprises the manufacturers and producers of the United States are invited to participate.

Commercial Union with Canada was Directly proposed by a resolution introduced in the House of Representatives last week by Mr. Butterworth, of Ohio. He movéd that the United States should "use all proper means to secure an honorable, speedy and permanent adjustment of all differences and controversies in regard to the fisheries, and, in aid and support of the permanency of such adjustment, to remove all obstacles and hindrances to complete and unrestricted trade and commerce between the United States and the Dominion of Canada." The subject is not new; it has been freely discussed on both sides the border. The main difficulty in any such project is to arrange a tariff to suit both countries, as, if the Canadian tariff were lower than ours, foreign goods would reach our markets *via* Canada. In Canada, as in the States, there is opposition to commercial union, but Mr. Butterworth has acted wisely in testing the opinion of Congress on the subject.

A Mining Horror is Reported from British Columbia. On January 24 there was an explosion in the Wellington Mines at Nanaimo, B. C. Two hundred men were in the mine at the time, and it is now certain that fully half of them have perished. An eye-witness states that when about one hundred yards from the pit he heard a loud report, and there instantly shot far into the air a dense mass of smoke and dust. This continued for five minutes and then subsided, leaving everything apparently as before. A rescue party was at once sent down, but had to be drawn up again on account of the after damp. They saw many dead bodies, which they were unable to bring up. About sixty of these were subsequently recovered. The rescue party returned to the task on Thursday, but were unable to penetrate the recesses of the mine. They saw fifteen dead bodies lying close together. No noises could be heard, and it is feared that all in the mine are dead.

The Sufferings of the Miners on Strike in Pennsylvania appear to be extreme. Harrowing reports of children without food, and sick women in houses where there is neither food nor fuel, are being published. A movement was made last week anonymously, but purporting to originate with some of the men, to incite a revolt from the Union, and a return to work individually. The circular urging this step was, however, declared by the Knights of Labor to be the work of the Company, and it does not appear to have had any influence. Mr. Corbin, the President of the road, issued a statement of the Company's side of the dispute, which statement held out no hope of a settlement. He insisted on "the right of the Company to manage its own property, and the right to employ labor in the mining of the coal, so that the Company will have an equal chance with its neighbors in competitive markets."

The Arrest of Mr. Cox, an Irish Member of Parliament, took place on January 23. The charge against him is of attending meetings of the League after they had been proclaimed. He had succeeded in outwitting the Irish police after the warrant for his apprehension was issued. He managed to get to London, but was arrested there and sent to Ireland for trial. He has been lodged in Ennis jail, where he bitterly complains of cruel treatment. It is expected that his case will form the subject of an attack on the Government when Parliament meets. Mr Cox is popular, and many members of Parliament who have no sympathy with his political opinions are said to be personally well disposed toward him and will support his cause. Mr. William O'Brien, who was released from prison on January 20, is being enthusiastically welcomed in Irish cities. At Mallow a banquet was tendered him on January 25, at which he was profusely complimented. Further arrests of prominent Irish leaders are threatened.

An Attempt to Assassinate Louise Michel, the famous French female communist, was made on January 22. She was making an address at a meeting of anarchists, when a man in the audience named Lucas suddenly arose, and pointing a revolver at the speaker, fired two shots at her. She received a serious wound in the head, and the lobe of one of her ears was torn away. Lucas had a narrow escape from lynching at the hands of the infuriated anarchists, and it was only the timely arrival of the gendarmes that saved him. He was locked up. Louise has advocated assassination herself as a legitimate political weapon, so she will not be able to protest on principle against her enemies employing it.

Another Complication on the Franco-German frontier occurred on January 22, but happily it has not aroused French hostility, though the frequently occurring irritation on the frontier forms an element of danger to peaceful relations. "A man named Barbaret, seventy-one years old, was boar shooting in the Erlux district, near the frontier line, when a German customs officer signalled to him to approach. No sooner had the man done so than the officer attacked him. After a severe struggle the German got possession of Barbaret's rifle and ran off with it." The Prefect of Nancy made a report of the affair, in which he says that the French frontier was not violated by Hahnemann when he took Barbaret's gun away. Barbaret has not made a formal complaint to the Government against Hahnemann, and therefore the incident cannot be the subject of diplomatic representations.

The German Military Preparations are watched with interest throughout Europe. Their extent and the urgency with which they are pushed forward awakens uneasiness, as the inference is drawn that Bismarck regards war as probable. On January 26 the Minister of War announced to the Reichstag committee that the loan required on account of the new Military bill would amount to 280,000,000 marks ($66,640,000). He believed the Government would be enabled by the bill to complete the military organization. The amount of the loan which the bill authorized would be a non-recurring charge, which in general would not involve further permanent expenditure except for the interest on the capital, and for the sums necessary to increase the staff of officials, and to maintain the new buildings provided for in the bill. In time of peace the new army would only exist on paper, but if a war should break out, it would become an army of flesh and blood.

Contributions to the Fund for Supplying Colored ministers in the South with this journal were received last week to the amount of $15. They were from: Burmah, India, $1; Crawfordsville, Ind., $1.50; Mill Green, Ind., $5; New Market, N. J., 25c.; McDonald's Corners, Ont., Can., 75c.; Philadelphia, Penn., $1; North Omaha, Neb., $2.50; New York, N. Y., $1; Norwood, Ill., $2. We gratefully acknowledge the above receipts, and regard them as an answer to many prayers which have been offered for the maintenance of this most useful fund.

The Death of the Venerable Mother of the late President Garfield occurred on January 21. She was over eighty-five years old; her death was really from old age and a failure of the vital powers. It resembled nothing so much as a child falling asleep from weariness. It took place at the Garfield home at Mentor, where she was staying in the absence of her daughter-in-law in Europe. Eliza Ballou Garfield was a direct descendant of Maturin Ballou, a Huguenot, who in 1685, upon the revocation of the Edict of Nantes, fled to this country and settled at Cumberland, R. I. He built a church there, and until his death acted as its pastor. Mrs. Garfield was a deeply religious woman. Her distinguished son had profound reverence for her. It will be remembered that his first act after his inauguration was to go to where she was sitting and give her a filial kiss.

Three Distinguished Clergymen Narrowly escaped a shocking death on January 27. The Rev. Phillips Brooks, D. D., the Rev. Charles D. Cooper, D. D., and Rev. William N. McVickar, D. D., were riding in a carriage with Miss McVickar, to take part in the dedicatory services of the new Church of the Holy Comforter at Twenty-seventh and Wharton streets, Philadelphia. In crossing the Pennsylvania Railroad tracks near the Arsenal, the driver did not observe the approach of an engine. Happily the latter was going at a slow rate of speed. It struck the rear wheels of the carriage, overturning it and splintering it to fragments. The three clergymen and the lady escaped with a few bruises, but the driver was badly cut about the head. The clergymen had a hairbreadth escape. One moment later and all must have been killed.

An Amusing Change of Attitude is Described in a letter from an Englishman published in a New York journal last Thursday. It was written to a private correspondent, who desired to know what were the principles of social distinction in a country which had neither king nor aristocracy. The person receiving the letter being a vigorous opponent of republican institutions, gave the letter to the press. The writer of it stated that when he arrived in this country he presented several letters of introduction, in which he was introduced as Mr. ——. He was treated courteously, but received no special attention nor invitations. After he had been here some months, however, he met a lady at a public reception who had known him in England, and who addressed him by the title he wears as the eldest son of an English peer. "From that moment," says the visitor, "I was overwhelmed with attentions, was absurdly complimented and flattered, and received more invitations than it was possible to accept." The time is coming when a similar change of attitude will take place as to the Christian. It will be when God acknowledges him before the universe as His son and a heir of Heaven (Ja. 2:5).

Twelve Children Tied Together with Cords were led by their teacher, a heroic young lady nineteen years old, who carried another six year old child in her arms through the blizzard of January 12, to a place of safety. The children were in a school-house at Mira Valley, near Ord, Neb., when the storm came on. It was a frail frame structure, and the wind shook it so that the children were terror-stricken. The teacher did her best to encourage them, but foreseeing that if the wind increased the building must be overturned, she found some cord and securely fastened it around the waists of the children, attaching the end of it to herself. She had scarcely done so when a terrific gust carried the roof of the school-house away bodily. Taking the youngest and frailest of her charges in her arms, with all the words of encouragement she could muster, the courageous teacher started with her "team" of frightened little ones out into the fury of the storm. Those who have braved the terrors of a Nebraska blizzard need not be told that the act of that young girl was one from which strong men might quail. Selecting her way carefully, following in the course of the storm, the brave girl led her little charges through snow-drifts and blinding blizzard a wearisome journey of three-quarters of a mile, to a farm-house, where the little band received a hearty welcome. But for the teacher's presence of mind in tying the children together one or more must have been lost. So in the storms of life those who have committed themselves to Jesus are saved, being bound in love to each other and to their Saviour and Guide. (1 John 4: 21.)

Fifty Hours on the Mast of a Sunken Ship were passed by a captain and a sailor recently. A fisherman of Havre de Grace, Md., was walking along the shore on January 16; he noticed a strange object just above the waves about half a mile out to sea. He made out after a time that it was two men clinging to a mast. He lost no time in getting help, and in a short time two small boats were on their way to the wreck. After a gallant struggle they reached the spot, and the two miserable men were taken on board. One of them, who proved to be the captain of the submerged vessel, said that three days before he had sailed from Baltimore on board a schooner. They had not been out more than six hours when they encountered a gale, which increased in severity until morning, when the mainsail was torn to shreds. While drifting before the gale she struck a heavy cake of ice, sprung a-leak and immediately filled. The men had to leap for their lives, climb on a spar, and only by the hardest work, gained the masthead, to which they clung until taken off. They had been there without food or water for fifty hours. When rescued, the captain's hands were frozen stiff, and his companion was also badly frostbitten. If relief had not come, as it did both men must have fallen off. Their joy, when they saw the boats coming to take them off the mast, may be imagined. Such joy would sinners feel on hearing of salvation through Christ, if they realized their danger of destruction, as the two shipwrecked men did. (Matt. 24: 37, 38.)

Either Marriage or Imprisonment was the alternative presented to a Polish immigrant by Judge Ehrlich in the New York City police court last week. A good-looking, intelligent Polish girl was the complainant in his case. She stated that he came from Rupin, in Poland, in which place she also was born. Two or three years ago, while living there, they became engaged to be married. At the time he suggested that America be their future home. As he was poor, he proposed that she proceed to New York, and, by work, save enough money to send for him. This she did. By manual labor she saved up enough money to pay for her lover's passage. He came, but knowing no trade, was not able to take care of himself. Undaunted, she sent him to a school, where he was to learn to make cloaks. She paid his board during this time, and gave him money from her own earnings. He rewarded her by running away, and, when captured, he refused to marry her. She then brought suit against him for $2,000 damages for breach of promise. He was arrested Tuesday and passed the night in jail, as he could not furnish $2,000 bail. The case was so clear against him that a lengthened period of incarceration seemed inevitable, and the judge explained to him that the only way to avert it was to marry the girl, as he had promised. The man preferred to do so rather than go back to prison, and the judge thereupon married them in court. A man so worthless as to desert a girl, who had made so many sacrifices for him, richly deserved imprisonment without the alternative of marriage. So it will be perceived at the Day of Judgment. Sinners who have rejected Christ and despised His sacrifice will deserve no pity. (Heb. 10: 29.)

A Leap Into Fire to Save a Comrade was taken by a fireman, in New York, on January 23. A large four-story brick building in Pearl Street was burning fiercely, and there being no alley-way at the rear, the firemen had great difficulty in getting water on that part of the structure, which appeared to be the centre of the conflagration. At length two men ventured on the roof and carried a hose across it from the front to the rear. Scarcely had they placed it in position when the roof fell in, carrying one of the men with it right into the raging flames. The other man clung to the cornice and quickly scrambled to the top of the wall. No sooner, however, did he perceive his comrade's danger than, seizing the end of a rope, he jumped down after him, dragged him out of the flames and tied the rope around his body, under his arms. Then climbing to the top of the wall again he hauled the unconscious man up. It was quickly done, and but for his promptitude the man must have burned to death, for he was completely overcome by the heat and his clothing was on fire. The rescuer also was severely scorched in his struggle. Many men who are enthusiastic when they hear of such a gallant rescue are indifferent when they are told of Him who, seeing a whole world in danger of perishing, descended to a life of hardship and a death of ignomy, that it might be saved. (Heb. 12: 2.)

BRIEF NOTES.

Dr. Justin D. Fulton delivered two lectures on the subject, "Why Priests should Wed," in Cooper Union, New York, on January 25 and 26.

The law passed by the present Tennessee Legislature prohibiting the playing of base ball on Sunday is pronounced constitutional by the Supreme Court.

Dr. Dorchester, in his "Latest Church Statistics in the United States," states that there are 4,601,416 Methodists in this country, and 3,729,745 Baptists.

A Women's Christian Temperence Union has been organized in Switzerland. Mdle. Frey, the daughter of the Swiss pastor at Aarau, is the secretary.

A lady who visits the inmates of jails and hospitals, would be grateful if subscribers to this journal would mail to her any old copies they may have to spare for distribution. Her address is, Mrs. E. Schwieman, 1225 Diversy Avenue, Chicago, Ill.

At Tokio, Japan, the Women's Christian Temperance Union recently celebrated its second anniversary. An eloquent address was delivered by Miss Shige Kushida. Two gentlemen in the audience gave fifty dollars each to the funds of the Union.

In France a movement is on foot which seeks the enforcement of the laws against the sale of immoral publications. A petition to be presented to the French Senate praying for the interference of the national legislature is being numerously signed.

A new mission for soldiers and sailors, to be known as the Mizpah Sailors' Rest, was opened at West Tenth and Washington streets, New York, on January 21. It is situated in a room formerly occupied as a bar-room, the owner of the building, it is said, refusing to lease it again for that purpose.

The value of the New York Society for the Prevention of Cruelty to Children is proved by the fact that during the past year 5,849 complaints were received and investigated by the Society, 1,900 cases prosecuted, 1,848 convictions secured, and 2,755 children were rescued and relieved. One hundred and fifteen children who were lost, stolen or strayed were returned to their parents.

The meetings conducted by the Rev. B. Fay Mills in Philadelphia have been wonderfully fruitful of results. Presbyterians Methodists, Baptists, Episcopalians, Lutherans, German Reformed and Congregationalists united in the work. Five hundred persons have made a profession of faith in Christ. On Sunday evening, January 15, from three to four hundred arose to ask for prayer.

Mr. D. L. Moody's meetings in Louisville, Ky., are stirring that city to its centre, and are having a wide influence. They are held in a tabernacle built for them at a cost of $10,000. It is warmed by steam and lighted by electricity, and has a seating capacity for four thousand persons. A telephone connected with the platform enables an invalid confined to her bed to hear the singing and sermon. The afternoon meetings are held in Warren Memorial Presbyterian Church, and there is an attendance of two thousand. Mr. Moody's next engagement is in California.

THE SECRET OF POWER.

A New Sermon by Pastor C. H. Spurgeon.

"If ye abide in Me, and My words abide in you, ye shall ask what ye will, and it shall be done unto you." John 15 : 7.

Degrees of Attainment Indicated—The Highest for Abiders in Christ—I. What the Special Blessing Is—Certain Exercise of Prayer—Liberty in Prayer—Success in Prayer—The Peerage of the Skies—II. How it is to be Attained—What Abiding Is—The Vine and the Branches—Abiding While Being Purged—And Afterward—His Words Also to Abide—III. Why it is So Attained—The Will Subdued—Safe to be Trusted—Sin a Bar to Success in Prayer.

THE gifts of grace are not enjoyed all at once by believers. Coming unto Christ, we are saved by a true union with Him; but it is by abiding in that union that we further receive the purity, the joy, the power, the blessedness, which are stored up in Him for His people.

There are these degrees of attainment among believers, and the Saviour here incites us to reach a high position by mentioning a certain privilege which is not for all who say that they are in Christ, but for those only who are *abiders* in Him. Every believer should be an abider, but many have hardly earned the name as yet. Jesus says, "If ye abide in Me, and My words abide in you, ye shall ask what ye will, and it shall be done unto you." You have to live with Christ to know Him, and the longer you live with Him the more will you admire and adore Him; yes, and the more will you receive from Him, even grace for grace. Truly, He is a blessed Christ to one who is but a month old in grace; but these babes can hardly tell what a precious Jesus He is to those whose acquaintance with Him covers well-nigh half a century! Jesus, in the esteem of abiding believers, grows sweeter and dearer, fairer and more lovely, day by day. Not that He improves in Himself, for He is perfect; but that as we increase in our knowledge of Him, we appreciate more thoroughly His matchless excellences. I call your earnest attention to the text, begging you to consider with me

Three Questions.

I. What is this special blessing? Let us read the verse again. Jesus says, "If ye abide in Me, and My words abide in you, ye shall ask what ye will, and it shall be done unto you." Observe that our Lord had been warning us that, severed from Him we can do nothing, and He does not now speak of what they should themselves be enabled to do, but of what should be done unto them: "it shall be done unto you." He does not say, "If ye abide in Me, and My words abide in you, ye shall do spiritual things;" but, "ye shall ask." By prayer you shall be enabled to do; but before all attempts to do, "ye shall ask." The choice privilege here given is a mighty prevailing prayerfulness. Power in prayer is very much the gauge of our spiritual condition; and when that is secured to us in a high degree, we are favored as to other matters.

One of the first results, then, of our abiding union with Christ will be the certain exercise of prayer: "Ye shall ask." If others neither seek nor knock nor ask, ye, at any rate, shall do so. Those who keep away from Jesus do not pray. Those in whom communion with Christ is suspended, feel as if they could not pray; but Jesus says, "If ye abide in Me, and My words abide in you, ye shall ask."

Prayer Comes Spontaneously

from those who abide in Jesus, even as certain Oriental trees, without pressure, shed their fragrant gums. Prayer is the natural outgushing of a soul in communion with Jesus. Just as the leaf and the fruit will come out of the vine-branch without any conscious effort on the part of the branch, but simply because of its living union with the stem, so prayer buds and blossoms and fruits out of souls abiding in Jesus. As stars shine, so do abiders pray. It is their use and their second nature. Habitual asking comes out of abiding in Christ. You will not need urging to prayer when you are abiding with Jesus: He says, "Ye shall ask;" and, depend upon it, you will.

You shall also feel most powerfully the necessity of prayer. Your great need of prayer will be vividly seen: Do I hear you say—"What! When we abide in Christ, and his words abide in us, have we not already attained?" Far are we, then, from being satisfied; it is then that we feel more than ever that we must ask for more grace. He that knows Christ best, knows his own necessities best. Prayer is now as much a necessity of our spiritual life as breath is of our natural life: we cannot live without asking favors of the Lord. "If ye abide in me, and my words abide in you, ye *shall* ask:" and ye shall not wish to cease from asking.

Note next, that the fruit of our abiding is not only the exercise of prayer, and a sense of the necessity of prayer, but it includes

Liberty in Prayer:

"Ye shall ask what ye will." Have you not been on your knees at times without power to pray? Have you not felt that you could not plead as you desired? You wanted to pray, but the waters were frozen up, and would not flow. You said mournfully, "I am shut up, and cannot come forth." The will was present, but not the freedom to present that will in prayer. Do you, then, desire liberty in prayer, so that you may speak with God as a man speaketh with his friend? Here is the way to it: "If ye abide in Me, and My words abide in you, ye shall ask what ye will." I do not mean that you will gain liberty as to mere fluency of utterance, for that is a very inferior gift. Fluency is a questionable endowment, especially when it is not attended with weight of thought and depth of feeling. Some brethren pray by the yard; but true prayer is measured by weight, and not by length. A single groan before God may have more fullness of prayer in it than a fine oration of great length. He that dwells with God in Christ Jesus, he is the man whose steps are enlarged in intercession. Thus shall you become Israels, and, as princes, have power with God. This is not all: the favored man has the privilege of successful prayer. There is a great breadth in this text, "Ye shall ask what ye will, and it shall be done unto you." The Lord gives the abider *carte blanche*. He puts into his hand a signed cheque, and permits him to fill it up as he wills.

Does this text mean what it says? I never knew my Lord to say anything he did not mean. I am sure that He may sometimes mean more than we understand Him to say, but He never means less. Mind you, He does not say to all men, "I will give you whatever you ask." Oh no; that would be an unkind kindness: but He speaks to His disciples, and says, "If ye abide in Me, and My words abide in you, ye shall ask what ye will, and it shall be done unto you." It is to a certain class of men who have already received great grace at His hands—it is to them He commits this marvellous power of prayer.

O my dear friends, if I may covet earnestly one thing above every other, it is this; that I may be able to ask what I will of the Lord, and have it. The prevailer in prayer is the man to preach successfully, for he may well prevail with man for God when he has already prevailed with God for men. This is the man to face the difficulties of business life; for what can baffle him when he can take all to God in prayer? One such man as this, or one such woman as this, in a church is worth ten thousand of us common people. In these we find

The Peerage of the Skies.

The text seems to imply that, if we reach this point of privilege, this gift shall be a perpetuity: "Ye shall ask," ye shall always ask; ye shall never get beyond asking, but ye shall ask successfully, for "ye shall ask what ye will, and it shall be done unto you." Here we have the gift of continual prayer. Not for the week of prayer, not during a month's conference, nor upon a few special occasions, shall ye pray prevailingly; but ye shall possess this power with God so long as you abide in Christ, and His words abide in you. God will put His omnipotence at your disposal; He will put forth His Godhead to fulfil the desires which His own Spirit has inwrought in you. I wish I could make this jewel glitter before the eyes of all the saints till they cried out, "Oh that we had it!" This power in prayer is like the sword of Goliath: wisely may every David say—"There is none like it; give it me." Oh, come, let us seek this boon. Listen, and learn the way.

II. The privilege of mighty prayerfulness—

How is it to be Obtained?

The answer is, "If ye abide in me, and my words abide in you." Here are the two feet by which we climb to power with God in prayer. Beloved, the first line tells us that we are to abide in Christ Jesus our Lord. It is taken for granted that we are already in Him. May it be taken for granted in your case, dear hearer? If so, you are to abide where you are. But abiding in the Lord Jesus does not only mean trusting in Him; it includes our yielding ourselves up to Him to receive His life, and to let that life work out its results in us. We live *in* Him, *by* Him, *for* Him, *to* Him, when we abide in Him. We feel that all our separate life has gone: for "ye are dead, and your life is hid with Christ." We have no reason for existence except that which we find in Christ; and what a marvellous reason that is!

As if to help us to understand this, our gracious Lord has given us a delightful parable. Let us look through this discourse of the vine and its branches. Jesus says, "Every branch in Me that beareth fruit, He purgeth it." Take care that you abide in Christ when you are being purged. "Oh," says one, "I thought I was a Christian; but, alas! I have more troubles than ever: men ridicule me, the devil tempts me, and my business affairs go wrong." Brother, if you are to have power in prayer you must take care that you abide in Christ

When The Sharp Knife is Cutting

everything away. Endure trial, and never dream of giving up your faith because of it. Say, "Though He slay me, yet will I trust in Him." Your Lord warned you when you first came into the vine that you would have to be purged and cut closely; and if you are now feeling the purging process, you must not think that some strange thing hath happened unto you. Rebel not because of anything you may have to suffer from the dear hand of your heavenly Father, who is the husbandman of the vineyard. No, but cling to Jesus all the more closely. Say, "Cut, Lord, cut to the quick if Thou wilt; but I will cling to Thee." Yes, cling to Jesus when the knife is in His hand, and so "shall ye ask what ye will, and it shall be done unto you."

Take care, also, that when the purging operation has been carried out you still cleave to your Lord. Notice the third verse: "Now ye are clean through the word I have spoken unto you."

Abide After Cleansing

where you were before cleansing. When you are sanctified, abide where you were when first justified. When you see the work of the Spirit increasing in you, do not let the devil tempt you to boast that now you are somebody, and need not come to Jesus as a poor sinner, and rest in His precious blood alone for salvation. Abide still in Jesus. As you kept to Him when the knife cut you, keep to Him now that the tender grapes begin to form. Do not say to yourself, "What a fruitful branch I am! How greatly I adorn the vine! Now I am full of vigor!" Our whole hope lies in Jesus at our best times as well as at our worst.

Yea, abide in Him as to your very life. Do not say, "I have been a Christian man now twenty or thirty years; I can do without continued dependence upon Christ." No, you could not do without Him if you were as old as Methuselah. Your very being as a Christian depends upon your still clinging, still trusting, still depending; and this He must give you, for it all comes from Him, and Him alone. To sum it all up, if you want that splendid power in prayer of which I spoke just now, you must remain in loving, living, lasting, conscious, practical, abiding union with the Lord Jesus Christ; and if you get to that by divine grace, then you shall ask what you will, and it shall be done unto you. But there is

A Second Qualification

mentioned in the text, and you must not forget it—"*and my words abide in you.*" How important, then, are Christ's words! He said in the fourth verse, "Abide in me, and I in you," and now, as a paralled to this, it is, "If ye abide in me, and my words abide in you." We must obey His precepts or He will not accept us as disciples. Especially that precept of love which is the essence of all His words. We must love God and our brethren; yea, we must cherish love to all men, and seek their good. Anger and malice must be far from us. We must walk even as He walked. If Christ's words abide not in thee, both as to belief and practice, thou art not in Christ. Christ and His gospel and His commands are one. If thou wilt not have Christ and His words, neither will He have thee nor thy words; but thou shalt ask in vain, thou shalt by and by give up asking, thou shalt become as a withered branch.

III. It is my last work to try to show why this privilege should be so obtained. This extraordinary power of prayer,

Why is it Given

to those who abide in Christ? May what I have to say encourage you to make the glorious attempt to win this pearl of great price! Why is it, that abiding in Christ, and having His words abide in us, we get to this liberty and prevalence in prayer? I answer, first, because of the fullness of Christ. You may very well ask what you will when you abide in Christ, because whatsoever you may inquire is already lodged in Him. Good Bishop Hall worked out this thought in a famous passage. I will give you the substance of it. Do you desire the grace of the Spirit? Go to your Lord's anointing. Do you seek holiness? Go to His example. Do you desire pardon of sin? Look to His blood. Do you need mortification of sin? Look to His crucifixion. Do you need to be buried to the world? Go to His tomb. Do you want to feel the fullness of a heavenly life? Behold His resurrection. Would you rise above the world? Mark His ascension. Would you contemplate heavenly things? Remember His session at the right hand of God, and know that He "hath raised us up together, and made us sit together in heavenly places." I see clearly enough why the branch gets all it wants while it abides in the stem, since all it wants is already in the stem, and is there for the branch.

The next reason for this is, the richness of the Word of God. Catch this thought, "If My words abide in you, ye shall ask what ye will, and it shall be done unto you." The best praying man is the man who is most believingly familiar with the promises of God. After all, prayer is but taking God's promises to Him, and saying to Him, "Do as Thou hast said." Prayer is the promise utilized. A prayer which is not based on a promise has no true foundation. Study what Jesus has said, what the Holy Ghost has left on record in this divinely inspired Book, and in proportion as you feed on the Word, and are filled with the Word, and retain the Word in your faith, and obey the Word in your life—in that proportion you will be a master-man in the art of prayer. You have acquired skill as a wrestler with the covenant angel in proportion as you can plead the promises of your God.

A Safe Promise.

Let us go a little further: you still may say you do not quite see why a man who abides in Christ, and in whom Christ's words abide, should be allowed to ask whatever he wills, and it shall be done unto him. I answer you again: it is so, because in such a man as that there is a predominance of grace which causes him to have a renewed will, which is according to the will of God. Suppose a man of God is in prayer, and he thinks that such and such a thing is desirable, yet he remembers that he is nothing but a babe in the presence of his all-wise Father, and so he bows his will, and asks as a favor to be taught what to will. Though God bids him ask what he wills, he shrinks and cries, "My Lord, here is a request which I am not quite clear about. As far as I can judge, it is a desirable thing, and I will it; but, Lord,

I am not Fit to Judge

for myself, and therefore I pray Thee, give not as I will, but as Thou wilt." Do you not see that, when we are in such a condition as this, our real will is God's will. Deep down in our hearts we will only that which the Lord Himself wills; and what is this but to ask what we will, and it is done to us? It becomes safe for God to say to the sanctified soul, "Ask what thou wilt, and it shall be done unto thee."

You clearly see that the holy God cannot pick up a common man in the street, and say to him, "I will give you whatsoever you will." What would he ask for? He would ask for a good drink, or permission to enjoy himself in evil lust. It would be very unsafe to trust the most of men with this permit. But when the Lord has taken a man, and has new-made him, has quickened him into newness of life, and has formed him in the image of His dear Son, then He can trust him.

I have not quite done. A man will succeed in prayer when his faith is strong; and this is the case with those who abide in Jesus. It is faith that prevails in prayer. The real eloquence of prayer is a believing desire. "All things are possible to him that believeth." A man abiding in Christ with Christ's words abiding in him, is eminently a believer, and consequently eminently successful in prayer. He has strong faith indeed, for his faith has brought him into vital contact with Christ, and he is therefore at the source of every blessing, and may drink to his full at the well itself.

O dear brother in Christ, if thy prayers speed not at the throne, suspect that there is

Some Sin That Hinders

them: thy Father's love sees a necessity for chastening thee this way. If thou dost not abide in Christ, how canst thou hope to pray successfully? If thou dost pick and choose of His words, and doubt this, and doubt that, how canst thou hope to speed at the throne? If thou art wilfully disobedient to any one of His words, will not this account for failure in prayer? But abide thou in Christ, and take fast hold upon His words, and be altogether His disciple, then shalt thou be heard of Him. Sitting at Jesus' feet, hearing His words, thou mayest lift up thine eyes to His dear face, and say, "My Lord, hear me now"; and He will answer thee graciously; He will say unto thee, "I have heard thee in a time accepted, and in the day of salvation have I succored thee. Ask what thou wilt, and it shall be done unto thee."

Unhappily, to a portion of this congregation my text says nothing at all; for some of you are not even in Christ, and therefore

Cannot Abide

in Him. O sirs, what shall I say to you? You seem to me to miss a very heaven now. If there were no hell hereafter, it is hell enough not to know Christ now, not to know what it is to prevail with God in prayer, not to know the choice privilege of abiding in Him and His words abiding in you. Your first matter is that you believe in Jesus Christ to the saving of your souls, yielding your souls to His cleansing, your lives to His government. God hath sent Him forth as a Saviour; accept Him. Receive Him as your Teacher; yield yourself up to Him as your Master. May His gracious Spirit come and do this work upon you now; and then, after this, but not before, you may aspire to this honor.

First of all—"Ye must be born again." I cannot say to you as you are now, "Grow," because you will only grow a bigger sinner. However much you may be developed, you will only develop what is in you: and that is, the heir of wrath will become more and more the child of evil. You must be made anew in Christ: there must be an absolute change, a reversal of all the currents of nature, a making you a new creature in Christ Jesus; and then you may aspire to abide in Christ, and let His words abide in you, and the consequent prevalence with God in prayer shall be yours. Gracions Lord, come Thyself, and uplift us to Thyself, for Thy mercy's sake. Amen.

[The prayers of the readers of this journal are requested for the blessing of God upon its Editors, and those whose sermons, articles or labors for Christ are printed in it; and that its circulation may be used by the Holy Spirit for the conversion of many sinners and the quickening of God's people. Dr. Talmage and Mr. Spurgeon especially request prayer every Sunday morning on behalf of their labors.].

GEMS FROM NEW BOOKS.

An Engineer's Vindication.*

A STRIKING instance, which illustrates the reign of necessity in these adjustments of physical elements, occurred some years ago, at Revere, Mass. The Beverly express ran into the Bangor accommodation, as it stood at the station, passing half-way through one car before it stopped. The engineer was arrested, and tried for manslaughter. He affirmed that he was running on the schedule time, fifteen miles an hour; the prosecution charged that he was running thirty miles an hour. The weight of the express was furnished to one of the professors in the Massachusetts Institute of Technology, who calculated the momentum of the train and the inertia of the car, and found that the momentum at fifteen miles an hour would be just enough to carry the express half-way through the car. At thirty miles an hour, the momentum would have carried it four times as far. The engineer was, of course, at once released.

The Kaffir's Problems.

It is almost a revelation of the working of the Heathen mind, that we have in the words of a Kaffir, Sekese, to the French traveller, M. Arbrouseille, on the subject of Christianity: 'Your tidings are what I want, and I was seeking, before I knew you, as you shall hear and judge for yourself. Twelve years ago, I went to feed my flocks. The weather was hazy. I sat down upon a rock, and asked myself sorrowful questions—yes, sorrowful, because I was unable to answer them. 'Who has touched the stars with his hands? On what pillars do they rest?' I asked myself. 'The waters never weary: They know no other law than to flow without ceasing from morning till night, and from night till morning; but where do they stop, and who makes them flow thus? The clouds also come and go, and burst in water over the earth. Whence come they? Who sends them? The diviners certainly do not give us rain, for how could they do it? And why do not I see them with my own eyes when they go up to heaven to fetch it? I cannot see the wind, but what is it? Who brings it—makes it blow and roar and terrify us? Do I know how the corn sprouts? Yesterday there was not a blade in my field: to-day I returned to the field, and found some. Who can have given the earth the wisdom and the power to produce it?' Then I buried my head in both my hands."

Mutinous Convicts Subdued.

The highest type of heroism is impossible without a grand moral ideal and moral courage. Instances are numerous of the control of large and infuriated masses of people by one man of great moral power.

Years ago, in a penitentiary in one of the Eastern States, the convicts, to the number of several hundred, mutinied one morning, and drove their keepers from the shop in which they were at work. The Warden sent, in affright, to the adjacent city for aid. A United States army officer was in the city, with a mere handful of troops—twenty-five or thirty—and

* From "The Gist of It," by Rev. Thomas E. Barr, B. A., a profoundly philosophical work for young students, proving more cogently and more conclusively than any book we know of, that Christianity alone is the solution of the problem of life, and is the best preparation a man can have for right living in the world of to-day: 350 pages; Price $1.50; published by *A. C. Armstrong & Son*, 714 Broadway, N. Y.

A School Teacher and a Pupil in Dakota in the Blizzard of January 12.

Two Victims of the Blizzard.

at once went to the prison. The convicts were all gathered at one end of the shop, a long building, armed with axes, hammers, chisels, and other tools of their work. Filing in at the opposite end of the building, the intrepid officer drew up his little company in line, bade them load their muskets in full view of the prisoners, and take careful aim at the crowd; then, taking out his watch, he said to the criminals, "The man that remains in this building at the end of three minutes shall be shot dead." What cared that throng of armed desperadoes, in the first flush of partial freedom, for the bunch of troops facing them? But a minute is a long, long time to stand and look quietly into the muzzle of a loaded gun, with no sound save the ticking of the watch whose moving hands determine the instant when the falling hammer will speed the ball on its errand of death. Ere it elapsed, some of the convicts nearest the door dropped quietly out; and, before half the allotted time had gone by, the entire number had left the shop, and returned to their cells.

Garfield's Control of a Mob.

On the morning of April 15, 1865, when the nation was thrilling in anger and indefinable dread at the assassination of President Lincoln, a mass of fifty thousand men gathered in New York City around the Exchange Building. General B. F. Butler addressed but was not able to disperse them. The crowd were armed, enraged. Suddenly, from the extreme right wing of the crowd rose a cry, "*The World!* The office of *The World! The World!*" and the mass began to move, as one man, toward that office. Where would this end? Destruction of property, loss of life, violence and anarchy, were in that movement, and apparently no human power could now check its progress. Then a man stepped to the front of the balcony, and held his arm aloft. His commanding attitude arrested universal attention. Perhaps he was going to give them the latest news. They waited. But while they listened, the voice—it was the voice of General Garfield—only said: "Fellow-citizens, clouds and darkness are round about Him. His pavilion is dark waters and thick clouds of the skies. Justice and judgment are the establishment of His throne. Mercy and truth shall go before His face. Fellow-citizens, God reigns, and the Government at Washington still lives." The tide of popular fury was stayed. The impossible had been accomplished. *The World* was saved, but that was not much. The safety of a great city was secured, and that was much. Such are the achievements of moral power, and well may one aspire to its possession and exercise.

THE BLIZZARD'S VICTIMS.

(See Illustrations.)

IT will be long before the blizzard of January 11–14 is forgotten in the Northwest. From Dakota, Minnesota, Wisconsin, Iowa and Nebraska the most distressing details of suffering and death continue to arrive. It is stated by one journal that when the list of the dead and missing is fully made up, the victims will be found to number *nearly one thousand*. Two hundred and thirty-eight bodies have already been found. Among the incidents reported are some that display heroism of a most exalted type. At Stoloff, Dak., a school teacher named Miss Jacobson observed the storm coming up, and fearing that one of her pupils, a delicate child, might be lost in the snow, started out to accompany her to her home. The blinding wind, laden with fine particles of snow, completely hid the path from them; they lost their way, and both perished. When their bodies were found, Miss Jacobson was found crouched in a hollow of the ground, the child tightly clasped in her arms and her dress skirt wrapped around the little one (*See Illustration*). Mary Connell, another teacher near Cavour, also attempted to convey a child to her home, and was lost; but, knowing the danger of standing still or resting a moment, she plodded with her little charge heroically all night long (*See Illustration*), and when morning came, was met by a party of searchers and conveyed to a house for shelter.

The searching parties who went out to look for missing friends were obliged to connect themselves with each other by ropes, so blinding was the storm, and so hopeless was any attempt to keep together in the teeth of the wind that tore across the prairie. But very few of the persons who were so unhappy as to be caught in the open by the sudden storm survived. A number of the dead had the appearance of having died from suffocation. Some had torn their clothing away from their throats, and others had thrown away their head-covering, and were clutching at their throats, as though struggling for breath. During a genuine blizzard such as this the air is filled with fine ice dust, driven with terrific force, which chokes the unfortunate victim in a short time if he attempts to stand against it. Several passengers on the trains died in the cars of cold after the trainmen found it impossible to go farther. The children especially succumbed, though it is worthy of note that the male passengers in many cases took off their overcoats and wraps to protect the little ones.

Sufferings from the intense cold are reported from other States and Territories, from Montana to Texas. In western Kansas the number of destitute people is said to be most alarming. Many have perished, and others are in an emaciated condition.

AGNES MENDON'S PICTURE.

(See Illustration on page 77.)

A LADY, neatly but inexpensively dressed, timidly entered a picture dealer's store in Philadelphia one cold winter's morning, and asked to see the proprietor. The clerk who spoke to her knew by her manner as well as by the flat, thin parcel she carried, what her business was. He was a sympathetic, kindly man, and he felt sorry for her.

"Poor creature!" he said to a fellow-clerk, when he reached the back part of the store, after placing a seat for her; "she is only just beginning, I think. It's awful to think what she will have to go through before she learns that she can't earn her living that way."

Agnes Mendon had plenty of time to look around her while she waited for the picture dealer, and what she saw did not tend to raise her spirits. Pictures infinitely superior to that she had brought to sell were scattered around in profusion. It seemed to her that purchasers rather than venders were the need there. Still she had built her hopes on the picture. Her work used to be much admired when she did it as an amateur, and the fact had encouraged her to hope that it might support her now that she was penniless. If she could get but a small sum for this, and an order for the other picture half-finished on her easel at home, she might hope. Her heart was throbbing with anxiety and suspense when the clerk told her that his principal had arrived and would see her at once.

A very few minutes sufficed to crush out the hope she had cherished. So many pictures were offered, the dealer said, some of them of real merit, as if hers had only the mere pretence of merit, that he had already a larger stock than he needed, and had stopped buying for the present. Agnes was too much crestfallen and the dealer's manner was too decisive to allow of any pleading, and she took up her rejected picture and left the store. The tears would come into her eyes, strive as she might, but she restrained them until she reached home, and then she let them have their course. They relieved her a little, but they brought no relief to her anxiety. She went into the little room where she had spent so much time over her work, and sat down before her unfinished picture. She took up her brush almost mechanically, but she could not proceed. Of what use was it to finish the picture, if she could not sell it? She sat gazing at it in a reverie, her mind wandering off into scenes far different from her present surroundings.

Life was very hard for poor Agnes. Up to a year ago her every want was supplied, and she had money in her pocket for charity. Her father was reputed wealthy, but when he died his executor was unable by the sale of all he possessed to discharge his indebtedness. Agnes was told the condition of affairs, and, rather than allow any reproach to attach to her dear, dead father's name, she placed her little fortune, the bequest of a distant relative, at the disposal of the executor, desiring him with that to pay every dollar of indebtedness. It was not just, it was not necessary, the executor said; the creditors had no legal claim upon her. But Agnes persisted, and the result was that she was penniless, and was trying to earn her bread with her pencil.

Agnes Mendon's Reverie.

As she sat motionless, looking sadly and wearily at her picture, all those years of happy youth passed before her mental vision. What misery her father would have endured could he have foreseen her present plight! He had been spared that sorrow, however, and on that account Agnes was thankful. She was still sure that she did right in sacrificing her own property to save his good name; she believed God would provide for her in some way. Still, cold and hunger were very dreadful things to this gently nurtured lady, and they appeared to be not so far away from her. She shuddered as she remembered the death of a poor girl who had been found one cold night near her father's house, and had been sheltered and cared for there, but too late to save her. The doctors had said she died of starvation. Agnes wondered if she would end like that. No; she thought not. Her faith in God was too strong to have such a fear. She would go to Him now and place her case in His hands; perhaps light would come. Light did come into her heart, though her mind had no light as to her plans; but she felt calmer, and having cast her burden on the Lord, could wait His time. None who put faith from them can realize what they lose in their own souls. Even if prayer brought no answer, its effect on the praying Christian cannot be overestimated. It gives peace, rest, confidence, hope.

It seemed for several weeks as if no other blessing was coming to Agnes. Every day the meagre store of money she had left grew smaller, though she husbanded it with the utmost vigilance. But she never ceased to pray, and her confidence that God would undertake for her eventually, never faltered. She answered advertisements, sought work of any kind, and made application to everyone who might be able to find her employment. Failure attended every effort. She had not the self-confidence and boldness that help some women to make their way, and as she had not been educated to earn her livelihood the qualities she could offer in the market were not marketable. One morning she changed her last dollar bill, and before doing so she spread it before God and with tears besought Him to look upon her in her extremity. She went out again on her pitiful quest, and there was no occupation now so menial that she would have refused it, if it would only bring her bread.

"Ah, Miss Mendon!" said a strong, cheery voice beside her, "how are you doing? I have not seen you for an age."

Agnes looked up and saw that her father's executor had overtaken her, and was by her side. He had warned her of this very trouble that had come upon her, when she insisted upon parting with her money, and now she shrank from letting him know that his predictions were fulfilled. But concealment was impossible; her worn, weary face told the story. "Not starved to death yet, you see," was the answer, which she tried to make gay, but with poor effect.

"No," he said, "but you look pretty near it. What are you doing?"

"Looking for employment."

"And failing, of course. You should have come to me before. I suppose your pride kept you away. You thought I should taunt you with being wrong after all. Well, I won't, for you are a brave woman. Now I think I can help you. I will see what can be done, and you come to me to-morrow and find out how I have succeeded. Good morning," and he hurried away.

Though there was no definite prospect of relief, yet Agnes instinctively felt that her troubles were near their end, and she returned home and offered thanks to God. He had heard her, she was sure; and in advance she poured out grateful words from her heart.

The next day, with a brighter look than her face had worn for many a day, she went to her friend's office.

"I have good news for you," he said, "and you will like it all the better because it is the result of your Quixotic self-sacrifice. One of your late father's creditors needs a lady to take charge of his house. He is a widower, and has had rather a painful experience with a variety of housekeepers—some of them dishonest, and some incapable. I told him I knew exactly the person to suit him, and when he heard who it was, and remembered how you behaved about that little matter of the deficiency, he was as eager to secure your services as you could wish. It is an easy position, and the pay is good. He is inundated with applicants, but he will listen to none until he knows if you will accept. Here is his address; either see him or write him, and arrange at once."

Tears of joy and thankfulness filled Agnes Mendon's eyes as she listened. Her long fight with poverty was ended, and her heart was full of gratitude. Her future was better than she hoped or knew at that time; for her refinement and pious cheerfulness so won upon her employer's heart, that he pleaded with her, and eventually succeeded in persuading her to enter into a closer relationship.

THE FAMILY OF TRIPE COURT.

By Brenda.

(*Continued from page 62.*)

THE TEMPERANCE PARTY.

No one of the neighbors who saw him depart with Bridget in the cab from Tripe Court that morning, expected Tom Mite to return at night in other condition than that of drunkenness. Jemmy Wiggles might make him "pass the corners" in his cab going to the Infirmary, but coming back Tom would be his own master, and it never occurred to any one of them to think that he would return sober. Neither did it enter, as a possibility, into the minds of Poll and Sue. They thought they could have told any person exactly what would happen. "Late in the evening, after saloon closing hours, their father would come staggering and shouting down the court, and make his way blunderingly up the stairs and into the room, and expect to find the bed all down, and ready for him as usual. But this evening he just won't," they would have said; "he'll have to get it and make it ready for himself, for we—*we* know what we're going to do, don't we? We won't tell, for it's a secret, but *we* know well enough!"

Poll and Sue, you remember, had agreed to run away, to be absent from home while their mother was absent, feeling that without her and the baby home would be intolerable. The plan of action settled upon by the miserable children was this—to leave Tripe Court in the evening, and to walk a long way westward, and get into the region of the nice stores; they planned to have a good look in at them, and then to have a supper of hot fried fish somewhere, payment for which they intended to provide themselves by taking half that three shillings with them that their mother had told their father the preceding evening he would find in the mug on the mantel-shelf. They reckoned it was fair that they should take this much of the money at least; they knew where it would all go to if they did not. And their father would have all those other sums their mother had said were owing to her. So they thought they might take half of this with a good conscience.

They could not quite settle beforehand where they would sleep at night—that would all have to depend upon circumstances—but it wouldn't be in a bed; of that they were pretty certain. Perhaps they would creep under a doorway or an arch and sleep, or perhaps they wouldn't sleep at all, but walk about till it was morning. And when morning came—well, they hadn't made many plans about the next day. They supposed they'd have to beg or do something to get bread, but their plans were very hazy as to living, after the supper of hot fried fish which they had promised themselves; the only thing they were certain of afterwards was this—that as long as mother was in the Infirmary they'd never go back to Tripe Court. The unhappy children had got their torn straw hats on, and had drawn their poor wraps around their shoulders, and were on the point of starting out on their runaway expedition to the West-end, when, to their dismay, they heard their father coming up the stairs. It had not entered into their heads to think he would be home so early.

"And there's not the bed got down, or anything!" cried out Poll in horror.

"Well, it's not a bit o' good trying to get it down now," said Sue with decision; "there's not time. We must dodge him round the table if he's angry, and fly out at the door and run, for in course we'll go, all the same."

The next minute their father had entered the room, and the children were gazing at him in amazement, for, contrary to all expectation, they saw in the dusky light that he was not only *sober*, but that he had brought back the *baby!* Their plans were changed in an instant. The hot fried fish, the thought of which had made them feel positively cheerful at starting forth, vanished into air. Without a word to each other, they both made up their minds at once what must be done *now*—they must stay at home, however miserable it was; they must stick by the *baby*, whatever happened. It flashed across them, at the same moment, that it must have been lack of money that had brought their father home sober. He would take the money in the mug, of course, and go out again and get drunk.

"You've brought Dinah back?" exclaimed the children in a breath.

"Yes; they wouldn't take 'er—too old," said their father. "But there ain't a moment to lose. I've got a hinvitation to a party to-night, and we're all a-goin', and must start quick."

"Whatever do you mean, father?" asked Poll, thinking he must have been drinking, after all.

"What I say: we're goin' to a party," repeated Tom, a little testily. "There'll be plum-cake at the party; what d'ye think o' that, children?" Then, producing the feeding-bottle, "Make this warm for the little 'un, will you? she can feed as we goes along."

"We've got no hot water, father," said Sue, beginning to grin at this very funny idea about the party. And she saw that Poll was beginning to grin too. Plum-cake, though not as good as hot fried fish, made them feel a little cheerful again, though they hardly believed in it. "Father," they thought, "*must* have taken a little and got fuddled, and was making all this up about a party."

"Look alive, then, and run and get Mrs. Job to give it a hot up," said their father. "The party begins at half-past seven, and it's a goodish step from here."

With quite a laugh this time at the mention of the party, Sue ran off with the bottle of milk to Mrs. Job's house, a few doors off. She found Mrs. Treeby there, consulting with Mrs. Job over her sick boy Billy.

"Father's come home," cried Sue, rushing in upon the two women as they stood talking over a paraffin lamp. "And he's sober, and he's brought back the baby; they wouldn't have her, she was too old."

"Ah," said Mrs. Treeby, nodding her head, "I told you so, Mary Job; she'd be over age."

"Well, I was *half* afraid, too," said Mrs. Job; "but it's such a scrap of a thing, and she was so bent on having it and all, I thought they *might* let it pass. Poor Bridget! How does your father say he left mother?"

"Oh, he didn't say; he can't wait to speak. He's a-hurrying of us up, me and Poll, to go out with him to a *party* to-night," said Sue, smiling again all over, "and he says there ain't a minute to lose. I'm just to get this 'ere bottle warmed up for baby to suck as we walks along, and I'm to be back at once."

Mrs. Job's countenance fell as she listened. "The party" seemed no joke to her. She had her own ideas about it, which, after she had warmed the milk and Sue had left, she communicated to Mrs. Trechy. She began putting on her shawl and bonnet in a hurry.

"I'm going to follow them," she said.

"What!" said Mrs. Treeby; "do you think —" and she stopped short in horror.

"Yes," said Mary Job, nodding, "it's my belief the party's a parcel of nonsense, and he's going out to make away with himself and those poor little dears!"

"Well, it never struck me," said Mrs. Treeby, "but you may be right. The river's handy, to be sure; yet, he's been and brought that feeding-bottle—that don't look like it. If he meant drowning it, poor dear, he wouldn't go feeding it first."

"That may be all a blind," said Mary Job; "it's just what one reads of in the newspapers every day in the week—men going off their heads when they're left alone; they are but poor things without us women after all—and doing away with themselves and children. It wouldn't surprise me one bit. Tom seemed just in the mood for doing it this mornin.' Bridget's leaving home seemed to prey on him dreadful. *There* they go!" she cried, as three figures passed the window quickly. "I'm off!" and Mrs. Job, with palpitating heart, rushed out into the keen air to follow them.

Rather to her surprise, Tom Mite did not lead his children riverwards. At a smart pace he led them into the most populated streets, going over the ground Mrs. Job knew that he had had to pass in the morning in the first stages of the journey to the Infirmary. "The Infirmary was in a retired district," reflected Mrs. Job; "it was quite possible he had seen a quiet spot there where he meant to carry out his dreadful intention tonight."

So she continued to follow them, having now and then almost to run to keep up with them, so fast did they go. As she hurried in pursuit, she made up her mind she would speak to a policeman, as soon as the way got lonely, and get him to join her, but they never reached the lonely parts. In the very heart of the bustle and crowd Tom suddenly stopped and consulted a paper he had in his hand. Then he went down a small side-street, called Blank Street, where there was a church, and next door to it a building with large windows all alight. Crowds of poor rough-looking people, men, women, and children, were pressing into this building, and Mrs. Job, full of surprise at this unexpected termination of her chase, saw Tom Mite and his children pass in with the crowd. Mary Job's curiosity was aroused. She determined to follow and find out what was the meaning of this large gathering. At the door there was a man stationed, taking from each person entering a paper of some sort. As Mary Job attempted to press past—

"Your invitation, ma'am?" he said.

"I haven't one, sir. What's going on?" sh replied.

"Never mind, ma'am, pass on; all's welcom to-night," said the man, hustling her forward and Mary Job found herself the next minute i a very large, lighted room, decorated with blu flags, and already packed with people sittin close together on the rows of benches filling th broad spaces on either side, with a narrow lan left as passage-way in the middle. At the en of the room there was a platform with a tabl on it, and chairs and some ladies and gentleme and a harmonium set open, and three blue flag depending from the wall.

As Mary Job crushed into a seat at the back—the front ones were all full—she perceived tha refreshments were being handed about by pe sons in the passage-way, carrying deep, broa wicker baskets piled with hunches of plum-cak and trays bearing mugs of some hot beverag which they were distributing as fast as the could go down each row of eager people. Th beverage was tea—the atmosphere was fragran with it; and Mary Job did not now require t ask the neighbor next to her what kind of gathering this was. She saw at a glance that i was a Temperance meeting.

She thought the world must have turne topsy-turvy, finding herself brought to a Tem perance meeting by Tom Mite! She wa anxious to see how he seemed to like it, an craned her neck aside to get a view of his fac as he sat on one of the benches in front, wit Poll and Sue beside him, and Dinah, the baby asleep in his arms. Oh, she could see he wa looking very glum, very low-spirited indeed and seemed not to be enjoying himself at al Poll and Sue, however, were looking radian each with a mug of tea in her hand and a larg hunch of cake; and the ragged little girl next t them said they would be allowed more tea an more cake when that was done.

"Really this was something like a party; was true, after all!" they were thinking; "an they were not sure that the tea and cake wer not as good as hot fried fish, and better."

But Tom Mite's thoughts were very differen *His* opinion of the party was that it was " thorough do"—a hoax of the worst descri tion; and I may tell you that he was very *angr* It wouldn't have required much to have mad him tip up the mug of tea that was offered t him, and throw his hunch of cake with all h might at the platform, whither all his blac looks were levelled; for on the platform, smi ing blandly, Tom discovered the young lad who had given him this invitation under th lamp-post, and who had so raised his hop about the prospects of beer and ale by disa pearing into a grog-shop immediately afte wards. Yes, he would have liked to throw h cake at her head, hoaxing him so shamefully.

"Drink in abundance"! he sneered inwardly "and what kind of drink?—*sloppy tea.*" (B this was not fair towards the tea; it was real good tea, and strong.) He wasn't sure that h wouldn't tell her father, if he could see hi about the grog-shop. She deserved to be show up. He'd like to give her into custody; week's imprisonment wouldn't be too much f her; and he was just marking his displeasu by getting up with a clatter, intending to dr the children out with him, to leave the buil ing, when he was arrested by Poll tugging his coat, and calling out:

"Oh, father, see; they've opened the thing —by *the thing* she meant the harmonium—"a they're going to sing!" whereupon Tom bum ed down again on the bench,

"The singing wouldn't be up to much mo than the *drink*, he'd bet," he thought to hi self; "still, if Poll and Sue wished to stay, w he supposed he might as well. There was not ing for them at home, nothing but darkness a wretchedness there! Here, at any rate, th was warmth and light and company, and he w *very* tired; his limbs ached—he didn't feel mu up to walking again for the present. The might be a row at the end," he thought.

saw men and women about him looking as discontented and angry at this joke as *he* was, and if there was to be a row he'd like to stay and join in it, and be able to tell the young lady what he thought of her playing them a trick like this. While the singing and the talking were going on he'd try and get a nap, and on the road home, as a salve to his outraged feelings, Tom promised himself again that pint of beer which he had been seeming to get so near to all day, and just missing. But have it he *would*. Two-pennyworth couldn't make a man drunk, and he'd leave the baby outside a moment with Poll and Sue while he went in to get it, and there'd be no harm done to anybody;" and so with all this in his mind Tom elected to stay for a space.

(*To be continued.*)

JESUS AND THE LITTLE ONES.

By Mrs. M. Baxter.

S.S. Lesson for February 12, Matt. 18: 1-14. Golden Text, Matt. 19: 14.

Ver. 1. The Disciples Still Dwelling on the Idea of an Earthly Kingdom—Ver. 2-4. Christ's Gentle Reproof—A Solemn Warning—Even Admission to the Kingdom Might be Refused—The Essentials for Entrance the Same as for Greatness—The Characteristics of a Child—Docility—Humility—Guilelessness—Ver. 5, 6, 7. How Childlike Believers Must be Treated—Representatives of Jesus—Consequence of Causing Them to Offend Ver. 8, 9. Darling Sins and Connections to be Renounced for Christ's Sake—Self-Purging Better Than Punishment—Ver. 10. The Powerful Protectors of the Humble—Ver. 11-14. A Mission of Infinite Compassion—Encouragement for the Erring and for Workers.

WHEN Jesus and His disciples were come to Capernaum, the public tax-gatherers came to Peter, and asked him, "Does not your Master pay tribute?" Why did they not come to Jesus Himself? How many there are who ask questions *about* Jesus, but will not go and ask Himself, who alone can fully answer them. In this case, the answer was a simple one, "Yes." Jesus did pay tribute, and He gave His reason for it when He said to Simon, "What thinkest thou, Simon? Of whom do the kings of the earth take custom or tribute? Of their own children, or of strangers?" Peter saith unto Him, "Of strangers." Jesus saith unto him, "Then are the children free. Notwithstanding,

Lest We Should Offend Them,

go thou to the sea, and cast an hook, and take up the fish that first cometh up; and when thou hast opened his mouth, thou shalt find a piece of money; that take, and give unto them for Me and thee." Jesus was the Son of David, and as such should have been exempted from taxation, but He would not stand upon His rights, or claim His privileges, lest He should offend.

"At the same time"—while occupied with this question of giving offence—the disciples came to Jesus with the question, "Who is the greatest in the kingdom of heaven?" How like a child of earth; how unbecoming an heir of heaven, is such a question! Man's greatness and God's greatness are the greatest contrast. The first of earth's "mighty men were, of old, men of renown," "corrupted [God's] way upon the earth," and "the earth was filled with violence." (Gen. 6: 4, 12.) It was these very men who brought the flood upon the earth through their sin! Nimrod was a "mighty hunter before the Lord," and he left behind him as his memorial a mighty city, and that was all! God did not say to him, as to Abraham, "I will bless thee....and thou shalt be a blessing." Men who conquer nations, and shed the blood of thousands, those who amass riches and oppress the poor, those who bear titles and pride themselves on family distinctions, those who rise into power politically—these are earth's mighty men! But Jesus "called a little child unto Him, and sat him in the midst of them, and said, 'Except ye be converted, and become as little children, ye shall not enter into the kingdom of heaven. Whosoever, therefore, shall humble himself as this little child, the same is greatest in the kingdom of heaven.'"

Who is the Greatest?

This is a question which more often agitates the hearts of the children of God than they allow, even to themselves. A child of God is used of Him in mission work, a great awakening breaks out, he leads all the meetings, and speaks with a power which is as much a marvel to himself as to others. He begins to think that he is a special instrument of God; he is much sought after, and his name becomes known. By and by, another star arises, a man whom God now blesses more than he. At first his whole will rises in rebellion, but when it is laid down, he is brought to the humbling but salutary conviction that God can do without him—and that, after all, he is not so needful to the works of God, as he thought. From being a mighty man in his own eyes, he becomes a little child, willing to be nothing, willing to be last, and then, unknown to himself, God makes him a power. Just so far as we value ourselves are we unfit for the work of God. "The last shall be first, and the first last" (Matt. 20: 16) is God's order.

While Moses set a value on *himself* as the most important Hebrew in Egypt, God could not use him; but when he had been a simple shepherd long enough to forget all his learning and all his assumption, God could use him. David's brethren were not little enough for God to use; Gideon, who accounted himself least in his father's house, was an instrument fit for God. Why is all this? "That no flesh should glory in His presence." (1 Cor. 1: 29.) "This people have I formed for myself; they shall shew forth My praise" (Isa. 43: 21); not their own. We were

Created in the Image of God.

The perfection of a portrait is that it sets forth the person it represents. If we set forth *ourselves*, we no more serve the purpose for which we were created and redeemed, than a beautifully executed portrait would serve its purpose if it was quite unlike the original. The wonder and glory of man's creation is that man is capable of containing God, of being a temple of the Holy Ghost, "an habitation of God through the Spirit." Christ dwelling in our hearts by faith. We are predestined "to be conformed to the image of (God's) Son," to be "partakers of the Divine Nature, having escaped the corruption that is in the world through lust." (Rom. 8: 29; II Pet. 1: 2.) How vain, then, is it for us to assume any personal honor, value ourselves on any personal holiness, or on any gifts which the Holy Ghost may use in us!

Having made the little child an example, Jesus began to speak about the little ones: "Whosoever shall receive one such little child

In My Name

receiveth Me." O how blessed are those who care for orphans, those who lead little children to Jesus, those who shield them from the awful snares laid for them in the world! Many enjoy the society of children for their own amusement. Is this to receive them in His name? Parents often make their own children ministers to their own pride; and they pride themselves on their children's beauty, wit, cleverness, learning, etc., etc., thus receiving them in their *own name* instead of Christ's. Again, in schools, how often those who teach, press forward the clever boys or girls, who will reflect credit on their teaching, and so recommend the school—forgetting that every dull, heavy, awkward child is to be received in the name of Christ. If every child born into the world of Christian parents were received in the name of Christ, if every pupil in a school were received in the name of Christ, if every young apprentice or workman, every young domestic servant were received in the name of Christ—what a different world it would be!

"But whoso shall offend [or cause to stumble] one of these little ones which believe in Me, it were better for him that a millstone were hanged about his neck and that he were drowned in the depth of the sea." The little ones have very keen eyes; they take everything on trust until they have been deceived; then

They Watch All the Time

and mentally take notes. They see mother lose her temper, and from that time they think it cannot be so very bad for them to have naughty tempers. They see father buy a paper on Sunday, and they think it can't be wrong for them to buy candies. An elder brother gets into debt, or a sister speaks of some impure story, and the little sentinel makes a mental note of it, and reproduces the same thing at another time. And Jesus takes notes too, and keeps an account of every one who has caused a little child to stumble. "Woe unto the world because of occasions of stumbling; for it must needs be that the occasions come (there must be trials of faith), but woe to that man through whom the occasion cometh" (R. V.). Jesus has just been paying the tribute money only to avoid an occasion of stumbling; now He urges that every occasion of stumbling should be cut off. If it is a hand, an eye or a foot, we are better without that, whatever it is, which causes us to stumble, or causes others to stumble; it is better to be blind or maimed than to sin or to cause others to sin. God gives us this

Wholesome Abhorrence of Sin,

that we may be willing to suffer anything rather than sin against our God. "Take heed that ye despise not one of these little ones"—a child or a child-like Christian—"for I say unto you, that in heaven their angels do always behold the face of My father which is in heaven. For the Son of man is come to save that which was lost." The angels are "all ministering spirits, sent to minister for them who shall be heirs of salvation" (Heb. 1: 14), and God lets them minister unseen to His little ones.

The Son of man did not come to build up man's goodness, and put His signature to that which is of man; but on the contrary, to seek that which was lost, and save it. Thus He said, "How think ye? If a man have a hundred sheep, and one of them be gone astray, doth he not leave the ninety and nine, and goeth into the mountains, and seeketh that which is gone astray? And if so be that he find it, verily I say unto you, he rejoiceth more of that sheep than of the ninety and nine which went not astray." God forbid that we should despise backsliders; if we had our eyes open to see the unseen, we should see Jesus after them all the time, and our hearts would go out with His towards them. "Even so, it is not the will of your Father which is in heaven, that one of these little ones should perish." All who perish, perish by their own perverse will, and not by God's will. Hell was not prepared for man, but "for the devil and his angels" (Matt. 25: 21), and all who go there go athwart the promises and the loving invitations of God. They must pass by a crucified Redeemer to reach everlasting death. He stands between.

O do not let us look on our children as existing for the position they may have in the world, but as being created for God, for His kingdom. He says, "*Suffer* little children, and forbid them not to come unto Me; for of such is the kingdom of heaven." How can we suffer them to come? Not by driving or forcing them, for this would make them hate the things of God, but by strengthening ourselves in God, who does not will that they shall perish, and who says, "Believe on the Lord Jesus Christ, and thou shalt be saved, and thy house." Perhaps there is no suffering to believing parents so keen as to have children unsaved. Therefore, there is nothing which so honors God as to trust Him with the salvation of our children. With some parents the very anxiety and fussiness which they manifest about their children's salvation is a cause of stumbling to the children, but God never faileth, in this or any other thing, those who put their trust in Him.

"COME TO ME."

Come to me, Lord, when first I wake,
As the faint lights of morning break;
Bid purest thoughts within me rise,
Like crystal dew-drops in the skies.

Come to me in the sultry noon—
Or earth's low communings will soon
Of Thy dear face eclipse the light,
And change my fairest days to night.

Come to me in the evening shade—
And if my heart from Thee has strayed,
Oh, bring it back, and from afar
Smile on me like Thine evening star.

Come to me in the midnight hour,
When sleep withholds her balmy power;
Let my lone spirit find its rest,
Like John, upon my Saviour's breast.

Come to me through life's varied way,
And when its pulses cease to play,
Then Saviour, bid me come to Thee,
That where Thou art Thy child may be.

Selected.

J. E. JEWETT, Publisher, 77 Bible House, New York will furnish the above poem in leaflet form at twenty cents per hundred. A *Sample Packet* of 50 leaflets assorted (no two alike), will be sent post-paid for ten cents. Postage stamps taken.

THE CHRISTIAN HERALD AND SIGNS OF OUR TIMES.

Entered according to Act of Congress in the year 1887, in the office of the Librarian of Congress at Washington.

Vol. XI., No. 6. Office, 63 Bible House. N. Y. THURSDAY, FEBRUARY 9, 1888. Annual Subscription, $1.50.

CONTENTS OF THIS NUMBER.

PORTRAIT OF THE PRINCESS CHRISTIAN OF SCHLESWIG-HOLSTEIN. and Sketch of her Philanthropic Work.
THE VEIL OF MODESTY. Dr. Talmage's Sermon to the Women of America last Sunday Morning.
ANECDOTES RELATED AT RECENT EVANGELISTIC MEETINGS.
THE PROPHETS AND THE APOCALYPSE.
A Physician's Mistake—A Chinaman's Prayers—A Dying Mormon's Song—A Prisoner's Dread—A Parisian Wife Beater—Life in the Zenana.
CURRENT EVENTS: The Growing Surplus—The Extradition Treaty with England—Congress to Investigate the Great Strike—The Mal-Administration in the Post-Office Department, Etc.
HEALING BY STRIPES. A New Sermon by C. H. Spurgeon.
Gems from New Books: Adrift at Sea in a Boat.
FEEDING THE DESTITUTE. (Illustrated.)
A CASE OF CONSCIENCE. (With Illustration.)
PICTURE OF THE MOSQUE OF KUTIBIA.
THE FAMILY OF TRIPE COURT. (Continued.)
A LESSON ON FORGIVENESS. By Mrs. M. Baxter.

THE QUEEN OPENING THE ROYAL HOLLOWAY COLLEGE.

THE PRINCESS CHRISTIAN, of Schleswig-Holstein—Ceremony of Unveiling the Queen's Statue.

THE PRINCESS CHRISTIAN,

OF SCHLESWIG-HOLSTEIN.

Her Philanthropic Work—Reminiscences of Childhood—Novel Occupations for Royalty—Visiting the Poor—Where Real Friends are Found—An Observant Visitor—Characteristics she Notes—A Modest Statement—Her Efforts for the Benefit of the Poor—Free Dinners for Children—Free Concerts—Organizing District Nurses—A Public Ceremony—Sage Counsel to Students—Euclid and Tacitus not to Exclude Domestic Habits—Alleviations of Monarchical Burdens.

THE lady whose portrait appears on the first page is the wife of Prince Frederick Christian, of Schleswig-Holstein, but she, with her husband, has made her home in England, where, as the third daughter of the Queen, she occupies a prominent position and enjoys a degree of social distinction which perhaps she would not have in her husband's land. Besides this, the bulk of his income is derived from lucrative offices about the English Court, most of which though sinecures could not be decently held by a non-resident. This is one of the abuses of royalty, but the English people have a profound regard for the present royal family, and only the radical party complain of the burden. Much of the discontent which might be provoked has been disarmed by the grace and tact of the Queen's daughters, whose husbands and families have become a national charge. This applies especially to the lady whose portrait appears on the first page, and she has just given a conspicuous proof of her kindliness and grace, comments on which have drawn forth other

Characteristic Personal Details

of a very creditable and interesting character. The Princess is forty-two years of age. She was born on May 25, 1846, and was named Helena Augusta Victoria. There is nothing recorded of her childhood and early days, beyond the fact that she was quick at learning her lessons, glad when the holiday seasons came round, possessed of a kindly and generous disposition, and brimful of merriment. The promise of her sunny girlhood has been abundantly fulfilled, for in these days she is beloved for her gentle kindliness and geniality wherever she is known. The domestics of her own modest household at Windsor are devotedly attached to her, and would do anything to prove their readiness to serve her. They have good reason for this, as the Princess is not only a kind mistress to them personally, but has shown her sympathy with their class, having taken an active part in organizing and managing the best institutions existing for the benefit of domestic servants.

It is a curious coincidence that in her early life she was brought into a somewhat humiliating connection with one member of the class which she has in maturer years done so much to aid. The story is worth telling because of the characteristic traits it displays, and the example it gives of the benefit of judicious early training, by which the royal little lady was taught to realize that birth and station do not confer the right to behave rudely to more lowly persons. It is narrated that the Princess Helena and her elder sister, Alice, when they were children, happened to go into a room in which a servant was engaged in polishing a grate. The girls, in a spirit of

Frolicsome Mischief,

insisted on helping her, and then when they had possession of the brushes left the grate and blackened the woman's face. The servant escaped at last from her little tormentors, and hurried to her room to wash her face, but on the way she met Prince Albert, who seeing the girl's disfigurement, insisted on knowing all about it. Presently the Queen was seen crossing the court towards the servants' quarters, leading the two child culprits. The woman, who by this time had washed her face, was brought forward, and the two girls had first to beg the servant's pardon, and then go to a store and purchase for her, out of their own pocket-money, a complete outfit in place of the dress, cap, etc., that had been soiled. The two Princesses afterwards declared that they rather enjoyed making presents to the woman, but asking her pardon they certainly did not like

The Marriage of Princess Helena

took place on July 5, 1866, the bridegroom being Prince Frederick Christian of Schleswig-Holstein, and she has now five children, three sons and two daughters. Prince Christian was born at Schleswig, Germany, January 22, 1831, and is therefore now fifty-seven years of age.

Royal Work

in the best sense of the word has been done for many years by the Princess. Romantic young ladies will be surprised to learn that pleasure and gaiety do not occupy the most prominent place in her life. Not long ago she gave an account of her philanthropic and benevolent occupations. It was done very modestly and only on fitting occasion, and her humble friends, it is said, would have drawn the picture in a far different way, throwing in colors mixed from feelings of profound gratitude to the lady whose gifts and personal labors have helped them in many a season of trouble. Of this the Princess said nothing. She gave the following brief sketch, which shows how sincere is her sympathy for the poor and afflicted: "Only those who really work among the very poor can fully understand and appreciate the real hardship of their lives, which so many, if not most of them, have to endure; and which, as a rule, are met so uncomplainingly and so bravely. Desirous of really being of more direct use, I obtained the consent of the Rector of Trinity Church, Windsor, to take a district in his parish under my especial care. It is situated in a very poor part of the town; the houses on the whole are good, the rents often high. When work is plentiful, they manage fairly well, but when times are hard, as was the case last winter, the distress is great. I, however, rarely heard complaints, unless I asked them to tell me how matters really stood. I generally visit my people twice a week, and it is a real pleasure to feel that my visits are looked forward to, and that they

Received me as a Friend,

so that by degrees I have learnt all their individual troubles and difficulties. I have endeavored from the first to encourage them to help themselves as much as possible, and then, when I found they could do no more, I have obtained help for them. I have found among them *my most real friends*. I am sure there are many who will understand the feelings which filled my heart when, on leaving Windsor for an absence of several weeks, one poor woman took both my hands in hers, and exclaimed, 'To whom shall I tell my troubles when you are gone?' To me the words were far more precious than any thanks that could have been offered me.

"It strikes me each time afresh how wonderful the poor are in helping one another, showing so much unselfish devotion, sitting up at night with the sick, looking after a neighbor's children, though they themselves have numbers of their own, and, above all, the childlike submission and resignation with which they take sorrow and trouble when they come upon them.

"During the last three years great efforts have been made to organize means of help in times of distress, and also harmless amusements, to bring some brightness into the lives of these poor people. As regards the first, I have started a fund, with the help of kind friends, for providing

Free Dinners for the Children

of the town during the winter. This fund also provides coals and the loan of blankets for those who most need them. I have been most generously helped by many in the town, and I sincerely trust this support will be continued to me. We now feed, on an average, 250 children twice a week, and care is taken that they are those who need such help. The dinners take place in the Town Hall (kindly lent by the mayor), and consist of soup and pudding, or meat, puddings, pies and stews.

I Am Always Present to Help

in serving the children, and am assisted by many kind ladies in Windsor. As there is nearly always more food provided than is consumed by the children, the surplus is given to a number of poor men out of employment, usually upwards of fifty, who are invited to come in and eat in the hall; these also have tickets, in order to be quite sure that they are not idle vagrants. These dinners commence the first week of January, and are continued till April."

Another kindly effort to cheer lives otherwise cheerless is *free concerts*. These the Princess described in detail, evidently hoping that other ladies would adopt similar means to brighten the lot of their poor neighbors. Harmonic societies and glee clubs have been easily induced by the Princess to give their services, and she being a skilled pianist, has always taken part in the concerts. They are extremely popular, and the Princess dwells with pleasure on the appreciation which the people have shown of the music

Nurses for the Sick Poor

are, however, probably the best blessing she has secured for her humble friends. She says: "I had long felt the extreme necessity there was for district nurses for the sick poor, and quite made up my mind, if possible, to establish them. Many and earnest were the conversations I had with some friends on this subject, without whose help I could scarcely have carried out my wish; for at first the obstacles I had to overcome were many, and seemed insurmountable. To begin with, there was the difficulty about money, and the conviction held by many that such a thing was useless, nay more, would be disliked by the poor. We fought our way by slow degrees; a meeting of influential members of the town was called, at which I got permission to engage a nurse for three months as an experiment, after which time, should it succeed, I asked that she might be established permanently. Before the three months were over, not only had the nurse proved herself an absolute necessity, invaluable in every sense of the word, but I was asked to find a second one; and I was enabled, by the generous gifts of friends and others in the town, to raise a fund for the permanent establishment of two district nurses. I am more than rewarded for any part I may have taken in this movement, by the fact that the poor clamor for these nurses, who are beloved for their unselfish devotion, and who bring help and comfort wherever they go.

An Infant Nursery

is another institution in this town which I should like to mention. It is the little crèche. It was started several years ago by a lady in this town, and I have taken a personal active interest in it for the last three years, and I am thankful to say that it is doing real good work. Of course, as for everything else, money is needed, and, though I have been more than generously helped till now, yet, with the winter coming on, the funds at our disposal will be severely strained. It is, therefore, no small source of anxiety to me; and I hope that assistance will still be forthcoming to enable us to go on with our work."

A Recent Public Ceremony

in which the Princess appropriately took a prominent part, was connected with a college for young women in which she took a deep interest. A prominent philanthropist built the college, and also directed the erection of a statue of the Queen in the quadrangle. When it was completed, it was felt that no more suitable person could be chosen to unveil it than the Princess Christian whose interest in every department of the college and its work was conspicuously manifested. Accordingly, with appropriate ceremonies the Princess inaugurated it on December 16 last (*See lower Illustration on first page*); at the conclusion of the day's exercises she made an address full of sound advice and womanly sympathy to the students, in the course of which she said:

"It is impossible for me to take leave of you without expressing my gratification at having been asked to come among you to-day, and perform the ceremony of unveiling my mother's statue. I note with pleasure the training in the institution is not confined to mere book learning, but that

Feminine Accomplishments

of varied description find a place here as well. It is no longer necessary, as was the case fifteen or twenty years ago, to lay stress on the importance of the higher education of women. It has, on the other hand, rather been a duty to warn against the almost exaggerated views that some are inclined to adopt on this subject. I should rather let a woman never forget that she is a woman, and that her chief attribute and the power she possesses lie in her womanliness. I certainly sympathize in the desire for learning and mental culture; but I do feel that sometimes the ambition which urges many to encroach on man's province causes them to underrate the importance of the many duties, and even privileges, which are given to women alone.

"I do not wish for a moment to suggest that the higher education of women and intellectual cultivation are incompatible with good housekeeping, and that women are of necessity worse wives, mothers or daughters because they have studied Euclid and read Tacitus. I am anxious to impress on you the consideration of how much the success of this great institution must depend on the character and tone which you, its first inmates, impress upon it. Women in England will look to you to ascertain what may be expected from female education in its highest development, and under the most favorable conditions. Be true to your college, your teachers, and your womanhood.

Be Gentle, be Courteous, be Religious;

and before many years are passed the anxious wish of the founder, to benefit the women of England by placing within their reach a complete course of education, will have been accomplished, and you will have shown that his bounty has not been expended in vain."

The upper illustration represents the opening ceremonies performed on another day at the inauguration of the college itself. The Queen was induced to attend them, doubtless at her daughter's solicitation. In a country where so much influence is exercised by royalty, the Queen's presence was a matter of great importance. Though it is difficult under a free Republic to understand the existence of such an influence among an intelligent people, the fact that it does exist cannot be overlooked; and, therefore, it is a matter for congratulation that it is beneficently exercised. Royal and imperial persons have been known to set an example of vicious and frivolous life; and other lands besides England have had unhappy experience of such cases. The present increase of intelligence and education, and the consequent transfer of power, first from the monarch to the aristocracy, and now from the aristocracy to the people, bodes ill for the permanence of monarchy; but the prejudice against royalty is to some extent disarmed when the monarch is personally lovable and is sincerely concerned for the welfare of the people. The most inveterate opponent of monarchical government cannot but feel that if all royal persons behaved themselves as does the Princess Christian, royalty would not be altogether a useless burden.

ANECDOTES RELATED AT RECENT EVANGELISTIC MEETINGS.

An Athlete Accepts Christ.—Mr. J. Arthur remarks: "About the finest man I ever knew was an athlete, but he did not know God. He was stricken down with fever. At that time a lady visited him, and told him of Christ, who was longing to save him. As she had ineffectually urged him to accept Christ when it was in his power, he now looked up into her face and said, 'Do you think I would be shabby enough to give up to God the dregs, the last of my days, that I may save my soul, when the devil has had the rest?' But he was shown that it was God's will and command that he should come, even at the eleventh hour, and John M'Farlane yielded to God, his only regret being he had not come to Christ sooner."

A Momentous Epoch.—Mr. Oatts Says: "I remember when the Spirit of the Lord first came very near to me. I felt that I was at one of the most momentous epochs in my life. I worked for God as much then as ever I have done since; all my spare time was given to it. People came to my office and said, 'Mr. Oatts, we never heard such addresses as you are giving!' And yet there were no conversions; I knew that there was something in me that was preventing the blessing from coming. So, going to the Lord one day, I gave myself wholly over to Him, and every day since then I have been near to Him. I am always floating on a full tide of blessing. We may work for the Lord, as we think, but unless He uses us, unless we give over ourselves wholly into His hands to be used by Him, there will be but little effect.'

Witnessing A Marriage.—Mr. T. Canning observes: "The other morning, when I was staying at the house of a minister in Scotland, we were surprised by a loud knock at the door. It proved to be a young man, who inquired if the minister were at home. Being told that he was, he turned away, saying that he would be back in five minutes. He returned within the specified time, but not alone; he brought a young lady with him. Then we discovered that the object of his visit was to be married. As I stood beside the pair, a witness to the ceremony, I thought what a fine picture it was of salvation. When to the question, 'Do you take this woman to be your wedded wife?' he answered, 'I do,' I thought *that* does not make a marriage; it takes two consenting parties to do so. But when the bride, in answer to a similar question, made the same reply, *then* it was done. It needed both sides. So with salvation; we have to take Christ as our Bridegroom, and Christ will take us as His Bride. He says, Him that cometh unto Me I will in no wise cast out.'"

A Reclaimed Infidel's Death.—A Friend related: "I was visiting, lately, an avowed infidel. Missionaries were chary of calling on him, for he had made it widely known that he kept a coal-hatchet handy for the special benefit of any missionary or minister who might visit him. A minister and myself thought we would give that man a trial. After earnest prayer we set out for the man's house, and, when we reached it, we knocked, but received no answer. The door was secured by a simple thumb latch, and, pushing it down, I walked right in, and my friend followed. We found the man in bed, dying of decline, and in a most miserable room, unfurnished and dirty; the grate had been taken from the fire-place and sold. I did indeed pity him and the poor little girl, who was his sole attendant. I spoke to him about his poor body, and the miseries he was undergoing, and remarked that he did not seem to have over much in the way of comfort. I slipped some money into the child's hand, telling her to go and get some food, and, when I turned to speak to the man about his soul, he completely broke down. All his boasted infidelity was worth nothing now. Soon he was resting his weary, starved soul on that Saviour whom he had so often reviled. Weak as he was, he was anxious to work for Christ, and he sent for his infidel friends that he might talk to them of Christ, but they would not come, and he had to content himself with praying for them. Not long afterwards he died a glorious death, praising that God who had not rejected him, when he sought Him even at the eleventh hour."

A Blasphemer's Conversion.—Mr. Cruikshanks related: "There lived in the north of Scotland an old man, who, before his conversion, was notorious for the bad language which he habitually used. At a time of revival he was converted. When it became known, many people watched him to see how he would bear himself, and if he would be able to overcome his besetting sin. On one occasion some people heard him use language which they did not like, and at once they began to ask themselves and each other if he were really converted. The minister was informed of their suspicions, and he, soon afterwards meeting the new convert, asked him, 'John, are you converted?' 'Yes,' he replied. 'Well, tell me all about it; how it happened!' 'Well,' the old man answered, 'it was just this way: *I did all I could, and the Lord did the rest.*' 'Ah,' thought the minister, 'I am afraid these people were right, and you are not converted. But,' he continued, 'John, tell me what you did?' '*Oh, Christ saved me, and I did all I could to hinder Him.*' That answer would not have been given by any but a saved man."

Capitulation at Last.—A Friend Relates the following: "I was visited by a companion who did not know of my conversion, but being very much troubled about religious matters he came to me to see if I could help him. I told him I was not learned in doctrine, but I could tell him about Christ, and this I did, urging him to accept Jesus as his Saviour. He was much affected, but did not decide. Next day I had a long talk with him, only to find that he had hardened his heart. After that he carefully avoided me, but once when I was preaching I met him. 'Man,' I said, 'have no more of this waiting, but come to Christ.' That night God touched his heart. He fairly broke down and wept, but still he would not sue for salvation. He went away unsaved. About two years passed, and one day I received a letter from him saying that he had at last come to Christ. He was in the habit of spending his Sundays drinking, but one Sunday the thought came vividly to him, 'How am I going to spend eternity?' He cried aloud for mercy, accepted Christ, and gave himself to His work. And now he is a successful preacher of the gospel."

A Well-spent Shilling.—Miss Cameron Relates: "Eighteen months ago, in one of our cottage meetings, a drunkard was brought to Jesus' feet. A few hours before he came in, he went to a young cripple girl, who was a Christian, and asked her if she would give him a shilling to get his dinner, for he was starving. The girl knew where her hard-earned money would go if she gave it to him, and she was not very able to spare it. She considered for a moment what she should do, for the giving up of the shilling meant that she must go without her own dinner; then, naming him, she said, 'I will give you the shilling if you will come to our meeting to-night.' He readily promised, glad to get away with the money. Meeting time arrived, and the girl's mother, hearing what her daughter had done, was determined that he should keep his word, and as the time went on, and the man made no appearance she went to the saloon in search of him. She found him there, and together they entered the meeting. At the close I asked him if he would like to sign the pledge; he replied that he would, but still looked dissatisfied. 'You want something more,' I said. 'I believe nothing short of Jesus Himself will satisfy you. Will you take Him to reign as king over you?' 'That I will,' was the earnest reply. We got on our knees, and there that poor unlettered man gave himself to Christ. From that night he has lived a most consistent and useful and beautiful life."

THE VEIL OF MODESTY,

Dr. Talmage's Fifth Sermon to THE WOMEN OF AMERICA.

Preached Last Sunday Morning, February 5, 1888.

"The Queen Vashti refused to come." Esther 1 : 12.

The Magnificence of Shushan—The Banquet in the Palace Garden—The Songs of Illustrious Revellers—The Summons to the Queen—I. Vashti as Queen—Uncrowned Queens—The School Teachers—The Death of a School Principal—A Criterion of Character—Contrast Between Goethe and Shakespeare—II. The Veiled Queen—Woman's Natural Modesty—Masculine Women—Divinely Called Women—An Outrageous Law—III. The Queen Sacrificed—Ruined Homes—The Mississippi Engineer's Heroic Death—IV. The Silent Queen—Magnificent Silence of Philosophers—A Frozen Crew on a Drifting Ship—A Traitress Crushed by Gifts.

IF you will accept my arm I will escort you into a throne-room. In this fifth sermon of the series of sermons there are certain womanly excellencies which I wish to commend, but instead of putting them in dry abstraction, I present you their impersonation in one who seldom gets sermonic recognition. We stand amid

The Palaces of Shushan.

The pinnacles are aflame with the morning light. The columns rise festooned and wreathed, the wealth of empires flashing from the grooves; the ceilings adorned with images of bird and beast, and scenes of prowess and conquest. The walls are hung with shields, and emblazoned until it seems that the whole round of splendors is exhausted. Each arch is a mighty leap of architectural achievement. Golden stars shining down on glowing arabesque. Hangings of embroidered work, in which mingle the blueness of the sky, the greeness of the grass, and the whiteness of the sea-foam. Tapestries hung on silver rings, wedding together the pillars of marble. Pavilions reaching out in every direction. These for repose, filled with luxuriant couches, in which weary limbs sink until all fatigue is submerged. Amazing spectacle! It seems as if a billow of celestial glory had dashed clear over heaven's battlements upon this metropolis of Persia.

In connection with this palace there is a garden, where the mighty men of foreign lands are

Seated at a Banquet.

Under the spread of oak and linden and acacia the tables are arranged. The breath of honeysuckle and frankincense fills the air. The waters of Eulæus filling the urns, and sweating outside the rim in flashing beads amid the traceries. Wine from the royal vats of Ispahan and Shiraz, in bottles of tinged shell, and lily shaped cups of silver, and flagons and tankards of solid gold. The music rises higher, and the revelry breaks out into wilder transport, and the wine has flushed the cheek and touched the brain, and louder than all other voices are the hiccough of the inebriates, the gabble of fools, and the song of the drunkards. In another part of the palace,

Queen Vashti

is entertaining the princesses of Persia at a banquet. Drunken Ahasuerus says to his servants: "You go out and fetch Vashti from that banquet with the women, and bring her to this banquet with the men, and let me display her beauty." The servants immediately start to obey the king's command; but there was a rule in Oriental society that no woman might appear in public without having her face veiled. Yet here was a mandate that no one dare dispute, demanding that Vashti come in unveiled before the multitude. However, there was in Vashti's soul a principle more regal than Ahasuerus, more brilliant than the gold of Shushan, of more wealth than the realm of Persia, which commanded her to disobey this order of the king; and so all the righteousness, holiness and

Modesty of Her Nature

rises up into one sublime refusal. She says: "I will not go into the banquet unveiled." Of course Ahasuerus was infuriated; and Vashti, robbed of her position and her estate, is driven forth in poverty and ruin, to suffer the scorn of a nation, and yet to receive the applause of after generations who shall rise up to admire this martyr to kingly insolence. Well, the last vestige of that feast is gone; the last garland has faded; the last arch has fallen; the last tankard has been destroyed, and Shushan is a ruin; but as long as the world stands there will be multitudes of men and women, familiar with the Bible, who will come into this picture-gallery of God, and admire the Divine portrait of Vashti the queen, Vashti the veiled, Vashti the sacrifice, Vashti the silent.

In the first place, I want you to look upon Vashti the queen. A blue ribbon rayed with white, drawn around her forehead, indicated

Her Queenly Position.

It was no small honor to be queen in such a realm as that. Hark to the rustle of her robes! See the blaze of her jewels! And yet, my friends, it is not necessary to have palace and regal robes in order to be queenly. When I see a woman with stout faith in God, putting her foot upon all meanness and selfishness and godless display, going right forward to serve Christ and the race by a grand and glorious service, I say: "That woman is a queen," and the ranks of heaven look over the battlements upon the coronation; and whether she come up from the shanty on the commons or the mansion of the fashionable square, I greet her with the shout: "All hail! Queen Vashti!" What glory was there on the brow of Mary of Scotland, or Elizabeth of England, or Margaret of France, or Catherine of Russia, compared with the worth of some of our Christian mothers, many of them gone into glory?—or of Ruth, who toiled under a tropical sun for poor old, helpless Naomi?—or of Mrs. Adoniram Judson, who kindled the lights of salvation amid the darkness of Burmah?—or of Mrs Hemans, who poured out her holy soul in words which will forever be associated with hunter's horn, and captive's chain, and bridal hour, and lute's throb, and curfew's knell, at the dying day?—and scores and hundreds of women, unknown on earth, who have given water to the thirsty, and bread to the hungry, and medicine to the sick, and smiles to the discouraged—their footsteps heard along dark lane, and in Government hospital, and in alms-house corridor, and by prison-gate? There may be no royal robe—there may be no palatial surroundings. She does not need them; for all charitable men will unite with the crackling lips of fever-struck hospital and plague-blotched lazaretto in greeting her as she passes: "Hail, Queen Vashti." Among the

Queens Whom I Honor

are the female day-school teachers of this land. I put upon their brow the coronet. They are the sisters and the daughters of our towns and cities, selected out of a vast number of applicants, because of their especial intellectual and moral endowments. There are in none of your homes women more worthy. These persons, some of them, come out from affluent homes, choosing teaching as a useful profession; others, finding that father is older than he used to be, and that his eyesight and strength are not as good as once, go to teaching to lighten his load. But I tell you the history of the majority of the female teachers in the public schools when I say: "Father is dead." After the estate was settled, the family, that were comfortable before, are thrown on their own resources.

It is hard for men to earn a living in this day, but it is harder for women—their health not so rugged, their arms not so strong, their opportunities fewer. These persons, after tremblingly going through the ordeal of an examination as to their qualifications to teach, half-bewildered step over the sill of the public school to do two things—instruct the young and earn their own bread.

Her Work is Wearing

to the last degree. The management of forty or fifty fidgety and intractable children, the suppression of their vices and the development of their excellencies, the management of rewards and punishments, the sending of so many bars of soap and fine-tooth combs on benignant ministry, the breaking of so many wild colts for the harness of life, sends her home at night weak, neuralgic, unstrung, so that of all the weary people in your cities for five nights of the week, there are none more weary than the public-school teachers. Now, for God's sake, give them a fair chance. Throw no obstacles in the way. If they come out ahead in the race, cheer them. If you want to smite any, smite the male teachers; they can take up the cudgels for themselves. But keep your hands off of defenceless women. Father may be dead but there are enough brothers left to demand and see that they get justice.

Within a stone's throw of this building there died years ago one of the principals of our public schools. She had been twenty-five years at that post. She had left the touch of refinement on a multitude of the young. She had, out of her slender purse, given literally thousands of dollars for the destitute who came under her observation as a school teacher. A deceased sister's children were thrown upon her hands, and she took care of them. She was a kind mother to them, while she mothered a whole school. Worn out with nursing in the sick and dying room of one of the household, she herself came to die. She closed the school-book and at the same time the volume of her Christian fidelity.

Queens Are All Such,

and whether the world acknowledges them or not, heaven acknowledges them. When Scarron the wit and ecclesiastic, as poor as he was brilliant, was about to marry Madame de Maintenon, he was asked by the notary what he proposed to settle upon Mademoiselle. The reply was: "Immortality! the names of the wives of kings die with them: the name of the wife of Scarron will live always." In a higher and better sense, upon all women who do their duty God will settle Immortality! Not the immortality of earthly fame, which is mortal, but the immortality celestial. And they shall reign for ever and ever! Oh, the opportunity which every woman has of being a queen! The longer I live the more I admire good womanhood. And I have come to form my opinion of the character of a man by his appreciation or non-appreciation of woman. If a man have a depressed idea of womanly character he is a bad man, and there is no exception to the rule.

The writings of Goethe can never have any such attractions for me as Shakespeare, because nearly all the womanly characters of the great German have some kind of turpitude. There is his Mariana, with her clandestine scheming; and his Mignon, of evil parentage, yet worse than her ancestors; and his Theresa, the brazen; and his Aurelia, of many intrigues; and his Philina, the termigant; and his Melina, the tarnished; and his baroness; and his Countess; and there is seldom a womanly character in all his voluminous writings that would be worthy of residence in a respectable coal cellar, yet pictured and dramatized, and emblazoned till all the literary world is compelled to see. No! No! Give me William Shakespeare's idea of woman; and I see it in Desdemona, and Cordelia, and Rosalind, and Imogen, and Helena, and Hermione, and Viola, and Isabella, and Sylvia, and Perdita, all of them with enough faults to prove them human, but enough kindly characteristics to give us the author's idea of womanhood; his Lady Macbeth only a dark background to bring out the supreme loveliness of his other female characters.

Again, I want you to consider

Vashti the Veiled.

Had she appeared before Ahasuerus and his court on that day, with her face uncovered, she would have shocked all the delicacies of Oriental society, and the very men who in their intoxication demanded that she come, in their sober moments would have despised her. As some flowers seem to thrive best in the dark lane and in the shadow, and where the sun does not seem to reach them, so God appoints to most womanly natures a retiring and unobtrusive spirit. God once in a while does call an Isabella to a throne, or a Miriam to strike the timbrel at the front of a host, or a Marie Antoinette to quell a French mob, or a Deborah to stand at the front of an armed battalion, crying out: "Up! Up! This is the day in which the Lord will deliver Sisera into thy hands." And when women are called to such out-door work, and to such heroic positions, God prepares them for it; and they have iron in their soul, and lightnings in their eye, and whirlwinds in their breath, and the borrowed strength of the Lord Omnipotent in their right arm.

But these are exceptions. Generally, Dorcas would rather make a garment for the poor boy; Rebecca would rather fill the trough for the camels; Hannah would rather make a coat for Samuel; the Hebrew maid would rather give a prescription for Naaman's leprosy; the woman of Sarepta would rather gather a few sticks to cook a meal for famished Elijah; Phœbe would rather carry a letter for the inspired Apostle; Mother Lois would rather educate Timothy in the Scriptures. When I see a woman going about her daily duty—with cheerful dignity presiding at the table; with kind and gentle, but firm, discipline presiding in the nursery; going out into the world without any blast of trumpets, following in the footsteps of Him who went about doing good—I say: "This is Vashti with a veil on." But when I see

Woman of Unblushing Boldness,

loud-voiced, with a tongue of infinite clitter-clatter, with arrogant look, passing through the street with a masculine swing, gayly arrayed in a very hurricane of millinery, I cry out, "Vashti has lost her veil." When I see a woman struggling for political preferment, and rejecting the duties of home as insignificant, and thinking the offices of wife, mother and daughter of no importance, and trying to force her way on up into conspicuity, I say: "Ah, what a pity: Vashti has lost her veil." When I see a woman of comely features, and of adroitness of intellect, and endowed with all that the schools can do for one, and of high social position, yet moving in society with superciliousness and hauteur, as though she would have people know their place, and an undefined combination of giggle and strut and rodomontade, endowed with allopathic quantities of talk, but only homeopathic infinitesimals of sense, the terror of dry-goods clerks and railroad conductors, discoverers of significant meanings in plain conversation, prodigies of badness and innuendo—I say: "Vashti has lost her veil."

But do not misinterpret what I say into a depreciation of the work of those glorious and

Divinely Called Women,

who will not be understood till after they are dead, women like Susan B. Anthony, who are giving their life for the betterment of the condition of their sex. Those of you who think that women have, under the laws of this country, an equal chance with men, are ignorant of the laws. A gentleman writes me from Maryland, saying: "Take the laws of this State. A man and wife start out in life, full of hope in every respect, by their joint efforts, and, as is frequently the case, through the economic ideas of the wife, succeed in accumulating a fortune, but they have no children: they reach old age together, and then the husband dies. What does the law of this State do then? It says to the widow, 'Hands off your late husband's property; do not touch it; the State will find others to whom it will give that, but you, the widow, must not touch it, only so much as will keep life within your aged body, that you may live to see those others enjoy what rightfully should be your own.' And the State seeks the relatives of the deceased husband, whether they be near or far, whether they were ever heard of before or not, and transfers to them, singly or collectively, the estate of the deceased husband and living widow."

Now, that is a specimen of unjust laws in all the States concerning womanhood. Instead of flying off to the discussion as to whether or not the giving of the right of voting to woman will correct these laws, let me say to men, be gallant enough, and fair enough, and honest enough, and righteous enough, and God-loving enough to correct these wrongs against women by your own masculine vote. Do not wait for woman suffrage to come, if it ever does come, but, so far as you can touch ballot-boxes and legislatures, and congresses, begin the reformation. But until justice is done to your sex by the laws of all the States, and women of America take the platforms and the pulpits, no honorable man will charge Vashti with having lost her veil.

Again: I want you this morning to consider

Vashti the Sacrifice.

Who is this that I see coming out of that palace-gate of Shushan? It seems to me that I have seen her before. She comes homeless, houseless, friendless, trudging along with a broken heart. Who is she? It is Vashti the sacrifice. Oh, what a change it was from regal position to a wayfarer's crust! A little while ago approved and sought for; now none so poor as to acknowledge her acquaintanceship. Vashti the sacrifice. Ah, you and I have seen it many a time. Here is a home empalaced with beauty. All that refinement and books and wealth can do for that home has been done; but Ahasuerus, the husband and the father, is taking hold on paths of sin. He is gradually going down. After a while he will flounder and struggle like a wild beast in the hunter's net—further away from God, further away from the right. Soon the bright apparel of the children will turn to rags; soon the household song will become the sobbing of a broken heart. The old story over again. Brutal Centaurs

Breaking up the Marriage

feast of Lapithae. The house full of outrage and cruelty and abomination, while trudging forth from the palace gate are Vashti and her children. There are homes represented in this house this morning that are in danger of such a breaking up. O, Ahasuerus, that you should stand in a home, by a dissipated life destroying the peace and comfort of that home. God forbid that your children should ever have to wring their hands, and have people point their finger at them as they pass down the street, and say: "There goes a drunkard's child." God forbid that the little feet should ever have to trudge the path of poverty and wretchedness. God forbid that any evil spirit, born of the wine-cup or the brandy-flask, should come forth and uproot that garden, and, with a blasting, blistering, all-consuming curse, shut for ever the palace gate against Vashti and the children.

Oh, the women and the men of sacrifice are going to take the brightest coronals of heaven! This woman of the text gave up palatial residence, gave up all for what she considered right. Sacrifice! Is there anything more sublime? A steamer, called the *Prairie Belle*, burning on the Mississippi River, Bludso, the engineer, declared he would keep the bow of the boat to the shore till all were off, and he kept his promise. At his post, scorched and blackened, he perished, but he saved all the passengers. Two verses of pathetic poetry describe the scene, but the verses are a little rough, and so I change a word or two:

"Through the hot, black breath of the burning
Jim Bludso's voice was heard.
And they all had trust in his stubbornness,
And knew he would keep his word.
And sure's you're born they all got off
Afore the smoke-stacks fell;
And Bludso's ghost went up above,
In the smoke of the *Prairie Belle*.
He weren't no saint, but at Judgment
I'd run my chance with Jim,
Longside of some pious gentleman
That wouldn't shake hands with him.
He'd seen his duty, a dead sure thing,
And went for it there and then,
And Christ is not going to be too hard
On a man that died for men."

Once more: I want you to look at *Vashti the silent*. You do not hear any outcry from this woman as she goes forth from the palace gate. From the very dignity of her nature you know there will be no vociferation. Sometimes in life it is necessary to make a retort; sometimes in life it is necessary to resist; but there are crises when the most triumphant thing to do is to keep silence. The philosopher, confident in his newly discovered principle, waited for the coming of more intelligent generations, willing that men should laugh at the lightning-rod and cotton-gin and steamboat—waiting for long years through the scoffing of philosophical schools, in grand and

Magnificent Silence.

Galileo, condemned by mathematicians and monks and cardinals, caricatured everywhere, yet waiting and watching with his telescope to see the coming up of stellar reinforcements, when the stars in their courses would fight for the Copernican system; then sitting down in complete blindness and deafness to wait for the coming on of the generations who would build his monument and bow at his grave. The reformer, execrated by his contemporaries, fastened in a pillory, the slow fires of public contempt burning under him, ground under the cylinders of the printing-press, yet calmly waiting for the day when purity of soul and heroism of character will get the sanction of earth and the plaudits of heaven. Affliction, enduring without any complaint the sharpness of the pang, and the violence of the storm, and the heft of the chain, and the darkness of the night—waiting until a divine hand shall be put forth to soothe the pang, and hush the storm, and release the captive. A wife abused, persecuted, and a perpetual exile from every earthly comfort—waiting, waiting, until the Lord shall gather up His dear children in a heavenly home, and no poor Vashti will ever be thrust out from the palace gate. Jesus, in silence, and answering not a word, drinking the gall, bearing the Cross, in prospect of the rapturous consummation when

"Angels thronged His chariot wheel,
And bore Him to His throne:
Then swept their golden harps and sung,
The glorious work is done."

An Arctic explorer found *a ship floating helplessly about among the icebergs*, and going on board he found that the captain was frozen at his logbook, and the helmsman was frozen at the wheel, and the men on the lookout were frozen in their places. That was awful, but magnificent. All the Arctic blasts and all the icebergs could not drive them from their duty. Theirs was

A Silence Louder Than Thunder.

And this old ship of a world has many at their posts in the awful chill of neglect, and frozen of the world's scorn, and their silence shall be the eulogy of the skies and be rewarded long after this weather-beaten craft of a planet shall have made its last voyage.

The Palace Gate of Heaven!

You can endure the hardships and the privations and the cruelties and the misfortunes of this life, if you can only gain admission there. Through the blood of the everlasting covenant, you go through those gates, or never go at all. When Rome was besieged, the daughter of its ruler saw the golden bracelets on the left arms of the enemy, and she sent word to them that she would betray her city and surrender it to them, if they would only give her those bracelets on their left arms. They accepted the proffer, and by night this daughter of the ruler of the city opened one of the gates. The army entered, and, keeping their promise, threw upon her their bracelets, and also their shields, until under the weight she died. Alas, that all through the ages the same folly has been repeated, and for the trinkets and glittering treasures of this world men and women swing open the portals of their immortal soul for an everlasting surrender, and die under the shining submergement.

Through the rich grace of our Lord Jesus Christ may you be enabled to imitate the example of Rachel and Hannah and Abigail and Deborah and Mary and Vashti. Amen!

A PHYSICIAN'S MISTAKE.

IN the current number of *Thy Healer* * is the following report of a testimony recently given at Bethshan by a Mr. Hobbs: "Bless the Lord for what He has done for me in respect of healing. I was taken ill last September twelve months, with blood poisoning. In two or three days I became delirious, and was so for six weeks. My life was trembling in the balance for several weeks. The doctor has told me since that he expected, when coming to see me, to see the blinds drawn; but my wife wrote to Bethshan, and asked the prayers of the Lord's people in my behalf, and from that time I began to get better. But there was a wound on my back that would not finally heal. The doctor said it would never heal. '*You will always*,' he said, '*have some little trouble with that*.' I spoke to another doctor. He said, 'You must have it burnt out.' I had it burnt, but it appeared again, and I had it burnt again. After this, I was at Mr. Allen's meeting, and was there led to trust the Lord for healing, and He has healed me. He has done for me what the doctors could not do."

A WARNING SIGNAL AT SEA.

A DISCUSSION of some interest to seamen has been carried on in the press as to the defects of the code of flag signals, by which conversation is carried on between passing vessels at sea. Instances have been cited in which a captain, who perceived that a vessel is in peril, has been unable to warn her captain, because there is no signal in the code expressing the warning he wished to give. One instance is that of the Guion steamship *Arizona*, which some eight years ago ran into an iceberg on the banks of Newfoundland. It is stated that she could have received warning of her danger on the previous day, had there been a signal which denoted that ice was ahead. The *Anchoria*, of the Anchor Line, which had sighted the iceberg, passed the *Arizona* about twelve hours before the accident, and the captain of the *Anchoria*, finding there was no signal in the code having reference to icebergs, suffered the *Arizona* to pass unwarned, and she afterward struck with such force that but for her water-tight bulkheads she must have sunk. The reply is made, that in that and similar cases, though there may be no specific signal, there is a general one which may be used with advantage. It is the signal, "*You are running into danger*," which is well known and often used. The same reply is often made to cavillers who insist that Bible teachings and warnings are of no use in the nineteenth century, as the conditions of life and the dangers and temptations are so different from those of the day in which the various inspired authors wrote. There can no temptation beset a man, no evil befall him, for which there is not an appropriate word of warning or which is not covered by some clear word of caution or direction in the Bible. (II Tim. 3:16.)

A CHINAMAN'S PRAYERS.

ONE of the most remarkable proofs of the divine origin of Christianity, is its adaptation to the condition of men of all stations and nationalities and the similarity of its effects upon all. An instance of this characteristic is mentioned in a letter from Mr. Hager, of Hong Kong, to the *Missionary Herald*. He says:

"We have several inquirers who are studying the Bible with us every evening, and one of these is a man who I think has a remarkably clear conception of what a Christian ought to be. It is a joy to instruct him further in the truths of the gospel. In telling me his experience a few days since, he said that he firmly believed the gospel, but that when he prayed he often felt that God was not present, and he thought that one ought to be conscious of the full presence of God before entering the church. 'Sometimes,' said he, 'I have felt that God was very near me, and I always desire to feel in this way.' As I listened to his simple and honest testimony of how he prayed that God might protect him during a typhoon which raged here a month ago, and how that *prayer was answered in a marvellous manner*, I could not but feel that God had revealed some things to this poor heathen soul, which many Christians of our home lands had to learn: namely, the confidence that a child of God may have in the Father's care. This man heard the gospel for the first time last year, when I was living in a Chinese inn, and some three or four months ago he came again into the chapel and heard me speak. Thinking that a tract upon the religions of China would be an excellent thing to give him, I gave him one, with which he afterward returned, and hearing the gospel more perfectly from our helper, he has been growing into the Christian life ever since.

* A monthly magazine edited by Mrs. M. Baxter, containing original articles on Holiness and Divine Healing. Annual subscription 75 cents. [illegible] be had from the office of this journal, 63 Bible House, New York.

A DYING MORMON BOY'S SONG.

IN a letter received from the Rev. J. D. Gillian, the devoted worker among the Mormons of Utah, he says: "All our mission schools are opened with singing gospel hymns, and scripture reading, followed with prayer, the school joining in the Lord's Prayer; so that thus the Mormons are taught spiritual songs, the fruit of which labor manifests itself in various ways. Here is one: Some years ago there entered one of our schools a youngest, 'ruined son' of a polygamous family, after he had been expelled from their own district school. Three winters he came to us and never caused us the least particle of trouble.

"At the close of the last winter of his attendance, he was taken suddenly ill with that dread disease, diphtheria, and, with three others of the family, carried to the grave.

"Their next door neighbor tells me that just before the spark of life fled, this young man opened his eyes and sung

"Rock of Ages, cleft for me,
Let me hide myself in Thee,"

and then closed them again, peacefully passing away.

"He never heard such songs in their Mormon meetings, and who knows but that the blessed Rock of Ages had revealed Himself to that poor boy, and at that last moment glory opened his lips in song."

A PRISONER'S DREAD.

RECENT scandals show that persons who lead double lives, indulging in secret sin while attending church regularly and professing to be strictly moral in their habits, run a terrible risk of exposure and disgrace. The fact that many do escape, however, is used by Satan to encourage them to go on in their hypocrisy, and they forget that a day is coming when exposure will be inevitable, and when those whom they love and whose love and respect they cherish will know them as they are. (Matt. 10: 26.)

An incident related by an ex-prison warden conveys a faint idea of the suffering such exposure will involve. He states that among the prisoners at one time under his care was a man who astonished him by declining to avail himself of the much coveted privilege of working in the garden of the prison on the Island. This privilege was accorded to prisoners as a reward for good behavior, and was much prized. This particular prisoner, however, declined it, and being pressed for his reason hesitated a moment, but finally told it. He had a wife and two children, who were ignorant of his being in prison. In the small yellow house, he said, directly *opposite his cell window* and just across the river where he would have to work, should he go outside, they were then living. He had watched his children all through the summer, playing in a vacant lot of land on the river-bank directly under his window, and so near him that he could hear the voices; and he could see his wife passing in and out of the house, or sitting at her window, little dreaming that he had been so near them for almost two years. His wife supposed he was in the West trying to obtain work, while he was really in prison for stealing. His feelings were respected, and he was allowed to serve out his sentence without being discovered. That prisoner said that his punishment had been aggravated by the sight of his dear ones so near him yet so separated by his sin. He thought he should die of shame if they knew where he was.

A PARISIAN WIFE BEATER.

AMONG the attendants of one of the McAll Mission stations in Paris was a woman whose dress was of the poorest, but it and the wearer were scrupulously clean. She was somewhat irregular in attendance, and being spoken to on the subject, said that her husband was violently opposed to her coming, and at times forbade it entirely. He was a drunkard, who beat her severely, and she was in terror of his outbreaks. She was advised to pray for him, and she said she did so continually.

"One night," says Mr. McAll, "he came home better disposed than usual, and, to the great surprise of his wife, he said to her, 'I am going to the meeting to-night with you; make haste!' The poor woman could hardly believe her ears. She prepared herself without delay, and all the way to the meeting she was praying inwardly that God would touch his heart. He listened very attentively, and seemed much interested. Going home his wife said nothing, for she was afraid of weakening the impression, but she prayed inwardly. The following evening he came back early and *sober*. While they were at supper, he asked where was the meeting that night, and, being told, he said he would go with her again. The poor woman could not imagine what it all meant. She did not dare hope that he was sincere. However, it was so, and when the service was over she said to me, 'This is my husband.' In shaking hands with me, he told me that with God's help he was a changed man, and had renounced his evil habits; he had asked pardon for his past life, and felt he had received it, and now he was determined to live for the Lord.

"I went to see them a fortnight ago, in their little room with its scanty furniture, but while I was there I could feel that it was sanctified by the presence of the Lord. He told me that now he was happy, that he had found the Saviour, and that his only desire was that his son, who is married and living in another part of the town, should be converted also. The wife was beaming with joy, her face still very pale, but no more sadness there; a quiet and extremely peaceful expression had taken its place."

LIFE IN THE ZENANA.

A STIRRING appeal for consecrated workers for India is made by Miss Easton, in a letter to the *Missionary Link*. She describes her own work in the homes of the people, and draws a touching picture of the benighted condition of the wives and mothers, who, being uneducated, and being kept in seclusion, are often mere nonentities in the home. In the course of her letter she says:

"It, a thing, is about the best description of her. Indeed, that is literally the way in which she is described in sacred books, unless she be fortunate enough to have a son, in which case she is known as his mother. It is sad, but true, that during all her early married life a woman is usually of not much more consequence in a family than a piece of furniture. After she has had children and becomes mistress of the house, she has some privileges that for years she never dreams of. To a good wife [as wives are esteemed there] her husband is a god, to whom she bows down and worships. I am led to this thought in connection with the women of this country by a conversation with my Munshi this morning, an unusually intelligent man, well educated, a tutor in one of the colleges; but his wife is a mere stick. He has a gentle disposition; so he is not unkind to her, but simply does not consider her at all; and how can he? While he has been out in the world, seeing its ways, reading its books, and getting his mind filled and furnished, she has been shut up in one room, or at the most has had the liberty of two or three in the same house; she never goes out, never sees anybody but her mother-in-law, who is more ignorant and superstitious than she. Until her baby came her life was a burden to her; now she has him to care for and love, and she is happy, but between husband and wife there is no ground of intercourse. What we need is more consecrated young women from home, to come out, and go in and out among these women, taking to them the work of God, helping them, lifting them up to a higher plane of living, comforting them 'with the comfort wherewith we ourselves are comforted of God.' They need just what American women would need under the same circumstances."

THE PROPHETS AND THE APOCALYPSE.

By Rev. N. West, D. D.

Difference Between Three Eras of Prophecy—The Discrimination of the Ends and Ages—The Essential Union of Prophecy—Israel in the Apocalypse—A Prominent Subject of all Prophecy—Her Final Triumph Assured—The Tableau of the End.

I HAVE said already* that the general and characteristic difference between pre-exile prophecy on the one hand, and exile and post-exile prophecy on the other, so far as the Ages and Ends are concerned, is that the former has only One End, One Advent and One Age succeeding that End, while the latter develop this End and this Age, first of all, into two Ends and Ages, and next into

Three Ends and Ages,

the last End in all cases being the Endless one. The whole future, undiscriminated, is seen in One End and Age in the earlier prophetic word. Turn to Isaiah, chapter eleventh, as a single illustration of this. Both Advents in that chapter are viewed as one, the whole future of grace and glory being foreshortened and seen as it were in perspective. The End or Epoch of Messiah's appearing is all-comprehensive of the whole development of the kingdom of God on earth. The prophet does not distinguish between a *Parousia* in humility and a *Parousia* in glory, but blends both, and describes the whole work of Messiah in one picture, without intervals, as a work complete. And so we find it in general everywhere. All the sufferings of the "Servant of Jehovah," and the glories after these, are commingled and focalized in the one End, and radiate into the age succeeding.

First comes the "*Day of the Lord,*" then the Messianic Age, Israel redeemed and glorious in front of it bringing life to the nations. In that Age, under the "New Covenant," sin is atoned and the sinner is pardoned, justified, renewed and sanctified, through faith in Messiah, the Spirit is poured out, the Gentiles are gathered, and showers of blessing fall in their season. The times of reviving and restitution enter history. The knowledge of the Lord is universal. The people are all righteous.

Jerusalem Restored

is transfigured, as is also the Holy Land. The precious things, the wealth of all nations, the glory of the Gentiles stream in to adorn it. The Temple is rebuilt in splendor unsurpassed. The Holy City is Jehovah's throne and dwelling-place. The land becomes fruitful. War ceases. Idolatry disappears. All nations are at peace, and man and nature too. The curse is gone. A painless, tearless, deathless state exists. The veil is removed from both Israel and the Gentiles. The Bridegroom rejoices over the Bride. Messiah reigns on David's throne forever and ever. A new Heaven and a new Earth crowns all. All belongs to the One End and One Age following it, in pre-exile prophecy.

But I showed you, also, how, in exile and post-exile prophecy this great and complex future began to be discriminated into various Ends and Ages, and how, by observing this discrimination, and by the help of New Testament light, reflected on the Old, we came to discover, not only our own present age, but the Millennial Age following, the "*Many Days,*" of Ezekiel 38 : 8. And now, allow me one brief word as to

Israel in the Apocalypse.

That wonderful book is capable of many "applications," but only of one organic "interpretation," based upon the entire unity and analogy of prophecy. We may "apply" its symbols to the times of early Pagan persecution, and also to later Papal persecutions. This is the figurative "application" based upon the equation of "Israel" with the "Christian Church." The Apocalypse was a book of comfort to the early Church. It was a comfort also to the witnesses of Christ in the Middle Age, and during the Reformation. But as surely as Israel "abides," Israel and Daniel's "people" are not the "Church," so surely is Israel the key for the true and final interpretation of the closing prophecy of the New Testament. It sums up in itself all the unfulfilled predictions respecting that chosen, predestined race. You meet Israel everywhere. The very announcement of the *Theme* of the book, viz., the Lord's Second Coming, refers us to Israel. "Behold, He *cometh with clouds*, and every eye shall see Him; *they also that pierced Him*" (Rev. 1: 7), i. e., the Jewish nation, as Zechariah assures us. The text is a combination of two passages, one from Zechariah, the other from Daniel, both in strict textual connection in the prophets with Israel's deliverance at the Second Advent of Messiah.

You meet Israel again in the promise made to the Philadelphian Church (Rev. 3: 7-11), by Him who is the "Lion of Judah's tribe," and has "the key of David."

Israel shall be Converted

in the last time, and in connection with the Coming of Christ. Again, you meet Israel in the Sealing of the 144,000 out of all their tribes (Rev. 7: 1-8), just before the Trumpet Judgments occur, and the Tribulation begins. Again, you meet Israel in Chapters 10, 11 and 12, chapters that place you in the very midst of Ezekiel's Valley of Dry Bones, and show you the prophetic word, and the Spirit of Life from God, with attending earthquake, beginning that work of spiritual, personal and national conversion and resurrection foretold by the prophets. The oath-taking Angel of the Covenant, Solar-faced and rainbow-crowned, whose shoulders are robed in cloud, and feet like pillars of fire, reminding you of the Pillar of Cloud in the Wilderness, and Him who dwelt in it, comes to His people again. The "little book" is the matter of the testimony of the "two witnesses." Their 1260 days of witness is the first half of Daniel's 70th week. The slaughter of the witnesses is in the middle of that week, and is the first public persecuting act of the last Antichrist. The succeeding 1260 days is the second half of that week, the time of the tribulation.

And again you see Israel triumphant in 15:3, 4, singing "the song of Moses, the servant of God, and the song of the Lamb," blending their first and last deliverances in one, and declaring that the time for national Christianity on earth has come, now that

Israel is Victorious,

and a nation converted to Christ. What you see in 14: 20 and 19 : 11-21 is the Armageddon conflict, closed out in the valley of Jehoshaphat, outside Jerusalem, the Lord Himself descending from "Heaven Opened," to destroy the Antichrist, bind Satan, raise the faithful dead, and begin the "thousand years'" blessed kingdom of glory on earth (Rev. 10: 1-7.) And what you see in Rev. 20: 9 is the "Beloved City," Jerusalem, restored, the home of the Daughter of Zion, which, for a "thousand years," has enjoyed the uninterrupted peace and glory and joy foretold by the prophets.

He who cannot see Israel here in this book, as distinct from the "Church" and the "Nations," will see nothing. After the 6th verse of the 1st chapter, in the 6th of the seven Epistles to the churches, between the 6th and 7th seals; between the 6th and 7th trumpets; between the 6th and 7th vials, in the wilderness here, on Mount Zion there, a worshipping part in the city now, a multitude pressing into the land from the East, a slaughter, a victory, a triumph, a glory, an effect on the nations, and all at the second coming of Christ; I say that he who cannot see this will see nothing! It is the eschatology of all the prophets. It is the eschatology of Christ. It is the eschatology of the Apostles—one eschatology from first to last, built and based on the one eternal plan and purpose of God with respect to Israel, an interpretation grounded in the unity, continuity, organic structure and genetic development of all prophecy, divine, infallibly sure, a light forever.

Look at it and see if it is not so. John has nothing the prophets have not. I have shown you this. He has nothing Christ has not, for the Apocalypse was given Him of God, and does not mean a literary production, but is

The "Revelation of Christ,"

as He comes the Second Time, to His covenant people, to fulfil the word of His promise to them, restore their state, and give them the kingdom. He has nothing the Apostles have not. His Eschatology is the same as that of Peter and Paul. Peter binds Israel's national repentance and the Second Coming of Christ together. (Acts 3: 19-21.) He tells of scoffers in the last days, of the world-judgment, the day of the Lord, the resurrection and the glory, the visible kingdom, and points to the New Heaven and Earth. (1 Pet. 3: 1-14.)

Paul also takes up each eschatological point and discusses it separately. In II Thess. 2 : 8 you have the Antichrist and the Second Coming of the Lord, but nothing is said of Israel. In Romans, chapter 11, you find Israel's conversion and the Second Coming, but nothing said about Antichrist. In 1 Cor. 15: 12-57, you hear him discussing the first resurrection at the Second Coming, but not a word about either Israel or Antichrist. In Romans 8: 17-23, you find him dilating upon the glorified inheritance on earth, to be received at the redemption of the body from the grave, when Christ comes, but nothing about any of the other points.

Now put all together, *combine* all that he says in one picture; what you get as a total result is Antichrist destroyed, Israel redeemed, the saints raised, the inheritance glorified and the Millennial interval between the Coming of Christ to assume the kingdom, and then the remote "End," when Christ surrenders the kingdom to the Father "that God may be all in all." 1 Cor. 15: 24—in short, you get precisely what John has given you in the Apocalypse, with this difference, that whereas Peter and Paul discuss the points separately, John discusses nothing, but combines all in a total

Tableau of the End

Time glowing under the highest light of the inspiration of the Holy Ghost. And so will every student of God's word find it, if only he comes to that word with a humble heart free from prejudice, and false theories of interpretation, and prays that God will open his eyes to see light in God's light alone, accounting all other light as but darkness. Blessed book is the Bible, the living word of the living God, one word from beginning to end, the work of one infinite mind, full of the wonders of wisdom, love and power! And from Moses to John, the Eschatology is one, because God's plan is one, the "*Thousand Years*" in John, following the Second Advent, and preceding the Last Judgment, being the very interval Paul himself has acknowledged in 1 Cor. 15: 24, and none other than the precise period of time, called by Hosea the "Third Day," by Isaiah a "Multitude of Days," and by Ezekiel "Many Days"—in every case, in both Old and New Testaments, associated with the glory of Israel in the Kingdom, and the redemption of the Nations accomplished by the Second Coming of Christ. The holy penmen mutually supplement each other. It is a demonstration, and true as the Book of God is true. The Lord open the eyes of His Church to see it, and love it, and teach it, and to Him be the glory forever.

---

* See last week's issue of this journal, page 71.

CHRISTIAN HERALD AND SIGNS OF OUR TIMES.

OFFICE, 63 BIBLE HOUSE, NEW YORK.
ENTERED AT THE POST-OFFICE AT NEW YORK, N. Y., AS SECOND-CLASS MATTER.

Published Weekly. Subscription price, $1.50 a year; $1 eight months; 75 cents six months; sent two months on trial for 25 cents; always payable in advance. Single copies for sale by, or can be ordered at, all newsdealers.

Remittances by Mail should be by Post-office money order, bank cheques, or drafts or express money order, and should always be made payable to THE CHRISTIAN HERALD.

Receipts are not sent, the receipt of the paper by a subscriber is a sufficient proof that his remittance has been received. If the paper does not arrive promptly, please advise us, that we may see if the address is correctly entered.

Change of Address. Name of Post Office and State, of both old and new address, should always be given in case of removal.

CURRENT EVENTS.

The Surplus in the Treasury Amounted to eighty-five million dollars on February 1. This shows a reduction in the balance against the Government for the month of January of over fifteen millions. The total reduction since the commencement of the fiscal year on July 1, 1887, is now sixty-nine millions. If that rate of reduction is maintained for the rest of the fiscal year it will reach a total or $144,000,000. There is, at present, no way in which this accumulation can be applied to the reduction of the debt except the purchase of bonds at a premium.

The New Extradition Treaty with Great Britain is arousing much public interest. It is stimulated by the refusal of the Senate to discuss it in open session. Mr. Riddleberger urged that course, but the Senate would not consent to publicity. It has been disclosed, however, that several amendments to the treaty have been proposed, among them one adding to the list of extraditable offences, assaults with explosives of any kind, and larceny and embezzlement. This would bring within the provisions of the treaty the Irish dynamiters who take refuge in the United States, and the American embezzlers who now find an asylum in Canada. The friends of the treaty express sanguine hopes of its ratification.

The Proposed Change in the Termination of the Presidential and Congressional terms, has again been endorsed by the Senate. On February 1, it adopted Senator Hoar's joint resolution proposing an amendment to the Constitution providing that the term of office of the President and of the Fiftieth Congress shall continue until April 30, 1889, at noon; and that in future April 30, at noon, shall be substituted for March 4, as the commencement and termination of the official term of the President, Vice-President, Senators, and Representatives in Congress.

The Nicaraguan Canal Expedition has Encountered a serious obstacle in the heavy rains, which have been almost incessant since its arrival on the Isthmus. A reporter who accompanied the expedition, writes that, with the exception of a few miles of transit line, the weather has been such that little beyond establishing a camping site accessible to wind and sun has been accomplished. He reports days of hard physical labor and exposure, and sleepless nights in damp forests, with only a rubber blanket and palm leaves for a bed. "Civil engineering," he says, "at its best is beset with many difficulties, but in a country of dense tropical vegetation, where primeval forest trees have stood for ages, and countless vines gnarled and twisted have matted themselves into an impassable barrier, from which the light of day is often hidden, the running of a transit line is attended with something more than ordinary hardship." A member of the expedition who acts as mail carrier between camps, set out one morning with a Nicaraguan for a camp but a short distance away. He expected to return in a few hours, but lost his way, owing to the clouds which obscured the sun. The two men wandered about for nine days in the forest with no food but the bark of trees. They were almost dead when they came upon a river, on which, floating on logs, they returned to the camp.

The Bad Mail Service in the West is Being investigated by a Senate Committee. Formalities about all Government inquiries are necessary, so possibly there is no other way of dealing with the evil than by the labor of an investigating committee. Investigation, however, seems a farce in a case that presents no mystery at all. Economy has been the object aimed at for some years past, and no particular desire to maintain efficiency has been displayed. The force of clerks in the chief offices is and has been ridiculously inadequate, and in many offices the clerks owe their appointments to politics, and not to intelligence or industry. It may be hoped that Mr. Dickinson will not wait for the report of the Committee before removing the abuses. As a case in point, this journal is now mailed fully *twenty-four hours earlier than formerly*, yet complaints of delay in delivery are numerous.

The Gigantic Strike in Pennsylvania is to be investigated by a special committee of the House. An effort was made to have it referred to the Inter-State Commerce Committee, but a strong appeal against that course was made by Mr. Rayner, of Maryland, who said the inquiry might as usefully be confided to the Chinese Embassy. The work of the Committee is to include an investigation into the grievances of the miners, collective and individual, and it is directed to ascertain the points in dispute between the miners and their employers, a trouble which Mr. Randall declared was a greater one than that between the railroad company and its employees. It was openly stated in the House by Mr. Rayner that the Reading Company defied the laws of Pennsylvania, that forbid a corporation doing business as a common carrier to engage in any other business. This had been done by incorporating within itself the Reading Coal and Iron Company, of which, and of the Reading Railroad, Mr. Corbin was President. In proof of his statement, he reminded the House that when called upon in Pennsylvania to pay a tax the Reading Company had maintained that it was an inter-State corporation.

The Effort to Secure Agreement Between authors and publishers on the details of an international copyright scheme has been renewed. The difficulty which has prevented an arrangement so far, and which is not yet solved, is the importation of copies printed abroad of a foreign work copyrighted here. The great body of American publishers are ready to accept a bill containing what is called a manufacturing clause, providing for the printing, etc., in this country, of all foreign books enjoying the protection of American copyright. Some influential publishers, however, want the absolute prohibition of all foreign editions of books copyrighted in America, which prohibition is contained in the Chace bill, which has been reintroduced in the Senate. On this point, the divergence is decisive. The Authors' League would prefer that matters should remain in their present condition to having international copyright burdened with such a prohibition.

A Marvellous Case of Juvenile Depravity has come to light in New York. A remarkable series of suspicious fires—six in a short space of time—have occurred in the Home for the Ruptured and Cripples in Forty-second Street. The last of these broke out on February 2, and a previous one on January 29. Happily, none of the patients perished, though in the fire of Sunday they were in great danger. Before the hook and ladder companies arrived, car conductors and drivers, and well-dressed men on their way to the Grand Central Depot or their homes, vied with each other in carrying the poor little cripples to places of safety. They were saved, but one of the domestic servants was suffocated before she was found by the firemen. The frequency of the fires at last aroused suspicion, and an investigation was made. It was discovered that the fires were all set by a little girl eleven years old, May Wilson, who, on being charged with the crime, confessed her guilt. She is herself a cripple, and has been tenderly cared for in the Home during the last three years. The nurses and attendants thought her a child of sweet disposition—the last in the Home likely to commit such a crime. It is supposed that she must be demented, as she seems to have had no motive for the fiendish act; but no other evidences of insanity are found in her.

Two Slight Shocks of Earthquake were Reported last week. One in this country and a second in England. On Monday, January 30, a tremor was distinctly felt at various places in Rhode Island. It was noticed at Providence and Newport by a large number of persons. They agree in stating that it was forty minutes past midnight when it occurred. Houses shook and articles on shelves were thrown down. A rumbling noise accompanied the vibration, as if a heavily laden wagon were being driven through the street. The shock at Newport was at first supposed to have been caused by a dynamite explosion in the harbor, but that theory was disproved. The British shock occurred on Thursday last. It was most severe in Scotland, notably at Dingwall, County Ross, and Inverness. In the English midlands, also, the shock was noticed. Coventry, Birmingham and its suburbs, and other towns in that locality, were shaken. No damage was done by the convulsion.

The Enforcement of the Coercion Act in Ireland continues with unabated vigor. The trial of Mr. Cox, member of Parliament, for making a speech at Kildysart, County Clare, in October, inciting tenants to conspiracy, has resulted in Mr. Cox being convicted and sentenced to one month's imprisonment. He was taken to Limerick and lodged in the jail there. There was no demonstration. It is stated that on the expiration of Mr. Cox's sentence he will be rearrested on a charge of making a speech at Schull inciting the people to conspiracy. The drift of public opinion in England is said by sagacious observers to be hostile to Home Rule in Ireland. This is especially so in London.

The Crown Prince of Germany is Stated by Dr. Mackenzie, his English physician, to be making encouraging progress. The doctor is extremely guarded in his reports, but he evidently cherishes the belief that the Prince's malady is not cancer. He paid his illustrious patient a visit at San Remo last week, and examined his throat. He pronounced it much better than when he saw it last in December. The improvement is due in a great measure to the separation of a piece of morbid tissue, surgically termed slough, which had become decayed and been thrown off. The curative process which has been taking place is an effort of nature to get rid of the disease, and is never seen in cases of cancer. Professor Virchow confirms this hopeful view of the case. He examined the piece of tissue under the microscope, and states that it contained no trace of cancer.

A Sensational Suicide has Occurred in St. Petersburg. An English journal states that it has authentic intelligence of the event, which the Russian Government, according to its custom, has kept a secret. An officer of the Russian army was found shot near the heart. He was taken to an hospital, and there, being assured that he was near death, he made a confession, which was taken down in writing. He declared that he was a member of a secret society which resolved to assassinate the Czar. A ballot was taken to decide who should undertake the task, and the lot fell upon him. Rather than commit the crime he determined to take his own life, and he had therefore shot himself.

Pastor C. H. Spurgeon Appears Anxious that his severance of connection with the Baptist Union should not be misunderstood. In a letter to the Union, cabled to the American press last week, Mr. Spurgeon says that every union, unless it is a fiction, must be based upon certain principles. The doctrine of baptism by immersion will not suffice as a groundwork. There are other doctrines, besides, which are essential. He is unable to feel fellowship with a man merely because of his adherence to the doctrine of immersion, if in other matters he is false to the teachings of Scripture. It is on the doctrine of the Inspiration and verbal infallibility of the Bible and on the Calvinistic theology that Mr. Spurgeon differs from some of his brethren in the Baptist ministry, but well-informed journals declare that the number of the heterodox is relatively very small. Mr. Spurgeon has been urged by the Baptist Union to relieve it of the stigma his withdrawal casts upon it. It appeals to him to state the names of the ministers with whom he objects to associate, but as such a statement would render him liable to a series of actions for libel, Mr. Spurgeon will act prudently in keeping silence.

A Clergyman's Tact in Dealing with a Lunatic recently, saved him from a conflict. The *Evening Star*, of Washington, D. C., states that about four o'clock on a Sunday afternoon a man rang the bell of the house where lives the Rev. Edward H. Swem, pastor of the Second Baptist Church. He was admitted and conducted to the pastor's study. He then declared wildly that he was the Lord Jesus Christ, and that a minister whom he named was the Apostle Peter. He also stated that the devil was confined over in the insane asylum. He ended by demanding a sum of money. "Step this way," said Mr. Swem, gravely but firmly, and conducted the maniac out on the front steps. "I want you," he continued "to go to the large building on the corner of E and Fifth streets and wait there until I come." Much to Mr. Swem's relief the maniac obeyed, and the building being a police station, he was taken care of until he could be returned to the asylum from which he had escaped.

A Man Repenting of Repentance is Described in a Boston journal. It appears that at the Vendome banquet to Gen. Sherman, on February 1, several extra waiters were employed. At the conclusion of the festivity they all feasted on the remains of the banquet, and one of them who had a partiality for ice cream, indulged in the delicacy to excess. He was taken sick in the night, and suffered excruciating pain. A physician was sent for, who upon his arrival was anxiously asked by the sick man if he were going to die, because if so he wanted to confess a crime. The physician, thinking that in any case the confession should be made, answered that he had seen many men die from a similar cause. The man then confessed that during the evening he had secreted spoons, forks and other silver articles in his bag, and had brought them home. The stolen articles were then handed to the doctor. The penitent thief did not die, and he will probably live to stand his trial for the theft. To a reporter the man said, with evident sincerity, that he felt himself to be the greatest fool in Boston. It may be hoped that he will yet be the subject of still another repentance, which will be "repentance unto salvation, not to be repented of" (II Cor. 7 : 10), or there will be no escape from that state where there is "no place for repentance, though it be sought carefully and with tears." (Heb. 12 : 17.)

The Swift Descent of a Steep Hill a Thousand feet long resulted in a fatal accident in St. Paul,, Minn., on January 27. A cable road is run on the hill, and that morning two cars were on the track going down the hill. The man who controlled the grip-apparatus found, when a few feet from the starting-point, that the grip had not a firm hold on the cable. He therefore applied the brakes, and in doing so, released the cable altogether. The tracks were icy, and the heavily laden cars began sliding down the hill by their own momentum, at a speed which increased every moment until it became frightful. There was no means of getting a fresh hold on the cable, and the brakes, though they prevented the wheels turning, could not prevent their slipping on the icy rails. At the foot of the hill there is a curve which, when the cars reached it in their mad descent, could not be safely turned. The second car swung outward and fell on its side with a crash. One passenger was killed outright, another had his hand torn off at the wrist, and all were injured more or less seriously. Some moral and spiritual wrecks in life result from an analogous cause. The church is often distressed by seeing persons who have made a profession of religion fall into grievous sin, and irretrievable ruin. They had not a firm hold on Christ at the beginning of their Christian life, and when trial and temptation came no power of their own could check their downward course. (Gal 5 : 7, 8.)

A Race for a Bride was Run at Fulton, Mo., on January 30. The young lady, who is the daughter of a farmer, was wooed by two lovers, one of whom is an opulent Texan farmer, and and the other, whom she preferred, is poor, but young and handsome. The Texan, finding his rival had a better prospect than himself of winning the prize, appealed to the girl's father, and promised to pay him five thousand dollars if the marriage could be arranged. Thus stimulated, the father sent his daughter on a visit to some friends, and warned the poorer suitor off. The girl temporized to gain time, and allowed her father and the Texan to suppose that she had yielded to them; but she secretly notified the poor suitor of her place of retirement, and suggested that he get a license and end the struggle by marrying her at once. The Texan, also, was prompted by the father to hasten matters, and he applied for a marriage license. He found that his rival had obtained one only half an hour before, and realizing that no time was to be lost, he ran at the top of his speed to the house where the girl was staying. He was too late, however, for his rival, learning that the Texan was in town, and guessing his business, had also run as hard as he could, and being the fleeter runner, had gained time enough to have the ceremony performed before the Texan's arrival. In the Christian race, happily, success does not depend on riches or strength. Union with Christ is secured by the poor and weak more frequently than by any others. (1 Cor. 1 : 26–28.)

The Arrest of Wealthy and Influential Citizens caused some surprise in Toronto on February 1. Four gentlemen of the highest respectability, at least one of whom is a millionaire, received summonses from the police magistrates to answer to the charge of compounding a felony. Three of the indicted men are respectively president, manager and solicitor of a well-known bank. Some time ago a note for $1,500 was presented at the bank for discount. The manager of the bank, examining the note after the depositor had left, noticed an informality in its wording, and sent it to the merchant by whom it purported to be signed, for him to rectify the error. The merchant at once denounced the signature as a forgery. Search was then made for the depositor, and he was found late at night at his home. He was brought to the bank, where he was informed by the bank's officers of the discovery that had been made. Finding the proof so clear he confessed his guilt, and said that he was engaged in a profitable business, but was short of capital. He would be able to redeem the note at maturity, and satisfied the officers of the bank that they ran no risk of loss in holding the note. Ultimately the culprit was allowed to go free, and no exposure took place at the time. Now, however, the persons who condoned his offence find that by doing so they violated the law. The forgery was a crime against the State which they had no power to forgive. It is this principle of inviolable justice which, applied to all sin, made the atonement of Christ necessary before pardon could be offered to the world. Only when the Redeemer had borne the penalty and satisfied justice could the sinner be held justified. (Rom. 3 : 26.)

A Remarkable Invention Called a Micro-Detector is described in a despatch from Houston, Tex. It states that on Wednesday of last week a number of scientists and reporters were invited to the jail, to test the efficiency of an electric machine, which not only conveyed noises to a distance, but increased their volume. When in working position, it will warn a jailer if prisoners in a distant part of the prison are attempting to escape by sawing, filing, or using any other adroit means. It was tested by a number of citizens posting themselves in a room in the back part of the prison, with doors closed. A clock was put in motion in a cell in one of the wings. Every click could be distinctly heard in the room. A saw was used gently on the bars of another cell, and the sound as heard by the party was a loud sawing noise. The instrument is worked by electricity on a single wire, the various noises of the cells coming over it distinctly. The invention is considered wonderful. And what is still more remarkable, it is the work of a prisoner, who has thus placed in the hands of the authorities the means of keeping a more vigorous watch over himself and his fellow-prisoners. Now the slightest whisper of a prisoner can be distinctly heard by the wardens on duty. Knowledge of this fact will doubtless make the men cautious, because in a jail, punishment is apt to follow promptly on an offence. Profane and mendacious persons are apt to forget that their words are not only so heard by the just God, but are registered against them. (Mat 12 : 36.)

BRIEF NOTES.

A large fire in Broadway, New York, on January 30, destroyed five buildings, containing property worth two million dollars. Two firemen were severely injured.

The Rev. Jackson Wray, the author of "The Friends of Aspendale," published in these pages last year, has received an invitation to become pastor of Zion Church, Toronto, at a salary of $4,000.

Two ladies have given a thousand dollars each toward the million dollar fund for Presbyterian ministers. They ask other ladies to join them in making a list of fifty subscribers of a like amount.

Arrangements for delegations from America to the International Missionary Convention to be held in London next spring, are being made; a series of meetings for the purpose have been held in New York and Brooklyn, the latter in Dr. Talmage's Tabernacle.

Dr. L. W. Munhall's meetings in Baltimore, Md., have stirred the whole city. On Sundays the meetings were held in Oratorio Hall, which was packed, and thousands were turned away for want of room. He is now holding meetings in Buffalo, N. Y.

Rev. E. Payson Hammond has been holding meetings in a tent at San Diego, Cal. It is unnecessary to say that the severe weather experienced in other parts of the country did not prevail there. All the churches of the city united in the work.

The estate of the late ex-Governor Washburn, of Massachusetts, amounted to $386,000, of which $159,000 is to be divided between the Commissioners of Foreign Missions, the Home Missionary Society and the Missionary Association.

The Rev. H. W. Brown and Mr. Avis are reaching large masses of the people in Nebraska. A correspondent at Grand Island states that in all the years of his residence there he never witnessed a movement so profound and extended. Mr. Brown is giving special attention to warnings against the sin of social immorality.

The Rev. H. S. Jenanyan and the Rev. Alexander McLachlan, two of last year's graduates from the Union Seminary, sailed on January 28 for Tarsus in the Ottoman Empire, where they are to superintend St. Paul's Institute, a newly founded Christian training school for the poor and orphan youth.

A religious canvass of the city of Minneapolis, Minn., is being made to ascertain the religious status of the people, and to stimulate attendance upon public worship and Sunday-school service. It is intended to hand every pastor a catalogue with residence of all attendants upon his church, and a list of non-church-goers, but who may express a preference for his church.

Clergymen and Evangelists who will Allow

Copies of the CHRISTIAN HERALD to be placed in the seats of churches, or will have them distributed at the doors, will be supplied with assorted parcels of back numbers if they will write to the Manager 63 Bible House, New York.

HEALING BY STRIPES.

A New Sermon, by Pastor C. H. Spurgeon.

"With His stripes we are healed." Isa. 53 : 5.

A Bible-Searcher Rewarded—Discovers the Means of Healing—I. Sin as a Disease—Deranges the System—Painful or Benumbing—Fatal—II. The Remedy—Christ's Physical and Mental Sufferings—What the Roman Scourge Was—How to Apply the Ointment—III. The Remedy Effective Wherever Applied—Heals Character—Conscience—A Personal Testimony—A Comparison of Walking-Sticks—A Soul-Saving Telegram—Conversion of a Murderer in Brazil—Four Lines of Poetry Blessed to a General, and an Officer.

BEING one evening in Exeter Hall, I heard our late beloved brother, Mr. Mackay, of Hull, make a speech, in which he told us of a person who was under very deep concern of soul, and felt that he could never rest till he found salvation. So, taking the Bible into his hand, he said to himself, "Eternal life is to be found somewhere in this Word of God; and if it be here I will find it, for I will read the Book right through, praying to God over every page of it, if perchance it may contain some saving message for me." He told us that the earnest seeker read on through Genesis, Exodus, Leviticus, and so on; and though Christ is there very evidently, he could not find Him in the types and symbols. Neither did the holy histories yield him comfort, nor the book of Job. He passed through the Psalms, but did not find his Saviour there; and the same was the case with the other books till he reached Isaiah. In this prophet he read on till near the end, and then in the fifty-third chapter these words arrested his delighted attention, "*With His stripes we are healed.*" "Now I have found it," says he.

"The Healing that I Need

for my sin-sick soul, and I see how it comes to me through the sufferings of the Lord Jesus Christ. Blessed be His name, I am healed!" It was well that the seeker was wise enough to search the sacred volume; it was better still that in that volume there should be such a life-giving word, and that the Holy Spirit should reveal it to the seeker's heart. I said to myself, "That text will suit me well, and peradventure a voice from God may speak through it yet again to some other awakened sinner."

I. In endeavoring to come to the full meaning of the text, I would remark, first, that God, in infinite mercy, here treats

Sin as a Disease.

"With His stripes"—that is, the stripes of the Lord Jesus—"we are healed." Through the sufferings of our Lord, sin is pardoned, and we are delivered from the power of evil: this is regarded as the healing of a deadly malady. The Lord in this present life treats sin as a disease. Our sin is our crime rather than our calamity: however, God looks at it in another way for a season. That He may be able to deal with us on hopeful grounds, He looks at the sickness of sin, and not as yet at the wickedness of sin. Nor is this without reason, for men who indulge in gross vices are often charitably judged by their fellows to be not only wholly wicked, but partly mad. Propensities to evil are usually associated with a greater or less degree of mental disease; perhaps, also, of physical disease.

Sin is a disease, for *it is not essential to manhood*, nor an integral part of human nature as God created it. It is a disease, because it puts the whole system of the man out of order. It places the lower faculties in the higher place, for it makes the body master over the soul. Sin is a disease which in some cases causes extreme pain and anguish, but in other instances deadens sensibility. It frequently happens that, the more sinful a man is, the less he is conscious of it. It was remarked of a certain notorious criminal that many thought him innocent because, when he was charged with murder, he did not betray the least emotion. In that wretched self-possession there was to my mind presumptive proof of his great familiarity with crime: if an innocent person is charged with a great offence, the mere charge horrifies him. The deeper a man goes in sin, the less does he allow that it is sin. Like a man who takes opium, he acquires the power to take larger and larger doses, till that which would kill a hundred other men has but slight effect upon him. By and by sin is sure to cause pain, like other diseases which flesh is heir to: and when its awakening comes, what a start it gives! Conscience one day will awake, and fill the guilty soul with alarm and distress, if not in this world, yet certainly in the next. Then will it be seen what an awful thing it is to offend against the law of the Lord.

This disease is fatal. Is it not written, "The soul that sinneth, it shall die"? "Sin, when it is finished, bringeth forth death." There is no hope of eternal life for any man unless sin be put away. This disease never exhausts itself so as to be its own destroyer. Evil men wax worse and worse. In another world, as well as in this present state, character will, no doubt, go on to develop and ripen, and so the sinner will become more and more corrupt as the result of his spiritual death. God, therefore, treats sin as a disease, because it is a disease; and I want you to feel that it is so, for then you will thank the Lord for thus dealing with you.

II. God treats sin as a disease, and He declares

The Remedy

which He has provided: "With His stripes we are healed." I ask you very solemnly to accompany me in your meditations, for a few minutes, while I bring before you the stripes of the Lord Jesus. The Lord resolved to restore us, and therefore He sent His Only-begotten Son, "Very God of very God," that He might descend into this world to take upon Himself our nature, in order to our redemption. He lived as a man among men; and, in due time, after thirty years or more of service, the time came when He should do us the greatest service of all, namely, stand in our stead, and bear the chastisement of our peace. He went to Gethsemane, and there, at the first taste of our bitter cup, He sweat great drops of blood. It is very rarely that a man sweats blood. There have been one or two instances of it, and they have been followed by almost immediate death; but our Saviour lived—lived after an agony which, to any one else, would have proved fatal. Ere He could cleanse His face from this dreadful crimson, they hurried Him to the high-priest's hall. In the dead of night they bound Him and led Him away. Anon they took Him to Pilate and to Herod. These scourged Him, and their soldiers spat in His face, and buffeted Him, and put on His head a crown of thorns. Scourging is one of the most awful tortures that can be inflicted by malice.

The Roman Scourge

is said to have been made of the sinews of oxen, twisted into knots, and into these knots were inserted slivers of bone, and buckle-bones of sheep; so that every time the scourge fell upon the bare back, "the plowers made deep furrows." Our Saviour was called upon to endure the fierce pain of the Roman scourge, and this not as the *finis* of his punishment, but as a preliminary to crucifixion. To this they added buffeting, and plucking of the hair; they spared Him no form of pain. In all His faintness, through bleeding and fasting, they made Him carry His cross until another was forced, by the forethought of their cruelty, to bear it, lest their victim should die on the road. They stripped Him, and threw Him down, and nailed Him to the wood. They pierced His hands and His feet. They lifted up the tree, with Him upon it, and then dashed it down into its place in the ground, so that all His limbs were dislocated.

There He hung, a spectacle to God and men. Now were all manner of bodily pains centered in His tortured frame. All the while His enemies stood around, pointing at Him in scorn, thrusting out their tongues in mockery, jesting at His prayers, and gloating over His sufferings. He cried, "I thirst," and then they gave Him vinegar mingled with gall. After a while He said, "It is finished." He had endured the utmost of appointed grief, and had made full vindication to divine justice: then, and not till then, He gave up the ghost.

To describe the outward sufferings of our Lord is not easy: I acknowledge that I have failed. But His soul-sufferings, which were the soul of His sufferings, who can even conceive, much less express, what they were? At the very first I told you that He sweat great drops of blood. That was His heart driving out its life-floods to the surface through the terrible

Depression of Spirit

which was upon Him. He said, "My soul is exceeding sorrowful, even unto death." When nailed to the cross He endured what no martyr ever suffered; for martyrs, when they have died, have been so sustained of God that they have rejoiced amid their pain; but our Redeemer was forsaken of His Father, until He cried, "My God, my God, why hast thou forsaken me?" That was the bitterest cry of all, the utmost depth of His unfathomable grief. Yet was it needful that He should be deserted, because God must turn His back on sin, and consequently upon Him who was made sin for us.

The remedy for your sins and mine is found in the substitutionary sufferings of the Lord Jesus, and in these only. These "stripes" of the Lord Jesus Christ were on our behalf. Do you inquire, "Is there anything for us to do, to remove the guilt of sin?" I answer: There is nothing whatever for you to do. By His stripes we are healed. All those stripes He has endured, and left not one for us to bear.

"But must we believe on Him?" Ay, certainly. If I say of a certain ointment that it heals, I do not deny that you need a bandage with which to apply it to the wound. Faith is the linen which binds the plaster of Christ's reconciliation to the sore of our sin. The linen does not heal; that is the work of the ointment. So faith does not heal; that is the work of the atonement of Christ. "But we must repent," cries another. Assuredly we must, and shall, for repentance is the first sign of healing; but the stripes of Jesus heal us, and not our repentance. These stripes, when applied to the heart, work repentance in us: we hate sin because it made Jesus suffer. When you intelligently trust in Jesus as having suffered for you, then you discover the fact that God will never punish you for the same offence for which Jesus died. Thus "with His stripes we are healed."

III. I have tried to put before you the disease and the remedy; I now desire to notice the fact that this remedy is immediately

Effective Wherever it is Applied.

The stripes of Jesus do heal men: they have healed many of us. It does not look as if it could effect so great a cure, but the fact is undeniable. I often hear people say, "If you preach up this faith in Jesus Christ as saving men, they will be careless about holy living." I am as good a witness on that point as anybody, for I live every day in the midst of men who are trusting to the stripes of Jesus for their salvation, and I have seen no ill effect following from such a trust; but I have seen the very reverse. I bear testimony that I have seen the very worst of men become the very best of men by believing in the Lord Jesus Christ. These stripes heal in a surprising manner the moral diseases of those who seemed past remedy.

The character is healed. I have seen the drunkard become sober, the harlot become chaste, the passionate man become gentle, the covetous man become liberal, and the liar become truthful, simply by trusting in the sufferings of Jesus. If it did not make good men of them, it would not really do anything for them, for you must judge men by their fruits after all; and if the fruits are not changed the tree is not changed. Character is everything: if the character be not set right, the man is not saved. But we say it without fear of contradiction, that the atoning sacrifice, applied to the heart heals the disease of sin. If you doubt it, try it. He that believes in Jesus is sanctified as well as justified; by faith he becomes henceforth an altogether changed man.

The fact that "with His stripes we are healed" is a matter in evidence. I shall take liberty to bear

My Own Witness.

Years ago, when I was a youth, the burden of my sin was exceedingly heavy upon me. I had fallen into no gross vices, and should not have been regarded by any one as being specially a transgressor; but I regarded myself as such, and I had good reason for so doing. My conscience was sensitive because it was enlightened; and I judged that, having had a godly father, and a praying mother, and having been trained in the ways of piety, I had sinned against much light, and consequently there was a greater degree of guilt in my sin than in that of others.

I tried to do as well as I could, and to behave myself aright; but in my own judgment I grew worse and worse. I felt more and more despondent. I attended every place of worship within my reach, but I heard nothing which gave me lasting comfort till, one day I heard a simple preacher of the gospel speak from the text, "Look unto Me, and be ye saved, all the ends of the earth." When he told me that all I had to do was to "look" to Jesus—to Jesus the crucified One, I could scarcely believe it. He went on, and said, "Look! Look! Young man, look!" I did look; and in that moment relief came to me, and I felt such overflowing joy that I could have stood up, and cried, "Hallelujah! Glory be to God, I am delivered from the burden of my sin!"

Many days have passed since then; but my faith has held me up, and compelled me to tell out the story of free grace and dying love. I can truly say:

"E'er since by faith I saw the stream
Thy flowing wounds supply,
Redeeming love has been my theme,
And shall be till I die."

I hope to sit up in my bed in my last hours, and tell of the stripes that healed me. I hope some young men, yea, and old men before me, will at once try this remedy; it is good for all characters and ages. "With His stripes we are healed."

I want to talk with those who have not tried

This Marvellous Heal-all.

Let us come to close quarters. Friend, you are by nature in need of soul-healing as much as any of us, and one reason why you do not care about the remedy is because you do not believe that you are sick. I saw *a peddler* one day, as I was walking out: he was selling walking-sticks. He followed me, and offered me one of the sticks. I showed him mine—a far better one than any he had to sell—and he withdrew at once. He could see that I was not likely to be a purchaser. I have often thought of that when I have been preaching. I show men the righteousness of the Lord Jesus, but they show me their own, and all hope of dealing with them is gone. Unless I can prove that their righteousness is worthless, they will not seek the righteousness which is of God by faith. Oh, that the Lord would show you your disease, and then you would desire the remedy!

Suppose, for a moment, you are not healed, let me ask the question, "*Why are you not?*" You know the gospel: why are you not healed by Christ? "I don't know," says one. But, my dear friend, I beseech you, do not rest until you do know. "I can't get at it," says somebody. The other day a young girl was

Putting a Button On

her father's coat. She was sitting with her back to the window, and she said, "Father, I can't see; I am in my own light." He said, "Ah, my daughter, that is where you have been all your life!" This is the position of some of you spiritually. You are in your own light; you think too much of yourselves. There is plenty of light in the Sun of Righteousness, but you get in the dark by putting self in the way of that Sun. Oh, that yourself might be put away! I read a touching story the other day as to how one found peace. A young man had been for some time under a sense of sin, longing to find mercy; but he could not reach it. He was *a telegraph clerk*, and being in the office one morning he had to receive and transmit a telegram. To his great surprise, he spelt out these words—"Behold the Lamb of God, which taketh away the sin of the world." A gentleman, out for a holiday, was telegraphing a message in answer to a letter from a friend who was in trouble of soul. It was meant for another, but he that transmitted it received eternal life, as the words came flashing into his soul.

I met this week with something that pleased me—how one man, being healed, may be the means of blessing to another. Many years ago I preached a sermon in Exeter Hall, which was printed, and entitled, "Salvation to the Uttermost." A friend, who lives not very far from this place, was in the city of Para, in Brazil. Here he heard of

An Englishman in Prison

who had in a state of drunkenness committed a murder, for which he was confined for life. Our friend went to see him, and found him deeply penitent, but quietly restful, and happy in the Lord. He had felt the terrible wound of blood-guiltiness in his soul, but it had been healed, and he felt the bliss of pardon. Here is the story of the poor man's conversion as I have it: "A young man, who had just completed his contract with the gas-works, was returning to England, but before doing so he called to see me, and brought with him a parcel of books. When I opened it, I found they were novels; but, being able to read, I was thankful for anything.

"After I had read several of the books, I found a sermon preached by C. H. Spurgeon, in Exeter Hall, on June 8, 1856, from the words, 'Wherefore he is able also to save them to the uttermost,' etc. (Heb. 7:25.) In his discourse, Mr. Spurgeon referred to Palmer, who was then lying under sentence of death in Stafford Goal, and in order to bring home this text to his hearers, he said that if Palmer had committed many other murders, if he repents and seeks God's pardoning love in Christ, even he will be forgiven! I then felt that if Palmer could be forgiven, so might I. I sought, and blessed be God, I found. I am pardoned, I am free; I am a sinner saved by grace. Though a murderer, I have not yet sinned 'beyond the uttermost,' blessed be His holy name!" It made me very happy to think that a poor condemned murderer could thus be converted. Surely there is hope for every hearer and reader of this sermon, however guilty he may be!

If you know Christ, tell others about him. You do not know what good there is in making Jesus known, even though all you can do is to give a tract or repeat a verse. Dr. Valpy, the author of a great many class-books, wrote the following simple lines as his confession of faith:

"In peace let me resign my breath,
And thy salvation see;
My sins deserve eternal death,
But Jesus died for me."

Valpy is dead and gone; but he gave those lines to dear old Dr. Marsh, the Rector of Beckenham, who put them over his study mantel-shelf. The Earl of Roden came in, and read them. "Will you give me a copy of those lines?" said the good earl. "I shall be glad," said Dr. Marsh, and he copied them. Lord Roden took them home, and put them over *his* mantel-shelf. General Taylor, a Waterloo hero, came into the room, and noticed them. He read them over and over again, while staying with Earl Roden, till his Lordship remarked, "I say, friend Taylor, I should think you knew those lines by heart." He answered, "I do know them by heart; indeed, my very heart has grasped their meaning." He was brought to Christ by that humble rhyme. General Taylor handed those lines to an officer in the army, who was going out to the Crimean War. He came home to die; and when Dr. Marsh went to see him, the poor soul in his weakness said, "Good sir, do you know this verse which General Taylor gave to me? It brought me to my Saviour, and I die in peace." To Dr. Marsh's surprise, he repeated the lines:

"In peace let me resign my breath,
And thy salvation see;
My sins deserve eternal death,
But Jesus died for me."

Only think of the good which four simple lines may do! Be encouraged, all of you who know the healing power of the wounds of Jesus. Spread this truth by all means. Never mind how simple the language. Tell it out: tell it out everywhere, and in every way, even if you cannot do it in any other way than by copying a verse out of a hymn-book. Tell it out that by the stripes of Jesus we are healed. May God bless you, dear friends!

GEMS FROM NEW BOOKS.

An Involuntary Voyage in a Frail Boat.*

IT was still early in the day, a good three hours before sundown, and Nathan would have an hour or more for himself out on the waters of the harbor before going to the evening reception of the president of the college. Between three and four o'clock of that July day, the sea in the harbor lay a calm, unbroken surface, reflecting every boat and white-winged ship that sailed its placid waters, with a distinctness that doubled the object, even to the repeating of mast-head, spar, lines of cordage and coil of rope. The air was sultry on land, and this made the life-giving, tarry, sea-weedy odors specially refreshing to him. With no thought of passing beyond the safe shelter of the bay, he looked half longingly over toward the misty gray line which meant the open sea.

Captain Pickett was on the watch for Nathan, and in five minutes the light, well-trimmed craft in which he had spent many an hour during the last months, was gliding over the blue water like a sea-gull. The old sea-captain had become fond of the youth who many a twilight had lingered to listen with never-failing interest to his tales of storm and shipwreck; and though he was not one to forecast trouble, just as Nathan was pushing off, his keen eye detected a shadowy, vapory cloud forming across the sky over toward the west. The sight of it caused him to raise a warning finger, as he called out to Nathan to keep a watch to westward, for there was a squall brewing.

Nathan meant to heed the old man's counsel; but his way was outward, and his mind was full of thoughts and hopes wide as the sea; and the calm was unbroken till within an hour of sundown; then he noticed a gentle stirring of the waves, while he felt the cool sweet touch of a fresh breeze from over the island, but he saw no cloud, though he looked skyward. The haze had spread and thickened, that was all, and so he let the little boat continue to float according to the guidance of wind and tide. It would be time to turn the helm and take the now idle oars in hand, half an hour hence; thus he thought, and then if the wind had freshened into a brisk breeze, he felt no fear. Had not his strong arm rowed in many a boat-race, and encountered many a head-wind and foam-crested wave? But even as he looked, the great even mass of floating clouds was riven by a flash of lightning, before the lurid red light of which the sunset colors grew dim, while suddenly he became conscious of a chill, and a darkening of the day. It was a wind storm—one of those sudden mid-summer showers that come and go so speedily. And yet, when the clouds broke and the darkness lifted, Nathan saw that it was already twilight on land and sea.

During the sudden fury of the gale, his one thought had been to keep the boat before the wind, and she still went dancing across the waves at a rate of many miles an hour. But as the squall abated, he had time to realize the peril that surrounded him, as in vain he strove to draw in the torn, rent fragment of the sail.

* From "A Modern St. Christopher," by Rose Porter. A beautiful story of New England life, full of excellent religious teaching, and well adapted to lead young men to make the Saviour the Guide of their lives. 231 pages. Price $1.25. Published by *Anson D. F. Randolph*, 38 West 23d Street, N. Y.

Feeding the Starving Poor in London.

Miss Rivers Interposing for Conscience' Sake.

that now hung like a rag; for, as he tried, he found his vaunted strength was as nothing, and then he turned to the oars, in which he had so confidently trusted; but as they touched the water, a great rolling wave dashed against the slender blades, snapping them in two. Meanwhile, the little pinnace continued courtesying on its way, keeping time to the rolling waves, one moment sinking into their receding trough, and the next bounding up on some foam-crested billow. All this time darkness was deepening, and Nathan knew he had crossed the harbor-bar, powerless to check the light craft, flying before wind and wave like a thistledown, blown it knows not where. And still the night darkened, and the great wide sea, the joyous sea of the morning, stretched now an ever-widening gulf between him and his dearest. But Nathan was not afraid; never once did his courage fail him all through the hours of the night. It was strange, knowing as he did that, humanly, all that was between him and a deep-sea grave was that frail boat. In one sense

He Did Not Pray

either, for there was that in his nature which held him back from seeking God in those hours of darkness and sore extremity, when he had closed his heart against the heavenly voice in the sunshine; but while his lips framed no uttered plea for mercy, there was a calm in his soul, for he was learning then the wonderful strength there is for weakness, in the knowledge that our names are borne up to the mercy-seat, buoyed on the wings of prayers offered for us ever since childhood. It was remembering this that led Nathan to repeat the strength-giving promise, "The everlasting arms are underneath."

These thoughts came trooping in his mind as rapidly as the clouds went scudding across the star-lighted sky; and as he thus mused, the short mid-summer night waned, the first early beams of day-dawn began to flush the east. Eagerly he watched for the increasing light, whilst something in the shadowy gray of the clouds above, and sea beneath, filled him with a sense of awe. Perchance, too, he realized his position with more reality when he saw the torn sail and broken oars that had been hidden by the darkness. He had cherished, also, the hope that morning would show the friendly shore of some near coast; but as the day brightened he looked in vain eastward and westward, to the north and to the south, scanning the outmost rim of the now clearly defined meeting-place of sea and sky; but not a rocky cliff or bold promontory reached out a kindly greeting to the sea-encompassed youth. By noon the strength of the morning was gone; he was hungry and thirsty; the rays of the sun beat down on him in hot and angry beams. What followed, Nathan Parret could not distinctly recall. He was dimly conscious of voices and a sudden rushing motion, as though he was being borne through the air, and then all became a blank.

When he woke to consciousness it was night again, but the dash of waves against a vessel's side told him that he was no longer out on the open sea, alone in a frail boat, for whose incoming Captain Pickett and a score of men, classmates and friends, had been watching for twenty-four hours now. He lifted his head and peeped into the gloom that was only broken by the dim burning of a swinging lamp, and then he stretched forth his hand, to feel the heavy folds of a sea-coat that was thrown across him, and then he slept again, a dreamless sleep, from which he did not wake till mid-day, when the story of his rescue was briefly told.

"It was noontime," thus the captain said, "of the day before, when the man at the wheel had caught sight of the little pinnace; his well-trained eye had discovered in it a prostrate figure, and with no delay the long-boat had been lowered by the strong New Bedford men, who had plied their oars with a steady stroke that speedily bridged the distance; and Nathan half an hour later had been lifted by friendly arms to the deck of the whaling vessel, *Mary Ann*, outward bound for a cruise among the northern waters."

FEEDING THE DESTITUTE.

(See Illustration.)

SAD stories of destitution and semi-starvation continue to arrive from newspaper correspondents in London. It is gratifying, however, to learn that Christian people are making an effort to alleviate temporarily some of the suffering. Among others, the Rev. M. Baxter has established a fund for providing meals to those who are absolutely without food or money. He has received assistance in this truly Christian undertaking from the public, and has thus been enabled to relieve some who might otherwise have perished for lack of food. The illustration on this page depicts the gathering in the hall, in which the meals are given. There is reason to hope that through the gospel addresses, given after the repast, some who have been fed with temporal food have been led to seek "the Bread of Life, whereof if a man eat he shall never hunger."

A CASE OF CONSCIENCE.

(See illustration on this page.)

"MR. STANFORD will see you at once, Miss Rivers," said a clerk to a young lady who, with an older lady of a somewhat crafty cast of features, was waiting in the outer office of Messrs. Stanford & Son, lawyers. The clerk looked a little suspiciously at the elder of the two. She did not receive a cordial welcome from the lawyer himself when, with Miss Rivers, she entered the office of the junior partner. He turned from the desk where he was standing talking with his father, and looked at her sharply and perhaps a little sarcastically as he greeted his young client.

"This person," Miss Rivers said, "has a claim against my aunt's property, Mr. Stanford."

"I think we must not go as far as that," said the lawyer. "We will say *she professes* to have a claim. I have had the honor of some visits from her already, and have heard all she has to allege. She has not a particle of foundation for her claim—some ridiculous story about being promised a thousand dollars for extra attention during the illness of your aunt, but she has no letter or paper to confirm her statement, and I do not believe the old lady ever made such a promise. It is simply a case of blackmail."

The woman whose assertions were so stigmatized set up a shrill and vociferous protestation, and inquired who the lawyer was that he should cast suspicion on the character of a respectable lady, who had boarded a great deal better people than he, in her time, and never had a word said against her. She had friends, and she would let him know that she was not going to be slandered by any one, lawyer or no lawyer. She only wanted her rights, etc.

Mr. Stanford listened to the outburst with growing impatience, and as the woman's tones grew higher and shriller, and she appeared to be working up to the point when hysterics only would convey her sentiments, he suggested to her, with mock politeness, that she leave the office, and took a step toward her, as if intending to hasten her exit. Miss Rivers, however, interposed.

"I should like her to have the money, Mr. Stanford," she said.

"Certainly I will follow your instructions, Miss Rivers, but excuse my saying that you are doing a very foolish and uncalled for thing. If she has any claim let her bring suit, as she proposes, and if she can substantiate it the courts will order payment. It will be quite time enough to pay then. You must allow me to protect you from imposition."

"I thank you for your advice, Mr. Stanford; I know you give it in my interest," said Miss Rivers, "but this is a matter in which I must have my own way, and I have quite decided. Will you tell her when she may come for the money?"

The lawyer shrugged his shoulders. "I am sorry for it," he said. "If she will come here on the first of next month, the money shall be ready for her."

"That's all I want," said the woman pertly. "I'm glad I haven't got to sue for it, which I should have done so sure as here I stand, for I'm not one as is going to be wronged without standing up for my rights. I wish you good morning, Mr. Stanford, and thank *you*, Miss Rivers." And she went out, closing the door with emphasis.

"This will reduce your inheritance considerably, Miss Rivers," said the lawyer. "You will not have more than five thousand dollars left, I think. Why do you suffer yourself to be imposed upon by such a person? Your aunt paid her well during her lifetime, I have no doubt. The claim is absurd; no judge on the bench would have admitted it."

"I believe my aunt did promise the money" said Miss Rivers. "She once make a remark in my hearing that convinces me that she did. I wonder she did not leave it in her will. She was dependent on this woman for her personal comfort, for she would not live with her relatives, and I think the prospect of the legacy may have had its effect in securing extra attention. But apart from all that, I would pay in such a case rather than go to law. I think that is my duty as a Christian."

"Indeed! Well it is a fortunate thing for us lawyers, that your principles are not common. What has religion to do with law?"

"It teaches us to resist not evil, and the Saviour explicitly enjoyed His followers to sacrifice their rights if they were sued. (Matt. 5: 40.) It is a case of conscience with me."

"It is very expensive to keep such a conscience," said Mr. Stanford. "A thousand dollars is a great deal to pay; I fancy most people would have found some cheaper way than that of satisfying conscience."

Miss Rivers despaired of convincing the lawyer that she had done right, but, though she knew he despised her for doing what seemed to him a foolish thing, she felt that the consciousness of duty done was a sufficient consolation for the loss of his respect and of her thousand dollars. The money was paid on the day appointed, and Miss Rivers supposed that she had heard the last of the affair. It was not so, however; it was about six weeks afterward that she received another visit from the woman whose claim she had paid. She brought with her a trunk which, as she said to Miss Rivers, "Your aunt kept in the storeroom. Books and letters in it, I guess. Nothing of any account, but you behaved honorable to me, and would not let the lawyers do me out of my rights, so I thought I would do as much by you. I should not have troubled to bring it if you hadn't stood my friend."

Miss Rivers thanked her, and a few days later sat down to examine the papers that the trunk contained. The eccentric old lady had saved every letter she had ever received, and there they were, neatly tied in bundles, with diaries, and records of business transactions. And there too, in a large package by itself, was a pile of bank-notes, which made the amount she had paid against the advice of the lawyer and at the dictates of conscience seem a very small sum in comparison.

The Mosque of Kutibia in Morocco.

A MOORISH MOSQUE.

(See Illustration.)

To see Mohammedanism in its full power, it is necessary to see it as it exists in Morocco. The Moor prides himself on being a far more faithful servant of Mohammed than the Turk, whom he regards as latitudinarian—a truckler to Christians and infidels. His hope is to extend his religion over the whole world, giving every man the choice of Mohammedanism or death. It is mainly through Moorish enthusiasm that the Koran is reverenced through northern and western Africa. So thoroughly has this fact been realized, that the Christian missionary societies, from the commencement of their labors down to the year 1881, made no systematic attempt to introduce the gospel among the Moors. In that year, however, Mr. George Pearse started on a mission to Morocco, and was so much encouraged by his success that he made an appeal for more missionaries, which was promptly responded to. There are now about twenty-five missionaries laboring there. It is chiefly among the poorer inhabitants that converts have been made. The oppression of the Government has rendered the lower classes discontented, and has produced an aversion to the Sultan and his officers which extends to the religion as well as the politics of the oppressors. This is very natural as the Sultan of Morocco is styled the Prince of the Believers, or, blasphemously, "the Vicegerent of God upon Earth."

The mosque of which a picture is here given is one of the most splendid in Morocco. From the gallery of its massive tower, five times in every twenty-four hours the call to prayer is issued. At sunrise, at noon, at three o'clock, at sunset and at *eshe*, or nightfall, the chant of the Muezzins is heard from the minaret. On working days the call is obeyed at home or in the street, or wherever the worshipper may happen to be, but on Fridays and holy days it is incumbent that the Mohammedan repair to the mosque, where portions of the Koran are read, and often a sermon is preached. Women are not encouraged to visit the mosques for prayer, though they are not absolutely forbidden. It is contended that their presence is liable to distract the thoughts of the male worshippers and impair the intensity of devotion.

THE FAMILY OF TRIPE COURT.

By Brenda.

(Continued from page 78.)

BRIDGET'S SURPRISE.

THE young lady whom Tom wished to give into custody, and who, I may now tell you, was the wife of the clergyman of the parish—he was in the chair to-night—continued to look very smiling and pleased, for all the while the hymn was being sung people were crowding in at the doors, and all the available chairs and stools were being got out for seats. She saw that her party—her Temperance meeting—was going to be a great success! And she had worked so hard at it for the last two days, she couldn't help being very pleased. Some of the work had been extremely trying—that of going into the saloons, as she had been doing all the afternoon; *not*, as Tom had imagined, to get a glass for herself, which he had fondly hoped would have made her "wonderous kind" to her guests in the matter of ale and rum, but to persuade the people she found there to come to her meeting this evening. And they were coming, and had come in such numbers as quite to astonish her.

Before her she saw seated men and women of the poorest class, whose faces, like Tom Mite's, told of habitual drunkenness, and who had got with them, also like Tom Mite, little undeveloped, white-faced children, clawing and tearing at the cake, whose appearance told as plainly as words how hungry and ill in health they were, because father's and mother's money all went to the grog-shops instead of to the butchers and bakers to buy wholesome meat and bread for them.

The Rector's wife wore the blue ribbon herself, and looked forward to pinning the same on many a coat to-night, as the Rector told the people when, after a hymn had been sung and prayer offered, he proceeded to address them on the subject of Temperance. "She'll never pin it on me, so she needn't think it," grumbled many a surly voice. And it did seem at the close of the evening as if that determination fixed itself upon every one in the meeting; for when the Rector, after earnest exhortation to them, called upon the people to come forward and sign the book, and have the ribbon pinned on, not one of the company made any response! Some were talking, some were staring stupidly in front of them, some were smiling jeeringly, as if *they* didn't mean to be caught, and others were snoring and too fast asleep to hear the appeal at all. The Rector's wife began to look quite downhearted, as she stood waiting behind her little table of badges.

"Come," said the Rector, good-naturedly, to the people, "don't be shy. Perhaps you *are* shy, and don't like to walk up to the table. Well, then, I told you to walk up to the table, but don't walk; sit where you are and hold up your hands. Those of you, my sisters and brothers, who wish to sign the pledge to-night, and bring brightness and happiness into your homes, hold up your hands!"

There was a pause; the Rector's eyes went quickly over the room; not an arm was raised.

"Not *one?*" he said sadly, letting his eyes roam over the heads over the people while he yet paused. "Yes," he cried, suddenly, with his face kindling, "I'm encouraged; there *is* one, just one!" and everybody was eager to see whose hand it was.

They followed the Rector's eyes, and many rose to their feet, because they could see nothing as they sat. There was quite an excitement, quite a sensation, when they saw that the clergyman's eyes were resting on the bare arm, uplifted, of a little baby! It had struggled out from a wrap that covered it, and, though the man holding the baby tried to suppress it and cover it up, the arm remained upraised in silent and most pathetic protest, it seemed, against the thing that had been under discussion—drink.*

"Well, at any rate, we have the *babies* on our side," exclaimed the Rector; and then he added thoughtfully, and with much feeling, "I dare say, if the owner of that little bare arm yonder could speak it would have to tell me something very pitiful about itself and—*drink*. I don't know its history; it's quite a stranger to me, but I can fancy what it might tell me: of a miserable home, and infant privations and sufferings, without mother to rock it, and sing to it, and soothe it; and, if I were to ask that little baby the cause, it would probably answer, 'Because somebody belonging to me *drinks*.'"

The Rector paused. There was a deep silence, some women sobbed, then a little movement amongst the audience, a slight sensation again. A miserable-looking man, with downcast face, and a baby in his arms, had advanced to the table; now he was bending down before the young lady writing his name in the book; now he and the baby—the baby was the one who had held its arm up—were having the blue ribbon pinned on them. And Mary Job, a moment later rousing herself suddenly from a nap in her quiet corner by the door, saw that the man and baby returning to their seats, wearing the blue ribbon, were *Tom Mite and little Dinah!* Wonder of wonders, Tom Mite had signed the pledge!

That night a little baby, with a blue ribbon on its arm, lay sleeping placidly in its cradle in Tripe Court, a shawl thrown over it to keep the draughts out, the cradle itself put on the table out of the reach of rats, a bottle of milk close handy and a sober father watching beside it, at the very moment that in the Workhouse Infirmary where poor Bridget was passing her first night away from home a voice was saying:

"I will wield that power for *you* to-night. I will pray that that eye, that arm, that love may reach and be around your little baby to-night, and I'm just as *sure* that no harm will be allowed to happen to it, and that it will be taken care of, as I am that there is a God in heaven."

Was Mrs. Cherry's confidence misplaced—does God ever disappoint?

The next morning—

"Poll and Sue," said Tom, "I'm off down to the docks to get work. Take care o' the little 'un, and let Mrs. Job know where I'm gone."

Right glad were they to carry such a message. It showed good intention at least on their father's part. Still they were not very hopeful. It was quite likely that Tom in his search for work might be overcome by thirst or get with some men who might invite him to drink—an invitation he had never been known to refuse—and he would come home drunk as usual. That was more likely than anything else, and the fact that the children thought so could be perceived by their father. Well, he could not expect anything else. They knew how often he had sworn off before. Still, he was sorry they had no more confidence in him, for he meant to hold on this time, and their belief in him might have strengthened his own, which was very weak. Never mind, he must prove his good resolution, and he did; he not only secured work, but came home sober.

It was a hard struggle, for now that Tom was working he felt the need of beer more than ever, but he would not give up. He could not look beyond the one day, but every morning he determined that he would not drink *that* day anyhow. As the days passed he grew stronger in his resolve, more confident of his own power, surprised that he had so much. Tom was a better man than he supposed he was, and the discovery pleased him; he began to respect himself. Then, what would Bridget say when she came out! How pleased her face would look when the children told her! Tom pictured the scene, and that gave him still more strength. Just then you could not have drenched him with beer if you had tried.

It was very dull at home, though, without Bridget. The children did what they could, and Mrs. Job looked in every day and helped them with the baby and the housework, but it was not like having Bridget. He did long for news of her, but none came for six weeks. Then it did come.

It was Sunday, and an unusual stir and flutter of expection was going on in all the wards of the Poorhouse Infirmary, increasing in degree as the afternoon approached. Some patients were not able to eat their dinner, they were so excited; some were crying for very joy on their pillows, because a notice had been issued in the week by the Workhouse authorities that that order of theirs forbidding visitors to the Infirmary during the prevalence of small-pox was now withdrawn: small-pox having abated outside, the old arrangements were to stand, and there were to be visiting days again.

This was Sunday, and therefore the first "visiting day," and, for very excitement, some couldn't eat, and, for very joy, some were crying at the prospect of seeing beloved home faces once more. Letters had been despatched in the week from almost every bed, bidding husbands, mothers, sisters, brothers, children, to come this Sunday afternoon without fail, and there was hardly a person in the great parish hospital to-day whose mind was not occupied with the thought of somebody's coming.

Amongst the expectant ones there was Bridget Mite, laundress, in the Victoria Ward. She was sitting up in bed, with her leg almost well, and her face shining with that new light that had come into it ever since that Sunday afternoon when she had accepted the Message of Consolation and Rest. She was one of those who had not been able to eat her dinner for excitement, thinking of seeing Tom and Poll and Sue, and oh! joy of joys, clasping her baby in her arms again; for she had written of course to Tripe Court in the week, telling them all to come this Sunday, and at two o'clock she was watching, with beating heart and anxious eyes, like everybody else, the door at the far end of the long ward, where would appear first her dear, shabby little group.

Every moment people were flocking in, singly or together, carrying either children or flowers, and in most instances with clean faces and respectable clothes. The visitors seemed all to have done their best to make a tidy appearance, "not to shame their friend" whom they had come to see. Even the granddaughter of the old cigar-light seller, Biddy, who was no better than Biddy had ever been, had spruced herself up with a clean white apron, and oiled her hair well, to do credit to Biddy on visiting day.

While she awaited it with all the love and affection possible, poor Bridget, it must be confessed, felt a little natural anxiety, a little tremulous as to how *her* party would look when it came. She expected to see Sue so smutty, and Poll so sooty, and Tom the shabbiest husband there, and her baby—oh! how she longed that it might come clean and nice to show to Mrs. Cherry, to whom she had talked of it so much, but she did not dare hope that it would. Mrs. Cherry had no one coming to see *her*—she had been in the Infirmary so long all her friends seemed to have forgotten her. But she was taking keen pleasure out of Bridget's anticipations.

"Let's see, dear; how many do you expect?" she asked of Bridget, as the time advanced, and yet Bridget's eyes were fixed on the door. "Husband, and how many little ones did you say?"

"Three," said Bridget: "a baby and two little girls. I dare say they'll be looking a bit rough to-day with me not there to brush them up," added poor Bridget, by way of preparing Mrs. Cherry for the shock of "Sooty's and "Smuts'" appearance when they should arrive.

"Well, now, *there's* a party; ain't those them?" cried Mrs. Cherry excitedly; "just them coming in now after that girl with the shawl over her head; it's the *number*."

Yes, a party answering in number to Bridget's family was just entering the ward; but Bridget shook her head. The party did not answer in appearance to hers; it was not the shabby, forlorn group of Tripe Court this. *This* was quite a creditable little party—the man with a good coat on his back. Tom hadn't such a coat, she knew. The baby in the man's arms had a white hood on, covered all over with crisp little satin bows, not like any hood Dinah possessed; and the other children, answering to Poll and Sue, were neither sooty nor smutty, they were perfectly clean and tidy.

"Oh, no, them's not *mine*," said Bridget slowly, shaking her head; but as they came nearer, her brown eyes got larger and larger with surprise. She looked doubtful, the blood rushed into her face, and she said under her breath, "Why, I almost think it *is* them," and the next minute there was not another doubt about it.

The clean, tidy little girls were at Bridget's bedside, with their arms round her neck, and the man and the baby were leaning over her too. They were Tom and the children, without a doubt.

"Whatever's happened, Tom?" whispered Bridget, after the first affectionate greetings were over, as with the baby pressed close to her she looked from one to the other of the little home group. That something *good* must have happened, she was sure.

Tom looked more like the fine dock laborer that she remembered of former years than tipsy Tom Mite of Tripe Court. He seemed not ashamed to look her in the face to-day. He had got that good coat on his back; he had the air of a *man* about him once more.

"It's *this*," replied Tom, touching proudly the bit of blue ribbon in his button-hole. "I've signed the pledge, Bridget, signed it the evening you come in here, and I've kept it, thank God, and been to work ever since."

"And baby wears it too, mother," cried Poll, pointing to the tiny badge on Dinah's shawl, "cos it was baby that made him sign it. It was 'er little h'arm that done it all! and in Tripe Court they calls 'er now the *Blue Ribbon Baby*. And father bought baby her hood and us our hats, mother," added Sue, "and he's as kind as ever he can be, and the home's changed, mother darling—just changed."

There was deep pathetic meaning in those last words. And Bridget fairly wept for joy.

(*To be Concluded.*)

* This incident actually occurred at a temperance meeting not long ago.

A LESSON ON FORGIVENESS.

By Mrs. M. Baxter.

S. S. Lesson for February 19. Matt. 18: 21—35. Golden Text, Matt. 6: 12.

Ver. 21, 22: The Common Desire to Set a Limit to Mercy—Christ Enjoining Unlimited Forbearance—Ver. 23, 24: A General Audit—The Servant an Embezzler—A Twelve Million Dollar Defalcation—Ver. 25: According to the Oriental Custom—Ver. 26: Obeisance Not Worship—Undertaking an Impossibility—Ver. 27: The King Better to Him than His Petition—Ver. 28: About Seventeen Dollars—Christ's Estimate of the Proportionate Debts to God and Man—Unnecessary Harshness in Making the Demand—Ver. 29, 30: Only Patience Asked For—Ver. 31: The Proper Course For Grieved Christians—Ver. 32-34: Forgiveness Revoked—A Terrible Possibility—Ver. 35: A Solemn Warning.

"FORGIVE us our trespasses as we forgive them that trespass against us." How can an unconverted or an unsanctified soul pray this prayer? We ask that the precise measure of our mercy to those who wrong us shall be the very measure of God's mercy towards us! If we only forgive those who we think are deserving of forgiveness, we ask God not to forgive us until we deserve it! If we forgive the undeserving by word, and yet cherish a spirit of antagonism against him in our hearts, we are praying God to cherish enmity in His heart against us! If we speak the word of forgiveness, and yet continue to tell out to others how much such an one has wronged us, we are asking God, in this prayer, to forgive us in word, and yet to bear witness against us. If we forgive and do not *forget* the injury, we are asking God to forgive us and yet to remember our sins against us! O how unsafe, how rash, it is to pray such a prayer, unless we

From Our Hearts

forgive "every one his brother their trespasses"! Paul teaches us to be "kind, one to another, tender hearted—forgiving each other, *even as* God also, in Christ, forgave you." (Eph. 4: 32, R. V.) God says, "I will forgive their iniquity, and I will remember their sin no more." (Jer. 31: 34.) Therefore, if we forgive as we are forgiven, we must remember the offence no more. If "He is kind unto the unthankful, and to the evil," we have not to wait until a person deserves it before we freely forgive.

Peter, who, with all his faults, was a very practical man, and a kind of economist in his way, was beginning to weigh the teaching of Christ against the resources he had in himself to live up to it. This set him calculating, and the result of his reflection was the question, "Lord, how often shall my brother sin against me, and I forgive him?" In order to have the thing very definite, Peter suggests what would seem to him a very great strain on his powers of endurance, "Till seven times?" O how utterly aghast must he have been at the answer of Jesus, "I say not unto thee until seven times: but, until

Seventy Times Seven!"

Four hundred and ninety times! Surely when we have forgiven the same person nearly five hundred times, we shall long ago have ceased to reckon our forgiveness; it will be the habit of our lives. True, our natural hearts would never be braced up to such a task, but Christ in us will live His own life of forgiveness, and repeat in our hearts, towards those who wrong us, what He said upon the Cross, "Father, forgive them, for they know not what they do." Our natural hearts instinctively turn to the wrong done to *us*, and they eloquently plead the injustice of it, and how it would be contrary to all the principles of justice to forgive the guilty. Christ in us, on the contrary, pities the sinning one, and, leading us to put ourselves out of the question, makes us willing to forego our own rights that that erring one may be restored.

"But," says one, "if you are to forgive every wrong, you put a premium on sin." So men said of Paul. (Rom. 3: 8.) But Jesus, in this parable, puts things on the right footing. He tells us of "a certain king, which would take account of his servants." Any direct allusion to the judgment-seat has become strangely unpopular in the present day; and yet the saved and unsaved must be judged; the saved, to "receive things done in his body, according to that he hath done, whether it be

Good or Bad"

(II Cor. 5: 10): the unsaved, to be judged before the great white throne "out of those things which were written in the books, according to their works." (Rev. 20: 11, 12.) But long before we shall be judged in another world, God brings His creatures from time to time to a little judgment-day on earth, when things come to a crisis with us, and the Spirit of God shows us what we are, and what we have done in the clear, searching light of God. This is what we call conviction of sin.

The king began to reckon. One after another his servants were brought before him, and strict and impartial investigation was made; old accounts were searched for and handed in, until one man was found who owed him ten thousand talents, i. e., about $12,000,000 (See Rev. Ver.). How could such a debt be ever met? There was nothing to be done but to confiscate his lands and goods. This scarcely met a fraction of the debt; the money had been utterly lost; the man himself, with his wife and children must be sold into slavery! O, if he had but faced the matter sooner, before such utter ruin came upon him, how different would everything have been! Now he had

No Hope in Himself;

he could do only one thing, and that was to throw himself on the mercy of his king and creditor. But was it not his king's money which he had lost? Had he not made his lord his greatest enemy? Yes, this was all true; yet it was all he could do to throw himself upon his mercy, and say, "Have patience with me, and I will pay thee all." A fair promise; thousands of debtors make it, but how can a bankrupt, who has nothing left, pay anything? The promise was of no value; it was but an impertinence. Yet the very turning to him at all touched the king's heart, and in his wonderful magnanimity, he "loosed him and forgave him the debt." How like God! And we know the other side—how, through the blood of Jesus, shed for us, God can be just and yet justify; without breaking His own holy law, He can yet forgive us all that debt.

The Small Debtor.

"But the same servant went out, and found one of his fellow-servants which owed him an hundred pence; and he laid hands on him, and took him by the throat, saying, Pay me that thou owest! And his fellow-servant fell down at his feet and besought him, saying, Have patience with me, and I will pay thee all." There was more sense in this promise than in his own to the king, for this debt was but a little over seventeen dollars as against twelve millions dollars; yet this man, this forgiven one, would not forgive, but "went and cast him into prison, till he should pay the debt." Do we realize that we are not in the world for ourselves, but for God? That if we are forgiven, we are to serve God's purposes first, as well as our own afterwards? God gives us life that we may live to Him; pardon, that we may reflect a forgiving God upon the world around us; love, that we may love the unlovely, as God has loved us, in the very midst of our sin and rebellion; and He would have us reflect Him as the moon reflects the sun. Thus the world can know His heart by what they see in us. It was true that his fellow-servant did not deserve forgiveness, but neither did he. His lord had dealt with him in grace when he was more undeserving. His fellow-servant had urged the same plea exactly that he had urged, yet he turned a deaf ear! But how can we know when to forgive? "If thy brother trespass against thee, rebuke him, and

If He Repent,

forgive him. And if he trespass against thee seven times in a day, and seven times in a day turn again to thee, saying, I repent, thou shalt forgive him." Why this excess of pardon? Because it is forgiving as God forgives. A poor woman had a drunken husband: he often beat her, and she would creep away up-stairs and pray, "O God, forgive him for beating me," and the words went like swords to his heart. He would bring very little money home, but if she had gone without food all day, she would always contrive to have something for him. It was not often, only now and then, that he turned to her, saying, "I repent." But whenever he did, there was as free a forgiveness as if it had been the first offence. That woman could pray from her heart, "Forgive us our trespasses as we forgive them that trespass against us." She forgave as God forgave, and those who knew her saw God in her. Another woman, in better circumstances outwardly, had a husband who made a great profession of religion. She was a tender, delicate woman,

A Second Wife,

and loved her husband with all her heart, and admired him, and looked up to him as being almost perfect. But, through the confession of a servant girl, she found he had been unfaithful to her, and the poor girl herself was ruined. Her only thought, at first, was to get away; he did not deserve forgiveness, truly; but he turned to her saying, "I repent," and, although with an almost breaking heart, for her disappointment in him, she took the God-like part of forgiving. A Christian merchant, an earnest worker for God, who, by his talents, with God's blessing, had come into a large way of business, had a superintendent in whom he fully trusted, to whom he confided everything, and whom he had raised from the lowest position in the business to the highest. Quite unexpectedly he turns round on his employer, shows him that he is in his power, sets up a similar business, and gains over the customers of his late employer. Money which once went into the work of God goes now to satisfy his pride. The man does not deserve forgiveness, but the impoverished employer has the opportunity to be God-like in forgiving. Such cases are always occurring. The drunkard, the unfaithful husband, the grasping man of business

Did Not Deserve Pardon,

but God gave an opportunity to the two suffering wives and to the merchant, to forgive as they had been forgiven.

The fellow-servants were grieved at heart, and told their lord all that had happened, and another judgment day took place. "His lord, after that he had called him, said, O thou wicked servant, I forgave thee all that debt, because thou desiredst me. Wouldst not thou also have had compassion on thy fellow-servant, even as I had pity on thee? And his lord was wroth, and delivered him to the tormentors, till he should pay all that was due unto him." And that was *never!* "So likewise," says our Lord, "shall My Heavenly Father do also unto you, if ye from your hearts forgive not every one his brother their trespasses." In heaven are those who are like God. The Lord teach us these lessons of love and forgiveness, lest, after having preached to others, testified of Christ, gloried in His love to us, we should, after all, become castaways.

For the *Christian Herald*.]

"FREELY YE HAVE RECEIVED, FREELY GIVE."—Matt. x, 8.

By LILLA M. ALEXANDER.

As the cloud, that heavenward rising,
Gathers moisture from the sea,
So my soul, by faith uplifted,
Draws its life and strength from Thee,
And is filled with all the fullness,
Of Thy love so rich and free.

For the ocean of Thy goodness,
In unmeasured mercy rolls;
And it fails not, though supplying,
Day by day our thirsty souls,—
For the fount from which it floweth,
Everlasting love controls.

And as rain-clouds, filled to bursting,
On the earth their fullness pour,
May I shed on those around me,
Something of my gathered store;
For the soul that giveth, groweth,
And oft emptied, holds the more.

Greenville, Conn.

J. E. JEWETT, Publisher, 77 Bible House, New York will furnish the above poem in leaflet form at twenty cents per hundred. *A Sample Packet of 50 leaflets* assorted (no two alike), will be sent post-paid for ten cents. Postage stamps taken.

STATEMENT
OF
The Mutual Life Insurance Company of New York
RICHARD A. McCURDY, President.

For the year ending December 31st, 1887.

ASSETS .... $118,806,851 88.

Insurance and Annuity Account.

	No.	Amount.		No.	Amount
Policies and Annuities in force, Jan. 1st, 1887	129,927	$393,809,202 88	Policies and Annuities in force, Jan. 1st, 1888	140,943	$427,0[illegible]
Risks Assumed	22,305	69,457,468 57	Risks Terminated	11,289	35,[illegible]
	152,232	$463,266,671 25		152,232	$463,26[illegible]

Dr. Revenue Account.

To Balance from last account	$104,719,784 51	By Endowments, Purchased Insurances, Dividends, Annuities and Death Claims	14,1[illegible]
" Premiums	17,110,901 69	" Commissions, Commutations, Taxes and all other Expenses	3,64[illegible]
" Interest, Rents and Premium on Securities Sold	6,009,020 84	" Balance to new account	110,0[illegible]
	$127,839,606 77		$127,8[illegible]

Dr. Balance Sheet.

To Reserve for Policies in force and for risks terminated	$112,430,096 00	By Bonds Secured by Mortgages on Real Estate	$49,6[illegible]
" Premiums received in advance	82,314 35	" United States and other Bonds	43,4[illegible]
" Surplus at four per cent	6,294,441 59	" Real Estate and Loans on Collaterals	20,1[illegible]
		" Cash in Banks and Trust Companies at interest	2,6[illegible]
		" Interest accrued, Premiums deferred and in transit and Sundries	2,3[illegible]
	$118,806,851 88		$118,8[illegible]

I have carefully examined the foregoing statement and find the same to be correct.

A. N. WATERHOUSE, A[uditor]

From the Surplus above stated a dividend will be apportioned as usual.

Year.	Risks Assumed.	Risks Outstanding.	Surplus.
1884	$34,681,420	$351,789,285	$4,743,771
1885	46,507,139	368,981,441	5,012,634
1886	56,832,719	393,809,203	5,643,568
1887	69,457,468	427,628,933	6,294,442

NEW YORK, January 25, 1888.

THE CHRISTIAN HERALD AND SIGNS OF OUR TIMES.

Vol. XI., No. 7. Office, 63 Bible House. N. Y. THURSDAY, FEBRUARY 16, 1888. Annual Subscription, $1.50.

CONTENTS OF THIS NUMBER.

PORTRAIT AND LIFE OF THE REV. H. LANSDELL, D. D., the Missionary Pioneer and Explorer of Siberia, Central Asia, etc.
WIFELY AMBITION, GOOD AND BAD. Dr. Talmage's Fifth Sermon to the Women of America, last Sunday Morning.
ANECDOTES RELATED AT RECENT EVANGELISTIC MEETINGS.
THE PYRAMID POINTING TO 1888-9 AS YEARS OF TROUBLE.
A CITY MISSIONARY IN A THIEVES' PARLOR.
CURRENT EVENTS—Treaties in Congress, etc.
PEACE WITHOUT OFFENCE. A New Sermon by C. H. Spurgeon.
Gems from New Books—Christian Heroism on the Operating Table.
DIAGRAM AND SECTIONAL PLAN OF PASSAGES IN THE GREAT PYRAMID.
A Brahmin's Interrupted Journey—A Captain's Dismissal—A Widow's Long Vigil.
PICTURE OF THE PAGEANT AT THE BLESSING OF THE RIVER NEVA.
FOUR INTERLOPERS IN HEAVEN. By Dr. Talmage.
THE FAMILY OF TRIPE COURT. (Concluded.)
THE RICH YOUNG RULER. By Mrs. M. Baxter.

THE REV. H. LANSDELL, D. D., Missionary Traveller in Siberia and Central Asia—Scenes in Asiatic Life.

REV. H. LANSDELL, D. D.,

The Distinguished Missionary Traveller.

Born in 1844—Enters a Divinity College in 1865—Ordained Curate in 1867—Interest in Mission Work—His Travels and Their Object—Journey through Siberia in 1879—Work in Russian Central Asia in 1882—Fears of Friends—Reception at St. Petersburg—Arrested as a Nihilist—Description of Bazaar Life on the River Irtish—Absence of Good Washing Accommodation—The Kalmucks—Marriage Custom—A Bazaar in Kuldja—The Kirghese Nomads—A Talk Inside a Tent—Visit to a Famous Mosque—Travelling in Siberia.

A MEMBER of the distinguished brotherhood of exploring missionaries, the Rev. Henry Lansdell, D. D., *whose portrait is given on ou. frontispiece*, was born at Tenterden, Kent, England, in 1844, we believe, and therefore is now about forty-four years of age. Having resolved to devote his life to the ministry of the Gospel, he entered the London Episcopal College of Divinity in 1865. After attaining considerable proficiency as a theological student, in 1867 he was *ordained as curate* to the late Canon Miller, at Greenwich. Mr. Lansdell's zeal in all kinds of purely *mission-work* was very marked from the outset of his public life, and in the year 1869 he was appointed Metropolitan Association Secretary to the Society for Irish Church Missions. Five years later he originated the Church Homiletical Society, of which he acted as secretary; and in 1875 he started and edited the *Clergyman's Magazine*. But it is

As a Traveller and Missionary

that Dr. Lansdell is best known, for he has not only journeyed round the world, and visited, with two exceptions, every country of Europe, but he has also visited parts of Siberia, Central Asia, Bokhara and Khiva, where no living Englishman had preceded him. In Dr. Lansdell's journeyings, which began in 1874, he has made *the distribution of gospel literature* his principal object. Each year he distributed thousands of pamphlets, tracts, etc., to the natives of the wild districts which he traversed. In 1878 he left St. Petersburg with two Russian *wagon-loads of Scriptures* and Gospel leaflets, which he gave away in a journey of 5,500 miles. In 1879 he travelled all across Asia to

The Prisons and Mines of Siberia,

leaving Bibles and evangelical tracts in every hospital and prison throughout that country, distributing by gift or sale nearly 56,000 books. On this occasion he continued his journey by way of Japan and San Francisco, and having crossed the American continent and the Atlantic Ocean, he completed a tour of 25,500 miles.

In 1880 Dr. Lansdell appears to have been content with a run of 700 miles to Mount Ararat in Armenia, returning by Constantinople, Athens and Rome; but in 1882 he made a very adventurous journey of 11,000 miles through Russian Central Asia, including Kuldja, Bokhara and Khiva, where he distributed 5,000 copies of the Holy Scriptures, and more than 1,000 gospel publications. Dr. Lansdell has published a fascinating volume entitled "Through Siberia," which has had a wide sale, and been translated into German and Swedish; and recently another, brimful of valuable information, with the title "Russian Central Asia," giving details of the journey of 11,000 miles, to which reference has been made. He has just prepared a popular edition of this last-named work bearing the new designation, "Through Central Asia," from which we proceed to summarize extracts chiefly explanatory of the five pictures accompanying the portrait, on our title-page. Like most travellers, Dr. Lansdell is a Freemason. In 1876 he was elected a Fellow of the Royal Geographical Society, and in 1880 a Member of the British Association; and in 1882 the late Archbishop of Canterbury conferred upon him the honorary degree of D.D., in recognition of his literary and missionary services.

Having matured his plans for his Central Asia journey, Dr. Lansdell says; "There were not wanting those who thought my project a hopeless one. Had not other Englishmen tried in vain to penetrate to Russian Central Asia? And was not one of them—a clergyman too, who proceeded by stealth as far as Tashkend—ordered to be off within four-and-twenty hours? Besides these there were some of my older friends who recalled that the last two Englishmen, Colonel Stoddart and Captain Connolly, who entered Bokhara in 1842, were put to death, and that Dr. Wolff, who went to ascertain their fate, nearly lost his life. By them I was thought to be entering on a dangerous enterprise; but I was able to assure them that I had not the slightest intention of putting

My Head Into the Lion's Mouth

merely for the satisfaction of saying that I had done so, and that, unless I had not only the permission but the cordial support of the Russians, I should probably not enter Bokhara. But to be candid, I realized it to be the most dangerous journey I had undertaken. I so committed myself into His keeping in whose name I was going forth, and—started." St. Petersburg was reached June 29, 1882, three days after the traveller left London; and within a couple of days he had virtually obtained of the Grand Duke Michael (uncle of the Emperor) and Count Tolstoi, the Minister of the Interior, permission to do exactly as he wished. Upon reaching Moscow an interpreter was secured, and a steamer taken for Perm. Here a tarantass, or travelling-carriage, was purchased, which was intended to be the travellers' dwelling and sleeping place for a long succession of days and nights, and to carry them 3,000 miles. The dreary journey from the Ural Mountains to Omsk having been safely accomplished, with no other incident than the arrest of Dr. Lansdell and his companion for a short time as Nihilists, occasioned by the free distribution of gospel tracts, they pushed forward to

Semipolátinsk,

an ancient city on the river Irtish, which was reached on August 24. "The buildings of Semipolatinsk," says Dr. Lansdell, "did not strike me as remarkable. The Russian and Tatar merchants of the place sell in the bazaars, tea, sugar and other groceries, cotton stuffs, Chinese silks, porcelain, furs, wax and honey. The principal trade, however, is carried on in winter, when the Cossacks and peasants come in from the neighboring districts, bringing skins, ropes and other produce. The Kirghese also—some on horseback and others in rumbling camel-carts (*as seen in frontispiece engraving No.* 1)—bring cattle and camel's hair, which they dispose of for flour, tobacco, iron ware, etc."

The next stage was to Sergiopol, a distance of only 180 miles, but comprising eleven stations and necessitating ten changes of horses. At this place a Sunday was spent, visiting the military hospital, prison and barracks, and leaving at each place some copies of the Scriptures, etc. "News of this soon spread," says the missionary, "and I was speedily visited, first by the Russian priest, who came to buy a Kirghese New Testament, and then by a Cossack schoolmistress, in pretty Russian costume and wearing the national head-dress known as the Kokoshnik, with which I fell in love; so, when the lady's purchases were completed, I ventured to ask her to sell it to me for a curiosity. She gracefully declined my request, but offered it as a gift. Accordingly, I made up its value in printed matter, which here I found highly prized, as everywhere else along my route."

At the various halting-stations along the road, Dr. Lansdell invariably managed to

Nail up in the Post-Houses

engravings of the Prodigal Son and Bible texts, while offering his books for sale. Blessings indeed they must have been in these solitary houses in the wilderness, and the post-masters seemed so to regard them. At the last station before Semipolatinsk an old man said, "The Lord must have sent these books for us."

One of the inconveniences of post travelling, in Asiatic Russia appears to be the absence of good lavatory accommodation. The common method among the Russian peasants of *washing the hands* is to place them beneath a bowl of water fixed at a height, out of which a stream of water slowly trickles (*as shown in front page picture No.* 2).

Describing the peculiarities of the different tribes whom he visited *en route* to Kuldja, Dr. Lansdell furnishes the following interesting items concerning the Kalmucks. He says: "The *lamas* are teachers, medical sorcerers and priests. Hence their services are called into requisition at a birth, to read prayers over the mother, and name the child; later to instruct the boy, to marry him when grown up, to treat him when ill to prayers and drugs, and after death to decide whether the corpse should be buried, exposed on the steppe to be eaten by dogs, or burned.

A Kalmuck Girl is a Shepherdess.

She is married early, without much attention to her predilections, even without her consent, but she is at liberty to leave her husband and return to her relatives. Whether she likes a suitor, is known by her leaving the tent as soon as the marriage negotiations commence; or the reverse, by her staying during the whole conference. The parents, however, seldom regard her taste, and the aspirant, with their consent, watches for an opportunity of seizing the girl and carrying her off by force, the parents considering their duty towards their daughter fulfilled *if only the man carry her off without their seeing it*."

There is a Buddhist pagoda in Kuldja, which was duly visited. "Crossing the courtyard," writes Dr. Lansdell, "we entered the joss-house and saw the idols. Against the wall was a large dais, with various eatables arranged thereon, and lamps and vessels for incense. Representations of dragons are displayed, as well as suspended banners and bells. On important occasions, instead of verbal prayers, papers with petitions written thereon are burnt, in the belief that the petitions will thus ascend to God more quickly.

The Bazaars.

On Sept. 4, 1882, the missionary and his interpreter, accompanied by the Consul's servant, visited the bazaars. Everywhere their eyes were met by ceaseless movement, bustle and noise, for the vendors of wares scream out to the purchasers, and there are crowds of children, some half-naked and others wholly so, chasing one another and increasing the general hubbub of the restless scene. Among the crowds of men there is a fair proportion of Chinese women, in national costume, who, owing to their compressed feet, sway from side to side, as if on stilts. The Sart bazaar, called in Russian, Bazaar ulitza, or "shop street," *an illustration of which we give under its winter aspect (on front page, engraving No.* 3), they found inhabited chiefly by a simple sort of people called Dungans. "Here," says the missionary, "it was amusing to see how every piece of old iron and tin was saved as precious, and exposed for sale, even to empty sardine and blacking boxes. They positively gave me 3 cents for an empty lobster tin."

Dr. Lansdell paid a visit to the Kirghese nomads, at Suigati, in the Ili valley, and tells us that he was so much interested in seeing a woman begin to put up her tent, that he would not stir from the spot till he had witnessed the whole operation. He says, "The component parts are felt and matting, wherewith to cover a framework, including a lintel and side-posts for a door, and ropes, made of horses' manes, hung from a hoop or corona inside to keep the tent down, and outside a stake was driven into the ground to windward for similar security. The floor was strewed with matting and felts, a space being left in the centre for the fire." The tent just described is *shown in our frontispiece picture No.* 4.

But the traveller was not contented with looking upon the erection of a tent, so he availed himself of an opportunity to visit one when it was "in full working order." He was entertained hospitably. After the meal, the host was asked if he would accept a copy of the New Testament, with the assurance that "it is the best book we have in England." He took it joyfully,

He was then asked what they—the Kirghese—thought became of us after death. Upon which the reply was given that "God had made good angels called *Mankir*, and bad angels called *Nankir* and that two of these angels sit invisibly on the shoulders of every man from his birth, Mankir being always on the right. Further, they see all the man does, and write the good and bad in their respective books, which at death are both taken to God, who decides whether the good or bad preponderates, and gives sentence accordingly; the bad being sent into the fire, and the others to the enjoyment of another life in the world of spirits, where the good find all they can desire." A simple but clear explanation of the truth followed, a hearty farewell was exchanged, Dr. Lansdell resumed his journey, and on September 15 entered Tashkend, the headquarters of the Russian administration in Central Asia, where he busied himself in his Master's work.

Arriving in course of time at Samarkand, he visited the celebrated tomb of Timur, and the Mosque of Shah-Zindeh, a Mohammedan local celebrity. *No. 5 frontispiece picture* illustrates the mode of travelling long distances in Siberia, through which country Dr. Lansdell journeyed in 1879, visiting the prisons, hospitals, barracks and penal settlements, and everywhere distributing the Word of life. He was invariably treated with cordiality and courtesy by the Russian officials, and he embodies the results of his visit in the volume to which we have already referred. It was while travelling through this lone land in winter that he conceived the purpose of traversing the dominions of the Czar in Central Asia. As in Siberia, so in St. Petersburg, Samarkand, Tashkend and every other place he touched at, he gave special attention to the needs of those in the prisons and mines, and his unvarnished relation has done much to

Dissipate Popular Misconception

concerning the general administration of the law in Russia. In his preface to "Through Siberia," Dr. Lansdell remarks: "Much has been written concerning the prisons and penal institutions of that country which is very unsatisfactory, and some things that are actually false. I do not believe that Russian prisons are what they might be, and I am sure they are not what those who are highest in authority would like them to be; but all this does not justify the representation of them to be what they are not."

He afterwards visited Bokhara, Khiva, Baku, Tiflis, Batoum, Odessa, etc. It may be stated, here, that when he was at Khiva he had *an interview* with the Khan, to whom he presented a Persian Bible and an Arabic New Testament. "I was of course keenly interested," he says, "as to how the Mohammedans would receive any attempts to convert them to Christianity. I say 'of course,' because I find it extremely hard to understand the position of those who say, 'Let the Mohammedans alone. Their religion is suitable for *them*. Converts can hardly be made, and, when made, do but follow the example of their Christian masters in eating pork and getting drunk.' Now, if this string of objections were true, *which it is not*, then I fail to see that a Christian would be released from obedience to

The Standing Orders of Christ

his Master, to 'make disciples of all nations, and preach the Gospel to every creature.' In 1883-84 the British and Foreign Bible Society sent colporteurs to both Bokhara and Khiva, where their success is of a very promising chareter.

This Long Journey of 20,000 Miles

came to an end on December 21, on which date Dr. Lansdell arrived in London, having been absent from England, 179 days, sleeping in his clothes half the number of nights. "I was somewhat exhausted," says the missionary, "by the journey, but not so much as I have been by writing my books. I commenced them with the thought that, having acquired information *possessed by no other Englishman living*, it was in a measure incumbent on me to offer it to the public. That uuty I have attempted to fulfil, and now I leave the results in higher hands.

ANECDOTES RELATED AT RECENT EVANGELISTIC MEETINGS.

A Sergeant's Story.—Speaking at a Testimony meeting, the man said: "It is about twenty years since the Lord found me and saved me. It was in Calcutta. It was at an evangelistic meeting there that I was deeply convicted of sin, but I did not at once find the Saviour. I went home very wretched, for I knew that if I were to die I should be lost. I was in an agony. I had no one to speak to, for I was on the staff; but taking up my Bible and kneeling down, I asked God to give me a text out of His own Word that would help me; and, bless His name, He did so. He showed me if I came to Christ as a helpless sinner, and gave myself to Him, He would take care of me; and He has done so from that time until now. He drew me to Himself. O that all men knew His beauty and matchless worth! 'And I, if I be lifted up from the earth, will draw all men unto Me.'"

From Donald Drunk to Donald Sober.—Mr. Dewar says: "When I was a boy, standing in a shop one day, a man very much under the influence of intoxicating liquor came in. He was an official person, and being appointed to lead others, should have been going the right road himself; but there he was, helplessly intoxicated. He went up to the shop-keeper, and began to speak to him in a quarrelsome and foolish manner. The shop-keeper, who was a friend of the man, turned to him and said, 'You are not Donald to-night; if you were I should speak to you at once. Go away, just now, and ask Donald to look in to-morrow and speak to me.' The man seemed to see the force of the remark, and went quietly away. And is it not true that the man who takes intoxicating drink ceases to be himself? It changes his character, and causes him to say and do things that in his sober moments he abhors."

A Surprised Railway Porter.—A Minister said: "A train was running into Glasgow from the south, one day lately, when a porter saw an old man on the line. He shouted to him to get out of the way, but the man was not within hearing. Then the porter, running to where he was, caught him by the coat and roughly pulled him off the track. As the train thundered past, the porter inquired, 'Another minute later, and what than?' The old man looked up into the porter's face, and smiling, answered, 'What then, do you ask? Then *glory*.' Taking the hand of the young man, who looked much astonished, he asked, 'If it had been *you*, what then?' The porter thought for a moment, then turned away without speaking. He knew that he could not say, 'Glory,' as the old man had done. But he determined that, without loss of time, he would become enabled to say that, whatever happened, he would be safe, and so forthwith he sought Christ."

A Good Day for Bess and Bob.—Mr. Hunter remarks: "A married couple whom I knew, were leading very ungodly lives. They were both stricken down by disease, and brought near to the gates of death. A Christian visitor called upon them, the result being the conversion of the woman to God. They were both restored to health; the one determined to live for Christ, the other more determined than ever to have his fill of sin. For two years this state of things went on, the wife's godly ways seeming only to increase her husband's brutal usage to her. One evening he found a new Bible in the house. He seized it, tore off the covers, then dashed the pages, a few at a time, into the fire. A few leaves, however, escaped the burning; these the poor woman afterwards gathered up and placed them on the mantel-piece. The next evening the man came home, and sitting down at the fire, he took one of the spare leaves to light his pipe. Beginning to fold it up, his eyes fell on the words, 'Father, forgive them, for they know not what they do.' The words took hold of his conscience. He replaced the leaf upon the shelf and went out. He returned after a short time, and his wife asked, 'Will you have supper, Bob?' 'No, thank you, Bessie,' he replied, 'I am not hungry.' She was surprised at the gentle answer, but greater was her surprise next morning when she came downstairs and found the fire alight, the kettle on the hob, and, better still, a new Bible on the table. At this moment Bob entered, and, with tears in his eyes, said, 'Bessie, will you forgive me?' This request was quickly and gladly granted. 'Will God forgive me?' he next inquired. 'Ask Him,' said his wife. This was also done, and now that home—once the scene of brutality and blasphemy—has become the home of love and of daily united prayer. 'Old things have passed away, and behold all things have become new.'"

A Highland Soldier thus Testifies: "When I was unconverted, I often lay awake, wondering how I was to get to heaven. I had been very wicked, both before and after I had joined the army, and I knew I could not hope to get there on the strength of my own good works, but I always delayed coming to Christ until I should be a little better, or until I had left the army. One night, as I was lying in bed, after 'lights out,' I heard a man—the first convert in our regiment, and who had been converted that night at the Soldiers' Home—telling his comrade who slept next to him, all about it. He did not know I was listening, but I heard every word, and resolved that next night I would go to the Soldiers' Home. I did not go with the intention of being saved, but the Holy Spirit of God led me there, and before I left I had given my heart to Jesus. And I have, from that night, through Divine help, been a Christian soldier.

Died at His Wife's Feet.—Mr. Thomson Observes: "A man was put into prison lately for deserting his wife and children, and they were taken to the poorhouse. After the fellow had been in prison for some time, the doctor told him that he had heart disease, and any great excitement might kill him. He at once resolved that what remained of his life would be very different from that which he had spent. When he was released, the first thing he did was to take his wife and children from the poorhouse and place them in lodgings. When he got his wife alone he knelt at her feet and exclaimed, 'Oh, Mary, I have been a bad husband to you, but in the strength of the Lord I will do better. I will do my duty as a man and as a Christian, if you will only say that you will forgive the past.' 'Yes, I do, with all my heart, Jack,' the wife replied. 'I am glad to hear you say that; there are brighter days in store for all of us now.' 'Mary, say that again,' he said, still kneeling at her feet; 'it does me good.' 'Get up, Jack; get up, I do forgive you,' replied the woman. She touched him as she spoke; *he was dead;* on his knees pleading for mercy. The excitement had been too much for his poor weak heart, and he was gone."

No Need to Shiver in the Corner.—"I remember a poor confirmed drunkard who had given himself to the Lord in one of our meetings. He was a strong-bodied man, and earned from two to three pounds a week. When he got home to his miserable, scantily furnished dwelling, he found his wife standing huddled together in a corner. When she saw he was sober, she came forward looking surprised, for it was the first time he had come home sober for months. 'What is the matter, that you stand shivering in that corner?' he asked. 'I thought you were drunk, and I was afraid of you,' she replied. The man, when he saw how he was feared by her whom he should have had only to love, broke down and wept. Looking up, he said, 'Mary, where are the children?' She went and fetched them. In the poor little creatures slipped one by one, looking fearfully in the direction of their father, as if he had been a wild beast whom they feared to arouse. Each fearful glance was like a stab to the father's heart, now that he was sober and in his right mind. Silently he embraced them, and resolved that from that night, they would have no reason to dread him. He says his home is now like a heaven since Christ came to dwell with him.

WIFELY AMBITION, GOOD AND BAD.

Dr. Talmage's Fifth Sermon to THE WOMEN OF AMERICA.

Preached last Sunday Morning, February 13, 1888.

"Arise and eat bread, and let thine heart be merry: I will give thee the Vineyard of Naboth." 1 Kings 21:7.

A Treasured Heritage—Its Sale to Ahab Refused—Jezebel's Plot to Gain it by Unjust Confiscation—The Victim—Retribution after Three Years—Fatal Results of a Wife's Bad Advice—A Wife's Power—Suggestion of the Ballot Test—Probable Effect of Female Suffrage on Burning Questions—Women Drinking in Restaurants—Cruelty of Female Employers—How Good Wives have Inspired Men—Illustrious Examples—Noble and Ignoble Ambitions—Social Distinction—Political Power—An Obliterated Family—The Brave Man Supported and Stimulated by his Wife—A Personal Statement—Famous Names Extinct—The Valor of Joan of Arc—An Empress Entertaining a Prince.

ONE day King Ahab, looking out of the window of his palace at Jezreel, said to his wife, Jezebel: "We ought to have these royal gardens enlarged. If we could only get that fellow, Naboth, who owns that vineyard out there, to trade or sell, we could make it a kitchen garden for our palace."

"Fetch in Naboth," says the king to one of his servants.

The plain gardener, wondering why he should be called into the presence of his majesty, comes in, a little downcast in his modesty, and with very obsequious manner, bows to the king.

The king says: "Naboth, I want to trade vineyards with you.

I Want Your Vineyard

for a kitchen garden, and I will give a great deal better vineyard in place of it; or, if you prefer money for it, I will give you cash."

"Oh, no," says Naboth, "I cannot trade off my little place, nor can I sell it. It is the old homestead; I got it of my father, and he of his father, and I cannot let the old place go out of my hands."

In a great state of petulancy, King Ahab went into the house and flung himself on the bed, and turned his face to the wall, in a great pout.

His wife, Jezebel, comes in, and she says: "What is the matter with you? Are you sick?"

"Oh," he says, "I feel very blue. I have set my heart on getting that kitchen garden, and Naboth will neither trade nor sell, and to be defeated by a common gardener is more than I can stand."

"Oh, pshaw!" says Jezebel, "don't go on in that way. Get up and eat your dinner, and stop moping. I will get for you that kitchen garden."

Then Jebezel borrowed her husband's signet, or seal—for then, as now, in those lands, kings never signed their names, but had a ring with the royal name engraved on it, and that impressed on a royal letter or document, was the signature. She stamped her husband's name on a proclamation, which resulted in getting

Naboth Tried for Treason

against the king, and two perjured witnesses swore their souls away with the life of Naboth, and he was stoned to death, and his property came to the crown, and so Jezebel got for her husband and herself the kitchen garden. But while the wild street dogs were rending the dead body of poor Naboth, Elijah, the prophet, tells them of other canines that will, after a while, have a free banquet, saying: "Where dogs lick the blood of Naboth, shall dogs lick thy blood, even thine."

And sure enough, three years after, Ahab, wounded in battle, his chariot dripping with the carnage, dogs stood under it lapping his life's blood. And a little afterward his wife, Jezebel, who had been his chief adviser in crime, stands at her palace window and sees Jehu, the enemy, approaching to take possession of the palace. And to make herself look as attractive as possible, and queenly to the very last, she decorated her person, and according to Oriental custom closed her eyes and ran a brush dipped in a black powder along the long eye-lashes, and then from the window she glared her indignation upon Jehu. As he rode to the gates in his chariot he shouted to the slaves in her room: "Throw her down!" But no doubt the slaves halted a moment from such

Work of Assassination,

yet, knowing Queen Jezebel could be no more to them, and the conqueror Jehu would be everything, as he shouted again, "Throw her down," they seized her and bore her struggling and cursing to the window casement, and hurled her forth till she came tumbling to the earth, striking it just in time to let Jehu's horses trample her and the chariot wheels roll over her. While Jehu is inside at the table refreshing himself after the excitement, he orders his servants to go out and bury the dead queen. But the wild street dogs had for the third time appeared on the scene, and they had removed all her body, except those parts which in all ages dogs are by a strange instinct or brutal superstition kept from touching after death—the palms of the hands and the soles of the feet.

All this appalling scene of ancient history was the result of

A Wife's Bad Advice

to a husband, of a wife's struggle to advance her husband's interests by unlawful means. Ahab and Jezebel got the kitchen garden of Naboth, but the dogs got them. The trouble all began when this mistaken wife aroused her husband out of his melancholy by the words of the text: "Arise, and eat bread, and let thine heart be merry: I will give thee the vineyard."

The influence suggested by this subject is an influence you never before heard discoursed on and may never hear again, but a most potent and semi-omnipotent influence, and decides the course of individuals, families, nations, centuries and eternities. I speak of wifely ambition, good and bad. How important that every wife have her ambition an elevated, righteous and divinely approved ambition.

And here let me say, what I am most anxious for is that woman, not waiting for the rights denied her or postponed, promptly and decisively employ the rights she already has in possession. Some say she will be in fair way to get all her rights when she gets the

Right to the Ballot-box.

I wish that the experiment might be tried and settled. I would like to see all women vote, and then watch the result. I do not know that it would change anything for the better. Most wives and daughters and sisters would vote as their husbands and fathers and brothers voted. Nearly all the families that I know are solidly Republican or Democratic or Prohibition. Those families all voting would make more votes but no difference in the result. Besides that, as now at the polls men are bought up by the thousands, women would be bought up by the thousands. The more voters the more opportunity for political corruption. We have several million more voters now than are for public good.

We are told that female suffrage would correct

Two Evils,

the rum business and the insufficiency of woman's wages. About the rum business I have to say that multitudes of women drink, and it is no unusual thing to see them in the restaurants so over-powered with wine and beer that they can hardly sit up, while there are many so-called respectable restaurants where they can go and take their champagne and hot toddy all alone. Mighty temperance voters those women would make! Besides that, the wives of the rum-sellers would have to vote in the interest of their husbands' business, or have a time the inverse of felicitous. Besides that, millions of respectable and refined women in America would probably not vote at all, because they do not want to go to the polls, and, on the other hand, womanly roughs would all go to the polls, and that might make woman's vote on the wrong side. There is not much prospect of the expulsion of drunkenness by female suffrage.

As to woman's wages to be corrected by woman's vote, I have not much faith in that.

Women are Harder on Women

than men are. Masculine employers are mean enough in treatment of women, but if you want to hear beating down of prices and wages in perfection, listen how some women treat washerwomen and dressmakers and female servants. Mrs. Shylock is more merciless than Mr. Shylock. Women, I fear, will never get righteous wages through woman's vote, and as to unfortunate womanhood, women are far more cruel and unforgiving than men are. After a woman has made shipwreck of her character, men generally drop her, but women do not so much drop her as hurl her with the force of a catapult clear out and off and down and under.

I have not much faith that woman will ever get merciful consideration and justice through woman suffrage, yet I like experiments, and some of my friends, in whose judgment I have confidence, are so certain that alleviation would come by such process that I would, if I had the power, put in every woman's hand the vote. I cannot see what right you have to make a woman pay taxes on her property to help support city, State and national Government, and yet deny her the opportunity of helping decide who shall be Mayor, Governor or President. But let every wife, not waiting for the vote she may never get, or, getting it, find it outbalanced by some other vote not fit to be cast, arise now in the might of the eternal God and wield the power of a sanctified wifely ambition for a good approximating the infinite.

No one can so inspire a man to noble purposes as a noble woman, and no one so thoroughly degrade a man as a wife of unworthy tendencies. While in my text we have illustration of wifely ambition employed in the wrong direction, in society and history are instances of

Wifely Ambition Triumphant

in right directions. All that was worth admiration in the character of Henry VI., was a reflection of the heroics of his wife Margaret. William, Prince of Orange, was restored to the right path by the grand qualities of his wife Mary. Justinian, the Roman emperor, confesses that his wise laws were the suggestion of his wife Theodora. Andrew Jackson, the warrior and President, had his mightest reinforcement in his plain wife, whose inartistic attire was the amusement of the elegant circles in which she was invited. Washington, who broke the chain that held America in foreign vassalage, wore for forty years a chain around his own neck, that chain holding the miniature likeness of her who had been his greatest inspiration, whether among the snows at Valley Forge or the honors of the Presidential chair.

Pliny's pen was driven through all its poetic and historical dominions by his wife, Calpurnia, who sang his stanzas to the sound of flute, and sat among audiences enraptured at her husband's genius, herself the most enraptured. Pericles said he got all his eloquence and statemanship from his wife. When the wife of Grotius rescued him from long imprisonment at Lovestein by means of a bookcase that went in and out, carrying his books to and fro, he was one day transported, hidden amid the folios; and the women of besieged Weinsberg getting permission from the victorious army to take with them so much of their valuables as they could carry, under cover of the promise shouldered and took with them as the most important valuables, their husbands—both achievements in a literal way illustrated what thousands of times has been done in a figurative way, that wifely ambition has been the salvation of men.

De Tocqueville, whose writings will be potential and quoted while the world lasts, ascribes his successes to his wife and says: "Of all the blessings which God has given to me, the greatest of all in my eyes is to have lighted on Maria Motley." Martin Luther says of his wife: "I would not exchange my poverty with her for all the riches of Crœsus without her." Isabella of Spain, by her superior faith in Columbus put nto the hand of Ferdinand, her husband, merica. John Adams, President of the United tates, said of his wife: "She never by word or ook discouraged me from running all hazards or the salvation of my country's liberties."

Thomas Carlyle

pent the last twenty years of his life in trying y his pen to atone for the fact that during his ife's life he never appreciated her influence on is career and destiny. Alas, that having taken er from a beautiful home and a brilliant career, e should have buried her in the home of a ecluse and scolded her in such language as only dyspeptic genius could manage, until one day hile in her invalidism riding in Hyde Park. her et dog got run over, and under the excitment he coachman found her dead. Then the liter- ry giant woke from his conjugal injustice, and rote the lamentations of Craigen-Puttock and heyne Row. The elegant and fulsome epi- aphs that husbands put upon their wives' tomb- tones are often an attempt to make up for lack f appreciative words that should have been ttered in the ears of the living. A whole reenwood of mounmental inscriptious will not o a wife so much good after she has quit the orld as one plain sentence like that which om Hood wrote to his living wife when he aid: "I never was anything till I knew you."

O woman, what is your wifely ambition, noble r ignoble? Is it

High Social Position?

hat will then probably direct your husband, nd he will climb and scramble and slip and fall nd rise and tumble, and on what level or in hat depth, or on what height he will, after a hile, be found, I cannot even guess. The con- est for social position is the most unsatisfac- ory contest in all the world, because it is so ncertain about your getting it, and so insecure posession after you have obtained it, and so nsatisfactory even if you keep it. The whisk f a lady's fan may blow it out. The growl of ne bear, or the bellowing of one bull on Wall Street, may scatter it.

Is the wife's ambition the political prefer- ment of her husband? Then that will prob- ably direct him. What

A God-forsaken Realm

is American politics, those best know who have dabbled in them. After they have assessed a man, who is a candidate for office, which he does not get, or assessed him for some office attained, and he has been whirled round and round and round and round among the drink- ing, smoking, swearing crowd, who often get control of public affairs, all that is left of his self-respect or moral stamina would find plenty of room on a geometrical point, which is said to have neither length, breadth or thickness. Many a wife has not been satisfied till her hus- band went into politics, but would afterward have given all she possessed to get him out.

I knew a highly moral man, useful in the church and possessor of a bright home. He had a useful and prosperous business, but his wife did not think it genteel. There were

Odors About the Business,

and sometimes they would adhere to his gar- ments when he returned at night. She insisted on his doing something more elegant, although he was qualified for no business except that in which he was engaged. To please her he changed his business, and, in order to get on faster, abandoned church attendance, saying, after he had made a certain number of hun- dreds of thousands of dollars he would return to the church and its services. Where is that family to-day? Obliterated. Although succeed- ing in business for which he was qualified, he undertook a style of merchandise for which he had no qualification, and soon went into bank- ruptcy. His new style of business put him into evil association. He lost his morals as well as his money. He broke up not only his own home, but broke up another man's home, and from being a kind, pure, generous, moral man as any of you who sit here to-day, has become a homeless, penniless libertine. His wife's am- bition for a more genteel business destroyed him, disgraced her, and blighted their child.

But suppose, now, there be in our homes, as thank God there are in hundreds of homes here represented, on

The Wife's Throne

one who says not only by her words, but more powerfully by her actions: "My husband, our destinies are united; let us see where industry, honesty, common sense and faith in God will put us. I am with you in all your enterprises. I cannot be with you in person as you go to your daily business, but I will be with you in my prayers. Let us see what we can achieve by hav- ing God in our hearts, and God in our lives, and God in our home. Be on the side of everything good. Go ahead and do your best, and though everything should turn out different from what we have calculated, you may always count on two who are going to help you, and God is one and I am the other." That man may have fee- ble health, and may meet with many obstacles and business trials, but he is coming gloriously through, for he is reinforced and inspired and spurred on by a woman's voice.

Some of us could tell of what influence upon us has been a wifely ambition consecrated to righteousness. As

My Wife

is out of town, and will not shake her head be- cause I say it in public, I will state that in my own professional life I have often been called of God as I thought, to run into the very teeth of public opinion, and all outsiders with whom I advised told me I had better not, it would ruin me and ruin my church, and at the same time I was receiving nice little letters threatening me with dirk and pistol and poison if I persisted in attacking certain evils of the day, until the Com- missioner of Police considered it his duty to take his place in our Sabbath services with forty officers scattered through the house for the preservation of order; but in my home there has always been one voice to say: "Go ahead, and diverge not an inch from the straight line. Who cares, if only God is on our side?" And though sometimes it seemed as if I was going out against nine hundred iron chariots, I went ahead cheered by the domestic voice: "Up! for this is the day in which the Lord hath delivered Sisera into thine hands."

A man is no better than his wife will let him be. O wives of America, swing your sceptres of wifely influence for God and good homes! Do not urge your husbands to annex Naboth's vine- yard to your palace of success, whether right or wrong, lest the dogs that come out to destroy Naboth come out also to devour you. Right- eousness will pay best in life, will pay best in death, will pay best in the judgment, will pay best through all eternity.

Extinct Families.

In our effort to have the mother of every household appreciate her influence over her children, we are apt to forget the wife's influ- ence over the husband. In many households the influence upon the husband is the only home influence. In a great multitude of the best and most important and most talented families of the earth, there have been no des- cendants. There is not a child or a grandchild, or any remote descendant of Washington, or Charles Summer, or Shakespeare, or Edmund Burke, or Pitt, or Lord Nelson, or Cowper, or Pope, or Addison, or Johnson, or Lord Chatham, or Grattan, or Isaac Newton, or Goldsmith, or Swift, or Locke, or Gibbon, or Walpole, or Canning, or Dryden, or More, or Chaucer, or Lord Byron, or Walter Scott, or Oliver Crom- well, or Garrick, or Hogarth, or Joshua Rey- nolds, or Spencer, or Lord Bacon, or Macaulay. Multitudes of the finest families of the earth are extinct. As though they had done enough for the world by their genius or wit or patriot- ism or invention or consecration, God withdrew them. In multitudes of cases all woman's op- portunity for usefulness is with her contempo- raries. How important that it be an improved opportunity!

While the French warriors on their way to Rheims had about concluded to give up attack- ing the castle at Troyes, because it was so heavily garrisoned,

Joan of Arc

entered the room and told them they would be inside the castle in three days. "We would willingly wait six days," said one of the leaders. "Six!" she cried out, "you shall be in it to- morrow," and under her leadership, on the mor- row they entered. On a smaller scale, every man has garrisons to subdue and obstacles to level, and every wife may be an inspired Joan of Arc to her husband.

What a noble, wifely ambition, the determi- nation, God helping, to accompany her com- panion across the stormy sea of this life and to- gether gain the wharf of the Celestial City! Coax him along with you! You cannot drive him there. *You cannot nag him there;* but you can coax him there. That is God's plan. He coaxes us all the way—coaxes us out of our sins, coaxes us to accept pardon, coaxes us to heaven. If we reach that blessed place, it will be through a prolonged and divine coax- ing. By the same process take your companion, and then you will get there as well, and all your household. Do just the opposite of your neigh- bor. Her wifely

Ambition All for this World,

and a disappointed and vexed and unhappy creature she will be all the way. Her residence may be better than yours for the few years of earthly stay, but she will move out of it, as to her body, into a house about five and a half feet long and about three feet wide and two feet high; and concerning her soul's destiny you can make your own prognostication. Her husband and her sons and daughters, who all, like her, live for this world, will have the same destiny for the body and the soul. You, having had a

Sanctified and Ennobled

wifely ambition, will pass up into palaces, and what becomes of your body is of no importance, for it is only a scaffolding, pulled down now that your temple is done. You will stand in the everlasting rest and see your husband come in, and see your children come in, if they have not preceded you. Glorified Christian wife! Pick up any crown you choose from off the King's footstool and wear it; it was promised you long ago, and with it cover up all the scars of your earthly conflict.

Sixteen miles from Petersburg, Russia, was one of the royal palaces, and there one night Catherine the Empress entertained Prince Henry. It was severe winter and deep snow, and

The Empress and the Prince

rode in a magnificence of sleigh and robe and canopy never surpassed, followed by two thou- sand sleighs laden with the first people of Russia, the whole length of the distance illumined by lamps and dazzling temples built for that one night, and imitations of mosques and Egyptian pyramids; and people of all nations, in all styles of costume, standing on platforms along the way and watching the blaze of the pyrotechnics. At the palace the luxuries of kingdoms were gathered and spread, and at the table the guests had but to touch the centre of a plate and, by magical machinery, it dropped and another plate came up loaded with still richer viands. But all that scene of the long ago shall be eclipsed by the greater splendors that will be gathered at the banquet made by the Heavenly King for those consecrated women who come in out of the winter and snowy chill of their earthly existence into the warm and illumined palaces of heaven. With the King himself and all the potentates, yourself robed and crowned, you will sit at a table compared with which all the feasts of Kenilworth and St. Cloud and the Alhambra were a beggar's crust. And the platter of one royal satisfaction touched at the centre shall disappear only to make room for a beggar's crust; and the golden plate of one royal satisfaction, touched at the centre, shall dis- appear only to make room for the coming up of some richer and grander regalement.

A THIEVES' PARLOR VISITED BY A CITY MISSIONARY.

THE Rev. James Wells, M. A., of Glasgow, in a recent address, said: "I entered a house where seven or eight men were playing at cards. As they were satisfied at a glance that I had nothing to do with the police, I at once announced myself as the missionary, and they with equal frankness announced their profession: they were regular thieves. I was *in a thieves' parlor*, or den of thieves. The house had scarcely a stick of furniture in it, for the householders held themselves ready to flit at a moment's notice. The men did not look like other men. Evidently their clothes had not been made for them, but had been got ready-made—probably at a pawn-shop. They had cropped heads, slouching round backs, and stunted, unhealthy-looking, back-boneless frames. They entered freely into conversation with me, and spoke quite respectfully. The oldest man among them—about forty—was an Englishman, called Friday; perhaps because, as in the case of Robinson Crusoe's man, some great event of his life had taken place on that day. He was a returned convict, and

The Chief of the Crew,

'by merit raised to that bad eminence.' He ruled them with a nod, and owed his undisputed authority apparently to the sheer intensity of his iniquity and his extraordinary force of character. His spirit seemed a compound of hatred of good and hatred of man—a compound of Cain and Ishmael, and I thought that I had never before met anyone so hardened and defiant. He gave me a disquieting idea of the meaning of the phrase 'the dangerous classes.' He had lustrous eyes, sunken cheeks, and a hollow, consumptive cough. I expressed regret at his poor health. 'Yes,' he said, 'I belong to a consumptive family, not one of whom has lived past forty-five, and I am now over forty.' I reasoned with them, and they all condemned themselves except Friday. 'No,' he said, sternly, 'society has wronged me, and I am just taking my revenge upon society; that's fair enough.' 'But,' I replied, 'you must be beaten sooner or later; for you are weak, man is strong, and God is stronger;

Both God and Man are Against You,'

'No,' he yelled, furiously, 'Friday will never give in.' He then described with admiration the death-bed of an old thief, whose name seemed a household word with them, and who, with his latest breath, ridiculed 'the parson,' who wished to pray with him, and died blaspheming.

"The next in point of age was 'Tommy,' who might be about twenty-seven. He had lately come out of prison, and was in bad health. Though brought up a Romanist, he had an extensive acquaintance with the Bible, which, he told me, he had gained in prison. He frankly admitted the truth of all I said, confessed his misery and self-dissatisfaction, but pleaded that he could not now keep himself. He deeply regretted that his father, who was also a thief, had not taught him a trade; he had been 'born in the business,' as another thief said; and no one could have added more feelingly than he did—'I am like the unjust steward in the parable. I cannot dig, and to beg I am ashamed.' His deep feeling drew out my sympathy, and subsequently I had friendly interviews with him.

"A well-dressed young fellow, who was master of the house, told me that he must be a Catholic, because his father had told him so. He said that as master of the house he levied blackmail on the rest. Four or five heavy-necked halflings completed the crew. They were apprentices at this thieves' college, though they had not yet taken out their degree, but they would soon be fit for it. They showed me some silk handkerchiefs which they had stolen, with the marks torn out. One showed me my own handkerchief *which he had abstracted from my pocket during conversation*. At my request he showed me how he had stolen it, and so I got

My First Lesson in Pocket-Picking.

They showed not a little hardened bravado, and a tendency to magnify their adventures. They had narrowly escaped detection the previous evening, as they had stolen, among other things, a basket with six bottles of brandy. They were revelling over their spoil when, roused by the alarm of the detectives, they threw up the window, and dashed the bottles in pieces against the wall. They described the episode with great animation and dramatic effect. They vowed a most intense hatred of policemen, and were quite sure that a thief had not so much to answer for on the Judgment Day as a policeman. I said, 'Is it fair or manly in you to take away from an honest workingman the money he has wrought for, and to do it by coming sneaking behind him?' They evaded the question, but maintained strongly that there was the strictest honor among thieves, and in proof of it quoted the case of the governor of Millbank Penitentiary, whose watch, stolen in London, was returned to him by post by the thieves, as soon as they knew that it was his, and all this in token of their respect for him. As I was leaving, Friday said, 'Well, you're the first stranger that has visited us to-day, and I take it for a good sign. I think we'll have good luck to-night,'—and a loud, rude laugh signified their hearty approval of the sentiment. Unwilling to let him have the last word, I made another appeal to him. 'Nay, nay,' he replied with piercing emphasis, 'none of your canting and praying for me; be sure Friday will die plucky; Friday will die plucky, and no mistake.' With these defiant tones ringing in my ears I came sadly down the stairs.

"Three or four months afterwards, when near the Tron steeple, some one gently touched my arm. Turning round, I found my friend Tommy, much excited. Courteously lifting his cap to me, he said: 'Do you remember that day when you saw us all in Princes Street?' 'Yes,' I said. 'Do you remember

What Friday Said to You?'

'Yes, he said that he would die plucky.' 'Well, he got seven years from Lord Ardmillan yesterday for stealing a watch; he never spoke a word after, nor lifted his head, and he was found dead in his cell this morning.' Poor Friday! after all, he did not die plucky. I told this story to a friend of mine, an advocate, who mentioned it to Lord Ardmillan. His lordship remembered Friday quite well, and, true Christian philanthropist that he was, he was profoundly affected."

A CAPTAIN'S DISMISSAL.

A CHRISTIAN captain held religious services on board his vessel every Lord's Day, wind and weather permitting, and many of his crew and passengers have been converted to God through his instrumentality. Some parties in New Zealand, connected with the firm which employed him, wrote home to complain of him, stating that Captain C. was too religious, and expressing a fear that the house would suffer, unless a check were put upon him. Accordingly, he was told that unless he altered his conduct in this respect he would be discharged on his return to England; and he was requested to take three days to consider the question, and then let the firm have his answer. The captain replied, "I do not want three days to consider; you can have the answer now." But no, he was to consider. On the third day he gave his answer, and it was to this effect: He would do his best for the owners, but if the passengers did not object to his preaching he must continue to do so. The reply was, "Very well, then; on your return you must leave the ship." The ship went out, and had a very prosperons voyage in every respect. Services were held on board morning and evening, and many were led to the Saviour. On reaching home, when all was settled, the captain was called into the office and told, "Well, captain, you have *not* done as we required you. You will remember what was said; you will have to leave the ship." "Sorry for it," was the reply; "she has had a good run and paid well?" "O yes; nothing to complain of," said the owner; "she has done well, never better. But there is our word, and that is our bond." "Well," said the captain, "I suppose you do not object to give me a letter to some other house; for I have done my duty as a servant to you ever since I entered your employ." "Do not be in a hurry," said the gentleman; "for although we never deviate from our word when it is given, and therefore you must leave the ship, yet—it is only to be removed to one of our best vessels, since we feel that a man who thus honors his God is too good to lose. And here is a cheque for £20, as an acknowledgment of our confidence." Such was the happy issue of one of the trials of a good man's life.

A WIDOW'S VIGIL.

SEVEN years in one room have been passed by a widow at Los Angeles, Cal. The *Alta* states that the efforts of the city council to have a house removed which stands on a city lot in Fort Street have been so steadily resisted that inquiries have been made as to the basis of the objections, and a remarkable story has been brought to light. Twelve years ago a man and his wife went from the East, and occupied the house. After five years the man, who was in a consumption, died. Thereupon his widow had her bed removed into the room in which he breathed his last, and has remained there ever since. During the whole seven years no one has seen her. She had a blind-door fixed to the room, and all business transactions have been made through its means. A faithful old woman has waited upon her, putting her meals inside the door, and receiving instructions there, the voluntary prisoner keeping carefully out of sight during the conversation. The explanation given by the widow for this extraordinary life is, that just before her husband died he told her that if it was possible for him to visit her after his death he would do so, and give her information about the world beyond the grave. On the night after his death she dreamed that he appeared to her, and told her to await his communication in his room, and that it might be eight years before she would receive it. She has accordingly waited there; and fully believing that her husband will come, has refused to leave the room lest he should come in her absence. She has displayed a constancy worthy of a better cause. If Christians were similarly minded there would be far more intensity in their work and consecration in their lives, as they would fear lest at their Master's coming, He should find them spiritually sleeping. (Mark 13: 35-37.)

A BRAHMIN'S INTERRUPTED JOURNEY.

THE death of a useful Scripture reader is reported from India by Rev. Thomas Tracy in a letter to the *Church*. He describes the man's death as not only peaceful but triumphant, and narrates the following account of his remarkable conversion.

Nandkishor, although a Brahmin, was so ignorant that he was unable to read. He was a young man, but had led such a life of sin that disease in one of its worst forms had made him a cripple, and threatened to soon end his days on earth. One who saw him at the time said that he was a living skeleton. Knowing as he did that he could not long live in such a condition, and with no hope of recovery, he decided that his best course was to reach, if possible, the sacred temple of Jagan Nith, and gain the merit of ending his life there. God, however, intended better things for him, and led him in a way he knew not. He had travelled fifty miles on his way, and there had left the carriage for some purpose, and was sitting near the entrance to the station, when he was observed by the civil surgeon of the town, who was accustomed to go or send to each passenger train, that he might be of service to any in need. This officer was an eminent Christian. Nandkishor was induced to give up his journey and go to the hospital in hope of being healed. At this hospital there was a Christian compounder, and at that time an inmate who was also a Christian. More than this, the missionary of the station and his helper were accustomed to visit the sick and tell them of the love of the Lord Jesus Christ. In these circumstances we see the loving hand of God in guiding this wanderer to Himself, for such favorable conditions could hardly have been found in all that region of country. Slowly the mind of Nandkishor was awakened, and slowly was he drawn to the Saviour who so lovingly held out His arms to receive him. Ignorance and prejudice and pride gave place to deep spiritual insight and firm faith and confidence in Jesus as the only Saviour of men. A good degree of health was granted to him as the result of care and skill, and he devoted it to the publication of the glorious news of salvation.

THE PYRAMID POINTING TO 1888-9 AS YEARS OF TROUBLE.

(*See Sectional Diagram on Page 108.*)

According to the Astronomer-Royal for Scotland, Professor Smyth's Period of 1,882 Years from the Nativity in A. D. 6.

THE Great Pyramid of Egypt is one of the acknowledged *Seven Wonders of the World*, on account of the Colossal Magnitude of its Height, Breadth and Length, and also its Antiquity and mysterious Origin.

Professor Piazzi Smyth, Astronomer-Royal for Scotland, spent a year in a visit of exploration to the Great Pyramid, and in writing a large book of 700 pages upon it, called "Our Inheritance in the Great Pyramid." In this book he, as well as the Rev. Dr. Seiss in his "Prophecy in Stone," and other writers, maintains that the Pyramid was

Constructed by Jewish Architects,

guided by a prophetic spirit, and that *the length of its interior passages in inches*, figuratively represents *periods of an equal number of years*, and that therefore, THE LENGTH OF THE GRAND GALLERY OF 1882 inches prefigures and represents A PERIOD OF 1882 YEARS FROM THE BIRTH OF CHRIST TO THE BEGINNING OF THE LATTER-DAY TROUBLOUS TIMES PREDICTED BY DANIEL TO PRECEDE THE SECOND ADVENT OF CHRIST. (Daniel 9: 26, 12: 1.)

After the Grand Gallery of 1882 inches, there follows a *low exit passage*, which is understood to represent the ensuing Troublous Times and Distress of Nations for a few years before the End of this Age, and accompanying considerable Depopulation of the Earth, which will take some years at the commencement of the Millennium to repair even measurably.

The true date of the Birth of Christ has been ably shown by the late Duke of Manchester in his learned book, "Times of Daniel," to be A. D. 5 or 6—the chronological evidence preponderating in favor of A. D. 6. Hence 1882 years commencing in A. D. 6 will end in 1888, as the commencement of Daniel's predicted Troublous Times and Distress of Nations. (Dan. 9: 25; Luke 21: 25.) And 1888, according to the Jewish Calendar, ends on April 1, 1889.

The Great Pyramid of Egypt is supposed to have been built about the year 2170 before Christ, and consists of an enormous solid mass of stones, covering an exactly square space of ground, which is 763 feet wide on each of the four sides of its base—about 13 acres. Each of its four sides gradually slants upwards until they reach their highest summit, which constitutes the apex of the pyramid, at a height of 486 feet from the earth.

In the very heart and centre of this gigantic mass of stone there is

An Interior Chamber,

called the *King's Chamber*, 412 inches long, 206 broad, and 230 inches high—that is to say, about 11½ yards in length, 6 yards wide, and 6⅓ yards high. This chamber is reached from the outside by a long, narrow passage, which is between 3 and 4 feet wide.

This *passage* from the outside first goes downwards for 985 inches, and this portion of it is called, for the sake of distinction, the *Entrance Passage*. The passage then proceeds *upwards* for 1,542 inches further, which portion is termed the *First Ascending Passage*. The passage then suddenly becomes about *seven times* higher, for it increases in height from 47 inches to 339 inches, and consequently from this point onward it is called

The Grand Gallery,

for a distance of 1,882 or 1,883 inches, at the end of which the passage abruptly decreases in height from 338 inches to 43 inches, i. e., about 3½ feet, so that a man has to stoop very much to creep onward. This very *low exit-passage* leading out of the Grand Gallery continues for 52 inches, and then comes what is termed the *Antechamber*, which is 116 inches long, 65 inches broad, and 149 inches high. After this, the passage becomes narrower and lower for a distance of 100 inches, and then enters at once into the spacious *King's Chamber*, inside which there stands a *granite coffer*, the *outside* measure of which is 90 inches long, 38½ inches broad, and 41 inches high.

The marked and superior height of the Grand Gallery, in contrast with the lesser height of the preceding *Entrance Passage* and *First Ascending Passage* is understood to typify the high and elevated character of the Christian dispensation in contrast with the inferior character of the preceding Jewish Dispensation.

It is an extraordinary fact that this

Pyramid Prefiguration

of the Troublous Times to commence about A. D. 1888-9 mainly agrees with certain chronological prophecies in Daniel and Revelation. For example, the 1,260 years (Daniel 12: 7; Revelation 11: 2), which is universally allowed to be the measurement of the Mohammedan as well as the Papal Antichrist, was calculated by the Rev. W. Girdlestone to commence in A. D. 630, the date of Mohammed's capture of Mecca, and therefore to end in 1890, by which time some tremendous blow will be inflicted on Mohammedanism and the Turkish empire (the mystic Euphrates) which is the principal stronghold and bulwark of the temporal power of Mohammedanism, although as the Mohammedans did not capture Jerusalem until 637, the 1,260 years of Mohammedanism cannot be expected to end fully until 1897.

The Rev. W. Girdlestone wrote in 1820 in his "Observations on the Prophecies:"—"The period of 1,260 years is to be dated from the establishment of Mohammedan imposture, which took place in the year A. D. 630, when Mohammed seized possession of the city of Mecca, which thenceforth became the sacred capital of Mohammedanism and synchronises therefore with the taking away of the daily sacrifice. (Rev. 11: 2, 3.) Mohammed did not establish his religion or his power till he was master of Mecca; from that time the Mussulman armies poured into Syria, and out of Syria they came upon Jerusalem."

Professor Smyth, in the fourth edition (in 1879) of his work, states that the Grand Gallery is 1,881 inches long, according to his measurement, but that Mr. Hiram Powers's measurement of it makes it to be between 1,881 and 1,882 inches; therefore Professor Smyth, in his detailed specifications of the measurements of the various *interior passages* of the Pyramid in his Chapter x. on page 222, specifies the length of this Grand Gallery to be 1,882 inches. He also states that Mr. Lane's measurement of it gives 1,894 inches as its length; so that after all its real length may be at least *one* or *two* inches longer than 1,882 inches, for it must be difficult to ascertain precisely to the amount of an inch the length of a long dark passage more than fifty yards long. In fact, Professor Smyth admits a marginal uncertainty to the extent of a *year* or two, i. e., an inch or two, for he says, on page 478: "So far as the final numbers of my actual Pyramid measurements are concerned, *I do not recommend any one to trust to them for so small a quantity as a whole year*," i.e., one inch. The Professor also says:

"For all those who have accepted the beginning of the Grand Gallery for the beginning of the Christian dispensation at the birth of Christ [Which the late Duke of Manchester, and Strauchius, hold to be in A. D. 5 or 6.—*Editor*.] there is nothing for it but also to accept that a period, distinct and finite, was appointed to that dispensation by God, and that that finite period is close upon us. Not an end of the world, or of nations, or of men, but of the dispensation.

"How Close, Then, is Such an End?

The answer to that question must depend on the length of the Grand Gallery by measure in pyramid inches, which symbolically represent *years*.

"As usual with the accounts of travellers at the Great Pyramid, there are various results in print. According to Mr. Lane's measurement of the Grand Gallery, its length is 1,894 pyramid inches. My own measures of the Grand Gallery, however, taken in 1865, amounted to, for the length up to the great step, 1,813.0 pyramid inches; and thence up to the end wall, in the line concluded for the slanting floor 68 inches farther—1,881.0 *pyramid inches in all*; or, as computed more exactly by Mr. H. A. Powers, of Cincinnati,* 1,881.4 *pyramid inches*.

"*Something*, then, seems to be appointed to take place at that particular time, and it is much easier to say what it *is not* than what it *is*. It is not, for instance, as just stated above, *the end of the world*, for there is a "passage floor" leading on from the Grand Gallery to the Antechamber; through that also, and onwards into the King's Chamber, the granite-lined and most glorious part of the whole interior of the building.

"In fact, it is rather like the *unexampled days of future trouble* which our Saviour Himself announced should immediately precede His second coming and terminate this dispensation of His first coming.

"O the unutterable anguishes of these most exceptional days to come! We read (Matt. 24: 21; Mark 13: 19) that "there shall be affliction such as there was not from the beginning of the creation which God created unto this time, neither shall be." But its duration will not be long, "for," continues our Saviour, "except the Lord had shortened those days, no flesh should be saved; but for the elect's sake, whom He hath chosen, He hath shortened the days."

"The Severities of These Times

are pyramidally expressed at this place by the *exit passage* from the south end of the Grand Gallery being *lower* still than any of the low passages, which indicate the troubles of the profane world in early times. Those passages were forty-seven inches in transverse, and fifty-two in vertical height; painfully low, therefore, for any full-sized men to creep through; but the *exit passage* leading from this end of the Grand Gallery is only forty-four inches in vertical height, and is the most trying part of the whole passage system."

* Professor Smyth says: "My measures ought to have been of the floor. For practical convenience they were taken on the surface of the ramps, and would have given the same result as the floor, but for the 'impending' of the south wall of the Grand Gallery, which makes the correction furnished by Mr. Powers. This I fully agree in: but I am not equally disposed to accept certain different modes of using my own measures, adopted either by Mr. W. Rowbotpm in his 'The Mystery of the Bible Dates Solved by the Great Pyramid;' nor, again, the rather different results brought out by Mr. Geo. N. Walsh, in his 'Israel's Chronology.' But I do not actively object to them, for some of their principles of divergence seem fair enough, in cases where it is difficult to maintain one opinion only, while the final and positive test for every one is the future. Mr. Walsh, I should perhaps add, by measuring *over* the surface of the Grand Gallery's step, in place of *through* it in continuation of the floor-line, increases the length of the whole from 1,881.4 to 1,910 pyramid inches."

CHRISTIAN HERALD AND SIGNS OF OUR TIMES.

OFFICE, 63 BIBLE HOUSE, NEW YORK.

ENTERED AT THE POST-OFFICE AT NEW YORK, N. Y., AS SECOND-CLASS MATTER.

Published Weekly. Subscription price, $1.50 a year; $1 eight months; 75 cents six months; sent two months on trial for 25 cents; always payable in advance. Single copies for sale by, or can be ordered at, all newsdealers.

Remittances by Mail should be by Post-office money order, bank cheques, or drafts or express money order, and should always be made payable to THE CHRISTIAN HERALD.

Receipts are not sent, the receipt of the paper by a subscriber is a sufficient proof that his remittance has been received. If the paper does not arrive promptly, please advise us, that we may see if the address is correctly entered.

Change of Address. Name of Post Office and State, of both old and new address, should always be given in case of removal.

CURRENT EVENTS.

The Extradition Treaty with Great Britain failed of confirmation in the Senate, last week. It was not finally rejected, but its further consideration was postponed until the first Monday in December. This decision was arrived at in secret session on February 8, and was adopted by a vote of 23 to 21. Senators have been moved to take this course, it is said, chiefly by two considerations. One of these is that though mutually advantageous, the treaty is more earnestly desired by Great Britain than America, and, therefore, that it is political to keep it in suspense pending the issue of the negotiation on the Fisheries. The chief cause, however, is doubtless an indisposition to confirm a treaty in which Irish refugees are vitally interested, until after the Presidential election, in which the Irish vote will be wanted by both parties.

An Important Mail Contract was Effected last week by the new Postmaster-General with the Chicago, Burlington and Quincy Railroad Company, by which the journey between New York and San Francisco will be performed in one hundred and twelve hours. By the new arrangement, which goes into operation at an early date, California mail leaving San Francisco in the evening after business hours and arriving at Council Bluffs in the afternoon of the third day will there be taken up by the new fast train, and will reach Chicago in time for the first morning delivery on the fourth day from the Pacific coast. A fast train is to leave Chicago on the arrival of the Pacific coast train, and to make New York in about twenty-five hours from Chicago, and about one hundred and twelve hours from San Francisco. And as the Pacific coast train will leave San Francisco in the evening, and as its connection, if established, will arrive in New York in the morning, it will make a practical saving of one full business day. This new contract is regarded by the Postmaster-General as the most advantageous, as well as the most important, ever entered into by the Post Office for a fast mail service.

The Possibility of an Agreement Between the parties on the Tariff question does not appear so remote as it did a few weeks ago. Prominent members of the Republican party are quoted by Washington journals as disposed to consent to a large increase in the free list, and important reductions in other cases. Senator Sabin, of Minnesota, has, it is stated, declared himself for free salt, free lumber and a reduction of the duty on steel rails. General Browne, Republican, of Indiana, declares for free salt, free lumber, free tin plates and a reduction on some hardware products. Mr. Nelson, Republican, of Minnesota, declares he is ready to go for tariff reduction. "Just as far as it is possible to go, I would like," he says "to have as many of the necessaries of life put on the free list as possible, and have the taxes retained on whiskey and tobacco." Other Republicans advocate reductions in articles which will not affect the business of the States they represent, and very few are opposed to some reduction. The aspect of affairs at the present stage suggests the expectation that the struggle on the question will be as much between sections of the country as between political parties.

The Agitation for the Admission of Utah into the Union is being vigorously prosecuted in Washington. The friends of morality should therefore be on their guard. The specious considerations urged by the Mormons are clearly deceptive. They point out that the constitution framed by Utah makes polygamy a crime, and undertakes never to revoke the article without the consent of Congress. Its power to do so, however, would be a question for the Supreme Court, and as the provision would place Utah on a different footing from other States, it is not difficult to predict how the Court would decide it. The plain fact is that if Congress surrendered its power to govern Utah by making her a State, she would be governed by the majority of her citizens, and they are Mormons, who, as their past record shows, are not to be trusted on the polygamy question, for they systematically set the law at defiance as long as they could. The demand for admission should therefore be strenuously resisted.

The Suspension of Another Bank in Cincinnati, the Metropolitan, caused some excitement last week. It was closed on February 7, and as in the case of the Fidelity Bank, arrests promptly followed. The President, Mr. William Means, and the Vice President, Mr. John R. Decamp, have both been arrested and placed under bonds. The President is charged with having loaned about a quarter of a million to himself without security. He contends, however, that although the amount appears against him on the bank's books, it was not a personal debt, but was used in protecting the bonds and stock of the institution. The bank examiner states that there is about $400,000 of bank funds of which he can find no trace at all. The money has simply disappeared without any record being made as to where it went. A not very reassuring opinion is that given on the case by Mr. Harper, of the Fidelity Bank, who is now in prison for his share in wrecking that institution. Mr. Harper denounces the lax methods of government examiners. He said: "The trouble is that these examiners do not call on a bank unless they hear rumors affecting its credit—the very time they should stay away and give the bank a chance to recover. Had the examiner done his duty the Fidelity would never have failed, and I would not now be in prison. The examination being careless and slack, I took the risk and lost. If the truth was known nine-tenths of all the bankers in the country would be in prison for the violation of the laws that I was convicted for."

An Important Speech by Prince Bismarck in the German Reichstag, on February 6, is variously interpreted in Europe as a general menace, and an attempt to establish a more pacific confidence than now exists. Probably it was intended as an intimation to all whom it might concern, that Germany was ready for war if war should be forced upon her, while herself desiring peace, and laboring zealously to promote it. The Chancellor, reviewing the past year's events, said that, "there has been very little change since then, when I feared war with France. Since then France has elected a peace-loving President, and, a pacific disposition has prevailed. I can therefore reassure the public that, so far as France is concerned, the prospect has become more peaceful. Regarding Russia, also, I am of no other opinion than when I said that we have to apprehend no attack from Russia. The situation must not be judged from press comments. The Russian newspapers I do not believe. I believe the Czar's word absolutely." Referring to the treaty with Austria, Bismarck declared that it was the expression of the community of interests of the two contracting parties. "This it was we wished the world to know. Not this treaty only, but also that with Italy is the expression of common interests and common efforts to avert common dangers." Finally, after sketching the effective strength of the German Empire, the Chancellor said: "When we undertake a war it must be a people's war which all approve, as in 1870. If we are attacked, then the *furor Teutonicus* will flame out. No one can make headway against that. Neither consciousness of our strength nor hope of victories can restrain us from continuing our peaceful efforts. I hope we shall remain at peace with our neighbors, especially with Russia, which has no pretext for a war."

The Opening of the British Parliament on Feburary 9, was marked by less excitement than usual. The Royal speech announced the settlement of the Afghan Boundary dispute with Russia, which so nearly precipitated war between the two countries a few years ago. Also the settlement of the disputes with France as to the Suez Canal and the New Hebrides. As to Ireland, the utterances are vaguely sanguine. The speech informs the legislators that "the measures which at great labor you passed last session for the benefit of Ireland have been carefully carried into effect during the period since elapsed. The result of the legislation, so far as tested by this short experience, is satisfactory. Agrarian crime has diminished, and the power of coercive conspiracies has sensibly abated. Measures tending to develop the resources of Ireland and to facilitate an increase in the number of proprietors of the soil will be laid before you." The Parliament also received an intimation that money is needed by the great spending departments, those of the army and navy, for fortifications and ships. The House will be asked "to provide for the improvement of the defences of the ports and coasting stations, rendered urgently necessary by the advance of military science, and also to sanction an arrangement providing for a special squadron to protect Australian commerce, the cost of which will be partially borne by the colonies." This with congratulation on an improvement in trade, and regret that there was no corresponding improvement in agriculture, completed the body of the royal communication.

An Operation on the Throat of the German Crown Prince was performed on February 9. The news caused disappointment to his friends the world over, who hoped that the favorable reports recently issued were an evidence that no operation would be needed. On the night of February 8, however the Prince experienced great difficulty of breathing. He spent the night walking briskly about his rooms, evidently suffering severely. Dr. Mackenzie and the other physicians held a consultation the next morning, and decided that it would not be safe to pass another night without an operation. It was accordingly performed, no chloroform being administered. The Prince bore it with fortitude, and experienced relief from its effects. The operation is technically known as *Tracheotomy*. It is a surgical operation by means of which an opening is made through the trachea, or windpipe, in which opening is introduced a small curved silver tube, which allows air to pass freely down into the bronchial tubes and thence to the lungs. This operation in itself, as a rule, does not carry any serious features with it, but is an operation which is used only in such disease as croup, where danger of suffocation arises from the filling up of the larynx and trachea.

The Irish Question from the Historian's standpoint is somewhat discouraging to the Liberals. Mr. James A. Froude, who is probably the greatest living historian, says in a letter recently published: "Any form of self-government which might be conceded to the Irish people, whether it be local councils or a parliament, would be used to increase England's difficulty in keeping Ireland attached to the kingdom. The Irish can be governed more easily than any other people in the world under military or quasi-military rule. The police are uniformly faithful and loyal. *England has never yet succeeded in governing Ireland constitutionally, and never will.*"

The Election of a President of Princeton in ccession to Dr. McCosh, whose resignation e trustees have reluctantly accepted, took ace on February 9. The choice fell upon Pro- ssor Francis L. Patton, D.D., LL. D., who ent to Princeton in 1881 to fill the Stuart Pro- ssorship on "the Relations of Philosophy and cience to the Christian Religion." Dr. Patton lso holds the chair of Christian Ethics in the ollege. His views are in decided agreement ith those of Dr. McCosh on philosophical and heological subjects, and if he accepts the Presi- ency it is believed that no material change will e made in the present methods. Dr. Patton is orty-five years old, having been born at War- ick, Bermuda, in 1843. He graduated from Princeton in 1865. His first charge was of the Eighty-fourth Street Church, New York. Dr. McCosh is to be President Emeritus of the Col- ege, with a salary of $2,500, and a further salary s Professor of Philosophy, if the high-spirited old gentleman will accept it. A bronze statue of him will be erected in front of the Marquand Hall, at a cost of $12,000.

The Death of the Rev. George Bowen is reported from Bombay, India. He has been forty-two years a missionary, and was known as the Nestor of the Indian Conference. He was born in this country in 1816, and was therefore seventy-two years old when he died. When a young man he read the writings of Gibbon, the infidel historian, and, falling under their influence, avowed himself an atheist. For eleven years he was an active oppenent of Christianity but he was converted at the death-bed of a lady to whom he was deeply attached, and after a short period of retirement and meditation resolved to sacrifice all his worldly prospects, which were very brilliant, and devote himself to Christ's service. In 1846 he went to India, where he supported himself by teaching, and preached the gospel *without salary*. He became the Secretary of the Religious Tract Society, managing its Indian depot *without pay* in addition to his other labors. He joined the MethodistConference, and continued to labor on until his death, never revisiting his native country, though often urged to do so.

Valuable Testimony to the Efficacy of the work for aiding discharged convicts was given at the anniversary of the Home of Industry, in New York. Some of the speakers had been old offenders, who had served various terms in penal institutions for serious crimes, and who had been reclaimed at the Home after their discharge from prison. Many of these have found profitable employment at trades or in business houses, while others are earning their living at the work done in the home itself. Since the establishment of the home, nine years ago, 2,311 convicts have been admitted as inmates, and of this number 1,061 have secured outside employment through the assistance of its officers.

A Quadrupedal Detective did Good Service to his owner at Middletown, N. Y., on January 21. A farmer residing in that town had business in a town across the New Jersey line, and drove there in his sleigh, behind a very valuable horse. He tied the horse and sleigh under a hotel shed, while he transacted his business, which he did not get through until long after dark. When he returned for the vehicle to drive home, that and the horse were gone. Evidently some thief had stolen them. As it was snowing heavily and blowing almost a gale, the farmer realized that it was useless attempting to search for his property, and remained for the night at the hotel. It appears that the thief thought he would baffle pursuit best by quitting the State, and so drove into New York State, where he meant to sell the horse and sleigh. The snow-storm caused him to lose his way, so he continued straight on, unaware that he was following the road which led directly to the home of the owner of the stolen property. When the horse arrived at the farm he stopped abruptly, and the thief applied the whip without avail. The struggle between man and beast for the mastery aroused the farmer's son, who came to the door, and recognizing the horse and sleigh, charged the man with the theft. He was so completely benumbed and subdued with cold that he did not deny the charge, but begged for warmth and shelter. The farmer's son saw that he was provided with them in the local prison, where he is awaiting trial. The instinct of the horse proved a better guide than does the reason of some men who have fallen under the power of the enemy. If they went to the Master He would deliver them. (Isa. 1 : 3.)

An Earthquake in Miniature Occurred Near Wilkesbarre early on the morning of February 10. It was caused by the explosion, from some unknown cause, of the powder works of Wapwallopen, in which were stored two thousand kegs of black giant powder. Every one of the fifty or more buildings that stood on the hillside above the station were wrecked. Men and women ran wildly in all directions; children cried, women moaned, men excitedly looked for missing men, sisters for their brothers, wives for their husbands, mothers for their sons. Wild confusion prevailed everywhere. Four men were literally blown to pieces, their heads and limbs being carried away from their trunks. Fourteen others were fatally injured, and about forty were severely cut and shaken. It was an astonishing fact that several men working near the scene of the explosion suffered no injury at all, while fellow-workmen almost at their sides received fatal wounds. Their escape seemed wholly inexplicable to them and to their families, who rejoiced over it. When the great day of severance comes, and one is taken and another left, there will be no difficulty in understanding the reason in each case, but then it will not be the one who is left, but he who is taken, who will be counted the happy one. (Matt. 24 : 40–44.)

An Athlete's Tears were an Unusual Specta- cle which was witnessed in the course of the six days walking match at Madison Square Garden, New York, last week. The miserable contest of endurance which took place excited the liveliest interest in the city. Large crowds watched the struggle in the Garden, cheering the respective favorites as they dragged their weary limbs around the track hour after hour, and still other crowds congregated around the bulletin boards in various parts of the city, eagerly noting the figures as they were posted, indicating the distance each of the men covered. To them, apparently, no event was of so thrilling an importance as whether this or that pedestrian was ahead of his competitors. One candidate who struggled hard for three days, broke down on the morning of the fourth day, and his physician told him it was of no use attempting to continue the race. Thereupon his manhood gave way and he *wept like a child*. This disappointment so keenly felt, showed how earnestly he had tried to win the prize. The ardor of the contestants, and the interest taken in the struggle, is significant when we consider how little there is to be gained in it compared with that race for an incorruptible crown, which the Apostle Paul describes, and about which there is too often so general an apathy. (1 Cor. 9 : 24–26.)

The Removal of a Dead Body from One grave to another has involved a suit at law which was decided on February 2. The Philadelphia *Ledger* states that some years ago a citizen purchased a burial lot of the McKeesport and Versailles Cemetery Company, and in it he buried several children and his wife. He married again, and a few years later he died. He requested that he be buried with his children and first wife in the family lot, and his request was complied with. The second wife and widow wanted to be buried there too when her time should come, but the surviving children of her husband would give her no promise of compliance, and she felt sure that, as the lot was already nearly full, her admission would probably be refused, as the children regarded her as an interloper in the family. She accordingly purchased a lot in another part of the cemetery and had her husband's body disinterred and removed there. The children of the man thereupon brought suit for the restoration of the body of their father. The suit has been granted in their favor, the Judge holding that the wife had no right to remove the body, and must restore it. The result is doubtless a severe disappointment for the widow, but she has the consolation of knowing that neither her stepsons nor the courts can prevent her after death rejoining her husband in the spirit, if he has gone to heaven, and she has a title through Christ to an inheritance there. (II Sam. 12 : 23.)

The Remarkable Deafness of an Engineer is the subject of interest in medical circles in Ohio. The *Journal*, of Columbus, O., states that an engineer on the Little Miami Railroad was suspended some time ago, because, having been examined by Dr. Clark, he was found to be so deaf that in a still room he could not hear ordinary conversation a foot away. The engineer lives at Cincinnati, and received treatment in that city for his disease, but without any special benefit. After being suspended eight months, the engineer again came to Dr. Clark and begged him to help him to reinstatement, insisting that he could hear perfectly while on an engine. The doctor thought he would test the case, and, accompanying the man to Cincinnati, made a number of experiments with him on engines. The result was, that the doctor found the engineer was not only telling the truth in regard to the matter, but also that the deaf man could hear low remarks and whispers on an engine, amid the roar of escaping steam, that even Dr. Clark's keen ear failed to catch. The doctor has, therefore, certified to his fitness for duty. It would be interesting to hear the aurists' explanation of so curious a fact as that of a man hearing tones when uttered in the roar and rattle of an engine cab, which would be inaudible to him in stillness. The Christian's experience, however, occasionally presents a similar phenomenon. The voice of God has been heard in the duties of life when it could not be recognized in the church or the closet. (Matt. 4 : 18.)

BRIEF NOTES.

Mr. E. J. Parker, one of Mr. C. H. Spurgeon's evangelists, with Miss Parker, is holding meetings at Sharon, Pa. Their meetings at Keyport, N. J., were blessed to the conversion of about forty persons and the revival of many dull Christians.

The International Council of Women is called to assemble in Washington, D. C., on March 25. It is under the auspices of the National Woman's Suffrage Association. Delegates from England, France, Germany and Denmark are coming. The sessions will continue a week.

Extensive preparations are being made for the annual convention of the "Christian Endeavor Societies," appointed to be held in Chicago next July. It is thought that no church in that city will hold the crowd that will attend, and that some large public hall will be required.

Rev. George C. Needham has commenced services at Springfield, Mass. During his recent visit to Philadelphia he conducted a daily noon meeting for business men and others, at the American Sunday-school Union Rooms, at which he gave a half hour's Bible reading. Much good resulted from this effort.

Dr. and Mrs. Munhall were not allowed to leave Baltimore without a permanent and substantial mark of the esteem of the churches. The six pastors of the Independent Methodist churches, who have taken prominent part in the work, presented them with a handsome silver tea set as an expression of appreciation.

The Rev. C. H. Yatman, of Newark, N. J., has been holding a one week's series of meetings in Mr. Moody's church in Chicago. Crowded audiences attended each service, and Mr. Yatman was successful in winning many souls to take their first step for God. The pastor (the Rev. Charles Goss) and people are urging him to return for another series of services.

Dr. N. W. Miner has received promises of money to the amount of $15,000 toward the erection of a new home for aged and infirm Baptist ministers. Promises to the amount of $20,000 have been given conditionally on a certain sum being raised. The home at West Farms, L. I., has now twenty-seven inmates. The building is utterly inadequate.

PEACE WITHOUT OFFENCE.

A New Sermon by Pastor C. H. Spurgeon.

"Great peace have they which love thy Law: and nothing shall offend them." Psalm 119: 165.

The Law of the Kingdom—I. A Spiritual Character—Founded on Love—Love of the Word—Life in it—Reverence for it—Scripture not like a Pack of Cards—The Scripture as a Revelation of God—II. A Special Possession—Great Peace—Not always with Men—Peace of Mind—Fresh Theology every Week—Peace of Conscience—III. A Singular Preservation—Stumbling-Blocks Removed—A Night in a Sheltered Bay.

BY the word "law" here is intended, not only the law of the ten commandments, but the whole of divine revelation, as it was in David's time, and as it is now. In David's day, the law was a smaller book than ours. We have that book at greater length, but it is one and the same. The New Testament is but an expansion of the same truth which the Old Testament contains.

Three things in the text are worthy of earnest attention. First, here is *a spiritual character*—"they which love thy law"; secondly, here is *a special possession*—"great peace have they;" and thirdly, here is *a singular preservation*—"nothing shall offend them"; or nothing shall be a stumbling-block to them. I. First, here is

A Spiritual Character

—"they which love thy law." Love lies deep, it is in the heart: it is not a thing of the surface, it is of the man's own self. As a man loveth, so is he. To love God's law is to have the very nature and essence of our manhood in a right condition. You cannot learn the law of God as you learn the laws of nature. Only he who does the will of God can know of the doctrine. Nothing in religion is sound till the heart goes with it. God says, "My son, give me thine heart," and He cannot be satisfied with anything short of it. Search, then, my hearers, and see if you really love the law of the Lord.

Form and Style.

He who loves the Word would not wish to have it altered, enlarged, or diminished: for he is content with what God chooses to teach him. If he finds any want of conformity in his own thought to God's thought, he throws his own thought away, and sets up the divine thought in its place. He loves every truth which the Lord declares; aye, and the very style and method of the declaration. As certain insects take their color from the leaves they feed upon, so have we become tinctured to the core of our nature with the living and incorruptible Word, which has proved its own inspiration by inspiring us with its spirit. Now

We Live in the Word

as the fish in the stream; it is the element of our spiritual life. This is the sort of people who obtain great peace from the law of the Lord, because, in the truest sense, they love it. The love of God's law includes a deep reverence for it. That man is blessed who trembles at God's Word. This Book is not to be compared with other books: It is inspired in a sense in which they are not; it stands alone, and is not one among other books. As towers an Alp above the mole-hills of the meadow, so Holy Scripture rises above the purest, truest, and holiest literature of man's composing. Other writings we feel free to criticise, but "My heart standeth in awe of thy Word."

This advances to *rejoicing in it.* We know that we love God's Word when

We Can Rejoice

in it. Fain would we gather up every crumb of Scripture, and find food in its smallest fragments. Even its bitter rebukes are sweet to us. *I would kiss the very feet of Scripture, and wash them with my tears!* If it be but God's Word, though some may call it non-essential, we dare not think it so. The little things of God are more precious than the great things of man. Truth is no trifle to one who has fought his way to it, and learned it in the school of affliction.

Further than this, we receive Holy Scripture with emotion. David says, "I hate and abhor lying: but thy law do I love." Those are

Hard Words,

David! Surely you are sinning against the charity of our cultured age! Yes, but when a man feels strongly, he cannot help speaking strongly. "I hate," says he, and that is not enough; he says, "I hate and abhor lying." His whole being revolts at it. He means not only that lying with which in common life men would deceive their fellows, and that is hateful enough; but he refers especially to that kind of teaching which gives the lie to the law of the Lord; for he adds, "But thy law do I love." He who worships the true God detests and loathes idols. In these days there are many men to whom the truths of Scripture are *like a pack of cards to be shuffled* as occasion suits. It does not matter to them what this man preaches and what that man writes. Hold your tongue; it will be all the same a hundred years hence; and, really, nobody can be quite sure of anything! To the man that is loyal to his Lord, and faithful to his convictions, it can never be so; he hates the teaching which belies his God. He that has never felt his blood boil against an error which robs God of his glory, does not love the law, nor will he know that great peace which comes by having the law enshrined in the heart.

One other virtue is included in the love of the Word. According to the context, great gratitude to God for His Word is formed in the believing heart. "Seven times a day do I praise thee, because of thy righteous judgments." God's judgments written in His Word are matters of praise. God's judgments actively going on in the world, which tally with those predicted in His Word, are also matters for adoring praise. The God of the word is the God of the deed. What He says He does, and every day and all the day we praise Him for it.

Beloved, God may do what He wills, and say what He wills, and we will praise Him. We read in His Word stern things, words of wrath and deeds of vengeance. Shall we try to soften them, or invent apologies for them? By no means. Jehovah our God is a consuming fire. We love Him, not as He is improved upon by

"Modern Thought,"

but as He reveals Himself in Scripture. It is not mine to improve upon the character of Jehovah, but to reverence and adore Him as He manifests Himself, either in judgment or in grace. I, who am less than nothing and vanity, dare not scan His work, nor bring Him to my bar, lest I hear a voice saying, "Nay, but, O man, who art thou that repliest against God?" Whatever God may be, or speak, or do—that is right: it is not mine to arraign my Maker, but to adore Him. Extenuations, explanations, and apologies may be produced from the best of motives; but too often they suggest to opposers that it is admitted that God's most holy Word contains something in it which is doubtful, or weak, or antiquated. Brethren, the Word of the Lord can stand alone, without the propping which many are giving it. Those props come down, and then our adversaries think that the Book is down too. The Word of God can take care of itself, and will do so if we preach it, and cease defending it. Let the pure gospel go forth in all its lion-like majesty, and it will soon clear its own way and ease itself of its adversaries.

The love of the law of God breeds *penitence* for having sinned against it, and *perseverance* in obedience to it. It also begets *patience* under suffering; and begets and fosters *holiness*. You cannot study the Scriptures diligently and love them heartily without having your thoughts and acts savored and sweetened by them. Let me commend to you, my beloved friends, that you live with the law of the Lord, till even men of the world perceive that you keep choice company. The

Trashy Lives

of most people are the fit outcome of the trash which they read. A life fed on fiction is a life of fiction: a life fed on divine fact will become a life of divine fact. I have not time in which to show you all the sweet uses of the law of the Lord.

This much, however, I must add: if in any of us there is a love of the law of the Lord, *this is a work of the Holy Spirit.* Nature does not love God, and hence it does not love God's law. If, then, thou lovest God and His holy law, the Holy Ghost has been at work in thee; and by this new love it is proven that thou art a new creature. Let thy love of the law be to thee a proof of thy regeneration; of thine election and the prophecy of thine

Ultimate Perfection.

If there be in thee a strong, passionate desire to accept and obey God's Word in everything, and to be conformed to it in thought and life, that desire will ultimately get the victory. Use well the sword of the Spirit, which is the Word of God, and by the force of thy love give sin sharp and heavy thrusts, and thou shalt conquer until every thought is brought into captivity to the law of Christ.

II. We have spent too long a time upon our first point, and shall have to be brief upon the other heads. Our second division is a very sweet part of the text; here is

A Special Possession,

"great peace have they which love thy law."

By peace here is not meant that a man who loves God's law will have great peace with everybody, for that is not at all true. If David penned this sentence, he certainly was not an instance of great peace with men flowing out of his love to the Lord's law. He was a man of war from his youth. He had peace as a shepherd boy, but even then he had to kill lions and bears; and soon after he had to meet a giant in single combat. Neither in his family nor in Saul's court was he at peace. He was hunted like a partridge upon the mountains, and had to run for it from day to day. He had not much earthly peace: for when he had done with Saul, the Philistines invaded the land. If it be possible, we are to live peaceably with all men; but He who has put enmity between the serpent and the woman never meant that we should enjoy the friendship of the world. The great peace which they have who love God's law refers to a peace which can exist when strife rages all around us.

Does not it meant this—first, great restfulness of the intellect? If we love God's law in the sense in which we have explained it, so as to stand in awe of it and rejoice over it, the result will be great

Peace of Mind.

Everybody must find infallibility somewhere. Some think it is with the Pope at Rome, others dream that it is in themselves: the second theory is no more true than the first. Others of us believe that infallibility lies in the Word of God: this book is to us the final court of appeal.

I care nothing what supposed philosophers may discover: they cannot discover anything true which is contrary to God's Word.

He who gave us the infallible Book has all the responsibility for its contents. If I believe what God tells me and do what He bids me, the results are with Him and not with me. He is the ruler of the universe and not I; and if there be any terrible mysteries, He must explain them and not I, if they ought to be explained. I am like a servant who is sent to the door with a message; if I deliver the message which my master gives me as I receive it, you must not be angry with me, for I did not invent the message, I only repeated it to you. Be angry with my master, not with me. That is how I feel when I have done preaching. If I have honestly preached what I believe to be in God's Word, I am free from all responsibility for my ministry. I have not before me the unbearable burden of composing a gospel. I remember well a minister, whom I much respect, saying to me: "I wish I could feel as you do. You have certain fixed principles about which you are sure, and you have only to state them and enforce them; but

I am in a formative state; I make my theology fresh every week." Dear me, I thought, what

A Hopeless State for Progress

and establishment! If the student of mathematics had no fixed law as to the value of numbers, but made a new multiplication table every week, he would not make many calculations. If a baker were to say to me, "Sir, I am always altering the ingredients of my bread: I make a different bread every week," I should be afraid the fellow would poison me one of these days. I cannot afford to experiment in the Bread of Life. Besides, there is an intellectual unrest in all this kind of thing, which is escaped from when we come to love the Word of the Lord as we love our lives.

Those who love God's Word have also a great peace which comes of a pacified conscience. Nothing will quiet conscience effectually and properly but the great doctrine of the substitutionary sacrifice of Christ. We see in the sacrifice of our Lord Jesus Christ that which must satisfy divine justice, and therefore our conscience receives a safe and holy quietus, and we have peace with God through our Lord Jesus Christ, by whom also we have received the atonement.

And the same conscience also brings great peace when it bears testimony to renewal of heart and life. If you have loved God's law and kept to the way of strict integrity, you will have within your own bosom an angel of peace to strengthen you in the hour of sorrow. "The testimony of a good conscience" is like the song of the angels to the shepherds at Bethlehem.

Peace to Our Desires.

You will not be grasping after wealth when the Word is better to you than the most fine gold. You will not be ambitious to shine among men when to you the Word of the Lord is a kingdom large enough. When our desires find their pasturage around the Great Shepherd's feet, our ambitions cease to roam, and we abide at home in peace.

When we love God's law also, we reach forward to the peace of *resignation* to God, acquiescence in His will, and conformity to it. It is of no use to quarrel with God. When we perfectly yield to God, our heart's sorrow is at an end. The sting of affliction lies in the tail of our rebellion against the Divine will. To love the law and the Lawgiver goes a great way towards loving all that He appoints and decrees; and this is a garden of peace to all who know it.

Besides, the love of the Word breeds a happy confidence in God as to all things in the past, the present and the future. When we love God's Word, we see God at the beginning of everything, God at the end of everything, and God in the middle of everything; and as we see Him present whom we love, we cease from anxious thought.

III. I am cramped for want of time; therefore I must, in a very few words, sum up what deserves to be spoken at length upon the third point. Here is

A Singular Preservation:

"Nothing shall offend them." There shall be no stumbling-block in their way. Intellectual stumbling-blocks are gone. One asks me, "Do you mean to say that you read the Bible and do not find difficulties in it?" I regard the Word of God as being infallibly inspired, and therefore if I find difficulties in it, which I must do from the very nature of things, I accept what God says about those difficulties, and pass on. The Word of God does not profess to explain all mysteries: it leaves them mysteries, and my faith accepts them as such. When out in a yacht in the Clyde, we came opposite the great rock called the Cock of Arran. Our captain did not steam right ahead, and rush at the rock; no, he did what was much wiser: he cast anchor for the night in the bay at the foot of it, so that we were sheltered from the wind by the vast headland. I remember looking up through the darkness of the night, and admiring its great sheltering wing. A difficulty was it. It became a shelter. Every now and then in Scripture you come before a vast truth. Will you steam against it, and wreck your soul? Will you not, with truer wisdom, cast anchor under the lee of it? Do we need to understand everything? Are we to be all brain, and no heart? What should we be the better if we did understand all mysteries? I believe God. I bow before His Word. Of course we are blessed, in this enlightened age, with some

Wonderfully Great Men,

who understand more than the ancients, and either know the unknowable, or think they do. In a sentence I will give you the result of my observation upon men and things: "*No man knows everything except a fool, and he knows nothing.*" If thou lovest the Word of God, thou wilt see no difficulties which will in the least cause thee to stumble. Things hard to be understood become stepping-stones on which to rise, not stumbling-blocks over which to fall.

"Nothing shall offend them." Does not this also mean that no moral duty shall be a cross to them which shall cause them to turn aside? They will not turn away from Jesus because a sin has to be abandoned, a lust denied, or a pleasure given up. Does Jesus say, "Do this?" They do it without demur. Does Jesus say, "Cease from that?" They withdraw their hands at the instant. Self-denial ceases to be self-denial when love commands it.

Moreover, the man who loves God's law, is not offended if he has to stand alone. He that truly loves God's law resolves that if all men forsake him he will cleave to the Lord and His truth. As for me, I am resolved not to follow a multitude to do evil. I will keep the old faith, and

The Old Way,

if I never find a comrade between here and the celestial gates. I do not think a man loves God's Word thoroughly till it breeds in him a self-contained peace, so that he is satisfied from himself, and drinks water out of the cistern of his own experience. What have we to do with other men as supporters of our faith? To their own master they stand or fall. As for our Master in heaven, let us follow Him through life, and unto death; for to whom else could we go? He only hath the words of eternal life.

Neither will such persons ever be so offended as to despair of God's great cause. The night grows darker and darker, but the man who loves the Divine law expects the sun to rise at his appointed hour. If he delay, we will not therefore doubt. Grace has produced, in past ages, men who were confident as to the triumph of truth when others feared for it. Look at the

Courage of Luther,

who, when everybody else despaired of the gospel, trusted his God and cheered his people, and would not hear of drawing back. He could not pronounce the word "despair." "Luther, canst thou shake Rome? The harlot sits enthroned upon her seven hills; canst thou hope to dislodge her, or loose the captive nations from her bonds?" "No," said Luther, "but God can." Luther brought his God into the quarrel, and you know which way the conflict turned. Not to-day, nor to-morrow, nor in twenty years, may God's truth win; but the Lord can afford to wait. His lifetime is eternity. O struggler for the truth, make thou sure that thou art with God and with the truth, and then be sure that God is with thee in truth, and will deliver thee. "Nothing shall offend them."

It is wonderful, if you love God's Word, how things which are stumbling-blocks to others cease to be injurious to you. Suppose you enjoy prosperity: if you love God's law, you will not be puffed up by deceitful riches or honors.

The same will be true of adversity. If you love God's law, you are the man to be poor, to be sickly, to be slandered; for you can bear it all, because you have meat to eat that the world knows not of. Your love to God's law will furnish you with a ceaseless stream of consolation. Nothing will damp the flame of your spirit, because the Lord feeds it secretly with a golden oil.

As for you who love not God's law, who know nothing of Jesus, because you have never submitted to the law of faith—there is no "great peace" for you. There may be the deceptive cry of, "Peace, peace, when there is no peace," but there is no hope for you till you are at one with God. As surely as God made thee, thou must yield to thy Maker, and accept thy Redeemer, and be renewed by His Holy Spirit, or thou art lost for ever. I pray the Holy Ghost lead thee to accept what God has revealed, and bow thyself to the Supreme Majesty of His Word, especially to the power and grace of the Incarnate Word, the Lord Christ Jesus; then wilt thou have great peace for this world and the next. God bless you, beloved, for Christ's sake. Amen.

GEMS FROM NEW BOOKS.

Christian Heroism in a Surgical Operation.*

IT was Sunday night, when, preparing for rest, I suddenly felt a large hard substance extending under my right arm. The conviction flashed upon me, "This is a cancer." I trembled a little, but knelt down and simply prayed my God that, if it was so, I might glorify Him, and patiently bear all that might be coming. It was a solemn night, with thoughts of eternity nearing, and oh, the peace of resting one's whole self on the word of Jesus, on His precious blood! In the morning kind Mrs. G. tearfully confirmed my idea, but I decided at once that I would not distress my dear sisters or friends, and only wrote to my doctor. His answer was reassuring; I might be mistaken, and of course he reserved opinion till he saw me. I was positively light-hearted, for had I not committed the whole burden to the Lord?

I had arranged for my nurse, M. Farrington, to meet me at Dr. Malins'. He told me I was looking in much better health. "And now, doctor, you must tell me candidly what is the matter." He looked grave, sat down silently, then most feelingly said. "It is stone cancer, and not a shadow of escape from this conclusion."

"So I thought; what do you advise?"

"Only two courses—operation, or, if it runs on, certain death." "Now, doctor, why can't you do it at once, this afternoon, and so save my friends?"

"Impossible; you don't know what an operation involves, and you would like to have a sister with you."

"Oh, dear, no; Mrs. Crane is abroad, and as to making my gentle sister Ellen suffer for me, oh never, never; Mary is quite enough, and you know He whom I trust in will be with me."

Sweet promises floated around me, and not a flutter of fear; verily it was the enfolding of His wing. Presently Dr. M. came in, and asked if he could do anything for me. I said, "Yes; will you kneel down with me?" I just committed myself into God's hand, asked for quietness, and that I might glorify Him; for skill to my doctors; and then, "Thy will be done" came gladly from my heart. My doctor's reverent "O Lord, grant this, for Jesus Christ's sake, Amen," was a sustaining clench to me. He left me.

Love, all love and faithfulness, and His strong arm closed around me as the doctor opened the door and said, "All is ready." Resolutely I inhaled the ether, the inevitable suffocating feeling was conquered, and then all was silence and darkness for three-quarters of an hour. Then the waking up—"Mary, when will it be over?" "It's all done; see, you are nicely in bed, and doctors gone." Then came the consciousness of utter weakness and helplessness. But truly, not one thing had failed me—not one word of all His good promises had been unfulfilled to me; and now underneath were the everlasting arms, in a manner only those know who have felt them.

I did not know till some weeks after how

---

*From the Autobiography of Maria Vernon G. Havergal. 336 pages; price $1 50; published by *Anson D. F. Randolph & Co*, 38 West Twenty-third Street, New York.

The Ceremony of Blessing the River Neva, at St. Petersburg, Russia.

graciously God had answered my prayer, that I might glorify Him before the doctors.

The next few days passed in excessive weakness, and the sultry weather was against me. But I believe my teetotalism of sixteen years greatly contributed to my recovery. A friend of mine who was operated on, and kept up afterwards with brandy and milk and opiates, could hardly walk on two sticks at the end of ten months, whereas in three months' I was walking to the top of Malvern Hill.

Secret Sin in a Cottage.

A strange impulse I had was the almost positive conviction that seemed given to me of people living in hidden sin. Once I was riding a pony in unfrequented lanes, and took a narrow turning, which led me to two cottages. Women and children were in both. Fastening the pony to the gate, I knocked at the first door, and was civilly asked to sit down while getting some tracts out of my bag. Then, asking God's guidance, I opened my testament to the fourth chapter of John. When I read the verse, "He whom thou now hast is not thy husband." I looked at the woman and exclaimed, "You must forgive me if I am wrong; I am a perfect stranger; I never heard of you or these cottages, but I think you are not married, and just living here to hide your sin. You cannot hide it from God, and He has sent me to tell you so. Let me be your friend, won't you?" The woman started, covered her face, saying, "You are right." I do not remember more sufficiently to write it down, but paid many more visits.

A Student's Mysterious Sickness.*

THE body is the mechanism of the manifestation and work of the spirit. It follows that any disturbance of the mechanism will interfere with that manifestation of spirit-activity. But that it does not follow that such interference actually impairs the spirit itself, is clearly shown by the numerous cases in which severe illness or accident enfeebles the body so as to injure its use by the spirit, but the activity of the spirit continues in full vigor. Not long since, in one of our Western colleges, a young man was prostrated by a severe attack of spinal meningitis. So serious was the attack that when, after several weeks' battle for life, he rose from his bed, the nervous system was so shattered as to be almost beyond the control of the spirit. It is probable that a very large part of the gray matter of his brain was actually destroyed by the fever, and for some months his memory was almost a total blank. Yet, during the entire period of illness and convalescence, all the spirit-powers were as intensely active as at any time of ordinary health; though frequently the physical mechanism wholly refused to obey the spirit, and an observer would have thought the spirit vitally injured. Professor Browen relates the remarkable case of James Kinnard, of Portland, Me., many years ago, who was attacked, while a young man, by anchylosis. Through several years his body gradually and completely ossified. Yet, up to the day of his death, his spirit-powers manifested perfect integrity and great vigor; and there are still extant literary essays of decided merit, composed by him in the intervals of comparative rest, during the tortures of a living death.

There is, then, no ground for affirming that the apparent decline of the spirit-action in old age is necessarily consequent upon the growing feebleness of the body. All that can logically be inferred, is that the condition of the physical mechanism prevents the manifestation of the spirit-activity; and the presumption is greatly in favor of the continuance of the full vigor of the spirit, even when the mechanism is falling into decay.

*From "The Gist of It," by Rev. Thomas E. Barr, B. A., 350 pages. Price $1.50; published by *A. C. Armstrong & Son*, 714 Broadway, New York.

BLESSING THE RIVER NEVA.

(*See Illustration.*)

EVERY year there is a singular and time-honored ceremony performed at St. Petersburg, the capital of Russia, called "The Blessing of the River Neva." It is generally timed to occur about January 18. It is attended by the Czar, and soldiers and courtiers and ladies, who crowd the saloons of the Winter Palace before proceeding to the Imperial Chapel, an ecclesiastical building sumptuously decorated in white and gold.

Everyone stands during the ceremony except the Emperor and Empress, for whom two State chairs are provided. The service consists of chanting, singing and prayers and other ceremonies, in which the Metropolites, or chief priests of the Russo-Greek Church, take the principal part. They are usually venerable bearded men, clad in robes richly bedecked with gold and silver, and surrounded by their crosier bearers and attendant clergy. At length the procession pours down the marble staircase of the Chapel, and ranges itself in a line from the Palace porch to a kiosk-like

Tabernacle Built Over the Ice.

There is a double line of clergy in square caps, from beneath which flows their long hair; choristers in purple and gold, and court pages in white trousers and gold-laced coats.

The supreme dignitary of the day is the Metropolite of Novgorod (St. Petersburg); before and after him are borne preciously bound books, gold crosses studded with jewels, the cup for the river water, on which are engraved sacred subjects, such as Moses striking the rock, and various pontifical insignia. The ceremony lasts only a few minutes. From an opening in the platform of the tabernacle a flight of wooden steps leads to the ice, and then, after the booming of guns across the ice-field, and much singing and chanting, the winter shield of the Neva is pierced, and the sacred cup dipped in the flowing water. *The crucifix is laid in the stream*, and the river is straightway pronounced blessed. The Czar and the Grand Dukes present kiss the hand of the Metropolite, a picture of our Saviour is carried along the quay, and the banners of the Russian armies are also blessed with the consecrated water. The cup of Neva water is next handed to the Czar, who touches it with his lips, and, according to immemorial custom, fills it to the brim with gold coins. As the Metropolite passes, officers run forward, kiss the sacred picture, and bow their heads to receive a sprinkling of the holy water, as it is now called.

At the conclusion of the ceremony, the parapet is crowned with a line of heads looking eagerly towards the hole where the Metropolite dipped the cross in the Neva. Men and boys climb over on to the ice, and run towards the spot. All hold bottles or vessels of some sort, to receive the blessed water. Those who cannot climb eagerly beseech the others to fill their bottles for them. Hands clutching bottles are stretched over the parapet to meet others straining upwards from the ice. Most are not content with obtaining a bottleful of the "holy water," but dip their hands in it, wash their faces, sprinkle their heads, and cross themselves with it, and even very young infants are saturated with the water by their anxious mothers, that they may not lose any supposed advantage.

The Established Religion of Russia

is that of the Greek church. This may be considered by many preferable to Roman Catholicism; but it leaves the masses of the population fearfully sunk in ignorance and superstition, as the ceremony of the blessing of the Neva shows. Hence the Bible Societies have for several years past been actively engaged in circulating the Scriptures among the people, and other evangelizing agencies have also been successfully employed in the dissemination of evangelical and saving truth. To these efforts the Russian Government makes no objection, but much more needs to be done by the enlightened followers of Christ in the way of missionary labor to meet the necessities of the vast Russian Empire.

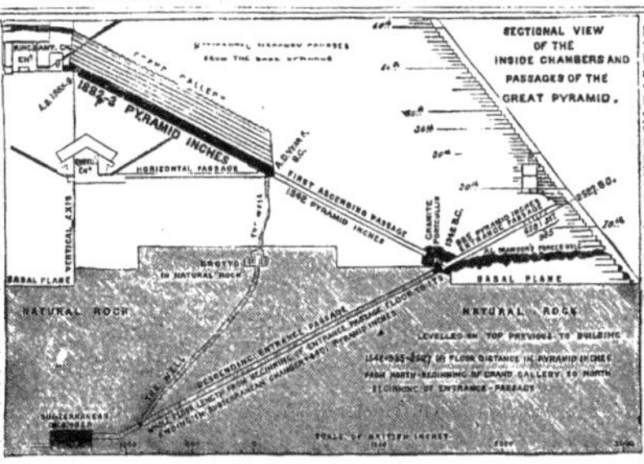

Sectional Diagram of the Great Pyramid. (*See page 103.*)

FOUR INTERLOPERS IN HEAVEN.

From Dr. Talmage's Talk Last Friday Evening, February 10, 1887.

A MESSAGE by the "Union Terrestrial and Celestial Telegraph" has just come. It announces the startling news that there is great excitement in the Celestial City. It seems that in the "House of Many Mansions" there was a great banquet and all the princes of heaven were present. In some burglarious way, as yet not found out, there were

Four Bigots got Through

the Shining Gate: a Presbyterian bigot, a Methodist bigot, an Episcopal bigot, a Baptist bigot. They found their way to the Banquet Hall, and pushed in upon the guests. The music ceased, the grapes of Eshcol dropped on the golden platter, and hands uplifted in shock of amazement. *The Presbyterian bigot* appeared with an armful of Westminister Catechisms and proceeded to distribute them among the banqueters. "What is that?" cried one of the princes of heaven, who turned out to be Robert Hall the immersionist. "Don't you know what that is?" cried out the Presbyterian bigot. "Then I move Robert Hall be expelled!" "No, no," cried a hundred voices; "that great soul has been here fifty-seven years, and brought up a great many with him from Bristol and Leicester." But the Presbyterian bigot said: "All this matters not, if he does not adopt the Westminster Assembly Catechism. I know from that he must have been elected to be damned. Out with him from the gates of heaven!"

At this moment *the Methodist bigot* broke in upon the excitement and demanded how many of those at the table had ever sat upon an "anxious seat," declaring that those who had not been converted in that way had no business in heaven. He brought an "anxious seat" with him, and sat on it himself very near the table, and rudely began to eat a cluster of grapes, throwing the skins into the face of a Scotch Presbyterian, who turned out to be John Knox. The bigot had

Hit the Wrong Man,

for John Knox, neither on earth nor in heaven, was of a temperament to take any impudence, and he gave the bigot very much such a look as he once did Queen Mary of Holyrood. The Methodist bigot moved that all those banqueters who had not come into the church militant by the "anxious seat," be denied the feast.

At this point *the Episcopal bigot* marched in with a great load of liturgies under each arm, and slammed them down on the table of the banquet, till all the goblets rattled. He said: "I propose to hold a service, just here and now. Each one of the banqueters will take one of these prayer-books and keep wide awake, and respond at the right place: 'Good Lord, deliver us.'" "No, no," said two of the best saints, who were found to be *Albert Barnes and Alfred Cookman*, "we never could on earth find the right place in the prayer-book, and we should even here make awkward work with the responses." At this the Episcopal bigot seized the white robes of Albert Barnes and Alfred Cookman, and pulled them violently toward the door; but there were so many who had been brought to heaven through the commentaries of the one, and so many through the preaching of the other, that there was a great rush of protectors around these great ones of heaven, and the bigot did not succeed in the expulsion.

At this point *a Baptist bigot* stepped into the excitement, carrying on his shoulders a burden that almost bent him double, so heavy was it. As he set down his load he took the lid off, and behold, it was a Baptistry. He said: "It does not seem as if some of you have been properly washed, and I shall proceed to put under the water all those who have neglected their ablutions. I shall take the first one I come to." This turned out to be Archbishop Leighton, who cried out: "Excuse me! My parents had me sprinkled when I was a baby, and I think that will do." "Sprinkled!" cried the Baptist bigot, "sprinkled! How dare you come here? *A spoonful of water on a man of your size* is nothing at all." The bigot, seizing the Archbishop, attempted to put him under the water, and in the resistance and struggle the Baptist got sprinkled and the Archbishop got immersed, and both would have drowned but for kindly interference on the part of bystanders. When the struggle was over, it was found that some of the white robes were as wet as though they had been diving in the River of Life for pearls.

Suddenly, from behind the curtains, a clarion blew, at which the banqueters laid hold of the four bigots and rushed them to the door, and rushed them through the street, and rushed them up to the battlements, crying "These Presbyterian, Methodist, Episcopalian and Baptist bigots have no business in heaven.

Throw Them Over the Wall!"

And down the battlements they were flung, now heads up, now heels up, over and over, down, down, till they came within sight of the earth. As they fell through among the stars, one came near being shoveled up by "The Dipper," and another just escaped being snatched by the paw of "The Bear," and another from being stung by "The Scorpion." The Presbyterian bigot had his bundles of Westminster Catechisms so tightly fastened to shoulders and arms that he was the more easily precipitated, and he struck headforemost in the graveyard back of Princeton. The Methodist bigot could not shake himself loose from his "anxious seat," and it beat him, bruised him and jerked him on the way down till he landed headfirst in the graveyard back of Middletown. The Episcopal bigot cried, as he was precipitated, to be delivered from the great weight of liturgical book-binding, and for the first time prayed without his notes as he went tumbling down swifter and swifter, till he fell transfixed on the spire of St. Alban's Cathedral. The Baptist bigot splashed into the middle of the Atlantic Ocean. When the expulsion was complete the banqueters again took their places in the "House of Many Mansions," and with lifted chalices, filled with water from under the throne, cried out: "Drink, one and all, to the communion of saints and the life everlasting."

My hearers, to-night let us rejoice that while once in a while there crops out something showing that the bigots are not all dead, the union revival meetings, now going on in many of the towns and cities, are proof that the boundary line between evangelical denominations is becoming of less and less importance.

THE FAMILY OF TRIPE COURT.

By Brenda.

(Continued from page 94.)

THE NEW LIFE.

IN all that Infirmary, with its long rows of beds, there was not one to which the long anticipated visiting day brought quite so much happiness as to that in which lay poor Bridget Mite, the laundress of Tripe Court. No wonder that when she heard the good news and saw in the children's faces and clothes the results of the reformation in Tom's habits, she could but weep. But they were almost the only tears Bridget had ever wept for joy. She had wept for woe with very good cause more frequently than most women of her age, but the end of all that was come, and the signs of sorrow were those that best relieved the joy of her full heart.

That night, when the visitors were all gone, Mrs. Cherry had to hear more about Tom than the loyal, suffering wife would tell before. The change in Tom was so marvellous to his wife, that Mrs. Cherry suspected that he was a pretty hard case. Bridget ventured now to tell her some of the things he had done under the influence of drink. Bridget could almost laugh at them now. But the talk was necessarily short, for excitement was bad for her neighbor, as Mrs. Cherry knew. So she tried to turn the few minutes left to profitable purpose.

"You'll go to church now, I presume?" she said. "Now you'll be less worried, and have better things to wear, church will be the proper thing."

"Yes, I'll never get into that way of life again that I was in when I came here," said Bridget. "It's worth all the pain to have broke it up. That's your doing, with the hymn you said to me, 'There is an eye.' You've been an angel to me, Mrs. Cherry; I'll never forget you."

"You know more what religion's worth to us poor folks now, don't you? Rich people can get along without it pretty easy, but when you are poor and troubled, and there seems no good left and no good ever likely to come, a hope of heaven is a thing one knows the value of. You'll never let it go again?"

"Never," whispered Bridget, firmly. "I'll have extra reason for church now, too, 'cause I've had such wonderful mercy; I never expected anything like this—Tom a new man and the children all so bright. When I get back among 'em there'll be no place so fit to go to as to church, I'm thinking."

It was easier work for Bridget now. The racking pain in her limb, the nights of restlessness and fever, had always been supplemented and aggravated by the mental agony which was wrung from her by every thought of that home in Tripe Court. Until the visiting day described in the last chapter, poor Bridget could only guess what was taking place there. What was likeliest to take place? Ah! Bridget knew that only too well. She pictured the scenes easily enough, but she never pictured the home in Tripe Court as it actually was. Had anyone hinted it to her, she would have said it was too good to be true. But now that she had actually seen Tom sober and the children clean and cheerful, all that heavy load of mental suffering passed away. Six long weeks she had borne the burden, and had escaped from it only when the more important physical torture claimed all her capacity of endurance. She need never have borne it at all, and that is the case with so many of the burdens we all carry.

The Infirmary doctors and nurses were surprised at the improvement that took place in their patient. It was so sudden and so thorough, no medicine, no liniment, in the pharmacopœia could have worked a change like that. It was almost miraculous. They thought so because they did not know how Bridget had worried about home. It was the harass and sorrow that had kept up the fever. Now those were relieved, only the physical ailment had to be dealt with, and that became benign at once. It was just the very opposite of a faith cure, yet many faith cures are like Bridget's. The faith that Mrs. Cherry tried to plant in the poor dark soul really failed to affect the body, however it might enlighten the soul. It was a "*Sight cure*" in Bridget's case; the life-giving mental ecstacy which effects the cure having been produced by sight and not by faith.

The doctors gave Bridget her discharge from the Infirmary, and she went back to Tripe Court. Bridget Mite did indeed find it to be a changed home; not much changed, outwardly—no new furniture had replaced the old; there were the same rickety chairs and tables, the blackened ceiling and mantel, the rat and the mice holes, the dilapidated safe; in outward aspect the home in Tripe Court remained as Bridget had left it. But "a changed home" she nevertheless felt it to be—changed, inasmuch as she felt God's peace and blessing now rested on it, since at its head there was a man engaged in honest toil every day, leaving them in the morning with kindly words, and returning at night with good money in his pocket, which he gave to his wife to buy meat and bread and coals, and coffee and cocoa, with never a black look or a murmur as in the old drinking days "that a fellow could never keep a penny to himself"—at whose coming the children no longer trembled, but ran with outstretched arms and joyful greeting, for the firm footstep on the stairs assured them night after night that father was returning perfectly sober.

Yes, Tom Mite kept the pledge; he could "pass the corners" now without "shying," and before very long, by dint of steady work at the docks, he was able to move into a little house in Inkerman Lane, a street farther removed from the river, and altogether a better spot than Tripe Court, where the Mites's home became happier and more prosperous still. Poll and Sue became members of the Band of Hope, and every Sunday Tom and Bridget and the children—no matter what the weather was or how hard the week's toil had been—wended their way riverward to take part in the services of St. Peter's Church. Poll and Sue continued to attend the Sunday-school at the Mission, where their changed appearance occasioned no little surprise among the children. Their teacher did not see it. She was the vicar's daughter, and had taken a great interest in them, but she was married now, and went away on her wedding trip the very week before Bridget went to the Infirmary. She was expected back soon, and the children felt that until she saw them and their new clothes, and heard of the cause, their triumph would not be quite complete. They were very eager to know when she would come, and one Sunday they were told that next Sunday afternoon she would be there, not to teach, but just to see them.

The children attending this Sunday-school were clearly very poor little ones. Children poorly clad and poorly fed, who would be glad, most likely, of the shabbiest cast-off clothes, and for anything else they could get. They were sorry when the school-bell rang for closing this afternoon, it was all so cold and dark outside, being gloomy November weather, and St. Peter's school-room, with its bright fire and gas-lights, was the nicest place they knew in winter. At home there was often no fire and no light, not even a "dip" candle to cast a cheering ray across garret or cellar. Their little pinched, red noses and chilblained hands and feet showed how sharply these river-side children suffered from scant food and fuel in the bitter November cold.

There was more noise and commotion than usual on this particular Sunday afternoon when the bell rang and the classes broke up. Teachers tried to control them and enforce some order in their manner of departure, but the children scrambled over the forms, and hustled and pushed, in wild hurry and eagerness to reach the doorway, where stood their dear friend, the vicar's daughter, who had come, according to promise, to see her poor little friends. She was smiling and nodding as the children surged round her, shouting and calling at the top of their shrill little voices, "How d'ye do, Miss Mary?" "Welcome back, dear Miss Mary!" as if they were just overjoyed at seeing her.

She was not "*Miss* Mary" any longer, but *Mrs.* Somebody now; but the children did not regard that. "Miss Mary" had crept in quietly, just while the last verse of the closing hymn was being sung; but she was quickly recognized, and as soon as the breaking-up bell had given its first testy little tingle, the children's enthusiasm broke loose, and, in spite of teachers, there they were, scrambling and rushing and crowding around "Miss Mary," shouting 'Welcome!' till they were hoarse. They were not content with merely shouting, they wanted "Miss Mary" to notice them each individually, and there were twenty and more little hands outstretched to be shaken, and a dozen others, not able to touch her in any other way, were patting her sealskin jacket, hoping she would feel them presently, and give them a nod. Amongst those most eager to be noticed were Poll and Sue, who seemed frantic in their efforts to make "Miss Mary" see them. They were on the outskirts of the small crowd, and, with all their pushing and scrambling, were unable to get any nearer for some time.

"Miss Mary's" eyes did rest on them once or twice, even at this distance, and she nodded; but the nod was not to their satisfaction, there was not hearty recognition in it, it was a puzzled nod, and the smaller one cried out to her sister at last:

"I don't believe she knows us, Poll, there! not a bit! She thinks we're some other children!"

"And of course she don't know you!" said a pert little school-fellow, scornfully, turning round close at her side. "Who'd ever know pigs if they changed into peacocks sudd*int*ly?"

There was a burst of laughter all round. The speech, though impolite, was forcible, and the two little sisters themselves joined in the laughter. There was so much truth in the insult, they resolved to let it pass.

The crowd was gradually thinning, aided by "Miss Mary," who had regard to the clock. Teachers were at last getting the children into some order, and making them file out at the door in proper order; and by-and-by, quite at the last, the two little sisters, who had been likened by their class-fellow to "pigs," got close up, and stood before "Miss Mary." Giving them her hand, she looked down at them with the puzzled look they had noticed before, and it seemed now to amuse the children very much. They stood smiling and twinkling up into her face as if it were the best joke in the world.

"Don't you know us, Miss Mary?" asked the elder one, pressing forward.

"Well, not *quite*. What are your names, children?" inquired Miss Mary.

"Why, '*Sooty*' and '*Smuts*'—we're 'Sooty' and 'Smuts' of course!" cried both children, in a breath. "*Now* don't you remember us?"

A sudden light came over "Miss Mary's" face, a look of great pleasure and wonderment. The mention of "Sooty" and "Smuts" brought up to her recollection a couple of children who, eighteen months ago, had been the shabbiest and wretchedest and most neglected-looking of all the children attending St. Peter's Schools. They used to come with their hair unkempt and tangled, their clothes hanging in rags about them, the brims of their hats half off, their bare toes showing at the ends of their boots, and their faces so disfigured and grimy with the dirt and smoke of the river-side, that their class-fellows—who were by no means spotless themselves—had nicknamed them "Sooty" and "Smuts."

And the *home* of these children!—Miss Mary thought of that too. A tenement in a dark place called Tripe Court, in which sometimes the little babies in their cradles were attacked by the rats infesting the river, and where there seemed no cleanliness and no peace and no security for any one. Looking down at the children now before her, Miss Mary's blue eyes grew larger and larger with surprise. She could scarcely believe her own senses. Where were the rags? where was the dirt? where the unkempt hair, and the torn boots, and the battered hats of the children she remembered? Gone! and in their places these two neatly dressed little people, with a good soap polish on their faces, and not a rag or a hole about them!

"'Sooty' and 'Smuts,' the Mites of Tripe Court—*really?*" exclaimed Miss Mary, as the delightful truth dawned upon her, at last, that they were those very same children, only changed.

"Yes, Miss Mary, 'Sooty' and 'Smuts' we are!" cried the children triumphantly; "but we don't live in Tripe Court any more, we lives in Inkerman Lane, and we feeds reg'lar every day, and we belongs to the Band o' Hope, and father's signed the pledge, and—and— 'Miss Mary!'" they shouted as they disappeared, "'*twas all along o' baby!*"

That was the cause to which then and ever afterward the two children ascribed the glorious change in their lives. Mrs Treeby always contended that Tom's reformation was due to that good talking to "she had given him that morning when Bridget went to the Infirmary. But the children knew better. They did not like Mrs. Treeby, who was always "lectorin" mother and reproving them. Besides, they had seen baby's little arm go up at the meeting, and knew what followed. They insisted that it was "all along o' baby," and they were right: that little arm had been a powerful instrument for good in God's hands, emphasizing afresh the truth of those words, "God hath chosen the foolish things of the world to confound the wise; and God hath chosen the weak things of the world to confound the things which are mighty; and base things and things which are despised hath God chosen." (1 Cor. 1 : 27.)

THE END

[This story may be had in book form, bound in cloth, price 90 cents, from Mr. Thomas Whittaker, publisher, 2 Bible House, New York.]

THE RICH YOUNG RULER.

By Mrs. M. Baxter.

S. S. Lesson for February 26. Matt. 19: 16-26.

Golden Text, Matt. 6: 24.

Ver. 16: What the Ruler Sought—An Inestimable Prize—His Mistake—Expecting to Earn It—Ver. 17: A Gentle Reproof (see Revised Version)—The Righteous Applying to the Sinners' Saviour—Reminded of the Rules in Vogue for His Class—Ver. 18-20: The Moral Man Conscious of Deficiency—Unaware of its Nature—Ver. 21, 22: The Flaw Revealed—Christ's Knowledge Clearer than Self-knowledge—Ver. 23-25: A General Observation—A Very Effective Bar Still—Ver. 26: A Warning Against Dogmatizing About Salvation—The Impossibility for the Finite not Impossibility for the Infinite.

"No man can serve two masters: for either he will hate the one and love the other, or else he will hold to the one and despise the other. Ye cannot serve God and Mammon." (Matt. 6 : 24.) What is Mammon? Some say, "Riches;" others, "The world." Is it not that which asserts itself as God's rival, whether it is in the form of riches, pleasure, fashion, the world in any form; or whether it be self in any of its multiplicity of forms? Jesus had just been blessing little children, children too young to be self-conscious; and He said of them, "Suffer *little* children to come unto Me, and forbid them not, for of such is the Kingdom of Heaven. And behold, one comer said unto Him, Good Master, what good thing shall I do, that I may have eternal life?" How little this man understood the Master! The little children were not received because they had done "some good thing." All they did was to receive, and they were blest. The ruler's ideas were those of all men until they are taught by the Holy Ghost. "*Good* Master, what *good* thing shall I do?"

Man's Goodness

was the thought which filled his heart. He was ready to *do* anything, *give* anything, if he might only inherit eternal life. He was fully convinced that eternal life was worth something; was, so to speak, a good investment; and he was ready to make a sacrifice to obtain it. But he began wrong; he did not see that it is man's badness, not man's goodness, which is his claim on God for salvation. No doubt his thought was, "This Jesus is a good man; if I can become as good as *He* is, I shall merit eternal life," and, no doubt, his heart swelled and beat high with the thought of the holy heroism which burned within him. There was no amount of gift he would think too great, so long as he might recognize himself, and be recognized by others, as the giver. There was no amount of self-denial or of austerity too great, so long as he might have the satisfaction of and take to himself the glory of being so devoted. He was ready to go all lengths, so long as he could get the credit for it, and have the sweet consciousness of his own goodness to rejoice in. Are there not many believers, even consecrated believers, who resemble him, and who luxuriate in the thought of how consecrated *they* are, how zealous and devoted *they* are, how deep is *their* love for souls, how perfectly consistent are *their* lives? Are there not many who think how much more true *they* are to God than some others who equally

Profess to be Cleansed

from all sin, and yet are unscrupulous in money matters, very loose with regard to truthfulness, or, it may be, still in bondage to light literature, smoking, snuff, etc.? Such will feel in their hearts something like the Pharisee when he said, "God, I thank Thee that I am not as other men are" (Luke 18: 11); I do not smoke, I do not read stories, I am true in all my dealings, my heart is pure, I love souls, I find no fault in myself, I am good, the blood of Jesus Christ cleanseth me from all sin, I am clean, I am good.

But what a complete revolution of all such thoughts lies in the words of Jesus, "Why callest thou *Me* good? There is none good but One, that is God." As much as to say, "If I am not God, I am not good; for only that which is God is good." Goodness does not grow in the soil of human nature; it is only as God comes in, and supersedes the human, that there is anything good in man; and then it is Christ in us which is good. We have known men the consistency of whose lives, judged by the law, was perfect; and yet, while sin was cleansed, self remained in them, and their very consistency and devotion to God became a snare to them, for, like Job, they gloried in it, and took satisfaction in it, instead of seeing goodness only in God. Job's mistake was

Not Sin, But Self.

He was "a perfect and an upright man;" according to the law, he did fear God and eschew evil. (Job 1: 1.) But he admired and gloried in his own goodness more than in God, and God was forced to keep him in such a position that self came to the surface; and then Job again and again blamed God, and justified himself rather than God. Thus God revealed Himself as the Creator, until Job shrank into nothing before such greatness; and the perfect man—who was none the less perfect as compared with his fellow-man—seeing himself in relation to God, cried out, "Behold, Lord, I am vile; what shall I answer thee? I will lay my hand upon my mouth." "I have heard of Thee by the hearing of the ear, but now mine eye seeth Thee; wherefore I abhor myself and repent in dust and ashes." (Job 40: 4; 42: 5, 6.) He did not say, "I abhor my *sin*, for, according to the law relating to his neighbor, he had not sinned, but he had served mammon, or self, more than he had served God.

The life of Jesus was

A Witness Against Self.

He came not to do His own will, and self loves its own will; He received not honor from man (John 5: 41), and self loves honor from man. He came to resist not evil, and to love His enemies, and taught us to do the same. He did not defend Himself, but "committed Himself to Him that judgeth righteously." Self always defends itself, and *will* have its rights. As long as we serve self, we are not serving God, however devoted we may be; for God put us into the world, not to show how good *we* are, but how good *He* is.

Jesus answered the young man, "If thou wilt enter into life, keep the commandments." He saith unto Him, "Which?" Jesus said, "Thou shalt do no murder; thou shalt not commit adultery; thou shalt not steal; thou shalt not bear false witness; honor thy father and thy mother; and thou shalt love thy neighbor as thyself." The young man saith unto Him, "All these things have I kept from my youth up; what lack I yet?"

Elastic Consciences.

Strange how elastic some people's consciences are. Jesus did indeed love His neighbor as Himself, and He showed it by taking upon Him our flesh, and bearing our sins and our sicknesses. He did most literally what He would have had another do for Him if He had been a lost sinner bearing the consequences of his sins. But some men will affirm unblushingly that they love their neighbor as themselves, while they take every opportunity of exposing the faults and skilfully pointing out the blemishes of that beloved (?) neighbor. Is it because they have an unusual relish for having their own faults exposed? Perhaps they will say like Job, that they have no faults. Let the bull's-eye lantern of God's discerning Spirit be turned full upon them, and O, how self comes out! It may be a good self, as with Job and the young ruler, or it may be a bad self, which shows itself in self-indulgence, tardiness, fretfulness, jealousy, spite, malice, etc. But whether good self or bad self it is not Christ, and if it is not God it is mammon. "What lack I yet?" said the young ruler. The man was honest; he had made an inventory of his own goodness, and thought he had passed the examination with flying colors, and perhaps he expected the Lord to say, "Thou art all fair, My son, there is no spot in thee." (Cant. 4: 7.) O how astonished must he have been at the reply, "If thou wilt be perfect, go and sell all that thou hast, and give to the poor, and thou shalt have treasure in heaven, and come follow Me."

Give All?

But that would be to cease to be a lordly benefactor, a renowned giver! That would be to put himself upon a level with ordinary men! He *could* not, for this involved the giving up of self. He could not serve God and mammon. O how many make a mammon of their Christian reputation! To them riches are nothing, comfort is nothing, all the world is nothing, but their reputation for consistency, for consecration, for uprightness, is dearer than life to them, and if anything assails it, and a doubt is thrown upon it, they will compass sea and land to prove themselves in the right. So did not Joseph in Egypt, it was enough for him that the Lord was with him, and He justified him by making him ruler over the whole land. We are converted and consecrated to show forth not our own praises, but "the praises of Him who hath called [us] out of darkness into His marvellous light." (1 Pet. 2: 9.) If we sell *all* that we have, we must be willing, if God so permits, to let our reputation go too, and let the Lord have that with all else. We are too apt to think that God's reputation is at stake with ours; but God is not dependent on us, He can do without any and all of us, blessed be His name. If we have, in very deed, sold all that we have, ourselves, our possessions, our reputation, our spirits, souls and bodies, then it becomes God's responsibility, not ours, to look after our reputation. He sometimes, yes, often, allows us to be misrepresented that we may be put to the proof whether we can trust Him with our good name, and then it ceases to pain us when we are wronged, for we know He cares for His own cause, and we live for no other.

The Needle's Eye.

The young man "went away sorrowful; for he had great possessions." "Then said Jesus unto His disciples, Verily, I say unto you, that a rich man shall hardly enter into the kingdom of heaven." So long as we *have* anything, or *are* anything in our own eyes, we are not small enough or empty enough to enter into the kingdom of heaven. "It is easier for a camel to go through the eye of a needle (i. e., the little postern gate which is left open when the great gates of a walled city are closed) than for a rich man to enter into the kingdom of God." The camel must be unloaded, and so must we, to get through the eye of the needle.

The disciples cried, "Who, then, can be saved?" and Jesus answered, "With men this is impossible;" man is so great in his own eyes that it is impossible to him to be small; "but with God all things are possible." Let God come into a man, and he feels small at once.

Peter thought he would show how much better he was than the young ruler, and said, "Behold, we have forsaken all, and followed Thee; what shall we *have*, therefore?" Poor Peter, he was still after mammon; still driving bargains for his own advantage; still self-seeking. Jesus showed that those who followed Him should indeed reign with Him; that those who left anything, or all, for *His* name's sake (not for their own holiness's sake) should receive an hundredfold and inherit everlasting life. But, He continued, "Many that are first shall be last, and the last first." Those who think themselves first, disqualify themselves by that very thought for the place they want—for to seek the first place is serving mammon, and not God.

LOVE'S HEIGHT.

I sometimes think God's tender heart must
ache,
Listening to all the sad complaining cries,
That from our weak, impatient soul's arise
Because we do not see that for our sake,
He answers not, or answers otherwise
Than seems the best to our tear-blinded eyes.
This is love's hardest task, to do hard things
For Love's own sake, then bear the murmurings
Of Ignorance, too dull to judge aright,
The love that rises to this wond'rous height.
He knows we have not yet attained; and so
He wearies not, but bears complaint and moan,
And shields each willing heart against His own
Knowing that some glad day we too shall know.

Selected.

MEXICO

Contributions in aid of Christian work in Mexico are most pressingly needed, and can be mailed to the address of
BISHOP H. C. RILEY,
Care of J. P. HEATH,
43 Bible House, New York.

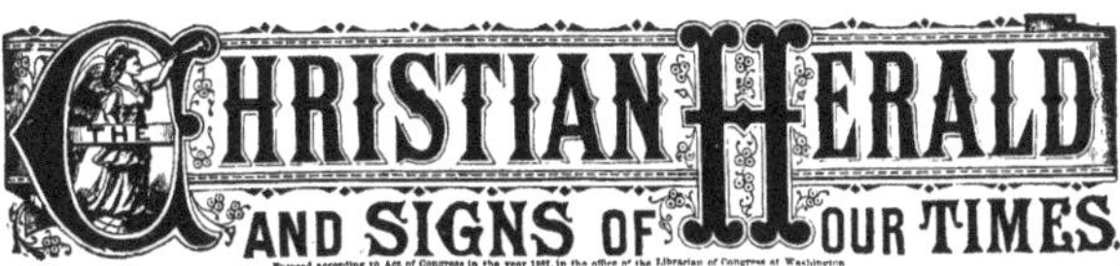

Entered according to Act of Congress in the year 1887, in the office of the Librarian of Congress at Washington.

Vol. XI., No. 8. Office, 63 Bible House, N. Y. | THURSDAY, FEBRUARY 23, 1888. | Annual Subscription, $1.50.

CONTENTS OF THIS NUMBER.

PORTRAITS AND LIVES OF THE LATE REVS. H. TOWNSEND AND T. J. COMBER, Missionaries in Africa.
WOMAN'S HAPPINESS. Dr. Talmage's Sermon to the Women of America, last Sunday.
THE GENTILE POWER: Its Rise, Culmination and Fall. By G. H. Pember.
An Indian Orphan Frozen—An African King Tested—A Spoiled Business—A Norwegian Missionary Healed—How a Lawsuit was Averted—Defective Life Preservers, etc.
PARAMOUNT EDUCATION. A New Sermon by C. H. Spurgeon.
PICTURE OF THE SULTAN'S PALACE AT ZANZIBAR.
DR. HEYWARD'S SUCCESS. (Illustrated.
MRS. TRANSOME'S PUPIL. A Serial Story.
CHRIST'S LAST JOURNEY TO JERUSALEM. By Mrs. M. Baxter.

MR. AND MRS. TOWNSEND CROSSING A RIVER IN AFRICA.

LIBERATED SLAVES LANDING AT SIERRA LEONE.

AKE CHURCH IN ABEOKUTA.

STREET BREAKFAST IN ABEOKUTA.

The Late Revs. H. Townsend and T. J. Comber, Missionaries in Africa—Scenes in Mission Work.

TWO BRAVE MISSIONARIES.

THE death of the intrepid young missionary to the Congo, Mr. T. J. Comber, has already been recorded in our news columns. We are now enabled to give his portrait, and with it that of the Rev. H. Townsend, another brave man whose life also was given to the service of Christ in Africa, and who has also entered into his reward. It is two years since Mr. Townsend died. But it is only now that his biography has appeared, that the full extent of the services he rendered to the cause of Christ in the Dark Continent is understood.

THE REV. HENRY TOWNSEND.

Founder of the Yoruba Mission.

Born in 1815—Dedicates Himself to Foreign Missions—Volunteers for Africa—Arrives at Sierra Leone in 1836—Marriage—Journey to Abeokuta—A Chief's Reception—The Yoruba Mission Begun in 1844—A Ride in a Tub—Progress—Orphanage Effort—An Army Dispersed—Escape from Death—Return Home.

MR. TOWNSEND was born on December 1, 1815, and died on February 25, 1886, at the age of seventy. In early life he gave his heart to God, and resolved to devote his life to the work of preaching the gospel to the heathen. Having been accepted by the committee of the Church Missionary Society as a catechist, he went to London, to undergo a fitting course of preparation for the work to which he believed the Lord had called him.

He had not been long a student, when there occurred a very serious mortality among the missionary staff at Sierra Leone, on the west coast of Africa, where the Society had a station; and the Society under these circumstances would only send *volunteers*. Henry Townsend, after prayer for Divine guidance, volunteered to go to the unhealthy field of service, and on the day preceding his twenty-first birthday, November 30, 1836, he

Landed at Freetown.

Having spent a few days with some missionaries and native Christians, he was appointed to Kissy as assistant in school and evangelistic work. Here, after two years' useful service, he was prostrated by yellow fever, and fears were entertained for his life. However, through the mercy of God, he was spared, and on his recovery he removed to Wellington, and labored abundantly, though weakened by frequent illnesses in the Sierra Leone district. After four years labor change of scene became imperative, and Mr. Townsend paid a brief visit to his native country. During this visit he became united in marriage to a lady of consecrated spirit, who during the remainder of his life proved a true helpmeet to him in his work. The marriage took place on October 1, 1840, and at the end of the same month the happy couple left their native land for Sierra Leone, where they labored until 1842, when a great movement took place which culminated in the establishment of the Yoruba Mission.

In that year two captured slavers were brought into Sierra Leone, and the captives set at liberty, to be returned to the Yoruba country, where they had been kidnapped. Their delight on being put ashore was intense (*See illustration on first page.*) The missionaries were enabled to converse with some of them, and it was learned that white teachers would receive a cordial welcome in the Yoruba country, if any dare venture thither in the face of the fatal climate and the enemies of the Yoruba people. Mr. Townsend volunteered to return with the liberated captives and ascertain what were the prospects of establishing a mission. He embarked on November 14, 1842, and landed at Badagry on November 29, whence he set out for the interior. During this journey he fell ill with ague and had to be carried in a litter.

His Arrival in Abeokuta

was attended with some ceremony. When Shodeki, the chief or king, was informed that a white man was coming with his liberated people, and that the white man was a teacher, he sent his son with an armed escort to bring in the distinguished visitor; for no white man had ever been seen in Abeokuta. "Sitting up in my basket litter," says Mr. Townsend, in his journal, "and carried on the shoulders of the men, at last we reached the presence of Shodeki.

"We alighted at the entrance into the king's yard, and I was led through a spacious yard to the place where the king sat, surrounded by his wives and retinue. He was clad in a scarlet velvet cloth, loosely thrown over him; he received me very kindly, and after the exchange of a few words, I was led away to the house appointed for my use. Soon afterwards he came to visit me, and sat down and had a little chat with those around him. He gave me a bag of cowries and a sheep.

"The few days of this interesting visit to Abeokuta were occupied in

Inspecting the Town.

The intercourse with the king was of the most friendly kind, who thankfully accepted a present brought for him—he said 'he hoped many white people would come and dwell with them.'"

In the afternoon of January 5, 1843, service was held in a shed in the king's yard, which was attended by the king, who had his mat spread near the speaker. On this occasion an immense number of spectators were assembled. After prayers Mr. Townsend expounded the parable of the great feast from St. Luke 14, and the people listened attentively. It was an impressive sight, and as the missionary looked from the eminence over his congregation and on over the vast town, he thought, "What a benefit it would be to them could there be at least six missionaries stationed in it. It would require many churches and schools in various parts to meet the real necessities of the people.

This hope of Mr. Townsend for six missionaries, besides churches and schools, has been more than realized, as at present Abeokuta and district has three native clergymen, seventeen lay teachers, 2,543 Christians, ten schools with 398 scholars.

Before leaving the country, Shodeki promised Mr. Townsend that he would give him any piece of land which might be chosen, and help to build a schoolhouse on it; that he would be glad even to get a native schoolmaster until white men came, and that he would find more children to teach than the missionaries could manage. As a farewell gift, he pressed on Mr. Townsend's acceptance a tusk of ivory, and sent after him other valuable offerings as tokens of sympathy, gratitude and good-will.

It was decided, on Mr. Townsend's report, to establish a mission in Abeokuta, and he was intrusted with the direction of it. On December 18, 1844,

A Farewell Meeting

was held in Sierra Leone of a most solemn character. Writing of it, Mr. Townsend remarks: "Thus were we sent forth by the Church in Sierra Leone, the clergy and laity together in prayer committing us to the care of Him who alone was sufficient to protect and sustain us in the work we were called on to do. The path before us, we knew, was beset with danger—perils among the heathen, perils from the Dahomians who periodically raided the country for slaves to send to the coast, perils by water, perils by land, and the perils of the climate were to be met, and could only be successfully met under the protecting and guiding care of our heavenly Father." The party embarked from the wharf amid a scene of extraordinary excitement, and with many a parting wish and blessing and affecting good-byes at the last moment. The party consisted of four missionaries and their wives, an interpreter, seven children, four carpenters, three laborers, and two native servants.

This party found the difficulties of travel far greater than Mr. Townsend had found them in his litter on his former visit. The following entry in the missionary's diary will show this: "This morning part of our escort returned. At 7 a. m. our tent was struck, and we were all ready to cross the Majuba water, called Ohre, for which, through the exertions of Mr. Gollmer, we were provided with a substitute for a canoe, *a large tub* (*See illustration*). This water was about four feet deep, and wide, having large stumps of trees sunk in it that rendered it very dangerous for persons to be carried across it. The tubs succeeded admirably, having men to drag them along, and to return for others, thus those unable to wade were comfortably conveyed across. This took an hour to accomplish, and at eight o'clock we left the banks of this water and proceeded on our way.

"Having been on horseback all of yesterday, to which I was not accustomed, I endeavored to make use of my carriers on starting, but after proceeding about a mile I gave it up, finding it quite impossible for the men to carry me. The road became almost impassable: it became dangerous for Mrs. Townsend to ride; she tried her carriers, but with no success, for with extreme difficulty she was carried 100 yards or so, and wus then obliged to remount her horse. Mine fell with me twice. The road was extremely slippery, and so narrow, having become a water course, that a horse could not stand with his feet together, high banks being on each side.

"Before reaching Imowo Otta, Mrs. Townsend's horse lay down with her through fatigue, and on reaching that place, although we had only gone over what was to me in my former journey four hours' walk, we were glad to encamp for the night. Our horses and people were worn out, and several of them already lame, and, to complete their sufferings, were in want of provisions, and ourselves in want of water, our encampment not affording that necessary of life. However, a heavy shower enabled us to catch water, with which we made tea, and after eating a good supper, for which the best of all sauces supplied the relish, and commending ourselves to the gracious protection of our Heavenly Father, we retired to rest."

The Work at Abeokuta

was from the first evidently and abundantly blest of God. Mission premises were erected on about three acres of land. Houses were constructed with mud walls and thatched roofs, which were a great improvement on the native huts of the locality. A small church, built of mud (*see illustration*), and a humble school-house, were added in time, and thus arose the first settlement of that Christian mission, which has already been so fruitful of good. Churches, school-houses, and missionary compounds were, formed; not indeed without hindrance or difficulty, arising in some cases from the heathens, or from the neighboring savage Dahomians, tribal wars, pestilence, frequent fires, and from deaths oft among the laborers, yet the work went on until, under God's blessing, the great African town of Abeokuta and regions beyond received the gospel in all its elevating and transforming influences.

Another useful institution was started in 1862 under Mr. and Mrs. Townsend's superintendence, viz., "The Ake Orphanage." "The heathen population of Abeokuta seldom or never attempt to bring up infants who have lost their mother. They are for the most part laid by the side of their dead mother to perish of want; or else, after some days, they are thrown away in some waste place." Hence the Christian effort needed for receiving these poor children. A notable instance of

A Rescued Orphan

is that of James Pearse, now the principal schoolmaster at Ake. When sixteen days old his mother died, and the child would have been buried with her, but a kind Christian woman, who had been *once a heathen priestess*, took charge of him, and thus rescued him from a premature death. In due time he was baptized, educated, and trained under Mr. and Mrs. Townsend's supervision, and eventually passed through the Training Institution at Lagos. He is about thirty-one years old, and hopes soon to be able to pass on to the College at Fourah Bay, Sierra Leone, for advanced education.

Pearse was named after Mr. Townsend's late father and brother, who often evinced an interest in him, by sending him suitable presents.

Extraordinary Escape From Death.

In the early part of 1864 the formidable and dreaded Dahomian army appeared again before Abeokuta. Its camp extended for two miles in length, on a rising ground. From the 7th of March to the 23d was a time of great anxiety, and many were the prayers presented to God for deliverance. To the surprise of all, the much dreaded foe departed, and one of the missionaries thus records the event:

"I consider the retreat of the Dahomians as one of the greatest victories the Church of God has obtained by prayer. The King of Dahomey has not come into this city, nor has he shot an arrow here, nor has he come before it with shields, nor has he cast a bank against it; by the way that he came, by the same has he returned, and has not entered into this city. There is great rejoicing among all people; and many heathens acknowledge that it is the arm of the Lord. We shall never be put to shame if we put our trust in the Lord."

Again, in 1873, the army appeared before Abeokuta, and, after being encamped thirteen days, suddenly disappeared. Mr. Cole, a native, who visited the deserted camp, says, "We thank God for our deliverance from the hand of that bloodthirsty man. Man proposes and God disposes. To Him be all the praise."

Mr. Townsend had the joy of witnessing the church at Abeokuta, which he had been instrumental in establishing, grow and thrive into vigorous life. When the infirmities of age came upon him he returned to his native land, leaving the work to be continued by younger hands. There he peacefully breathed his last, February 25, 1886, in the seventy-first year of his age.

THE LATE REV. T. J. COMBER.

THOMAS JOHN COMBER, *whose portrait appears on our frontispiece*, was born in 1852, and died in the Congo Free State, in September last, in his thirty-fifth year. His father, with a noble disinterestedness, has surrendered four of his children, three sons and one daughter, to the work of missions in Africa. Thomas Comber was led first to give himself to the work. How this came about may be given in his own words. Speaking at the valedictory service held in Plymouth in 1875, Mr. Comber stated: "I have no strange or startling account to give of my conversion. The chief influences which led me to the Saviour were those of a loving and loved mother, and an earnest Sunday-school teacher. When only about fifteen years of age I began to feel the powerful interest of my teacher, whose devotedness and earnestness in life were the grand secrets of his success amongst his pupils. Africa is my own choice, because that land has always seemed to me to have been the forgotten child of the mission family."

Mr. Comber was, as he said, fully bent on going to Africa, believing that God had called him to labor there. With this resolution—should the way be made possible—he entered Regent's Park College, having previously attended evening classes at the Metropolitan Tabernacle. In April, 1875, he was accepted by the Committee of the Baptist Missionary Society, and at the end of the year he reached the shores of Africa. For nearly three years he continued his labors at Cameroons and Victoria, on the dreaded West Coast, during which time he made important excursions, visiting especially the Bukundu region, in which, for some time now, a missionary station has been established.

The explorations of Mr. Stanley, resulting in the discovery and identity of the Lualaba and Congo rivers, and an immense extent of clear waterway reaching across the continent a thousand miles, at once attracted wide attention, and that not alone of geographers, but also of the friends of Christian missions. Messrs. Comber and Grenfell were among the first to move into the new ground. They proceeded on a preliminary expedition to San Salvador, the capital of the kingdom of the Congo in 1883. Mr. Comber, writing to the Home Committee in respect to this field, said: "I am not my own, nor am I out here for my own purposes and ends; and in all my movements, especially in such a deeply important one as I feel this to be, I look up to the gracious Master to fulfil His promise: 'I will guide thee with Mine eye,' and to make all things work together for the everlasting good of souls and His own eternal glory." The preliminary expedition having proved full of promise, Mr. Comber returned for reinforcements, and Messrs. Bentley, Hartland and Crudgington volunteered their services. Very soon after his arrival with the new missionaries at San Salvador in 1886, a heavy trial befell Mr. Comber. His dearly loved wife—but a few weeks previously a bride—was removed by death. The loss was almost paralyzing, but communion, to use his own words, with the Master, drove away the dead, blank despair from his heart, and as soon as possible we find him making an attempt to reach Stanley Pool by the Makutu route—an attempt which nearly cost him his life. The life thus spared fell, however, before the ravages of fever after a very short illness in the autumn of last year, 1887.

ANECDOTES RELATED AT RECENT EVANGELISTIC MEETINGS.

The Loyalty of Soldiers to Christ.—A Christian worker remarked: "Have you ever noticed what very fine Christians old soldiers make? How firmly many retired Indian officers stand up for Christ! I once asked an aged soldier the reason of this, and he replied, 'Oh, I know all about it. You see, in the Army you have to be out-and-out—either one thing or another, either plainly for Christ or plainly against Him.' Would that the Christians of this day saw the importance of being decidedly known as such. Why should they be ashamed of their uniform? Is not their party the winning party? Has it not the best Commander and the best pay? Then stand wholly up for Jesus."

A Tempter Defeated.—The Same Friend said: "When I was a very young man residing in London, I was tempted by one of my own sex to leave the paths of virtue. This young man tried to persuade me to go with him, but I refused. He persisted, and taking my hat off my head, said, 'If you do not come with me you will not get your hat.' But what value was my hat in comparison with my soul? I turned and left him with my hat in his hand, and seeing that I was not to be tempted he soon restored to me my hat. Young men, 'Resist the devil, and he will flee from you.' Beware of the commencement of evil. The best and only safe thing to do is to turn your back upon temptation when you see it approaching."

Billiard Players Converted.—The Rev. Mr. Stalker said: "I was once visited by a divinity student, whom I asked what had made him think of becoming a minister. In answer, he told me this strange story: 'At the age of eighteen I was master of a business in a country town. Some evangelistic meetings were started there. I went to one, and the arrow of God went straight to my heart. The wound was deep. I was in misery. I believed, but the difficulty was in confessing Christ. I was one of a number of young men who were in the habit of meeting every night to play billiards and bet. My first thought was—how can I tell of my conversion to my companions? In my trouble I did what too many do in their trouble—I resolved to go into the nearest city and have a spree. I was going to a theatre, when I met a young fellow belonging to my village. We spoke for a few moments, and, when we were about to part, the young man said, "There is a verse has been following me these two days," and taking out his Testament, he read, "If thou shalt confess Christ with thy mouth, and believe in thy heart, thou shalt be saved." My friend says he stood still. It was a bolt from heaven. He went back to his native village by the next train, and passing down in front of the inn he saw, standing there, his companions with whom he usually passed the night. Now was the moment of decision. Just then that text came back to his mind, and asking God to help him, he did confess his Saviour. When he left them, they stood looking after him as if too much astonished to say a word; but within one month, by the means of his example, God had brought every one of them to Himself."

A Delightful Cause of Agitation.—Mr. Stalker narrated: "I was staying with a brother minister, some time ago, and one night I noticed that he was very much agitated. I asked him what was the matter, for we had just been talking about his two boys, one of whom was at college, while the other had just taken a first prize at school, and I could see no cause for his agitation, but I soon learned what it was. In answer to my question, he replied, 'Every night I go up to my bedroom, and pray for my boys, and to-night, just as I was bending down my head, the elder one entered, and throwing his arms around my neck, exclaimed, "Do you know, father, that I have given myself to the Lord Jesus Christ?"' Then I did not wonder at his agitation. I am sure it must be like heaven begun on earth when a loved one comes to join you in the march heavenward."

The Peril of Putting Off.—An Evangelist said: "I went on Sunday week to see a young girl who lay dangerously ill. Most of the time she was unconscious, and as she lay there I tried to tell her how Jesus loved her, and how there was salvation for her if she would but trust Him. At length there came a short interval in which she was conscious, but all I had to tell her was that Jesus loved her, and an hour or two afterwards she was in eternity, whether saved or unsaved we could not tell. But what a solemn lesson! I was as if I had received a definite command, saying, 'Go, tell every man and woman while they have life to come at once to the Saviour, and not put it off till a dying day, when their frame is racked with pain, and their brain confused.'"

The Poacher and His Prey.—A Temperance worker testified: "Some years ago, before I knew Christ, I was out poaching a few miles from Edinburgh. I did not carry a gun for fear of detection, but a revolver, which could easily be concealed upon the approach of any one. On that day, the last which I ever spent poaching, I shot three birds, and jumping over a hedge secured them. Two were dead, but one only wounded. As it lay in my hand fluttering, I looked down upon the dying bird. I thought, 'What if that were *me*; where should I spend eternity?' I knew I should go to perdition, and God brought that conviction so forcibly home to my heart that I resolved to leave the ways of sin and seek the paths of righteousness. Not being very clear about the way of salvation, I went to a gospel meeting, and there I saw Christ as my Saviour, and thank God I could say that I had passed from death unto life."

A Brother's Apology.—A Successful Lay preacher remarked: "At the time of my conversion there was a revival in our neighborhood, and at the persuasion of my mother I consented to go to one of the meetings. But I paid no attention to the preaching; my whole interest was centred upon a young lady I saw there. I left the meeting worse than I went to it, having rejected God's offer of salvation. When I got home, my brother came to me and affectionately apologized for having lost his temper the last time he had spoken to me about my soul. As soon as my brother had left the room, I threw myself upon my knees, and tried to pray, but I could not; not a word would come. I rose, and going to my brother's room, burst in upon him with the words, 'Pray for me, for I cannot pray for myself!' He prayed with me, yet I could not get peace. I went and saw a Christian friend, who advised me to accept Christ there and then. After some hesitation I was able to do so, and I can assure you that I have never had cause to regret it. I went home and told my brother, and together we thanked God."

WOMAN'S HAPPINESS:

What Can and What Cannot Make a Woman Happy.

Dr. Talmage's Seventh Sermon to THE WOMEN OF AMERICA.

Preached last Sunday Morning, February 19, 1888.

"She that liveth in pleasure is dead while she liveth." 1 Timothy 5: 6.

An Editor's Question—Happiness Follows Usefulness—Cloudy Days in May—What Greenough and Barnes Thought of Life—Solomon's Two Opinions—Mistakes about Happiness—Not Dependent upon Social Position—A Grand Marriage—The Godless Mansion—A Night of Discontent—A Lord Envying a Dog—Neglect of Present Opportunities Irremediable—Make Your Father's Home Happy—Happiness not Dependent on Beauty—A Subtle Charm—The Hoof-Marks of Time—The Plain Woman in the Hospital—Mistaken for an Angel—A Wounded Drummer-Boy—Happines not Dependent on Masculine Flattery—Nor Fashion—The Jewish Fashion Plate—The World a Failure—A Dying Girl's Message to a Church.

THE editor of a Boston newspaper, a few days ago wrote asking me the terse questions: "What is the road to happiness?" and "Ought happiness be the chief aim of life?" My answer was: "The road to happiness is the continuous effort to make others happy. The chief aim of life ought to be usefulness, not happiness, but

Happiness Always Follows Usefulness."

This morning's text in a strong way sets forth the truth that a woman who seeks in worldly advantage her chief enjoyment, will come to disappointment and death. "She that liveth in pleasure is dead while she liveth."

My friends, you all want to be happy. You have had a great many recipes by which it is proposed to give you satisfaction—solid satisfaction. At times you feel a thorough unrest. You know as well as older people what it is to be depressed. As dark shadows sometimes fall upon the geography of the school girl as on the page of the spectacled philosopher. I have seen as cloudy days in May as in November. There are no deeper sighs breathed by the grandmother than by the granddaughter. I correct the popular impression that people are happier in childhood and youth than they ever will be again. If we live aright, the older the happier,

The Happiest Woman

that I ever knew was a Christian octogenarian; her hair white as white could be; the sunlight of heaven late in the afternoon gilding the peaks of snow. I have to say to a great many of the young people that the most miserable time you are ever to have is just now. As you advance in life, as you come out into the world and have your head and heart all full of good, honest, practical Christian work, then you will know what it is to begin to be happy. There are those who would have us believe that life is chasing thistledown and grasping bubbles. We have not found it so. To many of us it has been discovering diamonds larger than the Kohinoor, and I think that our joy will continue to increase until nothing short of everlasting jubilee of heaven will be able to express it.

Horatio Greenough, at the close of the hardest life a man ever lives—the life of an American artist—wrote: "I don't want to leave this world until I give some sign that, born by the grace of God in this land, I have found life to be a very cheerful thing, and not the dark and bitter thing with which my early prospects were clouded."

Albert Barnes, the good Christian, known the world over, stood in his pulpit in Philadelphia, at seventy or eighty years of age, and said: "This world is so very attractive to me, I am very sorry I shall have to leave it."

I know that Solomon said some very dolorous things about this world, and three times declared; "Vanity of vanities, all is vanity." I suppose it was a reference to those times in his career when his seven hundred wives almost pestered the life out of him. But I would rather turn to the description he gave after his conversion, when he says in another place: "Her ways are ways of pleasantness, and all her paths are peace." It is reasonable to expect it will be so. The longer the fruit hangs on the tree, the riper and more mellow it ought to grow. Hear, then, while I discourse upon some of the

Mistakes which Young People Make

in regard to happiness, and point out to the young women what I consider to be the source of complete satisfaction.

And, in the first place, I advise you not to build your happiness upon *mere social position*. Persons at your age, looking off upon life, are apt to think that if, by some stroke of what is called good luck, you could arrive in an elevated and affluent position, a little higher than that in which God has called you to live, you would be completely happy. Infinite mistake! The palace floor of Ahasuerus is red with the blood of Vashti's broken heart. There have been no more scalding tears wept than those which coursed the cheeks of Josephine. If the sob of unhappy womanhood in the great cities could break through the tapestried wall, that sob would come along your streets to-day like the simoon of the desert. Sometimes I have heard in the rustling of the robes on the city pavement the hiss of the adders that followed in the wake. You have come out from your home, and you have looked up

At the great House

and coveted a life under those arches, when perhaps, at that very moment, within that house, there may have been the wringing of hands, the start of horror, and the very agony of hell. I knew of such an one. Her father's house was plain, most of the people who came there were plain; but, by a change in fortune such as sometimes comes, a hand had been offered that led her into a brilliant sphere. All the neighbors congratulated her upon her grand prospects; but what an exchange! On her side it was a heart full of generous impulse and affection. On his side it was a soul dry and withered as the stubble of the field. On her side it was a father's house, where God was honored and the Sabbath, light flooded the rooms with the very mirth of heaven. On his side it was a gorgeous residence and the coming of mighty men to be entertained there; but within it were revelry and godlessness. Hardly had the orange-blossoms of the marriage feast lost their fragrance, than the night of discontent began to cast its shadow.

Cruelties and Unkindnesses

changed all those splendid trappings into a hollow mockery. The platters of solid silver, the caskets of pure gold, the head dress of gleaming diamonds, were there; but no God, no peace, no kind words, no Christian sympathy. The festal music that broke on the captive's ear turned out to be a dirge, and the wreath in the plush was a reptile coil, and the upholstery that swayed in the wind was the wing of a destroying angel, and the bead-drops on the pitcher were the sweat of everlasting despair. O, how many rivalries and unhappinesses among those who seek in social life their chief happiness!

All that this world can do for you in silver, in gold, in Axminster plush, in Gobelin tapestry, in wide halls, in lordly acquaintanceship, will not give you the ten thousandth part of a grain of solid satisfaction. *The English lord*, moving in the very highest sphere, was one day found seated with his chin on his hand and his elbow on the window-sill, looking out and saying: "O, I wish I could exchange places with that dog!" Mere social position will never give happiness to a woman's soul. I have had wide and continuous observation, and I tell the young women that they who build on mere social position their soul's immortal happiness are building on the sand.

Suppose that a youg woman expends the brightness of her early life in this unsatisfactory struggle and omits

The Present Opportunity

of usefulness in the home circle: what a mistake! So surely as the years roll around, that home in which you now dwell will become extinct. The parents will be gone, the property will go into other possession, you yourself will be in other relationships, and that home which only a year ago, was full of congratulation, will be extinguished. When that period comes, you will look back to see what you did or what you neglected to do in the way of making home happy. It will be too late to correct mistakes. If you did not smooth the path of your parents toward the tomb; if you did not make their last days bright and happy; if you allowed your younger brother to go out into the world unhallowed by Christian and sisterly influences; if you allowed the younger sisters of your family to come up without feeling that there had been a Christian example set them on your part—there will be nothing but bitterness of lamentation. That bitterness will be increased by all the surroundings of that home; by every chair, by every picture, by the old time mantel ornaments, by everything you can think of as connected with that home. All these things will rouse up agonizing memories. Young women, have you anything to do in the way of

Making Your Father's Home Happy?

Now is the time to attend to it, or leave it forever undone. Time is flying very quickly away. I suppose you notice the wrinkles are gathering and accumulating on those kindly faces that have so long looked upon you; there is frost in the locks; the foot is not as firm in its step as it used to be; and they will soon be gone. *The heaviest clod that ever falls on a parent's coffin-lid is the memory of an ungrateful daughter.* O, make their last days bright and beautiful. Do not act as though they were in the way. Ask their counsel, seek their prayers, and after long years have passed, and you go out to see the grave where they sleep, you will find growing all over the mound something lovelier than cypress, something sweeter than the rose, something chaster than the lily—the bright and beautiful memories of filial kindness performed ere the dying hand dropped on you a benediction, and you closed the lids over the weary eyes of the worn-out pilgrim.

Better that, in the hour of your birth, you had been struck with orphanage, and that you had been handed over into the cold arms of the world, rather than that you should have been brought up under a father's care and a mother's tenderness, at last to scoff at their example and deride their influence; and on the day when you followed them in long procession to the tomb, to find that you are followed by a still larger procession of unfilial deeds done and wrong words uttered. The one procession will leave its burden in the tomb and disband; but that longer

Procession of Ghastly Memories

will forever march and forever wail. O, it is a good time for a young woman when she is in her father's house. How careful they are of her welfare! How watchful those parents of all her interests! Seated at the morning repast, father at one end the table, children on either side and between, but the years will roll on, and great changes will be effected, and one will be missed from one end the table, and another will be missed from the other end the table. God pity that young woman's soul who, in that hour, has nothing but regretful recollections.

I go further, and advise you not to depend for enjoyment upon mere

Personal Attractions.

It would be sheer hypocrisy, because we may not have it ourselves, to despise, or affect to despise, beauty in others. When God gives it, He gives it as a blessing and as a means of usefulness. David and his army were coming down from the mountains to destroy Nabal and his flocks and vineyards. The beautiful Abigail, the wife of Nabal, went out to arrest him when he came down from the mountains, and she succeeded. Coming to the foot of the hill, she knelt. David with his army of sworn men came down over the cliffs, and when he saw her kneeling at the foot of the hill he cried, "Halt!" to his men, and the caves echoed it: "Halt! halt!" That one beautiful woman kneeling at the foot of the cliff had arrested all those armed troops. A dew-drop dashed back Niagara.

The Bible sets before us the portraits of Sarah and Rebecca and Abishag, and Job's daughters, and says: "They were fair to look upon." By out-door exercise, and by skilful arrangement of apparel, let women make themselves attractive. The sloven has only one mission, and that is to excite our loathing and disgust. But alas! for those who depend upon personal charms for their happiness. Beauty is such a subtle thing, it does not seem to depend upon facial proportions or upon the sparkle of the eye or upon the flush of the cheek. You sometimes find it among irregular features.

It is the Soul Shining Through

the face that makes one beautiful. But alas! for those who depend upon mere personal charms. They will come to disappointment and to a great fret. There are so many different opinions about what are personal charms; and then sickness and trouble and age do make such ravages! *The poorest god that a woman ever worships is her own face.* The saddest sight in all the world is a woman who has built everything on good looks, when the charms begin to vanish. O, how they try to cover the wrinkles and hide the ravages of time! When Time, with iron-shod feet, steps on a face

The Hoof-marks

remain, and you cannot hide them. It is silly to try to hide them. I think the most repulsive fool in all the world is an old fool! Why, my friends, should you be ashamed of getting old? It is a sign—it is *prima facie* evidence that you have behaved tolerably well, or you would not have lived to this time. The grandest thing, I think, is eternity, and that is made up of countless years. When the Bible would set forth the attractiveness of Jesus Christ, it says: "His hair was white as snow." But when the color goes from the cheek, and the lustre from the eye, and the spring from the step, and the gracefulness from the gait, alas! for those who have built their time and their eternity upon good looks. But all the passage of years cannot take out of one's face benignity and kindness, and compassion and faith. Culture your heart and you culture your face. The brightest glory that ever beamed from a woman's face is the religion of Jesus Christ. In the last war two hundred wounded soldiers came to Philadelphia one night, and came unheralded, and they had to extemporize a hospital for them, and the Christian women of my church, and of other churches went out that night to take care of the poor wounded fellows. That night I saw a Christian woman

In the Wards of the Hospital,

her sleeves rolled up, ready for hard work, her hair dishevelled in the excitement of the hour. Her face was plain, very plain; but after the wounds were washed and the new bandages were put round the splintered limbs, and the exhausted boy fell off into his first pleasant sleep, she put her hand on his brow and he started in his dream, and said, *"O, I thought an angel touched me!"* There may have been no classic elegance in the features of Mrs. Harris, who came into the hospital after the "Seven Days" awful fight, as she sat down by

A Wounded Drummer-boy,

and heard him soliloquize: "A ball through my body, and my poor mother will never again see her boy. What a pity it is!" And she leaned over him and said: "Shall I be your mother, and comfort you?" And he looked up and said, "Yes, I'll try to think she's here. Please to write a long letter to her and tell her all about it, and send her a lock of my hair and comfort her. But I would like you to tell her how much I suffered—yes, I would like you to do that, for she would feel so for me. Hold my hand while I die." There may have been no classic elegance in her features, but all the hospitals of Harrison's Landing and Fortress Monroe would have agreed that she was beautiful, and if any rough man in all that ward had insulted her, some wounded soldier would have leaped from his couch on his best foot, and struck him dead with a crutch.

Again: I advise you not to depend for happiness upon

The Flatteries of Men.

It is a poor compliment to your sex that so many men feel obliged, in your presence, to offer unmeaning compliments. Many capable of elegant and elaborate conversation elsewhere, sometimes feel called upon at the door of the drawing-room to drop their common sense and to dole out sickening flatteries. They say things about your dress and about your appearance, that you know, and they know, are false. They say you are an angel. You know you are not. Determined to tell the truth in office, and store and shop, they consider it honorable to lie to a woman. The same thing that they told you on this side of the drawing-room, three minutes ago they said to some one on the other side of the drawing-room. O, let no one trample on your self-respect. The meanest thing on which a woman can build her happiness is the flatteries of men.

Again: I charge yon not to depend for happiness upon

The Discipleship of Worldliness.

I have seen men as vain of their old-fashioned and their eccentric hat as your brainless fop is proud of his dangling fooleries. Fashion sometimes makes a reasonable demand of us, and then we ought to yield to it. The daisies of the field have their fashion of color and leaf; the honeysuckles have their fashion of ear-drop; and the snowflakes flung out of the winter heavens have their fashion of exquisiteness. After the summer shower the sky weds the earth with ring of rainbow. And I do not think we have a right to despise the elegancies and fashions of this world, especially if they make reasonable demands upon us; but the discipleship and worship of fashion is death to the body, and death to the soul:

I am glad the world is improving. Look at the fashion plates of the seventeenth and eighteenth centuries, and you will find that the world is not so extravagant and extraordinary now as it was then, and all the marvellous things thet the granddaughter will do will never equal that done by the grandmother. Go still farther back, to the Bible times, and you find that in those times fashion wielded a more terrible sceptre. You have only to turn to the third chapter of Isaiah, a portion of the Scriptures from which I once preached to you, to read:

The Jewish Fashion Plate,

"Because the daughters of Zion are haughty, and walk with stretched-forth necks and wanton eyes, walking and mincing as they go, and making a tinkling with their feet: In that day the Lord will take away the bravery of their tinkling ornaments about their feet, and their cauls, and their round tires like the moon, the chains, and the bracelets, and the mufflers, and bonnets, and the head-bands, and the tablets, and the ear-rings, the rings, and the nose-jewels, the changeable suits of apparel, and the mantles, and the wimples, and the crisping pins, the glasses, and the fine linen, and the hoods, and the veils." Only think of a woman having all that on! I am glad that the world is getting better and that fashion which has dominated in the world so ruinously in other days has for a little time, for a little degree at any rate, relaxed its energies.

All the splendors and the extravaganza of this world dyed into your robe, and flung over your shoulder, cannot wrap peace around your heart for a single moment. The gayest wardrobe will utter no voice of condolence in the day of trouble and darkness. The woman is grandly dressed, and only she, who is wrapped in the robe of a Saviour's righteousness. The home may be very humble, the hat may be very plain, the frock may be very coarse; but the halo of heaven settles in the room when she wears it, and the faintest touch of the resurrection angel will change that garment into raiment of exceeding white, so as no fuller on earth could whiten it. I come to you, young woman, to-day, to say that this world cannot make you happy. I know it is a bright world, with glorious sunshine, and golden rivers, and fire-worked sunset, and bird orchestra, and the darkest cave has its crystals, and the wrathiest wave has its foam wreath, and the coldest midnight its flaming aurora; but God will put out all these lights with the blast of His own nostrils, and the glories of this world will perish in

The Final Conflagration.

You will never be happy until you get your sins forgiven, and allow Christ Jesus to take full possession of your soul. He will be your friend in every perplexity. He will be your comfort in every trial. He will be your defender in every strait. I do not ask you to bring, like Mary, the spices to the sepulchre of a dead Christ, but to bring your all to the foot of a living Jesus. His word is peace. His look is love. His hand is help. His touch is life. His smile is heaven. O, come, then, in flocks and groups. Come, like the south wind over banks of myrrh. Come like the morning light, tripping over the mountains. Wreathe all your affections on Christ's brow, set all your gems in Christ's coronet, let this Sabbath air rustle with the wings of rejoicing angels, and the towers of God ring out the news of souls saved.

"This world its fancied pearl may crave,
'Tis not the pearl for me;
'Twill dim its lustre in the grave,
'Twill perish in the sea.
But there's a pearl of price untold,
Which never can be bought with gold;
O, that's the pearl for me."

The snow was very deep, and it was still falling rapidly, when, in the first year of my Christian ministry, I hastened

To See a Young Woman Die,

It was a very humble home. She was an orphan; her father had been shipwrecked on the banks of Newfoundland. She had earned her own living. As I entered the room I saw nothing attractive. No pictures. No tapestry. Not even a cushioned chair. The snow on the window casement was not whiter than the cheek of that dying girl. It was a face never to be forgotten. Sweetness and majesty of soul, and faith in God, had given her a matchless beauty, and the sculptor who could have caught the outlines of those features, and frozen them into stone, would have made himself immortal. With her large, brown eyes she looked calmly into the great eternity. I sat down by her bedside and said: "Now tell me all your troubles, and sorrows, and struggles, and doubts." She replied: "I have no doubts or struggles. It is all plain to me. Jesus has smoothed the way for my feet. I wish when you go to your pulpit next Sunday, you would tell the people that

Religion Will Make Them Happy.

"O death, where is thy sting?" Mr. Talmage, I wonder if this is not the bliss of dying?" I said: "Yes, I think it must be." I lingered around the couch. The sun was setting, and her sister lighted a candle. She lighted the candle for me. The dying girl, the dawn of heaven in her face, needed no candle. I rose to go, and she said: "I thank you for coming. Good night! When we meet again it will be in heaven—in heaven! Good night! good night!" For her it was good night to tears, good night to poverty, good night to death; but when the sun rose again it was good morning. The light of another day had burst in upon her soul. Good morning! The angels were singing her welcome home, and the hand of Christ was putting upon her brow a garland. Good morning! Her sun rising. Her palm waving. Her spirit exulting before the throne of God. Good morning! Good morning! The white lily of poor Margaret's cheek had blushed into the rose of health immortal, and the snows through which we carried her to the country graveyard were symbols of that robe which she wears, so white that no fuller on earth could whiten it.

My sister, my daughter, may your last end be like hers!

THE GENTILE POWER.

Its Rise, Culmination and Downfall.

By G. H. Pember.

God's Two-fold Division of Mundane Government—Satan Constituted Prince of the World—The Remote Period of His Inauguration—The Era of the Noachian Delegation—Its Failure—The Vicegerency of the Jew—His Recreancy—The Gentile Power—The Image Its Type—The Absolute Ruler—His Beneficent Reign.

THERE is one thing we must notice before we can understand the prophecies of God and the history of the world, and that is the very decided way in which God divides the government of this world into two parts, earthly and spiritual. Owing to the interaction of these two parts sin entered the world.

I do not intend to enlarge on the origin of sin. It is a vast and dreadful subject, going far back into past eternity, and of which we shall know nothing till we pass out of our present state. I will not speak of the hints given as to the past existence of man, and of the interval between the first and second verses of the first chapter of Genesis. Nor will I enter on the history of Satan and his angels and demons; only, remember, he is

The Lawful Prince of This World,

and prince of the power of the air. He would never have such titles given to him in God's Book were he a mere usurper. It seems that he was invested with the government of this world in past ages, and at some period thereafter became a rebel against God.

We begin, however, with our own race. When the earth was fitted, or, more properly, refitted, for our residence, the question arose, Who is to have possession? The Lord Himself answers, "The earth hath He given to the children of men." But temptation came from the rebellious race in the air, and it proved but too successful. It seems that after the Fall there was further intimacy between fallen man and supernatural beings, and the result was that God swept away the evil doers with a deluge.

Then followed the first covenant with man, which also involved the previous, or, as we may term them, the cosmic laws. For they were given to mankind, not to any election in particular. They include the laws of marriage, of the Sabbath, of the subjection of women, and of sacrifice as teaching that without shedding of blood there is no remission. To these the Noachian covenant added commands that flesh should be used as food, but not with the blood, and that the murderer should be punished with death. Such are the Divine laws given to the whole human race.

Now the signs which are connected with this covenant are two—

The Cherubim and the Rainbow,

Do not mistake as to the cherubim—there are so many strange notions respecting them. It is easy to interpret them if you take the Bible as its own interpreter. They stand before God as the representatives of the four great earth-tribes which He has pledged Himself to save. They first appeared after Adam was cast out of Paradise. Then the tree of life was guarded by a flaming sword turning every way and within its circle; nearer the tree, were placed the cherubim. Of the cherubim—four in number, because "four" is the number of terrestrial creation—we read that one had the face of a man, representing man redeemed; one the face of a lion, representing the beasts of the field; one had the face of an ox, representing the cattle; and one the face of an eagle, representing the fowls of the air. Thus are the four great earth-tribes represented.

God created two other tribes, but these—the fish and the creeping things—were not brought to man to be put under him and to be named. So also in Genesis 9 you find in the Noachian covenant mention is made of "the fowls, the cattle, and the beasts of the field," but none of the other two tribes. Why this is so we cannot tell; but we may venture to think that, as sin entered through the medium of the serpent, and as in the new earth there will be no more sea, these two earth-tribes will disappear. The other four will never, however, be destroyed from the earth. Thus we have the first hint of the truth brought out by Paul in Rom. 8, when he says that "the creature itself also shall be delivered from the bondage of corruption into the glorious liberty of the children of God." The other sign is the rainbow—always present where the real cherubim are seen; and always appearing as a token of the covenant.

Now how did this covenant of God with Noah work? It was God's call to the world to arrange its government in accordance with Divine principles. We have two great instances of how the covenant was disregarded, and why God took away the power from man. These are, the rebellion of Babel, and the wickedness of the cities of the plain. Then came the election of Abraham and his seed, which, you know, failed. Then God determined to give the world another chance. He put the Gentiles in power again, choosing out the civilized race, to which He gave power over the rest of men.

That took place when God determined to destroy Jerusalem: and he signified it by a vision to Nebuchadnezzar. In that vision the king saw, as you know, a great image, with four distinct parts, and of four various metals, representing the four great world empires—Babylon, Medo-Persia, Greece and Rome.

Now, the gold, the silver, the brass, and the iron, and iron and clay represent different kinds of government.

God's Ideal of Government

is absolute monarchy; therefore gold, the most precious metal, represents it. Man, however, has never succeeded in finding a righteous king who can be trusted with absolute rule. God will send a righteous King ere long, then earth will know happiness and peace again.

The second metal is silver, representing the limited monarchy of Medo-Persia, based upon an hereditary aristocracy. Thirdly, we have the brass, the limited monarchy of Alexander, based upon a military aristocracy. Fourthly, the iron, the strong Roman government, supposed to be democratic government, but democratic only in name, as any citizen who dared to oppose the will of the emperor soon discovered. Lastly, we come to the clay, which is democracy and no government at all; but iron is mingled with it, though the two cannot cohere. Therefore the Roman Empire will never be a pure democracy.

In Dan. 7 the vision of the four beasts goes over very much the same ground. The great image, however, represents human power from man's point of view, while the beast shows it from God's point of view. The beast represents human power reduced to bestiality by sin. And at the close there is One brought in "like a son of man," as the original reads; that is, man as God originally made him. The Lord Jesus is the only man now in God's universe who has preserved manhood as God gave it. The earth belongs to the sons of men, and the one Son of Man who remains intact must have it. The four beasts represent the world powers; the bodies, the masses of the people; the horns, or heads, the rulers.

Now, passing on to Rev. 4, please to pay attention to the situation. The Book of Revelation is divided into three parts. And while the first part describes a vision with which we have at present nothing to do, the second is devoted to "the things that are," the third to "the thing which shall be after these things." These

Two Divisions of Time

correspond to the indefinite, or Church-period of Daniel's seventy sevens, in which John was living, and to the seven years of judgment which are to follow it. Rev. 2 and 3 are occupied with the first of the two periods, after which the Church is mentioned no more until we come to the epilogue of the Book; the description of the second begins with chapter 4. The Church is then understood to have been taken away, and the question is, Can God at once restore the kingdom to Israel? No; because He has given the power to the Gentile, and He cannot take it back again till the Gentile is proved to have broken his trust. In chapter 4 we see the cherubim before the throne, and the rainbow surrounding it. God is preparing to judge the Gentile in accordance with the Noachian covenant, and to take the power from him, and give it back to the Jew. How will He do this? In Isaiah 24 (one of the most wonderful chapters in the Bible) we read, "Behold, the Lord maketh the earth empty, and maketh it waste." The figure is appalling: God destroys the inhabitants of earth by His plagues as rapidly as one would pour water out of a vessel. Now, why is this done? In verse 5 we are told, "The earth is also defiled under the inhabitants thereof; because they have transgressed the laws, changed the ordinance, broken the everlasting covenant." Now in Gen. 9:16 we have in the Hebrew the same word used, "the everlasting covenant," for the covenant with Noah.

Then in Rev. 5 the result of the judgment is given. The beasts have broken the covenant; therefore power is taken from them, and given to "One like unto a Son of Man," who is placed on the throne, and in the succeeding chapters is seen subjugating the world.

HOW A LAWSUIT WAS AVERTED.

AMONG some recently published reminiscences of Abraham Lincoln is one of the time when he was a practicing lawyer in Springfield, Ill. It is stated that a slight quarrel arose between two farmers who had up to that time been friendly neighbors. The quarrel grew more heated as time passed, and at last both men saw that a lawsuit would have to be tried before the difficulty could be settled. One morning Mr. Lincoln was seated in his office, when one of the farmers came to enlist his services. Lincoln heard his story with a serious face, and at its close said: "Now, if you and B—— go on with this suit, it will cost both of you your farms, and will entail an enmity that will last for generations, and perhaps lead to murder. Now B—— has just been here to engage me. He is in the other office now. I want you two to sit down here while I am gone to dinner, and talk it over and try to settle it; and to secure you from interruption I will lock the door." He did so, and did not return all the afternoon. The two men, finding themselves thus imprisoned, burst into a hearty laugh, which was the prelude to an amicable conversation. Lincoln had given them both the same warning, and advised a settlement and they took his advice. When the future President lounged in in his ungainly fashion late in the afternoon, he was pleased to find that the only use the litigants then had for a lawyer was to embody in a legal shape the settlement they had made. Mr. Lincoln probably missed a large sum of money in fees, by what he did, but he must have enjoyed the grateful respect of the farmers; and he took his place among the peacemakers, that very small company on whom Christ pronounced a blessing. (Matt. 5:9.)

A CIRCUS-RIDER'S CONVERSION.

IN his newly published work "Thirty-five years Among the Poor," Mr. Joseph Emery relates the following incident: "About twenty-five years ago, while visiting the women's hospital, I found one, recently admitted, who was quite sick and emaciated; her face betokened a dissipated life. Our conversation took the following direction: 'You are quite sick?' 'Yes, I am.' 'Are you a Christian?' 'That is none of your business.' 'True, but it is important to you.' 'I don't want to talk to you.' 'Very well, I will leave you.' So I left the room, and prayed God to change her mind. On my next visit she was very penitent, and, with tearful eyes, asked me to forgive her, and to read the Scriptures and pray with her. This I gladly did.

"Her history was a strange and sad one. When but a child six years old, she was persuaded to enter Dan Rice's circus, and performed many wonderful feats on horses. During many years she followed the circus throughout the land. All religious thoughts were soon dissipated; the very life she lived was one of gaiety, excitement and folly. Overtaken by sickness and poverty, she was admitted to the Infirmary, where she remained some seven years. On my second interview, I asked: 'Did you ever read through the New Testament?' 'No; only a little bit of it when I was in Sabbath-school.' 'If I bring one, will you read every word?' 'Indeed I will, and thank you for it.' The next time a Testament was given her. She began reading it carefully, and felt she was a sinner, and soon learned that Christ came into the world to save sinners.

"Desiring to be baptized, she came into the city and united with the High Street Baptist Church, of which I was the acting pastor. This convert was the first I ever baptized in the Ohio River. After her baptism, Ellen returned to the Infirmary, living a consistent Christian life; shortly before leaving, sickness prostrated her, but she was happy, trusting in Jesus.

DEFECTIVE LIFE-PRESERVERS.

PUBLIC attention has been called to the articles on ferry-boats and river steamers, which are placed there in compliance with the law requiring boats to carry life-preservers. It is stated that in many cases they are life-preservers only in name. On a Michigan steamer which was inspected, the life-preservers would not buoy up a weight exceeding seventeen pounds. On a Boston steamer they sank with a weight of twenty-four pounds. Experiments in other parts of the country reveal similar carelessness or fraud. The life-preservers are filled with worthless black cork or sawdust, and any persons trusting their lives to them in a wreck, would be miserably disappointed. It is a remarkable fact, however, that these fraudulent articles are in nearly all cases new. The old life-preservers, which might have been expected to deteriorate with age and exposure, are generally what they purport to be, and are capable of supporting a human body in the water. It is urged, in defence of the companies who have been putting these cheap and worthless life-preservers on board their boats, that the articles serve their main purpose—which is the moral one of averting panic and giving confidence in an emergency. The best life-preserver, it is said, cannot prevent a person drowning after a certain time in the water, and the poor ones fail a little earlier—that is all. It may be hoped that the Government Inspectors will listen to no such specious excuses, but insist on the requirements of the law being fulfilled. It is a cruel mockery to lead people to rely on life-preservers which will fail them in the time of trial. In a far more serious matter, there is reason to fear that reliance is being placed on resources which will fail. When death's dark river is to be crossed, the voyager who is trusting to good moral character, to regular church attendance, or to self-righteousness in any form, will be grievously disappointed, and only they who trust in Christ alone will be safe and triumphant. (Acts 4:12.)

A SPOILED BUSINESS.

IT is unusual for a teacher of religion to speak of his work as "a business." It is possible that men may be found even in the Christian ministry who think of their duties as business, but who have too much regard for decency to speak of them in that way. It appears, however, that Buddhist priests in Japan are not so particular. The Rev. J. P. Hearst, writing to the *Church* from Osaka, describes a business offer made on avowedly business motives to the missionaries by the Buddhist priests. He says:

"The Buddhist priests, finding that the 'Jesus people' had come into their midst, continued their policy of contempt until we had rented a suitable house, made the necessary changes in it, and held a couple of services, when they awakened to the danger of their situation, and began at once a system of persecution against the man who rented us the building. But fortunately for us the Japanese laws recognize the right of a tenant to remain in a house as long as he wishes to do so, provided the rent is paid; so the landlord told the priest he could not dislodge us if he wanted to, and what was more, he would not if he could. Finding no encouragement in that quarter, they changed their tactics and came to us, and told us that the people of the neighborhood were very much troubled that we had opened a preaching place there, and that they would give us 'five hundred yen' ($375). I replied that I was not particularly attached to that house, and if they would get us another just as good in that neighborhood and give me the five hundred yen besides, I would be very glad to exchange. 'But,' said they, 'another house in that neighborhood would be just as bad as this one.' It was to get us out of the neighborhood that they were willing to pay. I replied that in that case I would remain where I was; besides, the people in the community did not seem to object, so far as I could see. Then they acknowledged that the people did not care, but that they, the priests, wished us out of that place, because *we spoiled their business*. I think that Christianity must have begun to hurt Buddhism by this time, or the priests would not have made that offer. It is the first thing of the kind I ever heard of their doing."

AN INDIAN ORPHAN FROZEN.

THE blizzards of the past month have occasioned many fatalities, which have been reported in the newspapers, and have aroused much sympathy. There has been, however, much suffering and death which has not found a record in type. The Rev. W. F. Re Qua reports one pitiful case. It is that of a little Indian girl, an orphan, who had found refuge with a Choctaw, at Kielizco. She was but half-clad, and the Indian could find her no place to sleep in but an out-house. It was cold and miserable, but the child was so desolate that it seemed a home to her. She crept in out of the bitter storm, on the evening of January 14, and lay down to sleep. Poor child! the sleep was her last. In the morning she was frozen stiff.

Mr. Re Qua says that there are many of these poor little Indian orphans utterly unprovided for. Their little pinched faces look up to him so wistfully, as they plead for shelter. Some kind readers of this journal sent him a few barrels of cast-off clothing, which he distributed, and since then he has made many acquaintances among the children, who, hearing that clothing was given away, came, hoping to be in time for a garment. Mr. Re Qua believes that a great work might be done through them. If a rough building could be erected, and furnished with a few common beds or bunks, a number of the orphan children might be collected there, and their lives saved and education given to them. Government aid might be secured, if it could be shown that the work was actually being done. The Roman Catholics have already availed themselves of this provision, and have established boarding and day schools in various parts of the Territory, toward the support of which the Government allows $231,880, and an additional sum for food and clothing. The school Mr. Re Qua has opened now contains twenty children, but this is a different affair from the orphanage he is desirous of establishing. The Lord has provided for him and his devoted wife so wonderfully hitherto, that they believe this enterprise of the Orphanage, which they have laid before Him in prayer, will surely be realized.

AN AFRICAN KING TESTED.

AMONG the candidates for baptism whose names were given recently to Bishop Ferguson in Africa, was that of a king. The Bishop, in a letter to the *Spirit of Missions*, describes the influence which overcame the aged king's better desires, and also expresses his opinion on a vexed question which is perplexing some earnest workers in the field. He says:

"The next day we went to a heathen village to visit King Tayu Segbe. Brother Vinton had enrolled his name among the candidates for baptism; he having expressed a desire for the same, and manifested considerable earnestness. A favorable circumstance, too, was the fact of his having but one wife at the time, which was quite unusual for a man of his position. On introducing the subject of his intended baptism, and questioning him in reference to the same, we discovered that his mind had undergone a change. When his intention became known, some of his chiefs and kinsmen protested against it, on the ground that it would be lowering the dignity of his office for him to renounce polygamy; besides, he would be regarded as a poor man who could not afford to buy wives; and, to make sure their aim, they had already procured another woman for him. The king yielded the point.

"What he and all others need, is to have the heart really brought under the influence of the Holy Ghost. Polygamy and every other fancied obstacle will then vanish from sight. To my mind, a greater blunder could not be committed than to declare polygamy no barrier to Christian baptism. I regard its abandonment as a sure test of that complete surrender which the law of Christ demands. Remove it, and we may be able to number converts by scores; but we would soon find that the heart which clings to this evil will likewise hold fast to other concomitant ones. Polygamy has never been a barrier to any really converted soul; but it has undoubtedly kept many false professors out of the Church. We may, without any risk, say to a would-be convert who refuses to obey the divine law of monogamy: 'Thy heart is not right in the sight of God.'"

A NORWEGIAN MISSIONARY HEALED.

IN the course of an address at Bethshan, published in *Thy Healer*, Mr. Nestigaard, who was on the eve of his departure as a missionary to China, said: "I wish to give a little testimony as to how the Lord has led me. His way, which is not ours, has been wonderful to me. It is four years ago since Jesus saved me. I was then a schoolmaster in Norway, but I did not know what it was to be born again. It could be said of me similarly to what was said of Nicodemus, 'Art thou a teacher, and knowest not these things?' But when I was in that state, a dear man came to the house where I was staying, and showed me how I must pray. I did then begin to pray and to weep for my sin, and I made up my mind that I would try as earnestly in future to do good, as I had been in the past to do evil. Then I felt myself getting poorer and poorer in my heart, and at last I had to cry out that I was lost. I kept on praying all that night, and in the morning I remembered the precious words, 'The blood of Jesus Christ, the Son of God, cleanseth from all sin,' and my sins were then washed away. I saw a picture in the 'Pilgrim's Progress,' and I thought that picture was mine; and when I came to the cross, my burden went away, and ever since then Jesus has been faithful to me. I have since then preached the gospel in Norway, and God has blessed me and given me many souls. I have had letters from some who were converted.

"It is two years ago since the Lord showed me He could heal me. I was very sick at the time. I could pray, but could not believe He was my Healer. I was in pain all night, and was very ill in the morning; so I thought I must go to a physician. I did so, and got to the house at eight o'clock. The servant said I must come at nine o'clock, as the physician would not be there before. The pain was then very bad, and continued so on my way home. When I got there I went to my little room and opened my Bible, and I accepted the precious promise from the Lord: 'I am the Lord that healeth thee.' I thought, If the other promises of God are true, this must be too," and the Holy Ghost came down upon me, and I was healed, and from that time I have never had a return of the pain. I have been sick once since; but I took it to the Lord, and He at once healed me, and now I know that I need no other physician."

CHRISTIAN HERALD AND SIGNS OF OUR TIMES.

OFFICE, 63 BIBLE HOUSE, NEW YORK.

ENTERED AT THE POST-OFFICE AT NEW YORK, N. Y., AS SECOND-CLASS MATTER.

Published Weekly. Subscription price, $1.50 a year; $1 eight months; 75 cents six months; sent two months on trial for 25 cents: always payable in advance. Single copies for sale by, or can be ordered at, all newsdealers.

Remittances by Mail should be by Post-office money order, bank cheques, or drafts or express money order, and should always be made payable to THE CHRISTIAN HERALD.

Receipts are not sent, the receipt of the paper by a subscriber is a sufficient proof that his remittance has been received. If the paper does not arrive promptly, please advise us, that we may see if the address is correctly entered.

Change of Address. Name of Post Office and State, of both old and new address, should always be given in case of removal.

CURRENT EVENTS.

Mr. Blaine's Letter Supplied Politicians Last week with an absorbing subject for speculation and debate. It called forth an endless variety of opinion. Mr. Blaine, writing from Florence, Italy, to the chairman of the Republican National Committee, said: "I wish, through you, to state to the members of the Republican party that my name will not be presented to the National Convention called to assemble in Chicago in June next for the nomination of candidates for President and Vice-President of the United States. I am constrained to this decision by considerations entirely personal to myself, of which you were advised more than a year ago." While some politicians accepted these expressions as a decisive and final withdrawal from a candidacy which was within Mr. Blaine's reach, others refused to regard it in that light. It was pointed out that Mr. Blaine merely stated that his name would not be presented to the Convention, and did not pledge him to refuse a nomination offered spontaneously, or by acclamation. Unless Mr. Blaine before the assembling of the Convention issues another statement, in which he definitely, and explicitly declares that he will not accept a renomination if it is offered, the Florence letter evidently will not prevent his being nominated. It will, however, relieve the convention of some embarrassment, and if after all it should decide on making Mr. Blaine again the standard-bearer of the party, the letter will relieve him of individual responsibility for the nomination. In that case he would stand before the country in the strong position of having sacrificed his own inclinations at the call of the party.

The Blair Education Bill Again Passed the Senate on February 15, but by a reduced majority. The vote this year was 39 to 29. In 1886 the majority was 22. The reduction is due both to change of opinion and to change in the personality of the Senate. Four Senators who voted for the bill in 1886, voted against it last week, and one who voted against it in the former year voted in its favor now, explaining the change by a statement that he had given his pledge to his State. Of the affirmative votes 23 were cast by Republicans and 16 by Democrats, and of the negative votes 12 by Republicans and 17 by Democrats. The bill appropriates $77,000,000 to be distributed in the States and Territories during the next eight years, "in that proportion which the whole number of persons in each who, being of the age of ten years and over, cannot write bears to the whole number of such persons in the United States." Seven million dollars is to be distributed the first year, ten the second year, fifteen the third year; then thirteen, then eleven, then nine, then seven, and finally five millions. The money is to be used for educational purposes only, and an extra $2,000,000 is appropriated for the erection of schoolhouses in sparsely populated districts. The objection urged against the bill by it opponents in Congress and the country is that the Federal Government has no right to interfere, even for the public benefit, in a matter which is constitutionally under the control of the State governments.

The New Tariff Bill on Which the House Committee are at work is not, it appears, to be a bill embodying the recommendations in the President's message. The commitee realize that such a bill could not be passed, and prefers to produce a compromise measure which would enlist the support of all Democrats, rather than a bill which would be so radical in its changes that Mr. Randall and his section would oppose it. A member of the Commitee said last week that "an effort had been made to ascertain the opinions of the Democratic members, to learn who wants to have duties reduced, who will resist reduction, and how much reduction can be undertaken without provoking so much hostility as to make it impossible to pass the bill. There is no desire manifested by any members to menace or impair the industries of the country, but there is well-settled belief that many of the interests referred to would welcome just the relief we shall try to give them." And so it comes about that as the House is "sounded," it is found necessary to make changes in schedules.

The Fishery Commission Charged with the duty of settling the dispute with Canada arrived at an agreement which was signed at Washington on February 15. It goes unto operation at once as a temporary settlement, and will remain in force until the Senate either ratifies or rejects it. No authoritative statement of its provisions was given to the public last week, as courtesy to the Senate demanded that it should pass upon it before publication. It is, however, believed to be in the main a concession of the claims made by the United States. The statement is made that the headland theory has been abandoned by the British and Canadian Commissioners, and that therefore Americans can fish in the bays three miles away from shore. Also that a commission will survey and define the limits in the smaller bays. American fishermen, however, are prohibited buying bait in Canada, though they may continue to touch and trade in other commodities, and may send their catch to the United States in bond by rail from Canadian ports, which is a privilege long desired but hitherto refused. If these are really the terms of the settlement, the United States have gained important concessions by the treaty, and we may hope that the Senate will ratify it, and so end the vexatious and irritating controversy.

The Gigantic Strike of Miners in Pennsylvania which commenced on January 3, was "declared off" on February 17, by a circular issued by the three Master Workmen, Lewis, Thompson and Renn, and Chairman Davis. The twenty thousand idle miners were therein notified that they might resume work on Monday, February 20. The basis of agreement on which this issue was reached was that the men go to work on the old terms of $2.50, that none should be refused employment for their connection with the strike, and that a conference between representatives of the Company and the miners should be held to arrange a scale of prices in accord with those being paid by other firms. These terms were declared unsatisfactory by several assemblies of miners, and the railroad men who are still out did their utmost to prevent acceptance of them. The majority of the miners, however, appear to be convinced that the railroad strike is hopeless and that further self-sacrifice is useless.

A Significant Admission by a Representative of the coal owners was made on February 16 to the Congressional Committee appointed to investigate the labor trouble in Pennsylvania. The witness was the general manager of the Reading Coal and Iron Company, and he was requested by the Committee to explain the allotment system. He said its object was "to restrict the output;" practically it amounted to an ascertainment each month of the probable demand for coal; then each section or system or operator was allotted to supply his or its share of this demand and no more. This share was in proportion to the capacity of such operator or company, as compared with the total capacity of all. Under this arrangement the Reading's share was from eighteen to twenty per cent. This allotment was made to prevent overproduction and keep up prices. He went on to say that the system was advantageous to the Company, and in reply to the question of how it affected the consumers, he said "*Oh, we did not consider the consumer.*" The chairman of the House Committee then said that the committee meant, if possible, to pass a law that would protect the consumer.

An Ominous Cloud has Arisen in Venezuela, which may involve a dispute between our Government and that of England, as Venezuela claims that the Monroe Doctrine of the United States entitles her to expect our assistance in a contention with so powerful an antagonist. The difficulty has arisen about the boundary between Venezuela and British Guiana. Venezuela has granted a concession for the construction of a railroad to the famous Yuruari gold mines, but the governor of British Guiana issued a proclamation forbidding the making of the railroad, and declaring that the ground over which it was to run was British territory. Since then he has sent a force of soldiers to the mines and formally asserted the British claims to them. As the investors have hitherto paid tribute to Venezuela that Government contends that her claim to the mines is clear, and has instructed her consul at Washington to lay a statement of facts before Mr. Bayard.

A Vigorous Debate on Irish Affairs, Occupied the British House of Commons last week. The Government was severely arraigned by Mr. Gladstone, Sir G. O. Trevelyan, Mr. O'Brien, and other leaders of the Home Rule movement. The most severe strictures were on the arrest of members of Parliament, and their treatment in prison. Mr. Balfour, the Secretary for Ireland, defended the Government. Referring to a remark which had been made, that it was a sickening thing for members of Parliament to be imprisoned, he said it was a sickening thing that they should deserve it, and it would have been much worse if the Government had given the leading violators of the law a special privilege to defy it with impunity. A childish fuss had been made over the prison clothes, which was hardly worth while noticing. Regarding the alleged tortures in the prisons, he requested the prison inspectors to make a special inquiry, with the result of showing that it was utterly untrue that there was any harshness in treatment. As a matter of fact, Mr. O'Brien's health improved in prison. The debate showed that there was no change in the attitude of the two parties.

The French Foreign Secretary has Disturbed the feeling of security which Bismarck and other statesmen have so industriously labored to establish. M. Flourens, who has been recently elected to a seat in the legislature, said in the course of one of his campaign speeches that since other nations were concentrating their military forces, it behooved France to do likewise. As Russia is the only disturbing element in Europe, and as her movements are those which have produced all the anxiety, the remark of M. Flourens is significant, because his strength in France consists in the fact that he is the most earnest advocate of a Russian Alliance, and the man most likely to bring it about. It now appears clear to political observers, as it is to students of prophecy, that the next war, when it comes, will be in the nature of a stupendous duel, in which England also will be engaged. The evasive answers of the English Cabinet to questions put to them last week, convey the impression that England is secretly pledged to support the triple alliance in the event of war.

Sunday-school Superintendents and Teachers desirous of distributing copies of THE CHRISTIAN HERALD in their schools and classes, may have assorted parcels of back numbers by applying, stating number required, to the manager, 63 Bible House.

Contributions to the Fund for Supplying Colored ministers in the South with this journal have been received since our last acknowledgment to the amount of $24.75. They were from: Philadelphia, Pa., $5; Cornwall, Conn., $1; Warner, Ill., $2; Jackson, Ont., $2; Boston, Mass., $2.50; Dundas, Ont., $10.50; Minneapolis, Minn., 50 cents; Syracuse, N. Y., 25 cents; Hamilton, Ont., $1. We are sincerely glad to receive these amounts, which will enable us to add to our list names of preachers who, as they state, need just the kind of assistance this journal affords.

Pastor C. H. Spurgeon has been Further Encouraged in his bold stand for orthodoxy by the receipt of a resolution of approval passed by the Wesleyan Reform Union. In acknowledging it, Mr. Spurgeon said: "I am unable to remain longer quiet when *the war is for the authority of the Scriptures* and the great doctrines of man's ruin, his redemption and the finality of the Lord's judgment. Being zealous for the old evangelical faith, I may speak too sternly against the enemies of the truth, and my words may seem unnecessarily sharp swords. We will together fight for the Word and the Gospel. We will bear our outspoken witness against this modern purgatory."

A Convention of the National Reform Association is to be held in New York in April next. The call summoning it is signed by Bishop Huntington, the Rev. Joseph Cook, Felix R. Brunot, the Rev. J. C. K. Milligan, the Rev. Dr. Crafts, the Rev. Dr. Taylor, Horace Waters, Prof. McAllister, Prof. MacCracken, and many other prominent persons. The object of the convention is to secure "the united effort of Christian patriots to maintain all our civil and religious liberties and institutions, and secure for them a more permanent legal basis." The dangers which the Association recognizes as demanding united effort are the increasing desecration of the Sabbath, the growth of the power of the liquor interest, the bitter and determined purpose of Liberalists, Anarchists and Socialists to overthrow our civil institutions, the constant and increasing influx of foreign ideas wholly opposed to the Christian Republic, and the growing tendency to license moral evils, as gambling, liquor selling and the social evil.

A Man Died while Getting Insured in the Office of a Life Insurance Company, in New York, on February 13. He had applied for a policy securing a thousand dollars to his family at his death, and called at the office on that day to complete the transaction. The preliminaries were arranged, and the medical officer was completing the physical examination, when the man staggered across the room and fell down in a fit of apoplexy. The doctor went to his assistance and administered ammonia and other restoratives, but without avail. In five minutes the man was dead. The remarkable fact was, that, though death was so near, the doctor had discovered nothing wrong with the man, and was about to endorse his application. In another half-hour the insurance might have been completed, but the man had delayed his application for it just a little too long, and, in consequence, his family is now just a thousand dollars worse off than they would have been had he applied to the company earlier. It may be hoped that he had not similarly delayed, until too late, a still more important preparation for leaving the world. Every man has the opportunity of making his peace with God through Christ, and those who postpone availing themselves of it, for a single hour, incur the awful risk of losing it by death (II Cor. 6: 2.)

The Sale of a Man for a Yoke of Oxen, is a transaction recalled by the death, on February 12, at Middletown, N. Y. of a colored man of remarkable intelligence and physical power. He was eighty-four years old when he died, was possessed of considerable property, and was much respected for his sterling Christian character, by the citizens of the locality, both white and colored. In his youth, and not long before the passing of the act of 1827, which provided for the manumission of all the slaves in New York State, he was sold for fifty-five dollars. The deed of sale, executed in due legal form, transferring the negro boy Frank to his new owner, is still in existence, and is treasured as a relic of bygone times. It records that on the consummation of the sale, the consideration was changed from lawful currency to a yoke of oxen. After he was set free, his owner gave him a furnished cottage, in which he lived until his death last week. He was the last survivor of the Orange county freedmen. It seems strange to us now to think that a yoke of oxen should ever have been deemed equivalent to the value of a man, though even now an ox or a horse often receives more care and attention from its owner than a man does from his employer. But the actual value of a man cannot be computed. We know, however, how high a value his Maker places upon him, from the fact that to save men, He gave His only begotten Son to suffer and die. (John 3: 16.)

A Singular Case of Mistaken Identity was described by a deputy sheriff who, on February 14, passed through Omaha, Neb., in charge of a prisoner. He said that his prisoner, a young man of twenty-five years of age, was one of twin brothers, who so closely resembled each other that even intimate friends were in the habit of distinguishing them by their dress rather than by their features. Five years ago he dressed himself one night in his brother's clothes and committed a robbery on a farmer, whom he beat almost to death. He wore a mask, but in the scuffle it fell off and he was recognized, with the difference that, having on his brother's clothes, it was his brother who was arrested and tried for the crime. He was sentenced to ten years hard labor, and the guilty brother actually allowed him to go to prison, while he went out to Nebraska and invested the proceeds of his crime in a share of a ranch. Happily a friend of the imprisoned brother suspected what had occurred and made investigation, which has resulted in the release of the innocent prisoner and the arrest of the real culprit. It is feared, however, that he will escape punishment on the plea that the law has already pronounced his brother guilty of the crime. That plea cannot avail him when he stands at the bar of God to answer for all his sins. It may be hoped that before that time he will repent and seek mercy. Even to so unnatural a criminal it will not be refused, if he plead for it in the name of Christ, the Elder Brother of our race, who suffered—the innocent for the guilty. (1 Peter 2: 22, 24.)

A Society Man's Discomfiture is Reported in the Boston *Times*. It states, that recently a young man, living on Beacon Street, feeling it incumbent upon him to make a present to a certain lady, yet having but little money to devote to the purpose, made a tour of the jewelry stores in search of an appropriate gift. He happened to be in a bric-à-brac store on Washington Street, when a valuable vase was accidently broken. "How much was that vase worth?" he asked. "Before it was broken the price was $200," was the reply. "What is it worth now?" "Why, not much of anything; it cannot be mended." "Well, I'll give you $1.50 for it." "All right." "Now please place the pieces together as nearly right as possible, pack it up, and send it with this card to Miss Z., No.— Marlborough Street." The young man departed in great elation; an elegant vase, at so slight a cost! Soon afterward he called upon Miss Z., presumably all ready to be surprised and grieved at the accident she would tell him had befallen his choice gift. "How do you like my present?" he casually asked in the course of conversation. "O," said Miss Z., "we have had such a laugh over it. There was a receipted bill enclosed for one *broken* vase, $1.50." The young man's confusion and shame may be imagined. Instead of getting credit in the lady's eyes for making her a handsome present, he stood before her a detected trickster of a peculiarly mean type. There are many persons who, like Ananias and Sapphira (Acts 5: 1-10) have the audacity to practice such tricks in the church. Sometimes they succeed in getting honor from men by false pretences, but they cannot deceive God who reads all hearts and who will one day expose all hypocrites and workers of iniquity. (Isa. 29: 15.)

A Marriage has Been Solemnized in the Ice Palace of St. Paul. The *Globe* of that city says: "Under the glare of several hundred electric lights, and amid the joyous acclaims of thousands of interested spectators, a young couple stood upon a carpeted platform in the grand court of the ice palace last evening to plight their vows in holy wedlock. This feature of the carnival has been looked forward to with great eagerness, by residents of St. Paul and visitors alike, and crowds eager to witness it flocked into the great court of the domain of Borealis. There was an absence of the elaborate toilets usually visible at matrimonial events inside a sacred edifice. Heavy woollen mittens and coverings of the same material for the ears and faces of the assemblage were conspicuous, and gayly attired tobogganers and snowshoers added to the picturesqueness of the brilliant scene. As the ceremony closed and the bride and bridegroom walked to their carriage, the vast assemblage joined in chanting the wedding march. The walls and turrets of ice formed a strange but significant surrounding for a wedding." The young couple will find that the world in which they will live can be just as cold as those walls, but like them it will pass away. Happy will they be, then if, as on their wedding day, they have a home to go to, but that will be a house not made with hands, eternal in the heavens. (II Cor. 5: 1.)

BRIEF NOTES.

David R. Locke, the author of the famous war letters signed Petroleum V. Nasby, died February 15.

W. C. T. U. work is progressing in Arizona; $3,000 have been subscribed to build a temperance hall at Phœnix.

Mr. Charles Herald has received a pressing invitation to labor on the Pacific Coast. The phenomenal success of his work at Cooper Union, New York, will, however, prevent his accepting it.

A Prohibition journal, published at Emporia, Kan., gives each week a list of the names of those who purchase liquor at the drug stores of that city, with the ailments for which they claim to use them.

Mrs. Cleveland is making a strong personal effort to establish a ward for contagious diseases in the Child's Hospital in Washington. There is no place in that city where a child suffering from a contagious disease can be taken.

A prize of $100 is offered by a New York merchant for the best essay on "Christ, our Nation's King," to be sent, not later than May 31, to Rev. R. H. M'Cready, 252 Broadway, New York. The conditions of competition may be obtained from Mr. M'Cready by sending a stamped envelope.

Messers. Moody and Sankey have concluded their work in Louisville, Ky. At the last service thousands of persons were unable to obtain admission to the huge tabernacle. A collection of over three thousand dollars was taken up for the mission, conducted by "Steve" Holcombe, a reformed gambler. This is a mission very much after the pattern of the Cremorne and Florence missions in New York.

A Week of Prayer is called for by a circular of the National Woman's Christian Temperance Union, to continue from March 18 to 25. Miss Frances E. Willard and Mrs. Caroline B. Buell, who sign the call, recommend that the meetings be held quietly in the usual places of meeting, and the prayers be for wisdom and power.

Mr. E. P. Telford concluded yesterday an eight weeks' mission in Lynn, Mass. The first four weeks were spent in the church of which Dr. Knowles is pastor, and the latter four in the First M. E. Church, of which Dr. Pickles is pastor. This latter is the oldest M. E. church in the State, having been founded by Jesse Lee in 1791. On Sunday next Mr. Telford commences a mission in Wilmington, Del. The results at Lynn have been of a most remarkable character, calling for deep thankfulness.

A remarkable revival has taken place in the University of Wilberforce, O. It commenced in a few lady students holding private meetings for prayer in each other's rooms, and it quickly spread through the university. Recitations were suspended, and a day of fasting and prayer appointed. The faculty took a deep interest in the movement, and assisted it to the utmost. Forty students have made a profession of their faith, and the number of professing Christians in the university is now ninety-eight per cent. of the whole number.

PARAMOUNT EDUCATION.

A New Sermon, by Pastor C. H. Spurgeon.

"And they shall teach no more every man his neighbor, and every man his brother, saying, Know the Lord, for they shall all know Me, from the least of them unto the greatest of them, saith the Lord; for I will forgive their iniquity, and I will remember their sin no more." Jer. 31 : 34.

Grace Work in Dark Dress—The Effect of Knowing God—I. The One Essential Knowledge—A Common Misinterpretation—An Acquaintance with Bismarck—What it is to Know God—Knowing Him and Knowing about Him—On Speaking Terms with Him—A Divinely Imparted Knowledge—Regulates the Life—Is a Distinguishing Characteristic of the Regenerate—II. How the Knowledge is Obtained—Sin Produces Estrangement on Both Sides—Its Removal a Revelation—The King's Recognition—God Seen in Christ—A Personal Revelation.

TRUE knowledge of God is a covenant blessing. To know Jehovah as the only living and true God, to know Him personally and intimately, so as to say with David, "Thou art my God"—this is one of the choice blessings of the covenant of grace which grace bestows upon all the chosen. In this prophecy, Jehovah declares that He will yet give this knowledge to the house of Israel and to the house of Judah; and this is our hope for the long-wandering seed of Abraham, whom He will yet restore and save.

If we regard the passage before us as instructive in its order, the knowledge of God follows close upon the application of the law to the heart. Read, "After those days, saith the Lord, I will put my law in their inward parts, and write it in their hearts; and will be their God, and they shall be My people . . . . and they shall all know Me, from the least of them unto the greatest of them, saith the Lord." The work of grace usually begins, so far as we can perceive it, by the Holy Spirit's bringing the law into contact with the inner man. The law outside of a man is forgotten; he may profess a reverence for it, but it does not affect his desires and thoughts. But when the Holy Spirit begins to put the law into the inward parts, the immediate result is the discovery of our shortcomings and transgressions.

Law-Work is Grace-Work

in its darker dress. It is the axe which rough-hews the timber which grace goes on to fashion and smooth. By the operation of the law upon the conscience, convincing the man of sin, of righteousness, and of judgment, the Holy Spirit works towards the transforming of the heart. He takes away the stone out of it, and makes it to be a fleshy, tender, sensitive thing. Then with His own finger He writes the divine law upon the mind and the affections, so that the divine commands become the centre of the man's life, and the governing force of his action. The man now loves that law which before he, at his very best, only feared: it becomes his will to do the will of God. By a miracle of grace his nature is changed, so that its tendencies, which were all towards evil, are corrected by new tendencies, which are all towards good. As the law is written on the heart, a manifestation is made of God Himself. The man is made to know himself, to know God's law, and thus he is led to know the Lord. Now he acquaints himself with God, and is at peace. Of this gracious knowledge of the Lord I am going to speak this morning.

I. To begin with, we have here, first of all,

The One Essential Knowledge.

It is a great truth that, "This is life eternal, to know Thee, the only true God, and Jesus Christ, whom Thou hast sent." To know God, is to live in the light. This knowledge brings with it trust, peace, love, holiness, and acceptance. Do not read this passage as some do, and tear it up by its roots, and then use it as if it were a prophecy of the universal spread of religion. Do not dream of a day when we shall not need to teach our brother and our neighbor the great truths of our holy faith: at any rate, the text before us says nothing of the kind. This prophecy is to be read as it stands.

In the first place, as we have already said, it relates to the house of Israel and the house of Judah. At the present time these have forgotten the Lord as to a true spiritual worship of Him; for they have rejected the Messiah, in whose face God's glory is seen: this nation is to be brought back to its best estate; both portions of it shall be converted, and shall come under a new covenant of a very different tenor from that which their fathers so wantonly broke. The Lord will

Gather the Remnant

of Israel under a covenant of grace, by which He will work in them those things which, under the old covenant, He justly required of them. Under this covenant of grace they are to have their hearts inscribed with His law; Jehovah is to be their God, and they are to be His people. Then shall they, in very deed, know the Lord as their fathers knew Him in the days of Elijah, when the fire fell from heaven, and they cried, "Jehovah, He is the God. Jehovah, He is the God." Whatever else these converts shall not know, they shall know Jehovah, "from the least of them unto the greatest of them."

Refer the passage to the spiritual Israel, as you justly may, and you learn that when God deals with men in a way of grace, and impresses obedience upon their nature, then they all know Him, from the least unto the greatest of them. The universality of the text extends to all those who come under the new covenant, and are renewed in heart; these without exception know the Lord, and there is no need that they be instructed upon that important point. These people know the Lord, and never can forget Him: henceforth they are no more strangers to Him, but sojourners with Him.

Let us consider this knowledge, that we may see what it is. And to begin with: it is emphatically the knowledge of God: "They shall all know *me*." They may not know everything about God. Who could? Who knows the Lord in that sense but the Lord Himself? Only the infinite can comprehend the infinite. The intellectual comprehension of the attributes of God is beyond us: how, then, could we grasp His essence? The regenerate, however, know the Lord, though they do not, and cannot, understand His incomprehensible glories.

Observe, that the prophet speaks not of knowing facts about God, nor truths as to what God is, or has done, or will do—it is

Knowing God Himself.

Do you not perceive the difference? I may know, and I do know, a great deal about a certain renowned person; say, if you please, Prince Bismarck. I have read his biography, and I think I have some sort of an idea of his personal character: thus I know something about him. But if you were to ask me, "Do you know him?" I should at once answer, "No, I have not even seen him, I have never spoken with him, nor written to him, nor held any other communication with him; and therefore I cannot say that I know him."

Now, if this solemn question were passed round these pews, "Do you know God?" how would you answer it? Many would reply, "We have read the Scriptures, and so we know the attributes of God, and we remember with great reverence all that God has done, and promised to do; but still we cannot say that we know Him. Can any one say as much as that?" Let me break up the question—Have you ever spoken with God? Did He ever speak with you? Believers can say, "Truly our fellowship is with the Father;" can you say *that?* Were you ever conscious of the presence of God? Has He ever manifested Himself to you in any special way? Alas! many a very knowing man must honestly confess that he does not know the Lord in the sense contained in my questions. Even among professing Christians this may be sadly true; even as Paul said to the Corinthians: "Awake to righteousness, and sin not; for some have not the knowledge of God: I speak this to your shame."

I put this question to each one. Hast thou ever spoken to Him? Is it the habit to open thy heart to Him? Dost thou tell Him all thy secrets? I mean by this nothing bordering on fanaticism or superstition; but in sober earnestness I ask—Is God real to thee? Is He as real to thee as she that lieth in thy bosom, or as the friend who walketh with thee by the way? Is the invisible God as real to thee as any person that thou canst see, as much as actual fact as any substance which thou canst feel? Has the Lord ever spoken to thy soul? I will not put any special question about the medium of that speech. It may be, He has spoken through this Book, or through His minister, or by "a still small voice" within thy soul—but has the Eternal One ever spoken with thee?

Are you on Speaking Terms

with your God? If not, you cannot be said to know Him; and if you do not know Him, you are not among the renewed in heart; for of them the Lord saith in this Scripture, "They shall all know Me, from the least of them unto the greatest of them." Note, dear friends, in the next place, that it is a personal knowledge. Each renewed person knows the Lord for Himself. You cannot know God except for yourself. If I am asked whether I know such a person, it would be idle to answer, "Well, my brother knows him." That would be an admission that I did not myself know him. So with regard to God. No second-hand knowledge can be admitted here. You cannot know God through other people. Personal religion, and individual knowledge of God, are indispensable. Come, my hearer, what hast thou to say to this?

Next, this knowledge is one which is wrought in us by the Spirit of the Lord. It is the duty of every Christian man to say to his neighbor, and to his brother, "Know the Lord." It is the instinct of a new-born child of God to try and tell out what he knows. God uses this effort as His instrumentality for saving men. But the man who really knows the Lord, does not know Him solely by such instruction. This may be the means used, but the knowledge obtained comes from a higher source than brother or neighbor. When Peter confessed Christ, you remember how the Lord Jesus said, "Blessed art thou, Simon Bar-jona; for flesh and blood hath not revealed it unto thee." You may know a great deal intellectually by the teaching of men; but heart knowledge, the knowledge which is peculiar to God's elect, you can never receive except by the teaching of the Lord.

There are many truths, beloved brethren, which I feel always bound to teach to you so long as I am the pastor of this flock; but if I had an unmixed company gathered here of regenerated men and women, I should not think of saying to you, "Know the Lord"; for I should be

Sure that You All Knew Him,

from the least even to the greatest. We assume the presence of this knowledge when we preach to God's people: we take it for granted that they know the Lord, and, therefore, we do not again lay this foundation. A godly man's life is such that we perceive that he knows the Lord. Mark him when he gets into trade. He might take an unfair advantage; but he scorns it. Does he not want money? Yes, badly. But he has respect to One whom others cannot see. By a word of falsehood he might profit largely; he will not speak it. Why? "So did not I, because of the fear of the Lord." All who have been renewed in spirit, and have had God's law written upon the fleshy tablets of their heart, manifest to a greater or less degree that they know the Lord, and therefore their brethren perceive it, and cease to teach them what they are sure they know.

Next, this knowledge of God is universal among the regenerate. It is not universal among the sons of Adam, for multitudes know not God, and have no dealings with Him! But all those who are under the covenant of grace know the Lord. The regenerate man with one talent knows the Lord; the man with ten tal ents boasts not of them, but rejoices that he knows the Lord. This is the distinguishing mark of the regenerate, they know the Lord.

God is our hope, our confidence, our expectation; but we can have no hope in an unknown God. The knowledge of God lies at the bottom of every virtue and grace. The Lord is no more to us a stranger of whom we have heard—of whom a report has come to us through many hands. No; the Lord God is our personal Friend. This, in a large degree, is true of all those with whom the grace of God has dealt, to bring them under His covenant, and to give them new hearts and right spirits—they all know the Lord, from the least even unto the greatest.

II. And this leads me to the second point, whereon I ask your earnest attention: the one

Means of Obtaining This Knowledge

of God. Here it is: "For I will forgive their iniquity, and I will remember their sin no more." Do you catch the idea? The clearest knowledge of God comes out of pardoned sin. The most distinct, vivid, assured knowledge of Jehovah comes to us when our iniquity is blotted out.

Just think a little. Without the pardon of sin it is not possible for us to know the Lord. We run away from Him; we do not want to know Him. Like father Adam, we hide away among the trees of the garden; we do not desire to see our Maker; for we have offended Him. The thought of God is distasteful to every guilty man. It would be good news to him if he could be informed, on sure authority, that there was no God at all. He cannot know God, because his whole heart and mind and spirit are in such a state that he is incapable of knowing and appreciating the Holy One of Israel. Darkness covers the mind, because sin has blinded the soul to all that is best and holiest. The lover of sin does not know God, and

Does Not Want to Know Him.

While sin lieth at the door, there is a difficulty on God's part, too. How can He admit into an intimate knowledge of Himself the guilty man, as long as he is enamoured of evil? Shall the great king entertain rebels? Shall two walk together, except they be agreed? "God is angry with the wicked every day." He is of purer eyes than to behold iniquity. Hence the guilty man is, by reason of his own impurity of nature, and by reason of the holy nature of God, shut out from all knowledge of God.

But, beloved, we now speak a matter which we have proved by experience—in the pardon of sin there is made to the pardoned man a clear and unmistakable revelation of God to his own soul. I venture to say that there is a clearer revelation of God to the individual in the forgiveness of his sin than can be found anywhere else. God is to be seen in nature. Who among us would wish to question it? Walk abroad, and look around you, and above you, and behold your God! But while men are under the dominion of sin, nature does not reveal God to them; their eyes are holden, and they will not perceive Him. The most eminent students of nature have some of them remained without

The Discovery of a God.

The same is true of providence. God comes very close to many men by preserving their lives from imminent peril, or by providing them with things necessary in the moment of great need; and yet we have known men living in the centre of wondrous providences, and they have only thought themselves lucky fellows, or clever persons, and so have traced God's mercy to chance or self. But let me tell you, if you have ever felt the guilt and burden of sin, and God has come to you and brought you to the Saviour's feet, and you have looked up and seen the great Sacrifice, and put your trust in Him, and the Spirit has borne witness with your spirit that your sins and your iniquities have been forgiven you—then you know the Lord with emphasis and beyond all doubt. In such discovery of the Godhead there is a joyful conviction, an absolute certainty, a more than mathematical demonstration. The knowledge of God received by a distinct sense of pardoned sin, is more certain than knowledge derived by the use of the senses in things of this life.

In the thirty-third chapter of the Second Book of Chronicles, let me read to you concerning Manasseh, who had shed innocent blood very much: "Wherefore the Lord brought upon them the captains of the host of the king of Assyria, which took Manasseh among the thorns, and bound him with fetters, and carried him to Babylon. And when he was in affliction he besought the Lord his God, and humbled himself greatly before the God of his fathers, and prayed unto Him: and He was entreated of him, and heard his supplication, and brought him again to Jerusalem.

Then Manasseh Knew

that the Lord He was God." When Jehovah pardoned him, then the great sinner knew that Jehovah was God. There is no evidence like it. Infinite mercy personally received is a demonstration of the Godhead. The church of God, when she was in her praiseful frame of mind, and full of joy, what think you was her song? Micah 7:18 gives it to us: "Who is a God like unto thee, that pardoneth iniquity, and passeth by the transgression of the remnant of His heritage? He retaineth not His anger for ever, because He delighted in mercy. He will turn again, He will have compassion upon us; He will subdue our iniquities; and thou wilt cast all their sins into the depths of the sea." Hallelujah! Who is a God like unto thee? We wonder more at the God of pardons than at the God of thunders. There is a more vivid apprehension of the Godhead in obtaining mercy than in beholding works of power.

Beloved, you must bear with me a minute or two while I speak upon this delighful theme. How a man sees God when he comes to know in his own soul the fullness of pardon intended by this matchless word, "Their sins and their iniquities will I remember no more!" Can this be so? Does the Lord make a clean sweep of all my sins? Can it be that the Lord has cast them all behind His back? Has He blotted out the record which accused me? Has He cast my sin into the depths of the sea? Halleiujah! He is a God indeed. This is a God-like act. O Jehovah! who is like unto thee? When I know my sin to be forgiven, I need no one to say to me, "Know the Lord:" the fullness of His pardon has made Him known. Oh, the splendor of redeeming love! Does not every soul that knows the mystery of the Cross know the Lord? Jesus says, "He that hath seen me hath seen the Father."

Brethren, do not forget the great love which, when the plan was struck out, provided the august person for the working out of that plan? "He spared not His own Son, but freely delivered Him up for us all." When I think that the God who was offended by sin was Himself the sufferer on its account, my thoughts of God are raised far above any height to which the interesting facts of science have elevated them. As I see God in nature, I reverence Him; as I see Him in providence, I adore Him; as

I See Him in Christ Jesus,

pardoning my sin, I know Him. If God deal with thee, my brother, and thou knowest Him, this is sure knowledge. Neither time with its lapse, nor suffering with its fret, nor doubt with its venom, nor death with its terrors, can take from you that certainty of faith which comes with the pardon of sin. If you do not know the Lord by His personal manifestation of Himself in pardoning your sin, I do not wonder that you are easily turned about by every wind of doctrine; but if you do know the Lord by His appearing to you in grace, you are beyond the short-range guns of the enemy. Our memories must fail us, and our senses must leave us before we can doubt the glorious Godhead of our Jehovah. We may be beaten in argument by the sophistries of the new theologians; but we cling to the facts of our experience, and cannot be parted from them. When the God of the Old Testament is decried, we glory in Him, saying, "He has pardoned my sin, and thus He has proved himself to be God indeed." Our opponents may turn round and say, "That is no argument to us"; we only reply, "We dare say it is not; but it is argument enough for us, and we must leave you to judge for yourselves. If you will not believe our testimony, we are clear."

May the Lord renew to our souls, from day to day, our sense of pardoned sin, and we shall be happily established in His faith and fear, whatever others may have to say. Oh, how I desire that all my hearers may seek and find this sin-pardoning God in Christ Jesus! Look to your Saviour hanging on the tree, bearing the curse, that you might be blessed. Look, I say, and you also shall know the Lord. The Lord help you: Amen, and Amen.

GEMS FROM NEW BOOKS.

An Asiatic Home in Trinidad.*

THE second morning after my arrival in Trinidad, my host took me to a Coolie village, three miles beyond the town. The drive was between spreading cane fields, beneath the shade of bamboos, or under rows of cocoa-nut palms, between the stems of which the sun was gleaming.

Human dwelling-places are rarely interesting in the tropics. A roof which will keep the rain out is all that is needed. The more free the passage given to the air under the floor and through the sides, the more healthy the habitation; and the houses, when we came among them, seemed merely enlarged packing cases loosely nailed together and raised on stones a foot or two above the ground. The rest of the scene was picturesque enough. The Indian jewellers were sitting cross-legged before their charcoal pans, making silver bracelets and earrings. Brilliant garments, crimson and blue and orange, were hanging to dry on clothes-lines. Men were going out to their work, women cooking, children (not many) playing or munching sugar-cane, while great mango-trees and ceibas spread a cool green roof over all. Like Rachel, the coolies had brought their gods to their new home. In the centre of the village was

A Hindoo Temple,

made up rudely out of boards, with a verandah running round it. The boards were locked. An old man who had charge, told us we could not enter. A crowd, suspicious and sullen, gathered about us as we tried to prevail upon him. So we had to content ourselves with the outside, which was gaudily and not unskilfully painted in Indian fashion. There were gods and goddesses in various attitudes, Vishnu fighting with the monkey god, Vishnu with cutlass and shield, the monkey with his tail round one tree while he brandished two others, one in each hand, as clubs. I suppose that we smiled, for our curiosity was resented, and we found it prudent to withdraw.

Contrast of Races.

The coolies are useful creatures; without them sugar cultivation in Trinidad and Demerara would cease altogether. They are useful and singularly ornamental. Unfortunately, they have not the best character with the police. There is little crime among the negroes, who quarrel furiously, but with their tongues only. The coolies have the fiercer passions of their eastern blood. Their women, being few, are tempted occasionally into infidelities, and would be tempted more often, but that a lapse in virtue is so fearfully avenged. A coolie regards his wife as his property, and if she is unfaithful to him, he kills her without the least hesitation. One of the judges told me that he had tried a case of this kind, and could not make the man understand that he had done anything wrong. It is a pity that a closer intermixture between them and the negroes seems so hopeless, for it would solve many difficulties. There is no jealousy. The negro does not regard the coolie as

*From "The English in the West Indies," by James Anthony Froude, the record of a journey of observation, containing many facts of interest and importance, with sage reflections. Pp. 373. Price $1.75; Published by *Charles Scribner's Sons*, 745 Broadway, New York.

The Palace of the Sultan of Zanzibar, on the East Coast of Africa.

a competitor and interloper, who has come to lower his wages. The coolie comes to work, the negro does not want to work, and both are satisfied. But if there is no jealousy, there is no friendship; the two races are more absolutely apart than the white and the black. The Asiatic insists the more on his superiority, in the fear, perhaps, that if he did not, the white might forget it.

THE PALACE AT ZANZIBAR.

(See Illustration.)

THE edifice used by the Sultan of Zanzibar as a residence, and which is dignified by the title of palace, stands on the island of Zanzibar, which is about twenty-five miles from the country of that name, on the east coast of Africa. The island forms the capital of the Sultan's dominions, and is by far the most valuable part of them. The whole territory of the Sultan of Zanzibar extends eleven hundred miles along the coast of Africa, from Magdashooa on the north to Cape Delgado on the south, and as far inland as he can make his power felt. Over much of the country, a hundred miles or even less from the coast, his authority is only nominal. The Island of Zanzibar, however, with another island named Pemba, and a third, called Monfia, are completely under his sway, and are populous and prosperous. The chief inhabitants are the Arab merchants and farmers, who possess numerous slaves, and live in Zanzibar as a convenient centre for trade; while the fertility of the island renders farming a pleasant and profitable occupation.

The Sultan maintains an army of about fifteen hundred trained soldiers, whose quaint garb is seen in the illustration. With these and a few guns he is able to keep up his dignity and authority, collect his revenues and live in the state which an Oriental potentate deems necessary. In any sudden emergency recruiting and conscription would speedily raise the army to a formidable power as the whole male population is hardy and active and composed of the best fighting material. The Sultan's name is Seyyid Bargash Bin Said. He succeeded his elder brother, Seyed Majid, who died in 1870, and who was the first independent ruler of Zanzibar, the country prior to his reign having been a dependency of Muscat. His income is estimated at half a million dollars annually. The trade of the country is considerable for its size and location. It exports annually goods to the amount of about four millions and takes in exchange mainly from England, arms, machines, etc., to the value of three millions. The Sultan is bound by treaty with European powers to suppress the slave trade, but it continues to be carried on doubtless with his connivance.

DR. HEYWARD'S SUCCESS.

(See Picture on page 125.)

"MOTHER, it is five months to-day since you came to Linborough," said Dr. John Heyward, looking up from his newspaper one morning at the breakfast table. "A very short time it seems, doesn't it?"

"Yes, my son; and a very pleasant five months as well," replied Mr. Heyward, smiling across the table at her boy. "This *was* the place for you, after all.

"Of course it was; and, mother, I was looking up my books last night, and do you know, I have made a good deal of money since I came; not bad for a beginner, eh?" said the young doctor, gleefully.

"Very good, indeed; especially as your practice is increasing every day," said Mrs. Heyward, in a very satisfied tone.

"I think I can afford a holiday now, mother," continued the doctor. "I believe I'll run down to Kingsmead: our dear old home, for a couple of days."

"Do so, my boy, by all means. I am sure you must be wearying very much to see Edith."

Only a few months before, Mr. Heyward, who was a clergyman, highly esteemed by everyone, had died, leaving his widow dependent on the generosity and proper filial feeling of his two sons, Philip, the elder, who was in business, and Jack, the physician, with whom she was now living. Yes, five months had sped rapidly and pleasantly for the inmates of the villa, and the young doctor was now an established favorite in Linborough. But Mrs. Heyward's thoughts just now were so full of Philip, her other son, that she sat down by-and-by to write to him. He had been very selfish and unfeeling toward his mother, leaving the responsibility of her protection entirely to his brother Jack, while with all his heart and soul he devoted himself to making money.

On Christmas eve, Doctor Heyward and his mother accepted the invitation of a patient, and an influential friend of the physician—a Mrs. Lynne, to join a Christmas party at Lynnsday. They had come early by request and none of the guests had yet arrived. They found Mrs. Lynne in the drawing-room. "Good evening, dear Mrs. Heyward," she said, "My husband has been out with his gun all day, and is late with his toilet, Doctor Heyward will you please to go down to the library for a few minutes? I have left something there, which I should like you to bring up."

Considerably mystified, Jack retired downstairs and opened the library door, and there sitting in the dim twilight, clad in delicate evening dress, was the girl the young doctor loved best on earth. Evidently, Mrs. Lynne desired to give him a most delightful surprise.

"Why! my darling Edith, is it you or your ghost?" he stammered, in the greatness of his surprise, and the next moment she was clasped to his heart. A faint flush trembled on eithe cheek, and on the broad white brow every blue vein was distinctly visible. Her eyes had ever been wide and bright, but now they seemed unnaturally large, unnaturally bright. Also there was a darkening shadow about them, which Jack's professional eye did not like to see, but he was too much delighted with her presence to allow forebodings of evil to find a footing in his heart that night. As he quitted the hospitable mansion with his mother, shortly before midnight, he said to Mrs. Lynne, "I will be over early in the morning for a professional call."

"But I am not sick, Doctor Heyward," she said. "You mean a lover's call."

"No;" said Jack, "I must see Edith professionally. I am afraid she needs the physician more than the lover. At any rate I will come prepared to act in either capacity."

"You will be welcome in either, Doctor," said his friend.

A sad, uneasy feeling filled the young physician's heart, as he drove away, his mother by his side. Edith had lost her own mother, and a dear sister, by that insidious foe to youth and loveliness, consumption, and now the danger-flag was fluttering in her cheeks. No wonder Doctor Heyward's heart sank, and he felt that all the professional success which seemed to be gathering before him would be like Dead Sea fruit, if Edith did not live to share it with him. He drove home silently, and having assisted his mother to alight, he re-entered his carriage and drove on a mile farther to see a patient whose life was trembling in the balance, and by whose side he intended to pass an hour or two of the night.

As Mrs. Heyward entered the home the housekeeper met her.

"Mr. Philip is here, ma'am," said Martha, when she opened the door. "He came at nine o'clock." In much surprise Mrs. Heyward hurried into the dining-room, and Philip rose, smiling slightly at her evident consternation. "You are surprised to see me, mother," he said. "I only decided to come to-day, so there was no time to write. How are you and where is Jack?"

"Seeing a patient," answered Mrs. Heyward, throwing aside her cloak, and drawing in her chair to the fire, for a talk. "Now tell me something about yourself," she said. "Jack and I were speaking of you to-day, and wondering what had become of you that you did not answer my letter. You look years older than you did in the summer. My son, why will you work so hard? Why struggle for wealth at the cost of health and every other earthly blessing?"

Philip replied, "There will be no need for me to work so hard now, Mr. Gooderich has died, and I am his sole heir."

Mrs. Heyward held up her hands. "Dear son, how extraordinary! I do not know whether to congratulate you or not, my son," she said at length, in tones which were almost sad. "Riches are sometimes a great blessing, sometimes the reverse. And they always bring with them many cares." Presently Mrs. Heyward rose and laid a tremulous hand on his arm, as she said: "Since this wealth has thus strangely fallen into your hands, Philip, see that you use it aright. God will require from you an account of the uttermost farthing. Use it to make the world a brighter place than it is. Then it will bring its own reward, for in blessing others you will be unspeakably blessed yourself."

Dr. John Heyward and His Mother.

But not so did Philip propose to use his money. It was to be the nest-egg, the beginning of a great fortune, and he had no intention of using it for any one's happiness but his own. He sat still long after his mother left him, building castles in the air, and picturing himself the owner of many millions, controlling railroads, and vast financial enterprises. So he was sitting when his brother returned, and the two greeted each other and sat down to discuss the future.

It was all hidden from them then, but if they could have pierced the veil, they would have seen each other without recognition. Philip hard, selfish, rich; Jack toiling a medical missionary in a heathen land, looking forward to the time when his labor done he would enter heaven through the merits of Christ where he once more would see the angel girl whose influence had led him to sacrifice fortune and fame for Christ's sake.

MRS. TRANSOME'S PUPIL,

A SERIAL STORY.

How The Pupil Came.

If it would do anybody good to hear my story, they are welcome to it; ay! kindly welcome. I'm too old now to be of any use as a guide; but maybe I can still be useful as a finger-post, that points the way folks should follow.

I married out of my country; my people said, out of my station. For my father held a small farm, and the squire's lady had seen that I learned to read and write, and do fine sewing; but my husband was only a handloom weaver from the north, a man that could weave and sing right well, but never cared much for the inside of a book. But he was true and faithful to the backbone, till I learned from him something of his faithfulness, and knew it was the same as Abraham's, who was called the father of the faithful. Words that were always on his lips were, "Faithful in little, faithful in much;" and it seems to me, now he is gone, those words are my chief comfort. Wherever Transome is, he is faithful still.

It was a daring thing to marry so far away from one's own people in those days. There were no railroads, and the coaches were too dear for us, even the outside of them, where in the summer you were covered with dust and parched with thirst, and nipped with frost and wind in the winter. Transome and me did not once think of taking the coach after we were wedded. The canal ran almost straight from my village to his; and though the journey took us the best part of three days, and he was winning no money, it was the cheapest way of travelling. It seems to me, when I shut my eyes and think of it, as if it had all been in some other world, when Transome and me were young, and the warm sunny days were full of light and brightness, such as the sun never gives nowadays, as if the sun itself is growing old.

The boat floated slowly, slowly along the canal, while we walked together till we were tired, gathering the blossoms from the grassy banks, or sat on the boat, plucking the water-lilies up by their long roots. How gently we were rocked as the water rose beneath us in the locks! I can hear the rush and gurgling of the water now! And with my dim old eyes shut, I can see Transome looking upon me with a smile, such as I shall never more see again, till I behold his face on the other side of death's dark river, smiling down upon me as I reach the shore. Ah! there are no times now like those old times!

It was in the cool of the evening he brought me to his house, standing on the brow of a low hill, with what he called a clough, and I called a dingle, full of green trees and underwood, running down to a little sparkling river in the valley below. We could see far away from the door, and feel the rush of the fresh air past us, as it came over fields and meadows, and swept away to other fields and meadows. The cottage was an old one even then—built half of timber, with a thatched roof pitched very high and pointed, and with one window in it to light our up-stairs room. Down-stairs was one good-sized kitchen, with a quarried floor, and the loom standing on one side. Not a bit of a parlor or spare chamber, such as I'd been used to. I knew Transome thought often of that; but the place grew so dear to me, I ceased to care about any parlor.

As for the garden, we worked in it all our spare time, till many a passer-by would stop to look at the honeysuckle, and the travellers'-joy climbing up the wall, and hanging over our window in the roof; and at the posies in the garden, the hollyhocks and roses, and sweetwilliams, which made the air all sweet with their scent. After a while, when father and mother were dead, I forgot my old home; and it seemed as if I had never dwelt anywhere else, and must dwell there till the end of my days. Nothing happened to us; nothing save the birth, and the short, short life of a little child of ours, our only child, who died when he was seven years old, and could just read to his father at the loom.

It was that year the sky began to grow grayer and the wind to blow more chilly about the house. Transome was ten years older than me, and he began in some way to feel his age, now the boy was gone. And as time went on things became duller and duller; and his rheumatism grew worse and worse, till he had to give up his loom, and at last he could do little more than work out the rent by being odd man for our landlord, who knew he could trust him with untold gold.

But all this while the country-side was changing even faster than Transome and me. The railroads had been made, and machinery invented, and all the little villages were turning into towns as if by magic. There had always been a few mills along the course of our little river, but every year more and more sprang up with their tall smoky chimneys, and streets were made, and houses built, until the dingle itself became a row of straggling cottages, creeping up towards our pretty homestead. Perhaps it was because I belonged to another country, and spoke in a different fashion, but none of the country folks about there ever took heartily to me, and I always felt shy with them and their rough ways. Transome himself was a quiet man, and never cared to make many friends; so we dwelt like strangers among our neighbors, up in our thatched cottage, which was as different from the new red brick houses about it as we were to the factory people living in them.

But I never felt strange with children, nor they with me. So when Transome was laid up from his work, I opened a little dame school for the lads and lasses living in the houses down the dingle. They soon flocked to me like chickens at the cluck-clucking of an old mother hen, till I might have filled my kitchen twice over. But my outside number was thirty, and as they paid me, Transome and I managed to get along—what with him working out the rent, and me taking in fine sewing from the ladies of the town.

Transome was always proud of my learning, and now he was glad for me to earn money in that way, instead of by washing, as many a woman has to do when her man is ailing. But he did not like little ones as I did; they pottered him, he said, and he never knew how to manage them. So after a while whenever he could not go to work, he liked better to lie abed upstairs, till the evening school was over, than sit in the chimney-nook listening to the hum of their lessons, which always sounded in his ears like a score of hives swarming. I used to be afraid he would be dreary and sad in those long days, while I was as busy as could be downstairs. But he said he had thoughts come into his head that he could not put into words, for he had always been a man of few words, fewer than any I ever met with, and as he got older they became fewer still. Maybe he'll know how to tell me those thoughts of his when we meet in heaven.

I have only one thing to tell you about my little school; the only one strange thing that happened to me all the years I kept it.

It had been a sharp frost in the night, so sharp that the panes in the window, little diamond-panes, were frosted over with so many pretty shapes that I almost wished they could stay there always. I quite wished that the children were there to see them. When I opened the door all the great, broad sweep of country stretching before me was lightly powdered over with snow, and long icicles hung like a ragged fringe to the eaves. If the dingle had been there, how sparkling and beautiful every tree and shrub would have shone in the early light! But the last bit of the dingle was gone, and a new, red brick house stood at the end of our garden. Still, the low bushes about our place were silvered over, and glittered in the frosty sunshine, which they caught before it reached the houses below.

I had overslept myself that morning, for the night before I'd been poring over a book that had been lent me, till my candle burned down in the socket, and left me in the dark. I could not put that book down; it stirred my heart so. But now I began to feel as if I'd been wasteful, for candles were not plentiful with us, nor money to buy them, though I was loath to blame myself. At any rate I was behind time, and I could not tarry at the door but must hurry more than usual in getting breakfast over and redding up the kitchen in time for school. Inside the house the place seemed dark and dreary, and everything was cold to the touch of my fingers. I began to think of how ailing Transome was, and how the frost would bite him. He had not been to work for a fortnight, and the rent was running on all the while. The rent was my heaviest care. As long as that was paid, it did not matter much to me what I had to eat and drink, so that we made both ends meet, and kept out of every man's debt. But Transome's pains had been very bad all night; and I knew well he could not go out in such a bitter frost, if the rent was never paid.

Well! I was down-hearted that morning; and I felt as if I could not afford to put more than a spoonful and a half of tea in our little black teapot, which stood simmering on the hob. I'd been in such a glow over that book the night before, it seemed as if it made me all the lower that morning. I had wanted to be doing some good in the world; trading for the Lord, so as to offer Him something more than my mere day's work, which seemed to be all for myself and Transome. But now the glow was gone, I felt what a poor old creature I was, and that I could do nothing at all extra for Him.

"Ally!" I heard Transome calling from the room up-stairs, "are yo' asleep again? Aw'm fair parched wi' drought."

The floor between that room and the kitchen was nothing but boards and beams, so I could hear if he only turned over in bed. I had no need to stir from the fire to answer him; I only raised my voice a little.

"Coming, coming in a minute," I called back, "the tea's in the pot, and's only standing to get the strength out."

"Aw nivir see such a lass for a book," I heard him mutter to himself; "hoo forgets all when hoo has a book."

That was quite true. But hearing him say it to himself, and he in such pain, was ten times worse than if he had rated at me. Ay! I'd been selfish, all in my glow of wishing to do good in the world. What better good could I do than attend to the duties the Lord had given me? He had given me Transome to nurse, and take care of, and wait upon, and I'd set up late into the night, and overslept myself in the morning, while he was parched with thirst and racked with pain. Then there was the school; and the clock was pointing to not far from school-time, and me nothing like ready. If I could not fulfil these little duties, how could I ask the Lord to set me a greater one?

I poured out Transome's tea, and carred it up-stairs. He did not seem in the best of tempers. But I took no notice of his contrariness: for how could he be cheerful when he could not lift his hand to his mouth, and I had to feed him with every morsel and every sup he swallowed? At last he smiled upon me, a very little smile, and bade me go down to my own breakfast. I had hardly time to eat it, before my scholars came trooping up from the dingle: the mischievous little urchins bringing with them icicles hidded under their jackets, which soon melted and trickled down in pools on the floor. I had need of patience that morning.

After the water was well wiped away, I sat down behind my table in the chimney-nook, with my Bible and a Catechism, a Hymn-book and a primer before me. There were four benches across the floor, besides a small one at the end of the loom, where I put my best scholars, because they were out of my sight there. All were full, till there was scarcely elbow-room; and much care and thought it gave me how to scatter the most troublesome of them among the good ones, like the tares and the wheat growing together until the harvest. Not but that I could have picked out the tares well enough; but I knew it would never do to let them all congregate together. Maybe the Lord knows it is better for the wicked themselves to be scattered about among the good; so I set the tares about side by side with the wheat, but kept them all where I could have my eye upon them.

The snow was beginning to fall pretty thickly, with large, lazy flakes drifting slowly through the air, for there was no wind, when a boy near the door all at once broke in upon a spelling-class, that stood in a ring before me.

"There's somebry knockin' at th' door," he said, in a loud voice.

It must have been a quiet knock, for I had not heard it; but then my hearing was not as quick as it used to be when I could hear t bubbling of the river below the dingle. Besid the lads and lasses were all humming their tasl I told the boy to open the door; and he jump up briskly, glad to put down his lesson-book, only for a minute. Still, when the door w open I could see nothing but the large flak floating in, and the children catching at them

"Eh! but he's a gradely little chap!" cri the boy at the door in a tone of surprise.

"Tell him to come in," I called, bidding t class make way for our visitor.

Well, well! I never saw such a beautiful b before nor since. He was about seven, b rather small and delicate for his years. His e were as blue as the forget-me-nots that used grow along the river-side; and his brown h was sunny, as if it had a glory round it. Som how, I thought all in a moment of how the Lo Jesus looked when He was a blessed child earth. The little fellow had on a thin, threa bare sailor's suit of blue serge—so thin that was shivering and shaking with cold, for t snow had powerdered him over as well as eve thing else. He looked up in my face half sm ing, though the tears were in his eyes; and l little mouth quivered so he could not speak. held out my hand to him, and called him to in my softest voice, wishing it was as soft as used to be when I was young.

"What are you come for, my little man?" asked.

"I want to come to your school," he said, most sobbing; "but I haven't got any mone and Mrs. Brown says you'll not have me wi out money."

"Who is Mrs. Brown?" I asked, feeling heart strangely drawn to the child.

"She's taking care of me," he answered, " father comes back. Father'll have lots money when he comes home. But he's be away a long, long while; and nobody's kind me now. Sometimes Mrs. Brown says I m go to the workhouse. Father brought me parrot last time he came; but it flew away c night while I was asleep, and nobody ever it again."

I felt the tears start in my own old eyes as spoke, and all the scholars looked to me a there was a mist in the room.

"Poor boy!" I said. "And where is mothe

I might have spared him the question if I h thought a moment. His little mouth quive more than ever, and the tears slipped over eyelids, and ran down his cheeks.

"Never mind!" I said hastily, and draw him near to me, closer and closer till his c little head was on my bosom, "you shall c to school, my little lad."

Yet before the words were off my tongu began to wonder how it could be manag There was not a spare inch of bench, not e at the end of the loom, where my best scho sat. Only the day before I had refused stea to take in a boy for fourpence a week; ay! pence a week his mother offered me if I w only have him, and keep him out of misc Besides, there was Transome laid up, and rent running on, and sixpence a week ready me if I'd take it. Still, it would cost me n ing to teach the child, and it came across m if the Lord was saying, "This is what you do for me!" Yes, this was the extra wo had set me to do. After that, if anybody offered me five shillings a week to send child away to take another, I could not done it.

"I'll be sure to pay some day," said the anxiously; "when you've taught me to w I'll write and ask father to come home qui He went away in his ship a long while but he's sure to come home if I write hi letter. So I want to make haste and learn. I begin this morning?"

"You shall begin very soon," I answ ready to laugh and cry together at his way, and his belief that his father would back if he could only write him a letter. " me what your name is."

"My father's Captain John Champion," he aid, lifting his little head proudly, "and my ame's Philip; but father calls me Pippin, and ou may, if you like. Mrs. Brown calls me all orts of names."

"Creep in here, Pippin," I said, making a lace for him close beside me in the chimney-ook. There was barely room for me to stir; ut the little lad kept so still and quiet, with is shining eyes lifted up to me, and his face ll eager with hearkening to what I was teaching the other scholars that I did not care about eing crowded.

(To be Continued.)

CHRIST'S LAST JOURNEY TO JERUSALEM.

By Mrs. M. Baxter.

S. S. Lesson for March 4, Matt. 20:17-28. Golden Text, Matt. 20:28.

Ver. 17-19. A momentous Journey—Going Among Powerful Enemies—Christ Warns them of the Consequences—Knew He was Going to an Ignominious Death—A more Explicit Intimation of His End than the Last (Matt. 17:22) Given Six Months Earlier—Ver. 20-22. Salome a Sister of the Virgin Mary—Imagined His Kingdom would be Earthly—A Painful Request to Jesus on His Way to His Death—The Spirit of Selfish Rivalry—Ver. 23. Suffering Promised—Ver. 24-28. The Way to Eminence in Christ's Kingdom—Christ's own Exaltation Reached through Sacrifice.

PETER was a great bargainer. Jesus, in calling im, held out this inducement to him, and his rother Andrew, "Follow me, and I will make ou fishers of men." (Matt. 4:19.) Peter sought o bring the Lord to terms as to how often his rother should sin against him and he forgive im; and Peter it was who said, "Behold, we ave forsaken all and followed thee: *what shall e have*, therefore?" In Peter's renunciation of ll, there was still an anxiety to know what hould be the outcome; he had an eye to whether it was a safe investment, whether it ould answer in the long run, and so, in order o make sure, he asked:

"What Shall we Have, Therefore?"

esus answered, that they which followed Him, hould reign with Him, "joint heirs with Christ, f so be that, we suffer with Him:" "If we suffer, we shall also reign with Him." (Rom. 8:17; 1 Tim. 2:12.) But was Peter following Him? esus teaches us to "do good, and lend, hoping or nothing again" (Luke 6:35), and to repudiate the thought of any recompense on earth. Luke 14:12-14.) And while those who have rsaken any one or anything for *His* sake, shall ceive an hundred-fold; yet this reward is not ven to those who renounce anything for the ke of what they can get. In Peter's heart re was some thought of merit, some idea of much work or so much self-denial for so ch gain, and so much eternal reward.

So Jesus continued, "But many that are first ll be last, and the last first. *For* the kingm of heaven is like unto a man that is an uscholder, which went out early in the morn- to *hire* laborers into his vineyard; and when had agreed with the laborers for a penny a , he sent them into his vineyard." This was market-price of labor in that day, and the gain was a fair one on both sides. But it a bargain, a transaction in which each ght his own interest, and bound over the r to consider it. It was just on a par with r's question; it savored of the spirit of es unions, where class seeks to defend itself nst class, and to secure its own advantage. men who deal with men, as such, these gs may be necessary; but how little Peter erstood the heart of Christ when he introd this principle into his dealings with Jesus! little any one of us understands God's t when we apply this principle to our an s to prayer, when we say, "I have prayed believed as well as I knew how; I have all I can; what shall I *have*, therefore? not deserve to be answered? Is not God d to do what I ask Him?" And all the time the expectation in our hearts is grounded on what *we* are, what *we* do, and what amount of faith *we* render to God, rather than on what *He* is, on the faithfulness of *His* promises, and the riches of *His* grace toward us. There is so much of the bringing of God to terms, the driving of bargains with Him, the seeking to

Secure Our Own Interests,

that we don't give Him the chance to show how large is His heart of love toward us. He does not save us for the value of our repentance and our prayers, needful as they may be, but out of His own wondrous, measureless grace. He doesn't sanctify us because of the value of our consecration, needful as it is, but out of His own tender love; for it is His grace, and not our holiness, which keeps us from falling. He does not heal our bodies because of the intrinsic value of our faith, but because He "took our infirmities, and bore our sicknesses," and so secured us healing and health by grace, and not by merit. If we bring God to terms, and agree with Him for a penny a day, we shall get all we bargain for, but no more.

At the third hour, the sixth, and, once more, at the ninth hour, the householder went again into the market-place in his search for laborers, but none of them brought him to terms. "Go ye also into the vineyard, and whatsoever is right, that shall ye receive." This was all he said on the wages question, and the men trusted him, and were satisfied. Such trust might not answer with an unprincipled employer of labor; but is God unprincipled? Is He mean and miserly? Dare we not trust Him, and throw ourselves on the generosity of His great heart? At the eleventh hour the householder went again into the market-place, and found laborers standing idle, and on questioning them as to the reason, he received the answer, "Because no man hath hired us." O, how many wait for man's call to do God's work! How many fear to become missionaries without a university education! True, for the translation of the Scriptures and for advanced education, such a preparation may be needful, but for the simple preaching of the gospel, surely the anointing of the Holy Ghost and a thorough knowledge of the Word of God are the requisites; and surely we are now in the eleventh hour of this dispensation, and God is calling hundreds who have not been called of men, and is sending them into the vineyard!

The evening came, and with it the time for payment. The order of the householder was, "Call the laborers, and give them their hire, beginning from the last unto the first."

The Last First!

Was this just? Not if the householder had dealt with them on the ground of merit. But he dealt in grace. The eleventh-hour men received "every man a penny"—the very same sum for which the first-hour men bargained. The first-hour men thought within themselves, "Surely, if he is so liberal to those who have deserved nothing, he will be much more so to us!" But when their turn came, they received also every man a penny. They murmured, and were ready to go out on strike. But they had received all they bargained for—a fair day's wages for a fair day's work. They argued the point, "These last have wrought but one hour, and thou hast made them equal unto us which have borne the burden and heat of the day." "Equal unto us." They thought themselves superior to the eleventh-hour men, and all the pride and self-esteem of their nature rose up against being thought equal to the last-chosen workmen. Have none of us known this feeling of almost injustice in God when we have known prayer wonderfully answered to those who have known the Lord only a little time, and who have gone through none of the persecution which some of us have known? How we need to be confirmed in our knowledge of God's wondrous grace!

Jesus was about to take His last journey to Jerusalem, and, for the third time, He told His disciples of His coming sufferings Yet so little effect did it take upon them that, at the very time when He was occupied with this theme, the mother of two of them came to Him, with her two sons, to urge the request that they should be preferred to the highest honor in His kingdom. Did all His teaching go for nothing? Had He not just shown them that the first should be the last and the last first? Yes; but "the things of God knoweth no man, but the Spirit of God." (1 Cor. 2:11.) On the day of Pentecost all became clear, but as yet they were carnal and walked as men. (1 Cor. 3:3.)

All their Conceptions were Earthly,

and not heavenly. Yet Jesus did not lose patience with them; He only said, "Ye know not what ye ask. Are ye able to drink of the cup that I shall drink of, and to be baptized with the baptism that I am baptized with?" In their blindness and self-confidence "they say unto Him, We are able." They thought so, but how soon those very men "forsook Him, and fled!" Yet Jesus bore with them, and said, "Ye shall drink indeed of My cup, and be baptized with the baptism that I am baptized with; but to sit on My right hand and on My left, is not Mine to give, but it shall be given to those for whom it is prepared of My Father." These two disciples, James and John, did drink of His cup of suffering in persecution and death, and were baptized with His baptism of blood, when James was slain by Herod (Acts 12:2), and John, as tradition says, was cast into a tank of boiling oil.

When the ten remaining disciples heard of this request, they were indignant against James and John. "Who are *they* that *they* should have the pre-eminence?" "What have they done to merit such distinction?" Such were the thoughts which burned within them. "But Jesus called them unto Him." O, there is an atmosphere close to Jesus in which indignation dies, and bitterness flees away; only love can live near to Jesus. He gently explained matters. "Ye know that the princes of the Gentiles exercise dominion over them, and they that are great exercise authority upon them. But it shall not be so among you: but whosoever will be great among you, let him be your minister; and whosoever will be chief among you, let him be your servant; even as the Son of man came not to be ministered unto, but to minister, and to give His life a ransom for many." Jesus' greatness is in His love and self-sacrifice and mercy. Man's nature finds no difficulty in exalting itself, there is no greatness in that; but he who comes, like Christ, to minister and to give himself, is great in God's sight, for he is Christ-conquered, and the self which seeks to bargain with God has been displaced in him by the Christ who gives Himself. Man loves to rule, Christ came to minister; man loves to get, Christ came to give; and it is just in proportion to our appreciation of God's loving care for our interests that we shall find it easy, natural, to give all we can and all we have unreservedly to Him, that the question "What shall we have?" will cease; our interests are more than safe with Him. The question now is, "How can I rightly follow Him?"

THE VALLEY OF SILENCE.

In the hush of the valley of silence
  I dream all the songs that I sing;
And the music floats down the dim valley,
  Till each finds a word for a wing,
That to hearts, like the dove of the deluge,
  A message of peace they may bring.

But far on the deep there are billows
  That never shall break on the beach;
And I have heard songs in the silence
  That never shall float into speech;
And I have had dreams in the valley
  Too lofty for language to reach.

And I have seen thoughts in the valley,—
  Ah me! how my spirit was stirred!
And they wear holy veils on their faces,—
  Their footsteps can scarcely be heard;
They pass through the valley like virgins,
  Too pure for the touch of a word.

Do you ask me the place of the valley,
  Ye hearts that are harrowed with care?
It lieth afar between mountains,
  And God and His angels are there:
One is the dark mountain of sorrow,
  And one the bright mountain of prayer.

Selected.

CATALOGUES RECEIVED.

W. ATLEE BURPEE & CO.—Illustrated Farm Annual for 1888, of Vegetable and Flower Seeds, containing handsome colored plates, and full of valuable information as to the latest novelties in the seed line. It is mailed free on application to W. Atlee Burpee & Co., Philadelphia, Pa.

ROBERT SCOTT & SON.—Catalogue of Roses and other beautiful flowers, profusely illustrated with colored plates, and containing full description of all the latest novelties. Sent free on application to Robert Scott & Son, Philadelphia, Pa.

J. ROSCOE FULLER & CO.—Catalogue of Flower and Vegetable Seeds, sent free on application to J. Roscoe Fuller & Co., Floral Park, N. Y.

Vol. XI., No. 9. Office, 63 Bible House. N. Y. THURSDAY, MARCH 1, 1888. Annual Subscription, $1.50.

CONTENTS OF THIS NUMBER.

PORTRAITS AND LIVES OF REV. L. D. BEVAN, D.D., of Melbourne, and SIR H. PARKES, of Sydney, with Pictures.
THE GRANDMOTHER. Dr. Talmage's Sermon Last Sunday Morning to Women.
THE JUDGMENTS OF THE SEVENTIETH WEEK. By G. H. Pember.
Dr. Talmage on Hot Axles—The work of a Japanese Jailer's Wife—Boycotted Missionaries—A Moravian Missionary's Testimony.
HOLDING FAST THE FAITH. A New Sermon by C. H. Spurgeon.
PICTURES OF THE MARKET IN BAGDAD.
RIVER GARDENS IN CHINA. (Illust'd.)
MRS. TRANSOME'S PUPIL. (Continued.
CHRIST ENTERING JERUSALEM. By Mrs. M. Baxter.

SYDNEY, NEW SOUTH WALES, AS SEEN FROM PYRMONT.

BOURKE ST., MELBOURNE, AUSTRALIA

Rev. L. D. Bevan, D. D., of Melbourne (late of New York)—Sir H. Parkes, Premier of New South Wales.

REV. L. D. BEVAN, D.D., LL. B.

His Position in New South Wales—Birth and Early Consecration—Local Preaching and Call to the Ministry—Co-Pastorate with Mr. Binney—Call to New York—Characteristics of his Preaching—A Remarkable Sermon—A Testimonial of $8,000—Resignation and Return—Settlement in Melbourne.

THE astonishing progress of the thriving communities in the Southern Hemisphere was evidenced at the centenary of New South Wales recently celebrated. As very little is known in this country of that land, and few persons among us have any conception of the growing importance, and vigorous intellectual and commercial activity of its people, the pictures on the first page of this number, and a brief account of the rise and growth of the colony, will be welcome to the readers of this journal. With the pictures is the portrait of the Rev. Llewellyn D. Bevan, D. D., who was formerly the esteemed pastor of the Brick Presbyterian Church in New York, but is now one of the most prominent clergymen and leaders of religious thought in New South Wales. We give also with his portrait that of Sir H. Parkes, a man who, arriving in the colony nearly half a century ago a poor immigrant, has climbed up to the proud position of its premier statesman.

Llewellyn David Bevan is a Welchman. He was born at Llanelly, in South Wales, in 1841, and is now, therefore, forty-seven years old. He had the priceless advantage of a pious ancestry, and at a very early age he was led to give himself to Christ, and consecrate himself to His service. While still in his teens he frequently preached the gospel in the neighborhood of his native town, and with such acceptance and power that he was strongly and repeatedly urged by ministers and others to devote his whole life to the work of the Christian ministry. Happily this suggestion was perfectly congenial to the young man's inclinations, and once assured that it was of God, he embraced it with cordiality.

His Education

for his work was commenced in London, at University School, from which he passed to University College, where his course was remarkably gratifying. He then entered New College, to complete his preparation for the Congregational ministry. During his brilliant academic career he carried off several valuable scholarships, and took the degrees of B. A. and LL. B. at London University, with the highest honors. Subsequently, while in America, his learning and brilliant talents were recognized by the University of Princeton which sent him the diploma of D. D.

His First Engagement

was as co-pastor with the celebrated Rev. Thomas Binney, of the King's Weigh-House Chapel, in which he won golden opinions of a congregation accustomed to the most brilliant pulpit oratory of the day. After four years of this co-pastorate, during which his relations with Mr. Binney were of the happiest and most affectionate kind, he was induced in 1870 to accept the pastorate of the Whitefield Tabernacle, in London, which is now the scene of the ministerial labors of the Rev. J. Jackson Wray. There he was so pre-eminently successful that universal surprise and deep sorrow were experienced when it was announced that he had accepted an earnest

Invitation to New York.

But he felt that he was following the guidance of God, and at once relinquished all the bright prospects of usefulness and influence which were opening before him in connection with the Congregational Church of Great Britain. He commenced his labors in the Brick Presbyterian church at Fifth Avenue and Thirty-seventh Street, New York, in December 1876, and at once took a prominent position in the religious community of the Empire City. A large and intelligent congregation gathered around him, and listened with earnest attention to his teachings. These were of the most practical character. Dr. Bevan is a deeply observant man, and in studying the problems of American life he perceived that the great need of the nation is the acknowledgment of Christ's rule and obedience to His commands. Early in his ministerial labors in New York he had the courage, in

A Remarkable Sermon,

which attracted much attention, to denounce the growing greed of business men, and to declare that every Christian business man was bound to obey Christ's injunction, and recognize His rivals and competitors as his "neighbors." His subject was Esau selling his birthright (Gen. 25: 29–34). He said in the course of his sermon: "What are many of our modern tradings but this purchase of a birthright with nothing but a mess of pottage? We are placed in circumstances of exceptionally advantageous character. Knowledge and power on our side conspire with hard pressure and keen difficulty in the case of our fellow-man. He is perhaps fainting, dying, and appeals to us for help. 'Oh!' he cries, 'anything you please in my present emergency,' and he swears to us, and we go off with his birthright, bonds or lands, or houses, or jewels, or business advantages, or conditions of successful merchandise. How we chuckle to ourselves! How modest we look when friends congratulate us! How affectedly perhaps we even receive the thanks of the poor wretch himself, who has saved his life at that tremendous cost! And then, ah, what then? the miserable upbraidings of conscience and the loneliness of our midnight hours! Illgotten gain, every man knows and acknowledges, turns to rottenness and disappointment and loss in the very hands that were enriched. And yet the ill-getting of gains is no difficult problem to solve. There is not a conscience today in New York but could pass a very clear and far-reaching judgment upon what are gains ill got. I leave it to every conscience to point out the ill gain for and by itself."

This application of

Religion to Every-day Life

was a characteristic of all Dr. Bevan's sermons. He did not go out of his way to assail evils which were at a distance, but perceiving the dangers and temptations of his own hearers, told them what was their duty, whether they were offended or pleased. His courage and vigorous candor won for him the respect and admiration of God-fearing men, who were glad to find in him a guide and counsellor in the perplexing difficulties of business life. It was consequently with sincere regret that the church learned in 1882, after six years profitable association, that personal considerations had determined Dr. Bevan to sever his connection with the church, and return to England. It was not a question of money, or that would have been easily arranged, but of private and urgent necessity, which after listening to Dr. Bevan's explanation the church recognized. As a mark of their esteem they presented him with

A Testimonial of $8,000,

and sorrowfully bade him farewell. His last sermon was preached on May 7, 1882, to a congregation which filled the large edifice to overflowing. In it he warned his hearers of the dangers to which our beloved country is exposed, and earnestly besought them to labor aggressively against ungodliness in the State, in politics and in business.

On his return to England, Dr. Bevan became pastor of a new church in London, where, as in every sphere he has occupied, his labors were much blessed. He remained there four years, and then he was led to another change of sphere still more distant than that to New York.

A Call to Melbourne

was sent to him, and it was accompanied by such representations of the need of the young community, and the opportunities of usefulness which it afforded, that Dr. Bevan decided to renounce his lucrative engagement, his influential position as the leader of London Congregationalists, and go out to the onerous sphere in the Southern hemisphere. He has remained there until now, doing a grand work and enjoying the blessing of God on his labors. The church in which Dr. Bevan preaches, covers, with its adjacent buildings, an area of nearly two acres, will seat about 1,800 persons, is the centre of a population of more than 300,000 people, and occupies one of the most important positions in the colony. It is crowded on Sundays and on Thursday mornings with an intelligent and devout audience. Dr. Bevan's settlement in Melbourne has given an impetus there not only to Congregationalism, but also to the higher and worthier interests of our common Christianity, and it is having a beneficial influence in moulding the growing national life into a true Christian brotherhood.

SIR H. PARKES, K. C. M. G.

SIR HENRY PARKES is the Premier of New South Wales, and by his statesmanlike qualities has placed that Colony in the foremost position among the Australian provinces. His career is a notable illustration of the power of energy, industry and intelligence to raise a man in the social scale. In 1815, seventy-three years ago, he was born in a small farm-house, in a Warwickshire village. The boy's education was begun at a dame's school at Kenilworth, and so far as schools were concerned was completed at Gloucester, when he was eleven years old. His parents having fallen into poverty, he was obliged to earn his own living at a very early period of his life; but this early necessity of labor bred in him a spirit of independence, energy and self-reliance, to which, with the blessing of God, he owes the success of his subsequent career. He was apprenticed to a mechanical trade in Birmingham, where he married. Even in his days of

Heroic Struggle

and apparently hopeless prospects, he entered heartily into the political movements of the time, and educated himself in the study of political and social questions, and early identified himself with the Temperance movement, to which he has ever since been faithful. In 1839 he emigrated to Sydney, New South Wales, and so dependent was he then upon the labor of his hands for his daily bread that, as he told his hearers at a great public banquet given in his honor in 1881, he would one day have had to go without a dinner had he not found a sixpence on the street. He worked for some time in a hardware store, and then in a foundry; he afterwards established himself as a toy-maker, and then as a dealer in toys. He first took part in

Political Life

in 1848, when he acted as one of the secretaries to a committee formed to secure the election of Mr. Robert Lowe as member of the local Legislature for the city of Sydney. In the following year he interested himself prominently in the great agitations to compel the English government to cease sending the convicts to New South Wales, and for the introduction of a system of self-government. In December, 1850, he started the *Empire* newspaper, which he vigorously conducted for about seven years.

By this time Mr. Parkes had begun to make himself known in Sydney as a forcible public speaker and a political power to be reckoned with. In 1854 he was

Elected to the Legislature,

and in 1856 he was re-elected. He still represents Sydney in the Parliament of New South Wales. In May, 1872, he was entrusted by the Governor with the formation of a ministry, and he continued to hold office as Premier until February, 1875. In March, 1877, he became Premier for the second time, and in December, 1878, after a dissolution and re-election of Parliament, he took office as

Premier for the Third Time,

and has had the distinction of being at the head of the longest-lived Government of Australia. In June, 1877, the Queen recognized the value of his public services by conferring upon him the dignity of knighthood, and in 1882, King Humbert, of Italy, made him Knight

Commander of the Crown of Italy, in recognition of his philanthropic services to a large number of Italian emigrants who went out to New Ireland, and who arrived in Sydney in a state of great distress.

THE TWO CAPITALS.

(See Illustration on First Page.)

THE sister cities of Sydney and Melbourne are respectively the capitals of New South Wales and Victoria, the two southeast provinces of Australia. New South Wales comprises an area of about 310,700 square miles, which is about the size of Texas and Louisiana united. Its entire population is a little less than a million, of which 120,000 reside in Sidney and its suburbs. It was originally settled in 1788 as a penal colony, when Captain Arthur Philip arrived there having in charge seven hundred and fifty persons, who for various crimes had been condemned to transportation for seven years and longer periods. England continued to send her convicts there until 1850, when the protests of the free colonists induced her to choose another dumping-ground for her moral refuse.

Sydney

was a mere straggling village for several years after the settlement, but it has now grown into a stately and beautiful city. It stands on a long neck of land at the mouth of the Paramatta River, between two deep creeks, which form its inner harbor, where it has excellent wharves and docks. Access is gained to it by Port Jackson, which is the largest and grandest harbor in the world, having an average depth of fifty-four feet of water, with little variation from the tide.

The picture on the first page presents a side view of some of the older parts of the city, of which still older lie more towards the main harbor. Across the water, above the bridge and immediately in front of Pyrmont, rises a portion of the Brickfield Hill, on which are seen St. Andrew's Cathedral on the right, and the Town Hall to the left, with its massive buildings and lofty tower. The ridge, of which Brickfield Hill forms a point, is continued in a northerly direction by the Flagstaff Hill, where the city reaches its highest elevation in a flat precipitous rock. The city boasts a beautiful public garden, in which tropical plants flourish in the open air. It is laid out on ground sloping from the town to the sea and is a perfect paradise of beauty.

Melbourne

is the capital of the younger and more progressive province of Victoria, which lies to the south of New South Wales. Victoria comprises an area of 87,884 square miles, about equal to the combined area of Pennsylvania and Ohio. Its population now is a little over 900,000. It was settled in 1836, and fifteen years later the discovery of gold fields attracted to it crowds of immigrants from all quarters of the world, and placed the colony in the front rank of the Australian provinces for wealth and influence.

The illustration on the first page represents Bourke Street, one of the principal streets of Melbourne. It is a busy thoroughfare, having the Houses of Parliament at its eastern end, and containing numerous public buildings and fine business edifices. Bourke Street, and Collins Street, which is a more fashionable promenade, compare favorably with the best thoroughfares in American and European cities. They bear evidences, however, of their rapid and hasty growth. The people have built as they had occasion, and according to their means; the result being that intervening between blocks of handsome and imposing edifices are structures which can only be called sheds. These are the remains of the old city—that is, the city before 1851, which year is Melbourne's era. Before that the normal population was 25,000, and they were, for the greater part, poor, struggling tradesmen. In the thirty-seven years which have elapsed, the city has grown to 300,000, with a still greater increase of wealth. At its present rate of development a very few years will suffice to remove all traces of Melbourne's inglorious past, and make it one of the most splendid cities of the world.

ANECDOTES RELATED AT RECENT EVANGELISTIC MEETINGS.

An Unexpected Arrest by Death.—"I was hurriedly called lately to the death-bed of a young man who had suddenly fallen seriously ill. He said to me, 'I heard the gospel preached, yesterday and was sorely pressed to take Christ, but I put it off owing to something that I wanted to do to-day, and in which I could not indulge if I were a Christian, and now, here I am, dying, I fear. What am I to do?' I spoke to him a few encouraging words, and told him that Christ was still ready to receive him. He soon passed away, and, I hope, trusting in Christ. 'We know not what a day may bring forth.'"

The Record Inside the Hat.—Mr. Johnston observed: "There was a godly man in Belfast called Rev. Thomas Toye, who was very active in the Irish Revival of 1859. He died lately, and after his death there was found a slip of paper inside his hat containing the words, 'Born June, 1800; born again March, 1823.' He knew he had been born again, and was not ashamed to own it, but openly testified for his Lord on all possible occasions. Let us not forget that confession with the month, as well as belief with the heart, is one of the requisites of salvation. 'Whosoever therefore shall confess Me before men, him will I confess also before My Father which is in heaven.'"

An Arrow That Hit the Mark.—Mr. Arthur related: "I went into a church some years ago. There was an address, but I did not know what it was about; but after the address a young man rose and gave his testimony. He did not say much, indeed he could have scarcely said less. 'I am saved, and thank God I know it,' was his simple testimony. I for one could not say that I knew I was saved. But God's Holy Spirit sent that word home to my heart, and I resolved not to rest till I could say for myself as that young man had done, 'I am saved, and thank God I know it.' Going home that night I got face to face with that little text, 'Him that cometh unto me I will in no wise cast out,' and since then there has not been a day in which I did not rest assured of my salvation."

A Deistic Signalman Converted.—A Railway signalman says: "I was converted five years ago in a little garret. A poor widow lived there, and with her I went to lodge. She seemed to have taken me for a Christian, and at that time I had made some profession of regard for God, though in reality I was a deist, and on the highway to infidelity, and the first night in my new lodgings she asked me to read a chapter from the Bible. I was surprised, for I was not in the habit of doing so; but seeing no way to get out of it, I sat down and read the chapter. All the time I read I felt perfectly miserable, for the Lord showed me that I was doing wrong—pretending I was a Christian, when I was far from Christ. But it did me good; it brought down my pride, and was the means of bringing me at the feet of Jesus. I left all my false opinions about the Bible and God, and came simply to Christ, as an undone sinner. Bless His dear name, he accepted me and saved me. 'Except ye become as little children ye cannot see the kingdom of God.'"

Afraid to Confess Christ.—A Christian Soldier said: "When I joined the army I knew that I should at once have taken a decided stand for Christ, but I was cowardly enough not to do so, and one night I saw a comrade kneel down and pray. Some of the men laughed, and one naming me, said, 'You are in the religious room.' I was glad to hear that, but did not say so, for this remark made it worse than ever for me to acknowledge that I, too, was a Christian. Oh, I did feel mean, and hate myself for my silence. That comrade who had prayed asked me to come to the soldiers' gospel meeting. I consented, but even at the meeting I did not own Christ as my Master. On my return one of the men said to me, 'I say, don't you go to these meetings, or you will be getting converted, and we have got quite enough of that kind already!' But I continued to go, and one night God gave me courage to kneel down by my bed and openly show my allegiance to Him. Some of the others had quite a long talk over it. 'What does he need with conversion?' they asked one another, referring to me; 'he was always good enough, and a decent sort of fellow.' But one of them seriously said, 'I may be bad enough, but I am not so far gone as to laugh at a man thanking God for saving his soul. I know that it is the right thing to do, and I admire them for doing it.'"

Little Mary's Three Letters.—"I knew of a little girl who had given her heart to Jesus, and whose daily prayer was that her father might do the same. She sat down and wrote, 'Dear father, won't you be a Christian?' and she left the slip of paper on his table, where she knew he would find it. He saw it, read it, tore it into small shreds, and threw it on the floor. He said nothing about it, and the faithful child thought she would try again. 'Dear father,' she wrote, '*do* be a Christian,' and placed the slip as before on the table. This time he folded it up, and placed it in his pocket, and walked away, thinking of the words of his little monitor. The child was still unsatisfied, so, for the third time, she wrote, 'Dear father, won't you be a Christian? *Tell Mary*.' On the following morning, seeing the third note on the table, the father was overcome. He could stand it no longer. 'Where is Mary?' he called. Mary was in sight in a moment. He embraced her with an unutterable tenderness of feeling. His hard heart was completely subdued, and his little daughter was the means of bringing him to Jesus."

Result of Cowardice.—Mr. Hunter said: "In 1881 a young man came to my house seeking the way of life. After some conversation on the subject, we knelt in prayer. When we rose to our feet, I looked into his face and said, 'I think all is well with you now.' He merely smiled, and left the house. After that I always expected him to make a public profession, but he made none, and I was greatly disappointed. Time went on, and finally I got a letter from him, stating that he had indeed taken Christ that night, but through not openly confessing Him he had fallen away. Since then he had gone to hear a certain evangelist, who again had been the means of stirring up the desire within him to seek the face of his Saviour, but he also said that he had to undergo several weeks of fearful agony of soul before the smile of his Heavenly Father rested upon him. Oh, how important it is when Christ is received into the heart that an immediate profession of Him should be made, in order to indicate the convert's sincerity, and indicate his determination and hope to continue in the sunshine of God."

A Man with Diseased Blood—"A Gentleman was seized with a very peculiar disease. He tried many doctors, but not one could give him a remedy, or tell him what his trouble was. He went to Germany and put himself in the doctor's hands there. But it was of no avail. He returned home down-hearted, and rather worse than better. A friend advised him to obtain the advice of a certain well-known and skilful physician. He accordingly took his friend's advice, and the physician agreed to come. Entering the room where his patient sat, he looked keenly into his face. Then, taking hold of his arm, he extracted a drop of blood from it, which he carefully carried to the window and examined through a microscope. Then, turning to his patient he said, 'Your blood is diseased, but if you will promise to strictly obey me, and take the remedies I give you, you will recover.' The gentleman gladly promised that he would obey every command, which he did, and the result was, that under the care of that physician he was restored to perfect health in a few months. Dear friends, a Great Physician has come to heal the diseased soul of man, but if we do not put ourselves into His hands and obey His commands and accept of the remedy He offers, He can do nothing for us. Trust yourself to Him who forgiveth all thine iniquities, who healeth all thy diseases."

THE GRANDMOTHER.

Dr. Talmage's Eighth Sermon
TO THE WOMEN OF AMERICA.

Preached last Sunday Morning, February 26, 1888.

"The unfeigned faith that is in thee, which dwelt first in thy grandmother Lois." II Tim. 1: 5.

The Godly Influence of the Pious Ancestor—Statistics Wanted—The Dead Living for Good—American Women in the Last Century—Their Dress and Diet—A Glorious Race of Godly Women—The Grandmother in the Household—Two Eternities at One Cradle—The Mississippi-like Influence—To Outlast the World—The Legend of a Granite Column in Ceylon—The Mother's Unwise Training—Felt to the Fourth Generation—George W. Bethune's Grandmother—A Prayerful Letter—Grandmothers in Heaven—Make the Last Mile Easy—A Hard World for Women.

IN this love-letter which Paul, the old minister, is writing to Timothy, the young minister, the family record is brought out. Paul practically says: "Timothy, what a good grandmother you had! You ought to be better than most folks, because not only was your mother good, but your grandmother. Two preceding generations of piety ought to give you a mighty push in the right direction." The fact was that Timothy needed encouragement. He was in poor health, having a weak stomach, and was dyspeptic, and Paul prescribed for him a tonic, "a little wine, for thy stomach's sake"—not much wine, but a little wine, and only as a medicine. And if the wine then had been as much adulterated with logwood and strychnine as our modern wines, he would not have prescribed any.

But Timothy, not strong physically, is encouraged spiritually by the recital of grandmotherly excellence. Paul hinting to him, as I hint this day to you, that God sometimes gathers up, as in a reservoir away back of the active generations of to-day, a godly influence, and then in response to prayer, lets down the power upon children and grandchildren and great-grandchildren. The world is woefully in want of a table of statistics in regard to what is the protractedness and immensity of

Influence of One Good Woman

in the Church and world. We have accounts of how much evil has been wrought by Margaret, the mother of criminals, who lived near a hundred years ago, and of how many hundreds of criminals her descendants furnished for the penitentiary and the gallows, and how many hundreds of thousands of dollars they cost this country in their arraignment and prison support, as well as in the property they burglarized or destroyed. But will not some one come out with brain comprehensive enough, and heart warm enough, and pen keen enough to give us the facts in regard to some good woman of a hundred years ago, and let us know how many Christian men and women and reformers and useful people have been found among her descendants, and how many asylums and colleges and churches they built, and how many millions of dollars they contributed for humanitarian and Christian purposes?

The good women whose tombstones were planted in the eighteenth century are more

Alive for Good

in the nineteenth century than they were before, as the good women of this nineteenth century will be more alive for good in the twentieth century than now. Mark you, I have no idea that the grandmothers were any better than their granddaughters. You cannot get very old people to talk much about how things were when they were boys and girls. They have a reticence and a non-committalism which makes me think they feel themselves to be the custodians of the reputation of their early comrades. While our dear old folks are rehearsing the follies of the present, if you put them on the witness-stand and cross-examine them as to how things were seventy years ago, the silence becomes oppressive.

A celebrated Frenchman by the name of Volney visited this country in 1796, and he says of

Woman's Diet

in those times: "If a premium was offered for a regimen most destructive to health, none could be devised more efficacious for these ends than that in use among these people." That eclipses our lobster salad at midnight. Everybody talks about the dissipations of modern society, and how womanly health goes down under it, but it was worse a hundred years ago, for the chaplain of a French regiment in our Revolutionary war wrote in 1782, in his book of American women, saying: "They are tall and well proportioned, their features are generally regular, their complexions are generally fair and without color. At twenty years of age the women have no longer the freshness of youth. At thirty or forty they are decrepit." In 1812 a foreign consul wrote a book entitled, "A Sketch of the United States at the Commencement of the Present Century," and he says of the women of those times. "At the age of thirty all their charms have disappeared." One glance at the portraits of the women a hundred years ago and their style of dress makes us wonder how they ever got their breath. All this makes me think that the express rail train is no more an improvement on the old canal-boat, or the telegraph no more an improvement on the old-time saddlebags, than the women of our day are an improvement on the women of the last century.

But still, notwithstanding that those times were so much worse than ours, there was

A Glorious Race of Godly Women

seventy and a hundred years ago, who held the world back from sin and lifted it toward virtue, and without their exalted and sanctified influence before this, the last good influence would have perished from the earth. Indeed, all over this land there are seated to-day—not so much in churches, for many of them are too feeble to come—a great many aged grandmothers. They sometimes feel that the world has gone past them, and they have an idea that they are of little account. Their head sometimes gets aching from the racket of the grandchildren downstairs or in the next room. They steady themselves by the banisters as they go up and down. When they get a cold, it hangs on to them longer than it used to. They cannot bear to have the grandchildren punished even when they deserve it, and have so relaxed their ideas of family discipline that they would spoil all the youngsters of the household by too great leniency.

These old folks are the resort when great troubles come, and there is a calming and soothing power in the touch of an aged hand that is almost supernatural. They feel they are almost through with the journey of life, and read the old Book more than they used to, hardly knowing which most they enjoy, the Old Testament or the New, and often stop and dwell tearfully over the family record half way between. We hail them to-day, whether in the House of God or at the homestead. Blessed is that household that has in it a grandmother Lois. Where she is, angels are hovering round, and God is in the room. May her last days be like those lovely autumnal days that we call Indian Summer.

I never knew the joy of having a grandmother; that is the disadvantage of being the youngest child of the family. The elder members only have that benediction. But though she went up out of this life before I began it, I have heard of her faith in God, that brought all her children into the kingdom and two of them into the ministry, and then brought all her grandchildren into the kingdom, myself the last and least worthy. Is it not time that you and I do two things, swing open a picture-gallery of the wrinkled faces and stooped shoulders of the past, and call down from their heavenly thrones the godly grandmothers, to give them our thanks, and then persuade the mothers of to-day that they are living for all time, and that against the sides of every cradle in which a child is rocked beat

The Two Eternities.

Here we have an untried, undiscussed and unexplored subject. You often hear about your influence upon your own children—I am not talking about that. What about your influence upon the twentieth century, upon the thirtieth century, upon the fortieth century, upon the year two thousand, upon the year four thousand if the world lasts so long? The world stood four thousand years before Christ came; it is not unreasonable to suppose that it may stand four thousand years after His arrival. Four thousand years the world swung off in sin, four thousand years it may be swinging back into righteousness. By the ordinary rate of multiplication of the world's population in a century your descendants will be over three hundred and by two centuries at least over fifty thousand, perhaps two hundred thousand, and upon every one of them you, the mother of to-day will have an influence for good or evil. And if in four centuries your descendants shall have with their names filled a scroll of hundreds of thousands, will some angel from heaven to whom is given the capacity to calculate the number of the stars of heaven and the sands of the seashore, step down and tell us how many descendants you will have in the four thousandth year of the world's possible continuance?

Do not let the grandmothers any longer think that they are retired, and sit clear back out of sight from the world, feeling that they have no relation to it. The mothers of the last century are to-day in the senates, the parliaments, the palaces, the pulpits, the banking houses, the professional chairs, the prisons, the almshouses, the company of midnight brigands, the cellars, the ditches of this country. You have been thinking about the importance of having the right influence upon one nursery. You have been thinking about the importance of getting those two little feet on the right path. You have been thinking of your child's destiny for the next eighty years, if it should pass on to be an octogenarian. That is well, but my subject sweeps a thousand years, a million years, a quadrillion of years. I cannot stop at one cradle. I am looking at the cradles that reach all round the world and across all time. I am not talking of mother Eunice, I am talking of grandmother Lois.

The only way you can tell the force of a current is by sailing up stream; or the force of an ocean wave, by running the ship against it. Running along with it we cannot appreciate the force. In

Estimating Maternal Influence

we generally run along with it down the stream of time, and so we don't understand the full force. Let us come up to it from the eternal side, after it has been working on for centuries, and see all the good it has done and all the evil it has accomplished multiplied in magnificent or appalling compound interest. The difference between that mother's influence on her children now, and the influence when it has been multiplied in hundreds of thousands of lives, is the difference between the Mississippi River way up at the top of the continent, starting from the little lake Itasca, seven miles long and one wide, and its mouth at the Gulf of Mexico, where navies might ride. Between the birth of the river and its burial in the sea, the Missouri pours in, and the Ohio pours in, and the Arkansas pours in, and the Red and White and Yazoo rivers pour in, and all the States and Territories between the Alleghany and Rocky mountains make contribution. Now, in order to test the power of a mother's influence, we need to come in off of the ocean of eternity and sail up toward the one cradle, and we will find ten thousand tributaries of influence pouring in and pouring down. But it is, after all,

One Great River of Power

rolling on and rolling forever. Who can fathom it? Who can bridge it? Who can stop it? Had not mothers better be intensifying their prayers? Had they not better be elevating their example? Had they not better be rousing themselves with the consideration that by their faithfulness or neglect they are starting an influence which will be stupendous after the mountain of earth is flat, and the last sea been dried up, and the last flake of the ashes of a consumed world shall have been blown away, and all the telescopes of other worlds directed to the track around which our world once swung, shall discover not so much as a cinder of the burned-down and swept-off planet.

In Ceylon there is a granite column thirty-six square feet in size, which is thought, by the natives, to decide the world's continuance. An angel with robe spun from zephyrs is once a century to descend and sweep the hem of that robe across the granite, and when, by that attrition the column is worn away, they say time will end. But, by that process, that granite column would be worn out of existence before mother's influence will begin to give away.

Mothers Sowing Seed

If a mother tell a child he is not good, some bugaboo will come and catch him, the fear excited may make the child a coward, and the fact that he finds that there is no bugaboo may make him a liar, and the echo of that false alarm may be heard after fifteen generations have been born and have expired. If a mother promise a child a reward for good behavior, and after the good behavior forgets to give the reward, the cheat may crop out in some faithlessness half a thousand years further on. If a mother culture a child's vanity, and eulogize his curls, and extol the night-black or sky-blue or nut-brown of the child's eyes, and call out in his presence the admiration of spectators, pride and arrogance may be prolonged after half a dozen family records have been obliterated. If a mother express doubt about some statement of the Holy Bible in a child's presence, long after the gates of this historical era have closed and the gates of another era have opened, the result may be seen in a champion blasphemer.

But, on the other hand, if a mother walking with a child see a suffering one by the wayside and says: "My child, give that ten-cent piece to that lame boy," the result may be seen on the other side of the following century in some George Muller building a whole village of orphanages. If a mother sit almost every evening by the trundle-bed of a child and teach it lessons of a Saviour's love and a Saviour's example, of the importance of truth and the horror of a lie, and the virtues of industry and kindness and sympathy and self-sacrifice, long after the mother has gone, and the child has gone, and the lettering on both the tombstones shall have been washed out by the storms of innumerable winters, there may be standing, as a result of those trundle-bed lessons, flaming evangels, world-moving reformers, seraphic Summerfields, weeping Paysons, thundering Whitefields, emancipating Washingtons.

Good or bad influence may skip one generation or two generations, but it will be sure to land in

The Third or Fourth Generation,

just as the Ten Commandments, speaking of the visitation of God on families, says nothing about the second generation, but entirely skips the second and speaks of the third and fourth generation: "Visiting the iniquities of the fathers upon the third and fourth generations of them that hate me." Parental influence, right and wrong, may jump over a generation, but it will come down further on, as sure as you sit there and I stand here. Timothy's ministry was projected by his grandmother Lois. There are men and women here, the sons and daughters of the Christian Church, who are such as a result of the consecration of great-great-grandmothers. Why, who do you think the Lord is? You talk as though His memory was weak. He can no easier remember a prayer five minutes than he can five centuries.

This explains what we often see—some man or woman distinguished for benevolence when his father and mother were distinguished for penuriousness; or you see some young man or woman with a bad father and a hard mother come out gloriously for Christ, and make the church sob and shout and sing under their exhortations. We stand in corners of the vestry and whisper over the matter and say: "How is this, such great piety in sons and daughters of such parental worldliness and sin?" I will explain it to you if you will fetch me the old Family Bible containing the full record. Let some septuagenarian look with me clear upon the page of births and marriages, and tell me who that woman was with the old-fashioned name of Jemima or Betsy or Mehitabel. Ah, there she is, the old grandmother or great-grandmother, who had enough

Religion to Saturate a Century.

There she is, the dear old soul, grandmother Lois. In our beautiful Greenwood (may we all sleep there when our work is done, for when I get up in the Resurrection morning I want my congregation all about me)—in Greenwood there is the resting-place of George W. Bethune, once a minister of Brooklyn Heights, his name never spoken among intelligent Americans without suggesting two things—eloquence and evangelism. In the same tomb sleeps his grandmother, Isabella Graham, who was the chief inspiration of his ministry. You are not surprised at the poetry and pathos and pulpit power of the grandson when you read of the faith and devotion of his wonderful ancestress. When you read

This Grandmother's Letter,

in which she poured out her widowed soul in longings for a son's salvation, you will not wonder that succeeding generations have been blessed:

"NEW YORK, May 20, 1791.

"This day my only son left me in bitter wringings of heart; he is again launched on the ocean, God's ocean. The Lord saved him from shipwreck, brought him to my home and allowed me once more to indulge my affections over him. He has been with me but a short time, and ill have I improved it; he is gone from my sight, and my heart bursts with tumultuous grief. Lord, have mercy on the widow's son, 'the only son of his mother.'

"I ask nothing in all this world for him; I repeat my petition—save his soul alive, give him salvation from sin. It is not the danger of the seas that distresses me; it is not the hardships he must undergo; it is not the dread of never seeing him more in this world; it is because I cannot discern the fulfilment of the promise in him, I cannot discern the new birth nor its fruit, but every symptom of captivity to Satan, the world and self-will. This, this is what distresses me; and in connection with this, his being shut out from ordinances at a distance from Christians; shut up with those who forget God, profane His name and break His Sabbaths; men who often live and die like beasts, yet are accountable creatures, who must answer for every moment of time and every word, thought and action.

"O Lord, many wonders hast Thou shown me; Thy ways of dealing with me and mine have not been common ones; add this wonder to the rest. Call, convert, regenerate and establish a sailor in the faith. Lord, all things are possible with Thee; glorify Thy Son and extend His kingdom by sea and land; take the prey from the strong. I roll him over upon Thee. Many friends try to comfort me; miserable comforters are they all. Thou art the God of consolation; only confirm to me Thy precious word, on which Thou causedst me to hope in the day when Thou saidst to me, 'Leave thy fatherless children, I will preserve them alive.' Only let this life be a spiritual life, and I put a blank in Thy hand as to all temporal things.

"I wait for Thy salvation. Amen."

With such a grandmother, would you not have a right to expect a George W. Bethune? and all the thousands converted through his ministry may date the saving power back to Isabella Graham.

God fill the earth and the heavens with such grandmothers; we must some day go up and thank these dear old souls. Surely, God will let us go up and tell them of the results of their influence. Among our

First Questions in Heaven

will be, "Where is grandmother?" They will point her out, for we would hardly know her even if we had seen her on earth, so bent over with years once, and there so straight, so dim of eye through the blinding of earthly tears, and now her eye as clear as heaven, so full of aches and pains once, and now so agile with celestial health, the wrinkles blooming into carnation roses, and her step like the roe on the mountains. Yes, I must see her, my grandmother on my father's side, Mary McCoy, descendant of the Scotch. When I first spoke to an audience in Glasgow, Scotland, and felt somewhat diffident, being a stranger, I began by telling them *my grandmother was a Scotch woman*, and then there went up a shout of welcome which made me feel as easy as I do here. I must see her.

You must see those women of the early nineteenth century and of the eighteenth century, the answer of whose prayers is in your welfare to-day.

God Bless All the Aged Women

up and down the land and in all lands! What a happy thing, Pomponius Atticus, to say, when making the funeral address of his mother: "Though I have resided with her sixty-seven years, I was never once reconciled to her, because there never happened the least discord between us, and consequently, there was no need of reconciliation." Make it as easy for the old folks as you can. When they are sick, get for them the best doctors. Give them your arm when the streets are slippery. Stay with them all the time you can. Go home and see the old folks. Find the place for them in the hymn-book. Never be ashamed if they prefer styles of apparel a little antiquated. Never say anything that implies they are in the way. Make the road for the last mile as smooth as you can. Oh, my!

How You Will Miss Her

when she is gone. I would give the house from over my head to see mother. I have so many things I would like to tell her, things that have happened in twenty-four years since she went away. Morning, noon and night let us thank God for the good influences that have come down from good mothers all the way back. Timothy, don't forget your mother Eunice, and don't forget your grandmother Lois. And hand down to others this patrimony of blessing. Pass along the coronets. Make religion an heirloom from generation to generation. Mothers of America, consecrate yourselves to God, and you will help consecrate all the ages following! Do not dwell so much on your hardships that you miss your chance of wielding an influence that shall look down upon you from the towers of an endless future.

I know Martin Luther was right when he consoled his wife over the death of their daughter, by saying: "Don't take on so, wife; remember that this is a hard world for girls." Yes; I go further and say: It is

A Hard World for Women.

Aye, I go further and say: It is a hard world for men. But for all women and men who trust their bodies and souls in the hand of Christ, the shining gates will soon swing open. Don't you see the sickly pallor on the sky? That is the pallor on the cold cheek of the dying night. Don't you see the brightening of the clouds? That is the flush on the warm forehead of the morning. Cheer up, you are coming within sight of the Celestial City.

The Celestial City.

Cairo, capital of Egypt, was called "City of Victory." Athens, capital of Greece, was called "City of the Violet Crown;" Baalbeck was called "City of the Sun;" London was called "The City of Masts." Lucian's imaginary metropolis beyond the Zodiac was called "The City of Lanterns." But the city to which you journey hath all these in one, the victory, the crowns, the masts, of those that have been harbored after the storm. Aye, all but the lanterns and the sun, because they have no need of any other light, since the Lamb is the light thereof.

BOYCOTTED MISSIONARIES.

IN describing a recent tour, in a letter to the *Church* the Rev. J. G. Touzeau of Bogota in the United States of Colombia, thus refers to the action of the priest, or *cura*, of Panqueba: When we went, the cura prohibited all dealings with us—buying, selling, visiting, or even saluting on the street. The people generally obeyed, but gradually relaxed until nearly every one spoke in passing. All along a few principal families were friendly, and we bought all we needed, the ready money being more potent than the priest's threats. Certainly a large number, probably two or three hundred, were brought into direct personal contact with us in the region, and now know something about Protestant Christianity. On the journey in and out and during our stay we sold over thirty dollars' worth of literature, nearly all in very small amounts, cheap Testaments and tracts, perhaps about two hundred and fifty in number.

We were visited by the villagers, our neighbors: also by those who came from other towns, for Panqueba is a health resort. The foreigners were one of the sights, and these curious people are interested in something new in religion as well in other things; for if we did nothing else, we generally sang the gospel to them. Most of the work was done at night. Two of the principal men in Panqueba came nearly every evening to take lessons in English. Each evening we read in the Bible, sang and prayed, and very often there were earnest talks and questionings over what was read. One man showed great interest in us and our teaching, and finally, as he was leaving us and I pressed him to tell me if he were a believer, he told us he desired to join the church, but would come to Bogota, as he feared the fanaticism of his neighbors. He is one of the best natives with whom I have come into contact. His interest took the practical form of gifts of food for us and our beasts.

THE WORK OF A JAPANESE JAILER'S WIFE.

A WONDERFUL work of grace is reported from Yokohama, Japan, to the Presbyterian Mission Board by Rev. H. Loomis, in connection with the introduction of Christianity in Komatsu, a stronghold of Buddhism. He says: "About three years ago a Christian soldier was discharged from the army, and went to Kanazawa for the purpose of attending school. He obtained a room and board at the house of a person named Nakamura. They hated the Christian religion very bitterly, but the soldier was so pleasant and agreeable that he obtained permission to take their only child (a daughter about thirteen years of age) to the Sunday-school. At the same time he was very persistent in telling the mother about this religion he had found so full of comfort to himself.

After a while the mother and child began to attend church and prayer-meetings; and they were the most regular and punctual of all the attendants. The mother was eventually led to accept Christ as her Saviour. About three months afterward her husband, Nakamura, received an appointment as jailer at Komatsu, a town about twenty-five miles distant. The people of that place were very strong Buddhists and haters of Christianity. The priests had made their boasts that Christianity could get no footing in Komatsu, as their own religion was so well established. Two young evangelists went there to labor during their summer vacation, but could only get a few boys to attend their services.

While they were still there Mrs. Nakamura came with her husband and began to tell her friends and neighbors about this new and blessed way. They were at first offended at such talk, but she insisted that they should come and see for themselves. Then she invited the evangelists to her house, and many were thus induced to hear and study the Word of God.

When the evangelists left the city a little band was formed to meet for prayer and study of the Scriptures, with the jailer's wife as leader. This band grew to forty in number, and a Sunday-school was afterwards started. The Buddhist priests, of course, heard of the work, and they were so much afraid of the results that they put up notices that no one must go to hear this Christian woman, as it would bring upon them the wrath and vengeance of the gods. But this only helped the cause of Christianity, as it advertised it, and she was constantly beset by people who came to inquire about this strange doctrine. Christian workers were sent to help her, and a church has been formed. Recently seven converts were baptized at one service.

DR. TALMAGE ON HOT AXLES.

IN the course of his Friday evening talk, Dr. Talmage made the following remarks on an evil which is doing incalculable mischief in American life, causing men to become prematurely old, and many to break down and die in the midst of their usefulness:

We were on the lightning train for Cleveland. We had no time to spare. If we stopped for a half-hour, we should be greeted by the anathema of a committee. We felt a sort of presentiment that we should be too late, when to confirm it the whistle blew and the brakes fell, and the cry all along the train was: "What is the matter?" Answer: "A hot axle." The wheels had been making too many revolutions in a minute. The car was on fire. It was a very difficult thing to put it out; water, sand and swabs were tried, and caused long detention and a smoke that threatened flame down to the end of the journey.

We thought then, and think now, this is what is the matter with people everywhere. In this swift "express" American life, we go too fast for our endurance. We think ourselves getting on splendidly, when in the midst of our successes we come to a dead halt. What is the matter? Nerves or muscles or brains give out. We have made too many revolutions in an hour. A hot axle!

Men make the mistake of working according to their opportunities and not according to their capacity of endurance. "Can I run this train from Springfield to Boston at the rate of fifty miles an hour?" says an engineer. Yes. "Then I will run it, reckless of consequences." Can I be a merchant, and the president of a bank, and a director in a life insurance company, and a school commissioner, and help edit a paper, and supervise the politics of our ward, and run for Congress? "I can!" the man says to himself. The store drives him; the school drives him; politics drive him. He takes all the scoldings and frets and exasperations of each position. Some day at the height of the business season he does not come to the store; from the most important meetings of the bank directors he is absent. In the excitements of the political canvass he fails to be at the place appointed. What is the matter? His health has broken down. The train halts long before it gets to the station. A hot axle!

Literary men have great opportunities opening in this day. If they take all that open, they are dead men, or worse, living men who ought to be dead. The pen runs so easy when you have good ink, and smooth paper, and an easy desk to write on, and the consciousness of an audience of one, two or three hundred thousand readers. There are the religious newspapers through which you preach, and the musical journals through which you may sing, and the agricultural periodicals through which you can plough, and family newspapers in which you may romp with the whole household around the evening stand. There are critiques to be written, and reviews to be indulged in, and poems to be chimed, and novels to be constructed. When out of a man's pen he can shake recreation and friendship, and usefulness and bread, he is apt to keep it shaking. So great are the invitations to literary work that the professional men of the day are overcome. They sit faint and fagged out on the verge of newspapers and books. Each one does the work of three, and these men sit up late nights and choke down chunks of meat without mastication, and scold their wives through irritability, and maul innocent authors, and run the physical machinery with a liver miserably given out. The driving shaft has gone fifty times a second. They stop at no station. The steam chest is hot and swollen. The brain and the digestion begin to smoke. Stop, ye flying quills! "Down brakes!" A hot axle!

Some of the worst tempered people of the day are religious people, from the fact that they have no rest. Added to the necessary work of the world, they superintend two Sunday-schools, listen to two sermons, and every night have meetings of charitable and Christian institutions. They look after the beggars, hold conventions, speak at meetings, wait on ministers, serve as committee-men, take all the hypercriticisms that inevitably come to earnest workers, rush up and down the world and develop their hearts at the expense of all the other functions. They are the best men on earth, and Satan knows it, and is trying to kill them as fast as possible. They know not that it is as much a duty to take care of their health as to go to the sacrament. It is as much a sin to commit suicide with the sword of truth as with a pistol.

Our earthly life is a treasure to be guarded. It is an outrageous thing to die when we ought to live. There is no use in firing up a Cunarder to such a speed that the boiler bursts mid-Atlantic, when at a more moderate rate it might have reached the docks at Liverpool. It is a sin to try to do the work of thirty years in five years.

We need another proclamation of emancipation. The human locomotive goes too fast. Cylinder, driving-boxes, rock-shaft, truck and valve-gear need to "slow up." Oh that some strong hand would unloose the burdens from our over-tasked American life, that there might be fewer bent shoulders and pale cheeks and exhausted lungs and quenched eyes, the law and medicine and theology less frequently stopped in their progress because of the hot axle!

A MORAVIAN MISSIONARY'S TESTIMONY.

DURING the recent tour in the West Indies, taken by Mr. J. A. Froude, he inquired as to the truth of the reports circulated about the laziness of the colored race in the islands. He says:

I received a far pleasanter impression of the colored race from a Moravian minister, who called on me with a friend who had lately taken a farm. I was particularly glad to see this gentleman, for of the Moravians everyone had spoken well to me. He was not the least enthusiastic about his poor black sheep, but he said that, if they were not better than the average English laborers, he did not think them worse. They were called idle. They would work well enough if they had fair wages, and if the wages were paid regularly; but what could be expected when women servants had but three shillings a week, and "found themselves;" when the men had but a shilling a day, and the pay was kept in arrear, in order that if they came late to work, or if they came irregularly, it might be kept, or cut down to what the employer chose to give? Under such conditions any man of any color would prefer to work for himself if he had a garden, or would be idle if he had none. "Living" costs next to nothing, either to them or their families. But the minister said, and his friend confirmed it by his own experience, that the same fellows would work regularly and faithfully for any master whom they personally knew and could rely upon, and no Englishman coming to settle there need be afraid of failing for want of labor, if he had sense and energy, and did not prefer to lie down and groan. The blacks my friend said, were kindly-hearted, respectful and well-disposed, but they were children; easily excited, easily tempted, easily misled, and totally unfit for self-government. If we wished to ruin them altogether, we should persevere in the course to which, they were sorry to hear we were so inclined. The real want in the island was of intelligent Englishmen to employ and direct them, and Englishmen were going away so fast that they feared there would soon be none of them left. This was the opinion of two moderate and excellent men, whose natural and professional prejudices were all on the black man's side.

THE JUDGMENT OF THE SEVENTIETH WEEK.

By G. H. Pember.

Preparations Now Going on — Signs of its Near Approach — Antichrist Aided by Rome — Origin of Romanism in Babylon — Feminine Element in the Trinity — Relics of Pagan Superstition in Romish Churches — The Seventh Roman King — Napoleon a Probable Fulfilment — The Eighth to Ascend from the Abyss — Uses and then Overthrows his Romish Ally.

We see around us on all sides the preparatory stages of the events described in Rev. 17. The judgments of the Lord will soon come on the earth. These judgments are to take place in the last week, or the last seven years, as Daniel predicted. During that time the scene in Rev. 17 will take place, and the fact that the preparations are going on around us shows how necessary it is that we should be ready for the prior event, the coming of the Lord for His saints. We have in Scripture the description of the seven years which are to follow our Lord's coming; and if we see that these events are about to take place we know the Lord not only *may*, but must be

Near at Hand.

This chapter has been interpreted as having to do with a past age. One thing which leads people into mistakes is that they do not look at little words. For example, the parable of the ten virgins in Matt. 25 is introduced by the word "*then*," that is at the time of which our Lord has just been speaking—the time of the end. So here little words give the clue. John is called to see the *judgment*, or final destruction of the harlot. No doubt, the early Fathers were right in pointing out that the destruction of the harlot and the beast takes place during the last seven years. Antichrist gathers up his forces by the help of the harlot, but attains to his full power by destroying her. Thus his full manifestation is about three and a half years—just about the time Christ spent in His public ministry. Now the harlot is seen seated on the beast. Our Lord speaks about "the leaven of the Pharisees and Sadducees," the

Two Great Principles

of human thought and error. First, the devout spirit of the Pharisees. This often develops into a desire, not to find out God's will, but to build up some earthly system, creed, or philosophy. So men go astray on their own ideas, and soon begin to persecute those who disagree with them. The ultimate outcome of that school is seen in the harlot. Then, on the other hand, we have the liberal man of advanced thought, who ever wanders farther and farther away from God, until he strays into the land of fools, who say in their heart, "There is no God." But human nature won't stay long there; and bye-and-bye we may see the change from the present Atheism to the worship of man, or, rather, of the Man of Sin. These two principles working side by side in the world are soon to come into violent opposition.

Now the harlot is represented as the "mother of harlots and the abominations of the earth." Some suppose her to be Popery, but, while Popery is included, this goes farther, for the harlot is the great source of wickedness from earliest times. Therefore we must search for some system whence all others may have sprung. There is one such, and it is the Babylonian, the great feature of which is a Trinity in imitation of the blessed Holy Trinity. But

The Pagan Trinity

of Father, Mother and Son, which may be traced in all Pagan systems. This idolatry commenced with the worship of the sun-god, doubtless Satan himself. It is remarkable that the very name of Satan passes through its Chaldean form "Sheitan," into the Greek "Titan," the sun-god. And this Babylonish form of idolatry betrays itself in Theosophy and Romanism by the feminine element in the Trinity, Father, Mother and Child; but the Father soon passes out of notice, and everywhere is seen Woman and Child; moon goddess and sun-god.

Now you may have been astonished at some of the vestments in so-called Protestant churches. Whence do they come? Not from the Bible; not from any Jewish source. Whence then? Go to the museums and study the sculptured slabs, and signets and clay tablets; there you will discover the source.

These Robes are Babylonish.

When you understand this, then, if you see such in any church, you know whose service is going on. Again, if you see a tonsured priest, you recognize him as *attached to the sun*, and as a rebel against God, for God has commanded His priests *not* to make bald the head. The head of a picture or image surrounded with a circular halo reveals to you one of the minor deities or saints, invested with some attribute of the sun. The round wafer administered to the communicant is recognized as the sacrament of Mithras. Nor do you fail to notice how it breaks up the Christian symbolism, which demands that all the bread distributed be parted from one loaf.

The turning of worshippers towards the East reminds you of the

Universal Practice of Heathendom;

and you remember that the Creator commanded His holy of holies to be set towards the West, in order that He might at once distinguish between His worshippers and those of the sun and of Satan. Nor do you forget the incident of Ezek. 8:15, 16, where the greatest of all the abominations of Jerusalem is exemplified in the twenty-five men, between the porch and the altar, with their backs towards the temple of the Lord and their faces towards the East, worshipping the sun. Wherever you see these things, there is the finger of the harlot; the influence of Babylon, of Babylon in mystery it may be, but unmistakably of Babylon.

The harlot, then, is the organizer of this secret sect, the chief propagator of false religion. Her system of evil arose in Babylon, eventually found its seat in Rome, and, doubtless, will finally be transferred to Babylon at the time of the end. Rome is only part of it, though at present its headquarters.

So much for the harlot. As regards the beast, with his seven heads and ten horns, representing the Roman Empire, we must notice a canon of interpretation which is without exception. We may have a little trouble when symbols are not explained, but whenever God gives an explanation of the figure we are obliged to accept that as final. Now the beast has seven heads, and with regard to the woman these are said to be seven mountains on which she sits. So Rome, the seven-hilled city, is where she is sitting now; but Rome is her seat, not herself. And, with regard to Antichrist, the seven heads are said to be seven kings. That is

God's Own Explanation.

These seven kings are probably emperors of Rome, because "one was," that is to say, Domitian, in John's day. Hence some little clue to the others, though we can't be quite certain who they were. No doubt all were grand masters in the great conspiracy against God, resulting in Popery. Five had fallen: probably they were Julius Cæsar, Tiberius, Claudius, Caligula, and Nero; one was reigning at the time, that is Domitian: the seventh was yet to appear, and the expression, "and when he cometh" perhaps indicates that some time would previously elapse. It is likely that

He was the Emperor Napoleon,

who put an end to the long line of Roman emperors, and whose ideal would have made him the Antichrist himself could he have realized it, but the time had not then come.

We must avoid the mistake of supposing the Antichrist to be an eighth head of the beast. There is no eighth head, but one of the seven heads resuscitated will be the eighth king. "The beast that thou sawest was, and is not, and shall ascend out of the abyss," that is, he had passed through one earth-life when John saw the vision (A. D. 97), was then in the abyss, and should afterwards ascend out of it to play his part. He is said to be the beast himself; because, although properly a revived head, he will be so identified with the wishes and aspirations of the people that he may be regarded as their complete representative and exponent.

For his ascent out of the pit Satan is already preparing the minds of men by accustoming them to the supernatural in spiritualism, and especially to the idea of the return of the dead in the seances of the spiritualists and the revival of the doctrine of the transmigration of souls, now held by theosophists and Buddhists, who during the last three years have multiplied in America and England.

The Deification of Majorities.

Such are the two symbols: but how are we to connect them in the present time? The whole body of the beast is scarlet, and that is the imperial color. Compare Matt. 27:28. Hence when the vision is fulfilled the body politic will be sovereign, that is, the Government will be democratic. Similarly the whole body of the beast is full of names of blasphemy; whereas in Rev. 13:1 it is only his heads that are so: for in former times the Roman Emperor alone was called Divus, or God; and his bust was set up for worship in every magistrate's office. Thus he was the forerunner of the Antichrist, for the Pope never dared to do such a thing. But now we are being told that the "voice of the people is the voice of God," and the name of blasphemy is being transferred to the body politic. A majority of men is to outweigh everything.

Rome, then, is to regain, for a moment, her seat on the beast, her ascendency in Christendom, in democratic times such as the present. And she is already doing so. A change has taken place: she is beginning to seek

Power Through the People.

A few years ago she was opposed to Fenianism, and consequently many of her chapels were forsaken; now two of her archbishops are at the head of the conspiracy. An even more abrupt change of front has lately taken place in regard to the Knights of Labor in America, to the discomfiture of a bishop who had fulminated against them; and Rome is everywhere seeking popularity. Her community is increasing in the three Protestant countries, Germany, England and America. She has lately been called in to arbitrate between two European nations, as in the Middle Ages, and she has also received the public thanks of the German Emperor for her assistance in the matter of Prince Bismarck's Septennate Bill. On every side she is succeeding, and she is likely to, for in the autumn of last year she placed her affairs once more in the hands of the Jesuits. And as soon as she feels her power she will doubtless persecute, for at the time of her destruction John perceives that she is "drunken with the blood of the saints."

But her confidence will be the cause of

Her Downfall.

Secure on her seat, she will attempt to control the beast, and then there will be an explosion. A storm will arise in the Sadducean element, for the ten kings will hate the harlot, and make her desolate and naked, and eat her flesh, and burn her with fire. Thus the way will be cleared for Satan's blasphemous king, and the Great Tribulation will follow.

But the Lord does not wish His people to experience these miseries. Between the fall of the seventh king, which is now in the past, and the rise of the eighth, He will call for His own, and He has commanded, "Watch ye, therefore, and pray always, that ye may be accounted worthy to escape all these things that shall come to pass." Do we obey His command?

CHRISTIAN HERALD AND SIGNS OF OUR TIMES.

OFFICE, 63 BIBLE HOUSE, NEW YORK.

ENTERED AT THE POST-OFFICE AT NEW YORK, N. Y., AS SECOND-CLASS MATTER.

Published Weekly. Subscription price, $1.50 a year; $1 eight months; 75 cents six months; sent two months on trial for 25 cents; always payable in advance. Single copies for sale by, or can be ordered at, all newsdealers.

Remittances by Mail should be by Post-office money order, bank cheques, or drafts or express money order, and should always be made payable to THE CHRISTIAN HERALD.

Receipts are not sent, the receipt of the paper by a subscriber is a sufficient proof that his remittance has been received. If the paper does not arrive promptly, please advise us, that we may see if the address is correctly entered.

Change of Address. Name of Post Office and State, of both old and new address, should always be given in case of removal.

CURRENT EVENTS.

The Text of the Fishery Treaty was Given to the press on February 22. It appears to be less satisfactory to all parties, except England, than was the sketch of it referred to in this place last week. A Canadian member of Parliament declared in the Senate that Canada could have done much better for herself by negotiating directly than by sending to England for a diplomat, who came out with the sole object of securing peace between Great Britain and the United States. Senator Frye, of Maine, was equally emphatic in his disapproval of the treaty from the American standpoint. He claims that American fishermen ought to have the right to purchase in Canadian ports provisions, bait, ice, seines, lines, and all other supplies and outfits for a fishing voyage. He also dwells on the advantage it would be to American fishermen, and which, it was at first stated, was secured by the treaty, to land and transport their catch by land in bond. The much vexed question of the headlands, however, appears likely to be finally and definitely settled if the treaty is ratified.

The House Pension Committee Have Unanimously agreed upon a bill for granting pensions to prisoners of war during the rebellion. It provides that each man in the military or naval service of the United States, who was a prisoner of war for sixty days or more, and who is now suffering from any disability which can reasonably be presumed to be the result of exposure and hardships endured while in confinement as a prisoner of war, and not the result of his own misconduct or vicious habits, shall be paid the pension now provided by law for similar disabilities, provided that no person shall be allowed to receive more than one pension. It is stated that there are a considerable number of men who have been rendered, by the hardships of prison life, unable to earn an adequate support and who are now, in old age, suffering want or living on charity. The number is not very great, and it is likely to decrease rapidly in time.

The Admission of Four Territories as States is proposed under a bill introduced by Congressman Springer, of Illinois, reported favorably on February 23, by the House Committee on Territories. Mr. Springer's bill is to enable the people of Dakota, Montana, Washington Territory and New Mexico to form Constitutions and State Governments and to be admitted into the Union on an equal footing with the original States. The bill authorizes residents of these Territories to elect delegates to conventions proportionate in number with the population of the counties. They are to meet at the seat of Government of each Territory on the second Tuesday of September next, adopt the Constitution of the United States, and form Constitutions and State Governments. They are required to assume the Territorial debts, and provide and maintain a public-school system. The Constitutions are to be submitted to a vote of the people on the Tuesday after the first Monday in November next, and if a majority are in favor of it, the results shall be certified to the President of the United States. Until the next general census the new States, with the exception of Dakota, are to be allowed one representative each in the House of Representatives; Dakota is to be allowed two Representatives.

The Venerable and Highly Respected Philanthropist, Mr. Wm. W. Corcoran, passed away on Friday morning, Feb. 24, in the ninety-first year of his age. He was a native of Georgetown, D. C. For a short time he attended Georgetown College, but left in his sixteenth year. For several years he was engaged in the dry goods business, but failed; he obtained a situation as clerk in a bank, and finally opened a bank on his own account in Washington. It was there that he made his immense fortune by his loans to the Government. In 1835 he married Miss Louise Amory Morris, who died in 1840, leaving one son, who died soon after his mother, and a daughter, Louise, who became the wife of Mr. George Eustis, of Louisiana. Among Mr. Corcoran's many gifts, to his country, are the Corcoran Art Gallery, at Washington, and the Louise Home, in the same city, for "ladies who have seen better days."

The Devastation by a Tornado of Mount Vernon, a thriving town in southern Illinois, on February 19, has sent a thrill of horror through the country. The catastrophe was sudden and overwhelming, no premonitory signs prepared the inhabitants for the coming calamity. The day was fair and the sky clear; but about four o'clock in the afternoon a dense black cloud spread itself swiftly over the sky, and a distant rumbling, like the passing of a heavily laden freight train was heard. Almost instantly the dreaded cyclone struck the town. The funnel-shaped cloud with its terrible rotary motion swept across it, leaving in its track uprooted trees, overturned houses, and solid blocks of masonry which it tore out of substantial buildings. In five minutes it was gone and anxious people turned out to search for the dead and injured. From under the ruins thirty-nine dead bodies were recovered, and scores of persons, injured more or less seriously, were extricated from the débris. The wounded, maimed and bleeding sufferers presented a most pitiable spectacle. Over three hundred houses were utterly destroyed, leaving about a thousand persons homeless, and in many cases penniless. Distressing as the calamity was, it is a matter for thankfulness that it did not occur half an hour earlier, as at that time the Baptist and Methodist churches, which were laid in ruins, were filled with children at Sunday-school.

An Austrian Warning to Russia has been Indirectly administered. Roumania has notified Turkey that Austria gives her assurances that a Russian violation of Roumania territory would be considered a movement against Austria and a cause of war. The march of Russian troops into Roumania would not only be aggression of a positive kind, but would specifically threaten Austria's own defences. It is a safe conclusion, therefore, that it would be resented by the latter as a hostile movement. Still, to make a hypothetical case, and act upon it by a specific promise is noticeable, and Austria's purpose is presumably not only to warn Russia but to increase her friendly relations with Roumania. This kingdom must have an addtional bias toward Austria, as having voluntarily given her pledges of protection. Russia could convey forces to Bulgaria by sea without violating Roumanian soil, but in any extended war in the peninsula Roumania would find it almost an impossibility to preserve her neutrality.

Dr. Mackenzie Still Reiterates his Statement that the Crown Prince's disease is not cancer, and that no trace of cancer has ever been detected by microscopical examination. Other accounts are contradictory, but the fact remains, and it impresses the public both in Germany and elsewhere probably more than the reports of the doctors, that the Prince grows somewhat worse from month to month, and that a more formidable operation than the last one is now talked of. He may yet recover, as the whole civilized world hopes he may, but the present signs are ominous.

A Gladstone Candidate for Parliament was defeated at the polls last week. The election was at Doncaster, which was formerly represented in the House of Commons by Mr. Walter S. Shirley, a faithful follower of Mr. Gladstone. At the election last week both candidates were Liberals, but Mr. Fitzwilliam is a follower of Lord Hartington; but his opponent, Mr. Balfour, is a Gladstonian. A much larger vote was polled on both sides than at the previous election, when the Gladstonian was elected. But the Liberal Unionist developed a much larger increase than his opponent, and was elected by a majority of 211 in a vote of over 11,000. This will reduce the voting strength of the Home Rule party by two votes, on a division.

The Interior Department will Modify its order prohibiting the use of the Indian language in Indian schools. Ex-Justice Strong and a number of delegates from the Bible Society and the Missionary societies have waited on President Cleveland and explained to him the difficulties the order caused in giving religious instruction to Indian children and adults. It was represented that there are about 40,000 Indian children of school age, of which 15,000 are pupils and about 25,000 adult Indians, who cannot understand any language but their own. Consequently, to discontinue instruction in the Indian language will deprive them of any religious instruction. The delegates said they were heartily in sympathy with the Government's effort to teach the Indians English, but believed that an exception should be made in religious instruction until the Indians understand the English language. The President said the order had been construed more literally than was intended, and new instructions modifying it would be issued.

The Financial Condition of the Country, as indicated by the report of the Director of the Mint, published last week, is unique in the history of nations. When specie payments were resumed on January 1, 1879, the value of our gold coin was $275,000,000, and of our silver $95,000,000. The Government now reports the gold at $575,000,000, and the silver at $353,000,000. This is an increase of $558,000,000 since the Government resumed the payment of its obligations in hard money. The contraction in paper currency being insignificant, in comparison with this enormous increase, it is evident that there must have been a huge expansion of commerce, and a vast increment of accrued wealth, during the past nine years.

Anxiety about Mr. H. M. Stanley Continues. Whether he has penetrated to Emin Pasha's stronghold is not known. Explorers and persons who have some knowledge of the character of the country and people on this route are still hopeful of his safety. A Paris journal last week published an interview on the subject with M. de Brazza, who has recently returned from the Congo. In the course of it the French explorer expressed the opinion that after leaving the Aruwimi River, Stanley, in order to feed his men, would be required to make daily raids upon the tribes in the districts through which the expedition passed. This, of necessity, would have obliged him to push on with all possible speed. Stanley, M. de Brazza thinks, has probably joined Emin Pasha, and will return home via Khartoum or Suakim, as he would not return by way of Zanzibar, unless he felt that the strength of his expedition would enable him to force his way.

is Undoubtedly Difficult to Devise any amendment to the inter-Sate commerce law which the railroads shall be able to give reduced rates or free transportation to religious and charitable bodies without opening a door to fraud. Nevertheless the prohibition contained in the law will operate to the injury of many a beneficent work. A case in point is the Children's Aid Society. One of the most important features of the Society's work is the sending to suitable homes in the West of children rescued from lives of poverty and vice. Before the law was passed, the railroads gave these children and the Society's agents accompanying them free transportation. The society's officers desire to have this privilege restored, and they are to lay their case before the Senate Inter-State Commerce Committee. Various other charitable institutions have joined in the request for changes in the law, and Young Men's Christian Associations in several cities also ask for amendments which will enable their members to accept certain courtesies from the railroads.

The United States Evangelical Alliance proposes to conduct a canvass among the non-church-going classes of Brooklyn, N. Y. In regard to the direct methods by which the Alliance proposes to reach these masses of non-church-going people, Rev. Dr. Josiah Strong, Secretary of the Alliance, said that Brooklyn had been divided into thirteen sections, and that the churches of each section were being organized into branch Alliances. For every 100 members there was to be one supervisor, and for every supervisor ten visitors. Each community will be divided into as many districts as there are supervisors, and each district will be assigned to the care of one supervisor. Then each district will be subdivided into ten fields, and each field assigned to a visitor, who shall learn the church preference of the non-churchgoer whom he visits, and will extend to him in the name of the Alliance an invitation to attend the nearest church of that denomination, and his name will be sent to the pastor of the church. This plan is now being successfully worked in Mansfield, Ohio, and in Oswego, in this State.

A Southern Senator Confesses to a Ludicrous blunder. He had occasion to travel from Washington to New York, and, having purchased his sleeping-car ticket, he went to the depot and boarded a train. Being exceedingly tired and sleepy, he undressed immediately, went to bed, and was soon in a sound slumber. He awoke in the morning much refreshed, and proceeded to make his ablutions and dress, preparatory to crossing the ferry from Jersey City to the metropolis. When he issued from the car, however, he was overwhelmed with surprise. Washington's scenes were around him as they were when he went to bed the night before. On inquiry he learned that he had slept all night in the Washington depot, having entered a car which had not been attached to the New York train. Mortifying as the Senator's mistake was, it would have been still far worse if, instead of remaining still, he had been carried in an opposite direction. That mistake in a more serious matter is being made by many who "hope" they are Christians, and who "expect" to go to heaven when they die. When they awake to the discovery of their blunder their despair will be unbearable. (Luke 13: 26–28.)

Exclusion From a Grave in Calvary Cemetery, Brooklyn, N. Y., appears likely to involve a lawsuit. On February 19, an aged gentleman fell down dead suddenly of heart disease while attending a meeting in New York. The undertaker, to whom was confided the charge of the funeral, was informed that the deceased owned a grave in Calvary Cemetery, in which his wife was buried sixteen years ago, and in which, during his life, he had expressed a wish to be interred beside her. The undertaker, therefore, notified the authorities of the cemetery, but was astonished to learn that the interment would not be permitted. The body has, therefore, been temporarily deposited in Greenwood, to await the result of an appeal to the law, or to ecclesiastical authorities, whose mandate the cemetery officials will obey. The reasons for the refusal have not been divulged, but a clue to them is obtained, in the fact that Calvary is a Roman Catholic cemetery, and the meeting which the deceased was attending when he was stricken down was one to hear a discourse by the excommunicated priest, Dr. McGlynn. The issue of this case is a matter of public concern. Thousands of persons, who have purchased lots in cemeteries, want to know whether, after making provision for a last resting-place for their bodies, it is possible for any one to exclude them. Happily, no similar question can disturb the Christian about the destination of his soul. Though men may prevent his body lying in the resting-place he has provided for it, neither men nor demons can shut his soul out of the mansion which Christ has prepared for him. (John 14: 2.)

An Eccentric Widow's Death was Reported from Lewiston, Me., last week. She lived quite alone, in an old cottage in the business part of the town, avoiding all intercourse with neighbors and relatives, and never allowing any one to set foot inside her dwelling. Every window was closely curtained, and no signs of life were ever perceptible about the house. Her death was discovered almost by an accident, and no one could say exactly when it had taken place. Every room in the house, except the one in which she lived, was found covered with dust, no article of furniture having been moved since her husband died, thirty-three years ago. It was at that time that she commenced the hermit life, which continued till her death. Property to the amount of $30,000 in money and bonds was found secreted about the house. It was the carefully saved capital and its proceeds which her husband left her in his will, attaching to it the condition that she remain single. It is supposed that her motive for seclusion was an exaggerated and morbid desire to fulfil his wishes. It so, she probably misunderstood them, as no sane man would wish his widow to lead such a life. The whole system of monasticism is based on a similar error. Though Christ wishes His followers to be separate from the world, He does not wish them to neglect their duties, which they cannot fulfil when they seclude themselves. (John 17:15.)

A Bequest Contingent on Change of Name occurs in a will presented for probate in New York. This is the clause referred to: "I give and bequeath unto my godchild, Frederick Rudolph Peipers, the sum of $2,000, lawful money of the United States of America, for his own use, benefit and behoof forever; provided, however, and this legacy is upon the express condition, that my said godchild shall, from and after the time that this bequest shall have been made known to him, continue to so spell and write his name for all time forth, and in default of his so doing, this legacy to him shall be wholly void and of no effect, and the sum herein bequeathed shall fall into and become part of my residuary estate, and shall be disposed of according to the provision of the clause in this my will disposing of my residuary estate." The testator was evidently anxious that his name should be remembered after his death, and doubted whether his god-son would use it, unless it was clearly to his interest to do so. The desire that a family name be perpetuated is common, and the gratification of it was among the blessings promised in the Old Testament to those who keep His commands, "I will give them an everlasting name that shall not be cut off" (Isa. 56: 5), while we are assured that in spite of all precautions "the name of the wicked shall rot" (Prov. 10: 7).

A Self-Imposed Lenten Penance, Performed by a Brooklyn lady, was described recently by a police officer in the Eastern District. He said: "On the first day of Lent a lady presented herself at the police station in the evening and asked permission to sleep there. She was well dressed, modest-looking and sober, and I wondered at her request. I told her that I didn't think she could stand the place. 'Oh, yes, I can, and could if it were twice as disagreeable,' she replied. The next night she came again and stayed all night, and every night afterward until the end of Lent. When I found that she did herd with these drunken and dirty unfortunates who sleep here, I thought she would soon become as bad as the rest, and I watched her, to note the change which her associates would bring upon her. But no change showed itself. She preserved her tidy appearance and continued just as modest and well-behaved as when she first came." Some inquiries were made about her, and it was found that she belonged to a respectable family and had a good home, but that she had determined on sleeping among the wretched, drunken offscourings of the streets every night as a self-imposed penance. It was a vain effort, if undertaken with the idea that it would merit pardon for sin; but if having first obtained pardon through the merits of Jesus she went among the vicious and depraved to tell them of the Friend of sinners, it was an act of devotion which God would bless. (1 Cor. 13: 3.)

BRIEF NOTES.

It is reported that all the American missions in Burmah have incorporated total abstinence in their work.

Among the results of Rev. George C. Needham's work in Springfield, is the wonderful demand for Bibles. The number sold during and since his visit is unprecedented.

Mr. and Miss Parker's gospel mission at Sharon, Pa., closed on February 19. Over one hundred persons made a public profession of faith. They are now at Newcastle, Pa.

Senators Dingley and Frye, of Maine, are about to introduce into Congress bills for the better protection of women in the District of Columbia.

The Good Templars have entered actively upon the work of raising a fund for the erection of a suitable monument to the late John B. Finch. Circulars soliciting subscriptions have been sent out.

The Evangelical Alliance has prepared a form of constitution suitable for any branch Alliance. Copies can be had on application to the Secretary, the Rev. Josiah Strong, D. D., 42 Bible House.

It is proposed to commemorate the centenary of the birth of Adoniram Judson, which will occur August 9, 1888, by erecting a Judson Memorial Church in Mandalay, the capital of Upper Burmah.

Rev. Dr. Thomas S. Hastings has been elected President of the Union Theological Seminary. The seminary has been without a president since the death of Dr. Roswell D. Hitchcock, last summer.

At Nashville, Tenn., the Theatre Vendome was engaged for revival meetings recently, under the conduc of Mr. S. M. Sayford. Fully two thousand persons attended each night, and there were many conversions.

The police of Constantinople are closing all liquor shops kept by Europeans, on the ground that they are demoralizing the Turkish people. The Consulates are invaded by liquor-dealers complaining of the police.

Bishop Taylor's reports of his work in Africa are most encouraging. He has now a chain of stations far into the interior, the most advanced being located at a point on the Upper Kassai. Dr. Harrison, one of the two physicians who have joined the mission, is now at Luluaburgh, in the Congo State.

Twenty thousand dollars annually are paid by the city of Chicago to the support of the Washingtonian Home for Inebriates. The amount is derived from the proceeds of the licenses to saloon-keepers. The city is thus interested in the manufacture and reform of drunkards. Every city that issues licenses should also support such a home.

The fund now being raised by the Presbyterian Church for endowing a Board of Relief for aged ministers, widows and orphans, has been increased by a second gift of $10,000. This gift is anonymous, but it comes from St. Louis, Mo. The first gift of $10,000 was from an Eastern donor. The Committee engaged in the work of raising this fund believe that they will have a million dollars in hand by the time the Centennial of the Church is celebrated in May next.

Statistics of the Mormon Church show that there are 400 Mormon bishops in Utah, 2,423 priests, 2,947 teachers and 6,854 deacons. Salt Lake City is divided into wards of eight or nine blocks each, and a bishop is put in charge of each ward. Under him there are two teachers, whose business it is to learn the employment and income of every resident of the ward and report the same to the bishop. Then the bishop collects one-tenth of each man's income and turns it in to the Church.

HOLDING FAST THE FAITH.

A New Sermon, by Pastor C. H. Spurgeon.

"And to the angel of the church in Pergamos write; These things saith H. which hath the sharp sword with two edges; I know thy works, and where thou dwellest, even where Satan's seat is: and thou holdest fast my name, and hast not denied my faith."—Revelation 2: 12, 13.

Christ Coming Armed to the Church—Hypocrites There to be Purged out—The Circumstances of Christians Noted—Allowance Made for Evil Surroundings—I. The Fact about Pergamos—How the Faith may be Denied—By Keeping Silence—By Unholy Living—II. What Pergamos Did—Holding the Name of Christ—The Deity of it—Its Royalty—Its Saving Power—Its Immutability—III. What Christ's Name is to the Church—Comfort—Power—A Possession to be Defended—A Spurgeon in Jail.

SPECIALLY note, dear friends, at the opening of this morning's meditation, the character under which the Lord Jesus Christ presents Himself to the church at Pergamos. "These things saith He which hath the sharp sword with two edges." Does the Lord Jesus come to His church in that way? Does He at the door of the church bear a sword? a sword unscabbarded? a sharp sword? a sharp sword with two edges? Yes, even to His visible church this is how our Lord Jesus Christ appears. To His own spiritual and faithful ones He is to each one a husband, full of unutterable tenderness and love; but to the visible church, which at its best estate is never altogether pure, He appears in severer form. To a church He comes as Captain of the Lord's host, and He wields a sharp sword with two edges. It is the parallel of that passage where John the Baptist saith to Him: "His fan is in His hand, and He will thoroughly purge His floor, and He will gather His wheat into His garner; but He will burn up the chaff with unquenchable fire." We think of

The Coming of Our Lord

as a joy and a blessing; but, oh, remember that question, "But who may abide the day of His coming? and who shall stand when He appeareth?" The Lord bears the sword, and He beareth it not in vain. Time has not blunted its edge, it is "sharp;" and it hath two edges, as of old. But what will He do with that sword in reference to a church? We are not left in any doubt upon that point. Having mentioned some whose doctrines and lives were unclean, the Lord says: "Repent; or else I will come unto thee quickly, and will fight against them with the sword of My mouth." He turns the sword against those within the church who had no right to be there. It is no trifling thing to be a church member. I could earnestly wish that certain professors had never been members of a church at all; for if they had been outside the church, they might have been in far less peril than they are within its bounds. Outside, their conduct might have been tolerated; but it is not consistent with avowal of discipleship towards Jesus. I say this with deep sorrow. I introduce the subject as the Spirit Himself introduces it. I would make the sermon sweet to the saints, but the preface must be sharp, lest any seize upon comforts to which they have no right.

Notice that this blessed Saviour watches his church with an observant eye. He looks at the church in Pergamos, and He says, "I know thy works, and where thou dwellest, even

Where Satan's Seat is."

The Lord sees the position and the peril of the church at Pergamos, "where Satan dwelleth." Probably there were horrible idolatries, with obscene orgies in the city, or it may have been a place of peculiar licentiousness, or of special persecution. We cannot at this distance of time exactly tell what it was; but the Lord regarded it as the citadel of Satan. There are places in the world at this day where sin has so much the upper hand, or where error and unbelief reign so supreme, that the devil would seem to have there taken up his residence, and to have made it his capital city. You, dear friend, may be living in society where the evil one rules with undisputed sway. You are not favored to dwell with your fellow-Christians, but you go home to be met with blasphemies at the door; and all the week sights and sounds assail your eyes and ears which make you feel like Lot in Sodom. I am sorry for you; but let it comfort you that

Your Lord Knows All About It,

and He can either remove you from the trying position, or else He can still more glorify His grace by supporting you in it, and enabling you to overcome the enemy. He knows that "Satan desires to have you, that he may sift you as wheat;" and He prays for you that your faith fail not. He knows your perils, and He considers your trials. If you are holding fast His name and have not denied the faith, even *that* may be to Him a surer proof of your truthfulness of heart than works of labor and patience might be in other instances. When we have little strength, and are placed in positions of great difficulty, then the Lord thinks all the more of what we produce, and regards it as all the surer proof of fidelity. In the text it is commendation enough for Pergamos, under the circumstances that, dwelling so close to Beelzebub's own capital, close under the shadow of the throne of hell, that, church could earn this praise: "Thou holdest fast My name, and hast not denied My faith."

I. The first head will be, let us consider this fact. I hope it is a fact with many here present as surely as it was a fact with Pergamos. I trust it can be said of this church and of its members—"Thou holdest fast My name, and hast not denied my faith."

How May the Faith be Denied?

In several ways this may be done. Let me say it very tenderly, but very solemnly, some deny the faith, and let go the name of Jesus by never confessing it. Remember how the Lord puts this matter in the gospels: "Whosoever shall confess Me before men, him shall the Son of Man also confess before the angels of God; but he that denieth Me before men shall be denied before the angels of God." Here it is clear that to deny is the same thing as not confessing. I know people who almost boast of their neutrality. They have tried not exactly to hold with the hare and run with the hounds, but neither to hold with the hare nor yet to run with the hounds. These have hoped to find in their discretion the better part of valor; but, believe me, it is a valor which will be rewarded with everlasting contempt. This way you hope to lead an easy life. An easy life of such a kind will end in a very uneasy death. A life in which we have shunned the Cross of Christ will lead to a state in which we shall miss the crown.

But then it is very possible to deny the name and the faith

By Unholy Living.

Let none of us imagine that an orthodox creed can be of any use to us if we lead a heterodox life. No, Christ Jesus is to be obeyed as a Master, as well as to be believed as a Teacher. The disciple is to be practically obedient, as well as attentively teachable. "Without holiness no man shall see the Lord." Alas! we can deny the faith by actually forsaking it, and quitting the people of God. Some do so deliberately, and others because the charms of the world overcome them. We are told of some who went away from our Lord because of what He had taught. They cried, "This is a hard saying; who can hear it?" My friends, if you are not prepared to accept hard sayings, you need not profess to be disciples of Jesus. "Horrible doctrine!" cried one the other day. Granted that it is horrible, may it not also be true? Many horrible things take place around us, and yet none can deny the facts. You cannot exclude from your knowledge many things which are true, by merely crying, "Horrible!" It is not ours to judge of our Lord's teaching by our sentiment: we are to receive it by faith. He speaks terribly of the doom of the wicked, and He is not capable of exaggeration. What the Lord Jesus says is certain, for "He is the faithful and true witness," and therefore we will not turn from Him, whatever His teaching may be.

In what way may we be said to hold fast the name of Christ and the faith of Christ? I answer, by the full consent of our intellect, yielding up our mind to consider and accept the things which are assuredly believed among us. If we hold fast the name of Jesus, we must hold the faith *in the love of it*. We must store up in our affections all that our Lord teaches. We also hold it fast by holding it forth in the teeth of all opposition. We must confess the faith at all proper times and seasons, and we must never hide our colors. Only brave soldiers are worthy of our great Lord. Those who sneak into the rear, that they may be comfortable, are not worthy of the kingdom.

What Will our Captain say of Cowards

in that day when He distributes rewards to His faithful ones? Brethren, we must be willing to bear ridicule for Christ's sake, even that peculiarly envenomed ridicule which "the cultured" are so apt to pour upon us. We must be willing to be thought great fools for Jesus' sake. Some of us have forgotten more than many of our opponents ever knew, and yet they style us ignorant; we are bearing shame because we have the courage of our convictions, and yet they call us cowards. For my part, I am willing to be ten thousand fools in one for my dear Lord and Master, and count it to be the highest honor that can be put upon me to be stripped of every honor and loaded with every censure, for the sake of the grand old truth which is written on my very heart.

II. In the second place, having considered the fact, let us further enlarge upon it. What do we mean by holding fast the name of Christ? I reply, first, we mean holding fast

The Deity of that Name.

We believe in our Lord's real Godhead. "His name shall be called Wonderful, Counsellor, the mighty God." One of the names by which He is revealed to us is Immanuel. The word "El" is one of the great Oriental names of God. You get in Hebrew Elohim, and in Arabic "Allah." Our Lord Jesus is Immanu-*el*, that is, God with us; and we believe Him to be so. We also hold fast the name of Jesus, and the faith of Jesus, as to the royalty of His name. When we bow the knee in prayer, and say, "Thy kingdom come," we mean the kingdom of God, and we mean also the kingdom of Christ Jesus. He it is that as a Lamb is seen in the midst of the throne where saints and angels pay adoring homage. Soon shall the seventh angel sound his trumpet, and great voices shall be heard in heaven saying, "The kingdoms of this world are become the kingdoms of our Lord, and of His Christ; and He shall reign for ever."

We hold fast the name of Christ, as we believe in its saving power. "Thou shalt call His name Jesus: for He shall save His people from their sins." We hold fast the belief that Jesus saves us from the guilt of sin by having borne it in His own body on the tree. He died as a victim in our stead.

He Saves Us

from the power of sin by His Spirit, and by faith in His death; we overcome sin by the blood of the Lamb. Salvation in every department, salvation from its hopeful dawning to its glorious noontide in perfection, is all of Christ Jesus. He is Saviour, and He alone. "There is none other name under heaven given among men, whereby we must be saved." He is the unique Saviour, there is no other possible salvation now or in the world to come. Believest thou in Christ? Then thou hast salvation. "But he that believeth not shall be damned." Pronounce the word hard or soft as thou wilt, it will come to the same thing in the end—thou shalt be condemned, and condemned hopelessly, if thou believeth not in Jesus Christ, the one sole propitiation for the sins of men. This we hold fast.

Once, more we hold fast this name in its immutability. We are told to-day that this is an age of progress, and therefore we must accept an improved gospel. Every man is to be his own lawyer, and every man his own Saviour.

e are getting on in the direction of every an putting away his own sin, just as every himney should consume its own smoke. But, ear friends, we do not believe these idle reams. We want no new gospel, no modern lvation. Our conviction is that Jesus Christ "the same yesterday, to-day, and for ever." he way that Paul went to heaven is good ough for me. When I remember my dear rethren and sisters in Christ who have fallen leep, whom I saw die with triumph lighting p their faces, I feel quite content with the lvation which saved them, and I am not going o try experiments or speculations. To talk of mproving upon our perfect Saviour is to insult Him. He is God's propitiation; what would ou more? My blood boils at the idea of

Improving the Gospel.

There is but one Saviour, and that one Saviour s the same for ever. His doctrine is the same n every age, and is not yea and nay. What a trange result we should obtain in the general ssembly of heaven if some were saved by the ospel of the first century, and others by the ospel of the second, and others by the gospel f the seventeenth, and others by the gospel of he nineteenth century! We should need a different song of praise for the clients of these various periods, and the mingled chorus would be rather to the glory of man's culture than to the praise of the one Lord. No such mottled heaven, and no such discordant song, shall ever be produced. There is one church and one Saviour. This is what we mean by holding fast the name and faith of Jesus.

III. Thirdly, dear friends, to lead you a step further in the same road, let me show the practical place of the name and of the faith with us. The practical place of it is this: first of all, it is our personal comfort—The faith which we hold is our daily and hourly

Joy and Hope.

The doctrines which I believe in connection with the divine Person in whom I trust are the pillow of my weariness, the anodyne of my care, the rest of my spirit. Jesus gives me a look-out for years to come which is celestial, and at the same time I can look back with thankfulness on the years which are past. For all time the Lord Jesus is our heart's content. Nothing can separate us from His love, and therefore nothing can deprive us of our confident hope. Through this blessed name and this blessed faith believers are made glad and strong.

This also is our power in preaching; indeed, it is our power, our only power, in living before God. Brethren, the devil will never be cast out by any other name—let us hold it fast. If we conjure by eloquence, talent, music, or what not, the evil one will say, "Jesus I know, and Paul I know; but who are ye?" When we draw near to God, what is our strength wherewith to prevail *in prayer?* Is it not that we ask in the name of Jesus? That name prevaileth with God concerning everything, and so enables us to prevail with man; wherefore, hold it fast, and deny not the faith; for what can you do if the name of Jesus be given up?

Now, in closing, I will urge reasons for holding fast the name and faith of Jesus. I hope we hold it so fast that we can never give it up while reason holds its throne. There is an old Christian legend concerning Ignatius, that he never spoke without mentioning the name of Jesus, whom he loved. His speech seemed saturated with love to his Lord, and when he died, the name of Jesus was found to be stamped on his heart. It may not have been so literally, but no doubt it was true spiritually. The name of Jesus is, I hope, written in our hearts so as to be inseparable from our lives. That it may be so I will put the question thus:

Why Should We Give Up

the faith? I fail to see a reason. Why should I change my belief, or cease to hold fast the name of Christ Jesus my Lord? It is an irrational suggestion. "I am open to conviction," said a man who knew his ground. "I am open to conviction, but I should like to see the man that could convince me." I am in very much the same condition with regard to the gospel of my Lord Jesus: I am open to conviction, but I shall never see the man that can convince me out of my experience, my conviction, my consciousness, my hope, my all. Before I could quit my faith in the substitutionary work of the Lord Jesus Christ, and my confidence in the everlasting convenant ordered in all things and sure, I should have to be ground to powder, and every separate atom transformed.

We must defend the faith; for what would become of us if our fathers had not maintained it? If confessors, reformers, martyrs and covenanters had been recreant to the name and faith of Jesus, where would have been the churches of to-day? Must we not play the man as they did? If we do not, are we not censuring our fathers? It is very pretty to read of Luther and his brave deeds? Of course,

Everybody Admires Luther!

Yes, yes; but you do not want any one else to do the same to-day. When you go to the Zoological Gardens you all admire the bear; but how would you like a bear at home, or a bear wandering loose about the street? You tell me that it would be *unbearable*, and no doubt you are right. So, we admire a man who was firm in the faith, say four hundred years ago; the past ages are a sort of bear-pit or iron cage for him; but such a man to-day is a nuisance, and must be put down. Call him a narrow-minded bigot, or give him a worse name if you can think of one. Yet imagine that in those ages past, Luther, Zwingle, Calvin, and their compeers had said, "The world is out of order; but if we try to set it right we shall only make a great row, and get ourselves into disgrace. Let us go to our chambers, put on our night-caps, and sleep over the bad times, and perhaps when we wake up things will have grown better." Such conduct on their part would have entailed upon us a heritage of error. Age after age would have gone down into the infernal deeps, and the pestiferous bogs of error would have swallowed all. These men loved the faith and name of Jesus too well to see them trampled on.

Note What We Owe

them, and let us pay to our sons the debt we owe our fathers. It is to-day as it was in the Reformers' days. Decision is needed. Here is the day for the man; where is the man for the day? We who have had the gospel passed to us by martyr hands dare not trifle with it, nor sit by and hear it denied by traitors, who pretend to love it, but inwardly abhor every line of it. The faith I hold bears upon it marks of the blood of my ancestors. Shall I deny their faith, for which they left their native land to sojourn here? Shall we cast away the treasure which was handed to us through the bars of prisons, or came to us charred with the flames of Smithfield? Personally, when my bones have been tortured with rheumatism, I have

Remembered Job Spurgeon,

doubtless of my own stock, who in Chelmsford Jail was allowed a chair, because he could not lie down by reason of rheumatic pain. That Quaker's broad-brim overshadows my brow. Perhaps I inherit his rheumatism; but that I do not regret if I have his stubborn faith, which will not let me yield a syllable of the truth of God. When I think of how others have suffered for the faith, a little scorn or unkindness seems a mere trifle, not worthy of mention. An ancestry of lovers of the faith ought to be a great plea with us to abide by the Lord God of our fathers, and in the faith in which they lived. As for me, I must hold the old gospel: I can do no other. God helping me, I will endure the consequences of what men think obstinacy.

Look you, sirs, there are ages yet to come. If the Lord does not speedily appear, there will come another generation, and another, and all these generations will be tainted and injured if we are not faithful to God and to His truth to-day. We have come to a turning-point in the road. If we turn to the right, mayhap our children and our children's children will go that way; but if we turn to the left, generations yet unborn will curse our names for having been unfaithful to God and to His word. I charge you, not only by your ancestry, but by your posterity, that you seek to win the commendation **of your Master,** that though you dwell **where Satan's seat is,** you yet hold fast His **name, and do not deny His** faith. Stand fast, my beloved, in the name of God! I, your brother in Christ, entreat you to abide in the truth. Quit yourselves like men, be strong. The Lord sustain you for Jesus' sake. Amen.

[The prayers of the readers of this journal are requested for the blessing of God upon its Editors, and those whose sermons, articles or labors for Christ are printed in it; and that its circulation may be used by the Holy Spirit for the conversion of many sinners and the quickening of God's people. Dr. Talmage and Mr. Spurgeon especially request prayer every Sunday morning on behalf o their labors.]

GEMS FROM NEW BOOKS.

An Adventure with Wolves in Norway.*

THE last weeks before Christmas are in Norway always the busiest season in all trades, and coopers are no exception to the rule. They have so many orders that they are often in arrear with them. That was the case with a well-known cooper named Tollef Kolstad, one night about the middle of December. He had been at work since dawn on a huge tub, which had been ordered by Grim Berglund, the richest peasant in the parish. It was about ten o'clock at night when Tollef made the last stroke upon the tub, and placed it on the flat sleigh which with a swift horse he had borrowed of a neighbor. He was about to take his place on the sleigh, to drive to Berglund's house on the other side of the lake, with the barrel, for he knew Berglund would be glad to get it that night, when he heard a shrill voice call him.

"Father, do take me with you."

"No, my boy, there may be wolves out to-night, and they will eat little boys if they can get them."

"I am not afraid, father; do take me," and Tollef, who did not easily deny his little boy any innocent pleasure, consented. He lifted him up, wrapped him warmly in his little sheepskin coat and put him between his knees. Then taking the reins he urged the horse on toward the shore, beyond which was the broad expanse of ice that glittered like silver in the light of the moon and the spear-like gleams of the Aurora Borealis. They were soon on the frozen lake and speeding quickly across it. The wind cut them keenly; then it roared and whistled round their heads. But it was not that which made Tollef's heart stand still and clutch his boy convulsively in his arms. It was a terrible long-drawn howl which came floating toward him from the pine forest behind.

"What is that, father?" asked Thor, a little tremulously.

"It was wolves, my boy," said Tollef.

"Why do we not go back home?"

"Because they are behind us. Our only chance is to go on and try to get to the other shore before they overtake us."

The horse, sniffing the presence of wild beasts, snorted wildly as it ran, but electrified, as it were, with the sense of danger, strained every nerve in its efforts to reach the farther shore. The howls now came nearer and nearer, and they rose with a frightful distinctness in the clear wintry air, and resounded again from the border of the forest.

"Why don't you throw away the barrel, father?" said Thor, who strove hard to keep brave. "Then the sleigh will run so much the better."

"If we are overtaken, our safety is in the barrel. It is large enough for two, and will fit close to the ice." Tollef was still calm; but with his

---

*From "The Modern Vikings," by H. H. Boyesen, a collection of incidents of peasant life in Iceland and Norway. 274 pages with numerous illustrations; price $2; published by *Charles Scribner's Sons*, 745 Broadway, New York.

The Market-Place and Mosque of Bagdad.

one disengaged arm, hugged his little son convulsively.

"Now, keep brave, my boy;" he whispered in his ear, "they will soon be upon us." The horse was showing signs of exhaustion, and Tollef, seeing that only one chance was left, rose up with his boy in his arms, and, upsetting the barrel on the ice, concealed himself and the child under it. Hardly had he had time to brace himself against its sides, pressing his feet against one side and his back against the other, when the short, whining bark of the wolves told him that some had followed the horse, while the greater number remained to investigate the contents of the barrel. The howling and barking of these furious creatures without, was now incessant.

The father was less warmly clad than the son, and, moreover, was obliged to sit on the ice, while Thor could stand erect without knocking against the bottom of the barrel; and if it had not been for the excitement of the situation, which made Tolleff's blood course with unwonted rapidity, it is more than probable that the intense cold would have made him drowsy, and thus lessened his power of resistance. The warmth of his body had made a slight cavity where he was sitting, and whenever he remained a moment still, his trousers froze fast to the ice. It was only the presence of his boy that inspired him with fresh courage, whenever hope seemed about to desert him.

About an hour after the flight of the horse there was a lull in the attack, but a sudden increase of the barking noise around the barrel. From this, Tollef concluded that some wolves were hurt and their fellows were killing them.

But hark! what is that? It sounds like a song, or, rather, like a hymn. The strain comes nearer and nearer, resounding from mountain to mountain, flowing peacefully through the pure and still air:

> "Who knows how near I am mine ending;
> So swiftly time doth pass away."

Tollef, in whose breast hope was again reviving, put his ear to the ice, and heard distinctly the tread of horses and many human feet. He comprehended instantly that his only chance of life was in joining these people before they were too far away; and, quickly resolved, he lifted the boy on his left arm, and grasped the hatchet in his disengaged hand. Then, with a violent thrust, he flung the barrel from over him, and ran in the direction of the sound. The wolves saw him, and a pack of about a dozen immediately started in pursuit. They leaped up against him at once, while he struck furiously about him with his small weapon. Fortunately, he had sharp steel pegs in his boots, and kept his footing well; otherwise the combat would have been a short one. His voice, too, was powerful, and his shouts rose high above the howling of the beasts. He soon perceived that he was observed, and he saw in the bright moonlight six or eight men running toward him. Just then, perhaps in his joy, his vigilance was, for a fraction of a second, relaxed; he felt a pull in the fleshy part of his right arm. He was not conscious of any sharp pain, and was astonished to see the blood flowing from an ugly wound. But he only held his boy the more tightly, while he fought and ran with the strength of despair.

Now the men were near. He could hear their voices. But his brain was dizzy, and he saw but dimly.

"Hello, friend; don't crack my skull for my pains!" someone was shouting close to his ear, and he let his hatchet fall, and fell himself too, prostrate on the ice.

The wolves, at the sight of the men, had retired to a safe distance, from which they watched the proceedings, as if uncertain whether to return.

As soon as Tollef had recovered somewhat from his exhaustion and his loss of blood, he and his boy were placed upon a sleigh, and his wound was carefully bandaged. He now learned that his rescuers were on their way to a funeral, which was to take place on the next day, but, on account of the distance of the church, they had been obliged to start during the night. Hence their solemn mood, and their singing of funeral hymns.

After an hour's ride they reached the cooper's cottage, and were invited to rest, and share such hospitality as the house could afford.

THE MARKET-PLACE OF BAGDAD.

(See Illustration.)

THE name of Bagdad is so closely associated in the minds of young people with the famous wildly romantic but fascinating "Arabian Nights," that the fact of an actual city of Bagdad existing can scarcely be realized. Nevertheless Bagdad is a visible city on the banks of the Tigris, in Turkey in Asia, not far from the frontiers of Persia. Its ancient glory is departed, but sufficient of its ancient buildings still remain to convey to the visitor's mind an idea of the former grandeur of the city. The view depicted in the illustration of the market-place, with the magnificent mosque in the background, is a specimen of the general aspect of the city.

Bagdad is built on both sides of the river Tigris, its two portions being connected by a bridge of boats. It is a walled city, the walls of brick and earth being about five miles in circumference. Several large towers are built upon the wall, and it incloses many a large garden and date plantation. The present population of the city is about one hundred and fifty thousand.

Ancient Bagdad was founded by the Arabs about A. D. 762. They brought with them their religion, which had been given them by Mohammed, and which they thought their mission to carry by force of the word or the sword to the uttermost parts of the earth. For a time all was peaceful and prosperous in Mesopotamia, the land between the rivers Euphrates and Tigris, in which Bagdad is situated, and of which it is now the most important city. But in a few hundred years fresh hordes of barbarians broke in from the far East, of which the Turks now remain. Under their oppressive Government, everything is going to ruin and desolation, and Bagdad, though still the capital of the province, has dwindled into insignificance compared with what it once was, when it was said to rival Babylon in magnificence and power. It was the capital of the ancient Saracen Empire, and the principal seat of Mohammedan learning. For a long period this city recived all the trade of the surrounding countries, but now it has declined greatly, most of the products being carried by way of Trebizonde, partly on account of the hordes of robbers which infest Bagdad and the neighborhood, and partly on account of the frequent visitations of the plague, which finds a rich harvest in the filthy streets of the city.

The streets of the old town are narrow and irregular, and the majority o the houses are poor and meanly built Bagdad was greatly beautified and enlarged in the time of the famous caliph Haroun-al-Raschid, of whose work many fine structures still remain, among the most interesting of which are the renowned "Gate of the Talisman," a lofty minaret, built in 785, and the tomb of Zobedie, the beloved wife of Haroun-al-Raschid.

A CHINESE GARDEN.

(See Illustration.)

THE river gardens of China have interested all travellers in that strange country. Built out on piles driven in the bed of the stream, and connected with the owner's residence by a light bridge, they form a pretty yet somewhat fantastic feature of the landscape. There they rear their dwarf plants, which, to the eyes of a Chinaman, are far more beautiful than the stoutest oak or most graceful cedar.

A River Garden in China.

Such gardens as that depicted in the illustration belong, of course, to the wealthy classes, though the poorer classes make use of the rivers too, though in a more practical way. Some of them have actually built houses in this way on piles, regardless of the fact that a sudden rise in the river means certain death to them and their families.

The overcrowding of the Chinese cities has led other families to seek refuge in boats on the river, where they live from one year's end to another. These boat people constitute the lowest class of the Chinese people. They are found more or less in all districts, but most of all in the neighborhood of Canton, where they number about two hundred thousand. Their customs are somewhat different from those of the land people, and their worship is not the same. Another divergence is, that they never bind the feet of their women. This custom of foot-binding is almost as prevalent as ever. Absurd as it seems, the people cannot be induced to relinquish it. They regard natural feet as a badge of poverty. Mothers believe that small feet secure a life of ease; the woman with large feet, it is inferred, has to work for her living, and to go out in all weather. No man of good family would ever form an alliance with a lady having large feet. If such a thing should happen, his friends would make her life miserable.

No other land has such a wonderful system of waterways, but it was not until comparatively recent times that the Chinese fully realized their utility. There are thousands of miles of rivers and canals, the banks of which are now lined with thousands of towns and villages. There are few places in the empire, and none of any importance, but can be reached easily by boat—a mode of travelling offering many advantages to a people like the Chinese, but notably the one essential advantage of economy.

The houses are all built on the same plan, those of the wealthy having more rooms, and being easily distinguishable by the profusion of ornamentation. The rooms frequently open into a court filled with trees and shrubs, and having a small fish-pond or fountain in the centre.

The traveller is amazed wherever he goes, and the more, as he penetrates to the interior, at the extraordinary manners and customs of this wonderful people. To the Christian, however, the most distressing and awful consideration is, that this land teeming with immortal souls is still practically given over to the most degrading superstition. No generation has done so much as this to spread the knowledge of the Gospel in China, but, compared with the vast field, the progress made, encouraging as it is intrinsically, is but slight. Prayer, men and money are required of the Church, that the gospel should be preached even as a witness only in the cities of these perishing millions.

MRS. TRANSOME'S PUPIL.

A SERIAL STORY.

(Continued from page 127.)

A Parting.

THERE was a small, low chair of Willie's, my only boy who was dead, that was kept strung up to a hook in the strong beam by a bit of rope. It was a pretty chair, painted green, with roses along the back, and many a time my scholars had admired it. But no child had ever sat in it since Willie died. When morning school was over I climbed up on one of the benches, in spite of my stiff limbs, and unfastened it. The tears stood agin in my eyes, for I fancied I could see my boy sitting in it by the side of the fireplace, and watching me while I was busy about my work. But I dusted it well, and set it down just in Willie's own place in the chimney-nook, where Pippin was still quietly squatting on the floor; for he had not run away the moment school was over, like the other children.

"There!" I said, "that's your seat now, my little lad. It belongs to my Willie, who's been in heaven these twenty years, waiting for me and father. Nobody but a good boy ought to sit on a chair that belongs to him, now he's an angel.

"I'm going to be a good boy now, and an angel some day," said the child, smiling up into my face.

"The Lord help him and me!" I said to myself, as I put the room to rights after the lads and lasses; "it's not that easy to be good."

In the evening, after school was over, and I'd helped Transome to get up and come down-stairs, and had settled him quite comfortably in his own chair out of all draughts, I told him about my new scholar.

"Why, my lass!" he cried, aw do believe as it's oud measter's own nephew? He'd a gradely fine lass for's sister, and hoo wedded beneath her, like thee, Ally. Captain John Champion was na' captain o' one o' the bettermost sort o' ships; and oud measter swore 'at he'd never forgie' her."

I coaxed Transome to tell me all he knew about it, though his words were as scarce as silver. He had seen the little lad's mother scores of times before she was married, when she was living with her brother, our landlord. But when she had died, or how her poor child came to be living in our town, he could not tell.

"Transome," I said, as I poured out his tea, "if God had asked me what I wished for as He asked Solomon, I'd have chose to have written a book."

"Eh! but aw nivir did see sech a woman for a book!" he said again, looking across the table at me with such a pleasant look that I could not keep myself from going round to kiss him, He was sore changed since we came home together along the canal, and picked flowers from morning till night; but I loved him as much, ay! ten times more now than then.

"If I could write a book," I went on, as I sat down again in my chair, "I'd write one that would prick our old master's heart to the quick."

"Eh, lass! it u'd take a pen very long and very sharp to prick his heart," he answered.

"Yet," I said, half to myself, "he's a church member, and takes the sacrament; he's chairman at the meetings. If that boy belonged to me, and me rolling in riches like him, I'd give him the best schooling in all England. I suppose he's too proud to forgive his poor dead sister for marrying below her."

"He's a gradely rich man," said Transome, shaking his head gravely, "and aw reckon he can afford to have his likes and dislikes."

"No," I answered; "the Lord hasn't made any one rich enough for that."

"Aw were wrung," he said, "rich and poor are all alike to Him; but that's hard to mind, Ally."

Well! to go on with my story. Pippin came to school for nigh upon twelve months, never missing, morning or evening. I got so used to him being close beside me in the chimney-nook, that I should not have been myself if he was away. Never, no! never had I such a scholar as him. He learned as if he was hungry and thirsty for learning, and could never have enough. Many and many a question he asked that I could not answer, any more than if he had been a little angel come from heaven to learn all about this world. What little I knew I taught him; but I soon saw he would be quickly beyond me. He was like a young bird with unfleged wings nestling under my care for a little while; but soon his wings will be strong enough to carry him away, and he would fly out of my sight, and think no more of me than a bird thinks of last year's nest, left in the branches of a tree. As soon as he could hold a pen, or make an *a*, and a *b*, he was wild to write a letter to his father. And many a letter he wrote, and directed them all "To father, Captain John Champion, on the Sea." Even Mrs. Brown had not the cruel heart to tell him that his letters could never, never find his father.

But one night, when Transome and me were sitting quiet in the fire-light as usual, I heard a low rap at the door. Now it was an understood thing that none of the scholars were to come to the house of an evening, lest they should disturb Transome, being, as I said, a silent man, and not used to children's talk since Willie died. I opened the door by a hand-breadth, and who should be breaking the rule save Pippin himself! There he stood, panting as if he had been hunted up the hill. The cold air was rushing in upon Transome through the open door, and as the boy could not find his voice to speak, I drew him inside. His handsome face was crimson, and his eyes were glowing and sparkling with excitement. I took him up to the hearth, and poked the fire into a blaze for Transome to have a good look at him.

"This is Philip Champion," said I.

Transome put down his pipe, and wiped his glasses on his sleeve, before looking at him.

"He favors his uncle," he said, as the boy faced him; "but he's the born image o' his mother, poor lass!"

"I've come to say good-bye," cried Pippin, all eagerness and excitement; "I'm going a long way off to-morrow—to London."

"Going to London!" I repeated, in amazement; "is your father come back, Pippin?" I could not get rid of the notion that his father would come back some time, and that helped the boy to be so fond of me.

"No," he said, sorrowfully; "Mrs. Brown's sure he'll never come home now. So I'm going away."

"But where to?" I asked, drawing him within my arms to the very front of the fire. I felt my heart very heavy all at once; and the cold wind, whistling round the house, made it chilly even at the fireside.

"Why," he answered, squeezing my arm to his side, "it's partly because you taught me how to write letters. Just read this up, loud, Mrs. Transome."

He drew a crumpled bit of printed paper out of his little pocket. But I could not read the small print without my glasses, which were at the end of the mantel-shelf. When I had found them, and lit a candle, I smoothed out the bit of paper, and read these words—

"A lady wishes to adopt an orphan, the child of respectable parents, and will provide for the maintenance and education of the same. A boy preferred, must come for three months on trial. All expenses paid. Address: E. D. G., P. O., London."

"Well?" I exclaimed, more puzzled than before.

"I wrote to her out of my own head," said Pippin, "and she's sent money for me to go to London to-morrow."

"I never heard of such a thing!" I cried. "Don't you know any more about her, Pippin, my dear child?"

"No," he said. "Wrote of my own self, and she's sent the money to Mrs. Brown for me to go. Only if I don't do for her, you know, I'm to be sent back in three months; and Mrs. Brown says she doesn't know who's going to have me, for she can't. She says I must go to the union, and that's a dreadful place."

"Ay—so it is," said Transome, whose eyes were fastened on the boy.

"Couldn't you have me?" he asked, coaxingly, and putting his little arm around my neck. "You're kinder to me than anybody else." Don't you let me be sent to the union—please don't."

I looked across at Transome, and his face looked happy and pleasant, and he nodded his head at me. We had lived together so long there was no need for him to speak. It was as much as if he had said, "Ally, my lass, do as thee likes!" It was getting harder work than ever to win bread for him and me; but I could not bear to think of my clever, bonny boy being sent to the union; and his uncle rolling in riches.

"Yes, yes, my laddie," I said, "if you come back we'll find a corner for you, and a morsel to eat, and a sup to drink. The Lord, He'll provide for us all. But she won't send you back; the lady in London is sure to love you, if she hasn't a heart of stone."

"But I must come back some time to pay you," answered Pippin. "I'll not forget it, never. So I've brought you a bit of money father gave me long ago. That's all I've got now; but I'll pay you when I'm a rich man."

"That's reet and honest, lad," said Transome, "'faithful in little, faithful in much.'"

It was nought but a small foreign coin, with a hole bored through it, and hung on a blue ribbon, like a medal. But it was all Pippin had, and he would not take it back again, so I put it away carefully into a small box, where I kept a curl of Willie's hair, and the little Testament he had learned to read in.

"It's earnest money," I said. "The Lord will know when to give us the rest."

So we bid Pippin good-bye, not without tears even in Transome's eyes, though he was growing too old to shed tears at little things. And I stood to watch him, in spite of the searching bitter wind blowing over the brow of the hill, as he ran down the street until he was fairly out of my sight. That night I strung up Willie's chair again to the ceiling.

No, such another child ever came again to my school. I had good scholars and bad ones, and they were constantly changing, old ones leaving and fresh ones coming in; but never one like Pippin. Not one of them had his hungry brain and loving heart; and now he was gone, all the others seemed commonplace and at a distance from me. They could not creep into my heart as Pippin had done.

He did not come back at the end of three months. We never even heard of him. He was little more than a babe in years, and children cannot remember as old folks remember their friends. Mrs. Brown told me, when I made a purpose journey to inquire after him, that the lady had written to say he was safe and quite content, but she did not wish him to have any communication with his former home. Soon after that Mrs. Brown went away to live in Manchester, so we could ask for no more news about Pippin. I had, at times, an unsatisfied yearning when I thought of him; but, as years slipped away, I only recollected him as a child, who was dearest to me next to my own Willie.

Transome's rheumatism did not mend as he grew older and more infirm, and the burden of earning the rent as well as the living fell upon me. But times were very prosperous in the town just then, and trade was increasing every year. New mills were built along the river, and the mill-hands had constant work. Money was plentiful, and not a soul grumbled when I raised the school wage just enough to pay our rent.

Ah! I shall never, never forget that sunshiny evening early in May, when I followed my scholars down the garden, and stood for a moment or two leaning over the wicket. The broad open land lay all before me, with a great sweep of sky-line resting on the brows of distant hills. The sky was all blue; and the yellow stone-crop on the thatch shone like gold. The withy branches were covered with soft, fluffy little tufts, called goslings by children; and though the poplar-tree, growing so tall and slender at at the corner of the house, had no leaves yet, there were tassels of long crimson catkins hanging on its topmost twigs, and floating down when the soft pleasant spring breeze shook them a little. There were the rosemary and lavender bushes, that I had carried all the way from home when I was married, to plant under our kitchen window, and they were just coming into bud. I looked down what used to be the dingle, and thought of the primroses and hawthorn and bluebells, that used to grow in its green and grassy nooks. It was no wonder that I could not help shaking my head a little at the ugly houses that had sprung up in their place. Yet when I turned my back upon them, and could see nothing but our own home, with the blue sky only behind the thatched roof, I was more than content.

"The Lord knows exactly what I love best," I said to myself as I walked back up the garden path more slowly and toilsomely than when I was a young wife; "I wouldn't change it for the grandest house in all the town."

Transome had been hearty enough that afternoon to go down to his old master's to carry the month's rent. It was not far to go, but he would be weary and worn-out more than enough before he could climb up home again; so it would not do for me to loiter and tarry in the sweet air and sunshine. I hurried in to redd up the house, pile away the benches, and lay the tea all ready. The benches began to feel much heavier than they used to be. "It's the grasshopper," I thought, smiling to myself; "the grasshopper shall be a burden. Yes, yes! that time'll come to me as well as poor Transome. But God Almighty, He'll help me to bear the burden and heat of the day."

But I had not put everything as it should be before Transome came in slowly, slowly dragging one foot after another, and groaning heavily. Poor old man! I had not got my glasses on for fear of breaking them over my rough work, and I could not see his face clearly, but his groans went right to my heart. He had never given way so badly before, and I hastened to pull his arm-chair forward.

"Transome," I said, "is the pain so very bad this evening?"

"Ally!" he answered, in a stammering, choking voice; "Ally, lass! aw've gotten ablow."

All at once his old gray head fell on my shoulder, and he broke out into bitter sobbing and wailing, like a little child crying on its mother's bosom; only it was a thousand times more pitiful than a child, who can be hushed and sung to sleep in its worst trouble.

"What blow, Transome?" I cried; "who'd strike an old man like thee?"

"Th' oud measter," he said, amid his sobs; "we've got to go, Ally—to quit. He's goin' to sell th' oud place, to build bigger housen on; and we're bound to quit in a month's time. Oh, Ally, my lass!"

It fell upon me that sudden I was quite stunned and dazed at first, as if, as Transome said, somebody had struck me a heavy blow. All the house-place seemed swimming round me. I could hear his sobs and groans; but I felt as if I could not understand why he was in such trouble. Then all at once it came over me, like a great wave, and all the trouble stood out clear. I felt as if the house was crumbling away. Better it should fall upon us, and crush us to death, than we be driven out of it in our old age.

That was a night to be remembered. We sat down to the tea-table, but we could not swallow a morsel, though our throats were parched and our tongues dry. Whichever way we looked, all was darkness and blackness. There was no one to comfort him nor me, and no one to help. Neither had any hope of changing our master's mind. After we were gone to bed and both lay awake, making pretence to sleep, I could see no way—no way at all—out of our bitter sorrow and distress.

"Lord!" I heard Transome whisper, in the dead of the night, "only gie us strength to be faithful in little, and aw 'm sure thee'll gie us much when the reet time is come."

But how could we be faithful in little, if even that little was taken from us?

(To be Continued.)

CHRIST ENTERING JERUSALEM.

By Mrs. M. Baxter.

S. S. Lesson for March 11, Matt. 21 : 1-16. Golden Text, Ps. 118 : 26.

Ver. 1-3. The Close of a Momentous Journey—The Commission to the Disciples a Proof of Superhuman Knowledge—The Consent of the Owners Foreseen—Ver. 4, 5. The Prophecy of Zech. 9 : 9 Fulfilled—Christ's Usual Concern for the Fulfilment of Old Testament Prediction—Ver. 6-9. On the Colt (see Luke 19 : 30)—The Spread Garments a Usual Homage to Oriental Royalty (see II Kings 9 : 13)—Leaves Rather than Branches—Evidences of Popular Recognition—Ver. 10, 11. Citizens of the Capital Enlightened by Provincials—Ver. 12, 13. Probably the Next Day (see Mark 11 : 12-15)—A Second Cleansing—Executing a Law not Enforced by Proper Authorities—Ver. 14. A Fit Work for the Temple—Ver. 15, 16. Christ's Explicit Acceptance of Homage.

In the life of our blessed Lord there was no pressure, no hurry, no perplexity. He could say what very few of His disciples could say, "I do *always* those things which please Him." (John 8 : 29.) He lived in the consciousness of the truth, which is left in His Word, for us, "All things work together for good to them that love God." (Rom. 8 : 28.) Consequently, Jesus never recognized an interruption, and was never tried by it; it was permitted by His Father, and that was enough. On His way up to Jerusalem, having set His face as a flint (Isa. 50 : 7), He was teaching His disciples, and "as they departed from Jericho, a great multitude followed Him." Jesus did not complain of the distraction and noise, which necessarily accompanied such a throng, although it could not but have broken the thread of his discourse, and interfered with His teaching, which was so soon to come to an end. Jesus could trust the Holy Ghost, whom He would send to guide His own into all truth, and to bring to their remembrance whatsoever He had said unto them; and He could trust His Father's love, that whatsoever should seem to interfere with His teaching should, in the end, only go to illustrate and send home to heart and conscience all which He had said. Worry, vexation, impatience, hurry, are all

Manifestations of Self,

and are forms of unbelief. A Christian is worried, vexed, impatient, hurried, when he thinks that things are working together against his spiritual good, against his bodily health, and against the work of God in his hands. He beholds circumstances mightier than God, and frets against them. He does not *see* God in them, does not *feel* that God is in them, and so he walks in a vain shadow and disquiets himself in vain (Ps. 39 : 6), instead of confidently reckoning on God, and believing that He will extricate him from all perplexities and bring greater glory to Himself out of them.

On His way up to Jerusalem, Jesus passed through Jericho. There, in addition to the distraction of the multitude,

Another Interruption

awaited Jesus—"two blind men sitting by the wayside, when they heard that Jesus passed by, cried out, saying Have mercy on us, O Lord, Thou Son of David." The evangelists, Mark and Luke, say it was one blind man, but, wherever there is a man physically or spiritually blind, there is another, often many others, not far away. The multitude were not so patient under interruptions as Jesus was; they "rebuked them, because they should hold their peace." The multitude thought of *themselves*—they wanted to hear the words of the great Teacher, and they could not brook that two blind beggars should interfere with the comfort of such a large congregation. There are many congregations in churches and chapels whose one object is to enjoy the preacher; they sit in cushioned pews, in a nicely warmed and nicely appointed church, and expect an intellectual treat, or, maybe, a little spiritual comfort; and it would be most unseemly in such a congregation for a lost sinner, just alive to the fact that he was on the way to endless perdition, to cry out aloud, "Have mercy on me, O Lord." Yet the sympathies of the angels of God are not with the comfortable, cushioned hearers: there is not joy in heaven over every one who is at ease in Zion, but "there is joy in the presence of the angels of God over one sinner that repenteth."

The One in all that crowd who sympathized with the blind men was He who was most of all interrupted by them. Jesus could understand the intensity of earnestness with which they grasped the first opportunity they had had in their whole life-time to receive their sight. With them it was

Now or Never.

When a lost sinner comes to this point, when a believer in conflict about indwelling sin comes to this point, when one who is sick, blind, or deaf comes to this point, now or never, "*now* is the accepted time, behold, now is the day of salvation;" then something happens. "Jesus stood still and called them, and said, What will ye that I shall do unto you?" "What will ye?" Could it be that He who has all power, both in heaven and on earth, should put Himself and His Almighty resources thus at the command of two blind beggars? Yes; it was even so. They did not say, as hundreds of half-convicted souls say in inquiry meetings, "Not to-night." No; without a moment's hesitation, they cried, "Lord, that our eyes may be opened. So Jesus had compassion on them, and touched their eyes, and immediately their eyes received sight, and they followed Him." The opened eyes were used to keep them close to Jesus.

"And when they drew nigh unto Jerusalem, and were come to Bethphage, unto the Mount of Olives, then sent Jesus two disciples, saying unto them, "Go ye into the village over against you, and straightway ye shall find an ass tied, and a colt with her; loose them, and bring them unto Me. And if any man shall say aught unto you, ye shall say, The Lord hath need of them; and straightway he will send them." These were the simple orders for the triumphal entry into His own city of Him who was the King of kings and the Lord of lords! No wonder He was "despised and rejected of men," who look on the appearance, and judge from the outside. He had, "no form nor comeliness," in the eyes of such as see glory in waving banners, bands of music, triumphal chariots and flattering orations! The glory of Jesus was not in a manifestation of the greatness of man, but it was

God Manifest in the Flesh.

The glory was God's indwelling. Thus, in His triumphant entry into Jerusalem, there was nothing to distract the eye from God in Christ. Anyone who has an artist's eye shrinks from anything in the bonnet or the dress which attracts the eye from a beautiful face: the true artist instinctively dresses so that the face, and not the dress, may strike the eye. In the triumph of Jesus there was the same principle. The asses' colt, the coarse garments of the poor, in the place of lordly trappings, and the hurriedly cut branches of palm-trees, mingled with an extemporized carpet of yet more of the homely outer garments of the poor, did not distract the eye from Him who rode in meek and quiet dignity upon "an ass, and a colt the foal of an ass," as had been foretold (Jer. 9 : 9) more than five hundred years before. In the triumphs of kings and generals, the trophies of their victories were generally carried with them—kings in chains, slaves in chains, captive officers of the rival armies, captured horses, elephants, camels or lions, would be led in procession. *Jesus* had around Him souls saved from everlasting death, hearts set free from sin and misery, blind with restored sight, and deaf with restored hearing, those healed of all manner of diseases, and all of these acquainted with the living God. The kings of the earth exhibit their bound ones, but Jesus was surrounded with freed men, whom He, the Son of God, the Son of Man, had made free indeed. In the ready devotion which laid their garments at His feet, they spoke of devoted hearts surrendered to His service, and the palm branches told of a victory greater than that of the kings of the earth, a victory over sin and Satan for ever.

"I receive not honor from men," said our blessed Lord; but this sudden and most unwonted triumph was an exception. No doubt, those who looked that He should establish an earthly kingdom, were grievously disappointed; there was nothing in this strange procession to oppose the Roman power and rid the Jews of their hated subjection to a foreign power. No; Jesus was come to establish a kingdom which is "not meat and drink," nor yet horses and chariots, armies and landed possessions, but "righteousness and peace and joy in the Holy Ghost." (Rom. 14 : 17.) There was no sound of the trumpet in the triumph of Jesus, the human voice was the only music which reached His ear, but believing hearts took up the words of the Psalmist, and cried, "Hosanna to the Son of David! Blessed is He that cometh in the name of the Lord; Hosanna in the highest!" "Hosanna!" "Save now!" They thought of an outward deliverance, and knew not that, six days later, Jesus would indeed

Save a World

by bearing its sins in His own body on the tree! Does it strike any of my readers as strange that, while Jesus, in this moment of His greatest triumph, was so lowly, some of His followers are so hurt if people do not make a great fuss about them! Have we not all of us, some time or other, been hurt that we were not more appreciated and thought, in our foolish conceit, that it was the Lord's cause for which we were jealous. The yoke of Jesus makes us "meek and lowly in heart." (Matt. 11 : 29.)

When Jesus was come into Jerusalem, "all the city was moved, saying, Who is this?" "He was in the world, and the world was made by Him, and the world knew Him not. He came unto His own, and His own received Him not." (John 1 : 10, 11.) However great a work of God may be going on in a place, there are numbers of the people who know nothing about it: souls are saved and bodies are healed next door to them or in the very same street, but they know nothing about it; it is not in their line. But when the great day of account comes, will they not be held responsible? The multitude replied, "This is Jesus, the prophet of Nazareth of Galilee." Arrived in Jerusalem, Jesus did not ride on His lowly steed to the Sanhedrim or to the home of the Roman governor; the temple was the point of attraction to Him. It was His Father's house, and there He was at home. Those who had expected Him to restore the kingdom to Israel must have been strangely disappointed, when He occupied Himself in clearing the temple of the money changers, and all who were there for another purpose than to worship. He said, "It is written, My house shall be called the house of prayer; but ye have made it a den of thieves." Having cleansed the temple, He healed the blind and the lame there, ever occupied with others rather than Himself.

But even this little triumph of Jesus was sufficient to arouse the enmity of the chief-priests and scribes; they were mortified that so large a multitude had been attracted to Jesus, mortified that there were such manifest tokens of His power, and they reproached Him that the multitude and the children cried, "Hosanna to the Son of David!" Jesus referred them to Scripture, "Have ye never read, Out of the mouth of babes and sucklings Thou hast perfected praise." Such was the earthly triumph of the Son of God!

JESUS ALWAYS.

I always go to Jesus,
When troubled or distressed;
I always find a refuge
Upon His loving breast.
I tell Him all my trials,
I tell Him all my grief;
And while my lips are speaking
He gives my heart relief.

When full of dread forebodings,
And flowing o'er with tears,
He calms away my sorrows,
And hushes all my fears.
He comprehends my weakness,
The peril I am in,
And He supplies the armor
I need to vanquish sin.

When those are cold and faithless
Who once were fond and true,
With careless hearts forsaking
The old friends for the new,
I turn to Him whose friendship
Knows neither change nor end;
I always find in Jesus
An ever faithful Friend.

I always go to Jesus;
No matter when or where
I seek his gracious presence,
I'm sure to find him there.
In times of joy or sorrow,
Whate'er my need may be,
I always go to Jesus,
And Jesus comes to me.

Josephine Pollard.

J. E. JEWETT, Publisher, 77 Bible House, New York will furnish the above poem in leaflet form at twenty cents per hundred. *A Sample Packet* of 50 leaflets assorted (no two alike), will be sent post-paid for ten cents. Postages stamps taken.

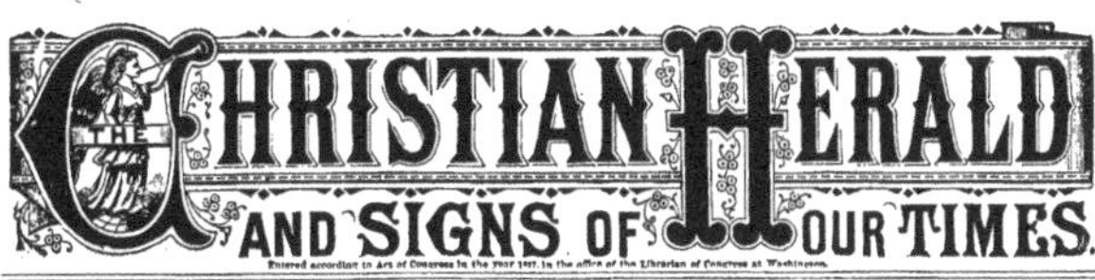

THE CHRISTIAN HERALD AND SIGNS OF OUR TIMES.

Entered according to Act of Congress in the year 1887, in the office of the Librarian of Congress at Washington.

Vol. XI., No. 10. Office, 63 Bible House, N. Y. THURSDAY, MARCH 8, 1888. Annual Subscription, $1.50.

CONTENTS OF THIS NUMBER.

PORTRAITS OF PRINCE OSCAR OF SWEDEN AND MISS MUNCK, HIS BRIDE-ELECT.

CHRIST, THE SONG. Dr. Talmage's Sermon Last Sunday Morning.

ANECDOTES RELATED AT RECENT EVANGELISTIC MEETINGS.

DISINTEGRATING FORCES. By Rev. A. C. Tris.

A Magical Rock in China—Paralysis Cured by a Dog—Mr. Mackay's Trials in Uganda, etc.

THE LORD AND THE LEPER. A New Sermon by C. H. Spurgeon.

Gems from New Bocks: A New England Home.

PICTURE OF AN INTERIOR OF A CHURCH IN STOCKHOLM.

ANTHONY HUNT AND THE LOST CHILD. (With Illustration.)

MRS. TRANSOME'S PUPIL. A Serial Story. (Continued.)

THE SON REJECTED. By Mrs. M. Baxter.

PRINCE OSCAR, of Sweden—MISS EBBA MUNCK, His Fiancee—A View in Stockholm.

PRINCE OSCAR OF SWEDEN,

And Miss Munck, his Bride-Elect.

Royal Prejudices Against Plebeian Marriages—The Origin of the Swedish Royal House—Lawyer Bernadotte, of the French Bar—Napoleon Making Kings—The Descendant of the Lawyer Scorning the Descendant of the Noble—Miss Munck's Circumspection and Modesty—Her Hospital Service—The Queen Won Over—The King's Opposition—Arrangements for the Wedding—Stockholm and Its People.

ANOTHER chapter is soon to be added to those love romances which have a man of royal lineage and a girl of humble origin for central figures. Such marriages of pure inclination are called mesalliances in monarchical Europe. Among royalty there exists a deep-rooted prejudice against such alliances, and, in order to prevent the dreaded admixture of plebeian blood with the blue blood of the kings, love-matches of the kind alluded to are always strenuously opposed. The latest case in point is the approaching marriage of Prince Oscar of Sweden, to Miss Ebba Munck. Prince Oscar, *whose portrait appears on our frontispiece*, was born at Stockholm in November, 1859, and is now therefore in the twenty-ninth year of his age. Miss Munck is about one year older. It is stated that the young lady's lineage is in reality more aristocratic than that of the Prince himself. The

Grandfather of the Present King

of Sweden was an obscure attorney named Bernadotte, in a small French town. When a young man, he wasted his affections on one of the maidens of the district, who, after giving his suit encouragement, jilted him for what she considered a better match, in the person of a neighboring farmer. But success did not smile on her, and she was reduced to such poverty as obliged her to become a laundress. Bernadotte meanwhile, from being a private in the French army, rose gradually in the favor of Napoleon I. until he attained the rank of general in the Emperor's victorious army. So much confidence had Napoleon in him, that when, desiring to strengthen his position in Europe, the latter gave his brother Joseph the throne of Spain, he gave Bernadotte the throne of Sweden. Hence, the family of the present King of Sweden was not royal until two generations ago, and the blood that flows in its veins is, therefore, not very strongly impregnated with the royal element.

The Swedish royal family has, however, some claims on

Public Esteem

higher than those of ancient lineage. Its members, especially the ladies of the House, have been famous for their love of the people, and their efforts to alleviate their sorrow and suffering. The mother of the present King was a conspicuous illustration. She was a grand-daughter of the beautiful Empress Josephine, whom Napoleon divorced. She married Oscar I., who was the second of the Bernadottes to reign over Sweden, and from the date of her settlement in the country grew in love and respect of the people. When her first child was born, the thoughts which were suggested to her mind by the comfort and luxury in which the royal babe was cradled, were of babes, just as much beloved, whose mothers could not provide common comforts for them. During her convalescence she thought out a scheme out of which grew a noble institution, to which many infants in poor homes all through the country owed health, if not life itself. She also introduced the home cultivation of silk, and had the necessary white mulberry-trees brought and planted at her own cost in Sweden. Aged and invalid women and delicate children were able by this industry to add to the family income, and lose their sense of dependence.

Diamonds Transformed.

Another noble lady of the Bernadotte house is the Princess Eugenie. She is the daughter of the last-mentioned lady, the sister of the present King, and therefore the aunt of the young man, whose portrait we give. A large fortune was bequeathed to her, when she was a child, by her grandmother. A part of it consisted in magnificent diamonds, collected at vast labor and with great care in matching them for color and shape. Many young ladies, especially those about a court, would have treasured these gems, but the Princess was interested in the erection of a great public hospital, and funds were lacking to make the institution the beneficent agency she had planned; she therefore sold her diamonds, and finished and endowed the hospital. She visited it incognita afterward but in one of the beds was a patient who recognized her. As tears of gratitude ran over his wan cheeks, the Princess said, "*Now I see my diamonds again.*"

The Prince and the Maid.

The acquaintance, which has developed into a romance and has distressed the family, originated in the household of the Crown Princess of Sweden, the wife of Prince Oscar's elder brother. She is a daughter of the Grand Duke of Baden, and a granddaughter of the Emperor William of Germany, and in October, 1885, she had amongst her maids of honor a young Swedish lady, Miss Munck, known for her beauty, grace and charming manner. Wherever she went she was admired; but although of high birth, Miss Munck was poor and an orphan. Her father, Colonel Munck, had left her an untarnished name, which had been borne by a long line of ancestors—all gallant soldiers—but very little money. Eventually, Miss Munck, yielding to the pressing advice of her friends,

Accepted an Offer of Marriage

from a wealthy young officer belonging to a crack cavalry regiment, and everything was prepared for the wedding. The day was fixed, the "trousseau" was bought, and presents had arrived, when Miss Munck suddenly broke off her engagement, for reasons which convinced her that she did not possess the exclusive affections of her suitor. She resisted all attempts at a reconciliation, and retired from court for some time. When she returned, her former high spirits had gone, and her face bore an expression of melancholy, which, however, enhanced her beauty.

It was then that she met Prince Oscar, who had been for a two years' trip round the world in the Swedish frigate *Vanadis*. After his return his friends discovered that he was in love with her, and the fact likewise became evident to Miss Munck herself. She could not fail to be complimented by the admiration of the young sailor Prince, but, being familiar with court laws and regulations, she was aware of the great gulf of caste which lay between them. According to the Swedish Constitution, a Prince marrying any lady but one of a royal family, forfeits his rights to the Throne and his privileges as a member of the Royal Family. Miss Munck had too much nobility of mind to be willing for her royal lover to make sacrifices for her sake, and she again left the Swedish court. She announced to her relatives her intention never to marry, and

Assumed the Garb of a Nurse,

and the charge of a ward in one of the large charity hospitals of Stockholm. Her conduct won the admiration of the King and Queen; and during several months she performed the services of one of the lady nurses at the "Home for the Sick," established by the Queen, in place of a lady who had become an invalid from overwork. Prince Oscar at length ascertained the occupation of the girl he loved, and discovered her retreat. By the time he found her, however, overwork and watching had laid her prostrate on a bed of sickness. He waited anxiously for her convalescence, and then renewed his suit. Miss Munck finally admitted that she reciprocated the Prince's love, but no pleadings could induce her to consent to marry him. On one condition alone would she yield, and that was, that the Queen herself should give explicit sanction to the match. This sanction the Queen, who had herself grown to love the girl, eventually gave.

The remaining obstacle to the union, and one that for a time seemed insuperable, was the opposition of the King. He was opposed to an alliance that would do nothing to strengthen his Throne, when many such alliances were attainable. In vain did Prince Oscar at first plead that as his brother, the Crown Prince, had already two sons, his own chances of ever ascending the throne, were practically *nil*, and that he therefore might be allowed to abandon the privileges of Royalty and renounce his interest in the succession without imperiling the perpetuation of the family dynasty; but as the time wore on, and the King saw his son could not be influenced in the matter, His Majesty was induced to yield, principally owing to the entreaties of the Queen, who was on the eve of an operation from which she was not expected to recover. The King could not resist the pleading of his beloved wife, whom he feared he was going to lose, and gave his consent.

In virtue of the Swedish Constitution, Prince Oscar will lose, besides his rights to the throne, his titles of "Royal Highness" and "Duke of Götland," the yearly allowance granted by the Swedish Diet, and his palace at Stockholm. He will in future be called

Prince Bernadotte.

He will retain his position as commander in the Swedish Navy, which rank he has earned fairly in the ordinary course of promotion. The Prince, it is said, seems the happiest of men. He and his affianced bride are now with the Queen of Sweden, who is travelling in England. The wedding is announced to take place on the 15th of this month, and the ceremony will be conducted by eminent Swedish clergymen. After their return from their honeymoon the young couple will settle at Carlskrona, a naval establishment in southern Sweden, where the Prince will be stationed.

The Bride-elect,

(*whose portrait appears on our frontispiece*) is described as of medium height, with fair hair, and large and expressive blue eyes. She has a certain dignity of manner, though quiet and unobtrusive, seeming to evade rather than court observation in any way. By the Queen she is treated with great kindness and affection, and Her Majesty and she are inseparable. Miss Munck's family belong to the lower order of Swedish nobility.

Precedents of Royal Mesalliances.

There are quite a number of precedents regarding so-called mesalliances within the recollection of the present generation. Prince Carl, the brother of the Grand Duke of Baden, married a plain Miss Von Beust; Prince Gustav de Saxe Weimer, Mlle. Marcocchia; the reigning Duke of Saxe Meiningen, a Mlle. Franz; the Count of Bari, a half brother of the last King of Naples, Francis II., a Mlle. Marconnay. The Princess Carl of Hesse was a Miss Von Grote; Princess Julius of Schleswig-Holstein, sister-in-law of the King of Denmark, was the charming Mlle. Riegsaer, whose father was only a captain in the Saxon army. The Princess Nicolas of Nassau was plain Mlle. Pouchkin; the widow of the late King of Portugal, Dom Ferdinand, was an American, a Miss Henules; Prince Louis de Bourbon gave his hand to a penniless creole beauty, Mlle. Hamel; and the Duchess Nicolas of Oldenburg was once known as Mlle. Bulazel. Nor have princesses hesitated to bestow their hand where their heart has already been given. It is a

Historical Fact

that Anne of Austria was secretly married to Mazarin; so was Marie Louise, after the death of Napoleon, to the Austrian colonel, Count Neipperg; and the Duchess of Berry left several children by her union with an Italian nobleman. The Princess Frederica of Hanover, a daughter of King George V., followed the advice of Queen Victoria to become the Baroness of Pawel-Rammingen. Princess Elizabeth o' Saxony, King John's daughter, mother of the present Queen of Italy, married, in the first instance, the Duke of Genoa, Victor Emanuel's brother, and afterwards the Marquis of Rapallo. Princess Frederica of Oldenburg is the Baroness de Washington. Princess Henietta of Schleswig-Holstein, the aunt of the future Empress of Germany, gave up rank and position to wed a simple professor, Dr. Esmarch, the eminent German surgeon.

THE CITY OF STOCKHOLM,

a picture of which is given on our first page, is the metropolis of Sweden, and is the centre of a large trade in pitch, tar and timber, which are exported to different parts of the world. It has some exceedingly handsome buildings, commercial, religious and philanthropic, and parks and gardens of considerable extent, and, during the summer-time, of much beauty. It stands in a situation remarkable for its enchanting scenery and for its favorable position; and from the fact that it is built upon seven rocky islands, it is often styled

The Venice of the North.

Near the Palace, which is a magnificent building, is the Church of St. Nicholas (*a picture of the interior of this church appears on page 157*). This ancient edifice derives its name from Nicholas Breakspeare, who was a missionary in the city, but was in 1154 made Pope of Rome, with the title of Adrian IV. He was the haughty prelate who compelled King Frederick I. to prostrate himself in the dust before him, kiss his foot, hold the stirrup of his saddle while he mounted, and then lead by the bridle the white palfrey on which he rode. In this building the Kings of Sweden and Norway are crowned. The Church of St. Catherine, not far off, is on the spot called Blood Bath, where ninety-seven eminent citizens were put to death by Christian II. in 1520, for some heinous but unproved offence against the laws.

The Kingdoms of Sweden and Norway

were united under one sovereign in 1815. The dual kingdom embraces the entire northwestern peninsula of Europe, usually called Scandinavia, and numbers about six million of inhabitants. The majority of the Swedes are Lutheran Protestants, and, owing to a system of excellent national iustruction, are well educated and intelligent. Agriculture is a favorite industry, a large number of the farmers being owners of the land they cultivate.

Every since the year 1559, the Swedes have made vigorous efforts to propagate the gospel in heathen lands. The special sphere of their operations was Lapland, and their work was conducted under royal auspices. Gustavus Vasa headed the missionary movement for the enlightenment of the Laps, and succeeding monarchs threw the weight of their influence into the Christian enterprise. In 1775 the New Testament, translated into the Lap dialect, was published. The mission was far from prosperous, however, and after years of hoping against hope, it was reluctantly abandoned. Nor is this to be wondered at, if the reports of the customs and propensities of both priests and people are true. After an interval of nearly three centuries, the spiritual needs of Lapland again engrossed the attention of the Swedes. In 1835,

The Swedish Missionary Society

was formed, and sent forth a young man of burning piety and irrepressible enthusiasm in the cause of Christ, named Carl Ludovic Tellstroem, a convert of the Wesleyan Mission in Stockholm, as a catechist to Lapland. He had many difficulties to encounter, from the migratory and dissipated habits of the people, but by following them to their markets and fairs, with his Bible, to instruct them in the truths of the gospel, there is reason to believe that with God's blessing his incessant and apostolic labors were productive of good results. Schools were afterwards established for the training of the rising generation, and the children were taught, fed and clothed at the expense of the society, and at the end of two years were sent home with tracts and books to interest and instruct their parents, families and friends. The British and Foreign Bible Society have for many years been doing a most gratifying work in the country.

ANECDOTES RELATED AT RECENT EVANGELISTIC MEETINGS.

Five Hundred Converts at Once.—The Pastor of a church in Scotland said: "At the town of Kirk O'Shotts, the minister who was to preach the communion sermon there thought to himself, 'How unfit I am to preach; I shall not go. There will be people gathered from all parts of the country to hear the gospel, and there will be present older and more experienced ministers than I; how much better they would deliver the Master's message, and if I do not go, some experienced pastor will break the Bread of Life to the people.' He rose from his knees, saying, 'I shall not go.' Just then the word of the prophet came to him, 'Have I ever been a dry place or a wilderness to thee?' He stopped, and turning, said, 'No, Lord, Thou hast never been a wilderness or a dry place to my soul. I will go in the strength of the Lord.' And he did go, trusting in Him who is the strength of the weak. That day, at the communion service, over 500 souls gave themselves to Christ, passing from darkness into the marvellous light of His kingdom. It is the weak things of this world that God uses to confound the strong, and a weak though trusting servant is one that can be made mighty for the purpose of God."

A Student and His Mother.—The Rev. Mr. Stalker narrates: "A short time ago a mother showed me a letter which she had received from her son, a student in one of the great colleges. He stated that one day a number of companions came into his room and asked if he would take part in a certain amusement. Without thinking, he answered good-humoredly that he would. But as soon as they were gone from his room he began to think of his Christian mother, and the godly home which he had so recently left. The mother had made a friend of her son; there had never been any secrets between them; and as he now thought of his home, and of her, he was not at all sure that the amusement in which he had promised to take part would be quite agreeable to his mother. Getting up from his desk he went to his friends, and said, 'You must consider that promise off until I hear from home.' The letter which I was shown was that in which he asked his mother's opinion concerning the purposed amusement, and promised that he would be guided by her advice and decision. What a grand thing it would be if Christians would just treat God as that student did his mother. Let us go to Him and ask His guidance on every point."

A Life Lost for a Pocketbook.—A Friend narrated the following: "I read lately about a shipwreck. The ship was slowly but surely going down, and the last lifeboat was being put off. The mate of the vessel was about to step in, when, starting back, he exclaimed, 'Oh, I have forgotten my purse.' The captain shouted to him to come away, and leave his purse; but the mate called out, 'I'll be back in a minute,' and dived below into his cabin for his much-loved purse. As he disappeared the vessel gave a lurch, and those in the boat were reluctantly compelled to push off, and they were only just in time, for with a roll the vessel sunk like lead beneath the waters. Next morning, the dead body of the mate was washed up on the neighboring beach. In his hand was rigidly clasped the purse of money for which he had risked and lost his life. It was opened, and what did it contain, think you? Only eighteenpence! For that paltry sum he had lost his life. Similarly, there are some men who are losing their souls for something of ridiculously small value. To gratify an evil passion, to gain the favor of some companion, to accumulate more or less wealth to obtain a certain social or commercial position—for these they rashly spurn the love of God, and sacrifice their never-dying souls."

A Sceptic on His Knees.—The Rev. Wm. Ross observed: "On New Year's morning, 1887, there came to me an intoxicated man, who boasted that he had never been overcome in argument by a believer in God, and glorified in the fact that he had turned some from being nominal Christians to declare themselves irreligious like himself. After speaking to him as kindly as I could for some time, I inquired, 'Can you tell me who it is that says, "To-day, if you will hear my voice, harden not your hearts"?' 'It is the Holy Spirit,' was his reply. 'And can you tell me who it is that says, "To-morrow, and at a more convenient season, I will hear you concerning this thing?"' He would not answer at first, but when I pressed him, he replied, 'It is the evil spirit.' 'Now,' I said, 'you have acknowledged that the Holy Spirit says, "To-day," and the evil one, "To-morrow." Now I hope that never again will you strive by ridicule to keep your fellow-creatures from coming to Christ at once. To do so, when you know the truth, would be inhuman.' Before I left him that morning he was upon his knees asking for mercy from that God whom, but lately, he had been despising and deriding, and he is now, I am happy to say, one of the most earnest and energetic Christians in the city where I live. 'Is there anything too hard for the Lord?'"

A Mother's Sad Disappointment.—Mr. R. B. Stewart said: "There was a friend of mine who was coming home from abroad with his son, who was unwell. His wife went to South Italy to meet them. She was there some time before them, and was anxiously awaiting their arrival. As soon as the ship came in sight she took a boat and was rowed out to meet them. When they got within shouting distance, they hailed the ship, and shouting the name of the lad, asked if he were on board and well. Answer came that he was there, but in a dying condition. The mother asked if she might come on board, but was told that the ship was under quarantine, and before she could get to see her son she must get an order from the consul. She pleaded, but the captain was firm; she could not come unless she had the warrant from the consul. 'Is he very ill?' she asked, as the boat was turned towards the shore. 'Yes, very ill,' was the reply. She procured the order and hastened back to the ship, and as they neared it they shouted, 'We have got the order.' The captain helped the mother on board and said, 'I am sorry that since you left the side of the ship your son has passed away; the dear lad is dead.' It was that she might get her boy's last words that the mother had struggled, and now she was too late. Does not this remind one of the parable of the ten virgins, five of whom found they had no oil, and going to buy oil, came back too late?"

A Most Risky Venture.—A Minister Related: "The local secretary of a Y. M. C. A. was dealing with a young man, who, in the course of conversation, said to him, 'And do you mean to tell me, sir, that I have to give myself wholly up to Jesus Christ?' 'Yes, that is it,' replied the secretary affectionately; 'and you have to do it at once if you would be saved. We have not a moment except the present that we can call our own.' The young man coolly answered, 'I do not believe that, and I will put this matter off, for a time at least.' At half-past one A. M. next morning the secretary's door-bell was violently rung, and a messenger breathlessly asked if he had spoken to a young man about his soul at a meeting last night. On being told that he had, the messenger said that the young man had hardly reached home when he was suddenly taken seriously ill, and was now very anxious about his soul, and wished the friend who had spoken to him but a few hours before to come to him at once. The secretary went, pointed out to him the way of salvation, but left without producing much impression. The young man lingered in much agony both in body and mind, but it seemed impossible for him to accept the Saviour. Just as he was at his last gasp, he almost shrieked, 'Lord Jesus, save me, I perish.' God only knows whether he was saved. It was a terrible risk to run. No one can reject the blessed Son of God and think to take Him up at any turn of the road. If you reject Him now, there is no promise for the future. 'Now is the accepted time: now is the day of salvation.'"

CHRIST THE SONG.

Dr. Talmage's Sermon, Preached Last Sunday Morning, March 4, 1888:

When one hundred and twenty new members were admitted to the Church at the Brooklyn Tabernacle. The present number of communicants is now four thousand one hundred and fifty.

"Now will I sing to my Well Beloved a song concerning my Beloved." Isa. 5.

The Grandest Pantheism—The Celestial Sounding-Board—An Electric Word—Christ Our Song—The Cradle Song—Echoes from Heavenly Gates—A Protective Influence—The Tears Over the Empty Cradle—The Old Man's Song—The Tune of Fifty Years Ago—The Song of Salvation—The Night Song—John Welch's Plaid—People who need a Song for the Night—The Sabbath-Song—His Birth Celebrated—The Everlasting Song—A Sailor's Song—The Children's Song—The Heavenly Song—Angelic Songs heard by the Dying Wife of a Clergyman—A Victorious King Prostrate on a Battle-field.

THE most fascinating theme for a heart properly attuned is the Saviour. There is something in the morning light to suggest Him, and something in the evening shadow to speak His praise. The flower breathes Him, the star shines Him, the cascade proclaims Him, all the voices of nature chant Him. Whatever is grand, bright and beautiful, if you only listen to it, will speak His praise. When I come in the summer-time and pluck a flower, I think of Him who is "the Rose of Sharon and the Lily of the Valley." When I see in the fields a lamb, I say, "Behold the Lamb of God that taketh away the sin of the world." When, in very hot weather, I come under a projecting cliff, I say:

"Rock of Ages, cleft for me,
Let me hide myself in Thee!"

Over the old-fashioned pulpits there was a sounding-board. The voice of the minister rose to the sounding-board, and then was struck back again upon the ears of the people. And the ten thousand voices of earth rising, find

The Heavens a Sounding-Board,

which strikes back to the ear of all the nations the praises of Christ. The heavens tell His glory, and the earth shows His handiwork. The Bible thrills with one great story of redemption. Upon a blasted and faded paradise it poured the light of a glorious restoration. It looked upon Abraham from the ram caught in the thicket. It spoke in the bleating of the herds driven down to Jerusalem for sacrifice. It put infinite pathos into the speech of uncouth fishermen. It lifted Paul into the seventh heaven; and it broke upon the ear of St. John with the brazen trumpets and the doxology of the elders, and the rushing wings of the seraphim.

Instead of waiting until you get sick and worn out before you speak the praise of Christ, while your heart is happiest, and your step is lightest, and your fortunes smile, and your pathway blossoms, and the overarching heavens drop upon you benediction, speak praises of Jesus.

The Electric Word.

The old Greek orators, when they saw their audiences inattentive and slumbering, had one word with which they would rouse them up to the greatest enthusiasm. In the midst of their orations they would stop and cry out, "Marathon!" and the people's enthusiasm would be unbounded. My hearers, though you may have been borne down with sin, and though trouble and trials and temptation may have come upon you, and you feel hardly like looking up, methinks there is one grand, royal, imperial word that ought to rouse your soul to infinite rejoicing, and that word is "Jesus!"

Taking the suggestion of the text, I shall speak to you of Christ, our song. I remark, in the first place, that Christ ought to be

The Cradle Song.

What our mothers sang to us when they put us to sleep is singing yet. We may have forgotten the words; but they went into the fibre of our soul, and will forever be a part of it. It is not so much what you formally teach your children as what you sing to them. A hymn has wings and can fly everywhither. One hundred and fifty years after you are dead, and "Old Mortality" has worn out his chisel in re-cutting your name on the tombstone, your great-grandchildren will be singing the song which this afternoon you sing to your little ones gathered about your knee. There is a place in Switzerland where, if you distinctly utter your voice, there come back ten or fifteen echoes, and every Christian song sung by a mother in the ear of her child shall have *ten thousand echoes* coming back from all the gates of heaven. Oh, if mothers only knew the power of this sacred spell, how much oftener the little ones would be gathered, and all our homes would chime with the songs of Jesus!

Preserving Power.

We want some counteracting influence upon our children. The very moment your child steps into the street, he steps into the path of temptation. There are foul-mouthed children who would like to besoil your little ones. It will not do to keep your boys and girls in the house and make them house-plants; they must have fresh air and recreation. God save your children from the scathing, blasting, damning influence of the streets! I know of no counteracting influence but the power of Christian culture and example. Hold before your little ones the pure life of Jesus; let that name be the word that shall exorcise evil from their hearts. Give to your instruction all the fascination of music, morning, noon and night; let it be Jesus the cradle-song.

This is important if your children grow up, but perhaps they may not. Their pathway may be short. Jesns may be wanting that child. Then there will be a soundless step in the dwelling, and the youthful pulse will begin to flutter, and little hands will be lifted for help. You cannot help. And a great agony will pinch at your heart, and

The Cradle will be Empty,

and the nursery will be empty, and the world will be empty, and your soul will be empty. No little feet standing on the stairs. No toys scattered on the carpet. No quick following from room to room. No strange and wondering questions. No upturned face, with laughing blue eyes, come for a kiss; but only a grave, and a wreath of white blossoms on the top of it; and bitter desolation, and a sighing at night-fall with no one to put to bed, and a wet pillow and a grave and a wreath of white blossoms on the top of it. The heavenly Shepherd will take that lamb safely, anyhow, whether you have been faithful or unfaithful; but would it not have been pleasanter if you could have heard from those lips the praises of Christ? I never read anything more beautiful than this about a child's departure. The account said, "She folded her hands, kissed her mother good-by, sang her hymn, turned her face to the wall, said her little prayer, and then died."

Oh, if I could gather up in one paragraph the last words of the little ones who have gone out from all these Christian circles, and I could picture the calm looks and the folded hands and sweet departure, methinks it would be grand and beautiful as one of heaven's doxologies!

I next speak of Christ as

The Old Man's Song.

Quick music loses its charm for the aged ear. The school-girl asks for a schottisch or a glee; but her grandmother asks for "Balerma" or the "Portuguese Hymn." Fifty years of trouble have tamed the spirit, and the keys of the music-board must have a solemn tread. Though the voice may be tremulous, so that grandfather will not trust it in Church, still he has the psalm-book open before him, and he sings with his soul. He hums his grandchildren asleep with the same tune he sang forty years ago in the old country meeting-house. Some day the choir sings a tune so old that the young people do not know it; but it starts the tears down the cheek of the aged man, for it reminds him of the revival scene in which he participated, and of the radiant faces that long since went to dust, and of the gray-haired minister leaning over the pulpit, and sounding the good tidings of great joy.

I was one Thanksgiving-day in my pulpit, Syracuse, New York, and Rev. Daniel Wald[illegible] at ninety-eight years of age, stood beside m[illegible] The choir sang a tune. I said, "I am sor[illegible] they sang that new tune; nobody seems to kn[illegible] it." "*Bless you, my son,*" said the old man, "*heard that seventy years ago!*"

There was a song to-day that touched the li[illegible] of the aged with holy fire, and kindled a glory [illegible] their vision that our younger eye-sight can n[illegible] see. It was

The Song of Salvation.

Jesus, who fed them all their lives long; Jesu[illegible] who wiped away their tears; Jesus, who sto[illegible] by them when all else failed; Jesus, in who[illegible] name their marriage was consecrated, and who[illegible] resurrection has poured light upon the graves [illegible] their departed. Blessed the Bible in whi[illegible] spectacled old age reads the promise, "I w[illegible] never leave you, never forsake you!" Bless[illegible] the staff on which the worn-out pilgrim totte[illegible] on toward the welcome of his Redeemer! Bles[illegible] ed the hymn-book in which the faltering tong[illegible] and the failing eyes find Jesus, the old ma[illegible] song. I speak to you again of Jesus as

The Night-Song.

Job speaks of him who giveth songs in the nig[illegible] John Welch, the old Scotch minister, used to p[illegible] a plaid across his bed on cold nights, and so[illegible] one asked him why he put that there. He sai[illegible] "Oh, sometimes in the night I want to sing t[illegible] praise of Jesus, and to get down and pray; th[illegible] I just take that plaid and wrap it around me, [illegible] keep myself from the cold." Songs in the nigh[illegible] Night of trouble has come down upon many [illegible] you. Commercial losses put out one star, sla[illegible] derous abuse put out another star; domest[illegible] bereavement has put out a thousand lights, a[illegible] gloom has been added to gloom, and chill [illegible] chill, and sting to sting, and one midnight h[illegible] seemed to borrow the fold from another mi[illegible] night to wrap itself in more unbearable darkne[illegible] but Christ has spoken peace to your heart, a[illegible] you can sing:

"Jesus, lover of my soul,
Let me to thy bosom fly,
While the billows near me roll,
While the tempest still is high.
Hide me, oh, my Saviour! hide
Till the storm of life is past,
Safe into the haven guide;
Oh, receive my soul at last."

Songs in the night! Songs in the night! F[illegible] the sick, who have no one to turn the hot pillo[illegible] no one to put the taper on the stand, no one [illegible] put ice on the temple, or pour out the soothi[illegible] anodyne, or utter one cheerful word—yet son[illegible] in the night!

For the Poor

who freeze in the winter's cold, and swelter [illegible] the summer's heat, and munch the hard cru[illegible] that bleed the sore gums, and shiver under bla[illegible] kets that cannot any longer be patched, a[illegible] tremble because rent-day is come and they m[illegible] be set out on the sidewalk, and looking into t[illegible] starved face of the child and seeing famine the[illegible] and death there, coming home from the bake[illegible] and saying, in the presence of the little famis[illegible] ed ones, "Oh, my God, flour has gone up[illegible] Yet songs in the night! Songs in the nig[illegible] *For the widow* who goes to get the back pay [illegible] her husband, slain by the "sharp-shooters," a[illegible] knows it is the last help she will have, movi[illegible] out of a comfortable home in desolation, dea[illegible] turning back from the exhausting cough, a[illegible] the pale cheek, and the lustreless eye, and r[illegible] fusing all relief. Yet songs in the nigh[illegible] Songs in the night! *For the soldier in the fie[illegible] hospital,* no surgeon to bind up the gun-sh[illegible] fracture, no water for the hot lips, no kind ha[illegible] to brush away the flies from the fresh woun[illegible] no one to take the loving farewell, the groani[illegible] of others poured into his own groan, the bla[illegible] phemy of others plowing up his own spirit, t[illegible] condensed bitterness of dying away from ho[illegible] among strangers. Yet songs in the nigh[illegible] Songs in the night! "Ah!" said one dyi[illegible] soldier, "tell my mother that last night the[illegible] was not one cloud between my soul and Jesus. Songs in the night! Songs in the night!

The Sabbath Song.

The Sabbath-day has come. From the altars of ten thousand churches has smoked up the savor of sacrifice. Ministers of the gospel are now preaching in plain English, in broad Scotch, in flowing Italian, in harsh Choctaw. God's people have assembled in Hindoo temple, and Moravian church and Quaker meeting-house and sailors' Bethel and kings' chapel and high-towered cathedral. They sang, and the song floated off amidst the spice groves or struck the icebergs or floated off into the Western pines or was drowned in the clamor of the great cities. Lumbermen sang it, and the factory-girls and the children in the Sabbath-class and the trained choirs in great assemblages. Trappers, with the same voice with which they shouted yesterday in the stag-hunt, and mariners with throats that only a few days ago sounded in the hoarse blast of the sea-hurricane, they sang it. One theme for the sermons. One burden for the song. Jesus for the invocation. Jesus for the Scripture lesson; Jesus for the baptismal font; Jesus for the sacramental cup; Jesus for the benediction. But the day will go by. It will roll away on swift wheels of light and love. Again the churches will be lighted. Tides of people again setting down the streets. Whole families coming up the church aisle. We must have one more sermon, two prayers, three songs and one benediction. What shall we preach to-night? What shall we read? What shall it be, children? Aged men and women, what shall it be? Young men and maidens what shall it be? If you chose to break the silence of this auditory, there would come up thousands of quick and jubilant voices, crying out, "Let it be Jesus! Jesus!"

We Sing His Birth,

the barn that sheltered Him, the mother that nursed Him, the cattle that fed beside Him, the angels that woke up the shepherds, shaking light over the midnight hills. We sing His ministry—the tears He wiped away from the eyes of the orphans; the lame men that forgot their crutches; the damsel who, from the bier, bounded out into the sunlight, her locks shaking down over the flushed cheek; the hungry thousand who broke the bread as it blossomed into larger loaves—that miracle by which a boy with five loaves and two fishes became the sutler for a whole army. We sing His sorrows—His stone-bruised feet, His aching heart, His mountain loneliness, His desert hunger, His storm-pelted body, the eternity of anguish that shot through His last moments, and the immeasurable ocean of torment that heaved up against His cross in one foaming, wrathful, omnipotent surge, the sun dashed out, and the dead, shroud-wrapped, breaking open their sepulchres, and rushing out to see what was the matter. We

Sing His Resurrection—

the guard that could not keep Him, the sorrow of His disciples: the clouds piling up on either side in pillared splendors as He went through, treading the pathless air, higher and higher, until He came to the foot of the throne, and all heaven kept jubilee at the return of the Conqueror. I say once more, Christ is

The Everlasting Song.

The very best singers sometimes get tired; the strongest throats sometimes get weary, and many who sang very sweetly do not sing now; but I hope, by the grace of God, we will, after a while, go up and sing the praises of Christ where we will never be weary. You know there are some songs that are especially appropriate for the home circle. They stir the soul, they start the tears, they turn the heart in on itself and keep sounding after the tune has stopped, like some cathedral bell, which, long after the tap of the brazen tongue has ceased, keeps throbbing on the air. Well, it will be a home song in heaven; all the sweeter because those who sang with us in the domestic circle on earth shall join that great harmony.

"Jerusalem, my happy home,
Name ever dear to me;
When shall my labors have an end
In joy and peace in thee?"

You know there is no such time on a farm as when they get the crops in; and so in heaven it will be a harvest song on the part of those who on earth sowed in tears and reaped in joy. Lift up your heads, ye everlasting gates, and let the sheaves come in! Angels shout all through the heavens, and multitudes come down the hills, crying, "Harvest home! harvest home!"

There is nothing more bewitching to one's ear than the song of sailors far out at sea, whether in day or night, as they pull away at the ropes—the music is weird and thrilling. So the song in heaven will be

A Sailor's Song.

They were voyagers once and thought they could never get to shore, and before they could get things snug and trim the cyclone struck them. But now they are safe. Once they went with damaged rigging, guns of distress booming through the storm; but the pilot came aboard, and he brought them into the harbor. Now they sing of the breakers passed, the light-houses that showed them where to sail, the pilot that took them through the straits, the eternal shore on which they landed. Ay, it will be

The Children's Song.

You know very well that the vast majority of our race die in infancy, and it is estimated that eighteen thousand millions of the little ones are standing before God. When they shall rise up about the throne to sing, the millions and the millions of the little ones—ah! that will be music for you! These played in the streets of Babylon and Thebes; these plucked lilies from the foot of Olivet while Christ was preaching about them; these waded in Siloam; these were victims of Herod's massacre; these were thrown to crocodiles or into the fire; these came up from Christian homes; and these were foundlings on the city commons—children everywhere in all that land; children in the towers, children on the seas of glass, children on the battlements. Ah, if you do not like children, do not go there. They are in vast majority, and what a song when they lift it around the throne!

The Heavenly Song.

The Christian singers and composers of all ages will be there to join in that song. Thomas Hastings will be there. Lowell Mason will be there. Bradbury will be there. Beethoven and Mozart will be there. They who sounded the cymbals and the trumpets in the ancient temples will be there. The forty thousand harpers that stood at the ancient dedication will be there. The two hundred singers that assisted on that day will be there. Patriarchs who lived amidst threshing-floors, shepherds who watched amidst Chaldean hills, prophets who walked with long beards and coarse apparel, pronouncing woe against ancient abominations, will meet the more recent martyrs who went up with leaping cohorts of fire; and some will speak of the Jesus of whom they prophesied, and others of the Jesus for whom they died. Oh, what a song! It came to John upon Patmos; it came to Calvin in the prison; it dropped to John Knox in the fire; and sometimes that song has come to your ear, perhaps, for I think it sometimes breaks over the battlements of heaven.

A Christian woman, *the wife of a minister* of the Gospel, was dying in the parsonage near the old church, where on Saturday night the choir used to assemble and rehearse for the following Sabbath, and she said, "How strangely sweet the choir rehearses to-night; they have been rehearsing there for an hour." "No," said some one about her, "the choir is not rehearsing to-night." "Yes," she said, "I know they are, I hear them sing; how very sweetly they sing!" It was not a choir of earth that she heard, but

The Choir of Heaven.

I think that Jesus sometimes sets ajar the door of heaven, and a passage of that rapture greets our ears. I wonder, will you sing that song? Will I sing it? Not unless our sins are pardoned, and we learn now to sing the praise of Christ, will we ever sing it there. The first great concert that I ever attended was in New York, when Jullien, in the "Crystal Palace," stood before hundreds of singers and hundreds of players upon instruments. Some of you may remember that occasion, it was the first one of the kind at which I was present, and I shall never forget it. I saw that one man standing, and with the hand and foot wield that great harmony, beating the time. It was overwhelming. But oh,

The Grander Scene

when they shall come from the East, and from the West, and from the North, and from the South, "a great multitude that no man can number," into the temple of the skies, host beyond host, and Jesus shall stand before that host to conduct the harmony, with His wounded hands and His wounded feet! Like the voice of many waters, like the voice of mighty thunderings, they shall cry, "Worthy is the Lamb that was slain to receive blessings, and riches, and honor, and glory, and power, world without end. Amen and Amen!" Oh, if my ear shall hear no other sweet sounds, may I hear that! If I join no other assemblage, may I join that!

I was reading of the battle of Agincourt, in which Henry V. figured; and it is said after the battle was won, gloriously won, the king wanted to acknowledge the divine interposition, and he ordered the chaplain to read the hundred and fifteenth Psalm of David; and when he came to the words, "Not unto us, O Lord, but unto thy name be the praise," the king dismounted, and all the cavalry dismounted, and all the great host, officers and men, threw themselves on their faces. Oh, at the story of the Saviour's love and the Saviour's deliverance, shall we not prostrate ourselves before Him now, hosts of earth and hosts of heaven, falling upon our faces, and crying, "Not unto us, not unto us, but unto thy name be the glory!"

A MAGICAL ROCK IN CHINA.

AN incident reported by Dr. Wilson, one of the Missionaries of the China Inland Mission, illustrates the superstition of the people. He says: "Mr. Pearse, Mr. Beauchamp and I, thinking that we should have a grand opportunity of preaching, visited a holy mountain about twenty miles to the north, which is frequented by many thousands of worshippers. About half-way, at the place where we left our mules and commenced the ascent, we rested at a temple, near to which was a small pool, and round it were congregated a number of pilgrims, watching the water very intently and then occasionally dipping their cups into it and drinking. I noticed a man who, with a large stone in his hand, was vigorously pounding away at a rock down by the waters edge. On asking what he was doing, he explained that the rock had magic virtue, and that if beaten for a few minutes water would flow from it. I watched' and, true enough, after a few minutes, water began to trickle from under it, and the whole surface of the pool quickly rose six or eight inches, and then as quickly receded. As soon as it began to rise all the people round the edge dipped in their cups and drank 'the holy water,' as they called it; others filled little earthenware bottles which they had brought with them on purpose, and corked them up to take home, believing in the magic efficacy of this water to heal diseases or keep away calamity. After watching a short time, one saw that the intervals were quite short, the water rising about every five minutes; so I persuaded them all to desist from pounding, assuring them that it had no effect whatever, and to leave the case to Nature; so they desisted, whilst we told them of the water of everlasting life, and they were no little surprised to see the water rise as before."

DISINTEGRATING FORCES

In the Church and the Family.

By Rev. A. C. Tris, of Howard, Kan.*

Restlessness a Prominent Sign of the Times—Deistical Tendencies in the Church—A Religion for the Times—One Wanted Giving More Authority to Man—Three Different Characters Developing as Predicted—Religious Communism—Changes in Family Life—Display and Extravagance—Children's Training Neglected—Parental Authority Ignored—False Views of Marriage.

It is not our purpose to speak of the forces of evil which will unite and bring about revolution and anarchy among the kingdoms of the Fourth world dominion, that great catastrophe which is drawing nigh. Our object is to speak of other forces of evil, which are doing a disintegrating work in church and family here and at the present time.

Restlessness

expresses the true character of this age. Not only the disturbances of terrestrial occurrences, the migration and emigration of nations, but, especially, the dislocated condition of church organizations and *secret workings* of revolutionary ideas and principles among all classes of society, warn us to pause and to take heed in regard to these ominous signs of the times. Let us not close our eyes to "the power of the forces," which under the leadership of Satan and his allies are shaking the very foundations of our holy religion and are working with irresistible energy to get dominion. The period in which we live is not only a time of dissatisfaction and uneasiness, but of change, of hankering after new ideas, of accepting strange doctrines, of "a new Christianity," and of cleaving to principles which must and will prepare the mind for Agnosticism and lawlessness. In II Tim. 3:1 it is emphatically declared: "That in the last days perilous times shall come, in which men shall have a form of godliness, but denying the power thereof."

Deistical Tendencies.

The present time has a tendency to embrace the religious tenets, both of Rome and of the Asiatic nations, and to make or compile a religion consisting in abstinence and works of devotion and charity, worshipping according to circumstances and to the precepts of men. Matt. 23:26. It is proposed to get rid of Christianity as a development of Judaism, and in its place have a religion in which the "whole world" can participate, and in which the Triune God is mentioned, nearly as *Amita Buddha* is mentioned in the Orient. A general idea has taken hold on the mind of the people that man has inalienable rights of freedom in will and choice, and that he has the prerogative to carve out his own way and select his future destiny at his own pleasure. This is an assumption of the sovereign rights of the Most High, and is called "rebellion" in I Sam. 15:23. It is dwelling deep in our depraved nature; it is becoming the spirit of the age, and is manifested in the wanton actions of nations, individuals and church members, is recognized in our universities and taught in our books of philosophy.

Before the Lord cometh with ten thousand of His saints. (Jude 11:15).

Three Different Characters

will be revealed: church members having *no brotherly love*, who "are going in the way of *Cain*;" church members, *unscrupulous* in word, thought and action, who like "*Balaam run greedily for reward*;" and church members seeking the honor and *ministerial offices* for money's-sake; who follow and "*perish in the gainsaying of Kore*." Every one of those three characters are pointed out as rebels or anarchists. Examining the state of the Church at the present day, we perceive grounds for suspecting their presence among us already. Religion has lost her pristine purity and chastity, which distinguished her from the world, from politics and from secular institutions. The Bride of Christ has lost "her veil" and is exposed to the gaze and the scorn of the world. Ministers have lost their prestige as ambassadors, accredited by the King of heaven, and the holy office is often looked upon as a secular office, and is graded in the scale of occupying "a position" in the community. How many of the clergy do not like to be questioned about their personal and inward calling to that holy office, and do not know what it is "*to be sent forth by the Holy Spirit*." History reveals the fact that the decay and the falling away of churches always did commence with uncalled, unscrupulous and unprincipled ministers.

Another great danger menacing the Church at the present time is that of *Centralization*, or

Religious Communism,

by which I mean that spirit of freedom and latitudinarianism which has permeated all denominations and all religious circles. The differences between churches and doctrines, are now too often regarded as consisting only in names, in small differences, in associations and in higher class, the *sharp edge of doctrinal differences* is blunted and worn away. In many families and religious circles is manifested a scoffing, contemptuous attitude toward church offices, which is so powerful in all its ramifications, that it defies and sets at naught all church rule and church government, so that the word excommunication has become, in Protestant churches, almost an obsolete word.

Seen in the light of history, we can easily discern how changed all this is from the practices of the early Christians and even from those of our own ancestors, only three or four generations back. The decadence is very manifest when the present religious exercises, attendance and spirit are compared with those of the former stern Puritans or Scottish fathers, with the former plain Methodists, or with the Bible-loving Huguenots; we fear, if those sainted fathers and mothers could attend the present religious meetings, that they would hardly recognize their spiritual descendants, and their unanimous cry would be heard: Ichabod: The glory is departed.

In Our Family Life

there is a mighty change in principles and habits. Taking a retrospect of only *eighty years*, we see a startling difference. *Then* the fathers and mothers of young and rising American States did enjoy more true love, joy and contentment, and above all, "more quietness of mind" (I. Peter 3:4), than the present generation. Indeed, they had more real trouble in the hard work of clearing the forests, marketing their products, educating their families and of vigilant watching their treacherous enemies, than this generation: and yet, they generally enjoyed life and lived to a good old age. Suicides, defalcations and bankruptcies were scarcely heard of. And what is now the condition in which thousands are? The struggle for social place and honor exhausts the energy on one side the house and the struggle for money the other side. Many families are spending more money than they really can afford, to keep up a false social position; and surrounded by associates, neighbors, friends, church and society connections, they follow the fashions lest they lose their standing in society, and *be left behind*. The consequences are that many families live in a feverish state, bearing a daily burden, harassed for the future, and worried about lacking so many things, real and imaginary, so that "the milk and sweet of life" is taken away; and rather than to curtail their expenses, or retrace their steps, they try to drown their apprehensions in excitement and worldly pleasure; in one word, they easily yield to *the inevitable*, silence their consciences, and set examples of folly for the rising generation. It is a sign of the last days, "that the *anxiety of the age*, and the *deceitfulness of riches* thoroughly choke the word, and *it* becometh unfruitful." Indeed, the word "Ichabod" (the glory has departed) can be written also on the family hearth—as an ominous word for the future.

Neglected Children

growing up without parental religious training is a consequence of this feverish family life, and from a consequence becomes itself a cause of further mischief. We are not unmindful that in the Sabbath-schools a great work is done *by proxy*, but taking this in due account, we say; after reflection, that the work of religious training has lost *its proper channel*, because the family altar, the daily reading of God's word, and family prayer, followed by parental admonitions and instruction, are commonly omitted, or entirely neglected. Parental authority is now not only on the wane, but, in many families it is set aside; and the consequences are that pride, callousness, indifference, irreverence and an unreligious spirit have taken its place, so that the children rule the household. The same spirit we find in many congregations, in which "*the young progressive party*" often rules the whole congregation. (I Kings 12:9-11.) It is a sure sign of the last days that men shall be *disobedient to parents*, unthankful, unholy, without natural affection, despisers of those that are good (II Tim., 3:2-4), and the history of the church and nations proves abundantly that the neglect of the family altar and family duties have always been the forerunners of lawlessness and destruction.

Godless Marriages

among young people is one of the results of this laxity of parental discipline. No civilized or Christian country on the globe has a young and rising generation which manifests so much self-will and unbridled liberty in choosing partners for life, and in marrying persons according to their choice, as this western New World. The sacred rights and prerogatives of parents are not regarded, as a common rule, in such engagements; neither is the word of the Most High consulted. The young people think that they possess all the required qualifications and wisdom needed to guide them in this most solemn affair of life, and the consequences are often deplorable, bringing misery on themselves and others. These are too numerous to be described at length; it is sufficint to enumerate the following: the favor and blessing of the Lord are withholden from many families; instead of true connubial love and fellowship, is manifested a disposition of wildness and negligence; wedlock has become unsavory, and marriage is regarded as little more than *a civil contract*, which can be broken or dissolved at will. It is an appalling fact to consider, what a myriad of separations and divorces are obtained for causes not sanctioned by divine law; and how *that evil* is growing rapidly. Remember, too, that laxity of the marriage ties is the sure forerunner of revolution and anarchy.

The Bible declares that *perilous times are in store for the world*. With the light of history to guide us we look at our own times, and we see that movements and tendencies which, working singly in past ages, have brought dire calamities on the nations, are now coming upon us together and with horrible unity. Thus we see how the warning of God's Word will be fulfilled, and fulfilled soon.

* Compiled from his new pamphlet, entitled "Ichabod: the Threatening Decay and Lawlessness."

PARALYSIS CURED BY A DOG.

An incident recently related by an eminent specialist on brain diseases, in the course of a lecture to medical students in Philadelphia, while illustrating his theory, also serves to illustrate the change which takes place in souls apparently insensible and incapable of Christian life and service, when the Holy Spirit removes the burden of sin and imparts the living energy of grave. (Ezek. 11:19, 20.)

The professor was explaining the affliction of paralysis, and said that cases apparently incurable, which the most skilful physicians had been unable to relieve, had been known to yield to sudden and violent emotion. He mentioned as an illustration, the case of a man who, for more than a year, had gone about on crutches, his left leg hanging a dead weight without feeling or power. There was no suspicion of shamming, for the leg had been examined and subjected to electricity and other tests. The man had not the slightest power or control over it. He abandoned hope of cure, but obtained such work as he could do to support himself. In going to and from his employment he had to pass a gate near which a savage dog was chained, and the cripple took care to keep well out of the dog's reach, as he hobbled by on his crutches. One day, however, the dog, making a sudden bound as the paralytic passed, broke his chain and rushed at him. The man looked around in terror, involuntarily dropped his crutches and ran like a deer. His paralysis was gone, and the use of his limb was restored to him. The helplessness of the leg, the professor said, was caused by the pressure of a clot of blood upon the brain, which the sudden emotion of fright expelled.

A HIDDEN CHINESE CONVERT.

"SOME time ago," says the Rev. Arthur Elwin, describing the Christian work in mid-China, "when persecution was raging, Andrew Chow, of the Chuchee district, was one who suffered much for the Lord's sake. The Chuchee magistrate found it necessary to visit Great Valley, Hang Chow, where Andrew lived, that he might see the damage done to the property of the Christians by the heathen. The heathen went out in a body to prevent his visiting their village; they waited for him at a village about three miles off, and when he came, told him there was no occasion for him to visit their village. The magistrate asked, 'Is there anyone here who belongs to this foreign religion?' Andrew stepped out before the magistrate, and in answer to questions, confessed his faith in the Lord Jesus Christ. The heathen followed Andrew to his house, determined to punish him severely for daring to speak as he had before the magistrate. They searched the house all through, but the bed in the room near the door, doubtless because it was in such a public position, they never thought of examining. The heathen left the house, declaring Andrew was not there. Young Andrew, quite unconscious of his danger, had slept soundly all the time, and awoke to find all the heathen had gone. When, some time afterwards, conversing with Andrew by the very bed on which he had slept, I asked him how it was the heathen had not found him; with a smiling face, the answer was given, 'The Lord hid me.' In the Church book at the Great Valley, there are three entries on three successive Sundays. On the first, Andrew's name is among those who received the Holy Communion at the hands of Bishop Moule. On the second, his name is down as having led the Christians at their service. The third Sunday there is note that on that day Andrew went home to heaven; so the event is expressed in the book. Now, far, far up on the lovely Chuchee hills he rests, and quietly awaits the Resurrection morn. Happy Andrew! hidden once for a time by the Lord on earth, and now hidden forever in the Saviour's presence in the glory."

ZULU GIRL FARMERS.

A PLEASANT surprise was experienced recently by Mr. Ireland, of Amanzimtote, who paid a visit to a seminary established for Zulu girls at Inanda, in Zululand. It seems that Mrs. Edwards, the Christian lady who is at the head of it, discovered that she could obtain a grant from the Government of Natal if she could make the school an "industrial school." Zulu girls and women are accustomed to field work, the warrior deeming it below his dignity to labor; the pupils therefore gladly co-operated in a scheme Mrs. Edwards mapped out to *work a farm*. Mr. Ireland, in a letter to the *Missionary Herald*, thus describes what has been accomplished:

"We found a beautiful little farm, comprising some fifteen acres or more, enclosed by wire fencing, and with the exception of a few acres, where the primeval sod was turned over once by the plow, the whole has been (or soon will be) brought into a fine state of cultivation by these Inanda schoolgirls. When the hour arrived for field work, we accompanied Mrs. Edwards and her girls to that part of the field not yet brought under cultivation. At a signal from their leader *the girls, some thirty-two of them, fell into line, each armed with a strong and rather heavy hoe*, and went lustily to work upon the greensward in front of them. During the hour and more they were at work they left some twenty yards behind them. Mrs. Edwards expects to raise, the present season, all the corn, pumpkins, beans, and potatoes that will be required for the year's consumption. A part of her plan of work is the planting of trees. Last year more than a thousand trees were planted, and this number will be more than doubled the present season if these energetic plans are carried out. Thus are this good lady and her coadjutors endeavoring to realize, in an indirect and individual way, not only morally but physically, the prophecy of Isaiah: 'The wilderness and the solitary place shall be glad for them; and the desert shall rejoice and blossom as the rose.'" (Isa. 35:1.)

THE TIGER AND THE MISSIONARY.

AMONG the remarkable stories related by the Rev. A. E. Haegert of his experience in Santhalistan, is the following, which he says occurred in February of last year: One evening, after tea we had worship, and commended ourselves and the Mission to God. After worship I had to go outside, and right under the window was a tiger, about twelve feet off. My first thought was to turn and flee, but fearing that he would jump on my back, I looked to the heavens and begged Jesus to help. Then I walked up to the tiger, who had already been to the cowhouse and scratched a hole to get at the cow and calves. The walls, however, were thick and hard, and he gave it up as a bad job. Now he walked round the house seeking his supper. I was unharmed as I approached him. On the verandah my dog was lying. He was from Scotland, and had never seen a tiger before, but he rushed at him and barked furiously. The tiger snarled at us and went a few steps on one side, so I passed quietly on. After walking about twenty yards, I realized that I was safe, and thanked God. I thought, 'Poor doggie, you will pay with your life for your master's safety.' So I whistled for him. To my great joy he came, wagging his tail, and still turning to bark at the tiger. 'The angel of the Lord encampeth round about them that fear Him.'"

THE FAMINE IN PERSIA.

HARROWING reports have been arriving now for two months past of suffering and death from starvation in Persia. Three calamities, either of which is much dreaded in Persia—inundation, drought and locusts — visited the country last year, and the food-supply finally harvested after the three visitations was utterly inadequate to maintain the people until next harvest. Among the appeals being made for help by the various missionary societies is one of much pathos, which is sent to us by Mr. Yaroo M. Neesan, the Persian missionary student whose portrait and life were published in this journal December 23, 1886. He is naturally deeply concerned about the peril of his countrymen, and is earnestly endeavoring, by lecturing and by the sale of Persian curiosities, to swell the fund in the hands of Dean Hoffman, of the General Theological Seminary, 426 West 23d Street, New York, where Mr. Neesan is being trained for missionary work. The following facts are extracts from his simple yet pathetic statement.

A journal published in Oroomiah, in Persia, says, "The famine that is now raging here and in Koordistan as far as Mosul, is very sore." Canon Maclean says, "This year the people in the mountain districts are suffering much from famine and from the destruction of their fields, houses and bridges by the great floods of last spring." A letter from the village of Sir says, "While writing, ——'s wife is in our house crying. She says, '*I have nothing in my house for my children to eat.*'"

Rabbi Abraham Moorbach, whose work was described in this journal of June 8, 1887, in an appeal to Mr. Neesan, written from Oroomiah, says, "The famine is very sore, and hundreds will die. We beg you to aid us in whatever way you can. In our village *of two hundred families, ten only of that number have provision for the winter*, and we do earnestly pray God that He will be merciful to our afflicted state."

Another writer says, "The keenness of the suffering increases with each day; many will perish if assistance does not come, many will perish even before assistance can reach us."

There are five months remaining before harvest time, the first opportunity the poor will have of helping themselves, and unless speedy assistance comes to them many will starve.

They are our brethren. They are suffering from hunger. Will you not help to save these Christian lives? *Twenty dollars will preserve one life* until the August harvests. "Verily I say unto you, Inasmuch as ye have done it unto one of the least of these my brethren, ye have done it unto Me."

Funds remitted to the Rev. E. A. Hoffman, D. D., Dean of the General Theological Seminary, will be forwarded by telegraph to Canon Maclean, the missionary in charge, at Oroomiah, Persia.

THE PEACE AT PONAPE.

THE events in Ponape, described in these columns on January 19 (page 39), naturally caused some solicitude to the friends of the missionaries. What course the Spanish Government might take toward the islanders who had slain the Governor and his soldiers was a question to be left in the hands of God, and doubtless that was what the missionaries did, for, in a letter from Mr. Doane to the American Board of Commissioners, he joyfully reports conduct on the part of Spain so magnanimous as to surprise everyone:

"A strong Spanish force of eight hundred men has," he states, "been sent to the island with a new Governor. The Spanish prestige being re-established, a proclamation was issued stating the terms on which the expedition would refrain from war. The proclamation began by offering a full, free pardon to all the chiefs, especially those called rebels. They were to meet at my house at Old Kenan, as neutral ground. This was the first point, with the further idea of complete submission on the part of the Ponapeans to the Spanish monarch. He demanded that all royal arms in the hands of the people should be given up; also, all the goods looted in July last during the *émeute*, the return of some runaway Manila soldiers, and the delivering over of some three natives accused of killing the Governor in July last.

"These five points were presented to the people, giving them a week to consider them. *We went to work in good earnest to save the people.* War, once opened, meant the destruction of all homes, farms, dwellings, the shooting of many men, and the deportation of many more. We plainly told the people there was no hope for them, and the sooner they were on their knees the better. Then we pushed out in drenching rains, threading paths almost impossible to walk in, running miles inland, scaling mountains buttressed by huge bowlders so slippery that they were difficult to climb.

"On the final day, four chiefs came in. One delayed, but grace was asked and granted, and the next day he came in. More time was asked for the accused natives. This was soon obtained, and it brought sunlight and joy; for the main features of the proclamation were met. My heart has ever since been singing her *Te Deum* and shouting her hallelujahs; for peace was brought back, not the demon of war.

"Now the old homes can be entered and re-occupied by natives who had fled to the mountains and forests for protection. We rejoice over what has been obtained. God be praised!"

CHRISTIAN HERALD AND SIGNS OF OUR TIMES.

OFFICE, 63 BIBLE HOUSE, NEW YORK.

ENTERED AT THE POST-OFFICE AT NEW YORK, N. Y., AS SECOND-CLASS MATTER.

Published Weekly. Subscription price, $1.50 a year; $1 eight months; 75 cents six months; sent two months on trial for 25 cents; always payable in advance. Single copies for sale by, or can be ordered at, all newsdealers.

Remittances by Mail should be by Post-office money order, bank cheques, or drafts or express money order, and should always be made payable to THE CHRISTIAN HERALD.

Receipts are not sent, the receipt of the paper by a subscriber is a sufficient proof that his remittance has been received. If the paper does not arrive promptly, please advise us, that we may see if the address is correctly entered.

Change of Address. Name of Post Office and State, of both old and new address, should always be given in case of removal.

CURRENT EVENTS.

An Important Financial Measure has Passed the House. It is a bill which authorizes the Secretary of the Treasury to use any part of the surplus that, in his judgment, is expedient for the purchase of bonds in the open market. The Senate has already practically committed itself to the financial policy embodied in this bill, and there is little doubt that it will become a law.

The Tariff Bill, Reported by the House Committee on Ways and Means, bears marks of the influence of the chairman, Mr. Mills, of Texas. It makes substantial additions to the free list, reducing the revenue on the basis of importations of the fiscal year 1887 by about $28,000,000. This includes the repeal of the duties on lumber, on salt, on wools, on flax, hemp, jute, and like fibres, and on some of their manufactures; on a considerable number of chemicals, embracing boracic acid and vegetable dyeing substances; on copper ore, tin plates and cotton ties; on books printed in foreign languages, or published for free distribution; on paintings and statuary, and on numerous articles yielding a small revenue. The reductions made in the duties that are not abolished, are expected, on the basis of the fiscal year 1887, to produce a decrease in revenue of about $24,000,000, in addition to the $28,000,000 mentioned above. The tariff issue is thus now officially before Congress, and—being the leading issue of the Presidential campaign—its progress will be watched with more than ordinary interest.

A National Art Commission is the Latest contemplated innovation proposed to Congress. A bill providing for such a commission, to consist of fourteen members, has passed the Senate. It provides that four of the commissioners shall be eminent sculptors, four eminent painters, three eminent architects, and the other three shall be selected from other employments, for their knowledge and good taste in art. It is to be their duty to report upon the character and value of such plans of public buildings, monuments, or works of art as shall be referred to them by Congress, and to select from designs offered by competitors for works of art ordered by Congress. Inasmuch as the members of the Commission are to serve without pay, there seems at least no harm done should the bill become a law.

Monopoly of the Public Lands is to be made impossible. The Committee on public lands has reported a bill to the House, by which it is sought to secure to actual settlers all the remaining public lands adapted to agriculture, and to protect the forests on the forest lands of the United States from destruction. The bill does not change the present mineral land laws, except to restrict the definition of such lands in the interests of homestead settlers, and to classify iron and coal lands together at a uniform rate of $10 per acre. In reporting the bill the Committee called special attention to the fact that every provision of the existing law under which public lands in large bodies have by fraudulent and dishonest methods been obtained by unscupulous parties is proposed to be repealed by the bill, and under its terms monopoly of the public lands will be impossible, and all public lands adapted to agriculture, even to a partial extent, or on which a citizen can establish a home, is made available in securing him a freehold estate. An official estimate places the public lands, excluding Alaska, classified as arable lands, on which crops can be raised without irrigation, at 75,000,000 acres.

The Bill to Incorporate the Maritime Canal Company of Nicaragua has passed the Senate, and it is said that its passage in the House is probable. It is claimed that the ship canal across Nicaragua, contemplated by this company, possesses vast advantages over M. Lessep's Panama scheme, which has already swallowed up much more capital than was originally expected, and which is in a bankrupt condition, with only a fraction of the work completed. As regards the Nicaragua canal, all that is asked of the United States Government is a charter of incorporation and political sanction for the enterprise. The Government is not asked to lend its credit, or give any financial guarantee. The canal will be constructed with private capital, and have the character simply of a commercial enterprise, unless contingencies should arise to give it unforeseen political importance.

The Will of the Late W. W. Corcoran, the Washington philanthropist, has been made public. He has added to his magnificent charities during his lifetime by bequeathing $100,000 to the Corcoran Art Gallery, to which he had already given $1,500,000; $50,000 to the Louise Home, to which he gave in life $500,000; $5,000 each to the three orphan asylums of the District, and $3,000 to the Little Sisters of the Poor. He makes many bequests, ranging from $100 to $15,000, to relatives, personal friends, and servants. The remainder of the estate is left in trust for his three grandchildren.

A Gigantic Strike of Engineers and firemen commenced on February 27, on the Chicago, Burlington and Quincy Railroad, which comprises in its system some of the most important arteries of travel, extending as far West as Omaha and comprising 6,000 miles of track. This inaugurates a strike of considerable magnitude. The strikers are all members of the Brotherhood of Locomotive Engineers and Firemen. The principle for which this organization is contending is the much vexed and disputed one, that those who do the same work for the same length of time shall be paid the same wages, without regard to degrees of skill and experience. The railroad company had followed the plan of classifying its engineers and firemen and paying different rates of wages, according to the difficulties of the work or the degrees of skill, experience and responsibility required, having its own examinations for employment and promotion. The strikers claim that this system is wrong, and want it abolished. They contend for a general schedule of wages, under which all shall be treated alike. The strike seems likely to be a long and stubborn one. A curious feature of it is, that among the men who have applied for places left vacant by the strikers are *said to be a number of Knights of Labor*. It is difficult to believe that members of an organization which has been so outspoken about "scab labor" should become "scabs." It is explained, however, that the Knights of Labor bear a grudge against the Brotherhood for not supporting them in the past by sympathetic strikes. The number of engineers and firemen on strike the first day was estimated at 1,600, but unless speedily settled it is feared that the strike will spread to other roads, and many more men will be idle.

An Unequivocal Vote of Approval of the British Government in the question of the Trafalgar Square Riots was given in the House of Commons on March 2. Sir Charles Russell proposed that the House appoint a committee to inquire into the conduct of the Government in prohibiting the meeting, and the police in suppressing it. He was powerfully backed up by Bradlaugh, and the Government, feeling sure that they had the support of the country, made the question one of confidence, meaning that they would stand or fall according as they were supported. The followers of Lord Hartington and Mr. Chamberlain therefore voted almost solidly for the Government, and for the suppression of the right of public meeting in crowded business thoroughfares. It is thus decided by a vote of 316 to 224 that the people have not the right to meet in Trafalgar square, but that is no deprivation, as they can meet in Hyde Park which is more convenient for those attending the meetings, and for those who wish to use the streets for business traffic.

The French Reply to the Great Speech of Bismarck in the German Reichstag was delivered by the Marquis de Breteuil in the French Chamber of Deputies, reviewing the situation in Europe caused by the triple alliance. He said he had no faith in its stability. France, he added, must wish the Czar to remain the arbiter of peace and France must seize every opportunity to show him sympathy and make him understand, without exaggerated demonstration, that the French are strong but discreet friends. In conclusion the Marquis said: "Let us show ourselves a nation desiring peace, but not fearing war. Let us reject all idea of an offensive war, and desire only to live and work, taking care that nothing shall compromise our honor and dignity."

The Fortifications of British Seaports was the subject of Parliamentary inquiry last week. To the American visitor, accustomed to the sight of defences so feeble as those of New York and other home ports, the defences of the naval strongholds of Great Britain appear formidable, but they are declared inefficient relatively. Mr. Stanhope, Secretary for War, has issued a memorandum, in which he admits that after a careful inquiry it has been ascertained that deficiencies exist in the defences of Portsmouth, Plymouth and the Thames, which render England's position dangerously insecure. This condition of affairs, he says, is mainly due, not to the misspending of credits, but to the rapid increase of the offensive power of other navies.

The Conviction and Sentence of M. Wilson, the son-in-law of Ex-President Grévy startled the French capital on Thursday last. As will be remembered, M. Wilson was charged with accepting money, in return for which he undertook to use his influence with the President, to secure contracts, decorations, titles, etc., for the persons paying him. As a matter of fact, several men were made members of the Legion of honor who had done nothing to merit the distinction, but had secured it by paying money to certain agents, who said, truthfully or falsely, that it went to Wilson. He was placed on his trial, and last week he was convicted and sentenced to two years' imprisonment, to pay a fine of 3,000*l.* ($600), and to be deprived of his civil rights for five years.

The Presidential Election in Mexico, Which takes place next June, appears to be decided in advance, as no one of the candidates yet named against Porfirio Diaz, the present incumbent, whose portrait and life appeared in this journal, on November 23, 1887, seems to be able to concentrate anything like an effective opposition. There seems to be no doubt that General Diaz will be re-elected by an overwhelming majority. He has made a strong and able President, and proved a sincere and dignified friend of the United States.

A Change for the Better in the Condition of the German Crown Prince is indicated by the latest bulletins. The *British Medical Journal* announces by authority that he is now slowly improving, though his windpipe is still in an irritated condition. On the other hand, however the *Lancet* comments upon the scarcity of official bulletins, and says it regrets that it is forced to the conclusion that the Crown Prince is proceeding from bad to worse.

A Request to Clergymen is Made by the National Women's Christian Temperance Union to which we are asked to give prominence. The Union, through its President and the Superintendent of its Sabbath Observance Department, Mrs. J. C. Bateham, of Painesville, O., asks ministers to preach on April 1, or on Easter Sunday, April 8, upon "the Christian Sabbath," calling special attention to the twofold peril threatening the Sabbath from adverse legislation and the growing desecration of the day. In this request the World's Sabbath Observance Prayer Union and similar organizations join, as also in asking that the first week in April be made a week of prayer for Sabbath observance.

A Boston Pulpit Relinquished for Foreign service, is an interesting fact communicated to a contemporary. It states that the exchange of a Boston church for pioneer mission labor is being made by the Rev. R. Henry Ferguson, pastor of the Dorchester Temple Baptist Church, Boston, who has decided to go to the Ka Chins, a people occupying the hills of northern Burma, southern China, and Thibet. The people have no written language, and Mr. Ferguson goes to reduce their language to writing, make the necessary grammars and dictionaries, and translate the Old and New Testaments for them. Bhamo, where he will make his home and station, is a city, inhabited chiefly by Chinese, Shans and Burmese, with some few English, and situated at the head of navigation of the Irrawaddi River. It is connected with Rangoon at the mouth of this river by a line of steamboats, making the distance by water 860 miles. Mr. Ferguson has resigned his pastorate in order to make special preparation for his work, and is now at work upon the Shemitic languages and medicine, and expects to sail in October.

A Tugboat, with no Engineer at the Levers, caused some excitement in the crowded East River a few days ago. The tugboat went into a slip for water about noon, and, having procured it, the engineer turned on steam and backed out into the river. Almost instantly another boat struck her near the stern, causing her to give a swift lurch. The engineer, who had stepped out to see what had occurred, lost his balance and fell into the river. He was rescued in a stunned condition by another boat. No one on his own boat saw him fall into the river, and the pilot was amazed, and then alarmed, to find no notice taken of his signals. The boat went forging on, and it required all the pilot's dexterity to keep her from collisions. He continued shouting to the deck hands to see what was wrong in the engine-room, and finally, the discovery was made that there was no engineer on board. The deck hands were a long time before they found out the lever with which they could shut off steam, and the boat damaged a pier and another boat, besides injuring herself, before her headlong course was stopped. Many souls, in their early efforts after salvation and before they surrender to Christ, are like that boat and her pilot—with good intentions and right resolves, but without power to execute them. (Rom. 7: 15, 19.)

A Supernatural Warning to a Mother is cited by a recent writer as evidence that natural law is not sufficient to explain even the events which occur within human experience. He states that a short time ago an inquest was held at New Albany, Ind., on the body of a boy killed at a railroad crossing. The boy's mother stated that, having sent her son, ten years old, on an errand, she distinctly heard him shriek and moan about half an hour after he left the house. Her daughter said that at the time named, her mother called her and bade her go and look for the boy, for she had heard him cry, and was sure he was hurt. Her daughter looked around the house, but could not see the boy, and concluded that her mother had been mistaken. Shortly afterward the mangled body of the boy was brought home. At the very time the mother heard his shriek, he had fallen under the wheels of a train of cars more than a mile away. It was impossible that his scream could have been heard at his home, yet the mother, who could have known nothing of what was occurring, evidently did hear it, as was proved by her solicitude in sending her daughter to search for him. Scientists, who cannot explain this phenomenon by any known law, yet who have to admit the fact, are inconsistent when they contend that the prayers of God's suffering children cannot reach His ears. (Isa. 65: 24.)

An Heir in Hiding is the Central Figure in a remarkable story given to the press last week. On February 24 a lawyer in Indianapolis received a telegram, inquiring if he would be in his office at a certain hour on the following day. The lawyer did not know the name attached to the telegram, but he sent an affirmative answer, and expected to receive a call from a new client. Instead of a client, a messenger waited upon him at the time indicated and placed a package in his hands containing $2,900. With the money the lawyer found a letter from a former partner, who eight years ago absconded, leaving a shortage in his accounts. This is the second amount that has been sent by the missing man, and it covers, with the sum before sent, the whole deficiency. He took extraordinary precautions to preserve the secrecy of his hiding-place, and in the letter he expressed his determination never to emerge from it, though there is now no charge against him. A remarkable fact is, that he has fallen heir to a large estate, but there is no way of communicating the fact to him. It is believed that he is working as a common sailor, or at some laborious occupation about ships or docks, and has been denying himself ordinary comforts to restore the money. Had he known of it, he need not have labored and denied himself, as the property which is waiting for him to claim it, would have paid the debt many times over. Many anxious souls are acting in the same way as to the eternal inheritance. They are toiling and striving to win salvation, when the perfect salvation of Christ is placed at their disposal, if they would only claim it. (Rom. 4: 4, 5.)

A Physician's Interdict on Kisses was among his most emphatic directions to his wife on leaving home sometime ago. "Remember," he said, "and do not let the children kiss any one." "Is it possible," asked a surprised third party who was present, "that you consider it necessary to give such instructions as that? Where is the danger?" "The danger is complicated and certain, said the doctor. "In my case, all kinds of people come to my house to consult me, and they often wait hours. If one of my children happens to come in they are almost certain to talk to it, and you know almost the first impulse with people who notice children is to kiss them. Bah! it makes me shudder—tainted and diseased breaths, lips blue with cancer, foul and decayed teeth. You would be tempted to kill a stranger who would waylay your daughter and kiss her by force, but the helpless, unsuspecting six-year-old child susceptible as a flower to every breath that blows, can be saluted by every one who chances to think of it. Hundreds of lovely children are kissed into their graves every year." The physician did not dread his children coming to harm through violence or hatred, but through a token of affection thoughtlessly given. Moral and spiritual evil is often similarly communicated. Young people are allured from the paths of religion and virtue, not by the hatred, but the false love of the world (II Peter 2: 18.)

An Amateur Matrimonial Agency of a Very successful kind is described in the Charleston *News and Courier*. It states that at its first introduction, at a large wedding reception, eleven marriages resulted from it. All the young people present selected a gentleman of known honor and reserve as president of a lovers' confidence bureau, and he was duly sworn to keep entirely secret all communications that should be forwarded to him in his official capacity that night. Each unmarried gentleman or lady not engaged nor resolved on celibacy, undertook to write his or her name on a piece of paper, and under it the name of the person they wished to marry, then hand it to the president for inspection; and if any gentleman and lady had reciprocally chosen each other, the president was to inform each of the result, and to keep strictly secret the communications of those who had not been reciprocal in their choice. After the appointment was made, communications were handed at intervals during the evening to the president, who at the close examined and sorted them. It was found that twelve young ladies and gentlemen had made reciprocal choices. In eleven cases the revelation of the mutual regard has, it is stated, led to marriage, and the young gentlemen of eight couples of the eleven have declared that their diffidence was so great that they certainly should not have addressed their respective wives had they not been apprised in this curious way that the ladies were favorably disposed toward them. It sometimes happens with souls anxious for salvation, that they are kept from peace by a similar lack of knowledge. When they realize that God is not hostile to them, but Himself desires their salvaton, they go to Him and find peace. (Ezek. 33: 11.)

BRIEF NOTES.

Mrs. John Wannamaker, of Philadelphia, has built a children's ward for the Pennsylvania Hospital of that city, at the cost of $35,000.

The American Church Missionary Society has received the names of twenty young men who volunteer for missionary work in either China or Japan.

Dr. Meredith's Tuesday evening Bible Class in Brooklyn is growing to the proportions of the one he conducted in Boston, Mass.; it is attended by at least 1,500 persons.

The Hon. J. V. Farwell, of Chicago, during his recent visit to London, conducted evangelistic services for Mr. Charles Cook, at the Metropolitan Music Hall.

In the Ontario Legislature, now in session, a bill has been introduced empowering municipal councils to pass by-laws defining the hours for closing any particular class or classes of retail shops.

Seven churches have united in the meetings conducted by Rev. B. Fay Mills, in Providence, R. I., Baptists, Presbyterians and Methodists are working together harmoniously in the harvest of souls.

The President has offered the post of Minister to Liberia to the Rev. J. O. Price, President of Livingston College, Salisbury, N. C. Mr. Price is one of the most cultured colored men in the United States.

Dr. William Ormiston, the famous and popular New York preacher, has resigned the pastorate in the Collegiate Reformed Church. Dr. Ormiston, after eighteen years of successful labor, resigns on account of obstinate throat trouble and loss of voice.

Messrs. Crossley and Hunter have been holding evangelistic services in the Dominion Methodist Church, Ottawa, Canada, for some time past. There have been a number of converts. Great interest has been taken in the work by Sir John and Lady Macdonald.

A series of evangelistic meetings at Dallas, Texas, have been commenced by Evangelist Harold F. Sayles, His first congregation numbered seven hundred. The Congregational, Second Presbyterian, Cumberland Presbyterian and First Methodist churches co-operated.

The Vienna correspondent of the London *Standard*, says: "Russia is promising concession to the Poles, and the Czar has been bestowing distinctions on the Polish noblemen of late—two ominous signs. An influential Pole, coming from Warsaw, where he had been visiting his estates, said to me, '*We shall have war in May*.'"

The union revival meetings, conducted by Dr. L. W. Munhall, in Buffalo, were blessed to an unprecedented degree in that city. More than seven hundred persons made a public confession of Christ, ascribing their conversion to God's blessing on the meetings. The influence of the meetings on the churches in quickening spiritual life has also been most evident.

Mr. Wm. McK. Gatchell, who died suddenly in Washington, D. C., on February 21, was an earnest and active worker in the Prohibition cause, was Secretary of the National Prohibition Bureau, but was acting at the time of his death as agent of the National Anti-Nuisance League. This League is organized to operate against the saloons, under the nuisance laws.

THE LORD AND THE LEPER.

A New Sermon by Pastor C. H. Spurgeon.

"And there came a leper to Him, and kneeling down to Him, and saying unto Him, If Thou wilt, Thou canst make me clean. And Jesus, moved with compassion, put forth His hand, and touched him, and saith unto him, I will; be thou clean. And as soon as He had spoken, immediately the leprosy departed from him, and he was cleansed." Mark 1: 40-42.

Healing Power Received in Communion—I. The Leper Eager to be Healed - Spiritual Lepers Who are not Eager The Despairing—The Indifferent—A Dreadful Confraternity—II. Believing he Could be Healed—Leprosy Incurable—The Basis of the Leper's Faith—III. His Faith Fixed on Christ—IV. A Real Cure—V. A Hesitancy—VI. His Earnest Action—VII. His Reward—The Cure Bearing Examination.

OUR Lord had been engaged in special prayer. He had gone alone on the mountain-side to have communion with God. Simon and the rest search for Him, and He comes away in the early morning with the burrs from the hill-side upon His garments, the smell of the field upon Him; He comes forth among the people, charged with power which He had received in communion with the Father; and now we may expect to see wonders. And we do see them; for devils fear and fly when He speaks the word; and by and by, there comes to Him one, an extraordinary being, condemned to live apart from the rest of men, lest he should spread defilement all around. A leper comes to Him, and kneels before Him, and expresses his confident faith in Him, that He can make Him whole. Now is the Son of Man glorious in His power to save. The Lord Jesus Christ at this day has all power in heaven and in earth. He is charged with a divine energy to bless all who come to Him for healing. Oh, that we may see to-day some wonder of His power and grace!

I. I will begin my rehearsal of the gospel narrative by remarking, first, that this leper's faith made him

Eager to be Healed.

He was a leper; I will not stay just now to describe what horrors are compacted into that single word; but he believed that Jesus could cleanse him, and his belief stirred him to an anxious desire to be healed at once. Alas! we have to deal with spiritual lepers eaten up with the foul disease of sin; but some of them do not believe that they ever can be healed, and the consequence is that despair makes them sin most greedily. "I may as well be hanged for a sheep as for a lamb," is the inward impression of many a sinner when he fears that there is no mercy and no help for him. Because there is no hope, therefore they plunge deeper and yet deeper into the slough of iniquity. Oh, that you might be delivered from that false idea! Mercy still rules the hour. There is hope while Jesus sends His gospel to you, and bids you repent. "I believe in the forgiveness of sins": this is a sweet sentence of a true creed. I believe also in the renewal of men's hearts; for the Lord can give new hearts and right spirits to the evil and unthankful.

We have a number of lepers who come in among us whose disease is white upon their brows, and visible to all beholders, and yet they are indifferent: they do not mourn their wickedness, nor wish to be cleansed from it. They sleep on upon the bed of sloth, and care neither for heaven nor hell. Indifference to spiritual things is the sin of the age. Men are stolid of heart about eternal realities. An awful apathy is upon the multitude. The leper in our text was not so foolish as this.

Lepers were obliged to consort together: lepers associated with lepers, and they made up

A Dreadful Confraternity.

How glad they would have been to escape from it! But I know spiritual lepers who love the company of their fellow lepers. Yes, and the more leprous a man becomes, the more do they admire him. A bold sinner is often the idol of his comrades. Though foul in his life, others cling to him for that very reason. Such persons like to learn some new bit of wickedness; they are eager to be initiated into a yet darker form of impure pleasure. Oh, how they long to hear that last lascivious song, to read that last impure novel! It seems to be the desire of many to know as much evil as they can. They flock together, and take a dreadful pleasure in talk and action which is the horror of all pure minds. Strange lepers, that heap up

Leprosy as a Treasure!

Lepers were not allowed to associate with healthy persons, except under severe restrictions. Thus were they separated from their nearest and dearest friends. What a sorrow! Alas! I know persons thus separated who do not wish to associate with the godly; to them holy company is dull and wearisome; they do not feel free and easy in such society, and therefore they avoid it as much as decency allows. How can they hope to live with saints forever, when they shun them now as dull and moping acquaintances?

II. In the second place, let us remark that this leper's faith was strong enough to make him believe that

He Could be Healed

of his hideous disease. Leprosy was an unutterably loathsome disease. As it exists, even now, it is described by those who have seen it in such a way that I will not harrow your feelings by repeating all the sickening details. The following quotation may be more than sufficient. Dr. Thomson, in his famous work, "The Land and the Book," speaks of lepers in the East, and says: "The hair falls from the head and eyebrows; the nails loosen, decay and drop off; joint after joint of the fingers and toes shrinks up and slowly falls away. The gums are absorbed and the teeth disappear. The nose, the eyes, the tongue and the palate are slowly consumed." This disease turns a man into a mass of loathsomeness, a walking pile of pests. Leprosy is nothing better than a horrible and lingering death. The leper in the narrative before us had sad personal experience of this, and yet he believed that Jesus could cleanse him. Splendid faith! Oh, that you who are afflicted with moral and spiritual leprosy could believe in this fashion! Jesus Christ of Nazareth can heal even you. Over the horror of leprosy faith triumphed. Oh, that in your case it would overcome the terribleness of sin!

Leprosy was known to be incurable. There was no case of a man being cured of

Real Leprosy.

by any medical or surgical treatment. This made the cure of Naaman in former ages so noteworthy. Observe, moreover, that our Saviour Himself, so far as I can see, had never healed a leper up to the moment when this poor wretch appeared upon the scene. He had cured fever, and had cast out devils, but the cure of leprosy was, in the Saviour's life, as yet an unexampled thing. Yet this man, putting this and that together, and understanding something of the nature and character of the Lord Jesus Christ, believed that he could cure him of his incurable disease. He felt that even if the great Lord had not yet healed leprosy, He was assuredly capable of doing so great a deed, and he determined to apply to Him. Was not this grand faith? For a real, conscious sinner to trust the Saviour is no mean thing. When you hope that there is some good thing in you, it is easy to be confident; but to be conscious of total ruin, and yet to believe in the divine remedy—this is real faith. To see in the sunshine is mere natural vision; but to see in the dark needs the eye of faith: to believe that Jesus has saved you when you see the signs of it, is the result of reason; but to trust Him to cleanse you while you are still defiled with sin—this is the essence of saving faith. His moral and spiritual miracles are often wrought upon cases which seem beyond all hope, cases which pity itself endeavors to forget, because her efforts have been so long in vain.

I like best about this man's faith the fact that he did not merely believe that Jesus Christ could cleanse a leper, but that He could cleanse *him!* He said, "Lord, if Thou wilt, Thou canst make *me* clean." It is very easy to believe for other people. There is really no faith in such impersonal, proxy confidence. The true faith believes for itself first, and then for others. Oh, I know some of you are saying, "I believe that Jesus can save my brother. I believe that He can save the vilest of the vile. If I heard that He had saved the biggest drunkard in Southwark, I should not wonder." Canst thou believe all this, and yet fear that He cannot save thee? This is strange inconsistency. If He heals another man's leprosy, can He not heal *thy* leprosy? If one drunkard is saved, why not another? If in one man a passionate temper is subdued, why not in another? If lust and covetousness and lying and pride have been cured in many men, why not in thee? Even if thou art a blasphemer, blasphemy has been cured; why should it not be so in thy case? He can heal thee of that particular form of sin which possesses thee, however high a degree its power may have reached; for nothing is too hard for the Lord.

The Only Healer.

III. Now notice, thirdly, that this man's faith was fixed on Jesus Christ alone. Let me read the man's words again. He said unto Jesus, "If thou wilt, thou canst make me clean." Throw the emphasis upon the *pronouns.* See him kneeling before the Lord Jesus, and hear him say, "If *thou* wilt, *thou* canst make *me* clean." He has no idea of looking to the disciples; no, not to one of them or to all of them. He had no notion of trusting in a measure to the medicine which physicians would prescribe for him. All that is gone. No dream of other hope remains; but with his eye fully fixed on the blessed Miracle-worker of Nazareth, he cries, "If *thou* wilt, *thou* canst make me clean." In himself he had no shade of confidence; every delusion of that kind had been banished by a fierce experience of his disease. He knew that none on earth could deliver him, and that by no innate power of constitution could he throw out the poison; but he confidently believed that the Son of God could by Himself effect the cure. This was God-given faith—the faith of God's elect, and Jesus was its sole object.

Heard Jesus Preach.

How came this man to have such faith? I cannot tell you the outward means, but I think we may guess without presumption. Had he not *heard our Lord preach?* Matthew puts this story immediately after the Sermon on the Mount, and says: "When He was come down from the mountain, great multitudes followed Him. And, behold, there came a leper and worshipped Him, saying, Lord, if thou wilt, thou canst make me clean." Had this man managed to stand at the edge of the crowd and hear Jesus speak, and did those wondrous words convince him that the great Teacher was something more than man? As he noted the style and manner and matter of that marvellous sermon, did he say within himself, "Never man spake like this man. Truly He is the Son of God. I believe in Him. I trust Him. He can cleanse me"? My hearer, have you not

Seen Jesus Save Others.

Have you not at least read of His miracles of grace? Believe Him, then, for His works' sake, and say to Him, "Lord, if thou wilt, thou canst make me clean."

O my dear hearers, cannot you trust the Lord Jesus Christ in this way? A divine Saviour must be able to cleanse thee from all sin. Only Jesus can do it, but He can do it—do it Himself alone, do it now, do it in thee, do it with a word. Say, "Lord, if thou wilt, thou canst make me clean." Faith must be fixed alone on Jesus. None other name is given among men whereby we must be saved. I do pray the Lord to give that faith to all my dear friends present this morning who as yet have not received cleansing at the Lord's hands. Jesus is God's ultimatum of salvation: the unique hope of guilty men both as to pardon and renewal. Accept Him even now.

IV. Now let me go a step further: this man's faith had respect to a real

Matter-of-Fact Cure.

He did not think of the Lord Jesus Christ as a priest who would perform certain ceremonies over Him, and formally say, "Thou art clean;" for that would not have been true. He wanted really to be delivered from the leprosy; to have those dry scales, into which his skin kept turning, taken all away, that his flesh might become as the flesh of a little child; he wanted that the rottenness, which was eating up his body, should be stayed, and that health should be actually restored. Friends, it is easy enough to believe in a mere priestly absolution if you have enough credulity; but we need more than this.

No sanctifying power comes with outward ceremonials in and of themselves. To believe that the Lord Jesus Christ can make us love the good things which once we despised, and shun those evil things in which we once took pleasure—this is to believe in Him indeed and of a truth.

None of us would imagine that this leper meant that the Lord Jesus could make him feel comfortable in remaining a leper. Some seem to fancy that Jesus came to let us go on in our sins with a quiet conscience; but He did nothing of the kind. His salvation is cleansing from sin, and if we love sin we are not saved from it.

Emancipation.

The man who frets under the yoke of sin will not long be a slave to it; if he can believe that Jesus Christ is able to set him free, he shall soon quit his bondage. Some sins which have hardened down into habits, yet disappear in a moment when Jesus Christ looks upon a man in love. I have known many instances of persons who, for many years, had never spoken without an oath, or a filthy expression, who, being converted, have never been known to use such language again, and have scarcely ever been tempted in that direction. This is one of the sins which seem to die at the first shot, and it is a very wonderful thing it should be so. Others I have known so altered at once that the very propensity which was strongest in them has been the last to annoy them afterwards: they have had such a reversion of the mind's action that, while other sins have worried them for years, and they have had to set a strict watch against them, yet their favorite and dominant sin has never again had the slightest influence over them, except to excite an outburst of horror and deep repentance. Oh, that you had faith in Jesus that He could thus cast out your reigning sins!

V. And now we will go another step: This man's faith was attended with what appears

A Hesitancy.

But after thinking it over a good deal, I am hardly inclined to think it such a hesitancy as many have judged it to be. He said, "If thou wilt, thou canst make me clean." There was an "if" in this speech, and that "if" has aroused the suspicions of many preachers. Some think it supposes that he doubted our Lord's willingness. I hardly think that the language justly bears so harsh a construction. What he meant may have been this: "Lord, I do not know yet that thou art sent to heal lepers; I have not seen that Thou hast ever done so; but still, if it be within the compass of thy commission, I believe thou will do it, and assuredly thou canst if thou wilt. Thou canst heal not only some lepers, but me in particular; Thou canst make me clean." Now, I think this was a legitimate thing for him to say, as he had not seen a leper healed: "If it be within the compass of thy commission, I believe thou canst make me whole."

See, also, how the leper, to my mind, really speaks without any hesitancy, if you understand him. He does not say, "Lord, if thou puttest out thy hand, thou canst make me clean;" nor, "Lord, if thou speakest, thou canst make me clean;" but only, "Lord, *if thou wilt*, thou canst make me clean:" Thy mere will can do it. Oh, splendid faith! If you are inclined to spy a little halting in it, I would have you admire it for running so well with a lame foot. If there was a weakness anywhere in his faith, still it was so strong that the weakness only manifests its strength. Sinner, it is so; and I pray God that thy heart may grasp it—if the Lord wills it He can make thee clean. Believest thou this? If so, carry out practically what thy faith will suggest to thee—namely, that thou come to Jesus and plead with Him, and get from Him the cleansing which thou needest.

VI. In the sixth place, notice his faith had

Earnest Action

flowing out of it. Believing that, if Jesus willed He could make him clean, what did the leper do? At once he came to Jesus. I know not from what distance, but he came as near to Jesus as he could. Then we read that he besought him; that is to say, he pleaded, and pleaded again. He cried, "Lord, cleanse me! Lord, heal my leprosy!" Nor was this all; he fell on his knees and worshipped; for we read, "Kneeling to Him." Now, poor soul, thou that art full of guilt, and hardened in sin, and yet anxious to be healed, look straight away to the Lord Jesus Christ. He is here now. In the preaching of the gospel He is with us alway: With the eyes of thy mind behold Him, for He beholdeth thee. Thou knowest that He lives, even though thou seest Him not. Believe in this living Jesus; believe for perfect cleansing. Cry to him, worship Him, adore Him, trust Him. Go home, and on thy knees say, "Lord, I believe that thou canst make me clean." He will hear you and will save you.

VII. Lastly, his faith had its reward. Have patience with me just a minute.

The Reward

of this man's faith was, first, that his very words were treasured up. Matthew, Mark, Luke, all three of them, record the precise words which this man used: "Lord, if Thou, wilt, Thou canst make me clean." They evidently did not see so much to find fault with in them as some have done; on the contrary, they thought them gems to be placed in the setting of their gospels. Three times over are they recorded, because they are such a splendid confession of faith for a poor diseased leper to have made. This man's first faith-words are folded up in the fair linen of three evangels, and laid up in the treasury of the house of the Lord. God values the language of humble confidence.

His next reward was, that *Jesus echoed his words*. He said: "Lord, if thou wilt, thou canst make me clean"; and Jesus said, I will; be thou clean." As an echo answers to the voice, so did Jesus to His supplicant. The Lord Jesus was so pleased with this man's words that He caught them as they leaped out of his mouth, and used them Himself, saying: "I will; be thou clean." If you can only get, then, as far as this leper's confession, I believe that our Lord Jesus, from His throne above, will answer to your prayer.

Christ's Compassion.

So potent were the words of the leper, that they *moved our Lord very wonderfully*. Read the forty-first verse: "And Jesus, moved with compassion." The Greek word here used, if I were to pronounce is in your hearing, would half suggest its own meaning. It expresses a stirring of the entire manhood, a commotion in all the inward parts. Oh, to think that a poor leper should have such power over the divine Son of God! Yet, my hearer, in all thy sin and misery, if thou canst believe in Jesus, thou canst move the heart of thy blessed Saviour. Yea, even now His bowels yearn towards thee.

No sooner was our Lord Jesus thus moved than *out went His hand*, and He touched the man and healed him immediately. It did not require a long time for the working of the cure; but the leper's blood was cooled and cleansed at once. To make Him quite sure that he was cleansed, the Lord Jesus bade him go to the priest, and seek a certificate of health. He was so clean, that he might be examined by the appointed sanitary authority, and come off without suspicion. The cure which he had received was a real and radical one, and, therefore, he might go away at once, and get the certificate of it. If our converts will not bear practical tests, they are worth nothing; let even our enemies judge whether they are not

Better Men

and women when Jesus has renewed them. If Jesus saves a sinner, He does not mind all men testing the change. Jesus does not seek display, but He seeks examination from those able to judge. Our converts will bear the test. Dear hearer, if thou believest on Jesus Christ, and if thou wilt trust Him, as the sent One of God, fully and entirely with thy soul, He will make thee clean. Behold Him on the cross, and see sin put away. Behold Him risen from the dead, and see new life bestowed. Behold Him enthroned in power, and see evil conquered. I am ready to be bound for my Lord, to be His surety, that if thou, my hearer, wilt come to Him, He will make thee clean. Believe thy Saviour, and thy cure is wrought. God help thee, for Jesus Christ's sake. Amen.

GEMS FROM NEW BOOKS.

YEARS OF DUTY AND SELF-DENIAL.*

EUNICE MARSH might well say that the first seventeen years of her life had been happy years. Her father, a man useful and much beloved, had during that time been minister of the only church in Hopeville, a town in the southern part of the State. She had lost her mother when she was a little child, but her loss had been well supplied by the love and care of her mother's mother, with whom she had lived, in the house that was now her home, till the time of her father's second marriage. Her new mother did not love her own little daughter, when she came, more dearly than she loved Eunice, and so the happy years moved on to

A Sorrowful Ending.

Suddenly, in the midst of happiness and usefulness, with no warning which those who loved him could understand, the minister died. Then Eunice returned to her grandparents' home, on the hill; and her stepmother, with her little daughter, came there also, to stay for a little while; and they never went away again. It was not a very large house, and the old people were far from being rich; but they offered the widow a home while she needed one. She did not need it long. She never quite recovered from the shock of her husband's death, and she died within the year, leaving her little girl to her sister Eunice, "to love and care for always—to be her very own." After a while

Happy Days

came again to Eunice. Why should she not be happy? Those who had gone from her had only "gone before," and those who remained were very dear; and life was before her—a mystery!—but a mystery of gladness and blessing, as she believed. Dr. Everett had been the minister's classmate in college, and his life-long friend; and when the minister died, he became the guardian and the life-long friend of his daughters. In his house they found a second home, and from him Eunice had the counsel and the guidance which, in their old age and with their failing powers, her grandparents could no longer give her. Strong, eager, ambitious, it would have pleased the girl well to be allowed to choose her own lot and work, and to make her own way in the world. But she was dutiful, and she loved her little sister dearly, and so she was willing to be restrained and guided, and to give herself to work, which seemed at first very humble work, which almost anyone might do, but which was

God-Given Work

—a blessing to others and herself; so time went on. Happy? Looking back over those first years, Eunice told herself that no one could have been happier than she was then. Yes, and afterwards also. For that which made much of the happiness was not taken from her at a single blow, nor was she called upon to choose

---

* From "Eunice," a plainly yet gracefully told story of domestic life in New England, by the author of "Janet's Love and Service," "Two Miss Jean Dawsons," etc., with eight full-page illustrations. Pp. 312, price $1.50. Published by *Anson D. F. Randolph*, 38 West Twenty-third Street, N. Y.

Interior of a Swedish Church.

between her duty and her happiness all at once. She knew there was no choice for her. When Justin Everett, the doctor's youngest brother—and like him, a physician—saw his way open to go West, to an uncle, to establish himself with him in his profession, Eunice might have gone with him as his wife, if circumstances at home had been different. But it was impossible. There was no choice to be made, and nothing to be said. Her grandfather had been stricken helpless, with little hope of ever being otherwise than helpless. Over her grandmother, younger than him by many years, hung an awful dread. She, too, must die; but she might be years in dying. Some one would have to watch by her dying bed, as she, in her youth, had watched by the dying bed of her own mother, till the slow months wore on to years, before her tired eyes closed at last in painless rest. No one needed to say to Eunice that she could not leave her grandmother to be cared for by others, while she went away to find her own happiness. She never even paused to consider the matter. It was impossible. Her lover thought quite otherwise, and pleaded with her with words which made her glad, and which hurt her sorely, but which did not move her from her purpose. Over one thing only she hesitated. Should she give him back his word before he went away? "No," said Dr. Everett; "you are both young. Wait." And so she waited, and was not unhappy. No woman can be unhappy whose life is lived not to herself but to others. Her service was truly willing service, and was

Its Own Reward.

She had cares, many and heavy, weary nights and anxious days, but she had kind friends, who took care for her and helped her; and her cares and labors and daily self-denials, and the hourly sight of her grandmother's faith and patience, and of her joyful release at last, did for heart and soul more than many prosperous years of untroubled happiness could have done.

A SWEDISH CHURCH.

(*See Illustration.*)

THE venerable building whose interior is depicted in our illustration, is familiar to all travellers in Europe, being interesting both intrinsically and from its associations. Among other churches of the capital of Sweden, are the wonderful old Cathedral and the Horsemen's, or Knights', Church, which is, perhaps, the most venerated and peculiar of all churches in the north of Europe. It is to the Swede what Notre Dame is to the Frenchman, and what Westminster Abbey is to the Englishman; for here the kings of the country have been buried for many a century. Only once every year is service held in it. The lofty stone spire, which was destroyed by lightning, has been replaced by one of cast iron; on each side the door are the equestrian statues which have given the church its name, both horses and riders being covered with solid armor. The building is one huge mausoleum. Every stone in the aisles forms the covering of a grave, and originally bore the name and style of the man whose prowess won for him the coveted distinction of burial in the Knights' Church. Now, however, the stones are broken, and the legends are undecipherable. The walls are adorned with ancient flags, drums, swords, and other implements of war. It is in this church that we find the tomb of Gustavus Adolphus, whose name is revered by every Protestant, and whose memory is cherished by the people of Sweden with the veneration and affection which Washington's name arouses in the breasts of the people of America. His body reposes in *a sarcophagus of green porphyry* placed on the right of the high altar, and inscribed with the short and fitting epitaph in Latin, "*Dying, he Triumphed.*" Since his time the established religion of Sweden has been Lutheran, and at the present time the King of Sweden is ineligible to the throne if he be not a Lutheran, as Queen Victoria would become incapable of wearing the English crown if she became a Roman Catholic. The clergy are not, as a rule, men of much learning, and have, in consequence, very little influence over the people. They are paid by the Government, which doles out to them very small salaries. There are in the entire kingdom about three thousand five hundred clergymen.

In travelling through Sweden, the visitor notices that every village has a church, conspicuous from a long distance by its tapering spire rising out of its nest of trees, and around its walls the green God's-acre in which lie the bodies of the villagers of past generations. On Sunday mornings fresh flowers are placed on most of the graves by the people who come from the surrounding country. As soon as they have entered the church the sexton locks the door, which he opens again after the invocatory prayer. Each of *the pews are locked* until the arrival of the owner, whose name is upon it. There are plenty of benches placed along the walls for strangers, or the poorest of the people, although there are but few who are actually in indigence, for the Swedish race, as a whole, is very thrifty, and, what is more important, of a devout and contented disposition.

A visitor to Sweden says: "In most of the churches the pulpits, always of wood, are elaborately carved with scriptural scenes and figures. These pulpits are often surmounted by a sounding-board, also carved. An old sounding-board in the village of Soderkoping has the word Jehovah in Hebrew letters inscribed on the most conspicuous part, while on top is an image of a human figure, very probably intended for the Saviour. As the people enter, they place what offerings they bring with them (and few come without anything at all) in receptacles near the door; often these are plain earthen pitchers placed on stools. All carry books of the service and the stranger would be impressed with the dignified and serious behavior of the congregations. The same variety of dress is seen as in our rural churches; rich and poor meet together. The fashionable ladies wear the French bonnet, but the majority have only a shawl or kerchief tied over the head, in a bow more or less elaborate. The men are for the most part rustic in garb and manner, and there are very few but are enthusiastic devotees of the snuff-taking habit. Boxes of the pungent stuff are passed from one hand to another, and even from pew to pew during service, and are freely used."

LOST AND FOUND.

(*See Picture on page 157.*)

MY name is Anthony Hunt. I am a drover and live miles and miles away upon the Western prairie. There wasn't a house in sight when we first moved there, my wife and I, and now we haven't many neighbors, though those we have are good ones.

One day, about ten years ago, I went away from home to sell some fifty head of cattle. I was to buy some groceries and dry goods before I came back; and, above all, a doll for our youngest, Dolly. She had never had a store doll of her own—only rag babies her mother had made for her.

Dolly could talk of nothing else, and went down to the gate to call after me to get a big one. Nobody but a parent can understand how full my mind was of that toy, and how, when the cattle were sold, the first thing I hurried off to buy was Dolly's doll. I found a large one, with eyes that would open and shut when you pulled a wire, and had it wrapped up in a paper and tucked it under my arm while I had the parcels of calico and tea and sugar put up. Then, late as it was, I started for home. It might have been more prudent to stay until morning, but I felt anxious to get back, and eager to hear Dolly's praises about her doll.

I was mounted on a steady-going old horse, and pretty well loaded. Night set in before I was a mile from town, and settled down as dark as pitch, while I was in the middle of the darkest bit of road I know of. I could have felt my way, though, I remembered it so well. When the storm that had been brewing broke, and the rain came down in torrents, I was five miles, or may-be six miles, from home.

I rode as fast as I could, but all of a sudden I heard a little cry like a child's voice. I stopped short and listened. I heard it again. I called, and it answered me. I couldn't see a thing, all was as dark as pitch. I got down and felt around in the grass—called again, and again was answered. Then I began to wonder. I'm not timid, but I was known to be a drover, and to have money about me. It might be a trap to rob and murder me. I am not superstitious, not very, but how could a child be out on the prairie in such a night, at such an hour? The bit of a coward that hides itself in most men showed itself to me then, but once more I heard the cry, and I said:

"If any man's child is hereabouts, Anthony Hunt is not the man to let it die."

I searched again. At last I bethought me of a clump of trees about fifty yards to the left of the road. In the stillness of the night I prayed to the Lord that he might guide me to the right path and lead me through the darkness of that stormy night to the spot where I thought a little child was in sore need of help. The Lord heard my prayer. Cuddled up under one of the trees, I found a little dripping thing that moaned and sobbed as I took it in my arms. I called my horse, and the beast came to me, and I mounted and tucked the little soaked thing under my coat as well as I could, promising to take it home to mamma. It seemed so tired, and pretty soon cried itself to sleep on my bosom.

It had slept there over an hour when I saw my own windows. There were lights in them, and I supposed my wife had lit them for my sake, but when I got to the doorway I saw something was the matter, and stood with a dread fear of heart five minutes before I could lift the latch. As last I did it, and saw the room full of neighbors, and my wife amid them weeping. When she saw me she hid her face.

"Oh, don't tell him," she said; "it will kill him."

"What is it, neighbors?" I cried, and one of the neighbors inquired:

"What's that you have in your arms?"

"A poor lost child," said I; "I found it on the road. Take it, will you? I've turned faint." And I lifted the sleeping thing and saw the face of my own child, my Dolly.

It was my own darling, and none other, that I had picked up on the drenched road. My little child had wandered out to meet papa and the doll, while the mother was at work, and they were lamenting her as one dead. I thanked the Lord on my knees before them.

It is not much of a story, neighbors, but I think of it often in the nights, and wonder how I could bear to live now if I had not stopped when I heard the cry for help upon the road, hardly louder than a squirrel's chirp.

That's Dolly yonder with her mother in the meadow—a girl worth saving, I think; the prettiest and sweetest thing this side of the Mississippi.

Anthony Hunt and the Lost Child.

MRS. TRANSOME'S PUPIL,

A SERIAL STORY.

(*Continued from page 148.*)

In the Almshouse.

How the days sped I do not know; but they seemed to pass by like the rushing of a river just before you come to a deep, dreadful waterfall, down which you must plunge into a flood that will drown you. Every morning and every evening carried us on to the terrible day when we must quit our old house for ever. I kept my school open till the very last; for this was no time to lose a single penny I could win. There was no other house near that place where we could move to. So my school would be lost, as well as our home, and I must try to begin again in a strange neighborhood, on the other side of the town, where the rents were lower. What was to become of Transome and me, baffled me whenever I looked forward. He did not lie in bed any more, but sat beside me in the chimney-nook, while I taught the children; now and then stretching out his hand—his poor hand—crooked and drawn together with rheumatism, just to touch me. I knew after a while what he was thinking of then, though he never put it into words.

Well, we had to sell some of our goods; the rest we carried with us to the other side of town, into a small house, in a close, pent-up street, where the wind never blew across one's face with a sweet, fresh breath. I did my utmost to gather together a few scholars; and sometimes I had a few, and sometimes none. Transome took to sitting always at my side; and if I was away for half an hour, doing a few errands, he'd welcome me back as though I had been away from him all day. He began, too, to talk more, at times quite eagerly, as if he was afraid he might some day want to tell me something, and would not have the chance. I never knew him talk so much as that long, dreary summer, when we were treading slowly down those steps poor folks know of, step after step, downwards and downwards, never stopping, till the last step crumbles away under one's feet, and all is lost!

We trod on the last step, and it crumbled away underneath our old feet when the first sharp touch of winter came. We had kept up till then, pawning and selling our few goods to buy bread. But when the biting cold came, and our blankets were in the pawnshop, and I had not a morsel of flannel to wrap about Transome's poor pained limbs, and no fire to give a little warmth to our worn-out frames, when I knew that all was lost! I was sorely bewildered and beset. Had the Lord been deceiving us all these years? Had He brought us to old age, and to the very gates of death, to forsake us at last? Transome had been faithful, if a poor ignorant man can ever be faithful to his God. If either of us had been unfaithful, it was me; and surely the Lord would not visit my sins and shortcomings upon him!

"Ally!" said Transome, one day, "bring th' book, and read me again how th' blessed Lord came to's end upo' th' cross."

So I opened my old Bible, and I read aloud to him, shivering and shaking with cold as I read. There was not a spark of fire in the grate, or a crust of bread in the cupboard. I had not a penny in the world, and did not know where to turn to find one. We had not any friends, Transome being such a silent man, and me a foreigner in that country; and all my kinsfolk were dead and gone. It was forty years since I had married away out of my county.

I was thinking all these thoughts, taking no heed of the blessed words my tongue repeated; for I had read those chapters so often to Transome, I did not need to think of them. How far even I had read I did not know, till all at once I heard Transome saying to himself—

"Scourged, and mocked, and crucified! God's own Son! That were ten times waur nor deein' i' th' poor house."

That word stung me to the core of my heart; though in my secret thoughts I had known it must come to that. But to hear Transome say so! I threw down the Bible, and cried with a loud and very bitter cry. It seems as if I could hear myself even now; and as if I could see Transome's thin, pale face, as he looks at me.

"Ally!" he says, "thee'rt a scholar. Is na' there a verse somewhere, 'faithful unto death.'"

"Ay!" I sobbed, "'be thou faithful unto death, and I will give thee a crown of life.'"

"That's it!" he cried; "learn it me, Ally, as yo' learn the little childer."

I could not say him nay, though my heart was like to break. He caught hold, fast, firm hold, of my hand, as I said it to him over and over again; him repeating it after me like the least of my scholars in our old house. It seemed hard to him; or maybe he wanted the lesson to be long, for it was growing dark in the afternoon, before he stopped saying it.

"We'll stay one other neet," he said. "We've been together many a long year. But to-morrow morn, Ally—"

There was no need for him to finish what he was saying. To-morrow we must go into the union workhouse. Nothing else lay before us. We had fought our fight; and this was the end of it! I could not believe that it was aught save a dream; only I was cold and hungry, and so was Transome; so cold and so hungry it could not be a dream.

"My lass!" he said tenderly, very tenderly, and my mind called back the sound of his voice as we came home picking flowers along the cannal-side, "we mun remember as't were God's own Son as deed upo' th' cross. If thee had to see me nang, it 'ud be far, far waur nor decin. i' th' union; but it would na 'be waur nor what He bore for us. No, no, Ally; God Almighty's dealin' wi' us is softer nor wi' Christ. And, Ally, His poor mother stood by to see him dee upo' th' cross."

"Oh! if it was only me," I cried, "I could bear it!"

"Ah, but thee'lt have to bear it for me," he said, smiling on me; "it's just the same wi' me. If it were na' for thee, Ally', aw could go cheerfu' and glad to th' union; for aw've noan so long to live. But never to hear thee say 'Good neet' as I fa' asleep, nor, 'Good day,' when th' morn breaks, that's th' hurt, lass, that's th' hurt."

In the dark cold night I took the few things we had left and pawned them, spending part of the money in coal and food; and thinking that with the rest we might come out of the poorhouse again in the spring, and I could get a little school together once again.

The long, long night wore away too soon; and then I went to the relieving-officer and got an order to go into the poorhouse.

There was a glimmer of pale sunshine in the sky as Transome and I crept along the streets toward the union workhouse, feeling as if everybody we met knew where we were going. He could not drag himself along save at a very slow pace; and here and there, wherever there was a doorstep to an empty house, we were forced to sit down and rest. Transome did not speak many words as we went along, for he was very weary with the journey; but every now and then his poor fingers clasped my arm more tightly, as if he meant to say, "Cheer up, Ally; it must come right in the end." But at length we reached the end, the long, blank wall, and the great black doors; and though we stood outside full five minutes, looking into each other's face, no help came. I was forced to ring the loud, clanging bell, and we crossed over the black doorsill into the poorhouse.

We stood inside the great black doors which swung to behind us, shutting us in as though they would never open again, save, maybe, when we were borne out through them in a pauper coffin. Transome leaned more heavily on my arm. A man in the poorhouse suit was sitting in a little room just within the doors, and as we stood staring about us he called out sharply,

"Na then! whatten yo' standin' there for?" he shouted; "canna' yo' come on and tell me whatten yo' want here?"

"I and my husband have brought an order to go into the house," I said.

"Inside birds, eh!" he said, laughing a little; "caught and caged! Go on then t' th' measter's office. First dur t' th' reet across th' yard."

I guided poor Transome across a large square yard, with nought to be seen save high walls on every side, with windows in them that had no curtains, like eyes without eyelids, looking down on us. But there was not a face to be seen at any of them; and a mournful stillness filled the place. It was Transome that knocked at the master's door, a quiet, feeble knock that could never have been heard if there had been much noise. We were called to go in, but we did not stay there many minutes; and the master sent a man with us to show us our separate wards.

Once more we had to cross the great yard, Transome clinging to my arm, till we came to a door in the wall, where we must say good-by to one another. We never had said good-by all those long years, those forty years, since he had taken me from my father's home in another county. How could I let him go out of my sight? It was not like him setting off for his day's work, sure of coming in again in the evening. How could him and me spend our time apart?

"Could na' yo' leave us for two or three minutes?" said Transome to the man, feebly. "She's been th' best wife as ever a man had these forty years; and I dunno how to bid her good-by. Gie us a minute longer to be together."

"That I will," answered the man, "but it canna be more nor a two or three minutes. Bless yo'! yo'll see one another at prayers morn and neet, if yo' chosen to go; and yo'll ha' half an hour o' Sunday, besides half a day out once a month. It's noan so bad, is th' house, so as yo' getten reet side o' th' measter."

He went off for a little while, leaving Transome and me against the door into the women's ward; with all those dark, staring windows looking down on us. I laid my head against the door-post, and broke out into heavy, heavy sobs.

"Na, Ally," cried Transome, "na, my lass! Hush thee! hush thee! God A'mighty's here as well as out yonder i' th' world. He knows where we are; and sure He loves us both, same as He's loved us all along. We mun put our trust in Him, and go through it; thee and me mun part. Eh! but I wonder if God A'mighty looks down on ony hearts sorer nor ours at this moment o' time?"

"Only promise," I said, through my sobbing, "promise me faithfully, you'll be careful of yourself, and keep up, so as we can get out again in the spring, when the warm weather is come. Oh! Transome, if I could only keep nigh you, and take care of you, I shouldn't mind."

"There's One as 'll take care on us both," he answered, his voice trembling; 'One as says, I'll never leave thee, nor forsake thee.' On'y think o' that, my lass. He's here i' th' poorhouse itsen; and nought'll part Him away from thee nor me. Good-by, Ally. Aw hear th' man comin' back to us."

He stretched out both his hands to me, and I put mine into them, and we kissed each other solemnly, as if we were both about to die, and enter into another world. I saw his face quiver all over, and then there came across it a patient and quiet look, which never left it again, never! I knocked at the door before me, and passed in; just catching a last sight of him turning away with nobody to lean upon. Then the door was thrust to between us, and I could see him no more.

I did not heed much what was said to me, and I did not look about my new dwelling-place; only I followed a woman, who passed through many rooms, where the windows were high up in the walls so that nobody could reach the sills, and where there were groups of women all dressed alike, chattering, most of them; and there was a strange close smell. Oh! how different from the sweet air in our old home! At last, when I came to myself, as it were, I found I was sitting on a chair at the head of a little narrow bed, in a long room, with two long rows of beds down the sides of it, and a narrow path up the middle. All the beds were alike, and the bare whitewashed walls closed us in, with nothing to be seen through the high windows, save a little bit of gray November sky. There were old women all around me; some of them many years older than me, even a few of them bed-ridden; but they seemed too dull to take any notice of me, as if everything that was like life had died out of them, save the bare life itself.

Well! there's no need to tell you much about the poorhouse. Most poor folks know more of it than they care to know, either through their own troubles, or the troubles of their friends. I don't say a word against it; only I could not be with Transome. There! think what it was to have been his wife forty years, with scarcely a brangle between us, and never a sulking quarrel, and all at once to be shut up in different parts of the same building with only a few walls and yards to part us, yet not be able to see him, or even send a loving message to him. I wet my pillow with my tears that night, ay! more than when my Willie died, as I wondered and wondered how he was faring, and if he was warmly wrapped up, and how his pains were. But I could do nothing for him, no more than if I was lying in my shroud and coffin. At last my loneliness and my trouble drove me to remember Him that is everywhere, and was with Transome as He was with me. "Lord," I said in my heart, for it was not altogether a prayer such as I had generally said to Him, "Lord, if they'd only make his bed comfortable, and wrap him up well in the blankets! Do put it into their hearts, Lord, for he's tried to serve Thee faithful all his life long."

After that I felt a little easier in my mind; I fell asleep, and dreaming of the days when Willie was alive, only sometimes the child was Willie, and sometimes Pippin. I suppose it was because I had close to my pillow the little box that held the curl of Willie's hair, and Pippin's piece of money. It was the only thing I had brought in with me, except a few bits of linen Transome had woven for me years ago.

Ah! how wearily the long hours of the day dragged by! I had been an active woman all my life; and now there was nothing for me to do. I begged that I might help to scour out the old men's ward, thinking I might get a word with Transome; but they said I was past the age at which women were set to work. I asked the matron to find me some sewing to do; but she told me that it was all done by the girls at school in the poorhouse. I saw then how the miserable old women about me had sunk lower and lower, till they were little better than idiots and nothing lay before me but the same fate.

The only time of the day when I felt myself alive was morning and night, when prayers were read in the big room. We old folks were not required to attend, for the room was cold and draughty; but I would not have missed it for anything less than the chance of getting out of the house again; not that I thought God would listen to me more there than in the ward; but Transome never missed going. We could neither speak to one another, nor sit side by side; but we could see each other's faces, and we felt that we were together while we were hearing the same prayers, and repeating the same words. When we said, "Our Father," I would have kept silent, hearkening if I could catch his voice, only I was afraid he might be hearkening for mine; and I said it, and listened said it, and listened, till at times I fancied I could hear a word or two from him amid all the hum of the other voices; just as a mother hears her baby sob in its sleep, though there may be a hundred louder noises about her. It was the rule for the women to go out from prayers first, and when I went by in my turn I could always see Transome looking towards me, with his patient smile upon his face. It used to go to my heart to think of him dragging himself across the yard when the rain was falling, or the snow was under foot, and him so weak with rheumatism. But then, it was our only comfort, his as well as mine; and he never missed coming morn and night.

(*To be Continued.*)

THE SON REJECTED.

By Mrs. M. Baxter.

S. S. Lesson for March 18, Matt. 21 : 33-46. Golden Text, John 1 : 11.

Ver. 33. The Owner's Omniscient and Exhaustive Provision—The Occupiers (see Ps. 115 : 15)—Ver. 34. Two Times of Fruit—Individual and Collective—The Owner's Messengers—From Noah to Malachi—Ver. 35-36. How they were Received—The Owner's Marvellous Forbearance—Ver. 37. His Condescension—Ver. 38, 39. The Rejection Actual and Spiritual—The Actual on Calvary—The Spiritual Continually Recurring—Ver. 40. An Appalling Question—Ver. 41-44. An Application not Limited to the Time—Ver. 45, 46. The Usual Combination of Malignity and Cowardice.

"HE came unto His own, and His own received Him not." It was strangely significant that Jesus, after His triumphal entry into Jerusalem, should have found no lodging-place within her walls! "He left them and went out of the city into Bethany, and lodged there." The stones of Jerusalem were as dear to Him as the stones of Bethany, but at Bethany were hearts which owned and loved Him, while Jerusalem said, "Who is this?" God had chosen Zion; He had desired her for His habitation ; He had said; "This is My rest forever : here will I dwell, for I have desired it." (Ps. 132 : 13, 14.) Yet Zion

Knew Him Not,

and found no beauty in Him that she should desire Him. He wept over her, yearned to save her, fain would have gathered her children as a hen gathers her chickens under her wings, but she *would not*.

On the following morning, as He took His way into Jerusalem, He saw a fig-tree, which, in its leafy promise, but real fruitlessness, was like Jerusalem, and like every human soul where Jesus does not dwell. Jesus said unto it: "Let no fruit grow on thee henceforward forever." And the word which called all things into being was as powerful in taking away life. "Presently, the fig-tree withered away! It was the exception when Jesus exercised His mighty power in destruction. Generally He spoke—sight, hearing, life, health, reason, comfort—into souls and bodies. But Jerusalem was courting judgment, rushing to destruction, and choosing the fate of the fig-tree. The disciples remarked on the suddenness of the fig-tree's withering, and Jesus took occasion to tell them that if they had faith, and doubted not, all things, whatsoever they should ask in prayer, they should receive. Jesus would encourage us to ask in faith, just as though He entreated us to stay Him from words and works of judgment, by showing the almightiness of real faith in God to stay it. It is as though He said, "I am powerless ; I must judge, but I put in your power authority to move mountains if you have faith and doubt not. Jerusalem was destroyed, but not before thousands of redeemed souls were safe in the arms of Jesus—men and women who, at this very time, took their part against Jesus, and, so soon after, swelled the cry, "Crucify Him, crucify Him."

When He was come into the temple, the chief priests and elders of the people, who always stood upon their dignity, came unto Him, as He was teaching, and said, "By what authority doest Thou these things?" What things? Jesus had never worshipped any God but One, His Father ; Jesus had made no graven image to worship ; Jesus had never taken His Father's name in vain ; had never really broken the Sabbath-day ; had never failed to honor His Father or His mother ; had not killed, but saved life, and healed disease ; had never done, thought or spoken impurely, but had saved many, many an outcast ; had never borne false witness, but was Himself the Faithful and the True ; had never coveted, for all things were delivered unto Him, both in heaven and on earth. And now the elders of the people want to know by what authority He lived a life so holy and so faultless.

By What Authority

He "went about doing good, and healing all that were oppressed of the devil." (Acts 10 : 38.) Alas, the same spirit is abroad to-day. A man swears, gambles, commits the most flagrant sins against common morality, and no one asks him his authority! But let this man be converted, and stand up in the street to warn others of the ruin he has escaped, and of the sin from which God has delivered him, and, very often, clergy and magistrates come and ask him "by what authority" he does these things! A so-called aristocract, who is really only a bond-slave of Satan, may ruin the life and break the heart of a fair young girl, but if any one pulls off the mask and exposes the hideous wickedness of her betrayer, the authorities compass sea and land to know "by what authority" sin is dragged to light, as though sin were not sin unless people know about it! As though the guilt did not lie in the breaking of God's law and the ruin of a fellow-creature, but only in the widely deserved shame of a man whose interest it is to walk about as a whited sepulchre! Man needs no authority for doing evil—alas, it is such a common thing!—but he needs authority for doing good! He may ruin souls, and no one interferes with him, but he must ask the clergyman, the minister, the magistrate, the mayor, the police, for leave to do what he can in saving them. Perhaps nothing more manifests the spirit of enmity to the gospel than this common interrogation, "By what authority" do you do this? O how men reject the Son of God! Men make up their minds that there is something unlawful in people being healed of disease by the hand of Jesus alone, and that it is absolutely wrong, sinful and "tempting Providence," as it is called, to go out as a missionary on apostolic lines, without purse or scrip or outfit, living on the food and wearing the clothing of the natives, and trusting God for supplies day by day. Whence comes this thought? Surely from an absolute disbelief in God, a putting of God out of the question. If God were shut out of the universe we should have to do the best possible for ourselves, but the terrible anomaly that we see around us is that God is outwardly acknowledged ; but when it comes to a practical issue, God is set aside, and man's devices take precedence.

Jesus answered by another question, "The baptism of John, whence was it? from heaven, or of men?" The elders, who were ready enough to assert their dignity when questioning Jesus, quite forgot themselves when He questioned them. There was no dignity, but quite the contrary, in their reasoning with themselves. "If we shall say, From heaven, He will say unto us, why then did ye not believe him? But if we shall say, Of men, we fear the people ; for all hold John as a prophet." These would-be administrators of justice and righteousness did not want to know what was true, or what would be a righteous answer, but only what would

Suit Their Purpose

best. *They would* not say, "From heaven," or they would condemn themselves ; they would not say, "Of men," because of the popular voice ; so they took neutral ground, and said, "We cannot tell." Whereupon He also said, "Neither tell I you by what authority I do these things." What a lesson for us in dealing with questioners. First prove them, as to whether they are real. Then, if they shuffle, simply refuse to enter into an argument. There is such a thing as casting pearls before swine. Jesus next spoke the parable of the two sons ; the professing Jew, who said, "I go, sir ; and went not" into the vineyard, and the converted Gentile, who said, "I will not," but afterward he repented and went. And Jesus showed them how publicans and harlots are the first to enter into the kingdom of heaven. These appreciated John the Baptist, whom the scribes could not condemn, and yet the rulers of the people received Him not.

Thus Jesus Was Rejected,

not only in His own person, but in that of His forerunner, and always because of the pride and self-sufficiency of those who rejected him. He then spoke another parable : "There was a certain householder which planted a vineyard, and hedged it round about, and digged a wine-press in it, and built a tower, and let it out to husbandmen, and went into a far country : and when the time of the fruit drew near, he sent his servants to the husbandmen, that they might receive the fruits of it." It was but his right ; it is true he was a non-resident landlord, but it was his due that he should get in the rents or the crops, at any rate a large share of them. But his claim was disputed, and his messengers killed. He sent again a larger deputation, but with a similar result. Last of all, he sent unto them his son, saying, 'They will reverence my son.' Now things came to a crisis, and the revolt in the vineyard grew desperate. They said 'This is the heir ; come, let us kill him, let us seize on his inheritance.' And they caught him, and cast him out of the vineyard, and slew him." It was a prophecy, in large part, already fulfilled. "This people have I

Formed For Myself,"

(Isa. 43 : 21), was God's claim, yet the house of Israel had gone astray from Him, turned every man to his own way, rejected God's rule, chosen them a king, and then fallen into idolatry. And now, centuries after their return from captivity in Babylon, their religion was all outside, they drew near to God with their lips, but their hearts were far from Him, and, whether in worldly matters or religious, self was still their centre ; if they prayed, it was to be seen of men ; if they did alms, it was to gain glory for their religiousness ; they disputed the fruit of the vineyard with the Owner, and persecuted all who asserted His claim! But is not this the spirit of the age in which we live? Is it not still a fact that, "all seek their own, not the things which are Jesus Christ's"? —from the comfortable minister who rides to church in his carriage, in spite of the fourth commandment, and when he gets there, enjoys the flattery of the people, to the millionaire who gives his thousands, and then expects to get the worth of it in flattery, or the luxurious hearer who enjoys the eloquence of the preacher, or the earnest worker who loves to be the idol of the souls which he has gathered. Where is God getting the fruits of the vineyard? Where is the evidence that He rules, and that He is Lord and Master? The object of the vineyard is that God shall have His due, and that Jesus the Son of God shall be glorified. "Whosoever shall fall on this stone shall be broken." Jesus has power to break down the pride and self-importance, and use His vessel to His own honor, "but on whomsoever it shall fall, it will grind him to powder." Christ must either break our hearts with His love now, or execute vengeance by and by.

IS THIS ALL?

Sometimes I catch sweet glimpses of His face,
But that is all.
Sometimes He looks on me and seems to smile,
But that is all.
Sometimes He speaks a passing word of peace,
But that is all.
Sometimes I think I hear His loving voice
Upon me call.

And is this all He meant when thus He spoke,
"Come unto me?"
Is there no deeper, more enduring rest
In Him for thee?
Is there no steadier light for thee in Him?
O come and see!

O, come and see! O, look, and look again!
All shall be right;
O, taste His love, and see that it is good,
Thou child of night!
O, trust thou, trust thou in His grace and power!
Then all is bright.

Nay, do not wrong Him by thy heavy thoughts
But love His love.
Do thou full justice to His tenderness,
His mercy prove;
Take Him for what He is; O, take Him all,
And look above!

Then shall thy tossing soul find anchorage
And steadfast peace;
Thy love shall rest on His; thy weary doubts
Forever cease,
Thy heart shall find in Him and in His grace
Its rest and bliss!

Christ and His love shall be thy blessed all
For evermore!
Christ and His light shall shine on all thy ways
For evermore!
Christ and His peace shall keep thy troubled soul
For evermore!

—*H. Bonar.*

J. E. JEWETT, Publisher, 77 Bible House, New York will furnish the above poem in leaflet form at twenty cents per hundred. *A Sample Packet of 50 leaflets* assorted (no two alike), will be sent post-paid for ten cents. Postage stamps taken.

Dry Goods for Spring Wear.

Messrs. James McCreery & Co. are now opening a large stock of Spring Styles, both in Silks and Woolens. There are many novelties, and a great variety of wearing material that is elegant and tasteful as well as moderate in cost.

A fine selection of faille Francaise Silks, made altogether in solid colors, deserves popularity. These silks wear well, and don't pull in the seams when made into waists. The firm has an endless variety of them in hand, among others a rousse, gray, chasseur, gobelin gray, golden brown, bismuth, golden brown; girofle, terra-cotta; canard, saphire blue; terra-cotta; templier, mousse green; acier, light gray; noyer, dark beige; and chandron, rich terra-cotta brown.

Plaid and striped surah silks are in demand to trim woolen goods for ordinary wear. Tussah silk is a nice silk for summer. It is not much heavier than India silk, yet stronger in point of wear.

The stock of draperies and trimmings which the firm now has on hand is a large one, and there is a variety to suit all tastes and all purses. In the line of woolen goods there is as much elegance and variety as in the silks, and the whole spring stock is well worthy of inspection.

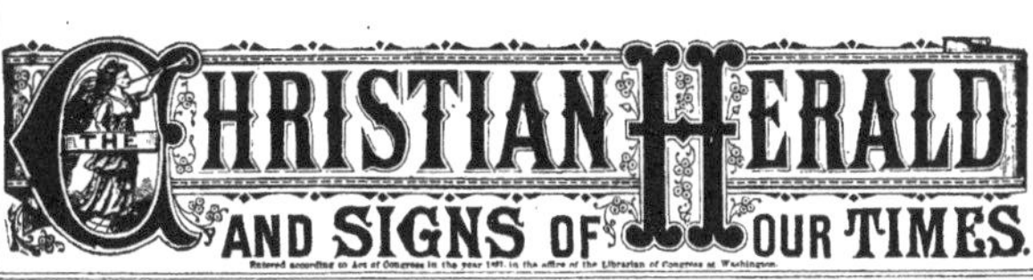
THE CHRISTIAN HERALD AND SIGNS OF OUR TIMES.

Vol. XI., No. 11. Office, 63 Bible House. N. Y. THURSDAY, MARCH 15, 1888. Annual Subscription, $1.50.

CONTENTS OF THIS NUMBER.

PICTURES OF THE LIFE OF THE CROWN PRINCE AT SAN REMO AND THE CONSULTATION OF PHYSICIANS.
THE AGE OF SWINDLE. Dr. Talmage's Sermon Last Sunday Morning.
ANECDOTES RELATED AT RECENT EVANGELISTIC MEETINGS.
THE EVOLUTION OF PROPHECY. By Rev. N. West, D. D.
A Day's Work in India—An Incensed Uncle Thwarted—Adrift on a Coffin—Little Lights in Heathen Homes—The Persecution in Mexico—A Sufferer's Claim on a Promise.
PORTRAIT OF THE LATE Mr. W. W. CORCORAN.
PICTURE OF JOSEF HOFMANN'S RECITAL.
JOB AMONG THE ASHES. A New Sermon by C. H. Spurgeon.
Gems from New Books: A Deranged Woman's Memory—The Close of a Useful Life—A Dying Soldier's Conversion, etc.
THE MINISTER'S PRODIGAL SON. (Illust'd.)
MRS. TRANSOME'S PUPIL. A Serial Story. (Con.)
SELF. By Mrs. M. Baxter.

THE PRINCE AND HIS DAUGHTERS VISITING A CURIOSITY SHOP.

THE PRINCE TAKING A DRIVE.

A CONSULTATION OF THE DOCTORS: DR. HOVELL; DR. SCHRADER; DR. KRAUSE; AND DR. MACKENZIE.

THE NEW EMPEROR OF GERMANY—His Invalid Life at San Remo.

THE CROWN PRINCE OF GERMANY.

Interest Taken in the Illustrious Patient — Dr. Lennox Browne's Opinion as to the Cause of His Condition—Life at San Remo—Medical Consultations—Dr. Mackenzie's High Opinion of the Crown Princess—The Importance of the Present Crisis Brought about by the Crown Prince's Illness—The Influence of Germany upon the Future of Europe.

THE attention of the civilized world is still concentrated in sympathetic sorrow and suspense on San Remo, where the struggle has been now for many weeks so gallantly waged between the Crown Prince of Germany and the mysterious malady which threatens his life. It is not the least painful feature of this momentous case that the differing opinions of the physicians have developed

Gloomy and Sanguine Feelings

in the public mind, and have led to painful public discussions. It is said that in diseases of this nature, whether the patient is tending toward recovery or decline, the course is rarely uniform, and there is nothing in an occasional return of suffering in the Prince's case that should compel us to believe the worst. The illustrious patient has seemed just as often on the point of recovery as he has seemed in serious danger. No one will have forgotten the alarm of December last, when Sir Morell Mackenzie, whose portrait and life we gave in the *Christian Herald* on January 12 (page 28), was hastily summoned to San Remo, and when, for a moment, many did not venture even to hope. The sufferer rallied so completely after that as to reassure those who had the keenest interest in his welfare, if any marked distinction on this point can be said to exist between his family and the vast majority of mankind.

The operation of tracheotomy, which was performed on February the 9th, was entirely successful in its immediate results, but as it was avowedly a measure of relief and not of a curative character, it has left the disease, whatever the disease may be, exactly where it was. The violent inflammation of the cartilages of the larynx continued for some time, but late reports describe it as subsiding, though it has proceeded so far that the larynx will never be of use to the Prince if he recovers. Probably if he were stronger, the surgeons would remove it by an operation; as it is, they may allow the disease to eat it away. This operation of Nature herself may, or may not, wear out the malady, and, while it goes on, the patient cannot hope to be free from lassitude and pain. As the

Doctors Disagree,

nothing seems to be positively known as to the true character of the Prince's mysterious affliction. Many of the German doctors seem to adhere to their earlier diagnosis of cancer; and though in November last Sir Morell Mackenzie seemed to yield a reluctant assent to their reasonings, he has since returned to his earlier and more hopeful view that the disease is *not* necessarily cancer. Professor Virchow is said to be positive that nothing submitted to his examination compels a belief in the worst, and his recent departure for Egypt has been taken by many persons to signify that he has no anticipation of any further call upon his services, while others believe that his departure was prompted by his reluctance to stand any longer between the English and German physicians in a position which must be painful to him.

Dr. Lennox Browne, the well-known author of several authoritative books dealing with the throat and its diseases has published

An Outspoken Letter

on the Crown Prince's case, in which he retorts on Dr. Mackenzie's German critics that his Imperial Highness's recent serious condition was largely due to previous mistreatment. He says the original cause of the irritation is undoubtedly *the attack of measles* "from which the Prince suffered early last year, and to this inflammation of the larynx following measles has to be added 'repeated traumatisms,' not by removal of the new growth by Sir Morell Mackenzie, but by the electric cauterizations which were employed even daily by one of the Prince's physicians for a period of several weeks before his Imperial Highness came under Sir Morell Mackenzie's hands at all."

The operation of tracheotomy recently performed with Dr. Mackenzie's sanction, by the German doctor, Dr. Bramann, consists in making an artificial opening into the wind-pipe, when, from obstruction by inflammation or otherwise of the natural air passages, the breathing is impeded to an extent threatening life. It is one of two operations adopted in such cases at the discretion of the physician. He may decide on *laryngotomy*, in which the opening is made in the membranous junction of the two principal cartilages of the larynx, and in which the tube has to remain in the passage but a short time, but is contra-indicated where, as in the case of the Crown Prince, there is already disease of the cartilages themselves. In such a case the opening is made as low as possible in the trachea or wind-pipe and this is the operation known as *tracheotomy*. Into the opening made in the windpipe a silver tube is introduced, with an inner tube that can be removed for cleansing. As air enters and passes out by the artificial opening, the voice is of course lost, because there is no breath passing through the natural passages to throw the vocal cords into sonorous vibration. If the patient wishes to speak, therefore, he is obliged to close up the external orifice of the tube with his finger.

After a time, an opening is made in the upper part of the silver tube as an experiment, for the purpose of endeavoring to re-establish the permanent breathway, and a valve is fitted to the external orifice so that the patient is able to speak at will. Although the operation is of some danger when performed for acute infantile diseases, as croup and diphtheria, there is *little or no immediate risk when performed on the adult*. An officer has been known to command his regiment with a tracheotomy tube in his wind-pipe, and there are many hack-drivers—a class peculiarly liable to inflammations of the throat—and other workingmen, who are going about their daily duties with this artificial auxiliary breathing-place in their throats, feeling but little inconvenience from it. They have, however, to cover the tube in the throat with the finger when they speak, but otherwise they are examples of the success of this beneficent operation.

LIFE AT SAN REMO.

(See Illustration on first page.)

THE Crown Prince's life at San Remo is essentially quiet and homely. His study is situated on the first floor of the Villa Zirio, as also the drawing-room and the sleeping-rooms of the Prince and Princess, and of the Countess Brull, the inseparable attendant of the Princess. The daily routine begins with early coffee at seven and breakfast at nine, after which, if fine, the Prince walks out with his wife and daughters. In *our illustration* he is shown *inspecting one of the curiosity shops of the town*. His eldest daughter is in front with him, the Princess and her youngest daughter being behind. Lunch is at one o'clock, and then *the Prince drives out*, always *sitting with his back to the horses*, so that the wind may not affect his throat. By his side in *our sketch* sits Dr. Schräder.. The Prince takes as much walking exercise as the weather and the state of his health will allow, but his daughters are constantly out of doors, while the Princess is an indefatigable walker. Their second son, Prince Henry, also frequently takes a sea-trip in the torpedo boat which has been courteously placed at the disposition of the Crown Prince and his family by the Italian Government.

Medical Consultations

are frequently held, and one such is *shown on our front page*. The doctors present are Sir Morell Mackenzie, and the German physicians, Dr. Mark Hovell, Dr. Krause, and Dr. Schrader.

The Crown Princess

has won golden opinions from the physicians, by her composure and the assiduity of her attention as a loving and tender nurse. Dr. Mackenzie's opinion of her has been admiringly expressed in an interview which he had recently with the representative of a society journal. The interviewer said: "That must have been an awful moment when you had to disclose the real state of things to the Prince." Dr. Mackenzie replied, "It was, for *me*. It is very seldom that we make such a communication to the patient himself; and even to the friends it is conveyed with all sorts of humane euphemisms. It was received with the most perfect calmness. The Prince, after an instant of silence, put out his hand with his usual winning smile, and grasping mine, said, 'I have been lately fearing something of this sort. I thank you, Sir Morell, for being so frank with me.' At dinner that evening he was the most cheerful of the party. In all my long experience, I have never seen a man bear himself, under similar circumstances, with such unaffected heroism." Sir Morell Mackenzie, who has a warm heart, though he does not exactly wear it on his sleeve, paused and locked rather sadly at the fire. After a few minutes I ventured to say, "And the Princess?" Sir Morell replied: "She is just such a wife as such a man deserves.

She is a Model Nurse,

having all her feelings under strict control, and suffering without making any sign. It is the simple truth that she is the most remarkable woman I have ever met. Her knowledge of science is something quite extraordinary, and she is now thoroughly posted in the pathology and surgery of the larynx. I consider that very few medical men not specialists would be able to acquit themselves so satisfactorily on these subjects as the Crown Princess. Her manner, when she cares to please, has an indescribable fascination about it which makes one understand the devoted feeling of personal loyalty that has sometimes been felt for Princes. I can only say that if all royal personages were like this exalted lady and her gallant husband, Republicanism would soon be an extinct tradition. You may easily conceive, therefore, that being still honored, as I have been throughout this sad case, with the fullest confidence of both these august persons—and, I may add, of their Royal relatives in this country—unfriendly criticism and unjust condemnation, alike pass by me like the idle wind.'"

A Life of Value to Europe

is that now hanging in the balance at San Remo. So far from thinking that the public exaggerates the importance which ought to be attached to the health of the German Heir-Apparent, we only wonder that Europe is not, during the period of suspense, hushed in alarm. There has hardly been in history a period when the future of Europe, and therefore of the world, appeared to hang, under Providence, more completely upon the health of a single man than it now does on this invalid.

The outbreak or the postponement of a war which, once begun, must cover all Europe, depends almost exclusively upon the attitude of Germany; and Germany, besides being a mighty State, is also an armed camp governed and directed by a hereditary Commander-in-Chief, whose will must be and is the ultimate motive-power in the gigantic machine. To every trained man—that is, to nine-tenths of all males in Germany between sixteen and forty—the Emperor has on certain subjects the legal right to give orders, enforced instantly and easily by the sovereign penalty of death. So strained is the situation of affairs, so deep the cleavage between the nations, that if the Emperor of Germany desires war, there will be war; and if he desires peace, war may be postponed, perhaps until a completely new condition of affairs has arisen either in France or in the East. The venerable Emperor has reached the confines of human life; he is satiated with victory and honor, and he notoriously desires peace; but he is so old, so feeble, so deeply affected by changes in the weather, that his life is admitted by his ablest physicians to hang upon a thread, which may be cut by the smallest accident, even by shock so light as a slip on an over-polished floor. His son, who must succeed him by law, and who would succeed him were the Monarchy elective, is at present prostrated by disease. If he dies, or is incapacitated, his reversionary power passes to

His Eldest Son, Prince William,

a young man of twenty-eight, as yet little known to the public, but believed by all who have access to him, and especially by his grandfather, who in his long life has never misjudged the powers of any man, to be a competent Hohenzollern; that is, a man who can and will govern strongly, and who is also believed to be, like his grandfather, before all things a soldier, with a confidence not unnatural in such a man, that all questions can be most easily solved by the sword. The army is his favorite occupation, and the long suspense of his nation under its heavy armor wearies and disgusts him. He would prefer a final, and therefore a military, solution of all difficulties. It is obvious that such a man will be more ready to give the signal for battle than either his grandfather or father, and this will probably continue his disposition even if he changes on becoming emperor, as much as history shows that the heirs to crowns have changed upon accession to the throne.

There would be, therefore, in the accession of Prince William, if he is as martial as he is believed to be, a positive increase in the liability of Europe to a war which, unless all calculations are at fault, might end in that awful calamity, a long-drawn contest between two nearly equal halves of the European continent. That under such circumstances Europe should be deeply moved, shows only its political judgment; while in Germany itself there is the additional cause of emotion, the personal regard which, explain it as we will, is evoked by crowned heads and those who may hereafter reign. The Crown Prince, on the steps of the highest throne in Europe, regarded with feeling of envy by the potentates of the European world, with the eyes of the peoples of the civilized world upon him, struck down at a crucial moment, physically helpless by disease, is a most pathetic figure, and one which brings home to men

The Vanity of Human Foresight,

the powerlessness of the wise to look forward for one day, with the most painful force. That, as Sir Arthur Helps once said, is the first of human disabilities.

The Crown Prince has some, at least, of his father's qualities—his moderation and his love of peace. His brief experience of the Regency, after Nobiling's dastardly attempt at assassination, gave him scant opportunity of proving his inheritance of the others. He would make a prudent ruler, and such a ruler, perhaps, is what is most wanted in the present crisis of the history of the world. Russia, France, Austria, Turkey—in short, all Europe is watching the events at San Remo with absorbing interest. Germany under a pacific Emperor could almost compel peace; but if that Power gave the signal, it is impossible to say in what remotest region it would fail to be heard. Even China is said to be attentively listening for the first shot to be fired on the Danube. If one thing is certain in a world of political illusions, it is that the Empire of Kaiser Wilhelm is peace, in so far as peace depends on his determined will, and wellnigh irresistible power. His son's influence would be exercised with no less energy in the same direction. His son's son, Prince William, would bring us at least to the unknown. It might, indeed, be the unknown of sagacity and perfect moderation, but where the event is necessarily so uncertain, every one must long for a continuance of the assurance of these precious influences which is involved in the preservation of the Crown Prince's life.

Such is the view of the statesman and the politician; to the Christian man who knows that the whole future is mapped out and controlled by his Heavenly Father, the anxieties of empires are unknown. All is in the hands of God, who ruleth all the kingdoms of the world.

ANECDOTES RELATED AT RECENT EVANGELISTIC MEETINGS.

The Rabbit Among the Cabbages.—Mr. Campbell White relates: "I remember a garden, one part of which was protected by a net, but the meshes of the net were rather large, and through one of them a tiny rabbit managed to squeeze. It was a little rabbit when it went through, but feeding on the cabbages it soon grew a big rabbit, too big to get back through the net, and there it stayed until the owner of the garden caught and killed it. Satan gets much of his prey in that way. The young people who venture into his meshes do not mean to stay, but they grow in sin until they cannot return by their own power, and they are ashamed or afraid to ask Christ's help."

A Saved Carter's Testimony.—Mr. Stewart says: "I stepped into a horse-car the other day and sat down beside an aged friend of mine, who held out his hand to me saying, with such a look of peaceful rest upon his face, 'My dear sir, I have almost reached the end of my journey, and even if it were possible to do so, not a day of my life would I live over again, and although I have often lost communion with my Heavenly Father, I have never lost union with Him. And now, I am going to everlasting glory, through the merits of that dear Saviour who died on Calvary for me, and whose precious blood purchased and cleansed me. Oh, how I long to be with Him and see Him!' I knew that man in his younger days when he was a swearing, drinking carter, who had earned a most unenviable notoriety for his daring and defiant blasphemies, but the Spirit of the Lord drew nigh to him, and he was constrained to give himself into Christ's keeping. Such is the power of God to save."

Losing the Power to Feel.—Mr. J. Campbell White remarks: "I was speaking some time ago to a young man who had recently yielded himself to the Lord Jesus Christ, and he told me that what made him think more of accepting Christ than anything else, more than even the earnest appeals and entreaties of earnest friends, was because he feared that slowly but surely his heart was being hardened, and spiritual death creeping upon him. He had heard so many impassioned addresses and solemn exhortations from the lips of Mr. D. L. Moody and other evangelists, and had stifled his convictions of sin, and resisted the affectionate strivings of the Holy Spirit so frequently and so long, that it was more and more difficult to move his feelings or excite his interest in any way. This fact vividly flashed into his mind one day, and he was appalled, and at once, cried to the Lord for mercy. The Lord answered his prayer, took away the heart of stone, and gave him a heart of flesh instead. To-day he is rejoicing in the salvation of Christ, and finds unspeakable delight in His happy service."

Called From a Sugar Refinery.—Mr. Johnson, missionary to the inhabitants of West Africa, wrought for his living until he was thirty-five years of age in a Scotch sugar refinery as a day laborer. When he was converted, he thought he ought to tell the Gospel of God's salvation to the heathen; but when he looked at himself, he said, "I am not fit to be a missionary." Again he felt, "I *must* go to the heathen in Africa," and again he stifled the voice by pleading his own inability. Yet again it was borne in upon his mind that it was God's will that he should go. He went to his minister and laid the case before him. The minister thought he was unfit for a missionary; he was so ignorant and illiterate. He next consulted his friends, but they were of the same opinion. He was in a quandary, but at last he determined resolutely to go, and after twelve months' schooling he and his wife set out for Africa. He thought, "I cannot preach, but I can tell them about Jesus." His first work there was to begin a school for children. That succeeded, and he started one for adults. His principal mode of teaching was by teaching all about Jesus. His pupils, young and old, were steeped in that knowledge only. When he examined them to see what progress they had made, he judged of their standing by the answers which they gave to the following questions: 'Who was Christ Jesus? What has Christ done? What is He doing? What will Christ Jesus do?' The result of the efforts of this unlettered laborer was indeed marvellous. Before he had been at the station five months there was a church formed, with a goodly number of members. Surely the Lord can use simple things to confound the wise, and the weakness of His servants to manifest His own infinite strength.

A Wife-beater's Home Changed.—Mr. Aaron Matthews, a converted Russian Jew, said: "For ten years I labored as a missionary in one of the lowest parts of Liverpool, and while there I knew a man who before his conversion to Christ was one of the worst, if not *the* worst, in that evil locality. One day, while visiting the people, I came unexpectedly upon him, and found him beating his wife. He was in a frantic rage; his hands were entwined in her hair, by which he dragged her about, while he belabored her in a most brutal manner. His wife was almost as wicked as himself; but what a change there was when Christ came into that family! No more wife-beating and drinking and blasphemy. Instead of constant misery and quarrelling, peace and joy and love reigned. That woman, who formerly had trembled at the approach of her husband, now listens eagerly for his footstep, that she may be ready to welcome him; for he now is a true husband, loving and protecting the wife whom God has given him. Christ in the heart not only gives us heaven in the future of eternity, but a sweet foretaste of it here."

How to Give Milk to a Calf.—Mr. Campbell White, speaking of the necessity for Christians to use a little tact when personally dealing with unsaved sinners, said: "One day, when walking in the country, I saw a maid giving a little milk to a calf. When she came with the pail of milk she placed the pail upon the ground, expecting the calf at once to drink. The creature looked at it, capered about, and, kicking up its heels, at length knocked the pail over, spilling its contents upon the ground. The second time the girl brought milk, but now she held the pail with one hand while she gave the calf the other, which had been dipped in milk, to suck. As it sucked, the hand was gradually lowered into the pail, and soon the calf was drinking freely. Some Christians, in dealing with anxious souls, often act as that girl did at first with the calf. They present the gospel in a way that seems to say, 'There it is, take it or leave it; it is nothing to me; I have done my duty.' Should we not rather try to gain their confidence, and persuade them to come, until, though they scarcely know it themselves, they are actually drinking in 'the sincere milk of the Word,' and accept Christ as their own Saviour."

No Pain in the Broken Leg.—Mr. King, an evangelist, says: "When I was down in Peebles not long ago, a lady told me of an accident which had occurred to a friend of hers. He had been out driving, when his horse ran off, and in attempting to get out of the vehicle he fell, and the wheels ran over his leg. He was not thought to be dangerously hurt at first, but as time went on he did not seem to recover nor his leg to mend. His friends at length became anxious. One day his wife entered the sick-room, and she found the invalid smiling and happy. 'Oh, I am ever so much better,' he said; 'the pain is all gone from my leg; I'll soon be about again now.' Just then the doctor came in, and being told of the sudden improvement he shook his head mournfully, for he knew that, now the pain was gone, mortification had set in, and there was no possible hope of recovery. In a very short time he was dead. Similarly there are people with whom the preaching of the Gospel arouses no pangs of conscience, no conviction of sin, and from that they argue that they are not in danger, and rest satisfied. Oh, take care that spiritual mortification has not set in, and that the soul be not already dead, and reprobate!"

THE AGE OF SWINDLE.

Dr. Talmage's Sermon preached last Sunday Morning, March 11, 1888.

"Whose trust shall be a spider's web." Job 8: 14.

The Two Skilful Architects—The Marauding Spider—A Type of the Unscrupulous Financier—Men who Watch and Prey—A Pestilence of Crime—Bankrupt Executors and Trustees—The Causes of the Epidemic—Careless Bank Directors—Their Character Attractive to Depositors—Producing Confidence—Their Responsibility—Orthodox Swindlers the worst of All—Ancient Banks—The Wheat Gamblers—Thwarting the Blessing of Providence—Advice to Financiers—Never Speculate on Borrowed Capital—Borrowing often only Stealing—Live within your Income—Be Careful of Trust Funds—Strange Effect of a Missionary's Sermon—A Cunning Abbot's Harvest—Thank God Harbor.

The two most skilful architects in all the world are the bee and the spider. The one puts up a sugar manufactory, and the other builds a slaughter-house for flies. On a bright summer morning, when the sun comes out and shines upon the spider's web, bedecked with dew, the gossamer structure seems bright enough for a suspension bridge for supernatural beings to cross on. But alas for the poor fly, which, in the latter part of the day, ventures on it, and is caught and dungeoned and destroyed. The fly was informed that it was a free bridge, and would cost nothing, but at the other end of the bridge the toll paid was its own life. The next day there comes down a strong wind, and away goes the web, and

The Marauding Spider,

and the victimized fly. So delicate are the silken threads of the spider's web that many thousands of them are put together before they become visible to the human eye, and it takes four million of them to make a thread as large as the human hair. Most cruel as well as most ingenious is the spider. A prisoner in the Bastille, France, had one so trained that at the sound of a violin it every day came for its meal of flies. Job, the author my text, and the leading scientist of his day, had no doubt watched the voracious process of this one insect with another, and saw spider and fly swept down with the same broom, or scattered by the same wind. Alas, that the world has so many designing spiders and victimized flies!

There has not been a time when the utter and black irresponsibility of many men, having the financial interests of others in charge, has been more evident than in these last few years. The unroofing of banks and disappearance of administrators with the funds of large estates, and the disorder amidst post office accounts and deficits amid United States officials, have made

A Pestilence of Crime

that solemnizes every thoughtful man and woman, and leads every philanthropist and Christian to ask: What shall be done to stay the plague? There is a monsoon abroad, a typhoon, a sirocco. I sometimes ask myself if it would not be better for men making wills to bequeath the property directly to the executors and officers of the court, and appoint the widows and orphans a committee to see that the former got all that did not belong to them.

The simple fact is that there are a large number of men sailing yachts, and driving fast horses, and members of expensive club houses, and controlling country-seats, who are not worth a dollar if they return to others their just rights. Under some sudden reverse they fail, and with afflicted air seem to retire from the world, and seem almost ready for monastic life, when in two or three years they blossom out again, having compromised with their creditors; that is, paid them nothing but regrets, and the only difference between the second chapter of prosperity and the first, is that their pictures are Murillos instead of Kensetts, and their horses go a mile in twenty seconds less than their predecessors, and instead of one country-seat they have three. I have watched and have noticed that nine out of ten of those who fail in what is called high life, have more means after than before the failure, and in many of the cases failure is only a strategem to escape the payment of honest debts and put the world off the track while they practice a large swindle. There is something woefully wrong in the fact that these things are possible.

First of all, I charge the blame on careless,

Indifferent Bank Directors

and boards having in charge great financial institutions. It ought not to be possible for a president or cashier or prominent officer of a banking institution to swindle it year after year without detection. I will undertake to say that if these frauds are carried on for two or three years without detection, either the directors are partners in the infamy and pocketed part of the theft, or they are guilty of a culpable neglect of duty, for which God will hold them as responsible as He holds the acknowledged defrauders. What right have prominent business men to allow their names to be published as directors in a financial institution, so that unsophisticated people are thereby induced to deposit their money in or buy the scrip thereof, when they, the published directors, are doing nothing for the safety of the institution? It is a case of deception most reprehensible.

Many people with a surplus of money, not needed for immediate use, although it may be a little further on indispensable, are without friends competent to advise them, and they are guided solely by the character of the men whose names are associated with the institution. When the crash came, and with the overthrow of the banks went the small earnings and limited fortunes of widows and orphans, and the helplessly aged, the directors stood with idiotic stare, and to the inquiry of the frenzied depositors and stockholders who had lost their all, and to the arraignment of an indignant public, had nothing to say except: "We thought it was all right. We did not know there was anything wrong going on." It was

Their Duty to Know.

They stood in a position which deluded the people with the idea that they were carefully observant. Calling themselves directors, they did not direct. They had opportunity of auditing accounts and inspecting the books. No time to do so? then they had no business to accept the position. It seems to be the pride of some monied men to be directors in a great many institutions, and all they know is whether or not they get their dividends regularly, and their names are used as decoy ducks to bring others near enough to be made game of. What first of all is needed is that 5,000 bank directors and insurance company directors resign or attend to their business as directors. The business world will be full of fraud just as long as fraud is so easy. When you arrest the president and secretary of a bank for an embezzlement carried on for many years, have plenty of sheriffs out the same day to arrest all the directors. They are guilty either of neglect or complicity.

"Oh," some one will say, "better preach the gospel and let business matters alone." I reply: "If your gospel does not inspire common honesty in the dealings of men, the sooner you close up your gospel and pitch it into the depths of the Atlantic Ocean the better.

An Orthodox Swindler

is worse than a heterodox swindler. The recitation of all the cathechisms and creeds ever written, and drinking from all the communion chalices that ever glittered in the churches of Christendom, will never save your soul unless your business character corresponds with your religious profession. Some of the worst scoundrels in America have been members of churches, and they got fat on sermons about heaven, when they most needed to have the pulpits preach that which would either bring them to repentance or thunder them out of the holy communion, where their presence was a sacrilege and an infamy.

We must especially deplore the misfortune of banks in various parts of this country, in that they damage the banking institution, which is the great convenience of the century, and indispensable to commerce and the advance of nations. With one hand it blesses the lender, and with the other it blesses the borrower.

The Bank was Born

of the world's necessities, and is venerable with the marks of thousands of years. Two hundred years before Christ the Bank of Ilium existed, and paid its depositors ten per cent. The Bank of Venice was established in 1171, and was of such high credit that its bills were at a premium above coins, which were frequently clipped; Bank of Genoa, founded in 1345, Bank of Barcelona, 1401; Bank of Amsterdam, 1699; Bank of Hamburg, founded 1619, its circulation based on great silver bars kept in the vaults; Bank of England, started by William Patterson in 1642, up to this day managing the stupendous debt of England; Bank of Scotland, founded in 1695; Bank of Ireland, 1783; Bank of North America, planned by Robert Morris, 1771, without whose financial help all the bravery of our grandfathers would not have achieved independence.

But now we have banks in all our cities and towns, thousands and thousands. On their shoulders are the interests of private individuals and great corporations. In them are the great arteries through which run the currents of the nation's life. They have been the resources of thousands of financiers in days of business exigency. They stand for accommodation, for facility, for individual, State and national relief. At their head and in their management there is as much interest and moral worth as in any class of men—perhaps more. How nefarious, then, the behavior of those who bring disrepute upon this venerable, benignant and God-honored institution!

We also deplore the abuse of trust funds, because they fly in the face of that divine goodness which seems determined to bless this land. We are having the eighth year of unexampled national harvest. The

Wheat Gamblers

get hold of the wheat, and the corn gamblers get hold of the corn. The full tide of God's mercy towards this land is put back by those great dykes of dishonest resistance. When God provides enough food and clothing to feed and apparel this whole nation like princes, the scrabble of dishonest men to get more than their share, and get it at all hazards, keeps everything shaking with uncertainty and everybody asking, "What next?" Every week makes new revelations. How many more bank presidents and bank cashiers have been speculating with other people's money, and how many more bank directors are in imbecile silence, letting the perfidy go on, the great and patient God only knows!

My opinion is that we have got near the bottom. The wind has been picked from *the great bubble of American speculation.* The men who thought that the Judgment Day was at least 5,000 years off, have found it in 1888, 1887, 1886; and this nation has been taught that men must keep their hands out of other people's pockets. Great businesses built on borrowed capital have been obliterated, and men who had nothing, lost all they had. I believe we are started on a higher career of prosperity than this land has ever seen, if, and if, and if.

If the first men, and especially Christian men, will learn never to speculate upon

Borrowed Capital.

If you have a mind to take your own money, and turn it all into kites, to fly them over every commons in the United States, you do society no wrong, except when you tumble your helpless children into the poorhouse for the public to take care of. But you have no right to take the money of others and turn it into kites. There is one word that has deluded more people into bankruptcy and State prison and perdition than any other word in commercial life, and that is *the word borrow;* that one word is responsible for all the defalcations, and embezzlements, and financial consternations of the last twenty years. When executors conclude to speculate with the funds of an estate committed to their charge, they do not purloin, they say

They Only Borrow;

when a banker makes an overdraught upon his institution, he does not commit a theft, he only borrows. When the officer of a company, by flaming advertisement in some religious papers, and gilt certificate of stock, gets a multitude of country people to put their small earnings into an enterprise for carrying on some undeveloped nothing, he does not fraudulently take their money, he only borrows. When a young man with easy access to his employer's money-drawer, or the confidential clerk by close propinquity to the account-books, takes a few dollars for a Wall Street excursion, he expects to put it back; he will put it all back; he will put it all back very soon. He only borrows. What is needed is some man of gigantic limb to take his place at the curb-stone in front of Trinity Church and when that word borrow comes bounding along, kick it clean through to Wall Street ferry-boat, and if, striking on that, it bounds clear over till it strikes Brooklyn Heights or Brooklyn hill, it will be well for the City of Churches.

Why, when you are going to do wrong, pronounce so long a word as borrow, a word of six letters, when you can get a shorter word more descriptive of the reality, a word of only five letters, the word steal?

There are times when we all borrow, and borrow legitimately, and borrow with the divine blessing, for Christ, in His Sermon on the Mount, enjoins "from him that would borrow of thee, turn not thou away." A young man rightly borrows money to get his education. Purchasing a house and not able to pay all down in cash, the purchaser rightly borrows it on mortgage. Crises come in business when it would be wrong for a man not to borrow. But I roll this warning through all these aisles, over the backs of all these pews,

Never Borrow to Speculate;

not a dollar, not a cent, not a farthing! Young men, young men, I warn you by your worldly prospects and the value of your immortal souls, do not do it! There are breakers distinguished for their shipwrecks—the Hanways, the Needles, the Caskets, the Douvers, the Anderlos, the Skerries—and many a craft has gone to pieces on those rocks; but I have to tell you that all the Hanways and the Needles, and the Caskets, and the Skerries, are as nothing compared with the long line of breakers which bound the ocean of commercial life north, south, east and west, with the white foam of their despair and the dirge of their damnation: The breakers of borrow!

If I had only a worldly weapon to use on this subject I would give you the fact fresh from the highest authority, that ninety per cent. of those who go into speculation in Wall Street lose all; but I have a better warning than a worldly warning. From the place where men have perished—body, mind and soul—stand off, stand off! Abstract pulpit discussion must step aside on this question. Faith and repentance are absolutely necessary, but faith and repentance are no more doctrines of the Bible than

Commercial Integrity.

Render to all their dues. Owe no man anything. And while I mean to preach faith and repentance, more and more to preach them, I do not mean to spend any time in chasing the Hittites and Jebusites and Girgashites of Bible times, when there are so many evils right around us destroying men and women for time and eternity. The greatest evangelistic preacher the world ever saw, a man who died for his evangelism—the peerless Paul—wrote to the Romans, "Provide things honest in the sight of all men;" wrote to the Corinthians, "Do that which is honest;" wrote to the Philippians, "Whatsoever things are honest;" wrote to the Hebrews, "Willing in all things to live honestly." The Bible says, that faith without works is dead; which being literally translated, means that if your business life does not correspond with your profession, your religion is a humbug.

Here is something that needs to be sounded into the ears of all the young men of America, and iterated and reiterated, if this country is ever to be delivered from its calamities, and commercial prosperity is to be established and perpetuated.

Live Within Your Means.

I have the highest commercial authority for saying, that when the memorable trouble broke out in Wall Street four years ago, there were $225,000,000 in suspense, which had already been spent. Spend no more than you make. And let us adjust all our business and our homes by the principles of the Christian religion. Our religion ought to mean just as much on Saturday and Monday as on the day between, and not be a mere periphrasis of sanctity. Our religion ought to first clean our hearts, and then it ought to clean our lives. Religion is not, as some seem to think, a sort of church delectation, a kind of confectionery, a sort of spiritual caramel or holy gumdrop, or sanctified peppermint, or theological anæsthetic. It is an omnipotent principle, all-controlling, all-conquering. You may get along with something less than that, and you may deceive yourself with it; but you cannot deceive God, and you cannot deceive the world.

The keen business man will put on his spectacles, and he will look clear through to the back of your head, and see whether your religion is a fiction or a fact. And you cannot hide your samples of sugar or rice or tea or coffee if they are false; you cannot hide them under the cloth of a communion-table. All your prayers go for nothing so long as you misrepresent your banking institution, and in the amount of resources you put down more specie and more fractional currency and more clearing-house certificates and more legal-tender notes and more loans and more discounts than there really are, and when you give an account of your liabilities you do not mention all the unpaid dividends, and the United States bank notes outstanding, and the individual deposits, and the obligations to other banks and bankers. An authority more scrutinizing than that of any bank examiner will go through and through and through your business.

I stand this morning before many who have trust funds. It is a compliment to you that you have been so intrusted; but I charge you, in the presence of God and the world, be careful, be as

Careful of the Property of Others

as you are careful of your own. Above all, keep your own private account at the bank separate from your account as trustee of an estate, or trustee of an institution. That is the point at which thousands of people make shipwreck. They get the property of others mixed up with their own property, they put it into investment, and away it all goes, and they cannot return that which they borrowed. Then comes the explosion, and the money market is shaken, and the press denounces, and the church thunders explosion. You have no right to use the property of others, except for their advantage, nor without consent, unless they are minors. If with their consent you invest their property as well as you can, and it is all lost, you are not to blame; you did the best you could,' but do not come into the delusion which has ruined so many men, of thinking because a thing is in their possession, therefore it is theirs. You have a solemn trust that God has given you.

In this vast assemblage there may be some who have misappropriated trust funds. Put them back, or, if you have so hopelessly involved them that you cannot put them back, confess the whole thing to those whom you have wronged, and you will sleep better nights, and you will have the better chance for your soul.

What a sad thing it would be, if after you are dead your administrator should find out from the account-books, or from the lack of vouchers, that you not only were bankrupt in estate, but that you lost your soul. If all the trust funds that have been misappropriated should suddenly fly to their owners, and all the property that has been purloined should suddenly go back to its owners, it would crush into ruin every city in America.

A Missionary's Sermon.

A missionary on one of the islands of the Pacific preached on dishonesty, and the next morning he looked out of his window, and he saw his yard full of goods of all kinds. He wondered, and asked the cause of all this. "Well," said the natives, "our gods that we have been worshipping permit us to steal, but according to what you said yesterday, the God of heaven and earth will not allow this, so we bring back all these goods, and we ask you to help us in taking them to the places where they belong." If next Sabbath all the ministers in America should preach sermons on the abuse of trust funds, and on the evils of purloining, and the sermons were all blessed of God, and regulations were made that all these things should be taken to the city halls, it would not be long before every city hall in America would be crowded from cellar to cupola.

Let me say in the most emphatic manner to all young men,

Dishonesty Will Never Pay.

An abbot wanted to buy a piece of ground, and the owner would not sell it, but the owner finally consented to let it to him until he could raise one crop, and the abbot sowed acorns—a crop of two hundred years! And I tell you, young man, that the dishonesties which you plant in your heart and life will seem to be very insignificant, but they will grow up until they will overshadow you with horrible darkness, overshadow all time and all eternity. It will not be a crop for two hundred years, but a crop for everlasting ages.

I have also a word of comfort for all who suffer from the malfeasance of others, and every honest man, woman and child does suffer from what goes on in *financial scampdom*. Society is so bound together, that all the misfortunes which good people suffer in business matters come from the misdeeds of others. Bear up under distress, strong in God. He will see you through, though your misfortunes should be centupled. Philosophers tell us that a column of air forty-five miles in height rests on every man's head and shoulders. But that is nothing compared with the pressure that business life has put upon many of you. God made up his mind long ago how many or how few dollars it would be best for you to have. Trust to his appointment. The door will soon open to let you out and let you up. What shock of delight for men who for thirty years have been in business anxiety, when they shall suddenly awake in everlasting holiday!

On the maps of the Arctic regions there are two places whose names are remarkable, given, I suppose, by some Polar expedition: "Cape Farewell" and "Thank God Harbor." At this last the *Polaris* wintered in 1871, and the *Tigress* in 1873. Some ships have passed the Cape, yet never reached the Harbor. But from what I know of many of you, I have concluded that though your voyage of life may be very rough, run into by icebergs on this side and icebergs on that, you will in due time reach Cape Farewell, and there bid good-by to all annoyances, and soon after drop anchor in the calm and imperturbable waters of Thank God Harbor—"Where the wicked cease from troubling, and the weary are at rest."

AN INCENSED UNCLE THWARTED.

MISS MACINTOSH, of the China Inland Mission, writing from Sa-kung-ling, says: "Hu Chin-fah is the son of a well-to-do farmer, and a sincere Christian. He was formerly a vegetarian, and very much opposed to the religion of Jesus Christ, and very earnest in the service of Satan. He is now as earnest in serving God as he was before in serving the devil. He has had a good deal of persecution since he believed. His father is an opium-smoker, and Chin-fah was most anxious that he should come here and worship God, and give up the opium. He consented, and we gave him some medicine. In a short time he had quite given the opium up, and came to worship one Sunday, looking so much better that the son's heart was filled with joy. But, alas! a bitter trial awaited him. A brother of his father's, who is very rich, hearing about this, was very angry, and told him he ought not to give up the opium, and that his 'son was very wicked for bringing him here, and not fit to live; he ought to go home and kill him.' The poor man listened to him, and one day *lifted a large knife to kill his son*, who happened to have a long pole in his hand, with which he defended himself, and escaped to his grandmother's house. The rich brother got the father more incensed against his son, so that he determined to go to the mandarin, and get him to take off his head. He came into the city for the purpose. The Christians in Sa-kung-ling met for prayer, and one of them followed the old man, and succeeded in persuading him to return home and be reconciled to his son, who was only seeking to do him good. On his return, Chin-fah came and knelt down before his father, asking his forgiveness if he had grieved him. Since then his father has been very good to him, and does not object to his coming to worship the Christians' God. We visited them lately, and were very kindly received. We believe God will yet hear and answer prayer for his father and mother."

A DAY'S WORK IN INDIA.

IN an interesting account sent by Mr. Hume to the *Missionary Herald* of a tour in the Ahmednagar district of the Bombay Presidency in India, he thus describes the programme generally followed for the day after the missionary tent is pitched:

"We go early in the morning, about sunrise, into the town proper, and preach to the people, who are usually seated at that time near the gate, around a fire; and those who are passing frequently stop to listen. Sometimes we have ten or twelve hearers, frequently from twenty to forty, and sometimes as many as seventy-five. We talk from half an hour to an hour there, and then go to the quarters of the lower caste, the Mahars, and do the same thing over again for from half to three-quarters of an hour. Then back to the tent for breakfast. The middle of the day is occupied with conversations with mission agents, Christians and Hindus who call, and with writing, etc. Sometimes in the early afternoon a company of people come and, we have a long talk with them. And at any rate, toward sunset we go again to the town and Mahar quarters, and again preach. Sometimes in the evenings I show in the village rest-house the pictures of a stereopticon, giving some general views, a few humorous ones, and many scriptural events and teachings. This lasts for an hour or more, and always attracts a large audience. If our tents remain many days in one place, then we visit the near villages and work in the same way, and return to our tents. Mrs. Hume and a Bible-woman visit the women, and I with a preacher go to the men. Though Mrs. Hume means to talk only to women, yet the baby-organ often draws quite a crowd of men also.

"Last Sunday I baptized two men and three children in this place, and one man and woman in another town near by. Some of these people are still exposed to a good deal of ridicule and opposition because they throw in their lot with Christ's people. For example: not long ago I had a long conversation with a large company of Hindus on 'Acquaintance with God.' Every one of them said he was *not acquainted with God*, and did not know how to get acquainted. I asked the government school-teacher and others to pray. But they said they did not know how. I then asked one of our Christians to pray. He rose and made a humble, suitable prayer. I said: 'This acquaintance with God, and freedom in speaking to Him, is what Christ has done for a plain man of your village, and what He wishes to give you.' Ever since then those people have made sport of the Christian. But I believe the incident will help both them and him."

ADRIFT ON A COFFIN.

A REMARKABLE deliverance from a watery grave is described by the saved man in this month's number of *Thy Healer*.* He says: "I was employed to convey an empty coffin to Moho Caye, in British Honduras, to bury a poor white boy who had died there of fever. Soon after leaving the wharf of our Belize Hospital, at 8 P. M., a squall came down, and our dory, being cranky, was turned over; thus Moore (my assistant) and I, were plunged in the sea.

"For four hours we were in this state, screaming for help, sharks around, night dark and dismal, and the Caye a long way off. Oh! how I did pray! I went down twice under the waves; but even under the sea, my spirit cried for help, and the Master answered me. Our boat drifted back, and we laid hold of it, getting a little rest, while we cried again for help, but we were very cold and worn out. Then the Lord gave fresh courage, and a strange thing happened. The coffin, which had drifted off a long way and time, came right up to us, just as we were giving up, briny, weary and cold-struck; but suddenly I got strength, and laying hold of the coffin, swam ashore on it to Moho Caye. As I reached the shore, the clock struck twelve, but I was too exhausted to get to the house, and so I laid down on the beach till I revived; then I crawled to the house, was taken in and warmed. Poor Moore, who was left on the dory, was also helped, for soon after my revival we heard a cry on the beach, and behold, it was Moore. Thank God!"

LITTLE LIGHTS IN THE HOMES.

A REPORT full of encouragement is published among some intelligence sent home by Miss Maltbie, from Bulgaria. She has been visiting the out-stations, and in the course of her tour paid special attention to the girl's schools and women's meetings. She says: "The first Sabbath was spent in Bansko, and the large, attentive congregation assembled in the pleasant church; the earnestness of the Christian women, who improved the time between services in seeking hungry souls that they might speak to them of the love of Jesus; the large number gathered at noon to hear the Word read and explained; the intensely interesting meeting of more than sixty children; the prayer-meeting late in the afternoon, led by the earnest, devoted preacher; and finally, the sweet half-hour with the dear little children who have lately given their hearts to the Saviour—all of these things left a deep impression upon me.

"Perhaps one of the most interesting features of the blessed work of grace which has been going on in Bansko for the past few months has been the awakening and conversion of about thirty children, who are now letting *their light so shine in their homes* that their thankful mothers gladly testify to the power of Jesus' love in the heart to change the worst of them into gentle, patient, obedient children. These young Christians gladly enlisted as soldiers against King Alcohol, and I put the symbolic ribbon of blue or white upon all the twenty-five who were gathered in Mrs. Ralu's room on that Sabbath evening. Mrs. Ralu leads the children's meetings, and the Holy Spirit has enabled her to accomplish a good work among the women and children the past year. These small lights set in these homes may become great lights, enlightening many souls, and I rejoiced much in this small beginning."

* A monthly magazine edited by Mrs. M. Baxter, containing original articles on Holiness and Divine Healing. Annual subscription 75 cents. May be had from the office of this journal, 63 Bible House, New York.

PERSECUTION IN MEXICO.

REPORTS from the Rev. Hubert W. Brown, in Mexico, to *The Church* show that the Presbyterian mission in that country is still struggling bravely, and now with some hope of success, against Romanist persecution and intrigue. The martyrdom of the two preachers Hurtado and Gomez, reported in these columns last year, has, it appears, caused apprehension among the aggressors. Mr. Brown says: "The offenders are in prison, fear has taken hold on the entire community, and some fifty of the participators in the riot have secretly stolen away. The relatives of those on trial came with every mark of respect to our minister, Rev. Felix Gomez, whose father and brother have been assassinated, and besought him to intercede in behalf of the men on trial. Catholics are learning that Protestantism is recognized, and is to be protected in its rights by the Chief Magistrate of the Republic."

By the side of these encouraging facts must be placed the darker picture supplied by other provinces. Mr. Brown says: "Persecution has scattered some of our congregations for the time being. This has been especially true in the province of Guerrero. Tuxpan, Platanillo and Ahuacuatitlan have suffered most, but other points also had to be temporarily abandoned. In the province of Tobasco, *Jesuit intrigue cost the life of a church-member* in Comalcalco, and through poison nearly deprived of reason our teacher in Paraiso, Miss Balcazar. Only five leagues from the capital, in San Lorenzo, the local authorities attempted to drive away the Protestants by false imprisonments. For three months only women and children attended the services. The matter was put into the hands of a trusted lawyer, Mr. Alfaro, who in the end secured the release of the imprisoned men. Near Ozumba similar methods were tried and with partial success. Only the other day I received word from Zitacuaro that the owner of the ranch of Colmena told the Indians that they must discontinue their Protestant services or leave the ranch. This widespread and determined persecution is a notable feature of the past year.

A SUFFERER'S CLAIM ON A PROMISE.

A TESTIMONY published in *Thy Healer* from a Mr. Grossmith, records his recovery from a malady which has many victims in this country. He says:

"I was attacked by my former enemy, *congestion* of the liver, two weeks ago. I was perfectly powerless, and could not even raise my hand to feed myself. I gave it to the Lord, but was still ill next morning. I thought then how the Lord appointed the Twelve to go forth to heal sickness and disease; and how they went and healed those who were sick, and then how at last, Jesus said: 'And these signs shall follow them that believe; In My name shall they cast out devils; they shall speak with new tongues; they shall take up serpents; and if they drink any deadly thing, it shall not hurt them; they shall lay hands on the sick, and they shall recover.' I thought, perhaps, it would be well to get some one to anoint me, but I did not know whom to get. My little boy, who went to the Sunday-school, was told by the deacon, who was Superintendent, that he would come and see me. He did so, and I asked him to anoint me, and pray according to God's word, but he was afraid to do so. I then sent for a niece of mine, who believes in Divine Healing. She is only about two or three and twenty, but she came and anointed me. She also prayed and believed, and I just rested on God's promise, but could not move. When night came on was still quite powerless, and continued in great agony all night, but rested in the Lord. My wife said, 'You had better send for a doctor,' but I kept on trusting. My wife came and fed me, for I could not raise my hand to my mouth. Just then, I lifted up my heart to the Lord, and asked if there was anything else I ought to do, and the thought at once came: 'Claim it.' I did claim it in the name of the Lord Jesus, and then I got up and went to business. I was pained just in the same way on the Tuesday, but claimed healing, and received it; and again there was the same thing on the Wednesday, and then it entirely left me, and I have been perfectly free since. I praise the Lord for His mercy."

THE EVOLUTION OF PROPHECY.

By Rev. N. West.*

The Classification of Old Testament Prophets—The Five Prophetic Epochs—Daniel's Far Reaching Vision—Ezekiel Still More Extended—Reaching Beyond the Millennium—John's Compilation—The Seventy Weeks—The Length of the Metallic Image—The Successive Recipients of the Apocalyptic Revelation.

THE catastrophe which broke Solomon's, or, rather, David's kingdom into two kingdoms, called Israel, i. e., the ten-tribed Israel, and Judah, i. e., the two-tribed Israel—the Northern Kingdom with Samaria as its capital, and the Southern Kingdom with Jerusalem as its capital—and prepared the way for the captivity of both, lays the foundation for all the prophecies we have in the Old Testament concerning Israel and Judah. The Babylonian Exile lays the foundation for our common

Classification of the Prophets

into Pre-exile, Exile and Post-exile prophets. There is another convenient and instructive division, if we group them around the epochs, or critical junctures and times of Israel's history. We get thus (1) the Pre-Assyrian prophets, or prophets of the Pre-Assyrian period. (2) The prophets of the Assyrian period. (3) Of the Transition period. (4) Of the Chaldean period, or time of the Exile; and (5) of the Persian period, or Post-exile prophets, the prophets of the restoration to the Close of the Old Testament Canon. The first are Obadiah, Joel and Jonah, Hosea and Amos. The second are Isaiah, Micah and Nahum. The third are Habbakuk, Zephaniah and Jeremiah. The fourth are Ezekiel and Daniel. The fifth are Haggai, Zechariah and Malachi. Sixteen in all; all speaking distinctly, save one or two, of Messianic times, all pointing to the last times, the Day of the Lord, and the Messianic redemption for Israel and the nations. They cover a period of 450 years of prophetic activity, from Joel to Malachi, and foretell the final triumph of the Kingdom of God on earth.

In the prophet Daniel, there is a coming of Messiah in humiliation, and to be "cut off" at a certain specified time. This you see in Daniel 9: 25. Then there is a coming of Messiah in the clouds of heaven, at the end of a long period following the first end. This you see in Daniel 7: 9, 22. Messiah comes at the beginning of the fourth prophetic empire. He comes also at its close. You have sailed up to your sky-line, and another one lies beyond it. You have reached the advent and find that it is parted into two advents with

An Intervening Age,

the age we ourselves are living in, the age when Israel is nationally cast away, the Church—historical period, the age of the Colossus or metallic image, the "times of the Gentiles," during the fourth or Roman empire in its various phases. Daniel has bequeathed to all succeeding time the great problem of Israel's future with respect to the nations, and of the nations also in relation to Israel throughout the whole course of history. It is here we learn what Israel's national condition is to be during the intermediate or parenthetic Age that has sprung up between these two ends, viz., our present Age, or the Roman portion of the "Times of the Gentiles." We find, also, that he has given us the *solution* of this great problem, in three different ways; first in the interpretation of the four-empired colossus or image Nebuchadnezzar saw; again, in the vision of the four beasts; and, once more, in the celebrated "seventy sevens," or "weeks of years," as found in the ninth chapter. In the first case, the Messianic Kingdom comes in its glory, and comes to Israel, only at the End of the fourth Empire; in the second case, only at the End of the life of the fourth beast, or, what is the same thing, at the overthrow of the "Little Horn," the last Antichrist into which the fourth empire runs out; and, in the third case, it comes at the close of the seventieth of the seventy weeks.

The Termini are Identical

in all these cases. The end point in all is the Second Coming of the Son of man. The solution of the great problem of the future history and final destiny of Daniel's people is just this, that, because of their national rejection of Messiah, they themselves will be rejected, and remain rejected, as a nation, during the times of the Gentiles, or until the Second Coming of Messiah, when they will, as a nation, be converted, and the Kingdom be restored to Israel, as the prophets have predicted.

Ezekiel sees farther than even Daniel does. Daniel sees an end following our present Age, and an Age following that End, an Age to him an endless one. Ezekiel, however, sees an End even to that last age. He sees the insurrection of Gog and Magog, not merely at the opening of the Age that follows the Second Coming of Messiah, but at its close. He sees Israel restored and in their land, dwelling safely "many days" in peace and blessedness, following the resurrection of the dry bones, and the overthrow of the Colossus, in judgment on the World-Power. He announces in a very remarkable prediction, that "*After many days*" Gog shall be visited for final punishment. Those "many days" are a long period of time, the time of restored Israel's blessedness in the Kingdom. They follow the Second Coming of Messiah, just because they follow Israel's resurrection and rehabilitation. You see what is done to Israel in Ezekiel, chapter 37—you see their blessedness and peace asserted in chapter 38, the full expansion of which is pictured in Old Testament colors in chaps. 40-48. But in 38: 8 you read that "*after*"

That Long Period

of "many days" Gog and Magog shall be visited for final punishment. This is precisely what John has in the Apocalypse. The "many days" of Ezekiel are the "Millennium" of John. It is folly to try and make the final judgment on Gog and Magog the last phase of the judgment on Antichrist and the world-power, at the Second Coming of Messiah. It is a different judgment altogether, and occurs "many days" *after* Israel's rehabilitation in their fatherland. It is post-millennial. Once for all, and in obedience to the fixed law of prophetic development, and building on Ezekiel, and guided by the Holy Spirit, John has made it sure that his "thousand years" are Ezekiel's "many days" and fall between the Second Advent and Gog's final destruction. What John does is to *combine*

The Eschatta of Isaiah,

Daniel, Ezekiel, Zechariah, in short, the Eschatta of all the Old Testament prophets, and arrange them in their temporal order and succession. In place of Isaiah's One End, and One Advent, and one Age following, we get three Ends, and three Ages, the last Age of course, being the endless age. Or, if we take into account the pre-Messianic or Jewish Age, then what we have is four Ages, and three Ends, viz., first, the Jewish or pre-Messianic with its End, viz., the first Advent; next our present Age, with its End, the Second Advent; third, the *Yamim Rabbin*, or "*Many Days*," i. e., the Millennial Age, with its End, in Gog's final Destruction; and fourth, the Endless Age, yet to be developed in the Apocalypse of John. And this is the whole evolution of the Ages and the Ends in the old Testament, reaching down from the Babylonian Captivity to the Last Judgment into which the Judgment on Gog expands itself, even down to the creation of the New Heaven and Earth.

If we put the whole Old Testament Chronological prophecy together concerning Israel, after David's Kingdom was broken, we shall get the formula of the combined 70 years Captivity, and the Seventy Year-Weeks, including the great interval between the 69th and 70th week, thus: 70 years, plus 483 years, or 69 weeks, plus the interval of our present age, *plus* the closing or seventieth week, i. e., seven years. And what is of special interest to the student of prophecy is this, viz.: that the formula 70 *plus* 7 *plus* 62 *plus* (our interval) *plus* 1 measures chronologically the whole

Length of the Metallic Image

from head to feet, and measures also the whole lifetime of the four beasts, the last of which ends in the last personal Antichrist. We get the total æonology and teleology of both Old and New Testament prophecy with respect to Israel and the nations; and in all we see how Israel, God's "choice forever," stands out, in rejection and in their calling and commission, recovery, death and resurrection, as the bringer, nationally, of Salvation to mankind. It is God's plan, and full, as Paul tells us, of the unsearchable wisdom of God. (Rom. 11: 33.)

Of post-exile prophecy I need only speak to you a word. We have Paul's word for it that Haggai's oracle, as to the shaking of the nations, of heaven, earth, sea and dry land, refers to the Second Coming of Christ. The prophet, moreover, connects the appearing of the "Glory" with the second temple then in existence, an appearing, however, only precursive of one more glorious, and in a temple built of all the wealth and treasure of the nations. Two advents are here, therefore. In Zechariah these Advents are so clearly predicted, Messiah riding on a colt, and again Messiah standing on the Mount of Olives, having come with all His holy ones, that it is impossible to mistake them, the one for suffering, the other for judgment and glory. In Malachi, also, you will find

Two Advents

separated by the period when, the Jews having rejected Messiah, His name becomes great among the Gentiles, while yet, before the final "*Day of the Lord*," Elijah is sent to restore Israel to a spiritual understanding of the words of Moses, after which, the storm having passed away, Israel redeemed at last, rejoices with gladness in the Kingdom, like calves let loose from the stall, upon the pasture refreshed and brightened with the beams of the rising sun. So ends Old Testament prediction. If we sum up the result, as to the development of the Ages and the Ends, what we get is the Jewish, the Christian, the Millennial and the Endless Ages; four Ages, three Ends and two Advents of Messiah. The Apocalypse assumes the truth of all Old Testament prediction concerning Israel and the Nations. I feel as certain of this as I do of any truth in the Bible, and it belongs to the reproach due to the superficial knowledge of so many, in our day of widespread Scripture study, that they have not recognized this fact, but still keep harping on the old and tuneless string that "the Millennium is found in only one passage of the Bible, and that in a very obscure book called the Apocalypse." Dear friends, the Apocalypse of Isaiah is a light. The Apocalypse of Daniel is a light. The Apocalypse of Ezekiel is a light. And the Apocalypse of John is a supreme and seven-fold unclouded light, which combines all other lights, and blazes like the sun at noon.

* From his recent lecture at Niagara, contained in full, revised by himself, in *The Word*, a pamphlet of 102 pages, comprising also prophetic lectures by Rev. H. M. Parsons, Rev. James H. Brooks, D. D., of St. Louis; Pastor E. P. Marvin, Rev. Albert Erdman, D. D.; Rev. S. H. Kellogg, D. D.; and other able expositors of prophecy. Owing to the large demand for this work, a supply of copies has been procured by *Mr. J. B. Jewett*, 77 Bible House, who will mail a copy to any address for fifty cents.

CHRISTIAN HERALD AND SIGNS OF OUR TIMES.

OFFICE, 63 BIBLE HOUSE, NEW YORK.

ENTERED AT THE POST-OFFICE AT NEW YORK, N. Y., AS SECOND-CLASS MATTER.

Published Weekly. Subscription price, $1.50 a year; $1 eight months; 75 cents six months; sent two months on trial for 25 cents; always payable in advance. Single copies for sale by, or can be ordered at, all newsdealers.

Remittances by Mail should be by Post-office money order, bank cheques, or drafts or express money order, and should always be made payable to THE CHRISTIAN HERALD.

Receipts are not sent, the receipt of the paper by a subscriber is a sufficient proof that his remittance has been received. If the paper does not arrive promptly, please advise us, that we may see if the address is correctly entered.

Change of Address. Name of Post Office and State, of both old and new address, should always be given in case of removal.

CURRENT EVENTS.

The Long Expected Bill for the Reduction of Internal Revenue taxes has been submitted by the Democratic majority of the Ways and Means Committee. It is supplementary to the Customs Tariff Reduction bill, the essential features of which were published in these columns last week; both measures combined will, it is claimed by the committee, reduce taxation to the extent of $75,000,000 annually. The bill repeals all the laws taxing tobacco growers and manufacturers of tobacco, except those of cigars, cheroots and cigarettes. The special license for retailers of spirits and malt liquors is also removed. The bill was consolidated with the Tariff bill, and will be so reported to the House.

The Promotion of Commercial Union With Canada is the object of a bill introduced in the House by Mr. Hitt, of Illinois, and referred to the Committee on Foreign Affairs. It provides that when the Dominion Government has declared a desire for commercial union, the President shall appoint three Commissioners to meet those who may be likewise designated to represent the Government of Canada, to prepare a plan for the assimilation of the import duties and internal revenue taxes of the two countries, and an equitable division of receipts in a commercial union.

Open Sessions for the Consideration of Treaties whenever a majority of the Senators are in favor of it, is a new rule adopted by the United States Senate. The immediate purpose is to secure a public consideration of the fisheries treaty with Great Britain, and there seems to be little doubt that this course will be followed. The correspondence which led to the appointment of a joint commission to settle the fisheries troubles, and protocols of the conferences which took place between the Commissioners, have been submitted to the Senate, accompanied by a letter from the Secretary of State. These documents show that an earnest effort was made by the representatives of both sides to reach an agreement which would secure the just rights of all parties. This is also apparent from the despatches received by the Foreign Office in London, from Mr. Chamberlain, during the progress of the negotiations at Washington, and made public last week. Mr. Chamberlain says the satisfactory result of the conference was due in a large degree to the spirit of conciliation manifested by both sides. Mr. Chamberlain has now returned to England.

The Dependent Pension Bill Passed the Senate on March 8. It provides that all persons who served in the military or naval services of the United States during the last war, and who are now, or may hereafter be, suffering from mental or physical disability, not the result of their own vicious habits, which totally incapacitates them for manual labor, and who have no other means of support, be entitled to $12 pension a month. In regard to dependent soldiers' parents, it is provided that they are entitled to pension in case they are without other means of support than their own manual labor or the contributions of others not legally bound for their support. The increase of pension for minor children is fixed at the rate of $5 a month instead of $2, as now provided. The assurance is given that the bill will also pass the House. Whether the President will approve, it is not known. The principal difference between this bill and the one vetoed by the President last year, is that "total disability" is now required, while in the vetoed bill the degree of disability was not definitely limited. It was on this point mainly that the President based his veto.

The Strike of Engineers and Firemen on the Chicago, Burlington and Quincy Railroad still continues. It is stated that the Brotherhood of Locomotive Engineers is prepared to spend a quarter of a million dollars, and stand out for weeks, to win the battle. On the 8th inst. they issued, however, an address to the public that they are willing to place the whole controversy in the hands of three railroad managers, and abide by their decision. It is rumored that the brakemen are also on the verge of a strike, getting discontented because of their fear to run with "green" engineers.

An Outrage on the Frontier Between Texas and Mexico was reported lasr week. The Texan account of the affair is, that a party of Mexican troops, consisting of a lieutenant and three soldiers, crossed the Rio Grande on March 3, in pursuit of a deserter. They caught the man near Eagle Pass, on Texan soil, and were endeavoring to drag him over the frontier when a deputy sheriff interfered, and warned the soldiers to desist, as they were violating international law. The Mexicans drew their pistols, and defied the officer, who, having obtained assistance, endeavored to arrest them. In the conflict that ensued, one of the Mexicans was killed, and the American deputy sheriff severely wounded. The case has been referred to Secretary Bayard for presentation to the Mexican Government.

A Two-fold Bereavement Has Befallen the literary world. Amos Bronson Alcott, one of the exponents of that mystic transcendental philosophy known as the Concord School, died on March 4, and his gifted and more renowned daughter, Louisa May Alcott, died on March 6, within forty-eight hours of each other, in their quiet home at Concord, Mass. Mr. Alcott was born in Wolcott, Conn., November 29, 1799. In early life he took up the profession of teaching, which he continued through life—in the schoolroom, on the lecturers' platform and through his writings, which latter, however, owing to the unpopular philosophy taught in them, were far from successful. His daughter entered upon a different and more congenial field. She was the children's friend *par excellence*, one of the most popular authors of juvenile stories we have had. Her fame rested chiefly on her first successful story, "Little Women," and it was that story which endeared her to so many thousands in this country and Europe alike. "An Old-fashioned Girl" and "Little Men" were nearly equal successes. Though she was the author of nearly a score of other books, her fame will rest chiefly on these three. Miss Alcott was born at Germantown, Pa., on November 29, 1832—the 29th of November was also her father's birthday—and removed with her parents to Boston when two years old, and in Boston and its immediate vicinity she made her home ever after.

Emperor William of Germany is Dead. After an illness of only a few days' duration the aged monarch was called hence at half-past eight on the morning of March 9. On the day previous the Court chaplain administered the last sacrament, and special services were held in many of the Berlin churches, when the edifices were crowded. The congregations joined fervently in the prayers for the Emperor's recovery, and many were so overcome as to give vent to their feelings in sobs. Divine services were also held in the palace. All the members of the Imperial family, the Court dignitaries and the members of the household were present. Hundreds of people stood bareheaded in the rain outside the palace and joined in the prayers offered by Chaplain Koegel. Eye-witnesses of the scenes at the Emperor's death state that during the last few hours of his life he suffered no pain. Half an hour before his death all the members of the family staying at the palace, the Court dignitaries, generals and ministers of State, were summoned to the chamber in which the Emperor lay dying. The Emperor was in a half sitting position on a camp bedstead. All the members of the royal family took places at the bedside. The room was crowded. Prince William stood nearest the Emperor, half bending over the couch. He earnestly watched the face of the dying monarch until he expired.

Frederick William of Prussia, Now King Frederick III. of Prussia and Frederick I. Emperor of Germany, is by no means out of danger, and most people expect the end to be reached before summer. Dr. Mackenzie and the German physicians attending him have issued a bulletin declaring that no divergencies of opinion regarding the nature of their august patient's illness exist. They emphasize that they do not maintain that a dangerous turn in the malady is imminent, and say that the sole responsibility for the conduct and treatment of the case remains, as prior to the recent operation, in the hands of Dr. Mackenzie. On receiving the sad news of the aged Emperor's death, Emperor Frederick III. and Empress Victoria made immediate preparations for leaving San Remo for Berlin.

The Motion for the Appointment of a Royal Commission to ascertain and report upon military measures necessary for the protection of Great Britain, was negatived in the House of Commons on the 8th inst., notwithstanding a strong speech in its favor by Lord Randolph Churchill, who contended that a rigid and vigorous inquiry and radical reforms were imperatively necessary. He could not, he said, vote confidence in the existing system; it was hopelessly bad. To this Mr. Stanhope, Secretary of War, replied that the Government would sanction an inquiry into any definite matter connected with the estimates, but would resist the appointment of a royal commission of a vague, general character.

An Important Letter from John Bright was read at a public meeting on March 7. The letter severely condemned the Gladstone wing of the Liberal party for "shirking discussion" of Mr. Gladstone's Irish policy generally, and his two bills in particular. Mr. Bright said: "They do not try to defend the bills. Nobody familiar with the details of the bills is able or willing to defend them. The Gladstonians prefer to attack the Government, to denounce Mr. Balfour, and to spread abroad extravagant falsehoods about the barbarous manner in which the Crimes act is enforced. They have great sympathy for disloyal Irish leaders, and for priests who forget that their true mission is one of peace, not of violence; but they say nothing in behalf of humbler men imprisoned for offences incited by gentlemen disturbes of the peace. The severity of the punishment inflicted for common offences in England is far beyond the severity of the sentences of the men whose writings and speeches have caused the terrorism, boycotting outrages, and murders that have disgraced Ireland and shocked mankind during the last seven years. Surely, in all modern history there is no instance of humiliation so great as that to which the bulk of the Liberals have been reduced by blindly following a leader who, toward the close of a great career, has committed the grievous error of adopting a policy to which the country will never consent."

The Installation of Dr. Talmage as Chaplain of the famous Thirteenth Regiment took place in the Brooklyn armory on March 7. The new chaplain was duly sworn in by Col. Austen, and took the oath to support the constitution of the State and the United States. The regiment hailed the conclusion of that ceremony by a loud shout, and a resounding blow with the butts of their rifles on the armory floor, which might have been a shock to nerves less strong than those of the new chaplain. His coolness aroused a fresh outburst of cheering. Dr. Talmage in a few graceful words thanked the regiment for its reception of him, and said he had accepted the office because it opened a new field of usefulness.

A Clergyman's Sudden Death at a Prayer-meeting is reported from Detroit, Mich. The First Presbyterian Church being without a pastor invited the Rev. Charles N. Waldron, D. D., to conduct the prayer-meeting on March 2. He had scarcely entered the room when he complained of feeling faint, and sat down in a chair. Friends came to his assistance, but he at once became insensible and died in less than two minutes. Dr. Waldron was a retired clergyman. His home was originally at Cohoes, N. Y., where he served as pastor of the Reformed Dutch Church of that city for thirty years. Dr. Waldron removed to Detroit in 1882, many members of his family having drifted westward. He was held in high esteem in the city, where he was in almost constant demand to supply pulpits, owing to his superior intellectual and oratorical gifts. He leaves a widow and three sons. He was in his sixty-sixth year.

A Remarkable Historical Sermon was preached on March 4, by Rev. C. E. Dunn, pastor of the oldest Presbyterian church in America. The church stands at Hempstead, Long Island, and its history runs back to the year 1644. It is not to be supposed, Mr. Dunn said, in tracing this wonderful record, that the church building, erected over two centuries ago, is standing to-day. That building was seized during the Revolutionary War by British soldiers, who converted it into a stable for a time, and it was afterward destroyed by fire. But the church organization, it is claimed, never died, and has existed until this day. The church was organized by the Rev. Richard Denton, and its members were a part of his old English congregation who followed him to America and settled in the peaceful Long Island hamlet. Mr. Denton remained at Hempstead and served the church there until 1659, when he returned to England. The building subsequently passed into the hands of the Congregationalists, and then of the Episcopalians, who had the support of the British Governor, but the Presbyterians built a smaller edifice near at hand, and of that site they have kept possession ever since, rebuilding and enlarging as occasion required.

Diamonds from the Skies were Exhibited in Philadelphia, on March 2, at a meeting of the Academy of Natural Sciences. Professor Lewis, who lectured that evening, produced a fragment of a meteorite containing diamonds, which fell in Siberia last October. He had extracted from the specimen two minute oval bodies, transparent, with traces of polarization, and having a high index of refraction. Having been able to scratch a sapphire with portions of the meteorite, he had come to the conclusion that it contained microscopic diamonds; and two Russian professors, who had examined it, agreed with him. The important bearing of this discovery upon the question of the origin of the diamond was dwelt upon, and attention was called to the similarity existing between the composition of meteorites and the diamond-bearing rock of South Africa. The facts and the theories founded upon them may be as important as the Professor thinks, but it will be by scientists rather than the general public that the importance will be perceived. The attention of the latter is too much absorbed by worldly affairs to think much of the bodies which come from the skies, and when their attention can be diverted in that direction, it is far more important that it be directed to another celestial visitant, whose value infinitely transcends diamonds — the Bread which came down from Heaven, whereof if a man eat he shall live forever. (John 6 : 51.)

The Value of an Arm Was the Subject of a dispute which came before the Supreme Court of New York for decision last week. A man had sued the Delaware, Lackawanna and Western Railroad in the Court below for the loss of one of his arms, and had gained a verdict for twenty-five thousand dollars. The Railroad Company contended that the amount was excessive, and appealed to the Supreme Court, but the appeal was dismissed. The judge, in handing down the judgment of the court, said: "There are other elements which enter into compensation for the destruction of an arm than pain and suffering and loss of power to earn money. Among them are the great deprivation of the capacity which follows to do many things essential to the common comforts of life, and the inexpressible sense of the want of that member. If the test were what any human being in full health would take for an arm, the sum named would be considered absurd." Unhappily the same test does not apply to the soul, which is of infinitely greater value than a limb. Multitudes of men are sacrificing their souls for money. (Matt. 16 : 26.)

Steel Filings Coated With Gold Were Sent to the Mint recently by some unsuspecting dealer. The officials at the Mint received a package by express from Little Rock, Ark., purported to be grains of gold. The size of the package, however, compared with its weight, convinced them that there was deception there in some form. The general appearance of the grains was much like that of the metal daily received, and they also bore successfully the acid test. Subsequently, a careful analysis was made to ascertain what the article really was and of what it was composed. The result was astonishing, revealing an ingenious device for the deception of parties dealing in gold bullion. The grains were found to be nothing more nor less than steel filings; and to give them the appearance of grains of the precious metal, they were covered with fine gold, which was made to adhere by the use of a composition of turpentine. The Church and the world are often similarly imposed upon. Men and women, who are really base metal, are often able to pick up a coating of cant phrases and wear a sanctimonious appearance, which is sufficient to deceive society and the Church. Though the deception may succeed here, and for a time, ultimate detection is inevitable. (Ezek. 33 : 31.)

An Astonished Captain and Crew Had a Narrow escape from death on March 7. They were on board a schooner, loaded with bricks, which was lying at the foot of West One Hundred and Twenty-ninth Street, New York. The schooner arrived the night previous, and made fast to the slip. There appeared to be no need for watching, as the vessel was safely at the end of her voyage, so the captain went to sleep in his cabin, and the crew also turned into their bunks below. Early in the morning a large ice floe came rapidly down the North River, borne by the receding tide toward the sea. As it was carried past the slip where the schooner lay, it received a swirling motion from the eddying water, and a sharp point projecting from it was driven into the schooner's side with mighty force. The ice floe passed on, leaving the schooner with a great hole in her timbers, through which the water was pouring. The vessel began to sink quickly, and as there was no one watching, no alarm was given to the sleeping captain and crew. They were, however, awakened by the shock and the deluge of water, and rushed on deck in their night-clothes. They managed to scramble on the slip, and so escaped with their lives, but they lost their clothing and all belonging to them on board. There are many Christians in a similar state of false security who are neglecting the Master's injunction to watch. A day of awakening is now near at hand, in which they will lament that they were found sleeping. (Mark 13 : 35, 36.)

A New York Belle's Disappointment was Described last week to a reporter by the baggage-master at the Central Depot. He said that one evening recently two trunks were checked by two young women. One trunk, a large Saratoga, belonged to the daughter of a millionaire, who was travelling to Washington. The other was a big, queer looking sea-chest, which was checked by a stout, healthy, immigrant girl from Sweden. In some inexplicable way, the checks were reversed and the trunks missent. The young lady, who had invitations to balls and dinner-parties, could not attend them, as she had nothing to wear but her travelling costume or the coarse woollen dresses and petticoats contained in the immigrant girl's trunk, while the immigrant girl, who had gone to Kansas, was mourning the loss of useful garments, for which the flimsy dresses and finery of the city belle were a poor substitute. It took three weeks to get the error rectified, and during that time both girls were much inconvenienced by the change inadvertently made. It may be hoped that at the end of the journey of life no such disappointment may await either of them. Then both will need the same garment—the robe of Christ's righteousness, which is offered alike to rich and poor, and without which there is no admission to eternal mansions. (Matt. 24 ; 11-13.)

BRIEF NOTES.

The Rev. George F. Pentecost, D. D., has been holding evangelistic meetings in Norwich, Conn., under the auspices of twelve churches of different denominations.

Dr. L. W. Munhall is announced to commence services in Macon, Ga., on March 14 (yesterday). He has accepted a united invitation from the churches of St. Paul, Minn., to visit that city at an early date.

Gen. Neal Dow, who ran as candidate for Mayor of Portland, Me., his own city, was defeated on March 5 by a Mr. Chapman, who had nearly 1,600 majority over Dow. The opposition to Dow is said to have been personal rather than political.

Rev. E. Payson Hammond's meetings for children, at Sacramento, Cal., have had good results; they were held in the Old Pavilion, and were very largely attended, the ministers of the various churches co-operating. A large number of children professed faith in Christ.

The great convention of Christian Endeavor societies, to be held in Chicago, in July, is already occupying the attention of the various committees. Arrangements have been made with the hotels for the reception of delegates at reduced rates, and appeals made to the trunk lines of railroad for special fares.

A bill passed by the House in the Ohio Legislature takes from the city councils the right to permit saloons to remain open on Sundays. By the provisions of the bill, all saloons throughout the State must be kept closed on Sunday. Democratic journals say that the Republican support given to this bill places Ohio among the doubtful States.

Evangelistic services are being held at Providence, R. I., by the Rev. B. Fay Mills. Two meetings are held each day, that in the afternoon in the First Baptist Church, and that in the evening in the Music Hall. Mr. Mills has held conferences with the Sunday-school teachers of the city, and on March 4 a gigantic mass meeting of the scholars, which has led to blessed results.

The first book ever printed in the Nbungoni dialect has been produced by Dr. Elmslie, the American missionary who has been stationed for some time among the Zulus, west of Lake Nyassa. The book was issued from the press of a neighboring mission station called Blantyre. It contains the decalogue, passages from the Psalms, Proverbs and the Gospels, with fourteen hymns.

Major Whittle's work in Iowa is being attended with great blessing in each of the cities he visits. In Cedar Rapids, Burlington and Sioux City the movement has astonished the citizens, who have never witnessed anything like it before. The Christian Convention held by Messrs. Moody and Sankey, at Burlington, gave an impetus to the work, which promises to render it a permanent missionary organization.

Mr. and Mrs. Willson have been assisting Dr. L. W. Munhall in his meetings at Buffalo, N. Y., during the absence of Prof. and Mrs. Towner. The wonderful success of the meetings has led the united churches to continue them after the conclusion of the four weeks for which arrangements had been made. One of the most important features of the services is the large number of youths who attend and have asked for prayers. They came in response to tickets of invitation sent to the houses of business.

JOB AMONG THE ASHES.

A New Sermon by Pastor C. H. Spurgeon.

"I have heard of Thee by the hearing of the ear: but now mine eye seeth Thee. Wherefore I abhor myself, and repent in dust and ashes." Job. 42 : 5, 6.

God's Revelation to Job—Inspires him with Awe—Yet Attracts him to God—I. Vivid Impressions of God Vouchsafed—Connected with Affliction—Prosperity a Painted Window—A Special Manifestation Necessary—II. Humility Produced—Christ the Standard of Righteousness—Sin an Impertinence—Pride and Culture Disappearing in God's Presence—III. Repentance Developed—What Job Had to Repent of—Despair—Impatience of Life—His Repentance a Sign and Precursor of his Deliverance.

JEHOVAH had spoken, Job had trembled. The Lord had revealed Himself, Job had seen Him. Truly, God did but display the skirts of His robe and unveil a part of His ways; but therein there was so much of ineffable glory, that Job laid his hand upon his mouth in token of his silent consent to the claims of the Everlasting One. God spoke to Job out of the whirlwind, concerning the greatness of His power, the wonders of His workings, the splendor of His skill, the infinity of His wisdom. Read the divine address, that you may see how Jehovah caused the afflicted patriarch to feel Him near.

In the confession which now lies before us, Job acknowledges God's boundless power; for he exclaims, "I know that Thou canst do everything, and that no thought can be withholden from Thee." He felt that whatever the Lord chose to think or desire, He could at once accomplish. Job had

A Glimpse of Omnipotence

of which the height and depth no mind can ever measure. Job sees his own folly. He speaks like a man in a maze or a muse, and he says, "Who is he that hideth counsel without knowledge?" Look at the second verse of chapter thirty-eight, and you will see that he is quoting what God had said to him. The Lord's words are ringing in his ears, and in his anguish he repeats them, accepting them as justly applicable to himself. It is not far from being right with us, when the words of God can fitly become our words. "The Lord answered Job out of the whirlwind, and said, Who is this that darkeneth counsel by words without knowledge?" And now Job replies, "I am that foolish one: I uttered that I understood not; things too wonderful for me, which I knew not." Many a holy prophet has done this, for inspired men are described as those who "enquired and searched diligently; searching what, or what manner of time the Spirit which was in them did signify, when it testified beforehand the sufferings of Christ, and the glory that should follow." It is not the thoughts of the prophet which have been inspired of God so much as their words; for frequently they were moved to speak prophecies which were quite beyond their own understanding. Hence I assert that there is a

Verbal Inspiration, or No Inspiration

at all worthy of the name. Job, as he comes before us in the text, is impressed with his own folly. He had to a large degree spoken what he felt sure was true, but he now feels that he did not understand what he said; and he at the same time tacitly confesses that he may have said in his bitterness many an unwise and unseemly thing, and therefore he bows his head before the Lord his God, and confesses that he has darkened counsel by words without knowledge, and uttered things that he understood not.

Notwithstanding, the man of God proceeds to draw near unto the Lord, before whom he bows himself. Foolish as he confesses himself to be, he does not therefore fly from the supreme wisdom. This was brave and wise action. Whatever Job might be or might not be, he was a firm believer in his God, and in every word which the Lord was pleased to speak. Let us do as Job did, and make our approach unto the Lord in childlike confidence even when He seems to frown. Let us get where Job was when he said, "Though He slay me, yet will I trust in Him." When we bow lowest before His throne, let not our humble bending have anything of distance in it. Lowlier before Thee, O Lord, would we be; but at the same time our cry is, "Nearer to Thee." Thus we come to the text, having used the connection as a step to its door.

I. First, then, we have sometimes very

Vivid Impressions of God.

Job had long before *heard* of God, and that is a great matter. He had been a reverent believer in the teachings of God, and an obedient servant to His commands; thus he had really heard God. The man who can say this can say a great deal. If God has ever been on speaking terms with you, you have much cause for gratitude. It is clear that you are not dead in sin, or if you were so when the Lord spoke to you, you are now alive; for His voice causes the dead to live. Job had heard God, but now he has more apprehension of Him. Of course, Job could not literally see God, he does not mean to assert that he did; for "no man hath seen God at any time;" but Job means that he now had a view of God very much more clear than any which he had obtained before; in fact, as much clearer as eyesight is more clear than hearing.

Notice, that in order to this close vision of God affliction had overtaken him. It was not till after he had scraped himself with the potsherd, nor till *his friends had scraped him with something worse than the potsherds*, that Job could say, "Mine eye seeth Thee." Not till every camel and every sheep had been stolen, and every child was dead, could the afflicted patriarch cry, "*Now* mine eye seeth *Thee*." Happy is that man who in prosperity can hear the voice of God in the tinkling of the sheep-bells of his abundant flocks, can hear Him in the lowing of the oxen which cover his fields, and in the loving voices of dear children around him. But

Prosperity is a Painted Window

which shuts out much of the clear light of God, and only when the blue and the crimson, and the golden tinge are removed, is the glass restored to its full transparency. Adversity thus takes away tinge and color and dimness, and we see our God far better than before, if our eyes are prepared for the light. The Lord had taken everything away from Job, and this paved the way to his giving Him more of himself. In the absence of other goods the good God is the better seen. In prosperity God is *heard*, and that is a blessing; but in adversity God is *seen*, and that is a greater blessing. Sanctified adversity quickens our spiritual sensitiveness.

Possibly, also, helpful to this was Job's desertion by his friends. Job's three friends! Ah me, I know their kindred! They were most devotedly attached to him, no doubt; and how warmly they proved it! They had met together with him, and said soft and sweet things to him in those days when he moved like a prince among the nobles of his people, and every eye that saw him blessed him. But when they found him sitting "down among the ashes," they had altered thoughts of him. They suspected him; and though they knew nothing against him, yet they perceived that he was not in the same honor as before. Between a prince in ermine and the same man in sackcloth there is, to some minds, a great difference.

Before Job could see the Lord, there was a special manifestation on God's part to him. "Then the Lord answered Job out of the whirlwind." God must really come and in a gracious way make a display of Himself to His servants, or else they will not see Him. Your afflictions will not of themselves reveal God to you. If the Lord Himself does not unveil His face, your sorrow may even blind and harden you, and make you rebellious. There must be a special revealing of the Lord to our own souls before we shall get such a clear apprehension of Him as Job intended by the words, "Now mine eyes seeth Thee." Read through the thirty-eighth chapter, and see how Jehovah declares His wisdom and His power: "Where wast thou when I laid the foundations of the earth? declare, if thou hast understanding. Who hath laid the measures thereof, if thou knowest? or who hath stretched the line upon it? Hast thou entered into the treasures of the snow? or hast thou seen the treasures of the hail? Canst thou bind the sweet influences of Pleiades, or loose the bands of Orion?" Here was a marvellous field for thought. The Lord speaks in nature, and it is done. His glory is seen in heaven and earth, in the sea and all deep places.

I need not tarry to say to you that all through that wonderful address of the Lord to His servant, He is saying, in so many words, "I am God; but who art thou?" The Lord is proving that nothing is impossible to His power and His wisdom. He had, after all, not allowed His servant to sink out of His reach. He was always able to rescue him. You learn here, also, that God is not amenable to our judgment. He giveth no account of His matters. He makes Job feel that He is God, and then there is an end to the matter. No apology is made to Job, and no explanation is given him; he must bow in unreserved submission, and surrender unconditionally; and he does so. Thus far he worshipped; but he must yet go further, until he cries, "I abhor myself, and repent in dust and ashes."

II. We have now reached our second point—when we have these apprehensions we have

Lowlier Views of Ourselves.

Why are the wicked so proud? It is because they forget God. Why did Pharaoh dare to say, "Who is the Lord, that I should obey His voice? It was because he did not know Jehovah: but after those ten plagues, he altered his tone, and cried out, "Intreat the Lord for it is enough." Even his great pride was forced to bow before Jehovah when judgments were let loose upon him. If men knew God, how it would change their thoughts and talk! If they could have even an indistinct idea "by the hearing of the ear," many of them would never be so irreverent as they now are, nor so lofty in their ideas of their own wisdom; but if they could "see" Him as Job did, and behold His inexpressible glory, they would become meek and lowly.

If you would know what God is, He sets Himself before us in the person of His dear Son. In every respect in which we fall short of the perfect character of Jesus, in that respect we sin. There is no better description of sin that I know of than this: "Sin is any want of conformity to the law of God," and God's law is the transcript of His own mind. Wherein in any moral or spiritual respect, we fall short of the divine character, we to that extent fall into sin. Permit me to suggest to each one here who has a high idea of himself, and has no sense of self-abhorrence, that such self-honor must arise from ignorance of God: for there is such an immeasurable distance between the perfection of God and our faultiness that our true position is that of

Penitent Humility.

Note, next, the impertinence of sin. How dare we trangress against God? O man, who art thou that rebellest against God? How darest thou to do to His face that which He forbids thee? How darest thou to leave undone in His very presence that which thy Lord commands thee to do? This makes sin a piece of presumption, a daring and glaring provocation of the Lord God. Although some of us can hold our heads high among our fellow-men, and we can say, "I am neither a drunkard, nor a thief, nor a liar, neither have I offended against the laws of integrity and charity," yet when we come before God, we perceive that we have not dealt towards Him as we ought to have done. To Him we have been thieves, robbing Him of His glory. "Will a man rob God?" To Him we have been liars: we have dealt treacherously, and we have broken our promises. To Him we have been ingrates, to Him we have been worse than brutes. Instead of equity, we have dealt towards God iniquity. Instead of love, we have dealt out enmity. Oh, when we think of this, we can understand why Job says, "Now mine eye seeth thee. Wherefore I abhor myself."

Once more, when God is seen with admiration, then of necessity we are filled with self-loathing. The more you appreciate God, the more you will depreciate yourself. While the thought of God rises higher and higher and higher, you also will sink lower and lower in your own esteem. The word used by Job, "I abhor myself," is a strong one. Do you know

What Self-Loathing Means?

Some of you do, I know. And I am sure that in proportion as you truly love, reverence and worship God, in that proportion you are full of abhorrence of self. You fine gentlemen, who often hold your heads so high that you can scarcely get through common door-ways, you know nothing of this! You high and mighty ladies, who cannot condescend to associate with any who are not of your superior rank; and you purse-proud men, who expect all to worship the golden calf which you have set up—you know nothing about this. O you wonderfully wise men, you intellectual persons, who so modestly dub yourselves "thoughtful and cultured," you snuff out a poor evangelical believer as if he were an idiot; may the Lord give you an hour of Job's "I abhor myself," and then you will be bearable; but as you now are, you are a trial!

III. Thirdly, I have to show you that such a sight fills the heart with

True Repentance.

Job says, "I abhor myself, and repent in dust and ashes." The word "myself" has been added by the translators; and they could hardly have done otherwise. Job's expression, however, refers to all that had come out of himself, or had lurked within himself. He abhorred all that he had been doing and saying. He says, "I abhor, and repent in dust and ashes." What did he repent of? I think Job repented, first, of that tremendous curse which he had pronounced upon the day of his birth. It was terrific. See third chapter. Next, Job heartily repented of his desire to die. In the sixth chapter he expresses it as he did several times: he says, "Oh that I might have my request; and that God would grant me the thing that I long for! Even that it would please God to destroy me; that He would let loose His hand, and cut me off! Do you wonder that he said this? Was ever man so tried? I do not wonder at all, even at his cursing the day of his birth, considering all the bodily pain and mental irritation he was enduring at the time.

I do not doubt but what Job repented of *his despair*. The ninth and tenth chapters, and many other passages wherein Job speaks, are tinged with hopelessness. He felt as if God had left him a prey to the enemy; but this was not true. The Lord has never deserted any one of His people. There is not on record, in all the history of the ages, a case in which God has failed them that trust Him. Has He not said, "I will never leave thee, nor forsake thee"? and He never has left nor forsaken any believer; yet Job evidently thought that He had done so, and he was greatly troubled.

His critics goaded him by cruelly charging him with hypocrisy and wickedness, and Job vindicated himself with great earnestness, appealing to God, and saying, "Thou knowest that I am not wicked." This was true. He could plead his innocence in the common courts of men, and there he could well enough defend himself; but when the matter came into the King's own court, he could not answer in the same strain, but felt compelled to plead guilty. Job has to retract all his pleadings and challenges. If the case is to be heard as

"Jehovah versus Job,"

then Job yields the point unreservedly. Job had also to confess that his statements had been a darkening of wisdom by words without knowledge. Sometimes we say, "I perfectly understand *that*; I could clear up that mystery." We define this and define that to our brethren; but when we get into the presence of God, we find that our definitions are the proofs of our ignorance. While we see not God, we fancy that we can read all the riddles of His word; but when we behold Him more nearly, we say with David, "So foolish was I, and ignorant: I was as a beast before thee." In the presence of God Job bowed his head and repented of all his suspicions and mistrusts; and this is what we must do if, in the day of our sorrow, we have been petulant and unbelieving.

Let me pass on. According to our text, repentance puts man into the lowest place. He says, "I repent in dust and ashes." "Dust and ashes"—that signifies the dust-heap, or what in Scotland they call the "midden." Job had made dust and ashes his headquarters. Repentance puts us in a lowly seat. You have heard sometimes, I dare say, among the beautiful nothings of the modern school, the mention of "the dignity of human nature." Behold a throne for the "dignity of human nature." Yonder dust and ashes are for this proud royalty. The dust-heap is for human nature in its glory, when it has on its richest robes. I say that when man wears *his*

Best Sunday Righteousness,

he is even then only fit for the midden; and every man of God that has been brought to true repentance, owns that it is so.

Next, note that all real repentance is joined with holy sorrow and self-loathing. I have read in the sermons of certain teachers that "Repentance is only a change of mind." That may be true; but what a change of mind it is! It is not such a change of mind as some of you underwent this morning when you said, "It is really too cold to go out," but afterwards you braved the snow, and came to the Tabernacle. Oh, no! repentance is a thorough and radical change of mind, and it is accompanied with real sorrow for sin and self-loathing. A repentance in which there is no sorrow for sin will ruin the soul. If thou canst look upon sin without sorrow, then thou hast never looked on Christ. A faith-look at Jesus breaks the heart, both for sin and from sin. Try thyself by this test.

But, next, repentance has comfort in it. It is to my mind rather extraordinary, that the Hebrew word, which is justly translated "repent," is also used in two or three places at least in the Old Testament to express comfort. Isaac, it is said, took Rebekah to his mother's tent, and was "*comforted* after his mother's death." Here the word is the same as that which is here rendered "repent." Isaac's mind was changed as to the death of his mother. As, then, there is in the Hebrew word just a tinge of comfort, so in repentance itself, with all its sorrow, there are traces of joy. Repentance is a bitter-sweet or a sweet-bitter.

The door of repentance opens into the halls of joy. Job's repentance in dust and ashes was

The Sign of His Deliverance.

God turned His wrath upon the three critics, but justified Job, and gave him the honorable office of intercessor on their behalf. Then "The Lord turned the captivity of Job when he prayed for his friends." "The Lord blessed the latter end of Job more than the beginning," and the turning-point was that sitting down in the dust and ashes. When you are brought as low as you can be, the next turn must be upward. Down with you, then! Off with the feathers of your pride, and the finery of your self-righteousness! Down with you among the useless and worthless things! From that point you will ascend. The more crushed, humbled, exhausted, and near death you are, the more prepared you are for God to raise you up.

Job was an unrivalled saint; none of us can compare with him; and if that perfect and upright man had to say, "I abhor myself," what will you and I say when we see God? We shall by and by behold Him on the judgment-seat; how shall we endure it? If you have no righteousness but your own, you will stand naked to your shame in the day when the Lord appeareth. You self-righteous men, dare you go before God in your own righteousness? If you dare, I marvel at your presumption. Job dared not. He could stand up boldly before his accusers, but when before God he was in another attitude. When it comes to dying and appearing before the Most High, you that have no righteousness but one of your own spinning, what will you do?

What shall you and I do? Brethren, we are not afraid; for there is a righteousness of God which is given to us by faith through Jesus Christ. God Himself cannot find any fault with His own righteousness; and if He gives me His own righteousness, even the righteousness of God which is by faith in Jesus Christ, which is to all and upon all them that believe, then I may hope to sit at last, not on the midden, but on the throne, rejoicing to find myself in Christ Jesus, crowned with a crown which I shall delight to cast at His feet.

GEMS FROM NEW BOOKS.

A DERANGED WOMAN'S MEMORY.*

"During the year, Mrs. Payne, an aged, afflicted woman, died. Her mind was somewhat deranged by a succession of heavy afflictions, yet she always evinced astonishing clearness and correctness in all religious truth. On asking her one day, 'Do you know Mr. R.? Mr. S.? Do you know me?' she said, 'No.' 'Do you know Jesus Christ?' 'I guess I do! I guess I do; I love Him! I ought to know Him! He died for a poor, guilty sinner like me.' She then gave vent to her feelings in cries, prayers and tears. Never was she bewildered about Christ and His salvation. Her affliction was of long duration, but her end was calm and peaceful as a summer evening."

Close of a Useful Life.

One of the last to die in the old hospital at Cincinnati, was the faithful nurse, Miss Van Alstin, who had watched over the sick nearly three years, and was so deeply interested that she left her earnings for the benefit of the Institution. Often she expressed fear of death, and at times doubted whether she was a child of God. One day our conversation took this turn: "Do you think a Christian should fear death?" "By no means; for to die is gain." "I've always had a dread of death." "So have many Christians; but when the last enemy comes, Jesus is with them, and they die in peace." "I've done so little in my life to glorify God!" "Are there not some things which give you pleasure?" "Yes; when I taught a class in a Sabbath-school in New York, that was one of the happiest parts of my life. Then, when I came to Ohio, and was in the nursery of the Orphan Asylum, the little children would come to me and say, 'You're my mother now; pray with me.' And I did, and God blessed me there. And the rest of my life has been spent among the sick and dying. Many a time at midnight I've kneeled by them and prayed."

The last months of her life were spent on a sick bed; she died of consumption. When near death, she wrote with a pencil these four lines, from a hymn which had been a great comfort to her in her illness:

"Jesus can make a dying bed
Feel soft as downy pillows are,
While on His breast I lean my head,
And breathe my life out sweetly there."

Her end was peace. She died happy in the Lord.

This slip of paper the dying nurse sent to another lady, dying of consumption in the next room. Thus one dear friend cheered the other, in view of crossing that mysterious stream we sometimes call the river of death. "I can trust Christ Jesus for time and eternity," was the expression of the last patient when dying.

Death of a Prodigal.

In 1854, William B., son of a minister of the gospel in South Carolina, was sick here many months, and died a sad death. He had been a profligate man, and though often urged to repent, kept on in his sins. He would say, "Ah! you may talk; when anybody's been as wicked as I have all their life, 'tain't so easy to repent."

---

* From "Thirty-five Years Among the Poor and the Public Institutions of Cincinnati." A deeply interesting volume of reminiscences, by the Rev. Joseph Emery, City Missionary. Pp. 350. Published by the author, *Joseph Emery*, 10 Pine Street, Cincinnati, O.

The Late Mr. W. W. Corcoran.

A Pianoforte Recital by the Boy Prodigy, Josef Hofmann.

He often deplored the life he had led, saying, "Ah, well! it's no use, it can't be helped, too late now!" His last words were, "Dark! all is dark; no hope! Too late! It's too late now!" Thus he died.

A Dying Soldier's Conversion.

On a Sabbath afternoon in April, 1862, Father Wright, of the Methodist Church, and four ladies accompanied me. By request of the soldiers, we sang the well-known hymn, "There is a fountain filled with blood," etc. Several men shed tears, and one man from Illinois wept aloud. On asking the cause, he said, "I'm the wickedest man in the army. I've broken every commandment except murder. Oh, what shall I do? The doctors have given me up. They say I can never get well."

We repeated to him the blessed invitations of the gospel, and reminded him that the "Blood of Jesus Christ, His Son, cleanseth us from all sin;" that He is able to save to the uttermost. "Though your sins be as scarlet, they shall be as white as snow; though they be red like crimson, they shall be as wool." He said, "I am too wicked a man to be saved." Father Wright spoke tenderly, and urged him to call upon Jesus, as did the dying thief, and he would be saved. We then sang:

"Just as I am, without one plea!
But that Thy blood was shed for me!"

The struggle continued, and the weeping. Then I said, "Will you now call on Jesus to save you?" He said, "I will, and he did. Most of that night he continued praying, and found peace in believing. He lived some two weeks longer, and died in peace, saved through the blood of the Lamb. He was shot through the thigh, and suffered great pain, but bore it all with resignation, after he had found peace. Many other soldiers were deeply affected by this service, and gave us the assurance that they would live better lives.

THE LATE MR. CORCORAN.

(See Portrait.)

THE venerable philanthropist and art patron, who died in Washington D. C. on February 24 had attained the advanced age of eighty-nine years, having been born at Georgetown, D. C. December 27, 1798. Mr. Corcoran spent his whole life in the District of Columbia, where his father settled shortly after the Revolutionary War, and became Mayor of the town. Young William was educated at the public school and college of Georgetown, and engaged in trade. In 1840 he formed a partnership in Washington with Mr. G. W. Riggs in the banking business. Henceforward his prosperity was continuous.

His financial services to the Government at the time of the Mexican War, when all other financiers avoided the loans, called out the thanks of Daniel Webester, then Secretary of State. He made a prodigious fortune, and during the latter years of his life devoted his time to the management of it and to its disposition in such ways as the owner believed would be a benefit to the public. No visitor to the national capital has failed to visit the Corcoran Art Gallery, at Pennsylvania Avenue and Seventeenth Street, over the door of which is the simple inscription "Dedicated to Art." This is a fine building filled with rich treasures of vast artistic and money value, which cost $350,000, and has on it an endowment of *two million dollars*, the gift of the munificent banker to the nation. The erection of the Gallery was begun in 1857.

Another and most touching expression of Mr. Corcoran's philanthropy, was the founding of the Louise Home for the sustenance of aged women left without means. The Home is named after Mr. Corcoran's only child, Louise, long since dead, whose memory he tenderly cherished.

Another instance of Mr. Corcoran's public spirit and liberality was his providing for the re-interment of the author of "Home, Sweet Home" and the erection of a monument over his grave.

It is stated with authority that Mr. Corcoran's gifts during his lifetime, which can be traced over and above the benefactions, which he succeeded in concealing, as he tried to conceal them all, amounted to over seven and a half millions, of which six millions were distributed ir sums of over $5,000 each.

JOSEF HOFMANN.

(See Illustration.)

THE precocious little genius for whose protection the Society for the Prevention of Cruelty to Children has interposed, is but a little over ten years of age, yet has kept large and critical audiencesin a state of delighted attention by his performances on the piano-forte. He is a native of Poland, having been born at Warsaw, June 20, 1877, but first attracted public notice in Germany, where critics of superior ability were electrified by his recitals. In the summer of last year his father took him to London, where he gave a series of concerts to large audiences, There Mr. Abbey, the New York manager, saw and heard him, and made a contract with his father for an Americen tour.

The boy was to give eighty-one performances in the United States, for which Mr. Abbey agreed to pay him $1,250 a week, the series to run from December, 1887, to April, 1888. The young prodigy gave fifty-three concerts, and was then withdrawn from the stage at the request of Mr. Elbridge Gerry; physicians examined the boy, and representations were made to his father as to the effect of the excitement and the laudation bestowed upon one so young. The result was that Mr. Hofmann cancelled the engagement for the remaining concerts, and has decided to keep his son away from the piano, even as an amusement, for several years. It is stated that the cerebral irritation, induced by the succession of concerts, threatened his reason, if not his life. The withdrawal is, of course, a disappointment to the public, as the reports of the earlier concerts were of so surprising a nature as to excite curiosity and a general desire to hear so precocious a performer.

THE MINISTER'S PRODIGAL SON.

(See Illustration on page 173.)

SOME years ago the Rev. Edward Darlington was in charge of one of the two churches in a small Long Island village. He and his good wife led a quiet, retired life in the comfortably furnished parsonage; and it would have been a happy life, too, if it had not been for Paul, their only child. Paul, though trained from infancy, by word and example, in the ways of meekness and obedience, showed at times a temper which spurned control. He had come to reflect—and the oftener his thoughts ran that way, the more the idea took hold on his boyish fancy—that he was only the son of a poor village parson, while his playmates were New York gentlemen's sons, who lived with their parents in handsome villas in the summer, and during the fall and winter in stately houses in the city. They wore fine clothes and had plenty of pocket-money, while he, the "parson's son," had scarcely ever any pocket-money; and as for clothes—his jackets were usually threadbare and his trousers garnished with patches.

Paul was a long way from being contented with his condition and his station in life. He dreamed of fame and riches; and though he was only fifteen years old, and knew very little, indeed, of the ways of the great world beyond the boundaries of his rural home and the precincts of the village academy, he fancied he could, unaided and alone, make his way successfully through life.

"The world owes everyone a living, and it will yield it to the brave," he said to himself. "I want to get away from this quiet country place. I am old enough to look out for myself, and when I return I'll be a rich man, perhaps a famous man—who knows?"

These thoughts filled Paul's mind more and more, until he resolved to make the experiment of facing the world alone. His preparations were necessarily few, and they were soon completed. The last evening came. Paul retired to his room earlier than usual that night. The hour was, however, far advanced before he laid down to sleep. He was remarkably taciturn at breakfast next morning, and his eyes wore a distracted, far-off expression. He lowered them whenever his father or his mother looked at him. He went out guiltily, giving his parents no intimation of his intention.

It was twelve years before anything more was heard of him, though his parents spent more time and money than they could afford in trying to trace him. The boy went West. Sometimes fortune smiled upon him and made him happy and hopeful; sometimes she went by on the other side, and he sighed for the peace and comfort of home. Sometimes he dined on plenty; sometimes the dinner-table was a stranger. Sometimes his raiment was of rich material, and he had showy jewelry, rings and breastpins; at other times he had to go ragged. The world was a great deal larger, a great deal colder, and a great deal less inclined to encourage the wild dreams of youth than he had ever imagined. Years of experience robbed him of the arrogance of youth, and taught him the truth that the four-leafed shamrock of fortune grows no more luxuriantly abroad than at home, and the glitter of gold is just as bright, when seen by one's own hearthstone.

The Prodigal Son's Interview With the Lawyer.

Wearying at last of the struggle in which he made no permanent advance but only lost one month what he had gained in the month before, Paul resolved to go home. He had been sick, and as he lay helpless and neglected in a strange boarding-house, where the hired girl came into his room once or twice a day to ask if he wanted anything, and always forgot to bring him the things he asked for, he thought longingly of his mother and his home. Fever consumed him, but no water was brought to him, and no one seemed to care whether he lived or died. Yes; like the Prodigal, he came to himself, and would go home. He hoped to have returned in wealth and style, but he did not mind that now; he would go in his rags. As soon as he was well enough he set out, and he arrived at the old village just twelve years after leaving it.

He made his way to the parsonage, but to his surprise and dismay it was untenanted. Were his father and mother dead? The thought startled and thrilled him; he had never thought of such a possibility. After a few minutes of anxious deliberation he resolved to seek out the village lawyer, who was his father's friend, and learn from him where his father and mother were. It was with some trepidation that he knocked at the lawyer's door, but he was not disappointed there. The lawyer was in and would see him presently—he was engaged just then. In a short time Paul heard the lawyer conducting his client into the house place from his office and then calling to his clerk to bring Paul in.

The lawyer looked at him searchingly through his spectacles, but evidently did not know him, and apparently did not like him, for he did not invite him to be seated. "Do you know—can you tell me—" Paul began—"I have come to find Mr. Darlington, the minister." His gaze wandered around the room, taking in the familiar objects, the iron safe, the legal almanac, the row of law-books, and all the furniture he knew so well when as a boy he had sat there while his father talked with the lawyer. But what was this? On a chair close to him was a hat, and, resting against it, a walking stick that Paul knew to be his father's.

"Mr. Darlington is not living here now," said the lawyer, but he is here on business this morning. In fact, he is in the house now. Do you wish to see him?

A great load was lifted from Paul's heart. His father was still alive. "Yes," he cried, "let me see him; I am his son."

A few moments more and the lawyer who had hurried away returned, with the minister. The old man could not believe that his long lost son had really returned, but as he scanned the lines of his face conviction came, and holding out his arms like the father in the parable, fell on his neck and kissed him. It was a happy journey to the village where Mr. Darlington now lived, for the old man was looking forward to the joy of restoring the prodigal son to his mother. Words cannot depict the joy of that meeting. Neither of them would listen to the son's self-reproaches. He was restored to them, and that was enough. Their magnanimity touched the heart of the wanderer more than any reproaches could have done, and he was completely broken down. It was not, however, until the next day which was Sunday that he fully realized how great had been his wrong-doing and how terrible his sin, not only against his parents but against God. His father preached from the text: "This my son was dead and is alive again, was lost and is found" (Luke 15:24), and in listening with bowed head to the story of Divine love he saw how shameful and wicked a thing it is to sin against a God so tender and long-suffering, and he sought and found pardon through the Saviour.

MRS. TRANSOME'S PUPIL.

A SERIAL STORY.

(Continued from page 158.)

Going Home.

ON Sunday afternoons, when Transome and I had our half-hour together, we had very little to say to one another. We sat side by side, silent for the most part, and strangers that had seen us would have thought we cared nought for one another. Our lives were so dull, with no change in them, that there was nothing to tell, and Transome could never get his thoughts shaped about in words. All I knew from him was that his ward was just like mine, filled with old men, with all the life gone out of them. He was warmed and clothed and fed as well as the rest, but that was all. There was nothing for us to talk about.

Yet when we had our afternoon out, and went outside the poorhouse walls, then our tongues seemed unloosed. We had got permission to go out on the same day, and Transome was waiting for me in his poorhouse clothes when I went through the great black doors. It was a chilly day in December, but it did not rain when we met, and we scarcely thought of the weather. Transome seemed more himself than he had done for a long, long while; and he crept along brisker, and with a brighter face than usual. We were like two birds that had been caged, and let out into freedom again for a little time, only with broken wings, and a string that would pull us back into the cage again.

The poorhouse was on the same side of the town as our old home, and because we had nowhere else to go to, we turned towards that, though we knew it would be gone, and had no more a place save in our hearts. The north wind blew coldly against us as we toiled up the steep street leading to the brow of the hill; but we scarcely took notice of it. We were together once more, out of the dark shadow of the poorhouse walls.

But when we reached the top of the street, where the dingle used to be, and turned the corner of the last house, to see the spot where our cottage had once stood, think what it was to find that it was standing there still! Not one whit changed! There was the poplar-tree, with a few brown leaves clinging still to its topmost boughs, and the thatched roof, just as we had left them! No, I could not believe my own eyes. I had been fretting and mourning over it in my secret heart as pulled down and and destroyed; and now I saw it unchanged, not a beam, not a handful of thatch gone; only there was no smoke from the chimney, and the kitchen-shutter was not taken down. Transome lifted the latch of the wicket, and we walked down the old path together. We sat down on the little bench beside the door, and looked in wonder at one another till I could not see him through my tears.

"Ally, lass!" said Transome, "it's like one o' my dreams—thee and me comin' home to th' oud house! Is it true, think's ta? Grip my hand hard if thee thinks it's true."

"Ay, it's true!" I answered, "and the old master might have left us alone in it all this time instead of driving us to the poorhouse."

"Hush, hush, lass!" he said; "it is na' a' together him. God sent us there, and we mun never set oursen again Him. But maybe He's keepin' it for us till we're ready to come out o' th' hous: again."

"We'd come out at once," I said, "if we could only have the old house again at the old rent; I could win bread for thee and me. Let us leave the house at once and come back."

"Nay, Ally," he answered, shaking his head, "we're boun' to wait th' Lord's pleasure. Th' winter's frost and snow are to come yet; and we've got nayther bed nor chair nor table left. But i' th' spring, lass!"

We sat there all the afternoon, chilled to the bone; yet happier than we had been since the evening Tramsome came home with the bad news that we were to quit. A lass from one of the houses hard by came to us and told us how one of the biggest mills about there had failed shortly after we left that part of the town; and now, as trade had begun to fall off, no one had taken to the mill and set the looms at work again. Many of the houses in the dingle were empty, she said. That was why our old landlord had not pulled down the cottage and built more in its place.

But we were forced to go away at last by the nightfall, though we lingered till it was quite dark, now and again plucking up a weed or binding up a flower in the old garden, where we had so often worked together in the cool of the day. As we made our way slowly back to the poorhouse, I talked over our plans as if I were a young wife again. As for Transome, he spoke but few words, as usual, only muttering to himself from time to time, "I' th' spring, my lass—i' th' spring!"

It began to rain fast when we were more than half a mile from the poorhouse; yet Transome, who was weary, could not quicken his lame feet. He bade me hurry on and get under shelter; but I begged and prayed him so to let me stay beside him as long as I could, that he could not say me no. For the rain did not take away the new hope from my heart, or the new plans from my head; and I scarcely felt it for myself, only for him, whose coat was getting soaked through and through. He was shivering with the cold; but still there was a bright light in his eyes, and a smile upon his face, as he kept saying, "I' th' spring, Ally—i' th' spring-time!"

All that night I could not sleep, and the next morning I found that the heavy rain of the evening before had brought on many pains in my old limbs. I had no power to lift myself from the bed; though when the bell rang for prayers, and I thought of Transome going, and how he'd feel at not seeing me there, I wept sore for trouble and sorrow. I begged everybody that came near me to take a message to him, but I got no answer back from him. Ah! they were a long three days that I lay there, not able to stir hand or foot without a groan wrung from me, spite of myself. But on the fourth morning I was able to get out of bed, and crawl across the floor to the fireplace at the far end of the ward, and take my place among the old women cowering about it. I was stretching out my stiff hands toward the blaze to gather all the warmth I could, when all of a sudden the door at the other end of the long room was thrown open, and a shrill voice called out to me, a sharp, shrill voice that rang through me, "Alice Transome, yo're to go quick to the sick-ward, for yo're man's dying."

All my pains were gone in an instant—swallowed up by a greater pain. I started from my chair, hurried down the room, and across the yard to the sick-ward, thinking of nothing, knowing nothing, hearing and seeing nothing, only the dree words ringing through and through my head, "Yo're man's deein!" The doctor met me at the foot of the stairs, and I could only cry out the name, "Transome!" He shook his head, and said something, but my ears were dull of hearing, and his voice sounded smothered and low. I almost ran as soon as I saw the door of the place where he was lying, and I knocked at the door, which had no latch on the outside, earnestly, earnestly, as if some terrible thing was hunting me, and I had fled there for safety. But the terrible thing was in there before me; though I pushed in eagerly as soon as the door was opened.

The place was exactly the same as the ward I came from, and the ward he came from—a long, narrow room, with narrow beds on each side, and the same coarse blue quilts over them. But every person lying on these beds was ill as well as poverty-stricken. I saw Transome the first moment—I saw no one save him. He was alone, no one near him; for he was passing away quietly, and the nurses had much to do, and were glad to leave him to himself. Quite alone, lying with his eyelids closed, and drifting away tranquilly out of this troublesome life, as if he did not know that he was going—just as a child falls asleep without knowing it. So quiet and still he was, that when I stole on tiptoe to his side, like I used to steal to Willie's cradle, he did not open his eyes, or move the poor hands that lay outside the quilt. I laid my hands softly upon them, and the icy chill that ran through me forced me to cry aloud.

"Oh, Transome!" I said, "are you going to leave me—to leave me behind you in this dreadful place?"

At that his face quivered all over, and his lips moved, and his eyelids opened. A smile came across his face, full of content, and his poor glazed eyes brightened as he saw me bending over him.

"Ally, my lass! Ally!" he whispered. I knelt down beside him, and put my arm under his old gray head; and he kept on whispering, "Ally, my lass! my poor Ally!" till I couldn't bear it a minute longer.

"Oh!" I cried, "the Lord is dealing very hard with us."

"No, no," he answered, "He's dealin' softer wi' us nor wi' His own Son, 'at were crucified upo' the cross. Nobry i' th' world has borne harder nor that. I'm a weary, sinfu' old man: but He were young, and there was no sin in Him, yet they put Him to death upo' the cross. No! Thee munna threep agen th' Lord, Ally."

"If He'd only let me come, too!" I cried again, feeling as if God must hear my cry, and take me along with Transome.

"Ay! aw'd bide for thee a while if aw could, for sure," he said, tenderly; "aw promised to bide wi' thee till death parted us; but 'twere the poorhouse first, and now it's death. But thee'lt not be long after me, Ally."

"No," I said; but my throat was so dry and choked I could say no more. If Transome died, all was over for me. I was a helpless, friendless old woman, with nothing before me but to live and die in the poorhouse, yet I could not be sure that I should die soon.

"Ally," he whispered again," I've gie'en thee mony and mony a cross to bear. But thee'lt forgie me a' now."

"Thou never gave me a hard word," I said.

"Th' Lord knows," he went on, "at aw love thee more now nor when we were wed. Dost remember, lass? But tell me, quick, what were those words thee learned me th' neet afore we came into th' house? 'Faithful unto death.' Quick, Ally."

No one knows how hard it was for me to make my voice speak through my sobs; but quietly and softly I repeated the words, putting my lips close to his ear:

"Be thou faithful unto death, and I will give thee a crown of life!"

"Gran' words," he whispered; "faithfu' unto death; crown o' life! Gran' words. Faithfu' unto death, Lord!"

His gray head fell heavier on my arm, and his eyelids dropped half over his eyes. His breath came feebler and feebler. I knew what it was. He tried to speak once more to me, but his poor tongue was stiff and cold. His fingers groped about a bit on the quilt, till I put my other hand into them. I would not stir or utter a cry, lest any of the strange women who were in the ward should come nigh us, and perhaps take me away from him. So quiet he was when he passed away forever, that even the sick man next to him, whom I could have touched with my hand without moving, did not know that Transome was dead. Only I knew.

Well, I cannot tell you any more. You have heard enough to know how Transome was faithful unto death. Maybe if I had been like him I should have been with him now in the presence of the Lord. But he has placed us here like children at school, who must stay till their tasks are learned by heart before they are let free into the holiday and the sunshine. I'd learned my lessons so as I might have forgotten them in the holiday time; and when Transome was called home from school the Lord left me here to get them better by heart.

All I saw of his funeral was the little plain hearse belonging to the poorhouse, with four of the poorhouse men riding outside it, ready to carry his coffin to the grave. After that I was like one dazed and bewildered; doing nothing of my own will and choice; but getting up and going to bed, eating and drinking, only when I was bid. Once I went to prayers seeking for Transome; but I never went again. The four bare white walls of the ward seemed nothing but a big grave, and I like one dead and buried in it; only it was a sort of living death, so dreadful that none but those who have felt it can know it. Nothing would ever change again. Summer and winter would be alike to me. I was there without pity, and without help; my heart dead within me. It seemed as if death itself had forgotten me, or would not have compassion on me.

It was one day in the spring that Transome had spoken of—"I' th' spring, Ally—i' th' spring time!" I was lying in my bed late on in the morning, for no one had bid me rise, though the sun was shining through the high windows, when the door near me was opened, and the matron and two gentlemen came through it. I had ceased to care to take any notice of visitors, for if they tried to comfort me, it was plain they knew nothing of my sorrow. So I closed my eyes wearily as they came in. But they stopped at the foot of my bed; and I thought maybe if I seem to be asleep they will pass on: for it troubled me for other folks to talk to me about Transome. But a voice, a strange voice, yet with a tone in it that somehow made me think of my school, said loud enough for me to hear:

"Surely this cannot be Mrs. Transome!"

"It's Alice Transome," answered the matron. "Her husband died four months ago, and she's never been herself since. She takes no notice of anybody, sir."

"*She'll take notice of me*," said the same strange, clear, pleasant voice, "I must make her know me; for I've come to pay a debt I owe her. Mrs. Transome, you have never forgotten your little scholar, Pippin?"

No, I had never forgotten him; yet I did not lift up my eyes all at once. I tried to recall his bonny face; but it was so mixed up with Willie's face, I could not. Then I felt a warm, strong hand take mine into its firm clasp; as firm as Transome's was when we were wed.

"It's Pippin!" said the voice, close to my ear. I made a great effort then to shake off the weight that had been crushing me down all those long months. I felt myself trembling all through me: and the warm hand clasped me more closely.

"Look at me!" said Pippin.

So I opened my eyes, and saw him standing beside my bed, a young, sunburnt man now, but with the same sunny hair and bright eyes that my little scholar had. I broke out into sobbing and weeping, so as I had never wept since Transome died.

"I am come to take you away from this place," he said, soothingly; "but you must not talk to me now. After dinner you shall get up and dress, and come away with father and me. *Father is come home* at last, Mrs. Transome!"

Then I looked, and saw behind him a man of middle age, whose hair was just going gray, and whose grave face bore the marks of bitter sufferings. But he looked kindly upon me as Pippin spoke, and said, "You were my boy's best friend when he had no one to care for him, and we will not leave you here." So they went away; and I lay quiet again, but feeling that the sun was shining still upon the world, and there was love and kindness in it yet, even for me.

That evening I had tea with them in a grand parlor in an inn in the town, and was waited upon as if I were a born lady. Pippin told me all his story, which is too long to tell here. How, like a child, the memory of me had died away from his mind, amid the many changes of his life. How, when he was a boy of sixteen, just leaving school, there came a rumor to him of his father's ship having been wrecked upon the coast of Africa nine years before, and how a white man was living among the black tribes there. It was no more than a rumor, but he could not rest until he had adventured himself to take help to that white man; and behold! it was his own father, Captain John Champion, who might never have escaped from that place, if his boy had not rescued him. They had only come back home a little while ago, and now, the memory of me having grown strong again, they had returned to our town to repay me for what I had done for him when a little child. Ah! if Transome had only lived to know it!

(*To be Continued.*)

SELF.

By Mrs. M. Baxter.

S. S. Lesson for March 25, Matt. 16:21–25. Golden Text, Rom. 15: 3.*

The Motive Principle of Worldly Lives—Its Manifestation in Education, Philanthropy and Social Life—Pharisaism in all Ages - Self Pity—Clinging to Creature Comforts - The Claims of Heathendom Ignored—The Divine Altruism of the Saviour—The Condition of Discipleship—Self to be Held Always Ready for Immolation—Christ's Teaching as to Self—Paul's Self was Crucified —The Changed Aspect of Personal Trials.

"Even Christ pleased not Himself." He was the only Man who ever lived a life totally free from self. "Every man for himself," or, as Scripture renders it: "All seek their own" (Phil. 2: 21.) is the motive-principle which governs every man who has not yielded himself to Christ; it is

The Very Essence of the World.

"Men will praise thee when thou doest well to thyself." (Ps. 49: 18.) Politics, religion and social life, as they generally exist, are all animated with this same principle; everybody expects, and is expected, to do the best for himself. Children are educated to look after their own interests; men go into business to secure a fortune for themselves; people build a church or a mission to secure the interests of the denomination to which they belong; nations go to war in order to exalt themselves, or to attain territory, or commercial advantages for themselves. Again, men enter into an argument to prove *themselves* in the right; they play a game to show *their* skill; they furnish a house to secure *their* comfort; they pray to God to ease *their* conscience; and, from first to last, self is the object of all. In a little country town, the squire cannot dine with the merchant, nor the merchant with the shopkeeper, nor the shopkeeper with the dressmaker, nor the dressmaker with the servant, nor the servant with the scavenger, because self would be supposed to lose some of its contemptible superiority! But surely, in religion self has no such place? Alas! there are the self-righteous. Were there not, in our Lord's time, such as "trusted in themselves that they were righteous, and despised others"? (Luke 18: 9) some who, "being ignorant of God's righteousness (which is without a flaw), and going about to establish their own righteousness, have not submitted themselves unto the righteousness of God (Rom. 10: 3.) And are there not Pharisees still, who thank God that they are not as other men are? Was not Cain such an one? Did not he seek to get standing-ground with God without any attempt to get the question of sin settled? There are the *self-holy*. Did not even the righteous or justified Job rejoice in

A Righteous Self,

justified, no doubt, by faith; for even in the Old Testament the just lived by his faith (Heb. 2: 4). Job yet gloried in his own integrity, and counted on his own righteousness, and greatly admired himself. He says, "I will maintain mine own ways before Him" (Job 13: 15), and so he would be independent of God. Again, "My face is foul with weeping, and on mine eyelids is the shadow of death; *not* for any injustice in *mine* hands: also, *my prayer is pure*" (16: 16, 17). "Till I die I will not remove mine integrity from me. My righteousness I hold fast, and will not let it go: mine heart shall not reproach me so long as I live." (27: 5, 6.) What was this but the setting up of a self, a righteous, holy self, as something to trust in? If the restraining grace of God had left him for a moment to himself, where would have been his purity, integrity and righteousness? And there are thousands like him, rejoicing in their own holiness, and boasting in it.

And then, even among Christians, how much we find of *self pity*, of being sorry for themselves, and nursing their own wrongs! Jonah was more ready to let the whole population of Nineveh perish than he was to endure the heat of the sun himself. There is something extremely revolting in his heartless selfishness. Yet how many of us are leaving hundreds of millions of heathen to perish, because we pity ourselves too much to leave comfortable homes and pleasant society, and a position where we are honored and respected! Jesus told His disciples that He "must suffer many things of the chief priests and scribes, and be killed, and be raised again the third day;" and Peter said, "Pity Thyself, Lord, this shall not be unto Thee." (Matt. 16: 21 margin.) "Pity thyself"! Self pity was as foreign to Jesus as sin was. He had not where to lay His head. He received not honor from men, and commissioned His disciples to live as He did. He came on earth to wage war against all the self which is in man, and to teach us to walk in

Newness of Life.

In Him was no self-righteousness, for He disclaimed power to do anything of Himself. (John 5: 19, 30; 14: 10) He fled from honor. (John 5: 34, 41; 6: 15.) He did not defend himself. "When He was reviled," He "reviled not again;" when He suffered, He threatened not, but committed Himself to Him that judgeth righteously, 1 Pet. 2: 23.) He sought not His own will, His own glory, His own comfort, that He might teach us the glory and beauty of a life lived out of self. Therefore, He answered Peter, "Get thee behind Me, Satan, for thou art an offence unto Me, for thou savorest not the things that be of God, but those that be of men." Then said Jesus unto His disciples, "If any man will come after Me, let him deny himself and take up his cross and follow Me." Not pity himself, not defend himself, not justify himself, not value himself; but deny himself; not make himself of importance, but let this mind be in him which was also in Christ Jesus, who "made Himself of no reputation. Not enrich himself, but sell all that he had and give to the poor, and he should have treasure in heaven. The world is full of self-assertion, self-importance, self-satisfaction, self-pity, self-righteousness, self-defence, self-indulgence. What of all this do we see in Jesus? His yoke—the yoke He bore and the yoke He puts on others—is that of a meek and lowly heart, where self is at a discount.

The whole teaching of Jesus is aimed at

The Destruction of Self.

Self will be first. Jesus teaches, "Whosoever will be great among men, let him be your minister; and whosoever will be chief among you, let him be your servant. Even as the Son of Man came not to be ministered unto, but to minister and to give His life a ransom for many." (Matt. 21: 26–28.) Self will defend self and have its rights. Jesus teaches, "I say unto you, that ye resist not evil" (Matt. 5: 39), and that His people are not to contend for a coat, nor to give blow for blow, nor to use resistance when compelled to go where they would not. Self naturally argues, but the Word of God teaches that "the servant of Christ must not strive." (II Tim. 2: 24.) Self is often a great economist, and has an eye to the future. Jesus says, "Lay not up for yourselves treasures upon earth." (Matt. 6: 19.) Self loves to be noticed and praised. Jesus says, "Woe unto you when all men shall speak well of you." (Luke 6: 26.) Self is a great grumbler, the Word of God teaches us "in everything' to "give thanks" (1 Thes. 5: 18), and to give "thanks always for all things" (Eph. 5: 20), because "all things work together for good to them that love God." (Rom. 8: 28.) Self likes good society. Jesus teaches, "When thou makest a dinner or a supper, call not thy friends, nor thy brethren, neither thy kinsmen, nor thy rich neighbors (the poor *may* be invited) *lest* they also bid thee again, and a recompense be made thee. But when thou makest a feast, call the poor, the maimed, the lame, the blind, and thou shalt be blessed; for they cannot recompense thee; for thou shalt be recompensed at the resurrection of the just." Self loves a handsome equipage or a first-class railway carriage. Jesus, when illustrating the command, "Thou shalt love thy neighbor as thyself," shows us a rich man getting off his ass, and putting the poor man to ride in his place, and says, "Go and do thou likewise." But if

Self is our very Nature,

our very personality, how are we to do violence to that which is our very being? Paul answers the question, "I am crucified with Christ; nevertheless I live; yet not I, but Christ liveth in me, and the life which I now live in the flesh, I live by the faith of the Son of God, who loved me and gave Himself for me." When Paul was converted he gave himself up to Jesus, not to keep himself in his own hands, and give from time to time so much service, so much love, so much time, etc. He gave himself, *out* of his own hands, as much as though he had died on the Cross of Jesus, and he counted Jesus as his new self, "Not I, but Christ." The Holy Spirit made Jesus real to him, and thus if anyone hurt him, he did not pity himself, but turned it over to Jesus, so that in the Philippian prison he could sing praises when he was persecuted. When, at Lystra, the people would have worshipped him as a god, Paul ran in among them, and far from being flattered, he cried out, "Sirs, why do ye these things? We also are men, of like passions with you, and preach unto you that ye should turn from these vanities unto the living God." The Holy Spirit which possessed Paul, showed him everything in the light of God. It ceased to be with Paul a question of how things touched *him*, pained *him*, inconvenienced *him*, honored or dishonored *him*. The question was, How did they touch Jesus? And this was no life of intense tension, or of unnatural strain; he let the Holy Ghost have him fully, and thus the blessed Spirit would

Glorify Jesus in Him.

Whenever a man is full of the Holy Ghost, the same fruits must follow. He has all the management, and He brings out the life and spirit of Christ. Where there is a constant contention within, as to how far to consider self, there the Holy Ghost is not allowed to have full sway, and self is disputing His rule. The Holy Ghost recognizes Jesus, but He does not recognize self. He teaches us how much more blessed is Christ's compassion than self-pity, God's Fatherly care than self-care, God's defence than self-defence, God's righteousness than self-righteousness, to please God than to be self-satisfied. O God, turn Thy hand upon us, and purge the leaven of self from us by the incoming and rule of Jesus Christ *Him*self.

* For use in schools where neither Review nor Temperance lesson is required, but choice of subject is left to the discretion of the teacher.

"HE KNOWETH ALL."

The twilight falls, the night is near
  I fold my work away,
And kneel to One who bends to hear
  The story of the day.

The old, old story; yet I kneel
  To tell it at Thy call;
And cares grow lighter as I feel
  That Jesus knows them all.

Yes all! the morning and the night,
  The joy, the grief, the loss,
The roughened path, the sunbeam bright,
  The hourly thorn and cross.

Thou knowest all—I lean my head,
  My weary eyelids close,
Content and glad awhile to tread
  This path, since Jesus knows.

And He has loved me! all my heart
  With answering love is stirred,
And every anguished pain and smart
  Finds healing in the Word.

So here I lay me down to rest,
  As mighty shadows fall,
And lean confiding on His breast
  Who knows and pities all.

Selected.

J. E. JEWETT, Publisher, 77 Bible House, New York will furnish the above poem in leaflet form at twenty cents per hundred. *A Sample Packet* of 50 leaflets assorted (no two alike), will be sent post-paid for ten cents. Postage stamps taken.

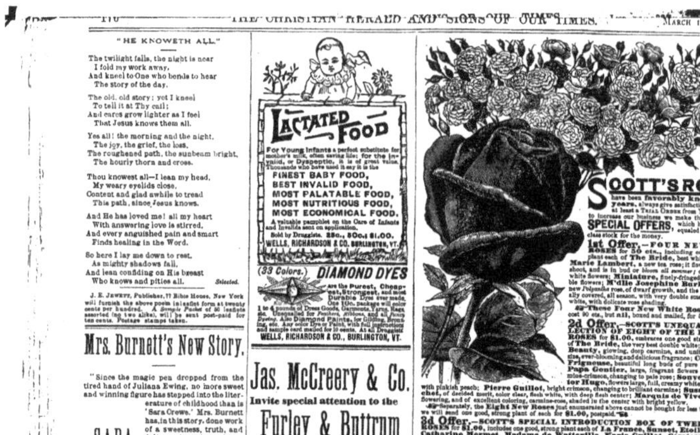

MEXICO

Contributions in aid of Christian work in Mexico are most pressingly needed, and can be mailed to the address of

BISHOP H. C. RILEY,
Care of J. P. HEATH,
43 Bible House, New York.

THE CHRISTIAN HERALD AND SIGNS OF OUR TIMES.

Vol. XI., No. 12. Office, 63 Bible House, N. Y. THURSDAY, MARCH 22, 1888. Annual Subscription, $1.50.

CONTENTS OF THIS NUMBER.

PORTRAIT AND LIFE OF REV. WARRAND CARLILE, of Jamaica, West Indies.
THE DECORATION OF THE SOUL. Dr. Talmage's Sermon last Sunday, at Fort Scott, Kan.
PORTRAIT AND LIFE OF THE LATE HENRY BERGH, of New York.
ANECDOTES RELATED AT RECENT EVANGELISTIC MEETINGS.
THE FATAL BLIZZARD IN NEW YORK.
THE WONDERFUL BIRTHDAY OF 144,000 CHRISTIANS. By Rev. M. Baxter.
HALF-WAY AND ALL THE WAY. A New Sermon by C. H. Spurgeon.
Gems from New Books: A Little Good Samaritan.
A PRAYER IN A CAVE. (With Illustration.)
A Swiss Clergyman's Lost Text.
PORTRAIT AND LIFE OF THE LATE MISS LOUISA M. ALCOTT.
SNOW-BOUND IN THE PARSONAGE. (With Illustration.)
MRS. TRANSOME'S PUPIL. A Serial Story. (Continued.)
THE MARRIAGE FEAST. By Mrs. M. Baxter.

THE LATE REV. WARRAND CARLILE, Thirty-eight Years Missionary in Jamaica—Scenes in His Life.

THE REV. WARRAND CARLILE,

Thirty-eight Years a Missionary in Jamaica.

A Remarkable Life—His Pious Home—School and University Life—Enters Business—Christian Activity—Marriage—Ride with Carlyle and Irving—Studies for the Ministry—Life in Ireland—A Momentous Dream—Sets Sail for Jamaica—Work and Blessing—Among the Negroes—A Fire—Building a Church—Dangerous Riding—Failing Health and Death.

A TRULY remarkable life was that of the veteran missionary whose portrait appears on the preceding page. It was remarkable in its length, for he was nearly eighty-five years old when he died, but still more remarkable for the variety and extent of Christian labors which it comprised. It began in a Scottish manufacturing town in 1796, and closed in 1881 among the colored population of Jamaica, W. I., to whose welfare he had consecrated nearly forty of his years. It was Mr. Carlile's privilege to give nearly all his life to Christ's service. It too often happens that the Christian, at the end of his course, looking back over his life, has reason to lament that his early years were given up to sin and pleasure; but Mr. Carlile was saved from that loss by the blessing of God on his

Christian Parentage.

He was the son of James Carlile, who, with his brother William, carried on the manufacture of sewing thread at Paisley, in Scotland, both men being noted for their eminent piety and large gifts to Bible and missionary societies. James Carlile, the father of Warrand, devoted a considerable portion of every day to the study of the Word of God, while engaged in the absorbing and prosperous business of the firm. For many years he met with the younger members of his family every Saturday morning, to read and explain a part of the Scripture, which he made as attractive to them as he could; and these weekly talks were a source of profit to both father and children (*See Illustration No. 1*). To Warrand especially they were blessed, for he was led, almost insensibly, in his tenderest years, to give himself to the Saviour; he himself could scarcely tell the time when he was not devoted to God. After completing the usual school education, he attended the Glasgow University for two years, and then became engaged in his father's business. He began to be an active Christian worker when hardly beyond the years of boyhood. He found scope for his activity in Sunday-school work at first, but when he became a man and was associated as a partner with his father, he turned his special attention to the workers employed in the factory. He had classes for them, and prayer-meetings with them, both in the mill and in his own house.

But the welfare of his own people did not engross the whole of Mr. Carlile's attention, or exhaust his Christian energy. He was a member of the Town Council, and the treasurer of the town for a time. This gave him

Access to the Prison,

which he regularly visited between the morning and afternoon services on Sundays, and frequently in the week when there were cases of special interest. He was a means of blessing to many of the prisoners, including two who were executed for stealing a horse. They were the last two to suffer the extreme penalty of the law in Scotland for any crime short of murder. He was thus engaged in a variety of Christian work for at least twenty years in his native town, and his name became famous there as a consecrated servant of Christ.

In the year 1820 he married Agnes Irving, daughter of Gavin Irving, of Annan, and youngest sister of the afterwards celebrated Edward Irving, who was at that time assistant to Dr. Chalmers, in Glasgow. The marriage was one of much happiness. Mrs. Carlile was in features like her brother, and her appearance attracted attention wherever she went. Her health, however, was not very good, even from her girlhood, and during her married life she was never strong. The winter before her death she was very ill, and was scarcely expected to recover. She became, during that illness, so enraptured with the study of the Prophets, especially of Isaiah and Revelation, that she felt it almost painful to return from her bright visions, to the commonplaces of life around her. Her return, however, was not for long, and after a married life of nine bright years, she passed into the deathless land.

To what extent Mr. Carlile came in contact with his famous brother-in-law we are not told in his biography, but an incidental reference in the reminiscences of Thomas Carlyle, "The Sage of Chelsea," shows that they were, at least on one occasion in familiar intercourse. Carlyle says that having, to go by Muirkirk in Ayrshire he and Irving, who was going back to Glasgow, set out together, Warrand Carlile going with them "with his fine riding-horse," which was of great service on the journey.

Warrand Carlile felt after his wife's death that life was quite changed for him. He consequently determined to relinquish his share in what had grown into a most prosperous business, and to

Study for the Ministry.

He had been at college in his youth for two years. He now returned to complete two years more of the literary course, and then four years of theology. He took a great interest in his studies, especially mathematics and Hebrew. Subsequently he was licensed as a preacher by the Presbytery of Paisley, and at once went over to Ireland on a visit to his brother, the Rev. James Carlile, hoping that he would find a sphere of missionary work in that country. He was invited to take charge of a Presbyterian congregation at Carlow, fifty miles south of Dublin, in the midst of a Roman Catholic population. He went there and remained six years, laboring among a people attached to him, though few in number. The poverty of the peasantry, although not so extreme as in the west of Ireland, was often very great. Mr. Carlile was untiringly and impartially active in relieving distress in times of scarcity. During a summer of

Real Famine

he took all the chief arrangements into his hands at the request of the local committee, got the supplies of food from Liverpool at a cheap rate, put up the boilers for preparing it, arranged the food that was to be cooked, had passages made for the orderly ingress and egress of the people, and presided in turn, with the priests and others, at the distribution. (*See Illustration No. 3.*) Thousands were relieved, and many of them ate eagerly, out of their tins, the food supplied them, before they left the building. He was thus a chief agent in saving the lives of many.

Mr. Carlile very soon felt that his work in Carlow was not to be his life work, and prayed earnestly to God for guidance. The Irish Presbyterian Church, with which he was connected, was then beginning its mission in India, and he was one of those suggested for this service. He was desirous to go. It was considered wiser, however, to send younger men. At length his prayer was answered, and light came in a very remarkable manner. One night he had a dream, in which he thought he saw the Lord Himself pointing him to the island of Jamaica as his place of service. This dream made so deep an impression on a mind predisposed for foreign service and only awaiting direction to a field, that it decided him, and he immediately sought a way of reaching it. He remembered that the Scottish Missionary Society, in which he had in Paisley taken a deep interest, had missions there. He waited not a single day, but wrote off in the forenoon to the Directors, offering himself at once for mission service in Jamaica. They wrote in a few days and accepted his offer, and he prepared speedily for his journey. His

Foreign Mission Life

was begun at the age of forty-six, an age when many missionaries are retiring, and it continued in activity for thirty-eight years, till his death at the age of nearly eighty-five. Mr. and Mrs. Carlile (for the missionary had married again) and their family sailed from Greenock in the ship *Isabella*. After a moderately fine passage of fifty days, the vessel arrived in the harbor of Montego Bay, one of the most beautiful harbors in the island, on January 2, 1843. (*See Illustration No. 5.*)

His first sphere of service in the island was Hampden, where he was at once brought face to face with some of the most revolting of the old African superstitions. Thence he went to Mount Zion, where he was gladdened in seeing many trophies of the saving power of God among the negroes. It was then decided that his particular charge should be Brownsville, a town named from the Rev. Dr. William Brown, son of Dr. John Brown, of Haddington, for many years Secretary of the Scottish Missionary Society. It is in the heart of a mountainous district, full of deep gullies and steep hillsides, down which flow the mountain streams, sometimes in raging torrents, while all around, imparting a quaint picturesqueness to the landscape, are dotted the cottages of the negroes. When Mr. Carlile

Settled at Brownsville,

the people had been emancipated only a few years. Few of the grown-up people could read well, though many could read imperfectly. All but the children had been slaves; and the old slave-overseers were still there, some of them being elders of the Church. A marvellous social as well as religious change had taken place in the few previous years, for whereas marriage had scarcely been known among the slaves, nearly all were now married, though there lingered many remnants of old sins and abuses. Among this simple people Mr. Carlile settled down to begin his second life-work, little expecting that he would spend so many years in Jamaica. His life henceforward was one of devotion to the cause he had espoused, and his efforts to lead the newly emancipated men and women into the true liberty of Christ were unremitting while life lasted. It was a life of quiet, steady usefulness, attended with much discouragement, but also with much success. Some stirring incidents of his life and work are worth recording. Among others, Mr. Carlile describes

A Fire

which took place, by which the cottage he was living in was endangered. The alacrity with which the people came to his aid much affected him. He says: "We were constrained to take possession of our present residence sooner than we intended, and, indeed, before it was prepared for our reception, by an accident which might have proved very serious. I was sitting writing in this house, which I had converted into my study, when a sudden clamor arose among the workmen around me, and on running to the window I perceived that the kitchen connected with the cottage was on fire. We all ran at our utmost speed to assist in extinguishing the flames, or in saving the cottage. Fortunately we had a little water in the house, in which I instantly steeped one or two blankets. A ladder was procured, and in the course of five minutes I was on the top of the roof. (*See Illustration No. 6*). While I was sitting on the top of the house shouting out for water at the top of my voice, I perceived that the thatch of the cottage had caught fire, and now I never doubted but that all was over, and that in five minutes more our frail tenement would be reduced to embers. I was preparing to descend and endeavor to save some of the furniture, when two men, wiser than myself, brought the ladder to the place where the fire had begun. I then threw to them the moist blankets, and by immediately applying these the fire was extinguished and the house preserved. Every one who saw the perilous condition of the house was amazed that it was saved.

"While I was busy on the top of the house, some of the people, who were rapidly collecting to our assistance, emptied the house of every article of furniture. Open drawers and boxes were lying about in all directions, and everything we had was exposed to the people.

While thus tossed about without any one to look after them, I do not think that even the most trifling article was abstracted."

The Building of a Church

was undertaken by Mr. Carlile to accommodate the increased congregations which had been gathered. The day at length came for *raising the spire*. The missionary relates: "When I told the carpenters that I intended rearing it without scaffolding, they shook their heads and declared it to be impossible. On the Monday morning after our Sacrament we assembled for worship, and having implored the Divine blessing, we proceeded to our work. The day was at first most unfavorable, as it blew strongly; but as I had already borrowed ropes from the neighboring estates, which could only be kept for a day, this being their busiest season, I resolved to proceed with the work. A goodly number of men were present to assist, to whom I was obliged to give the word of command like a sea-captain during a gale of wind. Just as I was proceeding to get the ropes fastened and the tackling prepared, I found, to my dismay, that the rope was too short for our purpose. I discovered that by placing the men who held the ropes on the top of the house, I could accomplish my purpose. One part of the spire we converted into a pole, by which we were enabled to raise up another. After a short time our anxieties were all at an end, and with a grateful heart we soon saw the building complete without injury or accident. The spire is octagonal, about sixty feet high, and constructed of the best and strongest Jamaica wood. (*See Illustration No. 7.*)

In 1863 Mr. Carlile visited his native country. He was full of vigor, and delivered many addresses on missionary work and triumphs, though at that time sixty-seven years of age. At the close of the year he returned to Jamaica, and continued to live there without any intermission until his death. Even in his

Later Years,

indeed, "up to the last," says his son, "he continued full of activity." After his eightieth year he was accustomed to take long rides, and diligently to visit the sick. The roads were often difficult, and even dangerous, but he was not to be daunted. Sometimes along a narrow path on a mountain side (*See Illustration, No. 8*), the horse or mule had to cautiously pick its steps, while steep, almost precipitous, slopes on the one side extended far down into the dark gullies. He used often to hold meetings in those scattered districts, accessible only by the mountain paths. A year or two before his death he had rather a severe fall from his horse, which caused him suffering for a time, but generally he appears to have met with scarcely any accidents, being upheld by the unfailing Hand.

His Health Began to Fail

somewhat rapidly in April, 1881. Though still physically active, he became bewildered, imagining himself back in the scenes of the past, in his old home in Paisley, surrounded by those who had long since departed. At length, in August, he was seized with a fever, and after a few days he "fell asleep in Jesus" at the age of eighty-four years and nine months. His wife, who had been his companion and stay during all these years, watched over him tenderly to the last. During the illness the negroes surrounded the cottage, full of anxiety, as of children for a loving father. (*See Illustration No. 9.*) His last conscious words, spoken in a solemn tone, and with clasped hands, were, "Blessed be God, blessed be God, for that peace which the world cannot take away." His countenance after death was peaceful and seraphic, and multitudes of the people all around came, with tears in their eyes, to have a last look at their dear pastor, who had watched over many of them from childhood upwards, and over all of them for more than a generation. He was laid to rest close to the manse where he spent so many years. Here, on the hillside, under the deep shadow of a mango-tree, a stone marks his last resting-place until the coming of the Lord.

ANECDOTES RELATED AT RECENT EVANGELISTIC MEETINGS.

A Hard Question Answered.—An Evangelist observes: "It is now six years since I came to Christ. I was asked by a friend to accompany him to a temperance meeting. I went, and there I was asked to take the pledge, and, to please my friend, I did so. I thought I was done with his importunities, but he would not let me be at peace. 'Would I come to a prayer-meeting?' he asked. Reluctantly I went, heedless, regardless of God. I entered the meeting without a thought of salvation, but ere I came out of it, it had pleased God by the Holy Spirit to bring me to Christ. The words of the apostle, 'How shall we escape if we neglect so great salvation?' filled me with alarm. I felt I was a poor, lost sinner. But God enabled me to answer the question. Seeing I could not escape, I fled for refuge to Christ, and found it in Him. I have now a joy which is unspeakable."

Curing the Missionaries' Languor.—Mr. Ludwig, of the U. P. Mission at Old Calabar, West Africa, relates: "In Africa we were often very much afflicted by a languor which is very difficult to bear, and for the time being renders one very useless. But we found that every Thursday and Sunday we were more cheerful, and had within us a joy for which we could in no way account. On these days we would say to each other, 'Surely there is someone at home praying for us.' And when we got home we found that it was on these very days that our friends had met especially to pray for us. This shows how every Christian can effectually help the foreign mission. Though all cannot go to preach to the heathen, yet all can pray for those who do go; and we read that 'The effectual, fervent prayer of a righteous man availeth much.'"

A Spree Prevented by Death.—A Fine, Well-built, intelligent youth, seventeen years of age, had been sitting listening to the gospel, and remained to the prayer-meeting. The preacher pleaded hard that he would that night accept the salvation offered him by our Lord. He was deeply impressed, but would not yield. He said, "It only wants a few weeks to Christmas. I have saved up thirty shillings in the bank, and I intend to have a spree with it; but I'll start the New Year a Christian." He was reminded, "Now is the accepted time," but it was no use; hardening his heart, he went his way. Two days after he was seized with a violent cold; he went out with some companions was caught in a heavy storm, and came home drenched with rain. Next day, he was unable to leave his bed, and on the day following he died—it is to be feared totally unprepared. Under his pillow was found his bank-book; and the very money that had caused him to reject Christ, and with which he intended to have a spree, bought him a shroud, and helped to pay the expenses of laying him in a Christless grave.

True to His Colors.—Mr. M'Gregor, Late an officer in the army, says: "When I joined the army my regiment was quartered at Gibraltar. I went out there determined to witness for Christ. I felt weak and somewhat timorous, and did not know how I should get on. My father sent me a religious paper, which arrived before I did, and was put into the letter-rack along with the other officers' papers. As I was standing near, one of the officers took it up, and, looking at it, said, 'Hillo, M'Gregor, are you a Christian?' 'I am,' I replied. 'And you take in this paper?' 'I do; and if you wish to read it you are welcome to it.' I had not been long in the army when the Lord, through two missionaries who visited Gibraltar, appeared to call me to follow Him more fully. I seemed to constantly hear the words: 'All that thou commandest we shall do, and wherever Thou sendest us we will go.' I prayed God to take me, young and inexperienced as I was, from the evil which surrounded me. But by-and-by I did not seem to care for the world, and in the army they were always against me; but soon they began to see that I did not care for derision and opposition—I even esteemed it an honor to be permitted to suffer for the sake of the Gospel. But I thank God that soon He made the way plain for me to resign my commission and go to China to serve Him there."

A Day and a Night in a Cave.—"Three months ago, in Lewis, at a communion season, a young Christian man and his friend were walking home together from one of the services. At parting, the Christian said to the other, 'I am grieved to think how little I have got after having the Gospel so fairly and fully preached to me for four or five days. What have I got to satisfy my hungry soul?' The other, who made no profession of religion, made no reply, but went home full of what his friend had said; and the thought of his own salvation so pressed upon his mind, that he was constrained to lift his Bible, and turn his way to one of a number of small caves on the rocks by the seashore, and there, alone with his Bible and his God, he spent all that day and all that night searching for something on which his soul could rest, but found nothing until in the morning, there in that lonely cave among the rocks, his eyes fell on the words, 'For God so loved the world that He gave His only begotten Son, that whosoever believeth in Him should have everlasting life.' He sprang to his feet with a shout of joy, and there on that verse he rested his weary soul."

A Great Secret Discovered.—Mr. Osborne remarked: "Six years ago I was summoned to the death-bed of my father. When I arrived I found he had been asking for me, and awaited me impatiently. I entered the sick-room, and had spoken to him for a while, when he asked to be lifted from his bed to the floor, and there, standing with one hand resting on my shoulder, and one on that of my mother, he solemnly said, 'Let us pray. It is probably the last time that we shall together send up our petitions to God.' I remember well how he used these words, 'Whom have I in heaven but Thee, and there is none on earth that I desire beside Thee, and goodness and mercy shall follow me all the days of my life, and I will dwell in the house of the Lord for ever.' All that night these words kept ringing in my mind. I asked myself, What is it my father has that I have not? Next morning, as I was going away, my father asked me if I were a total abstainer. I was not, but promised to become one as soon as I got home. But although I did so, that gave me no rest; for weeks I was miserable, but one night in a Gospel meeting I heard the hymn, 'There is a fountain filled with blood,' etc. Then I saw what it was I wanted; and there and then I closed with Christ, was saved by His grace, and am now happy in Him."

Choked While Intoxicated.—Mr. Mitchell Related: "I knew a woman who often came to our open-air meetings, and who was repeatedly spoken to about her soul by the workers. A short time ago she went to see some of her friends. In making merry they partook too freely of whisky, and, before she started for her home, she was helplessly intoxicated. When crossing the river in a ferryboat, her foot slipped and she fell into the water, from which she was rescued by the ferryman, but only just in time to save her life. Two policemen took her home, where, being completely sobered, she was asked by a Christian man who heard of the accident, 'If God had called you, where would your soul have gone?' Her answer was, 'God would not call me away in such a manner when He knew I was unprepared.' Next morning she went to procure more whisky, not touched in the least by her merciful escape from a watery grave, and soon she was as intoxicated as she had been on the previous night. But she had tasted no food, and was hungry; she set about preparing something, eating the while. As she was doing so, a piece stuck in her throat, and she died before help could come. Died under the influence of drink; died unprepared, after the fearful lesson of the previous day. 'He that being often reproved, hardeneth his neck, shall suddenly be destroyed, and that without remedy.'"

THE DECORATION OF THE SOUL.

Dr. Talmage's Sermon Preached last Sunday, March 18, 1888, at Fort Scott, Kansas.

"Put a ring on his hand." Luke 15 : 22.

A Ring for a Tramp—The Father's Recognition—God's Gift to the Forgiven Soul—I. The Ring of Adoption—A New York Waif in Philadelphia—Her Transformation—The Wardrobe of Heaven—Royal Privileges—II. A Marriage Ring—A Sacred Symbol—A Circle of Precious Memories—Christ the Husband of the Soul—No Divorce Possible—The Martyrdom of Margaret the Scotch Girl—III. The Ring of Festivity—A Gift of Gladness—Happy Christians—Their One Gold Ring—A Pillow of Rest—Life's Saturday Night—Messages to Heaven—An Unlimited Invitation—The People on the Threshold.

I WILL not rehearse the familar story of the fast young man of the parable. You know what a splendid home he left. You know what a hard time he had. And you remember how, after that season of vagabondage and prodigality he resolved to go and weep out his sorrows on the bosom of parental forgiveness. Well. there is great excitement one day in front of the door of the old farm-house. The servants come rushing up and say: "What's the matter? What is the matter?" But before they quite arrive, the old man cries out: "Put

A Ring on his Hand."

What a seeming absurdity! What can such a wretched mendicant as this fellow that is tramping on toward the house want with a ring? Oh, he is the prodigal son. No more tending of the swine-trough. No more longing for the pods of the carob-tree. No more blistered feet. Off with the rags! On with the robe! Out with the ring! Even so does God receive every one of us when we come back. There are gold rings, and pearl rings, and carnelian rings, and diamond rings; but the richest ring that ever flashed on the vision is that which our Father puts upon a forgiven soul.

I know that the impression is abroad among some people, that religion bemeans and belittles a man; that it takes all the sparkle out of his soul; that he has to exchange a roystering independence for an ecclesiastical strait-jacket. Not so. When a man becomes a Christian, he does not go down, he starts upward. Religion multiplies one by ten thousand. Nay, the multiplier is an infinity. It is not a blotting out—it is a polishing, it is an arborescence, it is an efflorescence, it is an irradiation. When a man comes into the kingdom of God he is not sent into a menial service, but the Lord God Almighty from the palaces of heaven calls upon the messenger angels that wait upon the throne to fly and "put a ring on his hand." In Christ are the largest liberty, and brightest joy, and highest honor, and richest adornment. "Put a ring on his hand."

I remark, in the first place, that when Christ receives a soul into His love, He puts upon him

The Ring of Adoption.

In my church in Philadelphia, there came the representative of a benevolent society in New York. He brought with him eight or ten children of the street, that he had picked up, and he was trying to find for them Christian homes: and, as the little ones stood on the pulpit and sang, our hearts melted within us. At the close of the services a great-hearted, wealthy man came up and said: "I'll take this little bright-eyed girl, and I'll adopt her as one of my own children; and he took her by the hand, lifted her into his carriage, and went away.

The next day, while we were in the church, gathering up garments for the poor of New York, this little child came back with a bundle under her arm, and she said: "There's my old dress; perhaps some of the poor children would like to have it," while she herself was in bright and beautiful array, and those who more immediately examined her, said that she had a ring on her hand. It was a ring of adoption.

There are a great many persons who pride themselves on their ancestry, and they glory over the royal blood that pours through their arteries. In their line there was a lord, or a duke, or a prime minister, or a king. But when the Lord, our Father, puts upon us the ring of His adoption, we become the children of the Ruler of all nations. "Behold what manner of love the Father hath bestowed upon us, that we should be called the sons of God." It matters not how poor our garments may be in this world, or how scant our bread, or how mean the hut we live in; if we have that ring of Christ's adoption upon our hand, we are assured of eternal defences.

Adopted! Why, then, we are brothers and sisters to all the good of earth and heaven. We have the family name, the family dress, the family keys,

The Family Wardrobe.

The Father looks after us, robes us, defends us, blesses us. We have royal blood in our veins, and there are crowns in our line. If we are His children, then princes and princesses. It is only a question of time when we get our coronet. Adopted! Then we have *the family secrets.* "The secret of the Lord is with them that fear Him." Adopted! Then we have the family inheritance; in the day when our Father shall divide the riches of heaven, we shall take our share of the mansions and palaces and temples. Henceforth let us boast no more of an earthly ancestry. The insignia of eternal glory is our coat of arms. This ring of adoption puts upon us all honor and all privilege. Now we can take the words of Charles Wesley, that prince of hymn-makers, and sing:

"Come, let us join our friends above,
Who have obtained the prize,
And on the eagle wings of love
To joy celestial rise.

"Let all the saints terrestrial sing
With those to glory gone;
For all the servants of our King,
In heaven and earth are one."

I have been told that when any of the members of any of the great secret societies of this country are in a distant city, and are in any kind of trouble, and are set upon by enemies, they have only to give a certain signal, and the members of that organization will flock around for defence. And when any man belongs to this great Christian brotherhood, if he gets in trouble, in trial, in persecution, in temptation, he has only to show this ring of Christ's adoption, and all the armed cohorts of heaven will come to his rescue.

Still further, when Christ takes a soul into His love He puts upon it

A Marriage-ring.

Now, that is not a whim of mine: "And I will betroth thee unto Me forever; yea, I will betroth thee unto Me in righteousness, and in judgment, and in loving-kindness, and in mercies." (Hosea 2: 19.) At the wedding altar the bridegroom puts a ring upon the hand of the bride, signifying love and faithfulness. Trouble may come upon the household, and the carpets may go, the pictures may go, the piano may go, everything else may go—the last that goes is that marriage-ring, for it is considered sacred. In the burial hour it is withdrawn from the hand and kept in a casket, and sometimes the box is opened on an anniversary day, and as you look at that ring you see under its arch a long procession of precious memories.

Within the Golden Circle

of that ring there is room for a thousand sweet recollections to revolve, and you think of the great contrast between the hour when, at the close of the "Wedding March," under the flashing lights and amid the aroma of orange-blossoms, you set that ring on the round finger of the plump hand, and that other hour when, at the close of the exhaustive watching, when you knew that the soul had fled, you took from the hand, which gave back no responsive clasp, from that emaciated finger, the ring that she had worn so long and worn so well. On some anniversary day you take up that ring, and you repolish it until all the old lustre comes back, and you can see in it the flash of eyes that long ago ceased to weep. Oh, it is not an unmeaning thing when I tell you that when Christ receives a soul into His keeping He puts on it a marriage-ring. He endows you from that moment with all His wealth. You are one—Christ and the soul—one in sympathy, one in affection, one in hope.

There is no power in earth or hell to effect a divorcement after Christ and the soul are united. Other kings have turned out their companions when they got weary of them, and sent them adrift from the palace gate. Ahasuerus banished Vashti; Napoleon forsook Josephine: but Christ is

The Husband that is True

forever. Having loved you once, he loves you to the end. Did they not try to divorce Margaret, the Scotch girl, from Jesus? They said: "You must give up your religion." She said: "I can't give up my religion." And so they took her down to the beach of the sea, and they drove in a stake at low-water mark, and they fastened her to it, expecting that as the tide came up her faith would fail. The tide began to rise, and came up higher and higher, and to the girdle, and to the lip, and in the last moment, just as the wave was washing her soul into glory, she shouted the praises of Jesus.

Oh, no; you cannot separate a soul from Christ. It is *an everlasting marriage.* Battle and storm and darkness cannot do it. Is it too much exultation for a man, who is but dust and ashes like myself, to cry out to-day: "I am persuaded that neither height nor depth nor principalities nor powers, nor things present, nor things to come, nor any other creature, shall separate me from the love of God which is in Christ Jesus, my Lord"? Glory be to God that when Christ and the soul are married they are bound by a chain—a golden chain, if I might say so—a chain with one link, and that one link the golden ring of God's everlasting love.

I go a step further, and tell you that when Christ receives a soul He puts on him

The Ring of Festivity

You know that it has been the custom in all ages to bestow rings on very happy occasions. There is nothing more appropriate for a birthday gift than a ring. You delight to bestow such a gift upon your children at such a time. It means joy, hilarity, festivity. Well, when this old man of the text wanted to tell how glad he was that his boy had got back, he expressed it in this way, Actually, before he ordered sandals to be put on his bare feet; before he ordered the fatted calf to be killed to appease the boy's hunger, he commanded: "Put a ring on his hand."

Oh, it is a merry time when Christ and the soul are united! Joy of forgiveness! What a splendid thing it is to feel that all is right between me and God! What a glorious thing it is to have God just take up all the sins of my life and put them in one bundle, and then fling them into the depths of the sea, never to rise again, never to be talked of again! Pollution all gone. Darkness all illumined. God reconciled. The prodigal home! "Put a ring on his hand!"

Every day I find happy Christian people. I find some of them with no second coat, some of them in huts and tenement houses, not one earthly comfort afforded them; and yet they are as happy as happy can be. They sing "Rock of Ages" as no other people in the world sing it. They never wore any jewelry in their life but one gold ring, and that was the ring of God's undying affection. Oh, how happy religion makes us! Did it make you gloomy and sad? Did you go with your head cast down? I do not think you got religion, my brother. That is not the effect of religion. True

Religion is Joy.

"Her ways are ways of pleasantness and all her paths are peace." Why, religion lightens all our burdens. It smooths all our way. It interprets all our sorrows. It changes the jar of earthly discord for the peal of festal bells. In front of the flaming furnace of trial it sets the forge on which sceptres are hammered out. Would you not like to-day to come up from the swine-feeding and try this religion? All the joys of heaven would come out and meet you, and God would cry from the throne: "Put a ring on his hand."

You are not happy. I see it. There is no peace, and sometimes you laugh when you feel a great deal more like crying.

The World is a Cheat.

It first wears you down with its follies, then it kicks you out into darkness. It comes back from the massacre of a million souls to attempt the destruction of your soul to-day. No peace out of God, but here is the fountain that can slake the thirst. Here is the harbor where you can drop safe anchorage.

Would you not like, I ask you—not perfunctorily, but as one brother might talk to another—would you not like to have a pillow of rest to put your head on? And would you not like, when you retire at night, to feel that all is well, whether you wake up to-morrow morning at six o'clock, or sleep the sleep that knows no waking? Would you not like to exchange this awful uncertainty about the future for a glorious assurance of heaven? Accept of the Lord Jesus to-day, and all is well. If on your way home some peril should cross the street and dash your life out, it would not hurt you. You would rise up immediately. You would stand in the celestial streets. You would be amid the great throng that forever worship and are forever happy. If this day some sudden disease should come upon you, it would not frighten you. If you knew you were going, you could give a calm farewell to your beautiful home on earth, and know that you are going right into the companionship of those who have already got beyond the toiling and the weeping.

Life's Saturday Night.

You feel on Saturday night different from the way you feel any other night of the week. You come home from the bank, or the store, or the shop, and you say: "Well, now my week's work is done, and to-morrow is Sunday." It is a pleasant thought. There is refreshment and reconstruction in the very idea. Oh, how pleasant it will be, if, when we get through the day of our life, and we go and lie down in our bed of dust, we can realize: "Well, now the work is all done, and to-morrow is Sunday—*an everlasting Sunday*."

"Oh, when, thou city of my God,
Shall I thy courts ascend?
Where congregations ne'er break up,
And Sabbaths have no end?"

There are people in this house to-day who are very near the eternal world. If you are Christians, I bid you be of good cheer. Bear with you our congratulations to the bright city. Aged men, who will soon be gone, take with you our love for our kindred in the better land; and when you see them, tell them that we are soon coming. Only a few more sermons to preach and hear. Only a few more heartaches. Only a few more toils. Only a few more tears. And then, what an entrancing spectacle will open before us!

"Beautiful heaven, where all is light,
Beautiful angels clothed in white,
Beautiful strains that never tire,
Beautiful harps through all the choir;
There shall I join the chorus sweet,
Worshipping at the Saviour's feet."

I approach you now with a general invitation, not picking out here and there a man, or here and there a woman, or here and there a child; but giving you

An Unlimited Invitation,

saying: "Come, for all things are now ready." We invite you to the warm heart of Christ, and the inclosure of the Christian Church. I know a great many think that the Church does not amount to much, that it is obsolete; that it did its work and is gone now, so far as all usefulness is concerned. It is the happiest place I have ever been in, except my own home.

I know there are some people who say they are Christians, who seem to get along without any help from others, and who culture solitary piety. They do not want any ordinances. I do not belong to that class. I cannot get along without them. There are so many things in this world that take my attention from God and Christ and heaven, that I want all the helps of all the symbols and of all the Christian associations; and I want around about me a solid phalanx of men who love God and keep His commandments. Are there any here who would like to enter into that association? Then by a simple, child-like faith, apply for admission into the visible Church, and you will be received. No questions asked about your past history or present surroundings.

Only One Test

—do you love Jesus? Baptism does not amount to anything, say a great many people, but the Lord Jesus declared: "He that believeth and is baptized shall be saved," putting baptism and faith side by side. And an apostle declares: "Repent and be baptized, every one of you." I do not stickle for any particular mode of baptism, but I put great emphasis on the fact that you ought to be baptized. Yet no more emphasis than the Lord Jesus Christ, the Great Head of the Church, puts upon it.

The world is going to, after a while, lose a great many of its votaries. There are to be revivals of religion that will shake the earth. We give you warning. There is a great host coming in to stand under the banner of the Lord Jesus Christ. Will you be among them? Will you be among the gathered sheaves? Some of you have been thinking on this subject year after year. You have found out that this world is a poor portion. You want to be Christians. You have come

Almost Into the Kingdom

of God; but there you stop, forgetful of the fact that to be almost saved is not to be saved at all. Oh, my brother, after having come so near to the door of mercy, if you turn back, you will never come at all. After you have heard of the goodness of God, if you turn away and die, it will not be because you did not have a good offer.

"God's spirit will not always strive
With hardened, self-destroying man;
Ye who persist His love to grieve
May never hear His voice again."

May God Almighty this hour move upon your soul and bring you back from the husks of the wilderness to the Father's house, and set you at the banquet, and "put a ring on your hand."

THE LATE HENRY BERGH.

(*See Portrait on page 188.*)

THE tender-hearted, earnest man to whom the brute creation of New York owes an incalculable debt of gratitude, was removed from the scene of his disinterested labors, on March 12. Henry Bergh was the champion of the distressed, ill-treated animals of all kinds. No lawyer ever espoused the cause of a wealthy client with more ardor than Mr. Bergh fought the case of a tortured dog or a cruelly-treated horse. He looked for no recompense, accepted no salary, but he labored with a vigor and an enthusiasm unexcelled by well-salaried officials. His very name was a terror to a cruel driver, or an inconsiderate owner of horses. Even the animals to be slaughtered for food were not beyond Mr. Bergh's thoughtful sympathy. He introduced more merciful methods at the city abattoirs, and secured legislation compelling their adoption. Dog-fighting, cock-fighting, rat-baiting, which were all common, when he began his labors, have now practically ceased, their patrons being forced by his efforts to hold their exhibitions in secrecy, under the ban of the law. A life full of self-denying, arduous and successful toil, on which he must have looked back with satisfaction, has come to its close, and the untiring worker rests from his labors.

Henry Bergh was born in 1823, in the city of New York; he was therefore in his sixty-fifth year when he died. His father was a ship-builder, and Henry with his brother Edward were in partnership with him and carried on the business after their father's death. They were of German descent, their grandfather having been a ship carpenter on the banks of the Rhine, who emigrated to this country in his youth. In 1842 Henry Berg sold out his share of the ship-building business, and entered himself a law student at Columbia College. Before the time for his graduation came he quitted college, married, and set out on a foreign tour. Eventually he and his bride settled down in Germany near the ancient home of the Bergh family. They remained in Europe for several years travelling extensively among its interesting historic localities. At length they returned to America, and then, in 1862, Henry Bergh received from President Lincoln the appointment of Secretary of Legation at St. Petersburg. Subsequently he was made American Consul in the same city, and was able to render efficient service in that office. Ill health, however, compelled his retirement in 1864, and he leisurely returned home. He remained a few weeks in England, where he made the acquaintance of the Earl of Harrowby, the President of the Royal Society for the Prevention of Cruelty to Animals. The facts he learned as to the society's work and the reforms it had effected, deeply impressed Mr. Bergh, and by the time the vessel on which he sailed reached Sandy Hook, he had resolved to make a similar society, in New York his life work.

The moral courage required for the undertaking was of the highest type. The sequel showed that Mr. Bergh possessed it to a degree hitherto unsuspected. He began his labor by seeking to arouse public opinion. He collected statistics with enormous difficulty, and then began lecturing and holding public meetings. He was ridiculed, called a fanatic and a visionary, but he was not discouraged. He succeeded in interesting a few men and women in his work, and at length, in 1866, after weeks of persistent lobbying as shrewd and crafty as if he were engineering a scheme to make himself a millionaire, he induced the Legislature at Albany to confide to an incorporated Society the powers of arrest and prosecution. Mr. Bergh was made President of the Society, and endowed it with a large share of his personal property. Shortly afterward Louis Bonard an eccentric Frenchman living in New York, bequeathed to the Society $150,000, and thus armed with ample funds Mr. Bergh went to work. At one time he directed his attacks to brutal dog-fighters, at another the hog slaughterers came under the ban of his displeasure. It made no difference in what station of life he found the offender. As soon as he had ascertained who was to blame he set in motion the machinery of his office and society. Assistant District-Attorney for life, and assistant to the Attorney-General, he was enabled to wield tremendous powers, and he never hesitated to make use of the opportunities thus afforded. He has more than once caused the suspension of the traffic on an important avenue, by removing horses from the street-cars when they were unfit for work, and arresting the drivers.

As a result of Mr. Bergh's labors, his Society has now four hundred officers at work in the State and its influence has spread throughout the country. Before he commenced his work there was not a State nor a Territory in the Union which had any law relating to the protection of animals from cruelty. Now thirty-four States have passed statutes bearing upon the subject. This excellent result was mainly due to a lecturing tour which Mr. Bergh undertook in 1873. During that tour he also availed himself of the opportunity of speaking before the Evangelical Alliance and the Episcopal Convention in furtherance of his pet projects. He was actually the means of having a new rule adopted by the Episcopal Convention, suggesting that Protestant Episcopal clergyman at least once a year preach a sermon on mercy to animals.

THE FATAL BLIZZARD IN NEW YORK.

A Day and a Night of Devastation—Wanderers in Snow and Darkness—Men Frozen Dead in the Streets — Traffic Suspended — Telegraphic Communication Cut Off—Telegraphing to Boston by Way of England—The Mercury Below Zero—Fifty Dollars for a Cab-Ride—Seventy-five Trains Snow-Bound.

THE storm which swept down upon New York City on the morning of March 12, will never be forgotten by any person who was in the city. The New York *Herald*, which pays special attention to all meteorological phenomena, states that it was the severest storm within the memory of living men, and that there is no record of any convulsion of nature bursting, as this did, upon New York, with a fury which arrested the resources of industry and civilization, paralyzed business, closed houses of amusement, interrupted traffic by steam or local transit, prevented telegraphic communication, and took over the great metropolis to its fierce, wanton will. The same goes on to say: "The day was one of confusing for many, business anxieties, embarrassments for some; fatal accidents, discomfort and interruption to all. There was a fierce, wild beauty in lower New York, its busy Broadway and that never ending roar, as silent and dead, but for the whirling gusts of banked and blinding snow, as

An Avenue in Buried Pompeii.

St. Paul's, with its memories of colonial days, wore a beauty of its own in the snows, while the sombre Astor, with the many-columned Post Office, might have been creations of the fancy, so strange were the freaks of the storm. But for every purpose, except to listen and wait, New York was *virtually a dead city*, business as completely dead as though it were under the guns of an invading army. It was a city in chaos, bowing before the awful Power which taught us—as it is well, perhaps, we should sometimes learn the lesson—how weak and frail we are in the presence of infinity. The following narrative, compiled from the voluminous reports of the daily journals, will give a faint idea of the dreadful visitation:

The storm started at about Sunday midnight. A gentle rain had been plashing on the pavements for several hours. Gradually it turned into a wet snow, and the gutters ran slush. The wind began to rise, and the thermometer fell rapidly. *Suddenly the whole city seemed to tremble* as the storm swept down upon it. Signboards were torn from the fronts of buildings, roofs were stripped, windows blown out, wagons overturned, and street-cars halted. When day broke the city presented an amazing appearance. Through the wild clouds of snow that were driven along the streets, could be seen loaded wagons given up by their drivers. At every turn could be seen these

Deserted Vehicles.

Their owners had fled for their lives, apparently regardless of what became of the property. Butchers' wagons piled high with meat, milk trucks crowded with cans, grocers' wagons, coal carts, street-cars, were scattered in the mountains of snow in all directions. There were thousands upon thousands of these abandoned wagons and carts, some overturned, some lying across the street, some half buried in the drifts. Here and there they formed enormous barricades, which caught the snow and rolled it up in solid barriers.

Long before daylight the horse-car lines gave up all attempts to carry passengers. The multitudes trudged through the storm to

The Elevated Roads,

and crowded every train. Even these trains were few and far between. The snow and wind made it almost impossible to work the switches, and the brakes were rendered useless. Finally the whole Elevated railway system came to a dead standstill. Then ensued scenes of excitement and suffering. There was a solid blockade of trains on the Sixth Avenue road, from Fourth Street to Twenty-eighth Street. The passengers were half frozen. They could not reach the stations except by walking along the narrow edge of the tracks, which was frightfully dangerous in such a high wind. Many of the men took off their overcoats to shelter the half perished women, while others went to the car platforms and called upon persons in the street below to bring ladders, offering sums of five dollars to any man who would bring one in five minutes. Ladders were soon brought, and train after train was emptied by that means.

So terrible did the storm become that men lost their way in the streets. The heavens darkened, and a great roaring sound came from the thundering clouds.

As the afternoon wore away men and women were blown flat on the ground or picked up in the air and thrown against buildings. Hundreds of pedestrians were cut and bruised. Many were run over. The very mail wagons had to be abandoned, in spite of the desperate struggles of the horses. They were left in all sections of the city. On Eighth avenue a hearse was deserted by its driver. A broker who had a fortune depending on his getting down-town, offered a cab-driver $500 for his horse, cab, and harness. "No," said the driver, "it ain't mine; but I'll take you down-town for fifty dollars, if ye'll pay in advance." And the broker paid. Many others succeeded in getting short rides of a mile or two for $25.

The storm increased in fury on Monday evening and through the night, and the mercury fell to one degree below zero. All through the wild night and far into the morning, the police were at work saving exhausted pedestrians from

Death in the Snow.

One well-known merchant at daybreak was found dead on Seventh avenue. Another man's rigid corpse was picked up in Central Park. An unfortunate woman was frozen to death in a hallway. Two other corpses were found not far off. Men were picked up senseless in all directions.

All the electric lights were out, and no attempt to light the gas lamps was made. Drunken men and women who were simply tired by long and severe struggles in the drifts were stumbled over in every neighborhood. The ambulances were overturned again and again, although some of them had extra horses attached by ropes to the shafts. A ghastly procession of wounded men and women began to file into the wards of the hospitals. Broken skulls, fractured arms, thighs and legs, frozen hands and feet—these were the things that kept the whole corps of every hospital up all night. Men were found bareheaded and insane in the tempest.

All telephone and telegraphic communication was suspended. Outside the city the wires were all down. The only telegraphic system in operation was the cable under the Atlantic, and messages were actually sent over that route to Boston, Mass., each message travelling six thousand miles.

Brooklyn was in a frightful plight, being completely cut off from New York. There was an effort made to run cars on the big Bridge, but one train was derailed on the west side, and further work in that direction was given up. To walk across the bare and unsheltered promenade in the storm that shrieked through the ponderous steel rigging meant suffering, and perhaps death. Many persons succeeded in walking across the river on a huge ice floe which became jammed in the river against the piers. There were several narrow escapes of passengers by that route, for the floe broke up and the pieces drifted down to the bay with their living freight, and but for the swift steam-tugs which followed the pieces many lives would have been lost.

The Buried Trains

on the trunk lines were an appalling feature of the storm, the results of which are not revealed at the time of writing. No less than *seventy-five trains were snow-bound* within a circle of fifty miles from the city. How the passengers, especially the women and children, must have suffered from hunger and cold may be imagined. The great trunk lines were all buried. Now and then some pale and half dead wanderer struggled into the mountainous outskirts and told dreadful stories of whole train-loads of passengers imprisoned in the snow, without food or the slighest means of escape. Rescue parties in sleighs were sent out in all directions to relieve the snow-bound unfortunates. The railway companies battled heroically with the snow, in their efforts to push through their trains. Here and there *engines were chained together* and hurled against the drifts at full speed. The New York Central company upset one of its heaviest locomotives while trying to butt a hole through the snow packed in the Fourth avenue tunnel. How many have died in the drifts while trying to reach help from these blocked trains will not be known for days.

A SWISS PREACHER'S LOST TEXT.

A REMARKABLE occurrence, illustrating the providential dealings of God in preparing a message for a soul in need, is described in a narrative translated from the German by Rev. S. F. Smith, D. D., and published in the *Watchword*. It refers to an experience in the life of a clergyman at Basle, in Switzerland, who had preached the gospel for many years.

One Sabbath he went as usual to the house of God, and on the way prayed earnestly that the word that day might be blessed to the salvation of at least one soul. He took his place in the pulpit, and during the singing opened the great Bible, and sought for the passage which he had selected for the theme of his discourse. But he was utterly unable to recall his text. He turned the leaves hither and thither again and again, but all to no purpose. But what seemed to him very remarkable, every time he turned over the pages of the Bible, his eye fell upon the words, "The Son of Man is come to seek and to save that which was lost."

His anxiety increased. The singing was ended; still his text did not come back to him, nor the plan of the sermon which he had prepared. Then came the prayer; the reader can imagine with what a troubled heart he approached the throne of grace. In his secret soul he cried out to God, "O Lord, help!" He opened the Bible again, and again his eye fell on the passage, "The Son of Man is come to seek and to save that which was lost." He took courage, read the passage aloud, and preached a very impressive sermon.

Returning to his home, he thought over the singular occurrence, and was unable to see why God had thus dealt with him. Several days passed, and he did not hear that the sermon had produced any effect. On Thursday morning he was sitting at work in his study. A knock was heard at his door, and an unknown man entered, with tears in his eyes. "Sir," said he, "I can no longer forbear to thank you for saving my life."

The pastor, unable to understand what he meant, begged him to sit down and tell him his story, when he related the following:

"For several months past I have been the most wretched man in the world. I am very poor, and have a numerous family, and in order to feed them I have been obliged to run in debt. My debts I could not pay, and my creditors were unwilling to wait any longer. I had reached the last point of necessity. Finding no comfort I was often tempted to drown my senses in strong drink, and thus for a few hours to forget my trouble. At last *I resolved to hang myself*, and last Sabbath was the day I had appointed. I put a rope in my pocket, and started for the woods not far away. As I passed by the church the bell was ringing, and the door stood open. A death-like solemnity seized me. I tried to go forward, but the bell would not let me. The more I tried, the louder the bell sounded in my ears. Then the thought came to me, 'Perhaps it can do you no harm to step into the church before you take your own life, and take along with you a good word.' So I turned and went into the church.

"As soon as the singing was ended, you, sir, read the text, 'The Son of Man is come to seek and to save that which was lost.' Then it seemed as if a haze came before my eyes. I began to shake and tremble, and said to myself, 'I am one of the lost, and there is no salvation for me, neither here nor there.' But when you told of the Lord Jesus Christ, and how He graciously seeks for the lost, hope sprang even in my heart, and the longer you spoke the more I was sure that He could and would save me. When you said, 'Amen,' I was so full of joy that I returned home gladly, threw the rope into the fire, fell upon my knees, and gave my heart forever to the Lord Jesus. So you see by the grace of God you have saved my body and soul."

The venerable minister heard the narration with deep emotion, and then said, "So God makes even church bells His messengers and servants, to seek and to save the lost."

Then the two fell upon their knees together and gave thanks to God.

THE WONDERFUL BIRTHDAY OF 144,000 TRANSLATED ONES ON THURSDAY, MARCH 5, 1896.

By the Rev. M. Baxter.*

Never in the history of this world, since the Creation until the present month of March, 1888, has it been known or recognized that the *fifth day of March* is destined to be a momentous anniversary-day, ranking in importance next to Christmas Day or Good Friday, because, as the latter were respectively the Birthday and Crucifixion Day of Christ at His First Advent, so the fifth day of March, 1896, is foreshown by Daniel's Prophecies to be the day of Christ's Second Advent, and, consequently, the Birthday of the Manchild in Revelation 12: 5—in other words, the formation and ascension of the Corporate body of the 144,000 watchful Christians to whom the Sun-clothed Woman (the Christian Church militant) is to give birth at Christ's Second Advent "in the air" at the distance of Sixty-nine Weeks of Literal Days after a future command to rebuild Jerusalem, as predicted in Daniel 9: 25.

Now, as these Sixty-nine Weeks are stated by Gabriel in Daniel 9: 24 (as learned expositors agree) to be "*determined*" or "*divided off*" from the commencing portion of the total period of 2,345 days, mentioned in the vision of Daniel 8: 14, as 2,300 days, with 45 days afterwards added to it in Daniel 12: 11, 12 (the excess of the 1,335 days beyond the 1,290 days),—therefore the Sixty-nine Weeks must begin at the same time as the 2,345 days, of which they are in fact the commencing section. And as the 2,345 days begin on November 8, 1894, inasmuch as they have to terminate with the End of this Age on April 11, 1901, therefore the Sixty-nine Weeks beginning simultaneously on November 8, 1894, will end on March 5, 1896.

The reason why April 11, 1901, is the End of this Age, as above stated, is because April 11, 1901, being

The Last Day of Passover Week,

is exactly 45 years distant from the last day of Passover Week in 1856, on which day the Crimean War Treaty of Peace was signed, which "cleansed the sanctuary" of the Holy Land from Turkish Mohammedan persecution at the end of the 2,300 *days* in their year-day fulfilment as 2,300 *years* (Daniel 8: 14); and also because April 11, 1901, is exactly 2,345 years distant from the last day of Passover Week in Nisan B.C. 444-5, on which day King Artaxerxes in the 20th year of his reign gave "the Command to Nehemiah to rebuild Jerusalem" in the 2d chapter of Nehemiah, exactly Sixty-nine Weeks of years before Messiah, the Prince, being made a Covenant at His Crucifixion in Passover Week A.D. 30.

There are Sixty-nine Weeks of years from Artaxerxes' "Command to rebuild Jerusalem" B.C. 444-5 up to the Crucifixion at Messiah's First Advent in A.D. 30, and there will be Sixty-nine Weeks of *days* from a future "Command to rebuild Jerusalem" on November 8, 1894, up to March 5, 1896, when Messiah the Prince will be "made a Covenant" to His waiting and watching people at His Second Advent. Thus

The Great Prophecy in Daniel 9: 25

will be fulfilled both in *year-days* and in *literal days*: "From the going forth of the commandment to restore and build Jerusalem unto Messiah the Prince shall be *seven weeks and threescore and two weeks*, and after threescore and two weeks, shall Messiah be *made a Covenant*."

The writer of these remarks did not discover until March or April 1887 that the day of the signing of the Crimean War Treaty of Peace in April, 1856, which ended the 2,300 years and commenced the remaining supplementary 45 years, was the *Last Day of Passover Week* according to the Jewish Calendar, and it is this discovery which enables us to be certain that the 45 years, starting on the Last Day of Passover Week in April, 1856, must necessarily end on the Last Day of Passover Week in April, 1901, which, according to Lindo's Jewish Calendar for 1901, will be April 11, 1901.

Previous to this discovery the writer had rested satisfied with the general fact that the 2,300 years ended with the Treaty of Peace which closed the Crimean War, without thinking of ascertaining what exact day it was in the spring of 1856, or what that day was according to the Jewish Calendar in reference to Passover Week. But it is evident that

The Sixty-nine Weeks of Years

having ended with the Crucifixion of Christ in Passover Week A.D. 30, must have begun in Passover Week B.C. 444-5, therefore the 2,300 *years*, which began at the same time as the Sixty-nine Weeks of years, or 483 years, must likewise have begun in Passover Week B.C. 444-5, and consequently must have ended in Passover Week A.D. 1856, and so indeed they did at the signing of the Crimean War Treaty of Peace, in Passover Week, April, 1856.

The writer of these remarks had not fully discovered all these particulars by March 5, 1887, and therefore did not then know that the Second Coming of Messiah the Prince, according to Daniel 9: 25, would be on March 5, 1896. Hence March 5, 1888, is the first periodical annual recurrence of the 5th day of March in the history of the human race in which any mortal man knows and recognizes it as the prospective anniversary day of the Second Advent of Christ. This knowledge now enables us to regard it with solemn reverence scarcely inferior to that with which we regard Christmas Day, or Good Friday, or Easter Day, because this fifth day of March will be the day in 1896 on which millions of deceased saints will arise from their graves, and 144,000 living, watchful Christians will be translated without dying to meet Christ in the air along with those resurrected saints.

We therefore begin this year to observe and commemorate every one of the eight remaining fifth days of March in 1888, 1889, 1890, 1891, 1892, 1893, 1894, 1895, with reverence and holy joy, as being the anticipative anniversary of Christ's Second Advent (in its earlier stage) and of the Resurrection and

Translation of Christians on March 5, 1896.

Thus four days from the date of the present number of the *Prophetic News* (March 1) will be the antecedent anniversary of the GLORIOUS BIRTHDAY of 144,000 living Christians, as March 5, 1896, because on that day THE MAN-CHILD WILL BE BORN on that eventful Day of days the Sun-clothed Star-crowned Woman, representing the Living Christian Church militant on earth, will give birth to the Manchild (the chosen body of 144,000 Wise Virgins or Watchful Christians) who will forthwith be caught up to God and to His throne at the first stage of Christ's Advent "in the air," as described in Rev. 12: 5, 14: 1-5; 1 Thess. 4: 16, 17.

Each of those 144,000 will enjoy the peculiar prerogative of having THREE BIRTHDAYS—a peculiarity which will not attach to any other of the human race. Each of them will have been (1) born at their natural birth; (2) born again at their spiritual conversion, concerning which Christ said, "Except a man be born again he cannot enter the kingdom of God" (John 3); (3) born a third time when, at their *translation* at Christ's Advent, they become part of the Manchild, i.e., one of the corporate body of

144,000 Watchful Christians,

to whom the Woman, the Christian Church on earth, is then to GIVE BIRTH. Perhaps scarcely any two of those 144,000 will have (1) the same natural or (2) the same spiritual birthday, but all of them will have the SAME TRANSLATION BIRTHDAY.

The Sun-clothed Woman will be delivered of the Manchild suddenly and instantaneously, so that all the 144,000 will be caught up alive to heaven at almost one and the same minute at Christ's Advent in the air. "The trumpet shall sound, and the holy dead shall be raised incorruptible, and we shall be changed" (1 Cor. 15: 51-2; 1 Thess. 4: 16). The Natal Day upon which this sublime and astounding TRANSLATION BIRTH will take place is clearly and conclusively foreshown by Daniel's Date to be

Thursday, March 5, 1896,

and the HOUR is also foreshown to be about the Ninth Hour—the Hour of the daily Evening Sacrifice—about *three o'clock in the afternoon* in Jerusalem—the same hour in which "Christ our Passover was sacrificed for us," and gave up the ghost.

In the *Prophetic News* for last month (February) a page was given showing the different times of the nations that correspond with 3 P.M. in Jerusalem. In London it is 38 minutes past 12 o'clock noonday, and in New York 43 minutes past 7 o'clock in the morning.

About nine years ago, in 1879, the writer published in the *Prophetic News* the great fundamental truth that there will be, according to the three passages in Daniel 8: 14; 9: 25; 12: 11-12, exactly 1,862 DAYS from the First Stage of Christ's future Advent in the air to its Second Stage at His descent on the earth upon the Mount of Olives.

Many expositors had long ago pointed out that the First Stage, when the Wise Virgins, who are ready, shall be caught up into the air without dying to meet Christ (as described in 1 Thess. 4: 16, 17; Rev. 12: 5; 14: 1-5), must be BEFORE the three and a half years of Antichrist's reign and persecution, and that the Second Stage is AFTER that three and a half years when Christ destroys Antichrist at the Battle of Armageddon, near Mount Olivet, as described in Zechariah 14, Ezekiel 39, Rev. 19.

But no expositor ever advanced beyond the general fact that at least three and a half years will intervene between

The Two Stages

of Christ's Second Advent, until the writer showed in his prophetic books, published in 1862-63, that the First Stage of Christ's Advent in the air to raise the deceased saints and translate 144,000 watchful Christians (1 Thess. 4: 16, 17; Rev. 12: 5; 14: 1-5) will be about FIVE YEARS before His descent on this earth at Mount Olivet at the battle of Armageddon.

One clear proof of this is that as the Manchild in Rev. 12: 5 (Christ Personal at His Ascension) was caught up to God's throne in A.D. 39, at the distance of 1862 *years* before the future End of this Age in 1901, so the Manchild (Christ Mystical—the corporate body of 144,000 living Christians) will be caught up to God's throne 1,862 *days* before the End of this Age on April 11, 1901. And March 5, 1896, will be exactly 1,862 days previous to April 11, 1901.

During the future Millennium of 1,000 years generations yet unborn will observe March 5 as a sacred holiday, and as the anniversary of the Second Advent of Christ and of the Translation of the 144,000, with a solemnity and rejoicing scarcely less than that with which they will observe and commemorate Christmas Day or Good Friday or Easter Day.

*From the *Prophetic News* for March; for sale, price 6 cents, at this Office, 63 Bible House, New York.

CHRISTIAN HERALD AND SIGNS OF OUR TIMES.

OFFICE, 63 BIBLE HOUSE, NEW YORK.

ENTERED AT THE POST-OFFICE AT NEW YORK, N. Y., AS SECOND-CLASS MATTER.

Published Weekly. Subscription price, $1.50 a year; $1 eight months; 75 cents six months; sent two months on trial for 25 cents; always payable in advance. Single copies for sale by, or can be ordered at, all newsdealers.

Remittances by Mail should be by Post-office money order, bank cheques, or drafts or express money order, and should always be made payable to THE CHRISTIAN HERALD.

Receipts are not sent, the receipt of the paper by a subscriber is a sufficient proof that his remittance has been received. If the paper does not arrive promptly, please advise us, that we may see if the address is correctly entered.

Change of Address. Name of Post Office and State, of both old and new address, should always be given in case of removal.

CURRENT EVENTS.

Mr. Randall's Tax and Tariff Reduction Bill, expected for some time, has at last been introduced in the House of Representatives. The estimated reductions under it will be $70,000,000 on internal revenue taxation and $25,000,000 on customs duties. The principle applied to the reduction of the tariff in this bill is stated to be the difference in cost of producing commodities in this and other countries where there are no climatic or other natural causes why they cannot be produced abundantly in this country. Mr. Randall does not propose, as it was expected he would, to abolish the whole Internal Revenue system. He limits himself to the repeal of the taxes on tobacco, fruit, brandy and weiss beer, and the reduction of the whisky tax from ninety to fifty cents a gallon. He also proposes to abolish dealers' licenses, wholesale as well as retail. It is difficult to see how Republicans can consistently support Mr. Randall's bill though they would undoubtedly prefer it to that of Mr. Mills. Practically, however, Mr. Randall's bill is an admission of the principle on which Mr. Mills bases his measure, though Mr. Randall is far more conservative than his colleague from Texas.

The Admission of Utah as a State was Formally proposed in a bill introduced in the Senate on March 15 by Senator Butler. It provides for the election of a Constitutional Convention in August next to meet in December. If after organization the Convention shall adopt the constitution of the United States, they shall have the right to frame a State Constitution, which shall contain among other things an irrevocable ordinance providing that perfect toleration of religious sentiments shall be secured, and that no inhabitant of the State shall ever be molested in person or property on account of his mode of religious worship. If the constitution formed by this Convention shall be ratified by the people of the Territory, the President is required to issue a proclamation admitting the State into the Union. So clear and emphatic have been the warnings to Congress against the admission of Utah that it may be hoped this bill will be rejected. Self-government once conceded to her, Congress would have no further power to prevent the continuance and legalization of polygamy.

The Approaching Meeting in Washington of the International Council of Women is arousing considerable interest in the Capital. The Council is called to celebrate the fortieth anniversary of the first public demand made for "women's rights," which was done in a convention held at Seneca Falls, N. Y., in 1848. Among the associations that will be represented are the following: American Woman Suffrage Association, National Temperance Hospital and Medical College Association, Knights of Labor Association for the Advancement of Women, Sorosis National Moral Education Society, Ladies of the Grand Army of the Republic, Women's National Indian Association, National Women's Christian Temperance Union, Women's State Fair Association, Indiana; Women's Centenary Association, and the Women's Baptist Missionary Society. Delegates will also attend from various foreign and international societies, among which are: The Red Cross Society, Edinburgh National Society for Women's Suffrage, Danish Women's Society, Finnish Women's Association, Norwegian Woman Suffrage Association, World's Woman's Christian Temperance Union, and several Women's Liberal Associations in England. Pundita Romabai will describe the condition of her sex in India, and an intelligent Chinese lady will speak of the women of China.

A New Treaty With China has been Negotiated with the object of settling the vexed immigration question. Its provisions, as published in the daily journals, indicate that China is ready to co-operate with the United States in stopping the migration of Chinamen to this country, and has already prohibited their embarkation from ports under the control of the Chinese government. It appears, however, that the bulk of immigrants come through Hong Kong, which, being under English control, is beyond the jurisdiction of the Chinese Government. The new treaty guarantees to the Chinese now in this country the rights and privileges which treaties, laws, and customs give to all foreigners, except to become citizens by naturalization. As to those Chinese now in this country who desire to go to China, and later return to the United States, the Chinese Government agrees, in the new treaty, that this re-entry shall be limited to such of them as can, before their departure from the United States, legally establish the fact that they leave in the country a wife, child, or parent, and that they possess here $1,000 worth of property. But the leave to return with this condition must be used within a year from their departure. The treaty, if ratified by the Senate, will give to our Government all the power to regulate Chinese immigration which China can concede.

The Gigantic Strike of Miners in the Lehigh region of Pennsylvania, is now practically ended. At a meeting of District Assembly 87, at Hazleton, last week, it was "declared off." It is reported that this action was the only course left to pursue, for the men, finding themselves and their children on the verge of actual death from starvation, were going back to work in large numbers. It is six months ago since the strike was inaugurated. And the suffering and want which have reigned in the region since then have been beyond power of words to describe. The men stood out firmly as long as possible, but they had reached the extremity when it was either to work or die of starvation and exposure. They went back to work at the scale of wages which ruled before the strike.

The Remarkable Feature of the Storm which visited the Middle Atlantic States on March 12, and whose greatest fury was spent in New York and the Hudson Valley, on Long Island, in Connecticut, New Jersey and part of Pennsylvania, was the combination of high winds and heavy snow. Continually for thirty-six hours it blew a gale of blizzardous proportions. The snow-fall was exceptionally heavy, and the high wind drifted the snow so badly, in the cities and in the open country, that for once the wheels of commerce were effectually clogged and the great American metropolis was isolated from the country. There were no trains arriving or departing; no mails; no telegraphic intercourse. After two days of untold hardships the snow embargo was partially raised by herculean efforts on the part of the authorities and private corporations and citizens, and the busy world began to assume its wonted aspect. The more prominent features of the visitation are described on page 182 of this issue. Serious disasters on the Middle Atlantic coast followed in the wake of the blizzard. The lives lost in shipwrecks at the Delaware Breakwater number thirty. A New York pilot-boat, the *W. H. Starbuck* No. 6," is believed to have gone to the bottom of the sea with six souls o[n] board, shortly after colliding with a Briti[sh] steamship, the *Japanese* 25 miles southea[st] of Barnegat and 95 miles from Sandy Hoo[k] during the gale. Grave fears are entertaine[d] for the safety of twelve other New York an[d] Sandy Hook pilot-boats which were out in th[e] terrible storm and have not yet been hea[rd] from. Each boat has on board, on an averag[e] eight persons.

The Remains of the German Kaiser, Whil[e] lying in state in the Berlin Cathedral, we[re] viewed by upwards of 300,000 people, belongin[g] to all classes of society. At the funeral o[n] March 16, there was a gigantic military displa[y] as well as an unprecedented collection of roya[l]ties, and there was no lack of visible signs o[f] grief. On the line of the funeral processio[n] cenotaphs and obelisks were erected at distance[s] of twenty-five feet. The Emperor Frederic[k] was not able to take part in the funeral cere[]mony. He surveyed the procession from a wi[n]dow of the palace as it passed. The solem[n] funeral service was held in the Cathedral a[t] noon, when the dead Emperor's grandson, a[s] chief mourner, walked up the nave and took h[is] place at the head of the coffin. Alongside o[f] him were the King of Saxony, the King of Be[l]gium, and the King of Roumania. Close b[y] stood the Grand Duke of Baden, Princes A[l]brecht and Henry and other princes of the roya[l] house of Prussia, the Prince Imperial of Austri[a] the Prince Imperial of Russia, the Grand Duke[s] Michael and Nicholas of Russia, the Prince o[f] Wales, the Crown Prince of Italy, the Crow[n] Prince of Denmark and the Crown Prince o[f] Greece, all in the uniform of their respectiv[e] countries. The princes of Bavaria, the Gran[d] Duke of Hesse, and other notables and foreig[n] representatives, including General Billot, o[f] France, and his suite, formed the next rows i[n] the nave. A sermon was preached by Dr. Koge[l] the Court chaplain, and the choir sang mus[ic] selected by the aged Kaiser for the occasio[n] shortly before his death. The coffin was the[n] taken up and carried by twelve stalwart off[i]cers to the hearse, and, followed by the processio[n] of illustrious personages, was taken to the mau[]soleum prepared for it at Charlottenburg.

General Boulanger has been Deprived of h[is] present command for breach of discipline, an[d] a decree to that effect has been approved b[y] President Carnot. The official journal state[s] that General Boulanger came to Paris on Fe[b]ruary 24, again on March 2, and again on Marc[h] 10, without permission from the War Offic[e]. The last two times, it says, he was in disguis[e] wearing dark spectacles and affecting lamenes[s]. The paper dwells on the serious nature of suc[h] breaches of discipline by a general officer. It [is] the popular opinion, however, that the condu[ct] of the Government is prompted by jealousy an[d] spite, and several demonstrations have take[n] place which show a dangerous tendency on th[e] part of the rougher classes to support the Ge[n]eral by force if necessary.

The Wedding of Prince Oscar of Swede[n] and Miss Ebba Munck (whose portraits we[re] published in this journal on March 8) too[k] place at Bournemouth, England, on the 15t[h] inst. The Queen of Sweden, Princess Carl an[d] Eugene of Sweden, the Crown Princes of De[n]mark, and the Duchess of Albany were presen[t]. Pastor Bestrow, of Stockholm performed th[e] marriage ceremony. The wedding was solemn[]ized with the Swedish Lutheran service in a[n] English Episcopal chapel, and has called for[th] protests from some of the high church clerg[y]men. Prince Oscar, who, now that he ha[s] resigned his royal privileges and station, t[o] marry the woman of his choice, is known a[s] Prince Bernadotte, came to the wedding in th[e] uniform of a Commander in the Swedish Nav[y]. The marriage service was essentially like th[e] English Protestant service. When it came to th[e] ring, both held it, he in the right hand, she the left, while they repeated the promises usu[al] in such cases. The happy couple went the Isle of Wight for the honeymoon.

A Terrible Calamity is Reported From Dakota. The Methodist Episcopal University at the town of Mitchell, has been destroyed by fire, and professors, students, and servants had to make their escape from the upper windows of the doomed building. One of the students was so seriously injured that he died within two hours; three others, among them Professor O. H. Taylor, sustained such severe injuries that they were not expected to live; and eight more are badly injured. Fortunately a snow-drift broke the force of the fall of some of the inmates, otherwise the calamity would have been still greater. One of the professors, Mr. Duncan, had a miraculous escape. He was driven to the roof by the flames. There was a deep snow on the roof, and it was bitter cold. He had secured a clothes-line, and fastening this to the waterspout he slid down through the flames. Both of his feet were frozen and he was scorched in the descent.

An Annuitant in Illinois has Recovered his lost health through his financial arrangement. Some time ago a citizen possessed of a small property lost his wife, and after her death fell into a condition of melancholia. He was still further depressed by money losses, as in his depressed condition he was imposed upon in business by unprincipled men. The attention of the county attorney was called to the case, and the man was taken care of. Finally he executed a deed transferring his property to the county, in return for which the county officers undertook to provide for him for life. He appeared to feel relief when the arrangement was complete, and since then has gradually recovered his health and spirits. He is relieved from all apprehension as to old age or sickness, having confidence in the integrity and capacity of the county to provide for his future. It may be hoped that he is equally at rest about his safety after the county has completed its contract by burying him. He will be still more dependent then, but if recognizing his helplessness in spiritual as he did in temporal matters, he has trusted his all with Jesus, he is safe. (II. Tim. 1 : 12.)

A Valetudinarian's Methodical Life is Described in the obituary column of a Boston journal. It states that a merchant of that city, who has died at the age of eighty-one, devoted the bulk of his life from his youth to the care of his health. He made that subject his continual study, and he devoted himself to it with a wonderful assiduity. He rode just so far each day, when the weather was fair, and at such an hour. He had a great variety of clothing, which he regulated with precision by the thermometer, sometimes changing his dress many times in a day, and selected for his overclothes when he rode out the very garments which the mercury indicated. He had a weathercock put upon his stable, within fair view from his bedroom and sitting-room: and that and his thermometer, and all possible signs of the weather, he was watching constantly, and found in these occupations an absorbing way of employing all his time. It is possible that his life may have been prolonged a few years by all this thought and care; but it is marvellous that any man conscious of possessing an immortal soul should have neglected its interests to give his supreme attention to his body, which must eventually die in spite of all his care. (Mat. 6 : 25.)

A Man Who Stole a Saw Mill has Astonished Baltimore, Md., by his audacity. A press despatch from that city states that in East Baltimore was an unused saw-mill belonging to a judge. The chief value of the mill consisted in the machinery, the building not being worth much. On March 5 a handsome, well-dressed stranger arrived, and examined the mill and the surrounding premises. He then summoned a man who does hauling, and informed him that he had decided to dispose of the machinery and "the old shanty," and wanted it removed at once. The man hired extra help and another dray and had the machinery packed the same afternoon, while the handsome stranger went to the junk dealers to arrange for a sale. Eventually he found a purchaser, and the machinery was carted to his place, and seven hundred dollars was handed over as purchase money. The stranger put the money in his pocket, and invited the carter to come to his hotel after the machinery was unloaded, dine with him, and receive the pay for his work. The carter, however, was unable to find the stranger at the time named, and the police, who were put on his tracked, have been similarly unsuccessful. The judge who owned the mill was presiding in the City Court when the theft took place, and when informed of his loss, was so amazed at the audacity of the thief that he burst into laughter. In a day when even property so cumbrous as the machinery of a mill is not safe from thieves, there can be no excuse for forgetting the injunction of the Saviour. (Matt. 6 : 19, 20.)

A Man Lost in Central Park, New York, Tells a thrilling story of his experience. He started on March 12 about noon, as usual, from his home in the up-town district to report at the Telegraph Headquarters where he was employed as an operator. He took his usual route across the corner of the Park at Seventy-third Street. The snow was deep, but he was wrapped up well, and did not mind the cold. He continued walking for nearly an hour, and began to wonder how it was he had not reached the east side of the Park, when he noticed that the location was unfamiliar to him. The snow was so deep that he frequently got in up to his waist, and his fingers began to show signs of frostbite. "Then," said he, "I got thoroughly frightened, and wandered about, floundering, rolling, and tumbling, rubbing my frozen fingers and ears till I was almost crazy. Not a familiar object in sight—nothing but snow, snow, snow! Oh! it was awful, I thought my time had come. When almost exhausted I stumbled up against a signboard. With my benumbed fingers I scraped the snow off and managed to read the directions to the nearest exit. At last—it seemed ages to me—I reached Fifth Avenue and fell on the sidewalk exhausted. I don't remember much more, except that I reached the office somehow, and they thawed me out. To a man in such peril the directions on the signboard were sufficient; he did not need that any one should urge him to follow them. Sinners in danger of perishing are not so wise. Not only do they ignore the directions to safety, but they are deaf to warnings and entreaties. (II Chron. 36 : 16)

Minute Mineral Missiles are Harassing Pedestrians on the avenues of New York which are used by the Elevated roads. Druggists and surgeons are visited by increasing numbers of persons who want some foreign object removed from the eye. Frequently the aid of experienced oculists is required before the painful intruder is extracted and the irritation and inflammation allayed. A member of the staff of a scientific and medical journal has been investigating the cause of this sudden increase in ocular affections. He was seen recently flourishing a large magnet about as he walked on the sidewalk, near the Elevated track. Being asked what he was doing, he explained that he was testing the floating matter in the air. He hung the magnet under the track of the elevated road, and when a few minutes later he took it down, it was coated with minute particles of iron dust. This dust, he believes to be the cause of the eye troubles. The swift passing trains grind off *showers of iron particles*, which often fall or are blown into the eyes of pedestrians. The microscope shows that the particles have jagged fringes, and many of them have barbs like a fish hook. When lodged in the eye they cause irritation, which is increased by rubbing, and they may lead to permanent injury if not removed by a skilled oculist. This adds another element of danger to life in the city. We have been told that germs of diphtheria, fevers, small-pox and other diseases float in the air; it appears now that our eyes are also threatened with flying darts. All these, however, are less to be dreaded, and do less harm, than the moral evil of the tainted atmosphere of vicious resorts, into which young men go voluntarily to see life. (Prov. 4 : 14, 15.)

The Kindness of a Farmer's Daughter in New Jersey promises to have a romantic issue. A despatch from New Brunswick, dated March 14, states that a farm-hand, employed on a farm four miles out of that city, has fallen heir to a large property in Scotland. Last October he was tramping through the State, in search of work. He was so utterly wearied and exhausted when he reached the farm where he now is, that he was in despair. Having applied for work, and being refused as usual, the tramp muttered, as he left the premises, "If I cannot get shelter to-night, I will kill myself." The words were overheard by the farmer's daughter, who interceded for the tramp, and induced her father to employ him. The man turned out well, and was evidently well educated and intelligent. He said that he belonged to a wealthy Scotch family, but had forfeited his claims on them. He fell in love with his employer's daughter, to whom he owed his engagement, and she reciprocated his affection. He was led to inform his family of his reformed habits and his changed prospects. In reply, he was notified that he and his brothers were joint heirs of a large estate, and that his share will be remitted to him. When the money arrives it is to be invested in the purchase of a farm, and he and the farmer's daughter are to marry and settle there. That the tramp should have turned out to be an heir, is a surprise to all, including his affianced wife. A similar surprise awaits the world when it is found that men and women whom it has despised, are heirs of God and joint heirs with Christ. (Matt. 25 : 37, 40.

BRIEF NOTES.

Revival services in the Methodist churches at St. John, N. B., have resulted in nearly 400 conversions.

The issue of a new version of the Bible in Spanish is projected. It is proposed to form a committee from the various missionary societies in Mexico to co-operate with the American Bible Society in preparing the book.

At the General Conference of the Methodist Episcopal Church to be held in May next in New York, delegates are expected from Germany, Italy, Sweden, India, China, Japan, and Africa.

Mr. D. L. Moody will, it is expected, take a brief period of rest at Northfield, at the conclusion of his work in Iowa, having decided to postpone the campaign on the Pacific coast to another year.

An effort is being made to gain the consent of the trustees of Columbia College to a scheme for founding an annex for women, affiliated to the college as Girton is to Cambridge in England.

An address exposing the errors of Evolution will be delivered by Mrs. Viola Gilbert, on Sunday next (March 25) at three o'clock in meeting room No. 24, of Cooper Union, New York.

A third foreign missionary is being supported this year by the students of Presbyterian College, Montreal. He is at Santo; the other two are respectively at Erromanga and Epate in the New Hebrides.

The Providence, R. I., Young Men's Christian Association has succeeded in raising funds for a handsome and commodious building, the erection of which will now be commenced.

The American Baptist Home Missionary Society is entitled, under a recent decision of Judge Haskell concerning the will of the late Governor Coburn, of Maine, to a legacy of $250,000, of which $150,000 is to be held in trust for the support of schools among the freedmen.

The evangelistic Services in Cooper Union, conducted by Mr. Charles Herald, are growing in interest and usefulness. The audiences gathered there are mainly of non-churchgoers. The inquiry-room on several Sunday nights recently has been thronged with anxious persons.

Rev. Thomas Harrison is now conducting revival services at the Central Methodist Church, Seventh Avenue and Fourteenth Street, New York. Over eight hundred persons made a profession of faith at the services which he held in the Jane Street church.

The State Convention of Colored Baptists in Tennessee has passed a resolution excluding from fellowship and from the pulpits of the State any minister who "fought Prohibition" in the recent campaign.

The ceremony of burning a $50,000 mortgage was recently witnessed by a large congregation in Bethany Presbyterian church, Philadelphia. The document having been redeemed, was brought into the church on a large tin waiter, a lighted match was applied to it, and it was soon reduced to ashes.

HALF-WAY AND ALL THE WAY.

A New Sermon by Pastor C. H. Spurgeon.

"And Terah took Abram his son, and Lot the son of Haran, his son's son, and Sarai his daughter-in-law, his son Abram's wife; and they went forth with them from Ur of the Chaldees, to go into the land of Canaan; and they came unto Haran, and dwelt there." Genesis 11: 31.

"And Abram took Sarai his wife, and Lot his brother's son, and all their substance that they had gathered, and the souls that they had gotten in Haran; and they went forth to go into the land of Canaan; and into the land of Canaan they came." Genesis 12: 5.

The Down-Grade After the Deluge—The Divine Silence—The Call to Abram—The Custodian of the New Revelation—The Called of this Dispensation—Separation Enjoined by the Spirit—I. The Call Often Only Half Obeyed—Abram's Difficulties—An Insidious Evil—His Companions—Compromise Demanded—Half Obedience, Whole Disobedience—II. The Peculiar Call—From God Himself—With Supreme Authority—Arouses Opposition—III. Obedience Leads to Special Ground—Separation from the World—Fellowship with God.

AFTER the flood, when men began to multiply and increase in the earth, it was not very long before they began to turn aside from the living and true God. At first, the sons of Noah walked in the light of divine knowledge, though even among them was found an evil seed. When scattered over the earth after the confusion of tongues at Babel, the earth's hoar fathers carried with them a measure of the knowledge of God which they had received from their sires; but after a while, the light grew dim, men began to worship the sun and the moon, and they adored fire as the mystic symbol of the mysterious and spiritual Lord. They sought out many inventions; and having once begun to quit their allegiance to the one God, they very rapidly travelled along the down-grade till they worshipped strange gods.

A long period passed without a voice from God. Man seemed left to himself, and in danger of being given up to idols. The nations wandered each a different way, but all the downward road. Yet grace had not ended its reign; and therefore, before the lamp of God had wholly gone out, the Lord determined to reveal Himself, and establish His worship in the world.

He Would Select a Family

to be His peculiar servants; He would manifest Himself to the father of that family, and would make with him a covenant. He would reveal to him the great things which He intended to do in the fullness of time, and He would bid Him hand down the revelation to His children from generation to generation. This family should grow into a nation, and to that nation should be committed the oracles of God. Out of that nation should come prophets and priests and heroes, who should believe in God and maintain the true faith against all comers, even until the Son of God Himself should come to manifest the glory of God.

In the wise sovereignty of His choice, the Lord chose Abram and his house. It was needful that the elect family should be led apart and

Abram Must Come Out

from Ur of the Chaldees, and all its associations of idolatry, and he must even leave his kindred and his father's house, and walk before the Lord in separation unto prompt obedience and complete consecration. Thus in his separation unto God would be fulfilled the gracious purpose of the Most High. The Lord's end and aim was to keep His truth alive in the world by means of a people who should be set apart for that service; and it was therefore essential that the person chosen to be the head of that family, the founder of that nation, should come right away from all connection with the corrupt world, and walk apart with God.

At this moment God is working in much the same manner in the midst of the world by His Church. A Church is an assembly called out. An *ecclesia* is not any and every "assembly:" a mixed crowd of unauthorized persons, having no special right to come together, would not be an ecclesia, or Church. The true Church consists of men who are called and faithful and chosen. They are redeemed from among men, and called out from among their fellows by effectual grace. God the Holy Spirit continues to call out, and bring to the Lord Jesus those who are chosen of God according to the good pleasure of His will. Practically, conversion is the result of the call, "Get thee out from thy country." It is a repetition of that searching word, "Come ye out from among them, and be ye separate, saith the Lord, and touch not the unclean thing." The Church is a repetition of the camp of Abram in the midst of Canaan. It is the Lord's portion among men, and it keeps His oracles.

In gathering instruction from the call and outcoming of Abram, I shall handle the matter by making three remarks. First, *this call is often only half obeyed.* In our first text we find the command of God very partially carried out. Secondly, *this call is of a very special character*, and I shall endeavor to show the manner in which it comes to us at this time. Thirdly, *this call, when it is really obeyed, puts the obedient upon a special footing:* they are henceforth peculiarly the Lord's.

I. In the first place, this call is

Often Only Half Obeyed.

It came to Abram when he dwelt in Ur of the Chaldees; but though he so far hearkened to it as to set out for Canaan, yet we read that "they came to Haran, and dwelt there." We do not know *how* the call came to Abram, whether by a voice which he heard with his ears, or by a mysterious impulse upon his mind, or by a dream or vision; but somehow or other, it was laid home to Abram's heart and conscience that he must go forth upon a journey he knew not whither; he must journey into another land, and no more dwell in city or town or village, but become a sojourner with his God, a tent-dweller, a stranger in a strange land.

His first step would naturally be to tell his friends that he must needs leave them, for the living God had called him to go to the land of Canaan. At once his difficulties began. His kindred could not bear to part with him. If they had distinctly opposed him, and said, "It is absurd; your talk is insanity; yet if you must be gone, go your way and welcome;" then he would have gone in sadness, but assuredly he would not have hesitated. A man possessed of Abram's wondrous faith would have torn himself away with great firmness, although with deep regret at the sorrow which he caused. Had they opposed him, his course would have been plain. But he had to meet with a much more

Insidions Evil.

Abram's friends consented to his zeal. Whether they agreed in his reverence for Jehovah or not, they felt that they could not cut themselves off from Abram, and therefore they resolved to go with him. The word to Abram was express, "Get thee out from thy kindred, and from thy father's house;" but how was this to be done when his kindred and his father's house clung to him, and yielded to him? Very naturally his loving spirit could see no other way but to bid them all come with him, and yield themselves to God. The father of the clan leads the way, and it is rather his migration than that of Abram. What was Abram to do? Instead of meeting opposition from his family, his own father is leading the way in the journey to Canaan. Did not this make his obedience easier? We shall see. Was not this happy union of the household, this undivided assent to the Lord's bidding, a great cause for rejoicing? It certainly appeared so; but all is not gold that glitters. What we think will help, may at length hinder. What looks like a work of grace, may turn out to be only the movements of unrenewed nature. Like the mixed multitude which came out of Egypt with Israel, we may have about us professed friends who may become our worst foes, in the secret of God's truth and grace.

In Abram's case the dreaded separation is spared: they start together for Canaan. So far, so good; at least, it looks so. The travelling is wearisome, and many are the murmurings. The huge caravan has not gone very far before the proposal is made that they should be satisfied with the move which they had made, and remain at Haran. True, it was not Canaan, but it might do as well. Did not the family reason: "We shall stay here. We have yielded a great many points to Abram in coming away from Ur. But we cannot yield to all his demands. We have proved our love to him and our reverence for the Lord, by coming thus far, and now we ask for a fair compromise. Abram

Must not be Bigoted.

Surely he will not be so foolish as to believe in verbal inspiration, and insist upon Canaan, when Haran quite meets the spirit of the command. There is no doubt that Haran answers every purpose, and we mean to stay here, and Abram must stay with us"? Abram and the rest settled down at Haran. He was conquered, not by open foes, but by compromising friends. My brethren, take ye good heed unto yourselves, that ye suffer not your feet to be entangled by the men of your own household. He that would follow the Lamb whithersoever he goeth, must not know his own kindred when he comes to the parting of the ways.

Let me describe the consequences of tarrying at any half-way house. To obey the Lord partially is to disobey Him. If the Lord bids Abram go to Canaan, he cannot fulfil that command by going to Haran. Haran was not mentioned in the call. You cannot keep God's command by doing something else which pleases you better. The essence of obedience lies in its exactness. Although something else may seem to you to be quite as good as the thing commanded, what has that to do with it? *This* is what God bids you, and to refuse the thing commanded, professing to substitute a better thing, is gross presumption. You may not think it so, but so it is, that half obedience is whole disobedience. Moreover,

Half-way Obedience

increases our responsibility, because it is a plain confession that we know the Lord's will, though we do it not. Abram had received the call, and knew that he had done so, else why had he come to Haran? He admitted, by going as far as Haran, that he ought to go the whole way to Canaan; and so, by his own action he left himself without excuse. Thus, you see, there was failure in obedience, and increase of responsibility. The result of this to Abram was the absence of privilege. God spoke not to His servant in Haran: neither dream nor vision nor voice came to him in the place of hesitancy.

Meanwhile, Abram was rendering an affliction needful. His father Terah must die, that the cord which held Abram might be broken. If the called one will not come out while the old man lives, Death must do his work, and remove the cause of disobedience. If Abram fears to weep at parting with a living father, he must weep over his grave. One way or another the Lord will cause His chosen to obey Him. Oh, that we would be tender of heart, and not be as the horse or as the mule, which have no understanding! Whips and rods would seldom be heard of if we were more promptly obedient.

All this while Abram was

Delaying the Great Blessing

which God was prepared to give unto him. He was keeping out of the promised land, and away from the place where Jehovah would manifest Himself to him, and enter into covenant with him. I fear that some true believers are depriving themselves of the richest joy and the most heavenly experience by their undecided conduct. Some of you have come away from your old sins, but you have not yet entered upon the new life in its fullness. You have left Ur of the Chaldees—the place of open sin; but you have not come to Canaan the holy. You are tarrying in the Haran of a partial obedience, which is neither here nor there—a sort of death in life, rebellion in obedience, unbelief in faith.

I know many professors who have left their

vicious habits, but they are not yet consecrated to the Lord Jesus: they are not absolutely in the world, and yet they are not abiding in the Lord. They are willing to be saved by the Cross of Christ, but they are not willing to take up Christ's Cross, and come right out decidedly upon His side at all times. This is a perilous state to be in. They have enough religion to make them miserable, but I fear not enough to fit them for joys eternal. They may ultimately get into heaven by the skin of their teeth; at least, I hope so; but they have no present joy, no immediate peace, no conscious fellowship with God. *Half-way-house godliness is wretched stuff: beware of it!*

II. Secondly, this call, especially

As it comes to us,

is of a very peculiar character. To us, of course, it is wholly *spiritual*. We are not called to-day to leave our country and our kindred, so far as our residence is concerned; but it seems to me that we are called to a much more difficult position than that; namely, to stay on the old spot, among old friends, and yet to lead a wholly new life. Of course, we are to quit all evil company; but we are not to leave the society of our fellow-men, nor to go out of the world. Even Abram was not called to be an ascetic, nor to live in a cave, nor to retire into the desert like a hermit. Within the borders of his own encampment Abram was a man among men, and pursued his daily calling as the keeper of great flocks of sheep and herds of oxen and camels, and so forth. As Abram was no Canaanite, though he sojourned in Canaan, so are we to prove ourselves to be of a totally distinct race. This is

A Difficult Business.

How great a wonder was asked by our Saviour's prayer: "I pray not that thou shouldest take them out of the world, but that thou shouldest keep them from the evil"! Not by difference in brogue, nor by peculiarity in dress, are we to be marked out as the servants of God; but our lives must be so Christ-like and pure, that men shall say of us, "Thou also wast with Jesus of Nazareth, for thy life betrayeth thee." This call, then, is of a deeply spiritual and peculiar character. My brother, have you heard it? My sister, have you heard it? Have you endeavored to obey it to the full?

See, dear friends, what the call is, and then remember that it comes to the believer from God Himself. The Lord calls His servants unto the separated life, and because of His authority they are bound to obey. He calls by His Word, either preached or read: it comes to the individual by an application of the Spirit of God, so that the man yields cheerful assent thereto. He is drawn, and therefore he runs. Such a person feels it a pleasure to take Christ for his example, and to put his feet down in the very tracks of the Lord Jesus. It is ours to follow the Lord's precept and example with great care and solemn determination, turning neither to the right hand nor to the left. It was so with Abram: is it so with you?

My brethren, if we thus separate ourselves unto obedience, we

Must Expect Opposition.

Severe criticism will not be spared us. Of course, some will say, "The man is mad;" others, more gently, will murmur, "He is sadly misled." Many will accuse you of a liking to be singular, or a weakness for going to extremes, or a self-righteous wish to excel others, or of having "a bee in your bonnet." Accusers will hint that you are seeking your own in some form or other; and if they cannot quite see a motive, they will imagine one. *What is the use of imagination if it will not help a man out when his facts run short?* Having once made up their mind that you are foolish and contemptible, they will view all your conduct through colored glasses, and condemn you up and down. Be not dismayed, but endure hardness for love of Jesus.

Suppose we do obey the divine call, what then? Will our course be smooth ever afterwards? Far from it. The walk of the separated believer *involves trial.* The trial of Abram in leaving his country was but one out of ten which are recorded. It is written, "In the world ye shall have tribulation." In the Lord's vineyard the knife is used, if nowhere else. The Lord tried Abram, and He will try us; it is a part of the process of love by which He prepares us for the eternal rest. The course of true faith never does run smooth. If thou wilt obey the divine call thou shalt be favored with more trials, thou shalt be honored with still greater tests of thy fidelity; but, then, thou shalt be known as the friend of God, and God shall make thee to be a blessing to others even to the end of time.

III. This brings me to my third and last point. This call, when it is obeyed, puts us

On Special Ground.

For, first, God is bound to justify the course which He Himself commands. When Abram went to Canaan at the Lord's bidding and remained there, the responsibility was with the Lord. If any evil had come of his conduct, he could not have blamed himself. It was neither his own wisdom nor his own folly which led him: God alone was his director. It is mine to obey, it is God's to prove that my obedience is wise. What peace this brings! We cease, also, from that moment to be of the world. God deals with the world one way, but with His separated ones in another way. "Them that are without, God judgeth;" but those who are within are not under law, but under grace. It is the joy of faith that there is no condemnation to them that are in Christ Jesus. There is discipline now within the house of God; but it is not that of a court of justice, but of love.

By coming out from the world and following the Lord closely, we come under the divine care and protection. How wonderfully Abram was screened from evil! Jehovah was his shield. He was a stranger in the midst of enemies, but they did not molest him: an awe was upon them, for Jehovah had said, "Touch not mine anointed, and do my prophets no harm." Wherever a true saint goes, the Lord lays His commands on all the powers of nature and all the angels of heaven to take care of him. When Abram was at peace, God blessed him in all things; and if he went to war, God gave his enemies as driven stubble to his bow. If we are with God, God is with us. When God's will is our delight, God's

Providence is Our Inheritance.

One more thought presses itself upon my heart; the man who for Christ's sake has cut all his moorings, and separated himself from the world, to follow the Lamb, has learned how to live, but he has also learned how to die. We die unto the world, and thereby learn to die. When we cease to trust in riches, when we resign our comforts, when we no longer lean on friends, when all things visible become as shadows to us, then we make a rehearsal of death. Unless the Lord Himself shall soon descend from heaven with a shout, we shall all die. Yes, the hour of our departure hastens on. Then we shall have to cut ourselves loose from our moorings, be they what they may. Soon shall we hear this word from heaven, "Get thee out of thy country, and from thy kindred, and from thy father's house, unto a land that I will shew thee." This will be our summons to the better Canaan, the land that floweth with milk and honey. We shall depart out of this world to face an unknown eternity; but we shall by no means dread the migration.

The one question I finish with is: Do you know anything about this? Have you ever felt this divine call? If so, make your calling and election sure. Carry out the separating ordinance to the full. Some of us had to take very decided steps at our first starting, but we began aright. We have been called since to equally painful courses, but we hope to keep right. Anything is better than a wound in the conscience. If we keep close to Christ, we shall find rest unto our souls. We look back without regret to what we may have suffered by decision; counting it less than nothing for the joy that was set before us. Oh you who by grace are beginners in the heavenly life, make a strong resolve: "We will be the servants of God, and endeavor in all things to obey Him." If you are now separated unto Him, you shall find your reward in that day when He shall divide the sheep from the goats, for then you shall be placed at His right hand, to hear Him say, "Come, ye blessed of my Father." May you be the children of believing Abram, for Jesus' sake! Amen.

GEMS FROM NEW BOOKS.

A LITTLE GOOD SAMARITAN *

IT was a dreadful afternoon. For several days it had rained continuously, the streets were chilly and sloppy; there was mud everywhere—sticky London mud—and over everything a pall of fog and drizzle. Sara was sent out again and again, until her shabby clothes were wet through. The absurd old feathers on her forlorn hat were more draggled and absurd than ever, and her down-trodden shoes were so wet they could not hold any more water. Added to this, she had been deprived of her dinner, because Miss Minchin wished to punish her. She was so cold and hungry and tired that her little face had a pinched look, and now and then some kind-hearted person passing her in the crowded street glanced at her with sympathy. But she didn't know that. She hurried on, trying to comfort herself in that queer way of hers, by pretending and "supposing." But really, this time it was harder than she had ever found it, and once or twice she thought it almost made her more cold and hungry instead of less so.

Some very odd things happen in this world sometimes. It certainly was an odd thing which happened to Sara. She had to cross the street—the mud was dreadful—she almost had to wade. She picked her way as carefully as she could, but she could not save herself much; only, in picking her way she had to look down at her feet and the mud, and in looking down—just as she reached the pavement—she saw something shining in the gutter. A piece of silver—a tiny piece trodden upon by many feet, but still with spirit enough left to shine a little. Not quite a sixpence, but the next thing to it—a fourpenny piece! In one second it was in her cold, little red and blue hand.

"Oh!" she gasped. "Is it true?"

And then, if you will believe me, she looked straight before her at the shop directly facing her, and it was a baker's, and a cheerful, stout, motherly woman, with rosy cheeks, was just putting into the window a tray of delicious hot buns, large, plump, shiny buns, with currants in them.

She knew that she needn't hesitate to use the little piece of money. "But I'll go and ask the baker's woman if she has lost a piece of money," she said to herself, rather faintly.

She crossed the pavement and put her wet foot on the step of the shop; and as she did so she saw something which made her stop.

It was a little figure, more forlorn than her own; a little figure which was not much more than a bundle of rags, from which small, bare, red and muddy feet peeped out—only because the rags with which the wearer was trying to cover them were not long enough. Above the rags appeared a shock of tangled hair and a dirty face, with big, hollow, hungry eyes.

Sara knew they were hungry eyes the minute she saw them, and felt a sudden sympathy. She clutched her little fourpenny piece and hesitated a few seconds, then she spoke to her:

"Are you hungry?" she asked.

The child shuffled herself and her rags a little more. "Ain't I, jist!" she said in a hoarse voice. "Jist ain't I!"

"Haven't you had any dinner?" said Sara.

"No dinner, nor yet no breakfas', nor yet no supper, nor nothin'."

"Since when?" asked Sara.

"Dunno'; never got nothin' to-day, nowhere. I've axed and axed."

---

* From "Sara Crewe" by Frances Hodgson Burnett. A beautiful, pathetic story, full of excellent teaching for girls. 83 pages; Price $1. Published by *Charles Scribner's Sons* 743 Broadway, New York.

The Late Henry Bergh. (*See Page 181.*)

Besieged Basutos Praying in a Cave.

The Late Louisa M. Alcott.

Just to look at her made Sara more hungry and faint. But those queer little thoughts were at work in her brain, and she was talking to herself, though she was sick at heart.

"Wait a minute," she said to the beggar child.

She went into the shop; it was warm, and smelled delightfully. The woman was just going to put more hot buns in the window.

"If you please," said Sara, "have you lost a fourpence—a silver fourpence?" and she held the forlorn little piece of money out to her.

The woman looked at it, and at her—at her intense little face, and her draggled, once fine, clothes.

"Bless us, no!" she answered. "Did you find it?"

"In the gutter," said Sara.

"Keep it, then," said the woman; "it may have been there a week. Goodness knows who lost it; *you* never could find out!"

"I know that," said Sara, "but I thought I'd ask you."

"Not many would," said the woman, looking puzzled and interested and good-natured all at once. "Do you want to buy something?" she added, as she saw Sara glance toward the buns.

"Four buns, if you please," said Sara; "those at a penny each.

The woman went to the window and put some in a paper bag. Sara noticed that she put in six.

"I said four, if you please," said Sara; "I have only the fourpence."

"I'll throw in two for make-weight," said the woman with her good-natured look. "I dare say you can eat them some time. Aren't you hungry?"

A mist rose before Sara's eyes. "Yes," she answered, "I'm very hungry, and I'm much obliged to you for your kindness, and," she was going to add, "there's a child outside who is hungrier than I am." But just at that moment two or three other customers came in at once and each one seemed in a hurry, so she could only thank the woman again and go out.

"See," she said, putting a bun on the ragged lap, "that is nice and hot. Eat it, and you will not be so hungry."

The child started and stared up at her; then she snatched up the bun and began to cram it into her mouth with great wolfish bites.

"Oh, my! Oh, my!" Sara heard her say hoarsly in wild delight.

"Oh, my!"

Sara took out three more buns and put them down. "She is hungrier than I am," she said to herself, "she's starving." But her hand trembled when she put down the fourth bun. "I'm not starving," she said—and she put down the fifth.

"Good-by," said Sara.

When she reached the other side of the street she looked back. The child had a bun in both hands and stopped in the middle of a bite to watch her. Sara gave her a little nod, and the child, after another stare—a curious, longing stare—jerked her shaggy head in response.

THE LATE LOUISA M. ALCOTT.

(*See Portrait.*)

CHILDREN in every English-speaking land knew that they had lost a friend when they heard of the death of Miss Alcott. Her book entitled "Little Women" has gone into every home here and abroad where intelligent children could beg, borrow, or buy it. Having read that, the young folks have wanted to read everything else that Miss Alcott wrote, and accordingly the announcement of a new book from her pen was always a source of eager, delighted anticipation to thousands of juvenile readers. Miss Alcott loved children, and the affection was ardently and gratefully reciprocated. Now, the last of her productions has passed through the press, and her congenial labor of delighting her vast audience is concluded.

Louisa May Alcott, though so closely identified with New England, was not a New Englander by birth. She was born at Germantown, Pa., on November 29, 1832. Her father was keeping a school there at the time, but two years later he removed to Boston, Mass., where he opened a school in the Masonic Temple. In 1840 the family went to Concord, with which place the name of Alcott was to be indissolubly identified. Miss Alcott began to write for the press when she was only sixteen years of age, though she was twenty-two when her first book, "Flower-Fables," saw the light. She had, however, written short stories and sketches for periodicals, for the first of which, published in 1851, she received five dollars. She began teaching, and was so engaged at the outbreak of the war, when she volunteered for hospital nursing. So assiduously did she devote herself to her hospital duties that she became ill, and narrowly escaped death by typhoid fever. She never afterward fully regained the health which characterized her earlier years. While in Washington, Miss Alcott wrote to her mother and sisters letters describing hospital life and experience, which in 1863 were revised and published in book form as "Hospital Sketches," attracting much favorable notice.

In 1867 appeared the first volume of "Litt[le] Women," the charming work which brought h[er] fame and money. In less than three years th[e] sales of this story amounted to 87,000 copie[s]. Her reputation was established. There was n[o] more need of teaching, and Miss Alcott coul[d] command her own price for her books. Amon[g] the best known of her later books were, "A[n] Old-Fashioned Girl," 1869; "Little Men," 187[1]; "Work: a Story of Experience," 1873; "Eig[ht] Cousins," 1874; "Rose in Bloom," 1876; "Si[l]ver Pitchers," 1876; "Under the Lilacs," 187[8]; "Jack and Gill," 1880; "Spinning-Wheel Sto[r]ies," 1884; "Lulu's Library," 1885; and "Jo['s] Boys," a sequel to "Little Men," 1886.

Miss Alcott was deeply attached to her fathe[r] and for many years made her home with him [at] Concord. She was suffering from illness whi[le] he was dying, but she dragged herself from h[er] bed to go to him to bid him farewell. It was [a] fatal effort; she caught cold, and died Marc[h] 6, surviving her father but a few hours.

A PRAYER IN A CAVE.

(*See Illustration.*)

DURING the disturbances in southern Afric[a] in 1880-81 a band of Basutos were closely pres[s]ed by their pursuers. There were only about [a] dozen of them, and they fled for their lives ov[er] the wild country west of East Griqualand. Su[d]denly they disappeared from view, and the pu[r]suing party, after a long search, concluded th[at] they must have found a place of concealmen[t] underground. A close examination was mad[e] of the land, and at length a hole was discovere[d] in a hillside, which evidently was the entran[ce] to a cave. Here, as was clear, the hunted me[n] had found a hiding-place. To the men on th[e] outside, the passage leading from the outer a[ir] into the cave was dark as night, and it neede[d] bolder spirits than any among them to ventu[re] into its recesses, where they might meet me[n] driven to bay and resolved to sell their liv[es] dearly.

Inside the cave there was a strange scen[e]. From within, looking toward the entrance the[re] was light, and the men hiding there could s[ee] their pursuers gather around the mouth of th[e] cave. They saw them hesitate, and felt that [a] struggle was imminent. With horror they sa[w] them bringing bundles of wood, and they kne[w] that the crafty men were going to set fire [to] them, and so fill the cave with smoke as to for[ce] them out by suffocation. Then ensued a se[p]aration in the besieged party. While som[e] watched the awful preparations with despa[ir], others who had listened in peaceful times to th[e] ching of the missionar- threw themselves on their es in supplication to "the e man's God."

he wood was kindled, the seemed to suck in the ke like a huge funnel, still the expected rush of besieged men did not e. Were they stoically osing to die of suffocation er than make a bold fight their lives? It appeared but when an investiga- was made some hours r, it was found that an- r exit from the cave had n discovered and that the tives had made their pe. They had prayed for verance in their desperate it, and they had gained it.

OW-BOUND IN THE PARSONAGE.

(See Illustration.)

IT must be a very urgent that could cause any one eave the comfort of a fire- this morning," said May wnell, as she entered the ery breakfast-room of the onage one morning when d and snow were render- travel a misery. The gyman, too, seemed to be is daughter's opinion, for hivered sympathetically as urned from the ice-cover- window to the breakfast-table, where May her two sisters were sitting. Mr. Brownell been several years a widower, but so success- / did his daughters try to fill the place of r dead mother that the clergyman used to he was in danger of being spoiled.

he girls would have been glad to keep him oors all day, but though there were many ugs in which the clergyman was governed by daughters, clerical duty was not one of them. of of that fact was furnished before the meal concluded. A message from Mrs. Durand, ck member of Mr. Brownell's flock, was de- red, begging the pastor to come to her with- loss of time, as she was much worse, and eved herself at the point of death. The young ple looked their protest, but Mr. Brownell esitatingly prepared for the journey.

May, my dear," he said, addressing his est daughter, "please bring my ulster and my tics."

But, papa," the girl ventured to interpose, ou'll certainly not go out until this terrible rm has abated a little!"

I must, my dear," Mr. Brownell replied with rm voice; "what are the fury of the ele- ets compared with the privilege of minister- to the peace of a dying Christian?"

May knew that further opposition would be less. So she got the ulster and the stout rshoes, and also an umbrella. Mr. Brownell the latter, however, in the hall, knowing t it would be worse than useless in the gale a blowing. He placed the umbrella against chair, remarking cheerily: "There, my old npanion, you and this book can keep com- ny." The book lying open on the chair was illustrated edition of Whittier's beautiful epic m "Snow-Bound." Grace, the minister's ond daughter, had just brought it down from library. She wanted to read to Frances, her nger sister, the Quaker poet's graphic word- tures, with the fierce snow-storm without as alistic accompaniment.

The good man opened the door and set brave- out on his errand of Christian duty. The rm raged around him and beat upon him, but held on his way nerved by the energy of the rit. His daughters watched him until he was of sight, and then turned to the morning's varied occupations. They noticed with uneasi- ness that the fury of the wind appeared to in- crease, and as the time passed and Mr. Brownell did not return, May and Grace became very anx- ious for his safety and peeped timidly through the window.

"Can you see anything of father?" asked Frances, who, with a feather duster in her hand, was coming down the staircase.

"No, dear," replied Grace, "the gale is whirl- ing the snow about so wildly and so high that it is not possible to see more than five feet ahead. Oh, what can we do! he will surely perish in such a storm!"

"Come, sisters," said May, "let us kneel down and pray to the Lord that he will shield our good father and lead him safely home."

All three knelt down and prayed silently, but fervently. Just then a tremendous gust of the high wind made the house tremble in its very foundation. A cry of terror escaped Frances and Grace. But May, more resolute and cour- ageous, admonished her younger sisters: "Do not fear; the Lord will protect our father and our house." The conviction was a stronger evidence of faith than might be supposed, for in that storm more than one house was over- thrown, and several persons perished in the drifts. The girls were too restless now to go on with their work, and stood around the window which overlooked the road by which their father would return. Though they could see so little, they were anxious to get the first glimpse of him that might be had.

Meanwhile the pastor had been engaged in a duty that made him oblivious of the tempest. Satan often molests the dying Christian in the hour of physical weakness and dissolution, and the faithful pastor was contending with the enemy of souls, cheering the poor, tossed and troubled spirit, by reminding her of the faithful- ness of her Saviour. At last the struggle was over; light came in the moment of leaving the world, and her lips uttered the word "Victory" with her latest breath.

With a heart full of thankfulness, the minis- ter left the chamber of death, which seemed to him a hallowed place, and descending, as from the Mount, prepared for his journey home. It was a more perilous undertaking than he knew.

The snow had been drifted by the fury of the gale until, in places, it was piled up twenty feet high. But the courageous minister pursued his way and struggled bravely on. After being on the road for about a quarter of an hour, he suddenly experi- enced a sensation as if his very vital power had been sapped, and fell down in the snow. The snow somewhat revived him. He arose and struggled on for another ten minutes. He was within sight of his own house, within view of that window from which his daughters were so eagerly watching, when his feet sank in an immense drift, and his exhausted powers utterly failed him. Had the girls not been watching, he must have perished within sight of his own door. Happily, however, his career of usefulness was not to be so cut short. Heed- less of the icy wind, mindful only of the treacherous drifts, all three girls ran to his aid and dragged him unconscious from the snow. He revived sufficiently to proceed with their support to the house, and there, under their minis- tration, he fully recovered. It was with earnest and sin- cere gratitude that the family gathered around the family altar, and praised God for His providential love which had led to the preservation of a life so precious.

Watching for the Clergyman.

MRS. TRANSOME'S PUPIL.

A SERIAL STORY.

(Continued from page 158.)

Poverty in Wealth.

I WENT back to my old cottage in May, having been away a whole year, and part of that time in the poorhouse, where Transome died; and where I should have died likewise, if it had not been for good friends who took me out and set me up in my old hime, and gathered scholars again for me. The cottage, with its half tim- ber walls and high-pitched roof and lattice win- dows had a very different look from all the new houses about it, built of red bricks, with sash windows and six rooms in each dwelling. When I was young, two rooms in a cottage were thought enough for a laborer's family. I recol- lect going once to the squire's hall, before I was married, and seeing the grand drawing-room, where there was every kind of costly furniture; but what everybody looked at first and longest was an old-fashioned carved oak chair, which had stood in that room over two hundred years. You could not help thinking of the children who had been nursed in it, and the old folks who had rested their weary limbs in it. The squire said he would not part with that old chair for the finest furniture in all London town; and I would not have exchanged my cottage for the best and newest of their six-roomed houses.

But now Transome was dead, and I there alone, how dreary it seemed at times! The wind sighed and wailed against the windows, and the rain beat, and the summer thunder- storms rolled over it, as they never used to do when he and I were young together; nor, for the matter of that, when we were old together, and sat in the chimney-nooks.

When the first rent-day came, and Tran- some was not there to take it, then I felt keener than ever that he had nothing more to do with the old place, where he and I had dwelt so long. I gave my little school a half-holiday, and the lads and lassies ran away shouting for joy, for it was a sweet, bright day in June, with not a cloud in the sky, and the wind that had been moaning and fretting from the east all through the month of May, was at peace again, and a soft breath, as quiet as a child's breathing when it is asleep, came up from the west with a touch of fresh sea-breeze in it.

It seemed to me, as I went slowly down the steep street which led to the town, that if Transome had only been there, the spring day would have made me young again. But there is always an if stealing in between us and perfect happiness, and always will be, till we stand before the throne of God, where the light is never dim, and where the very air we breathe is the breath of life. Transome was safely there already; while I was still in the world, with a rent to pay, and a poor, aching body, getting on for sixty years of age, which could never be made young again by June sunshine and westerly winds.

I could not get rid of a bit of fear in going to see my landlord, though I had my rent tied up in my pocket-handkerchief; and I had no thought that he would wish to disturb me again, like he had done before, in the hope of building more houses where our old cottage stood. But I had never had speech with him while Transome was alive; and I knew him to be a hard man, though he went regularly to church, and the sacrament, and was often chairman at the meetings. When I reached his door I was forced to wait a minute or two, for the tears would gather in my eyes as I thought how often Transome had been there before me, carrying the rent to the same hard landlord.

I knocked as soon as I was myself again, and a servant woman opened the door to me. She was a little under forty years of age, and looked weary and peevish. But Transome had told me what a life she had led for many a year, with no one about her but a close-handed, suspicious master; and I smiled, and spoke as pleasantly as I could.

"I am come to pay my rent," I said; "I'm Transome's wife. You remember him?" "Oh! ay, I remember him," she said, coldly, "so he died in the poorhouse at last!" There she hurt me. If he had only passed away peacefully in his own bed, under the old roof, I could have parted with him more willingly, seeing he was well on in years and racked with rheumatism. But to think of him driven to the poorhouse in his old age, and dying there, was almost more than I could bear at times.

"Ah, well!" she said, "master got no good out of it, that's one comfort. The house never let, and it vexed him sadly. He was glad enough to have you back again as tenant. Come this way; master never leaves me to take a penny for him."

She led the way along a dark passage, into a large, gloomy room, that looked as if no sunshine or fresh air could ever find their way into it. The curtains and carpet were worn threadbare; and everything seemed comfortless. It was getting towards evening, and though it was June, there was a sharp touch in the air, which old folks felt, in spite of calling the weather summer. At the far end from the door sat my landlord, cowering over a little morsel of fire, which was burning in a large grate. I could scarcely see him at the distance he was; but when he spoke, his voice was the piping, quavering voice of an old man.

"Mrs. Transome!" he repeated, when the servant shouted out my name, "old Transome's widow? Well! well! There's no need for you to stay, Rebecca."

Rebecca scowled at him, sure that he could not see her, and muttered something under her breath, which even I could not catch. But she slammed the door after her with a bang that made the old man half jump up from his chair, and cry, "Noisy huzzy!" But he sat down again without calling her back, as I thought he meant to do, and bade me go nearer.

When I was close enough to see him, I noticed a great change in him since I saw him last in church—more than a year ago. He had been stout enough then, and looked well-nourished and comfortable; but now his cheeks had fallen in, and all his body seemed shrunken and smaller. He gazed keenly at me, though, through his small, twinkling eyes, and his thin fingers clutched the few shillings I gave him, as tightly as if I might wish to have them back again.

"That's right," he said, after counting them twice over, "ten shillings a month! I should have been six pounds richer if I'd let you and Transome alone last year. But times are bad! times are bad!"

He never seemed to think of how much poorer I was by the loss of a home for twelve months, or by the death of Transome; nor how I might have been nothing but a pauper still, dying a slow death among other paupers, but for those dear friends who had found me out and set me up again.

"Times are bad, sir," I said, "and likely to be badder."

"Ah! ah!" he moaned.

"They do say," I went on, "that cotton will never be cheap again; and the mills will only work half time. But we must hope for the best."

"Ay!" he answered, "and Philip Champion is surety for your rent, you know."

"God helping me," I said, "I'll win my own rent, sir. I could have won it all this year, if you'd not turned us out of our cottage."

"It was a mistake," he answered, "a sad mistake; and I've lost money by it. Philip Champion told me you taught him for nothing when he was a boy; is that true, Mrs. Transome?"

"It cost me nothing," I said, "and he was the quickest scholar I ever had in my school; and see how he is paying me now, by setting me up again! He's your own nephew, sir, the only relation you've left, people say."

I was almost afraid to say that, for he had been very bitter against his sister, Philip's mother, who had left him to marry a poor man such as Captain John Champion was. But my landlord took it very quietly.

"Ah!" he said, looking into the smoldering fire, "I recollect the lad coming to me one morning: how Rebecca came to let him in, I don't know to this day! He was a pretty boy about seven, I think. "Uncle," he said, as bold as brass, "please to pay for me to go to school." I thought for a minute or two I'd take to the boy: but what an expense and upset it would have been! I should have had to alter my way of life completely: and his mother had been so selfish to leave me and get married, with no one to look after my interests, that I did not feel called upon to do anything for him. So I just bade him go about his business, for I had nothing to say to him. And he tells me you taught him for nothing."

"For love," I said, "he loved me dearly, and me him."

"Well," he went on, fumbling at the money, "I should not mind returning you sixpence out of the rent this once, as times are bad, and you gave my nephew schooling for nothing. But only this once, Mrs. Transome."

"No, no," I said, as he pushed a sixpence back towards me; "thank you kindly, sir, but I have no need of it. I have enough and to spare; it's other folks as times are bad with."

"Enough!" he repeated. "Why, woman! I have not enough: and now there's the money to save that I've lost by your cottage. Rebecca! Mrs. Transome says she has enough money."

The servant had just come into the room; and I saw him hide away the rent quickly out of her sight, pretending to laugh all the while at what I had said. I bid him good evening, and went my way, wondering how strange it was that a man rolling in money like him, and on the brink of the grave, where he could not take a farthing of it, should feel so much poorer than me, who had not been out of the poorhouse three months. Surely, there is none but God, whose blessing can make rich, and He addeth no sorrow with it.

I pondered it much that evening, as my fire burned briskly and cheerfully. The flames played and leaped as they had not done in the ri[ch] man's smoldering fire; and my mind was f[ull] of the difference betwixt him and us.

"Why, Transome," I said, "he's ten tim[es] poorer than us. All our riches are on the [other] side of the grave, where Jesus is preparin[g a] place for us. It doesn't matter what we ha[ve] here for such a little while."

But when I remembered, and lifted up [my] eyes, and saw the other chimney-nook emp[ty], then I found how poor this life can be, ev[en] though we know the Lord is laying up treasu[re] for us in heaven.

After that I went every month to carry [my] rent to my landlord; and pretty much the sa[me] conversation passed between us each time, o[nly] he never again offered to give me sixpence o[ut]. Now and then, when I had received a letter fr[om] his nephew, Philip Champion, I took care to t[ell] him about it, and how he was getting on w[ell] in the world, and how grand folks thought mu[ch] of him. The old man rather liked to hear of [it], especially when Philip sent me word how [his] father was making a great deal of money by [his] voyages out to foreign parts. Once I carri[ed] down a handsome shawl, far too fine for an [old] woman like me to wear, which Captain Jo[hn] Champion had brought for me all the way fr[om] India. My landlord told me I could sell it re[ad]ily but I would not lower myself by thinking [of] such a thing. Love is more than money.

Year after year I saw him growing more with[er]ed and shrunken, yet still in good health, a[nd] with his mind keen; ay, keener than ever wh[ere] money was concerned. He came by degrees [to] have a sort of liking for me, more becaus[e I] never missed going with my rent to the v[ery] day than for anything else I can think of. Th[ere] was never any change in the gloomy house, [not] even in the fire, which always seemed smold[er]ing sulkily in the big grate. How dree t[he] sameness was to me! As bad even as the sa[me]ness of the bare walls of the poorhouse, wh[ere] no change ever came. He, with his rich[es], lived a life as dreary and desolate as the po[or]est pauper in the parish.

I believe Rebecca liked me a little also. [I] felt very sorry for her, and it came into my he[ad] to take her each time a posy out of my gard[en], or an apple, or some early fruit, fresh gather[ed]; and she was pleased with them, for the mas[ter] kept such a close hand on all expenses, that [she] scarcely tasted a morsel of fruit. She lo[ved] flowers, she told me: but ever since Transo[me] had been forced to give up working in th[e] garden, the master had been afraid to [hire] another man, for fear of being cheated. So th[at] the garden lay overgrown with weeds, and [so] hard for want of digging that it could no[t be] otherwise than barren and useless.

I scarcely know how many years went [by]. When one is old the years pass by like mon[ths], and the months are shorter than weeks used [to] be. But year after year I saw a change creep[ing], creeping over my old landlord, till it becam[e so] marked and plain that nobody could help see[ing] it. I think, sometimes, that maybe he was [not] altogether given up to the love of money u[ntil] he turned Transome and me out of the cott[age] where we had lived under him so many ye[ars]. Even since then he had grown nearer and cl[ose]-handed, grudging even necessaries for him[self] and Rebecca. It was a very hard life for [her], for he was certainly growing childish and sim[ple], and would often and often make her sit up [in] the night lest robbers should break into [the] house. It was pitiful to see how thin and w[orn] and wrinkled she was growing before her ti[me], and she must have been a bonny lass in [her] youth, for her eyes were still dark and bri[ght], and when she smiled, which was very seld[om], poor thing! there was something kindly in [her] face that made it a pleasure to look at it.

Well! though I had seen my landlord grow older, the change startled me at last. His [love] of money had grown into a heavy bond[age]. For a long while he had complained of pov[erty], and to see him in an old worn-out brown [coat] and shoes with holes in the side, and linen [...]

ransome never put on in his life, you would taken him for one of the poorest beggars. had given up going out of doors; and no ors came to the house, except his lawyer. I d the lawyer, one day, if the old master was growing simple, but he said nobody in the was sharper or longer-headed. He was like I once saw, with every branch blighted and save one which grew green and strong the withered boughs, as if it drew all the that should have fed them to itself, and was ished by their barrenness. The love of money swallowed up all other love that, maybe, dwelt even in his heart.

(*To be Continued.*)

THE MARRIAGE FEAST.

By Mrs. M. Baxter.

Lesson for April 1. Matt. 22 : 1-14. Golden Text, Rev. 19 : 9.

racteristics of a Marriage Feast—The Joy Not rsonal—The Marriage of the King's Son—he Wonderful Bride—A Union of Choice—minently Practical—Who are Called—Friends the Family—The Garment Provided—The vited Guests—Their Preoccupation—The Persecuted Servants—The Destruction of the Persecutors—The Impending Crisis.

MARRIAGE feast is different from every . There are feasts where the guests come her for their *own* profit or enjoyment—the object for which they meet is to enjoy selves. But in a marriage feast the guests together to rejoice in the joy of another, rejoice with them that do rejoice." (Rom. 15) At a marriage feast, the united parties be centre of everything.

the parable before us, the king makes a riage *for his son.* God made salvation for ers, but He is preparing a bride out of sinsaved for the joy of the heart of Jesus.

The Wonder of Wonders

our glorious God is not content with simaving us, but He seeks to unite us to Himn a oneness which must be voluntary on part, and which is a union of choice. Jesus us when we were unlovable, unworthy, we are called to a union of heart and will purpose with Him who is the altogether y One and altogether worthy. And this a merely sentimental union, but one in we shall be conformed to the image of 's Son (Rom. 8 : 29), in which "we have the of Christ" (1 Cor. 2 : 16), in which we are with Him, as He is one with the Father (John 21-23), in which not *we* live, but *Christ* in us (Gal. 2 : 20), in which we are dead, our life is hid with Christ in God (Col. 3 : 3)! as in the life of Jesus, the Father which in Him did the works (John 14 : 10), and neither spoke nor did anything of Himself. our high, blessed calling, within reach of one of us, to be so united with Jesus that not be *we* who think and speak and act, hrist who dwells in our hearts by faith. —quite unconsciously to us at the time—emy of souls has used our unconverted and lips to think and speak his thoughts, od willing and able to make us His innts of thought and word, of love and g, to a lost world. It is very easy to get imental or a fanatical idea about union Christ which cannot fail greatly to injure use. But like all other truths of God,

ion with Christ is Eminently Practical.

ssed are they which are *called* unto the ge supper of the Lamb." (Rev. 19 : 9.) called? This is the question which will n the hearts of all who are God's true ren. Yes, thank God, He has no favorites. prayed for those whom His Father had Him out of the world, who had received words, and known surely that He came out God, "that they all may be one, as Thou er art in Me and I in Thee, that they also be one in us." (John 17 : 6, 8, 21.) It e saved, not the unsaved, who are called e marriage of the Lamb. It is not enemies, but friends of the family, who are invited to a marriage. God saves sinners, not because they are worthy, but because Christ is worthy to save them; and the more unworthy they show themselves to be, the more fit they are to be saved by Jesus. But they who come to the marriage supper must be *worthy*, not unworthy. A sinner must come to Jesus naked; all the covering he has is but filthy rags of his own righteousness (Isa. 64 : 6.), which must be torn off, that he may be saved. But the guest at the marriage supper must come in a wedding garment. The invitation to the marriage comes by many servants, while the invitation to the gospel feast (Luke 14 : 17, 21-23) is given by One alone, i. e., the Holy Ghost. The King "sent His servants to call them that were bidden, but they would not come." They were preoccupied. It was not sin that hindered them, they were not engaged in fomenting a rebellion against the king; it was simply self-seeking and self-occupation. He sent other servants; it was a pressing and repeated invitation, "Leave all for Jesus," with the inducement that, while the feast was, in the first place, for His Son, there was much for the guests, too: "My oxen and my fatlings are killed, and all things are ready; come unto the marriage."

"But they made Light of it."

They did not see the wondrous honor done to them. They "went *their* ways" instead of *His* way," one to his farm—a farm *in the Kingdom*—another to his merchandise—merchandise *of the kingdom:* they were doing the king's work in their own way, and were more occupied in the labor and the bartering than with knowing and carrying out the thoughts of the king! O how many of us are doing this in these days? We are full of work, and work for souls, the work of the Kingdom, increasing the number of missions and other agencies for evangelization, so that they tread one upon the other, and yet how little time we have to enter into the *King's* joys, or to weep with the *King's* sorrows. The Christian Church is as busy as an ant-hill, yet how little is accomplished in nearly two thousand years! How few, except the first disciples, have dared to go out without purse or scrip or staff! How little has been known of that self-renouncing spirit which led the first disciples to leave all claim to personal property outside the circle of the church! O how the farm,—whether the denomination or the little congregation; O how the merchandise—the gain of numbers or of influence for the kingdom, in exchange for so much effort or so much money laid out!—how it takes us away from the court of the King of Kings, the secret place of the Most High! The little farm of our own souls, if *we* bear the burden of it, is equally a hindrance. God wants us to take time to listen to Him, to take time to learn of Him.

Take Time to be Holy,

and real holiness is being God-possessed and God-occupied. Why make light of it? "Men do not make light of their own salvation when once the Holy Spirit has made eternal things real to them, and they have tasted "the powers of the world to come;" men do not make light of the work of winning souls when once they have apprehended their own danger and what God has saved them from, but O, how many of even devoted Christian workers make light of the privilege of close union with God! The majority of the invited guests went "*their* ways," and did not so much as ask to be excused! But the remnant broke out into open insurrection, and persecuted the faithful few who brought them the message. "They took His servants and entreated them spitefully and slew them." No doubt this was first fulfilled in the early persecutions of Christians by the Jews. But no persecution is so relentless as that which is provoked by a really holy life. The simple preaching of the gospel, if it does not, in its converts, contrast with the selfishness, the pride, the unreality, the hollow wickedness of the world, is easily tolerated. But when men and women are ready to sacrifice all for Christ; when they are ready to trust Him, without any arm of flesh, for food, clothing, health, &c.; when they can bear rebuke which is unmerited, and meet it with a smile; when they can return love for hatred, and prayers for curses—then the half-hearted in the kingdom begin to cry, "Down with such fanaticism;" and they will compass sea and land to prove that this transformation of character comes from beneath, and not from above, from the Devil, and not from God! The Jesuits, about two hundred and thirty years ago, persecuted the Port Royalist Christians, hunting them to death, and even digging their dead bodies out of their graves, for no other reason than that they were truly spiritual, Bible-loving Christians, and their lives wholly yielded to the Lord as living sacrifices; they came unto the marriage and suffered with Christ. The Waldenses were persecuted also by the Jesuits, thrown alive over frightful precipices, and subjected to the most horrible indignities and tortures, only because they did *not* make light of the invitation to the marriage, but Jesus and His Word were all in all to them!

"When the king heard thereof, he was wroth; and he sent forth his armies, and destroyed those murderers, and burned up their city." Surely this time is at hand. Things are

Coming to a Crisis.

Politics, commerce, religion, are all in a state of ferment, men's hearts are "failing them for fear, and for looking after those things which are coming on the earth." (Luke 21 : 25.) There is a general unrest and spirit of expectation, such as portends a coming earthquake. Men of science and of forethought may rack their brains to account for it, but the solution is given in God's Word. Christ is coming to take vengeance on those who know Him not, and obey not the gospel. (II Thes. 1 : 6.) But the same thing is enacted in miniature in the heart of every professing Christian who persecutes those who obey the call to the marriage. Disappointment, failure and vexation are the lot of such.

The time was pressing, and the King said to his servants, "The wedding is ready, but they which were bidden were *not worthy*. Go ye, therefore, into the highways, and as many as ye shall find, bid to the marriage." If the Jews had received Christ, He would have had a Jewish bride, but they would not; and now He is making up His elect from Jew and Gentile alike who believe in and yield themselves to Him. His general invitation brought together "bad and good," and this is the character of the dispensation under which we live. Wheat and tares, saved and lost, holy and unholy, bad and good, are joined together. But the King came in to see the guests, and at once a separation began to take place. There was a man which had not on a wedding garment, a garment provided for the guests; he had dared to appear in his own, but he was cast into outer darkness. It is an awful thing to tread on holy ground without God's preparation, to venture into a profession of union with God without the reality. For the marriage feast, "Many are called, but few are chosen." O, to be found among the few when Jesus comes!

THE SONG OF HOPE.

"The path of the just is as the shining light, that shineth more and more unto the perfect day."—Prov iv, 18.

A soft sweet voice from Eden stealing,—
Such as but to angels known.
Hope's cheering song is ever thrilling,
"It is better farther on."

I hear hope singing, sweetly singing
Softly in an under tone;
And singing as if God had taught it,
"It is better farther on."

By night and day it sings the same song,—
Sings it while I sit alone:
And sings it so the heart may hear it,
"It is better farther on."

It sits upon the grave and sings it,—
Sings it when the heart would groan;
And sings it when the shadows darken,
"It is better farther on."

Still farther on! O how much farther?
Count the mile stones one by one;
No! no! no counting—*only trusting*,
"It is better farther on."

—*Selected.*

J. E. JEWETT, Publisher, 77 Bible House, New York will furnish the above poem in leaflet form at twenty cents per hundred. *A Sample Packet* of 50 leaflets assorted (no two alike), will be sent post-paid for ten cents. Postage stamps taken.

Vol. XI., No. 13. Office, 63 Bible House, N. Y. THURSDAY, MARCH 29, 1888. Annual Subscription, $1.50.

CONTENTS OF THIS NUMBER.

PORTRAIT AND LIFE OF WILLIAM, LATE EMPEROR OF GERMANY.
REFORMATION OF EVIL HABITS. Dr. Talmage's Sermon in Chicago last Sunday.
ANECDOTES RELATED AT RECENT EVANGELISTIC MEETINGS.
THE PYRAMID POINTING TO 1888-89 AS YEARS OF TROUBLE, According to the Astronomer Royal of Scotland.
CURRENT EVENTS: The Proposed Fractional Currency—The Supreme Court on Prohibition—The Telephone Decision, etc.
Gems from New Books: A Puerperal Fever Cured, etc.
GRACE ABOUNDING. A Sermon by C. H. Spurgeon.
PICTURE OF THE SCENE OUTSIDE THE EMPEROR'S PALACE.
THE EMPEROR'S DYING MOMENTS.
A Pundit's Story—A Mexican Christian Disowned—A Jew's Conversion—A Chinese Shopkeeper's Testimony—Rev. W. F. Re Qua in the Indian Territory, etc.
REGINA'S RESTORATION. (With Illustration.)
MRS. TRANSOME'S PUPIL. A Serial Story. (Continued.)
CHRIST'S LAST WARNING. By Mrs. M. Baxter.

THE LATE EMPEROR OF GERMANY—BORN MARCH 22, 1797, DIED MARCH 9, 1888.

THE LATE EMPEROR OF GERMANY.

The Last of the Kings—The Death Scene—His Noble Mother—Delicate Boyhood—The Tutor Sergeant—An Officer at Ten Years Old—A Memorandum of Principles—Marriage—Exile in 1848—Becomes Regent—Accession to the Throne—His Policy—The Danish and Austrian Wars—The Leadership of Germany—The War with France—Closing Years.

THE late Emperor of Germany, whose portrait appears on the first page, has been called "*the last of the Kings*," and, in one sense, the title is appropriate. He held firmly and sincerely to the doctrine which lies at the root of kingship, but which has in these days become a subject for ridicule, that the king reigned by the divine selection and appointment. To a nation accustomed to choose its executive as well as its legislators by the popular vote, it seems incredible that any sane man should believe that God has given a nation into his hands to be governed by him according to his will, and to be handed over on his death to his eldest son as a successor appointed by Heaven. Yet that was Emperor William's profound conviction, and on many occasions he avowed it publicly, telling his people in plain words that he reigned, not by their will, but by the will of God. More than this, he acted upon his belief, for when, during many years, he and his people held conflicting views of national policy, William held by his own opinions, and in defiance of the popular will, and ignoring popular protests, governed Prussia on the principles which *he* believed to be conducive to her ultimate prosperity. Prussia is now convinced by the logic of facts that he was right, but there was a time when she was moved to a dangerous temperature of wrath by the thought that one man should have the power to impose his will on the whole nation. It must, however, be admitted that William fully accepted the logical consequences of his doctrine. Believing himself divinely appointed to govern, he recognized his responsibility to God for faithful service and, though he never regarded himself as accountable to his people for his conduct, he seems never to have lost sight of the fact that when his earthly course was run he would have to answer to the King of kings for the manner in which he had discharged his trust. The ruler who fully recognizes that fact may make mistakes, but he will surely be conscientious, and is likely to be great.

The Death Scene

appears, from the cable reports, to have been one of deep solemnity. The conviction had been growing all through the week that the end to the long grand life was near at hand. On Wednesday March 7, hope was abandoned; a fainting fit, so like death as to deceive all but the physicians, overcame the aged Kaiser, but he revived and was able to talk. On Thursday, after a night of sleeplessness and a forenoon of semi-unconsciousness, he again swooned, and the report went through Berlin, and was sent by telegram and cable all over the world, that he was dead. Again the pulse grew perceptible and the breath came back. He took nourishment and talked with his grandson Prince William, and with Bismarck. The old energetic spirit retained its power, though the frame it had animated was dying. "*I have no time to be tired,*" was his characteristic reply to his daughter, the grand Duchess of Baden, who urged him not to talk lest he tire himself. Soon after midnight the near approach of death became unmistakable. Gathered around him were his aged wife, the Empress, who was holding his hand, his grandson, Prince William and his wife, his daughter and the Princes of the Empire, while the Court preacher, Dr. Kogel, read the Psalms. One figure was absent, that of the stricken Crown prince lying in pain at San Remo. Toward six o'clock the venerable man made one last struggle for life, and spoke excitedly but in delirium. He soon sank into a stupor, and at twenty minutes past eight he passed away from the world without a struggle, and without pain. Lying in his customary half-raised position on his old soldier's camp bed, which had accompanied him in his campaigns, the Kaiser died so quietly that scarcely any one looking at him was conscious that he was dead. The only change was that his face lost its haggard, aged look, and became young again—a veritable Emperor in death even as he was in life.

A Career of Ninety-one Years

closed thus quietly, after scenes of storm, of warfare, and of popular turmoil. The aged potentate was born on March 22, 1797. He was the second son of Frederick William III., King of Prussia, and the celebrated Queen Louise, who was, in appearance and character, one of the loveliest women of her day, an affectionate wife, and a careful mother. There is a picture representing her sitting on a sofa rocking the baby William on her knee, while her elder son, Frederick William, is marching up and down the room in military style, brandishing a wooden sword, and the King is looking on with a complacent smile. Such scenes were not unusual in the domestic life of this happy royal family.

As a child William was very weak and delicate. His brother, the Crown Prince and heir to the throne, was much the stronger of the two. Referring to this, he himself said, soon after his brother's death: "I never thought that I would occupy this responsible position. I had no reason to believe I would outlive my dear brother. He was much stronger than I when we were both children, so that my succession to the throne was beyond my expectation. My life, I anticipated, would be spent in the Prussian army, and as an officer in that army I expected to fulfil my duties toward my King and country."

The two young princes were early initiated into the mysteries of military drill. An old sergeant named Bennstein was their tutor, and he was able to report Prince William as proficient at the age of eight years. He was made

An Officer at Ten Years Old,

as a second lieutenant of the Foot Guards. After this he attended drill regularly, and took part in parades. In 1813, when the Napoleonic war broke out, he was made captain, and went with his regiment to the field. On the 1st of January he crossed the Rhine, near the mouth of the Neckar, and a few days later he charged the French at the battle of Bar-sur Aube with the Cuirassiers, and was then ordered by his father, the King, to ride through a heavy fire for certain information—a mission he discharged with such coolness as to command the admiration of veterans, and to win from the Emperor of Russia the Cross of St. George, and from his father the Iron Cross. When Paris was taken and entered next year by the allied Princes of Russia and Prussia and Austria, William visited it in triumph for the first time.

An Interesting Memorandum,

written by the future emperor at this period of his life, deserves mention. It records the principles he established for the guidance of his life. Among them are the following: "I must be glad to have been born a prince, not because it gives me a position more exalted than that of others, but because it gives me greater opportunity to assist others. I must be friendly to all beneath me, and seek to make their duties as pleasant as possible. I must remember that what I would be ashamed to do as a man, I should be doubly ashamed to do as a prince. I must never forget a favor. I must never forget that my life and my duty belong to my country. I must always remember the many virtues of my mother with a grateful heart." In 1829, the future Emperor, who had by this time grown into a stalwart and handsome man,

Married the Princess Augusta

of Weimar at Berlin with great magnificence, the bridegroom, clad in silver armor, holding the lists in a tournament in honor of the bride, and presenting a striking appearance. The poor were not forgotten on the occasion. The royal bridegroom had a largess worth $3,000 judiciously distributed among the most needy and deserving families in the country.

After his marriage and until 1840 his life was comparatively uneventful, being passed in military studies, reviews and routine duties. He lost his father in 1840, and on the accession of his childless brother, Frederick William IV., he became known as heir apparent, with the title Prince of Prussia. At the coronation of his brother, he, as General of the Guards, rode at the head of this superb body of soldiers, and did homage to the new King. He was soon afterward put in command of the entire infantry, and in 1842, when Frederick William IV. visited England, he was placed in control of all the affairs of Government. Six years later he was

Driven Into Exile.

After the downfall of the Orleans dynasty in France, in 1848, the revolutionary feeling spread from France to Germany. Insurrections broke out in almost all the large German States, and the people became clamorous for a liberal government. This was especially the case in Prussia, whose Government had become a sort of patriarchal despotism. On March 16, 1848, a large crowd assembled in front of the royal palace in Berlin to parley with the King. The building was guarded by soldiers. When the King appeared, to address the multitude, his voice was drowned by the shouts of the assemblage. The King commanded them to be silent and to hear him, but the din grew louder. Then the soldiers were ordered to advance, and a sanguinary street fight ensued in which over two hundred persons were shot down. When order was somewhat restored it was charged that Prince William had ordered the soldiers to advance, and that they had first fired at his command. The feeling against him became so alarming that he was obliged to withdraw to England, where he remained until June, 1848, when he returned and took his seat as a Deputy in the National Assembly. There he avowed his readiness to work for the maintenance of a Constitutional Government, since his brother, the King, had seen fit to adopt one. But he was soon to have more congenial work.

Shortly after his return, the revolution in Wurtemburg and Baden assumed such alarming proportions that Prussian interference was asked. A detachment of the Prussian army, with Prince William in command, was at once sent to suppress the insurrection. One sanguinary conflict ended the uprising in Dresden, but that in Baden was not crushed until after a campaign of several weeks' duration. The Prince took an active part, being frequently under fire, and sharing the hardships of the campaign. It is said that once, when there was a scarcity of provisions, he divided his rations with a common soldier. In October, 1857 the King, his brother, having become mentally incapacitated, Prince William was made Regent, a position which he held until January 2, 1861, when the afflicted monarch died and William

Ascended the Throne

of Prussia as William I. He at once inaugurated a firm and determined policy, which aimed at consolidating Germany under Prussian leadership. He selected councillors who were fully in sympathy with his policy, among them Count Bismarck, Von Roon, and Moltke. He regarded a thorough organization of the army as an indispensable condition of success, and proceeded to place it upon a firm basis in the teeth of a strong Parliamentary opposition. When he ascended the throne his prerogatives were assailed by a powerful reactionary party, but he gathered around him the old Conservative leaders and gradually increased the influence and strength of the Conservative element.

The Danish War.

The efficiency to which King William had brought the Prussian army was first seen in 1864 in the war against the Danes, whose King had proclaimed Schleswig a part of Denmark. Notwithstanding Austria's jealousy of Prussia's growing power, King William's diplomatists prevailed upon Austria to unite with Prussia in this war, which resulted in the total defeat of the Danes. The Prussian soldiers and their leaders behaved with remarkable bravery, and after this war Prussia assumed a position among the first military powers of Europe. She had to settle accounts, however, with her ally, and that was not to be done without fighting. In the dispute Austria appealed to the Diet, which decided against Prussia, and called on all the States to arm against her. That was the beginning of

The Seven Weeks' War,

so called because in seven weeks Prussia prostrated Austria and her allies, and took the place, for which William and Bismarck had schemed, of leadership of Germany. At the final peace of Prague, August 23, 1866, Austria was excluded from Germany, and Schleswig-Holstein, Hesse-Cassel, Hanover, Nassau, and the free city of Frankfort were annexed to Prussia. A confederation was formed of the States north of the Main, with the King of Prussia as President and Bismarck as Chancellor. The other German States were left at liberty to form a new South German Confederation.

The War With France,

however, was the cause of making a united Germany. Soon after the battle of Sadowa, which ended the conflict with Austria, France began treating with Holland for the purchase of the Grand Duchy of Luxembourg. But King William was in a position to forbid the sale, with an army of 900,000 men to back him, and the Grand Duchy was declared to be neutral territory. Napoleon III. was humiliated. Not only France, but all Europe, was amused at the haughty emperor being obliged to retire from a negotiation at the command of the King of Prussia. It was evident that a deadly grapple between France and Germany must come. An occasion soon arose. In 1870, Prince Leopold of Hohenzollern refused the Spanish crown, and Napoleon, presuming that his candidacy was engineered by the King of Prussia, demanded a guarantee from Prussia that no prince of this house should ever again be a candidate for the crown of Spain. The King refused to give such a guarantee, and Napoleon made this refusal a pretext for declaring war. He relied upon the support of Austria and the south German States, which had fought Prussia in 1866; but Bismarck had formed alliances with them, and as result Napoleon found all Germany united against him. The magnificent perfection to which the King and Von Moltke had brought the Prussian army was now seen. *In eleven days* after Napoleon declared war, three armies, aggregating half a million men, were on their way to the frontier. Few kings have had in their lives a greater personal triumph than King William of Prussia in receiving the surrender of Napoleon III. at Sedan. But a prouder and a greater day for him was when he was made

Emperor of Germany.

Just as the victory of the Prussian armies over Austria in 1866 had filled the souls of William's subjects with a storm of patriotic enthusiasm, which swept away their resentment at the unconstitutional methods by which he made those armies superior to their adversaries, so the new and vastly greater triumphs of 1870 raised all Germany to a pitch of loyal ecstasy in which South Germans and North Germans, all that bore the German name, save Austria, melted into a single confederation and formed the German Empire. In the mirrored hall of the palace at Versailles, on the 18th of January, 1871, while the siege of Paris was still going on, William I., King of Prussia, was proclaimed Emperor of Germany.

The Constitution of Germany

was, after the French war, settled afresh; the legislative functions to be exercised by a Federal Council (Bundesrath) representing the various Governments of the States, and the Imperial affairs by a Diet (Reichstag) elected by the whole people. Every German of twenty-one years of age has a vote for the election of a member of the Reichstag, and each district of 50,000 has one member of that body; but Bundesrath, Reichstag, and Ministry are all practically so many tools in the hands of Bismarck, who might say with far more truth than the French monarch that did say it, that *he* was the State. The State is everything in Germany, the natural result being the spread of Socialism to an appalling extent. During William's long life no less than four attempts were made to assassinate him, besides the dynamiter's plot to blow up the National Memorial at Rudesheim on the occasion of his opening it in 1883. Through these, as on the field of battle, he was preserved, to die peacefully in his palace in Berlin, while crowds of his subjects filled the streets outside, weeping genuine tears for the dying old Emperor.

It should not be forgotten that the foundation of the dead Emperor's character was his religion. "The most important thing of all," he once told a deputation, "is the fostering of a living religious spirit." His piety was simple and sincere. He believed in God with all his heart and it was the confidence he reposed in His protection which kept him calm and steady under the bullet-hail of battle, and unswerving at the great crises of his memorable life.

ANECDOTES RELATED AT RECENT EVANGELISTIC MEETINGS.

A Tramp's Death by a Brick-Kiln.—"There was a poor tramp who wrongfully wasted in drink most of the money he could beg, and consequently was often forced to sleep out of doors. His favorite place on such occasions was a brick-kiln, where, coming as close to the fire as he thought prudent, he enjoyed the warmth. The brick-makers frequently remonstrated with him, saying it was unsafe, and he had better be careful or some accident would happen; but he heeded them not. One night, being more careless than usual, he lay down, and next morning he was found burned to death. As there was danger to that man in the neglect of repeated warnings, and his carelessness in exposing himself to the fire, so there is danger of eternal fire to the sinner, who ignores God's message of warning and salvation to him."

Unable to Look to Christ.—Mr. Thompson said: "A woman came to me in the street once, and said she wished me to visit her husband, who was ill, and with little hope of recovery. God had often spoken to him and sought to draw him to Himself, but in vain. I did visit him, and saw that he was very far gone. The doctor was present, but he could give no hope of life. Sitting down by the bedside, I tried to direct the dying man's eyes to Jesus upon the cross. I spoke for some time, but it was evident he did not understand me. I prayed, but still he was only semi-conscious, and quite incapable of apprehending the simple truths of the Gospel. There he was living, yet there was no help for him; he could not look to the Saviour, who has promised 'life for a look.' What a state in which to die! Come to Jesus while you have health and strength."

How the Funeral Expenses Were Met.—Mr. Bamford remarks: "I entered a house of mourning a few days ago, where a woman sat by her husband, who was in a dying condition. I spoke to her of her son, who had died only that day; he had been a bright lad of eighteen, and the hope and pride of his mother, until he fell ill. She was a mill-worker, and, although she wrought from six in the morning until six in the evening, it was all she could do to supply her invalid husband and son with the barest necessaries of life. Being now obliged to abandon her work at the mill, she was in the last extremity of poverty, and, as I looked on that calm, serene face, I said, 'How is it that you are able to maintain such calmness and peace under your present circumstances?' 'God is my Father; He knows my need,' she quietly replied. Then, pointing to the dead body of her son, she said, 'I have nothing with which to bury my son, but I know that every requirement will be met by my God.' Just as she had spoken a knock was heard at the door, and she remarked as she rose to open it, 'The Lord has sent what I need.' A young man entered, and placing a sum of money in the woman's hand, he said, 'I have been authorized by your son's companions to give you this money with which to meet the funeral expenses.' The funeral day arrived, but no one had come forward to offer to bury her son. Four of us went up to her house, and found the poor woman starting to go to the grave alone. Her face lighted up when she saw us, and she said, 'God has not failed me; He has sent four of His servants to take the remains of my dear son to their last resting-place!' What a remarkable embodiment of waiting on God was this poor woman!"

A Scotchman in Toronto.—Mr. Ross Relates: "When I was in Toronto, I was walking home one Sunday night with a young man. We had not gone far when we were met by a number of his companions, who stopped him, and asked him to come to the Park and make arrangements about something. 'No, I will not go,' replied the young man firmly; 'you know I told you I would not accompany you on Sunday for such a purpose.' After they were gone I remarked that I was glad to see him stand up so firmly for his Lord. 'You mistook me, sir,' he said, 'I am not saved. I belong to Scotland, and am the child of a godly household there. My parents were the happiest and purest people I ever knew. My conscience will not let me break the Lord's Day.' The moral influence which was brought to bear upon that young man by godly parents was good, but I am glad to say that before that day was gone, he had laid hold on eternal life by accepting Christ."

Two Dead Women.—Mr. Thompson Said: "I was preaching in Middlesboro-on-Tees, some time ago, and one day a woman came to my lodgings and said, 'Mr. Thompson, I am very anxious about my soul, but there is one verse in the Bible I cannot understand. It is that verse which says, "There is no difference."' I heard a story which illustrates this: There lay side by side the dead bodies of two women. The one had been a lady, had moved in the best society, was well-dressed, and wore a quantity of valuable jewelry. Her face was calm and beautiful even in death. But the other had been a fallen woman, and her face was a true index to the life she had led, and in the midst of her sin, she had been summoned to meet her God, having been killed when going home intoxicated the night before. There was no difference in that *both were dead.* The moral character, the past life, the immediate surroundings, did not affect the main question, the great similarity. Both were dead. So, while there may be difference in degree of iniquity in sinners, yet in the sight of God they are both alike, 'dead in trespasses and sins,' for 'All have sinned and come short of the glory of God.'"

A Mother's Dying Request.—Mr. Miller observed: "I came into this great city when I was fourteen years of age. I was the son of many prayers, but it seemed at one time as if they were all to be in vain. I was led away by evil companions, and wandered far from God, but sometimes, in my wildest moments, the Holy Spirit would strive with me and whisper, 'Remember your mother's prayers. Pray for salvation.' At last I was converted to Christ, and enabled to give up drink and my other besetting sins, leaning on Christ for strength to combat them, and to withstand the jeering of my companions. For some years I was a sleeping Christian, doing no work for Him who had saved me. Then my mother, to the instrumentality of whose prayers I owe my salvation, fell ill. As she lay in bed she had glorious visions of bright ones around her, waiting to bear her to heaven. I stooped over her bed to speak to her; she clasped my hand in hers, and whispered: 'Willie, work for Jesus; work for Jesus.' And there and then I pledged myself to give Him what strength I had, and will work for Him while I have any being. Oh, what happiness, joy and peace He gives to those who do His will!"

REFORMATION OF EVIL HABITS.

Dr. Talmage's Sermon Preached in Chicago last Sunday, March 25, 1888.

"When shall I awake, I will seek it yet again." Prov. 23 : 35

Solomon's Portrayal of a Mental Struggle — A Prodigal's First Impulse to Return—Obstacles in the Way of Restoration - Moral Gravitation—The Bonds of Habit – The Tippler Trying to Quit—A Smoker's Struggle – A Burning Ship Going Over Niagara—A Suggestive Statue in Paris—Obstacles in Society—A Prodigal's Reception in a Church—The Gospel in a Handshake—How to Overcome the Obstacles—Seek God—A Wounded Soldier at Antietam - Quit Bad Companions — Seek Christian Advice – A Night on the Old Farm – Returning Too Late.

WITH an insight into human nature such as no other man ever reached, Solomon, in my text, sketches the mental operations of one who, having stepped

Aside From the Path

of rectitude, desires to return. With a wish for something better, he says: "When shall I awake? when shall I come out of this horrid nightmare of iniquity?" But seized upon by uneradicated habit, and forced down-hill by his passions, he cries out: "I will seek it yet again. I will try it once more."

Our libraries are adorned with an elegant literature addressed to young men, pointing out to them all the dangers and perils of life—complete maps of the voyage, showing all the rocks, the quicksands, the shoals. But suppose a man has already made shipwreck; suppose he is already off the track; suppose he has already gone astray,

How is He to Get Back?

That is a field comparatively untouched. I propose to address myself this evening to such. There are those in this audience who, with every passion of their agonized soul, are ready to hear this discussion. They compare themselves with what they were ten years ago, and cry out from the bondage in which they are incarcerated. Now, if there be any in this house, come with an earnest purpose, yet feeling they are beyond the pale of Christian sympathy, and that the sermon can hardly be expected to address them, then, at this moment, I give them my right hand and call them brother. Look up. There is glorious and triumphant hope for you yet. I sound the trumpet of Gospel deliverance. The Church is ready to spread a banquet at your return, and the hierarchs of heaven to fall into line of bannered procession at the news of your emancipation. So far as God may help me, I propose to show what are the obstacles to your return, and how to surmount those obstacles.

The First Difficulty

in the way of your return is the force of moral gravitation. Just as there is a natural law which brings down to the earth anything which you throw into the air, so there is a corresponding moral gravitation. In other words, it is easier to go down than it is to go up; it is easier to do wrong than it is to do right. Call to mind the comrades of your boyhood days—some of them good, some of them bad. Which most affected you? Call to mind the anecdotes that you have heard in the last five or ten years—some of them are pure and some of them impure. Which the more easily sticks to your memory? During the years of your life you have formed certain courses of conduct—some of them good, some of them bad. To which style of habit did you the more easily yield? Ah! my friends, we have to take but a moment of self-inspection to find out that there is in all our souls a force of moral gravitation. But that gravitation may be resisted. Just as you may pick up from the earth something and hold it in your hand toward heaven, just so, by the power of God's grace, a soul fallen may be lifted toward peace, toward pardon, toward heaven. Force of moral gravitation in every one of us, but power in God's grace to overcome that force of moral gravitation.

The next thing in the way of your return is *the power of evil habit.* I know there are those who say it is very easy for them to give up evil habits. I do not believe them. Here is a man given to intoxication. He knows it is disgracing his family, destroying his property, ruining him body, mind, and soul. If that man, being an intelligent man, and loving his family, could easily give up that habit, would he not do so? The fact that he does not give it up proves it is hard to give it up. It is a very easy thing to sail down-stream, the tide carrying you with great force; but suppose you turn

The Boat up Stream,

is it so easy then to row it? As long as we yield to the evil inclinations in our hearts and our bad habits, we are sailing down-stream; but the moment we try to turn, we put our boat in the rapids just above Niagara, and try to row up stream. Take a man given to the habit of using tobacco, as most of you do, and let him resolve to stop, and he finds it very difficult. Twenty-one years ago I quit that habit, and I would as soon dare to put my right hand in the fire as once to indulge in it. Why? Because it was such a terrible struggle to get over it.

Now, let a man be advised by his physician to give up the use of tobacco. He goes around not knowing what to do with himself. He cannot add up a line of figures. He cannot sleep nights. It seems as if the world had turned upside down. He feels his business is going to ruin. Where he was kind and obliging he is scolding and fretful. The composure that characterized him has given way to fretful restlessness, and he has become a complete fidget. What power is it that has rolled a wave of woe over the earth and shaken a portent in the heavens? He has tried to stop smoking! After a while he says, "I am going to do as I please. The doctor doesn't understand my case. I'm going back to the old habit."

And he returns. Everything assumes its usual composure. His business seems to brighten. The world becomes an attractive place to live in. His children, seeing the difference, hail the return of their father's genial disposition. What wave of color has dashed blue into the sky, and greenness into the mountain foliage, and the glow of sapphire into the sunset? What enchantment has lifted a world of beauty and joy on his soul? He has gone back to smoking. Oh, the fact is, as we all know in our own experience, that

Habit is a Task-master;

as long as we obey it, it does not chastise us; but let us resist, and we find we are to be lashed with scorpion whips, and bound with ship cable, and thrown into the track of bone-breaking Juggernauts. During the war of 1812 there was a ship set on fire just above Niagara Falls, and then, cut loose from its moorings, it came on down through the night, and tossed over the Falls. It was said to have been a scene brilliant beyond all description. Well, there are thousands of men on fire of evil habit, coming down through the rapids, and through the awful night of temptation, toward the eternal plunge. Oh, how hard it is to arrest them! God only can arrest them.

Suppose a man, after five or ten or twenty years of evil-doing resolves to do right. Why, all the forces of darkness are allied against him. He cannot sleep nights. He gets down on his knees in the midnight and cries: "God help me!" He bites his lip. He grinds his teeth. He clenches his fist in a determination to keep his purpose. He dare not look at the bottles in the windows of a wine store. It is one long, bitter, exhaustive, hand-to-hand fight with an inflamed, tantalizing, and merciless habit. When he thinks he is entirely free, the old inclinations pounce upon him like a pack of hounds with their muzzles tearing away at the flanks of one poor reindeer. In Paris there is a sculptured representation of Bacchus, the god of revelry. He is riding on a panther at full leap. Oh, how suggestive! Let every one who is speeding on bad ways understand he is not riding a docile and well-broken steed, but he is riding a monster, wild and bloodthirsty, going at a death leap.

How many there are who resolve on a better life, and say: "When shall I awake?" but seized on by their old habits, cry: "I will try it once more; I will seek it yet again!" Years ago, there were some Princeton students who were skating, and the ice was very thin, and some one warned the company back from the air-hole, and finally warned them entirely to leave the place. But one young man with bravado, after all the rest had stopped, cried out: "One round more!" He swept around, and went down, and was brought out a corpse. My friends, there are thousands and tens of thousands of men losing their souls in that way. It is the one round more.

I have also to say that if a man wants to return from evil practices,

Society Repulses Him.

Desiring to reform, he says: "Now, I will shake off my old associates, and I will find Christian companionship." And he appears at the church door some Sabbath day, and the usher greets him with a look as much as to say: "Why, you here? You are the last man I ever expected to see at church! Come, take this seat right down by the door." Instead of saying: "Good morning; I am glad you are here. Come; I will give you a first-rate seat, right up by the pulpit." Well, the prodigal, not yet discouraged, enters a prayer-meeting, and some Christian man, with more zeal than common sense, says: "Glad to see you; the dying thief was saved, and I suppose there is mercy for you."

The Young Man, Disgusted,

chilled, throws himself on his dignity, resolved he will never enter into the house of God again. Perhaps not quite fully discouraged about reformation, he sides up by some highly respectable man he used to know, going down the street, and immediately the respectable man has an errand down some other street. Well, the prodigal, wishing to return, takes some member of a Christian association by the hand, or tries to. The Christian young man looks at him, looks at the faded apparel and the marks of dissipation; instead of giving him a warm grip of the hand, he offers him the tip ends of the long fingers of the left hand, which is *equal to striking a man in the face!* Oh, how few Christian people understand how much force and gospel there is in a good honest hand-shaking! Sometimes, when you have felt the need of encouragement, and some Christian man has taken you heartily by the hand, have you not felt thrilling through every fibre of your body, mind, and soul an encouragement that was just what you needed? You do not know anything at all about this unless you know when a man tries to return from evil courses of conduct he runs against

Repulsions Innumerable.

We say of some man, he lives a block or two from the church, or half a mile from the church. There are people in our crowded cities who live a thousand miles from church. Vast deserts of indifference between them and the house of God. The fact is, we must keep our respectability, though thousands and tens of thousands perish. Christ sat with publicans and sinners. But if there come to the house of God a man with marks of dissipation upon him, people almost throw up their hands in horror, as much as to say: "Isn't it shocking?" How these *dainty, fastidious Christians* in all our churches are going to get into heaven, I don't know, unless they have an especial train of cars, cushioned and upholstered, each one a car to himself. They cannot go with the great horde of publicans and sinners.

Oh! ye who curl your lip of scorn at the fallen, I tell you plainly, if you had been surrounded by the same influences, instead of sitting to-day amid the cultured, and the refined, and the Christian, you would have been a crouching wretch in stable or ditch, covered with filth and abomination. It is not because you are naturally any better, but because the mercy of God has protected you. Who are you that, brought up in Christian circles and watched by Christian parentage, you should be so hard on the fallen?

I think men also are often hindered from return by the fact that churches are too anxious about their membership and too anxious about their denomination, and they rush out when they see a man about to give up his sin and return to God, and ask him how he is going to be baptized, whether by sprinkling or immersion, and what kind of a church he is going to join. Oh! my friends, it is

A Poor time to Talk

about Presbyterian catechisms, and Episcopal liturgies, and Methodist lovefeasts, and baptisteries to a man that is comiug out of the darkness of sin into the glorious light of the Gospel. Why, it reminds me of a man drowning in the sea, and a life-boat puts out for him, and the man in the boat says to the man out of the boat: "Now, if I get you ashore, are you going to live on my street?" First get him ashore, and then talk about the non-essentials of religion. Who cares what church he joins, if he only joins Christ and starts for heaven? Oh! you ought to have, my brother, an illumined face and hearty grip for every one that tries to turn from his evil way. Take hold of the same book with him, though his dissipations shake the book, remembering that "he that converteth a sinner from the error of his ways shall save a soul from death and hide a multitude of sins."

Now, I have shown you these obstacles because I want you to understand I know all the difficulties in the way; but I am now to tell you how Hannibal may scale the Alps, and how

The Shackles may be Unriveted,

and how the paths of virtue forsaken may be regained. First of all, my brother, throw yourself on God. Go to Him frankly and earnestly, and tell Him these habits you have, and ask Him if there is any help in all the resources of omnipotent love, to give it to you. Do not go with a long rigmarole people call prayer, made up of "ohs," and "ahs," and "forever and ever, amens!" Go to God and cry for help! help! help! and if you cannot cry for help, just look and live. I remember, in the late war, I was at Antietam, and I went into the hospitals after the battle, and said to a man: "Where are you hurt?" He made no answer, but held up his arm, swollen and splintered. I saw where he was hurt. The simple fact is, when a man has a wounded soul, all he has to do is to hold it up before a sympathetic Lord, and get it healed. It does not take any long prayer. Just hold up the wound. Oh, it is no small thing, when a man is nervous and weak and exhausted, coming from his evil ways, to feel that God puts two omnipotent arms around him, and says: "Young man, I will stand by you. The mountains may depart, and the hills be removed, but I will never fail you." And then as the soul thinks the news is too good to be true, and cannot believe it, and looks up in God's face, God lifts His right hand and takes an oath, an affidavit, saying: "As I live, saith the Lord God, I have no pleasure in the death of him that dieth." Blessed be God for such a gospel as this! "Cut the slices thin," said the wife to the husband, "or there will not be enough to go all around for the children; cut the slices thin." Blessed be God, there is

A Full Loaf for Every One

that wants it! Bread enough and to spare. No thin slices at the Lord's table. I remember when the Master Street Hospital, in Philadelphia, was opened during the war, a telegram came, saying: "There will be three hundred wounded men to-night; be ready to take care of them;" and from my church there went in some twenty or thirty men and women to look after these poor wounded fellows. As they came, some from one part of the land, some from another, no one asked whether this man was from Oregon, or from Massachusetts, or from Minnesota, or from New York. There was a wounded soldier, and the only question was how to take off the rags the most gently, and put on the bandage, and administer the cordial. And when a soul comes to God, He does not ask where you came from or what your ancestry was. Healing for all your wounds. Pardon for all your guilt. Comfort for all your troubles.

Then, also, I counsel you, if you want to get back, to quit all your bad associations.

One Unholy Intimacy

will fill your soul with moral distemper. In all the ages of the Church there has not been an instance where a man kept one evil associate and was reformed. Go home to-day, open your desk, take out letter paper, stamp and envelope, and then write a letter something like this:

"My Old Companions: I start this day for heaven. Until I am persuaded you will join me in this, Farewell."

Then sign your name, and send the letter by the first post. Give up your bad companions or give up heaven. It is not ten bad companions that destroy a man, nor five bad companions, nor three bad companions, nor two bad companions, but one. What chance is there for that young man I saw along the street, four or five young men with him, halting in front of a grog shop, urging him to go in, he resisting, violently resisting, until after a while they forced him to go in? It was a summer night and the door was left open, and I saw the process. They held him fast, and they put the cup to his lips, and they forced down the strong drink. What chance is there for such a young man?

I counsel you also, seek Christian advice. Every Christian man is bound to help you. If you find no other human ear willing to listen to your story of struggle, come to me and I will by every sympathy of my heart, and every prayer, and every toil of my hand, stand beside you in the struggle for reformation; and as I hope to have my own sins forgiven, and hope to be acquitted at the Judgment seat of Christ, I will not betray you. First of all seek God, then

Seek Christian Counsel.

Gather up all the energies of body, mind and soul, and appealing to God for success, declare this day, everlasting war against all drinking habits, all gaming practices, all houses of sin. Half-and-half work will amount to nothing: it must be a Waterloo. Shrink back now, and you are lost. Push on, and you are saved. A Spartan general fell at the very moment of victory, but he dipped his finger in his own blood and wrote on a rock near which he was dying: "Sparta has conquered." Though your struggle to get rid of sin may seem to be almost a death struggle, you can dip your finger in your own blood and write on the Rock of Ages: "Victory through our Lord Jesus Christ!"

Oh! what glorious news it would be for some of these young men to send home to their parents in the country. They go to the post-office every day or two to see if there are any letters from you. How anxious they are to hear! Nothing would please them half so much as the news you might send home to-morrow that you had given your heart to God. I know how it is in the country. The night comes on. The cattle stand under the rack through which bursts the trusses of hay. The horses just having frisked up through the meadow at the nightfall stand knee-deep in the bright straw that invites them to lie down and rest. The porch of the hovel is full of fowl, their feet warm under the feathers. In

The Old Farm-House at Night

no candle is lighted, for the flames clap hands about the great backlog, and shake the shadow of the group up and down the wall. Father and mother sit there for half an hour, saying nothing. I wonder what they are thinking of. After a while the father breaks the silence and says: "Well, I wonder where our boy is in town to-night?" And the mother answers: "In no bad place, I warrant you; we always could trust him when he was home, and since he has been away there have been so many prayers offered for him we can trust him still." Then at eight o'clock—for they retire early in the country—at eight o'clock they kneel down and commend you to that God who watches in country and in town, on the land and on the sea.

Some one said to a Grecian general: "What was the proudest moment of your life?" He thought a moment, and said:

The Proudest Moment

of my life was when I sent word home to my parents that I had gained the victory." And the proudest and most brilliant moment in your life will be the moment when you can send word to your parents in the country that you have conquered your evil habits, by the grace of God, and become eternal victor.

Oh! despise not parental anxiety. The time will come when you have neither father nor mother, and you will go around the place where they used to watch you, and find them gone from the house, and gone from the field, and gone from the neighborhood. Cry as loud for forgiveness as you may over the mound in the churchyard, they will not answer.

Dead! Dead!

And then you will take out the white lock of hair that was cut from your mother's brow just before they buried her, and you will take the cane with which your father used to walk, and you will think and think, and wish that you had done just as they wanted you to, and would give the world if you had never thrust a pang through their dear old hearts. God pity the young man who has brought disgrace on his father's name. *God pity the young man who has broken his mother's heart.* Better if he had never been born—better if, in the first hour of his life, instead of being laid against the warm bosom of maternal tenderness, he had been coffined and sepulchred. There is no balm powerful enough to heal the heart of one who has brought parents to a sorrowful grave, and who wanders about through the dismal cemetery, rending the hair and wringing the hands, and crying: "Mother! mother!" Oh, that to-day, by all the memories of the past, and by all the hopes of the future, you would yield your heart to God. May your father's God and your mother's God be your God forever.

A PUNDIT'S STORY.

WHILE walking along the street a Pundit saw a man tearing up a book. He cried out to him to stop. The man said, "Why, it is a Christian book!" "Never mind," said the Pundit, "any literature is too precious for tearing." Seeing he wished for it, the man thought it an opportunity for money-making, and began to bargain. The Pundit gave him something, and took the torn book home. The book was St. Matthew's Gospel. He read it with keen interest, and it caused him much thought. He was "almost pursuaded." His wife had been taught in a zenana, and had died longing for baptism. Her dying testimony stayed in his mind; soon after he became very ill, and in his illness God dealt with him; he accepted Christ, and came for baptism, full of faith and full of joy. When all his friends found their clever leader had become a follower of Christ, they thought him mad, and said his illness had affected his brain. But he soon proved that his intellect was as good as ever. He wrote books; he went about preaching; but whereas before his position had been very high, and he had been held in honor, now he was an *outcast*. His friends forsook him; he was turned out of his family; he was penniless and hated. But after two years' grand testimony for Christ, he had a stroke of paralysis; one side was disabled. Still, his intellect was as clear as ever, his heart as true, ever since he has been confined to the house. He is quite invaluable to the missionaries; they send all inquirers to him; and as he lies there, his whole time is spent in pointing others to the Saviour he has found so precious, and in writing books and pamphlets on the truth of Christianity.

A JEW'S CONVERSION.

THE following extract from a personal narrative, published in the *Watchword*, furnishes a striking illustration of the superior power of prayer and tender appeal over argument, in dealing with opponents of Christianity:

"Brought up a Jew, I was instructed to follow the manifold ceremonial observances which have become so customary to Jews, but I was exceedingly unhappy. I experienced a void which I could not express; I realized a need which I could not define; I hungered and thirsted for I knew not what. After a time I fell in with some atheists. I eagerly devoured the poison contained in their writings, and listened to their blasphemous assumptions. The result was that my mind soon began to yield to their soul-destroying views. I doubted the inspiration of the Bible, and denied the possibility of Revealed Religion. At that time I came across a Christian whose consistent walk in the ways of God attracted me much. I saw he was real. I had to admit that he possessed a secret treasure which I did not. Being rather inclined to be argumentative I frequently reasoned with him about the claims of Jesus as the Messiah of Israel. The result of this was that I became very earnest in the Jewish religion, endeavoring to obtain salvation by my good works, seeking for peace by my own efforts.

"One Sunday afternoon I took a walk, and I heard three Christians singing that hymn:

"'Whosoever heareth—shout, shout the sound,
Send the blessed tidings all the world around,
Spread the joyful news wherever man is found,
Whosoever will may come!'

"The word "Whosoever" struck me forcibly, and one of the friends came up and said to me solemnly, 'Neither is there salvation in any other, for there is none other name under heaven given among men whereby we must be saved.' (Acts 4. 12.) But when I began to quibble and argue, he simply said, 'Friend, I will pray for you.' God in His infinite mercy answered that prayer."

A LADY'S WORK IN A VILLAGE.

IN a letter to the *Missionary Link*, Miss E. C. Eberle gives the following account of her visit to a village about five miles from Cawnpore, as a specimen of the way in which many Christian ladies are now engaged in spreading the knowledge of the gospel in the homes of India:

"We pass by Mohammedan mosques and Hindoo temples, also a railway station, and meet with buffalo, camels, and oxen, with pointed horns and strings of bells around their necks. We see men with almost every conceivable kind of costume, from a bed-quilt in the cool season to a bit of rag in the hot. Women are there too, with rings on their fingers, in their noses and ears, some of them as large as a tea-plate, and with uncombed hair streaming about their dark unwashed faces. Some of the men and boys have their heads shaved with the exception of one lock of hair, which is tied so as to stand out straight on the back of the head.

Reaching the village, I find myself surrounded by these poor ignorant and neglected ones. When I began my work in this and other villages I took with me a few simple medicines, with which I gained access to the houses of the inhabitants. At first they were very much frightened at the appearance of a stranger, one so unlike themselves, in their midst. Women appeared in the door-ways but to vanish at my near approach; others looked down upon me from their house-tops, while men, boys, and a few of the low caste less timid women followed me at every step; dogs came forth to greet me with a bark or growl, and altogether it was a new and strange experience. After one or two visits they were assured of my good intentions, and came to me for medicine with as much confidence as though I were their old family physician.

I am now always greeted by a number of boys, in whom I am greatly interested. Touching their foreheads, they say a salutation, and taking my basket of books they lead the way to one of the houses where I stop, and having called the family they are soon seated on the ground at my feet, these village houses having only the bare earth for a floor. Soon a number of women gather, and after a little pleasant conversation with them I ask them would they like to hear a hymn, and the answer is always the same, "Yes, we want to hear." Then there is silence while I sing. Afterward I teach them a Bible verse and explain it. In this way I visit a number of houses in the same day, and wherever I go the women and children are eager to hear, especially the women, who are not accustomed to learn anything.

A MEXICAN CHRISTIAN DISOWNED.

THE promise of the Saviour to any follower who on His account has lost family and possessions (Mark 10:29, 30) can be claimed just now by many Mexican converts. Dr. J. Wilton Greene, in the course of a long letter to *The Church*, mentions one case which is unhappily typical of a large number:

"A very intelligent young man, of excellent family, born and reared in Queretaro, on visiting this city, found his way to one of our services; his heart was touched by the Holy Spirit, and he was led not only to accept the Saviour, but also to dedicate himself to the ministry, in which he has been one of our most useful laborers. At once he was made to feel the displeasure of his sisters—he being an only brother, and both his parents having died. But, notwithstanding all the opposition directed against him, he held steadily on his way. Just before Christmas he resolved, after seven years of absence, to visit his family, and did so, being received cordially by his sisters and by the aunt with whom they live. During his stay he talked much of the gospel in its comforting and sustaining power, as he had proved it during the last year, when he was nigh unto death. The family heard him respectfully, and even eagerly, and he parted from them hoping that his testimony had been a blessing to them; but at the expiration of two weeks he received a letter from the aunt, in obedience to instructions given her by her confessor, discarding her nephew completely and disowning him for his evangelical faith and work. So that henceforth this noble servant of Christ is dead to his kindred, considered as the offscouring of the earth, and all simply for his faith in Jesus and disobedience to priestly authority."

REV. W. F. RE QUA IN THE INDIAN TERRITORY.

HOPEFUL and encouraging reports of Mr. Re Qua's work among the Indians continue to arrive. The promise for the summer is exceedingly cheering. Calls to labor have reached him from settlements in various parts of the Territory, some of them twenty-five and fifty miles distant from McAlister. He expects to make his way to these settlements during the spring and summer, and hold meetings, and, where schools are needed, to organize. Mrs. Re Qua, whose work among the Indian women has been attended with remarkable success, hopes to accompany her husband on these journeys. Her niece, also, who is an excellent singer and has had some experience in Christian work, has promised to assist. They ask the readers of this journal to pray that a large outpouring of the Holy Spirit may be granted, and that many of the Indians and white settlers may be brought out of darkness into God's light.

It would facilitate this work if a tent capable of holding one or two hundred persons could be obtained. At present there are no funds for this purpose, but Mr. Re Qua and his wife, whose faith seems unlimited, believe that before the time comes to set out on their journeys God will in some way provide them with a tent or the means to purchase one. It is gratifying to learn that these devoted missionaries have not been forgotten, during the winter, by our readers. Mr. Re Qua gratefully acknowledges in his last letter the receipt of gifts from some seventy-eight Christian friends, who, hearing of his work of faith, have ministered to the wants of the family. The bulk of them are strangers to him personally but they have given to him as a brother laboring for Christ, and one of those of whom Christ said, "Inasmuch as ye did it unto the least of these my brethren, ye did it unto me." (Matt. 25: 40.) Mr. Re Qua's address is McAlister Ind. Ter. The smallest contributions will be welcome, and will be gratefully acknowledged.

A CHINESE SHOP-KEEPER'S TESTIMONY.

MR. STEWART MCKEE, who is stationed at Ning-hsia, in China says: "You will be glad to know that God is blessing us. I have been on a tour round the district north of this, and had the opportunity of speaking for the Master to a great many people. I visited three markets, and at the largest had a very happy time. I was quite amused at the way one man showed his respect for the foreigner. I entered his shop, and, at his request, took a seat; I offered him a tract, and while we were talking, a man passing the door called me *a foreign devil*. I took no notice, but the shopman got into a perfect rage, and, leaping over the counter, went after the man and scolded him right thoroughly for daring to insult one who had come to do his people good. Then standing up in the street, he declared the doctrine of Jesus to be a good doctrine, and proved it by its fruits, telling them how the missionaries during the famine had distributed relief, and so saved thousands of lives; and of how, when he himself was at P'ing-yang, he had been cured of opium-smoking by a missionary, who refused to make one cash out of him, and who always instructed him in the way to be good. The result of this man's zeal was that I had an attentive audience for nearly two hours, while I told of the love of Jesus, and sold a number of Christian books."

A NOBLE SISTER OF A PROFLIGATE.

AN impressive instance of the power of Christian love and prayer for the reformation of the apparently incorrigible is related by Mrs. G. Sale Reany. She says: "In a very wealthy home a great sorrow gathered. The only son of that home was a drunkard. Again and again and again the father had forgiven him his wrong-doings, paid his debts, and started him afresh in life; but at the age of thirty he was so reckless, so unmindful of his father's wishes, that his parents banished him from home. They sent him abroad, only allowing him money so long as he stayed there. One year passed, two years passed, but Alexander grew no better, but rather worse. Now there were several sisters in that home. One, Margaret, was several years younger than Alexander. She loved her brother dearly, and deeply sorrowed over his wrong-doing. One day a new thought came to her. She would go and live with him abroad, and win him to love *her* Saviour! And after some delay and much pleading, Margaret gained consent to visit her brother, her absence from home being limited to twelve months.

Poor Margaret went with a brave heart, strong in love, and abounding in hope. It took her many weeks to reach him; then, when there, she found the life was rougher, harder, than the one she expected to live, but for Alexander's sake she bore everything patiently, prayerfully. Sometimes he would say to her:

"Maggie, I cannot understand it at all. Whatever makes you come away from home and live with a fellow here?" And Maggie would answer sweetly:

"One word will explain it all, Alec—love."

She did not say much *to* him, and I know she never talked *at* him, but she *lived her love*, and Alexander was softened by it. But he did not really alter; he drank as freely, and gambled whenever he had a chance.

The time passed quickly. Next week she must go home, to get back within the twelve months. Margaret was alone. She felt keenly, *bitterly* disappointed. It *seemed* as if her hopes were crushed, her love had failed. She threw herself upon her knees and poured out her soul to God. He must love Alexander much more than *she* did. . . . She was pleading His promises one by one; claiming them in the name of the Lord Jesus, when some one knelt down beside her and leant his head against her shoulder, weeping bitterly!

It was Alexander, who had heard her praying, and had crept in. His heart was truly broken in penitence for sin that night. . . . To-day Alexander is a brave, good man, doing his work in the world to help others to be good and brave. He says love saved him in those dark, dark days.

THE PYRAMID POINTING to 1888-89 AS YEARS OF TROUBLE.

According to the Astronomer-Royal for Scotland, Professor Smyth's Period of 1,882 Years from the Nativity in A. D. 6.

[In a previous article published in this journal, on February 16 (page 103), the measurements of certain chambers and passages in the Great Pyramid were quoted from Professor Piazzi Smyth's work, and their prophetic significance explained; the dimensions of other parts of the same marvellous structure, no less significant, are now given.]

PROFESSOR SMYTH writes: "The excruciating exit-passage from the end of the Grand Gallery, which, being only forty-four inches in vertical height, is painfully low for a full-size man to creep through, is exceedingly short, for after no more than fifty-three inches in length,* it enters into the freedom of the Antechamber, its quiet, peace, and presently *granite* protection. But the final reception into the Antechamber is not the only mode of mitigating the threatened horrors of that lower *exit passage;* for before entering that, there is a very peculiar mode of possible *entire escape*, from *the summit of the end* of the Grand Gallery itself, though *only for a few persons*, and not by their own power.

"This escape is by the doorway of exit into a small passage, at the upper southeast corner of the End (or, rather, upper southern end of the east wall) of the Grand Gallery, and is no less than twenty-seven feet above the history-recording floor, only, therefore, accessible to something approaching more to winged and flying rather than walking beings, and leading to

A Sort of Retreat,

more than apartment for earthly life, immediately over the grand final granite hall, the so-called King's Chamber. That said retreat is one of the five hollows of construction which Colonel Howard-Vyse found to exist above the King's Chamber, but while the upper four had been absolutely closed in and about with solid masonry, the fifth and lowest was furnished as above described with the passage-way leading to it from the almost inaccessible top of the southern end of the Grand Gallery, on its eastern side.

"Why it was so furnished there is nothing higher in the scientific or Egyptologic theories to show; though in the sacred and historic symbology *it immediately reminds us of what the evangelists in the New Testament promise, viz., of the elect being gathered in before the dread period of wars and tribulations on earth begins; and also of those elect thus saved meeting the Lord in the air* (1 Thes. 4. 17; Luke 17. 34-37; Rev. 3: 10: 12; 5), and being retained with Him in heaven for awhile before His Second Coming *to the earth itself* to establish His visible kingdom—the kingdom of the *Stone cut out without hands*, ordained to rule over *nations* in truth, righteousness, and universal extent, by grandly supernatural means of which the world under the present Christian dispensation knows nothing practically (Dan. 2. 34-44; 7: 13. 14.)

"The Rapture of the Saints

is necessarily, therefore, *one thing* perhaps *now impending*, but the return of Christ the Lord with His glorified saints to commence the Millennium is *quite another*, and perhaps a more certainly fixable, time—as indicated in the pyramid by the greater proximity of its markings to the chronicling floor-surface.

"But all these things," protest resistingly many devout readers, "have been continually expected every single year since the Ascension, eighteen centuries ago. Can, therefore, any special reason be now shown from Scripture, as well as from the Great Pyramid, why, at all events, this first of the latter-day miracles should be more likely to occur near to the present epoch than to any of the long past years? I reply that those who have studied prophecy earnestly must be aware that a very great number of results have been brought out, all converging to this epoch."

End of 1,260 Years of Mohammedanism about 1896-97.

In Revelation 11: 1-3 we read, "There was given unto me a reed like unto a rod (a measuring rod); and the angel stood, saying, Rise, and *measure* the temple of God, and the altar, and them that worship therein. But the court which is without the temple leave out, and measure it not; for it is given unto the Gentiles; and the holy city shall they tread under foot forty and two months." That is, this injunction implies, "The country outside, even Egypt and Palestine and all the land of Arabia, measure them not; no metrical consequence of any spiritual significance shall be found there by so doing; and they are further given over by God to the Mohammedans to have, to possess, and to tread under foot forty and two months of years (1,260 days,) i. e., 1,260 years." *Pasteur M. Rosselet* dates the 1,260 years from the taking of Jerusalem by the Saracens in A. D. 636-7, which would give A. D. 1896-7 for the close of Mohammedanism.

The Two Witnesses

to God (Rev. 11: 3) are supposed to be (at least in one fulfilment) the two houses of Israel—Judah and Joseph: and their testimony in sackcloth is the melancholy, though diverse, history of those branches of them in the eastern lands which have been, and are, under the iron-heeled domination of the Mussulman power for the appointed 1,260 years. But when that power shall fall at the end of the 1,260 years, the "drying up" of it, as the mystic Euphrates, by the action of the Sixth Vial being already begun—shall they, those witnesses, then reign on the earth? Far from it; the *low, extra low, passage-way* from the Grand Gallery to the Antechamber, as already mentioned, forbids the idea; and besides that, the revelation of St. John expressly says that it is at that moment, "when they shall have finished their testimony, the beast that ascendeth out of the bottomless pit shall make war against them, and shall overcome them, and kill them. And their dead bodies shall lie in the street of the city for three days and a half" (denoting in the year day fulfilment three *years* and a half). Though in a manner ineffectually, the next following verses declare, showing also, most effectually, that

God Will Interfere for Them.

But that final salvation is to be in Antechamber days, and the *troubles*, as the Pyramid's very low passage before that apartment indicates, are to commence previously on all who are left on the earth *after the Saviour shall have secretly and supernaturally removed His elect;* and after, too, that the

Seventh Vial

shall have been poured out into the air; for it is *after* that dread action, in accordance with the words of St. John (Rev. 16: 18), there shall be "voices and thunders and lightnings, and a

Great Earthquake,

such as was not since men were upon the earth, so mighty an earthquake and so great; and also the great hail out of heaven, every stone about the weight of a talent, to fall upon men."

These terms, as *Pasteur G. A. Rosselet* well remarks in his admirable work, entitled, 'L'Apocalypse et l'Histoire,' are *symbols* of prophecy, not vague, mystical, or fanciful, but most exact and truly descriptive to the very letter, when the meaning of the symbols is understood; just as the signs of operation of algebra in a mathematical work are anything or nothing to an ignorant person, but the most perfect expression for the things referred to that can be conceived when read forth by an educated analyst. Wherefore, by a wide inductive process, which in the end cannot fail to arrive exceedingly close to the truth, he proceeds to compare the words of St. John with accomplished history from the Apostle's days to these; and finds every jot and tittle capable of full explanation on one uniform system.

But what does the Pasteur say of the days which are still to come? His first note is, that "the rapture of the Church to the Lord in the air will take place *at or just before* the sound of the seventh trumpet. "*Let us hold ourselves ready*," says he, "*the time is very near.*"

Future Great Invasion of Southern Europe by Russian and North-German Armies.

Yet what does a "trumpet" mean in the book of Revelation? It means, says the Pasteur, AN OVERWHELMING INVASION OF FIERCE SOLDIERS. The first trumpet of the Apocalypse was that of the Goths, And could the words of the beloved disciple have been better chosen, or more expressive, when they are now found so strikingly confirmed by our greatest, though most sceptical, historian of those times (Gibbon), seeing that he has written in his Vol. V. p. 311, "On the 24th of August of the year A. D. 410, at midnight, the inhabitants of Rome were awakened by the tremendous sound of the GOTHIC TRUMPET: 1,163 years after the foundation of Rome, the imperial city, which had subdued and civilized so considerable a part of mankind, was delivered to the licentious fury of the tribes of Germany and Scythia"? Then follow the second trumpet for the invasion by the Vandals, the third for the Huns, the fourth the Heruli, the fifth the Saracens, and the sixth the Turks. But whom does the seventh trumpet, so soon to sound, announce?

Pasteur Rosselet replies: "The *Russians;* and when they are let loose, after the destruction of the Turkish Empire, and throw themselves on the more civilized surrounding nations, we shall know that the seventh trumpet has begun to sound, and

The Third 'Woe'

has commenced. But though both the first and second woes lasted many centuries, the third one is not to do so, for the Word of God tells us that the third woe shall be terminated in brief; or that the Russians shall merely be as a passing, though for the time heavy, Hail (Rev. 11: 19; 16: 21), a term also used in Revelation 8: 7.

Mr. Sydney Hall, a Pyramidal author, who is inclined to look upon the seven overlappings of the Grand Gallery as the seven times of each series of the Seals, Trumpets, and Vials, after expounding the Hail of the Seventh Vial as the future Russian plague, asks:

"'Is this fearful description of coming events to have no more weight with the mass of men than the warnings given to the old world by Noah? Surely the indifference which is shown to the signs of the times by mankind in general has been put on the record by our blessed Saviour Himself: 'As it was in the days of Noah, so shall it be in the days of the Son of Man. They did eat, they drank, they married wives, they were given in marriage, until the day that Noah entered into the ark, and the Flood came and destroyed them all. Even thus shall it be in the day when the Son of Man is revealed.''

*These fifty-three inches of exit-passage are understood by Professor Piazzi Smyth to symbolize fifty-three years following the 1,882 inches or years of the Grand Gallery. It is probable that the 1,882 years extend from A. D. 6, the date of the birth of Christ, to 1888 the present year, as the beginning of the Latter-day Crisis of Daniel's Troublous Times, lasting for thirteen years, from 1888 to 1901, this thirteen years being the first thirteen years of these fifty-three years, and then the remaining forty of the fifty-three years are commencing forty years of the Millennium from 1901 to 1941, being analogous to the forty years transition period of the Jews from their Exodus out of Egypt until their full entrance into the Promised Land.

CHRISTIAN HERALD AND SIGNS OF OUR TIMES.

OFFICE, 63 BIBLE HOUSE, NEW YORK.

ENTERED AT THE POST-OFFICE AT NEW YORK, N. Y., AS SECOND-CLASS MATTER.

Published Weekly. Subscription price, $1.50 a year; $1 eight months; 75 cents six months; sent two months on trial for 25 cents; always payable in advance. Single copies for sale by, or can be ordered at, all newsdealers.

Remittances by Mail should be by Post-office money order, bank cheques, or drafts or express money order, and should always be made payable to THE CHRISTIAN HERALD.

Receipts are not sent, the receipt of the paper by a subscriber is a sufficient proof that his remittance has been received. If the paper does not arrive promptly, please advise us, that we may see if the address is correctly entered.

Change of Address. Name of Post Office and State, of both old and new address, should always be given in case of removal.

CURRENT EVENTS.

The International Copyright Bill was Last week reported favorably to the Senate by the Committee on Patents. It has been amended in several particulars. The principal amendment is the insertion of a requirement that a copy of the book or article, or a description of the model, painting, or design, shall be deposited with the Librarian of Congress before publication in this country or the country of origin, and two copies of the book or article printed from type set in this country, or photographs of the work of art to be copyrighted, shall be deposited with the Librarian, and during the existence of the copyright the importation for sale of the book or article is prohibited. It is stated that the bill has the unanimous approval of the committee, and that its prospects of passing the Senate are regarded as favorable. A vigorous opposition to it is, however, expected in the House, which the advocates of the bill are endeavoring to disarm by convincing individual members beforehand of the benefits it is expected to produce.

The Construction of a System of Coast Defences is strongly urged in a report submitted last week by the Senate Committee on Coast Defences. The committee emphasizes that "the numerous cities upon the Atlantic and Pacific coasts and upon the lakes, with their large accumulations of agricultural and manufactured products, their thousands of millions of dollars of destructible property, are wholly defenceless and exposed to destruction or tribute in case of a foreign war with a nation possessing a modern navy." The committee points out that there is a surplus in the Treasury, and that the time is propitious for entering upon the work which has been so long delayed. There is a growing conviction in both parties that forts ought to be built, and that it is rash to leave our great cities at the mercy of foreign powers. The subject, however, demands mature consideration, not only on account of the enormous expenditure involved in fortifying the coast, but because opinion is divided as to the utility of forts when opposed to ironclads.

An Appropriation to Defray the Expenses of the Congress of American Nations, which is to be held in Washington in April, 1889, was made in a bill which passed the Senate on Thursday last. The bill originated in the House, but several changes have been made in it in the Senate. The proposed Congress is called for the purpose of carrying out the recommendations of the Commercial Commission which visited Central and South America during the administration of President Arthur. The bill requests and authorizes the President to invite the several governments of the Republics of Mexico, Central and South America, Hayti, San Domingo, and the Empire of Brazil, to join the United States in conference for discussing questions of mutual interest, and making such recommendations thereon as will tend, in the opinion of the Conference, to the general welfare. The topics to be discussed at the Conference are: The preparation of a code of international laws, and a mode of arbitration to settle disputes which may hereafter arise between the several American nations, without appeal to arms; a uniform system of weights and measures, Custom-house regulations, and methods for the appraisement of imported goods; a uniform code of copyright and patent laws, for the purpose of preventing the sale of fraudulent imitations of American manufactures; a customs union, regulating the admission of the peculiar products of each country into the others; and direct and regular lines of communication between the several nations.

A Revival of the Shinplaster Era, Contemporaneous with the Civil War, is contemplated. The House of Representatives, on March 19, by a vote of 170 to 67, passed a bill providing for the issue of silver certificates of the denominations of 25, 15, and 10 cents, redeemed, paid, and reissued in the same manner as silver certificates of larger denominations. The chief argument advanced for the passage of the bill was the necessity for providing a fractional currency which can be sent by mail, as inconvenience and loss arise in procuring postal money orders, or postal notes, especially to persons who do not live near a money-order office. It is expected that the bill will be opposed in the Senate, but that it may be passed there in an amended form.

The Telephone Monopoly, After Ten Years of litigation, has been sustained by a decision of the United States Supreme Court, rendered on March 19. The majority of the highest tribunal finds that Bell was the original inventor of the speaking telephone, and declares the validity of his patent. The decision has been so worded that it disposed of the charge of fraud, which was raised by Attorney-General Garland, in the Government suit brought to vacate the patent. Bell's original patent was granted in 1876, and a patent for an improvement the following year. In the infringement suits brought soon afterward by the Bell Company, the defence claimed that the telephone had been invented and used both in this country and in Europe, long before the date of Bell's patent, and submitted evidence that sound had been conveyed by electricity as far back as 1861. The first of these infringement suits was decided in the lower courts in 1881, and others at various times. All but one were won by the Bell Telephone Company, but six of the suits were appealed to the Federal Supreme Court. The main issue in all of them was whether Bell invented the telephone covered by his patent, or had used the discovery of some earlier inventor. The court of last resort has now decided in Bell's favor, by a majority of one, four judges pronouncing for Bell's patent, and three—Bradley, Field, and Harlan—dissenting. The telephone monopoly may therefore be regarded as established until 1893, when the original patent will expire.

The Death of Morrison Waite, Chief-Justice of the United States Supreme Court, on the morning of March 23, was a sad surprise to the public, as no intimation had been given of his illness being serious. The Chief-Justice was exceedingly popular, profound confidence being felt by men of all parties in his sterling integrity and legal ability. The Chief-Justice, though always identified in the public mind with Ohio, was really a New Englander by birth, having been born over seventy-one years ago, on November 29, 1816, in Lynne, Conn. He was the son of a prominent New England jurist. He graduated from Yale College in 1837, and after studying law with his father, he removed to Toledo, O., and there continued his legal education. He practiced law in Ohio until 1874, when President Grant nominated him to the position of Chief-Justice of the United States, made vacant by the death of Salmon P. Chase. The only important public appointment Justice Waite had previously held was that of counsel of the United States before the Tribunal of Arbitration at Geneva under the Treaty of Washington. In holding the highest judicial office in the land, Mr. Waite was careful to maintain its dignity. When in 1875 the suggestion of nominating him for the Presidency was made by some of his friends in Ohio, he wrote a letter declining to permit it, and expressing opinions on the subject which were highly approved throughout the country.

Emperor Frederick, of Germany, in Messages to the Reichstag and the Prussian Diet, declares he will follow the example of his father in maintaining the rights of the crown, while conscientiously observing the constitutions of the Empire of Germany and the Kingdom of Prussia. He expresses the hope that God will help him secure the welfare of the people. The Emperor also issued a proclamation addressed to the people of Alsace-Lorraine, expressing his determination to "preserve the rights of the Empire over the German territories reunited to the Fatherland after a long interval." He promises "an impartial administration of justice and benevolent government, conducted circumspectly, but with a firm hand." On March 22, the ninety-first anniversary of the late Emperor William's birth, Emperor Frederick attended a solemn memorial service in the chapel at Charlottenburg. The latest bulletin describes the Emperor's condition as "satisfactory."

Disastrous Storms are Reported from England and the Continent. In England, sheep have been frozen by hundreds, and many people have been injured or killed by the storms, which in many sections—in Westmoreland in particular—were the worst ever known. In central Germany there was a complete suspension of highway traffic, and in many districts the railways were snow-bound. In France, too, heavy snow-storms have prevailed, and seriously interfered with railroad traffic. In Spain, floods are doing enormous damage. In Italy the rivers have overflowed, and the rising of the Tiber has flooded the lower quarters of Rome. In Hungary thirty villages have been devastated by the floods. The severity of the weather in so many widely separated districts at the same time, is a most unusual characteristic of the season.

A Change in the System of Internal Government in England and Wales of a most radical character is proposed by the Conservative Cabinet now in office. On March 19 a bill was introduced in the House of Commons by Mr. Ritchie, President of the Local Government Board, to remodel the administration of the counties. It is proposed to establish councils, to be elected directly by the citizens, which are to have control of the police, to wield the powers now exercised by the local authorities over gas and water works, artisans' dwellings, the sale of food and drugs, and sanitary conditions, and to make advances in aid of emigration when there is reason to believe that the advances will be repaid. The councils will be under the control of a Government department, which will regulate the borrowing of money, audit the accounts, and also fix the number of members of the county councils. Other provisions give the councils the oversight of lunatic asylums, workhouses, reformatories and industrial schools, and the granting of licenses for the sale of intoxicating liquors. An important feature of the bill is the rearrangement of the country into urban and rural districts, making large cities into counties, with separate councils. It is the opinion of the London *Times* that the principle of the bill will probably be extended next year to Scotland. The measure is regarded as the most momentous that has been brought before Parliament in this generation, as it sweeps away time-honored methods which have been in operation for centuries, and substitutes an entirely new system of local government.

A Memorial Service in Honor of the German Emperor William was held on March 20, at Association Hall, New York, under the auspices of the German pastors. The German Consul-General was present as an invited guest. Resolutions were adopted, stating that since it had pleased the King of kings to recall Emperor William from the scene of his active life, after a long and blessed reign, though separated from their native hearths and incorporated into another political community, the assembly, as German evangelical Christians, sympathized with the Imperial household and the entire German people in their loss. At the same time they expressed their gratitude to God for His great mercy in allowing the Emperor to live so long among his people, to complete a glorious work, and on the eve of his life to breathe out his soul at the feet of the Prince of Peace, whose humble follower he was in life.

An Important Decision Adverse to Prohibition was handed down in the United States Supreme Court on March 19. The case arose out of the section of the Iowa Prohibition Law, which forbids any railroad company bringing liquor into that State unless armed with a certificate from the auditor of the county to which the consignment was destined, that the consignee had a lawful right to sell it. Acting under this section, the Chicago and Northwestern Railroad refused to accept five thousand barrels of beer unless the shipper would furnish such certificate. The latter sued for damages, and the railroad company pleaded the Iowa statute in defence. The Supreme Court, to which the dispute was carried, now declares the statute unconstitutional and holds the railroad company liable. It decides that while a State may regulate or prohibit the traffic within its own borders as it sees fit, it cannot *without the consent of Congress, expressed or implied,* regulate commerce between its own people and those of other States, nor prohibit the importation from another State of liquor or any other article of commerce. That, the court says, is an interference with inter-State commerce, the control of which is vested by the Constitution in Congress. Justice Matthews is the author of this opinion. It is worthy of note that Chief Justice Waite and Justices Harlan and Gray submitted a long dissenting opinion, maintaining the right of a State to protect the health, morals, peace, and good order of its citizens by prohibiting the bringing of intoxicating liquor into it from other States. It is obvious that the Supreme Court decision will prove a serious obstacle to the strict enforcement of State prohibitory laws.

The Marriage of a Dissipated Prisoner to a turnkey was arranged in the police station in Cincinnati, O., recently. A despatch from that city states that a Christian turnkey, employed there, is in the habit of expostulating with the prisoners, and urging them to repent and reform. He does this frequently in the still hours of the night, and when, through excitement or distress, prisoners reveal their wakefulness. On March 14 an intoxicated woman was brought in and incarcerated in the cells under his care. She was noisy at first, but under the turnkey's influence she quieted down and listened to his appeals. Finally, with genuine tears, she deplored her weakness and her sin, and told him the story of her life. The turnkey listened attentively, and, to his amazement, discovered that he was talking to a woman whose lover he had been many years before, when both were in a higher position in life. Being satisfied that the woman's repentance was genuine, the turnkey offered to marry her on the termination of the term of imprisonment to which she would be sentenced on the morrow. The story, however, reached the ears of the judge, who was so much interested that he suspended sentence, in order that the marriage might take place at once. The turnkey was deemed rash by his friends, but he has confidence in his wife, and believes that, through Christ's power, she will be kept from falling. How many of those whom Jesus will own as His bride, have been wooed and won in degradation as abject! (1 Cor. 6:9-11.)

A Fortune is Left to Buy a Tombstone by a recently deceased citizen of Frankford, Pa. The Philadelphia *Record*, in reporting the proceedings of the Probate Court, mentions the admission to probate of the will of an eccentric resident of Frankford. The testator leaves the whole of his estate, valued at twenty-five thousand dollars, to be expended in the erection of a magnificent monument over his grave. The will was executed on April 11, 1869, and attached to it is a codicil executed in 1886 giving explicit directions for the erection of the monument, which is to be upon his lot in Cedar Hill Cemetary. Three shares of the cemetery stock are bequeathed to the cemetery company, the income upon which is to pay for keeping the monument and lot in good repair. The testator probably hoped that the splendid monument would perpetuate his memory to succeeding generations. He thereby displayed his ignorance and folly. The day is near at hand when all such memorials will be overturned, and only "the righteous will be in everlasting remembrance." (Ps. 112: 6.)

A Chinaman's Dilemma was Pathetically described in Judge Howe's court in Indianapolis, Ind., on March 17. The man, whose name is Ah Sue, runs a laundry in that city. He has been nine years in this country, seven of which he spent in New York. Since he left Canton his father has died, and Ah Sue's brother inherited the paternal property, which is of considerable value. Recently the brother also died, and Ah Sue, being the next heir, is entitled to the property. He dare not, however, return to China, as, having left that country nine years ago without the permission of the authorities, he would, on his return, be thrown into prison and tried for his offence. His object in applying to the Court was to obtain naturalization papers, so that going back to China an American citizen, he might claim the protection of our Minister there. Judge Howe, however, was obliged to refuse the application, as under the enactment of 1881 no Chinaman can become a citizen. Ah Sue, therefore, will probably forego his inheritance in China, rather than acquire it at the cost of his liberty. Sometimes men do not act so wisely when they are confronted with a dilemma more momentous. Many are sacrificing their souls to gain a fortune. (Mark 8: 36.)

A Singular Case of Mistaken Identity is Reported from Minneapolis, Minn. Two years ago a builder left his home, saying that he was going to examine a piece of land with the view to erecting a house. That was the last seen of him by his family until ten days ago. Then he returned in a state of violent indignation and made an extraordinary statement. He said that he went to look at the land, as he had proposed, and sat down on a piece of rock to make his calculations. While there he was seized by two powerful men, and in spite of his protestations, he was carried off to St. Paul, taken before a judge, identified as one Henry Jones, an escaped lunatic and sent to the Rochester Insane Asylum. He was not allowed to communicate with his friends, but was detained there until, realizing that his wisest course was submission, he gained control over his exasperation and became calm and obedient to the keepers. After months of exemplary conduct, he was pronounced cured of insanity and released. He proposes to bring suit for damages for unlawful imprisonment. His sufferings were clearly due to his unfortunate resemblance to the escaped lunatic, which occasioned the mistake of the people at the asylum. The Christian has reason to be thankful for the assurance he has, that even after quitting the body his identity can never be misapprehended or lost. (II Timothy, 2: 19.)

Hospitality to a Bear was Rewarded in California recently. The San Pedro *Clipper* states that during the late inclement weather a farmer near that town took compassion on an Italian who with a trained bear was belated on his way to the town. The man was lodged in the farm-house for the night, while the bear was placed in the barn for safe-keeping. During the night the family was aroused by a terrible noise in the barn. Some one was screaming "Murder! Help!" and apparently engaged in a struggle for life. The farmer hastened to the spot, and found the bear with a man in his embraces, hugging him tightly, while the scared fellow struggled frantically to escape. The bear was muzzled, and could do the man no serious injury, though he was apparently doing his best to crush the life out of him with his powerful paws. The man proved to be a dishonest butcher, who had come to the barn to steal a fine calf. In the darkness he had stumbled over the bear, who had seized him and held him fast. The man would surely have been killed had not the farmer aroused the Italian, at whose command the bear released his hold on the thief. The farmer in obeying the apostolic injunction to entertain strangers was not among those who have thereby entertained an angel unawares (Heb. 13: 2); but his obedience was amply rewarded, as sooner or later the kindness of Christians to the poor and those in distress will be, according to the promise. (Luke 14: 14.)

BRIEF NOTES.

It is now definitely decided that the next National Convention of the United Society of Christian Endeavor will be held in the Armory Hall, Chicago, July 5-8.

It is announced that the Presbyterian Council has unanimously agreed to invite the Pan-Presbyterian Council to hold its meeting in 1892 in Toronto, Canada.

The Young Men's Christian Association of Cleveland, O., proposes to buy a $65,000 lot on which to erect a $100,000 building.

The Baptist churches of Louisville, Ky., have over three hundred new members, who ascribe their conversion to the blessing of God on Mr. Moody's recent visit to the city.

Four theological schools and colleges, besides Princeton, have now a foreign missionary in the field supported by the students. They are Knox, Union, Alexander, and Queens.

Peasants entombed by the recent avalanches in Spain and Italy were dug out alive after being buried in the snow, in some instances, for sixty hours. Many deaths are reported.

The new church for sailors in New York, for the erection of which the late Mr. Vanderbilt bequeathed $50,000, was dedicated March 18. Bishop H. C. Potter preached the sermon.

Mr. E. P. Telford's work at Wilmington, Del., has been of a very interesting character. The church has been crowded, and, at the earnest request of pastor and people, Mr. Telford has extended his stay two weeks longer.

At a recent discussion upon the religious condition of South London, a speaker said that in that portion of the city there were only 3,000 church-goers out of a population of 40,000. The chief causes mentioned were drink, overcrowding, and poverty.

A telegraphic despatch announces the sudden death, at Las Cruces, New Mexico, of the Right Rev. George K. Dunlop, Missionary Bishop of the Protestant Episcopal Church in that Territory. Bishop Dunlop was consecrated Missionary Bishop in 1880.

The Episcopal Church Convention of the Diocese of Ohio last week elected as Assistant Bishop of the diocese the Rev. Henry Y. Satterlee, D. D., of Calvary Church, New York. It is not certain that Dr. Satterlee will accept the office.

Gov. Lounsbury, of Connecticut, has appointed Thursday, March 29, as a day of fasting and prayer. The proclamation says: "I recommend to the people of this State that, abstaining from their usual vocations, they spend that day in penitential worship of God in their churches, and private fastings and prayer at their homes.

A cablegram has been received announcing the death, on March 17, at Shanghai, China, of the Rev. Dr. Mathew T. Yates, the celebrated Baptist missionary. Dr. Yates was in his seventieth year. Forty-five years ago he was sent to China, and has been there ever since, except for one short visit to this country about thirty years ago.

A cordial invitation to delegates to represent American Congregationalists at the forthcoming jubilee of Congregationalism, has been extended in a letter from the Secretary of the Congregational Union and Mission of Victoria. The jubilee meetings will be held in Melbourne at the same time as the International Exhibition, which it is expected will attract business men from the United States.

GRACE ABOUNDING.

A New Sermon by Pastor C. H. Spurgeon.

"Moreover the law entered, that offence might abound. But where sin abounded, grace did much more abound." Romans 5: 20.

The Effect of the Law—A Revelation of Corruption—Conviction of Conscience—As a Curative Agent—Inciting to Contrition—Grace Abounding According to Sin—I. As Seen in its Whole Work—At the Fall—The Ruinous Effects of Adam's Transgression—A Better Paradise Regained—Character Raised to a Higher Level—II. In Special Cases—On Sinai—On Calvary—In the Salvation of the Gentiles—III. In Individual Cases—Sinners Aged, Instructed, Despondent.

THE first sentence will serve as a preface; the second sentence will be the actual text. "Moreover the law entered, that the offence might abound." Man was a sinner before the law or Ten Commandments had been given. He was a sinner through the offence of his first father, Adam; and he was, also, practically a sinner by his own personal offence; for he rebelled against the light of nature, and the inner light of conscience. Men, from Adam downward, transgressed against that memory of better days which had been handed down from father to son, and had never been quite forgotten. Man everywhere, whether he knew anything about the law of Moses or not, was alienated from his God. The law was given, however, according to the text. "that the offence might abound." Such was

The Effect of the Law.

It did not hinder sin, nor provide a remedy for it; but its actual effect was that the offence abounded. How so? It was so, first, because it revealed the offence. Men did not in every instance clearly discern what was sin; but when the law came, it pointed out to man that this evil, which he thought little of, was an abomination in the sight of God. Man's nature and character was like a dark dungeon which knew no ray of light. Yonder prisoner does not perceive the horrible filthiness and corruption of the place wherein he is immured, so long as he is in darkness. When a lamp is brought or a window is opened and the light of day comes in, he finds out to his dismay the hideous condition of his den. He spies loathsome creatures upon the walls, and marks how others burrow out of sight because the light annoys them. He may, perhaps, have guessed that all was not as it should be, but he had not imagined the abundance of the evils. The light has entered, and the offence abounds.

The law causes the offence to abound by making an offender to stand without excuse. Before he knew the law perfectly, his sin was not so wilful. While he did but faintly know the commands, he could, as it were, but faintly break them; but as soon as he distinctly knows what is right, and what is wrong, then every cloak is taken away from him. Sin becomes exceeding sinful when it is committed against light and knowledge. Is it not so with some of you? Are you not forced to admit that you commit many sins in one, now that you have been made to know the law, and yet wilfully offend against it, by omission or commission? He who knows his Master's will and does it not, will be beaten with many stripes, because he is guilty of

Abounding Offences.

Why, then, did God send the law? Is it not an evil thing that the offence should abound? In itself it may seem so to be; but God dealeth with us as physicians sometimes deal with their patients. A disease which will be fatal if it spends itself within the patient, must be brought to the surface: the physician therefore prescribes a medicine which displays the evil. The evil was all within, but it did not abound as to its visible effects; it is needful that it should do so, that it may be cured. All this is with a view to his cure. God be thanked when the law so works as to take off the sinner from all confidence in himself! To make the leper confess that he is incurable, is going a great way towards compelling him to go to that Divine Saviour who alone is able to heal him. This is the object and end of the law towards men whom God will save.

Next, consider that there will be no seeking after grace where there is no sense of sin. We may preach till we are hoarse, but

You Good People,

who have never broken the law and are not guilty of anything wrong, will never care for our message of mercy. You are such kind people that, out of compliment to religion, you say, "Yes, we are sinners. We are all sinners." But you know in your heart of hearts you do not mean it. You will never ask for grace: for you have no sense of shame or guilt. None of you will seek mercy till first you have pleaded guilty to the indictment which the law of God presents against you. Oh, that you felt your sins! Oh, that you knew your need of forgiveness! for then you would see yourselves to be in such a condition that only the free, rich, sovereign grace of God can save you.

You see, then, the use of the law: it is to bring you where grace can be fitly shown you. It shuts you up that you may cry to Jesus to set you free. It is a storm which wrecks your hopes of self-salvation, but washes you upon the Rock of Ages. The condemning sentence of the law is meant to prepare you for the absolution of the gospel. If you condemn yourself and plead guilty before God, the royal pardon can then be extended towards you.

I. The doctrine of the text itself is this, that "where sin abounded, grace did much more abound;" and I shall try to bring out that truth, first by saying that this is

Seen in the Whole Work

of grace, from beginning to end. I would direct your attention to the context. The safest way to preach upon a text, is to follow out the idea which the inspired writer was endeavoring to convey. Paul has, in this place, been speaking of the abounding result for evil of one sin in the case of Adam, the federal head of the race. That one sin of Adam's abounded terribly. Concerning this, Paul says, "Where sin abounded, grace did much more abound."

Follow me when I notice, that sin abounded in its ruinous effects. It utterly destroyed humanity. In the third chapter of the Romans you see how, in every part of his nature, man is depraved by sin. Think of the havoc which the tyrant, sin, has made of our natural estate and heritage. Eden is withered—its very site is forgotten. Our life has lost its glory and immortality; for "Dust thou art, and unto dust thou shalt return." Every woman in her pangs of travail, every man in his weariness of labor, and all of us together in the griefs of death, see what sin has done for us as to our mortal bodies. Alas! it has gone deeper: it has ruined our souls. Sin has unmanned man. The crown and glory of his manhood it has thrown to the ground. All our faculties are out of gear; all our tendencies are perverted. The Lord Jesus Christ found us in a horrible pit and in the miry clay, and He not only lifted us up out of it, but he set our feet upon a rock, and established our goings. Raised from hell, we are lifted not to the bowers of Eden, but to the throne of God. Blessed be His name our Lord Jesus Christ can say, "I restored that which I took not away!" He restored more than ever was taken away from us; for He hath made us to be partakers of the divine nature, and in His own person He hath placed us at God's right hand in the heavenly places. Inasmuch as the dominion of the Lord Jesus is more glorious than that of unfallen Adam, manhood is now more great and glorious than before the Fall. Grace has so much more abounded, that in Jesus we have gained more than in Adam we lost. Our Paradise Regained is far more glorious than our Paradise Lost.

Again, sin abounded by

Degrading Human Character.

What a wretched being man is, as a sinner against God! Unchecked by law, and allowed to do as he pleases, what will not man become? See how Paul describes men in these progressive times—in these enlightened centuries: "This know also, that in the last days perilous times shall come. For men shall be lovers of their own selves, covetous, boasters, proud, blasphemers, disobedient to parents, unthankful, unholy, without natural affection, trucebreakers, false accusers, incontinent, fierce, despisers of those that are good, traitors, heady, high-minded, lovers of pleasures more than lovers of God; having a form of godliness, but denying the power thereof." Human nature was not at all slandered by Whitefield when he said that, "left to himself, man is half beast and half devil." I do not mean merely men in savage countries, I am thinking of men in London. Read human history, Assyrian, Roman, Greek, Saracenic, Spanish, English; and if you are a lover of holiness, you will be sick of man.

But now look on the other side, and see what the grace of God has done. Under the moulding hand of the Holy Spirit

A Gracious Man

becomes the noblest work of God. Man, born again and rescued from the Fall, is now capable of virtues to which he never could have reached before he sinned. An unfallen being could not hate sin with the intensity of abhorrence which is found in the renewed heart. We now know by personal experience the horror of sin, and there is now within us an instinctive shuddering at it. An unfallen being could not exhibit patience, for it could not suffer, and patience has its perfect work to do. When I have read the stories of the martyrs in the first ages of the Christian Church, and during the Marian persecution in England, I have adored the Lord who could enable poor feeble men and women thus to prove their love to their God and Saviour. What great things they suffered out of love to God; and how grandly did they thus honor Him! O God, what a noble being this grace has made man to be! I have felt great reverence for sanctified humanity, when I have seen how men could sing praises in the fires.

Again, dear friends, sin abounded to the causing of great sorrow. It brought with it

A Long Train of Woes.

The children of sin are many, and each one causeth lamentation. We cannot attempt to fathom the dark abysses of sorrow which have opened in this world since the advent of sin. Is it not a place of tears—yea, a field of blood? Yet, by a wonderful alchemy, through the existence of sin, grace has produced a new joy, yea, more than one new joy. The calm, deep joy of repentance must have been unknown to perfect innocence. This right Orient pearl is not found in the rivers of Eden. Yea, and that joy which is in heaven in the presence of the angels of God over sinners that repent is a new thing, whose birth is since the Fall. God Himself knows a joy which He could not have known had there been no sin. Behold, with tearful wonder, the great Father as he receives His returning prodigal, and cries to all about him "Let us eat, and be merry: for this My son was dead, and is alive again; he was lost and is found." God hath greater joy in man, and man hath greater joy in God, because grace abounded over sin. We are getting into deep water now! How true our text is!

II. I find time always flies fastest when our subject is most precious. I have a second head which deserves a lengthened consideration, but we must be content with mere hints. The great fact, that where sin abounded, grace did much more abound, crops up everywhere. This is to be seen in

Special Cases.

The first special case is *the introduction of the law.* When the law of Ten Commands was given, through man's sin, it ministered to the abounding of the offence; but it also ministered to the aboundings of grace. It is true there were ten commands; but there was more than tenfold grace. With the law there came forward a High Priest. The world had never seen a High Priest before, arrayed in jewelled breastplate, and garments of glory and beauty. The was the law; but at the same time there was the holy place of the Tabernacle of the Most High, with its altar, its laver, its candlestick, and its table of shew-bread. There was, also, the secret shrine where the majesty of God dwelt. God had, by those symbols and types, come to dwell among men. It is true, sin abounded through the law; but, then, sacrifices for sin also abounded. Sins of ignorance, sins of their holy things, sins of all sorts, were met by special sacrifices; so that the sins uncovered to the conscience, were also covered by the sacrifice.

The story of Israel is another case in point. How often the nation rebelled; but how often did mercy rejoice over judgment! Truly the history of the chosen people shows how sin abounded, and grace did much more abound.

Run your eye down history, and pause at the crucifixion of our Lord Jesus. This is the highest peak of the mountains of sin. They crucified the Lord of glory. Here sin abounded. But do I need to tell you that grace did here much more abound? You can look at the death of Christ till Pilate vanishes, and Caiaphas fades away, and all the clamor of the priests and Jews is hushed, and you see nothing and hear nothing but free grace and dying love.

There followed, upon the crucifixion of our Lord, the casting away of the Jewish people for a while. Sin abounded when the Lord thus came to his own, and His own received Him not. Yes; but the casting away of them was the saving of the nations. "We turn to the Gentiles," said the apostle; and that was

A Blessed Turning

for you and for me. Was it not? They that were bidden to the feast were not worthy, and the master of the house, being angry, invited other guests. Mark, "being angry"! What did he do when he was angry? Why, he did the most gracious thing of all; he said, "Go ye out into the highways and hedges, and as many as ye shall find, bid to the supper." Sin abounded, for Israel would not enter the feast of love; but grace did much more abound, for the heathen entered the kingdom.

The heathen world at that time was sunk in the blackest darkness, and sin abounded. You have only to study ancient history, and you will fetch a heavy sigh to think that men could be so vile. A poor and unlettered people were chosen of God to receive the gospel of Jesus, and they went about telling of an atoning Saviour, in their own simple way, until the Roman Empire was entirely changed. Light and peace and truth came into the world, and drove away slavery and tyranny and bestial lust. Where sin abounded, grace did much more abound.

If I were to ask you, now, to give the best illustrations of grace abounding in individuals, I think your impulse would be to choose men in whom sin once abounded. What characters do we preach of most, when we would magnify the grace of God? We talk of David, and Manasseh, and swearing Peter, and the dying thief, and Saul of Tarsus, and the woman that was a sinner. If we want to show where grace abounded, we naturally turn our eyes to the place where sin abounded. Is it not so? Therefore, I need not give you any more cases—it is proven that where sin abounded, grace did much more abound.

III. Lastly; and this is what I want to hold you to, dear friends, at this time: this

Holds True to Each One.

Let me take the case of the *open sinner*. What have you been? Have you grossly sinned? Have you defiled your body with unhallowed passions? Have you been dishonest to your fellow-men? Does some scarlet sin stain your conscience, even as you sit in the pew? Have you grown hardened in sin by long perseverance in it? Are you conscious that you have frequently, wilfully, and resolutely sinned? Are you getting old, and have you been soaking these seventy years in the crimson dye of sin, till you are saturated through and through with its color? Have you even been an implacable opponent of the gospel? Have you persecuted the saints of God? Have you tried by argument to batter down the gospel, or by ridicule to put it to reproach? Then hear this text: "Where sin abounded, grace did much more abound"; and as it was in the beginning, it is now, and ever shall be, till this world shall end. The grace of God, if thou believest in the Lord Jesus Christ, will triumph over the greatness of thy wickedness. "All manner of sin and blasphemy shall be forgiven unto men." Throw down your weapons of rebellion; surrender at discretion; kiss the pierced hand of Jesus which is now held out to you, and this very moment you shall be forgiven, and you shall go your way a pardoned man, to begin a new life, and to bear witness that "where sin abounded, grace did much more abound."

Perhaps this does not touch you, my friend. Listen to my next word, which is addressed to

The Instructed Sinner.

You are a person whose religious education has made you aware of the guilt of sin; you have read your Bible, and you have heard truthful preaching; and, although you have never been a gross, open sinner, yet you know that your life teems with sins of omission and commission. You know that you have sinned against light and knowledge. You have done despite to a tender conscience very often; and therefore you rightly judge that you are even a greater sinner than the more openly profane. Be it so; I take you at that. Do not run back from it. Let it be so; for "where sin abounded, grace did much more abound." Believe this! Give glory to God by believing it; and according to your faith, so be it unto you.

I address another, who does not answer either of these two descriptions exactly; but he has lately begun to seek mercy, and the more he prays the more he is *tempted*. Horrible suggestions rush into his mind; damnable thoughts beset and bewilder him. Ah, my friend, I know what this means: the nearer you are to mercy, the nearer you seem to get to hell-gate! When you most solemnly mean to do good, you feel another law in your members bringing you into captivity. You grow worse where you hoped you would have grown better. Very well, then; grip my text firmly as for your life. Look over the heads of all these doubts and devils, and inabilities, and see Jesus lifted on the cross, like the brazen serpent upon the pole; and look thou to Him, and the fiery serpents shall flee away from thee, and thou shalt live. Believe this text to be true, for true it is: "Where sin abounded, grace did much more abound."

For the Desponding.

"Ah!" saith another, "my case is still worse, sir; I am of a *despondent* turn of mind; I always look upon the black side of everything, and now if I read a promise I am sure it is not for me. If I see a threatening in God's Word, I am sure it is for me. I have no hope. It does not seem as if I should ever have any. I am in a dungeon into which no light can enter; it is dark, dark, dark, and worse darkness is coming. While you are trying to comfort me, I put the comfort away." Yes; I know you; you are writing bitter things against yourself; this morning you have been dipping your pen in gall; but your writing is that of a poor bewildered creature; it is not to be taken notice of. I see you writing, in text hand, great black words of condemnation: but there is nothing in them all. If thou canst grip it, and know it to be of a certainty the great principle upon which God acts, that grace shall outstrip sin, then there is hope of thee; nay, more than hope, there is salvation for thee on the spot. If thou believest in Jesus, whom God has set forth to be a propitiation for sin, thou art forgiven.

Oh, my hearers, do not despise this grace! Come, and partake of it. Does anyone say, as Paul foresaw that some would say, "Let us sin, that grace may abound"? Ah, then, such an infamous inference is the mark of the reprobate, and your damnation is just. He that turns God's mercy into a reason for sin, has within him something worse than a heart of stone; surely his conscience is seared with a hot iron. Beloved, I hope better things of you, for I trust that on the contrary, the sound of the silver bells of infinite love, free pardon, abounding grace, will make you hasten to the hospital of mercy, that you may receive healing for your sinfulness, strength for your feebleness, and joy for your sorrow. Lord, grant that in this house, in every case wherein sin has abounded, grace may yet more abound, for Jesus' sake! Amen.

GEMS FROM NEW BOOKS.

A PUERPERAL FEVER CURED.*

AFTER my own healing and sanctification, the thought of praying with others occasionally presented itself to me. I left it with the Lord, and bided His time. The day came when my own darling wife lay in a puerperal fever, with a pulse running to one hundred and eighty in a minute. I ventured to lay hands on her in the name of the Lord, and claim the promise in Mark 16: 18. In an hour the fever had gone, the pulse was nearly normal, and the skin moist. Shall not Jesus have the praise? After this, for some time, I had no call; but the matter lay upon my heart. Once I was asked to pray with a lady, and felt that I dared not refuse. God honored faith this time, also. At length I felt a constant pressure to call upon the subject, and prayed long and earnestly for light and guidance. Walking alone one day in the open country, the burden of my heart was "Lord, use me, if thou canst, in this work. I have been healed and the words keep ringing in my ears, 'freely ye have received, freely give.' Lord send me. It is a complete mystery how such a soul as mine can be fit for thy service, but I will take Thy word for it, and believe it. Yes, I will even believe that my heart and my body are actually fit to be a temple of the Holy Ghost, and to receive the 'gifts' of the spirit. Made so by the blood that cleanseth; how, I cannot comprehend, but fit for Thy service. Here I am; Lord, send me."

A Sign Given.

In a few days I received a note from a lady, unknown to me, asking me to call on her for prayer for healing. I prayed earnestly that if the Lord had really given me what He means by "gifts of healing," that I might have a certain specific sign while praying over this case, and in the event of this sign being given I solemnly promised never to doubt that God had really bestowed these "gifts" upon me. Suffice it to say that the sign asked for was distinctly given. From that day to this I have never entertained a doubt of God's "gifts." I have not been "called," very frequently, but that is a matter I leave with Jesus entirely. A single case will be all I can give here.

A Complicated Disease.

A man came to me, suffering intensely from a strange and complicated disease, which had absolutely baffled the combined skill of the physicians at the Jefferson Hospital at Philadelphia. He had shortly before sought and obtained the blessing of a clean heart, and was rejoicing in the grace of God. After some conversation, I prayed with him, with anointing and laying on of hands. He had come to my house with difficulty, pale and covered with a clammy perspiration. As soon as the prayer was ended, he arose from his knees, grasped his hat, shook my hand and abruptly departed, going off with a vigorous step. He at once began to tell of his healing; and from that day to this he has not had a symptom of the disease. After six months of health, he got into spiritual trouble, and was dangerously ill with another disease. So serious was this that the physician left word at the church for special prayer on his behalf. When I visited him, he was lying on a lounge, gasping for breath. His pain had been so severe that he could not bear the weight of a sheet on

* From "Divine Healing; or, the Atonement for Sin and Sickness" (enlarged edition) By Captain R. Kelso Carter. 180 pages. Price 50 cents; by mail, 57 cents. Published by *John B. Alden*, New York.

The Scene Outside the Royal Palace When the Emperor's Death Was Announced

his chest. His spiritual difficulties had been all removed, and his simple faith took hold of Jesus again for the Healer. After prayer he sat up at once, and shortly amazed his physician and family, beyond description, by rising and going about his business. The next day he walked upward of six or seven miles, and has been perfectly well ever since.

Modern Thorns in the Flesh.

It may be pertinently asked, whether the experience of those who believe for faith healing ever coincides with the theory, Are there any modern "thorns in the flesh?" I suggest this question intentionally, as I wish to open every possible point to the light of God's truth.

Yes, there are many instances of "thorns." This serves to show that cases like Paul's, and other Bible characters, are not rare exceptions, but rather types of a pretty general experience. In *Miracles of Healing* I related how I was led to trust God for my eye. Well, all these years He has kept me. I have used the eye constantly: teaching, reading, and writing, and have never taken my glass out of the case to this day. But whenever I close my normal eye, I find the old defect of dimness in the sight still there. This indicates that the astigmatism still remains. But at the same time it wonderfully speaks of God's power; for my physician said that, unless relieved by the glass, my eye would be unfit for use and give me great pain. Since I trusted the matter with Jesus, however, I have used it as much as I pleased and yet have not suffered any serious pain. Thus the Lord's power is constantly manifested in the continued miracle of healing, by which the natural consequences of using an astigmatized eye are entirely prevented. When both eyes are open, my sight is very good, and I am conscious of no defect whatever. Nevertheless I have prayed for its removal, many times. I have earnestly besought God to give me some indications, from the Word, that it is His will for me to retain it; but none such have ever been given. On the contrary, I have been directed to Scripture as explicit as possible for absolute healing. Therefore I claim this: by faith in the promise, it is mine potentially, in God's word; and I know it shall be in the physical fact. Meanwhile I keep constantly asking for light to see God's leading in the matter, and for apprehension to learn the lesson intended. When the lesson is fully learned, I know I shall be delivered, even from this.

THE EMPEROR'S DYING MOMENTS.

THE following narrative of the last hours of the Emperor's life has been published by one who was present, probably the Emperor's chaplain: Dr. Kogel repaired to the Emperor's sick-room at five o'clock on Thursday evening, March 8. After a few observations, in the course of which the chaplain spoke of the nation's prayerful sympathy with the august patient, he repeated the verse of Psalm 23: "Yea, though I walk through the valley of the shadow of death, I will fear no evil, for Thou art with me; Thy rod and thy staff they comfort me." Then the tenth verse of Isaiah 54. "For the mountains shall depart and the hills be removed, but my kingdom shall not depart from thee, neither shall the covenant of My grace be removed, saith the Lord that hath mercy on thee." And afterwards part of the first verse of Isaiah 43: "Fear not, for I have redeemed thee by thy name; thou art Mine." After each of the quotations the Emperor rejoined: "That is beautiful." When the chaplain continued, "I know that my Redeemer liveth; Christ is the resurrection and the life," the dying monarch broke in with, "*That is right.*"

During the evening a number of further Scriptures were repeated, among them Isaiah 14: 27; Rom. 5: 1; Mat. 28: 40; 1 John 1: 7; John 1.: 29; and Rom. 14: 7-9. These were not repeated at one time, but at intervals, so that the Emperor's strength might not be overtaxed. Verses were also read from the Emperor's favorite church hymns. When the chaplain repeated the words of Simeon, "Lord, now lettest Thy servant depart in peace, according to Thy word, for mine eyes have seen Thy salvation," the Grand Duchess of Baden, the Emperor's daughter, asked her father if he had understood what had been said. He gave an affirmative reply by repeating the last words of the passage, "Mine eyes have seen Thy salvation."

In one of the pauses the Emperor remarked spontaneously. "God has helped me with His name." At another time he said, like one dreaming, "We are going to have a devotional hour together." Then after an interval he said, on coming to himself, "I have had a dream; it was the last ceremony in the Cathedral." He evidently had in mind the picture of his own obsequies. At four o'clock on Friday morning, March 8, Court Chaplain Kogel offered up a prayer, and in the repetition of the Lord's Prayer, which followed, the Empress joined aloud. Then the chaplain began Psalm 27, The Lord is my light and my salvation; whom shall I fear? The Lord is the strength of my life: of whom shall I be afraid?" And the Grand Duchess of Baden again asked, "Papa, do you understand?" The expressive answer was, "It is beautiful." Upon this the devoted daughter inquired, "Do you know that mamma is sitting by your bed and holding your hand?" At these words the dying Emperor opened his eyes, and turned them for a long time upon his mournful consort. When he closed them again, it was forever. Thus his last looks were given to his wife.

REGINA'S RESTORATION.

(See Illustration on page 205.)

THE following incident is related in a work written in Danish by Pastor Rone, formerly of Elsinore. He says: "About a hundred years ago several German families left their native land and settled in America, among whom was a man from Wirtemberg, who with his wife and large family established himself on a grant of land which he cleared himself in the forest. There were no churches or schools in the neighborhood, but he did not on that account neglect the observance of the Sabbath. He always spent the day of rest at home with his family, instructing them himself to read the Bible and pray to God. Those were times of danger even for families living in towns, and much more for isolated districts. A tribe of Indians went on the warpath, and ravaged the country far and near. Eventually they reached the dwelling of the poor family from Wirtemberg, while the wife and one of the sons were absent, the husband, the eldest son, and two little girls named Barbara and Regina, were at home. The father and this son were killed by the savages, but they carried the two little girls into captivity, with a great many other children who were taken in the same manner. They were led many miles through the forest, the Indians taking care to cover the trail so that nobody might follow them. In this condition they were brought to the hunting-ground of the tribe, where the captured children were divided among the families.

"Barbara was at this time ten years old, and Regina nine. It was never known what became of Barbara, but Regina, and a little girl of two years old, whom she had never seen before, were given to an old widow, who was a very cruel woman. Her only son lived with her and maintained her; but he was sometimes absent for weeks together, and then the two white ch dren were forced to go into the forests to gather roots and anything they could find in the nature of food for the old woman; and when they did not bring her enough to eat, she would beat them in so cruel a manner that they were nearly killed. The little girl always kept close to Regina, and when she knelt down and repeated the prayers to the Lord Jesus, and the hymns which her father had taught her, the little girl prayed with her, and learned the hymns and prayers by heart.

"In this melancholy state these children remained nine long years, till Regina reached the age of eighteen, and her little companion was eleven years old. Regina continually repeated the verses from the Bible, and the hymns which she had learned when at home, and she taught them to the little girl. They often used to cheer each other with one hymn from the hymn-book used at Halle, in Germany:

"Alone, yet not alone am I,
Though in this solitude so drear."

They constantly hoped that the Lord Jesus would some time bring them back to their Christian friends.

"At last the hope of these children was realized. The Indians themselves sued for peace. The first condition was, that they would restore all the prisoners they had taken. Thus the two girls was released. It was an affecting sight to see the condition into which many of them had fallen in captivity. Some who were quite little when carried away, had acquired the habits of the Indians, and looked almost as wild as they. Scarcely any of them were recognizable at first sight. The news of the release soon spread, and parents who had lost their children long years before, hurried anxiously to see if their treasures were among the liberated crowd. Poor Regina's sorrowing mother came, among many other bereaved parents, but, alas! how could she tell whether, among those grown up girls, was the little nine-year-old child whom she had lost ten years before. Yes, her child had become a stranger to her; Regina had acquired the appearance and manner, as well as the language, of the natives. The poor mother went up and down among the young persons assembled, but by no efforts could she discover her daughters. She wept in bitter grief and disappointment. The Colonel in charge, pitying her distress, said, "Do you recollect nothing by which your children might be discovered?" She answered that she recollected nothing but a hymn which she used to sing with them, and which commenced:

"Alone, yet not alone am I,
Though in this solitude so drear."

The Colonel advised her to sing this hymn. Scarcely had the mother sung the first two lines of it, when Regina rushed from the crowd, began to sing it also, and threw herself into her mother's arms. They both wept for joy, and the Colonel gladly restored the daughter to her mother.

"It was a mutual recognition, but the hymn might not have availed to bring it about had not the daughter found in it precious comfort during her time of trial and suffering. There are many Christian men and women in the world who, looking forward to the time when, their earthly pilgrimage being over, they will enter into heaven, wonder if there will be recognition between them and loved ones who have preceded them many years. It may be that, if in no other way, by this community in some common joy and consolation, 'They will know even as they are known.'" (Cor. 13: 12.)

Regina Recognizes Her Mother.

MRS. TRANSOME'S PUPIL.

A SERIAL STORY.

(Continued from page 191.)

A Bargain.

It was a wonderful change for me, after that sad time in the poorhouse, to be back again in the dear old cottage, and I was thankful for it all the time. I used to thank God every morning and evening, and ask Him to bless Philip and his father, the good friends who had done it all for me.

Yes, they repaid me nobly. Captain John Champion had brought home with him stores of gold and ivory, not enough to make him rich, but ample and to spare for starting himself and Philip again in a way of getting more wealth. But first, they said, they were bound to provide for me; though I told them again and again I had done nothing to deserve it.

Well, by some means or other they prevailed upon our old landlord—who was Philip's uncle, you remember—to let me have my old cottage back again. He was more friendly with them now they had no need of any friendship from him. They bought furniture for me, as far as possible like that which Pippin could remember; though we could not have the old loom back, nor Willie's chair. And because I told them, and made them believe it, that I could not be happy to be idle and burdensome upon them, they set me up again with benches and books, and went themselves to the people living in the dingle, to ask them to send their lads and lasses to my school. There was only one great change.

But ah! that one change was almost more than I could bear. Never to have Transome sitting opposite to me in the chimney nook all through the long, lonely evenings; never to hear him move about in the room overhead, or see him pass by the window! When Pippin and Captain John Champion were gone, then I felt how desolate it was. There were the flowers, and the spring sunshine, and the fresh air blowing over the brow of the hill, but Transome was not there with me to enjoy them. He was dead. I could not get it out of my mind, and he had died in the poorhouse. Still, I was happy in my quiet way, and thankful; but there was another change coming for me, and it came in a strange way.

I had gone down to pay my rent one cold day in November, just such a day as that which drove Transome and me to seek shelter in the poorhouse for the winter. It made me feel very low and down, thinking of that bitter, bitter day. Rebecca opened the door for me, and took me into the kitchen, where there was the poorest pretence of a fire I ever saw. But when she sent me into the master's parlor, there was no fire at all there; and the old man sat with his feet on the fender, and a tattered shawl over his knees, shivering with the cold. He was hard upon eighty by that time; and the most withered skeleton of anatomy you could have found in all our country.

"Why, dear sir!" I cried, "you'll catch your death of cold, sitting without a fire a day like this! Whatever has Rebecca let the fire out for?"

He turned to me; his face was ghastly, with purple lips and watery eyes. I could hardly believe that so much misery could look out from a human creature's face; one of God's creatures, whom He loved, and for whom Christ died. Yet I had seen misery in my time.

"I've lost all my money," he said, in a weak, complaining voice; "every penny is gone, and there's nothing before me but the poorhouse."

He spoke so solemnly, that just at first I was quite taken aback. It all flashed across me how he had turned us out of our old home, and so forced us into the poorhouse, and I thought, Maybe the Lord's words are coming true, "With what measure ye mete, it shall be measured to you again." But do not think that I was glad. Nay; I felt grieved for the old man, who looked so desolate and forlorn, and I prayed silently, in my inmost heart, that he might not fall so low in his old age.

"How have you lost your money, sir?" I asked.

"I don't know," he said, with a trembling, sobbing voice, "only it's all gone, and I must go to the poorhouse to-morrow."

But just then I caught sight of Rebecca at the door, which stood ajar. She was tapping her forehead, and nodding at her master, as much as to say his head was not quite sound. So then I understood that it was only a notion that had taken possession of his brain, and troubled and distressed him as if it had been real.

"Ay, to the poorhouse!" he went on, "where you and Transome went once: but nobody will come to take me out, as Philip Champion took you. No, no. I shall die there, and be buried in a pauper's coffin and a pauper's grave."

Then I thought of Transome being buried in a pauper's coffin and a pauper's grave, all through our landlord's hard-heartedness and covetousness. But I knew well that through that gloomy door he had entered into God's house, where he was at home now, like a child gone home for his holidays. All the while my landlord kept on groaning and shivering, and lamenting that he must die in the poor-house.

Now when I came to ponder over it, it seemed a more dreadful thing for this rich man to lose the sense of being rich, and to suffer all the terror of poverty, than for us who were actually poor, and could feel that poverty was only a trial and a lesson sent us from our heavenly Father. For we were but like His Son, who for our sakes became poor, that we through His poverty might be made rich. But this rich man, with his hoards of money—how was he like the Son of God?

Still, it was not in my nature to stand quiet and see sorrow, without trying to comfort it. So I went up to my poor landlord, and put my rent in his numbed hand, which closed tightly over the money, as Transome's fingers closed over mine when he lay dying.

"There," I said, "that is enough to keep you nearly a week at least. Let Rebecca light a fire and get you some food, and you'll forget the poorhouse."

"You're a good woman," he said; "you'd be sorry to see me go to the poorhouse?"

"That should I," I answered; "but don't be afraid, sir. Turn your thoughts to God Almighty, who loves us all—"

"Ah!" he said, interrupting me with a long, long sigh, most pitiful to hear in one so old, "it's God who is taking away my money, no one else. Who can keep it, if He takes it away? I'm a poor man, Mrs, Transome—a friendless, penniless man."

"But how is God taking it from you?" I asked.

"I cannot tell how," he answered; "but it is melting away, melting away; and I cannot keep it. Every night and every morning I know it is going; but I cannot see or hear anybody taking it. It is God, I tell you; and who can help me, if He begins to take away my treasure?"

"But tell me," I urged, "how you know it is going?"

"I do not know," he said; "only I feel it. The moth and the rust have got at it, and I shall die in the poorhouse."

It was all in vain to argue with him, or try to comfort him. He hid the money I had brought in the breast of his ragged coat, and clasped both hands over it when Rebecca came to the door. I bade him good-day, and went out into the kitchen, grieved to the very core of my heart.

"A maundering old fool!" said Rebecca, "he's been going on like that the last week or more; and nothing 'ill put it out of his head. I sent on the sly for Mr. Saunders, the lawyer; but, thank you! master was too 'cute to say a word of it to him, and Saunders was quite naggy with me, though he'll take care to be paid for his trouble in coming. I don't know how to carry on, for I can't get a penny out of him."

"It's hard for you," I answered, "but you've been a good servant to him for many years, and you must bear on to the end now."

"Ay!" she said, with a long breath, "twenty good years, the best of my life. I should have been wedded long ago but for him. If he don't leave me the fortune he's promised me over and over again, I've made a bad bagain. But he's left it to me in his will; he'stold me so scores of times."

This was more than Rebecca had ever said to me; and I went home turning it over in my mind, and wondering how folks can do things for money that they would never do for love.

All through the coldest and darkest month of winter, my landlord was tormented by the dread of going to the poorhouse, and dying there. He stinted himself of necessaries even, often lying all day in bed to save a fire; as people are compelled to do, who are brought down to the lowest poverty. How Rebecca managed was a puzzle to me; but she had a hard time of it, you may be sure.

Many and many a time did the old man send for me, that I might tell him what the poorhouse was like: and every time I had to speak of it, my heart was made sore by the remembrance of Transome. Yet I could not refuse the poor rich man the only comfort he had in questioning me, and hearing my answers. For truly he would have been more cared for, and had better food and firing, in the poorhouse than he allowed to himself. Now and then I tried to turn away his thoughts from this miserable delusion, and to fix them upon God, and His Son, whose love can cover every sin, even the sin of covetousness. But he could not keep such things in his mind.

But one day when I was down there while Rebecca was gone out on some errand or other, though there were few errands to do in that house, the master tottered across the floor, opened the door, looked if anybody could be listening, and then came back to me, whispering in almost a frightened voice:

"She robs me," he said; "there is always money going; and nobody but her to steal it. But I dare not send her away, and have a stranger in the house."

"No, no, sir," I answered; "she's served you too long to rob you now. You must not get such a fancy into your head. Remember what a many years she's been with you."

"Yes," he said sharply, "because I said I'd make it worth her while to be faithful to me. But she's not to be trusted now, I tell you. She thinks my wits are going; but I'm sharp enough to know when I'm being robbed."

There was such a frightful, sneering look on the old man's withered face, that I could not bear to see it. I turned away my eyes to the dusty window, through which the sun was trying to shine into even that gloomy room; like God's grace into his gloomy heart, if he would but let it in.

"Ah!" he said, "I could have trusted Transome with untold gold, and you are like him. Come and live here, and keep your eye on Rebecca."

"Oh! no, no!" I cried hastily, thinking of my peaceful little cottage on the brow of the hill, with the flowers that would soon be blooming in the garden, and the birds chirping of a morning under the eaves, and my scholars trooping up merrily from the town. It made his large house seem a doleful prison.

"I'll make it worth your while," he began, but there I stopped him at once.

"You couldn't make it worth my while, sir," I said; "please God, I'm not long for this world, and my old home is better to me than any spot in the world; and your nephew, Philip Champion, has promised I shall have all I want, when I cannot win it for myself.

The old man sank down in his chair, almost in a heap, for he had very little strength left in him. But still I saw his sharp, glittering eye fixed upon me.

"Mrs. Transome," he said, after a while, "if you'll come and take care of me till I die, I'll leave all I have to Philip Champion."

That was different. I could not say no to that hastily. If I consented, Philip Champion, my little scholar Pippin, whom I loved more than anyone else in the world, would become a wealthy man. And I knew what Philip would do with riches—lay them, where he had laid himself, at the feet of Christ. Rather than see him grow like his uncle, I would have joyfully followed his coffin to the grave. But I had no fear of that. If Philip came into his uncle's money—and no one had a better claim to it—he would take it as a loan from God, to be laid out in His service.

"You must give me time to think of it," I said to my landlord.

And I did think of it, turning it over and over, till my poor head was fairly weary. Philip was gone away on a voyage with his father, and I could not write and ask him for counsel. Besides, if I did it, I should do it for his sake; and you cannot ask anyone you love how much you must give up for their sake. I had never thought I should be called upon to leave my old home again. But even my home spoke for Philip, who had taken me out of the poorhouse, and bought everything that was in it, and promised to take care of me when I was past work. It was but a little thing I could do in return; and it seemed as if I heard Transome's voice, saying, 'Ally, lass! Faithful in little; faithful in much!' After that I made up my mind to go, and quit my home a second time.

So the next day I dismissed my scholars, bidding them good-bye sorrowfully, and I went down again to my landlord's house. It looked more gloomy and dismal than ever: a large, square, dark house, of three stories, standing alone in a big garden, though there were plenty of other dwellings just beyond the garden walls; the windows were crusted over with dust and cobwebs, the only curtain they had, and here and there a pane was broken. The woodwork had not been painted for so many years that no one could guess what color it had been at first. All one side of the house was utterly desolate, for the rooms were unoccupied. But on the other side there was the master's parlor, with the kitchen behind it, his bedroom, and a spare room on the floor above, and Rebecca's bedroom and an attic over that. Yet even that side of the house seemed neglected and comfortless; for the sun was shining full upon it, making it look more dreary then it did on cloudy days. I thought of my own cheery home, and half turned away. But there was Philip to remember. I went on slowly down the gravel walk, overgrown with grass and dock-leaves, and was soon face to face with my landlord.

"You've made up your mind to come?" he said eagerly.

"Yes, sir," I answered; "but only on conditions. You'll leave your money to your own nephew, Philip Champion?"

"Ay, ay!" he said; "I'll send for Saunders at once, and alter my will; and I'll not forget you, Mrs. Transome. So now you must look sharp after Rebecca, you know, and see there's no waste or extravagance. You know what it is to be in the poorhouse, and I look to you to keep me out of it. I've very little money left to spend on housekeeping, and now I have three mouths to feed instead of two; so you must look sharp after Rebecca."

I had made up my mind he must promise a settled sum for every week's expenses; but we had a hard struggle before I won the victory. He beat me down, moaning over his poverty; and it was only when I threatened to leave him altogether, that he gave way. Then I went out to tell Rebecca; but, to my surprise, Rebecca knew all about it, and expected me to stay. Her story was, that she had told her master it was impossible for her to go on any longer without some help either in the day or at night; a nurse or charwoman they must have. He had grumbled at the expense, and refused to listen to her, till she suggested me. How he had prevailed upon me to go, paying no more than for my food, I have told you already.

"He knew a nurse 'ud ask such high wages," continued Rebecca, "and eat and drink so much; and as for me, I hate 'em. They give themselves such airs, and are no end of trouble. Besides, master's afraid to have any strangers in the house, for fear of 'em robbing him. I couldn't get him to hear of anybody, till I thought of you, and that suited him. He's as cunning as an old fox; and I'll be bound he's engaged you to come for next to nothing but victuals and lodging."

She waited for me to tell her what he was to pay me, but I had not given up my own home for money. I should be paid well enough when Philip came into the old man's property. Yet I felt downcast at the thought of so much cunning and deceit in a man so near the grave as he was. I went back to spend the last night in my house, and make arrangements for a neighbor to keep the key, and give an eye to it. For instead of being paid, I had made it a condition that I should keep on my cottage, and have every Sunday quiet to myself in it. Tha next morning I quitted it once more, not as when Transome and me were turned out of it, after living there nearly forty years, but still sadly, and with a great craving after the peace and quietness I was giving up for the sake of Philip.

(*To be Continued.*)

CHRIST'S LAST WARNING.

By Mrs. M. Baxter.

S. S. Lesson for April, 8. Matt. 23 : 23-39. Golden Text, Ps. 51 : 10.

The Religion of the Pharisees—A Religion of Empty Words—Avoiding Burdens—Craving Worldly Honors—The Woe Pronounced—Inconsistency and Hypocrisy the Bane of Religious Work—Proselytes Excelling the Teachers—The Other Side—The World Overcome—Sophistical Teaching—Scrupulous in Minute Details—Negligence in Weighty Matters—Persecution Foreseen—The Culmination—The Depth of Desolation.

WHEN God says blessed, "He creates blessing by His Word; then the Lord commanded the blessing." (Ps. 33 : 3); When He says, "Woe unto you," His word is equally creative. "He spake, and it was done; He commanded, and it stood fast." (Ps. 33 : 9.) Christ's last words to the multitude were words of warning, and the warning was against unreality. He spoke to the multitude *and* His disciples, for there is no lesson given to the unconverted from which the child of God can learn nothing. He said, "The Scribes and the Pharisees sit in Moses' seat;" i. e., they are in the place of authority, and are to be obeyed and respected for the sake of their office. "Obey them that have the rule over you." (Heb. 13 : 17.) "Let every soul be subject unto the higher powers." (Rom. 13 : 1.) "All, therefore, whatsoever they bid you observe, that observe and do; but do not ye after their works;

They Say, and Do Not."

for these leaders of the people's religion had no personal acquaintance with God; their religion was only empty words, only sounding brass or tinkling cymbal. Their unreality came out in the fact that they required of others what they would not do themselves. Others must deny themselves, while *they* lived in luxury; others must be humble, while *they* indulged in pride; others must be criticized and judged, imposed upon and wronged, but none must move a finger or speak a word against *them*. O how unlike Jesus! The Pharisees and Scribes took for granted that their very position made them superior to other people, and they presumed that everybody should know and acknowledge their superiority. Thus they expected their supposed inferiors to do all those things which they deemed unnecessary for such saints as themselves. How different from Jesus! Before He imposed a yoke upon His disciples, He bore it Himself; "Take *My* yoke upon you, for I am meek and lowly in heart" (Matt. 11 : 29); before He taught us to love our enemies, He loved us back from our enmity; before He taught us to deny ourselves, He "had not where to lay His head." What a glorious example for evangelists and missionaries! O let us *be* all which we teach others to be!

The Pharisees and Scribes, while professing to worship God, really worshipped themselves; "All their works they do, for to be seen of men;" they laid themselves out to attract admiration. They "love the uppermost rooms at feasts, the chief seats in the synagogues and greetings in the markets, and to be called of men, Rabbi, Rabbi." It was a matter of the last importance to them to be appreciated and honored by men. They were not satisfied in society without being made much of and introduced as the chief guests. In the very synagogue, they *must* be first; they went there, not to secure an audience with God, but to be well thought of among men. They loved titles, and could not exist without being distinguished some way or other.

O How Unlike Jesus;

"I am among you as He that serveth" (Luke 22 : 27); "the Son of man came not to be ministered unto, but to minister." (Matt. 20 : 28.) And again, "He that is greatest among you, shall be your servant, and whosoever shall exalt himself shall be abased, and he that shall humble himself shall be exalted." It is the very nature and spirit of the world to seek its own glory and to exalt itself; but this is altogether foreign to the spirit of Christ.

It was and is to those possessing such a spirit that Jesus said, "Woe unto you." When the woman taken in adultery was brought before Jesus, and no man was found without sin to condemn her, Jesus had said, "Neither do I condemn thee; go, and sin no more." (John 8 : 11.) It was urged against Jesus, "This man receiveth sinners, and eateth with them" (Luke, 15 : 2); yet this same Jesus said to the hypocrites who made such a profession of piety, "Woe unto you." First, "Woe unto you" because ye shut up the kingdom of heaven against men; for ye neither go in yourselves, neither suffer ye them that are entering to go in." Inconsistency and hypocrisy on the part of teachers do more to hinder the salvation of souls than any other one thing. O, what will be required at their hands on the great day of account! Another charge is, "Ye devour widows' houses, and for a pretence make long prayers;" defrauding the helpless of their little all under the garb of religion, and vaunting a communion with God which does not exist! "Therefore ye shall receive the greater damnation;" "ye compass sea and land to make one proselyte," to indoctrinate another into the miserable, wicked sophistry which dishonors God and ruins His blessed work with souls, and the proselyte soon exceeds his master in the work of religious deception. What a picture! But how strikingly lifelike! Who has worked for God in this generation without being almost broken-hearted at the very state of things here depicted. Thank God, there is

Another Side.

The same Jesus who thus draws aside the veil, and shows us things as they look on God's side, tells us "in the world ye shall have tribulation; but be of good cheer: I have overcome the world." (John 16 : 33.) Bad as is the heart of man, God can inhabit and transform it. Fear not, little flock; for it is your Father's good pleasure to give you the kingdom." (Luke 12 : 32).

His next accusation was of the unprincipled teaching of these false teachers, who made nothing of swearing by the temple, but everything of the gold of the temple, as though gold were more than God! He asks, "Whether is greater, the gift, or the altar that sanctifieth the gift?" and He shows that we cannot touch a holy thing without touching God Himself. Again, in the matter of tithes, these teachers were scrupulous; they gave the tenth even of the smallest herbs in their gardens, thus making a show of the greatest devotion to God, while they omitted all which involved the yielding up of their will, "judgment, mercy, and faith." There was no sacrifice of will in giving a tenth of their mint and sage, as well as of other fruit and vegetables, in that land where everything grew in such profuse luxuriance; but when it came to a question of actual justice between man and man, they shirked all responsibility which would make demands upon them, they would exact their own rights, but would not yield to the just claims of others. With them the law was, "I will have *my* rights; my neighbor must look after himself; I am a person of importance; he is nobody; why should I put myself to inconvenience for a person who is nothing to me?" Such is the hard, cruel, wicked spirit of the world, and of many professedly religious people too. "And faith." This, again, is neglected by the Pharisees. A man without faith is a man without God; his religion is like a hollow eggshell, which cracks and breaks into nothingness with the least pressure. Another charge was, "Ye make clean the outside of the cup and of the platter, but

Within

they are full of extortion and excess." A shop which is all outside, a beauty which is all made up of paint and finery, a character which is only surface-deep—O how despicable all these!—and such were the Scribes and Pharisees of those days; such are many professedly religious teachers of our day! God can see through the polished surface; His eyes, which are as a flame of fire, can detect the "extortion"—the wronging of others and the sinful oppression—which represents anything rather than the love of the Father; and the "excess" of self-gratification, self-love, self-exaltation, which accompanies it, and He styles it "full of hypocricy and iniquity." His last charge against them was, that they built the tombs of the prophets, and garnished the sepulchres of the righteous, and condemned their fathers for slaying just such as they were themselves daily persecuting. "Ye be witnesses unto yourselves that ye are the children of them which killed the prophets." Like father, like son; and then He prophecies that the prophets, the wise men and Scribes whom He will send unto them, will be slain by their hands, and persecuted from city to city. Jesus saw, in prospect, at that hour, Stephen stoned, James the brother of John slain with the sword, and the persecution against the Christians, both at Jerusalem and wherever there were Jews after He was risen from the dead.

Can a religious hypocrite ever become a true disciple of Jesus? Yes, praise God, with Him "all things are possible." "The blood of Jesus Christ, His Son, cleanseth us from all sin." (1 John 1 : 7.) He who made the heart, knows how to create in us clean hearts and to renew a right spirit within us, where there has been a wrong spirit.

Jesus closed His denunciation—His first and His last while on earth—by declaring that all the righteous blood which had been shed upon the earth, should be required of that generation. Why did He speak words of such terrible severity? He, the Son of God, was about to be slain by those very religious teachers; the crucifixion of Jesus would be the culmination of all the persecution of God's messengers, which had been perpetrated from the time that Cain had murdered Abel, and the generation or race of the Jews would be counted responsible for the blood of the Son of God! Having said this, He who would not, could not, force men to believe in Him and be saved, yearning with unutterable love to those whom He died for, but could not save, cried "O Jerusalem, Jerusalem, thou that killest the prophets and stonest them which are sent unto thee, how often would I have gathered thy children together, even as a hen gathereth her chickens under her wings, and ye would not!"

I Would, But Ye Would Not.

"Ye will not come to Me, that ye might have life." (John 5 : 40.) Such is the Lord's grievance. O that it might melt hearts! "Your house is left unto you desolate." So it is with the heart which does not receive Jesus, or does not receive Him in His fullness—there is nothing so desolate on earth as a heart where Jesus does not reign. "Ye shall not see Me henceforth, till ye shall say, Blessed is He that cometh in the name of the Lord." O sinner, why not say it now? Why not now accept a Saviour, a Cleanser, a Ruler? Why not gladden now the heart of Jesus and your own?

EASTER ANGELS.

God hath sent His angels
To the earth again,
Bringing joyful tidings
To the sons of men.
They who first at Christmas
Thronged the heavenly way,
Now beside the tomb-door
Sit on Easter Day.

In the dreadful desert
Where the Lord was tried,
There the faithful angels
Gathered at His side;
And when in the Garden
Grief and pain and care
Bowed Him down with anguish,
They were with Him there.

Yet the Christ they honor,
Is the same Christ still,
Who in light and darkness,
Did His Father's will,
And the tomb deserted,
Shineth like the sky,
Since He passed out from it,
Into victory.

God hath still his angels,
Helping at His word,
All His faithful children,
Like their faithful Lord,
Soothing them in sorrow,
Arming them in strife,
Opening wide the tomb-doors,
Leading into life.

Father send Thine angels
Unto us, we pray;
Leave us not to wander,
All along our way,
Let them guard and guide us,
Wheresoe'er we be,
Till our resurrection
Brings us home to Thee.

—*Selected.*

MEXICO

Contributions in aid of Christian work in Mexico are most pressingly needed, and can be mailed to the address of
BISHOP H. C. RILEY,
Care of J. P. HEATH,
43 Bible House, New York.

Entered according to Act of Congress in the year 1881 in the office of the Librarian of Congress at Washington.

Vol. XI., No. 14. Office, 63 Bible House, N. Y. THURSDAY, APRIL 5, 1888. Annual Subscription, $1.50.

CONTENTS OF THIS NUMBER.

PORTRAIT AND LIFE OF BENITO JUAREZ, the Patriot President of Mexico.

SPAIN AND THE SPANISH-AMERICAN REPUBLICS, by James Hosmer, M. A.

THE ANGELS OF THE GRASS. Dr. Talmage's Sermon last Sunday Morning.

PROPHETIC FEATURES OF THE GREAT PYRAMID, by Rev. M. Baxter.

A Young Bramin's Disappointment—A Ruined Speculator—A Japanese Idea of Christianity—Diamond Light—Preaching Under Fire—A Question at a Chinese Fair.

THE INFALLIBILITY OF THE BIBLE. A New Sermon by C. H. Spurgeon.

DR. DIX ON VICE IN MODERN SOCIETY.

PICTURE OF THE IMPERIAL MAUSOLEUM at Charlottenburg, Germany.

Gems From New Books: Mud by Measure, etc.

MRS. WILLOUGHBY'S FRIENDS. (With Illustration.)

PORTRAIT OF JOHN CURRIE, the Canadian Evangelist.

MRS. TRANSOME'S PUPIL. A Serial Story. (Continued.)

CHRISTIAN WATCHFULNESS, by Mrs. M. Baxter.

REFORMED CHURCH, MEXICO.

R. C. CATHEDRAL, MEXICO.

REFORMED CHURCH, SEVILLE, SPAIN.

INTERIOR OF REFORMED CHURCH, MEXICO.

BENITO JUAREZ, LATE PRESIDENT OF MEXICO.

BENITO JUAREZ.

The Patriot President of Mexico.

THE portrait on the preceding page is that of a man whose name is a hallowed memory in Mexico. Ever since his death, "*Juarez Day*" is kept as a holiday, his tomb is decorated with flowers, students and soldiers march in procession through the streets of the capital, and eulogistic orations are made. Accompanying his portrait is a picture of the interior of the principal church of the Mexican Church of Christ in the city of Mexico. Also on the left of the page a picture of the leading church building of the Spanish Reformation in Seville, Spain; and above that two small pictures, one of which represents the Church of San Jose in Mexico, which was given by Juarez to Bishop Riley, and the other the Roman Catholic Cathedral of the city of Mexico.

Juarez first became prominent in the country by his election in 1848 to the office of

Governor of Oaxaca,

his native State. He was at that time forty-one years old, having been born in 1807. His administration of the State, and still more his active Liberalism, gave him a national reputation, which was strengthened by the antipathy of the dictator, Santa Anna, by whom he was driven into exile. In 1855, however, he returned, was elected to the new Congress, and subsequently, by his appointment to the office of Chief-Justice of the Supreme Court, became practically Vice-President of the Republic. By the flight of President Comonfort in 1858, during the troubles arising out of the suspension of the Constitution,

Juarez Became President

by right, but he was unable to organize a government in the capital, which was in the hands of the reactionary Government. It was not until 1861, after a bitter struggle, during which he promulgated his famous "Laws of Reform," that Juarez succeeded by the aid of Diaz in capturing the City of Mexico, and assuming the duties of his office. The French intervention near the close of that year, and the struggle it precipitated, was the next episode in the eventful life of Juarez. Driven to Chihuahua, and thence across the frontier, Juarez never altogether lost heart nor abandoned the struggle for the independence of his country. It was not, however, until 1866, when, the Civil War being over, the United States were at leisure to interfere, that Juarez had any real ground for hope. Then Napoleon, heeding the protest of the Washington government, withdrew his troops, and the reign of Maximilian came to a tragic close. Juarez entered the City of Mexico in triumph, July 15, 1867. His conduct at that time showed the true greatness of the man: a train of provisions preceded the conquering army, and the famished inhabitants of the captured city, instead of being plundered by the victorious army, received from it gratuitous supplies of food.

Government and Death.

Only five years more of life remained to the gallant statesman and soldier, and they were passed in the work which he delighted to perform. To repair the waste of war, to reorganize the distracted country, and to carry out the enlightened policy embodied in the Laws of Reform, were congenial tasks. His countrymen elected him President for another term, and in 1871 he was re-elected, and on December 1, took the oath of office for the third time. That his third term would have been commenced in civil strife and bloodshed, seemed at first inevitable. Jealousy and fear lest Republican institutions might be imperilled by the continuous occupation of the Presidency by one man for so long a time aroused a strong opposition. Before it was thoroughly organized, however, the sudden death of Juarez occurred, July 18, 1872, and the movement collapsed. Even his strongest opponents could not refrain from joining in the national grief, and the dead hero and statesman went to his grave in his sixty-sixth year, amid signs of general mourning and public esteem, which has not diminished to this day.

SPAIN AND THE SPANISH-AMERICAN REPUBLICS.

By James Hosmer, M. A.

ALL lovers and students of God's Holy Word recognize His hand in the affairs of both individuals and nations, and, looking back over the history of the past, observe with what manifest design Almighty God has directed and controlled the course of human events, in consonance with His Divine plan for the fulfilment of His foreordained purpose; and all in perfect harmony with the free agency of men, and even through it.

It is my purpose, with God's help, to give some practical knowledge about Spain and Spanish America, and also about the great work which has been undertaken in the Spanish-American Republic of Mexico, toward conversion from error and the spread of pure religion among its people, and endeavor to show how marvellously the hand of our blessed Lord has been in the work from its beginning; tracing it, step by step, in its progress through national vicissitudes and changes of various character.

To understand fully the present condition of Spain and Spanish America, we must learn something of their past. Bear with me, then, while I go back to

Ancient Spain,

and recall to mind the fact that complete copies of the Old and New Testaments were *first printed* in the original languages under Ximenes, Archbishop of Toledo; and that the first Church Council, after the days of the Apostles, whose decisions have been carefully preserved and handed down to us—namely, that of the town of Elvira, situated near the modern city of Granada, which was held A. D. 305—bore the signature of the Bishop of Cordova in Spain as second on its canons; and that in the year of our Lord 325, the same distinguished ecclesiastic, Hosius of Cordova, helped to frame the Nicene Creed at the Council held at Nicea, the ancient capital of Bithynia. Spain having preserved the faith and order of the primitive Church, successfully resisted the intrusion of the Roman anti-canonical tyranny until the latter part of the 11th century, when the National Church was obliged to succumb to its baneful influence through the power of the throne. This was brought about by the importation of a French female sovereign, who succeeded in introducing the rites and ceremonies, as well as the ecclesiastical government, of the Romish usurpation. But it is a curious and most interesting fact, showing to my mind Divine interposition and manifest purpose of God's foreknowledge, that there still exists, as a part of the Cathedral of Toledo, a chapel in which the ancient Mozarabic liturgy of the primitive Spanish Church is used.

This grand cathedral, as may be known, is that of the Primate of the Spanish Church, standing in relation to Spain the same as Canterbury does to England. And when it was endowed with the immense wealth it now possesses, part of the endowment was made subject to the provision for the permanent chapel to which I have referred; so that at a certain hour, while the Latin mass is being celebrated in the main cathedral, the public worship of the ancient Church of Spain, according to the Mozarabic liturgy, is being carried on in the chapel which is a part of the same imposing structure, and within ear-shot of each other. Please mark this fact, and trace the analogy, that while the Jews were carried captive into Babylon, God "left not Himself without witness," speaking to His people even in the land of their exile by His servants the prophets! So while Romish error and idolatry have aggressively entered the primitive Spanish Church, the seed of her pure extraction was left to germinate within the very walls of the chief sanctuary, subsequently to bear fruit in a far distant soil, with a responsibility we may not overlook in its planting, and an earnest, consistent effort we must not neglect in its watering, that God may give it increase.

Passing over details in connection with the rapid colonization of the West Indies, I come to the period when Cortes fitted out vessels of war, and proceeded to

The Conquest of Mexico.

He finds his way to Vera Cruz, on the Gulf, founding and fortifying that city, and from thence penetrates to the heart of the country and establishes what is now its capital, the City of Mexico. He learns a tradition extant among the people, that they had been formerly visited by a white man, with long beard and flowing robe, who told them, as they described it, about heavenly things, and promised that white men should come among them again. Nor does Cortes fail to take due advantage of this tradition to aid him in his conquest. Thence he proceeds to the western coast of that country. Wherever he goes he plants the Cross and builds a church. His mission is that of a crusader, ostensibly at least, and such is the result; for in the hands of Almighty God he is evidently chosen and used as an instrument to spread some knowledge of the truth, and prepare the way for Christian civilization.

Next in prominence we trace in Spanish-American history the name of Pizarro. He lands on the Isthmus of Panama, and in the course of time finds his way down the Pacific coast to Peru. Here he subjugates the powerful native rulers, and founds on the site of the ancient city of Cuzco—the capital of the nation, where the Inca has his court and reigns in majestic splendor—the modern city of the same name. It may be reasonably inferred that the original inhabitants of Peru found their way there from Asia across the Pacific. Pizarro founds the city of Lima, the present capital of Peru. He captures rich treasures from the natives, and demonstrates the exceeding mineral wealth of the soil from which they had been obtained. Whatever may be the verdict of history as to the cruel means frequently employed to grasp their silver and gold, he was, at all events, consistent in his work for the Spanish Church, illustrating it by aiding to build church edifices on a scale of grandeur only to be equalled by the magnitude and opulence of those at home. He was a fierce and mighty conqueror, but at the same time justice demands his recognition as one who at least wished to be a hero of the Cross.

Thus Spanish power became firmly fastened on American soil, and the then mighty nation of Spain reaped the advantages of its wealth in mineral and other products. Thus

Spanish Colonial Rule

continued in America for a period of three hundred years. During this period the tide of immigration rapidly set in, until, at one time, many towns in Spain were largely depopulated of males, leaving, as it was said, wellnigh only the old men and women at home. Thus by intermarriages with the natives, in the course of time, a Spanish mixed race obtained pre-eminence; so that it is estimated there are now *over forty millions of people* speaking the Spanish language throughout Spain and Spanish America. Vast multitudes of native South American Indians, moreover, were driven, by conquest and occupation of their lands, to the interior, where they now exist in as pure a state of positive heathendom as many of the Africans of the so-called "dark continent."

In thus rapidly sketching the outlines of Spanish history in Spanish America it must be borne in mind that the ancient Spanish Church, perverted and enslaved by the Roman schism, kept pace with the growth of Spanish power and influence. The mainspring of that Church, to maintain ascendency and supremacy by material wealth, was not lost sight of. In Mexico its cathedrals were among the richest in the world, and the revenues of Church and bishopric were enormous. The Archbishop of Mexico rejoiced in a salary of $130,000 per annum; the Bishop of Puebla, $110,000; the Bishop of Valladolid enjoyed a similiar amount; and the Bishop of Guadalajara, $90,000.

At the beginning of this century the period of

South American Independence

was inaugurated by General Simon Bolivar, and that of Mexico by the famed Presbyter, Miguel Hidalgo. Between the years 1857 and 1861, in Mexico, the period of political reform set in. Then rapidly followed the Ecclesiastical Reformation, out of which is growing an evangelical work which may well rejoice the heart of every true Christian believer, and prompt in him an earnest desire to be in some way associated with its progress.

In regard to the period of political reform and material progress just referred to, I will confine myself chiefly to Mexico, although it may be stated generally that the same cause produced a similar effect, at different times, in many other parts of Spanish America. From the year 1821 to 1857 Mexico was greatly disturbed by a succession of conflicts growing out of the opposition of the Roman Catholic party to the constitutional government. On the one hand was a patriotic party favoring freedom, progress, and universal education; on the other, an intolerant and bigoted Romish Church organization that feared the dominance of principles which would destroy its power and influence.

Some of the Grand Results

which have marked the heroic struggle for political reform in Mexico are summed up by a writer as that of "National Independence; a Constitutional Republic; freedom of worship, opinion, speech, and of the press; open doors to the interchange of the benefits of modern civilization; and an earnest endeavor in behalf of national education." These are results of contesting principles from 1810 to 1857, culminating in the final establishment of the present constitution of Mexico. I have not referred in detail to the various struggles which, in the hands of an overruling Providence, have brought order and political reform out of the chaos of conflict, but have endeavored only to trace out, in the progress of history, the evident Divine purpose, in my humble judgment, in the preparation of the way for His work, in an unmistakable ecclesiastical reformation, by the more thorough purification and evangelization of a mass of people hitherto degraded and demoralized by bigotry and intolerance.

When the Mexican Government became emancipated from the rule of the Roman Catholic Church, and liberty of worship was enacted, a heavy burden of restraint seemed to be removed, and the path made clear for material progress. The Romish Church observances, hitherto so absorbing, became merely conventional and to a great degree voluntary. Hence, while no doubt infidelity increased for the time, the work of internal improvement manifested itself. English capital vied with that which found its way from the United States in opening up new avenues for trade, and the operation of the varied resources of land and climate. In this, however, England has maintained the lead and preference, owing to the very strong spirit of nationality which is jealous of interference from its close neighbor and great sister Republic, and which dreads the possibility of an attempted annexation. And it is this same spirit of intense nationality which prompts the more intelligent Mexican people, in the reformation of their religious observance, to demand an autonomous reformed Church in preference to foreign missionary effort.

Moreover, to England belongs the credit of having been privileged to sow the first seeds, which have now taken so deep root in Mexican soil, and which are bringing forth the fruit of a lasting reformation. As early as the year 1827 the British and Foreign Bible Society shipped

The First Lot of Bibles,

which fell into the hands of the people at a price which they could afford to pay. And for fifty years succeeding, the same good work was carried on. Since then Christian writings, by Church of England authors, translated into the Spanish tongue, have been freely distributed among some of the population of the City of Mexico. So that when the Mexican Presbyter, Manuel Aguilar, and a few devoted followers, took the first steps toward a National Church organization, during the year 1864, they found a number of people, with minds already prepared by a study and knowledge of God's Holy Word, to enter heartily into a pure and simple form of worship. Prior to this, however, in Santa Barbara, about the year 1861, a Mexican ecclesiastical organization was outlined by a former Roman Catholic Presbyter, Ramon Lozano, which he styled the Mexican Catholic Apostolic Church, but it was not until the year 1864–66 that a permanent Reformed Church was established.

Some four or five years later the Rev. Henry Chauncey Riley, a native of Chili, of American extraction, who was educated partly in the United States and partly in England, and who had been dovoted to Spanish Christian work for several years in New York, came to Mexico. It was at a period when to undertake

Evangelical Work

in that country was attended with no little personal danger; but trusting in the Lord, and confiding his safety to His care, he pursued a bold and heroic course in exposing the errors and fallacies of the Romish Church. With eloquent discourses and able publications in the Spanish tongue he fought down opposition. Having issued a powerful pamphlet, founded upon the unanswerable arguments contained in the writings of Bishop Ryle, of Liverpool, he aroused the pointed antagonism of the Romish Church, which called upon a certain Dominican friar, Manuel Aguas by name, noted for his ability, learning, and powerful eloquence, to reply to the arguments which had been so boldly set forth in this telling pamphlet. The friar read the pamphlet, pondered over it, studied it carefully and prayerfully, and, instead of attempting, to controvert, acknowledged that he was converted through its instrumentality.

Here manifestly was the Lord's Hand. Like Saul, "yet breathing out threatenings and slaughter against the disciples of the Lord," who, when his eyes were opened, became Paul the apostle to the Gentiles, so this Dominican friar, having realized the truth, became at once the most zealous and earnest worker in behalf of the Reformed Church. With all his mighty eloquence and untiring zeal, he worked indefatigably for evangelization, helping to gather, in the course of his earnest labors, during part of which he was the Bishop-elect of the native Mexican Church, some fifty congregations. Then he suddenly fell asleep, with the words—"yes, the precious blood of Jesus"—on his dying lips. He was one of the earliest workers of the Reformed Church in Mexico. The whole history of the self-sacrificing efforts to establish and maintain the work of the Mexican Branch of the Church has been marked by more or less of martyrdom and a succession of struggles, self-denials, and personal dangers, involving in some cases brutal murders, and therefore the saying, that "the blood of the martyrs is the seed of the Church," may not be inaptly applied to the reformed effort before us.

After the death of Manuel Aguas, Dr. Riley was

Consecrated Bishop

of the Valley of Mexico. He continued the work of his predecessor with zealous and untiring efforts, and, by the blessing of the Lord, numbers were added to the Church. He founded schools and orphanages, which, at one time, numbered nearly five hundred children. He had purchased and repaired, largely with his own private means, the magnificent Cathedral of San Francisco, and another church edifice in the City of Mexico. Besides this, Bishop Riley has expended the larger part of the income reserved from his patrimony for his own modest requirements in the support of the work confided to his care. He has been constantly advancing funds to meet the heavy expenditures of so large and important a work, and taking upon himself obligations to cover the current demand for means to carry it on. At present, the evangelizing effort in Mexico is crippled for lack of funds with which to continue it effectively, with the imminent danger of a possible sacrifice of some of its church buildings to meet outstanding obligations, in case the friends of the work do not rally in its behalf. Some of the schools have been disbanded, and most of the small band of heroic preachers have been at times left almost penniless.

If we properly regard the grand opportunity placed in our hands for an

Evangelizing Work in Mexico,

and the precious privilege afforded us of being co-workers together with Him, how shall we escape the responsibility if we neglect that which now appeals to us with such force? Fellow-Christians, think of it! Shall we withhold aid, when it may be that a large number of girls from the orphanage of the City of Mexico will be cast adrift upon the waves of immorality, amid an ocean of vice in that city? Such a danger confronts them. Shall we stand still and permit the opportunity of extending the work already commenced, by establishing a Divinity-school for the education of native preachers, to pass by unheeded? Unless pecuniary aid is at once afforded, such an opportunity may be lost. For if the work is stopped for lack of funds to carry it on, then the self-denying and earnest laborer in that vineyard of the Lord will be compelled to dispose of the church buildings and land, to meet accruing obligations. It must not be. If the true friends of the work of the Mexican Branch of the Church should now rally and make a combined and systematic effort to secure monthly, quarterly, and half-yearly subscriptions, the work will be revived and extended with all the grand possibilities which, by the blessing of God, may be expected in such a field where the harvest is already ripe; where the laborers are so few; and where the pathway has been so clearly marked out by the Lord.

Consider for one moment what a grand opportunity for evangelical work our Lord and Master places before us! Here is a pure and redeemed Church planted in the midst of Mexico, among the ruins of an institution which had lost not only its grasp of temporal power, but even the respect of a large number of its former adherents. Around it is clustered a tender vine bearing the fruit of youth reclaimed from misery and crime. A small sum, comparatively, will enable the earnest, zealous, and devoted little band of workmen to build up a school and college for instruction, by which many young Christian preachers and teachers may be sent forth to evangelize the Spanish-speaking nations.

Three Great Centres

of Christian effort, wide apart in geographical location, but united by a common tongue and sympathy of race and habits—namely, Madrid, in Spain; the City of Mexico; and Santiago, in Chili, the capital of the model republic of South America—present themselves to our consideration for the great work of the Lord in His Church, among the more than forty millions of Spanish-speaking people, as well as to bring the light of His Holy Word to the millions more of darkened heathendom now existing in South America. Out of this nucleus of the Mexican Branch of the Church, its schools and orphanages, may be developed the mighty work, by God's blessing, which I have but briefly outlined here. Let us remember that the Spanish race occupy one of the fairest portions of the whole globe. With the yoke of Romish thraldom cast off, a great future lies before it. In their midst a work of Christian faith has been commenced, restoring the purity and primitive simplicity of their early Apostolic Church, and a grand vantage-ground has been already gained. In the interest not only of Mexico, but of the entire Spanish race, this Christian evangelizing work in the Republic of Mexico should be effectively carried on. The danger of paralysis, for need of adequate means to maintain the work recently inaugurated, threatens. Shall the deadly disease be checked? Fellow-Christians, the case is in your hands! It is the work of the Lord!

THE ANGELS OF THE GRASS.

Dr. Talmage's Sermon Preached last Sunday morning, April 1, 1888.

"If then God so clothe the grass, which is to-day in the field and to-morrow is cast into the oven: how much more will He clothe you, O ye of little faith?" Luke 12: 28.

The Queen of Bible Flowers—Lilies as Teachers—Divinely Appointed—The Mission of the Flowers—I. Evidences of God's Providential Care—Prophetesses of Adequate Wardrobe—A Roman Emperor's Feast—The Flower on Luther's Desk—II. To Grace the Bridal—A Widow's Floral Relic—III. To Give Comfort at the Obsequies—The Dead Watching their Graves—Looking at Wild-Flowers in the Woods—Floral Pillows, Anchors, and Crosses—IV. As Religious Symbols—Almost Human—Symbols of Christ—Of Resurrection—The Trumpeters at Nelson's Funeral—The Archangel's Resurrection Blast.

THE lily is the queen of Bible flowers. The rose may have disputed her throne in modern times, and won it; but the rose originally had only five petals. It was under the long-continued and intense gaze of the world that the rose blushed into its present beauty. In the Bible train, cassia and hyssop and frankincense and myrrh and spikenard and camphire and the rose follow the lily. Fourteen times in the Bible is the lily mentioned; only twice the rose. The rose may now have wider empire, but the lily reigned in the time of Esther, in the time of Solomon, in the time of Christ. Cæsar had his throne on the hills.

The Lily had her Throne

in the valley. In the greatest sermon that was ever preached, there was only one flower, and that a lily. The Bedford dreamer, John Bunyan, entered the House of the Interpreter, and was shown a cluster of flowers, and was told to "consider the lilies."

We may study or reject other sciences at our option. It is so with astronomy, it is so with chemistry, it is so with jurisprudence, it is so with physiology, it is so with geology; but the science of botany Christ commands us to study when He says: "Consider the lilies." Measure them from root to tip of petal. Inhale their breath. Notice the gracefulness of their poise. Hear the whisper of the white lips of the Eastern and of the red lips of the American lily.

Belonging to this royal family of lilies is the lily of the Nile, the Japan lily, the lady Washington of the Sierras, the Golden Band lily, the Giant lily of Nepaul, the Turk's Cap lily, the African lily from the Cape of Good Hope. All these lilies have the royal blood in their veins. But I take the lilies of my text this morning as typical of all flowers, and this Easter day, garlanded with all this opulence of floral beauty, seems to address us, saying: "Consider the lilies, consider the azaleas, consider the fuchsias, consider the geraniums, consider the ivies, consider the hyacinths, consider the heliotropes, consider the oleanders." With deferential and grateful and intelligent and worshipful souls, consider them. Not with insipid sentimentalism, or with sophomoric vaporing, but for grand and practical and every-day, and, if need be, homely, uses, consider them.

The flowers are the angels of the grass. They all have voices. When the clouds speak, they thunder; when the whirlwinds speak, they scream; when the cataracts speak, they roar; but when

The Flowers Speak,

they always whisper. I stand here to interpret their message. What have you to say, O ye angels of the grass, to this worshipful multitude? This morning I mean to discuss what flowers are good for. That is my subject: What are flowers good for?

I. I remark, in the first place, they are good for lessons of God's providential care. That was Christ's first thought. All these flowers seem to address us to-day, saying: "God will give you apparel and food. We have no wheel with which to spin, no loom with which to weave, no sickle with which to harvest, no well-sweep with which to draw water; but God slakes our thirst with the dew, and God feeds us with the bread of the sunshine, and God has apparelled us with more than Solomonic regality. We are

Prophetesses of Adequate Wardrobe.

"If God so clothed us, the grass of the field, will He not much more clothe you, O ye of little faith?" Men and women of worldly anxieties, take this message home with you. How long has God taken care of you? Quarter of the journey of life? half the journey of life? three-quarters the journey of life? Can you not trust Him the rest of the way? God does not promise you anything like that which the Roman emperor had on his table at vast expense—five hundred nightingales' tongues—but He has promised to take care of you. He has promised you the necessities, not the luxuries—bread, not cake. If God so luxuriantly clothes the grass of the field, will He not provide for you, His living and immortal children? He will.

No wonder Martin Luther always had a flower on his writing-desk for inspiration! Through the cracks of the prison floor a flower grew up to cheer Picciola. Mungo Park, the great traveller and explorer, had his life saved by a flower. He sank down in the desert to die, but seeing a flower near by, it suggested God's merciful care, and he got up with new courage and travelled on to safety. I said the flowers are the angels of the grass. I add now they are the evangels of the sky.

II. If you insist on asking me the question, What are flowers good for? I respond, they are

Good for the Bridal

day. The bride must have them on her brow, and she must have them in her hand. The marriage altar must be covered with them. A wedding without flowers would be as inappropriate as a wedding without music. At such a time they are for congratulation and prophecies of good. So much of the pathway of life is covered up with thorns, we ought to cover the beginning with orange-blossoms.

Flowers are appropriate on such occasions, for in ninety-nine out of a hundred cases it is the very best thing that could have happened. The world may criticise and pronounce it an inaptitude, and may lift its eyebrows in surprise and think it might suggest something better; but the God who sees the twenty, forty, fifty years of wedded life before they have begun, arranges for the best. So that flowers, in almost all cases, are appropriate for the marriage day. The divergences of disposition will become correspondences, recklessness will become prudence, frivolity will be turned into practicality.

There has been many an aged widowed soul who had a carefully locked bureau, and in the bureau a box, and in the box a folded paper, and in the folded paper

A Half-blown Rose,

slightly fragrant, discolored, carefully pressed. She put it there forty or fifty years ago. On the anniversary day of her wedding she will go to the bureau, she will lift the box, she will unfold the paper, and to her eyes will be exposed the half-blown bud, and the memories of the past will rush upon her, and a tear will drop upon the flower, and suddenly it is transfigured, and there is a stir in the dust of the anther, and it rounds out, and it is full of life, and it begins to tremble in the procession up the church aisle, and the dead music of a half century ago comes throbbing through the air; and vanished faces reappear, and right hands are joined, and a manly voice promises: "I will, for better or for worse," and the wedding march thunders a salvo of joy at the departing crowd: but a sigh on that anniversary day scatters the scene. Under the deep-fetched breath, the altar, the flowers, the congratulating groups are scattered, and there is nothing left but a trembling hand holding a faded rosebud, which is put into the paper, and then into the box, and the box carefully placed in the bureau, and with a sharp, sudden click of the lock the scene is over.

Ah, my friends, let not the prophecies of the flowers, on your wedding day, be false prophecies. Be blind to each other's faults. Make the most of each other's excellences. Above all, do not both get mad at once! Remember the vows, the ring on the third finger of the left hand, and the benediction of the calla lilies.

III. If you insist on asking me the question, What are flowers good for? I answer, They are good to honor and comfort the obsequies. The worst gash ever made into the side of our poor earth, is the gash of the grave. It is so deep, it is so cruel, it is so incurable, that it needs something to cover it up. Flowers for the casket, flowers for the hearse,

Flowers for the Cemetery.

What a contrast between a grave in a country churchyard, with the fence broken down, and the tombstone aslant, and the neighboring cattle browsing amid the mullein stalks and the Canada thistles, and a June morning in Greenwood, the wave of roseate bloom rolling to the top of the mounds, and then breaking into foaming crests of white flowers all around the pillows of dust. It is the difference between sleeping under rags and sleeping under an embroidered blanket. We want Old Mortality with his chisel to go through all the graveyards in Christendom, and while he carries a chisel in one hand, we want Old Mortality to have some flower-seed in the palm of the other hand.

"Oh," you say, "the dead don't know; it makes no difference to them." I think you are mistaken. There are not so many steamers and trains coming to any living city as there are

Convoys Coming from Heaven

to earth; and if there be instantaneous and constant communication between this world and the better world, do you not suppose your departed friends know what you do with their bodies? Why has God planted "golden-rod" and wild-flowers in the forest and on the prairie, where no human eye ever sees them? He planted them there for invisible intelligences to look at and admire, and when invisible intelligences come to look at the wild-flowers of the woods and the table-lands, will they not make excursion and see the flowers which you have planted in affectionate remembrance of them?

When I am dead, I would like to have a handful of violets—anyone could pluck them out of the grass, or some one could lift from the edge of the pond a water-lily—nothing rarely expensive, or insane display, as sometimes at funeral rites, where the display takes the bread from the children's mouths, and the clothes from their backs, but something from the great democracy of flowers. Rather than imperial catafalque of Russian czar, I ask some one whom I may have helped by gospel sermon or Christian deed to bring a sprig of arbutus or a handful of China asters.

It was left for modern times to spell respect for the departed and comfort for the living in letters of floral gospel. Pillow of flowers, meaning rest for the pilgrim who has got to the end of his journey. Anchor of flowers, suggesting the Christian hope which we have as an anchor to the soul, sure and steadfast. Cross of flowers, suggesting the tree on which our sins were slain.

If I had my way, I would cover up all the dreamless sleepers, whether in golden-handled casket or pine box, whether a king's mausoleum or Potter's field, with radiant or aromatic arboresence. The Bible says, in the midst of the garden there was a sepulchre. I wish that every sepulchre might be in the midst of a garden.

IV. If you insist on asking me the question, What are flowers good for? I answer

For Religious Symbolism.

Have you ever studied Scriptural flora? The Bible is an arbetum, it is a divine conservatory, it is a herbarium of exquisite beauty. If you want to illustrate the brevity of the brightest human life, you will quote from Job: "A man cometh forth as a flower and is cut down." Or you will quote from the Psalmist: "As the flower of the field, so he perisheth; the wind passeth over it, and it is gone." Or you will quote from Isaiah: "All flesh is grass, and the goodliness thereof is as the flower of the field." Or you will quote from James the Apostle: "As the flower of the grass, so he passeth away." What graphic Bible symbolism!

All the cut flowers of this Easter day will soon be dead, whatever care you take of them. Though morning and night you baptize them in the name of the shower, the baptism will not be to them a saving ordinance. They have been fatally wounded with the knife that cut them. They are bleeding their life away: they are dying now. The fragrance in the air is their departing and ascending spirits. Oh, yes!

Flowers Are Almost Human.

Botanists tell us that flowers breathe, they take nourishment, they eat, they drink. They are sensitive. They have their likes and dislikes. They sleep, they wake. They live in families. They have their ancestors and their descendants, their birth, their burial, their cradle, their grave. The zephyr rocks the one, and the storm digs the trench for the other. The cowslip must leave its gold, the lily must leave its silver, the rose must leave its diamond necklace of morning dew. Dust to dust. So we come up, we prosper, we spread abroad, we die, as the flower—as the flower!

"Change and decay in all around I see;
O Thou who changest not, Abide with me!"

Flowers also afford mighty

Symbolism of Christ,

who compared himself to the ancient queen, the lily, and the modern queen the rose, when He said: "I am the rose of Sharon, and the lily of the valleys." Redolent like the one, humble like the other. Like both, appropriate for the sad who want sympathizers, and for the rejoicing who want banqueters. Hovering over the marriage ceremony like a wedding bell, or folded like a chaplet on the pulseless heart of the dead. Oh, Christ! let the perfume of thy name be wafted all around the earth—lily and rose, lily and rose—until the wilderness crimson into a garden, and the round earth turn into one great bud of immortal beauty laid against the warm heart of God. Snatch down from the world's banners eagle and lion, and put on lily and rose, lily and rose.

But, my friends, flowers have no grander use than when on Easter morning we celebrate the reanimation of Christ from the catacombs. The

Flowers Spell Resurrection.

There is not a nook or corner in all the building but is touched with the incense. The women carried spices to the tomb of Christ, and they dropped spices all around about the tomb, and from those spices have grown all the flowers of Easter morn. The two white-robed angels that hurled the stone away from the door of the tomb, hurled it with such violence down the hill that it crashed in the door of the world's sepulchre, and millions of dead shall come forth.

However labyrinthine the mausoleum, however costly the sarcophagus, however architecturally grand the necropolis, however beautifully parterred the family grounds, we want them all broken up by the Lord of the Resurrection. The forms that we laid away with our broken hearts must rise again. Father and mother — they must come out. Husband and wife — they must come out. Brothers and sisters—they must come out. Our darling children—they must come out. The eyes that with trembling fingers we closed, must open in the lustre of Resurrection morn. The arms that we folded in death must join ours in embrace of reunion. The beloved voice that was hushed must be returned. The beloved form must come up without its infirmities, without its fatigues—it must come up.

Oh, how long it seems for some of you! Waiting—waiting for the Resurrection! How long! how long! I make for your broken hearts today a cool, soft bandage of Easter lilies. Last night we had come in the mails a beautiful Easter card; on the top of it a representation of

The "Trumpet Creeper,"

and under it the inscription: "The trumpet shall sound, and the dead shall be raised." I comfort you this day with the thought of Resurrection.

When Lord Nelson was buried in St. Paul's Cathedral in London, the heart of all England was stirred. The procession passed on amid the sobbing of a nation. There were thirty trumpeters stationed at the door of the Cathedral, with instruments of music in hand, waiting for the signal, and when the illustrious dead arrived at the gates of St. Paul's Cathedral, these thirty trumpeters gave one united blast, and then all was silent. Yet the trumpets did not wake the dead. He slept right on.

But I have to tell you, what thirty trumpeters could not do for one man, one trumpeter will do for all nations. The ages have rolled on, and the clock of the world's destiny strikes nine, ten, eleven, twelve, and time shall be no longer!

Behold the Archangel Hovering!

He takes the trumpet, points it this way, puts its lips to his lips, and then blows one long, loud, terrific, thunderous, reverberating and resurrectionary blast. Look! Look! They rise! The dead! The dead! Some coming forth from the family vault. Some from the city cemetery. Some from the country graveyard. Here a spirit is joined to its body, and there another spirit is joined to another body, and millions of departed spirits are assorting the bodies, and then reclothing themselves in forms radiant for ascension.

The earth begins to burn — the bonfire of a great victory. All ready now for the procession of reconstructed humanity! Upward and away! Christ leads and all the Christian dead follow, battalion after battalion, nation after nation. Up, up! On, on! Forward, ye ranks of God Almighty! Lift up your heads, ye everlasting gates, and let the conquerors come in! Resurrection! Resurrection!

And so I twist all the festal flowers of this church with all the festal flowers of chapels and cathedrals of all Christendom into one great chain, and with that chain I bind the Easter morning of 1888 with the closing Easter of the world's history—Resurrection! May the God of peace that brought again from the dead our Lord Jesus, that great Shepherd of the sheep, through the blood of the covenant, make you perfect in every good work to do His will.

ANECDOTES RELATED AT RECENT EVANGELISTIC MEETINGS.

An Unexpected Answer.—Rev. Mr. Arthur says: "A minister not long ago was preaching in a place in the country, and as he came to the middle of his sermon he suddenly stopped and solemnly inquired, 'Is there anyone here who will come to Jesus now?' He did not expect an audible answer, but a man immediately rose in his pew and earnestly replied, 'I will, sir,' and with that 'I will' he passed from death unto life. If more people would make their acceptance of Christ as definite a transaction they would have a more robust Christian life."

A Seaman's Sad Doom.—"An Evangelist heard there was a sea-captain dying close at hand. He said he would visit him at once, but was told it was of no use, as none who had previously visited him had ever seen him touched by the power of God. However, the evangelist called on him, and told of the love of the Lord Jesus. The man listened to him quietly enough, but all unmoved. At last he said, 'Look here, young man, it is of no use speaking to me about these things. Nearly as far back as I can remember, God's Spirit was working with me, continually convincing me of my sin, but I always stifled His appeals. This went on for a long time, but during one long voyage I noticed He had left me. When I came ashore, and was going up a street, I came upon a crowd, in the centre of which was an evangelist. As I stood there listening, the Holy Spirit came upon me with redoubled power, urging me to give myself to God. I turned away muttering, "Oh, bother!" and walked straight into a liquor saloon, and got drunk to drown consciousness. God's Spirit left me, never to return.' Just then the man's wife came in; the evangelist remarked to her, 'This is, indeed, awful.' 'Awful,' she replied. They had spoken a few words, when the captain raised himself and said, 'It is getting dark, darker, dark—' He did not complete the word; he was dead."

Retribution in This Life.—About Fifty years ago there lived a gentleman, owner of a small property on the Welsh coast. Though a landowner, he was the leader of a band of men who lured vessels by false lights on the rocks, and stole their cargoes. One evening he heard that a Spanish trader was in sight and in distress. Immediately the false beacon fires were lit, and the poor seamen, thinking they were friendly guides, steered for them, and came right in among the breakers, where the ship was soon dashed to pieces. The wicked wrecker went down to the seaside, and the first body he saw on the shore, his face turned up and the moon shining full upon him, was his only son, to whom he was deeply attached. Unknown to the father, he had embarked on board this ship for home, little thinking that his own father would become the author of his destruction.

The Idols of the Heathen.—The Rev. John Thomas, missionary in India, was one day travelling through the country, when he saw a great number of people waiting near an idol temple. He went up to them, and, as soon as the doors were opened, he walked into the temple. Seeing an idol raised above the people, he walked boldly up to it, held up his hand, and asked for silence. He then put his finger on his eyes, and said, "It has eyes, but it cannot see! It has ears, but it cannot hear! It has a nose, but it cannot smell! It has hands, but it cannot handle! It has a mouth, but it cannot speak! Neither is there any breath in it!" Instead of doing injury to him for affronting their god and themselves, the natives were all surprised; and a Brahmin was so convinced of his folly, by what Mr. Thomas said, that he also cried out, "It has feet, but it cannot run away!"

Twenty Years "Thinking about It."—"A young lady was converted to Christ at a Gospel-meeting. As she was leaving the building, after the happy change, she felt so full of joy that she spoke to a woman about her soul. This woman was much older than she, and when asked, 'Have you come to Christ?' she replied, 'No; but I am thinking about it.' Twenty years passed. The young lady is married, and still she finds time, even among her household duties, to preach Christ. She was speaking at a meeting lately, and after the address went down among the audience. There she found that same woman, and again asked her the same question, and again got the reply, 'I am thinking about it.' Twenty years thinking about accepting the most gracious invitation that was ever offered! Twenty years considering if one should flee from danger, from certain destruction into peace and safety! How many souls are going to hell thinking of going to heaven! 'Turn ye, turn ye, for why will ye die?'"

Encouragement of a Brave Chief.—There is a touching fact related in the history of a Highland chief, of the noble house of M'Gregor, who fell, wounded by two balls, at the battle of Prestonpans. Seeing their chief fall, the clan wavered, and gave the enemy an advantage. The old chieftain, beholding this effect of his disaster, raised himself up on his elbow, while the blood gushed in streams from his wounds, and cried aloud: "I am not dead, my children, I am looking at you to see you do your duty." These words revived the sinking courage of his brave Highlanders. There was a charm in the fact that they still fought under the eye of their chief. It roused them to put forth their mightiest energies; and they did all that human strength could do to stem and turn the dreadful tide of battle. And is there not a more powerful charm for thee, O Christian, in the fact that you contend, in the battle-field of life, under the eye of your Saviour? Wherever you are, however oppressed by foes, however exhausted by the stern strife with evil—the eye of Christ is fixed most lovingly upon thee.

PREACHING UNDER FIRE.

A VISIT recently paid by the Rev. H. W. Rankin to Brighton, Colo., when he preached in a neat brick church, recalled to his memory his appalling experience on a previous visit to that town, which he describes in a letter to the *Church*. He says: "My first visit to this field was made four years ago, when I held the first service ever held in the place, preaching in a saloon, the only place that could be secured. That meeting will never be forgotten by those who attended it. A company of cow-boys, hearing that a meeting was going to be held, came galloping in on their ponies, with the determination to break up the meeting and run the preacher out of the place, as they had done in several others. They began by running their horses around the building, whooping like Indians, and firing their revolvers, then *running their revolvers through the broken panes of glass in the windows and firing through the building*. Many of the people became terribly frightened and ran out. I entreated the people to remain, saying that I was going to continue the service, with God's help, even if all left. This gave the people confidence, and many kept their seats. I went through with the service, and a few minutes before the meeting closed they jumped on their horses and rode off vanquished. The next day they rode into the place. I went and spoke kindly to the leader, and invited them to come to the meetings. The big tears rolled down his cheeks, and, taking me by the hand, he said, 'You are the greatest brick of a fellow we ever met, and we will never try to break up one of your meetings again. We will do anything you want done.' And they were my friends from that time."

A JAPANESE IDEA OF CHRISTIANITY.

A GOVERNMENT school at Sendai, in Japan, was closed a short time ago, but not until the step had been discussed in the provincial assembly. The discussion elicited several remarkable expressions of opinion. Mr. De Forest, who reports the debate to the *Missionary Herald*, says: "It is no small gain to have our school discussed in the provincial assemblies. Here, when the question of abolition of the Government Middle School was presented, it was strongly opposed by one member, who said that such a step would leave the city with nothing but that Christian school, where they had prayers every morning, and where there was so much religion that it might be called 'priest-ridden' or '*stinking with religion*.' To this the vice-governor replied that the school was doing a regular educational work that would compare well with other schools, and that the prayers were only two or three minutes long, the time, twenty-five minutes, being taken up mainly with addresses that conveyed useful information and *helped to make character*. A lawyer followed in the same strain; and the talk has cleared the track so that now it is fully understood that our school stands pledged to do all that is possible to develop character, as well as to quicken the intellect; and the means used are the principles of the Christian religion."

A QUESTION AT A CHINESE FAIR.

DURING a recent journey in China, to various places to the south of Tung-cho, where fairs were being held, Mr. Beach, a missionary of the American Board, preached at Sin Ling. In a letter to the *Missionary Herald*, he thus relates what occurred: "There was the densest crowd I have ever seen in my life, owing to its being a fair-day, and a theatre day too. The streets being full, the housetops were occupied by sightseers. The passage of our cart through this solid mass of humanity was an exciting and dangerous piece of business. Just outside the town was a hill, from which I preached to an immense crowd. One fine old man of seventy-three stood for more than an hour, listening intently, and then, owing to the infirmities of age, he came and sat down just behind me. In reply to *a man who wished to know whether I was explaining a method for getting rich*, and learning that I was not, went off disgusted, I tried to show that the reason why he wished to get rich was that he might attain happiness, and that he showed his unwisdom in not asking whether there was not a way to attain happiness that was eternal and not ephemeral. At this point the old gentleman took up the thought, and talked to the people very feelingly of the transitory nature of this world's joy. His words, being those of age and respectability, had effect. Later I talked personally to the old gentleman about his own relation to God, and his prospects for the other world, so soon to dawn upon him. I have some hope of the old man.

VICE IN MODERN SOCIETY.

IN the course of his Lenten lecture the Rev. Morgan Dix. D. D., the rector of Trinity Church, New York, startled his aristocratic hearers by a graphic portrayal of the dangerous habits and conditions of the upper ranks of society. Having deplored the vice of the lower classes, which has its origin in the crowded tenements, he asked: "But what shall be said of the higher classes, for those whose sins are without justification, and denote simply carelessness, irreligion, unbelief?

"Look how young girls are trained—in softness and luxury, with the one idea of making a figure in society, and a brilliant marriage; of making the most of their physical advantages, and alluring the other sex by the acts best adapted to that purpose. See them on the drive, through the troubled social sea, at their lunch parties, with a dozen courses and half as many kinds of wines; at the opera, immodestly attired; at the ball, giving the whole night to dissipation; at the summer haunts of fashion, without due oversight or sense of responsibility; treated with easy familiarity by careless men, and, apparently, without a vestige of an idea of what is due to a gentlewoman from a man. Listen to the low gossip among these young women, to the broad speeches and unclean stories by which they are prepared for that final surrender of the last ideas of propriety and of all faith in the honor and virtue of men.

"Then pass on, and let us look at the woman as married—married, perhaps, for her money, or marrying some man for his money, without love and without respect; married, but with no idea of living thereafter under bonds; resolved to be more free and enjoy life more; eager for admiration, athirst for compliments and flattery, so that the husband early drops into a secondary position, and some other man, who does the madly devoted for the time, engrosses the larger share of her thoughts. Follow out this subject till you come to the divorce suit and the separation, and thence to the next, and now adulterous marriage, when those whom Christ and the gospel forbid to marry so long as some one else liveth, snap their fingers at the attempted restriction, and commence a second partnership without fear and without remorse.

"We all know that these are the commonest things of the day. I have gone as far as I dare to go, and yet I have done no more that to skim the bubbling caldron and take off what comes to the top, leaving the black broth below, *a thing too foul to be described*. But the scum is an index to what is underneath: and if these things whereof we have spoken go on in sight, what, think you, goes on out of sight?"

DIAMOND LIGHT.

AN interesting question, in connection with diamonds, has been submitted to a practical experiment in Paris. It has long been asserted by some and denied by others, that the diamond has the power of retaining light and of afterward emitting it in the dark. The theory has been often stated, but has not been easy of test. All, or nearly all, the great diamonds—such as the Kohinoor, the Regent, the Grand Mogul—cannot be made the subject of experiment, and stones of a lesser size do not always give satisfactory results. Happily, a private individual, the owner of a gem of remarkable purity, lent his diamond for scientific investigations. These have been most satisfactory, and the "phosphorescence" of the stone may be regarded as proved. The diamond was exposed for an hour to the direct action of the sun's rays and afterward removed into a dark room. For more than twenty minutes afterward it emitted a light so bright as to render visible objects within reach of its rays. It then gradually paled until again submitted to the sun's rays. It is thus with God's jewels. The light they give in the world is derived from the Sun of Righteousness, and they would not give out light if they did not live always in "the light of God's presence." "The spirit of man is the candle of the Lord." (Prov. 29 : 27.)

A YOUNG BRAHMIN'S DISAPPOINTMENT.

IN an interesting autobiographical narrative published in the *Indian Witness*, a converted Brahmin describes the chagrin which he experienced when, as a youth, he *attempted to destroy a playmate* by a miracle and failed. He says: "Immediately after the performance of the sacred-thread ceremony—a ceremony consisting of putting the Brahmical badge round the neck, I was confined for three days in a closed room, and was not allowed to have intercourse with anyone except my grandmother, a venerable old lady, universally loved and respected. During these three days she became my teacher, and reminded me of my new duties and responsibilities, and what honor I could justly expect from the lower orders of society simply because I was a Brahmin. I thought that I was in possession of divine power, and could destroy anyone who would dare stand against me, simply by the breath of my mouth. I was very glad to have been told that I had this great power, and I thought of making an experiment, immediately after my release, on one of my playmates, who belonged to a caste next to the Brahmin, and with whom I was not always on good terms. So, after I was set free to walk about the village and join the company of my former playmates, one of the first things that I did was to find an occasion of a quarrel with the boy whom I wanted to destroy. I found the occasion very soon, and in the quarrel gave him two or three severe blows, and then warned him not to touch my person, as I had now *the power of reducing him to ashes*. Notwithstanding my warning, he retaliated and had given me the same number of blows, or perhaps more. I tried in vain to destroy him by the breath of my mouth, and at last threw my sacred thread at his feet, thinking that this time he would be burnt up with fire. But seeing that I was defeated in my attempt to destroy him, and all the magical power of my sacred thread failed, I ran crying to my grandmother."

A RUINED SPECULATOR'S CHANGE.

IN a new work, by the Rev. W. Haslam, the following incident is related: A wife and daughter who had received blessing at a mission, came to ask prayer for the husband and father at home. "He cannot come out," they said; "will you pray for his conversion?" As the mission went on, the ladies became more and more urgent for the object of their solicitude. The gentleman, it appeared, had been in a high station of life, and "well off," as it is called. Ultimately he lost all! After this he was obliged to work, and was fortunate in obtaining a lucrative situation, which provided a sufficiency for himself and family. It was very galling, however, to him to have to do this; and instead of humbling himself under God's hand, he tried to comfort himself by taking stimulants and smoking. Presently he lost his appointment, and in so doing brought poverty and destitution upon himself and his family. At length he fell ill, and before long was unable to leave the house, so that he could not obtain his accustomed stimulants. During this illness he was brought to a better mind. He was told that if he repented and prayed he would make his peace with God. He did repent, as he thought; that is to say, he was sorry for his wasted life and ruined state. I visited him. He was suffering from rheumatism, and consequently could not rise from his chair to welcome me. At last I said to him, "Do you think that your repentance and prayers can save you?" "Yes," he said; "I do not know of any other way." I pointed out to him God's way of salvation. A few days after this I called again, and, ringing the bell, waited for admittance. I had not waited long before I heard some one with a heavy footstep approaching the door. It was opened wide, and there stood my friend with a beaming face. "Come in," he exclaimed, "thou blessed! God has blessed you to my soul." I was taken all by surprise to see him up and walking about. "Oh, yes!" he said, "God has made me well. My burden of sin is gone, and my rheumatism is gone, too; I am quite another man. I cannot help thanking and praising God all day." I cordially thanked God with him, and then we walked back to the room where he used to be so dismal. "Everything," he said, "looks bright to me now; but," he continued, "the thing I wonder at most, is, why I did not see this simple and plain truth before."

PROPHETIC FEATURES OF THE GREAT PYRAMID.

By Rev. M. Baxter.*

Its Site—Its Plan—Its Astronomical Relations—The Ratio of the Cubit—The Pyramidal Inch—A Typical Coffer—A Perpetuated Measure of Contents—The Seven Overlappings of the Grand Gallery—A Summary of the Teachings.

THE question, "Why was the Pyramid built?" has been freely discussed of late years. The view maintained by Professor Smyth, and Dr. Seiss in his "Miracle in Stone," and by others, is, that the Pyramid was built not only for *scientific* purposes, but for *chronological* and *prophetical* also. Thus it is held that the object for which the Great Pyramid was erected, was to treasure up in its stone pages a record of Divine Wisdom relating to meteorological, astronomical, chronological, and other important truths. Further, that this storehouse of knowledge was kept perfectly sealed until the times we are living in, for the reason that it was to be a "witness unto the Lord of Hosts." (Isa. 19 : 19, 20.) The fact of its revelation being made now, also confirms the conviction that we are living in the last days—a truth that has been ascertained and proclaimed from numerous other standpoints in harmony with the Word of God.

In the *first place.*—In now pointing out some

Special Features in the Work

of the Pyramid's Oriental architect, with the best aids which modern science affords, we notice that *the site chosen* for the point of erection was eminently inconvenient for constructional purposes, as the rocky outcrop of the Ghizeh Hill had to be cut down and leveled; but it was essential to the grand design, it being in the 30th parallel of latitude, the very parallel which has to the north and south of it an equal distribution of terrestrial semi-surface. In this respect the Pyramid is absolutely unapproached by any other building, ancient or modern.

Secondly. We find that this structure was designed and *built* in its entirety on *a plan so scientifically perfect* that the sum of the measured four sides of the base bears, within the nearest possible practical approach, the same relation to the measure of its vertical height that the circumference of a circle bears to its radius. We find, moreover, that a certain standard measure was used in the construction of all the standard expressional features of the Pyramid. That standard was a cubit of 5×5 pyramid inches, and when one side of the square base is measured, it is found to contain this cubit 365 times with a fraction *plus*, thus giving *our sidereal year of 365 days*, and the plus fractions of the four sides giving, in their sum, the equivalent of *one day in four years, or showing leap year* in the cycle of four years, such cycle being indicated in the four pyramidal sides.

Thirdly. We discover that this huge pile of solid masonry was built to a microscopic nicety, *accurately squared, and*

Astronomically Oriented.

Nearer investigation reveals a still more impressive fact, viz., that the vertical height of this Pyramid, which has already spoken in its practical manner of the time of the earth's revolution around the sun, in its annual orbit, speaks likewise of the *length of radius* of the earth's orbit round the sun.

Fourthly. It appears that the cubit of 25 Pyramid inches bear an exact relation to the only true and unchanging standard in the knowledge of man, viz., the polar axis of the earth (8,000 miles) of whose semi-length or distance from the earth's centre to either pole (4,000 miles) this cubit of the pyramidal architect is the ten-millionth part precisely.

Fifthly. It is ascertained that the pyramid inch is critically the five-hundred-millionth part of the earth's axis length; also, that when the length of the diagonals of the base of the pyramid is found in such inches, the sum total of the length of one diagonal multiplied into the other, expresses the precession of the equinox in an inch to a year—namely, 25,827 years.

Sixthly. In the central King's Chamber, as already mentioned, there is a *Stone Coffer*, which is

A Marvellous Illustration

of the designer's skill and knowledge. The mass of its sides and bottom is cubically identical with its internal space-capacity, viz., 71,250 cubic inches; also the length of two of its adjacent sides is to its height as the circumference of a circle to its diameter. We find that this stone coffer corresponds and is commensurable with the sacred Ark of the Mosaic tabernacle in *space-capacity*, although much more massive and durable in its material, for the Coffer and the Ark each contain about 71,250 cubic inches as the total size of their interior space. The contents-capacity of the Coffer is also found to be precisely equal to the Hebrew laver, four chomers, and to that of the old Saxon chaldron, the quarter part of which is the ordinary *quarter* measure used by farmers for the *quarter of wheat*. It has also other indications of a remarkable character.

Seventhly. In the *Entrance Passage* from the outside of the Pyramid there is *a very significant angle*, which has been found to have a special astronomical use in indicating *the date of the Pyramid's erection*, and has, therefore, an axis-angle as tested by the most perfect scientific apparatus. Thirty years ago Sir John Herschell showed that such an angular position pointed to the transit of the *then* polar star, Draconis, below the pole, and at a measurable distance therefrom, and thereby enabled the building to tell its own absolute date of erection, which is thus inferred to have been about 2,170 years before Christ, because it was the exact point of time when that polar star, in its movements in the sky, would be in just such a position that its light would shine directly down the whole length of the tube of the *Entrance Passage*.

Eighthly. We find in that noble ascending passage, known as the "Grand Gallery," *seven* overlappings in the ascending walls, indicative alike of

Time-Division

into a week of days, visible to the naked eye, and the number of Pleiades, which constellation held so important a determining value in the adoption of the date of construction. Its angle, rising from north to south, is 26° 18' 10"; its length some 157 feet; its height 27 feet 5 inches; breadth varying from 3 feet 6 inches to 6 feet 10 inches—a truly grand passage, in itself commemorative of history, and leading to a notably symbolic and scientific chamber.

Thus this wonderful pyramid, computed to be built about B. C. 2170—nearly seventy years before the birth of Abraham, and 570 years before the Exodus led by Moses—is held to be an "altar in the midst of Egypt, even a pillar (or monument) in the border thereof, which shall be a *sign* and *witness* unto the Lord of Hosts in the midst of Egypt."

THE ETHICAL READINGS OF THE PYRAMID are of profound interest. The first *descending Eastern Passage* is 985 inches long, which are held to denote figuratively 985 years, beginning about eighty years before the Flood, and ending with the triumphant entrance of the Israelites out of the Wilderness into Canaan. At that point their comparative ascent to liberty and wealth becomes denoted by the commencement of the *Ascending Passage*.

The first Ascending Passage is 1542 inches in length, which are understood to represent figuratively 1542 years from the entrance of the Jews under Joshua's leadership into the full possession of the promised land until the birth of Christ.

Then at the end of 1542 inches of the first *Ascending Passage*, there commences the *Grand Gallery*, which is 1882-3 inches in length, which are understood to signify 1882-3 years of this Christian dispensation from the Birth of Christ in A. D. 6 at the end of which the *Troublous Times* and Distress of Nations will commence, as indicated by the Grand Gallery merging at that point into a low, narrow, difficult *exit passage*, and will run its course for an additional twelve years.

But this is not all, for at a distance of 33 inches from the beginning of the "Grand Gallery" we come upon a square

Sepulchral Aperture,

partly in its floor, from the bottom of which a passage leads westerly for a short space to the edge of a dark, almost perpendicular, abyssmal shaft, which leads down into the deep and dismal subterranean descending passage, just before it falls into the Hades chamber or pit, which lies some 180 feet down in the living rock. Now, taking the thirty-three inches along the line of the floor of the "Grand Gallery" to represent thirty-three years, this sepulchral chamber shows the date of the Crucifixion of Christ in A. D. 39 which was the 33d or 34th year in our Lord's life. The inhumation of His body in the tomb, and His resurrection, are thus thought to be exhibited in these mechanical features, which symbolize the fact that the grave could not detain Him beyond the appointed time.

The result of the learned labors of scientific men who have unfolded the mystery of the Great Pyramid, is that its chronology points to the duodecennial period of twelve years from 1888–9 to 1901, as an epoch of no common interest to the human family; but especially to that portion of it who love the truth and the God of truth, who serve "the living and true God," and wait for His Son from heaven, even Jesus, who delivered us from the wrath to come. Those who will candidly listen to the testimony, and have "an ear to hear what the Spirit saith unto the churches," will find enough in the conclusions drawn from the Pyramid concerning events in the near future, to fill the heart of every faithful child of God with joy and rejoicing, and to incite him to be ever on the alert, watching, hoping, praying, believing, and seeking daily, hourly, to be kept "unspotted from the world."

To sum up, then, the *scientific* features of the Great Pyramid are mathematically exact, and consist in part of the following: It squares the circle, tells its own latitude, its own age, the true shape of the earth, the distance of the sun, the law of gravitation, the density of the earth, the days in a year, the length of the precessional cycle, and contains a standard of weights and measures, temperature, etc.

* An extract from an exhaustive article in the March number of the *Prophetic News*. For sale, price six cents, at this office, 63 Bible House, New York.

CHRISTIAN HERALD AND SIGNS OF OUR TIMES.

OFFICE, 63 BIBLE HOUSE, NEW YORK.

ENTERED AT THE POST-OFFICE AT NEW YORK, N. Y., AS SECOND-CLASS MATTER.

Published Weekly. Subscription price, $1.50 a year; $1 eight months; 75 cents six months; sent two months on trial for 25 cents; always payable in advance. Single copies for sale by, or can be ordered at all newsdealers.

Remittances by Mail should be by Post-office money order, bank cheques, or drafts or express money order, and should always be made payable to THE CHRISTIAN HERALD.

Receipts are not sent, the receipt of the paper by a subscriber is a sufficient proof that his remittance has been received. If the paper does not arrive promptly, please advise us, that we may see if the address is correctly entered.

Change of Address. Name of Post Office and State, of both old and new address, should always be given in case of removal.

CURRENT EVENTS.

A Measure of Retaliation Directed Mainly against those countries prohibiting the importation of American hog products, is now before Congress. Senator Farwell, of Illinois, on March 29, introduced a bill reciting that products of the United States are unjustly discriminated against by certain foreign States, on various ill-founded pretexts, laying restrictions on the importation of such products, and that the diplomatic negotiations conducted through a series of years by the United States have failed to secure the removal of these unjust restrictions. It then provides that whenever the Minister or other chief diplomatic representative of the United States to any foreign State shall officially report the failure of the efforts of the United States to secure the removal of any discrimination by such foreign State against any product of the United States, the President shall be authorized to make proclamation directing that such products of the foreign State as he may deem proper shall be excluded from importation to the United States. The President may modify, revoke, or renew such prohibition as the public interests may require.

The Enlargement of the Yellowstone National Park, and the protection of the forests, game, and natural wonders within its limits, is enacted in a bill which passed the Senate on March 29. The area to be added to the park is about 2,000 square miles. This additional area abounds in large streams and lakes, the sources of the Columbia and Yellowstone, the waters running to both oceans. For the preservation of the water in this natural reservoir, the dense timber which covers the region is of immense value, and Senators believe that the best way to prevent its destruction is to include it within the park. The added country includes favorite resorts of deer, elk, bears, and mountain sheep, while the present limits of the park are said to be much too small for a satisfactory large-game preserve. The bill provides that roads are to be laid out and sites for bridges selected by an army engineer officer. Similar bills passed the Senate during the Forty-eighth and Forty-ninth Congresses; the House, however, failed to act upon them.

The International Council of Women, now in session in Washington, is attracting general public attention. The address of welcome was delivered on March 26 by Elizabeth Cady Stanton, who reviewed the history of the woman suffrage movement. "To celebrate our fortieth anniversary," she said, "we have here representatives in person, or by letter, from near every State in the Union, from Great Britain, France, Finland, Italy, Sweden, India, Denmark, and Norway. In welcoming representatives from other lands we do not feel that they are strangers and foreigners, for the women of all nationalities, in the artificial distinctions of sex, have a universal sense of injustice that forms a common bond of union between them." Among the papers read at the subsequent sessions, was one by Mrs. Julia Ward Howe, on "The Power of Organization." She recognizes three elements in society of which account must be made in any large plan of organization. First, she instances the class of leaders, small in number, powerful in its correspondence with certain needs of the body politic; secondly, the class of the led, strong in numbers and in the magnetic multiplication of sympathy. Between the two there is a class, moderate in extent, which neither aspires to lead nor asks to be led. This is a deliberative class, whose function is very important, intervening with deliberation between the few and the passion of the many. The "Legal Condition of Women in the Three Kingdoms" was the subject of a paper read by Mrs. Alice Scatcherd, one of the English delegates, who was sent by the Edinburgh Women's Suffrage and Women's Liberal Association. About thirty Women's Rights Associations are represented in the Council, and it is considered the largest gathering of notable women in the history of this country.

An Outbreak of Lawlessness in Connection with the strike on the Chicago, Burlington, and Quincy Railroad was a deplorable phase assumed last week in this gigantic strike of railroad employees. A band of men, regardless of the good name of the organization, and the advice of their best friends, attacked a switch engine on the track in Chicago, on March 29, threw the company's agents off the train, and maltreated the Superintendent of the road, who fell into their hands. It required a strong police force to scatter the rioters. Closely following these acts of violence, the yard force of the Chicago, Milwaukee, and St. Paul Railroad in Chicago, 200 men in all, went on strike, to show their sympathy for the Burlington men. Subsequently they listened to conservative advice, and returned to work again. Wise counsel, however, did not prevail long; for after a few hours the same men went on strike again. The strikers have added to their acts of violence by setting a railroad shop at Aurora, Ill., on fire, and attempting to burn a car standing on a side-track.

Master-Workman Powderly, the Head of the Knights of Labor, has issued a significant manifesto, in which he urges that the members work for the education of the rank and file to a higher standard, and discourage strikes. He confesses that the Knights of Labor strikes have not been successful, and that the time to call a halt has arrived. "It is agreed," he says, "that strikes do good. So does a fire. Strikes do good! Go to the coal fields of Pennsylvania and count the victims; go through the Lehigh region and count the sufferers; go into the homes of the brave, heroic men who waged the unequal battle, and ask of the wives and children you will find there if strikes do good, and note the answer. Let the ones who have felt the pangs of hunger testify. Do not go to those who, standing far from the scene of conflict, will say strikes do good." While Mr. Powderly is thus giving sound advice, a movement among his followers is gaining in strength, designed to bring about his removal from the chief office of the organization.

A Terrible Mine Disaster Occurred on March 29, at Rich Hill, a mining town of 5000 inhabitants, about 75 miles south of Kansas City, Mo., While the day men were at work in coal mine No. 6 about noon, and fifteen of them had just come up and were standing at the mouth of the shaft, an explosion took place that shook the earth for miles around, and was followed by a burst of flame from the mouth of the shaft that leaped fifty feet in the air. The men at the mouth of the shaft were badly burned. There were fifty-two men in the mine when the explosion occurred, of whom twenty-one were killed outright, and many others so severely burned as to render recovery almost impossible. It is a providential circumstance that the catastrophe occurred at a time of the day when a smaller number of men are down the mine than at any other time. A little earlier or later, over one hundred men would have been in the workings. The work of rescue was commenced as soon as it was possible to descend, and before danger of more explosions was past, the men showing marvellous heroism in volunteering for the perilous task. The superintendent and four men made up the first party of rescuers, and they had just found one injured man and put him on the cage to be drawn up when another explosion occurred, bruising and burning the brave rescuers at the foot of the shaft. They were soon drawn up, and after a brief interval another party descended. These extricated and brought up fourteen imprisoned men, who were more or less burned. The gallant men worked all night, and relaxed their efforts only when all hope of saving more lives was evidently futile.

The Financial Statement of Great Britian was presented to the House of Commons on March 26 by Mr. Goschen, the Liberal financier, who is now serving in the Conservative camp as Chancellor of the Exchequer. His financial proposals for the ensuing year are framed on Liberal principles, and the Conservatives, who will be bound in party honor to support them, will have to stultify many of their former votes. It appears that the total expenditure for the past year was over $437,000,000, and the income nearly $448,000,000. The *revenue from wine and spirits showed an increase* over the previous year of $1,500,000. The national debt had been decreased during the year by $38,000,000. Mr. Goschen proposes, for the coming year, to reduce the income tax, to increase the duties on wine, to put a tax on foreign securities, so as to prevent so much money going out of the country for investment, and to put a tax on horses. He stated that the Government intended to spend ten million dollars in adding to the fortifications on the coasts. An amusing result of this financiering is that the Liberals, to be consistent, must support it, though they so thoroughly detest Mr. Goschen for being a deserter that they would be glad to oppose any measure he advocated.

Empress Victoria of Germany, who is the eldest daughter of Queen Victoria, has made a speech which shows a gratifying sense of her responsibilities in her exalted station. Replying to addresses presented to her by seventeen associations of which she is a patroness, she said her foremost and most sacred duty will be the care of her suffering husband. She is conscious of the task devolving upon her as Queen and Empress, and will accomplish it to the best of her ability. At the same time, she is reminded that she has other social duties. The moral and intellectual education of women, the sanitary condition of the laboring classes, and the improvement of the facilities by which women may earn a livelihood, will constantly be before her. The noblest vocation of a princess, she says, is an untiring activity in the work of ameliorating the suffering of the masses. Owing to the difficulty of her task, she is doubtful whether she will succeed as well as her heart desires.

The Overthrow of the French Cabinet which occurred on Friday last is an event which has startled Europe. The Chamber of Deputies, by a vote of 268 to 237, carried a measure for the revision of the Constitution. The proposal was vigorously opposed by the Cabinet, and when it was carried the Ministers resigned. The advocates of the revision intend to make radical changes in the Constitution, one of the most important being the election of the President of the Republic directly by the people, as in the United States, instead by the Legislature, as conducted at present. General Boulanger has strongly advocated the revision, and this triumphant success of the scheme in the Legislature is consequently regarded as an ominous sign of his coming elevation to place and power.

Three Men in Strange Garb in a Church in New York on March 25 aroused the interest of the congregation. They were at the Methodist Episcopal Church in West Forty-first Street, and their object was to enlist the sympathy of the hearers in foreign mission work in their native lands. One of them was a Japanese named Takaki. He wore a flowing robe of gray silk. He described the good effected by Christianity in his country, and made his hearers smile by his unaccustomed English. Avac Cutujian was introduced as a Turk, but he subsequently explained that he was an Armenian. He gave an interesting report of mission progress in Turkey, and explained the urgent need existing for help in men and money. Mr. Cutujian was gorgeous in a green jacket, purple turban, and trousers of red and black stripes. He succeeded in persuading his audience that more money was needed in Armenia. The third, Marin Delchoff, a Bulgarian, wore a red fez, green waistcoat, cardinal jacket, and blue and silver trousers. His address was listened to with deep interest, as it dealt with the home life of Bulgarians, and presented in graphic words their sad need of Christian teaching.

The Home Missionary Society of the Congregational Church has made a vigorous protest against the admission of Utah as a State. The Rev. M. W. Montgomery, representing the Society, delivered an earnest address before the Senate Committee on Territories, on March 26. He spoke of the evils of Mormonism and said the 11,000,000 Protestants and 6,000,000 Roman Catholics of the country are a unit in condemnation of Mormonism. They asked that Congress shall break the delusions under which the Mormon people live—the delusion that their Church is stronger than the United States Government. He assured the committee that Congress could not legislate intelligently upon this question until it adopted as one of its fundamental principles that Mormonism is a lie and a fraud. The Committee evidently agreed with Mr. Montgomery, for on the same day Senator Cullom, on behalf of the committee, made a report declaring it to be the sense of the Senate that the Territory of Utah ought not to be admitted into the Union as a State until it is certain beyond doubt that the practice of plural marriages, bigamy or polygamy, has been entirely abandoned by the inhabitants of that Territory, and until it is likewise certain that the civil affairs of the Territory are not controlled by the priesthood of the Mormon Church.

The Discovery of a Hermit in a Cave on the Ramapo Mountains, in New Jersey, is reported in a despatch from Nyack, N. J. It is stated that some young men, who ventured, on March 17, into the forests in the wildest parts of Rockland county, observed a remarkable structure of rough planks on the mountain-side. They were curious as to what could be concealed there, and climbing up to it, they plunged through the snow-bank outside, and found a rude door, which they pushed in. Inside was a hut at the entrance to a cave, and there, on a pile of rags, lay a man, apparently in acute suffering. He was too weak to talk, but after the young men had lighted a fire and given him some nourishment, he revived, and yielding to their solicitation, consented to their wrapping him up and taking him to the nearest house, where he was hospitably received. Inquiries about him showed that he had lived in the cave for six or seven years. He is believed to have come from Pennsylvania about that time. It is known that such a man arrived at Suffern and purchased some planks, which he carried, one at a time, into the woods. He would give no information as to himself or his mode of life, and resented any attempts at conversation. There is reason to believe that he used the planks to build the hut around the cave, and lived there until he was found the other day. His motive for thus secluding himself cannot be imagined, but whatever it was, the narrow escape he had of dying from cold and hunger will probably overcome it. He owes his life to the fact that others did not neglect, as he has done for six or seven years, the duties every man owes to his fellow-man. It may be hoped that, as he realizes that fact, his life may be so changed as that he may be able to say in the apostolic sense, "None of us liveth to himself." (Rom. 14:7.)

Warnings of a Menacing Derelict have been brought to New York by the captain of the steamer *Caland*. He states that in his voyage here he narrowly escaped collision with an abandoned lumber-laden bark which had her mizzen-mast still standing. She was drifting in the great highway of transatlantic steamers, and was therefore liable to cause serious mischief. Calculations have been made of the probable effect on her course of the currents and of the winds, so as to locate as nearly as possible the position of the abandoned ship, and give warning to outgoing steamers. The reason is obvious: There is no one in command or controlling the movements of the derelict, and she may drift across the track of some other vessel, or run into another vessel and do serious damage and put lives in peril. It is probable that a cruiser will be sent from the navy-yard to take her in tow or blow her up. In the voyage of life much harm is done by human derelicts—men who drift along carelessly and heedlessly, not intending harm, but, being without God's guidance, going astray themselves and menacing the spiritual safety of others (Eccles. 9:18.)

The Discovery of Perpetual Motion is Again announced. An inventor at Lyons, Wayne County, N. Y., claims that a machine which he has patented and will place on exhibition on April 12, will run any length of time without the application of motive power. It consists of an ordinary chain, made of iron links two inches in length, running over a triangular framework. The chain runs on wheels placed at the three angles, and is so constructed that when descending the long side of the triangle the links double up, and the increased weight keeps up the motion. From the character of the motive power, the movement of the chain constantly increases in rapidity, and a brake is required to regulate it. The inventor states, that having determined to solve the problem which so many generations have believed to be unsolvable, he has spent thirty thousand dollars in experiments, and has given twenty-one years of labor to the task. He is confident that he has succeeded, but at present he cannot get practical men to believe in his success. It does not appear that any actual utility is accomplished by the machine, but the inventor will doubtless be satisfied if it renders his name famous. He is not the only man who has spent time and fortune to achieve that result, and he will probably learn, as others have done, that life so spent is wasted (Isa. 55:2).

A Dangerous Land-slide Occurred Near Kansas City, Mo., on March 26. A heavy rain fell on the two preceding days, which is supposed to have loosened a huge bluff, facing the Union Railroad Station. Fully fifteen hundred feet of the bluff appears to have been pushed forward by some irresistible agency, hundreds of tons of rock and earth sliding down the steep hillside. For several hours previous to the land-slide a peculiar snapping noise came from the face of the bluff, and this was followed by a crash which startled the whole city. Tons of earth and huge boulders had crashed down, demolishing the engine-house at the entrance of the street cable line tunnel. Along the face of the bluff, about half-way from the base to the top, is a ledge about thirty feet in width, on which are a number of shanties occupied by families of colored people. This ledge is now seamed with immense fissures, which extend its whole length, and houses are tilted in every direction. The residents were compelled to flee for their lives, and there was a general stampede from the houses which the bluff still overhangs. It would have been the wildest folly to remain in a dwelling that might be crushed at any moment. This was readily perceived, though preachers and Christian workers are unable to arouse men to similar alarm, though a far more terrible peril is impending, and though a way of escape is provided. (II Peter 3:10.)

The Daring Rescue of a Child From a Well is reported by an Indianapolis journal. It states that on March 26 a little two-year-old boy, while playing around his home, fell into a well thirty-seven feet deep, that had been cleaned out and left open. The mother heard the screams of the little one as he fell, and, rushing to the well, saw him floundering in two feet of water. Wild with desperation, the mother started to make the perilous descent to rescue her darling. At the risk of losing her life by falling to the bottom, she carefully but rapidly went down, and reached him none too soon. Clasping the child to her bosom, she called to her five-year old son to go to the neighbors, a half-mile distant, for help to rescue her from the well, it being walled with brick, and furnishing no footing for her to climb up. After nearly two hours of mental agony, the boy arrived with help, and she and the child were rescued. The child's head is terribly cut, but otherwise he was not hurt. As he grows older and hears of the act of devotion by which his life was saved, he will surely be inspired with more than ordinary filial affection. It will be well also if he is led to see in it a type of that infinite sacrifice on Calvary, by which his soul may be saved, and to render to his Saviour the consecration of his life. (Rom. 12:1.)

BRIEF NOTES.

Rev. Thomas Harrison has promised to visit Bloomington, Ill., at the conclusion of his labors in New York City.

The famous Hungarian patriot, Louis Kossuth, is seriously ill. He is now at Turin, Italy, and his death is daily expected. He is eighty-seven years of age.

The Young People's Societies of Christian Endeavor in the State of Rhode Island are doing effective work. During 1887 one hundred and eighty-nine joined the Church from those societies.

Rev. E. K. Love, pastor of the First African Baptist Church, Savannah, Ga., has baptized over fourteen hundred persons during his pastorate there of two and a half years. It has more than 5,000 communicants.

Revival services are being conducted in the Grand Army Republic building of Lynn, Mass., by Messrs. McLean and Willis. The building is densely crowded every evening. Over three hundred persons have made a profession of faith.

The physicians in attendance on Rev. J. Denham Smith, the well-known evangelist, who is dangerously sick, consider that he may pass away very soon. His sufferings are great, but his heart is filled with peace.

Rev. George C. Needham is continuing his work at Springfield, Mass. Last week he held four services each day but Monday. The young men of the College for Christian Workers, who are being trained for Y. M. C. A. secretaries, pastors' assistants, etc., attend the Bible readings, which are of spec[illegible] utility to them.

Rev. B. Fay Mills has c[illegible]nenced services in Indianapolis. He is assisted by [illegible] and Mrs. Towner, who not only conduct the singing, but labor personally in the meetings. The work just concluded by the evangelists, at Providence, R. I., is being continued by the churches, and by the Young Men's Christian Association.

Rev. J. Jackson Wray, of London, Eng., lectured last evening in the Broadway Tabernacle, New York, on Æsop, the Hunchback of Greece. The lecture was in aid of the funds of the N. W. C. T. U.

Rev. E. P. Hammond's work in California is being much blessed. Dr. Dwinell, of the Theological Seminary, at Oakland, who attended the Sacramento services, says: "There does not seem to be so much effort to collect names and count numbers as I have sometimes known, yet the hopeful conversions, I was told, reach into the hundreds. My own impression is that far larger blessings are now held out to the churches in that city than they have yet received."

An important conference of Christian Band Secretaries recently held in London, recommended "the summoning of a conference of ministers to take into consideration the formation of Young People's Societies of Christian Endeavor, in connection with their churches." The feature of the movement which especially commends it to the English clergymen, is the close and vital relation of the Society to the church, in this respect differing from any other young people's organization established there.

Sunday-school Superintendents and Teachers desirous of distributing copies of THE CHRISTIAN HERALD in their schools and classes, may have assorted parcels of back numbers by applying, stating number required, to the manager, 63 Bible House.

THE INFALLIBILITY OF SCRIPTURE.

A New Sermon by Pastor C. H. Spurgeon.

"The mouth of the Lord hath spoken it."—Isaiah 1:20.

The Old Testament Quoted by the Saviour—Reverenced by the Apostles—Five Inferences from its Divine Origin—I. A Warrant for Teaching—To be Taught with Awe—With Fidelity—With Courage—With Diligence—II. Is Entitled to Attention—Creation a Child's Picture-Book—Intrinsic Importance of the Bible—III. Has a Special Character—Unique Dignity—George Moore's Avowal—Absolute Certainty—IV. Is a Ground of Alarm—Its Threatenings Invariably Fulfilled—Babylon and Nineveh—A Visit to an Imprisoned Infidel—V. Gives Reason and Rest for Faith.

WHAT Isaiah said was, therefore, spoken by Jehovah. It was audibly the utterance of a man; but, really, it was the utterance of the Lord Himself. The lips which delivered the words, were those of Isaiah, but yet it was the very truth that "The mouth of the Lord hath spoken it." All Scripture, being inspired of the Spirit, is spoken by the mouth of God. However this sacred Book may be treated nowadays, it was not treated contemptuously, nor negligently, nor questioningly by the Lord Jesus Christ, our Master and Lord. It is noteworthy how He reverenced the written Word. The Spirit of God rested upon Him personally, without measure, and He could speak out of His own mind the revelation of God, and yet He continually quoted the law and the prophets, and the Psalms; and always He treated the sacred writings with reverence, strongly in contrast with

The Irreverence of "Modern Thought."

I am sure, brethren, we cannot be wrong in imitating the example of our divine Lord in our reverence for that Scripture which cannot be broken. The like valuation of the Word of the Lord is seen in our Lord's apostles; for they treated the ancient Scriptures as supreme in authority, and supported their statements with passages from Holy Writ. The utmost degree of deference and homage is paid to the Old Testament by the writers of the New. We never find an apostle raising a question about the degree of inspiration in this book or that. No disciple of Jesus questions the authority of the books of Moses, or of the prophets. If you want to cavil or suspect, you find no sympathy in the teaching of Jesus, or any one of His apostles. You and I belong to a school which will continue to do the same, let others adopt what behavior they please. As for us, and for our house, this priceless Book shall remain the standard of our faith and the ground of our hope so long as we live.

I. Coming closely, then, to our text, "The mouth of the Lord hath spoken it," our first head shall be—this is

Our Warrant for Teaching

Scriptural truth. We preach because "The mouth of the Lord hath spoken it." It would not be worth our while to speak what Isaiah had spoken, if in it there was nothing more than Isaiah's thought; neither should we care to meditate hour after hour upon the writings of Paul, if there was nothing more than Paul in them. We feel no imperative call to expound and to enforce what has been spoken by men; but since "The mouth of the Lord hath spoken it," it is woe unto us if we preach not the gospel! We come to you with, "Thus saith the Lord," and we should have no justifiable motive for preaching our lives away, if we have not this message.

The true preacher, the man whom God has commissioned, delivers his message

With Awe

and trembling, because "The mouth of the Lord hath spoken it." He bears the burden of the Lord, and bows under it. Ours is no trifling theme, but one which moves our whole soul. They called George Fox a Quaker, because when he spoke he would quake exceedingly, through the force of the truth which he so thoroughly apprehended. Perhaps, if you and I had a clearer sight and a closer grip of God's Word, and felt more of His majesty, we should quake also. Martin Luther, who never feared the face of man, yet declared that when he stood up to preach, he often felt his knees knock together under a sense of his great responsibility. Woe unto us if we dare to speak the Word of the Lord with less than our whole heart and soul and strength.

Dear brethren, because the mouth of the Lord hath spoken the truth of God, we therefore endeavor to preach it with absolute fidelity. We repeat the Word as a child repeats his lesson. It is

Not Ours to Correct the Divine

revelation, but simply to echo it. I do not take it to be my office to bring you new and original thoughts of my own; but rather to say, "The word which ye hear is not mine, but the Father's which sent me." It is not mine to amend or adapt the gospel. What! Shall we attempt to improve upon what God has revealed? The Infinitely Wise—is He to be corrected by the creatures of a day? Is the infallible revelation of the infallible Jehovah to be shaped, moderated, and toned down to the fashions and fancies of the hour? God forgive us if we have ever altered His Word unwittingly; wittingly we have not done so, nor will we. His children sit at His feet and receive of His words, and then they rise up in the power of His Spirit to publish the Word which the Lord has given.

Again, dear friends, as "The mouth of the Lord hath spoken it," we speak the divine truth with courage and full assurance. Modesty is a virtue; but hesitancy, when we are speaking for the Lord, is a great fault. If an ambassador, sent by a great king to represent his majesty at a foreign court, should forget his office and only think of himself, he might be so humble as to lower the dignity of his prince, so timid as to betray his country's honor. God forbid that he who speaks for God

Should Dishonor the King

of kings by a pliant subservience. We preach not the gospel by your leave; we do not ask tolerance nor court applause. We preach Christ crucified, and we speak boldly, as we ought to speak, because it is God's Word and not our own. *We are accused of dogmatism*; but we are bound to dogmatize when we repeat that which the mouth of the Lord hath spoken. We cannot use "ifs" and "buts," for we are dealing with God's "shalls" and "wills." If He says it is so, it is so; and there is an end of it. Controversy ceases when Jehovah speaks.

We are urged to be charitable. We *are* charitable; but it is with our own money. We have no right to give away what is put into our trust and is not at our disposal. When we have to do with the truth of God we are stewards, and must deal with our Lord's exchequer, not on the lines of charity to human opinions, but by the rule of fidelity to the God of truth. We are bold to declare with full assurance that which the Lord reveals. When we speak for the Lord against error, we do not soften our tones; but we speak thunderbolts.

I will also add, under this head, that, because "The mouth of the Lord hath spoken it," therefore we feel bound to speak His Word with diligence, as often as ever we can, and with perseverance, as long as ever we live. Surely, it would be a blessed thing to die in the pulpit; spending one's last breath in acting as the Lord's mouth. Dumb Sabbaths are fierce trials to true preachers. O my brethren, the Word of the Lord is so precious that we must in the morning sow this blessed seed, and in the evening we must not withhold our hands. It is a living seed and the seed of life, and, therefore, we must diligently scatter it.

Brethren, if we get a right apprehension concerning gospel truth—that "The mouth of the Lord hath spoken it"—it will move us to tell it out with great ardor and zeal. How can you keep back the heavenly news? "The mouth of the Lord hath spoken it"—shall not your mouth rejoice to repeat it? Whisper it in the ear of the sick; shout it in the corner of the streets; write it on your tablets; send it forth from the press: but everywhere let this be your great motive and warrant—you preach the gospel because "The mouth of the Lord hath spoken it."

II. Let us now row in another direction for a moment or two. In the second place, "The mouth of the Lord hath spoken it." This is

The Claim of God's Word

upon your attention. Every word which God has given us in this Book claims our attention because of the infinite majesty of Him that spake it. I see before me a Parliament of kings and princes, sages and senators. I hear one after another of the gifted Chrysostoms pour forth eloquence like the "Golden-mouthed." They speak, and they speak well. Suddenly there is a solemn hush. What a stillness! Who is now to speak? They are silent because God the Lord is about to lift up His voice. Is it not right that they should be so? It is He that made you; in His hands your breath is; and if He speaks, I implore you, open your ear, and be not rebellious. Hear what Jesus preaches from the tree. He says, "Incline your ear and come unto me: hear, and your soul shall live."

God's claim to be heard lies, also, in the condescension which has led Him to speak to us. It was something for God to have made the world and bid us look at

The Work of His Hands.

Creation is a picture-book for children. But for God to speak in the language of mortal men is still more marvellous, if you come to think of it. I wonder that God spoke by the prophets; but I admire still more that He should have written down His word in black and white, in unmistakable language, which can be translated into all tongues, so that we may all see and read for ourselves what God the Lord has spoken to us; and what, indeed, He continues to speak; for what He has spoken He still speaks to us, as freshly as if He spake it for the first time.

God's Word has a claim, then, upon your attention because of its majesty and its condescension, but yet, further, it should win your ear because of its intrinsic importance. "The mouth of the Lord hath spoken it"—then it is no trifle. God never speaks vanity. No line of His writing treats of the frivolous themes of a day. He speaks to thee of great things, which have to do with thy soul and its destiny. Treat not the Word of the Lord as a secondary thing, which might wait thy leisure and receive attention when no other work was before thee; put all else aside, but hearken to thy God.

Depend upon it, if "The mouth of the Lord hath spoken it," there is an urgent, pressing necessity. God breaks not silence to say that which might as well have remained unsaid. His voice indicates great urgency. Without reserve answer to His call, and say, "Speak, Lord; for thy servant heareth." When I stand in this pulpit to preach the Gospel, I never feel that I may calmly invite you to attend to a subject which is one among many, and may very properly be let alone for a time, should your minds be already occupied. No; you may be dead before I again speak with you, and so I beg for immediate attention. I do not fear that I may be taking you off from more important business by entreating you to attend to that which the mouth of the Lord hath spoken; for no business has any importance in it compared with this; this is the master theme of all.

III. And now, thirdly, this gives to God's Word a very special character. When we open this sacred Book, and say of that which is here recorded, "The mouth of the Lord hath spoken it," then it gives to the teaching

A Special Character.

In the Word of God the teaching has unique dignity. This Book is inspired as no other book is inspired, and it is time that all Christians avowed this conviction. I do not know whether you have seen Mr. Smiles's life of our late friend, George Moore; but in it we read that, at a certain dinner-party, a learned man remarked that it would not be easy to find a person of intelligence who believed in the inspiration of the Bible. In an instant George Moore's voice was heard across the table, saying boldly

"I do, for one!" Nothing more was said. My dear friend had a strong way of speaking, as I well remember; for we have upon occasions vied with each other in shouting when we were together at his Cumberland home. I think I can hear his emphatic way of putting it—"I do, for one!" Let us not be backward to take the old-fashioned and unpopular side, and say outright, "I do for one!"

Where are we if our Bibles are gone? Where are we if we are taught to distrust them? If we are left in doubt as to which part is inspired and which is not, we are as badly off as if we had no Bible at all. I hold no theory of inspiration; I accept the inspiration of the Scriptures as a fact. Those who thus view the Scriptures need not be ashamed of their company; for some of the best and most learned of men have been of the same mind.

There is also about that which the mouth of the Lord hath spoken

An Absolute Certainty.

Once spoken by God, not only is it so now, but it always must be so. The Lord of Hosts hath spoken, and who shall disannul it? The rock of God's Word does not shift like the quicksands of modern scientific theology. One said to his minister, "My dear sir, surely you ought to adjust your beliefs to the progress of science." "Yes," said he, "but I have not had time to do it to-day, for I have not yet read the morning papers." One would have need to read the morning papers, and take in every new edition, to know whereabout scientific theology now stands; for it is always chopping and changing.

The only thing that is certain about the false science of this age is that it will be soon disproved. Theories vaunted to-day will be scouted to-morrow. The great scientists live by killing those who went before them. They know nothing for certain, except that their predecessors were wrong. Even in one short life we have seen system after system—the mushrooms, or, rather, *the toadstools, of thought*—rise and perish We cannot adapt our religious belief to that which is more changeful than the moon.

Here let me add that there is something unique about God's Word, because of the almighty power which attends it. "Where the word of a king is, there is power," where the word of God is, there is omnipotence If we dealt more largely in God's own Word as "The mouth of the Lord hath spoken it," we should see far greater results from our preaching. I will say no more on this point, although the theme is a very large and tempting one; especially if I were to dwell upon the depth, the height, the adaptation, the insight and the self-proving power of that which "The mouth of the Lord hath spoken."

IV. Fourthly, this makes God's word

A Ground of Alarm

to many. Shall I read you the whole verse? "But if ye refuse and rebel, ye shall be devoured with the sword: for the mouth of the Lord hath spoken it." Every threatening that God hath spoken, because He hath spoken it, has a tremendous dread about it. Whether God threateneth a man or a nation, or the whole class of the ungodly, if they are wise they will feel a trembling take hold upon them, because "The mouth of the Lord hath spoken it." God has never yet spoken a threatening that has fallen to the ground. When He told Pharaoh what He would do, He did it; the plagues came thick and heavy upon him. When the Lord at any time sent His prophets to denounce judgments on the nations, He carried out those judgments. Ask travelers concerning Babylon, and Nineveh, and Edom, and Moab, and Bashan; and they will tell you of the heaps of ruins, which prove how the Lord carried out his warnings to the letter. Depend on it, then, that when Jesus says, "These shall go away into everlasting punishment," it will be so. When He says, "If ye believe not that I am He, ye shall die in your sins," it will be so. The Lord never plays at frightening men.

"Alas," says one, "I shudder at the severity of the divine sentence." Do you? It is well! I can heartily sympathize with you. What must he be that does not tremble when he sees the great Jehovah taking vengeance upon iniquity! The terrors of the Lord might well turn steel to wax. Let us remember that the gauge of truth is not our pleasure nor our terror. It is not my shuddering which can disprove what the mouth of the Lord hath spoken. It may even be a proof of its truth. Did not all the prophets tremble at manifestations of God? One of the last of the anointed seers fell at the Lord's feet as dead. Yet all the shrinking of their nature was not used by them as an argument for doubt.

The Cause of Unbelief.

O my unconverted and unbelieving hearers, do remember that if you refuse Christ, and rush upon the keen edge of Jehovah's sword, your unbelief of eternal judgment will not alter it, nor save you from it. I know why you do not believe in the terrible threatenings. It is because you want to be easy in your sins. A certain sceptical writer, when in prison, was visited by a Christian man, who wished him well, but he refused to hear a word about religion. Seeing a Bible in the hand of his visitor, he made this remark: "You do not expect me to believe in that book, do you? Why, if that book is true, I am lost forever!" Just so. Therein lies the reason for half the infidelity of the world, and all the infidelity in our congregations. How can you believe that which condemns you? Ah! my friends, if you would believe it to be true, and act accordingly, you would also find in that which the mouth of the Lord hath spoken, a way of escape from the wrath to come; for the Book is far more full of hope than of dread. Therefore, I pray you, treat the sacred Scriptures with respect, and remember that "These are written, that ye might believe that Jesus is the Christ, the Son of God; and that believing ye might have life through His name."

V. And so I must finish, for time fails, when I notice, in the fifth place, that this makes the word of the Lord

The Reason of Our Faith.

"The mouth of the Lord hath spoken it," is the foundation of our confidence. There is forgiveness; for God has said it. Look, friend; you are saying, "I cannot believe that my sins can be washed away, I feel so unworthy." Yes, but "The mouth of the Lord hath spoken it." Believe over the head of your unworthiness. "Ah," says one "I feel so weak I can neither think, nor pray, nor anything else, as I should." Is it not written, "When we were yet without strength, in due time Christ died for the ungodly"? "The mouth of the Lord hath spoken it"; therefore, over the head of your inability still believe it, for it must be so.

I think I hear some child of God saying, "God has said, "I will never leave thee, nor forsake thee," but I am in great trouble; all the circumstances of my life seem to contradict the promise": yet, "The mouth of the Lord hath spoken it," and the promise must stand. "Trust in the Lord, and do good; so shalt thou dwell in the land, and verily thou shalt be fed." Believe God in the teeth of circumstances. If you cannot see a way of escape or a

A Means of Help,

yet still believe in the unseen God, and in the truth of His presence; "For the mouth of the Lord hath spoken it." I think I have come to this pass with myself, at any rate, for the time present, that when circumstances deny the promise, I believe it none the less. When friends forsake me, and foes belie me, and my own spirit goes down below zero, and I am depressed almost to despair, I am resolved to hang to the bare word of the Lord, and prove it to be in itself an all-sufficient stay and support.

By and by we shall come to die. The death-sweat shall gather on our brow, and perhaps our tongue will scarcely serve us. Oh that then, like the grand old German Emperor, we may say, "Mine eyes have seen Thy salvation," and, "He hath helped me with His name." When we pass through the rivers He will be with us, and the flood shall not overflow us; "For the mouth of the Lord hath spoken it."

Brethren, we have not followed cunningly devised fables. We abide where heaven and earth are resting; where the whole universe depends; where even eternal things have their foundation; we rest on God Himself. If God shall fail us, we gloriously fail with the whole universe. But there is no fear; therefore, let us trust, and not be afraid. His promise must stand; for "The mouth of the Lord hath spoken it." O Lord, it is enough! Glory be to Thy name, through Christ Jesus! Amen.

[The prayers of the readers of this journal are requested for the blessing of God upon its Editors, and those whose sermons, articles or labors for Christ are printed in it; and that its circulation may be used by the Holy Spirit for the conversion of many sinners and the quickening of God's people. Dr. Talmage and Mr. Spurgeon especially request prayer every Sunday morning on behalf of their labors.]

GEMS FROM NEW BOOKS.

THE MUD BY MEASURE.*

People waste their time in mud-measuring. One says, "My foot is only covered with the mud; but look at that fellow, he is ankle deep in it." The one who is ankle deep in mud says, "Look at that man! he is up to the knees in mud;" while he in his turn says, "I am not so bad as that man; he is up to the neck in mud." It is of no use to talk like that: here is a rope-ladder to help you all up from the pit. "Oh," says one, "I am as good as my neighbor and better than many." Very true, perhaps, but that is only the difference between being up to the knees in mud or up to the neck; if you are in the pit, you need a rope-ladder that you may get out and place your feet on a rock, for there is no difference. One man with decent boots on, and only one foot a little muddy, says, "I do not believe there is no difference. Do you mean to say I am no better than that fellow there up to his neck in mud?" No, my friends; and very likely that fellow up to his neck will get hold of the ladder first, for he is so shocked at the mud that he is glad to get out of it; while the respectable man spends his time in arguing about the depth of mud he is in. It is not mud-measuring, but salvation, we have to do with, for "There is no difference, for all have sinned and come short of the Glory of God."

The Prisoner's Plea.

Think of the day and ordeal of judgment. Will you plead guilty or not guilty? Guilty, not as leading a wretchedly bad life as a thief or a murderer, but of breaking God's law in *one* point? You say, "I must acknowledge breaking it in one point." Then you are guilty. Have you any excuse to make? "Yes, much." Have you prayed? "Yes, all my life." Then pray on. Have you been charitable? "Oh yes, I give to the infirmary and to the famine fund." Then sell all you have and give to the poor. You say, "That is very hard." Yes, but I cannot help it: such is the way you have chosen with your excuses, prayers, and good works. Another man pleads "guilty" at once. Have you any excuses, any prayers, any good deeds, any endeavours to do right, to plead in your behalf? "No." Have you nothing good to say for yourself? Are you only fit to be cast away from God? "I have not a single excuse or palliation to present." Then God says, "I have nothing but a Saviour for one so bad as you are." If you come as a sinner alone,

* From "The Seeking Saviour and other Bible Themes" by the late Dr. W. P. Mackay, M. A., of Hull. This work was commenced by Dr. Mackay before he died, and has been completed by other hands, from his papers. Among the series is one sermon entitled "the Glory of God," which has a mournful interest from its being the last sermon the sainted man ever preached. Had Dr. Mackay lived to prepare the volume for the press, there might have been more polish in its style, but it would not have breathed, as it now does, the very spirit of the man as if he were speaking. 343 pages. Price $1.25. Published by *Anson D. F. Randolph*, 38 West Twenty-third St., New York.

John Currie, the Canadian Evangelist.

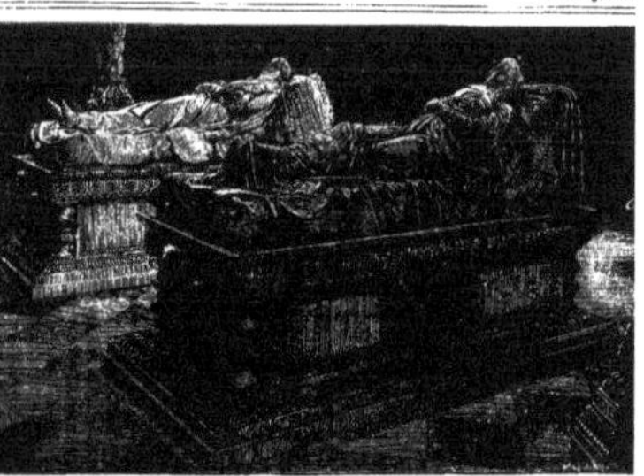

The Imperial Mausoleum at Charlottenburg, Germany.

not sinner and company, God will give you Christ, for it is grace now, as it will be judgment then. The righteousness which is of faith is for any man who will take the place where righteousness can flow. The place of the lost sinner now; for "behold, now is the day of salvation."

The Missing Line.

I remember when at school we used to work out long problems; and I have often worked out some problem in algebra, and at the end come to some most absurd result. What was the reason? Merely one line left out. Our great rationalistic thinkers have brought out a wondrously stupid result with all their thinking, a very unscriptural result; and why? They forget one factor, and that factor is sin. The Bible is the history of *sin*, and the doctrine of the Bible is the doctrine of *sin* put away, from Genesis to Revelation. "Without shedding of blood" (*blood, blood and sin*) "there's no remission of sin." They tell us that we preach the theology of the shambles; let us stand by the blood theology and sound it in every ear. God first shed blood in providing a covering for the sinner Adam; God last shed blood in sheathing His sword in the Man His Fellow. He is the Alpha and the Omega, the beginning and the ending, the first and the last, the author and finisher, of the blood theology.

JOHN CURRIE.

(See Portrait on this Page.)

JOHN CURRIE, whose evangelistic labors among the poor in the United States and Canada have been much blessed, was born in Glasgow, Scotland, on December 2, 1843. He is therefore now in his forty-fifth year. His father was foreman in a baker's shop, and his mother was a dressmaker. For some six years after his birth the family were in comfortable circumstances, but at the end of that time the father began to drink heavily, and soon all the money that had been saved by the joint earnings of himself and his wife were spent. The young mother was almost heartbroken. She would sit for hours and cry over John and his little sister, who needed clothes and food, while she waited for her husband's return, wondering if he would bring home any money. Things grew worse and worse, until at last Mrs. Currie went wrong in her mind through grief, and after much suffering she died. She recovered her reason a short time before her death, and in her last moments was able to commend to God's keeping the two orphans she was leaving behind.

The boy passed under the care of his grandmother, but appears to have had no education, or to have derived no profit from such as he had. He had been a sufferer by the dissolute habits of his father, and had by painful experience proved how much misery indulgence in liquor involves, yet, strange to say, he was not deterred by the awful example. Foot-racing, boxing, dancing, and drinking occupied his time, and he soon sank into degradation. Hoping to get rid of his evil habits and associations, he in 1869 left his native country and crossed the Atlantic. Many have tried this experiment without success, for change of scene without change of heart is but a vain remedy. Currie found it to be so, and the first five years of his residence in America were marked by dissipation as debasing as that of his life on the other side the Atlantic.

At length, while he was in Montreal, he was induced by a Christian worker to visit the Young Men's Christian Association, and there he was persuaded to sign the pledge. Three nights afterward he attended a religious service and heard the testimonies of converted men. He was so deeply impressed that he became anxious to secure the same blessing for himself. Finally he made a profession of his faith in Christ and began a new life. Six months' experience of the blessing of Christianity moved him to testify of them to others. He began a work in the slums of Montreal in a saloon known as *Joe Beef's Canteen*, the proprietor of which not only allowed him to talk with the poor degraded creatures who haunted the place, but actually set up a platform from which he could give gospel addresses. The work succeeded from the outset. Currie was in earnest, and the people who came to the Canteen were not fastidious about the language or grammar of the preacher. Many were rescued from vice and misery, and Currie was fairly launched in his career as an evangelist. Since that time he has travelled extensively in the United States and Canada, holding successful meetings in many of the large cities. He has worked in Boston, New York, Brooklyn, Albany, Detroit, Chicago, St. Louis, San Francisco, and Leadville; and everywhere his labors have been attended with blessed results.

THE IMPERIAL MAUSOLEUM.

(See Illustration.)

THE final resting-place of the remains of the deceased Emperor William is a familiar spot to the citizens of Berlin. It stands in Charlottenberg (Charlotte's town), the western suburb of Berlin named after Queen Charlotte. The visitor to Berlin always goes to the pretty subur see it and the park and the castle. In less half an hour the "Stadtbahn" takes him o the heart of Berlin to the "West End," w eminent politicians and illustrious person have their residence.

So deeply is the mausoleum hidden by trees which surround it, that the visitor keep steadily to the main road, bordered mighty pines and firs, or he easily loses his among the winding paths. Down that William I. was borne to his grave on Fri March 16, to take his place in the silent t side by side with his venerated mother and noble father. It is a place of tender and lowed associations with him, for there in most solemn hours of his life he was accust ed to go for meditation and prayer.

Outside its gates stands day after day a v an sentinel of stalwart frame, guarding chamber of death. The pines whisper my riously overhead, but no harsh, loud sound turbs the solemn peace. Every head is bare the door at the top of the broad steps is ope and visitors enter the mausoleum.

MRS. WILLOUGHBY'S FRIENDS.

(See Illustration on page 221.)

"YOU are my adviser-general," said a newly come to reside in Greenburg, to Mrs. loughby, the clergyman's wife, "perhaps can tell me if there is anyone within a mi two, who can make a dress for me, well quickly?"

"Oh yes," was the reply; "that is a mat shall be very glad to arrange for you. I will come with me this morning I will intro you to a family thoroughly worthy of confid I am deeply interested in them, and have a sincere respect for each one. When you them I think you will be glad to put wor their hands."

"Not a charitable arrangement, is it? quired the lady. "I have always preferr give money rather than work in cases of ity. One always pays a high price for work to persons whom one employs be one is sorry for them."

"Come and see," said Mrs. Willoughby. you think the girls look incompetent, you say nothing about employing them. I a friendly with them that I can call with a f without their expecting a commission."

Mrs. Willoughby was content to let the ter depend on the impression the Misses F would make on a prospective employer, wi uttering any further eulogy. And her confi as justified. Entering the uiet home in which they ved, the clergyman's wife assed unannounced into the orkroom with the easy confidence of an intimate friend, ad her new acquaintance accompanied her. They paused n the threshold, unnoticed y the four bright-looking rls within. One of them was olding up a bonnet for the miration or criticism of others, and each seemed be deeply interested in the hibition.

"You have succeeded to a arvel, Marion," said one o was seated at a sewing achine. "That is exactly at the old lady ought to into ecstacies about. I am re she will like it." Mrs. lloughby and her compan entered the room as this nion was given, and it was to see by the welcome four sisters gave to the ergyman's wife, that a very arm friendship existed beeen them. Marion would ave retired with the bonnet, at her sisters would not ermit it. Mrs. Willoughby's oinion must be had; for is was, in fact, Marion's rst achievement in that line, ad was the result of a very tief experiencein a city miller's workroom. Praise uld be given very conscientiously, and the ung lady was cheered by the unstinted enmiums of her friend and the strange visitor. he latter at once proceeded to the object of r visit, evidently satisfied by the manner and ds of the young people that incompetence d high charges were not the characteristics their business.

'Who are they? How did you come to know em?" were the questions she put to Mrs. illoughby when, after a long and pleasant conrsation with the four girls, the two ladies left eir busy home.

'I have known them many years," said the gyman's wife, "in fact, from their school-girl ys. Their father was a warm friend of my band's, and one of his most zealous supports, and their mother was one of the most saintly men I ever knew. Husband and wife were a affectionate couple, and very proud of four pretty, intelligent daughters and their ."

"They seem to be well-educated, ladylike how is it they have to earn their living s way?"

Ah! that is a sad story," said Mrs. Willough- "I suppose their present condition was the last thing Mr. Francis expected for ughters. He was a physician, with a large ce, and had accumulated a considerable e before he died. He left it entirely in e's hands, and she, after his death, allowson to manage it for her. Poor lady! lieved him to be one of the best, as he ly was one of the smartest, young men of rcle. During his father's life he had be-, but when that restraint was removed, he had control of so large a sum of money, gan to develop evil tendencies, of which mother had no suspicion. Reports of fast g and lavish expenditure began to circulate, eventually we had to believe them, but Mrs. ncis would not. I think his sisters must have wn soon afterward, and at last even his poor, owed mother was horror-stricken to find that son was surely a villain. The discovery was death-blow, and it did not come until every ar of the fortune was gone. These four girls left actually penniless, with their mother dead in the house, and their brother a fugitive in a foreign land.

"It was saddening to see how their relatives and friends fell away from them. It seemed as if no one would help them. Finally, I suppose the family name and honor was thought to be at stake, and their uncles found money for funeral expenses, and proposed to place the four girls in different families connected with them by distant relationship. That kind of semi-pauperism, and more than all, the separation from each other, killed the project. One or two friends assisted them, and they were enabled to get some instruction and commence business, with such success as you see. It is now two years since the experiment was first made, and they are earning a comfortable livelihood, with satisfaction to themselves and those who employ them. They are a thoroughly united, happy family, and I am happy to say they are all treading in their mother's footsteps, loving and serving their Saviour with full purpose of heart."

Mrs. Willoughby's Friends.

MRS. TRANSOME'S PUPIL.

A SERIAL STORY.

(Continued from page 207.)

A Tragedy.

IF I had not loved my dear Philip so much, if his image when he came to me begging me to take him as a pupil had not been all the time before me, along with that later aspect of him as my friend and benefactor, I could not have endured the wretchedness of my position. Nothing supported me but the old man's promise to leave all his wealth to Philip Champion. I knew it would be a blessing to Philip; it was anything but a blessing to its present owner. That was one of the many things I learned in that sad time. Do you want to know what they were?

Well! then I learned what a cruel bondage the love of money is. It was a bondage, not only to our old master, but to Rebecca and me. To get a shilling from him was as painful to him as giving a drop of his life's blood. He grudged himself every morsel he ate; and he could not bear to see the fire burning bright, and clear from ashes, but he must have the grate choked up with them, and a little handful of live embers on the top. That spring-time he would have no fire kindled in the kitchen, because of the extra expense my living was to him; and we sat with him in his parlor, and did what little cooking was done there. He was the poorest man I ever knew.

But it was at night that the bondage pressed upon him most cruelly. As soon as it grew dark, he was tormented with fears of robbers, which prevented him from falling asleep, until he was quite worn out with weariness. He never knew what it was to lay his head down on his pillow, and sleep soundly and peacefully. His money kept him waking worse than rheumatism ever kept poor Transome. He would not hear of Rebecca and me both going to bed, but one of us must sit up in the spare room joining his, within call of him. Dreary hours of darkness were those. Never a night passed by, but he cried out in his troubled sleep that thieves were breaking in to steal his treasure. Many a time I found him crying and wringing his hands, as he sat up in bed, between waking and sleeping; and it was harder to pacify him than a frightened child who has been awaked by some terrifying dream. Yet as soon as he could recover himself he would vow and declare that he had no money in the house, and thieves would be finely disappointed if they came. I never knew what to believe.

"Tell me," I said to him, one day when we were alone, "why you are so full of fear. If there is no money in the house, how is it you cannot sleep for terror?"

"I cannot tell," he answered, with a troubled face, "but as soon as I fall asleep it seems as if all my money, all I ever had, was hoarded up in my room. There's gold under my pillow, and in all the boxes, and all the drawers, and hidden under the flooring; gold everywhere; and thieves are always trying to break in to steal it. I hear them whispering, and creeping about; and boring stealthily at the door to get in, till I cry out; and that wakes me, and you or Rebecca come in and tell me I've been dreaming. But it is not like a dream. I wish the night would never come, for it is always the same thing."

"Every night?" I said.

"Every night," he repeated, with his wavering, trembling voice.

"But you should ask God to deliver you from these terrors," I said, for I felt grieved for the miserable old man. "He is ready to help all those who cry to Him. He brought me out of all my troubles, and He can save you."

"I dare not," he answered, his shaking head falling lower on his breast, "if I ask Him for anything, He will require me to give up my money. I know it; I tried it years ago. I wished to be safe, and be a Christian, but I could not give up my money. It is too late now. I cannot part with it."

He spoke slowly, and as it were unwillingly, in a low tone, as though he were thinking aloud, not talking to me. So awful the words sounded to me that I trembled and shivered.

"No," he said, "no! it is too late."

He was silent for a few minutes. Then a cunning look came over his wrinkled face, and he looked at me sharply with his small, sunken eyes.

"I've been talking nonsense," he said. "I've no money to give up. I'm a poor, penniless old man, with nothing before me but to die in the poorhouse."

He began to groan over his poverty, and mutter about the poorhouse. But I could bear it no longer, and I rose up, and left him to groan and mutter to himself. The dark, gloomy house seemed like a prison to me, and the air in it stifled me. I went out into the wilderness of a garden, and walked up and down its grass-grown walks, thinking of the wretched man who was tossed from one delusion to another: at night tormented with fears for his riches, by day burdened with dread of the poorhouse. Truly, he had pierced himself through with many sorrows.

How gloomy were the long nights of the next winter! Before it was dusk in the afternoon our master would begin to worry about the doors being locked, and the shutters fast; and there was no rest until Rebecca and I had been all round the house to see if every place was safe. Even then he would send us again and again during the night, to make sure that no fastenings had been forgotten; and sometimes when he was well enough he would go round to satisfy himself. I can see him now—his poor, bent body, hardly strong enough to bear its own weight, and his shaking head, and his searching eyes peering into the darkest corners, where he fancied some robber might be lurking. I begged him often and often to have some honest, decent man to sleep in the house for our protection, for what could I or Rebecca do if his fears came true? But he would not give ear to my words. He could trust no man, he said. I knew that he could not trust God.

Philip Champion had been once in England since I had left my cottage to dwell with his uncle; but he had not had time to visit me, and I did not tell him what I was doing for his sake. My landlord had told me that his will was altered, and all was right for Philip. Without that I think I could not have borne up.

I was beginning to be a little timorous myself; though I had never known what fear meant when Transome and I lived in our little home, even when it stood quite close at the head of a clough that had no very good name. The poor food, and bad nights, and the prison-like feeling of the place, began to tell upon me almost as much as the poorhouse did. It seemed as if there was nothing in the world to be thought of, or talked about, or cared for, but money. Rebecca was constantly telling me of her expectations from her old master, and what she meant to do with her thousand pounds. So both in parlor and kitchen, whenever I was alone with either of them, all the talk and all the thought was money. Nay, my mind began to dwell upon it, though it was for Philip's sake; and I seemed to forget the sunshine, and the fresh air, and the singing of birds, and the love one of another, even God's love.

Whether I should have grown like Rebecca and our master, I cannot tell. But after Christmas was past—a Christmas with no good-will or gladness in it—and while the nights were still long and dreary, the end came. It was almost as if a voice had come from God, "Thou fool, this night thy soul shall be required of thee!"

I had fallen asleep for very weariness one night in the large old chair, where I kept watch in my turn for our master. It was more of a doze than a sleep; for he had been quiet only for a little while, after crying out once or twice that he could hear thieves trying all the doors and shutters in the house. It was so old an alarm, like the boy's cry of "Wolf!" that it had not disturbed me at all; and when he went quiet, I fell off into an uneasy doze in my chair. The back of it was toward the door, a high back, which kept my head free from draughts, and hid me from the sight of anybody in the master's room. Just before me, over the mantel shelf, there stood an old cracked looking-glass, in a tarnished gilt frame, where, when I looked up, I could see dimly the light in my master's bedroom.

Suddenly, as I was dozing, a bright gleam from the looking-glass shone across my face, and I woke up, broad-awake, as though some voice had called me; but there was no sound. Only in the dim glass I could see a fuller light than ever was given by a farthing rush-light, and it was moving about in the room beyond. Yet I kept still, why, I scarcely know, watching the flitting of the light in the dim glass above me. But all in an instant a shrill, wavering, terrified cry ran through the house, and I saw a man's figure cross hastily to my master's bedside.

What was I to do? A poor, feeble old creature like me! I had not strength to contend with a child; and how could I defend my master and his money from a thief? There were but two courses open to me. I might either go into the chamber, and do whatever I could to protect the poor old man, or I could steal quietly and wake Rebecca, and try to get help from my neighbors. I was not long in deciding. Before the thief turned away from my master's bedside I crept noiselessly, quaking with fear, across the floor, and made my way up-stairs to Rebecca's room.

She was sleeping soundly, for though her room was above the master's, she was too much used to hear him cry for help, to be disturbed by that last cry of his. But when I put my hand on her, she awoke in a moment, and looked at me with eager eyes.

"Hush!" I whispered, the thieves are here at last. Be quiet, Rebecca. Steal out of the back door, and call for help. You will be quicker than me."

"Thieves!" she said, in a scornful tone; "are you out of your mind, too?"

"No," I said, "it's true this time. Get help, Rebecca, quickly. They may murder him. Hark! he is as quiet as death now."

For in the room below, our master's cries had ceased entirely, and all was still. That frightened Rebecca. She sprang up, and throwing on a cloak that hung behind the door, she stole silently down the stair-case. I followed and saw her tarry for a moment or two, peering in through the open doors, through which the light was shining brightly; and then very swiftly, but very steadily, she sped on her way; and presently the click of a latch down-stairs told me she was fairly out of the house. I was alone with the thieves!

But those were terrible minutes! Never shall I forget them. I hid myself in a dark corner of the stair-case, listening and watching with all my might. The house was so still I could hear their footsteps moving about the room, and the hurried opening and shutting to of boxes and drawers. There were more boxes in that chamber than anywhere else in the house, but nobody had seen the contents of them except the master. There was also an old-fashioned desk, full of little drawers, and secret recesses, which I have often and often seen since, that gave the thieves a world of trouble. They were not so quiet now, and I could hear two voices speaking; but the master's voice I could not hear, though I hearkened for it anxiously. A great dread came over me, lest he should have been murdered.

I could hear the thieves at work with their tools, just as the master had described it to me, sawing and boring, and breaking open locks, with very little precaution against noise now. It seemed so long that I began to think Rebecca must have fled away in her fright, and left me and her poor old master to their mercy. To be sure I might have followed her; the way was free, and the house-door open. But I could not make up my mind to go, and leave the old man quite alone, even though I could give him no help, save to stand there behind the door, praying that Rebecca might come back soon.

At length—but oh, how long it seemed!—I heard footsteps treading cautiously along the gravel walk towards the house; and I held my breath to listen, and trembled the more, lest the thieves should catch the sound. But they had grown too secure, having been so long undisturbed, and they were too busy with their tools to hear so slight a noise as that. Nearer and nearer, into the hall below, and quietly up the dark stair-case, came three or four of our near neighbors, with Rebecca leading them, and so, quietly, without wavering, they broke in up on the thieves, and caught them almost befor they knew they were in danger.

What a sight that room was when I went in I told you there were more locked-up boxes an drawers there than anywhere else in the hous which no one had ever seen opened; but now a their contents were strewed and scattered abou the floor. Well! the old master's mother mu have been as fond of hoarding as he was: bu she had hoarded clothing, and there were a her old satin dresses and petticoats, and high heeled slippers, and laces and linen, all fade and mildewed. There was also good war clothing that might have kept many a poo creature from dying of cold, but now it wa moth-eaten and useless. I saw packets of ye low letters, and a miniature portrait or two ly ing among them. But I could not wait to loo well at these things. I pressed on to the hea of the bed, and drew the old tattered curtai aside, and looked down at the master's face.

Was he dead? The poor withered face lay o the pillow, with its mouth fallen half open, an its filmy eyes staring with a look of terror, suc as I never saw before or since. I spoke to hi softly, then loudly; and laid my hand upon th bent and crooked fingers, which seemed to b grasping at something. After that I knew was true. He was dead!

There was no one in the room with me; fo there had been a little scuffle with the thieve and they had been dragged by our neighbo into the room beyond. But at my sudden c one of them came running in quickly. He sa in a moment what had happened; and quietl as if awe-struck at the terrible face of the corps he drew me away out of the room, and himse locked the door, and said he would carry th key at once to the police-station.

How it was I cannot tell. Neither he nor spoke a word of it; but whether it was from o faces, or from him locking the door so silentl the truth seemed to flash upon all the re The thieves themselves were struck dumb fo minute; and then one of them cried out with loud and terrified voice:

"We never laid a finger on him!" he said swear 't. Rebecca, speak for me! Thou kno aw could na' have th' heart to kill an oud m like him. Rebecca, doesn't thee know m See! I'm Robin Cherrick, thy sweetheart i' oud time, as th' oud mester persuaded thee turn off. Eh! lass, if thee had been true to I should never ha'e come to such a pass as thi

I turned about to look for Rebecca, and th she stood, with a face like death; only her d eyes were fastened upon the man that h spoken, and her lips moved as if she were spe ing, only no sound came through them. All once, before any of us could run to her, she down on the floor like one dead.

Some of them carried her up-stairs, and her on her bed; and I was left alone with to bring her back to her senses. I could h many strange sounds down in the house bel voices and footsteps echoing through the de late room, and such a stir, and noise, and c fusion all about him, as would have brought old master to life again if there were any of stepping back over the threshold he had crossed. My own mind seemed to be w dering, as if I were only passing throug frightful dream: only there was Rebecca's f white and rigid, with lips close set, under very eyes, and her heart scarcely beating w I laid my hand upon it.

I almost thought she was dead too; but a a long while I saw her eyelids quiver a little, a deep, heavy sigh came through her pa lips. I had no light save a small candle, as had been burning in the master's room; her face looked ghastly, with the hair all ru about it. I did not speak to her, but I ba her forehead again with some cold water.

"Mrs. Transome?" she whispered.

"Ay, it's me," I said, "you're very ill, Rebe Lie quiet, my dear."

She lay still, as I bade her, for a few minu

ut she was busy thinking and remembering hat had happened. All at once she started up, nd clung to me like a child that has been scared nd frightened.

"Was there anybody robbing the master?" he asked, in a hurried but faint voice.

"Hush! my dear," I said. "Yes, there have een thieves in the house; but they're taken way now."

"Did one of them say his name?" she asked gain.

"Ay!" I answered.

"Tell me what it was," she said eagerly, don't be afraid to tell me."

"Robin Cherrick," I answered; "who is he, ebecca? Tell me all about it, my poor dear!" She had fallen back again upon the bed, and ad hidden her face in the pillow; but all her ody was shaken by her heavy sobs. It was a ng time before she could speak to me again.

(*To be Continued.*)

CHRISTIAN WATCHFULNESS.

By Mrs. M. Baxter.

. B. Lesson for April 15, Matt. 24: 36-51. Golden Text, Mark 13: 37.

hat Watchfulness Implies—The Watchman's Duties—The Call to Christians—To Watch for the Lord's Coming—The Signs Accumulating—The Gospel Being Preached as a Witness—The Coming Tribulation—The Classes of Mourners—Lovers of Nature—Of Architecture—Vain Attempts at Suicide—Mistaken Ideas of Prophetic Dates—The Doom of the Indifferent—The Advent Surely Pre-Millennial—The Functions of True Watchmen.

"What I say unto you, I say unto all, Watch." ark 13: 37.) To watch is to be awake, to be guard, to observe and take account of all ings around us. A good watchman does not much, lest he should fail to notice someing which is taking place. The duty of a tchman, in old times, was to keep watch on top of a tower, or some elevated place, from ich he could perceive the approach of an eny; he was awake when others were sleeping; could observe what others saw not, and his was to apprise them. The world is lying darkness and death; eight hundred million athens, as well as the larger number of people so-called Christian lands, are on their way to rdition, but they are asleep to things eternal, d the apostle Paul says to us: "Let us not , as do others, but let us watch and be so-." God calls His children as He did Ezekiel, He said to him, "I have made thee a tchman unto the house of Israel; therefore, the word of My mouth, and give them ing from Me."

our chapter for to-day, we are exhorted by Lord Himself to

Watchfulness in Relation to His Coming

. After speaking of those things which uld mark the whole dispensation till He again—false Christs, false prophets, wars, of wars, famines, pestilences, earth-in divers places—all which things He "the beginning of sorrows," saying "the not yet"—He goes on to speak of the dis-signs of the end itself. "This gospel of Kingdom shall be preached in all the world witness unto all nations; and then shall d come." Thank God, the impetus to nary zeal has increased enormously the years; let us watch, let us look up and our heads, for our redemption, as well as of the Jews "draweth nigh;" Christ is , even at the doors." Another sign is abomination of desolation" (translated by "the idols of the desolator" Dan. 9: 27.) standing in the holy place, i. e., the of Jerusalem, which is to take place at same time as the great tribulation, "When shall see the abomination of desolation ding in the holy place . . . *then* shall great tribulation, such as was not since the inning of the world unto this time, no, nor shall be. And except those days should be tened, there should no flesh be saved; but the elect's sake those days shall be shortened. . . . Immediately after the tribulation of those days shall the sun be darkened, and the moon shall not give her light, and the stars shall fall from heaven, and the powers of the heavens shall be shaken: and *then* shall appear the sign of the Son of Man in heaven; and *then* shall all the tribes of the earth mourn, and they shall see the Son of Man coming in the clouds of heaven with power and great glory." Such are the signs of the end of this age, and the coming of the Lord.

The Gospel is Being Preached as a Witness,

but idols have not yet been set up in the "holy place," for the temple is not yet rebuilt, so that the idols cannot yet have been set up there. But we are taught to watch, because when we see all these things we may "know that He is near (see margin, v. 33), even at the doors."

The tribulation is the terror of the world; for where their treasure is, there will their hearts be also. The merchants will mourn in those days, "for no man buyeth their merchandise any more." (Rev. 18: 11.) The great men of the earth shall mourn, the "kings of the earth, and the great men, and the rich men, and the chief captains, and the mighty men, hid themselves in the dens, and in the rocks of the mountains; and said to the mountains and rocks, Fall on us, and hide us from the face of Him that sitteth on the throne, and from the wrath of the Lamb. For the great day of His wrath is come; and who shall be able to stand?" (Rev. 6: 15-17.) Those who have lived for the lust of the eyes in beautiful scenery, shall mourn, for "Every island fled away, and the mountains were not found." Those whose pride and admiration have been set upon the architecture of grand cathedrals, or proud public buildings, shall mourn, for "there was a great earthquake, such as was not since men were upon the earth, so mighty an earthquake, and so great; and the cities of the nations fell." (Rev. 16: 18-20.) Men who die unsaved have to leave behind them all they have lived for, men who live to the time of the tribulation, will behold all they have lived for vanish from their grasp while they are yet alive. Some of them, in their terror, will "seek death, and shall not find it; and shall desire to die, and death shall flee from them." (Rev. 9: 6.)

But while the world thus loses its all, the expectant bride of the Lamb has everything to gain from the coming of the Lord. "But of that day and hour knoweth no man." Many sit down under these words, and make them an excuse for not understanding the book of Revelations, of which Christ has said, "Blessed is he that readeth—and they that hear the words of this prophecy.'" (Rev. 1: 3.) And also "Seal not the sayings of the prophecy of this book: for the time is at hand." (Rev. 22.) God would have us search His word and watch for the fulfilment of what He has predicted. Paul says to the Thessalonians, "Ye, brethren, are not in darkness, that that day should overtake you as a thief." It will overtake, as a thief, all who are living for things present. As the days of Noe were, so shall also the coming of the Son of Man be. For as in the days that were before the Flood, they were eating and drinking, marrying and giving in marriage, until the day that Noe entered into the ark, and

Knew Not

until the flood came and took them all away; so shall also, the coming of the Son of Man be." And this exhortation is especially strong to believers. (Luke 21: 34) "And take heed to *yourselves*, lest at any time your hearts be overcharged with surfeiting and drunkenness, and cares of this life, and so that day come upon you unawares . . . Watch ye, therefore, and pray always, that ye may be accounted worthy to escape those things that shall come to pass, and to stand before the Son of Man." There is a spirit of bitter opposition abroad, to any who, having given their lives to the study, think they have arrived at a knowledge of the time. May it not be that those who are altogether indifferent about the matter, may be put to shame when Jesus finds they have not so much as troubled themselves to inquire about the time of His coming, and so were taken unawares? "Then shall two be in the field—the one taken and the other left"—similarly occupied with their hands, but the affections of the one set on things above, and of the other on things upon the earth! "Two grinding at the mill"—the one taken and the other left. "Watch, therefore." What for? That we may know how and when to expect our Lord, and to be ready for Him. "Ye *know* not (but it does not follow that we never shall know) what hour your Lord doth come." "If the goodman of the house had known in what watch the thief would come, he would have watched." If we have some idea of the time when we may expect a visitor, we make up the fire, lay the table, and make ready, and say, "He may be here any moment, now." "Therefore, be ye also ready; for in such an hour as ye think not, the Son of Man cometh."

The majority of Christians believe that Jesus will not come again until after the Millennium, and that the Millennium is to be brought about by the earnest preaching of the gospel; and to them the exhortations to watch for the coming of Christ have no meaning, except as applied spiritually, or understood to mean the final judgment. But these are such as have not studied the Word of God about the coming of the Lord. If the world were all to be converted before Christ came, how then do we find that the state of things when Christ comes is likened to the time before the Flood, when God was obliged to destroy the world because of the sin which dwelt in it?

Our blessed Lord shows that

The True Character of the Watchman

is not only that of warning the sinner, as in Ezek. 3: 18-21, but also to be "a faithful and wise servant, whom his Lord hath made ruler over His household, to give them meat in due season." God's rule is a rule of giving, of supply. Just as Jesus fed the multitudes by the hands of His disciples, so would He now have every true child of His to be a dispenser of the blessings of His kingdom, a dispenser of salvation in the name of Jesus, of liberty from the power of sin, of freedom from anxiety, from sickness, and from misery by faith in Him. Blessed is that servant whom his Lord, when He cometh, shall find so doing. Verily I say unto you, "That He shall make him ruler over all His goods;" just as Pharaoh made Joseph ruler over all Egypt. He that is faithful in that which is least, is faithful also in much; and he that is unjust in the least, is unjust also in much. (Luke 16: 10.) There may be a sentimental talking about expecting the Lord, but unless we are in word and deed setting forward the interests of His kingdom, such an expectation can only condemn. A man living in every luxury, and spending most of his income upon himself, is surely not a "faithful and wise servant," for he is appropriating to himself what God gave him in trust for His kingdom. There are servants, evil servants, who say, "My Lord delayeth His coming;" and the effect of such a belief leads to oppression of their fellow-servants, and to their own gross self-indulgence. But "the Lord of that servant shall come in a day when he looketh not for Him, and in an hour that he is not aware of, and shall cut him asunder and appoint him his portion with the hypocrites: there shall be weeping and gnashing of teeth."

"A SOLITARY WAY."

PSALM cvii., 1 TO 9.

Proverbs xiv. 10; I Corinthians ii. 11.

There is a mystery in human hearts,
And though we be encircled by a host
Of those who love us well, and are beloved,
To every one of us, from time to time,
There comes a sense of utter loneliness.
Our dearest friend is "stranger" to our joy,
And cannot realize our bitterness.
"There is not one who really understands,
Not one to enter into *all* I feel:"
Such is the cry of each of us in turn.
We wander in "a solitary way,"
No matter what or where our lot may be:
Each heart, mysterious even to itself,
Must live its inner life in solitude.

Job vii. 17; Matthew x. 37.

And would you know the reason why this is?
It is because the Lord desires our love,
In every heart He wishes to be *first.*
He therefore keeps the secret-key Himself,
To open *all* its chambers, and to bless
With *perfect* sympathy, and holy peace,
Each solitary soul which comes *to Him.*
So when we feel this loneliness, it is
The voice of JESUS saying, "Come to Me:"
And every time we are "not understood,"
It is a call to us to come *again;*
For Christ alone can *satisfy* the soul,
And those who walk with Him from day to day
Can never have "a solitary way."

Isaiah xlviii. 16; Psalm xxxiv. 22.

And when beneath some heavy cross you faint,
And say, "I cannot bear this cross alone,"
You say the truth. Christ made it purposely
So heavy that you must return to Him.
The bitter grief, which "no one understands,"
Conveys a secret message from the King,
Entreating you to come to Him *again.*
The Man of Sorrows understands it well,
In *all* points tempted, HE can feel with you;
You cannot come too often, or too near,—
The Son of God is infinite in grace,
His presence *satisfies* the longing soul,
And those who walk with Him from day to day.
Can never have "a solitary way."

Farmers and others who have a little leisure time for the next few months will find it their interest to write to B. F. Johnson & Co., of Richmond, whose advertisement appears in another column. They offer great inducements to persons to work for them all or part of their time.

SPECIAL NOTICE.—*Any readers of the Christian ... who wish to procure the above book or any other publicati... Mr. J. B. Alden, can send their orders to me at his published ... and the books will be sent promptly and guaranteed to rea... safely.* **J. E. JEWETT, 77 Bible House, New Y...**

Vol. XI., No. 15. Office, 63 Bible House. N. Y. THURSDAY, APRIL 12, 1888. Annual Subscription. $1.50.

CONTENTS OF THIS NUMBER.

PORTRAITS AND LIVES OF DR. T. J. BARNARDO AND REV. ARCHIBALD BROWN.
CURSING AND SWEARING. Dr. Talmage's Sermon Last Sunday Morning.
ANECDOTES RELATED AT RECENT EVANGELISTIC MEETINGS.
PROPHETIC CONFERENCE IN PARIS.
HEARING AND SIGHT. A New Sermon by C. H. Spurgeon.
PORTRAITS OF MISS DOUGLASS AND HER BURMESE LADY MEDICAL STUDENTS.
PICTURE OF THE GREAT PYRAMID.
MRS. TRANSOME'S PUPIL. (Continued.)
THE TEN VIRGINS. By Mrs. M. Baxter.

BRINGING IN THE BEEF

THE PUDDING

THE TE

ENTERTAINMENT BY THE PIPERS

SONGS BY LADY FRIENDS

DR. T. J. BARNARDO and REV. ARCHIBALD G. BROWN—Scenes at the Recent Dinner to the London Poor.

DR. T. J. BARNARDO.

The Benefactor of Homeless Children.

Character of his Work—Birth and Medical Education—Preparing for the Foreign Mission Fields—A Visit to a City Slum—Carrying a Boy to a Hospital—Nightly Exploration—Seventy-three Children under a Tarpaulin—His Institutions—2,430 Children Sheltered—A Supper for the Aged.

WORLD-wide fame has been attained by the work being done for the homeless waifs of the British metropolis, by the indefatigable philanthropist, whose portrait, with that of Rev. Archibald Brown, his fellow-laborer in the same cause, appears on the preceding page. His visits to this country have made him known to the public of the United States and Canada, and many of our readers in the latter country have been brought into closer and pleasant relations with him, by taking into their homes boys rescued from the streets and trained in his institutions. His portrait and a brief account of

His Work

will therefore be acceptable to his many friends who are readers of this journal. Briefly stated, Dr. Barnardo does a work which the Government of his own and other countries has neglected, that of prevention of crime. In all the great cities of the world there are to be seen boys who have no home; some who have not even a shelter, and many others who have a place they call home, but which has none of the associations about it which give to the word its meaning and true import. Such boys soon become criminals. Their necessities, their associations, their companionships, all tend in that direction. But in London, Dr. Barnardo has been led to interpose between them and their apparent destiny, so far as his strength and means would allow. As the result of his efforts, many a young man is now earning a livelihood by his honest labor, who a few years ago was just commencing in sheer desperation a life of crime. The methods Dr. Barnardo employs, and the origin and progress of the work, form a very interesting and suggestive narrative.

Dr. Barnardo is an Irishman. He was *born* in Dublin, in 1845, and is now in the forty-third year of his age. When he was about nineteen years old, he was brought to a knowledge of Christ as his Saviour, and after prayerful deliberation, he resolved to devote himself to the Lord's service as a medical missionary in China, and removed to London for the purpose of preparing himself for the vocation he had chosen.

At London Hospital.

Accordingly, in 1866, he entered the London Hospital as a student of medicine. It was at this time that he became acquainted with the necessitous condition of the children of the London streets; and utterly oblivious of all apprehension that the work of helping and rescuing these unfortunate ones would prove an obstacle in the way of realizing his early hopes, he magnanimously devoted the whole of his leisure to an attempt to effect their reclamation.

The finger of God soon indicated with unmistakable clearness that his life and energies were to be occupied and expended in the interests of the hapless youth, whose destitute and perilous condition he so deeply commiserated, and, as time wore on, the conviction that *this* was the pathway of duty and service which his Heavenly Father would have him adopt, at length led him to unreservedly give himself to the colossal task, in which he has been blessed in a remarkable manner.

In 1876 he obtained the diploma of the Royal College of Surgeons, Edinboro', and subsequently proceeded to the fellowship. But although a properly qualified medical man, and always taking a keen interest in professional matters, he has for more than twenty-one years been almost wholly absorbed in his present large and growing work.

Gratuitous Service.

It is a noteworthy fact that Dr. Barnardo has given his life to the work without any hope of worldly remunerations. He commenced it in faith, and though large sums of money have been given him to enable him to carry it on he has not used any of it for his own support, but has given it all to the work. It has now grown to vast proportions, but still he has accepted neither fee nor reward for all he has done. (Heb. 11 : 26.) Referring to this fact, which is not generally known, the late Lord Cairns who was Lord High Chancellor of England, remarked in the course of an address which he made at a public meeting in connection with the work: "Dr. Barnardo has given to this arduous labor an energy and ability and constant care which no money could have purchased, and no money could pay for—he has done all this *without money and without price*."

A Visit to a City Den

was the occasion of his attention being first called to the need for such a work as he has done. In 1866, while Dr. Barnardo was preparing to qualify himself for the medical profession, he happened to visit a miserable lodging-house of the lowest type, in one of the densely crowded thoroughfares of the East End of London. The apartment was a horrible den, and it was filled with men and women whom in many instances destitution had made criminals, and who now seemed to be beyond the possibility of amelioration, and to whom the approach of death and the sheltering darkness of the grave might prove the greatest of blessings.

In this lodging-house Dr. Barnardo found a boy in the very extremity of sickness, and whose only hope of recovery lay in immediate removal to a neighboring hospital. The owner, or lessee, of the lodging-house, a very virago of a woman, in the most peremptory manner, intimated her determination to prohibit the departure of the lad until he had paid his arrears of rent, and at once seized upon his tattered clothing as a security for the liquidation of the debt. The young medical student, however, was quite equal to the emergency, and taking off his great-coat, snatched up the lad from the filthy pallet on which he was helplessly lying, and, wrapping him in it, speedily carried him in his arms to the hospital, and had the satisfaction there of seeing him gradually gather strength, and finally recover.

Nightly Explorations.

Having thus commenced the Christ-like work of "rescuing the perishing," he continued his labor of love, and every night after his hours of study were over, instead of visiting the theatres or spending the evening in dissipation, as was the habit of many of his fellow-students, Dr. Barnardo started off on a tour of exploration in the abodes of the poor, looking for sick people to whom his skill might be of service. Once, on a moonless night, in the very depth of midwinter, he saw no fewer than seventy-three children, lying one upon another, packed like sardines, the small fellows above, and the bigger below, under a tarpaulin by a wharf, on the bank of the river Thames. He heard of thousands of city Arabs whose hand, even in youth, was against every man, and every man's hand against them, and with the determination of his naturally resolute character, made more intense by his prayerful waiting upon God, he resolved that whatever loss of ease, strength, or money it might entail, a home should be found for these destitute ones, for whom no man seemed to have the least solicitude. He has been faithful to his mission, and it has grown so vigorously in his hands that now he has in his Home no less than

2,430 Rescued Children.

Notorious lodging-houses and haunts of vice were visited with nightly regularity. Sometimes the genial visitor was made the target of scorn, and at other times he might be seen confronting peril from those who had every reason to fear the invasion of their immoral lairs. But, at last, having secured a dilapidated house in Stepney Causeway, which has since developed, under his administrative ability and persistent purpose, into the present Home for Destitute Lads, he deliberately, and with true nobility of character, resolved that henceforth it should be the work of his life to work for the salvation, both temporally and spiritually, of the crowds of half-famished, half-naked children who were to be found prowling about the narrow alleys, and railway arches, fruit-markets, and the river foreshore, graduating in vice, becoming adepts in criminality, and constituting an increasing danger in the midst of an apathetic community.

The Institutions

which have gradually grown up in connection with Dr. Barnardo's work are of a three-fold character, the leading departments of which may be thus described: The *first*, or *Preventive Department*, for the rescue and reclamation of orphan, destitute, or neglected children, includes the Boys' Home, which was founded in 1870; the Girls' Village Home, which was opened in 1873; the Little Boys' Home; the Infirmary for Sick Children of the destitute class, founded in 1876; the Labor House for Destitute Youths, opened in 1882; and Leopold House Orphan Home for Little Boys in 1883. The *second*, or *Industrial and Educational Section*, for the instruction and employment of boys and girls not absolutely helpless, comprises the various brigades of boys who are employed out of doors, Shoeblack Brigade, City Messengers, etc.; the Ragged and Day School work; Factory Girls' Mission; the Free Dinner-Table to Children; and the Young Workmen's Hotel. The *third*, or the *Adult Mission Section*, embraces the Mission Halls and Coffee Palaces, of which he has several in operation; Deaconess House, Medical Mission, and all the network of beneficent agencies—Evangelistic, Temperance, and Medical—at work among the laboring poor.

A Dinner for the Aged Poor,

to the number of twelve hundred, is depicted in the various panels of the first page illustration. It was recently given at one of Dr. Barnardo's institutions, through the munificence of Mr. John Howard Angas, of Angastein, South Australia, who, desiring to do something for the relief of the distress in London, decided on this method of feeding the poor, and wisely chose Dr. Barnardo's as his almoner. The guests were of the poorest class, from fifty years old and upwards, were composed of the entirely destitute, homeless, and friendless, many of whom had doubtless moved in respectable society. The system adopted on this occasion to obtain guests, was the appointment of a number of friends to visit the lodging-houses, the casual wards and night refuges, and give the tickets to the most destitute, with a kind and hearty invitation. A company of Dr. Barnardo's boys acted as waiters, and showed almost as much delight in placing the hot roast beef and potatoes, and plates of steaming pudding before the guests, as the latter did in their consumption.

After the dinner there was an entertainment, to which a number of boys in the institution contributed. They were dressed as Scotch pipers, and their peculiar music seemed to delight the guests. Genial speeches from several distinguished visitors followed, among which was one from *Mr. Farwell, of Chicago*, who appeared intensely interested in the gathering.

REV. ARCHIBALD G. BROWN.

THE eminent Baptist clergyman, whose portrait accompanies that of Dr. Barnardo on the first page, is the intimate friend of that gentleman, and is in his own sphere doing a similar work. He believes that Christianity is a practical power to be used for the physical as well as the spiritual benefit of the masses, and he has acted on that belief. Mr. Brown was born at Brixton Hill, London, on July 18, 1844, so that he is now in his forty-fourth year. His father and mother were sincere Christian people, and he enjoyed all the priceless advantages of a pious home. During the period of his school-life, at Brighton, he attended the ministry of the late Rev. Mr. Sortain, which proved of immense value to him.

His First Public Service

was at the meeting of a city missionary, who had invited him to go and read to the people.

This piece of service he readily undertook, as he had given some considerable attention to the art of elocution. He reasonably supposed that the reading-book would be the Bible; but on arriving at the meeting-place, he was told that nothing was wanted beyond a few extracts from the "Pilgrim's Progress." "Is that *all* you are to give the people?" asked the young man with characteristic warmth; "there should be preaching—preaching Christ." "If you think so," the missionary dryly replied, "you'd better preach." Mr. Brown replied, "Well, I've never done such a thing: but, rather than simply read the 'Pilgrim's Progress' to them, I'll try."

Not content with preaching the good news to about twenty people, he sallied forth into the streets, and into several saloons, and succeeded in inducing between thirty and forty of those who were "taking their glass" to come and attend the service. His text on the occasion was, "Thou shalt call His name Jesus." Soon after this, his first sermon, Mr. Brown saw that he could be useful as a Sunday-school teacher, and without hesitation he once more went into the streets and gathered for himself

A Class of Young Arabs

for whom no one seemed to care. All these efforts were made while he was "diligent in business," and before he had thought of devoting himself to the ministry. His father was a deacon at the Metropolitan Tabernacle, and when in 1860, the son felt that he had been called to pulpit labor, he entered the Pastor's College, to study under Mr. C. H. Spurgeon. There he spent two years in preparing for his future life-work. At the end of his academical course he accepted an urgent invitation from a church in Kent, where he labored with success for about four years. In 1867 he accepted an invitation from a church

In the Eastern District

of London, and ever since he has labored in that poverty-stricken locality. The church soon had to be rebuilt on a larger scale to accommodate the crowds which were drawn to his ministry, for his preaching, which strikingly resembles that of Mr. Spurgeon, has the same charm for the people, and enjoys the same success. The new building was called the East London Tabernacle, and like the Metropolitan Tabernacle, has become a centre of a wide circle of blessing in the neighborhood. It holds a congregation of 3,500, and cost $66,500. Since he has labored there, 4,000 members have been added to the church.

The question was once put to Mr. Brown, "Can you tell me any sermon of yours which you have known to be specially useful in conversion of sinners?" His reply was: "The largest number I have known to be converted by one sermon was upwards of a hundred. It was the night when I preached on the text, 'Young man, I say unto thee, Arise.'" The sermon was almost an extemporaneous one, but he felt, even while preaching it, that it was being accompanied with power from on high.

In addition to the ordinary Church work which Mr. Brown directs, may be mentioned an Orphan Home, a Soup Kitchen; a depot for free meals, with distribution of food, fuel, and clothing; and a Seaside Home at Herne Bay.

Like the majority of successful evangelists, Mr. Brown is a firm believer in the Pre-millennial Second Coming of Christ, His personal reign for 1,000 years over the nations of the earth, and in the future literal restoration of the Jewish nation to Palestine. His hope for the world's salvation and happiness depends on the predicted Personal Advent of the Prince of Peace Himself.

ANECDOTES RELATED AT RECENT EVANGELISTIC MEETINGS.

A Frenchman's Dream.—Mr. Thompson Said: "On one occasion we had a testimony-meeting, and a Frenchman rose and said, 'Some years ago I had a dream that Jesus was coming round among men, and I offered my hand to Him, but He would not have it. That dream made such an impression on me that I came to Christ. And though in my dream Christ refused my hand, it was only a dream: in the reality He did not refuse me. Christ casts out none that come to Him.'

The Danger of Avarice.—A Servant of an Indian rajah was ordered to keep away from a cave near the rajah's residence, and to keep all others away. The servant began to consider the probable reason of his having been forbidden to enter the cave. He made up his mind that his master must have great treasure hid there, and resolved to get it. Taking a fellow-servant with him to secure the prize, they rolled away the stone at the mouth of the cave, when a tiger sprang upon them and tore them to pieces.

The Gates Closed upon the Captain.—"There was a captain serving with his regiment in India. His colonel was a true Christian, and many times spoke plainly to the young man about coming to Christ. But the captain would reply, 'What is the use of speaking to a young fellow about that? Wait till I am old and gray-haired.' By and by they were separated, and the younger man, the captain, was sent to a station where there were very few white people. He continued his old godless life for a time, but disease came suddenly upon him. His wife attended to his every comfort, but he manifestly grew worse, until at length the doctor told him there was no hope of recovery. Just at that time his old colonel was passing through a neighboring district, and when the sick man heard this he sent to see him. The colonel quickly came. He strove to comfort and point the dying man to Jesus, and as he was by the bed-side praying, the patient opened his eyes and exclaimed, 'Oh! I see the gates of heaven open. Oh! what a glorious sight.' Then he shut his eyes again, but suddenly shrieked out, 'Oh! I am lost! I am lost! I am lost! They are shutting the gates; I am too late.' The next minute he was dead."

Moral Suicide Prevented.—Mr. Knox, an evangelist said: "Some time ago I casually met an old friend in the street. In earlier life we had been very close companions, and had walked into town every morning to business. But a time of spiritual change came to me, bless the Lord. I was led to give my heart to Christ, while my companion remained in the world doing the devil's service. From that time our companionship was broken, for 'how can two walk together except they be agreed?' We had been separated for some years, when I again met him. We grasped each other warmly by the hand as I asked him, 'How are you getting on, George, my dear fellow?' 'Oh, well enough; doing the best I can—an angel cannot do more,' was the half-hearted but flippant reply. 'George,' I said, 'that is not right; it is nothing less than moral suicide. Let there be no more putting off of this matter; you may die any minute, and be lost forever. Come to Christ at once.' The poor fellow's eyes filled with tears; he was only too willing to come, for evidently he was heartily tired of the world and its amusements. And, thank God, he now no longer rests his hope of salvation on *the best he can do*, but on what Christ has done for him."

A French Pastor's Story.—Pasteur Barnier remarks: "I was the child of Christian parents, my father being a missionary, and my mother his faithful helper in all his work. It is about thirty-five years ago that there was a great evangelistic revival in my father's district in the south of France. I remember well one of the speakers addressing the young, and asking them to try the love of Christ, and see if it did not make up for all the pleasures of the world. In the middle of that crowded meeting, without any one knowing of it, I resolved to come to Him, and bowing my spirit at the foot of His cross, shed tears of repentance, but thinking the while of the many years I had given to the enemy. What a happy night that was! but the communion that followed was still more blessed. When my father saw me, for the first time, at the Lord's Table, he said in surprise, 'Harold, why are *you* here?' 'Because Christ has touched my heart, I replied. He took me by the hand and praised God. At that meeting over two hundred young people were brought to the Lord. What a mighty meeting that was! Fourteen societies arose from it, besides home and foreign missionaries. When the Holy Spirit comes in power, we can yet have Pentecostal blessing."

A Successful Prescription.—A Christian worker relates: "A doctor in a country district was, one very stormy night, quietly sitting by his room fire, and hoping, as he listened to the wind and rain without, that he would not be called out. A minute or two later a servant entered with a note. Looking at it, the doctor said, 'Seven miles' ride; I suppose I must go.' Silently he rode for the first six miles without meeting any one, then he noticed a cart drawn by a half-starved looking horse. He looked for a driver, but found none. On he went for another mile, when he noticed a dark object staggering along in the middle of the road. As the doctor came up, the owner of the lean horse stammered out, 'I say, doctor, is that you? I want you to give me a prescription; they say you are real good to the poor; perhaps you will give it to me for nothing.' 'Well, my friend, what is it that ails you?' said the doctor. 'I want *a prescription for keeping my legs from turning into the saloon*.' 'I cannot give you it my man, but there is a Great Physician, a Friend of mine, who will give you what you want.' 'Oh tell me where he lives, that I may go to him, for I am in danger of losing both body and soul.' Months passed, and again the doctor saw the same figure on the road, but not intoxicated this time. He came up, caught the doctor by the hands, and with tears rolling down his face, he said, 'God bless you!' That was all, but the doctor understood that the Great Physician had dealt with him, and had effected a cure of both body and soul. For Him no case is too desperate; He can save unto the uttermost."

The Unopened Letter.—Mr. Scroggie relates: "I heard only lately of a poor lad who, getting among fast companions, began to go to the theatre. Having once begun, he felt he must keep it up. He could not afford it, but in order to pander to his evil desires, he took some money from his master's till; then fearing he would be found out, he ran off and joined the army, and soon, to the distress of his widowed mother, was ordered to India. His mother wrote to him regularly, filling her letters with good advice and motherly love. This so annoyed her son that at length he wrote, telling her that as there was nothing but religion in her letters, he would not open them again; and when the next letter came it was tossed unopened into his box. Some time afterwards he was attacked by fever, and brought very low. A Christian comrade sat down by the sick man's bed, and opening his Bible began to read. His sick comrade interrupted him, saying, 'Oh, if you are going to read, just get my mother's letter out of my box.' He got it, and the first words it contained were to the effect that now she had saved enough money to buy his discharge, and enclosed was an order for the money. When he heard this the poor soldier exclaimed, 'Is it true? is the money there?' Being told that it was, he exclaimed, 'If I had only known, I might have been in Scotland now instead of lying here dying of the fever. Oh! if I had but known.' Like that mother's letters the Bible is lying neglected in many a house, and those who might learn from it that Christ has purchased their discharge from sin and Satan, remain in bondage, unconscious of the blessing within their reach."

CURSING AND SWEARING.

Dr. Talmage's Sermon Preached Last Sunday Morning, April 8, 1888.

"So went Satan forth from the presence of the Lord, and smote Job with sore boils from the sole of his foot unto his crown. And he took him a potsherd to scrape himself withal; and he sat down among the ashes. Then said his wife unto him, Dost thou still retain thine integrity? Curse God, and die." Job 2:7-9.

A Series of Catastrophes—A Foolish Wife's Counsel—Job's Better Sense—Blasphemy a Prevalent Sin—A Two Days' Awful Record in a Car—How the Habit Grows—Children Thinking it Manly—The Example of Fathers and Bosses—From Infirmity of Temper—From Profusion of Bywords—Leads to Perjury—What is the Cure?—Entreat God to Deliver—Often Punished in this World—A Scotchman's Awful Death—A Blasphemer at Catskill—An Appalling Oath—Who is Blasphemed—The Dark Day in New England—A Rainbow Arch.

A STORY oriental and marvellous. Job was the richest man in all the East. He had camels and oxen and asses and sheep, and, what would have made him rich without anything else, seven sons and three daughters. It was the habit of these children to gather together for family reunion. One day, Job is thinking of his children as gathered together at a banquet at the elder brother's house.

While the old man is seated at his tent door, he sees some one running, evidently from his manner bringing bad news. What is the matter now? "Oh," says the messenger, "a foraging party of Sabeans have fallen upon the oxen and the asses, and destroyed them, and butchered all the servants except myself." Stand aside! Another messenger running. What is the matter now? "Oh," says the man, "the lightning has struck the sheep and the shepherds, and all the shepherds are destroyed except myself." Stand aside! Another messenger running. What is the matter now? "Oh," he says, "the Chaldeans have captured the camels, and slain all the camel-drivers except myself." Stand aside! Another messenger running. What is the matter now? "Oh," he says, "a hurricane struck the four corners of the tent where your children were assembled at the banquet, and they are all dead." But

The Chapter of Calamity

has not ended. Job was smitten with elephantiasis, or black leprosy. Tumors from head to foot—forehead ridged with tubercles—eyelashes fall out—nostrils excoriated—voice destroyed—intolerable exhalations from the entire body, until, with none to dress his sores, he sits down in the ashes with nothing but pieces of broken pottery to use in the surgery of his wounds. At this moment, when he needed all encouragement and all consolation, his wife comes in, in a fret and a rage, and says: "This is intolerable! Our property gone, our children slain, and now you covered up with this loathsome and disgusting disease! Why don't you swear? Curse God and die!"

Ah, Job knew right well that swearing would not cure one of the tumors of his agonized body, would not bring back one of his destroyed camels, would not restore one of his dead children. He knew that profanity would only make the pain more unbearable and the poverty more distressing, and the bereavement more excruciating. But, judging from

The Profanity Abroad

in our day, you might come to the conclusion that there was some great advantage to be reaped from profanity. Blasphemy is all abroad. You hear it in every direction: The drayman swearing at his cart, the sewing girl imprecating the tangled skein, the accountant cursing the long line of troublesome figures. Swearing at the store, swearing in the loft, swearing in the cellar, swearing on the street, swearing in the factory. Children swear. Men swear. Women swear! Swearing, from the rough calling on the Almighty in the low restaurant, clear up to the reckless "O Lord!" of a glittering drawing-room; and the one is as much blasphemy as the other.

There are times when we must cry out to the Lord by reason of our physical agony or our mental distress, and that is only throwing out our weak hand toward the strong arm of a father. It was no profanity when James A. Garfield, shot in the Washington depot, cried out: "My God, what does this mean?" There is no profanity in calling out upon God in the day of trouble, in the day of darkness, in the day of physical anguish, in the day of bereavement; but I am speaking now of the triviality and of the recklessness with which the name of God is sometimes used.

The Whole Land is Cursed

with it. A gentleman coming from the far West sat in the car day after day behind two persons who were indulging in profanity; and he made up his mind that he would make a record of their profanities, and at the end of two days several sheets of paper were covered with these imprecations, and at the close of the journey he handed the manuscript to one of the persons in front of him. "Is it possible," said the man, "that we have uttered so many profanities the last few days?" "It is," replied the gentleman. "Then," said the man who had taken the paper, "I will never swear again."

But it is a comparatively unimportant thing if a man makes record of our improprieties of speech. The more memorable consideration is that every improper word, every oath uttered, has a record in the book of God's remembrance, and that the day will come when all our crimes of speech, if unrepented of, will be our condemnation. I shall not to-day deal in abstractions. I hate abstractions. I am going to have a plain talk with you, my brother, about a habit that you admit to be wrong.

The habit grows in the community, by young

People Thinking it Manly

to swear. Little children, hardly able to walk straight on the street, yet have enough distinctness of utterance to let you know that they are damning their own souls, or damning the souls of others. It is an awful thing the first time the little feet are lifted, to have them set down on the burning pavement of hell! Between sixteen and twenty years of age, there is apt to come a time when a young man is as much ashamed of not being able to swear gracefully as he is of the dizziness of his first cigar. He has his hat, his boots, and his coat of the right pattern, and now, if he can only swear without awkwardness, and as well as his comrades, he believes he is in the fashion. There are young men who walk in an atmosphere of imprecation—oaths on their lips, under their tongues, nesting in their shock of hair. They abstain from it in the elegant drawing-room, but the street and the club-house ring with their profanities. They have no regard for God, although they have great respect for the ladies! My young brother, there is no manliness in that. The most ungentlemanly thing a man can do is to swear.

Fathers Foster This Crime.

There are parents who are very cautious not to swear in the presence of their children; in a moment of sudden anger, they look around to see if the children are present when they indulge in this habit. Do you not know, O father, that your child is aware of the fact that you swear? He overheard you in the next room, or someone has informed him of your habit. He is practicing now. In ten y a he will swear as well as you do. Do not, O father, be under the delusion that you may swear and your son not know it. It is an awful thing to start the habit in a family—the father to be profane, and then to have the echo of his example come back from other generations; so that generations after generations curse the Lord.

The crime is also fostered by master mechanics, boss carpenters, those who are at the head of men in hat factories and in dock-yards, and at the head of great business establishments. When you go down to look at the work of the scaffolding, and you find it is not done right, what do you say? It is not praying, is it? The employer swears—his employee is tempted to swear. The man says: "I don't know why my employer, worth $50,000 or $100,000, should have any luxury I should be denied simply because I am poor. Because I am poor and dependent on a day's wages, haven't I as much right to swear as he has with his large income?" Employers swear, and that makes so many employees swear. The habit also comes

From Infirmity of Temper.

There are a good many people who, when they are at peace, have righteousness of speech, but when angered they blaze with imprecation. Perhaps all the rest of the year they talk in right language, but now they pour out the fury of a whole year in one red-hot paragraph of five minutes. I knew of a man who excused himself for the habit, saying: "I only swear once in a great while. I must do that just to clear myself out."

The habit comes also from the profuse use of bywords. The transition from a byword, which may be perfectly harmless, to imprecation and profanity, is not a very large transition. It is "my stars!" and "mercy on me!" and "good gracious!" and "by George!" and "by Jove!" and you go on with that a little while, and then you swear. These words, perfectly harmless in themselves, are next door to imprecation and blasphemy. A profuse use of bywords always ends in profanity.

The Habit is Creeping Up

into the highest styles of society. Women have no patience with flat and unvarnished profanity. They will order a man out of the parlor indulging in blasphemy, and yet you will sometimes find them with fairy fan to the lip, and under chandeliers which bring no blush to their cheek, taking on their lips the holiest of names in utter triviality.

Why, my friends, the English language is comprehensive, and capable of expressing all shapes of feeling and every degree of energy. Are you happy—Noah Webster will give you ten thousand words with which to express your exhilaration. Are you righteously indignant—there are whole armories in the vocabulary, righteous vocabulary—whole armies of denunciation, and scorn, and sarcasm, and irony, and caricature, and wrath. You express yourself against some meanness or hypocrisy, in all the oaths that ever smoked up from the pit, and I will come right on after you and give a thousand-fold more emphasis of denunciation to the same meanness and the same hypocrisy, in words across which no slime has ever trailed, and into which the fires of hell have never shot their forked tongues—the pure, the innocent, God-honored Anglo-Saxon in which Milton sang, and John Bunyan dreamed, and Shakespeare dramatized.

There is no Excuse for Profanity

when we have such a magnificent language—such a flow of good words, potent words, mighty words, words to suit every crisis and every case.

Do you know that this trivial use of God's name results in perjury? Do you know that people who take the name of God on their lips in recklessness and thoughtlessness are fostering the crime of perjury? Make the name of God a foot-ball in the community, and it has no power when in court-room and in legislative assembly it is employed in solemn adjuration! See the way, sometimes, they administer the oath: "S'help you God—kiss the book!" Smuggling, which is always a violation of the oath, becomes in some circles a grand joke. You say to a man: "How is it possible for you to sell these goods so very cheap? I can't understand it." "Ah!" he replies, with a twinkle of the eye, "the Custom-house tariff of these goods isn't as much as it might be." An oath does not mean as much as it would were the name of God used in reverence and in solemnity. Why is it that so often jurors render unaccountable verdicts, and judges give unaccountable charges, and useless schemes pass in our State capitals?

What is an oath? Anything solemn? Anything that calls upon the Almighty? Anything that marks an event in a man's history? Oh, no! It is kissing the book! There is no habit, I tell you plainly—and I talk to hundreds and thousands of men to-day who will thank me for my utterance—I tell you, my brother—I talk to you not professionally but just as one brother talks to another on some very important theme—I tell you there is no habit that so depletes a man's nature as the habit of profanity. You might as well try to raise vineyards and orchards on the sides of belching Stromboli, as to raise anything good on a heart from which there pours out the scoria of profanity. You may swear yourself down; you cannot swear yourself up. When the Mohammedan finds a piece of paper he cannot read, he puts it aside very cautiously, for fear the name of God may be on it. That is one extreme. We go to the other.

What is the Cure

of this habit? It is a mighty habit. Men have struggled for years to get over it. There are men in this house of God who would give half their fortune to get rid of it. An aged man was in the delirium of a fever. He had for many years lived a most upright life and was honored in all the community; but when he came into the delirium of this fever he was full of imprecation and profanity, and they could not understand it. After he came to his right reason he explained it. He said: "When I was a young man I was very profane. I conquered the habit, but I had to struggle all through life. You haven't for forty years heard me say an improper word, but it has been an awful struggle. The tiger is chained, but he is alive yet."

If you would get rid of this habit, I want you, my friends, to dwell upon

The Uselessness of It.

Did a volley of oaths ever start a heavy load? Did they ever extirpate meanness from a customer? Did they ever collect a bad debt? Did they ever cure a toothache? Did they ever stop the twinge of the rheumatism? Did they ever help you forward one step in the right direction? Come now, tell me, ye who have had the most experience in this habit, how much have you made out of it? Five thousand dollars in all your life? No. One thousand? No. One hundred? No. One dollar? No. One cent? No. If the habit be so utterly useless, away with it!

But you say: "I have struggled to overcome the habit a long while, and I have not been successful." You struggled in your own strength, my brother. If ever a man wants God, it is in such a crisis of his history. God alone, by His grace, can emancipate you from that trouble. Call upon Him day and night, that you may be delivered from this crime. Remember, also, in the cure of this habit, that it arouses God's indignation. The Bible reiterates, from chapter to chapter, and verse after verse, the fact that it is accursed for this life, and that it makes a man miserable for eternity. There is not a sin in all the catalogue that is so often peremptorily

Punished in This World

as the sin of profanity. There is not a city or a village but can give an illustration of a man struck down at the moment of imprecation. A couple of years ago, briefly referring to this in a sermon, I gave some instances in which God had struck swearers dead at the moment of their profanity. That sermon brought to me from many parts of this land and other lands statements of similar cases of instantaneous visitation from God upon blasphemers. My opinion is that such cases occur somewhere every day, but for various reasons they are not reported.

In Scotland a club assembled every week for purposes of wickedness, and there was a competition as to which could use the most horrid oath, and the man who succeeded was to be president of the club. The competition went on. A man uttered an oath which confounded all his comrades, and he was made president of the club. His tongue began to swell, and it protruded from the mouth, and he could not draw it in, and he died, and the physicians said: "This is the strangest thing we ever saw; we never saw any account in the books like unto it; we can't understand it." I understand it. He cursed God and died.

At Catskill, N. Y., a group of men stood in a blacksmith's shop during a violent thunderstorm. There came a crash of thunder, and some of the men trembled. One man said: "Why, I don't see what you are afraid of. I am not afraid to go out in front of the shop and defy the Almighty. I am not afraid of lightning." And he laid a wager on the subject, and he went out, and he shook his fist at the heavens, crying, "Strike, if you dare!" and instantly he fell under a bolt. What destroyed him? Any mystery about it? Oh, no.

He Cursed God, and Died.

Oh, my brother, God will not allow this sin to go unpunished. There are styles of writing with manifold sheets, so that a man writing on one leaf, writes clear through ten, fifteen, or twenty sheets; and so every profanity we utter goes right down through the leaves of the book of God's remembrance. It is no exceptional sin. Do you suppose you could count the profanities of last week—the profanities of office, store, shop, factory? They cursed God, they cursed His Word, they cursed His only Begotten Son.

One morning, on Fulton Street, as I was passing along, I heard a man swear by the name of Jesus. My hair lifted. My blood ran cold. My breath caught. My foot halted. Do you not suppose that God is aggravated? Do you not suppose that God knows about it? Dionysius used to have a cave in which his culprits were incarcerated, and he listened at the top of that cave, and he could hear every groan, he could hear every sigh, and he could hear every whisper of those who were imprisoned. He was a tyrant. God is not a tyrant; but He bends over this world, and He hears everything—every voice of praise, every voice of imprecation. He hears it all. The oaths seem to die on the air, but

They have Eternal Echo.

They come back from the ages to come. *Listen! listen!* "All blasphemers shall have their place in the lake which burneth with fire and brimstone, which is the second death." And if, according to the theory of some, a man commits in the next world the sins which he committed in this world—if unpardoned, unregenerated—think of a man's going on cursing in the name of God to all eternity!

The habit grows. You start with a small oath, you will come to the large oath. I saw a man die with an oath between his teeth. Voltaire only gradually came to his tremendous imprecation; but the habit grew on him until, in the last moment, supposing Christ stood at the bed, he exclaimed, "Crush that wretch! Crush that wretch!" Oh, my brother, you begin to swear, and there is nothing impossible for you in the wrong direction.

Who is this God whose name you are using in swearing? Who is He? Is He a tyrant? Has He pursued you all your life long? Has He starved you, frozen you, tyrannized over you? No! He has loved you. He has sheltered you. He watched you last night. He will watch you to-night. He wants to love you, wants to help you, wants to save you. He was

Your Father's God,

and your mother's God. He has housed them from the blast, and He wants to shelter you. Will you spit in His face by an imprecation? Will you ever thrust Him back by an oath?

Who is this Jesus whose name I heard in the imprecation? Has He pursued you all your life long? What vile thing has He done to you that you should so dishonor His name? Why, He was the Lamb whose blood simmered in the fires of sacrifice for you. He is the Brother that took off His crown, that you might put it on. He has pursued you all your life long with mercy. He wants you to love Him, wants you to serve Him. He comes with streaming eyes and broken heart, and blistered feet to save you.

Where is the hand that will ever be lifted in imprecation again? Let that hand, now blood-tipped, be lifted, that I may see it. Not one. Where is the voice that will ever be uttered in dishonoring the name of that Christ? Let it speak now. Not one. Not one. Oh, I am glad to know that all these vices of the community, and these crimes of our city, will be gone. Society is going to be bettered. The world, by the power of Christ's Gospel, is going to be saved, and this crime, this iniquity, and all the other iniquities, will vanish before the rising of the Sun of Righteousness upon the nation.

There was one day in New England memorable for storm and darkness. I hardly ever saw such an evening. The clouds which had been gathering all day unlimbered their batteries. The Housatonic, which flows quietly, save as the paddles of pleasure-parties rattle the oarlocks, was lashed into foam, and the waves hardly knew where to lay themselves.

Oh, What a Time It Was!

The hills jarred under the rumbling of God's chariots. Blinding sheets of rain drove the cattle to the bars, or beat against the window pane as though to dash it in. The grain fields threw their crowns of gold at the feet of the storm-king. When night came in, it was a double night. Its mantle was torn with the lightnings, and into its locks were twisted the leaves of up-rooted oaks and the shreds of canvas torn from the masts of the beached shipping. It was such a night as makes you thank God for shelter, and open the door to let in the spaniel howling outside with terror. We went to sleep under the full blast of heaven's great orchestra, the forests with uplifted voices, in chorus that filled the mountains, praising the Lord. We woke not until the fingers of the sunny morn touched our eyelids. We looked out the window, and the Housatonic slept as quiet as an infant's dream. The trees sparkled as though there had been some great grief in heaven, and each leaf had been God-appointed to catch an angel's tear. It seemed as if our Father had looked upon the earth, His wayward child, and stooped to her tear-wet cheek and kissed it. So will

The Darkness of Sin

and crime leave our world before the dawn of the morning. The light shall gild the city spire, and strike the forests of Maine and the masts of Mobile, and all between. And one end resting on the Atlantic coast and the other resting on the Pacific beach, God will spring a great rainbow arch of peace, in token of everlasting covenant that the world shall nevermore see a deluge of crime.

"But," says some one, "preaching against the evils of society will accomplish nothing. Do you not see that the evils go right on?" I answer, we are not at all discouraged.

It seemed insignificant for Moses to stretch his hand over the Red Sea. What power could that have over the waters? But the East wind blew all night; the waters gathered into two glittering palisades on either side. The billows reared as God's hand pulled back upon their crystal bits. Wheel into line, O Israel! March! March! Pearls crash under the feet. The shout of hosts mounting the beach answers the shout of hosts mid-sea; until, as the last line of the Israelites have gained the beach, the shields clang, and the cymbals clap; and as the waters whelm the pursuing foe, the swift-fingered winds on the white keys of the foam play the grand march of Israel delivered, and the awful dirge of Egyptian overthrow. So we go forth, and stretch out the hand of prayer and Christian effort over these dark, boiling waters of crime and sin. "Aha! Aha!" say the deriding world. But wait. The winds of divine help will begin to blow; the way will clear for the great army of Christian philanthropists; the glittering treasures of the world's beneficence will line the path of our feet; and to the other shore we will be greeted with the clash of all heaven's cymbals; while those who resist and deride and pursue us will fall under the sea, and there will be nothing left of them but here and there, cast high and dry upon the beach, the splintered wheel of a chariot, and, thrust out from the surf, the breathless nostril of a riderless charger.

PENITENTIAL STONE CARRYING.

A CURIOUS penance was undergone recently in Brazil by the inhabitants of Larangeiras, at the instigation of two monks, who succeeded in convincing them that they had committed sin in allowing the Protestant preachers to hold services in the town. The monks characterized the preachers as thieves and assassins, and so excited the people that the native Protestants petitioned the local judge for protection for their lives and property. The Rev. J. B. Kolb, in a report to the *Church*, thus describes the tactics of the two so-called "Holy men:"

"The monks had what is called a 'day of penitence,' when the inhabitants of the town, almost to a man, followed the monks to a stone quarry, and, each one putting a stone on his head, carried them for more than a mile. The president of the province, the judges of the courts, and everybody almost were found in the procession. As they passed our home and that of some believers, they were not sparing in their remarks."

After this came the crowning act of the "mission," an "auto da fe," or burning of books. The monks ordered the people to bring their Bibles, and whatever tracts they had in their houses, and have a grand festa in burning them. Two large baskets, it is said, were brought, and as the Bibles and other printed matter were thrown into the fire, the people would cry "death" to this or that member of our church. All this was done at the foot of a great cross which the monks had had the people set up.

About a week after this had happened we arrived at Larangeiras. There was a large crowd of people at the steamer landing, which had been gathered to give us a warm reception. It had been arranged that certain persons were to have met us and warn us not to land at the peril of our lives, but they did not have the courage to do so. We landed, and, as the good Lord would have it, we were welcomed home by some persons of the highest consideration in the city. Thus was the wrath of our enemies frustrated. "It is encouraging to read that, although the missionaries were absent, the native Protestants never wavered or showed signs of faltering."

A BRAHMIN'S TRICK.

A CONVERTED Brahmin, who has recently been lecturing in Calcutta, in the course of his remarks described an incident which he says first shook his faith in the doctrines and ceremonies of the native religion. He said:

"At the annual festival in connection with the worship of the god *Mohadeva*, whose name you may have heard, I was selected to officiate at his altar. My duty consisted in placing a few leaves of the *Tulshi* tree on the head of the god, *Mohadeva*, and repeating a verse from the *Veda*, the sacred book of the Hindus, until the leaves would fall down. I was told that the leaves would fall of themselves, which would be taken as a sign that the god had been pleased, and the worshippers received his favor. I did as I was directed, and the women, who fasted all the previous day, prostrated themselves on the ground, in the belief that they would accelerate the falling down of the leaves thereby. Having placed the leaves of the *Tulshi* tree, I began repeating the verse from the *Veda*, and the women remained inside the temple in the position I have described, while a number of men stood outside calling on the name of their god, and asking him to bestow his favor on them. Well, I continued repeating the verse for full two hours, and anxiously waiting for the falling down of the leaves, but the leaves would not fall. The women, who thought that a great calamity would soon take place in our village, began to strike their heads against the ground, while the men busied themselves in the discussion of the cause or causes which might have led the god, *Mohadeva*, to show his disfavor in this way.

"At this juncture a priest, more experienced in the art of worshipping the gods and goddesses, came to our rescue. He was provided with a cushion near the god, and began to repeat the same verse that I was repeating. To my great surprise, he finished the business in five minutes, and there was great joy in the company of the worshippers. You might ask, How did he do it? Well, I shall tell you how he did it. Having taken his seat near the god, he in the pretence of repeating the verse from the *Veda*, lowered his head a little towards the altar, and blew away the leaves by the breath of his mouth. I was near him, hence I was able to detect the deception. This act of the priest shook my faith in the Hindu gods."

A CHINESE INFIDEL'S EXPERIMENT.

THE disinterested kindness of a missionary has been the cause, under God, of the conversion of a Chinese infidel and his wife. One of the missionaries of the China Inland Mission says: "I visited an out-station, and met a Chinese gentleman there. He came to me, not to inquire about the truth, but about foreign science, railways, and telegraphs, etc. After I had satisfied his curiosity, I took the opportunity to speak to him about spiritual things. He said he did not believe there was a God, and if a God did exist, he did not think it was possible He would hear and answer prayer. He had tried to read the Word of God, but had found it very uninteresting. I told him, 'If you wish to read it and to understand it you must pray to God, you must have the Holy Spirit. Then you will be able to understand that book; and I can tell you that you will find it the most wonderful book you ever read.' I urged him very earnestly to come to Christ. I felt a special responsibility, and as he went away I said I would pray for him. He said to himself, 'This is very strange; here is a *foreign devil*, who is so interested about my salvation and my eternal welfare that he will pray for me—it is very odd, to say the least of it.' The more he thought of it the stranger it became. He said, 'I will pray as an experiment.' He went into his room and prayed—he had no idea that anything would come of it, it was a mere experiment—and then he read a few verses of Scripture. He kept on for months, and he found the Word of God became more and more interesting, until he found he was a new creature in Christ Jesus, and that light had come into his soul. He was afraid to tell anyone about it, but at last he decided to speak to his wife, and told her the story of God's love. He expected that she would be angry; but, instead of that, she said, 'That is exactly what my heart has been longing for all my life.' She too became a true Christian."

A HUSBAND'S FAITH.

THE following testimony to Divine Healing recently given at Bethshan is reported in *Thy Healer*:*

Mr. J. Harris, a Gospel Union evangelist, said: I came to Bethshan five weeks ago to hear about Divine Healing. I did not seem to get much satisfaction to my mind, but I came again. I was something like Thomas, and could not believe unless I had seen; and when I had seen some slight cases, Satan tempted me as regards their genuineness. But the Lord's will was to show me something very definite. Last Wednesday morning I received a telegram from my dear mother, telling me to go home at once, as my wife was seriously ill. The enemy said, "What about your Divine Healing now? Your wife will be dead before there is a train for you to go and see her." I went on my knees, and said: "Lord, tell me what Thou art going to do with my wife?" The words of Christ came to me with much force: "This sickness is not unto death, but for the glory of God, that the Son of God might be glorified thereby." I did not then trouble about the train, but went by the first one possible.

My friends met me at the station, and said: "I am afraid you are too late." We hurried home as fast as the horse could take us. My dear mother said: "You are too late." The doctor also told me I was too late. Another doctor met me on the stair, and said: "Ah! Mr. Harris, you are too late." Another doctor—for there were three engaged in the case—met me higher up, and said: "You cannot come higher up at present; it is too late." The enemy said: "What about your faith now? What about your Healer now?" But the words kept ringing in my soul, "Not unto death." The third doctor then said: "You may just come in." I went in and took my wife's cold, icy hand in my own. "The enemy said: "What do you think now?" There was not a word from her lips. She was cold, yet my faith still claimed from God.

Presently my wife opened her eyes. I said: "You are very sick." "Yes," she said, "I am going to die." "No, my dear," I said, "God is going to bring you through, He is going to bring you off more than conqueror." I said to the three doctors and hospital nurse: "Can you do any more?" "Nothing," they said. "Now, God," I said, on my knees, "it is Thy turn now;" and God did answer prayer in a wonderful way. I left my wife on Saturday morning, progressing most wonderfully. I have to thank Him for the lesson, and for what He is teaching me. My prayer is that I may know more of God.

* *Thy Healer and Faith Witness*, a monthly magazine, edited by Mrs. M. Baxter, contains original articles on Holiness and Healing, Authentic Testimonies of Divine Healing, and Items of Intelligence from Heathen Lands where Missionaries are laboring in faith, soliciting no help from man, but relying solely on God for support. Annual Subscription, 75 cents, may be sent to the Manager of CHRISTIAN HERALD, 63 Bible House, New York.

A STOLEN SON RESTORED.

A DISCOVERY which has made several persons happy is reported in a despatch from Camden, N. J., to the New York *World*. It appears that a Philadelphia reporter recently made the acquaintance of a young man, whose history interested him, and which he published in his journal. The young man, who is twenty years old, has been wandering over the United States for nearly twelve twelve years, not knowing where he came from. He never had a name until the Centennial year, when he was abandoned in Philadelphia by a man whom he knew as "Jim." At the direction of this man he called himself John Burns, and by that name he has known himself since that time. The first he remembers of his existence is of his wandering over Pennsylvania with this "Jim" and two other men, who he says were thieves, and who tried to make a thief of him. When he refused to steal, they beat him and treated him like a dog.

After being cast adrift, he wandered to Bath, Me. From there he went to Bangor, where a kind-hearted farmer took him in and gave him all the schooling he ever got. He drifted from there to Lowell, Mass., to towns in New York State, and then to a Pennsylvania town within half a dozen miles of Beaver Falls. Then he went down to Philadelphia and over to Camden. That was about two years ago, and he has resided there ever since, working in Anderson's canning factory. He is a sober, industrious, and honest young man, and has gained lots of friends who have become deeply interested in his life's story. A few days after the history of his case was published in the Philadelphia newspaper, the young man got a letter from a gentleman at Beaver Falls, urging him to send on his picture, and as many details of his history as were possible. He replied to this letter, inclosing his picture. Three days after, there came another and longer letter from his correspondent. He and all his friends remarked the strong family resemblence of Burns's picture to themselves and their children. They said their boy was stolen when he was two and a half years old, or about eighteen years ago, and that in spite of all their efforts they could never get a clue to him. They are satisfied that he is their son, as he bears a peculiar mark on his neck, which, in addition to his resemblance of feature, is a convincing proof of his identity. The young man set out the next day to visit them. He said that all that night he was unable to sleep for joy at the thought of finding his family. His separation was involuntary, and he had only to be informed of his father's home to seek reunion; but those voluntary wanderers from their heavenly Father may be assured that they would experience still greater joy if they would seek His face. We know, too, that in Heaven also, there is rejoicing over the returning wanderer. (Luke 15:10.)

A COLPORTEUR'S WORK IN AUSTRIA.

IN the report sent to the American Bible Society, by its agent in Prague, several incidents are mentioned of an encouraging character. One Colporteur writes: "Entering a poor dwelling, I saw the father lying very ill on a miserable bed. Offering the Scriptures at the usual price, a feeble voice from the bed replied: 'What can I do with that? My children need food.' Upon this the poor mother began to weep. There stood the children, just home from school, begging for bread, but there was no bread nor any money in the house. The words of Christ, 'Give ye them to eat,' came to me with such force that I could not do otherwise than go to the nearest bakery and purchase bread for the hungry family. Then sitting down by the bedside of the poor man, I found a willing listener to the words of Jesus. On leaving I gave him a Testament, which he received with marked gratitude, kissing the book tenderly and then weeping as I went away."

Another Colporteur writes of two recent cases that have given him pleasure. Several months ago he sold a workman a Bible. It was a new book to him and he read it earnestly for truth and light. Meeting him not long since, the man told him of his joy and faith, and of Christ's help in emergency. In the factory where he worked there was something very difficult to be repaired. All hesitated to undertake it. The foreman asked this man if he would attempt it. "With God's help, I will." While others were preparing to help him, he went to a quiet corner for earnest prayer. The divine blessing was not withheld, and the difficult task was soon accomplished.

"The other case was of *a man of bad reputation* who had long abused and neglected his family, who had, in frequent absences from home, indulged in all forms of sin and vice. He returned to the village where I was stopping. Seeing him one day walking away from town, I followed him, and soon persuaded him to buy a Bible, which he promised to read diligently. After some weeks I had the pleasure of meeting him again and of finding he was quite a changed man, penitent for his sinful life, and fully resolved to live according to the good book that had brought him light."

A SEPTUAGENARIAN BUDDHIST.

AN earnest old lady, on the verge of three-score years and ten, waited on the Rev. J. W. Stevenson, one Sunday afternoon, during his residence in a town of eastern China, where he was the only Christian missionary among nearly 300,000 heathen. She introduced herself as "a very religious person," and, with the air of a connoisseur, asked to have the new religion explained to her. She said: "Every religion I have heard of I have attached myself to. Will you please tell me about this religion? How much money shall I have to pay? what journeys shall I have to make? and what prayers shall I have to offer?" "I could see the woman was intensely in earnest," says Mr. Stevenson, "and I listened to her story. She told me she had abstained from animal food for eighteen years, and she had a room fitted up full of idols, and she had got up every morning at four o'clock, and on her knees, counting over her beads, kept on repeating the name of Buddha. Every hundred beads counted would reckon ten cents to her credit in the next world, and lessen her sufferings in purgatory. Poor woman! I told her about the Lord Jesus Christ coming down from heaven, and I explained it to her, but she could not understand it. The gracious character of the gospel was utterly opposed to her ideas, and she went on mumbling Buddha's name, counting her beads and plying me with questions. Months afterwards she came again and said, "I cannot understand this religion of yours—it seems a puzzle. I have been trying to believe, but I cannot—it is the most difficult task I have ever attempted." At last she got light, and the Holy Spirit revealed the Lord Jesus Christ and His perfect work. Then peace flowed into her soul; she laid aside her beads, her idols, and other things, and gave up her trust in her good deeds. She came to live near to us, so that she might attend all the services and the prayers, morning and evening.

NOTES OF THE RECENT PROPHETIC CONFERENCE IN PARIS.

WHAT is supposed to be the first Advent Conference ever held in the French capital, was convened in Miss De Broen's Mission Hall, Belleville, on Wednesday March 14. The Revs. Messrs. Pym, H. Gill, J. Anderson, M. Wood, Dr. Anderson, from Sweden, etc., spoke.

The *Rev. Melville Pym* said that this gathering was not for the purpose of bringing forward any special or minute prophetic views, but of meditating upon the general fundamental truth of the speedy Second Advent of Christ. The first promise to this effect was given in the Garden of Eden, "The Seed of the Woman shall bruise the Serpent's Head." About 4,000 years afterwards this promise began to be fulfiled, when the Babe of Bethlehem was born, and in due time died for the ungodly upon the Cross, but before doing so, He said to His disciples, "I go away to prepare a place for you, and I will come again to receive you to Myself." And then after His crucifixion and resurrection two angels announced to His disciples, "This same Jesus which is taken from you, shall so come in like manner as He has been taken." The Jews for the most part neglected to discern

The Signs of the Times,

and to recognize that the time of Christ's First Advent was arrived. Many are committing the same mistake now with reference to His Second Advent. Surely it is our duty to strive diligently, with God's help, to do His Will, to prepare for our Saviour's Advent, and to show forth the praises of Him who has called us out of darkness into light. I once saw the Sandwich Islands, so fertile and beautiful, the hill from which the idolatrous natives in this century cast their idols into the sea. Now we, too, have an idol, if there is anything in our hearts which takes a place above the Lord Jesus. And it is impossible for us to be in a proper attitude of waiting for the Lord from heaven, if we have any cherished idol in our heart. Do we show love to all our other brethren in Christian work? Let us ask ourselves, is our work a labor of love? Do we manifest the same love as was exhibted towards the prodigal son by his Father? Are we humble, like Him who is meek and lowly? A gentleman travelling in America was kind to a little girl travelling with her mother. At the end of the journey she asked him, "Does my gentleman love Jesus?" The question followed him till it led to his conversion. Let us similarly be zealous to win souls to Christ, and to aim to have the same mind in us which was in Christ Jesus.

The *Rev. Howard Gill* contended, and in proof cited and explained the second chapter of Titus, that the subject of the Lord's Second Coming is the most practical in the Bible. The servant who believes his Master is at the door will be

In Readiness for His Return.

The Old Testament, the Epistles, the Apocalypse, are full of the snbject, and this Scriptural attitude was much more attained by the early Church than by the Church of the present day.

The *Rev. Mr. Lewis* said: To the child of God, although not to the man of the world, the Second Advent is full of practical importance, exerting an influence upon his actions every day of his life. The Book of Revelation, which is tabooed and shunned by so many, is the only book in the Bible commencing with a spiritual blessing upon its perusal. The Early Church were ever looking for Christ *from* heaven, but modern Christians are looking for Him *in* heaven, expecting to leave this earth to meet Christ *in* heaven. The *Seventh Day* of 1,000 years is now about to dawn, as we are, according to the most reliable chronology, arrived

Nearly at the End

of the Six Days of 1,000 years each, as typified by the Six Days of Creation, according to the general belief of the Primitive Church. What manner of persons should we be in all holy conversation in view of these things?

The *Rev. Mr. Anderson*, minister of the Congregational church meeting in the Rue Royale, Paris, said: Some affirm that Christ will come only spiritually—that He comes in dispensations of His providence, or in the infliction of judgments, or in the bestowment of spiritual and temporal blessings, such as the abolition of slavery, and the removal of abuses, and to destroy the Man of sin, who will soon be desolating the earth; and that thus the world will grow better and better. But the Word of God says that Christ will come personally and visibly to restore all things (Acts 3:21) to a state of comparative purity and innocency, and to set up His throne of temporal government over the House of David and over all the Gentiles. Instead of the world growing better, it will deteriorate and retrogress until Christ's Second Coming, to the state it was in in the days of Noah, when the whole earth was full of violence and all flesh had corrupted its way upon this globe; and its wickedness provoked the wholesale destruction of the Flood. In

The Last Days

evil men and seducers are to wax worse and worse, deceiving and being deceived. The Apostle Paul also says that in the last days perilous times shall come, and scoffers arise, saying, Where is the promise of His Advent? If the world is to become good and righteous before the return of Christ, we could never hope to see Him come back at all. But it is His personal return that will cause righteousness to cover the earth, as the waters cover the channels of the great deep

Now we are not to wait in idleness and inactivity for Christ's Second Coming; but the command is, "Occupy till I come". There were many types given in the Bible by which the manifold character of that occupation is made clear. We should imitate Noah, who warned the Antediluvians as a preacher of righteousness. We should be diligent Christian *preachers*, and at the same time *builders*, in a sense, of an ark of refuge for our perishing fellow-creatures, by bringing salvation to their very doors, and compelling them to come in, and sit down at the Marriage Supper of the Lamb. We should

Imitate the Angels

in Sodom, who laid hold of Lot and his family, and brought them out of the city of destruction to the hill of safety. We should be laboring to snatch sinners as brands from the burning and to rescue the perishing, if we truly believe in the speedy Advent of Christ. We should resemble the wise virgins of the Parable, holding forth the lamp of light, and of Scriptural instruction to our fellow-men. We should be like the diligent servants, putting out the pound entrusted to us to usury, so that it may become ten pounds. We should be found in the attitude of the Bride waiting for the Bridegroom. Like sheep waiting for their shepherd to lead them into green pastures, and beside still waters. Like obedient subjects, willing that this Man should reign over us. And like good seed, not tares, furnishing spiritual food for others.

CURRENT EVENTS.

The Important Financial Measure Authorizing the Secretary of the Treasury to use any part of the surplus that, in his judgment, is expedient for the purchase of bonds in the open market, which, as stated in these columns on March 8, has passed the House, also passed the Senate last week, but in an amended form. The most important of the amendments provides for buying silver bullion to the amount of bank circulation that may be surrendered, if not taken out again by other banks within thirty days, and coining it into standard dollars in excess of the minimum of $2,000,000 per month, now required by law. Senator Beck, of Kentucky, was the author of this proposition. Its adoption by a vote of thirty-eight to thirteen, is considered a decided victory of the advocates of unlimited silver coinage. It is taken for granted by Senators of both parties that the House conferees will accept the bill as passed by the Senate, and that it will go to the President in that shape. If so, Mr. Cleveland is very likely to veto it, unless his views have changed very much since 1885, when, before his inauguration, he wrote to Congressman Warner and others his famous anti-silver letter.

A Change of the Day of Inauguration of the President from March 4 to April 30, and a change of the date of the meeting of Congress, so as to bring that body together two months after its election, instead of thirteen months, as now, was the object of a joint resolution introduced in the House of Representatives in the early part of the present session. It was called up last week, and defeated by a vote of 80 to 154. The Republican members strongly opposed the inauguration day change, because it would extend the term of the President nearly two months; and the Republicans and Democrats alike objected to the Congressional change, on the ground that it would involve changes in Senatorial as well as Representative terms, and produce confusion; and by one member the suggestion was made that thirteen months was not too long a time to give a newly elected member to arrange his own business concerns, so as to admit of his attending Congress and become familiar with the rules of the House and the business that would come before it. Thus the constitutional provision regarding the Presidential term and the meeting of the national legislature, will remain undisturbed for the present.

The Education of the Indians is the Subject of a letter written by President Cleveland in response to a resolution adopted by the Philadelphia Annual Conference of the Methodist Episcopal Church protesting "against the recent action of the Government in excluding the use of native languages in the education of the Indians, and especially the exclusion of the Dakota Bible among those tribes where it was formerly used." The President says this protest must have been based upon a misconception of the Government policy and the rules of the Indian Bureau. "It will not do," he explains, "to permit these wards of the nation, in their preparation to become their own masters, to indulge in their barbarous language because it is easier for them or because it pleases them." This rule, however, applies only to secular teaching, and "surely there can be no objection to reading a chapter in the Bible in English, or in Dakota, if English could not be understood, at the daily opening of those schools, as is done in very many other well-regulated secular schools." As regards missionary schools, moral and religious instruction may be given in the Indian language as an auxiliary to English. The President then says that provision is made for the theological training of young men in missionary schools to fit them as Indian preachers, and the possession and use of the Bible, so far as it does not interfere with the secular English teaching, insisted upon, is especially secured. As to the rules of the Indian Bureau, the President thinks "there need be no fear that in their execution they will at all interfere with the plans of those who sensibly desire the improvement and welfare of the Indians. At any rate, until it is demonstrated that these rules operate as impediments to Indian advancement, they will be adhered to, while the Government will continue to invoke assistance of all Christian people and organizations in this very important and interesting part of the labor intrusted to it."

The International Council of Women, recently in session at Washington, previous to final adjournment formulated its objects, aims, and demands, as follows: It is the unanimous voice of the Council that all institutions of learning and of professional instruction, including schools of theology, law, and medicine, should, in the interests of humanity, be as freely opened to women as to men; that opportunities for industrial training should be as generally and liberally provided for one sex as for the other; and the representatives of organized womanhood in this Council will steadily demand that in all avocations in which both men and women engage, equal wages shall be paid for equal work; and, finally, that an enlightened society should demand the only adequate expression of the high civilization which is its office to establish and maintain—an identical standard of personal purity and morality for men and women.

The Great Railroad Strike in the West, which has of late been attended by various acts of violence, is again confined to the Chicago, Burlington and Quincy Railroad. The workmen on the other roads connecting with the "Burlington," who had refused to handle trains or cars containing freight for its lines, have raised this boycott and returned to work, with the understanding that they will refrain from any discrimination in the handling of freight. The withdrawal of these "sympathetic" strikers from their brothers of the "Burlington" is a heavy blow for the latter. Chief Arthur is reported having favored the raising of the boycott. The strike on the Burlington road has now been in force since February 27.

A Terrible Railroad Accident Occurred on April 5, four miles west of New Hampton, Iowa, on the Milwaukee and St. Paul Railroad. A passenger train plunged into a swollen creek, the bridge of which was washed out. A scene of the wildest confusion ensued, and it was with great difficulty that the passengers could be reached, owing to the rushing of the waters through the car windows. Nine persons lost their lives, and about twenty were injured, some of them so dangerously that it is feared they cannot recover. There had been nothing to show that there was danger ahead, and the train plunged into the swollen stream while running at full speed.

The Probability of the Resignation of Prince Bismarck as Chancellor of the German Empire is announced by no less an authority than the Cologne *Gazette*. It is officially denied, but little credence is placed in these denials. The motive for Bismarck's intended retirement is said to be the proposed marriage of Prince Alexander of Battenberg and Princess Victoria of Prussia, the second daughter of the Emperor of Germany. "Until the Bulgarian question shall have been settled," says the Cologne *Gazette*, "the projected marriage can only be judged from a political point of view, and on that account the marriage is an impossibility. The German policy has its root in the endeavor to avoid anything that would be likely to arouse the slightest inducement for suspicion. As long as Bulgaria is in question, this course of action affords the only means of retaining the full confidence of the opposing Governments. That confidence would be disturbed in an instant if the Czar's most detested antagonist were to become the son-in-law of Emperor Frederick." It is believed in Germany, that the arrangement of the marriage is to be charged to Queen Victoria, the mother of the Empress, who has become infatuated with the Battenbergs; and with the tenacity characteristic of her race clings to her infatuation the more firmly for the opposition it excites. She is about to visit, her daughter at Berlin, and it was expected that the betrothal would be announced during her visit but as such an announcement will involve the resignation of Bismarck, it is likely to be postponed.

Emperor Frederick of Germany is Reported gaining in strength. The London *Lancet* says that while the condition of the larynx is unchanged, the Emperor's general strength has increased. He is able to perform some official acts, and has issued an amnesty decree. The offences to which it applies are: insulting the sovereign; crimes and misdemeanors in the exercise of civil rights; insulting or resisting officers of the law; disturbing the public order; press offences; infractions of the law of public meeting, &c. The Emperor has also addressed a rescript to the Minister of War, recommending changes in army tactics in keeping with the progress made in the art of manufacturing fire-arms. Another rescript, addressed to Prince Bismarck, is to the effect that he desires to follow his father's example and to labor with his entire strength for the welfare of the German people.

The Appalling Earthquake in China, a brief report of which was received in January, shortly after its occurrence, appears to have been more disastrous to both life and property than was then supposed. A lengthy despatch from China was published by the New York *Herald* on April 2, from which it appears that not less than *fifteen thousand persons were killed* during the four days during which at short intervals the shocks continued. The capital district of Yunnan is absolutely one mass of ruins. At Lainon, another Chinese town, the effect on buildings has been almost as terrible, with the additional horror of the earth yawning till a frightful chasm was produced, from which red-colored water was ejected. Further north, at Lo Chan, where ten thousand met their doom, the aspect of the country has been completely changed. Large tracts of land suddenly disappeared in the course of the visitation, and in their place lakes formed.

One of Those Brutal Mexican Exhibitions, a bull fight, was given in the town of Zelaya on Easter Sunday. It ended in a frightful catastrophe. Some prisoners who had obtained permission to attend the savage performance set fire to the amphitheatre, which was rapidly enveloped in flames. Eighteen persons were burned to death, and sixty-eight others so seriously injured that some of them are not expected to survive. Fifty other persons were knocked down and trampled upon by the panic-stricken audience and badly injured. The bulls, maddened by the roaring of the flames, broke loose from their stalls and rushed wildly through the surging mass of humanity, tossing aloft and knocking over all who stood in their way. Among the eighteen dead were two women, who were first gored to death by the bulls and their bodies afterward burned. The prisoners who had caused the disaster made their escape. Surely, the desecration of the Sabbath by such a vile exhibition had fearful consequence for those making the Lord's Day a season of wicked sports.

Sunday-school Superintendents and Teachers desirous of distributing copies of The Christian Herald in their schools and classes, may have assorted parcels of back numbers by applying, stating number required, to the manager, 63 Bible House.

The Rev. Jacob Freshman's Tour in the South has resulted in stirring up the Christian public to an increased interest in the evangelization of the Jews. He held large meetings in Philadelphia, Baltimore, Md., Washington, D. C., and extended his tour to Richmond, Va. In all the cities he visited, he made his way to the quarters chiefly occupied by the Hebrew residents, and distributed large quantities of Hebrew-Christian literature and conversed with the people. He returned in time to hold his services in the Hebrew-Christian Church in St. Marks Place, New York. The work going on there is of a most encouraging character. Inquirers increase in number and baptisms are frequently taking place of Jews who, under Mr. Freshman's earnest preaching and private conversation, have come to recognize in Jesus of Nazareth their Messiah. Mr. Freshman has excellent plans for extending his work in New York and other cities, but at present, lack of funds prevents his executing them. He depends solely on voluntary contributions, and would be grateful for help, however small. His address is 17 St. Mark's Place, New York.

An Interesting Wedding was Solemnized last week at the Florence mission for fallen women in New York. Both bride and bridegroom are described as being from "the salvage of the big city." The bride, Miss Kitty Eagan, was converted at the Florence mission, and the bridegroom, Mr. James Edwards, who is a Scotchman, was converted at the Jerry McAuley mission. The latter is a reformed drunkard. He hasn't touched a drop of liquor for two years, and though before his reformation he was in abject poverty, he is now earning his $4.50 a day as a bricklayer. His wife also has given good evidence of her change of heart and life; she has entirely reformed, and for six months past has been the assistant matron at the Florence mission. The wedding ceremony was performed by the Rev. Stephen Merritt, who presented the happy couple with a fine illuminated Bible as a wedding gift. The young couple, as they received the congratulations of their friends, looked the picture of happiness.

Ignorance was Punished as a Crime by a Judge in Newark, N. J., on April 4. The prisoner brought before him for sentence was a practicing physician, who, in treating a patient, had blundered so grossly that the patient died. Medical witnesses had testified that under proper treatment she would have recovered, and the jury, believing their evidence, convicted the physician of manslaughter. The Judge, in passing sentence of six months' imprisonment, said: "You were actuated, doubtless, by good motives. If you had known the right you would gladly have done it. Your crime was ignorance. As a result of your ignorance and incompetence the life intrusted to you was lost, and the law holds you accountable. The public must be protected, and those who are ignorant and unskilful made to understand that they cannot, with impunity, trifle with human life." There are men occupying our pulpits, who, at the day of final account, will discover that this principle applies to them. Through ignorance of God's Word they are preaching error, and the souls of their hearers, being deluded, are being lost. Though their motives may be good, they will be held accountable. (Ezek. 33: 6.)

The Construction of an Alien-Sifting Machine is a work urged on Congress by Senator Palmer, of Michigan, and seven other statesmen, who have each attempted the task in definite measures. Senator Palmer in a recent interview said it was "about time we as a nation went out of the asylum business," as already the inmates of lunatic asylums and prisons were chiefly of foreign birth; and in New York State, of the foreign born population, one in every thirty-five was supported by the people in the almshouses, while they contained only one in a hundred and sixty-eight of the native population. Senator Palmer's project is to refuse admission to every immigrant not provided with a certificate from the United States consul of the district from which he comes, and to compel the consul, under penalties, to make diligent inquiry before granting the certificate as to the antecedents of the intending immigrant, to satisfy himself that the man is neither criminal, lunatic, pauper, anarchist, Mormon, nor laborer under contract. This system, the Senator thinks, would sift out undesirable immigrants, and give us *only the best.* If it should go into operation it will exclude even those wrongdoers who desire to reform, and begin a new life in the New World. Happily for them no such system excludes them from that better kingdom, the Founder of which sought for His subjects, not "the best," but the lost (Matt. 9: 13.)

A Perilous Escape from a Desert Island was accomplished by a citizen of Michigan recently. He and a friend went on a yachting expedition along the coast of the Gulf of Mexico. During a storm they were cast on the rocks of a small uninhabited island about two miles from the mainland. Their boat was wrecked, and after three days they began to give up all hopes of rescue, no boats passing near the island. Some wild berries which grew there served to prevent starvation. On the fifth day one of them decided to try and reach the mainland by swimming. After a severe struggle he succeeded in reaching the shore at a point several miles from any habitation. He was nearly naked, and had to walk along the flinty coast for six miles before he saw a human being, to whom he related his story. He was taken in charge, and after several hours a boat was found to bring off the other man, who had by this time given his companion up for dead and resigned himself to his fate. If a vessel had come to the island before the desperate expedient of swimming was tried, how gladly the two men would have welcomed the means of escape! Yet spiritual castaways, though in worse danger, reject the offer of salvation brought to them by the life-boat of the gospel (Heb. 2: 3).

The Practice of Shanghaeing Will Probably receive a check from a sentence pronounced on a ship's captain in the United States Court at Baltimore, Md., on April 5. It appears that some time ago three young men passed through Baltimore on their way from New York to Atlanta, Ga. They went out in the evening for a walk and were met by a stranger who invited them to drink, and they accepted his invitation. He afterward invited them to go for a sail in his pleasure yacht, and took them on board that night, as he said the yacht would sail early in the morning. They were too stupefied with liquor to perceive the character of the vessel when they went on board, but the next morning they found they were on an oyster vessel. They state that they were brutally treated, and were forced to work like galley-slaves at the oyster grounds, and narrowly escaped with their lives. On their complaint the captain was arrested on his return to Baltimore, and being convicted, was last Thursday sentenced to sixty days imprisonment and to pay a fine of one hundred dollars. It is hoped that this exemplary punishment will serve as a warning to other captains who are in the habit of recruiting their crews by stealing men in our ports. It will be well also if the account the victims give of their sufferings saves others from being similarly entrapped. Unhappily the painful experience of one person does not always suffice to put others on their guard, or the testimonies of those who have been delivered from Satan's bonds would have long ago kept men from falling into his snares. (Job. 12: 5.)

A Mammoth Hotel Drawn by Locomotives, was a spectacle which attracted thousands of spectators to Coney Island on April 3. The Brighton Beach Hotel—an edifice 460 feet long and 130 feet wide, covering nearly an acre and a half of ground, and worth a quarter of a million dollars—was in danger of being swept away by the sea, which is rapidly encroaching on the island. During the winter the waves have undermined the hotel, and it was determined to move it bodily to a site nearly six hundred feet farther from the water. Excavations were made, and huge beams placed under the building. Underneath these were placed a hundred and twelve iron platform cars, which rested on twenty-four railroad tracks previously laid from the hotel to its proposed site. Heavy cables, rove on tackles, were then attached to the hotel and connected with six powerful locomotives. When all was ready for the journey the signal was given, and the six engines, pouring out volumes of steam, applied their strength to their five thousand ton burden. There was a straining and snapping of the cables, but soon the building was seen to be moving slowly, and before night it had travelled one-fourth of its journey without the fall of a bit of plaster or the disturbance of a board. The expense of moving the hotel is estimated at fifty thousand dollars. Men who build on the sand are not always so successful in saving their property from destruction. In this case skill and ingenuity have averted the catastrophe for the time, but for those persons whom the Saviour compared to such builders, there are no means of escape available, and their eternal ruin is inevitable. (Matt. 7: 26, 27.)

BRIEF NOTES.

Every man on the Kansas City police force is, it is said, a church member. Two of the officers are elders in the church, and a number of them are deacons.

The local option campaign in Michigan has closed for the summer. Of thirty-seven counties that have voted on the question, all but two gave majorities for prohibition.

The Franz Brewery, in Sioux City, Ia., managed by John Arensdorf at the time of Rev. Haddock's murder, has become a butter and egg depot since the adoption of Prohibition in Iowa.

Mr. and Miss Parker, the evangelists from Mr. C. H. Spurgeon's church, have been holding revival meetings at Bristol, Pa. During the fifteen days of their mission large numbers were led to Christ.

The Woman's Christian Temperance Union of Cleveland had been invited by the Common Council of that city to name two women who shall act as janitor and matron at the Central Police Station.

In the recent elections in Massachusetts, out of 102 towns, 82 voted against and 20 for license. In a total vote of 33,908, the majority against license is 7,826; an increase of more than 1,000 over the majority last year.

At St. James Episcopal Church, Chicago, Ill., an entirely silent service was recently conducted. It was the baptism of the child of two deaf mutes, and the sermon was preached in the sign language by a clergyman who was a deaf-mute.

Major J. H. Cole commenced services at Warrensburg, Mo., on the conclusion of his work at Carthage. In the latter town nearly seven hundred persons gave their testimony to faith in Christ, as the result of God's blessing on his labors.

A Parisian astrologer has cast the horoscope of General Boulanger, and had the result sold by peddlers in the Paris streets. He asserts that the General is destined to overthrow Germany on November 7, 1890, and to become President of the Republic in May, 1891.

The present Prime Minister of the Sandwich Islands is an earnest Christian. When he visited Berlin, in connection with a commercial treaty, it was his practice to attend Bible readings on Sunday nights, and he found it easy to decline diplomatic invitations on the Lord's Day.

Judge Wm. A. Cheney, of California, says, that during his term as a criminal judge, out of every one thousand cases which came before him, whisky had something to do with making the criminal in nine hundred. He adds that, in his opinion, it is the greatest evil on earth, and that he will die before another drop passes his lips.

Messrs. Brown & Avis have been enabled to do an excellent work at Central City, Neb. Not only have large numbers been converted at the meetings in the Opera House, but a spirit of unity and brotherly feeling has been seen rapidly growing in the churches, as the ministers and members have been brought into contact as fellow-laborers in the revival.

The oldest man in the world is said to be James James, a colored citizen of the United States, who resides in Santa Rosa, Mexico. He is 135 years old. He was born near Dorchester, S. C., in 1752. He was one of the laborers at Fort Moultrie during the unsuccessful attack by the British fleet in 1776. He was then twenty-four years old. His master, James James, manned one of the guns during the fight. His last owner was Henry James, who moved to Mexico in 1858 in order that his slaves might become free before his death.

HEARING AND SIGHT.

A New Sermon by Pastor C. H. Spurgeon.

"As we have heard, so have we seen in the City of the Lord of Hosts, in the City of our God: God will establish it for-ever." Psalms 48 : 8.

Sight not Always Confirming Hearing—Reports That do not Bear Investigation—When Sight Surpasses Hearing—I. Importance of Listening to True Witnesses—The Voice of the Bible—Of the Prophets—Of the Fathers—A Misunderstood Test—A Universal Taster—II. Good Hearing Leading to Seeing—Inviting to See by Examining Facts—Testing the Promises—Cheques Needing Presentation—III. The Truth Confirmed—Experience of Repentance—Of Regeneration—Of Answered Prayer—IV. Seeing Leads to Witnessing—V. Brings Fuller Assurance.

"As we have heard, so have we seen:" this is seldom true. In many places we see what we have not heard, and what we have heard we do not see. Time was when many simpletons believed that the streets of London were paved with gold. Ten thousand idle tales there are in every country, of mines where fortunes may be dug out of the earth, and plains where wealth forces itself on the immigrant; but how seldom do we hear the good news, "As we have heard, so have we seen."

But when you come into the "City of the Lord of Hosts, in the City of our God," the reports about it are true, and the truth exceeds the report; for, like the Queen of Sheba, we cry, "The half was not told me." When we speak of the privileges of the Church of God on earth it is impossible to exaggerate. And if we speak of the city of God as it shines in full splendor above, words fail us to set it forth. I doubt not when we arrive at its blest abodes, and tread its golden streets, and wear our crowns of immortality, we shall not only say, "As we have heard, so have we seen," but we shall be lost in wonder and surprise at the overwhelming revelations of divine love.

It is always true of the things of God, and of the Church of God—"As we have heard, so have we seen." What His Word promises, His Work performs. This thought will be the clue of my sermon, and my line of discourse will be guided by the text.

I. Our first observation upon the text is this—it is most important that we

Listen to True Witnesses;

for, else, we shall not be able to say, "As we have heard, so have we seen." If we listen to false witnesses, the more we believe them the worse for us: it will not be faith but credulity, and in due time there will be a sad awakening from the dreams. It is of the first importance to you all that you should hear the word of God, and receive the truth as it is in Jesus; so that, both in the throng of life, and when you stand upon the borders of death, and in the changeless state of eternity, you may be able to say, "We thank God for the gospel which we heard; for what we heard with our ears has been verified in our lives.

The Israelites who sang this forty-eighth Psalm had heard of Jerusalem and its Temple; of Jehovah, and of His sure defence of His chosen city: how had they heard of it?

They had heard of it by reading for themselves, or listening to the reading of the Word of God. They had five books of Moses, and other writings. In these books they read marvellous stories of what Jehovah had done for His people. They would remember well how the Lord wrought for His chosen in Egypt, and how He brought them out of the house of bondage with a high hand and outstretched arm. My brethren, attend carefully to what this Book records and reveals. It is now enlarged for your greater edification. Let this record be the report which you hear, concerning the Lord our God and His ways of grace. Let us give earnest heed to prophets and apostles and evangelists, who wrote in the name of the Lord; for in that case we shall hear truths which shall be so verified by experience, as to make us joyfully exclaim, "As we have heard, so have we seen."

These good people had also listened to *the ministers of God*. The priests, when they were not engaged in actual attendance at the Temple, were expected to teach the people. It is said of the tribe of Levi, "They shall teach Jacob Thy judgments, and Israel Thy law." Prophets also went through the land declaring the mind of God, and when the people heard these messengers, whom the Lord had sent to speak in His name, they heard that which the Lord fulfilled; for none of the words of His servants were suffered to fall to the ground. How necessary it is that you should hear the truth spoken by those that are sent of God; for many false prophets have gone forth into the world. That which a man fetcheth out of his own mind may or may not be true; in any case, you have a right to criticise and discuss it; but he that speaketh with "Thus saith the Lord" at the back of his words, stands on another platform.

No doubt, also, these good people had

Listened to Their Fathers.

In these days the proud notion is abroad, that our fathers cannot have been so wise as their highly cultured sons. Yet in the long run, these same youths will alter their opinions as their years increase. Wisdom is neither in age nor in youth, but in God alone; yet I love to hear what gray-headed men have to say, who are further advanced in the journey of life than I am; for there is weight in their testimony. They may not speak with all the brilliance and fire of youth; but their speech has salt in it, derived from the certainty of actual experience.

Some, nowadays, are inclined to hear everything, bad, good, and indifferent. I believe that hearing everything will end in hearing nothing. That text is often quoted and misunderstood, which says, "Prove all things."

False Doctrines Cannot be Proved,

and you need not make the attempt. It is only the truth which is capable of proof. The text does not mean "experiment upon everything"; but receive nothing until it has been proved to be true and good. The most of us are not appointed to the office of Universal Taster: we are not commissioned to taste all deadly things that we may know their precise effect: we are far better employed in holding fast that which is good. The truths which we have already proved to be the truth of God, we hold as with a death-grip; and, as we hold them fast, we also hold them forth.

II. Secondly, good hearing leads on to seeing—"As we have heard, so have we seen." You cannot all use those words. Some of you have heard, and heard, but have never yet seen. The man who is

Content with One Inlet

to his mind, namely, his ears, but never uses his eyes, must imagine that God has made a mistake, and has given him more senses than he needs. Surely this argues a want of sense. Dear friends, you are not only invited to hear the gospel, but the Lord Jesus says to you, as He said to His first disciples, "Come and see." "O taste and see that the Lord is good." You are invited to see for yourselves whether these things be so. You will ask, How can a hearer of the gospel become a seer of it?

Note first, that he can do this by examining the facts which he hears stated, and judging whether they are really so. The Scripture tells you that your heart is deceitful—see whether it be not so. It tells you that there is a natural inclination in man towards evil—study yourself, and see whether this is not the case. It tells you that there is in human nature an impotence towards that which is truly good, and an aversion to God. Seriously consider whether your own life, as a natural man, does not prove the truth of these charges. There are some things about yourself, while as yet you are unconverted, which you have heard of in the Scriptures, and I would urge you to see whether they are not true in your own case. It will be a great help to you if you will examine into these things in reference to your own self. The subject for consideration is near at hand, and it will be, in many ways, useful to yourself to know whether Holy Scripture gives a true description of human nature, as you find it in yourself.

We further see what we hear, when we obey the commands and receive the blessings promised upon obedience. For instance, you are bidden to confess your sins; now see whether this is true. "If we confess our sins, He is faithful and just to forgive us our sins"—not only hear the precept, but see whether

The Promise is True.

Here is another test: "Come unto me, all ye that labour and are heavy laden, and I will give you rest." You have heard it hundreds of times; come and see for yourself whether rest is given.

We also turn hearing into sight when, receiving the blessings which are promised to faith, we enter into a new life. Some of us can bear witness that we have entered into a new world; that things which are now everything to us, were nothing to us a little while ago. As to a deaf man there is no sound, as to a blind man there is no light, so to us a few years ago there were no spiritual things; for we were devoid of those spiritual faculties by which spiritual things are discerned. But, now that we have believed in Jesus, we have passed into another universe; and we now possess a life as much above the life of our former state as the mental life is above that of the brute, which perisheth. The promises of God are of little service to a man if he merely hears them or reads them, and has no further dealing with them. They are like a cheque which is kept for months and years in a drawer, and never presented at the bank.

III. I beg your attention to the third point, which is this: that seeing wonderfully

Confirms the Truth

of what we hear. We are bound to believe God, even when we cannot see. That the Lord has said it, would be quite enough for us if we reverenced Him as we ought. But it does help us very much when, having implicitly believed in God's testimony, He grants us grace to see that what we have believed is most surely true. Let me show how the experience of a believing man confirms the truth of what he has heard.

To go back to where I was just now, all that Holy Scripture says about *our ruin* may be seen to be true. Many of us have not only heard, but we have felt the evil result of sin upon our minds and hearts. We know that sin dwelleth in us, and strives for the mastery. We can never doubt that our natural tendencies are faulty, and that our best desires are imperfect. It does not matter what modern deceivers preach; you may depend upon it, that men when they come to die, if their consciences are at all awake, are persuaded that the threatenings of Holy Scripture are true. Sentiment kicks against eternal punishment; but conscience cries "Amen" to the righteous sentence of the law.

We believe in our personal desert of the wrath of God, for we are sure it is so, and our only comfort is that the sentence of death has been fulfilled in us in the death of the Lord Jesus Christ, our Substitute. All that the Holy Scripture saith about sin and its results, we do from our heart of hearts confirm, for, "As we have heard, so have we seen,"

Brighter things, however, have we heard and seen. Brethren, we heard that if we came to Jesus as we were, *He would receive us;* and He did receive us. We heard that He would graciously forgive; and He did forgive. We heard that in forgiveness, He would give us peace, and

We have Found it So.

"Being justified by faith, we have peace with God through our Lord Jesus Christ," We heard that poor sinners, justified by faith, received a joy unspeakable, and we have received that joy. We bear our testimony that "This man receiveth sinners": we bear witness that He casts out none that come to Him. We declare to you that, in the fullness of His grace, He puts rebels in the children's place. Yes, "As we have heard, so have we seen."

Then we heard that there was such a thing as *regeneration*. We used to hear with wonder that declaration, "Ye must be born again."

We were told that we must pass from death unto life: that old things must pass away, and all things must become new. We heard it attentively and believingly; but now we have gone further —we have seen it. Many of you know the great and radical change, because you have experienced it. You can say, "One thing I know, that, whereas I was blind, now I see." We have passed out of a dead world into

A Living World.

Having been buried with Christ, we have also risen with Him, and our life dwells and flourishes in a new world. We are conscious that a new heart beats within us; a new life looks out of our eyes, and moves in our members. The new birth is a fact.

Further, to show you how experience supports the Word of God, we were told many times over that *God hears prayer*. There are numbers of persons here whom any lawyer would be glad to put in the witness-box on any matter of fact; for their statements would be questioned by nobody, since they are well known for integrity and truth. These persons are prepared to bear solemn witness, as in the presence of God, that many a time God has as distinctly heard their prayers as if He had thrust His hand through yonder skies. As we have heard about prayer, so have we seen; and none can drive this faith out of us, since it is confirmed by what we have seen over and over again in actual experience. So long as reason holds her seat, we must and will believe in prayer.

Yes, let me remind you, also, that we heard with our ears, that there is a God of *Providence* who rules and over-rules all things. We were glad to sing, "The Lord will provide." We believe in a gracious providence, and we have also seen it! Time does not suffice this morning for us to narrate personal incidents, but assuredly

My Own Experience

teems with them: in times of need the Lord has showed Himself quite as able and willing to supply the needs of His servant in these days as He was to feed the nation in the wilderness when He rained manna from heaven for them, day by day. All things have worked together for good to them that love God, even until now. We can look back upon experiences which, at the time, were especially bewildering and perplexing; and of those very experiences we can now say, "Blessed be God for them!"

One thing more I will notice, and have done with these verifications which sight gives to hearing. We have often heard that those who believe in God have *hope in their deaths*. We have been told over and over again, that

> "Jesus can make a dying bed
> Feel soft as downy pillows are."

Now, we have not seen this for ourselves, for we have not yet forded the last river; but we have seen it in others. I suppose that the most of you have distinctly seen that the end of the righteous man is peace. I, from my calling have many scores of times seen saints in their last hours. This is the witness I put on record—the very happiest persons I have ever met with have been departing believers. I have not met at weddings, nor at jubilee feasts, nor in moments of singular prosperity, such joyful persons as I have seen amid weakness and pain upon their dying beds. The only sons of men for whom I have felt any envy have been dying members of this very church, whose hands I have grasped in their passing away. Saintly death-beds are grand evidences of Christianity. It is something to say in our last hours, "As we have heard, so have we seen."

I can truly say that hitherto my own experience and observation have confirmed the teachings of the Word of God. I have not yet met with anything which could shake my confidence in the divine revelation. I trust I am neither an absolute fool nor a blind bigot, who would shut his eyes to reason: I would not ignore a certified fact, either in science or history, or in the world of mental life; and yet I know of no fact which can disprove so much as one of the solemn declarations of God, nor even cast a shadow of suspicion upon a doctrine of Holy Scripture. I have *heard* much, but I have *seen* nothing of the science which disproves the Scriptures: there is no such science; it is an imposture which has stolen the name. Our knowing is far better than our theorizing; and whatever our theorizing may have done our actual knowledge has never been on the side of the baptized infidelity of the advanced school. All our experience makes us say, "As we have heard, so have we seen in the city of the Lord of hosts."

On this point I have spent the strength of my discourse; the remaining two heads shall be treated briefly, although they are of great practical value.

IV. When hearing turns to seeing, and is confirmed by it, then it

Leads to Witnessing.

The text, you see, is itself a testimony: "As we have heard, so have we seen." In these days every man that can witness for the truth ought to do so: even if he stammers, he must not be silent. So many are decrying the truth, that, if in your heart and conscience you have proved it true, you are bound to give to the Lord the testimony of even a stammerer. I suppose Moses could do no more than that, for he was a man slow in speech; but when he would have preferred to be quiet, the Lord said to him, "Who hath made man's mouth?" Your mouth is as God made it: use it as best you can, and speak up for His name and cause.

Such testimony as that of our text is *sometimes involuntary*, and is none the less precious on that account. When you have tasted and handled of the good things of God, I am sure yon will have to tell others of your glorious discoveries! your mouth will be filled with laughter, and your tongue with singing, till those who are round about you will be compelled to say, "The Lord hath done great things for them," and you will answer, "Yes, the Lord hath done great things for us; whereof we are glad." Jesus said, "Out of the mouth of babes and sucklings hast thou ordained strength," when the children were shouting in the Temple. Young converts, if they have newly tasted that the Lord is gracious, must sound out their joys. Who would stop them? If these should hold their peace, the stones would cry out. But your involuntary witnessing must lead up to constant *voluntary* witnessing for your Lord, and His holy cause. O ye who are on the Lord's side, awake, arise, or be condemned as traitors!

Our testimony should be *very frequent*. Believers would do a thousand times more good if they were not so particularly careful to avoid offending men of the world. If Christ Jesus offends people, they ought to be offended; for He is sure to be a "stumbling-stone and rock of offence" to those who stumble at the Word, being disobedient. We have heard of a great warrior, who was more at home on the field of battle than amid the ceremonies of courts; his sword nearly tripped him up when walking backwards from the throne, and his majesty remarked that his sword seemed very much in the way. "Yes," said the brave man, "*and your majesty's enemies find it so*."

V. For lastly, hearing, seeing, witnessing, God will give you a yet

Fuller Assurance

than you have as yet. Permit me to read the text again: "As we have heard, so have we seen in the city of the Lord of hosts, in the city of our God: God will establish it forever." That is the conclusion which the saint comes to when he has tried the truth for himself, and borne witness to the result of his trial. God will never leave His church. God will never forfeit His word. God will never desert His Gospel. Because He is Jehovah of hosts and changes not, and has all power at His disposal; because He is our Lord, our God in covenant. He cannot desert the work of His own hands, nor leave the people of His love. Because His honor is bound up in the whole enterprise that Christ undertook, He must go through with it, and He must arrive at a glorious conclusion. God will establish it forever. Come, my brethren, let us cast aside all doubts about what the future is to be. The battle rages, the foe is as furious as he is subtle, while we are weak as water and can do nothing by ourselves; but let us not despond; for, if the gospel be God's gospel, He will take care of it; if the church be Christ's Church, the gates of hell cannot prevail against her. The battle is not ours, but the Lord's: in His name let us set up our banners and cry with full confidence of victory, "The Lord of hosts is with us; the God of Jacob is our refuge." Hallelujah, hallelujah. Amen.

GEMS FROM NEW BOOKS.

THE FOUNDER OF MORMONISM*

AN unpleasing picture has been drawn of Joseph Smith by one who knew him as a boy, and by another, who perhaps studied his character at closer range and from a more intimate personal acquaintance. Between twelve and thirteen years of age he is remembered by this witness as "a dull-eyed, flaxen-haired, prevaricating boy, noted only for his indolent and vagabondish character, and habits of exaggeration and untruthfulness. He seldom spoke to anyone outside of his intimate associates, except when first addressed by another, and then, by reason of his extravagances of statement, his word was received with least confidence by those who knew him best. He could utter the most palpable exaggeration or marvellous absurdity with the utmost apparent gravity. He nevertheless evidenced the rapid development of a thinking, plodding, evil-brewing mental composition—largely given to inventions of low cunning, schemes of mischief and deception, and false and mysterious pretensions. He was, however, proverbially good-natured, very rarely, if ever, indulging in any combative spirit toward any one, whatever might be the provocation."

As the boy advanced in years he developed a mental attitude that, amid more favoring circumstances, and under the stress os some moral encouragement, might have grown to fullness. His reading took a theological turn, and the Bible became a book of daily study. His mind was retentive; he was possessed of a rude eloquence of speech, and had that rare power of expression that, to the strangers or the simple, would seem the outward form of a sincere belief within.

A Remarkable Document.

It has been again and again quoted that even Brigham Young declared that "the prophet was of mean birth; that he was wild, intemperate, even dishonest and tricky in his youth." Smith's neighbors gave the same testimony. Eleven of the most prominent and respectable citizens of Manchester, N. Y., under date of November 3, 1833, affixed their names to this emphatic declaration: We, the undersigned, being personally acquainted with the family of Joseph Smith, Sen., with whom the so-called Gold Bible originated, state: that they were not only a lazy, indolent set of men, but also intemperate, and their word was not to be depended upon; and that we are truly glad to dispense with their society."

As if the above did not cover the ground with force and exactness, a supplemental declaration was made on December 4, 1833, and signed by sixty-two residents of Palmyra: "We, the undersigned, have been acquainted with the Smith family for a number of years, while they resided near this place, and we have no hesitation in saying that we consider them destitute of that moral character which ought to entitle them to the confidence of any community. They were particularly famous for visionary projects; spent much of their time in digging for money which they pretended was hid in the earth, and to this day large excavations may be seen in the ground

---

* From "Early Days of Mormonism" by J. H. Kennedy. A narrative compiled from original sources, clearly showing how the pernicious fraud originated and the circumstances that fostered its growth. 275 pages; Price $1.50. Published by *Charles Scribner's Sons*, 745 Broadway New York.

Dr. Maria Douglass, Director of the Countess Dufferin Medical College of Rangoon, Burmah, and Her Pupils.

not far from their residence, where they used to dig for hidden treasures. Joseph Smith, Sen., and his son Joseph, were in particular considered destitute of moral character, and addicted to vicious habits."

Smith's Own Confession.

Despite the attractive ingenuity of the story Smith gave to his followers about the revelation and discovery of the gold plates, there is substantial reason for the belief that the whole fabrication grew out of an impromptu jest on the part of young Smith, which was received in such earnest, that his subtle cunning saw in it a new way to distinction and possible gain. The story is told plainly and fully by Peter Ingersol, a near neighbor of the Smiths, and at that time one of Joseph's most intimate friends. He declares that one day the future founder of Mormonism called upon him, his countenance and manner betraying evident enjoyment of some hidden jest. Upon being questioned he made the following statement: "As I was passing yesterday across the woods after a heavy shower of rain, I found in a hollow, some beautiful white sand that had been washed up by the water; I took off my frock and tied up several quarts of it and then went home. On entering the house I found the family at the table eating dinner. They were all anxious to know the contents of my frock. At that moment I happened to think of what I had heard of a history found in Canada, called the 'Golden Bible,' so I very gravely told them it was the 'Golden Bible. To my surprise they were credulous enough to believe what I said. According, I told them I had received a command to let no one see it; 'for,' said I, 'no man can see it with the naked eye and live.' However, I offered to take out the book and show it to them, but they refused to see it, and left the room. 'Now,' said Jo, 'I have got the fools fixed, and we will carry out the fun.'"

The Seeking Saviour and Other Themes. by the late Dr. Mackay, of Hull. This work has been published since Dr. Mackay's death, but the greater part was ready for publication when he died, and to that has been added the striking discourse which he delivered the last time he entered the pulpit, and a few manuscripts found among his papers. 247 pages, cloth cover; Price 75 cents. For sale at this office, 63 Bible House, New York.

A MOTHER'S VOW.

THE conversion of a woman in China, through the recovery of her son from a dangerous sickness, is a remarkable incident related by Rev. J. W. Stevenson, one of the China Inland Missionaries. He says: "A young workingman heard the Gospel; he was naturally quick—a fiery, enthusiastic youth. He believed in the Lord Jesus Christ with all his heart. When he went about his business he talked about Christ; he c[illegible] not help speaking of Christ and His great l[illegible]

He had a great desire to see his mother saved. He spoke to her with tears, prayed with her, and entreated her to come to the Lord, that she might share in the joy and peace that filled his heart. She said, 'I am too old; you young people may take up this new religion; the religion of my ancestors will do for me.' This distressed his heart; and when he was talking to others he often thought of his own mother. He was burdened with the fact that his mother was quite indifferent to the claims of Christ, and he cried to God for her. God was sure to hear such prayers. How did He do it? He laid that young man on a bed of sickness prostrated with typhus fever.

The mother went to the doctor, she went to the temples; she did all she could, but it was of no avail—the young man got worse, till all hope was gone. Then, in her distress and despair, she came to the chapel, and said, 'O, sir, will you come and pray for my son? He is dying.' We went, and knelt down by the bedside, and we prayed to God there and then. The woman rose with tears streaming down her cheeks, and said, 'If your God will save my son, I vow that I will serve Him in future.'

God did graciously restore him, and this woman became an inquirer, then a candidate for baptism, and is to-day a consistent member of the church. The Chinese are not so different from us, they have hearts; and though this woman's spiritual nature was dead, there was a tender chord in her heart, and God could put His finger on that chord. Through her love for her son an entrance was found for the Gospel, and she was saved."

LADIES' MEDICAL CLASS, OF BURMAH

(See Illustration.)

MENTION has already been made in these co[lumns] of the deep interest taken by Lady Du[fferin] in the welfare of the women of India, an[d] the effort she made to organize a corps of train[ed] female physicians and nurses, who could b[e] admitted to the jealously guarded homes of th[e] women who were dying of maladies which medical science could cure or alleviate. In February 1886, when the Earl of Dufferin was Viceroy of India, he and the Countess of Dufferin visited Burmah. Her ladyship received at Rangoon the committee and active supporters of a society formed under the presidency of Sir Charles Bernard then Chief Commissioner, to establish in tha[t] province a branch of the National Associatio[n] which she had organized. A public meeting was held in the Rangoon Town Hall on Apr[il] 14 in that year; grants of money were promise[d] by the Government of Burmah and the Municipality of Rangoon; a large bungalow was rente[d] on lease for a hospital, and Dr. Maria Douglas[s] was appointed Resident Medical Officer an[d] Superintendent.

The instruction of Burmese native women i[n] nursing and midwifery is an essential part o[f] this institution; and classes for that purpose hav[e] been formed by Dr. Maria Douglass, *whose portrait, with those of her first pupils,* we are gla[d] to be able to give this week to our readers. Th[e] president of the Rangoon Association is no[w] Mr. C. H. T. Crosthwaite, who has succeeded Sir Charles Bernard as Chief Commissioner o[f] Burmah. The Bishop of Rangoon, Mrs. Spear[-]man, and Mr. F. A. Gillam, well-known loc[al] philanthropists, are on the managing committe[e] and subscriptions, private donations, and grant[s] from local municipalities, contribute to th[e] funds. The work of the past year has been of [a] most satisfactory and promising character, an[d] the Gospel of Christ is being read and studie[d] on all hands, for the people have learned tha[t] they are indebted to the teachings and influence of Christ for this splendid agency and vehicle of blessing in their midst.

The late Lady Brassey, when she and Lor[d] Brassey, in the yacht *Sunbeam,* visited Rangoon, in March, 1887, took much interest [illegible] this undertaking, and presented a set of anatomical charts and obstetric diagrams to serve in teaching the native pupils. Since the hospital was opened, in April of last year, 142 patients were treated, to November 30, of which eighty-eight were cases in childbirth; and there were only five deaths, three being those of new-born children. Eighteen students are being trained, and books for their learning are translated into the Burmese language.

In a recently published volume, "The Coming of the Great Queen," by Major E. C. Browne, are some extracts from Dr. Pedley's able treatise on Burmese midwifery, showing the barbarous treatment suffered by the women of that country from the stupid ignorance of their ordinary attendants. They are stewed or baked and smoked almost to death, in close, airless chambers, made as hot as possible, and filled with steam, during some days and nights before and after childbirth; many die, and the health and strength of many more are destroyed. We are glad to learn that, through the National Association and the Hospital over which Dr. Maria Douglass presides, measures are being taken to correct these deplorable practices in Burmah, and very soon, with God's blessing, they will be numbered with the things that are no more.

The Pyramids of Cheops, Chephren and Mencheres, from the Nile.

THE PYRAMIDS.

(*See Illustration.*)

MUCH interest has been manifested by our readers in the articles on the prophetic significance of the Great Pyramid, published in recent numbers of this journal. Herewith is an illustration depicting the exterior view of it and its two smaller companions, which are known as the pyramids of Chephren and Mencheres. They stand about six miles west of the river Nile, and ninety miles from the Mediterranean, and are built on a hill two hundred and fifteen feet above the sea-level, and one hundred and fifty feet above the level of the desert. It is a remarkable fact, proved by incontestable evidence, that this whole region was once covered by the sea. The traveller, to this day, finds at the base of the hills quantities of the shells of fishes which live only in the bed of a deep sea, and pebbles which could only have obtained their present shape by the action of tidal water. The work of levelling the top of the hill, digging the foundation to the solid rock, and erecting the Great Pyramid, must have occupied an army of one hundred thousand men for twenty years. This is exclusive of the time and labor required for cutting a canal from the Nile to the site chosen for the Pyramid, by which alone the vast blocks of granite could have been brought from the quarry to the hill. How these blocks were raised from the base of the hill to the elevation which they now occupy, is still a puzzle to civil engineers.

The area prepared for the base was 750 feet square, or thirteen and a half acres, which is larger than the area of Union Square in New York. The second and each succeeding tier was of course smaller than the one below it, receding like the steps of a stairway. There are now two hundred and two of these tiers. But originally there were two hundred and twenty tiers, varying in height from twenty to fifty-six inches, and on the top, the apex, a magnificent block was placed at a height of 486 feet, which is within seventy feet of the height of the Washington Monument, and nearly twice the height of the towers of the Brooklyn Bridge. Its bulk is enormous—fully eighty million cubic feet. Its workmanship displays consummate ability. Practical men who have carefully examined it say that the tools used must have been long straight saws, circular saws, and drills of various kinds *pointed with jewels.* Previous to the commencement of the recent careful study of the construction of the Pyramid, it was supposed that the work of building it was continuous during the lifetime of one or more kings, a casing of stone being added as a covering to an original small nucleus at stated periods; but that theory was speedily abandoned when careful examination proved the unity of design and the conception of plan from the beginning of the work of construction. It is now clearly proved that when the building was commenced the architect had the design of the present gigantic structure drawn out in all its majestic proportions. The position of "the King's Chamber," and the evident intention to make that apartment the grand focus of the entire structure, is a convincing proof of the unity of design from the beginning.

The building was completed 2,170 years before Christ, and therefore had already been standing four hundred years when Joseph became chancellor of Egypt, and sent the wagons to fetch Jacob his father, and his brethren, to Egypt. Doubtless the priests of that day were acquainted with the road into the interior of the Pyramid, but the secret was lost, and it was not until 820 years after Christ, or about three thousand years after the Pyramid was built, that the entrance was found. The Caliph Al Mamoun was convinced that the structure was not solid, as was supposed, but contained rooms, which might be filled with treasure. He therefore determined to pierce it, and had it carefully examined for traces of any stone which had the appearance of a door. He decided to attempt the north face, and fixed upon a spot to commence operations. The point selected proved to be twenty-five feet lower than, and about twenty feet west of, the true entrance, but as the tunneling proceeded horizontally, the workmen struck into the descending passage, with its regular walls, leading to the interior and exterior. The excited workmen ran along the passage with flaming torches into the Grand Gallery under the beautiful arch with its granite portcullis, and on into the King's Chamber, in the very heart of the mountain of stone. There the famous coffer was found, but it was empty. As there was no treasure there, explorations were discontinned, and eight hundred years elapsed before interest in the interior revived. Even then, little was done, and it was not until this generation that, through the efforts of Professor Piazzi Smyth, the full beauty and prophetic significance of the vast structure were made known to the world.

MRS. TRANSOME'S PUPIL.

A SERIAL STORY.

(*Continued from page 223.*)

Rebecca Disappointed.

DOWN-STAIRS there was a concourse of strange people about. Two or three policemen, a doctor, and Mr. Saunders, the lawyer. Mr. Saunders called me into the parlor.

"You are as likely as anybody to tell us where Philip Champion can be found," he said. "He is your master's next relative and heir-at-law, if he has made no will."

"But I thought you had made his will, sir," I answered.

"Not I," he said. "He was often talking about it; but I could never persuade him to give me the necessary instructions."

Down, down sank my heart; for I knew nothing of law or inheritance. The old man had not kept his promise to me, or to Rebecca.

"If there is no will," said the doctor, "young Champion takes every penny, I suppose?"

"Yes, yes, Philip Champion comes into it all!" answered Mr. Saunders.

I think it frightened me to hear there was so much money coming to my Philip—Pippin, my little scholar. I sank down on the nearest chair.

A strange Sabbath-day was that; so different from any other in my life! I had been used to escape from the weary care of our master's dismal house to the quiet of my own cottage, where I could gather strength and comfort for the week. But that Sunday I could not quit the house, with all those strange men about it. As for finding a nook for myself, where I could collect my thoughts a little, and have a quiet spell over my Bible, that was out of the question, save for a few minutes, by the side of Rebecca's bed, while she still slept. But she roused up soon after noon-tide, and gave me no rest with asking questions about Robin Cherrick, who by this time was fast bound in Lancaster jail, or in some secure place, maybe, nigh at hand. All I could tell her was that there would be a coroner's inquest early the next morning.

"Rebecca," I said, "our old master is gone where he can do nothing for himself or you with all his riches."

She stared at me for a few moments with glaring eyes; and after that she screamed again and again like a maniac, till the doctor came up from the floor below to see what was the matter with her. It was a long while before he could control her; and then he gave her a draught, which presently threw her into a sound sleep.

I was free now to go down-stairs. Through the long, narrow window on the stair-case, I saw the dawn breaking, in clear gray light, with rosy clouds floating across the east already bright from the shining of the unrisen sun.

But after nightfall the place grew quiet. Mr. Saunders, who had been searching through every desk and drawer for a will, was gone; and that room was locked up carefully, as though it contained some precious treasure. One policeman alone remained to guard it. Then—but how can I tell you the awful stillness that seemed to gather and brood over the place which held the corpse of the poor miser? Rebecca, who had been wailing and weeping all day, fell into silence, as though she dared not hear the sound of her own voice. The wind moaned through the empty rooms in the other part of the house, and whistled through the key-hole, but there was nothing else to be heard; though we held our breath, and listened—listened as though we might perhaps catch the old man's foot-fall, or the jingling of his keys, in the locked-up room overhead. It grew fearsome at last—that silence like the grave.

"Rebecca," I said, "I'll read a verse or two up loud."

My voice sounded through the stillness as if I had shouted out the words. I opened my Bible at random, as I remember mother used to do when I was a girl, if she lacked special comfort or direction. I had never been used to do it myself, but that night it came natural to me. Surely if my mother ever needed special comfort through the common troubles of her country life, I needed it more sorely in that trouble. But my eye fell upon these words, and I kept silence, and did not read them aloud to Rebecca. "The rich man shall lie down, but he shall not be gathered: he openeth his eyes, and he is not.

"Terrors take hold on him as waters; a tempest stealeth him away in the night.

"The east wind carrieth him away, and he departeth; and a storm hurleth him out of his place.

"For God shall cast upon him, and not spare: he would fain flee out of his hand.

"Men shall clap their hands at him, and shall hiss him out of his place."

The next morning early an inquest was held by the coroner and twelve jurymen. All the doctors that had come in on Sunday to look at the master's corpse, were of one mind as to his death. No one had laid a hand upon him. He had waked up suddenly from his dreams of terror to find they were no longer dreams, but real. His life had been nothing better than the flickering flame of a candle, ready to go out if a puff of wind reached it; and the sudden shock had come upon him as if a door had opened, and a mighty rushing wind, had swept over his soul, carrying it away like a leaf into the other world. There was no reason to think that Robin Cherrick and his mate had any direct hand in his death.

But they were carried from the town-jail, where they had been locked up, and taken before the magistrates; and both me and Rebecca were forced to go, and witness against them. Poor Rebecca! It was years since she had seen Robin: and now she had to look him in the face, a sullen, evil face, and swear to him being the man who had courted her in old times, and how he used to come about the place, and knew the house well, and the master's riches, and his lonely way of living. He scarcely looked at her after the first minute; but she could not keep her eyes away from him; and even when she was speaking to the magistrate, answering the questions he put to her, her white face was turned toward Robin, and her frightened gaze fastened upon him. We heard him and his mate sentenced to jail, there to wait till the next assizes, when they would be tried by the judge. Then we returned to our dismal dwelling-place, which could never be called a home, where preparations were being made, under Mr. Saunders's directions, for the funeral of the dead man.

No news came of Philip Champion, except that the lady in London who had adopted him and brought him up, wrote word that she did not expect him home from his voyage with his father for several weeks to come. The old master had made no friends in the town, or such as he once had had forgotten him, and did not care to come to his burial. Even Rebecca refused to go. So it came to pass that there was none but me, save Mr. Saunders and one doctor, who would both be paid for their trouble, to follow him to the grave.

I went into the death-room just before the coffin-lid was fastened down upon the poor, wrinkled, withered face. The men were gone away; for they had forgotten to bring the proper nails with them; so the room was empty, but for me and the corpse. So still it lay, so lifeless, that I could hardly believe that somewhere apart from it the soul was living yet! Then the remembrance came across me how once I said to Transome "If God would ask me what I wished for, like He did Solomon, I'd have chosen to write a book that would prick our old master's heart to the quick." Ay! but God Himself had written a book for him that ought to have pricked his heart to the quick over and over again. I wondered how he could have read about God's own Son being a poor man, and all His blessed words against the love of riches, and yet go on loving money till it cast out all other love. And I thought of Jesus and His great sacrifice of Himself, and His dying upon the cross, and how all this had been cast aside, and counted as nothing by the side of gold. He had known it all; once he professed to believe it all. He had put Christ and his own soul into the balance with money; and he had chosen *money!* "And so I saw the wicked buried, who had come and gone from the place of the holy; and they were forgotten in the place where they had so done."

I was very sorrowful that evening; but Rebecca was more lively, and inclined to talk more than she had done while the corpse was in the house. She was restless, too, and made herself busy about the kitchen, doing first this thing and then that, for the mere sake of moving about, and keeping her face away from me.

"I suppose the will won't be read till the heir comes back," she said to me from the far end of the kitchen.

"There is no will," I answered; "for Mr. Saunders had told me for certain, as we drove home from the burial, that there could not have been one made.

"No will!" she repeated, coming swiftly across the floor, and looking down upon me with eyes all aflame, "no will!"

"No," I said; "Mr. Saunders says he's searched everywhere, and there isn't one."

"But how shall I get my thousand pounds?" she cried, in a shrill voice.

There it cropped up again—that terrible love of money, which had destroyed our poor old master, body and soul. It was almost as though I saw some devil glaring at me through her eyes. I got up from my chair, and stood opposite to her, trembling like a leaf.

"My poor lass!" I said, for she would be as poor as I now, "God is too good to you to let you have the money you've sold yourself for. He'll give you something better than that. He has given you His own Son, who for our sakes became poor, though He was very rich, that we through His poverty should become rich."

My voice was choked and unsteady; but I felt as though God gave me the words to speak. Rebecca stood staring at me for a minute, as if she did not fairly hear me; and then she flung her apron over her face, and sank down in my chair, and broke out into a passion and a fit of sobs and crying.

"Poor Robin!" I said, after a while, "if you had the thousand pounds, it 'ud be the price of his soul."

"Ay!" she sobbed, "it would. I've been the ruin of him. I'm a wicked woman, and very foolish, Alice Transome. Tell me what I can do now."

So, in the firelight, I told her as well as I could, of what our blessed Lord and Saviour did to prove His love to every one of us, and to teach us how little count He set upon what we are apt to prize most. He never cared for money; what He looked for was love. She listened and listened, sobbing now and then, and catching her breath so as not to lose what I was saying about Him. And I spoke also to her about Transome and me, how we had lived together forty years, learning more and more about God's ways, until we came to know that we were nothing, no more than helpless little babes in His hand, but that He was all, Master, King, Father. And I began to say how it might have been the same with her and Robin; but there she cried out as if my words wounded her sorely.

"If I could but have my time over again!" she said.

But not one of us can have our time over again. I thought of Transome, and our early days; and how if those could come again I would take care so that he should not have to die in the poor-house. No, no. Only one moment at a time belongs to us; and we have no more power over yesterday than over to-morrow.

Thank God, Philip reached us before Robin's trial came on. I was so rejoiced to see his face that I was ready to say, "Lord, now lettest Thou thy servant depart in peace." Yes; peace came back with him. I went home to my own cottage, and lighted a fire on my own hearth; and sat in my own chimney-nook again. Philip was close at hand; and no more charge or anxiety rested upon me.

Yet when the time came, I was obliged to go to Lancaster Assizes, and appear before the judge, and bear witness against the prisoners who stood for trial before him at the dreadful bar. Rebecca was forced to be there too. It was not a very long trial, so they told us afterwards; but to her and me it seemed as if it would never, never be ended. We sat together in a little room, not far from the great hall where the trial was going on, hearkening for some one to come with news. At last Philip opened the door just as the daylight was growing dim, and we could not clearly see his face. He sat down on the bench beside Rebecca, and put his hand kindly upon hers.

"Rebecca," he said, in that voice of his which always seemed to go straight to one's heart, "it is a heavy sentence."

"Tell me;" and she whispered, in a hoarse tone.

"Remember," he went on, "that my uncle's death was caused by their crime; and that Robin has been in prison for theft before, five years, for stealing a letter with money in it. Now he is sentenced to transportation for fifteen years."

"It was me that did it," she said again, in the same loud whisper, and she burst into uncontrollable weeping.

"Yes!" Philip answered, for he knew all about it, "yes! in one sense, you did it. You loved money more than you loved him. If men and women were only true to one another, faithful to one another, whom they have seen, they would be more faithful to God, whom they have not seen."

"What can I do?" she asked, "what can I do? There is no way now that I can make it up to him. And I do love him, spite of all; I do, indeed."

But there did not seem to be anything she could do for Robin. Philip found out for her that he was to be transported to some place in Australia, where there was a convict settlement for prisoners with long sentences like his. By his influence he got an order for Rebecca and me to visit him before he went away; though we were only allowed to see and speak to him through a double grating, with a warder standing by, who could hear all we said.

(To be Continued.)

THE TEN VIRGINS.

By Mrs. M. Baxter.

S. S. Lesson for April 22. Matt. 25 : 1-13. Golden Text, Matt. 25 : 10.

Why the Second Advent is to be Longed for—The Utilitarian Conception of Religion—Who will Go Forth to Meet the Bridegroom—What They Leave—Their Vocation—The Slumber of the Church—The Recent Awakening—The Division Among the Virgins—The Long-Expected Cry—The Five Exhausted Lamps—The Essential Oil—Varieties of Lamps—No One Possessing Surplus Oil—A Lesson for Sinners and Unsanctified Believers—Fatal Procrastination.

"Then." This word connects this parable of the ten virgins with the preceding chapter. "*Then*," when the signs of the Lord's coming begin to appear, "shall the kingdom of heaven be likened unto ten virgins, which took their lamps, and went forth to meet the bridegroom." Some will say, If His word is true, Lo, I am with you alway;" if He dwells in our hearts by faith and is never a moment absent from us—why should we think so much about His second coming? The same objection might have been urged about the first coming of Christ. Souls were saved and sins forgiven before He came, but O how dark were the gleams of light which then visited man, compared to the very presence, the very words and deeds of Jesus, as He walked in person upon earth! The Lamb slain from the foundation of the world, and represented in every sacrifice, was not understood as was Jesus, "who His own self bore our sins in His own body on the tree" (1 Pet. 2 : 24)—the God-man victim. And though our hearts rejoice to rest in the glorious fact that He dwells with us and in us, yet how transcendently glorious will be the moment when we shall see Him as He is in all His glory, King of kings and Lord of lords, manifested to the eyes of all!

The general idea of religion is

A Kind of Utilitarianism.

Apart from God, men cannot be saved, and so they make use of Jesus to save their souls from everlasting destruction, and there they stop, many of them, and go no further. There are others who, being saved, ask God to make use of *them*. This is a step higher, and this is an instinct to every one who is really saved, really a new creature" in Christ Jesus, with whom "old things are passed away; behold all things are become new." (II Cor. 5 : 17). But this also savors of Utilitarianism. But there are some who, while quite as ready to serve as any, are far more taken up with God than with His service; the thought of their own devotedness is abhorrent to them; they hold Jesus in such esteem that to do anything for Him is only too great a privilege, and it brings its own reward with it. It is these who shall go "forth to meet the Bridegroom"—not only go forth from sin, but forth from self, from worldly conventionalities, from everything else, to Jesus. Their hearts are not set on the reward they shall obtain, nor the honors they shall have when Jesus comes. They say with Mephibosheth, "Yea, let [others] take all, for as much as my Lord the king is come again in peace unto His own house" (II Sam. 19 : 30). Yet even of these which go forth—virgin souls, set apart for the Bridegroom—five are "wise," and five are "foolish." Every virgin went forth with a lamp. Those who are most absorbed with God, and are in communion with Him, are more noticeable for the light of Christ which they shed upon the world than for any remarkable talents or wonderful works which they do. They shine, they are "the light of the world," men take knowledge of them that they have been with Jesus; when hypocrisy, false doctrine, heresy, and indifference rend the Church of Christ, the light shines on unhindered. To shine is

Their Vocation!

They go forth, the Bridegroom before them, and all else behind them. In the early Church, the going forth to meet the coming Bridegroom was such that Paul had to write to the Thessalonians, "Now we beseech you, brethren, by the coming of our Lord Jesus Christ, and by our gathering together with Him, that ye be not soon shaken in mind, or be troubled, neither by spirit, nor by word, nor by letter as from us, as that the day of Christ is at hand. . . For that day shall not come, except there come a falling away first, and that man of sin be revealed, the son of perdition" (II Thes. 2 : 1-3). Thus the Bridegroom has tarried, and all the virgins have "slumbered and slept." The earnest expectation of the early Church that Christ was coming faded away, and few, even of the most devoted of God's children spoke of His coming during the Middle Ages. But for more than half a century, God has been waking up His children, and through literature and Bible readings, a large number have been aroused to believe in the coming of the Bridegroom, if not to go forth and meet him. Perhaps only one of these witnesses has given his life to warn the unconverted of the fearful judgments which accompany the revelation of "the man of sin," and "the coming of the Lord." God bless his testimony!

The virgins are not all alike, although they appear so. There were wise and foolish amongst them. All of them had lamps, which were easily lit, and all, for the moment, gave light. "At midnight there was a cry made, Behold the Bridegroom cometh; go ye out to meet Him." It was the long-expected sound, the culmination of all their hearts' desires. No more sleep, no more slumber. He was at the doors. With beating hearts and trembling hands they trimmed their lamps, and one by one the little lights began to shine. But now came the testing time—some of the lamps, which had flickered for a moment, until the heat had attracted a supply of oil into the wick, began to burn with a steady and increasing brilliancy. Others which burned with a brillant light for a moment, suddenly collapsed, smoldered for a moment, and went out.

What Was The Matter?

The lamps were all right, but they had taken no oil; there was nothing to feed the light. It was the last moment, the procession was starting: in despair, they cried to the virgins who held their burning lamps aloft, "Give us of your oil, for our lamps are going out" (margin). But the wise answered, saying: "Not so; lest there be not enough for us and you; but go ye rather to them that sell, and buy for yourselves." How many there are who attempt to keep up the light and the life of God without the Holy Ghost. God has blest them in a meeting, and used them in winning souls; the fire has been kindled, but there is no fuel, and the fire dies out. They preach still, but the words fall powerless; they pray still, but the prayer of earthly manufacture is like a balloon without its gas; it will not rise. They testify, but the testimony is stale, these are cold, lifeless ashes instead of fire; there is no heat to warm, nor light to cheer. In order to have the light of God burning in our own souls, we need to give the Holy Ghost full access to all parts of our being. If the oil is there, the lamp will burn. Where the Spirit of the Lord is, there is liberty." There are many who are most particular about the kind of lamp they have. Some prefer an Episcopal Church lamp, some a Methodist lamp, some a Presbyterian lamp, some a Baptist lamp, some a Congregational lamp, some will only have a mission lamp. But

The Great Matter

with all is to get the oil supply—without it all is a failure. But the wise virgins have no surplus oil to bestow upon others. "Go ye rather to them that sell, and buy for yourselves." Alas, it was too late! They had slept unprepared. While the wise virgins had lamp and oil ready to their hands, the unwise had procrastinated, and, at the same time, had formed a most erroneous opinion of what was essential: they put the lamp first, the light last. O, how many are doing this! They put their denomination, or, may be, their talents or their efforts first, and strange to say, God the Holy Ghost last. They think that any moment they may run for the oil. But it was an unaccustomed journey for the foolish virgins; they had never been that way before. While they went in search of oil, "the Bridegroom came; and they who were ready went in with Him to the marriage, and the door was shut." Never, throughout an endless eternity, would the foolish virgins be called again to the marriage of the Lamb.

Whether we have here a lesson to believers to live yielded up to the Holy Ghost continually after having once been filled with the Spirit, or to the sinner, who will find himself shut out from God for ever and ever, if he is not found ready, the lesson is equally solemn. There may be some true children of God who yet have not so received the Holy Ghost as to be burning and shining lights.

O, Why Delay?

Jesus says, "Receive ye the Holy Ghost," (John 20 : 22.) The coming of the Bridegroom will be a testing time; He sits as a Refiner and Purifier of silver; He tests the metal, searches the hearts, and tries the reins of the children of men. No unreality can live in His presence. His presence will show which are the manufactured and which are the Holy Ghost prayers. His presence will discover which messages come direct from God through the speaker, and which were made discourses. He will find out every unreal profession, every untrue sentiment, everything which savors of hypocrisy.

"The door was shut." The virgins who were too late to join their companions went to buy oil, and they obtained what they went for; their lamps were now as brilliant as the others, but it was too late, they had lost their chance. They were virgins, they had left all for the Bridegroom, but when they knocked at the door, He said to them, "I know you not." We can only know Jesus by the Holy Ghost. "No man can say that Jesus is the Lord, but by the Holy Ghost;" but has it ever dawned upon us that Jesus will not know *us* but by the Holy Ghost dwelling in us? that the point of contact between us and Jesus is the Holy Ghost indwelling? "Watch therefore, for ye know neither the day nor the hour wherein the Son of Man cometh." It is said of the Queen of England that she never keeps anybody waiting. Many people make a habit of being late for every engagement. Do they consider that this habit of procrastination, if indulged in, may cost them their part at the marriage supper of the Lamb? Procrastination is a selfish habit, but it is a guilty one, too. We have no more right to steal a person's time than we have to steal his money. But,

O, How Awful,

if we should sin against our own souls by this thing! Let us accept the "unction from the Holy One" (1 John 2 : 20), and live yielded up to God moment by moment, that when the cry goes forth, "Behold the Bridegroom cometh," there may be no rush for oil at the last, but we may have nothing else to do but to enter into the joy of our Lord.

THE GREAT REFINER.

"And He shall sit as a refiner and purifier of silver."—MAL. iii. 3.

'Tis sweet to feel that he who tries
The silver, takes his seat
Beside the fire that purifies,
Lest too intense a heat—
Raised to consume the base alloy,
The precious metals, too, destroy.

'Tis good to think how well He knows
The silver's power to bear
The ordeal to which it goes;
And that with skill and care
He'll take it from the fire, when fit,
With His own hand to polish it.

'Tis blessedness to know that He
The piece He has begun,
Will not forsake till He can see—
To prove the work well done—
An image by its brightness known,
The perfect likeness of His own.

But ah! how much of earthly mould,
Dark relics of the mine,
Lost from the ore, must He behold—
How long must He refine,
Ere in the silver He can trace
The first faint semblance of His face?

Thou great Refiner! sit Thou by
Thy promise to fulfil;
Moved by Thy hand, beneath Thine eye,
And melted at Thy will,
O may Thy work forever shine
Reflecting beauty pure as Thine.

—*Selected.*

J. E. JEWETT, Publisher, 77 Bible House, New York, will furnish the above poem in leaflet form at twenty cents per hundred. A *Sample Packet* of 50 leaflets assorted (no two alike), will be sent post-paid for ten cents. Postage stamps taken.

Entered according to Act of Congress in the year 1887, in the office of the Librarian of Congress at Washington.

Vol. XI., No. 16. Office, 63 Bible House, N. Y. THURSDAY, APRIL 19, 1888. Annual Subscription, $1.50.

CONTENTS OF THIS NUMBER.

PORTRAIT AND LIFE OF THE LATE REV. WILLIAM G. SCHAUFFLER, D. D.

JEALOUSY. Dr. Talmage's Sermon Last Sunday Morning.

ANECDOTES RELATED AT RECENT EVANGELISTIC MEETINGS.

THE KEY TO ALL THE PROPHECIES. By George H. Pember, M. A.

Gems from New Books: The Roman Punishment—The King's Thread—The Parson Converted—A Son Puzzled, etc.

THE RENT VEIL. A New Sermon by C. H. Spurgeon.

A Divorce Averted—Blood Poisoning Cured—An Anxious Night in Africa. Real Estate in Palestine—A Wail in Babylon—A Midnight Interview on the Elevated Railroad.

PICTURE OF THE WEDDING OF PRINCE OSCAR, OF SWEDEN, TO MISS MUNCK.

A STREET SCENE IN CAIRO, EGYPT. (With Illustration.)

MRS. TRANSOME'S PUPIL. (Continued.)

THE TALENTS. By Mrs. M. Baxter.

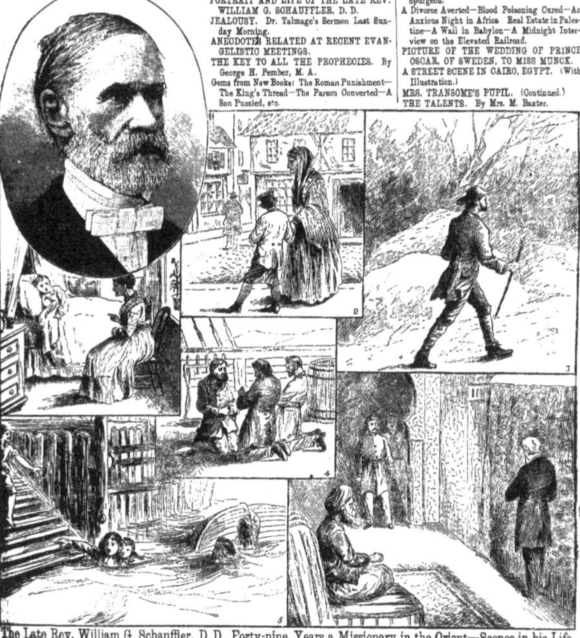

The Late Rev. William G. Schauffler, D. D., Forty-nine Years a Missionary in the Orient—Scenes in his Life.

WILLIAM G. SCHAUFFLER, D. D.

Forty-nine Years a Missionary in the Orient.

Birth in Germany in 1798—Removal to Russia—A Critical Illness—A Blind Instructress—An Evangelical Roman Catholic Priest—Conversion Under his Preaching—A Journey of Relief—In Peril of Wolves and Robbers—Meeting With Dr. Wolff—Fog Lifted in Answer to Prayer—Journey to America—Welcome at Andover—Marvellous Linguistic Achievements—Ordination—Visit to Paris—Arrival in Constantinople—Marriage—A Remarkable Escape From Drowning—Translation of the Bible—A Rescue From a Harem—Return to America—Death in 1883.

A WORK of a deeply interesting character* has just been published, containing the record of well-nigh half a century of arduous and successful missionary labor in eastern Europe. It is a simple statement, in which there is not a trace of self-glorification, yet the reader is astonished, not only by the character and quantity of the work accomplished, but by the strong faith and complete self-devotion of the man who was enabled to perform it. As the study of such a life cannot fail to be both interesting and suggestive, we this week give, with his portrait, a brief sketch of Dr. Schauffler's work, compiled from his autobiography.

William G. Schauffler was born in Stuttgart, Germany, August 22, 1798, and died in New York on January 26, 1883, in the eighty-fifth year of his age. In 1804, his father removed to Odessa, in Russia, his trade as a wood-turner having a better prospect of success in that town. He had three children besides William, and the journey was a long and toilsome one. In Odessa the future missionary received his early education in a school, taught by his father's clerk, in the sheriff's office. Though his father and mother were not at that time pious, they were a model of morality, and very careful to show outward respect for religion. Prayers were read in the household every morning, and while there was no divine service in Odessa, a sermon was read on the Sunday; but of conversion to Christ no one in the family, or in the city, seemed to know anything.

A Serious Illness

came upon the boy when he was seven years old, and his nurse, a German neighbor, calmly told him that he would surely die. He was naturally startled (*See illustration on first page, No.* 1), but as at that time he had learned nothing of his condition as a sinner, but, only in general terms, of Christ being the Saviour of the world, he was not greatly concerned, as he thought he would go to heaven where he would be happier than in this world. He recovered, however, and the easy assurance which had comforted him in his sickness was soon disturbed. In mingling with the street boys, quarrelling with his playmates, and disobeying his parents, he recognized a degree of sinfulness, which rendered him uneasy about his eternal destiny.

A Blind Woman

appears to have been his first religious instructor. She belonged to a band of pilgrims who, under a mistaken interpretation of prophecy, quitted their homes and passed through Odessa on their way to the Caucasus. Her husband died on the way, and the pilgrims left her behind, in Odessa. The boy's mother formed the acquaintance of the blind woman, through the latter selling off her books and some small articles of property for her support. Mrs. Schauffler bought from her a copy of Bogatzky's "Golden Treasury," and that the boy read with interest. The blind woman was invited to visit the Schauffler home, and William, being the youngest of the family, used to be sent to fetch her, and guide her back to her home. (*See Illustration No.* 2.) During those walks she would talk earnestly to him about his soul, but without imparting any light that he could use.

An Evangelical Catholic Priest,

named Lindl, was ultimately the agent used of God for the lad's conversion. He arrived in Odessa, from Bavaria, where his evangelical preaching had brought him into trouble with his ecclesiastical superiors, and with the Government. The Emperor of Russia having heard of him, and learned that he was imprisoned, used his influence to obtain his release, and invited him to Russia. Mr. Lindl rented a house in the same street as the Schauffler family, and William soon made his acquaintance, and went to hear him preach. "I remember," he says, "neither text nor subject; I only remember that it swept away, in the first part, all worthiness and claim of the sinner, and in the second part it opened wide the door of free grace in Christ." Mr. Lindl was soon called away from Odessa to Sarata, a village at some distance, but the good work was continued.

A Perilous Journey

was taken by the young man shortly after his conversion, which was a labor of love and gratitude. Mr. Lindl was as much hated by the Catholic priests and bishops of Russia as he had been by those of Bavaria. They were prevented molesting him by the knowledge that he enjoyed the esteem and friendship of the Czar, but they did all they could to prevent him receiving support from the people. On one occasion, being in sore straits for money, Mr. Lindl sent an appeal to St. Petersburg, which elicited a prompt response. A large sum of money, in gold, was sent for him to Odessa, but there were no means of sending it forward to its destination. The road was a long and dreary one. It was infested with wolves and robbers, and beyond the Dneister, which was the greater part of the journey, it degenerated into mere bog and morass, the only safe footing being on certain hillocks covering the bones of ancient Moldavian chiefs. The journey was one from which all shrank. Young Schauffler, however, volunteered to carry the money to his friend and teacher. Fastening the gold in a girdle around his waist, and commending himself to God, he set out briskly (*See Illustration, No.* 3) to meet the wolves, or robbers, or whatever other dangers might await him. "My arrival," he says, "was as an angel's visit to Mr. Lindl and his people, who were even then at prayer."

Desires for Christian Work

began to rise in the young man's mind immediately on his conversion. At one time he thought of hiring himself out as a shepherd, in order to reach the shepherds of Moldavia and Bessarabia, who were notorious for their ignorance; at another he contemplated becoming a servant among the Tartars; but in each case he was shown by Divine guidance that his way was not there. At length, in 1825, Joseph Wolff, the eminent missionary, visited Odessa, and young Schauffler went to hear him; and, making his acquaintance, became his guide around the neighborhood. Dr. Wolff learned the desires of his young companion, and set himself to the work of furthering them. By this time, owing doubtless to the influence of William Schauffler's consistent Christian life, a change had come in his home: one sister and his elder brother were converted, and his aged mother was prepared to give up her youngest boy to Christ's service. Dr. Wolff found little difficulty in the family in arranging for the departure. The plan was for the two to go together to Palestine, where Mr. Schauffler was to labor among Mohammedans, and Dr. Wolff among Jews.

On February 8, 1826, after an affectionate farewell to his family, he accompanied Wolff

On Board a Ship

bound for Constantinople. The wind being favorable, the passage across the Black Sea was made in less than the usual time, but on approaching land the fog became dense. The captain became alarmed, and in conversation with Dr. Wolff and Mr. Schauffler, admitted that there was serious danger of running aground. "If, with this wind aft, we do not make the Bosphorous," he said, "we shall fare badly." "Come, captain," said Dr. Wolff, "let us ask Divine direction." The captain said he should be glad to have his passengers pray, but he must be on duty, looking out for the channel. It was about noon, and the two missionaries joined in prayer for guidance. In a short time they went on deck, and were told by the captain that just at twelve o'clock the fog lifted and showed them the mouth of the Bosphorous. "We are running right ahead for it," he said, "and now, gentlemen, if you will give thanks to God for this deliverance, I shall be happy to join you." No second suggestion was needed; the three knelt on the ship's deck and gave hearty thanks (*See Illustration, No.* 4).

Comes to America.

Dr. Wolff decided on spending some time in Constantinople, and, accordingly, arrangements were made for Mr. Schauffler commencing at once the study of Turkish. He was an adept in the art of learning languages, and had already acquired French, Italian, and English, before leaving Odessa, having exchanged lessons with travellers of those nationalities who had visited Odessa. German and Russian he knew of course, as the former was the language of his native land, and the other of his adopted country. He had also commenced the study of Latin and Greek, in which he afterward became proficient. Before attaining middle life, he could *preach fluently in six languages, and could read and understand twenty-six.* He studied earnestly while in the Turkish capital, and continued the work, when, owing to a change in Dr. Wolff's plans, they removed to Smyrna. There Dr. Wolff finally decided to abandon his Palestine project for that time and return to England. He advised Mr. Schauffler to go to America for the needful preparation for missionary work; and, giving him letters of introduction to Mr. Evarts, then secretary of the Board of Commissioners, and to other prominent persons, saw him safely on board a vessel bound for Boston, Mass. Mr. Schauffler says that when he landed at that port on September 7, 1826, after a voyage of four months, he had but one dollar in his pocket.

By the advice of Mr. Evarts the young traveller went to Andover, where he was kindly received by both professors and students. For some months Mr. Schauffler supported himself by turning bed-posts for a wood-turner in the village, that being the best work available; but at length a student in the senior class, who knew his worth, returning from a visit to Boston, brought him the welcome intelligence that the Ladies' Society for Promoting Christianity among the Jews would defray his expenses for three months. He then gladly relinquished the production of bed-posts and gave his whole time to study, working regularly at his books sixteen hours a day, to the amazement of the professors and students, who did not know the capacity of his iron constitution. During his five years residence at Andover he acquired Arabic, Chaldee, Syriac, Samaritan, Persian, and Spanish, with a fair knowledge of Ethiopic and Coptic. At the conclusion of his Andover course Mr. Schauffler was ordained a

Missionary to the Jews

in Turkey, in a solemn service at Park Street Church, Boston, on November 14, 1831. The Board of Commissioners for Foreign Missions had invited him, without his application, to enter their service, and suggested to him that he should stay in Paris on his way to his field of labor, to attend lectures on Arabic and Turkish. As his knowledge of those languages was all self taught he gladly accepted the suggestion, and spent three months in the French capital under the best teachers in Europe. On April 9, 1832, he quitted the brilliant city to commence his life's labors, praying earnestly, as he recommends every Christian traveller to do, for the salvation of its Godless inhabitants. From Paris to Strasbourg he made the journey by diligence, thence crossing the Rhine to Kehl, and so to his native town of Stuttgart. He preached there, and thence, accompanied a part of the way by several missionary companions, he travelled on to Odessa, where he had the happiness of seeing his aged mother and brother and sisters. On the following Sabbath he preached in the Lutheran

*The Autobiography of William G. Schauffler. Edited by his Sons. Pp. 258; Price $1.25. Published by *Anson D. F. Randolph & Co.*, 38 West Twenty-third Street, New York.

church to an overflowing congregation, people having come from all the villages around to hear their old friend. After a very brief stay among them he set out for Constantinople.

Very arduous and discouraging was the work among the Jews of that city, but Mr. Schauffler labored earnestly, with his heart strong in faith. After some time, business of the Society required him to visit Smyrna, and there he met, earnestly and devotedly laboring in missionary work, Miss Mary Reynolds, the lady who afterward became his loving wife and valued fellow-worker. He returned to Constantinople, and after prayer and consideration wrote her an offer of marriage, which she accepted. Shortly afterward they were married, and together engaged in the work at Constantinople.

An Escape from Drowning

was an incident which occurred about a year and a half after the marriage. The providential rescue made a deep impression upon them, for so dire was the danger, that death to the whole party seemed inevitable. Mr. and Mrs. Schauffler had remained in Constantinople during the ravages of the Plague, ministering to the sick and continuing their mission work until rest and change became absolutely necessary. It was decided that they should go to Odessa for recuperation. Accordingly the missionary and his wife and child, with a nurse and a lady friend, went to the shore to go on board the Russian steamer, to which they were to be taken in a caique, or row-boat. The nurse, who stepped into the caique after the ladies, being unaware of the frail character of the boat, stepped aside and heavily. Instantly the boat tipped, throwing out all who were in it, and Mr. Schauffler, who had his foot on the edge, steadying it. They sank in twenty feet of water, but happily Mr. Schauffler was able to rescue his wife and her companion; and the nurse, bravely holding on to the babe, supported herself by clinging to one of the posts of the jetty, until he could go to her assistance. Thus in God's mercy, all were saved. (*See Illustration No.* 4.)

Arrived in Odessa, they found a great revival work commenced, in which they were delighted to assist. Health of body was recovered by both while engaging in this congenial work, which refreshed and invigorated their souls. Their friends begged them to remain through the winter, as there had been a fresh outbreak of the Plague at Constantinople, but this Mr. Schauffler and his wife regarded rather as a reason for their return; and though death in all human probability awaited them, they went back. The trying scenes through which they passed it is impossible to describe here. One after another of their household attendants was seized with the sickness and died. A dear friend and fellow-worker lay at the point of death, but still the brave missionary and his wife continued at their post, faithful and devoted in their labor and mercifully preserved from the scourge until the time of trial had passed.

The Triumph of His Life,

by which Dr. Schauffler became known the world over, was commenced shortly after his return from his Odessa visit. It was the translation of the Bible into Hebrew-Spanish. He labored unceasingly on this work, and at length was privileged to complete it. His success was so remarkable that the chief Rabbi, to whom a copy was presented, spoke of it in the highest praise, and it is still the standard work used by both English and American missionaries in Jewish work. It was printed in Vienna, Dr. Schauffler superintending the operation. While residing in that city he held evangelistic services, which brought him under the ban of the police. The services were summarily closed, but Dr. Schauffler escaped imprisonment, and before leaving he was admitted to an audience with the emperor, who graciously accepted a copy of the Bible, and expressed the hope that it would prove beneficial to the people. The fame of this work brought Dr. Schauffler prominently into the notice of the Bible Societies; and when the American Board decided to transfer the Jewish work he entered the employ of the American Bible Society and the British and Foreign Bible Society, and under their auspices translated the New Testament into Turkish.

It would be impossible even to summarize the work of the forty-nine years which Dr. Schauffler spent in labor for Christ in Constantinople, Vienna, Odessa, and other cities. Perils from the Plague, from fanatical priests and Mohammedans, from Jewish Rabbis, and in conflicts with the Turkish officials, would have worn out any ordinary man; but he was supported by an unwavering faith which carried him triumphantly through all.

A Rescue From a Harem,

which he undertook and effected, will show the indomitable character of the man, and how ready he was to engage in any good work, though it might lie outside his legitimate sphere. Word reached him in Constantinople that an attack had been made by Mohammedans, aided by Persian troops, on a village near the Russian frontier and that a German named Meyer, with his wife and child, had been carried into captivity. The man succeeded in making his escape in the night, carrying his child with him, but his wife was too closely guarded, and it was believed that she had been sold as a slave in Constantinople. Dr. Schauffler determined to find her. He earnestly prayed for direction, and then set out on a tour of the city, which must have seemed hopeless in such a place. In almost the first street he searched he heard of a man who had a German woman in his harem. He went to his house and demanded an interview with the woman. The Turk refused to let him see her, but allowed an interview to take place, a curtain being hung between Dr. Schauffler and the woman, while he jealously watched (*See Illustration No.* 5.) She was not the woman he sought, and she had no desire for deliverance, but she gave Dr. Schauffler a clue to where Mrs. Meyer might be found. He went there, and, aided by the Russian Minister, succeeded in liberating her and restoring her to her husband.

The simple, modest record of Dr. Schauffler's life contained in his autobiography is so full of thrilling incidents that it is difficult to realize their having been compressed into one life. To that volume we must refer our readers for the record of a grand career of noble self-sacrifice. He did not quit the scene of his labors until 1874, when he was seventy-six years of age. Then he, with his devoted wife, returned to America to spend the remainder of their lives with their sons. Dr. Schauffler continued to preach in the home churches and to stimulate the interest of the Christian public in the work to which he had given his life until 1883, when he peacefully fell asleep in Jesus.

ANECDOTES RELATED AT RECENT EVANGELISTIC MEETINGS.

The Stone in the Courtyard.—A Worker relates that "A few years ago a servant of Christ went into a castle courtyard in the north of England, and saw there a large stone, upon which were engraved the words, 'Turn me over and I will tell you the truth.' He thought he would see what the stone had to tell. So he put out his strength to the utmost, and found on the other side was cut the sentence, 'Kindly actions never die,' and beneath this, 'Turn me over again.' So the man went on his way, feeling he had learned a lesson worth remembering. For Christ's sake go forth and do what you can; where you expect least, you may sometimes find the greatest blessing; and whether you see it or not, the kind action shall never die. The kindest action ever done was Christ dying to save man. 'Greater love hath no man than this, that a man lay down his life for his friends.'"

A Publican's Conversion to God.—"Some years ago, I was conducting evangelistic services in Hartlepool. They were held in a theatre, and two of the most regular attendants of the meeting were the little daughters of a publican of that town. They were invariably accommodated with a seat beside the singers, and one night their hearts were touched with the love of Jesus, and they gave themselves to Him. Next morning, as they were sitting down to breakfast, one of them said to her father, 'Papa, why do you not ask a blessing from God?' The man did not answer, but afterwards he told a friend that the thought that his child had never seen him ask a blessing went deep into his heart. She had often heard him swear, but never thank God. She had often seen him stagger in drink, but never bend the knee to the Most High God; and there and then, he resolved that he would leave his old life, come to Christ, sell out from the whisky trade, and live for the God whom he had so long neglected, and he speedily did so. What a wonderful result through a single, simple question, of a little girl! Let us all speak for Christ, no matter how feebly, for we know not what a power it may become, under the influence of the Holy Spirit."

The Yellow Placard on the Wall.—"A Poor woman was standing at her window and saw on the opposite side of the street a great yellow placard, announcing a gospel meeting that was to be held that night in a certain hall. The woman considered for a moment, and then, happily for herself, determined to go. She went, and the speaker spoke of that great salvation that reaches down to the very worst of God's creatures. And that night, even as the morning light shines suddenly into a darkened room, lighting it up with the glorious rays of the sun, God gave that woman His great salvation. On the following night she got her mother to accompany her. The mother's heart was also filled with wonder and joy; and, turning to her daughter, she asked, 'Mary, will it last?' 'Aye, mother, it will last, for it is an everlasting salvation,' Mary replied."

A Widow Opportunely Supplied.—A Christian friend and worker writes: "I am a believer in special providences, as I have seen them illustrated in various instances. Here is one: I was going one day to call at the house of a poor widow and her daughter on some errand, and just as I was starting a strong impression came in my mind to take them some food, and as I had just been baking some bread, I thought I would take some to each one. I wrapped it up and started again, when something seemed to say to me, 'Go back and get some more.' I stopped, for I knew the Voice; but I did not want to go back, being in a hurry. But after a moment's thought I went back and got a good supply of food, and again started on my way. When I arrived at the place and gave them what I had brought, the daughter said, 'Oh, what a mercy! We had not anything in the house to eat to-day!' 'It is more blessed to give than to receive;' but how often we miss the blessing because we do not know and heed the Voice that speaks to us."

An Evangelist Rebuked by a Ferryman.—Mr. Graham says: "There was among our workers a young man who lived on the other side of the river. This was no great inconvenience, as there was a ferry near the mission by which he could cross. But what troubled him was the crossing the ferry on Sunday; he tried to persuade himself it was quite right, but there was always an uneasiness experienced about it. However, as it saved him a long walk to and from the mission he continued to use the ferry. One Sunday, as he was crossing with some tracts in his hand, he offered one to the ferryman. The man took it, and looking first at the tract, then at the distributer, said, with a sneer curling his lip, 'If it were not for the like of you I might get away on Sunday, and learn the gospel for myself. These words struck home to the young man's heart, and he resolved that that would be the last time he would use the ferry-boat on the Lord's Day. Since then he has bravely walked the long distance every Sunday. 'If thou turn away thy foot from the Sabbath, from doing thy pleasure on My holy day, and call the Sabbath a delight. . . I will cause thee to ride upon the high places of the earth'" (Isa. 58: 13, 14.)

JEALOUSY.

Dr. Talmage's Sermon Preached last Sunday Morning April 15, 1888.

"Jealousy is the rage of a man." Prov. 6: 34.

A Combination of Vices—A Strong Infusion of Envy—Its Antediluvian Results—Its Long Record of Crime—Voltaire's Maniacal Rage—Napoleon's Disgraceful Bequest—The Root of European Perturbation—Its Influence in Politics—In the Occupations and Professions—Medical Jealousy—Dr. Mackenzie and the German Physicians—Garfield's Physicians—Jealousy in the Pulpit — The Ecclesiastical Barbecue — The Offence of Albert Barnes—No Expulsion Unaided—A Duke as a Target—Merlin Saved by a Hen—Persecution a Blessing.

Some subjects a religious teacher touches a thousand times, now coming on them from one direction, now from another. But here is a Bible theme that for some reason is left totally alone. This morning, asking your prayers, and in the strength of God, I want to grapple it.

There is an old sin, haggard, furious, monstrous, diabolical, that has for ages walked and crawled the earth. It combines all that is obnoxious in the races human, quadrupedal, ornithological, reptilian, and insectile, horned, tusked, hoofed, fanged, stinged; the eye of a basilisk, the tooth of an adder, the jaws of a crocodile, the crushing folds of an anaconda, the slyness of a scorpion, the tongue of a cobra, and the coil of the worm that never dies. It is

In Every Community,

in every church, in every legislative hall, in every monetary institution, in every drawing-room levee, in every literary and professional circle. It whispers, it hisses, it lies, it debauches, it blasphemes, it damns. My text names it when it says, "Jealousy is the rage of a man." It is grief at the superiority of others; their superiority in talent or wealth or beauty or elegance or virtue or social or professional or political recognition. It is the shadow of other people's success. It is the shiver in our pocket-book because it is not as fat as some one else's pocket-book. It is the twinge in our tongue because it is not as eloquent as some one else's tongue. It is the flutter in our robes because they are not as lustrous as some one else's robes. It is the earthquake under our house because it is not as many feet front and deep as our neighbor's house. It is the thunder of other people's popularity souring the milk of our kindness. It is the father and mother both of one-half of the discontent and outrages and detractions and bankruptcies, crimes and woes of the human race.

It Was Antediluvian

as much as it is postdiluvian. It put a rough stick in the hands of the first boy that was ever born, and said to him: "Now, Cain, when Abel is looking the other way, crush in his skull; for his sacrifice has been accepted and yours rejected." And Cain picked up the stick as though just to walk with it, and while Abel was watching some bird in the tree-top, or gazing at some waterfall, down came the blow of the first assassination, which has had its echo in all the fratricides, matricides, uxoricides, homicides, infanticides, and regicides of all ages and all nations.

This passion of jealousy so disturbed Caligula at the prominence of some of the men of his time, that he cut a much-admired curl from the brow of Cincinnatus, and took the embroidered collar from the neck of Torquatus, and had Ptolomaeus killed because of his purple robe, which attracted too much attention. After Columbus had placed America as a gem in the Spanish crown, jealousy set on the Spanish courtiers to depreciate his achievement, and aroused animosities till the great discoverer had his heart broken. Urged on by this bad passion, Dionysius flayed Plato because he was wiser than himself, and Philoxenius because his music was too popular. Jealousy made Korah lie about Moses, and Succoth depreciate Gideon.

Jealousy made the trouble between Jacob and Esau, that hurled Joseph into the pit, that struck the twenty-three fatal wounds into Julius Cæsar, that banished Aristides, that fired Antony against Cicero. Tiberius exiled an architect because of the fame he got for a beautiful porch, and slew a poet for his fine tragedy. That set Saul in a rage against David. How graphically the Bible puts it when it says:

"Saul Eyed David."

It seems to take possession of both eyes and makes them flash and burn like two port-holes of hell. "Saul eyed David." That is he looked at him as much as to say: "You little upstart, how dare you attempt anything great? I will grind you under my heel. I will exterminate you; I will, you miserable homunculus. Crouch, crawl, slink into that rat-hole. I will teach those women to sing some other song, instead of 'Saul has slain his thousands but David his tens of thousands.'" When Voltaire heard that Frederick the Great was forgetting him, and putting his literary admiration on Bacaulard d'Arnaud, the old infidel leaped out of his bed and danced the floor in a manical rage, and ordered his swiftest horses hooked up to carry him to the Prussian palace.

That despicable passion of jealousy led Napoleon the First to leave in his will a bequest of five thousand francs to the ruffian who shot at Wellington when the victor of Waterloo was passing through Paris. That stationed the grouty elder brother at the back door of the homestead when the Prodigal Son returned, and threw a chill on the family renunion while that elder brother complained, saying: "Who ever heard of giving roast veal to such a profligate?" Aye, that passion rose up, and under the darkest cloud that ever shadowed the earth, and, amid the loudest thunder that ever shook the mountains, and amid the wildest flash of lightning that ever blinded or stunned the nations, hung up on two pieces of rough lumber back of Jerusalem the kindest, purest, lovingest nature that heaven could delegate, and stopped not until there was no power left in hammer or bramble or javelin to hurt the dead Son of God.

That passion of jealousy, livid, hungry, unbalked, rages on, and

It Pierces the Earth

like a fiery diameter and encircles it like a fiery circumference. It wants both hemispheres. It wants the heavens. It would, if it could, capture the palace of God, and dethrone Jehovah, and chain the Almighty in eternal exile, and after the demolition of the universe would cry: "Satisfied at last, here I am! Alone! the undisputed and everlasting I, Me, Mine, Myself." That passion keeps all Europe perturbed. Nations jealous of Germany, of England, of Russia, and those jealous of each other, and all of them jealous of America.

In our land this passion of jealousy keeps all

The Political World A-boil.

There are at least five hundred people who are jealous of Governor Hill and would like to be his successor, about five thousand who are jealous of Grover Cleveland and would like to relieve him of the cares of office; and after the nominations of next summer have been made, a whole pandemonium of defamation, scurrility, hatred, revenge, falsehood, profanity, and misrepresentation will be turned upon this land. The tariff, about the raising or lowering or reformation of which many of them care nothing except as to its effect on votes, will be discussed from a thousand platforms; and the people of Louisiana will be told that the tariff must be arranged for the advantage of American sugar, the people of Virginia will be told that the tariff must be arranged for the advantage of American tobacco, and the people of Pennsylvania will be told that the tariff must be arranged for the advantage of American iron, and the people of Kentucky will be told that the tariff must be arranged for the advantage of American whisky, and the people of Ohio that the tariff must be arranged for the advantage of American wool, while Massachusetts and Connecticut will be promised protection for manufactures, and all the monetary interests, North, South, East and West, will be told in each neighborhood that the taxes and *tariff will be fixed to suit them, irrespective of anybody else*; and, the Presidential election over, all will settle down as it was before. If you think that all this discussion in public places is from any desire of the welfare of the dear people and not for political effect, you are grievously mistaken. Go into all

Occupations and Professions,

and if you want to know how much jealousy is yet to be extirpated, ask master builders what they think of each others houses, and merchants what their opinion is of merchants in the same line of business in the same street, and ask doctors what they think of doctors, and lawyers what they think of lawyers, and ministers what they think of ministers, and artists what they think of artists. As long as men and women in any department keep down and have a hard struggle, they will be faintly praised, and the remark will be: "Oh, yes; he is a good, clever sort of a fellow." "She is rather, yes, somewhat, quite—well, I may say, tolerably nice kind of a woman." But let him or her get a little too high, and off goes the aspiring head by social or commercial decapitation.

Remember that envy dwells more on small deficits of character than on great forces: makes more of the fact that Domitian amused himself by transfixing flies with his penknife than of his great conquests; of the fact that Handel was a glutton than of the fact that he created imperishable oratorios; more of Coleridge's opium habit than of his writing "Christabel" and "The Ancient Mariner"; more of the fact that Addison drank too much than of the fact that he was the author of "The Spectator"; more of a man's peccadilloes than of his mighty energies, more of his defeats than of his victories.

Look at the sacred and heaven-descended science of healing, and then see Dr. Mackenzie, the English surgeon who prolonged the life of the Crown Prince of Germany until he became Emperor, and I hope may yet cure him, so that he may for many years govern that magnificent German nation, than which there is no grander. Yet so great are the

Medical Jealousies

that Dr. Mackensie dare not walk the streets of Berlin. He is under military guard. The medical students of Germany can hardly keep their hands off of him. The old doctors of Germany are writhing with indignation. The fact is that in saving Frederick's life Dr. Mackenzie saved the peace of Europe. There was not an intelligent man on either side the ocean that did not fear for the result if the throne passed from wise and good old Emperor William to his inexperienced grandson. But when, under the medical treatment of Dr. Mackenzie, the Crown Prince Frederick took the throne, a wave of satisfaction and confidence rolled over Christendom, what shall the world do with the doctor who saved his life? "Oh," cried out the medical jealousies of Europe, "destroy him; of course, destroy him!"

What a brutal scene of jealousy we had in this country

When President Garfield Lay Dying!

There were faithful physicians that sacrificed their other practice and sacrificed their health for all time, in fidelity to that deathbed. Doctors Bliss and Hamilton and Agnew went through anxieties and toils and fatigues such as none but God could appreciate. Nothing pleased many of the medical profession. The doctors in charge did nothing right. We who did not see the case knew better than those who agonized over it in the sick-room for many weeks. I, who never had anything worse than a run-round on my thumb, which seemed to me at the time was worthy all the attention of the entire medical fraternity, had my own ideas as to how the President ought to be treated. And in proportion as physicians and laymen were ignorant of the case, they were sure the treatment practiced was a mistake. And when in post-mortem the bullet dropped out of a different part of the body from that in which it was supposed to have been lodged, about two hundred thousand people shouted: "I told you so!" "There, I knew it all the time!" There are some doctors in all cities who would rather have the patient die under the treatment of their own schools than have them get well under some other pathy. Yea; look at

The Clerical Profession.

I am sorry to say that in matters of jealousy it is no better than other professions. There are now in all denominations a great many young clergymen who have a faculty for superior usefulness. But they are kept down and kept back and crippled by older ministers, who look askance at these rising evangelists. They are snubbed. They are jostled. They are patronizingly advised. It is suggested to them that they had better know their place. If here and there one with more nerve and brain and consecration and divine force go past the seniors, who want to keep the chief places, the young are advised, in the words of Scripture: "Tarry at Jericho till their beards are grown." They are charged with sensationalism. They are compared to rockets that go up in a blaze and come down sticks, and the brevity of their career is jubilantly prophesied. If it be a denomination with bishops, a bishop is implored to sit down heavily on the man who will not be moulded; or if a denomination without bishops, some of the older men with nothing more than their own natural heaviness and theological avoirdupois are advised to flatten out the innovator.

In Conferences and Presbyteries

and associations and conventions there is often seen the most damnable jealousy. Such ecclesiastical tyrants would not admit that jealously had any possession of them, and they take on a heavenly air, and talk sweet oil and sugar plums and balm of a thousand flowers, and roll up their eyes with an air of unctuous sanctity, when they simply mean destruction of those over whom they pray and snuffle. There are cases where ministers of religion are derelict and criminal, and they must be put out.

But in the majority of cases that I have witnessed in ecclesiastical trials, there is a jealous attempt to keep men from surpassing their theological fellows; and as at the Presidential elections in country places the people have

A Barbecue,

which is a roasted ox round which the people dance with knives, cutting off a slice here, and pulling out a rib there, and sawing off a beefsteak yonder, and having a high time—so most of the denominations of Christians keep on hand a barbecue in which some minister is roasted, while the Church courts dance around with their sharp knives of attack, and one takes an ear, another a hand, another a foot, and it is hard to tell whether the ecclesiastical plaintiffs of this world or the demons of the nether world most enjoy it. Albert Barnes, than whom no man has accomplished more good in the last thousand years, was decreed to sit silent for a year in the pew of his own church while some one else occupied his pulpit; the pretended offence that he did not believe in a limited atonement, but the real offence the fact that all the men who tried him put together would not equal one Albert Barnes.

Yes: amid all professions and businesses and occupations and trades, and amid all circles, needs to be heard what God says in regard to envy and jealousy, which, though not exactly the same, are twins: "Envy is the rottenness of the bone;" "Where envy and strive is, there is confusion and every evil work;" "Jealousy is the rage of a man." My hearers, if this evil passion is in any of your souls, cry mightily unto God for

Its Expulsion.

That which has downed kings and emperors and apostles and reformers, and ministers of religion and thousands of good men and women, is too mighty for you to contend against unaided. The evil has so many roots, of such infinite convolution, that nothing but the enginery of omnipotence can pull it out. Tradition says that when Moses lifted up his hand to pray, it was all encrusted with manna; and no sooner do you pray than you are helped. Away with the accursed, stenchful, blackening, damning crime of jealously! Allow it to stay, and it will eat up and carry off all the religion you can pack into your soul for the next half-century. It will do you more harm than it does any one it leads you to assail. It will delude you with the idea that you can build yourself up by pulling somebody else down. You will make more out of the success of others than out of their misfortunes. Speak well of everybody. Stab no man in the back. Be a honey bee rather than a spider; be a dove rathar than a buzzard.

Surely this world is large enough for you and all your rivals. God has given you a work to do. Go ahead and do it. Mind your own business. In all circles, in all businesses, in all professions, there is room for straightforward successes. Jealousy entertained will not only bedwarf your soul, but it will flatten your skull, bemean your eye, put pinchedness of look about your nostril, give a bad curl to the lip, and expel from your face the divine image in which you were created. When you hear a man or woman abused, drive in on the defendant's side.

Watch for Excellences

in others, rather than for defects, morning-glories instead of nightshade. If some one is more beautiful than you, thank God that you have not so many perils of vanity to contend with. If some one has more wealth than you, thank God that you have not so great stewardship to answer for. If some one is higher up in social position, thank God that those who are down need not fear a fall. If some one gets higher office in Church or State than you, thank God there are not so many to wish for the hastening of your obsequies.

The Duke of Dantzig in luxurious apartments was visited by a plain friend, and, to keep his friend from jealousy, the Duke said: "You can have all I have if you will stand twenty paces off and let me shoot at you a hundred times." "No, no," said his friend. "Well," said the Duke, "to gain all my honors, I faced on the battle-field more than a thousand gunshots fired not more than ten paces off."

A minister of small congregation complained to a minister of large congregation about the sparseness of his attendants. "Ah," said the one of large audience, "My son, you will find in the Day of Judgment that you had quite enough people for whom to be held accountable."

Substitute for jealousy an everlasting emulation. Seeing others good, let us try to be better. Seeing others industrious, let us work more hours. Seeing others benevolent, let us resolve on giving a larger percentage of our means for charity. May God put congratulations for others into our right hand, and cheers on our lips for those who do brave and useful things. Life is short at the longest; let it all be filled up with

Helpfulness For Others,

work and sympathy for each other's misfortunes, and our arms be full of white mantles to cover up the mistakes and failures of others. If an evil report about some one come to us, let us put on it most favorable construction, as the Rhone enters Lake Leman foul and comes out crystalline. Do not build so much on the transitory differences of this world, for soon it will make no difference to us whether we had ten million dollars or ten cents, and the ashes into which the tongue of Demosthenes dissolved are just like the ashes into which the tongue of the veriest stammerer went.

If you are assailed by jealousy make no answer. Take it as a compliment, for people are never jealous of a failure. Until your work is done you are invulnerable. Remember

How Our Lord Behaved

under such exasperations. Did they not try to catch Him in His word? Did they not call Him the victim of intoxicants? Did they not misinterpret Him from the winter of the year 1 to the spring of the year 33; that is, from His first infantile cry to the last groan of His assassination? Yet He answered not a word! But so far from demolishing either His mission or His good name, after near nineteen centuries He outranks everything under the skies, and is second to none above them, and the archangel makes salaam at His footstool. Christ's bloody antagonists thought that they had finished Him when they wrote over the cross His accusation in three languages, Hebrew and Greek and Latin, not realizing that they were by that act introducing Him to all nations, since Hebrew is the holiest language, and Greek the wisest of tongues, and Latin the widest spoken.

You are not the first man who had his faults looked at through a microscope, and his virtues through the wrong end of a telescope. Pharaoh had the chief butler and baker endungeoned, and tradition says that all the butler had done was to allow a fly in the King's cup, and all the baker had done was to leave a gravel in the King's bread. The world has the habit of making a great ado about what you do wrong and forgetting to say anything about what you do right, but the same God will take care of you who provided for *Merlin, the Christian martyr*, when hidden from his pursuers in a hay-mow in Paris, and a hen came and laid an egg close by him every morning, thus keeping him from starvation. Blessed are they that are persecuted, although persecution is a severe cataplasm. Ointment may smart the wound before healing it. What a soft pillow to die on if when we leave the world we can feel that, though a thousand people may have wronged us, we have wronged no one; or, having made envious and jealous attack on others, we have repented of the sin and as far as possible made reparation! The good resolution of Timothy Poland in his quaint but exquisite hymn, entitled "Most Any Day," we might well unanimously adopt;

We'll keep all right and good within,
Our work will then be free from sin;
Upright we'll walk through thick and thin
Straight on our way.
Deal just with all; the prize we'll win
Most any day.

When He who made all things just right
Shall call us hence to realms of light,
Be it morn or noon or e'en or night,
We will obey;
We'll be prepared to take our flight
Most any day.

Our lamps we'll fill brim full of oil
That's good and pure, that would not spoil,
And keep them burning all the while
To light our way;
Our work all done, we'll quit the soil
Most any day.

The Death of Benjamin Harris Brewster,

who was Attorney-General of the United States during President Arthur's administration, occurred April 4, at his home in Philadelphia. He was 72 years of age having been born in Salem County, N. J., in 1816. He was a graduate of Princeton College. His national reputation dates from the time when he conducted the notorious Star Route trials, as public prosecutor. Though those trials resulted in a miscarriage of justice, it was through no fault of Mr. Brewster, who did his utmost, and displayed the highest ability in his efforts to get the evildoers convicted. Mr. Brewster was not only a good jurist, but learned on many subjects besides the law, especially on ecclesiastical history, on which he frequently lectured for the benefit of charities. Mr. Brewster's face was conspicuous wherever he went, on account of its being deeply scarred and drawn by burns received when a mere child, in the rescue of his baby sister from a fire. He was extremely sensitive to any reference to this disfigurement, and on one occasion administered a severe reproof to a lawyer who, during the trial of a case, had the bad taste to allude to it. Mr. Brewster, in dignified and simple language, told of a faithful nurse, wearied with untiring labors, who fell asleep while holding a little child; the tired arms relaxed the precious burden fell on the hearth—and when the little one was saved, the face of her rescuer "was burned as black as the heart of the man who could twit another of a personal deformity."

A DIVORCE AVERTED.

AN incident reported from Japan is worthy of wide publication in this country. The rapidly increasing number of divorces here might be checked if husbands would follow the example of the Japanese gentleman concerned. It is stated that this gentleman, who is a dignitary of some kind, was much distressed by the exceeding bad temper of his wife; so he called together some of his friends and asked their advice in the matter. They decided that he ought to put her away, and find some one with a more agreeable disposition. But he said that he was much attached to her, and that, as she had only this one fault, he was not willing summarily to send her off. About this time one of his friends became a Christian, and as a result of this change, a great difference was observed in his temper. He was formerly accustomed to get angry, and abuse his family and others in a fearful manner. But this new religion had so changed his heart that he was gentle and kind to every one at all times. So the Japanese dignitary thought over the matter very seriously; and when he was about to leave home for three months, he gave directions that his wife should attend the Christian service every Sabbath. On his return, he found that a great change had taken place in her also, and he was highly delighted. She was so impressed with the power and truth of Christian teaching, that she became a believer in Jesus Christ at once. Her violent temper had disappeared, and she was now one of the most amiable and gentle of wives. Her husband is not a Christian, but he testifies most emphatically to the value and truth of the religion that has wrought such a blessed change in his home.

BLOOD POISONING CURED.

A LETTER published in *Thy Healer** reports a remarkable case of recovery from blood-poisoning, which is one of the most obstinate maladies known to physicians. The sufferer, Miss E. A. Hopwood, of 61 Ashmead Road, London, says: "The Lord has just tenderly healed me of what seemed like a strained muscle in my arm, but which developed into serious blood poisoning, malignant pustules breaking out on my right arm and other parts of my body; my throat, too, was bad, and threatened to be malignant. When Dr. McKillian came to see my mother, I asked him to anoint me; he did so, and in less than two days, healing was manifest in the arm. A film over my eyes, and other serious symptoms, disappeared, and on the ninth and tenth days I almost watched delicate pink skin replacing the offensive pustules. How I praise our Father for His unspeakable Gift, Jesus, 'by whose stripes we are healed.' Neither medicine nor lotions did I use; He sent *His Word* and healed me. May He be glorified in my renewed powers!"

AN ANXIOUS NIGHT IN AFRICA.

IN a letter from Cape Palmas, Africa, to a contemporary, a Methodist lady missionary there describes a painful experience in the course of a journey she and other missionaries tried to make up the River Cavalla. She says: "There is a tribe near the mouth of the river who are not friendly with the Liberians, and they said we should not go up the river. But they are great cowards themselves, so they hired the next tribe above to stop us. We had heard all this, but we were ready, and so we could only go and try. Well, when we got up to this tribe they came out in canoes, each man with gun and knife, and blowing the war-horns. Such a frightful noise! They surrounded us and took us ashore. They unloaded one of our boats on the bank, and then held what they call a 'palaver'—a talk as to what next to do. We were told that if we stayed all night, we could go up the river in the morning; so the head man, next to the king, took all us women to sleep in his house, a new one he was building and had not used. It had two small windows and a door in it, and a part of the boards were down for the floor. He laid the rest down, and we put two mattresses down, and three women and four children did the best they could to rest on that. Two more rested in shipboard chairs, and Mrs. Astley and myself sat up on camp-chairs. We had left two of our young men at Cape Palmas, sick with the fever, and now Annie Whitfield was taken shortly after she left the Cape. So I spent the most of the night down on the floor, bathing her head as best I could by pouring water out of a bottle on a cloth, and when the bottle was empty I went to the river and filled it. It was a long night. I never closed my eyes; and when the moon went down, and it was dark, I could only feel, for we had no light. How I looked up to God for help in our hour of need! Taken by a savage tribe, no light, and fever among us!"

The missionaries were not allowed to proceed in the morning, but after a day of suspense were informed that they must return to Cape Palmas, as they would on no account be allowed to go higher up the river.

* *Thy Healer and Faith Witness*, a monthly magazine, edited by Mrs. M. Baxter, contains original articles on Holiness and Healing, Authentic Testimonies of Divine Healing, and Items of Intelligence from Heathen Lands where Missionaries are laboring in faith, soliciting no help from man, but relying solely on God for support. Annual Subscription, 75 cents, may be sent to the Manager of CHRISTIAN HERALD, 63 Bible House, New York.

REAL ESTATE IN PALESTINE.

A REMARKABLE fact, the significance of which will be recognized by students of prophecy, is mentioned in the *Watchword* in an article by Professor Kellogg. He says: "Within the past twenty years, the price of building sites about Jerusalem has risen fifty per cent., and is still increasing; while in twenty years the population has doubled. A later writer from Jerusalem, in *The Jewish Chronicle*, says, that about the Jaffa gate the price of building sites has increased fourfold in the last five years. The population of Haifa has doubled in ten years, the value of exports and imports has largely increased, and land has increased threefold in value since 1878.

Almost every acre of the great plain of Esdraelon is in a high state of cultivation, and "presents one of the most striking pictures of luxuriant fertility which it is possible to conceive." In 1882, the cost of transporting the Sursock's share of the wheat crop of this fertile plain to the seaport was $50,000. The Bedouin raids which made the fruits so uncertain a few years ago throughout eastern Palestine, have become a thing of the past. Roads are being constructed in a land where, till lately, there were none. In Haifa, a few years ago, a cart had never been seen; but lately, an omnibus was running four or five times a day to Acre, and a good road had been finished to Nazareth. A road is also in progress from Jerusalem to Hebron. Similar accounts reach us from other points. On this, besides many others, we have again the valuable testimony of Mr. Oliphant, who says: "*It is a remarkable fact, that while every province in Turkey has been steadily retrograding during the last few years, Palestine alone has been rapidly developing in agricultural and material prosperity.*" The modern world is at a loss what to do with the Jews, and the Jews are at a loss what to do with themselves. Slowly the idea of restoring the people to the land, and the land to the people, is taking shape and form in the minds of increasing numbers both of *Jews and Christians*.

A WAIL IN BABYLON.

IN a recent lecture by Mr. Boscawen, he surprised his hearers by the news that, a few months ago, a discovery had been made of two hundred thousand Babylonish tablets, which formed an enormous library. Some of them were the clay tablets on which children had written their exercises five thousand years ago, and they could still be easily read by persons who had learned the cuneiform character. But the most interesting part of the library was the theological department, in which were found hymn-books containing wonderful religious hymns, in one of which there is an eloquent and touching aspiration after perfect purity. In the library of Kutha, which is buried beneath the mound of Tel Ibrahim, and out of which city the Samaritans originally came, there have been discovered tablets which prove that here was chiefly taught the religion of Babylon, and from them we learn something of its eschatologic doctrines. The tablet called the "Descent of Ishtar," which records her descent into the city of the dead, is of singular beauty and power, and many of its passages are strikingly similar to well-known passages in our own loved Bible. "I go down the death road; I go to that place whence there is no return, to that place wherein is no light, and where I shall ever sit in thick darkness." How sublime in its simplicity, how touching in its pathos, and how gloomy is the valley of the Shadow of Death when we walk therein unaccompanied by Him who is the Life from the dead and the Light that shineth unto the perfect day!

How essentially mathematically and analytically minded the Babylonians were, is proved by the exact manner in which they arranged and catalogued these enormous libraries; a system so thorough and so perfect that to this day the authorities of the British Museum can find no better, and they docket and tabulate these very Babylonian inscriptions exactly as they were docketed and tabulated 5,000 years ago.

A MIDNIGHT INTERVIEW AT A STATION.

THE following incident, related in the New York *Telegram*, shows the value of a kind word spoken in season: "A *Telegram* reporter was on the platform of the Houston Street station, after midnight, one night this week, when two flashily-dressed young women, with bruised faces, and hair disheveled and flying in the damp air, came staggering up the narrow stairs of the station, followed soon afterward by a party of boisterous, half-drunken young men, who immediately began to bandy words with them.

"At that moment two elderly gentlemen entered the station and approached the women.

"'Go away,' said the younger, warningly, as her companion replied to one of the young men, with a loud oath, that she would not take another drink that night.

"'That's right, friend,' said one of the elderly gentlemen, encouragingly; 'but wouldn't it be better if you had God to help you?'

"Then opening their eyes wide, and for the first time distinguishing the two gentlemen from the crowd of well-dressed roughs about her, the older woman uttered a surprised exclamation, and both women, suddenly sobering up, conversed in low tones with their new-found friends until the arrival of the uptown train, boarding which, they were all soon lost to sight.

"At first the reporter did not take in the situation, and, turning to the ticket-seller, inquired who the gentlemen were.

"'Oh, everybody knows them around here,' was the reply; 'they were Mr. Crittenton and his friend, from the Florence Night Mission and Home, on Bleecker Street, off the Bowery. They'll go up now where the girls live, and pray with them awhile on the door-steps. Mr. Crittenton used to be a big druggist, on Fulton Street.'

"The Florence Mission, on Bleeker Street, which the reporter visited the next night, was packed to the very sidewalk with women and men, the occasion being of unusual attractiveness, because of the regular weekly 'sociable' that was to be held after the meeting that night.

On one side of the little chapel sat *the Home-girls*—those who have abandoned their lives of shame; and on the other the 'street girls,' whom the 'missionaries' had just brought in.

"A recently converted Bowery saloon-keeper was just giving a testimony as the reporter entered. Said he, 'I've gone into my back room and made a bottle of whisky while my bar-tender was selling some of you a drink. I made it as much out of poison as anything else, and yet you couldn't tell the difference between it and eight-year-old liquor.'

"After the momentary commotion had subsided, an Irishman got on his feet ahead of somebody else who was rising, and told how he was reclaimed from drunkenness, and then a young woman, and after her a middle-aged woman got up, and told how they had been reclaimed from drunkenness and lives of shame.

"A fine-looking man, who bore traces of dissipation, then said that on the night before, crazed by drink and overcome with remorse at the thought of the wife and children he had left destitute in the South, he was on his way to the East River to drown himself, when he staggered into the Mission, attracted by the word 'Florence,' the name of one of his little daughters, over the door-way.

"Away in the corner, *among the 'Home' girls, the reporter recognized the two young women* whom he had seen in the Houston Street station the night before."

THE KEY TO ALL PROPHECY

By G. H. Pember.*

Daniel's Perplexity—Enlightened by an Angel—The Rule of Interpretation Imparted—Daniel's Difficulty Solved—The Key of Universal Application The Seventy Weeks—Divided into Three Parts—Commencement of the First Seven—The Date Known—The End of the Sixty-Two Weeks also Known—The Interval Following—The Missing Week—The Sign of its Commencement Clearly Defined—The Close of the Week of Years.

THE great revelation granted in answer to Daniel's confession and prayer (Dan. 9:20-27) is a key to all Hebrew prophecies. Until he had received it he could not understand his own previous visions. After that of the Four Wild Beasts we find him saying: "As for me, Daniel, my cogitations much troubled me, and my countenance changed in me." And at the end of the eighth chapter also, he remarks: "And I, Daniel, fainted and was sick certain days; afterward I rose up and did the king's business; and I was astonished at the vision, but none understood it." But

The Disclosure

of the Seventy Weeks, which was vouchsafed to give him skill and understanding, enabled him to comprehend the purposes of God; and, consequently, in His preface to the next revelation, he tells us that he understood the thing, and had understanding of the vision. Surely that which enlightened Daniel is of the greatest importance to us also, upon whom the ends of the ages are come; nor should we forget those pregnant words: "And none of the wicked shall understand; but the wise shall understand." (Dan. 12:10.)

But what sign would mark the commencement of the four hundred and ninety years? And, when they had commenced, would their course be unbroken to the end of the period, or would it be interrupted. These questions the angel now proceeds to answer.

The Appointed Time

would begin at the going forth of a command to restore and build Jerusalem—not the temple, of which there is no mention, but the city, the street, and the wall. From this date until the appearance of an Anointed One, who should also be a Prince—that is, a Royal Priest—seven weeks and sixty and two weeks, that is, sixty-nine weeks, were to elapse; or in other words, there should be forty-nine and four hundred and thirty-four, or in all, four hundred and eighty-three years between the edict and the coming of the Messiah as a Prince. At this point it seems there is a gap separating the Four Hundred and Eighty-third Year from the last Seven. For God had given up the sinful nation which rejected His Son: His covenant was suspended, so that they were no longer His people: and, consequently, the course of the Four Hundred and Ninety Years had ceased to run on.

We have thus found from the prophecy of the Seventy Weeks that there has now been for more than eighteen hundred years an entire cessation of God's dealings with the Jews as a nation. A great gap extends—as we understand by the words of Daniel, Zechariah, and the Lord Himself—from Messiah the Prince to the false prince that shall come; from the good Shepherd, Whom the flock abhorred and rejected, to the idol shepherd, whom the majority of them will follow to their own destruction; from Him Who came in His Father's name to that other who shall come in His own name.

And during the interval between the true Messiah and the false, Hebrew prophecy is almost entirely in abeyance, and there remain in present operation only one or two fearful utterances which stretch, as it were, here and there across the whole

Width of the Chasm.

Such is the cry of Hosea, which startled the prosperous and haughty times of Uzziah with the fateful words: "For the children of Israel shall abide many days without a king, and without a prince, and without a sacrifice, and without an image, and without an ephod, and without teraphim."

Such is the mournful burden of Micah that, because of the smiting of the Judge of Israel upon the cheek, God would give up His people, until the travailing woman should bring forth.

And such, especially, are the terrible fulminations in Leviticus and Deuteronomy, those words of fear: "And the Lord shall scatter thee among all people, from the one end of the earth even unto the other; and there thou shalt serve other gods, which neither thou nor thy fathers have known, even wood and stone. And among those nations shalt thou find no ease, neither shall the sole of thy foot have rest: but the Lord shall give thee there a trembling heart, and failing of eyes, and sorrow of mind: and thy life shall hang in doubt before thee; and thou shalt fear day and night, and shalt have none assurance of thy life."

With the exception of such passages as these, and the few predictions respecting the Gentiles, all Old Testament prophecy—which invariably refers to the literal Judah, Jerusalem and Israel—centres upon the events immediately connected with the two advents. For, as Peter tells us, the Spirit, through the prophets, "testified beforehand the sufferings of Christ, and the glory that should follow"—that is, the first coming to suffer and die, and the consequent rejection of the Jews; and the second coming to rule with power, and the consequent restoration of all Israel.

The knowledge of this fact is indispensable to a right understanding of prophecy; for events connected with the two great but now widely separated eras, are often mentioned together, even in the same sentence. Nor is there any confusion in such an arrangement: for had the Jews received Christ at His first coming, John the Baptist would have been Elijah to them, the last Seven Years would have followed immediately, and then the kingdom would have been restored to Israel. But the unbelief of the Jews separated those things which might have been joined together, and, consequently, the marvellous events of the last Week have not yet begun to take place.

Lest, however, we should feel any perplexity in regard to the interpretation of Old Testament prophecy, the Lord Himself has given us

A Clue.

In the fourth chapter of Luke we may find an account of His visit to the synagogue at Nazareth, where He read a passage from Isaiah, and declared it was fulfilled on that day in the ears of His audience. The passage runs as follows: "The Spirit of the Lord is upon Me: because He hath anointed Me to preach the Gospel to the poor; He hath sent Me to heal the broken-hearted, to preach deliverance to the captives, and recovering of sight to the blind; to set at liberty them that are bruised, to preach the acceptable year of the Lord." When He had read so much, He closed the book; and if we turn to the sixty-first chapter of Isaiah, we shall see in what manner He extracted the passage. He ceased reading in the middle of a sentence, because its next clause leaps the wide chasm between the first and second advents, and speaks of "the day of vengeance of our God." Unless, therefore, He had closed the book when He did, He could not have said, "This day is this Scripture fulfilled in your ears."

Before, however, we deduce

A Canon of Interpretation

from our Lord's method of procedure, we should be careful to notice that prophecy must always, when it is possible, be taken literally. The Bible is not a riddle, but a revelation. Written to suit the mean capacities of our race while still in the flesh, it is easily intelligible to those who surrender themselves to the guidance of the Spirit. It presents but few difficulties, if we are willing to receive it just as it has been delivered to us, and do not wish to avoid that which is supernatural. And with a few avowed exceptions—such as when the mind that hath wisdom is challenged, or when he that hath ears to hear is bidden to hear—if it does speak figuratively, it employs plain and obvious figures, the purpose of which is to illustrate and make clear, and not to mystify.

There is no reason to doubt that the prophecies of the second advent will be fulfilled as literally as those of the first. From this consideration, and from the example given above of our Lord's way of dealing with Scripture, we would suggest the following method of interpretation:

In any prediction of the Old Testament, regard that which has been exactly fulfilled at the first advent as already past.

Apply all else to the times of the second advent, as literally as the case will allow.

By way of example we may cite the words of Isaiah: "For unto us a Child is born, unto us a Son is given: and the government shall be upon His shoulder." Now the Child was born, and the Son was given, at the first advent; but the Government did not then devolve upon Him, for He was cut off and there was nothing for Him. He left our world as a nobleman going into a far country to receive for Himself a kingdom and to return. At the second advent therefore, will the government be placed upon His shoulder. It is only *after* the Fourth Beast has been slain, and his body destroyed and given to the burning flame, that the Son of man shall be brought to the Ancient of days, and invested with dominion and glory, and a Kingdom.

So in the thirteenth chapter of Zechariah, the seventh verse refers to the first advent, but the eighth and ninth to the second; for the destruction of Jerusalem by Titus resulted in the dispersion of the whole Jewish nation, not in the deliverance of one-third of them.

If, then, we apply this process, of which our Lord Himself gives us an example, the Bible becomes a plain revelation, and is no longer a tissue of enigmas. Its every page sparkles with glory, and it is found to be filled with disclosures and instructions which Paul might well compare to gold, silver, and precious stones.

*From the third edition of his excellent work. "The Great Prophecies concerning the Jews, the Gentiles and the Church of God"—a book remarkable for the learning and wide research it displays, yet so simple in style and diction that any reader can understand it, and under its guidance perceive the meaning of the prophecies of the Bible. 458 pages. Price by mail, $1.50. For sale at this office, 63 Bible House, New York.

Complaints of Irregularities in the Post Office are forwarded to headquarters as soon as they are received at this office, and the officials there assure us that a thorough investigation is made in each case. These irregularities have increased enormously during the past few months, and the proprietors of other journals besides this are inundated with complaints from their subscribers, who rashly conclude that because they do not receive their papers they have not been mailed to them. We shall be glad to hear promptly from any subscriber whose copy of this journal goes astray, and we will at once notify the Postal authorities.

CURRENT EVENTS.

A Deadlock of Eight Days' Duration in the House of Representatives had brought public business in the lower branch of Congress to a perfect standstill, but the wheels of legislation, which had been clogged for over a week, were set in motion again on April 12. The cause of this deadlock was a measure known as the Direct Tax Bill. This bill provides to pay to the several States and Territories all the moneys collected under an act of Congress passed as a war measure in 1861, and levying a direct tax. The amount involved is $17,000,000. The bill to refund this tax was strenuously opposed by a determined minority, who asserted that the passage of such a bill would be tantamount to a legislative declaration that there is no limit or constitutional inhibition on Congress in the matter of appropriating public money. The minority resorted to every parliamentary device to prevent the consideration of the bill, and it was finally agreed to postpone it until December next.

The Twenty-fifth Anniversary of the Emancipation of the colored people from slavery in this country is to be celebrated by an Exposition on a large scale, to be held at Atlanta, Ga., and to continue from November 12, 1888, to February 12, 1889. The Exposition is intended to illustrate the progress and achievements of the colored race, and to furnish information as to their educational and industrial status. Early in the present session of Congress, a delegation of prominent colored men submitted this Exposition project to the Senate Committee on Education and Labor. They asked the Government to aid them in their enterprise, and to extend a loan to enable them to assure its success. As a result of this appeal the committee last week recommended the passage of a bill providing for a loan of $400,000, under restrictions similar to those contained in the acts in aid of the Centennial and New Orleans Expositions. The committee in its report says that the Exposition is to be conducted by a body corporate composed of representative colored men, known as the "Colored World's Fair Association of America," incorporated under the laws of the State of Georgia. The General Assemblies of Georgia, Alabama, and Tennessee have, by joint resolution, cordially indorsed the proposed Exposition, as has the New Orleans Chamber of Commerce; and memorials and petitions from many representative men and associations in the Southern States have been sent to Congress in favor of it. The city of Atlanta has tendered 200 acres of land and suitable buildings, free of rental charges. The colored population of the United States, according to the report of the Senate committee, is now upwards of 7,000,000. It was 6,518,793 by the census of 1880.

The Dependent Pension Bill, Which, as Stated in these columns on March 15, has passed the Senate, is being essentially changed and modified by the House Committee on Invalid Pensions. The most important changes relate to the amount of pension to be paid and the degree of dependency required. For the uniform rate of $12 a month provided for in the Senate measure, the House has substituted the monthly rate of one cent per day for each day of service preformed by the beneficiary. This, in some cases, would yield more than the $12 a month provided in the original bill, while in many others it would produce much less. The House Committee also changes that provision of the Senate bill which made a dependence on manual labor for support a prerequisite to receiving the pension. The result of the proposed alteration in many cases would be to make total disability for manual labor sufficient to secure the pension, even where there is no dependence on manual labor at all. The bill is made to apply to soldiers of all wars and their widows. These changes so materially change the character of the bill that its final passage, if achieved at all, will be considerably delayed.

An Important Decision of the United States Supreme Court was handed down on April 9. Its significance consists in its concession of State rights. The question in dispute was as to the right of a State to prohibit the manufacture and sale of oleomargarine. This the Court definitely sustained by upholding the Pennsylvania anti-oleomargarine law. That statute makes it unlawful for any person to manufacture or sell any butter or cheese or other article designed to take the place of these products, made from any compound other than unadulterated milk or cream. The opponents of this law asserted that it was in violation of the Fourteenth Amendment to the Constitution, and that oleomargarine was a new invention, not deleterious to the public health. The Supreme Court holds, however, that it is entirely within the police powers of the State to protect the public health, and that the questions whether the manufacture of oleomargarine is or may be conducted in such a way as to involve such danger to the public health as to require the suppression of the business rather than its regulation, are questions of fact and of public policy, which belong to the legislature of the State to determine.

The Arrest of a Prominent Spiritualistic medium, with her husband and two friends, took place in New York on April 11. Three weeks ago Luther R. Marsh, a well-known lawyer, who holds a responsible office in the city government, astonished the editors of the daily journals by inviting them to his house to see a number of paintings which he said were the work of Raphael, Rembrandt, and other eminent artists, who were induced to exercise their art in the spirit world by Madame Diss Debar, a medium residing with him. Reporters were sent to examine the paintings, and declared them to be miserable daubs, all evidently the work of one hand, and that not a skilful one. Mr Marsh, on being pressed, admitted that he had given Madame Diss Debar a deed of his house for the purpose of making it a "Temple of Spiritualism," and so strong was his belief in her powers, that he was evidently prepared to transfer other portions of his property to her. In order to save him from his own infatuation, several of his legal friends interfered, and having obtained evidence of the medium's previous operations of a similar kind, had her and her accomplices arrested for conspiracy.

Labor Troubles in the Brewing Trade Culminated last week in a strike in Chicago and a lock-out in New York. The principle involved is the same in both cases. In Chicago the employers have made a stand against recognition of the Unions. For more than a year the employers have been irritated against the Central Union, and a struggle was seen to be inevitable. One of the firms recently employed a non-Union man, and refused to dismiss him when called upon to do so. The Union men then quitted work, and as there was an evident intention on the part of other firms not to renew the annual agreement with the men, all the brewers' men in the city went on strike, involving the closing of the breweries and the idleness of two thousand men. *In New York* the dispute has arisen over the annual agreement hitherto made between the employers and the Unions. The Union wished a clause inserted pledging employers to use no kegs, malt, or coal but such as were produced by Union men. The employers not only refused to insert the clause, but to sign the same agreement as last year, and a lock-out was declared. It throws over three thousand men out of employment. This is one of the very few trade disputes which may benefit the public. If it restricts the production of beer it will be a blessing rather than a calamity.

An Important Letter from Emin Pasha, for whose rescue Mr. Henry M. Stanley is conducting an expedition, was received by the Anti-Slavery Society last week. It is dated August 16. In it he says: "I will certainly remain here when Stanley arrives. I could not desert my work just at the dawn of better times. Once provided with necessaries, I do not deem it difficult to open a direct road to the coast through Lango and Masai. It is only necessary to conquer the fierceness of the Lango people. Camels and donkeys form ample means of transportation. The death of Gordon was a great blow to civilization in Africa. Upon me, his last surviving officer in the Soudan, devolves the honor of developing his intentions." Still later information is published in an Italian journal, in two letters from an Italian traveller named Casati. They are dated respectively September 21 and 24, stating that he had been taken prisoner by King Traxiore, whom he finally persuaded to become friendly to Emin Bey. Eventually Traxiore charged him with a mission to negotiate an alliance with Emin Bey. The letters state that Stanley had not arrived at Wadelai up to the time of their despatch. These letters, though reassuring as to Emin, cause concern as to Stanley, who expected to arrive at Wadelai before the dates mentioned.

Disorders are Again Reported from Ireland. The determination of the Government to suppress the League and to disperse all its meetings seems to have revived the antipathy to English rule with increased violence. At a large League meeting at Kilrush on April 8, a riot became imminent, and a regiment of militia, with fixed bayonets, charged the crowd, and several persons were injured. At Ennis, on the same day, a meeting had to be broken up by the police and fifty persons were arrested. At Loughrea, where Mr. O'Brien was to speak, the crowd assumed a threatening attitude, and had to be dispersed by the police. At Miltown Malbay three thousand persons assembled, but dispersed quietly on the advice of their leaders when the police threatened to charge. A meeting at Ramsgrange was postponed for a week on account of the presence of a formidable police force.

A Significant Speech Dealing with the General European situation and the condition of Ireland was made by Lord Salisbury, the English Premier, at Carnarvon, Wales, on April 10. He expressed the conviction that all the rulers of Europe were struggling to prevent the calamity that might result from race conflicts, in which circumstances might arise that would involve their peoples. There was now reasonable hope that the life of Emperor Frederick would be continued.. His life would be a pledge for the advancement of mankind and the maintenance of peace. Referring to the fisheries treaty, Lord Salisbury said that he had sent Mr. Chamberlain to America unfettered with orders, beyond informing him of the broad views of the Government. The treaty was a monument, and would stamp a peaceful feeling upon both nations.

Contributions to the Fund for Supplying colored ministers in the South with this journal have been received since our last acknowledgment to the amount of $15.05. They are from: Pingree, Ill., $2; Fairmount, Minn., $2; Byesville, O., $5; Sierra City, Cal., 25c; Baltimore, Md., 50c; Newark, N. J., $1; Leeds, Ala. $1; Chicago, Ill., 50c; Woodhaven, N. Y., $3. On behalf of the beneficiaries of this fund we sincerely thank our friends who are supporting it. Each dollar has a wide-reaching influence, as it affords, under the blessing of God, direct assistance to some preacher who sorely needs it, and through him all to whom he ministers. We should be sincerely glad if the fund grew to such an extent that every colored minister in the country could receive the journal every week, and have the benefit of reading the sermons and other religious articles it contains.

Mr. E. P. Telford, the English Methodist evangelist, commenced a thirteen days' mission in the Fifth Street Methodist church, Philadelphia, on April 8. He expects to conclude his work in this country on May 1, and sail for England on May 15. He has accepted an engagement to hold a series of services in London in the Great Assembly Hall built by Mr. F. N. Charrington, commencing June 1. Mr. Telford trusts that the many friends he has made on this side the Atlantic will pray for a blessing on these services, as the opportunity is a grand one, the hall having a capacity for 5,000 persons.

Wonderful Jubilee Services to Commemorate the reception of *one thousand converts* were held in the Jane Street Methodist Episcopal Church last week. During the revival meetings conducted there by the Rev. Thomas Harrison, scenes of unprecedented enthusiasm have been witnessed, and at last the number of persons making a profession of faith, as the result of God's blessing on the services, reached one thousand. An all-day meeting, commencing at six o'clock in the morning, for praise and rejoicing, was called for April 13, and immense crowds assembled to take part in the glad celebration. Among the prominent clergymen who spoke during the day were Rev. T. De Witt Talmage, D. D., Rev. J. M. Buckley, D. D., Rev. J. H. Vincent, D. D., LL. D., and Rev. Stephen Merritt, the pastor of the church. The services continued all night; and Mr. Harrison and Mr. Merritt, though physically exhausted by their protracted labors, continued their efforts with undiminished ardor.

A Midnight Search for a Physician in New York, was graphically described by a poor barber to a reporter last week. He said that late on the night of April 5 his wife complained of severe pain, which, toward twelve o'clock, became alarming. She was in agony, but could not tell what was the cause, though she felt sure that, unless soon relieved, she must die. Her husband was scared, and ran out to find a doctor. He lived in a rear tenement in Mulberry Street, and knew of no physician whom he could call. He, therefore, went to the nearest police station, where the officer gave him the address of several physicians, and sent a patrolman with him to guide him in his search. At the first address the house was empty—the doctor having changed his residence; at the second and third the doctors were not at home; and at the fourth and last the doctor was himself sick in bed with rheumatism, and unable to move. The policeman then accompanied the barber to his home, and finding the woman still alive, but in excruciating agony, he called an ambulance. It was nearly four o'clock when the ambulance arrived, and then the surgeon would not take the patient, as it was not a hospital case. The search for a physician was then renewed, and at last, after several calls, a doctor responded and administered remedies, which almost instantly gave relief. "I am glad my wife recovered," said the poor man, "but I never want to pass another night like that." If the man had lived in his own mansion on Fifth Avenue, he would, probably, have found less difficulty in his search; but he, and all who are poor, need have no dread of such an experience in their spiritual maladies. The ear of the Great Physician is ever open to them. (Isa. 41: 17.)

A Philadelphia Belle's Scarred Shoulders are the result of a ludicrous but painful accident reported in a local journal. It states that a beautiful and charming young lady, who is a great favorite in fashionable society, a few evenings ago undertook to perform her toilet without her maid's assistance. She thought it would enhance her charms if she could curl the short locks of golden hair growing on the nape of her neck. To do this nicely she used an ordinary slate pencil, heated in the gas jet to such a degree that it almost singed the tresses as she turned them around it. Part of the stray locks had been treated, and, the pencil having been heated again, she proceeded to curl the remainder, when, to her horror, the hot pencil slipped from her fingers and rolled over her shoulders underneath her garments and lodged on her back beyond her reach. Her pitiful screams as the pencil burned into her delicate flesh soon brought her mother to her assistance, but not until she had suffered acutely and blisters had been raised that will be long in healing. The heated slate pencil, it is said, is regularly used for the hair by thousands of young ladies. This accident will probably lead those of them who hear of it to take extra care in the operation. It is much to be wished that they would also heed another warning of still greater moment. "Branding instead of beauty" was one of the threatenings pronounced against the daughters of Zion "who were haughty and walked with stretched forth necks and wanton eyes." (Isa. 3: 16, 24.)

A Clergyman Preaching His Own Funeral sermon was the strange spectacle witnessed at a church in Clark County, Georgia, on April 8. A coffin was brought into the church the day before, and the pastor, who is eighty-four years old, tested it by placing himself in it. On Sunday morning, fully three thousand persons assembled to hear what the eccentric preacher would say. Taking as his text (Eph. 2: 9), "Not of works, lest any man should boast," he gave a brief history of his life, and a modest account of his labors, from which it appeared that he was born in North Carolina, and in the course of his ministry had occupied pulpits in eleven different States. He had heard many funeral sermons preached, and had grieved as he listened to the praising of bad men and the over-lauding of good men. "I know my own faults," he said, "and my own good points. I have determined not to have men talking over my dead body about things they do not know, so I made up my mind to preach my own funeral sermon to-day. When at last my eyes are closed in death I want my body to be put away quickly under the blessing which I pronounce over myself to-day." Whatever may be thought of the discretion of the venerable preacher, his sermon afforded his hearers the spectacle of a man not afraid to think of his own death, and set before them the way by which they might attain that assurance. (II Cor. 5: 5, 6.)

The Rejection of a Wife's Petition Led to Her attempted suicide in New York, on April 11. Three years ago she listened to the wiles of a wicked man, who induced her to leave her home, and her husband and child, and live with him in Boston, Mass. As is invariably the case, the man tired of her, and neglected her. Conscience, too, continually reproached her, and finally she returned to New York, and going to her husband, confessed her sin, expressed her contrition, and begged his forgiveness. She found him obdurate; he would not forgive her nor allow her to stay in his home. She went to live with her widowed mother, but after a few weeks they were unable to pay for their board, and were in want. The wife then made another appeal to the husband she had wronged, and he gave her money and clothing, but would not reinstate her nor forgive her. She returned to her mother's home in acute agony of mind, and on Wednesday, during her mother's absence, she procured poison and drank it. Providentially her mother returned soon afterward, and discovering what she had done, had her removed to the Hospital, where by skilful treatment her life was saved. She is so melancholy, however, that it is feared she will make another attempt to kill herself. It is probable that she is partially demented, or she would dread death instead of seeking it. Her life even without her husband's pardon would be bearable if she would seek the forgiveness of God which is freely offered to her through Christ. (Isa. 55: 7.)

BRIEF NOTES.

Rev. A. T. Pierson, D. D., has resigned the pastorate of the Bethany Presbyterian Church, Philadelphia.

The New York Conference of the Methodist Episcopal Church pledged the members not to vote for a candidate for any office who was not a Prohibitionist.

The Baptist anniversary will be held in Washington, D. C., on May 16, immediately after the close of the Southern Baptist Convention in Richmond.

The Rev. Henry Y. Satterlee, rector of Calvary Episcopal Church, Fourth Avenue and Twenty-first Street, has declined the call to the assistant bishopric of Ohio.

The Rev. J. F. Campbell, who went into the Pine Mountains of Tennessee in 1886, says that he found there 700 square miles without a single church edifice or Sunday-school.

The United States Senate has passed a measure to establish a commission of five persons to investigate very fully, and from all sides, economical, political, and moral, the traffic in alcoholic liquors.

Urgent requests have come to Rev. F. E. Clark, President of the United Society of Christian Endeavor, to present the subject of the Society to the English public at the annual May meetings in London.

A second National Conference of the Anti-saloon Republicans is to be held in New York May 2 and 3. Its purpose is to induce the Republican National Convention to put an anti-saloon plank in its platform.

The Treasury Department of the Presbyterian Foreign Board has a very favorable outlook. The total receipts for eleven months to April 1 are $675,287, which is $92,270 over receipts last year for the same time.

The new French chapel at Springfield, Mass., which will be ready for dedication in May, makes the fifth French Congregational church in Massachusetts, one at Springfield, Holyoke, Ware, Fall River, and Lowell.

Messrs. Pratt and Birdsall have been recalled, after six weeks' labor, to the churches in Taunton, Mass., Wakefield and Cambridge. So encouraging were the results of the meetings that there was a desire for more of them.

Mr. Elliot F. Shepard, who recently purchased the well-known evening journal, the New York *Mail and Express*, publishes a text of Scripture at the head of its editorial columns every night, and says that he intends to do so as long as he shall control them.

At Mr. D. L. Moody's meetings in Denver, Col., over three hundred persons made a profession of faith. At Leadville and Colorado Springs the services were crowded beyond any religious service ever held in that locality. The inquiry meetings were thronged

Mr. C. H. Yatman has been holding meetings at Charleston, S. C. There was a very large attendance, and judging by the reports in the secular papers, which are of a flippant, sneering character, the results are very hopeful. When the world cries out that the conversions will not hold, we may be sure that it has been hurt.

The meetings conducted by Rev. B. Fay Mills in Indianapolis have been signally blessed. On Sunday, April 1, at the suggestion of Mr. Mills, instead of the regular Sabbath-school lesson being taught, each teacher had personal conversation with the members of his class, following it up with prayer and exhortation. A correspondent says it was a reaping time.

At a recent meeting in Pittsburgh, Pa., in St. Andrews Protestant Episcopal Church, eleven clergymen of different denominations sat in the chancel and took part in an evangelistic service. The secular journals are astounded by the fact that there was no clashing in the service. They all appeared to agree as to the main doctrine to be inculcated, and as to the way of salvation.

The eleventh Triennial Conference of the Young Men's Christian Associations of all lands is to be held in Stockholm, Sweden, August 15–19. Arrangements are being made for special rates to delegates and their friends. The party will sail *via* the *City of Berlin*, Inman Line, July 21. This will give an opportunity for a brief tour in Great Britain or on the Continent, as well as attendance upon the Conference.

Clergymen and Evangelists who will Allow Copies of the CHRISTIAN HERALD to be placed in the seats of churches, or will have them distributed at the doors, will be supplied with assorted parcels of back numbers if they will write to the Manager, 63 Bible House, New York.

THE RENT VEIL.

A New Sermon by Pastor C. H. Spurgeon.

"Jesus, when he had cried again with a loud voice, yielded up the ghost. And, behold, the veil of the temple was rent in twain from the top to the bottom."—Matt. 27: 50, 51.

"Having therefore, brethren, boldness to enter into the holiest by the blood of Jesus, by a new and living way which He hath consecrated for us, through the veil, that is to say, his flesh."—Hebrews 10: 19, 20.

Miracles a Fit Accompaniment of the Crucifixion—The Veil of the Temple Untearable by Human Hands—The Way Open to the Holy of Holies—I. What Has Been Done—The Separating Ordinance Abolished—Separating Sin Removed—Separation in Nature Bridged—A God-made Way of Access—II. What is Imparted—Boldness of Entrance—Right to Perform Priestly Functions—Shaking Hands With an Apostle—III. How to Exercise the Grace—Use the Way of the Atonement—Characteristics of the Way.

The death of our Lord Jesus Christ was fitly surrounded by miracles; yet it is itself so much greater a wonder than all besides, that it as far exceeds them as the sun outshines the planets which surround it. It seems natural enough that the earth should quake, that tombs should be opened, and that the veil of the temple should be rent, when He who only hath immortality gives up the ghost. The more you think of the death of the Son of God, the more will you be amazed at it. As much as a miracle excels a common fact, so doth this wonder of wonders rise above all miracles of power. That the divine Lord, even though veiled in mortal flesh, should condescend to be subject to the power of death, so as to bow His head on the cross, and submit to be laid in the tomb, is among mysteries the greatest. The death of Jesus is the marvel of time and eternity, which, as Aaron's rod swallowed up all the rest, takes up into itself all lesser marvels.

Yet the rending of the veil of the temple is not a miracle to be lightly passed over. It was made of "fine twined linen, with cherubim of cunning work." This gives the idea of

A Substantial Fabric,

a piece of lasting tapestry, which would have endured the severest strain. No human hands could have torn that sacred covering; and it could not have been divided in the midst by any accidental cause; yet, strange to say, on the instant when the holy person of Jesus was rent by death, the great veil which concealed the holiest of all was "rent in twain from the top to the bottom." What did it mean? It meant much more than I can tell you now.

According to the explanation given in our second text, the rending of the veil chiefly meant that the way into the holiest, which was not before made manifest, was now laid open to all believers. Once in the year the high priest solemnly lifted a corner of this veil, with fear and trembling, and with blood and holy incense he passed into the immediate presence of Jehovah; but the tearing of the veil laid open the secret place. The rent from top to bottom gives ample space for all to enter who are called, of God's grace, to approach the throne, and to commune with the Eternal One. Upon that subject I shall try to speak this morning, praying in my inmost soul that you and I, with all other believers, may have boldness actually to enter into that which is within the veil at this time of our assembling for worship.

I. First, think of

What Has Been Done.

In actual historical fact the glorious veil of the temple has been rent in twain from the top to the bottom: as a matter of spiritual fact, which is far more important to us, the separating legal ordinance is abolished. There was under the law this ordinance—that no man should ever go into the holiest of all, with the one exception of the high priest, and he but once in the year, and not without blood. If any man had attempted to enter there, he must have died, as guilty of great presumption and of profane intrusion into the secret place of the Most High. Who could stand in the presence of Him who is a consuming fire? This ordinance of distance runs all through the law; for even the holy place, which was the vestibule of the Holy of Holies, was for the priests alone. The place of the people was one of distance. All this is ended. The precept to keep back is abrogated, and the invitation is, "Come unto Me, all ye that labor and are heavy laden." "Let us draw near" is now the filial spirit of the gospel. How thankful I am for this! what a joy it is to my soul!

Some of God's people have not yet realized this gracious fact, for still they worship afar off. Very much of prayer is to be highly commended for its reverence; but it has in it a lack of childlike confidence. I can admire the solemn and stately language of worship which recognizes the greatness of God; but it will not warm my heart nor express my soul until it has also blended therewith the joyful nearness of that perfect love which casteth out fear, and ventures to speak with our Father in heaven as a child speaketh with its father on earth. My brother, no veil remains. Why dost thou stand afar off, and tremble like a slave? Draw near, with full assurance of faith. The veil is rent: access is free. Come boldly to the throne of grace.

This rending of the veil signified, also, the removal of the separating sin. Sin is, after all,

The Great Divider

between God and man. That veil of blue and purple and fine twined linen could not really separate man from God: for He is, as to His omnipresence, not far from any one of us. Sin is a far more effectual wall of separation: it opens an abyss between the sinner and his Judge. Sin shuts out prayer, and praise, and every form of religious exercise. Sin makes God walk contrary to us, because we walk contrary to Him. Sin, by separating the soul from God, causes spiritual death, which is both the effect and the penalty of transgression. Our Lord Jesus Christ put away sin by the sacrifice of Himself. He taketh away the sin of the world, and so the veil is rent. By the shedding of His most precious blood we are cleansed from all sin, and that most gracious promise of the new covenant is fulfilled: "Their sins and their iniquities will I remember no more." When sin is gone, the barrier is broken down, the unfathomable gulf is filled.

Separating Nature.

Next, be it remembered that the separating sinfulness is also taken away through our Lord Jesus. It is not only what we have *done*, but what we *are*, that keeps us apart from God. We have sin engrained in us: even those who have grace dwelling in them have to complain, "When I would do good, evil is present with me." Difference of nature hangs up a veil, but the new birth, and the santification which follows upon it, through the precious death of Jesus, remove that veil. He that hates sin, strives after holiness, and labors to perfect it in the fear of God, is in fellowship with God. It is a blessed thing when we love what God loves, when we seek what God seeks, when we are in sympathy with divine aims, and are obedient to divine commands: for with such persons will the Lord dwell. When grace makes us partakers of the divine nature, then are we at one with the Lord, and the veil is taken away.

"Yes," saith one, "I see now how the veil is taken away in three different fashions; but still God is God, and we are but poor puny men; between God and man there must of necessity be a separating veil, caused by the great disparity between the Creator and the creature. How can the finite and the infinite commune? Although this is a much thinner veil than those I have already mentioned, yet it is a veil; and it is hard for man to be at home with God. But *the Lord Jesus bridges*

The Separating Distance.

The gulf is completely filled by the fact that Jesus has gone through with us even to the bitter end, to death, even to the death of the cross. He has followed out the career of manhood even to the tomb: and thus we see that the veil, which hung between the nature of God and the nature of man, is rent in the person of our Lord Jesus Christ. We enter into the holiest of all through his flesh, which links manhood to Godhead.

Now, you see what it is to have the veil taken away. Solemnly note that this avails only for believers; those who refuse Jesus refuse the only way of access to God. God is not approachable, except through the rending of the veil by the death of Jesus. Come this way, and you may come freely. Refuse to come this way, and there hangs between you and God an impassable veil. Without Christ you are without God, and without hope. Jesus himself assures you, "If ye believe not that I am he, ye shall die in your sins." God grant that this may not happen to any of you!

The rent is not in one corner, but in the midst, as Luke tells us. It is

Not a Slight Rent,

through which we may see a little, but it is rent from the top to the bottom. There is an entrance made for the greatest sinners. If there had only been a small hole cut through it, the lesser offenders might have crept through; but what an act of abounding mercy is this, that the veil is rent in the midst, and rent from top to bottom, so that the chief of sinners may find ample passage! This also shows that for believers there is no hindrance to the fullest and freest access to God. Oh, for much boldness, this morning, to come where God has not only set open the door, but has lifted the door from its hinges, and removed it, post and bar.

I want you to notice that this veil, when it was rent, was rent by God, not by man. It was not the act of an irreverent mob; it was not the midnight outrage of a set of profane priests; it was the act of God alone. Nobody stood within the veil; and on the outer side of it stood the priests, only fulfilling their ordinary vocation of offering sacrifice. It must have astounded them when they saw that holy place laid bare in a moment. How they fled, as they saw that massive veil divided without human hand in a second of time! Who rent it? Who but God Himself? God Himself has set the ladder between earth and heaven. Come to him now, ye humble ones. Behold, he sets before you an open door!

II. And now I ask you to follow me, dear friends, in the second place, to an experimental realization of my subject. We now notice

What We Have:

"Having therefore, brethren, boldness to enter into the holiest." Observe the threefold "having" in the paragraph now before us, and be not content without the whole three. We have "boldness to enter in." There are degrees in boldness; but this is one of the highest. When the veil was rent, it required some boldness to *look* within. If any did look into the holiest when the veil was rent, they were among the boldest of men; for others must have feared lest the fate of the men of Bethshemesh would be theirs. (1 Sam. 6: 19.) Beloved, the Holy Spirit invites you to look into the holy place, and view it all with reverent eye; for it is full of teaching to you. Look, look boldly through Jesus Christ, but do not content yourself with looking! Hear what the text says: "Having boldness to *enter in*."

Let us follow the example of the high priest, and, having entered, let us perform the functions of one who enters in. "Boldness to enter in" suggests that we act as men who are in their proper places. To stand within the veil filled the servant of God with an overpowering sense of the divine presence. If ever in his life he was near to God, he was certainly near to God then, when, quite alone, shut in, and excluded from all the world, he had no one with him except the glorious Jehovah. O my beloved, may we this morning enter into the holiest in this sense. Jesus hath made us nigh by His precious blood. Try day by day to live in as great nearness to God, as the high priest felt when he stood for a while within the secret of Jehovah's tabernacle. The high priest had a sense of communion with God; he was not only near, but he spake with

God. Beloved, do you know what it is to commune with God? Words are poor vehicles for this fellowship; but what a blessed thing it is! Fellowship with the Most High is elevating, purifying, strengthening. Enter into it boldly. Enter into his revealed thoughts, even as he graciously enters into yours; rise to his plans, as he condescends to yours; ask to be uplifted to him, even as he deigns to dwell with you.

This is what the rent of the veil brings us when we have boldness to enter in; but, mark you, the rent veil brings us nothing until we have boldness to enter in.

Why Stand We Without?

Jesus brings us near, and truly our fellowship is with the Father, and with his Son Jesus Christ. Let us not be slow to take up our freedom, and come boldly to the throne.

But the high priest, if you recollect, after he had communed and prayed with God, came out and blessed the people. That is what you will do if you have the boldness to enter into the holiest by the blood of Jesus: you will bless the people that surround you. The Lord has blessed you, and He will make you a blessing. Your ordinary conduct and conversation will be a blessed example; the words you speak for Jesus will be like a dew from the Lord: the sick will be comforted by your words; the despondent will be encouraged by your faith; the lukwarm will be recovered by your love. May we each one have boldness to enter in, that we may come forth laden with benedictions!

Why is it that we have boldness? Is it not because of our relationship to Christ which makes us "brethren"? "Having therefore, *brethren*, boldness." The feeblest believer has as much right to enter into the holy place as Paul had; because he is one of the brotherhood. I remember a ryhme by John Ryland, in which he says of heaven:

"They all shall be there, the great and the small;
Poor I shall shake hands with the blessed St. Paul."

I have no doubt that we shall have such a position, and such fellowship. Meanwhile, we do shake hands with him this morning as he calls us brethren. We are brethren to one another, because we are brethren to Jesus. Where we see the Apostle go, we will go; yea, rather, where we see the Great Apostle and High Priest of our profession enter, we will follow. "Having, therefore, boldness."

Our boldness arises from the perfection of His sacrifice. Read the fourteenth verse: "He hath perfected for ever them that are sanctified." We rely upon the sacrifice of Christ, believing that He was such a perfect substitute for us, that it is not possible for us to die after our substitute has died; and we must be accepted, because He is accepted. Moreover, we have this for certain, that as a priest had a right to dwell near to God, we have that privilege; for Jesus hath made us kings and priests unto God, and all the privileges of the office come to us with the office itself. We have a mission within the holy place; we are

Called To Enter

there upon holy business, and so we have no fear of being intruders. A burglar may enter a house, but he does not enter with boldness; he is always afraid lest he should be surprised. You might enter a stranger's house without an invitation, but you would feel no boldness there. We do not enter the holiest as house-breakers, nor as strangers; we come in obedience to a call, to fulfil our office.

I cannot leave this point until I have reminded you that we may have this boldness of entering in at all times, because the veil is always rent, and is never restored to its old place. The Lord said unto Moses, Speak unto Aaron thy brother, that he come not at all times into the holy place within the veil before the mercy-seat, which is upon the ark; that he die not;" but the Lord saith not so to us. Dear child of God, you may at all times have "boldness to enter in." The veil is rent both day and night. Yea, let me say it, even when thine eye of faith is dim, still enter in; when evidences are dark, still have "boldness to enter in"; and even if thou hast unhappily sinned, remember that access is open to thy penitent prayer. Come still through the rent veil, sinner as thou art. What though thou hast backslidden, what though thou art grieved with the sense of thy wanderings, come even now! "To-day, if ye will hear His voice, harden not your hearts," but enter at once; for the veil is not there to exclude thee, though doubt and unbelief may make you think it is so. The veil cannot be there, for it was rent in twain from the top to the bottom.

III. My time has fled, and I shall not have space to speak as I meant to do upon the last point—how we exercise this grace. Let me give you the notes of what I would have said.

Let us at this hour enter into the holiest.

Behold The Way!

We come by the way of atonement: "Having therefore, brethren, boldness to enter into the holiest by the blood of Jesus." I have been made to feel really ill through the fierce and blasphemous words that have been used of late by gentlemen of the modern school concerning the precious blood. I will not defile my lips by a repetition of the thrice-accursed things which they have dared to utter while trampling on the blood of Jesus. Everywhere throughout this divine Book you meet with the precious blood. How can he call himself a Christian who speaks in flippant and profane language of the blood of atonement? My brothers, there is no way into the holiest, even though the veil be rent, without blood. We have always to plead the atonement. As without shedding of blood there is no remission of sin, so without that blood there is no access to God.

Next, the way by which we come is *an unfailing way*. Please notice that word—"by a *new* way"; this means by a way which is always fresh. Then the apostle adds, it is a "*living way*." A wonderful word! The way by which the high priest went into the holy place, was of course a material way, and so a dead way. We come by

A Spiritual Way,

suitable to our spirits. It is *a dedicated way*: "which He hath consecrated for us." When a new road is opened, it is set apart and dedicated for the public use. Sometimes a public building is opened by a king or a prince, and so is dedicated to its purpose. Beloved, the way to God through Jesus Christ is dedicated by Christ, and ordained by Christ for the use of poor, believing sinners, such as we are. Lastly, it is *a Christly way*; for when we come to God, we still come through His flesh. There is no coming to Jehovah except by the incarnate God. God in human flesh is our way to God; the substitutionary death of the Word made flesh is also the way to the Father.

Beloved, I have done when I have just remarked upon the next two verses, which are necessary to complete the sense, but which I was obliged to omit this morning, since there would be no time to handle them. The apostle tells us that we may not only come with boldness, because our high priest leads the way, but because we ourselves are prepared for entrance. Two things the high priest had to do before he might enter: one was, to be sprinkled with blood, and this we have; for "our hearts are sprinkled from an evil conscience."

The other requisite for the priests was to have their "bodies washed with pure water." This we have received in symbol in our baptism, and in reality in the spiritual cleansing of regeneration. To us has been fulfilled the prayer:

"Let the water and the blood,
From Thy riven side which flowed,
Be of sin the double cure,
Cleanse me from its guilt and power."

We have known the washing of water by the Word, and we have been sanctified by the spirit of His grace; therefore, let us enter into the holiest. Why should we stay away? Why not begin to-day that sweet enjoyment of perfect reconciliation and delight in God, which shall go on increasing in intensity until you behold the Lord in open vision, and go no more out? Heaven will bring a great change in condition, but not in our standing, if even now we stand within the veil. It will be only such a change as there is between the perfect day and the day-break; for we have the same sun, and the same light from the sun, and the same privilege of walking in the light. "Until the day break, and the shadows flee away, turn, my beloved, and be thou like a roe or a young hart upon the mountains of Division." Amen, and Amen.

GEMS FROM NEW BOOKS.

THE ROMAN PUNISHMENT.*

IT is observable that the Roman magistrates, when they gave sentence upon any one to be scourged, a bundle of rods tied hard with many knots was laid before them. The reason was this: that whilst the beadle, or flagellifer, was untying the knots, which he was to do in a certain order and not in any other hasty or sudden way, the magistrate might see the carriage and deportment of the delinquent, whether he were sorry for his fault, and showed any hope of amendment, that then he might recall his sentence, or mitigate the punishment; otherwise he was corrected the more severely. Thus God in the punishment of sinners, how patient He is; how loath to strike; how slow to anger if there be but any hopes of recovery! How many knots doth He untie? How many rubs doth He make in His way to justice? He doth not try us by martial law, but pleads the case with us, "Why will ye die, O House of Israel?" And all this to see whether the poor sinner will throw himself down at His feet, whether he will come in, and make his peace and be saved.

The King's Thread.

It is reported of the old kings of Peru, that they were wont to use a tassel or fringe made of red wool, which they wore upon their heads, and when they sent any governor to rule as viceroy in any part of their country, they delivered to him one of the threads of their tassel, and for one of those simple threads he was as much obeyed as if he had been the king himself—yea, it hath so happened that a king hath sent a governor only with this thread to slay men and women of a whole province, without any further commission. For of such power and authority was the king's tassel with them, that they willingly submitted thereunto, even at the sight of one thread of it. Now, it is to be hoped that if one thread shall be so forcible to draw heathen obedience, there will be no need of cart-ropes to haul on that which is Christian.

The Parson Converted.

Mr. Haslam, telling the story of his conversion, says, "I do not remember all I said, but I felt a wonderful light and joy coming into my soul. Whether it was something in my words, or my manner, or my look, I know not; but all of a sudden a local preacher, who happened to be in the congregation, stood up, and putting up his arms, shouted out in Cornish manner, "The parson is converted! The parson is converted! Hallelujah!" and in another moment his voice was lost in the shouts and praises of three or four hundred of the congregation. Instead of rebuking his extraordinary "brawling," as I should have done in a former time, I joined in the outburst of praise; and to make it more orderly I gave out the doxology—"Praise God from whom all blessings flow"—which the people sung with heart and voice, over and over again.

A Son Puzzled.

An ungodly youth accompanied his parents to hear a certain minister. The subject of the discourse was the heavenly state. On returning home, the young man expressed his admiration of the preacher's talents. "But," said he, turn-

* From Spurgeon's Sermon Notes: Volume IV., Romans to Revelation. The outlines of sermons which this volume contains are useful to preachers, Sunday-school teachers, and all Bible students: being a commentary of a most practical character, with anecdotes and quotations illustrative of the texts. Pp. 408; Price $1; Published by *Robert Carter & Brothers*, 530 Broadway, New York.

The Marriage of Prince Oscar of Sweden to Miss Ebba Munck.

ing to his mother, "I was surprised that you and my father were in tears." "Ah, my son!" replied the anxious mother, "I did weep, not because I feared my own personal interest in the subject, or that of your father; but I worried for fear that you, my beloved child, would be forever banished from the blessedness of heaven." "I supposed," said the father turning to his wife, "that those were your reflections; the same concern for our dear son made me weep also." These tender remarks found their way to the young man's heart, and led him to repentance.

A Hindoo Mother.

Away over in India a poor native woman—like Naomi—"was left of her two sons." She did not, perhaps, know enough to think about God at all in her grief; but she would take no comfort. To everything that could be said, she had but one answer: "I had but two, and they are both gone."

Day after day she pined and fretted, going listlessly about, her life "empty" of all but a blank despair. One morning, as she wandered here and there among the people of the mission, one of them again remonstrated. But the poor thing gave her old reply: "I had but two, and they are both gone." "Look!" said the worker, turning, and pointing towards a group near by, where a white lady of the mission stood directing some dusky natives; "Do you see her?" The woman looked and saw a sweet, pale face; patient, gentle, glad, as clear as a sky washed blue with storms, but wearing that unmistakable look which tells that storms have been. "Yes," she said, "I see her." "Well," said the other, "she has lost her sons too!"

The poor native mother gazed for a minute, spellbound, then she sprang towards her. "Oh, lady," she cried, "Did you have two sons? Are they both gone?"

And now the white mother on her part turned and looked. "Yes," she said, "I had two."

"Are they both gone?"

"Both."

"But they were all I had," cried the other, "and they are both gone!"

"And mine are both gone," said the white lady, clasping the hands of her poor sister in sorrow. "But Jesus took them; and they are with Jesus, and Jesus is with me. And by and by I shall have them again."

And from that hour the native woman sat at her white sister's feet, followed her about, and from her would take comfort—"the comfort wherein she herself was comforted of God."

THE ROYAL SWEDISH WEDDING.

(*See Illustration.*)

THE marriage of Prince Oscar of Sweden and Norway and Mlle. Ebba Munck, whose portraits appeared in this journal on March 8, took place at St. Stephen's Church, Bournemouth, England, on March 15. It was a day of brilliant sunshine, and the air was fragrant with the aroma of the surrounding pine forests. The church was decorated with flowers, and filled with a fashionable assemblage. The chancel-steps were draped with ruby velvet. The first of the wedding party to arrive were the Crown Princess of Denmark and the Duchess of Albany, the former attired in a costume of old gold velvet, the latter wearing a dress of gray-striped silk. The Queen of Sweden was dressed in ruby velvet, with white bonnet and feather-plume. The bride entered with her cousin, Colonel Munck. The bridegroom wore the gold and blue uniform of a naval commander. The bride wore a dress of ivory satin trimmed with lace and feathers, and had on her head a coronet of myrtle and orange-blossoms surrounded by a veil. *Bridesmaids there were none.*

The service, which was according to the rites of the Swedish Lutheran Church, was conducted by Pastor Gustaf Reskow, one of the Swedish court chaplains. It began with the singing in English of the Psalm commencing, "I will lift up mine eyes unto the hills from whence cometh my help." The singing over, the pastor delivered an address in Swedish to the pair, who now stood before him. Dwelling on the words, "If we walk in the light," he spoke of the eternal light that could illumine this world of darkness. The address was brief, and then came the questions according to the Lutheran ritual, "Wilt thou, Oscar Charles Augustus, have this woman to be thy wife, to love her always, in good days and in evil days?" The Prince made answer, "Yes," as also did the bride to the reciprocal question. Then bridegroom placed the ring on the open b in the pastor's hands, and, turning to the br said in Swedish, "I take you to be my la wife, for good times and bad times, and in to I give you as a symbol this ring." Both the golden circle, and the bride repeated same formula, substituting the words, "an token I accept this ring." After Psalm had been sung in Swedish, the blessing pronounced over the married pair, who k together on a gold-embroidered cushion. hymn, "Jesus is my best friend," followed, service terminating with two verses of English marriage hymn. "How welcome the call, and sweet the festal day."

During the singing Prince Oscar led bride to his Royal mother, who kissed embraced her several timer with much ten ness. Then the bridegroom himself was war embraced by her, and from the Queen passed on to the Crown Princess of Denm who kissed both, and so on to the Duches Albany and Prince Oscar's two brothers. service occupied twenty-five minutes. Su quently Prince and Princess Bernadotte, name by which the newly married couple be known, left for the Isle of Wight, where were to spent the honeymoon.

A STREET IN CAIRO.

(*See Illustration on page 253.*)

A RECENT traveller in Egypt has calle "the land of contrasts." The name is ap priate, for two civilizations are there side by s The ruins of magnificent temples, built of sto quarried under the lash of the Pharaohs, w derful statuary and the remains of edifices unequaled grandeur, stand there in sharp c trast with the mean, almost squalid, erection a race as incapable of appreciating the bea of the ancient edifices as they are of constr ing them. The traveller finds it difficult realize, as he looks upon the people and cities sunk in lazy indifference to all but wants of the hour, that Egypt was once mig among the ruling nations of the world. pecially in Cairo, the capital of Egypt, is contrast conspicuous. There the impo randeur of the achievements of ygone generations in close proximity to the tawdry work of modern times, renders the latter still more contemptible.

The city of Cairo covers about three square miles and is surrounded by a wall. Ismail Pasha, the former Khedive, spent enormous sums in beautifying the city according to his notions. New streets were opened, gorgeous buildings erected, and a system of mains laid down. Yet even these modern improvements could not make Cairo a modern city. The antipathies of race and religion existing among its people rendered it unsafe to open the city to free intercourse. The quarters inhabited respectively by Christians, Jews, Turks, &c., are all separated by huge gates, at which a guard of soldiers is placed every night. The street represented in the illustration is in the most ancient part of the city, and forms a connecting link between the remote past and the present. The majority of the recent buildings of the poor are of mud only. To get an idea of the city and surrounding country, as a whole, it is only necessary to ascend to the summit of the citadel, and it is then spread out before the spectator like a map. The following is a graphic description of the scene as described by Dr. James Ludlow: That silver gleam winding down at our left is the Nile, whose source has been the geographical enigma of all centuries, whose annual overflow redeems from the desert a narrow ribbon of fertility, which has nourished the mightiest empires, whose combined mysteries and beneficence drew men to worship it in one of the earliest and most influential religions of mankind.

A Street in Cairo, Egypt.

Beyond the river, beneath the sands of the Libyan desert, lie the buried ruins of ancient Memphis, where the prostrate colossal statue of Rameses II., like some giant guard asleep at his post, has been on duty for *three thousand years*. A little to the north, and within an easy carriage drive of a morning, rise the great Pyramids, the largest and *oldest works of man*. So vast are they, that though they have been frequently used as quarries for palaces, fortifications, and mosques, they are not from this distance visibly diminished. Around them are tombs and temples in which are buried the secrets of remotest antiquity, over which the Sphinx watches with motionless lips.

On this side of the river lies the suburb known as *Old Cairo*, by many believed to be the Babylon mentioned in the first Epistle of Peter, certainly that Babylon to which Strabo refers, and whose old Roman fort is still visible among the débris of two thousand years.

Directly before us as we look north from the citadel lies Cairo proper. The city was founded by the Fatemite princes in 969 A. D. The planet Mars, or Kaher, being then ascendant, they called the city El-Kaherah, from which the present pronunciation, Cairo, is derived. The forest of minarets and domes, houses and tombs, marks every generation since.

A natural division of the city would be into two sections, the one of the dead, the other of the living; for large districts of it are given up to tombs. Many of these are really memorial mosques, in which lie the bodies of the Caliphs and Mameluke princes. Here and there is *a woman's tomb*, at the window of which is a running stream of water and a cup, that the thirsty may drink and bless the memory of the departed. Most of the tombs are unsightly slabs or plastered mounds, hardly distinguishable in color from the deep dust which, unlike our green grass, glares around them. These cemeteries are perfect Tophets of filth, the lair of mangy dogs and lazared men. The city of the living is majestic from a distance, with its homes of nearly 400,000 people, and its 400 mosques. But when we descend into it we will find it compact with as much squalor and misery as can be found elsewhere within the same limits on the globe.

MRS. TRANSOME'S PUPIL.

A SERIAL STORY.

(Continued from page 230.)

Philip's Friend.

I THOUGHT in the prison Rebecca would say nothing, and the fifteen minutes given to us would pass in silence. She stood, holding fast by the iron bars, and looking at Robin with fixed eyes; all her face quivering, and her lips twitching; while he stared back at her, sullen and miserable, with his felt mask pushed up over his forehead, ready to be pulled down again so as to hide his face, when he went back among his fellow-convicts. How many minutes had gone I could not tell, but I felt as though we had been there a long, long while, gazat one another, before Rebecca found voice to speak to him.

"Robin," she said, "forgive me."

"No," he answered, gruffly.

"Harken to me, Robin," she went on, "I've made up my mind what I'll do. I'll come out to Australia, and I'll get a place as servant near where you are; and if ever I can see you, I'll go through fire and water to get a sight of you; and whenever yo're let out, I'll be there ready to take hold of your hand the moment you come through the jail-door. Ay! I will, if there's a breath of life in my body."

I saw a gleam come over Robin's miserable face, and into his sullen eyes; and he stretched out his hand through the bars, as if he could take hold of hers there and then. But he could not reach her, nor her hand touch his.

"You'll forgive me, if I'll do what I say!" asked Rebecca earnestly; "it's many a year to bide, but I'll do it, if the Lord keeps me alive. I'll be at thy prison door ready for thee to come out; and we'll begin a new life, my dear, thee and me. You had a good mother, Robin."

"Ay!" he said with a sob, and the tears rolled down his face.

"Oh! if I'd only been a good woman like her!" cried Rebecca, "but God's forgave me, Robin, and He'll forgive you too. Only think of your mother, and ask God to forgive you, and help us to be good till we meet again. I must go away now, and may never see you for a long while; maybe not till your time's over; but I'll be there, in Australia; and you say to yourself till then, 'She's true to me at last.' Tell me if you forgive me before I go."

"Ay! I forgie' thee fully and freely," he answered. "God bless thee, lass! I'll look out for thee to be watin' for me out yonder."

"Time's up!" said the warder, throwing down his newspaper, and coming close to us.

"Good-bye, Robin! Good-bye, my dear!" cried Rebecca; "I'll be there!"

"Good-bye!" he said; but there was no time for another word from either of them.

So Rebecca and I went our way, leaving Robin within those dreary walls, with but a spark of hope shining in the far-off years. We told Philip Champion of the pledge she had given to him; and his face glowed, and his eyes sparkled with joy, as he said it was a true thing, and a noble thing to do. And he called Rebecca his friend and sister, and promised to use all the influence he had at home or abroad on behalf of Robin Cherrick, though it was little anybody could do for him; for the sentence was passed, and he must bear it as the due punishment for his crime. But Philip made every arrangement for Rebecca, so that she could go out to Australia with ease and comfort; and, though it did not come to my knowledge until I heard from her months afterwards, he settled upon her the thousand pounds which had been promised to her by his uncle. So she was a rich woman in that distant country; and being clever and quick, she opened a small business, and began to make a home for herself and Robin when his time was up.

I went to Liverpool with Rebecca to start her on her long voyage. The ship lay in the middle of the river, with a flag floating from the masthead. There was a crowd of emigrants waiting on the pier, for the pilot-boat to put them on board of her; and one little child in the throng, who looked up into Rebecca's face saw something there that took her fancy, and would cling to her, till Rebecca took her up in her strong arms, and held her there, kissing her fondly from time to time. Then I knew she would not be lonely or dull on board ship, through the long, idle months. I went across in the boat with them, and saw the berth where she was to sleep. But I was dazed by the bustle about me, and hardly knew what I said or did, till there came the clang of a bell, and a shout of "All friends ashore!" and Rebecca clasped me about the neck, and burst out crying. They hurried me along, and down into the boat again; and when my eyes were clear from tears I saw the ship lying behind us, with its masts against the light of the setting sun; and the blue flag was being lowered from the mast-head.

And I said to myself, "There isn't a truer heart than hers on board yon ship. God grant she and Robin may win through to a good old age yet, like Transome and me."

* * * * * * *

It is I, Milicent Carr, who have written down the foregoing narrative, from the lips of Mrs. Transome herself, scarcely venturing to alter a word in them; yet now and again retouching them, as fondly and carefully as one brushes away a speck from a portrait that we love.

And now that the time is come when the whole is complete, and the past has "orbed into the perfect star, we saw not when we dwelt therein;" and I can look back at it, with eyes still dimmed with tears, and see it shining with a brightness that grows more and more unto the perfect day—now I am ready to tell you myself all that is lacking to finish the history Alice Transome began.

First of all, then, you must be told how empty and dreary my own existence had become, even before I had fairly passed through my girlhood. My brother, George Carr, was suffering from a spinal complaint, which would make him for life a prisoner in his own room. My father and mother had made every arrangement for the future with a view to his comfort solely; and I was left in charge of him, in solemn charge, by both of them. His illness kept us in so utter a seclusion that I had no friends, no acquaintances even, besides the busy physician, who spent a few minutes with us occasionally, not in the hope of effecting a cure for George, but to render to him any alleviation of his pain which was possible. Two old servants, a middle-aged man and his wife, who had no wish to change their condition, formed our household.

Our house was a detached dwelling; one of those places in Brompton presenting a blank side to the road, and surrounded by high walls over which no passer-by can catch a glimpse of the interior. It had been bought by my father purposely for George, who could be carried out upon the lawn, when the summer was hottest, and lie there under the rustling leaves of the poplars, or the thick branches of the elms, where the birds chirped drowsily from their hiding-places amidst the foliage. But after some years even this change became too trying for him; and all he could bear was to have the windows flung wide open, and lie with his pale face watching the summer clouds floating across the little field of blue which could be seen from his sofa. Sometimes for hours together he could not suffer the sound of my voice, nor the turning of a leaf in my book; and all I could do for him was to sit in perfect stillness, where, if his languid eyelids opened for an instant, he could see my face, and feel that he was not forsaken.

But all this wore out my girlhood. The long seclusion made me shy and formal; and it had become difficult, if not impossible, for me to form any friendship, should the chance come across me. I did not know how to respond if any stranger spoke to me, except on mere matters of business. By the time I was five-and-twenty I felt as old as many women are at fifty. All the possibilities of my life seemed exhausted; and only a vast barren wilderness stretched before me, which made me shudder as I looked forward, and saw nothing between me and the far horizon except a level flat, threatening a perpetual monotony and weariness.

"Milly," said George to me, one day when he was unusually well, "you and I need more interest in our lives. What do you say to adopting a child?"

"Adopting what?" I cried, feeling sure I had not understood him aright.

"A child!" he repeated: "a boy, I think; for if he were too noisy and boisterous, we might send him out of the way when I could not bear with him."

"If you had a child to think of," he went on, "you would feel younger again; and perhaps I should as well. I fancy I should like to watch a boy playing in the garden, or hear him whistling about our quiet house, or coming in from school every evening."

"But there are your bad days," I objected.

"Well! I really think I give way to my bad days," he said: "but when I cannot bear a noise, he must stay out of hearing somewhere, or learn to be quiet for a while. At any rate, we could try it for three months; we should know by the end of that time."

We talked it over for a day or two; and the plan took deeper hold of us both, until at last I wrote out an advertisement, similar to some I had seen in the *Times*, and sent it to that paper. I had often been struck by the number of benevolent persons who offered to adopt children; so I followed their example, and waited with great anxiety for the answers.

Nearly all the children offered to us were babies. I had to reply, stating more particularly what we were looking for. After that I had several very extraordinary persons coming to the house, with boys of different ages, who did not at all answer my expectations. I began to think that our plan must fall to the ground.

But one morning a letter in a child's writing, a large, round hand, with very shaky upstrokes and downstrokes, slanted all ways, came to me by post. I opened it with some curiosity, and read it aloud to George.

"My father is Captain John Champion, and he's gon to see a long wile ago, and never came back. i am living with Mrs. brown in castle street, Burn Ston, lankysheir, and go to School, were i lerne to rite and read. I will try to be good, for i no Jesus loves me, and wants me to be good. Pleas let me cum for 3 months, and see how you like me, and if i am a good boy. i was eight years old last berthday, and father's been away 3 yeres, a long wile. he told me be good and tell the truth, till i come back, and i am goin to do it. i want to lern a grate deal before he comes back again. i havent any mother, or brother, or sister, only father; and mrs. brown ses she must send me to the yuneon if father dosant come home soon. i am very sorrie and fritened."

Poor little letter! and poor little writer! We laughed; but we did not care to meet each other's eyes, for fear of seeing tears in them. It happened that my brother's doctor came that very day; and it turned out that he had some friend in Burnstone, to whom he offered to write about the boy. This gentleman saw Mrs. Brown and Philip Champion, learned the boy's story, and gave us so favorable an account of him, that I forwarded money and directions to the woman to send him up at once to me in London.

I remember that the day Philip came was one of George's worst days. From early in the morning he had been lying in a stupor, if it could be called a stupor which was miserably sensitive to every sound; and I had been sitting with him, at his feet, facing him, so that he could see me without stirring. Both of us heard Thomas leave the house, about the time when the train which brought the child was due in London; and both of us heard him come in again about an hour afterwards. But neither of us spoke or moved. George lay like one dying, and I sat still with a sinking heart, as I dreaded to hear the shrill voice of a child breaking through the profound silence. I began to fear that neither of us had counted the cost as we should have done.

But the silence was not broken. The twilight came on, and George slept a little while. When he woke up again, he spoke in quite a blithe and cheerful tone.

"It's past, Milly," he said; "one more day is gone for ever, thank God! Now run and look at your boy, and send my tea."

I was glad to move, for I was stiff and cramped with my long watch. Very weary and bowed down I felt; and my heart was heavy with the thoughts that had passed through my brain during the day. How many days there were in every year! and how many years in a lifetime! My spirit seemed cramped as well as my body, and I could not force it out of its attitude of dull melancholy and foreboding. How long were we to bear the burden of such lives as ours?

I could not even wish to see the child I had sent for. I went into my own room, and had tea there alone, shrinking from the charge I had undertaken. I felt a desire to send him away again without seeing him. It seemed to me, perhaps because I was brought into personal contact with so few people, that to see any of our fellow-creatures involved us in a new and stronger relationship toward them. When we awake from our dream of death, and our open eyes look upon Him who has loved us, and in whom we have believed though we saw Him not, what new tenderness and discipleship, strengthened a thousand-fold, will spring up in our hearts for Him!

But I could not send the boy away unseen. Martha waited upon me very slowly, and coughed a short, irritated cough now and then, as if about to speak, but I would not give her the opportunity. After I had finished my tea I put off going down-stairs as long as I could; and then I went reluctantly, looking forward with dismay to the three months' trial we had partly promised to the boy.

I opened the door of the dining-room so gently, from long habit, that the child did not hear me. A blazing fire filled the grate, but there was no other light. He was sitting in my father's large old armchair, drawn in front of the fire; and his curly little head was resting on his hand, as he gazed dreamily at the glowing embers. There was a wistful, subdued quiet about his face and posture that went straight to my heart. He was waiting patiently, that was evident, for something unknown to come to him. I did not think, as Mrs. Transome did, of the one Blessed Child, who has made all children's lives sacred; but his face called to my mind those angel faces to be seen in the pictures of the old religious painters.

As I paused on the threshold the boy became conscious of my presence, and slipped down from his high seat, crossing the room on tiptoe, and speaking in a whisper almost too low for me to hear.

"Is he better now?" he asked; "I have not made any noise."

The earnest, uplifted face was so winning that I bent down, and pressed my lips to the soft cheek as fondly as if it were no new face to me. Nor did it seem new. That odd trick of the brain, which makes us feel as if we could dimly remember the present in the long-forgotten past, brought to me the sensation of having looked upon it, and caressed it in some former life.

"Yes; he is better now," I said, sitting down in the chair he had left, and taking him on my knee, "and you've been as quiet as a little mouse."

"I knew he'd be better soon," he answered, with a beaming glance at once shy and merry, "because as soon as that man told me he was ill, I asked God to make him better. I knew God would do it."

"Are you sure of it?" I asked; for it had been plain to me long ago that our prayers were too feeble to reach the ear of God.

"Sure!" said the child, "why! isn't he better? My mother told me God is everywhere, and I must ask Him for what I want, just as I asked her. I was a very little boy then; but I've never forgotten it."

"You must never forget it, Philip," I said. But had not I forgotten it? Was there not within me the lurking unbelief that God was so near as to catch every whisper; nay, even to see my thoughts afar off? I leaned back in the chair, with my arm about the child, who kne o little of me, yet trusted me so simply, that lready his face was bright with a smile as he ooked up to me. Was it possible that I might o lean upon God, of whom I knew so little, and ok up into His unseen face with a trust as ull? Was His arm really about me, as mine as about Philip?

"If you love me," he said, "and let me live ere till father comes home, I'll try to be very uiet and good. Mrs. Transome said you'd be ure to love me if you hadn't a heart of stone. 'ou haven't a heart of stone, have you?"

"I hope not," I answered, stroking his wistul face.

(*To be Continued.*)

THE TALENTS.

By Mrs. M. Baxter.

, S. Lesson for April 29, Matt. 25: 14-30. Golden Text, Rev. 2: 10.

'he Owner of the Talents Entrusted for Use—The Money in the Stewards' Hands—A Law of the Kingdom—The Trust Unequally Distributed—The Rule of Distribution - Excuses Inadmissible—A Selfish Life Inexcusable—The Typical Man of One Talent—The Coming Reckoning Time—The Servants Becoming Rulers—Misconceptions of the Character of God.

"Be thou faithful unto death, and I will give hee a crown of life." (Rev. 2: 10.) In the parble of the virgins, the Church, at the time of Christ's coming, is likened to virgin bride-souls aiting for the bridegroom. But the children f God must not *only* shine and look for their ord. This is indeed the highest kind of serice, and few are they who answer to this decription of the wise virgins. But there are also ervants (literally slaves) who wait for their Lord ith consciences quickened by the Holy Ghost, nd with a high sense of the responsibility hich devolves upon them. Christ is represented "as a man travelling into a far country, ho called his own servants and delivered unto em his goods." Let us not forget that whatver power or talent we possess is not our own, ut God's. St. Paul asks: "Who maketh thee differ from another? and what hast thou at thou didst not receive? Now, if thou didst ceive it, why dost thou glory, as if thou hadst ot received it?" (1 Cor. 4: 7.) St. Peter says, As every man hath received the gift, even so inister the same one to another, as

Good Stewards

f the manifold grace of God." (1 Pet. 4: 10.) tewards act for another, and are responsible, at ll times and for all things, to their master. As ewards, we cannot look upon our time as ours be planned out and used as *we* like. It is od's time, and if He chooses to break up our ans and disorganize them, or if He permits at we shall be interrupted, He has a perfect ght to do so; the time is His. If we have oney, we have it but as stewards for Him; we ve no right to make investments, or to buy tates on our own account. Nor have we any ght to give to a pertinacious beggar, on the me principle as the unjust judge avenged the or widow: "Because the woman troubleth me, will avenge her, lest by her continual coming, e weary me." (Luke 18: 5.) It is the Lord's oney, and He never gives because He is wored into it; neither can we, as His stewards. e avengeth speedily, and "giveth to all men erally, and upbraideth not." (James 1: 5.) If has given us a good voice, it is not in order at we may gain glory for our singing, or readg, or speaking; it is God's voice, and we are t stewards to use it as He directs. If we have sition, it is not that we should make use of at position to assume superiority over others, d thus gratify our pride and despise others. o; the position is God's, to be held for Him; it does not serve to the increase of His kingm, it is misappropriated.

In the laws of His kingdom, the great ones the readiest to serve, and their dignity is own in their likeness to their Master, who me, "not to be ministered unto, but to minisr, and to give His life a ransom for many." e often see in people who have risen from poverty to riches, a vulgar assumption of superiority; they think they would lose caste if they were to ride third-class, or wash the tea things, or make a bed, or carry a parcel; whereas those who are of gentle birth always, by instinct, do what they can to help others. It is so in the spiritual life. Many who are put in some position of authority over others, in churches or missions, set themselves up as being something superior, and lord it over those who are placed under them; but the bark of the wolf betrays them beneath the sheep's clothing. If we have a house, the house is God's property, to be used for Him, to receive His messengers, and to serve for the purposes of His Kingdom. Again, whatever knowledge of God we possess is not given to us only for ourselves, it is God's property, of which we are but stewards. Paul so felt his responsibility that he said, "For though I preach the gospel, I have nothing to glory of; for necessity is laid upon me; yea, woe is unto me, if I preach not the gospel." (1 Cor. 9: 16.) If we are true stewards, it will be so with us, and our hearts will say, "Woe is unto me, if I do not win souls for Jesus."

The man who went into a far country did not make an equal distribution of his goods among his servants; "Unto one he gave five talents, to another two, and to another one; to every man

According to His Several Ability."

God is severely criticised by His own children regarding the distribution of His talents. How often we hear it said: "If only I had your energy, how much I could do for God!" "If only I had your zeal, how much I could do!" "If I had the wealth of so and so, how much I would give to missionary work!" O how men dishonor God in this way, saying by such words, "God has made it possible for others to serve Him, but impossible for me," while He says, "It is accepted according to that a man hath, and not according to that he hath not"! (II Cor. 8: 12.) We do not read of Peter and John saying to Paul, "Paul, if we had your education, how much we might do for God!" No, they placed themselves, unlearned and ignorant as they were, at the disposal of the Holy Ghost, and He used them mightily. It is dishonest and sinful when children of God excuse themselves from any kind of usefulness, because God has not made their talents and opportunities just the same as those of some others. No child of God has a right to

A Selfish, Useless Life.

Those of us whose family claims or necessary work keeps us at home or in the shop, can make that home or shop our mission hall, and pray for all who go out and come in. The milkman, the dustman, all have souls to be saved. The woman who comes for a dozen of matches, or a reel of cotton, or a penny's worth of blacking has a soul to be saved. If we have not the five talents which make us useful among the heathen or in a mission hall at home, let us make use of all which God does trust us with in the family; that our houses may be consecrated by all which God does in them through us.

One of the servants received but one talent; his Lord could trust him with no more, but, like many men with small brains, he was very conceited, and, taking offence because more had not been committed to him, he "went, and digged in the earth, and hid

His Lord's Money."

O how many are like this man! They want to do some great thing, something which would be spoken of, and get into the papers; and because their talents do not reach out so far, they despise the day of small things, and think, "What is the use of coming out from the world at all if you don't get any credit for it?" And so they drag the world into the Church, and have concerts, bazaars, etc., and do as the world does. They hold their membership, and somewhere, buried away in the past, they have some remembrance of a time when God forgave them their sins, but no such thing has power over their life in the present; their Lord's money is hidden.

"After a long time, the lord of those servants cometh and reckoneth with them."

The Reckoning Time is Coming:

let us live and walk and speak in the light of our coming Lord. The servant who had received the five talents came with bold step and head erect: he knew that his lord would be glad when he brought forth the double of that which was entrusted to him. And he which had received the two, had traded with the same and increased them in equal proportion. To each of these the lord said, "Well done, thou good and faithful servant; thou hast been faithful over a few things, I will make thee ruler over many things." No more a slave, but a ruler; no longer occupied with little things, but with great! "Enter thou into the joy of thy lord." All that which is really stewarded yields increase: it is only that which we hold as our own which yields hay, straw, stubble, which the first fire of trial or temptation burns to ashes. But how trade with our talents? "Yield yourselves unto God, as those that are alive from the dead, and your members as instruments of righteousness unto God." (Rom. 6: 13.) Let God have the use of you, yield to God every moment in every detail of life, and accept Him for that moment, and He will see to it that this commerce will yield its increase in your own soul, in the church, and in the world. What God wants, is men in whom and through whom He finds room to manifest Himself, and these shall enter into the joy of their Lord; "heirs of God, and joint heirs with Christ, if so be that we suffer with Him, that we may be also glorified with Him." (Rom. 8: 17. R. V.) What have we won for Jesus? What has been the result of our lives up to the present time? If we take stock, how much is there in souls won? How much in Christ-like influence? How much in the love of enemies? How much in self laid down? How much in intercession? Is our life just such that when Jesus comes we may give account with joy and not with grief?

Last of all came the servant who had buried his one talent in the earth. He came and said, "Lord, I knew thee, that thou art an hard man, reaping where thou hast not sown, and gathering where thou hast not strawed, and I was afraid, and went and hid thy talent in the earth; lo, there thou hast that is thine." It is an awful thing when men judge God by themselves. "Thou thoughtest that I was altogether such an one as thyself." (Ps. 50: 21.) When men, especially converted men, know nothing of God but hardness and exaction, it is a clear proof how little acquaintance they have made with Him, whose very name is love; all they have known of Him was when their perverse will crossed His. But this is wilful ignorance, and God gives it no quarter. The servant had as full an opportunity as the two others, and he had lost it. Therefore the decree went forth, "Take, therefore, the talent from him, and give it unto him which hath ten talents. For to every one that hath shall be given." All that we have in Jesus is grace for grace; all that we hold in Jesus is a pledge for more. "But cast ye the unprofitable servant (servant though he be) into outer darkness; there shall be wailing and gnashing of teeth."

ABBA FATHER.

Strength for to-day, Father, strength for to-day,
Strength to be holy, to walk in Thy way;
Strength for the keeping my robes undefiled,
Strength to be humble, as seemeth Thy child.

Strength in temptation to turn from the snare,
Strength to be constant and earnest in prayer;
Patient in well doing, faithful in heart,
Never, O Lord, from Thy truth to depart.

Strength for the crosses Thou giv'st me to bear,
Resting my heart on Thy Fatherly care,
Trusting, although I may not understand;
Knowing that Thou all my goings has planned.

Strength to shun evil, to cleave to the right,
Strength that my rushlight burn clearly and bright;
Strength that I bring no reproach on Thy name;
"Looking to Jesus," Thy promise I claim.

Still be Thou near me, whatever betide,
Let me not wander away from Thy side;
In life or in death be Thou with me alway,
Strength for to-day, Father, strength for to-day.

—*Mrs. M. P. Handy.*

A SERMON BY Rev. T. DeWitt Talmage.

"Let him appoint officers over the land, and take up the fifth part of the land of Egypt in the seven plenteous years."—Gen. xli. 34.

These were the words of Joseph, the president of the first life insurance company that the world ever saw. Pharaoh had a dream that distracted him. He thought he stood on the banks of the river Nile, and saw coming up out of the river seven fat, sleek, glossy cows, and they began to browse in the thick grass. Nothing frightful about that. But after them, coming up out of the same river, he saw seven cows that were gaunt and starved, and the worst looking cows that had ever been seen in the land, and in the ferocity of their hunger they devoured their seven fat predecessors. Pharaoh, the King, sent for Joseph to decipher these midnight hieroglyphics. Joseph made short work of it, and intimated that the seven fat cows that came out of the river were seven years with plenty to eat; the seven emaciated cows that followed them were seven years with nothing to eat. "Now," said Joseph, "let us take one-fifth of the corn crop of the seven prosperous years, and keep it as provision for the seven years in which there shall be no corn crop."

The King took the counsel, and appointed Joseph, because of his integrity and public spiritedness, as the president of the undertaking. The farmers contributed each one-fifth of their income. In all the towns and cities of the land there were branch houses. This great Egyptian life insurance company had millions of dollars as assets. After awhile the dark days came, and the whole nation would have starved if it had not been for the provision they had made for the future. But now these suffering families have nothing to do but go up and collect the amount of their life certificates. The Bible puts it in one short phrase: "In all the land of Egypt there was bread." I say this was the

First Life Insurance Company.

It was divinely organized. It had in it all the advantages of the "whole life plan," of the "endowment plan," and all the other good plans. We are told that Rev. Dr. Inhate of Lincolnshire, England, originated the first life insurance company in 1638. No, it is as old as the corn cribs of Egypt, and God himself was the author and originator. If that were not so, I would not take your time and mine in a Sabbath discussion of this subject. I feel that it is a theme vital, religious, and of infinite import—the morals of life and fire insurance. It seems to me that it is time for the pulpit to speak out. But

What does the Bible say in regard to this subject?

If the Bible favors the institution I will favor it; if the Bible denounces it I will denounce it. In addition to the forecast of Joseph in the text, I call to your attention Paul's comparison. Here is one man who, through neglect, fails to support his family while he lives, or after he dies. Here is another man who abhors the Scriptures, and rejects God. Which of these men is the worst? Well, you say the latter. Paul says the former. Paul says that a man who neglects to care for his household, is more obnoxious than a man who rejects the Scriptures. "He that provideth not for his own, and especially those of his own household, is worse than an infidel."

Life Insurance Companies help most of us to provide for our families after we are gone.

But if we have the money to pay for insurance and do not have it, we have no right to expect mercy at the hands of God in the judgment. We are worse than Tom Paine, worse than Voltaire, and worse than Shaftesbury. The Bible declares it; we are worse than an infidel. After the certificate of death has been made out, and the thirty or sixty days have passed, and the officer of a life insurance company comes into a bereft household and pays down the hard cash on an insurance certificate, that officer of the company is performing a positively religious rite, according to the Apostle James, who says: "True religion, and undefiled before God and the Father, is this: to visit the fatherless and the widow in their affliction," and so on.

* * * * * *

When men think of their death, they are apt to think of it only in connection with their spiritual welfare, and not of devastation in the household, which will come because of their emigration from it. It is meanly selfish for you to be so absorbed in the heaven to which you are going that you forget what is to become of your wife and children after you go. You can go out of this world not leaving them a dollar, and yet die happy if you could not provide for them. You can trust them in the hands of the God who owns all the harvests and the herds and the flocks; but if you could pay the cost of a life certificate and neglect to do so,

It is a mean thing for you to go up to Heaven while they go to the Poorhouse.

You, at death, move into a mansion, river front, and they move into two rooms on the fourth story of a tenement house in a back street. When they are out at the elbows and knees, the thought of your splendid white robe in heaven will not keep them warm. The minister may preach a splendid sermon over your remains, and the quartette may sing like four angels in the organ loft, but your

Death will be a Swindle.

You had the means to provide for the comfort of your household when you left it, and you wickedly neglected it.

"O," says some one, "I have more faith than you: I believe when I go out of this world the Lord will take care of my family." Yes, He will provide for them. Go to Blackwell's Island, go through all the poorhouses in the country, and I will show you how often God provides for the neglected children of neglectful parents. That is, He provides for them through public charity. As for myself, I would rather have the Lord provide for my family at a private home, and through my own industry and parental and conjugal faithfulness. "But," says some man, "I mean in the next ten or twenty years to

Make a Great Fortune,

and so I shall leave my family, when I go out of this world, very comfortable." How do you know that you are going to live ten or twenty years? If we could look up the walk of the future we would see it crossed by pneumonias, and pleurisies, and consumptions, and colliding rail trains, and runaway horses, and breaking bridges, and funeral processions. Are you so certain you are going to live ten or twenty years that you can warrant your household any comfort after you go away from them? Besides that, the vast majority of men die poor.

Two only out of One Hundred Succeed in Business.

Are you very certain that you are going to be one of the two? There are men who die solvent who are insolvent before they are under the ground, or the estate is settled. How soon an auctioneer's mallet can knock the life out of an estate! A man thinks the property worth $15,000, under a forced sale it brings $7,000. The business man takes advantage of the crisis, and compels the widow of his deceased partner to sell out to him at a ruinous price or lose all. * * Or the administrator is ordered by the Surrogate Court to wind up the whole affair. The estate is supposed to be worth $20,000, but after the indebtedness has been met, and the bills of the doctor and the undertaker and tombstone cutter have been paid,

There is Nothing Left.

That means that the children are to come home from school and go to work. That means the complete hardship of the wife, turned out with nothing but a needle to fight the great battle of the world. Tear down the lambrequins, close the piano, rip up the Axminster, sell out the wardrobe, and let the mother take a child in each hand and trudge out into the desert of the world. A life insurance would have hindered all that.

"But," says some one—

"I am a man of small means, and I can't afford to pay the premium."

That is sometimes an awful and genuine excuse, but rarely. The answer [illegible] it is this: If you are too poor to support [illegible] family and pay for a policy on your life [illegible] are too poor to take the chance of dyin[illegible] leaving them deprived of the support [illegible] brain and hands supply them. In nine [illegible] out of ten, when a man says that, he sm[illegible] up in cigars, and drinks down in wine, [illegible] expends in luxuries enough money to ha[illegible] paid the premium on a life insurance p[illegible] which would have kept his family from [illegible] ary when he is dead. A man ought to [illegible] himself down on the strictest economy unt[illegible] can meet this Christian necessity. You hav[illegible] no right to the luxuries of life until you have made such provision. I admire what was said by the Rev. Dr. Guthrie, the great Scottish preacher. A few years before his death he stood in a public meeting and declared: "When I came to Edinburgh the people sometimes laughed at my blue stockings and at my cotton umbrella, and they said I looked like a common ploughman, and they derided me because I lived in a house for which I paid thirty-five pounds rent a year, and ofttimes I walked when I would have been very glad to have had a cab; but, gentlemen, I did all that because I wanted to pay the premium on a life insurance that would keep my family comfortable if I should die." That I take to be the right expression of an honest, intelligent, Christian man.

The Utter Indifference of Many People on this Important Subject accounts for Much of the Crime and Pauperism of the Day.

Who are these children sweeping the crossings with broken brooms, and begging of you a penny as you go by? Who are these lost souls gliding under the gaslight in thin shawls? Ah! they are victims of want, and in many of the cases the forecast of parents and grandparents might have prevented it. God only knows how they have tried to do right. They prayed until the tears froze on their cheeks, they sewed on the sacks until the breaking of the day, but they couldn't get enough money to pay the rent; they could not get money enough to decently clothe themselves, and one day in that wretched home the angel of purity and the angel of crime fought a great fight between the empty bread-tray and the fireless hearth, and the black-winged angel shrieked "Aha! I have won the day."

Say some men: "I believe what you say:

It is Right and Christian,

and I mean some time to attend to this matter." My friend, you are going to lose the comfort of your household in the same way the sinner loses heaven—by procrastination. I see all around me the destitute and suffering families of parents who meant some day to attend to this Christian duty. During the process of adjournment the man gets his feet wet, then come chills and a delirium, and the doleful shake of the doctor's head, and the obsequies. If there be anything more pitiable than a woman delicately brought up, and on her marriage day, by an indulgent father given to a man to whom she is the chief joy and pride of life until the moment of his death, and then that same woman going out with helpless children at her back to struggle for bread in the world where brawny muscle and rugged soul are necessary—I say if there be anything more pitiable than that, I don't know what it is; and

Yet there are Good Women who are Indifferent in Regard to their Husbands' Duty in this Respect,

and there are those positively hostile, as though a life insurance subjected that man to some fatality. There is in this city to-day a poor woman keeping a small candy-shop, who vehemently opposed the insurance of her husband's life, and when application had been made for a certificate of $10,000, she frustrated it. She would never have a document in the house that implied it was possible for her husband ever to die. One day in the quick revolution of machinery his life was instantly dashed out.

What is the Sequel?

She is with annoying tug making the half of a miserable living. Her two children have been taken away from her in order that they may be clothed and schooled, and her life is to be a prolonged hardship. O man, before forty-eight hours have passed away, appear at the desk of some of our great life insurance companies, have the stethoscope of the physician put to your heart and lungs, and by the seal of some honest company decree that your children shall not be subject to the humiliation of financial struggle in the dark days of your demise.

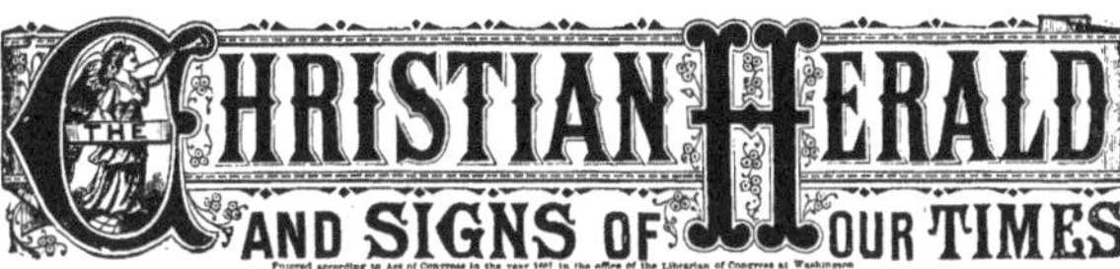

Entered according to Act of Congress in the year 1887 in the office of the Librarian of Congress at Washington

Vol. XI., No. 17. Office, 63 Bible House, N. Y. THURSDAY, APRIL 26, 1888. Annual Subscription, $1.50.

REV. DR. ANDREW A. BONAR.

CONTENTS OF THIS NUMBER.

PORTRAITS AND LIVES OF DRS. HORATIUS AND ANDREW BONAR.
BRILLIANT BITTERNESS. Dr. Talmage's Sermon last Sunday Morning.
ANECDOTES RELATED AT RECENT EVANGELISTIC MEETINGS.
THE STORM CLOUDS GATHERING. A Prophetic Article.
Perils Among Indians—A Bible in a Blanket—An Execution Prevented—Called by the Great Spirit—High Caste Learners—A Thankful Congregation—Mr. Be Qua's Work in the Indian Territory.
JESUS AFFIRMED TO BE ALIVE. A New Sermon by C. H. Spurgeon.
Gems from New Books: A German Captain's Order—A Meal of Carrion.
PORTRAIT AND LIFE OF THE LATE AMOS BRONSON ALCOTT.
MRS. PINFOLD'S ILLUMINATION. (Illustrated.)
PICTURE OF THE VILLA PALMIERI, FLORENCE, Queen Victoria's Italian Retreat.
MRS. TRANSOME'S PUPIL. A Serial Story. (Continued.)
THE JUDGMENT. By Mrs. M. Baxter.

REV. DR. HORATIUS BONAR.

The New Tay Bridge, View from the South-east. 2. Inside the Bridge. 3. The New Tay Bridge, from East Tayport, Two Miles distant.

DRS. ANDREW AND HORATIUS BONAR, the famous Scotch Preachers and Authors—New Tay Bridge.

REV. DR. ANDREW A. BONAR.

His Early Years from 1810 to 1839—Journey to Palestine—Revival in Dundee—Secedes with the Free Church—Writes M'Cheyne's Memoirs—Elected Moderator of the Assembly in 1878.

ONE of the best-known and most highly esteemed pastors in the Free Church of Scotland is the Rev. Andrew Bonar, whose portrait appears on the preceding page in company with his distinguished brother, Dr. Horatius Bonar. He was born in Edinburgh in 1810, so that he is now seventy-eight years of age. His father was a man of high Christian character and extensive knowledge. Andrew was favored in his youth with the best educational advantages, and he availed himself of them to good purpose. The fruit of his application soon became apparent; he won the proud position of Dux of Edinburgh High School. The same success attended his academic career at the University, where he received the approbation of his professors, and the esteem of his class-mates.

He had already, when quite a boy, accepted Christ as his Saviour, and as a consequence he resolved, with his brother, Horatius, to consecrate his life to the ministry of the gospel. This resolution once made, he subordinated all his reading and thinking, and all that he did, to qualifying himself for this work. He was

Licensed to Preach

by the Presbytery of Jedburgh, in 1835, when he was twenty-five years old. Dr. Candlish, of Edinburgh, then in the zenith of his fame, having had his attention directed to the promising licentiate, invited him to assist him as parish missionary. Mr. Bonar consented, and consequently was brought under an influence which must have helped to mould his methods of pulpit preparation, as well as to implant in him a lofty conception of the work he had undertaken. In 1838, he was ordained as colleague in the pastoral charge of Collace, in Perthshire.

In 1839 he was one of a Mission of Inquiry to the Jews, chosen partly on account of his familiarity with the Hebrew Scriptures, and partly also on account of his affectionate intimacy with M'Cheyne. On his return home he was joyfully welcomed by his flock, and at once assisted with unreserved enthusiasm in

The Revival

which had originated in Dundee, and was spreading like a wave of blessing in all the district round about. The revival was destined to effect great changes in the religious life of Scotland. Ministers were stirred up to a sense of their responsibilities, and the influence they could wield as ambassadors for Christ. The people, feeling the need of gospel preaching, saw that they could not be sure of having it so long as the choice of their ministers was vested in the hands of men often indifferent to the best interests of the congregations. They thought they had the right to choose their own teachers in spiritual things, and demanded it; for they believed that the appointment of pastors by careless patrons was the source of the deadness and blight of the Scottish Church. So the conflict began which ended in

The Disruption

of 1843. Mr. Bonar, on the day of final decision, threw in his lot with the Free Church party, and left the church in which he had hitherto ministered. The majority of his parishioners followed him. A new place of worship was erected, and the work of grace went on; sinners were pricked to the heart, and believers were instructed in the things of God.

In 1856 Mr. Bonar felt it to be his duty to accept a call to Finnieston, Glasgow. It was simply a mission station. Ten persons constituted his first congregation; but Finnieston Free Church grew under his preaching and influence, until now the members number more than 1,000. In 1874 Edinburgh University conferred upon him the degree of D. D., in recognition of his scholarship and his many valuable contributions to theological literature. In 1878 he was elected Moderator of the General Assembly of the Free Church. When Messrs. Moody and Sankey visited Scotland he gave them his warmest sympathy and co-operation. In 1881 he was a welcome and honored guest and speaker at Mr. Moody's Conference at Northfield, and he returned home with all the glow and fervor of "youth renewed"; and even now, though advancing in life, his activity and enthusiasm are unimpaired, and as in the days of his youth, he is able to do the duties of a strong man.

The Memoirs of M'Cheyne

is the book by which Dr. A. Bonar will be best remembered. It is a model biography, and has had a circulation of nearly 140,000 in Great Britain, besides being widely read in the United States. His work entitled "Christ and His Church in the Psalms" proves how profound is his Hebrew scholarship, and is marked throughout by rare spiritual insight which no linguistic acquisitions can supply; while his "Commentary on Leviticus," brings to light in a very wonderful manner the New Testament verities which lie enshrined in Old Testament rites. He has also written a large number of tracts and little gospel books, which have done excellent service and been blessed to many in both hemispheres. Like his brother Horatius, he believes in the pre-millennial advent of the Saviour, and looks for it as an event likely soon to occur.

REV. DR. HORATIUS BONAR.

Born in 1808—Becomes Presbyterian Minister at Kelso in 1839—The Dundee Revival—Publishes His Kelso Tracts and Popular Hymns and Other Books—Joins the Free Church—Becomes Minister of the Grange Church, Edinburgh—Moderator in 1882—Pre-millennial Doctrines.

THE noble octogenarian preacher, whose portrait appears on the first page, in company with that of his younger brother, has recently received a substantial mark of the esteem of his fellow-countrymen, who have presented him with a purse containing five thousand dollars. At the presentation, attention was called to the fact that the family has long held an honored place among the churches of Scotland. Two centuries ago, one of its representatives was a distinguished minister, preaching the truth at the risk of martyrdom.

Horatius Bonar was born at Edinburgh, in 1808, so that he has attained the ripe age of eighty years. His father was Solicitor to the Government in all business relating to Excise, an office which is now abolished. The lad received his early education at the Edinburgh High School and the Edinburgh University, and while he was pursuing his studies he formed

A Memorable Friendship

with the saintly Robert Murray M'Cheyne, whose "Life and Remains" have been given to the world by his brother the Rev. A. Bonar. In early life he resolved to enter the Christian ministry. Among his instructors was the famous Dr. Chalmers, whose influence upon him was of the most beneficial and abiding character, and to this day he speaks of him in terms of enthusiastic and grateful admiration. Before he had finished his academical course he had published a little volume entitled "Christian Essays" which obtained a fair measure of publicity, and gave promise of the literary distinction which the author has since attained.

In 1839, at the age of thirty-one, the student became a minister, and the interesting old town of Kelso was

His First Field of Labor.

It is picturesquely situated on the banks of the silvery Tweed, and surrounded by a country justly famous, both in song and story. Nearly every stone and tree in the locality was associated in the minds of the residents with some memorable personage or deed which still lives in history. Here, in the full vigor of his early manhood, he gave himself to his work of winning souls with prayerful and unflagging assiduity. His sermons were full of fire and unction; and his pastoral visitation, especially in the homes of poverty or the abodes of suffering, was highly prized for his marked tenderness and sagacity in giving comfort or guidance.

Dr. Bonar has from the very outset of his career been an ardent believer in the power of the Press in the world-wide distribution of the truths of salvation. In spite of the many and varied calls upon his time, he managed while he was at Kelso to devote some portion of the week to edit the *Presbyterian*, a magazine which did magnificent service in contending for "the faith once for all delivered unto the saints." About the year 1839, when the revival occurred in Dundee, under the preaching of his friend M'Cheyne, none rejoiced more intensely or thanked God more than he did. He entered into the movement with heart and soul and did his best to spread it, and wherever he went many conversions were effected. But even then "What more can be done?" was his earnest inquiry by day and night. He thought that his pen might possibly reach those who were beyond his voice, so he wrote

"The Kelso Tracts."

His threefold object was to arouse the careless, to make plain the way of salvation, and to strengthen and instruct and gladden the children of God everywhere. These messengers of life were scattered far and wide, they gained entrance into thousands of Scottish homes, and everywhere they were cordially welcomed and eagerly read. In Scotland and England the number circulated was said to be very large, while in America they became popular and highly appreciated. And their work of mercy is not ended yet, for to this day they continue to receive the blessing of God.

Dr. Bonar had, in the earlier days of his ministry, and still in his eightieth year retains, a most benignant influence over children and young people. His winning manner and gentle tones arrested and enchained their attention, and his weighty words savingly impressed their hearts. His Sabbath-school services in Kelso are still remembered by many of the old scholars with undiminished delight.

His Hymns,

one of which he wrote for each service, were sung by the boys and girls. These hymns are now to be heard in many Sunday-schools with which Christian zeal and consecration have girdled the globe. Among some of the special favorites may be mentioned: "I Lay my Sins on Jesus," "A Few More Years shall Roll," "I was a Wandering Sheep," and "I Heard the Voice of Jesus Say." After the singing, the pastor would give an address, in which "the story of Jesus and His love" was told, and which even the youngest child present could understand.

When the "disruption" of 1843 occurred, there were many stirring changes. Many of the families of the Presbyterian Church were sorely perplexed by the difficulties which surrounded them, but the pastor of Kelso was not. For conscience sake, and to show his practical sympathy with his brethren in distress, he at once cast in his lot with the Free Church. He had not, like most of those who left the Established Kirk, to leave his church on leaving the denomination. It was secured to him and his congregation by some special clauses in the title deeds, and so, as the years rolled on, it became increasingly a centre of light and usefulness.

As an Author,

Dr. Bonar has attained world-wide fame. He has written much and well. He had read much, and had a retentive memory; his heart was on fire with love to Christ and souls; and, as a natural consequence, his were winged words, and his books have enjoyed merited popularity. His "Night of Weeping" has been as balm to many bereaved and lonely hearts, comforting them in the presence of the newly opened grave; while his "Morning of Joy" has in many instances lifted the thoughts of the sorrowful to that radiant land where suffering and death are unknown. "God's Way of Peace" has still a friendly hand for those who are seeking increased light. "The Land of Promise," "The Desert of Sinai," "Light of Truth," are among the best known of his other books, which go on teaching lessons in Christian experience, and unfolding the truths of the kingdom of the Redeemer. In all he wrote, as in all he said, Dr. Bonar was swayed by his life purpose—God's glory and the profit of souls. He did not seek earthly honor, but it came to him. His name has become a household word, and his writings have won a high place in the devotional literature of our century.

In 1856, the strain of long labors having so impaired his energy that rest was imperatively needed, he went on a tour through the Desert of Sinai and the Holy Land. He returned with health and energy renewed, and continued his labors of voice and pen. The year 1865 brought a change in his life though not in his work. It was the year of his

Removal to Edinburgh.

As the reputation of Dr. Bonar grew, many efforts had been made to induce him to leave his beloved Kelso for a larger sphere of ministry, and at length, after twenty-seven years of earnest and successful labor, he yielded. A new church was built in the suburb of Edinburgh, called The Grange, and he was asked to fill its pulpit. He consented. Like-minded men and women flocked around him, and he became as dear to them as he had been to his church at Kelso; while to many visitors from different parts of the world who wished to see and listen to the sweet singer, a Sabbath spent at The Grange remains a treasured and inspiring memory. In 1882 he was honored in being elected Moderator of the Assembly.

In 1886, through age and feebleness, Dr. Bonar having become unequal to the heavy duties of the pastorate, was furnished with a colleague. He is now quietly awaiting his Master's call to the mansions and rest of which he has so often and so melodiously sung; but while the natural force of the venerable servant of God may be abated, his mental vigor and power to discern the signs of the times are still in fullest exercise. A striking proof of that fact is furnished in a letter which he wrote to Mr. J. E. Mathieson on the occasion of the Mildmay Conference on the Second Advent, in March, 1886. He said:

"**The Poison of the Last Days**

has penetrated everywhere: unbelief, error, strong delusion, self-will, ambition, pride, hatred of God and of His Christ—these are the deadly forces that are operating all over earth and disintegrating society, making all human rule impossible, and demonstrating the necessity for the arrival of Him who is to end all these overturnings, and to introduce the reign of peace, the kingdom of everlasting order.

"Antichrist is rising rapidly and gaining strength. Multitudes are enlisting unconsciously under his banner, and adopting his watchword—*Liberality*, reckoning it illiberal to believe in judgment to come, or in hell, or in the wrath of God, or in the sinner's eternal doom. To meet all this we look for the arrival of the Christ of God; and as the confusion increases, and the rebellion waxes stronger and stronger, we raise more and more loudly the Church's cry, 'How long, O Lord, how long?'"

Dr. Bonar has been a well-known advocate of pre-millennarian views for many years. He embodied his opinions in "Prophetic Landmarks," a very valuable hand-book for those who are beginning the study of prophecy. He holds that the Personal Advent of Christ is not far distant, and that although Popery and Mohammedanism are Antichrists for 1,260 *years*, yet the Great Personal Antichrist of the last days will persecute the Christian Church finally for 1,260 *days*. His advocacy of these beliefs has also been eloquently promoted in the *Quarterly Journal of Prophecy*, which he conducted with singular skill for some years. His "Hymns of Faith and Hope" are the fruit of thirty years' thought and feeling. Their title is very appropriate, for they sing of faith triumphant in difficulties, and of hope that never grows old. In them will be found a music to silence earth's discords, and a loving trust to throw a rainbow of hope over the sorrows of life.

THE NEW TAY BRIDGE.

THE new bridge, a picture of which appears on the first page, is the structure erected to supply the place of the one which is identified with sorrow and bereavement in many a home. The terrible disaster on the night of Sunday, December 28, 1879, when the iron railway bridge over the Tay estuary, at Dundee, suddenly collapsed while a passenger train was crossing, amidst a violent hurricane of wind, falling into the raging waters below, with its burden of upwards of ninety lives, cannot yet have been forgotten. The old bridge, which had taken six years to construct, cost $1,750,000, and was opened for traffic in May, 1878. The new bridge, which was opened in July, 1887, was constructed by Messrs. W. Arrol & Co., of Glasgow. The length of it is 10,780 feet, or 3,593 yards—rather more than two miles; the width of the river Tay just where it crosses being 9,580 feet. The quantity of wrought iron used is 19,000 tons, of steel 3,500 tons, and of cast-iron 2,500 tons; with 3,000,000 rivets, averaging five inches in length; 10,000,000 bricks, weighing 37,500 tons; and 70,000 tons of concrete, used in the foundations. It has cost somewhat more than five million. The new structure was first used for ordinary passenger traffic on the Queen's Jubilee Day, in 1887. The public advantage gained by the railway for which the bridge is built is that of shortening the journey from Dundee to Edinburgh by one hour, and from Aberdeen to Edinburgh by two hours. Its advantages are well appreciated, for since its opening the traffic between Dundee and the East of Fifeshire is doubled. It is the property of the North British Railway.

ANECDOTES RELATED AT RECENT EVANGELISTIC MEETINGS.

An Ex-Policeman's Trophy for Christ.—Mr. William Clyde, a Scotch evangelist, said: "We had among the members of our Mizpah Band a Highland-man who had formerly been a policeman, and now that he was converted, his heart was warm towards those who used to be his companions, and he took every opportunity to set before them the Gospel of Christ. Coming home from his work, daily, he crossed Glasgow Green, and made it a point to speak to the policeman on duty there. He resolved to win that man for Christ. Repeatedly he invited him to come to the gospel meeting in the evening, when he was off duty, and at last he did come, and was brought to Christ. In testifying afterwards, the new convert said, 'Before I came to this meeting I was half converted by the quiet and gentle, yet zealous bearing, of my friend, who induced me to come here, and I was quite prepared to go the other half.' Personal dealing is much honored by God. It is one of the Christian's highest privileges to lead men and women to the Saviour."

Forty Faithful Soldiers Frozen. — "There was a Roman emperor who had among his soldiers forty Christian men. Being informed of the fact, he flew into a passion, and said, 'I will have no Christians among my men! Go, tell them that if they will not turn from serving their God they will be stripped and sent forth upon a frozen lake to perish there.' But the forty soldiers were faithful to Christ, and nothing would induce them to forsake Him. So they were taken down to the side of a frozen lake and there stripped of their garments. Not far from the lake was a hut, in which was a large blazing fire, robes, large sums of money, and also a sumptuous feast spread, all placed there by order of the emperor to tempt the men to forsake Christ. They were told that even yet if they would but forsake their God they would be taken to this hut, and all that was in it would at once belong to them. All stood firm, and they were sent forth upon the lake. They gathered together, and the whole forty raised their hands to heaven and prayed: Dear Lord, grant that we may be found faithful to Thee.' But one of the number proved unfaithful, he forsook the lake, fled to the hut, where he obtained all that was promised. The centurion of the band was so struck with the noble action of these nine and thirty men that he resolved to join them. He, too, was stripped by his own men, and went forth to join the brave soldiers in the middle of the lake. Again forty hands were raised to heaven, while they prayed, 'Oh, Lord, grant that we may be found faithful to Thee.' Their prayer was answered, for forty frozen bodies were found next morning."

Found Dead in Bed.—Mr. Robert Service observes: "I arrived at a gospel meeting one evening rather late. As I entered, a woman who had been taken slightly ill was coming out. Another lady accompanied her to a side room, and there spoke to her about her soul, urging her to accept Christ at once. She resented being spoken to in so direct and personal a manner. Ill as she was, she scowled angrily upon her kind friend. Presently, however, she listened respectfully, and as well as she was able, to the message of Christ's love to her. I do not know if she did close with the offer of salvation, but I trust she did, for on the second night after her illness she was found dead in bed." A similar sudden end overtook two wealthy gentlemen lately, who were both found dead in their bedrooms, without any previous illness, namely, Mr. Charles Hengler, the owner of some circuses, and Lord Wolverton, who died worth fifteen million dollars, and whose previous day had been spent at races and a theatre."

The Elder and the Blacksmith.—A Scotch evangelist related: "There was in one of our churches an elder who was very anxious about the salvation of a certain blacksmith in the neighborhood. One day, while visiting his minister, he felt that man's salvation laid more heavily on his heart than ever. The minister and he both prayed about the man, and as the good elder left the manse it was snowing heavily, just one of those nights in which everyone who has a home would wish to be there; but disregarding the fury of the elements, he mounted his horse and rode to the blacksmith. As he came up he could hear him working. Tying his horse to a ring at the door, he entered, and walking straight up to the smith, said, as he grasped his horny hand, 'Oh, my friend, I am very anxious about your salvation, about your soul.' That was all he said, and going out he rode home. Half-an-hour later the smith came to him and said, 'Sir, I am very anxious about my own soul.' And soon, by the Holy Spirit, he was led to accept Christ, and found salvation."

A Young Lady Paralyzed after Dancing. —Mr. Thompson said: "I heard of a young lady in London, who was engaged to be married to an officer in the British army. By the grace of God he became converted, and immediately wrote to the young lady telling her of the great change that had taken place, and offering to her the cup of salvation from which he himself had drunk, that they might together travel Zionwards. She wrote back saying, 'The winter season is just beginning, and I have many engagements; besides, we have a dance on Thursday to which I must go, but if you call on Friday, I will tell you.' She had a whole winter's engagements, and she could not make up her mind to give them up even to secure eternal life. She was at the ball on the Thursday, and returning home tired and worn out, she seated herself by the open window, for she was very warm. Next morning her maid went to wake her as usual, but as she got no response to her repeated knocks at the door, she entered, and there the young lady lay over the side of her bed, paralyzed. A doctor, who was summoned, pronounced her to be dying, and with only one or two hours to live. Word was at once sent to the officer to whom she was engaged. He hastened to her home, thinking there might still be time for her to be saved through a penitent faith in Christ. There *was* time, but whether she was able to make her peace with God or not must remain unknown. The tongue that would have spoken, or the hand that might have written the answer, were both stricken with paralysis."

BRILLIANT BITTERNESS.

Dr. Talmage's Sermon, Preached last Sunday Morning, April 22, 1888.

"There fell a great star from heaven, burning as it were a lamp, and it fell upon the third part of the rivers, and upon the fountains of waters; and the name of the star is called Wormwood." Rev. 8: 10, 11.

An Extraordinary King of the Fifth Century—Legend of a Heaven-sent Sword—The Three Divisions of his Captives—His Three Coffins—Embittered Lives—Their Baleful Influence—Morning and Evening Stars in Society—Wormwood in Parental Thrones—Stars of Wit—The Humorist a Public Benefactor—Stars of Worldly Prosperity—Often Overbearing—The Bitter Water Sweetened—The Only Means—Star Nations of the Past—The Star of the Free Nation—Magnificent Possibilities and Awful Perils.

PATRICK and Lowth, Thomas Scott, Matthew Henry, Albert Barnes, and some other commentators say that the star Wormwood of my text was a type of Attila, King of the Huns. He was so called because he was brilliant as a star, and, like wormwood, he embittered everything he touched. We have studied the Star of Bethlehem, and the Morning Star of the Revelation, and the Star of Peace, but my subject this hour calls us to gaze at the star Wormwood.

A more extraordinary character history does not furnish than this man,

Attila, the King of the Huns.

One day a wounded heifer came limping along through the fields, and a herdsman followed its bloody track on the grass to see where the heifer was wounded, and went on back, further and further, until he came to a sword fast in the earth, the point downward as though it had dropped from the heavens, and against the edges of this sword the heifer had been cut. The herdsman pulled up that sword and presented it to Attila. Attila said that sword must have dropped from the heavens from the grasp of the god Mars, and its being given to him meant that Attila should conquer and govern the whole earth. Other mighty men have been delighted at being called liberators, or the Merciful, or the Good, but Attila called himself, and demanded that others call him,

The Scourge of God.

At the head of seven hundred thousand troops, mounted on Cappadocian horses, he swept everything, from the Adriatic to the Black Sea. He put his iron heel on Macedonia and Greece and Thrace. He made Milan and Pavia and Padua and Verona beg for mercy, which he bestowed not. The Byzantine castles, to meet his ruinous levy, put up at auction massive silver tables and vases of solid gold. A city captured by him, the inhabitants were brought out and put into three classes: The first class, those who could bear arms, who must immediately enlist under Attila or be butchered; the second class, the beautiful women, who were made captives to the Huns; the third class, the aged men and women, who were robbed of everything and let go back to the city to pay heavy tax.

It was a common saying that the grass never grew where the hoof of Attila's horse had trod.

His Armies

reddened the waters of the Seine and the Moselle and the Rhine with carnage, and fought on the Catalonian plains the fiercest battle since the world stood. On and on until all those who could not oppose him with arms lay prostrate on their faces in prayer, and, a cloud of dust seen in the distance, a bishop cried: "It is the aid of God; and all the people took up the cry: "It is the aid of God;" As the cloud of dust was blown aside, the banners of reinforcing armies marched in to help against Attila, the Scourge of God. The most unimportant occurrences he used as a supernatural resource, and after three months of failure to capture the city of Aquileia, and when his army had given up the siege, the flight of a stork and her young from the tower of the city was taken by him as a sign that he was to capture the city; and his army, inspired with the same occurrence, resumed the siege and took the walls at a point from which the stork had emerged.

Slain on the evening of his marriage by his bride Ildico, who was hired for the assassination, his followers bewailed him, not with tears but with blood, cutting themselves with knives and lances. He was put into three coffins, the first of iron, the second of silver, and the third of gold. He was buried by night, and into

His Grave

were poured the most valuable coin and precious stones, amounting to the wealth of a kingdom. The grave-diggers and all those who assisted at the burial were massacred, so that it would never be known where so much wealth was entombed. The Roman empire conquered the world, but Attila conquered the Roman empire. He was right in calling himself a scourge, but instead of being the Scourge of God, he was the scourge of hell. Because of his brilliancy and bitterness, the commentators were right in believing him to be the star Wormwood of the text. As the regions he devastated were parts most opulent with fountains and streams and rivers, you see how graphic my text is: "There fell a great star from heaven, burning as it were a lamp, and it fell upon the third part of the rivers, and upon the fountains of waters; and the name of the star is called Wormwood."

Have you ever thought how many

Embittered Lives

there are all about us, misanthropic, morbid, acrid, saturnine? The European plant from which wormwood is extracted, *Artemissa Absinthium*, is a perennial plant, and all the year round it is ready to exude its oil. And in many human lives there is a perennial distillation of acrid experiences. Yes, there are some whose whole work is to shed a baleful influence on others. There are Attilas of the home, or Attilas of the social circle, or Attilas of the church, or Attilas of the State, and one-third of the waters of all the world, if not two-thirds the waters, are poisoned by the falling of the star Wormwood. It is not complimentary to human nature that most men, as soon as they get great power, become overbearing. The more power men have the better, if their power be used for good. The less power men have the better, if they use it for evil.

Birds circle round and round and round before they swoop upon that which they are aiming for. And if my discourse so far has been swinging round and round, this moment it drops straight on your heart and asks the question:

Is Your Life a Benediction

to others, or an embitterment, a blessing or a curse, a balsam or a wormwood?

Some of you, I know, are morning stars, and you are making the dawning life of your children bright with gracious influences, and you are beaming upon all the opening enterprises of philanthropic and Christian endeavor, and you are heralds of that day of gospelization which will yet flood all the mountains and valleys of our sin-cursed earth. Hail, morning star! Keep on shining with encouragement and Christian hope!

Some of you are evening stars, and you are cheering the last days of old people; and though a cloud sometimes comes over you through the querulousness or unreasonableness of your old father and mother, it is only for a moment, and the star soon comes out clear again and is seen from all the balconies of the neighborhood. The old people will forgive your occasional shortcomings, for they themselves several times lost their patience with you when you were young, and slapped you when you did not deserve it. Hail, evening star! Hang on the darkening sky your diamond coronet.

But are any of you the star Wormwood?

Do You Scold and Growl

from the thrones paternal or maternal? Are your children everlastingly pecked at? Are you always crying "Hush!" to the merry voices and swift feet, and their laughter, which occasionally trickles through at wrong times, and is suppressed by them until they can hold it no longer, and all the barriers burst into unlimited guffaw and cachinnation, as in high weather the water has trickled through a slight opening in the mill-dam, but afterward makes wider and wider breach until it carries all before it with irresistible freshet. Do not be too much offended at the noise your children now make. It will be still enough when one of them is dead. Then you would give your right hand to hear one shout from their silent voices, or one step from the still foot. You will not any of you have to wait very long before your house is stiller than you want it. Alas that there are so many homes not known to the Society for the Prevention of Cruelty to Children, where children are put on the limits, and whacked and cuffed and ear-pulled, and senselessly called to order, and answered sharp and suppressed, until it is a wonder that under such processes they do not all turn out Modocs and Nana Sahibs!

What is your influence upon the neighborhood, the town, or the city of your residence? I will suppose that you are

A Star of Wit.

What kind of rays do you shoot forth? Do you use that splendid faculty to irradiate the world or to rankle it? I bless all the apostolic college of humorists. The man that makes me laugh is my benefactor. I do not thank anybody to make me cry. I can do that without any assistance. We all cry enough, and have enough to cry about. God bless all skilful punsters, all reparteeists, all propounders of ingenious conundrums, all those who mirthfully surprise us with unusual juxtaposition of words. Thomas Hood and Charles Lamb and Sidney Smith had a divine mission, and so have their successors in these times. They stir into the acid beverage of life the saccharine. They make the cup of earthly existence, which is sometimes stale, effervesce and bubble. They placate animosities. They foster longevity. They slay follies and absurdities which all the sermons of all the pulpits cannot reach.

They have for examples Elijah, who made fun of the Baalites when they called down fire and it did not come, suggesting that their heathen god had gone hunting, or was off on a journey, or was asleep, and nothing but vociferation could wake him, saying: "Cry aloud for he is a god; either he is talking or pursuing, or peradventure he sleepeth and must be awaked." They have an example in Christ, who with healthful sarcasm showed up the lying, hypocritical Pharisees by suggesting that such perfect people like themselves needed no improvements, saying: "The whole need not a physician, but they that are sick."

But what use are you making of your wit? Is it besmirched with profanity and uncleanness? Do you employ it in amusement at physical defects for which the victims are not responsible? Are your powers of mimicry used to put religion in contempt? Is it a bunch of nettlesome invective? Is it a bolt of unjust scorn? Is it fun at others' misfortune? Is it glee at their disappointment and defeat? Is it bitterness put drop by drop into a cup? Is it like the squeezing of Artemisia Absinthium into a draught already distastefully pungent? Then you are the star Wormwood. Yours is the fun of a rattlesnake trying how well it can sting. It is the fun of a hawk trying how quick it can strike out the eye of a dove.

But I will change this, and suppose you are

A Star of Worldly Prosperity.

Then you have large opportunity. You can encourage that artist by buying his picture. You can improve the fields, the stables, the highway by introducing higher style of fowl and horse and cow and sheep. You can bless the world with pomological achievement in the orchard. You can advance arboriculture and arrest the deathful iconoclasm of the American forest. You can put a piece of sculpture into the niche of that public academy. You can endow a college. You can stocking a thousand bare feet from the winter frost. You can build a church. You can put a missionary of Christ on that foreign shore. You can help ransom a world. A rich man with his heart right—can you te me how much good a James Lenox or a George Peabody or a Peter Cooper or a William E. Dodge did while living, or is doing now that he is dead? There is not a city, town, or neighborhood that has not glorious specimens of consecrated wealth.

But suppose you grind the face of the poor. Suppose when a man's wages are due you make him wait for them because he cannot help himself. Suppose that, because his family is sick and he has had extra expenses, he should politely ask you to raise his wages for this year, and you roughly tell him if he wants a better place to go and get it. Suppose by your manner you act as though he were nothing and you were everything. Suppose you are selfish and

Overbearing and Arrogant.

Your first name ought to be Attila and your last name Attila, because you are the star Wormwood, and you have embittered one-third, if not three-thirds, of the waters that roll past your employees and operatives and dependents and associates; and the long line of carriages which the undertaker orders for your funeral, in order to make the occasion respectable, will be filled with twice as many dry, tearless eyes as there are persons occupying them.

There is an erroneous idea abroad that there are only a few geniuses. There are millions of them; that is, men and women who have especial adaptation and quickness for some one thing. It may be great, it may be small. The circle may be like the circumference of the earth or no larger than a thimble. There are thousands of geniuses here this morning, and in some one thing you are a star.

What Kind of a Star are You?

You will be in this world but a few minutes. As compared with eternity the stay of the longest life on earth is not more than a minute. What are we doing with that minute? Are we embittering the domestic or social or political fountains, or are we like Moses, who, when the Israelites in the Wilderness complained that the waters of Lake Marah were bitter and they could not drink them, their leader cut off the branch of a certain tree and threw that branch into the water, and it became sweet and slaked the thirst of the suffering host? Are we with a branch of the Tree of Life sweetening all the brackish fountains that we can touch?

Dear Lord, send us all out on Thy mission. All around us embittered lives—embittered by persecution, embittered by hypercriticism, embittered by poverty, embittered by pain, embittered by injustice, embittered by sin. Why not go forth and sweeten them by smile, by inspiring words, by benefactions, by hearty counsel, by prayer, by gospelized behavior! Let us remember that if we are wormwood to others we are wormwood to ourselves, and our life will be bitter and our eternity bitterer. The gospel of Jesus Christ is

The Only Sweetening Power

that is sufficient. It sweetens the disposition. It sweetens the manners. It sweetens life. It sweetens mysterious Providences. It sweetens afflictions. It sweetens death. It sweetens everything. I have heard people asked in social company: "If you could have three wishes gratified, what would your three wishes be?" If I could have three wishes met this morning I tell you what they would be. First: More of the grace of God. Second: More of the grace of God. Third: More of the grace of God. In the dooryard of my brother John, missionary in Amoy, China, there is a tree called

The Emperor-Tree,

the two characteristics of which are that it always grows higher than its surroundings, and its leaves take the form of a crown. If this emperor-tree be planted by a rose-bush it grows a little higher than the bush, and spreads out above it a crown. If it be planted by the side of another tree, it grows a little higher than that tree and spreads above it a crown. Would God that this religion of Christ, a more wonderful emperor-tree, might overshadow all your lives! are you lowly in ambition or circumstance, putting over you its crown; are you high in talent and position, putting over you its crown. Oh, for more of the saccharine in our lives and less of the wormwood!

What is true of individuals is true of nations. God sets them up to revolve as stars, but they may fall wormwood.

Star Nations.

Tyre—the atmosphere of the desert fragrant with spices coming in caravans to her fairs: all seas cleft into foam by the keels of her laden merchantmen: her markets rich with horses and camels from Togarmah, her bazaars filled with upholstery from Dedan, with emeralds and coral and agate from Syria, with wines from Helbon, with embroidered work from Ashur and Chilmad. Where now the gleam of her towers, where the roar of her chariots, where the masts of her ships? Let the fishermen who dry their nets where once she stood, let the sea that rushes upon the barreness where once she challenged the admiration of all nations, let the barbarians who set their rude tents where once her palaces glittered, answer the question. She was a star, but by her own sin turned to wormwood and has fallen.

Hundred-gated Thebes—for all time to be the study of antiquarian and hieroglyphist; her stupendous ruins spread over twenty-seven miles; her sculptures presenting in figures of warrior and chariot the victories with which the now forgotten kings of Egypt shook the nations; her obelisks and columns; Carnac and Luxor, the stupendous temples of her pride. Who can imagine the greatness of Thebes in those days when the hippodrome rang with her sports, and foreign royalty bowed at her shrines, and her avenues roared with the wheels of processions in the wake of returning conquerors? What dashed down the vision of chariots and temples and thrones? What hands pulled upon the columns of her glory? What ruthlessness defaced her sculptured wall and broke obelisks and left her indescribable temples

Great Skeletons of Granite?

What spirit of destruction spread the lair of wild beasts in her royal sepulchres, and taught the miserable cottagers of to-day to build huts in the courts of her temples, and sent desolation and ruin skulking behind the obelisks and dodging among the sarcophagi and leaning against the columns and stooping under the arches and weeping in the waters, which go mournfully by as though they were carrying the tears of all ages? Let the mummies break their long silence and come up to shiver in the desolation, and point to fallen gates and shattered statues and defaced sculpture, responding: "Thebes built not one temple to God. Thebes hated righteousness and loved sin. Thebes was a star, but she turned to wormwood and has fallen."

Babylon—with her two hundred and fifty towers and her brazen gates and her embattled walls, the splendor of the earth gathered within her palaces, her hanging gardens built by Nebuchadnezzar to please his bride Amyittis, who had been brought up in a mountainous country and could not endure the flat country round Babylon—these hanging gardens built, terrace above terrace, till at the height of four hundred feet there were woods waving and fountains playing, the verdure, the foliage, the glory, looking as if a mountain were on the wing. On the tip-top a king walking with his queen, among statues snowy white, looking up at birds brought from distant lands, and drinking out of tankards of solid gold, or looking off over rivers and lakes upon nations subdued and tributary, crying: "Is not this

Great Babylon

which I have built?" What battering-ram smote the walls? What ploughshare upturned the gardens? What army shattered the brazen gates? What long, fierce blast of storm put out this light which illumined the world? What crash of discord drove down the music that poured from palace window and garden grove, and called the banqueters to their revel and the dancers to their feet? I walk upon the scene of desolation to find an answer, and pick up pieces of bitumen and brick and broken pottery, the remains of Babylon, and as in the silence of the night I hear the surging of that billow of desolation which rolls over the scene, I hear the wild waves saying: "Babylon was proud. Babylon was impure. Babylon was a star, but by sin she turned to wormwood and has fallen."

The Star of the West.

From the persecutions of the Pilgrim Fathers and the Huguenots in other lands, God set upon these shores a nation. The council-fires of the aborigines went out in the greater light of a free government. The sound of the war-whoop was exchanged for the thousand wheels of enterprise and progress. The mild winters, the fruitful summers, the healthful skies charmed from other lands a race of hardy men, who loved God and wanted to be free. Before the woodman's axe forests fell, and rose again into ships' masts and churches' pillars. Cities on the bank of lakes begin to rival cities by the sea. The land quakes with the rush of the rail-car, and the waters are churned white with the steamer's wheel. Fabulous bushels of Western wheat meet on the way fabulous tons of Eastern coal. Furs from the North pass on the rivers fruits from the South. And trading in the same market is Maine lumberman, and South Carolina rice merchant, and Ohio farmer, and Alaska fur-dealer. And churches and schools and asylums scatter light and love and mercy and salvation upon sixty millions of people.

I pray that our nation may not copy the crimes of the nations that have perished, and our cup of blessing turn to wormwood, and, like them, we go down. I am by nature and by grace an optimist, and I expect that this country will continue to advance until the world shall put on millennial era, and that when Christ comes again He will set His throne somewhere between the Alleghanies and the Sierra Nevadas. But be not deceived!

Our Only Safety

is in righteousness toward God and justice toward man. If we forget the goodness of the Lord to this land, and break His Sabbaths, and improve not by the dire disasters that have again and again come to us as a people, and we learn saving lesson neither from civil war nor raging epidemic, nor drouth, nor mildew, nor scourge of locust and grasshopper; if the political corruption which has poisoned the fountains of public virtue, and beslimed the high places of authority, making free government at times a hissing and a byword in all the earth; if the drunkenness and licentiousness that stagger and blaspheme in the streets of our great cities, as though they were reaching after the fame of a Corinth and a Sodom, are not repented of, we will yet see the smoke of

Our Nation's Ruin;

the pillars of our National and State capitols will fall more disastrously than when Samson pulled down Dagon; and future historians will record, upon the page bedewed with generous tears, the story that the free nation of the West arose in splendor which made the world stare. It had magnificent possibilities. It forgot God. It hated justice. It hugged its crime. It halted on its high march. It reeled under the blow of calamity. It fell. And as it was going down, all the despotisms of earth, from the top of bloody thrones, began to shout, "Aha, so would we have it!" while struggling and oppressed peoples looked out from dungeon bars, with tears and groans, and cries of untold agony, the scorn of those and the woe of these uniting in the exclamation, "Look yonder! There fell a great star from heaven, burning as it were a lamp, and it fell upon the third part of the rivers, and upon the fountains of waters; and the name of the star is called Wormwood!"

THE STORM CLOUDS GATHERING.

Two Momentous Cablegrams—The Struggle Predicted by the Inspired Writers—Its Result Outlined—The Map of Europe Rearranged—The Materials of the Conflagration—The Pacific Situation Suddenly Disturbed Boulanger Come to the Front—Journalistic Portraits of Him—His Rumored Napoleonic Descent—The Fighting Kaiser—A Woman's Description of Him—The Rising Waiting his Call.

THE cable last week, brought almost simultaneously two startling communications, the significance of which every student of prophecy cannot fail to appreciate. They were (1) the sudden crisis unexpectedly developed in the physical condition of the Emperor of Germany, which was of so serious a nature, that a decree was hastily issued, making the Crown Prince regent or virtually Emperor, and (2) the triumphant election of General Boulanger in France, as a deputy of the Legislature, by the Department of the North. The momentous meaning of these two events, which in one week have come upon Europe like a thunder clap, is realized when we remember the warnings which prophetic expositors have uttered in this and past times, which were based upon the conclusions derived from their study of the prophecies.

The Warnings

were to the effect that a gigantic upheaval of European nationalities was imminent, and that it would probably be opened by a fierce struggle between Germany and France. The Rev. M. Baxter explained fully in these columns last year, and with greater detail in his pamphlets,* the reason which had led him and many eminent expositors, notably "the prince of commentators," Matthew Henry, to believe that this struggle could not be delayed much, if at all, beyond next year. The chief of these reasons was, that the twenty-three kingdoms which now occupy the area of Cæsar's Roman Empire are, by annexation, conquest, or diplomatic re-arrangement, to be transformed into ten kingdoms in fulfilment of the type which Nebuchadnezzar saw in the image with ten toes (Daniel 2: 41, 42) and which Daniel, by Divine illumination, explained as a kingdom divided into ten. In a later vision granted to Daniel himself, the same type was seen (Daniel 7: 23, 24) in the fourth beast with ten horns, which, as the angel informed him, represented a kingdom out of which ten kings should arise. As this fourth kingdom is clearly

The Roman Empire,

which in the zenith of its greatness girdled the Mediterranean Sea, and included England, too, it is evident that when the prophecy is fulfilled it will become a decem-regal power, cohering by iron-bound treaties, and eventually controlled and directed by one diabolically possessed monster, the Napoleonic Antichrist, who, either in his own person or dynastically, would present to the world the unique spectacle of a being miraculously raised to life after being slain by the sword. The result of this impending gigantic international struggle is thus revealed, but not the process. It is not, however, difficult for any reader of history to arrive at the conclusion that it will be by war; and the precision with which Daniel fixes the dates as revealed to him, renders it clear that the time for the commencement of those wars is now at hand.

The student of prophecy, therefore, being sure that God saw all things from the beginning, and revealed the future to His servant for the enlightenment and preparation of His people, looks around for signs of its fulfilment. A few weeks ago few of those signs were recognizable. France had just peaceably elected a President of pacific disposition, who took pains to assure the nations in general, and Germany in particular, of his amity and cordiality. His assurances were accepted in good faith, and the statesmen of Germany congratulated themselves on his elevation to the Presidential chair. Boulanger, the firebrand, the one centre about which the warlike elements of France clung, was in disgrace in a remote province, the subject of the gibes and sneers of the party in power.

A similar peaceful aspect was seen in Germany. The warlike Emperor, the man who, guided by Bismarck, had with the sword in hand won glory and increased territory for the Empire, was dead, and in his place stood his son, a man of peace, notoriously disinclined to be guided by Bismarck, and opposed to the policy known as that of blood and iron. To-day both aspects are changed, and the change has come with astounding suddenness. The Emperor is reported to be dying—may even be dead before these lines are read—his son and successor, a young hot-headed aspirant to the fame of his ancestor, Frederick II., who deluged Europe with blood, is appointed regent; and in France the whilom despised Boulanger has returned to Paris with the confidence of an enormous section of the French people, publicly and emphatically declared in him. The gravity of the situation is realized when we examine the respective characters and aims of

The Champions

of the rival nations. Boulanger who was dismissed from his military command by the Government, and was then triumphantly elected to the French Parliament by the Department of the North, in a contest in which he received 172,272 votes, being nearly 100,000 more than those polled for his chief antagonist, is now the most prominent figure in France. Of his elevation a French journal, the *Evenement* says: "The success of Boulanger is very great. What will the member-elect of the Nord do now? He has declared that he would go on to the end. *The end is the dictatorship* of a soldier raised up by a coalition of the enemies of the Republic.

M. Blowitz, the French correspondent of the London *Times*, who has achieved a world-wide reputation as a sagacious observer of current events, says, in reference to the address by which General Boulanger endeavored to allay the suspicions prevalent respecting him: "Louis Napoleon talked exactly in this strain from 1848 to 1851. He, too, wished only to be President of the Republic; but when President, he made himself Emperor; and, as President, Boulanger might become Emperor. The causes of this success defy analysis. It cannot be explained nor combated. Universal suffrage has its freaks, and to try to stem it is hopeless. General Boulanger and his satellites have invented nothing—they simply imitate precedents, and universal suffrage asks nothing else. They demand, like Louis Napoleon, revision and dissolution; they are ready, like him and his abettors, to risk everything. There is still an alliance of anarchists and absolutists, and just as Louis Napoleon said that the Empire was peace, so General Boulanger says he desires the peaceful regeneration of the country."

According to M. Joffrin, the socialist municipal Councillor, who went down to oppose General Boulanger, "the peasants are led to believe that he is a natural son of Napoleon, by a Russian princess. *Prophetical almanacs are distributed which fix the 7th of May*, 1890, *for his defeat of the Germans.*" When we add to all this the rumor that he is *a close friend of Prince Jerome Napoleon*, though, for prudential reasons, the friendship is a secret one, and that one of Prince Jerome's sons disbursed money and canvassed for him in his election, General Boulanger's popularity and probable return to power become increasingly significant.

The German Champion,

the son of the Emperor, is a young man of twenty-nine, who has openly espoused the cause of Prince Bismarck in antagonism to his father. He has had no training as a statesman, but has become familiar with all military details, and has already displayed a remarkable genius in the manœuvering of large bodies of troops. The Berlin correspondent of the New York *Times*, in describing him, says: "Prince William is, in truth, as purely North German by heredity, as wholly a product of Wend and Saxon and Goth and Borussian intermixture, as can be found. One may call him, indeed, a culmination of the Hohenzollern type of soldier-statesman, reached, curiously enough, by the same crossing of blood which produced Frederick the Great. The mother of that wonderful warrior was also a Guelph—Sophie Dorothea—the sister of George I. It is passing strange that when, a century and a half later, a Hohenzollern Crown Prince next again takes a wife from the Brunswick House, the eldest son should again be marked by nature for a world fighter. Why this result should follow is not clear. Whatever else the Guelphs may be, they distinctly are not a military family. Yet when a Sophie Dorothea or a Victoria Adelaide is wedded by a Frederick William of Hohenzollern, lo! the issue is

A Born Captain of Men.

I think I have related before in these columns a remark which I heard made here in Berlin two years ago, during the Congo Conference. It was at a state function, and I stood beside an elderly lady who had been in Berlin for many years, and who had been in a position to know the younger members of the imperial family as well and closely as she could have known her own nephews and nieces. In the course of talk I asked her: "What kind of a man is the young Prince William?" "*I don't call him a man at all,*" she replied quickly and with emphasis. "*He is a brute.*" I can fancy an elderly woman of a couple of generations back, who was attached to the suite of the Empress Josephine, speaking in precisely the same words of the first Napoleon.

Apparently all the women who have had to do with the bringing up of Prince William hold him in horror and detestation. I have had numerous proofs of this, although I have never been able to fasten upon any specific reasons for it. Their dislike for him is based on a general conception of his character. This view is that he is *utterly cold, entirely selfish, wantonly cruel, a young man without conscience or compassion, or any softening virtues whatever.* That he has great abilities they all admit; but they stop there. Heart he has none, upon their reckoning. And I am bound to say that if you look into his face with this preconceived notion of the young man's character, you can find plenty of signs which seem to substantiate it.

Nobody with eyes in his head could have passed the week just ended in Berlin without recognizing that if a firebrand comes to the throne, the materials are close-crowded for

A Terrible Conflagration.

The army here in Germany will utterly swamp what organized pacific instincts there are in the empire the moment a young fighting Kaiser draws his sword and cries out: "Who will follow me?" The fact of the existence of Bismarck's colossal army will magnify itself in the popular mind; the spirit in which he built it up, the peaceful intent, the patriotic aim—will all vanish like steam on a lamp chimney.

"The military class is all-powerful in the upper, middle, and higher grades of German society. Very little of provocation, or popular appeals to national feeling, would make it master of nine-tenths of the German people. Kaiser William II. in the glamor of his youthful distinction of face and figure, of his deep Teutonic prejudices, of his all-controlling belief in himself and his race and his destiny—could hurl a practically united Germany in warfare east, west, or south a month after he had ascended the Hohenzollern throne. The whole German nation from Basil to Königsberg would rise to his enthusiastic support. This is not a pleasant or humane conclusion, but it is a necessary one.'

The materials of confederation are thus vividly portrayed as existing in the rival nations,

* The three pamphlets—1. Coming Wars from 1888 to 1891, and Translation of 144,000 living Christians on March 5, 1896, before the 3½ years' persecution by Napoleon, etc. 2. Twenty Predictions about Coming Wars, by Twenty Learned Expositors. 3. End of this Age by the Descent of Christ in Passover Week, April, 1901, being 45 years from the Crimean War Treaty of Peace in Passover Week, April, 1856, and 2,345 years from Passover Week, April, B. C. 444-5, as shown by Daniel's Dates; sold altogether, in one colored cover at 20 cents, 144 pages, at *Christian Herald* Office, 63 Bible House, New York.

and it is not only students of prophecy, but secular journalists, who foresee the impending storm. The New York *Herald* asks: "Is history to repeat itself with Boulanger as

Napoleon the Fourth?

Is France to pass under a new military despotism? As a general proposition, the political adventures of Boulanger, or of any French commander, would concern us little. But the relations of Continental Europe are so unfortunate, that imminent war hangs over the nations like one of those impending avalanches which the cry of a chamois hunter might dislodge and send raging down the mountain. A breath, a murmur, may bring war—and with war misfortune to mankind. Since Sedan, eighteen years ago, public opinion has been dreading lest that word came from France. General Boulanger may say what he will—his election in this Department of the Nord can only mean a moral declaration of war. We may see the Napoleon experiment repeated."

IN PERIL AMONG INDIANS.

AMONG the thrilling incidents related in the *Minnesota Missionary*, by that devoted laborer for Christ among the Indians, Bishop Whipple, is the following, which occurred during the awful Sioux outbreak of 1862: "The Sioux attacked the trading-posts and killed the employees. When they came to Major Forbes's place, the clerk in charge, Mr. George Spencer, was wounded and fled up-stairs. The store was filled with goods, so they would not burn it. Wakeautawa, 'His Thunder,' a friend of Spencer's, passed through the Indians, and went up-stairs, and taking Spencer in his arms carried him to his lodge. He then sat by his side with a double-barrelled gun, and as the Indians came to kill him said, 'Kill him, if you dare; two of you shall die for one! He is my *codah* (friend). I said I would save his life, and I will.' For days and weeks that faithful man guarded his friend until rescued. Wakeautawa was afterward a scout under General Sibley, and was killed; and to the credit of Mr. Spencer, he showed his gratitude by caring for the wife and children of his Indian friend.

A Bible in a Blanket.

"Lorenzo Lawrence rescued Mrs. Sweet and her children. Other Day saved good Dr. Williamson, the missionary families and employees of Yellow Medicine. Wakashaw, Good Thunder, Taopi, and others planned the deliverance of all the captives. Simon Angmani and others performed deeds of heroism in defence of prisoners. Wahchaucamaza, at the risk of life, carried a message through the hostile camp, creeping through the grass until he could deliver it to Robertson, who carried it to Fort Ripley. Good Thunder's present wife, Sarah Farnum, took the Bible from the mission chapel, and wrapped it in a blanket, and when she could, sent me word, 'The words of the Great Spirit are safe. I send you the good news to make your heart glad.'

An Execution Prevented.

"Time would fail me to recall all the incidents which showed the fidelity of our friends. They were surrounded by savage foes, mad with hate, and drunk with blood. In some cases these Christian Indians were threatened with death. It did not move them. 'Kill me, if you wish; but you cannot keep me from doing what is right. I am not afraid to die.' Taopi and about 100 friendly Indians came to Faribault. The people were indignant, and some foolish threats were made to kill Taopi. He came one day to see me with Alexander Faribault. He handed me a paper and said, 'Read this.' It was a certificate of General Sibley's. 'The bearer, Taopi, or "Wounded Man," is a civilized chief of the Sioux, who is entitled to the gratitude of the nation for having, with others, rescued over 200 white women and children during the Sioux war. H. H. Sibley, Colonel commanding.' Said Taopi, 'I saved your people from death. If you Christians have the same law as the Sioux, that when one man dies another shall die in his place, and for this your people would kill me, tell them not to shoot me like a dog, but to send for me to come down into the square, and I will show them how a man can die.' This interview was printed in the village paper, and we heard no more of killing Taopi.

Called by the Great Spirit.

"Brave, noble Taopi; he would have suffered had I not been able, through the kindness of friends, to care for him. One day I received a letter. 'Come quick, I can't see plain; the Great Spirit has called me for the last journey. I am not afraid to go, for His Son, Jesus, is going with me, and I shall not be lonesome on the road. Come, for I want to see you, and hear you once more.' I cannot forget that death-bed, where the very peace of God rested on the dying Christian. He sleeps in Maplelawn Cemetery, with his faithful wife Nancy, and I have placed a white tombstone over the grave of one of the truest men I ever knew.

"A few of these Indians still live at Faribault. Most of these women were removed to the mission a few years later. We bade them good-by at the Lord's Table. After the service these women came one by one and took my wife's hand, and with tears kissed it, and said, 'In Heaven to meet you I hope.' Blessed words for us all, that after a little more work, a little more sickness, a little more sorrow, there will come 'the rest for the weary' in the home where all partings are over."

IN THE INDIAN TERRITORY.

A MERCIFUL preservation, in a time of peril, is reported in a letter received last week from Rev. W. F. Re Qua, who, as our readers are aware, is laboring among the Choctaws, in the Indian Territory, relying solely on God for his support. On Sunday, April 1, he held a meeting at a considerable distance from his home, having travelled thither in a lumber-wagon which the "head-man" kindly drove over to convey Mr. and Mrs. Re Qua, their little daughter and their niece. After the night service they were returning by the same conveyance, when, the night being very dark, the "head-man" mistook the way, drove up on the side of a bad crossing and came in contact with a huge branch, which threw the whole party out of the wagon. The terrified team started off at a mad gallop, but providentially missing the prostrate missionary and his family. They were all severely shaken, though all escaped without serious injury, except Mr. Re Qua, who was badly lamed. This is the second accident of the kind which the missionary has met with in the course of his perilous work, but, as he thankfully acknowledges, he has been wonderfully kept from many other dangers.

Mr. Re Qua desires us to thank the friends who are contributing toward the purchase of the tent and organ for the summer work. Thirty-eight dollars toward the hundred and fifty have already been sent to him, and he is full of faith and confidence that the balance will come in time for the campaign which he has planned. It has been suggested to him that if another edition of Mrs. Re Qua's poems, "Stones for the Temple," were issued and sold at one dollar, and seven cents for postage, the profit on it might help them considerably in their work. The book is heartily commended by Mr. Ira D. Sankey, Miss Frances E. Willard, Mrs. Ella Wilcox, and other well-known authors.

A THANKFUL CONGREGATION.

IN a communication to the *Spirit of Missions* from Bishop Ferguson of Cape Palmas, Africa, whose portrait and life appeared in this journal on March 18, 1886, he thus describes his visit to a village of Congoes near the settlement of Gardnerville: "After a rather tedious journey on foot of two and a quarter hours, we reached the village, and proceeded at once to an unfinished thatched building, intended for a place of worship. From that spot not a house was to be seen; but a messenger was despatched to announce our arrival, and very soon several men and women made their appearance from among the bushes in different directions. The assembly was composed of Methodists, Baptists, and members of our Church. [Protestant Episcopal.] On introducing ourselves, stating that we had come to see the religious state of things, three of the men stood up and addressed us by turns; one of whom, a Baptist brother, spoke in a most pathetic strain. He said they were glad that we had come to see their sad condition; they were living like heathen: no church, no school, no training for their children, who were growing up in wild ignorance; that some of them had undertaken to build the house under whose roof we were assembled; that it was not intended for any particular denomination, only that they might have a place to meet in on Sundays.

A Bargain.

"Our hearts were deeply moved by this address. Appeal for help was never more urgent anywhere! It was no fancied picture; for there the facts stood before our eyes in all their startling realities. I could not avoid promising that if they would complete the house and have the land on which it stood deeded to the mission, I would give them a school-teacher and arrange for regular services. Could our Church people in America have witnessed the scene which immediately followed this announcement, the women raising their hands to heaven and exclaiming, 'Thank God, our prayers are heard! Our poor children will go to school now instead of spending all day fishing in the mangrove swamp! Praise the Lord!' I am sure they would make it possible for me to fulfill this promise!"

Contributions to the funds of the Board of Missions of the Protestant Episcopal Church should be sent to the Mission Rooms, 22 Bible House, New York. Cheques being made payable to R. Fulton Cutting.

HIGH CASTE LEARNERS.

AN unprecedented work in India is described in a letter from Miss Lyman, of Bombay, to the *Missionary Herald*. She says: "Nearly a year ago a high-caste Hindu woman living in Parell, three miles from here, came to request Mrs. Hume to open a Sabbath-school in her house. This Mrs. Hume did, having as many as fifty-four scholars, with an average attendance of thirty women and girls each Sabbath. The boys also were so eager to hear the gospel stories that Mr. Abbott and a native helper opened a class for them on the veranda, where as many as seventy-five men and boys gather to listen to them. After a while this woman came again to beg Mrs. Hume to open a day-school in her house, and the week after our arrival it was started. Yesterday the school was closed for a week's vacation. I wish that some of our friends in America could have been there to hear those girls, after six weeks' instruction, read so well, and repeat Scripture verses and tell Bible stories which Mrs. Hume had taught them in the Sabbath-school. Some of the native Christians were present, and one of them said afterwards that hitherto he *had not had sufficient confidence in the work to pray for it; but when he saw it he had to pray to God then and there*, for it was so wonderful. Now, the women in Parell beg for a teacher for themselves, and thus two teachers and an assistant are needed for the work there.

"This is a wonderful opening—an unheard-of thing in the past, for a Hindu house of a very high caste to be opened to Christians.

"The work going on here has been a constant source of surprise to me. I came from a Christian church in a Christian country, but I have been forced to own to myself that it is not doing more than half the work for the Master that this little church of one hundred and ten members is doing, and here they are all poor, many of them living in only one room."

CURRENT EVENTS.

An Adverse Report on the Fisheries Treaty between the United States and Great Britain, the features of which were explained in our issues of February 23 and March 1, has been decided on by the Republican majority of the Senate Committee on Foreign Relations. This action did not cause any great surprise, as it was evident, even before the provisions of the treaty were published, that opposition to its ratification would be organized. Concern for the Irish vote in the Presidential election, party jealousy, and the natural inferences to be drawn from Mr. Chamberlain's silly boasting on his return, all operate against the treaty. The committee's decision was reached on a strict party vote. Messrs. Sherman, Edmunds, Frye, Evarts, and Dolph, Republicans, voting against a favorable report, and Messrs. Morgan, Brown, Saulsbury, and Payne, Democrats, supporting the treaty. The committee has also reported adversely the resolution providing for the discussion of the treaty in open session. This action as to secret sessions was also supported by the Democratic Senators, though only by a small majority. In connection with this matter, Mr. Hoar, of Massachusetts, a Republican Senator, introduced a resolution on the 19th inst., providing that one of the official reporters of debates should be present when the treaty was taken up, and make a full report of the proceedings, and that such portions should be made public as a majority of the Senate should order.

The Bond Purchasing Bill which, as stated in these columns on April 12, the Senate returned to the House, with a scheme to substitute silver for surrendered national bank circulation tacked to it, will, in all probability, remain undisturbed in the pigeon-holes of the Ways and Means Committee room. There is no longer any necessity of acting upon it, the House having disposed of the question in another and more simple way last week. It passed a resolution declaring it to be the sense of the House that the Secretary of the Treasury has the authority, under the act of 1881, to purchase bonds with the surplus. Immediately following this Congressional action the Secretary of the Treasury issued a circular inviting proposals for the sale of United States bonds to the Government. Being asked in regard to it, he said he had not made up his mind as to the amount of bonds he would purchase, though the fact that proposals will be received daily, without limit as to time, might imply that he wanted to buy a large amount. The amount to be purchased, however, he said, depended almost entirely upon the amount offered and the prices asked. The surplus, as estimated at the Treasury Department, is now $105,000,000.

The Great Tariff Debate, Which Has Been awaited with so much interest, and which will engage the attention of Congress and of the country for at least several weeks, was begun in the House of Representatives on April 17. The special measure under consideration is the Mills Tariff Reduction Bill, a synopsis of which was given in these columns on March 8. Mr. Mills, of Texas, who, in his capacity as Chairman of the Ways and Means Committee, led the debate, as he had reported this bill, and also the bill for the reduction of Internal Revenue taxes, consolidated with it. The burden of his speech was the declaration that it was the cheaper cost of raw materials in England that enabled that country to compete with the United States. It was, he contended, the high tariff on the raw materials that made the cost of our manufactures high, and kept us from being the best manufacturing people in the world, as we were the best agricultural people. It was a suicidal policy that closed to us the markets of the world. Venerable Mr. Kelley, of Pennsylvania, the champion of the protectionists, replied to Mr. Mills's argument. He spoke strongly in support of the policy of protection, and asserted that the enactment of the pending bill would paralyze the industry and enterprise of the American people and overthrow their manufacturing supremacy.

The Bill to Divide the Territory of Dakota, and to admit the southern portion as a State, passed the Senate on April 19, by the votes of 26 Republicans, who were opposed by 23 Democrats. The latter were in favor of admitting Dakota as one State, but all were opposed to dividing the Territory. The bill as passed declares the State of South Dakota a State of the United States of America, and ratifies the constitution which the people of South Dakota have formed by themselves. It fixes the boundaries of the State, and give the State concurrent jurisdiction of the Missouri River, and every other river bordering on the State. It provides that until the next census and apportionment South Dakota is to have two representatives in the House of Representatives, and, as a matter of course, like any other full-fledged State, two representatives in the United States Senate. That portion of the former Territory not within the State of South Dakota is to continue as a Territory under the name of North Dakota, with Bismarck as its capital.

The Death of Ex-Senator Roscoe Conkling, which occurred on April 18, has elicited expressions of profound regret—from his adversaries as well as from his friends. Since his resignation of the Senatorship in 1881, he has devoted himself exclusively to his legal practice, and declared himself out of politics, but to the last he exercised a power which was felt in the councils of his party, and at the polls. His masterly abilities, his polished eloquence, and above all, his unimpeachable integrity, won for him the ardent admiration of the masses. Though wielding immense power during the two terms of President Grant, and controlling the patronage of the Empire State until his resignation, he was known to have kept his hands clean; and that fact, standing out in marked contrast to the character of the men who antagonized him, was not overlooked by the people, even when his course did not have their approval. The deceased statesman was under sixty years of age, having been born in Albany, N. Y., October 30, 1828. He was in splendid physical health, and his mental powers were in full vigor, until within a month of his death. The collapse was caused by his being caught in the fatal blizzard of March 12, when he walked from Wall Street to Union Square. He caught a severe cold in the head, which developed an abscess at the base of the brain, causing him acute suffering. After a critical operation, he appeared to rally, but after a brave struggle finally succumbed.

Anarchy in Cuba, with Horrible Atrocities, is reported in despatches, which were preceded by sinister rumors last week. It is stated that the administration of Captain-General Marin is equivalent to a reign of terror; murders, kidnapping, robberies, and plunder by high Government officials, are said to be the fruits of General Marin's despotic reign. A Havana correspondent of the New York *Sun* indignantly writes: "Death stalks, grim and unopposed, through a once flourishing island, and, handcuffed and outraged by her cruel masters, Cuba is fast sinking into a condition of utter lawlessness, despair, and ruin." The Madrid Government has declared the provinces of Pinar, Del Rio, Villa Clara, and Havana under martial law. It is reported that in consequence of this action an emeute has broken out. Great disturbances are supposed to exist, but as the cable is under the censor's control, no reliable news can be obtained. It is stated that three Havana newspapers have been suppressed, and also that the Madrid Government would remove General Marin at once.

Lord Hartington Was Honored last Week by being presented with the freedom of the city of London. After the presentation a banquet was given at the Mansion House. Lord Hartington, recounting the arguments against the Gladstone policy, said he was unable to predict the result of the Irish struggle, but he was confident that the problem would not be solved by the compromise of 1886. Ireland could not be dealt with as a colony. The decision rested with the democracy. If they were weak and weary of the struggle, Ireland might obtain independence. If they were strong and had the spirit of their kinsmen across the Atlantic, they would not permit Ireland to be separated. In order that the struggle might be carried to a successful issue the Unionists must not flinch, as there was still much work to do. The Government had wisely shown that they did not fear the widest extension of local government.

Emperor Frederick of Germany is Rapidly sinking, and his death may be momentarily expected. A very alarming crisis has set in, and the gravest fears are entertained of a speedy fatal ending of the unhappy monarch's disease. He said to Court Chaplain Koegel: "*You pray for my preservation; rather pray for my release.*" The anxiety and display of personal interest on the part of the population of Berlin, and in fact of the whole of Germany, are much greater than they were in the case of old Emperor William. An eminent Berlin throat physican has expressed the opinion that the Emperor is suffering from soft cancer, and the development has arrived at a point where no operation can avail to postpone death beyond a few days.

A Peasant Revolt has broken out in Roumania. The houses of land-owners and farmers have been sacked and wrecked, granaries pillaged, and the local officials barbarously treated, a number of them having been killed. The territorial troops joined in the pillage and fired upon the troops of the line. Since instructions were sent to the troops to adopt severe measures for the suppresion of the revolt, a host of the insurgents have been killed and wounded or taken prisoners. The prisons are crowded. Fugitives continue to pour into Bucharest. It is believed that stringent measures adopted by the Government will speedily suppress the uprising. One of the Bucharest papers says that if the Government desires to effectually quell the revolt it should demand the immediate recall of M. Hitrovo, the Russian Minister, whom it accuses of originating the rising.

The Sudden Death of Matthew Arnold, the accomplished English critic, poet, and essayist, occurred on Sunday, April 15, in Liverpool. Mr. Arnold was a son of the famous Dr. Arnold of Rugby, and was sixty-six years of age. Probably no Englishman of his day exercised so strong an influence as he on the literary life and work of the country. Scholarly and refined in manner, his society was eagerly sought, and highly appreciated. His works were extensively read, but it was chiefly by the upper classes and university men that their excellences were most valued. His aim was to convince men of position, and especially young men, that gross pleasures and sensual delights were degrading, and that in purity, truth, and benevolence there were greater joy and happiness than the gratification of the senses could ever afford. Such teaching was sorely needed, and was productive of good, though it is greatly to be regretted that it did not reach a still higher plane. Mr. Arnold twice visited America, and on the second occasion came to attend the marriage of his daughter to a citizen of New York.

A Question of Great Interest to the American Presbyterian Board of Foreign Missions has been satisfactorily settled by Mr. Oscar Straus, the United States Minister at Constantinople. The Board has fifteen schools in Syria, which the Turkish authorities summarily closed in 1886. Of these Mr. Straus secured the reopening of ten during his stay at Beyrout a fortnight ago, and secured a pledge that the remaining five would be opened as soon as the new Governor-General of Syria arrives. Mr. Straus was last week at Jaffa, on his way to Jerusalem. His energy and zeal in the cause of Christian missions are all the more noteworthy from the fact that he is a Jew.

A Prayer-Meeting in a Broadway Hotel was described by Rev. Thomas Harrison at the recent jubilee at the Jane Street Church, New York. He said: "Last night the proprietor of a prominent hotel in Broadway broke an engagement to a card party to come to this meeting. He had been here before. He was converted. His wife had been here before. She was converted. They found God here last night. They went home, and there at midnight they two began a prayer-meeting in one of the rooms of the hotel alone by themselves. Two guests dropped in to see what they were about, and were converted. Then an actress came in to find out what they were shouting for, and she was converted. Here are the cards of all, here in my hand. They sent them round to me to-day. And they—they are probably in this house praising God."

A Fatal Pride has been Displayed by a Family of sisters in New Jersey. For some years past a house at Mount Holy, N. J., has been occupied by three ladies, daughters of a Baptist clergyman, who, at his death, left that and another small property to them. They lived a secluded life, and their neighbors knew nothing of their circumstances or their means of support. It was surmised, however, from the rigid economy they evidently practiced, that they were poor. A discovery made recently proved that their poverty was far more abject than was imagined. It was learned that one of the sisters was dead, and an investigation revealed the fact that she had *died of starvation*. Kindly neighbors who then went to the house, ascertained that there was neither food nor fuel there, nor had there been any for some time. The ladies had been too proud to make their destitution known, and their reserve had cost one life and placed the other two in peril before it was broken. The case excites much sympathy. It is stated, however, that relief might have been easily obtained had the sisters asked for it; and the survivors are, therefore, blamed for not doing so, and so averting their sister's death, and their own suffering. To many churches and individual Christians in spiritual destitution the same reproach applies. The Giver of all grace is ready to respond to all who ask in faith. (Mal. 3: 10.)

The Lace Cuffs of the Late Attorney-General Brewster were frequently the subject of ridicule, and the favorite jest of his rivals, who tried to represent the great lawyer as effeminate and foppish in his tastes. No explanation was ever publicly vouchsafed by Mr. Brewster, on the matter, but he continued to wear the cuffs in spite of all the raillery which they cost him. Since his death, however, the reason for his indulging in a habit apparently so inconsistent with his vigorous character has been given to the press by a personal friend. It appears that when he first went to the bar, he had to undergo a bitter struggle with poverty. His learning and splendid talents were long in receiving recognition, and the young lawyer was often in sore straits for money to maintain a respectable appearance. His mother, whom he loved with rare devotion, knew of his hardships, and presented him with a set of shirts of her own handiwork. The old lady, intent on her son's having the best she could produce, had made the shirts on the pattern in vogue in her youth, and had ornamented the cuffs with a delicate ruffle, on which she had expended infinite pains. The gift touched the tenderest susceptibilities of Mr. Brewster's nature, and though he must have shrunk from appearing with his wrists so garnished, he would rather have cut his hands off than have refrained from wearing the ruffles, which were a proof of his dear mother's love. Later, when death had robbed him of that venerated parent, he continued to wear the ruffles in touching regard for her memory. It is much to be wished that a similar spirit was more generally to be found among Christians. Too often, the reproach of Christ has been found too heavy a cross, and ridicule has driven them to conceal their love. (Luke 6: 22.)

A Mechanical Device for the Prevention of railroad collisions was exhibited in New York last week. It consists of an arrangement of levers on the locomotive, which, in connection with a rod in the centre of the track, enables the engine-driver to set the signals himself. On approaching a signal-post the engineer by pressing a treadle with his foot lowers the bar under the engine, and this, striking the rod on the track sets in motion a compress apparatus which moves the signal and keeps it in place for a definite time, which may be regulated beforehand. By an extension of the system a starting train gives automatically a signal one mile to the front, and, arriving at that point, gives a similar signal another mile to the front and one mile to the rear, stopping any following train at the first block signal until the first train is clear of the second block signal. The working of the signals being thus confided to the man who, as engineer, occupies the place of greatest danger, it is supposed that the duty would never be neglected. Experience, however, proves that men are sometimes careless, even when they are aware that their carelessness puts their own lives in peril. Multitudes in every Christian land are well acquainted with the means God has provided for their eternal safety, yet neglect to avail themselves of them, though they know the awful consequences of dying in their sins. (Prov. 18: 10.)

A Valuable Series of Photographs is Being prepared by Professor Davidson, of the coast Survey. Some time ago he made a number of pencil drawings, from the deck of a cruiser, of some of the prominent headlands along the Pacific coast. They were necessarily imperfect, as they were taken while the cruiser was in motion, and the outlines were therefore constantly changing. Every sketch had to be taken in five minutes and under unfavorable circumstances, yet they were found to be of more use to navigators than the most elaborate descriptions in the old charts. He has therefore been commissioned, at his own desire, to take a series of photographs of the coast of California, Oregon, and Washington. They are to be taken at two distances, one at twenty miles from the coast and the other at ten miles. In addition to these two series, there would be a set of three views of every headland, as seen when approaching it from the southward, when abreast of it, and when approaching it from the northward. The value of these views can only be understood by persons who have seen the wild and rocky mass of dangers to the navigator which the Pacific coast presents. A captain to whom the coast was unknown, would find these pictures of inestimable service. But if he had them on board and did not study them he would be deemed foolish and reckless. Yet it is precisely this course that men take who sail on into the unknown, future leaving unstudied the revelation God has given in His Word. (Rev. 1: 1-3.)

Twenty-five Criminals Arrested by a Dog is a record on the books of a police precinct of New York. A reporter who saw the record recently, asked who was "Jack," to whom twenty-five arrests were credited. He was informed that Jack was a dog, who had voluntarily attached himself to the station, and had made himself useful. He presented himself there one cold night about five years ago. The dog was hungry, and the policeman on duty fed him. After that night the dog made the police station his home, and he was named "Policeman Jack." Jack is about the station in the day, but at night he patrols the precinct, rain or shine. Many of the patrolmen have found him a ready helper in running down escaping thieves or ruffians, and for such services the dog is credited on the books of the precinct. Not long ago a policeman saw thieves attempting to rob a drunken man, and started to arrest them. They fled, and he pursued. Suddenly Jack rushed past him, sprang upon the back of one of the thieves, and fastening his teeth in the man's collar, forced him to the ground. The other thief surrendered, and both prisoners were marched to the police station. Many other remarkable anecdotes are related of his intelligence and prowess. His example may be commended to many who are lacking in gratitude for benefits received. It is not uncommon to see men profess faith in Christ and receive a welcome into His Church, who never make any effort to serve Him by bringing in sinners from the world. (Matt. 4: 19.)

BRIEF NOTES.

The Old Testament in Japanese, recently completed, has had a large sale. One thousand six hundred copies were called for within a month of its publication.

It is proposed to observe the week preceding June 9, as a week of special prayer all over the world for the blessing of God on the World's Missionary Conference which meets in London from June 9 to 19.

The Ohio Senate, on April 13, passed a bill to close saloons on Sunday. The vote stood twenty-five to two, and the spectators cheered loudly as the result was announced.

The annual report of the Young Men's Christian Union of Boston, shows that it counts on its roll a total of 5,148 members. During the past year, among its philanthropic work was the provision of 2,000 "rides for invalids."

A successor to Dr. Meredith, now of Brooklyn, N. Y., in the pastorate of the Union Congregational Church, Boston, Mass., has been found in Rev. M. R. Boynton, of Haverhill—a young man of remarkable preaching ability. His salary will be $5,000.

An example of practical philanthropy has been set by the Baroness Burdett-Coutts, who has established, in London, work-shops equipped with sewing-machines, where poor seamstresses can go and use them at a low charge.

The need of a more stringent extradition treaty with Canada is becoming apparent to all but the men who profit by the present absurd system. Within the last two years Canada has lost $3,000,000 through embezzlers, who have escaped to the United States with the money. During the same time American embezzlers have taken more than $20,000,000 into Canada.

A generous member of Grace Episcopal Church, New York City, has promised to build a beautiful church on Blackwell's Island. It will be located on a commanding site near the almshouse, and will be under the charge of the Rev. William G. French, who has given more than fifteen years of faithful and devoted service to religious work on the island.

The programme for Chautauqua has been issued. The grounds will open for the season on July 3d. The School of the English Bible, the College of Liberal Arts, and the Teachers' Retreat immediately follow. The popular Sunday-school Assembly is to open on the 7th of August, Phillip Brooks, Joseph Cook, Drs. E. E. Hale, L. T. Townsend, W. R. Harper, and other eminent men have promised to take part.

A missionary in South Africa sends a very interesting account of a Society of Christian Endeavor among the Zulus. The organization is modified, necessarily, to meet the needs of the natives, but the main features are the same as in America. The Zulu young people take much delight in their Society, are instructed by the missionaries in Bible truth, and learn to pray and work by actual experience, as do their young brethren on the other side of the globe.

The fifth annual meeting of the International Missionary Union will be held at Bridgeton, New Jersey, July 5-12, 1888, inclusive. Ministers and others interested in foreign missionary work are invited to be present. All foreign missionaries of either sex, temporarily or permanently in this country, are eligible to membership in the Union, and will receive free entertainment during the meeting. For information address the President of the Union, the Rev J. T. Gracey, D. D., 202 Eagle Street, Buffalo, N. Y.

Sunday-school Superintendents and Teachers desirous of distributing copies of THE CHRISTIAN HERALD in their schools and classes, may have assorted parcels of back numbers by applying, stating number required, to the manager, 63 Bible House.

JESUS AFFIRMED TO BE ALIVE.

A New Sermon, by Pastor C. H. Spurgeon.

"Against whom, when the accusers stood up, they brought none accusation of such things as I supposed: but had certain questions against him of their own superstition, and of one Jesus, which was dead, whom Paul affirmed to be alive."—Acts 25: 18, 19.

The Roman Governor Puzzled—The Charge Referring to Questions and Speculations—The Prisoner's Bold Affirmation—I. Real Gospel Preaching Full of Jesus—Unknown to the Multitude—Despised by the Many—His Death Admitted—Unpopularity Assured—The Please-Everybody Gospel—II. Affirms the Resurrection—Infers the General Resurrection—A Doctrine of Sweet Inferences—III. Affirms that Jesus is Still Alive—Paul Had Seen and Spoken to Him—He is Preparing Heaven for the Redeemed.

FESTUS is giving to King Agrippa a brief account of the matter between Paul and the Jews. It may not be a very accurate account; for Festus did not profess to understand the business. He was a Roman governor newly come to Judæa; he had no acquaintance whatever with Jewish Scriptures nor with Jewish laws; he is, therefore, merely giving to King Agrippa a rough outline of the affair as it struck him.

He Was Puzzled

how he should represent the matter to Cæsar, to whom Paul had appealed. Festus is represented by our translators as calling the Jewish religion a "superstition." I hardly think he would have used so harsh a term before Agrippa, who professed to be of the Jewish faith. But yet, as he probably knew that Agrippa's religion did not lie very deep, and was the mere appendage of a man of fashion, Festus was not very particular about the word which he used; and he lighted upon one which may mean "superstition" as the Authorized Version has it, or "religion" as the Revised Version has it. "Well, well," he seems to say to Agrippa, "*I do not know much about it.* I supposed when the Jews brought this man before me, that he would be charged with a breach of the Roman law, and I was prepared, of course, to deal with the prisoner; but when I listened to their accusation, and found that there was nothing in it but some disputes about their religion, I hardly knew what to say. Their controversy is important to them, I dare say; but it can be of no consequence either to you or to me, for it turned very much upon a person of the name of Jesus, which was dead, whom Paul affirmed to be alive."

I want you to notice that, rough-and-ready as this description is, and neither full nor deep, yet on the surface we see that in the controversy we have the same condition of things as we usually see in such conflicts. On the one side Paul's opponents fought with the weapons of "certain questions," and on the other hand he defended himself with a bold affirmation. This is the old story of

Speculation Against Dogmatism.

It is always the way: the adversaries of the cross of Christ assert nothing, but they question everything. They will not lay down a basis, nor define their opinions. If they would do this, we might soon demolish their fabrics of falsehood; but all that they propound is "certain questions." On the other hand, those who are witnesses for the Lord Jesus have little care about questions, speculations, and the boasted outcome of cultured thought; but they affirm certain definite facts: they affirm these to be a revelation from God, and there they stand.

I. To begin with:

True Gospel Preaching

is full of Jesus. Jesus is the most notable figure in Christian testimony. The apostle Paul, whom we may regard as a model in preaching, exercised a ministry which was always full of our Lord Jesus Christ. Following the historical connection of the verse before us, we note that he preached "Jesus to multitudes unknown." Festus evidently knew not Jesus, for he speaks of Him as "one Jesus." He mentions the name as belonging to some obscure individual of whom he knew nothing, and cared less. The great ones of the earth know nothing of the King of kings. Beloved, to this day this is the wonder of wonders, that the incarnate God is not known. His birth is the starting-point of the age; and yet it was almost unanimously ignored by those who wielded the recording pen of history. His was the most extraordinary life that ever passed before mortal eyes; and yet how little notice was taken of it! Beyond Palestine it seems not even to have awakened curiosity. He died, and then to the people most concerned in Him He became "one Jesus, which was dead." The new Roman procurator, and myriads like him, well informed upon other matters, hardly knew His name, and only mentioned half of it when they spoke of "one Jesus, which was dead."

Jesus Little Known.

Brethren, this is why we must keep on preaching Jesus Christ, because He is still so little known. The masses of this city are as ignorant of Jesus as Festus was. You can never have a congregation in any of our places of worship and feel sure that they all know Jesus. If you gather in the outsiders from the street, you may be sure that the story of Jesus will be news to them. We call this a Christian country; but it would be very difficult to prove that it is so. If we took certain lines of observation as to the moral and religious conduct of our fellow-men, we should logically arrive at the conclusion that we live in a heathen rather than in a Christian city. Still the world knoweth Him not.

Paul preached Jesus, who was despised by many. The language of Festus is not only that of ignorance, but in a measure that of contempt. He speaks of "one Jesus, which was dead." Jesus is evidently nothing to Festus, and Festus does not imagine that Jesus is very much to King Agrippa. Probably he was quite right: Jesus was nobody among the

Rank and Fashion and Culture

of the period. Behold the unlearned of the day, if you speak to them of the great Sacrifice, and the wondrous atonement made by blood, they scarcely hearken to you, for such high things are not for them: they are so hardly pressed with daily labor and slender pay that they cannot think of sin and sacrifice and salvation; but they ask, "What has the poor workingman to do with religion?" Alas, that this folly should be so prevalent!

Then you turn to the learned, and hope that here, at any rate, due attention will be given to the great marvel of reconciling love. Alas! it is not so. To these more educated ones the doctrine of the cross is foolishness. They ask for something new; something more philosophical. Substitution and sacrifice—they will have none of them. Ths story of the league of justice with grace, the reconcilement of holiness with mercy, is beneath their notice. They are too cultured to believe the common faith, too wise to accept that which God hath revealed unto babes. Beloved brethren, it should never cause us doubt when we see many despising our Lord, for this is nothing new, and nothing unexpected. Did He tell us that if we preached in His name all men would receive us? Nay, He warned us that the contrary would follow.

Gospel preaching is also full of Jesus Christ in this respect, that we do not conceal His death. Festus notes that the conflict was concerning "one Jesus, which was dead." The Jews said He was dead, and Paul also confessed that He was dead: there was no disagreement between them over that matter. Hear, then,

The Debate.

"What! did your Leader die?" "Yes, He was crucified." "Did you not say He was divine?" "Yes." "Yet is He dead?" "It is even so." "Yet you spoke of His leading you on to victory?" "So we did." "Yet He is dead?" "Yes, He died at Calvary." "How, then, can your boasting stand?" "We believe that by His death He has gained the victory and accomplished His great purpose." "But how did He die?" "He died the death of a felon upon a gibbet. His enemies nailed Him to a cross, and put Him to a death which was reserved for slaves. We confess this; yea, and glory in it!" We glory that our Lord Jesus was put to death as bearing the sin of many. This we hold and teach; not defending it, nor apologizing for it: but affirming it with all boldness, with the desire that we may be understood. If any cavil at this teaching, we do not therefore conceal it; we expected that it would be cavilled at. We desire more and more to obtrude this truth of substitution whenever we preach, and to make it the head and front of our gospel. Even people who are not saved by it should yet be made to know that we preach Christ crucified. In such a case, we have done our work successfully, even if souls are not saved; for we are unto God a sweet savour of Christ, as well in them that perish as in them that are saved, if we have exalted the Lord Jesus, and borne witness to His power to save.

Beloved, I would have you further note that true gospel preaching will be full of Jesus as He is revealed in the Old Testament. Our apostle, when he spake before King Agrippa, went on to declare that he had said "none other things than those which the prophets and Moses did say should come: that Christ should suffer, and that He should be the first that should rise from the dead, and should shew light unto the people, and to the Gentiles." Paul's teaching paid as much deference to the ancient Scriptures as did that of the Jewish rabbis who were opposed to Him; nay, in very truth He paid a far more real homage to the Bible than they did. As for us,

The Old Testament is Prized

by us as much as the New. We do not preach Jesus as a fresh arrival, the inventor of a new religion, the founder of a novel way of salvation. No: we preach the Messiah of the Old Testament, whose gospel is set forth in the types and in the teachings of Moses and the prophets: "Jesus Christ the same yesterday, and to-day, and for ever." Every gospel sermon should set forth Jesus scripturally; for it is not the Christ of fancy, but the Christ of fact that saves the souls of men.

Let me add that where the Gospel is faithfully preached the reproach of Christ will not be shunned by the preacher. Read in the fifth verse of the twenty-fourth of Acts how Paul won this reproach. His adversaries said: "We have found this man a pestilent fellow, and a mover of sedition among all the Jews throughout the world, and a ringleader of the sect of the Nazarenes." This was the reputation of Paul. Well did Mr. Whitefield say, "There is no going to heaven as a minister except in a fool's cap and a fool's coat." There is no hope of preaching Christ faithfully without being called by disrespectful titles, regarded as a fool and reckoned among the vulgar and ignorant. Some kind of ugly name will always be appended to the gospeller. Brethren, expect it, and accept it! Bid farewell to a quiet life, if you resolve to be true to Jesus. I know a minister of whom one said, "He is a truly good man and nobody ever says a word against him." Upon inquiry, I heard a judicious person say "He preaches no error, but he avoids the obnoxious side of truth. What he preaches is true enough, no doubt, but it is not easy to say what it is. Nine out of ten of his hearers could not say what his precise opinion may be, but he has a fine flow of words. Those who do know what he is preaching about usually say that, take it for all in all, there is nothing in it." Of course nobody opposes an indistinct, colorless,

Please-Everybody Gospel:

it is not worth while. But speak clearly and distinctly the doctrine of the great Sacrifice, and you will bring upon your head a shower of opposition: you will be "a pestilent fellow" and "a ring-leader of the sect of the Nazarenes." Gospel preaching does not cry, "Peace, peace," when there is no peace; but it is the sword which the Lord Jesus came to send upon the earth. Now beloved, as I resolve, God helping me, in my preaching to preach to you nothing else save Jesus Christ, so I beseech you, in your schools, in your families, in your public ministries of an and every kind, begin and end with Jesus, who was dead and is alive. Declare His blessed name, and proclaim the glory of His cross! God forbid that you should place anything in front of your testimony save Jesus crucified! Your gospel is a golden frame, let Jesus be the portrait which is hung up in it.

II. Secondly: gospel preaching

Affirms The Resurrection.

Please notice, that Paul did not argue the resurrection, but affirmed it. He did not prove it philosophically, but he affirmed that Jesus rose from the dead, because such and such persons saw him alive after he had risen. He did not merely say that it was probable, that it was possible, that it was reasonable, but that it was so, for witnesses proved it. Two saw him, eleven saw him, four hundred saw him. He dealt with the resurrection as common-sense persons deal with any other fact of history; he quoted his authorities, and affirmed that it was so. His witnesses were honest and true men, who dared to go to prison, and even to die, on account of their statements. They had nothing whatever to gain, and everything to lose by their testimonies. They stated that Jesus, whom they knew to have been dead, had risen again, and had given clear proofs that he was alive. This corner-stone of our faith is sure, and upon the certainty of it we build our faith.

Moreover, *Paul*—and he, I say, is a model among gospel preachers—teaches us to preach in our gospel all the

Sweet Inferences

which flow from the resurrection of Jesus Christ. Here they are. He rose from the dead, and therefore His sacrifice has been accepted. God has brought again from the dead our Lord Jesus, that great Shepherd of the sheep, by the blood of the everlasting covenant. The work He has done has pleased the Father, and therefore he has brought him back from among the dead. His acceptance is ours: we are "accepted in the Beloved." Now, also, we live unto God. Our Lord Jesus died unto sin once; but in that He liveth, He liveth unto God: so is it with us. This is our joy: His work is accepted, His bearing of our curse is finished, life in us is made manifest.

I must repeat what I have said already, that from the resurrection of our Lord we draw the comfortable inference of the resurrection unto eternal life of all who are in Christ. We said farewell, a little while ago, to him whom we loved so well, but we shall see the honored one again. We laid our sister in the grave with many tears. Oh, how we miss her! But we shall meet her again when the trumpet shall sound. We preserve a long list of departed ones, of which we scarcely dare to think, for tears drown our eyes; yet will we refrain from weeping, for as the dew of herbs causes them to spring up again, so the rising again of our Lord restores to us the beloved ones who have fallen asleep. The broken circle of our fellowship shall be renewed, for Jesus, its centre, has risen again.

III. But now, alas for me! I have scant time for the point which I wanted most fully to discuss—gospel preaching affirms that Jesus is alive. We do not preach to you a dead Christ, but one who is able to save to the uttermost, seeing He ever liveth. Jesus died, Jesus rose again, Jesus is now alive. Paul

Knew that Jesus Lived,

for He had spoken to him out of Heaven. Paul had both seen and heard the Lord Jesus, and thus he had been turned from a persecutor into an apostle. His entire being was transformed by what he saw and heard; assuredly he was no deceiver, and he was not the sort of person to have been deceived. Jesus Christ is then alive, for Paul saw him. Beloved, receiving the witness of our apostle, and remembering many other infallible proofs which we have not time to mention, we also believe that Jesus, who was dead, is alive. What follows from this? Why, first, He is alive *to bestow the Holy Spirit*. Many blessings come from our Lord's death, but the Holy Spirit was an early gift of His resurrection life: especially was it the outcome of his ascended life. The gift of the Holy Spirit is the ascension gift of our living Lord. The life and light and liberty of the Spirit are with us, because Jesus lives. Beloved, do you think the times are dark and dreary? Be not afraid: while Jesus lives the Holy Spirit is always obtainable, the Holy Spirit is always ready to work in and with us. What more do we want?

Jesus is also in heaven making preparation for our coming. What has to be done to make heaven ready I am sure I do not know, though I have often tried to guess; but Jesus says, "I go to prepare a place for you." Heaven, when we get there, will prove to be the exact place for us. Jesus is living—living on purpose to keep heaven for us, and make it in all respects ready for us. Furthermore, lay hold of this thought, that Jesus is

Alive to Intercede

for us. I am most rich, beloved, when I have your prayers. If I might have a part in the prayers of all thé saints on earth, I would not envy a Kaiser his dominions. Yet what are all the prayers of saints compared to the prayers of the King of saints? We trust not in a dumb, dead Christ, who could not speak for us, but we rest in an advocate whose eloquent pleadings before the throne of God can never be denied.

O child of God, I would have you further remember that Jesus is still alive, to commune with you. You bend not over His corpse, but you sit at His feet. Carnal men would think me dreaming if I were to tell of our spiritual intercourse with our living Lord.

Still Doth He Speak

to our hearts. Pearls may not be cast before swine, nor the love secrets of our souls declared in the streets; but we have been conscious at times of influences other than those which are natural and common. Jesus has made Himself known to us: He has stood behind us, and His shadow has fallen over us. He has manifested Himself to us as He does not to the world. You know what I mean. Jesus does not forget us. He has not allowed a great gulf to open between us and Himself. He is still the loving, living, active Jesus to us and with us.

How I wish that every child of God here who is in trouble would go at once with that trouble to the living Christ! Oh that every sinner who is crushed beneath his load of sin would bow at once before the living Christ, whose voice speaks pardon! You cannot perceive Jesus, but He is present where His gospel is preached. Eye cannot see Him, nor hand touch Him, but He is visible and

Tangible to Faith.

Bow before Him! I know you have often thought, "If, instead of seeing Mr. Spurgeon on the platform, I could see Jesus, I would confess my sin to Him, and ask His pardon." I pray you do so, even though you see Him not, *for He sees you.* Fain would I cease to be seen of you, that your hearts might see my Lord, for He is here. Bow before Him, confess to Him, and trust Him.

"Oh!" cries a loving one, "If Jesus were visibly here, I would take Him home with me and entertain Him." Do so, I pray you, though you do not see Him. Constrain Him to abide with you. Treat the Lord Jesus, not as a phantom, but as a real Christ. Paul affirmed that He was alive; believe Paul's affirmation, and speak to the living Jesus. I will give you a text: "Whom having not seen, ye love." You cannot love a dead person as a dead person. You may love the memory of the dead; but if you love them, you regard them as living. Love is for life; it cannot dwell with death. We have not seen Jesus, but we love Him, and this proves that to our hearts He lives.

Oh that our Lord would now appear! Oh that His silver trumpets would ring out while yet I speak to you! Oh that His feet would once more touch this earth! The second coming of our living Lord is the ultimatum of our faith. He is alive, and as surely as He lives, He will open wide the golden gate, and come again to take His people up to be with Him for ever. Has He not said, "I will come again, and receive you unto Myself"? They that have been faithful to him in this evil generation, through the dark as well as through the light, and have followed at His heel through mire and slough—these shall partake of His glory. "These are they which follow the Lamb whithersoever He goeth." Who is on the side of the living Christ at this hour? Let him come out and boldly say so. Hold not back, lest ye be found traitors. Confess your Lord, take up your cross, and be the living servants of the living Jesus. Amen.

[The prayers of the readers of this journal are requested for the blessing of God upon its Editors, and those whose sermons, articles or labors for Christ are printed in it; and that its circulation may be used by the Holy Spirit for the conversion of many sinners and the quickening of God's people. Dr. Talmage and Mr. Spurgeon especially request prayer every Sunday morning on behalf of their labors.]

GEMS FROM NEW BOOKS.

How Conviction Came.*

Once a mother told her pastor that she was troubled about her daughter, who was going to join the church. "She has not conviction enough," was the complaint; "and yet I have talked to her about her sins over and over again, setting them all in order before her, till we were both of us in tears: Oh, what can I do more?" Then he gave her in her own hands a Bible, and he read aloud to her slowly, Isaiah 6: 1-5. She saw, without any word of his, that the prophet became intelligent as the sight of God flashed upon him, and grew penitent as the moment when the seraphim cried "Holy." Then he turned to Job 42: 5, 6. She saw in silence that the patriarch repented, not when his exasperating friends pelted him with accusations, but when his eyes were opened to see God. She went away quietly to talk, with a wondering and awe-struck heart, about the holiness of Jehovah; thus her child melted into contrition before the vision, and wept.

A German Captain's Order.

I heard some time ago of a German captain, who was drilling a company of volunteers. The parade-ground was a field by the seaside. The men were going through their exercises very nicely, but the captain thought he would give them an exercise in obeying orders. They were marching up and down in the line of the water, at some distance from it. He concluded to give them an order to march directly towards the water, and see how far they would go. The men are marching along. "Halt, company," says the captain. In a moment they halt. "Right face," is the next word, and instantly they wheel round. "Forward march," is then the order. At once they begin to march directly towards the water; on they go, nearer and nearer to it. Soon they reach the edge of the water. Then there is a sudden halt. "Vat for you stop? I no say halt," cried the captain. "Vhy, captain, here is the vater," said one of the men. "Vell, vot of it," cried he, greatly excited; "vater is nothing; fire is nothing; everything is nothing. Ven I say, forwart martch, then you must forwart martch." The captain was right; the first duty of a soldier is to learn to obey.

A Meal of Carrion.

A member of his congregation being in the habit of going to the theatre, Rowland Hill went to him and said, "This will never do—a member of my church in the habit of attending the theatre!" Mr. so-and-so replied that it surely must be a mistake, as he was not in the habit of going there, although it was true that he did go now and then *for a treat.* "Oh!" said Rowland Hill, "then you are a worse hypocrite than ever, sir. Suppose any one spread the report that I ate carrion, and I answered, 'Well, there is no wrong in that; I don't eat carrion every day in the week, but I have a dish now and then for a treat.' Why, you would

*From Spurgeon's Sermon Notes: Volume IV., Romans to Revelation. Pp. 408: Price $1: Published by *Robert Carter & Brothers*, 530 Broadway, New York.

The Late Amos B. Alcott.

Mrs. Pinfold's Illumination.

say, 'What a nasty, foul, and filthy appetite Rowland Hill has, to have to go to carrion for a treat!' Religion is the Christian's truest treat, and Christ is his enjoyment."

THE LATE A. BRONSON ALCOTT.

(See Portrait.)

THE kindly, lovable old man who won the name of the American Socrates had no Plato to make him known to the world, and his own efforts as an author have had but little success in that direction. All who knew him personally, however, recognized in him a bright, ardent spirit, eagerly bent on discovering the great secret of human life in this world, and how it might be made a blessing to its possessor and to the race.

Amos Bronson Alcott was born in Wolcott, Conn., November 29, 1799, and he was therefore in his eighty-ninth year on March 4, last, when he died. Owing to the poverty of his parents, his school education was brief and irregular. School in the winter and farm labor in the summer was the rule in the Alcott as in so many New England homes of those days. He learned to write with a piece of chalk on his mother's kitchen floor, and as soon as he had mastered the art of reading he devoured such books as came in his way. "Bunyan's Pilgrim's Progress" was his favorite book in his boyhood, and to the last the venerable philosopher continued to love and admire that matchless volume. At the age of thirteen, he finally quitted the school at Spindle Hill, and being equipped with a small stock of wares he set out as a peddler in the South. He tramped through Virginia and North and South Carolina, but succeeded in selling only a few dollars' worth of goods.

Trade was evidently not his vocation, and on his return he entered on the work which occupied the largest portion of his life—that of an educator of the young. He had a profound belief in the purity and spiritual penetration of little children, and delighted to listen to their talk and lead them to think and reason. His method of education was fatherly, and always had the moral training and development as its primary object, as being far more important than intellectual acquirement. The idea of corporal punishment was abhorrent to him, and under his gentle, discriminating system he had no occasion to resort to it.

All his leisure time was devoted to hard study, chiefly of metaphysics, philosophy, and theology. He contributed extensively to the *Dial*, and became a recognized leader of the Transcendental School, if not its actual founder. In 1842 he was induced to visit England, to consult with the prominent thinkers in the ranks of social and educational reformers. He lectured extensively, and on his return he was accompanied by two English friends, who aided him in establishing his ideal community, at Frudlands, near the town of Harvard. The scheme was not a success, and was soon abandoned.

The famous "Conversations" commenced shortly afterward, and were continued for nearly forty years. By these Mr. Alcott was best known to the American public. Often they were simply lectures on Character, Love, Poetry, Nature, or some kindred subject, but Mr. Alcott was always at his best when his audiences accepted his invitation to take part in the proceedings by asking questions and expressing their opinions. Since 1857 he resided at Concord, Mass., and there a circle of warmly attached friends gathered around him. His days were spent in study and literary work, and his evenings in congenial society. The works by which he is best known are "Conversations with Children on the Gospels," "Table Talk," and "Concord Days."

MRS. PINFOLD'S ILLUMINATION.

(See Illustration.)

ANY person passing the cottage in which Mrs. Pinfold lived would have thought it a picture of peace and calm contentment, in complete harmony with the surrounding fields and the summer sunshine which flooded them and the cottage with glorious light. The door was set wide open, and the widow, as she passed it in the course of her household duties, could see the cattle lazily grazing in the fields, and, in the distance, the laborers toiling at their work, and though she could not make them out distinctly, she knew that her two boys were among them. The sweet peace and tranquility without, had not, however, its reflection on Mrs. Pinfold's countenance. She was in deep trouble, and red eyes and furrowed brow showed that tears had not long ceased flowing, and would soon flow again.

"I d' know 't I've any call t' worry," she had said some days before, when an earnest Christian visitor had tried to arouse her to a consciousness of her state before God; "I've done my duty all through. I guess there ain't anybody I've had dealings wi' 'ts ever complained o' me. Father and mother and husband are gone, but they all allowed I'd done what was right, and the boys wouldn't hear anything against their mother, I guess. No; I aint such a sinner as you'd make out. There's many 's be though, if you're looking for work."

Still, the visitor was convinced that the old woman had been moved, and, in spite of her assumption of security, was not so much at ease under his words as she wished him to think. He therefore deemed it wise to leave her to the work of the Spirit, that she might be enlightened as to the state of her own heart by His omnipotent power. He acted wisely. Mrs. Pinfold had plenty of time to think as she worked, and she would not have been herself if her thoughts had not been occupied with an accusation that she had failed in her duty. It was her cherished pride—she had nothing else to be proud of—that she had never failed in that. A good mother, a good wife, a good daughter; yes, so far her conscience, which was a rigid one, acquitted her. But as to her duty to God? The more Mrs. Pinfold thought, the more guilty she grew in her own eyes.

The next Sunday she went to church as usual, but with an object that was not usual with her. Formerly she had gone as a duty; now she went to learn what she could do. It was not punishment she dreaded, but she was oppressed with a terrible sense of guilt, of meanness, of base ingratitude. To her surprise the regular clergyman was absent, and in his place was the very man who had visited her, and disturbed her peace of mind by his talk. That was well; he might tell her what she wanted to know. The text was, "Justified *freely* by His grace" (Rom. 3: 24), and the preacher showed how the sinner, having broken the law, was without hope of acquittal, except in the righteousness of Christ, which was offered to him. The distressed woman listened, but could not realize it.

The next day her burden grew heavier, and she wept as she worked. She knew, in a general way, that Christ died to save sinners, but there were great sinners—drunkards, thieves, and the like—to whom she had always applied the fact, not to herself. Suddenly, as if by a flash, she saw herself in the same category, and therefore with the same glorious hope. The thought overcame her. She put down her work, and sitting down on the rough bench in the kitchen, clasped her hands, while the joy flowed through her whole being, like a river. It was bewildering, enrapturing joy, such as none know but those who have felt it—a joy the world can never give nor take away.

THE ROYAL RETREAT IN FLORENCE.

(See Illustration on Page 269.)

SEVERAL royal personages are just now ruralizing at Florence, recuperating after the arduous labors which are said to be incidental to the vocation of a monarch. The Queen of England was the first to take up her abode there, and she has now been joined by the King and Queen of Sweden and other minor royalties. The illustration here given represents the villa in which

Queen Victoria is living. It is the property of the Earl of Crawford and Balcarres, who placed it at her disposal during her stay in the fair Italian city.

Florence, as is well known, is one of the most interesting cities of Italy, and scarcely inferior to Venice in historical renown, in the beauty of its architectural edifices, and of its collections of art, more especially of sculpture, while far superior in its associations with Italian literature. The Villa Palmieri is nearly two miles from the Porta San Gallo to the northeast of the city, on the road to Fiesole. The adjacent valley of the Mugello was always a favorite rural retreat of the rich Florentine citizens; and it was somewhere in this pleasant valley that Boccaccio, the author of the "Decameron; or, Ten Days' Tales" placed the fancied assembly of ladies and gentlemen, whom he supposed to have left their houses in the city on account of the plague, in the summer of 1347, and to have amused each other by telling the series of stories which he relates.

The Villa Palmieri, Florence. Queen Victoria's Present Residence.

Not far up the hill is the Villa Mozzi (now Villa Spence), which was the favorite residence of Lorenzo the Magnificent, and Careggi. The villa built by Cosmo dei Medici—in which Cosmo died, in 1464, and Lorenzo, in 1492, expired after his famous interview with the famous monk and preacher Savonarola—is among the hills on this side of Florence. The ancient Roman town of Fæsulæ, now Fiesole, from which Florence "descended," is a place of much antiquarian interest.

The villa constructed by the Palmieri family, at a spot called the Fonte dei Tre Visi, originally bore the name of Schifanoia, which meant "Avoid Disturbance." The Palmieri owned it for centuries; they built an arch or bridge over the public road, connecting the gardens with a terrace which commands a delightful view. An Italian, who had purchased the villa of the Palmieri, bequeathed it to the ex-grand Duchess of Tuscany, and her trustees sold it, some years ago, to the Earl of Crawford and Balcarres. A new road was then made round the hill, and an expenditure of about $50,000 was incurred in various improvements.

MRS. TRANSOME'S PUPIL.

A SERIAL STORY.

(Continued from page 255.)

A Light in a Dark Home.

IN a short time Thomas came to say that my brother wished to see the boy. I waited a minute or two to tell Philip whom he was going to visit; and how many years he had been ill; and how he had been suffering that very day. His bonny face grew grave and serious; and he trod along the carpeted hall with a careful and silent step. I wondered what he would think of George's white, worn face and low voice. He entered the room with me, unconsciously clasping my hand more tightly; but the moment he saw George, he stole forward on tip-toe again, and put his hand down softly on his pillow.

"Are you very ill?" he asked, in a low tone.

"Very," answered George; "and so you are come to be our boy, are you?"

"If you love me, and let me stay," he answered. "Have you never asked God to make you quite well again?"

"Yes, thousands of times," said George, as gravely as the child had spoken.

"Then He knows it's best for you to be ill," said Philip, "but He loves you all the same, you know. Mrs. Transome says He wont give us just what we ask for; and we must learn to be content, because He knows best. I asked Him for a pony ever so long, and He did not give me one: but it isn't because He does not love me. He chooses for old Transome to have bad pains, and old Transome says he'll be faithful to God in spite of them, for God had been faithful to him. When God chooses, it's all for the best, Mrs. Transome says."

"Yes," said George, holding the boy's small brown hand in his thin white fingers, "and I must learn to be content too."

"It's like learning lessons," Philip went on, in his clear young tones. "Mrs. Transome told me so. It's just like learning our A B C. It took me a whole week to learn all the letters; that was a long while."

"Yes, it is a long while," said George; but I knew he was not thinking of the child's lesson in the alphabet. No, it was his own harder task he was looking at. I am afraid we had both forgotten our first faith in God's love: and now we were sent back to it by the simple teaching of Philip, so that we might begin again a childlike life in His kingdom.

"Milly," said George, after the boy had gone away under Martha's care, "God has sent us one of His own little ones."

Yes, of a truth Philip was one of God's own children. Do not misunderstand me. The boy showed at times self-will, and sudden passion, and a spark of vanity now and again. All these were in him, and his simple nature could not hide them; though it could and did conquer them in the long-run. But there was no swerving of his inmost heart from a true and loyal love to Christ, whose life on earth became the pattern for his own. When I studied Philip's character in its transparent simplicity, the words that came most often to my mind were those of our Lord's speaking: "If therefore thine eye be single, thy whole body shall be full of light." There seemed to be no darkness, no dissimulation, in Philip at all. He loved the light, and always came to the light, even when he brought to it deeds to be reproved.

How life changed to George and me! The blankness and emptiness were gone. The future lay before us, with the promise of a beautiful life outside our own, that would link us again to the busy world. Year by year our interest in it grew deeper. There were masters to choose for Philip; a day-school to find for him, where he could have the wholesome companionship of other boys. We sent him to a large public school, where his brilliant gifts and insatiable thirst for knowledge would find full scope. George was himself a good classical scholar, and his old love for study revived, now there was a young brain, quick and eager, at work beside him. The hours that had been wont to drag so wearily along began to "glide with down upon their feet." Philip's studies, Philip's sports, Philip's friendships, absorbed us both.

Before he had completed his seventeenth year he won a scholarship. The head-master of his school, with whom he was a favorite, strongly urged him to remain another year under his tuition, and then to go to college. But the boy's mind was set upon studying as a medical student in one of the hospitals. The loyal spirit that was within him, longing to serve God diligently, and to tread closely in the footsteps of his Lord, could point out no better way than this.

"I can go among the very worst and poorest then," he said to us, earnestly, when we were trying to dissuade him. "You think I am too good for it? Why, if I were a hundred times better and more clever I should be hardly fit for such work! When I think of them down there, in their misery and ignorance and sin, I feel as if it would be treason for me to forsake them, just to grow rich or famous. I should choose to be a popular doctor at the East End, among the very worst, if I may have my choice."

My heart felt somewhat heavy with disappointment, for I had built many a castle in the air for my boy; and it had never entered my thoughts that he should bury himself and his great gifts among the very low and ignorant. As for George, his face was lit up with a smile that was almost heavenly.

"We shall have very little to leave you, Philip," I said.

"Are you going to die soon, Aunt Milly?" he asked laughing; "when I'm an old man of fifty, you'll not be seventy years of age; think of that! It's scarcely worth while for me to consider what you can leave to me. No, no; I shall be sure of more than Jesus Christ ever had. If I'm only clever enough to make a good doctor, and it comes true of me, 'He went about doing good,' that's enough for me."

His expression softened into a grave tenderness, and his voice grew low as he spoke. He did not often talk in this way to us; and I can see again his boyish, handsome face, half turned away from our eyes. It was a summer's evening, and we had the window open, that the fitful western wind might come in, rustling the papers on my brother's table, and breathing softly across his feverish face. George had taken Philip's hand into his, and was holding it fast as he looked at him with his strange smile. Just then we heard the distant tinkle of the house-door bell, a sound that had become frequent since Philip had gone to school, where he had formed many friendships. We knew our quiet talk was over; and so it proved. In a few minutes Thomas came in with a message.

"There's a shabby sort of a woman," he said, in a disparaging tone, "asking if Master Philip Champion is living here still. She won't tell me her business, but she says it's very particular; for she's come all the way from Liverpool a-purpose to see him."

"What's her name, Thomas?" asked my brother.

"Mrs. Brown, sir," he replied.

"That is the woman your father left you with, Philip," I said, with a quick throb of my heart. I could not hear the name without an undefined dread that it foreboded some change: and any change now would be an evil and a sorrow. The boy's face flushed crimson, and a glow spread over it, full of eager hope and gladness.

"My father's come back!" he cried.

He had not spoken of his father for years, and I had hoped that he had slowly reconciled himself to the idea that he had been lost at sea. But the eager, excited face before me contradicted the hope. The childish faith and expectation had never died; and now they sprang up in full vigor and life at the mere mention of this woman's name. "My father's come home!" he cried again, in a tone that brought tears into my eyes, and my brother's.

"Philip," said George, in his low, patient, measured voice, "remember! it is over twelve years since your father went away."

"I shall look for him to come back," he exclaimed, vehemently, "as long as it is possible for him to be alive, unless I find out for certain that he is dead."

"Twelve years!" repeated George, as though his thoughts were dwelling upon all that Captain John Champion must have suffered, if he were still alive; "twelve years, my dear boy!"

"Sailors have been lost longer than that," said Philip, moving toward the door, where Thomas was still standing. It was not a minute since he had uttered the woman's name; but it seemed to me already as if our hold upon Philip were slackened, and our close relationship with him were lost. He was not our boy after all, but belonged to some other—a stranger. Yes; I own to it; a strong and bitter feeling of jealous disappointment seized upon me.

"Let me come with you, Philip," I cried, as he was passing out of my sight.

Was there any tone in my voice that betrayed me? I cannot tell; only I know that my boy turned back again quickly, and stooped down to kiss me, and George held out his worn, hollow hand, as if to draw me nearer to him. I believe both of them felt a quick, instinctive sympathy for me, as deep as men can ever feel for a woman whose hand is forced to loose its grasp of her chief treasure. But neither of them knew what that moment was to me.

I had time, while Philip and I went to the dining-room, and Thomas fetched the woman in from the hall, to consider how very improbable it was that she should bring any intelligence about Captain John Champion, after so many years. This somewhat reassured me, though the glimpse I had had into Philip's heart could never be forgotten. Through all these years there had been a deep want, a profound, passionate longing, which no love or care of ours could satisfy. George and I could not be to him what his own father and mother would have been; so different, in the hidden root of things, must adopted relationships be from real ones.

Mrs. Brown came in; and Philip placed a chair for her. He was trembling with agitation, and could not command his voice to speak. She gazed critically at him, as if on her oath as to his identity.

"You're fairly like your father," she said, after this survey, "but you're more like your poor mother. It's a hard world, this is, for poor folks like me, and I've had a heap of trouble, but I've not forgot him or her. You've forgot him, I'll be bound!"

"No, never!" cried Philip. But he could say no more. He leaned his hand on my shoulder, and I felt how his strong young frame trembled, while his color came and went as fitfully as a delicate girl's.

"I've brought some news of Captain John Champion," continued the woman, in cold, hard tones. "May be you'll not think it worth much, but it's the last we've heard.

"It's a long story," she went on, with no change either in voice or face. "I've been knocked about a good deal ever since Master Philip left me, nine years ago now, as you'll recollect, ma'am, and never stayed more than a year, or eighteen months at the longest, in one place; so it were no wonder folks lost sight of me, and couldn't find me out, let them want ever so much. It might have been Captain John Champion hisself seeking after me, he'd have found it just as hard work; for I gave him up entirely after being away more than three years. But it wasn't Captain John Champion hisself, poor fellow! However, it were a seafaring man, as had gone out with him in his ship, and been wrecked with him, and saved with him, and brought home news of him, if he could only have lit upon me."

"How long ago?" cried Philip.

"It's four years pretty nigh since *he* came back," said Mrs. Brown, "and he did his best to find me out; but he couldn't, and he gave up at last, and went another voyage, and another, and another, searching for me whenever he was ashore, but never hearing a word of me till three months ago, when one of his old mates came lodging at my house in Liverpool, and heard me tell how I'd once had a captain's son to take care of, and how some grand folks in London had taken to him. 'What was the little chap's name?' he said. 'Philip Champion,' I said. 'That's Dan Sterne's old captain,' he said; 'him as was shipwrecked off the Ivory Coast somewhere.' So he went looking for him next day, and found Dan Sterne at death's door in the hospital, for he was quite worn out with following the sea, and was fallen into a waste, with no more than a few days' life in him. He sent for me as soon as ever he'd heard his shipmate's story, and I went there not much too soon to hear what he'd got to say."

Philip had sunk down on his knees at my side, with his eyes fastened upon the woman's face, as if he could look through hers into the brain beyond, and read what was there more quickly than he could learn it from her slow utterance.

"I'm not sure I rightly recollect it all," she said, "but he told me how the ship was broken to pieces on the rocks, and all aboard her were drowned, save him and the captain, and they two got on shore, and lived for a few days watching for a sail on the sea, till some of the savages came down and carried them up the country, and made slaves of them. Ah! he said, they knew what sufferings were, but they bore up under them, and the negroes treated them better when they found how clever the captain was. Only they never let him out of their sight; never, night or day. Dan Sterne wasn't watched so close, and he managed to escape; and he made his way through forests and bogs and jungles, and wild beasts, and wild men, day after day, night after night, till he reached a place where there were civilized folks—Portuguese, he thought; and after he'd been there a few months a ship brought him home to Old England. That's nigh upon four years ago, and he did his utmost to find me out, as he promised the captain he'd be sure to do if he ever saw England again; but he couldn't find me; and I only found him dying in the hospital."

"Is he dead?" asked Philip; "is that all?"

"Ay! he's dead," she answered; "and that's all, save a little bit of a map he gave me, where the place is that they were cast ashore upon. He pricked the place with a pin as near as he could guess, and he said they went east from there. I was to be sure and say they journeyed east from there, neither north nor south, but due east. Captain John Champion, he said, was pretty middling in health, but he was a close prisoner among them, and could not get a chance of escape."

(*To be continued.*)

THE JUDGMENT.

By Mrs. M. Baxter.

S. S. Lesson for May 6. Matt. 25:31-46. Golden Text, ver. 46.

Folly of Ignoring the Subject—A most Momentous Fact—Universal and Individual Application—The Christian in the Day of Judgment—Responsibility Measured by Privilege—Questions Left for Settlement at the Judgment-Seat—When it will Take Place—After the Millennium—The Sentences—Motives Taken into Account—Present Rewards to be Abjured—A Proverb Reversed—Eternal Destiny Self-Controlled—An Awful Temerity.

It has become an unfashionable and unusual thing in many congregations to speak of the Day of Judgment. Yet, surely, if it is true that we are hastening every moment to the "judgment-seat of Christ, that every one may receive the things done in his body according to that he hath done, whether it be good or bad," it is a most momentous fact, one which we should do well to face, and which it is the utmost folly and wickedness to ignore! "God shall bring every work into judgment, with every secret thing, whether it be good or whether it be evil." (Ecc. 12:14.) "Every idle word that men shall speak, they shall give account thereof in the day of judgment. For by thy words thou shalt be justified, and by thy words thou shalt be condemned." (Matt. 12:36, 37.) If this is so, how utterly mad and rash it is to live without regard to the fact that every word and every deed has a bearing on the endless eternity to which we are all hastening! Oh, how we need to pray in faith, with the Psalmist: "Set a watch, O Lord, before my mouth: keep the door of my lips." (Ps. 141:3.) "We must *all* appear before the judgment-seat of Christ."

No One can Escape.

Many a subterfuge may succeed in escaping an earthly court of law, but who can escape the just judgment of God? Some believe that for the Christian there is no judgment, but Paul says, "*We*," including himself, "must all appear before the judgment-seat of Christ." True "there is, therefore, no condemnation (i. e., final condemnation to be lost) to them which are in Christ Jesus," but we must all receive according to that we have done; we must all reap that which we have sown. If we, who are God's children, lived more in the light of coming judgment, the poor lost souls around us would more readily credit that there is a judgment for them.

Many of God's children think that because they are saved, and believe in Jesus, they will come off lightly at the time of judgment, while they are quite willing to admit that lost sinners deserve eternal damnation. But it was *Moses*, the man of all others, who knew God best in his time, who might not enter the promised land; it was not some poor reprobate Israelite who knew not God. "That *servant*," that one who is in the service of God, "which knew his lord's will, and prepared not himself, neither did according to His will, shall be beaten with many stripes. But he that knew not, and did commit things worthy of stripes, shall be beaten with few stripes. For unto whomsoever much is given, of him shall be much required; and to whom men have committed much, of him they will ask the more." (Luke 12:48.)

It is not without purpose that our loving Lord, before speaking of the final judgment, when He shall separate the sheep from the goats, speaks first of the ten virgins, and then of the servants who are entrusted with the talents. Much as God's Word teaches us of faith, it also teaches much of responsibility, and we break the harmony of His Word, and lose its balance, when, in learning to trust God, we ignore our responsibility; or when, under the presence of responsibility, we trust ourselves rather than God. The right thought of coming judgment is that of all others which is calculated to lead us into a life of trust, since *we* cannot keep ourselves or guide ourselves aright, but He has promised to be our Keeper, and to guide us with His eye. We are responsible to trust Him as Moses did in the desert, and Paul did in his journeys, and are responsible to do whatsoever He tells us. But if we, who are God's children, take upon ourselves to judge and choose what we shall do, how will it appear at the judgment-seat? "Well, *I* don't see that there is any harm in reading novels," says a luxurious young Christian lady. Well, sister, are you willing to let that question be

Settled at the Judgment-seat,

and then receive of your just Judge what He considers due for such an employment of His time and strength? "Well, I don't see that there is any harm in telling out how so-and-so has treated me," says a deeply injured child of God. "I think I ought to expose him." Well, brother, shall we leave it to the searching light of the judgment-seat, although the Word of God says, "I say unto you, That ye resist not evil." (Matt. 5:39.) "Why do ye not rather take wrong. (1 Cor. 6:7.) "It is better, if the will of God be so, that ye suffer for well doing than for evil doing." (1 Pet. 3:17.) Oh how small, how infinitesimal, will all wrongs received from man appear when we stand before the judgment-seat of Christ! Let us lay up for ouselves treasures in heaven by making all our calculations in view of that great day of account. Some may say, "But if we serve God, and walk so as to please Him now, is not this the best preparation possible for the judgment-seat?" Certainly it is so, but as the consciences of some are very lax about that which does or does not please God, He has also given us the coming judgment as an incentive to live to His glory.

After the marriage of the Lamb, after the distribution of rewards to His servants, after the millennium (or thousand years of Christ's reign, Rev. 20:6), comes the final Judgment Day. "When the Son of Man shall come in His glory, and all the holy angels with Him, then shall He sit upon the throne of His glory: and before Him shall be gathered all nations; and He shall separate them one from another, as a shepherd divideth his sheep from the goats." No other hand but the hand of Jesus can be trusted to do this work of separation. "I am the good Shepherd, and know My sheep, and am known of Mine, *as* the Father knoweth Me, and I know the Father." (John 12:15, Gr.) "He shall set the sheep on His right hand, but the goats on the left." While the saved of this dispensation are reigning with Him in glory for a thousand years on earth (Rev. 20:4), the wicked shall still be left awaiting the judgment, and they, and those who have lived during the time of the Millennium, will be judged together. First, He will say to them on His right hand, "Come, ye blessed of My Father, inherit the kingdom prepared for you from the foundation of the world, for I was an hungered and ye gave Me meat; I was thirsty and ye gave Me drink: I was a stranger, and ye took Me in; naked, and ye clothed Me; sick and in prison, and ye visited Me." This announcement will come with a burst of surprise upon the righteous. The virgins *expected* to enter into the marriage feast, the servants *expected* a reward for their service, but the sheep

Expected Nothing.

"Lord, when saw we Thee an hungered, and fed Thee? or thirsty, and gave Thee drink? When saw we Thee a stranger, and took Thee in? or naked, and clothed Thee? Or when saw we Thee sick or in prison, and came unto Thee?" And the King shall answer and say unto them, "Verily I say unto you, inasmuch as ye have done it unto one of the least of these My brethren, ye have done it unto Me." "Whosoever shall give to drink unto one of these little ones a cup of cold water only, in the name of a disciple, verily, I say unto you, he shall in nowise lose his reward." (Matt. 10:42.) It is not so much the things we do, in themselves, which shall tell in the great account, but the motive from which we do them; whether in our own name, for the sake of our own reputation, or in the name of Jesus, to increase His glory. "Whatsoever ye do, in word or deed, do all in the name of the Lord Jesus," i. e., in the character of the Lord Jesus, acting for Him, by His authority, as His representatives. Now, if we seek credit from man for any kindness which we may have the privilege of doing, and desire to be considered benevolent, we are doing it in our *own* name, and not in Christ's; we have our reward on earth, and we miss it at the great day of account. It is a law of the kingdom of heaven that we are not to seek our recompense in this world. "Take heed, that ye do not your alms before men, to be seen of them: otherwise ye have no reward of your Father which is in heaven. Therefore, when thou doest thine alms, do not sound a trumpet before thee, as the hypocrites do in the synagogues and in the streets, that they may have glory of men. Verily, I say unto you, they have their reward." (Matt. 6:1, 2.) They have it now. Poor, miserable reward is glory of men! Again, Christ warns us not to seek for glory among men when we pray and when we fast, lest in reaping the miserable reward of glory among men, we should miss the reward of our Father which is in heaven, who "shall reward thee openly." (Matt. 6:6.) Again, "When thou makest a dinner or a supper, call not thy friends nor thy brethren; neither thy kinsmen, nor thy rich neighbors, *lest they also bid thee again, and a recompense be made thee.*"

Flee Present Rewards,

"be afraid of quick returns," in the work of God. "But when thou makest a feast, call the poor, the maimed, the lame, the blind: and thou shalt be blessed; for they cannot recompense thee; for thou shalt be recompensed at the resurrection of the just." (Luke 14:12-14.) There is a well-known proverb, "a bird in the hand is worth two in the bush," and for men of the world who count God out in their lives, and in all their prospects, there is wisdom in it. But with the child of God it is the exact reverse. A recompense in hand is the worst investment possible. "Lay not up for yourselves treasures upon earth" (Matt. 6:19)—gold, position, reputation, honor—where all things change, "where moth and rust doth corrupt, and where thieves break through and steal; but lay up for yourselves treasures in heaven, where neither moth nor rust doth corrupt, and where thieves do not break through nor steal." "Set your affections on things above, not on things on the earth." (Col. 3: 3.) God is our portion on earth—heirship of God and joint heirship with Christ, our treasure in heaven. Just as we have to avoid a bargaining spirit, so, also, a greedy, grasping spirit. And then in the great time of account we may be surprised that God accounts some little thing done for one of His children, something long forgotten—something which we never counted, as having been done unto Him.

Rewards or punishment are according to the value which Jesus, the King of Glory, has had in our eyes. Oh, now we see, that having been saved by Jesus and redeemed by His precious blood, all that we do and say must be more or less connected with Him. "To me to live is Christ," said Paul. (Phil. 1: 21.) "None of us liveth to himself, and no man dieth to himself." (Rom. 14: 7.) Men may not like to retain God in their knowledge (Rom. 1: 28), and may seek to ignore the Lord that died for them, but, by doing so, they do not shut out Jesus from their lives—there he figures as a Saviour rejected and despised: ignoring Christ does not make Him cease to be; ignoring the judgment will not prevent it! Oh, how demented are men who, in their childish and wicked folly, say with the fool, "No God," while the very unrest of soul which comes out in such a declaration fulfils the very words of the God whom they reject. "The wicked are like the troubled sea when it cannot rest, whose waters cast up mire and dirt." (Isa. 57: 20.) Oh, how precious is it for the child of God to know that the kingdom to which he is welcomed has been prepared for him from the foundation of the world. It was destined for man before Adam fell; man was created for it, and adapted for it! God never created men for hell; never adapted them for companionship with demons. No; hell was prepared for the devil and his angels, and all men who, through rejecting Jesus, force themselves thither, must not wonder if they find themselves out of joint with their surroundings, for an endless eternity. Oh, it is an awful fact that every living man holds his eternal destiny in his own hands!

"Thus shall He say, also, unto them on His left hand, Depart from Me, ye accursed, into everlasting fire, prepared for the devil and his angels; for I was an hungered, and ye gave Me no meat; I was thirsty, and ye gave Me no drink; I was a stranger, and ye took Me not in; naked, and ye clothed Me not; sick and in prison, and ye visited Me not." Many of those who shall be lost eternally will have done many benevolent actions, but there was no Christ in them: they did them in their own name, and for their own sake, and they were not done unto Him. Their life has told against Jesus instead of for Him. A life without Christ is a lost life; philanthrophy without Christ is but among the works of the law by which no flesh shall be justified before God—righteousness which is but filthy rags after all. The wicked will be taken by surprise. It is astonishing how little men believe that the wrath of God abideth on them, if they do not believe. (John 3: 36.) God tells them that he that believeth not shall be damned, and they coolly set down God's declaration as though it were a mere matter of human opinion! Daringly they go on in their

Unsaved and Unsafe Condition,

and take the fearful risk of leading their lives according to their own perverted judgment, ignoring the just claims of God! They fail to submit themselves unto His righteousness, and at the last, when the Judge of all the earth shall judge them according to the Word which He has spoken, they will be taken aback, and say, "Lord, when saw we Thee an hungred, or athirst, or a stranger, or naked, or sick, or in prison, and did not minister unto Thee?" They did not see Him where He was to be seen, in the least of His earthly brethren. They had despised the people of God, failed to honor, failed to help, failed to recognize the people of God, and the Master makes the cause of His people to be His own. "Inasmuch as ye did it not to one of the least of these, ye did it not to Me." God expects His people to be such as can be recognized: "A peculiar people, zealous of good works." (Tit. 2: 14): He looks that men shall take knowledge of them that they have been with Jesus. And then He expects that the unsaved shall see Him in them, and treat them as the brethren and kinsmen of the Son of God. There is no appeal from the sentence of the King. It is final. Everlasting fire, "prepared for the devil and his angels." God never exaggerates. Fire means fire, and everlasting means everlasting. Men try to explain away the Word of God, and make it mean more or less than God intended. If this word "everlasting" does mean "age upon age," it does not fix any limit to that punishment; that everlasting punishment which awaits the lost. "These shall go away into everlasting punishment, but the righteous into life eternal."

NO ROOM FOR JESUS.

O pleading life, crowded so full
Of earthly toil and care!
The body's daily need receives
The first and last concern, and leaves
No room for Jesus there.

O busy brain! by night and day
Working with patience rare,
Problems of worldly loss or gain,
Thinking, till thought becomes a pain:
No room for Jesus there.

O throbbing heart! so quick to feel
In others' woes a share,
Yet human loves each power inthrall,
And sordid treasures fill it all;
No room for Jesus there.

O sinful soul! thus to debase
The being God doth spare!
Blood-bought, thou art no more thine own,
Heart, brain, life, all are His alone;
Make room for Jesus there—

Lest soon the bitter day shall come
When vain shall be thy prayer,
To find in Jesus' heart a place;
Forever closed the door of grace.
Thou'lt gain no entrance there.

—*Selected.*

J. E. Jewett, Publisher, 77 Bible House, New York, will furnish the above poem in leaflet form at twenty cents per hundred. *A Sample Packet* of 50 leaflets assorted (no two alike), will be sent post-paid, for ten cents. Postage stamps taken.

"CURIOSITIES OF THE BIBLE;" Test questions and answers pertaining to Persons, Places and Things, including Bible Readings and Studies, Prayer Meeting Outlines, Concert Exercises, Chalk Talks and Seed Thoughts illustrated. *The Detroit Christian Advocate* says:—"This unique publication is already in the hands of many pastor's, students and Sunday-school teachers. It is a veritable cyclopædia—full to the very brim of good things. The volume will prove a real treasure in any Christian home." 606 pages illustrated. Price $2. Teachers and Agents wanted to introduce it. E. B. TREAT, Publisher, 771 Broadway, New York.

"I want to thank you," writes a young man to B. F. Johnson & Co., Richmond, Va., "for placing me in a position by which I am enabled to make money faster than I ever did before." This is but a sample extract of the many hundred of similar letters received by the above firm. See their advertisement in another column.

Vol. XI., No. 18. Office, 63 Bible House. N. Y. THURSDAY, MAY 3, 1888. Annual Subscription, $1.50.

REV. CHARLES WESLEY, M.A.

CONTENTS OF THIS NUMBER.

PORTRAITS OF CHARLES WESLEY AND HIS MOTHER.
MODERN SPIRITUALISM. Dr. Talmage's Sermon Last Sunday morning.
ANECDOTES RELATED AT RECENT EVANGELISTIC MEETINGS.
THE THREE PROPHETIC PERIODS. By G. H. Pember, M. A.
A Fisherman's Monday Catch.—Congo Boys in a London Fog—Jewish Inquirers in Palestine—Emin Pasha and the Missionaries—A Disgusted Immigrant.
CURRENT EVENTS: Congressional Notes—Queen Victoria in Berlin, etc.
DAVID'S SPOIL. A New Sermon by C. H. Spurgeon.
Gems from New Books: A Pioneer Missionary.
PICTURE OF THE SUPPOSED SARCOPHAGUS OF ALEXANDER THE GREAT.
THE BLACKSMITH'S ARGUMENT. (With Illustration.)
PICTURE OF A SCOTTISH CROFT.
MRS. TRANSOME'S PUPIL. A Serial Story. (Continued.)
THE LORD'S SUPPER. By Mrs. M. Baxter.

MRS. SUSANNAH WESLEY: HIS MOTHER.

THE "HOLY CLUB." OXFORD: THE ORIGIN OF METHODISM.

THE "FOUNDERY": FIRST HEAD-QUARTERS OF METHODISM.

MR. WESLEY WITNESSES THE CALMNESS OF THE MORAVIANS IN A STORM.

A PERSECUTOR CONVERTED WHILE HIDING IN A SACK.

REV. CHARLES WESLEY, M. A., the Poet of Methodism—MRS. SUSANNAH WESLEY, his Mother.

THE REV. CHARLES WESLEY, M. A.

The Quadrennial General Conference—Birth at Epworth—His Mother's Piety—Life at Westminster School and at Oxford—The "Holy Club" and the Name "Methodist"—Embarkation for Georgia—The Moravians in a Storm—Return to England—Work among the Convicts in Newgate—Opposition and Persecution—Opening the "Foundry"—Two Visits to Ireland—A Persecutor in a Sack—Last Days and Death—His Hymns.

THE General Conference of the Methodist Episcopal Church, which is this week holding its sessions in New York, attracts the attention of the religious world, not only by the importance of the business to be transacted, but by the eminence and fame of the men who are assembled. The bishops, missionaries, editors, and able preachers who are to take part in its proceedings, are men convoked from widely scattered spheres of labor to give their counsel and aid in conducting the business of a Church which has no equal in the army of Christendom for energy and earnestness. Many prayers are being offered that the record of the achievements of the past four years which have elapsed since the last General Conference assembled, may stimulate all who hear to still more consecration and self-sacrificing labor, and that God will guide the deliberations to the increasing usefulness of this branch of His church.

It is appropriate at a time when Methodism occupies so large a share of the thoughts of religious people that the portrait of one of the fathers of Methodism, with that of his sainted mother, should occupy the place of honor in this journal. It is given to one the value of whose services to the cause is apparent in every Methodist church the world over, as its walls echo with the tuneful words which his pen inscribed.

The Poet of Methodism

was born December 18, 1708, in the old parsonage at Epworth, Lincolnshire, England, where his father, Rev. Samuel Wesley, was rector. He was about five years younger than his famous brother John, and sixteen years younger than Samuel, his eldest brother. The parsonage was the scene during the early years of the boys of a continual struggle with poverty, the father's income being small, and his family large. Sometimes even suitable food and clothing were lacking in the home, and there was always need of the most rigid economy.

Charles Wesley received the rudiments of his education under the tuition of his mother, *whose portrait accompanies that of her son on the first page.* She was a woman of sincere piety and of a cultured mind. She died in London on July 23, 1742. When, as she was dying, her sons and daughters stood around her bed, she said, "Children, as soon as I am released, sing a psalm of praise to God." Her interment took place in Bunhill Fields, and many thousands of mourners stood around her grave, for she was a woman greatly beloved, and her memory is blessed. Charles was sent in 1716, when he was about eight years old, to Westminster School. He was placed under the care of his brother Samuel, who was then one of the ushers in the establishment, and for a time generously bore the cost of his little brother's maintenance, whom he succeeded in making an excellent classical scholar. At Westminster, Charles was sprightly and active; his aptitude, however, was conspicuous in fighting, and it procured for him the admiration of the boys, and the title of

Captain of the School.

At the end of about five years he was elected one of the King's scholars, and his expenses were defrayed out of the endowment of the school. In 1726 he was entered a student at Christ Church College, Oxford. His brother John had lately left the same college, having obtained a fellowship in Lincoln college, Oxford, and had just resolved by the grace of God to be a Christian in heart and soul, unlike so many in that classical institution, who were going forth to preach merely for a livelihood. At this time, however, Charles would not listen to anything that was said to him on the subject of religion, but three years later, in 1729, he became much concerned about his state before God as a sinner, and began to seek the way of salvation. About this period, and while John was absent from Oxford,

The Name of "Methodist"

was first given to Charles Wesley and his thoughtful companions. In November, 1729, John Wesley, who for three years had been serving his father in the curacy of Wroote, attached to Epworth, returned to Oxford, that he might undertake the education of some young gentlemen, in whose welfare Dr. Morley, the Master of the University, was interested. Charles and his pious companions were rejoiced at his arrival, and immediately formed themselves into a "society" under his superintendence, "that they might promote each other's intellectual, moral, and spiritual improvement." Their entire number at first only amounted to four. Charles Wesley had just completed his twenty-first year, taken his B. A. degree, and become a Tutor.

The number of Methodists in the University soon began to increase, but not rapidly. They were objects of ridicule and censure, and were known and spoken of as the Reforming Club, the Godly Club, the Holy Club, Bible Moths, and so on; so that some of them found it difficult to maintain their ground amidst the raillery and invective with which they were treated. (*See Illustration.*) On April 25, 1735, the venerable rector of Epworth died, and the Wesley family was deprived of its head. John and Charles were both present, and the dying sayings of their beloved parent made a permanent impression upon their hearts. The following year they embarked as

Missionaries for Georgia.

The Colony of Georgia was formed under the sanction of a royal charter, which was granted in 1732. It was to be an outlet to the redundant population, especially of London, and to be an asylum for such foreign Protestants as were harassed by Popish persecution. Mr. John Wesley was prevailed on to undertake a mission among the Indians in the neighborhood of the colony. His brother Charles accompanied him as Secretary to Governor Oglethorpe. Up to this time Charles Wesley had declined entering the ministry; but he was now ordained, that he might be able to officiate as a clergyman in the colony, where the spiritual interest of the people had been neglected. They set sail from the Thames on October 14, 1735.

The ship in which the Wesleys embarked, the *Simmonds*, contained 124 persons—men, women and children—among whom was the Governor himself, and twenty-six Germans, members of the Moravian Church, with David Nitschman, their Bishop. Throughout their voyage, they occupied every hour with some useful work connected with the object to which their lives were unreservedly devoted. They were detained in the Downs by contrary winds, during which time Mr. Charles Wesley complied with the request of the clergyman at Cowes, and preached three or four times in his church.

The conduct of the Moravian Brethren, when on their voyage to Georgia, showed how thoroughly their hearts were filled with faith and love. It made a deep impression upon the susceptible and observant minds of the two Wesleys.

A Storm

came upon the emigrants when they were within about ten days' sail of the American continent. The waves of the sea were mighty; the winds roared fearfully; and the ship not only rocked to and fro with violence, but threatened every minute to be engulphed, or to break in pieces. "In this state of things," says John Wesley, "I went to the Germans. Of their humility they had given a continual proof, by performing those servile offices for the other passengers which none of the English would undertake; for which they desired and would receive no pay; saying it was good for their proud hearts; and their loving Saviour had done more for them. There was now an opportunity of trying whether they were delivered from the spirit of fear, as well as from that of anger, pride, and revenge. In the midst of the psalm wherewith their service began, the sea swept clean over the deck, split the mainsail in pieces, covered the ship, and poured in between the decks, as if the great deep had already swallowed us up. A terrible screaming began among the English. The Germans calmly sang on. I asked one of them afterwards, 'Were you not afraid?' 'I thank God, no,' was his reply. 'But,' I asked, 'were not your women and children afraid?' 'No,' he answered mildly, his face bright, 'our women and children are not afraid to die.'" (*See Illustration.*)

On landing upon the American shore, on February 5, 1736, one hundred and fourteen days after their voyage began, the people united in praise and thanksgiving to their Almighty Preserver. For five weeks the two brothers remained together; but early in March Charles

Removed to Frederica,

in the island of St. Simon, where he was to have spiritual charge of the people, and where the Governor, to whom he was secretary, had fixed his residence. Charles's mission, like that of his brother, was an utter failure; conspiracies were formed to discredit him with the Governor, and attempts were even made to get rid of him by assassination. It was not due, however, to the cause which afterward brought the two brothers into persecution, as they had not then begun to preach the distinctive doctrines of Methodism. On the 15th of May some duties connected with his secretaryship called Charles to Savannah, and from thence, much to his glad surprise, he was sent with despatches to England, and he never again visited Frederica. "I was overjoyed," he says, "at my deliverance out of this furnace, and not a little ashamed of myself for being so."

In 1737 and 1738 the Wesleys (for John had also returned to England as well as his brother) had frequent interviews with the good Count Zinzendorf and Peter Böhler, and through the efforts and teachings of Böhler, they were led to see the depths of peace and joy into which the Christian is privileged to enter through faith in the finished atoning work of Christ.

For several weeks after his conversion, Charles Wesley was very ill, but his heart burned with love to Christ his Saviour, and with zeal for the advancement of His work and glory. Scarcely a day passed but one or more persons were by means of his labors convinced of the truth, and believed to the saving of their souls. Not only was this the case in different parts of London among the poor and uninstructed, but also among some of the clergy. Mr. Stonehouse, the Vicar of Islington, received the truth through him, and at once began to preach it. Mr. Charles Wesley became Mr. Stonehouse's curate, and after reading prayers nearly every day in the church, he would go forth to hold private meetings in various directions. In behalf of no class were his sympathies more deep than of condemned culprits. He was

A Frequent Visitor at Newgate Prison.

In those times the criminal law of England was horribly sanguinary. Thefts and highway robberies were generally punished with hanging. In this state of the law, the execution of eight, or ten, or even more men on one day was no uncommon occurrence. Many a poor condemned convict did Charles Wesley teach the way of salvation through faith in Christ and commend in prayer to the pity of the Saviour. Among the churches which were opened to him for preaching his favorite doctrine was Westminster Abbey, in which he was once permitted to hold forth the lamp of salvation.

Meanwhile John Wesley had visited the Moravian church at Herrnhut, in Germany, and on his return home in September, 1738, felt convinced that similar societies might be raised up in Great Britain. From this time the brothers began to co-operate with each other for the advancement of true religion; John adopting

Charles's mode of procedure, preaching in such churches as were open to him, and holding meetings for conversation, mutual exhortation, and scriptural exposition. On October 28, this same year, Charles Wesley first delivered an entire sermon without notes in the church of St. Antholin, London. Eventually he became one of the most fluent and impressive extempore preachers of the last century.

Opposition Soon Arose.

The doctrine of salvation by faith was objectionable to the majority of those who attended the churches; and so great were the crowds which attended the ministry of the Wesleys that regular seat-holders were subjected to much inconvenience; they could not bear so much heat and crowding! Charles was dismissed from his curacy at Islington, and sought other fields for the exercise of that ministry which he felt he had received of the Lord. Then commenced that long itinerant career, as a preacher in the open air, and in all sorts of buildings wherever they could be obtained, in the course of which the gospel was proclaimed in all its fullness and power throughout the length and breadth of England, and by means of which multitudes were led into the kingdom of God, and united in the fellowship of a brotherhood which has its representatives and agencies to-day in all parts of the world. The subsequent history of Charles Wesley is interwoven with the spread of Methodism, and into this, interesting as it undoubtedly is, we have no space to enter.

In November, 1739, the brothers Wesley opened their first separate place of worship in London. This "preaching-house," was

The Foundery,

in Moorfields. It was a large and shapeless brick building, formerly belonging to the Government, and used for the casting of cannon for the army. An explosion having occurred, in which some lives were lost, the establishment was removed to the neighborhood of Woolwich. The Foundery was the birth-place of "The United Society." (*See Illustration.*) The lease of this property expired about the year 1777, when the commodious chapel in the City Road was built, and the congregation removed thither. In this house of worship, now commonly referred to as "The Cathedral of Methodism," Charles Wesley generally preached in the morning and afternoon of nearly every Sunday until his ministry closed.

In September, 1747, Mr. Charles Wesley paid his first visit to Ireland. He spent six months in Dublin, preaching twice a day, and strengthening a newly formed "Society" there. In the summer of 1748 he again crossed the Channel, and for nearly three months labored with apostolic zeal and marvellous blessing at Dublin, Cork, Kinsale, Bandon, and many other places. His meetings excited a strong opposition, especially among the Roman Catholics, and often his opponents resorted to violence. The incident of

The Man in the Sack,

which has been often related, occurred during one of these visits. Some Romanists discovered that there was a little company of Methodists meeting in secrecy and caution in a barn near Wexford. One of the persecutors agreed to conceal himself before the service began, and then suddenly open the door for his accomplices to enter. He found nothing to hide in but an old sack, in which he lay quiet and unnoticed. The hymn went so well that he waited to hear it all before disturbing them; and the prayer which followed sent the arrow of conviction into his heart, so that he groaned and wept. The terror of the simple worshippers, when such unexpected sounds were heard from the sack, may be easily imagined. They took courage, however, helped the man out, prayed with him, led him to Christ, and soon welcomed him into the "Society." (*See Illustration.*)

Mr. Charles Wesley survived most of his early religious companions. He had seen such saintly men as Hervey Grimshaw, Whitefield, and Perronet, "the Archbishop of the Methodists," pass away, together with Fletcher, the devoted Vicar of Madeley, and the time was rapidly approaching when he perceived that he also must die. His treasure and his heart were already in heaven. As the months rolled away he became weaker and weaker, until on March 29, 1788, *one hundred years ago* this year, he yielded up his spirit into the hands of his Saviour, after fifty years of laborious and effective ministry, and at the age of seventy-nine years.

As a Sacred Hymn-Writer

the name of Charles Wesley is enshrined in the hearts of many, both on earth and in heaven. A universal favorite with all evangelical denominations is his hymn commencing "Jesu, lover of my soul." So also are "He dies! the Friend of sinners dies!" and "Hark, the herald angels sing" and "Lo, on a narrow neck of land," which last was composed on the promontory of the Land's End, in Cornwall. Some of the most valued of the Wesleyan hymns are translations from the German. Of these, the finest of them all is from a hymn of Count Zinzendorf, the Moravian:

"Jesus, Thy blood and righteousness
My beauty are, my glorious dress."

Of the hymns in the Wesleyan hymn-book and supplement, 769 in number, about 600 are ascribed to Charles Wesley, and thirty to forty to John Wesley. Of the remainder, sixty-six are taken from Dr. Watts, ten from Dr. Doddridge, and the rest from eighteen different hymn-writers.

ANECDOTES RELATED AT RECENT EVANGELISTIC MEETINGS.

Miserable Excuses for Refusing Christ.—Mr. Thompson said: "I met two young men lately whose excuses for not accepting Christ were characterized by much frivolity. One of them refused because he was engaged to go to a ball with a young lady, and to disappoint her might give unpardonable offence; while his companion also declined the gospel invitation because he had been put upon a dance committee, and it might cause confusion and disappointment if he withdrew. Miserable excuses these for declining the invitation to the marriage supper of the Lamb! Yet it is for similar trifles that sinners fritter away their opportunity of securing eternal life, and consign themselves to a lost eternity. 'How shall we escape if we neglect so great salvation?'"

A Surprised Preacher.—Mr. Richard Weaver relates: "Not long ago my son was speaking on a platform about the Jews demanding that Barabbas should be released to them and Christ crucified. Standing up, he cried, 'Christ or Barabbas! Christ or Barabbas! Choose ye this day whom ye will have.' He did not expect an immediate answer, but, much to his surprise, a young man in the centre of the hall jumped up and enthusiastically cried out, 'Christ, Christ for me!' That was settling the question of salvation and eternity at once. He saw by the light and teaching of the Holy Spirit that there was no time for procrastination. Are there not many unsaved sinners around us with whom it would be well were they also to answer with all the earnestness that this young man did, 'Christ for me!'"

A Blaspheming Scoffer Struck Dead.—Mr Thompson said: "I was preaching in a certain place in the North not very long ago, where I heard a terrible story of three young fellows. It was a communion Sunday, and they were out taking a walk. They went into a liquor saloon for some refreshments, and while there one of them said, 'Let us have a communion of our own!' He knelt, and taking a glass in his hand, said in mock solemnity, 'This is the cup of my blood, shed for the remission of sins,' and handed it to his companion, who drank, and handed it back again to him. The words were repeated, and the glass handed to the other young man, who also drank. For the third time he repeated these holy words with blasphemous tongue, and was about to raise the liquor to his own lips, but God, who will not be mocked, arrested the action, and the scoffer fell dead upon the spot. Fear and horror fell upon his companions. They ran out and told the bartender what had happened, but he was afraid to enter the room. In haste they went to a chapel close by, and got some Christians to come. There they found the dead man, with the glass in his hand. I said to the friend who told me this, 'Can you vouch for the truth of this story?' 'Yes,' he replied, and he told me the address of the man from whom he had heard it, and who was the first man from the chapel to enter the room. God's judgment often seems deferred, but it sometimes descends upon the mocking sinner, and he is hurled into eternity with the mockeries still upon his lips."

Converted at the Sewing Machine.—"There was a woman sitting at her sewing machine in her kitchen. Her hands held the cloth. As she worked she was singing that hymn, 'Take me as I am.' When she came to the verse,

'Behold me, Saviour, at Thy feet,
Deal with me as Thou see'st meet;
Thy work begin, Thy work complete,
And take me as I am,'

she stopped her machine, and looking up to God with a weary, longing heart, she prayed, 'Yes, Lord Jesus, take me as I am; I do come to Thee.' I saw her at the meeting afterwards, and noticing her joyful face I spoke to her. It was then she told me the story of her conversion, and thanked God that He *did* take her. That Saviour is ready to be your Saviour, too."

A Lady's Singular Dream.—"The Wife of an Episcopalian minister in Plymouth, who has written many books, saw that there was a fullness of blessing that she had not yet obtained, and she set her heart upon attaining it. She searched diligently, but it seemed as if she were to be baffled. One night she learned in a dream what was wanting. She dreamt that she saw her heart, in the middle of which was a great tumor, and while that was there she could not have close communion with God. But she heard that the blood of Christ could remove the tumor. She went to Christ, and had her heart washed in His blood. When she awoke she knew what it meant. The tumor was the figure of sin. Sin, no matter how secret, or how small, must be washed away in the blood of Christ before she could have communion with Him. She gave herself into Christ's hands to be kept clean, and soon afterwards the Lord put the completeness of her surrender to the test. Two of her children were brought to the valley of the shadow of death, but yet she was able to say, 'Thy will be done.' She could not have done that before, but now she could give to God what she loved better than herself."

Money in Answer to Prayer.—Dr. W. Wood Smyth observes: "A Christian, who had long been employed as a trusted servant by a well-known American firm, thought of setting up in business for himself in a rising town in the West. He told his employers of his intention, and where he purposed going. They replied, 'Go, and we will never oppose you.' He went, but had scarcely started, when his old firm, instead of keeping their promise, actually opened a branch in the same town, close to his place, where they tried by every means in their power to occasion his downfall. He took the matter to the Lord, and laid all the circumstances before Him, and pleaded His promise of help in the day of trouble. One day he found himself with $500 to pay, and an empty safe. 'That is not much,' he thought; 'it may come in before the bank closing time.' But the time crept on, and there was no money; he began to be anxious, and went out to see if he could procure a loan of that amount, but failed. He returned to his office, and knelt in prayer. As he prayed, the name of a person whom he had forgotten came into his mind. Up he arose, and almost ran to that man's office, and asked the loan of the sum needed. He got it at once, and hurrying to the bank paid it in, but only just in time. He trusted in the Lord, and the Lord did not fail him. 'Cast all your care upon Him, for He careth for you.'"

MODERN SPIRITUALISM.

Dr. Talmage's Sermon, Preached last Sunday Morning, April 29, 1888.

"Behold, there is a woman that hath a familiar spirit at En-dor. And Saul disguised himself, and put on other raiment, and he went, and two men with him, and they came to the woman by night: and he said, I pray thee, divine unto me by the familiar spirit, and bring me him up, whom I shall name." I. Sam. 28: 7, 8.

The Nocturnal Visit to the Medium—The Awful Apparition—The Warning to the King—I. Spiritualism an Old Religion—Its Introduction to America—The Hydesville Spirits—Ancient Varieties of Witchcraft—God's Curse on them All—II. How Men Fall into the Snare—Its Victims Among the Troubled—An Ill-Spelled Letter Through a Medium—III. Affairs of Darkness—A Dream of a College President—IV. Brings Doom and Death—V. A Social and Marital Curse—VI. A Cause of Insanity—The Fatal False Revelation About the "Atlantic"—VII. It Ruins the Soul—A Christian Seance.

I HAVE recently become a spiritualist. At least so some of the journals of that belief declare. This, together with the fact that "mediums" are now being tried in the criminal courts, setting millions of people to make inquiry in regard to communication between this world and the next, leads me to preach this sermon.

Trouble to the right of him, and trouble to the left of him, Saul knew not what to do. As a last resort, he concluded to seek out a spiritual medium, or a witch, or anything that you please to call her—a woman, who had

Communication with the Spirits

of the eternal world. It was a very difficult thing to do, for Saul had either slain all the witches, or compelled them to stop business. A servant one day said to King Saul, "I know of a spiritual medium down at the village of En-dor." "Do you?" said the king. Night falls. Saul, putting off his kingly robes, and putting on the dress of a plain citizen, with two servants, goes out to hunt up this medinm.

Saul and his servants after awhile reached the village, and they say, "I wonder if this is the house"; and they look in, and they see the haggard, weird, and shrivelled-up spiritual medium sitting by the light, and on the table sculptured images, and divining-rods, and poisonous herbs, and bottles, and vases. They say, "Yes, this must be the place." One loud rap brings the woman to the door; and as she stands there, holding the candle or lamp above her head, and peering out into the darkness, she says, "Who is here?" The tall king informs her that he has come

To Have His Fortune Told.

When she hears that, she trembles, and almost drops the light, for she knows there is no chance for a fortune-teller or spiritual medium in all the land. But Saul having sworn that no harm shall come to her, she says, "Well, who shall I bring up from the dead?" Saul says, "Bring up Samuel." That was the prophet who had died a little while before. I see her waving a wand, or stirring up some poisonous herbs in a cauldron, or hear her muttering over some incantations, or stamping with her foot, as she cries out to the realm of the dead, "Samuel! Samuel!" Lo, the freezing horror! The floor of the tenement opens, and the gray hairs float up, and the forehead, the eyes, the lips, the shoulders, the arms, the feet, the entire body of the dead Samuel, wrapped in sepulchral robe, appearing to the astonished group, who stagger back, and hold fast, and catch their breath, and shiver with terror.

The Dead Prophet,

white and awful from the tomb, begins to move his ashen lips, and he glares upon King Saul, and cries out, "What did you bring me up for? What do you mean, King Saul?" Saul, trying to compose and control himself, makes this stammering and affrighted utterance, as he says to the dead prophet, "The Lord is against me, and I have come to you for help. What shall I do?" The dead prophet stretched forth his finger to King Saul and said, "Die to-morrow! Come with me into the sepulchre. I am going now. Come, come with me!" And lo! the floor again opens, and the feet of the dead prophet disappear, and the arms, and the shoulders, and the forehead. The floor closes. O, that was an awful séance!

I. I learn from this subject that Spiritualism is

A very Old Religion.

Spiritualism in America was born in the year 1847, in Hydesville, Wayne County, New York, when one night there was a loud rap heard against the door of Michael Weekman; a rap a second time, a rap a third time; and all three times, when the door was opened, there was nothing found there, the knocking having been made seemingly by invisible knuckles. In that same house there was a young woman who had a cold hand passed over her face, and there being seemingly no arm attached to it, ghostly suspicions wtre excited.

The excitement spread. There was a universal rumpus. The Hon. Judge Edmunds declared, in a book, that he had actually seen a bell start from the top shelf of a closet, heard it ring over the people that were standing in the closet; then, swung by invisible hands, it rang over the people in the back parlor; and floated through the folding doors to the front parlor, rung over the people there, and then dropped on the floor. N. P. Talmage, Senator of the United States, afterwards Governor of Wisconsin, had his head quite turned with spiritualistic demonstrations. The tables tipped and the stools tilted, and the bedsteads raised, and the chairs upset, and it seemed as if the spirits everywhere had gone into the furniture business! Well, the people said: "We have got something new in this country; it is a new religion!" Oh no, my friend, thousands of years ago we find in our text a Spiritualistic séance.

Nothing in the spiritualistic circles of our day has been more strange, mysterious, and wonderful, than things which have been

Seen in Past Centuries

of the world. In all the ages there have been necromancers, those who consult with the spirits of the departed; charmers, those who put their subjects in a mesmeric state; sorcerers, those who by taking poisonous drugs see everything, and hear everything, and tell everything; dreamers, people who in their sleeping moments can see the future world and hold consultation with spirits. Yes, before the time of Christ the Brahmins went through all the table-moving, all the furniture excitement, which the spirits have exploited in our day; precisely the same thing over and over again, under the manipulations of the Brahmins. Now do you say that spiritualism is different from these? I answer, all these delusions I have mentioned belong to the same family. They are exhumations from the unseen world.

What does God think of all these delusions? He thinks so severely of them that He never speaks of them but with livid thunders of indignation. He says: "I will be a swift witness against the sorcerer." He says: "Thou shalt not suffer a witch to live." And lest you might make some important distinction between spiritualism and witchcraft, God says, in so many words: "There shall not be among you a consulter of familiar spirits, or wizard, or necromancer; for they that do these things are an abomination unto the Lord." The Lord God Almighty, in a score of passages, which I have not now time to quote, utters His indignation against all this great family of delusions. After that be a Spiritualist if you dare!

II. Still further: we learn from this text how it is that people come to fall into Spiritualism. Saul had enough trouble to kill ten men. He did not know where to go for relief. After awhile he resolved to go and see the witch of En-dor. He expected that somehow she would afford him relief. It was his

Trouble Drove Him There.

And I have to tell you now that Spiritualism finds its victims in the troubled, the bankrupt, the sick, the bereft. You lose your watch, and you go to the fortune-teller to find where it is. You lose a friend; you want the spiritual world opened, so that you may have communication with him. In a highly wrought, nervous, and diseased state of mind, you go and put yourself in that communication. That is

Why I Hate Spiritualism.

It takes advantage of one in a moment of weakness, which may come upon us at any time. We lose a friend. The trial is keen, sharp, suffocating, almost maddening. If we could marshal a host, and storm the eternal world, and recapture our loved one, the host would soon be marshalled. The house is so lonely. The world is so dark. The separation is so insufferable. But Spiritualism says: "We will open the future world, and your loved one can come back and talk to you." Though we may not hear his voice, we may hear the rap of his hand. So, clear the table. Sit down. Put your hands on the table. Be very quiet. Five minutes gone. Ten minutes. No motion of the table. No response from the future world. Twenty minutes. Thirty minutes. Nervous excitement all the time increasing. Forty minutes. The table shivers. Two raps from the future world. The letters of the alphabet are called over. The departed friend's name is John. At the pronunciation of the letter "J," two raps. At the pronunciation of the letter "O," two raps. At the pronunciation of the letter "H," two raps. At the pronunciation of the letter "N," two raps. There you have the whole name spelled out. J-o-h-n, John. Now, the spirit being present, you say: "John, are you happy?" Two raps give an affirmative answer.

Pretty soon the hand of the medium begins to twitch and toss, and begins to write out, after paper and ink are furnished, a message from the eternal world. What is remarkable, the departed spirit, although it has been amid the illuminations of the heaven, cannot spell as well as it used to. It has lost all grammatical accuracy and cannot write as distinctly. I received

A Letter through a Medium

once. I sent it back. I said: "Just please to tell those ghosts they had better go to school and get improved in their orthography." Now, just think of spirits, that the Bible represents as enthroned in glory, coming down to crawl under the table, and break crockery, and ring tea-bells before supper is ready, and rap the window-shutter on a gusty night! Is there any consolation in such poor, miserable work compared with the thought that our departed Christian friends, got rid of pain and languishing, are in the radiant society of heaven, and that we shall join them there, not in a stifled and mysterious half-utterance, which makes the hair stand on end and the cold chills creep the back, but in an unhindered and illimitable delight?

> "And none shall murmur or misdoubt,
> When God's great sunrise finds us out."

III. I learn, still farther, from this subject that Spiritualism and necromancy are

Affairs of Darkness.

Why did not Saul go in the day? He was ashamed to go. Besides that, he knew that this spiritual medium, like all her successors, performed her exploits in the night. The Davenports, the Fowlers, the Foxes, the spiritual mediums of all ages, have chosen the night or a darkened room. Why? The majority of their wonders have been swindles; and deception prospers best in the night.

Some of the performances of spiritual mediums are not to be ascribed to fraud, but to some occult law that after awhile may be demonstrated. But I believe that now nine hundred and ninety-nine out of every thousand achievements on the part of spiritual mediums are arrant and

Unmitigated Humbug.

The mysterious red letters that used to come out on the medium's arm were found to have been made by an iron pencil that went heavily over the flesh, not tearing it, but so disturbing the blood, that it came up in great round letters. The witnesses of the séances have locked the door, put the key in their pocket, arrested the operator, and found out, by searching the room that hidden levers moved the tables. The sealed letters that were mysteriously read without opening, have been found to have been cut at the side, and then afterwards slyly put together with gum arabic, and the medium who, with a heavy blanket over his head, could read a book, has been found to have had a bottle of phosphoric oil, by the light of which anybody can read a book; and ventriloquism, and legerdemain, and sleight of hand, and optical delusion account for nearly everything. Deception being the main staple of Spiritualism, no wonder it chooses the darkness!

You have all seen strange and unaccountable things in the night. Almost every man has at some time had a touch of hallucination. Some time ago, after I had been over-tempted to eat something indigestible before retiring at night, after retiring I saw the president of one of the prominent colleges astride the foot of the bed, while he demanded of me a loan of five cents! When I awakened I had no idea it was anything supernatural. And I have to advise you, if you hear and see strange things at night, to stop eating hot mince pie, and take a dose of bilious medicine. It is an outraged physical organism, enough to deceive the very elect after sundown, and does nearly all its work in the night. The witch of En-dor held her séances at night; so do they all. Away with this religion of spooks!

IV. Still further: I learn from my text that *Spiritualism is doom and death* to its disciples. King Saul thought that he would get help from the "medium"; but the first thing that he sees makes him swoon away, and no sooner is he resuscitated than he is told he must die. Spiritualism is doom and death to everyone that yields to it.

It Ruins the Body.

Look in upon an audience of spiritualists. Cadaverous. Weak. Nervous. Exhausted. Hands clammy and cold. Voices sepulchral and ominous. Bewildered with raps. I never knew a confirmed Spiritualist who had a healthy nervous system. It is *incipient epilepsy and catalepsy*. Destroy your nervous system and you might as well be dead. I have noticed that people who are hearing raps from the future world have but little strength left to bear the hard raps of this world. A man can live with only one lung or with no eyes, and be happy, as men have been under such afflictions; but woe be to the man whose nerves are shattered. Spiritualism smites first of all, and mightily, against the nervous system, and so makes life miserable

I indict Spiritualism, also, because it is

A Social and Marital Curse.

The worst deeds of licentiousness and the worst orgies of obscenity have been enacted under its patronage. The story is too vile for me to tell. I will not pollute my tongue nor your ears with the recital. Sometimes the civil law has been evoked to stop the outrage. Families innumerable have been broken up by it. It has pushed off hundreds of young women into a life of profligacy. It talks about "elective affinities," and "affinital relations," and "spiritual matches," and adopts the whole vocabulary of free-lovism. In one of its public journals it declares "marriage is the monster curse of civilization." "It is a source of debauchery and intemperance." If Spiritualism could have its full swing, it would turn this world into a pandemonium of carnality. It is an unclean, adulterous, damnable religion, and the sooner it drops into the hell from which it rose, the better both for earth and heaven. For the sake of man's honor and woman's purity, I say let the last vestige of it perish for ever. I wish I could gather up all the raps it has ever heard from spirits blest or damned, and gather them all on its own head in thundering raps of annihilation!

I further indict Spiritualism for that it is

A Cause of Insanity.

There is not an asylum between Bangor and San Francisco which has not the torn and bleeding victims of this delusion. Go into any asylum, I care not where it is, and the presiding doctor, after you have asked him, "What is the matter with that man?" will say: "Spiritualism demented him"; or, "What is the matter with that woman?" he will say, "Spiritualism demented her." It has taken down some of the brightest intellects. It swept off into mental midnight judges, senators, governors, ministers of the gospel, and one time came near capturing one of the Presidents of the United States. At Flushing, near this city, a man became absorbed with it, forsook his family, took his only fifteen thousand dollars, surrendered them to a spiritual medium in New York, attempted three times to put an end to his own life, and then was incarcerated in the State Lunatic Asylum, where he is to-day.

A Fatal Falsehood

Many years ago the steamer *Atlantic* started from Europe for the United States. Getting mid-ocean, the machinery broke, and she floundered around day after day, and week after week; and for a whole month after she was due people wondered, and finally gave her up. There was great anguish in the cities, for there were many who had friends aboard that vessel. Some of the women, in their distress, went to the spiritual medium, and inquired as to the fate of that vessel. The medium called up the spirits, and the rappings on the table indicated the steamship lost, with all on board. Women went raving mad, and were carried to the lunatic asylum. After awhile one day a gun was heard off Quarantine. The flags went up on the shipping, and the bells of the churches were rung. The boys ran through the streets, crying: "Extra! The *Atlantic* is safe!" There was the embracing as from the dead, when friends came again to friends; but some of those passengers went up to find their wives in the lunatic asylum, where this cheat of infernal Spiritualism had put them.

A man in Bellevue Hospital, dying from wounds made by his own hand, was asked why he tried to commit suicide, and he said: "The spirits told me to." Parents have strangled their children, and when asked why they did it, replied: "Spiritualism demanded it." It is the patronizer and forager for the madhouse. Judge Edmonds, in Broadway Tabernacle, New York, delivering a lecture in behalf of Spiritualism, admitted, in so many words: "There is a fascination about consultation with the spirits of the dead that has a tendency to lead people off from their right judgment, and to instill into them a fanaticism that is revolting to the natural mind."

It not only ruins its disciples, but it ruins the mediums also, only give it time. The Gadarean swine, on the banks of the Lake of Galilee, no sooner became spiritual mediums than down they went, in an avalanche of pork, to the consternation of all the herdsmen. The office of a medium is *bad for a man, bad for a woman, bad for a beast*.

VII. I bring against this delusion a more fearful indictment:

It Ruins the Soul

immortal. First it makes a man a quarter of an infidel; then it makes him half an infidel; then it makes him a whole infidel. The whole system, as I conceive it, is founded on the insufficiency of the Word of God as a revelation. God says the Bible is enough for you to know about the future world. You say it is not enough, and there is where you and the Lord differ. And although the Scriptures say: "Add thou not unto His words, lest He reprove thee, and thou be found a liar," you risk it, and say, "Come back, spirit of my departed father; come back, spirit of my departed mother; of my companions; of my little child—and tell me some things I don't know about you, and about the unseen world." If God is ever slapped square in the face, it is when a spiritual medium puts down her hand on the table, invoking spirits departed to make a revelation. God has told you all you ought to know, and how dare you be prying into that which is none of your business? You cannot keep the Bible in one hand and Spiritualism in the other. One or the other will slip out of your grasp, depend upon it. Spiritualism is

Adverse to the Bible

in the fact that it has in these last days called from the future world Christian men to testify against Christianity. Its mediums call back Lorenzo Dow, the celebrated evangelist, and Lorenzo Dow testifies that Christians are idolaters. Spiritualism calls back Tom Payne, and he testifies that he is stopping in the same house in heaven with John Bunyan. They call back John Wesley, and he testifies against the Christian religion, which he all his life gloriously preached. Andrew Jackson Davis, the greatest of all the Spiritualists, comes to the front, and declares that the New Testament is but "the dismal echo of a barbaric age," and the Bible only "one of the pen-and-ink relics of Christianity."

"But," says some one, "wouldn't it be of advantage to hear from the future world? Don't you think it would strengthen Christians? There are a great many Materialists who do not believe there are souls; but if spirits from the future world should knock and talk over to us, they would be persuaded." To that I answer, in the ringing words of the Son of God: "If they believe not Moses and the prophets, neither will they be persuaded, though one rose from the dead."

I believe these are the days of which the Apostle spake when he said: "In

The Latter Times

some shall depart from the faith, giving heed to seducing spirits." I think my audience, as well as other audiences in this day, need to have reiterated in their hearing the passages I quoted some minutes ago: "There shall not be among you a consulter of familiar spirits, or wizard, or necromancer, for they that do these things are an abomination unto the Lord"; and, "The soul that turneth after such as have familiar spirits, I will set Myself against them, and they shall be cut off from their people."

But I invite you this morning to

A Christian Seance,

a noonday séance. This congregation is only one great family. Here is the church table. Come around the church table; take your seats for this great Christian séance; put your Bible on the table, put your hands on top of the Bible, and then listen, and hear if there are any voices coming from the eternal world. I think there are. Listen! "Secret things belong unto the Lord, our God, but things that are revealed belong unto us and to our children." Surely, that is a voice from the spirit world! But before you rise from this Christian séance, I want you to promise me you will be satisfied with the Divine revelation until the light of the eternal throne breaks upon your vision. Do not go after the witch of En-dor. Do not sit down at table-rappings, either in sport or in earnest.

Teach your children there are no ghosts to be seen or heard in this world, save those which walk on two feet or four—human or bestial. Remember that Spiritualism, at the best, is a useless thing; for if it tells what the Bible reveals, it is a superfluity: and if it tells what the Bible does not reveal, it is a lie. Instead of going out to get other people to tell your fortune, tell your own fortune by putting your trust in God and doing the best you can. I will tell your fortune: "All things work together for good to them that love God." Insult not your departed friends by asking them to come down and scrabble under an extension-table. Remember that there is only one Spirit whose dictation you have a right to invoke, and that is the holy, blessed, and omnipotent Spirit of God. Hark! He is rapping now, not on a table, or the floor, but rapping on the door of your heart, and every rap is an invitation to Christ and a warning of judgment to come. Oh, grieve Him not away! Quench Him not. He has been all around you this morning. He was all around you last night. He has been around you all your lives. Hark! There comes a voice with tender overmastering intonation, saying: "My Spirit shall not always strive."

THE THREE PROPHETIC PERIODS.

By G. H. Pember.*

The Entire Course from the Beginning of the Seventy Weeks to the Second Advent—The Angel's Separation—The first Period of 483 Years—The Second Indefinite—The Third of Seven Years——The Four Key Verses—The Work of the First Period—The Destruction to Follow—The Missing Week—Its First and Second Half—The final Consummation.

THERE is a fact, the knowledge of which is indispensable to those who would comprehend Divine revelations of the future. Prophetic time, from the commencement of the Seventy Weeks to the Second Advent, is divided into three grand periods, which are plainly marked out in the book of Daniel, and as plainly recognized in the Apocalypse.

In glancing through the book of Daniel we observe that the prophet could not understand his earlier visions in the seventh and eighth chapters; that in the ninth chapter an angel is sent, in answer to his earnest prayer, to give him "skill and understanding"; and that, after receiving this communication, he readily comprehended the final vision, which is narrated in the tenth and following chapters. It is clear, then, that the four verses (Daniel, 9: 24-27) which contain the angel's words are the key to the whole book.

Now the purport of these verses is, that God had divided what was then future time into three periods.

I. The first, a definite time of four hundred and eighty-three years, beginning with the issue of a mandate for the rebuilding of the city and walls of Jerusalem, and ending with the presentation of Messiah as her King to the daughter of Zion, four days before His death.

II. The second, an indefinite period, beginning immediately upon the close of the first, and ending with the resurrection of the dead in Christ and their translation, together with all waiting believers who are then upon earth, to meet the Lord in the air. This is the present age, the time of the Church, during which all

Jewish Prophecies are Suspended.

III. The third, a brief period of but seven years, beginning on the day when Antichrist shall make a seven years' covenant with the majority of the Jewish nation, and ending with the glorious appearing of the Lord Jesus to set up His Kingdom. This is a time of judgment, God's strange and short work, during which He will resume His dealings with the Jews by casting them into the refining furnace, carry on His controversy with the Gentiles, and permit the fulfilment of the prophecies concerning Antichrist and the Great Tribulation.

Now with these three distinctly marked times before us, let us remind ourselves of two facts.

First: the Scriptures cannot be broken or disagree. We may, therefore, justly expect to find in the Apocalypse a recognition of the periods disclosed to Daniel.

And, secondly, John wrote many years after Christ's entry into Jerusalem. Therefore, the first of Daniel's periods had then passed away, and the apostle was living in the second or Church period.

Turning now to the Apocalypse, we shall find that its contents are given to us by the Lord Himself in the nineteenth verse of the first chapter, where He says: "Write, therefore, the things which thou sawest, and the things which are, and the things which shall be after these things."

We have, then, the following harmony with the scheme of the Seventy Weeks:

I. Daniel's first period had passed by.

II. What John had already seen is written in the first chapter, which describes his vision of the sanctuary arranged for the present dispensation. Then, occupying the second and third chapters, come "the things that are," or prophecies of the age in which John was living, which is still going on, and which answers to Daniel's second and indefinite period.

III. Lastly, stretching from the fourth to the nineteenth chapter, come "the things that shall be after these things," that is, in Daniel's third period, the seven years of judgment.

A careful application of this Divinely revealed scheme will dispel confusion, and enable us to range the predictions of the two great prophets, as well as those of all others, in their proper order.

We must now examine these verses [Daniel 9: 24-27] minutely. *Seventy Weeks.* Literally,

Seventy Sevens.

The word "week" is retained, because we have no exact equivalent for the Hebrew original,* which signifies a period of seven, but does not decide whether the seven are hours, days, months, years, or any other measure of time. That point must always be determined by the context; and in the present passage periods of seven *years* each are doubtless intended, because Daniel's mind is dwelling on the Seventy *Years* of Jeremiah.† The meaning of the angel seems to be: The Seventy Years of probation will not suffice; nay, after them must come seven times seventy other years. We should remember that the Sabbatical years and the Jubilee made the idea of a week of years very familiar to Israelites.

Have been severed off. That is, from the times of the Gentiles, from the age during which their four World-empires should hold sway. *Upon thy people and upon thy holy city.* This prophecy, then, is concerned with Israelites, and not with Christians. Seven times seventy, or four hundred and ninety years, are to be taken out of the times of the Gentiles for the special dealings of God with the Jews and Jerusalem; that is, of course, with the Jews at Jerusalem: for the people must during the time be dwelling in their own country.

To shut up the transgression. That is, to arrest and restrain it so that it can no longer work and spread. The article probably indicates the whole course of Israel's transgression or breaking away from God.

To seal up sins. The figure of sealing is connected with that of shutting up in prison or restraining. So Darius seals the stone which is put at the mouth of the lions' den, with his own signet and that of his lords.

The Sealing Up

of sins consequently signifies their restraint under safe custody. There is a good illustration of both figures, and probably a clue to the interpretation of the passage in the twentieth chapter of the Revelation, where an angel, after binding Satan and casting him into the abyss, shuts him up and sets a seal upon him, that he may deceive the nations no more.

To cover iniquity. That is, according to the well-known Scriptural figure, to make atonement for it. *To bring in everlasting righteousness.* When the transgression is shut up and the sins are sealed, then everlasting righteousness shall be brought in. This will be done by the introduction of the New Covenant, in accordance with which God will no longer write upon tables of stone, but put His law in the inward parts of His people and write it in their hearts.

To seal up vision and prophet. When sins are sealed up, vision and prophet shall also be laid aside as being no longer needed. For it was only after sin had come into the world that prophecy was introduced as a great instrument of God in the war against it; and so when sin is put away prophecies also shall fail. *To anoint a Holy of Holies.* Lastly, in the place of the Tabernacle and former temples in which the covering or atonement was wont to be typified, a new Holy of Holies shall be anointed.

The prophecy then speaks of vengeance which should follow for the cutting off of Messiah: the city and the Sanctuary, Jerusalem and the Temple, should be destroyed. This was fulfilled by the Romans under Titus, about forty years after the death of Christ: but still there is no mention of the missing Seven Years.

Lastly; we are told that, after the destruction of the city and Sanctuary, there should be wars and desolations until the end, during a period fixed by God. Terribly has this been verified; and so frequent have been the captures of Jerusalem by Roman, Persian, Saracen, and Turk, that the city of our Lord's time has become deeply buried beneath successive

Layers of Ruin

and *débris*, and is now found from fifty to eighty feet below the level of the soil. All these destructions are included in the words, "And until the end there shall be war, that which is determined for desolations;" and yet there is no mention of the final Seven Years.

Thus, from the appearing of Messiah, the Prince, there occurs an undefined interval, a great interruption in the progress of the Seventy Weeks, which is not unnoticed in other parts of Scripture.

But, to retrace our steps for a moment, the city and Sanctuary were to be destroyed by the people of a prince that should afterwards come; and since it is added that this prince will meet his doom in the last great outpouring of God's wrath, it is manifest that he cannot have appeared in past time. Now the Romans destroyed the city and Sanctuary: so far, therefore, we gather that the prince will be a head of the Fourth Empire; but the time of his end shows us further that he will be the last head—that is, the Antichrist.

In the final verse of the prophecy we are told that he will confirm a covenant with the majority of the Jewish people for One Week. And so at length we find

The Missing Seven Years,

the Seventieth Week. Now the Jews must by this time have settled again in their own land, because the prophecy is expressly connected with the people and the city. Possibly the prince may himself have restored them: but, at any rate, he will find them in some trouble, or terrified by some impending danger, and will undertake their protection in Palestine for seven years. The compact may, perhaps, be similar to that by which Napoleon III. promised to maintain Maximilian as emperor of Mexico for a fixed time. But whatever the covenant may be, it will only be accepted by a majority of the people, and not by the whole nation: God will again leave Himself a remnant which shall not bow the knee to Baal.

Thus restored and settled in their own land, the Jews will rebuild their Temple and renew the sacrifices and services; but, probably, in a proud and atheistical spirit, and certainly in a way very displeasing to God. The last chapter of Isaiah represents them as engaged in these works not long before the appearing in glory of the Lord Jesus, a description of which begins with the fifteenth verse.

But the Jews will go their own ways during

The First Half of the Seven Years,

and then there will be a change. In the middle of the Week—that is, at the end of Three Years and a Half—Antichrist will cause the sacrifices to cease, and transfer the worship of Jehovah to himself, exalting "himself above all that is called God, or that is worshipped; so that he as God sitteth in the Temple of God, showing himself that he is God."

In such a mockery of Godhead the prince will

* From the third edition of his excellent work, "The Great Prophecies concerning the Jews, the Gentiles, and the Church of God"—a book remarkable for the learning and wide research it displays, yet so simple in style and diction that any reader can understands it, and under its guidance perceive the meaning of the prophecies of the Bible. 458 pages. Price by mail, $1.50. For sail at this office, 63 Bible House, New York.

* Some commentators use "heptad," or "hebdomad"; either of which words would do, if it could be considered English.

† If Christians be suspected of bias in interpreting "the sevens" as weeks of years, because the end of the sixty-ninth seven is thus made to synchronize with the time of Christ's death, it is impossible to bring such a charge against Jews. And yet, until the Middle Ages were far advanced, the Jews invariably adopted the same explanation, although by so doing they convicted themselves of rejecting the Messiah, and placed a formidable weapon in the hands of their Christian opponents.

continue, until the hour allotted to the powers of darkness has come to its full end. Then that which has been decreed will have been poured upon the desolate city of Jerusalem, and the time of the consummation will have arrived. Down from heaven will the flood of God's indignation be poured: the blasphemous pretender will be confounded by a brightness—far above that of the sun—which, lighting up the whole globe with the speed of the storm flash, will proclaim the advent of the King of kings.

A FISHERMAN'S MONDAY CATCH.

IN a letter to the *Missionary Herald* from Tillipally, in Ceylon, Mr. S. W. Howland, thus refers to the public interest in a native Christian fisherman who abstains from his occupation on the Lord's Day: "Next Sabbath is to be communion at Chavagacherry, and two are to be received, one the wife of a Christian, the other a cousin of a Christian in a fisher village. His cousin is part owner of a fishing-net, or seine, costing about twenty-five dollars, and this man, with others, uses it. They pray every morning before setting out, and they think that their catch is on the whole greater than that of the nets used seven days in a week. On several occasions their heathen neighbors, seeing their large catch on a Monday, have declared their intentions of keeping the Sabbath, and several of them seem really interested.

"We were recently invited to hold a meeting in a school held just in front of a large temple. I am told that a meeting has never been held there before. We never had better attention, and they asked us to come again. A short time before, we were invited to a meeting in the rest-house attached to a temple. We preferred to hold it in the open air under a large tree. The temple musician played a pipe quite skilfully, and quickly joined in the tunes of our lyrics, most of which are adapted from temple music. *The hand-drum and the cymbals* also added their noise to the music of the baby-organ, and we sang tune after tune in a style quite pleasing to the large crowd that gathered, who listened attentively to the earnest address that followed. We would not have such instruments in a Christian place of worship, but they did not seem out of place there."

CONGO BOYS IN A LONDON FOG.

Two boys from the Congo were recently brought to London by a missionary, and one morning to their amazement they could see neither sun nor sky; nothing was visible from the window of their room but brown murky fog. It was what is known as "a London particular." The missionary says: "It was really a terrible fog. Day by day, and night after night, without break or lifting, or any intermission, it hung like a yellow pall, solid and stifling, over the great metropolis. Each morning we awoke with a gleam of hope that the longed-for change had come; each morning we found, on straining our eyes through the darkness, that our view was still yesterday's view, and the view of the day before—a dense, grimy, yellow wall of fog, massed up against the window, beyond which no object could be seen, and through which daylight had scarcely strength to penetrate.

"To our Congo boys, who had just arrived in England, this was a new and very strange experience. Sitting by the fire hour after hour, and glancing up every now and then at the grimy prospect without, M'Teva and Bompole were quite at a loss to comprehend, or in any wise account for, the unwonted aspect of things, which bore to them the appearance of a new phenomenon. At last M'Teva said, in a very grave voice, 'What time this chimney will finish?' 'What chimney?' I asked, looking up surprised from my desk to see if the chimney was on fire. 'What time this chimney will finish?' he repeated, pointing out of the window with a decisive brown finger that left no doubt as to the meaning of his words. To which I answered smiling, that of course we could not tell, but that we hoped it would finish soon! Next morning, there being no alteration in the aspect of affairs, the boys came to us once more with: 'When will sun shine again?'"

Ah, M'Teva, with your simple Central African ideas, it is not in the outer world alone that such "chimneys" are apt to hide the sun! How often are heart and soul befogged with the heavy clouded atmosphere of earth's great metropolis. How often every-day work and weariness, trifling and pleasure and sin, physical weakness! love of ease, and temptation yielded to, combine to shut out from the soul the light of the Sun of Righteousness! And we look up, but cannot see Him shine. We catch no ray of His splendor and reflect none to the world.

EMIN PASHA AND THE MISSIONARIES.

THE brave lieutenant of Gen. Gordon whose situation in the heart of Africa has so long been the cause of anxiety in civilized lands, and for whose relief or rescue Mr. H. M. Stanley started out with a large expedition early last year, has written a cheerful letter to his friends in England. He says: "I cannot speak too highly of the untiring exertions and valuable assistance afforded me by Mr. Mackay, the missionary in Uganda. At great personal inconvenience, he has not only provided for the despatch of our posts from and to Zanzibar, and done his utmost to facilitate our transactions in Uganda, but he has actually deprived himself of many valuable things to assist myself and g[illegible] me comfort. He has done splendid work in Uganda; but lately his labors have been somewhat interfered with by the Arabs trying to have him turned out of Uganda. In the interest of the Uganda Mission, I am very glad that Mr. Stanley chose the Congo road for his expedition. He will there encounter numberless difficulties, arising mostly out of the soil to go across, yet he will without doubt succeed in vanquishing them; while, coming by Uganda, he would never have obtained permission to come here, except by sheer force, besides imperilling the life and work of the missionaries.

"As to myself, if ever I wanted an encouragement to pursue my work, the acknowledgment of what, by God's permission, I was allowed to do until now will spur me to go on and to do my duty cheerfully. I am sorry to disappoint your kind wish that your letter may find me safely arrived at Zanzibar; and I may as well tell you that I have been greatly amused by the doubts expressed in some papers if I would stay or leave when Mr. Stanley arrives. I think there can be no doubt that I shall stay, and I wonder how anyone could suppose the contrary. I need not dwell on the reasons for my decision. Would you desert your own work just at the dawn of better times? Since my last letter to you I have been able to resume the regular turn of affairs, relaxed somewhat by the events you know. I have inspected our stations and erected two new ones. I have put order everywhere, and our native chiefs have been consulted."

A DISGUSTED IMMIGRANT.

THE number of immigrants arriving in this country this year is greater than it has been for several years past, and is just now averaging a thousand a day. The majority of them—especially those that come from England and Norway and Sweden—are strong and healthy people, with a little capital, and are, therefore, the kind of immigrants likely to prosper, and help in the development of the country. The clerks at Castle Garden say that a large proportion start immediately for the West. As a rule, the best do so; the loafers and undesirables prefer to remain in New York. They say that the immigrants are generally in excellent spirits, pleased with the attention they receive, and full of hope for the future. One remarkable exception, however, is mentioned. It is that of an Englishman, with gray hair and whiskers, about fifty years old, who came by the Inman steamship *City of Montreal*. His face wore a gloomy expression when he first caught sight of America. When quarantine was reached, he sniffed the air with a look of disgust, and when the *Montreal* reached her dock, the old man announced that he thought America was a disgusting country. "What's wrong about it?" he was asked. "Oh, the air don't agree with me. It's not what I looked for. I'm going straight back to the old country." The old man was duly inspected by representatives of the Commissioners of Emigration, and was obliged to go to Castle Garden. But he stubbornly refused to penetrate the country any further. He went to the clerk and stated that he was anxious to return home by the *City of Montreal*, and gave him money for a return passage ticket. The old man decided to live in the Garden during his stay in America, and during the time he waited for the steamer to return, he would not venture outside the Castle walls. It is strange that, having taken so long a voyage, the man should have returned without further investigation. Some men, however, habitually act on first impulses. It is so with some who are brought to revival meetings and evangelical services. The air of heaven does not agree with them if they are still in love with sin. But to those who are ready to sever their connection with the world, and are prepared by the Holy Spirit for the heavenly life, the idea of return is never entertained. (Heb. 11:15, 16.)

JEWISH INQUIRERS IN PALESTINE.

A MISSIONARY laboring in the Holy Land, chiefly among Jewish residents and visitors, states that recently he met a Jew from Hamadan, whom he noticed listening intently while he spoke of man's sinfulness, and man's great need of atonement. Tracing the sacrificial system under the old covenant, and showing that the appointed way of approaching God has always been by a sacrifice, since without the shedding of blood there could be no remission, he showed that since the destruction of the second Temple up to the present time Judaism lacked this principal thing, while Christianity had in Jesus of Nazareth a Temple, a Priest, and a Victim. Seeing him attentively listening, the Jew was asked whether he had ever read the book called the "Old Paths." "No, but I should like to do so;" and so he was given a Hebrew copy. After a few days he returned to the Dispensary with a friend, also a Jew of Hamadan, expressing his gratitude for the very interesting book, which he had read. He asked to take it to Hamadan. His friend having also read it with much interest, eagerly begged for a copy. He returned another day to receive it, and at the same time took tracts and portions of Scriptures, which were thankfully received, with the promise they should be read.

A Christian lady who has devoted her life to this work, is receiving much encouragement. She visits the Christian Hospital on Sunday and Thursday in each week, the Enquirers' Home Tuesdays and Fridays, and reads in the workroom each day but Wednesday, and holds a Mothers' Meeting. Friday is set apart for visiting converts, and Saturdays exclusively to going among the Jews in their houses. Being the Jewish Sabbath, both men and women are found at home, and a greater welcome given than on other days. Her Jewish acquaintance has now become so large that it is impossible to keep pace with the visiting. The Mothers' Meeting now numbers forty-five Jewesses, and has been divided, one half being taken in each alternate week, from the difficulty in finding work for them. The meetings last two hours, the second hour being devoted to reading the Old and New Testament, explanation and prayer. All the women display eager interest.

CURRENT EVENTS.

An Experimental Trial of the Fisheries treaty is suggested. At a caucus of Democratic Senators, to consider the subject of the treaty, the impossibility of its ratification at the present time was admitted, the Republican majority in the Senate being opposed to it. It was therefore decided to ask the Republicans to let the treaty lie over until next winter. The request will be made on the ground that the American fishermen directly interested in the subject can give the provisions of the treaty a practical trial during the coming fishing season, under the terms arranged for the prevention of disputes pending the ratification of the treaty. It was pointed out in the caucus that by the provisions of this protocol, American fishermen can obtain substantially all the benefits of the treaty for the coming two years by the payment of a small license fee, and it was argued that such a test would be the best possible method for the fisher men to follow in deciding whether or not the treaty would be helpful or harmful to their interests.

International Copyright Occupied the Attention of both Senators and Representatives last week. In the Senate, the measure for securing it having been favorably reported, there was a vigorous debate on its merits. Senator Morrill, of Vermont, offered an amendment to insert a provision that publishers of American newspapers or other periodicals should be allowed to copy articles from any foreign paper or periodical, and for that purpose to import such publications. Mr. Vance, of North Carolina, promptly proposed to put in a clause withholding the right to copyright from foreign newspapers, magazines, and periodicals. No action was taken on these amendments. Two days previous to the Senate proceedings on the copyright bill, an identical measure was reported favorably in the House by the Judiciary committee, which, in its report, said that the passage of the bill will be "just to our authors, publishers, and artists—beneficial to our literature, and honorable to our civilization."

The Christian Principles of Civil Government were the subject of an interesting discussion at a conference of the National Reform Association held in Washington last week. Resolutions were adopted, declaring the strength and glory of the American system of education lay in the freedom with which it is thrown open to all children, and that to remove the Bible from the schools would be subversive of the ends for which they have been established and maintained.

The Outrage on the Frontier between Texas and Mexico mentioned in these columns on March 15, has been investigated by the Mexican Government and two of its officers concerned in it have been sentenced to ten years' imprisonment. One of these officers, under orders from his superior, had crossed the Rio Grande with three men in pursuit of a deserter. The Mexicans became involved in a dispute with American officials, and in the conflict that ensued one of the Mexicans was killed and an American deputy sheriff severely wounded. The Mexican court-martial acquitted the private soldiers, as they were only obeying orders, but made the officers suffer for having failed to preserve the inviolability of the frontier. In a similar case some time previous to this occurrence, the Mexican offenders were sentenced to death.

The Indians are to be Benefited by a Measure proposed to Congress by the Indian Rights Association, and their rights under the laws of the several States and Territories are to be secured by it. The bill defines the legal standing of the reservation and other Indians, and creates special courts for the trial of cases in which Indians are concerned. An officer, to be known as the Next Friend, is to be appointed by the court of each district: he is charged with the duty of instituting suits on behalf of the Indians, or to defend them in prosecutions begun against them. The broad principle is laid down in the proposed new law that the Indians are entitled to the full protection secured by the Constitution to persons other than citizens. The bill also provides for the appointment of a committee to recommend to Congress a general plan for a common-school system on the Indian reservations. It is thought that the passage of this bill will bring the Indian problem much nearer a satisfactory solution.

The Two Hundred and Fiftieth Anniversary of the founding of an American city is an event of rare occurrence. Such an anniversary was, however, celebrated in New Haven, Conn., on April 25. On that day it was 250 years since John Davenport and a small band of faithful followers landed at what is now the corner of College and George streets, and there, under a wide-spreading elm-tree, they founded New Haven, known throughout the country as the "City of Elms." In honor of the anniversary, New Haven was bright with decorations, and had a great parade in the morning, and commemorative services at Centre Church in the afternoon. The committee in charge of the celebration placed a tablet on the building which now stands on the spot where John Davenport and his followers landed, bearing the following inscription: "The founders of this town landing near this spot, assembled for the worship of God on the first Sunday, April 25, 1638."

Horrible Atrocities Have Been Committed in Brazil, according to a report published in the London *Times*. A Rio de Janeiro correspondent of that usually reliable journal, under date of March 21, writes that a wealthy Brazilian poisoned 3,000 Indians in one of the western provinces of Brazil, and 800 in another, because they occupied land which could be much better employed by the whites. It is said that the massacre was accomplished by poisoning all the wells with strychnine and chlorate of mercury. The story rests on the authority of an important Rio journal.

A Papal Condemnation of Irish Methods has been promulgated. The Roman correspondent of the London *Chronicle* states that the Pope has signed a document in reference to the Nationalists' plan of campaign and boycotting in Ireland, both of which the head of the Roman Church condemns as illegal. He says he is convinced that the land courts will reduce all unfair rents, and condemns boycotting as a practice contrary to justice and charity. The Irish members of Parliament are somewhat agitated over the Pope's decree, and are eagerly conferring as to what steps are necessary, in view of its appearance. The Dublin *Freeman's Journal* urges the people to exercise calmness and patience, and to receive the Papal decree with profound respect and loyalty to Rome. It declares that boycotting is rare.

A Sensation in the British House of Commons was produced on April 25, during a debate on Irish affairs, by an attack of Lord Randolph Churchill on the Government. He charged his former colleagues with being unfaithful to pledges distinctly made to the Irish, and was the more indignant because, as he alleged, he had been made the mouthpiece of the Cabinet in giving those pledges when in office. He said that the Government in 1886 pledged themselves to extend to Ireland the same amount of local liberty as was enjoyed by other parts of the British Isles. If the Government relied merely upon their executive powers and if they were going to preach that the Irish must be looked upon as inferior, they might for a time hold that position, but only for a very short time. There was not sufficient interpretation of the Government policy. If Ireland had to wait in the hands of the executive, the Conservatives must take care that they did not expose themselves to a well-directed indictment of reaction. When the division was taken, Lord Randolph Churchill and several Conservatives and Unionists left the House in order to avoid voting. The bill, however, was lost by a vote of 282 to 195. It proposed to extend to Ireland the same system of local government which the Government proposes to give to England. Mr. Balfour, the Irish Secretary, said he would gladly vote for such a bill when the present social conflict ceased, but the time had not come.

Queen Victoria has Left the Villa Palmieri, near the Italian city of Florence, a picture of which appeared in our previous issue, and returned to England, after remaining three days at Berlin. On her way to the German capital she was met at the Tyrolese city of Innsbruck by Emperor Francis Joseph of Austria. The meeting between the two sovereigns was very cordial. At Munich she was greeted at the railway station by Prince Regent Luitpold, Queen Marie, and other members of the royal family of Bavaria. The reception at Berlin was cordial, without being specially enthusiastic, the population of the capital city of Prussia being known to harbor a feeling akin to antipathy to the august mother of their present Empress. Queen Victoria spent some time in prayer at the tomb of Emperor William, and placed a wreath on his coffin. The meeting with Emperor Frederick, her sorely afflicted son-in-law, is described as having been very affectionate. A pleasant feature of her visit was her friendly conversation with Prince Bismarck, who shook hands heartily with her. The Queen, accompanied by her daughter, the Empress, reviewed the flower of the German army, the White Life Guard Cuirassiers, on an immense plateau about a mile from the imperial palace. The Queen has been made chief of this renowned regiment, which is considered one of the highest honors in the gift of the German Emperor.

The Welcome Intelligence of an Improvement in the condition of Emperor Frederick of Germany was received last week. His marvellous constitution has again rallied from what appeared to be a fatal crisis in his disease. His temperature is again almost normal, and his sense of taste, which he lost during the critical period, has returned. This is regarded as an exceptionally favorable sign, and the physicians are of the opinion that the dangerous crisis has passed. He has again begun to hear State reports. One of his recent official acts was the appointment of Count Herbert Bismarck, the oldest son of the Chancellor, to the position of a Prussian Minister of State, and to place him at the head of the Prussian—not German—Ministry of Foreign Affairs.

General Boulanger Received a Marvellous ovation on April 19, in going through the streets of Paris to take his seat in the Legislature, to which the Department of the North has elected him by a majority of nearly 100,000 votes. The press correspondents cable that no such demonstration has been witnessed in the French capital since the fall of the empire. The mob in their enthusiasm made an effort to unharness the horses and drag the carriage in which Boulanger was seated; he dissuaded, however, his admirers from doing this. In the Chamber of Deputies Boulanger took his seat at the extreme left. The excitement in France over the spread of the Boulanger movement is intense.

Sunday-school Superintendents and Teachers desirous of distributing copies of THE CHRISTIAN HERALD in their schools and classes, may have assorted parcels of back numbers by applying, stating number required, to the manager, 63 Bible House.

Pastor C. H. Spurgeon's Return to the Baptist Union was announced in a brief telegram to the New York *Tribune* from its London correspondent. Mr. Smalley says that on April 23, the Union met in Dr. Parker's Tabernacle and passed a report which satisfied Mr. Spurgeon, as certain clauses were omitted from it. Mr. Spurgeon's brother, who was understood to act for him, seconded the adoption of the report and intimated that his brother would resume his membership. The announcement is vague, but is probably substantially correct, and the mail will doubtless bring more complete details.

A Secession From the Church of Rome, as important in its bearing and its influence as was years ago the bold stand taken by Père Hyacinthe, the renowned French ecclesiastic, has just occurred. This time, too, the seceder is a French priest—the Right Rev. Leon Bouland. He has renounced his allegiance to the Roman hierarchy, and applied for admission to the Protestant Episcopal Church. Mgr. Bouland, who is now forty years of age, studied for the priesthood under the personal direction of Cardinal Lanigérie, Archbishop of Algiers and Primate of Africa. In 1881 he received the honorary appointment of Canon of St. Michael the Archangel, Rome, and in 1882 that of President-General of the Society of the Avocats de St. Pierre, in North America. In the same year he was made a member of the "Académie des Arcade," in Rome; Canon of the Metropolitan Church of Rheims; Commander of the Order of the Holy Sepulchere; and Private Chamberlain to Pope Leo XIII. In June, 1886, Mgr. Bouland was also appointed by the Pope, General Director of the organization in North America of the Society of Peter's Pence. It is stated that he will be received into the Protestant Episcopal Church by Bishop Potter, in New York, in a few days.

A Temporary Advance in the Line of Court Precedence, which was contemplated by the Queen of England, is said to have caused some perturbation in royal circles. An English journal states that her Majesty was extremely desirous of having her favorite son-in-law, Prince Henry, of Battenberg, attend the funeral of the late Emperor of Germany. He has, however, no rank in Germany at all equivalent to that he has in his adopted country. He would, therefore, have been placed in a very humble position in the procession, and have been required to give place to the crowd of royalties, serenities, highnesses, and other dignitaries who would have been entitled in Berlin to a better place than he. The Queen, however, decided to save him this humiliation by making him her special representative at the obsequies, which would thus have invested him with a dignity that would have secured him one of the first places. She was eventually induced to abandon her project by the information that such an act would be very distasteful to the German court and nation, but had she persisted, the temporary and reflected dignity of the Prince would have been recognized. It is thus that the humble follower of Christ will be glorified in the universe, not for himself but for Christ's sake. (John 17: 21, 22.)

A Desperate Fight in a Burning Building took place in St. Louis on April 19. There were about seventy lodgers sleeping on the fourth and fifth floors of a "home" in that city, when the night watchman discovered a fire under the stairway of the second floor. He at once sent a call over the wires for engines, and then ran through the building awaking the sleepers. They found, however, that their escape by the stairs was cut off, and they rushed to the windows. Soon the cry was raised that a rope had been found, and there was a general rush to the window from which it hung. One after another descended safely, but time pressed, for the crowd in the street below could see the figures of the men around the window grow more distinct every minute as the fire reached the room where they were, and formed an awful background to the group. To add to the horror of the spectacle, the men were seen to be fighting for their turn with the rope, and the struggle grew fiercer as the flames rose. The last man to come down on the rope had his clothes on fire. He was the watchman who first discovered the fire, and he bore in his arms a cripple, who was unable to descend alone. Several men were burned in the building, having fallen in the struggle to get to the rope. There being but one way of escape, it was not surprising that every man tried to avail himself of it with that horrible death by burning as the alternative. There was no apathy or procrastination there, as there is with sinners who are in far worse danger, and who know that for them also there is but one way of escape. (Hos. 13: 4.)

An Electrical Homicide Occurred in New York on April 26. A young man who was employed in a clothing store in the Bowery, having closed the store for the night, stood talking to a friend under the electric light suspended in front of the door. As he started home he casually reached up, according to a habit he is said to have had of touching the lamp when he passed near it. His hand must have rested upon the lightly insulated wire connected with the upper carbon, or the carbon itself, which projects slightly above the top rim of the globe. He will never tell exactly what he did touch, as he was killed instantly. He fell with a gasp into the arms of a passer-by, and with a shudder which convulsed his body from head to foot breathed his last. It appears that he generally jumped when he touched the lamp, but on Thursday it is supposed that he must have reached it by placing his foot on the iron casing in front of the store, thus completing the electric circuit with the earth and making a conductor of his body. Whether he had ever been warned of the danger of his habit, is not stated, but it is possible that if he had been he would not have heeded it, as he had touched the lamp so many times with impunity. That is how men act in regard to sin, seeing that "sentence upon an evil work is not" always" executed speedily." (Eccles. 8: 11.)

A Lady's Struggle with a Mad Dog is De-scribed in a press despatch from Nashville, Tenn. It states that on April 23, the children in a school at Cyprus Creek were busy at their lessons when a shaggy dog, his eyes flaming, and foaming at the mouth, snapping and biting, dashed in at the door and made toward the pupils. Miss Mollie Green, a young lady of eighteen years, who teaches the school, thought only of the children in her care, and sprang between them and the intruder. She kicked at it, her skirts protecting her, and by the aid of a heavy ruler, kept the dog at bay until all the children had fled. The infuriated animal repeatedly sprang at her throat, but she was agile and warded him off. When all the little ones were gone, she desperately fought off the dog until she reached the door, which she pulled to after her, and fell fainting outside. The children in the mean time ran to the nearest house, an eighth of a mile distant, and gave the alarm. Two men soon came and killed the dog. Miss Green's clothes were torn to ribbons during the encounter. What pain and misery might have been caused in the homes of the village had the young teacher been less self-forgetful and brave, it is dreadful to imagine. Her heroism elicits the most enthusiastic admiration even from those who listen unmoved, when they are told of One, who, to save them from becoming the prey of the great enemy of man, interposed on their behalf, and died to save them. (Heb. 2:10-15).

Four Days Trying to Get Married Have wearied a young couple in West Virginia. They started out on April 23, from their respective homes in Williamstown to find a clergyman to unite them in wedlock. They made several applications, but not being able to offer evidence of their parents' consent, they were refused in each case. The next day they crossed the Ohio, and took the cars for Wheeling, where they applied in regular course for a marriage license. The civil official looked them over, and guessing their ages, declined to issue a license. Nothing daunted, they sought the necessary aids to matrimony in Pennsylvania, but were twice refused—once by the clerk of the court, and once by the justice, who, having given them some fatherly advice about premature matrimonial ventures, bid them return to their parental roof. One more effort was made in Ohio, but it was also futile. Weary and disconsolate the boy took his companion to the home of a relative. He then telegraphed his father for permission to marry, but did not receive it. On the other hand, a brother of the lady started after them, intending to fetch his sister home. He succeeded in inducing them both to return. Their disappointment is just now doubtless hard to bear, but they may derive consolation from the fact that the experience of others has proved that very early unions scarcely ever produce anything but trouble and regret. It is the reverse of this, however, in the case of union with with Christ, of which marriage is a type. That cannot be premature, and those have most happiness who enter into that union early in life. (Prov. 3: 1-4.)

BRIEF NOTES.

Rev. H. Varley has arrived at Melbourne, where he will remain some weeks with his sons.

Mr. Richard Weaver, the famous English evangelist, has been sick, but is now restored, and engaged in work.

The Rev. T. Spurgeon, son of the Rev. C. H. Spurgeon, and President elect of the New Zealand Baptist Union, has just been married to Miss Rutherford, of Auckland.

The Episcopalians of Los Angeles, Cal., have opened a church-room in that city, where visitors may find religious papers, directories, and a list of desirable boarding and lodging houses.

The receipts of the Presbyterian Board of Foreign Missions up to March 23, amounted to $589,970, leaving a large sum to be raised before the close of the financial year.

Stephen Green, a rich Philadelphia printer, has cancelled the debt against the Methodist Episcopal Church of Wenonah, N. J., and also presented it with a new parsonage, valued at $9,000.

During last year Dr. Dowkontt was enabled to carry on seven missionary dispensaries in New York City, in which forty-seven students were trained for medical missionaries in heathen lands. A house for lady students has now been opened.

It is proposed to raise $100,000 for an American church building in Berlin. A number of $1,000 subscriptions have already been secured, and pews are to be offered to American colleges and other institutions at $1,000 each for the free use of their graduates.

The Secretary of Foreign Missions Committee of the Southern Church stated, in an address before Maryland Presbytery, April 19, that nine missionaries have been sent out during the past ecclesiastical year; that foreign mission work is free from the burden of debt; and that there is a balance of $7,000 in the treasury.

Rev. E. E. Davidson, the evangelist, closed his labors in Rockville, Ill., on April 19. More than twelve hundred people were present at the concluding service. A list of over four hundred names of seekers after Christ is now in the hands of the pastors of the four churches specially interested.

A General Christian Conference, similar to the Congress of Churches held in Washington last year, is to be held in Montreal in October next. The list of subjects to be considered includes the following: "Current Unbelief," "Capital and Labor," "National Perils," "Co-operation in Christian Work," etc.

The negotiations for the union of Congregationalists, Congregational Methodists, and Free Methodist Protestant churches in Georgia have been successfully concluded. The result is called the United Congregational Conference of Georgia. The Conference embraces about fifty churches, with a membership of 3,500.

A pilgrimage to Rome by 135 Mexican Roman Catholics has been commenced. The pilgrims sailed from New York on the *Bolivia*, taking with them presents for the Pope valued at more than $200,000. One article, a cross of gold set with diamonds and opals, is valued at $60,000.

Rev. George C. Needham, the evangelist, has been holding a series of meetings in the Clarendon Street Baptist Church, Boston, Mass., of which the Rev. A. J. Gordon, D. D., is pastor. The meetings are held under the joint auspices of the Committee of the church and the Evangelistic Association. Mr. Needham has also given Bible readings every noon, for ministers and Sunday-school teachers, in the Park Street Congregational Church, which were well attended.

DAVID'S SPOIL.

A New Sermon by Pastor C. H. Spurgeon.

"This is David's spoil." 1 Sam. 30: 20.

David's Disaster Retrieved—The Additional Spoil—His Portion—A Type of Christ—I. Jesus a Channel of All Good—Recovers the Spoils from Satan—Victory for His Sake—Through His Leadership—II. The Recovery Greater than the Loss—The Surplusage—Sonship and Heirship Redemption—Resurrection—Refined Materialism—I.I. The Spoil of Consecrated Offerings—The Heart—The Special Talent—Property—A Millionaire's Contribution.

WE have aforetime gathered spoil for ourselves out of David's behavior in the hour of his sorrow at Ziklag, and we will now turn to the other side of this leaf in his history, and receive instruction from the time of his victory. But we must not do this till we have refreshed our memories with the story of his conduct under distress. When he came to the city he found it burned with fire, the property of himself and his comrades carried away, and, what was worse, all their wives, and their sons, and their daughters gone into captivity. In the madness of their grief the people turned upon their leader, as if he had led them into this calamity. He was the only calm person among them, for he "encouraged himself in the Lord his God." With due deliberation he waited upon the Lord, and consulted the oracle through the appointed priest, and then, under divine guidance, he pursued the banditti, took them at unawares, recovered all his people's goods, and captured

A Large Booty

which the Amalekites had collected elsewhere. David's men, in the moment of their despair, had spoken of stoning him; but now, in the morning of their victory, with general acclamations they determine that David shall have, as his portion of the spoil, all the cattle which belong to the Amalekites themselves; and so, driving these in front, as they return to Ziklag, they say, "This is David's spoil." I think I hear them, as they drive the bullocks and the sheep before them, shouting right lustily, "This is David's spoil!"

Now, using David as the type of Christ, I want, if I can, to set all David's men—all Christ's men—shouting with all their hearts, "This is Jesus' spoil!" He it is of whom Jehovah saith, "I will divide Him a portion with the great, and He shall divide the spoil with the strong." He has a grand reward as the result of the great battle of His life and death. We will even now award to him the spoil, and cry, "This is David's spoil"; feeling, all the while, as the Psalmist did, when he said, "Thou art more glorious and excellent than mountains of prey."

I. We begin with the first observation that, practically, all the spoil of that day was David's spoil, and in truth, all the good that we enjoy comes to us through our Lord Jesus. He has been given as a Leader and a Commander to the people, and every victory they win is

Due to Him,

and to Him alone. Without Him we can *do* nothing, and without Him we can *obtain* nothing. All that we once possessed by nature, and under the law, the spoiler has taken away. By our own efforts we can never regain what we have lost; only through our great Leader can we be restored and made happy. We ascribe unto Jesus all our gains, even as David's men honored their captain.

For, first, David's men defeated the Amalekites, and took their spoil, but it was for David's sake that God gave success to the band. God's eye rested upon his chosen servant, the Lord's anointed, and it was not for the warriors' own sakes, but for David's sake, that God guided them to the hosts of Amalek, and gave them like driven stubble to their sword. How much more true it is to us that every blessing, every pardoning mercy, every delivering mercy, is given to us through Him who is our shield and God's anointed! It is for the sake of Jesus that we are pardoned, justified, accepted, preserved, sanctified. Only through this channel does the mercy of God come to us. On this blessing, and on that favor, yea, on them all, we see the mark of the cross. These are all fruits of our Redeemer's passion, the purchase of His blood. again we say, "This is David's spoil."

Moreover, David's men gained the victory over Amalek because of David's leadership. If he had not been there to lead them to the fight, in the moment of their despair they would have lost all heart, and would have remained amidst the burning walls of Ziklag, a discomfited company. But David encouraged himself in the Lord, and so encouraged all his desponding followers. Drawing his sword, and marching in front, he put spirit into them: they all followed with eager step because their gallant leader so courageously led the way. This is exactly our case, beloved, only we are even more indebted to our Lord Jesus than these men were to David.

Following at his feet we, too, fight with sin. Treading in His footsteps we, too, overcome the world, the flesh, and the devil. Have you never heard Him say, "Be of good cheer, I have overcome the world"? And you, dear brothers and sisters, whatever victories you win, whatever spoils you divide, will own that it is through Jesus that you have conquered. They said of Waterloo that it was a soldiers' battle, and the victory was due to the men; but ours is

Our Commander's Battle,

and every victory won by us is due to the great Captain of our salvation. Let the crown be set upon His head, even on the battle-field, and let us say of every sin that we have overcome, every evil habit that we have destroyed, "This is David's spoil." We had never won this victory if Jesus had not led us: we have it for His sake. We have it under His leadership. Without exception, all the saints on earth and in heaven confess this to be true.

Yes, and our Lord Jesus has recovered for us the future as well as the past. Our outlook was grim and dark indeed till Jesus came; but oh, how bright it is now that He has completed His glorious work! Death is no more the dreaded grave of all our hopes. Hell exists no longer for believers. Heaven, whose gates were closed, is now set wide open to every soul that believeth. We have recovered life and immortal bliss. We are snatched like brands from the burning, and made to shine like lamps of the palace of the great King. We are set up to be for ever trophies of the conquering power of Jesus, our glorious David. Look at all the saints in heaven in their serried ranks, and say of them all, "This is David's spoil."

II. But the most interesting part of our subject is this: all the booty was practically David's spoil, but there was a part of it which was not recovered, but was

A Clear Gain.

They recovered all they had lost, and over and above there was a surplus of spoil from the defeated foe. Now, in the great battle of Christ on our behalf, He has not only given us back what we lost, but He has given us what Adam in his perfection never had. And I want you to dwell upon that, because this part of it is peculiarly our Lord's spoil. Those good things which we now possess, over and above what we lost by sin, come to us by the Lord Jesus. Now that the Son of God has come into the field, He is not content with restoration, He turns the loss into a gain, the fall into a greater rising.

And first, dear friends, think: In Christ Jesus human nature is lifted up where it never could have been before. Man was made in his innocence to occupy a very lofty place. "Thou madest him to have dominion over all the works of thy hands; thou hast put all things under his feet." Man would have enjoyed that dominion had he never fallen, but he never could have obtained what he has now gained, for "we see Jesus, who was made a little lower than the angels for the suffering of death, crowned with glory and honor." And we see in Jesus human nature joined in mysterious union with the Godhead. It is a wondrous honor this—that manhood should be taken into intimate connection, yea, absolute union with God! For listen: through Jesus Christ we are this day made the sons of God, which angels never were. The most glorious being next to God is man. A sinner most shameful once, but now in Christ a child accepted and honored! What can I say of this but "This is David's spoil"? This is what Jesus brought us. It came to us by no other way or method. Neither do we know in what way or method it could have been given to us, but by the will of God

Through our Lord

Jesus Christ. It is given to us through Jesus Christ, our elder Brother and our covenant Head, and unto Him let the glory of it be ascribed world without end.

Another blessing which was not ours before the fall, and therefore never was lost, but comes to us as a surplusage, is the fact that we are redeemed. You sang just now that verse,

"Never did angels taste above
Redeeming grace and dying love."

It is clear that you could never have known free grace and dying love if Jesus had not come to redeem you. Unfallen intelligent spirits will say in eternity: "Do you see those beings bowing nearest to the eternal throne? Do you see those well-beloved creatures? Who are they?" Spirits that have lived in other worlds will come crowding up to the great metropolis, and will say one to another, "Who are those courtiers—those that dwell nearest to God? Who are they?" And one spirit will say to another: "They are beings whom God not only made as He made us, but whom the eternal Son of God redeemed by blood." And one shining one will say to his fellow: "What is that? Tell me

That Strange Story."

Then will his companions delight to say, "They were saved because the Son of God took their nature, and in that nature died." "Wonderful! Wonderful!" his friend will answer; "How could it be? Was there suffering for them, and pain for them, and bloody sweat for them, and death for them on the part of the ever-blessed Son of God?" The answer, "It was even so," will be news full of astonishment even to the best instructed celestial mind.

We shall be creatures who have known sin, and have been recovered from its pollution. There will be no fear of our being exalted with pride, or drawn away by ambition as the now-apostate angels were; for we shall constantly remember what sin did for us, and how grievous was our fault. We shall for ever remember the price at which we were redeemed; and we shall have ties upon us that will bind us to an undeviating loyalty to Him who exalted us to so glorious a condition. It seems to me wonderful beyond expression: the more I consider, the more I am astonished.

Again, to my mind it is a very blessed fact that you and I will partake of a privilege which would have been certainly

Unnecessary to Adam,

and could not by Adam have been known, and that is, the privilege of resurrection. We shall die unless the Lord should suddenly appear. I would not have you, brothers and sisters, look upon the prospect of death with any sort of dread. I know that death is associated with pain, but nothing can be more absurd. There is no pain in death: pain belongs to life; death, even naturally, puts an end to pain. But death to the believer is undressing as his Lord undressed—putting off garments of which, I trow, we need not be so very fond, for they do fit us ill; and oftentimes, when our spirit is willing, it is hampered by these garments of clay, for the flesh is weak. "Where should the dying members rest but with their dying Head?" "That grave of our blessed Lord, if he had not meant us to enter it, would have been left an empty tenement when He came away; but when He came out of it, He left it furnished for those that should come after Him. See there the grave-clothes folded up for us to use! The bed is prepared for our slumber.

The napkin is laid by itself, because it is not

for the sleeper, but for those who have lost his company. Those who remain behind may dry their eyes with the napkin, but the grave-clothes are reserved for others who will occupy

The Royal Bed-Chamber.

When great men removed in the olden time, their servants took away the arras, or hangings of their chambers; but if those hangings remained, it was for the convenience of guests who were invited to occupy my lord's rooms. See, then, our Lord expects us to lie in his royal bed-chamber, for He has left the hangings behind Him! To the retiring-room of the tomb we shall go in due time. And why should we be grieved to go? For we shall come forth again: we shall rise from the dead. "Thy brother shall rise again," was Mary's consolation from the Master's lips. It is yours.

Children of the resurrection, dread not death! Your faces are turned to the sun. Press forward to the light eternal, and fear not to pass through the death shadow; it is no more than a shadow. If you cannot leap over the grave, you can pass through it. It shall be your joy to rise when the morning breaketh, and to be satisfied; for you shall wake up in His likeness. As for the resurrection, "This is David's spoil," this is Christ's gift and boon. The resurrection from the dead is the peculiar glory of Christianity. The immortality of the soul had been taught and known before, for it is a truth which even reason itself teaches; but the resurrection of the body comes in as the last and crowning comfort: and "this is David's spoil."

Let me not weary you. The topic might well interest us on several occasions; it is too large to be confined to one discourse. Our singular relation to God, and yet to materialism, is

Another Rare Gift

of Jesus. God intended, by the salvation of man, and the lifting up of man into union with Himself, to link together in one the lowest and the highest—his creation and Himself. Shall I make it very plain? These poor substances—earth, water, and the like—they seem far down in the scale. God makes a being that shall be, as an old Puritan used to say, half soul and half soil; even man, who is both spirit and dust of the earth. We find in him water, salts, acids, all sorts of substances combined, to make up a body, and married to this is a soul, which is brother to the angels, and akin to Deity. Materialism is somewhat exalted in being connected with spirit at all. When spirit becomes connected with God, and refined materialism becomes connected with a purified spirit, by the resurrection from the dead, then shall be brought to pass the uplifting of clay, and its junction with the celestial.

Our manifestation of the full glory of God is another of the choice gifts which the pierced hands of Jesus alone bestow. Principalities and powers shall see in the mystical body of Christ more of God than in all the universe besides. They will study in the saints the eternal purposes of God, and see therein His love, His wisdom, His power, His justice, His mercy, blended in an amazing way. They will admire for ever those whom God loves and delights in, those whom He keeps as the apple of His eye, those whom He rejoices over, and of whom He hath said that He will rest in His love, and He will rejoice over them with singing. Truly it hath not entered into the heart of man to guess at the glory of God in the saints, the exceeding glory which shall be revealed in us through Jesus Christ our Lord. "This is David's spoil." Oh, come, let us sing unto the Lord, let us magnify the name of Jesus Christ!

III. I close with the practical part of my sermon:

That Which We Willingly Give

to Jesus may be called his spoil. There is a spoil for Christ which every true-hearted follower of His votes to Him enthusiastically. We have already seen that all things which we have are of Christ, and that there are certain special gifts which are peculiarly of Christ; and now, what shall be David's spoil from you and me? First, our hearts are His alone for ever. Of every believing heart it may be said, "This is David's spoil." You and I must give ourselves to-morrow to earning our daily bread, and our thoughts must go, to a large extent, after earthly things in the common pursuits of every-day life. But our hearts, our hearts, are as fountains sealed for our Well-beloved. O mammon, thou shalt not have them! O pleasure, thou shalt not have them! These are David's spoil. Let it be so that our whole heart is the sole possession of Jesus! We will neither rend it nor cast lots whose it shall be, for "this is David's spoil."

Now there is another property I should like King Jesus to have, and that is, our special gifts. I know one who, before his conversion, was wont to sing, and he often charmed the ears of men with the sweet music which he poured forth; but when he was converted, he said, "Henceforth my tongue shall sing nothing but the praises of God." He devoted himself to proclaiming the gospel by his song, for he said, "This is David's spoil." Have you not some gift or other, dear friend, of which you could say, "Henceforth this shall be sacred to my bleeding Lord"? Some peculiar faculty? Some choice piece of acquirement not generally possessed? Something in which you excel? I would that you had at least some little garden of flowers or herbs which you could so reserve that only Jesus should pluck the fruits. Say of the best gift you possess, "This is David's spoil."

Lastly, have you not something of your own proper substance that shall be David's spoil just now? That was a blessed act when the woman broke the most precious thing she had—her box of alabaster, and let the perfumed nard stream down the Saviour, anointing Him for His burial. She felt that the precious perfume was David's spoil.

There Was No Waste:

in fact, no other gift ever went so completely to its purpose *without being taxed on the road*, for Jesus had it all. Kindly did He observe the loving honor which she paid Him. What if the ointment were sold, and given to the poor? Yet it could never be so economically used as when it was all devoted to Him. I do think it so pleasant sometimes to give Jesus Christ distinctly a gift from yourself of somewhat that you will miss. It is good to give to the poor, but it has a daintier sweetness in it to do somewhat distinctly for Him, for the spread of His own glory, and the making known of His own fame. "The poor ye have always with you": abound towards them in your charity whenever you will; but to your Lord at special seasons dedicate a gift, and say, "This is David's spoil."

There was a poor woman once, whose little fortune could be carried between her finger and her thumb—her fortune I said, for it was all that she had. Two mites, I am told, was all it came to. She took it, it was her all, and she put it in the treasury; for this was "David's spoil." It belonged to the Lord her God, and she gave it cheerfully. I do not know whether since the days of the apostles anybody has ever given so much as that woman. I have not. Have you? She gave all her living. Not all her savings, but all her living. She had nothing left when she gave her farthing; she loved so much that she consecrated all her living. There was a man who, in the providence of God, had been enabled to lay by many thousands. He was a very rich and respected man. I have heard it said that he owned at least half a million; and at one collection, when he felt specially grateful and generous, he found a well-worn sixpence for the plate, for that was David's spoil! That was David's spoil! Out of all that she possessed, that sixpence was David's spoil! This was the measure of his gratitude! Judge by this how much he owed, or at least how much he desired to pay. Are there not many persons who, on that despicable scale, reward the Saviour for the travail of his soul? I shall not upbraid them. I shall not urge them to do more, lest I spoil the voluntariness of the large gifts they mean to bring.

For us, who are deep in the Redeemer's debt, who have had much forgiven, who every day are bankrupt debtors to the measureless mercy of infinite love—for us, no paltriness will suffice. We must give something which, if it be not worthy of Him, shall, at least, express the truth and warmth of the gratitude we feel. God help us to be often setting aside this and that, and the other choice thing, and saying, "This is David's spoil, and it shall be a joy to my heart to give it!"

God bless you, dear friends. May we come to the table of communion, and meet with our glorious David there, and feel his praises making music in our hearts! Amen.

[The prayers of the readers of this journal are requested for the blessing of God upon its Editors, and those whose sermons, articles or labors for Christ are printed in it; and that its circulation may be used by the Holy Spirit for the conversion of many sinners and the quickening of God's people. Dr. Talmage and Mr. Spurgeon especially request prayer every Sunday morning on behalf of their labors.]

GEMS FROM NEW BOOKS.

A KING'S AWAKENED CONSCIENCE.*

On a March evening, in the year 1705, King Frederick IV. of Denmark sat in deep thought in his palace. As he looked over the papers on the table, his eye rested on the petition of a poor widow. Her husband and eldest son had been murdered in a native outbreak at Tranquebar, and she sought redress and help. The circumstance was slight, and might have made little impression on a mind preoccupied, but that the heathen population, added by adventure or conquest to Denmark, had already weighed upon the king. They could be found at many points of his dominions—in Greenland, India, and St. Thomas—and they had filled him with misgivings that he had not acted fairly by them, that, as a Christian Prince, he ought to have sent messengers to preach the gospel to them. He was engaged in war with Sweden, and perhaps the seriousness of his position at the time made his conscience sensitive; a sudden conviction smote through his mind, and, like a famous king before him, his countenance was changed and his thoughts troubled him. For ninety years there had been a Danish East India Company under charter and protection of the crown; for ninety years Danish ships had sailed to Tranquebar, Danish merchants had traded and grown rich in it, Danish soldiers had defended it, and Danish governors had ruled it; but no ship had ever carried a Danish missionary to preach the gospel. For these ninety years the Christian conscience of the land had been asleep, and it was now high time to awake. Penitent, perplexed, and restless, he summoned Dr. Lutkens, his chaplain, who found him poring over a map of the coast of Coromandel. Could the chaplain procure him men, he would send out

Apostles to the Indies.

He had taken his decision with hasty energy, for while he was musing the fire had burned, and Lutkens, with a joy he did not hide, heaped fuel on the fire. Yet he could not answer the king's question. The Church of Denmark was no more alive to mission work than other churches of that time, and such men as were wanted were scarcely to be found. He paused for a moment, and then said: "Send me." The king was moved by the old man's self-sacrifice, but he could not part with him. He reckoned on his counsel; he must have him by his side; it was younger men he wanted, who could face the hardships and the climate with less risk. "Get us the men," he said; whereupon Lutkens went out to seek.

He found that he had undertaken a difficult task; himself a German, he naturally turned to

---

* From "The Dawn of the Modern Mission," by the late Rev. W. Fleming Stevenson, D. D., showing the characteristics of heathen religions, and what they had come to be when the gospel touched them, and how the first contact occurred. 188 pages. Published by *A. C. Armstrong & Son*, Broadway, New York.

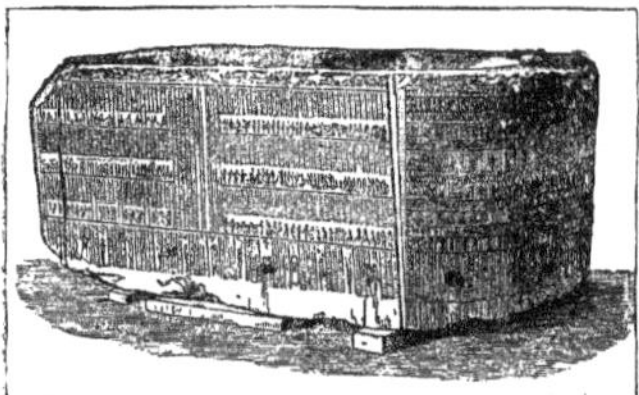

The Ancient Coffin Supposed to be that of Alexander the Great.

The Home of a Scottish Crofter.

two of his old colleagues at Berlin. His correspondents took the matter up with warmth, and, on consulting with their brother ministers, it appeared they might return a favorable answer. The man who had been unconsciously trained for this work was at the moment in their neighborhood, and was about to leave it. One more illustration of the curious exactitude with which God's plans fit into one another.

Lange was commissioned by his brother ministers to write to a young minister named

Ziegenbalg,

and propose that he should go as a missionary either to Africa or St. Thomas, telling him of the king's desire, and that their choice had fallen upon him and his old fellow-student Plutschau. Ziegenbalg's first impulse was to draw back; it was impossible he could be fitted for so peculiar a calling—then characteristically he yielded. If it was God's doing, he would not resist Him, but only prayed that he might be convinced he was right. The two young students were accepted, and a small sum was enclosed to each for travelling expenses. The hasty preparations were soon made, and they reached Copenhagen on October 16, to find that it was neither Africa nor St. Thomas they were to sail for, but Tranquebar!

A SCOTTISH CROFT.

(*See Illustration.*)

MUCH has been heard during the past few months of the Scottish Crofters, who have at length drawn public attention to their condition. As is commonly the case with poor people, their grievances, real or fancied, were ignored by legislators and the public, until crimes and outrages stirred the authorities to action, and people began to inquire how it was that such crimes were being committed. The reply was very simple: the crofters said they were slowly dying of starvation, as their farms, or crofts, did not produce sufficient to support them and their families. They wanted more land, for which they were willing to pay rent, but it was refused to them, because the wealthy lords who owned it wanted it as a preserve for deer to amuse themselves in the shooting season. The law, of course was with the lords, who stood calmly on their clear "rights of property." The question now is, whether the laws shall be changed so that the lords shall be required to sell or rent the land to the crofters.

The crofts are small holdings on the Outer Hebrides, some small islands off the western coast of Scotland. Thither a commission has been despatched to hear the complaints of the people and report to Parliament. One of the cases which the commissioners examined was that of a family living in a hut about twenty feet long, with no window, having light only from the door; and with no chimney, so that the smoke from a peat fire on the floor, thickly filling the hut, comes out either by the door, or through the thatch of the roof. It is said that the thatch, becoming charged with soot and with carbon from animal exhalations, when stripped off the roof makes valuable manure. *A wooden box in the corner is the only bedstead, which serves for the whole family of five persons.* The floor is deep in mud. At the other end is kept the live-stock, which consisted, at the time, of a cow and two ducks. The croft near Ballallan (which is the one *represented in the illustration*) is a more prosperous establishment, the owner possessing several stacks of grain, and many sheep and cows; this croft is inclosed with a "dry stane dyke." The view of Loch Erisort, looking southwest, with the snow-clad hills of Harris in the distance, is taken from the village of Ballallan. Mr. Platt is the owner of the deer forest nearest this croft. The crofters, when driven almost distracted with hunger, made a raid on this man's forest and killed some of his deer, whereupon he had them arrested, and they have been tried in Edinburgh, but acquitted by the jury.

THE COFFIN OF ALEXANDER THE GREAT.

(*See Illustration.*)

ANOTHER sarcophagus is added to the list of those which the respective discoverers contend once held the remains of the mighty conqueror, Alexander the Great. A few weeks ago the newspaper reports announced that the true and identical coffin had been found at Saida, or Sidon, in Syria. The evidence in its favor has not yet been produced, and until it is the report cannot be credited, as all the known circumstances connected with Alexander's death and burial forbid us to believe that the coffin could have ever been removed to Syria. The monarch died in Babylon November 12, 323 B. C., and his remains were carried with great pomp to Alexandria, and there interred. It is therefore much more probable that the stone coffin in the British Museum (*a picture of which is given on this page*) is the true coffin of Alexander, as it was found at Alexandria, and had all the evidence of the traditions of generations on its side.

The modern history of this ancient relic is soon told. Napoleon I. took possession of it during the French occupation of Egypt in 1799. Two years later the British acquired possession of Alexandria, and promptly shipped the sarcophagus to London and deposited it in the British Museum, where it still remains. An investigation satisfied Edward D. Clark, LL. D. of the identity of the coffin, and he wrote a book, which was published in 1805, giving his reasons for the belief. He quotes Strabo, Suetonius, and Leo Africanus, in support of his theory. He states that the Emperor Augustus, when at Alexandria, paid a special visit to the tomb of Alexander, and when the body was taken from the sarcophagus, placed a golden crown upon it. Dr. Clark tells how the alleged tomb continued to be an object of reverence to the Mohammedan conquerors, who would not even allow Christian to see it.

The sarcophagus was brought to England i the government ship *Madras*, and before th vessel sailed the Capitano Bey, with his suit and many Turks of distinction, came on boa to render a last act of devotion to this reli which they all solemnly touched with their to gues, the Capitano Bey declaring that Prov dence would never suffer the tomb to arri safely in England. Turks identify Alexand under his Egyptian deification as the son Jupiter Ammon with the two-horned "Dhu lkarnein" of the Koran. The student of pr phecy however identifies him with *the "notab horn"* between the eyes of the he-goat in Da iel's vision (Dan. 8: 5.) who attacked the ra with two horns (Media and Persia) and "ca him down and stamped upon him," as Alexand did; and when the notable horn was broken, Alexander's death, four notable ones came i its place; that is, Alexander's empire was divide among his four generals, as history records.

THE BLACKSMITH'S ARGUMENT.

(*See Illustration on page 285.*)

"YOU'RE like this iron, Bob," said Ezra Mi ler, the blacksmith, as he held the piece in que tion in his great pliers, for the inspection of sa Bob, while he put his foot on the block, accor ing to his habit when entering on an argumen

Bob looked at the heated metal earnestly, if to discover some portraiture of his simple fe tures, or some resemblance in it to his figur and then, as if giving up a conundrum, sai "Well, I ain't red-hot, anyhow!"

"No, I guess not, this morning," Ezra rejoi ed, "but it's like you for all that, and I'll te you why. Before it went in the fire, I could d nothing with it, but now I can turn it to mo any use it's big enough for. That's just lik what you've been telling me. You wouldn have cut up as you did last night, and foug with Jem, that's always been your friend, you'd been sober. You allow that?"

Bob nodded assent.

"Well, the devil uses you as I do this iron he gets you red-hot mad, and then you're fit f any job he wants done. There's this differen though: he never puts you to a good use, an the iron has the better of you there. Your us is always bad, because he never has any goo jobs on hand. Do you suppose if you hadn been heated up with rum you'd ha' done th bit o' devil's work last night? Not you! Th ain't your line. You're a kind-hearted cha and I shouldn't wonder if you ain't thinkin now of taking a dollar or two to Jem's wife t help her out while Jem's laid up. That's rig enough; you take it, and don't get heated u again. Quit, dead!"

Bob had not thought of taking that dollar o two Ezra had credited him with intending but he thought of it now, and resolved t it. Jem was a good llow, but terribly ovoking to a man liquor. Still, he d not mean to hit m so hard as to lay m up, and, as he ew well enough, he ould not have done if he had not been inking. "I guess u're right," he said last, "I will take e money to Jem's ife. She'll let me ve the rough side her tongue, I pre- me. That's no more an any woman ould do. I'll have quit the liquor, o; I always make a ol of myself."

"It's worse than hat," said Ezra; you're real wicked to the bargain. ou're a fool, first of l, for taking the liq- or, and putting your- lf into a condition which the devil can -look here," and iting the action to e word, Ezra pound- d away on the iron, hich was again hot.

"It'll be a hard job o quit," said Bob uefully, "but I'll try."

The Blacksmith's Argument.

"Oh, well, you're man enough for that, Bob, guess," said Ezra. "Ask God to help you; He will."

"I ain't one of the religious sort," said Bob, "but I'm proud enough not to be the devil's tool, and I allow I've been that."

"You'd be a deal safer, my lad, if you did not trust to yourself quite so much. I know you ain't one of the religious sort, and I'm sorry for it; you'd be improved if you were."

Bob sauntered out of the shop, ill at ease, with an aching head and an accusing conscience. Ezra was a good fellow, who had helped him out of more than one scrape, and who always gave him good advice. He did not feel like going to work, but he knew he must go. Last night's expenses, and that dollar or two for Jem's wife, would make a hole in his week's money big enough without losing time. How his head did ache! He must have just one glass before he could do any work, and after that he would quit. So Bob had his glass to brace himself, and then dragged himself off to his work.

Somehow it was harder to quit than even Bob had estimated. He certainly did try two or three nights; he went right home, and would not go out again. It was pretty dull, he thought. His wife was at her work, but Bob could not settle to anything. He tried to read, but reading was never easy to him; he tried doing a bit of carpenter work in-doors, but he yawned and stretched himself, and looked at the clock. It seemed the longest evening he had ever passed. And how thirsty he was! At last he gave it up, and late on the third evening he found himself in his old corner in the saloon. A man was there with a violin, and the remainder of the evening passed pleasantly.

Bob felt a little ashamed of himself in being beaten in his attempt to quit, and avoided the blacksmith's shop on his way to and from his work. He did not like having to tell Ezra that he had failed. Ezra would be sure to preach again. He would limit himself firmly, and would not exceed the allowance he knew he could stand. But even there he failed—he had not reckoned on treating. One night, having taken his usual modicum, an old friend dropped in, and Bob was easily persuaded to drink at his friend's expense. Then, of course, he had to treat his friend, and after that Bob was not under his own control. He was, as Ezra told him, in the heated condition when the devil could put him to any bad use. Unhappily, a bad use was soon found for him. Lurching from side to side of the sidewalk as he went home, Bob stumbled and fell against a window. I was the window of a saloon, and the bar-tender, knowing well that Bob's condition showed that he had been at a rival establishment, had no compunction in administering punishment. Bob was not the man to take it meekly. He struck out, and with fatal effect.

The next morning he was awakened in a cell, and wonderingly inquired how he came there. Murder, he was told, had led to his position. It was reduced to manslaughter at the trial, mainly by the energetic efforts of his friend Ezra, but it meant ruin to the poor, weak creature, who trusted in his own strength. During his long imprisonment, and the years it took him to work up again in a strange town, where he went to escape the name of "a jail bird," Ezra's lecture on the hot iron needed no new illustration to imprint itself on his memory.

MRS. TRANSOME'S PUPIL.

A SERIAL STORY.

(*Continued from page 270.*)

A Call to Work.

MRS. BROWN searched in her basket for the map, and drew it out at last; a yellow sea-stained chart, crumpled in many folds. Philip could not take it from her, but I took it, and smoothed it out on my lap, for her to point out the pin-mark made by the dying seaman. As she laid her finger upon it, a deep heavy sob broke from my boy's lips.

"Philip!" I said, "Philip!" and I drew his head down to rest upon my shoulder, and laid my cheek against his forehead. I think he felt then how dearly I loved him, for he clasped his arms round me, and wept as passionately and unrestrainedly as though I had been his mother. I made a sign to the woman to leave us, and so we two were alone, filled with one thought, and partly one sorrow.

"Aunt Milly," he whispered, "this is almost worse than if my father were dead."

Not almost, but quite, I said to myself. But I did not speak it aloud: and by and by Philip roused himself, and leaned over the old chart to look at that pin-mark. It seemed only a week or two since he was standing at my knee to learn his first lesson in geography, and now! Ah! I foresaw that moment what lay before me; and how the restless, faithful love of that young heart would carry him far away from me.

At last Philip carried off the chart to George's room, while I went to dismiss Mrs. Brown. I followed him as quickly as possible, grudging every moment I must be away from him just then. He was kneeling by the side of George's sofa, with the chart open before him, and was telling him rapidly all that we had heard. The eager, sorrowful, boyish face! The tremulous, vibrating voice! The imploring, penetrating gaze, with which he met our eyes! It is all present to me now; and once more I feel the pang after pang that pierced my heart that night, and for many a long night to follow.

"My soul doth magnify the Lord," said Mary. "Yea, a sword shall pierce through thine own soul also," said Simeon, as if in answer. It seems to me as though that must be said of every deep love, whose birth we welcome with songs of gladness, and which we cherish as a heavenly gift, till the sharp, poignant anguish comes in its train. Yet not for centuries upon centuries of grief would Mary have forgone the blessedness of calling the Lord her Son.

Even from that night I knew that we could not keep Philip at home, with the idea of his father's sad captivity brooding in heart and brain. The perils of the search, the uncertainty of its issue, only fired the boy the more. There was his scholarship to give up, for it was granted only for purposes of study, and that grieved him a little; but it did not shake his resolution for a moment.

We obtained all the information we could, and procured letters of introduction to European missionaries and traders dwelling in that unhealthy region; and when that was done, nothing seemed left to George and me but to sink back into the dreary stillness of our former life.

I accompanied Philip to Liverpool, where we saw Mrs. Brown again, who was loud in her protests against the fruitless expedition; but she could tell us no more and give us no better clue than we had learned from her before. Until we were on the deck of the steamer which was to carry Philip away from me, I could scarcely believe that I was not in a dream. But the parting was too near at hand now for me to doubt the truth of it; and once the vessel had sailed away, there could be no return for him. But he had no wish to change his mind; that was evident. Whatever lay before him of peril, or pain, even unto death, he was prepared to meet. His face seemed to have lost for ever the last expression of boyhood, and to have taken the resolute, self-contained aspect of manhood. Yet the tears stood in his blue eyes, and he clasped my hand fast in his own, as we leaned over the bulwarks, our faces turned away from those who were standing by, looking at each other for the last time.

"Aunt Milly," he said, "God sent me to you."

"Yes, Philip," I answered; "but He is taking you away again."

"Only for a little while," he said. "I begin to see now that a whole lifetime is but a little while. We shall talk about this in Heaven. If I should never come home again, I shall tell you all about it there."

"Oh, my boy!" I cried. "It will be more than I can bear if you don't come back to me, and I never know what is become of you. Life is very long, Philip, and what am I to do through all the years, if you are lost to me, as your father has been lost to you, and I do not even know whether you are happy in heaven or in horrible slavery on earth!"

He answered me only by repeating in his low, pleasant voice a verse from one of my favorite hymns:

"Christ leads us through no darker room,
Than He passed through before;
He who into God's house would come,
Must enter by the door."

"But it is darker than I expected," I cried; and so it was. There was a dense darkness over that moment; and as I looked into the future I could not see a ray of light. I was sending my boy out upon a wild mission, into unknown dangers, which could not be exaggerated, and with no brilliant result to follow upon a successful ending. The most he could do was probably to satisfy himself of his father's death, amidst a savage tribe of native Africans. If I could have been sure that he would have found his father, I could have let him go more willingly.

"It seems to me," he said, his voice faltering a little, "as if I could almost feel Christ's hand clasping mine. He can lead us through any darkness."

Those were the last words he spoke to me, except a hurried good-bye as he left me in the boat which was to separate us. I looked up, and saw his grave, loving face looking down upon me from over the bulwarks—as I was to see it once more in after years—and a smile came across it, as he met my eyes. So we gazed, until we lost sight of one another in the distance.

There is one burden, one oppression, in life to me; the stern, inexorable regularity of time—the unhasting, unlingering beat of the moments, which pause for no fever of our pulses, nor hurry for no dreary languor of our hearts. When I reached home again the loud ticking of the time-pieces in the quiet house harassed me more than I can tell, now there was no need to watch for the hour when Philip would be coming in. Oh! the countless rounds those hour-hands must make before they point again to the moment he returns!

There were not many opportunities of hearing from him. He wrote when he landed at Sierra Leone, telling us he should join a caravan going south for the Ivory Coast, as soon as one started. Then we heard again, three months later, that a rumor of a white man kept in captivity, who was still alive, had decided him to go on with a few adventurous traders, who were venturing farther into the interior than the rest. After that all was silence, month after month. The African mails came in, and I waited, sick with hope deferred, for the coming of a letter; but there was none. Think of that; and remember that we had no personal interest in his father, he was of no kin to us, was altogether unknown to us; so that there was no special affection for him to counterbalance our anxiety for Philip. Moreover, if he found his father, he would belong to us no more. It was difficult to reconcile one's self to this.

Yet my brother George did it. Whether men are less exacting and less selfish in their love than we are, or whether he had entered more fully than I into the spirit of Christ, I hardly know. He waited with a patient hope, month after month, for tidings; and he spoke of Captain John Champion as if he was willing to give up Philip for him.

"The boy could do nothing else," he said, one day; "would you have had him remain at home in comfort, while he believed his father was in captivity among savages? Better a thousand times for the lad to perish in his brave enterprise than own such a selfish spirit as that."

"But it is very hard upon us," I answered, "after all we have done for him."

"Milly," he said quietly, "were we bringing him up for ourselves, or for God?"

I had no answer to give. My conscience spoke out loudly, but my voice could not. I had been bringing him up for myself; and centring all my love and hopes and pride in him. It was a hard struggle to pass through. I had looked upon myself as one of Christ's disciples; and so long as Philip's faith in Him, and loyal service to Him, had not crossed my own plans, I had rejoiced in both. But now that they were broken through and scattered, I could almost have wished that the boy had been less faithful to his Master.

Two years had gone by; more than twelve months had passed bringing no tidings of Philip. Our hopes had long since grown faint; though I learned at last to reconcile myself to the will of God. June was come again; and once more George and I sat with his window open, watching the flickering of the sunshine through the leafy trees. A chart of the western coast of Africa, on a large scale, lay within reach of my brother's hand; though he knew every line upon it. We seldom spoke of Philip now. But as I leaned back in my chair, with half-closed eyes, my thoughts were far away, in those strange regions which had grown familiar to me. I heard Thomas knock at the door, and open it only the space of an inch or two; and his voice came to my ear as if from a long distance.

"Miss Carr is wanted," he said.

What there was in his tone or manner, I cannot describe. My heart gave a sudden, great throb of expectation. I sprang from my chair, pushed past him as he tried to speak a few words to me, ran towards the dining-room, and caught Philip in my arms as he stood watching for me in the doorway.

I look back upon that day as perhaps the most gladsome of my life. He was changed; it was no boy who had come back; but there was the same voice, and the same sunny smile upon the face. The story he had to tell was so foreign to our life at home, that we listened with wonder and with trembling. His father was with him; but now, after the lapse of years, the recollection of him, as he sat by silent and almost melancholy, has faded from my mind: I see only Philip; I hear his voice, and once more the conviction deepens upon me that, all the perilous journey through, he had felt, as he said, Christ's hand clasping his. So close had grown his communion with Him in the dangers he had confronted, that never more could he be satisfied with the low level of the Christian life, where we were dwelling.

And now that Captain John Champion was in England again, what was to be done with him? He had brought home with him a small store of ivory and gold-dust, sufficient for his own immediate wants, and to pay for Philip's training in the hospital for a year or so; but he was not a man willing to be dependent upon others. His health had suffered severely during his captivity, with its innumerable hardships, and George urged him to get the best medical advice in London. Philip went with his father to consult the physician recommended by George's doctor, and we waited with some anxiety for their return.

They came in at once to my brother's room; their faces graver than they had been since that day they had come home. Yet Captain John Champion's was the saddest; for Philip's wore an expression so like the one I had seen when we parted on board the steamer at Liverpool, at once tender and resolute, that I felt a vague foreboding in my heart.

"Well?" said George, for neither seemed inclined to speak first.

"Bad news! bad news! answered Captain John Champion. "I'm little better than a useless old hulk."

"No," interrupted Philip. "Dr. Croft says my father may live many long years yet, and be in tolerable health. But he must not leave the sea; and, if possible, some one belonging to him must be with him, for his death might be sudden, or possibly very painful."

"That cannot be," said the father, looking sorrowfully at the son. "I cannot have anybody belonging to me with me."

"That must be," said Philip, cheerfully. "I have no calling or profession. I am as free to study navigation, and become a seaman, as I am to study diseases, and become a doctor. And what is more, uncle George, we met an old friend of my father's in the city; and when we told him the doctor's verdict, he offered my father on the spot the command of a ship chartered for Madeira, with a first-class mate and a capital crew. I've made up my mind to become a sailor."

"But, Philip," I cried, "you will throw away all your talents and your prospects; even your own wishes!"

"That's what I say," resumed his father, half eagerly. "I cannot consent to him sacrificing everything for me. No, no; my boy. God has given you great gifts; and He looks for you to use them in His service, not to follow the sea with a broken-down old man."

"His father!" said Philip.

There was silence among us for a few minutes after that. Captain John Champion sank wearily into a chair, and leaning his head on his hands, concealed his face from us; but the light fell upon his hair, which was going white and thin. The firm, loving expression on Philip's face strengthened as he looked at his father. As for me, I could not bear the thought of him becoming a sailor.

"Philip is right," said my brother's feeble voice, breaking the silence at last.

"Thank God, you think so!" exclaimed Philip. "Why! did not our Lord Jesus Christ take up Joseph's trade for some reason or other? Though it seems to me only a fancy, you know, but it seems to me just now it could not be exactly what He would choose. That has been in my mind since I've been thinking of going to sea with my father. And, Aunt Milly, I daresay His mother would be very much disappointed and grieved, when her wonderful child had to go into the workshop, and busy His hands with the carpenter's tools. It would seem to her as if He were thrown away, with all His marvellous gifts. If ever I begin to weary of the sea, I will think of His weariness in the carpenter's shop."

What could Captain John Champion, or I say against that? I had never thought of that; but Philip had quickly caught sight of the footsteps where Christ had gone before, and now there was no other path for him to tread. His father and I were dumb before his truer discipleship.

And I found when he was gone away again there was not the same blank there had been before. We heard from him pretty often. Letters came dropping in unexpectedly, posted at different ports, or forwarded by vessels that had crossed their course upon the sea. Their voyages were not very long; and sometimes there would be the pleasant bustle of expectancy and preparation for their arrival, and sometimes the almost pleasanter surprise of their unforeseen return. They seemed to bring fresh sea-breezes into our town-built house; and we scarcely lost the sense of new life and vigor that one visit gave before another followed. Philip was studying navigation with nearly as much ardor as he could have studied medicine, that he might pass an examination in it, and get appointed as mate to his father's ship.

understood then how Mary "kept all these ngs, and pondered them in her heart"; message of the angel, and the songs of the ole host of heaven over her child's birth; sayings of Simeon and Anna in the temple, the astonishment of the doctors and elders His understanding and answers. And I also olved to wait until I saw what God meant to with my boy Philip.

(*To be continued.*)

THE LORD'S SUPPER.

By Mrs. M. Baxter.

S. Lesson for May 13, Matt. 26: 17-30. Golden Text I Cor. 5:7.

e Most Difficult of all Sciences—Beyond the Capacity of the Disciples—Passover in Christ's Time—An Unreal Celebration—The Passover Christ Prepared—The Honor Conferred on a Host —The Feast Prepared—Divine Food for Supernatural Life—The Startling Announcement—Snares for Consecrated Christians—The Apostacy Abroad—A Remembrance of Deliverance.

AFTER His words to the disciples about His ming, and His speaking the parables of the gins, the talents, and the sheep and the goats, sus said to His disciples, "Ye know that after o days is the Feast of the Passover, and the n of man is betrayed to be crucified." Oh how tle the disciples understood what He said! ain and again He had declared to them that must suffer, but they had never taken it to art. They knew His goodness, believed in s power, admired His teaching, but could not derstand that He was about to die to redeem eir souls. There is no science or knowledge any kind which is so difficult for the natural an to grasp as the fact of Christ's redemption, cause it goes counter to all the pride and self-liance of our nature. Only the Holy Spirit n make us believe how utterly lost we are; ly He can show us what a Saviour Jesus is.

The Sacred Season

the Passover had come. This feast, neglected the ungodly kings of Judah, was now strictly served, but there were no such manifestations in the old revivals which took place in the ys of Hezekiah, when all Judah was moved, d they kept the Passover fourteen days instead of seven, and the priests and scribes received such a plentitude of offerings that they laid them by heaps" (II Chron. 30; 31 : 10); or the days of Josiah, when "There was no assover like to that kept in Israel from the ys of Samuel the prophet; neither did all the ngs of Israel keep such a passover as Josiah pt." (II Chron. 35: 18.) *Now* things were different; an outside, unreal religion had set in, d Jesus likened the religious people of this me to "whited sepulchres, which indeed appear beautiful outwardly, but are within full of ad men's bones, and of all uncleanness." (Matt. ; 27.) To Jesus the Passover had a meaning hich it could not have to any other. Since at first Passover in Egypt, when the destroyg angel passed over every blood-sprinkled orway, because God had said, "When *I* see e blood, I will pass over you," Jesus had been own forth in every Passover—the crucified amb, the sprinkled blood, the bitter herbs, all oke of Jesus and His atoning work; and it ust have been with strange feelings that He swered the question of the disciples, "Where lt Thou that we prepare for Thee to eat the ssover?"

"That we Prepare for Thee?"

sus was preparing for *them* a Passover of hich they little dreamt, although He had so ainly declared it to them. Oh, how our human hearts say to Jesus, "Let me prepare for hee," and how often some thought of patroning God lays hold of us, and we act as though e could, some way or other, enrich God! Yet sus did not criticise; He did not come "to ondemn the world, but that the world through lim might be saved." (John 3: 18.) He accepted eir desire to serve Him, while His own renounced will was preparing a Passover which ould serve, not a nation, but a world. "He said, o into the city to such a man, and say unto him, the Master saith, my time is at hand; I will keep the Passover at thy house with My disciples." "My time is at hand." None of the disciples appeared to notice His words. It was the time for slaying a lamb for every house in Israel, "*My time.*" Oh how it spoke of His coming sacrifice! The apostles, Mark and Luke, tell us that Jesus said a man should meet them bearing a pitcher of water, that they should follow him, and say to the master of the house, "Where is the guest-chamber where I shall eat the Passover with My disciples?" When He sent forth His disciples without purse or scrip, He directed them, when they entered into a city, to inquire who in it was worthy to receive them. (Matt. 10:11-13.) It was just in the same spirit that He honored His host with His presence. When the lives of Christians reflect the light and heat of God, His love and holiness, on those with whom they meet, everyone who knows the Lord feels it a privilege to entertain them; for they give far more than they take; they bring, and leave behind them a blessing which endures. It is quite another thing with those who make it a practice of living on religious people, and who thus bring the cause of Christ into reproach. A true follower of Jesus will never give trouble in a house, but rather be willing to help: he will never inconvenience his host or hostess whenever it is possible to avoid it; he will not complain of inconveniences, but be grateful for everything, and he will take the inmates of that house on his heart in prayer. Oh how privileged should any of us have felt if the Master had sent His two disciples to *our* house, there to keep the Passover!

The disciples did as Jesus had appointed, and made ready the Passover. The unleavened bread was baked, the bitter herbs were gathered, the lamb was slain and roasted, or, rather, crucified (for the Jewish spit was in the form of a cross), the blood was taken in a basin, and sprinkled on the lintel and the door-posts, and He whose blood was so soon to be shed sat down with His disciples. When the Passover was first instituted, the children of Israel were commanded to eat it with their loins girded, their shoes on their feet, and their staff in their hand, and they were to eat it in haste, for they were in an enemy's land, and on their way to the Land of Promise.

"Christ Our Passover

is sacrificed for us"; not only has He shed His blood, but He says, "My *flesh* is meat indeed, and My blood is drink indeed." The Passover lamb was the last food which the children of Israel ate in Egypt; it strengthened them for that miraculous journey in which the hand of God was so manifest throughout, where their very bread was to come from heaven, their water out of the stony rock, their pathway was to be in the depths of the sea, their raiment was to last untorn and unworn for forty years, and their shoes or sandals were to need no repair! What a picture of the Christian life, lived "by the faith of the Son of God"! Truly, we need divine food for the supernatural life to which God has called us. The children of Israel were made independent of the ordinary necessities of life by the fact that God undertook their every temporal need, and proved Himself sufficient. But the true Christian's life has to be as truly a life of faith as the life of the children of Israel was. The children of Israel had the pillar of clouds of fire to manifest the presence of God, but we have to take it on trust; and when we do so the Holy Spirit reveals Him. God spoke to them by a voice which their outward ears could hear. He speaks to us most often by His Word. Oh how we need divine sustenance for a life which is above nature, and which no struggles or efforts of our human nature can either produce or sustain!

Jesus sat down with the twelve. As they ate, Jesus said, "Verily, I say unto you, that one of you shall betray Me."

"One of You,"

One of the chosen twelve, called to "be with Him" (Mark 3:12) one who was selected from among other disciples to be a special witness for Jesus! Satan aims high: all the modern delusions have drawn out the worldly, half-hearted Christians, but the enthusiastic, the devoted, the consecrated, who yet wanted to *be* something superior to others, those whose self-life has taken such a spiritual turn that few could recognize that it was self at all. There was deep sorrow among the little band, and each one turned to the Master, saying, "Lord, is it I?" Peter and John were the most desirous to know who it was. Peter beckoned John to ask Jesus. He was the

Nearest to His Master,

and lay on His breast at supper. When he asked, "Lord, who is it?" Jesus answered that it was he to whom He should give a sop when He had dipped it, or who should dip his hand with His in the dish; and He added, "The Son of man goeth as it is written of Him (nothing could hinder that which was coming to pass), but woe unto that man by whom the Son of man is betrayed! It had been good for that man if he had not been born."

God keep His own disciples from betraying Jesus! There are fearful forms of apostasy abroad, many saying, "I am Christ," and deceiving many, setting up themselves as some great one. If ever it behooved Christians to be little, and to know their nothingness, it is now. Judas at last said, "Lord, is it I?" Jesus said, "Thou hast said." And *yet* Judas consummated the deed of betrayal! He had gone too far to stop, he was bound in honor to the chief priests, and this bond was stronger than his love to Jesus. He was bound hand and foot by Satan, and was no more his own master. Probably he justified his deed by imagining that Jesus would exert His power on His own behalf, and thus he did evil, counting on the evil being turned to good—a kind of sophistry with which Satan catches many. And as they were eating —not after a fast, as the sacerdotalists teach now—Jesus took bread, and blessed it, and gave it to the disciples, and said, "Take, eat, this is My body," and, as Paul adds, "which is broken for you; this do in remembrance of Me." The Passover was to be a remembrance of *their deliverance*, the Lord's Supper a remembrance of

The Person of our Deliverer.

The one was to lead them to rejoice in *their freedom*, the other to rejoice in *Him* who died to set them free. "And He took the cup, and gave thanks, and gave it to them, saying, Drink ye all of it: for this is My blood of the new testament, which is shed for many for the remission of sins"; and Paul adds, "this do ye, as oft as ye drink it, in remembrance of Me." When the Passover lamb was slain, the blood was not to be eaten, "for the life of the flesh is in the blood" (Lev. 17 : 11), but the blood of Jesus, His very life, is the life of our souls and bodies as we trust Him. "As the living Father hath sent Me, and I live by the Father, so he that eateth Me, even he shall live by Me. Jesus is as necessary to our souls as is food to our bodies; we cannot continue to live spiritually but as we draw upon Him. His flesh was given for the life of the world. All flesh has been condemned to die. "The end of all flesh is come before Me" was not only for the days of the Flood. Jesus has passed through death, and He breathes into us His own life; just as we let our self-life die, just as we deny ourselves and ignore ourselves, His life replaces ours.

"If You Love Me, Lean Hard!"

The following incident in the missionary life of Miss Fidelia Fiske, in Oroomiah, Persia, suggested the accompanying lines:

A few Sabbaths since, I went to Geog Tapa with Mr. Stoddard. It was afternoon, and I was sitting on a mat near the middle of the church, which had no seats, and only a floor of earth. I had been to two exercises before, and was weary, and longed for rest; and with no support, it seemed to me that I could not sit there till the close of the service. But finding that there was some one directly behind me, I looked, and there was one of the sisters, who had seated herself so that I might lean upon her. I objected; but she drew me back to the firm support she could give, saying, "If you love me, you will lean hard." And then there came the Master's own voice. "If you love Me, you will lean hard;" and, I leaned on Him, too. I was surprised to find that I was not at all weary that night, nor in the morning, and I have rested ever since, remembering the sweet words, "If you love me, lean hard."

CHILD of my love, lean hard,
And let me feel the pressure of thy care.
I know thy burden, for I fashioned it—
Poised it in my own hand, and made its weight
Precisely that which I saw best for thee.
And when I placed it on thy shrinking form,
I said, "I shall be near, and while thou leanest
On me, this burden shall be mine, not thine."
So shall I keep within my circling arms
The child of my own love; here lay it down,
Nor fear to weary him who made, upholds,
And guides the universe.
Yet closer come;
Thou art not near enough. Thy care, thyself
Lay both on me, that I may feel my child
Reposing on my heart.
Thou lovest me?
I doubt it not; then, loving me, lean hard.

J. E. JEWETT, Publisher, 77 Bible House, New York, will furnish the above poem in leaflet form at twenty cents per hundred. A Sample Packet of 50 leaflets assorted (no two alike) will be sent post-paid, for ten cents. Postage stamps taken.

TEN THOUSAND "Curiosities of the Bible." By a New York Sunday-school Superintendent. 600 pages. Illustrated. Price $2. Send for it. *The St. Louis Christian Advocate* says:—"This is one of the most remarkable books out. Not so much for the matter it contains, as that it is mostly from the Bible or directly referring to it, but for the ingenuity and skill with which that matter is arranged. We have not for a long time, if ever, seen anything more cleverly done, and are not at all surprised that sixty thousand copies have been disposed of. It will please and delight every reader." Teachers and Agents wanted to introduce it. E. B. TREAT, Publisher, 771 Broadway, New York.

The success of some of the agents employed by B. F. Johnson & Co., Richmond, Va., is truly marvellous. It is not an unusual thing for their agents to make as high as $20 and $30 a day, and sometimes the profits run up as high as $40 and $50—even more. But we hesitate to tell you the whole truth, or you would scarcely believe we are in earnest. Write them and see for yourself what they will do for you.

GOSPELS OF YESTERDAY.

DRUMMOND. SPENCER. ARNOLD. By ROBERT A. WATSON, M.A. 327 pages, 12mo, cloth. Price $1.25.

"The attempt to refute these three influential and very different writers in one small volume is a bold one. But we must declare it successful. . . . By 'Gospels of Yesterday,' Mr. Watson means Gospels that, till yesterday, were unheard of. He has done much to make his title true in another sense, namely, that whatever claim these Gospels had set up to be listened to yesterday, the ground is cut from under them to-day."—*Church Bells.*

"The many attractive features of Professor Drummond's book, and its great popularity and influence make it all the more necessary for those who dissent from its teaching to state with courtesy, yet with firmness, their reasons for dissent. Mr. Watson has done this part of his work with great incisiveness and power. So thorough is the criticism, so powerfully does he set forth the inconsistencies of the writing under his notice, that we are inclined to feel sympathy with the author and to ask whether he has not misinterpreted the meaning of Professor Drummond. But no; he gives chapter and verse, and each proposition he combats is fully given. . . . If Mr. Watson had done nothing more in this book than his criticism of Mr. Spencer, he would have done most effective service. . . . His criticism of Mr. Arnold is simply an attempt to bring some of Mr. Arnold's statements to the bar of history and of criticism. The attempt is successful; and the seemingly solid reasoning of that distinguished poet and critic becomes a dissolving view, such stuff as dreams are made of."—*British Weekly.*

☞ Sent post-paid for $1.25.

THOMAS WHITTAKER,
2 & 3 Bible House, N. Y.

MEXICO

Contributions in aid of Christian work in Mexico are most pressingly needed, and can be mailed to the address of
BISHOP H. C. RILEY,
Care of J. P. HEATH
43 Bible House, New York.

New Catalogue. Now Ready.

BEFORE YOU BUY ANY BOOKS FOR YOUR SUNDAY-SCHOOL LIBRARY

Send to me for a full Catalogue of the **cheapest** and **best** Sunday-School Books ever offered, and our

Special Offer to Sunday-Schools.

Satisfaction guaranteed or money refunded.

J. E. JEWETT, Publisher,
77 Bible House, New York.

WOMAN:
HER POWER AND PRIVILEGES.

A series of Sermons by Rev. T. DeWitt Talmage. Just published. 12mo. 200 pages, paper cover. Sold by all dealers for 25 cents; or sent to any address by mail, post-paid, on receipt of price. Address
J. S. OGILVIE & CO., Publishers,
P.O. Box 2767. 57 Rose Street, New York

OUR YOUTH
J. H. VINCENT, Editor.
Weekly. Illustrated.
Till Dec. 1, on trial, for SIXTY CENTS.
Mention this paper.
Phillips & Hunt, Pub'rs,
805 Broadway, N. Y.

A TWELVE-ROOM MODERN HOUSE OF LOW COST.

The floor plans, full description and cost (for different localities) of the above h[illegible] AND OF 60 OTHER BEAUTIFUL HOUSES AND COTTAGES, ranging in cost from $650 to $3,000, are given in Shoppell's latest pamphlet of designs [illegible] pages), which will be mailed to any address, post-paid, on receipt of 25 cents (stamps [illegible]). Address R. W. SHOPPELL, ARCHITECT, 63 BROADWAY, NEW YORK. (Mention this paper.)

A Most Appropriate Gift Book for "THE OLD FOLKS AT HOME."

Fifty Years and Beyond;
OR
OLD AGE AND HOW TO ENJOY IT.

A Book of Incalculable Value as well as Interest to all who have passed the Meridian of Life.

Compiled by Rev. S. G. LATHROP,
INTRODUCTION BY
Rev. ARTHUR EDWARDS, D.D.,
Editor N. W. Christian Advocate.

The object of this volume is to give to that great army who are fast hastening toward the "great beyond" some practical hints and helps as to the best way to make the most of the remainder of *the life that now is*, and to give comfort and help as to the life that is to come.

"They are the writings of the most eminent men, living and dead. It is by no means a gloomy book, and can be marked as excellent on every page."—CHICAGO INTER-OCEAN.

"It is a tribute to the Christianity that honors the gray head and refuses to consider the oldish man a burden or an obstacle. The book will aid and comfort every reader."—NORTHWESTERN CHRISTIAN ADVOCATE.

"The selections are very precious. Springing from such numerous and pure fountains, they can but afford a refreshing and healthful draught for every aged traveller to the great beyond."—WITNESS.

A lady who received a copy of this book writes: "Fifty years and Beyond" was bought for my aged parents, they are perfectly delighted with it, say 'it is a gem.' It is the very book I have been looking for, many, many years."

Price, Bound in rich cloth, 400 pages, $1.00.
" Presentation Edition, gilt edges, 1.50.
Sent by mail, postpaid, on receipt of price.

J. E. JEWETT, Publisher,
77 Bible House, - - New York.

A long-needed book. Thoroughly practical

Young People's Prayer Meetings

HOW TO CONDUCT THEM; TOGETHER WITH A GREAT MANY CHOICE THEMES AND TEXTS USED IN MANY SUCCESSFUL MEETINGS.

By REV. F. E. CLARK.

Founder and Originator of "The Society of Christian Endeavor." A book that fills a long felt want. Just the thing for "Societies of Christian Endeavor." 12mo, cloth, 75 cents.

"It is an unusual combination of Christian common sense, with a broad and also minute knowledge of the Needs, Desires, Tastes and Feelings of young people. The training of young converts, and the making of them before they are trained, the place and work of the young people's meeting, the best methods of conducting it, and its relation to the development and power of the Church—these, under various heads, are considered fully and wisely. . . . We commend it heartily. It is especially indispensable to every live minister."—*The Congregationalist*, Boston.

Sent, post-paid, on receipt of price.

J. E. JEWETT, 77 Bible House, New York.

Facts Stranger than Fi[ction]

A REMARKABLE BOOK

The Wonders of Pra[yer]

A BOOK OF WELL AUTHENTICATED AN[D WON]DERFUL ANSWERS TO PRAYER, AS NARRATED BY

D. L. Moody, C. H. Spurgeon, Newman Hall, D.D., Bishop T. Bowman, Chas. G. Finney, George Muller, Abraham Lincoln, W. W. Patton, Chas. Cullis, [illegible] S. I. Prime, D.[D.], Bishop Simpson, F. Krummacher, Martin Luther, John Knox, And hosts of others.

New Edition. Revised by Maj. D. W[illegible]
12mo, Handsome cloth binding. Price, [illegible]

To a greater extent than any other book, [illegible] extraordinary recital of facts and incidents, it fully answers that all-important [question] "DOES GOD ANSWER PRAYER?"

It also shows that the promises of the Bi[ble are ab]solutely true, and faithfully fulfilled in the [experience] of those who are constantly trusting in the[m to] ask His help in their daily anxieties and ex[illegible]. It is a book of great comfort and encoura[gement to] Christians, in their doubt, fear, sorrow, or [illegible] trust Him more fully in faith, and shows ho[w He has] delivered others in times of distress, peril, [illegible]tude, can hear and deliver them also.

To those who are not Christians, it is a rec[ord of un]doubted facts from the experiences of [illegible] now living, proving the real existence and [illegible] God, in controlling circumstances, directi[ng the] wills, and all things of earth, showing His [illegible] and power in daily events of life, and demo[nstrating] that He is not a distant Creator, but ever ne[ar].

This book should be in every Christian [illegible] invaluable to all Sabbath-school teachers [illegible]ars. It should be given to every child, for [illegible] pure and healthful instruction to encourage [illegible] of every one, and aims to lead all to come [illegible] willing minds to learn of the *Great Comfor[ter]*. Sent by mail, postpaid, on receipt of price.

J. E. JEWETT, Publisher,
77 Bible House, - - New [York].

"THE WORD FOR THE [DAY]"

Text, Hymn and Prayer for [every] day in the year. Compi[led] by A. J. A. R.

"The word for the day" has been compile[d with ref]erence to real every-day needs not fictitious [senti]mental ones. Its thoughts are very well sel[ected], its brief prayers are prayers indeed; for dev[otion it] is admirable.—*New York Evangelist.*

"The word for the day" is one of those a[ids] to a true Christian life.

16mo, Cloth, plain, 75c.; Gilt, $1.00; Amer[illegible] $1.75; Calf, flex., $2.50.
Sent by mail, postpaid, on receipt of pr[ice.]

J. E. JEWETT,
77 Bible House, N[ew York].

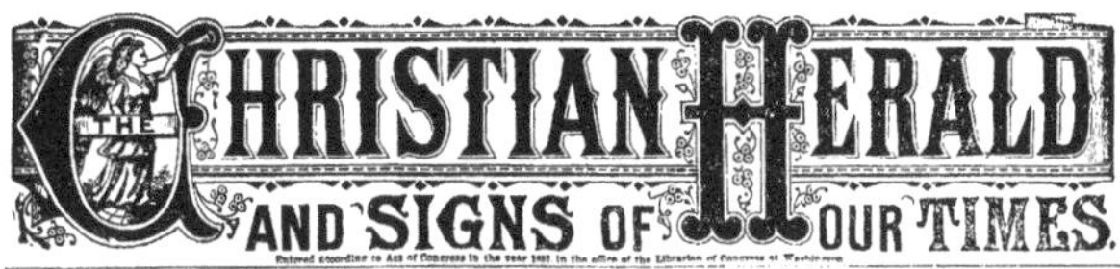

Entered according to Act of Congress in the year 1887, in the office of the Librarian of Congress at Washington.

Vol. XI., No. 19. Office, 63 Bible House. N. Y. THURSDAY, MAY 10, 1888. Annual Subscription, $1.50.

CONTENTS OF THIS NUMBER.

PORTRAITS OF PRINCE ALEXANDER OF BATTENBERG AND PRINCESS VICTORIA OF GERMANY.

LOSS AND GAIN. Dr. Talmage's Sermon Last Sunday Morning.

ANECDOTES RELATED AT RECENT EVANGELISTIC MEETINGS.

THE COMING CRISIS. By Dr. J. A. Wylie.

A Smoker Emancipated—A Bible Class of Judges—The Ornaments of a Goddess—A French Mechanic in a Hospital—The Horrors of Chinatown—A Magic Wand Superseded—A Telegram to buy a Sheep.

THE COMING OF THE BRIDEGROOM.

CURED AT LAST. A New Sermon by C. H. Spurgeon.

Gems from New Books: Mr. Beecher at School, etc.

PORTRAIT OF CORNELIA SORABJI; RESCUING PEOPLE FROM THE GERMAN INUNDATIONS (With Illust.)

ISAAC BOURNE'S BIRTHDAY MOTTO

MRS. TRANSOME'S PUPIL. (Continued.)

JESUS IN GETHSEMANE. By Mrs. M. Baxter.

Prince Alexander of Battenberg, and Princess Victoria of Germany—The Palace of Charlottenburg.

ROYAL MATCHMAKING.

THE three Victorias—Victoria, Queen of England; her daughter, Victoria, Empress of Germany; and her granddaughter, the Princess Victoria, have managed together to produce a grave international crisis, which at one time promised very serious results, and which, even now must be a sore subject in the imperial palace of Germany. It seems ridiculous that the love affairs of a young couple should imperil the peace of Europe, and involve the possibility of millions of men being arrayed in hostile conflict; yet so delicate are the relations of the Governments of Europe, and so sensitive are they to the slightest disturbance, that even so apparently trivial an affair as the suggested marriage of a princess sufficed to produce excitement little short of a panic.

The Project of the Marriage

is said to have originated with the Queen of England. She has become infatuated with the Battenberg young men, one of whom (Prince Henry) is married to her daughter Beatrice, and another (Prince Louis) to her granddaughter, the daughter of the late Princess Alice. She then favored the espousal of the third prince (Prince Alexander) to another granddaughter—the daughter of the Empress of Germany. The young lady herself, who is not remarkable for her beauty, is said to have fallen wildly in love with the handsome prince, who, on his part, was not averse to so splendid a match as that of becoming son-in-law of the Emperor of Germany. Thus, all the principal parties to the affair were in accord, when the intervention of Prince Bismarck put an obstacle in the way, and taught the wooers that even where royalty is concerned, "true love does not run smooth." Germany and Russia have for years been on anything but cordial terms, and Bismarck perceived that if the Emperor's daughter were married to a man whom the Czar regards as his enemy, the act would be regarded as a deliberate affront to Russia, and would inflame the animosity already existing between the two Governments. The Czar would naturally expect that the Emperor of Germany had, by this act, definitely cast in his lot with those statesmen who favor the restoration of Prince Alexander to the throne of Bulgaria.

Bismarck's Protest

was made the moment the affair was broached, but he evidently failed to carry his point, for he resorted to the two measures which he always carries up his sleeve. He threatened to resign, and he published the fact in the Cologne *Gazette*. For so great a man, Bismarck is curiously limited in devices for getting his own way. All through his career, whenever he struck a snag he has done these two things. Sometimes he uses the Berlin *Post*, or the *Kreuz Zeitung*, instead of the Cologne organ, but it is always a threat to resign, and the rumor of it appears in some papers close to him. The central and controlling idea of his foreign policy has always been to keep friends with Russia. How much of this has been due to his own conception and wisdom, and how much to the fanatical affection of the late German Emperor for the family of the Czar, is not clear, but it is patent to the world that Germany for years has been deferring to the Czar's likes and dislikes in an almost servile fashion. The whole European concert, as it exists, may be said to rest on Bismarck's proved anxiety to do nothing which can give the Czar offence. The situation really puts the present Emperor

In a Dilemma.

If he allows the marriage to proceed he runs the chance of losing the services of Bismarck, though the chance is not great, and he formally notifies the Czar that the season of Germany's deference to Russian wishes and designs is at an end, which would be only another way of saying that if the Czar wants anything more in Europe, he will have to fight for it. If Frederick, on the other hand, breaks off the match, he publishes to the world that, so craven is Germany's attitude before Russia, it dares not even marry one of its Princesses to the man she loves because the Czar happens not to love him. Some way of escape has apparently been found, but it is generally believed that the project has been postponed, not abandoned. It will be an interesting question to watch, for the three ladies who are pitted against the iron Chancellor are not of the character accustomed to give up a project on which they have set their hearts.

That Prince Bismarck had good ground for protest, however it may result, was evident from the tone of the Russian press when the idea of the marriage was first made public. A prominent St. Petersburg journal said: "Who knows but that the placing of Prince Alexander in a new high position might rekindle thoughts of his return among the leaders of the Bulgarian revolution, and, notwithstanding assurances to the contrary, defer the establishment of tranquillity in the Balkans, and also of pacific relations between the Powers? The question is how to reconcile these possible consequences with Prince Bismarck's programme and Emperor Frederick's pacific views and friendly assurances. We are certain that the German policy will know how to weigh the consequences, and prevent possible dangers to the relations between Russia and Germany and to the general peace."

The Crisis of the Love Story,

says the Berlin correspondent of an English journal, arrived at the end of March last, when Bismarck first heard that Prince Alexander was to be recognized as a German Prince, to receive the Order Pour le Mérite, and to be appointed to the command of an Army Corps. These projects the Emperor Frederick, however, after consultation with Prince Bismarck, abandoned. The second stage of the crisis was reached a few days later, when Prince Bismarck was officially informed of their Majesties' desire that Prince Alexander and Princess Victoria should be betrothed, and that the former would come to Berlin in a few days for that purpose. Then Bismarck spoke. He prepared an elaborate statement, and laid it before the Emperor.

Of this document, which is thirty pages in length, the following is the substance: The Chancellor first points out the changes in the relations between Russia and Germany which he considered would be brought about by the betrothal and by the bestowal of the above-mentioned military distinctions on Prince Alexander. On the ground of his own personal observation, Prince Bismarck then described in detail the irreconcilable differences between the Czar of Russia and Prince Alexander. He pointed out the fact that Prince Alexander's name was removed from the Russian Army List, and thence inferred the undesirable consequences of the Prince's appointment to the command of a German Army Corps. Among these the chief, Prince Bismarck thought, would be that the Czar would feel such an appointment as a deep personal affront.

Prince Bismarck's statement then discussed the possibility of Prince Alexander again becoming connected with the Bulgarian people, and described the complications which could not fail to ensue in the event of the resumption of the connection, which would deprive Germany of her present neutral position in the Bulgarian Question. A Franco-German war, the Chancellor pointed out, would by no means necessarily entail the support of France by Russia; whereas, on the other hand, in the case of a Russo-German war, the participation of France against Germany would be quite certain. The Chancellor concluded by remarking that, for the before mentioned reasons, the projected betrothal would appear to be a complete departure from the system of German policy built up during the past twenty years; that he would, therefore, no longer be able to bear the full responsibility, but must lay down his office as Chancellor if, contrary to his advice, the projected betrothal should take place. It is almost needless to add that the Chancellor had the cordial support of the Crown Prince. That young man, if he had no other reason for opposing the marriage, would have found it in the fact of its being favored by his mother and grandmother—the English influence which he so heartily detests.

PRINCE ALEXANDER.

THE Prince whose portrait appears on the preceeding page has had a romantic career, in which he has displayed remarkable personal heroism and a degree of statesmanship which is honorable to him. When he was affectionately and enthusiastically urged by the Bulgarians to hold his position in defiance of Russia he firmly refused to allow the blood of his people to be spilled in his personal interests, and resolutely insisted on abdicating his throne rather than bring on his country a disastrous war. Such conduct must be recorded to his credit; and it contrasts favorably with that of many potentates, who have not hesitated to deluge with blood the countries they ruled rather than waive their personal interests.

Prince Alexander is thirty-one years of age having been born April 5, 1857. He is the second son of Prince Alexander of Hesse, who was a brother of the late Empress of Russia and he is, consequently, a first cousin of the Czar. His great grandfather, on his mother's side, was a journalist, named Haucke, who ingratiated himself with the Russian grand-duke Constantine. Haucke's son, with the grand-duke's influence, was appointed a colonel in the Russian service, and when he was killed during the Polish riots in 1830, Constantine had his little daughter educated at his own expense. She grew up a beautiful and accomplished lady, and while at the Imperial Court, won the affections of the brother of the Empress, who married her and took her to his home at Hesse, in Germany, where his brother was reigning duke. The Battenburg young men are the offspring of that marriage. Two of the three are supported by the British taxpayers, having no income whatever of their own. Louis, the eldest, has a snug place in the British Navy, and the third, Henry, has a still better place as husband of the Queen's favorite daughter and the holder of lucrative sinecures in the British establishment.

Prince Alexander was, in April, 1879, elected to the throne of the newly formed State of Bulgaria which by the treaty of Berlin was carved out of Turkey, and in 1885 assumed the sovereignty of Eastern Roumelia, when he proclaimed the union of the two Bulgarias. During his reign, however, he maintained a perpetual quarrel with the Russians concerning the tutelage which they sought to maintain over Bulgarian affairs, civil and military. In 1881 he committed a serious error in suddenly suspending the Democratic Constitution of Tirnova, which had been promulgated by the former Russian Regent Governor, Prince Dondoukoff-Korsakoff, and the Russians were not slow to take advantage of this, and intrigued for his overthrow.

In 1883, however, Prince Alexander not only restored the Constitution, but, turning upon the Russians, asked why the Bulgarians should not be allowed to have a Bulgarian Home Minister instead of having to submit to the dictation of a Russian official? This won the devotion of the Bulgarians, who supported him heart and soul, and Russia was obliged eventually to recall the Ministers who were thwarting the Prince at every turn, and to replace them by more impartial men. However, at the instigation of Russia, the Prince was removed by a *coup d'état* on August 21, 1886, when he resigned his crown.

THE PRINCESS VICTORIA.

THE young lady whose portrait accompanies that of Prince Alexander on the first page is the second daughter of the Emperor and Empress of Germany. Her full name is Frederica Amelia Wilhelmina Victoria. She was born April 12, 1866, and she is therefore twenty-two years of age. While but little of a biographical nature is known of her, a very favorable impression of her character is prevalent in Berlin. It is known that her mother, who is the eldest daughter of the Queen of England, and a woman extraordinary learning and ability, has devoted special pains to the training of the Princess, and has every reason to be gratified with the result. One report sums up the prominent characteristics of the young lady in the words, "A favorite daughter in a Christian and intellectual family, she exhibits in a high degree the graces of refined and cultivated maidenhood." It is sad for the Princess that her love affair should be so ruthlessly thwarted, and that having the approval of father and mother, which in humbler circumstances would be deemed sufficient for the match, she must be disappointed for reasons of state. She has thus had to learn that an exalted station involves its penalties, and that self-sacrifice for the good of others becomes all the more imperative for her, because of the momentous concerns with which her lot is bound up. It may be hoped that, if the obstacles to the marriage should not be removed, grace may be given her to bear her disappointment bravely and cheerfully, and that she may be led to follow in the footsteps of the Prince of Heaven, of whom it was written that "He pleased not Himself."

THE PALACE OF CHARLOTTENBURG,

a picture of which appears on the first page, and where the Emperor and Empress of Germany are now residing, together with the Princess Victoria and her sisters, is situated on the west side of Berlin. Charlottenburg itself is a small, quiet town. Since the death, in 1873, of the Dowager Queen Elizabeth, Charlottenburg has not, until now, been the abode of Royalty. It has been a favorite resort of visitors from the neighboring city. The public road from Berlin is on the south side of the Palace. The Royal Mausoleum in the Park contains the body of Queen Louisa, the late Emperor's mother. Here the venerable Kaiser used to come every year on the day of his mother's death, and engage in solemn communion; and here he himself now rests until the morning of the Resurrection shall summon him, and all who sleep, both small and great, to appear before the King of kings.

A LITTLE HERO.

The heroism of a twelve-year old boy is mentioned by a surgeon in Georgia, as among the most memorable incidents of his practice. The doctor was called to attend the daughter of a railroad employee, whose lower limbs had been caught in the turn-table, and terribly cut and mangled. For some time amputation was contemplated but it was eventually decided to try to save the limbs. The effort was successful up to a certain point, but the wound would not heal. The doctors at last informed the family that it would be necessary to ingraft pieces of skin from a healthy person upon the lacerated surface, if the girl's limbs were to be saved. The brother of the girl, a boy twelve years of age heard what was said, and promptly offered the doctors as much of his skin as they needed. The little fellow was warned that the operation would be painful, but he said he guessed he could stand it if it would do Belle any good. There being no doubt of that, he stripped of his coat, and stood unflinchingly, while four strips of skin were taken from his arms, and transplanted to his sister's legs. The operation was completely successful, and the skin grew healthily, covering the wounds. The surgeon says that though he has performed many operations, he has never performed one that so impressed him with the power of the mind over the body, as that of taking the skin from the arm of the brave little boy whose love for his sister made him superior to pain. Nothing is said of the sister's gratitude, but it may be presumed she would never forget this proof of her brother's love. If through carelessness or perversity, she had obstructed the cure, and, losing her limbs after all, had rendered the boy's suffering fruitless, she would have been deemed crazy as well as wicked. Yet when sinners for whose salvation Christ gave His life die in their sins they are guilty of far worse turpitude. (Rom. 5: 7.)

ANECDOTES RELATED AT RECENT EVANGELISTIC MEETINGS.

Letting Their Finger-Nails Grow.—A minister observed: "Some people foolishly consider it to be beneath their dignity to work. The literary men in China, for instance, are very much afraid that the people will think they labor for a livelihood, so they let their finger-nails grow very long in order to produce the impression that they do not work. One literary man was so anxious about this matter that he tied splints upon his fingers to make his finger-nails grow very long and straight. And what was the result? When he took off the splints and bandages, certainly his nails were grown; he gained what he wanted, but his hand was paralyzed and perfectly powerless. Do not some Christians think it beneath their dignity to work among the poor and do humble services for Christ? They certainly are members of His body, through the faith which unites them to Him, but they are unfruitful, useless members, a very shame and reproach to the name which they bear."

Making A Public Choice of Christ.—Mr. D. J. Findlay remarked: "Some time ago, at a series of gospel meetings which were being held, a gentleman attended them night after night, and each night he came most distinctly under the influence of the Holy Spirit. At the close of one of these meetings the chairman asked those who were anxious about their souls to come forward to the front bench. This gentleman felt strongly moved to go, but he thought, 'There is not so much necessity for going to that particular seat; I can be saved at home just as easily as here!' He went home, and sought to close with Jesus, but could not. The several following nights were just the same, but one night the Holy Spirit was so importunate that the man was ready to find peace. In the meeting he rose to go to the front, but had scarcely gone three steps when he fell upon his knees in the aisle, and there God saved his soul. Yes, it is true God can save a perishing sinner anywhere, but one of the conditions of salvation is that we confess the Saviour before men, and our persistent refusal to publicly make our choice of Christ may be nothing else but a persistent shirking of that condition. Of all such will Christ be ashamed, and will not confess their names when He comes in glory."

Refusing to Let Go the Rope.—A Christian worker says: "A ship was recently on the rocks on the Scottish coast. The wind was high and the waters rough. Every minute she was expected to go to pieces. The boats were lowered, and the sailors by means of a rope were lowering the passengers over the side into the boats. Most had gone in safety, and they now came to a lady, who was told to hold on tightly to the rope until she got the word, 'Let go,' and then at once to obey, and she would fall into the boat beneath. She was lowered, the boat floated below, the word to let go was given, but the woman spasmodically held on, and the boat floated away. Again they tried her, and again at the critical moment her courage failed. They drew her up, and gave the rope to her little daughter, who, simply obeying instructions, was soon safe in the boat. They gave the mother another chance, but though she had seen her own child saved she was still afraid to follow, and when the ship went to pieces she was drowned. Similarly, there are men and women who will not let go the habit, the pleasure, or some other rope which prevents them entering the gospel life-boat, though by doing so they would ensure their eternal safety. And too many cling to such things to the last hour of life, and then go down to a lost eternity."

A Physician on a Bed of Straw.—A Temperance lecturer observed: "I was addressing a meeting in the West of Scotland a short time ago, and at the close the wife of the chairman asked her husband to visit a doctor who was dying. He looked annoyed, and declined to go. I offered to visit the dying man, and after a minute's hesitation my chairman agreed to accompany me. While on the way thither he told me a little of the life history of the man whom we were going to see. At one time he was one of the leading men in the town, rich and respected by all. But in an evil hour he gave way to strong drink, and under its fell influence rapidly lost position, money, and respectability, until he had fallen to the miserable state in which we found him. In an attic at the top of a narrow, shaky, dingy stair we found him, his room almost without a chair, and the learned and once reputed physician lying on a bed of straw. We spoke to him, and bending over him whispered the text, 'This is a faithful saying,' etc. But I fear he had lost the power to apprehend what was said. His feet were already in the cold waters of the river of death. This is a sample of what strong drink does for its devotees. What fine capabilities has it not withered? And what brilliant careers has it not blasted? And once having given way to its influence, few there are who ever overcome it. But God's arm is not shortened that He cannot save, neither is His ear heavy that He cannot hear."

Mr. Spurgeon Throws a Stick at a Dog.—Mr. Lakin said: "When the Rev. C. H. Spurgeon was living at Nightingale Lane, Clapham, he was much troubled by a most unwelcome guest, in the shape of a dog, that frequently visited his garden, and destroyed his flower-beds and borders. Mr. Spurgeon resolved to watch and give the intruder a warm reception. One morning he saw the dog in his garden at its old trick. Picking up a stout walking-stick, he slipped out and got behind some trees to watch his opportunity. When the dog came near enough he took careful aim and threw his stick at it. But his aim was not of the best, and instead of hitting the dog, the stick spent its force on the air. The dog looked up, and seeing the stick and the man, it drew its own conclusions, and running to the stick, picked it up, and brought it to Mr. Spurgeon. His wrath was disarmed; he could not strike the dog who thus humbly brought the stick that was thrown at it. So taking the stick with one hand, with the other he patted the dog's back and said, 'Good fellow, good fellow!' This may illustrate how sinners, like that dog, have been disobeying God's law. He has caught us in the very act, and hurled at us the condemnation for our misdeeds. Let us accept the position, and own our condemnation just, and present ourselves before Him, pleading for mercy, and He will receive and pardon us."

A Sad Love Disappointment.—Mr. W. Thomson, relates: "I heard a minister tell this very pathetic story. He said: 'I had a sister whom I loved dearly, and I also had a companion with whom I was specially intimate. We had been together at school, and together at the same college, and both were studying for the ministry. He visited our house very frequently, and I suppose it was natural enough that he should fall in love with my sister. After some time they were engaged. Towards the end of his university course he accepted a situation as tutor in a gentleman's family, and accompanied them on the Continent. From that time his feelings seemed to have changed. His letters grew very frigid, and when he returned to England he had no scruple in telling me that he wanted a rich wife, and the first time he saw my sister he told her that their engagement must be considered at an end. That night my sister became a maniac, and within a week leaped out of a three-story window, and was killed. And to-day the cause of this catastrophe fails to see that he has done anything wrong, and cannot be made to understand why I can be no longer a friend of his. But that is impossible until he acknowledges that he was the means of my dearly loved sister's death. God, says that we must confess our sins before we can obtain His forgiveness. Before He can save us we must acknowledge we are sinners, and then, for Christ's sake, He freely forgives.'"

LOSS AND GAIN.

Dr. Talmage's Sermon Preached Last Sunday Morning, May 6, 1888.

"What shall it profit a man if he shall gain the whole world, and lose his own soul?" Mark 8: 36.

A Question for Bargain-Makers—The Value of the Two Properties—I. The World a Grand Property—Impossible to Get a Good Title to It—Contingent on Life and Sensibility—Subject to Writ of Ejectment—No Fire Insurance on It—Thirteen Worlds Consumed—Always Involves Trouble—Thackeray Pitying His Own Reflection—II. The Soul as a Property—Its Majestic Silence—Capacity for Happiness—The Price Paid for It—The Home Prepared for It—Values Compared—Satan's Bid for the Soul.—A Sailor's Heroic Death.

I AM accustomed, Sabbath by Sabbath, to stand before an audience of bargain-makers. There may be men in all occupations sitting before me, yet the vast majority of them, I am very well aware, are engaged from Monday morning to Saturday night in the store. In many of the families of my congregation, across the breakfast-table and the tea-table, are discussed questions of loss and gain. You are every day asking yourself: "What is the value of this? What is the value of that?" You would not think of giving something of greater value for that which is of lesser value. You would not think of selling that which costs you ten dollars for five dollars. If you had a property that was worth fifteen thousand dollars, you would not sell it for four thousand dollars. You are intelligent in all

Matters of Bargain-Making.

Are you as wise in the things that pertain to the matters of the soul? Christ adapted his instructions to the circumstances of those to whom He spoke. When He talked to fishermen, He spoke of the gospel-net. When He talked to the farmers, He said: "A sower went forth to sow." When He talked to the shepherds, He told the parable of the lost sheep. And am I not right, when speaking this morning to an audience made up of bargain-makers, that I address them in the words of my text, asking: "What shall it profit a man if he shall gain the whole world, and lose his own soul?"

I propose, as far as possible, to estimate and compare the value of the two properties.

I. First, I have to say that the world is

A Very Grand Property.

Its flowers are God's thoughts in bloom. Its rocks are God's thoughts in stone. Its dew-drops are God's thoughts in pearl. This world is God's child—a wayward child, indeed: it has wandered off through the heavens. But about eighteen hundred and eighty-eight years ago, one Christmas night, God sent out a sister world to call that wanderer back, and it hung over Bethlehem only long enough to get the promise of the wanderer's return, and now that lost world, with soft feet of light, comes treading back through the heavens. The hills, how beautiful they billow up, the edge of the wave white with the foam of crocuses! How beautiful the rainbow, the arched bridge on which heaven and earth come and talk to each other in tears, after the storm is over! How nimble the feet of the lamp-lighters that in a few minutes set all the dome of the night ablaze with brackets of fire! How bright the oar of the saffron cloud that rows across the deep sea of heaven! How beautiful the Spring, with bridal blossoms in her hair! I wonder who it is that beats time on a June morning for

The Bird Orchestra.

How gently the frail harebell tolls its fragrance on the air! There may be grander worlds, swarthier worlds, larger worlds than this; but I think that this is a most exquisite world—a mignonette on the bosom of immensity! "Oh," you say, "take my soul! give me that world! I am willing to take it in exchange. I am ready now for the bargain. It is so beautiful a world, so sweet a world, so grand a world!"

But let us look more minutely into the value of this world. You will not buy property unless you can get

A Good Title

to it. After you have looked at the property, and found out that it suits you, you send an attorney to the public office, and he examines the book of deeds, and the book of mortgages, and the book of judgments, and the book of liens, and he decides whether the title is good before you will have anything to do with it. There might be a splendid property, and in every way exactly suited to your want; but if you can not get a good title, you will not take it. Now, I am here this morning to say that it is impossible to get a good title to this world, If I settle down upon it, in the very year I so settle down upon it as a permanent possession, I may be driven away from it. Ay, in five minutes after I give up my soul for the world I may have to part with the world; and what kind of a title do you call that? There is only one way in which I can hold an earthly possession, and that is through the senses. All beautiful sights through the eye, but the eye may be blotted out; all captivating sounds through the ear, but my ear may be deafened; all lusciousness of fruits and viands through my taste, but my taste may be destroyed; all appreciation of culture and of art through my mind, but I may lose my mind. What a frail hold, then, I have upon any earthly possession!

In courts of law, if you want to get a man off a property, you must serve upon him

A Writ of Ejectment,

giving him a certain time to vacate the premises; but when Death comes to us and serves a writ of ejectment, he does not give us one second of forewarning. He says: "Off of this place! You have no right any longer in the possession." We might cry out: "I gave you a hundred thousand dollars for that property"; the plea would be of no avail. We might say. "We have a warrantee deed for that property"; the plea would be of no avail. "We have a lien on that storehouse"; that would do us no good. Death is blind, and he cannot see a seal, and cannot read an indenture. So that, first and last, I want to tell you that when you propose that I give up my soul for the world, you cannot give me the first item of title.

Having examined the title of a property, your next question is about insurance. You would not be silly enough to buy a large warehouse that could not possibly be insured. You would not have anything to do with such a property. Now, I ask you what assurance can you give me that this world is not going to be burned up? Absolutely none. Geologists tell us that it is

Already on Fire;

that the heart of the world is one great living coal; that it is just like a ship on fire at sea, the flames not bursting out because the hatches are kept down. And yet you propose to palm off on me, in return for my soul, a world for which, in the first place, you give no title, and in the second place, for which you can give no insurance. "Oh," you say, "the water of the oceans will wash over all the land and put out the fire." Oh, no. There are inflammable elements in the water—hydrogen and oxygen. Call off the hydrogen, and then *the Atlantic and the Pacific oceans would blaze like heaps of shavings.* You want me to take this world, for which you can give no possible insurance.

Astronomers have swept their telescopes through the sky, and have found out that there have been thirteen worlds, in the last two centuries, that have disappeared. At first they looked just like other worlds. Then they got deeply red—they were on fire. Then they got ashen, showing they were burned down. Then they disappeared, showing that even the ashes were scattered. And if the geologist be right in his prophecy, then our world is to go in the same way. And yet you want me to exchange my soul for it. Ah, no; it is a world that is burning now. Suppose you brought an insurance agent to look at your property for the purpose of giving you a policy upon it, and while he stood in front of the house he should say, "That house is on fire now in the basement," you could not get any insurance upon it. Yet you talk about this world as though it were a safe investment, as though you could get some insurance upon it, when down in the basement it is on fire.

Brings Trouble.

I remark, also, that this world is a property, with which everybody who has taken it as a possession has had trouble. Now, I know a large reach of land that is not built on. I ask what is the matter, and they reply that everybody who has had anything to do with that property got into trouble about it. It is just so with this world; everybody that has had anything to do with it, as a possession, has been in perplexity. How was it with Lord Byron? Did he not sell his immortal soul for the purpose of getting the world? Was he satisfied with the possession? Alas! alas! the poem graphically describes his case when it says:

"Drank every cup of joy, heard every trump
Of fame, drank early, deeply drank, drank draughts
That common millions might have quenched; then died
Of thirst, because there was no more to drink."

Oh yes, he had trouble with it; and so did Napoleon. After conquering nations by the force of the sword, he lies down to die, his entire possession the military boots that he insisted on having upon his feet while he was dying. So it has been with men who had better ambition. Thackeray, one of the most genial and lovable souls, after he had won the applause of all intelligent lands through his wonderful genius, sits down in a restaurant in Paris, looks to the other end of the room, and wonders whose that forlorn and wretched face is; rising up after awhile, he finds that it is Thackeray in the mirror! Oh,

This World is a Cheat.

Talk about a man gaining the world! Who ever gained half of the world? Who ever owned a hemisphere? Who ever gained a continent? Who ever owned Brooklyn? Talk about gaining the world! No man ever gained it, or the hundred-thousandth part of it. You are demanding that I sell my soul, not for the world, but for a fragment of it. Here is a man who has had a large estate for forty or fifty years. He lies down to die. You say, "That man is worth millions and millions of dollars." Is he? You call up a surveyor, with his compass and chains, and you say, "There is a property extending three miles in one direction, and three miles in another direction." Is that the way to measure that man's property? No! You do not want any surveyer, with his compass and chains. That is not the way you want to measure that man's property now. It is an undertaker that you need, who will come and put his finger in his vest-pocket, and take out a tape-line, and he will measure five feet nine inches one way, and two feet and a half the other way. That is that man's property. Oh no, I forgot; not so much as that, for he does not own even the place in which he lies in the cemetery. The deed t[o] that belongs to the executors and the heirs,

Oh, What a Property

you propose to give me for my soul! If yo[u] sell a bill of goods, you go into the counting room and say to your partner, "Do you thin[k] that man is good for this bill? Can he giv[e] proper security? Will he meet this payment? Now, when you are offered this world as a po[s]session, I want you to test the matter. I d[o] not want you to go into this bargain blindly. [I] want you to ask about the title, about the i[n]surance, about whether men have ever had a[ny] trouble with it, about whether you can keep [it], about whether you can get all, or the ten tho[u]sandth, or one hundred-thousandth part of it.

There is the world now. I shall say no mo[re] about it. Make up your mind for yourself, as [I] shall, before God, have to make up my mind f[or] myself, about the value of this world. I cann[ot] afford to make a mistake for my soul, and y[ou] cannot afford to make a mistake for your sou[l].

II. Now, let us look at

The Other Property

—the soul. We cannot make a bargain witho[ut]

seeing the comparative value. The soul! How shall I estimate the value of it? Well, by its exquisite organization. It is the most wonderful piece of mechanism ever put together. Machinery is of value in proportion as it is mighty and silent at the same time. You look at the engine and the machinery in the Philadelphia Mint, and, as you see it performing its wonderful work, you will be surprised to find how silently it goes. Machinery that roars and tears soon destroys itself; but silent machinery is often most effective. Now, so it is with the soul of man, with all its tremendous faculties—it moves in silence. Judgment, without any racket, lifting its scales; memory, without any noise, bringing down all its treasures; conscience taking its judgment-seat without any excitement; the understanding and the will all doing their work. Velocity, majesty, might; but silence—silence! You listen at the door of your heart. You can hear no sound.

The Soul is all Quiet.

It is so delicate an instrument that no human hand can touch it. You break a bone, and with splinters and bandages the surgeon sets it; the eye becomes inflamed, the apothecary's wash cools it; but a soul off the track, unbalanced, no human power can readjust it. With one sweep of its wing it circles the universe and overvaults the throne of God. Why, in the hour of death the soul is so mighty, it throws aside the body as though it were a toy. It drives back medical skill as impotent. It breaks through the circle of loved ones who stand around the dying couch. With one leap it springs beyond star and moon and sun, and chasms of immensity. Oh, it is a soul superior to all material things! No fire can consume it; no floods can drown it; no rocks can crush it; no walls can impede it; no time can exhaust it. It wants no bridge on which to cross a chasm. It wants no plummet with which to sound a depth. A soul so mighty, so swift, so silent, must be a priceless soul.

I calculate the value of the soul, also, by its

Capacity for Happiness.

How much joy it can get in this world out of friendships, out of books, out of clouds, out of the sea, out of flowers, out of ten thousand things; and yet all the joy it has here does not test its capacity! You are in a concert before the curtain hoists, and you hear the instruments preparing—the sharp snap of the broken string, the scraping of the bow across the viol. "There is no music in that," you say. It is only getting ready for the music. And all the enjoyment of the soul in this world, the enjoyment we think is real enjoyment, is only preparative; it is only anticipative; it is only the first stages of the thing; it is only the entrance, the beginning of that which shall be the orchestral harmonies and splendors of the redeemed.

You cannot test the full power of the soul for happiness in this world. How much power the soul has here to find enjoyment in friendships! but oh, the grander friendships for the soul in the skies! How sweet the flowers here! but how much sweeter they will be there! I do not think that when flowers die on earth, they die forever. I think that the fragrance of the flowers is the spirit being wafted away into glory. God says there are palm-trees in heaven and fruits in heaven. If so, why not the spirits of the dead flowers? In the sunny valleys of heaven, shall not the marigold creep? On the hills of heaven, will not the amaranth bloom? On the amethystine walls of heaven, will not the jasmine climb? "My beloved is come down in his garden to gather lilies." No flowers in heaven? Where, then, do they get their garlands for the brows of the righteous?

Christ is glorious to our souls now, but how much grander our appreciation after awhile! A conqueror comes back

After the Battle.

He has been fighting for us. He comes upon the platform. He has one arm in a sling, and the other arm holds a crutch. As he mounts the platform, oh, the enthusiasm of the audience! They say: "That man fought for us, and imperilled his life for us"; and how wild the huzza that follows huzza! When the Lord Jesus Christ shall at last stand out before the multitudes of the redeemed of heaven, and we meet Him face to face, and feel that He was wounded in the head, and wounded in the hands, and wounded in the feet, and wounded in the side for us, methinks we will be overwhelmed. We will sit some time gazing in silence, until some leader amidst the white-robed choir shall lift the baton of light, and give the signal that it is time to wake the song of jubilee; and all heaven will then break forth into: "Hosanna! hosanna! Worthy is the Lamb that was slain."

I calculate further the value of the soul by

The Price Paid For It.

In St. Petersburg there is a diamond that the Government paid two hundred thousand dollars for. "Well," you say, "it must have been very valuable, or the Government would not have paid two hundred thousand dollars for it." I want to see what my soul is worth, and what your soul is worth, by seeing what has been paid for it. For that immortal soul, the richest blood that was ever shed, the deepest groan that was ever uttered, all the griefs of earth compressed into one tear, all the sufferings of earth gathered into one rapier of pain and struck through His holy heart. Does it not imply tremendons value?

I argue, also, the value of the soul from the home that has been fitted up for it in the future. One would have thought a street of adamant would have done. No; it is a street of gold. one would have thought that a wall of granite would have done. No; it is the flame of sardonyx mingling with the green of emerald. One would have thought that an occasional doxology would have done. No; it is a perpetual song. If the ages of heaven marched in a straight line, some day the last regiment, perhaps, might pass out of sight; but no, the ages of heaven do not march in a straight line, but in a circle around about the throne of God; forever, forever, tramp, tramp! A soul so bought, so equipped, so provided for, must be a priceless soul, a majestic soul, a tremendous soul.

Now, you have seen the two properties—the world, the soul. One perishable, the other immortal. One unsatisfying, the other capable of ever-increasing felicity.

Will You Trade?

Will you trade even? Remember, it is the only investment you can make. If a man sell a bill of goods worth five thousand dollars, and he is cheated out of it, he may get five thousand dollars somewhere else; but a man who invests his soul, invests all. Losing that, he loses all. Saving that, he saves all. In the light of my text, it seems to me as if you were this morning offering your soul to the highest bidder; and I hear you say: "What is bid for it, my deathless spirit? What is bid for it?" Satan says: "I'll bid the world." You say: "Begone! that is no equivalent. Sell my soul for the world? No! Begone!" But there is some one else in the audience not so wise as that. He says: "What is bid for my immortal soul?" Satan says: "I'll bid the world." "The world? Going at that, going at that! going! Gone forever!

> "What is the thing of greatest price,
> The whole creation round?
> That which was lost in Paradise,
> That which in Christ is found.
>
> "Then let us gather round the cross,
> That knowledge to obtain;
> Not by the soul's eternal loss,
> But everlasting gain."

Well, there are a great many people in the house who say: "I will not sell my soul for the world. I find the world is an unsatisfying portion." What, then, will you do with your soul? Some one whispers here: "I will give my soul to Christ." Will you? That is

The Wisest Resolution

you ever made. Will you give it to Christ? When? To-morrow? No; now. I congratulate you if you have come to such a decision. Oh, if this morning the eternal Spirit of God would come down upon this audience, and show you the vanity of this world, and the immense importance of Christ's religion, and the infinite value of your own immortal souls, what a house this would be! what an hour this would be! what a moment this would be? Do you know that Christ has bought your soul? Do you know that He has paid an infinite price for it? Do you know that He is worthy of it? Will you give it to Him now?

I was reading of a sailor who had just got ashore, and was telling about his last experience at sea. He said: "The last time I crossed the ocean we had a terrific time. After we had been out three or four days, the machinery got disarranged, and the steam began to escape, and the captain, gathering the people and the crew on deck, said: "Unless some one shall go down and shut off that steam, and arrange that machinery at the peril of his life, we must all be destroyed." He was not willing to go down himself. No one seemed willing to go. The passengers gathered at one end of the steamer waiting for their fate. The captain said: "I give you a last warning. If there is no one here willing to imperil his life and go down and fix that machinery, we must all be lost."

A Plain Sailor

said: "I'll go, sir;" and he wrapped himself in a coarse piece of canvas and went down, and was gone but a few moments, when the escaping steam stopped, and the machinery was corrected. The captain cried out to the passengers: "All saved! Let us go down below and see what has become of the poor fellow." They went down. There he lay dead. Vicarious suffering! Died for all! Oh, do you suppose that those people on the ship ever forgot, ever can forget, that poor fellow? "No!" they say; "it was through his sacrifice that I got ashore." The time came when our whole race must die unless some one should endure torture and sorrow and shame. Who shall come to the rescue? Shall it be one of the seraphim? Not one. Shall it be one of the cherubim? Not one. Shall it be an inhabitant of some pure and unfallen world? Not one. Then Christ said: "Lo! I come to do thy will, O God"; and He went down through the dark stairs of our sin and wretchedness and misery and woe, and He stopped the peril, and He died, that you and I might be free. Oh, the love! oh, the endurance! oh, the horrors of the sacrifice! shall not our souls this morning go out toward him, saying: "Lord Jesus Christ, take my soul. Thou art worthy to have it. Thou hast died to save it."

God help you this morning rightly to cipher out this sum in gospel arithmetic: "What shall it profit a man if he shall gain the whole world, and lose his own soul?"

A Jewish Rabbi Offering Prayer in the United States Senate, attracted considerable attention in Washington last week. The incident is described, as follows: The Senators, who were in their seats when President Ingalls rapped them to order, were somewhat surprised to see standing before them, in the place usually occupied by the Chaplain of the Senate, a little black-whiskered man who had neglected to remove his hat. He wore a long, black coat and a white cravat, and looked very ministerial all except the hat. It was at first supposed that he had forgotten to remove it, but when the Senators arose he began to ask the blessing without uncovering his head. By his side stood the Rev. Dr. Butler, the regular chaplain of the Senate, who did not seem to be at all surprised at the personal appearance of his friend. The man with the hat on was Dr. H. Pereira Mendes, a Jewish rabbi of New York. It is not the custom of rabbis to uncover their heads when offering prayer, and so Dr. Mendes did not do it even in the presence of the United States Senate. This is the second instance, probably, in the history of the Government when a Jew offered prayer in the Senate.

A SMOKER EMANCIPATED.

The difficult achievement of breaking off the long continued habit of tobacco-smoking was described in a testimony recently given at Bethshan, and reported in *Thy Healer*.* He said: "'All things are possible to them that believe': and so it proved in my case in relation to smoking. Unknown to me, our friends on the platform, when building the hall, laid my case before the Lord. I had *smoked for about fourteen years*, and I felt it was absolutely necessary on account of my health, and because it eased my chest. After that the Lord exercised me with these words which Mrs. Baxter was speaking from one Sunday afternoon: 'Know ye not that your body is the temple of the Holy Ghost, which is in you, which ye have of God? And ye are not your own.' I had such an exercise that afternoon as never since the Lord revealed Himself to me twenty-five years ago. The question would come: 'Cannot I trust Him with my nerves and chest and everything?' I shall not forget going home with Mr. Boardman and telling him about the exercise of my soul. He said: 'Yes, brother, and so was I exercised, for I have been a smoker, and it was by seeing the detriment it was to me.' What I passed through that week, no one but God knew. The next Sunday Miss Murray took the same words: 'Know ye not that your body,' &c. I was just looking to the Lord, and I saw Him and no one else, and these words came distinctly to my heart as though God spoke them: 'I have come down to deliver you—I have come down to deliver you.' And He is the Deliverer, and if we do but accept the deliverance from Him, no matter what the bondage is, He will free us from it when we ask Him.

I can now say to the glory of God I have not been troubled with phlegm since. Satan has tempted me, but God helped me. I belong to the Lord, and He has redeemed me, spirit, soul, and body. And since He healed me I have scarcely spit any phlegm, and that is nearly four years ago."

A BIBLE CLASS OF JUDGES.

In spite of the recent outbreak of persecution in Japan the missionaries are much encouraged, and the work is making progress. Mr. Atkinson, who writes from Kobe to the *Missionary Herald*, says: "A new building for an English night-school was begun two years ago in a rented building. It has had to move several times, but now has a building erected expressly for its use. It is established by Christian men, and the teachers are Christians. Most of the work is done by Japanese. The school has a Christian basis, and is intended to act as an evangelizing agent. The number of students is a little over sixty. Financially, it is entirely sustained by the Japanese.

"I have been invited by some judges of the Prefectural Court to give them instruction in the New Testament. This is *a very interesting class*, I can assure you. The coming Saturday afternoon they have notified me that nine are coming. Saturday afternoon is a half-holiday at the court. They come to my study at two o'clock, and leave a little before four. Miss Dudley has services at the house of one of these men. Lately he offered prayer there, and once at a union prayer-meeting of the three churches. I think the interest may date from last summer. At that time the Vice-Minister of Justice was here, examining this and other Prefectural Courts. He is a member of one of our Congregational churches in Tokoi. Mr. Kozaki is his pastor.

"The Kobe church building, which seats four hundred, is now too small for the congregation. Adjoining lots have been bought, and it is hoped that a building capable of holding at least a thousand people will be up before many months go by. A couple of Sundays ago I preached for pastor Harada. On a front seat half a dozen young Buddhist priests were seated. Some of them took full notes of my sermon, and all listened with evident interest. The following Sabbath the same men were there again, I was told, each man having a New Testament with him."

THE ORNAMENTS OF A GODDESS.

An interesting offering has recently been handed into the treasury of the mission in Madura in the Indian Archipelago. Mr. Tracy, who is laboring there, says: "On Christmas day there were brought to me by a new convert some ornaments which in days gone by he and his brother had caused to be made in honor of their family goddess. The ornaments are made of copper, heavily plated with gold, and are made in four pieces, being the head, feet, body, and crown ornaments in which they were wont annually to set the goddess forth for special worship. Recently in the division of family property among the brothers, these fell to the lot of this young man, and he has brought them to me. The work and overlaying of gold must originally have cost no small sum, and he offered them on Christmas morning as his pledge of fidelity to a Saviour and a religion whose adornment is not external, but that of a meek and lowly spirit."

A FRENCH MECHANIC IN A HOSPITAL.

At the McAll Mission Station at Rochefort, France, encouraging progress is being made. M. Durrleman, who is in charge, reports one case of especial interest. He says: "There is a man here about fifty years of age, who, after his conversion, brought his wife, his daughters, his son-in-law, and his son to the meetings. They had not been many times when the father met with a serious accident; his hand was caught in the driving-wheel of an engine, and for several days it was thought that he would lose it. I feared that, by this accident, his faith might be shaken, but, on the contrary, the trial led him to trust God even more implicitly, and when his hand was saved he did not cease to bless God, considering that it was a miracle. The family was troubled by the insinuations of the neighbors, and some of them said: 'It is not astonishing that such things happen to you when you change your religion.' But afterwards, when his wife and children saw what a comfort his Bible was to him, and what a source of strength his 'new religion' was, they returned to the meetings. A few days since the mother said to me, 'Monsieur, I owe you much; now I know that Jesus died for me.' During the time that the father was in the hospital he was permitted to lead to the Saviour a young soldier who occupied the cot next his."

Subscriptions for the support of the McAll Mission, in France, may be sent to Miss Frances Lea, 1622 Locust Street, Philadelphia, Penn.

THE HORRORS OF CHINATOWN.

In a communication to the *Church*, Miss M. R. Cable, who is laboring among the opium-dens and gambling-houses of the Chinese quarter of San Francisco, reports appalling details of the cruelties and immoralities of that abode of darkness and heathenism. Beginning six years ago, with the teaching of one little girl, she has now over one hundred whom she is permitted to teach and visit in their homes. In the course of her description of this work she says: "Opium-dens, gambling-dens, and houses of prostitution abound. In one of these houses we have a class of five little girls whom we have been teaching. These children are being raised for immoral purposes. The oldest of them, about eleven years of age, has, I think, been already bought by a procuress; and although we have reported her case several times to the officials, yet the law is evaded, and it now remains for Christian women to so arouse public opinion that these things cannot exist in our country. It is a burning disgrace to our boasted civilization.

"One little waif has been rescued. She had been made to sit up every night until one or two o'clock sewing on buttons; and when she became so weary that she could no longer work, her ears were nipped with scissors to arouse her. Her hands and face are covered with scars, giving unmistakable evidence of cruelty. She is in the mission home, where her 'wrinkled old face, that looked as if there was no joy on earth,' has begun to freshen and brighten under the kindly influences of love and Christian training."

A MAGIC WAND SUPERSEDED.

During the visit of a medical missionary to Telarbes, in Syria, and while he was dispensing medicines to the sick poor of the town, in the school-yard, a Moslem magic medicine man entered the village, and came immediately to pay his respects to the sheikh who was in the company. The missionary says: "This travelling quack presented a strange appearance, dressed in bright-colored baggy pants, short coat, tight sleeves, and an immense turban on his head. He seated himself on the ground, and called his servant to bring him his pipe. This servant, very poorly dressed, carried a bag in one hand, and in the other a stick about five feet long, on the end a large brass object covered with strange-looking figures and Arabic characters. The man carefully placed *the magic wand* (for this staff is supposed to possess wonderful powers of healing) in a safe place. From the bag he extracted a hookah, or water-pipe, which he proceeded to fill with tobacco and light for his master, who sat and smoked and criticised western methods of practicing medicine. When we had prescribed for all the sick and had loaded our medicine chest on a mule, the Arab doctor asked if any one was in need of his services. When answered in the negative, he ordered his servant to bring his donkey, saying he would go where he was wanted. The animal was brought, his master mounted, gave his legs a swing, and was off. His servant, with bag and magic staff followed after."

A TELEGRAM TO BUY A SHEEP.

In the Missionary Training Institute in London there come, it appears, trials of faith as in George Muller's Institutions, and others which are dependent on God for support. Miss L. Guinness mentions one or two cases. She says: "We have become vegetarians in practice, if not in principle, more than once. We well remember, about ten years ago—when lack of funds made the reduction of current expenditure imperative—students, household, and all going without meat for several days. Happy they who, under such circumstances, are able to retrench sufficiently! With a family of a hundred or more members looking to one for daily support, the matter is not so simple! However we did our best, and amongst other items reduced the butcher's bill at a sweep, by dispensing altogether with butcher's meat. Our party of missionary students began to realize that mutton and beef do not grow on dining-tables by means of natural law. Soon after this, at our weekly prayer-meeting, we were interrupted one day by a telegram, and on opening the envelope discovered the somewhat startling direction: "Buy a sheep, and charge to———." It was not long before our dining-hall again saw wholesome legs of mutton, vegetarianism being over for the time. Ten years have passed since then; ten years in which the lesson of faith has often been repeated. We have known the living from hand to mouth, which, one has well said, is a blessed life if the hand that feeds the mouth is the hand of God. We have learned to understand very practically the meaning of the words, 'My God shall supply all your need.' And the lesson has at times been no easy one to con. But lately, for the same sufficient reason as of yore, we have re-adopted vegetarianism on certain days each week. And so we are vegetarians again, and day by day are reminded by the simple fare before us that 'Man doth not

* *Thy Healer and Faith Witness*, a monthly magazine, edited by Mrs. M. Baxter, contains original articles on Holiness and Healing, Authentic Testimonies of Divine Healing, and Items of Intelligence from Heathen Lands where Missionaries are laboring in faith, soliciting no help from man, but relying solely on God for support. Annual Subscription, 75 cents may be sent to the Manager of Christian Herald, 63 Bible House, New York.

ve by bread alone, but by every word that proecdeth out of the mouth of God.'

"Strangely enough, on opening the letters one iorning recently, we came across one from an ld friend, containing, with a welcome gift of ;5, the words, 'Will you accept the enclosed onation towards your butcher's bill, which iust be a serious item in so large a household?' 'he gift seemed to us doubly *a propos*, as funds 'ere even more than usually wanting."

THE COMING CRISIS.

By Dr. J. A. Wylie.

'he Commencement of the Twelve Hundred and Sixty Years—Its Close in Revolution—The Beginning of the Seven Vials—Daniel's Extended Periods—The Sanctuary Beginning to be Cleansed—The Predicted Period of Repose—The Froglike Spirits Appear—The Symbolic Hail.

The Roman Emperor, Justinian, promulgated is celebrated Code of Laws throughout the hole of his reign, from A. D. 529 to 565. This ode gave a legal standing to the Papacy, and nacted persecuting laws against the spiritual hristian Church. This Code of Laws we fix on s the probable commencement of the 1,260 ears of the Papacy's chief power, and of the hristian Church prophecying in sackcloth. Rev. 11 : 2, 3.) Hence, adding 1,260 years to ie Era of Justinian—529 to 565—we are brought own to 1789 to 1825, the epoch which included ie Era of the French Revolution. We find iat Revolution abrogating the Justinian Code, lienating to State purposes the Church's property, and declaring the temporal power of the ope to be finally abolished. In these events e find what appears to be

The Termination of the 1,260 Years.

'he Seven Vials commenced to be poured out t that French Revolutionary epoch. In 1821–26 ie waters of the mystic Euphrates began to be ried up at the pouring out of the Sixth Vial t the Greek insurrection. To the 1,260 years, 'aniel adds a total period of 75 years, namely, rst 30 years (the 1,290), and then an additional eriod of 45 years (the 1,335 in Daniel 12 : 11, 12). 'he first 30 bring us down to the time when astern Christendom began to be cleansed of ie Mohammedan desolation, and its cleansing so far advanced that Protestant congregations re already numerous, and every year becoming iore so. They now enjoy legal toleration in urkey. "Blessed is he that waiteth and ometh to the one thousand three hundred five nd thirty years."

The Appearance of the Frog Spirits.

Western Europe has been enjoying a period f repose, which it is plain from the prophecy it as to do. Peace has been so lengthened and rofound as to have excited the astonishment of tatesmen. And meantime we have seen the hree identical froglike spirits predicted under ie Sixth Vial in Rev. 16 : 13, secretly plotting r an agitation that will exceed anything ever nown, for when the Seventh Vial shall be oured out into the air, there shall be "voices, hunders, and lightnings, and a great earthuake such as was not since men were upon the arth; so mighty an earthquake and so great." hese are the usual apocalyptic symbols of tuults, insurrections, wars and revolutions. The reat national changes introduced by the politial earthquake are further described by the eference to "islands and mountains," the symbol of great and small monarchies. "And every land shall flee away, and the mountains shall ot be found." And a great hail shall be poured own from the firmament. Hail is the emblem f warlike armies from the north. The fall both f the little kingdoms and the great monarchies f Europe is plainly predicted in these apocalypic representations; because in the earthquake very island is to flee away, and the mountains ot to be found. *This revolution will be accompanied by a war of unexampled severity and horror.* The symbolic hail falling from the northern egion indicates its fall from France or Russia. The winds of popular fury, bursting in terrific orce, will soon sweep the fragments of the Prophetic Image away, and efface every trace of its existence. Such is

The Catastrophe

which prophecy reveals as awaiting the kingdoms of modern Europe. The prophecy of Daniel 2 synchronises with the Seventh Vial of Revelation, and throws light upon it. Both portend an entire change in the social and political fabric of Europe—the fall of its kingdoms, the extinction of its dynasties, the alteration of its laws and forms of government, the abolition of its offices and dignities, the dissolution of its armies, the destruction of all the symbols of its authority, and the obliteration even of the territorial boundaries of its States. Nothing short of this can fulfil the figures of Daniel and the symbols of the Apocalypse. In the one we not only behold the Prophetic Image ground to powder, but its last particles swept away by the tempest. In the other we see the earthquake burying cities, overthrowing mountains, and so agitating the ocean that its islands are submerged by its tumultuous waves. If figures have any meaning, these must import the total overthrow of all the powers that now bear rule in Europe, and the utter extinction of the last vestige of their authority. It is a new creation which the world is to undergo, and dreadful convulsions will usher it in.

THE COMING OF THE BRIDEGROOM.

By Mr. W. Birch.*

Britain's Menace from Ireland—National Sins to be Judged—The Rise of the Napoleonic King—His Seven Years' Covenant—The Formation of the Decem-Regal Confederacy—The Rapture of the Waiting 144,000—The Ascendancy of Antichrist.

As this Age is shown by Daniel's 2,345 years, dated from the Command to rebuild Jerusalem in Passover Week, B. C. 445, to end in Passover Week 1901, and as the ten-kingdomed confederacy is to be formed by about ten years before the End of this Age, that is to say, by about 1891, therefore the European wars necessary to change the present *twenty-three* kingdoms into these *ten*, and in which France will annex the territory up to the Rhine, may be anticipated to break out before the close of 1888. Britain will be drawn into the conflict, and Ireland, taking advantage of the opportunity, will obtain Home Rule, and become practically independent of England. When it is remembered that about one-fourth of the British Army consists of Irish Romanists, and that there are many thousands of Irish Roman Catholics in each of our large towns, it will be seen that if, at a time of European war and bad trade, they join with the socialists and the thousands of unemployed or discontented, the consequences to Britain may be most disastrous. As a nation, we have forgotten God, and merit His indignation. One among many of

Our National Sins

is the widespread disregard of the injunction to "keep holy the Sabbath Day." Notice the many public-houses and shops open for buying and selling on the Lord's Day; the fashionable dinners and amusements of the rich, and the debasing pleasures of many of the poor on that sacred day; together with no inconsiderable number of the "cultured classes" looking upon the written word of God as antiquated and obsolete, upon the Judgment Day as a superstition.

When the allied ten nations have been formed within the territories of the Roman Empire, there will arise about 1891-92 an eleventh little horn or king of

Napoleon Name or Nature,

called "the king of the *North*" or Syria; Egypt being called the *South*. This little king will climb into power as King of Syria, by flatteries (Daniel 7: 24; 11: 21), and after having first arisen as a little monarch over some lesser State, such as Macedonia for instance, inside the present Turkish Empire, he will then make a covenant or league for seven years with the Jews—probably from Passover Week, 1894, to Passover Week 1901—giving them the right of free worship in Jerusalem, where they will build a temple, and offer morning and evening sacrifices as in ancient times—probably about November 8, 1894, exactly 2,345 literal days before the Last Day of this Age, which is shown by Daniel's dates to be Thursday, April 11, the last day of Passover Week in 1901. This little king will then wage three wars against the king or ruler of the South (Egypt), and in the second war be hindered by the ships of Kittim; but in about two years and a half after the signing of the covenant with the Jews, he will conquer Egypt; and after heading a red-republican revolution in Europe (Rev. 17. 3), he will become its Military Dictator, about April, 1897.

The *first* form of

The Ten-kingdomed Confederacy,

about 1891, will have been purely *monarchical* and *liberal*, but this *second* of *scarlet* form in 1897 will be *Red-republican* and *Ultramontane*. Then the *third* form of the confederacy of the ten nations about three and a half years from the signing of the Jewish Covenant will be that of the little king advanced to supreme power as Universal Emperor. The Pope will then be his obsequious servant, and, looking upon him as a God, shall command the world to worship him under pain of death. This shall last about three and a half years until our Lord descends on Olivet.

Nearly two years after the signing the seven years' term of the Jewish Covenant, the Lord Jesus shall suddenly appear in the clouds, but His presence will be felt only by the Christians who, like the five Wise Virgins, are ready and watching for Him. Though there may be several millions of Christians, yet only 144,000 of them will be ready

To Ascend in the Air

to be with the Lord. We read in Daniel 9: 25, "From the going forth of the commandment to restore and build Jerusalem UNTO Messiah, the Prince, shall be seven weeks and threescore and two weeks" (Daniel 9: 25), or sixty-nine weeks. A future Commandment to restore and rebuild Jerusalem will go forth at the same time as when the Jewish sacrifices shall be restored, in a rebuilt temple at Jerusalem, about November 8, 1894; and in sixty-nine weeks afterwards, namely, about March 5, 1886, our Lord may be expected to come as a Bridegroom to call His waiting disciples to His side. At the same time "the dead in Christ shall rise first," that is, all the saints who have died since the world began shall be raised.

After this *Firstfruits* Translation of the 144,000, business and political affairs will proceed on the earth as usual.

The King of Syria

will cast covetous eyes on Egypt, and seek to obtain control of the Suez Canal; but though the ships of Kittim (probably meaning Britain) shall hinder him, he will eventually take possession of Egypt, and, having previously overcome three of the ten nations (Daniel 7 : 24), the remaining six will submit to his victorious arms, and acknowledge him as their Head. He will break his covenant, and stop the morning and evening sacrifice. Having overcome the Jews and other nations, his navy being the combined fleets of Europe, he will rule the world, including America. Those who refuse to receive his mark or to worship his image, he will order to be beheaded upon huge scaffolds erected in every town of Europe. But at last, after his reign of three and a half years, the Lord Jesus will appear on the Mount of Olives, Antichrist and the false prophet will be seized, and cast alive into a lake of fire. (Rev. 19 : 19.)

* An extract from a sermon preached in Free Trade Hall, Manchester, England, where he has a regular congregation of from one to two thousand persons. He has published his sermons every week for over fourteen years. The one from which this extract is taken is No. 776.

CURRENT EVENTS.

The Highest Judicial Honor of this Country was conferred last week on Melville Weston Fuller, a Chicago lawyer—the President having nominated him Chief Justice of the United States Supreme Court, to succeed Chief Justice Morrison Waite, whose death was chronicled in these columns on March 29. Mr. Fuller is fifty-five years of age. He has held a prominent place at the Illinois bar for over a quarter of a century, and has been an active member of the State Legislature. As he has never held a judicial position, considerable surprise is expressed at his selection for the highest judicial office in the land, where judicial ability is needed in a greater degree than political partizanship. Politically, Mr. Fuller is a Democrat. Washington reports agree in stating that he did not seek the Chief Justiceship. There were no papers of application in his behalf, but there were many letters of recommendation coming from some of the most prominent and influential men of the East and West. Mr. Fuller gained a high reputation as an ecclesiastical lawyer some years ago, by his defence of Mr. (now Bishop) Cheney, of the Reformed Episcopal Church, who was prosecuted for leaving the word "regenerate" out of the Protestant Episcopal service of Infant Baptism. Mr. Fuller conducted the case through several years of tedious litigation, and rendered valuable assistance in the organization of the Reformed Episcopal Church.

Important Amendments to the Interstate Commerce Act have been proposed by the Senate Committee, which has had the apparent defects of this law under consideration. One of these amendments provides that a reduction in the published railroad rates shall only be made after three days *public notice*, instead of without previous notice, as at present. Another and more important amendment makes it the duty of the railroad companies to keep the printed schedules open to the public. The law is to be made stricter, and its violation is to be more efficiently guarded against, by the insertion of a clause which makes violation punishable, in the discretion of the court, by *imprisonment as well* as by the fine already provided for. This would certainly make railroad officials more careful, and prevent more effectively than is now the case, the practice of unjust discriminations in the matter of freight charges.

Another Unseemly Wrangle in the United States Senate took place on May 1. As usual, Mr. Ingalls, of Kansas, was conspicuous in it, and also, as usual, Mr. Voorhees, of Indiana, opposed him, and lost his temper in doing so. Mr. Ingalls renewed his attack on the late Generals, Hancock and McClellan, denounced the appointment of Mr. Lamar to the Supreme Court bench, and declared that Mr. Cleveland was never elected to the Presidency, but was counted in by a partnership of "footpads and sneaks," and declared that the Democratic Senators who had resented his (Ingalls's) attack on the dead generals were, from the beginning, the enemies of the Union, and, like Senator Voorhees, avowed in sympathy with the South, Copperheads, Butternuts, Knights of the Golden Circle, and all their degraded allies. This tirade caused much excitement, and Senator Voorhees, in reply, declared that the charge made by Mr. Ingalls was a base lie, so infamous a falsehood that the black walls of perdition could produce nothing like it. "I spit upon it!" he shouted. "I spurn it! I kick it from me! I despise it! The Senator from Kansas cannot fish up from the filth of the sewers these old, stale lies, and make them respectable in the Senate of the United States, but it is possible for him, with a short step, to put himself upon a level with them." For some time it seemed that the interference of the police would be required to keep the peace. This was a scene, not in a low pot-house, where it would have been appropriate, but in the dignified Senate of the United States, which is supposed to be composed of the most cultured statesmen in the country.

The New Treaty Regulating Chinese Immigration, whose salient features were explained in our issue of March 22, is now before the Senate, having been reported last week by the Committee on Foreign Relations, with the recommendation that it be ratified. The Committee has added two amendments. One provides that the prohibitive features of the treaty shall apply to those Chinamen who are now absent from the country, regardless of any certificates they may hold, and the other requires that the classes privileged to return to the United States shall only be permitted to land upon presenting certificates issued subsequent to the present time. There seems to be little doubt that the treaty will be ratified, although the Pacific coast Senators are not unanimous in its favor. Senator Mitchell in particular is opposed to any treaty at all with the Chinese. He thinks the existing treaty should be abrogated, and a law passed absolutely prohibiting any Chinaman from coming to this country. There are other Republican Senators who are not enthusiastic for the new treaty, but they are too few to secure its rejection. A new anti-Chinese bill has been introduced in the House of Representatives, prohibiting Chinamen from coming into the United States after three months subsequent to the passage of the act, the provisions of which are to apply to all persons of Chinese descent, whether subjects of China or any other foreign power, and the words "Chinese laborers" shall be construed to mean both skilled and unskilled laborers, and Chinese employed in the mines.

Destructive Floods Have Visited Northern Texas and part of the Indian Territory. Houses, fences, and crops on the bottom-lands have been completely swept away, and in some places houses had to be held in place by strong ropes. Men went in wagons to rescue helpless women and children who had become water-bound, and were unable to save themselves. Miles of railroad track were washed away, and traffic was seriously interrupted. At Lehigh, ten miles west of Ataka, Ind. Ty., forty families were compelled to abandon their homes. There was much suffering, but fortunately no lives were lost, so far as known.

The Condition of the Emperor of Germany somewhat improved last week, though it as yet affords little ground for hope of complete recovery. The bulletins are extremely vague. One of the latest said: "The Emperor was free from fever this morning and was able to rise. His strength is gradually increasing. The present favorable symptoms indicate that he will soon overcome the weakness remaining from the recent crisis. The weakness especially affects his legs. He made slight attempts to walk today. The weather still prevents his taking outdoor exercise. The Emperor makes himself understood more than formerly by whispers and signs, but he uses no phonetic system." The *Vossische Zeitung* says it has learned from a reliable scource that the local disease in the Emperor's throat has increased but little since the Emperor left San Remo.

The War Between Italy and Abyssinia has not been closed by the good offices of England. The well meant attempt at mediation has however been appreciated by the Italian Government. Prime Minister Crispi stated in the Italian Chamber of Deputies last week that the Italian Government had felt bound to accept the offer, it having received proofs of England's friendship. "England has no interests opposed to ours," continued the Premier, "and knows well that we shall never injure her, and that we may, under certain circumstances, aid her. Although the mediation mission undertaken by England did not succeed in accomplishing its object, still, its services were useful, in that it apprised King John of the pacific intentions of Italy." Motions were made demanding the recall of the Italian troops who are fighting against Abyssinia, but they were not acted on.

The Problem of the Scottish Crofters is to be dealt with through assisted emigration. The British Government proposes to grant them land in Canada, pay their passage out, and lend them a little capital. On May 1 Mr. Macdonald, who is judge-advocate for Scotland, stated in the House of Commons that $50,000 would be appropriated to increase the fund raised by private subscription for the relief of the crofters. This would give to each family $600, which they would be expected to repay in twelve annual installments. A free grant of Government land would be made in each case. It is stated that the crofters have the same objections to emigration that are manifested by the Irish, and cling to their wretched crofts in spite of their hardships. Whether love of their old homes will be stronger than the tempting offer of the Government, remains to be seen. What they wish is more land from the deer forests around them, but a Conservative Government could not consistently interfere in that direction.

The Attitude of the Pope towards the Nationalist, agitation in Ireland, mentioned in our last issue, has caused the leaders of the Irish National League to prepare a circular, which has been distributed throughout Ireland to every branch of the league, calling upon the members to be firm in their adherence to that body, and arranging for the simultaneous meetings of twenty League branches at a time, until all the members have met and conferred upon the line of action to be adopted in respect to the Papal rescript and other emanations of Rome. It is reported from Rome that a special congregation of the Propaganda, composed exclusively of Cardinals, is now examining several questions relative to the Irish agitation, upon which it will formally vote. Cardinal Simeoni has submitted at least ten points to the congregation. The Vatican appears resolved that those opposing its decisions will place themselves "outside the pale of moral and Christian law." The Vatican does not doubt that the Irish bishops will feel the necessity of adopting the line of conduct the Pope prescribes.

Warlike Disturbances in Macedonia Were reported last week. They show that Russia still continues her meddling policy, and is endeavoring to find an excuse for further hostilities against Turkey. The outbreak occurred at Monastir, in Macedonia. The Servian and Greek portions of the population are said to have united to oppose the authority of Turkey. A part of the same plot was a raid on Turkey by Montenegrins. Should the Macedonian rising grow menacing, diplomatic representations will be made by the British Minister at Athens, and if they do not result in satisfactory assurances, England, Austria and Italy will send a squadron to the Piræus. It is evident from many signs that the European atmosphere is becoming highly charged with dangerous elements, and generals and statesmen are foreboding a general conflict. In an interview with a French journalist General Gourko, the Russian Governor of Warsaw, denied that Russia was desirous of war, but said it was impossible to predict events. He hoped that, should an outbreak of hostilities occur, France would not remain neutral. He hinted that in such case France, as Russia's ally, would have to deal with England as Italy's ally. Nobody could count on England's neutrality, and this, he said, was a matter for serious reflection.

The General Conference of the Methodist Episcopal Church assembled in New York on May 1. Ex-Judge Fancher made an address of welcome to the delegates. Bishop Bowman read the statement prepared by the Board of Bishops. The burning question of the admission of lady delegates was delicately handled in this statement. Attention was called to it as an innovation, but the bishops did not apparently wish to influence the Conference either for or against the admission. Neither did the address of the Bishops, which was read on the following day by Bishop Merrill, deal with the question in a partisan spirit. On Thursday, however, the Committee appointed to consider the question made its report, and it was against the admission of the ladies. It ran: After serious deliberation and serious discussion for several hours they are firmly convinced that the church contemplated the admission of men only as lay representatives, and that it never has consulted or expressed its desire upon the admission of women to the General Conference. *Resolved.* First, that under the constitution and laws of the church, as they now are, *women are not eligible* as lay delegates in the General Conference. On the presentation of this report, an animated debate ensued. How closely it touches the conference, may be inferred from a test vote taken on the question whether the ladies might be allowed to occupy seats among the delegates pending the decision of the Conference. The courtesy was refused them by a vote of 106 to 103.

The Evangelical Alliance is Extending With remarkable rapidity, and the number of its branches is multiplying almost daily. Dr. Russell, whose clear and forcible address at Washington, D. C., was recognized as a masterly presentation of the aim and methods of the Alliance, has yielded to the solicitation of the Board of Managers to resign his charge at Oswego, N. Y., and devote himself exclusively to the work of the Alliance. In a recent interview at Kingston, N. Y., Dr. Russell thus summarized the benefits to be derived in a city from organizing a branch of the Alliance: First, a local branch would unite all the churches in evangelical work; second, it would give laymen something to do; third, it "would work the city clean," that is to say, that every house in it would be visited, and the subject of religion and morality would be presented to every person; fourth, it would keep the churches constantly at work, and there would be a constant centralization of religious influence brought to bear upon the people.

A Man Chased to Death by a Shadow caused some excitement on board the French steamer *La Champagne*, which arrived in New York on April 29. Among the passengers on board when the steamer left Havre was a young Swiss gentleman, who was returning from a pleasure trip in Europe. He had lived in New York five years, and was in prosperous circumstances. Six months ago he returned to his old home in Switzerland, and spent a pleasant time with his family and friends, and afterward travelled about through Germany and Austria. He appeared to enjoy his trip immensely, and set out on his return to America, in good health and spirits. After the steamer had been two days at sea a change came over him. He grew melancholy, and seemed to be suffering from nervous trouble. He complained that he was being followed around the ship by some one who wanted to do him a mischief, and when anyone approached him he shivered and trembled like a frightened child. It was hoped that the invigorating sea-air would rid him of his hallucination, but it did not. On the morning of April 23, the passengers on deck were startled by seeing him rush on deck clad only in shirt and trousers, shrieking to them to stop the man who was after him. He reached the vessel's side before he could be stopped, and jumping on the rail plunged overboard. The vessel was stopped, and a boat lowered for his rescue, but he was never seen again. Men in sound health find it difficult to understand any one being so terrorized by an imaginary foe, but nervous sufferers know how possible it is for a man to be driven to frenzy by nervous disorder. It is a dreadful affliction, before which the stoutest heart quails; yet scoffers, and men who live in sin in defiance of God, forget that it is one of the scourges with which their Maker threatens them. "They are to flee when no man pursues." (Lev. 26: 17.)

The Transplantation of an Eye was an Operation performed in Philadelphia on April 28. It is the first time such an operation has been performed in this country, and there is a record of only two cases in which it has been successfully performed in Europe. These were at Giessen, Germany. The patient in the Philadelphia case was a young lady who was suffering from cenconma, which is the formation under the pupil of the eye of an opaque tissue which renders the sufferer totally blind. Dr. Fox, who had witnessed one of the operations at Giessen, decided to treat her by the same method. A piece of the pupil of the eye, one-sixth of an inch in width, and the fourteenth of an inch thick, was cut out, and replaced by a piece exactly the same size, from the eye of a rabbit, and the eye was then covered by the eyelids and bandaged. The operation was skilfully done, and it is believed that the patient will be able to see. If, happily, that should be the result, the achievement will be one of the greatest in the history of surgical science, and many poor, sightless creatures will rejoice in hope. One can but wish that the spiritually blind who hear of the cures wrought by the Great Physician of souls were similarly moved, and would come to Him and receive their sight. (John 9: 39.)

A Convict Marriage was Celebrated in Atlanta, Ga., on April 30. Several years ago two convicts in the State Penitentiary—a young woman of twenty years, and a man of thirty, were brought in contact in the course of prison duties. They grew attached to each other, and eventually a sincere and ardent love sprang up between them. It had a remarkable effect on both; they changed from being disobedient and unruly to model convicts. The man was a carpenter by trade, and he made himself useful about the prison and won the good opinion of the officials by his cheerfulness and industry. The woman also listened to the appeals of Christian visitors, and her penitence and evident anxiety to receive the forgiveness of God convinced them that her heart was changed. They made an appeal to the Governor on her behalf, and eventually secured a pardon for her. She was received into the Christian Home in Peters Street, where she led an exemplary life. On April 28, her lover's term expired, and he immediately sought her out, and with the consent of the manager of the Home, they were married. It may be hoped that the love which transformed their characters in the Penitentiary will continue to exercise its potent influence over them and keep them from returning to their evil ways. They will be safe from such a relapse if their hearts are filled with a still holier love for Him who died to deliver Satan's prisoners. (II Cor. 5: 14, 15.)

A Thrilling Adventure with a Panther is reported in the *Evening Wisconin*. It states that a few nights ago a farmer while driving home from Hot Springs, noticed that his horses while passing through the woods became uneasy. Finally they came to a standstill, and showing symptoms of fear, would advance no farther. The farmer whistled to his large and trusty bulldog, which was but a short distance in advance of him. Just as the dog started to return, in obedience to the alarm, his owner heard a noise in the branches of a tree which stood near the roadside, and when the dog had got within twenty-five yards of the wagon, he was pounced upon by a hugh panther, which leaped from the tree upon him. A terrible fight ensued. The farmer's team, became frightened and ran home with him. As soon as he reached his home he tethered his team, ran into the house, picked up his Winchester rifle, and returned to the spot to take a hand in the battle. He found his faithful dog torn to pieces, but no signs of the panther were visible. He probably owed his life to the courage and valor of his faithful hound who had died in his defence. The poor animal will always have a place in his grateful recollection, for men appreciate a devotion which saves their lives. It is marvellous that an infinitely greater love so seldom fills their hearts when they hear of One who to save their souls from eternal death met their enemy in deadly conflict and laid down His life in their cause. (Heb. 2: 14,15.)

BRIEF NOTES.

Vital statistics just published show that the annual death rate in New York city is about 26 to every 1,000 persons. In London it is a little less than 20.

At the fifth annual meeting of the American McAll Association, recently held in Brooklyn, it was stated that the contributions to the mission from America last year were $38,856.41.

Ground has been broken for a new Congregational church in Northfield, Mass. It will have a seating capacity of over a thousand. Mr. Moody has contributed $5,000; Mr. Sankey, $1,000.

Dr. Rainsford, rector of St. George's Protestant Episcopal Church, this city, states that the church, which is wholly free, is receiving more, by $10,000 a year, than when it depended on pew rents.

Joseph Rabinowitz, the Christian reformer among the Jews, has recently been warned by the Russian Government to cease from his missionary labors among his brethren in the South and West of Russia.

The condition of the Rev. J. Denham Smith, the successful revivalist, is said to have improved, some of the more serious expressions of his malady having disappeared, and this has been accompanied with a corresponding rally in his strength.

On the second birthday anniversary of the baby King of Spain, 12,000 meat pies, as many cakes and oranges, and 1,500 pounds of sweets, have been ordered to regale the school children of Madrid, who will sing hymns and odes to their young sovereign.

Dr. George F. Pentecost's revival services at Schenectady, N. Y., were remarkably blest. They were held in the Opera House, which, though it has a seating capacity of 2,000, was not large enough to hold all who came. The number of converts was enormous.

A clue to the cause of the distress in London is given by a lady who has taken a prominent part in the efforts to relieve the sufferers. She says that 150,000 of them have come before the board, and of the whole number only two were abstainers from strong drink.

The revival services of Messrs Crossley and Hunter at Belleville, Ontario, have produced a profound effect. So widespread are the interest and religious feeling manifested that balls have been stopped, and the engagements of theatrical troupes cancelled, owing to the sparse attendance, and lack of interest taken in them.

Dr. L. W. Munhall and Prof. and Mrs. D. B. Towner are at present conducting a series of meetings in St. Paul, Minn. A thorough organization of the churches of the city was made prior to their arrival, a choir of two hundred voices collected, and a band of Christian workers trained to assist in the services. A week is to be spent in each of four central churches.

Mr. William Noble has been spending a few days in Paris on his way home from a trip through Southern France and Northern Spain. He spoke at the Y. M. C. A., where he enrolled a number of pledges and put the blue ribbon on the superintendent of the Paris City Mission. He also addressed a meeting of Mr. McAll's workers, and spoke at Miss De Broen's mission at Belleville.

Nicholas Carriger, one of the leading wine men of Sonoma County, Cal., recently wrote to a veteran temperance worker as follows: "I am convinced that I made a mistake when I entered into the wine and brandy business. This day I can say that all my vines, and wines, and brandy, and costly works, and wine-cellars—all would I now gladly give if I could only say just what you can to my boys and to all the children."

A cordial invitation to the World's Conference of Young Men's Christian Associations, to be held in Stockholm, Sweden, on July 21, has been extended by the King of Sweden, who takes a special interest in the proposed Conference. Any further details in regard to this Conference can be secured from the International Secretary, Mr. Richard C. Morse, at the Y. M. C. A. Building, 52 East Twenty-third Street, New York City.

Clergymen and Evangelists who will Allow Copies of the CHRISTIAN HERALD to be placed in the seats of churches, or will have them distributed at the doors, will be supplied with assorted parcels of back numbers if they will write to the Manager, 63 Bible House, New York.

CURED AT LAST.

A New Sermon by Pastor C. H. Spurgeon.

"And a woman having an issue of blood twelve years, which had spent all her living upon physicians, neither could be healed of any, came behind Him, and touched the border of His garment: and immediately her issue of blood stanched." Luke 8:43. 44.

A Sufferer and an Outcast—A Timid, Silent Seeker—I. What she had Done—Had Resolved to be Cured if she Could—Diseased Souls kept from the same Resolve—By Indifference—She Sought the Physicians—Persevered in the Treatment—Absurd Prescriptions of Ancient Times—Doctors Ceremony and Morality—Money All Gone—II. What had Come of It—A Sad Result—Yet Led to the Cure—III. What She Did at Last—The Simplest Thing—The Most Free—The Only Effectual Thing—IV. The Thing for the Convicted Sinner to Do.

THOUGH I take Luke's statement for a text, I shall constantly refer to the version of the same story which we find in Mark 5:25 to 29.

Here we have one of the Lord's hidden ones: a case not to be publicly described because of its secret sorrow. We have here a woman of few words and much shamefacedness. Her malady subjected her to grievous penalties according to the ceremonial law. There is a terrible chapter in the Book of Leviticus concerning such a case as hers. So that, in addition to her continual weakness, she was made to feel herself an outcast, under the ban of the law. This created, no doubt, great loneliness of spirit, and made her wish to hide herself out of sight. In the narrative before us she said not a word until the Saviour drew it out of her, for her own lasting good. She acted very practically and promptly, but she was

A Silent Seeker;

she would have preferred to have remained in obscurity, if so it could have been. The immediate cure of this woman is the more remarkable because it was a wayside miracle. The Saviour was on the road to restore the daughter of Jairus; this woman's healing was an extra of grace, a sort of over-splash of the great fountain of mercy. The cup of our Lord's power was full—full to the brim—and He was bearing it to the house of the ruler of the synagogue; this poor creature did but receive a drop, which He spilt on the way. The episodes of the Lord Jesus are as beautiful as the main run of His life's poem.

I. Consider, therefore, concerning this woman,

What She Had Done.

She had been literally dying for twelve years. What had she been doing? Had she resigned herself to her fate, or treated her malady as a small matter? Far from it. Her conduct is highly instructive. First, she had resolved not to die, if a cure could be had. She was evidently a woman of great determination and hopefulness. She knew that this disease of hers would cause her life to ebb away, and bring her to the grave; but she said within herself, "I will have a struggle for it. If there is a possibility of removing this plague, it shall be removed, let it cost me what it may of pain or payment." Oh, what a blessing it would be if unsaved ones here would say, each one for himself, "I am a lost soul; but if a lost soul can be saved, I will be saved!" Alas, it is not so with many! Indifference is the rule—indifference about their immortal souls! Many are sick with dire spiritual disease, but they make no resolve to have it cured; they trifle with sin and death and heaven and hell.

Insensibility has seized upon many, and a proud conceit; they are full of sin, and yet they talk of self-righteousness. They are weak, and can do nothing; yet they boast of their ability. They are not conscious of their true condition, and hence they have no mind to seek a cure. How should they desire healing when they do not believe that they are diseased? May the Holy Spirit show every unregenerate person the fatal nature of his soul's disease; for this, I trust, would lead to the making of a firm resolve to find salvation, if salvation is to be had.

Alas! many have never come to this gracious resolution, because they cherish a vain hope, and are misled by an idle dream. Some fancy that in the article of death they may cry, "God be merciful to me a sinner," and so may leap into salvation. It seems to them a very slight business to be reconciled to God. They imagine that they can be converted just when they will, and so they put it off from day to day, as if it were of no more consequence than going to shop to buy a coat or a gown. Believe me, the Word of God does not set forth the matter in this way. It tells us that even the righteous scarcely are saved, and it rouses us to strive to enter in at the strait gate. God save you from every false confidence which would prevent your being in earnest about the healing of your souls!

Let us next note, that this woman having made her resolve, adopted the likeliest means she could think of. This woman went to gentlemen who were supposed to understand the science of medicine. Was it not natural that she should look for help to their superior wisdom? She cannot be blamed for looking to the

Men of Light and Leading.

Many, in these days, do the same thing. They hear of the new discoveries of professedly cultured men, and hear their talk about the littleness of sin, and the larger hope, and the non-necessity of the new birth. Poor deceived creatures! they find in the long run that nothing comes of it; for the wisdom of man is nothing but pretentious folly. We cannot blame the woman that, being a simple soul, and anxious for healing, she went to those first who were thought to know most. Let us not, with Christ so near, go roundabout as she did, but let us touch our Lord at once.

No doubt the sufferer also tried men who had diplomas, or were otherwise authorized to act as physicians. How can you blame her for going to those who were in the succession, and had the official stamp? Many sin-sick souls nowadays are, at first, very hopeful that the ordained clergy can benefit them by their duly performed services and duly administered sacraments. At least, good men, eminent in the church, may be looked to for aid; surely these know how to deal with souls! Alas! It is vain to look to men at all, and foolish to depend on official dignity, or special repute. Some teachers do not know much about their own souls, and therefore know less about the souls of others. Vain is the help of man, be the man who he may. There is no medicine beneath the sky that can stay the palpitations of a heart which dreads the judgment to come. No earthly surgery can take away the load of sin from the conscience. No hand of priest or presbyter, prophet or philosopher, can cleanse the leprosy of guilt. The finger of God is wanted here. There is one Heal-all, one divine *Catholicon*, and only one. Happy is he that hath received this infallible balm from Jehovah Rophi—the Lord that healeth.

What perseverance that woman must have had! I am not going to say anything about our doctors nowadays; no doubt they are the most learned and skilful that can be: but in earlier times

Surgery was Murderous,

and medicines poisonous. Many of the prescriptions of those days are sickening, and yet ridiculous. I read yesterday a prescription, of our Saviour's time, warranted to cure many diseases, which consisted of *grasshopper's eggs*. These were supposed to exercise a marvellous influence, but they are no longer in the list of medicines. *The tooth of a fox* was said to possess special powers; but I noticed that one of the chief drugs of all, the most expensive, but the surest in its action, was *a nail from the finger of a man who had been hanged*. It was important that he should have been hanged; another finger-nail might have had no efficacy. Poor creatures were made to suffer most painfully by cruel medicines, which were far worse than the disease. As for surgical operations, if they had been designed to kill, they were certainly admirably arranged for their purpose. The wonder is that for twelve years poor human nature could stand out, not against the disease, but against the doctors. Brethren, the case is much the same spiritually.

Have you been to *Doctor Ceremony*? He is, at this time, the fashionable doctor. Has he told you that you must attend to form and rules? Has he prescribed you so many prayers, and so many services? Ah! many go to him, and they persevere in a round of religious observances, but these yield no lasting ease to the conscience. Have you tried *Doctor Morality*? He has a large practice, and is

A Fine Old Jewish Physician.

"Be good in outward character," says he, "and it will work inwardly, and cleanse the heart." A great many persons are supposed to have been cured by him and by his assistant, *Doctor Civility*, who is nearly as clever as his master; but I have it on good evidence that neither of them apart, nor even the two together, could ever deal with an inward disease. Do what you may, your own doings will not staunch the wounds of a bleeding heart. *Doctor Mortification* has also a select practice; but men are not saved by denying themselves until they first deny their self-righteousness. *Doctor Excitement* has many patients, but his cures seldom outlive the set of sun. *Doctor Feeling* is much sought after by tender spirits; these try to feel sorrow and remorse; but, indeed, the way of cure does not lie in that quarter. Let everything be done that can be done apart from our blessed Lord Jesus Christ, and the sick soul will be nothing bettered. You may try human remedies for the space of a lifetime, but sin will remain in power, guilt will cling to the conscience, and the heart will abide as hard as ever.

Golden Ointment.

But this woman not only thus tried the most likely means, and persevered in the use of them, but she also spent all her substance over it. That was perhaps the chief thing in ancient surgery! this golden ointment which did good to the physician, whatever became of the patient. *The most important point was to pay* the doctor. This woman's living was wasting away, as well as her life. She continued to pay, and to pay, and to pay; but she received no benefit from it all; say, rather, that she suffered more than she would have done had she kept her gold. Thus do men waste their thought, their care, their prayer, their agony, over that which is as nothing: they spend their money for that which is not bread. At last she came to her last shekel. In the end, there was an end to her means; but so long as the silver lasted, she lavished it out of the bag. What would not a man give to be saved? I never wonder that dying men give their estates to priests in the hope that they can save their souls. If gold could purchase pardon, who would withhold it? Beloved, you see where this woman was. She was in downright, desperate earnest to have her mortal malady healed, and so she spared neither her labor nor her living. In this we may wisely imitate her.

II. We have seen what the woman had done; now let us think of

What had Come of it.

We are told that she had suffered many things of many physicians. That was her sole reward for trusting and spending: she had not been relieved, much less healed; but *she had suffered*. She had endured much additional suffering through seeking a cure. That is the case with you who have not come to Christ, but, being under a sense of sin, have sought relief apart from Him. You have been trying to feel good, and to do good, that so you may be good; but the very effort has made you feel how far off you are from the goodness you so much desire. Your self-denial has excited cravings after evil, and your mortifications have given new life to your pride. Efforts after salvation made in your own strength act like the struggles of a drowning man, which sink the more surely. As the fruit of your desperate efforts, you have suffered all the more. In the end, I trust this may work for your good, but up till now it has served no healing purpose: you are now at death's door, and all your praying, weeping, church-going, and sacrament-taking do not help you one bit.

There has been this peculiarly poignant pang about it all, that

You are Nothing Bettered.

Cheerily did you hope, but cruelly are you disappointed. You cried, "I have it this time," but the bubble vanished as you grasped it. The evil of your nature, when repressed in one place, broke out in another. You dealt with the symptoms of your disease, but you did not cut off the root of the mischief: it only showed itself in another form, but it never went away. You gave up one sin only to fall into another: you watched at the front entrance, and the thief stole in at the back door. Up till now, O soul, thou hast not come to Jesus, and after all thy goings elsewhere, thou art nothing bettered.

We read of this woman, that though she suffered much, she was nothing better, but *rather grew worse*. No better after twelve years of medicine? She bought disappointment very dearly. Friend, is this your condition? You are anxious to be right, and, therefore, you are earnest in every effort to save yourself; but still you are nothing bettered. You climb a tread-mill, and are no higher after all your climbing. You drift down the river with one tide, and you float up again when it turns. Night after night you pull up in *the same old creek* that you started from. Oh, pitiful condition! Getting gray, too; becoming quite the old gentleman; and yet no nearer eternal life than when, as a lad, you used to attend the house of God, and wished to become a child of God. Nothing bettered? No;

She Grew Worse?

Fresh mischief had developed: other diseases fed upon her weakness; she was more emaciated, more lifeless, than ever. Sad result of so much perseverance! And is not that the case with some of you who are in earnest, but are not enlightened? You are working, and growing poorer as you work. There is not about you so much as there used to be of good feeling, or sincere desire, or prayerfulness, or love for the Bible, or care to hear the gospel. You are becoming more careless, more dubious, than you once were. You have lost much of your former sensitiveness. You are doing certain things now that would have startled you years ago, and you are leaving certain matters undone which once you would have thought essential. Evidently you are caught in the current, and are nearing the cataract. The Lord deliver you!

This is a sad, sad case! As a climax of it all, the heroine of our story had now spent all that she had. She could not go now to the Egyptian doctor, or to the Syrian doctor, or to the Hebrew doctor, or to the Roman doctor, or to the Greek doctor. No; now she must do without their flattering unction in the future. As for those famous medicines which raised her hopes, she can buy no more of such costly inventions. This was, perhaps, her bitterest grief: but—let me whisper it in your ear—this was the best thing that had yet happened to her; and I am praying that it may happen to some of you. At the bottom of your purse,, I trust, you will find wisdom. When we come to the end of self we come to the beginning of Christ. That last shekel binds us to the pretenders, but absolute bankruptcy sets us free to go to Him who heals diseases without money and without price. Glad enough am I when I meet with a man who is starved out of self-sufficiency. Welcome, brother! Now you are ready for Jesus. When all your own virtue has gone out of you, then shall you seek and find that virtue which goeth out of Him.

III. This brings to our notice, thirdly,

What She Did At Last.

Weaker and weaker had she become, and her purse had become lighter and lighter. She hears of Jesus of Nazareth, a man sent of God who is healing sick folk of all sorts. She hears attentively; she puts the stories together that she hears; she believes them; they have the likeness of truth about them. "Oh," says she, "there is yet another opportunity for me. I will get in the crowd, and if I can only touch the bit of blue which he wears as the border of his garment, I shall be made whole." Splendid faith! It was thought much of in her own day, and we may still more highly prize it now that faith has grown so rare.

After all, this was the simplest and easiest thing that she could do. Touch Jesus. Put out thy finger and touch the hem of His garment. The prescriptions she had purchased were long; but this was short enough. The operations performed upon her had been intricate; but this was simplicity itself. Not only was this the simplest and easiest thing for the poor afflicted one, but certainly *it was the freest and most gracious*. There was not a penny to pay. It is so this morning, dear hearer. Come, and receive grace freely. Bring no good works, no good words, no good feelings, no good resolves, as the price of pardon; come with an empty hand, and touch the Lord by faith. The good things which you desire, Jesus will give you as the result of His cure; but they cannot be the cause or the price of it. Accept His mercy as the gift of His love! Come empty handed, and receive! This is

The Only Effectual Thing.

Touch Jesus, and salvation is yours at once. Simple as faith is, it is never-failing. A touch of the fringe of the Saviour's garment sufficed: in a moment she felt in her body that she was healed of that plague. "It is twelve years ago," she said to herself, "since I felt like a living woman. I have been sinking in a constant death all this while, but now I feel my strength come back to me." Blessed be the name of the great Healer! She was exceeding glad. Tremble she did, lest it should turn out to be too good to be true; but she was most surely healed. O my dear hearer, do trust my Lord, for he will surely do for you that which none other can achieve. Leave feeling and working, and try faith in Jesus. May the Holy Spirit lead you to do so at once!

IV. And now, poor convicted sinner! here comes the driving home of the nail. Do thou as this woman did. Ask nobody about it, but do it. She did not go to Peter, James, and John, and say, "Good sirs, advise me." She did not beg from them an introduction to Jesus, but she went of her own accord, and tried for herself the virtue of a touch. You have had advising enough; now come to real work. There is too much tendency to console ourselves by conversations with godly men: let us get away from them, and speak to their Master. Talks in the inquiry-room, and chats with Christian neighbors, are all very well; but

One Touch of Jesus

would be infinitely better. I do not blame you for seeking religious advice; this may be a half-way house to call at, but do not make it the terminus. Press on till, by personal faith, you have laid hold on Jesus. Yield to the sacred impulse which is just now operating upon you. Do not say, "To-morrow may be more convenient." In this woman's case, there was the Lord before her; she longed to be healed at once, and so, come what may, into the crowd she plunged. She was so enfeebled, that one wonders how she managed to get near Him. However, there was her chance, and she seized it. There was the fringe of the Lord's mantle; out went her finger; it was all done. Oh, my friend, you have an opportunity now, by God's great grace, for you are in His house of prayer. Jesus of Nazareth passeth by at this moment. He who speaks to you is not trying to say pretty things, but he is pining to win your soul for Jesus. Oh, how I wish I could lead you to that saving touch!

O Lord, save this people! Why do you come, Sunday after Sunday, in such crowds? and why must I stand here and bleed my heart away in love to your souls? Is the sole result to be that I help you to spend an hour and a half in a sort of religious amusement? What a waste it is of my labor, and of your time, unless some gracious work is done! Oh, sirs, if you are not brought to Christ, my preaching will prove a curse to you! It appalls me to think that the preaching of the gospel will be a savor of death unto you unless it brings you life. Put not the day of grace from you. By the living God, I do implore you, trust the living Redeemer. As I shall meet you all, face to face, before the judgment-seat of Christ, I do implore and beseech you, put out the finger of faith, and trust the Lord Jesus, who is so fully worthy to be trusted. The simple trust of your heart will stay the death which now works in you. Lord, give that trust, for Jesus' sake! Amen.

GEMS FROM NEW BOOKS.

MR. BEECHER LEARNING GRAMMAR.*

THE school-book was divided into two divisions in Grammar, under leaders on either side, and the grammatical reviews were contests for superiority, in which it was vitally important that every member should be perfected. Henry [Mr. Beecher] was generally the latest choice, and fell on his side as an unfortunate accession, being held more amusing than profitable on such occasions. The fair leader on one of those occasions took the boy aside to a private apartment, to put into him, with female tact and insinuation, those definitions and distinctions on which the honor of the class depended.

"Now, Henry, *A* is the indefinite article, you see, and must be used only with a singular noun. You can say *A Man*, but you can't say *A Men*, can you?" "Yes, I can say amen too," was the rejoinder. "Father says it always at the end of his prayers."

"Come, Henry, now don't be joking! Now, decline *He*. Nominative He, possessive His, objective Him. You see His is in the possessive. You can say His book, not Him book." "Yes, I say Hymn-book, too," said the scholar, with a quizzical twinkle. Each one of these sallies made his young Mentor laugh, which was the victory he wanted. "But now, Henry, do be serious; just attend to the active and passive voice. Now, I strike, is active, you see, because if you strike you *do* something. But I am struck is passive, because if you are struck you don't do anything, do you?" "Yes I do—I strike back again."

He Resolves to be a Sailor.

He made up his little bundle, walked the wharf, talked with sailors and captains, hovered irresolute on the verge of voyages, never quite able to grieve his father by a sudden departure. At length he wrote a letter announcing to a brother that he could and would no longer remain at school; that he had made up his mind for the sea; that if not permitted to go, he should go without permission. This letter was designedly dropped where his father picked it up. Dr. Beecher put it in his pocket and said nothing for the moment, but the next day asked Henry to help him saw wood. Now the wood-pile was the Doctor's favorite debating ground, and Henry felt complimented by the invitation, as implying manly companionship.

"Let us see," said the doctor; "Henry, how old are you?" "Almost fourteen!" "Bless me! how boys do grow! why it's almost time to be thinking what you are going to do. Have you ever thought?" "Yes; I want to go to sea." "To sea! of all things! well, well! after all, why not? Of course you don't want to be a common sailor. You want to get into the navy?" "Yes, sir, that's what I want." "But not merely as a common sailor, I suppose?" "No, sir; I want to be a midshipman, and after that a commodore." "I see," said the Doctor cheerfully. "Well, Henry, in order for that you know you must begin a course of mathematics and study navigation and all that." "Yes, sir, I'm ready." "Well then, I will send you up to Amherst, next week, to Mount Pleasant, and then you'll begin your preparatory studies, and if you are well pre-

* From "A Biography of Rev. Henry Ward Beecher; By William C. Beecher and Rev. Samuel Scoville, assisted by Mrs. Henry Ward Beecher; 713 Pages, with numerous portraits and illustrations. Price, $3.00, cloth. Published by *Charles L. Webster & Company*, New York.

Cornelia Sorabji, the Indian Girl Graduate.

Isaac Bourne's Birthday Motto.

pared I presume I can make interest to get you an appointment." And so he went to Mount Pleasant, at Amherst, Mass.; and Dr. Beecher said shrewdly: "I shall have that boy in the ministry yet."

A Providential $100 Bill.

While Henry and Charles were at college, Dr. and Mrs. Beecher were very much straitened for money. One evening particularly they were talking about it, and did not know what they should do to keep the boys along. At last Dr. Beecher said: "Well, the Lord always has taken care of me, and I am sure He always will." The mother lay awake and cried. She cried because she did not see how they should get along; but what most troubled her was, that her husband had so much faith and she had not any. The next morning was Sabbath morning. Some one rang at the door and a letter was handed in, containing a one hundred dollar bill and no name. They did not know then who gave it, but learned afterward that it was Mr. Homes—a thank-offering at the conversion of one of his children.

CORNELIA SORABJI:

The First Girl-Graduate of West India.

MUCH interest has been aroused in the young lady whose portrait appears on this page, from the fact that she was the first lady in India to avail herself of the advantages of a University education. She entered the Deccan College at Poona in 1884, and like all pioneers had much to contend with. She felt keenly her isolated position among upwards of 300 men, who, with the exception of two Englishmen and a few Parsees, were all Hindus, and who naturally looked with no kindly eye upon this innovation. It is needless to dwell upon the annoyances to which she was subjected, or to the unfriendly criticisms among her own countrymen on her unprecedented course, but, with the goal of her ambition always in view, she went bravely on, winning golden opinions from Principal and Professors alike.

To all who have watched her course with interest, not unmixed with curiosity, it is no small gratification to find that she has, even at this early period of her life—for she is only just out of her teens—done her part in elevating the position of her countrywomen. Her brave, high-souled, gentle behaviour and influence, cannot fail to raise the character and ability of women in the estimation of the Parsee and Hindo young men with whom she daily came in contact. Among her own sex, her example has already borne fruit, two Parsee ladies and one Jewess having sought for admission into the Colleges in Bombay and Poona. In Miss Sorabji's case no concessions were made on account of her sex. She studied Latin in common with the men. She was "top of her year" in the previous examination, has held a scholarship each year of her course, was "Hughlings Scholar" in 1885, having passed head of the University in English, "Havelock prizeman" the end of the same year, being top of the Deccan College in English, has taken honors each time, and in the final B. A. examination of the Bombay University, held in November, 1887, she was one of the four in the entire Presidency, and the only student from her own College, who suceeded in gaining First Class honors. Miss Sorabji is a Parsee Christian lady, the daughter of a native missionary.

ISAAC BOURNE'S BIRTHDAY MOTTO.

(See Illustration.)

WHO has not seen homes in which two mighty influences are at work—the children growing up in doubt whether they shall follow the example of their pious mother, or the example of a careless, scoffing father? Isaac Bourne's home was one of that kind. He was a hard worker and had won a good position as foreman in the employ of a firm of contractors. In his youth he had been a scholar in the Sunday-school, and though never identifying himself with a church, had been regular in attendance on religious service. Latterly, however, he had grown careless in such matters, and from association with infidels, had contracted a habit of sneering at the Bible and religious teachers, much to his godly wife's distress.

"What book is that you have there?" he said one Sunday evening, as his two little girls hastily left the supper-table to resume their examination of a little volume which seemed to be regarded as a great treasure.

"Only a birthday-text book," said the younger: "Mamie's Sunday-school teacher gave it to her."

"What's a birthday-text-book?" asked the father. "I never heard of such a thing."

"It's a book with a text for every day in the year," said Mamie, "and we find out where our birthdays are and then we have a text for a motto. See, here's mine: 'Wisdom is more precious than rubies.'"

"That's sense," said Isaac, "though I suppose it is a Bible text. It's a pity religious folks don't remember it. They'd be of more use if they did. Let me have a look at the book. See, my birthday is March 25; now let us see what sort of a motto they give me." Isaac turned over the pages till he found the date, and read: "Be not deceived; God is not mocked; for whatsoever a man soweth that shall he also reap." Isaac was silent. He changed color as he handed the book back to Mamie, and leaving his cup of coffee only half drunk went out.

Mrs. Bourne had not been unobservant while clearing the table; she heard the text read, and noticed her husband's embarrassment and his sudden departure. She knew from his manner that he was deeply moved, and going up-stairs to her bedroom, she fell on her knees and prayed for him as she often did, but this time with a spark of hope in her breast.

Isaac meanwhile was walking out in the fields to think it out, as he said. He knew well enough that in the natural world the crop was like the seed, and he had had enough experience in managing the rough gang of men under his control to be aware that in the moral world the same rule held good. Young fellows who took to drink and evil ways were no good in the work, and could not be got rid of too soon. What if the law held in the spiritual world! "Whatsoever a man soweth," Ah! what a harvest would be his in that case! The big strong man actually trembled as he thought of the life he had lived for the last ten years.

It was after ten o'clock when he once more entered his home. He had been walking and thinking all the time, and had made up his mind. The children were gone to bed and Mrs. Bourne was sitting up for him, reading the Bible, which she closed when he entered, lest it should lead him to utter one of those sneers which always cut her to the heart. There was no danger of that to-night, however.

"Wife," said Isaac, "I am going to turn over a new leaf. I guess I have been on the wrong track a considerable time. I want to get back to the old route; the times we had when we were married first. You'll have to help me, for I'm a long way out."

Ah, glad was the pious woman to avail herself of the opportunity! Knowing well his weakness and his temptations, she led him to abandon the hope of getting back by his own strength and directed him to the Source of the only power that could transform his heart and life.

RESCUING PEOPLE IN THE INUNDATIONS IN PRUSSIA.

(*See Illustration.*)

THE disastrous floods in Prussia, caused by the overflowing of the Elbe, the Oder, and the Vistula, with their tributaries, have rendered one hundred thousand people homeless, and have caused misery and immense loss of property. To the east of Berlin, and especially in the province of Posen, where the peasantry are mostly of Polish race, the destitution is severely felt, as the means of relieving it are deficient; and Her Majesty, the Empress Victoria, in her journey to that province, on purpose to see the condition of the distressed inhabitants, and to supervise the efforts of public charity, performed a a royal office which has won for her deserved applause. In the opposite direction, on the banks of the lower Elbe, between Hanover and Mecklenburg, several towns were inundated, especially Domitz and Lenzen; it was in the latter town that the scene was witnessed which is depicted in the illustration.

Rescuing People in the Inundated Districts of Germany.

Domitz, which belongs to Mecklenburg, was entirely isolated, and had all communication with the rest of the world cut off, until steamboats of the Magdeburg line arrived. Lenzen and Seedorf were so flooded that the water reached *the roofs* of the lower and smaller houses, and the first-floor windows of the others. At Eldenburg two hundred persons were drowned, and there was great loss of life in other districts; the bursting of the dykes suddenly overwhelmed the farm-houses and cottages built in the meadows below them, and many families perished, as well as much cattle. Huge blocks of drifting ice and congealed snow came down from the hills and floated to a great distance; in some instances with beasts, and even human beings, carried away upon them.

A famine is threatened in Posen, Pomerania, and Silesia, and the number of persons emigrating to America will soon be enormously increased. The alluvial lands of the Vistula are now a single field of destruction, affecting seventy-nine villages with about thirty thousand inhabitants. The whole of this vast tract about the town of Elbing, from three hundred to four hundred square miles, is under water. There is no possibility of either harvest this year or of spring cultivation, as the submerged land lies below the river and the Baltic. Experts say it will take months of labor to steam pump the water away. These alluvial soils are the best agricultural land. It has for the most part been cultivated by yeomen farmers, who were, till floods overwhelmed them, in fair circumstances.

The Emperor has handed 40,000 marks (about $10,000) from his own purse to Herr Achenbach, the head of the relief committee, who accompanied the Empress to Posen to inquire into the distress by the floods. The money is to be used for the relief of the sufferers. The Empress on her arrival in Posen was enthusiastically cheered by the people. She first visited the asylum, a large school-house where the homeless are temporarily lodged, and thence went to the Governor's house, where she took lunch. Addressing Councillor Jacobs the Empress said: "I commission you to express to all taking a helpful part in the present danger the thanks of the Emperor and myself. The calamity that has befallen you arouses our deepest sympathy, and we hope to alleviate your sufferings as far as human help can alleviate them." The persons who have been prominent in helping the sufferers by the floods were presented to the Empress, who thanked them for their efforts to alleviate the distress among the people.

MRS. TRANSOME'S PUPIL.

A SERIAL STORY.

(*Continued from page 287.*)

A Glorious Occupation.

PHILIP had been between four and five years at sea, when, one wild December evening, just as I was thanking God in my heart that he was safe ashore, and his father's ship in the Liverpool docks, Philip suddenly burst into our quiet room with an unusual vehemence, which startled both George and me.

"Quick! quick! Aunt Milly!" he cried breathlessly; "put on your bonnet and cloak in a moment, and come with me! I've a cab waiting at the door. Come quickly; for it is a wild night, and people may die out of doors, if they do not find shelter soon. Wrap yourself up warmly, my dear."

Of late Philip had assumed a masterful tone towards me, which amused me; and now he hurried me like a whirlwind out of the sitting-room, and up-stairs to my chamber-door, while he continued speaking, without giving me an opportunity for asking a question. He ran back to George while I dressed myself; but he stood at the open door, and at the first sight of me closed it, and, as if eager not to lose a moment, hastened through the hall to the cab at the door. He helped me in, sprang in after me, and the next instant we were rattling along the street, through the storm of rain and wind.

"But where are you taking me, Philip?" I asked, with increasing anxiety.

He did not answer; and there was something in his silence, and the wildness of the night that stirred me to the heart. A faint, vague dread awoke within me. During the whole of my stagnant, uneventful life I had never been out of doors in such a night and such a storm as this. The streets were almost deserted, and sudden, violent gusts of wind roared along them, with driving showers of rain and hail. Great masses of black clouds, torn into long and ragged pennons, drifted across the dark sky. I wished he would tell me where we were going, and what he wanted me to do; but I felt almost afraid of asking him.

"My dear little Aunt Milly!" was all he said; "the best little woman in the world!"

We stopped at length before a dark and narrow passage, not far from the river: for I could just catch the gleam of distant lights twinkling across its troubled current. He led me down this passage to an open space, beyond, where I could distinguish the strip of sky overhead only by the little rifts in the black clouds which covered it. He paused for a moment, and listened beside an old door, but there was not a sound to be heard; and with a hurried exclamation of fear, he lifted the latch, and opened it. There was no glimmer of light; but Philip drew out a little pocket-lantern from under his rough seaman's coat, and turned it full upon the interior of the place.

It was a mere shed; and one corner of the wall had either given way, or it was in the course of being pulled down, for the wind was blowing, and the rain and hail beating in through a great gap. Under the wall farthest from this wide opening, and upon the damp, unpaved floor, there was crouching a figure, upon which the light of Philip's lantern shone fully. It was that of a miserable girl, very young, as I knew afterwards, but old-looking to my eyes, that had never seen a face like hers; the hollow cheeks were painted, and the thin, wasted arms and shoulders were hardly covered by the dingy finery that could not shield her from the storm. Her wild, bright eyes glared at me fiercely; or, rather, they gazed past me, at Philip. I thrust myself between him and her, as if to hide her from him, with a vague sense of aversion and terror in my heart.

"Aunt Milly!" said his pleasant, pitiful voice behind me, "this is work for you, not me, to do."

"Philip!" I cried, half angrily, turning round to look into his face. It was pale and sorrowful, so as I had never seen it before, with an expression of deep pain and pity in his eyes, as they looked back at me earnestly. Yet it seemed to me, in spite of its sadness and pain, almost like the face of an angel.

"Save her!" he said, "God sent me to save her from the river; and he sends you now to save her from sin. I give her into your hands."

"Leave us," I said. I could not bear to see him so near to her, or know that her eyes were fastened upon him. Yet when he was gone I did not know what to do. The terrible, painted face looked up at me with the sullenness of despair, yet with a dumb pleading in the solemn eyes that was irresistible. I saw that her poor, tawdry clothing was drenched with rain, or perhaps with the troubled waters of the river, and that she was shivering violently. A short, dry cough shook her. We gazed at one another in painful silence. "God help me!" I cried, in my own heart; "if I cannot love her, I can do nothing for her." Then I came to know, as I never knew before, that Christ Himself could not save us from our sins, if He did not love us with a love that passeth knowledge. Love alone wins the victory over sin. I drew nearer to the crouching girl. I laid my hand, which had never touched any one like her, upon her forehead, and found it burning with fever. The fierce, questioning eyes were fixed upon me, without blenching an instant.

"Will you come home with me?" I asked gently.

"Your own home?" she said.

"Yes, with me," I answered; "come. You shall have some food first, and a night's rest; and then we will talk together."

But the girl bent down her head till it almost touched my feet, hiding it from me. "Not your home!" she repeated, sobbing.

"Yes," I said; "there is a little room inside mine. You shall sleep there; and to-morrow you shall tell me all."

"You ought not to have me," she cried; "you never would, if you knew all."

"There is no need for me to know," I answered; "our Lord Jesus Christ knows it, yet He sends me to take you home."

Perhaps, I thought, He will let me take her to another home some day, in His Father's home, where she has the same right to enter that I have. I lifted the miserable girl from the ground, though she made a feeble effort to withstand me; and I drew her cold hand through my arm. The storm beat vehemently against us as I opened the door! but Philip had been standing outside in the rain and hail, and without uttering a word, he led the way to the street, and put us both into the cab, where the girl sank down on the floor, and hid her face in the folds of my dress.

The little room, where Philip had slept when a child, did not need much preparation, and before an hour was gone by, the poor, forlorn, lost girl was sleeping there, with the painted cheeks washed clean, and the feverish head resting peacefully on the pillow. The last thing, before I went to bed myself, I stole in softly to look at her, shading the candle with my hand, as I had been wont to do when my little Philip was lying there. When I came away, I opened my Bible, and read with misty eyes, before which the words swam confusedly, the story of the woman who "stood at the feet of Jesus, behind Him, weeping, and began to wash His feet with her tears, and did wipe them with the hairs of her head, and kissed His feet, and anointed them with ointment." "Wherefore," said the Lord, "her sins, which are many, are forgiven: for she loved much; but to whom little is forgiven, the same loveth little."

But the next morning the girl was sullen, and would say nothing except that she must go, and she could not live the life we led. I reasoned with her, and laid before her the awful death from which Philip had rescued her the night before, and the remorse which would again drive her to self-destruction. She listened, and shuddered, and wept; yet she persisted that she must go—the stillness and quiet of our life would kill her. I seemed to have no power to cast out the wayward and sullen spirit that had entered into her. What was I to do! Must I summon Philip to speak to her? I shrank, why I hardly knew, from that.

Then all at once a light broke in upon my perplexity, shining down the years that had gone by, as though they had been years of long training for some special work God would have us do for Him. There was my life of monotony, and separation from those ties most women have, and George's years of pain, and slowly purifying chastisement. Now Philip had guided us into the field, white unto the harvest, where we two, consecrated by suffering, might reap, and receive wages, and gather fruit unto eternal life, until we should be called to rejoice together with our Lord.

No; Philip was not the one to win the stubborn girl back to God. But I could take her to George. Without telling her where we were going, I bade her come with me. I can see her now—the weary young creature, standing on the threshold, and peering forward with searching, hollow eyes into his room. And his face worn and wasted with pain, and his thin hair white as snow, and his hand stretched out to her, as if he knew why I brought her to him, and needed no word of explanation.

"Come," he said, in a tone as if he were speaking to some wayward child, "come and talk to me, and let us see what we can do to get right again."

The girl stepped softly into the room, her face changed from stubbornness to pity. I heard him ask her to give him a draught of water, and to lower the blinds for him; and she did so with womanly gentleness, moving as quietly as I could have done. Then I waited no longer; for I saw there was a link between them there could never be between her and me. It may be that it was the travel-stained feet, and the unanointed head of the Lord, that first stirred hope in the heart of the woman that was a sinner. There was something that even she could do for Him.

How happy we were that evening! Captain John Champion's sunburnt face wore a look of great content. Philip whistled gayly as he wandered about the house and garden. George lay upon his sofa, glad at heart, for he had found work to do for God and his fellow-creatures. And I felt that life had new possibilities, and could never again sink into an insignificant monotony.

I remember that when Captain John Champion left us to go to his lodgings, which were near at hand, he put both his hands on Philip's shoulders, and looked into his eyes with a steadfast, profound look of love.

"God bless thee, my lad!" he said. "Never was father better pleased with his son!"

Yes; that was our work, given at last directly into our hands. It seemed strange to me at first, and I shrank from it a little; but it was never strange to George. There was with him some unseen power, which never failed of victory. After awhile we were compelled to take a house near to us, near enough for his influence to be felt in it. Other persons, who had the same work at heart, joined themselves to us; and before long we found ourselves too busy for life to be monotonous, or pain unendurable.

Philip was still with his father upon the sea, when his uncle's great fortune fell to him as heir-at-law. I knew of it some weeks before he did, for he had just set sail when his uncle died, and could not be recalled. I occupied myself, in such spare moments as I had, in building castles in the air for him, as I was wont to do when he was a clever boy at school.

I should like to have seen him when he first heard the news of his inheritance; but this could not be, for a letter from the lawyer found him at one of the ports they touched at, where they expected news from us. So I did not see him in the first flush of his change of fortune. When he reached home, seven weeks later, there was no difference in him that I could discover.

"You are a rich man now, Philip," I said, after I had kissed him, and held him near to me for a minute or two, scanning his face closely.

"Yes," he answered, "and I am glad of it."

"You can become whatever you please now," I said, with a thrill of exultation, for I wanted all the world to know what he was; "you will become a great man, and make yourself a famous name."

"No," he answered, so quietly that I felt checked and quieted also, "I can do nothing but what God has chosen for me. This money does not set me free from the work He has given me to do."

"What do you mean?" I asked. "This great fortune changes your position and circumstances altogether. You cannot remain a mate on board a merchant vessel; that would be absurd with wealth like yours. Remember, it brings its own responsibilities and duties."

"It brings no duty greater than that I am already fulfilling," said Philip, "you forget my father cannot live except on the sea; and that no one can take my place with him. The chief difference my uncle's money could make to us, if it were ten times as much, would be that our cabins might be more luxuriously fitted up. The sea and the wind care little whether one is rich or poor; there are the same storms and the same risks for us seamen."

"But, Philip!" I exclaimed.

"Well," he said, smiling, "there is my father in one scale, my fortune in the other. Which is to kick the beam, Aunt Milly? No, no. I gave up my profession for his sake, and it is a light matter to give up this. But I am glad to be rich, too; for if any whim or fancy should come into this dear head, I can gratify it to the utmost. Tell me what my money shall do for you?"

But it could not do anything for me to compensate for the disappointment I suffered in seeing him push aside the golden opportunities offered to him. My brother upheld him in his resolution. I know now that George and he, in their close friendship, had climbed nearer up to God than I, and looked down, as though they were already sitting in heavenly places with Christ Jesus, upon the glittering accidents of time, which dazzled my eyes with their lustre. Captain John Champion sided with me, and at times poured into my ear his bitter regrets at being a hindrance to his son's career. But there was no remedy for it; none that we could see. We never saw a cloud on Philip's sunny face, nor heard a syllable of dissatisfaction with his lot. If he felt any, the thought of our Lord in His uncongenial work checked it. What then was of gloom, and of natural disappointment, was fought out in loneliness, with no eye to witness but his Master's.

One thing would prosper from his wealth, that was certain. Our work would no more be limited for want of funds. He made, too, an arrangement that was good for us all. One evening, before he went away again, after all the law-business connected with his inheritance was settled, he found me weary, rather with the anxieties than with the labor of our work, which was increasing almost beyond my strength. I had good assistants under me, but not one who could share the special cares crowding upon me. He stood looking at me that evening with a very thoughtful face.

"Aunt Milly," he said, "you seem scarcely older than when I came to you nearly twenty years ago."

That was true; for I had had no girlhood, and his life had brought back youth and hope and gladness to mine. I hardly felt older than when he was a child, standing at my knee to say his lessons.

"But you will soon be old if this goes on," he continued. "I must find a mother for your girls."

"I wish you would," I said, almost despondently.

"I will coax Mrs. Transome to come," he answered; "she's lonely in her little place, now Transome is gone, and she will soon enter heart and soul into our work here. Don't suppose she is too old; she is a sharp, active, little woman; besides, what you want is not another person to work, but some one to share your anxiety. You must recollect I am a rich man now, and what money can buy I can pay for."

"Money cannot buy what I want," I said.

"No; you want Mrs. Transome," he went on, "and she will come. She will trot about the house, and give a kind word to this one and that; and they'll learn to look upon her as a kind of mother, with her bright, natty, old-fashioned ways, and her pleasant face. Wouldn't such a woman be a comfort to you, Aunt Milly?"

"I think so," I answered, yet doubtfully; but he would not heed the hesitation in my tone.

"She shall come," he said. "I will set about it at once. We must set apart a little room for her own; and you'll find it will become a haven for the girls in their worst moments. Yes; we must have Mrs. Transome; the home is not complete without her."

When Philip had any idea like that in his head, he could not rest till it was worked out. The next day the little room was chosen; and the day after it was so furnished that you felt, as you put your foot into it, that it was the very place where an old woman would find herself at home and comfortable. He hurried down to Lancashire, and before a week was over he brought Mrs. Transome back in triumph.

(To be Concluded.)

JESUS IN GETHSEMANE.

By Mrs. M. Baxter.

S. S. Lesson for May 20, Matt. 26: 31-46. Golden Text, Heb. 5: 8.

Jesus Singing—Conscious of His Approaching Agony and Death—Supported by His Loving Confidence in His Father—His Veneration for the Written Word—The Betrayal Predicted—Peter's Self-Confidence—Self a Broken Reed—Jesus Pressed by the World's Sin—The Witnesses Prepared by the Transfiguration—The Vicarious Suffering—His Prayer Heard—Strengthened for Propitiation—Failure of the Disciples.

AFTER Jesus had commemorated the Passover with His disciples, at the Last Supper, they sang a hymn, probably one of the Psalms, which were in special use at the Passover season. Jesus had been, so to speak, anticipating the commemoration of His own death, in that last supper and first communion. To a carnal mind there was nothing to sing about, but Jesus was the great pioneer of all renounced wills. He came down from Heaven, not to do His own will, but the will of Him that sent Him. (John 6: 38.) A renounced will leaves the heart at liberty to praise; a renounced will is never crossed, never disappointed. It says:

"Ill that He blesses is our good:
And unblest good is ill:
And all is right that seems most wrong,
If it be His sweet will."

Thus they sang a hymn. There is always something wrong with a heart which cannot praise God; it is not in full health. Just because, in His every step towards the cross, Jesus was pleasing His Father, He could, in the midst of His deep suffering, sing a hymn. But while in peace as regarded Himself, even at such an hour, Jesus spoke with sadness to His disciples. They went out into the Mount of Olives, a place consecrated by the prayers and tears and teachings of Jesus. He spoke prophetically: "All ye shall be offended because of Me this night, for it is written, I will smite the Shepherd, and the sheep of the flock shall be scattered abroad,"

For it is Written,

"Jesus, though He was the Son of God, did not give special, personal revelations as His authority for what He said, but He spoke with absolute certainty of the fulfilment of what was written. Oh, how daring is the assumption of those who exalt what they suppose to be direct revelations above the written and inspired word of God!

Peter, the ever ready man of impulse, answered Him, "Though all men shall be offended because of Thee, yet will I never be offended." And Peter meant it, and believed all he said. He believed in his own integrity, his own devotion and zeal and love, and thought it was to be counted on; but Peter little knew, or little understood, the strain to which it would be put. How many have we known who have yielded themselves, as far as they knew, to the Lord, and believed themselves utterly incapable of ever being angry again, or ever feeling proud or envious or light or unkind; and yet, in a time of sore temptation, the very sins from which they have believed and asserted they were saved, have returned again upon them, and they have been broken-hearted and despairing.

Self is but a Broken Reed,

and cannot be relied on. But when, in the full consciousness of our own weakness and liability to sin, we trust the Lord to keep us, we *do* experience the blessed truth, "None of them that trust in Him shall be desolate." (Ps. 34: 22.) Jesus could see far into the future, and with His prophetic eye looking on into the next few hours, He said, "Verily, I say unto thee, that this night, before the cock crow, thou shalt deny me thrice." Peter knew Jesus as little as he knew himself, and he took upon himself to contradict his Master flatly, and say, "Though I should die with Thee, yet will I not deny Thee." He could not believe anything bad about himself. We never know God until we are

Thoroughly Disappointed With Ourselves,

and come to expect nothing more from ourselves, but everything from God. Oh, what a comfort it is to know that He knows the very worst of us, and *yet* loves us, yet trusts us, yet uses us, yet desires that we should be one with Him, as He is one with the Father! Our safety is not in something in *us* that we can count on, but it is in His keeping power.

It was *then*, just at the very hour when the foremost of the disciples manifested so little understanding of the truth, at the hour too in which there was a strife as to which of them should be the greatest (Luke 22: 24), that "Jesus came to Gethsemane." Gethsemane means *an oil press*; and truly Jesus was to be pressed like the olive berries with the weight of a world's sin. He knew all that was coming upon Him, and said to the disciples, "Sit ye here, while I go and pray yonder." Although He was God, yet Jesus as man began everything with prayer. How often we have failed in something which we have undertaken, because we did not first wait to ask and obtain the wisdom strength, grace, or resources which we needed for the occasion; and on the other hand, when we *have* recognized and acted on the knowledge of our absolute dependence upon Him, how wonderfully have we been carried through indescribable troubles!

And He took with Him Peter and the two sons of Zebedee: the same disciples who had witnessed the first resurrection from the dead by the hand of Jesus, and the same who had been witnesses of the transfiguration. We receive grace for grace, i. e., to prepare for more grace, and knowledge *for* knowledge. What we know of God makes us capable of and fits us to know more still. Thus the disciples who had been nearest to Him in His glory, were those who could be trusted to witness His agony. Jesus began to be

Sorrowful and Very Heavy.

This was unlike Jesus. No burden of conscience, no conflict of will, no murmuring against His Father, darkened the spirit or clouded the brow of Jesus. He had no remorse for the past, no gloomy forebodings for the future, to make Him "very heavy." But he was now, as the Son of man, as the Man of men, as the Representative of all mankind, to enter into the shadow. Jeremiah, in his Lamentations, speaks prophetically of the sufferings of Jesus. "See, O Lord, and consider: for I am become vile. Is it nothing to you, all ye that pass by? behold, and see if there be any sorrow like unto my sorrow, which is done unto me, wherewith the Lord hath afflicted me in the day of His fierce anger." (Lam. 1: 11, 12.) Sorrows which were not His own, but man's; sins which He knew not, for He "knew no sin" (II Cor. 5: 21); shame which we sinners had brought upon ourselves; remorse for sins not His own. All these, were adopted sufferings of Jesus in that hour. Sin and all its consequences lay heavy upon Him. It was more than human strength could stand, and He said to His disciples, "My soul is exceeding sorrowful, *even unto death*." Jesus never exaggerated, He felt death creeping over Him, and He had not yet fulfilled His mission, and carried our sins to the cross. He made one request to the disciples, "Tarry ye here, and watch with Me."

"He went a little farther"—He must be alone—and cried, "O, My Father, if it be possible, let this cup pass from Me! nevertheless, not as I will, but as Thou wilt." Was the prayer answered? Was he spared in Gethsemane when death crept over Him, that He might expiate our sins in Gethsemane? Surely, yes. "Who, in the days of His flesh, when He had offered up prayers and supplications, with strong crying and tears, unto Him that was able to save Him from death, and *was* heard in that He feared" (Heb. 5: 7): *was* saved from death, *was* strengthened by an angel in Gethsemane (Luke 22: 43), that He might fully do His work upon the cross. He did not shrink from suffering; with Him it was an understood thing from the foundation of the world, that He should be the Lamb slain; had He died in Gethsemane, it would have been

A Martyrdom, but not a Propitiation.

He was not yet judged, not yet condemned. God had laid upon Him our sins, but man had not yet sealed Him as the sacrifice, by executing the Holy One of Israel. Yet even before the prayer was heard, before the angel strengthened Him, Jesus yielded up His will, even about redeeming the world, and said, "O, My Father, if this cup may not pass from Me, except I drink it, Thy will be done." The last request which Jesus made of His disciples before He suffered, was disregarded. Instead of watching with Him, they were asleep. The mightiest battle which ever took place on earth was being fought, and they were all unconscious! He said to Peter, "What, could ye not watch with Me *one* hour?" Thou, Peter, who hast declared thou couldst go with Me to prison and to death, couldst thou not watch *one* hour? Oh how soon human nature fails! "Watch and pray," the Master said, "lest ye fall into temptation; the spirit, indeed, is willing, but the flesh is weak." What is this? An excuse? And made for the sleeping disciples at the very hour when the bloody sweat was rolling in drops from every pore? Could Jesus *so* forget Himself for others! O wondrous, unutterable love!

He went away the second time and prayed, as we have seen, and a second time He found the disciples sleeping. This time He said no words to them, but went back to speak the same words to His Father. "Then cometh He to His disciples, and saith unto them, Sleep on, now, and take your rest: behold, the hour is at hand, and the Son of Man is betrayed into the hands of sinners. Arise, let us be going; behold he is at hand that doth betray Me." The first phase of His sufferings—that which took place alone with God—was over; the outward aspect, when He should be a spectacle to men and angels, was yet to come. Oh how

We Need our Gethsemane

before every cross! Oh how we need to settle matters alone with God before we are set in the front of the battle! Now Jesus was ready for the cross; now He could face men and devils as the Sin-bearer; now He who was Life itself could go through death without shrinking. But the disciples? Oh how they failed at the supreme moment! Had they been faithful in Gethsemane, they would probably not have forsaken Him on His way to the cross. The Lord teach us to watch with Him, and so to be ready for whatsoever shall come upon us. If *we* fail to watch and pray, we shall surely fall into temptation, as the disciples did when they forsook Him and fled.

"THOU WILT GUIDE ME."

PSALMS XXXII. 8.-XLVIII. 14.-LXXIII. 24. ISAIAH LVIII. 11.

Thou wilt guide me, kind and gentle Father,
Through this life, stormy, wild;
I ask not for its gayest joys, but rather
That I may be Thy child.

I cannot go alone, unlov'd, untended,
Through life's untrodden way,
For oft into forbidden paths I've wended,
And still may go astray.

My future journey looks so dark and dreary,
Its hills so steep and long;
But oh, it's sweet when very faint and weary,
To lean upon the Strong.

And though I cannot see a step before me—
Though clouds my pathway hide—
I fear not while Thy gentle love shines o'er me,
My kind, unerring Guide!

And so I close my eyes to other voices,
And listen unto Thine:
My spirit drinks Thy counsels, and rejoices,
Tasting of life Divine.

Then lead me on, dear Saviour, in Thy kindness,
Through paths Thy feet have worn,
Unspotted by all this world's sin and blindness,
Into that glorious bourne,

Where seraphs, crowned with glory will receive me,
And take me to Thy breast,
No more to *disobey, forget*, or *grieve* Thee,
But bathe in perfect rest.

J. E. JEWETT, Publisher, 77 Bible House, New York, will furnish the above poem in leaflet form at twenty cents per hundred. *A Sample Packet* of 50 leaflets assorted (no two alike), will be sent post-paid, for ten cents. Postage stamps taken.

X

THE CHRISTIAN HERALD AND SIGNS OF OUR TIMES.

Vol. XI., No. 20. Office, 63 Bible House, N. Y. THURSDAY, MAY 17, 1888. Annual Subscription, $1.50.

CONTENTS OF THIS NUMBER.

PORTRAITS AND LIVES OF SIR WILFRID LAWSON, REVS. J. T. WIGNER, CANON ELLISON, AND C. H. SPURGEON.
OBSCURATION. Dr. Talmage's Sermon Last Sunday Morning.
ANECDOTES RELATED AT RECENT EVANGELISTIC MEETINGS
PICTURE OF THE CHINESE TEMPLE OF THE EARTH AT PEKIN.
SCENES AT THE SECOND ADVENT. By Rev. Nathaniel Starkey.
A Victim Rescued—An African Chief's Dilemma—An Idol Beheaded—In a Calcutta Orphanage—A Widow's Help in Nice.
LITTLE JEMMY'S FATHER. (With Illustration.)
SHE WAS NOT HID. A New Sermon by C. H. Spurgeon.
Gems from New Books: A Professor Puzzled—A Mistaken Chase of a Cow—Early Hardships.
PORTRAIT AND LIFE OF BISHOP WILLIAM TAYLOR.
MRS. TRANSOME'S PUPIL. (Concluded.)
PETER'S DENIAL. By Mrs. M. Baxter.

SIR WILFRID LAWSON, PRESIDENT OF U.K. ALLIANCE.

REV. J. T. WIGNER, VICE-PRESIDENT OF BAPTIST UNION.

REV. CANON ELLISON, CHURCH OF ENGLAND TEMPERANCE SOCIETY.

REV. C. H. SPURGEON, PASTOR OF METROPOLITAN TABERNACLE.

PROMINENT SPEAKERS AT THE RELIGIOUS ANNIVERSARIES IN LONDON.

SIR WILFRID LAWSON.

The Prohibition Leader in England—The Lawson Family—Sir Wilfrid Born in 1829—Succeeds to the Title in 1867—Elected to Parliament in 1859—Introduces his Permissive Bill in 1864—Carries his Local Option Resolution in 1880—Popularity as a Speaker—Remarks at Mr. Spurgeon's Tabernacle.

PROMINENT among the leaders of the great religious and philanthropic organizations which are just now celebrating their anniversaries in London, are the four eminent men whose portraits appear on the first page. Three of them are clergymen, and the fourth, Sir Wilfrid Lawson, is the valorous champion of the movement which in England corresponds to the Prohibition movement here. "Ye are the salt of the earth," said the Saviour, addressing His few followers, and in every age of the world such salt has been needed, and has been found. In England, as in this country, drunkenness, immorality and irreligion are corrupting society, and there is, therefore, weighty reason to honor such men as these, whose lives and teachings exercise the beneficent influence of moral salt, and to thank God for raising them up and giving them the courage and talents to perform their work.

Sir Wilfrid Lawson, *whose portrait is one of the four*, is the son of the late Sir Wilfrid Lawson, of Aspatria, Cumberland, a family which has been prominent in the county for nearly 300 years, and received its baronetcy from James I. He was born September 4, 1829, so that he is now in the fifty-ninth year of his age. He succeeded to the title and estates on his father's death, in 1867. From an early age he has been an enthusiastic advocate of the Temperance movement, and is now the leader of the United Kingdom Alliance, organized to promote temperance legislation in Parliament, and is its spokesman in the House of Commons.

At the General Election of 1859 he ran in conjunction with his uncle, the late Sir James Graham, as a candidate for the representation of Carlisle, and was elected by only a very narrow majority over his opponent, Mr. Hodgson, a gentleman of great influence in the locality. In March, 1864, he first moved for leave to introduce the measure now so well known as

The Permissive Bill,

the main principle of which is the giving to two-thirds of the inhabitants of any parish or township of Great Britain an absolute power to prohibit the issue of licenses for the sale of intoxicating liquors within their districts. It was supported by only forty members out of six hundred and sixty-five.

In 1865, Sir Wilfrid was displaced at the General Election by his former opponent, Mr. Hodgson; but at the General Election three years later, on appealing to the enlarged constituency as a supporter of Mr. Gladstone, he was elected at the head of the poll. He succeeded on June 18, 1880, in gaining a vote of the House of Commons endorsing the principle of his measure. It carried no legislative power, but was an expression of the opinion of the House that such a measure would be beneficial. It was known as the

Local Option Resolution

and was passed by a majority of twenty-six. In 1885, he was a Parliamentary candidate for the new Cockermouth division of Cumberland, but was defeated by a Conservative majority of ten. In 1886, as a Gladstonian Liberal, he gained the seat by a considerable majority. He is a familiar figure in the House of Commons, where, as in the country districts, he is very popular. His speeches, enlivened with humorous touch and racy anecdote, are appreciated even by those who differ with him. His opposition to war and perpetual pensions, is well known. He also consistently opposes every year the custom of the House of Commons to adjourn on the day of the Derby, the great English horse-race, though he is never successful in inducing the House to sit. It is, however, of some value to have one man courageous enough to raise a protest against the habit, When members see him rise from his place with his conspicuously bald forehead, long brown beard, and twinkling eyes, brimming over with good humor and harmless drollery, they involuntarily prepare to laugh.

Doubtful Temerity.

Sir Wilfrid also maintains a persistent opposition to the annual votes in Parliament for the Army and Navy; and his constant assertion that England has nothing to fear from the colossal armies of Europe, and need not go to the expense of preparing to resist a possible invasion by them, is consistent with his principles if not in harmony with facts. His remark that England's only enemies are "the Pope and the Colorado Beetle" is amusing, but he forgets that Steam Navigation has practically bridged the English Channel and that England could not mobilise 100,000 soldiers in sufficent time to prevent 100,000 French soldiers landing on the English coast and seizing London.

At the annual meeting of the Baptist Total Abstinence Association recently held

At Mr. Spurgeon's Tabernacle,

Sir Wilfrid made a most efficient chairman, and in the course of other appropriate and highly-appreciated remarks, said he hoped they had all read the debate of the previous night in the House of Commons, when fourteen speakers had condemned the extension of the liquor traffic to the native races of India; in fact, they were ready to protect everyone but their own countrymen. He was glad they had got as far as protecting native races, but they should protect their own land. The House of Commons had said that no man should deal in alcohol unless he had a good moral character, and that put them on a separate footing from other people, and the magistrates were very particular. Well, he was sure if he applied to a bench of Tory magistrates *he* should not get a license. The licensed victuallers were respectable—they said so themselves. They congratulated themselves at all their anniversaries and dinners that they had got through another year respectably

Without Getting Into Jail.

Referring to Local Option, he said Parliament had sanctioned his scheme several times. They said they would give him what he wanted in the Local Government Bill, but instead of doing so they offered a sham and a snare.

Sir Wilfrid is an evangelical churchman, a generous landlord, and beloved by his tenants.

REV. J. T. WIGNER.

Born at Harwich—Early Profession of Christ—Enters Stepney College—His First Pastorate—His Present Sphere of Work.

A SECOND prominent leader is the Vice-President of the Baptist Union, the Rev. John Thomas Wigner, *whose portrait appears on the first page.* He was born at Harwich, Essex, about seventy-three years ago. Shortly after the death of his mother, which took place when he was a mere child, he removed with his father to Burnham, in the same county, in which town he was apprenticed. He early made a profession of Christ, and when he was only about eighteen years of age he entered Stepney College, as a student for the gospel ministry, and here he was the contemporary of many men who have since become distinguished in the denomination. Here also he had as a fellow-student the judicious and scholarly Dr. Angus, who now presides over the College in which he was formerly a pupil, although the College, which was instituted in the year 1810, has been removed to Regent's Park. Mr. Wigner entered on his

First Pastorate

in December, 1839, at King's Lynn, Norfolk, and there he remained until 1865. During his ministry a new place of worship was built and paid for; another edifice was built at West Lynn for the people in that locality, mainly through his exertions; and throughout the entire county his influence was felt in the various efforts put forth to further the interests of the kingdom of Christ and to reach non-churchgoers.

In 1866 he removed to London, and entered on his second pastorate, where his ministry has realized a gratifying measure of success. He has more than once been elected President of the London Baptist Association, in which office he has been energetic in establishing new churches, and collecting funds for philanthropic enterprises. The cost of building two of Mr. Spurgeon's Orphan Houses at Stockwell was defrayed with funds raised by his efforts. It is generally felt that the Baptist Union, which is a national organization, has acted wisely in making the London president its vice-president.

A prominent religious journal says of Mr. Wigner, "It is given to but few men to be able to carry on the Lord's work after the age of seventy years has been attained and passed, but Mr. Wigner has been graciously permitted to continue in the service of his Master, and to be doing good service when most men would be seeking repose, which to the majority of men is simply imperative; and we should pray that he may be spared a season longer to preach the glad tidings of the Gospel of Christ, and at last hear the Master's 'Well done, good and faithful servant, enter thou into the joy of thy Lord.'"

REV. CANON ELLISON.

Temperance Pioneers in the Protestant Episcopal Church—Eulogium by a Church Paper—Personal Career—Scholastic and Official Honors.

The Temperance cause in Great Britain has no warmer friend than Canon Ellison, *whose portrait appears on the first page.* Though the early band of Temperance pioneers in the Protestant Episcopal Church included many clergymen of honor and well-won distinction for their services on behalf of the Gospel of Christ, like Dean Close, Canon Bardsley Rev. Stopford Ram, Dr. Maguire, and Canon Babington, who stood shoulder to shoulder in the hard fight against prevalent drunkenness and consequent poverty and immorality, the name of Canon Ellison has, from the outset, been conspicuous as

A Leader of the Temperance Movement

within the church. One of the organs of the denomination, says: "It would be impossible to speak too highly of Canon Ellison's labors as a founder—one might almost say *the* founder—of the Church of England Temperance Society. At Church Congresses, conferences, public meetings, and in the pulpit, he has been, from the first, its chivalrous champion, through evil report and keen criticism, and happily lives to see his labors crowned with a success far exceeding the most hopeful anticipations of those who were associated with him during the exceedingly difficult course of its early history."

Henry John Ellison is rather more than sixty-six years of age, but happily possesses the vitality and strength of many a far younger man. His duties are multifarious and onerous, but he discharges them with a readiness and ease which demonstrates the versatility of his genius and the cordiality and thoroughness of his devotion to the work in which he is engaged. He graduated at Oxford about 1838, when he took his M. A. degree. His first benefice was the perpetual curacy of All Souls, Brighton, which he held from 1840 to 1843. From 1845 to 1855 he was vicar of Edensor, Derbyshire, and in 1854 was made Prebendary in Lichfield Cathedral. In 1855 he was appointed to the vicarage of New Windsor, and the following year made

Reader to the Queen

at Windsor Castle. In 1875 his active work for the Temperance cause generally, and for the Church of England Temperance Society in particular, induced him to seek a less onerous parochial charge, and he therefore resigned the vicarage of New Windsor and accepted the Rectory of Great Haseley, Oxfordshire, where he still remains; and as a result of the appreciation of the University authorities for his invariable urbanity, ripe scholarship, and conscientious ministry, he had the distinction conferred upon him, in 1873, of an honorary canonry in connection with his *alma mater*, Christ Church College, Oxford. He is also a Chaplain in Orditary to the Queen, and has been for many years past the trusted and enterprising Chairman of the Church of England Temperance Society.

THE REV. C. H. SPURGEON.

His Recent Stand for Evangelical Truth—His 2,000th Sermon—Success of His College—The Stockwell Orphanage—Personal Career.

It is unnecessary to repeat here the details of the life of the great preacher whose sermons appear from week to week in this journal, as a full biography has been more than once published in these columns. He has, however, recently passed through an experience which has awakened increased interest in him throughout the religious world, and has enhanced the respect and esteem in which he is held. As our readers are aware, he has felt it his duty to make an emphatic protest against doctrines being preached which are in conflict with Evangelical theology, and has even gone so far as to withdraw from the Baptist Union when he found that the Union as a body was not prepared to insist on all its members being faithful to the orthodox creed. He was much cheered in taking this painful step by receiving from large numbers of clergymen in his own and other denominations expressions of sympathy and approval, showing how large a number of ministers are still faithful to the Gospel. Happily, too, the Council of the Baptist Union was able at its meeting on April 23 to announce the termination of what has come to be named the "Down-grade" controversy, by the emphatic manner in which the evangelical character of the basis and constitution of the Union had been officially declared, and with which declaration the Rev. J. A. Spurgeon, as representing his brother, expressed himself satisfied.

Mr. Spurgeon's 2,000th Printed Sermon

was published at the beginning of this year—an event, we need not say, absolutely without parallel in the history and work of any minister of the Christian Church, and constituting a sufficient cause, if any were needed, for our once again calling attention to one who has perhaps done more than any man living during the last quarter of a century, and over, to stir the religious vitality, not in London only, but throughout the world.

Besides his pastoral work, his labors as an author, and his grand work in founding and supporting his orphanages, Mr. Spurgeon has, in conducting

His Pastors' College,

established a claim on the gratitude, not only of his brother Baptists, but on the Evangelical world generally. His students are to be found at the uttermost ends of the earth. In New Zealand we find his son, Thomas, and other students. On the Congo his missionaries are laboring for Christ. Not in Australia, nor in tropical Africa only do we find successful and earnest preachers who have received their training in his college; in our own land, in Canada, and other countries beside Great Britain his spiritual sons are preaching the gospel in its purity and power. Missionary work, however, forms but a small portion of Mr. Spurgeon's self-imposed labors for the glory of God.

The Stockwell Orphanage

is another splendid testimony of his sagacious and unceasing efforts to execute his Divine Master's command, "Feed my lambs." Here nearly 600 children are fed both physically and spiritually, and trained for useful service in the world. Mr. Spurgeon was born at Kelvedon, Essex, in 1834, and is now fifty-four years old. He first preached before a London congregation at New Park Street, in 1853. The Metropolitan Tabernacle was opened in 1861, and is always full to overflowing. Mr. Spurgeon has published a sermon weekly since the first week in 1855. "A book fund," carried on in Mr. Spurgeon's house, and superintended by Mrs. Spurgeon, has supplied indigent clergymen and ministers, free of charge, with over 100,000 volumes. In 1879, Mr. Spurgeon received a "Silver Wedding" testimonial of over $30,000. In 1884, on his attaining his fiftieth year, another sum of about $25,000 was presented. The whole of these funds were distributed in charity, $25,000 having been devoted to the endowment of the Tabernacle Almshouses.

It is stated that some time ago these works of charity were effectively used as an argument in a discussion with a blatant scoffer at Christianity, who expressed a profane wish that all preachers, and especially Mr. Spurgeon, were swept off the face of the earth as a useless load of rubbish. "Well," said his Christian opponent, "suppose to oblige you Mr. Spurgeon could be removed, would you undertake to support the six hundred orphans in his homes and the aged people in his almshouses? That is pure philanthropy which you approve." The scoffer made no reply, but turned away abashed.

ANECDOTES RELATED AT RECENT EVANGELISTIC MEETINGS.

An Old Drunkard's Debt Paid.—Mr. Henry Lakin narrates: "There was a man at a meeting in this hall the other night, upon whom I pressed the claims of Christ, and urged him to accept salvation. He replied, with a smile at the idea, and said, 'Oh sir, I am nearly seventy years of age, and I have been a great sinner and a great drunkard the most of my life.' And he looked as if he had settled the matter, and that there could be no salvation for him. 'Any more to say?' I asked. 'No,' he replied, 'but I do not believe God would forgive me all that. I have so much standing against me, and I cannot see that God could or would forgive me.' 'Man,' I answered, 'it is just as easy for God to forgive you with all that load of sin upon you, as if you had only committed one sin. Christ bore all your sins upon Calvary!' The light broke in on the poor man's mind, and, though late in life, he was led to trust himself to Christ, the Almighty Saviour, who invites all weary and heavy laden ones to come unto Him, and saves 'even unto the uttermost' all who come unto Him."

An Infidel's Prayer Answered.—"There was a father, an infidel, who had an only daughter lying dangerously ill. He had not prayed for long, but as he knelt at the bedside of his daughter, he thought, 'Oh, if there were only a God, and I knew it, I would pray Him to give me back my daughter.' Then the fearful thought rushed upon him, 'What if there be a God after all!' The thought preyed upon his mind; and, in an agony of doubt, he clasped his hands, and exclaimed 'Oh, God, for the first time since my childhood, I pray to Thee! Oh, if Thou be, if there in truth be a God, then, I beseech Thee, let this little child raise her hand.' He had scarcely finished this prayer, when his little girl slowly withdrew her hand from under the clothes, and pointed upwards. The nurse, entering the room at that moment, tried to put it down, but the man cried out, 'Do not touch that hand; it is pointing the way to God.' Again, as if to show there had been no mistake, the tiny hand was slowly raised. This some time infidel accepted this as a direct message from God to himself, and from that time he became not only a consistent Christian, but a most zealous worker for the Lord."

A French Captain's Dilemma.—Rev. W. H. Burton said: "A story which my dear father once told me reminds me exactly of the condition of many anxious souls. During the war which raged between England and France in the early part of this century, a French convoy sailed from a distant land, bound for their native shores. The first part of the voyage was prosperous, and all went well, until one night a heavy storm scattered the ships, and some of them, altogether missing their companions, had to do the best they could to get home alone. One of these, being thus left, made very slow work, and it was a long time before, in a crippled state, she made the English Channel. But just then a heavy southwest gale sprang up, and, in a half sinking state, the poor Frenchman realized the impossibility of making a French port. There was Plymouth directly under his lee, and war-ships and privateers almost within gunshot. His dilemma was great. He looked upon himself already as a prisoner, and his ship as a prize in the hands of the enemy. And yet his fears were utterly groundless. There was no enemy to fear. Unknown to him, a treaty had been signed, and peace had been declared between the two nations, and when the pilot approached him with the good news, his joy was overflowing. He ran into Plymouth and was safe. Troubled soul, I want to assure you that thus you may have rest. The treaty is signed, and by 'the blood of the everlasting covenant,' it was sealed at 'the place called Calvary.' The blessed gale against which you are struggling should not be resisted. Come, and find the peace which awaits the trusting heart."

The Safer Shelter of the Harbor.—Seafaring is a dangerous calling, and the mariner often runs to the haven for shelter and safety, as well as for repose. I remember thus once running for Kingston Harbor. The sensation of calm and of safety which suddenly possessed us as we entered that place of quiet rest I cannot describe. We had had very rough weather in the Irish Sea, and were earnestly longing for the port, when, most of us being below in the cabins, and ignorant of our nearness to land, the vessel, which had been rolling and pitching so that we could scarcely keep our seats, suddenly became as apparently motionless as the house in which we sit. The change was marvellous. Glad voices all around began to say, "It is the harbor!" All care vanished! Timid people became brave, the weak became strong, and in a few moments we were all on deck, delighted for the haven and thankful for the granite ramparts behind which we were safely moored. Still the storm raged on outside. The boisterous surges of St. George's Channel, through which we had come, still continued their wild commotion. Other vessels, some of them laboring heavily under the gale, could be seen making for port: but within the haven all was calm—all was safe. Motionless, our good ship lay snugly berthed beside the jetty, and we knew that as long as that stout sea-wall stood, nothing could possibly hurt us. *What a shelter!* with what peace the sailor rests when he has made the haven!

Who Saved the Sentinel's Life?—"A Party of tourists were on board a great steamer on one of the American rivers, when one of their number began to sing in a deep, rich voice, that beautiful hymn beginning with

'Jesus, lover of my soul,
Let me to Thy bosom fly.'

He had scarcely finished, when a gentleman—not one of the party—came forward to him, and said, 'Excuse me, sir, were you in the late war?' 'I was,' replied the other. 'Tell me, were you in such an army, in such a place, at such a time?' 'I was,' the singer answered. 'Ah! I thought I recognized the voice and the hymn. Do you remember being sentinel on a particular night of great danger?' continued the questioner. 'Well do I remember it,' was the reply. 'When I was told that I had to be sentinel on that terrible night, my heart was in a great tremor, because I knew my life was in imminent peril. I went out with that song, that I have just been singing, upon my lips, and when I came to

'Cover my defenceless head,
With the shadow of Thy wing,'

suddenly I felt a sense of inexpressible safety, and from that moment my fears fled.' 'Wonderful!' said the gentleman. 'We were on the Southern side, and that night orders were given that the sentinel on your side must be shot. I was sent to do the work, and when I came right opposite to you, you were walking up and down singing that hymn. I prepared to take aim, but you just then sang the words mentioned. My rifle dropped; I could not touch you.'"

OBSCURATION.

Dr. Talmage's Sermon, Preached Last Sunday Morning, May 13, 1888.

"The sun shall be turned into darkness." Acts 2: 20.

An Awful Hypothesis—The Natural Sun Extinguished—The Earth Freezing—Christianity the Sun of Mankind—The Effort of Atheism to Extinguish It—What Would Result from their Success—I. The Degradation of Womanhood—The Condition of Woman in Non-Christian Lands—A Question of Dynamics—II. The Demoralization of Society—The Death of an Infidel—Christianity a Mighty Restraint—Churches Overthrown—Sunday-Schools Scattered—Asylums Abolished—Eclipse not Destruction.

CHRISTIANITY is the rising sun of our time, and men have tried with the uprolling vapors of scepticism, and the smoke of their blasphemy, to turn the sun into darkness. Suppose the archangels of malice and horror should be let loose a little while, and be allowed to extinguish and destroy the sun in the natural heavens! They would take the oceans from other worlds, and pour them on this luminary of the planetary system, and the waters go hissing down amid the ravines and the caverns, and there is explosion after explosion, until there are only a few peaks of fire left in the sun, and these are cooling down and going out until the vast continents of flame are reduced to a small acreage of fire, and that whitens and cools off until there are only a few coals left, and these are whitening and going out until there is not a spark left in all the mountains of ashes, and the valleys of ashes, and the chasms of ashes.

An Extinguished Sun!

A dead sun! A buried sun! Let all worlds wail at the stupendous obsequies. Of course, this withdrawal of the solar light and heat throws our earth into a universal chill, and the tropics become the temperate, and the temperate becomes the Arctic, and there are frozen rivers, and frozen lakes, and frozen oceans. From Arctic and Antarctic regions the inhabitants gather in toward the centre, and find the Equator as the poles. The slain forests are piled up into a great bonfire, and around them gather the shivering villages and cities. The wealth of the coal mines is hastily poured into the furnaces, and stirred into rage of combustion, but soon the bonfires begin to lower, and the furnaces begin to go out, and the nations begin to die. Cotopaxi, Vesuvius, Etna, Stromboli, Californian geysers, cease to smoke, and the ice of hail-storms remains unmelted in their crater. All the flowers have breathed their last breath. Ships with sailors frozen at the mast, and helmsmen frozen at the wheel, and passengers frozen in the cabin;

All Nations Dying,

first at the North and then at the South. Child frosted and dead in the cradle. Octogenarian frosted and dead at the hearth. Workmen with frozen hand on the hammer, and frozen foot on the shuttle. Winter from sea to sea. All-congealing winter. Perpetual winter. Globe of frigidity. Hemisphere shackled to hemisphere by chains of ice. Universal Nova Zembla. The earth an ice-floe grinding against other ice-floes. The archangels of malice and horror have done their work, and now they may take their thrones of glacier, and look down upon the ruin they have wrought. What the destruction of the sun in the natural heavens would be to our physical earth, the destruction of Christianity would be to the moral world. The sun turned into darkness!

Infidelity in our time is considered a great joke. There are people who rejoice to hear Christianity caricatured, and to hear Christ assailed with quibble and quirk and misrepresentation and badinage and harlequinade. I propose this morning to take infidelity and Atheism out of the realm of jocularity into one of tragedy, and show you

What Infidels Propose

and what, if they are successful, they will accomplish. There are those in all our communities who would like to see the Christian religion overthrown, and who say the world would be better without it. I want to show you what is the end of this road, and what is the terminus of this crusade, and what this world will be when Atheism and Infidelity have triumphed over it, if they can. I say, if they can. I reiterate it, if they can.

In the first place, it will be the complete and unutterable

Degradation of Womanhood.

I will prove it by facts and arguments which no honest man will dispute. In all communities and cities and states and nations where the Christian religion has been dominant, woman's condition has been ameliorated and improved, and she is deferred to and honored in a thousand things, and every gentleman takes off his hat before her. If your associations have been good, you know that the name of wife, mother, daughter, suggest gracious surroundings. You know there are no better schools and seminaries in Brooklyn or in any city of this country than the schools and seminaries for our young ladies. You know that while woman may suffer injustice in England and the United States, she has more of her rights in Christendom than she has anywhere else.

Now, compare this with woman's condition in lands where Christianity has made little or no advance—in China, in Barbary, in Borneo, in Tartary, in Egypt, in Hindostan. The Burmese sell their wives and daughters as so many sheep. The Hindoo Bible makes it disgraceful and an outrage for a woman to listen to music, or look out of the window in the absence of her husband, and gives as a lawful ground for divorce a woman's beginning to eat before her husband has finished his meal. What mean those white bundles on the ponds and rivers in China in the morning? Infanticide following infanticide. Female children destroyed simply because they are female. Woman harnessed to a plow as an ox.

Woman Veiled and Barricaded,

and in all styles of cruel seclusion. Her birth a misfortune. Her life a torture. Her death a horror. The missionary of the cross to-day in heathen lands preaches generally to two groups—a group of men who do as they please and sit where they please; the other group, women hidden and carefully secluded in a side apartment, where they may hear the voice of the preacher, but may not be seen. No refinement. No liberty. No hope for this life. No hope for the life to come. Ringed nose. Cramped foot. Disfigured face. Embruted soul. Now compare those two conditions. How far toward this latter condition that I speak of would woman go if Christian influences were withdrawn and Christianity were destroyed? It is only a question of dynamics. If an object be lifted to a certain point and not fastened there, and the lifting power be withdrawn, how long before that object will fall down to the point from which it started? It will fall down, and it will go still further than the point from which it started. Christianity has lifted woman up from the very depths of degradation almost to the skies. If that lifting power be withdrawn she falls clear back to the depth from which she was resurrected, not going any lower because there is no lower depth. And yet, notwithstanding the fact that the only salvation of woman from degradation and woe is the Christian religion, and the only influence that has ever lifted her in the social scales is Christianity—I have read that there are women who reject Christianity. I make no remark in regard to those persons. I make no remark in regard to them. In the silence of your own soul make your observations.

If infidelity triumph and Christianity be overthrown, it means

The Demoralization of Society.

The one idea in the Bible that atheists and infidels most hate, is the idea of retribution. Take away the idea of retribution and punishment from society, and it will begin very soon to disintegrate; and take away from the minds of men the fear of hell, and there a great many of them who would very soon turn this world into a hell. The majority of those who are indignant against the Bible because of the idea of punishment, are men whose lives are bad, or whose hearts are impure, and who hate the Bible because of the idea of future punishment, for the same reason that criminals hate the penitentiary. Oh, I have heard this brave talk about people fearing nothing of the consequences of sin in the next world, and I have made up my mind it is *merely a coward's whistling to keep his courage up.* I have seen men flaunt their immoralities in the face of the community, and I have heard them defy the Judgment Day, and scoff at the idea of any future consequence of their sin; but when they came to die, they shrieked until you could hear them for nearly two blocks, and in the summer night the neighbors got up to put the windows down, because they could not endure the horror.

I would not want to see a rail-train with five hundred Christian people on board, go down through a drawbridge into a watery grave. I would not want to see five hundred Christian people go into such disaster, but, I tell you plainly, that I could more easily see that than I could for any protracted time stand and

See an Infidel Die,

though his pillow were of elder-down and under a canopy of vermilion. I have never been able to brace up my nerves for such a spectacle. There is something at such a time so indescribable in the countenance. I just looked in upon it for a minute or two, but the clutch of his fist was so diabolic, and the strength of his voice was so unnatural, I could not endure it. "There is no hell, there is no hell, there is no hell!" the man had said for sixty years; but that night when I looked in the dying room of my infidel neighbor, there was something on his countenance which seemed to say, "There is, there is, there is, there is!"

The Mightiest Restraints

to-day against theft, against immorality, against libertinism, against crime of all sorts—the mightiest restraints are the retribution of eternity. Men know that they can escape the law, but down in the offender's soul there is the realization of the fact that they cannot escape God. He stands at the end of the road of profligacy, and He will not clear the guilty. Take all idea of retribution and punishment out of the hearts and minds of men, and it would not be long before Brooklyn and New York and Boston and Charleston and Chicago became Sodoms. The only restraints against the evil passions of the world to-day are Bible restraints.

Suppose now these generals of Atheism and Infidelity got the victory, and suppose they marshalled a great army made up of the majority of the world. They are in companies, in regiments, in brigades—the whole army. Forward, march! ye hosts of infidels and atheists, banners flying before, banners flying behind, banners inscribed with the words: "No God! No Christ! No punishment! No restraints! Down with the Bible! Do as you please!" The sun turned into darkness!

Forward, march! ye great army of infidels and atheists. And first of all you will attack the churches. Away with those houses of worship! They have been standing there so long deluding the people with consolation in their bereavements and sorrows. All those churches ought to be extirpated; they have done so much to relieve the lost and bring home the wandering, and they have so long held up the idea of eternal rest after the paroxysm of this life is over. Turn the St. Peters and St. Pauls and the temples and tabernacles into club-houses. Away with those churches!

Forward, march! ye great army of infidels and atheists, and next of all

They Scatter the Sabbath-Schools

—the Sabbath-schools filled with bright-eyed, bright-cheeked little ones who are singing songs on Sunday afternoon, and getting instruction when they ought to be on the street corners playing marbles, or swearing on the commons.

Away with them! Forward, march! ye great army of infidels and atheists, and next of all they will attack Christian asylums—the institutions of mercy supported by Christian philanthropies. Never mind the blind eyes and the deaf ears and the crippled limbs and the weakened intellects. Let paralyzed old age pick up its own food, and orphans fight their own way, and the half reformed go back to their evil habits. Forward, march! ye great army of infidels and atheists, and with your battle axes hew down the cross and split up the manger of Bethlehem.

On, ye great army of infidels and atheists, and now they come to the graveyards and the cemeteries of the earth. Pull down the sculpture above Greenwood's gate, for it means the Resurrection. Tear away at the entrance of Laurel Hill the figure of Old Mortality and the chisel. On, ye great army of infidels and atheists, into the graveyards and cemeteries; and where you see "Asleep in Jesus," cut it away, and where you find a marble story of heaven, blast it, and where you find over a little child's grave: "Suffer little children to come unto Me," substitute the words "delusion" and "sham," and where you find an angel in marble, strike off the wing, and when you come to a family vault, chisel on the door: "Dead once, dead forever."

But on, ye great army of infidels and atheists, on! They will attempt to scale heaven. There are

Heights to be Taken.

Pile hill on hill, and Pelion upon Ossa, and then they hoist the ladders against the walls of heaven. On and on until they blow up the foundations of jasper and the gates of pearl. They charge up the steep. Now they aim for the throne of Him who liveth forever and ever. They would take down from their high place the Father, the Son, the Holy Ghost. "Down with them!" they say. "Down with Him from the throne!" they say. "Down forever! Down out of sight! He is not God. He has no right to sit there. Down with Him! Down with Christ!"

A world without a head, a universe without a king. Orphan constellations. Fatherless galaxies. Anarchy supreme. A dethroned Jehovah. An assassinated God. Patricide, regicide, deicide. That is what they mean. That is what they will have, if they can, if they can, if they can. Civilization hurled back into semi-barbarism, and semi-barbarism driven back into Hottentot savagery. The wheel of

Progress Turned the Other Way

and turned toward the dark ages. The clock of the centuries put back two thousand years. Go back, you Sandwich Islands, from your schools and from your colleges and from your reformed condition to what you were in 1820, when the missionaries first came. Call home the five hundred missionaries from India and overthrow their two thousand schools, where they are trying to educate the heathen, and scatter the one hundred and forty thousand little children that they have gathered out of barbarism into civilization. Obliterate all the work of Dr. Duff in India, of David Abeel in China, of Dr. King in Greece, of Judson in Burmah, of David Brainerd amid the American aborigines, and send home the three thousand missionaries of the cross who are toiling in foreign lands, toiling for Christ's sake, toiling themselves into the grave. Tell these three thousand men of God that they are of no use. Send home the medical missionaries who are doctoring the bodies as well as the souls of the dying nations. Go home, London Missionary Society. Go home, American Board of Foreign Missions. Go home, ye Moravians, and relinquish back into darkness and squalor and death the nations whom ye have begun to lift.

Oh, my friends, there has never been such a nafarious plot on earth as that which Infidelity and Atheism have planned. We were shocked a few years ago because of the attempt to blow up the Parliament Houses in London; but if Infidelity and Atheism succeed in their attempt,

They Will Dynamite a World.

Let them have their full way, and this world will be a habitation of three rooms—a habitation with just three rooms: the one a madhouse, another a lazaretto, the other a pandemonium. These infidel bands of music have only just begun their concert—yea, they have only been stringing their instruments. I today put before you their whole programme from begining unto close. In the theatre the tragedy comes first, and the farce afteward; but in this infidel drama of death the farce comes first and the tragedy afterward. And in the former, atheists and infidels laugh and mock, but in the latter God Himself will laugh and mock. He says so. "I will laugh at their calamity and mock when their fear cometh."

From such a chasm of individual, national, world-wide ruin, stand back. Oh young men, stand back from that chasm! You see the practical drift of my sermon. I want you to know

Where That Road Leads.

Stand back from that chasm of ruin. The time is going to come (you and I may not live to see it, but it will come, just as certainly as there is a God, it will come) when the infidels and the atheists who openly and out and out and above-board preach and practice Infidelity and Atheism, will be considered as criminals against society, as they are now criminals against God. Society will push out the leper, and the wretch with soul gangrened and ichorous and vermin-covered and rotten apart with his bestiality, will be left to die in the ditch, and be denied decent burial, and men will come with spades and cover up the carcass, where it falls, that it poison not the air, and the only text in all the Bible appropriate for the funeral sermon will be Jeremiah 22:19: "He shall be buried with the burial of an ass."

A thousand voices come up to me this morning, saying: "Do you really think Infidelity will succeed? Has Christianity received its death blow? and

Will the Bible Become Obsolete?"

Yes, when the smoke of the city chimney arrests and destroys the noonday sun. Josephus says about the time of the destruction of Jerusalem the sun was turned into darkness; but only the clouds rolled between the sun and the earth. The sun went right on. It is the same sun, the same luminary as when at the beginning it shot out like an electric spark from God's finger, and to-day it is warming the nations, and to-day it is gilding the sea, and to-day it is filling the earth with its light. The same old sun, not at all worn out, though its light steps one hundred and ninety million miles a second, though its pulsations are four hundred and fifty trillion undulations in a second. Same sun with beautiful white light made up of the violet and the indigo and the blue and the green and the red and the yellow and the orange—the seven beautiful colors now just as when the solar spectrum first divided them.

At the beginning God said: "Let there be light," and light was, and light is, and light shall be. So Christianity is rolling on, and it is going to warm all nations, and all nations are to bask in its light. Men may shut the window-blinds so they cannot see it, or they may smoke the pipe of speculation until they are shadowed under their own vaporing; but the Lord God is a sun! This

White Light of the Gospel

made up of all the beautiful colors of earth and heaven—violet plucked from amid the spring grass, and the indigo of the southern jungles, and the blue of the skies, and the green of the foliage, and the yellow of the autumnal woods, and the orange of the southern groves, and the red of the sunsets. All the beauties of earth and heaven brought out by this spiritual spectrum. Great Britain is going to take all Europe for God. The United States are going to take America for God. Both of them together will take all Asia for God. All three of them will take Africa for God. "Who art thou, oh great mountain? before Zerubbabel thou shalt become a plain." The mouth of the Lord hath spoken it. Hallelujah, amen!

THE TEMPLE OF THE EARTH.

(*See Illustration on page 317.*)

THE Chinese have more gods and less religion than any other nation on the globe. Almost everything in nature is deified, and the spirits of the dead emperors are added to the long list. The edifice represented in the illustration is the Temple of the Earth, the second in size and grandeur in the empire. It is surpassed only by that to the Supreme Ruler of Heaven. Sacrifices of beasts are offered there annually, being slain the day before presentation, and after presentation divided among the worshippers.

The present condition of religious observance in China affords the best opportunity there has been for centuries for the preaching of the gospel, and it is a remarkable fact that it has come at a time when the Government has declared for toleration. Christian missionaries are permitted to teach and preach without incurring legal penalties, and the people are on their side yearning for a new system of religion. Confucianism, Buddhism and Taoism, the three systems of China, still number among their adherents the conservative classes, but the younger generation, and the more honest and intelligent of the elder people, have now revolted from the corruption and fraud and superstition which flouish in the three systems. A suspicion is growing up that the priests themselves do not believe what they teach, and that such zeal as they display is not zeal for truth, but for the maintenance of a system by which they get gain. That may be the explanation of the anomaly of three national religions flourishing side by side.

The earliest religion was Confucianism, which is a system of morality concerning itself with the relations of men to each other, rather than with their relations to a Divine Being. There was sufficient sound morality in it to keep it alive in spite of its defects, from its birth in 551 B. C., to the present time. But a system that had in it no recognition of God, was not sufficient, and Buddhism was introduced about 63 A. D. Finally Taoism, with its worship of many gods and demons, came and spread throughout the country. All three systems have their adherents, and the devotees of one are often found in the temples of the others, as if it did not matter very much one way or the other which was true.

A WIFE-BEATER CONVERTED.

IN a letter from a lady-missionary in China to the *Missionary Herald* she thus describes a noteworthy baptism at Pas-ting-fu: "For several weeks it has been evident that the Spirit was working in the hearts of the people about us, and the interest culminated in the meetings which were held. A week ago yesterday was communion Sunday, and twenty were added to our number, some being received into full membership and others into the 'Christian Congregation.' I had never before been present at the baptism of a heathen convert, and the scene was an impressive one. This acceptance of Christ must mean so much to those who have come out of the darkness and joylessness of heathenism. As one looks into the earnest, happy faces of these redeemed ones, and contrasts them with the faces of those without hope in the world, he gains a new conception of the power of Christ's gospel. Among those who joined the 'Christian Congregation' was a man who a year ago was beating his Christian wife and trying in every way to get her to give up her religion. She was very anxious that her son should come to our school here, and prayed that some way might open which would make it possible. One day her husband surprised her by giving up his opposition and offering to come himself to Pao-ting-fu to place his boy in the school. The father was invited to join the station class, and has been one of the most earnest listeners."

A VICTIM RESCUED.

THE recent death of a beautiful and accomplished lady renders it possible to publish the sad story of her life without causing pain to the parties concerned. A few years before the war, a wealthy gentleman, named Golden, owning a large number of slaves, resided in Southern Georgia. He was a widower, with one son and two daughters, whom he passionately loved. The younger daughter especially, he almost idolized, and lavished on her education and amusements large sums of money. She was small and slight of figure, with dark eyes and hair, sprightly in manner, but extremely proud of her beauty and aristocratic blood. After the war, Mr. Golden, utterly ruined, came North, to earn a livelihood. He was, however, unused to work, and the restraint and confinement of an office in the city, were irksome to him. More than all, his poverty and loss of station oppressed him; he fell sick and died. His son obtained a clerkship, which only just sufficed to maintain him, and the elder daughter married an old admirer, who knew her in better days.

Anda, the younger daughter, was alone and penniless. She was glad to accept an asylum offered her in the home of a kindly old uncle, living in the country. It was not easy for the proud, haughty beauty to adapt herself to the ways of a quiet country home. It was so different to the old life of luxury, when every wish was anticipated and slaves obsequiously waited her bidding. If she had been a Christian she would have known where to go for the strength she needed to live this new and uncongenial life, and would have found in the love of God an influence that would have raised her above the petty vexations and humiliations of her surroundings. Unhappily, she had no conception of happiness but in worldly pleasure and fashionable amusements, which were now beyond her reach.

After some time a change came. A young man, whom Anda Golden had met during her brief residence with her father in the city, visited her, and it was easy to see that she was fascinated with him. His fashionable attire, his easy air of gentility won her admiration. Her protectors, honestly desiring her welfare only, sought to learn the character and occupation of her friend, but though he talked freely enough of his aristocratic acquaintances, and appeared to be living in good society, he was reticent about himself. His manner excited suspicion, which was cautiously and delicately communicated to the girl. But Anda was head-strong. She knew her own business; she desired only to be let alone; her city friend was worth a hundred of the country farmers who came around her with their clumsy, boorish admiration. She had always had her own way, and it was impossible to open her eyes to the vain frivolous character of the admirer of whom she knew nothing.

The visitor remained a few weeks, and then took his departure. Anda grew nervous and anxious. She received a few letters, but they became gradually less frequent, and finally ceased altogether. Then the haughty little beauty broke down utterly. She was in an agony of despair. With bitter tears and lamentations she confessed to her friends that she had surrendered a woman's most precious possession, and that her wicked admirer had worked her ruin. He had promised her speedy marriage, but had cast her off, and she did not know where he was living nor even his real name. Some families would have cast her out to save themselves from social disgrace; they had warned her, and she had rejected their warning and affectionate counsel with scorn; she herself was conscious that she had no further claim upon them. They, however, had learned of Christ compassion for the sinner, and they stood by her.

Out of the trouble Anda rose a new woman. The unexpected tenderness and love shown to her after her wayward and ungrateful behaviour, moved her first and most, but she was led to see the spring of conduct which seemed to her more than human. Her friends were followers of Christ, and it was from Him that they had learned compassion for the fallen. She was led to study His character and herself to become a Christian. It was astonishing to see the wonderful change that came in her character. She became humble, softened, gentle, childlike, and was never so happy as when performing some humble work that would minister to the happiness of others. She visited the cottages of the village, sat by the bedside of the sick, and was a ministering angel to any who were in trouble. Her old nature was completely gone, leaving not a trace of the former faults. Her life for years was filled with deeds of love and kindness, and her relative, from whom these facts have been obtained, and who vouches for their truth, states that when she died two weeks ago, the whole neighborhood mourned, and at her funeral there was a scene of weeping such as is rarely witnessed.

AN AFRICAN CHIEF'S DILEMMA.

IN the course of a sermon in St. Paul's M. E. Church, New York, on April 29, Bishop William Taylor related a remarkable incident in connection with one of his stations in Central Africa. Among those who came to the station, and received instruction were some children who were so eager for teaching that they attended regularly, though in order to do so they had to make a toilsome journey on foot from the village where they lived, which was seven miles from the mission-building. After a time they beguiled the way with singing the hymns they had learned in the school, and so became proficient in that accomplishment. They also took to singing them around their home, and so excited the interest of the family. Their old grandfather, though apparently not particularly remarkable for his spiritual-mindedness, was especially impressed with the singing, and at last resolved on paying the missionaries a visit. The journey was a long one for him, but he accomplished it, and God blessed the interview to his conversion.

Not long afterward, when the question of his baptism came up, the old man, who was chief in his tribe informed the missionaries that *he had two wives*. This difficulty is a common one in African mission work. It is extremely painful to break up family relations, and it is the most severe test of a convert's sincerity that he is called upon to make. The old chief in this case was in terrible distress, and knew not how to sever the tie he had made in accordance with heathen customs. The missionaries, at his request, agreed to see the two wives, and to explain to them why it was necessary that one of them should be put away.

The old man brought them to the mission and then a clue to his perplexity presented itself. One of the women was elderly, not much younger than himself; the other was young and strong. In a society in which all the work is done by the wife, and the husband takes his ease while his wife digs and delves for his support, it was easy to see that he would gain by retaining the young woman and discarding the old one. Still the husband clung to the elder woman, but feared the consequences of putting the younger away. As gently and delicately as possible the missionaries told the two women how the case stood, and that the chief had decided to make his choice between them. The elder woman was not slow to realize the advantages her rival had over her, and, expecting that her husband would prefer the young and strong woman to herself, burst into tears. The weeping, however, soon gave place to joy when the old chief embraced her and told her that he should cleave to the wife of his youth. The missionaries anticipated some trouble with the younger woman, who seemed to have considerable temper and spirit; but to their surprise she accepted her lot with satisfaction. The chief had been a hard master, and she was even glad to learn that she would have to toil for him no more. She had little faith in the transformation of his character, and was more than willing to separate. Thus the dreaded interview ended to mutual satisfaction, and the three departed to begin their new lives under changed conditions. It is not often that matrimonial difficulties have so mutually agreeable an ending in that or another land.

AN IDOL BEHEADED.

A MISSIONARY at Hang-chow, China, reports a strange incident of Chinese superstition. He says: It is well-known that the Chinese are a nation of gamblers; only those who have lived among them can tell the extent to which it is carried on. During the last few years Manilla lottery tickets have offered a new and inviting field of action. A few months ago a man not far from here bought one whole ticket for six dollars. Was the number a lucky one? Who could tell? He would ask the gods to help. He therefore bought a small "god of wealth." Having put this up in his house he spread the ticket before it and prayed for success. Time went on, the lottery was drawn at Manilla, and lo! our friend drew a blank; his number did not win. What did he do? He took his god and with a knife, deliberately cut off its head because it had not answered his prayers. Strange to say, after a few days the man seemed to think he had dealt rather hardly with his god. He therefore *fastened its head on again* and the last I heard of it, about a fortnight ago was that he and his friends were worshipping it again. Surely these people need the Gospel.

IN A CALCUTTA ORPHANAGE.

IN the *Indian Witness* of March 31, is the following account of a day in the Orphanage at Calcutta: It was *the Children's Day*, and, therefore, it was proper that everything connected with the day and its service should pertain to these noble little folk. Hence, three orphan boys (two of Mahommedan and one of *Thakur* parentage) were baptized; and, best of all, thirty-one lads of all heights and sizes were recommended by their several class leaders and received into full membership in the Church. All departments of the Orphanage contributed this fine long list: the gardens and fields three, the boot and shoe department (Industrial School) ten, the various classes of the Day-school thirteen, and resident Christian families the balance. One of the above was a *pahari* boy from Pauri, who was received into the Orphanage only a few weeks ago; but he has behaved himself so nicely (to Pauri's credit) and won all our hearts that his leader recommended him for membership. Another—and the youngest of all—was the son of a *fakir*. He and his aged father were the first in their village, two years ago, to come out and accept Christianity. Soon after the old father died and Gunga Das, an only son—was left an orphan, the only Christian in that village of some 500 inhabitants. But *Gunga Das* was to be the small beginning of what is now a growing Christian community there

A WIDOW'S HELP IN NICE.

THE mission workers in connection with Rev. R. W. McAll's work in France, have received unexpected but very welcome aid from a widow at Nice. In their report they say: "We came to Nice, leaving on our way back the gambling hell of Monaco, the curse of the country and shame of the civilized world. Nice suffers much from that neighbor. The moral tone of the city is lower than anywhere in France, and probably in the rest of the world. For a long time our work here was almost hopeless, though very expensive; it seemed as if we were throwing pearls before swine.

"But there was in Nice a simple English widow, living modestly in a quiet lodging house, where she stayed until the heat compelled her to go to Switzerland. For twenty-five years she had spent the winter in Nice, and as she was a thorough Christian, she had done all she could to bless the city in which she dwelt. As we were discouraged, and told her one day of the great expense and the little results, she said: 'Have faith in God. I know a blessing will come on this city, and I wish you to continue the work; I promise to give you 5,000 francs ($1,000) a year as long as I am spared, on condition that you do not publish my name.'

"She kept her promise for seven years, until the Lord recently called her to Himself. She died suddenly, but not without having seen something of the expected blessing. Nice has become one of our most encouraging stations. The hall, situated in the best street, is well attended; conversions have taken place. Our friend, M. Borel, who had the management of the station, received a great blessing in his own soul through his intercourse with Mrs. Humphreys; the result was that a little revival has been produced, about thirty new converts have formed together a band of *volunteers*, for the purpose of evangelizing, of distributing tracts, etc. The meeting we attended was excellent. In the hearty prayers of those dear people, we felt the Spirit Himself praying."

SCENES AT THE SECOND ADVENT.

By Rev. Nathaniel Starkey.

The Coming Translation of Saints—Its Results upon Those Who are Taken and Those Who are Left—Our Lord's Intimation of the Event—The Raising of the Righteous Dead—The "Foolish Virgins" Shut Out—Their Experience of the Great Tribulation—Meeting the Bridegroom after the Translation—The Great Melchizedek—The Dead Who were raised at Christ's Resurrection—The Glorious Change.

THAT "moment" spoken of by the Apostle in I Corinthians 15: 52, must become presently realised by millions of our race. Something unprecedented in the world's history must soon take place, and we shall lose nothing, but possibly make a gain, by attempting to realise the result consequent upon the rapture, first to them that are taken, and next to them that are left. Concerning

Them That are Taken

but little can be said. The apostle is content with saying, "And so shall we ever be with the Lord." What is expressed in the words "with the Lord," not only does language fail to utter, but the imagination fails to conceive. To be "caught away with them (the raised ones) in the clouds to meet the Lord in the air," and seeing Him to be made like Him, is altogether beyond our conception. Well might John say, "We know not what we shall be, but we know that when He shall appear we shall be like Him," and so much as we can grasp of that suffices us to know.

But this leads to reflection upon the relative

Ties and Dependents

of those who share in the rapture. We have it from the lips of our blessed Lord Himself that, '*Two men shall be in the field, the one shall be taken and the other left.*' Let us suppose, then, that the one taken will be the proprietor or tenant of the field, and that at the homestead there will be a wife and several young children. How the case may be with the wife may depend upon the measure of sympathy in which she has been to her husband. If an enemy of the truth or careless about her state Godward, she may find herself left bereaved of husband. Again, let us suppose that "the other left" in the field has in his homestead a wife in readiness for her Lord's coming, and caught away at the same moment that he missed his friend. He will return to his house to report that some strange thing has happened when, to his amazement, he finds his home bereft of his wife, and the servants in consternation to know what has become of their mistress.

Again, we learn from our blessed Lord, that "Two women shall be grinding at the mill," possibly fellow-servants, the one deriding, the other enduring for His name's sake, whose coming she anticipates, the one reckoning on her earthly prospects, the other looking for her Lord from heaven. No wonder that one is taken, and the other left, and where will be her derision then?

Again, "In that night also there shall be two men in one bed," possibly brothers in one family, and fellow-Christians, too. Ere they fall asleep one may be found saying to the other, "Who knows but the Lord may come before morning! How delightful to wake and find oneself 'for ever with the Lord!'" To which the other may respond, "Ah! there you are again, riding your favorite hobby; I expect to live and die and be buried many long years before then." What wonder that the one shall be taken while the other is left?

In like manner we might extend our thought to the exchange, the market-place, the crowded hospital, the lonesome sick room, or the thronged thoroughfare, where two shall be speaking together, walking together, negotiating some more or less important business matter together; when lo! in a moment, one is gone and the other remains alone. Or it may happen when believers are gathered at a table of the Lord, remembering Him until He come, and we have often thought it may be the happy experience of some to be so overtaken. But

What Empty Spaces

may be seen then! The minister, with one of the deacons, and a score or two of the members gone, while the rest are left in blank astonishment to self-examination and inquiry whether, after all, they have known anything savingly, or whether their faith has been only fancy. In other cases possibly the minister and the deacons, with the bulk of the congregation, may be left to see that those two or three among them that held strange pre-millennial views, and were always talking about the importance of being ready, were, after all right, while the rest were wrong. Let us then be of the number who daily say, "Thou shalt guide me with Thy counsel, and afterwards receive me to glory" (Psalm 73: 24). The change of the living and

The Raising of the Dead

are to happen simultaneously, "in the twinkling of an eye"—the briefest point of time that can be expressed. We will here just hazard the expression of a thought we have entertained for years on this matter, for which we have indeed no express revelation, but which in the very nature of things appears to us not only likely, but reasonable that, whenever the time draws near—say, within a year, or two, or three—the Lord may spare many loved ones the pain of dying by detaining them on the earth to partake at length in the rapture of the living and changed saints. Where He has seen an earnest (perhaps a life-long) looking and longing for His appearing, coupled with a hope to escape the last enemy, we think it not improbable that His love towards them may be shown after this order; and surely the thought that such might possibly be, should prove an additional incentive to entertain the lively hope and expectation. We see in Matt. 25

The Foolish Virgins

"shut out," which, to our understanding, means, in the case of the living—that they will *not be changed*—but left behind to seek what sooner they ought to have found, "oil in their vessels with their lamps." They will doubtless seek it at once, by "going to them that sell," having recourse to means of grace ordinary and extraordinary, turning to the Lord with weeping and supplication, repentance and confession, crying, "Lord, Lord, open unto us," hoping that He may grant unto them a second rapture. But no, the door is shut, that day of grace is past, that degree of acceptance and approval is lost; but they may yet attain unto the *second degree*, if then they keep the faith, and overcome the beast, his image, his mark, and the number of his name, which must then presently rise out of the sea of trouble, emphatically called the Tribulation, the Great One.

Then will be better understood than hitherto (Luke 21: 36), "Watch ye, therefore, and pray always, that ye may be accounted

Worthy to Escape

all these things that shall come to pass, and to stand before the Son of Man." Their brethren comprising the little flock, or flock of little ones, that have gone up, have been accounted worthy to escape, and will be then standing before the Son of Man in His revealed glory. Those who have had their life for the most part in the earth, must remain on the earth, while those who have found their life in Christ, and lived it, shall be caught away to meet Him, having (it may be) seen this to be the hope of their calling, and followed after it, if they might apprehend that for which they had been apprehended of Christ Jesus, and so pressed towards the mark for the prize of their high calling of God in Christ Jesus.

And now let us contemplate

The First Meeting

in person of the Bridegroom with his Bride. We think the first sight the Church matured and made meet for marriage shall obtain of her Lord, will in some sort agree with the last sight she had of Him when "lifting up His hands He blessed them, and while He blessed them He was parted from them, and a cloud received Him out of their sight." For now, as their great Melchizedek, He shall meet them fresh from the battle-field, as the true seed of their father Abraham, returning from the slaughter of kings, having fought a good fight, and kept the faith to the end: now as slain ones, yet more than conquerors, they have, as His true followers, ascended up on high, leading captivity captive, and He, their great Fore-runner, comes forth with uplifted hands to bless, and with the bread of satisfaction and the wine of joy in His hand, blesses them, pronouncing them "blessed of the Most High God, possessor of heaven and earth," and as heirs of that God and joint heirs with Himself in His Father's possession—now becomes His own and their inheritance—invites them to bless the Most High God who hath delivered them thus from all their enemies and given them a final victory. Thus as King of righteousness and King of peace, He shall invite them to share dominion with Him, and as priest of the Most High God "He shall come down from offering the sin-offering, the burnt-offering, and the peace-offering,"—all in His own person fulfilled—and forth from the right hand of the Majesty on high 'shall come out and bless the people, and the glory of Jehovah shall appear." (Leviticus, 9: 22, 23.)

Nor must we forget the many risen saints who then must bear Him company, who for 1,800 years and more have been in glory with their risen Lord. What their number may have been or who, we are not told, but Matthew says, "Many bodies of the saints which slept arose,

Came Out of their Graves

after His resurrection, and went into the holy city, and appeared unto many." Now, that which alone is certain of them is, that their burial-place was at Jerusalem, that the earthquake disturbed their resting-place and consequently them, and that when by the Spirit of Holiness the Father raised Jesus from the dead, it pleased Him to raise these also, and by their appearing to many in Jerusalem, "the holy city," to give our faith assurance that not our Lord alone, but all His saints, should with Him share in risen life. If we might indulge our fancy ever so little, it would be to imagine that Zacharias and Elizabeth, Simeon and Anna, and possibly John the Baptist, forerunner of our Lord, were among this favored company, who, we doubt not, tarried only the "forty days," and then as our blessed Lord's escort ascended with Him, comprising in antitype the wave sheaf (Lev. 23 10: 11), earnest, and first-fruits of the great harvest of risen ones, which at the period we are considering shall have been at length reaped to share the glory with them. "And so shall we ever be with the Lord," said the apostle; and well may he add, "Wherefore comfort one another with these words."

* From his article in the *Prophetic News*, a monthly magazine, for sale, price six cents, at this office, 63 Bible House, New York.

NEW EDITION OF REV. M. BAXTER'S PAMPHLETS.

THREE PAMPHLETS IN ONE.

1. Coming Wars from 1888 to 1891, and Translation of 144,000 living Christians on March 5, 1896, before the 3½ years' persecution by Napoleon, etc.

2. Twenty Predictions about Coming Wars, by Twenty Lerned Expositors.

3. End of this Age by the Descent of Christ in Passover Week, April, 1901, being 45 years from the Crimean War Treaty of Peace in Passover Week, April, 1856, and 2,345 years from Passover Week, April, B. C. 444-5, as shown by Daniel's Dates.

The Three Pamphlets in an Illuminated Cover, 144 Pages.

Price Twenty Cents.

For sale at this office, 63 BIBLE HOUSE, NEW YORK.

CURRENT EVENTS.

The Adverse Report on the Fisheries Treaty between the United States and Great Britain, was made public last week, the injunction of secrecy having been removed by the Senate: It appears from it that the majority of the Committee on Foreign Relations bases its objections partly upon the fact that the Administration undertook the negotiations without first consulting the Senate. As regards the treaty itself, strong objections are made to the provisions in regard to the delimitation of the waters over which Canada has exclusive jurisdiction. The Republican majority of the committee arrived at the conclusion that the treaty, "instead of diminishing sources of irritation and causes of difficulty, arising from different interpretations and disputes, will very largely increase them." The minority of the committee, on the other hand, in a carefully prepared report, express the opinion that it is better for our country that the treaty should be ratified, and they are equally convinced that the en[illegible] class of our people who are actively engaged in our North Atlantic fishing industry will be benefited by its ratification. The minority declare that "the protocol to the treaty is an honorable and friendly overture of the British Government, and should be allowed to develop by actual experience whether this treaty will be beneficial to our fisheries and commerce."

The New Chinese Treaty was Ratified by the United States Senate, on May 7, after the two important amendments mentioned in these columns last week, had been adopted. By the addition of these amendments, the features of the treaty providing for the exclusion of Chinamen from the United States for the next twenty years, have been rendered still more stringent than was originally designed. Notwithstanding these very strict provisions, some of the Pacific coast senators expressed the opinion that the treaty was not strong enough to suit the requirements of their section of the country. The other senators thought, however, that the treaty fulfilled all reasonable expectations, and when the vote was taken, the treaty was ratified by the almost unanimous consent of the Senate. In other countries, too, the agitation against Chinese immigration is becoming very strong. The Government of New Zealand last week proclaimed all Chinese ports to be infected, in order to put a stop to the entrance into the colony of Chinese immigrants. The Government of South Australia has proposed that an intercolonial conference be held for the purpose of arranging for united measures to exclude Chinese immigrants.

The Passage of the International Copyright Bill through the Senate, was secured on the 9th inst., by a vote of 35 to 10. It was passed practically as reported from the Committee on Patents, and the amendments, which proposed to withhold the copyright from foreign newspapers, magazines, and periodicals, and to insert a provision that publishers of American newspapers or other periodicals should be allowed to copy articles from any foreign paper or periodical, were promptly rejected. It is considered certain that the bill will pass the House if it can be reached in time. The measure is not looked upon favorably in England. At a conference in London, on May 4, between representatives of the printing and allied trades and a section of the London Chamber of Commerce, the International Copyright Bill was denounced. The Right Hon. Mr. Ritchie, President of the Local Government Board, who received the deputation, was asked to invite other Chambers of Commerce to co-operate with them to prevent the adoption of such a law. It is thought that the opposition in England is caused by the clause which was inserted at the instance of the American Typographical Union, providing that copyrighted books, must be printed from type set within the limits of the United States. This expression of English disapproval causes considerable surprise and may render the House less disposed to pass the measure. To pass it in the form the English desire, would arouse the antagonism of the whole printing trade of the United States.

The River and Harbor Bill Which is Designed to take 20 millions of dollars out of the public treasury, was last week rushed through the House of Representatives under a suspension of the rules. Only 21 Democrats and 48 Republicans had their votes recorded against the proposed wasteful expenditures of public monies. Mr. Sowden of Pennsylvania, voiced the opinion of the minority when he emphatically declared that the House was not justified in making the extraordinary appropriations carried by the bill, and he asked whether the President, pledged to the honest and economical administration of the Government, would approve the measure if it was passed by Congress. It was high time to call a halt, and cease the reckless expenditure of the people's money. There never had been a more wasteful piece of legislation before Congress. It is apprehended that, extraordinary as the appropriations are, they will receive additions in the Senate. If the bill serves no other purpose, it will be instrumental in reducing the much-complained-of surplus in the treasury.

The Destruction of the Beautiful Cathedral of Buffalo, N. Y., on May 10, has caused general regret. It was caused by an explosion of the natural gas which is generally used in the city. It is supposed that there was too great a pressure on the mains, and the meter burst. A gas jet being alight near the meter, supplied the final element of destruction, and, in a minute, the great tongue of flame shot upward, setting on fire all the wood-work within reach The firemen were quickly on the spot, but were puzzled how to deal with a fire that was fed with burning gas. Before a plumber could be found to cut off the gas, the cathedral was gutted, and its two magnificent organs burned. The walls and tower still stand, but the interior is a mass of blackened ruins. There were many other explosions of natural gas in various parts of the city at the same time, and several fires were started. Among them was one in the Westminster Presbyterian chuch, but the janitor being able to turn off the gas, that building was saved.

A Terrible Catastrophe Occurred on the night of May 5, on the Philadelphia and Reading Railroad near Locust Gap, Pa. A freight train of seventy-five cars became disconnected by the breaking of a coupling, and the engine and three cars ran half a mile before the crew discovered that the train was divided. The first section awaited the arrival of the second at the foot of a heavy grade, but the two brakemen lost control of the second section, and it dashed into the first section, causing an explosion in two cars which were loaded with dynamite and giant powder. At the scene of the accident the railroad runs along a steep hill, at the bottom of which stood two rows of houses occupied by the Philadelphia and Reading Coal and Iron Company's employees. The force of the tremendous explosion wrecked these buildings, seventeen in all, and the stoves set fire to the ruins Eight persons, among them six children, suffered a horrible death, and twenty were badly injured. In addition to the homes, twelve cars were de troyed. All the windows in the Locust Ga churches and schools were broken and the doo blown off. In Mount Carmel, two and ha miles distant, large store windows were broke The explosion was distinctly felt in Shamok six miles away. None of the train hands we injured, although one of them was blown considerable distance.

The Affairs of Bulgaria are Again Attractin general attention. It is reported that Bismarc in accordance with the formally expressed de sire of Emperor Frederick and the Czar, will as the Porte to depose Prince Ferdinand. Th latter, however, seems to be determined t maintain his position on the Bulgarian thron In the course of a speech at a banquet in th hall of the Sabranje, (the Legislature), at Ti nova, he emphatically declared: "Here, in th building, I swore to lead Bulgaria to the go marked out for her in history. I now repe that oath, assuring you that, without sparin myself, I shall with heart and soul adhere to th promise I made before God and the people."

The Necessity of Placing England in a Pro er state of defence, was urged by a deputatio of members of Parliament, who, last week, pr sented an address to that effect to the Rig Hon. Edward Stanhope, Secretary of State f War. Mr. Stanhope declared that there was n occasion for a panic. England's preparations, h said, compared favorably with those of forei powers. Still, the Government recognized th necessity for immediate action. At all the mi itary ports and coaling stations the work strengthening the defences was being carrie on with renewed activity, and at the leadi mercantile ports every effort was being made complete the submarine mining defences." A attack upon London by way of the Tham would be made an absolute impossibility. Mu tifarious forces of regulars, militia and volu teers, were about to be organized, and the Go ernment would be able to produce at short n tice a field army sufficient to defend Englan and primarily to protect London. The Lond *Daily Telegraph*, in a column article heade "England in Danger," asserts on "the highe military authority," which is supposed to mea Lord Wolseley, that the strength of the army entirely insufficient, and declares that "the n tion ought to demand that instant attention given to our army and navy."

The Papal Rescript Relating to Boycottin and the Nationalists plan of campaign have n at present operated favorably in Ireland. Th tenants of a number of estates in the Coun Clare have adopted this plan, and "moo lighters" have raided four farms, because th occupants had paid their rents. They destro ed property and injured the tenants. On M 10, exciting struggles took place at Carmac near Thurles, between a strong force of eme gency policemen and tenants whom they soug to evict. The police used a battering ram effecting an entrance to some of the house They met with a stout resistance, the tenan throwing boiling water at them and assulti them with sticks and stones. Some of the i tended evictions were effected. The others, is believed, will be abandoned. Mr. Parnell h taken occasion to express his opinion on th action of the Vatican. At a banquet given hi by the Eighty Club in London last week h said, Irish Catholics knew their political du and how to vindicate themselves. They woul not allow anybody, however, high or influenti to influence them a jot in their political duty t their country—a thing that had been repeated tried from Rome, but had always failed. Th opinion is gaining ground that the action of th Pope will have disastrous results as the mo desperate and lawless classes of agitators hav hitherto been checked by association with th priests, who to some extent restrained them. the influence of the priests is withdrawn i obedience to the Papal rescript the Nationali organization will fall into the hands of the wor elements of the people.

The Exclusion of the Lady Delegates from the Methodist Episcopal General Conference was voted on May 7. The debate grew warmer as it proceeded, and at last Dr. Buckley, who was the leader of the members opposed to their admission, declared that if the conference admitted the lady delegates it would exceed its powers, and he and a hundred other ministers would move for impeachment. The question was at last settled by the adoption of an amendment to the committee's report, adding to the clause against admission these words: "But since there is great interest in this question, and since the church generally should be consulted in regard to such an important matter; therefore, Resolved. That we submit to the annual conferences the proposition to amend the second restrictive rule by adding the words, 'And said delegates may be men or women,' after the words, 'two lay delegates for an annual conference,' so that it will read, 'Nor of more than two lay delegates for an annual conference, and said delegates may be men or women.'" So amended, the report of the committee excluding the ladies from this conference was adopted. The ministers and lay delegates voted separately. The former stood 159 yeas, and 122 noes. The laymen were more favorable: their vote was yeas 78, noes 76. So this question which has long agitated the church, was decided for the time, and referred to the local conferences for final settlement.

An Octogenarian Sailor Wept as He Told the story of his conversion in Sands Street Church, Brooklyn, on Sunday May 6. It was at the last service held in the old church, which is now to be pulled down to make way for the Bridge improvements, and many persons who were deeply affected, recalled incidents and scenes of the hundred years of the church's existence. Among these was Mr. Frazier, who was converted through the blessing of God on the labors of a band sent out from Sands Street Church to work among sailors: "I used to be one one of the worst boys in the Sunday-school," said gray-haired Mr. Frazier, "and they decided to put me out. But there was a little man who wore knee-breeches and a queue who said, 'No, bring him to me.' He was a glorious little man, and he put his hand on my head, and talked to me in such a loving manner that I melted there and then. I was wicked after that, but finally I gave my heart to Jesus in the old church."

A Beautiful Prodigal Girl Received a Prodigal's welcome last week at her father's home in St. Louis. Two years ago she was the pride of her family and the centre of an admiring circle of friends. Amateur theatricals were a favorite amusement of the social circle, and this young lady was successful in her parts, and she was so highly praised as to convince her that she had dramatic talent and would make a popular actress. Accordingly she left home, secretly, and joined a travelling theatrical company passing through St. Louis. She received a salary of fifteen dollars a week, which was subsequently raised as her talent developed. The company did not succeed when it came East, as it had done in the West, and finally on reaching New York, was disbanded, and the manager was unable to pay salaries. All this time the girl's parents had been sorrowfully searching for her and receiving letters at long intervals, saying that she was doing well and was perfectly contented. A gentleman at Newark, N. J., who was a friend of the family, had promised to keep a look out for the girl if the company came East and when he heard of its being disbanded, he made a search for her, but failed. Two weeks ago, however, he heard of a girl being in distress, and charitably went to her relief. He was agreeably surprised to find that she was the girl from St. Louis. He immediately telegraphed to her father, and was authorized to promise her full forgiveness and a welcome home if she would come. At first the girl had obstinately refused to go home, when urged to do so, refusing to believe that she would be received, but on reading her father's telegram, she broke down completely, and was eager to go. On May 7, she set out and was met with demonstrations of joy. The same assurance of forgiveness and welcome God holds out to every repentant prodigal, and none have ever been rejected who have trusted in it. (Isa. 55 : 7.)

A Gigantic Lumber Raft is being Constructed at Finger-Board, on the Bay of Fundy. It is being built by the same man who made the raft which caused so much trouble last year. The new raft is to contain *over thirty thousand logs*, and will be seven hundred feet long. It will be worth about $60,000. This second attempt to solve the problem of cheap transportation of lumber to New York will, the owner predicts, be successful. The first attempt failed, because the tug was not strong enough to manage the stupendous floating mass, and being obliged to cut it adrift, was unable to regain hold upon it, and the raft having no steering apparatus, nor any one upon it to guide it, drifted out to sea. This time the constructor will put huge masts and sails upon it, to reduce the labor of the tug; a house to accommodate fourteen men will be built upon it, and it will be fitted with a rudder. The logs will be connected with strong chains, and spiked together, and it is thought that it will be manageable and cannot be disintegrated. It will be, therefore, like a huge ship, but unlike other ships, it will be ship and cargo in combination, and its component parts will constitute its value. It is thus with the Church, which is being gathered out of the world, and which cannot be disintegrated, but which Christ will bring into the eternal haven. It will bear no earthly treasure, but its individual members are each and all precious to Him who gave Himself for them. (Eph. 4 : 16.)

The Discovery of a Cave a Mile in Length is reported from Tully, N. Y. A press despatch from that place states that on May 8, a farmer employed a number of men to dig a well near his house. When his men had excavated a few feet the bottom suddenly fell out of the well, at a time when, happily, all the men were in places of safety. There was left in the bottom of the shallow well a broad hole leading into utter darkness, apparently of unfathomable depth. In a short time an exploring party was formed, ropes and windlasses were procured, and several daring men were lowered to the bottom. It was found that the bottomless well led into a cave, whose bottom was about forty feet below the well. The explorers went over the cave with torches and lanterns, and found it to be about a mile long. It extends directly under a lake, but is entirely dry, no water whatever having been found. A number of stone columns and some *fine stalactites and stalagmites* were found, with fossil formations, and Mr. English, the geologist, who subsequently descended, found two very fine specimens of trilobite. Another explorer found a number of fern formations. The farmer had been living for many years over these wonderful natural beauties, utterly unconscious of their existence. It is just so with the wonders of grace. Every Christian after his conversion, is astonished that he could have lived so long ignorant of the glories revealed to him. (Rom. 11 : 33).

A Brave Girl Rescued a Whole Family from a burning house in a village near Tower City, Dak. Ter., on May 1. About six o'clock in the morning Miss Greenough, a girl only sixteen years old, was passing a lonely cottage, when she noticed smoke issuing from a window, soon followed by a tongue of flame. No one was in sight, but the girl raised a loud cry which was heard by some men at a distance, Realizing that no time was to be lost, she forced open the door of the cottage and wakened a woman who had a babe sleeping by her side. The woman ran down stairs with the infant in her arms, and escaped with slight burns received on the stairway which had by this time caught fire. She hurriedly told Miss Greenough that two other children were sleeping in the room overhead, and the brave girl ran up-stairs to save them. She brought both down, but when she came to the place where the stairs were burning they halted. Escape seemed cut off, but Miss Greenough quickly decided on her course. Calling to the men who had come to the rescue to be ready, she raised one child in her arms, and threw it over and through the flames to a man who caught it. She did the same with the second child and finally leaped herself. She was severely burned, but all the others were only slightly injured. But for her efforts the whole family would probably have perished. None who hear of the noble girl's heroism can fail to admire and honor her for it; but what must be the feelings toward her of that mother and her children! It would be strange if they were ungrateful. Yet men for whose salvation Christ suffered and died hear the story of His death with indifference. (Acts 13 : 40, 41)!

BRIEF NOTES.

Rockford, Ill., with a population, of about 20,000, will have no licensed saloons during the coming year.

A great revival at Crawfordsville, Ind., followed the labors of Rev. B. Fay Mills. His services were preceded by united preparatory meetings, and the pastors are now continuing the work.

On Sunday Evening, May 6, Dr. Talmage, clad in regimental uniform, preached the annual sermon in the Tabernacle, to the Thirteenth Regiment, of which he was recently elected Chaplain.

By a recent decision of the Supreme Court of Pennsylvania, saloon-keepers are made responsible for any injury, loss or damage suffered by their patrons in the saloons, or as a consequence of their visits there.

At the Seventy-second Annual meeting of the American Bible Society, it was announced, that by the efforts of Dr. Hepburn, the Bible in Chinese had been completed. The receipts last year amounted to $557,340.

Plymouth Church, Brooklyn, has decided to invite Dr. Lyman Abbott to become permanent pastor of the Church, in succession to the late Rev. Henry Ward Beecher. Dr. Abbott's services as temporary pastor have been highly appreciated by the Church.

Ben Hogan, the Ex-Pugilist, has been holding services in the M. E. Church, East Syracuse, N. Y. The building has been crowded to excess, and much good has been done. At the first service, after Mr. Hogan's plain, earnest talk, fifty persons rose to ask for prayer.

Three prominent members of the National Women's Christian Temperance Union, who were negotiating recently for the hire of a hall in New York, were assured by the Irish janitor that the profits of the liquor sold at the bar would defray more than half the cost of the hall.

At the annual meeting of the National Temperance Society in New York, on May 8, it was stated that the receipts for the past year were $60,675.65. Eight colored men are now employed by the Society in the Southern States, and are doing good work among their brethren. Dr. Cuyler was elected President.

At the Conference on the Christian Principles of Civil Government, recently held in Philadelphia, a resolution was passed, declaring, "That we regard 'Sunday mails,' 'Sunday railroad trains,' and 'Sunday newspapers' as a triple unholy alliance, against the sanctity of the Sabbath and the rights of the people to a day of rest."

Two respectable farmers named Primley, living near Seneca, Kan., state that on May 3, a farm-hand named Althous, during a heated discussion on the Sacrament of the Lord's Supper, uttered an appalling blasphemy. The words were scarcely out of his mouth, when he became violently insane, rushed around with awful groans, and, despite their efforts, made his escape into the woods.

During the first two weeks of Dr. L. W. Munhall's meetings in St. Paul, Minn., fully one thousand persons publicly confessed Jesus as their Saviour. Seven hundred and eighty-three handed in their names and declared their church preferences. The services on Sundays are held in Market Hall, which seats two thousand persons, but large numbers were unable to obtain admission.

The Christian Chapel at 344 Central Avenue, Brooklyn, N. Y., is making encouraging progress. The work was commenced about a year ago by Mr. George Lusty, who, remarking the need of the locality, opened a Sunday-school there. There were only 20 children at first, but the school now contains 130, and there are regular preaching services, the congregation, composed chiefly of non-church goers, filling the room. Mr. Lusty had no promise of support, but relied solely on God, and he has been enabled to maintain the work.

"SHE WAS NOT HID."

A New Sermon by Pastor C. H. Spurgeon.

"And when the woman saw that she was not hid, she came trembling, and falling down before Him, she declared unto Him before all the people for what cause she had touched Him, and how she was healed immediately."—Luke 8:47.

The Divine Purpose in the Woman's Healing—A Confession Required—I. Hiding in Her Case very Excusable—She was Weak and Timid—Her Cure would be Known Without Confession—Not Essential to the Cure—II. Hiding not Permitted—Needed for the Lord's Glory—For the Sake of Others—For Her Own Good—Became a Daughter—III. Christians in Hiding should Come Out—For the Sake of the Church—The Family—Neighbors—Lady Burgoyne's Confession—Objections Answered.

LAST Sabbath morning we spoke upon the woman who was healed of her issue of blood. After having spent all her living upon physicians, and being disappointed in them all, she touched the Saviour's garment, and was healed immediately. She came behind Him, for she did not wish to be seen. She said not a word: she had not the courage to ask for the blessing in an open manner. When cured, she slunk away into the crowd: she was anxious to be unobserved.

If the narrative had ended where we left it last Sunday, what a quietus it would have afforded to those good, peace-loving people who, in these days of blasphemy and rebuke, will take no sides at all! "Anything for a quiet life." They are very comfortable, and mean to remain so. What does it matter to them though the whole Church should be rotten with error? They hope to go quietly to heaven—indeed, they feel they are going there; and, if they are not soldiers of the cross, yet they trust they are followers of the Lamb; if they do not contend earnestly for the faith once delivered to the saints, yet still they eat the fat, and drink the sweet, and enjoy the privileges of a comfortable religion. That is the present policy of many, and gladly enough would they have sheltered themselves behind this woman. She, however, was not hid, nor may they be.

I. First, then, we say concerning this woman,

Her Hiding

seemed very excusable. I have already said, that if, in any instance, a cure might have been concealed, this was one; and it was so for many reasons. First, because of this woman's natural timidity, and because of the nature of her malady. It would appear that if in any case the thing might have been done in a corner, or if done in a crowd, might have been passed over without remark, this was an evident case in point. Yet the Saviour, tenderly considerate as He is, will not have it so. And you, dear friend, may say, "I am naturally so very timid and retiring: pray, excuse me." This woman was not only bashful, but her sickness made her rightly wish to remain in obscurity. "I should not like my story to be known," says one. She might have justly said the same; it must have been hard, indeed, for her to confess what the Lord had done. Yet she had to acknowledge His grace openly, and so must you.

In addition to this, remember that the Saviour did not court publicity. He laid no injunction upon those whom He healed that they should tell everyone of the marvel. He did not seek fame or observation: He did not strive nor cry, nor cause His voice to be heard in the streets. In several cases He bade the healed ones tell no man what was done; and in this case He had given the cure without any open request for it. Might she not from this conclude that her secret act of faith was approved, and that it might continue secret, since it had gained the boon? You may reason in that way about yourself, and say that Jesus does not need that you should testify for Him. Indeed, it is true, that He does not need anything of any of us; but is this a fit way of treating your Lord? You may say that quietude on your part would be excusable; but as the Saviour did not think so in this woman's case, I believe that He will not think so in your case. I trust that in His mercy He will deal with you as with her, and compel you to come out and own the wonders of His grace.

Excuse might also have been found for the healed woman, in the fact that her cure would make itself known by its results. When she reached home everybody would see that she was quite another person; and when they asked how it came to pass, she could tell them all about it. They would see in her life the best evidence of the work of our Lord upon her. Is it not better to speak by your life than by your lips? Exactly so, and herein lies the apparent force of this excuse for disobedience. It needs some truth to keep

A Falsehood on its Legs.

Note well that this woman was not permitted to withhold the open avowal of her indebtedness to Christ, even though it was certain that her health and her conduct would witness to His power. I know what you say: "I need not join a church: I can be a Christian at home. Better live a Christian life than wear a Christian name." My friend, we never proposed to you that you should put the wearing of a Christian name in the place of a Christian life—we have solemnly spoken the reverse of such a notion. We would earnestly remind you of our Saviour's words: "These things ought ye to have done, and not to have left the other undone."

Another pretext might have served this woman, if she desired an excuse. She might truthfully have said, "It is evident that an open confession is not essential to my cure, for I am cured." She was healed immediately, and it is added, that she felt in her body that she was healed of that plague; so that she knew that she was healed, and it was clear that

An Avowal

of her faith was not necessary to her receiving that great boon from the Lord. Hence, many argue, "To confess Christ and join with His people is not necessary to my salvation." Who said it was? Open confession is not necessary; nay, is not permitted, till you are saved. How could this woman have made any confession of a cure till she was cured? But being cured, it then became necessary that she should confess it; not necessary to the cure, that is clear; but necessary because of the cure.

Thus I have shown you that in her case many excuses might have been made; and yet, after all, it would not have been a fitting thing if she had stolen away in the crowd, and gone home cured without praising and blessing her Lord. It would have been to her everlasting dishonor. Within herself she felt that it was a marvellous cure which had come to her by a touch of Him, and she could not praise Him enough. The stones would have cried out against her if she had not confessed His miracle of gracious power, and the earth would have refused to bear up such a monster of ingratitude. Instantly she fell down before Him, and told all the truth.

II. Secondly, her

Hiding Was Not Permitted

by the Saviour. For, first, an open confession on her part was needful in reference to the Lord's glory. If this woman concealed her cure, others might do the same; and if they all did it, then Christ's commission would have no visible endorsement from the Lord God. I should like to impress this idea upon those of you who do not confess your Lord: whatever is right for you to do is right for other people to do. If it is right for one Christian not to confess Christ and join a church, it must be allowable for other Christians to do the same. If *you* may go to heaven by the backstairs so may I, and God's grand entrance to the kingdom may be deserted. Who will care to go to heaven by the open way, with all its responsibilities and opposition, if you can just as easily take the snug road behind the hedges, and slink into glory without observation? The change wrought in the spiritual and moral condition of the saved is God's attestation of the gospel; and if this is not to be spoken of, how is the world to know that God has sent the gospel at all?

As God is seen in his works of creation, Jesus is seen in His miracles of grace. Shall we rob Him of His glory? God forbid that we should do Him this serious dishonor. When first I knew the Lord, if anybody had said to me, "You will be ashamed to confess Christ although He has saved you. The day will come when you will blush to own His name," I should have felt indignant at the suggestion. Why, I wanted to tell everybody of the Saviour's love. If there had been nobody else to hear me, *I should have had to tell the cat.* I felt like Bunyan did when he said he wanted to tell the crows on the ploughed land all about it. I cannot understand how it is that you who know the Saviour, or think you do, can imagine it to be right to hide away, and cover up the glory of Christ. Oh, tell it! Tell it all the world over that He has healed us, forgiven us, and saved us.

But the confession had to be made

For the Sake of Others.

Do any of you wish to live unto yourselves? If you do, you need saving from selfishness. I have seen it brought as a charge against evangelical religion that we teach men to look to their own salvation first, and that this is a kind of spiritual selfishness. Ah, but if that salvation means salvation from selfishness, where is the selfishness of it? It is a very material point in salvation to be saved from hardness of heart and carelessness about others. Do you want to go to heaven alone? I fear you will never go there. Have you no wish for others to be saved? Then you are not saved yourself. Be sure of that. What is the most natural plan to use for the salvation of others but to bear your own personal testimony?

But especially she had to do this

For Her Own Good.

The Saviour had designs of love in bringing this poor trembler forward before all the people. By this He saved her from a host of fears which would have haunted her. Suppose she had gone home healed, and had never confessed it; surely she would have felt uneasy? A sense of having stolen the boon without leave or license would have caused her uneasy dreams and sad apprehensions. She would worry herself with the fear that the disease would soon return again, or that she would die from a fearful judgment. All such fears were rendered impossible by her open confession, and that which followed upon it. Jesus assured her that He had taken no offence; He wished her to have no fears, for, said He, "Thy faith hath saved thee. Go in peace."

Our Lord also gave her an increased blessing after her confession. Perhaps the Lord is reserving some great favor for some of you when you avow His name. You hide indoors, and *He allows you milk enough to live upon;* but if you would come out and confess Him, He would feed you with the strong meat of the kingdom. You would become a braver and more useful person if you would take up your cross. Confess what Christ has done for you. For what did the Saviour give her?

He gave her clearly to know her relationship to Him. He said, "Daughter!" I do not know that the Saviour ever called any other woman daughter, for He was guarded in His speech to women; but to this one woman

He Said, "Daughter."

Oh, may the Lord give trembling ones to see and feel the near and dear relationship which exists between Christ and their souls! May your sonship come up before your minds most vividly, as a reward of obedience. May Jesus say to some of you, "Son, be of good comfort"; or to another, "Daughter, be of good cheer, thy faith hath saved thee." "What would I give," says one, "if Jesus would call me 'daughter'"! Give Him your whole self by believing in Him, and confession of Him, and see if He does not reveal to you His love."

Next notice that He gave a commendation to her faith: "Thy faith hath made thee whole." Why, it was not her faith which made her whole.

was it? No, but Jesus puts His own crown upon the head of faith. It is always safe for Jesus to crown faith, because faith always crowns Jesus. Her faith would answer, "Lord, I did nothing, thou didst it all," and, therefore, Jesus ascribes her healing to her faith. How much I desire that you, who are now afraid of your own faith, would win your Lord's praise by coming out and bearing witness to what He has done for you! Then will you not only believe, but also know that you have believed, and end for ever your present state of miserable doubt.

III. Thus I have already reached my last point: your

Hiding Ought to be Ended.

"Whom are you speaking to, sir?" Well, not to you, dear friends, who are always to the front, lifting the banner of the cross. "Whom are you speaking to, sir?" To you, my friend, if you are really a disciple, but secretly, for fear of the Jews. If you keep yourself to yourself, it is to you that I am speaking, and I desire to press upon you your obligations. *What owest thou to my Lord?* You are washed from your uncleanness. You are clothed with the robe of righteousness. You are accepted in the Beloved. You know that you have passed from death to life. Unless fearfully mistaken, you know that you are the Lord's. Well, then, own it. Do not be ashamed to take your place in

The Cross-Bearing Procession,

and follow the Lamb whithersoever he goeth. This is still the way to honor and immortality.

Do you not think you owe something to the church of God, which kept the gospel alive in the world for you to hear? Did not a band of godly men and women meet together, and see that the gospel was preached? Was it not so that you were saved? Should you not help to keep that church going by whose means you were brought to Jesus? May I be permitted also to say, I think you owe something to the minister who led you to Jesus? What a cheer it is to us when we get a letter from one who has found the Lord through our teaching; and better still, when face to face we meet one who has trusted the Saviour through our poor instrumentality! Those who are sowers of the seed know what a joy it is to see it spring up. Besides, you owe it to yourselves. Are you going to be mere bats, fluttering out when none will observe you, and hiding from the light? Are you going to be like mice, which only come out at night to nibble in the pantry? Quit yourselves like men! You owe it to your family. You should tell your household what grace has done for you. Many a person wonders that his sons and daughters do not turn out well, when he himself has never been openly on the Lord's side. Do you not think you owe it to your neighbors to show your colors. O ye saved ones, fly them at the mast-head, nail them there; and never let the enemy take them down.

Now let me hear some of

Your Objections,

and answer them. I hope I have been answering them all through my sermon. Here is one. "Well, you know, Mr. Spurgeon, I am such an insignificant person. It cannot make any difference what I do." Yes, and this woman was a very insignificant person—only a woman! When I speak thus in English, it is a very ungallant speech, but if a Rabbi had said it in Christ's day, it would not have seemed at all out of place, for they taught that no holy person ought, in the streets, to allow a woman's dress to touch him, lest he should be defiled thereby. They thought that if a scribe tried to teach a woman the law, he dishonored the law by doing so. Religious men lightly esteemed women in the Saviour's day. Our divine Lord never gave the slightest sanction to such an abominable spirit, and I am not going to lend any sanction to your saying "I am only a poor feeble woman." God thinks much of the lowly: you must not talk so. Besides, many of you do not think so meanly of yourselves as you pretend to do when you want to avoid your duty. Do not excuse yourselves through pretended humility.

Jesus does not excuse one of His healed ones from owning the work of His grace. A dear lady, who has long since gone to glory, was once an honored member of this church; it was

Lady Burgoyne,

and when she wished to unite with us she said to me, "Dear sir, I cannot go before the church. It is more than I can manage to make a confession of Christ before the members." I told her that we could make no exception for anybody, and especially not for her, who was so well established in the faith that she could surely answer a few questions before those who were brethren and sisters in the Lord. She came bravely, and spoke most sweetly for her Lord. Some of you may remember her, with her sweet countenance, and venerable bearing. When she had owned her Lord, she put both her hands on mine, and said emphatically, "With all my heart I thank you for this; I shall never be ashamed of Christ now. When aristocratic friends call upon me I will speak to them of my Lord." She did so constantly. You never found her slow to introduce the gospel, whoever might be with her. She frequently said to me, "Oh, what a training that was for me! I might have been a timid one all my days if I had not made that confession before the church." Now I say to you, if it be an ordeal, undergo it for Christ's sake. But, indeed, it should be a pleasure to own your Lord among His own disciples.

False Shame.

"Alas!" says one, "I could not tell of what the Lord has done for me, because mine is such a sorrowful story. You know what I used to be, sir, sovereign grace has made me to differ, but my former life silences me!" Was it not so with this woman? How could she tell her story? But then it was to the glory of God, and so "she told Him all the truth." Whatever you were before you were converted, never boast of it; but at the same time do not deny it, but honor your Saviour. Remember how often Paul tells us what he was before conversion. If any rake up your old sin, answer that it is sadly true, but you have been washed, and much has been forgiven you. Own that you were the chief of sinners, and that even now you are less than the least of all saints, but the Lord has brought you from death to life to the glory of His name.

"Ah!" says one, "but suppose after I had confessed Christ I should become as bad as ever." Suppose that this woman had supposed such a sad thing, and had said, "O Lord I cannot confess that thou hast healed me, for I do not know how I may be in six months' time." She was not so mistrustful. "But suppose the Lord should leave me, and suffer me to leave Him." Yes, and suppose you were to leave off supposing anything of the sort, and just take His promise as it stands. "He that believeth in Him hath everlasting life." "He that believeth and is baptized, shall be saved." Do you believe His word? Then lay aside such suspicions. Jesus does not give us

A Trumpery, Temporary Salvation;

He does not save us for a quarter of a year and then leave us. If saved by Him, you will be forever saved! He is the Author of eternal salvation. If He gives you a new heart, it is a new heart, and will never become an old one. When I trusted Christ, I did not trust Him to save me for a year or two, but for ever. When you go the heavenly journey, *take a ticket all the way through.* Some of our friends take a ticket to the next station, and then rush out to get another. Take your ticket for the New Jerusalem, and not for a half-way-house. The train will never break down, and the track will never be torn up. If you can trust Jesus Christ to carry you through to glory, He will do it. Let not that fear disturb you.

"Ah!" says one more, "it seems too good to be true. I cannot think that such a one as I may dare to link myself with the Lord Jesus Christ, who is so great and so glorious." Yet this is your only hope. You are only saved through being in Christ. This may be too great, too good for us to imagine, but then we need not imagine it; it is clearly revealed in the infallible Word of God. He that believeth in Jesus is one with Him. Come, then, and own that blessed oneness.

Be one with Christ to-day in his humiliation, and you shall be one with Him by-and-by in His glory. Be despised and ridiculed for His sake, and you shall be honored and glorified with Him in the day when He appeareth. God bless you for Christ's sake! Amen.

GEMS FROM NEW BOOKS.

A MISTAKEN CHASE OF A COW.*

LIVING in the outskirts of the city, where the fences were poor, and straying cattle often gave them great annoyance, Henry [Mr. Beecher] one day, to his immense disgust, found a cow quietly resting in the middle of the barn floor. With the accumulated indignation aroused by numerous chases which these poachers of the highway had led him, by many tramplings across flower-beds and destruction of garden vegetables, he drove her out and chased her down the street. Coming in hot and tired from his run, he threw himself on the sofa, saying, "There, I guess I've taught one old cow to know where she belongs." "What do you mean?" said his father, looking up apprehensively from his paper. "Why, I found another cow in the barn, and I have turned her out and chased her clear down the street, and I think she will stay away now." "Well," said Dr. Beecher, "you have done it. I have just bought that cow, and I had to wade the Ohio River twice to get her home; and, after I have got her safely into the barn, you have turned her out. You have done it now, and no mistake." And the chasing of that cow was renewed.

A Professor Puzzled.

Mr. Beecher roomed, while at college, with Professor Stowe, who was the soul of punctuality, and was continually pained at the failure of his young room-mate to be on time at morning prayers in the seminary chapel. Having done his best to wake him up one morning, apparently without success, he had gone down-stairs with many expressions of disgust. No sooner was he out of the room than Mr. Beecher sprang up, dressed himself as only college students can, ran to the seminary by a back way, and when the Professor entered, was sitting demurely in front of the desk. The amazement of the teacher at this unexpected appearance, rubbing his glasses and peering at him again and again, to determine whether it was real or he only saw a vision, was always remembered by Mr. Beecher with a chuckle of merriment.

Early Hardships.

Of his first pastorate, at Lawrenceburg, Ind., Mr. Beecher wrote at a later date: "I had no idea that I could preach. I never expected that I could accomplish much. I merely went to work with the feeling, 'I will do as well as I can, and I will stick to it, if the Lord pleases, and fight His battle the best way I know how.' And I was thankful as I could be. Nobody ever sent me a spare-rib that I did not thank God for the kindness which was shown me. I recollect when Judge —— gave me his cast-off clothing; I felt that I was sumptuously clothed. I wore old coats and second-hand shirts for two or three years, and I was not above it, either, although sometimes, as I was physically a somewhat well-developed man, and the Judge was thin and his legs were slim, they were rather a tight fit.

"You can form some conception of that field when I tell you that it was a place where they had four gigantic distilleries, from which was carried to market a steamboat-load of liquor every day. When I went there, I entered upon my vocation of preaching; I found a church—a little red-brick building—with nineteen or

* From a Biography of Henry Ward Beecher, by William C. Beecher and Rev. Samuel Scoville, assisted by Mrs. Henry Ward Beecher. 713 pages, with numerous portraits and illustrations. Price, $3. Published by *Charles L. Webster & Company*, New York.

Bishop William Taylor.

Jemmy's Friend Exhibited the Shoes.

twenty members. There was one man, and the rest were women. With the exception of two persons, there was not one of them who was not obliged to gain a livelihood by the labor of the hands. So you will understand how very poor they were.

"I was sexton as well as minister. There were no lamps, so I went and bought some, and filled them and lit them. *I swept the church and lighted my own fires. I did not ring the bell, because there was none.* I opened the church before every meeting, and shut and locked it after every meeting. I took care of everything in the church. Here, in this little frontier village, then on the very borders of civilization, I began my real work."

BISHOP WILLIAM TAYLOR.

(See Portrait.)

THE most conspicuous figure, and by far the most interesting, in the throng of eminent men assembled in the Methodist Episcopal Quadrennial Conference in New York, is that of Bishop Taylor, whose life and labors have made his name known all over the world. William Taylor *was born* May 2, 1821. He is therefore now sixty-seven years of age, but his manly, upright figure, his quick, nervous energy, and his elastic step give the impression to a stranger that he is still in his prime. The place of his birth was a city at the base of North Mountain, Rockbridge County, Virginia. His father was a tanner, and until he was twenty years of age the future Bishop spent his working hours in the tannery. The family were Presbyterians; but the father, having attended a camp-meeting at Cold Sulphur Springs, in 1833, profited so much under the preaching of a Methodist minister that he resolved on joining a Methodist church.

William Taylor was converted while a youth, and it became his highest ambition to preach the gospel, especially as an evangelist. He applied for and received an exhorter's license from the Baltimore Conference, and was subsequently licensed as a preacher and appointed missionary to San Francisco, Cal. His work, "California Illustrated," gives a vivid picture of his life in that State. He evidently entered upon his duties in an apostolic spirit, and devoted himself without reservation to the service of his Master. So earnest was he, and so widely did God bless his labors, that the name "California" Taylor is that by which, even at this day, he is best known.

In 1862 Mr. Taylor commenced his first foreign evangelizing tour. His destination was Australia. Dr. Buckly, writing of Mr. Taylor's labors in that country, says that at the Ecumenical Council he inquired of the Wesleyan ministers there from Australia as to the success of the different American and European evangelists who had visited the scene of their labors, and without exception they stated that the permanent effects of the evangelistic labors of William Taylor in Australia were greater than those of any man who visited that country.

From Australia Mr. Taylor went to Africa, and labored in Cape Colony, Natal, and Caffraria, where great additions were reported, both among foreigners and natives, 1200 colonists and 7000 Kaffirs professing conversion.

India is probably the land nearest to Mr. Taylor's heart. For that country he has labored and prayed incessantly since the first time he set foot in it, in 1870. He had no salary, but he set to work in faith, believing that God would feed him as long as He had need of him. He had written one or two books, which were selling well in America, and they supplied him with funds for travelling expenses. He preached throughout Southern India, opening preaching-stations everywhere, and where churches already existed doubling and trebling the number of the worshippers. He left India in 1875, to *assist Mr. Moody* in England; but the condition of India has been a burden on his heart.

Space will not permit a description of his work in Palestine, Ceylon, Canada and South America. The Bishops' address at the General Conference at Cincinnati thus referred to his work in the last-named sphere: "The western coast of South America was visited a few years since by the Rev. William Taylor, and under his influence several young men and women have gone to that region, chiefly as teachers, *risking their support* among the people and also endeavoring to preach the Gospel of Christ."

At the Conference, in May, 1884, Mr. Taylor was present as a delegate from Southern In and when it was resolved to elect a Bishop the African field, he was chosen for the of Since that time he has labored zealously in Dark Continent, planting stations and direct the labors of the missionaries who have g out at his invitation.

LITTLE JEMMY'S FATHER.

(See Illustration.)

IN one of the poorest and most squalid tricts of a great city a few workingmen w assembled in their dinner-hour in a salo They brought their dinners with them, and saloon-keeper, with an eye to custom, allo them to eat them in his place.

They were all chatting amicably except man, who sat on a barrel reading the newspa which the proprietor thoughtfully provided the use of his customers. He was not a c tomer though he would like to have been, was he in the strict sense of the word a worki man, though he ought to have been, as he a wife and children who were in sad need money. Simon had no money either, and bar-tender had just apprized him that he no credit, but Simon wanted a drink badly, was waiting in the hope of some friend com in who would treat him.

Now and again the saloon-door was pus open an inch or two, and a little curly head w two bright eyes could be seen. One of the d ers caught sight of it at last, and beckon the child in, said to his companions, "Look this pretty little lad. Come here, boy; what you want?"

"Want a piece o' bread," was the brief rep

"Well, you little scarecrow, you do lo hungry. See what you can do with a cracke And he lifted the child on the counter, a handed him a big cracker out of the dish. T child had on a ragged shirt and pants, no soc and his little bare feet were thrust into a p of boots so much too large for him that it m have been difficult to keep them on. There a general laugh at these boots when they came conspicuous from the child's position.

"Where did you get your boots from, little man?" said his friend, who was hold him on the counter.

They ain't *my* boots," the child. "They'm er's Sunday boots; her said I could wear 'cause I ain't got e."

"Now, ain't that a e?" said the man, ing an arm around child. "Fancy what n must be to let a as pretty and smart is go around in this And these are his ay boots, too; he look a nice respect- kind of a man if his ay clothes match his ay boots." And he the thin little leg up he inspection of his anions.

"ather's out o' work," in the child, as if in ce of his parent.

should think so," the man, "and judg- y your looks, I should e generally is. I'll bet as his beer every day, gh. If I'd a lad like I'd see if I couldn't bit better for you. I my little un when he about his age, and I got over it yet, though a good many years I guess his father ld get over it easier. don't seem to take h stock in him."

"Don't I, though?" said n, who all this time kept his position on cask, hiding his face nd the newspaper, lest child should see and gnize him. That last oach, however, cut to the quick; and, ping down, took the in his arms. "He's the dearest thing I in the world, and he loves his father, you, Jemmy? But you are about right, , in what you've said beside that. I aint od father, but please God I'll make a ge."

non started out before the men had recov- from their surprise. The thought that he t lose his boy, and deserved to lose him, kened his steps. He went right to a place e he could sign the pledge; signed it, took boy home, and then set about looking for with an energy that ensured success.

MRS. TRANSOME'S PUPIL.

A SERIAL STORY.

(*Continued from page 309.*)

The Wreck.

HEN I saw Mrs. Transome I knew that Philip right, and that he had brought me what ey cannot buy. She had once been rather but she was bent into a small woman. Such asant, wholesome, motherly old dame she ked, that I stooped down and kissed the pla- sweet face, which was smiling at me.

"Thank you kindly, my dear," she said; "there's welcome in it."

She stroked my hand with her wrinkled gers, and before I could prevent her, lifted it her lips, and kissed it. I followed her and ilip to the room he had prepared for her, and tched him point out to her all the little things had chosen for her himself, with a boyish dness that I had not seen in him since he s a boy.

"You are to be a mother to us all," he said, ting her in a cushioned, old-fashioned chair had found somewhere, just suited for her; d she sat in it, smiling at us both, with her spectacles pushed up to the white border of her cap; "we're a set of rebel children," he went on, "and you'll find us harder to manage than your little school. As for me, I intend always to have my own way."

"Aye!" but thee has chose the Lord's way, Pippin," she answered, "and now thee canst have thine own way. Only, mind thee, He chose thee first."

"And you'll be at home here?" I asked.

"Sure!" she replied; "as much at home as in any place where Transome isn't? I shall go home where he is some day; but never fear me not being happy till the time comes."

That was true; for there was a quiet cheerful- ness, which was almost merriment in her, that never seemed to flag. The storm of life was over with her, and she was in the haven where she would be. Even the sorrow and the sin with which we had to deal did not disturb her deep tranquillity and profound trust in the im- measurable love of God. And this came into our refuge as a calm and pacifying element, which breathed itself over the passionate and stubborn hearts among whom our work lay. There was not one among the poor, miserable, lost girls, whom we sought and gathered into our home, who did not learn, before many days had passed, to call her "mother."

I know now that this was the perfect hour of my life. I had almost said, "Would to God I had known it then!"

One thing I grudged—that Philip should gain so little personal advantage from his wealth. Certainly he bought a vessel of his own, and he and his father went hither and thither as they pleased. They came in home oftener; but every time that they staid on shore longer than a few weeks, it became more evident that as long as Captain John Champion was living, Philip must still spend the best portion of his time on the sea.

It was about two years after Philip came into his inheritance, that at last a plan for sending out to America some of our rescued girls became practicable and advisable. It was a new step for us, and gave us much anxiety. But Philip had already joined in some emigration movements, and had given free passages to many a poverty-stricken artisan and his family to Canada. For the times were bad in England just then; and there was a great clamor of distress and want, which reached our ears more directly than it could have done in former days. George and Philip and I discussed the matter in and out, from every possible point of view.

"Milly," said George, "what would you say to going out yourself to America, and seeing the ladies who are to take charge of our girls?"

Such a question positively made my heart cease to beat for some seconds. It opened such vast changes, such undreamed-of revolutions in the habits of my life, that I shrank back frightened.

"Could you spare her!" cried Philip, all aglow with excitement.

"To be sure," said George, calmly, as if it were no unusual thing, "I should like her to go, if you promise to bring her home safely in two months or so."

"There is nothing I should like so much," exclaimed Philip; "you shall have no trouble at all, Aunt Milly; and we shall be back in two months at the latest, with three or four weeks to spare on the other side. You will know something of the sea, then! Say you will come."

"You might just as well take Mrs. Transome," I said; "I am too old now."

"I will take her," answered Philip; "she will come if I ask her, and you cannot say you are too old then. Say no more, Aunt Milly, I shall run down to Liverpool this very night, and see that everything is made comfortable for you.

I made some faint remonstrances; but it was impossible to me to oppose him when George was on his side. There were only a few days for me to prepare in; for all our arrangements had been made, and our emigrants were waiting to go. After all it was far less trouble and exertion than I had expected. Philip came back from Liverpool to fetch Mrs. Transome and me; and I had simply to leave myself in his hands, and have everything done for me. It was I who obeyed now, not Philip. I bade George farewell, and left home, with a strange sensation of losing almost my own identity.

But there were no good-byes at Liverpool. All we had to do was to cross over to the steamer, which lay in the river, ready to start, for we must get over the bar at the next tide, and the last hour was come. As we drew near, I was surprised to see how large it was.

"That is not your own ship, Philip?" I said.

The Temple of the Earth, Pekin, China. (*See page 309.*)

"No," he answered, "ours is much smaller, and not as steady a sailer as this is. So we are all going as passengers only; and I shall have nothing to do but take care of you both."

"Why wouldn't you let us rough it with you?" I asked, disappointed that we were not to cross the Atlantic in Philip's ship, and under Captain John Champion's command.

"Nothing rough should come near you, if I could help it," he said tenderly.

Certainly he had no intention to let us meet with any hardships on the sea. The stateroom he had chosen was the best on board, and was furnished luxuriously. The saloon upon which it opened was fitted up at a still greater cost, with a magnificence that astonished me, and still more amazed Mrs. Transome.

We had been out seven days, and more than two-thirds of the voyage were over; yet the same unvarying, shimmering, tossing plain of water stretched round us to the unbroken circle of the horizon. From the first the sky had been almost cloudless, and the vast dome of it bent over us like an hospitable roof, which would shelter us from all storms; for no one could dream of change in heavens so clear and calm.

"What are you looking at so earnest, Captain!" asked Mrs. Transome on the seventh evening, as we watched the solemn setting of the sun into the crimson sea. A low streak of livid purple, with a line of gold on its ragged edge, lay along the horizon southward; and Captain John Champion, with his brown hand shading his eyes, was searching the sky above it with keen glances. I asked Philip what it meant.

"A change in the weather," he said lightly; "you must get ready for some slight hardships, Aunt Milly."

We lingered late upon deck that night, so late that Mrs. Transome, who felt chilly with the night air and dew, left us. The moon was at the full, and we watched it rising in the clear eastern sky.

We bade one another good-night then, but after he had taken me down to my cabin, I heard him go up on deck again. Even to me there was a difference that night in the sound of the waves, as they beat against the thin planks between me and them. There came, too, all at once, a low, long, suppressed moan of the wind across the sea; the first sigh of the storm that was driving towards us. I shall hear it to my dying day; a sound never to be forgotten, sad and inexpressibly mournful.

All the next day, and the night following, did the storm rage. At first the passengers took little heed of it; but as hour after hour passed by, and the tossing of the sea did not lull for a moment, they grew frightened. The steerage-passengers were almost unmanageable. Whenever we saw the Captain, he looked grave and anxious; but he remained on deck most of the time, as did Philip and Captain John Champion. After the night set in, I sat with Mrs. Transome in our cabin, listening to the heavy roar of the storm, and the groaning timbers of the vessel, till Philip opened the door.

"Lie down," he said; "but do not undress to-night."

"Is there any danger?" I asked.

"Yes," he answered, "there is some danger, but my father and I are here to take care of you. You must trust yourself to me, and promise to obey me implicitly, and at once, whatever I may tell you to do."

"Philip?" I said, questioningly.

"Obey me like a child," he continued. "We have sprung a leak, and if the danger increases, there will be mad confusion on board among the steerage-folks. Your only safety will rest in simple obedience, even if we have to be parted for a little while. Do you understand me?"

"Oh, Philip!" I cried, "do not let me be parted from you."

"Not if I can help it," he said. "But it may be our duty to be separated. Will you leave me when I bid you go? Promise me, my darling."

"You will not leave me if you can help it?" I asked.

"Not for a moment," he answered, cheerfully. "And you promise me the same, mother?"

"No," said Mrs. Transome; "no, Pippin."

She was gazing at him earnestly, with a placid smile. Philip gazed back at her; and a solemn, steadfast, happy expression passed over both their faces.

"God bless thee, my boy Pippin!" she said. I think I see thee like thee was when I saw thee first! God bless thee!"

"We watched the daybreak dawning slowly over the whirl of waters that washed against the cabin-window. It strengthened very slowly into a dull, leaden light. There went a shiver suddenly all through the great ship; and a cry, as of one voice, rang through all the roaring of the tempest. Captain John Champion ran down to us. All the saloon was thronged with hurrying and frightened people. We struggled up the ladder on to the deck; some hands helping us, and others dragging us back again. All the deck was covered with panic-stricken men and women, fighting for their own safety. Captain John Champion pushed a way for me through the crowd; and all at once I felt Philip's arms about me.

"Shall we all be saved?" I cried.

"Not all," he said, "not all. But I promised George you should go home safely. I must do all I can for you."

"Will you be saved yourself?" I asked.

He did not speak. But the look upon his face, the young, beautiful, solemn face, was answer enough for me.

"He saved others: Himself He cannot save."

"Let me die with you," I cried, clinging to him.

"No! there is George at home," he said, "you must go for his sake."

He unclasped my hands from about him, and carried me across the deck to the place where the last boat was filling rapidly with passengers. I looked over the sea, heaving and swelling still, though the fierceness of the storm was over. Here and there peaks of black rock, against which the white foam was tossing. Some of the boats were already hurrying away, so heavily laden that they sank dangerously in the water. Underneath the deck there was a mingling of fearful sounds, of cries and shrieks for help which none could give. Every face about me wore a terrified aspect; except Philip's and Mrs. Transome's, who looked at me sorrowfully indeed, yet peacefully, as though they were thinking of me, not of themselves.

"Isn't she coming?" I said to Philip.

"No, she may stay with me," he answered.

"Good-bye, my dear," she said. "To-day I shall be with Him, and with Transome."

"There is not another moment!" cried Philip; "good-bye, my darling. God keep you."

I know nothing of the next few minutes. Only as the boat cast off from the ship's side I heard Philip's voice again calling to me. God gave me strength to look up and see his face once more. He was standing apart from the throng now, for there was no more work for him to do, and his father and Mrs. Transome were beside him. I could see their faces clearly, their eyes following me, and their hands waving a last farewell to me. The sun was breaking through the mass of drifting clouds, and shone full upon them. "Is there no hope?" I asked from one of the crew beside me, who was putting all his strength to his oar.

"No; she is settling down fast," he answered; and I saw that the seamen were urging the boat onward, to get well out of the swirl of the water when the ship went down.

Oh Christ! thou knowest how much anguish a human heart can bear without breaking. For though thine own heart was broken, it was not under the burden of thy sorrows but under the weight of our sins.

A few hours after we left the steamer we were picked up by a vessel homeward bound. I know very little of the voyage back. Fortunately I could tell the captain and the doctor, who attended me assiduously, who I was, and where I lived; but all else seemed blotted out of my memory. All was a blank to me, a dreary emptiness, through which I vainly tried to get at some realization of my sorrow.

It was not three weeks from the time I left home, when I landed in Liverpool again. I remember the long journey up to London, solitary and desolate, as if it had been yesterday. There was still the confused sense of a terrible grief hanging over me; but when I rang the bell of our own house door, that bell Philip had so often rung when I was listening for him to come home, the cloud upon my brain began to lift itself. Before the door was opened to admit me, all was clear and distinct; I knew that his foot would never cross the threshold again. I beckoned to our servant to keep silent as I entered the house, where henceforth life would be for me a solemn waiting for death. At the farther end of the hall was the door of my brother's room, which stood partly open; and as I drew nearer to it I heard a quiet voice reading aloud. I had no thought of going in, though I was longing to weep the bitter tears that were burning under my eyelids. But I must be careful of George. The sudden shock of my return now might be dangerous for him. The quiet voice fell upon my ear in these words—

"And I saw a new heaven and a new earth; for the first heaven and the first earth were passed away; and there was no more sea."

I sank down on the ground beside the door, and my tears came like a flood; still my brother's low, calm voice went on reading:

"And God shall wipe all tears from their eyes; and there shall be no more death, neither sorrow, nor crying, neither shall there be any more pain: for the former things are passed away."

I could see him from where I knelt at the half open door. He had lifted up his eyes from the book, and was looking across the room with almost a smile upon his face. Who could it be he was looking at, out of my sight? What was it that made my heavy heart leap with a hope springing from the very darkness of my sorrow?

"If we only knew that Aunt Milly was safe!" said the other voice;

I could not, for the first moment, believe it was Philip who was speaking.

I cannot tell you how we met. I only remember that after a while I found myself in my own chair, on my brother's hearth, with Philip beside me, my hand grasping his, as if we were again in a sinking ship, and I had nothing else to hold as the waters were closing over us.

Philip had to tell me how, when the steamer went down, his father and Mrs. Transome sank at once with it, and he lost sight of them for ever; while he, who was young, caught a floating spar, and was upheld by it for a time while the vessel settled. The shock I had felt in the cabin, and the shiver that ran through all the timbers of the ship, had been caused by its striking, though lightly, upon a sunken reef, and there was but little swirl of the waters, such as had been anticipated. The upper portion of the rigging had even remained above the surface; and Philip with a few others had found safety amongst it. They did not remain there long, for they lay in the course of vessels, and before night came on they were rescued by a steamer, which had brought him home yet more quickly than I had been brought myself. He had reached London only the day before I did.

There is little more for me to tell you. In the course of a few weeks we heard that our emigrants, the girls we were taking out to settle in American homes, had all reached New York in safety. They wrote to us in the hope that we had also been rescued, telling how Philip and Captain John Champion had quietly marshalled them to their boat, through a crowd of passengers frenzied with terror.

[T]here is now no longer a necessity for Philip [to l]ive upon the sea. His life has grown fuller [in i]nfluence and of power over his fellowmen. [Th]e one duty has been faithfully discharged; [and] broader, perhaps grander duties are rising in its place. What he will become, what [spe]cial work he will do here for God, I do not know. But it is no more as a servant that he [wor]ks, it is rather as a son. There is a perfect[nes]s and unity in his obedience which is not [the] obedience of a hireling.

THE END.

PETER'S DENIAL.

By Mrs. M. Baxter.

[Sunday School] Lesson for May 27, Matt. 26: 58-75. Golden Text, 1 Cor. 10: 12.

[The] Astonishment of the Disciples—Their Master [R]efraining from Using Miraculous Power—[T]heir Flight—Peter Following at a Distance—[A] Suffering Believer in Dakota—Peter Hindered [fr]om Faith by Self-Confidence—The Depletion [o]f Strength by Small Unfaithfulnesses—Peter as [a] Spectator of his Master's Trial—His Silence a [D]enial—The Three Challenges—His Remorse.

[J]UDAS had already betrayed Jesus, and He [wh]o came to preach, and to bring "deliverance [to t]he captives" (Luke 4: 16) was arrested like a [com]mon criminal, and conducted by armed [offi]cials to the High Priest. In spite of His re[pea]ted assertions that He should be delivered into the hands of wicked men and crucified, [the] disciples had never believed that it would [rea]lly be so. They were so set on their own [ide]as—formed, indeed, from Scripture, but [Scr]ipture only partially understood—that they [had] never yet abandoned the hope that Jesus [wou]ld become the reigning Messiah, and rid the [Hol]y Land from the Roman yoke. Now that [the]y saw Him apprehended, and led away for [tria]l, without exercising His wonderful power to [del]iver Himself, their

Hopes Were at an End,

[and] in the despair of the moment, they, who [had] declared that they would follow Him to [pri]son and to death, all "forsook Him and [fle]d." They had seen Him conquer the waves [and] the wind, multiply the loaves, overcome [sic]kness, and prove Himself Master of death it[self]—how, then, in this supreme moment should [He] let His cause fail; how yield just now, when, [if] He had but smitten down His enemies, and [pl]uck Herod from the throne, He might have [bee]n proclaimed King of the Jews by a devoted [and] grateful crowd of followers, and Galilee, [Sa]maria and Judea might so easily have come [un]der His sceptre. But they did not under[sta]nd that His kingdom was "not of this [wo]rld"; if it had been, *then* would His servants [hav]e fought that He should not be delivered to [the] Jews. (John 18: 36.) "But Peter followed [Hi]m afar off." Peter must be a leader; for, [goo]d or bad, he was always foremost. Zealous, [ad]venturous, daring to a degree, it was he who [ste]pped out upon the water to go to Jesus; he [wh]o sought to drive bargains with the Master; [he] who attempted to dictate to the transfigured [Sa]viour. And now when all had forsaken Jesus, [he] was the only one who at first turned back, [an]d followed Him. But still he

Followed Afar Off.

[O]h how many disciples there are who follow [Jes]us at a distance! *A poor sufferer*, in Dakota, [wa]s in the greatest suffering. All human reme[die]s had failed to cure her terrible disease—in[ter]nal scrofula. Through a copy of THE CHRIS[TI]AN HERALD, she was led to see the Lord as [he]r Healer, and reading in her Bible (James 5: [14]-16) God's command to the sick that they [sh]ould send for the elders of the Church to [an]oint them in the name of the Lord, she sent [for] a minister of one of the churches, who re[fus]ed to anoint her, giving as his reason that [pe]ople would talk so if she were not healed! [Sh]e then sent for another minister, who told [he]r that her body should first be purified of the [di]sease by medicines, and then she might be [an]ointed. Surely these men, who cannot take God [at] His Word are following afar off! There are some who need to be met in church to be known as Christians; elsewhere the difference between them and the world is not sufficient to be distinguished. They speak the language of the world; they have the spirit of the world; their interests, their tastes, their houses, their appearance, all betoken a heart set on things below rather than on things above. Peter was not aware how long he had been following Jesus

Afar Off in Spirit.

He had not learned the lesson which Jesus would have taught him when he walked upon the water, and was for the moment lifted above things seen and temporal. He had not seen how liable he was to fail, or recognized, in his ready fear of the winds and waves, how little real confidence he had in Jesus. True, his faith had ventured further than that of the other disciples, but he was still full of self-confidence, and this came between him and a continuous confidence in the Lord. As long and as far as we reckon upon ourselves at all, just so far we lack confidence in Jesus. Peter had not learned the lesson which Jesus would have taught him when in answer to his Master's prediction of His coming sufferings, Peter suggested that he should pity Himself. True, Peter had just previously acknowledged Jesus as "the Christ, the Son of the living God," but, in his spirit, both upon the water, and in his rebuke to Jesus, he was found *afar off* from the spirit which animated Jesus, and He said to him, 'Get thee behind me, Satan, thou art an offence unto Me; for thou savorest not the things that be of God, but those that be of men." (Matt. 16: 16-23.) Again, upon the Mount of Transfiguration, Peter failed; he again presumed to bring forward his own ideas; "Lord, it is good for us to be here; let us make here three tabernacles, one for Thee, one for Moses, and one for Elias." (Matt. 17: 4.) How far off was all this from the spirit of the Master! Jesus had no resting-place on earth, He had "not where to lay His head." When again Peter bargained with Jesus saying, "We have forsaken *all* and followed Thee; what shall we have, therefore?" O, how far off was his spirit from that of Jesus! Before any child of God comes to have a grievous fall, there must have been many

Small Unfaithfulnesses

leading up to it. There have been lessons only half learned, warnings of God which have not been laid to heart. There have been many circumstances which appealed to the conscience, and which were calculated to arouse the attention, but they have not been laid to heart, and at last there is nothing for it, but that God should let His child go on, until the fall comes which fills him with shame, confusion, and remorse. All the teachings, all the hints, all the warning which Jesus gave Peter never taught him as much as he learned, when at last he found by bitter experience that he was capable of denying his Lord.

Peter followed afar off, but at last he "entered into the high priests' palace and went in and sat with the servants to see the end." He took the place of a mere spectator, who looked on from simple curiosity. He it was who had asserted, "Though I should die with Thee, yet will I not deny Thee." (Matt. 26: 35.) Yet his very position at that hour was in itself a denial of Jesus. Peter was witness to all that happened. He heard them seeking for false witnesses, yet

Peter Did Not Stand Up

as a true witness in his Lord's defence! He heard their wresting of His words, yet he did not state the facts, or tell the exact words which Jesus uttered about the temple! He heard the high priest ask Jesus: "Answerest thou nothing? What is it which these witness against Thee?" And he saw his Master as a sheep dumb before her shearers! It was perhaps the first time Peter had ever seen an innocent person unwilling to defend himself. There was nothing in Peter's nature which responded to, or understood such forbearance, and when, at last, Pilate put the question, "Art thou the Christ, the Son of God?" Peter heard Him say, "Thou hast said. Nevertheless, I say unto you, hereafter ye shall see the Son of Man sitting on the right hand of power, and coming in the clouds of heaven." Had not God revealed unto Peter that Jesus was "the Christ, the Son of the living God"? How came it, then, that now, when the question was raised before the priestly tribunal, Peter had not a word to say? Oh, how easy it is to speak of what we believe among those who understand us, and who themselves believe! But to witness for Christ among His enemies is no light task; it needs the power of the Holy Ghost to do it. The high priest said, "He hath spoken blasphemy;" the people, "He is guilty of death!" And Peter heard it all, and yet

Never Confessed his Lord!

Then did they spit in His face, and buffeted Him; and others smote Him with the palms of their hands." And Peter was like one paralyzed or stupefied; he saw, he heard, but as though he saw and heard not. And why? Because he still clung to his former idea that Christ was to assume earthly sovereignty at this time, and with this idea in his mind, and the knowledge he had of Christ's power over the elements and over man, it would seem to Peter a waste of suffering, and a needless endurance, for Jesus to suffer thus. Perhaps he was awaiting a moment when Christ would, in one instant, change the whole scene, and the high priest would bend on his knees abashed before the revealed Messiah. Oh, how dangerous it is for us to run away with certain ideas from Scripture, and then, blind to its general tendency, strain every point, and disregard the teachings of God in the course of events which happen around us, in order that we may establish our theory! All heresies begin thus.

Peter sat without, in the palace, as far from Jesus as he could well be. A damsel came unto him, saying, "Thou also wast with Jesus of Galilee." It was a name of scorn; it meant reproach, and was

A Well-directed Sneer.

Peter was no longer, by faith and by choice, under the keeping of Jesus. It is a fearful thing to say, but it is true, that when a child of God does begin to sin, he sins more terribly and goes down more rapidly than one who is unconverted. The unconverted have a certain power of will and conscience which keeps them; the child of God has yielded himself unto the keeping of another, and when he wrests himself out of the hands of his keeper, he has no ballast, but rushes madly downwards. Peter denied, before them all, saying, "I know not what thou sayest." The deed was done, yet Peter was not alive to it. Another maid saw and recognized him as a follower of Jesus. With an oath, Peter again denied, saying, "I do not know the man." Many of us would shrink from words such as these, but what does our life say? Does it say to all around us, "I know Jesus"? After a while, others who stood by said, "Surely, thou art one of them; for thy speech betrayeth thee." The more determined the assertion was, the more vehemently Peter contradicted it. "Then began he to curse and to swear, saying, I know not the man. And immediately the cock crew." Till that moment he thought Jesus in the wrong, and might, perhaps, have tried to excuse himself. But now the word of his condemned Master was fulfilled: "The cock crew." All was changed. He did not understand Jesus, but he would no longer disbelieve Him. But oh, his sin! Peter's heart was broken; he went out, and wept bitterly.

"THY WILL."

Teach me to do Thy will; for Thou art my God. Psalm cxliii. 10.
I delight to do Thy will, O my God; yea, Thy law is within my heart. Psalm xl. 8.

Take Thine own way with me, dear Lord,
Thou canst not otherwise than bless;
I launch me forth upon a sea
Of boundless love and tenderness.

I could not choose a larger bliss
Than to be wholly Thine; and mine
A will whose highest joy is this,
To ceaselessly unclasp in Thine.

I will not fear Thee, O my God!
The days to come can only bring
Their perfect sequences of love,
Thy larger, deeper comforting.

Within the shadow of this love,
Loss doth transmute itself to gain;
Faith veils earth's sorrows in its light,
And straightway lives above her pain.

We are not losers thus; we share
The perfect gladness of the Son,
Not conquered—for, behold, we reign;
Conquered and Conqueror are one.

Thy wonderful grand will, my God!
Triumphantly I make it mine;
And faith shall breathe her glad "Amen."
To every dear command of Thine.

Beneath the splendour of Thy choice,
Thy perfect choice for me, I rest;
Outside it now I dare not live,
Within it I must needs be blest.

Meanwhile my spirit anchors calm
In grander regions still than this;
The fair, far-shining latitudes
Of that yet unexplored bliss.

Then may Thy perfect, glorious will
Be evermore fulfilled in me,
And make my life an answ'ring chord
Of glad, responsive harmony.

Oh! it is life indeed to live
Within this kingdom strangely sweet
And yet we fear to enter in,
And linger with unwilling feet.

We fear this wondrous rule of Thine,
Because we have not reached Thy heart;
Not venturing our all on Thee,
We may not know how good Thou art.

—*Jean Sophia Pigott.*

J. E. Jewett, Publisher, 77 Bible House, New York will furnish the above poem in leaflet form at [illegible] cents per hundred. *A Sample Packet of 50 leaflets* assorted (no two alike), will be sent post-paid, for ten cents. Postage stamps taken.

The above beautiful poem printed in booklet form on extra heavy bristol board, 18 pages, with a delicate spray in tint on each page, ribbon-tied, and enclosed in titled envelope, will be sent post-paid for 20 cents, or three together for 50 cents.

THE CHRISTIAN HERALD AND SIGNS OF OUR TIMES

Entered according to Act of Congress in the year 1887 in the office of the Librarian of Congress at Washington.

Vol. XI., No. 21. Office, 63 Bible House, N. Y. THURSDAY, MAY 24, 1888. Annual Subscription, $1.50.

CONTENTS OF THIS NUMBER.

PORTRAIT AND LIFE OF CAPTAIN ALLEN GARDINER, THE PIONEER OF SOUTH AMERICAN MISSIONS.

A CASE OF LOVE AT FIRST SIGHT. Dr. Talmage's Sermon Last Sunday Morning.

ANECDOTES RELATED AT RECENT EVANGELISTIC MEETINGS.

THE SIGNS OF CHRIST'S COMING.

A Persecuted Christian Widow—Consecrated Saturdays in the East—Remarkable Cure of a Diseased Hip—A Long Search Ended—A Remarkable Movement in India.

THE PROPHETIC CRISIS IN EUROPE.

A MISSIONARY HERO'S PERIL. (Illustrated.)

A YOUNG LAWYER'S DECISION. (Illustrated.)

THE RAPID BELIEVER. A New Sermon by Pastor C. H. Spurgeon

Gems from New Books: Lost in the Mountains, etc.

PORTRAIT AND LIFE OF W. H. HOWLAND, Esq., Ex-Mayor of Toronto.

THE EPOCHS OF A LIFE. A New Serial Story by Rev. L. S. Keyser.

JESUS CRUCIFIED. By Mrs. M. Baxter.

CAPTAIN ALLEN GARDINER—Finding His Body—Scene on the Shores of Patagonia.

COMMANDER ALLEN GARDINER.

Pioneer Missionary to Terra del Fuego.

Birth and Boyish Predilections—Voyages and Appointments—A Memorable Era in his Life—Death of his Wife—Consecration to Pioneer Missionary Work—Explorations in Africa—Among the Indians of South America—Difficulties—Crosses over to Patagonia—An Unpatronized Expedition—Among Hostile Natives—Accumulated Disasters—Starved to Death—The Present South American Mission.—Bishop Riley's Efforts.

THE prediction of Charles Darwin, that missionaries would never do any good with the natives of Terra del Fuego, has long been falsified. Even before the death of the eminent scientist much progress had been made, and he was manly enough to admit that he had been mistaken, and as a practical evidence of his change of opinion he made a handsome donation to help the missionaries to carry on their work. "I am now convinced," he said, "that you were right and I was wrong in our respective estimates of the native character." But in making that admission, Darwin did not rightly perceive his mistake. It was not so much in his estimate of the native character that he was mistaken as in failing to rightly appreciate the power of the Gospel of Christ to change character, savage as well as civilized. The work begun by the noble pioneer, Captain Allen Gardiner, *whose portrait appears on the first page*, has extended through the whole southern section of the South American Continent, and, in spite of obstacles in climate and human character, is being vigorously pressed. *A steamer* bearing the honored name of Allen Gardiner now carries the missionaries from place to place, and fifty thousand dollars have been raised as an endowment fund to support a Bishop, and secure

Efficient Organized Effort.

Residents in Paraguay, who formerly despaired of ever introducing the gospel among the Indians, now speak most hopefully of the work, and, impressed by what has already been accomplished, now confidently predict the happiest results. That the obstacles were of a character to dishearten any man but one permeated with living faith in the omnipotence of God may well be conceived. The people were sunk in the lowest barbarism, and seemed destitute of the elements of character to which Gospel appeals could be made. Mr. R. Stewart Clough, whose portrait appeared in this journal on July 17, 1887, gives an appalling description of their condition as he saw it. He states that as the steamer on which he travelled passed along the coast, and the passengers gazed in wonder and delight on the forests and luxuriant foliage, they saw men and women *almost destitute of clothing moving like wild animals* among the trees or clustered on the water's edge gazing in wonder on the steamer. (*The illustration on the first page* is taken from a sketch made by this devoted missionary during his journey.) As we read the hopeful reports of the missionaries now in the field, our thoughts are carried back to the gallant man who laid down his life to found the work which is now thriving—Captain Allen Francis Gardiner, the pioneer of South American Missions.

He was born at Basildon, England, on June 28, 1794, and died, in 1851, at the age of fifty-seven. His father, Samuel Gardiner, was a God-fearing man, and early instilled into the mind of his sons, of whom Allen was the fifth, principles of truth, which subsequently developed and ripened into abundant and widespread fruitfulness and blessing.

Boyish Predilections.

Very early in life Allen chose the navy as his profession. His boyish imagination was fired by a desire for adventure, which manifested itself in various ways, some of them amusing, and all of them significant. On one occasion he was found asleep on the floor, when he ought to have been in bed, giving as his reason when aroused that it was his intention to travel all over the world, and that he therefore wished to accustom himself to hardships, of which his hard bed was the first in order. These incidents were carefully noted by the family, and in after years, when he became famous, they were published as proofs of his early ardor.

He Entered the Naval College

on February 13, 1808, at the age of fourteen. There he remained for two years, and became proficient in the theory of his chosen vocation. He first went to sea as a *volunteer* in the Fortune, on July 20, 1810, and was transferred to the Phœbe, in March of the following year. The following year he exchanged into the Dauntless, and sailed to Madras, Penang, Malacca, Singapore, Manila, and Macao. A little later the ship sailed to Australia, and thence to Chili and Peru, and eventually Allen Gardiner invalided from the ship, while she was at Sydney, and took passage to the Cape of Good Hope.

Allen Gardiner's connection with the Dauntless, marks

A Memorable Era in his Life,

for it includes the time in which he steadily set his face toward the service of God, and in which he began to take that deep interest in the aborigines of South America, and especially of Chili, which never afterward left him. It was on this voyage, moreover, that he made his first acquaintance with Christian missionaries, and had an opportunity of acquainting himself with the blessed effect of their devoted and self-denying labors at Singapore, and again at Tahiti. From his journal at this period, we extract the following, under date, "Cape Town, August, 1822: The last time I visited this colony, I was walking in the broad way, and hastening by rapid strides to the brink of eternal ruin. Blessed be His name, who loved us, and gave Himself for us,

A Great and Blessed Change

has been wrought in my heart, and I am now enabled to derive pleasure and satisfaction in hearing and reading the Word of God, and in attending the means of grace. I trust that this alteration has indeed been effected by the Holy Spirit of God."

On July 1, 1823, he was *married* to a lady of high Christian character, and in the following year was again called to active service in his profession. He served three years more, visiting various ports in the Old and New World. He obtained his promotion as commander September 13, 1826; but though he retained his early fondness for the service, and often applied for employment, he was never after this period actively engaged in it.

Mrs. Gardiner's health had never been robust, but in 1833 consumption developed itself with an ominous rapidity. Though everything was done that love and skill could suggest, she gradually declined, and on May 24, 1834, died full of hope and peace through faith in the atoning sacrifice of Christ. Her last days were most bright and happy, and writing of the event a year later, the bereaved husband says: "Oh, what assurance of pardon, what joy, and peace, and heavenly tranquillity, and ardent desire to be with her Saviour did He infuse into her soul!" From this time he devoted himself afresh to the service of God, and with all the force of his strong character, set himself upon a new course. He chose the work of

A Missionary Pioneer,

and went first of all to Africa, explored the Zulu country, and started the first missionary station at Port Natal. A few years later he devoted many months to an attempt to obtain entrance into New Guinea. Animated with love to Christ, and full of apostolic fervor, he went from island to island of the Indian Archipelago, endeavoring to find opportunity of introducing Christianity; but all his efforts were baffled.

Having devoted his time and fortune for more than three years to the cause of the Gospel at Port Natal and in the Zulu country, he left South Africa when the breaking out of war between the Zulus and the Boers rendered missionary work impracticable. But with characteristic energy he sought another sphere of work. His mind reverted to

The Indians of the Pampas

and of Chili, whose heroic maintenance of their own independence had, years before, excited his admiration, while their continued Paganism was, in his view, a standing reproach to the Christian world. Captain Gardiner left Table Bay, in South Africa, on May 15, 1838, and conducted his family to Rio Janeiro, thence to Buenos Ayres, and across the Pampas to Mendoza, and as soon as the season was sufficiently advanced, they crossed the Cordillera into Chili.

From 1838 to 1841 Captain Gardiner visited one tribe of Indians after another, his self-imposed mission being attended with

Imminent Perils

at every turn. Many of these people he found friendly to himself, and favorable to his purpose of planting the standard of the cross of Christ among them; but much of his effort was succeeded only by disappointment through the machinations of the Spanish padres, or priests, of the Roman Catholic Church. Being at Chiloe, July 31st, 1841, he writes:

"Having at last abandoned, with great reluctance, all hope of reaching the Indian population in the part where they are most civilized and least migratory, my thoughts are necessarily turned toward the south. I purpose going to the Falkland Isles and from thence crossing over in a sealing vessel, and, if possible, bringing back with me two or three

Patagonian Lads

in order to teach them English, and thus prepare them to become interpreters to the missionaries who, we trust, may eventually settle among them. Who can tell but that the Falkland Islands, so admirably suited for the purpose, may become the key to the aborigines both of Terra del Fuego and of Patagonia!"

In consequence of the peaceable and friendly demeanor of the Patagonians, Captain Gardiner was encouraged to believe that a good work might be carried on among them, with every hope of blessing. In 1844 a special society was formed for South America alone. Its headquarters were established, and soon afterward the principal of a public school, Mr. R. Hunt, volunteered to go out and become the first catechist in Patagonia. He and Captain Gardiner were landed at Oazy Harbor, in the Strait of Magellan, with three small huts, and necessary provisions for three months. This was in the month of February, 1845. Before long, however, it was necessary to abandon Patagonia, at least for a time.

Swimming with an Indian.

But Captain Gardiner was not to be daunted by difficulties. He heard the Saviour's command to preach the Gospel even to the ends of the earth, and, at his own expense, penetrated with unabated heroism into Bolivia and Terra del Fuego. The difficulties he had to encounter were not spiritual and moral only; there were natural obstacles to overcome. One of these was met and successfully overcome during a journey in Bolivia. On March 23, 1846, he came to the banks of the river Pilcomayo, which he had to cross. He had no boat and the river was too high to ford. He therefore engaged an Indian to swim across with him, and away they went, leaning together on a bundle of reeds. The current was very rapid, but the captain assisted by the Indian, breasted it gallantly and at length stood safely on the opposite side.

We must turn now to the final effort which ended Captain Gardiner's exertions for the benefit of the Indians in the extreme south of the Continent. Anxiously did he desire that some branch of Christ's Church would evangelize the immense territory; but he failed to enlist the support of his own countrymen, or of the Moravian Church, to which he applied. At length mainly through the generosity of a private lady

A Missionary Expedition

was fitted out under Gardiner's superintendence and the little company sailed from Liverpool on September 7, 1850. Three months later the party were landed at Picton Island, Terra del Fuego, one of the group of islands separated from the mainland of South America by the Straits of Magellan. All the islands are bleak and almost barren, mere rocks, the highest of which are covered with perpetual snow. Here little beside disappointment and danger attended them. Affairs reached a crisis in the following December, when food began to run short, and the attitude of the Indians became menacing.

Winter was coming on, and in the missionaries' quarters there was an almost

Utter Absence of Food.

Sickness also had prostrated some of the number, and death had invaded their ranks. A vessel had been long expected with provisions for the party, but it did not arrive. The anxious glances cast seaward took in no welcome sail. They watched, but it was all in vain. In January, 1852, the English Government ship *Dido* went to their relief. She left the Falklands, and arrived at Banner Cove on the 19th. The captain of the *Dido* says: "Our notice was first attracted by a boat lying upon the beach about a mile and a half inside of Cape Kinnaird. I sent Lieutenant Pigott and Mr. Roberts to reconnoitre and return immediately. They returned shortly, bringing some books and papers, having discovered

The Body of Captain Gardiner

and that of Mr. Maidment unburied. On one of the papers was written legibly, but without date, "If you will walk along the beach for a mile and a half, you will find us in the other boat, hauled up in the mouth of the river at the head of the harbor on the south side. *Delay not, we are starving.*"

"I landed early next morning, January 22d, and visited the spot indicated, where we found the wreck of a boat with part of her gear and stores, and the remains of two bodies. They were those of Mr. Williams, a surgeon, and John Pearce, a Cornish fisherman, and papers which show the death and burial of all the rest of the mission party, *seven in all*. The two boats were about a mile and a half apart. Near the one where Captain Gardiner was lying was a large cavern, called by him Pioneer Cavern, and in it Mr. Maidment's body was found. Captain Gardiner's body was lying beside the boat, which apparently he had left, and being too weak to climb into it again, had died by the side of it. We were directed to the cavern by a hand painted on the rock, with 'Psalm 62: 5-8,' ['My soul, wait thou only upon God for my expectation is from Him,' etc.,] under it." (*See Illustration.*) Thus the whole party had perished in their endeavor to carry the Gospel to the benighted people. While we mourn the sad circumstances of their death, we cannot but rejoice that their sacrifice was not in vain.

The South American Mission

is now successfully at work, and in Terra del Fuego, the Falklands, and the Fuegian Archipelago, the Gospel is being preached, and many of the natives have gladly accepted Christ, and been baptized in His name. This mission was definitely founded in 1854, and ten years later chaplaincies were appointed on the east and west coasts of South America. The earnest prayerful efforts which Bishop Riley is now making to build up evangelical work in Mexico and to make it a centre from which to reach the Spanish American peoples of South America will we trust be blessed to the same object. If the Christian Churches of the United States respond to his appeals and furnish him with the necessary funds, his missionaries from the North may yet join hands with those of the South American Mission from the South, and so the whole of the great South American Continent may ring with the glad tidings of salvation. As this work of Bishop Riley's is the branch identified with the United States, it has the first claim on American Christians, who realize the responsibility of the church for the heathendom in our hemisphere. *Subscriptions in aid of it may be sent to the Treasurer, Mr. J. P. Heath, 43 Bible House, New York.*

ANECDOTES RELATED AT RECENT EVANGELISTIC MEETINGS.

A Cry that Brought Salvation.—An Evangelist said: "I was once addressing a Gospel meeting, and at the close of it a little girl came to me and earnestly said, 'Please, sir, I want to come to Jesus.' 'Then come in here and just kneel, and ask Him to take you,' I replied, pointing to the ante-room. We went in together, and the child knelt and prayed this short, effective, and most personal prayer, 'Jesus Christ save me.' As she pleaded, the tears flowed freely; but at length, as on an April day, the sun shone forth in the midst of the shower. And, rising from her knees with a most radiant face, she joyously exclaimed, 'Jesus has heard me; Jesus has saved me.' And she left the hall 'a new creature' in Him. For a long time I could not forget that prayer, the pointedness of it; there was no going round about, but simply 'Jesus—me.'"

Prayer in a Thunderstorm.—"I was once preaching," said Mr. Richard Weaver, "in a country district, and after the service I had to go twenty miles before I reached the farmhouse where I was staying. The night was very stormy, and as we went along, the farmer's son, who was driving, would exclaim after each vivid flash of lightning, 'Lord protect us.' 'No, Lord,' I rejoined, 'keep on thundering.' 'Why do you say that?' the young man asked in a trembling voice. 'Do you not wish the storm to stop?' 'Yes,' I replied, 'but I wish much more than that you might keep on praying.' On our arrival at the house the farmer's wife was glad to see us safe home. 'Yes, I am right glad to be home,' I said; 'yet I would not have missed that storm for a good deal. Do you know, it made your son pray? and I hope that having approached God in the time of trouble, he will stay there all his life, for there alone is perfect peace and safety.' The young man did accept Christ as his Saviour.'

A Sceptic Collier's Fear.—Richard Weaver said: "When I was a working collier, I remember working alongside a great boastful sceptic, who was engaged removing the supports from certain parts of the workings. It sometimes happens, as on this occasion, that a stone gets loose, and comes crashing down upon the miner. This particular stone was only a small one, but quite large enough to frighten my brave sceptic. I was not a Christian myself then, yet I always abhorred his braggart scepticism. When I went up to him he was lying under the stone and moaning, 'Lord help me.' Putting my hand upon the the stone I pressed it down so as to make it appear heavier. 'What are you going to do?' I asked; but his only answer was, 'The Lord help me.' As I pressed heavier, and heavier, his fear increased, and he redoubled his cries to the Lord whom he had affected to despise. At length I took off my hand, and showed him the size of the stone, saying, 'See there! What is the worth of all your infidelity, when a stone that size can drive it all out of you in half a minute?' Atheism cannot stand the approach of death."

The Silk-Weaver's Prodigal Daughter.—A noted Evangelist said: "Early one morning there came to the farm at which I was staying, a poor girl. Her clothes were saturated with rain, and she was faint with fatigue. During the night she had walked twenty miles through all the storm to see me. She wanted to be shown the way of salvation. She was furnished with dry clothes, and food was set before her, but she would not eat. She asked if there were any promises in the Bible for a sinner like her. Many were pointed out to her, and soon in that room the seeking sinner passed from death to life. Poor girl, her story was a sad one; she had left her home five years before, and had walked in the downward path. Her mother was dead, and her father was a silk-weaver. After having placed her under the protection of a Christian lady, I sought her father. When I met him I told him of the conversion of his daughter, and asked him if he would be reconciled to her. 'She can never enter my house again,' he said. 'If she did, her brothers and sisters would leave it.' 'The Lord has forgiven her,' I said, 'will not you? If her mother could speak from heaven, would she not plead with you to take her back?' Here he suddenly exclaimed, 'Send her home.' I took her home that night. The door was opened by her brother, who held out his hands to her, saying, 'Welcome home, my sister.' It was indeed a welcome she got, but not to be compared with that accorded to the returning and penitent sinner when he seeks his Father's face."

A Boy's Anxiety for His Parents.—"I was preaching in Sheffield not long ago," says Richard Weaver, "and at the end of the meeting I noticed a man, woman, and little boy sitting in the centre of the hall. The boy was crying bitterly. Going up to him I inquired the reason of his tears. 'Did he wish to be saved?' 'Oh, no,' he answered, 'Jesus pardoned *me* last night; but here are my father and mother, and I want Jesus to save *them*. Turning to the father, I said, 'You should thank God for such a son.' here the boy looked up into his father's face, and said, 'Father, do you give God your heart?' The father appeared to be about to tell his son to be still, but the child continued, 'Do come into the ante-room, and mother, do you come, too,' and taking each by the hand they walked into the room together. There the little fellow prayed, 'Oh God, Thou hast saved me, save my father and mother.' The father interrupted him, saying, 'But I am too bad to be saved, my son; I am too great a sinner.' But the little home-missionary answered, 'God commendeth His love towards us in that while we were yet sinners, Christ died for us.' God blessed these words, and the earnestness of that son, and they left the hall together rejoicing in the Lord Jesus as their Saviour."

A Perilous Ride.—Some Years ago the bridge over the Usk, near Caerleon, Monmouthshire, was washed away, and a new one had to be constructed. While the buttresses were being built, a commercial traveller, who had been absent some time from the place, drove up one night in his gig to the riverside, where the bridge used to be. It was a very dark night, and he gave the reins to his horse, who, he knew, was well accustomed to the road. They crossed safely over what he took to be the bridge, and came to an inn near the river. The landlady asked him, being an old acquaintance, what part of the country he had come in from. "From Newport," he answered. "Then you must have crossed the river?" said the woman in astonishment. "Yes, of course. How else could I have come?" "But how did you manage it, and in the dark, too?" "The same as usual; there is no difficulty in driving over the bridge, even though it be dark." "Bless the man!" said the landlady, "there is no bridge to drive over. You must have come along the planks left by the men." "Impossible," was the answer; and nothing could persuade the traveller that night that there was no bridge. But early next morning he went to the river-side, and found, as he had been told, that the bridge was gone. His horse had taken him safely over three planks, left by the workmen, where one false step, to the right or to the left, would instantly have plunged him into the swollen river beneath. The man stood aghast at the dreadful danger he had gone through, and so marvellously escaped.

A CASE OF LOVE AT FIRST SIGHT.

Dr. Talmage's Sermon Last Sunday Morning, May 20, 1888.

"And she went and came and gleaned in the field after the reapers; and her hap was to light on a part of the field belonging unto Boaz, who was of the kindred of Elimelech." Ruth 2 : 3.

An Eventful Day in the Harvest-Field—A Beautiful Gleaner—The Ancestress of Jesus—I. Trouble Develops Character—A Pastor's Sermons Improved by Bereavement—The Fountain of Hippocrene—The Nation Purified by its Trials—II. The Beauty of Unfaltering Friendship—The Poor Deserted in Misfortune—Ruth's Fidelity—III. A Joyful End of a Dark Path—The Road from Sinai to Calvary—IV. The Insignificant May be Momentous—Luther's Discovery of the Bible—A Long Succession of Conversions—V. The Beauty of Female Industry—Madame De Stael's Boast—VI. Value of the Gleanings.

THE time that Ruth and Naomi arrive at Bethlehem is harvest-time. It was the custom when a sheaf fell from a load in the harvest-field for the reapers to refuse to gather it up; that was to be left for the poor who might happen to come along that way. If there were handfuls of grain scattered across the field after the main harvest had been reaped, instead of raking it, as farmers do now, it was, by the custom of the land, left in its place, so that the poor, coming along that way, might glean it and get their bread. But, you say: "What is the use of all these harvest-fields to Ruth and Naomi? Naomi is too old and feeble to go out and toil in the sun; and can you expect that Ruth, the young and the beautiful, should tan her cheeks and blister her hands in the harvest-field?" Boaz owns a large farm, and he goes out to see the reapers gather in the grain. Coming there, right behind the sun-browned reapers, he beholds

A Beautiful Gleaner

—a woman more fit to bend to a harp, or sit upon a throne, than to stoop among the sheaves. Ah, that was an eventful day! It was love at first sight. Boaz forms an attachment for the womanly gleaner—an attachment full of undying interest to the Church of God in all ages; while Ruth, with an ephah, or nearly a bushel of barley, goes home to Naomi to tell her the successes and adventures of the day. That Ruth, who left her native land of Moab in darkness, and travelled through an undying affection for her mother-in-law, in the harvest-field of Boaz, is affianced to one of the best families in Judah, and becomes in after-time

The Ancestress of Jesus

Christ, the Lord of glory. Out of so dark a night did there ever dawn so bright a morning?

I learn in the first place from this subject how *trouble develops character*. It was bereavement, poverty and exile that developed, illustrated and announced to all ages the sublimity of Ruth's character. That is a very unfortunate man who has no trouble. It was sorrow that made John Bunyan the better dreamer, and Dr. Young the better poet, and O'Connell the better orator, and Bishop Hall the better preacher, and Havelock the better soldier, and Kitto the better encyclopedist, and Ruth the better daughter-in-law.

I once asked an aged man in regard to his pastor, who was a very brilliant man: "Why is it that your pastor, so very brilliant, seems to have so little heart and tenderness in his sermons?" "Well," he replied, "the reason is our pastor has never had any trouble. When misfortune comes upon him, his style will be different." After awhile the Lord took a child out of that pastor's house; and though the preacher was just as brilliant as he was before, oh the warmth, the tenderness of his discourses. The fact is that

Trouble is a Great Educator.

You see sometimes a musician sit down to an instrument, and his execution is cold and formal and unfeeling. The reason is that all his life he has been prospered. Bnt let misfortune or bereavement come to that man, and he sits down at an instrument, and you discover the pathos in the first sweep of the keys. Misfortune and trials are great educators. A young doctor comes into a sick-room where there is a dying child. Perhaps he is very rough in his prescription, and very rough in his manner, and rough in the feeling of the pulse, and rough in his answer to the mother's anxious question; but years roll on, and there has been one dead in his own house; and now he comes into the sick-room, and with tearful eye he looks at the dying child, and he says: "Oh, how this reminds me of my Charlie!" Trouble, the great educator.

Sorrow, I see its touch in the grandest painting; I hear its tremor in the sweetest song; I feel its power in the mightiest argument. Grecian mythology said that the fountain of Hippocrene was struck out by the foot of the winged horse Pegasus. I have often noticed in life that the brightest and most beautiful fountains of Christian comfort and spiritual life have been struck out by

The Iron-shod Hoof

of disaster and calamity. I see Daniel's courage best by the flash of Nebuchadnezzar's furnace. I see Paul's prowess best when I find him on the foundering ship under the glare of the lighting in the breakers of Melita. God crowns his children amid the howling of wild beasts and the chopping of blood-splashed guillotine and the crackling fires of martyrdom. It took the persecutions of Marcus Aurelius to develop Polycarp and Justin Martyr. It took the world's ánathema to develop Martin Luther. It took all the hostilities against the Scotch Covenanters and the fury of Lord Claverhouse to develop James Renwick, and Andrew Melville, and Hugh McKail, the glorious martyrs of Scotch history. It took the stormy sea, and the December blast, and the desolate New England coast, and the war-woop of savages, to show forth the prowess of the Pilgrim Fathers—

"When amid the storms they sang,
And the stars heard, and the sea;
And the sounding aisles of the dim wood
Rang to the anthems of the free."

It took all our past national distresses to lift up our nation on that high career where it will march along after the foreign aristocracies that have mocked, and the tyrannies that have jeered, shall be swept down under the omnipotent wrath of God, who hates despotism, and who, by the strength of His own right arm, will make all men free. And so it is individually, and in the family, and in the Church, and in the world, that through darkness and storm and trouble men, women, churches, nations, are developed.

II. Again, I see in my text the beauty of

Unfaltering Friendship.

I suppose there were plenty of friends for Naomi while she was in prosperity; but of all her acquaintances, how many were willing to trudge off with her toward Judæa, when she had to make that lonely journey? One—the heroine of my text. One—absolutely one. I suppose when Naomi's husband was living, and they had plenty of money, and all things went well, they had a great many callers; but I suppose that after her husband died, and her property went, and she got old and poor, she was not troubled very much with callers. All the birds that sung in the bower while the sun shone have gone to their nests, now the night has fallen. Oh, these beautiful sun-flowers that spread out their colors in the morning hour! but are always asleep when the sun is going down! Job had plenty of friends when he was the richest man in Uz; but when his property went and the trials came, then there were none so much that pestered as Eliphaz the Temanite, and Bildad the Shuhite, and Zophar the Naamahite.

Life often seems to be a mere game, where the successful player pulls down all the other men into his own lap. Let suspicions arise about a man's character, and he becomes like a bank in a panic, and all the imputations rush on him and break down in a day that character which in due time would have had strength to defend itself. There are reputations that have been half a century in building, which go down under some moral exposure, as a vast temple is consumed by the touch of a sulphurous match. A hog can uproot a century plant.

In this world, so full of heartlessness and hypocrisy, how thrilling it is to find some friend

Faithful in Adversity

as in days of prosperity! David had such a friend in Hushai; the Jews had such a friend in Mordecai, who never forgot their cause; Paul had such a friend in Onesiphorus, who visited him in jail; Christ had such in the Marys, who adhered to Him on the cross; Naomi had such a one in Ruth, who cried out, "Entreat me not to leave thee, or to return from following after thee; for whither thou goest I will go, and where thou lodgest I will lodge; thy people shall be my people, and thy God my God; where thou diest, will I die, and there will I be buried; the Lord do so to me, and more also, if aught but death part thee and me."

Joy out of Sorrow.

III. Again, I learn from this subject that paths which open in hardship and darkness often come out in places of joy. When Ruth started from Moab toward Jerusalem, to go along with her mother-in-law, I suppose the people said, "Oh, what a foolish creature to go away from her father's house, to go off with a poor old woman toward the land of Judæa! They won't live to get across the desert. They will be drowned in the sea, or the jackals of the wilderness will destroy them." It was a very dark morning when Ruth started off with Naomi; but behold her in my text in the harvest-field of Boaz, to be affianced to one of the lords of the land, and become one of the grandmothers of Jesus Christ, the Lord of glory. And so it often is, that a path which starts very darkly, ends very brightly.

When you started out for heaven, oh, how dark was the hour of conviction—how Sinai thundered, and devils tormented, and the darkness thickened! All the sins of your life pounced upon you, and it was

The Darkest Hour you ever Saw

when you first found out your sins. After awhile you went into the harvest-field of God's mercy; you began to glean in the fields of divine promise, and you had more sheaves than you could carry, as the voice of God addressed you, saying, "Blessed is the man whose transgressions are forgiven, and whose sins are covered." A very dark starting in conviction, a very bright ending in the pardon and the hope and the triumph of the gospel.

So, very often in our worldly business, or in our spiritual career, we start off on a very dark path. We must go. The flesh may shrink back, but there is a voice within, or a voice from above, saying: "You must go;" and we have to drink the gall, and we have to carry the cross, and we have to traverse the desert, and we are pounded and flailed of misrepresentation and abuse, and we have to urge our way through ten thousand obstacles that must be slain by our own right arm. We have to ford the river, we have to climb the mountain, we have to storm the castle; but, blessed be God, the day of rest and

Reward Will Come.

On the tip top of the captured battlements we will shout the victory; if not in this world, then in that world where there is no gall to drink, no burdens to carry, no battles to fight. How do I know it? Know it? I know it because God says so: "They shall hunger no more, neither thirst any more, neither shall the sun light on them, nor any heat, for the Lamb which is in the midst of the throne shall lead them to living fountains of water, and God shall wipe all tears from their eyes."

It was very hard for Noah to endure the scoffing of the people in his day, while he was trying to build the ark, and was every morning *quizzed about his old boat* that would never be of any practical use; but when the deluge came, and the tops of the mountains disappeared like the backs of sea-monsters, and the elements, lashed up in fury, clapped their hands over a drowned world, then Noah in the ark rejoiced in his own safety and in the safety of his family, and looked out on the wreck of a ruined earth.

Christ, Hounded of Persecutors.

denied a pillow, worse maltreated than the thieves on either side of the cross, human hate smacking its lips in satisfaction after it had been draining His last drop of blood, the sheeted dead bursting from the sepulchres at His crucifixion. Tell me, O Gethsemane and Golgotha! were there ever darker times than those? Like the booming of the midnight sea against the rock, the surges of Christ's anguish beat against the gates of eternity, to be echoed back by all the thrones of heaven and all the dungeons of hell. But the day of reward comes for Christ; all the pomp and dominion of this world are to be hung on his throne, uncrowned heads are to bow before Him on whose head are many crowns, and all the celestial worship is to come up at His feet, like the humming of the forest, like the rushing of the waters, like the thundering of the seas, while all heaven, rising on their thrones, beat time with their sceptres: "Hallelujah, for the Lord God omnipotent reigneth! Hallelujah, the kingdoms of this world have become the kingdoms of our Lord Jesus Christ!"

"That song of love, now low and far,
Ere long shall swell from star to star;
That light, the breaking day which tips
The golden-spired Apocalypse."

IV. Again: I learn from my subject that events which seem to be most

Insignificant May be Momentuous.

Can you imagine anything more unimportant than the coming of a poor woman from Moab to Judah? Can you imagine anything more trivial than the fact that this Ruth just happened to alight—as they say—just happened to alight on that field of Boaz? Yet all ages, all generations, have an interest in the fact that she was to become an ancestor of the Lord Jesus Christ, and all nations and kingdoms must look at that one little incident with a thrill of unspeakable and eternal satisfaction. So it is in your history and in mine: events that you thought of no importance at all have been of very great moment. That casual conversation, that accidental meeting—you did not think of it again for a long while; but how it changed all the phase of your life!

It seemed to be of no importance that Jubal invented rude instruments of music, calling them harp and organ; but they were the introduction of all the world's minstrelsy; and as you hear the vibration of a stringed instrument, even after the fingers have been taken away from it, so all music now of lute and drum and cornet is only the long-continued

Strains of Jubal's Harp

and Jubal's organ. It seemed to be a matter of very little importance that Tubal Cain learned the uses of copper and iron; but that rude foundry of ancient days has its echo in the rattle of Birmingham machinery, and the roar and bang of factories on the Merrimac. It seemed to be a matter of no importance that Luther found a Bible in a monastery; but as he opened that Bible, and the brass-bound lids fell back, they jarred everything, from the Vatican to the furthest convent in Germany, and the rustling of the wormed leaves was the sound of the wings of the angel of the Reformation.

It seems to be a matter of no importance that a woman, whose name has been forgotten, dropped a tract in the way of a very bad man by the name of Richard Baxter. He picked up the tract and read it, and it was the means of his salvation. In after-days that man wrote a book called "The Call to the Unconverted," that was the means of bringing a multitude to God, among others Philip Doddridge. Philip Doddridge wrote a book called: "The rise and Progress of Religion," which has brought thousands and tens of thousands into the kingdom of God, and among others the great Wilberforce. Wilberforce wrote a book called: "A Practical View of Christianity," which was the means of bringing a great multitude to Christ, among others Legh Richmond. Legh Richmond wrote a tract called: "The Dairyman's Daughter," which has been the means of the salvation of unconverted multitudes. And that tide of influence started from the fact that one Christian woman dropped a Christian tract in the way of Richard Baxter—the tide of influence rolling on through Richard Baxter, through Philip Doddridge, through the great Wilberforce, through Legh Richmond, on, on, on, forever, forever. So the insignificant events of this world seem, after all, to be most momentous. The fact that you came up that street or this street seemed to be of no importance to you, and the fact that you went inside of some church may seem to be a matter of very great insignificance to you, but you will find it the turning-point in your history.

V. Again: I see in my subject an illustration of

The Beauty of Female Industry.

Behold Ruth toiling in the harvest-field under the hot sun, or at noon taking plain bread with the reapers, or eating the parched corn which Boaz handed to her. The customs of society, of course, have changed, and without the hardships and exposure to which Ruth was subjected, every intelligent woman will find something to do.

I know there is a sickly sentimentality on this subject. In some families there are persons of no practical service to the household or community; and though there are so many woes all around about them in the world, they spend their time languishing over a new pattern, or bursting into tears at midnight over the story of some lover who shot himself! They would not deign to look at Ruth carrying back the barley on her way home to her mother-in-law, Naomi. All this fastidiousness may seem to do very well while they are under the shelter of their father's house; but when the sharp winter of misfortune comes, what of these butterflies? Persons under indulgent parentage may get upon themselves habits of indolence; but when they come out into practical life their soul will recoil with disgust and chagrin. They will feel in their hearts what the poet so severely satirized when he said:

"Folks are so awkward, things so impolite,
They're elegantly pained from morning until night."

Through that gate of indolence how many men and women have marched, useless on earth, to a destroyed eternity! Spinola said to Sir Horace Vere: "Of what did your brother die?" "Of having nothing to do," was the answer. "Ah," said Spinola, "that's enough to kill any general of us." Oh! can it be possible in this world, where there is so much suffering to be alleviated, so much darkness to be enlightened, and so many burdens to be carried, that there is any person who cannot find anything to do?

Madame de Stael

did a world of work in her time; and one day, while she was seated amid instruments of music, all of which she had mastered, and amid manuscript books which she had written, some one said to her: "How do you find time to attend to all these things?" "Oh," she replied, "these are not the things I am proud of. My chief boast is in the fact that I have seventeen trades, by any one of which I could make a livelihood if necessary." And if in secular spheres there is so much to be done, in spiritual work how vast the field! We want more Abigails, more Hannahs, more Rebeccas, more Marys, more Deborahs consecrated—body, mind, soul—to the Lord who bought them.

VI. Once more: I learn from my subject

The Value of Gleaning.

Ruth going into that harvest-field might have said: "There is a straw, and there is a straw, but what is a straw? I can't get any barley for myself or my mother-in-law out of these separate straws." Not so said beautiful Ruth. She gathered two straws, and she put them together, and more straws, until she got enough to make a sheaf. Putting that down, she went and gathered more straws, until she had another sheaf, and another, and another, and another, and then she brought them all together, and she threshed them out, and she had an ephah of barley, nigh a bushel.

Elihu Burritt learned many things while toiling in a blacksmith's shop. Abercrombie, the world-renowned philosopher, was a philosopher in Scotland, and he got his philosophy, or the chief part of it, while, as a physician, he was waiting for the door of the sick-room to open. Yet how many there are in this day who say they are so busy they have no time for mental or spiritual improvement; the great duties of life cross the field like strong reapers, and carry off all the hours, and there is only here and there a fragment left that is not worth gleaning. Ah, my friends, you could go into the busiest day and busiest week of your life and find golden opportunities, which, gathered, might at least make a sheaf for the Lord's garner. It is the

Stray Opportunities

and the stray privileges which, taken up and bound together and beaten out, will at least fill you with abounding joy. There are a few moments left worth the gleaning. Now, Ruth, to the field! May each one have a measure full and running over! Oh, you gleaners, to the field! And if there be in your household an aged one, or a sick relative that is not strong enough to come forth and toil in this field, then let Ruth take home to feeble Naomi this sheaf of gleaning: "He that goeth forth and weepeth, bearing precious seed, shall doubtless come again with rejoicing, bringing his sheaves with him." May the Lord God of Ruth and Naomi be our portion!

A MISSIONARY HERO'S PERIL.

(See Illustration on Page 332.)

The courage which sustains the good man who is engaged in his Master's service, and is sure that God will preserve his life until his work is done, was marvellously displayed in a moment of supreme peril by the late Robert Moffat in the early days of his work in Southern Africa. The ignorant and superstitious savages by whom he was surrounded regarded the white man with suspicion, and many of them were convinced that his residence in their midst would surely bring evil on the tribe. It was, therefore, not surprising that when a season of protracted drought occurred, the missionary's enemies charged him with being the cause of the trouble. The professional rain-makers were set to work, but without success, and then a band of natives with their chief at the head went to the mission to demand the departure of the white men.

Moffat was in his garden repairing a wagon when the deputation arrived, but he was quickly on the scene when he heard of his visitors. "We stood patiently to hear the message," he said, when relating the story in after years, "and we expected the worst. The principal speaker informed us that it was the determination of the chiefs that we should leave the country, and, referring to our disregard of threatenings, added what was tantamount to the assurance that measures of a violent character would be resorted to, to carry their resolutions into effect, in case of our disobeying the order. While the chief was speaking, he stood quivering his spear in his right hand.

"Mrs. Moffat was at the door of our cottage, with the babe in her arms, watching the crisis, for such it was. I replied: 'We have indeed felt most reluctant to leave, and are now more than ever resolved to abide by our post. If you are resolved to rid yourselves of us, you must resort to stronger measures, for our hearts are entirely with you. You may shed blood, or burn us out. We know you will not touch our wives and children.'" Then throwing open his coat, Moffat stood erect and fearless. "Now, then," said he, "if you will, drive your spears to my heart; and when you have slain me, my companions will know that the hour has come for them to depart."

At these words the chief man looked at his companions, remarking with a significant shake of the head, "These men must have ten lives, when they are so fearless of death; there must be something in immortality."

A PERSECUTED CHRISTIAN WIDOW.

How much it costs to make a profession of faith in Christ in heathen lands may be seen by the following narrative from Rev. S. Knowles, the well-known missionary in India: "A *Kshatri* widow at Mahadeva, who had been virtually treated as a slave, and then greatly neglected and almost starved to death by her high caste friends, had been instructed in the truths of the gospel by our people, when she made up her mind to fully accept Christ, and cast in her lot with the Christians. For this purpose she came with her son and daughter—the one aged thirteen, the other eleven years—and asked our people to receive them. As soon as her caste relations, who had despised and treated her as a poor wretch under a heavy curse, found out that she and her two children wanted to connect themselves with us, they at once began their persecuting annoyances. The first thing they did was to confine the widow and her two children to their huts, and make them prisoners; and then they betrothed her daughter to the son of a distant relation. Not satisfied with this, on the morning of March 27 the chief man of the village headed a mob and proceeded to the place where our Christian families resided. There this excited crowd began wildly shouting and gesticulating, and giving the women the foulest abuse, which latter the Hindus, on the festival, know only too well how to give in all its ugly filthiness; threatening to burn down their houses and cut off their feet if they ever came near any of the Kshatri homes again. The next day they formally ostracised our people by excluding them from the village well, and from visiting any of their families. In a hundred petty ways they daily annoyed and disturbed the peace of these Christian families. They appealed to us for help, and we endeavored to settle the question by calling the Kshatris to our tent and quietly reasoning with them; but only a few leading Brahmans responded to our call. These were men whom we had met on former visits, and who again listened to the gospel patiently and with apparent favor. After these friends had left us, we sat down and wrote out an account of the Mahadeva affair to the Agent of the Balrampur Estates, and in whose charge this village happens to be placed."

CONSECRATED SATURDAYS IN THE EAST.

THE remarkable devotion of a Christian church in Koordistan has recently been shown in the erection of a place of worship. It was mainly accomplished by the manual labor of its members, who are too poor to give much money, but were willing to work. The account of the work is given in a report from Mr. Browne, of the Eastern Turkey Mission, to the American Board. In the course of it he says: "As I approached Haine I saw the white walls of their new chapel, the most conspicuous building in the town. The undertaking of building it seemed at first preposterous, but it has been accomplished. After various disappointments the pastor secured a large but very cheap lot on the edge of the town, and also an old ruin, with stone for building. The firman, the Sultan's permission to build, a document not easy to obtain, and which it was thought would require a long time, and perhaps a large expense, 'was granted at the first request, and at a cost of a single postage stamp.' This has not ceased to be a marvel to the whole community. The stone from the ruin was soon exhausted, and the Government gave the pastor permission to open a quarry wherever he could find one. After prayer one was found where the stones readily came out in blocks just suited to the building, thus saving expense.

"Henceforward the building proceeded without interruption. All through the long summer 'the people had a mind to work' as well as give and pray. *Every Saturday they dedicated entire* to the work of the Lord's house. Long before day ox-carts and beasts of burden, men and women, left the town for the quarry, where they toiled joyfully till evening. Going and coming and while at work their songs were borne into the town, which seemed stirred to its centre in sympathy and admiration for these brave toilers for Christ and the church. In the fall the building stood completed.

"So much were the Gregorian priests and ecclesiastics impressed that again and again they were forced to say to their people: 'If these Protestants, so few and so poor, can do a work like this, what ought we to be able to do?' Two leading Gregorians, master workmen employed on the chapel, became so impressed by the zeal and spirit of our people that before the building was finished they had become 'persuaded,' and with eight other Gregorian houses joined the Protestant community."

REMARKABLE CURE OF A DISEASED HIP.

IN the current number of *Thy Healer** Mrs. Baxter publishes the following remarkable narrative which was sent to Bethshan by a friend at Plymouth, England: "A dear girl, Sarah Vanstine, of not yet twenty summers, has been a great sufferer with hip-disease for seven years, and went first to the hospital at Newton Abbot; from there to Exeter Hospital for two years, and last to Plymouth Hospital for seventeen months. Here an operation was performed, diseased bone extracted, and thigh bone scraped. This caused great inflammation, which broke out in several very large abscesses. She could eat no food, her life appeared ebbing out fast. They discharged her from the hospital incurable, with a certificated nurse to dress her wounds. We shall not soon forget that emaciated form as we entered that room for prayer; but as we anointed and prayed, the power of the Lord was present to heal, and in her own words, she felt as though His hand touched every wound and all soreness was gone; and the next morning the dear girl, that had not moved for seventeen months, got up in her bed, got to the window, raised it, and stood looking out. She improved rapidly, the leg that was so much shorter began to develop in length and strength with the other. One crutch soon went, and then the other, and now she is the strongest, and, her mother says, the heartiest in the family; praise the Lord. Is there anything too hard for the Lord?"

A BROTHER RECOGNIZED BY A SCAR.

CAPTAIN CHARTERS, of Stanley Pool, commander of the Mission ship *Peace*, relates an affecting incident which he witnessed during his recent voyage in Africa. He says: "In the month of July, 1887, we reached the mouth of the Arameni. We had on board a boy of fifteen years of age. He was a personal attendant of Mr. Stanley. The boy had been captured a number of years previously to our arrival, by Arabs. The town had been burned, and he, together with many others, had been sold into slavery. He had met with Stanley, and the explorer, finding him intelligent, had taken him into his service. As we approached the mouth of the Arameni, you could see the boy, just like any other boy, when he sees home after a long absence. He began to get excited, and could scarcely keep himself still. As we approached, the natives looked at the *Peace*. They saw us on board, and, thinking the Arabs had come back again, they took to their canoes and paddled away as quickly as they could; and then we saw one or two canoes coming nearer, until one came right alongside of the *Peace*. The moment it touched, the boy said to one of these wretched looking men, 'You are my brother.' But the savage would not be persuaded. By and by he looked at him and said, 'Yes, you are my brother; you have a mark on your arm that you got while we were bathing in the river one day, and *a crocodile bit you*.' The moment he said that, you should have seen how that poor boy acted. He threw his arms around his brother, and the two wept for joy. As the two embraced, Stanley was touched. He pointed to the pathetic sight, and said: 'Some people say the African has no love, has no gratitude. There is a sight that speaks for itself.'"

* *Thy Healer and Faith Witness*, a monthly magazine, edited by Mrs. M. Baxter, contains original articles on Holiness and Healing, Authentic Testimonies of Divine Healing, and Items of Intelligence from Heathen Lands where Missionaries are laboring in faith, soliciting no help from man, but relying solely on God for support. Annual Subscription, 75 cents, may be sent to the Manager of CHRISTIAN HERALD, 63 Bible House, New York.

A LONG SEARCH ENDED.

A LADY missionary in India was speaking in a village to some native women, and, at the close of the address, an aged man who had listened intently to her words, accosted her and asked: "Would you come and visit my wife at my home?" He was one of a religious order, an elderly man, past seventy, and this lady said, "Oh, gladly!" and she followed him home, where he had a tank and a grove—a sort of religious establishment. He listened and listened and believed, and while his wife was taught the lesson, he was the chief learner. He related his history afterward to the lady. He said, "From the time I was a youth I have been seeking after God, longing that I might find Him. I was willing to dare anything if only I could know God. I went and joined myself to an order of monks, and went through their course of austerities. In summer time I have sat in the jungle, lighted four fires, and sat between them, with the burning sun overhead, enduring much suffering; then I would plunge into a tank in the bitter colds of winter, and there I would stand for hours until life almost fled. Oh! I sought after God for years in different places, and by all manner of austerities, but I never found Him, and, at last, I said, I have sought Him so long that I shall wait until He reveals Himself to me. But now, as I listened to your words, I have found that which I have been seeking all my life." He was baptized, on a profession of his faith in Christ. And now we see this aged man, with tears streaming down his cheeks as he weeps, because, he says, so short a time is left to him in which to serve on earth this Saviour whom he had sought so long.

A REMARKABLE MOVEMENT IN INDIA.

THE Rev. M. J. Coldron, of Chandbally, thus describes in the *Indian Witness* a remarkable movement begun by a native teacher:—There is a very interesting case of a native "Guru," who about eight years ago, got a tract, most probably the one entitled "The Confuter of Caste." This gave a new tendency to his mind, and he began preaching the doctrine of no caste, that all men are the children of one Supreme Father, and that the Son of God is the only Person who is authorized or has the power to save sinners.

This Guru has shown such earnestness and such adaptation to his work, that he now has about 5,000 followers. He told me his experience, how he came to enter upon this work. He was formerly rich, owned lands, and one year he had a large amount of rice in his godown, and the Lord appeared to him in a dream and told him to sell all his rice, and give the proceeds to the poor; then the Lord came to him again and said, sell all your land and give to the poor and I will make you rich in *dharma*; he said it took him a long time to be willing to give up everything, but since he did he has found the Lord's promise true.

The Spirit has evidently been teaching him many things regarding the principle of Christianity, but his two most prominent features are "one caste," and the Son of God the Saviour of sinners. He holds to some superstitious ideas, and probably will, but the real essence of the plan of salvation seems to be in him, and I believe he is called of God to further the cause of Christ. One peculiarity about him is that he claims to be especially called of God to preach this new doctrine, and brings as his proof *three* "birth marks; the print of a foot," a mark in the form of a lotus, and that of a sea-shell," all of which are recognized by the lower classes of Hindus as positive proof that he is a teacher from God, and they feel bound to obey his words. So he asked me to have these signs published in an Oryia tract, stating that he proclaimed that all people were to be in one caste, and to accept the Son of God as the Saviour from sin. He is a man about thirty-eight years old, and all that his enemies can say against him is that he is teaching the "Sahibs' religion" and his followers disregard the Hindu religion. His followers are in forty different villages.

The Zemindars and Brahmins tried to stop his preaching by threatening to stop his barber and dhobie, but he simply replied, they belong to my disciples. Although in his present state of development he has some ideas, which we with a clearer vision could not accept, still I believe God is leading him, and that if properly managed he will come with all his followers; and that this may yet prove an opening for the people of Orissa to receive the Gospel.

THE SIGNS OF CHRIST'S COMING.

By Rev. E. Bullinger.

AT Christ's second coming there shall be signs from heaven, great and terrible, but we have already and now the signs of the "sure word of prophecy." We desire to show from these signs of the Scriptures, that we are fast approaching the time when there "shall appear the sign of the Son of Man in heaven." The second advent of Christ will consist of

A Series of Events,

of which the visible and personal appearing of Christ will be the great central point. His first coming consisted of many events, and extended over a period of about thirty-three years. A Jew read of this coming in Micah 5:2, "Thou Bethlehem Ephratah . . . out of thee shall He *come* forth unto me that is to be uler in Israel;" and he also read of this same coming in Zech. 9:9. "Rejoice greatly, O daughter of Zion; shout, O daughter of Jerusalem; behold, thy King *cometh* unto thee," &c. But there was nothing in these prophecies to tell him that there were to be more than thirty years between these two events, which were both Christ's *coming*. So likewise in the prophecies of *Christ's second coming*, we read, "I will come again and receive you unto Myself" (John 14:3), and "The Lord my God shall come, and all the saints with Thee." Some interval is clearly implied between

The Rapture and Reception

of the saints by Christ and their *return with* Him in glory. And so when we read that the saints are to be caught up "to meet the Lord in the air" (1 Thess. 4:17), there is nothing in that passage to tell us how long they shall be with Him there, before they return with Him in glory; whether it is to be momentary or prolonged. We learn, however, from many Scriptures that at least seven years will run their course. All the events that are recorded in the book of "The Revelation of Jesus Christ" are connected with and form part of that Revelation, and go to make up the Second Advent; while the personal appearing of Christ will of course form a definite act in that series of events, as definite as the lightning's flash. (Dan. 7:25.)

The Return of the Jews

will not be accomplished in a day or a week. There will be a preliminary, or partial, gathering: and there will be also a "second" complete and miraculous gathering. The return from Babylon occupied more than forty years. The re-building of the street and the wall was to be in "the strait of times." (Dan. 9:25, margin) i. e., the smaller interval of the two named, viz., in "seven weeks," or seven sevens of years, i. e., forty-nine years, The dispersion of the Jews likewise was not completed until the destruction of Jerusalem, till forty years after Christ foretold it in Luke 21. So that we might expect the gathering of the Jews to their city and land to be accomplished *gradually* in the course of years, and by apparently natural causes; when the Antichrist shall be revealed in his time, and first by flatteries and deceit, then by violence and persecution shall lead up to his own destruction by the glory of Christ's coming with His saints—the saints having been previously caught up to meet Him in the air.

In a work by Dr. Kellogg entitled, "*The Jews: or prediction and fulfilment*," there is a mass of evidence, and a collection of facts showing how in the past history of the Jews the most minute predictions have been *literally fulfilled*, and pointing the most powerful argument to a like literal fulfilment of prophecies in the present, and in the near future.

Their Restoration Will be Gradual

(Ezek. 37:7-14.) The restoration is not to be the one work of a moment, but it is marked by successive stages. (1) "a noise," (2) "a shaking," (3) "the bones came together, bone to his bone," (4) "the sinews and flesh came up upon them," (5) "the skin covered them above," (6) "the breath came into them and they lived," and (7) they "stood up upon their feet."

Now as the Restoration of Israel cannot be the work of a moment or a day, or of a mere brief period, is it too much to ask whether we may not call present movements, the "noise" and the "shaking," even if not the coming together of bone to bone.

THE PROPHETIC CRISIS IN EUROPE.

Turkey in Extremis.

THE condition of Turkey is thus described by a contemporary: "Not for years has the couch of the 'sick man' been so prickly. A quarrel with Greece; Roumania veering towards revolution and anarchy; Crete boiling up; Bulgaria quiet with the dull quietness which usually precedes a storm; even Armenia daring to make public protest about her grievances—such are some of the troubles which torment the poor invalid at Constantinople. Nor can he flatter himself that he possesses a single friend on whose assistance he could rely, were Russia to pick another quarrel with him. And *that* is the chief danger which is even more acute than it was two months ago. The spectacle of this helpless and fatuous Power vainly endeavoring to gain its ends by the obselete chicaneries of old-fashioned diplomacy is a standing temptation to the heirs-expectant to make an end of the business. Events seem moving to the partitioning of Turkey between Russia and Austria, or to a great European war." The end of Turkish Mohammedan rule in Europe—or in prophetic phraseology—"*the drying-up of the river Euphrates*" is one of the predicted signs of the end of this dispensation.

France and Boulanger.

There is a pause in what is called in derision "the Boulangist craze," but in the opinion of those best qualified to form an opinion on the subject the pause is on the surface only. The fact is clearly perceived by unprejudiced observers who mix with the masses of the people. The able correspondent in Paris of the London *Record* says: "The fear of an immediate appeal to the country, and, as the result of this, of the revision of the Constitution and the establishment of a Dictatorship, drove the innumerable sections of the Republicans together, and caused them to support the Floquet Cabinet. Even if this spasmodic concentration, the mere creation of terror, could be developed into a loyal, patriotic, and consistent upholding of the Republic, I believe it would come too late. The discontent with the existing state of things is now far too deep-seated and wide-spread to be appeased with anything short of revision. Were it otherwise, I do not see any satisfactory indications that partyism is inclined to give way to patriotism. Imagine the existence of no less than fourteen parties, or groups, in the Chamber, each with its duly constituted chairman and committee! For this reason, therefore, because the forces that would oppose Boulangism are so pitiably incapable of rising above their petty differences, and uniting for the good of the commonwealth, and still more, perhaps, because of the extraordinary hold which Boulangism has taken upon the popular mind throughout France, my belief is that *its success is inevitable*. A French lady residing in one of the central Departments told me the other day that you cannot buy a pound of sugar or coffee in the little town near her home, but the paper in which it is wrapped up bears the portrait of Boulanger; and one of the Directors of the Western Railway assures me that almost every guard and engine-driver on their line carries the *brav' General* in his pocket!" We have already pointed out that Boulanger will in all probability play the part of forerunner to the Napoleonic Antichrist that is to arise very shortly; hence the importance of observing the steps he takes in order to realise his ambition—the military dictatorship of France.

Affairs in Eastern Europe.

The omens in Eastern Europe are becoming increasingly disquieting and portentous. A large body of Montenegrins have crossed the river Lim into Servia, and the Mussulman population of Nova Warosch in the Sandjak of Nova Bazar, fled precipitiously on the approach of the invaders. The evident determination of Greece to extend its activity to Macedonia, and the undisguised encouragement it is receiving from the agents of Russia, leads the Bulgarians to conclude that if they allow the Greeks to proceed unhindered in that direction, Macedonia will for ever be lost to them. If the Bulgarians connive at any movement in Macedonia they will be putting themselves in flagrant opposition to the stipulations of the Berlin Treaty, and will at once call down upon themselves the anger of the Turkish Government; yet it is believed that they would risk that, rather than abandon Macedonia to Greece. Meanwhile intelligence received at Belgrade from Yranji states that "disturbances of some magnitude have broken out in the vilayet of Monastir, and that Servians and Greeks have united to oppose the Turkish authorities." Should this trouble develop into a triangular quarrel between Greece, Servia, and Bulgaria, the strong sympathies of both Russia and Austria will involve them in the struggle, and when once the dogs of war are unchained, the weakest will go to the wall. The London *Times* says:—"Although nothing is happening of a distinctly alarming character, the condition of European affairs at this moment inspires widespread uneasiness, if not actual apprehension.

Minor Portents.

Numerous unsettled questions exist which taken singly might be ignored, but collectively involve no small peril to the general tranquillity. Wherever we turn we find unsettled weather, and although no storm has actually burst, the political meteorologist cannot but confess that he has little ground for a confident forecast. Statesmen, however, indulge the hope that peace may be maintained through the summer. Beyond that time they do not venture to build. The London *Standard* says: "The rival interests of Russia and Austria-Hungary are not to be reconciled by the wit of man. It may be that the main crater of the volcano has not yet opened, and that it is only a subsidiary and transitory eruption in the little outbreak in Macedonia that is now beginning to attract the attention of Europe. But what if we are now *on the eve of the long-threatened explosion?* The thought is a terrible one; but it is one which wise men will not shrink from on that account. From some quarter or other, by some agency or other, the Eastern Question must at no distant day be reopened. Has the day come? Is it near at hand? No one knows for certain. All we know is, that the elements of mischief are once more in an ominous state of activity."

CURRENT EVENTS.

The Change Made in the Chinese Treaty by the Senate before ratification, will delay its going into execution if it does not annul it altogether. The Senate treated it as if it were a bill from the House and ratified its own amendment inserted without the consent of the sovereign power of the second part. The Senate recollected that there were Chinamen who had left the country with the right to return, and they wished to prevent those from getting back. So the treaty was changed and the assent of the Chinese Government to the changes must be obtained before any part of the treaty can take effect. The assent of the Chinese Government cannot be obtained, if it is obtained at all, before the end of the summer, and it is probable that by that time the Chinamen who wish to return will hasten back to avoid the exclusion with which they are menaced in the amendment.

Another Whole Week has Been Devoted by the House to the interminable Tariff debate. A remarkable feature of the proceedings, which, however, is by no means unique, is that in a matter in which the interests of the whole country are so seriously involved, the members of the House occupy their time in making speeches which are only useful as campaign documents, and are not adapted or designed to aid in the solution of a difficult and momentous problem. The statesmen in Washington seem to be content to have the question decided at the polls by the votes of men who cannot be supposed to have the time or facilities for gaining an intelligent comprehension of the subject, rather than to accept the responsibility belonging to them of dealing with it in a dignified and statesmanlike manner. The majority appear to consider how their action on the tariff will affect their prospects of re-election, rather than how their action will affect the interests of the nation. One important fact was brought out during last week's debate which shows that the Ways and Means Committee did not treat the bill in so sectional a spirit as was supposed. Mr. Breckinridge of Arkansas, declared that although the committee had put wool on the free list, the number of sheep in the South had increased during the past twelve years from three to nine millions, while in New England and the middle States the number had decreased from nine to eight millions. The main difficulty in dealing with the question is evidently caused by its being approached in a party rather than a patriotic spirit.

An Uninstructed Delegation to the Republican National Convention, in Chicago, is to go from New York. At the State Convention, held in Buffalo on May 16, it was resolved that "the Republicans of New York, in convention assembled, certain that the National Convention at Chicago will present candidates for President and Vice-President whose devotion to American ideas, and to the protection of labor, agriculture and manufactures, will command the approval of the people, pledge to the Republican standard-bearers, in the national contest their united and zealous support, and enter upon the canvass confident of victory." This resolution would not, however, have been passed, had it not been understood that the delegation would support Mr. Blaine's candidacy. Mr. Depew's friends were numerous in the convention, but in the face of the action of conventions in other States, the presentation of Mr. Depew's name might have involved the New York delegation in embarrassment. This was especially considered unwise, because it was evident that, as in 1880 and 1884, New York will be the battle-ground on which the Presidential election will be decided. The fact that the delegation is headed by the names of United States Senator Frank Hiscock, ex-United States Senator Warner Miller, Chauncey M. Depew, and Thomas C. Platt, shows how the State's vote in the National Convention will be cast. The tariff resolution was worded with extreme caution. It did not afford "the guiding light" which legislators in Congress had expected, as an indication of the extent to which the party in New York is prepared to go in tariff reduction. It simply approved "the action of the Republican members of Congress in opposing the Mills tariff bill, so-called," and urged "them to persevere in defeating every device intended to place upon the statute book the free-trade theories of Mr. Cleveland's annual message."

The New York State Democratic Convention, which has been the subject of much anxiety in the Party throughout the country, assembled in New York city on May 15. It was generally understood that upon the action of this Convention depended the question of the renomination of Mr. Cleveland. If the opposition manifested toward him by a large and influential section of his party proved strong enough to prevent his receiving the endorsement of his own State, the prospect of a renomination would be very small. The Convention, however, appeared from the outset to be entirely in the hands of the President's friends. Not only was there selected a delegation to St. Louis wholly in favor of Mr. Cleveland's renomination and instructed to do all in their power to bring this about, but most of Mr. Hill's supporters in the State Committee were forced to make way for pronounced Cleveland men. Mr. Cleveland's name was received with the heartiest enthusiasm, and the plank in the platform commending his message to Congress on the surplus met with more enthusiasm from the delegates than any other utterance. The portion of the platform which refers to the tariff gave trouble to the committee having the matter in charge. After much discussion, it was simply determined not to be too pronounced on the subject, and the matter was dismissed with the indorsement of the recommendations contained in the President's message to Congress. The convention could not decently avoid endorsing Gov. Hill's administration: but it did so in a perfunctory manner which must have been very discouraging to those friends of the Governor who have been advocating his nomination for the Presidency.

The Great Flood now Prevailing along the Mississippi river, exceeds in horror all that have preceded it since 1851. The water reached the danger point at Quincy, Ill., on May 9, and since that day it has risen steadily. On May 13, the first break occurred in one of those great embankments known as the Indian Grove Levee. During the day other crevasses were made, and within a few hours thousands of acres of winter wheat were laid waste. The farmers had been working on the embankment night and day, in the hope of saving their homes, and when the flood came a majority of them had barely time to save their families, so sudden and overwhelming was the rush of the torrents. The next day the Sny Carte levee gave way, causing still greater destruction. That was followed by the Alexandria levee and it is now feared that not an acre of ground in this vast territory can escape the flood. At the close of the week cattle and horses in the fine wooded pastures were overwhelmed in many localities and drowned. The river above and below the city was from ten to fifteen miles broad, covering all the farms on both sides and extending from the bluffs on the Illinois side to the high bluffs in Missouri. On the dry places on the embankment hundreds of cattle, horses, and hogs stood without food, and no prospect of drink except when in danger of being swallowed up by the floods. Far across on the opposite bluffs were gathered hundreds of men, women, and children, many of them utterly destitute, without sufficient clothing, and some suffering for want of food.

The Irish Members of Parliament have issued a formal protest against the rescript which the Pope recently launched against boycotting and the plan of campaign. They flatly contradict, seriatim, each of the assertions made by the Pope, and say, in conclusion: That the demand of the Irish people for agrarian reform and political liberty is dictated by necessity, sustained by natural justice, and conducted by modes of action and methods of organization prescribed or allowed by the constitution to which the Irish people owe whatever they have won of civil and religious freedom; that the force of this national movement against unconstitutional coercion and organized calumny *will continue to be exerted* until we shall have achieved success. While unreservedly acknowledging the spiritual jurisdiction of the Holy See, we, as guardians of those civil liberties which our Catholic fore-fathers resolutely defended, feel bound to solemnly reassert that Irish Catholics can *recognize no right of the Holy See to interfere* with the Irish people in the management of their political affairs."

A Combination in the French Chambers has been arranged which promises to cause a serious crisis in the affairs of the Republic. The Bonapartist group in the Chamber of Deputies have resolved to combine with the Right in an effort to bring about a dissolution of Parliament. Whether this resolution has been formed with the pure idea of causing embarrassment to the Government, and so leading the nation to believe that tranquillity and security are not to be expected under Republican Institutions, or that some concession of value to the Bonapartists has been made by the Right, is not stated, but it is certain that the crisis which the combination will produce is one of a very serious character. In the meantime Gen. Boulanger becomes more outspoken in his ambitious appeals to the people. Speaking at a luncheon at Douai, Gen. Boulanger called the Constitution a "ridiculous compromise between a pseudo-monarchy and a false republic." Those who feigned to propose revision, he said, refused it now because they feared to lose their seats.

The Suffering Emperor of Germany has entered on another period of improvement. The intense weakness which followed his last crisis has gradually disappeared under the careful treatment of his physicians. The cable report on Friday last stated that he was able to take an airing in the park, dividing the time between resting in the tent, and driving about in the pony-carriage. The consultation of the doctors was held in the tent. On leaving the park the Emperor walked up the steps of the Schloss supporting himself by the balustrade. He was also able to visit the chapel. Another encouraging feature of the case is that the matter taken from his throat has been submitted to microscopical examination by Professor Virchow, who declares that it does not contain any cancerous cells. Dr. Mackenzie, however, does not speak hopefully of the case, though he persists in his assertion that if an operation had been performed when the German doctors recommended it the Emperor would surely have died. He says that his present condition proves that he had not the recuperative power which would have been necessary to recover from it. Dr. Mackenzie said recently to a press correspondent "The Emperor is certainly suffering from perichondritis, which with disease of the cartilage is very dangerous, though not necessarily fatal. If he also has cancer, that will necessarily prove fatal sooner or later."

Contributions to the Fund for Supplying Colored Ministers in the South with this journal have been received since our last acknowledgment to the amount of $13.30. They are from: East Line, N. Y., $1; Seymour, Ind., $1.80; East Des Moines, Iowa, $2.50; No. Greenfield, N. Y., $1; Philadelphia, Pa., $2 and $5. Testimonies to the value of this agency are continually coming to hand. Many colored ministers have no commentaries, nor theological works, and they gratefully acknowledge the benefits they have derived from the sermons and other exegetical matter published in these pages. Thus every dollar subscribed is a benefit not only to the preacher, but to his hearers. Christians who have the welfare of the colored race at heart, may materially promote it by enabling us to extend the benefits of this fund.

A New and Powerfully Written Story by Rev. L. S. Keyser is commenced in this number of THE CHRISTIAN HERALD. It is gratifying to learn that his previous story, "The Way Out," published two years ago in these columns, was blessed of God to the conversion of several young men who were known as sceptics and that others were led by reading it to abandon their attitude of hostility to Christianity. The rapid and alarming increase of scepticism among the young men in our colleges is a most serious omen for the country, which is causing anxiety to true and enlightened patriots. We earnestly hope that our readers will pray that the publication of Mr Keyser's story will be blessed even more abundantly than his former one.

The Methodist General Conference Decided on Thursday last to add five bishops to the list. There are twenty-five candidates for the vacancies so that the announcement led to increased activity among the friends of the clergymen whose names are prominent. Complaints have been made to the Conference of the methods adopted by enthusiastic partizans. They savor, it is alleged, too much of the political system, and requests have been made that lobbying shall be prohibited. The vexed question of the Status of Bishop Taylor has been submitted to a sub-committee, which, in a series of resolutions, defines the position of a missionary bishop. It is declared that his functions and jurisdiction are limited to the mission field to which he is appointed, and his salary is to be paid out of the foreign mission fund, and not out of the general treasury.

Rev. Thomas Harrison's Meetings at the Eighteenth Street Methodist Episcopal Church in New York, are being blessed in a remarkable manner. The church is densely crowded at every service by men and women of all classes. Among those who last week made a profession of faith, were a wealthy Wall Street broker and his wife, who were in deep grief over the death of their little daughter. The scene when the wife, who first found peace, discovered that her husband was in the church, and was also seeking the Saviour, was most affecting. She joined in the prayers for his conversion, and when, after a period of much distress and conflict, he finally gave himself to God, her joy was greater than she could express. The number of persons who have made a profession of faith through the blessing of God on Mr. Harrison's labors in New York, is now over fourteen hundred.

The Discovery of a Miser's Hoard is Reported in the Pittsburgh *Despatch*. It states that as the owner of a sawmill was engaged in halving a big cypress log, the teeth of the saw began to grate harshly on his ear. He stopped the machine to ascertain the cause, and, to his surprise, he discovered a box, measuring about four by eight inches. After much difficulty he got the box out and pried the lid open, his eyes almost starting from their sockets when he saw that it was filled with coin. After satisfying himself that it was real gold, the sawyer put his treasure in a place of safety. He refused to tell the neighbors the amount of his find, but satisfied their curiosity to some extent by displaying several twenty-dollar gold pieces. When the man from whom the sawyer obtained the log learned of the discovery, he laid claim to the box, and when his claim was not recognized he threatened a lawsuit. It is supposed that the money was placed in the tree many years ago, by a man named Spencer, an old miser, who lived near where the tree was cut down. When he accumulated the hoard he could have had no idea that it would ever fall into the hands of a stranger or he would have been greatly distressed. If he knows now it will cause him no concern. The only matter of moment to him now on his side of the grave is whether in this life he was rich toward God. (Luke 12: 20, 21.)

The Disposal of Soldiers' Clothing was the subject of newspaper discussion last week. A complaint was made in a daily journal that recruits were required to sell their civilian dress immediately on enlisting, and that the recruiting officer introduced them to a second-hand clothes dealer, to whom they were obliged to sell their clothes, and who gave the recruiting officer a commission on the transaction, of course paying the recruit an inadequate price. The other side of the story soon found its way to publication. It appears that it is true that the recruit on entering the army is not allowed to keep his civilian's clothes, but he is allowed two weeks in which to dispose of them and can make his own bargain with a purchaser of his own choice. Experience, however, proves that the transaction has not much profit in it for any one. The men who offer themselves, do so generally as a last resort. They are often coatless, and their other garments are seldom worth a dollar; very often they are given away. It is with them very much as it is with the sinner who enters the service of Christ. He, too, is driven to his last resource, and his own righteousness has to be discarded before he takes on the robe which Christ provides for him, but he knows it is only filthy rags, of no value to any one. (Isa. 64: 6.)

Terror at a Waving Wire Caused a Block of traffic on Broadway, New York, on May 12. It was one of the Brush Illuminating Company's wires, and hung from a pole near Howard Street. The wire parted close to its connection with a pole on the east side of Broadway and fell across the roadway. The end of the wire, from which the insulation had been torn when it parted, struck the railroad tracks in the centre of the street and there was at once a vivid display of daylight pyrotechnies which attracted a great crowd. The wire in its fall narrowly escaped striking a man and horse passing beneath it, Every time the naked end of the wire touched the steel rails, there were emitted long streaks of blue flame and showers of brilliant sparks All travel on Broadway was stopped, and no one had the temerity to touch the wire, in view of recent experiences in that direction. The police captain of the Precinct sent a messenger to the station of the Illuminating Company in Elizabeth street, and linemen were soon on the spot. The current was shut off and the wire was removed. Then, after a delay of nearly an hour, traffic was resumed. A few months ago a score of hands would have been thrust out to remove the obstruction, but so many persons have been killed of late by touching electric wires that more caution is exercised now. Would that a similar result were produced by the moral and spiritual catastrophes which occur! Men see their companions go to a fate worse than death through liquor and the indulgence of vicious propensities, yet they heed not the warning (Job. 12: 5).

An Important Lawsuit was Closed by a Practical experiment, in Brooklyn, N. Y., on May 15. A druggist was sued by a customer for ten thousand dollars in compensation for injuries she claimed that she had received as a result of his blunder. She said that she had taken a prescription to his store to be made up, and, when she received the medicine, she took one dose and was soon afterwards seized with severe pain in the stomach, with a burning sensation and a copious hemorrhage from the mouth. She had submitted some of the medicine to an analyst who had tested it, and who stated that caustic potash had been used in it instead of iodide of potassium. After the plaintiff and the analyst, had given their evidence, the druggist was called to the stand. He declared that the prescription was accurately dispensed, and that the medicine was not poisonous, and could not have produced the results described. "Should you be afraid to take the medicine yourself?" asked the Judge. "Not at all," said the druggist, and, before any one could prevent him, he took a large dose in the presence of the court. Several doctors, who were witnesses, wanted to administer antidotes, but the witness would not have it, and he showed no bad effects from swallowing the mixture. The jury thereupon gave him a verdict. The personal testimony and practical evidence had more weight with them than the scientific reasoning of the experts. It is so with the world in spiritual matters. Neither cogent reasoning nor eloquent appeals are so efficacious in the conversion of sinners, as the personal witness of men whom religion has blessed (1 John 4: 13, 14).

BRIEF NOTES.

Mr. Thomas Whitley, of England, whose son recently died in the missionary work on the Congo, has paid the outfit and passage of a man to take his son's place.

Rev. Eynon Davis, a Welsh clergyman, recently stated that there is not a single atheistic book published in the Welsh language.

Pundita Ramabai's appeal for funds to found a school for high-caste Hindoo women has met with such favorable response that the school will open next January.

A pastor of Columbus, O., estimates that the number of church accessions resulting from the meetings held in that city by Dr. L. W. Munhall, number 1,000.

The Baptist Year Book, just issued, records a membership of 2,917,315 in the 31,891 churches. During the year 158,373 were added to the membership, and 608 new churches were established.

The union meeting of the Young People's Societies of Christian Endeavor of the various churches in New York was held at the Central Presbyterian church, last Thursday afternoon and evening.

Mr. Charles Herald is now conducting services in Bethesda Chapel, Brooklyn, N. N., the mission in connection with the Central Congregational Church, of which Dr. Behrends is pastor. The attendance is of an encouraging character, and much good is being done.

Bishop Littlejohn, of Long Island, is preparing a memorial to Congress on the subject of the spiritual destitution in the Army. The memorial asks for the appointment of more chaplains, and of men of greater efficiency.

The American Baptist Home Mission Society received the past year $551,596, of which $145,603 was received by contributions for general purposes; $41,579 for schools and buildings, and $39,629 for church extension. The receipts from legacies were $245,485.

The Rev. Edward Judson announces that he has received subscriptions amounting to $135,000 for a Judson Memorial Church for the benefit of the masses in New York. The site is the southwest corner of Washington Square and Thompson Street. The amount yet to be raised is $65,000.

The Springfield *Republican* says: "A Boston notion in church work is called a House Committee, and its members scatter themselves among the congregation. Each one is responsible for the five pews in front of him, to whose occupants he speaks and shows the attentions which will make them feel at home."

During the hearing of a case before the referee in New York last week, a witness desired to be sworn instead of affirming. Five hours were spent by the messengers in a fruitless search for a Bible. The referee wanted the witness to swear on a volume of the Civil Code, but he declined, and the case was adjourned to the next day.

The leading Hebrew congregation of New York have now added a Sunday service to their long-time Sunday-school; they sit in pews, ladies and gentlemen together, instead of the women being compelled to climb upstairs into the "court of the women;" the gentlemen remove their hats, instead of donning them as heretofore. A synagogue in Chicago, and another in Philadelphia, also now have Sunday services.

Pastor C. H. Spurgeon, it is now stated, declines to resume his membership in the Baptist Union. The concessions which satisfied his brother were not sufficiently explicit to remove Mr. C. H. Spurgeon's scruples. He said: 'All has been done that can be done, and yet without violence to conscience we cannot unite; let us not attempt it any more, but each one go his own way in quiet, striving honestly for that which he believes to be the truth of God.'

THE RAPID BELIEVER.

A New Sermon by Pastor C. H. Spurgeon.

"Jesus answered and said unto him, Because I said unto thee, I saw thee under the fig-tree, believest thou? Thou shalt see greater things than these."—John 1:50.

The Plain-Speaking, Honest Man—No Dissimulation in Him—The Password between Jesus and Nathanael—I. One who Believed Readily—Was Not a Suspicious man—Meant Business—Satisfied with Evidence—II. A Man Highly Commended—Received a Promise—Men with Eyes and no Eyes—III. A Man with Peculiar Temptation—Ready Believers Doubting the Reality of Conversions—Reasons Why Some Escape Severe Conviction—A Talk with a Scotchwoman—A Despairing Hearer Saved.

NATHANAEL was by nature a man free from cunning and deceit. He was a specimen of that "honest and good ground" of which our Saviour speaks in the parable, upon which, when the seed fell, a hundredfold harvest was produced. We have some such men about us, thank God, in this country; regular John Blunts, as we say, clear as crystal, true as the sun in the heavens. Speech is not to them the medium for concealing their thoughts. When they have a mind to speak,

They Speak their Mind.

You know where they are. They may have a great many faults, but they have not the faults of deception and dissimulation. They are Israelites indeed, in whom is no guile. You know the kind of people: they may at times speak too harshly, and hurt your feelings; they may put things in an ugly shape, and tread on people's corns; but they are as straight as a plumb-line, and you may be sure you know them when you have heard what they say.

Now, when the good brethren who had joined the Saviour came to tell Nathanael that they had found the Christ, he blurted out his objection at once. They said, "We have found Him of whom Moses in the law and the prophets did write, Jesus of Nazareth"; but he did not take everything for gospel which his friends told him. He does not beat about the bush, but he says at once, "Can there any good thing come out of Nazareth?" It is always a good thing, when a man has a prejudice, if he will but state it, and "out" with it. You can always deal with this kind of fellow. If he will say what is troubling him, and tell you what keeps him back from faith, why, then you can put your finger on his difficulty, and try to remove it.

Nathanael's question was met at once by his comrades, who said to him,

"Come and See";

and, like the honest man that he was, he took up their challenge. He would "come and see"! How many there are who make objections, but they will not "come and see"! They have heard concerning a certain preacher, perhaps, such and such absurd things; but another says, "It is not so. Come and see." Not they. They do not want to come and see: for they are unfair, and prefer to cherish a bad opinion of the man. They know so much that they do not wish to learn any more. Nathanael was not of that sort. "Come and see," was an invitation which commended itself to his judgment. "Oh, yes," said he, "by all means."

Nathanael is on his way to see for himself, when the Lord Jesus Christ, turning to those around Him, says, in a voice loud enough for him to hear, "Behold an Israelite indeed, in whom is no guile!" Here comes a man with no craft, no cunning in him. Nathanael is startled to find his real character so clearly read, and somewhat bluntly asks, "Whence knowest thou me?" I must do him the justice of believing that he said it respectfully; yet, nevertheless, he curtly said "Whence knowest thou me?" As much as to say—"Thou hast hit the nail on the head; but how camest Thou to know this?"

"Jesus answered and said to him, Before that Philip called thee, when thou wast under the fig-tree, I saw thee." What Nathanael was doing under the fig-tree I do not know. Some think that he was there in meditation; others say in prayer. Very possibly, but I do not know, and the wisest expositors do not know, and you do not know. Anyhow, Jesus mentioned to him a something which he remembered, and thought much of, though it was entirely between God and his own soul. Between Jesus and Nathanael, "under the fig-tree" served as a pass-word. They were known to one another by that; and at once Nathanael cried, "Rabbi, Thou art the Son of God; thou art the King of Israel." He is fairly won, and by an open confession he commits himself at once to what he believes. He is

Not Ashamed of his Convictions,

He has enlisted beneath the banner of the King of Israel once for all. Forth he comes without a moment's reservation with that blessed confession of faith—"Rabbi, Thou art the Son of God; Thou art the King of Israel." Our Lord Jesus, charmed with the grace which He had Himself given, delighted with the faith which He had Himself created, answers, "Because I said unto thee, I saw thee under the fig-tree, believest thou? thou shalt see greater things than these." This ready convert, so speedily convinced, was very acceptable to the Lord Jesus.

I. First, then, here is

One who Believed Readily.

The first time he saw the Saviour he was converted to the faith. The first sentences that were addressed to him by the Lord Jesus Christ fairly won him to hearty faith and loyal service. Why was that? Why was he so soon brought to discipleship?

I think, perhaps, it was because he was such a true man himself that the element of suspicion was not in his character. Persons who are remarkably suspicious and constantly incredulous, are seldom very truthful themselves. If you follow them home, you will discover that they are suspicious of others, because they are not true to themselves, and their difficulty in believing others arises from the fact that they measure other people's corn with their own bushel. They imagine that other people are as big liars as they are themselves. I believe this is the bottom of much of the distrust and questioning which seethes around us. Sometimes that suspiciousness comes upon men's minds through long dealing with deceptive persons. But if you find that a man began life with a general suspicion and doubt of others, you may conclude that he was a born deceiver, radically false from his birth. Nathanael had never taken anybody in nor tried to mislead anyone in his life, and, therefore, he did not expect to be deceived. He was just as honest as the day; and so he came to the Saviour with a heart that was open to faith, ready to believe Him.

An Expectant Believer.

But, further, this Nathanael, this rapid believer in the Lord Jesus Christ, had, I have no doubt, been seeking guidance beforehand, and that guidance he had honestly followed. I should think that he had for years been expecting the coming of the Messiah. The tone of his language argues that. Therefore, when Philip came to him, and told him that he had found the Messiah, and indicated to him that he had better come and see for himself, he was willing at once to come, and without delay he came with the view of seeing for himself whether this Jesus of Nazareth was the promised one. He was not only candid, but he was interested. He was concerned about divine things, and in thorough earnest to know the truth in reference to them. So that he came to Jesus with solemn intent and eager desire. Oh, dear friends, if you came to hear the gospel, meaning business, we should expect to see more of you converted.

Observe that he was satisfied with one piece of clear evidence. That one item of evidence convinced him. The Lord Jesus said, "Before that Philip called thee, when thou wast under the fig tree, I saw thee." Nobody knew that he had been under the fig tree, except the Lord who sees all things. No mortal living was aware of what Nathaniel had done, or thought, or purposed in that shady retreat. When Jesus, therefore, with a peculiar look, said "I saw thee," Nathaniel also saw Him that spake to him. "Godhead alone could speak thus," said he "there is the Spirit of God in that man. He knows the secret things of my life. He has revealed me to myself." "Rabbi," said he, "Thou art the Son of God; Thou art the King of Israel." The conclusion was a sound one, but how speedily it was reached!

II. In the second place, here is one who

Was Highly Commended.

The Lord Jesus owned his faith to be the true faith. He said, "Believest thou?" but He meant that He perceived that he truly believed. He owned that, though his faith was born then and there, it was the genuine article. Chris[t] owns, as true faith, that faith which is not lon[g] in coming. Fear not, dear hearer, that if tho[u] believest off-hand at this very moment thy fait[h] will be any the less sincere and effectual.

Jesus did more than own it to be faith. H[e] commended it as rarely excellent. He spoke a[s] if He were astonished, and was so pleased wit[h] this ready faith, that He made a promise t[o] Nathanael. Said He, "Thou shalt see greate[r] things than these. If thou canst see so muc[h] in My one saying, that I saw thee under the fi[g] tree, thou hast the kind of eyes that are fit t[o] see great sights." He that will see shall see, bu[t] he that closes his eyes shall be blinded. Man[y] are the people in this world who, if you sho[w] them the greatest marvel, do not wonder. The[y] look at it, and see nothing. When you mee[t] with such an unobservant person, you say t[o] yourself, "I shall not show that man anythin[g] more. It does not pay to unveil rarities to hi[m] he has no appreciation of them." But here [is] another who, when you show him some curi[o] that you have in your house, is pleased with i[t] and spies out at once the excellence and beaut[y] of it. You say, "I have something more which [I] will gladly show you!" Oh, you that readil[y] believe in Christ, you are the men to who[m] Christ will make known His secrets! Oh, m[y] beloved hearers, may it be so with you! B[e]cause your faith so readily chimes in with wh[at] Christ reveals, may you have visions of Go[d] and may none of you be so dull of heart that [it] shall be said, "He could not show them ma[ny] mighty works because of their unbelief"!

III. I come, thirdly, to notice that here is man who might possibly be troubled with

A Peculiar Temptation.

People of this kind are subject to a speci[al] trial, with which I will now deal. In th[is] church a considerable number of us, beginni[ng] with the pastor, came to Christ after an aw[ful] amount of conviction and despondenc[y]. We are none the better for this, but we are [not] least free from one particular temptation of t[he] evil one. Oh, how I look back upon those tim[es] in which I felt my bondage, but could not atta[in] to liberty—those days in which Christ w[as] preached to me, but I could not hear Him, a[nd] I wandered up and down everywhere before [I] found peace! In this church, and in the office[rs] of the church among the deacons, there is esp[e]cially one dear brother who sometimes c[an] hardly understand me when I speak about t[he] difficulties some have in coming to Christ, [f]or he never experienced them. You all know hi[m], one of the sweetest and best of men; but [he] came to Jesus Christ as a boy readily enoug[h]. He heard the gospel, and he believed it, a[nd] without any sort of terror he rejoiced in t[he] Lord, and he continues to do so to this d[ay]. He is none the worse saint for this, but in so[me] respects all the better.

Satan's Sophistry.

I know, however, what is the peculiar temp[ta]tion of those who come so readily to Chri[st]. The devil comes to them, and he says, "No[w] look you. You have read Mr. Bunyan's 'Gra[ce] Abounding,' have you not?" "Yes," says t[he] good man. "Well," says he, "you never we[nt] through the like battle and struggle." "No[, I] never did." "Then," says he, "you are [not a] child of God. You see, you were easily co[n]verted; there was no deep work in your so[ul]

You came to Jesus Christ one sunshiny day, and you will go away from him one dark day. You are like the stony-ground hearer, the seed sprang up in you on a sudden, because there was no depth of earth, and you will soon die away when the sun is risen with fervent heat." Now, the next time the devil comes to any of you with that, I want you to talk to him, if he is worth it, for your own good. I want you to

Quench that Fiery Dart.

Let me help you with a few considerations. Those you have read of, who came to Christ under so much terror, it may be that they had some other trouble at the same time, as well as the trouble of their conscience. Perhaps, in addition to being convinced of sin, they were suffering from poverty, or sickness, or dyspepsia, or remorse, or some other vexation of spirit. Discern carefully between spiritual trouble and temporal trouble. Temporal trouble may help to aggravate the spiritual, but it is not a necessary part of it, but very much the reverse. It may increase the apparent depth of the work of repentance, but it may detract from its real worth.

May it not also be that these who are so hard put to it in coming to Christ are without the helps that you have? Perhaps they cannot read. Possibly they have nobody to explain the Scriptures to them. They may be misled by their religious guides, and have no one to keep them out of the ditch. It may be that they are placed where they are rather hindered than helped; they have no Sunday-school teacher, no Christian friend to sympathize with them; and so they have a hard fight of it. Many a man who is wounded in battle is soon restored, because the surgeon takes him up as soon as the bullet lays him low; whereas the wound of another, who has to lie and bleed for hours, will prove far more serious. Do you not think that you ought to be very thankful that you have so many things to help you, and that thus you the more readily come to Christ?

Very possibly, too, many of those who had those terrors and horrors in coming to Christ, as I had myself, must lay them to the door of their unbelief. Had they believed, they might have had comfort long before; but they went to the law for comfort, or they looked to feelings instead of looking to Christ, and so they remained in darkness. Now, if you have the privilege of believing at once, as I pray you may have, should you not be glad of it, and, instead of envying those others, should you not thank God that you were brought to find Jesus Christ by so sunny and speedy a route.

There is a story that I have told you before, but I must tell it to you again, for I do not know anything better. A young man in Edinburgh went out, and he thought he would speak about Jesus to the first person that he met with. He met

A Musselburgh Fishwife

carrying a great load on her back. I cannot speak Scotch: I have not that useful acquirement; so I will put the conversation into English. He said to her, "Here you are with your burden." "Ay," said she. "Well," he said, "did you ever feel a spiritual burden?" "Ay," said she, "that I did, long ago, long ago, and I soon got rid of it; for I did not go the same way to work that John Bunyan's pilgrim did." "Oh," thought the young man, "I hoped that I had met with a Christian woman, but she must be a great heretic to talk in that way." "Now," said she, "Bunyan's Evangelist that he speaks of was *not half a gospel preacher*. He was one of the usual sort. He was not clear in the gospel; for when he met with the poor pilgrim, weary with his burden, he said to him, 'Do you see that wicket-gate?' 'No' said the man, 'I do not see it.' 'Do you see that light over the gate?' 'Well,' he said, 'I think I do.' 'Now,' he said, 'you run that way with your burden.'" "Why man," said she, "that was not the way to do at all. What had that man to do with the wicket-gate or with the light over it? The gospel does not say run to a gate or a light. What he should have said was, 'Do you see that cross? Look at that, and your burden will fall from your shoulder.' I looked straight away to the cross, and not to the wicket-gate; and at the cross I lost my burden.

"Now," said she, "what did the pilgrim get by going round to the wicket-gate? He tumbled into the Slough of Despond, and was like to have lost his life there." "Ah!" said the young man, "did you never go through the Slough of Despond?" "Ah, yes!" she said, "I have been through that slough many a time; but, let me tell you, it is much better to go through it with your burden off than it is with your burden on." And so it is. I do not want any of you to attempt to flounder through the Slough of Despond with your burden on. I want you to have done with the Slough of Despond, and the wicket-gate, and all that bother, and just look to Christ alone; for salvation lies in a look at Him, and there is salvation in none other. Peace comes to sinners by nothing else but faith in Jesus. All else is vain, be it what it may. Frames and feelings, sinkings and risings, doings and frettings—all these may go for nothing. Believe in Jesus Christ, and thou shalt be saved. This is *God's short way to heaven*, and blessed is he who knows how to take it.

A Desperate Man.

Again, the Lord may deal roughly with some because he means to qualify them for comforting despairing souls. He puts His servants through the furnace when He means them to work at pulling others out of the fire. He chastens them every morning because He means to make Barnabases of them, that they may be sons of consolation to souls in distress. I have been through the thick darkness at times for your sakes. If ever a soul was in a horror of great darkness, I was one day when I preached in this pulpit from "My God, my God, why hast thou forsaken me?" I could not understand why I felt in such an awful state as I did, till that evening there came into the vestry a man whose hair seemed to stand on end. He looked at me, and said, "I have never found a preacher that met my experience before." We sat down, and he told out his tale of woe. I rescued that man, by seasonable comfort, from being sent to a lunatic asylum, and perhaps from committing suicide; and then I said to the Lord my God, "Let me go through the fire again, if it will help me to meet the case of thy poor afflicted children." But you, my dear brother, my dear sister, may not be called thus to cut your way through the

Forrests of Sorrow

as the pioneer of others. You are not sent to be a guide to thousands, but quietly to pursue your own lowly way; and, why do you want all this painful experience? You cannot make use of it; be thankful that you are spared the ordeal.

I was going to have another head, but I think that I will not; I will venture no further, but close with a word to sinners, although I have in truth been speaking to them all through.

Here me, thou that wouldst be saved. The way of salvation is by believing in the Lord Jesus Christ; that is, by trusting Him. There are two things I have to say to thee. First, God commands thee to believe in Jesus Christ: and, secondly, nothing thou canst do will please God so much as for thee at once to believe in His Only-begotten Son, whom He has set forth to be the propitiation for sin. Look at the sixth chapter of John's Gospel, and the twenty-eighth and twenty-ninth verses. There you have it. "Then said they unto him, What shall we do, that we might work the works of God?" They meant, "What are the best works, the works most pleasing to God?" "Jesus answered and said unto them, This is the work of God, that ye believe on him whom he hath sent." If you could build a row of alms-houses, or endow a church, or pay the salaries of a hundred missionaries, it would not half so well please God as for you to believe on His Son Jesus Christ.

Thou poor guilty man, thou poor guilty woman, humble, unknown, obscure, a nobody God bids thee trust His Son, and assures thee that this will please Him more than all else thou canst do! Wilt thou not do it? Oh, end your ramblings; end your strivings; end your seekings. Come and trust my Lord Jesus, and thou shalt receive eternal life. Your frettings, and your hopings, and your doubtings, your comings, and your goings—end them all by simply trusting Jesus, and it is finished: thou art saved from wrath, and the life of holiness has begun in thee. Now shalt thou live after a nobler sort. Now shalt thou be filled with good works to the praise of His glory, seeing thou art no more trusting in them. I beseech thee trust in the Lord Jesus Christ alone, and thou shalt receive power to become a child of God. Amen.

[The prayers of the readers of this journal are requested for the blessing of God upon its Editors, and those whose sermons, articles or labors for Christ are printed in it; and that its circulation may be used by the Holy Spirit for the conversion of many sinners and the quickening of God's people. Dr. Talmage and Mr. Spurgeon especially request prayer every Sunday morning on behalf of their labors.]

GEMS FROM NEW BOOKS.

LOST IN THE MOUNTAINS.*

"OUR next stage," says Dr. Grant, "was over the mountain pass of Dohar, the most difficult between Constantinople and Persia. The recollection of what Messrs. Smith and Dwight experienced in their passage over this mountain, together with the fact that three natives had perished in the snow not long before, prepared me to expect a toilsome and difficult ride. But delay was not likely to make any improvement for many days to come; and moreover a storm of rain had set in on the plain, which would soon quite obstruct the road, as the horses would sink almost to their stomachs at every step. As we began to ascend the mountain we found the rain changed to snow, and accompanied by a strong wind, which soon increased to a gale. When about two-thirds of the way up the mountain, the guide, who professed to be well acquainted with the road, led us into such deep snows that our hardy horses were unable to proceed, and it became evident that we had wandered from the path. After much difficulty we succeeded in finding it, but it was soon lost again; and the guide, after a fruitless search, declared it impossible to proceed. To turn back was nearly as hopeless, as the snow had filled our tracks as soon as they were made, and the wind would then be in our faces. Under these circumstances I felt that our hope was in God alone; but with His assurance that He would direct the path of those who acknowledge Him in all their ways, I felt that He would order all for the best, though in what manner or to what end I could not foresee. Just then, as unexpected as if an angel had descended from heaven, four hardy mountaineers came tramping over the snow from the opposite side of the mountain. With much difficulty we prevailed on one of them to act as our guide; and by breaking down the high drifts of snow with our feet, and leading our horses where we could not ride, we at length succeeded in passing the mountains."

A Providential Ride.

Dr. Grant was suffering from malarial fever during his stay at Mardin, in Eastern Turkey, and seemed likely to die. Skilful treatment and careful nursing, however, saved his life, and when he became convalescent, he was persuaded by Mr. Homes to go out one morning for a ride. In their absence the Koords mutinied and slew the Governor and several others of the local authorities, massacred some of the native Christians, and then proceeded to the residence of the missionaries bent on murdering them.

* From "Light in Darkness," by Rev. J. E. Godbey, D. D., and A. H. Godbey, A. M. A valuable and comprehensive survey of mission work in heathen lands, from the organization of the missionary societies to the present time, with numerous illustrations; 768 pages. Sold by subscription only. Published by *Holloway & Company*, St. Louis and San Francisco.

W. H. Howland, Esq., Ex-Mayor of Toronto.

Robert Moffat's Heroic Answer to the African Chief. (See page 325.)

When Dr. Grant and Mr. Homes returned to the city after their ride, they found the gates closed to prevent the escape or rescue of the intended victims, especially of themselves, who were supposed by the Koords to be somewhere within the walls. Hearing the fearful uproar, and guessing the cause, they went to a Syrian convent a few miles from the city, and were hospitably received by the inmates until they could find a place of safety.

W. H. HOWLAND, ESQ.

(See Portrait.)

THE energetic and public spirited gentleman whose portrait appears on this page is one of those rare examples of high Christian principles united with vigorous administrative capacity in municipal life. Mr. Howland has twice occupied the mayoral chair of Toronto, and in both cases his administration has been a public benefit to the city. As an earnest Christian, a strong temperance advocate and a munificent philanthropist he has won an enviable position in the esteem of his fellow citizens.

William H. Howland was born at Lambton Mills, in the County of York, Ontario, in 1844, and is therefore now forty-four years old. His father, Sir Wm. P. Howland, was first Lieutenant-Governor of the new Province of Ontario, when the Dominion was formed.

In 1860, when Sir W. P. Howland entered public life, his son, who was then sixteen, left school to take his father's place in the large business institution of which that gentleman was head. The steady and persevering lad at once found himself at home in his new sphere of life, and speedily developed business traits and talents that have ever since kept him a successful member of the mercantile community.

Mr. Howland was first led to seriously think of the things of God in 1876. Up to that time he had been like most young men moving in the higher circles of society, a lover of pleasure. In that year he visited England, and being invited to spend a few days at the residence of a friend, he complied. After dinner on the first day of his visit, on retiring to his room his eyes were directed to a Scripture text worked by one of the ladies of the house, and placed over a mirror. The text was "Fear not, I have redeemed thee; thou art Mine." The Holy Spirit carried home the silent message, and the young man was led to think, "Fear—What have I to fear? Whom have I to fear?" These were the changes which kept ringing through the chambers of his heart. Get rid of that text he could not. It was a nail fastened in a sure place by the Master of Assemblies. Jesus Christ was accepted, and the young convert stepped from the thought of "fear" to that of "love."

On his return to Canada, he found the country aroused upon the great question of Intemperance, and into this great movement he threw his whole energies. He at once became a total abstainer, and from that day Canada has not known a more courageous advocate of the principles of Total Abstinence. Mr. Howland is a man of action. He must work, and when as an unconverted man he was ever to be found meeting his share of the demands made on him by fashionable society, so now as a child of God he promptly entered into Christian activity. His first Christian effort was in connection with Hospital work, which came in his way as a member of the Trust Board of the Hospital, of which he subsequently became chairman. His duties in that office were not in his opinion confined to mere administration, but included earnest effort for the spiritual welfare of the patients. In his church work he was equally energetic, and his Bible-class soon became one of the largest in the city. Its numbers, indeed, increased so rapidly that it was deemed advisable to organize it on an independent, undenominational basis and make it an agency for mission work. A Hall was secured and fitted up, and the class has since become a prominent feature in the Christian work of the city. From it really sprang the "Toronto Mission Union," an organization which has accomplished untold good among the poor of Toronto.

While working in those and many similar efforts for the salvation of souls and the elevation of his fellows, there came in 1886 a call from his fellow-citizens to offer himself for election to the office of chief magistrate of the chief city of the Dominion. Many hours were spent in prayer before he gave his consent. By a vote previously unparalleled in the history of the city, he was elected; and when, at the end of his first term of office, he was requested to offer himself for another term, his opponent being backed by all the money which the liquor interests could supply, the result was Mr. Howland's re-election by a majority far exceeding that of the previous year. To the great regret of the citizens, he declined a re-election in 1888, owing to the claims pressing upon him as a son, for his father, through ill-health, felt unable to care for the interests of the large and growing business carried on by the firm.

A YOUNG LAWYER'S DECISION.

(See Illustration on page 333.)

"WHERE can Frank be?" said the elder of two ladies—mother and daughter—as they looked at the clock on the mantel-piece of a luxuriously furnished room where the morning m[eal] was spread. "He has not been in all night. [I] never knew him stay out before."

Mrs. Belton was not kept long in suspen[se], for as she spoke a ring at the bell was hea[rd], and in a few minutes a stalwart young man [of] five and twenty years entered the room, a[nd] affectionately saluted his widowed mother a[nd] his sister.

"I am very glad you have come, Frank; I w[as] worrying about you dreadfully," said t[he] mother. "Where have you been all night?"

There was an unwonted pallor on the you[ng] man's face and a gravity in his manner that w[as] not habitual with him, which both ladies n[o]ticed. He leaned heavily on the table as [he] answered in solemn tones: "Mother, Ernest [is] dead. I have just come from his bedside."

"Poor fellow," said Alice; "how very sa[d]. Such a promising young man, and so wealt[hy] too. It must be a terrible blow to his fath[er]. All his hopes were centred in his heir."

"Yes," said Frank Belton, "and they a[re] shattered now. The poor man is almost besi[de] himself with grief, and I think the mother [is] worse still. She is a good Christian woma[n], but it will take some time to reconcile her [to] this loss."

"I do not doubt that," said Mrs. Belto[n], looking fondly at the speaker, the thought ev[i]dently crossing her mind of what her own fe[el]ings would be if she were to lose *her* son. "[I] can sympathize with her sincerely, though [I] knew little of him. It is a melancholy end [to] so much anticipation; but I should not be su[r]prised if his death improved your prospect[s], Frank. I know it appears selfish to say so, b[ut] it is not really selfish, for I wish with all m[y] heart the young man had lived. It is of no u[se] wishing in such matters, and it does seem like[ly] that his father's firm will offer you a partnersh[ip] instead of a salary now."

"Ah, mother," Frank answered, "you a[re] always thinking of me, but I am afraid you w[ill] be disappointed. Mr. Meritt will offer me t[he] partnership, I believe; but I shall not accept [it]. I shall never be a lawyer now."

"Not accept it! Never be a lawyer!" repea[t]ed Mrs. Belton, rising in astonishment a[nd] clasping her hands to keep down her excit[e]ment. "What can you mean, Frank?"

"Simply, mother, that grand as the profe[s]sion is, I cannot follow it. I must preach t[he] Gospel. It is my duty, and I dare not trifle wi[th] it. I never saw it clearly until now."

Mrs. Belton stood aghast. She was speec[h]less for a moment, and stood looking reproac[h]fully at her son. At last she said: "Fran[k]

you lost your senses? Do[
mean that you will give u[
ntarily a prospect that does
come to one man in a thous-
? With your talents and
a position at your age there
o office beyond your reach.
might sit in the Senate yet,
ven become President, be-
you die. Do you know what
are giving up to be a clergy-
, with a small salary, and
precarious?"

Yes, mother," he said, "I
counted the cost; I had a
talk with Ernest last night.
know we have been very
mate friends, almost like
thers, and have often talked
ther of our brilliant future,
ugh not so much lately, since
knew what religion really
nt. But last night Ernest
ted to see me principally on
matter. He wanted to tell
that, standing, as he did, on
brink of the grave, the bril-
t career we had sketched
ther had lost all its roseate
. He said he could see noth-
satisfactory in it at all, and
ld not follow it if he were
ecover. He begged me with
dying breath to give my life
lly to God's service, and,
ther, with God's help I will
it."

Frank, you astonish me."
. Belton said: "I thought
had too much manliness to
on the impulse of a moment.
is feeling will pass away, and
n you will regret this insane
."

No, mother, never, God help-
me. It is not the impulse of
moment; I have often medi-
ed this course. Ernest's ap-
l only confirms me."

His sister Alice had sat looking at Frank
iously while this dialogue was going on; she
rose, and throwing her arms around his
k kissed him, and told him she would ever
y that God would give him strength to keep
resolution. "You are right, Frank," she said;
is a far nobler thing you do than anything
you could have done. May God bless you."
The worldly mother, thus deserted by the
y ally who could have inflenced her son, sat
wn in despair, weeping tears of disappoint-
nt. But the time came when she too rejoiced
Frank's decision, and was content when she
r him a useful and successful minister of the
spel, even though she knew his name would
er become famous, nor his wealth and station
society attain the eminence she had hoped for.

The Young Lawyer Declares His Resolution. (*See page 332.*)

THE EPOCHS OF A LIFE.

A NEW SERIAL STORY.

By Rev. L. S. Keyser.

A Mind Disquieted.

IT is only when middle age is reached, and perhaps not quite fully until near the close of , that the epochs of a career can be identified their momentous nature appreciated. Then easy to lay the finger on the day, even the ur, when, standing at the parting of the ways, choice was made which determined all the ure. Or it may be that no choice was made, some influence entered into the stream of turning it imperceptibly into a channel herto unknown, rendering its onward course ooth and tranquil, or troubled and tumultu-. Most frequently that influence comes by ociation with some other life in friendship or love. It may come gradually, or it may come denly without warning or premonition, but comes, and life is not the thing after its ad- nt that it was before. Such an epoch arrived the lives of two young men, one lovely morning in May, as they strolled through a country clad in all the glories of luxuriant verdure.

"I want to tell you, Hadley," said one of them, "about a lecture I heard a few weeks ago. It was a revelation to me. It threw a new light on subjects that I have been familiar with from infancy, but never looked at from the lecturer's standpoint. I daresay it will be new to you too."

"There is nothing new under the sun, George," returned the other." We have Biblical authority for that fact. Still, I am sufficiently conscious of my own ignorance to be aware that there are many old things, and especially old ideas, that I should think new. Anyway, whether your light is new or old it will be welcome if it is useful, so I shall be glad to get your account of it."

"I believe I could almost reproduce the lecture verbatim if I had time," said the one addressed as George," for it has made an indelible impression on my mind. It was so striking, so piquant, so unique, and the lecturer's bold, forcible style was so convincing, that every sentence seems to be burned into my brain. But, of course, I shall not attempt to rehearse the whole. A few of the salient points will be enough."

"But had you not better tell me first what was the theme of the address?"

"The subject was—'Logic *versus* Christianity.'"

"Ah! it was an infidel lecture, was it?" said Hadley, with a gesture of impatience. "I do not think that I care to hear about harangues of that character. The less attention we pay to discussions on anti-religious themes the better, I'm inclined to think."

"Why, Hadley, you are not so narrow as that, are you?" returned George, almost scornfully. "That is precisely what the lecturer told us—that the devotees of Christianity are prejudiced, mentally-contracted and bigoted, and do not want information; that they are opposed to free discussion, because they fear that their faith in their cherished dogmas might be disturbed. Surely you and I, Hadley, who are seeking to extend the horizon of our knowledge, ought to welcome light from every source. Truth can be attained only by free, untrammeled investigation and by keeping the mind in a receptive attitude. Come, friend Hadley, we must not be so dense and narrow-sphered as the people around us. I thought that you, at least, had made sufficient progress on the highway of knowledge to get beyond believing blindly in what may prove to be effete traditions."

The young man called Hadley looked up at his companion with an eye that flashed momentarily with anger and wounded vanity; for he had just reached that degree of mental culture, when a precocious youth cannot brook a reflection on his intellectual acquirements, and therefore his friend's suggestion that he shrank from investigation through fear or prejudice piqued his pride of intellect and was decidedly humbling to his self-esteem, especially as he was, though not a professing Christian, a believer in the Divine origin of the Scriptures. By dint of considerable effort he succeeded in getting his ruffled feelings partially under control before he spoke.

"I wish you to understand, George," he said, presently, "that I am not biassed on the subject of religion, but am open to conviction. Let us sit down here on the hill-top, and with that panorama before us"—pointing toward the broad valley below them, bounded by sloping hills on each side—"we shall be in a good position to examine an argument to prove that all this glorious beauty came into existence without a God. I will persunate the chairman and you the infidel acrobat and gymnast. I now call on Mr. George Tomlinson Dane to favor us with an epitome of a grandiloquent disquisition."

"Dick Swiveller *redidivus*," laughed George.

The young men were warm friends, having many traits of character in common. Hadley C. Madelling had from early youth manifested a more than ordinary aptitude for learning, and was ambitious to secure an education. At the time of which we speak, he was attending a preparatory school, called "The Academy," in the village of Banesville, near his home, and in another year he would be fitted for college. Which of the institutions of learning in his own State or those adjacent he would make his *Alma Mater* he had not as yet fully determined.

The evolution of his spiritual life up to this time demands a brief notice. He had been reared by pious parents in the tenets of the Christian religion, and until the period of our meeting him he had never entertained any doubts as to the divine authority of the Bible. It is true, he had never experienced a revolution of character through the converting power of Christianity, nor had he made a public profession of religion; yet he had accepted intellectually the faith of his father and mother as a matter of course. Nothing in his history had occurred to suggest doubt. Indeed, so busy had he been in the pursuit of his technical studies that he had bestowed very little attention upon the subject of religion, scarcely enough to lead him into scepticism.

Like others reared in Christian households, he had been frequently importuned by his parents to yield himself to Christ, but owing to that perversity of the human heart, so familiar to all careful students of man's natural state, he had persistently disregarded these earnest admonitions, although more than once he had to fight against the convictions of conscience. And having steeled himself against the counsellings of his friends and his better nature, he had just arrived at that period of life and that stage of mental attainment when he might easily be swayed one way or the other, according to the hands into which he fell.

It was at this critical time of his moral and spiritual development that his intimate friend, George Dane, heard the cavilling lecturer against the Christian religion who had stopped in his peregrinations at a neighboring town, and Dane had listened to him with the rapt enthusiasum peculiar to young persons.

Dane, like Hadley, was preparing for college. The homes of the young men were about three miles apart, so that they were not regarded as belonging to precisely the same neigborhood; yet on account of their community of ambition and employment, a warm friendship had sprung up between them, which frequently brought them into each other's society. George was also a student of remarkable natural gifts. In the country school he had outstripped all competitors, and had gone far beyond his teachers, and at the early age of sixteen he had himself undertaken a school, carrying it through with gratifying success. The country could not boast of a more ready debater or a more eloquent public speaker than George Dane, among all its young knights of the school-room. He would traverse the country for miles to attend a lyceum, if there was any prospect of an exciting intellectual tournament.

Religiously, the little experience he had had was unfortunate. In a time of religious awakening while he was quite young, he had, without any very defined ideas of his undertaking, united with the church, in company with a number of his associates; but not finding his experience satisfactory, and lacking perhaps in moral earnestness, he had finally abandoned the church; for which act of disloyalty he had been "disciplined" by the official board and lectured with a little want of tact by the minister. These circumstances had stirred not a little hostility in him toward churches and religion itself. Howbeit, no well-defined scepticism had taken possession of his mind until he heard the aforesaid lecture. That was one of the epochal events in *his* religious history.

It must not be supposed that these neoplastic sceptics were capable as yet of profound philosophic thought or research. Metaphysics was still a *terra incognito* to them, nor would they have been able to comprehend a scholarly work on speculative theology, even if they had had access to one. They were just at the age when young students are most likely to be impressed and captivated by the scepticism of the lower type intellectually, with its dashing style, its gorgeous diction, its scurrilous mode of assault and its proneness to ridicule all sacred institutions. More than one popular representative of this grade of infidelity will be thought of in this connection. Unfortunately many talented young persons during the formative period of their lives fall into the hands of these superficial carpers at the Christian religion, and thenceforward the arid life of infidelity or agnosticism begins with them.

A popular writer of the day speaks as follows of the period of life now under consideration: "I call it the period of *transition*. Every young person, especially if engaged in reading and study, comes to a time when the powers of reason are growing fast, and habits of independent thought begin to start inquiry. The growing mind asks a reason for things." If at "this transition state between the intuitive and rational periods" of the young investigator's development, he is *not* firmly grounded in the faith, "he begins to say of one thing after another which he may have been taught, 'That is not true; I can no longer believe it.' He begins to untie from one stake, but has no other to tie to, and so he drifts away from all fastenings into a general doubt, if not denial, of all truth. His faith suffers wreck." It may be added, that this is especially true if the infidel tracts that are scattered broadcast over the country happen to fall into the hands of the neophyte in unbelief.

It was a radiant morning when the colloquy just described took place. From their elevated point of observation the young men looked below them into a deep hollow, filled with willows and dense underbrush, which formed the wedge-like beginning of the valley that widened out into broad upland fields and green meadows farther away, while to the right and left the ridge-like hills towered up to a considerable altitude. The scene, stretched out in perspective before them, was an enchanting one. Melodious sounds also added to the gay joyfulness of the day. All about them could be heard the lyrical trills of the birds. Upon the topmost twig of a willow-tree the robin heaved his red bosom in tuneful vocalization. In the bushes below, the brown-thrush and the cat-bird were vying with each other in their efforts at melodious mockery. A cardinal grossbeak interlarded the more continuous music with an occasional outburst of clear, resonant notes, while at frequent intervals a little goldfinch shot through the air in an irregular course, like a flake of gold from the sun, now falling, now rising in graceful arcs, with a burst of fine, quickly repeated notes at every downward movement.

"It was a joy to watch the gleam
Of tender sky and tinted leaf;
The wind scarce stirred the placid stream—
It was a day for sweet belief."

But the minds of the young men were not in harmony with the sweet aspects of nature. It was strange that on a morning like this they should start out on the weary, arid, unsatisfactory pilgrimage of doubt, with its shadowless stretch of barren wastes. Nature herself might have admonished them, had they listened to her voice, that the way of trust and faith in God was the way of mental tranquillity. It must be remembered, however, that the young intellectual adventurers were not aware of the sterility into which they were about to plunge. For one of them, at least, no mirage of the desert, no promised lands, ever appeared more green and refreshing to the weary traveller than the land of "independent research" appears to him.

"As I said," began George Dane, "I shall rehearse only the most telling points of the lecturer. Here is the one that occurs first to my mind. The Bible, said the speaker, tells us that *all* things are possible with God. That is not a true statement. It is not in accordance with the constitution of things. God cannot do all things. There are natural impossibilities which can never be made possible. For instance it is impossible to place two hills near to gether without having a valley between, or to *turn a grindstone two ways at once*."

"Shades of Chesterfield!" exclaimed Hadley, nonplussed for a moment, "who would have thought of such absurdities? But what point did he make against the Bible by that poor witticism?"

"Do you not see? He meant to show that the Bible is inaccurate and unscientific in its statements. A clear and exact writer would have said, 'All things that are possible in the nature of things, are possible with God, if there is a God.' The evident conclusion is this: If the Bible speaks so loosely, so unphilosophically, of one matter touching ultimate principles, can we repose confidence in *any* of its *ipse dixits*, and above all, can we believe it to be an inspired and infallible book? Mistaken in one point, may it not be mistaken in many others? I tell you, Hadley, as the speaker put these questions, in clarion tones and with flashing eyes, his argument seemed conclusive."

"I never thought—" began Hadley. But he was soon lost in reflection. His eye was b upon the valley before him, but so preoccup was his mind, that he only gazed into vaca A terrible tremor of uneasiness thrilled thro his being; it seemed as if something had gi way, as if the foundations of a building l been partially undermined and the struct were trembling, tottering, poised on the un ble air.

"Ah! there are many things of which and I have never thought," said George, wh he noted his friend's look of perplexity. "W you hear more?"

"Yes; let us have the facts," assented H ley, becoming more willing to listen now th at the beginning of their dialogue.

"At one point in his lecture," resumed Geor "the speaker dilated on the miracles of Bible. 'A wonderful book for prodigies!' said. Now, these supernatural occurrences contrary to all experience. We never witn now-a-days anything like the dividing of Red Sea; ships and boats must be used in m ern times for transporting armies across la bodies of water. Neither are warriors at pres able to blow down the fortifications of th enemies with horns and trumpets, as it is s was done with the walls of Jericho. We never permitted to witness the spectacle of descending miraculously from heaven in answ to a modern Elijah's prayer. Then the lectu became daring. 'If you believe in the God of t Bible,' he said, 'come out here on the rostru and pray that fire may be sent down into t hall to devour the enemies of Jehovah! Eve thing occurs according to the sway of inex able law. The rain descends, the winds blo the waves dash, men are born, they survive a perish—all things take place in accordance w the unchanging laws of nature, without t intervention of a supernatural agency. If m acles were necessary in Scriptural times bolster up a faltering faith, they are necess now, for there is as much doubt now as ever the world's history.'

And then the lecturer lifted his hands in m supplication to heaven and said, 'Lord, give one miracle to-night, just one little miracle, a it will accomplish more good than all the prea ers and Bibles in Christendom!' He waited moment, as if to see if the daring prayer wou be answered. I confess that his words and the trical attitude made my blood curdle."

A look of pain crossed Hadley's face as listened to the recital "That was horrib sacrilegious," he said, with a shudder.

(To be Continued.)

JESUS CRUCIFIED.

By Mrs. M. Baxter.

S. S. Lesson for June 3, Matt. 27: 33-53. Gold Text Phil. 2: 8.

The Discussion of Christ's Enemies—The Awf Remorse of Judas—What He had to See to Jesus Lineally King of the Jews—Arraigned b fore Pilate—His Majestic Silence—The High Indictment as Man's Substitute—Pilate's R luctance to Sentence a Law-Abiding Man—H Futile Expedient—A Pertinent Momento Question—The Great Scapegoat—The Crowd Calvary—Mocking the Dying Saviour—The A palling Darkness—Without God in Death—T Last Cry.

THE morning broke upon Jerusalem, b neither Jesus nor His enemies had sle Strange that His disciples could sleep in t Garden while His enemies were so awak strange that to this day, while the enemies God's truth are so on the alert, the disciples Christ are so asleep! Which of us is awake we should be awake to the danger of perishi millions, at home and abroad? Who is awa to the deadening encroachments of Rome our schools and churches? Who is alive to o national responsibility regarding India and t drink traffic? China and the opium? Th morning opened upon a council of men who souls were in danger of eternal death, and t subject they discussed was how to put Jes Christ, the Son of God, who alone could sa em. to death! In order to do this, they must liver Him to Pontius Pilate, the Roman vernor. It was just at this time that Judas scovered his fatal, fearful mistake, and in his ter remorse, he who might have gone to Jesus ce, went to the chief priests, threw down the irty pieces of silver, the price of Jesus, the ual price of a slave, "a goodly price that I was ised of them" (Zec. 11 : 13), and cried, "I have nned, in that I have betrayed the innocent ood," but the unhappy man made his confession man, not to God, and he was met with the solent, heartless rejoinder, "What is that to us?

"See Thou to That."

Is there one reading these pages who runs e awful risk of passing day after day with all e burden, guilt and stain of his life's sins, uncansed and unforgiven, on his own soul? Jesus ready now to see to that, and to take the hole responsibility upon Himself. He offers to swer for you. But if, like Judas, you leave it l it is too late, then the very enemy of your ul, who has led you into sin, will say to you, he taught the chief priests to say unto Judas, What is that to us? See thou to that." Could iests, religious leaders, be so indifferent to a ul broken with remorse? Yes; and God says them, "The diseased have ye not strengthed, neither have ye healed that which was k, neither have ye bound up that which was oken, neither have ye brought again that hich was driven away, neither have ye sought at which was lost." (Ezek. 34 : 4.)

Jesus stood before the Governor, He who as "from the beginning," who was "with God," d "was God," from all eternity, stood bere the Roman ruler of the country! He who knew no sin," "neither was guile found in His outh," stood there accused before a sinner! late asked Him, "Art Thou the King of the ws?" And Jesus said unto Him, "Thou sayt." The Jews had but to search the pediees to find that He was lineally descended n David, and was therefore by birth the ing of the Jews. But they wanted no such ing, they sought the greatness of this world: king who received not honor from man ould not suit them. The chief priests and ders were the chief accusers of Jesus! They ho of all men should have received, and made im known were loud in their accusations gainst Him! Why was this? Their religion d degenerated into a mere form, and the wer and works of Jesus was such a reflection n their powerlessness that it found them out be mere hypocrites, if He were really proved be the Son of God, and thus their religious putation hung on the hope that they might ove Jesus to be an impostor. They accused im of many things, but as He was speechless fore the chief priests, so was He also before late and Herod too. (Luke 23 : 8, 9.) Jesus as not there to carry out His own cause, but e cause of lost undone sinners. Pilate maryled at His silence, for he could not tell all that as taking place in that hour, how that Man ho stood dumb before him, was arraigned at e same moment before the bar of God as

The Man

ho of His own free will and by His own divine thority, included in Himself all men of all tions, and all generations. And there, as He ood silent, the accumulated history of the sin f man came up, and dark, mighty waves of ccusation rolled over Him, until in spirit He ried, "All thy waves and thy billows are gone ver me (Ps. 42 : 7). Thou hast made the iniuities of us all to meet on Him" (Isa. 53 : 6 argin). He adopted, He the great sin offerg, all the sins of the world, and His pure and nsitive spirit, which could not respond to a ingle breath of sin, was dumb before man and umb before God. God keep us from making ght of sin which cost Jesus so much! "*Fools* ake a mock at sin" (Pro. 14 : 9).

Pilate was not envious of Jesus; He had lways been subordinate to the laws of the ountry, and had in no way assumed other than piritual authority, and authority over disease and death; He neither sought money, land nor honor; and Pilate was deeply impressed by what He saw and heard of Jesus. He was

Unwilling to Pronounce Sentence

against Him. He thought of an expedient. It was the custom at the feast to release one prisoner who should be the choice of the people. There was in custody at this time, a notorious man who had been the dread of many, a murderer and disturber of the peace. Pilate gave a choice to the people whether he should release Barabbas or Jesus, the murderer or the Prince of Life. There were many living in Jerusalem who had personally benefited by the ministry of Jesus; only three days ago the blind and the lame had been healed in the temple (Matt. 21 : 14). Surely the people would choose the great Healer! But the chief priests were exerting all their influence and using their strongest arguments to get the people on their side, and they choose Barabbas. Pilate was sorely perplexed; his wife had sent warning him not to condemn Jesus, but he plainly saw that if he did the right thing and acquitted Jesus, he should lose his popularity and probably his office. "What shall I do then with Jesus which is called Christ?" A strange question for a judge to ask of the people; but it is a question which every man must answer. Reader, have you answered it! Pilate knew that Jesus was innocent, but he thought he would shift the responsibility so he took water, and washed his hands before the multitude, saying, I am innocent of the blood of this just Person; see ye to it." Was he innocent? When we say so often, "He suffered under Pontius Pilate," do we count him innocent? The people replied in their rash fanaticism, "His blood be on us and on our children." "By thy words thou shalt be justified, and by thy words thou shalt be condemned." (Matt. 12: 37.) In the scattered, persecuted, despised race of Jews, we see how this fearful challenge has been accepted of God.

Then Barrabas was released, and Jesus was delivered to be crucified. Man had his choice, but he did not do as he chose with Jesus. God had measured the cup He was to drink.

All Had Been Foretold.

Pilate, his conscience all uneasy, scourged Jesus, but he could have had no power at all against Him, except it had been given him from above (John 14 : 11.) "I *gave* My back to the smiters, and My cheeks to them that plucked off the hair; I hid not My face from shame and spitting" (Isa. 50 : 6.) Of His own free will, our most loving Lord yielded Himself to be mocked, and scourged, and spit upon, that all the world might know how hateful sin is in the eyes of a holy God. But all this contumely from man was little in comparison with the awful shadow which He was entering when the Father's wrath came upon Him as the one eternal Scapegoat. Aaron, on the great day of atonement, laid both his hands upon the head of the live goat, and confessed "over him all the iniquities of the children of Israel, and all their transgressions in all their sins, putting them upon the head of the goat," and then sent him "away by the hand of a fit man into the wilderness." And the goat bore upon him all their iniquities, unto a land not inhabited (Lev. 16 : 21, 22.) And just so, sin after sin of man was transferred to Jesus, who His own self bore our sins in His own body on the tree, that we, being dead to sins, should live unto righteousness. (1 Pet. 2 : 24.) The Messianic Psalms, especially Ps. 22 : 35-69, express much of the agony of Jesus, when sin, sickness, sorrow, lay there upon Him for our sakes.

Scarcely was the cross raised with its wondrous burden, than the unconscious and mercenary soldiers claimed their perquisites in the clothing of Jesus, parting His garments and casting lots upon His vesture, as had been foretold. (Ps. 22 : 18.) Jesus was the centre of all eyes: "sitting down, they watched Him there." Yet how little of what really was taking place did any of them see! Two thieves were crucified with Him, but again it was to fulfil the Scripture, "And He was numbered with the transgressors." (Isa. 55 : 12.) Satan was abroad among the crowd, and

The Roughs and Idlers,

who form the largest part of every crowd, eagerly took their cue from the chief priests, and saw that it was "the thing" to revile Jesus. Oh, how unlike His own spirit, His wonderful compassion! He lifts up the fallen and seeks the lost. The cry that ran through the crowd was, "Thou that destroyeth the temple and buildest it in three days, save Thyself! If Thou be the Son of God, come down from the cross!" The chief priests, forgetting their own dignity in their mad and bitter hatred of Jesus, added, "He saved others (they would not deny that), Himself He cannot save. If He be the King of Israel, let Him now come down from the cross, and we will believe Him." "Himself He cannot save!" No, the whole spirit and mission of Jesus ran counter to self-saving; He *gave* Himself, He saved others. Had He saved Himself at that hour, and accepted the impious challenge of these so-called spiritual guides, a world's salvation would have been lost! He could have caused the earth to open and swallow them up, like Korah, Dathan and Abiram, but "the Son of Man was not come to destroy men's lives, but to save them (Luke 9, 56), and instead, He looked up to His Father before His communion with Him was shut out by the intense blackness of man's sin, and prayed, "Father, forgive them, for they know not what they do." Torn with intense agony, He yet would remember others, and commended His mother and his beloved disciples to each other's care. After three long hours—how long to Him we know not, for a thousand years to Him may be as one day (II Peter 3 : 8)—the eyes which looked on in vulgar curiosity were to be disappointed. No earthly eye might see Jesus die. "From the sixth hour there was darkness over all the earth until the ninth hour." Darkness stills the ignorant, and doubtless the scoffing jests grew fewer and fewer, and one and another of the gazers went away. But the climax came at last. "About the ninth hour Jesus cried with a loud voice, My God, My God, why hast Thou forsaken Me?" He must taste as man even that awful bitterness, that blackness of hell itself,

To be Without God!

One more cry, and the soul of the Redeemer left His lacerated body and broken heart until, three days later, he claimed them from the grave! His murderers were forced to hear the last cry, "Father, into Thy hands I commend My spirit," and around the cross all was still. But away on Mount Moriah the same hand which received His spirit rent the veil of the temple from the top to the bottom, shook the earth, and it quaked, rent the rocks, and broke open the sepulchres of many of the saints. Two hearts were rent, if not more; one thief passed into Paradise quickly after his Lord, and the centurion, a heathen Roman, put the Jews and the disciples to shame by saying, "Truly, this was the Son of God!" Thus Jesus died, and thus He died for me.

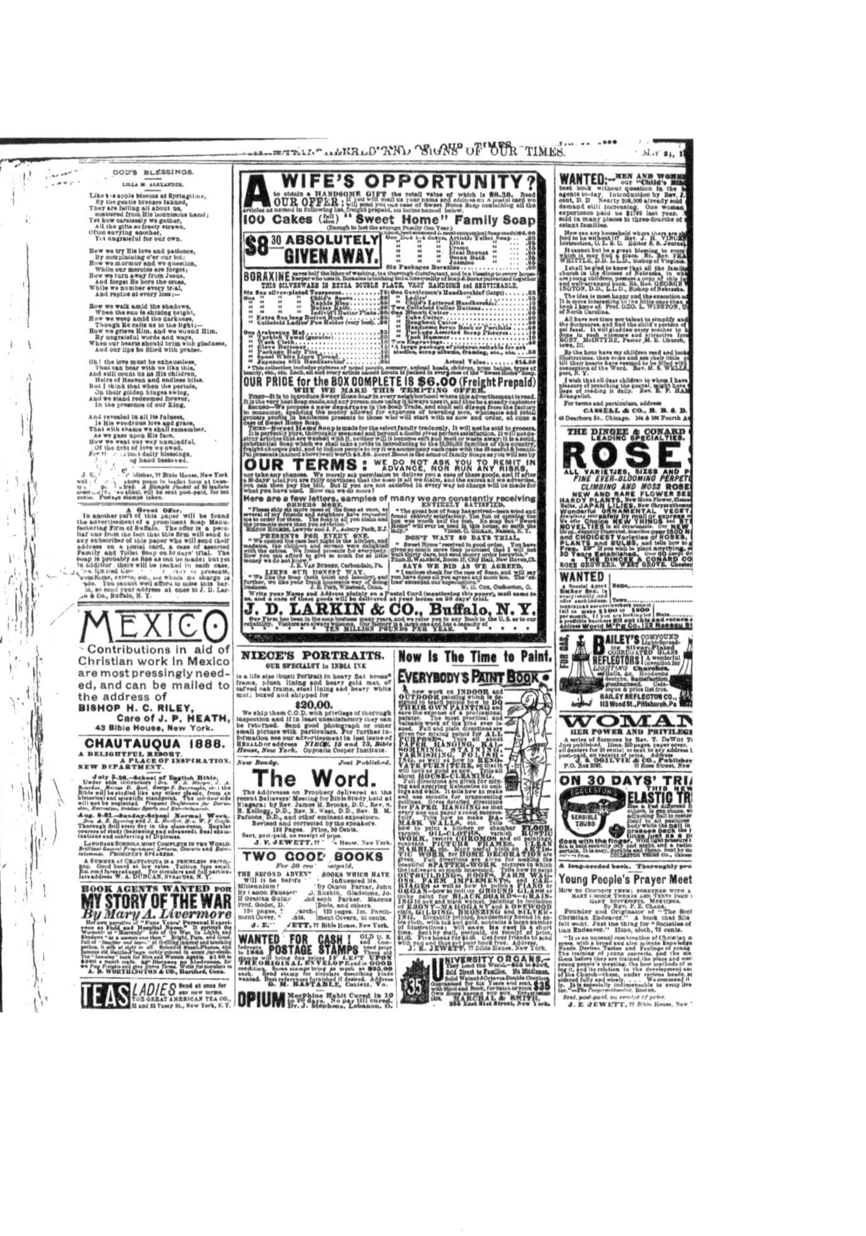

GOD'S BLESSINGS.

LILLA M. ALEXANDER.

Like the apple blooms at Springtime,
By the gentle breezes fanned,
They are falling all about us,
scattered from His bounteous hand;
Yet how carelessly we gather,
All the gifts so freely strewn,
Often envying another,
Yet ungrateful for our own.

How we try His love and patience,
By complaining o'er our lot;
How we murmur and we question,
While our mercies are forgot;
How we turn away from Jesus,
And forget He bore the cross,
While we number every trial,
And repine at every loss;—

How we walk amid the shadows,
When the sun is shining bright,
How we weep amid the darkness,
Though He calls us to the light;—
How we grieve Him, and we wound Him,
By ungrateful words and ways,
When our hearts should brim with gladness,
And our lips be filled with praise.

Oh! the love must be exhaustless,
That can bear with us like this,
And still count us as His children,
Heirs of Heaven and endless bliss.
But I think that when the portals,
On their golden hinges swing,
And we stand redeemed forever,
In the presence of our King,

And revealed in all its fulness,
Is His wondrous love and grace,
That with shame we shall remember,
As we gaze upon His face,
How we went our way unmindful,
Of the debt of love we owed,
For th[illegible] daily blessings,
[illegible]ng hand bestowed.

J. E. [illegible] Publisher, 77 Bible House, New York will [illegible] above poem in leaflet form at twenty [illegible] red. *A Sample Packet of 50 leaflets assorted [illegible] will be sent post-paid, for ten cents.* Postage stamps taken.

A Great Offer.

In another part of this paper will be found the advertisement of a prominent Soap Manufacturing Firm of Buffalo. The offer is a peculiar one from the fact that this firm will send to any subscriber of this paper who will send their address on a postal card, a case of assorted Family and Toilet Soap on 30 days' trial. The soap is probably as fine as can be made; but yet in addition there will be packed in each case, [illegible] limited time [illegible] presents, premiums, extras, etc., for which no charge is made. You cannot well afford to miss this bargain, so send your address at once to J. D. Larkin & Co., Buffalo, N. Y.

A long-needed book. Thoroughly pra[ctical].

Young People's Prayer Meet[ings]

HOW TO CONDUCT THEM; TOGETHER WITH A [list of] MANY CHOICE THEMES AND TEXTS USED [in] MANY SUCCESSFUL MEETINGS.

By REV. F. E. CLARK.

Founder and Originator of "The Soc[iety of] Christian Endeavor." A book that fills [a] felt want. Just the thing for "Societies of [Chris]tian Endeavor." 12mo, cloth, 75 cents.

"It is an unusual combination of Christian c[ommon] sense, with a broad and also minute knowledge [of the] Needs, Desires, Tastes and Feelings of young [people]. The training of young converts, and the [illegible] them before they are trained, the place and [illegible] young people's meeting, the best methods of [conduct]ing it, and its relation to the development and [life] of the Church—these, under various heads, a[re con]sidered fully and wisely. . . . We commend it [heart]ily. It is especially indispensable to every live [pas]tor."—*The Congregationalist*, Boston.

Sent, post-paid, on receipt of price.

J. E. JEWETT, 77 Bible House, New [York].

Entered according to Act of Congress in the year 1887, in the office of the Librarian of Congress at Washington.

Vol. XI., No. 22. Office, 63 Bible House, N. Y. THURSDAY, MAY 31, 1888. Annual Subscription, $1.50.

CONTENTS OF THIS NUMBER.

PORTRAITS AND LIVES OF GENERALS O. O. HOWARD AND "STONEWALL" JACKSON.
DISABLED HUNTERS. Dr. Talmage's Sermon last Sunday Morning.
THE BURDENSOME STONE. By Rev. A. C. Tris.
A Girl Waif Rescued—A Nobleman's Testimony—A Chinese Christian Beheaded—A Superstitious Exhumation—Bright's Disease Cured, etc.
INVITATIONS TO THE WEDDING. A Sermon by C. H. Spurgeon.
PICTURE OF MERCHANT STREET, MANDALAY.
AN INJURED WIFE'S RESOLVE.
THE EPOCHS OF A LIFE. A New Serial Story by Rev. L. S. Keyser.
JESUS RISEN. By Mrs. M. Barter.

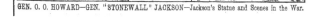

GEN. O. O. HOWARD—GEN. "STONEWALL" JACKSON—Jackson's Statue and Scenes in the War.

GEN. OLIVER OTIS HOWARD.

The Havelock of America.

THE observance this week throughout the Northern States, of Decoration Day, turns all our thoughts back to the bitter struggle which a quarter of a century ago desolated homes and filled the land with mourning. No patriotic citizen desires to revive the memories of that time in an angry spirit, or to inflame passions which the years of peace have happily tranquillized; but we cannot, and it would not be honorable to human nature if we could, forget the dead heroes who took part in that desperate struggle. We decorate their graves and cherish their memories, the tributes of affection and personal sorrow mingling with the floral offerings which public reverence places on their last resting-place. In harmony with the emotions which are aroused through the community by the day, THE CHRISTIAN HERALD this week bears upon its first page the portraits of two Christian men who were leaders in the long strife, each of whom, while taking opposite sides, honestly and sincerely, we cannot but believe, acted conscientiously in thus choosing the flag under which they fought—General Oliver Otis Howard,

"The Havelock of America,"

and General Stonewall Jackson, the Christian hero of the South, are to Christians of all names and denominations the two representative men who, without invidious distinctions, will be recognized as fitting types of what was best and noblest in the two armies.

Oliver Otis Howard, who is now the general commanding on the Pacific slope, and whose continuance in that position recently evoked strong expressions of gratification from men of all parties in that section, was born at Leeds, Maine, in 1830, and is now therefore fifty-eight years of age. He was descended from an English family which settled at Bridgewater, Mass., where for several generations the name held an honored place in the esteem of the citizens. His great grand-father, Seth Howard, had so far abjured his English prejudices that he fought in the Revolutionary War and attained the rank of Captain. His youngest son, who during that heroic conflict remained at home caring for his mother, and carrying on the work of the farm, was the grandfather of Gen. O. O. Howard, the subject of this sketch. Rowland B. Howard, the father of the General, married Eliza, daughter of Oliver Otis of Scituate, Mass., from whom our hero derives his first names.

Early in Life

the future general gave evidence of Christian character. It is recorded of him that during his father's last illness, the boy, then only nine years old, one day, looked earnestly up in his father's face and put to him the solemn question. "*Father, do you ever pray?*" "Sometimes, my son," said the sick man; "would you like to have me pray now?" "Yes," said the boy, and there and then, father and son knelt together at the throne of grace. Not many weeks afterwards the father died, and the boy was left to the care of his noble Christian mother. He acquired the rudiments of education at a school in the neighborhood, after which he was sent to the Academy at Hallowell, residing in the house of his uncle, the Hon. John Otis, member of Congress. Subsebuently, he studied at Monmouth and Yarmouth Academies, until he was ready to enter Bowdoin College, from which he graduated in 1850. Thence he went to West Point, graduating there in 1854.

Strong Temperance Principles

characterized him in those days. In his first term he declined to join a companion on some festive occasion in a bottle of wine, and being reminded that great men had always had a liking for intoxicants, replied that if it were necessary to drink to be a great man, he would rather never be great. He has steadfastly adhered to that resolution through his distinguished career, and has successfully demonstrated the possibility of a temperance man becoming great. Throughout his career at West Point he was known, not only as a total abstainer in a society where it was the fashion to drink, but as a young man abhoring profanity, and as a Bible-reader and a praying man.

His first position after leaving West Point was at Watervliet, N. Y. Shortly after attaining the rank of second lieutenant he secured a twenty days' leave of absence, and running down to Maine in February, 1855, he was married to a lady whom he fell in love with in his boyhood, and who has been to him ever since the best wife and the staunchest friend man ever had. little more than a year afterward—a year spent in pleasant association with congenial friends, at the arsenal at Kennebec, Me., and at Watervliet, the young husband and wife were separated by the call to military service. Mrs. Howard went home to her friends, and her husband went to Florida to serve against the Seminoles, During that conflict the gentleness and humanity which have distinguished his later years were first observed, and were all the more remarkable by being united with daring and valor. At the close of the Seminole war he received the appointment of mathematical instructor at the military academy, and had the happiness of again enjoying the society of his wife.

His Conversion

he has himself frequently described. His brother had a sweet-heart, a simple fragile girl, who had been brought under the influence of the Holy Spirit and had a yearning desire to know more of the great truths unknown to any one. She visited a minister and shortly became an ardent believer and true Christian. Gen. Howard's brother soon felt the influence of his lady friend, and through him the General himself was led to Christ, "and the cause of all," said General Howard in the course of an address a few weeks ago to the prisoners in the State prison at San Quentin, Cal., "was the tender, simple girl. And what is the result? My brother has been ministering to thousands for years, and thank God! with success." He commenced Christian work at West Point, immediately organized a cadets' prayer meeting, regularly visited the soldiers' hospital, and every Wednesday held a meeting for soldiers and their wives and families, at which he gave religious addresses.

The Outbreak of War

interrupted this life of happy usefulness. In May, 1861, he received the appointment of Colonel of the Third Maine Regiment of volunteers, and resigned his commission in the regular army to accept it. At the dinner given at the Astor House, New York, to the officers of the regiment, the health of the Colonel was proposed, and the guests raised their bumpers of wine to drink it. The Colonel duly responded, but his glass was filled with water. "The true beverage of a soldier," he said, "is cold water, and in this I pledge you." Every glass was lowered and his health was drunk in water. How many lives might have been saved if every officer in that army had been similarly minded! The regiment marched on to Washington, and shortly afterwards—in September 1861 Colonel Howard received his star, and became Brigadier General of volunteers. He took part in the first battle of Bull Run, and after that disaster to the Union arms went into camp near Alexandria Va., to drill and instruct his men.

The Empty Sleeve.

In the succeeding campaign General Howard was assigned to the duty of making a reconnoissance from Warrenton Junction to the Rappahannock, and acquitted himself with so much sagacity as to win special praise from Sumner, who was in command of the Second corps. The bloody battle of Williamsburg was fought before Howard could reach the scene of action, though he marched all night through a drenching rain. The sight of the field with its heaps of dead filled him with sorrow, but he exerted himself in aiding and directing the men engaged in the removal of the wounded. (*See Illustration No* 1.) He also visited the hospital and prayed with the dying. It was, however, with the battle of Fair Oaks that General Howard's name was to be most closely identified. The battle had gone against McClellan all through the first day, when toward evening Sumner's corps crossed the bridge, which was trembling under the pressure of the swollen waters, and attacked Johnston's flank. Howard gallantly led the attacking force (*See Illustration No* 2) and fought with dauntless courage. He was wounded in the right arm, but tying a handkerchief about it to stop the bleeding he was soon again in the thick of the fight. His horse was shot under him, but another was secured, and he was waving his wounding arm aloft to cheer on the men when a second shot struck it and shattered it. Then he was compelled to leave the field and go under the care of the surgeons who quickly amputated the injured limb. He went home to be nursed back to health, but even there he sought to serve his country by stirring speeches delivered in the chief centres, pleading for volunteers and arousing patriotic enthusiasm.

At Chancellorsville.

After two months' rest, General Howard insisted that he was well enough to return to duty, and in spite of the urgency of his friends, he rejoined McClellan as the army was returning from the Peninsula. He was assigned to the command of "the California Brigade," but after Antietam he was transferred to the command of Sedgwick's division, and subsequently of the Eleventh Corps. A month later, on May 3, 1863, occurred the incident depicted in the lower left of the illustration on the first page. It was at Chancellorsville and the corps was overwhelmed with the panic which sometimes seizes troops on the field when without shelter, they are exposed to the enemy's fire. Howard, careless of his own danger, rode toward the retreating men earnestly trying to check the stampede. Seizing the colors and holding them under the stump of his maimed arm he rode in front of the troops, that had become a mere mob, with voice and gesture vainly striving to induce them to make a stand. For some time the disgrace of this panic reflected on General Howard, but those who knew all the circumstances praised instead of blaming him, and the public has long since given him the honor he deserved.

Our space does not permit of our tracing, in detail, the heroic actions which marked General Howard's career in the later years of the war. He was conspicuous at Gettysburg, and bore a worthy part in the conflict before Chattanooga. He was placed in command of the Fourth corps shortly afterward, and made the campaign from Chattanooga to Atlanta. As commander of the army of the Tennessee, he led the right wing of Sherman's army from Atlanta to Savannah, and thence northward in the march which terminated in the surrender of Johnston. The administrative capacity and sterling

Christian Principles

for which he was noted, led to his being chosen Commissioner of the Freedmen's Bureau, an appointment which he accepted in deference to the wishes of President Lincoln though conscious of the enormous labor and responsibility it entailed. Since that time, his life has been one of continuous activity. In command against the Indians and in his duties on the Pacific slope, where he is now stationed, he has won the good opinion of the military authorities and the general public. It may be mentioned as a striking proof of the energy and devotion of the General that though engaged so constantly in the duties of his profession he has found time to study the Bible in the original languages, and has neglected no opportunity of conducting religious services and visiting the hospitals and prisons wherever he might be placed.

GENERAL "STONEWALL" JACKSON.

On the Southern side of the terrible conflict the name of General Thomas Jonathan Jackson occupies a place second to none in military ability, as well as in the Christian graces of character, and his tragic death on May 10, 1863, has invested him almost with the glories of martyrdom. He was born at Clarkesburg, Va., on January 21, 1824, and was therefore only thirty-nine years old when he died. He was left fatherless at the early age of three years, and his mother after a hard struggle of three years, at length found it necessary to accept the offer of her husband's family to take charge of her children. Thomas and his brother Warren were received into the home of an uncle. The parting with their mother was a very bitter one, and Thomas especially could never speak of it even after he had attained manhood without tears. He loved her with a passionate devotion rare in so young a boy, and when one year afterward he was recalled to her bedside during her last illness, the earnestness with which she pleaded with him to love the Saviour, and trust only in Him, was never effaced from his memory.

In June, 1842, Jackson, then eighteen years of age, was admitted to West Point, where he devoted himself most earnestly to his studies. Owing partly to his own restless temperament and his impatience of the control which his uncle wisely endeavored to exert over him, he was behind most of his fellow students in acquirements when he entered the institution. He graduated, however, in 1846 with distinction and when asked afterward by an aunt, whom he loved tenderly on account of her resemblance to his dear, dead mother, how he had managed to learn so much in so short a time, said, "*By weeping, study and prayer.*"

The War With Mexico

was raging when Jackson graduated, and he went at once to the front with the brevet rank of Second Lieutenant of artillery. His bravery in that war, and notably his intrepidity at the capture of the City of Mexico won him considerable fame, and he rose to the rank of Captain, and at the close of the war to that of major. From Mexico, Major Jackson was sent with his command to Fort Hamilton, Long Island. There he remained two years, his thoughts dwelling much upon religious subjects. In July, 1851, having been elected Professor of Natural Philosophy and Artillery Tactics in the Virginia Military Institute at Lexington, he resigned his position in the army, and went thither. A few months later he joined the Presbyterian Church. His perfect and childlike faith in God's goodness, as revealed most fully in Christ, made him cheerfully confident that nothing could happen except for the best.

He had been in Lexington a little over two years, when he married Miss Eleanor Junkin, on the 4th of August, 1853. After spending fourteen months of uninterrupted happiness with his young wife, she was torn from him by death, in the autumn of 1854. His grief for her was so great that his friends were alarmed about him; yet in his moments of bitterest agony his resignation to God's will was unshaken. His duties as professor might well have satisfied the appetite of any ordinary man for teaching, but Jackson longed for more distinctively Christian work, and he accordingly

Opened a Sunday-School

at Lexington, in which he labored with all his heart. His thoughts often turned longingly to the Foreign Mission field, and in his letters to his aunt he frequently referred to missionary work as that which seemed to him the grandest occupation in which a man could engage. For the present, however, the way was not open, and he was content to labor in the sphere in which he was placed, until God should indicate His will by clear leading. His grief over the loss of his wife lightened under constant occupation, and eventually he married a second time. The lady was Mary, second daughter of Dr. Morrison, an eminent Presbyterian clergyman of North Carolina. A quiet summer vacation spent in New England in 1860, was probably the happiest period in Jackson's life; but its calm enjoyment was ended by

The Cry of Secession,

the meaning of which, and all it involved, none knew better than he. He declared that war was inevitable, "but," said he, "it seems to me that if our people would unite in prayer, even yet peace might be preserved." The decision of Virginia could not be ignored by such a man as Jackson. Nor was he one to stand idle in such a crisis. Robert E. Lee, on his appointment of Commander-in-Chief of the Virginia forces, called out at once the senior cadets in the Virginia Institute, and it devolved on Jackson to lead them to Richmond. Before setting out he retired with Mrs. Jackson, and devoted two hours to reading the Bible, and prayer. After a few days in drilling the raw levies, Jackson was appointed major in the engineer department, but almost immediately it was exchanged for that of colonel at Harper's Ferry.

The events which followed in rapid succession are too well known and too numerous to have description here. His valor and his extraordinary strategic ability did much to secure for the Southern armies the victories which marked the early stages of the gigantic struggle. No more able nor daring a General rode under the Southern flag, and his firmness and determination soon won for him the love and ardent admiration of his men, and the significant title of Stonewall Jackson. The circumstances of

His Death

will never be forgotten while American history is read. They form so romantic and pathetic a picture that the interest and sympathy of the reader dwell upon them with unfailing zest. It was at Chancellorsville, on May 3, 1863, that the memorable attack of Lee on the Union army was made. In that dreadful charge Jackson was the impersonation of military enthusiasm. Onward he dashed at the head of his column, as much carried away by the success of his men as the most thoughtless soldier in the ranks. "Forward!" "Press on!" were his answers to every question. His enthusiasm was contagious, but the men had marched twenty miles and were weary. They received a check and began to retreat. After endeavoring to restore order to his lines, he rode along the turnpike to make a reconnoissance. On both sides the skirmishers were firing, and Jackson's escort was mistaken for a body of Federal cavalry and received a volley from the Confederate line of battle. General Jackson was struck and received three balls, one in the right hand and two in the right arm, one of which shattered the bone and cut the artery about two inches below the shoulder. Captain Wilbourne, one of his escort, and Wynn, his assistant, ran up to him as he reined up his horse on the plank road near the spot where he had received the fatal fire, and stood gazing at his troops as if dumbfounded at what they had done. The firing had ceased, but around him were lying the dead and wounded, while their horses, dashing riderless and terrified through the woods, added to the confusion and horrors of the scene.

The wound was dressed and he was placed in a litter (*see illustration*), and though firing had recommenced he was carried through the leaden storm to the rear. It is thought that his wound would not have proven fatal had it not been for an accident. One of the men who was helping to bear the litter, caught his foot in a trailing vine, and fell. The General was thrown out and fell heavily on his wounded shoulder. On reaching the hospital the arm was amputated, and for a day or two hopes were entertained that he would recover. He grew worse, howeve , and on Sunday, May 10, he peacefully passed away. The illustration in the centre of the front page is a representation of the statue which his sorrowing fellow citizens have erected to his memory.

ANECDOTES RELATED AT RECENT EVANGELISTIC MEETINGS.

Lost in the Alps.—A Minister in the North says: "Two young men were one day going up a narrow pass in the Alps. One of them lost his footing and slipped, and was falling, when the other caught hold of him firmly, and, looking over the icy precipice, said, 'It is all right, brother; I have you, and, God helping me, I will tightly hold you.' He did his best, but the weight was too great, and after much vain struggling, he had to let his brother slip from his weakening grasp as if torn from him by the strength of a giant. But Christ can keep us. His arm is all powerful; not the weight of our own evil nature, nor the strength of the great giant sin, nor anything on earth or in hell, is able to pluck us from His omnipotent hand."

A Lady's Last Look at Her Children.—Mr. W. Thompson relates: "A lady who had something the matter with her eyes consulted a doctor, and was told that at any moment she might lose her sight for ever. In great distress she went home, and dressed her children, a boy and a girl, in their best clothes, and as they stood she seated herself before them, and gazed at them, feasting her eyes upon them, and fixing every line of their features upon her memory. Eventually, as the doctor had said, her sight utterly failed, and she became blind. But she treasured the images of her darlings in her heart. It is with such a look as that of the mother on her children that we should look to Jesus—a look that will imprint His image for ever on our hearts, so that whatever happens we may not forget the beauty of His dear face."

Last Visit to the Billiard Saloon.—A worker relates: "About sixteen years ago, when I was sitting alone in my lodgings, one night, the thought came to me most forcibly, 'On which side of the great white throne shall I stand?' The thought was oppressive; I knew I was then unsaved. I could not get rid of the question, and at last in desparation I lifted my hat and went to a billiard saloon, and there, amid the click of the balls and general excitement, hoped, for a time at least, to deaden the clamour of my awakened conscience. But God was too kind to let me run far from Him, and that same night He was found of me who sought Him not. I never visited a billiard saloon again. Now I know when I stand before that once dreaded 'great white throne,' I shall be on the right side, for I am trusting in Christ for salvation. Brother, sister, on which side will you stand in the last day?"

An Aged Woman's Battle with a Fiend.—"I was once preaching in Edinburgh," says Richard Weaver, "and, at one of the meetings there, a young lady said to me, 'There is a poor old woman who wants to speak to you.' As soon as I saw her I knew she had seen better days. 'Mr. Weaver,' said the wretched woman, 'I have been to hear you every night, but my besetting sin is drink, and I cannot overcome it. Last night I resolved to give it up, and what a fearful battle I had to keep from the rum shop, but I begin to fear the Lord will not pardon me.' 'But God is love,' I said, 'and loves with a love far beyond anything which we can apprehend. Perhaps you have had some one who loved you.' The woman produced a little card, upon which was wrought in delicate letters the very words I had quoted, 'God is love.' 'That,' she said, 'was wrought by my daughter, who, as she lay dying, said, "Mother, when I am gone and there is no one to love you on earth, remember, 'God is love.'"' Looking at me she inquired, 'Is God love?' 'God is love,' I repeated. The woman knelt, and, ere she rose, she had given herself to Christ. About a year afterwards I was in Edinburgh, where I met this woman, well-dressed and happy-looking. I asked if she still had the card. In answer she pulled it from her breast. Ah, she carried the declaration of God's love *near* her heart, and the love itself *in* her heart. That was a sinner saved by Divine grace, and plucked from the talons of the fierce fiend of strong drink."

DISABLED HUNTERS.

Dr. Talmage's Sermon Preached Last Sunday Morning, May 27, 1888.

"The lame take the prey."—Isa. 33 : 23.

Maimed Winners of Life's Prizes—Blind Poets—Famous Invalids—Eminent Christian Sufferers—A Deaf Mute's Answer—A Legend of St. Modobert—Cure of a Blind Boy—A Man on Crutches—Orphaned Children—Men of Small Talent—Unknown Gospel Workers—A Child Rescued by an Engineer—Men off the Track—A Sinner Cut Down—A Tremendous Gospel—Doubtful of Sympathy—A Pilot's Ring on a Moonlight Night.

THE utter demolition of the Assyrian host was here predicted. Not only robust men should go forth and gather the spoils of conquest, but even men crippled of arm and crippled of foot should go out and capture much that was valuable. Their physical disadvantages should not hinder their great enrichment. So it has been in the past, so it is now, so it will be in the future. So it is in all departments. Men labor under seemingly great disadvantages, and amid the most unfavorable circumstances, yet making grand achievements, getting great blessing for themselves, great blessing for the world, great blessing for the church, and so "the lame take the prey."

Blind Poets.

Do you know that the three great poets of the world were totally blind? Homer, Ossian, John Milton. Do you know that Mr. Prescott, who wrote that enchanting book, "The Conquest of Mexico," never saw Mexico, could not even see the paper on which he was writing? A frame-work across the sheet, between which, up and down, went the pen immortal. Do you know that Gambassio, the sculptor, could not see the marble before him, or the chisel with which he cut it into shapes bewitching? Do you know that Alexander Pope, whose poems will last as long as the English language, was so much of an invalid that he had to be sewed up every morning in rough canvas in order to stand on his feet at all?

Do you know that Steuart, the celebrated painter, did much of his wonderful work under the shadow of the dungeon, where he had been unjustly imprisoned for debt? Do you know that Demosthenes, by almost superhuman exertion, first had to conquer the lisp of his own speech before he conquered assemblages with his eloquence? Do you know that Bacon struggled all through innumerable sicknesses, and that Lord Byron and Sir Walter Scott went limping on clubfoot through all their life, and that many of the great poets and painters and orators and historians and heroes of the world had something to keep them back, and pull them down, and impede their way, and cripple their physical or their intellectual movement, and yet that they pushed on and pushed up until they reached the spoils of worldly success, and amid the huzza of nations and centuries, "the lame took the prey"?

You know that a vast multitude of these men started under the disadvantage of

Obscure Parentage.

Columbus, the son of the weaver. Ferguson, the astronomer, the son of the shepherd. America the prey of the one; worlds on worlds the prey of the other. But what is true in secular directions is more true in spiritual and religious directions, and I proceed to prove it.

There are in all communities many invalids. They never know a well day. They adhere to their occupations, but they go panting along the streets with exhaustion, and, at eventime, they lie down on the lounge with achings beyond all medicament. They have tried all prescriptions, they have gone through all the cures which were proclaimed infallible, and they have come now to surrender to perpetual ailments. They consider they are among many disadvantages; and when they see those who are buoyant in health, pass by, they almost envy their robust frames and easy respiration.

But I have noticed among that invalid class those who have the greatest knowledge of the Bible, who are in nearest

Intimacy With Jesus Christ,

who have the most glowing experiences of the truth, who have had the most remarkable answers to prayer, and who have most exhilarant anticipations of Heaven. The temptations which weary us who are in robust health they have conquered. They have divided among them the spoils of the conquest. Many who are alert and athletic and swarthy loiter in the way. These are the lame that take the prey. Robert Hall, an invalid, Edward Payson, an invalid, Richard Baxter, an invalid, Samuel Rutherford, an invalid. This morning, when you want to call to mind those who are most Christlike, you think of some darkened room in your father's house from which there went forth an influence potent for eternity.

A step farther: Through raised letters the art of printing has been brought to the attention of the blind. You take up the Bible for the blind, and you close your eyes, and you run your fingers over the raised letters, and you say: "Why I never could get any information in this way. What a slow, lumbrous way of reading! God help the blind." And yet I find among that class of persons, among the blind, the deaf and the dumb, the most thorough acquaintance with God's word. Shut out from all other sources of information, no sooner does their hand touch the raised letter than they gather a prayer. Without eyes, they look off upon the kingdoms of God's love. Without hearing they catch the minstrelsy of the skies. Dumb, yet with pencil, or with irradiated countenance, they declare the glory of God.

A large audience assembled in New York at the anniversary of the Deaf and Dumb Asylum, and one of the visitors with chalk on the blackboard wrote this question to the pupils: "Do you not find it very hard to be deaf and dumb?" And one of the pupils took the chalk and wrote on the blackboard

This Sublime Sentence

in answer: "When the song of the angels shall burst upon our enraptured ear, we will scarce regret that our ears were never marred with earthly sounds." Oh! the brightest eyes in Heaven will be those that never saw on earth. The ears most alert in Heaven will be those that in this world heard neither voice of friend, nor thrum of harp, nor carol of bird, nor doxology of congregations.

A lad who had been blind from infancy was cured. The oculist operated upon the lad, and then put a very heavy bandage over the eyes, and after a few weeks had gone by, the bandage was removed, and the mother said to her child: "Willie, can you see?" He said: "Oh! mamma, is this Heaven?" The contrast between the darkness before and the brightness afterward was overwhelming. And I tell you the glories of Heaven will be a thousandfold brighter for those who never saw anything on earth. While many with good vision closed their eyes in night, and many who had a good, artistic, and cultured ear went down into discord, these afflicted ones cried unto the Lord in their trouble, and He made their sorrows advantage, and so "the lame took the prey."

In the seventh century there was

A Legend of St. Modobert.

It was said that his mother was blind, and one day while looking at his mother he felt so sympathetic for her blindness that he rushed forward and kissed her blind eyes, and, the legend says, her vision came immediately. That was only a legend, but it is a truth, a glorious truth, that a kiss of God's eternal love has brought to many a blind eye eternal illumination.

A step further: There are those in all communities who toil mightily for a livelihood. They have scant wages. Perhaps they are diseased, or have physical infirmities, so they are hindered from doing a continuous day's work. A city missionary finds them up the dark alley, with no fire, with thin clothing, with very coarse bread. They never ride in the street-car; they cannot afford the five cents. They never see any pictures save those in the show-window on the street, from which they are often jostled, and looked at by some one who seems to say in the look: "Move on! what are you doing here looking at pictures?" Yet many of them live on mountains of transfiguration. At their rough table He who fed the five thousand breaks the bread. They talk often of the good times that are coming. This world has no charm for them, but heaven entrances their spirit. They often divide their scant crust with some forlorn wretch who knocks at their door at night, and on the blast of the night-wind, as the door opens to let them in, is heard the voice of Him who said: "I was hungry and ye fed me." No cohort of Heaven will be too bright to transport them. By God's help they have vanquished the Assyrian host. They have divided among them the spoils. Lame, yet they took the prey.

I was riding along the road one day, and I saw

A Man on Crutches.

I overtook him. He was very old. He was going very slowly. At that rate, it would have taken him two hours to go a mile. I said: "Wouldn't you like to ride?" He said: "Thank you, I would. God bless you." When he sat beside me, he said: "You see, I am very lame and very old, but the Lord has been a very good Lord to me. I have buried all my children. The Lord gave them, and the Lord had a right to take them away. Blessed be His name. I was very sick, and I had no money, and my neighbors came in and took care of me, and I wanted nothing. I suffer a great deal with pain, but then I have so many mercies left. The Lord has been a good Lord to me." And before we had got far, I was in doubt whether I was giving him a ride or he was giving me a ride! He said: "Now, if you please, I'll get out here. Just help me down on my crutches, if you please. God bless you. Thank you, sir. Good morning. Good morning. You have been feet to the lame, sir, you have. Good morning." Swarthy men had gone the road that day. I do not know where they came out, but every hobble of that old man was toward the shining gate. With his old crutch he had struck down many a Sennacherib of temptation which has mastered you and me. Lame, so fearfully lame, so awfully lame; but he took the prey.

A step further: There are in all communities

Many Orphans.

During our last war, and in the years immediately following, how many children we heard say: "Oh! my father was killed in the war." Have you ever noticed—I fear you have not—how well those children have turned out? Starting under the greatest disadvantage, no orphan asylum could do for them what their father would have done had he lived. The skirmisher sat one night, by the light of fagots, in the swamp, *writing a letter home*, when a sharpshooter's bullet ended the letter which was never folded, never posted, and never read. Those children came up under great disadvantage. No father to fight their way for them Perhaps there was in the old family Bible an old yellow letter pasted fast, which told the story of that father's long march, and how he suffered in the hospital; but they looked still further on in the Bible, and they came to the story of how God is the Father of the fatherless, and the widow's portion, and they soon took their father's place in that household. They battled the way for their mother. They came on up, and many of them have in the years since the war, taken positions in church and State. While many of those who suffered nothing during those times have had sons go out into lives of indolence and vagabondage, these who started under so many disadvantages, because they were so early bereft, these are the lame who took the prey.

A step further: There are those who would like to do good. They say:

"Oh! if I had Wealth,

or, if I had eloquence, or if I had high social position, how much I would accomplish for

God and the church!" I stand here to-day to tell you that you have great opportunities for usefulness. Who built the Pyramids? The king who ordered them built? No; the plain workmen who added stone after stone and stone after stone. Who built the dikes of Holland? The government that ordered the enterprise? No; the plain workmen who carried the earth and rung their trowel on the wall. Who are those who have built these vast cities? The capitalists? No; the carpenters, the masons, the plumbers, the plasterers, the tinners, the roofers, dependent on a day's wages for a livelihood. And so in the great work of assuaging human suffering and enlightening human ignorance and halting human inquity. In that great work, the chief part is to be done by ordinary men, with ordinary speech, in an ordinary manner, and by ordinary means. The trouble is that in the army of Christ

We all Want to be Captains

and colonels and brigadier-generals. We are not willing to march with the rank and file and to do duty with the private soldier. We want to belong to the reserve corps, and read about the battle while warming ourselves at the campfires, or on furlough at home, our feet upon an ottoman, we sagging back into an arm-chair. As you go down the street, you see an excavation and four or five men are working, and perhaps twenty or thirty leaning on the rail looking over at them. That is the way it is in the church of God to-day: where you find one Christian hard at work, there are *fifty men watching the job.*

Oh! my friends, why do you not go to work and preach this Gospel? You say: "I have no pulpit." You have. It may be the carpenter's bench, it may be the mason's wall. The robe in which you are to proclaim this Gospel may be a shoemaker's apron. But woe unto you if you preach not this Gospel somewhere, somehow! If this world is ever brought to Christ, it will be through the unanimous and long-continued efforts of men who, waiting for

No Special Endowment,

consecrate to God what they have. Among the most useless people in the world are men with ten talents, while many a one with only two talents, or no talent at all, is doing a great work, and so "the lame take the prey." There are thousands of ministers of whom you have never heard—in log cabins at the West, in mission chapels at the East—who are warring against the legions of darkness, successfully warring. Tract-distributors, month by month undermining the citadels of sin. You do not know their going or their coming; but *the foot-falls of their ministry are heard in the palaces of Heaven.* Who are the workers in our Sabbath-schools throughout this land to-day? Men celebrated, men brilliant, men of vast estate? For the most part, not that at all. I have noticed that the chief characteristic of the most of those who are successful in the work is that they know their Bibles, are earnest in prayer, are anxious for the salvation of the young, and Sabbath by Sabbath are willing to sit down unobserved and tell of Christ and the resurrection. These are the humble workers who are recruiting the great army of Christian youth—not by might, not by power, not by profound argument, not by brilliant antithesis, but by the blessing of God on plain talk, and humble story, and silent tear, and anxious look. "The lame take the prey."

An engineer on a locomotive going across the western prairies day after day, saw a little child come out in front of a cabin and wave to him; so he got in the habit of waving back to the little child, and it was the day's joy to him to see this little one come out in front of the cabin-door and wave to him, while he answered back. One day the train was belated, and it came on to the dusk of the evening. As the engineer stood at his post he saw by the headlight

That Little Girl on the Track,

wondering why the train did not come, looking for the train, knowing nothing of its peril. A great horror seized upon the engineer. He reversed the engine. He gave it in charge of the other man on board, and then he climbed over the engine, and he came down on the cowcatcher. He said, though he had reversed the engine, it seemed as though it were going at lightning speed, faster and faster, though it was really slowing up, and with almost supernatural clutch he caught that child by the hair and lifted it up, and when the train stopped, and the passengers gathered around, to see what was the matter, there the old engineer lay, fainted dead away, the little child alive, and in his swarthy arms.

"Oh!" you say, "that was well done." But I want you to exercise some kindness and some appreciation toward those in community who are snatching the little ones from under the wheels of temptation and sin—snatching them from under thundering rail-trains of eternal disaster, bringing them up into respectability in this world and into glory for the world to come. You appreciate what the engineer did; why can you not appreciate the grander work done by every Sabbath-school teacher this afternoon?

Oh! my friends, I want to impress upon myself and upon yourselves that it is not the number of talents we possess, but the use we make of them.

God has a Royal Family

in the world. Now, if I should ask, "Who are the royal families of history?" you would say, "House of Hapsburg, House of Stuarts, House of Bourbons." They lived in palaces, and had great equipage. But who are the Lord's royal family? Some of them may serve you in the household, some of them are in unlighted garrets, some of them will walk this afternoon down the street, on their arm a basket of broken food; some of them are in the almshouse, despised and rejected of men; yet in the last great day, while it will be found that some of us who fared sumptuously every day, are hurled back into discomfiture, there are the lame that will take the prey.

One step further: There are a great many people discouraged about getting to Heaven. You are brought up in good families, you had Christian parentage; but you frankly tell me that you are a thousand miles away from the right track. My brother, you are the one I want preach to this morning. I have been looking for you. I will tell you

How You Got Astray.

It was not maliciousness on your part. It was perhaps through the geniality and sociality of your nature that you fell into sin. You wandered away from your duty, you unconsciously left the house of God; you admit the Gospel to be true, and yet you have so grievously and so prolongedly wandered, you say rescue is impossible. It would take a week to count up the names of those in Heaven who were on earth worse than you tell me you are. They went the whole round of iniquity, they disgraced themselves, they disgraced their household, they despaired of return because their reputation was gone, their property was gone, everything was gone; but in some hour like this they heard the voice of God, and threw themselves on the divine compassion, and they rose up more than conquerors. And I tell you there is the same chance for you. That is one reason why I like to preach this Gospel, so free a Gospel, so tremendous a Gospel. It takes a man all wrong, and makes him all right.

In a former settlement where I preached, a member of my congregation quitted the house of God, quitted respectable circles, went into all styles of sin, and was slain of his iniquity. The day for his burial came, and his body was brought to the house of God. Some of his comrades who had destroyed him were overheard along the street, on the way to the burial, saying: "Come, let us go and hear Talmage damn this old sinner!" Oh! I had nothing but tears for the dead, and I had nothing but invitations for the living. You see I could not do any otherwise. "Christ Jesus came to seek and save that which was lost." Christ in his dying prayer said: "Father, forgive them," and that was a prayer for you and for me. Oh! start on the road to Heaven to-day.

You Are Not Happy.

The thirst of your soul will never be slaked by the fountains of sin. You turn everywhere but to God for help. Right where you are, call on Him. He knows you, He knows all about you, He knows all the odds against which you have been contending in life. Do not go to Him with a long rigmarole of a prayer, but just look up and say: "Help! Help!"

But you say: "My hand trembles so from my dissipations, I can't even take hold of a hymn-book to sing." Do not worry about that, my brother; I will give out a hymn at the close so familiar you can sing it without a book. But you say: "I have such terrible habits on me, I can't get rid of them." My answer is, Almighty grace can break up that habit, and will break it up. But you say: "The wrong I did was to one dead and in Heaven now, and I can't correct it. By the grace of God, go into the presence of that one, and the apologies you ought to have made on earth make in Heaven.

"Oh!" says some man, "if I should try to do right, if I should turn away from my evil doing unto the Lord, I would be jostled, I would be driven back, nobody would have any sympathy for me." You are mistaken. Here, in the presence of the church on earth and in Heaven, I give you to-day the right hand of Christian fellowship. God sent me here to-day to preach this, and He sent you here to hear this: "Let the wicked forsake his way, and the unrighteous man his thought, and let him return unto the Lord, who will have mercy, and unto our God, who will abundantly pardon." Though you may have been the worst sinner, you may become the best saint, and in the great Day of Judgment it will be found that "where sin abounded, grace does much more abound," and while the spoils of an everlasting kingdom are being awarded for your pursuit, it will be found that the lame took the prey. Blessed be God that we are, this Sabbath, one week nearer the obliteration of all the inequalities of this life and all its disquietudes.

The Pilot's Ring.

Years ago, on a boat on the North River, the pilot gave a very sharp ring to the bell for the boat to slow up. The engineer attended to the machinery, and then he came up with some alarm on deck to see what was the matter. He saw it was a moonlight night and there were no obstacles in the way. He went to the pilot and said: "Why did you ring the bell in that way? Why do you want to stop? there's nothing the matter." And the pilot said to him: "There is a mist gathering on the river; don't you see that? and there is night gathering darker and darker, and I can't see the way." Then the engineer, looking around and seeing it was a bright moonlight, looked into the face of the pilot, and saw that he was dying, and then that he was dead.

God grant that when our last moment comes we may be found at our post doing our whole duty; and when the mists of the river of death gather on our eyelids, may the good Pilot take the wheel from our hands and guide us into the calm harbor of eternal rest!

"Drop the anchor, furl the sail,
I am safe within the vale."

A NOBLEMAN'S TESTIMONY.

LORD BRASSEY'S personal testimony on the subject of Christian missions in distant lands, which he gave recently at a public meeting, speaks volumes when we remember that it comes from a cultured man, and a shrewd observer. He said: "I can give you the personal testimony of an old sailor, and a wide traveller, to the good and noble work which is being done in distant lands under the auspices of this and kindred societies. I have been on board the storm-tossed vessel in which a good bishop of the Anglican Church was engaged in carrying the gospel to the distant and storm-bound and ice-bound shores of Labrador; I have been in the stormy waters of the Straits of Magellan, and have seen at what sacrifice and by what efforts the gospel is carried to the savage people of Terra del Fuego; I have seen the devoted missionaries who are sent forth by the United States at their work at Beyrout and Lahore. On the occasion of a recent journey, both at Umritzur and Agra, I saw what devoted men, and not less devoted women, were doing in the great cause of the education of heathen children. I have had the privilege at the Island of Tahiti of listening to a French Protestant pastor, a man of great culture, a man who had formerly held the post of teacher to one of the most distinguished nobles of our land, and I have heard that man deliver a sermon which was listened to with great attention by his native audience. The last missionary station which I visited was that established in Darnley Island, and we had the privilege of taking the wife of a missionary, Mr. Hunt, in the *Sunbeam*, from Thursday Island to Darnley Island. We spent a most interesting day with Mr. Hunt and Mr. Savage at Darnley Island. We saw the place of worship on the island—a humble, but picturesque building; we saw much of the native teacher and his wife, persons whom it was impossible to know without feeling the greatest admiration and respect for them. We heard a most interesting narrative of the difficulties and efforts which are involved in carrying the gospel to the savage races of New Guinea. We heard, and it was impossible to hear the story without a thrill of admiration, of the devotion which is shown by the native teachers acting under the guidance of their English leaders in this great cause. The greater the peril, the more imminent the prospect even of death in the great cause, the more earnest is the enthusiasm of the native teachers to go forth into this dangerous field."

A CHINESE CHRISTIAN BEHEADED.

DURING the excitement aroused in China over the French campaign in Tonquin, all Europeans were in peril through the prejudices of the people, who were unable to discriminate between the French and other foreigners. Mr. Whitehead, a missionary there, relates that there was a still stronger antipathy to Chinamen who had become converts to the Christian religion. "They had," he says, "to pass through a very severe ordeal. One man, a native assistant, went through a town called Kau-Kong, when a reward of fifty dollars was posted in the market-place for his head, and yet he entered the place and preached Christ's Gospel. Some of the Christian women even had naked swords held over their heads and crossed over their throats, and still remained firm. At a place called Tin-Un, the mandarin positively sat in his chair and watched the mob pull down the houses and shops of the Christians, carry off their goods, and then turn the poor men and women half-naked into the street, never lifting a finger unless the mob touched a heathen man's shop; and all he did was to provide them a boat to take them away in their half-naked condition, and when they left he clenched his official fist in their faces, and said, 'Never, let me see you here again.' These men lost their home, lost their business and property—all with the exception of bare life—for the sake of the Lord Jesus Christ. A native assistant was dragged off with violence to the temple, and ordered to worship the idol there. 'No,' he said, 'I am a Christian, I cannot worship an idol.' 'You worship the idol or you die,' they said. 'I can die,' said the courageous man, 'but I cannot deny my Lord and Master.' He did die. They led him to the top of a hill near which the city was built, and there they deliberately severed his head from his body; they took his mangled remains and threw them over the precipice, far into the river running at its foot, and he died a martyr for his Lord."

A GIRL WAIF RESCUED.

THE beneficent work Dr. Barnardo is doing for the homeless children of London has no better illustration than in the following sorrowful incident which recently occurred: "Among the candidates who were admitted during the last month to our Home," says the philanthropist, "was Kate, a girl of fourteen, whose story was told in a few words by the lady who brought her under my notice. This child, my correspondent wrote, was born in an immoral home. She seems to have known nothing but cruelty and want, and had been in a *drunken fighting household* all her life. She actually never slept in a bed till she came to our town one year ago. Her mother was a bad character all her life, an inveterate drinker, and openly immoral. Kate used occasionally to coax her mother out of the saloon, and when she could, obtained money for food, taking it from her mother's dress while the woman was drunk, and telling lies to screen herself from the thrashings that the man whom she called father gave her. From this man poor Kate suffered a course of systematic cruelty until the wretched mother died. Then he put her into a train to get rid of her. On arriving at J. she was supposed to be a girl for whom there was a look-out, so she was kept in the workhouse until identified. When the truth leaked out she was sent to me and placed in our temporary Home. I found her emaciated, forlorn and ragged. This poor girl-waif, with none in the world to help her, was at once admitted to our Home."

BRIGHT'S DISEASE CURED.

THE disease which has carried off so many eminent men, and is believed to be incurable, and which is known as Bright's Disease, is the subject of a testimony which Miss Carrie F. Judd publishes in her *Triumphs of Faith*. The sufferer, who dates from New Marlborough, Mass., and signs herself Mrs. Ellen E. Hall, says: "During the summer of 1885, my limbs were swollen to the knees so badly that I could not button my shoes. I had a bad cough, and my heart troubled me. If I moved about quickly my heart would beat so rapidly that I could hardly breathe. The latter part of August I went to see a physician, and he told me that I was in a very bad condition, but did not tell me how badly off I was, but told my friends that I had Bright's Disease, and it was impossible for me to live through the year. This doctor moved away, so I employed another excellent doctor, but I grew rapidly worse, a good deal of the time not able to wait upon myself. I was in this condition for about seven months.

I had read accounts of prayers being answered for sick and troubled ones at the Fulton street prayer-meetings and thought I would write and ask them to pray for me that I might be spared and well enough to see my children. *I did not ask to be cured*, as I knew that my disease was called incurable. I began to be better from that time, so that I could do a little light work and ride out in warm, pleasant weather. I told a friend about writing to the Fulton street prayer-meeting, and she gave me your little book to read, entitled "The Prayer of Faith." This was the first that I had ever known about being healed by the prayer of faith, but it was several months before I could accept healing in this way for myself. I was taking very powerful medicine all this time, nearly every hour during the day and sometimes at night. My physician had told me that he was afraid that I might be worse when cold weather came on, as the cold was very bad for my disease, and that it would take but a very little to make me worse than I was before, and in the fall of 1886, as cool weather came on some of my symptoms were worse.

November 16, 1886, Dr. Charles Cullis of Boston offered prayer for my recovery, and Miss Judd and several of my friends also united in prayer for me. Our pastor also offered prayer for me at the same time, and anointed me with oil according to James 5:14, 15. The Lord heard and answerd the prayers that were offered for me, and healed me. I left off taking medicine that day, and have not taken a drop of any kind of medicine since. That night I slept all night like a child, something I had not done for a long time. And from that time my cough left me, my strength began to return. At first I was only able to do light work, but in about three months I was able to do all my work, washing included. I have not been sick since.

A SUPERSTITIOUS EXHUMATION.

AT a recent missionary meeting the Rev. T. Bramfitt, of the Wesleyan Missionary Society, said: "I will illustrate some of the difficulties under which we labor in China. At Kwang-Chi I have not only preached, but have played the part of a medical man. One day a woman came to me with two children, both being very ill. She asked me to prescribe for them, and I did so successfully. She returned, giving thanks to God and the missionary, and became a constand attendant at our chapel. Her home was about two miles from the town, and notwithstanding her cramped feet, every Sunday for two or three years she was found in the house of God. In the course of time she was converted, and was the means of bringing into the Church the whole of her family. As years went on the work of God developed in her village round about, and I was enabled to accomplish the work of enlarging the chapel, and building a minister's house. Whilst building the minister's house the woman came to me in sad distress and said, 'What do you think the people in the village have done? You remember having interred the brother of my husband? Well, the head man of the village has gone to the grave and *exhumed the coffin and thrown it by the roadside.*' It seems that a man in the village has become suddenly ill—it was said in consequence of the evil influences proceeding from that grave. I went to see the offending head man, and pointed out that he had committed a capital crime against his country's laws, personally offended against me, and illegally injured the Christians. The man was very determined, and refused to reinter the body or apologize to the family. I threatened to send a petition to the mandarin. I gave the head man of the village till 12 o'clock the next day before I sent in my petition, and at that time I did so. The mandarin came immediately in his robes of office, and very soon the headman of the village was before me, kneeling and asking me to dictate my terms. A little firmness on that occasion assured the rights of our friends in the village. The cause of God all around has progressed in consequence."

A TWENTY YEARS' PENANCE.

A MISSIONARY in India sends to the *Indian Witness* a description of a valuable work in which the leaders are a former devotee and his Christian wife. He says: We are encamped under the trees where for over twenty years Jhandula Ram (the banner of Ram) did severe penance, imposed on himself both as a supposed adequate punishment for sins of the present and past births, and as an expression of penitence and the highest virtue. Five years ago he heard the Gospel of Christ preached in the open air, when he believed, and was baptized. His name was then changed to Jhandula Masih [the banner of Christ] and a true banner his has been, read and known of all about Mahadeva. He was married to his *chelin*, or female disciple, who chastely attended him through all the long years of his self-inflicted tortures, and both were induced to remain in the place where they had been called to work for the Great Master according to the light they had received. And the Lord has blessed and owned their labor of love and work of faith and patience of hope. Three other families have been brought out and baptized through their agency; and two schools, one for boys and the other for girls, have been established. A year ago a Christian teacher and his wife were sent for the latter, and they have both rendered good service. So that, here, in this centre of a great village population there is a small Christian community growing up and taking form.

THE BURDENSOME STONE.

By Rev. A. C. Tris, of Howard Kans.*

The Stone Quarried—Now Temporarily Cast Away—Always Burdensome—Pharaoh's Experience—Supremacy in Asia Minor—A Burden in Babylon—A Burden in the Dispersion—Persecution Futile—A Burden to Turkey—I the Future—A Financial Burden—A Theological Burden—The Key to the Eastern Question—A Loadstone.

AMONG the prophecies of the seers of Israel a remarkable expression of deep significance is used respecting Jerusalem. Zechariah says: (12: 3): "In that day I will make Jerusalem *a burdensome stone* for all peoples. All who burden themselves with it shall be cut in pieces, though all the people (nations) of the earth be gathered together against it"—a prophecy which sets before us in bold relief the future condition and the deliverance of God's ancient people, restored in their land Canaan.

In these words we have a panorama of the past, and a vista of the future before us, and a most unique exhibition of the most singular character of Israel through the ages, which is represented as "a stone" taken by the Almighty from the quarry of the creation, as a stone which in itself possesses no worth above other stones or nations, and yet which is set apart by election, and chiselled by the hand of the Great Architect to be the greatest wonder of grace, mercy, and judgment ever known among nations; yea, as

A Stone Cast Away

for a time, which shall be restored to such a glory that its "dust" shall be precious in the eyes of the Church of God. (Ps. 102: 14). Israel is not only as a stone of strength, it is also like a golden thread interwoven in the web of nations, beautiful in its design and visible to all nations, so that the spirit of the age cannot close their eyes in seeing the yellow golden fabric intermixed in the affairs of nations. It is an obvious fact that Israel from its beginning has been "a burdensome stone" for all the peoples, a firebrand (Zech. 3: 2) to many nations—a factor or medium placed on earth to try men, that the thoughts of many hearts may be revealed, and to be a dispenser of blessings unique to any nation on the globe.

A cursive review of the past and present time will place our suggestion above all contradiction. In the history of the Patriarchs we see all the particulars of the text verified: Abram called and taken from the Chaldean quarry, was placed in the land of Ham, was loaded with earthly and heavenly blessings (Ps. 68: 30), migrated in the midst of mighty nations, lived as a stranger and sojourner, and yet as "a mighty Prince" (Gen. 23: 6), being indeed a burdensome stone in the eyes of the Canaanites, and so protected by Jehovah that not any one dared to burden himself with him.

In Egypt the children of Israel were "burdensome stones;" being shepherds of sheep, they were loathsome stones in the eyes of Mizraim, and their servile occupation was to burn "brick."

Pharaoh's Experience

was another instance of the truth of the words of Zechariah: "He shall be cut in pieces," while the host of Israel sung the anthem of praise and deliverance on the borders of the Red Sea. As long as Israel had no idols in their camp, Balaam could not curse (Num. 24: 17), and the prowess of the Nations of Canaan melted "like snow in Salmon. (Ps. 68: 14). In the theocracy and in the kingly rule of Israel and of Judah, the children of Abraham were "a most burdensome stone" for the nations of the East—divided, and yet strong, small in territory and resources, and yet exercising a supremacy in Asia Miner.

In the captivity the tribes of Israel were like burdensome stones: a people who would not sing one of the songs of Zion to please their captors in Babylon (Ps. 137: 1-6)—a people who did not bow before the Amalekite Haman, the highest officer of the court of Artaxerxes—a nation always resembling the burning bush of Sinai (Exod. 3: 2), and yet, the angel Jehovah was in the midst of them.

Jerusalem, as a city, had the reputation of being: "A rebellious city, hurtful unto kings and provinces" (Ezra 4: 15), and was in many respects "a burdensome stone"

For Eastern Nations,

and when the fullness of time came, and the Christ of God was born, the City of the Great King did not receive "the born King of the house of David," but rejected the Prince of life, and nailed Him on the tree (Acts 3: 14-15; 1 Peter 2: 24); and, consequently, Jerusalem lost the Divine favor, and had to endure the burning wrath of Jehovah.

But, let us see in what respect Israel is left in the Diaspora. Their covenant God has never yet repudiated His own covenant people; they are still a people of one origin and blood. In religious matters they have lost the acumen of mental qualifications of discernment in regard to their own prophecies (Rom. 2: 7); their sharp-minded philosophers and Talmudistical expositors are going around their own prophetical oracles, and can see nothing of the Logos, and of the Son of David, Jesus our Lord; and, this fact is the more remarkable because, in all other things, the Jews have naturally acute mental powers, and a quicker perception than ever their fathers had. In the deep recesses of their being, powers are slumbering and burning, which cause

The Envy of the Nations.

and from this is springing forth the anti-Semitic agitation in our day, and the hatred of the Teutonic-Muscovite Turko-Slavonic persecutions. The Jews are an enigma in the world, a stone of contention, and a rock on which the radical philosophical and agnostic delusions of the age have suffered shipwreck. Jerusalem, the gate city, leading to three continents, has been for many years past the burdensome political stone, which has burdened the greatest statesmen of the age. The Eastern Question has become a household word, and that question can only be solved, and this Gordian knot cut by the restoration of Israel to Canaan, and

The Fall of the Moslem Power.

If we recall the sufferings of the Jews in the East, in Spain, in England, in the middle ages, and those of recent times, and how Old Jewry, Jewish Strasse, and the Ghetto, are names familiar to every one; and how many among Christians look upon the Jews as a people of the weary breast and wandering foot, who can claim only a grave! Can any one doubt the truth of the prophecy: "That Jerusalem is called a burdensome stone," and the Jews are yet in the Diaspora, but thank God, the exiles scattered in all the world are to come home (Ezek. 37: 1-12; Zech. 12: 7.)

The Future.

At that day, says the prophet, Jerusalem shall be "a burdensome stone." That day is yet future; it will be when the Jews will come from the north (Jer. 3: 18,) from the east and west, and take possession of their fatherland. No nation on earth has better claim than Israel to call it by that name; then, Israel shall dwell in peace (Ezek. 39: 11,) and only outward circumstances shall make Jerusalem to be a burdensome stone. At that day Jerusalem shall be *financially a burdensome stone*, and shake the money centres of the world, as never happened before, when Israel shall draw their wealth (Isa. 60: 17,) marvellous sums, from the Exchanges and Bourses, to be placed in the land of their fathers. Values of properties must consequently suffer a depletion, and a money crisis will be experienced.

At that day Jerusalem shall be

A Burdensome Theological Stone,

and bring to naught the doctrine told for many ages—that the Christian Church is Zion and Jerusalem, and that Israel must first be converted in their exile condition. All nations will hear that Zech. 12: 10 is fulfilled, and that the Jews have seen Him who has come to save and to bless them in their own land (Ps. 118: 26-29.) Oh, what a stone of confusion will be the return of Israel for the religious and political world at that day, the far-seeing English statesmen, and the rulers of the New Western world, as the islands of the sea (Ps. 72: 10) shall send their ships and their presents (Isa. 66: 19), and the work will be done speedily (Acts 12: 41).

At that day, when Israel shall dwell safely and quietly in Jerusalem and in the lands of their fathers, the Eastern and European nations especially will look upon Jerusalem as

A Coveted Golden Stone,

the bonanza of the world, and especially the Prince of the mighty Empire of Russia, with a multitude of allies (Ezek. 38, 39), will think of pillaging the treasures of Palestine, and will actually go up with greater armies than ever were gathered on the earth, to destroy Jehovah's band; but the Watcher and Holy One coming down from heaven will hew down the "Muscovite" and "Gomer's" armies by earthquakes, fiery devastation, and pestilence, so that the prowess of Russia will be annihilated, and our text will be literally fulfilled: "All shall be cut in pieces, though all the nations of the earth be gathered together against it."

At that day Israel shall be a burdensome stone for all peoples when it shall stand as the head of nations, pre-eminently above all the nations of the earth (Ps. 110: 2, 3).

Finally, at that day, Jerusalem shall be

The Loadstone

of all the religious magnetic desires of the nations. The needle of this compass will not point to Mecca for the Eastern nations, neither to the Lady at Loretto for the Western nations; it will have only one centre—Jerusalem the Golden, the Cross and the Crown of King Jesus, the throne of the Son of David, "and the nations will go up from year to year to worship the King, the Lord of hosts, and to keep the feast of Tabernacles." (Zec. 14: 16). Then the fulness of earth's resources and of the mental development of all nations shall be on exhibition, because the veil of darkness now covering all nations will be swallowed up. The caravan of worshippers, led by their kings, shall bring their wealth, honor and glory in the New Jerusalem (Matt. 2: 11; Rev. 22: 24-27), and shall sit down with Abraham, Isaac and Jacob in the kingdom of God (Luke 13: 28, 29) to keep the feast with all who have been counted worthy to inherit the first resurrection. (Rev. 20: 6). Indeed, the state of Jerusalem in the ages to come is beyond description, and no wonder that the holy soul of John, seeing the glory, exclaimed: "Blessed are they who 'may enter in through the gates into the city.'" (Rev. 22: 14).

* From his article in the May number of the *Prophetic News*; for sale, price six cents, at this office, 63 Bible House, New York.

CURRENT EVENTS.

The Prospects of a Settlement of the International copyright question materially improved last week. On Thursday last the Judiciary Committee of the House of Representatives decided to report the bill recently passed by the Senate instead of the House bill on the same subject, so that if the bill passes the House without important changes, it will not have to be sent back to the Senate but can go to the President at once. It is, however, very low on the list, and unless reached by a suspension of the rules, it is not likely to be dealt with at this session. The opponents of the measure have employed an active firm of agents to work against it, and much capital is being made out of the dissatisfaction with which the bill is regarded in England.

The Necessity of Passing the Appropriation bills has caused the House to close the debate on the Mills' Tariff Reduction measure. The appropriations are exhausted by June 30, and it was consequently imperative that that business should be speedily dealt with, June being a month broken by Presidential Conventions. No final vote has been taken on the bill, and it will therefore be within the power of the Conventions to give expression to party feeling on the subject. There appears to be little doubt that the tariff will be the issue of the Presidential campaign. The fact cannot be ignored by the Conventions, and it now seems probable that the Democratic party will go before the country pledged to tariff-reduction on the lines of the Mills bill. It will be a distinct gain if this important question should supersede the personal one, which has too often rendered a Presidential campaign a disgrace to politics.

The Serious Illness of General Philip Sheridan was reported last week. It was at first stated that the General had been seized with apoplexy, but later reports, authenticated by the physicians in attendance, attribute his illness to an affection of the heart. The trouble first became alarming on Monday, May 21, when the General was thought to be dying. He recovered, however, from that attack, but had a relapse the next day, and on Friday a third seizure prostrated him. For some seconds his heart ceased to beat entirely, and those around him feared that the end had come. By immediate hypodermic injections and other restoratives a slow, but feeble, palpitation of the heart was brought about. For an hour or more he lingered in this uncertain condition, but his pulse finally grew stronger, and his breathing became somewhat easier. The disease from which he is suffering is valvular disease of the heart. He is fifty-seven years of age.

The Democratic State Convention of Pennsylvania, which met at Harrisburg, on May 3, has caused a sensation by its emphatic endorsement of President Cleveland, and the Mills Bill. It was so decisively in unanimity with the policy of the Administration, that it instructed the State delegation to the national Convention to vote for the renomination of the President. The tariff plank of the platform was also of an unmistakable character. It declared that revision of the tariff laws is necessary with a view to their simplifications, the correction of their incongruities and inequalities, the regulation of duties in such manner as will put American industry on a firm and permanent basis covering the difference between wages in this country and in foreign countries, the abolition of taxes on raw materials for manufactures, and the relief of the people from useless and onerous taxes, and from extortion by trusts and monopolies controlling the prices of the common necessaries of life, and requested the Democratic Congressmen of Pennsylvania to give the Mills bill "their earnest and undivided support." It is evident that whatever Mr. Randall may do, there is in his State a powerful section of the party which does not sympathize with his utterances on this crucial question.

The Fatalities Caused by the Floods from the Mississippi have not yet been accurately ascertained, and it will be impossible to ascertain how many deaths were due indirectly to the exposure and hardship entailed. Several very sad cases are reported. One of them relates to a farmer named Johnson, who lived in the Sny levee district. He was on the levee working with other farmers when the embankment gave way. Mounting his horse, he had *a mad race with the advancing waters* for his home, where his three little children were sleeping. Reaching there just as the water struck the house, he placed the children in a wagon and started for the bluffs. The rapidly advancing flood floated with the wagon box from the wheels and two of the children were drowned, Johnson saving himself and one little daughter. The child is all he has left of a happy home and a farm of 200 acres. While Samuel Moore was taking his two children out of the Indian Grove district in a boat, the boat was capsized and Moore was drowned. The children saved themselves by climbing upon a log. Two families in the Sny district, near Fall Creek, are unaccounted for, and no trace of them can be found. Rumors of still further loss of life are current. The waters began falling on May 19, and by the 22d had been reduced sufficiently to allow of the resumption of traffic on some of the railroads.

The Importation of the English Rector for Holy Trinity Church in New York, is declared by the United States Circuit Court to be an infringement of the Contract Labor law, and the church is therefore called upon to pay the *fine of one thousand dollars* provided by the law. Judge Wallace, on May 22, pronounced judgment in the case. He said that the corporation of Holy Trinity offended against the law in that it hired the Rev. M. Warren, of England, a clergyman of the Church of England, to become its rector at a salary of $10,000 a year. Judge Wallace held that the law was plain, and that while its framers presumably did not intend to have it affect clergymen, there was no escape from its language. The statute excepts actors, singers, lecturers, and artists only, and hence leaves no possible interpretation as regards clergymen, except that they are included in the interdicted classes. An effort is to be made to have the law amended, so as to include clergymen among the classes privileged to make agreements across the Atlantic.

The Delay in Getting the Electric Wires under ground in New York, involved no less than twenty-two serious fires in the city last year, not one of which, says the chief of the fire department, would have occurred if the law had been complied with. Beside this several lives have been lost by contact with wires broken or imperfectly insulated. In addition to this the firemen have been impeded in their efforts to extinguish fires in various parts of the city by the network of wires, which prevented the raising of the water-tower and the moving of the ladders. It is gratifying to learn that an opportunity has at last occurred for making the mayor explain his share of the responsibility. Coroner Levy is inquiring into the cause of death in a case directly attributable to the hanging wires, and he has subpenæd the mayor as a witness. It may be hoped that such questions will be put to him as will elicit the cause of his opposition to a project which directly concerns the safety of life and property in the city. Of the manifold evils from which the city has suffered under the rule of Mayor Hewitt, this at least should be removed.

A Royal Wedding took place in Berlin on May 24. Prince Henry, the second son of the Emperor of Germany, was married to Princess Irene, third daughter of the Grand Duke of Hesse and the late Princess Alice, of England. Thus bride and bridegroom are first cousins—both being grandchildren of Queen Victoria. Both Emperor Frederick and Dowager Empress Augusta were present during the ceremony, and the Prince of Wales represented the Queen of England. Thousands of people were assembled outside the castle at Charlottenburg, where the ceremony took place. When the aged General von Moltke arrived, he was enthusiastically greeted by the multitude. The Emperor, in the uniform of a grand marshal, walked in erect, with a firm gait and movement. He gazed calmly over the assembled company, smiling and bowing graciously. Approaching his mother, he bowed low and kissed her hand, and then seated himself beside the Empress. Altogether, it was an impressive and touching scene.

The Improvement in the Condition of the Emperor of Germany continued last week. He was able to take daily drives and to attend to official business. The Berlin correspondent of the New York *Herald*, who had an interview with Dr. Mackenzie, sends a cable despatch which shows, however, on how slight a tenure the valuable life of the Emperor depends, and how soon he may be succeeded by the young man whose accession to the throne is regarded in Europe as the signal for war. Dr. Mackenzie is reported as saying that the Emperor will soon go to Potsdam, and after about a fortnight's rest he will go to Homburg. "If he can go to Homburg, there is no reason why the patient may not live a month, three months or more, but if the corrosive sore should eat inward it would, of course, be fatal. But it is not doing so now. The Emperor's constitution and the absence of nervousness are favorable for recovery, but they are simply splendid for resistance against disease." Being asked if recovery were possible, the Dr. said: "Most certainly. I still maintain that recovery is within the limits of possibility."

The Relations of Germany and France have been strained by the report of a decree, affecting Alsace and Lorraine. The charge is made that Germans entering France have been subjected to annoyance, and that Frenchmen visiting Alsace and Lorraine, have been endeavoring to stir up disloyalty to Germany. The result has been the preparation of a decree which was issued on May 25. It requires that all Frenchmen going to Alsace-Lorraine be provided with passports issued by the German Embassy in Paris—after careful inquiry. This passport, which the traveller will have to show every time he may be asked to do so, must also bear the *visé* of the Governor of Alsace-Lorraine. The *North German Gazette* says that it is high time to make clear, in a manner admitting of no misunderstanding, that Alsace-Lorraine belongs entirely to Germany.

Anxiety About the Safety of Mr. H. M. Stanley was not allayed last week; not the slightest intelligence about him came to hand. This, however, gives some slight comfort, for had he been overwhelmed by a hostile attack or perished of starvation, news of the event could scarcely have failed to be sent. His importance is so clearly recognized, even among African savages, that such a circumstance would speedily have passed from tribe to tribe. Dr. Schweinfurth says there is no reason to be uneasy about Stanley's fate. He is probably waiting half way for Tippoo Tib's reinforcements and stores, without which it is useless to reach Wadelai. The government of the Congo State has received advices that Dr. Mangold, of Kiel, is about to start in search of Stanley.

The Centennial of the Presbyterian Church was held in Philadelphia on Thursday last. On May 24, 1788, one hundred years ago, the General Assembly of the Presbyterian Church of America was founded and instituted in the same city. The centennial anniversary of this event was celebrated with ceremonies, impressive and interesting, by the general assemblies of the two great divisions of the Church. The ceremonies were held in the Academy of Music and in Horticultural Hall, a building not unlike a Presbyterian church itself. The interiors of both these edifices were profusely decorated with flowers, shrubs and banners gay. During each meeting each auditorium was crowded, in spite of the continuous rain, and a large number of well known Presbyterian clergymen sat on the platform. Mrs. Cleveland was present among the audience.

The Methodist Episcopal General Conference completed on Thursday last the election of five bishops, which it was decided to add to the Episcopate. There was no diminution in the lobbying and log-rolling complained of during the earlier days of the Conference. The first two ballots were taken on May 22, but they were fruitless, the Conference having decided that two-thirds of the votes cast were necessary to a choice. On the third ballot two bishops were elected—*Dr. John H. Vincent* of Plainfield, N. J., and *Dr. James N. Fitzgerald*, of Newark, N. J. The votes were distributed among eighty-one candidates. The fourth ballot had no decisive result, but on the fifth *Dr. I. W. Joyce* of Cincinnati was elected. Eight more ballots were taken without result, but on the fourteenth *Dr. J. P. Newman* of Washington, D. C., was chosen. *Dr. D. A. Goodsell*, of the New York East Conference, was elected on the sixteenth ballot. On Friday *Dr. J. M. Thoburn* of Calcutta was made a missionary bishop. The most momentous change effected by the conference was made on Wednesday, when it was decided to change the maximum term of pastorate from three to five years.

A Weird Celestial Phenomenon was Witnessed at Findlay, O., on May 21. A despatch from that city says that about eleven o'clock that night a light which had been visible all the evening in the northern skies suddenly concentrated in the formation of a clear and vivid representation of a hand of giant proportions, through which pulses of flame, red as blood, throbbed and bounded as in human arteries, and then fell back and were swallowed up in the darkness below. The hand reached from the horizon, through which it seemed to be thrust, half way up the sky, the wrist and fingers being particularly well defined, and perfect in form and proportion, the index finger pointing to the city. For more than an hour this impressive and mysterious exhibition was visible, and then slowly the hand began to fade away and become shadowy. The fire behind the scene appeared to go down and gradually die out; and finally, soon after midnight, the sky resumed its normal appearance. The despatch adds that several notoriously wicked persons were much alarmed by the spectacle Doubtless the phenomenon can be explained from natural causes, but a day is coming in which there will be an appearance in the sky that every one will recognize as supernatural, and all impenitant sinners will see with well-grounded alarm. (Rev. 1 : 7).

A Physician's Twenty-four Hours' Tramp through rain and storm was graphically described by himself on the witness-stand in the course of a trial in New York last week. He stated that he prescribed for a patient, but, inadvertently wrote, "Squills's Solution," instead of "Squills's Mixture," in a prescription. He knew that if the man took two teaspoonfuls of the solution, as directed, he would fall asleep and die, as it was a strong dose of opium. He, therefore, went immediately to the patient's house, accompanied by another practitioner. But they were too late—the patient had that minute swallowed the dose. He was dizzy and sleepy already; the drug was doing its deadly work. "I knew," said the physician, "that there was a human life at stake, and I gave no thought to the awful storm that was raging that night. The man must be kept walking, or die. The hours sped on, and the storm increased in fury, and still we three plodded on through the rain. We had to drag the man along. It was a heavy burden, and there was danger of our becoming exhausted. Occasionally, as a brief respite, we would jump on to a car, but always on the front platform, so that the rain could beat in the face of our involuntary companion. We took him into the basement of the New York Hospital, in Fifteenth Street, and gave him some new remedies. In a few minutes we were out in the storm again, and the walk was continued all night, and till the evening of the next day, by which time the man was out of danger." It is a pity that the same persistence and heroic treatment cannot be applied to those who, having drunk of the cup of sin, are in danger of sinking into the spiritual sleep of callousness. (Eph. 5 : 14.)

A Child Sleeping with a Bear is an Extraordinary incident reported from Kingston, New York. A press despatch from that city, states that on May 9, a little girl three years old, the daughter of a farmer of Boiceville in the Catskill mountains wandered away from home. She was missed toward evening, and a search was commenced for her which continued all night. No trace of her could be found, and the parents were distracted with grief. They never expected to see her alive again, for it seemed impossible that so small a child could live through the night in the woods. On Thursday morning, however, to their intense delight, the child was found alive and well, in a ravine between two mountains, two miles away from home. She gave a rational account of her wanderings, but when her father asked her how she spent the night and if she was not dreadfully cold, the child said that she saw a big bear and she crept close up to it and its fur kept her warm all night. Of course the story was not believed, but as the child is singularly truthful, and under close questioning adheres consistently to her story, it is now thought that she did really sleep with the bear, who for some reason refrained from hurting her. In these days it is natural to doubt the truth of the child's story, because the nature of bears is to kill and devour, but the time is not many years distant when such a story will cease to be improbable, for under the millennial reign of Christ upon earth, the nature of the brute creation as well as human nature will be changed. (Isa. 65 : 25.)

* **The Inoculation of a Man for Leprosy is an** experiment described by Mr. John M. Putnam, the United States Consul General to Hawaii, in a despatch to the Department of State, received last week. Mr. Putnam makes the alarming statement that when a white man of means is stricken with leprosy, in the Sandwich Islands, he emigrates to the United States, to escape imprisonment on the Island of Death. Mr. Putnam also assures the Government that, in spite of all that has been said to the contrary, the malady is certainly contagious, and, in proof, cites a remarkable experiment. He states that a native was condemned to death in Hawaii for the crime of murder. His sentence, however, was commuted to imprisonment for life on condition that he submitted to leprous inoculation. The experiment was made by a German specialist, who removed a tubercle from a man in an advanced stage of leprosy, and inserted it in an incision in the arm of the condemned man. The tubercle adhered, and now forms a hard purple cicatrix sensitive to the touch, being thoroughly incorporated in his system. No evidence of the effect of the virus was seen for some time, but now symptoms have appeared which satisfy all the doctors that the man is suffering from leprosy, and that the disease is surely contagious. It may be hoped the knowledge thus gained, at the cost of a life, will save the lives of some who might otherwise have contracted the disease. Those who are delivered from the "leprosy of sin," likewise owe their rescue to the sacrifice of a life, but that was not a life already forfeited and risked from selfish motives. Christ voluntarily suffered and died for the joy of saving a world (Heb. 12 : 2).

A Man Wanting to be Imprisoned, Made an ineffectual endeavor to get arrested, on May 8, at Rochester, N. Y. About four years ago a boathouse-keeper at Black Rock, Buffalo, was convicted of smuggling goods from Canada, and sentenced to a year's imprisonment. While being taken to the penitentiary, he escaped, and reached Canada in safety. Finally he determined to return, and being able now to obtain legal assistance, which he did not have at his trial, he decided to surrender himself, and then, by a writ of habeas corpus, secure a new trial. He presented himself at the penitentiary on Tuesday of last week, when, to his surprise, the authorities refused to admit him. It had been discovered since his flight that his trial was illegal, and to imprison him at this time might involve an action for damages. The man, however, did not wish to lie under the stigma of the sentence, and, therefore, applied to the marshal for an arrest. The marshal, however, like the prison-wardens, refused to arrest him, and an application was then made to the United States Court, equally without success. The man is, therefore, free, though under sentence. It is a curious situation, but as the sentence is never likely to be executed, the man will doubtless not trouble himself further about it. That unconcern is displayed by sinners against God who are also under sentence, but, unlike that man, are in constant danger of having it executed, as it surely will sooner or later, unless they avail themselves of the Atonement. (Eccles. 8 : 11.)

BRIEF NOTES.

The Chinese Government is about to erect monuments to General Gordon on the scenes of his victories over the Taiping rebels.

Dr. Washington Gladden has been appointed to represent Ohio Congregationalists at the World's Missionary Conference in London, in June.

Since the commencement of Dr. George F. Pentecost's labors in Schenectady, N. Y., 383 additions have been made to the membership of six churches in the city.

The New York State Sunday-School Association will hold its thirty-third annual Convention in the city of Rochester, commencing Tuesday morning, June 12.

The Rev. B. Fay Mills has been holding services in the Central Congregational Church, Chelsea, Mass. All the evangelical churches united in the meetings. The church, which holds twelve hundred persons, has been crowded every day.

Mayor Robinson, of Gloucester, Mass., having refused to sign more liquor licenses, and the Supreme Court having decided that he is legally bound to sign such as are granted by the Aldermen, declares that he will resign his office rather than sign them.

Rev. Sidney G. Law, Chaplain of the Tombs prison, New York, had 32,767 prisoners under his spiritual oversight last year. He preaches in the prison every Sunday from the cross gallery, where he can be heard in all the cells, and visits the prisoners during the week. Several remarkable conversions have taken place.

The sad news has reached London that Bishop Parker died on the 26th of March, of sickness, in the Unyoro country, to the southeast of the Albert Nyanza. Bishop Parker was the successor of the lamented Bishop Hannington, who was put to death by the orders of the King of Uganda.

Mr. John Wanamaker, of Philadelphia, who has adopted the system of sharing his profits with his employees, has informed them that, in addition to $59,000 already distributed in monthly dividends as a per centage on the sales, a further sum of $50,000 was to be divided among those who had been with the firm for seven years.

The meeting conducted by D. L. W. Munhall, in St. Paul, Minn., have been much blessed. A St. Paul pastor says it is the most wonderful movement he has ever witnessed there or elsewhere. The night meetings in the Market Hall have been full of interest and power. Great crowds have been present, and the inquiry room has been full at each service. At one service upward of one hundred and fifty persons made a profession of faith.

Canvassers Wanted to Sell, from House to House, THE CHRISTIAN HERALD. Any man, woman or youth may easily add to their income every week by selling the paper in their spare hours in their own neighborhood. One man has sold one hundred copies on a Saturday. For terms address Manager of CHRISTIAN HERALD, 63 Bible House, New York

THE INVITATIONS TO THE WEDDING.

A New Sermon by Pastor C. H. Spurgeon.

"The Wedding was furnished with guests." Matt. 22: 10.

The First Invitations—Disloyalty Abroad—I. It Seemed as if None Would Come—Various Characters Invited—Curt Refusals—Levity of Some—Violence of Others—II. A Mournful Prospect—The King Dishonored—The King's Son Grieved—The Bride Disappointed—III. The Catastrophe Prevented—By a Fuller Invitation—More Publicly—Power with the Messengers—IV. The Feast a Success—A Ragged Regiment—Had to Wear the King's Livery—Washing Also Provided.

OUR discourse will follow the lines of the parable. A king desired to honor his son right royally. He loved his son well, for he deserved richly of him; and therefore, as the most fitting time had come, he resolved to honor him. His son was about to take to himself a spouse; should not his marriage, which is a great event in life, be celebrated with honor? The father determined to honor his son on the joyful occasion by inviting a large number of guests to a sumptuous banquet. Not by the infliction of pain, or the pressure of taxation, but by liberality and festivity, would the king honor the Crown Prince. It should be

An Extraordinary Feast.

Surely, it would be the simplest thing in the world to gather together a grateful company of guest. One would expect a competition for admission; everybody in the royal domain would eagerly ask for an invitation. But it fell out otherwise; there was a disloyal feeling abroad, and it now expressed itself; those who were bidden would not come, and means had to be used to secure the result spoken of in the text, so that "the wedding was furnished with guests."

The parable is plain. The great Father delights to honor Jesus, His Only-begotten Son. The Father loves the Son, with whom He is one. The Son has deserved well at the Father's hands, for He has been "obedient unto death, even the death of the cross." It is the Father's aim in the work of grace to glorify His Son, who, as God and man in one nature, is the channel of grace to fallen men. He proposes to do this now that the Lord Jesus takes His church into marriage union with Himself.

One would have thought that every man hearing that manhood was thus to be honored by union with Godhead would flock towards the marriage-feast. It would have seemed certain that all would desire to know this heavenly mystery, and as soon as they knew it would press forward to be partakers in its bliss. Alas! this is not the case; and this morning my business is to tell you the story of how the purpose of divine love appeared in peril, but how, in the end, it is accomplished; and, according to the language of the text, "the wedding was furnished with guests."

I. Our first point is, that it

Seemed as if None Would Come.

The wedding-feast was prepared: oxen and fatlings were killed, all things were ready; but where were the guests? Those first invited, and naturally expected, would not come. Previons notice had been given them of the festival, and afterwards a summons had been sent to say that the hour was come; but, instead of joyfully responding, they would not come. These were, first of all, the Jews, to whom the gospel had been given by the law and the prophets long beforehand. 'He came unto His own, but His own received Him not." Israel was not gathered: few out of the chosen nation recognized the Messiah. He came with a feast of mercy for them, but they would have none of it. He called, and they refused.

To-day this same class will be found among the children of godly parents; dedicated from their birth, prayed for by loving piety, listening to the gospel from the childhood, and yet unsaved. We look for these to come to Jesus. We naturally hope that they will feast upon the provisions of grace, and like their parents will rejoice in Christ Jesus; but, alas! how often it is the case they will not come! Dear hearers, some of you are not privileged with godly parents, but you have been for many years willing listeners to the Word of life and yet you do not accept Christ Jesus as yours, nor accept the provisions of his grace. You do not joy with Him in His union, with His chosen, for you do not love Him. How sad is this! Well may the dispirited preacher mourn, and fear in his heart that the great festival of love will prove a failure! If such as you are will not come, how will the wedding be furnished with guests?

The Invitation Pressed.

The outlook grew worse still when they came not though they were reasoned with. When they would not come, the king sent other servants to bring them to a better mind; and this was the form of his reasoning: "Behold, I have prepared my dinner; my oxen and my fatlings are killed, and all things are ready: come unto the marriage." No kinder argument could have been used: there was an appeal to all that was noble in them, and had they been worthy they would have come at once. Still they made light of it. You have been invited to Jesus many a time; tearful earnestness has pleaded with you, and yet men of God have had to return to their Master, saying, "Who hath believed our report?" it becomes a sorrowful business, and our anxious fears cannot see how the wedding will be furnished with guests.

The case looks darker still when we notice that, though reasoned with by new messengers, they did not come. It it said, "He sent forth other servants." I tell you from my very soul that, if my Lord will only bring you to the banquet of His grace, I mind not who shall be the successful messenger. If you will not believe in the Lord Jesus Christ unto eternal life through what I have to say, may the Lord remove me, and send some one else, to whom He will give power by His grace to reach your hearts. "He sent other servants." A preacher may be too rhetorical: let a plain-speaking person be tried. He may be too weighty: let another come with parable and anecdote. Alas! with some of you the thing wanted is not a new voice, but a new heart. You would listen no better to a new messenger than to the old one. If you look at

The Various Characters

who would not come, you will see more and more cause for sorrow. Of some we simply read that "they would not come." They made no excuses or apologies, but curtly said they would not come. There was an end of the matter. Many dismiss the gospel at once; they are not to be reasoned with: they do not want it, and will not have it. A large class of the community have heard of the way of salvation, but they care nothing for it. It is not with them want of information, but want of inclination. They have neither mind nor will for heavenly things.

A second class made light of it. They were indifferent to royal honors and duties. They were taken up with the care of what they had in possession, and went their way, each man to his farm, saying, "I have worked hard to get my farm, and I cannot afford to let it lie idle." Another was taken up with the care of getting an estate, and went to his merchandise, saying, "I have nobody to keep my shop. I must mind the main chance. If you do not look alive, everybody will run over you. I must attend to my buying and selling." The worldly-wise make up a very numerous class. The rich man cannot be religious, his position in society prevents; the poor man cannot mind the things of God, he is worn out by earning his daily bread. Thus they all make excuse. Lord, when so many are unwilling, and so many more are occupied with other things, how shall the wedding be furnished with guests?

A third class were violently opposed: they would not be bothered, they had no patience with religious cant; they "took His servants and entreated them spitefully, and slew them." These are not so numerous as the others; but yet they are found among us. Sceptics, swearers, revilers of godliness, and "modern thought" men: these revile the cross, and are ferocious against the gospel. When we see these raging and raving, we are apt to ask very mournfully—How can the wedding be furnished with guests?

II. Secondly, it was

A Mournful Prospect.

Imagine that there had been no guests at the wedding feast: what then? First it would have been greatly to the king's dishonor. The Crown Prince is married, and nobody comes to the wedding! The feast is free, costly, plentiful, but nobody will come to it. What an insult! The banqueting-hall is lighted, and the minstrels are in their place, but no eyes or ears are charmed. What a wretched spectacle! Empty halls, unfurnished benches, meat untasted carried out to the dogs! History does not record a more deliberate and unmistakable insult. Let me translate the parable. If no souls are saved, if the great plan of redemption does not save, what a farce the whole business will be! What a dishonor to the name of the great God! Look at the supposition, that you may see the impossibility of it.

In the next place, suppose none had come to the wedding feast; then the king's son would have been grieved. His wedding, and nobody there! If it were your own, perhaps you could put up with it; for you do not stand in so public a position as the king's son, and you have not provided so vast a banquet. But the king's son! Only imagine that

It is His Wedding-Day,

and the servants are mustered in the hall, but not a single guest arrives. He has no one to congratulate him upon the happy day, no one to wish him well, no one to welcome the bride. Now, the same is true of our Lord Jesus Christ: Look at the dreadful supposition, and think whether it can be. I am sure, as you gaze upon it, you will say "Impossible! A bleeding Saviour cannot die in vain.

If no guests had arrived, how disappointed would the Bride have been! She, too, would have had to share in the failure of the day. Her bridal would have been remembered with no pleasure. She would have been happy in the bridegroom, but also unhappy because of the unkindness shown to him. In vain her rich apparel, and her costly ornaments, for there are no eyes to gaze upon them. If souls are not saved the church misses her greatest joy. But if sinners are not saved, if the preaching of the gospel is in vain, if they will not come to Christ, then are saints full of heaviness, and the church cries out, "Hast thou forgotten to be gracious?"

Would it not have meant, also, the enemy's triumph? The king's foes would have heard of it, and laughed him to scorn. At a royal wedding he could not command guests! How they would scoff at his wasted provision! "Ha, ha! Ha, ha!" The story would have been told on every ale-bench. The sons of Belial would make rare mirth of it. The King, the Prince, the Bride, would all have been ridiculed, because of a wedding in empty halls, a feast with phantom guests! I do not believe that God intends to let Satan triumph in this way. I cannot imagine that He will allow the powers of darkness thus to open their wicked mouths against Him.

III. Let us go a step further and notice this

Catastrophe Graciously Prevented.

"The wedding was furnished with guests." We are very much in the same case to-day as the servants were in when the invited ones would not come. We preach and teach the gospel, but we have to complain that so many will not come to the banquet of grace. God gives us many souls, but not so many as we desire. We are eager for many more, and we begin to be afraid lest, after all, God should not be glorified as we wish that He should be. In the parable an unfurnished banquet was prevented, and so it will be in the reality. How was the calamity averted?

It was prevented, first, by a fuller invitation. At first the heralds only called those who had been previously bidden, a sort of aristocracy of hopeful persons. As these would not come, we read, "Go ye therefore into the highways, and as many as ye shall find, bid to the marriage." They went out,

Not to a Select Band,

but to all whom they might find. It is a grand thing when we get a clearer idea of what the gospel really is. The more evangelical our notions become, so that we are prepared to preach the gospel to every creature under heaven, and to say, "He that believeth and is baptized shall be saved," the more we may hope for large success.

Again, the invitation was now given more publicly. They had simply gone to the houses of the invited guests, and said, "All things are ready: come." But now the servants go to the chief places of concourse; and they cried aloud, and spare not among the crowds of men. One has gone to the market-cross; another is preaching where four ways meet. Hark to the voice of one upon the village green, and to the songs of others as they traverse the back slum! You cannot now go along a street without hearing the news of the great wedding feast. Many will be brought in when many are eager to bring them in. It came to pass that the king's message was more widely made known, and thus "the wedding was furnished with guests."

Again, the calamity of a wedding without guests was prevented by a certain secret power which went with the messengers. We read that they "gathered together all, as many as they found, both bad and good." They did not merely invite them, but they gathered them in. An influence went with the words of those servants which drew the people together; they could not wish to stay away; they came gladly. Beloved, all the hope of our ministry lies in the Spirit of God operating upon the spirits of men. If the Holy Ghost be with us we shall see thousands flocking to Jesus.

IV. I close by noticing that in the end

The Feast was a Success.

"The wedding was furnished with guests." Guests are a part of the furniture of a wedding feast. You may pile on your gold and silver plate, hang up your banners, load your tables, and sound your music; but if you have no guests the feast is a failure. The feast was more of a success than it would have been had there been no opposition. The persons who came to the wedding were more grateful than the first invited might have been if they had come. The richer sort had a good dinner every day. But these poor beggars picked off the streets, they had not tasted meat for months. Their half-starved bodies welcomed the fatlings. How glad they were! I warrant they were thankful for such a feast. They said it was an ill wind that blew nobody any good; because their betters have refused to come, there was now room for them. When the Lord saves great sinners, such as you and me, He wins warm hearts for Himself. When the Lord saves unlikely ones, He gets unusual thankfulness. When He brings in the drunkard and the profane, the unclean and the hardened, and makes them pure and holy, and puts them among the children, what gratitude He gets! If some of you moralists get saved—and God grant you may!—you will never prize the precious blood so much as those who are washed by it from foulest stains.

The joy that day was much more expressed than it would have been had others come. Those ladies and gentlemen who were first invited, if they had come to the wedding, would have seated themselves there in a very stiff and proper manner. Dear me, what a fine thing propriety is! And yet, what a dead thing it is! One said to me the other day, "I have gone to my place of worship for many years, and nobody ever did speak to me that I know of, and nobody ever will; for we are all too respectable to know one another." You know the dignified style of self-satisfied people. Among such there is no cordiality, no freshness, no sweet naturalness. Did you ever attend a breakfast or dinner of beggars? Did you ever see a company of very hungry people feeding to their heart's content? The dull monotony of respectability knows no joy like that which comes to poverty when it feasts to the full at the table of bounty. Let the Pharisee and the moralist refuse the gospel: there are those about who, in accepting it, will do it greater honor than their dull souls could ever render it. Thus the wedding was furnished with guests, who expressed their joy enthusiastically.

How the provisions were relished! It does one good to see a hungry man eat his food. He does not act the critic, and cavil at this expression and that. He is too sharp-set to be particular about the dishes and the carving. We marvel sometimes at the capacity of hungry men; there is no end to it; and it is the same with spiritual as well as natural hunger. The king himself that day was gladdened, as he saw what a gallant company of trenchermen they were, and how there was

No Niggling, Nor Finding Fault,

but only unbroken enjoyment and gratitude. The choicest kind of guests had been collected if the object was to give joy. Ah dear friends! if you have a deep sense of sin, you will greatly love free grace and undying love. This is the lack of certain gentlemen who are always finding fault with the gospel: they never knew their own state by nature and by practice, and therefore do not prize salvation.

Certainly, the occasion became more famous than it would otherwise have been. If the feast had gone on as usual it would have been only one among many such things; but now this royal banquet was the only one of its kind, unique, unparalleled. To gather in poor men off the streets, laboring men and idle men, bad men and good men, to the wedding of the Crown Prince—this was a new thing under the sun. Everybody talked of it. There were songs made about it, and these were sung in the king's honor where none honored kings before. To many it seemed like a story out of the Arabian Nights. It did not read like a piece of common history at all, but

Like a Fairy Tale

of the age of gold. Dear friends, when the Lord saved some of us by His grace, it was no common event. When He brought us great sinners to His feet, and washed us, and clothed us, and fed us, and made us His own, it was a wonder to be talked of for ever and ever. We will never leave off praising His name throughout eternity. That which looked as though it would defame the King turned out to His honor, and "the wedding was furnished with guests."

One thing more: the king's liberality was all the better seen. If those who were first bidden had put in an appearance, they would have come arrayed in their own scarlet and fine linen. Now these fine clothes would have been more for the glory of those who came in them, than for the honor of the King. There was nothing of this among those who were gathered from the highways.

They Were in Sorry Gear.

It was difficult, perhaps, in some cases, to tell which was the original stuff of their garments, so patched and mended were they. Anyhow, they were *a ragged regiment;* and what was the consequence? Why, then they must all be dressed in the Prince's own livery, and all the glory of their apparel must be unto Him. Everyone that came in to the feast was invited to put on the king's wedding garments. It was a grand sight to see so many all in one royal livery; every guest wearing the uniform of mercy. So is it with us poor sinners.

How I wish that I could gather in many this morning, both bad and good! I mean by good those who are comparatively so as to their moral conduct. You are bidden to come to the wedding-feast of love. But even if you are bad, and obliged to own that you are so, I am equally anxious to gather you in to the feast. Do you ask me: What are we to do? What were these persons to do? To come just as they were, and freely receive what the king had freely provided. You are to bring nothing. Still, everybody must go home and wash, must he not? No, the washing and the clothing shall all be done for you at the King's palace. Come as you are. "But what do you mean by coming?" We mean trusting: trust your soul with Jesus Christ, and He will save it. Trust Him, and you shall know that He died in your room, place, and stead, so that, believing in Him, you shall not perish, but have everlasting life. May the Holy Spirit lead you to believe in Jesus, that is, trust Him. Amen and Amen.

GEMS FROM NEW BOOKS.

AN ENCOUNTER WITH A MAD BULL.*

AN incident connected with my experience when I was a little boy may come in to illustrate the goodness of God. I was born in Liverpool, England. One day when I was about six years old, as I was going home from school, there was quite an excitement in the street. It happened that a bull had been taken into a slaughter-house in that neighborhood to be killed. They had fastened a rope around his horns in the usual way. The rope was then put through an iron ring in the floor of the slaughter-house, the bull's head was drawn down to the floor, and a man standing by hit it a heavy blow with an axe which he held in his hands. It generally happened that the blow thus given would cause the animal to fall to the ground, where he would be slaughtered. But in this case it was not so. The blow of the axe, instead of killing the bull, or knocking him down, only made him angry. He gave a violent jerk, which broke the rope that bound him, and ran off into the street. Then he went racing down the street as fast as he could go, swinging his tail about, and bellowing as loud as he could. This made a great excitement. I remembered to have seen men go out into the middle of the street, when a horse was running away, and stop him by swinging their arms. Then I thought I would try to stop the bull in the same way. So I went into the middle of the street when the bull was coming near, and tried to stop him by swinging around my arms, but the bull never minded me at all. He came bellowing on. When he got quite near I turned and ran away from him. After running a few steps, I looked around to see how near he was to me. But just as my head was turned toward him, he struck me on the forehead with one of his horns. This knocked me down to the ground. Then he took hold of my jacket and tore it off and went on his way. The horn struck my forehead about an inch above my left eye. If it had struck but a little lower it would have gone through the eye, into the brain and would have killed me. The mark of that wound is here on my forehead now, and has been there ever since. When in shaving, or brushing my hair, I stand before the mirror and see that mark, it always makes me think of the goodness of God in preserving my life when I was a little boy.

A Little Christian's Strike.

Richard, (Dr. Newton) when a boy was employed in his father's store and he was required to keep the store open on Sunday mornings. This was his first struggle with himself. He made it a matter of prayer for some time—and the opening of the shutters on the Lord's day morning for the neighbors to come and get their provisions, tried him sorely. At last his position was taken. One Saturday evening he kindly and gently, but firmly, told his father that he could no longer work upon the Sabbath, and that if his father insisted upon his doing so, he would be compelled to leave his store. The father flew into a violent rage, and told his son that if he refused to do as he was bid he should leave his home. A week later, when Saturday night came round, after the

* From "The Heath in the Wilderness," with Biographical Reminiscences by the late Rev. Richard Newton, D.D., Rector of St. Paul's Church, of Philadelphia. The twenty sermons which make up this volume are in Dr. Newton's rich and beautiful style, full of gospel truth. 374 Pages; Price $1.25. Published by *Robert Carter and Brothers* 530 Broadway, New York.

Scene in Merchant Street, Mandalay, Burmah.

time of closing up, Richard, with a few clothes in his bag, without any formal adieu, left his father's house and went to a neighbor's to pass the coming Sunday.

His father banished him from home on this proof of his determination not to conform to the habit of Sunday store-keeping. By the help and advice of his friends, the young aspirant to the ministry went to the manual labor-school, at Wilmington, Delaware, then under the charge of the Rev. Mr. Clemson. One class-mate, whom the affectionate letters of that period termed "dear Tommy," still survives in the person of the Rev. Thomas F. Fales, of Waltham, Mass. It was a hard school this of the manual labor, for the fare was scant and the work heavy. Some of the students objected to driving home the cows from the pasture lot, as beneath their dignity; but not so with this zealous boy. Beside, he had to pass the door of his distant relatives, the Greatorex family, in their quiet old mansion on the Brandywine; and even then there was one daughter whose heart went out for the ruddy faced boy, who to earn his way to the ministry was not ashamed to be seen driving home the teacher's cows. It is ever thus that we are helped by unconscious ministries over the hard places of life, when we are in the path of duty; and in that path the pity which is akin to love grew into the sacred relationship of husband and wife.

A PREACHER THREATENED.

IN the life of the late Rev. Henry Ward Beecher, published by Charles L. Webster & Co., the following incident, which occurred during Mr. Beecher's residence in Indianapolis, is related:

A man in the City Hotel, not a little feared because of his brutality, had done something more brutal than usual, and, the facts coming to Mr. Beecher's knowledge, in his sermon on the following Sunday, he expressed in no gentle terms his abhorrence of the act, and in very strong language rebuked the man. Many of his hearers were alarmed lest the man would, when he heard of the sermon, do Mr. Beecher some injury. Of course, before the day was over, the substance of the sermon had been reported throughout the town, and did not fail to reach the man's ears.

On Monday morning Mr. Beecher went to the post-office immediately after breakfast, and must go right by the hotel around which this man would most likely be hanging. He got his mail and turned to go home. As he passed the hotel there were several men standing by, evidently waiting for some development. At that moment the man came down the steps with a pistol in his hand.

"Did you say thus and thus in your sermon yesterday?"

"I did."

"Did you intend those remarks for me or meaning me?"

"I most certainly did."

"Then take it back, right here, or I will shoot you on the spot."

"Shoot away," was the reply, as looking the ruffian sternly in the face, Mr. Beechsr calmly, with deliberate step, walked past the man. With pointed pistol and fierce oaths, the man followed for a few paces, when, baffled by the imperturbable coolness of his opponent, he slunk away down a side street, ashamed to return to the hotel.

STREET SCENE IN MANDALAY.

(See Illustration.)

THE business street of Mandalay, the capital of Burmah, is Merchant Street, a typical block of which, as sketched by a recent visitor, is represented in the illustration on this page. While retaining the style of business, and the customs of the country, it is evident from the inscriptions on the signs that the store-keepers are anxious to cultivate the business of the English officers and soldiers now in Burmah, who doubtless have more money to spend than the natives. The curious vehicle, however, drawn in the foreground, is an indication that the Burmese ladies also make their purchases there. The vehicle is *a private carriage*, such as is used by the highest aristocracy of Burmah. They are commonly drawn by oxen, as represented in the illustration. The coachman, who does not appear to entail a heavy expenditure on his employers in the matter of livery, is very skilful in getting good speed and a tolerably level gait from his steeds.

The principal trade of Mandalay has now fallen into the hands of the Chinese, who keep stores of all kinds, as well as run laundries and mechanical shops. Their enterprise, energy, and industry make them formidable rivals to the Burmese, who are lazy, as a rule, and not particularly civil or obliging to their customers. The Chinese have made a permanent settlement in the country, and when they have made a fortune do not return to China, as do their countrymen who emigrate to other lands, but marry a Burmese lady, and set up their country houses in Burmah. Their matrimonial proposals find favor with the Burmese girls, who prefer them as husbands to their own countrymen.

Beside falling behind in business competition, the Burmese have suffered from the drinking habit, which has become more prevalent since the English occupation of the country. The English government has adopted in Burmah the system of licensing, which has been found financially successful in India. They sell to some contractor the exclusive right of liquor dealing over a defined section, and he is allowed to open as many drinking booths as he chooses. It was introduced in India in 1876, and the revenue increased under the system from three million dollars to five millions. The result, however, was less beneficial to the morals of the natives than to the government treasury. The lower classes degenerated into sots and loafers, and earnest protests were evoked from the more intelligent classes. It is astounding that the English government, having witnessed the result of the system in India, should have introduced it into Burmah. An effort is now being made by the temperance men in Parliament to bring them to account and compel a reformation.

AN INJURED WIFE'S RESOLVE.

(See Illustration on page 349.)

ON the upper floor of a house of the better class a lady was busily engaged in packing a few trunks which stood open around her. Evidently she was not preparing for a pleasure excursion, for her face was tearful, and several times in the course of her work she sat down to vent her grief in weeping. It was sad to see one so young and beautiful in such bitter sorrow, but there was no one there to see, and she was glad of that. The pauses in her occupation did not change her plans, for when tears had relieved her overburdened heart she resumed her work with new energy. She was despoiling the rooms of their prettiest adornments. There were articles there for masculine use, but those she left in their places; it was the lighter objects which accompany a lady's sojourn in a home that she was gathering together and depositing in the trunks. It was sorrowful work and the tears would come, blinding her eyes so that she could scarcely see what she was doing but she persevered until all was done and the trunks locked and addressed. Then sitting down and looking around the room, so changed, she burst into a fresh torrent of weeping.

Mrs. Temple was leaving the home which, only three years before, she had entered as a happy bride. She was going back to her fath er's house, sick at heart, humiliated, despairing. The gentle, affectionate disposition, which her face indicated, must have been sorely tried before a step so decisive could have been possible to her. If her husband had been dead, the despair in her heart would not have been so crushing as it was, as she realized that he was only dead to honor and to character. The man himself was living; it was her idea of him as a noble, honorable man that was dead. A few months after their marriage he had been brought home intoxicated from some convivial gathering, and had horrified her and frightened her by his strange talk and manner. The next day he begged her to forgive him, and promised that it should never occur again. But the promise was soon broken, and it became a frequent occurrence. The past two years had been a constant succession of miseries and humiliations. Time and again her husband had vowed to break with his set, and abstain from liquor, but he failed, She had borne with him patiently, had forgiven him again and again, and encouraged him in his efforts to reform, but patience was exhausted now. One outrage had filled up the cup of bitterness which he had compelled her to drink. He had entertained a party of his friends in his own home—having faithfully promised his wife that there should be no excess. This promise he, as a host, could not keep. The party grew hilarious, and scenes of tipsy foolery had occurred. Finally, Mrs. Temple had been insulted by one of the guests, and her husband had been too incapable himself to protect her. Then she determined to go to her father; and on telling her husband the next morning of her resolve, he, in the surly mood which unfailingly followed a debauch, bade her go her way. That accounted for the packing, the tears, and the despair.

An Injured Wife's Magnanimity.

Only a few more minutes remained for her to spend beneath her husband's roof, when she heard a ring at the bell, and the servant came to inform her that the Rev. Herbert Vaughan was below, desiring to speak to her. She would gladly have excused herself, but Mr. Vaughan was an old friend, and at any rate she would like to wish him farewell before leaving.

"I have come from your husband, Mrs. Temple," he said. "I want you to forgive him once more. He has told me of all that has occurred, and begged me to plead with you for pardon."

"If he has really told you all," Mrs. Temple answered, "I wonder that you should have come."

"It was my duty in the circumstances, and I sincerely believed that I should be promoting your own happiness in gaining your consent."

"It is too late, now," said Mrs. Temple shaking her head. "I have determined to go back to my father; my husband knows of it, and in a short time I shall be on my way. Nothing now could change my resolution. I have been deceived too many times already."

"If you were sure that your husband had really reformed, had become a new creature in Christ, and was endued with God's strength to resist temptation in the future, I think I know enough of your nature to say that you would not be obdurate."

"Ah, Mr. Vaughan, if I knew that," said Mrs. Temple, "I should not wish to go. I should have hope then; but I never expect to hear that now."

"I solemnly assure you, Mrs. Temple, that I have the happiness to be the bearer of that good news," said the clergyman. "I am convinced from a pretty extensive experience that your husband is really converted. I recognize unmistakable signs of it, and you know what the grace of God can do."

The look of joyful intentness in Mrs. Temple's face as she strove to realize the good news was almost painful to witness, revealing as it did the despair from which she was slowly emerging. The clergyman rose and extended his hand. "Is it really true?" the poor wife asked. "Where is he? Will you not take me to him?"

"I will send him to you, Mrs. Temple," was the answer. "He is yearning to come to you; he will be here in less than an hour, and I venture to predict that your meeting will be the beginning of a new union between you, that will no more be marred by your husband's faults."

And Mr. Vaughan's prediction was fulfilled.

THE EPOCHS OF A LIFE.

A NEW SERIAL STORY.

By Rev. L. S. Keyser.

Author of "The Way Out," etc.

(*Continued from page 334.*)

SAPPING THE FOUNDATIONS.

IT was, as George quickly perceived, not so easy as he had expected to get Hadley to share his admiration for the infidel lecturer. Bold, blasphemous utterances revolted him, being repugnant alike to his spirit and training. Intellectual conceit, the longing for mental independence, and the confidence that young men so often cherish in their own penetration and logical acumen, were Hadley's weak points, and by these he was most easily moved. Therefore, when Hadley denounced the infidel's utterance as sacrilegious, George rejoined:

"It did sound terrible; but the question is not one of sentiment, but of fact."

"I must admit," said Hadley, "that I have often been puzzled by the supernatural occurrences recorded in the Bible; but I never realized the—the difficulty of believing in them until now. Can it be that we have been clinging to a delusion all our lives? It is a fact that we never see any thing in nature or human experience corresponding to the miraculous healing of lepers or the opening of the eyes of the blind, and other prodigies of which we read in the Bible."

"Why, no; common sense teaches us that the laws of nature are immutably fixed. Of course, every superstition has been supported and disseminated by means of pretended miraculous wonders, and Christianity seems to be no exception to the rule. But, to continue; the lecturer called our attention to the morality of the Scriptures, especially of the Old Testament. He spoke of Abraham's inhumanity in turning Hagar and her babe into the desert, of Jacob's chicanery, of David's licentiousness and wife-stealing; and yet these men, he said, were the objects of God's special favoritism. He also spoke of the gross narratives in certain parts of the Bible, which he said he would not dare to read before a refined audience, which no preacher ever reads before his congregation, which are not fit to be read in the family circle or even in the closest privacy. The polygamy of the patriarchs of Bible times was also made the object of the most caustic derision by the lecturer. They were magnificent specimens of the *genus homo* to hold up as paragons of perfection for our imitation. 'No wonder,' he cried, 'that our country is cursed with Mormonism and Oneida Communities, priest-ridden as it is and dominated by the teachings of such a Book!'"

The cold drops of perspiration stood on Hadley's forehead as he listened. "I have often wondered," he said "that those passages are contained in the Bible. To be sure, the evil deeds of good men are held up to reprobation, and we are told how Jacob and David and the others suffered for them. Still, I wonder these things were not suppressed. They do harm, But you do not think that it is true that our national immorality can be traced to the Bible.

"I am afraid it is. I do not believe that the speaker exaggerated. At the risk of wearying you," George continued, "I must call your attention to another well-taken point of the lecture. The speaker maintained that Christians are kept down in the thralldom of ignorance by their religious teachers, who cow and browbeat them by the most terrific denunciations if they dare to question a single article of faith. These teachers are either as ignorant as their dupes, or else they are misleading the people for purposes of gain. 'The priests are making their living out of you!' he exclaimed, as if he were addressing the adherents of religion."

"George, I don't believe that," interrupted Hadley, with a scowl of displeasure. "It is mean to impute unworthy motives to those who differ with us. I have an uncle in the west who is a preacher, and I believe that he is honest in his beliefs."

"Is he educated?"

"Well—no; I cannot say that he is."

"Then he comes into the category of the uninformed and deluded. I believe that many professors of religion are sincere enough, but they are unenlightened. 'You Christians,' said the lecturer, 'remind me of a nest full of half-fledged young robins, who open their mouths from ear to ear, ready to gulp down any thing that is flung into their æsophagi.'"

"Ha! ha!" laughed Hadley; "he was inclined to be facetious. That jest must have fallen flat on the audience."

"On the contrary, it was greeted with a volley of vociferous applause."

Hadley sat for awhile wrapped in deep reflection. The leaven of scepticism had been p into his mind, and it was already beginning to foment and diffuse itself through his being, filling his heart with a vague dissatisfaction, or, to change the metaphor, he was like Ixion on his wheel, whirling around and around, until his head was dizzy with the continuous revolution.

Milton's apostrophe to Eve, as the arch-enemy of mankind lay in wait for her, aptly portrays the subtile despoliation that skepticism was beginning to effect in the young student's spiritual life:

"Such ambush, hid among sweet flowers and shades,
Waited with hellish rancor imminent,
To intercept thy way, or send thee back
Despoiled of innocence, of faith, of bliss."

Is it possible that we have been duped so scandalously by our religious teachers?" thought Hadley. Then he passed in review before his mind a large number of his religious acquaintances in the village of Banesville and the surrounding country, and it was astonishing how many of them were found wanting when weighed in the balances of his criticism. It was true, most of them were men and women of ordinary common sense, but very few of them made any pretensions to breadth of culture, or to an acquaintanceship with the science of the day. And as to the preachers to whom he had listened, they appeared to be men of very meagre abilities. True, some of them seemed to be fairly educated, but he had never become sufficiently acquainted with them to learn whether they knew anything about the great questions which men of science discuss and the arguments which learned sceptics use in their efforts to undermine belief in the Scriptures. He was inclined to think that they simply accepted the Bible without question. As for quite a number of these clerical gentlemen, he had often been disgusted with their grammatical lapses, their stilted, unnatural manner, and their "nasal twang," as he called the offensive intonations that are sometimes heard in the pulpit.

On the other hand, there was Professor Borst, Principal of the academy which he attended—he was at least neutral on the subject of religion, never having committed himself, *pro* or *con*; and there was one of the acutest and most successful teachers of the country, who was an avowed infidel. Why had he never thought of these things before?

Could it be possible that the old, venerated Book was a fraud foisted upon the credulous by designing men for mercenary purposes? If so, it ought to be known, and the imposture should be exposed. Yet what an unsettling that would make in his previous assurance and peace of soul! With England's laureate he could say: "I falter where I firmly trod." But every sacrifice should be cheerfully made in the interests of truth, reasoned the young iconoclast, becoming enthusiastic.

"A little leaven leavens the whole lump." This adage of inspiration is as true of the process of unbelief in the soul as of the progress of grace. The doubtful suggestion, the sly innuendo, crept stealthily into Hadley's soul, on that fair spring morning, and, from that time, it began to pervade his being, diffusing itself through mind and heart, until he was ultimately led to the abandonment of all faith in religion.

"Hadley, we must be truth-seekers and free-thinkers," said George, after a brief pause of silence.

"Truth-seekers and free-thinkers! Where did you pick up those terms? Yon must have learned them since our last conversation a few months ago."

George drew a number of well-worn pamphlets from his pocket, and having selected one of them, whose pages were well-embellished with pencil-marks, he laid the rest on the grass by his side, saying, as he did so: "I always carry my commentaries with me, and find them convenient for reference."

They bore upon their title-pages the impress of a well-known book-making firm which has sent out its publications far and wide to undermine the honest faith of the young, and often sapping the foundations of virtue simultaneously with the destruction of faith. Many a young person, at that critical period of life, when the mind is most plastic, secretes the literature of this character from the eyes of parents and pious friends, and pores over it on the sly, until his heart is filled with bitterness, and his moral nature is unhinged.

At that moment Hadley happened to glance toward the valley below, and, as he did so, his attention was caught by a man walking leisurely up the by-road which wound transversely down the slope of the hill. As he came nearer the place where the young men were sitting, one of them recognized him.

"It is my father," said George. "I suppose that he is on his way to Banesville."

When the pedestrian came to the brow of the hill, he glanced casually across the field and caught sight of the young men, who were seated on the grass a few rods from the road. He halted a moment, and then, with a familiar salutation, he scrambled over the rail-fence, and came towards the boys. As he approached, George hurriedly gathered up the pamphlets that were lying on the grass by his side, and with an air of embarrassment which he could not conceal, he hustled them into the inner pocket of his coat, while a painfully guilty flush colored his face. Hadley, too, felt that his cheeks were turning crimson, as his friend's father came up.

"How are you, boys?" said Mr. Dane. After Hadley returned the greeting, Mr. Dane turned to his son and said: "You have chosen a pleasant place for study. I did not know, at first, who the two students were, so busy with their books on the hill-top. The books have disappeared though, I see. What science were you studying? What text books were you reading?"

George looked distressed for a few moments, and it was obvious that a painful struggle between his natural truthfulness and the fear of incurring his father's displeasure, was going on in his mind. It was foreign to his disposition to falsify, but he dreaded the consequences of making an honest confession to his father, and so the evil impulse within him was allowed to prevail, and he replied, hesitantly:

"Oh—they are— they are—only a few school-journals that I have just received through the mail, with some special pamphlets on — on — algebra."

The father looked doubtfully at his son, for a moment; but as the latter had always been, so far as his parents knew, a boy of strict veracity, Mr. Dane was unwilling to question the truthfulness of George's answer, although the halting manner of his son did not escape his notice. So he said: "You seemed to be very much interested in your reading; would you allow me to see the journals of which you speak?"

The deception having been begun, had to be kept up. For answer, George reached into another pocket of his coat, and, producing several pamphlets, he handed them to his father, and sure enough, on the outside of the paper-bound volumes, appeared, in large type, the name of a popular journal on pedagogics, several copies of which George happened to have with him at that time. The young man loathed himself for his duplicity, but he had not the moral courage to confess the truth. Mr. Dane took the journals, but, as he turned the leaves, he still felt himself nonplussed, for he could not understand why his son should have been so anxious to secrete literature of so useful a character. However, he thought best to say no more about it, and, after chatting awhile with the boys, he resumed his walk, saying that he was on his way to the village to get some medicine for a neighbor who had been taken ill.

As soon as he was gone, Hadley said, somewhat severely: "It was too bad to deceive your father in that way, George; it was outrageous."

"I acknowledge that it was not quite brave, and I do feel mean over it," replied George; "but it was the best way out of a dilemma. That was the first time I ever got into such a pickle, and I was thrown off my balance for a minute or so, and I am afraid that I did not extricate myself in an honorable way. But, see here, Hadley, wasn't it better to use a little strategy than to hurt the old man's feelings and make an unpleasant scene in the family, when I get home? Of two evils I was merely choosing the least. We must be governed by policy in these things."

"That is a dangerous philosophy," protested Hadley, whose love for the truth had not been undermined.

"But it has the support of a high authority in free-thinking circles. Only the other day I was reading an eloquent lecture by an infidel orator, in which he argued such questions of casuistry. He says that the man who sacrifices his life for a faith, or an ideal, is a fool. He thinks that it would be better to *lie* than to *die*. The Pilgrim Fathers, he maintains, were fanatics for leaving their own country, to cross the sea, and take up their abode in the inhospitable forests of the New World, merely for the privilege of worshipping God as they thought best. If they had had a little sense, they would have stayed in Old England, and made themselves comfortable, ready to swear to the Thirty-nine Articles, 'or forty, if necessary,' as he wittily says. The little *ruse* of which I have just now made use, and which seems to shock you so, is of a piece with the instances cited by the lecturer. I am not unconscionable, but I don't like to get into trouble with my venerable sire."

It did not occur to Hadley then as it would have done to an older and wiser man, that George had practically proved the dangerous character of the influence under which he had fallen. Well would it have been for him had he, recognizing in the lie he had just told, evidence of the demoralizing effects of his new philosophy, refused for himself to join in its pursuit. The poor, shallow fellow, however, merely answered: "Well, well, suppose we say no more about it. You were just about to read from one of your pamphlets, I believe, when your father interrupted us."

Hadley threw himself into a recumbent position upon the grass, and George began reading a chapter on the so-called "discrepancies of the Bible," in which the ingenious author attempted to prove that the accounts of the Crucifixion and Resurrection of Christ, as given by the Evangelists, were absurdly contradictory. The argument was elaborate, and to the young novitiates in Biblical learning, it appeared unanswerable. When the perusal was finished, George turned and looked into the anxious and troubled face of his friend.

"What do you think?" he inquired.

"Well, I am in a dilemma," said Hadley. "If the Bible is not true, it is a colossal fraud. But I cannot give it up on such evidence alone; and so I intend to investigate it further."

"That is right, and in order to help you in your investigations I will give you a catalogue of the publications of the publishers of this pamphlet. You may wish to secure some of them."

"But if I put that kind of literature into my library, I fear that mother, who as you know is religious, will trouble herself about it," said Hadley, doubtfully.

"Oh, she need not know you have the books. You can secrete them in some out-of-the-way niche—that is the way I do, to keep them out of the reach of my parents."

"But I do not conceal my text-books on German, or Latin, or mathematics from my mother," suggested Hadley, rather acutely.

George looked puzzled for a moment. "But that is—a—a different matter," he put in, at length.

"Why?"

"Oh, the—the—because it would pain her unnecessarily, and, as you know, we must exercise a little charity toward the old people's crotchets."

"But if the books contain the truth?"

"Well, well, we are only investigators as yet:

we are truth-seekers, eclectic philosophers, and do not assert anything dogmatically just now. At any rate, others need not be informed in regard to all the processes by which we reach our conclusions."

This sophistry acted as a sedative upon Hadley's conscience.

(*To be Continued.*)

JESUS RISEN.

By Mrs. M. Baxter.

S. S. Lesson for June 10. Matt. 28 : 1-15; Golden Text I Cor. 15: 20.

The Mighty Conqueror Unable to Hold the Saviour—His Resurrection an Unanswerable Proof of Divinity—A Woman the First to See Him—Became the First Preacher of the Resurrection—The Worshipping Disciples—Feeling Granted to Those of Little Faith—Not Called Blessed—The School of Faith—The Trial of an Author's Wife—The Bribe to the Watch.

"Now is Christ risen from the dead, and become the first fruits of them that slept." (1 Cor. 15: 20.) The "First fruits," inasmuch as "Christ, being raised from the dead, dieth no more; death hath no more dominion over Him." (Rom. 6: 9.) "Whom God hath raised up, having loosed the pains of death: because it was

Not Possible

that He should be holden of it." (Acts 2: 24.) Death could claim Lazarus, although he was once raised; the widow's son and Jairus' daughter died again; the Shunamite's son, and the son of the widow of Zarepta all died again after they were raised from the dead. Against all these, death had a rightful claim; "By one man sin entered into the world, and death by sin; and so death passed upon all men, for that all have sinned." (Rom. 5: 12.) All these were sinners, but Jesus, even when He had borne our sins, "knew no sin" and "did no sin, neither was guile found in His mouth." (2 Cor. 5: 21; 1 Pet. 2: 22.) Death had no grip on the sinless One, "it was not possible that He should be holden of it." It is the glorious witness of our acceptance with God that He who "bare our sins in His own body on the tree" is risen from the dead, and sitteth on the right hand of God, ever living to make intercession for us. The story of the Jews, that His disciples stole His body while the keepers slept, the idea of the Rationalists that Jesus was only a moral reformer, the plea of the Agnostics that they cannot know anything which is not subject to their human reason—all are answered by the glorious fact of the resurrection of Jesus. We can say to one and all, "I know that my Redeemer liveth, and that He shall stand at the latter day upon the earth: and though after my skin, worms shall destroy this body, yet in my flesh shall I see God." (Job. 19: 25, 26.)

The First to See Him.

Only one of the disciples had understood the sacrifice of Jesus; it was a woman, the same who anointed Him for His burial; and that same Mary Magdalene was the first to whom the risen Jesus appeared. (John 20: 1-16; Mark 16: 9.) While it was yet dark, and others were sleeping, Mary had groped her way to the sepulchre, and, finding the stone rolled away, she had fetched Peter and John, who saw the empty grave, and went away. But to Mary, who had drunk more deeply into the spirit of Jesus, and had understood more of His mission than any other, there was no place on earth like the place where she had last seen Jesus. He had said that He should rise again; the empty grave was witness to the fact. But where *was* Jesus? She lingered there until He manifested Himself to her, and sent her with glad news of His resurrection to the other disciples. Her report brought other women with her, Mary the mother of James, Salome and Joanna; but they had been preparing to anoint a dead Jesus, and they brought with them spices and ointments. Mary had brought nothing with her but simple faith in His word. They saw an angel, the same who had burst the sepulchre, scattered the keepers, and rolled away the stone. Mary had seen the Lord, but the women saw only an angel. When we make preparation and bring our spices to anoint a dead Saviour, we may be pleased with our own devotion and gratified that we do so much for Him who died for us; but

He Lives.

Jesus is not a poor dead corpse who needs our care to keep Him from corruption, and our earnestness and zeal to keep His work alive in the world: He is the living, risen Son of God, able to give us infinitely more than we can give Him. Mary was not taken up with her own devotion, but with her Lord, and so, when He wanted a messenger to His disciples, Mary was at hand, and became *the first preacher of the Resurrection* to the Apostles themselves. It is blessed to see an angel in the tomb, and to get the message of Jesus second-hand; but how much more blessed to see Jesus Himself! The keepers had been so terrified that they "became as dead men," but the angel said to the women, "*Fear not ye:* for I know that ye seek Jesus which was crucified. He is not here, for He is risen. Come see the place where the Lord lay. And go quickly, and tell His disciples that He is risen from the dead: and, behold, He goeth before you into Galilee; there shall ye see Him; lo, I have told you." True, they had not understood, as Mary had, the message of the resurrection, but they did the next best thing; as soon as they heard of Jesus risen, they came to see for themselves. Thus they had nothing to fear, and they met with their reward. "As they went to tell His disciples, Jesus met them." "He is not far from every one of us," and every one that seeketh Him findeth. He said "All hail." And they came, and held Him by the feet, and worshipped Him." He would not let Mary Magdalene touch Him; why then should these women? He had said to her

Touch Me Not

for I am not yet ascended to my Father:" yet now these women "held Him by the feet," and He did not rebuke them. Mary's faith was far in advance of theirs. When, again and again, He had told His disciples that He should be delivered to the Gentiles, mocked and crucified, and should rise again the third day (Matt. 16: 21; 17 22; 23: 20: 18: 19; Mark. 8: 31; 9: 9; 10: 32; Luke 9: 22; 13: 33; 18: 32), "they understood none of these things: and this saying was hid from them, neither knew they the things which were spoken." (Luke 18: 34). And even at the time of His resurrection, "as yet they knew not the scripture, that He must rise again from the dead." (John 20: 9). But Mary knew, and understood. There was no need for Mary to verify the fact of His resurrection by touching Him with her hands: her soul had bowed before her risen Lord when she said to Him, "Rabboni," *my* Lord. She had *given herself* in that word, and she asked nothing for herself. Faith does not want feeling to make it more sure. There are thousands of believers kept back from blessing because they want to feel before they believe. In heart they say, "Except I shall see in His hands the print of the nails, and put my finger into the print of the nails, and thrust my hand into His side, I will not believe." (John 20: 25). Jesus comes down to these. He invited Thomas to do this very thing, and He let the women hold his feet that they might have the evidence of their senses that He was risen. But He did not call them blessed; blessed are they that have *not* seen (nor felt), and yet have believed. (John 20: 29). We are in

The School of Faith,

all day long, and every day. Circumstances, health, weather, friends, business, all are pressed into God's service to teach us lessons of faith. He calls us to see Him in everything, and tells us that all things are for our sakes, and that "all things work together for good to them that love God." Yet how often do we meet with believers in a mourning spirit, going with their spices to anoint the dead and to groan over impossibilities, rather than glorying in the midst of untold difficulties, because a risen Christ is greater than them all! How many mourn over their failure, their natural nervousness, their poor physical constitution, or some trying turn of circumstances! And they take for granted that Christ has no more to do with all these things, than if He were still lying in the grave. They don't feel He can be pleased with them, they don't think He can care about such trifles, they don't think they have that great faith which they suppose He requires. O, if they saw that He was risen, and "ever liveth to make intercession for us." If they could only see the intense interest He takes in all our family, household, and business concerns, their hearts would go out to Him as Mary's did; and just in the most trying moments, instead of floundering about with the vain effort to extricate themselves, their hearts' glad, restful acknowledgment would be, "*My* Lord."

A Certain Author

was compiling a book which needed considerable care and time in the arrangement. His wife sometimes rendered him what assistance she could, but being herself extremely occupied, every moment was of importance to her. The book was just completed when her husband said that a new thought had struck him, and the whole of the labor must be gone through again. In order to do this she must give up some important engagements. She went to the Lord, and asked Him what was to be done. Time was when she would have chafed and fretted at the loss of time. The work was done over again, and a third time thrown over. And then the precious lesson was learned. The Lord showed her that *her* education in recognizing a risen Christ, who ruled over all things, and who was sole Proprietor of the hours and moments which seemed so wasted, was far more important than the actual moments as they fled; He could employ time better than she could. Let us live all day, and every day, in full view of a living, risen, ascended, glorified Jesus, who loves us with an everlasting love; and then things and people will all be seen as subject to Him.

While the women went on their errand, "some of the watch came into the city, and shewed unto the chief priests all the things that were done." They had seen the darkness, and felt the earthquake when Jesus died, and now the keepers told them of how another earthquake had taken place, and how the angel of the Lord had come down from heaven, and rolled away the stone from the door of the sepulchre, and how they had shaken and become as dead men. Would they now acknowledge the Son of God? Alas! they were playing a fearful game, and they kept it up till the last. For the sake of their religious reputation, they still dared to fight against God! They made lies their refuge, took counsel with others like themselves, and bribed the soldiers to say that the disciples stole the body of Jesus while they slept. If a Roman soldier slept at his post he must die. But the priests promised to secure their safety. Miserable delusion! Who believes the story? Jesus and the Resurrection has been preached, and has turned the world upside down!

WHEN WILL IT BE?

"That day and that hour knoweth no man."—MARK xiii. 32.

When will it be?
Just at the nightfall, when all work is done,
And rest comes, following the vanished sun,
Bringing its peace to those who weary grew
With labor lasting all the long day through?
Will it be then?

Or will it be at midnight's solemn hour
When earth seems sleeping like a folded flower?
Then will there come a knocking at the door,
And the soul start at sounds unheard before,
And listen for a voice in terror dumb,
The dreaded voice of Death, that says "I come;
Art ready for the journey thou must take
Before the cock crows and thy friends awake"?

Or will it be at morning, when the sun
Rises on golden tasks anew begun?
Will I be standing at the plow when he
Whose face we dread so much shall come to me
And say, "Give o'er thy labor. Say good-bye
To these thy comrades?" Will I shrink and cry,
"Oh! spare me yet a little while, I pray.
I am not ready. Wait till close of day"?
Ah, soul? not ready? Will the plea avail
Uttered by lips that terror has made pale?
No! He will say, "Thou knewest soon or late,
My feet would tarry at thy soul's closed gate,
Wast Thou not bidden to be ready? Lo!
I come and find thee unprepared to go.
Thou ask at time. Was time not given thee?
Too late regret, and all in vain thy plea!"

Rise, soul, and set thy house in order, lest
At any moment Death should be thy guest.
Be ready for the journey thou must go
At morn or midnight. If he finds thee so,
Brave with a faith in things thou canst not see,
What does it matter when he comes to thee?

—*Eben E. Rexford.*

J. E. JEWETT, Publisher, 77 Bible House, New York will furnish the above poem in leaflet form at twenty cents per hundred. *A Sample Packet of 50 leaflets* assorted (no two alike), will be sent post-paid, for ten cents. Postage stamps taken.

THE CHRISTIAN HERALD AND SIGNS OF OUR TIMES.

Entered according to Act of Congress in the year 1887, in the office of the Librarian of Congress at Washington.

Vol. XI., No. 23. Office, 63 Bible House, N. Y. THURSDAY, JUNE 7, 1888. Annual Subscription, $1.50.

CONTENTS OF THIS NUMBER.

PORTRAITS OF THE LATE BISHOP PARKER AND THE SULTAN OF ZANZIBAR.
THE ASSASSINATION. Dr. Talmage's Sermon Last Sunday Morning.
THE CLOSING SCENE OF ANTI-CHRIST'S REIGN. By G. H. Pember.
A Sunday in Colombia—A Mud Idol in China—A Luxurious Opium Den—A Night of Prayer Against Cholera—A Family Saved from Death, etc.
A DESIRABLE POSSESSION. A New Sermon by C. H. Spurgeon.
PICTURE OF A JAPANESE INTERIOR.
A BEATEN AFRICAN CHRISTIAN. (With Illustration.)
A WIDOW'S SON RESCUED. (With Illustration.)
THE EPOCHS OF A LIFE. (Continued.)
THE GREAT COMMISSION. By Mrs. M. Baxter.

The Late Bishop Parker, of Equatorial Africa—The Late Sultan of Zanzibar—An African Slave Market.

THE LATE BISHOP PARKER.

Second Bishop of Equatorial Africa.

Born in 1851—Cambridge Life—Ordained in 1876—Becomes Curate at Exeter—Goes to Calcutta—Return to England in 1885—His Work Among the Gonds of India—Consecrated Bishop of Central Africa in 1886—His Journeys—His Death.

MUCH has been said of the hardihood, the persistence and determined resolution of the Anglo-Saxon race in pursuing any object when pursuit has once been commenced, no matter what obstacles are encountered, nor what reverses attend the earlier stages of the enterprise. An example of those qualities, consecrated to the service of Christ, is witnessed in the mission work in Central Africa. No sooner had the news of the martyrdom of Bishop Hannington (whose portrait appeared in this journal on January 27, 1887) been received, than other consecrated men volunteered to take the vacant place, knowing well that they too might fall as he fell. One was selected whose portrait appears on the preceding page, and he went full of faith to take up the work that Bishop Hannington had left undone. As was briefly mentioned in these columns last week, he, too, has fallen in the field after a brief period of eighteen months' labor. The full details of his death have not yet been received, but there is, unhappily, no reason to doubt the truth of the main sad fact. The post of danger is again vacant, but already offers are being made by valiant Christian men, who are ready to go out to fill the vacancy in the ranks of Christ's army.

The Right Rev. Henry Perrott Parker, B. A., was second Bishop of Eastern Equatorial Africa. He was born in 1851, and was, therefore, only thirty-seven years old when he died. He was a graduate of Trinity College, Cambridge, England. Amongst his most intimate friends at Cambridge, was the Rev. Jani Alli, who exerted a strong influence over him, and it is believed that the constant intercourse that took place between the two, first led Henry Parker to turn his mind to foreign missionary work. On graduating from Trinity, the young student was ordained, and for nearly three years served as curate in Exeter. In 1878, however, the claims of the foreign mission field could no longer be resisted, and he offered himself to the Church Missionary Society, and was accepted. At first it was proposed that he should go to Bombay, where Mr. Jani Alli was then stationed; but just then the Rev. J. Welland, the Secretary of the Church Missionary Society in Calcutta was sick, and it became necessary that a joint secretary should be associated with him, and to this post Mr. Parker was appointed. Just a year afterwards Mr. Welland died, and Mr. Parker became sole secretary. He remained

Six Years at Calcutta,

doing the Society most valuable service. In the early part of 1885 he paid a brief visit home, but was soon back in India. At this time, however, it was not to Calcutta that he was assigned, but at his own desire to direct evangelistic work among the aboriginal Gônd people of the Central Province. To receive such a comrade (in addition to two young brethren) was a great encouragement to the Rev. H. D. Williamson, who had been laboring among the Gônds for six years. Mr. Parker's special object was to form a Mission which, from the first, should be self supporting. He thoroughly believed that this could be done, and that a Native Christian community gradually built up on such a system would be more stable than the dependent congregations that look to the missionary to provide churches and schools.

The Death of Bishop Hannington

in 1885 imposed on the Missionary Society the task of selecting a successor from numerous missionaries ready to take up the work. Ultimately the Committee offered the Bishopric to Henry Parker. He was very young, being at the time only thirty-four years of age, but it was felt that his practical missionary experience rendered him specially qualified for that arduous and difficult post. But so intensely interested was he in his work amongst the Gônds that he only consented to be nominated for the Bishopric on condition that another missionary should be sent out in his place. He took farewell of his friends in Calcutta on August 2, 1886, when a special service was held in the Cathedral. The Bishop officiated, and gave an address, in the course of which he spoke of the sacrifice Mr. Parker's Indian friends were then making.

A Fellow Worker's Testimony

to the value and efficiency of Mr. Parker's service was given by a missionary of the Church Missionary Society, who worked for some months with him in India. He said:

"I was associated with Mr. Parker for some seven months during the year 1879, living in the same house and sharing in the pastoral work at the old Church, Calcutta. I need hardly say that to hear of his death was a severe shock, for during our short intercourse I had learned to know and love him as a dear brother in Christ. Many and many a time have we knelt together and besought God for our work, and what seems to me now, as I look back, the most prominent point in his character was his earnest spirit of prayer. He never undertook anything, however trivial, without first seeking the Divine guidance and blessing. His temper and disposition were singularly sweet and loving, and his manner most winning, his influence being most powerful among young men.

His One Aim

and object was to preach Christ and Him crucified. I can recall many a case when his faithful testimony was blessed to the edification of Christ's Church in Calcutta. But his desire was to enter upon more direct missionary work; and when I returned to my station in Santalia, where I was doing medical work at the time, Henry Parker often came to visit me, and told me how much he longed to be promoted to labor more directly for the evangelization of the heathen. He seemed especially to be drawn towards the aboriginal tribes. And at length, after some years' excellent and faithful service as Secretary in Calcutta, and pastor of the old church, he was called of God to enter the Gônd Mission. Of this part of his life I can say little, as I left India in 1882; but I have heard how the same spirit of earnestness and self-sacrificing labor was exhibited there too; and I know well what a struggle it must have been to him to leave his Gônd Mission to undertake the more onerous duty of superintending

The Central African Church.

Few men could have been more fitted for this the last scene of his labors. His experience in the Secretariat in Calcutta had eminently adapted him for Africa, and during the short period of his episcopate he was enabled to show his wonderful power of organization. His character was indeed a singularly beautiful one, and its Christian fragrance will not soon be lost. Eminently a man of prayer, he loved to know that others too prayed for him; and how touching a sentence in his last letter to me, 'I wept tears of gratitude when I thought how many in England were praying for me!' He possessed a very clear judgment, and was wonderfully prudent and sagacious. His temper, too, was so even and calm that he never appeared in the least degree ruffled, even when the most trying circumstances and difficult positions confronted him. He was bold and fearless, yet never rash or headstrong, a loving and most sympathizing friend." Mr. Parker was

Consecrated Bishop

on Monday, October 18, 1886, in St. James' Church, Paddington, the officiating Prelates being the Archbishop of Canterbury, the Bishops of London, Carlisle, Mauritius, and Sierra Leone. The sermon was preached by his friend, the Rev. Handley C. G. Moule, of Cambridge, who, in glancing at the characteristics of the diocese which that day received its second bishop, alluded in pathetic terms to the murder of Bishop Hannington. "And now," he added, "his successor is before us ready in the same cause, for death or for life, in this great sacred field."

Although Bishop Parker's Episcopate has lasted only eighteen months, it has not been in vain. He arrived at Frere Town on November 27, 1886; at once visited Zanzibar; was presented to the Sultan, and took counsel with Bishop Smythies. Then in December, 1886, returning to Frere Town, he visited Rabai Kisultini, of the Girlama country. Taita and Mr. Wray, Chagga and Mr. Fitch welcomed the Bishop in the succeeding January. The same month saw him, accompanied by his friend and companion, Mr. Blackburn, set out on a more extensive journey of four hundred miles through Usambara and Unguru to Mamboia, which was reached on August 5. From Mamboia their route lay to Mpwapwa, and on through Ugogo to Uyui, which was reached on September 19. There a month was spent, when the Bishop moved on to Wusambiro, west of Jordan's Nullah, at

The South End of Victoria Nyanza.

On November 15 he left Wusambiro, still in company with Mr. Blackburn, to explore the country south of Speke Gulf, with the object of selecting a new station. Having found what seemed a promising position at Nasa, he returned to Wusambiro. Here Bishop Parker met his band of missionaries, and for a fortnight (from December 13 to 28) considered, in company with Messrs. Ashe, Mackay, Blackburn, Walker, and Hooper, all the problems connected with their work. Writing soon after the end of this Conference, at least one of the missionaries present recorded in very thankful terms his sense of the Bishop's tact and love throughout this time, and of the spiritual profit derived from a little time in his company. Bishop Parker's plan was to pass on around the lake in the direction of Kavirondo, and to explore that country in connection with his plan for a more direct route to and from the coast. He had expected to leave Nasa, early in February, hoping to complete the journey and get back in time to start on the homeward route about the middle of April. Mr. Blackburn seems to have fallen ill upon March 5; consequently the Bishop and he had probably been travelling for three or four weeks, and the fatal sickness may have been contracted in the district either west or north of Speke Gulf. On May 1 a brief telegram announced the death of both the Bishop and his Chaplain after an illness of ten days.

Bishop Parker is said by those who best knew him to have combined in an exceptional degree the qualifications needed for his arduous work. Of deep spirituality, intense devotion, sound judgment, and withal of a loving and tender personal disposition, he exercised

A Remarkable Influence

upon the noble little band of missionaries under his supervision, every one of whom was ready to follow him with devoted loyalty. Nor was it only within that circle alone that his remarkable personality made itself felt. A Wesleyan missionary came across the Bishop's path, and went on his way, strengthened and uplifted by communion and conference with him. All the characteristics which won the admiration and love of the missionary who writes of Henry Parker as he knew him in India, were observed and their influence felt in Africa. Nor were the organizing and administrative qualities of the man less conspicuous than those which go to form his more personal character. A clear thinker, he grasped with remarkable rapidity the situation in his vast diocese, the steps which seemed essential to success, and the best way of setting about their realization. The need of more men he saw and felt keenly; and the paramount necessity of giving the people

The Word of God in the Vernacular

he had but recently given an expression to in a letter to the secretary of the British and Foreign Bible Society. Writing on January 12, 1888, from Wusambiro, he showed how helpful it would be to the missions in Mombassa, Frere Town, Girima, Shimba, Kisulutini, Taita, and Chagga, if the Bible Society were to establish a depot for Scriptures in Frere Town; and the Bishop asked that this should be done. He considered that mission work, in the part of Africa to which he referred, had suffered because inadequate attention had been given to the preparation of vocabularies, grammars, and to the translation of the Scriptures, &c., into the languages understood by the people. There is now a consensus of opinion, he said, amongst the laborers in the field that more must be attempted, and there are already a printing press in Ferre Town and a translation committee. The Rev. W. E. Taylor, of the Church Missionary Society, had been set apart at his suggestion to make translation work his first duty.

THE LATE SULTAN OF ZANZIBAR.

Born in 1837, and Died in 1888—Extent of His Father's Territory—The Slave Trade Treaty—Diminution of the Sultan's Dominion—Size and Population of Zanzibar—Commercial Importance.

SEYYID BARGASH BIN SAID, *whose portrait* accompanies that of the late Bishop Parker *on the first page*, was born in 1837, and died on March 27, 1888, at his palace at Zanzibar (a picture of which appeared in these columns on February 23, last). His death breaks the only remaining link connecting Zanzibar with her political past. When he was born, his father, Seyyid Said, ruled over Zanzibar, Muscat, and a huge territory of Eastern Africa as far as Lake Tanganyika. He was, therefore, a very considerable potentate; the most considerable by far in those parts. But when he died his *fifteen sons* quarrelled over the inheritance, until England intervened as mediator and persuaded one son to be content with Muscat, and another, Majid, with Zanzibar. When Majid died, in 1870, he was succeeded by his brother Seyyid Bargash, who was then thirty-three years of age. At that time Dr. (now Sir John) Kirk was Acting-Consul at Zanzibar; he acted as Bargash's mentor, and made British influence all-powerful at his court. It was he who succeeded, where Sir Bartle Frere had failed, in persuading the Sultan to sign a treaty which, if fully carried out, would have abolished the slave-trade in Zanzibar. This it has not done, but it has modified its worst features.

The Sultan had considerable trouble with the inland chiefs some four or five years ago, who, encouraged by German settlers, asserted their independence. War, however, was averted by a Convention held in London two years ago, by which England and Germany agreed that the Sultan's dominions should be confined to the islands and a strip of coast ten miles wide, and the Sultan prudently assented to this arrangement. Though a Wahabi, or member of the strictest Moslem sect, the late Sultan was always most considerate to Christian missionaries and travellers. Syud Khalifah, his elder brother, now succeeds to the throne.

The Territory of Zanzibar

is situated on the east coast of Africa. It consists (1) of the island of Zanzibar, fifty-five miles in length and twenty-five miles in breadth, with an area of 625 square miles, with a population of 300,000; (2) the isles of Pemba and Mafia, and the African coast from Warsheik to Tungue, which is properly called the Suaheli coast. The population of Zanzibar island, in which the Sultan's palace is situated, is composed of Arabs, intermixed with various East African races, Hindi and Malagasy traders, free negroes and numerous foreigners; but chief among them are the Arab landowners, and slave-holders, and employers. The commercial importance of Zanzibar has been recently increasing, and its situation will doubtless lead to continued progress. European enterprise is becoming more and more engaged in this region, which, until Henry M. Stanley opened up the Congo river, was scarcely known except as the starting place of explorers.

HE OLD SLAVE MARKET

at Zanzibar is *shown on the picture on the first page*. It is an irregular, unpaved, oblong space, 50 yards by 30 yards in extent, three of its sides consisting of palm-thatched huts, the fourth presenting stone buildings of more respectable pretensions. In the days of the recognized existence of the slave trade, the sale generally took place between four and five o'clock in the afternoon. The centre of the market was occupied by the slaves, seated in rows upon the ground. Walking about and criticising the various "lots," might be seen men of every race belonging to Eastern Africa and Arabia. Apart from the other slaves, and standing up, in our picture, are to be seen the choice female specimens. Those who have witnessed it, say it was a revolting sight to watch a lascivious Arab, wishing to add to his harem, handling and examining the objects of his purchase before closing a bargain. There is grave reason to believe that, notwithstanding all that the British Government have done from time to time for the suppression of the traffic, it is still being carried on, with the connivance of the Zanzibar authorities, though not to the former extent.

ANECDOTES RELATED AT RECENT EVANGELISTIC MEETINGS.

A Forty Years' Rest.—"When the Beloved Rev. Ebenezer Erskine lay upon his death-bed he was visited by a member of his congregation, who said to him, 'During your ministry among us, sir, you have given us many precious words and directions, but now, when you are dying, and your own soul about to be ushered into eternity, it would give me and many others great help to know assuredly upon what you are resting for your soul's salvation.' 'Ah,' said the dying minister, 'I am resting my soul where it has rested these forty years, upon Him who has said, "I will never leave thee nor forsake thee."' Yes, that is the God upon whom we rest, and we have the well-founded assurance that though we walk through the valley of the shadow of death our God will be with us and we need, therefore, fear no evil."

The Pattern on the Wall Paper.—A Worker among the poor narrated: "I once visited a woman who was just recovering from a severe illness. She said that, as she lay in bed, looking at the paper on the wall, which was of a red and white pattern, she thought of that passage in God's Word, 'Come, now, and let us reason together, saith the Lord; though your sins be as scarlet, they shall be as white as snow' (Isaiah 1: 18). Then, pointing to the red, she would say, 'I have had sin as red as that, but I thank Thee, Lord, that Thou hast made them as white as that,' pointing to the white portion of the pattern. Yes, dear friends, God lets His people know that they are saved, that they may rejoice in the knowledge. As soon as she herself was saved through faith in the cleansing blood of Christ, this woman called her family around her, and for the first time had family worship. And what a heartfelt service it was, being presided over by one just snatched from the jaws of death, and who could not praise and thank her Saviour enough for His wonderful goodness to her."

"Plucked" at the College Examination.—Rev. Wm. Ross observed: "It was the last few days of the University session. Large crowds of excited students were gathered in the quadrangles; for upon that day the results of the various examinations had been made known, and there, affixed to the notice boards were long lists, upon which were the names of the successful candidates, ranged alphabetically. Every student, as he came near, anxiously scanned the names ranged under his initial, then retired with his face radiant with joy, or sunk in despondency, according to the published result of the examination. Among the last of the excited group there came up one somewhat elderly student. He had entered college very late, but had studied hard, and strained every nerve to qualify himself. As he approached, it was apparent to all that he was greatly agitated. He walked up to the list, and at one glance saw his name was not there. Instantly he became ashy pale; some feared he was about to faint, but recovering himself, he muttered, 'I am done for,' and walked away. He was too old to try again, and he looked upon himself as beaten in that pursuit in which he had been so earnest. But I see before me another crowd, larger than that of the students, to which every people, and tribe, and kingdom, have contributed. They stand before the great white throne, and the roll of Lamb's book of life is being read. And all whose names are not inscribed therein are lost for ever; it is too late to try again."

The Bridge That Spans the Chasm—A young student said: "One day, as I was walking in the country, I wished to go from one field to another, but they were separated by a stream too broad to be jumped with safety. I walked up the stream some distance, until at length I I came to a tree which was lying across the water, but I was afraid to risk myself upon it, and continued to walk on until I met a laborer going towards the stream. I stopped him and asked if it were safe to cross by that tree. He replied that it was, and seeing that he was a big, strong fellow, I asked him if he had used the tree as a bridge. He had. Then his opinion had more weight with me, because it was backed by personal experience. And I trustingly walked over the bridge in safety. And now I, who have walked over the Bridge, Jesus Christ, that spans the gulf of sin between fallen man and a righteous God, can assure you of the stability of the Bridge. I have crossed over, burdened with as heavy a load of sin as any one, and from my experience I can tell you that your faith in Him will not be misplaced."

Miserable in Heaven.—"The Rev. Mr. Keevill, when out walking one day, met a man to whom he said, 'I hope, friend, you have an interest in Christ?' 'That I have, now,' was his reply, 'but it was not so when you spoke to me last about twenty years ago.' 'Have I seen you before?' the minister inquired. 'Yes, sir,' said the man, twenty years ago: I was standing at the head of my horses after a spell of ploughing. I was swearing hard. You stood silently by for a minute, then solemnly said, 'I do not know what you would do in heaven, supposing you went there. There will be no bad language there, for all is pure and good, and as you hate that which is pure and good you would hate Christ, and it would be a misery for you to be there in heaven without loving Christ. When you went sadly away I saw myself to be so wicked, and unfit to be where Christ was, that I wept, and resolved, in God's strength, that from that night there should be a change. I came to Jesus in all my sinfulness and shame, and was washed in His precious blood, which cleansed every impurity, and now I know that when I go to heaven my chief joy will be to dwell where Jesus is, and gaze upon His glorious face.

Dying for His Soldier Brother.—Mr. Hamilton says: "There is a story told in connection with the decimation of the Strelzi by the then Czar of Russia. When that rebellious corps was drawn up in the Grand Square of Moscow, they were disarmed, then told to number off, and every tenth man to step out. Too well they knew what was to be the fate of those who were taken out. They were to be shot, to die for themselves and their comrades. All the men deserved to die, but only each tenth man was to receive the punishment. Side by side in that corps stood two brothers. As the numbering approached, the elder glanced anxiously down the rank. To his joy he saw he was safe, he was a ninth man; but the next instant a pang of horror shot throught his heart, for his brother, who stood next to him, was a tenth man. Instantaneously the thought flashed upon him, how could he meet his parents if he went home alone, to tell the sad fate of their favorite son, whom he himself had enticed to join that ill-fated corps? Swiftly and silently he glided behind his brother, and taking his place, gently pushed him into that which he had vacated. Steadily the numbering went on, the younger answered to nine, and the elder to ten, and, stepping out, died that his brother might live. Does this not remind us of Christ's great sacrifice for us? And if He died for us should we not live to Him?"

THE ASSASSINATION.

Dr. Talmage's Sermon Preached Last Sunday Morning, June 3, 1888.

"Whosoever doth not bear his cross, and come after me cannot be my disciple." Luke 14 : 27.

Crucifixions Under Darius—An Ordinary Mode of Punishment—A Forest of Crosses—One Sublimely Conspicuous—The Sufferer Upon It—Exhausted by Previous Scourgings—A Thrilling Picture at Antwerp—The Cross on Christ's Shoulders—The Stripping—The Crown of Thorns—The Cross Set Up—Suffering Aggravated by Absences—The Death Hours—A Test for Love—A Cross for Every One—Confession a Cross Like a Gate—A Young Man's Confession in a Store—A Greek Architect's Bold Announcement—Scars Won in Battle—The Fiery Cross.

THE cross was a gibbet on which criminals were put to death. It was sometimes made in the shape of the letter T, sometimes in the shape of the letter X, sometimes in the shape of the letter I—a simple upright; sometimes two cross-pieces against the perpendicular bar, so that upon the lower cross-piece the criminal partially sat. But whatever the style of cross, it was always disgraceful and always agonizing.

When Darius conquered Babylon, he put two hundred captives to death on the cross. When Alexander conquered Tyre, he put two thousand captives to death on the cross. So it was just

An Ordinary Mode of Punishment.

But in all the forest of crosses on the hills, and in the valleys of the earth, there is one cross that attracts more attention than any other. It is not higher than the others, it is not made out of different wood, there is nothing peculiar in the notch at which the two pieces are joined, and as to the scene, they witnessed crucifixions every few weeks, so that I see a reckless man walking about the hill, and kicking carelessly aside a skull, and wondering who the villain was that had so flat and misshapen a head; and here is another skull, and there on the hillside is another skull. Indeed, the Bible says it was "a place of skulls." But about the victim on one of these crosses all ages are crying: "Who is He? Was He a man? Was He a God? Was He man and God?"

Through the darkness of that gloomy day, I come close up enough to the cross to see who it is. It is Jesus. How did He come there? Had He come up on the top of the hill to look off upon the beautiful landscape, or upon a brilliant sunset? No. He came there ill and exhausted. People sometimes wonder why Christ expired so quickly on the cross, in six or seven hours, while other victims have been on the cross for forty-eight hours before life was extinct. I will tell you the reason. He was exhausted when He came there. He had been scourged. We are horrified at the cruelties of the whipping-post, but those cruelties were mercy as compared with the scourging of Jesus Christ.

I saw at Antwerp a picture made by Rubens—

Rubens' Picture of the Scourging

of Jesus Christ. It was the most overmastering picture I ever looked at, or ever expect to see. As the long-frocked official opened the door that hid the picture, there He was—Christ with back bent and bared. The flagellator stood with the upper teeth clenched over the lower lip, as though to give violence to the blows. There were the swollen shoulders of Christ. There were the black and blue ridges, denied even the relief of bleeding. There was the flesh adhering to the whips as they were lifted. There were the marks where the knots in the whips gouged out the flesh. There stood the persecutor, with his foot on the calf of the leg of the Saviour, balancing himself. O! the furious and hellish look on those faces, grinning vengeance against the Son of God. The picture seized me, it overwhelmed me; it seemed as if it would kill me. I do not think I could have looked at it five minutes and have lived. But that, my friends, was before Christ had started for Calvary. That was only the whipping. Are you ready for your journey to the cross?

The carpenters have split the timber into two pieces. They are heavy and they are long pieces, for one of them must be fastened deep down in the earth lest the struggling of the victim upset the structure. They put this timber upon the shoulder of Christ very gradually, first, to see whether He can stand it, and after they find He can stand it, they put the whole weight upon Him. Forward now, to Calvary. The hooting and the yelling mob follow on. Under

The Weight of the Cross,

Christ being weary and sick, He stumbles and falls, and they jerk at His robe, indignant that He should have stumbled and fallen, and they cry: "Get up, get up!" Christ, putting one hand on the ground and the other hand on the cross, rises, looking into the face of Mary, His mother, for sympathy; but they tell her to stand back, it is no place for a woman—"Stand back and stop this crying."

Christ moves on with His burden upon His shoulders, and there is a boy that passes along with Him, a boy holding a mallet and a few nails. I wonder what they are for. Christ moves on until the burden is so great He staggers and falls flat into the dust, and faints dead away, and a ruffian puts his foot on Him and shakes Him as he would a dead dog, while another ruffian looks down at Him, wondering whether He has fainted away, or whether He is only pretending to faint away, and with jeer and contempt indescribable says: "Fainted, have you? fainted? get up, get on!"

Now, they have arrived at the foot of the hill. Off with His clothes. Shall that loathsome mob look upon the unrobed body of Christ? Yes. The commanding officers say: "Unfasten the girdle, take off the coat, strip Him." The work is done. But bring the coat, for here are

The Gamblers

tossing up coin on the ground, saying: "Who shall have the coat?" One ruffian says: "I have it, I have it—it is mine!" He rolls it up and puts it under his arm, or he examines it to see what fabric it is made of. Then they put the cross upon the ground, and they stretch Christ upon it, and four or five men hold Him down while they drive the spikes home, at every thump a groan, a groan! Alas! Alas! the hour passes on and the time comes when they must crucify Him.

Christ has only one garment left now, a cap, a cap of thorns No danger that it will fall off, for the sharp edges have punctured the temples and it is sure and fast. One ruffian takes hold of one end of the short beam of the cross, and another ruffian takes hold of the other end of the short beam of the cross, and another ruffian puts his arms around the waist of Christ, and another ruffian takes hold of the end of the long beam of the cross, and altogether they move on until they come to the hole digged in the earth, and with awful plunge it jars down with

Its Burden of Woe.

It is not the picture of a Christ, it is not the statue of Christ, as you sometimes see in a cathedral; but it is the body of a bleeding, living, dying Christ. They sometimes say He had five wounds, but they have counted wrong. Two wounds for the hands, two wounds for the feet, one wound for the side: they say, five wounds. No, they have missed the worst and they have missed the most. Did you ever see the bramble out of which that crown of thorns was made? I saw one on a Brooklyn ferry-boat, in the hands of a gentleman who had just returned from Palestine, a bramble just like that out of which the crown of thorns was made. O! how cruel and how stubborn were the thorns. And when that cap of thorns was put upon Christ, and it was pressed down upon Him, not five wounds, but ten, twenty, thirty—I cannot count them. There were

Three or Four Absences

that made that scene worse. First, there was the *absence of water*. The climate was hot, the fever, the inflammation, the nervous prostration, the gangrene, had seized upon Him, and He terribly wanted water. His wounds were worse than gunshot fractures, and yet no water. A Turk, in the thirteenth century, was crucified on the banks of a river, so that the sight of the water might tantalize him. And oh! how the thirst of Christ must have tantalized, as He thought of the Euphrates and the Jordan and the Amazon and all the fountains of earth and Heaven poured out of His own hand. They offered Him an intoxicating draught made out of wine and myrrh, but He declined it. He wanted to die sober. No water!

Then, my friends, there was the *absence of light*. Darkness always exasperates trouble. I never shall forget the night in the summer of 1873, in the steamer *Greece*, mid-Atlantic, every moment expecting the steamer to go down. All the lights in the cabin were blown out. The captain came crawling in on his hands and knees, for he could not stand upright, so violently was the vessel pitching, and he cried out: "Light up, light up!" The steward said: "We can't light up; the candles are gone and the holders are gone." The captain said: "I can't help that; light up!" The storm was awful when the lights were burning, worse when the lights went out.

Then there was the absence of faithful nurses. When you are ill, it is pleasant to have the head bathed, and the hands and feet rubbed. Look at the hands and feet of Christ, look at the face of Christ.

There Were Women There.

who had cared for the sick, but none of them might come up near enough to help. There was Christ's mother, but she might not come up to help. They said: "Stand back, stand back; this is no place for you." The high priests and the soldiers wanted it their own way; they had it their own way.

The hours pass on, and it is twelve o'clock of the Saviour's suffering, and it is one o'clock, and it is two o'clock, and it is almost three o'clock. Take the last look at that suffering face; wan and pinched, the purple lips drawn back against the teeth, the eyes red with weeping, and sunken as though grief had pushed them back; blackness under the lower lid, the whole body adroop and shivering with the last chill, the breath growing feebler and feebler and feebler, until He gives one long, deep, last sigh.

He is Dead!

Oh, my soul, He is dead! Can you tell why? Was He a fanatic, dying for a principle that did not amount to anything? Was He a man infatuated? No; to save your soul from sin, and mine, and make eternal life possible, He died. There had to be a substitute for sin. Who shall it be? "Let it be Me," said Christ; "let it be Me." You understand the meaning of that word, substitution. You were drafted for the last war; some one took your place, marched your march, suffered your wounds, and died at Gettysburg. Christ comes to us while we are fighting our battle with sin, and death, and hell, and He is our Substitute. He marches our march, fights our battle, suffers our wounds, and dies our death. Substitution! Substitution!

How do you feel in regard to that scene described in the text, and in the region around about the text? Are your sympathies aroused? or are you so dead in sin, and so abandoned, by reason of your transgressions, that you can look upon all that tearless and unmoved? No, no; there are thousands of people here this morning who can say in the depths of their soul, "No, no, no; if Jesus endured that, and all that for me, I ought to love Him. I must love Him, I will love Him, I do love Him. Here, Lord, I give myself to Thee; 'tis all that I can do."

But how are you going to test your love, and test your earnestness? My text gives a test. It says, that while Christ carried

A Cross for You,

you must be willing to carry a cross for Christ. "Well," you say, "I never could understand that. There are no crosses to be carried in this land; those persecutions have passed, and in all the land there is no one to be crucified, and yet in the pulpit and in the prayer-meetings you all keep talking about carrying a cross. What do you mean, sir?" I mean this: that is a cross which Christ calls you to do, which is unpleasant and hard. "Oh," you say, "after hearing the story of this Christ, and all that He has endured for me, I am ready to do anything for Him. Just tell me what I have to do, and I'll do it. I am ready to carry any cross."

Suppose I should ask you at the close of a religious service, to rise up, announcing yourself on the Lord's side—could you do it? "Oh, no," you say, "I have a shrinking and a sensitive nature, and it would be impossible for me to rise before a large assemblage, announcing myself on the Lord's side." Just as I feared. You

Cannot Stand that Cross.

The first one that is offered you, you reject. Christ carried a mountain, Christ carried a Himalaya, Christ carried a world for you, and you cannot lift an ounce for Him.

But here is a man whose cross will be to announce among his business associates to-morrow morning on Exchange, that he has begun a new life; that while he wants to be faithful in his worldly duties, he is living for another world, and he ought to advise all those who are his associates, so far as he can influence them, to begin with him the Christian life. Could you do that, my brother? "Oh, no," you say, "not just that. I think religion is religion, and business is business, and it would be impossible for me to recommend the Christian religion in places of worldly business." Just as I feared. There is a second cross offered you, and you cannot carry it. Christ lifted a mountain for you; you cannot lift an ounce for Him.

There is some one whose cross will be to present religion in the home circle.

Would You Dare to Kneel

down and pray if your brother and sister were looking at you? Could you ask a blessing at the tea-table? Could you take the Bible and gather your family around you, and read of Christ and heaven and your immortal soul? Could you then kneel and pray for a blessing on your household? "Oh," you say, "not exactly that. I couldn't quite do that, because I have a very quick temper, and if I professed religion and tried to talk religion in my household, and then after that I should lose my temper, they would scoff at me and say: 'You are a pretty Christian!'" So you are cowed down, and their sarcasm keeps you out of heaven and away from Christ, when, under God, you ought to take your whole family into the kingdom. Christ lifted a mountain, lifted a world for you; you cannot lift an ounce for Him. I see how it is: you want to be favorable to religion, you want to support Christian institutions, you like to be associated with those who love Jesus Christ; but as to taking a positive step on this subject, you cannot—you cannot, and my text, like a gate of a hundred bolts, bars you away from peace on earth and glory in heaven.

There are hundreds of men and women here brave enough in other things in life who simply for the lack of manliness and womanliness stay away from God. They dare not say: "Forever and forever, Lord Jesus, I take Thee. Thou hast redeemed me by Thy blood, here is my immortal spirit. Listen, all my friends. Listen, all the world." They are lurking around about the kingdom of God—they are lurking around about it,

Expecting to Crawl in

some time when nobody is looking, forgetful of the tremendous words of my text: "Whosoever doth not bear his cross, and come after Me, cannot be My disciple." An officer of a neighboring church told me that he was in a store in New York—just happened in—where there were many clerks, and a gentleman came in and said to a young man standing behind the counter: "Are you the young man that arose the other night in the Brooklyn Tabernacle and asked for prayers?" Without any flush of cheek, he replied: "I am. I haven't always done right, and I have been quite bad; but since I arose for prayers, I think I am better than I was." It was only his way of announcing that he had started for the higher life. God will not cast out a man who is brave enough to take a step ahead like that.

I tell you these things this morning because, my dear friends, I want to show you how light the cross is that we have to carry compared with that which Christ carried for us. You have not had the flesh torn off for Christ's sake in carrying your cross. You have not carried the cross until it fetched the blood. Under His there was a pool of carnage that plashed the horses' fetlocks. You have friends to sympathize with you in carrying the cross: Christ trod the winepress of God's wrath alone, alone! The cross that you and I ought to carry represents only a few days or a few years of trial. The cross that Christ carried for us had compressed into it the agonies of eternity.

There has some one come here to-day whom you have not observed. He did not come through the front door; He did not come down any of these aisles; yet I know He is here. He is from the East, the far East. He comes with blistered foot, and with broken heart, and cheeks red, not with health but with blood from the temples. I take hold of His coat and I say: "It does not seem to fit Thee." "No," He says, "it is not mine; it is borrowed; it does not belong to me now. For my vesture did they cast lots." And I say to Him: "Thine eyes are red as though from loss of sleep." He says: "Yes, the Son of man had not where to lay His head." And I touch the log on His back and I say:

"Why Carriest Thou This?"

"Ah!" He says, "that is a cross I carry for thee and for the sins of the whole world. That is a cross. Fall into line, march on with Me in this procession, take your smaller crosses and your lighter burdens, and join Me in this march to Heaven." And we join that procession with our smaller crosses and our lighter burdens, and Christ looks back and He sees some are halting because they cannot endure the shame, or bear the burden, and with a voice which has in it majesty and omnipotence, He cries until all the earth trembles: "Whosoever doth not bear his cross, and come after Me, cannot be My disciple."

O! my brethren, my sisters—for I do not speak professionally, I speak as a brother would speak to a brother or sister—my brother, can you not bear a cross if at last you can wear a crown? Come now, let us divide off. Who is on the Lord's side? Who is ready to turn his back upon the Lamb of God that taketh away the sin of the world? A Roman emperor said to

A Greek Architect:

"You build me a coliseum, a grand coliseum, and if it suits me, I will crown you in the presence of all the people, and I will make a great day of festival on your account." The Greek architect did his work, did it magnificently, planned the building, looked after its construction. The building was done. The day for opening arrived. In the coliseum were the emperor and the Greek architect. The emperor rose amid the plaudits of a vast assembly and said: "We have gathered here to-day, to open this coliseum, and to honor the Greek architect. It is a great day for the Roman Empire. Let this building be prosperous, and let honor be put upon the Greek architect. O! we must have a festival to-day. Bring out those Christians and let us have them put to death at the mouth of the lions." The Christians were put into the centre of the amphitheatre. It was to be a great celebration in their destruction. Then the lions, hungry and three-fourths starved, were let out from their dens in the side of the amphitheatre, and they came forth with mighty spring to destroy and rend the Christians, and all the galleries shouted: "Huzza, huzza! Long live the emperor!" Then the Greek architect arose in one of the galleries and shouted until in the vast assemblage all heard:

"I too am a Christian!"

and they seized him in their fury and flung him to the wild beasts, until his body, bleeding and dead, was tumbled over and over again in the dust of the amphitheatre. Could you have done that for Christ? Could you, in a vast assemblage, all of whom hated Christ, have said "I am a Christian," or, "I want to be a Christian?" Would you have had the ten thousandth part of the enthusiasm and the courage of the Greek architect? Nay, I ask you another question: would you in an assemblage where they are nearly all Christians—in an assemblage a vast multitude of whom love Christ and are willing to live, and if need be, to die for Him—would you dare to say: "I am a Christian," or, "I want to be a Christian?" Would you say in the presence of the friends of Christ as much as the Greek architect said in the presence of the enemies of Christ? O! are there not multitudes here this morning who are ready to say: "Let the world look on, let all the galleries of earth and heaven and hell look on, I take Christ this day. Come applause or abuse, come sickness or health, come life or death, Christ forever."

Are You for Christ,

are you against Him? The destinies of eternity tremble in the balance. It seems as if the last day had come and we were gathered for the reckoning. "Behold, He cometh with clouds, and every eye shall see Him." What I say to one I say to all. What are you doing for Christ?

O! Christian man, O! Christian woman? Have you any scars to show in this conflict? When a war is over the heroes have scars to show. One hero rolls back his sleeve and shows a gunshot fracture, or he pulls down the collar and shows where he was wounded in the neck. Another man says: "I have never had the use of my limb since I was wounded at that great battle." When the last day comes, when all our battles are over, will we have any wounds for Christ? Some have wounds for sin, wounds for the devil, wounds gotten in fighting on the wrong side. Have we wounds that we can show—wounds gotten in the battle for Christ and for the truth? On that Resurrection day Christ will have plenty of scars to show; Christ will stand there and show the scars on His brow, the scars on His hands, and the scars on His feet, and He will put aside the robe of His royalty and show the scar on His side, and all heaven will break down with emotion and gratitude in one great sob, and then in one great hosanna. Will you and I have

Any Scars to Show?

There will be Ignatius, on that day showing the mark of the paw and teeth of the lion that struck him down in the Coliseum. There will be glorious John Huss, showing just where on his foot the flames began on that day when his soul took wing of flame and soared up from Constance. There will be Hugh McKail ready to point to the mark on his neck where the axe struck him. There will be McMillan and Campbell and Freeman, the American missionaries who with their wives and children were put to death in that awful massacre at Cawnpore, showing the places where the daggers of the Sepoys struck them. There will be the Waldenses showing where their limbs were broken on the day when the Piedmontese soldiery pitched them over the rocks. Will you and I have any wounds to show? Have we fought any battles for Christ? O! that we might all be enlisted for Christ, that we might all be willing to suffer for Christ, that we might all bear a cross for Christ. When

The Scottish Chieftains

wanted to raise an army, they would make a wooden cross, and then set it on fire, and carry it with other crosses they had, through the mountains, through the highlands, and among the people, and as they waved the cross the people would gather to the standard and fight for Scotland. So to-day, I come out with the cross of the Son of God. It is a flaming cross—flaming with suffering, flaming with triumph, flaming with glory. I carry it out among all the people. Who will be on the Lord's side? Who will gather to the standard of Emmanuel? "Whosoever doth not bear his cross, and come after Me, cannot, cannot be My disciple."

THE CLOSING SCENE OF ANTICHRIST'S REIGN.

By G. H. Pember, M. A.*

Antichrist's Last Resource—The Vast Army Around Jerusalem—The City at Its Last Extremity—On the Verge of Capture—The Praying Inhabitants—Sudden Darkness—The Glory of the Descending Christ—Antichrist's Doom—The Cloven Mountain—The Refuge of the Jews—The Triumphal March Into the City.

THE closing scenes of Antichrist's reign will probably be terrible to himself as well as to the world. As to the plagues of the locusts, and the demon-horsemen, they come from below, and are, apparently, under his own direction and control. But with their disappearance his resources are exhausted, and then the fingers of Him, who is the Last as well as the First, begin to write the doom of the Beast, and the False Prophet upon the sky. For

The Vials are Filled

with "the wrath of God, Who liveth for ever and ever," and their contents are poured down from heaven by His agents issuing from the celestial Temple. Just as when the Lord looked out from the pillar of cloud, and took off the chariot-wheels of the Egyptians, immediately before the utter overthrow of Pharaoh and his host; like the smiting of the Sodomites with blindness, which, after an interval of but a few hours, was followed by the descent of the fiery deluge; so these appalling plagues will be premonitory of the final, the irresistible, and the all-destructive, stroke. Upon the human inhabitants of the world they will be sent in mercy as a last appeal: but men will only blaspheme God's name the more, and will not repent to give Him glory; while the Antichrist, goaded to blasphemous insanity, will dare—in spite of the threatening signs of Omnipotent interference, and the sudden catastrophe of his great city—to make war upon the Lamb.

But as soon as that conflict begins, it is ended. The saints upon earth have

Long and Painful Struggles

with the Powers of Darkness, and often do they need to remember the prophet's cry of faith—"Rejoice not against me, O mine enemy: when I fall, I shall arise; when I sit in darkness, the Lord shall be a light unto me." (Micah 7:8). Nay, even the angels have their one-and-twenty days of agonizing with the fallen High Ones that are still on high. (Dan. 10:13). But the instant that the glorious Lord appears, the foe will be paralyzed, and all resistance cease.

The last scene is sketched for us in the fourteenth chapter of Zechariah and the nineteenth of the Apocalypse.

The Armies of Antichrist

will have marched from Armageddon, in the north of Palestine, to besiege Jerusalem; and so numerous will they be that they will literally overspread the land. They will have closed in upon the Holy City, and the anxious eyes of those who peer from its loftiest watch-towers will be able to discern nothing but the serried ranks of splendid infantry and cavalry, and the long and heavy trains of artillery, covering the ground. Yet, although the inhabitants of Jerusalem are defenceless so far as carnal means are concerned, the spirit of grace and supplication is at last poured out upon them, and, as the cruel faces of the foe advance upon their city, fervent prayer is ascending from its midst; and, from no feigned lips, the cry goes up to God—"Oh that Thou wouldst rend the heavens, that Thou wouldst come down!"

There is, however, no interference: the foremost companies of the enemy are on the point of entering the streets: another moment, and the voice of prayer will be drowned by the outcries of terror and the shrieks of the wounded and the ravished. But, just at this awful crisis, the noon-day sun suddenly withdraws its light, and becomes black as sackcloth: the city is snatched from the view of those who are already sure of their prey: thick night enshrouds them:

A Horror of Great Darkness

paralyzes every eagerly advancing foot. An instant of silence, and then, swiftly as God's arrows speed from East to West, the blackness of heaven is cloven asunder, and the dazed earth flooded with a light such as it has never beheld since the sin of Adam. In the midst of the refulgent splendor the hosts of heaven are revealed descending towards Jerusalem, and at their head, conspicuous far beyond all, glorious in His apparel, and moving in the greatness of His strength, rides the Christ, at last confronting Antichrist.

Hitherto proud boastings have issued from the lips of Satan's king: but now he falls helplessly to the ground, blasted by the red lightning which streams from the King of kings; and, together with the False Prophet, and in full sight of his countless armies, he is seized by the angels of the Lord, to be hurled alive into the lake which burneth with fire and brimstone.

Christ Alights Upon the Earth,

and His feet stand upon the Mount of Olives, which is before Jerusalem on the East: there is a mighty earthquake, and the mountain cleaves asunder, one half moving towards the North and the other half towards the South, so that there is a great valley between them. (Zech. 14: 4.) Then the Jews, guided by a Divine impulse or command, pour out of their city and run into the newly formed valley, with such haste as they have never shown since they fled from before the earthquake in the days of Uzziah, king of Judah. (Zech. 14: 5.) For it is the place where the meek of the land are to be hidden: (Zeph. 2: 3) it is the rock cleft and the chamber prepared for them. (Isa. 26: 20, 21.). And as soou as they are safely enclosed within it, the Lord will destroy His irrepentant foes throughout the whole length of Palestine, from Armageddon to Bozrah; so that when the children of Abraham come forth from their covert, the multitudinous forces of the enemy, which would have devoured them, will be ashes beneath the soles of their feet. (Mal. 4: 2,3.) The merciless countenance of the Antichrist, "that opened not the house of his prisoners," (Isa. 14: 17) will have vanished for ever, and in his stead the Christ will be standing before them, their Redeemer and Saviour, who loved not His own life that He might bring them peace. How fair will He then appear to them: with what rapture will their hearts respond to the invitation to lead Him into Jerusalem as their King. For while the Lord will break in pieces all His persistent foes, He would have the hands of those who love Him to open their doors, that He may enter in.

How Glorious a Procession

will that be which will move from the cloven Mount of Olives to the Holy City. Along the very way, over the Brook Kidron and up to the gates of Jerusalem, which the Lord once trod in sorrow as He went to His death, He will now pass in triumph as the King of kings and Lord of lords, to see at length of the travail of His soul. It is for this time, probably, that the twenty-fourth Psalm was written: at least it marvellously expresses what must be the feelings of those Jews who will conduct their Messiah to the place which He has chosen, and who will not forget the command—"Cry out and shout, thou inhabitant of Zion: for great is the Holy One of Israel in the midst of thee."

Too often they will have heard the worshippers of the Antichrist denying, not merely the sovereignty, but even the very existence of the Father and the Son: they will be sufficiently acquainted with those evolutionary theories which have been already invented to demonstrate, on a basis of fiction, that the world was able to form itself, and had no need of a Creator. But after the wondrous things which their eyes have seen, with how full a heart will they sing:

"The earth is the Lord's, and the fulness thereof;
The world, and they that dwell therein.
For He hath founded it upon the seas,
And established it upon the floods."

Then, as they begin to ascend the hill toward the citadel, they will bethink them—The Holy One of Israel is in our midst; what manner of men must we be who are henceforth to dwell in His presence for ever!

By the prophet Daniel the Jews are called "the people of the Saints of the High Places," and these Saints with whom they are so closely connected are

The Glorified Church,

whose members will both accompany their great Head when He returns to Jerusalem, and will also watch over His earthly people during the Millennium. There is, then, no reader of these pages whom the Lord Jesus has not invited to be with Him, and to share His joy, on that wondrous day, when, after the lapse of so many weary centuries, He shall appear as the Deliverer, to turn away ungodliness from Jacob. And the day is fast approaching: for already the children of Abraham are being barried out of their dwellings among the Gentiles, and are beginning to gather to their own land.

* From his new work entitled, "Antichrist; Babylon and the Coming Kingdom"; a volume of remarkable originality and power, showing much scholarly research. 171 pages. Price in cloth, including postage, 50 cents. For sale at this office, 63 Bible House, New York.

A MUD IDOL IN DANGER.

THE effort to raise female character in the East is obstructed by a prejudice which is founded on the immorality associated with education in the only class of women who, prior to missionary work, had any learning at all. Mr. Gutterson who is laboring in the island of Madura in the Indian Archipelago, mentions two facts in a letter to the *Missionary Herald*, which show how dark is the present state of women there. He says that one of the Bible women employed by the American Board, noticed a woman worshipping an idol near her house. "Won't the next rain injure that god?" said the Bible-woman. "Yes; but so I've been taught to do, and I know of no better way; what is your way?" replies the woman. "For a long time many of the high-caste Hindus have objected," said the Bible-woman, "to my teaching their wives to read, it being the custom to teach only the temple dancing-girls." Such has been the state of society for generations; the idea of female education has been associated with the temple service, which was not that of a vestal. No wonder that civilization lags in the East. In England a woman takes a senior wrangler's prize in Greek, nor are American girls behind. In India men think it a disgrace to educate their daughters, and point with scorn to the life of those who have been taught to read.

A NIGHT OF PRAYER AGAINST CHOLERA.

AT the recent meeting of the International Medical Missionary Society in New York, of which the indefatigable Dr. Dowkontt is the founder and director, an interesting speech was made by Dr. George E. Post, who has labored for a quarter of a century as medical missionary in Syria. He said that as a clergyman he could never gain an entrance among these people, who would gladly welcome him as a Medical Missionary. He had himself been decorated by the Sultan, had ridden in state on the Pasha's own horse, attended by envoys and troops, and had lodged in the very palace. Moreover, hundreds of Moslem women had come to him in their times of sickness, who would never go to one of their own countrymen.

A poor Moslem woman, upon whose arm the Doctor had operated, was afterwards seen by him at her house surrounded by a lot of young girls. The Doctor read from Isaiah 53, and asked, "Who wrote these words?" "God." "Of whom were they spoken—of Mahomet?" "No, of Christ; it would not be true of anyone but Him." So they replied, and then fell on their knees in tears, and prayed with the Doctor to that Christ. A few years since Dr. Post was resting at Mount Lebanon, when a messenger came five days' journey asking for some medicine for cholera, as many were dying. There was a church of native converts in that city, and they had sent the man to Dr. Post. Instead of sending the medicine he decided to go himself. It was in August, the heat intense, but the Doctor and his faithful attendant went

His man, however, confessed fear of the cholera, and as they neared the city he begged the Doctor to let him stay outside all night to pray. But the Doctor stayed with him, and in the morning the man's fear was all gone, and they went in together, their self-sacrificing spirit causing all the people to forget their differences, leading them to meet to pray, and praise, and weep together. Not one of the Christians died from cholera.

A SUNDAY IN COLOMBIA.

In the course of a tour in the United States of Colombia which the Rev. J. C. Caldwell describes in a letter to the *Church*, he spent a Sunday in Zenza, which he was told was a very religious town. This is the way that Sunday was spent there: At last we arrived at the town, and inquired for lodgings at an inn. A tall, rough-looking fellow came out and said we might stop there, so we entered the house back of the saloon, glad to get any place to sleep, and after disposing of our beasts asked for dinner, and sat down to talk to curious people who began to gather about us. Next morning, Sabbath, when we came to take our chocolate and bread, we found our host with other gamblers seated at the dining-room table gambling. That day we rested and read and observed the habits of the people. I never saw such a "religious" place. Every little while the bells would ring for mass; people from all directions flocked from the surrounding country to the Catholic church. Between one mass and the next one the people spent the time either drinking and chattering, or quarrelling in the big square in front of the church, whilst our host, with many others among the principal men of the place, spent the time in gambling; at least we found them thus engaged when from time to time we had occasion to return to the dining-room, a miserable, filthy gambling-room.

A LUXURIOUS OPIUM DEN.

The following description of the most famous resort of opium smokers in China—the *nan-gin-tsen*, at Shanghai, appeared originally in the *North China Herald*. "This den," the report says, "is known throughout the length and breadth of the empire to the Chinese, and it helps to make Shanghai regarded as a city affording exceptional opportunities for pleasure and dissipation. It is situated in the French concession in Shanghai, within a stone's-throw of the wall of the native city, within which no opium shops are supposed to exist. The character of the place could not be guessed from its external appearance, although the air of the people passing in and out might suggest it. The throngs visiting it represent all stations of life, from the coolie to the wealthy merchant or the small mandarin. It is with difficulty that one gets inside through the crowds of people hanging round the door. Those who have not the requisite number of copper cash to procure the baneful pipe watch with horrible wistfulness each of the more affluent pass in with a nervous, hurried step, or totter out wearing that peculiar dazed expression which comes after the smoker's craving has been satisfied and his transient pleasure has passed away.

"One requires a strong stomach to stand the sickening fumes with which the air inside is thickened. The clouds of smoke, the dim light from the numerous colored lamps, the number of reclining forms with distorted faces bent over the small flames at which the pipes are lighted, cause the novice a sickening sensation. But as soon as the eye becomes accustomed to the scene, it is noticed that the place is got up on an expensive scale. In the centre of the lower room hangs one of the finest of Chinese lamps, the ceiling is of richly carved wood, while the painted walls are thickly inlaid with a peculiarly marked marble, which gives the idea of unfinished landscape sketches. Numerous doors on all sides lead to the smokers' apartments. In the outer portion of the building stands a counter covered with little boxes of the drug ready for smoking, which a dozen assistants are kept busy handing out to the servants who wait upon the *habitués* of the place. The average daily receipts are said to be about $1,000.

"The smoking apartments are divided into four classes. In the cheapest are coolies, who pay about eight cents for their smoke. In the dearest the smoke costs about fourteen cents. The drug supplied in each class is much the same both in quality and quantity; it is the difference in the pipes that regulates the price. The best kinds are made of ivory, the stem being often inlaid with stones and rendered more costly by reason of elaborate carving; the cheapest kinds are made simply of hard wood. The rooms also are furnished according to class. In the most expensive the lounge upon which the smoker reclines is of fine velvet, with pillows of the same material; the frames of each couch are inlaid with mother-of-pearl and jade, and the whole air of these rooms is one of sensuous luxury. There is also a number of private rooms.

"In the poorer section will be seen many wearers of the tattered yellow and gray robes of the Buddhist and Taoist priests. Women form a fair proportion of the smokers. The common belief is that the opium sleep is attended by a mild pleasurable delirium, with brief glances of Elysium; but this is the exception, not the rule. People smoke to satisfy the craving begotten of previous indulgence. There is accommodation for 150 smokers at a time, and there is seldom a vacancy very long. The stream of smokers goes on from early morning till midnight, when the place closes."

A FAMILY SAVED FROM DEATH.

One of those horrible tragedies comprising murder and suicide which occasionally startle the whole community, was averted recently by the timely visit of a Christian physician. Dr. Dowkontt, who is doing a grand work among the poor of New York by sending out the young men whom he is training for medical missionaries into the tenement house districts and slums of the city, to begin their work among the heathen at home, relates the incident. He says that word was brought to the dispensary that a family was in sickness and destitution, and a doctor was sent to investigate. He found a family of five persons under very painful circumstances. The father and husband had been trying in vain to get work, and the entire family had been two whole days without food. The wife and mother and one of the children were very sick, and all were in a starving condition. Some suitable food was soon obtained by the doctor, and appropriate medicine given, by which means their pressing needs were met.

During conversation had with them, the fact of the father having decided on the morning the doctor came to their aid, *to take the children's lives, his wife's and his own*, was made known. Temporary aid was given them for a time, work obtained for the man, and better still, both man and wife were led to the Saviour. Thus they were not only saved physically, the sick being healed, and the hungry fed and cared for—but we trust, and believe, that they were also saved spiritually, thus *saved body and soul.*

A MISSIONARY PIONEER.

One of the noble band of missionary pioneers whose names are now almost forgotten, save by those who, laboring in the same fields, find their labors lightened by the toil of their predecessors, was Bartholomew Ziegenbalg, whom Frederick IV., King of Denmark, sent out to labor for Christ, in Tranquebar. In a recently published work, reprinted in this country, by A. C. Armstrong & Son, of New York, Dr. Wm. Fleming Stevenson tells the story of his heroic labors under difficulties which would have crushed any man not supported by unwavering faith in God. He says:

The journey to India was then a serious matter. Sailing on November 29, they did not reach Tranquebar till July 9, 1706. It was early in the morning when they arrived, and they were ordered to remain in a house before the gate till the Governor had leisure to come in the afternoon. On his arrival, assuming the utmost roughness, he asked what brought them there. They were a mere nuisance. Had they any authority? What could he do? That was no place for missionaries. They were not wanted. What could the king know about such things? And so turned upon his heels and withdrew with his suite to the fort.

The sun had set, and as already the houses were shrouded in gloom the strangers could not tell what turn to take, but watched and waited under the silent stars—the first Protestant missionaries that ever stood on Indian soil, wondering much what would happen next, and bethinking themselves that even the Son of man had not where to lay His head.

Ziegenbalg and his friend owed their shelter for the next few days to the pity of one of the Governor's suite. Afterward they were permitted to occupy a house upon the wall, close by the heathen quarters, and here they settled down to their work, with patience and trust, a confession of their weakness and shrinking, and a quiet, manly resolution that are very touching. Six days after his arrival we find Ziegenbalg busy acquiring the first rudiments of Tamul, without books, grammars, dictionaries, or even an alphabet! By extraordinary industry he was able to speak the language intelligibly in eight months. In 1709 he could speak in Tamul as familiarly as in his native German. He had scarcely been two years in India when he began the translation of the New Testament. It was finished within three years, and then, with characteristic tenacity of purpose, he took the opportunity of a serious illness which interrupted his other labors, to commence the Old Testament, a much more formidable enterprise, and which he only succeeded in carrying as far as the end of Ruth. So this young priest who could preach in Tamul (he was only twenty-six) had already become a great power in southern India, and was shaking the heathen mind by his "incessant speaking about the things of God."

A DESCENDANT OF MOHAMMED REVILED.

A notable inquirer in Kurdistan was recently met by Rev. S. G. Wilson, the well-known Presbyterian missionary in Persia, during a tour among the Koords, which he describes in a letter to the *Church*. The man, he says, is a very intelligent and apparently sincere inquirer. He is owner of three villages, and the chief of a band of "Dervish penitents," while at the same time *a descendant of Mohammed*. His near relatives hold the chief religious offices in the district. He has long been a reader of the Bible, and has had much intercourse with preachers and missionaries. He is a frequent attendant at preaching, and has the name of being a Christian in the community. His relatives neglect and oppose him, and the boys in the street use his name as they would the devil's. Once he had the names of the apostles on a paper in his pocket, and it accidently fell out in the court-room. One of the judges picked it up, and with others began to assail him for his opinions. He boldly maintained the divinity of Christ, and with such ability that they were unable to answer him, and closed the discussion, saying, "Let him go; he is an infidel." At another time he and some Armenians were caught in a fierce snow-storm, and were greatly alarmed. The Kurd was heard by the Armenians to cry out, "Eli, Eli, lama sabachthani?" The Armenians, not recognizing the prayer, thought he was becoming demented; but he chided them for their ignorance of their own Scriptures. He says that *three times in distress he has prayed this prayer and been delivered.*

PUBLISHER'S NOTICE.

The whole edition of the Christian Herald was mailed last week to subscribers during Tuesday, May 29. The last delivery at the New York Post Office, duly receipted for, was made at 11.46 P. M. This information is given to enable subscribers whose copies of the paper are delayed, to make definite complaint to their Postmasters.

CURRENT EVENTS.

A Caucus of Democratic Members of the House held on May 30, pledged the party to united support of the Mills Tariff Bill, as it should be finally presented by the Committee on Ways and Means and to vote for no amendment unless proposed by a member of that committee. This decision of course will not be regarded as binding by Mr. Randall and his friends. A large number of amendments have also been presented by Democratic members which will probably receive a considerable amount of Democratic support. Against this, however, must be reckoned some Republican defections. That this element will have weight, there can be no doubt. In the vote that was taken on Thursday last, on the proposal to defer the operation of the free list until November 1889, the Democrats received the support of five Republicans—Messrs. Nelson and Lind, of Minnesota, Anderson and Fuller, of Iowa, and Smith of Wisconsin.

The Fisheries Treaty With Great Britain was debated last week in open Executive Session in the Senate. Mr. Frye, of Maine, who is the recognized leader of the opposition to ratification, condemned the treaty in strong terms. His speech was wholly devoted to denunciation of the treaty and the Government. The strong arguments which were expected from him were not adduced, but there is no doubt that they will be formulated by other Republican Senators in the course of the debate. Mr. Frye was apparently carried away by his indignation. He characterized the treaty as a cowardly betrayal of American interests—"the most disgraceful and humiliating surrender which the American Republic has ever made in its whole history." He admitted, however, that the retaliation act passed last session, went too far, and ought not to be carried out in its full terms. It is expected that Mr. Frye's speech will be effective as a campaign document.

An Important Letter From Mr. James G. Blaine was published on May 30. It was addressed to Mr. Whitelaw Reid, who with other friends of Mr. Blaine cherished the hope that in spite of the famous Florence letter, Mr. Blaine would accept a nomination to the Presidency if spontaneously and unanimously offered by the Republican National Convention. Mr. Blaine perceives that the uncertainty as to his course, which Mr. Reid's efforts have produced, was injurious to Republican prospects, and also embarrassed other candidates. He therefore reiterates in plainer terms his determination not to be a candidate. He says: "If I should now by speech or by silence, by commission or omission, permit my name in any event to come before the Convention, I should incur the reproach of being uncandid with those who have always been candid with me. The misrepresentations of malice have no weight, but the just displeasure of friends I could not patiently endure." Several Republican journals still urge that Mr. Blaine should be nominated, and insist that if the nomination were made by acclamation he would not refuse it. The majority of the Party, however, appear now to favor the nomination of Mr. Walter Q. Gresham, of Indiana, who was Postmaster-General, and subsequently Secretary of the Treasury in President Arthur's Cabinet. Most of the States have their "favorite sons," but Mr. Gresham seems to be the only one whose boom extends beyond his own State.

That the Mormons of Utah Have Not Abandoned Polygamy is evident in spite of recent declarations. Politicians who are advocating the admission of Utah to Statehood will therefore be grossly deceived if they imagine that the pledges made by the Mormons will be observed. Speaking last week at the dedication of a new temple at Manti, Lorenzo Snow, who glories in the title of "Apostle," plainly showed that the prosecutions for polygamy were in his opinion religious persecution. He said: "There never was a time when we were moving more swiftly in the path of exaltation. Some of the Elders have been to the penitentiary, and they came out better looking, and they will grow better looking. How far these persecutions may go it is not for me to know. It is not for me to care. Persecutions become a pleasure to those who suffer for righteousness. It was so with the three Hebrew children. There is no point at which we can say we have suffered enough to receive the rewards that God has promised us. We ought never to say we have had enough."

The Prohibition National Convention Assembled at Indianapolis, Ind., on May 30. Tomlinson Hall, in which the sittings were held, was densely crowded, though it has a seating capacity of five thousand. The permanent organization was made with Mr. John P. St. John, of Kansas, as chairman, and the Rev. Sam Small, the noted revivalist, as Secretary. On the following day the nominations were made. The Convention did not need to ballot for its candidate for President. *General Clinton B. Fisk*, of New Jersey, was nominated for that office by acclamation, as had been foreseen before the Convention met. The *Rev. John A. Brooks*, of Missouri, was nominated for Vice-President. The platform adopted, beside its most prominent plank on Prohibition, explicitly endorses female suffrage. As to the tariff question the platform says: "That an adequate public revenue being necessary it may properly be raised by import duties and by an equitable assessment upon the property and the legitimate business of the country, but import duties should be so reduced that no surplus shall be accumulated in the Treasury, and that the burdens of taxation shall be removed from foods, clothing and other comforts and necessaries of life." The only plank on which there was marked division was that relating to Female suffrage, and there were only sixty-three votes cast against that.

The Meetings of the National Civil Service Reform League, in New York last week, were anticipated with unusual interest, in view of the probability of Mr. Cleveland's renomination for the Presidency. There was general curiosity to learn whether, in the event of his being a candidate, the members of the League would support him, as they did in 1884. To that question the League gave no definite answer; but Mr Curtis, in his opening speech, did not conceal the fact that Mr. Cleveland's course had been a disappointment to civil service reformers. Beside this, he strongly advocated an amendment to the Constitution, making the President ineligible for re-election, which he contended would relieve him of the temptation to make appointments of an improper character for the sake of the support he would gain. By its resolutions, also, the League expressed its disappointment with the Administration, declaring that in many instances the forms of the civil service reform law have been so abused by appointees of the Administration, who are not in sympathy with reform, as to bring about widespread distrust in reform methods. The League, however, is not dismayed by the acknowledged failure of reform. Mr. Curtis contended that public opinion is being educated, and has made solid progress. Contrasting the present date with 1881, he showed that practices which then excited no comment, would now be generally condemned, and would place any party adopting them in a critical position at the polls.

A New Scheme for the Pacification of Ireland has been framed. The author is Mr. Chamberlain, whose opposition to Mr. Gladstone's plan was the most serious obstacle it encountered. Mr. Chamberlain's scheme, in brief, proposes to give each county in Ireland a governing board controlling county affairs, the police, and poor laws. The four provinces, Ulster, Munster, Connaught, and Leinster, are to be given provincial Parliaments. The object of this divergence from Mr. Gladstone's plan is to prevent the Protestants of Ulster being swamped in an Irish Parliament. The fact, however, of its conceding the principle of Home Rule in any shape must make it distasteful to the Conservatives and the bulk of the Unionists. So far the scheme has been received with ridicule, but as Lord Randolph Churchill's attack on the Government for breaking its pledges to Ireland has influenced public opinion, it is considered probable that Lord Salisbury may grant some concessions to Ireland on the basis of Mr. Chamberlain's proposals.

The Boulanger Movement in France Appears to be growing to proportions that are intoxicating to the General. In an interview published in a French journal last week he said: "I have been pushed to the front. There I am, and so long as I am wanted there I shall stay. Whatever people may tell you, I have promised only two things—the revision by means of a dissolution and the reform of the social laws, or, perhaps, I should say of the social manners. Where my promises are concerned *I shall go all lengths.* I cannot succeed at once, you object. Learn that it would be quite possible for me to precipitate events, but I have regarded it as my duty not to engage the country in disquieting adventures. Industry and commerce dread anything like a crisis. I hope to gain my ends calmly and logically by the mere force of things. What is called Boulangism if spreading like a tree with almost mathematical regularity, I am striving, I assure you, to pull back my too impetuous partisans by the coat-tails."

Reports from Zanzibar were Received in London, on May 28, professing to give reassuring intelligence of Mr. H. M. Stanley. They stated that messengers from Tippoo Tib, have arrived there with letters from Major Barttelot, dated Singatini, on the Congo, October 25. Major Barttelot says that deserters from Henry M. Stanley's camp had arrived at Singatini after a twenty days' canoe voyage. They reported that Stanley and all his party were well and had a plentiful supply of food. Major Barttelot's party is also well. The letters further say that the behavior of Tippoo Tip has not been satisfactory. No details are given regarding Stanley's route. An official of the American Geographical Society, on being shown the cable message, declared that the report was contradictory and evidently designed to mislead. He feared that Tippoo Tib had proved false to Stanley, and had conspired with African chiefs on his route to cut off the explorer's supplies of food and starve him and his party to death. The fact that Mr. Stanley expected to have reached Emin long ago, and that direct intelligence from him ought in that case to have been received, occasions serious apprehension as to the fate of the explorer.

The International Committee of Young Men's Christian Associations, at 40 East Twenty-third Street, New York, has just issued the Association "Year Book for 1888." From this pamphlet of 200 pages, it appears that there are now 1,240 Associations in America, and 3,804 in the world. The American Associations have a membership of 175,000; they own buildings valued at $5,609,265, and have a total net property of $7,261,658; last year they expended $1,181,338 in local work and $104,949 in general work. 752 men are devoting their entire time to the local, State, and International work as Secretaries and Assistants; there are 23 State Committees, that employ one or more travelling Secretaries, and the International Committee's secretarial force numbers 14; 77 of these Associations are engaged specially in work among railroad men; 10 among German-speaking young men; 273 are in colleges; 29 are colored, and 18 Indian.

The Great Methodist Conference in New York closed its business on May 31. The delegates in separating to their various spheres of labor expressed their gratification with their reception in the city. The total cost of the Conference including the travelling expenses and entertainment of delegates and the $5,000 paid for hire of the Opera House amounts to *Seventy thousand dollars*. The chief point of interest, to the Methodist community through the country, which was left to be decided at the conclusion of the Conference, was the assignment of the Bishops to the various sections for the ensuing four years. This was arranged according to the old precedent, each bishop having the choice in the order of his election. *Bishop Bowman*, the senior bishop, chose to remain at St. Louis. *Bishop Foster* is to be in Boston, and *Bishop Merrill* in Chicago. *Bishop Andrews* comes from Washington to New York, *Bishop Warren* remains in Denver, *Bishop Foss* goes from Minneapolis to Philadelphia, *Bishop Hurst* goes from Buffalo to Washington, *Bishop Ninde* remains at Topeka, *Bishop Walden* goes from Chattanooga to Covington or Cincinnati, *Bishop Mallalieu* remains at New Orleans, and *Bishop Fowler* remains at San Francisco. Of the five newly elected Bishops, *Bishop Vincent*, who was first elected, had first choice, and selected Buffalo, *Bishop Fitzgerald*, next in order, took Minneapolis, and *Bishop Joyce* chose Chattanooga, *Bishop Newman* selected the Omaha or Lincoln residence, and signified a strong probability that he would decide on Omaha. This left Texas only, and this section will be under the Episcopal charge of *Bishop Goodsell*.

A Cruising Evangelist has been Furnished with a vessel commissioned for Christian labor by the Congregational Sunday-school society. Five years ago a young man named George Lane, who used to be a Maine fisherman, having been converted, attempted to do some evangelistic work along the coast in his leisure time, travelling from place to place in his small skiff. Gradually he extended his work to the South, and succeeded in establishing many Sunday-schools, and his labors were greatly blessed. The attention of the Congregational Society was recently directed to his work, and a fine sloop, which he named *The Pilgrim*, has been purchased for his use. In the summer he will work along the east coast, and in the winter in the South. The boat that he formerly used was small and frail, but in the *Pilgrim* he will have a better floating house. There is a great deal of room for storage of Christian literature, as well as room to enjoy the comforts of life. In the summer his wife goes about with him, and he will carry one man for a sailor.

An Insect was Photographed by its Own light in Connecticut recently. The parents of a young lady in a school at Bridgeport, Conn., sent to her a few weeks ago a collection of beetles from Cuba. Among them were two or three specimens of the bug known as *Elater Noctilucus* or fire beetle of the West Indies. They measure about an inch in length and resemble in shape the New England spring beetle. On each side of the thorax is a large, oval velvety black spot, like an eye, and some of them have in place of the oval spot two translucent, opal-like spots on the sides of the thorax and from these at night the insect throws at will a strong light, resembling two tiny electric lamps in full glow. The light from one insect is sufficiently strong to enable one to read fine print with ease. When agitated the insect also gives out a similar light from the tissue between the segments on the under side of the body. The beetles were taken to a photographic artist in the city, who found that the light emitted from them though of a greenish hue, contained abundant actinic rays by which with a sensitive plate he could obtain negatives. After a few experiments he succeeded in taking a picture of one of the beetles by no light but that emitted by the beetle itself. It is too often forgotten that pictures of human character are taken in the same way: every man is judged by the light he gives. It is well for the world around him as for the man himself when that light is clear and heavenly coming from "the spirit of man which is the candle of the Lord." (Prov. 20: 27.)

A Cabin for Respectable People is Reserved on a ferry-boat plying between New York and the Brooklyn Navy Yard. Last week there was a dispute on board the boat, which belongs to the receiving ship *Vermont*, about the admission to the starboard cabin of some men who were going to the *Vermont* to enlist in the Navy, and it was said that the captain of the *Vermont* had ordered the cabin to be reserved for officers of the Navy. When, however, an appeal was taken to the captain by the men, he said: "I have issued no such order. There has always been a rule that visitors to the ship, and respectable people, shall occupy one side of the boat. The crowds of men who come over, desiring to enlist, and many other undesirable persons, are expected to stay on the other. The officers were merely enforcing this rule. No respectable person is kept off the boat." It is well for the world that no such distinction is made against those desiring to enlist in Christ's service, as is made against the men desiring to enlist in the service of the United States. Though they may not be respectable—may even be undesirable—the Great Captain of Salvation assures them of a cordial welcome, and they all enter His service by the same door. "There is no difference." (Rom. 3: 22.)

Houses are Kept for Ornament, not for Use, by a tribe of Indians near Black River Falls, Wis. A newspaper correspondent who visited the settlement which is occupied by the Winnebago Indians, says that many of them have little frame houses on their farms, with log stables for their ponies. All of the houses have some furniture, and some of them have become so far advanced as to have strips of carpet on the floor, and one high-toned family had a lounge and a hammock, while they nearly all have chairs or benches in their h[illegible] They seem to be there for ornament, [illegible] they are rarely used, for the people prefer to sit on the floor. During the summer, and in some cases during the winter, they build their wigwams in the yard near the houses, and occupy them in preference to the houses. They like to tell about their houses, and take pride in their possessions, but the habits of a life-time are too strong for them to surrender, and while the house is a good thing to talk about, the wigwam is their ideal home. To the white men it seems a crazy thing for a man to sit on the floor when he has chairs, and to live in a wigwam when he has a house, but there are many Christian men who show a similar perversity in their spiritual life. God has placed at their disposal His Almighty provision, yet they persist in worrying and harassing themselves about their temporal concerns, instead of living in peace and faith in the promises. (1 Peter 5: 7).

A Young Man Trying to Discover his Own name, applied to an official of the Board of Health, in New York, on May 30. The young man said that he always believed that his name was Louis Wilson. He had just arrived from Germany, from which country he had escaped to get evidence to prove to the German Government that he is an American, and that he is not subject to be drafted for service in the German army. His mother, who, before her death, resided in Nuremberg, had told him that he was born in New York eighteen years ago. He started for America, and was put under arrest at Bremerhaven for seeking to avoid military duty, but was released, with a warning that he must not attempt to leave the country. He escaped to Scotland, whence he made his way back to America. He searched the records of the Board of Health to no purpose, but at Bellevue Hospital he found a record that in 1870 a female patient, named Wilson, had given birth to a male child. The doctor who attended the case is dead, and the young man does not know how to establish his identity. He was advised to write to the Secretary of State, and place himself under the protection of the Government. It is doubtful, however, whether Mr. Bayard can protect him without some evidence of his having been born in this country. It is well for the young man that only his physical interests are thus embarrassed. If he has been born again, his King is able to keep his soul from the clutches of his enemies (John 10: 28).

BRIEF NOTES.

An examination of the records of the penitentiary at Joliet, Ill., shows that ninety-two per cent. of the prisoners brought there used intoxicants.

The will of Mrs. J. S. Waterman, of Sycamore, Ill., leaves her residence and sixty acres of land for a school for girls, with a fund of $200,000 for its maintenance.

The general agent of the John F. Slater Fund reports that during the past year $45,000 has been distributed among forty-five educational institutions in the South.

Rev. C. H. Yatman commenced on June 1, a series of union young people's meetings in Washington, D. C. by invitation of the superintendents of the Sunday-schools.

The Hartford (Conn.) Young Men's Christian Association has been authorized by General Charles T. Hillyer to buy a site for their new building, not to cost over $30,000, which he would contribute.

Mrs. Lizzie D. Johnson desires us to thank the friends who have supplied her with copies of this journal to distribute in the Texas prisons. Much good has resulted from it, and she earnestly hopes the friends will continue so to aid her.

Rev. B. Fay Mills went from Chelsea, Mass., to Gloversville, N. Y., to hold meetings. The mission at Chelsea has left abiding results in that place. Over 700 persons have united with the various churches who were brought to decision at Mr. Mills' services.

At the Methodist General Conference it was stated that connected with the various M. E. churches there are 24,225 Sunday-schools, 268,391 officers and teachers, 2,008,328 scholars, an increase during the quadrennium of 2,772 schools, 38,826 teachers, 312,708 scholars.

The Woman's Christian Temperance Union of Monroe County, N. Y., has presented Mrs. Cleveland with an elegant Griffith Club microscope and accessories, in recognition of her temperance views. The microscope was made specially, and is of the finest workmanship.

It is proposed to establish in Bethany ("the town of Mary, and her sister, Martha") a home which shall form a centre of Christian work. The village has to-day about five hundred inhabitants. A piece of land has been secured, and the prospect is said to be encouraging.

Major Whittle's meetings in Winona, Minn., have been very successful. The number of converts is said to be over three hundred, and among them were several of the most prominent men of the city. Dr. L. W. Munhall paid a visit to Winona from St. Paul, to give one day to the work.

The number of delegates from the United States to the general Conference on Foreign Missions, to be held in London, June 9-19, is one hundred and sixty-eight. Most of them have already sailed. The London committee earnestly hope that the meetings be made the subject of prayer during their continuance.

Mr. Moody's College Student's Summer School and encampment at Northfield, Mass., is announced to begin on June 30, and continue to the 15th of July. The course of Bible study is to be conducted by Mr. Moody, who has invited a number of prominent men from the United States and elsewhere to take part in the meetings.

Pascal Porter, a boy only eleven years of age, whose parents live in Jefferson County, Ind., has been delivering gospel addresses in that State, and in Kentucky. The Louisville *Courier Journal* says, He shows a wonderful acquaintance with the Bible, is modest in deportment, and has been very successful among children.

A DESIRABLE POSSESSION.

A New Sermon by Pastor C. H. Spurgeon.

"These things have I written unto you that believe on the name of the Son of God, that ye may know that ye have eternal life, and that ye may believe on the name of the Son of God."—1 John 5:13.

Why the Bible is Read with Indifference—A Legatee's Interest in a Will—I. John's Special Purpose Threefold—To Implant Full Assurance—A Minister Dependent on the Wind—The Three Witnesses—Intensive Faith Wanted—Courageous Faith—Joyful Faith—II. John's Purpose Followed—A Religion Hardly Worth Keeping—A Blind Child's Confidence—A Caviller in an Omnibus—Mr. Dodd's Dying Words.

JOHN wrote to believers—"These things have I written unto you that believe on the name of the Son of God." It is worthy of note, that all the epistles are so written. They are not letters to everybody, they are letters to those who are called to be saints. It ought to strike some of you with awe when you open the Bible and think how large a part of it is not directed to you. You may read it, and God's Holy Spirit may graciously bless it to you, but it is not directed to you. You are reading another man's letter: thank God that you are permitted to read it, but long to be numbered with those to whom it is directed. Thank God much more if any part of it should be used of the Holy Ghost for your salvation.

We do not wonder that certain men do not receive the epistles, for they were not written to them. Why should they cavil at words which are addressed to men of another sort from themselves? Yet we do not marvel, for we knew it would be so. Here is a will, and you begin to read it; but you do not find it interesting; it is full of words and terms which you do not take the trouble to understand, because they have no relation to yourself; but should you come upon a clause in which

An Estate is Left to You,

I warrant you that the nature of the whole document will seem changed to you. You will be anxious now to understand the terms, and to make sure of the clauses, and you will even wish to remember every word of the clause which refers to yourself. Oh, dear friends, may you read the Testament of our Lord Jesus Christ as a testament of love to yourselves.

This leads me to make the second remark, that as these things are written to believers, believers ought especially to make themselves acquainted with them, and to search into their meaning and intent. John says, "These things have I written unto you that believe on the name of the Son of God." Do not, I beseech you, neglect to read what the Holy Ghost has taken care to write to you. It is not merely John that writes. John is inspired of the Lord, and these things are written to you by the Spirit of God. Give earnest heed to every single word of what God has sent as His own epistle to your hearts. This much is the porch of my sermon; let us now enter more fully into our subject, noticing:

I. First, that John wrote with a special purpose. Men do not write well, unless they have some end in writing. To sit down, with paper and ink before you, and so much space to fill up, will ensure very poor writing. John knew what he was at. His intent and aim were clear to his own mind, and he tells us what they were. According to the text, the beloved apostle had

One Clear Purpose,

which branched out into three. To begin with, John wrote that we might enjoy the full assurance of our salvation. "These things have I written unto you that believe on the name of the Son of God, that ye may know that ye have eternal life." Many who believe on the name of Jesus are not sure that they have eternal life; they only hope so. Occasionally they have assurance, but the joy is not abiding. They are like a minister I have heard of, who said he felt assured of his salvation, "*except when the wind was in the east.*" It is a wretched thing to be so subject to circumstances as many are. What is true when the wind is in the soft south or the reviving west, is equally true when the wind is neither good for man nor beast. John would not have our assurance vary with the weather-glass, nor turn with the vane. He says, "These things have I written unto you, that ye may *know* that ye have eternal life."

I speak affectionately to the weaker ones, who cannot yet say that they know they have believed. I speak not to your condemnation, but to your consolation. Full assurance is *not essential to salvation*, but it is

Essential to Satisfaction.

May you all get it—may you get it at once; at any rate, may you never be satisfied to live without it. You may have full assurance. You may have it without personal revelations: it is wrought in us by the Word of God. These things are written that you may have it; and we may be sure that the means used by the Spirit are equal to the effect which he desires. Under the guidance of the Spirit of God, John so wrote as to attain his end in writing.

He begins thus: "Whosoever believeth that Jesus is the Christ is born of God." Do you believe that Jesus is the anointed of God? Is He so to you? If so, you are born of God. "How may I know this?" Brethren, our evidence is the witness of God Himself as here recorded. We need no other witness. John has thus positively declared the truth, that you may know that you have eternal life. Can anything be more clear than this?

The loving spirit of John leads him to say, "Every one that loveth Him that begat, loveth Him also that is begotten of Him." Do you love God? Do you love His only begotten Son? You can answer those two questions surely. I knew a dear Christian woman who would sometimes say, "I know that I love Jesus; but my fear is that He does not love me." Her doubt used to make me smile, for it never could have occurred to me. Love to Jesus is an effect which proves the existence of its cause.

John goes on to give another evidence: "By this we know that we love the children of God, when we love God, and keep His commandments." Obedience is

The Grand Test of Love.

If you are living after your own will, and pay no homage to God, you are none of His. If you never think of the Lord Jesus as your Master, and never recognize the claims of God, and never wish to be obedient to His will, you are not in possession of eternal life. If you desire to be obedient, and prove that desire by your actions, then you have the divine life within you. Judge yourselves. Is the tenor of your life obedience or disobedience? By the fruit you can test the root and the sap.

But note, that this obedience must be cheerful and willing. No doubt some for a while obey the commands of God unwillingly. They do not like them, though they bow to them. They fret and grizzle because of the restraints of piety; and this proves that they are hypocrites. What you wish to do, you practically are doing in the sight of God. If there could be such a thing as holiness forced upon a man, it would be unholiness. O my hearer, it may be that you cannot fall into a certain line of sin; but if you could, you would: your desires show what you really are. I have heard of Christian people, so-called, going to sinful amusements, just, as they say, to enjoy a little pleasure. Ah well, we see where you are! Where your pleasure is, your heart is. If you enjoy the pleasure of the world, you are of the world, and with the world you will be condemned. If God's commands are grievous to you, then you are a rebel at heart. Loyal subjects delight in the royal law. "His commandments are not grievous."

I said to one who came to join the church the other day, "I suppose you are not perfect?" and the reply was, "No, sir, I wish I might be." I said, "And suppose you were"? "Oh, then," she said, "that would be heaven to me." So it would be to me. We delight in the law of God after the inward man. Oh, that we could perfectly obey in thought, and word, and deed! This is our view of heaven. We would scarce ask to be rid of sorrow, if we might be rid of sin. We would bear any burden cheerfully if we could live without the slightest fault of omission or commission. When we are without spot we shall also be without grief. His commandments are not grievous, but they are ways of pleasantness and peace to us. Do you feel that you love the ways of God, that you desire holiness, and follow after it joyfully? Then, dear friends, you have eternal life, and these are the sure evidences of it.

John then proceeds to mention

Three Witnesses.

Now, dear hearers, do you know anything about these three witnesses? "There are three that bear witness in earth; the spirit, and the water, and the blood: and these three agree in one." Do you know "the Spirit"? Has the Spirit of God quickened you, changed you, illuminated you, sanctified you? If so, you are alive unto God. Next, do you know "the water," the purifying power of the death of Christ? Does the crucified Lord crucify your sins? Is the water applied to you to remove the power of sin? Do you now long to perfect holiness in the fear of God? This proves that you have eternal life. Do you also know "the blood?" Do you know the power of the blood to take away sin, the power of the blood to speak peace to the conscience, the power of the blood to give access to the throne of grace? Do you know the quickening, restoring, cheering power of the precious blood of Christ, which is set forth in the Lord's Supper by the fruit of the vine? Then in the mouth of these three witnesses shall the fact of your having eternal life be fully established.

Not Transient.

Furthermore, John wrote that we might know our spiritual life to be eternal. Please notice this, for there are some of God's children who have not yet learned this cheering lesson. The life of God in the soul is not transient, but abiding; not temporary, but eternal. Some think that the life of God in the believer's soul may die out; but how, then, could it be eternal? If it die, it is not eternal life. If it be eternal life, it cannot die. Beloved, our Lord Jesus Christ calls the life of His people eternal life. How often do I quote this text! It seems to lie on the tip of my tongue; "I give unto My sheep eternal life; and they shall never perish, neither shall any pluck them out of My hand." And again, "He that believeth in Him hath everlasting life." It is not temporary life, not life which at a certain period must grow old and die, but everlasting life. "It shall be in him a well of water springing up into everlasting life."

Once more, according to the Authorized text, though not according to the Revised Version, John desired the increase and confirmation of their faith. He says, "That ye might believe on the name of the Son of God." John wrote to those who believed, that they might believe in a more emphatic sense. As our Saviour has come not only that we may have life, but that we may have it more abundantly, so does John write, that having faith

We May Have More of It.

Come, beloved, listen for a moment to this! You have the milk of faith, but God wills that you should have the cream of assurance! He would increase your faith. May you believe more extensively. Perhaps you do not believe all the truth, because you have not yet perceived it. Perhaps your doctrinal belief has been poor and thin. Many of you live upon milk, and yet your years qualify you to feed on meat. Why keep to babes' diet?

It will be well for you if your faith also increases intensively. Oh that you may more fully believe what you do believe! We need deeper insight and firmer conviction. We do not half believe, as yet, any of us. Many of you only skim the pools of truth. Blessed is the wing which brushes the surface of the river of life; but infinitely more blessed is it to plunge into the depths of it. This is John's desire for you. that you believe with all your heart, and soul, and strength.

He would have us trust courageously. Some can believe in a small way

About Small Things.

Oh for a boundless trust in the infinite God! We need more of a venturesome faith; the faith to do and dare. Often we see the way of power, but have not the faith which would be equal to it. See Peter walking on the sea! I do not advise any of you to try it, neither did our Lord advise Peter to do so; we do well enough if we walk uprightly on land. But when Peter had once taken a few steps on the sea, he ought to have known that his Lord could help him all the rest of the way; but alas! his faith failed, and he began to sink. He could have walked all the way to Jesus if he had but believed right on. So is it with us: our faith is good enough for a spurt, but it lacks staying power. If the Lord bids you, you may go through fire and not be burned, through the floods and not be drowned. Such a fearless, careless, conquering faith may the Lord work in us!

We need to believe more joyfully. Oh, what a blessed thing it is when you reach the rest and joy of faith! If we would truly believe the promise of God, and rest in the Lord's certain fulfilment of it, we might be as happy as the angels. I notice very early in the morning how the birds begin to sing; before the sun is up or even the first gray tints of morning light are visible, the little songsters are awake and singing. Too often we refuse to sing until the sun is more than up, and noon is near. Shame on us! Will we never trust our God? Will we never praise Him for favors to come? Oh, for a faith that can sing through the night and through the winter! The Lord give you such faith.

II. Thus I have gone through my first head, and taken nearly all the time. I must now come to push of pike, as the old soldiers used to say. We must drive our teaching home. The purpose which John had in his mind,

We Ought to Follow Up.

Our conscience tells us that we ought to seek full assurance of salvation. It cannot be right for us to be children of God, and not to know our own Father. How can we kneel down and say, "Our Father which art in heaven," when we do not know whether He is our Father or not? Will not a life of doubt tend to be a life of falsehood? Can you rest? Dare you rest, while it is a question whether you are saved or not? Can you go home to your dinner to-day and enjoy your meal, while there is a question about your soul's eternal life? Oh, be not so foolhardy as to run risks on that matter! I pray you, make sure work for eternity. If you leave anything in uncertainty, let it concern your body or your estate, but not your soul.

Listen, as I close, to this mass of reasons why each believer should seek to know that he has eternal life. Here they are. Assurance of your salvation will bring you "the peace of God which passeth all understanding." If you know that you are saved, you can sit down in poverty, or in sickness, or under slander, and feel content.

Assurance is the Koh-i-noor

amongst the jewels wherewith the heavenly Bridegroom adorns His spouse. Full assurance will sometimes overflow in cataracts of delight. Peace flows like a river, and here and there it leaps in cascades of ecstatic joy. There are seasons when the plant of peace is in flower, and then it sheds a perfume as of myrrh and cassia. Oh, the blessedness of the man who knows that he has eternal life! That religion which sets no sweetmeats on the table is a niggardly housekeeper. I do not wonder that some people give up their starveling religion: *it is hardly worth the keeping*. The child of God who knows that he has eternal life goes to school, but he has many a holiday; and he anticipates that day of home-going when he shall see the face of his Beloved forever.

Full assurance gives a man a grateful zeal for the God he loves. These are the people that will go to the Congo for Jesus, for they know they are His. These are the people that will lay down their all for Christ, for Christ is theirs. These are the people that will bear scorn and shame and misrepresentation for the truth's sake, for they know that they have eternal life. These are they that will keep on preaching and teaching, spending and working, for theirs is the kingdom of heaven, and they know it. Men will do little for what they doubt, and much for what they believe. If you have lost your title deeds, and you do not know whether your house is your own or not, you are not going to spend much in repairs and enlargements. When you know that heaven is yours, you are anxious to get ready for it. Full assurance finds

Fuel for Zeal to Feed Upon.

This also creates and sustains patience. When we know that we have eternal life, we do not fret about the trials of this passing life. I could point to brethren here this morning, and I could mention sisters at home, who amaze me by their endurance of pain and weakness. They know that they are the Lord's, and so they say, "Let Him do what seemeth him good." *A blind child* was in his father's arms, and a stranger came into the room, and took him right away from his father. Yet he did not cry or complain. His father said to him, "Johnny, are you afraid? You do not know the person who has got hold of you." "No, father," he said, "I do not know who he is, but you do." When pain gives us an awkward nip, and we do not know whether we shall live or die, when we are called to undergo a dangerous operation, and pass into unconsciousness, then we can say, "I do not know where I am, but my Father knows, and I leave all with Him." Assurance makes us strong to suffer. This will give you constant firmness in your confession of divine truth. You who do not know whether you are saved or not, I hope the Lord will keep you from denying the faith; but those who have a firm grip of it, these are the men who never will forsake it.

A Caviller in an Omnibus

said to a Christian man one day, "Why, you have nothing after all to rest upon. I can prove to you that your Scriptures are not authentic." The humble Christian man replied, "Sir, I am not a learned man, and I cannot answer your questions; but I believe in the Lord Jesus Christ, and I have experienced such a change of character, and I feel such joy and peace through believing, that I wish you knew my Saviour, too." The answer he received was a very unexpected one: the unbeliever said, "You have got me there; I cannot answer *that*." Just so: we have got them there. If we know what has been wrought in us by grace, and know assuredly the sustaining power of that grace, they cannot overcome us. *The full-assurance man baffles the very devil.*

Dear brethren, this is the kind of thing that will enable you to bear a telling testimony for your Lord. It is of no use to stand up and preach things that may or may not be true. I am charged with being a dreadful dogmatist, and I am not anxious to excuse myself. When a man is not quite sure of a thing, he grows very liberal; anybody can be liberal with money which he cannot claim to be his own. The broad-school man says, "I am not sure, and I do not suppose that you are sure, for indeed nothing is sure." Does this sandy foundation suit you? I prefer rock. The things which I have spoken to you from my youth up have been such as I have tried and proved, and to me they wear an absolute certainty, confirmed by my personal experience. I have tried these things: they have saved me, and I cannot doubt them.

Brethren, if you know that you have eternal life, you are prepared to live, and equally prepared to die. How frequently do I stand at the bedside of our dying members! I am every now and then saying to myself, "I shall certainly meet with some faint-hearted one. Surely I shall come across some child of God who is dying in the dark." But I have not met with any such. Brethren, a child of God may die in the dark. One said to old Mr. Dodd, the quaint old Puritan—"How sad that our brother should have passed away in darkness! Do you doubt his safety?" "No," said old Mr. Dodd, "no more than I doubt the safety of Him who said, when He was dying, 'My God, My God, why hast thou forsaken me?'" God grant that you may have this assurance, all of you! May sinners begin to believe in Jesus, and saints believe more firmly, for Christ's sake! Amen.

GEMS FROM NEW BOOKS.

A CANDIDATE'S BLUNDER.*

SOME years ago a young aspirant for office in Iowa drove up to a hotel, alighted and engaged a room. He desired his trunk taken to his room; and, seeing a man passing whom he supposed to be the porter, he imperiously ordered him to take it up. The porter charged him twenty-five cents, which he paid with a plugged quarter, worth only twenty cents. He then said, "You know Governor Grimes?" "O yes, sir!" "Well, take my card to him, and tell him I wish an interview at his earliest convenience." "I am Governor Grimes," said the supposed porter, "at your service, sir." "You—I—that is, my dear sir, I beg a thousand pardons!" "None needed at all, sir," said the Governor. "I was rather favorably impressed with your letter, and had thought you well suited for the office specified; but sir, any man who would swindle a working man out of five cents would defraud the public treasury if he had opportunity. Good evening sir."

The Artist's Warning.

There was an old German father who tried to make something good and useful out of his boy. But the son was an artist and he liked to dream and paint and skip his day's work on the farm whenever he could do so. At last, just before his son left him to go to Paris, where he was about to study art, the old father said to him: "Tony, my son, remember this last advice of your old father: our passions are our greatest enemies. What we want to do is to be able to command them. The discipline of the human will is the secret of durable conquests and long happiness. Tony, I have always loved the crowing of the cock. It announces the day and chases away the phantoms of the night. The sound resembles a war-cry. It admonishes us to spend our lives in fighting against ourselves."

A year or two after this, when his father had died, Tony, then a rising young artist in Paris, was tempted by his companions to join a band of gamblers, who were making money at the expense of foreigners in Paris. One night when he was lying awake thinking over in his mind whether or not he should go with these bad companions he heard a cock crow. Like the crowing of the cock which brought to Simon Peter's memory the words of Jesus, the sound of the crowing brought back to Tony the last words of his honest old father. That morning crow sounded like a voice from his father's grave, and it turned the scale of his will. He said no to his tempters and gained the victory over the evil passions within him.

A Friendless Boy.

There was a boy at school named Carl who quarrelled with all his companions, and he made up his mind that he would cross off his list of friends every one he quarrelled with. At last, in the midst of the long winter term, he found that he had quarrelled with them all, and that there was really not one left for him to play with. At last one day the teacher found him looking through a knot-hole in the fence at the other boys playing ball in the play-ground. "What are you doing, Carl?" asked the teacher. "I am looking at the boys playing, sir," answered Carl. "Why don't you play with

---

* From "A Father's Blessing," and other Sermons for Children, by William Wilberforce Newton, an excellent volume of pithy, bright thoughts in plain language, with incidents from history and current events. A valuable volume for a father to put into his boy's hands. 343 pages. Price $1.25. Published by *Robert Carter & Brothers*, 530 Broadway, New York.

Interior of a Japanese Home.

A Father's Merciless Beating of His Christian Daughter in Africa.

them?" the teacher asked. "Because I'm mad at them all, and vowed I wouldn't play with them again," said the boy. "Well then," said his teacher why do you look at them instead of playing by yourself?" Carl was silent a moment and then replied, "Because I'm so awfully tired of myself."

We very soon get tired of ourselves in this world, and it is a great help to us at times to feel that we can play with other people and can have them comfort us. Do not despise other people; other people often bring great blessings to us, as they did to the tribe of Zebulon with his haven for ships.

A PERSECUTED AFRICAN CONVERT.

(See Illustration.)

A NATIVE Christian of the Cameroons, Africa, passing through a village inhabited by a heathen tribe, remained there a few days, that he might speak of Christ to the people. The message apparently bore no fruit, but after a short time one girl gave evidence of having heard the truth with saving power. Under further instruction, she became a believer in Christ and renounced the idols of the tribe. Her father was exasperated with her conduct, and conceiving that he himself was disgraced by his daughter's renunciation of her ancestral religion, resolved to punish her publicly. At first his persecution was limited to solitary confinement. She was shut up in a hut alone without food or water. The girl, however, remained firm, and the father then abandoning hope of conquering her by that means, took her out into the middle of the village, and there beat her severely in the presence of the whole tribe. Not even then did the girl's fidelity to Christ waver. She was supported by the power of the Holy Spirit, and continued to testify to the truth of the White Man's Religion. But, while her soul strengthened, her body sank under the cruelty to which she had been subjected. The beating might not have been fatal had it not followed close confinement and fasting. As it was, she sank, and, after a short illness, passed away, declaring to the last her faith in Christ. The missionary who relates the incident states that the hut in which she was imprisoned is now used as a place of Christian teaching, and the father whose cruelty caused her death has himself become a Christian.

A JAPANESE HOME.

(See Illustration.)

IT is only in comparatively recent times that trustworthy information about Japan and the Japanese has been available. So closely was the country closed against Western intrusion that the manners and customs of the people were completely unknown. Now, however, a more enlightened policy has been adopted by the Government, and a strong desire is manifested for the introduction of Western civilization.

Our illustration represents the interior of a home occupied by a middle class family in Japan. It is the time of the customary evening meal, which in Japan is usually of the lightest and most digestible kind.

The people bear a strong resemblance to the Chinese, both in appearance and in their way of life. They are rather under middle size, well made, and robust, with complexion either brown or pale; but their distinctive feature is the eye, which is small, oblong, or almond-shaped, and deeply sunk in the head. They have the head large, the neck short, the nose large, black hair, thick and shining from the oil they rub into it.

As lately as 1870, the whole nation, of *thirty-five millions* of inhabitants, was sunk in spiritual darkness. In that year, however, Mr. Goble, an American missionary, went there in faith, and supporting himself by his own labors, learned the language and began preaching the gospel. Now, several missionary societies, both American and English, are represented in the work, and are making encouraging progress.

THE RESCUE OF THE WIDOW'S SON.

(See Illustration on Page 365.)

"ARTHUR, you will have to earn your own living, my boy," said a dying man, who had called his son, a youth of some sixteen years, to his bedside. "I meant to have sent you to college and put you in the way of entering professional life; but the Lord has ordered things differently. I am going to die, and your mother and Lottie will have only just enough to support them. The little I leave, with the insurance, must be safely invested, and safe investments do not pay very high interest. Still they can live on the income, for your mother is economical. But you must not be a burden upon them. You must get a clerk's position and do your best."

"I will, father, I will," said Arthur.

"And be a comfort to your mother, Arthur, and take care of Lottie. You must take my place as far as you can. Be a good son and a good brother. I leave them to you. Look to God for help and guidance, and He will be a Father to you."

Arthur promised that he would, and after his father's death, he lost no time in seeking work. Unhappily the only available place offered him was in a city some two hundred miles off. His mother would have had him decline it and wait for some opportunity near home, but Arthur was anxious to set to work at once, and, moreover, was fascinated by the prospect of city life. He was a country lad, and as is usual his ideas of the grandeur of a city were far beyond the reality. Very sorrowfully Mrs. Edgerton packed his trunks, saw that his outfit was thoroughly complete, and bought a new Bible, which she put in with a prayer that it might be blest to him. Then commending her boy to the care of God, she bade him good-bye with many tears.

Arthur felt that he was going out to seek his fortune. How many men, now millionaires, had gone as he was going, a poor lad, from the country to the city. He would work hard, would find out how money was made, and some day he would come back rich, and then his mother should see what he would do for her. What would she like him to do? Arthur's castles in the air sprang up quickly. Before he reached his destination he saw himself taking his mother and Lottie to a grand mansion of his own and installing them there, surrounded with every luxury that money could buy. He saw himself honored by his father's friends, elected Mayor of his native town, perhaps sent to Congress. Who could tell what he might not rise to! Some of the Presidents had not had any greater advantages than he.

Poor lad! If he had known a little more of

city life he might have been less sanguine. The country stamp was so plainly written on his face and form and dress, that his fellow-clerks chaffed him, and as he thought, despised him. He was dull and lonely and miserable. Everything was so different from what he had expected. It was not surprising that in his eagerness to shake off his country manners and to make friends, he should have fallen into snares set for the unwary. He was anxious to familiarize himself with city life and city ways, and the guidance he had was of the worst kind. If some earnest Christian had made his acquaintance, he might have been kept from the evil, but none such reached him.

It was about two years after Arthur's leaving home that Mrs. Egerton received a letter in a handwriting with which she was not familiar, saying that her son was seriously ill, and suggesting that she should come to nurse him. Of late letters from him had been growing less and less frequent, and she had become more and more uneasy about him. She knew that he was doing well in his employment, for each half year his salary had been raised, and Arthur had reported to her the favorable terms in which his employers spoke of him, but of his social life she knew nothing. This letter, therefore, filled her with forebodings, and she set out on her journey with an aching heart.

Arthur was delirious when his mother arrived and did not know her. The doctor who attended him spoke doubtfully of his recovery, and hinted that the difficulties in the case were largely due to the irregular life he had been leading. One or two men came, who said Arthur owed them money, and wanted her to pay them. Arthur's own talk, in his delirium, confirmed her fears, for it was evident that he fancied himself in drinking circles and among betting men. Mrs. Edgerton did not understand much of his talk, but she understood enough to know that he had wandered far away from the paths of temperance and virtue. Still he was her own boy, and his sins seemed to appeal to her heart for her greater love, that she might win him back to righteousness.

It was a long weary time of anxiety and distress, but Arthur's naturally good constitution triumphed at last over his disease, and with the first sign of convalescence his mother carried him off to her country home. There he rapidly regained strength, and was able to get around the house and garden with daily increasing vigor. Mrs. Edgerton had forborne to say anything to him of his life, or of what she had learned from his own lips in his sickness. He was often lost in thought, and she trusted that repentance was in his heart. But she waited for him to confide in her.

One evening, the trio sat in the cozy parlor, Mrs. Edgerton at her needlework, Lottie reading aloud a volume of religious biography, and Arthur sitting in a fit of abstraction. He had been unusually silent all day, and more than once Mrs. Edgerton had gone to her room, and prayed that God would lead him to make the confession which she hoped was almost upon his lips. Lottie laid her book down at last, and said she was tired out, and would go to bed. Then, when mother and son were alone together, Arthur spoke. The whole sorrowful story was told. He did not know that she was prepared to hear it, and was surprised that her joy so quickly overcame the distress it naturally caused her. Together they knelt to beseech God's forgiveness, and Arthur solemnly consecrated his future life to the Saviour.

The Widow Awaiting Her Son's Confession.

THE EPOCHS OF A LIFE.

A NEW SERIAL STORY.

By Rev. L. S. Keyser.

Author of "The Way Out," etc.

(Continued from page 351.)

IN THE PUBLIC ARENA.

AFTER a little more interchange of thought, the young men separated, promising to meet and compare notes as frequently as possible. George walked rapidly down the hill, pursued the valley for nearly a mile, crossed the creek on a log that had fallen from bank to bank, and then leaving the bottom-lands, he made his way across the hills to his home, unconscious of the harm he had done himself and his friend.

But he experienced no pleasure in his walk. A feeling of compunction and self-contempt on account of the falsehood he had told, oppressed him, and it was many days before he could again look his father full in the face. George resolved that he would thereafter employ no "strategy" to relieve himself of embarrassments. It must be said for him that he was a young man of high moral ideals, and, except in the instance just described, he had always been scrupulously truthful.

Hadley, engrossed in deep thought, walked slowly through the orchard back to the house. From that day a great change came over him, and the change was not for the better. Terrible doubt and rebellion rankled in his heart, destroying his peace for many years.

Here was the home of his childhood, a spot made sacred by the associations that clustered around it; and yet, after that day, it was different, and he was dissatisfied with it. What if it had been a nursery of error and delusion for him? the school in which he had been made the dupe of a monstrous and enslaving imposture? The thought chafed and irritated him.

And yonder were the hills over whose slopes and summits he had often rambled, and from which he had often watched the setting sun depart through a gate-way of chromatic glory; there were the valleys, curling between the hills, along whose streams he had often threaded his way with hook and line; and here and there were the secluded glens, into whose shadows he had often stolen to read a favorite book, or listen to the song of the thrush and oriole. Those had been days of mental quietude and delight. But now he looked upon all these scenes with changed eyes. In the days of his faith in religion it had seemed to him that nature had always spoken to him of the God of revelation; but now he suspected that in this it had led him into error, had become accessory to the teachers who, perhaps, had deceived him, and, therefore, he felt that he could no longer place implicit confidence in its testimony.

The next autumn he and his confederate in unbelief, George Dane, returned to the academy to complete the last year of their preparatory training, before going to college. As they were bosom friends and possessed many tastes in common, they cheered and abetted each other in the war upon Christianity, and, therefore, made swift progress down the rapids of unbelief. As the year passed, they became more confident and out-spoken, until many of their friends saw with regret that they had deserted "the old paths, where is the good way," and haughtily refused to "walk therein" any longer.

At first Hadley was uneasy and restive, for he could not lightly cast aside the faith in which he had been reared. He grew sullen and morose, listening with impatience to the well-meant admonitions of his mother, frequently walking out of the room while she was speaking to him.

"Oh, Hadley," cried his mother, "what is wrong with you? You seem to have lost faith in everything. Why are you so different from what you used to be?"

But Hadley was averse to discussing the subject of religion with his mother, and her tears irritated him beyond measure. So he rose, and suddenly left the room, without deigning to give her a word in reply.

Yet deep down in his consciousness the arrow penetrated, and made him uneasy. However much he tried to banish the thought of death, it would come to him again and again. Amid the casualties to which men are liable, life is very uncertain, and the young sceptic could not entirely waive the feeling that, should he be brought to the test, he would not fancy taking a "leap into the dark," if he were summoned hence. "Give me no guess for my dying pillow," said one who has looked deeply into the problems of existence. However much men may flout at the confessions of the dying, and however much they may soothe themselves by speculations concerning death and the future, there still remains in every breast, not dead to all good, not only an inward shrinking from the prospect of physical dissolution, but also a "dread of something after death."

"For in that sleep of death what dreams may come,
When we have shuffled off this mortal coil,
Must give us pause."

"And after death the judgment," says the Scripture, and the conscience of every man responds to the dictum. If there are men who never feel this tremor of the soul at the prospect of dying, they either never think at all, or they have despoiled and debauched their moral nature beyond recovery, or both.

For a long time subsequent to this conversation with his mother, Hadley could not shake off the thoughts that she had suggested to his mind. He struggled against them, but they weighed heavily upon him. It was evident that he could not easily throw off the restraints of his early training. But he continued to stifle the disagreeable feeling until, at last, as the days went by, he brought himself back to a life of comparative serenity.

When one has once launched his bark upon the sea of scepticism, there are many winds and waves that continue to hurry him onward in his misguided course. In midwinter, one night, Hadley and George Dane drove in a sleigh to a village, about four miles distant, to attend a meeting of "The Eureka Lyceum," a flourishing debating society of the place. A question of special interest was to be discussed that evening, and the young men went with the expectation of engaging in an intellectual tilt, and, perhaps, return with colors flying. At this gathering an event occurred which accelerated their descent into uncompromising infidelity.

After an exciting discussion by the regularly appointed debaters, an opportunity was given for all who wished to do so to participate in the general discussion which was to follow. Our young heroes were not slow to act upon the suggestion. As the question for discussion bordered on the subject of religion, Hadley, who had gradually grown bolder and had less compunction in his hostility to the Bible, dragged his scepticism into the debate, making several remarks that tended to cast odium on the cause of Christianity. Of course, he did not speak discourteously, but still he expressed his sentiments with no little emphasis, not to say asperity.

A number of persons sprang to the floor, claiming the right to speak, as Hadley concluded, and it was some minutes before the chairman could quell the confusion that the speech had aroused.

"I have stirred up a hornet's nest," whispered Hadley to his friend Dane.

"Yes, and you had better prepare yourself for the puncturing," was Dane's rejoinder.

Hadley compressed his lips, and held himself in readiness for the reception of a vigorous fusillade upon the objectionable sentiments which he had uttered.

The man who succeeded in securing the floor was unhappily a man of hasty and impatient temperament, prone to regard an expression of opinion opposed to his own, as a wilful advocacy of error, due either to ignorance or perversity. He denounced Hadley as an infidel, and proceeded to declaim on the evil that atheistic teaching would work in society, robbing the Christian of his Bible, taking away his hope of heaven, and removing the restraints which kept man from crime. The speech was eloquent and forcible, but it was denunciation, not argument, and was in no sense a reply to Hadley's address.

The young man listened with impatience; he winced when the epithet of infidel was applied to him, conscious that whatever name he might bear in the future, he certainly was not an infidel at that time. The attack upon him was so personal that his request to be allowed to make an explanation was readily granted by the chairman. "My, friends," he said, with a strong effort to control the passion which prompted him to reply in angry tones, "you have heard me denounced as an infidel, and you have listened to the delineation of the evils which I am to bring on society by my teaching. You will of course form your own opinion on that subject, but it appears to me that our friend has somewhat mistaken the situation. A pope conscious of infallibility might so have spoken of some heretic brought up before him for judgment, but here, on common ground, and with a presumption of equality, it seems to me that it would have been in better taste to have shown wherein the opinions I expressed were wrong, and whether I had erred in my premises or in reasoning from them. If he had done so successfully, I should, I hope, have had the grace to acknowledge my error, and you certainly would have been saved from the danger of adopting theories so demolished. As it is, I am resolved to pursue truth wherever she leads, and am not scared by the awful results which our friend predicts. Let us have the actual truth, even though it may cost us some happiness and comfort; anything is better than leaning on a false, delusive hope. If Christianity is true, let us accept it, and I, for one, will do so right gladly; if it is not true let us reject it as any other error, whatever the consequence may be. But do not imagine that any honest truth-seeker will halt in his course or keep silence when some timid soul shrieks vile epithets after him, and tries to scare him with fearsome prognostications. Argument may enlighten and convince him, vituperation never."

There was a marked sensation in the audience as Hadley concluded, and a number of persons clamorously applauded him; for, by his courteous bearing, he had won the sympathy of many of them, and that was almost tantamount to gaining their sympathy for the cause he advocated. Hadley's rejoinder produced a complete recoil in the audience against his antagonist, and it availed nothing for the latter to rise and reiterate, "I am not angry! I am not angry! I am only in earnest!" For all who heard him knew that the violent language that had fallen from his lips was not the expression of an amicable feeling. It is too often the case that Christian people, who are really honest in their convictions, do harm to their own cause by carnal weapons in their warfare against sin and unbelief.

The two young champions of free thought drove home that night more strongly intrenched than ever in their positions of antagonism to Christianity, and more determined to carry on the war "to the death," as they tragically expressed it. When they were alone they gave expression to the real feelings that stirred them, and their hot words were strangely at variance with the outward suavity that had characterized their behavior during the debate.

In the evolution of a sceptic's character, it must be remembered that many composite elements combine to make him what he is. After the events above described, Hadley began to watch the conduct of believers with the eye of a critic, and, of course, excrescences were easily found. One professed Christian mistreated his farm hands. Another was quarrelsome. Another was accused of overreaching in trade. A "loud" professor was the greatest gossip in the neighborhood. And, worst of all, a minister of the village was found to be guilty of falsehood, and a distressing church trial was the result. And so it happened that whenever Hadley's mother or Christian friends appealed to him to become a Christian, he pointed scornfully to the "bright and shining lights," as he called them, just mentioned. By degrees, therefore, he became more impervious to all saving influences.

Meanwhile, study was going on vigorously at the academy, and one triumph after another was won. Spring—the season of color and song—had opened gloriously. The academy days of the young students were rapidly drawing to a close. They had shared the honors about equally between them, there being only one of their classmates who disputed the palm with them. This was a clever young girl who lived near Hadley's home, and with whom he had attended the district school in their childhood. This girl, whose name was Mabel Richardson, had too much native talent to allow herself to be outstripped in the race for honors by her masculine competitors, and the outcome proved that she had kept pace with them to the last. Hadley had taken a boyish fancy to her, admiring her opening beauty, and bright intellectual gifts, and she seemed to reciprocate his friendly interest in her.

One evening, after the recitations of the day were over, Hadley joined Mabel on the steps of the academy building, and walked by her side down the street of the village. There was a bright smile on the girl's lips and a flush of color on her cheeks, as Hadley spoke to her. It was plain that she felt a peculiar interest in her talented classmate.

"You are succeeding remarkably well in your studies, Mabel," he said, making use of her first name with the familiarity which long acquaintance allowed him.

The tone of patronage did not irritate the girl, who replied with a bright smile: "Young men are apt to think that they have monopolized all the intellect of the country, and I have been trying to disabuse their minds of that mistake."

"Ah! no one here will make that mistake now. I suppose you intend to go to college after you are through the academy, do you not?"

"That is not decided yet," Mabel answered. "Circumstances are rather against my doing so. Perhaps after a year of rest, I shall go to a ladies seminary in the east."

"Oh! I believe in co-education, nothing is gained and much lost by the separation of the sexes in our schools," said the young wise-acre. "You have proven that young ladies can keep pace with their masculine rivals, and I have no doubt from what you have done here that you would out-distance most of the young men in a first-class college."

"Well, my father prefers that I should go to a seminary," she returned. "But it is still a question whether I shall carry on my studies any longer after I leave the academy. I presume," she added, looking at him slyly, "that *you* are going to college."

"Yes; George Dane and I will go somewhere; but we have not yet decided where. However, we shall come to a conclusion by and by. "I wish," he subjoined, "that you could attend the same college we do. We three would make a creditable delegation from this section."

She looked at him with a bright blush, as she answered, "It certainly would be very pleasant."

"You see," Hadley continued, "if three of us went from the same place, it would help us also in our—in our—social life. We would form a sort of coterie of our own, and could encourage one another in many ways."

"Oh! I should be no credit to you," she laughed.

"You would be a credit to the academy from which you go, and the college of which you were a student," returned Hadley, with sincere emphasis.

The girl, it could plainly be seen, was pleased with the outspoken compliment, perhaps not so much for its own sake, as on account of its author. Then a shadow passed over her face, as if an unpleasant thought had occurred to her, and she said, in a tone in which there was a note of sadness: "Thank you for your compliment, Mr. Modelling; but I think you and Mr. Dane will have to represent the rising talent of the section, and I may return the compliment by saying that it is safe in your hands. We shall expect to hear of your triumphs, and shall be proud of you. I think there is no prospect of my joining you. I wish there were."

The two young people had by this time reached the crossing where their ways separated, and they wished each other good by with mutual good feelings. What the outcome would have been had they been associated in their studies and social relations during the next three years who can say. As it was, time and distance exerted their wonted influence, and mutual regard that might have ripened into love, faded into a mere pleasant memory.

(*To be Continued.*)

THE GREAT COMMISSION.

BY Mrs. M. Baxter.

. S. Lesson for June 17. Matt. 28 : 16-20. Golden Text. Ps. 68 : 11.

he Full Text of the Commission from the Four Evangelists—Not Limited to the Eleven—No Christian Uncommissioned—The Promised Support Still Available—Almighty Power Still Given—The Lethargy of the Churches—Persecution May be Needed to Arouse them—The Main Outfit of a Missionary—The Name of Jesus a Power, not a Charm—The Gospel Seen as Well as Heard—Where to Begin Missionary Work.

"THE Lord gave the word: great was the company of those that published it" (Ps. 68 : 2), or ev. Ver., "The Lord giveth the word: the omen that publish the tidings are a great host." 'hat word? What tidings? This Psalm is pposed to have been used when David brought the ark of God to Jerusalem from the house Obededom. But these words well fit the ibject which we have before us—Christ's great ommission to His followers before He ascended to heaven. If we make

A Harmony of this Charge

om the four Gospels, it would read somewhat follows: All power is given unto Me both in eaven and in earth; go ye therefore and teach l nations. Preach the gospel of repentance ıd remission of sins to every creature, beginng at Jerusalem, baptizing them in the name of e Father, and of the Son, and of the Holy host; teaching them to observe all things hatsoever I have commanded you. As My ather hath sent Me, even so send I you. Reive ye the Holy Ghost. Whomsoever sins ye mit, they are remitted unto them—and whomever sins ye retain, they are retained. He that elieveth and is baptized shall be saved, and he at believeth not shall be damned. And these gns shall follow them that believe. In My ame they shall cast out devils; they shall speak ith new tongues: they shall take up serpents; ıd if they drink any deadly thing it shall not urt them; they shall lay hands on the sick, ıd they shall recover. Lo, I am with you way, even unto the end of the world [Gr. Age"] (Mark 16. 15-18; Luke 24: 64-7.

This commission was given to the eleven, but so to all the disciples. (Luke 24: 33-48; comp. cts 1: 12-15). O, if we really believed that all ower was given to Him both in heaven and in rth, and that as the Father sent Him, even so e sent us, and if, moreover, we believed that e *is* with us, individually, and always, how ould we be occupied with difficulties and hinrances as we are? God calls for a witness to l nations. He

Excuses No Man From Being a Missionary,

he has himself been brought to Christ. "He at gathereth not with Me scattereth abroad." latt. 12: 30). Every living man or woman ho is not winning souls to Christ is doing the evil's work in scattering them from Him. It as not to the eleven, but to the assembled and of believers, that He said, "*Ye* are witesses of these things," and "As My Father ath sent Me, even so send I you" (comp. uke 24: 33-48; and John 20: 21-23). "As very man hath received the gift, even so minster the same one to another, as good stewards f the manifold grace of God." (1 Pet. 4: 10). 'he equipment for the service is this, "Lo, I am ith you alway." The God of Pentecost with s, why should we not have Pentecostal times? et us know that we are in His will, going when nd where He sends us, and, in the company of ehovah Jireh, we do not need to be backed by Society lest, our means should fail, with or ithout a Society "the Lord will provide." Vhen He sent Elijah on a journey, He cared or his temporal supplies. With the God of onah on our side, the God who turned the ing and people of Nineveh to repentance in ne day, we have the power which the idolarous heathen want. Christ never contemplatd such a state of things as exists amongst us—he forming of little societies of Christians, who sit down comfortably in their churches and "enjoy religion" as they call it. If every believer is called to be a missionary, the least we can do is for every congregation at home to send at least *one* missionary abroad, and to support him in the field. Two thousand two hundred students in American colleges have this year devoted their lives to missionary work; shall England do less? Last year, the China Inland Mission sent out one hundred additional missionaries, thank God. But what are they among so many?

The Time is Short.

"The devil has come down unto you, having great wrath, because he knoweth that he hath but a short time." (Rev 12: 12.) If the Church of Christ is ever to awake from her guilty lethargy, it must be now. When the infant Church at Jerusalem began to settle down and rest upon her lees, God allowed persecution to break out, so that all the disciples were scattered abroad except the apostles. (Acts 8: 1.) If the Jesuits continue to make the advances they have been making in England the last few years, it will not be long before unspiritual Christians will be called again to undergo persecution. Perhaps nothing else will arouse us from our selfishness and our littleness. Here in England churches and missions are struggling with each other which shall succeed in our densely populated towns and cities. There will be three or four churches and as many mission halls in a single street, while whole provinces in China, India, and Africa are crying out for the bread of life.

Numbers of Christians are feeling the call to preach the gospel, and yet how few are willing to undergo the disheartening scoffs which their want of education and the Societies' lack of funds occasion! Let us get on to higher ground. When God wanted an Amos to testify for Him against an idolatrous Israel, He did not first send him to a school of the prophets. "I was no prophet, neither was I a prophet's son, but I was an herdman, and a gatherer of sycamore fruit, and the Lord took me as I followed the flock, and

The Lord said unto me, Go

prophecy unto My people, Israel." (Amos 1: 14, 15). Yet this same Amos, who had perhaps never learned a lesson in geography, seems to have been well acquainted, not only with his own land and its cities, but also with those of neighboring countries (Amos 1: 4), and also to have some knowledge of history. Either God had been preparing him beforehand, unknown to himself or any one else, or He must have quickened his intellect at the time. After all, intellectual culture is by no means the essential thing in the outfit of a missionary, but rather that he should be filled with the Holy Ghost, and know how to commune constantly and really with his God. "All power is given unto *Me*; go ye therefore." "Receive ye the Holy Ghost." "As My Father hath sent Me, even so send I you." This is the main outfit of a missionary. If he knows that he is sent of God, and that the all power of God is with him, he does not need to be troubled about his own lack of qualification. But if he wants to be a missionary because he cannot succeed in anything else, he has mistaken his vocation. David was a shepherd, and God called him from the flock; Amos was a herdman, and Peter a fisherman. Those who have not proved themselves to be industrious, persevering, obedient, etc., in their earthly calling, are not likely to do much as missionaries.

God wants men and women of faith, such as can count upon Him for everything. When He sent out the twelve without purse or scrip, nothing to hold either money or food, by their own confession they lacked nothing (Luke 9: 35); the Lord looked after their needs as He did after the needs of His people in the wilderness. And if in our own times this is not exactly the course which He would have His missionary children adopt, still this is the spirit of faith which should actuate them. There is a great deal of talk about faith in these days, which is only a head-knowledge faith; for instance, a certain man of God who preaches and writes that the coming of the Lord is at hand, and who says that he trusts God for everything, is the greatest stickler we know for his own rights, his own comforts, his own position, and his own possessions; while another, who holds the same views, but is not so loud in his profession, gives away to the last penny of his income, and avoids holding any property because the Lord is coming; that which is a mere doctrine to the one man, is a power in the life of the other. God has promised those who go into all the world, and preach the gospel to every creature, that "these signs shall follow them that believe; In My name they shall cast out devils." The name of Jesus is a power but not a charm. When the sons of Sceva attempted to use it as a charm, the demons prevailed against them. We can only use the name of Jesus

Under His Direction.

"In My name they shall speak with new tongues." We believe the time is not far distant when these words shall be fulfilled as they were on the day of Pentecost. There is already a wonderful quickening of intellect among missionaries in the learning of language, but "ye shall see greater things than these." And so in the authority over poisonous reptiles, and poisonous or malarious atmosphere, the drinking of "any deadly thing," we have yet to see the promise claimed in its fulness. "The Word of God is not bound," we are not straitened in Him. Praise the Lord, "they shall lay hands on the sick, and they shall recover" is being fulfilled in thousands of cases, and shall be yet more as the end draws near.

The Lord would have us first proclaim the message of "repentance and remission of sins," and then teach "them to observe all things whatsoever I have commanded you"—all the teaching of Jesus. This is the true gospel: none can be spared. Paul said to the Ephesian elders, "I have not shunned to declare unto you all the counsel of God" (Acts. 20: 27), and for this reason he claimed that he was pure from the blood of all men. Paul's teaching and his life corresponded, and consequently his words had weight. A heathen Chinese said to a missionary, "I have not only heard the gospel, I have seen it; a man who has become a Christian is in my employ, and he has become so truthful, so honest, so obliging, that I can see the gospel of Christ is a power which changes a man. A man may shut his ears to what we say, but he cannot shut his eyes to what we are."

But how long are we to wait until we can become missionaries? Here is the answer—"Beginning at Jerusalem." Begin at home. If the Holy Ghost possesses us and leads us to do all we can, just where we are, we shall soon want a wider field, and as we are ready for it, God will open it before us, if we are living sacrifices ready to His hand. No one who is really trusting God needs to force a door of usefulness open. The open doors are plentiful enough, but the laborers, the fitted ones, the men sent of God, and the women sent of God, are few. In the Revised Bible the rendering of Ps. 68: 11 is "The women that publish the tidings are a great host," and this word seems to be having its fulfilment in our day. Perhaps never in the history of the Church, since the days of the apostles, were there so many women engaged, some way or other, in proclaiming the blessed gospel of Christ. So shall it be in the last days. Again, let us encircle the world in our prayers, "Ask of Me, and I shall give thee the heathen for thine inheritance, and the utmost parts of the earth for thy possession." (Ps. 2: 8). "Pray for Africa," was the constant greeting of the late Major Malan, and O how God has been opening up Africa since he was taken to glory. God teach us to pray for the heathen.

"MY TIMES ARE IN THY HAND."

I need not care
If days be dark or fair,
If the sweet Summer brings delight
Or bitter Winter chills the air.

No thought of mine
Can penetrate the deep design
That forms afar, through buds and bloom,
The purple clusters of the vine.

I do not know
The subtle secret of the snow,
That hides away the violets
Till April teaches them to blow.

Enough for me
Their tender loveliness to see,
Assured that little things and large
Fulfil God's purpose equally.

How this is planned
Or that, I may not understand;
I am content, my God, to know
That all my times are in Thy hand.

Whatever share
Of loss, or loveliness, or care
Falls to my lot, it cannot be
More than Thy will for me to bear.

And none the less,
Whatever sweet thing comes to bless
And gladden me; Thou art its source—
And sender of my happiness.

Add this to me,
With other gifts so free—
That I may never turn my face
In any evil hour from Thee;

Nor on the sand
Of shifting faith and feeling stand;
But wake and sleep with equal trust,
Knowing my times are in Thy hand.

—*Mary Bradley*

J. E. JEWETT, Publisher, 77 Bible House, New York will furnish the above poem in leaflet form at twenty cents per hundred. *A Sample Packet of 50 leaflets* assorted (no two alike), will be sent post-paid, for ten cents. Postage stamps taken.

WORKS OF J. W. KIMBALL.

How to See Jesus with Fulness of Joy and Peace.

250 pp. Cloth. Price, 75 cents.

This precious book has been the means of comfort to many a weary soul, and hoping that many more may be led to read its sweet exhortations, we give a few out of the many commendations we have received. A new edition has just been printed, and we send it forth earnestly hoping that it may be even more blessed in its ministration than the former ones.

"I have been fifty years a member of the Presbyterian Church. Your 'How to See Jesus' has helped me to a better understanding of some things, and to a deeper interest in the Scriptures. Your words are so plain and simple that they come at once to the heart as food in season."—*E. T., Utica, N. Y.*

"I have read 'How to See Jesus' with much joy; it brings so much help to me."—*Oakland, California.*

"I find in 'How to see Jesus' just the reading we invalids need."—*M. M., Earlville, N. Y.*

"'How to See Jesus' is such a good book I want it to be comforting many who need it."—*Holyoke, Mass.*

"While in Des Moines, Iowa, I found your book 'How to See Jesus.' I have thought many times since the good Lord must have led me to it, as I found in it just the comfort I needed. It will be a benefit to many of my friends; have decided to make them a present of it; so please send me twelve."

"Thanks for the precious book 'How to See Jesus.' I have never read a book that has done me any more good."—*E. A., Colorado.*

"Many thanks for calling my attention to 'How to See Jesus.' I find it grandly helpful."—*W. J., South Pueblo, Col.*

"Next to the Bible, the best book I ever saw."—*W. E., Maine.*

"I cannot tell you how pleased I am with 'How to See Jesus.' It seems written for me, and I take great comfort from it."—*Newfoundland.*

"I find 'How to See Jesus' very instructive. As I read I personate the person spoken to. My trouble is not worldliness, but a fearful heart. This suits my case exactly."—*L. S., N. Salem, N. Y.*

"Words seem inadequate to express my deep sense of obligation to you for your precious book."—*F. I., New York.*

"I think I will get more real help, just the kind I need, from 'How to See Jesus.'"—*Mrs. J. L., Indianapolis, Ind.*

"I am much pleased with 'How to See Jesus,' and instructed. Your style holds attention without weariness—good for invalids."—*C. W., Mass.*

"If you were to get all the words of thanks and combine them together, you would not then get half the true feelings of my heart for that precious book, 'How to See Jesus.' I feel that you have been to me what Great Heart was to the Pilgrims, cheering and showing them the way to the Celestial City."—*E. A., Abbeville, S. C.*

Heaven: My Father's House.

250 pp. Cloth. Price, 75 cents.

It is often said we know nothing of heaven, but Jesus says, "All things that the Father hath are mine: the Comforter shall take of mine and show it unto you." True to his promise, from the day I knew the Lord, the Comforter began to show me heavenly things. What I freely received, He bade me freely give. The kind approvals here recorded increased my obligation, and not less my delight to share these joy-inspiring things with as many as I may. I pray God that each reader may find them his Lord's own revelations to himself.—*Preface.*

"I can surely say that, excepting my Bible, no book has ever done me so much good as 'Heaven: My Father's House.' After a day spent in the sick room trying to calm the fevered brain and ease the aching limbs, you cannot imagine with what eagerness I turn to that book for rest, and it never fails to bring it, and with it the prayer, 'Not as I will, O Father.'"—*E. E., Iowa.*

"Death, as seen from Mr. K.'s point of view, is a natural event in the order of the Christian's life. Instead of recoiling from the inevitable destiny, we are led by this more familiar view to look upon the change without fear, yea, with cheerfulness."—*Rev. Dr. H. B. Hackett, Newton Theological Seminary.*

"Full of pointed illustrations, fresh, vigorous writing; nothing dull; short, crisp sentences; the reader is borne on rapidly; the writer speaks as though his thoughts rushed upon him. A fulness of nature, and joy in life runs through it."—*S. K. B.*

"It is one of the most interesting books I have ever perused. I purpose that many of my friends and neighbors shall read it. No one can read it, certainly no Christian, without profit."—*Rev. E. Bridgman, Shanghai, China.*

"I have read Mr. K.'s book with no small pleasure. It is full of thought, and there is much beauty both of sentiment and words; and no one will be wearied with its chapters nor think them too many, nor too long."—*Rev. Dr. Horatius Bonar, Edinburgh, Scotland.*

"Pray accept my heartiest thanks for your sound common-sense book on 'Heaven.' I seldom read any purely religious book except the Bible, but have read and re-read yours with growing satisfaction. It is the only book upon the subject I would recommend a friend to buy, after a good Bible. I wish every church member would read your 'Heaven,' for it would free his brain from so much popular nonsense."—*Antioch, Syria.*

**** Either of the above books will be sent, postpaid, to any address on receipt of price.*

Address *J. E. JEWETT, Publisher, 77 Bible House, New York.*

RECENT BOOKS BY D. L. MOODY.

A New Edition in new binding of the following Popular Works of D. L. MOODY, has just been issued:

JUST IS[illegible]ED.

PREVAILING PRAYER; WHAT HINDERS IT?
As e[illegible] solemn work, full of helpful hints on t[illegible] and hindrances to prevailing prayer.

[illegible]ENTH THOUSAND (NEW).

[illegible]E WORK! TO THE WORK! A Trumpet [illegible]ll. Exhortations to Christians.

T[illegible] new work, by Mr. Moody, is in the line of his most successful effort, that of stirring Christians to active, personal, aggressive work.

SIXTIETH THOUSAND.

SECRET POWER; or, the Secret of Success in Christian Life and Work.

"A deeply earnest and helpful book for the use of Christians on the work of the Holy Spirit in the believer, inciting to more diligent effort and to a more perfect use of the privileges of the 'Sons of God.'"

SIXTY-FIFTH THOUSAND.

THE WAY TO GOD, AND HOW TO FIND IT.

"It puts the way so plainly that 'he who runs may read.'"—*Religious Telescope.*

"Full of pathos, point and power. Cannot fail to be the means of quickening and blessing wherever read."—*Methodist.*

NINETY-SECOND THOUSAND.

HEAVEN; its Hope; its Inhabitants; its Happiness; its Riches; its Reward.

"While adapted to the humblest capacity, it will command the attention of the mature and thoughtful."—*National Presbyterian.*

ONE HUNDRED AND THIRTIETH THOUSAND.

TWELVE SELECT SERMONS.

"With the effect of these addresses, when spoken, the whole land is acquainted, and now that they are printed, they will tend to keep in force the impression they have already made."—*Methodist.*

The above works, the combined sale of which has already reached over Three Hundred and Fifty Thousand are now issued in a new dress, known as the STANDARD EDITION.

Bound in Rich English Cloth, beveled edges, and put up in Neat Box, six vols. Price, per set, $3.60.

The former bindings "The People's Edition" may also be had. Cloth, neat gold and ink dies, 60 cents per vol. Cheap edition in paper cover, 30 cents per volume.

Sent postpaid on receipt of price. Address

J. E. JEWETT, 77 Bible House, New York.

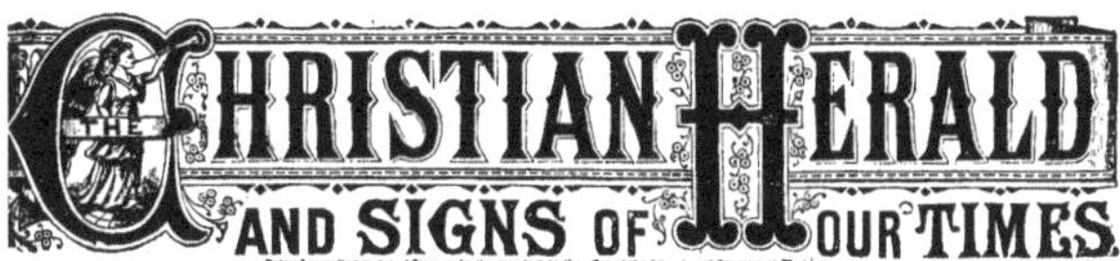

This Journal contains every week a Portrait and Biography of some eminent person; a new Sermon by the Rev. C. H. SPURGEON, of London, and the Rev. Dr. ALMAGE'S latest Sunday morning Sermon; also always a Prophetic Article, and a Summary of Current Events, as well as Stories, Anecdotes, etc.

ol. XI., No. 24. Office, 63 Bible House, N. Y. THURSDAY, JUNE 14, 1888. Annual Subscription, $1.50.

CONTENTS OF THIS NUMBER.

RTRAITS AND LIVES OF THE SIX NEW ISHOPS OF THE METHODIST EPISCOPAL HURCH.
GEVITY. Dr. Talmage's Sermon last Sunday forning.
ECDOTES RELATED AT RECENT EVANGELISTIC MEETINGS.
THE CONVERSION OF THE WORLD. By Dr. L. W. Munhall.
The Chief Priesthood Renounced—A Physician's Explanation of Divine Healing—An African's Abstinence—A Service in Madagascar—Unappreciated Rewards—A Lawyer's Conversion in a Church Vestibule—A Scoffer's Confession.
MARY MORGAN'S DARLING. (With Illustration.)
THE WEDDING GARMENT. A New Sermon by Pastor C. H. Spurgeon.
Gems from New Books: Buddha's Early Life, etc.
PICTURE OF THE EMPEROR OF GERMANY IN HIS STUDY.
THE EPOCHS OF A LIFE. A New Serial Story by Rev. L. S. Keyser. (Continued.)
NEWNESS OF LIFE. By Mrs. M. Baxter.

REV. J. N. FITZGERALD, D. D. — REV. J. H. VINCENT, D. D., LL. D. — REV. ISAAC W. JOYCE, D. D.

REV. J. M. THOBURN, D. D. — REV. JOHN P. NEWMAN, D. D., LL. D. — REV. DANIEL A. GOODSELL, D. D.

SIX BISHOPS ELECTED at the RECENT METHODIST EPISCOPAL GENERAL CONFERENCE.

THE SIX NEW M. E. BISHOPS.

THE Metropolitan Opera House, New York, was the scene of an impressive ceremony on May 29. The five Bishops, and the Missionary Bishop for India and Malaysia, were there and then consecrated for their work. The stage was set for the interior of a cathedral, and six small tables were placed there, one for each Bishop. After the hymn, "The Morning Light is Breaking," had been sung. Bishop Bowman passed from one candidate to another, a friend of each saying, as the senior Bishop approached, "We present unto you this holy man to be consecrated a bishop." After the usual questions had been answered by each candidate, a Bible was given to each, with the injunction to give heed to its teachings, and the ceremony of laying on hands was performed. The singing of a hymn, and the benediction, pronounced by Senior Bishop Bowman, concluded the simple but impressive ceremony. As the election of these ministers to episcopal functions will have an important influence on a numerous and respected section of the Christian Church, their portraits, which appear on the first page, and a brief sketch of their lives, cannot fail to interest our readers.

THE REV. J. H. VINCENT, D. D., LL.D.

HOWEVER it may be with the present generation, there is no question as to the first place among the new men in the estimation of the rising generation in the Methodist Church. The interest of the young people has been the chief thought of Dr. Vincent's life, and to promote that, he has given the best of his years and the most of his labor. To thoroughly organize the Sunday school system, and to render it efficient in all its details, has been his predominant desire, and he has devoted himself to that task with unflagging zeal.

John Hoyt Vincent is a native of Tuscaloosa, Ala., where he was born February 23, 1832. He is, therefore, now fifty-six years of age. When he was six years old his parents removed to Northumberland County, Pennsylvania, and sent him for his education to Milton and Lewisburg academies, and subsequently to the Wesleyan Institute, Newark, N. J. At the early age of seventeen, he received the "exhorter's" license, and the following year he was made a local preacher. His sphere of labor was the Luzerne Circuit in the Baltimore Conference, but in 1853 he entered the New Jersey Conference, where he remained until 1857. In that year he was transferred to the Rock River Conference, and was stationed successively at Joliet, Mount Morris, Galena, Rockford, and Chicago. While at Galena, and before the importance of the fact had dawned upon him or any one else, he was the pastor of U. S. Grant, then in business in that town as a tanner. With the future General, he formed a pleasant friendship, and has among his most treasured possession several friendly letters from General Grant, written in the days of his early struggles.

Dr. Vincent's remarkable adaptation to Sunday-school work was first publicly recognized during his labors in Chicago. He succeeded after much exertion in getting a uniform system of lessons adopted for the Chicago schools, thus recognizing the advantages of the system now in use under the title of the International Lessons. He also commenced the publication of two journals for Sunday school teachers and scholars, which had a wide circulation. With that promptitude for recognizing special adaptation and merit for which the Methodist Church is noted, the value of Dr. Vincent's labors was perceived by the General Conference, and in 1868 he was elected editor of Sunday School Literature, and corresponding Secretary of the Sunday-school Union. So energetically and efficiently did he discharge the duties of those offices that he was four times re-elected by General Conferences, and has only now laid them aside at the call to "Come up higher." One enterprise alone established Dr. Vincent's fame in America. In the line of his special work he, in conjunction with Lewis Miller, inaugurated the Chautauqua assembly, which has done so much for the promotion of religious education, and which owes its existence and growth largely to his genius and fostering care.

REV. J. N. FITZGERALD, D. D.

THE second bishop elected by the Conference, and on the same ballot with Dr. Vincent, was Dr. Fitzgerald, who, though not so widely known outside his Conference as the famous Sunday-school worker, is a man of mark in his denomination. Tall and commanding in frame, and with a mind of masculine vigor, Dr. Fitzgerald is a man fitted by nature for a leader of men—a force to be counted upon as of no slight importance either by friend or foe.

James N. Fitzgerald was born at Newark, N. J., in 1838, and is now in his fiftieth year. In his early years it might have been predicted of him that he would become a famous general, or a Senator, or even President of the Republic, but a prophecy that he would become a bishop would have struck all who knew him as extremely unlikely to be fulfilled. He chose the profession of the law, and studied in the office of Frederick T. Frelinghuysen, who was Secretary of State in President Arthur's Cabinet. He was admitted to the bar in 1858, and at once entered upon a prosperous career. His association with Chancellor Runyon of New Jersey was a guarantee of his ability and learning, which marked him out for early and high advancement. To the young lawyer, deeply read, fluent of speech, and with great oratorical gifts, life opened very brightly, and he might naturally have looked forward to the acquisition of a large fortune, and the attainment of exalted official position. Three years, however, after his entrance on professional life, an event occurred which completely changed his future.

In 1861 a powerful religious awakening took place in the Central Methodist Episcopal Church of Newark, and, among the converts, was Mr. Fitzgerald. As was to be expected in a temperamen so positive and decisive as his, conversion was the turning-point in his temporal as well as his spiritual life. He promptly relinquished his professional practice and entered at once on study for the ministry. He was admitted to the Newark conference in April, 1862, and was appointed to the East Newark Station. There his powerful, cogent sermons, delivered in a melodious baritone voice, and with marked oratorical power, drew large numbers to hear him, and much good was done. He was clearly a man to fill a larger sphere, and, after a year, he was removed to Elizabeth. Subsequently he was appointed to Hudson city, and then successively to Newton, Paterson, and Jersey City, and for two years he was presiding elder in the Newark district. He also held the office of secretary to the Newark Conference for eleven years. In the General Conferences of 1876, 1880, and 1884, he was an assistant secretary, and all who came in contact with him at those great assemblies, were impressed by the singular lucidity of his mind, his aptitude for organization, and his clear and convincing arguments. In 1881, when a successor was needed to the late David Terry, as Recording Secretary of the Missionary Board, these qualities marked him out as the man for the responsible post, and he was appointed. He is now called to the highest position in the gift of his brethren, and enters upon its duties with the good-will and confidence of all.

REV. ISAAC W. JOYCE, D. D.

THOUGH Dr. Joyce was not among the men whose names were popularly discussed for the Episcopate, he was the third to be elected at the General Conference, and he received a larger number of votes than were cast for any of the successful candidates. He brings to his new duties a wide experience of an analagous character as presiding elder in an exceptionally difficult district, and a reputation for judicial acumen, which has secured him a place on the judiciary committee of more than one General Conference.

Isaac Wilson Joyce is a native of Ohio. He was born on October 11, 1836, and is therefore now in his fifty-second year. He comes of Irish parentage, and has inherited a hearty, genial, disposition, no little wit and humor, and the faculty of making warm friends wherever he goes. He was converted when he was only sixteen years of age, while he was residing with his parents in Tippecanoe County, Indiana, and united with the church near Lafayette. His earliest ministerial work was done in that city. He spent a term there in each of the two churches, and subsequently four years as presiding elder. His next appointment was at Greencastle, where he succeeded in raising funds for the erection of a beautiful church. In 1880 he was a delegate to the General Conference at Cincinnati, and his stay there led to his being transferred to the Cincinnati Annual Conference with St. Paul's Church in that city, as his first appointment. At the conclusion of his term he was appointed to Trinity Church, in the same city, and then, his influence being so strong, and his work so extensively blessed, he was granted a second term at St. Paul's. He is pre-eminently a pastor in the strict sense of the term, looking vigilantly after the spiritual interests of the people committed to his care, while not neglecting the duties of the pulpit. Dr. Joyce enjoys the cordial respect of hi brethren in the ministry, and the only person who will regret his elevation to the Episcopat are those who have sat under his ministry, bu must now part with their beloved pastor for th general good of the church.

REV. JOHN P. NEWMAN, D. D., LL. D.

IT is difficult even now to realize that th noted man has been made a bishop. It wa only on the fourteenth ballot, and after th most strenuous efforts of his friends, that th result was achieved. The leading journal the Methodist Church says of the election "More than two-thirds of the General Confe ence have elected him bishop. This makes hi not the bishop of those only who voted for hi but of the Methodist Episcopal Church; a all will wish for him a career which will crow the closing chapter of his life with lasting ho ors, and demonstrate by its usefulness to t Church the wisdom of the choice." This sk fully worded paragraph will also, it may hoped, form a basis for amicable adjustment all that is past of an unpleasant nature.

Dr. Newman, by his political relations, h occupied so prominent a position in the publ view, that only a brief summary of the leadi events in his career is necessary in this plac He was born in New York, September 1, 18 and is therefore now in his sixty-second ye He was received in the Oneida Conference 1848, and in 1855 was transferred to the Tr Conference. Three years later he became member of the New York Conference, and w appointed to the Bedford Street Church. the expiration of his term there, he went on tour in Europe and the East, writing descri tive letters to the press, and, on his retu publishing a book entitled, "From Dan to Be sheba," which commanded a large sale. 1862 and 1863 he was pastor of the Washingt Square Church, in New York.

Dr. Newman spent the following five ye in the South, having accepted a commissi from Bishop Ames to reorganize the Church the ground newly occupied by the Union armi Of his work there much has been said and wr ten on both sides of the question, which it unnecessary now to recall. A more congen field was occupied by Dr. Newman when, G Grant having become President, he obtain the appointment to establish the Metropolit Church in Washington, D. C. Dr. Newm was also made Chaplain of the Senate, and three years in the Federal Capital were prof ably spent. In 1873 General Grant appoint him Inspector of Consulates. This post enabl him to visit, under the most agreeable auspic the chief points of the world where the Unit

States is officially represented. On his return he published another book entitled "Thrones and Palaces of Babylon and Nineveh." He was again appointed to the Metropolitan Church, where he continued to labor until 1878, when he returned to New York as pastor of the Central Church. At the end of his term he accepted the pastorate of a Congregational Church, [illegible]ded in maintaining his personal con[illegible]with the Methodist Conference. In [illegible] a variety of disagreeable experiences with the leading member[illegible] the Congregational Church, he was again [illegible]or of the Metropolitan Church in Washington, which he now leaves for the Episcopate.

REV. DANIEL A. GOODSELL, D. D.

THE last of the bishops elected for the American field was Dr. Goodsell, who, though not elected until the sixteenth ballot, received a larger number of votes than the two first elected. He thus has the gratification of knowing how large a number of his brethren reposed confidence in his qualifications for the office.

Daniel Ayers Goodsell was born in Newburg, N. Y., on November 5, 1840. He is consequently the youngest of the Bishops elected at the recent Conference. His father, the Rev. Buell Goodsell, was one of the best known and most respected among the early laborers in the Methodist Episcopal Church. His term as presiding Elder in the New York East Conference was one of remarkable success. The future Bishop was educated at the New York University, and in 1859, joined the Conference of which his father was an honored member. Though at that time only nineteen years of age, he was nearly six feet high and of good proportions. At his first two charges, according to established rule he remained only one year, but since that time he has been induced at the request of the official board to continue the full term. He has been stationed at Riverhead, Glen Cove, Greenpoint Tabernacle, Brooklyn, South Norwalk, Conn., Meriden, Conn., and since 1878 successively at Washington Street and New York Avenue, Brooklyn. He has served his Conference as secretary for sixteen years with great efficiency, and has won the general esteem of its members.

Dr. Goodsell is one of the most unassuming of men, yet he is a man of profound learning and of considerable literary ability. He is chiefly remarkable, however, for his energy and industry and the unselfish spirit in which he gives time and labor to tasks which can bring him neither gain nor renown. His one desire seems to have been to be useful, and few know how thoroughly he has succeeded. Men who have worked with him, or who have had the advantage of sitting under his ministry, alone know his inestimable worth. It is certain that if his life is prolonged the Methodist Church will have no more solid and conscientious work from any of its Bishops than from Dr. Goodsell.

REV. J. M. THOBURN, D.D

THE decision of the Conference to elect a Missionary Bishop for India could have but one result in the circumstances. Dr. Thoburn has so long been identified with the Indian work that no other name than his was in the minds of the majority of the delegates. As pastor, presiding elder, and editor he has labored successfully in that distant land, and it is fitting that he should become its first Methodist bishop.

James M. Thoburn is fifty-two years of age, having been born at St Clairsville, Ohio, March 7, 1836. His early years were years of hard work. He lost his father by death when he was fourteen years of age, and it was only by his own exertions and frugal life as a school teacher that he was enabled to secure a college education. He entered Allegheny College, from which he graduated in 1857, and after one year's service in the Pittsburg Conference he offered himself as a missionary to India. He sailed for that country on April 11, 1859, in company with Messrs. Judd, Waugh, Parker, and Downey, and their wives. Landing in Calcutta, he was appointed to Nynee Tab, a well-known station in the Himalayas; then at Garhwal, where he preached in Hindi; next to Moradabad, where he preached in Hindustani; afterward at Lucknow, where both English and Hindustani were used; and lastly in Calcutta. There, not only among the white residents, but with the natives and the sailors in the port, Dr. Thoburn labored successfully, and has had the gratification of seeing the church grow and increase to a marvellous degree since his first connection with it. He is best known in this country and in Europe by his editorial work on the *Indian Witness*, a journal from which extracts have often been published in these columns, and which is recognized as the reliable organ of the Methodist Church in India.

ANECDOTES RELATED AT RECENT EVANGELISTIC MEETINGS.

"Run Over on the Railway.—Two Young women had gone on the railway lines for the purpose of gathering coals, and were warned by a man of their danger; but, it is said, they only laughed at and scoffed him. The engine came along at its appointed time, and before they could get off the line they were dashed down upon the ground, run over, and ushered into eternity. They, doubtless, at the last moment, realized their danger, but it was then too late. You, too, dear friends, are on the railway of life; the appointed time of the engine of death approaches, and, perhaps, like the two young women, you have often laughed and scoffed when you heard the warning voice of coming danger. Oh, flee to the refuge which God has provided for you in Jesus. He that believeth on the Son hath everlasting life (John 3: 36).

Afraid of Being "Given Up" by a Lover— Mr. Thompson said: "A little while ago a young woman came to me and said she wished to be saved. Some time before she had professed conversion, but it had only been profession, and now she wished to become possessed of the reality. What hindered her from coming forward and making a bold stand for Christ was a young man to whom she was attached, and whom she feared she would have to give up if she made an avowal of Christ. I told her that the loss of any earthly friend, however dear, would be as nothing in comparison with what she would find in Christ. This young woman by some would be termed a backslider, but in reality she was not; she had never been truly converted, and knew it herself. I besought her to prove her preference for Christ by accepting Him without any further delay. The struggle was long and severe, but at last, through the power of the Holy Spirit, she triumphed, and received the Saviour. It was not long before the young man himself, instead of 'giving her up,' as she had feared, expressed sympathy with her in the step she had taken, and took his place in the ranks of those who follow Jesus."

Overtaken by the Tide.—A Christian Worker relates: "There were two boys, the sons of a naturalist, and themselves, though still young, very enthusiastic in that interesting department of science. They were at the sea-shore gathering specimens of sea-weed. Being in a part where the rocks jutted out on either side, the tide came in very swiftly, and they were so intent on their occupation, that they did not notice it until it was too late to get away. 'Never mind,' said the older to his smaller brother, 'if you get upon my back I'll save you, and we will be safe round the corner in no time.' The younger obeyed, and they started through the water, but they had not gone far, when relaxing his hold he fell from his brother's back. The other dived after him, and placing him as before, re-commenced his struggle. 'If you try to save me,' said the little fellow, 'you will be lost yourself, let me go.' 'No,' was the firm reply, 'I can and will save you.' But the younger felt that that was impossible, so throwing up his arms he slid off his brother's back and sank. His brother tried to recover him, but ineffectually. At last, scarcely caring whether he himself was saved or not, he struck out for the shore alone, bearing the sorrowful tale of his brother's death to his parents. That brave lad did his best to save his brother, but was unable. But, thank God, our Elder Brother, Jesus Christ, is not only willing but can save to the uttermost, and none are lost who trust in Him."

Ropes Round Twelve Necks.—"A Certain English king laid siege to the French town of Calais. The garrison made a most stubborn defence, and so enraged the king that on the capitulation of the city he determined to sack the place; but his Queen, whom he dearly loved, pleaded for the people, and he consented to spare their lives if the chief men came to him very penitently, and besought mercy. Twelve men, with ropes round their necks and heads bent low, came from the town, and, approaching the king, cried for clemency. So too the sinner must cast off his own righteousness and, clothed in the sack-cloth of repentance, approach the Most High, pleading for mercy. These twelve men had only their lives spared, but we, in the greatness, of His love, are taken into the family of the King, and clothed in royal robes, and invited to partake of the marriage supper of the Lamb."

A Young Hindoo Scapegrace, of Some Education, fell into very bad habits, and finding himself one day in financial extremity, he stole some money, about three dollars, from his aunt, with whom he lived. 'Passing along the road one evening," says the missionary, who relates the incident, "he found lying in his path a small Christian book, entitled, 'The Heart Book,' translated and printed in his own language. On reading it his attention was arrested, and his conscience aroused. He went home, humbly confessed his theft, and restored the money. For six months he read and re-read the graphic description of his own heart-workings in the little book. His conscience, so seared and dead before, now gave him no rest. His aunt advised him to go to a friend in a near village, who had a larger book, which they called 'God's Word.' He went, borrowed the friend's Bible, and read it as he had read the Heart Book. The Holy Spirit wrought upon him as he read. He was converted, accepted Christ, ceased all idolatrous worship and rites, and was baptised. His family persecuted him, as a matter of course, and cast him out, and even performed his funeral rites, but he lives, an earnest, happy Christian, rejoicing in the salvation he has found."

The Unexpected Beauty of the Scene.— "There was a poor blind boy—not poor in circumstances, but poor because of his affliction—whose mother took him to all the most eminent doctors, and oculists, to see if anything could possibly be done for him. Only one practitioner gave him any hope. He said if the lady left the boy under his charge for so long, he thought he could enable her son to see. The mother gladly agreed. The boy was left, and at the end of the time was taken home by his mother. On a certain day the bandages were to be taken from his eyes. The day came, a glorious day of sunshine, and there were many friends gathered at the house. The bandage was at length taken from the lad's eyes. He gave one look around him, then running to the couch he hid his face and wept. His mother asked him why he wept. 'Oh mother,' he said, 'why did you not tell me it was all so beautiful?' 'But I tried to tell you, my boy,' she replied. 'Not that it was *so* beautiful,' persisted the boy.' No matter how faithfully he was told, for want of vision he could not apprehend it; he must see for himself. Similarly, when we tell the sinner of the beauty of Christ, His love and mercy and grace, in a manner they seem to understand, but they cannot realise it in anything of its fulness, until they have seen Him for themselves."

LONGEVITY.

Dr. Talmage's Sermon Preached Last Sunday Morning, June 10, 1888.

"With long life will I satisfy him." Ps. 91 : 16.

Religion a Chariot, not a Hearse—Conducive to Long Life—I. By making Care of Health a Duty—The Caligraphy of God—The Whispering-Gallery of the Soul—An Ill-used Watch—II. By Protesting Against Dissipation—Lives of Genius Curtailed by Sin—Illustrious Examples—III. By Relieving Worry—A Twenty-Millionaire Friend—The Wheels of a Carpet Factory—An Almighty Sedative—IV. By Assuring Post-Mortem Happiness—Four Experiments—The Voice of the Rainbow.

THROUGH the mistake of its friends, religion has been chiefly associated with sick-beds and graveyards. The whole subject, to many people, is odorous with chlorine and carbolic acid. There are people who cannot pronounce the word religion without hearing in it the clipping chisel of the tombstone cutter. It is high time that this thing were changed, and that religion, instead of being represented as a hearse to carry out the dead, should be represented as a chariot in which the living are to triumph.

Religion, so far from subtracting from one's vitality, is a glorious addition. It is sanative, curative, hygienic. It is good for the eyes, good for the ears, good for the spleen, good for the digestion, good for the nerves, good for the muscles. When David, in another part of the Psalms, prays that religion may be dominant, he does not speak of it as a mild sickness, or an emaciation, or an attack of moral and spiritual cramp; he speaks of it as "the

Saving Health

of all nations"; while God, in the text, promises longevity to the pious, saying: "With long life will I satisfy him." The fact is that men and women die too soon. It is high time that religion joined the hand of medical science in attempting to improve human longevity. Adam lived nine hundred and thirty years. Methuselah lived nine hundred and sixty-nine years. As late in the history of the world as Vespasian, there were, at one time, in his empire forty-five people one hundred and thirty-five years old. So far down as the sixteenth century, Peter Zartan died at one hundred and eighty-five years of age. I do not say that religion will ever take the race back to antediluvian longevity, but I do say the length of life will be increased.

It is said in Isaiah: "The child shall die a hundred years old." Now, if according to Scripture, the child is to be a hundred years old, may not the men and women reach to three hundred and four hundred and five hundred? The fact is that we are mere dwarfs and skeletons compared with some of the generations that are to come. Take the African race. They have been under bondage for centuries. Give them a chance, and they develop a Frederick Douglass or a Toussaint L'Ouverture. And if the white race shall be brought from under the serfdom of sin, what shall be the body? what shall be the soul? Religion has only just touched our world. Give it full power for a few centuries, and who can tell what will be the strength of man, and the beauty of woman, and the longevity of all?

My design is to show that practical religion is the friend of long life. I prove it, first, from the fact that it makes the care of our health

A Positive Christian Duty.

Whether we shall keep early or late hours, whether we shall take food digestible or indigestible, whether there shall be thorough or incomplete mastication, are questions very often deferred to the realm of whimsicality; but the Christian man lifts this whole problem of health into the accountable and the divine. He says: "God has given me this body, and He has called it the temple of the Holy Ghost, and to deface its altars, or mar its walls, or crumble its pillars, is a God-defying sacrilege." He sees God's caligraphy in every page—anatomical and physiological. He says: "God has given me a wonderful body for noble purposes."

That arm with thirty-two curious bones wielded by forty-six curious muscles, and all under the brain's telegraphy; three hundred and fifty pounds of blood rushing through the heart every hour, the heart in twenty-four hours beating 100,000 times, during the twenty-four hours overcoming resistances amounting to 224,000,000 pounds of weight, during the same time the lungs taking in fifty-seven hogsheads of air, and all this mechanism not more mighty than delicate and easily disturbed and demolished.

The Christian man says to himself: "If I hurt my nerves, if I hurt my brain, if I hurt any of my faculties, I insult God and call for

Dire Retribution."

Why did God tell the Levites not to offer to Him in sacrifice animals imperfect and diseased? He meant to tell us in all the ages that we are to offer to God our very best physicial condition, and a man who through irregular or gluttonous eating ruins his health, is not offering to God such a sacrifice. Why did Paul write for his cloak at Troas? Why should such a great man as Paul be anxious about a thing so insignificant as an overcoat? It was because he knew that with pneumonia and rheumatism he would not be worth half as much to God and the Church as with respiration easy and foot free.

An intelligent Christian man would consider it an absurdity to kneel down at night and pray and ask God's protection, while at the same time he kept the windows of his bedroom tight shut against fresh air. He would just as soon think of going out on the bridge between New York and Brooklyn, leaping off and then praying to God to keep him from getting hurt. Just as long as you defer this whole subject of physical health to the realm of whimsicality or to the pastry-cook, or to the butcher, or to the baker, or to the apothecary, or to the clothier, you are not acting like a Christian. Take care of all your physical forces—nervous, muscular, bone, brain, cellular tissue—for all you must be brought to judgment.

Smoking your nervous system into fidgets, burning out the coating of your stomach with wine logwooded and strychnined, walking with thin shoes to make your feet look delicate, pinched at the waist until you are nigh cut in two, and neither part worth anything, groaning about sick headache and palpitation of the heart, which you think came from God, when they came from

Your own Folly.

What right has any man or woman to deface the temple of the Holy Ghost? What is the ear? Why, it is *the whispering-gallery of the human soul*. What is the eye? It is the observatory God constructed, its telescope sweeping the heavens. What is the hand? An instrument so wonderful that when the Earl of Bridgewater bequeathed in his will $40,000 for treatises to be written on the wisdom, power, and goodness of God, Sir Charles Bell, the great English anatomist and surgeon, found his greatest illustration in the construction of the human hand, devoting his whole book to that subject.

So wonderful are these bodies that God names His own attributes after different parts of them. His omniscience—it is *God's eye*. His omnipresence—it is *God's ear*. His omnipotence—it is *God's arm*. The upholstery of the midnight heavens—it is the work of *God's fingers*. His life-giving power—it is the breath of the Almighty. His dominion—"the government shall be upon *His shoulder*." A body so divinely honored and so divinely constructed, let us be careful not to abuse it.

When it becomes a Christian duty to take care of our health, is not the whole tendency toward longevity? If I toss my watch about recklessly, and drop it on the pavement, and wind it up any time of day or night I happen to think of it, and often let it run down, while you are careful with your watch, and never abuse it, and wind it up just at the same hour every night, and put it in a place where it will not suffer from the violent changes of atmosphere, which watch will last the longer? Common sense answers. Now, the human body is God's watch. You see the hands of the watch, you see the face of the watch; but the beating of the heart is the ticking of the watch. Oh, be careful and do not let it run down!

Again: I remark that practical religion is a friend of longevity in the fact that it is *a protest against dissipations*, which injure [illegible] the health. Bad men and women l[illegible] short life. Their

Sins Kill

them. I know [illegible] of good old men, but I do not know [illegible] dozen bad old men. Why? They do not get old. Lord Byron died at Missolonghi at thirty-six years of age, himself his own Mazeppa, his unbridled passions the horse that dashed with him into the desert. Edgar A. Poe died at Baltimore at thirty-eight years of age. The black raven that alighted on the bust above his door was delirium tremens—

"Only this and nothing more."

Napoleon Bonaparte lived only just beyond mid-life, then died at St. Helena, and one of his doctors said that his disease was induced by excessive snuffing. The hero of Austerlitz, the man who by one step of his foot in the centre of Europe shook the earth, *killed by a snuff-box!* Oh, how many people we have known who have not lived out half their days because of their dissipations and indulgences! Now practical religion is a protest against all dissipations of any kind.

"But," you say, "professors of religion have fallen, professors of religion have got drunk, professors of religion have misappropriated trust funds, professors of religion have absconded." Yes; but they

Threw Away Their Religion

before they did their morality. If a man on a White Star line steamer bound for Liverpool, in mid-Atlantic jumps overboard and is drowned, is that anything against the White Star line's capacity to take the man across the ocean? And if a man jumps over the gunwale of his religion and goes down never to rise, is that any reason for your believing that religion has no capacity to take the man clear through? In the one case, if he had kept to the steamer his body would have been saved; in the other case, if he had kept to his religion, his morals would have been saved.

There are aged people who would have been dead twenty-five years ago but for the defence and the equipoise of religion. You have no more natural resistance than hundreds of people who lie in the cemeteries to-day, slain by their own vices. The doctors made their case as kind and pleasant as they could, and it was called congestion of the brain, or something else, but the snakes and the blue flies that seemed to crawl over the pillow in the sight of the delirious patient showed what was the matter with him. You, the aged Christian man, walked along by that unhappy one until you came to the golden pillar of a Christian life. You went to the right; he went to the left. That is all the difference between you. Oh, if this religion is a protest against all forms of dissipation, then it is an illustrious friend of longevity. "With long life will I satisfy him."

Again: religion is a friend of longevity in the fact that

It Takes the Worry Out

of our temporalities. It is not work that kills men, it is worry. When a man becomes a genuine Christian he makes over to God not only his affections, but his family, his business, his reputation, his body, his mind, his soul—everything. Industrious he will be, but never worrying, because God is managing his affairs. How can he worry about business when in answer to his prayers God tells him when to buy and when to sell; and if he gain, that is best, and if he lose, that is best?"

Suppose you had a supernatural neighbor who came in and said: "Sir, I want you to call on me in every exigency; I am your fast friend

I could fall back on $20,000,000; I can foresee a panic ten years; I hold the controlling stock in thirty of the best monetary institutions of New York; whenever you are in trouble, call on me and I will help you; you can have my money and you can have my influence; here is my hand in pledge for it." How much would you worry about business? Why, you would say: 'I'll do the best I can, and then I'll depend on my friend's generosity for the rest."

Now more than that is promised to every Christian business man. God says to him: "I own New York and London and St. Petersburg and Pekin; and Australia and California are mine; I can foresee a panic a million years; I have all the resources of the universe, and I am your fast friend; when you get in business trouble or any other trouble, call on me and I will help; here is my hand in pledge of omnipotent deliverance." How much should that man worry? Not much. What lion will dare to put his paw on that Daniel? Is there not rest in this? Is there not

An Eternal Vacation

in this? "Oh," you say, "here is a man who asked God for a blessing in a certain enterprise, and he lost five thousand dollars in it. Explain that." I will. Yonder is a factory, and one wheel is going north, and the other wheel is going south, and one wheel plays laterally and the other plays vertically. I go to the manufacturer and say: "O manufacturer, your machinery is a contradiction. Why do you not make all the wheels go one way?" "Well," he says, "I made them to go in opposite directions on purpose, and they produce the right result. You go down-stairs and examine the carpets we are turning out in this establishment and you will see." I go down on the other floor and I see the carpets, and I am obliged to confess that though the wheels in that factory go in opposite directions, they turn out a beautiful result; and while I am standing there looking at the exquisite fabric an old Scripture passage comes into my mind: "All things work together for good to them who love God." Is there not rest in that? Is there not longevity in that?

Suppose a man is all the time worried about his reputation? One man says he lies, another says he is stupid, another says he is dishonest, and half a dozen printing establishments attack him, and he is in a great state of

Excitement and Worry

and fume, and cannot sleep; but religion comes to him and says: "Man, God is on your side; he will take care of your reputation; if God be for you, who can be against you?" How much should that man worry about his reputation? Not much. If that broker who some years ago in Wall Street, after he had lost money, sat down and wrote a farewell letter to his wife before he blew his brains out—if instead of taking out of his pocket a pistol he had taken out a well-read New Testament, there would have been one less suicide. O nervous and feverish people of the world, try this almighty sedative. You will live twenty-five years longer under its soothing power. It is not chloral that you want, or morphine that you want; it is the gospel of Christ. "With long life will I satisfy him."

Again: practical religion is a friend of longevity in the fact that it removes all corroding care about a future existence. Every man wants to know what is to become of him. If you get on board a rail train, you want to know at what point it is going to stop; if you get on board a ship, you want to know into what harbor it is going to run, and if you should tell me you have no interest in what is to be

Your Future Destiny,

I would, in as polite a way as I know how, tell you I did not believe you. Before I had this matter settled with reference to my future existence, the question almost worried me into ruined health. The anxieties men have upon this subject put together would make a martyrdom. This is a state of awful unhealthiness. There are people who fret themselves to death for fear of dying.

I want to take the strain off your nerves and the depression off your soul, and I make *two or three experiments.* Experiment first: When you go out of this world it does not make any difference whether you have been good or bad, or whether you believed truth or error, you will go straight to glory. "Impossible," you say; "my common sense as well as my religion teaches that the bad and the good cannot live together forever. You give me no comfort in that experiment." *Experiment the second:* When you leave this world you will go into an intermediate state where you can get converted and prepared for heaven. "Impossible," you say; "as the tree falleth, so it must lie, and I cannot postpone to an intermediate state reformation which ought to have been effected in this state." *Experiment the third:* There is no future world; when a man dies, that is the last of him. Do not worry about what you are to do in another state of being; you will not do anything. "Impossible," you say; "there is something that tells me that

Death is Not the Appendix

but the preface to life; there is something that tells me that on this side of the grave I only get started, and that I shall go on forever; my power to think says 'forever,' my affections say 'forever,' my capacity to enjoy or suffer, 'forever.'"

Well, you defeat me in my three experiments. I have only one more to make, and if you defeat me in that I am exhausted: A mighty One on a knoll back of Jerusalem one day, the skies filled with forked lightnings and the earth filled with volcanic disturbances, turned his pale and agonized face toward the heavens and said: "I take the sins and sorrows of the ages into my own heart. I am the expiation. Witness earth and heaven and hell, I am the expiation." And the hammer struck him, and the spears punctured him, and heaven thundered: "The wages of sin is death!". "The soul that sinneth, it shall die!" "I will by no means clear the guilty!" Then there was silence for half an hour, and the lightnings were drawn back into the scabbard of the sky, and the earth ceased to quiver, and all the colors of the sky began to shift into

A Rainbow

woven out of the falling tears of Jesus, and there was red as of the bloodshedding, and there was blue as of the bruising, and there was green as of the heavenly foliage, and there was orange as of the day-dawn. And along the line of the blue I saw the words: "I was bruised for their iniquities." And along the line of the red I saw the words: "The blood of Jesus Christ cleanseth from all sin." And along the line of the green I saw the words: "The leaves of the Tree of Life for the healing of the nations." And along the line of the orange I saw the words: "The day-spring from on high hath visited us."

And then I saw the storm was over and the rainbow rose higher and higher until it seemed retreating to another heaven, and planting one column of its colors on one side the eternal hill, and planting the other column of its colors on the other side the eternal hill, it rose upward and upward "and behold there was a rainbow about the throne.' Accept that sacrifice and

Quit Worrying.

Take the tonic, the inspiration, the longevity of this truth. Religion is sunshine; that is health. Religion is fresh air and pure water; they are healthy. Religion is warmth; that is healthy. Ask all the doctors and they will tell you that a quiet conscience and pleasant anticipations are hygienic. I offer you perfect peace now and hereafter.

What do you want in the future world? Tell me and you shall have it. Orchards? There are the trees with twelve manner of fruits, yielding fruit every month. Water scenery? There is the River of Life, from under the throne of God, clear as crystal, and the sea of glass mingled with fire. Do you want music? There is the oratorio of the Creation led on by Adam, and the oratorio of the Red Sea led on by Moses, and the oratorio of the Messiah led on by St. Paul, while the archangel with swinging baton controls the one hundred and forty-four thousand who make up the orchestra.

The Other Side of the Grave.

Do you want reunion? There are your dead children waiting to kiss you, waiting to embrace you, waiting to twist garlands in your hair. You have been accustomed to open the door on this side the sepulchre. I open the door on the other side the sepulchre. You have been accustomed to walk in the wet grass on the top of the grave. I show you the under side of the grave; the bottom has fallen out and the long ropes with which the pall-bearers let down your dead, let them clear through into heaven.

Glory be to God for this robust, healthy religion. It will have a tendency to make you live long in this world, and in the world to come you will have eternal life. "With long life will I satisfy Him."

A SCOFFER'S AVOWAL.

A LADY who is doing Christian work among the garrison at Gibraltar, relates a remarkable incident which occurred a few weeks ago. She says: "One evening a Rifleman, well known in the regiment as an atheist, came in to do Satan a service. He meant to snatch away the seed sown, to refute the speaker's arguments in the barrack-room, and throw ridicule upon the whole mission. My subject was, 'What think ye of Christ?' The unbeliever remained to the after-meeting, for the purpose of obtaining a knowledge of our proceedings, and that he might deter some anxious inquirer or 'chaff' a comrade. I asked him, 'What think *you* of Christ?' 'Thank you, I don't believe, and I don't want to,' he replied. 'Whether you believe or not, here is a fact, that you will have to meet God and render to Him an account. Now, what answer will you give Him to the truth you have heard to-night?' 'If there be a God, I'll take my chance," he answered flippantly, and then added, 'As for hell, I don't believe in it.' After a few more solemn words I left him. He attended regularly, and his presence was by no means cheering to us, as we feared he was undoing the good work among his comrades. God had purposes of grace towards him, and, while we refrained from speaking to him again, His Spirit was dealing with his soul. One evening, on inviting anxious seekers to stand up, our unbelieving friend rose, evidently in much emotion. Prayer was made for him; he was then personally dealt with. 'I confess that I came the first night to mock; but the words haunted me. All next day I was unhappy. I came again and again. I have felt miserable; but to-night I seem to feel there is hope for me.'

"As one who had publicly denied his Creator, and through whose influence a Bible-reader had apostatized, it was thought fitting that he should make a public confession of Christ. Accordingly, one Sunday evening at the large meeting, in the presence of many unconverted who knew him as an atheist and blasphemer, he told the story of his change in a few simple words: "I denied there was a God, I ridiculed the Bible, I gloried in infidelity, but now I do love Jesus. He has saved me, and I wish all my comrades would come to Him and be saved too. *I only wish I could undo the harm I have done.*' It was a scene calculated to draw tears of thanksgiving and sympathy."

THE CONVERSION OF THE WORLD.

By Rev. L. W. Munhall, M. D.*

The Scripture Millennium — Events Antedating the Predicted 1,000 Years' Reign of Christ— State of the World When Christ Comes to it — The Days of Noah and of Lot—The Parable of the Wheat and the Tares—The Virgins and the Leaven — The Progress of Christianity.

SOME inquire, "Do not the Scriptures teach that the world is to be converted?" I answer, Not by a single word! But how about these prophecies?

"Ask of Me, and I shall give thee the heathen for thine inheritance, and the uttermost parts of the earth for thy possession." (Psalm 2:8). "The wolf also shall dwell with the lamb, and the leopard shall lie down with the kid; and the calf and the young lion and the fatling together; and a little child shall lead them. And the cow and the bear shall feed: their young ones shall lie down together: and the lion shall eat straw like the ox. And the sucking child shall play on the hole of the asp, and the weaned child shall put his hand on the cockatrice's den. They shall not hurt nor destroy in all My holy mountain: for the earth shall be full of the knowledge of the Lord, as the waters cover the sea. (Isaiah 11:6-9).

"But this shall be the covenant that I will make with the house of Israel: After those days, saith the Lord, I will put My law in their inward parts, and write it in their hearts; and will be their God, and they shall be My people. And they shall teach no more every man his neighbor, and every man his brother, saying. Know the Lord, for they shall all know Me, from the least of them unto the greatest of them, saith the Lord: for I will forgive their iniquity, and I will remember their sins no more." (Jeremiah 31:33-34.)

I answer that pre-millennialists believe in the

Literal Fulfilment

of them. They believe in a Millennium during which the devil is really bound, with nothing to "hurt nor destroy in all my holy mountain," when "the earth shall be full of the knowledge of the Lord as the waters cover the sea." Not the sort of Millennium some think we are having now. Not even a Millennium where Christian principles will dominate the civil governments of earth, as some post-millennialists claim; but a Millennium where all bow to the mild sway of the sceptre of the King of Heaven. The post-millennialists hold that the Church is to march forward in its conquests until the world is converted, or, at least dominated by the principles of the doctrines of Christ, and thus shall these prophecies be fulfilled. The pre-millennialists believe that through the Church, by the preaching of the gospel, all who are to be saved during this dispensation, will be by accepting Christ as Saviour; and then, when God's purposes in grace for this dispensation are accomplished,

Christ Comes to Take His Bride Away

to save her from the fires of the great tribulation, at the end of which time He returns with His bride to judge the world in righteousness and destroy the antichrist and his armies, the man of sin "with the brightness of His coming. (II Thess. 2:8.)

A careful contextual examination of the above mentioned and similar prophecies, will reveal the fact that their fulfilment will be accomplished by terrible judgments. For instance: the things prophesied of in Ps. 2:8, are thus introduced in the following verse: "Thou shalt break them with a rod of iron; thou shalt dash them to pieces like a potter's vessel." (Ps. 2:9.) The context to Isa. 2:6-9 indicates the same thing: "But with righteousness shall He judge the poor, and reprove with equity for the meek of the earth: and He shall smite the earth with the rod of His mouth, and with the breath of His lips shall He slay the wicked" (Isa. 11:4. Jer. 31:33, 34) has reference to Israel and Judah only, as the context clearly shows: "Behold, the days come, saith the Lord, that I will make a new covenant with the house of Israel, and with the house of Judah: not according to the covenant that I made with their fathers, in the day that I took them by the hand to bring them out of the land of Egypt; which my covenant they brake, although I was a husband unto them, saith the Lord" (Jer. 31:31, 32). The stone cut out of the mountain in Dan. 2:35, that shall ultimately fill the whole earth, smites the feet of the image (the image represents the world powers) and dashes it to pieces, and it becomes "like the chaff of the summer threshing floors," and so on of the rest of these prophecies to the last.

The renowned Dr. Chalmers was once lecturing to some students on the closing scenes of this dispensation. As he was nearing the conclusion of the lecture, he was interrupted and compelled to leave the class hastily in answer to an imperative summons. As he gathered his hat and coat hurriedly in leaving, he said, "Young gentlemen, think as you will about these matters, one thing is absolutely certain, the dispensation of the Spirit will close with a smash."

But how about Phil. 2:10, 11: "That at the name of Jesus every knee shall bow, of things in heaven, and things in earth, and things under the earth; and that every tongue shall confess that Jesus Christ is Lord, to the glory of God the Father." Is the bowing of the knee and confessing that Jesus is Lord equivalent to salvation? If so, then the "final restorationists" are right when, chiefly upon the testimony of these verses, they claim that not only all the inhabitants of earth shall at last be found among the "blood-washed throng" in heaven, but of hell also, together with the devil and all demons. But they are not right, for this Scripture teaches no such thing. The time is coming when the devil and all atheists, infidels, and blasphemers will be obliged to kneel and confess that Jesus Christ is Lord, to the glory of God the Father;

When "He Cometh With Clouds,

and every eye shall see Him, and they also which pierced Him, and all kindreds of the earth shall wail because of Him" (Rev. 1:7), but it will avail them nought.

The Word of God does not teach that the world is to be converted. It teaches most explicitly that it will *not* be. Let it speak for itself as to what will be the condition of affairs when He shall return:

"But as the days of Noe were, so shall also the coming of the Son of Man be. For as in the days that were before the flood, they were eating and drinking, marrying and giving in marriage, until the day that Noe entered into the ark, and knew not until the flood came and took them all away; so shall also the coming of the Son of Man be." (Matt. 24:37-39.) Surely, no one will claim that the world was converted in the days of Noah. Yet as it was then, so shall it be when Christ returns.

"Likewise also as it was in the days of Lot; they did eat, they drank, they bought, they sold, they planted, they builded. But the same day that Lot went out of Sodom, it rained fire and brimstone from heaven, and destroyed them all. Even thus shall it be in the day when the Son of Man is revealed." (Luke 17:28-30.) Sodom didn't look much like it was converted in Lot's time. No more will the world be when Christ is revealed. See Jude, verse seventh.

"This know also, that in the last days perilous times shall come. For men shall be lovers of their own selves, covetous, boasters, proud, blasphemers, disobedient to parents, unthankful, unholy, without natural affection, trucebreakers, false accusers, incontinent, fierce, despisers of those that are good, traitors, heady, highminded, lovers of pleasure more than lovers of God; having a form of godliness, but denying the power thereof; from such turn away." (II Tim 3:1-5.) Here is

An Explicit Description

of the condition of affairs immediately preceding the advent of the Lord; but we find nothing at all resembling a converted world in the narrative.

"Then Jesus sent the multitude away, and went into the house, and His disciples came unto Him, saying, Declare unto us the parable of the tares of the field. He answered and said unto them, He that soweth the good seed is the Son of Man; the field is the world; the good seed are the children of the kingdom; but the tares are the children of the wicked one; the enemy that sowed them is the devil; the harvest is the end of the world, and the reapers are the angels. As therefore the tares are gathered and burned in the fire, so shall it be in the end of this world" (age). Matt. 13:36-40.

This parable, and the Lord's own interpretation of it, leaves no doubt whatever but that when He returns there will be multitudes of unsaved people on the earth:

Tares Growing with the Wheat.

If the parable of the ten virgins represents the professing church, half of it will be found unregenerated when the Lord returns, and the other half asleep. The exegetes are pretty well agreed that "leaven," in the Scriptures, signifies corruption, and the kingdom of heaven the professing church, in part. If these conclusions be true in every other case, why not in Matt. 13:33? "Another parable spake He unto them: The kingdom of heaven is like unto leaven, which a woman took, and hid in three measures of meal, till the whole was leavened." In this case this passage would signify that corrupting influences will work in the visible church until the whole is corrupted. Is not such interpretation justified by the question of the unjust judge, "Howbeit when the Son of man cometh, shall He find faith (the faith) on the earth?" (Luke 18:8, R. V.) Do not the sixth and nineteenth chapters of Revelation, inclusively, justify such interpretation? Has not this view of the case already come to pass once? Was not the professing church as corrupt as Satan could ever wish it to be for nearly a thousand years? Is man, naturally, any better that this condition of affairs should not occur again?

Let it be said there is nothing, save the word of inspiration, so convincing, that the church is a divine Institution, and, "that the gates of hell shall not prevail against her," as that she has lived and accomplished so much, to the glory of God, despite the formality worldliness, ignorance, and schisms that have marred her beauty and hindered her progress. She shall yet look "forth as the morning, fair as the moon, clear as the sun, and terrible as an army with banners," (Song of Solomon 6:10.)

But, while this is so, it should not be forgotten that the Word of God, nowhere, by a single sentence, intimates that the world is to be converted before Christ comes. It does, however, teach that, "This Gospel of the Kingdom shall be preached in all the world (Greek, inhabited earth), for a witness unto all nations, and then shall the end come." (Matt. 24:14).

* From his work entitled "The Lord's Return, and Kindred Truth," 190 pages. The Willard Tract Depository, Toronto, Canada.

UNAPPRECIATED REWARDS.

No clearer evidence of the degradation of the Central African races and the difficulties of missionary work among them has been given than that contained in a report from Mr. Ousley, the missionary of the American Board at Kambini, who has been trying to stimulate the children in the schools by rewards, and describes the disappointing results in a letter to the *Missionary Herald:* He says: "We have noticed the desire, on the part of a number of the pupils, to absent themselves from the religious part of the schoolwork. One would not suspect small children of such a spirit, but we have noticed it too prominently of late to continue to offer a little work to those who come regularly to school, whereby they may earn a wrap or garment, at the close of school.

"As yet very few appreciate the value of clothes, even after they have secured them. We naturally thought that the parents of the chil dren would be glad to have us furnish their children with work sufficient to earn something to wear. But it is the reverse. They prefer, seemingly, to have their children about them in an almost nude condition, rather than that they secure garments or wraps by working for them. In view of our desire to help them get something to cover their bodies, we have required of our scholars only three full hours' work per day for five days, which is the equivalent to about one fourth or one fifth of the market value of such articles in this part of the world. To our surprise and disappointment the parents of some of the children ceased to come to our services, as also to the school exercises, and their excuse is that we have not given them any clothes or anything to eat for coming. Not one in a hundred of the girls and the women would wear clothes even if they could get them as a free gift, and the men who really desire clothes generally contrive to buy them from the traders."

THE CHIEF PRIESTHOOD RENOUNCED.

A YOUNG man in Persia has voluntarily chosen to be a teacher, when, by abjuring the Christian faith, he might have been made chief priest of his sect. The Rev. S. G. Wilson, in the course of a letter to the *Church*, thus describes the case: During a recent tour in the southern portion of our field, I was impressed with the manifestations of the power the gospel is exerting upon Mussulmans. Our first stage brought us to a village of Ali-Alahis, a sect so heterodox as to be almost outside the pale of Islam. They always give a ready ear to Christian teaching. We have a convert here who belongs to the priestly family. His father was chief priest of the sect, but consented to put his son in our Tabriz school, where he received the truth. The son might have inherited the office if he had not rather chosen to suffer affliction with the people of God. He was known to all as a Christian. Last spring the school was reopened under his charge. He had offers of employment as teacher in their mosque, with a good family, if he would teach from their books, but he was desirous of doing the Lord's service. His instruction is largely from distinctly Christian books. After awhile the mujteheed (chief mollah) of Tabriz, who has the village tax for his perquisite, sent a demand that he give an account of himself for teaching from "American books," and the mollah, who was instrumental in closing the Mussulman department of our school at Tabriz, came to vex him; so that he has scarcely been able to keep his school together, and many of the people have broken off intercourse with him.

A PHYSICIAN'S EXPLANATION OF DIVINE HEALING.

PHYSICIANS as a rule are more sceptical about Divine Healing than other persons, as their training leads them to believe that only by medical treatment can disease be overcome. One case, however, of a physician frankly ascribing a cure to the intervention of Divine power is related in *Thy Healer** this month. Mrs. Hudson, speaking at Bethshan said:

"A young girl named Mary Parker, living in Birmingham, suffered from spinal complaint, and was quite unable to sit up in bed. She had heard of the Lord's healing, and thought He might do for her as He had done for others. She saw the promise and believed it, and then she had a desire to be anointed. A clergyman was willing to anoint her, and she was anointed nine months before the healing came; but during that time she trusted perfectly in the Lord. The friends said it was fanaticism, and the doctors said she was incurable, but she kept on trusting. Yet, after the anointing she became worse. She had an attack of paralysis, and was cramped up in bed with her ancles one across the other. Her speech was also affected, her vocal organs seemed paralysed, but she went on trusting the Lord all the time. There was no anxiety whatever, but she was just resting in His promise, and knowing that when the time came she would be healed. One lady said to me: 'If Mary Parker is healed I shall believe in Divine Healing.' She came to me afterwards and said, rejoicing: 'O! Mary Parker is healed.' Well, this young girl went on in this state. First, her speech came back in four or five months, and she knew the Lord was working; and, at the end of nine months, after a day of great suffering, it seemed as if every joint in her body had become loosed, and she was suddenly made to sit up in bed. She told me this herself. She called to her mother and said: 'Mother, don't be frightened, the Lord's time is come,' and to her mother's glad surprise she rose from her bed and walked. 'When I turned the sheet down,' she said, 'I was surprised to find my legs perfectly straight, and then I walked.' Then the father and other members of the family were called up to rejoice with her. Mrs. Hudson described the visit of the doctor two days afterwards, and how he made her walk up and down the room and saw it was a perfect cure. He said: 'I have had nothing to do with this, *it is a miracle of the olden times.*'"

**Thy Healer and Faith Witness*, a monthly Magazine, edited by Mrs. M. Baxter, contains original articles on Holiness and Healing, Authentic Testimonies of Divine Healing, and Items of Intelligence from Heathen Lands where Missionaries are laboring in faith, soliciting no help from man, but relying solely on God for support. Annual subscription, 75 cents, may be sent to the Manager of CHRISTIAN HERALD, 63 Bible House, New York.

AN AFRICAN'S ABSTINENCE.

IN an encouraging report from the West Central African Mission of the American Board, published in the *Missionary Herald*, Mr. Currie mentions an incident which gave the missionaries much comfort. He says: An effort has been made in almost every place visited to sow some seeds of gospel truth. Many people have thus heard for the first time about Jesus and His love. Many have learned that there are white men in the country who seek to do them good and not evil. One of my boys, while on a journey for the first time, took his stand for Christ; and he has since shown that he was in earnest about what he then did. One of the men, on my last trip, refused to drink beer when it was presented to the carriers, and attended worship every night. Two others attended worship regularly, and frequently lingered, after the exercises were over, to ask questions about what they had heard. Often, while on the march, I could hear some of the men trying to sing the hymns they had heard us sing at worship. In one place, almost seven days' journey from here, I found that some of the people, while on their way to the *ombala*, had stopped at our schoolhouse, and learned a few truths from the preaching of one of the brethren, which they carried back to their own village and made known to others. These are small items, but they all have a bearing on the future of our work; and while we look for a large crop from bountiful sowing, it is not impossible to get a good plant from a single mustard seed.

A SERVICE IN MADAGASCAR.

THE character of the work done by missionaries in heathen lands, as well as an evidence of the power of the truth, may be seen in the following extracts from a report of the effort Mr. Shaw is making to reach the dark places of the island of Madagascar:

It was not without difficulty that he reached the benighted region of his labors; shipwreck was escaped as by a miracle, and many perils by sea and land were braved, both by the missionary and his devoted wife. The people of one dark village were "the whole of them more or less drunk." During Mr. Shaw's temporary absence from the village in which he settled, war broke out, and on his return home he found his medical and surgical skill in great demand, and soon became known far and near as a true friend of the people.

In an account of his work in a third village, he tells of the very tardy assemblage of men and women to listen to the gospel, as he preached under the shadow of some fine spreading trees. "I begin," he says, "in a chatty way, to tell them of the character of the God whose name they know, but only to fear, as the Creator and punisher. It is a grand new view to them that He is a God of love, and that He has sent His Son that those who believe on Him should have eternal life. We finish our impromptu service by my telling them I am going to speak to this great God but loving Father, and ask them to follow me in their thoughts with bowed head. In a few words, asking for light for them and blessing, we joined in the first prayer ever offered in that village. Before leaving them, they had promised to put up a building in which I could more conveniently talk to them than in the open air; and so we may hope that before very long a rough but commodious chapel will be erected there.

A LAWYER'S CONVERSION IN A CHURCH VESTIBULE.

AN incident which should encourage preachers who are apt to think that their sermons are wasted, is related by Dr. A. J. Gordon, of Boston, in his *Watchword*. He states that a clergyman had devoted great pains to the preparation of a sermon, which he hoped would be blessed to some members of his congregation who had hitherto been deaf to his appeals. He prayed earnestly over that sermon, and went to his church in a very intense frame of mind. But the night was stormy, and of those whom he was longing to reach, only three were present, and one of them slept through the sermon. He returned home in a dispirited mood. "That sermon was utterly wasted," he said to his wife, as they sat down after the service.

He was mistaken. The next morning a well-known lawyer came to see him, and told him his experience. He had started out that evening without an umbrella, and when the storm came on, he turned into the church vestibule to shelter. The door leading from the vestibule into the church was ajar, so he heard every word of the sermon. He listened with an interest that he was surprised at. It was his boast that he could live, and had always lived and prospered, without religion. He was a successful lawyer, with genial manners, which made him universally popular. He was charitable and generous, not from any sense of duty, but from a kindness of heart that made him willing to do anything to alleviate suffering or distress in others.

He believed himself to be thoroughly sincere, and he was merciless in discovering inconsistencies in the lives of those who professed to be Christians. He was the leader of a large circle of young men, who, admiring his character and talents, followed his example implicity in regard to religious matters. He had not entered the doors of a church for years, and it was only the fury of the elements that had driven him to seek a temporary shelter there this evening. Had the sermon been argumentative he would have sought arguments to refute it. But it was nothing of the kind; it was an earnest appeal to all to come to the Saviour, and he could not doubt that the speaker spoke from his heart.

A strange longing to know somewhat of this joy and peace in believing came over him, as he stood there alone in the darkness. He began to pray, and after he went home he was unable to rest until he had given himself to God, and the next morning he went to the preacher to tell him the joyful news.

PUBLISHER'S NOTICE.

The whole edition of The Christian Herald was mailed last week to subscribers during Tuesday, June 5. The last delivery at the New York Post Office was made at 10.50 P. M.

CURRENT EVENTS.

The Renomination of President Cleveland for the Presidency, and the nomination of Mr. Allen G. Thurman, of Ohio, for the Vice-Presidency, by the Democratic National Convention, at St Louis, last week, were both more unanimous than the political prophets had led the country to expect. In spite of the dissatisfaction of a section of the party with the attempt Mr. Cleveland made in the early part of his term to fulfil his pledges to the civil service reformers who supported him, and in spite of the disapproval of another section with his message on the tariff, he was nominated with an enthusiasm truly remarkable. There was no balloting, no show of opposition; the wave of enthusiasm carried the Convention away, and the nomination was made by acclamation. When the time came for filling the second place on the ticket, there was but little less unanimity. Gen. Black formally withdrew his name by telegraph, in the interest of harmony, as the Convention was evidently overwhelmingly in favor of Mr. Thurman. The name of Gov. Isaac P. Gray, of Indiana, was duly presented, and his nomination urged, on the ground that Mr. Thurman being already seventy-six years of age, there was a possibility of his dying before the completion of his term, when "the Senate might be cursed by another Ingalls." But even that possibility did not weigh with the Convention, and Thurman was nominated at the first call of States.

The Platform Adopted by the Convention was not constructed without a protracted struggle in the Committee on Resolutions. It would, however, have been a stultification if the Convention, after re-nominating Mr. Cleveland, had failed to give a clear expression of its adherence to the principles of his tariff message. Mr. Edward Cooper, of New York, did his utmost, it would appear, to prevent this, doubtless realizing how difficult it will be to carry New York and other doubtful States on any platform tending even slightly in the direction of free trade. But he was outvoted, though not convinced, and he took the precaution of having his dissent from the action of his fellow-members of the Committee publicly announced by the Chairman of the Convention. As finally agreed upon, the tariff plank of the platform not only endorses the President's message, but accepts the Mills' Bill as its practical outcome. It declares that "The Democratic Party in the United States in National Convention assembled, renews the pledge of its fidelity to Democratic faith, and reaffirms the platform adopted by its representatives in the convention of 1884, and indorses the views expressed by President Cleveland in his last earnest message to Congress as the correct interpretation of that platform upon the question of tariff reduction, and also indorses the efforts of our Democratic representatives in Congress to secure a reduction of excessive taxation." The Committee appear to have had a prevision of the application which will be made of the plank in the campaign, and endeavoured to disarm it in advance, by contending that "a fair and careful revision of our tax laws, with due allowance for the difference between the wages of American and foreign labor, must promote and encourage every branch of such industries and enterprises by giving them assurance of an extended market and steady and continuous operations." That the Republican party will join issue on this question, there can be no doubt, and the campaign promises therefore to be fought this time on principles rather than on the personal records of the candidates.

The Decisive Republican Victory in Oregon last week is hailed by the party as an augury of success in the Presidential campaign. An election took place on June 4. of a member of Congress, and members of the State Legislature, who will choose a United States Senator. The election turned entirely on the Tariff question, and the result is unequivocal. The normal Republican majority is 1200, but this year the recent heavy increase of the immigration ran up the figures considerably on both sides. Though the official returns were not published last week, the Democrats concede a Republican majority of at least seven thousand. This year only one county has returned a Democratic plurality, and that was under 50. The change in eastern Oregon was greater than was generally expected. Of the 75 new members of her Legislature, the Republicans elected 63, the Democrats 10, and 2 are in doubt. So the next Legislature in joint ballot will stand at least 71 Republicans to 19 Democrats. Senator Dolph will therefore be his own successor. There is not one county in the State where the Democrats have elected their county ticket. The increase in the Republican vote is more marked in manufacturing and wool-growing districts than in purely agricultural counties. There was a large increase in the Prohibition vote.

The Abolition of Executions by Hanging in New York State was effected on June 4, when Governor Hill signed the bill passed by the Legislature, substituting the electric spark for the rope as the instrument of death. The bill also contains a number of provisions intended to reform the abuses connected with the death penalty which have become a scandal. The condemned criminal now holds a daily levee, and reporters publish the most minute details as to his demeanor, conversation, and habits, which give him a notoriety highly esteemed by the criminal classes. The new bill which now becomes law and applies to crimes committed after January 1, 1889, provides that the prisoner sentenced to death shall be immediately conveyed by the Sheriff to one of the State prisons and there *kept in solitary confinement* until the day of execution, to be visited only by officers or by his relatives, physician, clergyman, or counsel. The court imposing sentence shall name merely the week within which the execution is to take place, the particular day within such week being left to the discretion of the principal officer of the prison. The execution is required to be practically private, only officials, clergymen, physicians, and a limited number of citizens being allowed to be present.

A Severe but Just Arraignment of the liquor trade of New York, and of the Police and prosecuting officials who neglect their duty, was made on June 4, by Judge Barrett in his charge to the Grand Jury. He said: "It seems to be a very disgraceful state of things that there should be 5,000 presentations of violations of a particular law not attended to. It warrants the conclusion that there is either deliberate and open defiance of the law by those engaged in the liquor business, or that there is a most decided and inexcusable inefficiency on the part of the officers of the law. It does not seem within the bounds of possibility that the law should be so flagrantly and openly defied as that there should be 5,000 excise cases to be presented to you. Why it should be so, I cannot say. Why persons engaged in the sale of intoxicating liquors cannot do their business in strict obedience to the laws as other citizens do, is something that I cannot understand." He then proceeded to express his contempt for the system of spasmodic raids and the conduct of the police at the trials, which prevented convictions. What was needed, he said, was to have a few of the proprietors of the large saloons in the Penitentiary, which would do more good than the arrest of small barkeepers and the other petty acts of the police.

The New Governor-General of Canada, Lord Stanley, of Preston, arrived by the steamer *Sarmatian* on June 2. In an interview with a reporter he said that he had acquired while in the Colonial Office considerable knowledge of Canada's vast resources, and had been greatly impressed with the future in store for the country. He would not go to his new post with preconceived ideas, and did not wish to force any policy upon a country possessing a responsible government. The Marquis of Lansdowne, the late Governor-General of Canada, on leaving the Dominion said he had been deeply moved by the warmth of the farewell given him at Ottawa and Toronto. He had great hopes for the future of the Dominion, owing to the good harvests in the Northwest and the large number of people immigrating into the country.

Another Ministerial Crisis in Germany developed last week, and was only averted by the concession of the Emperor. The interference exercised by Prince Bismarck with the freedom of election during the reign of the late Emperor, was always deplored by the present Emperor when he was Crown Prince. To him and to his English wife it appeared scandalous that the votes of the people should be controlled and manipulated by the Government. In giving his assent to the Quinquennial Landtag Bill which extends the existence of the Legislature from three to five years, the Emperor, therefore, took occasion to write to Herr Von Puttkamer, directing him to refrain from using Government influence in the elections. The Emperor also resolved to publish this letter in the official journal an appendix to the bill. Bismarck was so deeply mortified by the project that he threatened to resign if the letter were published. So acute became the crisis that the Emperor's disease was aggravated, and finally he consented to withold the letter from publication. It is stated, however, that an Imperial rescript will be issued warning the local authorities against interfering in the elections. Herr Von Puttkamer has in consequence resigned his office as Minister of the Interior.

A New Irish Programme of a More Hopeful character is said to have been arranged by Mr. Balfour, the Secretary for Ireland. The New York *Sun* publishes a despatch from its London correspondent, describing an interview which he has had with Mr. Balfour. The correspondent reports the Secretary as saying: "that the Government is now maturing a great policy of public works in Ireland. It is a scheme of much importance. I purpose to introduce three bills, involving a very large outlay of public money, for the purpose of a scheme of arterial drainage. I hope to follow this up next year by schemes of a similar character. I do not believe that these plans will involve the building of piers and so on, for I am not sure that this sort of work would be advisable. But a very great sum of money will be spent, and this will tend to relieve Ireland. Concerning the prevalent distress, we have found it worst in the Arran Islands. The Government has distributed a large amount of seed potatoes there, sufficient for the whole need of the population. No relief works have been begun on the islands, as they are not considered necessary." The Government will doubtless find schemes of this character, if wisely executed, more effective in pacifying Ireland than coercion.

A Judge Exchanging the Bench for the Pulpit, has surprised a Western city. The Portland *Oregonian* announces that "Ex-Chief-Justice Roger S. Greene, late of the Washington Territorial Supreme Court, is now closing up his legal business, preparatory to devoting his entire time to the ministry. He is one of the leading members of the Baptist Church, and has always been prominently identified with religious movements connected with it. Judge Greene is senior member of the law firm of Greene, McNaught, Hanford & McGraw, and is ranked as one of the leading attorneys in the Territory. He was Chief-Justice of the Supreme Court for sixteen years, having been succeeded by Chief-Justice Jones. Judge Greene says he finds himself unable to give the amount of time he desires to religious work, and at the same time practice law, and his explanation suggests that in his opinion the two callings are not sympathetic."

Deeply Interesting Services were held Last week at St. George's Church, New York, of which Rev. W. S. Rainsford is rector. On Sunday, June 3, thirteen young men, who have been energetic and devoted workers in the missions of the church during the past four years, were ordained "lay helpers" by Bishop H. C. Potter. These young men, who appeared very intelligent and refined, are empowered to deliver sermons in any Protestant Episcopal church in the diocese, and to read the services. Mr. Rainsford spoke highly of the value of their past services, and was full of hope for the future. On Thursday, June 7, another gratifying service, in connection with the same church, was held. This was the presentation to the church of the beautiful memorial building erected at the expense of Mr. and Mrs. John Pierpont Morgan in memory of the late Mr. and Mrs. Charles Tracy. The building will be used as a clergy house and as the centre of evangelistic and mission work in the parish.

An Unconscious Heir is Wandering About the country, while the executors of his grandfather's estate are looking for him. About fifteen years ago an old farmer died, leaving, among other possessions, a farm on the outskirts of Brooklyn, N. Y. All the property went to the widow for her life, and at her death, to her six children. It was not a large estate when the farmer died, but the land on the outskirts of Brooklyn has now become very valuable, owing to the rapid growth of the city. There is, therefore, a large sum to be divided among the children—the widow being now dead. One of the daughters is also dead, and her share goes to her son, a young man of restless, shiftless disposition, who, five years ago, wandered away from home, pedling coal in scattered villages, and has not been heard of since. If the family had expected much benefit from the farmer's estate, the young man would probably have taken care to keep his relatives informed of his whereabouts; but, as he has not done so, he can have no idea how large a sum is awaiting his return to claim it. It is stated that he was always in a needy, impoverished condition, and exactly the kind of man to appreciate such a sum of money as he is now heir to. In his poverty and vagrancy he resembles the Christian, who, though an heir of God, fails to apply for the riches of grace promised to all who ask. (Mal. 3: 10.)

Three Bears were Killed by a Boy only Fourteen years old, in Monroe County, Pennsylvania, a few days ago. The boy was sent by his father to a clearing in the woods near his house to chop up some trees that had been felled. In about an hour he returned with his axe and his clothing covered with blood, and stated that he had killed three bears. His father was sceptical, but on going to the clearing he found that the boy had told the truth. The lad said that he had commenced chopping on the fallen tree, when a big bear jumped out from beneath it and made a rush for him. He buried the axe in the animal's skull, and another blow killed the bear. The boy then looked in under the tree and discovered the two smaller bears. He routed them out and attacked them. One of the bears showed fight, but the other one slouched away. He killed the young one as quickly as he had the old one, and then gave chase to the other and dispatched it in the same way. After the bodies of the dead bears had been taken home the boy returned to his work as if nothing had happened. The old bear weighed over three hundred pounds. The father is very proud of his young son's prowess. It may be hoped that he will teach him to be equally valiant in the battle he will have to fight with that "roaring lion," the great enemy of souls, and also to tell him that in that battle those are most likely to fail who rely on their own strength, and those sure to succeed who trust wholly in Christ. (Rom. 12: 11.)

A Disastrous Visit to a Lunatic Asylum has been made by a reporter at Milwaukee, Wis. A daily journal of that city states that a brilliant young man engaged in newspaper work was detailed to write an article on the asylums of the State. In order to prepare himself for the work he secured permission to examine the county asylum, and while being shown through the building manifested unmistakable signs of insanity. He became very angry when taken away by the Superintendent, who thought the sights were affecting his brain. The reporter was very indignant and threatened to make a public denunciation of the Superintendent. He was so persistent in his demands to the Governor for an investigation of what he called abuses that one was finally ordered, which resulted in the proof that he is himself insane, and he has now been committed to the asylum. This young man is entitled to sympathy because the investigation which brought the calamity upon him was undertaken not out of curiosity, but in the line of his duty. There are many cases, however, of a still more deplorable disaster coming upon investigators when sympathy must be mingled with blame. The young men who go into the haunts of dissipation "to see life" too often themselves fall into a snare and become as vicious as those whom they go to see. (Prov. 4: 14,15.)

A Silent Marriage took Place in the Office of a Justice of the Peace in Jersey City on Saturday, June 2. A young man entered the office, and held out to the Justice a pad on which was written, "Can you give me a marriage license?" "Cannot you speak?" wrote the Justice. The visitor shook his head. The Justice then wrote "No license is required; I can marry you now." The young man seemed pleased, and going away, soon returned with a young lady, quietly but tastefully dressed. The Justice greeted her cordially, but she stopped his talk by producing a pad on which she wrote that she too was a deaf mute. The usual questions and answers were then given in writing, and finally the Justice wrote, "I pronounce you man and wife." The couple were immediately clasped in each other's arms. The young husband informed the justice that he had a sufficient income to support his wife, and that they had lived in the same town, and had loved each other from childhood. As they went away the Justice said he had never married a more happy looking couple. They were probably attracted to each other by their common affliction. The revelations of the divorce courts prove that many marriages are made in which the parties have nothing in common but an unregenerate spirit. Such marriages are not likely to be happy, and still less promising are those marriages in which one of the parties is a Christian and the other is not. In that case the command of God is violated. (II Cor. 6: 14-15).

Hanged with a Woman's Hair is the fate which befell a sparrow whose body has been sent to the Natural History Society at Worcester, Mass. The *Spy* of that city states that a gentleman whose house is surrounded with pine trees, recently noticed a sparrow suspended from the end of a limb of one of these trees. He could see nothing by which the bird was hung, and it was a very curious sight. His son, who was called, went up into the tree and carefully sawed off a small portion of the limb. The whole secret was then revealed. On the twig was a neatly built nest, in which were three speckled eggs. When examined they were found to be cold, which showed the home had been broken up for some time. The male sparrow was hung by a woman's hair, which was knotted around his neck just as neatly as though it had been done by human hands. The other end was fastened to the nest, being a part of it. The eggs were on one side of the nest, while on the other side was a hole just large enough for the bird to go through. It is supposed that the bird, in leaving its nest by the hole, became entangled in the hair, which, becoming a noose around its neck, proved strong enough to hold the bird until it died. It is marvellous that so slight a thing as a hair from a woman's head should cause the death even of a bird, but then, the bird was so entangled that it could not use its strength. It is so with many of the habits and temptations that hold men in their sins. They appear slight and trival, but they prove fatal to spiritual life unless the victim is delivered by Christ's Almighty power. (Isa. 61: 1.)

BRIEF NOTES.

The Rev. Sam Jones has been holding successful meetings at Fulton, Mo. He is now preaching at Rome, Ga., after which he goes to Chillicothe, Mo.

An extensive revival in St. Thomas is reported as the result of the Divine blessing on the labors of Messrs. Crossley and Hunter, the Evangelists.

Fully fifty centenarians are said to be living in New England, Maine leading the list with sixteen, and Connecticut coming next, with eleven.

A recent report states that there are 130,000 Mormons in Utah, of whom 80,000 are under eighteen years of age; one-third of them are living in polygamy.

Rev. Reuben Saillens, associate manager of the McAll Mission in France, is also pastor of the Baptist Church in Paris, which has one hundred and sixty members.

A playhouse is to be erected in Newark, N. J., for the use of children who have no place but the streets to play in. Mrs. Dr. Smith has given $12,000 for the purpose.

Major Geo. A. Hilton lately closed a series of meetings at Piqua, O., where one hundred and twenty-nine new members were added to the Women's Christian Temperance Union.

Between five and six hundred representatives were present at the women's meeting of the Society of Friends, and about three hundred representatives at the men's meeting, both of which were held in New York recently.

A summer Union Service for persons whose churches will be closed has been commenced in the large open Pavilion, 90th St. and 9th Ave., New York. Rev. C. C. Goss and other ministers will assist in conducting the services during the summer.

At the General Conference of the African Methodist Episcopal Church, recently held at Indianapolis, Ind., the sessions were opened with prayer by the Rev. David Smith, who is 104 years old, and has been a professing Christian ninety years.

The faculty of Cornell College have added an amendment to the rules of that institution, to the effect that students found guilty of intoxication, gambling, or other gross immorality, or of interference with the personal rights of any student, shall be expelled.

Rev. Dr. Somerville, of Glasgow, has returned to Scotland, having conducted gospel services in Buda Pest for both Jews and Gentiles, at Debreczin, Szolnok, Szegedin, Bekes, Gyoma, Gro-swardein, and other places in Hungary. On Jan. 30 he entered his seventy-sixth year.

A reputable citizen of New York, returning home late at night on Wednesday of last week, carrying a parcel under his arm, was ordered to stop by a policeman, but as the officer was not in uniform, and did not show his shield, the citizen mistook him for a thief, and ran. Thereupon the policeman fired, wounding him seriously.

At the annual meeting of the Young Woman's Christian Association, of the City of New York, the report showed a valuable year's work, which is summarized as follows: 13,000 women in the classes, 11,000 volumes in the library, 1,600 positions secured for young women, out of 2,000 applications. The total expense of the work has been a little less than $24,000.

The Christian Home for Intemperate Men, at 1175 Madison Avenue, New York, has received, since its opening in 1877, more than 2,440 men, and the results have been most encouraging. Within a year three hundred and forty-six persons have been admitted, of whom three-fourths have reformed and are in situations secured by the Home.

THE WEDDING GARMENT.

A New Sermon By Pastor C. H. Spurgeon.

"And when the king came in to see the guests, he saw there a man which had not on a wedding garment: and he saith unto him, Friend, how camest thou in hither not having a wedding garment? And he was speechless. Then said the king to the servants, Bind him hand and foot, and take him away, and cast him into outer darkness; there shall be weeping and gnashing of teeth."—Matt. 22:11-13.

The Loyal and the Rebellious Separated by Preaching—A Further Discrimination—I. What is Meant by the King's Coming In—The Crown of the Feast—A Season of Gracious Visitation—Augustine's Prayer—A Time of Discovery—II. The Meaning of the Wedding Garment—A Distinguishing Mark of Grace—The Gift of the King—Mourning Garb, an Insult at a Wedding—The Robe of Righteousness—III. The Guest Without the Garment—Preferring his Own Dress—IV. Why He was Speechless.

Two Sabbath mornings ago I preached from this parable, and I trust many were encouraged by it; but I noticed among inquirers who came to see me afterwards, a desire to know about the wedding garment; for they feared lest, in coming to join the church, they should come like the man of whom I shall now speak. Many true hearts are extremely sensitive to the impression of fear, and they seem to be on the watch for reasons for anxiety. I do not condemn them; on the contrary, I wish there were more of such holy tremblers. It is much better to be afraid of being wrong than to be indifferent as to what you are.

My chief object this morning will be to allay the fears of gracious ones, If they understand what the wedding garment really is, they will probably discover that they are wearing it; and, if not, they will know in whose wardrobe that garment of joy is to be found, and they will gladly ask to be arrayed therein. Immediately after our text, we find these solemn words: "Many are called, but few are chosen." This is a conclusion drawn from the whole parable, in which we see processes at work, which separate the chosen few from the many who are called.

A Distinction Was Made

by the summoning of the invited guests. The simple delivery of the invitation set a difference between the loyal and the rebellious—a distinction most marked and decisive. So it is in the preaching of the gospel: we preach it to every creature within our reach. Lovingly, tenderly, earnestly; not so well as we would, but still with all our heart we call men to the royal feast of grace; and straightway the very invitation begins to gather out the precious from the vile. When men will not have Christ and His grace, the Word preached by His humble servant drives them away, and they go with the chaff.

But the work of discrimination is not finished after the gospel has been heard and men have been brought into the church. Alas! even in the church division has to be made; indeed, it is there that this is most fully carried out. "His fan is in His hand, and He will throughly purge His floor." If He uses a scourge nowhere else, He will be sure to use it in His own temple. In our text we see a man who has hearkened to the invitation and has come into the feast, and thus has passed the first test; and yet he is unable to abide the second; he has been received by the servants, but he cannot deceive their Master. The King detects him as a spot in the feast, and he is cast out from the palace of mercy into the outer darkness, where there is weeping and wailing and gnashing of teeth. May none of us be of this sort!

I. May the Holy Spirit help us while we consider, first, what is meant by

The King's Coming In.

"The king came in to see the guests." They were all reclining at the tables, for "the wedding was furnished with guests." They gathered while the sun was up, but darkness covered the world outside when "the king came in to see the guests." They had feasted, and now the king came to honor the assembly. It was the crown and the culmination of the feast. No matter how dainty the viands, nor how bright the hall, the feast has not reached its height till his majesty appears in gracious condescension. It is so with us, beloved, in reference to our greater King.

These are seasons of gracious visitation: times of refreshing from

The Presence of the Lord.

When the King comes into the assembly, the preaching of the word is in demonstration of the Spirit, and in power. Then the day of Pentecost has fully come; the Spirit is abundantly outpoured, souls are saved, saints are edified, and Christ is glorified. The wedding would have been a failure without guests; but what would the feast have been if the host had refused to come in and see the guests? But the King came in in due time. Ay, came in among that crowd of wayfarers gathered from the highways at a moment's notice, and His presence crowned the festival with honor and rapture.

This coming in to see the guests indicates a glorious revelation of Himself. When the King saw the guests, the guests saw *Him;* but, inasmuch as His sight of them was the more important sight of the two, the chief thing is mentioned while the minor matter is implied. Do we know what it is to see God? This is the special privilege of the pure in heart. When the Lord's way is in the sanctuary, then His sanctified ones behold Him. Spiritual eyes have looked to Jesus by faith, and He saith, "He that hath seen Me hath seen the Father." When Augustine read those words, "Thou canst not see My face and live," he was bold enough to answer, "Let me die to see Thy face."

But here is the solemn point to which I call your attention: this visitation brings with it a time of discovery and searching of heart. When the King comes in to see the guests, the light grows stronger, and all things are revealed: for all things are naked and open to the eyes of Him with whom we have to do. If the Lord our God were to come into His church to-day there would be an awful shrinkage among the number of His guests; a panic would seize the assembly, and the door would be blocked with men hastening to escape His eye.

Look how the King's discernment is recorded in the text. One man only had refused to put on a wedding garment, but the king at once fixed his eye upon him. The Saviour, by a kind of heavenly charity, mentions only

One Intruder,

but I fear we must regard the one as the type of many. If the King should come in at the time of our communion, I am afraid He would detect more than one. This is a solemn matter. It will not make the true-hearted wish the King to stay away, but those who are wilful deceivers may well tremble. The King does come to this church. He is specially present in the midst of this people, and the consequence is that His judgment is strict with us. I have seen the rod of his discipline here in a very striking manner. I have seen the fair professor wither in the heat of love, and the rootless Christian dried up in the noontide of grace. He might have gone on very well in any other church, but he has not been able to abide the brandished sword of the Spirit, and its dividing asunder soul and spirit, joints and marrow. He has not been able to sit it out, but has been obliged to go away and find an easier rest.

II. Now I would answer the second question:

What is the Wedding Garment?

You are probably aware that this has been a point greatly disputed among theologians. Is the wedding garment justification, or sanctification, or what? I am not going to be theological and bring doctrinal matters to the text; but I shall read the parable as it stands, and interpret its details by its general run. It is called a "*wedding* garment"—a garment suitable for a marriage feast. Let us translate the figure, rather than attempt to rivet a doctrine to it. What does a wedding garment mean? What is that which we must have in connection with our Lord's marriage, or be cast out forever?

I think I may say plainly that it must signify a distinguishing mark of grace. Everybody does not wear a wedding garment: he who wears it has put it on because he is a wedding guest. You know the wedding guest at once by his attire. True members of the church of God wear a distinguishing mark. If you are not different from other people, you have no right in the church of God. If a servant can live with you for years and never discover your love to God, I should think there is none to discover. There ought to be a something about us which sets us apart—a something which can be seen and understood by common people, even as a wedding garment could be seen, and

Its Meaning

at once perceived. Your religion must not require a microscope to perceive it, nor should it be so indistinct that few can discover any meaning in it. It should be as visible as the white garment worn by Easterns at a marriage.

I may boldly add here that the wedding garment was a distinguishing mark of grace; for as these people were fetched in from the highways they could not have provided themselves with wedding garments. It is the custom in the East for a king to provide robes for his guests; therefore this wedding garment was a mark of grace, freely given and received. Is there, then, a something about you which the Lord in love has given you? Do you differ from others, not in natural attainments, but in spiritual grace? Does the difference mainly lie in what God Himself has done for you? That is the question involved in the symbol of the wedding garment.

In the next place, it was

A Symbol of Respect

for the king. To be fit for his company, the dress must be special. The absence of such a dress was, in the case before us, the badge of irreverence and disloyalty. This man said to himself: "I will feed at the feast without acknowledging its intent. Whoever stops me, I will push my way in, and I shall sit there in my every-day garments, to let the king know that I do not respect him in the least, and will not wear the robes he provides." It is as if you had lost a son, and some wretched man should say, "I will attend the funeral in a wedding suit. I shall thus wound the feelings of the mourners, and show my contempt for the whole affair." What an insult it would be! To turn the picture. Suppose you were being married, and somebody forced his way into the wedding dressed in mourning, with crape upon his hat, and black kid gloves upon his hands. What a wanton insult! If such impudence were met with a horse-whip, who would be surprised? Now, this man acted in that fashion: he had no respect for the king: he showed his traitorous nature in the worst possible manner, spiting the king in his own halls upon a tender occasion. Dear friends, I trust that you can truly say, "I have on the wedding garment of reverence."

A Token of Honor.

The wedding garment was, moreover, a token of honor for the Prince. My hearers, do you feel a love to the Lord Jesus Christ? Many do not. I grieve to say we have a race of men sprung up nowadays who call themselves Christians, who pour contempt upon His precious blood, and ridicule the substitutionary sacrifice. Dreadful assertion! but it is a matter of fact. The name of Jesus, why, it is to our lives what the sun is to the skies, what the rivers are to the plains. Nothing makes us so glad as thoughts of Jesus. I am sure when I hear a sermon about Christ, my Master, my very heart grows warm within me. Is it so with you? Well, then, you have on the wedding garment; that is to say, you do truly, though it be but in a simple way, pay homage to the Prince of Peace; you love the name and person of Jesus, and you come into His church because you do so.

The wedding garment means, in a word, *conformity to the requirments of the occasion* It was a wedding, and the guests must put on a suitable dress. This man refused to put it on. He was proud, and would not wear the gift of grace; he was self-willed, and must needs be singular, and show his independence of mind. The regulation was by no means irksome, and to the rest of the guests the commandment was not grievous; but this man would have his own way in defiance of the Lord of the feast. What could come of such folly? Now, one of

The Requirements of the Feast

is, that you with your heart believe on the Lord Jesus, and that you take His righteousness to be your righteousness. Do you refuse this? If you will not accept the Lord Jesus as your substitute, bearing your sins in His own body on the tree, you have not the wedding garment. Another requirement is that you should repent of sin and forsake it; and that you should follow after holiness, and endeavor to copy the example of the Lord Jesus. You are to possess, as the work of divine grace, a godly and upright character. Have you such a character? Even though you are not perfect, yet, inasmuch as you follow after righteousness, you have the wedding garment. You say that you are a Christian; do you live like a Christian? Are you in a position and condition which agree with the gospel feast? If so, you have on the wedding garment.

Those who came unto the feast were, when they came, both bad and good; so that the wedding garment does not relate to their past character, but relates to something with which they were invested when they came to the banquet. The putting on of a wedding robe cannot refer to an elaborate ceremony, or a feat of the intellect, or to a deep experience of the heart; and yet it involved joining in the wedding, or not joining in it. It involved reverence for the King, and homage to the Prince, and sympathy with the whole matter. Look well to yourselves, and see whether you truly yield yourselves to the Lord, and agree with Him in the whole matter.

The Man Without the Garment.

III. Thirdly, who is the man that has not on the wedding garment? I should say, first, he is the man who rejects God's revealed gospel that he may follow his own thought and his own wisdom. He says that he is loyal to Christ, and he expects all his fellow guests to be firm friends with him, for is he not in the banquet as much as they are? But he does not mean by loyalty what they mean by it. He is among believers, but he is not truly of them. He talks about atonement; he does not mean substitution. He talks about the divinity of Christ; he does not mean the Godhead of Christ. He talks about justification by faith; but he does not mean the old-fashioned doctrine. He speaks of regeneration, but means evolution. He girds himself with the garment of philosophy, but he refuses the robe of revelation, for the cut of it is too old-fashioned for him. His robe is not of God's provision; it is from his own wardrobe. He glories in his own culture, and not in the revelation of God, nor yet in the work of divine grace upon the heart. He is in the church, but he is not in Christ. He has a name to live, but he is dead.

The next person who has not on the wedding garment is *the man who refuses the righteousness of God* because he has a righteousness of his own. He thinks

His Dress Good Enough

for Christ's own wedding. What does he want with imputed righteousness? He scouts it as immoral. He who is himself immoral! What does he want with the precious blood of Jesus? He does not need to be washed from crimson stains. His own righteousness, though it be of the law, and such as Paul rejected, he esteems so highly that he counts the blood of the covenant an unholy thing! Ah me, the insolence of self-righteousness! Its pride is the very chief of sins, for it slights the righteousness of God.

Why, some dare to come into the church who have not even common morality. It is shocking we should have to say it, but nowadays, we meet with those who call themselves Christians who can drink upon the sly, who can commit uncleanness with their bodies, who can be dishonest in their trading, who can be liars, who can hate their own flesh and blood and be at enmity with their brethren, and yet dare to come to the communion table. In the highlands of Scotland it was at one time difficult to get Christian people to come to the Lord's Table, for they so trembled under a sense of their unworthiness. We do not want to push this too far, but that is a great deal better than that unholy daring, which is to be found in the minds of so many who serve Christ and Belial. God save His church from degradation!

I do not see how that man can be said to have on a wedding garment who takes no interest in the work of the church. You see, when a man puts on the wedding garment, he did as good as say, "I am interested in the wedding. I wish God's blessing to the bride and bridegroom." But many come in now to the King's feast who do not care a snap of the finger for the church of God, nor for Christ either. They come in because a sort of selfishness makes them anxious to be saved; but as to the bride, the Lamb's wife, they do not care whether she starves or flourishes. Sad and wretched business this!

IV. To close, why was this man speechless? We do not often meet with people who have no excuse. Excuse-making is the easiest trade out. A man can make an excuse out of nothing at all, or out of what is less than nothing—out of a direct lie. But here was

A Man Who Could Not Speak.

Why was that? Well, I think, first, the affront was too bare-faced. "How camest thou in hither?" If he did not like the king he could have kept outside. There was no need why he should come in at all, and there display his malice. If any of you are resolved to be lost, you need not add to your eternal ruin by making a profession of religion, for hypocrisy is a superfluity of naughtiness. Next, the affront was so audacious. "How camest thou in hither?" said the king. He must have pushed by the deacons at the door. The fellow would come in. When the king said, "Bind him hand and foot," I think it was because he had used hand and foot to get in. He would get in; he said, "I will get in. I will defy the king to his face, and sit in among his guests without a wedding garment." You, dear friend, do not wish to do that: I am sure it is the last thing you would do. Why, we have to persuade you to come in at all; for you are so tenderly jealous lest you should be mistaken. Do not let this parable condemn you.

Lastly, the reason why he was speechless was because, even if he could have spoken and been free from terror, there was

Nothing to be Said.

He could not cry, "Lord, I did not know it." He saw all the rest with wedding garments on. He could not say, "Lord, I could not get a wedding garment": each one had received a garment gratis, and he might have received the same. He could not say, "Lord, I was pushed in here by somebody else." No, he had willingly chosen to come, and to defy the rule. I do not wonder that the King said, "Bind him hand and foot, and cast him into outer darkness; there shall be weeping and gnashing of teeth."

I have been accused of representing the state of the lost in too horrible a manner. I have never gone beyond the dreadful descriptions given by our Lord Himself. Do not risk your eternal future. Come to the Church of God and join it, but do not join it unless you love the Lord. Do not come to the gospel feast unless you reverence the King; unless you love the Prince; unless you are in sympathy with the great work of grace which is pictured as a wedding feast. If you have sympathy with the wedding, love to the Bridegroom, and delight in the bride, then come and welcome; for you have the wedding garment. I am thinking just now of all those other hundreds of people at the wedding, all of them clothed with the wedding garment. What joy they felt! Many had been bad, and all had been poor: but they all had the wedding garment, and not one of them was cast out. If you will but put your trust in Jesus, and so honor the Son; and rest in the love of the Father, and so honor the King, it is written, "Him that cometh to me I will in no wise cast out." God bless you for Jesus' sake!

GEMS FROM NEW BOOKS.

BUDDHA'S EARLY LIFE.*

BUDDHA was born at Kapelavastu, the capital of the kingdom of that name, at the foot of the mountains of Nepaul. His father, the King of Kapelavastu, was one of the family of the Sakyas, and belonged to the clan of the Gautamas. His mother was Mayadevi, the daughter of King Suprabuddha. Buddha was therefore by birth of the Kshatriya, or warrior caste, and he took the name of Sakya from his family and that of Gautama from his clan. Endowed with all the gifts of genius and physical beauty, he easily outstripped all his comrades and even his masters, in feats of bodily and intellectual strength. But from childhood he was possessed by a deep melancholy, from which nothing could divert him. Those around could see no cause for it, but it was in truth the sorrow of the world, the insoluble problem of life, which was weighing on his soul. In the hope of turning the current of his thoughts he was married to the beautiful Gopa, the daughter of Danapam. The marriage proved one of the happiest, but Buddha remained as he had been before, absorbed in meditation on the problems of life and death. "Nothing is stable on earth," he used to say, "nothing is real. Life is like the spark produced by the friction of wood. It is lighted and it is extinguished; we know not whence it came nor whither it goes. It is like the sound of a lyre, and the wise man asks in vain from whence it came and whither it goes. There must be some supreme intelligence where we could find rest. If I attained it I could bring light to man; if I were free myself I could deliver the world." The king, who perceived the melancholy mood of the young prince, tried everything to divert him, but all was in vain.

The Renunciation.

At length the decisive day came. One morning, when the young prince with a large retinue was driving through the eastern gate of the city, he met on the road an old man, broken and decrepit. One could see the veins and muscles over the whole of his body; his teeth chattered, he was covered with wrinkles, bald, and hardly able to utter hollow and unmelodious sounds. He was bent on his stick, and all his limbs and joints trembled. "Who is that man?" said the prince to his coachman, "he is small and weak, his flesh and his blood are dried up, his muscles stick to his skin, his head is white, his teeth chatter, his body is wasted away; leaning on his stick he is barely able to walk, stumbling at every step. Is there something peculiar in his family, or is this the common lot of all created beings?" "Sir," replied the coachman, "that man is sinking under old age. His senses have become obtuse, suffering has destroyed his strength, and he is despised by his relations. He is without support, and useless, and people have abandoned him, like a dead tree in the forest. But this is not peculiar to his family. In every creature youth is defeated by old age. Your father, your mother, all your relations, all your friends will come to the same state. This is the appointed end of all creatures."

* From "The Ancient World and Christianity," By E. De Pressensé, D. D. Translated by Annie Harwood Holmden. This work is an attempt to show how in the ancient world everywhere, the greatest men were found seeking a God greater than local and national divinities, and uttering bitter lamentations over their failure. Also to show what must be the gloomy future of a democracy without God, and that the only hope of society is in the Light which broke on the world eighteen centuries ago. 470 Pages. Published by *A. C. Armstrong & Son*, 714 Broadway, New York.

The Emperor Frederick III. of Germany in his Study at Potsdam.

"Alas," replied the Prince, "are creatures so ignorant, so weak and foolish, as to be proud of the youth by which they are intoxicated, not seeing the old age which awaits them. As for me, I go away. Coachman, turn my chariot quickly. What have I, the future prey of old age, to do with pleasure?" And the young prince returned to the city without going to his park.

His resolution was taken: kingdom, power, glory, wife, all must be abandoned, while he shut himself up to lead in solitude the life of an ascetic. So far he had not gone in practice beyond the ideal of the Brahmans, who looked upon the life of the Anchorite as the final goal to be reached. But he had already risen to a much fuller and higher conception of the religious life than theirs. He saw more clearly than any before him the intensely sorrowful side of life. To him it appeared, indeed only as a transparent veil cast over the death to which it leads, and which is therefore the only abiding reality. Hence he was not long satisfied with the teaching the Brahmans had to give him. Having learned all that the most illustrious of them could impart, he went away disappointed.

THE SUFFERING EMPEROR.

(See Illustration.)

THE whole civilized world watches with sympathy and admiration the brave strnggle for life now being waged by Frederick III., Emperor of Germany. The reports of the physicians and nurses describing his patience and fortitude under suffering, prove him to be a man of true nobleness of character, worthy of the exalted position which he occupies. He has now been removed from Charlottenburg to Potsdam, some twenty miles off, where he occupies the palace built by his illustrious predecessor, Frederick the Great, which was formerly known as "the New Palace," but which the Emperor has named "Friedrichskron," in memory of its builder. There he continues to utilize every interval of relief from pain in attention to public business, as he did at Berlin, and appears conscientiously desirous of leaving no duty unperformed. On the days when he is too weak to sit up he occupies the invalid's lounge provided for him, the head of which can be so adjusted as to allow him to read or write in a reclining posture.

Another contribution to his comfort is the reading-stand shown in the illustration. This was a gift from his mother-in-law, Queen Victoria, and is of much service to him. Standing by his couch, the Emperor can, by stretching out his hand, swing the arm of the stand so as to bring the book it holds to the proper focus, and so enjoy reading without the fatigue of holding the book. As the Emperor is something of a student, this gift is appreciated by him.

It is gratifying to learn that the German doctors now agree with Dr. Mackenzie that his disease is not cancer, though they admit that it is of so serious a nature as to render the prospect of complete recovery very doubtful.

MARY MORGAN'S DARLING.

(See Illustration on page 381.)

NEVER was there a more welcome arrival in a home than that of little Eddy in the home of Edward and Mary Morgan. Mary's home before her marriage was full of brothers and sisters, and merry voices were heard in it from morning to night. The little cottage in the country to which Edward took her after their wedding was as pretty as hands could make it, and for the first month or two Mary's time was fully occupied in adorning it and making it home-like. After that, however, the hours hung heavily. Edward had to leave early to be at his office in the city in time for business, and it was not until seven o'clock in the evening, and sometimes later, that he returned. Mary shortened the evening by going to meet his train, thus discounting his coming by the half hour it took her to walk to the station. But the days were very long and very lonely to her.

The baby's birth changed all that. Mary had plenty to do then. Besides, it was such a pleasure to sit and look at him while he was asleep, watching the strange little smiles that flitted across the tiny face, telling of dreams which it was impossible for her to conceive of, so little experience could there be in that short life to make the basis of a dream. Her work even drifted into arrear, baby being so inexhaustible a subject of interest. He was the most wonderful baby, too, so bright and intelligent, and actually seemed, as Mary believed, to understand her talk before he was a month old. Edward had to listen when he came home at night to the account of some extraordinary evidence baby had given during the day of his surprising qualities. The young mother brightened under the new circumstances of her life, and the little cottage was no longer dull.

Eddy's coming, too, had another good result; it led Mary to pray. As a girl she attended church, but she had never given her heart to God. Her mother and father were Godly people, but Mary had always been indifferent in religious matters, and when she and Edward were married and lived in the country there was no church near, so they had spent their Sundays at home or in little excursions. Even the form of religion was abandoned. Now, however, a sense of responsibility was upon her. She began to pray, first for her child and then for herself. She said nothing of it to her husband, for, in his case, indifference to religion had developed into opposition to it. She wanted her boy to grow into a good man, and she instinctively recognized that there was no preservative that could keep him from the world's evil as religion could. Therefore she began to pray, and most earnestly, that she might be enabled to train him aright. Poor mother! had she but realized that the first step was to give herself unreservedly to God, her heart might have been saved its worst pang.

As little Eddy grew, his mother's love became more intense. A singularly bright, lovable child, gentle and affectionate, he was loved by all who knew him; but he was his mother's idol. When he was three years old she taught him the Lord's Prayer, a simple prayer for his mother and father, and a verse of hymn, and as he knelt at her knee every night, and went through the little ritual, Mary thought his face looked so like the face of an angel, that she would clutch him to her breast and clasp her arms around him with a passionate fervor that told of a love which overmastered her.

What was her terror, then, when little Eddy fell sick! The doctor was summoned, and his diagnosis awaited with agonizing suspense. It was a relief when she found that he did not apprehend danger; but she could know neither peace nor rest till her little darling was running around as usual. Her husband made light of her fears, but even he grew anxious when little Eddy continued to grow worse. The little fellow would recover, he felt sure, but it seemed a long while about. At length even the doctor began to look grave, and was more careful in his examination of the child's condition. There was no disease in the child's perfect organism, but there was a lack of vitality that puzzled him. Gentle as he was before, Eddy seemed now to be almost angelic in disposition, and his patience touched the mother's heart more than anything had done.

Mary Morgan's Anxious Caress.

One beautiful bright morning Mary set the window of his little bedroom open that he might enjoy the sunlight and the songs of the birds. The child lay looking at the bright prospect for a short time, but at last announced that "Eddy is tired; Eddy wants to go to sleep." He turned over and settled himself comfortably, but presently said that before he went to sleep he must say his prayers. His mother, fearing his weakness, persuaded him to say them in bed, telling him that God could hear them there just as well as kneeling at her knees. The little fellow said the simple words correctly as usual, and then satisfied, dropped into a gentle slumber with his cheek resting on his clasped hands. Mary took her work and sat at the open window to be near him if he waked, but the calm, and summer heat overcame her, and she too dozed. She could not have slept more than half an hour, when she woke up suddenly, with the sensation of something cold passing over her. Her eyes turned to the bed, but there was no change. Eddy had not moved. Still she felt uneasy, and going to the bedside, bent over, and kissed him. There was no response; the child was dead. He must have died in his sleep without a pain or a struggle. The little head lay upon the pillow with the hands clasped just as Mary had seen them before she fell asleep. But the soul was gone.

A neighbor coming in a short time afterward to inquire after the child, found the bereaved young mother in a swoon beside the body, and for a long time it was feared that she too would die. But God mercifully preserved her. Very slowly, through many weeks, she struggled back into life, but her heart seemed crushed within her. As she reclined in her invalid's chair in the room where her darling died, her thoughts full of her loss, she began to ask herself why this trouble had fallen upon her. She asked the question fiercely at first, as if reproaching God, but self-examination followed and reproaches died away out of her mind. Then, she thought of her little child as he must be in the presence of God, and the longing to go to him, and the thought that in her present state there would be eternal separation, overcame her, and for the first time she wept penitent tears. They were the beginning of a new life for her. At first the desire to be re-united with her darling was the supreme motive, but as she realized the cause of her dreaded exclusion better, love to the Saviour, whose death and atonement had made reconciliation with God possible, eclipsed every other feeling, and so Mary entered into peace.

THE EPOCHS OF A LIFE.

A NEW STORY F AMERICAN COLLEGE LIFE.

By Rev. L. S. Keyser.

Author of "The Way Out," etc.

(*Continued from page 367.*)

The First Term in College.

"How is it," asked Hadley one day of his friend George Dane, "that our parents and teachers never told us of these objections to the Bible? Of course they must have known that there were many men who rejected the book, and a still larger number who doubted its inspiration. It seems to me that a wiser course, if they wished us to become believers like themselves, would have been for them to have said to us, 'Such and such arguments are brought against the Bible, but they are unsound,' and then have given us the refutation, if refutation is possible."

"Ah!" said Dane, "I have thought of that. It was *the novelty* of these arguments that first attracted me. If I had gone over the ground before, under the guidance of some Christian believer, I suppose the lecturer who opened my eyes would have found a less willing disciple. The Christian Church, however, seems to prefer a policy of silence. So much the worse for it, I should say."

And how many young men have had cause to make the same remark! Yet it is still the policy pursued in families and churches. The fatal difficulty with this policy of silence and repression is, that when the young inquirer by some means is brought face to face with the objections of sceptics, as he surely will be, he is unprepared for them; he knows not how to meet them; he has not even been apprised of their existence, and consequently he regards himself as the dupe of his teachers, who have kept the facts hidden from him. In such a case to be forewarned might have been to be forearmed.

The anti-Christian campaign is carried on with more vigor than many persons suppose. Publishing firms in New York and Boston send out their tracts and books in vast quantities to the young men and women of the land, who often read them and brood over them until they are led astray by their specious arguments. The fact must be faced, and as far as possible the influence of this literature must be countervailed. How can this be done if we refuse to investigate the facts, and even close our eyes to their existence?

Early in June, extensive preparations were made for the commencement exercises of the academy. As the young men and women about to graduate were allowed the privilege of choosing their own themes for their addresses, subject, of course, to the approval of the Principal, our two half-fledged sceptics had the presumption to select topics of a decidedly anti-Biblical character. The Principal, however, objected, saying that such a course would damage their prospects in that vicinity for life. They replied, with their usual bravado, that they were not governed by motives of sordid policy and self-interest, but that they were willing to immolate themselves, if necessary, upon the altar of truth. But Professor Borst contended that it would be hurtful to the academy, if they were allowed to utter infidel sentiments under its auspices. Many Christian parents, he said, were sending their sons and daughters to him to be prepared for college, and he could not afford to lose their patronage. When the young men were about to protest, he told them curtly that if they would not accede to his wishes, he would refuse them certificates of graduation, and would not allow any of them to speak at all. So these knights of free-thought concluded to let "the interests of truth" take care of themselves, and finally chose themes for their orations that were tame and harmless enough for the most orthodox taste. They yielded, however, with ill grace, and sneered contemptuously at Professor Borst's "time serving spirit."

During the week of commencement another epoch-making event in their history occurred. The Principal had engaged the Rev. Dr. J. H. Hartridge, President of Grand Central College, of a neighboring State, to deliver an address before the students of the academy, and the people of the village.

On the evening of the lecture the two young men went to the church in which the address was to be delivered. The audience-room was filled to its utmost capacity, there being scarcely standing room in the aisles. A reserved seat had been provided for the graduating class, and to this seat they were conducted.

The Rev. Dr. Hartridge was a man of strong "bodily presence," largely built, and muscular. His face, which was closely shaven, and especially his large jaws, indicated firmness, if not obstinacy, of purpose; his lips were large, almost sensuous, his eyes flashing, his forehead high and receding, and his voice strong and sonorous. Our young students were favorably impressed with him before he arose to speak.

From the beginning of the lecture to its close the audience was held spell-bound. The Doctor was the master of a strong, perspicacious style, with a happy faculty for concise, epigrammatic statement, and a peculiar genius for building up thought, stratum upon stratum, until a mountain of truth seemed to rise, Alp-like, before his auditors. That evening he had a great deal to say about moral character.

"All things must be made to contribute to the formation of moral character," he maintained. "Whatever does not add something to the ethical development of man's being is sin. The earth has been filled with beauty and glory, Alp on Alp, wide valleys, deep cañons, majestic rivers, stretching plains; and wherefore was all this magnificence wrought out by the divine Sculptor? To aid in building us up in moral grandeur of soul. We are to develop and expand into the moral largeness of which these majestic scenes and operations in nature are the prototype. Last evening I climbed one of the hills that sentinel your beautiful village, and looking toward the sky, I beheld Venus, star of the twilight, glowing upon me like the eye of God. I was held enchanted by the scene of earth and sky. 'Why all this sweet and tranquil beauty?' I asked myself. To suggest cheer and help and incentive to man in his struggle for the attainment of moral perfection. As that star glows yonder in heaven's vault, so must I strive to make my character glow and sparkle and gleam in moral effulgence. As that star shines serenely yonder, so must I possess my soul unmoved above the toil and moil and upheaval of earthly passion and carking care. Mr. Ruskin has told us of 'The Ethics of the Dust;' he might also write about the ethics of the mountains and the valleys, of the sea and the sky; for all nature is full of ethical suggestions. Thus, my young friends, I would have you listen to all the voices around you and within you, to all the suggestions of beauty and goodness in the worlds of nature, of thought, of religion, and I beseech you to let every fact that touches your lives become an incentive to nobler deeds and higher aspirations."

The above excerpt, which is rather a paraphrase than a quotation, is sufficient to indicate the general character of the address. The young men were captivated by the speaker's thought and earnest manner. When the address was concluded, and they had taken the Doctor's hand in a warm, grateful pressure, they started arm in arm toward Hadley's home. Their course took them by a well-worn path across the fields and through the woods, and as they walked along they whiled the time in conversation.

"He is the grandest man I ever saw," said Hadley, enthusiastically, for he had arrived at that age when one is inclined, if ever, to be a hero-worshipper.

"I acquiesce in your verdict," responded George. "It is true, he seems to believe in religion, but I'll wager that he does not accept it in the credulous style of the ignorant people with whom we are acquainted."

"Of course not; a man of his calibre cannot be the slave of superstition. He is too broad-minded for that. I was fascinated by what he said of the formation of moral character. Of course, we believe in morality as much as the votaries of religion do. It is only their absurd tenets that we object to; they are not essential to morality, but are rather inimical to it."

"Ah, but you forget," laughed Hadley, "that Christians think that an infidel is almost as bad as a cutthroat, and is fit only to be tortured over a slow fire in a world of a very tropical climate."

"Pooh! that is because they are so dense and do not understand us. They think that a religionless morality is insufficient for the needs of fallen human nature."

The young men walked on awhile in silence

"Tell you what," said Hadley, presently, "I've made up my mind to become a student of the Grand Central College, if you will go along with me next fall. It will be invigorating, intellectually and morally, to live in the atmosphere of such a man as Dr. Hartridge. What do you think about it?"

"It is a happy thought—an inspiration, in fact," replied George, "Yes, yes, I shall go with you, and shall follow you like your shadow. You know that I am your *vade mecum* every time. Give me your hand on our compact."

The resolution formed so suddenly by the young men was found not to be ill-advised, and it was carried out in the following September. The opening day of the fall session found them pleasantly domiciled in their new college home, ready for the active duties of under-graduate life. The desire to acquit themselves well and achieve academical honors was the all-absorbing ambition with them, as they entered upon their college work, and they, therefore, applied themselves sedulously to their studies. They had not come to college to fritter away their time, or to spend their hard earnings foolishly. Like many other young men from country districts, they brought with them robust bodies and vigorous minds to their college work, and it was not long before they were regarded as students of the brightest promise, on account of which they were shown marked favors by their preceptors.

Their spiritual experiences were exceedingly checkered during the next three years. Even at the threshold of their college career they found themselves sadly disappointed in their instructors, at least in one respect.

"It is inexplicable," remarked George, one day, half to himself.

"What are you dreaming about now?" asked Hadley, looking up from his books.

"Well, you know that we supposed that these intellectual Samsons at the head of an institution like the G. C. C. would accept the Scriptures, if they accepted them at all, in a modified form; in a sort of allegorical sense, rather than as historically and literally true; but most of them actually pride themselves on being what is called 'evangelical,' which means, I suppose, that they gulp down the Bible entire, in regular orthodox fashion. Did you not hear what Dr. Hartridge said the other morning at chapel in regard to 'hacking the Bible to pieces with a rationalistic penknife'? I confess that I am mystified and disappointed."

"I have been puzzling my brain over the same conundrum," replied Hadley. "Is it pusillanimity or lack of information that makes them so credulous? It certainly cannot be the result of honest conviction."

"Tell you what I think," put in George, after a moment's reflection; "I believe that cowardice is at the bottom of it. These men dare not antagonize public sentiment, for fear of losing patronage, or being ousted from their positions. Don't you remember what Professor Borst told us when we wanted to give our opinions an airing at our commencement exercises?"

"But, George," said Hadley, "I think that you are a little ungenerous, and I believe that I have a more probable explanation of the phenomenon. Perhaps these men have been so exclusively devoted to the pursuit of technical studies, burrowing after Greek roots and solving mathematical problems, that the new light which has burst upon others, has not yet dawned upon their mental firmament."

"Well that is an ingenious and charitable theory, and I half believe that you are right."

"There is one fact that confirms my hypothesis," Hadley went on. "Our Professor of natural science, Dr. Busentide, is of course conversant with the advanced thought of the times, and must be acquainted with the disagreements of science and the Bible; and have you not noticed that he is about the only member of the faculty who does not make a profession of religion? He never leads in the devotions at chapel exercises. I'll wager that he has gotten into the current of advanced thinking, while the other professors are still floundering in the stagnant pools and bogs of superstition."

"Yes, that is a more generous view than the other," acquiesced George; "I cannot believe myself that our teachers are a pack of hypocrites and cowards; their investigations have been confined to a narrow field, that is all. Well, that makes our duty clear," said George in a superior way; "we must make up for their deficiencies by disseminating the new light and giving the college a propulsion in the direction of advanced thought."

"And we shall not be afraid of the frothy rage of the bigots, either," declared Hadley. "I despise toadyism above all things."

And so our two college sciolists imposed upon themselves the easy and delightful task of enlightening the Grand Central College on the great problems of Christian theology, and in their conceit and enthusiasm they did not for a time doubt their ability to do so. But soon their enthusiasm received a check, for only a few weeks' stay at the College sufficed to convince them that their instructors were very superior men, and were not the dry pedants that they had thought them.

On several occasions these rash young unfetterers of thought ventured to express their opinions relative to religion in the class-rooms, but they were rather curtly dismissed, or their remarks were entirely ignored by their professors, and in the literary societies, when they undertook to ventilate their views, they soon found that the opinions of college novitiates were regarded by the more advanced students as exceedingly crude, and their splenetic thrusts at religion were greeted with contemptuous outbursts of laughter. It was not so easy, after all, to put a quietus on the religious sentiment of the college. The young men were cowed, but as they were compelled by the force of circumstances to repress the expression of their unbelief, its fire only smouldered within them, and continued to gather force for a violent ebullition by and by. It is needless to say that the treatment they received made them all the more acrimonious against religion.

Finally they made a compact to maintain silence on the subject, both in the recitation rooms and in the literary halls, until they had reached a higher academical standing, and in the meantime they would investigate every department of anti-religious literature, and so strengthen and fortify their positions that they could not be overthrown by a few jeers. They believed that the time would come when their contemporaries would listen to them with respect.

During the first three years of their college life they searched the Scriptures with some degree of assiduity for the purpose of unearthing the "discrepancies." They also poured over the agnostic and anti-Christian scientific literature of the day, passing to the study of a higher class of sceptical writings than those which they had read before their entrance into college. It is true, their libraries received occasionally an accession from those New York and Boston publishing houses that print and circulate the literature of a rampant and vituperative character; but in the main the young investigators had lost their relish for such writings by becoming acquainted with works of higher scientific value. For a time they basked in the light of Spencer and Huxley, until they were filled with agnostic dogmatism. Then they devoured the late Professor Clifford's "Scientific Basis of Morals," with its sly insinuative thrusts at faith and its indefinite and fanciful "Religion of Humanity." Having heard a great deal of that brilliant Frenchman, Renan, they purchased his "*Vie de Jésus*," and became more strongly intrenched in unbelief by its romantic fancies. Thus while their unbelief was passing to a higher, at least a more respectable stage, it was none the less bitter and uncompromising, but was daily gaining in strength.

Meanwhile they were advancing in mental power and becoming more matured in character. They mastered their technical studies with an ease that astonished their fellow-students, and at the end of the third year it was found that Hadley Madelling stood at the head of his class, and his talented friend, George Dane, was next to him on the roll of honor.

(*To be Continued.*)

NEWNESS OF LIFE.

By Mrs. M. Baxter.

S. S. Lesson for June 24. Eph. 4:20-24. Golden Text, Rom. 6:4.

What Newness of Life is—The Sublime Altruism—How Jesus Lived—Not Sensitive to Unkindness or Insult—Self a Great Bargainer—The Crucified Self—How it is to be Attained—In One Definite Act—The Property Transferred—The Mental Spirit Renewed—Newness of Life as a Testimony—Christ's Life a Model.

"ARE ye ignorant that all who were baptized into Jesus Christ were baptized into His death? We were buried, therefore, with Him through baptism into death: that like as Christ was raised from the dead through the glory of His Father, so we also might walk in newness of life." (Rom. 6:3, 4. R. V.) What, then, is this newness of life? Is it forgiveness of sins? But forgiveness of sins is not new, it is as old as David, for he says, "Blessed is the man whose iniquity is forgiven, and whose sin is covered. Blessed is the man unto whom the Lord imputeth not iniquity." (Ps. 32:1, 2.) It is not cleansing, for that, too, is as old as David, for he says, "Purge me with hyssop, and I shall be clean: wash me, and I shall be whiter than snow... Create in me a clean heart, O God, and renew a right spirit within me." (Ps. 51:7, 10.) It is not the work of winning souls, for David says, "Restore unto me the joy of Thy salvation; and uphold me with Thy free Spirit, *then* will I teach transgressors Thy ways, and sinners shall be converted unto Thee." (Ps. 51:12, 13.) All these things are new to unconverted sinners. But Paul is writing of something which is new to God's children, when he speaks of "newness of life." A *new* thing is a thing which has not been before; and, praise God, Jesus brought into our nature in His own person, a life such as had never been lived on earth before. "Behold, I make all things new." (Rev. 21:5.)

A new life is not a life only free from sin, but

A Life Set Free from Self.

When Jesus came into the world, He would not have sinned had He been born as a prince, with all the attendants of royalty; but He would have done as human nature generally does., He would in this way have sought His own interests; it would not have been "newness of life." When, at the age of twelve years, He sat among the doctors in the temple, He, who knew all things, would not have sinned if He had taken the position of Teacher among them; but this would have been self-assertion, and self-assertion is not newness of life: Jesus never forced Himself upon the notice of any. When His enemies said of Him, "He casteth out devils through Beelzebub, the prince of the devils," Jesus might have resented such an insult in the spirit of the law, which says, "An eye for an eye, and a tooth for a tooth." But resentment is not newness of life, it is self defending itself. Jesus, "when He was reviled, reviled not again; when He suffered, He threatened not, but committed Himself unto Him that judgeth righteously." (1 Pet. 2:23.) This is newness of life. When one of the chief Pharisees invited Him to his house, on purpose to watch Him with critical eyes, Jesus did not expose him, but made use of the opportunity to speak words of life to the guests and to His host, and taught that parable of the gospel feast which has been blessed to thousands of souls. (Luke 14:1-24.) Jesus was not proud, therefore He was

Not Sensitive

to that which touched only Him. Sensitive people are always self-filled people; they do not know newness of life. When the Samaritan woman, who, with all her impurity of life, yet had a kind of zeal for her sect, refused a drink of water to Jesus, instead of His turning from her with the thought that she deserved nothing at His hands, He patiently opened to her the glorious truth about the living water: this was newness of life.

Jesus always acted quite irrespective of the way in which He was treated. The majority of men, even of professing Christians, make their conduct to others to depend upon the conduct of others towards them. But this is not newness of life; the very heathen can do as much. "If ye love them which love you, what reward have ye? do not even the publicans the same? (Matt. 5:46.) Self is

A Great Bargainer.

"We have left all and followed Thee: what shall we *have* therefore?" is the language of self towards God. "You have never done anything to benefit me; why should I help you?" is the language of self toward man. All this belongs to the old man; it is not newness of life. Jesus taught that we are not to do anything with a view to recompense from man. (Luke 14:13, 14.) "Love ye your enemies, and do good and lend, *hoping for nothing again*, and your reward shall be great, and ye shall be the children of the Highest; for He is kind to the unthankful, and to the evil." (Luke 6:35.) This is newness of life; a kind of life never lived before Jesus came on earth; a life in which self has no place. Most people who know something of the gospel, live as though they did right to trust Jesus for the salvation of their souls; but they care for themselves, defend themselves, are anxious about themselves, assert themselves, as though no "newness of life" had ever been made possible to them.

Paul teaches the Ephesians that newness of life is learning Christ. "Ye did not so learn Christ; if so be that ye heard Him, and were taught in Him as the truth is in Jesus: that ye put away, as concerning your former manner of life, the old man, which waxeth corrupt after the lusts of deceit." Surely, the "old man" is our self-life, that of which Paul said, "I am crucified with Christ." (Gal. 2:20.) Paul had not died so that his body was laid in the grave, but he had yielded up his self-life, to be nailed to the cross of Christ, so that its claims and hopes and fears and wills were to be no more regarded; but the

Wills, Purposes, Desires

and thoughts of Jesus, were to take its place. "Nevertheless I live; yet not I, but Christ liveth in me; and the life which I now live in the flesh, I live by the faith of the Son of God, who loved me, and gave Himself for me." This was newness of life—Christ taking the place of self all along. Paul's life was no patchwork, no mended-up affair; he could say boldly, and none could deny it, "Christ liveth in me." "To me to live is Christ." (Phil. 1:27.)

But how are we to "put off the old man" and to "put on the new?" There is but one way: "Yield yourselves unto God as those that are alive from the dead. (Rom. 6:13). Let God have His way with you, own Him in everything, and never resist Him. It may be done, and ought to be done in

One Definite Act

of making ourselves over to God, just as definite as the transfer of property by the signing of the title deeds. But then there comes the perpetual claim of self, "the old man," upon the renounced property; and here self has to be denied, "put off" as it is called, or "counted out" continually. For instance, we may be workers much owned of God; we attend a meeting, people know we are there, but take no notice of us. Self says, "That is an intentional affront! Why should I be treated thus?" Christ in the heart says, "Thank God that I am left in quiet and not noticed; for I have such a blessed opportunity to pray for all these people." Christ in us does not mark the affront, or, if it is perceived, puts it off, denies it, will not notice or remember it. This is newness of life.

"And be renewed in the spirit of your mind." We cannot renew ourselves, any more than we can create ourselves. It is the prerogative of Him without whom "was not anything made that was made" (John 1:3) to renew us. "Behold *I* make all things new." The renewing is the renewing of the Holy Ghost." (Tit. 3:5). We read of this renewing that it is daily; "the inward man is renewed day by day" (II Cor. 4:16), and that the "new man" is "renewed in knowledge after the image of Him that created him." (Job 3:10). The renewing is never in our own power—it is ever, "*Be* renewed," submit yourselves to the renewing; "Be renewed in the spirit of your mind, and put on the new man, which after God hath been created in righteousness and true holiness." (R. V.). How are we to "put on the new man"? Just as we deny self we are to acknowledge Christ. Just as we count out the old man we are to count in or reckon in, the new man. Christ dwells in our hearts by faith (Eph. 3:17), and we take and maintain our position of being crucified with Christ by faith, we reckon on God's renewing to work out in our lives that newness of life which God wants to be

A Testimony to a Lost World.

The world is full of self. God wants self to have no voice in His little flock. And yet religious selfishness is the most common, the most degrading, selfishness which there is. It seems as though Satan, when he finds a soul escaping from his bondage of sin, would move heaven and earth to keep that soul under the bondage of self, that so God should be frustrated, and that the very principle of self which governs in the world, and which is a theatre for sin to act upon, should be united to a certain amount of spiritual life, as though God should be made to contradict Himself in the people who believe in Him!

Few believers seem to take in that we are called to walk as Christ walked, and that the divine precepts of the Sermon on the Mount are as binding upon us as the Old Law was upon the Jews. Retaliation and resentment reign in rival factions of the church just as in the spirit of Zechariah, whose dying word was, "The Lord look upon it, and require it" (II Chron. 24:22), and few there are who possess the spirit of Stephen, "Lord, lay not this sin to their charge" (Acts 7:60). Yet surely only such as serve "in newness of spirit, and not in the oldness of the letter" (Rom. 7:6) can rightly claim the name of "Christian" or "Christ-man!" It is our privilege to live the life and bear the character of another, and that other the Son of God. Otherwise though we may be converted and cleansed from sin; though we may be wise to win souls and possessed of great zeal, we are not fulfilling the purpose for which God created, redeemed, and sanctified us. "Neither circumcision availeth anything, nor uncircumcision, but a new creation." (Gal. 6:15). The world has had enough of self—whether heathen self or Jewish self, whether Romish self or Protestant self, whether natural self or spiritual self, is alike hateful. What the world wants is Christ, the new creation. A charitable spirit, Christ-like words, Christ-like deeds; a spirit that will ask nothing and give all; which, like the sun, will shine down upon the evil and the good, and give blessing of some kind to the just and to the unjust. A spirit which will rebuff none but hypocrites from its fountain of love in God, can afford to breathe out love upon all. Newness of life is the clothing of the bride when she makes herself ready. (Rom. 19:1). The Holy Spirit produce in us this newness of life!

"THE SECRET OF HIS PRESENCE."

BY ELLEN LAKSHMI GORCH.

—A Native of India.—

In the secret of His presence
  How my soul delights to hide!
O how precious are the lessons
  Which I learn at Jesus' side!
Earthly cares can never vex me,
  Neither trials lay me low;
For when Satan comes to tempt me
  To the secret place I go.

When my soul is faint and thirsty,
  'Neath the shadow of His wing
There is cool and pleasant shelter,
  And a fresh and crystal spring;
And my Saviour rests beside me,
  As we hold communion sweet:
If I tried I could not utter
  What He says when thus we meet.

Only this I know: I tell him
  All my doubts, and griefs, and fears;
O how patiently He listens!
  And my drooping soul He cheers.
Do you think He ne'er reproves me?
  What a false friend He would be,
If He never, never told me
  Of the sins which He must see.

Would you like to know the sweetness
  Of the secret of the Lord?
Go and hide beneath His shadow:
  This shall then be your reward.
And whene'er you leave the silence
  Of that happy meeting-place,
You must mind and bear the image
  Of the Master in your face.

J. E. JEWETT, Publisher, 77 Bible House, New York, will furnish the above poem in leaflet form at twenty cents per hundred. *A Sample Packet* of 50 leaflets assorted (no two alike), will be sent post-paid, for ten cents. Postage stamps taken.

THE MARVEL OF THE AGE.

50,000 Words 1,000 Illustrations Over 700 Pages.

THE REVISED NEW AMERICAN DICTIONARY

—IS THE—

CHEAPEST DICTIONARY IN THE WORLD, Because it is revised and corrected to the present year, and contains all needed words in the English Language, with the true phonetic spelling of every word, based upon the World's lexicographer Webster, and other standard authorities, besides which it gives

A COMPLETE LIBRARY OF UNIVERSAL KNOWLEDGE, Useful alike to old and young, rich and poor, Farmers, Merchants, Bankers, Doctors, Storekeepers, Railroad and Telegraph Operatives and all who can read. OVER 100 VOLUMES are epitomized in this work. It contains in addition to the ordinary Dictionary an APPENDIX to the Dictionary which gives hundreds of words not found in any other work, and is corrected down to 1885. Specimens of the English Language from the year 450 to the present time. Foreign words and phrases, Popular Names of American cities and states, Scripture, Proper Names, Slang and Vulgar Phrases. How to speak and write correctly, Rule for Pronunciation; words mispronounced &c. Seperate Nautical, Musical, Geographical, Geometrical, and Mythological Dictionaries.

GUIDE TO BUSINESS, giving everything necessary to be known relating to the management of business, book keeping, weights, measures, values of coins, banking laws, how to tell counterfeits, tests for gold and silver, Laws relating to Landlord and Tenant, Interest, Usury, Homestead, Insolvent and Contract Laws, How to make Wills, etc.

THE POLITICAL AND HISTORICAL SYNOPSIS is the result of the labors of over one hundred experts, and contains more information and Statistical History of our Country than any other volume of the kind. Census Returns, Population of leading Cities, Number of Indians, their tribes and location; Principal officers of the Government with their salaries.

Declaration of Independence with autographs of the signers of that basis of our liberties; Constitution of United States and a thousand other useful items of information, carefully selected and reliable. The Armies and Navies of the world; the Troops of the Revolution, &c., &c. Epitomized Statistics of the Churches and Religious Denominations; Councils of the Christian World; Newspapers and Periodicals; Railroads of the World, their Length and Cost; Rulers of every Country; Revenues of every Nation; Shipping of the World; the Public Debt of the United States, and five thousand other interesting statistics.

A BIOGRAPHICAL DICTIONARY containing interesting information concerning nearly three thousand Men and Women who have distinguished themselves in Art, Science, Literature, Statesman-ship, the Pulpit, Platform Judicial Courts, or War. Rules for the Organization of Public Meetings, Farmers Clubs &c., are given full and explicitly.

Over 1000 Illustrations several of them colored in the highest style of art including the Flags of all Nations printed in all the colors which distinguish the emblems of the Countries. Pilot Signals of all the principal nations; the various Flags of the United States; Autographs of all the Presidents from Washington to President Arthur;

ANCIENT ALPHABETS OF THE WORLD, in large plates on plate paper; Single and Double hand Deaf and Dumb Alphabets; Maps showing the meaning of geographical terms, and one showing the Center of Population at the close of each decade from 1790-1 to 1880. Diagrams, Sectional Sketches, &c., THE BROOKLYN BRIDGE with full particulars of the greatest Engineering work of the Century, relating thereto. HOW TO MAKE KNOTS, with 48 illustrations. Mechanical Movements, illustrated by 140 wood engravings, and over 800 other illustrations of Natural History, Botany, Geology, Mechanics, Architecture, Astronomy, &c.

This book is everybody's VADE MECUM, and is indispensable in every home. For the purpose of examination we will send this wonderful work, containing 50000 WORDS, and Over 1000 ILLUSTRATIONS, handsomely bound in cloth, gilt lettered, on receipt of ONE DOLLAR, TWO COPIES ONE DOLLAR AND SEVENTY FIVE CENTS. Send One Dollar for a sample copy and see what you can do. We desire Agents to sell this book, because they can make money quick as a wink. Over 300,000 of the New American Dictionaries have been sold in 2 years. The Revised New American Dictionary has 100 pages more of valuable matter over 700 pages total.

EXTRAORDINARY OFFER! If any person will get up a club of Seven at One Dollar each we will send FREE a premium the American Waterbury Stem Winding Watch; for a CLUB of 15 we will send free a Solid Silver Hunting Case Watch; for a CLUB of 25 we will send free a Ladies' Solid Gold Hunting Case Watch; for a CLUB of 45 we will send free a Gent's Solid Gold Hunting Case Watch. You can easily secure one of these watches in a day or two or during your leisure time evenings.

Send Money by Post Office Money Order or Registered Letter. Mention this Paper

World M'f'g Co, 122 Nassau Street, New York.

The New American ROLLER ORGAN

is operated similar to the finest French Music Boxes and PLAYS 260 TUNES, from a waltz to a hymn, with perfect tune and time. Gives better satisfaction than A HUNDRED DOLLAR PARLOR ORGAN and ten times more pleasure. This Organ is the perfection of musical instrument is and the grandest and most marvellous instrument ever presented to the public. It plays SACRED MUSIC, MARCHES WALTZES, POLKAS, JIGS Reels, Opera Selections, Popular Songs, Church music, as well as any organ. Nothing grander, or combining so many features can be found in French or Swiss Music Boxes, cost ing $100. WE WANT A SPECIAL AGENT, EITHER SEX, IN EVERY LOCALITY, AND OFFER SUCH INDUCEMENTS THAT EARNEST WORKERS CANNOT FAIL TO MAKE $100 TO $200 PER MONTH. When you order a sample instrument get Special Terms. Price Only Six Dollars in BEAUTIFULLY CARVED CASES with music.

PERFECTION ATTAINED AT LAST

ONLY $6 WITH MUSIC

260 TUNES

Get 6 for one. It will fill you with astonishment and delight. If you want it sent C.O.D. send $0.50 when you order and pay balance $5.50 when you get organ. Send P.O. order Registered Letter or by Express. Address

WORLD M'F'G CO. 122 Nassau Street, New York

Notice.

THE NEW AMERICAN ROLLER ORGAN should be had by every familly for it is a source of endless pleasure and is appreciated by every one. If you do not feel like paying the cash for it you can easily get it **free** if you will devote a few hours time to getting up a club of **nine** at One Dollar each, for the **New American Dictionary**, the best book of the kind ever published, and sold at One Dollar.

If you will try to get up a Club we will send you a sample copy by mail, post-paid, **for only Forty Cents** if you will fill the blank below, or copy it and mention the **CHRISTIAN HERALD.**

ORDER BLANK.

WORLD MA[illegible] CTURING CO.,
122 Nassau Street, New York.

Please [illegible] me at once, by mail post-paid, the **NEW AMERICAN DICTIONARY**, for which I [illegible] FORTY CENTS.

I her[illegible] agree to do my best to get **NINE** subscribers for the **NEW AMERICAN DICTIONA[RY]** [illegible] **One Dollar Each**, with the understanding that when I send you **NINE DOLLARS** [illegible] to receive **Nine Dictionaries** and the New American Roller Organ **free** for my troub[le].

NAME ....

TOWN ....

COUNTY ....

STATE ....

DATE ....

Horsford's Acid Phosphate:
Ill Effects of Tobacco
relieved by its use.

The readers of the CHRISTIAN HERALD are often requested to cut out the advertisements, or order blanks when writing to advertisers when notices appear in this paper. Many of our readers do not wish to do this as they wish to [pre]serve the paper entire. The World Manufacturing Co., whose notice and order blank appear in another column, inform us, that if you will *mention that you saw the notice* in the CHRISTIAN HERALD, and copy the order blank, it will answer the purpose as well.

A Wife's Opportunity.

Write your name and address plainly on a postal card (mentioning this paper), sending same to J. D. Larkin & Co., Buffalo, N. Y., and they will send you, on 30 days trial, one of their **Great Boxes** (advertised in a recent issue of this paper), of "Sweet Home" Soap and presents. Better accept the offer at once, as you run no risk.

Teachers during vacation, farmers' sons when work is slack on the farm, and any others not fully and profitably employed, can learn something to their advantage by applying to B. F. Johnson & Co., Publishers, 1009 Main St., Richmond, Va.

MEXICO

Contributions in aid of Christian work in Mexico are most pressingly needed, and can be mailed to the address of
BISHOP H. C. RILEY,
Care of J. P. HEATH,
43 Bible House, New York.

MISS JONES' QUILTING.

Written by
JOSIAH ALLEN'S WIFE.

This is one of the best stories ever written by this popular author, full of fun and good humor. 12mo., [illegible] pages; paper cover, 25 cents; cloth, 50 cents. Sold by all newsdealers or mailed to any address, post-paid, on receipt of price, by
J. S. OGILVIE, Publisher,
57 Rose Street, New York.

AGENTS! Send for [CAT]-A-LOG. A. H. TREAT'S of New Books. The National Hand-book of American Progress. 1492 to 1890. The Boss Campaign Book, $3; also, The Bow in the Cloud, or Words of Comfort, by 200 Authors. $1.75. E. B. TREAT, 771 Broadway, New York.

Missionary Libra[ry]

For Sabbath-Schools, Mission Bands, and the [Home] Circle.

Koan and Saijiro, or Life in Japan. Carrothers 440
Glimpses of Maori-Land. Butler 318
Life and Adventure in Japan. Clark 247
From Hong Kong to the Himalayas. Clark 368
Jottings from the Pacific. Gill 304
Along the River and Road in Fuhkien. Dukes 362
Home Life in China. Bryson 314
Among the Mongols. Gilmour 382
Madagascar and France. Shaw 438
Every-Day Life in India. Rowe ....4[illegible]
Scenes in Southern India. Mitchell 372
Old Highways in China. Williamson 293

This set of 12 vols., 12mo, all of recent [issue], containing 4,280 pages and 276 cuts, and [hand]somely bound in cloth, all in a polished c[hest]nut case, at

ONLY TEN DOLLARS *NET.*

Single copies at list prices, postage prepa[id].

AMERICAN TRACT SOCIE[TY]

150 Nassau Street, New York.

BOSTON, 54 Bromfield Street; ROCHES[TER], N. Y., 93 State St.; CHICAGO, 122 Wabash A[ve.]; PHILADELPHIA, 1512 Chestnut St.; CIN[CIN]NATI, 176 Elm St.; SAN FRANCISCO, 735 Ma[rket] St.

An Illustrated Hand book on Afric[a]

GIVING AN ACCOUNT OF ITS PEO[PLE], ITS CLIMATE, ITS RESOURCES, ITS DISCOVERIES, RIVERS, LAKES, AND SOME OF ITS MISSIONS.

CLOTH, 50 cts. PAPER, 25 cts.

Testimonials.

Rev. Daniel Steele, D.D., writes: "I have read [your] ILLUSTRATED HAND BOOK ON AFRICA with great [in]terest. Not many people have time to read Stan[ley's] large volumes, and a still smaller number can affo[rd to] own them. Your Hand Book, scattered widely am[ong] Christian people, will awaken our interest in the g[reat] enterprise of the evangelization of the dark contin[ent]. I hope you will be called upon for a hundred thou[sand] copies."

"We have read this book several times, studied [the] newly made map, looked at the striking pictures, [and] it is surprising to see the amount of valuable infor[ma]tion he has gathered so rapidly together." And ag[ain]: "Not one person interested in Bishop Taylor's w[ork] ought to be without this Hand Book. It contains large pages of excellent reading, ten illustrations, a map of the New Congo State." Rev. E. I. D. P[e]per, in *Christian Standard.*

Sent, post-paid, on receipt of price.

J. E. JEWETT, 77 Bible House, New Yor[k].

BOOK AGENTS WANTED F[OR]

MY STORY OF THE WA[R]
By Mary A. Livermo[re]

Her own narrative of "Four Years' Personal Exp[eri]ence as Field and Hospital Nurse." It portray[s the] Womanly or "Heavenly" side of the War, its Lights [and] Shadows "as a woman saw them." Bright, Pure, and G[ood], full of "laughter and tears," of thrilling interest and touc[hing] pathos, it sells at sight to all. Splendid Steel-Plates, famous old Battle-Flags, richly colored in exact fac-si[mile]. The "booming" book for Men and Women Agents. $10[0 to] $200 a month made. Distance no hindrance, [as] we Pay Freights and give Extra Terms. Write for circula[rs to] A. D. WORTHINGTON & CO., Hartford, Conn.

WANTED FOR CASH! OLD U[nited States] and [Con]federate POSTAGE STAMPS used [prior] to 1865. These stamps will bring fine prices IF LEFT [ON] THE ORIGINAL ENVELOPE and in GO[OD] condition. Some stamps bring as much as $25 each. Send stamp for circulars describing [kinds] wanted. Best references furnished if desired. Add[ress] G. M. BASTABLE, Catlett, V[a].

"Demonology or Spiritualism Ancient and Modern."—"An effective weapon."—"[A] sword of fire."—"Only unanswerable work on [the] subject."—Startling disclosures.—History, facts, data.—Scores saved already. Whole communi[ties] rescued. Every family, preacher and christian wo[rker] needs one. 316 pp. 12mo, cloth. Price reduced [to ...] Sent by mail, postpaid, on receipt of price. Add[ress] J. E. JEWETT, 77 Bible House, New Y[ork].

PRICE $180.

UNIVERSITY PIAN[OS] FROM $180 TO $[illegible] FINEST PIANOS IN THE WOR[LD]. SOLD DIRECT TO FAMILIES, sav[ing] the enormous expenses of [illegible]. Sent with beautiful cover, st[ool] and book, for trial in your own home before you buy. Guaranteed six years. Send for catalogue. Marchal & Smith Piano Co., 235 E. 21st st., N. [Y.]

$75.00 to $250.00 A MONTH can be m[ade] working for us. Agents p[re]ferred who can furnish a horse and give their wh[ole] time to the business. Spare moments may be profit[ably] employed also. A few vacancies in towns and cities. [B.] F. Johnson & Co., Pub's, 1009 Main St., Richmond, [Va.]

TEAS LADIES Send at once f[or] our new terms. THE GREAT AMERICAN TEA C[O.], 31 and 33 Vesey St., New York, N[.Y.]

THE CHRISTIAN HERALD AND SIGNS OF OUR TIMES.

Vol. XI., No. 25. Office, 63 Bible House, N. Y. THURSDAY, JUNE 21, 1888. Annual Subscription, $1.50.

CONTENTS OF THIS NUMBER.

PORTRAIT OF PRINCE HENRY, OF PRUSSIA, AND HIS BRIDE.
PULPIT AND PRESS. Dr. Talmage's Sermon last Sunday Morning.
ANECDOTES RELATED AT RECENT EVANGELISTIC MEETINGS.
THE GLORIOUS APPEARING. By Rev. W. Fuller Gooch, M. A.
Rev. W. F. Re Qua Among the Indians—A Dying Girl's Message—The Reformation of a Colored Convict—The Growing Work in China—A Singular Indian Rite—A Dishonest Chinawoman's Confession.
A MESSAGE TO SLAVES. A New Sermon by Rev. C. H. Spurgeon.
Gems from New Books: The Administration of the Bastinado—Escape from Savage Darfurians, etc.
PORTRAIT OF MGR. LEON BOULAND, the Converted Roman Catholic Bishop.
PICTURE OF THE PROMENADE IN HAVANA.
FRED HOLDEN'S DEFALCATION. (Illustrated.)
THE EPOCHS OF A LIFE. A New Serial Story by Rev. L. S. Keyser. Continued.)
GOD'S COVENANT WITH ISRAEL. By Mrs. M. Baxter.

PRINCE HENRY, of Prussia, and his Bride PRINCESS IRENE, of Hesse—The Royal Wedding Cortege.

THE ROYAL WEDDING IN BERLIN.

The Houses United—The Bridegroom—Born in 1862—An Expert Wood-Carver—Arrested by a Park-Keeper—A Connoisseur of Queens—Enlisted in the Navy—The Unpleasantness of Discipline—Voyage Around the World—The Bride—Her Illustrious Mother—A Wonderful Sick-Nurse—Her Service in the Military Hospitals—Her Conversion—The Wedding Ceremony—The Welcome to the Bride—A Courtier Chaplain—An Affectionate Family.

THE interesting royal marriage briefly chronicled in these columns two weeks ago, uniting as it does in another bond of union the heads of the two European nations with which our own people are most closely allied by descent and sympathy, deserves a more extended notice, and we therefore give this week portraits of the bride and bridegroom, and a picture of the wedding cortége.

The Bridegroom

is Prince Henry, second son of Frederick III., Emperor of Germany, and the bride is the third daughter of Louis, Grand Duke of Hesse. They are cousins on the mother's side—the bridegroom's mother, the Empress of Germany, being sister to the bride's mother, Princess Alice, respectively the eldest and second daughters of Queen Victoria. They are also related, on the paternal side: King Frederick William I. of Prussia being their common great, great-grandfather. Prince Henry is in his twenty-sixth year, having been born August 14, 1862. As a boy, he was somewhat careless, and not particularly devoted to study; but he was so amiable and persuasive in manner that he generally turned aside the intended scolding. Like all German princes, he learned a trade, and thus became a finished amateur carpenter, delighting in wood-carving, and turning out charming little presents for his family and friends. His restless disposition often brought him into trouble. Among the incidents of

His Boyhood

now recalled, is a story of his delight at the consternation with which he filled a park-keeper who did not know him. It seems that one day the lad slipped out with his elder sister, Princess Charlotte, into the gardens at Potsdam, and began picking the flowers. A park-keeper promptly pounced on the delinquent, scolded him furiously, and when the boy replied that he had a right to take the flowers, the irate keeper bade him come to the police station. "All right," said Prince Henry, "but I must tell papa first." "And where does this papa live?" growled the keeper. "Papa is the Crown Prince, and he lives in that palace," was the answer.

He had, too, a boy's lack of reverence for dignities. In the course of his studies he was engaged on one of those histories written by fulsome panegyrists of royalty, who represented all queens as beautiful, graceful, and witty. The lad had seen but two queens—his grandmothers, the queens of Prussia and England—neither of whom could be honestly so described. His quiet comment was: "I think this man never saw a queen."

It is stated that his mother's ardent desire that one of her sons should be a sailor was so frequently expressed that her husband determined to gratify it in Prince Henry's case. Having obtained the consent of the old Emperor William, the boy was received into the navy, and with the true Prussian spirit of discipline, was to be treated as an ordinary cadet. When his turn came for an extended voyage, the mother had a natural feeling of concern for the safety of her boy. But she overcame her maternal reluctance and agreed to his going. During his absence, the royal family had two bereavements. He was at Singapore when the Grand Duchess Alecia died, and off Japan when he heard the news of the death of his younger brother, Prince Waldemar. His mother entreated that he be recalled home to console her, but the old Emperor William was inflexible. "You consented to part with him for two years," he said, "and now he must do his duty, too." He is the first of his line who has ever sailed round the world as representative of the new German name and guardian of the new German rights. It was on board the *Prince Adalbert* under Captain MacLean, a man of Scottish descent, that Prince Henry familiarized himself with the rules of naval discipline and the risks of the sea by circumnavigating the globe; and a subsequent voyage to the West Coast of Africa on board the ironclad *Olga* added to his experience as a seaman.

The Bride,

Princess Irene, had the inestimable advantage of a good mother. Every one who knew the late Princess Alice, loved her. She was gentle, affectionate, and unwearying in devotion to her loved ones. During the illness of her father, Prince Albert, she was his constant nurse, and her self-possession and thoughtfulness were as astonishing as her affection. In 1871, after her marriage, when her brother the Prince of Wales was stricken down with the disease which had proved fatal to his father, Princess Alice left her German home, and during his long fight for life devoted herself with the same unselfishness to the task of nursing him. Again, in the Franco-German War, the Princess showed herself an angel of mercy in sickness. The crowded hospitals at Darmstadt were under her superintendence, and the post in her hands was no sinecure. Nearly all her time she was in the wards, personally looking to the welfare of the wounded soldiers, and speaking to them gentle words of sympathy and encouragement.

Her conversion came through the blessing of God on a season of sorrow and bereavement. On June 29, 1873, her little son, Prince Frederick William, then a little more than two and a-half years old, fell from an open window in the palace of Darmstadt, and received such injuries that he died almost immediately afterwards. At first this heavy calamity seemed to have produced only "the sorrow of the world that worketh death"; but gradually it became, by God's inscrutable mercy, the means of leading her to think, so that she finally came to seek and find peace in a firm faith in Jesus Christ revealed in the Scriptures of truth, as the only Saviour of sinners. Herr Bergsträsser, in his "Memoirs," says: "The lamented Princess was for several years a disciple of German Rationalism. She seems, in fact, to have come very near to openly denying the Divine existence. All the while, however, she was a devoted wife and mother, and a pattern of every moral virtue. The loss of a child under circumstances which are still well remembered in England, proved the turning-point in the Princess's life. She said to a friend: 'The whole construction of philosophical conclusions which I had formerly built up I now find to be based on nothing; nothing has remained; and what should we be in life if we had no faith and no conviction that there is a God who governs the world and each single one of us? I feel the necessity of prayer; I like to sing hymns with my children, and each has its favorite hymn.'"

From such a mother, so wise, amiable, and tender, the Princess Irene must have had the best of training, and must have learned, from her example, what a good wife and princess should be. She is in her twenty-second year, having been born July 11, 1866. That was the year of the war between Prussia and Austria; and the ceremony of "christening" the baby Princess was performed on the very day when the treaty of peace was signed. She was appropriately named Irene, the Greek word signifying Peace.

The Marriage

was celebrated on May 24 last. On the previous day the bride was brought to Berlin by her father, and the bridal party was met and conducted to Berlin by the Crown Prince of Germany and a brilliant staff. After the usual greetings had taken place, the Crown Prince introduced the distinguished men by whom he was accompanied, to Princess Irene, and then conducted his future sister-in-law to a carriage. Mourning dresses for the late Emperor were discarded for the occasion, and all the younger princesses appeared in white. Princess Irene, in an open victoria drawn by four black horses, with outriding postilions, looked beautiful in her ivory white silk dress. She was completely overcome by the hearty enthusiasm of the reception. Twenty thousand people lined the route, shouting, "*Hoch!*" "*Wilkommen!*" &c. She was pale, though she smiled occasionally. A thousand torches of electric light reflecting on the cuirassiers' helmets and on the Gardes du Corps were all toned down to a full-moon ideal. The bridal reception was in the Blue Salon of the palace. The Prince of Wales, who is uncle of both bride and bridegroom, and distinguished guests awaited the arrival of the royal party, who were driven into the courtyard between lines of the Foot Guards. Afterward the bride and bridegroom held a reception in the palace. The park in front was like fairyland, illuminated by electric lights.

From an early hour on the wedding-day the beautiful Unter den Linden and

The Road to Charlottenburg

were lined with people eager to catch a glimpse of the wedding guests as they drove from the capital to the royal palace in the suburb. The Russian Grand Duke Sergius, who represented the Czar on the occasion, appeared in an open carriage, who was closely followed by the Russian Ambassador, and the Russian Military Plenipotentiary, Count Kutusoff. The German Crown Princess, who was accompanied by the Princess Albert, Consort of the Prince Regent of Brunswick, came next, and behind her Royal Highness's coach followed a closed carriage with her little sons, all dressed in white. The eldest, Prince William, stood up and acknowledged the cheers of the people by raising his right hand to his hat, as if giving a military salute. The Prince of Wales, wearing the scarlet uniform of his Blücher Hussars, also drove out to Charlottenburg in an open carriage. The German Crown Prince, in honor of his brother, the bridegroom, appeared in the uniform of the Naval Battalion. Both he and Prince Henry were greatly cheered by the crowd, as was also Count Moltke, who drove out alone in an open carriage.

Meanwhile the royal family and the most distinguished of the guests had assembled in

The Spacious Blue Hall,

once the bedroom of Frederick the Great. In this apartment the Empress performed the first act in the proceedings by fastening on the head of Princess Irene, the bride, the Wedding Crown of the Prussian Princesses, consisting of circlets of brilliants resting on a cap of purple velvet. The bride wore a magnificent *moiré antique* wedding dress, which was adorned at the neck with several diamonds as large as nuts. Like the splendid diamond necklace, the bridal fan of gold work adorned with diamonds, and the diamond bracelets, these precious gems belong to the treasure of the Prussian Crown. Round her neck Princess Irene wore a fourfold chain of magnificent pearls, the wedding gift of the Emperor and Empress. The Indian shawl, which was *the gift of the Queen of England*, being unsuitable for a bride's attire, was not worn at the ceremony.

After the fastening on of the Crown the civil ceremony of the marriage was performed, and upon its conclusion the Royal persons

Proceeded to the Palace Chapel.

The bridegroom conducted the bride on his right arm, and they entered the chapel punctually at noon. Behind the bridal pair came the Grand Duke of Hesse, walking with the Empress, the Prince of Wales with the German Crown Princess, and the Crown Prince with the Grand Duchess Sergius. Meanwhile the other guests had assembled in the chapel, a pleasing little structure, adorned with a fine painting of Faith, Love, and Hope, and numerous medallions and reliefs, representing Biblical scenes, the colors, among which blue and gold predominate, blending in admirable harmony. All chairs had been removed in preparation for the present ceremony, with the exception of six large armchairs, placed before the altar, and intended for the highest personages present. Upon the altar, a carved and gilded table, with a cover of red velvet, stood two burning candles and a Bible. The whole space behind and beside the altar, was covered with roses of all colors, the exquisite perfume of which filled the chapel. Just as the bride and bridegroom were stepping up to the altar the Empress Augusta, in deep black with white trimming, entered the chapel in a bath chair. The Empress Victoria stepped up to her mother-in-law and kissed her hand, the other members of the Royal Family following her example.

The service was opened by the choir singing a hymn, "Praise the Lord, the mighty King of Honors," in which the assembly joined. At this point, through a doorway near the Empress Victoria's chair,

The Emperor Entered,

in Grand General's Uniform, with the ribbon of the Hessian Order, walking erect and with elastic step, attended by General Winterfeld. He bowed urbanely in all directions, and, after kissing his mother's hand, sat down beside the Empress Victoria. The service was conducted by Dr. Kögel, first Court Chaplain, who was assisted by the Rev. Herr Persius, of Potsdam, the bridegroom's religious instructor, Superintend- Müller, of Charlottenburg, and Dr. Sell, of Darmstadt. Dr. Kögel took as his text John 14: 27, "Peace I leave with you, My peace I give unto you."

In the course of his address, he said: "After days of deep mourning and anxious care a May day of happiness and splendor greets our Royal house. Your hearts, devoted in deepest affection to one another, will seal the covenant with a marriage-ring and the oath of fidelity before God's altar. The two illustrious fathers lay on your heads the blessing by which the houses of children are built up; a deeply moved mother draws the child of an early sainted sister to her heart; our Empress Mother, amid the sorrow of isolation, is full of tenderest sympathy for your young happiness, for which the late Emperor folded his hands in blessing; and England's good Queen, who was present lately in this house of God, remembers the wedding-day of her grandchildren in her prayers. Supported by so much love and fidelity, surrounded by the blessings and good wishes of brothers and sisters, relations and friends, yourselves full of ardent gratitude, you enter this memorable sanctuary, and receive the gracious promise of the eternal Prince of peace, 'Peace I leave with you, my peace I give unto you.'"

At the conclusion of the chaplain's address a chorale was sung, whereupon the Emperor, who had apparently resolved to forget his illness for that day at least, made a sign to Prince Henry to kneel down for

The Exchange of the Rings,

which was announced to the outer world by thundering salvos of artillery, and for the prayer and blessing. Handel's "Hallelujah Chorus" concluded the ceremony. The aged Empress Augusta, grandmother of the Bridegroom, embraced and kissed the Prince and Princess. The Empress Victoria then kissed the Bride, while the Emperor embraced his son with much affection. At the *déjeuner* which followed in the Schloss the Crown Prince proposed the only toast—the health of the Bride and Bridegroom. Prince and Princess Henry drove at three P.M., in a carriage drawn by four horses to the railway station through an outburst of parting cheers from the tens of *thousands of spectators lining the streets*. They travelled by railway to Ermansdorf, in Silesia, where they are spending the honeymoon.

ANECDOTES RELATED AT RECENT EVANGELISTIC MEETINGS.

The Young Woman's Notion of Prayer.—"'I should not know what to say,' observed a poor young woman in the East of London, when I asked her to pray to God. 'I might make a mistake, and, oh, how dreadful that would be!' To which I replied, 'God knows your heart, and well He knows what you mean, though you cannot express yourself as you would like.' 'Oh, I am so glad to know that!' she answered; 'but I thought I must pray to God like the clergyman, who uses a book, and says things in such a nice and beautiful way. I know I could never pray like that, sir.' It was not long ere with streaming eyes and a plaintive voice this poor penitent exclaimed, 'Oh, have mercy on me, hear me, and save me, for Jesus Christ's sake,' and God answered her prayer, and filled her with the joy of His salvation."

Twenty-five Christians in a Cave.—Mr. McDonald, a Scotch missionary of South Africa, says: "I first went to South Africa immediately after the close of one of our little wars, and great was the desolation it had occasioned. Mission stations demolished, the people scattered, and years of good undone in as many weeks. When I got to what had once been a flourishing mission station, I found only twenty-five Christians left, and they were meeting in a cave to worship God away from the notice of the other natives. But in the course of a few years God has wrought wonders, and the twenty-five Christians have increased to six hundred and twenty-four, no longer meeting in a cave, but with two mission centres having twenty-six preaching stations each. There is room for a great work in Africa, but the difficulty is the scarcity of missionaries. Why are there so many preachers in Great Britain and so few in Africa? God did not mean the Bread of Life to be kept in one corner of the earth while men and women were starving."

An Instance of Divine Retribution.—"Vengeance is mine; I will repay, saith the Lord." So reads the well-known passage of Scripture, and the Christians in Kanye, Bechuanaland, South Africa, are learning that the words are true. Six months ago they were cruelly attacked by their heathen neighbors; their houses were burnt down, and their property stolen or destroyed. But they did not retaliate, preferring patiently to suffer wrong-doing. The hand of God, however, has overtaken the wrong-doers, and one after another of the ringleaders has died from drink and other evil practices. In relating these facts the Rev. James Good says that both the heathen people and the Christians are alike deeply impressed. Not only so, but more than forty new members have been received into the native church, and they have a larger number of inquirers than in any past year. At their New Year's gathering nearly fifty wagons came in from the out-stations. The church was full, and they had a large gathering on the mountain on the site of their burnt-down church. In the evening 250 rejoicing Christians sat together at the Lord's Table.

Dead on the Doorstep.—"There was a Poor old Scotch woman, who lived in a village in the far North. She had a daughter who resided in a valley at some distance off. One day in winter she went on a visit to her daughter, and as she was taking some refreshment preparatory to returning home, a blinding snow-storm came on, and her daughter advised her to stay where she was for the night; but the old woman insisted on going home at once, so she put on her plaid and set out. Her daughter was very anxious about her all that night, and getting up early in the morning went to her mother's house; but she did not find her there. In great alarm she ran to the nearest neighbor, and procuring help, they searched the hills, but in vain; nowhere could the aged woman be found. They went to her home again, this time by the front door, for they had gone to the back before, and there they found her dead, frozen on the doorstep. She had struggled bravely through the snow, on, on, on; nearer and nearer, until victory seemed within her grasp and safety at hand. Then, just at the doorstep she sank exhausted, and there she died. And are there not many persons who are almost saved, who almost trust in Christ, who will almost get to heaven? But *almost* is of no use. The individual who is almost a Christian will be lost as irretrievably as the blackest sinner."

A Native Pastor on His Son's Death.—The Rev. Ruttonji Nowroji, native pastor at Aurangabad, Western India, thus writes to the Rev. W. S. Price, in reply to a letter of sympathy on the death of his son from cholera: "I must thank your for your kind expressions of sympathy in my recent loss. It was my second son, a lad about sixteen years of age. The attack was very strong and severe. He struggled for nearly five days, and suffered much in body; but oh! I cannot tell you how completely happy he was in mind. There was no fear—no doubt; all was light and peace. His mind would wander upon all earthly things; but Christ—His atoning sacrifice, His love, His glory—heaven, and heavenly fecility, were deep realities to him. He would quote passage after passage from the Bible without a mistake. He prayed much. He offered a beautiful prayer in which was much praise, commending us all to our Father in heaven. Never before have I ever witnessed so happy and so peaceful a death. It was a sweet sleep. I praise the Lord for this great comfort and consolation. Our hearts have sorely bled, but we have been greatly comforted."

A Climb in the Rocky Mountains.—Mr. McCaul, a Christian worker, of Canada, relates:,"I remember spending two weeks in the Rocky Mountains. There were many fine views to be had, but one especially from a certain point which stood high above the surrounding peaks, but the roads to it were so precipitous and dangerous that few cared to risk the dangers. A party of us, however, determined to attempt the ascent, that we might obtain this gorgeous view. Our guide directed us to follow him closely, to put our feet in the marks he left by his feet, to stop where he stopped, and when he caught hold of a tree and swung himself forward, to wait till it swung back, and then one by one follow his example. I happened to be immediately behind him, and with what earnestness did I watch his every movement, that I might follow it! When we reached the top we were amply rewarded for all we had had to endure. Similarly, dear friends, the only way to reach the heights and view the glory-land which we shall soon enter, is by steadily, earnestly, and watchfully following Jesus, our Divine Guide, and if we endure to the end, what a glorious reward! a crown of life that fadeth not away, and to dwell with Christ forever."

The Young Man With the Blue Ribbon.—Mr. Thomson said: "I once met a young man in his own home who wore the blue ribbon of abstinence. In the course of conversation I inquired of him. 'Are you a Christian, my dear friend?' Replying in the negative, as I had feared, I then said, 'You know, my dear fellow, your blue ribbon will never take you to heaven, glad as I am to see you with it; you must turn your back upon all your sins and seek mercy through Jesus Christ. Are you willing here and now to kneel and confess your sins and find pardon?' He immediately gave his assent, and we both knelt. After I had prayed for him and he himself had asked for forgiveness, we rose from our knees. I then asked, 'Has He forgiven you?' 'I do not know,' was the doubtful reply, to which I responded, 'If we confess our sins, He is faithful and just to forgive us our sins. His business is forgiveress, and your business is confession. So He has not proved faithful to you, has He?' Holding out his hand to me, he exclaimed, 'Oh, yes; the Lord has forgiven me for Christ's sake, but it really seems too good to be true.' I have watched that young man during the years that have since passed, and he is still walking in the light and love of God."

PULPIT AND PRESS.

Dr. Talmage's Sermon Preached Last Sunday Morning, June 17, 1888.

"The children of this world are, in their generation, wiser than the children of light." Luke 16 : 8.

A Golden Opportunity—The Aid the Press Might Render to the Pulpit—Estranged by Indiscriminate Hostility—Justice Sure in the End—Painful Personal Experiences—The Reaction—Christian Courtesy to be Extended to Reporters—A New View of Armageddon—The Evil of Sunday Newspapers—A Bible the First Book Printed—Pointed Sermons Wanted—A Treaty Proposed—Benjamin Franklin's Epitaph—Luke a Reporter—Conversion of a Reporter—Unappreciated Work—A Proposed Marriage.

SACRED stupidity, and solemn incompetency, and sanctified laziness are here rebuked by Christ. He says worldlings are wider awake for opportunities than are Christians. Men of the world *grab occasions*, while Christian people let the most valuable occasions drift by unimproved. That is the meaning of our Lord when He says: "The children of this world are, in their generation, wiser than the children of light."

A marked illustration of the truth of that maxim is in the slowness of the Christian religion to take possession of the secular printing press. The opportunity is open, and has been for some time open, but the ecclesiastical courts, and the churches, and the ministers of religion are, for the most part, allowing

The Golden Opportunity

to pass unimproved. That the opportunity is open, I declare, from the fact that all the secular newspapers are glad of any religious facts or statistics that you present them. Any animated and stirring article relating to religious themes they would gladly print. They thank you for any information in regard to churches. If a wrong has been done to any Christian church, or Christian institution, you could go into any newspaper of the land and have the real truth stated. Dedication services, ministerial ordinations and pastoral installations, corner-stone laying of a church, anniversary of a charitable society, will have reasonable space in any secular journal, if it have previous notice given. If I had some great injustice done me, there is not an editorial or a reportorial room in the United States into which I could not go and get myself set right: and that is true of any well-known Christian man. Why, then, does not our glorious Christianity embrace these magnificent opportunities? I have before me a subject of first and last importance: How shall we secure the secular press as a mightier reinforcement to religion and the pulpit?

The first thing toward this result is cessation of

Indiscriminate Hostility

against newspaperdom. You might as well denounce the legal profession because of the shysters, or the medical profession because of the quacks, or merchandise because of the swindling bargain-makers, as to *slam-bang newspapers* because there are recreant editors, and unfair reporters, and unclean columns. Guttenberg, the inventor of the art of printing, was about to destroy his types and extinguish the art, because it was suggested to him that printing might be suborned into the service of the devil; but afterward he bethought himself that the right use of the art might more than overcome the evil use of it; and so he spared the type, and the intelligence of all following ages. But there are many to-day in the depressed mood of Guttenberg, with uplifted hammer, wanting to pound to pieces the type, who have not reached his better mood, in which he saw the art of printing to be the rising sun of the world's illumination.

If, instead of fighting newspapers, we spend the same length of time, and the same vehemence, in marshalling their help in religious directions, we would be as much wiser as the man who gets consent of the railroad superintendent to fasten a car to the end of a rail-train, shows better sense than he who runs his wheelbarrow up the track to meet and drive back the Chicago limited express. The silliest thing that a man ever does is "to fight" a newspaper, for you may have the floor for utterance perhaps for one day in the week, while the newspaper has the floor every day of the week. Napoleon, though a mighty man, had many weaknesses, and one of the weakest things he ever did was to threaten that if the English newspapers did not stop their adverse criticism of himself, he would, with four hundred thousand bayonets, cross the Channel for their chastisement.

Don't Fight Newspapers.

Attack provokes attack. Better wait till the excitement blows over and then go in and get justice, for get it you will if you have patience, and common sense, and equipoise of disposition. It ought to be a mighty sedative that there is an enormous amount of common sense in the world, and you will eventually be taken for what you are really worth, and you cannot be puffed up, and you cannot be written down, and if you are the enemy of good society, that fact will come out, and if you are the friend of good society, that fact will be established.

I know what I am talking about, for I can draw on my own experience. All the respectable newspapers, as far as I know, are my friends now. But many of you remember the time when I was the most continuously and meanly attacked man in this country. God gave me grace not to answer back, and

I Kept Silence

for ten years, and much grace was required. What I said was perverted and twisted into just the opposite of what I did say. My person was maligned, and I was presented as a gorgon, and I was maliciously described by persons who had never seen me as a monstrosity in body, mind, and soul. There were millions of people who believed that there was a large sofa in this pulpit, although we never had anything but a chair, and that during the singing by the congregation I was accustomed to lie down on that sofa and dangle my feet over the end. Lying New York correspondents for ten years misrepresented our church services, but we waited, and people from every neighborhood of Christendom came here to find the magnitude of the falsehoods concerning the church and concerning myself. A reaction set in, and now we have justice, full justice, more than justice, and as

Much Over-praise

as once we had under-appreciation; and no man that ever lived was so much indebted to the newspaper press for opportunity to preach the gospel as I am. Young men in the ministry, young men in all professions and occupations, wait. You can afford to wait. Take rough misrepresentation as a Turkish towel to start up your languid circulation, or a system of massage or Swedish movement, whose pokes and pulls and twists and thrusts are salutary treatment. There is only one person you need to manage, and that is yourself. Keep your disposition sweet by communion with the Christ, who answered not again, the society of genial people, and walk out in the sunshine with your hat off, and you will come out all right. And don't join the crowd of people in our day who spend much of their time damning newspapers.

Again: in this effort to secure the secular press as a mightier reinforcement of religion, let us make it the avenue of religious information. My advice, often given to friends who propose to start a new paper, is: "Don't! Don't! Employ the papers already started." The biggest financial hole ever dug in this American continent is the hole in which good people throw their money when they start a newspaper. It is almost as good and as quick a way of getting rid of money as buying stock in a gold-mine in Colorado. Not more printing-presses, but the right use of those already established. All their cylinders, all their steam power, all their pens, all their types, all their editorial chairs and reportorial rooms, are available if you would engage them in behalf of civilization and Christianity.

Again, if you would secure the secular press as a mightier reinforcement of religion and th[e] pulpit, extend widest and highest

Christian Courtesies

to the representatives of journalism. Gi[ve] them easy-chairs and plenty of room when th[ey] come to report occasions. For the most pa[rt] they are gentlemen of education and refin[e]ment, graduates of colleges, with families [to] support by their literary craft, many of the[m] weary with the push of a business that is pr[e]carious and fluctuating, each one of them t[he] avenue of information to thousands of reader[s,] their impression of the services to be the im[pression] adopted by multitudes. They are con[]necting links between a sermon, or a song, or [a] prayer, and this great population that tramp [up] and down the streets day by day and year [by] year with their sorrows uncomforted and the[ir] sins unpardoned. More than eight hundr[ed] thousand people in Brooklyn, and less th[an] seventy-five thousand in churches, so that o[ur] cities are not so much preached to by ministe[rs] of religion as by reporters. Put all journalis[ts] into our prayers and sermons. Of all the hu[n]dred thousand sermons preached to-day, the[re] will not be three preached to journalists, a[nd] probably not one. Of all the prayers offer[ed] for classes of men innumerable, the praye[rs] offered for the most potential class will be [so] few and rare that they will be thought

A Preacher's Idiosyncrasy.

This world will never be brought to God un[til] some revival of religion sweeps over the la[nd] and takes into the kingdom of God editors a[nd] reporters, compositors, pressmen, and newsbo[ys.] And if you have not faith enough to pray f[or] that and toil for that, you had better get out [of] our ranks and join the other side, for you a[re] the unbelievers who make the wheels of t[he] Lord's chariot drag heavily. The great fi[nal] battle between truth and error, the Armage[d]don, I think, will not be fought with swor[ds] and shells and guns,* but with pens—quill pe[ns,] steel pens, gold pens, fountain pens, and, b[e]fore that, the pens must be converted. T[he] most divinely honored weapon of the past h[as] been the pen, and the most divinely honor[ed] weapon of the future will be the pen; prophe[t's] pen and evangelist's pen and apostle's pen, f[ol]lowed by editor's pen and reporter's pen a[nd] author's pen. God save the pen! The wi[ng] of the Apocalyptic angel will be the print[ed] page. The printing-press will roll ahead [of] Christ's chariot to clear the way.

"But," some one might ask, "would you ma[ke]

Sunday Newspapers

also a reinforcement?" I have learned [to] take things as they are. I would like to s[ee] the much-scoffed-at old Puritan Sabbaths co[me] back again. I do not think the modern Su[n]day will turn out any better men and wom[en] than were your grandfathers and grandmoth[ers] under the old-fashioned Sunday. To say no[th]ing of other results, Sunday newspapers a[re] killing editors, reporters, compositors, and pre[ss]men. Every man, woman, and child is entit[led] to twenty-four hours of nothing to do. If t[he] newspapers put on another set of hands, th[at] does not relieve the editorial and reportor[ial] room of its cares and responsibilities. C[ur] literary men die fast enough without killi[ng] them with Sunday work.

All things are possible with God, and my fai[th] is up until nothing in the way of religious v[ic]tory would surprise me. All the newspa[pers and] printing-presses of the earth are going to be t[he] Lord's, and telegraph and telephone and ty[pe] will yet announce nations born in a day.

The First Book Ever Printed

was the Bible by Faust and his son-in-l[aw] Schoeffer in 1460, and that consecration of ty[pe] to the Holy Scriptures was a prophecy of t[he] great mission of printing for the evangelizati[on] of all the nations. The father of the Americ[an] printing-press was a clergyman, Rev. Je[sse] Glover, and that was a prophecy of the religi[ous] use that the gospel ministry in this coun[try] were to make of the types.

*Rev. 16 : 16–21.

Again: we shall secure the secular press as a mightier re-inforcement of religion and the pulpit, by making our religious utterances more interesting and spirited, and then the press will reproduce them. On the way to church some fifteen years ago, a journalist said a thing that has kept me ever since thinking: "Are you going to give us any

Points

to-day?" "What do you mean?" I asked. He said: "I mean by that anything that will be striking enough to be remembered." Then I said to myself: What right have we in our pulpits and Sunday-schools to take the time of people if we have nothing to say that is memorable! David did not have any difficulty in remembering Nathan's thrust: "Thou art the man;" nor Felix in remembering Paul's point-blank utterance on righteousness, temperance, and judgment to come; nor the English king any difficulty in remembering what the court preacher said, when, during the sermon against sin the preacher threw his handkerchief into the king's pew to indicate whom he meant.

The tendency of criticism in the theological seminaries is to file off from our young men all the sharp points and make them too smooth for any kind of execution. What we want, all of us, is more point, less humdrum. If we say the right thing in the right way, the press will be glad to echo and re-echo it. Sabbath-school teachers, reformers, young men and old men in the ministry, what we all want if we are to make the printing-press an ally in Christian work is that which the reporter spoken of suggested—points, sharp points, memorable points. But if the thing be dead when uttered by living voice, it will be a hundred-fold more dead when it is laid out in cold type.

Now, as you all have something to do with the newspaper press, either in issuing a paper or in reading it, either as producers or patrons, either as sellers or purchasers of the printed sheet, I propose on this Sabbath morning, June 17, 1888,

A Treaty to be Signed

between the church and the printing-press, a treaty to be ratified by millions of good people if we rightly fashion it, a treaty promising that we will help each other in our work of trying to illumine and felicitate the world, we by voice, you by pen, we by speaking only that which is worth printing, you by printing only that which is fit to speak. You help us, and we will help you. Side by side be these two potent agencies until the Judgment Day, when *we must both be scrutinized for our work, healthful or blasting*. The two worst off men in that day will be the minister of religion and the editor if they wasted their opportunity. Both of us are the engineer of long express trains of influence, and we will run them into a depot of light or tumble them off the embankments.

What a useful life and what a glorious departure was that of the most famous of all American printers,

Benjamin Franklin,

whom infidels in the penury of their resources have often fraudulently claimed for their own, but the printer who moved that the Philadelphia convention be opened with prayer, the resolution lost because a majority thought prayer unnecessary, and who wrote at the time he was viciously attacked: "My rule is to go straight forward in doing what appears to me to be right, leaving the consequences to Providence," and who wrote this quaint epitaph showing his hope of resurrection, an epitaph that I hundreds of times read while living in Philadelphia:

"The Body of Benjamin Franklin, Printer, like the cover of an old book, its contents torn out, and stript of its lettering and gilding) lies here food for worms. Yet the work itself shall not be lost, for it will (as he believed) appear once more in a new and more beautiful edition, corrected and amended by the Author."

That Providence intends the profession of reporters to have a mighty share in the world's redemption is suggested by the fact that Paul and Christ took a reporter along with them, and he reported their addresses and their acts.

Luke was a Reporter,

and he wrote not only the book of Luke, but the Acts of the Apostles, and without that reporter's work we would have known nothing of the Pentecost, and nothing of Stephen's martydom, and nothing of Tabitha's resurrection, and nothing of the jailing and unjailing of Paul and Silas, and nothing of the shipwreck at Melita. Strike out the reporter's work from the Bible and you kill a large part of the New Testament. It makes me think that in the future of the Kingdom of God, the reporters are to bear a mighty part.

A Reporter at The Tabernacle.

About thirteen years ago a representative of an important newspaper took his seat in this church, one Sabbath night, about five pews from the front of this pulpit. He took out pencil and reporter's pad, resolved to caricature the whole scene. When the music began, he began; and with his pencil he derided that, and then derided the prayer, and then derided the reading of the Scriptures, and then began to deride the sermon. But, he says, for some reason, his hand began to tremble, and he, rallying himself, sharpened his pencil and started again, but broke down again, and then put pencil and paper in his pocket, and, his head down on the front of the pew, and began to pray. At the close of the service he came up and asked for the prayers of others, and gave his heart to God; and, though still engaged in newspaper work, he is an evangelist, and hires a hall at his own expense, and every Sabbath afternoon preaches Jesus Christ to the people.

And the men of that profession are going to come in a body throughout the country. I know hundreds of them, and a more genial or highly educated class of men it would be hard to find, and, though the tendency of their profession may be towards scepticism, an organized, common-sense, gospel invitation would fetch them to the front of all Christian endeavor. Men of the pencil and pen, in all departments, you need the help of the Christian religion. In the day when people want to get their newspapers at three cents, and are hoping for the time when they can get any of them at one cent, and, as a consequence,

The Attaches of the Printing Press

are, by the thousand, ground under the cylinders, you want God to take care of you and your families. Some of your best work is as much unappreciated as was Milton's Paradise Lost, for which the author received twenty-five dollars; and the immortal poem "Hohenlinden" of Thomas Campbell, when he first offered it for publication, and in the column called "Notices to Correspondents," appeared, the words: "To T. C.—The lines commencing 'On Linden when the sun was low,' are not up to our standard. Poetry is not T. C.'s forte."

O men of the pencil and pen, amid your unappreciated work you need encouragement, and you can have it. Printers of all Christendom, editors, reporters, compositors, pressmen, publishers, and readers of that which is printed, resolve that you will not write, set up, edit, issue, or read anything that debases body, mind, or soul. In the name of God, by the laying on of the hands of faith and prayer, ordain the printing-press for righteousness and liberty and salvation. All of us with some influence that will help in the right direction, let us put our hands to the work, imploring God to hasten the consummation. A ship with hundreds of passengers approaching the South American coast, the man on the lookout neglected his work, and in a few minutes the ship would have been dashed to ruin on the rocks. But a cricket on board the vessel, that had made no sound all the voyage, set up a shrill call at the smell of land, and the captain, knowing that habit of the insect, the vessel was stopped in time to avoid an awful wreck. And so, insignificant means now may do wonders, and the scratch of a pen may save the shipwreck of a soul.

Are you all ready for the signing of the contract, the league, the solemn treaty proposed between Journalism and Evangelism? Let it be

A Christian Marriage

of the pulpit and the printing-press. The ordination of the former *on my head*, the pen of the latter *in my hand*, it is appropriate that I publish the banns of such a marriage. Let them from this day be one in the magnificent work of the world's redemption.

"Let thrones and powers and kingdoms be
Obedient, mighty God, to Thee;
And over land and stream and main,
Now wave the sceptre of Thy reign.

"O, let that glorious anthem swell,
Let host to host the triumph tell,
Till not one rebel heart remains,
But over all the Saviour reigns."

THE TEXT AMONG THE FLOWERS.

IN Mr. C. H. Spurgeon's magazine for this month, Captain Meldrum relates the following: "A young man, named Robert Reyner, belonging to Hartlepool, whom I know personally, told me the following story a short time ago, and I am sure I can rely upon its truth, he being a thoroughly sincere Christian, as well as a good worker for God's cause. He was by trade a driller in the iron shipbuilding, which is very hard, laborious work. Having to be in all positions at work, he found his labor to be very trying to his constitution; and it ultimately brought on a dreadful malady in the form of a double rupture. The poor fellow toiled on as long as he could, but at last he had to cease his work. He became worse and worse, and was advised to go to London, to see what could be done for him there. After much prayer, he consented to go to the great city, and went to Guy's Hospital. After having been examined by the principal doctors, he was told that there was nothing for him but to undergo a very dangerous operation.

"The surgeons intimated at the same time that they required his own consent, for the operation would be peculiarly full of risk. They gave him a week's consideration, and at the end of the week he gave his consent that in three days the operation should be performed. With much prayer he committed his case in a child-like manner to his heavenly father, in whom he had strong faith. Then he thought of his dear young wife being left in this hard, unfeeling world, without any earthly friend, and this was a sharp trial to his loving heart. This gave him great trouble for the first two out of the three days of waiting. Sometimes, also, his faith wavered at the prospect of premature death. No wonder, for life had its holy pleasures for him.

"He said to himself that he would never again have the privilege of standing up to preach the glorious gospel of the blessed God. This sudden end of his happy service gave him some trouble of mind. However, the day before the operation, lying on his bed meditating, the Lord sent a message from the throne. A delicate-looking lady came to his bedside with a basket of flowers. She talked with him some little time; and, upon leaving, she presented him with a little bunch of flowers, and in the midst of them he found a tiny card, bearing the somewhat singular text of Scripture—we mean singular to be put to such a use: 'He trusted in God; let Him deliver Him now.' (Matt. 27:43.)

"When he read these words they filled him with holy joy, and he cast himself deliberately upon his God, and cried, 'Come on, you doctors!' The following morning the principal doctor was much surprised to see him so full of joy; and was still more taken aback when he told them that he would not be chloroformed, as he intended going to heaven in his sober senses. In the presence of the four doctors he exclaimed, 'Lord, deliver me now! Nevertheless, Thy will be done.' He bore up under the terrible pain like a true hero, for the Lord sustained him. The operation was skilfully performed, and he recovered, and is still preaching the glorious gospel of the ever-blessed God."

REV. W. F. REQUA AMONG THE INDIANS.

A VERY hopeful letter from Mr. ReQua has come to hand. He has been on an evangelistic journey into the Cherokee nation, and has been much encouraged by the result. There is reason to believe that many souls were converted at the meetings held. A local journal published at Muscogee, Ind. Ter., says: "The meetings at Tahlequah were well attended—sometimes the house was crowded—on one or two occasions some could not find seats. These meetings were among the most spiritual ever held at Tahlequah. Christians were greatly benefited, and some led, as it seemed, to trust the Saviour. Brother ReQua's visit will long be remembered by those who attended the meetings, and listened to his earnest words and inspiring gospel songs. He is expecting to procure a tent and conduct gospel meetings at different places in the Territory during the coming summer. If he succeeds in carrying out his plan, we feel sure that wherever he goes the people will be not only interested, but greatly benefited by the services of this earnest faithful servant of God."

On reaching Fort Gibson he found the intertribal convention assembled, and he was enabled to speak to representatives of five tribes: the Choctaws, Cherokees, Creeks, Chickasaws, and Seminoles. Ex-chief Bushey-head, attended the meetings held by Mr. ReQua, and manifested a deep and serious interest in the gospel message. He came to the preacher for personal conversation, and assured him that if he is enabled to carry out his project of tent-work for the summer he will be warmly welcomed, and hundreds of Indians who have never heard of Christ, will flock to his meetings. Bushey-head was also enthusiastic about the idea of an orphanage for the Indian children, those who have lost their parents being in a deplorable condition. He promised to give it his hearty support and to do anything in his power to promote it.

Mr. ReQua has now *received sixty-eight dollars* toward the tent, and a brother at Eau Claire has promised him a set of harness when he is ready for it. He is confident that God will answer his prayers in this matter. The urgent need of the work among these heathen tribes being so clear, and the blessing that has attended his labors being so manifest, he is assured that in some way God will incline His people to give him the funds still needed. Every dollar brings him nearer to the object of his hope. *His address is Rev. W. F. ReQua, Box 14 McAlister, Indian Territory.*

A DYING GIRL'S MESSAGE.

AN incident connected with one of Rev. E. P. Hammond's meetings has recently come to light. A Christian gentleman, who attended the meeting to speak to the inquirers, devoted all his attention to one girl, who after a long conversation at last perceived the truth, and joyfully made a profession of her faith. The worker, anxious that she should, as it were, nail her colors to the mast, gained her promise to go right home, and tell her parents, who were godless persons, that she had become a Christian, and was resolved with God's help to lead a Christian life. Whether the girl did so, or what was the result, the Christian worker did not hear for many years, as he left the town, and did not return to it until business took him there. It so happened that at the same time evangelistic meetings were again being held there, and it was stated on the bills that he would speak. After the meeting he was asked to speak to a man who had just made a profession of faith. On going to him the man asked if he was really the person whose name was on the bills, and on being answered in the affirmative, asked if he remembered speaking to a girl named Jeanie many years ago at one of Mr. Hammond's meetings. The Christian worker remembered the incident and said so.

"I am Jeanie's father," said the big man with tears in his eyes. "My wife and I were very angry with poor Jeanie when she told us about joining the church, and it was a sore subject for a long while. Jeanie was true and faithful though, and she was a good girl. Not long ago she fell ill, and when she was dying she made me promise to find you, and tell you that she died quite happy, trusting in Jesus. I never heard of you till I saw the bills of these meetings. I hated to come to the meeting, and my wife would not come, but I would not break my promise to poor Jeanie. I came just to give you her message, and while I sat and listened, waiting to speak to you, the Lord laid hold of me, and I have given myself to Him. I'm so happy, and I want you to pray for my wife. Poor Jeanie! I wish she knew."

THE REFORMATION OF A CONVICT.

A REMARKABLE instance of the power of kindness to overcome desperate natures is related in the *Youth's Companion*. It says: One of the most hopeless cases ever brought into the great Moyamensing Prison in Philadelphia was a negress, who was convicted of a crime of violence. She was a huge, fierce animal, who had been born and had lived in the slums of Alaska Street. She was a drunkard and dissolute from childhood.

The chaplain, after she had been under his charge for six months, shook his head hopelessly and passed by her cell without a word.

One day the matron, taking a bunch of soiled scarlet flowers from her hat, threw them to "Deb" carelessly, with a pleasant word or two. The woman started in astonishment, and then thanked her earnestly. The next day the matron saw the flowers, each leaf straightened and smoothed, pinned up on the wall of the cell. Deb, in a gentle voice, called attention to them, praised their beauty, and tried, in her clumsy way, to show the pleasure they had given her.

"That woman," said the matron to the chaplain, "has the rarest of all good qualities. She is grateful. There is one square inch of good ground in which to plant your seed."

The matron herself planted the seed. Every day she showed some little kindness to the poor, untamed creature, who was gradually softened and subdued simply by affection for this, her first friend, whom she followed like a faithful dog.

By and by the matron took her as a helper in the ward, a favor given only to the convicts whose conduct deserved reward. Deb was orderly, quiet, and neat from her sheer gratitude only. The matron's hold upon the woman grew stronger each day. At last she told her the story of the Saviour's sacrifice. Deb listened with wide, eager eyes.

"He died for me—*me!*" she said.

The matron gave up her position, but when Deb was discharged she took her into her house as a servant, trained, taught her, cared for her body and soul, always planting her seeds in that "one square inch of good ground."

Deb became a humble, faithful Christian. "He died for *me*," was the thought which lightened her darkened soul.

THE GROWING WORK IN CHINA.

SOME idea of the work accomplished by the China Inland Mission through faith and prayer, may be gained from a recent statement made by its founder, Rev. J. Hudson Taylor. He said that twenty-two years ago, on May 26, 1866, there were only three Protestant Mission stations, and these were in two provinces. But now stations had been opened in ten provinces. There were now in connection with all Protestant societies 500 more missionaries, not counting their wives, in the country than there were twenty-two years ago. Four thousand souls at least have been gathered into the fold by the agency of the China Inland Mission. The present staff of the China Inland Mission numbered 294, *viz.*, missionaries and their wives, 112; unmarried missionaries, 169; associates, 13. The native helpers—pastors, evangelists, colporteurs, Bible-women, etc.—number 132. Some of the missionaries have gone out at their own expense. The others have all gone out in dependence upon God for temporal supplies, and with the clear understanding that the Mission does not guarantee any income whatever, and knowing that, as the Mission does not go into debt, it can only minister to those connected with it as the funds sent in from time to time may allow. There are now sixty-six organized churches, eighteen schools, three hospitals, five dispensaries, and sixteen opium refuges. The Rev. E. O. Williams, who is about to give himself up to the missionary work in China, and who was lately vicar of a large parish in Leeds, England, said the question was not, Why should I go? but, Why should I *not* go? not, Have I a call to the heathen? but, Have I *a call to stay at home?* Last year Mr. Taylor prayed that he might be enabled to place one hundred more missionaries in the field, and that he might have $50,000 more money for the work. He now announces that 103 missionaries have been sent out, and the income for the year was $168,588, being $55,000 more than the income of the previous year. Mr. C. T. Studd the famous English cricketer, who through Mr. Moody's instrumentality was led to give up all the advantages resulting from a university career and devote himself to missionary work in China, was married on April 7. His wife was Miss Priscilla Stewart, who is also a missionary in China.

A SINGULAR INDIAN RITE.

THE consciousness of inward sin, yet the deplorable ignorance of the only effectual means of cleansing it by the blood of Christ, which cleanseth from all sin, were betrayed in a strange rite recently witnessed by a missionary in India. He saw a young man attempting to cleanse his stomach and intestines by swallowing a piece of cloth about two inches broad and eight yards in length. It is one of their purificatory rites, and great religious merit is attached to it. The Hindus seem to have gone a step further than the Pharisees in this respect. The cloth was, at first, soaked in water, and then, little by little, it was swallowed in a few minutes, and by several spasmodic movements of the stomach and intestines, the washing was effected, and after washing, the cloth was drawn out. The young man who performed this feat has taken to it since the last four months. This rite shows to what extent the Hindoo mind has exerted itself to cleanse itself from the impurities of sin. "I have spoken to him," says the missionary, "and left some Christian books with him to show him the true way of life, and how he may really attain, through Christ, the purity which He requireth who, as the man evidently perceives, 'desires truth in the inward parts.'" (Ps. 51 : 6.)

A DISHONEST CHINAWOMAN'S CONFESSION

A LADY missionary in China—Mrs. Broumton—relates a striking answer to prayer which recently occurred in the mission work. She says: "Mr. Ts'en, the school-teacher and evangelist at Kwei-yang, who is the first-fruits of the work there, has suffered much persecution from his friends and relatives for being a Christian; his wife also has been a great trial to him, through her deceitful and indolent habits, and many prayers have gone up on her behalf, that she might be led to repentance and salvation. Some time ago Mrs. Andrew wrote telling us Mrs. Ts'en was ill; and lately she has written again, and tells us that the disease (dropsy) seems to be on the increase, and has affected Mrs. Ts'en's mind considerably. She behaved very strangely and talked incoherently, saying she had been charged with theft, etc. Mr. and Mrs. Andrew and others often prayed in her room, that the Lord would have mercy on her, and *lead her to repentance*. The following morning, when her husband and Mrs. Andrew were with her, she spoke of having committed thefts at different times. The recital of her misdeeds appeared to relieve her mind somewhat. She confessed to having stolen food, clothing, and money from different persons, and at different times, extending over a period of several years. After several hours Mrs. Andrew called again, and

Mrs. Ts'en a second time enumerated the thefts she had committed. She wished the people whom she had wronged to come, that she might ask their forgiveness. Her husband went to the people and told them what his wife had done, and promised to repay them. His relatives wished him to hush up the matter, but God gave him the grace to do what was right. Mrs. Andrew writes, 'She has been weeping, and praying, and confessing her sin, and in those matters her mind has been quite clear.' At other times she would say, 'Ah, to think of the love of God in giving His Son Jesus to die for me!' She had been exhorting those about her to believe in Jesus; she seems penitent and humble, and Mr. Andrew says: 'She appears to realize to some extent the enormity of her sins against God and man.' She says she could not help but confess. We believe not a few, both at home and in China, who take a prayerful interest in Mr. Ts'en, have been praying also for his wife, and we trust this is but the beginning of the answer."

THE GLORIOUS APPEARING.

By Rev. W. Fuller Gooch, M. A.

Three Distinct Appearings Spoken of—The Third Near at Hand—The Pole Star of Hope—A Personal Appearing—His Glory not yet Revealed—The Veil Lifted on the Mount—The Glorious Kingdom—A Confusion of Terms—A Greater Kingdom than Solomon's—Designed to Comfort—And to Quicken Effort.

AMONG the blessed teachings of grace in reference to the salvation wrought out for us by our Lord, the Apostle Paul, in writing to Titus, places this: "Looking for that blessed hope, the glorious appearing of our great God and Saviour Jesus Christ." (Tit. 2:13.) A consideration of this joyous prospect may serve to quicken our faith and animate our joy.

There are three definite and distinct appearings of our Lord spoken of in Scripture. They are all referred to in the ninth chapter of Hebrews; the first is past, and is set forth in verse 26; then in verse 24 we read, "Christ is not entered into the holy places made with hands, which are the figures of the true, but into heaven itself, now to appear in the presence of God for us." This refers to the present, and points to the position He occupies while absent from earth, hidden from mortal sight within the veil; but in verse 28 we read, "Unto them that look for Him shall He appear the second time without sin unto salvation." It is to this latter, future, and

Nearing Manifestation

our subject, as set forth by Titus, alludes. Christ is gone into heaven only for a time; so soon as this present dispensation of faith has passed away He will again be revealed to sight, in order that the earth, which as yet has only been the scene of His humiliation and suffering, may be the sphere of His glory and complete triumph over all the works of the devil. Hence we read in Acts 3:20, "He shall send Jesus Christ, who before was preached unto you, whom the heavens must receive *until* the times of restitution of all things which God hath spoken by the mouth of all the holy prophets since the world began." There is nothing more sure and certain than the fact that Christ shall come again, and be made manifest as the King of kings and Lord of lords. As surely, and as personally, as He came the first time to suffer and to die shall He come the second time "to reign, and to prosper on the earth."

The second advent is as much a part of God's purpose as the first, and is essential to the completeness of that redemption which He came to obtain. No spiritual influence connected with the gospel dispensation, however widespread or blessed it may be, can answer the great ends of His promised appearing in the glory of His kingly power, nor can anything He does in heaven as the Aaronic Priest within the veil, or as seated on His Father's throne on high, answer to, take the place of, or render needless, His Melchisedek priesthood, as the One who is to be "a Priest upon His throne," in the day when "He shall reign in Mount Zion and in Jerusalem, and before His ancients gloriously."

This glorious appearing of Christ is the great object of Christian hope,

The Pole-Star

which cheers and guides the earnest watchers whose place it is during the night of time to watch for the dawn of the coming day. Grace teaches us that here we are only strangers and sojourners, called to be followers of our Lord in His rejection by the world, and to suffer with Him, treading the same path of self-sacrifice and consecration to the Father's will He so constantly and perfectly pursued. He assures all who faithfully do so that, if they suffer with Him, they shall also reign with Him; sharing His cross, they shall share His crown; thus animating their hearts with hope and inspiring them with courage to do battle with every foe, and to resist steadfastly all that impedes their course. It is well for us, therefore, to have a clear knowledge of the hope set before us in the gospel, and to acquaint our minds with Scripture teaching on a subject so closely allied with our present experience and future prospects as "heirs of God, joint-heirs with Christ."

Let us consider this appearing in reference to the glory of Christ, which shall then be revealed. The Revised Version, instead of "the glorious appearing," reads, "the appearing of the glory of our great God and Saviour, Jesus Christ." Hitherto the world has only beheld His humiliation. "He was in the world, and the world was made by Him, and the world knew Him not." Once, for a brief space,

The Veil was Withdrawn,

and to the favored three, Peter, James, and John, a glimpse was given of His glory; they were allowed to be "eyewitnesses of His majesty, when they were with Him in the holy mount," so that they were enabled to make known with certainty "the power and coming of our Lord Jesus Christ." But full soon the splendid vision passed away, and gave place to revelations of the sufferings and death their Lord was to undergo at Jerusalem. After His resurrection no eyes saw Him but those of disciples and chosen witnesses. He appeared at intervals to those who knew and loved Him, by many infallible proofs assuring them that He had risen, and then ascended to heaven without making any sign or manifestation of His kingly glory or power. The men of Galilee who watched His ascension were comforted as He vanished from their sight by the promise that, "This same Jesus shall so come in like manner as ye have seen Him go into heaven," and went their way to learn that the glory which He was to have in accordance with the predictions of the Old Testament was to follow (not precede) this present dispensation of faith during which their Lord would be hidden from view, remaining absent from the earth until the time should come for His glory to be revealed.

Then too shall the glory of His kingdom be revealed.

The Kingdom and the Church

have often been confounded, one with the other, as though they were one and the same, but Scripture does not so speak of them. The prophets of the Old Testament continually set before us a far different state of things, under the reign of Christ, to that which obtains in connection with the Church. The era of Solomon is typical of a time far brighter than any that has been known upon earth, or than can be known while "the King of Glory" is absent. Psalm 72, brings before us a King and a kingdom of which Solomon's palmiest days were but a shadow and figure. Israel shall under His sway be no longer scattered and peeled, but regathered, restored to Divine favor, and made a blessing and a praise in all the earth.

In that day He who is now rejected and disowned by the vast majority in every land shall be universally adored, and His "name be set up for an ensign of the people; to it shall the Gentiles seek, and His rest shall be glorious." It is for this we are taught to pray, saying, "Thy kingdom come, Thy will be done on earth, as it is in heaven." Glory beyond compare shall then be seen upon the Son of Man, the ruler whose coming shall be bright "as the light of the morning when the sun riseth, a morning without clouds, as the tender grass springing out of the earth by clear shining after rain." Then shall all that God has decreed for men in connection with the work of Christ be accomplished, and His solemn oath be performed, "As truly as I live, all the earth shall be filled with the glory of the Lord."

But we must turn from this part of our subject to consider what is the attitude grace teaches us to maintain in reference to this bright appearing of our Lord. It is to be cherished by us as a blessed hope. Hope is one of the three chiefest of the Christian graces, and is as important to the completeness of the Christian character as faith or love. It is

Designed to Comfort

and soothe in the midst of sorrow and trial ever incident to mortal life. Its province is to soar beyond things seen and temporal, and to rejoice in the things not seen and eternal. It animates the heart and nerves the soul for conflict and endurance, and by its ever-increasing confidence and assurance, begotten of experience, it enables the believer to sing and triumph even though the clouds be dark and all surroundings adverse. The object of our hope is clearly defined to be one and distinct in its nature, "We are called in one hope of our calling," so that there need be no mistake as to what it is we are to be yearning after and aspiring to. The teaching of our text is uniform with that of the New Testament throughout. The appearing of the Lord, His return in glory and in power to reign as King of kings, and Lord of lords, is the one sure and blessed end and consummation to which we are to look forward. Not death, or its results to the unclothed spirit, not heaven in the technical sense of the word, but Christ Himself; perfect salvation is only attained when He appears.

We are to be *looking* for this blessed hope. The words are significant and suggestive. They denote *eager desire*. We do not look for that for which we have but little concern, or on which we set little value. Well may we long for the appearing of our Lord; all that is brightest and best in our calling and destiny as believers depends upon it, is attained when it takes place.

One of the Truest Tests

of our regard for the Saviour is found in this, if our hearts are full of faith in Him, and of joy in His service, we shall "love His appearing," the period of His absence will be to us a season of earnest longing for His return; while if we are, on the other hand, taken up with the world, and living to ourselves, we shall have little desire for His coming, being consciously unready to meet Him. Diligent preparation is also involved in looking for His return. What manner of persons ought those to be who expect His speedy approach? The only fitting reply is found in the words of II. Peter, 3:14. "Wherefore, beloved, seeing ye look for such things, be diligent, that ye may be found of Him in peace, without spot and blameless." This "blessed hope" is intended to exert a holy influence upon our hearts and lives, kindling a flame of sacred devotion, and arousing to zeal and fidelity in every sphere of life. It is impossible to cherish it and be careless, worldly, and half-hearted, for "every man that hath this hope in Him purifieth himself, even as He is pure." May the Holy Spirit so reveal Christ in us, "the hope of glory," that under its blissful inspiration we may indeed "live soberly, righteously, and godly in this present world."

PUBLISHER'S NOTICE.

The whole edition of The Christian Herald was mailed last week to subscribers during Tuesday, June 5. The last delivery at the New York Post Office was made at 11.45 P. M.

CURRENT EVENTS.

Four Large Ships are to be Added to the Navy if the Naval Appropriation Bill prepared by the House Committee is adopted by Congress. The bill makes an appropriation of $6,000,000, of which $4,000,000 are for construction and $2,000,000 for armament. Strong efforts have been made to induce the committee to provide for a lot of small vessels, which could be quickly built and would afford more places for commanding officers, but these efforts have not been successful. The bill authorizes the construction of four ships: two unarmored cruisers, each to have a guaranteed speed of nineteen knots, one unarmored cruiser with a guaranteed speed of twenty knots, and one armored ship of about 7,500 tons, with no guarantee of speed, but planned to make not less than seventeen knots. One of the four must be built in a navy-yard, and all may be built in such yards if the President is satisfied that none of the bids made by contractors is reasonable. The six ships in process of construction are expected to be ready for service before the end of this year. Four of these are double turreted monitors.

International Arbitration was Indorsed by the Senate on Thursday last, by the adoption of a concurrent resolution reported by Mr. Sherman, requesting the President, from time to time, as fit occasions may arise, to invite negotiations with foreign Governments, "to the end" that any disputes that cannot be adjusted by diplomatic agency, may be referred to arbitration, and be peaceably adjusted by such means. Ths resolution, however, was taken up for reconsideration, when Mr. Riddleberger pointed out that probably the first use to which it would be put by the Government would be the settlement of the Fisheries dispute.

The Fisheries Treaty Occupied the Attention of the Senate on two days last week. On Monday, Senator Gray, of Delaware, made an eloquent speech in its defence. He contended that the only ground there could be for objecting to the treaty was based on the theory that the bays of Canada, Nova Scotia, and Newfoundland, which were more than six miles wide, were not territorial waters. That theory the United States could not afford to lay down on account of the valuable fisheries of Behring Sea. Discussing each clause of the treaty, he argued that it gave to American fishermen the right to enter Canadian ports on all occasions to purchase all the supplies ordinarily asked for trading vessels, the only exception being supplies distinctively peculiar to fishing vessels, and asked whether it was not the part of statesmanship to secure impartial privileges by the ratification of the treaty. The treaty secured every right of American fishermen and left the tariff on fish where it ought to be left—as a subject to be dealt with by the legislative branch of the Government. On Wednesday, Senator Hale, of Maine, made a strong speech against ratification. He said that the American fishermen were opposed to the treaty to a man. He also insisted that it was a device on the part of Great Britain to get Canadian fish admitted free. Further consideration was postponed until June 25. As matters now stand, the probabilities are that the treaty will not be ratified.

The Progress Made in the Preparations for cutting the Nicaragua Canal, encourages the hope that this gigantic enterprise will be completed at no distant day. Four of the surveyors who have been at work on the route, returned to New York on June 14. They were last on the western division of the canal, to which they were transferred a few weeks ago, after completing their work on the San Juan River. The entire expedition enjoyed excellent health, and all were happy over the successful results of their work. The hydrographic party completed the off-shore soundings at Brito, and the work in the lake, at the mouth of the Rio Lajos, and went to the San Juan about the middle of May. After a few days' work at Don Carlos, the party were to proceed to Greytown, to finish the survey of the harbor. Of the two large parties to which the four surveyors belonged, there was not one man sick during the three months they were on the ground. This is a remarkable fact, proving conclusively the superiority of the Nicaragua over the Panama route.

The New Governor-General of Canada, Lord Stanley of Preston, took the oath of office at Ottawa, on June 11. The ceremony took place in the Senate chamber, in the presence of a brilliant and distinguished assemblage. In reply to the civic address of welcome, Lord Stanley returned hearty thanks for the kindly welcome that had been accorded him on his first coming to reside among them as Her Majesty's representative. Although only in Canada a few hours, he thought he could already say that he experienced, even before his arrival, that hospitality, kindness, and cordiality which made the name of the Dominion proverbial. In regard to the question of federal union in Australia, no one who had ever been connected with important interests of great colonies could fail to perceive the advantage of that movement when it proceeds spontaneously and when the feeling that dictated it was genuine.

A New Expedition for the Exploration of the Ruins of Babylon and other Old Testament cities is to sail on June 23, from New York. It is under the auspices of the University of Pennsylvania. The expenses of the expedition will be defrayed by Mr. George W. Childs, Messrs. Clark, the bankers, and other prominent citizens of Philadelphia. Professor Peters, Ph. D., Dr. R. F. Harper, of Yale, and Mr. J. D. Prince, of Columbia College, are to be among the explorers. In an interview with a reporter, Dr. Peters said: "The field is full of ruins of the most ancient cities of the world, only one or two of which have ever been explored, and those only in the very least degree. We know the names of fifty or sixty cities which existed there—cities of importance—and the sites of not one dozen of these have been determined. It will give some idea of how little work has been done when the sites of these cities have been left undetermined. The actual site of digging cannot be definitely stated before departure. It depends primarily upon the permission granted by the Turkish authorities, and, secondarily, upon information to be obtained on the spot. The region in which these ancient cities lie is comprised between the rivers Tigris and Euphrates." The expedition is to follow the preliminary work performed by the Wolfe expedition of 1885, the cost of which was defrayed by the late Miss Catherine Wolfe, of New York.

The Melancholy Intelligence of the Death of the Emperor of Germany on Friday last has caused world-wide regret. The cheering reports of his condition, recently published, encouraged the hope that his valuable and useful life would be prolonged, even if his complete recovery was impossible. The wise and liberal principles which have marked his brief reign, and his evident desire to enlarge the constitutional liberties of the people, were so acceptable to th masses in Germany that, apart from the person love and sympathy with which he inspired them they ardently hoped that he might be spare for a few years. Other European nations, too recognizing the immense interests that hun upon his life, and how enormously the dange of war would be increased by his giving place t the fiery young man who is his son and succe sor, were no less anxious than the Germa people for him to live. God in His wisdom however, decided otherwise, and the Emper bowed in resignation to His will. On Thur day, when he was no longer able to speak h wrote upon a pad: "I have tried my best to d my duty to my God and to my country. I fe that the end is now near. God's will be done. It would appear that the fear expressed by D Mackenzie a month ago, and published in thes columns on May 31, that the corrosive sore i the Emperor's throat might eat inward and pro duce fatal results, was realized. The wall an cartilages between the gullet and the windpip were on June 12, found to be impaired, and pa ticles of food consequently passed into the a passages. The physicians then abandone hope, and informed the family that death wa near at hand. The patient was kept alive b food artificially administered until Friday, whe he succumbed to the dreadful disease, and abou 11 A. M. he peacefully passed away. He was i his fifty-seventh year.

The Austrian Government Proposes to Rai the sum of eight millions dollars for extraord nary military and naval expenditure for the cu rent year, in addition to the ordinary outla There is a curious preamble to the appropri tion bill, in which these expenses are propose It states that, though all the European cabine are united in desiring peace, circumstances, ne ertheless, indicate that an increase in Austri Hungary's defences is the surest safeguard o peace. Remarks of the same tenor were mad by the Emperor Francis Joseph, in receiving th Delegations. He said he was satisfied with th amicable relations existing between Austria an the powers. The great military credits demand ed did not mean that trouble was impendin They were asked because other States had aug mented their forces. He declared that he ea nestly desired peace. Genial and pacificator as these statements were, they did not impres Russia to any great extent, though they wer probably uttered mainly for the benefit of th country. A prominent Russian journal som what cynically observes, in commenting upo them, that if Austria's intentions were tho oughly pacific, it would rest with her to init ate a settlement of the Bulgarian question.

The Panic in England Produced by the A sertion of eminent military authorities that would be quite practicable for an enemy to in vade the country, gains increased force fro disclosures now being made of official corru tion. The London correspondent of the Ne York *Herald*, who is a Member of Parliamen states that the public as yet do not know on half of the disgraceful details. The Duke o Cambridge complains that the army is no strong enough, and Lord Charles Beresford wh is in the navy, declares that the navy is ineff cient, but independent Members of Parliamen contend that the hundred and fifty million do lars a year now spent on those two departmen is ample to make them all that they should b if the money were economically spent. Th charge is made that the Queen's relatives hold ing offices in the army and navy absorb larg sums annually without adding to the efficienc of the service, that contracts are not honestl awarded, and that wholesale corruption exist Bayonets of tin, ships imperfectly armored guns that burst, and shells that will not burn are supplied by contractors who, having to pa bribes, try to come out with a profit by furnish ing material of the cheapest and poorest kin Meanwhile Lord Salisbury's government rid cules the agitation, and insists that the pan has been excited for political purposes.

Contributions to the Fund for Supplying Colored ministers in the South with this journal have been received since our last acknowledgement to the amount of $36. They are from: Montreal, Can., $5; Orange, Mass., $1; Bethel, Me., $5; "Adventist," Cambridgeport, Mass., $25. Our friends will be glad to learn that letters are being sent from some of the ministers who have received the paper through their kindness, speaking in terms of warm gratitude of the help they derive from its pages, and saying that God is blessing their labors now more abundantly than even before.

The Mother of the Rev. C. H. Spurgeon Died at Croydon, on May 23, at the age of seventy-three. An English journal says: "It is impossible to tell how much of the blessing that has rested upon the ministry of her sons is to be attributed to the training they received at their mother's knee. We have heard that, on one occasion, as her husband, the Rev. John Spurgeon, was on his way to fulfil a preaching engagement, it suddenly occurred to him that possibly he was neglecting his own family while going away from home to do the Lord's work. Returning to the house, and seeing no one about, he went up-stairs, and, listening outside the bedroom door, he heard his wife pleading with and for their children. He came down without disturbing her, feeling that he could safely leave his family with such a mother." She was a Congregationalist.

The Great International Missionary Conference in London opened on June 9 and was in session throughout last week. Each day has been devoted to a separate field of foreign missions. When the work in Africa was under consideration, Gen. Fisk, who presided, urged the necessity of opposing the liquor traffic in that country, and of inculcating higher standards of morality in commercial dealings. He said that nothing was so calculated to prejudice the natives and retard the work of the missions as fraudulent commercial transactions. The recent remarkable revival of Islamism was anxiously considered by the Conference on June 11. Mr. Schrieber, of Berlin, said that throughout the Dutch possessions in the East, Moslem schools had been established to oppose Christian missions. Dr. Post, who is one of the American delegates, spoke of the destructive social and political influence of Islamism in perverting individual morality and crushing the life out of the people. He also referred in strong terms to the success of medical mission work in Syria. He said the benefits derived by the people from the medical treatment by the missionaries greatly helped in gaining their attention to the gospel. The Lord Mayor of London has shown civic hospitality to the delegates by entertaining them at a sumptuous luncheon at his official residence.

Six Weeks on a Coral Reef were Spent by a shipwrecked crew and passengers recently. The oceanic steamer Mariposa, which arrived at San Francisco on June 9, rescued a number of shipwrecked people whom she picked up from Palmyria Island, a coral reef, north of Samoa. They belonged to the British bark Henry James, which had been wrecked on April 16, while on a voyage from New South Wales to San Francisco. The Henry James struck on a reef, and the captain, finding the vessel sinking, got his people into the boats. After a perilous voyage of twelve hours they reached Palmyria, where they found some abandoned huts, but no inhabitants. They had but little provision with them, and it was, at first, feared they would starve to death. Among the passengers were several women and children, who were likely to suffer severely from hardship and exposure. Happily, however, an exploration of the island led to the discovery of good water. Cocoanuts, also, were found in abundance, and these, with birds, land crabs, and peppergrass, formed their diet. Six long weeks of weary waiting were passed, and they had begun to despair, when, on May 29, to their great delight, the Mariposa came in sight, took them all on board and carried them safely to Honolulu. Had any of those castaways neglected to go on board the Mariposa when it came to their rescue, they would have been thought crazy; yet when men, shipwrecked of sin—moral castaways, in imminent danger of perishing, are invited on board the gospel ship and offered eternal salvation, comparatively few accept it. (Heb. 2: 3.)

An Aristocratic Young Shoeblack is Pursuing his occupation in Newark, N. J. A reporter in that town noticed recently a lad of sixteen, who, with two colored boys under his leadership, has set up a shoeblacking establishment in a shanty on one of the Newark streets. The boy's manner and educated talk led the reporter to believe that there was some mystery about him, and, on questioning the boy, he heard a strange story. The lad asserted that he was the son of a well-known political leader, who is at present Lieutenant-Governor of a Western State. The father wanted to send him to college, but the boy, who hated books, and was of a restless, roving disposition, shrank from that arrangement. Finally, being unable to change his father's mind, he ran away from home. He beat his way to Portland, Ore., and from there went to Omaha, where he got a blacking outfit. Since then, he says, he has made a living by blacking boots, and has been in Memphis, New Orleans, Atlanta, and all the larger Southern and Western cities, and in New York, Philadelphia, Brooklyn, and Newark. Several times, he says, some of his father's friends have recognized him, and urged him to go home, but he is not ready to do so yet, because he thinks he has not yet seen enough of the world. The undutiful youngster has had many hardships, but they have not subdued his rebellious spirit. He is like those older wanderers with whom the voice of mercy pleads to return and be reconciled to their Heavenly Father, but who prefer the ways of the world, with its sins and miseries, to the delights of their Father's house. (Jer. 18: 11, 12.)

A Neglected Corpse Lay in the Grand Central depot, New York, nearly the whole of last week. It came from Pittsfield, Mass., in a common stained coffin on Monday night and was placed in the baggage room. No one came to claim it until Thursday, when a man called and said it was the body of his wife, and he was going to send it on to Philadelphia when he had obtained the necessary permit. He removed the address label from the box in which the coffin came, and also took away the trunk that accompanied the corpse. He did not return, however, and at length the Board of Health was notified and the corpse was sent to the Morgue. A clue to its identity was discovered there, and word was sent to Pittsfield. This brought some relatives of the deceased woman to New York, who took charge of the body and sent it on to Philadelphia to be interred in the family lot in the cemetery there. They said that they had furnished the money for embalming and burying the body, and had placed it in charge of the husband, whose neglect was probably due to his dissipated habits. His apparent indifference and negligence must have been painful to the friends, but, happily, his wife, who could she have known of it must have been sorely pained, was beyond reach of that affliction. It may be hoped that she had given her soul into Christ's keeping and if so, that being safe, the disrespect shown to her body would be a matter of no concern to her. (II Tim. 1: 12).

Two Lovers Were Unexpectedly Reunited in a hospital in Quebec recently. A despatch from Chicago to the New York *Tribune* states that in a suburb of that city a newly married couple have come to live whose history is a romance. The husband is the son of an Episcopal rector in Yorkshire, England, and he for a time was curate of the parish. Adjoining his home a landed proprietor, one Molineux, of French descent, lived. He was a Catholic. The young clergyman fell in love with Mr. Molineux's daughter and proposed for her hand, but the father drove him from the premises. The daughter was sent away where he could not find her. The young curate, heart-broken, gave up his work and came to America, obtaining a situation as book-keeper in a New York wholesale house. He was made travelling salesman. One day, while in Quebec, he was run down by a heavy omnibus, picked up and conveyed to a hospital. During his sickness, as much to his surprise as to his delight, he discovered that one of the Sisters of Charity in the hospital was none other than the girl he had loved in Yorkshire. Miss Molineux's parents had sent her to a convent in France, and from there she was transferred with other French nuns to Quebec. He renewed his suit, and she joyfully consented to marry him. As soon as he recovered, the marriage took place, and they have settled near Chicago. Thus the prize for which the young man longed came to him through misfortune. Had he not been run over by the omnibus he might never have found his bride. The man who has faith in God's providence ought never to count anything that happens to him an evil. God designs every event to be the means of good to His children. (Rom. 8: 28.)

BRIEF NOTES.

The Rev. C. H. Yatman, who has recovered from his long sickness, expects to commence daily meetings for young people at Ocean Grove, on July 1.

At the anniversary of the Upper Canada Bible Society the Rev. John Hall, D. D., was the chief attraction. The services were held in the Metropolitan Church, Toronto.

The Rev. Jackson Wray, London, England, has sent a cablegram to the congregation of Zion Church, Toronto, declining the call which was so cordially presented to him to become their pastor.

Rev. James Freeman Clarke, died on June 8, at his residence in Jamaica Plain, Boston. Dr. Clarke was critically ill about a year ago, but he partially recovered his health and resumed a part of his work.

Letters of inquiry in reference to Mr. Moody's Bible School for Y. M. C. A. members and associates, to be held at Northfield, June 30–July 15, should be addressed to C. K. Ober, 52 East Twenty-third Street, New York.

The centennial of colored Baptists of Georgia began in Savannah on June 6, and continued two weeks. Five thousand negro Baptists were present. At the opening of the celebration over 300 preachers were in attendance.

A Prohibition meeting to ratify the nomination of General Clinton B. Fisk and Rev. John A. Brooks for President and Vice-President, will be held in the Metropolitan Opera House, New York, on June 22, at 8 P. M.

Mr. R. T. Booth has arrived at Sydney in excellent health, having completed his tour round the world. Speaking of his visit to England, he said he was surprised at the stability of his former work, especially at Sheffield and Newcastle.

Mr. Charles Cook reports that the past month's services in Hyde Park, London, have been crowned with much blessing, scores of persons having professed to have received Christ. His work at Dorking and in Ireland has also been very cheering.

A double wedding in the Garfield family took place at Mentor, June 14. Miss Mollie Garfield, only daughter of the late President, was married to her father's Secretary J. Stanley Brown. Harry Garfield, the eldest son, was married to Miss Belle Mason, of Cleveland, O.

An American lady in Russia writes regarding the persecution of Lutherans in the Baltic provinces, as follows: "Between sixty and seventy Lutheran clergymen have been arrested, and a part of this number have already received sentence of banishment to Siberia, while others are held to bail awaiting trial."

The Protestant Episcopal Diocese of Delaware has chosen for its bishop in succession to the late Rev. Alfred Lee, the Rev. Leighton Coleman, S. T. D., Rector of the Church of the Redeemer, Sayre, Penn. The Diocese of Fond Du Lac has elected the Rev. George McClellan Fiske, of Providence, R. I., its bishop, to succeed the late Bishop Brown.

The arrangements for the National Convention of Christian Endeavor Societies, to be held in Chicago, July 5–8, are now completed. Among the speakers announced are Rev. James H. Brookes, D. D., of St. Louis, Mo., Professor, W. R. Harper, Mrs. G. R. Alden ("Pansy") and Miss Frances E. Willard. For further particulars, address U. S. C. E. 50 Bromfield St., Boston, Mass.

A MESSAGE TO SLAVES.

A New Sermon By Pastor C. H. Spurgeon.

"And Moses spake so unto the children of Israel: but they hearkened not unto Moses for anguish of spirit, and for cruel bondage." Ex. 6 : 9.

The Importance of a Monosyllable—The Responsibility of a Messenger—The Message Moses Delivered—I. Salvation from Bondage—Spoke of God—Of the Covenant—Of God's Pity—Of His Coming Deliverance—II. The Message Rejected—Disappointment at First—Discomfort of Rebuilding a House—Poverty and Misery Producing Spiritual Indifference—John Newton's Wonderful Transformation—III. The Rejected Message True—A Notice in a Shop Window.

LITTLE words often contain great meanings. It is often the case with that monosyllable "*so*." In the present instance we must lay stress upon it and read the text thus, "Moses spake *so* unto the children of Israel." That is, he said what God told him to say. He did not invent his message. He did not think out the gospel that he had to carry to the people. He was simply a repeater of the divine message. As he received it, *so* he spake it. "Moses spake *so* unto the children of Israel." If he had not done *so*, the responsibility must have rested upon himself, whether the nation was moved by his words or not; but when he was

Simply God's Ambassador,

saying only what God would have him say, his responsibility was limited. If he delivered the Lord's own word and it failed to win the heart of Israel, he could not be blamed. Although it was a great sadness of heart to him that the people did not, and even could not, receive the divine message, yet as far as he was concerned, his conscience was clear. It is ever so with the preacher of the gospel: if he declares the word of the Lord as he has received it, whether men will hear or whether they will forbear, he is clear before God, whatever his hearers may do or may not do.

When a man-servant goes to the door with a message from his master, if you do not like what he tells you, do not be angry with him. What has he to do with it? Has he said what his master told him to say? If he has, then be angry with his master if you must be, or accept what his master says if you think fit; but let the poor man that brought the message be held clear if he has faithfully reported his master's words. I claim that if I have preached my Master's gospel, whether men are saved or lost, whether they accept it or reject it, I must leave that with themselves, and not have their sin laid at my door. How heartily do I cry to God that the Word may not be a savour of death unto death, but a savour of life unto life; but oh, my hearers, if you perish after hearing the gospel of God, do not think that you can cast the blame on me.

Now, the message Moses brought was rejected, and he knew

Why it Was Rejected.

He could see the reason. The people were in such bondage, they were so miserably ground down, they were so unhappy and hopeless, that what he spake seemed to them to be as idle words. There are hundreds of reasons why men reject the gospel. We will not go into them now. Oh that men were less cunning in making apologies for refusing the Lord Jesus!

Amongst all the reasons, however, that I ever heard, that with which I have the most sympathy, is this one—that some cannot receive Christ because they are so full of anguish, and are so crushed in spirit, that they cannot find strength enough of mind to entertain a hope that by any possibility salvation can come to them. It is to their sad case that I desire to speak. I think that I can speak to the case, if God help me, for I have felt the same. I do remember when I could not believe even Jesus Himself by reason of sore anguish and straitness of spirit; and, therefore, as one who has worn the chains, I speak to those who are still in chains. I know the clanking of those fetters, and what it is to feel the damp of the stone walls, and to fear that there is no coming out of prison, and to be so despairing that even when the emancipator turned the great key in the lock, and set the door wide open, yet still my heart had made for itself a direr cage, and I could not believe in the possibility of liberty, and therefore I sat bound in a dungeon of my own creation. Ah! there is no Bastille so awful as that which is built by despair, and kept under the custody of a crushed spirit. Many are the desponding ones whose eyes fail so that they cannot look up, or look out. To such I speak.

I. And first, will you notice that what Moses brought to these people was glad tidings. It was a free and full gospel message. To them it was the gospel of

Salvation from a Cruel Bondage,

the gospel of hope, the gospel of glorious promise. It is a very admirable type and metaphorical description of what the gospel is to us. Moses' word to them was singularly clear, cheering, and comforting; but they could not receive it. "They hearkened not unto Moses for anguish of spirit and cruel bondage."

First, Moses spoke to them about their God. He said, "You have a God, and His name is Jehovah, the God of your fathers, the God of Abraham, of Isaac, and of Jacob." They looked up from their bricks, and they seemed to say, "God? What have we to do with Him? Oh, that the straw were given us to make our bricks! we are up to our necks in this filthy Nile mud making the bricks, and you come and talk to us about God. Go, and preach to Pharaoh and the taskmasters that rule us; but as for us poor creatures slaves that we are, we do not understand you. What do you mean by JAH, Jehovah, our God? Bring us more garlic and onions, or lessen our daily tasks, or take away the sticks from our drivers, and then we will listen to you." And so they shook their heads, and said that such mysteries and theologies were not for them.

What a poor reason for refusing light because the night is so dark! Man's best hope lies in His God. O you whose lives are bitter with toil and want, there is something for you after all, much better than the hard saying, "What shall we eat, and what shall we drink?" There is an inheritance above

The Grinding Toil

of every-day life. There is a portion much better than this killing care which frets so many of you, and makes life a calamity to you. Do not, therefore, because of the heaviness of your lot, refuse to hear about God, your Maker, your Benefactor. In that direction lies your only real hope. Have this God for a father and a friend, and life will wear another aspect, and you will be another man.

So Moses went on to speak yet more about God's pity to them. He reported that Jehovah had said, "I have also heard the groaning of the children of Israel whom the Egyptians keep in bondage, and I have remembered My covenant." I fancy that those words opened their eyes a little. They looked up and said to one another, "Is there, indeed a God who has heard our groanings? Oh, but," they muttered, "look at the many years we have been groaning. Why, it is forty years since this man Moses first came out and saw our burdens! What is the use of pity that is so

Tardy in its Movements?"

And yet, dear sirs, if you are inclined to talk so, it may be that if God be slow He is sure; and if He be slow to you, it is out of patience and long-suffering to others. He knows best when and how to save His people. Remember that when the tale of bricks was doubled then Moses came; and when you are getting to your very worst, and your night is darkening into a sort of hellish midnight, it may be that your darkness is coming to an end.

And then Moses went on further with his blessed gospel message to tell them about the Lord's resolve to rescue them by a great redemption. The Lord had said, "I am Jehovah, and I will bring you out from under the burdens of the Egyptians, and I will rid you out of their bondage." Do you notice that all along the Lord uses strong words, and speaks like a great king? "I am Jehovah. I will. I will. I will." When you go home, just notice what a number of "I wills" there are in this declaration of the great God. When God says, "I will," he means it; depend upon it. God means to save you. Poor, troubled, confessedly guilty sinner, believe in Jesus Christ the Son of God, and trust yourself with Him, and the Lord will save you.

He Will Deliver You

from all the guilt of your past life, the evil habits of your present life, and from the temptations of your future life.

Moses told them about the Lord's ways of grace and the inheritance which He had prepared for them. My message is after the same sort. God will take you, poor guilty ones, to be His children. He will promote you to be His willing servants. He will use you for His glory though now you dishonor His name. He will sanctify you and cleanse you, and He will bring you to heaven, even you who have lien among the pots and have been defiled in the brick-kilns of sin. He will never rest till He makes you sit upon his throne with Him, where He is glorified, world without end. This I speak to you who are in bondage. Believe you in Christ Jesus, and He who has come to save the lost will give you as clear and clean a deliverance from the power of sin as Jehovah gave Israel deliverance from the power of the Egyptian tyrant. He will bring you out of bondage and guide you through the wilderness till you come into the rest, even to a goodlier land than Canaan, though it flowed with milk and honey.

II. We come now to note, that it was

Received With Unbelief

caused by anguish of heart. The message was from the Lord, and it was full of hope for them, but they were too much broken down to receive it. We can quite understand what that meant. Let us look into the case. They could not now receive this gospel because *they had at first caught at it, and had been disappointed.* They were under a misapprehension, for they expected to be free at once, as soon as Moses went to Pharaoh; and as they did not get immediate relief, they fell back into sullen despair. When Moses came to them and said that God had appeared to him at the bush, and had sent him to deliver them, they bowed their heads, and worshipped. Great things they looked for on the morrow, for they were at the end of their patience; but after that when Moses went in unto Pharaoh, and the tyrant doubled their labor by denying them straw, then they could not believe in God or in his messenger. The man who judges with shortness and straitness of judgment, demands a remedy that will cure his soul of all evils on the spot, and if it does not evidently and immediately do this, he cries, "Away with it!"

Grace may truly and effectually come to a heart, and for a while cause no joy, no peace; but the reverse. I have known many a man coming to this Tabernacle, who has been prospering in business, and so on, and yet he has been going down to hell as fast as ever he could travel. Well, he has come and heard the gospel and he has made a great many improvements in his conduct, and has become a regular and attentive hearer; and at that very time he has fallen into an affliction the like of which he had never experienced before; and he has consequently complained, "Why, I am

Worse Instead of Better.

I find my heart grows more rebellious against God than ever it was before." I do not wonder that it should be so, for I have seen so many examples of it. The discipline of the household of God begins very early. But a present increase of sorrow has nothing to do with what the main result will be, except that it works towards it in a mysterious manner. Perhaps what you at first thought was genuine faith, was not faith and God is going to knock down the false before He builds up the true.

If you had an old house, and any friend of yours were to say, "John, I will build you a new house. When shall I begin?" "Oh!" you might say, "begin next week to build the new house." At the end of the week he has pulled half your old house down "Oh," say you, "this is what you call building me a new house, is it? You are causing me great loss, I wish I had never consented to your proposal." He replies, "You are most unreasonable: how am I to build you a new house on this spot without taking the old one down?" And so it often happens that the grace of God does seem in its first work to make a man even worse than he was before, because it discovers to him sins which he did not know to be there, evils which had been concealed, dangers never dreamed of. Thus the work of grace even makes his bondage seem to be heavier than ever it was; and yet this is all done in wisdom, in love, and in fulfillment of the promise which God has given. The work of deliverance began very grimly, but it ended very gloriously.

The inability of Israel to believe the message of Moses arose also from the fact that

They were Earthbound

by heavy oppression: the mere struggle to exist exhausted all their energy, and destroyed all their hope. The extreme hardness of their lot made them despondent and sullen. I do not wonder that a great many are unable to receive the gospel in this city of ours, because their struggle for existence is awful. I am afraid that it gets more and more intense, though even now it passes all bounds. If any of you can do anything to help the toil-worn workers, I pray you do it. The poor workwoman, who sits so many hours with the candle and needle, and does not earn enough, when she has worked all those hours, to more than just pay the rent and keep body and soul together, do you wonder that she thinks that this gospel of ours cannot be for her, and does not care to listen to it? I know that it would be her comfort, but her soul refuseth to be comforted, she is so crushed. The dock laborer, who comes home five days out of the six having earned nothing, and hears his little children crying for bread—is it any wonder that he cannot hear about heavenly things?

It is all very easy to say that it ought not to be so; but it is so; and it is so with multitudes in London. And yet, dear friend—if such a one has come in here to-night—I pray you do not throw away the next world because you have so little of this. This is sheer folly. If I have little here, I would make sure of the more hereafter. If you have such a struggle for existence here, you should seek that higher, nobler, better life, which would give you, even in penury and want, a joy and a comfort to which you are a stranger now. May the Holy Ghost come upon you, and raise you out of this present evil world to newness of life in Christ Jesus!

But worst of all, there are some who seem as if they could not lay hold on Christ because their sense of sin has become so intolerable, and the wretchedness which follows upon conviction has become so fearful, that they have sunk down almost to be contentedly despairing. I hardly know any condition of mind that is worse than

Chronic Despair,

when, at last, that which seemed alarming enough to drive to madness settles down into a hopeless, sullen moroseness. These Israelites had at last sunk so low that they said, "Let us alone, that we may serve the Egyptians." Oh, it is a dreadful thing when a heart gets to that, when a man desires that Christ would depart from him, and let him alone to perish. Do not some men virtually say, "I know I am lost. Let me enjoy myself as well as I can; I cannot—I cannot enjoy sin; but don't vex my conscience. Do not worry me with your talk here, for I shall suffer enough hereafter. Do not tantalize me about saving faith, for I shall never believe. Do not begin talking to me about repentance. I shall never have a soft and tender heart; I know I never shall." A man who has begun to be numbed with cold, cries to his comrades, "Leave me to sleep myself to death"; and thus do despairing ones ask to be left in their misery. Dear soul, we cannot, we dare not, desert you.

I will tell you what you shall do; do give me a hearing. In the name of God, believe that there is hope yet—that even now Christ Jesus invites men, and especially such as you, to put their trust in Him. O, you who are burdened with sin, He calls you to let Him be your Saviour. If there is a man in the world He died for, you are the man. If there is one man here that is worse than any other, more sad, more sick, more sorry, more despairing, than another, my Lord Jesus Christ, who is here, has come to meet with such a one. Oh troubled heart, Jesus has come to seek and to save *you!* Did you never hear

The Story of John Newton,

on the coast of Africa? He had got himself into such a state by his sins, his drunkenness, his vice, that at last he was left on the coast of Africa, and virtually became a slave. Did John Newton dream, when he wandered up and down with a hungry belly, full of fever, and at death's door, that the day would come when he would be the companion and dear friend of Cowper, and when the church of St. Mary Woolnoth, over there in the city, would be crowded every time he stood up to preach of free grace and dying love? He did not think it, but it was so predestined. Something equally gracious may be ordained for you.

III. I have many more things to say, but I might weary you with them rather than bless you. The message was at first not received by Israel by reason of their anguish, but it was

True for all That,

and the Lord made it so. What did the Lord do when He found that these people did not hearken to Moses for anguish of spirit, and for cruel bondage? What did the Lord do? He was not going to give them up because of their wretched condition. He had said, "I will bring them out," and he meant to do it. The first thing the Lord did to prove His persevering grace was to commission Moses again. (Ex. 6:1; 7:2.) So the Lord God, in everlasting mercy, says to His minister, "Again proclaim My grace." It seems a terrible thing to have to pour our souls into deaf ears. Yet I shall not give it up, for I have done it with some here for nearly thirty-three years, and I may as well go on. Why should I lose so much labor? I will try again, like Peter, who, after toiling all night and taking nothing, yet let down the net at the Lord's bidding. One of these days those dead ears will be made to live.

It is a grand point when the Lord lays the conversion of men on the hearts of His ministers, and makes them feel that

They Must Win Souls.

Moses was bound to bring out Israel. God has issued His royal decree, and be you sure it will stand. I believe that God is saying to His church, "You have to do it. You have to gather out mine elect out of every nation under heaven." To the church in London He says, "Bring this people out of the bondage of sin." "Oh," says one man, who lives down some street near this place, "Sir, I can hardly live in this street. It teems with ill-living women." You have to save them. Passing a little shop as I did the other day, I saw written up in the window, "*If any poor girl that wishes to lead a better life will only step inside she will find a friend.*" That is one of our dear members. I felt so pleased as I saw it. I should like to see such a notice in a great many windows. I would like to see you live among the wicked, and put up in your windows, "If anybody wants a friend, there is one inside. Come in." You are called to save them! They must not be *lost.*

Somebody says, "What are you talking about, Mr. Spurgeon? We cannot save them." I am talking as God said, when He told Moses and Aaron that He gave them a charge to bring His people out of Egypt. They could not do it, but yet they did it. Anyone can do what He can do, but it is only *God's servant that can do what he cannot do.* We, my brethren, are called to perform the impossible; we are to be familiar with miracles. To the eye of reason there is no use in preaching to men dead in sin. I freely admit *that;* but if it is a commission from God, then it is not ours to raise questions, but to do as we are bidden. Oh that He may give us grace to tell out the gospel, and to keep on doing it till He has brought His own elect out of the bondage of sin and Satan, and saved them with an everlasting salvation! The Lord bless you for His name's sake. Amen.

[The prayers of the readers of this journal are requested for the blessing of God upon its Editors, and those whose sermons, articles or labors for Christ are printed in it; and that its circulation may be used by the Holy Spirit for the conversion of many sinners and the quickening of God's people. Dr. Talmage and Mr. Spurgeon especially request prayer every Sunday morning on behalf of their labors.]

GEMS FROM NEW BOOKS.

THE BASTINADO.*

WHILE in Egypt, Dr. Lansing visited the sugar plantations of Mustapha Pasha. While talking to Markus a Copt, who had bought a number of books, and to whom Dr. Lansing was anxious to sell a Bible, the missionary's attention was attracted by a cry of distress, and on looking out of the window to learn the cause, he beheld for the first time, the judicial administration of the bastinado. A number of the night watch on one of the cane plantations had gone to sleep at their posts, and were being punished therefor. The sentence was carried out in the presence of the judge, in front of the village café. Each man stepped forward in turn, and apparently without reluctance, and, lying down on his face, raised the soles of his feet. Two men sitting on the ground, one on each side of the culprit, firmly grasped his extended hands, and then placed their feet against his sides. Two others, likewise sitting on opposite sides of his knees, held his feet in place by means of a stick about four feet long, with a noose in the middle, which was wound around the ancles, they also steadying themselves by placing their feet against his sides, so that he was held as if in a vice. The torturers were two strong men, who had their flowing sleeves tied up so as to give their arms free play, and the instrument of torture was a koorbash, which is a heavy whip, much like our cowhide, about five feet long and made of hippopotamus skin. Each man struck the foot of the culprit. The whip was raised high in air, and came heavily down with a crash that reminded the missionary of our old-fashioned threshing with flails. The number of strokes was twenty-five. Some, whose hardened feet did not seem to suffer so much, received a few more; others, who squirmed very much and besought the Effendi very piteously for mercy, were let off with less. Most of them did not move, and when they rose, after limping a few steps, put on their shoes, and walked off as if nothing had happened.

An Escape from Darfurians.

During the afternoon, Dr. Lansing, while taking a stroll through the town, met with an adventure which came very near terminating his missionary career. Passing near a large factory, he observed in the yard some strange-looking black fellows, quite different from the tawny or dusty brown Copts and Arabians. On stepping in to look about, he found himself surrounded by twenty or thirty of them, violently gesticulating and vociferating, and evidently bent on mischief. One huge, ferocious fellow was on the point of striking, when the missionary sternly demanded to be let alone. Another then asked him what he wanted, and Dr. Lansing replied, "Nothing; I only walked in to look about me." The fellow at once, with no gentle

* From "Light in Darkness," or Missions and Missionary Heroes, by Rev. J. E. Godbey, D. D., and A. H. Godbey, A. M. An illustrated work on foreign missions in all quarters of the globe. 764 Pages. Sold by Subscription only. Published by Holloway & Company, St. Louis, and San Francisco.

Mgr. Bouland, the Converted R. C. Bishop.

The Promenade in Havana, Cuba.

grasp, laid hold of him, offering to show him about; but the doctor did not relish such friendliness; and on observing some others closing the huge gate, he wrested himself free, and walked out as fast as dignity would permit. On inquiring of a man whom he met, who the black fellows were, he was told that they were savage Darfurians, who had been brought from their native land to be trained as soldiers, and were detained at Esneh to be partially acclimatized. The man added, without knowing anything of Dr. Lansing's adventure, "They kill people when they can get them inside."

A Maronite Martyr.

Asaad El Shidiak, a talented Maronite priest, was employed to reply to the teachings of the missionaries in Syria, and began his preparations for the work by a course of research. While so engaged, the truth dawned upon him, and he became an advocate of the religion he had attacked. This drew upon him persecution, threats of excommunication, and twenty members of his family assembled to carry him by force to the Patriarch, his second elder brother being the leader. Asaad's expostulations and his mother's tears were alike in vain. He was taken to the convent of Alma and afterward to Canobeen. The place where he was destined to wear out the remainder of his days was one of the wildest and least accessible recesses of Lebanon. On his arrival there he was subjected by the order of the Patriarch to the most cruel treatment. With a heavy chain around his neck, the other end of which was attached to the wall, he had to lie on the bare floor. When he died, or how, is not definitely known. When Ibrahim Pasha captured Acre, Mr. Tod, an English merchant, procured from him ten soldiers, and searched the convent, but Asaad could not be found. The Patriarch asserted that he had been dead two years, but though this was doubted, nothing reliable could be learned.

MGR. LEON BOULAND.

(See Portrait.)

THE remarkable letter sent to the Pope by the distinguished ecclesiastic, whose portrait appears on this page, will win for him the respect of all Protestants. Though so highly placed in the Romish Church he has voluntarily severed himself from her communion on conscientious grounds. He wrote: "My decision to withdraw from the Roman Church is not a thought of recent origin. It is the mature result of convictions forced upon me during my travels in both hemispheres, and of my study for ten years of the chief religious and social questions which agitate our time—questions to which the Christian fathers furnish solutions wholly at variance with the Syllabus, and the policy of the Ultramontane Court."

Leon Bouland is about forty years of age. He is a Frenchman, and a graduate, with the highest honors, of the University of Paris. His studies for the priesthood were carried on under the personal direction of Cardinal Lavigerie, Archbishop of Algiers and Primate of Africa. In 1881 Monsignor Bouland received the honorary appointment of Canon of St. Michael the Archangel, Rome; and in 1882, that of President-General of the Society of the "Avocats de St. Pierre" in North America. The same year he was made a member of the "Academie des Arcades" in Rome; Canon of the Metropolitan Church of Rheims; Commander of the Order of the Holy Sepulchre; and *Private Chamberlain to Pope Leo XIII.* In June, 1886, Monsignor Bouland was also appointed by the Pope General Director of the organization in North America of the Society of St. Peter's Pence. He first visited this country in 1875 for the purpose of writing a history of the French in North America, a work now nearly completed.

While preparing his book for the press Monsignor Bonland has occupied himself with the charge of a French Roman Catholic church at Central Falls, R. I., and with the founding of another French church in Boston.

THE PROMENADE IN CUBA.

(See Illustration.)

THE Queen of the Antilles, as the island of Cuba is called, has an estimated population of about a million and a half, of whom the whites, including the coolies, number about 800,000. It has an area of 43,000 square miles, which is about the size of the State of Virginia. Its climate is one perpetual summer, of which August and September are the hottest months. In the lovely uplands of the south alone are those two months tolerable. In the low-lying districts the yellow fever scourge is then fearfully active, and annually carrries off its large percentage of victims. The illustration on this page represents the promenade in Havana, the capital, which is almost the only amusement at the command of the Cuban ladies. The strange, awkward-looking vehicles appear early in the day, and, as the sun grows hot, they disappear, and the ladies resume their monotonous life within doors. The men do not often join in these promenades. Their time is divided between their offices and the numerous cafés and restaurants, which are declared to be the most sumptuous in the world. Religious life in Cuba is at the lowest ebb. Nominally, it is Roman Catholic, but, especially among the males, practical Atheism is the rule.

FRED HOLDEN'S DEFALCATION.

(See Illustration on page 397.)

TWO men were seated in the smoking-room of a hotel, in a large city, one dull, drizzly January afternoon. The one whose name was Frederick Holden was a middle-aged man, dressed somewhat expensively, but in excellent taste. His companion, Alfred Willett, was much more homely in appearance; evidently not a city man, judging by the provincial cut of his clothes and his quieter, more sluggish manner. They smoked for some time in silence, or talking on impersonal matters; but as the last of the other occupants of the room rose and went out, they drew their chairs near together.

"Now, then, Fred," said Willett, "what did you mean in your telegram? What is the urgent matter that you wanted me to decide for you?"

"Well, Alf," said Holden, "I have no real friend besides you, and I want you to advise me in the worst strait a man can be in. I am in a desperate fix, and I do not know which way out of it involves the least risk."

"I am sorry to hear that," said Willett; "as a general principle, however, I do not think it is best to look at a difficulty from that standpoint. When a man is cornered, I believe he ought to ask what is the *right* course, and not trouble himself about the risk. However, let me hear what the trouble is."

"Well it is money trouble of the worst kind. You remember that five years ago, when I was married, marriage seemed to be the most desirable thing on all hands. Daisy's father was dead, and she had decided to seek a situation as governess. I was earning enough as confidential clerk to support us comfortably, though living alone I was spending the greater part of my salary. If I had possessed about five or six hundred dollars to furnish a home, we might be married immediately. Daisy would be spared the humiliation of earning a livelihood, and I should be better and happier in married life. The advantages were undeniable, but then I did not possess the requisite five hundred dollars, and I fretted considerably over that miserable deficiency. Finally I could bear it no longer, and as I had a large sum belonging to the company always passing through my hands, I concluded to borrow what I needed, and repay it gradually out of my salary. It was easily done, but to repay it was difficult. We had many expenses at first, Daisy's sickness and my own, and then the children came. The first three years the salary did not cover expenses, and the ice being broken, I borrowed more money to make up the deficiency. So it has gone on, until now my shortage is fully two thousand dollars."

Willett raised his hands in horror. "I hoped you were going to say it still stood at five hundred. I would have made an effort to let you have that, but two thousand is hopeless."

"Thank you, old man," said Holden, "I knew I could count on your good will, but I did not expect you could lift me out of this. The worst feature of the affair is that discovery is inevitable. There is a new element in the Board of Directors. Two or three of them are troubled with conscientious scruples about their duty, and there is to be a thorough audit next week; I shall have to show that my balance is correct to a cent. Now what am I to do?"

"Oh, you can have no doubt of that. You should confess the whole case; tell the Directors the circumstances, and offer, if they will forgive you and retain you in office, to work on half pay till the shortage is repaid."

"Ah! there your country training leads you astray. No director would do that. He dare not, in view of what would be said if the thing leaked out. No, I should be dismissed without a character; Daisy would break her heart, and we should all starve. No that would not do. What is generally done, is for the clerk to seize all he can lay his hands upon, and make tracks for Canada, sending for his family afterward."

"I would rather die than do that, Fred," said Willett; "you would never be happy again. Your conscience would torment you continually. No; be persuaded; do the right thing, whatever the consequence may be. Make your peace with God by repentance and entreat His forgiveness through Christ, and He will see you through, somehow. You may have to suffer; sin involves that, but you will be supported."

"Frankly," said Holden, "I have not the courage to confess. I know what the result would be. Is there nothing else you can think of? Do you know any one who would advance the two thousand dollars?"

Willett shook his head. "No, my dear boy," he said, "there is only the one course open to you. Depend upon it, any other will involve you in deeper sin and misery."

Holden was not convinced. The other way was so much smarter and had so often succeeded. He sighed heavily, and the two friend separated never to meet again on earth. Many years afterward Willett heard the end of his friend's tragic story. An unfinished letter in Holden's hand came to him enclosed in one from Mrs. Holden. In his own letter Holden said that the money he took with him to Canada, as he decided, had been lost within a year. That despairing of earning a living there, he had gone to England, only to meet with new disappointment. He was then in utter destitution, living in a wretched garret, earning a scanty subsistence by copying law documents. "I wish," he wrote, "I had taken your advice. I have found it true that the way of transgressors is hard." The letter ended there, and Mrs. Holden wrote that she found him dead in his chair, his head resting on his arm, the pen still in his hand, and the unfinished letter before him on his desk. His last words were those written to his friend.

Holden's Last Letter.

THE EPOCHS OF A LIFE.

A NEW SERIAL STORY.

By Rev. L. S. Keyser.

(*Continued from page 382.*)

WHEN the third summer vacation was over the two students were back again in their old college haunts shaking hands with the friends who had returned, like themselves, to their academical duties At the close of the first day of the session, George and Hadley sat in their old study, talking in a desultory fashion.

"By the by, George," said Hadley at length, "did you notice that we have a new accession to our class this term?"

Dane gave vent to a sarcastic snort, as he replied, "Oh, yes, I saw him, and I amused myself by fixing the category he belongs to."

"Well, in what sort of a gauge did you succeed in putting him?"

"He is rather a priggish, starchy character, and his mental diamond is not of the first water. Forehead too smooth and narrow. No danger that he will snatch the honors from us. Rather handsome, though, and may be a ladies' man."

"You are quite an analyst. But did you learn anything about him?"

"I played the part of Paul Pry, I acknowledge, and learned that he studied under a private tutor before he came here, and has passed a creditable examination for admission to the Senior Class. And more than that, thanks to my inquisitive proclivites, I have found out that he is designed for the ministry."

"Wh-e-e-w!" whistled Hadley, intensely interested in these facts. "There is some fun in store for us at last. This embyro parson will make a splendid target for our wads of humor. We shall see how much of an expert he is at intellectual fencing. If you have gauged him correctly, we need not be afraid of discomfiture. Of course, we might know that he is not a man of much calibre, or he never would have chosen the ministry as his profession. No one with a sound, healthy brain would throw away his manhood and his prospects in life for a useless and puerile vocation like that."

"Hold, there!" interfered Dane, "let us be fair. Dr. Hartridge, President of the College, is a preacher—a D. D., you know—and I understand that he served a number of congregations very acceptably before he was hoisted to his present position. So is Dr. Battinger, our Professor of Latin, a clergyman, and yet you think him the most brainy man of the Faculty."

"Yes that is so," Hadley admitted. "They are shining examples of able men in the pulpit; but you must remember that they have abandoned the profession now, and you may depend that their present occupation is much more congenial. It is not unlikely that they were glad to find a way of escape from regular preaching that did not necessitate a confession of change of view."

"Still, they were able men, and I should think as young men as they were, to use your reprehensible slang, brainy men and they chose the profession of the ministry, so we must not be too hasty in concluding that the same choice in another young man is a clear proof of semi-imbecility. I base my opinion of the new student on more philosophical grounds."

"Well we shall see how he acts: I think we shall have some fun with him."

The fun commenced not many days afterward. In some colleges it might have begun earlier; but in the Grand Central hazing was not permitted. There are methods, however, of trying a man's power of self-control quite as severe as the rough horse-play of hazing. An insult, a withering sarcasm, a brutal taunt, may goad into fury a man who could bear physical pain with the endurance and unruffled composure of an Indian. Harrison Duneman, the new student, was a man peculiarly susceptible to such treatment. He was a dull man, whose strong animal nature was proof against pain, but whose mental nature was weak and undisciplined. He was morbidly sensitive to slights, as most dull men are, and had none of the nobleness of spirit which can bear to see another's superiority recognized by society. Conscious of mental power, and proud too of acquirements which his sluggish nature had gained only by severe labor, it mortified him when a company which had been bored by his serious remarks was charmed by the light jests of some witty humorist. He could not forgive a man who so eclipsed him, and he hated with vindictive hatred a man who made him the butt of his raillery. Duneman took life seriously, and a good-humored joke to which he could find no repartee stung him like a blow. It was a cruel fate that threw him into rivalry with Madelling and Dane, who, having none of the instincts of good breeding, which keep a true gentleman from wantonly hurting the feelings of another, had no compunction about wounding him wherever he might be vulnerable.

It was in the class-room of the Professor of mathematics that the campaign opened. A difficult problem was submitted, and Duneman, with some show of confidence, undertook its solution on the black-board. He worked rapidly and without hesitation for some minutes, to the surprise of some members of the class who had confessed their inability to solve it. But then his hand wavered; he had lost the thread of calculation, and stood before the board in evident embarrassment. An audible titter went through the class, in which Duneman would have joined if he had been less conceited or more self-possessed.

Madelling was then called upon to essay the solution of the problem. Mathematics had long been his favorite study, and he was perfectly familiar with the problem in hand. He saw where Duneman had gone astray, and with easy celerity the figures were displayed on the board and the correct result underscored with a flourish. Hearty applause broke out on all hands except from Duneman, who stood glaring at the board, the prey of chagrin and mortification. Hadley glanced at him, saw his suffering, and with a spirit of wicked mischief took up the crayon again and wrote at the foot of the blackboard: "*For the benefit of the unevolved Parson.*" It was a cruel blow, applied with the dexterity of the Dublin hackney coachman who prided himself on his ability to rouse his beast to a gallop by applying his whip to "a raw." The class, however, thought it witty and burst into loud laughter. Duneman winced, his face flushed, and he turned angrily on his tormentor. But the words would not come, and he gnashed his teeth in impotent rage. Finally he turned to the Professor and said: "Am I to be insulted by a country bumpkin? The sacred calling I have chosen has nothing to do with this matter, and it ought to be protected from coarse, boorish, and sacrilegious indignities."

It was Hadley's turn now to lose temper. The reference to his rusticity brought the blood to his face and showed that he too had "a raw." It was a gratuitous insult, like his own, and the tormentor who had felt no compunction at giving pain, quivered from head to foot when he received punishment in kind. He advanced with clenched hand as if to strike. By a violent effort, he controlled himself sufficiently to allow his partly lifted hand to fall by his side, and then the two angry students stood glaring at each other. At length Hadley hurled out from between his teeth a speech of vulgar abuse, which he afterward thought of with shame. He said: "You show more of the spirit of a wild-cat than of a man! I suppose that you are cultivating yourself for the pursuit of your 'sacred calling,' as you term it. Like most of your set, you have the spirit that built the inquisitorial fires in the Dark Ages. It is a pity that you can't take a joke, but must bristle up like a hyena! A pretty specimen of a pulpit exhorter, *you* are!"

"Gentlemen, gentlemen," interposed the Professor, with as much seriousness as he could command under the circumstances, "be seated, and do not quarrel over a harmless joke."

The class tittered.

"I do not think it a joke," said Duneman. "The fellow meant to insult me"; but he obeyed the Professor by taking his seat.

The class tittered louder.

"And I am persuaded that he is too much of a torpedo to make a good parson," put in Hadley, sarcastically.

The class broke into a loud guffaw.

"I insist that this interchange of words be stopped at once," broke in the Professor, sternly, and all knew that he meant what he said. "Gentlemen, I regret that this undignified passage has taken place in my recitation-room, and hope that such an offence against decorum will not be repeated. Since it is your first offence, I will not report you to the President, but a repetition of the scene shall be summarily dealt with. The class is excused."

Hadley walked sullenly to his room in company with his friend Dane, who was still laughing over the encounter and was amused as much by his friend's tragic mood.

"What is it that is so ludicrous?" Hadley asked. "I see nothing to laugh at. The fellow is a regular porcupine. Don't you think he disgraced himself?"

"Oh! there was not much difference between you, I think," said Dane; "you called each other names, that was all. You began it, you know, and I thought you were going to hit him. I am glad you stopped in time. It was grand, though, to see you both there on exhibition like a couple of wild beasts. Oh, Oh!" and Dane went off into another explosion of laughter.

"Well you are not very sympathetic," said Hadley." "I should have thought my friend would have resented such an insult to me. A country bumpkin indeed!"

"Oh! there is no need for me to take up the cudgels; you showed yourself fully a match for our clerical friend. You forgot, I suppose, when you began throwing stones that you live in a glass-house. Well, well get the panes replaced and think no more about it."

Repairs, however, were not easily made on either side. The dislike engendered between the two students increased rather than diminished. Duneman, too, having discovered that Madelling held sceptical opinions, came to regard the quarrel as in a sense a religious dispute and to regard himself as a martyr suffering for conscience sake. He spoke of Madelling as "the infidel student," and it was not difficult in a community of the kind in which they lived to arouse a prejudice against him on that ground. He began to meditate on plans for humiliating him, and with Jesuitical spirit to think that it did not much matter whether the means employed were quite honorable, so desirable did it seem that the enemy of religion should be put to shame. So on each side the enmity between them grew and intensified.

In the mean time other events of importance were occurring. It was thought advisable by the college authorities to give the undergraduates an opportunity for frequent practice in public speaking. Besides many special days and anniversaries, when speaking was in order, every third Saturday forenoon was devoted to the reading of essays and the delivery of orations by the young men and women of the college. The exercises were held in what was called "Chapel Hall," which, although a large, commodious room, was almost invariably filled to overflowing by an interested audience. In this way the young aspirants for literary or oratorical distinction had excellent opportunities for the exercise and display of their budding talents, and it must be confessed that many of the productions delivered there were above a mediocre quality. There was the embryonic promise of the future essayist, poet, lawyer, or legislator.

On the first Saturday morning devoted to these exercises after the beginning of the new session, there was a general rush for Chapel Hall. Our two friends, Hadley and George, sat together as usual, on one of the seats occupied by the Senior class. The hum of conversation was heard through the hall before the exercises began. Suddenly Hadley's attention was arrested by the entrance of a young lady, through the doorway at the side of the room, whose appearance impressed him.

"Do you see that young lady?" he whispered to Dane. "The one just entering the door."

The young men watched her, as she stepped up the aisle along the wall, and then turning, found a seat near them, a little in front and to their right. Courtesy would not allow them more than a brief occasional glance at her, but those furtive glances were sufficient to convince them that she was a fascinating girl, with dark-blue eyes, and pearly, slightly pale cheeks. Yet there was an element of hauteur and imperiousness in her bearing, and a kind of reckless abandon characterized the toss of her head, as if she cared very little for the good or bad opinion of others, and as if her thinking was carried on with entire independence.

"Mr. Analyst," said Hadley, touching his friend's arm, "there is another specimen upon whom to exercise your critical faculty. What is your opinion of that young lady, eh?"

Dane scrutinized her closely for a few minutes before he answered.

"She is certainly very beautiful," he said, "and appears to be intellectual. No doubt she is a cultivated girl, and there is something charming about her apparently easy and careless carriage. She is a girl, too, who will not swallow every kind of teaching she hears. You can read her independence in her physiognomy, and in every movement of her graceful head. Yet I cannot say that my admiration of her is unqualified. I am afraid that she is too haughty and too indifferent to public opinion, and probably a little 'strong-minded' for a woman. She reminds me of a certain forward female I once met, who was an arrant scoffer at religion, and I could not help but feel that such raillery came with an ill grace from her lips. It seemed so out of harmony with that modest femininity which is the peculiar heritage of woman. I wouldn't be surprised to learn that this girl entertains some opinions not in accord with reigning ideas, and that she has the courage to assert them. Nevertheless, I confess that I admire her blonde beauty."

"Well, you have characterized her very happily," returned Hadley. "You have put in apt phrases what I had indefinitely in my mind. It remains to be seen whether your analysis is correct."

During the progress of the exercises, Hadley divided his attention about equally between them and the young lady who had arrested his attention. While some well-digested and thoughtful production was being delivered, he noticed that she was an attentive and appreciative listener; but when the performance was crude and puerile, she could not conceal her impatience. A frown of displeasure would contract her brow and her eyes would wander restlessly over the audience.

"She has no patience with immature thought," reflected Hadley. "Evidently she is a thinker herself. At any rate, she has gotten beyond the crude state. The question is where does she belong? I shall start out on a voyage of discovery as soon as the exercises are over."

No sooner was the last speech delivered and the audience dismissed, than Hadley proceeded to put his resolve into execution; but his inquiries only proved that his fellow-students were as ignorant of the girl's name and whereabouts as he was himself. It appeared that she was a stranger. Not many of the young men of the class had observed her in the crowd, and none of them could give him a clue. But Hadley was a resolute young man, and he was not to be thwarted easily.

"Tell you what, Dane," he said, taking his friend's arm, "I have a plan by which we may ferret out her hiding-place. Come along, let us follow her—accidentally, of course—until we find out where she lives."

In the crowd passing down the stairs to the ground floor they had some difficulty in keeping the girl in the range of their vision, but by dint of considerable effort they got closer to her, and then, assuming a careless manner which one of them at least did not feel, they sauntered along in the crowd a few paces in her rear. As the people dispersed to the right and left, the young men had to be more careful lest their surreptitious pursuit should be discovered. The young lady, accompanied by a friend, continued her walk along Main Street through the heart of the town, and by the time she had reached the suburbs beyond, there were very few persons besides herself upon the sidewalk. Presently she turned aside, opened the gate in front of an elegant residence, surrounded by tall poplars and maples, and waving her friend adieu, she stepped lightly up the stone walk and entered the house with that familiar freedom which says, "This is my home."

(*To be Continued.*)

GOD'S COVENANT WITH ISRAEL.

By Mrs. M. Baxter.

I. S. Lesson for July 1, Exodus 24: 1-12. Golden Text, Heb 8: 10

Moses Called Up to the Mount—The Old and the New Dispensations—The Vow of the People—The Signification of the Offering—Something Lacking—Power Given Through Christ—Moses Supernaturally Sustained—The Indispensable Element of Worship—The Plan of the Tabernacle Imparted—Its Types—The Emblematic Stones—The Anointing of the Priests.

THE children of Israel were still in the Wil- lerness of Sinai. The law had been spoken to hem from the mountain by the voice of God, vith attendant circumstances which were calcu- ated to inspire awe and terror, so that they had aid to Moses, "Speak thou with us, and we will ear; but let not God speak with us lest we lie." (Ex. 20: 19.) "And Moses drew near unto he thick darkness where God was." It was arkness to the people, but it was light to Moses. It was there that the directions and romises of the next three chapters were given. and then God said to Moses: "Come up unto the ord, thou, and Aaron, Nadab, and Abihu, and seventy of the elders of Israel; and worship ye

Afar Off,

nd Moses alone shall come near the Lord; but hey shall not come nigh; neither shall the eople go up with him." Oh, how different from he invitations of the New Testament! "Come nto Me, all ye that labor and are heavy laden, nd I will give you rest." (Matt. 11: 28). Hav- ng therefore boldness to enter into the holiest y the blood of Jesus . . . let us draw near." Heb. 10: 19-22.) The law says, "Stand off;" he Gospel, "Draw nigh."

Moses came and told the people all the words f the Lord, and all the judgments: and all the eople answered with one voice and said, "All he words which the Lord hath said, will we o." It was the second time they had made his declaration (see Ex. 19: 8), but how little id they realize that they had not in themselves ower to do all that they now engaged to do! And Moses wrote all the words of the Lord." Whether he wrote upon a rock, as was often the use at that period, or whether, as in Deuteron- my 27: 23, upon stones, plastered with plaster, hich would harden when the writing was fin- hed, we know not. As the writing seems to ave formed a portable book, perhaps it was on a ax tablet, or on the papyrus leaf, which was much sed in Egypt later. After writing God's mes- ages, Moses built an altar, with twelve pillars, hat all the tribes of Israel might be represented here. And then he sent young men, which of- ered burnt offerings, and peace offerings, as a eal of the people's pledge of obedience. The urnt offering signified the offering of them- elves to God, and the peace offering, their vows nd thanksgiving to God." (Lev. 7: 12-17.) nd Moses took half of the blood, and ut it in basins; and half of the blood he prinkled on the altar. And he took the book f the covenant, and read in the audience of he people: and they said (for the third time), All that the Lord hath said, will we do, and e obedient." But there was

Something Still Lacking:

an may have the best intentions, but without he precious blood of Christ he cannot carry hem out. "The blood of Jesus Christ, His Son, leanseth us from all sin"; the unclean might ot enter into the tabernacle. We "were not deemed by corruptible things, such as silver nd gold . . . but with the precious blood of hrist." (1 Pet. 1: 18.) Moses took the blood nd sprinkled it on the people, and said, "Be- old the blood of the covenant which the Lord ath made with you concerning all these words." was but a type—man's imperfect offering to od. But He saw through it His beloved Son, an high priest of good things to come," who neither by the blood of goats and calves, but y His own blood . . . entered in once into the oly place, having obtained eternal redemption r us." (Heb. 9: 12.) Jesus pleads for us that He has been slain as the one great Offering, and on this ground He makes it possible for man to enter into covenant with God. How many have said, not three times, but fifty times, a hundred times, "All that the Lord saith unto me, I will do, I will walk so as to please God, I will not turn aside," and yet, again and again, there have been failures. "But what the law could *not* do, in that it was weak through the flesh," God did. How? He sent "His own Son in the likeness of sinful flesh and for sin." He sent Him to shed His blood, and so "condemned sin in the flesh, that the righteousness of the law might be fulfilled in us who walk not after the flesh, but after the Spirit." (Rom. 8: 3, 4.) The law says, "You *ought* to walk so as to please God." The precious blood says, "You *can* walk so as to please God; your sins are atoned for, they condemn you no more. The life is in the blood, life for you to *enable* you to do the will of God." "I will put My laws into their mind, and write them in their hearts." (Heb. 8: 10.) Praise God, it is not only our duty, but a blessed possibility, to do the will of God. "Almost all things are by the law purged with blood, and without shedding of blood is no remission." (Heb. 9: 22.) Life purges death. The law is the "ministration of death, written and engraven in stones (II Cor. 3: 7); the precious blood is the very life of Christ, not only poured out, but imparted to us as our life.

Having thus mediated God's covenant with the people, Moses went up into the mountain with Aaron, Nadab, Abihu, Joshua, and seventy elders of Israel, "and they saw the God of Israel." It was "devouring fire" to all who were below, but on the mountain all was glory and the effulgence of light. After eating and drinking together in the mountain, Moses and Joshua arose, and "Moses went up into the mount" that he might be permitted to enter into the thoughts of God, and into His plans and purposes as never before. Moses was content, at the call of God, to leave the people, much as his presence seemed necessary; God was responsible. Forty days and forty nights, without eating, drinking, and probably without sleeping, too, Moses was in the mount with God; but he was breathing in an atmosphere of life itself from his close contact with God; and no doubt He who breathed into Adam's nostrils the breath of life, had some means of sustaining Moses supernaturally.

God was about to teach Moses His will about worship. The first element of worship (now that the people had been sprinkled with the blood) was the spirit of sacrifice. "Speak unto the children of Israel that they bring Me an offering; of every man that giveth it willingly with his heart shall ye take my offering." There is no real worship without

Giving to the Lord.

The right order is, They "first gave their own selves to the Lord," (II Cor. 8: 5), and then, according to our value for Jesus, will be our further giving to Him. Some count *themselves* worthy of a richly furnished house, horses, carriages, and servants, and *Christ* worth about as much as the wages of their kitchen maid. The first disciples were in a hurry to get rid of all that belonged to them, "Neither said any of them that aught of the things which he possessed was his own, but they had all things common." (Acts 4: 32.) They counted Jesus worthy of their all. Then God gave Moses the pattern of an ark of testimony which was to contain the law within, and the manifest presence of God without. "And then I will meet with thee, and I will commune with thee from above the mercy seat, from between the two cherubims which are upon the ark of the testimony, of all things which I will give thee in commandment unto the children of Israel." Then God commanded Moses to make a table on which the shew-bread should be placed before Him always; and a candlestick of pure gold with seven branches. All this was to speak of Christ. He is the ark, God's meeting-place with man; He is "the Bread of Life" typified by the shew-bread; He is "the Light of the world," God's golden candlestick. Then the tabernacle was to be made of many parts, pillars, boards, curtains, tables, loops and sockets to make "one tabernacle" (Ex. 26: 6.) It was to be thus a beautiful picture of the Church of Christ. "For as the body is one and hath many members, and all the members of that one body, being many, are one body, so also is Christ." "For by one Spirit are we all baptized into one body. . . For the body is not one member, but many." (1 Cor. 12: 13-14.)

He next commanded him to make holy garments for Aaron, "for glory and for beauty" (Ex. 28: 2), and above the holy garments Aaron was to wear two onyx stones upon his shoulders with the names of the children of Israel graven upon them, "And Aaron shall bear their names before the Lord upon his two shoulders for a memorial" (Ex. 28: 12). His strength was to bear their weakness! Oh! What a type of our beloved Lord who bears our unworthy names upon His Almighty shoulder. "The government shall be upon *His* shoulder (Isa. 9: 6.) And then Moses was to make a breast-plate with the names of the children of Israel also engraven upon it. "And Aaron shall bear the names of the children of Israel

Upon His Heart

when he goeth in unto the holy place, for a memorial before the Lord continually." (Ver. 29.) But he was not only to bear the judgment of the children of Israel upon his heart, but also Aaron must have a plate of pure gold upon his forehead with the inscription "Holiness unto the Lord," "that Aaron may bear the iniquity of the holy things . . . that *they* may be accepted before the Lord." (Ver. 38.) Oh how wondrous! The sin which we have committed so lightly, lies heavy on the heart of our great High Priest. Then God commanded Moses to clothe Aaron and his sons with the holy garments and consecrate them. But before they could be anointed, their right ear, right hand, and right foot must be marked with blood, in token that they were a blood-bought and ransomed priesthood. (Ex. 29: 20.) Are not we too priests unto God? Then they might be anointed with the holy oil made for no other purpose, and none like it must be made, on pain of death. "Upon man's flesh shall it not be poured," but only on the holy garments. (Ex. 30: 30-33.) There must be no imitation of the Holy Ghost, God's true anointing; and the Spirit cannot rest upon the flesh; God's Spirit comes on Christ in us, and not upon our self-life. And God commanded also that when a census of the children of Israel was taken, every man should give "a ransom for his soul unto the Lord," an acknowledgement that his life was forfeited, yet redeemed. And He also ordained that a continual burnt offering should be offered, a morning and an evening sacrifice, "at the door of the tabernacle of the congregation before the Lord; when I will meet you, to speak there unto thee. And then I will meet with the children of Israel, and the tabernacle shall be sanctified by My glory . . . And I will dwell among the children of Israel, and will be their God. And they shall know that I am the Lord their God, that brought them forth out of the land of Egypt, *that* I may dwell among them: I am the Lord their God." This was the purpose of all—that God might dwell among them. The purpose of His dealings with us is that He may dwell *in* us.

"NEVER MIND."

What's the use of always fretting,
At the trials we shall find
Ever strewn along our pathway?
Travel on, and "Never Mind."

Travel onward; working, hoping;
Cast no lingering glance behind,
At the trials once encountered;
Look ahead and "Never Mind."

What is past, is past forever.
Let all fretting be resigned.
It will never help the matter,
Do your best and "Never Mind."

And if those who might befriend you,
Whom the ties of nature bind,
Should refuse to do their duty,
Look to heaven, and "Never Mind."

Friendly words are often spoken,
When the feelings are unkind,
Take them for their real value,
Pass them by, and "Never Mind."

Fate may threaten, clouds may lower,
Enemies may be combined,
If your trust in God is steadfast,
He will help you, "Never Mind."

—*Mary E. McCleary.*

J. E. Jewett, Publisher, 77 Bible House, New York, will furnish the above poem in leaflet form at twenty cents per hundred. *A Sample Packet* of 50 leaflets assorted (no two alike) will be sent post-paid, for ten cents. Postage stamps taken.

Christian Work in Mexico.

Through the reading of the Holy Scriptures translated into Spanish some earnest souls in Mexico have, by God's blessing, been led to a clear knowledge of the Gospel. From their numbers able preachers of the Christian faith in its primitive purity have been raised up, around whom congregations have been gathered from among the humble poor, who have been the first to publicly welcome and defend the pure Gospel in Mexico. The members of these congregations, rich in faith, have worked earnestly and bravely for Christ and his truth among their fellow countrymen in that beautiful Southern portion of North America called Mexico. Schools have been established by them, in which large numbers of bright boys and girls have received a good secular education and been carefully taught the Christian faith. From the children thus educated faithful Christian workers have been raised up. A Mexican Church of Christ, that maintains the faith in its purity and integrity, has been organized among these native Christians in the Republic of Mexico. The members of this Mexican Church of Christ, though gathered mostly from among the poor, are yet doing a most important Christian work in Mexico. To continue that work, we need to pay a few leading workers small monthly salaries, and also to defray some current expenses. To raise the needed funds we have formed a society with an office at 43 Bible House, New York, U. S., and should be pleased to have many of our fellow Christians join this society by becoming regular contributors to its treasury. We are trying to secure monthly or quarterly contributions to meet the regular monthly expenses of the work. In order to continue and extend the work, we wish to raise four hundred dollars a month, by endeavoring to have four hundred persons each give on the average *one dollar every month* to this object, leaving the donors to give less or more as they may be able and willing.

We earnestly invite all who will, to join us in this systematic effort in behalf of the cause of Christ in Mexico, by becoming monthly subscribers to this fund. We have already regular subscribers whose gifts amount monthly to over eighty dollars, and a growing circle of friends who are forwarding us occasional donations.

This Mexican Church of Christ is a very effective instrumentality through which to do Christian work among the 50,000,000 who speak the Spanish language, few of whom have ever had a Bible in their hands. A beautiful church building has been secured in the City of Mexico as the centre of the activities of this Mexican Church of Christ. Through the workers connected with that centre more than forty congregations have been gathered from among the poor. We have some faithful and able preachers now in the field, but more young men need to be trained for the ministry. Multitudes of Protestant children in Mexico, some of them orphans, need to be educated. We make three requests of you, Christian reader: *first*, that you will become a monthly or quarterly subscriber in behalf of this Christian work; *second*, that you will try and induce your friends to do the same; *third*, that you will remember this precious work in Mexico in your prayers.

I most sincerely thank all who are already generously contributing to this Christian work for their timely and generous gifts, and I earnestly invite many others, to unite with us in aiding this important Christian work by also becoming monthly subscribers in its behalf. Those who may not feel that they can give as much as a dollar a month are earnestly asked to give what they can, whenever they are able—EVERY LITTLE HELPS. If you will generously consent to contribute a dollar a month or more or less to the work, will you kindly inform me of the fact? Contributions either large or small can be mailed directly to my address as follows:

BISHOP H. C. RILEY, care of J. P. HEATH,
No. 43 Bible House, New York, U. S.

Vol. XI., No. 26. Office, 63 Bible House. N. Y. THURSDAY, JUNE 28, 1888. Annual Subscription, $1.50.

CONTENTS OF THIS NUMBER

PORTRAIT AND LIFE OF THE LATE FREDERICK III., EMPEROR OF GERMANY.
HUMAN CONSTELLATIONS. Dr. Talmage's Sermon Last Sunday Morning at Winfield, Kans.
ANECDOTES RELATED AT RECENT EVANGELISTIC MEETINGS.
THE SPIRIT IN THE COMING AGE.
PICTURE OF A MEETING OF WALDENSES.
How Bishop Parker Died—A Night on a Mountain—A Fact for Statesmen—One Bible in a Chilian Home—A Vicious Religious Festival—A Singular Testimony in India—Political Progress in Japan.
CURRENT EVENTS: The Republican National Convention—Congressional Notes—The New Emperor's Proceedings, Etc.
THE SLUGGARD'S FARM. A New Sermon by Rev. C. H. Spurgeon.
Gems from New Books: A Needlewoman's Gift—A Tatterdemalion's Self-Denial, Etc.
ROSA'S CROSS (With Illustration).
THE EPOCHS OF A LIFE. A New Serial Story by Rev. L. S. Keyser. (Continued).
THE GOLDEN CALF. By Mrs. M. Baxter.

THE LATE FREDERICK III., EMPEROR OF GERMANY—Born Oct. 18, 1831—Died June 15, 1888.

THE LATE EMPEROR FREDERICK III.

A Mysterious Providence—The Lamented Emperor—His Childhood—Education—First Meeting with the Princess Victoria—How He Proposed to Her—Marriage in 1858—Protest Against Despotic Government—The Schleswig-Holstein War—Good Generalship at Sadowa—His Triumph at Sedan—A Characteristic Incident—Illness—The Death Scene.

THE death of the Emperor of Germany on Friday, June 15, should remind us that we walk by faith, not by sight. Were it not so, such an event would be altogether grievous and lamentable. Happily the Christian is assured that in public affairs, as in the events of his own life, God is ordering everything according to His own wise purposes. The world is not controlled by chance, nor by the caprices of a malevolent fate. At times we are confronted by events which we cannot understand; success and failure are not distributed according to our ideas of merit, and the ills that flesh is heir to fall more heavily upon one whose life appears to us the most blameless, while the evil-doer escapes them. So is it with the end of life. A man whose career promises to be a blessing to the world is cut off before his beneficent projects are realized, while others live on, working mischief and causing misery, into old age. We feel as the disciples did on the road to Emmaus, as they talked together, and were sad, and are inclined to say with them, "We trusted that it had been He which should have redeemed Israel." At such times even prayer seems to be of no avail, and our spirits are depressed by the taunts of the enemy, who uses their apparent failure as a reproach. As a nation we have had to bear those taunts,

As When Lincoln Died,

and again when Garfield was taken away. It is so now in Germany when the enlightened Prince, from whose wisdom and justice so much of good was expected, is removed at the commencement of his reign, and his place occupied by one whose character and principles are antagonistic to national liberty and progress. Disappointment is natural, but its voice is hushed by the thought that some wise purpose surely underlies the mysterious event and will become manifest when all mysteries are explained. In this special case it may be that the sagacious, peace-loving ruler has been called to give place to the headstrong, ambitious youth who succeeds him, in order that in

The Events Which are Coming

upon the world Germany may play the part marked out for her by divine wisdom, and the impending calamities may be brought down by an appropriate instrument. "Thou shalt be gathered to thy grave in peace," said the Lord to the good King Josiah, "because thine heart was tender, and thou didst humble thyself before God, and thine eyes shall not see all the evil that I will bring upon this place." (II Chron. 24: 27, 28.) God in His providence works by natural means: the curse causeless does not come: it may therefore be that in the final crisis is this world's history on which we are about to enter—a period of wars and tumults—there is work appointed for Emperor William II. to do, which he will do from the promptings of his own ambition, unconscious that he is fulfilling the purposes of the King of kings. Thus it will be seen that it was in mercy that Emperor Frederick was gathered to his fathers and Emperor William reigns in his stead.

Frederick's Childhood

was passed in a time of general European unrest. He was born at Potsdam on October 18, 1831. His grandfather, Frederick William III., the grand-nephew of Frederick the Great, was then King of Prussia. The country was menaced by Austria from without, and by the discontented people within. England was passing through the throes of a great political convulsion. France had just driven out her weak king, and filled his place by one still weaker. Russia was crushing out, with cruel, ruthless hand, the last embers of the Polish revolt. Spain and Portugal were in anarchy, and Turkey was sullenly bowing before the inexorable logic of the events of 1827-29. Two lives—those of his uncle and father, lay between the child and the throne, and those two lives covered a momentous but glorious period of national history. Of the Prince's boyhood not much is related. His mother, who was a pupil of Goethe, devoted herself, unremittingly, to his training, and she was aided by Ernst Curtius, the historian of Greece.

In 1840 Frederick William III. died, and was succeeded by his eldest son, Frederick William IV., the uncle of the late Emperor. His reign was chiefly remarkable for the civil commotions which, in common with all Europe, agitated Prussia. The part which Prince William, the father of the late Emperor, took in suppressing the rising in Berlin rendered him obnoxious to the people, and it was deemed advisable that he and his family should leave Prussia for a time. They went to England, and then it was that the young prince Frederick, then a youth of seventeen, who quitted the university to accompany his father, first saw the little girl who afterwards became his wife. It was the hope of both families that these two might be united, and ten years later that hope was realized. The story of

His Marriage

opens in so simple and natural a manner that, though it has often been told, it deserves reproduction here. In September, 1855, when all England was rejoicing over the capture of Sebastopol, Frederick paid a visit to the Queen at Balmoral. He went thither with the consent of his parents and of his uncle, the King, Frederick William IV., to ask for the hand of Princess Victoria, a young maiden of fifteen years.

Writing in her journal, on September 29th, the Queen says: "Our dear Victoria was this day engaged to Prince Frederick William of Prussia. . . . He had already spoken to us, on the 20th; but we were uncertain, on account of her extreme youth, whether he should speak to her himself, or wait till he came back again. However, we felt it was better that he should do so, and during our ride up Craig-na-Ban, this afternoon, he picked *a piece of white heather* (the emblem of good luck), which he gave to her, and this enabled him to make an allusion to his hopes and wishes as they rode down Glen Girnock, which led to this happy conclusion." A pretty story, simply told. Writing on Oct. 2, the Prince Consort says that Prince Fritz left Balmoral on the previous day, and speaks in ardent praise of the childlike simplicity and candor of his daughter. "The young people are ardently in love with one another," he adds, "and the purity, innocence, and unselfishness of the young man have been, on his part, equally touching." It was this engagement in 1855 which was fulfilled on January 25, 1858, when the gallant soldier-prince was married to the Princess on whom his heart was set.

The bride and bridegroom were heartily welcomed in Berlin, and in August of the same year Queen Victoria and the Prince Consort visited them in their new home. A great change was impending over Prussia. The then King was stricken with a painful malady, and after the royal travellers from England had returned to her shores, Prince William was formally declared Prince Regent. He had acted in that capacity since the autumn of 1857; but in October, 1858, he was appointed Regent with full powers, his brother's dementia being declared incurable. Three years later, January 2, 1861, the afflicted monarch died, the Prince Regent became King, and our hero

Crown Prince.

The King, under the guidance of Bismarck, at once set himself to the thorough reorganization of the army, which in spite of the resistance of his people he enormously increased. He insisted on the old feudal prerogatives of royalty and though he was faithful to the letter of the Constitution, he took advantage of all his resources to render it powerless and to defeat the checks it imposed upon him. That slowly but surely brought on a constitutional crisis. During the long persistent struggle with the majority in the Lower House, which had taken England for a model, Herr Von Bismarck fought the King's battle with a force and dexterity totally unexpected, and the temper of the combatants rose to such a pitch that quarrels and duels were frequent. Prince Frederick William was imbued with English opinions; his wife's influence, which was paramount with him to the end of his life, having already operated upon him. In 1863 the strife had reached a critical stage, the policy of the Government became harsh, and the Crown Prince was so moved that he addressed words of strong remonstrance to his father. He did so in a memorable letter, in which he respectfully but earnestly besought the King to yield to the wishes of his people and warned him that the fate of the dynasty would be imperilled by his despotic policy. He even offered to resign his command in the army and the offices he held about the court, if his father desired.

The Outbreak of War,

however, put an end to this controversy, and also showed that the King's persistence in strengthening the army was justified by results. The Crown Prince was disgusted with the unequal struggle between Prussia and Austria combined, and the little Kingdom of Denmark, but his duty as the first subject of the realm was clear, and he went through the one short campaign, which sufficed to end the struggle, on the staff of Marshal Wrangel. The conflict with Austria, in which this Danish war culminated in 1866, appealed much more forcibly to the Crown Prince's patriotism, and it also established his reputatiou as an able general. Scarcely had the declaration of war been heard when he was marching through the mountains of the Silesia frontier with 125,000 men at his back. Once over the mountains into Bohemia the Crown Prince's successive blows—Trautenau, Nachod, Skalitz—fell upon the bewildered Austrians like thunder from a clear sky, while Prince Frederick Charles fought his way toward the same point from the other side, sweeping away all obstacles with a rapidity which gave to this strange campaign its now historical name of the Seven Days' War. But before the two invading hosts could unite, the Austrian commander-in-chief fell upon Frederick Charles with a superior force, hoping to overwhelm him before the Crown Prince could come up. The scene was the field of Sadowa, and at first it seemed lost to the Prussians, for the pressure of the Austrian masses was tremendous, and all the valor of the Northern army could barely hold its own against such odds. Suddenly the smoke rolled aside, for a moment from the hard-fought field; and the Crown Prince, who had made a circuit to take the Austrians in the rear, was seen approaching. His arrival decided the day and won him the applause of all Europe. At the close of the day the Crown Prince joined his father on the meadows of Problus, where the delighted veteran took off his breast the Order of Merit and gave it to his son. The King has recorded the affecting incident: "At last I came upon Fritz, with his staff. What a moment, after all we had gone through, and upon the evening of such a day! I gave him the *Ordre pour le Merite* with my own hands, so that the tears ran down his cheeks."

The Franco-Prussian War,

four years later, rendered the Crown Prince still more illustrious. The victories of Weissenburg and Wörth, the investment of Strasburg, the passage of the Vosges, followed each other like claps of thunder, and he was pursuing his victorious advance when he learned that his late opponent, McMahon, was marching towards Metz to join Bazaine against Prince Frederick Charles. It was the situation of Sadowa over again, and once more the Crown Prince turned the scale. Although McMahon had nearly four days' start, the indefatigable German leader overtook him at Sedan, where a second Waterloo placed at the mercy of the conquerors 80,-

000 French soldiers, 4,000 officers, 400 guns, and the Emperor himself. After this he took part in the investment of Paris, and held his position until the capitulation was signed. During both these wars the Prince was the idol of his troops. It was not only his skill and valor that won their love, but his own regard for their comfort.

A Characteristic Incident

related by a press correspondent illustrates this interest. He wrote: "I have been the accidental and unseen witness of a little scene just now which is worth recording. A country cart was rumbling down the street with two wounded officers—young men—on their way to the station. An officer on foot beckoned to the driver to stop, and went up to the cart, the occupants of which tried to salute him, but he made a gesture, and leaning over, entered into conversation with them for ten minutes, evidently asking after their wounds. On parting, he shook each by the hand and continued his way up the street, accompanied by two other officers. He halted at my quarters and inquired if there were any wounded inside—they had been removed, some to their last resting-place—then went on, and, meeting a cart full of wounded soldiers, talked to them each in turn, and so went on; visiting the hospitals and the wounded in the most unostentatious manner. *It was the Crown Prince.* No wonder his men are fond of him."

The Years of Peace

which succeeded the war of 1870 were occupied by Frederick in the work allotted to capable men in his station; and he frequently represented the King in visits and ceremonials. Before that period, he was at the opening of the Suez Canal, and visited Palestine. After it, he went to Vienna, in 1873, to be present at the opening of the Exhibition; and subsequently travelled in Sweden, Norway, and Denmark. He paid a visit to Victor Emmanuel at Naples in 1875, and attended the funeral of that King in Rome in 1878. He presided over the Commission organized when the assassins Nobiling and Hödel endeavored to slay the Emperor William; and in 1881 it was his sad duty to witness the funeral of Alexander II., at St. Petersburg. On many other occasions he took part in public business, and was always ready to foster education, literature, and art. The excavations at Olympia, which yielded such fruit, owed much to him; and he did not forget his student days at Bonn. He was Rector of that University, and he presided over one of its great student celebrations. In addition to his scholastic rank at Bonn, the degree of Doctor was conferred on him by the Universities of Königsberg and Oxford. Moreover, he wrote one or two books; one on his Eastern tour, and another on the war of 1866.

His Fatal Malady

first appeared in January of last year. It was then thought to be only an inflammatory affection of the throat, with a cough and hoarseness. The affection, however, not yielding to treatment, Dr. Mackenzie, the famous specialist in throat diseases, was consulted, and in May he removed a foreign growth from the Prince's throat. The operation caused general uneasiness in Europe, which was not allayed by the report of Professor Virchow that cancer cells were not found in the part removed. Subsequent operations were performed, until at length the disease appeared so low down in the throat that it was no longer possible to operate from the mouth. By Dr. Mackenzie's advice the illustrious patient went to Italy to spend the winter. Varying reports of his condition appeared, but when, in February of this year, tracheotomy was finally resorted to, to save him from suffocation, the prospect of his recovery faded in gloom. On March 9, while he was still in Italy, his aged father died, and the Prince became

Emperor.

His address to his people, and the dignities he conferred on eminent men, confirmed the good opinion previously entertained of his character. His last official act was a still more decisive evidence of the enlightened policy he would have pursued had he lived. It was an indignant reproof to Government agents who interfered in the elections in the interest of the Government, and of Herr Puttkamer, the Secretary of the Interior, who directed them.

Meanwhile, however, his disease was making rapid progress. He became unable to take solid food, and his strength speedily declined. On June 14 it became evident that

His Death

was close at hand. The disease had affected the lungs, and the inflammation there could not be otherwise than fatal. Still, the Emperor maintained the tranquillity of mind which had characterized him throughout his affliction, and which did not desert him at the trying moment when he first learned the nature of his disease. He continued to write loving messages for his friends long after the power of speech had left him. Ever mindful of others, and knowing the jealousy with which the German physicians regarded Dr. Mackenzie, he wrote on one of his slips: "I feel that Dr. Mackenzie has done all that human science, watchfulness and skill, could do to prolong my life. I thank him." The Empress was promptly at his bedside when the dangerous symptoms appeared, and during the remaining hours of his life would not quit her post. The Emperor lay with her hand clasped in his, and once, when Bismarck appeared at his bedside, he placed it in that of the grim old chancellor, as if commending her who was soon to be a widow to his powerful protection. He remained perfectly conscious during the day and night, though the fatal symptom of coma occasionally asserted its sway. On the morning of Friday, June 15, the intervals of unconsciousness grew longer, and the members of the family grouped around the bed perceived that he was rapidly sinking. At eleven o'clock Dr. Mackenzie signed to the Empress, who fervently kissed the hand of the dying Emperor, and it was observed he drew it to him and kissed it—his last act. At twelve minutes past eleven o'clock Sir Morell took out his watch, and declared that life had passed away. So ended a life singularly noble and useful, and Germany now mourns in her dead Emperor, the soldier, the scholar, and the statesman, whose love for her, and concern for her welfare, ended only with his life.

ANECDOTES RELATED AT RECENT EVANGELISTIC MEETINGS.

A Condemned Murderer's Despair.—An Evangelist remarks: "Not long ago there was a man who for murder was condemned to die, and was in one of the prisons awaiting the day of his execution. An old friend happening to visit the governor of the State, was being shown around the city, and among other places was taken through the prison and shown the condemned cell. After they were gone a warder attending the felon, said to him, 'Do you know who that was that was visiting you?' 'No, he gloomily replied. 'That was the governor of the State,' replied the warder. Then the condemned man stamped his foot in a paroxysm of despair, and exclaimed, 'Why did you not tell me before? If I had but known I would have knelt before him and prayed him to save me; but now it is too late.' Why does not every sinner kneel and ask pardon of the Saviour and Governor of the Universe, *now*, while He is passing by."

A Farmer's Death Foreshadowed.—"A farmer went almost daily into a market town to buy and sell. He regularly dined in a certain hotel in that town. One night he dreamt that he had entered the hotel, and when he was passing through the hall, he saw a door that he had never noticed there before. He turned the handle and walked in. The door immediately closed behind him, and to his horror he found himself in a room with a great number of his friends who had died. He tried to get out, but his efforts were in vain. 'You cannot get out,' said one of his skeleton friends; 'you, also, shall be dead in eight days.' In the morning the farmer awoke, much disturbed about his dream, and went at once to his minister and related it to him. 'You are an unsaved man,' said the minister, solemnly. 'You ought to come to Christ at once; a distinct call may have come to you through this dream.' 'No,' replied the farmer, 'I will not be whipped into the kingdom, but have no objection to be wooed and won by Christ.' 'Friend, don't let your proud folly ruin you for ever,' the minister exclaimed; 'God has been trying to win you for years.' 'And do you mean to tell me that I shall be a dead man in a week? It is all fancy; I will take my chance.' Next day, when the farmer was in the hotel, he looked for the door of which he dreamed, but he did not see it, and he went on living as before, until the eighth day arrived, when he entered the hotel to partake of his dinner, at which he drank a bottle of wine—perhaps more. Presently he mounted his horse, to go home; but on the road he fell from it, and was killed. How shocking is the end of all who obey not the gospel of Christ!"

The Smuggler's Cargo.—The Rev. Mark Guy Pearse told, in a recent sermon, of a boatman with whom he went fishing and who joined him in greeting the daylight with the morning hymn. "Ah," said the man, "I could not have done that in the past; I did not feel like singing hymns when the day was breaking." And he told how in the past he had belonged to a smuggling crew, and how one day they saw the Government boat giving chase, and their one hope was in throwing the cargo overboard, lest that which would convict them should be discovered; they preferred to surrender the cargo rather than run the risk of imprisonment. At last, just as they were thinking that nothing that could lead to trouble would now be found on board, the hopeless cry was raised, "It's floating—it won't sink!" And there, in the wake of their vessel, and in sight of the Government officials, floated the incriminating cargo that the waves would not engulf! But it is not so with the evil that the heart abandons as it looks up to Christ. The tempter sometimes whispers to us that our sins are unpardonable, and such as must drive us to despair. But, whatever the tempter or our own depressed natures may suggest, there is nothing between the seeking soul and the Redeemer. "Their sins and iniquities will I remember no more." "He will subdue our iniquities; and Thou wilt cast all their sins into the depths of the sea."

The Bank Manager's Investment.—Mr. Hamilton remarked: "A late very popular manager of a bank was visited by a friend, who said to him, 'Oh, Mr. B., I know of a first-class chance for making a fortune, if I had but a few hundred pounds to invest.' 'May I ask what it is?' replied the manager. His visitor then went into the details of the contemplated transaction, and Mr. B. said, 'I think it will be very profitable. Do you not mean to touch it?' 'I cannot,' said the other, despondingly, 'I have not sufficient capital just now.' That was all that was said, and the bank manager's friend took his departure. Some time afterwards, as he had drawn several rather heavy checques, this gentlemen sent his bank-book to be made up, and when it was returned to him he was surprised to find that there was an entry of £500 in his favor, which he did not remember having paid into the bank. He immediately went to the bank and inquired concerning it. The clerk could give him no information other than that the entry had been made at the instance of the manager. He went to his friend, the manager, about the mistake. 'It is not a mistake,' replied Mr. B., 'I directed it to be put there. When you were here last you gave me some information on a certain subject. I thought your views were right, and acted upon your advice, with the result that I have cleared a considerable profit, and the £500 paid in to your account is your share of it.' That man took his religion into practical business, and rendered to every man his due. Nothing would have been easier than for him to keep the whole profits, and few, knowing the circumstances, would have dared to find fault; but he loved his neighbor as himself."

HUMAN CONSTELLATIONS.

Dr. Talmage's Sermon Preached at Winfield, Kansas., last Sunday Morning, June 24, 1888.

"They that turn many to righteousness shall shine as the stars for ever and ever." Dan. 12:3.

Every Man has Influence—Is Peopling Heaven or Hell—How to Turn Many to Righteousness—I. By a Right Example—Result of a Little Child's Ablutions—The Best Kind of Binding for a Bible An Intrepid General in the Mexican War—II. By Prayer—A Mother's Prayer for a Wayward Boy—III. By Christian Admonition—IV. The Reward.—To be as Stars—Shining with Borrowed Light—A Light Independent—Unknown Graves at Richmond—Like Stars in Clusters—In Swift Motion—In Magnitude—In Duration.

EVERY man has a thousand roots and a thousand branches. His roots reach down through all the earth; his branches spread through all the heavens. He speaks with voice, with eye, with hand, with foot. His silence often is thunder, and his life is an anthem or a doxology. There is no such thing as negative influence. We are all positive in the place we occupy, making the world better or making it worse, on the Lord's side or on the devil's, making up reasons for our blessedness or banishment; and we have already done work in

Peopling Heaven or Hell.

I hear people tell of what they are going to do. A man who has burned down a city might as well talk of some evil that he expects to do, or a man who has saved an empire might as well talk of some good that he expects to do. By the force of your evil influence you have already consumed infinite values; or you have, by the power of a right influence, won whole kingdoms for God.

It would be absurd for me to stand here, and, by elaborate argument, prove that the world is off the track. You might as well stand at the foot of an embankment, amid the wreck of a capsized rail-train, proving by elaborate argument that something is out of order. Adam tumbled over the embankment sixty centuries ago, and the whole race, in one long train, has gone on tumbling in the same direction. Crash! crash! The only question now is, by what leverage can the crushed thing be lifted? By what hammer may the fragments be reconstructed? I want to show you

How we may Turn Many

to righteousness, and what will be our future pay for so doing.

First. We may turn them *by the charm of a right example*. A child coming from a filthy home, was taught at school to wash its face. It went home so much improved in appearance that its mother washed her face. And when the father of the household came home, and saw the improvement in domestic appearance, he washed his face. The neighbors happening in, saw the change, and tried the same experiment, until all that street was purified, and the next street copied its example, and the whole city felt the result of one school-boy washing his face. That is a fable, by which we set forth that the best way to get the world washed of its sins and pollution, is to have our own heart and life cleansed and purified. A man with grace in his heart, and Christian cheerfulness in his face, and holy consistency in his behavior, is a perpetual sermon; and the sermon differs from others in that it has but one head, and the longer it runs, the better.

There are honest men who walk down Wall Street, making the teeth of iniquity chatter. There are happy men who go into a sick-room, and, by a look, help the broken bone to knit, and the excited nerves drop to a calm beating. There are pure men whose presence silences the tongue of uncleanness.

The Mightiest Agent

of good on earth is a consistent Christian. I like the Bible folded between lids of cloth, of calfskin, or morocco, but I like it better when, in the shape of a man, it goes out into the world—a Bible illustrated. Courage is beautiful to read about; but rather would I see a man with all the world against him, confident as though all the world were for him. Patience is beautiful to read about; but rather would I see a buffeted soul calmly waiting for the time of deliverance. Faith is beautiful to read about; but rather would I find a man in the midnight walking straight on as though he saw everything. Oh, how many souls have been turned to God by the charm of a bright example!

When, in the Mexican War, the troops were wavering, a general rose in his stirrups and dashed into the enemy's lines, shouting, "Men, follow me!" They, seeing his courage and disposition, dashed on after him and gained the victory. What men want to rally them for God is an example to lead them. All your commands to others to advance amount to nothing so long as you stay behind. To affect them aright, you need to start for heaven yourself, looking back only to give the stirring cry of, "Men, follow!"

Again: We may turn many to righteousness

By Prayer.

There is no such detective as prayer, for no one can hide away from it. It puts its hand on the shoulder of a man ten thousand miles off. It alights on a ship mid-Atlantic. The little child cannot understand the law of electricity, or how the telegraphic operator, by touching the instrument here, may dart a message under the sea to another continent; nor can we, with our small intellect, understand how the touch of a Christian's prayer shall instantly strike a soul on the other side of the earth. You take ship and go to some other country, and get there at eleven o'clock in the morning. You telegraph to New York, and the message gets here at six o'clock in the same morning. In other words, it seems to arrive here five hours before it started. Like that is prayer. God says: "Before they call, I will hear." To overtake a loved one on the road, you may spur up a lathered steed until he shall outrace the one that brought the news to Ghent; but a prayer shall catch it at one gallop. A boy running away from home may take the midnight train from the country village, and reach the seaport in time to gain the ship that sails on the morrow; but

A Mother's Prayer

will be on the deck to meet him, and in the hammock before he swings into it, and at the capstan before he winds the rope around and on the sea, against the sky, as the vessel ploughs on toward it. There is a mightiness in prayer. George Muller prayed a company of poor boys together, and then he prayed up an asylum in which they might be sheltered. He turned his face toward Edinburgh and prayed, and there came a thousand pounds. He turned his face toward London and prayed, and there came a thousand pounds. He turned his face toward Dublin and prayed, and there came a thousand pounds. The breath of Elijah's prayer blew all the clouds off the sky, and it was dry weather. The breath of Elijah's prayer blew all the clouds together, and it was wet weather. Prayer, in Daniel's time, walked the cave as a lion-tamer. It reached up, and took the sun by its golden bit, and stopped it.

What Prayer can Do.

We have all yet to try the full power of prayer. The time will come when the American Church will pray with its face toward the West, and all the prairies and inland cities will surrender to God; and will pray with face toward the sea, and all the islands and ships will become Christian. Parents who have wayward sons will get down on their knees and say: "Lord, send my boy home," and the boy in Canton shall get right up from the gaming-table, and go down to find out which ship starts first for America.

Not one of us yet knows how to pray. All we have done as yet has only been pottering. A boy gets hold of his father's saw and hammer, and tries to make something, but it is a poor affair that he makes. The father comes and takes the same saw and hammer, and builds the house or the ship. In the childhood of our Christian faith, we make but poor work with these weapons of prayer, but when we come to the stature of men in Christ Jesus, then, under these implements, the temple of God will rise, and the world's redemption will be launched. God cares not for the length of our prayers, or the number of our prayers, or the beauty of our prayers, or the place of our prayers; but it is the faith in them that tells. Believing prayer soars higher than the lark ever sang; plunges deeper than diving-bell ever sank; darts quicker than lightning ever flashed. Though we have used only the back of this weapon instead of the edge, what marvels have been wrought! If saved, we are all the captives of some earnest prayer. Would God that, in desire for the rescue of souls, we might in prayer lay hold of the resources of the Lord Omnipotent!

We may turn many to righteousness

By Christian Admonition

Do not wait until you can make a formal speech. Address the one next to you. You will not go home alone to-day. Between this and your place of stopping you may decide the eternal destiny of an immortal spirit. Just one sentence may do the work. Just one question. Just one look. The formal talk that begins with a sigh, and ends with a canting snuffle, is not what is wanted, but the heart-throb of a man in dead earnest. There is not a soul on earth that you may not bring to God if you rightly go at it. They said Gibraltar could not be taken. It is a rock, sixteen hundred feet high and three miles long. But the English and Dutch did take it. Artillery, and sappers and miners, and fleets pouring out volleys of death, and thousands of men reckless of danger, can do anything. The stoutest heart of sin, though it be rock, and surrounded by an ocean of transgression, under Christian bombardment may hoist the flag of redemption.

The Reward.

But is all this admonition and prayer and Christian work for nothing? My text promises to all the faithful eternal lustre. "They that turn many to righteousness shall shine as the stars forever." As stars, the redeemed have a borrowed light. What makes Mars and Venus and Jupiter so luminous? When the sun throws down his torch in the heavens, the stars pick up the scattered brands, and hold them in procession as the queen of the night advances; so all Christian workers, standing around the throne, will shine in the light borrowed from the Sun of Righteousness—Jesus in their faces, Jesus in their songs, Jesus in their triumph.

Christ left heaven once for a tour of redemption on earth, yet the glorified ones knew He would come back again. But let Him abdicate His throne, and go away to stay for ever, the music would stop; the congregation disperse; the temples of God be darkened; the rivers of light stagnate; and every chariot would become a hearse, and every bell would toll, and there would not be room on the hillsides to bury the dead of the great metropolis, for there would be pestilence in heaven. But Jesus lives, and so all the redeemed live with Him. He shall recognize them as His comrades in earthly toil, and remember what they did for the honor of His name, and for the spread of His kingdom. All their prayers and tears and work will rise before Him as He looks into their faces, and He will divide His kingdom with them; His peace—their peace; His holiness—their holiness; His joy—their joy. The glory of the central throne reflected from the surrounding thrones, the last spot of sin struck from the Christian orb, and the entire nature a-tremble and a-flash with light, they shall shine as the stars for ever and ever.

Again: Christian workers shall be like the stars in the fact that they have

A Light Independent

of each other. Look up at the night, and see each world show its distinct glory. It is not like the conflagration, in which you cannot tell where one flame stops and another begins. Neptune, Herschel, and Mercury are as distinct as if each one of them were the only star; so our individualism will not be lost in heaven.

great multitude—yet each one as observable, as distinctly recognized, as greatly celebrated, as if in all the space, from gate to gate, and from hill to hill, he were the only inhabitant; no mixing up—no mob—no indiscriminate rush; each Christian worker

Standing Out Illustrious—

all the story of earthly achievement adhering to each one; his self-denials and pains and services and victories published. Before men went out to the last war, the orators told them that they would all be remembered by their country, and their names be commemorated in poetry and in song; but go to the graveyard in Richmond, and you will find there six thousand graves, over each one of which is the inscription, "Unknown." The world does not remember its heroes; but there will be no unrecognized Christian worker in heaven. Each one known by all; grandly known; known by acclamation: all the past story of work for God gleaming in cheek and brow and foot and palm. They shall shine with distinct light as the stars, for ever and ever.

Again: Christian workers shall shine like the

Stars in Clusters.

In looking up, you find the worlds in family circles. Brothers and sisters—they take hold of each other's hands and dance in groups. Orion in a group. The Pleiades in a group. The solar system is only a company of children, with bright faces, gathered around one great fireplace. The worlds do not straggle off. They go in squadrons and fleets, sailing through immensity. So Christian workers in heaven will dwell in neighborhoods and clusters.

I am sure that some people I will like in heaven a great deal better than others. Yonder is a constellation of stately Christians. They lived on earth by rigid rule. They never laughed. They walked every hour anxious lest they should lose their dignity. But they loved God; and yonder they shine in brilliant constellation. Yet I shall not long to get into that particular group. Yonder is a constellation of small-hearted Christians—asteroids in the eternal astronomy. While some souls go up from Christian battle, and blaze like Mars, these asteroids dart a feeble ray like Vesta. Yonder is a constellation of martyrs, of apostles, of patriarchs. Our souls, as they go up to heaven, will seek out the most congenial society.

Yonder is a constellation almost merry with the play of light. On earth they were full of sympathies and songs and tears and raptures and congratulations. When they prayed, their words took fire; when they sang, the tune could not hold them; when they wept over a world's woes, they sobbed as if heart-broken; when they worked for Christ they flamed with enthusiasm. Yonder they are—circle of light! constellation of joy! galaxy of fire! Oh, that you and I, by that grace which can transform the worst into the best, might at last sail in the wake of that fleet, and wheel in that glorious group, as the stars for ever and ever!

Again: Christian workers will shine like the stars in swiftness of motion. The worlds

Do not Stop to Shine.

There are no fixed stars save as to relative position. The star most thoroughly fixed flies thousands of miles a minute. The astronomer, using his telescope for an alpenstock, leaps from world-crag to world-crag, and finds no star standing still. The chamois hunter has to fly to catch his prey, but not so swift is his game as that which the scientist tries to shoot through the tower of observatory. Like petrels mid-Atlantic, that seem to come from no shore, and be bound to no landing-place—flying, flying—so these great flocks of worlds rest not as they go—wing and wing—age after age—for ever and ever. The eagle hastes to its prey, but we shall in speed beat the eagles.

You have noticed the velocity of the swift horse under whose feet the miles slip like a smooth ribbon, and as he passes, the four hoofs strike the earth in such quick beat your pulses take the same vibration. But all these things are not swift in comparison with the motion of which I speak. The moon moves fifty-four thousand miles in a day. Yonder, Neptune flashes on eleven thousand miles in an hour. Yonder Mercury goes one hundred and nine thousand miles in an hour. So like the stars the Christian shall shine in swiftness of motion.

You hear now of father or mother or child sick one thousand miles away, and it takes you two days to get to them. You hear of some case of suffering that demands your immediate attention, but it takes you an hour to get there. Oh, the joy when you shall, in fulfilment of the text, take starry speed, and be equal to one hundred thousand miles an hour! Having on earth got used to Christian work, you will not quit when death strikes you. You will only take on more velocity. There is a dying child in London, and its spirit must be taken up to God: you are there in an instant to do it. There is a young man in New York to be arrested from going into that gate of sin: you are there in an instant to arrest him. Whether with spring of foot, or stroke of wing, or by the force of some new law that shall hurl you to the spot where you would go, I know not; but my text suggests velocity. All space open before you, with nothing to hinder you in mission of light and love and joy, you shall shine in swiftness of motion as the stars for ever and ever.

Again: Christian workers, like the stars,

Shine in Magnitude.

The most illiterate man knows that these things in the sky, looking like gilt buttons, are great masses of matter. To weigh them, one would think that it would require scales with a pillar hundreds of thousands of miles high, and chains hundreds of thousands of miles long, and at the bottom of the chains basins on either side hundreds of thousands of miles wide, and that then Omnipotence alone could put the mountains into the scales and the hills into the balance. But puny man has been equal to the undertaking, and has set a little balance on his geometry, and weighed world against world. Yea, he has pulled out his measuring line, and announced that Herschel is thirty-six thousand miles in diameter, Saturn seventy-nine thousand miles in diameter, and Jupiter eighty-nine thousand miles in diameter, and that the smallest pearl on the beach of heaven is immense beyond all imagination. So all they who have toiled for Christ on earth shall rise up to a magnitude of privilege, and a magnitude of strength, and a magnitude of holiness, and a magnitude of joy; and the weakest saint in glory become greater than all that we can imagine of an arch-angel.

Brethren, it doth not yet appear what we shall be. Wisdom that shall know everything; wealth that shall possess everything; strength that shall do everything; glory that shall circumscribe everything! We shall not be like a taper set in a sick man's window, or a bundle of stick kindled on the beach to warm a shivering crew; but you must take the diameter and the circumference of the world, if you would get any idea of the greatness of our estate when we shall shine as the stars for ever and ever.

Lastly—and coming to this point my mind almost breaks down under the contemplation—like the stars, all Christian workers shall

Shine in Duration,

The same stars that look down upon us looked down upon the Chaldean shepherds. The meteor that I saw flashing across the sky the other night, I wonder if it was not the same one that pointed down to where Jesus lay in the manger, and if, having pointed out His birthplace, it has ever since been wandering through the heavens, watching to see how the world would treat Him! When Adam awoke in the garden in the cool of the day, he saw coming out through the dusk of the evening the same worlds that greeted us last night.

In Independence Hall is an old cracked hell that sounded the signature of the Declaration of Independence. You cannot ring it now; but this great chime of silver bells that strike in the dome of night, ring out with as sweet a tone as when God swung them at the creation. Look up at night, and know that the white lilies that bloom in all the hanging gardens of our King are century plants—not blooming once in a hundred years, but through all the centuries.

The star at which the mariner looks to-night was the light by which the ships of Tarshish were guided across the Mediterranean, and the Venetian flotilla found its way into Lepanto. Their armor is as bright to-night as when, in ancient battle, the stars in their courses fought against Sisera. To the ancients the stars were

Symbols of Eternity.

But here the figure of my text breaks down—not in defeat, but in the majesties of the judgment. The stars shall not shine forever. The Bible says they shall fall like autumnal leaves. As, when the connecting factory-band slips at nightfall from the main-wheel, all the smaller wheels slacken their speed, and with slower and slower motion they turn until they come to a full stop; so this great machinery of the universe, wheel within wheel, making revolution of appalling speed, shall, by the touch of God's hand, slip the band of present law, and slacken and stop. That is what will be the matter with the mountains. The chariots in which they ride shall halt so suddenly that the kings shall be thrown out. Star after star shall be carried out to burial amid funeral torches and burning worlds. Constellations shall throw ashes on their heads, and all up and down the highways of space there shall be mourning, mourning, mourning, because the worlds are dead. But the Christian workers shall never quit their thrones—they shall reign for ever and ever.

CONVERTED IN THE CATACOMBS.

IN an introduction to a lecture by Prof. de Launay, formerly Professor of ancient and modern languages in the State College of Louisiana, Canon Christopher recently gave an interesting account of the Professor's conversion from Roman Catholicism. It appears that M. de Launay, who is a native of Paris, after graduating at the University of Angers, was placed by his relatives under the care of the Vicar-General of the Jesuits, at Rome, as his spiritual adviser. He studied under Cardinal Mezzofanti, the most reputed linguist of his day. He was joined to the company of Jesus, and was sent to Fribourg. There, while preparing to enter as a novice, an attack of typhoid fever brought him to the verge of death. In his anguish of soul he sent for a priest to bring him the Viaticum, or last Communion. The priest, whilst lifting up the host, exclaimed in Latin, "Blessed are they who hunger and thirst after righteousness, for they shall be filled"; "Come unto Me all ye who are weary and heavy laden, and I will give you rest." These words were a light in the darkness to his agonized soul, but the clear, bright sun of simple trust in Christ was not yet apparent.

After recovering he returned to Rome, and he frequently visited the catacombs. Among these tombs of the martyrs his troubled spirit found peace, joy, light, and repose, in beholding, reading, and sketching the pictorial records and inscriptions on these tombs. Here he learned how far Popery had wandered away from the truth and teachings of Christ. In the first three centuries of bloody persecution he found nowhere a prayer for the dead, nor to the dead; nowhere a crucifix, but the signs and symbols of the Resurrection; nowhere among the miles and miles of graves a prayer to the blessed mother of our Lord; she is not even named. Here there was no grovelling devotion to sculptured images of wood and stone. M. de Launay perceived that the religion of the early Christians and martyrs buried in the catacombs was what the New Testament taught, but not what the Church of Rome taught. He felt that he could not conscientiously remain a Roman Catholic. He came to America, and after laboring for some time in the College of Louisiana, went to Paris, where he is now laboring with much success as a Protestant missionary.

THE SPIRIT IN THE COMING AGE.

By Pastor E. P. Marvin.*

His Progressive Work—Pentecost to be Eclipsed in the Coming Outpouring—At the Bringing in of the Fullness of the Gentiles—Bodies of the Saints Redeemed—The Brute Creation to Share—The Timely Watch-Cry—The Duty of Watchfulness.

THE Holy Spirit has been constantly at work in the world from the creation. He brooded over chaotic creation, Gen. 1 : 2, inspired prophets, II Pet. 1 : 21, filled them with power, Micah 3 : 8, and wrought wonders through Moses, Joshua, Samson, and Elijah. He co-operated continually with Christ on earth in all His wondrous works, Matt. 12 : 28. Christ was filled with the Holy Spirit, Luke 4 : 1. He was conceived, Matt. 1 : 20, anointed, Acts 10 : 28, and raised from the dead by the Holy Spirit, I Pet. 3 : 18. He breathed the Spirit on His disciples, John 20 : 22. The present is "the special dispensation of the Holy Spirit" only in its

Progressive and Varied Work.

It is really a dispensation of the Trinity. All three persons were represented at the Baptism of Christ. The Holy Spirit, as the Executive of Divinity, applies the purchased Redemption, and calls out the Bride elect. Christ, the Prince of Life, imparts life through the Holy Spirit. The promise and potency of all regeneration and restitution resides in the Spirit of God—"As it was in the beginning, is now, and ever shall be, world without end, Amen." As the work of the Spirit has been progressive in power and permanence in ages past, we may expect the same divine progress in ages to come.

Many prophecies of the Spirit's power and work await a more complete fulfilment at and after the Coming of the Lord. The blessing at Pentecost and afterward, is repeatedly called an "earnest," that is a sample and pledge of more to follow, II Cor. 1 : 22, and 5 : 5; Eph. 1 : 14. The earnest is but a small portion of the promised abundance. A careful study of Joel 2 : 28-32 reveals that this prophecy does not find its complete and final fulfilment in Acts 2 : 15-20. Verses 12, 17, 18, 27, in Joel, interpret "*afterward*" in v. 28. After the repentance and restoration of God's ancient people, will come the Great Outpouring. Besides, the Spirit was not poured out on "all flesh" at Pentecost, but only on Jews in Jerusalem, and there were no celestial "signs." Every prophecy must find its mate, and Pentecost does not fully meet and complete this. Again, in Acts 3 : 19, 21, it is declared that when God's ancient people repent, refreshing shall come, Christ shall return, and

Prophetic Restitution

be ushered in. We cannot separate these events widely, and they are all in the future. They are called times or seasons of refreshing, and they are directly related to the Coming of the Lord. We also read of these in James 5 : 7 as "the early and latter rain." Pentecost then was but an increase of blessing over the past, and an earnest of the future.

A more powerful, conspicuous, and wonderful outpouring of the Holy Spirit will come when the Fullness of the Gentiles is brought in, Christ returns, and the Jews are restored. The first work is to evangelize the world and gather in the "election of grace," the fullness of the Gentiles, the Bride of Christ. Then the Spirit will work with seven-fold power. There shall be showers and floods of blessing. Ps. 72 : 67; Isa. 44 : 3; Ezek. 34 : 46. A new heart will be given, and Israel shall come forth from the charnel house. Ezek. 36 : 4-28, and 37 : 1-13. Israel shall be honored among the nations, and wonders shall be wrought. Zech. 8 : 21-23; Acts 15 : 14-17; Rom. 11 : 15, 26. We have in the order of redemption: 1. An election of Jews. 2. An election of Gentiles. 3. The nation of Jews. 4. The nation of Gentiles.

God chose the Jew first to preserve and transmit His truth and grace. Upon his failure,

A Gentile Remnant

is called. After this election of grace is complete, the Jew must come again upon the scene to be blest, and to bless the world. Gen. 12 : 3. The Jews were the first missionaries, and they will be the last, up to the "Coming Day." They are God's Mediatorial People, destined to fill the world with the knowledge of God. Pentecost must be repeated with seven-fold power before the millennium, acting upon the long-rejected people, and through them upon the nations.

Prophecy forecasts blended scenes of judgment and mercy, love and wrath, rewards and punishments. Ps. 2 : 8, 9; II Thess. 1 : 8; Jude 14. See the Book of Revelation. Until then we shall win no general and decisive victory. This is true divine evolution from age to age. The "good time is coming," not by human wisdom and worldly progress. Professor Guizot used often to speak in foreign tongue of "*developpment*," and this foreign-coined word fitly characterizes the general progress of the race for the whole 6,000 years.

Then will the Holy Spirit redeem the bodies of the saints from the grave, and transfigure those of the living saints. No one ever died in the presence of Christ on earth; and some were raised to life as an earnest of the future. Our bodies, fashioned like unto the glorious body of the Son of God, will be the everlasting temple of the life-giving Spirit. John 6 : 63; Rom. 8 : 11; I Cor. 15 : 42-53; I Thess. 4 : 16-18.

The Inferior Creation,

cursed by sin and made subject to vanity, shall be regenerated and restored by the Holy Spirit. The Spirit will flood the earth, operating again on matter, eradicating the curse, renewing the face of the earth, and causing the desert to rejoice and blossom like the rose. Job 26 : 13; Ps. 104 : 30; Isa. 35 : 1; Rom. 8 : 10, 11.

This is the "regeneration," the bloom-time, when new life shall spring and beauty smile on every side. The earth is linked with man in both humiliation and glory. Soul, body, and earth are all redeemed. Man's original inheritance, usurped and damaged by the usurper. Satan, is then to be renovated and restored. Even the brute creation share in the restitution, Their savage nature is eradicated, and they dwell in peace with man and each other. Isa. 11 : 6-9. The Spirit can tame savage beasts as easily as savage men. Thus Satan's world becomes the Lord's again, and this is a prelude to the eternal state. Ps. 24. The Spirit, in co-operation with our Messianic King, erects and manifests the promised Kingdom, and

Jerusalem, the Metropolis,

becomes the centre of the world's peace. Isa. 32 : 1; Hag. 2 : 9. And we, as fellow-heirs, shall share in the glory and authority of the heavenly department of this kingdom. II Tim. 4 : 18. Israel on earth, as the head of nations and the source of blessing, shares the glory of the terrestrial. At the close of this millennial stage, we have the last judgment, and the complete renewal of the earth as the eternal home of the saints, underneath the new heavens, all plainly revealed. We may see, then, that Christ and the Holy Spirit do not make a failure, because the world is not all converted in this dispensation. Indeed, if the conquest of the world had been the dispensational promise and purpose, we might well call the last 1800 years a failure. But the true purpose (Acts 15 : 14) has been, and is being clearly fulfilled, and it is no failure that the spirit does not finish up all His work in our time. A glorious and final triumph is sure in ages to come.

Ministers of the Word who neglect the careful and prayerful study of Dispensational Truth, may well fear that a blight will come upon their spiritual life, and failure on their ministry. And especially must those who wilfully shut their eyes to the flood of light now poured upon their pathway concerning the present truth and blessed hope of the Lord's Coming, totally misunderstand "the signs of the times," blunder much in fruitless services, lack the supreme inspiration of revelation, and "be ashamed before Him at His Coming.' "Maranatha" is

The Timely Watch-cry,

and this is more and more testing and assorting the hearts, lives, and labors of the professing Church. We are not following a forlorn hope because we do not now "take the world for Christ," but allow Him the glory of taking it for Himself, in co-operation with the blessed Holy Spirit. Constantine first conceived the unscriptural scheme of erecting the Church into a kingdom, taking the world, and reigning in the absence of its rejected sovereign, and he thus inaugurated the greatest apostacy the Church ever saw. The Post-millennial error, "My Lord delayeth His coming," causes no small part of the worldliness and apostacy of the Church to-day. We are cheered by a bright hope, stimulated by an ever-imminent triumph, and encouraged by a reward insured by fidelity. II Tim. 4 : 7, 8.

Corporate testimony in holy living, apart from the world, seems almost gone. The spiritual grace of wisdom and corporate soul-winning by the stated means of grace, has fearfully declined. As a pastor, I am compelled to confess that the Spirit seems to use the professing Church less and less, as if corporate fellowship service were ending. As pastors we seem to be gathering the few grape gleanings after the vintage is done! We are resolved into individual testimony and service. Rev. 3 : 20. Evangelists, who look for that Blessed Hope, seem to be doing most of the soul-winning. It is supper-time. We must go to the streets and lanes, the highways and hedges.

Finally, how frequently we should pray, and how eagerly we should watch for the speedy Coming of the Lord! Christ prayed for the Spirit to come, John 14 : 16, 17; and the Spirit prays for Christ to return, Rev. 22 : 17. Revelation closes with a promise from heaven, which is wafted back in a prayer. Rev. 22 : 20.

* From his recent lecture at Niagara, contained in full, revised by himself, in *The Word*, a pamphlet of 192 pages, comprising also prophetic lectures by Rev. H. M. Parsons, Rev. James H. Brooks, D. D., of St. Louis; Rev. Albert Erdman, D. D.,; Rev. S. H. Kellogg, D. D.; and other able expositors of prophecy. Owing to the large demand for this work, a supply of copies has been procured by *Mr. J. E. Jewett*, 77 Bible House, New York, who will mail a copy to any address for fifty cents.

A NIGHT ON A MOUNTAIN.

A FAMILY on the brink of a precipice in the dark had a hairbreadth escape from death on June 9. That afternoon, a farmer living in Sullivan County, Penn., set out in a light spring wagon with two horses from Williamsport to go to Eagle's Mere. He was accompanied by his wife and his two small children. Just as it was growing dusk, and when within a few miles of their destination, the farmer in crossing the rough mountain path took a wrong turn. They travelled on without discovering the mistake for two hours. It grew very dark, and the overhanging branches of trees shut out even starlight. Yet they went on until suddenly the woman broke silence with, "I hear a noise like rushing waters." The farmer was loth to believe it, but lest there might be danger he stopped the horses. He then heard the ominous roar of a waterfall. The man was unnerved for a minute, when he lighted a piece of paper and to his horror discovered that they were on the brink of a precipice. Two more steps and the entire party would have been hurled down into a stream of water threading a sharp and rugged bed of rock two hundred feet below. Towering above them on the other side of the pathway was a straight wall of rock as high above them as the roaring falls beneath. It was a moment of awful suspense. As quickly as he could, the farmer had his wife and children out of the vehicle, and then, finding there was not room enough to turn, he unharnessed the horses and took out the pole. He reversed the wagon inch by inch, fearful every moment of its turning over the precipice; the horses were again hitched to, and they began to retrace their steps, the farmer walking at their heads. In this way they travelled over rough and dangerous roads, infested with bears and panthers, until the welcome dawn greeted their eyes. Not far off they heard the tinkle of cow bells and the barking of a dog. A loud shout brought a man to them who put them in the right road for Eagle's Mere. When they arrived the lady was so prostrated by the fearful experience of the night that for five hours she was unable to speak. Their peril was a fit type of the lives of thousands. Lost on the mountains of unbelief, in spiritual darkness, they are tending toward the precipice of death. But for all such God's Spirit waits to guide them to the path of peace and safety. (Ezek. 33: 11.)

HOW BISHOP PARKER DIED.

THE brief cablegram announcing the death of Bishop Parker, the successor of the martyred Bishop Hannington, which was all the intelligence we had of the sad event, when his portrait was published in this journal on June 7, has now been supplemented by a letter from Dr. Mackay. Writing from Usambiro, Eastern Equatorial Africa, Dr. Mackay says: "At our evening meal on March 26, the Bishop seemed fairly well, and was quite cheerful. His room was next to mine, and between two and three o'clock in the morning I heard him call his servant, Robert. I got up, thinking there was something wrong, and found him in bed shaking with a sharp attack of ague. He said that he had just taken a glass of quinine, but feared he had done so too late to ward off the attack. Ashe and I got him a hot bottle for his feet, and stayed with him a short time until the second or hot stage had begun to yield to slight perspiration. He begged us to retire, but bade his boy to sleep in the room by him, so as to be ready to call any of us should he feel worse. Soon after six o'clock on Monday morning, I went in to see him. He seemed to be in a very high fever, and completely jaundiced in appearance. Towards evening the fever passed off and coma set in. We arranged to divide the night in watching him, the hours till midnight falling to me. He seemed to sleep fairly quietly till about half-past nine, when breathing became irregular, and he began to groan. I sent for Ashe quickly, and just as he arrived breathing stopped, and our dear Bishop ceased to be with us. He died at 9: 45, just an hour of a fortnight since Blackburn expired. The loss to us is, indeed, great, but Africa has lost a true friend.

A FACT FOR STATESMEN.

THE uneasiness produced in all countries now by the anarchic tendencies of workingmen is on both sides of the Atlantic calling for the attention of statesmen. Not only in our own country, but in Germany, France, England, Belgium, and other lands, the governments are aware that the most difficult problem, but the most urgent is the Labor Question. As a rule, however, they overlook the fact that the most successful preventive of anarchy and social disorder is the gospel. Nowhere is the revolutionary spirit so active as among the artisans of France, among whom the Rev. R. W. McAll's mission is successfully laboring, and this is the testimony of one of its most prominent workers: "The result of the services of the mission halls is most hopeful. Restless, discouraged, desperate hearts are the very ones for whom it has a message, and, go where it will in France, it finds such hearts to-day. So much the greater, then, is the need of carrying the work forward into places where it has not yet penetrated. For while the Spirit of God is moving in the hearts of this people, discontented with their present lot, though not yet realizing their need of the gospel, the time is most propitious to present to them that which is their best and sufficient help. If any proof were needed that the gospel is a true panacea, even for the social woes under which the common people of France, as of all Europe, are suffering, it comes to us from the report of the Protestant pastors of Belgium, who have publicly stated that not one of the members of their churches (principally laboring men, whose poverty is deep, and whose outlook is dark and discouraging) took any part in the violent labor disturbances which a year or more ago agitated all Liege aud the district of Charleroi; but conducted themselves throughout as Christians."

ONE BIBLE IN A CHILIAN HOME.

A DEEPLY encouraging incident is reported in a Bible Society's report. It states that a Bible in Spanish was given, some time ago, to a Chilian sailor serving on board a steamer. The donor was a passenger, who said it was of no use to him, and the sailor was welcome to it. The young Chilian was deeply interested in it, and without any human agency whatever he became a true Christian. On his return trip he brought the Bible home with him to Talcahuano, where his parents and brothers and sisters resided. His eldest sister commenced a study of the book, and in a short time she gave up the confessional and the mass, and became a true Christian. In the course of two years the whole family, including her parents, three sisters, two brothers, and a brother-in-law, all embraced the truth as it is in Christ Jesus, and gave up all connection with Rome. This great work of God was performed without any instrumentality except His own Word and Spirit. The Rev. Dr. Swaney, a missionary in Chili, on his arrival there, met this Christian family.

A VICIOUS RELIGIOUS FESTIVAL.

A NATIVE Christian missionary in India, sends to the *Indian Witness* a sickening account of the scenes at a *mela* as he witnessed them, and in the midst of which he preached the gospel. He says: "Last week, hoping to reach the masses of our benighted countrymen, I started in company with my two assistants to the Dhulian Mela (fair), held in honor of Krishna, eleven miles from our station. I think it will not be uninteresting to state why these melas are held. To avert calamity and to bring down blessings, an image of Krishna, who is called by the people a *living* Sham Chand (supposing him always ready to grant their wishes) is brought by the wealthy classes from its shrine on the payment of a large sum of money. The image comes, attended by a *Mohanto*, who is respected and dreaded more than the god himself. The people flock to all parts to beg his blessings. It is a painful sight to see the *Mohanto* surrounded on all sides by the superstitious devotees, who remain on their knees until the food which was given to the god is distributed to them. To meet the wants of the immense concourse of people, the shop-keepers come; to gratify the lusts of the dissolute, prostitutes flock; to please the senses of hearing and seeing, of the poor as well as the rich, the dancing men and women resort; to amuse the children, players get together; and to cheat the innocent, gamblers assemble. These are the constituent parts which compose a *mela*. Thus is the most sacred shrine of the Hindus turned into a den of wickedness.

A SINGULAR TESTIMONY IN INDIA.

A STRIKING testimony to the effect of gospel preaching is mentioned in a letter from the Rev. W. A. Moore, a missionary in India to Dr. Cullis, who publishes it in his *Times of Refreshing*. He says: "Yesterday Goolab Sing went to the small-cause court to preach to the persons who gather there. He met an old friend, who said, 'Wherever I go, I hear you Christians preach, and no matter what we may say against your doctrines, yet *the truth sticks*. Until recently I did not think anything about doing wrong, but lately, when I lie, the thought, "What will I do should death overtake me?" makes me tremble and makes me afraid to do wrong."' Mr. Moore goes on to say: "A few days ago I sent out Bhkum Sing with some vernacular books for sale. He went to the house of *our old Marathi teacher* and found him reading the Bible. This teacher takes three Christian papers, and seeing the Bible advertised in one of them, sent for one and is studying. The Christian papers taken by him are eagerly read by several educated Hindus. Last Sunday, while preaching in the bazaar, *a brazier* listened very attentively. After we finished preaching, I gave away a few Gospels. This brazier was very anxious to get one, but as a man from a distant village wanted one we gave it to him, and told the brazier he would get one if he went to Goolah Sing's next day. Next day he went to G. S's place, and brother Namajee had a long talk with him. The man is convinced of the truth, but does not know how to earn his livelihood if he became a Christian."

POLITICAL PROGRESS IN JAPAN.

THE interest excited throughout the civilized world in the condition of Japan, especially among Christians, who hear with gladness of the opportunities afforded in that country for the preaching of the gospel, is gratified by the publication in the New York *Evening Post* of a lengthy letter from Rev. T. S. Tyng, the Protestant Episcopal missionary at Osaka. The facts which he there gives show a remarkable advance in civil liberty, and indicate that in the matter of elections the Japanese are at least as far advanced as ourselves. He says: "Another straw, showing the movement of the current, is shown in a case now pending in the superior court of this city. An election to fill a vacancy in the assembly of a recent prefecture, was recently held. Party spirit ran high. The sub-prefect, who had the counting of the votes, was of the minority party, and, if report is true, threw out, on the ground of mistake in the writing of a name, votes enough to elect his candidate, and reported to the prefect accordingly. The prefect accepted his report, and declared his candidate elected. For this he has been indicted, at the instance of the opposite party, and, appointee of the central government though he is, must now stand his trial in the ordinary courts of law, for accepting and giving effect to the report of his subordinate. This is but one of many indications that the power of popular government as already established in Japan, is growing stronger day by day."

The impression of Japan, recently produced by the popular representation of the humorists, is also declared by Mr. Tyng to be erroneous. He says: "Assassination or beheading may be the Asiatic method of asking for the resignation of obnoxious cabinet officers, but it is certainly not the method now or lately in vogue in Japan. Of recent ministers of state, Kuroda, in 1882, or thereabouts, and Inouye, in 1887, were driven from office by popular opinion—the former for alleged corruption, the latter for too great concession to foreign powers in the negotiations for treaty revision; but neither has met with any tragical fate. Okuma, Itagaki, Tani, and Soyeshima are names of some who have quietly withdrawn because of disagreement with the party in power; Okuma and Itagaki becoming leaders respectively of the moderate and advanced liberals. There has been no instance of a cabinet minister beheaded since the revolution which established the Mikado's government in 1868, and no beheading of anybody since that form of punishment was abolished in 1873. Capital punishment in any form is now reserved for cases of high treason, murder, and sometimes arson, and can be inflicted in no case whatever, except by due process of law, through the agency of the courts, as in the case, also, with all punishment for felony. A good instance (one out of many) of the absence of bloodthirstiness in the treatment of political offenders, is Mr. Mutsu. He was convicted of complicity in Saigo's rebellion, condemned to five years' imprisonment, released at the end of two years and a half; in eighteen months more put into office, and now goes to represent his country as Minister at Washington."

CHRISTIAN HERALD AND SIGNS OF OUR TIMES.

OFFICE, 63 BIBLE HOUSE, NEW YORK.

ENTERED AT THE POST-OFFICE AT NEW YORK, N. Y., AS SECOND-CLASS MATTER.

EVERY NUMBER CONTAINS:

The Portrait and Biography of some eminent person.
The Sermon Dr. Talmage preached the last Sunday morning.
An Exposition of Unfulfilled Prophecy.
A Summary of the Events of the Week. Notes of Religious and Temperance Movements, etc.
A Sermon by Rev. C. H. Spurgeon, of London, from advance sheets sent by special arrangements.
Pictures of Missionary Life, etc., and Descriptive Articles.
An instalment of a Serial Story.
An Exposition of the International Sunday-School Lesson, by Mrs. M. Baxter.

ANNUAL SUBSCRIPTION, $1.50.

Remittances by mail should be by bank cheques, Post-office orders, or Express money-orders whenever possible. If currency is sent it should be in a registered letter. Cheques and money-orders should be made payable to THE CHRISTIAN HERALD. Making them payable to individuals often causes delay.

New subscriptions may commence at any time. When subscribers do not indicate their wish, they commence with the first number of the month in which the subscription is received.

PUBLISHER'S NOTICE.

The whole edition of The Christian Herald was mailed last week to subscribers during Tuesday, June 19. The last delivery at the New York Post Office was made at 11.56 P. M.

CURRENT EVENTS.

The Republican National Convention which assembled at Chicago on June 19, joined issue with the Democratic party, as was expected, on the Tariff question. It stands squarely, explicitly, and emphatically for Protection, with a tariff not for revenue, but for the nurture of American industries. If a large surplus continues to accumulate therefrom, the Convention was in favor of the abolition of the Internal Revenue, or large expenditures for the national welfare, in preference to any reduction of the tariff. As the plank of the platform adopted by the Convention on Thursday last is likely to become the subject of discussion in every city in the country, and as it is an unequivocal declaration of the political faith of the Republican party, it may be well to quote it in full. The Convention declared: "We are uncompromisingly *in favor of the American system of protection.* We protest against its destruction as proposed by the President and his party. They serve the interests of Europe; we will support the interests of America. We accept the issue, and confidently appeal to the people for their judgment. The protective system must be maintained. Its abandonment has always been followed by general disaster to all interests except those of the usurer and the sheriff. *We denounce the Mills Bill* as destructive to the general business, the labor and the farming interests of the country, and we heartily indorse the consistent and patriotic action of the Republican Representatives in Congress in opposing its passage. We condemn the proposition of the Democratic party to place wool on the free list, and we insist that the duties thereon shall be adjusted and maintained so as to furnish full and adequate protection to that industry. The Republican party would effect all needed reduction of the national revenue by *repealing the tax upon tobacco*, which are an annoyance and burden to agriculture, and the *tax upon spirits* used in the arts and for mechanical purposes; and by such revision of the tariff laws as will tend to check imports of such articles as are produced by our people, the production of which gives employment to our labor, and releases from import duties those articles of foreign production (except luxuries), the like of which cannot be produced at home. If there shall still remain a larger revenue than is requisite for the wants of the Government, we favor the entire repeal of internal taxes rather than the surrender of any part of our protective system, at the joint behest of the Whisky Trusts and the agents of foreign manufacturers." The platform also advocates the bi-metallic standard of money, the reduction of letter postage to one cent an ounce, and condemns the Fishery treaty.

The Balloting for Candidates for the Presidency was commenced by the Convention on Friday last. The number necessary to a choice was 417. In the first ballot the candidates and numbers stood as follows: Sherman 229; Gresham, 114; Depew, 99; Alger, 84; Harrison, 79; Allison, 72; Blaine, 31; Ingalls, 28—(These were 17 from Kansas, 10 from Arkansas, and 1 from South Carolina. The names of the men who thought Ingalls fit for the Presidency have not been published.) -Phelps, 25; Rusk, 25; Fitler, 24; Hawley, 13; Lincoln, 3; McKinley, 2. On the second ballot Sherman made a gain of twenty; Alger, of thirty-two; and Harrison, of sixteen. The third ballot, which was the last taken on Friday showed no material changes.

The Modification of the Order of the Indian Bureau, in regard to the use of native languages in the Indian schools has been so made as to be entirely satisfactory to the religious societies interested in the improvement of the Indians. The purpose of the Government in insisting upon the use of the English language in the Indian schools, was that young Indians might be brought up to the familiar use of the language which is necessary to them in adopting the arts and ways of civilization, and to their self-dependence and protection in their contact with white men. The President, however, perceives that the missionaries and religious teachers, who render great assistance to the Government in the work of making the Indians tractable and self-reliant, and preparing them for a better social and industrial condition, find it difficult to reach their understanding and feelings effectually by the use of any dialect except their own in their religious instruction. The order, therefore, remains in force, but exceptions are made in favor of religious teachers.

The General Conference on Foreign Missions in Exeter Hall, London, ended June 20. Among the speakers were Rev. Dr. Ellenwood and Rev. Dr. John Hall, both of New York. The following American ministers, among others, were seen in the audience: Dr. Pierson, Dr. Murdock, and Dr. Gordon, Boston; Dr. Dowkontt, F. Emerson, G. Post, D. Langford, Dr. Boardman, and Dr. Chambers. The speakers contended that mission work was one of the duties of a nation, and that the country that refused to obey the Lord's command to preach the gospel to all people would certainly have to look to the morals of its own inhabitants. A high tribute was paid by Dr. Murdoch, of Boston, to the King of the Belgians for his efforts to suppress the sale of liquor in the Congo State. A committee, including Mr. Murdoch, was appointed to present an appropriate address to King Leopold. Mr. Pierson, of Philadelphia, made the concluding address. He testified to the deep impression that the Conference had made on the delegates.

The New Kaiser has Issued his Proclamation to the German people. It lacks the ring of spontaneity which characterized his addresses to the army and navy. It probably indicates the effect recent public criticisms have had upon the young monarch. He cannot fail to have noticed that while his father was admired and beloved, he himself is regarded with distrust, and his accession to the throne as a ground for apprehension. He evidently makes an effort to disarm those feelings by his proclamation. After a glowing tribute to his father's memory, he says: "Called to the throne of my fathers, I have assumed the government, looking up to the King of kings, and have vowed to God that, after the example of my fathers, I will be a just and clement prince to my people; that I will foster piety and fear of God; that I will protect peace and promote the welfare of the country, and that I will be a helper of the poor and distressed and a true guardian of the right." The Emperor appears to have mistaken his century. Feudalism is dead. Such utterances on the part of his grandfather were pardonable in an aged king who had won distinction on the battle-field; but in a youth, they indicate notions which this century has outgrown.

The Burial of Emperor Frederick III. of Germany took place June 19, with impressive ceremonies and amid signs of sincere national grief. A spectator says: "Everyone seemed as if going to the funeral of one's own father or brother. The music was exquisite, and all the arrangements were in perfect taste and simplicity. The religious services were brief and went straight to the heart." Even Von Moltke, the venerable soldier, shed tears as he looked on the coffin of his sovereign. A first semi-private service was held in Friedrickskron Castle, where the Emperor died, and a more public service in Friedenskirche. The new Emperor followed with the Prince of Wales and the King of Saxony. Prince Henri, the late Emperor's second son, the Prince of Saxe Meiningen, Prince Bismarck, Von Moltke, and many other distinguished personages were in the procession. Dr Mackenzie had, at the new Emperor's request made a formal report of the case, and the autopsy which the Emperor ordered to be made in defiance of the wishes of his widowed mother fully confirmed the surgeon's statement.

The Pope's Rescript on Irish Affairs has produced so strong an antipathy to him among the Roman Catholic Nationalists in Ireland that Archbishop Walsh has made an attempt to allay it by an interview published in the *Freeman's Journal* last week. The archbishop said that nothing was further from the Pope's thoughts than to put any obstacle in the way of the success of the Nationalist Cause. On the contrary, it was the Pope's firm conviction that the rescript, by condemning those points of practical working which evoked hostile criticism, would be of most decided assistance in the advancement of the programme. It may be so but at present the Nationalists appear to think that a little more of such assistance would be fatal to their cause, and they are by no means grateful for the old gentleman's attempt to help them.

An Attempt to Reform the British House of Lords is being made by Lord Salisbury. He has prepared a bill for the purpose, which on June [illegible] he introduced in Parliament. The measure proposes that not more than three life peers shall be appointed yearly, these to be drawn from the judges of the superior courts, rear-admirals, major-generals, ambassadors, and privy councillors, the Queen also having the power to appoint two others yearly not so qualified. The changes are of a very feeble and ineffective character, but that any measure of the kind should be endorsed by a Conservative Government, is matter for astonishment.

Disquieting News of Mr. H. M. Stanley reached this country on Friday last. The cable brought a despatch from St. Paul de Loando which reported that several deserters from Stanley's expedition have reached Camp Yambunga. They state that after traversing the Upper Aruwhimi, Stanley struck into a rough, mountainous country, covered with dense forests. The natives, who were excited by reports spread by the Arabs, disputed the passage of the expedition and there was continuous fighting. Stanley was severely wounded by an arrow. He was compelled several times to construct camps in order to repel attacks, and was obliged to use the reserve provisions that were intended for Emin Pacha. The Soudanese attached to the force had all died or disappeared. The deserters estimate that the caravan had lost one-third of its men, and they say that many of those remaining were ill, including the Europeans. Stanley was encamped when the deserters left. He was surrounded by hostiles, and was unable to send news to Emin or directly to Yambunga. Letters from Emin Pacha, dated November 2, 1887, have been received, in which he says that up to that date he had received no news of Stanley. A powerful expedition, under Major Barttelot, had gone to the relief of the explorer early in May.

The Reception into the Protestant Episcopal Church of Mgr. Bouland, the converted Roman Catholic Bishop, whose portrait and life appeared in this journal last week, took place on June 17, at Grace Church, New York. Various slanderous reports affecting his moral character were put in circulation when his conversion was announced, but Mgr. Bouland invited the most thorough investigation. Two committees were therefore appointed to sift the charges to the bottom, and both, after searching inquiries, pronounced the charges false. The convert was formally welcomed by Bishop Potter. He and the Bishop sat in the chancel during the prayers, and at their conclusion Mgr. Bouland, in the presence of two presbyters, the Rev. Dr. Miel, of Philadelphia, and the Rev. J. McD. Bottome, of Grace parish, stood before the Bishop, who delivered an allocution declaring the reception and charging him to observe the duties of his new allegiance. Mgr. Bouland declared his faith and his reasons for leaving the Catholic Church. It is expected that he will labor in Paris, France, after a brief period of rest.

A Jewish Rabbi's Blessing on a Christian church is published in a St. Louis journal. The Jewish congregation of Temple Israel, in that city, has been rebuilt recently, and, during the time that the congregation was excluded from its home, it was hospitably received in the building of the First Christian Church, where it held its services every Saturday. Its Synagogue being now completed, the Rabbi, Dr. S. H. Sonneschein, has written a letter of thanks to the Christian pastor, expressing the gratitude of the congregation for Christian hospitality. It concludes with the following patriarchal benediction: "This, your kindness, was one more of those precious links in the golden chain of mutual recognition which, under the fostering arms of true American civilization, reconciles the disciples of Moses to the disciples of Jesus. May this Godly spirit of a free fraternization abide and increase as the years roll on! May the Eternal Lord of Hosts, the God of Israel, bless your church and all your hopes and plans! 'For my brethren's sake and friends' sake, I speak peace for thee. For the sake of our God's house I solicit thy weal.' (Psalm 122: 8–9.)" Surely, among the Church's hopes which the Rabbi prays God to bless, is one that every disciple of Moses may be led to see in his writings the Messiahship of Jesus of Nazareth.

A Disappointed Wife Who Carried her wrongs to the United States Supreme Court for redress, had her case decided on the last day of the recent term. She stated that while on a visit to Portland, Oregon, ten years ago, she met a man in society, who eventually asked her to marry him. He promised to convey to her, after marriage, two blocks of property in Portland. She consented to marry him, and her mother, who at first objected to the match, also agreed to it when she heard of the promised property. They were married, but the husband postponed, on one plea and another, making the formal conveyance. Finally, after some years of married life, he persuaded his wife to make a visit to Europe, taking their daughter with her to be educated. During her absence he had dealt with the property as his own, and had in fact settled it on another woman. The wife, thereupon, filed a bill of complaint, and carried her case to the Supreme Court. She was defeated, however, the Court holding that as she had never received a written agreement, nor received the rents of the property, nor exercised any of the rights and privileges of ownership, there was no evidence of transfer. Women who are about to marry for money will doubtless take warning from this case, and see to it that the property promised to them is legally conveyed, or in some way their ownership is acknowledged. The Christian, as part of the Bride of Christ, has exceeding great and precious promises, and he can have no fear that faith will not be kept with him; but his life would be happier and more useful if he availed himself of his privileges and took up the earnest of his possession. (Eph. 1: 14.)

A Narrow Escape from Death by Suffocation occurred at Saccarappa, Me., recently. The Lewiston *Journal* says that a lady from Boston who was visiting that town, after spending a pleasant evening with her friends retired for the night. In her home in Boston the electric light was used, and in a fit of absent-mindedness she went to the gas burner and turned the tap, as she did that of the electric light in her own chamber at home. Of course there was in this case no brilliant arc of light, and in her abstraction she concluded that there was something wrong for the moment with the dynamo, and it would be all right presently. She therefore left the tap turned and retired to rest. Happily for her the smell of the escaping gas aroused some of the other inmates of the house and her life was saved, but it was with difficulty that she was aroused from unconsciousness. It used to be supposed that the blunder of turning on the gas without lighting was limited to persons who had not kept up with the times. It appears, however, that familiarity with the very latest triumphs of civilization is just as effectual in leading to the same blunder. It is so in religion. Among those who will be lost, the learned sceptics will stand side by side with the ignorant and vicious. (1 Cor. 3: 18-20.)

The Suicide of an Eleven-Year Old Boy has overwhelmed a family in New York with grief. The boy was exceedingly bright and intelligent. His teacher in the public school states that he made more progress than any boy in her class. He had, however, an unconquerable dislike to the study of the German language, which his father, who is a native of Germany, insisted on his learning. The boy was sent in the evenings to a German institution in the city for special instruction in the language, but early this year he absented himself and spent the evenings in play. The father supposed that he was attending regularly, and was not notified of his absense, because the teachers supposed the family had moved away. But last week a teacher met him in the street, and at once wrote to the father about his truancy. The boy felt sure he would receive a severe whipping, and one of his companions says he was in terrible distress about it. He procured some rat-poison on June 21, took it, and died the same night. If the boy could only have believed it possible that his father would forgive him, his wicked act might not have been committed. That is the awakened sinner's case, and when once he sees that through the atonement of Christ pardon is secured, despair gives place to joy. (Rom. 5: 11.)

A Verdict for a Wedding Present has Made a young couple in South Carolina happy. Some time ago, a family comprising a mother, her son and two daughters fell into extreme poverty through the death of the husband and father. Eventually, driven to their last resources, they contracted to work for a citizen of Abbeville. The laws of South Carolina are strict about the fulfilment of these contracts, and laborers under contract are held to implicit observance of them. One of the girls, however, who was very beautiful, won the affections of a prosperous young farmer of the neighborhood, and at his earnest solicitation consented to marry him. The ceremony was performed, but as the bride was still under contract, the young farmer was prosecuted for enticing her off the place. A despatch from Columbia, S. C., says, "The case was fought hotly on both sides, but the jury could not be induced to decide against the young couple, and has given them a verdict of not guilty as a wedding present." The verdict, if the despatch correctly states the case, appears to have been prompted by mercy rather than justice, as in law the bride's services were due under her contract. This is not the only case of an engagement being broken by marriage. A more serious one, which too often occurs, is that of persons who have given themselves to Christ, but when they are married becoming so absorbed in their new relation as to do nothing more in His service. This is the more inexcusable, because work in the Saviour's cause exalts and sanctifies married life. (1 Peter 3: 1 and 7).

A Living Necklace Around the Throat of a lady nearly caused her death last week. A telegram from Seymour, Ind., to the New York *Herald* states that the principal of the public school in that town heard screams from the children in the playground during recess. She ran out to learn what the trouble was, and was horrified to see a black racer snake, four feet in length, in possession of the yard. Quick as thought the snake turned upon her, ran up her back, and twisted itself around her neck so tightly that she was almost strangled. She was unable to cry out, but the children screamed lustily and their cries were heard by a man who was passing. He responded promptly, and succeeded in killing the snake before it seriously injured the lady. The nervous shock, however, has prostrated her, and she has been unable to attend to her duties since. Though the bite of this variety of snake is said to be harmless, its attacks are so treacherously made, and the strength of its coil is so great, that the victims cannot liberate themselves. It is so with the treacherous attacks of man's great enemy, that old serpent, the devil. The only sure way of escape is in the help of Christ, who has overcome him by Almighty power. (Heb. 2: 14. 15.)

BRIEF NOTES.

A contemporary states that Mrs. Hastings, a missionary in Ceylon, is a sister of President Cleveland.

Thirty thousand rupees (about $15,000) have been promised by American Young Men's Christian Associations toward establishing a Young Men's Christian Association in each university town in India.

The Rev. A. B. Simpson, of the Gospel Tabernacle Church, New York, announces that the annual summer convention and school will be held at Old Orchard Beach, Me., from August 10 to 20, 1888.

Inquiries as to the formation of clubs of King's Daughters, which are doing so much good in connection with the Evangelical churches, should be sent to Mrs. B. Whitman, Lawrence Avenue, Dorchester, Mass.

Pundita Ramabai joined the King's Daughters during her stay in this country. Ramabai goes to her Indian home ready to extend the welcome to her sisters there. She takes with her the silver cross for her daughter, and hopes to form a "ten" immediately on her return.

Dr. Geo. F. Pentecost's series of meetings in Atlanta, Ga., were chiefly directed to revival work in the strict acceptation of the term, namely, to members of churches; the meetings were large, and many of all denominations attended, though the union meetings were not held.

A series of evangelistic meetings for young men has been commenced in Association Hall, Fourth Avenue and Twenty-third Street, New York, and will continue for one month. They are under the leadership of J. W. Dean, the former Secretary of the Association of Iowa.

Rev. Jacob Freshman recently visited Toronto, and was warmly welcomed by his large circle of friends. He preached in the morning (June 3) in St. James Square Church (of which Dr. Kellogg is pastor), and in the evening in Elm Street Methodist Church. The encouragement he received, both there and in Montreal, leads him to believe that he will be able to locate a missionary to the Jews in each city.

The services conducted by Messrs. Crossley and Hunter, St. Thomas, Ontario, have been the means of a wonderful revival, extending for many miles around. Men and women came from long distances to attend the meetings, and going home with a blessing, told their neighbors, who came too. The evangelists took the names of more than nine hundred persons during the month who were anxiously seeking salvation.

Mr. "Ben" Hogan, well known throughout the United States as a converted prize-fighter, is now holding services in Mr. and Mrs. Naylor's Berachah Mission, in West Thirty-second Street, New York. He has recently made a successful evangelistic tour on the Pacific Coast. In Oregon, Washington Territory, California, Montana, Utah, New Mexico, and in fact nearly every State and Territory in the Far West, he has held meetings which God has blessed to the conversion of some notoriously immoral characters.

THE SLUGGARD'S FARM.

A New Sermon by Pastor C. H. Spurgeon.

"I went by the field of the slothful, and by the vineyard of the man void of understanding; and, lo, it was all grown over with thorns, and nettles had covered the face thereof, and the stone wall thereof was broken down. Then I saw, and considered it well: I looked upon it, and received instruction."—Proverbs 24: 30-32.

A Wise Man Learning—Weeds as Teachers—I. A Definition of a Lazy Man—Not His Own Opinion—Antinomian Sluggards—Cultured Uselessness—The Sluggard's Neglected Opportunities—His Interests Trifled With—His Loss Incalculable—Reflections Upon Christ—II. His Land—Producing Weeds—Sure to Produce Something—The Soul's Natural Produce—The Thorns in the Sluggish Christian's Heart—In his Home—In the World—III. The Lesson of the Land.

No doubt Solomon was sometimes glad to lay aside the robes of state, escape from the forms of court, and go through the country unknown. On one occasion, when he was doing so, he looked over the broken wall of a little estate which belonged to a farmer of his country. This estate consisted of a piece of ploughed land and a vineyard. One glance showed him that it was owned by a sluggard, who neglected it; for the weeds had grown right plentifully, and covered all the face of the ground. From this, Solomon gathered instruction. Men generally learn wisdom if they have wisdom. The artist's eye sees the beauty of the landscape because he has beauty in his mind. "To him that hath shall be given," and he shall have abundance; for he shall reap a harvest even from a field that is covered with thorns and nettles.

We may find instruction everywhere. To a spiritual mind nettles have their use, and

Weeds have Their Doctrine.

Are not all thorns and thistles meant to be teachers to sinful men? Are they not brought forth of the earth on purpose that they may show us what sin has done, and the kind of produce that will come when we sow the seed of rebellion against God? "I went by the field of the slothful, and by the vineyard of the man void of understanding," says Solomon; "I saw, and considered it well: I looked upon it, and received instruction."

I. First, think of Solomon's description of a slothful man. Solomon was a man whom none of us would contradict, for he knew as much as all of us put together; and besides that, he was under divine inspiration when he wrote this Book of Proverbs. Solomon says a sluggard is

"A Man Void of Understanding."

The slothful man does not think so; he puts his hands in his pockets, and you would think from his important air that he had all the Bank of England at his disposal. You can see that he is a very wise man in his own esteem, for he gives himself airs which are meant to impress you with a sense of his superior abilities. The proverb is not complimentary to him, but I am certain that Solomon was right when he called him "a man void of understanding." Solomon was rather rude, according to the dainty manners of the present times, because this gentleman had a field and a vineyard, and as Poor Richard saith, "When I have a horse and a cow every man biddeth me good morrow." How can a man be void of understanding who has a field and a vineyard? Is it not generally understood that you must measure a man's understanding by the amount of

His Ready Cash?

At all events, you shall soon be flattered for your attainments if you have attained unto wealth. Such is the way of the world, but such is not the way of Scripture. Whether he has a field and a vineyard or not, says Solomon, if he is a sluggard he is a fool, or if you would like to see his name written out a little larger, he is a man empty of understanding. Not only does he not understand anything, but he has no understanding to understand with.

I am glad to be told by Solomon so plainly that a slothful man is void of understanding, for it is useful information. I have met with persons who thought they perfectly understood the doctrines of grace, who could accurately set forth the election of the saints, the predestination of God, the firmness of the divine decree, the necessity of the Spirit's work, and all the glorious doctrines of grace which build up the fabric of our faith; but these gentlemen have inferred from these doctrines that they have to do nothing, and thus they have become sluggards. Do-nothingism is

Their Creed.

They will not urge other people to labor for the Lord, because, say they, "God will do His own work. Salvation is all of grace!" The notion of these sluggards is that a man is to wait, and do nothing; he is to sit still, and let the grass grow up to his ancles in the hope of heavenly help. How shall we survive the censures of this dogmatic person? How shall we escape from this very knowing and very captious sluggard? Solomon hastens to the rescue and extinguishes this gentleman by informing us that he is void of understanding. The sluggard, whether he is sluggish about his business or about his soul, is "a man void of understanding."

As a rule, we may measure a man's understanding by his useful activities; that is what the wise man very plainly tells us. Certain persons call themselves "cultured," and yet they cultivate nothing. True wisdom is practical: boastful culture vapors and theorizes. Wisdom ploughs its field, wisdom hoes its vineyard,

Wisdom Looks to its Crops,

wisdom tries to make the best of everything; and he who does not do so, whatever may be his knowledge of this, of that, or of the other, is "a man void of understanding." Why is he void of understanding? Is it not because *he has opportunities which he does not use?* His day has come, his day is going, and he lets the hours glide by to no purpose. Let me not press too hardly upon anyone, but let me ask you all to press as hardly as you can upon yourselves while you inquire each one of himself—Am I employing the minutes as they fly? This man had a vineyard, but he did not cultivate it; he had a field, but he did not till it. Do you, brethren, use all your opportunities? I know we each one have some power to serve God; do we use it? If we are His children He has not put one of us where we are of necessity useless.

You are not asked to do in the service of God that which is utterly beyond you, for it is expected of us according to what we have, and not according to what we have not. The man of two talents is not required to bring in the interest of five, but he is expected to bring in the interest of two. Solomon's slothful man was too idle to attempt tasks which were quite within his power. Many have a number of dormant faculties of which they are scarcely aware, and many more have abilities which they are using for themselves, and not for Him who created them. Dear friends, if God has given us power to do good, pray let us do it, for this is

A Wicked, Weary World.

As for a sluggard in soul matters, he is indeed void of understanding, for he trifles with matters which demand his most earnest heed. Man, hast thou never cultivated thy heart? Has the ploughshare never broken up the clods of thy soul? Has the seed of the Word never been sown in thee? or has it, taken no root? Hast thou never watered the young plants of desire? Hast thou never sought to pull up the weeds of sin that grow in thy heart? Art thou still a piece of the bare common or wild heath? Poor soul! Thou canst trim thy body, and spend many a minute at the glass; dost thou not care for thy soul? You take care of the worse part, and leave the better to perish through neglect. This is the height of folly! He that is a sluggard as to the vineyard of his heart, is "a man void of understanding." If I must be idle, let it be seen in my garden, but not in my soul.

Or are you a Christian? Are you really saved, and are you negligent in the Lord's work? Then, indeed, whatever you may be, I cannot help saying you have too little under standing; for surely, when a man is saved him self, and understands the danger of other men' souls, he must be in earnest in trying to pluc the firebrands from the flame.

A Christian Sluggard!

Is there such a being? A *Christian* man on hal time? A Christian man working not at all fo his Lord; how shall I speak of him? Surely w must be void of understanding if, after bein saved by the infinite love of God, we do nc spend and be spent in His service. The eterna fitness of things demands that a saved ma should be an earnest man.

The Christian who is slothful in his Master service *has no idea what he is losing;* for th very cream of religion lies in holy consecratio to God. Some people have just enough relig ion to make it questionable whether they hav any or not. They have enough godliness t make them uneasy in their ungodliness. *The have washed enough of their face to show the di upon the rest of it.* "I am glad," said a servan "that my mistress takes the sacrament, fc otherwise I should not know she had any reli ion at all." You smile, and well you may. wish some professors would do Christ the ju tice to say, "No, I am *not* one of His disciple do not think so badly of Him as to imagine th I can be one of them." We ought to be refle tions *of* Christ; but I fear many are reflectio *upon* Christ. When we see a lot of lazy servant we are apt to think that their master must be very idle person himself, or he would never p up with them. Oh, let not the world think th Christ is indifferent to human woe, that Chri has lost His zeal, that Christ has lost His ene gy! yet I fear they will say it, or think it, if the see those who profess to be laborers in the vin yard of Christ, nothing better that mere sluggard

II. Now, secondly, let us look at the slu gard's land: "I went by the field of the slot ful, and by the vineyard of the man void of u derstanding; and, lo, it was all grown over wi thorns, and nettles had covered the face the of." Note, first, that *land will produce so thing.* Soil which is good enough to be ma into a field and a vineyard must and will yi some fruit or other; and so you and I, in o hearts, and in the sphere God gives us to occ py, will be

Sure to Produce Something.

We cannot live in this world as entire blank we shall either do good or do evil, as sure as are alive. If you are idle in Christ's work, y are active in the devil's work. The sluggard sleeping was doing more for the cultivation thorns and nettles than he could have done any other means. If it be not farmed for G the soul will yield its natural produce; a what is the natural produce of land if left to self? What but thorns and nettles, or so other useless weeds? What is the natu produce of your heart and mine? What b sin and misery? What is the natural prod of your children if you leave them untrained God? What but unholiness and vice? Wh is the natural produce of this great city if leave its streets and lanes and alleys witho the gospel? What but crime and infamy? So harvest there will be, and the sheaves will the natural produce of the soil, which is s death, and corruption.

In many instances there will be a great d of this evil produce; for a field and a viney will yield more thistles and nettles than a pi of ground that has not been reclaimed. Negl is all that is needed to produce evil. If you sire to bring forth a harvest unto God, I m need long to instruct you in ploughing, sowi and watering; but if you wish your mind to covered with Satan's hemlock, you have o to leave the furrows of nature to themselves

While we look upon the lazy man's vineya let us also peep into the ungodly sluggar heart. He does not care about repentance a faith. To think about his soul, to be in earn about eternity, is too much for him. He wa to take things easy, and have a little more fo ing of the arms to sleep. What is growing in his mind and character? In some of the spiritual sluggards you can see drunkenness, uncleanness, covetousness, anger, and pride, and all sorts of thistles and nettles; or where these ranker weeds do not appear, by reason of the restraint of pious connections, you find other sorts of sin. The heart cannot be altogether empty; either Christ or the devil will possess it.

Friend, if you believe in Christ, I want to peep over the hedge into *your heart* also, if you are a sluggish Christian; for I fear that nettles and thistles are threatening you also. Some have sadly morbid forebodings; they are discontented, fretful, selfish, murmuring, and all because they are idle. The.e are

The Weeds that Grow

n sluggards' gardens. I have known the sloth·ul become so peevish that nothing could please :hem; the most earnest Christian could not do ·ight for them; the most loving Christian could not be affectionate enough; the most active :hurch could not be energetic enough; they letected all sorts of wrong where God Himself aw much of the fruit of His Spirit. This cenoriousness is one of the nettles that are quite sure o grow in men's gardens when they fold their .rms in sinful ease. If your heart does not yield ruit to God it will certainly bring forth that rhich is mischievous in itself, painful to you, .nd injurious to your fellow-men.

May I next ask you to look into *your own ouse* and home? It is a dreadful thing when a aan does not cultivate the field of his own amily. What is the use of zeal abroad if there s neglect at home? How sad to say, "My own ineyard have I not kept!" Have you never eard of one who said he did not teach his chilren the ways of God, because he thought they vere so young that it was very wrong to prejudice them, and he had rather leave them to hoose their own religion

When They Grow Older?

)ne of his boys broke his arm, and while the ergeon was setting it the boy was swearing all ıe time. "Ah!" said the good doctor, "I old you what would happen. You were afraid) prejudice your boy in the right way, but *the vil had no such qualms;* he has prejudiced him ıe other way, and pretty strongly too." It is ur duty to prejudice our field in favor of corn, r it will soon be covered with thistles. Cultiate a child's heart for good, or it will go wrong f itself, for it is already depraved by nature.

As it is with homes, so it is with *schools.* You unday-school teachers can make your classes) tiresome to the children that they will hate unday. You can fritter away time in school ithout bringing the lads and lasses to Christ, ıd so you may do more hurt than good. I have nown Christian fathers who by their severity ıd want of tenderness have sown their family eld with the thorns and thistles of hatred to ligion, instead of scattering the good seed of ve in it. Oh, that we may so live among our ildren that they may not only love us, but ve our Father who is in heaven! May fathers ıd mothers set such an example of cheerful ety that sons and daughters shall say, "Let tread in our father's footsteps, for he was a appy and a holy man. Let us follow our moth's ways, for she was sweetness itself."

I beg you once more to look at

The Great Field of the World.

o you see how it is overgrown with thorns and ettles? If an angel could take a survey of the hole race, what tears he would shed, if angels ould weep! What a tangled mass of weeds the hole earth is! Yonder the field is scarlet with e poppy of popery, and over the hedge it is llow with the wild mustard of Mahometann. Vast regions are smothered with the thises of infidelity and idolatry. The world is ll of cruelty, oppression, drunkenness, rebelon, uncleanness, misery. What the moon sees! hat God's sun sees! What scenes of horror! ow far is all this to be attributed to a neglectl church? Nearly nineteen hundred years are ne, and the sluggard's vineyard is but little improved! What has the church been doing all these years? She ceased after a few centuries to be a missionary church, and from that hour she almost ceased to be a living church.

However, instead of asking what the church has been doing for these nineteen hundred years, let us ask ourselves what are we going to do now? Are the missions of the churches always to be such poor, feeble things as they are? Are the best of our Christian young men always going to stay at home? We go on ploughing the home field a hundred times over, while millions of acres abroad are left to the thorn and the nettle. Shall it always be so? God send us more spiritual life, and wake us up from our sluggishness, or else when the holy watcher gives in his report he will say, "I went by the field of the sluggish church, and it was all grown over with thorns and nettles, and the stone wall was broken down, so that one could scarcely tell which was the church and which was the world: yet still she slept, and slept, and slept, and nothing could waken her."

III. I conclude by remarking that there must be some lesson in all this. I cannot teach it as I would, but I want to learn it myself. I will speak it as though I were talking to myself. The first lesson is, that

Unaided Nature

always will produce thorns and nettles, and nothing else. My soul, if it were not for grace, this is all thou wouldst have produced. Beloved, are you producing anything else? Then it is not nature, but the grace of God that makes you produce it. Those lips that now most charmingly sing the praises of God would have been delighted with an idle ballad if the grace of God had not sanctified them. Your heart, that now cleaves to Christ, would have continued to cling to your idols—you know what they were—if it had not been for grace divine. And why should grace have visited you or me—why? Echo answers, why? What answer can we give? "'Tis even so, Father, for so it seemed good in Thy sight." Let the recollection of what grace has done move us to manifest the result of that grace in our lives.

We see here, next, the little value of natural good intentions; for this man, who left his field and vineyard to be overgrown, always meant to work hard one of these fine days. To do him justice, we must admit that he did not mean to sleep much longer, for he said—"Yet a little sleep, a little slumber, a little folding of the hands to sleep."

Only a Little Doze,

and then tuck up his sleeves and show his muscle. Probably the worst people in the world are those who have the best intentions, but never carry them out. In that way Satan lulls many to sleep. They hear an earnest sermon; but they do not arise and go to their Father; they only get as far as saying: "Yes, yes, the far country is not a fit place for me; I will not stay here long. I mean to go home by-and-by." They said that forty years ago, but nothing came of it. When they were quite youths they had serious impressions, they were almost persuaded to be Christians, and yet they are not Christians even now. They have been slumbering forty years! Surely that is a liberal share of sleep! They never intended to dream so long, and now they do not mean to lie in bed much longer. They will not turn to Christ at once, but they are resolved to do so one day. When are you going to do it, friend? "Before I die." Going to put it off to the last hour or two, are you? And so, when unconscious, and drugged to relieve your pain, you will begin to think of your soul? Is this wise? Surely you are "void of understanding."

"Surely you do not object to my having a little more sleep?" says the sluggard. "You have waked me to soon. I only ask another little nap." "My dear man, it is far into the morning." He answers, "It is rather late, I know; but it will not be much later if I take just another doze." You wake him again, and tell him it is noon. He says, "It is the hottest part of the day: I dare say if I had been up I should have gone to the sofa and taken a little rest from the hot sun." You knock at his door when it is almost evening, and then he cries, "It is of no use to get up now, for the day is almost over." To-morrow is only to be found in the calendar of fools; to-day is the time of the wise man, the chosen season of our gracious God. Oh that the Holy Spirit may lead you to seize the present hour, that you may at once give yourselves to the Lord by faith in Christ Jesus, and then from His vineyard—

"Quick uproot
The noisome weeds that without profit suck
The soil's fertility from wholesome plants"!

GEMS FROM NEW BOOKS.

A NEEDLEWOMAN'S GIFT.*

ORGANIZATIONS of women for the relief of sick and wounded soldiers, and for the care of soldiers' families, were formed with great spontaneity at the very beginning of the war. There were a dozen or more of them in Chicago in less than a month after Cairo was occupied by Northern troops. They raised money, prepared and forwarded supplies of whatever was demanded, every shipment being accompanied by some one who was held responsible for the proper disbursement of the stores. Sometimes these local societies affiliated with, or became parts of, more comprehensive organizations.

A poor girl, who called herself a "tailoress," came one day to the rooms of the Commission.

"I do not feel right," she said, "that I am doing nothing for our soldiers in the hospitals. I must do something immediately. Which do you prefer—that I should give money, or buy material and manufacture it into hospital clothing?"

"You must be governed by your circumstances," was the answer made her. "We need both money and supplies, and you must do that which is most convenient for you."

"I prefer to give money, if it will do as much good."

"Very well, then give money. We need it badly, and without it cannot do what is most necessary for our brave men."

"I will give the Commission my net earnings for the next two weeks. I would give more, but my mother is an invalid, and I help support her. Usually I make but one vest a day, as I do 'custom work,' and am well paid for it. But these next two weeks, which belong to the soldiers, I shall work earlier and later."

In two weeks she came again, the poor sewing-girl, with a radiant face. Opening her portemonnaie, she counted out nineteen dollars and seven cents. She had stitched into the hours of midnight on every one of the working days of those two weeks.

A Five-Dollar Gold Piece.

A little girl, not nine years old, with sweet and timid grace, entered one afternoon, and laid a five-dollar gold piece on my desk. Half frightened, she told its story. "My uncle gave me that before the war, and I was going to keep it always; but he's got killed in the army, and now mother says I may give it to the soldiers, if I want to—and I'd like to. Will it buy much for them?"

I led the child into the storeroom, and pointed out to her how much it would buy—so many cans of condensed milk, or so many bottles of ale, or so many pounds of tea or codfish, etc. Her face brightened with pleasure; but when I explained that her five-dollar gold piece was equal then to seven and a half dollars in greenbacks, and told her how much comfort could be carried into a hospital with the amount of stores it would purchase, she fairly danced for joy. "Why, my five dollars will do lots of good, won't it?"

A Tatterdemalion.

A little urchin, who often thrust his unkempt pate into the room, with the shrill cry of

* From "My Story of the War: A Woman's Narrative of Four Years' Personal Experience as Nurse in the Union Army," by Mrs. Mary A. Livermore. Illustrated with numerous portraits and scenes; 700 pages. Published by *A. D. Worthington & Company*, Hartford, Conn.

A Prohibited Meeting of the Early Waldensian Church.

"Matches! matches!" had stood a little apart, watching the girl, and listening to the conversation. As she disappeared, he fumbled in his pockets and drew out a small handful of crumpled fractional currency, such as was then in use. "Here," said he, "I'll give yer suthin' for them sick fellers!" and he put fifty-five cents in my hand, all in five-cent currency. I was surprised, and hesitated.

"No, my boy, don't give it; I'm afraid you cannot afford it. You're a noble little fellow; but that is more than you ought to give; you keep it, and I'll give fifty-five cents for you—or somebody else will." "Git eaut," was his disgusted commentary on my proposal; "yer take it, now; p'haps I ain't so poor as yer think. My father, he saws wood, an' my mother, she takes in washin', an' I sells matches, an' Tom, he sells paper, an' p'haps we've got more money than yer think. Our Bob, he'd gone to the war hisself, but he got his leg cut off on the railroad, in a smash-up. He was a brakeman, yer see. Yer take this, now."

I took the crumpled currency. I forgot the boy's dirty face and tattered cap; I forgot that I had called the little tatterdemalion a "nuisance" every day, for months, when he had caused me to jump from my seat with his shrill, unexpected cry of "Matches!" and I actually stooped down to kiss him.

He divined my intention, and darted out on the sidewalk, as if he had been shot.

"No yer don't!" he said, shaking his tangled head at me, and looking as if he had escaped a great danger. "I ain't one o' the kissin' sort!"

Ever after, when he met me, he gave me a wide berth, and walked off the sidewalk into the gutter, eyeing me with a suspicious, sidelong glance, as though he suspected I still thought of kissing him. If I spoke to him he made no reply; but if I passed him without speaking, he challenged me with a hearty "Hullo, yer!" That brought me to an instant halt.

THE HEROIC WALDENSES.

(See Illustration.)

THE European religious press is chronicling the earnest, consecrated effort now being made by the Waldenses to evangelize the city of Rome. There is a deep significance in this movement, to every student of history, for it is a striking evidence of the extent to which the teaching of the Saviour has permeated the hearts of this wonderful people. They are now rendering to Rome the highest service in returning the grandest good for the bitterest evil.

The Waldenses were among the earliest sufferers for the gospel in Europe when the fierce rage of papal persecution burst upon those who would not acknowledge the supremacy of the Pope, and chief among the foremost of the earnest propagandists of the pure religion of Christ. *The illustration on this page* represents a preaching service among their native rocks and valleys when they were denied the privilege of meeting in a sanctury, under threat of imprisonment and death.

The country of Waldensia, which thus became a cradle for the truth, is but twenty miles in length, and some eighteen broad. It is situated among the mountains between France and Italy, in the valleys called Lucerna, San Martino, and Perosa, the streams of which ultimately gather themselves into the river Po. The sufferings of this venerable Church are written in blood. On the way to La Tour, the little capital of the Waldensian valleys, as their wooded mountains rise to view, the traveller approaches "consecrated ground." "Almost every rock is a monument, and every meadow witnessed executions, and every village had its roll of martyrs." They recount thirty-six distinct persecutions, some designed actually to exterminate them from the face of the earth.

Every visitor to La Tour must be struck by the picturesque rock that rises behind the little town. This is the Monte Castelluzzo, with the Waldensian temple in the foreground. We look on it as on the old tower in Paris, where the bell hung that signalled the massacre of St. Bartholomew. Their valleys have had many "St. Bartholomews," and it was from Castelluzzo that, on April 27, 1655, the signal was given to execute the orders of Christina, regent of Savoy, who, acting for her son Charles Emanual II., and under her holy father the Pope, sent 15,000 soldiers to massacre every Protestant the valleys contained. "Children," says Leger, an eye-witness, "torn from their mothers' breasts, were seized by the feet and dashed in pieces against the rocks or walls, while their tender bodies were cast on the common heaps. The sick, the aged, both men and women, were either burnt in their houses or literally cut in pieces, or were rolled over the rocks."

It is the descendants of those martyrs wh are now carrying to Rome the precious news c salvation through Christ alone.

ROSA'S CROSS.

(See Illustration on page 413.)

"ROSA, Rosa, here is a letter from papa, cried two childish voices at the foot of the parsonage stairs. A tall, slender girl came quickl from her room, and hurried down to join he brother and sister in the breakfast-room.

Rosa Erndale was mother and sister, both, t the two children, who were respectively seve and nine years her junior. The natura mother of the family had been dead now fiv years, and Rosa had done her utmost to fill he place to her father and little Effie and Herbert in fulfilment of the promise she gave to he mother when she was dying. It had been severe trial to the girl, for Mr. Erndale wa overwhelmed with grief at his wife's death, an he did not conceal from Rosa how far she wa from performing her mother's duties with he mother's skill. Yet she had not been unsuccessful. Kind friends in her father's church gav her advice and help; she was diligent an thoughtful; and after the first year of bereavement, the parsonage was as well manage as under the reign of its dead mistress. Sh won the affection of the two children, wh obeyed her cheerfully, and she had the satisfac tion of seeing that her father less and less fre quently compared her management to her di advantage with that of his dead wife.

Mr. Erndale was absent now on his annu vacation, an opportunity that Rosa had seize for a thorough house-cleaning and general reno vation. The last touches were put to it now and if, as was probable, the letter in the hand of the children announced her father's almo immediate return, Rosa would be ready for hin every carpet down, the furniture again in it place, and the new paint all dry and odorles.

The letter was a long one, which was contrar to Mr. Erndale's habit. Rosa sat down to rea it while breakfast waited, and the two childre climbed on the back of her chair to read over her shoulder. But suddenly she crushe the paper between her hands and rose to he feet. The weight of the two children was to much for the chair after Rosa's weight was o it, and they went backward with it with a crash They had to be comforted, their bruised head bbed, and the tears dried first of , and then Rosa insisted on break- t before any further attention was en to the letter.

"What for you crying, Rosa?" ked little Herbert, presently. "You n't hurt your head."

"And you have not eaten a morsel, sa," put in Effie. "What is in pa's letter; is not he well?"

Oh, yes, papa is well, and he is ming home soon. I will tell you about it by and bye."

"Tell us what makes you cry, sa?" persisted the boy.

"Yes, yes, I will tell you all about presently. I have not read all pa's letter yet."

As soon as the meal was finished sa sought her own room, and re, in quiet and with many tears, e read the paternal epistle through. . Erndale, with some circumlocu- n, informed his daughter that he ntemplated marrying again. In t, he had already proposed and en accepted by a lady of suitable e. Finally he told his daughter the me of the lady, a member of his n church, and one to whom, as he s aware, Rosa did not entertain e kindliest feelings. In fact, Rosa d been subjected to her criticism, d she had at last been goaded into imating to her, politely and deli- tely, but explicitly, that she pro- sed managing the domestic affairs the parsonage without outside terference. This rebuff had not en pleasant for either party; and sa's aversion had been increased the suspicion that the lady pired to succeed her dear mother. r. Erndale probably understood mething of the trouble, for he ok pains, in many words, to culcate on his daughter her duty the new circumstances.

"If she would only make him happy," moaned or Rosa, as she read the letter, "I should not ind. But I am sure he will be miserable. Why, e will want to write his sermons, I believe; e will want to manage everything. And the ildren! Oh, my poor children! If it were t for them I could go away; but I cannot de- rt them."

She sat and wept for some time, but at length e rose and wandered disconsolately through e house. She went into her father's study, d there a fresh burst of weeping overcame r, for standing by the minister's desk in the ace it had occupied ever since the bereave- ent was her mother's portrait. The gentle, ving face in the picture seemed now to have ken on an expression of reproach or of mute otest against what seemed to Rosa a profana- n; but it also reminded her of her mother's vice, which in this bitter sorrow she had for- tten, to go to God for help in trouble. She e and opened the minister's Bible, which was ng on his desk. The first words that met her e were, "If any man will come after Me, let n deny himself and take up his cross and fol- v Me." (Matt. 16: 24.) Rosa did not need y one to make the application for her. She w her duty, and she knelt down and asked d to give her strength to do it.

When she rose from her knees her heart was htened of its heavy load. The children were tonished, when she told them the unwelcome ws, that Rosa was not angry about it, so eerfully did she speak and so calmly did she about her ordinary duties. But the sweetest y she had came from a friendly visitor who d, "Why, child, how like your mother you e growing! You have just her sweet spiritual pression. I never noticed it before to-day."

Rosa's cross proved a heavy one; but so con- nually did she go to God for strength, and so constantly was it given to her, as it is to all who ask in faith, that she was enabled to bear it with joy until it was graciously removed.

Rosa Learns How to Bear Her Cross.

THE EPOCHS OF A LIFE.

A NEW SERIAL STORY.

By Rev. L. S. Keyser.

(Continued from page 308.)

A Meeting in the Woods.

THE lady in whose house the young men had taken lodgings was an old resident of the town, and as it was evident that the strange girl in question was also a resident of the place, they concluded that their hostess might be able to give them information concerning her. Before the day was passed, the woman was adroitly catechised and some interesting information was elicited. The young lady's name was Belle Havelock. She was the daughter of one of the prominent bankers of the town, a man who had accumulated considerable wealth, and who, as they knew, took a great interest in the college. They were already aware of the last fact, but had never taken the trouble to ascertain where Mr. Havelock lived.

Belle, his only daughter, was a young lady of versatile talents, and the reason the young men had never met her was because she had been attending a young ladies' seminary in the State of New York, for a number of years, and, of course, while she was at home during the summer vacations, they were absent from town enjoying their rest from college work. However, she had graduated from the seminary in the previous June, and had now come home to stay. All who knew her admitted that she was a bright, clever girl, although her naturally haughty mien had made her slightly unpopular among the young women of the town.

"I took her to be a rather unique girl," remarked Hadley, when they had gained this cue to her character. "I am determined to secure an introduction to her and cultivate her acquaintance."

"You can do as you like," replied George, "but as for me, I believe that I shall steer my frail bark clear of this remarkable female. I am a little afraid of her."

"Pooh! you are a timid youth, destined to die an old bachelor. Be careful that you don't turn into a paleozoic fossil. We have been living like a couple of anchorites since we have been in college, and have neglected the amenities of social life. Yes, I am persuaded that we have, and so I propose to allow myself some of the pleasures of society, even if you do carry off the honors of the class. A little brightening up in our manners wouldn't come amiss if we intend to become public reformers, and would free us from the charge of boorishness."

"And get us into a labyrinth of trouble, without an Ariadne's thread to help us out," said George. "However, if you have a mind to start out on a 'flirting' expedition, I shall not object; only don't hold me responsible for the consequences."

"Ah, you are too cowardly for your own good," declared Hadley, with an impatient gesticulation. "No good of that kind is ever gained except at some risk. Every young fellow must have his love-troubles sooner or later. I believe that I shall choose to have mine sooner."

Hadley was bent on obtaining an introduction to Miss Havelock as soon as possible. But he did not find it so easy to compass his wish as he supposed it would be; for she had been away from town so many years that she was a stranger to nearly all the students of the college, and Hadley was unable to make her acquaintance for several weeks. In the meantime he had seen her several times at one of the churches of the town, and observed that she listened to the sermons with ill-concealed impatience, a shadow of disgust passing over her features when the divine claims of Christianity were presented. She was obviously not a Christian. Perhaps she was an unbeliever. Somehow, bitter as he was against religion himself, the thought that this girl might be animated by like sentiments did not please Hadley. He would have thought better of her if she had been more devout, and less hostile.

"It is impossible for me to stay indoors on a day like this," said Hadley, early one Saturday morning. "I am going out on an ornithological jaunt. Your company will be acceptable, Dane, if you have a mind to go with me."

"I cannot go to-day," George answered. "I have promised to speak next Saturday morning, and this will be my only opportunity to prepare. I know I cannot do any great things, but I must do the best I can. I am going to get a few facts together and arrange them in order. If it were not for that I should enjoy an excursion immensely."

"Then I must go alone, for I feel the outdoor mood coming on. Hark! I can hear the birds trilling in the groves yonder, 'calling me away, calling me away,'" said Hadley, humming the last words of a familiar chorus.

And seizing his hat, and putting a small blank-book with a pencil-case into his pocket, he was off to the woods. He wandered east the town for several miles, exploring the hedges, forests, meadows, and deep rocky valleys with their rippling streams, in search of feathered songsters. True, there was not the abundance of woodland music that characterizes the season of spring, but on the whole, he was amply repaid for his efforts.

In the afternoon he took a circuitous course homeward, continuing his observations. By the time he reached the woods into which he had first entered, half a mile from town, he had taken a large number of notes on "bird-ways," and had almost decided to go to his study without delay. At that moment his mind was suddenly changed by the whistle of a cardinal-grossbeak in a dense thicket near the edge of the woods, on a rocky slope. His faculties were instantly on the alert, as is always the case with a bird-lover when his ears are greeted by a song from the throat of a feathered favorite.

He stole slyly to the edge of the copse, so as not to disturb the cardinal-plumed piper, and then, quietly pushing aside the bushes, he peered into the thicket, determined to gain a sight of the bird and watch him in his singing attitudes. After considerable effort, and at the cost of a few scratches from the sharp briers, he pressed his way into the midst of the underbrush, and at last descried the cardinal bird-form perched on a twig, and at intervals piping his lively tune. It was a beautiful specimen.

Presently the crested vocalist shifted his position, and Hadley in pursuit pushed his way through the thicket almost to the other side. While he was peering sharply in every direction to catch another view of the bird, he stopped suddenly in embarrassed surprise; for as he glanced toward a small opening among the bushes, his sharp sight detected a pair of blue eyes peering at him with curious interest, while a laughing face was photographed in the aperture. He started up in astonishment, and as he did so his hat was caught by some "pesky" briers and lifted from his head, while a thorny branch came into uncomfortable proximity with his scalp. It was an embarrassing situation, making him conscious of a flow of blood along the arteries of his face, giving it the hue of the cardinal-bird which he had just been watching.

Who was the owner of that pair of blue eyes? Were they the property of a male or female spy? He would investigate. Obeying the first impulse that seized him, he scrambled through the tangled mass of bushes and briers, to the edge of the thicket, determined to solve the mystery of the blue orbs that had been watching him.

What was his consternation when he came out into the clear space to find himself face to face with a young lady, and to make the situation more perplexing, his first glance at her face told him that she was the girl in whom he was interested and whose name he had learned was Belle Havelock!

The young man was disconcerted. He had made his exit from the underbrush in an impetuous style and rather the worse for contact with the briers, only a few paces from the spot where the girl was standing; and he stood looking at her in a dazed and helpless way. He was ashamed to beat an unceremonious retreat. It would have been the quintessence of ludicrousness to turn his back on the young lady and walk away without a word. Evidently she was sharing his embarrassment to some extent, as was indicated by the rosy color that mounted to her cheeks. To Hadley's unspeakable relief, her lips parted and she burst into a ringing, merry laugh. The droll nature of the situation and the girl's ebullition touched Hadley's sense of the ridiculous, and he joined spontaneously in the merriment. There was no other alternative but to speak. The girl obviously felt that an apolgy was due the young man for watching him.

"Mr. Madelling," she said, with a slight courtesy.

Hadley lifted his hat and bowed to her, as he said: "I believe I have the pleasure of making the acquaintance of Miss Havelock."

"Ah! you know me, I suppose, as I know you," she said, with a smile. "You will wonder how I learned your name. Well, 'an honest confession is good'—you know the rest. I saw you on your way to college several times and noticed you in church, and I had the curiosity to inquire what your name was. You perhaps ascertained mine in the same way."

"I plead guilty," he answered, "though I hope neither of us is so finical as to think it a very grave offence."

"Oh, no, there is no need of being so conventional," laughed Miss Havelock. "But I do owe you an apology for watching you just now. You will think me a veritable Paul Pry. But it came about in this wise. You see, I am troubled, like yourself, with an occasional out-door *furor*, and that is what brought me out here to-day. While I was sitting under the trees reading, I heard the whistle of the cardinal-bird in the thicket, and I was seized with a desire to reconnoitre. As I was peering about, for the bird, I heard a crackling in the bushes, and begun to wonder if I had been tracked by a bear. I waited, however, and saw you."

"Ah! well I was a less alarming sight, I trust. At all events you will not be afraid of my making a meal of you."

"No, not exactly that, though from something I heard of you the other day, I should fancy you must have some of the bear element in your nature."

"I suppose all men have a little of it; I think I know what you refer to, and if you have heard the whole story you must be aware that I had severe provocation."

"Oh! do not apologize to me, Mr. Madelling; I assure you I was not hurt. Your antagonist is able to take care of himself, I have no doubt. Believers are generally ready for fight against unbelievers, though they do not always win. I have just been watching an encounter with a good deal of interest" and she held up a volume of Huxley's Essays which she had been reading.

They were standing by a shady bank, and at Hadley's suggestion they seated themselves and he took the book from her hand.

"Rather an abstruse companion for a summer day in the woods, is it not, Miss Havelock? he said. "I should have expected if I met a young lady out here, to find a novel in her hands, if she had a book at all."

"I do not read much fiction," she replied. "Once in a while I read a novel when I hear it strongly recommended, and when I am in a special mood for it."

"Conscientious scruples?" asked the young man.

"Oh no, not at all. I do not care for novels. They weary me. The charactèrs are so seldom natural. They are either utterly bad or so saintly that we doubt if they can be human. The men and women we know have all natures in which good and evil is mixed, but the majority of novelists are so clumsy that they cannot paint them so. They must make them either angels or fiends."

"And so you give such works a wide range and turn to the scientists and philosophers for recreation," said Hadley. "There is Huxley, for instance," pointing to the volume in her hand. "Do you find him interesting?"

"Intensely."

"Is that so? Well, at one place he speaks of the immortality of the soul. Is it in that collection of his Essays?"

She turned the leaves of the book rapidly. "Yes, here it is," she said presently. "I have marked it as one of his most striking paragraphs."

"Would you read it? My memory is not retentive enough to enable me to quote it verbatim."

For answer she read as follows: "If a man tells me that the soul is immortal, I would say to him, How do you know it? And if he were to say to me, The soul is not immortal, I should be still obliged to repeat the question: How do you know *that?*"

"Yes, that is the paragraph I referred to," said Hadley. "That is agnosticism pure and simple."

"But it is entirely honest," returned the girl, with a gleam in her eye.

"Ah! but does he not leave you in the san mist-land in which certain writers of fictio leave you?" questioned Hadley, looking at h smilingly, but intently.

Her eye dropped, and a flutter of embarras ment was perceptible in her manner for a m ment, but her discomposure did not last lon "Let us have definiteness where definiteness possible; but where the truth is not yet di covered, it is better to acknowledge our igno ance than to assert error or blindly accept figment of the brain as truth. But, Mr. Mad ling," she added, smiling, "these are rath abstruse questions for a hungry man to discu Perhaps you had better try to secure somethi a little more substantial."

The young man could not find it in his hea to leave her yet, so congenial did he find h society.

"In my debilitated state perhaps it would n be wise for me to venture to town alone," he h the temerity to say, with a peculiar circumf upon the last word.

"That is a hint, is it?" laughed the gi "Well—I might return with you, if you thi that you are in a serious state of weakness," s said, a little hesitantly, but there was a pleas smile on her lips. "The sun will soon be dow any way. Yes, it is my duty to go with you —to—take care of you. Perhaps you rememb what Wordsworth says in his 'Ode to Dut apostrophizing that virtue, which he calls 'ste daughter of the voice of God.

"'I myself commend
Unto thy guidance from this hour;
O, let my weakness have an end!
Give unto me, made lowly wise,
The spirit of self-sacrifice;
The confidence of reason give;
And in the light of truth thy bondman let me live.'

As she concluded she rose.

"It would be so much pleasanter if you we with me because you—you like to, than becau you feel it your duty," he ventured to s audaciously.

A bright vermillion went to her cheeks a clung there as she replied: "We ought alwa to like to do our duty."

On their way to town Hadley encouraged M Havelock to talk of herself. He found that t report of her having been educated in an ea ern seminary was correct. He could not he but admire her easy self-possession and lig and gay manner. And yet on her forehead we a few lines that indicated an active and serio mind, and her dark-blue eyes at times seem very deep and thoughtful. No doubt she wa girl of moods, gay and serious by turns. At a rate, notwithstanding her light badinage, Ha ley was convinced that she was not a lay figu but a girl of real color and force of character.

As they walked up the street toward h home, she looked up at him with a *naïve* sm and said: "It was rather queer—I mean the w in which we became acquainted."

"Do you think that we are now on speaki terms?" he asked, with some show of anxiet

"Oh, yes; I do not see any use in being co ventional."

"No use at all."

"Then you will call and see—us, will you she said, as she put her hand into his at t gate, adding: "My parents will be glad to ma your acquaintance. They are warm friends the students, and always welcome them into o home. Toward the college boys," with a rogui emphasis on "boys," "they throw off all prudi formality."

"I shall call with pleasure," was Hadley ready rejoinder, as he lifted his hat, and ba her good evening.

(*To be Continued.*)

THE GOLDEN CALF.

By Mrs. M. Baxter.

S. Lesson for July 8, Exodus 32: 15-26. Golden Text 1 John 5: 21.

Lengthened Absence Provided for—Moses Thought to be Dead—The Sin of Impatience—Aaron's Weak Submission to Popular Clamor—The Sin Repeated in These Days—God's Offer to Moses—A Man Regardless of Self-Interest—His Success—His Indignation at Sight of the Calf—Aaron's Unmanliness—The Massacre—Moses Returns to the Lord—A Self-Immolatory Prayer.

WHEN Moses had gone up into the mountain God's command, he had made provision for absence: "He said unto the elders, 'Tarry here for us, until we come again unto you; d, behold, Aaron and Hur are with you; if y man have any matters to do, let him come to them.'" (Ex. 24:14.) Forty days and forty hts was a long time to wait, and human soning would, no doubt, suggest that Moses st long ago have died in the mountain; he st have fallen over some precipice, or have cumbed to the pangs of hunger. But such mises were nothing short of sin in the people om God had taken under His immediate e and protection. God had sent Moses to their leader, He had manifested His power ough Moses as He never had done before ough any mortal man, and He was responle alike for Moses and for them. Oh, how ch we lose through

The Sin of Impatience.

lessed are all they that wait for Him." (Isa. 13.) There is perhaps no one with whom are so impatient as God. How often we r it said, "I have asked God to direct me, I have no answer, and I am *obliged* to decide." o obliges you? Is not God your Master? ely He will not make you wait, and n blame you for waiting. The children of el had received the command, "Tarry ye e for us until we come again unto you;" they took upon themselves the responsibilof disobeying. "When they saw that Moses ayed to come down out of the mount, the ple gathered themselves together unto on, and said unto him, Up, make us gods ch shall go before us; for as for this Moses, man that brought us up out of the land of pt, we wot not what is become of him." doubt they had imagined that his interrse with God would consume only a few rs, and when day after day passed and they e disappointed, it seemed never to occur to m to inquire of the Lord, or to ask Aaron nquire of Him—they acted on human reason- and turned their backs on God. Oh, how understand that

Transactions with God

of more moment, and are worth more time, n any amount of preaching and outward acty for God! But Aaron! Surely he who was ed to be the High Priest, the type of Jesus, man nearest to God in the worship which l was teaching Moses—surely he would not part with the people against God? Yes, the Aaron who when under Moses' influence so true to God, now fell under the influence opular feeling, and was led away so far as to e a graven image for the people to worship! material of the golden calf was the golden ings which God was willing to accept as rings for the tabernacle. Whatever we keep urselves becomes a snare to us; as long as we l ourselves, and all we are and have as the d's, and unquestionably submit to His disposal , it is no snare to us. If those useless earrings been given to the Lord, the golden calf d not have been made. Imagine *Aaron* ding at the dedication of the image, and ng, "These be thy gods, O, Israel, which ght thee up out of the land of Egypt!" then Aaron proclaimed a feast to the Lord mixing up his service with idolatry), in which y offering except the sin and trespass offer- were offered. When men sin most they the farthest off from any confession of sin, the conscience loses its sensitiveness. We wonder at the idolatry of the children of Israel, and that they should have desired any graven image of a God who had made His power so manifest among them, but is not England sinning the same sin, in those idols which are being placed in St. Paul's Cathedral? What have we Protestants to do with crucifixes and images of the Virgin Mary? Is it not our glory that God Himself is with us, and that He dwells and walks in us? What have we to do with idols?

While the scene of revelry was transpiring below, God was acquainting Moses with the matter up in the Mount Sinai. "Go get thee down, for *thy* people, which thou broughtest out of the land of Egypt, have corrupted themselves." "*Thy* people?" Were they not the Lord's? They were not acting as such just now, and God puts Moses to a severe test. He says, "I have seen this people, and behold, it is a stiff-necked people. Now, therefore, let Me alone, that My wrath may wax hot against them; and I will make of thee a great nation." The choice was given him by God Himself, whether he would be a great man in himself, or a living sacrifice! Thank God, the Spirit of Christ was beforehand in some of these saints of old (1 Pet. 1:11, 12), and signally so in Moses. Utterly

Regardless of His Own Interest,

he argued the matter with God, "Why doth Thy wrath wax hot against *Thy* people whom *Thou* hast brought forth out of the land of Egypt? .... Wherefore should the Egyptian speak and say, For mischief did He bring them out?" Oh, this self-ignoring spirit, how rare it is! "Turn from Thy fierce wrath," he says, "and repent of this evil against Thy people." God had prayed Moses, "Let Me alone." But Moses refused, and prevailed with God! What a lesson of intercessory prayer! Was not he doing in the mountain with the Lord more than he could do in the plain? Moses reminded the Lord of His promises, and "the Lord repented of the evil which He had thought to do unto His people."

Until Moses had settled the matter with God, he was not prepared to meet the people. And when he went down from the mount he held in his hand the two tables of the testimony, "written on both sides, on the one side and on the other were they written. And the tables were the work of God, and the writing was the writing of God, graven upon the tables." Joshua accompanied Moses. Where he had been during the time of Moses' communing with God in the mount we know not, or what had become of the seventy elders; but, in any case, Moses found Joshua waiting for him. What we see makes more impression on us than what we hear. Moses *saw* the calf and the dancing (probably resembling the licentious orgies observed in heathen festivals to this day), and Moses' anger waxed hot, and he cast the tables out of his hands, and brake them beneath the mount. He had been occupied forty days and forty nights, without eating or drinking, and perhaps without sleeping, in ascertaining the mind of God, that he might teach the people the will of the God whom they had three times promised to obey. And now that he had brought them the very writing of God Himself, he finds them, with Aaron at their head, worshipping an idol! He had obtained God's mercy for them, but his own indignation was stirred up. He gave their sin no quarter, but "took the calf which they had made, and burnt it in the fire, and ground it to powder, and strewed it upon the water, and made the children of Israel drink." Then he called Aaron to account: "What did this people unto thee, that thou hast brought so great a sin upon them?" Priest, and brother to Moses,

Aaron was Unmanly,

just as Adam was when he cast the blame of his sin upon Eve. Instead of making a clean breast of it, Aaron excused himself by casting all the blame upon the people. It is very probable that Aaron may have acceded to their request from the best of motives, thinking to retain his influence over them until Moses should return, and so mixing up the worship of God with idolatrous rites. But why did he not inquire of the Lord?

Moses did not argue the matter; he saved all his reasonings for God; and, when dealing with man, his actions went further than his words. He "stood in the gate of the camp, and said, who is on the Lord's side? let him come unto me." The whole tribe of Levi, with, no doubt, Aaron at their head, ranged themselves on Moses' side, and then the command to slay went forth, and three thousand perished. The law has no mercy. "the soul that sinneth, it shall die" (Ezek. 18: 4). Now that sin was recognized as sin, and punished with death, Moses called on the people for a general consecration of themselves to the Lord, "that He may bestow upon you a blessing this day." Probably there was little sleep in the camp of Israel that night, and on the morrow Moses said to the people: "Ye have sinned a great sin; and now I will go up unto the Lord; peradventure, I shall make an atonement for your sin." What, must Moses leave them again? Yes; their very sin necessitated it. How unwise, how mad it is to lose patience with God! He is a better economist of time than we are. "And Moses returned unto the Lord,"

A Wonderful Type of Jesus,

entering within the veil. He pleaded, "Oh, these people have sinned a great sin, and have made them gods of gold. Yet now, if Thou wilt, forgive their sin; and if not, blot me, I pray Thee, out of Thy book which Thou hast written." Another such prayer is hardly anywhere on record, except it be that of Paul, "I say the truth in Christ. I lie not; my conscience also bearing me witness in the Holy Ghost, that I have great heaviness and continual sorrow in my heart. For I could wish that myself were accursed from Christ for my brethren, my kinsmen according to the flesh." (Rom. 9: 1-3.) Moses and Paul did not live for themselves in any sense; soul and body, will and desire, reputation, and all else, was sacrificed for others. God gives every Christian the privilege of so following Him. "None of us liveth to himself, and no man dieth to himself." (Rom. 14: 7.) "If any man will come after Me, let him deny himself." (Matt. 16: 24.) "And the Lord said unto Moses, whosoever hath sinned against Me, him will I blot out of My book." God will not do unrighteously. There is a very general making light of the heinousness of sin in our day. The gospel has been very fully preached, and the way of salvation made very easy. But many who profess to find peace, have never seen their sinfulness in the light of God, and groaned under the consciousness that they deserved nothing but God's wrath. Sure, He can convert a soul as rapidly as the jailer at Philippi, but it is the real sinner whom God saves from real sin and real condemnation. It is no simple thing of the feelings or imagination. A soul which has been consciously a lost soul, undone, and justly condemned by a righteous God, can never forget the first smile of God, or the horror of the horrible pit, and the miry clay from which he has been rescued. God is a Holy God; no man can break His law with impunity. He hates sin, He is of purer eyes than to behold evil, and yet He forgives, and blots out our sins by the blood of Jesus Christ, His beloved Son.

MY THREEFOLD REST.

I.

"Come unto Me, all ye that labor, and are heavy laden, and I will give you rest."—Matt. xi., 28.

From sin and sins, dear Lord I rest—
 Altar and Priest and Sacrifice Thou art;
By law and sin no more opprest,
 I share in Thy beatitude a part.
My yesterdays are covered by Thy blood;
 To-day my only shelter is Thy power;
To-morrow Thou wilt be as strong and good
 As in the past most gracious hour.

II.

"Take My yoke upon you, and learn of Me; for I am meek and lowly in heart; and ye shall find rest unto your souls."—Matt. xi. 29.

I rest by serving at Thy will—
 Thy yoke is easy and Thy burden light;
And peace grows deep and deeper still,
 As my obedience proves Thy might.
I hold my powers alone for Thee—
 Use them in loving errands of Thy grace;
And calm me, though I may not see
 Thy methods, as before Thy face.

III.

"There remaineth, therefore, a rest to the people of God."—Heb. iv., 9.

And yet the noblest rest remains
 In sweet reserve for hope and love;
It hath no place for sighs or pains,
 'Tis kept a glad surprise above.
Oh, rest untroubled and serene,
 In Thy bright presence, spotless Lamb!
Fit me each day, by every scene,
 For robe and harp, for crown and palm.

—*Stone.*

Christian Work in Mexico.

Through the reading of the Holy Scriptures translated into Spanish some earnest souls in Mexico have, by God's blessing, been led to a clear knowledge of the Gospel. From their numbers able preachers of the Christian faith in its primitive purity have been raised up, around whom congregations have been gathered from among the humble poor, who have been the first to publicly welcome and defend the pure Gospel in Mexico. The members of these congregations, rich in faith, have worked earnestly and bravely for Christ and His truth among their fellow countrymen in that beautiful Southern portion of North America called Mexico. Schools have been established by them, in which large numbers of bright boys and girls have received a good secular education and have been carefully taught the Christian faith. From the children thus educated faithful Christian workers have been raised up. A Mexican Branch of the Church of Christ, that maintains the faith in its purity and integrity, has been organized among these native Christians in the Republic of Mexico. The members of this Mexican Church of Christ, though gathered mostly from among the poor, are yet doing a most important Christian work. To continue that work, we need to pay a few leading workers small monthly salaries, and also to defray some current expenses. To raise the needed funds we have formed a society with an office at 43 Bible House, New York, U. S., and should be pleased to have many of our fellow Christians join this society by becoming regular contributors to its treasury. We are trying to secure monthly or quarterly contributions to meet the regular monthly expenses of the work. In order to continue and extend the work, we wish to raise four hundred dollars a month, by endeavoring to have four hundred persons each give on an average *one dollar every month* to this object, leaving the donors to give less or more as they may be able and willing.

We earnestly invite all who will, to join us in this systematic effort in behalf of the cause of Christ in Mexico, by becoming monthly subscribers to this fund. We have already regular subscribers whose gifts amount monthly to over eighty dollars, and a growing circle of friends who are forwarding us occasional donations.

This Mexican Church of Christ is a very effective instrumentality through which to do Christian work among the many millions on this Western Hemisphere who speak the Spanish language, comparatively few of whom have ever had a Bible in their hands. A beautiful church building has been secured in the City of Mexico as the centre of the activities of this Mexican Church of Christ. Through the workers connected with that centre more than forty congregations have been gathered from among the poor in different parts of the Republic of Mexico. We have some faithful and able preachers now in the field, but more young men need to be trained for the ministry. Multitudes of Protestant children in Mexico, some of them orphans, need to be educated. We make three requests of you, Christian reader: *first*, that you will, if possible, become a monthly or quarterly subscriber in behalf of this Christian work; *second*, that you will try and induce your friends also to contribute to it; *third*, that you will remember this precious work in Mexico in your prayers.

We most sincerely thank all who are already generously contributing to this Christian work for their timely and generous gifts, and we earnestly invite many others, to unite with us in aiding it by also becoming monthly subscribers in its behalf. Those who may not feel that they can give as much as a dollar a month are earnestly asked to give what they can, whenever they are able—EVERY LITTLE HELPS. Fellow Christian, if you will generously consent to contribute a dollar a month or more or less to the work, will you kindly inform me of the fact? Contributions either large or small can be mailed directly to my address as follows:

BISHOP H. C. RILEY, care of J. P. HEATH,
No. [illegible] ...le House, New York, U. S.

Vol. XI., No. 27. Office, 63 Bible House, N. Y. THURSDAY, JULY 5, 1888. Annual Subscription, $1.50.

CONTENTS OF THIS NUMBER.

PORTRAIT AND LIFE OF SIR JAMES KING (Lord Provost of Glasgow) AND VIEW OF THE GLASGOW EXHIBITION.
NONE LIKE JESUS. Dr. Talmage's Sermon at Crete, Neb., Last Sunday Morning.
ANECDOTES RELATED AT RECENT EVANGELISTIC MEETINGS.
THE LITERAL RESTORATION OF THE JEWS. By Rev. S. H. Kellogg, D. D.
The McAll Mission in Corsica—Female Beer Drinkers—A Centenarian's Comfort—The Martyrdom in Mexico—A Madura Woman's Emotion.
AN APOSTOLIC PRAYER. A New Sermon by Pastor C. H. Spurgeon.
CURRENT EVENTS: The Republican Candidates—Congressional Notes—The Emperor's Inaugural Speech—Rumors of Mr. H. M. Stanley—A Debate on Ireland, etc.
Gems from New Books: A Three Days' Bride, etc.
PICTURE OF THE PRINCE AND PRINCESS OF WALES OPENING GLASGOW EXHIBITION.
THE TWO SCHOOL FRIENDS. (With Illust.)
THE EPOCHS OF A LIFE. A New Serial Story by Rev. L. S. Keyser. (Continued.)
GOD'S PRESENCE PROMISED. By Mrs. M. Baxter.

SIR JAMES KING, Lord Provost of Glasgow—THE GLASGOW INTERNATIONAL EXHIBITION.

THE LORD PROVOST OF GLASGOW.

THE International Exhibition, recently opened in the great Scottish city is a matter of interest in the United States, inasmuch as this country is well represented among the exhibits, and travelling Americans in large numbers are visiting it. Besides this, a large number of our citizens are of Scottish birth or descent, and though Scotchmen of energy and grit are apt to leave their country for more promising fields, they never lose their love for their native land. In their voluntary exile their thoughts turn with affectionate interest to Scotland, and their dearest and most intimate friends are their fellow-countrymen. Thrifty, energetic, honest, and reliable, as a rule, they have been among the best of our transatlantic settlers; and some of our best statesmen, generals, lawyers, and clergymen owe their success here to the Scottish strain in their blood. The picture of the Exhibition on the first page, and the portrait of the Lord Provost, will be of interest therefore to a large class of the readers of this journal.

Practically the office of Lord Provost is equivalent to that of mayor. The title, which comes from the Latin term *præpositus* (set over), is usually of ecclesiastical or academical association, but in Scotland the duties of the Provost are only civic. He presides as chief magistrate in the police courts, as the mayors of English towns do, and he occupies the chair of the city council. In Glasgow, Edinburgh, Aberdeen, and Perth the Provost is entitled to the prefix of "Lord," though the title is retained only during his term of office.

Sir James King, the present Lord Provost of Glasgow, is one of the Jubilee Knights raised in common with other mayors of important cities to knighthood in honor of the year of the Queen's Jubilee. He is a native of the city which he now rules, and is extremely popular there in spite of the fact that he is a Conservative in politics, and an Episcopalian in religion—two characteristics which are apt to create a prejudice against a man in Scotland. Sir James was educated in the High School of the city, and subsequently graduated from the University of Glasgow. He then entered the office of his father, who was chief of an alum company, and has now been succeeded by his son. Sir James became a member of the city council in the spring of 1886, and in November of that year he had the honor of being elected Lord Provost without a dissentient voice. In returning thanks for this honor he remarked that: "To one who is proud of being a native of Glasgow, who knows well its varied interests and industries, who has during his whole life watched the rapid strides it has made in population and in material prosperity, there can be no distinction so great as to be chosen its civic head." The highest hopes held regarding his occupancy of the Chief Magistrate's chair have been more than realized—whether in his conduct of the Council conclaves or in social courtesies and entertainments.

The office of Lord Provost is not the only honor which has been conferred upon Sir James King. In 1875 the members of the Merchants' House elected him Dean of the Guild, and, in 1877, the Chamber of Commerce elected him Chairman. In 1879 he was made Dean of the Faculties of the University of Glasgow, and some six years later the Senatus honored him with the degree of LL. D. Sir James has been a Justice of the Peace of the counties of Lanark, Renfrew, and Stirling for close upon a quarter of a century, and in 1879 he was created Deputy Lieutenant of Stirling County.

The city over which he rules has a population of more than half a million, and is the second city of the empire. Its claims to antiquity are well established. There is a tradition that a bishopric was founded there by St. Mungo in 560, and it is known that the foundations of its cathedral were laid in 1115. During the next five hundred years the progress made by the town did not keep pace with its rivals, but in the early days of American colonization, it made rapid strides. It was the chief emporium for the Virginia tobacco trade, and subsequently dealt largely in cotton and sugar. It has held an important place in the annals of British history. Probably few of those who witnessed the other day the entry of the Prince and Princess of Wales into the city to open the exhibition, remembered anything of another Royal entry into Glasgow—that of the last hope of the Stuart kings, 143 years ago. A very different aspect the city wore on December 25, 1745, when it received Prince Charles Edward, the last of the despicable royal Stuarts, an unwelcome guest, no friend to the men of trade, and already a waning star. When he left his lodging at the foot of Glassford Street, on January 3, 1746, and marched eastward on his way to Falkirk and Culloden, he carried with him $50,000 of the honest burghers' money; the remembrance of which may lend greater interest in the eyes of these burghers' descendants to the relics of the Prince which have been brought together in the Glasgow Exhibition.

The citizens of Glasgow, however, do not much concern themselves with historical associations. More do they glory in the sight of the great ocean fleets coming up to their wharves laden with the wealth of East and West. And little do they care for the smoke-cloud that overhangs their roofs while they know that their furnace blasts are forging the navies, the iron walls, of half the world. Sheltered within her college walls from his rivals, the instrument-makers of Glasgow, *James Watt*, like the magicians of the "Arabian Nights," evoked from his kettle the white genius Steam. Since then, Electricity, another of the Titan brood, has been born upon earth. Like too many of the Arab genii, these mighty powers have made slaves of their discoverers, and as "he who increaseth knowledge, increaseth sorrow" (Eccles. 1:18), it has turned out that the increase of labor-saving appliances has increased labor.

THE GLASGOW INTERNATIONAL EXHIBITION.

(*See Illustration on first page.*)

THE citizens of Glasgow have made great efforts to produce an exhibition worthy of the position of their city as the largest in Scotland, and as the second city of the Empire, and they have been successful. Their exhibition is the largest organized within the British dominions since that of London in 1862. They have raised the largest guarantee-fund yet subscribed for such a purpose. They have

Expended $350,000 on Buildings,

which are convenient and commodious, covering an area of nearly sixteen acres. They secured for these buildings a magnificent site in the midst of the most beautiful natural surroundings. They are much more picturesquely treated than is usual with such edifices, the style chosen being Saracenic. The dome and minarets have a striking appearance, and form a very pleasing group, especially when seen in combination with the spire of the University, or the tall tower of a neighboring church.

The General Design

resembles that of the first International Exhibition in London in 1851, as it has a great central avenue or nave, sixty feet in width, with a transept of equal width intersecting it at the centre. Right and left of the main avenue the various courts, thirty-seven in number, are ranged. They have a uniform width of 50 feet, and vary in length from 50 feet to 135 feet. The Grand Hall is an imposing structure, capable of accommodating 3,000 persons. The section of the building allotted to *the fine arts* has been designed and constructed with a view to its being retained as a temporary home for the fine-art collection belonging to the corporation. There are in all seven picture-galleries, also a sculpture-gallery, and two upper corridors for architecture and photography. The *machinery department* is a conspicuous feature of the Exhibition. It is laid out in parallel courts, nine in number. Among the outside buildings the most important is the "Bishop's Palace." It is an exact reproduction of the old Bishop's Castle, which formerly stood near the Glasgow Cathedral, and the ruins of which were removed a century ago. The building is erected on the slope below the University, and is used for the exhibits of the archæological and historical section. It is surmounted by a gallery and promenade, which commands a view of the grounds.

The structure is, for the most part, of wood, with an iron and glass roof covering. The main feature is a central dome, which rises to a height of 150 feet, and is flanked by lofty minarets and towers of Oriental form. It is internally richly decorated in the style of the Alhambra. The principal entrance is in the centre of the building, and opens into the great central dome. In front is a statue of the Queen, who thus, in effigy at least, seems to preside over the Exhibition. She looks toward the Kelvin, and over the beautiful grounds, with kiosks, trees, and the sloping banks, surmounted on one side by the University, and on the other by the houses of the West End Park. In front of the main entrance are two bridges, communicating with the grounds on the right bank of the Kelvin.

The Foreign Section

comprises articles of various kinds from New York, Chicago, and other cities of the United States, Paris, Lyons, Vienna, Bohemia, Bremen, Berlin, Hamburg, Leipsic, Cologne, Milan, Florence, Turin, Amsterdam, Denmark, Norway, Russia, Turkey, the West Indies, and Australia. The Artisan Section consists mainly of models and specimens of work by individual working-men in Glasgow and the neighboring towns. Three courts are allotted to the Women's Arts and Industries of the United Kingdom. The Dominion of Canada occupies a special Court; India fills three Courts, and Ceylon one Court. The Grand Hall is decorated with a collection of national flags. The Queen's Jubilee presents, numbering 799 articles, are exhibited in the Museum.

One very interesting section of the Exhibition is that of specimens of woman's arts and industries. The ladies by whom the arrangement was superintended worked with a will and have made one of the most successful collections of the kind ever seen. Among them are conspicuous several exhibits from the Queen's daughters. The Empress of Germany exhibits a cushion and table-cover; and at her request the Duchess of Albany has forwarded for exhibition in this section a water-color drawing done by the Empress as a present to her brother, the late Duke of Albany. Princess Christian sends a chair in curious burnt leather and embroidery.

Interesting Archæological Exhibits

in large numbers have been sent in and are exhibited in the Bishop's Palace. Mr. Matthew Brownlie, of Strathaven, sends a flag which was *carried by the Covenanters* at Drumclog. The Duke of Montrose lends two portraits of his ancestor, "The Great Marquis"; also a portrait of Viscount Dundee, otherwise Graham of Claverhouse. Many will gaze with interest upon the sword which he wielded at the battle of Killiecrankie, where he met his death. Mrs. Erskine sends miniatures in Limoges enamel of *Queen Mary and her first husband*, King Francis II. of France. Further, two rat-tail table-spoons, dated 1686, which belonged to the Earl of Mar, who raised the Jacobite "standard on the Braes o' Mar" in 1715. The Earl of Mar and Kellie has lent *the cradle of King James VI.*, a substantial article of carved oak with inlaid panels. The high chair in which the King sat when a child is a solid piece of oak furniture. The Earl also sends a fine miniature of Mary Queen of Scots, a leaden badge of a King's bedesman, dated 1725; the lock and key of Kirkcudbright Tolbooth; Mr. Greenshields sends a collection of *weapons which belonged to the Covenanters*; and various exhibitors have sent remarkable specimens of silver coins—the whole making an exhibition of extraordinary interest.

THE OPENING CEREMONY.

(*See Illustration on page 428.*)

In order that nothing might be wanting to the success of the Exhibition that patronage could give, the Prince and Princess of Wales were induced to take part in the inaugural ceremony. The city was elaborately decorated to receive them. The streets traversed by the official procession were fenced on both sides with strong barricades, and were decorated with Venetian Masts from which hung festoons and streamers. The length of streets treated in this way for the journey to the Exhibition and back by a different route extended to five miles. Over the whole distance private houses and public buildings were tastefully decorated with draperies, flags, shields, and heraldic devices. In many cases balconies were thrown out and areas were covered over with extemporized platforms, while on the wide vacant spaces in Sauchiehall Street several grand stands had been erected for the accommodation of spectators, and were largely taken advantage of. At every opening in the main street were lorries, carts, and omnibuses covered with people, while the steep streets sloping northwards were used as natural galleries, and were filled, as far as the eye could reach, with eager crowds.

The Prince and Princess were received at the Glasgow Central Railway Station by the Lord Provost, Sir James King, and Lady King, who conducted them to the Corporation Chambers. There a large company was assembled. The royal visitors then went to the residence of the Lord Provost in Claremont Terrace, passing under a triumphal arch as their carriage approached the house. Sir James and Lady King entertained them with luncheon, after which they went to the Exhibition. Sir Archibald Campbell, President of the Executive Committee, there handed to the Prince

A Gold Key

of remarkable workmanship, specially devised by Mr. John C. Chubb. The wards in the lower part of the key are so arranged as to form the letters "G. E.," for Glasgow Exhibition. The stem is a Gothic arrangement of four clustered columns, above which, on a shield, is the Scottish Lion, and on the reverse the arms of the Prince of Wales, in enamel; from this springs a thistle-bloom, while the two large leaves of the national plant rise and form the bow of the key; an inner border is formed by tracery work, with fleur-de-lys finials at intervals, rising in the centre to the Maltese cross at the top. The bow of the key bears the crest of St. Mungo and the arms and fish supporters of the City of Glasgow in full heraldic colors. The reverse has a fac-simile of the badge of the Exhibition, showing an emblematic figure of Glasgow, and an inscription recording the presentation of the key to the Prince of Wales. It was inclosed in a handsome velvet case with gold monogram. On receiving the key, the Prince, amid cheers, opened the east door of the vestibule, and entered the Exhibition. The Prince and Princess walked to the front of the platform of the Grand Hall, the Glasgow Choral Union singing the national anthem, and the artillery on the neighboring heights firing a salute of twenty-one guns.

After their Royal Highnesses were seated, and prayers had been read by the Rev. Dr. Donald M'Leod, Sir Archibald Campbell presented an address, *as shown in our picture*, to which the Prince made a graceful reply.

When the inaugural ode had been sung, the Prince declared the Exhibition open amid much enthusiasm. The choir gave the "Hallelujah Chorus." The royal party entered the Picture-Galleries and Women's Industries Section, where the Princess was presented with a handsome piece of sewed work by Lady Campbell. After the royal party had partaken of tea in the reception-room, the Prince visited the Indian Court, and then, with the Princess, re-entered the carriage and drove to the Central Station, where he took train for Hamilton.

ANECDOTES RELATED AT RECENT EVANGELISTIC MEETINGS.

Stimulating the Soldiers.—Mr. McCaul says: "It is said of Napoleon I. that before he led his soldiers into any action that was more than usually hazardous, he would mount his white charger, and galloping up and down the ranks, cheerily shout, as he made his sword ring in its sheath, 'Come on, men, and I will lead you to victory!' This greatly encouraged the men, who, when under the eye of their general, or as they humorously called him, 'The Little Corporal,' felt that they could accomplish almost anything. Similarly, Christ, our great Captain, calls to the Church Militant, 'Come on, men, and I will lead you to victory!' Nothing withstands the Great Conqueror of sin and death and hell, our Leader: 'For he must reign till He hath put all enemies under His feet.'"

"Old Mortality" and the Covenanters' Tombs.—The Rev. J. S. Balmer observed: "Sir Walter Scott, in his story of 'Old Mortality,' tells how that worthy showed his veneration and love for the Covenanters of Scotland. He went from graveyard to graveyard in the old country, seeking the resting-places of the heroes and heroines of the Covenant. When he found a grave without a stone, he placed one upon it, and chiselled an inscription there, that the name of the Covenanter who fell in the cause of truth might not be forgotten. When he found a stone where the inscription was wearing away, he restored it with hammer and chisel, and from graveyard to graveyard went forth seeking to make the names of the Covenanters known in the coming days. It has often seemed to me that an occasion like this brings before us work something of the same kind—only our work is not upon gravestones, for the missionary cause is not dead; there never was in it more vitality than there is to-day—our work is not upon gravestones, but upon living minds and living hearts."

A Bottle of Whisky under the Pillow.—An evangelist relates: "I was taking tea with an ex-saloon-keeper the other day, and in course of conversation I remarked, 'Surely a spirit merchant's business must be a money-making one when you were enabled to retire from it so young.' 'Oh,' he replied, 'I did not leave it because I was rich, but because I was afraid to remain in it. There was a time I never went to bed without a bottle of whisky under my pillow. My conscience often kept me awake at night, for I knew I was ruining my own soul, and all those who came into my shop, and,' he continued, 'when in bed, I could see around me the spectres of people who had come to my shop for drink, and whom I knew to have died as drunkards—some in *delirium tremens*, some from want, some from accidents, but the death of all occasioned by drink; and I was heartily glad to get out of the business.' That man was not converted until after he left the business, and ever since he has been unfailing in his efforts to win other liquor-dealers to Christ."

Smitten on Both Cheeks.—An Evangelist said: "When I was preaching on an English racecourse one day, a man standing by said, 'Look here, if you say I'm a sinner, I'll give you a blow.' 'Very well,' I said, 'if it will do you any good, do so.' He struck the blow, but he did not seem to benefit by it. Again, at Liverpool, when one of our gospel sandwich-men was walking along with texts of Scripture upon his boards, a big, burly fellow, also a betting-man, walked up to him. I saw there was going to be trouble, so I stepped between them. 'What are you?' he angrily inquired. 'A sinner saved by grace.' 'And what am I?' he inquired. 'A sinner not yet saved by grace,' was my answer. 'Oh, you are a saint; now the Bible says, "If any man smite you on the one cheek, turn the other." Now I am going to try you,' and he struck me on the cheek. What was I to do? I had often had that cheek struck in the devil's service; should I not bear to have it smitten for Christ's cause? I turned the other, which he treated as he had done the first. 'Now it is my turn,' I said, and I dropped on my knees, and prayed to God to save that man. He stood beside me, and I could hear him mutter, 'Ah, that is a true Christian prayer.' When I rose to my feet he offered me five shillings, but, of course, I refused the money. He did not know what to do, that he might in some way atone for his conduct. He stood by us as we preached all day, and, whenever men of his own class threatened to molest us, he stepped forward in our defence. That is God's way; He kills all His enemies by converting them into friends."

Testing the Quality of the Iron.—Mr. Berry said: "We had an exhibition two or three years ago of iron products in Wolverhampton, and one of the most interesting of the exhibits was a large bar of iron, ten feet long and six inches thick, twisted as you have seen iron twisted into a series of crescent ribs. But the curious thing about the piece of iron was that it had been twisted cold, gripped at one end by a vice, at the other by a revolving engine, and twisted cold. I found upon inquiry that *the poorest iron* made was capable of being twisted and kneaded and done anything with, according to the worker's will, *when it is hot* fresh out of the furnace, but that *only the best iron will twist cold*. Therefore, as a test of the quality of the iron they twist it cold, and if it will stand that test it is sterling metal. Now, our churches were hot enough fifty years ago, and though they have lost that early heat of excitement, they are showing the quality of the metal which is in them by going on with the work, promoting all its branches and interests now, though it has lost its novelty."

The Spartan's Wreath of Triumph.—"There was an old law among the ancient Spartans that forbade any but one who had been crowned at the athletic games to stand beside their king in front rank in the day of battle. A youth entered at the games one day, and was disciplining himself carefully for the struggle. Large sums were offered him if he would withdraw, but he scorned them all. The day of trial came, and to him it was a day of triumph, as he anticipated. His perseverance was rewarded, and the crown of victory was his. When he received it, it was only a wreath of green parsley and bay-leaves. A friend near him remarked that, and asked him what he thought of it. 'I look not on it,' was the reply, 'but because of it I can stand by my king in the van!' That is one of the greatest honors and rewards that Christ, the King of glory, gives to His servants, that they may stand by Him in the van during the fight with sin and Satan; and is it not a high position to occupy, honorable to ourselves and helpful to our fellows?

Bad Choice of a Young Lady.—"A servant of Christ concerned about the spiritual welfare of the youth of his congregation, met a young lady about whose soul he was specially interested. He urged upon her the necessity of coming to Christ and giving up the world and its pleasures. But the young lady frivolously replied, 'I mean to have both Christ and the world.' 'Impossible,' said the minister, solemnly; 'you cannot serve God *and* mammon,' and he redoubled his efforts to induce her to choose between Christ and the world. At length the young lady deliberately replied, 'Well, if I *must* have my choice, I choose the world.' With a sorrowful heart, the aged minister left her, saying, 'Well, if you choose the world, go and make the best of it. But, oh, remember this world is only for time. What will you do in eternity?' The young lady followed up her choice. One night as she was singing the well-known song based on the parable of the Ten Virgins, and was rendering the words, 'Too late, too late! ye cannot enter now,' her slumbering conscience suddenly awoke. She vividly saw she was like one of the foolish virgins, and there was no more rest for her; days of sorrow succeeded nights of darkness, until at length light broke in upon her mind, and she saw that there was still time to repent and accept Christ. This she did, and found in Him a ready and loving Saviour.

NONE LIKE JESUS.

Dr. Talmage's Sermon Preached Sunday Morning, July 1, 1888.

"Unto you therefore which believe, He is precious." 1 Pet. 2 : 7.

The Cause of Hard Times—Different Kinds of Faith—Head Faith and Heart Faith—A Mining Disaster in Pennsylvania—Personal Interest in a Rescue—Christ's Rescue from the Mine of Sin—Christ Precious to the Believer—I. As a Saviour—Omnipotent Chemistry—One Unforgiven Sin—II. As a Friend—In Business—In the Family—A Sailor's Confession in New York—III. As a Final Deliverer—A Talk on Risks—Laughter in Heaven—The World's Food for the Soul—A Second Crucifixion—A Young Man's Letter Answered.

WE had for many years in this country commercial depression. What was the matter with the stores? With the harvests? With the people? Lack of faith! Money enough, goods enough, skilful brains enough, industrious hands enough, but no faith. Now what damages the commercial world, damages the spiritual.

Our Great Lack

is faith. That is the hinge on which eternity turns. The Bible says we are saved by faith. "O," says some one in the audience, "I have faith. I believe that Christ came down to save the world." I reply that in worldly matters, when you have faith you always act upon it. For instance, if I could show you a business operation by which you could make five thousand dollars, you would immediately go into it. You would prove your faith in what I tell you by your prompt and immediate action. Now, if what you call faith in Christ has led you to surrender your entire nature to Jesus and to corresponding action in your life, it is genuine faith, and if it has not, it is not faith at all.

There are some things which I believe with the head. Then there are other things which I believe with the heart. And then there are other things which I believe both with the head and heart. I believe, for instance, that Cromwell lived. That is a matter of the head. Then there are other things which I believe with the heart and not with the head. That is, I have no especial reason for believing them, and yet I want to believe them, and the wish is the father to the expectation. But there is a very great difference between that which we believe about ourselves, and that which we believe about others. For instance, you remember not a great while ago there was

A Disaster in Pennsylvania,

amid the mines; there was an explosion amid the damps, and many lives were lost. In the morning you picked up your newspaper, and saw that there had been a great disaster in Pennsylvania. You said "Ah, what a sad thing this is; how many lives lost! O, what sorrow!" Then you read a little further on. There had been an almost miraculous effort to get those men out, and a few had been saved. "O," you said, "what a brave thing, what a grand thing that was! How well it was done!" Then you folded the paper up, and sat down to your morning repast. Your appetite had not been interfered with, and during that day, perhaps, you thought only two or three times of the disaster.

But suppose you and I had been in the mine, and the dying had been all around us, and we had heard the pickaxes just above us as they were trying to work their way down, and after a while we saw the light, and then the life-bucket let down through the shaft, and, suffocated and half dead, we had just strength enough to throw ourselves over into it, and had been hauled out into the light. Then what an appreciation we would have had of the agony and the darkness beneath, and the joy of deliverance. That is the difference between believing a thing about others and believing it about ourselves.

We take up the Bible and read that Christ came to save the world. "That was beautiful," you say; "a fine specimen of self-denial. That was very grand indeed." But suppose it is found that we ourselves were down

In the Mine of Sin

and in the darkness, and Christ stretched down His arm of mercy through the gloom and lifted us out of the pit, and set our feet on the Rock of Ages, and put a new song into our mouth: O, then it is a matter of handclapping; it is a matter of congratulation; it is a matter of deep emotions. Which kind of faith have you, my brother?

It is faith that makes a Christian, and it is the proportion of faith that makes the difference between Christians. What was it that lifted Paul and Luther and Payson and Doddridge above the ordinary level of Christian character? It was the simplicity, the brilliancy, the power, and the splendor of their faith. O, that we had more of it! God give us more faith to preach and more faith to hear. "Lord, we believe; help Thou our unbelief!" "To you which believe, He is precious."

First: I remark Christ is precious to the believer,

As a Saviour from Sin.

A man says: "To whom are you talking? I am one of the most respectable men in this neighborhood; do you call me a sinner?" Yes! "The heart is deceitful above all things and desperately wicked." You say: "How do you know anything about my heart?" I know that about it, for God announces it in His Word; and what God says is always right. When a man becomes a Christian, people say: "That man sets himself above us." O, no! Instead of setting himself up, he throws himself down. He cries out: "I was lost once, but now I am found. I was blind once, but now I see. I prostrate myself at the foot of the cross of the Saviour's mercy."

What a grand thing it is to feel that all the bad words I have ever uttered, and all the bad deeds I have ever done, and all the bad thoughts that have gone through my mind, are as though they had never been, for the sake of what Christ has done. You know there is a difference in stains. Some can be washed out by water, but others require a chemical preparation. The sin of the heart is so black and indelible a mark that no human application can cleanse it, while the blood of Jesus Christ can wash it out for ever. O, the infinite, the

Omnipotent Chemistry

of this glorious gospel! Some man says: "I believe all that. I believe God has forgiven the most of my sins, but there is one sin I cannot forget." What is it? I do not want to know what it is, but I take the responsibility of saying that God will forgive it as willingly as any other sin.

> "O'er sins like mountains for their size,
> The seas of sovereign grace expand,
> The seas of sovereign grace arise."

There was a very good man, about seventy-five years of age, that once said: "I believe God has forgiven me, but there was one sin which I committed when I was about twenty years of age that

I Never Forgave Myself

for, and I can't feel happy when I think of it." He said that one sin sometimes came over his heart, and blotted out all his hope of heaven. Why, he lacked in faith. The grace that can forgive a small sin can forgive a large sin. Mighty to save! Mighty to save! Who is the God like unto our God, that pardoneth iniquity? O, what Jesus is to the soul that believes in him! The soul looks up into Christ's face, and says: "To what extent wilt Thou forgive me?" And Jesus looks back into his face, and says: "To the uttermost." The soul says: "Will it never be brought up again?" "Never," says Christ. "Won't it be brought up again in Judgment Day?" "No," says Christ, "never in the Judgment Day." What bread is to the hungry, what harbor is to the bestormed, what light is to the blind, what liberty is to the captive, that, and more than that, is Christ to the man who trusts Him.

Just try to get Christ away from that Chr tian. Put on that man the thumb-scre Twist it until the bones crack. Put that fo into the iron boot of persecution until it mashed to a pulp. Stretch that man on t rack of the inquisition, and, louder than all t uproar of the persecutors, you will hear h voice like the voice of Alexander Le Cro above the crackling faggots as he cried out: " Jesus! O, my blessed Jesus! O, divine Jesu who would not die for Thee?"

Again: I remark that Christ is precious the believer,

As a Friend.

You have commercial friends and you have fam ily friends. To the commercial friend you g when you have business troubles. You can loo back to some day—it may have been ten twenty years ago—when, if you had not had th friend, you would have been entirely overthrow in business. But I want to tell you this mor ing of Jesus, *the best business friend* a man ev had. He can pull you out of the worst perplexiti There are people in this audience who have g in the habit of putting down all their world troubles at the feet of Jesus. Why, Christ mee the business man on the street and says: " business man, I know all thy troubles. I will with thee. I will see thee through." Look o how you try to corner or trample on a man wh is backed up by the Lord God Almighty! Loo out how you trample on him!

O, there is a financier that many of our bus ness men have not found out. Christ owns the boards of trade, all the insurance comp nies, and all the banking houses. They say th the Vanderbilts own the railroads; but Chri owns the Vanderbilts and the railroads, and the plottings of stock gamblers shall be put confusion, and God with His little finger sha wipe out their infamous projects. How ofte it has been that we have seen men gather u riches by fraud, in a pyramid of strength an beauty, and the Lord came and blew on it an it was gone; while there are those here to-da who, if they could speak out in this assemblag or dared to speak out, would say: "The be friend I had in 1837; the best friend I had 1857; the best friend I had at the opening the war; the best friend I ever had—has been th Lord Jesus Christ. I would rather give up a other friends than this one." But we have als

Family Friends.

They come in when we have sickness in th household. Perhaps they say nothing; bu they sit down and they weep as the light go out from the bright eyes, and the white petal of the lily are scattered in the blast of death They watch through the long night by the dy ing couch, and then, when the spirit has gone soothe you with great comfort. They say "Don't cry. Jesus pities you. All is well. Yo will meet the lost one again." Then, when you son went off, breaking your heart, did they no come and put the story in the very best shape and prophesy the return of the prodigal? Wer they not in your house when the birth ange flapped its wings over your dwelling? And they have been there at the baptisms and at th weddings. Family friends! But I have to tel you that Christ is the best family friend. O blessed is that cradle over which Jesus bends Blessed is that nursery where Jesus walks Blessed is that sick brow from which Jesus wipes the dampness! Blessed is that table where Jesus breaks the bread! Blessed is that grave where Jesus stands with His scarred feet on the upturned sod, saying: "I am the Resurrection and the Life; he that believeth in Me, though he were dead, yet shall he live"! Have you a babe in the house? put it into the arms of

The Great Child-Lover.

Is there a sick one in the house? Think of Him who said, "Damsel, arise." Are you afraid you will come to want? Think of Him who fed the five thousand. Is there a little one in your house that you are afraid will be blind or deaf or lame? Think of Him who touched the blinded eye, and snatched back the boy from pileptic convulsion. Oh, He is the best friend. ook over your family friends to-day, and find nother that can be compared to Him. When e want our friends, they are sometimes out of wn. Christ is always in town. We find that me will stick to us in prosperity who will not adversity. But Christ comes through darkt night, and amid ghastliest sorrow, and across ughest sea to comfort you.

There are men and women here who would ave been dead twenty years ago but for Jesus. hey have gone through trial enough to exhaust n times their physical strength. Their propty went, their health went, their families were attered. God only knows what they suffered. hey are an amazement to themselves that they ave been able to stand it. They look at their ce happy home, surrounded by all comfort. one! They think of the time when they used rise strong in the morning, and walk vigorsly down the street, and had experienced a ealth they thought inexhaustible. Gone! verything gone but Jesus.

He Has Pitied Them.

is eye has watched them. His omnipotence s defended them. Yes. He has been with em. They have gone through disaster, and e was a pillar of fire by night. They have ne across stormy Galilee, but Christ had His ot on the neck of the storm. They felt the aves of trouble coming up around them gradlly, and they began to climb into the strong ck of God's defence, and then they sang, as ey looked over the waters, "God is our refuge d strength, an ever-present help in time of ouble; therefore we will not fear though the rth be removed, though the mountains be rried into the midst of the sea, though the aters thereof roar and be troubled, though the ountains shake with the swelling thereof.

The other day there was *a sailor who came to the Bethel* in New York, and said: "My ds (he was standing among sailors), I don't ow what's the matter of me. I used to ar a good deal about religion, and about Jesus rist. I don't know that I have any religion, that I know anything much about Christ; t when I was in mid-Atlantic I looked up one y through the rigging, and there seemed to me light through my soul. I have felt differt ever since, and I love those that I once ted, and I feel a joy I can't tell you. I really n't know what is the matter of me." A ugh sailor got up, and said, "My lad, I know at's the matter of you. You have found sus. It is enough to make any man happy."

"His worth if all the nations knew,
Sure the whole earth would love Him too."

I remark again: Christ is precious to the liever, as

A Final Deliverer.

u and I must after awhile get out of this rld. Here and there one perhaps may come to eighty, to ninety years of age, but your mmon sense tells you that the next twentye years will land the majority of this audience eternity. The next ten years will thin out reat many of these family circles. This day y do the work for some of us. Now why do ay this? To scare you? No; but just as I uld stand in your office, if I were a business n, and you were a business man, and talk er risks. You do not consider it cowardly to k in your store over temporal risks. Is it e in us this morning to talk a little while r the risks of the soul, that are for eternity? n every congregation Death has the last year en doing a great deal of work. Where is ur father? Where is your mother? Your ild? Your brother? Your sister? O, cruel es Death seem to be! Will he pluck every wer? Will he poison every fountain? Will put black on every door-knob? Will he p every heart-string? Can I keep nothing? e there no charmed weapons with which to out and contend against him? Give me ne keen sword, sharpened in God's armory, h which I may stab him through. Give me ne battle-axe that I may clutch it, and hew him from helmet to sandal. Thank God, thank God, that he that rideth on the pale horse hath more than a match in Him who rideth on the white horse. St. John heard the contest, the pawing of the steeds, the rush, the battle-cry, the onset, until the pale horse came down on his haunches, and his rider bit the dust, while Christ, the conqueror, with uplifted voice declared it: "O death, I will be thy plague: O grave, I will be thy destruction." The sepulchre is

A Lighted Castle

on the shore of heavenly seas, and sentinel angels walk up and down at the door to guard it. The dust and the dampness of the grave are only the spray of the white surf of celestial seas, and the long breathing of the dying Christian, that you call his gasping, is only the long inhalation of the air of heaven. O, bless God for what Christ is to the Christian soul, here and hereafter!

I heard a man say, some time ago, that they never laugh in heaven. I do not know where he got his authority for that. I think they do laugh in heaven. When victors come home, do we not laugh? When fortunes are won in a day, do we not laugh? After we have been ten or fifteen years away from our friends, and we greet them again, do we not laugh? Yes,

We will Laugh in Heaven.

Not hollow laughter nor meaningless laughter, but a full, round, clear, deep, resonant outbreak of eternal gladness. Oh, the glee of that moment when we first see Jesus! I think we will take the first two or three years in heaven to look at Jesus; and if, in ten thousand years, there should be a moment when the doxology paused, ten thousand souls would cry out: "Sing! Sing!" and when the cry was, "What shall we sing?" the answer would be, "Jesus! Jesus!" Oh, you may have all the crowns in heaven! I do not care so much about them. You may have all the robes in heaven; I do not care so much about them. You may have all the sceptres in heaven; I do not care so much about them. You may have all the thrones in heaven; I do not care so much about them. But give me Jesus—that is enough heaven for me. Oh, Jesus! I long to see Thee, thou "chief among ten thousand, the One altogether lovely."

There may be some here who have come, hardly knowing why they come. Perhaps it was as in Paul's time—you have come to hear what this babbler sayeth; but I am glad to meet you face to face, and to strike hands with you in one earnest talk about your deathless spirit. Do you know, my friend that this world is not good enough for you? It cheats. It fades. It dies. You are immortal. I see it in the deathless spirit looking out from your eye. It is a mighty spirit. It is an immortal spirit. It beats against the window of the cage. I come out to feed it. During the past week the world has been trying to feed it with husks. I come out this morning to feed it with that bread of which if a man eat he will never hunger.

What has the World Done

for you? Has it not bruised you? Has it not betrayed you? Has it not maltreated you? Look me in the eye, immortal man, and tell me if that is not so. And yet, will you trust it? Oh, I wish that you could forget me, the weak and sinful man—that I might vanish from your sight this morning, and that Jesus might come in! Aye, He comes here this morning to plead for your soul—comes in all covered with the wounds of Calvary. He says, "O, immortal man! I died for thee. I pity thee. I come to save thee. With these hands, torn and crushed, I will lift thee up into pleasures that never die." Who will reject—who will drive Him back?

When Christ was slain on the cross, they had a cross, and they had nails, and they had hammers. You crucify by your sin, O impenitent soul! the Lord Jesus Christ. Here is a cross; but where are the nails? Where are the hammers? "Ah," says some one rejecting Christ, some one standing a long way off, "I will furnish the nails. I don't believe in that Jesus. I will furnish the nails." Now we have the nails, who will furnish the hammers? "Ah," says some hard heart, "I will furnish the hammers." Now we have the nails and the hammers. We have no spears; who will furnish the spears? "Ah," says some one long in the habit of sin and rejection of Christ's mercy, "I will furnish them." Now we have all the instruments: the cross, the nails, the hammers, the spears: and the crucifixion goes on. Oh, the darkness! Oh, the pang! Oh, the tears! Oh, the death! "Behold the Lamb of God, that taketh away the sins of the world!" Lord Jesus

Help that Man.

He sits far back to-day. He does not like to come forward. He feels strange in a religious assemblage. He thinks perhaps we do not want him. O Jesus, take that trembling hand. Put thine ear to that agitated heart, and hear how it beats. O, lift the iron gate of that prisonhouse, and let that man go free.

Lord Jesus, help that woman. She is a wanderer. No tears can she weep. See, Lord Jesus, that polluted soul, see that blistered foot! No church for her. No good cheer for her. No hope for her. Lord Jesus, go to that soul. Thou wilt not stone her. Let the red-hot chain, that burns to the bone till the bloody ichor hisses in the heat, snap at Thy touch. O, have mercy on Mary Magdalene!

Lord Jesus, help that young man! He took money out of his employer's till. Didst Thou see it? The clerks were all gone. The lights were down. The shutters were up. Didst Thou see it? O, let him not fall into the pit. Rememberest Thou not his mother's prayers? She can pray for him no more. Lord Jesus, touch him on the shoulder. Touch him on the heart. Lord, save that young man! There are many young men here.

I Got a Letter

from one of them who is probably here to-day, and I shall have no other opportunity of answering that letter. You say you believe in me. O, do you believe in Jesus? I cannot save you, my dear brother. Christ can. He wants and waits to save you, and He comes to-day to save you. Will you have Him? I do not know what our young men do without Christ—how they get on amid all the temptations and trials to which they are subjected. O, young men, come to Christ to-day, and put your soul and your interest for this life, and for the next, into His keeping. In olden times, you know, a cup-bearer would bring wine or water to the king, who would drink it, first tasting it himself, showing that there was no poison in it, then passing it to the king, who would drink it. The highest honor I ask is that I may be cup-bearer to-day to your soul. I bring you this water of everlasting life. I have been drinking of it. There is no poison in it. It has never done me any harm. It will do you no harm. O, drink it, and live forever. And let that aged man put his head down on the staff, and let that poor widowed soul bury her worried face in her handkerchief, and these little children fold their hands in prayer, while we commend you to Him who was wounded for our transgressions, and bruised for our iniquities; for to you which believe, He is precious.

THE LITERAL RETURN OF THE JEWS.

By Rev. Samuel H. Kellogg, D. D.*

Temporal and Spiritual Blessings Foretold by the Same Prophets—Not the Return Under Ezra—Reasons for Believing it Still Future—I. To be in the Latter Days—II. To Include all the Twelve Tribes—III. To be Final—IV. Complete—V. In National Independence—VI. Two Restorations Predicted, of Which One Only Has Taken Place.

THE same prophets who predict a future reversal of the *spiritual* curse of hardening which has for ages rested on the Jew, no less plainly and explicitly predict the reversal of all *temporal* curses which were denounced, and have so literally fallen upon the nation, the land, and the Holy City. Thus, for example, we read in Jer. 30:3: "Lo, the days come, saith the Lord, that I will bring again the captivity of my people Israel and Judah, and I will cause them to return to the land that I gave unto their fathers, and they shall possess it." So we read again in Ezek. 37:21: "Say unto them, thus saith the Lord God, 'Behold, I will take the children of Israel from among the heathen, whither they be gone, and will gather them on every side and bring them into their own land!'" Such examples, as every Bible reader knows, might be multiplied indefinitely.

It is utterly impossible to apply all such predictions of return to the land, as some have sought to do, to the return under Ezra from the Babylonian exile. Whatever they mean, it is absolutely certain that they refer to an event which is *yet in the future.* This will be perfectly clear from the following considerations:

1. The Scriptures undoubtedly predict a return which is to take place

"In The Latter Days."

To "the latter days" is expressly referred, e. g., the prophecy of Jeremiah, in chapter 30. What this expression means, every Bible student knows. It is never used with reference to any period before the first advent of our Lord. Least of all is it ever used in any of those prophecies which by common consent refer to the restoration from Babylon. The return of "the latter days," therefore, whatever it be, cannot be understood of the restoration from Babylon, nor of any event before the first coming of our Lord. Hence, as nothing since the first advent has occurred which could be so understood, it is plain that the promised return is an event yet in the future.

2. Another proof that the Babylonian restoration cannot be intended in all these predictions of a regathering of Israel in the land, is found in the fact that the restoration of

The Ten Tribes,

under the names of Ephraim, Israel, etc., as well as that of the two tribes of Judah and Benjamin, is distinctly predicted. Thus, for example, in the prophecy of restoration in Jer. 30:31, the restoration of the house of Israel or Ephraim, as distinguished from that of Judah, is as specifically the subject of chapter 31 as is the restoration of Judah the subject of the chapter preceding. Very explicit is the language of the prophet Ezekiel in this matter: "Say unto them, thus saith the Lord, God, Behold, I will take the stick of Joseph, which is in the hand of Ephraim, and the tribes of Israel his fellows, and will put them with him, even with the stick of Judah, and they shall be one in mine hand. . . . And I will make them one nation in the land upon the mountains of Israel, and one king shall be king to them all, and they shall no more be two nations, neither shall they be divided into two nations any more at all." (Ezek. 37: 19-22). It is very plain, again, that, whatever these words mean, they were not fulfilled in the restoration from Babylon, nor have been at any time since. They *must* refer to an event yet in the future.

3. In the third place, whereas the restoration from Babylon, and the rebuilding at that time of the city of Jerusalem, was followed again and again by dispersion and by a yet more complete overthrow of the city, this restoration of the latter days is uniformly represented as being absolutely *final.* Thus we read of

A Rebuilding of Jerusalem,

after which "*it shall not be plucked up, nor thrown down, any more forever.*" (Jer. 31: 40.) So also, by Amos, the Lord says, "I will plant them upon their land, and they shall *no more* be pulled up out of their land which I have given them." (Amos 9: 15.)

These words assuredly cannot be referred to the restoration from Babylon, after which they were again pulled up out of their land, and scattered more widely and fearfully by the armies of the Romans than they ever were by the power of Nebuchadnezzar.

Final and Complete.

4. Again, we read of a restoration which shall not only be final, but *complete.* Thus, the Lord said by the prophet Ezekiel, "O mountains of Israel! . . . . I will multiply men upon you, *all* the house of Israel, even *all* of it." (Ezek. 36: 8-10.) So also by Isaiah the Lord promised, "Ye shall be gathered *one by one*, O ye children of Israel." (Isa. 27: 12.) Surely no one will insist that the restoration from Babylon satisfies such language as this. So far from all returning at that time, we are told that only 42,360 of the captives ever returned. (Ezra 2: 1, 64.) Anything approaching to a universal restoration of Israel to their own land the world has never yet seen. So, again, it is plain that whatever these predictions mean they cannot refer to the return from Babylon, but to an event which is yet in the future.

5. This is, if possible, made still more clear by what we are told of the *condition* of Israel thus restored. As regards

Their National Life,

they are to be in a state of *independence.* "Strangers shall *no more serve themselves* of Jacob." (Jer. 30: 8.) But since the Babylonian restoration the Jews have had to wear the yoke of the Gentiles almost without interruption. The brief *quasi* independence of the Jews, under the Asmonean kings, was soon followed by the beginning of a more complete subjection than ever, from which they have never yet recovered. And then, in the second place, it is always added that after that future restoration to the land the long history of Israel's apostasies shall end. Thus we read in the prophecy of Ezekiel that after the final reunion of Ephraim and Judah on the mountains of Judah, they shall not "*defile themselves any more* with any of their transgressions." From that time on the sanctuary of God "shall be in the midst of them *forevermore.*" It is needless to say that such words as these cannot be applied to a restoration which, if it cleansed them from idolatry, only brought them for a while into their own land, there to commit after a time the greatest crime of their whole history, in the crucifixion of the Son of God.

6. Finally, the prophets themselves recognize the fact that there shall be

Two Restorations.

In the book of Isaiah this is said in so many words, thus: "It shall come to pass in that day that the Lord shall set his hand again *the second time* to recover the remnant of his people, which shall be left, from Assyria, and from Egypt, and from Pathros, and from Cush, and from Elam, and from Shinar, and from Hamath, and from the islands of the sea. . . . And He . . . shall assemble the outcasts of Israel, and gather together the dispersed of Judah from the four corners of the earth." (Isa. 11: 11, 12.)

But the Babylonian restoration was the first, and not the second; and as there has certainly been no restoration since, it follows, according to the explicit teaching of the prophet, a second restoration of Israel is yet in the future.

Here then we have no less than six independent proofs that the Scriptures do predict a regathering of the Jews into their own land, such as the world has never yet seen. Do the words of Scripture which foretell that this shall be, mean what they undoubtedly say, or are they, one and all, to be understood as merely figurative descriptions of the prosperity of the church in the latter days, or, at most, as poetic amplifications of the prophecies of Israel's conversion?

Strange, indeed, that such a question should ever have been raised! If such words as those which we have cited do not teach that Israel, the

Literal, Historical, National

Israel, shall yet be gathered into their own land, to be rooted out no more forever, we ask, with all earnestness, what words could possibly have been substituted which should have taught this? The very same terms are used in Jer. 29: 10, in predicting the return of the Jews from the Babylonian captivity, which are elsewhere employed to predict the return of the latter days. As every one knows, the event proved that these words were to be taken in their plain and evident literal sense; they meant precisely what they said, nothing more and nothing less. How, then, on any sound principles of exegesis, can any one be justified in denying that the self-same words in the same prophets, foretelling a "second" restoration, also mean exactly what they meant in the former case, namely, a literal return of the Jewish nation to their own land? We insist, on principles of interpretation which seem to us little less than axiomatic, that the the presumption in this case, for the literal interpretation of these temporal promises to Israel, is wellnigh irresistible.

* From the new edition of his work entitled "The Jews, or Prediction and Fulfilment; an Argument for the Times." Pp. 329. Price $1.25. Published by *Anson D. F. Randolph & Company*, 38 West 23d St., New York.

TWENTY YEARS IN EGYPT.

THE Rev. A. Crombie says: "There are cases where individual mission work has been successful. I especially refer to the work of Miss Whately among the Mohammedans of Egypt for the last twenty years. She went there to recruit her health, and to return after the winter months; but the ignorance and degradation of the females aroused her sympathy, and made her wishful to do something for their enlightenment. Finding no schools for Mohammedan girls, she set herself the difficult task of establishing them. She commenced to teach them to read and sew in her own sitting-room, and the number soon rose to over twenty. Quietly and steadily the work advanced. In 1862 Miss Whately returned to England, and the work was placed in other hands; but failure of health and many discouragements caused it to be abandoned. On hearing that, Miss Whateley resolved to return. On reaching Cairo she proceeded to the deserted school-room, and, finding a well-known teacher at the door, she was sent to tell former scholars 'School is open.' Soon there was a rush of scholars on the stairs shouting the cheering words, 'Welcome, welcome, teacher! Our teacher is come back! God be praised!' By patient labor Miss Whately achieved success. She has labored, also, much among the women, visiting them in the lanes of the city, and in the fields while at work in connection with the maize, sugar-cane, and other products of the country, and testifies that she found them eager to listen to the gospel message when delivered in a kindly spirit."

THE LAST MAN ON THE WRECK.

A FEW years ago a homeward bound vessel was wrecked on the southwest coast of England. The lifeboat was lauuched, and away the men went, and were a long while at sea. Darkness set in, but the people on the coast lighted great fires so that the lifeboat might be guided on its return to shore. After awhile they saw it returning, and a great strong man, of the name of John Holden, who was on the coast, cried aloud to the captain of the lifeboat, 'Hi! hi! have you saved the men?' The captain answered, 'Ay, ay, I have saved the men'; and all hearts were filled with gladness. But when they reached the coast it was found that *one man was left clinging to the mast.* 'Why did not you save him?' said Holden—'why did you not save him?' 'Because we were exhaust-l,' said the captain, 'and we should all have rished if we had remained another five minutes attempting to save one man.' 'But you ill go back—you will go back to the rescue?' hey said they had not the strength, the storm as so fierce. Holden threw himself on the shin-, and lifted up a prayer to God louder than e storm, that God would put it into the hearts some of those people to go to the rescue of is one man, just as Jesus Christ came to rese one lost world. When he had ceased prayg six men volunteered to accompany him, and hn Holden, with six men, were prepared to and rescue that one man. They were preparing to start, when the good old mother of hn Holden threw her arms around his neck nd said, 'John, you must not go. What can I o if you perish? You know your father was rowned at sea, and it is just two years since our brother *William left*; we have never heard word of him since. No doubt he, too, has erished. John, what shall I do if you perh?' John said, 'Mother, God has put it ito my heart to go, and if I perish He will take are of you.' And away he went; and after while the lifeboat returned, and when he neard the coast a loud voice was raised, 'Hi! hi! ohn, have you saved the man?' John answerd, in a trumpet voice, 'Yes, we have saved the an; and tell my mother *it is my brother William we have saved*.' Now, there is your broher man the wide world over; haste to the scue even if you perish in the attempt."

THE McALL MISSION IN CORSICA.

ONE of Mr. McAll's mission workers, who has one to Corsica to carry on the work so wonerfully blessed in Paris, gives a sad account of e deplorable ignorance existing on the island. he says: "In order to reach those who never me to meetings I generally take my meals in staurants, where I enter into conversation ith all sorts of educated men. It would surise you to hear their questions about Protestnts, as they are utterly ignorant of the fact at seven countries of Europe had shaken off e yoke of the Pope, acknowledging the Scripres as their only standard.

"A country schoolmaster, who for years had een wishing to know the truth, came up to me ne day at luncheon time, and most cautiously pproached the subject of salvation. The Lord sed my testimony, and saved that hungry soul. You have, indeed, opened heaven to me,' he id in one of his letters, 'and it is now my appy privilege to influence my pupils, in order lead them to Jesus, that they may grow up, nd not only be good citizens, but faithful hristians.' This schoolmaster lives now in a llage near Sartène, where vengeance and murer bring about great distress.

"At the Government Training College I was sked last year to give courses of modern lanuages. As these normal schools are non-professional, I take advantage of this liberty to introice the gospel.

"Last summer, when spending my vacation at artène, I found an open door in many rich famies, where prejudice had hitherto prevented all tercourse with evangelical Christians. Even ldiers came up to my room to get gospels, and anted to hear about the finished work of our ord."

FEMALE BEER DRINKERS.

AN alarming sign of the times is mentioned the *National Temperance Advocate*. It quotes om a Chicago journal the statement of a resurant keeper in that city that many women in hicago are becoming great beer-drinkers. He ys: "Ten years ago the spectacle of a woman inking beer while lunching was so rare as to use comment. Now they come in droves, and der with the familiarity of veterans their favite brands, and many of them have so far culvated the failing of their masculine brethren at they are not happy unless they also have a ate of limburger. Wines and stronger drinks e little called for, but the growth of the beer-drinking habit is astonishing, and although I am in the business, to me it is really alarming." The beer propagandism of the present period, especally among women, as in Chicago, and among the young of both sexes, is the greatest obstacle the temperance reform now has to contend with. The doctrine enunciated by the Supreme Court of the United States, that the brewery and the beer-saloon are nuisances which the people of any State may cause to be abated and destroyed, should be everywhere and unceasingly proclaimed and enforced.

A CENTENARIAN'S COMFORT.

IN a volume of reminiscences, recently published, the Rev. Joseph Emery, who has been thirty-five years a city missionary in Cincinnati, Ohio, describes a visit which he paid to a Christian centenarian. He says: One of the happiest men I ever visited was old Father Cox. He lived in his own house on Elm Street, near Liberty. During my first visits, some thirty years ago, his wife was living; she was over eighty years of age, very infirm. Nothing pleased this aged pair more than to hear the Word of God and prayer, with singing. They were a happy couple, and for many years belonged to a Methodist church. After a brief illness, Mrs. Cox died, leaving her aged husband to mourn his loss. He preferred to live in his own house, and so remained for some years, lonesome, but always happy. Concerning all temporal things his memory failed, but never on spiritual things. He would forget the names of his long-tried and true friends, but he never forgot that name which is above every name. The name of Jesus was written on his heart; it could not be erased. His Book of Psalms, and Testament, and Hymn-book, were always on the table. These he would read every day.

Entering his room one day I said, cheerily: "Well, Father Cox, how are you to-day?" "Thank God, I'm as well as usual; nothing to complain of." "Don't you at times feel lonesome?" "Not very; I've always my Bible and Hymn-book, and I can draw nigh to God in prayer. The neighbors come in now and then." "Suppose death should come in some day, what would you say?" Without a moment's hesitation the aged man replied: "I'd say, Come, welcome death, I'll gladly go with thee!" "Then you feel ready to die?" "Yes, indeed; any day the Lord sees fit, I'm ready to meet Him." "You seem to be a happy man?" "Indeed I am; why shouldn't I be? I have Jesus here every day, and I love to pray to Him. I know He's forgiven all my sins, and I shall soon be with Him."

This venerable man continued in this happy frame of mind to the end of his life.

THE MARTYRDOM IN MEXICO.

IT will be remembered that last August three Protestant teachers in Guerrero, Mexico, were assassinated in a riot stirred up by a Roman Catholic priest, named Vergara. The Rev. J. Milton Greene, D. D., has recently visited the scene of martyrdom, and sends an account of his journey to the *Church*. In the course of it, he says: "Passing the cemetery where the precious dust of the three martyrs reposes, we were met at the entrance to the town by several brethren, who, with open arms and tearful eyes, welcomed us with a hearty Mexican embrace, and accompanied us to the residence of the widow Zaragoza, where Abraham and Felipe were murdered. Touching as was my reception, it did not absorb my attention, which was rather fixed upon the battered and broken doors, and the blood-stained walls, which remained as most impressive reminders of the awful tragedy which had occurred seven months before. There on the wall hung the book-shelves from which his murderers snatched one of the largest volumes, tore off the covers, seated himself on the helpless form, and beat it with the book, which he afterward placed in mockery under the bleeding head as a pillow, then left his poor victim, still in the agony of death, to rush with his comrades to the house of Miguel Cipriano, and complete the bloody, sickening task. Oh! as I looked at the mutilated book, which I preserve as *a sacred relic still stained with that consecrated blood*, and as I lay down at night on that bed where the summons to a martyr's death reached my poor boy, I realized as never before what martyrdom is in all its hideous reality, not as we paint it to ourselves afar from all shadow of danger, not as we sing of it in our moments of Christian ecstacy, not as we imagine to ourselves the white-robed blessed ones around the throne, but as it came to our dear brethren, mocking at the love of life and blasting the hopes of continued existence and usefulness in the world, breaking the hearts of loving wife and children, accompanied by physical agony and blood, nervous torture and bodily dissolution, the shrieks and groans of the dying mingling with the heart-piercing lamentations of wife and children, and the pitiless, diabolical butchery of demonized, infuriated religious fanaticism. I have never seen elsewhere such a pall of desolation as rests on the village. Scarcely a house exists, apart from those occupied by our brethren, from which the husband or the sons, or both, are not absent. Twenty-two of those who took part in the massacre have been consigned to the army and sent to Yucatan—most of them to die on its burning sands; fifteen are in the district jail at Teloloapan, one league away, of whom 'four at least,' says Governor Arce, 'will be shot,' while another fifteen are fugitives from justice, and among them the priest, Vergara, whose photographs, a hundred in number, with a circular urging his arrest, have been sent all over the republic."

A MADURA WOMAN'S EMOTION.

ALL the missionary reports dwell on the wonderful results of women's work among the heathen. One of the most remarkable comes from Madura, in the Indian Archipelago, and is published in the *Missionary Herald*. It appears that a Bible-woman gathered a little class of native women together, and used to speak to them about Jesus, reading to them, and explaining His life of love. One day a woman who had been a most attentive listener interrupted her with: "Are all the things you read and tell us about Jesus written in that book?" "Yes, and much more than I have yet told you." "I want a book like it; will you bring me one to-morrow?" "Yes, I will bring one, but of what use will it be to you? You cannot read it." "But I must have the book that tells about Jesus." The next day when the book was given to her, she clasped it eagerly with both hands, and touched it lovingly with her lips. Then opening the book she said, "*Show me the place where Jesus' name is.*" As soon as it had been pointed out to her she kissed the sacred page reverently. Before the Bible-woman left the house the happy owner of the book asked that the place might be marked so that she would always find the name of Jesus.

Another woman, who has only been under instruction a few months, has been much impressed with the thought that it is her duty to go from house to house, like the Bible readers, teaching and telling of the love of Jesus. She is very anxious to read in the New Testament, and has persuaded her husband to help her, so that she may learn more rapidly. Not long since she came early in the morning, and entreated the Bible-woman to go with her to a neighboring village to preach, saying she wished to begin to tell what she had learned about Jesus, but was afraid to teach in her own village, where she was well known, for the people would laugh at her because she knew so little. Surely God has blessed this branch of the work in answer to many earnest prayers.

THE CHRISTIAN HERALD AND SIGNS OF OUR TIMES.

OFFICE, 63 BIBLE HOUSE, NEW YORK.

ENTERED AT THE POST-OFFICE AT NEW YORK, N. Y., AS SECOND-CLASS MATTER.

EVERY NUMBER CONTAINS:

The Portrait and Biography of some eminent person.
The Sermon Dr. Talmage preached the last Sunday morning.
An Exposition of Unfulfilled Prophecy.
A Summary of the Events of the Week, Notes of Religious and Temperance Movements, etc.
A Sermon by Rev. C. H. Spurgeon, of London, from advance sheets sent by special arrangement.
Pictures of Missionary Life, etc., and Descriptive Articles.
An instalment of a Serial Story.
An Exposition of the International Sunday-School Lesson, by Mrs. M. Baxter.

ANNUAL SUBSCRIPTION, $1.50.

Remittances by mail should be by bank cheques, Post-office orders, or Express money-orders whenever possible. If currency is sent it should be in a registered letter. Cheques and money-orders should be made payable to THE CHRISTIAN HERALD. Making them payable to individuals often causes delay.

New subscriptions may commence at any time. When subscribers do not indicate their wish, they commence with the first number of the month in which the subscription is received.

PUBLISHER'S NOTICE.

The whole edition of The Christian Herald was mailed last week to subscribers during Tuesday, June 26. The last delivery at the New York Post Office was made at 11.12 P. M.

CURRENT EVENTS.

The Candidate of the Republican Party for the Presidency, as stated in part of our edition last week, is General Benjamin Harrison, of Indiana. This result was reached on Monday, June 25, on the eighth ballot. The inside history of the operations which led to the Convention's choice, is probably known to very few. It appears probable, however, that it was due mainly to an urgent cablegram from Mr. Blaine, requesting his friends to cease voting for him. The tactics of the Blaine men were devoted to the maintenance of the deadlock, in the hope that the candidates, despairing of a nomination, would withdraw and leave the way open for the nomination of Mr. Blaine by acclamation. Mr. Sherman, however, had clung too long to the hope of being the candidate to withdraw while a chance remained, and as Mr. Blaine would accept nothing short of a unanimous and uncontested nomination, Mr. Sherman's persistence rendered such a nomination impossible. Realizing the fact, Mr. Blaine sent his cablegram, and his friends, perfectly understanding who was responsible for their defeat, went over to Harrison rather than Sherman. Gen. Harrison's record, both as a soldier and a statesman, is clean, and we may therefore hope that the campaign will be free from the odious personalities which disgraced the campaign of 1884. He is a grandson of William Henry Harrison, who was elected ninth President of the United States in 1840, and died one month after his inauguration. He is fifty-five years of age, and has served one term in the United States Senate. He is a member of the Presbyterian Church, and has for many years conducted a large Bible class in the Sunday-school of the First Presbyterian Church in Indianapolis.

Mr. Levi P. Morton, the Republican Candidate for the Vice-Presidency, was chosen on the first ballot. The importance of carrying New York State, and the difficulty of doing so with a Western man at the head of the ticket, in the face of a Democratic ticket headed by a New York candidate, doubtless led to this choice. He is a native of Vermont and is sixty-four years of age. His father was a Congregational minister, and his mother's brother was the Rev. Levi Parsons, the first American Missionary to Palestine. From the latter, the candidate derives his first names. Until 1863 Mr. Morton was in the dry-goods business, but in that year he established a bank in New York in partnership with Mr. George Bliss. Five years later, in partnership with Sir John Rose, for some time Finance Minister in Canada, he opened a bank in London under the name of Morton, Rose & Co. In 1878 he was elected to Congress and took a prominent part in financial discussions. President Garfield appointed him Minister to France, where he became exceedingly popular. He has made several large charitable gifts, one of the best known being a quarter share in the freight of the ship *Constellation*, which in 1880 was sent laden with food for the starving people of Ireland. Like Gen. Harrison, Mr. Morton is a strong Protectionist.

President Cleveland was Formally Notified of his nomination on June 26, by the Committee appointed by the St. Louis Convention. In the course of his reply, accepting the nomination, he said: "Familiarity with the great office which I hold has but added to my apprehension of its sacred character, and the consecration demanded of him who assumes its immense responsibilities. It is the repository of the people's will and power. Within its vision should be the protection and welfare of the humblest citizen, and, with quick ear, it should catch from the remotest corner of the land, the plea of the people for justice and for right. For the sake of the people, he who holds this office of theirs, should resist every encroachment upon its legitimate functions, and for the sake of the integrity and usefulness of the office it should be kept near to the people, and be administered in full sympathy with their wants and needs." Republicans will probably disagree with the President as to the other parts of his speech, but this passage is one that will commend itself to patriots of both parties. Whether Mr. Cleveland is re-elected or General Harrison succeeds him, this conception of the President's responsibilities and duties is that which the American people will like to see dominant in the White House.

Judge Kelley's Suggestion in the House on June 27, that the Mills Tariff Bill be dropped, produced more amusement than was reasonable. No one imagines that it can be enacted, as, if it should pass the House, it would be thrown out by the Senate. Mr. Kelley contended that as the Democratic National Convention had endorsed the bill, and the Republican National Convention had explicitly condemned it, the issue between the parties was fairly joined and might await the national verdict at the polls in November. His suggestion, however, was not accepted, and the Democratic leaders stated that they were determined to proceed with the bill even if it involved sitting until March 4. There are probably more amendments to come from the Democratic side yet, and it is possible that some of the Republican amendments may be accepted. In any case the Republicans wish to go on record in the details of the bill, and neither party is justified in casting on the people the responsibility of deciding a question which lies within the jurisdiction of Congress.

The Formation of an Indian Territory With Indians in the principal offices, is the logical outcome of the recent Indian Council at Fort Gibson. Important steps were taken to unite the five civilized tribes. The main difficulty, however, arises in their own opposition to the holding of lands in severalty. So long as the tribes hold the lands in common, the chief men will be rich in comparison with others, and will exercise an influence which must repress individual effort, and retard civilization. If the projected union of the tribes is realized, a partition of the lands and individual ownership will become a necessity, and in that result lies the one hope of settling the vexed Indian problem.

The New Emperor of Germany Delivered two important speeches last week. On Monday he opened the Reichstag with imposing ceremonies, and his speech on that occasion somewhat relieved the apprehensions of war excited in other lands by his accession to the throne. He said: "In foreign politics I am resolved to maintain peace with every one, so far as it lies in my power. My love for the German army, and my position in it, would never induce me to attempt to endanger for the country the benefits of peace *unless the necessity for war is forced upon us* by a hostile attempt on the Empire or one of its allies. Our army will assure us peace, or if peace be broken it will enable us to fight for it with honor. That, with God's help, will be possible for it to do by reason of the strength it has derived from the army laws you recently unanimously voted." The assurance is welcome, though it is extremely guarded, and bears marks of having been revised, if not dictated, by Bismarck. Unhappily, monarchs who have large armies at their disposal are apt to think that "war is forced upon them," and history shows that both parties to all wars have made that their plea. Therefore, though the statement that the Emperor desires to maintain peace is reassuring, the general tone of his remarks does not inspire strong confidence in his pacific intentions. A second speech which he made on Thursday, at the opening of the Landtag, has caused considerable uneasiness among German liberals at home. He plainly intimated that his policy would be on the lines of that of his grandfather, between whom and the Landtag there were numerous disputes. He also hinted that constitutional government was an experiment, which might be abandoned if found irksome. The impression his remarks produced was that he would hold tenaciously to all his prerogatives, and that constitutional liberty in Prussia would be a very precarious and exceedingly limited privilege.

Reports of Disastrous Floods Along the Line of the Mexican Central Railroad have been published. It is possible that the loss of life is exaggerated, but the estimates range from 700 to 1,500, and from El Paso comes the statement that 1,000 bodies have been recovered. The adobe houses at Silao and Leon were easily undermined, and swept into ruins, and the water rose so rapidly that many of the occupants were overwhelmed without realizing their danger. The Mexican Central Railroad has suffered much, and 100 miles of it is said to be under water. Thousands of people have been rendered homeless, and much property has been destroyed. The National and State Governments are rendering aid to the sufferers.

A Parliamentary Defeat has Befallen the followers of Mr. Gladstone, in the House of Commons. On June 25, Mr. John Morley, who was Secretary for Ireland in the Gladstone administration, directly challenged the Government's procedure in Ireland. He moved a vote of censure on the Government for its administration of the Irish Crimes act, as calculated to undermine respect for the law, estrange the people of Ireland, and prove injurious to the interests of the Empire. In the course of the debate on the proposal, Mr. Chaplin, a conservative member, had the bad taste to taunt Mr. Gladstone with his advanced age in making a vigorous personal onslaught on the venerable Liberal leader. Mr. Gladstone's retort must have convinced his assailant that age had not diminished his powers as a ready speaker. Mr. Gladstone said that undoubtedly he felt in some respects the encroachment of age, but added, amid loud cheering, "I shall be able for a little while, I hope, to cope with antagonists of the calibre of the right honorable gentleman." Apart from this personality the debate was adverse to the Liberals, and Mr. Balfour, the present Irish Secretary, evoked great enthusiasm by declaring that the Government had succeeded beyond their expectations in suppressing lawlessness in Ireland. Whether they would be allowed to proceed, he did not know, but he did know that the future of Ireland could only safely rest on foundations of honesty, liberty, and law. When the vote of the House was taken the vote of censure was rejected by a majority of ninety-three, showing that the alliance between the Unionists and the Tories was still in full force.

Young Ladies Driving Horses and Phaetons in which young men were being conveyed to the polls was the novel sight witnessed at Independence, Mo., on Monday of last week. The question at issue was the sale of liquor for four years in Jackson County, of which Independence is the county-seat. A despatch from that city states that women were the most active among the workers on the Prohibition side. On the voting day they were everywhere at the polls, at the lunch-stands, and on the street corners, wearing silk badges and with "dry" ballots in their hands. Girls stood at the polls, and at every voting place was a banner on which was inscribed: "Temperance beaus or no beaus at all." Hundreds of children carried banners through the streets, and about the voting precincts. Some of these were inscribed: "Sow whisky ballots and reap drunken boys." The legend, "We can't vote, but we can suffer," was carried by the women in a parade, and occupied a prominent place in each ward precinct. Many of the best people of the town were interested in the contest, and it was no infrequent sight to see young girls with horse and phaeton covered with streamers, bringing in young gentlemen to vote for local option. It was mainly due to this activity that the prohibition of the sale of liquor in Jackson County for the ensuing four years was carried by over 200 majority.

A Mother's Strange Bequest Came Before the Surrogate of New York, last week, on the protest of her brother-in-law, who contended that it was invalid. The woman, who died recently in a charity hospital in New York, made and executed her will in due form a few weeks before her death. She had no lands or houses or money to give away; no stock or securities of any kind; no jewelry or silver plate, or books or pictures or heirlooms to leave to surviving kindred. She had but one bequest to make—her little nine-year-old daughter Harriet, who would be left an orphan at her death, her father having died six years before. Her bequest was the gift of this child to the Society of St. John, and till she became of age. She appointed the Society as her executor and trustee. The child's uncle, with whom she is living, is strongly attached to her, and is disputing the will in the hope of retaining her in his family. It is said that the uncle's objection caused some surprise in court. If it had been the will of a millionaire that was disputed there would have been no surprise, but that any one should contend over a legacy so valueless as a child, astonished the officials. That is the fault of this mammon-worshipping age. Money is held in higher esteem than souls. We have only to think of the cross to realize what is the true value of one soul. (John 3: 16.)

Red Fire on the Mountain Peaks of Oregon as an illumination in celebration of the Fourth of July was a project under discussion at Portland, Ore., last week. It was decided, on June 4, to raise a subscription to illuminate the whole chain of snow-covered peaks stretching from northern California nearly to the British Columbia line, a distance of seven hundred miles, with red fire. The Portland committee in charge of the celebration undertook the task of illuminating Mounts Hood, St. Helen's, and Adams. A party from Eugene promised to illuminate the Three Sisters, near the head of the Willamette Valley, about 120 miles south, and a party from Ashland to illuminate Mount Pitt, a peak forty miles north of California. Arrangements were made with the citizens of Sissons, Cal., to burn red fire on the summit of Shasta, the grandest of Pacific coast snow-peaks. The citizens of Seattle, W. T., agreed to illuminate Mount Rainier, and the Port Townsend people to take care of Mount Baker. It was stated that if the night proved cloudless a person on any of the hills back of Portland would be able to see the fire burning on five mountains, namely, Rainier, St. Helen's, Adams, Hood, and the Three Sisters. Each illuminating party would be able to see the work of at least one of the others. From Rainier to see Hood, Hood to see the Three Sisters, and so on down to Shasta. As more than one of these peaks are over twelve thousand feet high, the illumination, if carried out yesterday, must have been a wonderful spectacle. It reminds us of that more awful scene which is yet to take place in the days of the final convulsion, which many now living will witness. (Rev. 8: 8.)

A Tailor's Broken Promise Led to a Suicide in Boston, Mass., last week. A young couple were to have been married in that city on June 27. The bride was ready at the appointed time, the minister was at the house, and the guests assembled, but the bridegroom did not come. After waiting two hours, a messenger was sent to his home to ascertain the cause of his delay. It was found that the young man had ordered his wedding suit from his tailor, who had failed to send it at the time appointed. The young man fumed and fretted over the delay, and at last, being of a very excitable temperament, the thought of the wedding party waiting for him, of his bride's vexation, and the disgrace which he imagined would fall upon him, overthrew his reason, and he shot himself. He was taken to the hospital, where he received skilful treatment, but he died the next day. That disappointment over the non-arrival of the clothes at such a time should have caused chagrin is not surprising, but to have caused it to a degree prompting self-destruction argues a mind without stability. Had the young man been a follower of Christ his faith would have raised him above the power of the tempter. The trials and vexations of life cannot unbalance the mind of one who trusts in God, for he has the promise that he will be kept in perfect peace. (Isa. 26: 3.)

A Boston Philanthropist's Blunder has Defeated his benevolent intentions. Mr. T. W. Higginson, the historian, in describing the Harvard University in the columns of a contemporary, last week, calls attention to a serious decrease in the income it derives from a philanthropist's bequest. Some twenty years ago a Boston merchant left about half a million dollars to the University for special purposes. He did not wish the principal to be touched, but to be invested, and the income applied to the support of professors, and the maintenance of students. To avoid the risk of loss he eventually decided to invest it himself. In his will he stated that having long observed the fluctuations of real estate in Boston he had taken pains to invest this property in a manner approaching absolute certainty, i. e., in improved real estate in the very heart of Boston. This was all that could be done for safety, it then seemed, by the most experienced investor. For a time the result was all that the testator wished; but then came the fire, which destroyed the very property which he had chosen as the one absolutely safe investment. The structures were rebuilt, but the cost has so depleted the original bequest that the income derived from it is now less than one-fourth of the amount needed to carry out the testator's designs. Thus the effort to attain absolute certainty, though conducted with skill, experience, and purity of motive, has failed, and becomes another warning to all who are making this world's wealth their trust. (Matt. 6: 19, 20.)

A Train was Attacked by a Bull on Staten Island, N. Y., on June 25. For some time past, a bull, belonging to a farmer there, has been the terror of women and children. During the recent hot spell the temper of the animal has become worse, and it was difficult to confine him to his pasture. On Monday he broke loose and strayed on the railroad track, and resisted all attempts to drive him off. Soon a train came along, and the engineer, on seeing the valuable beast on the line, blew a shrill whistle, to scare him out of the way. The bull faced the engine, and answered with a resounding bellow. The engineer slowed up, but saw that he could not bring his train to a standstill before reaching the animal. He blew a second whistle, but it only seemed to excite the bull, who lowered his head, pawed the ground, and replied by another defiant bellow. The locomotive struck him, and rolled him about sixty feet, the train slowing all the time. With the agility of a cat he regained his feet, and furiously charged the engine. This time he was crushed under the wheels, and half the train passed over his body. Charging a train was a very different business from that of scaring women and children. The notion that led the bull to his destruction is dangerous for men as well as animals. Previous successful exploits over weak opponents is apt to engender the belief that the victor is invincible. Then his downfall is near. An awful illustration of that fact will be witnessed in the near future when Antichrist, grown arrogant and blasphemous by conquest, falls beneath that Stone which grinds those on whom it falls to powder. (Luke 20: 17, 18.)

BRIEF NOTES.

A large number of deaths from sun-stroke occurred in New York, during the unprecedented heat last week.

Secretary Fairchild received recently a conscience contribution of $1,600 in an envelope postmarked Washington, D. C.

The McAll meetings in Paris have a total attendance of about 43,000. The American McAll Association raised the past year nearly $39,000 for the work.

A branch of the Christian Endeavor has been formed in Burmah. It is known by the name of "Kyo-zah-thaw-ah-thin"—literally, "The Society Which Tries."

Sunday-school children of Richmond Hill Church, L. I., are cultivating half an acre of ground, planted with potatoes for the benefit of the destitute children in the Five Points Mission, New York.

The Puritan Congregational Church of Wilkesbarre, Pa., was struck by lightning on Sunday evening, June 24, while service was being held. Many of the audience were prostrated by the shock, but no one was killed.

Tent services have been commenced in Chicago by Mr. W. F. Bischoff, at the corner of Harrison and Desplaines streets. He will probably spend the summer in Chicago, in the tent work, under the direction of the Chicago Evangelization Society.

The Rev. J. Sharpe, an English Congregational minister, who is now visiting this country, would be glad to receive invitations to occupy vacant pulpits during his stay. Letters may be sent to him at the office of this journal, 63 Bible House, New York.

Rev. F. E. Clark, President of the United Society of Christian Endeavor, who has just returned from England, reports great interest in the movement in all parts of Great Britain. A section has been formed under the auspices of the Sunday-School Union.

Mrs. Warnes Huntly, the English evangelist, has been conducting a series of gospel meetings at the M. E. Church, Dawson, Fayette Co., Pa. They were well attended, and as the result of the Divine blessing on her labors, many souls were added to the church.

General Gonzales, the former President of the Mexican Republic, and at present governor of the State of Guanajuato, has recently prohibited bull-fights within his territory as demoralizing, and because the money spent in this sport could be much better employed.

Mr. Ferdinand Schiverea has received invitations to labor in Canada during the summer and fall. As he is sure of a cordial welcome there, he has accepted them. Any of our readers in Ontario desiring to secure his services should write him at Ozone Park, Woodhaven, Long Island, N. Y.

An Inter-Denominational Bible Conference, conducted by Dr. L. W. Munhall, will be held at Ocean Grove, N. J., July 25–31, 1888. Among those who are expected to take part are, Bishop Nicholson, Professor W. G. Moorehead, Luther T. Townsend, S. L. Bowman, James H. Brooks, Nathaniel West, and W. J. Erdman.

The Rev. Jacob Freshman celebrated on June 24 the twenty-first anniversary of his ordination to the Christian ministry. He gave a brief history of his work, and of the difficulties he had met with as the son of a Jewish Rabbi, in carrying on a mission to the Jews. Several ministers of New York and Brooklyn took part in the services. At the close another Jewish convert was baptized by Mr. Freshman.

The emigrants, during twelve months from Great Britain and Ireland, including foreigners, numbered 396,494, of whom 281,487 were of British and Irish origin. In 1886, the total was 330,801, and in 1885 it was 264,385. On the other hand, the country received immigrants in 1887 to the number of 119,013, of whom 33,538 were foreigners, against 108,879 in 1886, and 114,549 in 1885.

Clergymen and Evangelists who will Allow Copies of the CHRISTIAN HERALD to be placed in the seats of churches, or will have them distributed at the doors, will be supplied with assorted parcels of back number if they will write to the Manager, 63 Bible House, New York.

AN APOSTOLIC PRAYER.

A New Sermon by Pastor C. H. Spurgeon.

"And the Lord direct your hearts into the love of God, and into the patient waiting for Christ." II Thess. 3 : 5.

A Difficult Voyage Proposed—To the Innermost Recesses of the Sacred Fatherland—Paul Prays God to Direct Them—A Parallel Translation—I. Two Precious Things—The Love of God—A Gateway into Paradise—Its Central Importance—Its Infallible Constancy—The Patience of Christ—II. Two Eminent Virtues—What Characters will be Produced—Patience in Waiting for the Lord's Coming.

For the moment, Paul in spirit is coasting the purple shores of the celestial country. With his Thessalonian friends he is making a joyful voyage within hail of Emmanuel's land. The sail is bright with the sunlight, and the keel is marking a silver track behind it. The apostle's happy soul has left far in the stern the deceivableness of unrighteousness and the rocks of error. It comes into his heart that he would gladly steer his friends into certain of those lovely creeks which run up far into the inner recesses of the sacred fatherland. Shall he turn the helm that way? He pauses; for the navigation is difficult. One must be greatly expert to thread the streams which descend from the sunny fountains. It is not given even to all saints to follow all the windings of the rivers of delight.

Paul had been with his brethren at sea in the place where the Lord sank all their transgressions in the depths, and he had been with them in sore affliction, when neither sun nor moon appeared, and in all such seafaring he was in his element; but, brave pilot as he was, he could not pretend to penetrate all the richer and rarer experiences which bring elect souls nearest to the heart of the great Father; and therefore, instead of offering to be their pilot, he bowed his head, and prayed, "The Lord direct your hearts into the love of God, and into the patient waiting for Christ."

The Special Entrance

into the goodly land, which the apostle desired for his friends, was one which mere insight, wit, knowledge, or instruction could never give them. If so, he would have directed their minds that way at once. But the perception of the heavenlies is only given to heavenly faculties. The attainments which Paul desired for his friends were not beliefs of the head, but indwellings of the heart. To return to our figure of sailing up the creeks and rivers into the centre of the glorious country—that delicious voyage was only possible to the more refined and spiritual powers of the soul. Those sweet waters could only be navigated by the heart, and the heart itself would need divine direction before it could find the entrance to them.

Paul could give his converts external directions, he could guide his more advanced brethren in the work, walk, and warfare of life; and he did so with all simplicity and earnestness. He urged them to abound in this grace, and to avoid that folly; but he felt that his exhortation would be inefficient unless their hearts were touched. Here he felt

His Own Powerlessness,

and so he cast the grand matter of heart-work upon the Lord Himself. As the heart naturally baffles all physicians, so spiritually it is far beyond our knowledge. Who among ministers can guide you? Therefore may "the Lord direct your hearts." God alone knows the heart, and God alone can rule it; for this ruling Paul makes request. "The Lord direct your hearts." Let us borrow his prayer, and turn it to our own personal use: "*Domine dirige nos.*"

But here we must do a little translating or interpreting. Observe in the Revised Version a difference of translation. There we read "into the patience *of* Christ." This is a great improvement upon our former translation; but, although it is accurate, it is not complete: it does not take up the whole of the meaning. In our Authorized Version we have "the patient waiting for Christ"; but in its margin we find "into the patience of Christ"; showing that the earlier translators felt that "the patience of Christ" would be a good translation; and yet, after considering it in all its bearings, they thought that Paul did not quite mean the patience *of Christ*, but that he meant a patience which we exert *towards Christ*. It there not weight in this? Does not the context support it? As the love into which we are to be directed is love to God, so the patience into which we are to be directed must be towards Christ.

I. To begin, then, here are

Two Precious Things

for us to enter into. The first precious thing which we are to enter, is the love of God. Beloved, we know the love of God in various ways. Many know it by having heard of it, even as a blind man may thus know the charms of an Alpine landscape. Poor knowledge this! Others of us have tasted of the love of God, have talked about the love of God, have prayed and have sung concerning the love of God. All very well, but Paul meant a dove of a brighter feather. To be directed into the love of God is quite another thing from all that we can be told of it. A fair garden is before us. We look over the wall, and are even allowed to stand at the door, while one handeth out to us baskets of golden apples. This is very delightful. Who would not be glad to come so near as this to the garden of heavenly delights? Yet it is something more to be shown the door, to have the latch lifted, to see the gateway opened, and to be gently directed into the Paradise of God. This is what is wanted—that we may be directed *into* the love of God. Oh, that we may feel something of it while we meditate upon it!

Beloved, we come, when we are taught of the Spirit, to enter into the love of God by seeing

Its Central Importance.

The love of God is the source, centre, fountain and foundation, of all our salvation, and of all else that we receive from God. At the first we are much taken up with pardoning grace. We are largely engrossed with those royal robes of righteousness with which our nakedness is covered. We are delighted with the viands of the marriage banquet: we eat the fat and we drink the sweet. What else would you expect from starving souls admitted to the abundant supplies of heavenly grace? Afterwards we begin more distinctly to think of the love that spread the feast, the love that provided the raiment, the love that invited us to the banquet, and gently led us to take our place in it. This does not always come at first; but I pray that none of us may be long receiving the gifts of love without kissing the hand of love; that none of us may be content to have had much forgiven without coming and washing the feet of our forgiving Lord with our tears, and declaring our deep and true love to Him.

Again, I pray that we may be directed into the love of God as to its infallible constancy. The unchangeable Jehovah never ceases to love his people. It would be

A Wretched Business

to be directed into the love of God only to find it a thing of the past. Oh, believing soul, thou hast not to deal with things which once were gems of the mine, but now are dreams of the night. Oh, no! the love of God abides for ever the same. When thou wast without strength, "in due time Christ died for the ungodly." Since thou hast known Him He has never varied in His love. When thou hast grown cold, He has loved thee; when thou hast grown cruel, He has loved thee. Thou hast grievously provoked Him till He has taken down His rod and made thee smart; but He has loved thee in the smiting. With God there is as much love in chastening as in caressing. He never abates in fervor towards His ancient friends. Has He not said, "I am the Lord; I change not; therefore ye sons of Jacob are not consumed"?

This love we ought to know, and if the Lord will lead us into it we shall know that it is omnipresent. I mean by this, that whatever condition we may be in, the Lord is still active in love towards us. Thou hast come out alone: time was when thou didst come to the house of God in company; but it may be that graves and desertions furnish sad reasons for thy present solitude. Still, thou art not alone; thy Father's love is with thee. Thou art, to-night, perhaps, in a very strange part of thy spiritual experience: thou hast not gone this way heretofore.

The Road is Not New

to eternal love. Go where thou mayest, the air is still about thee; go where thou mayest, thy Father's love is all around thee. Higher than thy soarings, deeper than thy sinkings, is all surrounding love. Thou art going home, perhaps, to a bed from which thou shalt not rise for months. Thou hast no apprehension, just now, of what lies before thee in the immediate future. It is as well thou shouldst not know. I should be slow to lift the curtain of merciful concealment, even if it were in my power to do so. There is no necessity to know details when one or two grand facts provide for all contingencies. Trouble not thyself about the morrow. If thou art to be sick, or if thou art to die, thy Father's love will be with thee still. Therefore go on, and fear not.

I have thus spoken a little upon a vast theme. I fear it will seem to you mere surface-work; and yet I pray that it may lead you to deep knowledge of divine things, so that you may apprehend God's love as yours, and then may feel the power, the unction, the savor, which comes out of His love, making all your heart as sweet and aromatic as a chamber in which a box of precious ointment has been broken. Oh, that you might be led into the innermost secret of the Lord's love till it shall saturate you, take possession of you, carry you right away! The Lord direct you into the love of God.

The second part of the prayer upon which we shall have to dwell is, "The Lord direct your hearts into the patience of Christ." Now, beloved, I have another great sea before me, and who am I that I should act as your convoy over this main ocean? Here I am lost. I cannot take my bearings. I am a lone speck upon the infinite. I will imitate the wise apostle, and pray, "The Lord direct your hearts into the patience of Christ."

What a patience that was which Jesus exhibited for us in our redemption! To come from heaven to earth, to dwell in poverty and neglect, and find no room even in the inn! Admire the patience of Bethlehem. To hold His tongue for thirty years—who shall estimate

The Patience of the Carpenter's Shop?

When He spoke, to be despised and rejected of men, what patience for Him whom Cherubim obey! Oh, the patience of the Christ to be tempted by the devil! One can hardly tell what patience Christ must have had *to let the devil come within ten thousand miles of Him!* There is not much in a patience which cannot help itself; but you well know that all the while Christ could have conquered all foes, chased away all suffering, and kept off all temptation; but for our sakes, as Captain of our salvation, that He might be made perfect through suffering, His patience had its perfect work, right on to Gethsemane. Do you need that I tell you this? Golgotha, with all its woes, its "*lama sabachthani*," its abyssmal griefs, do I need remind you of the patience of Christ for us when the Lord laid on Him the iniquity of us all?

Oh, the patience within Christ Himself! God never seems so like a God as when He divinely rules Himself. I can understand His shaking earth and heaven with His word; but that He should possess His own soul in patience is far more incomprehensible. Marvel that omnipotent love should restrain omnipotence itself. In the life and death of our Lord Jesus we see almighty patience. He was very sensitive—very sensitive of sin, very sensitive of unkindness, and yet, with all that sensitiveness, He showed no petulance, but bore Himself in all the calm grandeur of Godhead. He was not quick to resent an ill, but he was patient to the uttermost. He spoke burning words sometimes: His mouth could be like the red lips of a volcano as He poured out the burning lava of denunciation upon "scribes and Pharisees, hypocrites"; but the resentment was never aroused by any injury done to Himself. When He looked that way it was always gentleness: He cried, "Father, forgive them; they know not what they do." Oh, the wondrous patience of Christ!

Elevating Not Sensuous.

Now, beloved, what is wanted is, that we be directed into this patience of Christ. The choicest saints in different ages of the world have studied most the passion of our Lord; and although nowadays we hear from the wise men that it is sensuous to talk about the cross and the five wounds, and so forth, for my part I feel that no contemplation ever does me so much real benefit as that which brings me very near my bleeding Lord. The cross for me! The cross for me! Here is doctrine humbling, softening, melting, elevating, sanctifying. Here is truth that is of heaven, and yet comes down to earth: love that lifts me away from earth, even to the seventh heaven.

O friends, I can wish you no greater blessing than to be directed into these two things—the love of God, and the patience of your Saviour. May the Lord lead us into both of them at this hour, and continue upon us the heavenly process all the rest of our lives, in all experiences of sorrow and of rapture, and in all moods and growths of our spirit!

II. But now I must ask your attention, for the few minutes that remain to me, to what is, perhaps, still the real gist of the text: Here are

Two Eminent Virtues

to be acquired. "The Lord direct your hearts into the love of God." Beloved, let the love of God to you flow into your hearts, and abide there till it settles down and bears on its surface the cream of love to God, yielded by your own heart. The only way to love God is to let God's love to you dwell in your soul till it transforms your soul into itself. Love *to* God grows out of the love *of* God.

Well, now, concerning love to God: if you receive it fully into your souls it will nourish the contemplative life. You will want to be alone. You will prefer to sit silently at Jesus' feet, while others wrangle over the little politics of the house. You will *give up being busy-bodies*, talking in six peoples' houses in an hour: quietude will charm you. You will love no company so much as the society of Him who is the Best and the Most. It will also animate the active life if you love God. You will feel that you must yield fruit unto your Lord. Your soul, when full of the love of God, will cry, "I must go after the wanderer; I must care for the poor; I must teach the ignorant." You cannot love God and be lazy.

Love to God will also arouse enthusiasm. We want more persons in the church who will be a little daring—rash men and women who will do things which nobody else would think of doing, such as will make their prudent friends hold up their hands and say, "How could you? If you had consulted with me, I could have given you

Many a Wise Hint

as to how it ought to have been done." This has been my lot of late. I have been surfeited with notions as to how I should have acted. Yes, my friend, I know you of old. You have wisdom at your fingers' ends. But let me quietly whisper that you would have done nothing at all; you would have been too anxious to save yourself from trouble. There was never a child that was near drowning but what the man that plunged in and drew him out of the river ought to have done it in a better way. He wetted himself too much; he waited too long, or he handled the drowning one too roughly. Alas, for silly criticisms of gracious deeds! If you come to love God with all-consuming zeal you will not be hindered by criticisms.

And this love, better still, will transform the character. It is wonderful what a difference love makes in the person that is possessed with it. A poor timid hen that will fly away from every passer-by loves its offspring, and when it has its chicks about it, it will fight like a very griffin for its young. And when the love of Christ comes into a timid believer, how it changes him! It takes the love of sin away, and implants a sublime nature. God only knows what a mortal man can yet become. Of women sunken in sin, what saints the Lord has made when He filled them with His love!

When the sun shines on a bit of glass bottle far away, it flashes like a diamond. A little fleecy vapor in the sky rivals an angel's wing when the sun pours itself upon it. Our Lord can put so much of Himself, by means of His love, into the hearts of His people, that they may be mistaken for Himself.

John Made a Blunder

in heaven, when he fell at the feet of one of his brethren, the prophets; for he had come to be so much like his Lord, that John could hardly tell the one from the other. Had he forgotten that word, "We shall be like Him; for we shall see Him as He is"? It doth not yet appear what we shall be, but love is the transfiguring power in the hand of the Holy Spirit. If the heart be directed into the love of Christ, it is on the highway to holiness.

Lastly—I am sorry that time will fly so fast just now—we want our hearts to be directed into *patience towards Christ*. What a subject is this! Beloved, if our hearts are directed into patience towards Christ we shall suffer in patience for our Lord's sake, and we shall not complain. Those about us will say, "It is wonderful how resigned he seems"; or, "How gladly she bears grief for love of Christ!" And if it be the suffering of reproach and scorn for Jesus' sake, if we are directed into the patience of Christ, it will not seem to be any trouble at all. We shall bear it calmly, and in our hearts we shall laugh at those who laugh at us.

Yet it is not all patience of suffering that we want. We want

The Patience of Forbearing.

We must learn not to answer those who blaspheme. "Bear, and forbear, and silent be." Chew the cud in peace. Put up with much. When reviled, revile not again. The Lord direct your hearts into the patience of Christ. We shall also want the patience of working—working on when nothing comes of it—pleading on with souls that are not converted—preaching when preaching seems to have no effect—teaching when the children do not care to learn. We need the patience of Christ, who set his face like a flint, and would accomplish his work, cost what it may. He never turned aside from it for a moment. The Lord direct our hearts into patient working!

Then there is the patience of watching in prayer—not giving it up because you have not received an answer. What? Did a friend say she had prayed for seventeen years for a certain mercy, and now meant to ask it no more? Sister, make it eighteen years, and when you have got to the end of eighteen, make it nineteen. May the Lord direct our hearts into the patience of Christ in prayer! We long kept Him waiting; we need not complain if He makes us tarry His leisure. Still believe, still hope, still wrestle, until the break of day.

We want to be directed into patience towards Christ, and especially in patience in

Waiting for His Coming.

That, no doubt, is very justly inferred, and so it is put in our translation very prominently: "Patient waiting for Christ." He will come, brothers; He will come, sisters; He will come at the appointed hour. To the jots and tittles God's word will stand. He will come to the tick of the clock. We know not when; we need not ask; but let us *wait*.

I am sorry, very sorry, that there are persons here to whom all this must seem a strange lot of talk. They know nothing about it. Dear souls, you cannot at present know anything about it. You must first be born again. A total change of heart must come over you before you can enter into the love of God or the patience of Christ. May that change take place to-day, before you go to sleep! If the Lord shall lead you to seek his face, this is the way to seek it: *trust His dear Son*. Lifted on the cross is Jesus Christ, the great Propitiation for sin. Look to Him, and looking alone to Him you shall be saved. He will give you the new heart and the right spirit with which you shall be enabled to enter into the love of God and the patience of Christ. The Lord direct you at this very hour, for Jesus' sake! Amen.

GEMS FROM NEW BOOKS.

A THREE DAYS' BRIDE.*

A YOUNG captain in the officers' ward interested me greatly, and I went daily to visit him. A refined and delicate fellow, with a very sensitive nervous organization, he had suffered severely. He had endured two amputations of the arm, which still refused to heal, and a third was ordered. He had become so reduced that the surgeon feared the result, and so informed the patient. Then the young officer telegraphed the girl who was to be his wife, and who had only delayed coming to him because of his earnest entreaty that she would not encounter the horrors of a hospital, unless he sent for her. She came as fast as the lightning express could bring her, and, at her own desire, before he submitted to another operation, they were married by the chaplain. The arm was removed to the shoulder. For a day or two there was hope of him, and then he sank rapidly.

I entered the ward about two hours before his death, and found his three days' bride ministering to him with inexpressible tenderness. There were no tears on her cheek, no lamentations on her lip, but her face shone with unnatural brightness, and she seemed to be lifted above the depressions of her surroundings. Mrs. —— and myself were about to pass them by, not thinking best to intrude on their privacy or sorrow, but the look in the husband's eyes invited us, and we moved softly toward the couch of death. He was conscious, and understood, but could only speak in occasional whispers.

"You are ready to go?" asked Mrs. ——, my hostess, who had seen much of him.

For answer, he looked at his young wife, who was gazing in his face. She understood him, and answered:

"Yes, we are both ready—he to go, and I to stay." And turning to us, she added, "When he enlisted I gave him to God and the country. I expected this, and am prepared for it."

And next morning I met her embarking for home, with the body of her beloved. Her own relatives were a married sister, and a brother in the Army of the Potomac. She was taking the coffined remains to the widowed mother of the dead man, who lived near Centralia, Ill., and who had two other sons in the army, and a son-in-law. The exaltation of her spirit still upbore her, and I saw that nature would not assert itself till her duties to the dead were over.

A Methodist Backslider.

I had nearly completed the tour of this ward, making memoranda for letters which the men desired written, or of some want to be gratified, or some errand done—every bed being occupied by a very severely wounded man—when I halted beside one on whose handsome face the unmistakable look of death was settling. He labored painfully for breath, and large drops of perspiration stood out on his forehead.

"You are suffering a great deal," I said.

"Oh, yes! oh, yes!" he gasped, "I am! I am! But not in the body; I can bear that; I don't mind pain, I can bear anything, but I can't die! *I can't die!*"

"But perhaps you may not die; it is not certain but you may recover. While there is life there is hope, you know."

*From "My Story of the War," by Mary A. Livermore. A deeply interesting narrative of her experience in the army hospitals during the war, containing numerous anecdotes and incidents, and reminiscences of thrilling scenes, with numerous illustrations. 700 pages. Price $3.50, by subscription only. Published by *A. D. Worthington & Co.*, Hartford, Conn.

The Prince and Princess of Wales at the Inauguration of the Glasgow Exhibition. (*See page 419.*)

"Oh, no, I can't live—I know it—there's no chance for me. I've got to die—and I *can't* die! *I am afraid to die!*"

I drew a camp-stool to his bedside, and, sitting down, I told him of Christ's mission on earth, and assured him that however great had been his sins, they would be forgiven of God, since he was penitent, and sought forgiveness.

"Can't you get a Methodist minister?" he asked. "I used to belong to the Methodist church, but I fell away.

One of the attendants remembered that the hospital steward was also a Methodist minister, and hastened to find him. To him I communicated the particulars of the case, and besought him to assist in allaying the anguish of the dying man, which was distressing to witness. The announcement that the steward was a Methodist minister was beneficial to the sufferer. To him he listened eagerly. "The love of Christ," was the chaplain's theme. "He had only to trust in the Saviour, only to ask for forgiveness, and God, who was always ready to pardon, would grant his prayer. Christ had died to save just such conscience-smitten, stricken, penitent souls as he"—thus ran the chaplain's talk.

"Can't you sing, chaplain?" I inquired.

Immediately, in a rich, full, clear tenor, whose melody floated through the ward, and charmed every groan and wail into silence, he sang hymn after hymn. All of them hymns so well known to his dying auditor that I saw he followed the singer, verse after verse. The music affected him, as I had hoped. The burden rolled from the poor boy's heart, and in feeble, tender tones he said, "It's all right with me, chaplain! I will trust in Christ. I can die now!"

"Sing on, Chaplain!" I suggested, as he was about to pause to make reply.

Patients, attendants, surgeons, all in the ward, glowed under the soaring melody, and the dying man's face grew rapturous. Then the chaplain was summoned away by a call from his office. It was getting late in the afternoon, for I had tarried a couple of hours at this bedside, when my friends came from the other wards of the hospital to say that it was time to return.

"Don't go! stay!" whispered the fast sinking man. The words rushed to my memory, "Inasmuch as ye have done it unto one of the least of these, ye have done it unto Me," and I promised to remain with him to the end. The end came sooner than any one thought. Before the sun went down, he had drifted to the immortal shore.

THE TWO SCHOOL-FRIENDS.

(*See Illustration on page 429.*)

THE vows of life-long friendship interchanged between school-girls when they separate at the end of school life, the promises to write every week to each other without fail, and the interest they are to take in each other's doings as long as they live, are apt to pass into forgetfulness in less than a year. New associations and relations in life drift them apart, and though the kindly recollection remains, communications become rare, until they cease altogether. With Helen Dysart and Amy Morton it seemed probable that there would be an exception, for between them the bond was more than one of mere personal regard. They were both converted about a year before leaving the seminary, and happened to be the only girls there who made a profession of religion. This tended to isolate them from the others, though they grieved that it should be so, and strenuously endeavored to draw the other girls, not only into their friendship, but to lead them into the joy and peace of the gospel. They failed, and their failure drew them closer to each other, as there was a tendency in the seminary to ridicule their religion. When they separated, a regular correspondence began, and was kept up for some months.

It was a letter from Amy Morton that brought a sudden ending to the correspondence. "Do not, I entreat you, dear Helen," she wrote, "make the engagement you are thinking of. You admit that your lover has no sympathy with your religious life; how, then, can you hope for happiness? Though, as you say, he pledges himself never to interfere with your church-going and your religious duties, you will naturally feel a constraint in all that. He may be as exemplary in his life as you think, and as devoted to you as he professes, but as he cannot enter into the highest and best of your thoughts and hopes, he will inevitably draw you aside into worldliness, or he will become estranged from you. I solemnly warn you that this match, brilliant as it is, will be a misery to you, and I beg of you for you own sake to break the engagement if you have pledged yourself."

Amy received no answer to this letter, and rightly concluded that Helen Dysart was offended by her faithfulness. A short time afterward, the engagement against which she had protested was made public, and a year later she saw the announcement of the marriage.

Amy Morton's own life during the next few years was one of busy usefulness. In the world, yet not of the world, her light shone steadily, guiding many of her poorer friends, and not a few among her fashionable acquaintances, into the channels of joy and peace. More than once suitors had sought her hand only to retire before the vigorous life and purpose which subordinated all to her work. She was derided by some, and pitied as a fanatic by others, but she persevered, and she had the joy of seeing some who had ridiculed her come to her in their troubles, in preference to all others, for consolation and advice. "She may be peculiar, my dear," said one who knew her, and had not always been her friend, to another who spoke slightingly of Amy Morton's fanaticism. "She may be peculiar, but her peculiarity is one that many of us could ill spare. She is the only girl I know of, who utterly forgets herself for the sake of others. Amy does not know what selfishness is, and self-denial is a pleasure to her. I suppose it is her religion that does it for her, and I honor her for it." Certainly Amy's life was leading her friends to believe that there was power in "the love of Christ that constraineth."

It was about five years after the writing of that letter to Helen Dysart that Amy Morton was one of a large party assembled at a well-known hospitable mansion in the holidays. "Mr. and Mrs. Plymdale are coming to-morrow," said her hostess to Amy on the night of her arrival. "I am so glad that you will be here to meet them. Mrs. Plymdale is quite one of the queens of society now. She distanced all her rivals in Washington last season. A little reckless and imprudent, perhaps, but always charming." Amy did not recognize the name, but the next day, when Mrs. Plymdale arrived, she recognized the lady with delighted surprise as no other than her old friend Helen Dysart. She was very different now from the school-girl Amy had known. Her self-possession, ready wit, and vivacious manner made her the life of the brilliant circle. All eyes were attracted to her, and the incense of delicate flattery which was offered to her seemed to be her ordinary atmosphere. Amy was astonished that so plain and simple a girl could have developed into the brilliant creature who fascinated all within her reach.

Another side to the picture was disclosed, however, to Amy, that night. Throwing a light shawl over her shoulders, Mrs. Plymdale made her way to Amy Morton's bedroom. "I am so glad to see you again, my dear girl," she said, in her old impulsive way. "You are just the same darling creature as ever. What have you been doing all these years? They have made more difference to me than to you."

"Yes, you have developed wonderfully; I should scarcely have known you. Have you been happy?"

"I have had a great deal of pleasure; that is the nearest approach I have made to happiness. It is not quite the same thing, I find. Oh! Amy, I have sold myself for pleasure, and I am a long way from happiness. You were quite right in that dreadful letter you wrote me. I have become a worldling. The temptation was too strong. You do not know the life I led the first year. I did try to be good; it was impossible. The kind of men and women that came to the house, and the continual urging to go to this place and the other, made me yield. I was flattered, dazed, excited; my ambition stimulated, and gradually I gave up all. Amy, it is nearly three years since I prayed! What is to become of me? I dare not be alone; I dare not think. Sometimes I feel as if I should become demented. When I looked at your pure, innocent face to-night, and thought of what I had become, I trembled. Oh! I can never get back to the right again: I am lost, utterly." The brilliant, worldly woman bent her head on her friend's shoulder and sobbed hysterically.

Amy had comforted many a poor waif of the streets, and pointed her to the Saviour. She had stood by the bedside of degraded women in despair, and had led them to trust in the atoning blood of Christ, but she had never had so difficult a task as to lead back this backslider to God. She resisted all appeals. She had no desire to return. A life of pleasure was the only life open to her now. God had cast her off as she deserved, she said, and there was no hope for her. Amy would not believe such things, and she continued pleading with her for a long time; but even she, who had seen the most degraded turn from their evil ways and repent, had less hope of this beautiful, fascinating woman, whom Satan had enticed with the cup of worldly pleasure. One resource only—that of prayer—was left to her; and feeling her own utter powerlessness, she committed her friend's case to God, praying that she might even yet be rescued, even though it might be as by fire.

Helen's Pitiful Confession.

THE EPOCHS OF A LIFE.

A NEW SERIAL STORY.

By Rev. L. S. Keyser.

(Continued from page 414.)

The Syren's Enchantment.

THE entrance of Belle Havelock into Hadley Madelling's life was an epoch of momentous importance. She was very beautiful, and that fact has a mighty influence in the relations of the sexes, no matter how studious and pre-occupied a young man may be. But the charm Belle cast over Hadley was due still more to the piquancy of her manner, the incisiveness of her remarks, and the keen intelligence she showed in dissecting the characters of mutual acquaintanees. She seemed to be destitute of reverence altogether. Neither age nor social standing protected any one from her caustic ridicule. It was delicious to listen to her witty raillery, but it occurred to Hadley more than once, during the early days of their acquaintance, that she would have been more charming had she been more gentle and womanly. Still, even in her most cynical moods, she was fascinating; and an evening in her society could not be dull.

At his first call upon her at her home, she received him with unconcealed pleasure, and evidently was glad that he had availed himself of the permission she had given him to visit her. The evening was passed in vivacious conversation, chiefly on matters connected with the college. Belle gave no clue to her religious condition, but, from the glances Hadley took at her library, he inferred that her favorite authors were agnostics and avowed unbelievers, from which he concluded that there would be no difference of opinion between them on religion.

That she attended church, however, he knew, for he had seen her there; and he therefore, according to the custom in vogue at the college, asked the pleasure of accompanying her on the following Sunday evening. The request was granted cheerfully.

It was with some degree of impatience that he waited for Sunday evening. Undoubtedly it would be regarded as a triumph in the college, if he should be the first young man to appear in public with this beautiful and intelligent girl, who had already attracted considerable attention among the students. It was, therefore, with a feeling very like exultation that he walked down the street by her side before the time for the evenning service.

"What church do you propose to attend?" she inquired, after they had gone a few blocks.

"I have no preference, and will leave it to you to choose," he replied.

"A stranger is to preach to-night at the Jefferson Street Church. Perhaps we might have a mental tonic there, if such a thing is to be had in a church service. If you have no choice, we will go there."

He readily assented, for he, the sentimental egotist, was not so anxious that the services should be profitable, as that he might display the social triumph he had won. As the last bell was ringing, they stepped into the church, and were politely ushered to a pew.

It was an unfortunate service for them. Unhappily, the "strange" clergyman who was to deliver the discourse was one of those crude, silly, conceited declaimers who find their way occasionally into a Christian pulpit. Gifted with a voluble flow of words, and possessed of a retentive memory, crammed with a mass of unassimilated knowledge, while lacking the logical faculties for its arrangement and use, the poor man talked as one beating the air.

In the first place, he chose a sensational text—one that might be made to point in any direction that suited the preacher's unbridled fancy, instead of one that would admit of a practical and logical development. And this text was tossed about and played with in the most capricious fashion. That class of persons who are excited by claptrap might have thought it a splendid sermon, but to thinking people it was painful to listen to his rambling, incoherent declamation and fanciful interpretations.

The preacher, being saturated by an immense amount of vanity, thought that, as he was preaching in a college town, it would be a good opportunity to parade his knowledge of "science" and "philosophy." He proceeded to deliver a wordy diatribe against science as the enemy of the Bible. In several passionate outbursts, he denounced the hypothesis of Darwin, calling it *Darwinianism*, greatly to the amusement of the students present. Then he made a lunge at the "evolution theory," speaking of the ape as "the undeveloped grandpapa" of a number of eminent scientific men, several of whose names he mispronounced. Some of the students in the audience gave way to convulsive laughter. All this vituperation was dashed off in an apparently pugnacious and ill-humored spirit.

But worst of all, he made several very ungenerous assaults on scepticism, calling it abusive names, instead of pointing out its errors. It was denominated "senseless," "blatant," "corrupt," and even "devilish." Scepticism, he said, was a crime. Sceptics were rebels. They dared to doubt the word of God Himself. Fancy the blasphemous impiety of the created being doubting the word of the Creator! Apparently, the poor man could not conceive of honest doubt, had no idea that the sceptic whom he abused only required to be convinced that the Bible really is the word of God to believe and obey. Evidently this would-be preacher was more of an expert at browbeating than at argument. He was more anxious to parade his unsystematized knowledge than to reclaim the wanderer.

From the corners of his eyes, Hadley furtively watched the changing expressions on the face of the girl beside him, and was almost pained to see her hard, angry look. She could not hide her deep disgust, and turned away with an impatient curl on her lip. It was barely possible for her to endure the speaker's puerile and high-flown peroration.

When they were clear of the dispersing crowd after the service, Miss Havelock burst into a ringing laugh, which did not seem to be the expression of real merriment, but there was an intonation of irony in it.

"Mr. Madelling, that was an intellectual banquet, was it not? 'A feast of reason and a flow of soul,'" she said, with an effort at good-humor.

"Now," thought Hadley, "is the time to get an insight into her theological views." So he said, tentatively: "Do you not think that it was on a par with the usual quality of the sermons we hear?"

"I have heard better," was her rejoinder; "but, it is true, there is very little mental nutriment in the effusions of the pulpit." And then, pausing a moment, as if in doubt whether her next remark would meet with a favorable reception on the part of her interlocutor, she added: "But it is no wonder, when we consider the subject-matter of their discourses. That is sufficient to cramp and dwarf any mind."

"Ah! you mean that their text-book furnishes very little mental stimulus, do you?"

"Mr. Madelling, I shall stop this circumlocution at once," she said, earnestly. "I have the courage of my opinions, and I think it cowardly to conceal them. It is impossible that one who has thought and read as much as you have should accept these Hebrew legends as the word of God. If I am rightly informed, your attitude toward the Bible is not altogether friendly. Allow me to say that I sympathize with you. My intellect rebels against such inane teaching as that to which we listened to-night.

While Miss Havelock was making these observations, Hadley could see by the light of the moon that her face was flushed with feeling. Here was a girl, bright and winsome, having an intellectual affinity with him cultivated literary tastes, and surrounded with all the advantages of wealth; what could there be lacking to render them entirely congenial? Yet the feeling of warmth and ardor that had been aroused in him when he first saw her in Chapel Hall, and afterward when he met her in the grove, was becoming cooled by degrees. She was just as beautiful as before; he still admired her intellectual acumen; but when he saw that she rejected religion with cold scorn, and ventured out boldly into a rigid intellectualism, he felt chilled. A woman destitute of tender, reverent sympathies would never awaken his love. Yet she charmed him, and he was loath to quit her society so early; and, therefore, when she politely asked him to step into the cosy room that she called her study, he was not slow to accept the invitation.

"And so you think," he said, when he was seated, "that these gospel stories are all a myth!"

"Not exactly that," she replied, quickly; "but I think them the ideas of men of bygone ages, which their successors are trying to impose upon an age that has outgrown them. I do not pretend to account for the hold that they have taken on the minds of many people, any more than I account for the remarkable spread of Buddhism, or Mohammedanism. And I am willing to grant that there are many valuable things, historical, ethical, and practical, in the Bible; but when the churches want to saddle it upon us as the only revelation of God, and as the only guide of life, and especially when they threaten us with a most fearful doom if we discard it, then it is time to call a halt to their assumptions. Such dogmatic claims fill me with indignation, and make me almost hate the Bible." She sat looking at him with a flushed face, her eyes flashing with a deeper color than their usual azure.

"Ah! she could hate with a vengeance," thought Hadley. Then he said aloud: "Miss Havelock, you have been travelling the same road that I have travelled, and I can fully sympathize with you. But what is to be done? The Church holds its thousands in thralldom, and by some means has captured nearly all our institutions of learning, so that our hands are tied, and our mouths closed. Everything is against us. What can we do?"

The girl rose, and said with feeling, "Go and teach them better—these deluded people. Why should Christians monopolize the pulpits, the platforms, and the press of the country? Give the new light to the world. Disseminate it with tongue and pen, and show the slaves their chains. If I were a *man*, I should employ every agency available for that purpose. It is a mission of which a man of staunch moral fibre might well be proud."

"But are you aware of the obstacles in the way of such an undertaking?" objected Hadley, in melancholy tones. "Why, Miss Havelock, only three years ago my colleague, Mr. Dane, and myself tried, in the lyceum halls and class-rooms of the college, to gain a hearing in behalf of free-thought, but were sneered at as mere tyros in learning, or were summarily hushed up."

"You are older now," urged the girl; "you are more matured in character, your intellectual gifts are recognized and respected, your compeers in the College will not undertake to cow you now; and if they do, rise to the occasion, as Gambetta did when he was hissed, or Wendell Phillips when he was threatened with mob-violence—turn on your opponents, and overwhelm them with logic and vehement earnestness. You and your friend have had your eyes opened, and it is your duty to open the eyes of others."

"Do you wish us to become martyrs?"

"Mr. Madelling, are you too—too timid to give expression to your honest convictions from the platform of yonder college? Will you let the cause of truth suffer, merely because you lack the courage or fortitude to advocate it, and endure the consequences?"

She seemed taller than her natural stature as she stood imperiously beside him. She was not the same girl as the one he had met a week ago, *naïve*, rollicking, careless. She looked older, but she was almost as peerless as a queen in that majestic attitude.

He sat before her too nonplussed to answer, and she resumed: "They allow sentimental utterances there that are favorable to religion. It was said, only last Saturday morning, by some flamboyant young orator, that 'the Bible is the bulwark of our nation, the ægis of our liberties.' The Professors looked on with a smile of approbation—some of them did. Nobody said 'Stop! we cannot have such sentiments advanced here.' Why should one phase of the question be discussed, and not the other? If this religious balderdash is tolerated by 'the powers that be,' ought they to object when the plain, unvarnished truth is told? Some one must be the pioneer of every new truth. A few strong, eloquent appeals would revolutionize the college, and open the eyes of the blind votaries of religion."

"You have certainly put in a strong plea," acknowledged Hadley. "But there is one thing that has troubled me of late. What good will it do to open people's eyes? Will it make them better men and women to teach them that the Bible is not true? Will it put a more substantial foundation under our social structure? Will it comfort anybody's sorrow to tell them, in our Huxleyan way, that we do not know whether there is a heaven or not? Will it be salutary, in any respect, to disabuse people's minds of their religious errors, and tell them that our ignorance is as dense as their presumption is nauseating?"

There is a queer psychological feature about the thinking of many self-styled sceptics, that deserves to be noted. They can, when they *feel* so disposed, state the case of the Christian as tersely and strongly as their own. The reason of the ease with which they shuffle their position is because they themselves are in uncertainty as to what they shall believe. Yet there was considerable sincerity in Hadley's questions, as well as in what he added: "These considerations cut the nerve of my enthusiasm sometimes, and make me pessimistic."

For a moment the girl's eyes dropped, and she sank into a chair, with a deep flush in her face. But in a few moments she rallied.

"Mr. Madelling, error is never really beneficent. What we want is truth, whether it brings happiness or sorrow. People ought to face the truth bravely. It can never be healthful for the mind to be held in superstition and error. Here is a mother whose idolized child is dead. Though her heart break, it is better for her to face the truth, and bear it with fortitude, than console herself with the delusion that her child is yet alive. It is the hallucination of dupes and fools to cling to error because it affords them a little temporary relief from sorrow. So it is the work of a disordered brain to believe in heaven because it affords comfort, when we know nothing about it. The desire for heaven, as Spencer says, is, with most people, only a kind of 'other worldliness.' It is putting a premium on virtue, appealing to mercenary motives to incite people to its practice."

"I am at one with you there," exclaimed Hadley, admiringly. "We ought to practice virtue for its own sake. In the same spirit we ought to welcome truth. My conscience responds to your counsel. But who shall run the gauntlet of unpopularity by becoming the pioneer of these new truths?"

"Why should not you and your friend?"

"Ah, but—"

"But what?"

"One naturally shrinks from incurring public disfavor."

"You will not, sir, to any great extent," declared the girl, emphatically. "It is the sure road to true popularity. You will receive the plaudits of the *élite* of thinkers, those who are governed by reason and intelligence. Besides, you will be the spokesman of a large class of persons, whose sentiments you will voice and enunciate, and become the deliverers of a class of honest souls who are chafing under the thraldom of religious intolerance."

"Perhaps you are right. There are, no doubt, more infidels than Christians suppose. But why do not *they* express their opinions?"

"Because they have no leader," said the girl. "They will follow a valiant and competent champion. You are the man for that position in the college."

"I will think of what you have said," he rejoined, rising and looking at his watch.

(*To be Continued.*)

GOD'S PRESENCE PROMISED.

By Mrs. M. Baxter.

S. S. Lesson for July 15, Ex. 33: 12-23; 34: 1-7. Golden Text, Matt. 28: 20.

The People without God's Presence—The Tabernacle Removed—God Conversing with Moses—Moses' Desire to Know God's Way—Spurious Revelations in Modern Days—The Test of Revelation—The Presence Promised to Moses—His Desire to See God—Dying to See Him—The Revelation Granted.

THE glory of our holy religion is a present God. "Lo I am with you alway, even unto the end of the world" (Matt. 28:20), is an inspiration for every moment of a true Christian's life. When Moses was interceding with God for the people, God said to him, "Depart and go up hence, thou and the people which thou hast brought up out of the land of Egypt, unto the land which I sware unto Abraham, to Isaac, and to Jacob, saying, Unto thy seed will I give it,

And I will Send an Angel

before thee . . . for I will not go up in the midst of thee, for thou art a stiff-necked people; lest I consume thee in the way." Moses brought this message to the people, and when they "heard these evil tidings, they mourned, and no man did put on him his ornaments." The ornament and glory of Israel was the pillar of cloud and the pillar of fire: let that be absent, and every other ornament was a mockery. Painted and gilded churches, vestments, beautiful architecture, fine music—O how hollow they all are, when the Lord is absent. Let us put off all our ornaments until it can be said, "The Lord is there." (Ezek. 48:35.)

Then "Moses took the tabernacle," the place of meeting with God, "and pitched it without the camp, afar off from the camp, and called it the "Tabernacle of the Congregation." God could no longer be met in the midst of His people. God is not found in the midst of those whose hearts are after golden calves, music and dancing, and other self-indulgence or self-glory. "Every one which sought the Lord, went out unto the tabernacle." Moses was the first to go out, and the people, who dared not themselves draw near, stood at their tent-doors, watching him. But the sin of the people did not hinder Moses from communion with God. As he "entered into the tabernacle, the cloudy pillar descended and stood at the door of the tabernacle." The people knew that God and Moses were entering into conversation, and every man of Israel arose and worshipped (i. e., prostrated himself) in his tent door.

And the Lord Talked with Moses.

"The Lord spake unto Moses face to face, as a man speaketh unto his friend." Oh, how many formal, useless prayers there are, because men throw prayers into the air, and do not first wait in reverent awe to know that the cloud descends, and that God is there. Moses' intercourse with God was no experiment, no hap-hazard work; he spake with Jehovah face to face. He was deeply and personally acquainted with God, and he communed with Him without any constraint. This is the privilege of every child of God who is reconciled to Him by the death of His Son, and who is yielded up to Him in living sacrifice, "alive unto God," and his members "instruments of righteousness unto God."

Here, again, we have a sample of Moses' communion with God. He "said unto the Lord: See Thou sayest unto me, Bring up this people: and Thou hast not let me know whom Thou wilt send with me." Moses was familiar with the guidance of God, he understood God, and was at home with Him; but he could not accept a second-hand guidance—an angel could never take the place of God with him. The people had said, "Speak *thou* with us, and we will hear: but let not God speak with us, lest we die." (Ex. 20:19.) Moses, on the contrary, would have God guide him, but let not an angel, or any other being, come between him and God. Moses knew God face to face; the people knew God only through Moses. Oh, let us have first-hand dealings with our God! Moses went on to plead: "Thou hast not let me know whom Thou wilt send with me, yet thou hast said, I know thee by name, and thou hast also found grace in My sight. Now, therefore, I pray Thee, if I have found grace in Thy sight,

Shew Me Now Thy Way,

that I may know Thee, that I may find grace in Thy sight; and consider that this nation is Thy people." "The wisdom of the prudent is to understand His way." (Prov. 14:8.) That Moses knew as well as Jeremiah, that "the way of man is not in himself: it is not in man that walketh to direct his steps." (Jer. 10:23.) He had learned by his own experience in the mistake he made in Egypt, when he took matters into his own hands and slew the Egyptians and when he had to be put to school by God in the land of Midian, that truth of God, "My thoughts are not your thoughts, neither are your ways My ways, saith the Lord. For as the heavens are higher than the earth, so are My ways higher than your ways, and My thoughts than your thoughts." (Isa. 55:8, 9.) Jesus says to us, "I am the Way," and He is indeed the Way into all that is of God. "Show me now Thy way," said the same Moses who had once so signally taken his own way. No one is fit to be a leader of others who has not learned to let God guide him. And yet the question of guidance is perhaps more caricatured by Satan than any other, and perhaps there is nothing in which we are more apt to make mistakes. The Roman Catholic and the Ritualist shirk all the responsibility by casting it on the priest or "spiritual director," but the judgment-seat will prove whether God is a party to this arrangement. The Mormon takes his guidance from

Pretended Revelations

which pander to the desires of licentious men, who all the time crushed the womanhood and dignity out of woman, and declared polygamy to be the guidance of God. The Agapemonites, Shakers, and the few followers of Mr. Wood, of Brighton, declare, on the contrary, that it is wrong to marry, and they separate husband and wife. A considerable number of self-called religious teachers of the day give out that they are called to live a faith life, and, caricaturing real faith, they quarter themselves on some hospitable Christian and tell him God guides them to stay on with him! Now all these diverse and perilous teachings cannot be really the guidance of God. How, then, shall we know the true from the false, how discern that which is of God and that which is not of Him? "To the law and to the testimony (the *whole* council of God, not a few isolated passages), if they speak not according to this word it is because there is no light in them." Read the Bible as a whole, with a will yielded up, and God will never let it confuse. True, all erroneous teaching is claimed by its disciples to come from the word of God, but it is the word of God read in the light of self-will.

God answered Moses, "My presence shall go with thee, and I will give *thee* rest." But Moses was speaking for the people as well as for himself, and he said, "If Thy presence go not with me, carry *us* not up hence. For wherein shall it be known here that I and Thy people have found grace in Thy sight? Is it not in that "Thou goest with us?

So Shall we be Separated,

I and Thy people, from all the people that are upon the face of the earth." It is our calling and privilege to be a peculiar people (Tit. 2:14), but the peculiarity must not consist in oddity or eccentricity, but in the presence of God with us. This distinguished Joseph, whether in the family in Potiphar's house, in the prison or the court; this distinguished Elijah, and made him superior to King Ahab, and all the assembled prophets of the idolatrous Jezabel. This made Paul so to speak and act that jailers, judges, and kings fell down and trembled before him.

Again Moses prevailed with God. It was not by "vain repetitions," not by urgent and desperate appeals, but by his quiet, unalterable confidence in the goodness of God. He could not accept that God would break a promise or go back from His word. The Lord said unto him, "I will do this thing, also, that thou hast spoken: for thou hast found grace in My sight, and I know thee by name." Then Moses grew bold, and made a further request, this time for himself: "I beseech Thee, show me Thy glory." What is the glory of the Lord? God is our glory, but there is none greater than the Lord, to be His glory." "And He said, I will make all My goodness pass before thee." The glory of the Lord is what He is, His goodness. But to see the face of God, man must die;

"Thou Canst Not See My Face;

for there shall no man see Me and live." "Sirs, we would *see* Jesus," said some Greeks to Philip; but when Philip told Jesus, He said, "Except a corn of wheat fall into the ground and die, it abideth alone: but if it die, it bringeth forth much fruit." (John 12:21-24.) "Blessed are the pure in heart; for they shall see God." Paul saw God in everything, and believed that all things worked together for good; but, then, Paul was crucified with Christ, nevertheless he lived; yet not he, but Christ lived in him. (Gal. 2:20.)

Then the Lord said to Moses, "Behold, there is a place by Me, and thou shalt stand upon a rock; and it shall come to pass, while My glory passeth by, that I will put thee into a cleft of the rock, and will cover thee with My hand, while I pass by: and I will take away Mine hand, and thou shalt see My back parts; but My face shall not be seen." The only safe place for a sinner in the presence of God is hidden in the rock Christ Jesus. All Moses' faithfulness to God could never put away sin. Only hidden in the cleft rock, in the wounds of Jesus who died for him, could he stand before God.

But before Moses could see God, he must remedy his rash act of breaking the tables of stone in his anger at the sight of the golden calf. God said, "Hew thee two tables of stone, like unto the first (the tables were to be no longer the work of God, but only an imitation), and I will write upon the tables the words that were on the first tables, which thou breakest." Moses had given way to anger and hopelessness when he broke the tables. He had pleaded with God to have patience, but he had lost patience himself; therefore he must make the tables anew. At God's command, he presented himself with the unwritten tables in his hand, and then God answered his prayer. The Lord descended in the cloud, and stood with him there, and proclaimed

The Name of the Lord.

And the Lord passed by before him, and proclaimed, "The Lord, the Lord God, merciful and gracious." It is the glory of God to be merciful and gracious—"long-suffering, and abundant in goodness and truth. Keeping mercy for thousands, forgiving iniquity and transgression and sin." All this is the glory of the Lord. But it is His glory to be just, also; that will, by no means, clear the guilty; "visiting the iniquity of the fathers upon the children, and upon the children's children, unto the third and to the fourth generation." Moses had known enough of God to trust Him before this; he was acquainted with His power and His faithfulness; he knew Him as a Holy God, but this overwhelming revelation of His goodness was more than all he knew before. He had always felt safe with God. All the thunders of Sinai had not the terror for him which the absence of God would have had; and again he prostrated himself, and, in the light of the new revelation of God, which he now had, he urged anew. "If now I have found grace in Thy sight, O Lord, let my Lord, I pray Thee, go among us; for it is a stiff-necked people; and pardon our iniquity and our sin, and take us for Thine inheritance." God let Himself be conquered by the faith of His servant, and He reneweth His covenant.

NOT KNOWING.

I know not what shall befall me.
God hangs a mist o'er my eyes,
And so at each step of my onward path,
He makes new scenes to rise,
And ever joy He sends me, comes
As a sweet and glad surprise.

I see not a step before me,
As I tread on another year,
But the past is still in God's keeping,
The future His mercy shall clear,
And what looks dark in the distance,
May brighten as I draw near.

For perhaps the dreaded future
Has less bitter than I think;
The Lord may sweeten the waters
Before I stoop to drink.
Or, if Marah, must be Marah,
He will stand beside its brink.

It may be He keeps waiting
Till the coming of my feet,
Some gift of rare blessedness,
Some joy so strangely sweet,
That my lips should only tremble,
With the thanks they cannot speak.

O, restful, blissful ignorance!
'Tis blessed not to know,
It holds me in those mighty arms
Which will not let me go,
And hushes my soul to rest,
On the bosom that loves me so.

So I go on not knowing,
I would not if I might;
I would rather walk in the dark with God,
Than go alone in the light:
I would rather walk with Him by faith,
Than walk alone by sight.

My heart shrinks back from trials
Which the future may disclose,
Yet I never had a sorrow,
But what the dear Lord chose;
So I send the coming tears back,
With the whispered words "He Knows."

—*Selected.*

J. E. JEWETT, Publisher, 77 Bible House, New York will furnish the above poem in leaflet form at twenty cents per hundred. *A Sample Packet* of 50 leaflets assorted (no two alike), will be sent post-paid, for ten cents. Postage stamps taken.

Christian Work in Mexico.

Through the reading of the Holy Scriptures translated into Spanish some earnest souls in Mexico have, by God's blessing, been led to a clear knowledge of the Gospel. From their numbers able preachers of the Christian faith in its primitive purity have been raised up, around whom congregations have been gathered from among the humble poor, who have been the first to publicly welcome and defend the pure Gospel in Mexico. The members of these congregations, rich in faith, have worked earnestly and bravely for Christ and His truth among their fellow countrymen in that beautiful Southern portion of North America called Mexico. Schools have been established by them, in which large numbers of bright boys and girls have received a good secular education and have been carefully taught the Christian faith. From the children thus educated faithful Christian workers have been raised up. A Mexican Branch of the Church of Christ, that maintains the faith in its purity and integrity, has been organized among these native Christians in the Republic of Mexico. The members of this Mexican Church of Christ, though gathered mostly from among the poor, are yet doing a most important Christian work. To continue that work, we need to pay a few leading workers small monthly salaries, and also to defray some current expenses. To raise the needed funds we have formed a society with an office at 43 Bible House, New York, U. S., and should be pleased to have many of our fellow Christians join this society by becoming regular contributors to its treasury. We are trying to secure monthly or quarterly contributions to meet the regular monthly expenses of the work. In order to continue and extend the work, we wish to raise four hundred dollars a month, by endeavoring to have four hundred persons each give on an average *one dollar every month* to this object, leaving the donors to give less or more as they may be able and willing.

We earnestly invite all who will, to join us in this systematic effort in behalf of the cause of Christ in Mexico, by becoming monthly subscribers to this fund. We have already regular subscribers whose gifts amount monthly to over eighty dollars, and a growing circle of friends who are forwarding us occasional donations.

This Mexican Church of Christ is a very effective instrumentality through which to do Christian work among the many millions on this Western Hemisphere who speak the Spanish language, comparatively few of whom have ever had a Bible in their hands. A beautiful church building has been secured in the City of Mexico as the centre of the activities of this Mexican Church of Christ. Through the workers connected with that centre more than forty congregations have been gathered from among the poor in different parts of the Republic of Mexico. We have some faithful and able preachers now in the field, but more young men need to be trained for the ministry. Multitudes of Protestant children in Mexico, some of them orphans, need to be educated. We make three requests of you, Christian reader: *first*, that you will, if possible, become a monthly or quarterly subscriber in behalf of this Christian work; *second*, that you will try and induce your friends also to contribute to it; *third*, that you will remember this precious work in Mexico in your prayers.

We most sincerely thank all who are already generously contributing to this Christian work for their timely and generous gifts, and we earnestly invite many others, to unite with us in aiding it by also becoming monthly subscribers in its behalf. Those who may not feel that they can give as much as a dollar a month are earnestly asked to give what they can, whenever they are able—EVERY LITTLE HELPS. Fellow Christian, if you will generously consent to contribute a dollar a month or more or less to the work, will you kindly inform me of the fact? Contributions either large or small can be mailed directly to my address as follows:

BISHOP H. C. RILEY, care of J. P. HEATH,
No. 43 Bible House, New York, U. S.

A NEW BOOK
BY AN EXPERIENCED AUTHOR.

The Life of
REV. JOHN WESLEY, A.M[illegible]
By Rev. EDWARD DAVIES.
Introduction by DR. CHARLES CU[illegible]

12mo. 261 pages and five illustrations, bound [illegible] cloth. Price, 75 cents. Paper cover, 50 ce[illegible]

OPINIONS OF THE PRESS.

"Mr. Davies has produced a most readable b[illegible] furnishes a good outline of early life, college [illegible] spiritual experience and evangelistic labors [illegible] Wesley, and of the Church organization wh[illegible] petuates his name and work."—*The Wesleyan*, [illegible]

"It is compiled from the latest biographi[illegible] makes a very entertaining and profitable vol[illegible] will be read with interest and profit."—*Zion's* [illegible] Boston.

"We have just finished reading Rev. E. Davi[illegible] of Wesley.' It is glorious, reading of God's w[illegible] dealings with his servant. The power of G[illegible] do we as I finished reading the book, and I [illegible] and praised the Lord."—Capt. R. KELSO CART[illegible]

THE BOY PREACHER;
OR,
The Life and Labors of Rev. Thomas Ha[illegible]

With sketches of the wonderful revivals in w[illegible] has been engaged. Enlarged edition, includ[illegible] sermon on THE BAPTISM OF FIRE with a ful[illegible] of the late jubilee in New York, and sketche[illegible] sermons of Dr. Buckley and Vincent, and Dr. T[illegible] with a fine steel portrait of Mr. Harrison.
Price, gilt-top, $1.25. Sent by mail, post-[illegible] receipt of price.

J. E. JEWETT, Publisher and Books[illegible]
77 Bible House, New York

Vol. XI., No. 28. Office, 63 Bible House. N. Y. THURSDAY, JULY 12, 1888. Annual Subscription, $1.50.

The New Empress of Germany.

CONTENTS OF THIS NUMBER.

PORTRAITS AND LIVES OF THE NEW EMPEROR AND EMPRESS OF GERMANY, AND PICTURE OF THE LATE EMPEROR'S DEATH CHAMBER.
SOUR EXPERIENCES. Dr. Talmage's Sermon in the West Last Sunday.
PICTURES OF THE RIO POLOCHIC, GUATEMALA.
Timid Passengers on a Steamer—How a Quarrel Ended—Practical Religion in China—A Happy Christian Leper—An American Pompeii—The Returned Chinese Immigrants.
THE TWO TRANSLATIONS. By G. H. PEMBER, M. A.
AN IMPIOUS TAUNT. A New Sermon by C. H. Spurgeon.
Gems from New Books: A Baltimore Policeman's Conversion—A Young Captain—The Dying Sister—Fifteen Wicked Men.
PORTRAIT OF THE NEW CROWN PRINCE OF GERMANY.
A MATRIMONIAL BURDEN (With Illustration.)
THE EPOCHS OF A LIFE. A New Serial Story by Rev. L. S. Keyser (Continued.)
THE GIFTS FOR THE TABERNACLE. By Mrs. M. Baxter.

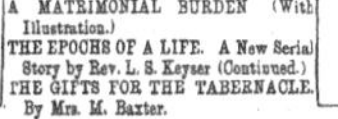

William II., Emperor of Germany.

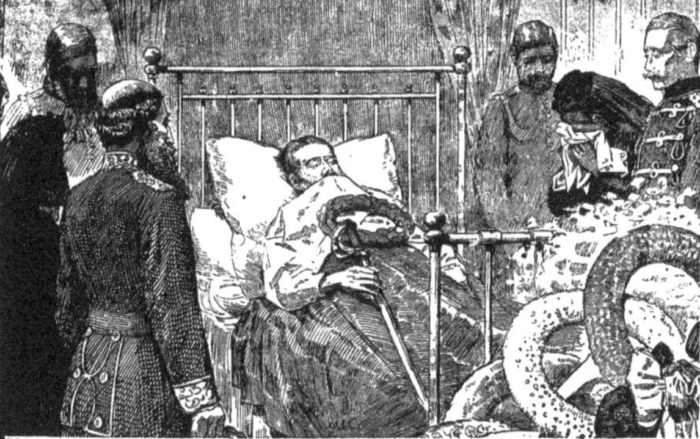

SCENE IN THE DEATH CHAMBER OF THE LATE EMPEROR FREDERICK III. OF GERMANY.

WILLIAM II., EMPEROR OF GERMANY.

HAVING already described somewhat extensively in previous numbers of this journal the character of the young monarch whose portrait appears on the first page, it is only necessary here to summarize briefly the events of his life, and to note the new indications furnished by his recent public utterances.

Frederick William Victor Albert was born on January 27, 1859, and is consequently twenty-nine years of age. Like all Hohenzollern heirs to the throne, he has received a most careful military education, having been given a commission as second lieutenant in the Guards *on his tenth birthday* by his grandfather, the late Emperor William I. His military education, moreover, was in no way mere child's play, for he was subjected to the strictest discipline, and, as he evinced an ardent love for military matters, he eventually became one of the smartest officers in the service, and thoroughly acquainted with all the minute and manifold details of military administration. He served in turn with infantry, cavalry, artillery, and engineer regiments, passing examinations of efficiency in each branch; and neglected nothing which could contribute towards making him fit to take command in the field. Not that

His Education

was wholly military; for he studied for some time at Bonn, and subsequently spent several years in mastering the complete machinery of the Civil Service, under the eye of Dr. Asschenbach, President of the Province of Brandenburg. Moreover, in order to fit the young Prince for his future position, his grandfather requested Prince Bismarck to take him in hand, and initiate him into the mysteries of statesmanship and foreign diplomacy, and thus Prince William, whose force of character greatly resembles that which distinguishes the Iron Chancellor, early conceived a reverence for the great statesman and his policy, which has had a marked effect upon his character.

Before all, however, the Prince showed an all-engrossing devotion to the pursuit of arms; so much so as to inspire the prophecy in more than one quarter that he would in later years develop that military genius which characterized his famous predecessor, Frederick the Great. Indeed, he has never concealed his desire to win laurels for himself and soldiers on the field of battle—a desire which has been encouraged by many of his seniors, and which has made him immensely popular with the army. The new Emperor, since the death of his grandfather, has had a considerable share in the affairs of the state; his father, by a special rescript on March 29, empowering him to "take a direct part therein." In all things he has shown himself a staunch disciple of Prince Bismarck.

The Emperor's first words, on his accession, were addressed to the army and navy, in proclamations which were issued so promptly as to suggest a suspicion that the young man actually wrote them while his father was still alive.

His Proclamations

were conceived in a spirit of despotic principle, indicating his conviction that he was accountable to God alone for his conduct as Emperor, and was in no sense responsible to the nation. This was held by his grandfather, and was excusable in the veteran of ninety, but is ridiculous in the hot-headed young man of twenty-nine. In his address to the army, he alludes to the sense of honor and duty which his glorious ancestors had implanted in the army, and declares that he and the army will stand together in an indissoluble bond, in peace and storm. In the navy his Majesty states that he has, since his earliest youth, felt a warm and lively interest, and he knows that every member of it is prepared to give his life for the honor of the German flag, wherever it may be. The tone of both proclamations implies that he relies on his fighting men to execute any project, righteous or wicked, which he forms. But notwithstanding his martial ardor, it is generally considered that the weight of responsibility which now rests upon him, together with the counsels of Prince Bismarck, will act as a wholesome check upon the warlike propensities which are attributed to him, though it is evident that he will be more ready to rush into war than was either of his immediate predecessors.

To the Reichstag,

as to the Landtag on June 25 and 27, the Emperor used language of similar tenor. As an influential journal remarked: "The Emperor's speech to the Reichstag means, if it means anything, that, with Austria, and Italy, the German Empire will continue to maintain international relations based upon treaty stipulations, but that with Russia the personal relations between Czar and Kaiser will stand for the interests of Germany. This is personal government indeed. It is something so boldly tyrannical and irresponsible that it takes the breath away. The old Emperor might have exercised the power implied by the young Emperor's words, but he would not have avowed the purpose. Never in the nineteenth century has the imperial prerogative been so bluntly asserted; and what makes it worse is the fact that the peace of Europe may at any time depend on the whims of a madcap and a madman. So far as the immediate effect of his words is concerned, his utterances have no significance. But they are important in showing that this young man has no sympathy with modern ideas of government. He wants to be not only as absolute as William I. or Frederick II., but to exercise an absolutism as barbarous as that of the Great Frederick's father. William II. would carry Germany back to the middle of the last century."

The young man's admiration for Prince Bismarck may lead him to rely on that statesman's guidance for a time, and so he may be kept from egregious folly, but should he in some crisis act as did King Rehoboam (1 Kings 12: 1–16), whose spirit he has, he, too, may find that "a haughty spirit goeth before a fall." (Prov. 16: 18.)

THE EMPRESS OF GERMANY.

(See Portrait on first page.)

THE new Empress was married to the present Emperor, on February 27, 1881, when he was but little more than twenty-two years of age. Her name is Augusta Victoria Fredericka Louisa Fedora Jenny, and she was the eldest daughter of Duke Frederick of Schleswig-Holstein Sonderburg, Augustenburg, who had died the year before, a disappointed, aggrieved, and dejected man, because he had been despoiled of his inheritance and expelled from his realms by the King of Prussia. The alliance in question, which had been arranged by his Royal Highness's most influential female relatives, was welcomed with sincere approval throughout the Fatherland. Four sons have been born of this marriage, the eldest of whom, now the "German Crown Prince and of Prussia"—that being the official version of his actual title—came into the world on May 6, 1882. *(His portrait, in his miniature military uniform, appears on page 444.)* He bears the names of Frederick William Victor Augustus Ernest.

An important factor in

The Social Rule

of the new Empress has its rise on this side of the Atlantic. She has formed a close and intimate friendship with an American lady, the daughter of Mr. David Lea, the wealthy banker. Miss Mary Lea is now the wife of Count Waldersee, an officer of distinction in the German army, and a great favorite of Von Moltke. The pretty American lady has unbounded influence over the Empress, and scandal hints that the Emperor himself is more apt to take her advice than that of his wife, with whom he does not lead an ideal life. "Like all persons of hot head and somewhat self-sufficient disposition," says the New York *Tribune*, "the new Emperor is as soft as wax in the hands of a clever and clear-headed woman. Now that the young William has succeeded to his father's crown, and the Crown Princess has become Empress, the *rôle* of the fair American may become a commanding one, and the 'power behind the throne' vested in the person of Mary Lea, Princess of Noer and Countess of Waldersee."

As explaining in some degree the influence of the Countess Waldersee over the Empress, it is stated that when the latter was married she did not enjoy the favor of her mother-in-law, the English Princess, who is now the Dowager Empress of Germany. This placed her at some disadvantage in the Court, as the mother-in-law is admitted to be one of the ablest and most brilliant women in Europe, while the daughter-in-law is not highly gifted with natural talent, nor burdened by book knowledge or accomplishments. The mother-in-law is somewhat intolerant of "stupid women," and perhaps a little too plainly classed her daughter-in-law in that category. The Princess William therefore was only too glad to seize the helping hand held out to her by Count Waldersee's wife, and to avail herself of the relations between them to turn to her for guidance.

Count Waldersee is now placed in the exalted position of deputy to Von Moltke, as that great general's advanced age necessitates his having an assistant in his duties. His own choice fell on Count Waldersee, and the Emperor naturally approves of the arrangement. Some high office at court will probably be found for the Countess, who will doubtless be able to aid her pupil now to repay with interest some of the humiliations she suffered at the hands of the brilliant but somewhat caustic English Princess. A recent cablegram intimates that the English court is to be taught that under the brief reign of the late Emperor there was too much English influence exerted in German affairs, and that for the future the Queen of England and her daughter the Dowager Empress will not be encouraged to give their advice, or to meddle in any way in social or political life in the German court.

THE DEATH-CHAMBER SCENE.

(See Illustration on first page.)

IN accordance with German custom, an artist was summoned to the Palace of Friederichskrohn immediately the late Emperor breathed his last, to take photographs of the chamber, the silent figure on the bed, and the mourning group around it. Scarcely a shade paler than he had been during the last days of his illness the dead Emperor's face reclined on the snowy pillows, framed by hair and beard, light brown rather than gray in color. The expression of that face was peaceful beyond description. The spectators could not restrain their tears as they gazed on those placid features. The Emperor's bed stood removed from the wall, in which there is an alcove that would not allow the air to circulate. It was a common iron bedstead with brass ornaments. Besides the snowy linen, nothing was visible but a dark counterpane. The Emperor had a small silk kerchief tied round his neck to hide the disfiguring hole where the canula had been inserted, upon which rested a golden chain with three lockets, the central one containing the Empress Victoria's miniature when a child. Upon the breast rested a small laurel wreath entwined with scarlet ribbon, and having two white roses in the centre. This laurel wreath was sent to the Emperor by his wife the Empress Victoria after the battle of Woerth. The roses were the last she gave him. The Emperor's hands were laid upon the cavalry swore he used in 1870. He was placed in the coffin in the same position.

Behind the bed there stood a shabby gray arm-chair, prized by the Emperor far above his other belongings. It is the arm-chair in which Frederick the Great breathed his last. At the lower end of the bed stood a small table supporting a beautiful wreath of laurels.

An Autopsy

was subsequently held by order of the new Emperor William, although the Dowager Empress Victoria was averse to it. Public feeling in

Berlin distinctly favored the holding of such an examination, and the supposed abandonment of the plan caused the revival of the excitement against Dr. Mackenzie, who was charged with omitting an autopsy in order that he might prevent a final authoritative report as to the true malady from which the Emperor died. Besides the doctors who conducted the autopsy, Count von Stolberg-Wernigerode, Court Chamberlain, remained during the examination, which proved the existence of cancer. The physicians who performed the post mortem examination, formally announced that death resulted from "cancer of the larynx and inflammation of the minor bronchial tubes, due to the introduction of foreign morbid substances." The cartilage of the larynx had totally disappeared, leaving a huge cavity, so that portions of food flowed over into the trachea and lungs. Thus, "the direct cause of death is attributed to paralysis of the lungs." Further, the report states that the presence of perichondritis and caries of the cartilages contributed to the difficulty of fixing the nature of the disease until recently.

Dr. Mackenzie's friends state that he concurred in the holding of the post-mortem. They also say that he knew the character of the disease from an early period, but took the best course possible with the patient.

The Vienna *Neue Freie Presse* publishes a letter from Professor Virchow, dated Berlin, March 27, dealing with the attacks upon Dr. Mackenzie, wherein he declares that he (Dr. Mackenzie), with his great experience, certainly agreed with the diagnosis of his German colleagues, and in concealing the nature of the malady from the Emperor, acted as a man and a physician should act in such a case.

The Funeral

took place on June 18. All the way from the castle to the Fridenskirche, where the body was placed, torches and cressets were seen. Every here and there rose huge flagstaffs and poles bearing banners with mourning devices. The troops who were to take part in the funeral ceremony comprised the entire garrison at Potsdam and a portion of the Berlin and Spandau garrisons. Prince Bismarck and Count von Moltke, and a number of foreign princes—notably the Prince of Wales, who was deeply attached to his brother-in-law, and the King of Saxony, also an intimate friend—appeared among the mourners.

The railway stations at Berlin and Potsdam were closed against the public. Crowds gathered outside these buildings, and soldiers and police were posted all around the station to keep back the crowds. The Friedrichskron Palace was guarded like a fortress.

At nine o'clock in the morning the bells were tolled, and at half-past ten o'clock the ministers who were to officiate took their places around the coffin in the palace. The choir sang the hymns, "Soon Thou callest me to higher joys," and "Jesus is my trust." As the last strains died away, Chaplain Kögel arose and offered a prayer, in which he alluded in feeling terms to the double grievous visitation upon the imperial house and upon the nation. He thanked God for all He had done for the departed monarch, and implored heavenly consolation for the sorely tried members of the imperial family, and for the nation. Then the choir sang the hymn, "If I am to die." The commanders of twelve regiments, of which the late Emperor was the chief officer, carried the coffin to the hearse, the choir meanwhile singing, "I know that my Redeemer liveth." Eight majors then took the horses by the bridles, and the procession started for the church.

Upon arriving at the church the mourners took the seats assigned to them. After the service, Chaplain Kögel pronounced the benediction. There was no sermon. After the firing of volleys and minute guns by the troops, the mourners took their departure.

Before leaving, the widowed Empress bent over the coffin, and took a solemn farewell look at her dead husband's face.

ANECDOTES RELATED AT RECENT EVANGELISTIC MEETINGS.

The Voice Gideon Ouseley Heard. — Mr. Balmer said: "When Gideon Ouseley was impressed with the thought that he ought to preach Jesus Christ to the people he hesitated for a time, but a voice came to him as if saying, '*Gideon, do you know the nature of the evil?*' and he said, 'Yes, I do; I know the nature of the sin.' '*Do you know the remedy for the evil?*' Gideon said, 'Yes, I do.' 'Then go and tell it; go and preach it.' Now that is the simple story. We know the nature of the disease. We know the only remedy is in Jesus Christ, and we must go and make the remedy known to those who are in the dark valley of the shadow of slavery and death."

The "Headman" and His Warriors.—"Some time after I went to Africa," said a Scotch missionary, "a heathen headman sent for me to pay him a visit. This invitation he many times renewed; but as the object of his visit was only political, I declined. By and by I thought, 'Have I any right to refuse this invitation? May not the Lord overrule this for good?' I determined to go, and sent word accordingly. My assistant and I soon arrived at this man's village, and he sent his son to bid us welcome, and give us a place where we might hold a meeting. We soon had a good service, the chief himself coming to hear us, with two hundred of his warriors. This was one of the greatest honors that could be shown to us. After the meeting we had a long conference, which ended by his giving us liberty to choose a site for a church in any part of his country. We made our choice, and there is now a good work being done in that place. That is how God holds the hearts of kings and rulers in His hand, and causes them to do as He pleases. It also shows how doors are being opened for the spread of the gospel in heathen lands."

A Promise of Money—An Evangelistic Worker in the North observes: "One day I received a letter from a gentleman, the tenor of which ran thus: 'Understanding that you are engaged in a good work, and one with which I am in hearty sympathy, I shall be happy to give you £100 towards the furtherance of the cause. If you call at my office I shall have pleasure in handing you a cheque for that amount.' When I got that letter there were three things to be settled. First, Was there such a person as the writer represented? Yes, there was. Secondly, is he able to give so large a donation? Yes, he is wealthy. Thirdly, can he be relied upon to fulfil his word? He can. He is a Christian and a man of honor. These three things being settled, I am richer by the amount promised, though I have it not actually in my possession. I believe in the letter, and the man's fulfilment of his promise. At the time appointed I called, and at once was handed a cheque for the amount promised. Similarly God has promised us salvation, if we will accept it. God has promised, and He will fulfil. Why then do not men come and claim that which He has said He will give? Call upon Him, and you shall be saved."

From the Ship to the Shore.—The Son of a sea-captain said: "We had been many days 'beating' up the English Channel, when, one morning, the wind changed to 'fair,' and my father said, 'If this wind lasts, we shall be at home to-night.' How glad I was to hear the news! Towards evening, however, the breeze died away; and, although we had entered the Needles passage, yet with an 'ebb' tide against us, our hopes began to wane. Soon the 'darkness thickened,' and weary with watching, I went down into my little cabin and tried to sleep. Meanwhile the ebbing tide ceased; and presently the fair flood began to flow, upon the bosom of which, apparently without a motion, the vessel was carried into the roadstead. The first intimation I had of our arrival home, was the noise of the cable running out as the anchor was cast. As I ran on deck in the midnight darkness, I shall never forget how I shrank from getting into *the small boat that was waiting to take us to the harbor*. Scarcely awake, I remember seeing, about a mile distant, the lights on the shore, the black waters—as black as night—between; my father sitting in the stern of the boat, waiting to receive me, and the sailors ready with their oars waiting to pull away. I was but a little fellow, and remember a strong man carried me down the gangway and deposited me in my father's arms. Father at once threw his greatcoat around me, and beyond hearing his orders to start, and the first splash or two of the oars, I am utterly oblivious of all that happened. I fell sound asleep in his arms. When I opened my eyes again, I found myself in my own little room, the morning sun shining brilliantly, and my mother and the family waiting to give me a welcome home. And may not the landing in heaven be similar? Death, after all, is but the little boat that takes us to the shore. The Pilot who has been our guide all through, will be our strength then. Our eyes will soon close to the darkness and open to the light. The dark waters 'between,' will soon be behind forever."

A Customer "in the Horrors."—Mr. Stewart observes: "A saloon-keeper well known to myself, entered his shop one morning, and proceeded to clear up the place as usual. He had scarcely begun to do so, when a man rushed in, and, leaning over the counter, said, hoarsely, 'Quick, quick, give me a glass of whisky, for pity's sake.' The publican lifted a glass, and knelt down to fill it. While doing so he heard a knock, and, looking up to see what it was, beheld his customer *in the horrors*. As he looked at the poor slave of Satan standing there, trembling from head to foot, he imagined he saw the very Evil One himself looking from his eyes. The man redemanded his whisky, but the publican dropped the measure, saying, as much to himself as to the man, 'No, never; never again to you or any other man, God helping me.' His intending customer was surprised, and noticing that the tap was still running, he drew the publican's attention to it, who replied, 'Yes; it is running, and so will all the others be in a minute.' And at once he turned on every tap in the shop. When telling me of this, he said, 'That man thought me mad, but I had only then come to my senses, and seen for the first time that the traffic in which I was engaged was ruining immortal souls."

The Medical Student's Leap.—Mr. Campbell said: "I was present at a Gospel meeting not long ago, and when the service had just ended, and the workers were gathered together in groups talking, there entered the hall a young medical student. He walked slowly up to the first knot of workers, and said, very seriously, 'Can you tell me how to be saved?' One of the number answered, 'Just believe.' 'I have heard those words, believe and faith, so often,' replied he impatiently, 'yet I do not know what they mean; can you not use any other word to make plain what is meant?' He then walked towards me, to whom he put his question in a new form, 'can you tell me how to trust?' I said, 'You are now standing beside me here; but suppose instead of being in safety, the house were on fire, and we were encircled with flames. There is no safety for us in the house; but in the street below the firemen are ready with a life-saving apparatus, upon which is spread a large sheet. They call upon us to leap, and they will catch us. We hesitate; the flames draw nearer. Again they cry, 'Leap, men, leap.' We look at the distance between, and cry, 'The risk is great,' but the reply comes, 'There is no risk; trust yourselves to us.' We leap, and are caught. That is an illustration of saving trust.' The young man remained quiet for a minute, then, grasping me by the hand, he said, 'Thank God, I have taken the leap.' Then he shook hands with everyone in the hall, and rather astonished some by asking if *they had taken the leap*. At length he left for home, full of the joy of trusting in a newly-found Saviour."

SOUR EXPERIENCES.

Dr. Talmage's Sermon, Preached at Chicago Last Sunday Morning, July 8, 1888.

"When Jesus, therefore, had received the vinegar." John 19: 30.

Christ's Cry of Thirst—The Agony Implied in the Complaint—The Vinegar an Insult—Lives in which Acids Predominate—A Story of King George—Christ Able to Sympathize with the Troubled—His Own Experience of Sourness—The Sourness of Betrayal—Of Physical Disabilities—Of Poverty—Genius Inadequately Paid—Wilkie, Gainsborough, and Goldsmith—Christ's Life of Poverty—Sourness of Bereavement—Christ's Tears Over Lazarus—The Sourness of Death—Christ in Sympathy with the Dying—A Crew Dying of Thirst—Nana Sahib's Ruby.

The brigands of Jerusalem had done their work. It was almost sundown, and Jesus was dying. Persons in crucifixion often lingered on from day to day—crying, begging, cursing; but Christ had been exhausted by years of maltreatment. Pillowless, poorly fed, flogged—as bent over and tied to a low post, His bare back was inflamed with the scourges intersticed with pieces of lead and bone—and now for whole hours, the weight of His body hung on delicate tendons, and, according to custom, a violent stroke under the armpits had been given by the executioner. Dizzy, nauseated, feverish—

A World of Agony

is compressed in the two words: "I thirst!" O skies of Judea, let a drop of rain strike on His burning tongue! O world, with rolling rivers, and sparkling lakes, and spraying fountains, give Jesus something to drink! If there be any pity in earth or heaven or hell, let it now be demonstrated in behalf of this royal sufferer. The wealthy women of Jerusalem used to have a fund of money with which they provided wine for those people who died in crucifixion—a powerful opiate to deaden the pain; but Christ would not take it. He wanted to die sober, and so He refused the wine. But afterward they go to a cup of vinegar and soak a sponge in it, and put it on a stick of hyssop, and then press it against the hot lips of Christ. You say the wine was an anæsthetic, and intended to relieve or deaden the pain. But

The Vinegar was an Insult.

I am disposed to adopt the theory of the old English commentators, who believed that instead of its being an opiate to soothe, it was vinegar to insult. Malaga and Burgundy for grand dukes and duchesses, and costly wines from royal vats for bloated imperials; but acids for a dying Christ. He took the vinegar.

In some lives the saccharine seems to predominate. Life is sunshine on a bank of flowers. A thousand hands to clap approval. In December or in January, looking across their table, they see all their family present. Health rubicund. Skies flamboyant. Days resilient. But in a great many cases there are not so many sugars as acids. The annoyances, and the vexations, and the disappointments of life overpower the successes. There is

A Gravel in Almost Every Shoe.

An Arabian legend says that there was a worm in Soloman's staff, gnawing its strength away; and there is a weak spot in every earthly support that a man leans on. King George of England forgot all the grandeurs of his throne because, one day, in an interview, Beau Brummel called him by his first name, and addressed him as a servant, crying: "George, ring the bell!" Miss Langdon, honored all the world over for her poetic genius, is so worried over the evil reports set afloat regarding her, that she is found dead, with an empty bottle of prussic acid in her hand. Goldsmith said that his life was a wretched being, and that all that want and contempt could bring to it had been brought, and cries out: "What, then, is there formidable in a jail?" Correggio's fine painting is hung up for a tavern sign. Hogarth cannot sell his best paintings except through a raffle. Andrew Delsart makes the great fresco in the Church of the Annunciata, at Florence, and gets for pay a sack of corn; and there are annoyances and vexations in high places as well as in low places, showing that in a great many lives are the

Sours Greater Than The Sweets.

"When Jesus therefore had received the vinegar." It is absurd to suppose that a man who has always been well can sympathize with those who are sick, or that one who has always been honored can appreciate the sorrow of those who are despised, or that one who has been born to a great fortune can understand the distress and the straits of those who are destitute. The fact that Christ Himself took the vinegar, makes Him able to sympathize to-day and for ever with all those whose cup is filled with sharp acids of this life. He took the vinegar!

In the first place, there was

The Sourness of Betrayal.

The treachery of Judas hurt Christ's feelings more than all the friendship of His disciples did Him good. You have had many friends; but there was one friend upon whom you put especial stress. You feasted him. You loaned him money. You befriended him in the dark passes of life, when he especially needed a friend. Afterward, he turned upon you, and he took advantage of your former intimacies. He wrote against you. He talked against you. He microscopized your faults. He flung contempt at you when you ought to have received nothing but gratitude. At first, you could not sleep at nights. Then you went about with a sense of having been stung. That difficulty will never be healed, for though mutual friends may arbitrate in the matter until you shall shake hands, the old cordiality will never come back. Now I commend to all such the sympathy of a betrayed Christ. Why, they sold Him for less than our twenty dollars! They all forsook Him and fled. They cut Him to the quick. He drank that cup to the dregs. He took the vinegar.

There is also the sourness of pain. There are some of you who have not seen a well day for many years. By keeping out of draughts, and by carefully studying dietetics, you continue to this time; but oh, the headaches, and the sideaches, and the backaches, and the heartaches which have been your accompaniment all the way through! You have struggled under a heavy mortgage of

Physical Disabilities;

and instead of the placidity that once characterized you, it is now only with great effort that you keep away from irritability and sharp retort. Difficulties of respiration, of digestion, of locomotion, make up the great obstacle in your life, and you tug and sweat along the pathway, and wonder when the exhaustion will end. My friends, the brightest crowns in heaven will not be given to those who, in stirrups, dashed to the cavalry charge, while the general applauded and the sound of clashing sabres rang through the land; but the brightest crowns in heaven, I believe, will be given to those who trudged on amid chronic ailments which unnerved their strength, yet all the time maintaining their faith in God. It is comparatively easy to fight in a regiment of a thousand men, charging up the parapets to the sound of martial music; but it is not so easy to endure when no one but the nurse and the doctor are the witnesses of the Christian fortitude. Besides that, you never had any pains worse than Christ's. The sharpnesses that stung through His brain, through His hands, through His feet, through His heart, were as great as yours certainly. He was as sick and as weary. Not a nerve or muscle or ligament escaped. All the pangs of all the nations of all the ages compressed into one sour cup. He took the vinegar!

There is also the

Sourness of Poverty.

Your income does not meet your outgoings, and that always gives an honest man anxiety. There is no sign of destitution about you—pleasant appearance, and a cheerful home for you; but God only knows what a time you have had to manage your private finances. Just as the bills run up, the wages seem to run down. But you are not the only one who has not been paid for hard work. The great Wilkie sold his celebrated piece, "The Blind Fiddler," for fifty guineas, although afterwards it brought its thousands. The world hangs in admiration over the sketch of Gainsborough, yet that very sketch hung for years in the shop-window, because there was not any purchaser. Oliver Goldsmith sold his "Vicar of Wakefield" for a few pounds, in order to keep the bailiff out of the door; and the vast majority of men in all occupations and professions are not fully paid for their work.

You may say nothing, but life to you is a hard push; and when you sit down with your wife, and talk over the expenses, you both rise up discouraged. You abridge here and you abridge there, and you get things snug for smooth sailings, and lo! suddenly there is a large doctor's bill to pay, or you have lost your pocketbook, or some debtor has failed, and you are thrown abeam-end. Well, brother, you are

In Glorious Company.

Christ owned not the house in which He stopped, or the colt on which He rode, or the boat in which He sailed. He lived in a borrowed house; He was buried in a borrowed grave. Exposed to all kinds of weather, yet He had only one suit of clothes. He breakfasted in the morning, and no one could possibly tell where He could get anything to eat before night. He would have been pronounced a financial failure. He had to perform a miracle to get money to pay a tax-bill. Not a dollar did He own. Privation of domesticity; privation of nutritious food; privation of a comfortable couch on which to sleep; privation of all worldly resources! The kings of the earth had chased chalices out of which to drink; but Christ had nothing but a plain cup set before Him, and it was very sharp, and it was very sour. He took the vinegar.

The Sourness of Bereavement.

There were years that passed along before your family circle was invaded by death, but the moment the charmed circle was broken everything seemed to dissolve. Hardly have you put the black apparel in the wardrobe before you have again to take it out. Great and rapid changes in your family record. You got the house and rejoiced in it, but the charm was gone as soon as the crape hung on the door-bell. The one upon whom you most depended was taken away from you. A cold marble slab lies on your heart to-day. Once, as the children romped through the house, you put your hand over your aching head, and said: "Oh, if I could only have it still!" Oh, it is too still now. You lost your patience when the tops, and the strings, and the shells were left amid floor; but oh, you would be willing to have the trinkets scattered all over the floor again, if they were scattered by the same hands. With what

A Ruthless Ploughshare

bereavement rips up the heart. But Jesus knows all about that. You cannot tell Him anything new in regard to bereavement. He had only a few friends, and when He lost one it brought tears to His eyes. Lazarus had often entertained Him at his house. Now Lazarus is dead and buried, and Christ breaks down with emotion, the convulsion of grief shuddering through all the ages of bereavement. Christ knows what it is to go through the house missing a familiar inmate. Christ knows what it is to see an unoccupied place at the table. Were there not four of them—Mary and Martha, and Christ and Lazarus? Four of them. But where is Lazarus? Lonely and afflicted Christ, His great loving eyes filled with tears, which drop from eye to cheek, and from cheek to beard, and from beard to robe, and from robe to floor. Oh, yes, yes. He knows all about the loneliness and the heartbreak. He took the vinegar!

The Sourness of Death.

Then there is the sourness of the death-hour. Whatever else we may escape, that acid-sponge will be pressed to our lips. I sometimes have a curiosity to know how I will behave when I come to die; whether I will be calm or excited;

whether I will be filled with reminiscence or with anticipation. I cannot say. But come to the point I must and you must. In the six thousand years that have passed, only two persons have got into the eternal world without death, and I do not suppose that God is going to send a carriage for us, with horses of flame, to draw us up the steeps of heaven; but I suppose we will have to go like the preceding generations. An officer from the future world will knock at the door of our hearts, and serve on us the writ of ejectment, and we will have to surrender. And we will wake up after these autumnal and wintry and vernal and summery glories have vanished from our vision; we will wake up into a realm which has only one season, and that the season of everlasting love.

But you say: "I don't want to break out from my present associations. It is so chilly and so damp to go down the stairs of that vault. I don't want anything drawn so tightly over my eyes. If there were only some way of breaking through the partition between worlds without tearing this body all to shreds! I wonder if the surgeons and the doctors cannot compound a mixture by which this body and soul can all the time be kept together? Is there no escape from this separation?" None; absolutely none. So I look over this audience to-day—the vast majority of you seeming in good health and spirits—and yet I realize that in a short time all of us will be gone—gone from earth, and gone for ever. A great many men tumble through the gates of the future, as it were, and we do not know where they have gone, and they only add

Gloom and Mystery

to the passage; but Jesus Christ so mightily stormed the gates of that future world that they have never since been closely shut. Christ knows what it is to leave this world, of the beauty of which He was more appreciative than we ever could be. He knows the exquisiteness of the phosphorescence of the sea; He trod it. He knows the glories of the midnight heavens, for they were the spangled canopy of His wilderness pillow. He knows about the lilies; He twisted them into His sermon. He knows about the fowls of the air; they whirred their way through His discourse. He knows about the sorrows of leaving this beautiful world. Not a taper was kindled in the darkness. He died physicianless. He died in cold sweat, and dizziness and hemorrhage and agony, that have put Him in

Sympathy With all the Dying.

He goes through Christendom, and He gathers up the stings out of all the death pillows, and He puts them under His own neck and head. He gathers on His own tongue the burning thirsts of many generations. The sponge is soaked in the sorrows of all those who have died in their beds, as well as soaked in the sorrows of all those who perished in icy or fiery martyrdom. While heaven was pitying, and earth was mocking, and hell was deriding, He took the vinegar!

To all those in this audience to whom life has been an acerbity—a dose they could not swallow, a draught that set their teeth on edge and a-rasping—I preach *the omnipotent sympathy of Jesus Christ*. The sister of Herschel, the astronomer, used to help him in his work. He got all the credit; she got none. She used to spend much of her time polishing the telescopes through which he brought the distant worlds nigh; and it is my ambition now, this hour, to clear the lens of your spiritual vision, so that looking through the dark night of your earthly troubles you may behold the glorious constellation of a Saviour's mercy and a Saviour's love. O, my friends, do not try to carry all your ills alone. Do not put your poor shoulder under the Apennines when the Almighty Christ is ready to lift up all your burdens. When you have a trouble of any kind, you rush this way, and that way; and you wonder what this man will say about it, and what that man will say about it; and you try this prescription, and that prescription, and the other prescription. O, why do you not go straight to the heart of Christ, knowing that for our own sinning and suffering race He took the vinegar!

There was a vessel that had been tossed on the seas for a great many weeks, and been disabled, and the supply of water gave out, and the crew were

Dying of Thirst.

After many days, they saw a sail against the sky. They signalled it. When the vessel came nearer, the people on the suffering ship cried to the captain of the other vessel: "Send us some water. We are dying for lack of water." And the captain on the vessel that was hailed responded: "Dip your buckets where you are. You are in the mouth of the Amazon, and there are scores of miles of fresh water all around about you, and hundreds of feet deep." And then they dropped their buckets over the side of the vessel, and brought up the clear, bright, fresh water, and put out the fire of their thirst. So I hail you to-day, after a long and perilous voyage, thirsting as you are for pardon, and thirsting for comfort, and thirsting for eternal life; and I ask you what is the use of your going in that death-struck state, while all around you is the deep, clear, wide, sparkling flood of God's sympathetic mercy. O, dip your buckets, and drink, and live forever. "Whosoever will, let him come and take of the water of life freely."

Yet, my utterance is almost choked at the thought that there are people here who will refuse this Divine sympathy; and they will try to fight their own battles, and

Drink Their own Vinegar,

and carry their own burdens; and their life, instead of being a triumphal march from victory to victory, will be a hobbling-on from defeat to defeat, until they make final surrender to retributive disaster. O, I wish I could to-day gather up in my arms all the woes of men and women—all their heart-aches—all their disappointments—all their chagrins—and just take them right to the feet of a sympathizing Jesus. He took the vinegar. Nana Sahib, after he had lost his last battle in India, fell back into the jungles of Iberi—jungles so full of malaria that no mortal can live there. He carried with him also a ruby of great lustre and of great value. He died in those jungles; his body was never found, and the ruby has never yet been recovered. And I fear that to-day there are some who will fall back from this subject into the sickening, killing jungles of their sin, carrying

A Gem of Infinite Value

—a priceless soul—to be lost forever. O, that that ruby might flash in the eternal coronation! But no. There are some, I fear, in this audience who turn away from this offered mercy, and comfort, and Divine sympathy; notwithstanding that Christ, for all who would accept His grace, trudged the long way, and suffered the lacerating thongs, and received in His face the expectorations of the filthy mob, and for the guilty, and the discouraged, and the discomforted of the race, took the vinegar. May God Almighty break the infatuation, and lead you out into the strong hope, and the good cheer, and the glorious sunshine of this triumphant Gospel.

THE RIO POLOCHIC, GUATEMALA.

(*See Illustration on page 444.*)

As with other Central American republics, Gautemala has two distinct lands and climates. The lowlands, near the coast, covered with luxuriant tropical vegetation, where the heat is intense, are fatal to the white races; but on the high table-lands, some of which are four thousand feet above the sea-level, the trade-winds lower the temperature, and the air is fresh and pure. The rivers vary greatly with the seasons. In the rainy season they carry a large volume of water to the sea, but in the dry season they are not navigable far from their mouths. The Polochic, a part of which is shown in the illustration, is for a considerable distance choked up by the soil it filters from its banks, and is impeded at its mouth by a dangerous sand-bar. The scenes along its banks are the amazement of the visitor, who gazes enraptured at the beauty of its trees and flowers, its trailing plants and rare growths.

The population of Guatemala is believed to be about a million and a quarter, of whom 360,000 are whites. The others are made up of Indians and negroes, ladinos and Sambos. The ladinos are a mixed race of Spanish and Indian origin, while the Sambos—a physically strong race, but morally weak—are a cross of Indian and negro blood. All are nominally Roman Catholics, the Spanish settlers having taken care that there is no lack of priests; but the priests do not understand the native languages, and are therefore powerless to impress their charge even with the doctrines of Romanism. The natives consequently cling to their debasing superstitions, and are, for the most part, living in idleness, immorality, and drunkenness. The earth produces, without cultivation, sufficient to furnish them with food, and a day or two of work, at long intervals, easily supplies them with money to buy whisky, while their clothing is so scanty that a few cents will buy them all that they wish to wear.

Education, even among the whites, is at a low ebb. The immorality and ignorance of the priests have disgusted them with religion, and they are, consequently, fast tending toward open infidelity. There is urgent need of earnest, self-denying Christian work among them. The most hopeful plan to reach the country and the other Spanish-American lands, is that which Bishop Riley is laboring so indefatigably to carry into operation. It is that of training, in Mexico, young Christian men and women to go there, not to make proselytes for any denomination, but to preach in their own language the pure gospel of Christ. The work has been carried on as far as the funds would permit. Dr. Riley has devoted to it the whole of his private fortune, and he is now working on in faith that God will incline the hearts of Christians in the United States to support and extend the effort he has begun, and to which he has devoted so many years of his life.

Subscriptions in aid of the Church of Jesus, in Mexico, it pastors, evangelists, church and orphanages, will be thankfully received by the Rt. Rev. H. C. Riley, 43 Bible House, New York.

A CAPTIVE GAMBLER PREACHING.

AT the recent International Missionary Conference in London, the Rev. J. McGowan related the following incident of mission work in China: "In Amoy, was a Chinese gambler, whose wife and father entreated him to give up that ruinous practice; but the passion was too strong for him, and even attemps to shame him could not drive him from it. But one day he came within the sound of a preacher's voice. The demon of gambling was from that time driven out of him. He became a Christian, and, not only that, but a preacher of the gospel. Soon after that he was seized by the members of a predatory village, carried thither, and his goods and money distributed, and he himself held to ransom. But he gladly seized the chance of preaching the gospel where it had never been heard before, with the result that his goods, etc., were given back to him by those who had been impressed by his excellent words. This man had formed a church."

TIMID PASSENGERS ON A STEAMER.

THE following incident in connection with Captain Dutton, the Christian seaman, well known to our Canadian readers, is narrated in the *Faithful Witness*, as an illustration of the love and wisdom of God's providential dealings with his people: During a voyage of the S. S. *Sarmatian*, of which Captain Dutton was commander, we had entered the River St. Lawrence, when suddenly a heavy fog arose which completely hid the shore and all objects from view; the ship, which was going at full speed, continued on her course without relaxing in the least; the passengers became rather frightened, and considered it extremely reckless on the part of the captain; finally one of them went and remonstrated with the first mate, telling him of the fears of the passengers. He listened and then replied, with a smile: "Oh, do not allow them to be frightened; they need not be the least uneasy; the fog only extends a certain height, and the captain 'is up above the fog,' and it is he that is running the vessel." When this was reported to the passengers, the change on their countenances, from fear and uneasiness to quiet satisfaction, was wonderful. Oh, what cheer and comfort it would bring to our hearts on our voyage of life, if, when surrounded by the mists of doubt or sorrow, and unable to see our way, we could always remember that our Captain "is above the fog," that He is guiding our way, and will bring us at last, if we only wait and trust Him, to the "haven where we would be."!

HOW A QUARREL ENDED.

AN excellent method of dealing with a vituperative enemy was recently described by Rev. Moses D. Hoge, D.D., of Richmond, Va. He states that two friends had a misunderstanding which developed into a quarrel. Both were Christian men, and there was general regret over the affair in the religious community. At length one of them heard that the other was talking against him, and he went to him and said, "Will you be kind enough to tell me my faults to my face, that I may profit by your Christian candor, and try to get rid of them? "Yes, sir," said the other, "I will do it." They went aside, and the man who had made the request, said, "Before you commence telling me what you think wrong in me, will you please kneel down with me, and let us pray over it, that my eyes may be opened to see my faults as you will tell them. You lead in the prayer." It was done, and when the prayer was over, the man who had sought the interview, said, "Now proceed with what you have to complain of in me." But the other replied, "After praying over it, it looks so little that it is not worth talking about. The truth is, I feel now that in going around talking against you, I have been serving the devil myself, and have need that you pray for me, and forgive me the wrong I have done you." How many a quarrel that causes scandal in the church might be settled, if the injunction of the Great Teacher (Matt. 18: 15) were thus similarly obeyed!

PRACTICAL RELIGION IN CHINA.

THE commands of Christ as to the kind of life a Christian ought to live, though not always obeyed in Christian lands, are never obeyed there or in heathen countries without producing good effects on others. A remarkable illustration of that fact is mentioned by the Rev. Frank V. Mills in a letter to the *Church*. He says: "The gospel has power over the lives of some Chinamen, as I learned from a heathen the other day. I was standing on one of the bridges in the city, trying to interest the bystanders in the tracts I was selling, when a stranger asked if a Christian did not live in a house near by. I replied I thought one did, but I did not know him, as he was not a member of our communion. 'Well,' said the questioner, '*he is a wonderful man. He does not get angry nor quarrel with his neighbors, and when you revile him he does not talk back*.' I felt I had accomplished a great deal in just being the cause of bringing out this heathen testimony to the value and power of the religion we are trying to promulgate. Another day I was standing in front of a shop with my bag of tracts. Some one came from the shop and bought an illustrated tract. Pretty soon he came again and bought another. Then he brought the first back and wanted to exchange it. Later on he brought out two more books, asking to exchange them, but, said I, 'You did not get these books from me; they are old ones.' 'But we have read them and want to see some others.' They were Christian tracts, the same as some I was selling, so I willingly gave him others in exchange."

A HAPPY CHRISTIAN LEPER.

ONE of the most remarkable illustrations of the power of Christianity to give happiness under the most distressing circumstances is related by Mr. W. C. Bailey, the secretary of the Mission to Lepers in India, who has recently travelled through that country. He says: "When I was passing through an asylum one day, I came to the hut of one leper, whom I had known as a Christian for many years. He crawled out of his hut, as best he could, into the pleasant sunshine outside—sunshine which he could not see, for his eyes had gone long since—just as I passed, and I said to him: 'Do you remember me?' I had to repeat my question before he recognized my voice, and gladly welcomed me as 'Padri Bailey Sahib.' He was very much worse than when I had last seen him, and in fact in such a shocking condition that I commiserated him upon his sufferings. Very quietly he answered me, 'No, Sahib, no! Since I trusted Christ, nineteen years ago, I have known neither pain of mind or body. God is very good to me.' I turned, astounded, to my companion, the head of the asylum. 'Did you ever hear anything like that?' I asked, knowing that, at times especially, the poor fellow must suffer frightfully. Not only was the man himself one of the brightest Christians I ever met, but nearly all the good that is done in the asylum is done through him. He used to compose hymns to Jesus that all the lepers sing." Ah, friends! Think of the spirit prisoned in that sightless, mutilated body, singing unceasing praises to its God! "God is very good to me!"

AN AMERICAN POMPEII.

IT is not uncommon to hear sceptics ridicule the idea that the world has to pass through the judgments described in prophecy. There are, however, abundant examples of the sudden destruction, in the past, of advanced civilization, from which the inference is legitimate that what has occurred in the past, in isolated cases, may occur in the future universally, as the Apostle Peter says it will. (II Peter 3. 10.)

One example has recently been found in the shape of a magnificent city in the midst of lava and ashes, by the railroad engineers and surveyors who are surveying the route for the Kansas City, El Paso and Mexican Railroad, which will be built in a diagonal direction through New Mexico from northeast to southwest. The surveying party has just reached that part of the line which lies between the thirty-third and thirty-fourth parallels of latitude at their intersection with the one hundred and sixth degree of longitude. They passed along the lava flow which by the local population is called the Molpais, which is probably the most unique of its kind in America. It consists of *a sea of molten black glass*, agitated at the moment of cooling in ragged waves of fantastic shapes. These lava waves or ridges are from ten to twelve feet high with combing crests, and the whole formation presents the appearance of having been made at a comparatively modern period.

This lava flow is about forty miles long from northeast to southwest, and from one to ten miles wide. For miles on all sides the country is the most desolate that can be imagined. It has been *literally burned up*. It consists of *fine white ashes* to any depth which, so far, has been dug down. To the north of the lava flow, and lying in a country equally desolate and arid, the surveyors have come upon the ruins of Gran Gulvera, known already to the early Spanish explorers, but which have been visited by white men less often even than the mysterious ruins of Palenque in Central America. Only a few people at Socorro and White Oaks have been at Gran Guivera, because it is at present forty miles from water. The surveyors found the ruins to be of gigantic stone buildings, made in the most substantial manner and of grand proportions. One of them was four acres in extent. All indications around the ruins point to the existence here at one time of a dense population. No legend of any kind exists as to how this great city was destroyed or when it was abandoned.

THE RETURNED CHINESE IMMIGRANTS.

THE self-denying Christian ladies who have been teaching Chinese immigrants in the Sunday-schools in San Francisco, and other large cities, and have, in consequence, had to bear much ridicule and obloquy from our own people, who ought to know better, will be consoled and encouraged by the letter which the Rev. H. V. Noyes, Presbyterian missionary in Canton, sends to the *Church*. He says, that among the Chinamen who came to America to make a fortune, and have returned, are many who have brought with them, in addition to their fortune, something better than gold. They have come back true Christians, and instead of spending the remainder of their days in idle luxury, as they probably intended when they left China, they have come back to spend both time and money in spreading the knowledge of Christ among their neighbors.

"There are," says Mr. Noyes, "few places in southern China where there is not a mission chapel within fifteen miles, a distance the Chinese easily walk. Of these chapels, the Presbyterian mission has six. *Every one of these six locations was obtained by the help of Christians returned from California*. Of the thirteen native assistants who have labored at these stations, *six were converted in California*, one in Australia, and one received his first serious impressions and religious instruction from a member of the Chinese church in California, on the steamer crossing the Pacific. The work in these localities has resulted in the establishment of two churches, one of which has been almost entirely self-supporting from the beginning. The members of this latter church have already established places, in private houses, for religious services and instruction, in two outlying villages.

Besides the faithful laborers mentioned above, we can point, with great satisfaction, to others *converted in California*, to Rev. Kuan Loy, the earnest pastor of the Second Church, Canton; to another faithful man, now preaching in the chapel of the First Church; to the two most valuable medical assistants in the Canton hospital; to Dr. Thomson's right-hand man at Yeung Kong, the faithful Bible student and intelligent preacher, Lam Tai. These men are among our very best native helpers, commencing their Christian course in the United States, and continuing their studies and work in China.

A MAHARAJAH'S PREJUDICE OVERCOME.

HOW a Maharajah in India, who had persistently refused to allow any Christian missionary to settle in his country, was led to urge one to come and preach, was told at the International Missionary Conference in London by Dr. Sutherland of Canada. He said that a Dr. Valentine, being out of health, was recommended to go to the Himalayas in hope of restoration. He had to pass through Jeypore, and in the way of courtesy called upon the Maharajah. In conversation this ruler told him that his wife was ill, and that the doctors had given her up. Dr. Valentine said he would like to see her; the Maharajah was pleased, and made every effort, at length with success, to get him an interview with the Maharanee. Under his treatment she was restored to health, and the Rajah said, "What can I do to thank you?" Dr. Valentine answered, "Let me preach the gospel in Jeypore." The other answered, "Yes, if you will settle here and be my private physician." "But," said Dr. Valentine, "I am a missionary. I will stay if you will allow me to preach the gospel from one end of the province to the other without let or hindrance." To this the Maharajah consented; and Dr. Valentine remained for fourteen years, and now the United Presbyterian Church has a large and very prosperous mission there.

THE TWO TRANSLATIONS.

By G. H. Pember, M. A.*

The Finishing of the Great Mystery—The Time of General Assembly—Three Different Classes of Glorified Believers—The Raptured, the Martyrs, and the Faithful Survivors—To Reign in the Millennium—The Reward of Being in the First Rapture—Not for all Christians—Holiness Essential—Watching and Prayer Necessary.

IN writing to the Corinthians, the Apostle Paul bids them regard himself and his colleagues as "stewards of the mysteries of God"—an expression often twisted by sacerdotalists into accord with their own views, and interpreted to mean "dispensers of the sacraments." But neither Baptism, nor the Lord's Supper, is ever called a mystery in the New Testament; the term is invariably applied to revelations given by the Spirit for communication to the Church.

The mystery of the Church—the great mystery of the present dispensation—is the most frequently mentioned of all. It is said to have been hidden from the ages, and its secret was that God would invite Jews and Gentiles, without distinction, to be one in Christ, to become members of His body, of His flesh and of His bones, and to be partakers of a heavenly destiny. The Lord began to reveal some of its details in the Seven Parables, and in so doing is said to have fulfilled the prophecy: "I will utter things which have been kept secret from the foundation of the world."

Of its termination we are told that, "in the days of the voice of

The Seventh Angel,

when he is about to sound, then is finished the mystery of God. (Rev. 10: 7.) For, at that time, the last member of the Church of the First-born will have been made ready, and, at the blast of the seventh trumpet, its general assembly will take place.

But now the question arises, Is this event the same as that which is described by Paul in the First Epistle to the Thessalonians?

Several reasons induce us to think that it is not.

And, first, Paul does not preface his description with any notice of the violent persecutions, or supernatural judgments, which are to take place just before the mystery is finished.

Again: in the first five verses of the next chapter he manifestly treats the rapture as the introduction to the Day of the Lord, just as Christ Himself gives it us

The Sign of His Presence

in the air. So, too, in the Second Epistle, when he adjured the Thessalonians, by the coming of Christ, and our gathering together unto Him, not to be persuaded that the Day of the Lord was then in progress (II Thess. 2: 1, 2), he clearly implied that the coming and the gathering must take place before that Day.

On the other hand, the blast which signals the conclusion of the mystery sounds just at the close of the time of judgment. For the seventh angel's period includes the final outpouring of wrath from the vials, the plagues of which are of such a nature that their duration must be very limited, or no flesh would be saved. Moreover, their horrors appear to be cumulative; since, under the fifth vial, men are represented as blaspheming God for what they are still suffering from the first. (Rev. 16: 2, 11.)

It would seem, then, that the rapture of which Paul speaks, and the

Fulfilment of the Mystery

of God, are distinct events, and there is no lack of proof that the Church will be gathered to the Lord *in two translations*, one taking place before, and the other after, the Great Tribulation and the persecutions of Antichrist. In the twentieth chapter of Revelation the full assembly of the Church of the First-born is described in these terms: "And I saw thrones, and they sat upon them, and judgment was given to them; and I saw the souls of them which had been beheaded for the testimony of Jesus, and for the word of God, and such as worshipped not the Beast, neither his image, and received not the mark upon their forehead and upon their hand; and they lived and reigned with Christ a thousand years. The rest of the dead lived not until the thousand years should be finished. This is the first resurrection." Now, in this passage we can discern

Three Different Classes

of glorified believers. There are, first, those who are seen sitting upon thrones, and who are probably the company which will be caught up to the Lord at the beginning of the Presence. Then there are those who, being left behind, will be martyred for the testimony of Jesus during the Seventieth Week; and, lastly, those who will be faithful witnesses for Christ in the times of trial, neither worshipping the Beast nor his image, but will, nevertheless, escape death, or, at least, death by persecution. The first class appears to occupy a higher position than the others, but all live and reign with Christ for a thousand years, while the rest of the dead are not recalled to life until the end of that period.

Thus the glorified saints which John saw are those who, in the Lord's words, shall be accounted worthy to obtain that age, and resurrection out of the dead. For they will live and

Reign during the Millennial Age,

while others are still confined to the abode of disembodied spirits; they will not wait for the general awakening, but be raised up from the great multitudes of the dead, and have part in the First Resurrection.

We should not omit to notice that their reign is limited to a fixed time; therefore, this kingdom is not identical with eternal life, nor yet with the inheritance which, as Peter tells us, "fadeth not away." It is something additional to both of these, and special. And, whenever it is mentioned in the New Testament, it appears to be connected rather with the fruits of faith than with faith in the abstract.

The expression, the *souls* of them that had been beheaded, is peculiar, and its possible meaning not very apparent to the merely English reader. In Greek the same word signifies "soul" and "life"—that kind of life which enables us to rejoice in all that God has created. Now this word is used by the Lord in the oft-quoted saying: "Whosoever would save his life—or soul—shall lose it: and whosoever shall lose his life for My sake shall find it." Of the promise in the last clause, all who spend and are spent in His service are inheritors, and especially those whose love urges them forward on the path of obedience, even though Death appear standing in the way.

There is a gracious recognition of this in a previous vision, in which

The Souls of Martyrs

were seen lying under the great altar, poured out as the blood of a sacrifice which had been offered to God. Such a sacrifice, with which He is well pleased, was presented by those who had been beheaded for the testimony of Jesus; at His command they had cast their lives upon the ground, and now, in return for the few and evil years of mortal existence, He has given them length of days, even life for evermore.

It is, then, the manifest teaching of Scripture that the Church will ascend to the Lord in two divisions, the first of which will leave the earth at the beginning of the Presence, the other toward its close. But it is most important to remember that the set time for its full assembly is at the sounding of the seventh trumpet. Then the mystery of God will be finished, and the invitation to Jew and Gentile to become one in Christ, as a heavenly people, be withdrawn.

Hence, so far, at least, as the living are concerned, to have part in the first rapture is a reward and privilege given only to those whom the Lord, when He comes, shall find watching. It involves

Immunity from The Terrific Woes of The End;

it is that blessing for which the Lord urges us to strive, when He bids us take heed, lest, coming suddenly, He find us sleeping. And those who obtain it will have secured the fulfilment of His promise: "Because thou hast kept the word of My patience, I also will keep thee from the hour of temptation, which shall come upon all the world, to try them that dwell upon the earth." (Rev. 3: 10.)

Surely such a promise is of vital interest to us, standing, as we seem to be, hard by the end of the age. It cannot be misunderstood: it has nothing to do with Jews, but occurs in one of the Epistles to the Churches; it is not given unconditionally to mere believers, but only to those who walk consistently, and are willing to endure with Christ. To them it brings assurance of escape from a temptation by which all other men must be tried, since it is to come upon the whole world. And, as the next verse intimates, their deliverance will be wrought by the personal advent of the Lord.

And how earnestly He is longing to rescue His own from the frightful ordeal through which they otherwise must pass, we may see by the memorable but much neglected command in the Gospel of Luke, which He uttered just after He had been portraying the terrors of the Last Week: "Watch ye, therefore, and pray always, that ye may be accounted worthy to escape all these things that shall come to pass, and to stand before the Son of Man."

Of these words also it is impossible to mistake the meaning, unless we do so wilfully. They certainly intimate that a Christian, though sure of eternal life, is

Not Sure of Being Removed

from the earth before the troubles of the Last Week. This favor will be granted only to those who have progressed in holiness, only to those who have been so strengthened with might in the inner man that they can watch and pray. Such a growth in grace *may*, indeed, be attained by all believers; the *power* of watching and prayer is given to every man at his conversion; but if he would be able to bring it into action, he must be willing to deny himself, to take up his cross, and to follow his Master. Then there will be no doubt as to the issue; for faithful is He that calleth you, Who will also do it."

But the Lord has no thought of translating worldly-minded believers from the toils of life into the joy of His Presence, of admitting them to honor and immortality by the gate of glory instead of by the dark valley of Death. Those who vainly expect such a thing are like the Jews, who would have had Christ put Himself at their head as the all-victorious King, when as yet He had not saved them from their sins. But He will not grant to the careless and slothful servant that blessing which Paul craved, yet did not receive, the joy of being clothed upon, without the necessity of shuffling off this mortal coil, and so He bid us watch and pray always, that we may be accounted worthy to escape the time of greatest trouble, and to stand before Him while it is going on.

* From his work, entitled "The Great Prophecies concerning the Jews, the Gentiles, and the Church of God," for sale at this office, 63 Bible House, New York. It is written in a most popular and eloquent style, and describes the impending fulfilment of Revelation and Daniel, and is illustrated by a colored chart. 458 pages. Price, including postage, $1.00.

CHRISTIAN HERALD AND SIGNS OF OUR TIMES.

OFFICE, 63 BIBLE HOUSE, NEW YORK.

ENTERED AT THE POST-OFFICE AT NEW YORK, N. Y., AS SECOND-CLASS MATTER.

EVERY NUMBER CONTAINS:

The Portrait and Biography of some eminent person.
The Sermon Dr. Talmage preached the last Sunday morning.
An Exposition of Unfulfilled Prophecy.
A Summary of the Events of the Week, Notes of Religious and Temperance Movements, etc.
A Sermon by Rev. C. H. Spurgeon, of London, from advance sheets sent by special arrangement.
Pictures of Missionary Life, etc., and Descriptive Articles.
An instalment of a Serial Story.
An Exposition of the International Sunday-School Lesson, by Mrs. M. Baxter.

ANNUAL SUBSCRIPTION, $1.50.

Remittances by mail should be by bank cheques, Post-office orders, or Express money-orders whenever possible. If currency is sent it should be in a registered letter. Cheques and money-orders should be made payable to THE CHRISTIAN HERALD. Making them payable to individuals often causes delay.

New subscriptions may commence at any time. When subscribers do not indicate their wish, they commence with the first number of the month in which the subscription is received.

PUBLISHER'S NOTICE.

The whole edition of The Christian Herald was mailed last week to subscribers during Tuesday, July 3. The last delivery at the New York Post Office was made at 11.00 P. M.

CURRENT EVENTS.

The Ceremony of Notifying Gen. Harrison of his nomination for the Presidency took place on July 4. Thirty-three gentlemen, each representing a separate State or Territory, waited upon the candidate at his home, in Indianapolis, Ind., and Mr. M. M. Estee, of California, as chairman, formally informed him that the Convention had unanimously chosen him as the standard-bearer of the party in the coming contest. Gen. Harrison displayed becoming modesty in his reply, accepting the nomination, referring gracefully to "the more eminent men who divided with him" the suffrages of the Convention. He went on to say: "I accept the nomination with so deep a sense of the dignity of the office, and of the gravity of its duties and responsibilities, as altogether to exclude any feeling of exultation or pride. The principles of government, and the practices in administration, upon which issues are now fortunately so clearly made, are so important in their relations to the national and to individual prosperity, that we may expect an unusual popular interest in the campaign. Relying wholly upon the considerate judgment of our fellow-citizens, and the gracious favor of God, we will confidently submit our cause to the arbitrament of a free ballot." The platform adopted by the Convention was, the General stated, in harmony with his views.

Congress has Beaten its Record in the Construction of this year's River and Harbor Bill. The Senate concluded its labors upon it on July 2, and sent it back to the House for consideration in its extended shape. The bill as it has gone back to the House appropriates the enormous sum of $22,474,783.77. As originally reported to the House from committee, it carried a little over nineteen millions, which would have been a larger appropriation for this purpose than any ever before made. It left the House increased to nearly twenty millions. The Senate committee added a million and a half, and then the Senate a net amount of nearly a million more. The largest sum ever before appropriated in a river and harbor measure was $18,738,875, contained in the act of August 22, 1882, passed over President Arthur's veto. Hence the bill now pending proposes to expend $3,735,908 more than the amount which caused such a storm of public indignation six years ago. In its present shape the bill includes several items rejected in former years by the House, and which the House will probably again eliminate. They included the Hennepin Canal appropriation, the purchase of the Green and Barren River property, and the purchase of the Portage Lake and Lake Superior canals. If Congress adheres to the principle of this bill it is evident that there need be no fear of the Treasury being too full.

The Treasury Statement Just Issued Shows that the national debt, less cash in the Treasury, on June 30, when the fiscal year closed, was $1,165,584,656, being a reduction during the month of June of $14,429,502. This brings the total reduction of the debt for the year up to $113,844,080. It leaves a net cash balance on hand of $103,220,464, which is an increase despite the purchase of bonds. The statement of the Treasury shows that the amount already paid out for premiums on the bonds—that is, through purchasing them of the holders instead of waiting for them to mature, when the holders must accept their face value—has amounted to over $8,000,000. Against this has to be set the sum that would have been paid in interest on the bonds if they had not been bought.

The Trouble Over the South American Mails appears likely to be renewed, Posmaster-General Dickinson being apparently as much opposed to subsidies as his predecessor. In reply to a request for his opinion from the Chairman of the House Post Office Committee, Mr. Dickinson declares that the subsidy provision "would not be advantageous to the service, but the disadvantages would be positive." He would be compelled to contract with the owners of American vessels for the transportation of the mails to the ports of Central and South America and the West Indies for a period of not less than five years, with a compensation of $1 for each mile sailed on the outward trip, regardless of the amount of mail carried. Considering the number of companies available for the service and their relations to each other, there would be practically no competition, and the maximum rate would have to be paid in each case. It would not encourage the development of new lines, but on the contrary would secure advantages to those now in existence which they would be sure to confine to themselves. Practically it would be a mandate to distribute the appropriation among certain companies, which could be easily named beforehand.

Cincinnati Celebrated her Centennial by a double pageant on July 4. In the morning the magnificent exposition which during the past few months has been brought to completion, was formerly opened by Gov. Foraker. He was supported by the Governors of Nebraska, Indiana, Pennsylvania, and ex-Governor Bryan, of Kentucky, with Senator Sherman and Congressman Butterworth. The exposition is intended to celebrate not only the settlement of Cincinnati, but of Ohio and the whole Northwest. Accordingly Indiana, Michigan, Illinois., and Wisconsin have taken part in the celebration. The General Government assisted with an appropriation of $50,000 and the loan of collections from the Smithsonian Institute and the Patent Office. The signal for opening the exposition and setting the machinery in motion was given by the widow of President Polk, who, by touching an electric button at her home in Nashville, Tenn, sounded a gong in the exposition building. In the evening a grand pageant, illustrating the progress of science, art, and manufactures of the past century, passed before the Governor and his distinguished guests. The exposition will remain open for ten weeks.

The Reunion on the Battle-field of Gettysburg on three days of last week was the occasion of hearty fraternization of North and South. Fully a thousand Southern veterans were present at the opening exercises to meet the Northern regiments, and many more came later. A feature of the celebration was the dedication by the various States, notably New York, New Jersey, Pennsylvania, and Wisconsin, of a large number of monuments in memory of the brave men from each State who fell in the battle twenty-five years ago. On Monday the corner-stone of the Memorial Church of the Prince of Peace was laid on the battle-field with impressive ceremonies by Bishop Howe, of the Protestant Episcopal Church. A large number of stones to be used in its erection have been given by veterans, or friends of men who perished in the battle, and their names are inscribed on the stones. The manœuvres of the battle were rehearsed with the joining of hands as at former reunions, and Generals Sickles, Gordon, Longstreet, and Slocum were seen in friendly converse, taking interest in the various movements.

The Long-Anticipated Suit for Libel, of O'Donnell against the *London Times*, was tried last week, and resulted in a verdict for the newspaper. Mr. O'Donnell was formerly editor of *United Ireland*, and a member of the Parnellite party. He claimed that he had been injured by a series of articles published in the *Times*, under the heading of "*Parnellism and Crime*," in which the Parnellites were charged with associating with murderers and instigating crime. As he is not now a member of the party, O'Donnell's case was that he had suffered by the imputation, and claimed $250,000 damages. The case was conducted in a feeble manner, and, as the judge who tried it said, really served the cause of the *Times* more than that of the plaintiff. In defence the newspaper produced letters purporting to be written by Mr. Parnell implying that he was in association with the men who perpetrated the Phœnix Park murders, and that he approved of the crime. Mr. Parnell did not go upon the witness-stand, but in the House of Commons he denounced the letters as forgeries.

The Approaching Meeting between the Emperor of Germany and the Czar of Russia has taken Europe by surprise. For months past the relations of the two countries have been, if not strained, anything but cordial, and the newspapers of each country have attacked each other with bitter upbraidings. Now it is announced that the young Emperor proposes to pay a visit, the first of his reign, to his northern neighbor. The event is significant and the French nation, which hoped to have Russia's assistance in the next struggle with Germany, is unable to conceal its disappointment. It is believed to be Kaiser Wilhelm's intention about the 15th, or at the latest on the 18th inst., to leave Dantzic in the royal yacht *Hohenzollern* for Peterhof, where the two monarchs will greet one another. Count Herbert von Bismarck, among others, is to accompany the Kaiser. By August 1 His Majesty will be back again in the German capital. From St. Petersburg news comes that considerable preparations are already being made for a worthy reception of the German Kaiser. That the Emperor should visit the Czar before visiting the Emperor of Austria is also regarded as an ominous fact, as the triple alliance into which Germany entered was regarded as a pledge to protect Austria against Russia.

The Unanimous Vote of the French Senate to grant the extraordinary army appropriation demanded by the Secretary of War, indicates that France feels little confidence in the pacific assurances of the Emperor of Germany. The amount appropriated for the army alone was ninety-four million dollars. In asking for this sum the Secretary of War said to the Senate that it was intended to perfect the armament of the French troops and the completion of fortresses. "We must face manfully, added the Minister, "the eventualities in the presence of which we may find ourselves." These significant words produced a marked effect upon the Senate. It is somewhat remarkable that M. Boulanger has recently been gaining friends among the royalists, who appear to think that his destiny is to overthrow the Republic.

The Pan-Presbyterian Council Met in London n July 4. At its first session a general report ras read by Mr. Matthews, of Quebec. He tated that the church now numbered four mil-ion communicants, equivalent to twenty million dherents. He said that education was much ooked after, as the principles they held did not ommend themselves to persons without educa-ion. Respecting missions, sixty thousand com-nunicants had been gathered into the Presby-erian Church from heathenism, and over five undred ministers had been sent to preach the ospel to the heathen. At the evening session Ir. Van Norden, of New York, who presided, ead a paper on the need of home missionary fforts. He said that the Presbyterian Church n America was never more prosperous or ag-ressive, freer from unbelief and heresy or more piritual than to-day, because it was never more live to missionary effort. Mr. Pierson, of Philadelphia, delivered a stirring address on or-anized Christian work. The next Council is o be held at Toronto.

Another Effort is to be Made to Gain the Re-ase of the Rev. W. F. Davis, of Boston, Mass., ho is in prison for preaching on the Common. lis counsel has presented a petition for a writ f habeas corpus in the Supreme Judicial Court efore Judge Field, in Boston, stating that he ntended to raise a question as to the constitu-onality of the city ordinance prohibiting reaching on the Common, in order to carry the ase before the Supreme Court of the United tates at Washington. Judge Field took the apers in the case under consideration.

Another Death in the Niagara Rapids took ace on July 4. A man named Robert W. lack, of Syracuse, N. Y., undertook to navigate e rapids in a boat of his own construction. e had built it of white pine lined with oak, d had fitted it with a propeller which could worked by hand. It was shod with iron and s made expressly to stand the strain of the ughest water. Flack had the utmost confi-ce in his boat, and assured the reporters that ere was not the slightest doubt of his ssing through the dangerous waters safely. e was buckled by a strap around his waist to s seat in the boat, so that if the boat capsized would be in his place when it righted again. wice after entering the rapids the boat made a mersault and came up right side uppermost, d the man could be seen using his steering paratus. Once more it turned when opposite e Deveaux College grounds, but this time it ated on keel uppermost. The fatal strap pt Flack under the boat and held him there, ile the boat floated into the whirlpool and cir-d around. It was nearly an hour before some venturous swimmers succeeded in catching e boat and dragging it to land. Flack was ll in it, held by the middle, his head and els hanging limply together like the ends of a lf empty sack. His face and body had been unded until they were almost unrecognizable human remains. The same spirit of adven-e and unwarranted confidence in his own re-urces which led to his losing his life, have led many others losing their souls. The rapids pleasure and the whirlpool of sin are more to dreaded than Niagara. (Prov. 5: 22, 23.)

The Discovery of a Long Lost-Mother Will ke the recent Republican convention in Chi-go memorable to one of the delegates. The legation from California entertained each er on their way East with personal reminis-ces. Among them, one of the delegates m San Francisco, said that he had not been Chicago since he was twelve years old. His ily had lived in Baraboo, Wis., and when father died he had started with his mother New York. In the crowded railroad station Chicago he had become separated from his ther, and had never seen her since. By mis-e he got into an excursion train for Niagara lls and was carried to Buffalo. There a be-volent man in the station helped him to New rk, where he hoped to find his mother. He not find her, but got work as errand boy in a store, and supported himself for six years. Then he went West, and turned up in a miners' camp in California. He struck "pay dirt," invested his earnings in San Francisco, and made money rapidly. He had written often to people to ask about his mother, but never obtained tidings of her. The delegate was in the convention the day Harrison was nominated. Just as he was coming out a patrol wagon went by with an old woman in it. The police were taking her to the poorhouse. He looked at her, stopped the wagon, and found his mother. She accompanied him the next day to his home in San Francisco. Doubtless the mother also, during the long years of their separation, had vainly sought her lost son. Happily for the wandering sinner separation from his heavenly Father need never continue long. To the seeking soul God is always near. (1 Chron. 28 : 9.)

A Charity Girl's Fortune was Announced to her foster-father at Breslau, L. I., last week. About three years ago a tailor happened to see among the children in the poorhouse of Hudson County, New Jersey, a bright little girl, who impressed him so favorably that he asked permission to adopt her. The child's parents, who were in indigent circumstances, gave their consent and the authorities of the poorhouse accordingly transferred their charge to the tailor. She has been tenderly cared for and educated, her foster parents treating her as their own child. To their astonishment, last week a lawyer waited upon them and announced that the little girl was heiress to $125,000. Her mother, it appeared, was the daughter of wealthy parents in London, but they had cast her off because she had married against their wishes. They are now dead, and though they were unable to forgive their daughter, they so far relented as to leave this fortune to her eldest child. The poor little charity child, the adopted daughter of the tailor, is now therefore a wealthy little heiress, much to her own surprise and that of her foster-parents. Greater surprises even than that are in store when God acknowledges His children before the assembled world. Then it will be found that among the poor and despised are some who are "heirs of God and joint heirs with Christ." (James 2 : 5.)

Two Astonished Prisoners Stood before the Judge in a New York Police Court on July 2. They had been brought into the station-house the previous evening, charged with "loitering," and had been kept there all night. When confronted with the judge the man and his female companion expressed considerable indignation at the treatment they had received for "loitering," which certainly did not appear a very heinous offence to commit on the evening of a day in which the thermometer had been registering nearly a hundred degrees in the shade. The man especially seemed to expect that they would be immediately released and the officer who had arrested them severely reprimanded. The case, however, assumed a different aspect when the policeman told his story. He had looked up the record of the prisoners. He showed that the man had committed crimes in Galveston, Tex., and in St. Louis, Mo., and that the woman's record was not clean. The prisoners had doubtless forgotten that the police had facilities for learning the past life of criminals, and producing it at the proper time. A similar mistake is made by men who, when alarmed about the prospect of death and judgment, think that all they have to do is to "turn over a fresh leaf" and become reformed characters. Unless their past sins are blotted out by the blood of Jesus, through faith, they cannot stand in the judgment. (Prov. 20:9).

The Purchase and Sale of a Husband for two hundred dollars are recorded in the Chicago *Times*. It is stated that a young married man living at Montreal, Canada, contracted expensive habits, and though he was earning considerable income as book-keeper in a wholesale house, he contributed nothing to household expenses, but spent all his money on fashionable clothes, expensive jewelry, and personal indulgences. His wife was reduced to painful straits, and expostulated with him frequently. Ultimately he became enamored with another lady, and deserted his wife. She followed him to Chicago, where she had the pair arrested. Before the trial came on, the prisoners pleaded with the injured wife, begging her to refrain from prosecuting them. The husband even promised to return to his home if the case were dropped. The wife, however, was not moved by that inducement, as the return of her husband did not promise to conduce to her happiness. Finally, the woman for whom her husband had deserted her agreed to give the wife two hundred dollars if she would abandon the prosecution and all claims on the husband. This the wife consented to do, and the transaction was completed. The disgraceful immorality of the bargain will surely work its own retribution, and the purchaser of the husband will probably be the worst sufferer. Though she had the money to purchase him, it is unlikely that she has the power to reform him. But for that power even the incalculable price with which Christ purchased His bride, when He redeemed her with His precious blood, would have been wasted. He is able to make her "holy and without blemish." (Eph. 5 : 25–27.)

BRIEF NOTES.

The National Temperance Camp-meeting, at Ocean Grove, N. J., will be held August 1–5.

The Young Men's Christian Association of Cleveland, Ohio, has received a gift of $25,000 toward the erection of its new building, from Mr. John D. Rockefeller, President of the Standard Oil Company.

The Rev. Thomas Harrison closed his labors at the Jane Street M. E. Church, New York, on July 1, when a grand thanksgiving jubilee was held, to rejoice over the conversion of seventeen hundred souls.

Mr. George W. Vanderbilt has given a commodious building to the city of New York to be used as a circulating library, and has furnished it, and equipped it with six thousand volumes of standard literature.

The American Institute of Christian Philosophy will hold its eleventh Summer School at Round Lake, N. Y., July 26–August 1; and the Twelfth School at Key East, N. J., August 7–11. Full information may be obtained of the Secretary, Mr. C. M. Davis, 4 Winthorp Place, New York.

The Rev. H. G. Pendleton, the veteran Congregationalist minister, familiarly known as "Father Pendleton," died on July 3 at Chenoa, Ill. He was eighty-seven years of age, and during his long life had been the founder or organizer of a large number of Congregational churches in Illinois.

The Rev. E. Walpole Warren requested the trustees of Holy Trinity Church, New York, to hoist the Stars and Stripes on July 4 from the flagstaff over the porch. Though the Doctor is an imported pastor, and the church has been fined for importing him, he is evidently in sympathy with American patriotism.

Mr. George Muller was in Auckland, New Zealand, at the close of April. On the 23d of that month he had been twelve weeks in New Zealand, but the openings for service were so abundant that he thought it likely he might be detained three, four, or six weeks longer in Auckland, besides visiting other places in the North Island.

A noble monument to the memory of Helen Hunt Jackson, is to be erected at Santa Fe, New Mexico. It will be a thirty-thousand dollar building, to be used for an Indian girls' school. One hundred and fifty pupils will be accommodated. The school will bear the name of the devoted friend of the Indians, the author of "A Century of Dishonor."

Mr. Araki Miyake, a native Japanese, and a graduate of Rutgers College, delivered an address on Sunday evening, June 3, in Emanuel Reformed Episcopal Church, Newark, N. J., under the auspices of the Cawnpore Mission Band of that church, on "Japan and Christianity." He gave a very encouraging account of the progress and prospects of Christianity in Japan.

A delegation from the English Universities of Oxford, Cambridge, Trinity College, Dublin, and Utrecht University, Holland, arrived last week in New York and proceeded to Northfield, Mass., to take part in the Conference on Christian Work and Bible Study being held by Mr. Moody. About four hundred delegates from the various branches of the Young Men's Christian Associations of America are also in attendance.

AN IMPIOUS TAUNT.

A New Sermon by Pastor C. H. Spurgeon.

"He trusted in God; let Him deliver Him now, if He will have Him: for He said, I am the Son of God." Matt. 27: 43.

The Sin Bearer Taunted—I. The Acknowledgment of His Faith—The Mockers Said He Trusted in God—How They Knew—By His Life—A Personal Faith—Makes Men Strong—The Mentonese and the Prince of Monaco—II. The Test the Essence of the Taunt—Logical—An Item for the Devil's Gazette—A Brave Patient in Guy's Hospital—All Faith Must be Tried—III. The Answer—God Does Deliver—By Sustaining—In His Own Way.

IT is very painful to the heart to picture our blessed Master in His death-agonies, surrounded by a ribald multitude, who watched Him and mocked Him, made sport of His prayer and insulted His faith. Nothing was sacred to them: they invaded the Holy of Holies of His confidence in God, and taunted Him concerning that faith in Jehovah which they were compelled to admit. Beloved, the treatment of our Lord Jesus Christ by men is the clearest proof of total depravity which can possibly be required or discovered. Those must be stony hearts indeed which can laugh at a dying Saviour, and

Mock Even at His Faith

in God! Compassion would seem to have deserted humanity, while malice sat supreme on the throne. Painful as the picture is, it will do you good to paint it. You will need neither canvas nor brush nor palette nor colors. Let your thoughts draw the outline, and your love fill in the detail; I shall not complain if imagination heightens the coloring. The Son of God, whom angels adore with veiled faces, is pointed at with scornful fingers by men who thrust out the tongue and mockingly exclaim, "He trusted on the Lord that He would deliver Him: let Him deliver Him, seeing He delighted in Him."

While thus we see our Lord in His sorrow and His shame as our substitute, we must not forget that He also is there as our representative. In Him we see what we have in our measure to endure. "As He is, so are we also in this world." We also must be crucified to the world, and we may look for somewhat of those tests of faith and taunts of derision which go with such a crucifixion. "Marvel not if the world hate you." You, too, must suffer without the gate. Not for the world's redemption, but for the accomplishment of divine purposes in you, and through you to the sons of men, you must be made to know the cross and its shame.

I. First, then, my beloved brethren, you who know the Lord by faith, and live by trusting in Him, let me invite you to observe

The Acknowledgment

which these mockers made of our Lord's faith: "He trusted in God." Yet the Saviour did not wear any peculiar garb or token by which He let men know that He trusted in God. He was not a recluse, neither did He join some little knot of separatists, who boasted their peculiar trust in Jehovah. Although our Saviour was separate from sinners, yet He was eminently a man among men, and He went in and out among the multitude as one of themselves. His one peculiarity was that "He trusted in God." This was the one thing which distinguished him among men—"He trusted in God," and He lived such a life as naturally grows out of faith in the Eternal Lord. This peculiarity had been visible even to that ungodly multitude who least of all cared to perceive a spiritual point of character. Was ever any other upon a cross thus saluted by the mob who watched His execution? Had these scorners ever mocked any one before for such a matter as this? I trow not. Yet faith had been so manifest in our Lord's daily life that the crowd cried, "He trusted in God."

How did they know? I suppose they could not help seeing that He made much of God in His teaching, in His life, and in His miracles. Whenever Jesus spoke it was always godly talk; and if it was not always distinctly about God, it was always about things that related to God, that came from God, that led to God, that magnified God. A man may be fairly judged by that which he makes most of. The ruling passion is a fair gauge of the heart. What a soul-ruler faith is! It sways the man as the rudder guides the ship. When a man once gets to live by faith in God, it tinctures his thoughts, it masters his purposes, it flavors his words, it puts a tone into his actions, and it comes out in everything by ways and means most natural and unconstrained, till men perceive that they have to do with a man who makes much of God. To our Lord Jesus, God was all in all; and when you come to estimate God as He did, then the most careless onlooker will soon begin to say of you, "He trusted in God."

In addition to observing that Jesus made much of God, men came to note that He was a trusting man, and not self-confident. Certain persons are very proud because they are

Self-Made Men.

I will do them credit to admit that they heartily worship their Maker. Self made them, and they worship self. We have among us individuals who are self-sufficient, and almost all-sufficient; they sneer at those who do not succeed, for *they* can succeed anywhere at anything. A vat of sufficiency ferments within their ribs! There was nothing of that sort of thing in our Lord. The words that He spake He spake not of Himself, and the great deeds that He did He never boasted of, but said, "The Father that dwelleth in Me, He doeth the works." He was a truster in God, not a boaster in self.

It is evident that the Lord Jesus trusted in God openly, since even yonder gibing crowd proclaimed it. Some good people try to exercise faith on the sly: they practice it in snug corners, and in lonely hours, but they are afraid to say much before others, for fear their faith should not see the promise fulfilled. They dare not say, with David, "My soul shall make her boast in the Lord: the humble shall hear thereof, and be glad." This secrecy robs God of His honor. Brethren, we do not glorify our God as He ought to be glorified. Let us trust in Him, and own it. Oh, I want you so to live that those who dislike you most may, nevertheless, know that you do trust in God! When you come to die, may your dear children say of you, "Our dear mother did trust in the Lord!" May that boy, who has gone furthest away from Christ, and grieved your heart the most, nevertheless say in his heart, "There may be hypocrites in the world, but my dear father does truly trust in God!" Oh, that our faith may be known unmistakably!

Faith Must Begin at Home.

Of what use were the longest arm if it were not fixed to the man himself at the shoulder? If you have no faith about yourself, what faith can you have about others? "He trusted in the Lord that He would deliver Him." Come, beloved, have you such a faith in the living God? Do you trust in God through Christ Jesus that He will save you? Yes, you poor, unworthy one, the Lord will deliver you if you trust him. Yes, poor woman, or unknown man, the Lord can help you in your present trouble, and in every other, and He will do so if you trust Him to that end. May the Holy Spirit lead you to first trust the Lord Jesus for the pardon of sin, and then to trust for all things.

Certainly, dear friends, it is extremely *comfortable* to trust in God. I find it so, and therefore speak. To roll your burden upon the Lord, since He will sustain you, is a blessed way of being quit of care. We know Him to be faithful, and as powerful as He is faithful: and our dependence upon Him is the solid foundation of a profound peace. If you trust in men—the best of men—you are likely to be lowered by your trust. We are apt to cringe before those who patronize us. If your prosperity depends upon a person's smile, you are tempted to pay homage even when it is undeserved. The old saying mentions a certain person as "knowing on which side his bread is buttered." Thousands are practically degraded by trusting men. But when our reliance is upon the liv[ing] God, we are raised by it, and elevated both m[or]ally and spiritually.

This confidence in God makes men *strong*. [I] should advise the enemy not to oppose the m[an] who trusts in God. In the long run he will [be] beaten, as Haman found it with Mordecai. [He] had been warned of this: "If Mordecai be of [the] seed of the Jews, before whom thou hast beg[un] to fall, thou shalt not prevail against him, [but] shalt surely fall before him." Contend not w[ith] a man who has God at his back. Years ago [the] Mentonese desired to break away from the [do]minion of the Prince of Monaco. They the[re]fore drove out his agent. The prince came w[ith] his army—not a great one, it is true, but s[till] formidable to the Mentonese. I know not wh[at] the high and mighty princeling was not goi[ng] to do; but the news came that the King of S[ar]dinia was coming up in the rear to help [the] Mentonese, and, therefore, his lordship of M[o]naco very prudently retired to his own ro[ck]. When a believer stands out against evil, he m[ay] be sure that the Lord will not be far away.

II. Secondly, I want you to follow me brie[fly] in considering the test which is

The Essence of the Taunt

which was hurled by the mockers against [our] Lord—"Let Him deliver Him now, if He w[ill] have Him." Such a test will come to all [be]lievers. It may come as a taunt from enemi[es]; it will certainly come as a trial of your faith. T[he] arch-enemy will assuredly hiss out, "Let H[im] deliver Him, seeing He delighted in Him."

This taunt has about it the appearance [of] being very logical, and indeed in a measure it is. If God has promised to deliver us, and [we] have openly professed to believe the promise, [it] is only natural that others should say, "Let [us] see whether He does deliver him. This m[an] believes that the Lord will help him; and [He] must help him, or else the man's faith is a de[lu]sion." This is the sort of test to which we o[ur]selves would have put others before our conv[er]sion, and we cannot object to be proved in [the] same manner ourselves. Perhaps we incline [to] run away from the ordeal, but this very shri[nk]ing should be a solemn call to us to quest[ion] the genuineness of that faith which we are afr[aid] to test. "He trusted on the Lord," says [the] enemy, "that He would deliver him: let H[im] deliver him"; and surely, however malici[ous] the design, there is no escaping from the lo[gic] of the challenge.

The taunt is specially pointed and perso[nal]. It is put thus: "*He* trusted on the Lord t[hat] He would deliver *Him:* let Him deliver *Him*." "Do not come to us with your fiddle-fad[dle] about God's helping all His chosen. Here i[s a] man who is one of His people; will He help *hi[m]*? Do not talk to us big things about Jehovah [at] the Red Sea, or in the Desert of Sinai, or C[anaan] helping His people in ages past. Here is a [liv]ing man before us who trusted in God that [He] would deliver him: let Him deliver *him* no[w]." You know how Satan will pick out one of [the] most afflicted, and pointing his fingers at h[im] will cry, "Let Him deliver HIM." Brethren, [the] test is fair. God will be

True to Every Believer.

If any one child of God could be lost, it wo[uld] be quite enough to enable the devil to spoil the glory of God for ever. If one promise [of] God to one of His people should fail, that [one] failure would suffice to mar the veracity of [the] Lord to all eternity; they would publish it [in] the *Diabolical Gazette*, and in every street [of] Tophet they would howl it out. "God has fail[ed]. God has broken His promise. God has cea[sed] to be faithful to His people." It would th[en] be a horrible reproach—"He trusted in God [to] deliver him, but He did not deliver him."

Much emphasis lies in its being in the pres[ent] tense: "He trusted in God that He would [de]liver Him: let Him deliver Him *now*." I [thank] Thee, O Lord Jesus; Thou art not now in the w[il]derness, where the fiend is saying, "If Thou [be] the Son of God, command that these stones ade bread." No. Thou art nailed to a tree; hine enemies have hemmed Thee in. The gionaries of Rome are at the foot of the cross. e scribes and Pharisees and raging Jews comss Thee about. There is no escape from ath for Thee! Hence their cry: "Let Him eliver Him *now*." Ah, brothers and sisters! is is how Satan assails us, using our present d pressing tribulations as the barbs of his arws. Yet here also there is reason and logic the challenge.

I told you a story the other day of *the brother Guy's Hospital* to whom the doctors said that must undergo an operation which was exemely dangerous. They gave him a week to nsider whether he would submit to it. He as troubled for his young wife and children, d for his work for the Lord. A friend left a nch of flowers for him, with this verse as its otto, "He trusted in God; let Him deliver im now." "Yes," he thought, "*now*." In ayer he cast himself upon the Lord, and felt his heart, "Come on, doctors, I am ready for u!" When the next morning came, he refused take chloroform, for he desired to go to aven in his senses. He bore the operation anfully, and he is yet alive. "He trusted on e Lord that He would deliver him" then and ere, and the Lord did so.

A Christian man may be beaten in business, may fail to meet all demands, and then San yells, "Let Him deliver him *now*." The or man has been out of work for two or ree months, tramping the streets of London til he has worn out his boots; he has been ought to his last penny. I think I hear the ugh of the Prince of Darkness as he cries, Let Him deliver him *now*." Or else the beever is very ill in body, and low in spirit, and en Satan howls, "Let Him deliver him *now*." ome of us have been

In Very Trying Positions.

e were moved with indignation because of adly error, and we spoke plainly, but men resed to hear. Those we relied upon deserted ; good men sought their own ease and would t march with us, and we had to bear testiony for despised truth alone, until we were oulves despised. Then the adversary shouted, Let Him deliver him *now*." Be it so! We do t refuse the test. Our God whom we serve ll deliver us. We will not bow down to modn thought nor worship the image which huan wisdom has set up. Our God is God both hills and of valleys. He will not fail his servts, albeit that for awhile He forbears that He ay try their faith. We dare accept the test, d say, "Let Him deliver us *now*."

Beloved friends, we need not be afraid of this unt if it is brought by adversaries; for, after , the test will come to us apart from any alice, for *it is inevitable*. Brethren, we have t a tithe of the faith we think we have. But hether or not, all our

Faith Must Be Tested.

d builds no ships but what He sends to sea. living, in losing, in working, in weeping, in ffering, or in striving, God will find a fitting ucible for every single grain of the precious th which He has given us.

Yes, the test will come again and again. May gibes of adversaries only make us ready for sterner ordeals of the judgment to come! O dear friends, examine your religion. You ve a great deal of it, some of you; but at of its quality? Can your religion stand the t of poverty, and scandal, and scorn? Can it nd the test of scientific sarcasm and learned ntempt? Will your religion stand the test of g sickness of body, and depression of spirit used by weakness? What are you doing amid common trials of life? What will you do in swellings of Jordan? Examine well your th, since all hangs there. Some of us who ve lain for weeks together, peering through e thin veil which parts us from the unseen, ve been made to feel that nothing will suffice but a promise which will answer the taunt, et Him deliver us *now*."

III. I shall finish, in the third place, dear friends, by noticing

The Answer

to the test. God does deliver those who trust in Him. God's interposition for the faithful is not a dream, but a substantial reality. "Many are the afflictions of the righteous; but the Lord delivereth him out of them all." All history proves the faithfulness of God. Those who trust God have been in all sorts of troubles; but they have always been delivered. They have been bereaved. What a horrible bereavement was that which fell to the lot of Aaron, when his two sons were struck dead for their profanity in the presence of God! "And Aaron held his peace!" What grace was there! Thus will the Lord sustain you also, should He take away the desire of your eyes with a stroke. Grave after grave has the good man visited, till it seemed that his whole race was buried, yet his heart has not been broken; but he has bowed his soul before the will of the ever-blessed One. Thus has the Lord delivered His afflicted one by sustaining him. In other ways the bush has burned, and yet has not been consumed.

But God's ways of deliverance are His own. He does not deliver according to the translation put upon "deliverance" by the ribald throng. He does not deliver according to the interpretation put upon "deliverance" by our shrinking flesh and blood. He delivers, but it is in His own way. Let me remark that, *if God delivers you and me in the same way as He delivered His own Son, we can have no cause of complaint.*

What Kind of a Deliverance

was that? Did the Father tear up the cross from the earth? Did He proceed to draw out the nails from the sacred hands and feet of His dear Son? Did He set Him down upon that "green hill far away, beyond the city wall," and place in His hand a sword of fire with which to smite His adversaries? Did He bid the earth open and swallow up all His foes? No: nothing of the kind. Jehovah did not interpose to spare His Son a single pang; but He let Him die. He let Him be taken as a dead man down from the cross and laid in a tomb. Jesus went through with His suffering to the bitter end. O brothers and sisters, this may be God's way of delivering us. We have trusted in God that He would deliver us; and His rendering of His promise is, that He will enable us to go through with it; we shall suffer to the last, and triumph in so doing.

Anyhow, He will deliver His chosen: the taunt of the adversary shall not cause our God to forget or forego His people. I know that the Lord will no more fail me than any other of His servants. He will not leave a faithful witness to his adversaries. "I know that my Avenger liveth, and that He shall stand at the latter day upon the earth: and though after my skin worms destroy this body, yet in my flesh shall I see God: whom I shall see for myself, and mine eyes shall behold, and not another; though my reins be consumed within me." Is this also your confidence? Then do not sit down in sorrow, and act as though you despaired. Quit yourselves like men. Be strong, fear not.

There are times when we may use this text to our comfort. "Let Him deliver Him now," saith the text, "if He will have Him." You, dear friends, who have never believed in the Lord Jesus Christ before, how I wish you could try Him now! You feel this morning full of sin, and full of need. Come, then, and trust the Saviour *now*. See whether He will not save you *now*. "Oh," you say, "I am in such an unfit state; I am in all the deshabille of my carelessness and godlessness." Come along, man, come along, just as you are. Tarry not for improvement or arrangement, for both of these Jesus will give you; come and put your trust in the great Sacrifice for sin, and He will deliver you—deliver you *now*. Lord, save the sinner, *now!*

It may be that some of us are in trouble about the church and the faith. We have defended God's truth as well as we could, and spoken out against deadly error; but craft and numbers have been against us, and at present things seem to have gone wrong. If we have not spoken in God's name we are content to go back to the dust from whence we sprang; but if we have spoken God's truth, we defy the whole confederacy to prevail against it. Let us drown the taunts of the adversary with our shouts of Hallelujah! The Lord shall reign for ever and ever. Hallelujah. Amen!

GEMS FROM NEW BOOKS.

A BALTIMORE POLICEMAN'S CONVERSION.*

A POLICEMAN was appointed to guard the doors of the church during the services held by Rev. Thomas Harrison, at Baltimore, owing to the pressure of the crowds who sought admission. On one occasion a young man came after the church was full, and was refused admission by the policeman. He urged his request with importunity, and said that Mr. Harrison had invited specially, that night, such as he to attend. The policeman had been duped on a previous occasion by a similar plea, and still objected to let the young man in. At length he consented to appeal to Mr. Harrison, as to the truth of the statement, and the policeman and the young man entered together. While waiting to speak to the evangelist, the power of the Holy Spirit operated on the hearts of both, and that night the policeman and his charge were both rejoicing in the Saviour.

A Young Captain.

There was living in Baltimore, at the time, a young soldier, who had been a captain in the army. He was an intelligent man, and something of a wit. He was the leader of a circle of godless young men, whose chief delight consisted in caricaturing religion and religious teachers, and he was deputed to hear "the boy preacher," and report to his associates. He made his way into one of the meetings, with this wicked object. Mr. Harrison's first words that night were: "My text is but one word, and I have but a very few words to say about it. My text is '*Eternity*,' and I ask you where you will spend it?" The man heard no more; with the question ringing in his ears he left the building. He found his associates, and said, "That man has asked me a question I cannot answer. He wanted to know where I was going to spend eternity, and I believe I shall spend it in hell. I am going back to talk to him." He returned to the meeting, accompanied by his friends, and before Mr. Harrison left Baltimore, he had the pleasure of seeing them all publicly profess their faith in Jesus, and their joy in His salvation.

The Dying Sister.

A pure-minded invalid sister was exceedingly anxious for the salvation of her wicked brothers. She invited them around her dying bed, and besought them to come to Christ for salvation. One of them was deeply affected, and in a few days he sent a letter to the ringleader of the company of wicked men that he mingled with, asking for a private interview. The letter was answered in person; and after inquiring as to the great secret for which he sent for him, he was surprised to find that he was sent for because his friend was in earnest for the salvation of his soul, but he did not want to go forward for prayers without having his companions go with him. After hearing his simple story, he said to his friend:

"I am glad for you. I hope you will go on with your good purpose. I do not know what I shall do; but we will write letters of invitation, and have a meeting in my parlor." The letters were sent, and some

Fifteen Wicked Men

met to decide what they would do in relation to the salvation of their souls. Not a Christian among them! But they had told a Christian man to be ready if they should call for his help.

* From "The Boy Preacher; or, The Life and Labors of Rev. Thomas Harrison, together with Sketches of the most Remarkable Revivals in which he has been Engaged.' By Rev. E. Davies. Pp. 250, with portrait. Price $1.25. Published by the Holiness Book Concern, Reading, Mass.

New Crown Prince of Germany. (*See page 434.*)

Scene on the Rio Polochic, Guatemala. (*See page 437.*)

They discussed this great subject till nine o'clock, P. M. There was one noted drunkard among them, who had made his home more like hell than heaven. He arose and said:

"Boys, you all know me, and you know what a wicked man I have been, and how miserable I have made my family. I have decided that it is time for me to change my course of life. I am going to the Union Square Church, and am going forward for prayers, if I go alone."

This settled the matter with eight more, and they all, nine, went to the church to seek salvation. The pastor had expected them all the evening, and met them at the door of the church, and made a way for them to go to the altar. They pressed their way through the crowd, and cried mightily to God for mercy, and found salvation.

The next day they sent out letters in every direction, inviting their companions to meet in the vestry of the church, and about fifty responded to the call—not a Christian among them, except the converts. But Dr. France stood ready to go down and help them, when they gave the signal.

After the pastor went down to the vestry, Mr. Oran, the miserable drunkard I wrote about, arose, and said. "Gentlemen, you all know me—what an awful sinner I have been. But God has wrought a great change in me. He has forgiven all my sins, and renewed my heart after His likeness; and if you cannot believe me, who have been so wicked, then go and ask my wife."

This was conclusive evidence that he was truly converted, and fully determined to be faithful to God and man.

Something to Lean on.

'An old gentleman rose for prayers one night during Mr. Harrison's service at the Brooklyn Tabernacle. He was accompanied by his two daughters, who had been converted during the services, and who had with difficulty persuaded their father to attend *just once*. To the intense joy of his children, he listened attentively; and when those desiring prayer were asked to stand up, he arose. In conversing with him at the after-meeting, he said he was *seventy-five years of age*, and had led 'a fair sort of life,' and had 'not been a very bad man'; he was old now, and, as he quaintly expressed it, '*wanted something to lean on*.' By the blessing of God he was brought to see that his boasted righteousness counted for nothing, and he learned that in Jesus he had a support on which he might lean in time and in eternity. His day of indifference was over, and in the eventide of his life he has light.

A MATRIMONIAL BURDEN.

(*See Illustration on page 445.*)

"Ah! Mrs. Thornton, I am glad to see you here," said a society man, as he languidly seated himself beside a lady at a fashionable party. "It is such a bore to talk to those simpering girls. *You* are always piquant and charming. Shall we see Mr. Thornton here to-night?"

"No; he is immersed in his books, as usual. He would only be miserable if he came, and would make me miserable, so I did not urge him to come. He regards all evenings spent in society as a waste of time, I believe."

"Well, he is quite right about that, but what is one to do with one's time? One must get rid of it somehow, and this is a very delightful way of wasting it. Cannot you get him to look at it in that light?"

"Not at all, Mr. West. Mr. Thornton is so desperately in earnest about his work that his difficulty is, not to get rid of time, but to get time enough. He works all night, sometimes, when he has been interrupted in the day."

"What a strange life his must be! Quite refreshing in these days when no one seems to be in earnest about anything. Then you have to idle for two?"

"I have to come alone to such places as this, if that is what you mean. I do not choose to retire altogether from the world yet, and of course, if my husband will not come with me, I *must* come alone. It is very dull for me; I suppose there are many who think I am a widow, or have quarrelled with my husband."

"That mistake might lead to results more agreeable to you than to Mr. Thornton."

"Oh! I do not think he troubles. I often tell him that his books and his literary reputation are dearer to him than his wife is. They certainly occupy more of his attention."

"I cannot think that is possible with such a wife," said Mr. West, gallantly: "I expect he prefers to have your society when he can have it altogether. If he came out with you he would have to share it with your friends. It may be an excess of devotion on his part."

"You are very ingenious, Mr. West; you should have been a lawyer. Your clients would have risen in their own esteem when they heard your pleading. But I know too much to be influenced. When Mr. Thornton and I do spend an evening alone we have the *dullest* time. I cannot interest him in *anything*. I wanted his advice about re-furnishing the drawing-room, a[nd] gave up an evening last week to deciding abo[ut] it; but he said he would rather leave it entire[ly] to me. He offered me a cheque for the expen[se] but he would not help me to decide anythin[g]. He is just *absorbed* in his work, and is quite d[is]traught when he is on any other track."

"What a doleful picture! How did he ev[er] succeed in making love? Did he bring his boo[ks] and read to you?"

"Not exactly, but I read them for myse[lf]. They helped to fascinate me, and Mr. Thornt[on] was more fascinating himself as a lover than [as] a husband. I had no idea then that he wou[ld] think of shutting himself up in his study all da[y] and leaving me to just *die* of loneliness a[nd] monotony."

"Still, you can amuse yourself; he does n[ot] object to that, I suppose?"

"Oh, no; but it is dreary work. When I s[ee] other ladies escorted by their husbands, and r[e]ceiving attention from them all the time, I a[m] just ready to cry with vexation. Of course, [I] know that an income has to be earned, but M[r.] Thornton is so easy with the people he dea[ls] with. He ought to be better paid for his wor[k]; then he would not have to do so much."

"I suppose rather a large sum is required i[s]," said Mr. West, glancing at the handsome dre[ss] which Mrs. Thornton wore, and the jewels th[at] glistened on her fingers.

"Oh, no; Mr. Thornton likes me to dre[ss] well, and to have the house as I like it; [he] never objects to give any money I need. But [I] am very careful. A great many ladies spe[nd] more than double what I do."

"That point of providing the funds amiab[ly] is a decided merit," said Mr. West sententiou[s]ly. "I think I have heard more complaints o[n] that score than on any other. Generally it [is] quite an ordeal for a wife to extract a chequ[e] from her husband. As a bachelor I have [no] personal knowledge, but I have certainly hea[rd] ladies refer to it as a very painful experienc[e]. You should be thankful that you are spare[d] that."

"Oh! it is not quite all gloom. If Mr. Thorn[ton] would only be more sociable, and take a[n] interest in ordinary affairs I would be conten[t]. His connecting himself with that church wa[s] the turning-point. Things were not so bad be[fore] that. It takes his time, and I think h[e] does a great deal of gratuitous work for it, an[d] it increased his expenses too. I am sure of that, for I have heard his liberality praised, and [I have] lectured him about it. How can he provid[e] ing for a rainy if he gives away oney? He has no te fortune."

e conversation was n up at this point ome ladies who getting up some ur theatricals and d Mrs. Thornton Mr. West to help ranging parts. It ong past midnight the arrangements completed and Thornton's car- brought her to home. She us- retired to rest ce, but this even- her wrongs, and eglect she was en- g, were more viv- her mind through g dwelt upon them onversation with old friend. She onsequently in the d to expostulate bly with her hus- , and she therefore straight to his ; where she felt of finding him at work. He was , but at that mo- not at work. The ent lamp was burn- and its shade cast light down on the er's head, which d on his arms fold- n the table. Mrs. rnton entered so elessly that he was aware of her pres- ,and she thought he asleep. She went quietly behind him and ed him on the shoulder with her fan. He startled, and rose instantly to his feet, look- at his wife with a dazed expression as if cely recognizing her.

Why, Edward," she said, "I caught you ping. Work is over for to-night I infer."

No, no, my dear, not yet. I have more to Must get it done, the full tale of bricks know, and my case is worse than the Israel- ; I have the straw but nothing else at ent. Go to bed, dear; you have had a sant evening, I hope."

he man's face was so pale and his eyes so dshot with long poring over his task, that Mrs. Thornton felt some compunction it upbraiding him then. She went to her n in silence and Mr. Thornton resumed seat. Once more his head fell upon his s and he resumed his pleading with God for ngth, for help in his weary work, and for a sing on his thoughtless, frivolous wife. It a dreary lot—that of the hard uncomplain- worker. His profession tasked his brain to the ost limit of endurance; he must work early late continuously, lest debt, the enemy he ded, should overtake him. And he was out sympathy; that was worst of all. That r he had done all, his wife should not be py, should complain of his neglect, should perceive that his work was for her, was as a ght around his neck, rendering every burden vier. Still more distressing to him was it she had not gone with him when a year or ago he had gone to Christ, weary and heavy n, and had found the promised rest. Hith- he had borne his burden cheerfully, had ned to reproaches without retort, had ed to reason or defend himself, and was fully doing his duty. "O God, help me, for ist's sake," he prayed. "In thee alone is hope." How many thousands of God's children are uttering the same prayer, daily, hourly, almost crushed beneath burdens that their fellows know nothing of, yet sustained in the path of duty by God's strength, and learning day by day the faithfulness of Him who has said, "My grace is sufficient for thee"!

Mr. Thornton Oblivious of His Wife's Return.

THE EPOCHS OF A LIFE.

A NEW SERIAL STORY.

By Rev. L. S. Keyser.

(*Continued from page 430.*)

A Better Light.

THE earnestness with which Miss Havelock urged Hadley to enter upon an anti-Christian crusade in the college moved him powerfully. No man likes to admit that he lacks courage, and especially to a charming girl who declares that if she were a man she would not be afraid. Belle Havelock's words had almost stung the young student, but her friendly grasp of the hand at parting and her bewitching smile took away any personal pain he might have felt.

On his way to his rooms he could still feel the thrill of her touch. His emotions were in a flurried state. It was impossible to analyze them. Her cynicism repelled him, while her intelligence and beauty attracted him. In her opposition to revelation she evinced so much earnestness and sincerity, and withal seemed to have so high a regard for the truth, that he could not but respect her.

Her enthusiasm was contagious. Before Hadley retired that night, he had given his roommate an epitome of his conversation with the brilliant girl, and though George was less infected by her intensity, the two young doubters resolved that the policy of repression had dominated them long enough, and that they would avail themselves of the first opportunity to begin a vigorous campaign against Christianity.

This resolution would perhaps have been carried out immediately had not a new star crossed the orbit of Hadley's life, which for a time made a new centre for his thoughts diametrically opposed in its influence to the star whose brilliant but baleful rays would lead him into the arena of anti-Christian conflict.

That, also, sprang from a woman's nature. Oh, if women only realized their power and their responsibility, how different a world this would be! How the power before which men bow might be used to guide, to stimulate, to guard the lives of lovers and husbands, and to develop the good that is in them! It would be difficult to gauge the power that one beautiful, consecrated woman has at her disposal. No more mighty influence do we know of in this world, below that of the Spirit of God.

Such a woman it was upon whom the eyes of Hadley and his friend rested as they entered the class-room of the Professor of Languages on the morning after Hadley's interview with Belle Havelock. She was sitting quietly and modestly there as a student, utterly devoid of self-consciousness and apparently oblivious of the fact that many eyes were bent on her in mute admiration.

"Look at that young lady, Hadley," said Dane. "Did you ever see so spiritual a face? If I were a painter wanting a model for an angel I should look no further."

"Yes, she is very beautiful," said Hadley. "Who is she?"

"I do not know," Dane replied. "I think I had rather not know. She is a being I should prefer to worship afar off. I never saw such exquisite grace and purity embodied in a human face before. It would ruin the charm to hear her utter the young lady frivolities that probably are all that she can produce. I should not like to have my conception marred."

"Nonsense!" said Madelling; "you are too sentimental. If I can get to know her I shall. She is only human, after all, and I daresay is amenable to masculine influence."

When the new-comer's turn came to recite both young men listened intently. Her voice was singularly clear and melodious, and in translating the Latin verse she used well-chosen and correct words. A question or two from the professor as to idiom and construction she answered intelligently and with ease.

The class passed from room to room until at last they were in the presence of their instructor in mathematics. This was the last recitation of the morning. The professor seemed to be perfectly confident of the abilities of the new girl student, for, addressing her, he said: "Miss Winters, will you go to the board and solve the eighth problem?" Hadley noticed that it was one of the most difficult problems of the lesson. His own name was mentioned in conjunction with hers, and as he went to the board to solve the problem assigned him, he stood by her side.

Their hands came into close propinquity more than once. It was with pleasure that he furtively watched the easy grace and mastery with which the girl drew her figures and manipulated her signs. Presently it happened that he was putting down a column of figures near the place on the board where she was drawing a mathematical diagram. By an accident their hands touched. She glanced up at him innocently. As their eyes met, a thrill ran through him, causing the blood to mount, as if propelled by the piston of an engine, to his forehead and temples.

"Of course, she might disappoint one on nearer acquaintance, as you say," remarked Hadley to his friend, when they had reached their study. "One cannot always trust his first impressions. I have had some recent experience confirmatory of that fact, for when I first saw Belle Havelock I thought that I had received an attack of the 'grand passion'; but, while I admire her as much as ever, I have been disappointed in her in some respects. She is not the kind of girl I should choose for a lady-love. Too cynical. While it is perfectly proper to be bold and outspoken against the Christian errors, I still should not be able to love a girl who shows so much contempt for sacred institutions—who doesn't even believe in heaven or immortality. Perhaps Miss Winters would be disappointing in other respects. But I think not. If I mistake not, she is a believer in the Christian religion. The opinion is forced upon me intuitively when I look at her. But we will keep ourselves on the *qui vive* for a few days and see whether we can find out anything about her."

"One thing seems to be obvious," replied George, "and that is, she is very bright intellectually. With what clear, confident tones she gave the explanation of her problem! It was thrilling. But how modest she is! Did you see how she blushed when the class applauded her? I doubt whether she really liked it. I do not know that I should fall in love with her, but I believe that I should enjoy her society."

"As for myself, I am not so sure about not falling in love," said Hadley, doubtfully. "Perhaps I am too impressionable, but if I had any objection to taking that plunge, I should avoid her company. Under the circumstances, however, I shall keep my eye on her for a few days, and if she proves to be what her *début* promises, I shall seek an introduction."

The week, with its studies, recitations, and social enjoyments, passed. The oftener Hadley saw Miss Winters the more he was fascinated by her grace, beauty, and mental brilliance. As his restive mind was continually harassed more or less by theological questions, he was more than curious to learn what was her attitude toward religion. His curiosity was destined to be gratified before long.

It happened one day in the recitation-room of the Professor of Mental Philosophy, that a question was put to Miss Winters in such a way as to require an unequivocal declaration of her views on a cardinal doctrine of Christianity. In firm, clear tones, without a moment's hesitation, and yet without dogmatism, her conviction was expressed; so that all knew that she was a firm believer in evangelical truth. A moment of silence followed her declaration. Then some one began to applaud. Hadley glanced around and saw that it was Duneman. The next moment the room vibrated with the hearty applause of the whole class, in which the two sceptics, almost against their own volition, found themselves joining. Afterward, as a sort of emollient for their consciences, they explained that they had not acclaimed the girl's sentiments, but the girl herself.

It was now clear to the young sceptics that Miss Winters was a Christian girl. There is perhaps something paradoxical in every nature. Much as Hadley detested the tenets of religion for himself, he experienced no special revulsion of feeling when he discovered that Miss Winters accepted the Scriptures with an acquiescent faith. One thing was "a foregone conclusion." She was incapable of hypocrisy. If she accepted the gospel, she also tried to conform her life to its principles. How she could accept it mystified him, but the fact that so intellectual a girl believed it, was, in a measure, a presumption in its favor. So that for a day or two he rather oscillated toward a favorable view of the gospel.

However, it was unfortunate that the divinity student noticed the applause bestowed by the two young sceptics upon Miss Winters' statement in the recitation-room. As he had once suffered humiliation at Hadley's hands, he improved the occasion at the next meeting of the Athenian Society, on the following Friday evening, to deliver him a severe castigation. It may be remarked that this organization was made up of young men only, and gave but one or two public exhibitions during the year. The meeting referred to was an ordinary one. Mr. Duneman appeared to feel it his duty to make an invidious thrust at "the insincerity of infidels," as he entitled his speech. After speaking awhile he said: "We had an exhibition of the lack of sincerity among opposers of the Bible in one of our class-rooms the other day. A member of the class made an emphatic statement of her belief in evangelical doctrine, and when the class expressed its appreciation, several young men, whose anti-Christian views are well known, joined vigorously in the applause. Is not that *prima facie* evidence that they do not believe what they advocate? Or does it prove that they are like straws that are carried in any direction that the wind blows—that they want to be on the popular side? I pity men who court a cheap notoriety in that way. Those of us who are sincerely attached to the Bible would not applaud a statement that was averse to it. No; even if we are, in the opinion of certain quasi wise-acres, narrow-minded and bigoted, we can at least lay claim to the merit of being sincere. We do not howl with every pack of wolves, or give our acclamations to sentiments that we reprobate."

Of course, while this harangue was being delivered, there were many furtive side-glances cast at Hadley and George, and at the close a loud guffaw, accompanied by the clapping of a few hands, burst from the lips of the young men of the society. They cared very little for the real points at issue, but it was regarded as a good joke that the two honor men of the class should receive such an unmerciful scoring.

The charge of dishonesty did not set well with Hadley. It stirred his irascibility into a blaze, and it was fortunate for the divinity student that the rules of the Society did not permit an immediate reply. Duneman's speech proved to his opponents that he was not too scrupulous, with all his vaunted piety, to retain a grudge, and wait for an opportunity to resent an insult. Hadley knew that the speech had a personal reference to himself, and was meant in repayment for the humbling that Duneman had received some time before.

After the exercises were over the fencing began. Walking up to the divinity student, Hadley said: "You charged me the other day with boorishness; do you not think that you have acted the part of a boor yourself this evening?"

"I do not know what you mean," Duneman replied.

"Well," said Madelling, "you are more obtuse than I thought. I will tell you what I mean. I know that in your remarks, this evening, you were making a personal allusion to my friend and me. Every one knew to whom you were referring." Hadley looked inquiringly around the circle that had gathered about them, and received several confirmatory nods.

"Yes, and what then?" said Duneman; "what I said was true."

"That may or may not be; I am not going into that. The point I make is, that in dragging these personal matters into a public speech, and at a time when no reply was possible, you did a very ungentlemanly thing. In fact, it was a mean and cowardly thing, and you ought to be ashamed of it."

"I am not ashamed, and there is no cause for shame," said Duneman, hotly. "You are doing a great injury to the students of the college by your infidel notions, and I was perfectly just in opposing your influence, and showing you, in common with other infidels, are in[...] cere. Your opposition to the Bible is m[...] put on to impress the college with your cou[...] and independence. It is only skin-deep."

"Like your religion!" retorted Madel[...] his temper rising. "If your religion gove[...] your tongue and life, you would not be so [...]cious and vindictive. I know enough of [...] Bible to see that you do not obey its teach[...] You lack spirituality as much as you do [...] manners, and I am afraid you have too [...] temper to make a useful clergyman."

The charge went home. Duneman's [...] science told him that he had erred, that he [...] not so acted as to commend the religion he [...]fessed to his friends or his enemies, and h[...]proached himself even more bitterly than [...] his accuser. Wounded self-esteem, howe[...] would not let him confess his fault. "[...] brought it on yourself," he muttered, sullen[...]

"Well," said Hadley, "you have certa[...] taught us how a Christian acts in these da[...] he thinks himself injured." And he tu[...] on his heel and left the room. "I suppose," [...] said to Dane, when they were alone, I [...] have to accept the situation. Duneman a[...] are enemies. I expect he will do me all th[...] jury he can. But he will find that I can [...] him blow for blow."

Dane laughed. "You will not be gover[...] by the Scripture which you quoted to him[...]"

"Not much! Nobody practices those max[...] nowadays, not even the Christians themsel[...] so far as I can see. They are as touchy [...] vindictive as other people, and I don't see [...] I should be molded by a book which I re[...]diate."

"Hadley, it seems to me that you are bec[...]ing terribly acrimonious," said Dane, with so[...] concern. "You must not let your scepticism [...] your temper, or you will prove its unethical [...]ture at once. The question is not whether a [...]tain code of morals is taught in the Bible, [...] whether it is in harmony with the laws of ri[...] If it is wrong to hold a grudge or take reven[...] it is *wrong*, Bible or no Bible. The moral [...] is above all—"

"The moral law"! echoed Hadley, reflect[...]ly. Then turning upon his companion wi[...] look of concern, he said: "George, do you kn[...] that I cannot see where we are to draw the l[...] of demarkation between the moral and the th[...]logical! Since I have been reading the writi[...] of these agnostic authors, ethical distincti[...] are fading more and more from my mind. W[...] should we call one thing right *per se*, a[...] another wrong? If there is no God, with [...] power of volition, where is there any basis [...] moral relations? Everything is the result [...] evolution, and cannot be changed by the wil[...] man, if he has a will. There can be no mora[...] where there is no freedom, for the power [...] choose is the very root of the ethical. If th[...] is no God, but the world is the outcome of [...] blind laws of development, where is the se[...] of calling one thing right and another wrong[...]"

"But we agnostics do not say that there is [...] God; we simply say that we do not know [...] cannot know."

"Well, that is simply plunging farther i[...] the labyrinth. It is to say that we do not kn[...] and cannot know whether there is any basis [...] our moral distinctions."

"That is dangerous doctrine to sow bro[...]cast."

"If it is the truth, it ought to be disseminate[...]"

But George was flurried. He did not like [...] logical conclusions of his philosophy of the [...] known and unknowable. If all moral disti[...]tions were obliterated, the result would be a [...]pletion of all the moral energies of man. [...] looked fallacious. Perhaps there was some f[...] in the reasoning. He would, some time, [...] over the ground again. But his lids were g[...]ting heavy, and he abandoned the attempt [...] solve the abstruse problem for that evening.

(To be Continued.)

HE GIFTS FOR THE TABERNACLE.

By Mrs. M. Baxter.

Lesson for July 22, Ex. 35: 20-29. Golden Text, II Cor. 9: 7.

to Estimate a Gift—A Wife's Gift of Herself ystematic and Impulsive Giving—The True inciple—Moses' Face Illuminated—A Voluny Offering Asked—Personal Ornaments Conrated—The Work of the Women—Jewels m the Leaders—Special Skill Imparted.

EVERY man according as he purposeth in eart, so let him give; not grudgingly, nor ecessity; for God loveth a cheerful giver." Cor. 9: 7.) God takes no gift from the hand, h is not given from the heart. "Speak the children of Israel, that they bring an offering: of every man that giveth it *ingly with his heart* ye shall take My offer-" (Ex. 25: 2.) A gift is an expression of estimation of a thing. If our heart is in hing, we give to it time, strength, or money. an sets his heart on getting a fortune, and gives to this object time, strength, talent, ing, money: you see his heart is in it, he for it, it absorbs him. The affections of a an are drawn out to the man she loves, and gives all she has and is when she gives her- her name, her property, to be united to This is the kind of giving which becomes nsomed, redeemed, saved, sanctified sinner.

"What is Jesus Worth to Me?"

e question which decides the giving of the d of God. If a man has $5,000 a year, and spends on house rent, furniture, house exes, clothing, schooling, etc., $4,900, and $100 a year directly on the work of God, heart values himself fifty times more than ! O how terrible are those words: "With t judgment ye judge, ye shall be judged; with what measure ye mete, it shall be sured to you again!"

e need to have an established principle ut giving. There are many who give from e impulse, just when some pressing claim ches their heart; but they do not look upon they have and are as God's, and so they do think of inquiring of Him what His mind is o the disposal of their property. When they e put down their names on a subscription it has been because they think it will be ected of them; it is done "grudgingly," and necessity," and they make the task of the ector very hard by always assuring him or that they cannot afford it; and yet, if he e asked to dinner, he might find that they *ld* afford the first salmon which was in season, first asparagus, the first green peas, etc. If spent a few days in the house he might find the finest brand of cigars, expensive dresses, expensive journeys, parties, and amusets, etc., could be afforded. In excuse they urge, "Well, one *must* do as others do." gine a company of the primitive Christians king into such an establishment! A Barnaand his friends, who counted nothing that possessed as his own, and reckoned nothing of any value except as it served his Lord! true principle of giving is, that all we have God's already, and He has a right to all: ow, therefore, our God, we thank Thee, and ise Thy glorious name. But who am I, and at is my people, that we should be able to r so willingly after this sort? For all things ne of Thee, and

Of Thine Own

e we given Thee." (1 Chron. 29: 13, 14.) ne will ask, "What proportion of our income uld we give to the Lord?" It is impossible make a rule. The rule under the law was -tenth, and this may be a good beginning unconverted people and legal Christians; as the heart gets filled with Jesus it is wonful how earthly possessions become an enbrance, and the privilege of giving all to s is more and more seen. Some may say, hat would you do if you were a laboring , earning only about $5 a week, with a family ix children?" I think I would ask the Lord show me what to do under such circumstances. Perhaps such a man could not honestly give more than five or ten cents a week, unless he did some extra work at home in the evening, and earned thereby a little store for the Lord; and yet his whole life might be a gift, his children trained for God, and his house a witness for Him.

"Do you think we ought to give to the Lord's work while we are in debt?" How can you? You would be robbing of one to give to another. If you owe the shoemaker for a pair of boots, and then you give money to the work of God, you are getting credit for loving God's work with the shoemaker's money; it is just the same as though you stole the boots from him, and put them into the collection.

"Provide Things Honest

in the sight of all men." (Rom. 12:17.) Perhaps the shoemaker may love God's work as much as you do, but, while you give *his* money to the collection in your own name, *he* is prevented from giving anything, although the money is rightly his! God put an end to this unrighteousness! "How much can I afford?" is the world's question. "How much will God accept from such as I?" is the question of His humble, loving child.

When Moses came down from the mountain, his face shone with the reflected light of God, and he was obliged to put a veil on his face. He had been communing with God, and his first message to the people was to enforce the observance of the Sabbath day, and then there immediately follows: "This is the thing which the Lord commanded, saying, 'Take ye from among you an offering unto the Lord: whosoever is of a willing heart, let him bring it, an offering of the Lord." There was no compulsion, no constraint, no urging; to give unto the Lord was a wondrous privilege. We have seen in various missions a most unseemly urging upon the people to give, showing that the faith of the worker was in the people, and not in the Lord. "And they came every one whose heart stirred him up"; not one unwilling, grudging grumbler, saying, "I cannot afford it." There were no collectors, the people brought their offerings themselves, "every one whom His spirit made willing, and they brought the Lord's offering to the work of the tabernacle of the congregation, and for all His service, and for the holy garments." They all brought what they had, "bracelets and earrings and rings and tablets, all jewels of gold," showing plainly that they thought God's service of more value than the ornamenting of their persons; these were

Willing Hearted.

Sometimes it costs a young Christian girl something to put a handsome bracelet aside to be sold for the Lord's work. But oh how much more lovely, in God's sight, the hand which gives for the conversion of the heathen, or the work of God in our own land, than the hand which looks like a stand in a jeweller's shop, encumbered with useless rings and bracelets! How much more to God's glory is the ear which hearkens to his voice, than the ear which is dragged out of shape by useless and unnatural earrings. "Every one offered unto the Lord an offering of gold. They gave their best to Him. This is the true principle of giving—God the first, God the best. Then every one who possessed blue, purple, scarlet, fine linen and goat's hair, red skins of rams and badger skins, brought them; not because they had no use for them: perhaps not one of these offerings was lying by useless. Probably the skins formed their covering for the night, and the fine linen was ready to make into clothing when their present clothing was worn out, but God provided that they should not be at a loss, and Moses could bear testimony at the end of their wilderness wanderings: "Thy raiment waxed not old upon thee, neither did thy foot swell, these forty years." (Deut. 8:4.) Silver, brass, and shittim wood were among the offerings; the tals were brought, doubtless, from Egypt, the od perhaps felled in the more fertile parts of wilderness.

Many of the women could give more that was valuable by their work than any other way. "All the women that were wisehearted did spin with their hands, and brought that which they had spun, both of blue, and of purple, and of scarlet, and of fine linen. And all the women whose hearts stirred them up in wisdom spun goat's hair." But what kind of wisdom was this? It was a kind of wisdom which is very rare, but very precious; the wisdom to do the will of God in common things; yet all had its bearing on the direct service of God. There must have been large spinning meetings and sewing meetings there under the tents of the wilderness; and if any passer-by had wanted to know why there was all this industry in the wilderness, the answer would have been, "It is for the Lord." All was freewill work, as well as freewill offering. God provided their food, they were fed with bread from heaven; God kept their clothing from wearing out; all their labor was for Him, and all was voluntary.

The rulers brought the most costly gifts. This is not always the case in our day. They "brought onyx stones, and stones to be set, for the ephod and for the breastplate; and spice, and oil for the light, and for the anointing oil, and for the sweet incense." We can imagine the gladness of heart with which the people, who had been saved through all the plagues of Egypt, brought through the sea, and miraculously maintained, testified their gratitude in the giving of willing offerings, and in their work for the tabernacle. "The children of Israel brought a willing offering unto the Lord, every man and woman whose heart made them willing to bring for all manner of work, which the Lord had commanded to be made by the hand of Moses."

Just as God had called Moses and fitted him to be the leader of the people, so He called Bezaleel to be master of the works in the wilderness. Moses said, "See, the Lord hath called by name Bezaleel, the son of Uri, the son of Hur, of the tribe of Judah; and He hath filled him with the spirit of God, in wisdom and in understanding, and in knowledge, and in all manner of workmanship; and to devise curious works, to work in gold, and in silver, and in brass, and in the cutting of stones, to set them, and in carving of wood, to make any manner of cunning work. And He hath put in his heart that he may teach, both he and Aholiab." What wisdom of God is here! He not only provided for the worship of the tabernacle, and so gave the people an object for work in their wilderness life, but taught them, through these two men, all kinds of trades which should fit them for their possession of the Promised Land; and He imparted dignity to the labor by making it voluntary, so that every day's service was a willing gift to the Lord. If we are altogether His, and live for Him alone, He will make all we give to Him a precious investment which will bring us rich returns.

MRS. M. BAXTER'S WORKS.

COMPLETE IN JESUS.

"Complete in Him."—Col. ii. 10.

Complete in Jesus! O how full
  Of heavenly peace the thought,
Our souls redeemed—our pardon sealed!
  Since Jesus' blood hath bought.

Complete in Jesus! have our souls
  In bitter anguish cried?
'Tis Jesus hears and gives relief,
  'Twas for our souls He died.

Complete in Jesus—blissful thought!
  'Tis ours, whate'er befall;
Our Jesus is our Saviour, Friend,
  Our Life, our Hope—our All.

O let us place our hand in His,
  As on through life we go;
Like little children, trusting all
  To Him, come weal or woe.

Thus shall our trembling hearts be filled
  With love which grows not dim,
If "Jesus only" be our peace
  And this—'Complete in Him.'

—*T. C. Whittemore.*

Lawrence, Mass.

J. E. Jewett, Publisher, 77 Bible House, New York will furnish the above poem in leaflet form at twenty cents per hundred. *A Sample Packet* of 50 leaflets assorted (no two alike), will be sent post-paid, for ten cents. Postage stamps taken.

B. F. Johnson & Co., Publishers, of Richmond Va., have an advertisement in another column that may interest you. Read it.

TWIN BABIES.

This is the heading of a large advertisement appearing in this issue of Christian Herald. Those who read it will no doubt be anxious to know whether it is true that all of the articles named in the list of presents are sent in each box of the "Sweet Home" Soap. Yes, it is true, and the firm who make the offer are reliable and well established. "Sweet Home" Soap is of an extraordinary fine quality, and no one is disappointed who uses it. It bears no comparison with the cheap soaps with which our markets are flooded. The method of selling the soap is a novel one, and readily commends itself to every one, since those who buy it get all the profits usually paid out to traveling salesmen, wholesale and retail grocers, etc. Besides, no payment is asked until the goods are received and have been on trial in the house for thirty days. The soap is delivered right at the door, all freight charges prepaid, and arrangements made so that if one is not satisfied after seeing the presents and using the soap, the box will be taken away without expense or outlay of any kind. A postal-card sent to J. D. Larkin & Co., Buffalo, N. Y., will bring a box on trial. A short time ago a gentleman connected with this paper sent a postal-card requesting a trial case, in answer to which a box of "Sweet Home Soap, containing all of the articles promised, was promptly delivered at his office door, all freight and delivery charges prepaid, thus verifying the promises made in the advertisement. The soap was of excellent quality, and the presents were as described. All you have to do is to send your name and address on a postal-card, ordering a trial box. Address J. D. Larkin & Co., Buffalo, N. Y. They are worthy of your confidence, and when you get the goods you will not be disappointed.

This Journal contains every week a Portrait and Biography of some eminent person; a new Sermon by the Rev. C. H. SPURGEON, of London, and the Rev. Dr. TALMAGE'S latest Sunday morning Sermon; also always a Prophetic Article, and a Summary of Current Events, as well as Stories, Anecdotes, etc.

Vol. XI., No. 29. Office, 63 Bible House, N. Y. THURSDAY, JULY 19, 1888. Annual Subscription, $1.50.

CONTENTS OF THIS NUMBER.

PORTRAITS AND LIVES OF SIX OF THE PRINCIPAL SPEAKERS AT THE INTERNATIONAL MISSIONARY CONFERENCE.
IN GOOD HUMOR WITH OUR LOT. Dr. Talmage's Vacation Sermon.
ANECDOTES RELATED AT RECENT EVANGELISTIC MEETINGS.
THE SEVEN PROPHETIC PARABLES. By G. H. Pember, M. A.
A Child's Crippled Foot Cured—A Sister Missed—A Physician's Angel—Dr. Summers in an Epedemic in Africa—A Fugitive Child-Wife, etc.
PORTRAIT OF DR. TALMAGE AS CHAPLAIN OF THIRTEENTH REGIMENT, N. G. S. N. Y.
DOROTHY'S CHARGE. (With Illustration.)
MOSES: HIS FAITH AND DECISION. A New Sermon by C. H. Spurgeon.
Gems from New Books: A Wise Mother, etc.
PICTURE OF A STREET SCENE IN ALEXANDRIA, EGYPT.
THE EPOCHS OF A LIFE. A New Serial Story by Rev. L. S. Keyser. (Continued.)
THE TABERNACLE. By Mrs. M. Baxter.

REV. H. GRATTAN GUINNESS.

REV. A. T. PIERSON, D.D.

REV. MARMADUKE C. OSBORN.

REV. A. J. GORDON, D.D.

MR. A. H. BAYNES.

SIR JOHN H. KENNAWAY, BART.

Six of the Principal Speakers at the Recent International Missionary Conference.

THE INTERNATIONAL MISSIONARY CONFERENCE.

Six of the Leaders.

THE lively interest taken throughout Christendom in the great International Missionary Conference which has just concluded its sittings in London, has nowhere been more marked than in the United States. The delegates from this country were representative and able men, and their reception and the attention with which their speeches were listened to were eminently gratifying to our people. There is good reason to believe that a new impetus was given by the Conference to missionary enthusiasm, and we may hope that in the future there will through its influence be more union and fraternal feeling in the work among the various societies which are laboring to extend the knowledge of Christ throughout heathendom. The portraits on the preceding page are of six of the men who took a prominent part in the Conference, and who are fairly representative of its various component elements.

REV. H. GRATTAN GUINNESS.

THE founder of the East London Missionary Institute is well known in this country by his personal visits and by his works. He came first into prominent notice by an evangelistic tour he made in 1859 through Great Britain, Ireland, Canada, and the United States. Subsequently, he settled in Bath, England. Being impressed with the inadequacy in number and acquirements of the missionaries for the wide field of heathendom, he advised and was aided to establish a missionary training institute at Harley House, in London. The Institute was opened in March, 1873. It trains men of all evangelical denominations, of all nationalities, and of all classes; and it trains them for all societies, all lands and all spheres of Christian effort. It is as comprehensive as it is possible to be, within the limits of evangelical truth. The students have been of various nationalities; not only English, Scotch, Irish, and American, but French, German, Italian, Spanish, Swedish, Danish, Russian, Bulgarian, Syrian, Egyptian, Kaffir, Negro, Hindoo, Parsee, Koordish, and Jewish, and they have been of various denominations. Those of them who have gone forth as missionaries are now connected with about twenty different societies and associations.

The first Christian mission on the Congo was originated by Mr. and Mrs. Guinness, and was, until recently associated with their work, but has been transferred to the American Baptist Missionary Union.

Mr. and Mrs. Guinness's valuable works on Prophecy, "The Approaching End of the Ages," and "Light for the Last Days," are well known.

THE REV. A. T. PIERSON, D. D.

THE Rev. Dr. Pierson, who was one of the American delegates to the Conference, is the author of a very valuable article entitled "The Apparent Waste of Missions." He was one of the speakers on June 11, on "The Condition and Increase of the Heathen, and their Claims upon the Christian Church." He is pastor of Bethany Presbyterian Church, Philadelphia, and was born in New York City in the year 1837, so that he is now fifty-one year old. At the age of fifteen he was converted to Christ, and became a member of the Presbyterian Church. Having passed through college, and received the usual theological training, he was licensed to preach by the New York Presbytery, and shortly afterwards, at the age of twenty-three, he accepted the charge of the Congregational Church at Binghampton, N. Y. Three years later he returned to the Presbyterian communion, and successively filled pastorates at Waterford, N. Y., Detroit, Mich., Indianapolis, Ind., and Philadelphia, his present charge.

Dr. Pierson's Work in Philadelphia

is chiefly amongst the working classes. The church and Sunday-school hall, each capable of accommodating more than 2,000 persons, cost about $250,000. The fame of Bethany Sunday-school for size and excellence of arrangement has gone over the United States. In the Sunday-school hall a lay college is maintained from September to May, and some effort for the improvement of the people is going on almost every evening. There is an assistant pastor and a large body of earnest unpaid workers. The church is practically under the free and open system, and is generally crowded. And in addition to these agencies evangelistic services are carried on the greater part of the year in a mission tent, and conversions are constantly reported.

Dr. Pierson is an expository preacher, and in this, to a large extent, is the secret of his pulpit power and usefulness. Among the men deeply instructed in the Word of God who gather around Mr. Moody, in his conferences at Northfield, none exceed Dr. Pierson in close acquaintance with the Scriptures, or in clearness and fullness of expository teaching. His studies are confined, almost wholly to the Bible in the original tongues, and if ever a preacher might be described as

"A Man of One Book,"

that preacher is Dr. Pierson. His mind seems saturated with the Word of God, both in the letter and spirit. And busy as he is as a speaker, his pen is nearly as busy. It is said that he is a regular contributor to some thirty religious magazines and papers. In 1886 he published two books—one entitled "Many Infallible Proofs; a Series of Practical Chapters on the Evidences of Christianity, or the Written and Living Word of God"; and the other, "The Crisis of Missions." On the subject of missions Dr. Pierson is intensely in earnest. He is also a firm believer in the Speedy Second Advent of Christ, and at the International Prophetic Conference at Chicago, in November, 1886, gave an able and impressive address on the "Imminent Second Advent of Christ a Motive to Evangelism."

RFV. MARMADUKE C. OSBORN.

MR. OSBORN is one of the foremost men of the Wesleyan Methodist Connexion—popular as preacher and lecturer, uniformly esteemed as a Christian pastor, and possessing, moreover, a share of administrative power which, especially in his own missionary work, has been of signal service to the denomination. He has long been one of the chief officials of the Wesleyan Missionary Society—a society whose fame is worldwide. He was born in 1827, and is therefore sixty-one years old. It was his privilege to be born of godly parents and to be brought up in the nurture and admonition of the Lord. At a very early age he accepted Jesus as his Saviour and Master. In his boyhood he had a notion that he should preach the gospel of Christ, and he could never shake off the impression.

He was educated for the ministry at Richmond College, under the Revs. Thomas Jackson and John Farrar, of whom he always speaks with enthusiastic gratitude. Leaving the theological institution, he was appointed in 1850 to Cambridge, and subsequently to Bradford, York, Liverpool (Pitt Street), Liverpool (Brunswick Street), Bristol, London (City Road), in each circuit remaining the full three years—a striking testimony to uniform good feeling between pastor and people. On the platform and in the pulpit he speedily made his mark. His ministrations were largely in request throughout the whole Wesleyan Connexion, and the high estimation entertained concerning him was displayed in his appointment to visit and report on the Wesleyan Missions in the West Indies.

Not only is he an eloquent minister and a popular speaker, but also an able administrator, as he has proved by the valuable services he has rendered to the Missionary Society in his official capacity. Missionary service requires quenchless zeal as well as tact, skill, and general knowledge of human nature. The highest order of man is required for a missionary, and this fact has been all along strongly impressed on the church by Mr. Osborn.

Missionary enterprise may be said to have been the work of Mr. Osborn's life-time. To this he has devoted all his energies, all his abilities, all his heart and soul, and he has lived to see some of the fruits of his labors. He has taken an active part in the International Missionary Conference.

REV. A. J. GORDON, D. D.

ADONIRAM JUDSON GORDON, the pastor of the Clarendon Street Baptist Church, Boston, Massachusetts, is well known to our readers. He was one of the most honored members of the American delegation. He was born at New Hampton, on April 19, 1836, and is therefore now fifty-two years of age. His father was a deacon eminent for his piety, who for many years had been an enthusiastic supporter of foreign missionary work, and an ardent admirer of the devoted men who leave home and country to preach the Gospel of Christ to those who sit in heathen darkness. One heroic man especially had won his respect, the pioneer American missionary, Adoniram Judson, "the apostle of Burmah." To him he tendered a tribute of homage by naming his infant child after him, and there is reason to believe that the pious father offered many prayers that he might prove worthy of the name given to him. It is certain that in his religious life and work, and notably in his interest in foreign missionary work, Dr. A. J. Gordon has been and is a living testimony of the power and influence of early training, and of the results of parental prayers.

He was Converted to Christ

at the age of sixteen, and united with the church at New Hampton. Almost immediately afterwards he was strongly influenced to become a preacher of the gospel. He entered a preparatory school with the distinct object of fitting himself for a theological training in college. Thence he went to Brown University, where he entered with zest, even while a student, into active Christian work, teaching in the Sabbath-school and helping in missions in the neighborhood around.

In 1860, at the age of twenty-four, Mr. Gordon *graduated*. He then proceeded to Newton Theological Seminary, for a more special course of training for ministerial and pastoral work. Before the completion of his studies there, he had already entered upon his life's labor, by accepting, at the earnest solicitation of the people of Jamaica Plain, Mass., the office of pastor of the Baptist church in that place. His *ordination* took place in June, 1863, and until the year 1869 Dr. Gordon continued there. He then received a call from Boston, to become the minister of the Clarendon Street Baptist Church in that city. He accepted the call, and went to his new sphere with the expectation of doing vigorous and energetic work. He was not disappointed in that expectation, nor in the anticipated results. A new edifice was erected, which was soon filled with worshippers. Dr. Gordon is an

Earnest Student of Prophecy,

and a firm believer in the Premillennial Advent of Christ. He took a prominent part in the Prophetic Conference at New York in 1878, and in that at Chicago in 1886. As an author he has become favorably known to English-speaking Christians the world over. Among his best known works are "In Christ," "Grace and Glory," "Congregational Worship," "The Ministry of Healing" and "Two-fold Life."

ALFRED HENRY BAYNES, ESQ.

The name of Alfred Henry Baynes is a familiar name among British Baptists, who know him in many honorable connections, but chiefly as Secretary of their Missionary Society. His father was the Rev. Joseph Baynes, who was the pastor of the Baptist Church at Wellington, Somersetshire, for the long period of upwards of forty years. Alfred Henry was born at Wellington in 1838, so that he is just now fifty years of age. He was educated at Devonshire College, Bath. At first it was intended that he should enter the medical profession, but that project was abandoned on account of ill-health. Subsequently he became associated with several of the public undertakings of Messrs. Peto, Brassey, and Betts, the well-known railway and building contractors. In 1860, at the request of Sir Morton Peto, he undertook temporarily the finances of the Baptist Missionary Society. What was intended to be but a very temporary engagement has continued now twenty-eight years and promises to continue for years to come.

In 1881, at the request of the society, Mr. Baynes visited India and Ceylon, and inspected all the Baptist Mission Stations in that quarter of the globe. In connection with the missionary society Mr. Baynes has made several pleasant trips to Italy, which perhaps may be regarded as the most important part of the European field occupied by the society. He has also visited Belgium, and conducted negotiations in connection with the Baptist Congo mission with the King of the Belgians. In December, 1884, Mr. Baynes visited Berlin in connection with the sittings of the West African and Congo Conference, which met in that city. He was also charged to conduct negotiations relating to the annexation by Germany of the Cameroons and Bimbia on the West Coast of Africa, and the interests and property of the Mission at various stations in these districts. These negotiations were conducted with the German Chancellor and the authorities of the German Foreign Office, and were brought to as satisfactory a conclusion as was possible under the circumstances. He was one of the Executive Committee of the International Missionary Conference.

SIR JOHN H. KENNAWAY, BART., M. P.

For seventy years the name of Kennaway has been prominent in the Missionary Society of the Protestant Episcopal Church of England. His grandfather Sir John Kennaway was the first president of the Devon and Exeter auxiliary, which was founded in 1816; the next baronet, also Sir John, held the same office for many years; and the Sir John of to-day succeeded to it in the year 1872.

Sir John was born at Escot, Ottery St. Mary, Devonshire, in 1837, and is a little over fifty years of age. He was educated at Harrow, proceeding thence in due course to Balliol College, Oxford, where he took first-class honors in Law and History. He was called to the Bar at the Inner Temple in 1864. He has represented the Eastern Division of the county of Devon in Parliament since April 1870. From a very early period he evidenced deep sympathy with missionary and philanthropic enterprises.

He presided at a largely attended meeting in connection with the International Conference, on June 11, when the subject for consideration was the promotion of missionary effort in China. He said that though Britain had for a long time stood alone in that field of labor, America was now her rival there. He pointed out how minor differences of creed or form disappear in the face of missionary work, just as a disagreement between two naval officers who served under Nelson was speedily reconciled by Nelson's command in the presence of the enemy. He expressed pleasure at seeing American friends present, as well as some from France and Germany. He claimed that missions had been successful, and their indirect benefits great. Sir John described the considerable progress of the work of late, not only in China, with which land that meeting was concerned, but bade his hearers not forget the earlier labors of Morrison and others. The eleven months of seed-sowing in China were well advanced, and who could say how much the Lord of the harvest would give them in the remaining months of harvest?

ANECDOTES RELATED AT RECENT EVANGELISTIC MEETINGS.

Red Eyes and Green Spectacles. Mr. McCaul, of Canada, said: "In England, some time ago, a Quaker friend of mine was travelling through the country. He stopped at a roadside inn, and while he sat there, a gentleman, a rural land-owner in the district, came in and ordered a glass of liquor. When the gentleman turned round towards him my friend noticed that he had very red eyes and wore large green spectacles. Whether or not there was something special in the Quaker's gaze I do not know, but the gentleman seemed very uneasy about it, and remarked, as he made his way to a seat, 'I have very bad eyes and have required to wear glasses for a long time, though they do not seem to do me much good.' 'My friend,' replied the Quaker, 'I will tell thee what I think. *If thou wearest spectacles on thy mouth, thine eyes will soon improve.*' Strong drink does not get credit for half the evil it does. If it takes away the sight, we blame study; if it ruins business, we blame the bad times; if it ruin a man's Christian life, we blame the bad example of professing Christians. But it is drink, the fiery fiend, that every year destroys its thousands of victims."

Happy Consequences of a Shower.—W. F. Green, said: "I remember, some twenty years ago, a lady was going home from a love-feast on Sunday afternoon, and was driven by a passing shower to take refuge in a court. A working man saw her and invited her into his house. She went in; her heart was full of the love of God, and she began to speak to this man about the Saviour. She found his wife was ill. 'May I see her?' she asked. 'Certainly,' he replied, and she went up-stairs, prayed with the woman, came down again, continued her conversation with the man, and obtained from him a promise to come to the house of God. 'Well,' she said, 'I will call for you.' 'Never mind that,' he said, 'I will be there.' She, however, did call for him, and looked after him for about a week; the result was that he eventually found peace, and became one of the most successful sick-visitors and one of the happiest Christians I ever met with in my life. It was quite a pleasure to meet him, for his face used to shine like an angel's. There is a bit of work done—done casually, just by the wayside."

Devils Adjured to Enter Eggs.—Rev. Silvester Whitehead related at the annual meeting of a missionary society that "In Canton, a father brought his son to the Taouist priest, saying that he was possessed of the devil. They consulted the idol, and then they announced that in the body of the child there were no fewer than five devils, intimating that for a consideration *in silver* they could expel them all. They placed the boy in front of the deity, and they placed on the ground at his feet five eggs, into which they adjured the devils to enter. Having done this a vase was placed over the eggs, while the high priest sounded a loud blast upon a horn. It was then lifted, and it was found that the eggs were no longer on the ground, but by act of legerdemain had been transferred to the vase. This, of course, was regarded as an undoubted proof that the devils had entered into the eggs. They then drew blood from an incision in the boy's arm, and dipping the seal of the temple into the blood, stamped the name of the deity upon his forehead, wrists, neck, and back. He had been suffering all the while from nothing but fever and ague. It is in this way that the people are deluded, impoverished, and priest-ridden."

A Victim of Drinking and Gambling Rescued. Richard Weaver said: "I had been preaching in a certain town for some days, when, one morning, two little barefooted boys came to the house at which I was staying. They were brought into the room in which I was sitting, and coming up to me the elder said, 'Sir, we were at your meeting last night, and we heard you say that God loved every one; now, we have an awful wicked father; do you think God would save *him?*' At the boys' request a friend and I accompanied them to their miserable home. We were guided by the boys, who kept saying to each other, 'If God saves father won't we be happy!'" We reached their home, where we found their broken-hearted mother. As I looked at her I recognized a former acquaintance. I had known her when she was young and happy in her father's house. By-and-by her husband came in, a poor, drunken-looking fellow. 'What!' I exclaimed, for I recognized him also. 'My old master's son! Is it possible he can have come to this?' 'You see,' said the man, 'to what drinking and gambling have brought me.' Here one of the little fellows whispered to me, 'Pray for father.' I knelt at once and the dear lad prayed, 'Oh God, you love my father, save him for Jesus' sake.' The father dropped upon his knees beside us, and cried, 'Oh God, be merciful to me a sinner.' And soon he found peaee in Christ. He turned to his wife, and said, 'Oh, Mary, can you ever forgive me?' She was only too willing to do so, and I left them happy with each other in Christ."

The Drunkard and His Dead Wife. "When I was eight years of age, I heard a story from the late Mr. John B. Gough, which greatly affected me, and caused me, even at that early age, to pledge myself as a total abstainer. The great orator told in glowing terms the scenes that had been enacted in his own home, and how at last his base conduct and brutality had brought his wife to her death-bed. Even then her thoughts were of her husband, and she got him to promise that never again would he touch intoxicating liquor. Her words were, 'Now John, you will never touch strong drink again, never until I give it to you with my own hands.' He promised. She thought she had completely won his heart, and died contentedly. Her illness had sobered him, but when she was gone, the craving came back to him with redoubled force. Vainly he fought against it, he *must* have liquor. But how could he have it, and still keep his promise to his dead wife. He left the house, and quickly returned with a bottle of rum. He poured some into a glass, and carrying it over to where the dead body of his wife lay, he knelt, and lifting the thin, lifeless hand, *he forced the cold fingers round the glass, and lifted both her hand and it to his mouth* and drank the contents of the glass; nor was he content with one glass, but he drank until he fell helplessly intoxicated beside the corpse of his wife. That is what a man will do for drink. Oh, you moderate drinkers, who see no evil in a glass, tamper not with it, for it is full of subtlety and venom!"

How the Leak Was Stopped. "Some Few years ago, a sailing vessel was caught in a great storm; for some time it successfully combated the elements, but the strain upon all parts was excessive; and every moment the crew feared that the vessel would spring a leak. At last their fear was realized. The vessle *was* leaking. A search was made, and the leak was discovered; it was just at the water-line, but there was no way to get at it except over the side. Would any one venture? Would any face almost certain death in the chance of saving his comrades? No one could be *ordered* to such a duty. Volunteers were called for. Two or three men stepped forward, but one of them said, 'No, mates, let me go; I am a Christian, and better prepared to die than any of you. Let me go.' The other men looked at him in surprise, but silently acquiesced. He was lowered over the side, on a thin scaffolding. The waves broke over him, and every instant threatened to carry him into the raging waters, but He who stilled the tempest was with him, and, strong in His strength, the sailor was enabled to nail a board over the leak, and the ship was saved. The heroic sailor was drawn safely up, and soon afterwards gave himself entirely to the work of his Master, and to-day is an active missionary among the sailors. Nor was his testimony in the hour of peril without effect upon his mates. They saw that Christianity, instead of lessening, increased and ennobled manhood, and the event was blessed to the souls of some of them."

IN GOOD HUMOR WITH OUR LOT.

Dr. Talmage's Vacation Sermon.

"Be content with such things as ye have." Heb. 13: 5.

People who Get no Vacation—Common-Sense View of Social Differences—Reasons for Contentment—I.—The Poorest have the Indispensables of Life—The Originals of Famous Pictures—II.—Happiness not Dependent on Externals—A Study of Faces in Wall Street—A Happy Apple-woman—A Shipwrecked Woman's Song—III.—All Conditions Transitory—Kings Turned into Guano—The Sceptres Transferred—The Roll-Call of the Great—IV. God Knows what is Best—The Cry of the Threshed Wheat—V. The Lord will Provide—VI. A Grand Indemnity—A Glorious Vacation.

If I should ask some one, "Where is Brooklyn, to-day?" he would say, "At Brighton Beach, or East Hampton, or Shelter Island." "Where is New York. to-day?" "At Long Branch." "Where Philadelphia?" "Cape May." "Where is Boston?" "At Martha's Vineyard." "Where is Virginia?" "At the Sulphur Springs." "Where the great multitude from all parts of the land?" "At Saratoga," the modern Bethesda, where the angel of health is ever stirring the waters. But, my friends, the largest multitude are at home, detained by business or circumstances. Among them all newspaper men, the hardest worked and the least compensated; city railroad employees, and ferry masters, and the police, and the tens of thousands of clerks and merchants waiting for their turn of absence, and households with an invalid who cannot be moved, and others hindered by

Stringent Circumstances,

and the great multitude of well-to-do people who stay at home because they like home better than any other place, refusing to go away simply because it is the fashion to go. When the express wagon, with its mountain of trunks, directed to the Catskills or Niagara, goes through the streets, we stand at our window envious and impatient, and wonder why we cannot go as well as others. Fools that we are, as though one could not be as happy at home as anywhere else! Our grandfathers and grandmothers had as good a time as we have, long before the first spring was bored at Saratoga, or the first deer shot in the Adirondacks. They made their wedding-tour to the next farmhouse, or, living in New York, they celebrated the event by an extra walk on the Battery.

Now, the genuine American is not happy until he is going somewhere, and the passion is so great that there are Christian people, with their families, detained in the city, who come not to the house of God, trying to give people the idea that they are out of town, leaving the door-plate unscoured for the same reason, and for two months keeping the front shutters closed while they sit in the back part of the house, the thermometer at ninety! My friends, if it is best for us to go, let us go and be happy. If it is best for us to stay at home, let us stay at home and be happy. There is a great deal of

Good Common Sense

in Paul's advice to the Hebrews: "Be content with such things as ye have." To be content is to be in good humor with our circumstances, not picking a quarrel with our obscurity, or our poverty, or our social position. There are four or five grand reasons why we should be content with such things as we have.

The first reason that I mention as leading to this spirit, advised in the text, is the consideration that *the poorest of us have all that is indispensable* in life. We make great ado about our hardships, but how little we talk of our blessings. Health of body, which is given in largest quantity to those who have never been petted and fondled, and spoiled by fortune, we take as a matter of course. Rather have this luxury, and have it alone, than, without it, look out of a palace window upon parks of deer stalking between fountains and statuary. These people sleep sounder on a straw mattress than fashionable invalids on a couch of ivory and eagles' down. The dinner of herbs tastes better to the appetite sharpened on a woodman's axe or a reaper's scythe, than wealthy indigestion experiences seated at a table covered with partridge and venison and pineapple. *The grandest luxury God ever gave* a man is health. He who trades that off for all the palaces of the earth is infinitely cheated. We look back at the glory of the last Napoleon, but who would have taken his Versailles, and his Tuilleries, if with them we had to take his gout?

"Oh," says some one, "it isn't the grosser pleasures I covet, but it is the gratification of an artistic and intellectual taste." Why,

You Have the Original

from which these pictures are copied. What is a sunset on a wall compared with a sunset hung in loops of fire on the heavens? What is a cascade, silent on a canvas, compared to a cascade that makes the mountain tremble, its spray ascending like the departed spirit of the water slain on the rocks? Oh, there is a great deal of hollow affectation about a fondness for pictures on the part of those who never appreciate the original from which the pictures are taken. As though a parent should have no regard for his child, but go into ecstasies over its photograph. Bless the Lord to-day, O man! O woman! that though you may be shut out from the works of a Church, a Bierstadt, a Rubens, and a Raphael, you still have free access to a gallery grander than the Louvre, or the Luxemburg, or the Vatican—the royal gallery of the noonday heavens, the King's gallery of the midnight sky.

Another consideration leading us to a spirit of contentment, is the fact that our *happiness is not dependent upon outward circumstances.* You see people happy and miserable amid all circumstances. In a family where the last loaf is on the table, and the last stick of wood on the fire, you sometimes find a cheerful confidence in God; while in a very fine place, you will see and hear discord sounding her war-whoop, and hospitality freezing to death in a cheerless parlor. I stopped one day on Broadway, at the head of Wall Street, at the foot of Trinity Church, to see who seemed the happiest people passing. I judged, from their looks,

The Happiest People

were not those who went down into Wall Street, for they had on their brow the anxiety of the dollar they expected to make; nor the people who came out of Wall Street, for they had on their brow the anxiety of the dollar they had lost; nor the people who swept by in splendid equipage, for they met a carriage that was finer than theirs. The happiest person in all that crowd, judging from the countenance, was the woman who sat at the apple-stand, knitting. I believe real happiness oftener looks out of the window of an humble home, than through the opera-glass of the gilded box of a theatre.

I find Nero growling on a throne. I find Paul singing in a dungeon. I find King Ahab going to bed at noon, through melancholy, while near by is Naboth contented in the possession of a vineyard. Haman, prime minister of Persia, frets himself almost to death because a poor Jew will not tip his hat; and Ahithophel, one of the greatest lawyers of Bible times, through fear of dying, hangs himself. The wealthiest man, forty years ago, in New York, when congratulated over his large estate, replied, "Ah, you don't know how much trouble I have in taking care of it!" Byron declared, in his last hours, that he had never seen more than twelve happy days in all his life. I do not believe that he had seen twelve minutes of thorough satisfaction. Napoleon I. said, "I turn with disgust from the cowardice and selfishness of man. I hold life a horror; death is repose. What I have suffered the last twenty days is beyond human comprehension." While, on the other hand, to show

How One may be Happy

amid the most disadvantageous circumstances, just after the *Ocean Monarch* had been wrecked in the English Channel, a steamer was cruising along in the darkness, when the captain heard a song, a sweet song, coming over the water, and he bore down toward that voice, and found it was a Christian woman on a plank of the wrecked steamer, singing to the tune of St. Martins:

"Jesus, lover of my soul,
Let me to Thy bosom fly,
While the billows near me roll,
While the tempest still is high."

The heart right toward God and man, we are happy. The heart wrong toward God and man, we are unhappy.

Another reason why we should come to this spirit inculcated in the text, is the fact that all the *differences of earthly condition are transitory.* The houses you build, the land you culture, the places in which you barter, are soon to go into other hands. However hard you may have it now, if you are a Christian

The Scene will Soon End.

Pain, trial, persecution, never knock at the door of the grave. A coffin made out of pine boards is just as good a resting-place as one made out of silver-mounted mahogany or rosewood. Go down among the resting-places of the dead, and you will find that though people there had a great difference of worldly circumstances, now they are all alike unconscious. The hand that greeted the senator, and the president, and the king, is still as the hand that hardened on the mechanic's hammer, or the manufacturer's wheel. It does not make any difference now, whether there is a plain stone above them, from which the traveller pulls aside the weeds to read the name, or a tall shaft springing into the heavens as though to tell their virtues to the skies.

In That Silent Land

there are no titles for great men, and there are no rumblings of chariot-wheels, and there is never heard the foot of the dance. The Egyptian guano which is thrown on the fields in the East for the enrichment of the soil, is the dust raked out from the sepulchres of kings and lords and mighty men. O the chagrin of those men if they had ever known that in the after ages of the world they would have been called Egyptian guano!

Of how much worth now is the crown of Cæsar? Who bids for it? Who cares now anything about the Amphitryronic Council or the laws of Lycurgus? Who trembles now because Xerxes crossed the Hellespont on a bridge of boats? Who fears because Nebuchadnezzar thunders at the gates of Jerusalem? Who cares now whether or not Cleopatra marries Antony? Who crouches before Ferdinand, or Boniface, or Alaric? Can Cromwell dissolve the English Parliament now? Is William Prince of Orange, king of the Netherlands? No; no! However much Elizabeth may love the Russian crown, she must pass it to Peter, and Peter to Catherine, and Catherine to Paul, and Paul to Alexander, and Alexander to Nicholas. Leopold puts the German sceptre into the hand of Joseph, and Philip comes down off the Spanish throne to let Ferdinand go on. House of Aragon, house of Hapsburg, house of Stuart, house of Bourbon, quarrelling about everything else, but agreeing in this: "The fashion of this world passeth away." But have all these dignitaries gone? Can they not be called back? I have been to assemblages where I have heard the roll called, and many distinguished men have answered. If I should

Call the Roll

to-day of some of those mighty ones who have gone, I wonder if they would not answer. I will call the roll. I will call the roll of the kings first: Alfred the Great! William the Conqueror! Frederick II.! Louis XVI.! No answer. I will call the roll of the poets: Robert Southey! Thomas Campbell! John Keats! George Crabbe! Robert Burns! No answer. I will call the roll of artists: Michael Angelo! Paul Veronese! William Turner! Christopher Wren! No answer. Eyes closed. Ears deaf. Lips silent. Hands palsied. Sceptre, pencil, pen, sword, put down forever. Why should we struggle for such baubles!

Another reason why we should culture this

spirit of cheerfulness is the fact that *God knows what is best* for His creatures. You know what is best for your child. He thinks you are not as liberal with him as you ought to be. He criticises your discipline, but you look over the whole field, and you, loving that child, do what in your deliberate judgment is best for him. Now, God is the best of fathers. Sometimes His children think that He is hard on them, and that He is not as liberal with them as He might be. But children do not know as much as a father. I can tell you why you are not affluent, and

Why You have not been Successful.

It is because you cannot stand the temptation. If your path had been smooth, you would have depended upon your own surefootedness; but God roughened that path, so you have to take hold of His hand. If the weather had been mild, you would have loitered along the water-courses; but at the first howl of the storm you quickened your pace heavenward, and wrapped around you the robe of a Saviour's righteousness.

"What have I done?" says the wheat-sheaf to the farmer, "what have I done, that you beat me so hard with your flail?" The farmer makes no answer, but the rake takes off the straw, and the mill blows the chaff to the wind, and the golden grain falls down at the foot of the windmill. After awhile, the straw looking down from the mow upon the golden grain banked up on either side the floor understands why the farmer beat the wheat-sheaf with the flail.

Who are those before the throne? The answer came: "These are they who, out of great ribulation, had their robes washed and made white in the blood of the Lamb." Would God hat we could understand that our trials are

The Very Best Thing

or us. If we had an appreciation of that truth, hen we should know why it was that John oyra, the martyr, in the very midst of the lame, reached down and picked up one of the aggots that was consuming him, and kissed it, nd said, "Blessed be God for the time when was born for this preferment!" They who uffer with Him on earth, shall be glorified with Him in heaven. Be content, then, with such hings as you have.

Another consideration leading us to the spirt of the text, is the assurance that *the Lord will rovide* somehow. Will He who holds the waer in the hollow of His hand allow His chilren to die of thirst? Will He who owns the ttle on a thousand hills, and all the earth's uxuriance of grain and fruit, allow His children o starve? Go out to-morrow morning at five 'clock, into the woods, and hear the birds hant. They have had no breakfast, they know ot where they will dine, they have no idea here they will sup; but hear the birds chant t five o'clock in the morning. "Behold the owls of the air: for they sow not, neither do hey reap, nor gather into barns, yet your heavnly Father feedeth them. Are you not much etter than they?"

Seven thousand people, in Christ's time, went nto the desert. They were the most

Improvident People

ever heard of. They deserved to starve. They ight have taken food enough to last them ntil they got back. Nothing did they take. A d, who had more wit than all of them put toether, asked his mother that morning for some aves of bread and some fishes. They were ut into his satchel. He went out into the desrt. From this provision the seven thousand ere fed, and the more they ate the larger the aves grew, until the provision that the boy rought in one satchel was multiplied so he ould not have carried the fragments home in x satchels. "Oh," you say, "times have hanged, and the day of miracles has gone." I eply that, what God did then by miracle, He oes now in some other way, and by natural ws. "I have been young" said David, "and ow am I old; yet have I never seen the rightous forsaken, nor his seed begging bread." It high time that you people who are fretting bout worldly circumstances, and who are fearing that you are coming to want, understood that the oath of the Eternal God is involved in the fact that you are to have enough to eat and to wear.

Again: I remark that the religion of Jesus is

The Grandest Influence

to make a man contented. Indemnity against all financial and spiritual harm! It calms the spirit, dwindles the earth into insignificance, and swallows up the soul with the thought of heaven. O ye who have been going about from place to place, expecting to find in change of circumstances something to give solace to the spirit, I commend you this morning to the warm-hearted, earnest, practical, common-sense religion of the Lord Jesus Christ. "There is no peace, saith my God, for the wicked," and as long as you continue in your sin, you will be miserable. Come to Christ. Make Him your portion and start for heaven, and you will be a happy man—you will be a happy woman.

Yet, my friends, notwithstanding all these inducements to a spirit of contentment, I have to tell you this morning the human race is divided into two classes—those who ɪcold, and those who get scolded. The carpenter wants to be anything but a carpenter, and the mason anything but a mason, and the banker anything but a banker, and the lawyer anything but a lawyer, and the minister anything but a minister, and everybody would be happy if he were only somebody else. The anemone wants to be a sunflower, and the apple orchards throw down their blossoms because they are not tall cedars, and the scow wants to be a schooner, and the sloop would like to be a seventy-four pounder, and parents have the worst children that ever were, and everybody has the greatest misfortune, and everything is upside down, or going to be. Ah, my friends, you never make any advance through such a spirit as that.

You Cannot Fret Yourself Up;

you may fret yourself down. Amid all this grating of tones I strike this string of the Gospel harp: "Godliness with contentment is great gain. We brought nothing into the world, and it is very certain we can carry nothing out; having food and raiment, let us therewith be content."

Let us all remember, if we are Christians, that we are going after awhile, whatever be our circumstances now, to have

A Glorious Vacation.

As in summer we put off our garments, and go down into the cool sea to bathe, so we will put off these garments of flesh, and step into the cool Jordan. We will look around for some place to lay down our weariness, and the trees will say: "Come and rest under our shadow;" and the earth will say: "Come and sleep in my bosom;" and the winds will say: "Hush! while I sing thee a cradle hymn"; and while six strong men carry us out to our last resting-place, and ashes come to ashes, and dust to dust, we will see two scarred feet standing amid the broken soil, and a lacerated brow bending over the open grave, while a voice, tender with all-affection, and mighty with all-omnipotence, will declare: "I am the Resurrection and the Life; he that believeth in Me, though he were dead, yet shall he live." Comfort one another with these words.

REV. T. DE WITT TALMAGE, D. D.

Chaplain of the Thirteenth Regiment, N.G.S.N.Y.

(*See portrait on page 460.*)

THE familiar face of Dr. Talmage appears in a new setting in the picture inserted in this number of THE CHRISTIAN HERALD. It is engraved from a photograph recently taken of the popular preacher in his uniform. As previously announced in these columns, the famous Thirteenth Regiment, which is Brooklyn's crack corps, decided last spring to invite Dr. Talmage to fill the post of regimental chaplain, made vacant by the death of Rev. Henry Ward Beecher. Dr. Talmage accepted, and has been formally installed.

The ceremony of inducting the new chaplain was the occasion of a gala night at the Hanson Place Armory. Both the galleries were filled by ladies and gentlemen who were interested in the evening's entertainment, and the main drill-room had to be called into requisition to make room for the large number of people present. The reviewing stand was tastefully decorated, and the band, under the leadership of W. C. Bowen, gave a concert for half an hour preceding the military programme. The regiment turned out ten companies of sixteen files front, and, under command of Colonel Austen, were put through a battalion drill, embracing manœuvres in company, battalion, and division movements. After the drill, which occupied three-quarters of an hour, the battalion was dismissed, and shortly thereafter reformed for dress parade. At this parade there were on the floor: The regiment, four hundred strong; the veteran corps, thirty-five strong, and the new company from the Brooklyn Tabernacle, forty-two strong.

Swearing the Chaplain.

After the men had been brought to parade rest, Colonel Austen escorted Dr. Talmage to the front, and said: "It is with great pleasure I welcome you as chaplain and captain of the soldiers of this regiment. May the teachings you give us enable us to take higher rank in the armies of the future. While, in accepting the command, you sacrifice some things, yet we hope to show you and the people of Brooklyn that we will discharge our duties as becomes the members of the Thirteenth Regiment."

Then Colonel Austen swore in Dr. Talmage as chaplain, after which he presented him with his commission.

In accepting the commission, Chaplain Talmage said: "Colonel Austen, men of the Thirteenth Regiment, and all their friends here gathered—I take this commission in my hand with two feelings—an appreciation of the honor done me, and a realization of the new duties that with it will roll upon my already busy life. Why do I accept it? Because I like to be intimately associated with public-spirited men, and believe it is another door of useful opportunity opened. I want to do my humble part toward hastening the time when Brooklyn, which is commonly called the best city of the Union, shall be recognized as second to none.

The First Time He Took the Oath.

"But, oh, the contrast between the first and second taking of the oath of office as chaplain! On the first occasion the North and South were in rage of battle, our institutions seemed going into eternal dismemberment, and in the barns and farm-houses around Sharpsburg and Hagerstown, all turned into hospitals, I saw scenes of suffering that I will not try to recount now. All that compared with the brilliant and lovely spectacle to-night, when the land is full of peace, and there is no prospect that any of these soldiers will ever be called to draw the sword or shoulder the musket in the defence of our institutions. And the occasion is adorned by the presence of womanhood, without whom life would not be worth living."

Then Chaplain Talmage introduced the new company, which he hoped would in a short time be one of the strongest in the regiment.

After the chaplain had finished his address, he was presented by Colonel Austen to the field and staff officers, and then the dress parade took place. Chaplain Talmage, however, failed to follow the officers when the parade was dismissed, and upon this being remarked, said that if there were any mistakes in drilling, he had not made any, for he took care to drop out before any drill took place.

A CHILD'S CRIPPLED FOOT CURED.

A REMARKABLE case of Divine Healing is related by Mrs. Brodie, of British Honduras, in this month's number of *Thy Healer*.* She says: "I have a precious testimony from Liverpool, which I have been asked to give out. When God took me there some weeks ago, I went to the house of a woman that had a little fellow two or three years of age under her care. He was not well, and she was anxious, because he was not her own, and she had promised, in case of anything coming to this child, she would have a doctor immediately, though she believes in the Lord's Healing. She was much troubled, and I asked her what was the matter. She said that a week before I got there, the little fellow began to limp and said that his foot hurt him. She had the day before called in a medical man and he had said the tendons were getting diseased, and this had increased her anxiety. I said, 'Let us put him into the Lord's hands,' and we did so. I went to the little fellow's cot and prayed for him. I have since received this letter, in which she says: 'My heart is full of praise to Him who loved us, and gave Himself for us. On Friday morning my dear little "Sonnie" got up on the sofa on which he had been sitting, and said: "Sonnie can walk." Kate, who was with him, said: "No, darling, you must sit still;" but in a moment he was on the floor, standing quite straight, with his heel down on the ground, and, before he could be prevented, he *ran* along the hall to tell "mamma," "Sonnie quite better.' Praise His holy Name, He *has* glorified His Name in this case. When the doctor called in the afternoon, the dear child ran to meet him. I felt I must give my Lord *all* the honor; so I told him of your visit and of having asked the Lord to heal him. The dear man had a long talk with me about means, about our Lord using the clay; so I said: "Well, sir, I do praise Him for what He has done." "So do I," he said, "for I can assure you I came this afternoon with great misgivings." "Bless the Lord, O my soul, and all that is within me, bless His holy Name!'"

DR. SUMMERS IN AN EPIDEMIC.

Two interesting letters have been sent home by Dr. W. R. Summers, from the Congo. His many friends in New York will be concerned to learn that he has been suffering from pleurisy and septic fever. At the time of writing, January 3, 1888, he was recovering after five weeks' suffering. In the course of his letter he refers to an epidemic of small-pox, which carried off a native king and led to barbarous cruelty, in accordance with African rites in such cases. He says: "Lieutenant Le Marinel, of the Belgian service, in the Congo Free State, has returned from Nyangwe, his immense caravan burdened by about eight hundred slaves, bought either by the Bashilange tribes or by the Angola carriers, who were tacitly allowed to do this business in return for the poor payment they received. Of course, with such a caravan, the lieutenant could not stop the traffic, if he had tried. His return journey was made quickly, but hundreds died of small-pox, or of great ulcers, on the road, and many of the slaves fled. When the caravan arrived here it was in a miserable condition, as, in addition to sickness, they had had much hunger on the road. No doubt most would have died of small-pox had not Lieutenant Le Marinel acted with praiseworthy caution, in making a second caravan of small-pox cases, and ordering this to remain a good distance behind the others. *I had much work with these people.* A small-pox reservation was made on the other side of the river Lulua, and all new cases were immediately sent there. Chinguengue, the king second in importance, was attacked by the pest, and refused to cross the river, and in a few days died. His body was placed on a bedstead, and five slaves built a mud and wattle house over it. *His principal wife was then beaten to death by sticks*, and her body cast into the Lulua, while the five slaves were beheaded, and their remains left to guard the body of Chinguengue. Chinguengue was by far the most intelligent man of the Bashilange, and his death was felt by all."

* *Thy Healer and Faith Witness*, a monthly Magazine, edited by Mrs. M. Baxter, contains original articles on Holiness and Healing, Authentic Testimonies of Divine Healing, and Items of Intelligence from Heathen Lands where Missionaries are laboring in faith, soliciting no help from man, but relying solely on God for support. Annual Subscription, 75 cents, may be sent to the Manager of CHRISTIAN HERALD, 63 Bible House, New York.

A PHYSICIAN'S ANGEL.

THE writer of the Epistle to the Hebrews in enjoining hospitality to strangers, reminds his readers (Heb. 13: 2) for their encouragement that "*some have entertained angels unawares.*" There are some, too, whose kindness to the poor and afflicted have, much to their own surprise, led to rich reward. An illustration is furnished by the life of Sir Andrew Clark, who was recently elected President of the Royal College of Physicians in England and who has probably the largest and most lucrative practice in London. It appears that he owes the first step into public notice, which is always the most difficult for a young physician, to the persistency of an old pauper woman in a charity hospital, to whose case he gave gratuitously the most constant thought and attention. The old woman was deeply grateful and was greatly impressed by his skill and kindness. One day Mrs. Gladstone visited the hospital where she lay, accompanied by her son Herbert, then a little boy and in very delicate health. The poor woman reciprocated Mrs. Gladstone's kindly interest in her by a keen anxiety about the youthful Herbert, and begged Mrs. Gladstone so persistently to let her doctor see the boy that at last she won her point. "But who is your doctor?" asked Mrs. Gladstone. "Young Mr. Clark," replied the woman. And so it came about that "young Mr. Clark" obtained an introduction to the Gladstone family, treated his young patient with success, and at once became famous among the London aristocracy. The now celebrated and wealthy physician himself related the story at a meeting of the organizers of the Hospital Sunday Fund in the Mansion House, London.

A FUGITIVE CHILD-WIFE.

IN a letter from India which Miss Gardner sends to the *Missionary Link*, she tells a pathetic story of a fugitive girl who, with her mother, is now under the care of the missionaries in Calcutta. The girl, whose name is Ahmadi, was married according to the native custom when she was seven years old to a boy of twelve. The boy took a dislike to her from the first, and would strike her frequently as they played in the house of his father. But as time went on, and the boy grew older and stronger, the beatings became more and more frequent, and the cries of the little girl more pitiful, if there had been anybody to be moved with pity for her, but there was not. As she grew older, she was delicate and sickly, the constant state of fear in which she lived not being a good way to bring about a healthy physical condition. Her father-in-law joined with his son, and lent the energy of his stronger arm when that of the younger man seemed not sufficient for their cruel purpose. At length, however, the poor child's condition reached the ears of her mother, and the mother-heart, moved with love and pity, went to her child, and finding things even as she had heard, she took her little one away, back to her own home. But this did not suit the brutal instincts of the young husband: He must have her near him. The mother refusing to let the little one go back, he took the case to law and lost it, being bound over to "hold the peace" for six months. During this time Ahmadi lived with her mother, enjoying her care and love.

But by and by the six months passed away, and again the going back stared them in the face. They could not bear the thought; the child clung to the mother and cried, "Don't let me go!" But what could she do? The law could no longer afford them a protection. If they stayed where they were, the husband would claim his wife, and go she must. So they resolved to go away, and helped by the missionaries, who had been their friends through all this heavy trial, they fled to Calcutta, to them a foreign land. Here she is, with her mother, and has been here for the last two months. The little Ahmadi is getting to be bright and cheery, but the mother carries about a weary, sad face, that it makes one's heart ache to see. She has not learned of Christ, and of course the burden of this great affliction must seem heavy indeed.

A PATHETIC PROTEST FROM AN AFRICAN.

THE heart of every Christian must be touched by the pathos of an appeal sent for transmission to England. The Mohammedan emir of Nupe, West Africa, has sent the following stirring message to Bishop Crowther, of the Niger mission:

"It is not a long matter; it is about barasa (rum). Barasa, barasa, barasa! It has ruined our country; it has ruined our people very much; it has made our people mad. I beg you, Malam Kip, don't forget this writing, because we all beg that he [Crowther] should beg the great priests [committee of the Church Missionary Society] that they should beg the English queen to prevent bringing barasa into this land.

"For God and the prophet's sake, for God and the prophet his messenger's sake, he must help us in this matter—that of barasa. We all have confidence in him. He must not leave our country to become spoiled by barasa. Tell him, may God bless him in his work. This is the mouthword from Malike, the emir of Nupe."

A SISTER MISSED.

IN the course of an address at a recent convention, Dr. A. J. Gordon, of Boston, quoted an incident related by a minister, who said: "I knew two sisters, one of whom was saved, but the other was not saved, and the saved one could not help thinking, again and again, of the words 'the one shall be taken and the other left,' and she said, '*I* shall be taken and my sister left.' And she was so impressed by this that she could not help telling her sister about it. They retired to rest, but each of them had only a troubled sleep, because of the great thought which had taken possession of their hearts. Sleep at length came to the unsaved one, and then her sister rose from her couch and began to plead with God to change her dear sister's heart. Presently the sleeping one awoke, and, missing her sister, was greatly troubled, and she said, 'It is midnight, and the Lord *has* come. He has taken my sister and I am left.' She sprang from her couch, and then she saw her kneeling in prayer; she threw her arms around her, and they prayed together. Then they went back to their couch and slept peacefully until the sun rising came forth as a bridegroom from his chamber. And peace through believing now filled the heart of the sister who had been unsaved, and she said: 'Dear sister, if the Lord comes to-day we shall both be taken, and neither will be left.'" Let the truth sink into your hearts. May God lead you to Christ, so that when He comes there may be no separation between you and those you love.

THE SEAMAN'S GUIDE.

MARKING the mariner's way is an occupation in which the Coast and Geodetic Survey Department of the Government has been for some time engaged. The volumes resulting from its efforts are now nearly ready for publication. The greater part of the data for the Atlantic coast has been collected, and in accordance with instructions of F. M. Thorn, Superintendent, is rapidly being placed in a comprehensive shape. Thus in giving sailing directions for any harbor or river, an effort has been made to include them in a continuous statement, carrying the navigator from entry to his destination. Much practical information will also be given, the most important concerning the greatest draught of vessels which are actually taken to particular places; the depth of water in channels; depth alongside wharves; pilots, whether necessary and where obtained; the best anchorages, most available harbors of refuge; harbor regulations, anchorage limits, if fixed by regulations; the ports at which supplies, fresh water, coal, &c., can be obtained; hospitals available for mariners, and other information of value to seamen. These facts have been collected at enormous labor and expense, and will doubtless be appreciated by the captains of vessels. They will be useless, however, to any captain who merely carries the volumes with him but does not study them. That is the case with many who are in danger of making shipwreck on the voyage of life. They do not study the Book which God has given them to guide them safely to the heavenly shore. (II Tim. 3:16.)

THE SEVEN PROPHETIC PARABLES.

By G. H. Pember, M. A., author of "Earth's Earliest Ages," "The Great Prophecies," etc.

THE seven parables as given in the thirteenth chapter of Matthew's Gospel, are not primarily intended for practical teaching—in the other gospels they are so intended, but in Matthew they are *a great prophecy of the history of the Church*—that is the professing Church, within which are found the true members of Christ. They appear to be arranged in chronological and consecutive order, and to trace in outline the entire course of the Church's history. Let us glance at them briefly.

I. The Sower and the Seed.

The parable of the sower represents *the first period of the Gospel age*. The sowing is the preaching of the Word by the Lord and His disciples, perhaps to the end of the first century. The showers of blessing were then copious; there has been nothing like them since, until our times, in which the latter rain warns us of the approaching harvest. How rapidly the Gospel was spread in those early times is indicated by Paul when he tells the Colossians that the Gospel "is preached to every creature under heaven." I do not wonder at it. You will remember how active Paul and the other apostles were; and how converts no sooner accepted the Gospel than they were off to preach it to others. The church at Colosse was so founded, and Paul had never seen it when he wrote his letter to it. So also was it with the Church at Rome. Paul had never been there when he wrote the Epistle to the Romans; but when he was on his way as a prisoner to the great city, and saw the brethren coming to meet him, he thanked God, and took courage. The spread of Christianity was so rapid that even the heathen writers noticed it. Tacitus speaks of an "immense number of Christians" at Rome itself, and that only a year or two after the date of the Epistle to the Romans. And a few years later Pliny speaks of the temples of Bithynia and Pontus being forsaken, because such multitudes had received the Gospel.

II. The Tares and the Wheat.

The next parable is that of the tares sown upon the wheat. It seems to refer specially to the history of the second and third centuries, *the great time of heresy*. When Satan saw what the preaching of the gospel was accomplishing everywhere, he adopted the most effective measures to undo the work. A flood of insidious false doctrines was let loose upon the Church to such an extent that all the heresies of later times, in whatever guise they appear, are merely revivals of those of this period. Two books which have come down to us contribute their evidence to this fact. One is a volume "Against Heresies," written by Irenæus of Lyons, a disciple of Polycarp, who himself had sat at the feet of the Apostle John. The other is from the pen of Hippolytus, a pupil of Irenæus, and entitled, "A Refutation of all Heresies." Satan seems to have put forth all his ingenuity and all force in endeavoring to poison the fountain of truth. Alas! the taint remains to this day in the tenets of many of the sects. And strange to say, this time of heresy was *also a time of terrible persecution*. Satan knew what he was about. He subtilely devised errors not easily distinguished from truth, and held out the hope of escaping persecution to those who would accept them. Nothing is said respecting the persecutions in this parable, but their occurrence is indicated by a warning to the Lord's people not to retaliate upon their persecutors. Though the tares are the children of the wicked one, His servants are not to root them up from the field, which is the world, not to put to death those who propagate error. Even at the harvest, it is the angels who are to be the reapers and to gather out the tares; we shall not have that sorrowful task.

III. The Mustard-Tree.

The third parable is that of the mustard-tree, which seems to deal with *the fourth century*. The mustard plant is a pot-herb and an annual, but, like other annuals in Palestine, it sometimes becomes perennial, and so grows into a tree with great branches, which afford shelter to the fowls of the air. But by this development beyond the limits of its kind *it violates the creation-law of the third day*. What the fowls of the air represent is indicated by our Lord in His explanation of the parable of the sower.

Now all this exactly corresponds with what happened in the fourth century, when the Church, having passed through ten persecutions, and having only increased and become stronger, was assailed by Satan in another way. Constantine, who checked the last persecution, became the patron of the Church. He has been generally represented as a Christian; but that is a perversion of history. He never was a Christian at all—at least, not until within a few days of his death. He simply put Jesus

Christ in the Pantheon

of Rome, together with the other gods, and did this in deference to his soldiers, many of whom were professing Christians. But the Lord Jesus will not accept this. He claims sole worship and allegiance. Constantine's religion was no Christianity. This is obscured through the falsification of Church history, but many facts remain to attest it. The very names of the days of the week remind us of it; for the first of them is called "Sunday," an extremely Pagan appellation connected with Apollo, the Sun God. Constantine had observed that the chief difference between Christian and heathen lay in the observance of the first day of the week, and as his object in patronizing the Church was to amalagamate her with heathenism, he issued a decree that the heathen were to keep the first day of the week in honor of the sun, while the Christians devoted it to the worship of Christ. Hence the name; and very soon Christ and Apollo came to be identified, more or less. The worship of the Sun God came from Babylon. In this way, then, the mustard seed, contrary to the law of its existence, became a great tree—or, in other words, the Church *became great and popular*, and instead of the presence of the Holy Spirit, the wicked spirits of the air found lodgment in her branches.

IV. The Leaven in the Meal.

But we must pass on, leaving you to study out these thoughts. The next parable is that of the leaven. Strangely enough some have interpreted the leaven as a good influence. How any readers of the Bible could entertain such an idea seems inexplicable. *Not once in the whole of the Scriptures is leaven used for anything save corruption*, for, as known to the ancients, it was itself something which had become corrupt. It was indeed put into bread, but the bread had to be carefully baked, else it would have become sour. Indeed, the Hebrews spoke of unleavened bread as "sweet," of leavened bread as "sour." Leaven was expressly forbidden to be offered in any sacrifice. The parable seems to be founded on the meat offering; and the woman, representing an apostate church, mingles it with fine meal, thus rendering the latter unfit for an offering to the Lord. The parable thus seems to have reference to *the Apostate Greek and Latin Churches*.

V. The Treasure Hid in the Field.

At the close of the parable of the leaven there is a pause: our Lord retires with His disciples into a house. The remaining three parables are spoken to the disciples alone, and, therefore, perhaps, had a more restricted meaning. The first is that of the treasure hid in a field. Many think that Christ is the husbandman, and the Church the treasure; but surely our Lord did not light by accident on His Church when He was about some other business! The husbandman is ploughing or digging, and his spade or plough strikes against something. He digs and finds treasure; for the sake of which he gives up all that he has and buys the field. The Lord seems to be describing *the conditions of the Churches of the Reformation*, upon which a strange deadness fell soon after their establishment. Each of them had the treasure, the Gospel of the Lord Jesus, surrounded by a larger or smaller field of other doctrines; and each of them had their doctrines sharply defined, like a fenced field. In one of these communities a man would hear the gospel preached, and, for the sake of it, would embrace all the tenets of the sect at whatever cost to himself.

VI. The Pearl of Great Price.

In the next parable the condition of things is altered. The treasure is not hid in a sharply defined field, but beneath the shifting waves of the sea: it sinks as a pearl to the bottom. That seems to me to represent *the state of things upon which we are now entering*. A man may say he belongs to this or that sect, but his statement is no indication of his opinion of doctrine. Every man has his own ideas. The countless creeds, sects, heresies and philosophies are all mingled in a confused and ever-shifting mass like the waters of the sea. Soon the truth of God will not be lighted upon accidentally as it were, but only by patient search—the merchantman is "seeking goodly pearls." But even in these perilous times of the end God will always have witnesses who will be able to bring up the priceless pearl from beneath the waters of human speculation and to offer it to those who are honestly seeking the truth. But perhaps it may not be long before he who would obtain it will have to give up all that he has for the prize.

VII. The Net Cast Into the Sea.

The last parable is that of the drag-net, which represents *the circle within which the Gospel is preached;* while *the shore is the end of the age.* A net does not inclose all the fish of the sea, and when the Lord returns there will be many who will not have heard of His name nor seen His glory, and with them He will not deal in final judgment. But we may notice that, although the net contains all sorts of fish, only two classes are recognized when they are separated. The good are gathered into vessels and the bad cast away. The good are first picked out, and to some this has seemed a contradiction of the parable of the tares. It is not so, however: for there is no note of time in the latter. The apparently contradictory command should be rendered, "First collect the tares, and then bind them in bundles to burn them; but as to the wheat, gather that into thy barn."

In these seven parables the Lord reveals the whole history of the Church, from the first sowing to the gathering of His coming.

CHRISTIAN HERALD AND SIGNS OF OUR TIMES.
OFFICE, 63 BIBLE HOUSE, NEW YORK.
ENTERED AT THE POST-OFFICE AT NEW YORK, N. Y., AS SECOND-CLASS MATTER.

EVERY NUMBER CONTAINS:

The Portrait and Biography of some eminent person.
The Sermon Dr. Talmage preached the last Sunday morning.
An Exposition of Unfulfilled Prophecy.
A Summary of the Events of the Week, Notes of Religious and Temperance Movements, etc.
A Sermon by Rev. C. H. Spurgeon, of London, from advance sheets sent by special arrangement.
Pictures of Missionary Life, etc., and Descriptive Articles.
An instalment of a Serial Story.
An Exposition of the International Sunday-School Lesson, by Mrs. M. Baxter.

ANNUAL SUBSCRIPTION, $1.50.

Remittances by mail should be by bank cheques, Post-office orders, or Express money-orders whenever possible. If currency is sent it should be in a registered letter. Cheques and money-orders should be made payable to THE CHRISTIAN HERALD. Making them payable to individuals often causes delay.

New subscriptions may commence at any time. When subscribers do not indicate their wish, they commence with the first number of the month in which the subscription is received.

PUBLISHER'S NOTICE.

The whole edition of The Christian Herald was mailed last week to subscribers during Tuesday, July 10. The last delivery at the New York Post Office was made at 11.20 P. M.

CURRENT EVENTS.

A New Treaty with Mexico to Prevent border troubles has been negotiated. Mr. Secretary Bayard and Don Matias Romero have had under consideration a scheme to obviate for the future the difficulties which have frequently arisen in the past through the passage of unguarded grazing cattle across the border line from Mexico to this country, or oftener from the United States into Mexico. In such cases the return of the wandering cattle raised claims for duties. The new treaty is expected to enable cattle owners on both sides to avoid trouble hereafter. The Senate will have no compunction about ratifying such a treaty.

The Evils of the Present Immigration System have at length compelled the attention of Congress. On Thursday last the House unanimously adopted a resolution, introduced by Mr. Ford, of Michigan, that "the Speaker shall appoint a committee of five members who shall, within thirty days after the adjournment of this House, begin an investigation into the causes and methods of excessive, artificial, and injurious immigration to the United States, and the effect of such immigration upon the general health and prosperity of the several State commonwealths. The committee may employ counsel, a clerk, an interpreter and a stenographer. The committee shall report, at the next session of the Fiftieth Congress, a bill to correct and control the evils arising from the present conditions and methods of immigration." There is no intention to restrict legitimate immigration, but only to check the operations of padrones, agents of transportation companies, and other persons who make a business of stimulating and assisting immigration from selfish motives.

The Submission to the States of a Prohibition amendment to the Constitution is advocated in a report of the Senate Committee on Education presented by Senator Hoar on July 9. The Committee says: "The agitation for national legislation for the extirpation of the traffic in alcoholic poison made and sold to be used as a beverage will never cease to disturb, and finally to destroy, the great political parties until they submit to the States the question of the enlargement of national, constitutional jurisdiction, so as to include control of the subject. When decided, if adversely to the ratification, the subject will be eliminated from national politics, at least for many years. If, on the other hand, the proposed amendment should be ratified, and become a part of the national law, the chief curse of the world would be summoned to the block of national justice, and die by the hand of the only power which can wield an axe big and sharp enough to cut off its hydra head. Then we shall have peace." The Committee is over-sanguine about the elimination of the question, if the amendment is not ratified. The Prohibitionists are not the people whom one failure discourages.

An Important Extension of the Civil Service Reform Rules has been made. They are now to operate in the appointment of all employees in the Federal and District Governments, except unskilled laborers, and in the Customs and Postal Service outside Washington. Hitherto, all offices in which the salary was over $2,000 or under $900 were not filled by competitive examination, but in future they will be filled as other offices are, except in a few specified cases where the service required is of a technical character. The extension is a practical testimony to the value and efficacy of the much-maligned law, and is a safe indication that the Departments in which it has been operative have benefited by the system. It has now been so long in force that if it had failed to secure its object in providing the Government with efficient employees the failure must have been discovered. The curtailment of patronage which it assures is a distinct gain, and this extension implies that it promotes efficiency also.

Over a Million Dollars Damage was Done last week by the sudden rise of the River Monongahela. The freshet extended from the head of the river to below Pittsburg, Penn. It commenced so suddenly on July 9, as to take the river-men unawares, and they were not prepared when the great volume of water burst upon them. Millions of feet of lumber, scores of coal craft, fences, out-houses and coal tipples floated down the swift current during the following two days. At every point between Greensboro and Pittsburg the low lands were under water, and the residents were compelled to live in the upper stories of their houses; and in some cases to seek the hills for safety. Many had not time to remove their goods, as *the water rose at the rate of a foot an hour*, and at Greensboro thirty-two feet of a rise was recorded in less than twenty-four hours. Among the wreckage was a saw-mill with all its machinery, which was swept from Belle Vernon, Penn., to a point sixty miles below Pittsburg. It is feared that several persons must have been drowned, and that others will die from damp and exposure. *The Valley River* also overflowed its banks on July 10, and caused much damage at Grafton and Wheeling, W. Va.

The German Physicians who were Consulted in the case of the late Emperor Frederick, have issued a medical report strongly condemnatory of Dr. Mackenzie, the English physician. They assert that as far back as May 15, 1887, Dr. Gerhardt pronounced the illustrious patient's disease to be cancer, and his opinion was confirmed by other German physicians. After a consultation they recommended an operation. They consented, however, to await the examination of Dr. Mackenzie, who at that time expressed his doubts as to the accuracy of their diagnosis, and was opposed to an operation until the disease should be proved to be cancer. They submitted the decision to the then Crown Prince, who declined to subject himself to the operation in the face of Dr. Mackenzie's opinion. They then appealed to the Prince's father, Emperor William, who said that his son was old enough to judge for himself, and refused to interfere. Later, when the cancer was clearly proved, it had spread too far to be extirpated by the knife. The report of the physicians shows a strong animus against the English physician, and not a little detracts from its value as a scientific document. Dr. Mackenzie has made no formal reply. He hints that he maintains silence in deference to the wishes of august persons, presumably the ex-Empress and her mother. He declared, however, that he has an elaborate answer prepared, which will be published at the proper time, and will show the German report to be "a tissue of falsehoods." The Doctor speaks also of disgraceful scenes in the patient's sick-room, and of one occasion when his chief assailant came to perform his duties in a state of intoxication.

An Earthquake Shock was Felt in Several districts of Canada on July 8, about seven in the evening. It was most severe in the district between Belleville and Kingston. In the vicinity of Napanee and Deseronto the earth vibrated and houses shook so vigorously that people were awakened, and hastily fled outside. Accompanying the shock was a low rumbling roar as of far off thunder. It was accompanied by a rattling sound that filled people with fear. Goods in stores were knocked off the shelves by the violence of the quake. Similar shocks were experienced at Enterprise, Newburg, Moscow, and Yarker. At Northport and Picton the residents thought that there had been an explosion.

Mr. Parnell's Scheme for the Government of Ireland is on the Federation principle, which has long been advocated by statesmen who are not Irishmen. In an interview published in the *Pall Mall Gazette*, the Irish leader sketches his chief features. His idea is that England, Ireland, Scotland, and Wales shall each have a Parliament for the administration of local affairs. Thus the London Parliament will become purely an English, the Cardiff Parliament a Welsh, the Dublin Parliament an Irish, and the Edinburgh Parliament a Scotch body. The House of Lords, however, will be replaced by a congress of members from all the four kingdoms and from each of the colonies to form an imperial Parliament which will legislate on all national affairs. This plan is practically that of the Constitution of the United States so far as legislation is concerned. It has often been suggested before as a practical solution of the problem, but the Irish party has never been authoritatively committed to it, and Mr. Parnell in thus speaking out has answered a great many questions, particularly concerning the retention of the Irish members at Westminster, to which no one could obtain a satisfactory response hitherto.

The Duel in France on Friday last between General Boulanger and Prime Minister Floquet is discreditable alike to the two men and to their country. That the two most prominent statesmen in the nation should quarrel like two schoolboys, and should afterward meet in murderous combat, argues not only a low type of statesmanship, but a deplorable lack of morality. The example thus set to the people cannot but be pernicious. The fight grew out of a scene in the Legislature on Thursday. General Boulanger, whose inordinate vanity has made him the laughing-stock of Europe, proposed the dissolution of the Chamber. He grandiloquently declared that the country was trembling with emotion at always having presented to it as an enemy a citizen who only desired the welfare of the Republic. M. Floquet, in his reply, taunted General Boulanger with being a lingerer in sacristies and the ante-chambers of princes. The taunt went home, and Boulanger responded by calling out the usual retort of a blackguard, "*It is a lie.*" The Chamber rejected his motion, and Boulanger thereupon resigned his seat. At ten o'clock the next morning he met Floquet by appointment in a retired spot about two miles out of Paris, and there a duel with swords took place. General Boulanger proved inexpert with the soldier's weapon, and his antagonist, though a civilian, succeeded in wounding him severely in the throat. The soldier fell to the ground unconscious, and was ignominiously carried from the field. His wound is said to be serious.

The Pan Presbyterian Council in London closed its sittings on Thursday last. The council adopted a proposal made by Professor Charteris, of Edinburgh, that women be enrolled under the kirk session and the sanction of the Church courts, as deaconesses, and set apart by the Presbytery to assist in the service of the church. The subject of a liturgy for the church was revived by Dr. T. G. Apple, of Lancaster, O. In the course of the discussion on the question, the Rev. Donald Fraser, of London, suggested that the Westminister directory be thoroughly revised and rendered suitable to modern times. The services should be so arranged as to be complete without sermons, and the number of short prayers should be increased. The congregation should utter the responses and join audibly in the prayers. The council decided to appoint a permanent Secretary in London, and Dr. G. D. Mathews, of Quebec, was elected. Dr. W. H. Roberts, of Cincinnati, was elected Secretary for America.

An Improvement on the Practice of Closing the churches during the hot weather has been made this year by several pastors, and it may be hoped will be widely adopted. Rev. W. E. Needham, of Westchester, Pa., has closed his church on Sunday evenings and taken the congregation into the open air. The result has been highly gratifying. Vast audiences have gathered to hear the word. Men and women who rarely go to a place of worship have flocked out and listened attentively to the story of the Cross. Rev. Thomas Needham has pitched a large tent on Broad Street, Philadelphia, for the summer months.

An Actress was Wounded on the Stage at Staten Island, N. Y., on July 11. A play is being performed there in which a gladiatorial combat occurs. A girl who takes one of the parts interposes at one stage of the combat, to plead for the life of her lover, who is one of the gladiators. Failing in this, her part requires her to fling herself into the arms of her brother, another gladiator, and entreat him to kill her, that she may die with her lover. The actress who usually takes this part was sick on Wednesday night, and another actress, who has understudied the part, took her place. She was somewhat nervous and excited, and at the critical time anticipated the action, and threw herself into the arms of the gladiator before he was aware of her intention. The dagger which he held in his hand was poised at the moment, and instead of *pretending* to stab her, he really did so inadvertently. The weapon entered her side, inflicting a severe wound, which bled copiously, and necessitated her removal to the infirmary. The daily journals say that the performance went on as if no catastrophe had occurred, and the spectators thought that the girl's shriek was only that required by her part. There are many besides professional actors and actresses who regard the solemn realities of life and death as a fit subject for mockery and sport. To such death will bring an awful disillusion. They will then learn how serious are the matters that they have treated with levity. (Prov. 1 : 25, 26.)

A Woman's Interference in a Quarrel led to her death in Long Island City, N. Y., on July 7. It appears that a large building in that city is let out to a number of families, who occupy two or three rooms each. A widow and a widower who lived in the building decided on getting married, and they invited all their fellow-occupiers to a wedding supper. Both bride and bridegroom were well known in the building, and one or two of the guests had reasons for being disappointed by the marriage. Considerable liquor was consumed, which did not foster reticence about grievances. Finally a quarrel was evolved, and from angry words the men passed to fighting. Two of the men engaged in a desperate battle which seemed likely to end in the death of one of them. They left the room where the wedding festivities had been held and continued to fight in the hall-way, where the noise attracted the attention of the woman who owned the building. She had not been at the reception and did not know the cause of the fight; but fearing that murder would be done, she rushed between the combatants to part them. They both resented her interference, and their wrath turned upon her. They took her up and flung her into the area, where, falling upon her head, she broke her neck and died instantly. This is not the first time by many that peacemaking has proved a dangerous vocation. Doubtless, anxious as the woman in this case was to make peace, she would not have interfered could she have foreseen the fatal result of her effort. It was not so with the great Peacemaker by whom men may attain eternal peace. He voluntarily laid down His life that the world through His death might be reconciled with God. (Eph. 2 : 14–16.)

A Beauty Doctor is Gaining a Lucrative Practice in New York. Every day she has patients coming to her to be treated for ugliness. They may be in perfect health, physically, but not quite at peace in their minds because of defects which they think render them unpleasing in the eyes of their fellow-mortals, and as far as possible she undertakes to eradicate the complaint of plainness. Women go to her to be made thinner or stouter, to have their color heightened or reduced, to be treated for ugly complexions, red eyes, thin hair, round shoulders, and all the physical faults which make the difference between beauty and the lack of it. This "Beauty Doctor," as she is called, has effected some wonderful cures of plainness by a course of diet and exercise, and in several cases has taken entire charge of a woman for six months, with the result that at the end of that time her friends scarcely knew her, so greatly had her appearance changed. Some of her patients complain of the rigor of her treatment, but they undergo it cheerfully for the sake of the result. One can but wish that there was the same anxiety to attain beauty of character, the imperishable beauty which is a blessing to the possessor and to the world. For this there is an infallible recipe. (1 Peter 3 : 3, 4.)

An Extraordinary Epidemic of St. Vitus' dance is reported to exist in Duquoin, Ill. The press despatch on the subject, received in New York, caused some doubts as to the truth of the report, that disease not being regarded as one that could become epidemic. A reporter, therefore, was sent to interview Dr. Spitzka, a physician who has made nervous disorders a special study. He said that St. Vitus' dance might certainly be epidemic, and he had known cases in which it had become so in public schools. If a child afflicted with it was not isolated, but allowed to continue at school, then an epidemic is quite apt to follow from imitation. Sometimes the other children will imitate the one suffering from St. Vitus's dance from pure mischief, and will find that they have lost the power to control their own movements. But more often the imitation is of that unconscious sort which makes a whole school restless from the presence of a single restless individual, or which makes you inclined to yawn when the man with whom you are talking yawns. The defect of stuttering, which is a kindred disorder, is often caught in that way. We have Scriptural authority for the fact that a still worse disorder may come from association. The man who associates with wicked men is apt to become wicked. (1 Cor. 15 : 33.)

Seventeen Dead Voyagers for China Were despatched from New York last week. On July 9 three Chinaman arrived in the city from San Francisco, and having made proper application to the health authorities, proceeded with an undertaker and a Chinese laborer to the Cemetery of the Evergreens. There a grave was opened and the coffin lifted out. The Chinese assistant removed the lid, and disclosed a skeleton which must have been interred many years ago. The bones were taken out of the coffin, and placed in one of a number of oblong tin boxes which the party had brought with them. Some Chinese hieroglyphs were scratched upon the box, and it was closed. It was noticed that while American laborers were employed to do the digging, they were not allowed to touch the coffin or to handle the bones. This part of the work was done by the Chinese laborer whom the party had brought them. When the work was done they proceeded to another grave, where the same process was gone through. Seventeen graves in all were opened, and the skeletons removed. The tin boxes had evidently been made to contain just one skeleton without crowding and no more. They were stacked upon the wagon, and taken back to the city, where they were expressed to San Francisco to be there shipped to China. The three Chinamen who superintended the exhumation and removal were representatives of "the Six Companies," who conduct Chinese emigration. A superstition prevails among the Chinese that if their dead bodies are buried out of China their souls cannot enjoy happiness in Paradise, hence every Chinaman insists upon having a contract from responsible persons to carry his bones back to China within a specified time after his death, if he should die abroad. It is a pity that men who are concerned about their happiness after death should not know how that object may really be attained. Among ourselves those who have that knowledge, too often feel so little concern about their eternal state that they neglect to make use of it. (Matt. 7 : 24–27.)

BRIEF NOTES.

Absinthe drinking is said to be increasing to an alarming extent in New York.

Topeka, Kas., has more churches than any city of the same size in the country, and has not a single saloon or drinking-place. There were, four years ago, 140 saloons.

The Naval Temperance Union is making encouraging progress. At its meeting last week on the receiving ship *Vermont*, it was stated that there are now 2,500 members, nearly all of whom are man-of-war's men.

Lane Theological Seminary has been doing good work. Since 1836 it has sent out 800 graduates, half of whom entered the home field, and 80 became foreign missionaries. At the close of the late session 16 young men graduated.

Bishop Williams, of the Protestant Episcopal Diocese of Connecticut, though seventy-one years of age, delivers twelve lectures every week to the divinity students at Middletown, beside preaching nearly every Sunday, and attending to his episcopal duties.

A foreign journal announces that two Jews of Paghdad have purchased Babylon, and now own all that remains of the palaces and hanging gardens of the city where Daniel was thrown in the den of lions, and Shadrach, Meshach and Abednego into the fiery furnace.

At the recent convention in Chicago of Societies of Christian Endeavor, it was stated that there are now in the United States eighteen hundred and ninety-nine societies, having a total of 125,000 members. The receipts last year were $18,890, and the expenditures, $16,855.

The total amount of money embezzled in the United States last year, so far as a disclosure was made by the losers, was, according to the New York *Herald*, $4,546,468. Two men took a million each. The total number of defalcations in the past ten years was 465, and the aggregate loss. $48,513,466.

A large party from Dr. Talmage's church will go to Europe for their annual trip. It is proposed to spend seven weeks in visiting Great Britain, France, Germany, Austria, and Italy. The expense will be about $250 for each person. Dr. Talmage's lecture engagements will not permit of his accompanying the party.

The Legislature of Louisiana has under consideration a bill prohibiting, under penalty, the manufacture, sale, or use of fire-arms. A heavy special tax is to be placed on those now owned in the State, the proceeds to go to the public schools. A person convicted of carrying concealed weapons is to be punished by imprisonment.

The Chicago Evangelization Society, of which Mr. D. L. Moody is President, will hold a summer school for Bible study for men only, during the month of August, at Chicago. Major D. W. Whittle, and other eminent evangelists, will take part. For full particulars, address the Secretary, Mr. F. G. Ensign, 154 Madison Street, Chicago, Ill.

The congregation assembling in St. Paul's Cathedral, Buffalo, N. Y., which was recently destroyed by fire, has accepted the invitation of the trustees of the Jewish Temple to meet there during the rebuilding of their house of worship. At the first service held in the synagogue, the gospel appointed for the day contained the words: "They shall put you out of the Synagogues." (John 16 : 2.)

MOSES: HIS FAITH AND DECISION.

A New Sermon by Pastor C. H. Spurgeon.

"By faith Moses, when he was come to years, refused to be called the son of Pharaoh's daughter; choosing rather to suffer affliction with the people of God, than to enjoy the pleasures of sin for a season; esteeming the reproach of Christ greater riches than the treasures of Egypt: for he had respect unto the recompense of the reward."—Hebrews 11: 24-26.

A Correction in the Idea of Moses—Not a Representative of Law Only—I. Moses had Faith—Believed in God—Believed Israel was His People—Believed in a Future Judgment—II. His Clear Decision—What He Gave Up—A Princely Status—Natural Affection—Apparent Leading of Providence—Opportunities of Doing Good—Prisoners in a Bishop's Coal-Hole—Moses' Choice of Affliction—III. Moses to be Imitated—A Personal Declaration.

WE generally picture Moses with beams of glory rising from his brow, and the two tables of the law in his hand; a stern man holding forth a sterner law. But we must correct our idea. Moses is as much an example of faith as he is a representative of law. What he did was as much due to his faith as were the acts of Paul or John. In describing Moses, the summary must begin "By faith," as much as if we were describing Abraham. Continue to regard Moses as a representative of the law, but also view him as a man of powerful faith.

I need scarcely remind you that the faith of Moses was peculiarly active and operative. I might apply the words of James to him, and say, "Likewise also was not Moses justified by works when he refused to be called the son of Pharaoh's daughter, and chose to endure affliction with the people of God?" The faith of Moses was what ours must be, a faith which worked by love—even love to God, and love to His people. It was no mere belief of a fact; but that fact had an overpowering influence upon his life. Moses believed, believed firmly and intensely, believed for himself, so that he took fast hold of that which is invisible. Moses showed the reality of his faith in his life, by what he refused to do, and by what he chose to do. Both the negative and the positive poles were made right by his faith. Everything about Moses proved the vigor of his faith in God.

I. First, then,

Moses had Faith.

It is very clear that Moses believed in God. He was learned in all the learning of the Egyptians, he had been brought up in the very best academies of the period; but he had not been seduced from faith in his God. There were gods many in Egypt; but Moses worshipped the one God, the God of his fathers; and though he may have known comparatively little of Him, he knew enough to have no other God but the God of Abraham, Isaac, and Jacob. I would that all of you believed in the living, personal, working, ever-present God! In these days many do not believe in a personal God, but in some sort of force or mystic energy, they know not what. This is virtually to have no God at all. To Moses the existence and ruling power of God were the greatest facts of life. Although the pomp and power and glory, and wisdom of the ruling nation were all on the side of idols, Moses worshipped the one God; for in His power and Godhead he solemnly believed.

In the next place, Moses believed that the Israelites were the chosen people of God. This, of course, he had learned from his parents, and he heartily believed it, though it certainly did not look to be true. For this cause Moses loved them, and desired to be numbered with them. Certainly, they were not in themselves a very lovable people: there was much about them that must have saddened the heart of Moses. They were ignorant, while he was educated: they had been debased by slavery, while he was of that brave disposition which is nourished in freedom. When he himself attempted to be their champion, they did not receive him. He found two of them striving together, and when, with gentle words he would have made peace between them, one of them replied, "Who made thee a prince and a judge over us?" Yet Moses said, "Whatever they may be, they are the people of God, and I will be one of them."

Even to this day the Lord has a chosen people, a remnant according to the election of grace.

Looking Critically at the Church

of God, we soon detect much that is faulty, many shortcomings and many grievous evils; yet the church of God is God's choice, and we may not despise it. *If they are good enough for God, they are good enough for me.* If you never join a church till you find a perfect church, you must wait till you get to heaven; and if you could go there as you are, they would not receive you into fellowship. Consider who are the people that acknowledge God in their lives, who hold the truth as it is revealed, who believe the Holy Scriptures, and worship God in the Spirit, having no confidence in the flesh. Cast in your lot with these people, however poor and commonplace they may be.

Next, dear friends, note this—Moses had faith in a future judgment. He looked beyond the present; for he "had respect to the recompense of the reward." It is dangerous to be always looking at things from one point of view. If we could go quite round, and see things from the future, looking back upon them rather than forward to them, how differently they would appear! "Oh!" said a lady to her minister, "I find great pleasure in going to the play. There is the pleasure of anticipation, there is the pleasure of enjoying it, and there is the pleasure of thinking it over afterwards." "Yes," said her minister, "I know all that, madam; but there is one pleasure you have forgotten, namely, the pleasure of meditating upon it on a dying bed." She shrugged her shoulders; she could see no pleasure there. I wish that men would estimate their pleasures by that rule. How will they look when we lie dying? How will they appear when we stand before the judgment-seat of God?

Let me not quit this point till I have said that Moses had a personal faith by which he realized the whole business for himself. His faith led him on to personal action. He did not say, "I am placed by Providence in the palace of Pharaoh, and so I am not called upon to suffer like the rest of my race." No, no, but he refused to be called the son of Pharaoh's daughter. He did not say, "I am so circumstanced that I need not suffer, and, therefore, I will keep out of the general trouble as well as I can." You know how men feel, that there is nothing like keeping on the warm side of the hedge. Moses resolved that he would suffer affliction with the people of God.

This was the faith of Moses, a real personal faith. Come, dear friends, ask yourselves, have you all such a personal faith in God? I tell you, if your faith is not personal and practical faith, it is not worth two-pence. It will do you no good, either here or hereafter. It will leave you lost to God if it leaves you still a friend to the world, and an alien from the people of God. Oh, that you may say from your heart, "This God is my God for ever and ever. He shall be my Guide even unto death."

II. Our second point is this: Moses exhibited

A Clear Decision.

Note, first, the time of his choice: "When he was come to years." We do not know the exact time to which this refers. When he was forty years of age he visited his brethren, but his mind may have been made up long before. It was "when he was come to years." I suppose that means early in life, so soon as he was of full age. Still, it is said, "when he was come to years," as much as to say, that whatever his decision was while he was yet young, that decision was carried out more practically when he was come to years. We do wish to see young people converted, but we wish it to be as thoughtful a conversion, as clear and deliberate a change, as if they were advanced in age. We trust that their following years will confirm what they do in their youth. Moses decided for God early in life; but he decided also when he was capable of forming a mature judgment.

Moses went about arranging his life like a man of business, and decided wisely; but we must note well

The Prospect which He Gave Up.

He "refused to be called the son of Pharaoh's daughter." To be the son of Pharaoh's daughter made him a prince of Egypt. Some have thought that the Pharaoh then reigning had no other child but this daughter, and that her son Moses would have succeeded to the throne of Egypt. We cannot be sure of that, though it may have been so. The son of a princess had noble rank and grand opportunities. Wealth was evidently to be had; the treasures of Egypt were before him. Honor was his already, and as he grew older, titles would multiply upon him. But "He refused to be called the son of Pharaoh's daughter."

A great many would say, What a fool he was to give up what others covet! I fear that many of you professors would not lose a situation for Christ. Some of you could not lose a shilling a week of extra pay for the Lord. Ah me, this is a miserable age! Go with a lancet throughout these Isles, *and you could not get enough martyr-blood to fill a thimble.*

Backbones are Scarce,

and grit is a rare article. Men do not now care to suffer for Christ; but they must be respectable, they must vote in the majority, they must go with the committee, and be thought well of for their charity. As to standing up and standing out for Christ, it is looked upon as an eccentricity, or worse.

For a moment, I will show you some of the arguments which Moses must have had to meet in his own mind, when having come to years he began to think the matter over, many arguments would arise and demand reply. The first argument would be, "*You will be acting very unkindly to your adopted mother*—What will she say? She drew you out of the water when you might have been drowned; she took you home; she saw that you were nursed and cared for, she has had you trained and educated. She has spent no end of money on you; there is nothing you could wish for but what she has supplied; her heart is entwined in yours: and now, having come to years, if you refuse to be called her son it will be a very sad return for her love." Natural affection has often proved a serious difficulty in the way of grace. The Lord Jesus has said, "He that loveth father or mother more than Me is not worthy of Me; and many are thus unworthy." Moses thus proved his faith to be stronger than that of many who are mastered by family ties, and held captive by the bonds of earthly love.

Next, there would come before the mind of Moses the plausible argument, "Providence has led you where you are, and you ought to keep your position." When he looked back he saw

A Remarkable Providence

watching over him in the ark of bulrushes, and bringing the Egyptian princess down to that particular part of the Nile to bathe. How singular that she should see the ark, and save the life of the weeping babe! Could he fly in the teeth of providence by relinquishing the high position so specially bestowed? Thus would flesh and blood reason. How often have I heard people excuse themselves for doing wrong by quoting what they call providence! Arguments from providence against positive commands are ingenious deceptions. Providence is of God, but the lesson which we draw from it may be of the devil. When Jonah wanted to flee to Tarshish he went down to Joppa, and found a ship going to Tarshish. How providential! Nothing of the sort. Whenever a man wants to do wrong he will find opportunities at hand; but let him not excuse his wickedness by the apparent opportunity for it. Be afraid of that kind of providence which makes sin easy. Our rule of life is the commandment of the Lord, not the doubtful conclusions which may be drawn from providences.

Yet another argument may have met Moses, r it is one which I have heard repeated till I n sick of answering it. *Moses could do a deal good by retaining his position.* What oppor- nities for usef. lness would be in his way! See ow he could help his poor brethren! How of- n he could interpose at the court to prevent justice! Moreover, what a bright light he ould be in his high position: his example ould commend the faith of the true God to the ourtiers and great ones; nobody could tell hat an influence would thus be exercised up- n Egypt. Pharaoh himself might be convert- d, and then all Egypt would bow before Jeho- h. Thus have we met with brethren who say, Yes, I am in a church with which I do not gree; but then,

I can be Useful."

I know that a certain religious Union is foster- g evil; but then, I can serve the cause by aying in it." Another is carrying on an evil ade, but he says, "It is my livelihood: and esides, it affords me opportunities of doing ood!" This is one of the most specious of ose arguments by which good men are held bonds of evil. As an argument, it is rotten the core, We have no right to do wrong, om any motive whatever.

But, dear friends, do you not think that Moses ight have made a compromise? That idea is ery popular. "Now, then, Moses, do not be o strict! Some people are a deal too particu- r. Those old-fashioned puritanical people e narrow and strait-laced: be liberal and ke broader views. Cannot you make a com- romise? Tell Pharaoh's daughter you are an raelite; but that, in consequence of her great indness, you will also be an Egyptian. Thus ou can become an Egypto-Israelite—what a ne blend! Or say an Israelito-Egyptian—with e better part in the front. You see, dear iends, it seems a simple way out of a difficulty, hold with the hare and run with the hounds. saves you from unpleasant decisions and sep- rations. Besides, Jack-of-both-sides has great raise from both parties for his large-hearted- ess. I admire this in Moses, that he

Knew Nothing of Compromise;

ut first he refused to be called the son of Pha- oh's daughter; and, secondly, he made a de- berate choice rather "to suffer affliction with e people of God, than to enjoy the pleasures f sin for a season." My hearers, come out, I ray you, one way or the other. None of your imming. It will go hard with trimmers at e last great day. When Christ comes to di- ide the sheep from the goats, there will be no iddle sort. There is no place for trimmers. odern thought is trying to make a purgatory, ut as yet the place is not constructed, and, eanwhile, you border people will be driven own to hell. May God grant us grace to be ecided!

Notice the lot which Moses chose. He refused be called the son of Pharaoh's daughter, but e chose to take his portion with the oppressed, proached, and ridiculed Israelites. I want you see the terms in which his judgment is ex- ressed; for no doubt the Holy Spirit tells us xactly how Moses put it in his own mind. He ose rather to suffer "affliction *with the people God.*" Does not that alter it wonderfully? Affliction" nobody would choose; but "afflic- on *with the people of God*," ah, that is another usiness altogether. "Affliction with the peo- le of God" is affliction in glorious company. was reading the other day the life of John hilpot, who was shut up

In Bishop Bonner's Coal-Hole,

Fulham Palace. There he and his friends ng psalms so merrily that the Bishop chided em for their mirth. They could have quoted postolical authority for singing in prison. hen there were seven of them, Philpot wrote: I was carried to my Lord's coal-house again, here I, with my six fellow-prisoners, do thank od, as others do in their beds of down." To with the people of God, one would not mind ing in the coal-hole. No one wants to be in Bonner's coal-hole; but better be there with the martyrs than up-stairs in the palace with the Bishop. "*With the people of God*"; that is the sweet which kills the bitter of affliction.

Now, notice what he said about the baits upon the other side: "Choosing rather to suffer affliction with the people of God, than to enjoy the pleasures of sin for a season." See! he calls the pleasures of the court "the pleasures of sin." Why, Moses, you need not fall into vice. You could be an Egyptian, and yet be chaste and honest and sober and just and good. Yes, but he regards his proposed life as the son of Pharaoh's daughter as full of "the pleasures of sin." Now, mark this: If you believe in the Lord Jesus Christ, it becomes your duty decidedly to come out and stand on His side; and if you do not do so, the pleasures derived from your sin of omission will be the pleasures of sin. You are living a life of disloyalty to Christ, and that is a life of sin. Then note the word, "*For a season.*" Did you hear the tolling of a bell? It was a knell. It spoke of a new-made grave. This is the knell of earthly joy—"*For a season!*" Honored for doing wrong—"*For a season!*" Merry in evil company—"*For a season!*" Prosperous through a compromise—"*For a season!*" What after that season? Death and judgment.

III. I want, in the last place, to say that

Moses Should be Imitated.

First, brethren we should have Moses' faith. The things which Moses believed are true; and therefore ought still to be believed. They are as important to-day as when he believed them; let us lay hold upon them, and feel their practical bearings this very morning. Young men especially, I entreat you to believe in God, and in His work of grace among His people, that you may be numbered with His chosen now, and in the day of His appearing.

Next, we must imitate Moses in this, that if we do believe we must come out on the Lord's side. Now that you have "come to years," do let it be seen on whose side you are. Let there be no doubt, no hesitation, no vacillation; but let those who see you in the house or in business know that you are on the Lord's side. Let me exhort you also to see things in the eternal light. Do not look at things in their bearings upon to-day, or to-morrow, or the next few years. Judge by eternity. For the present the good man may be a loser. You must look further than your foot. Take the measuring line of the sanctury, and use it when you judge of spiritual things.

Note another important matter: I pray that you may get into fellowship with Christ. Oh to know Christ and love Him, to have Him to be your Saviour, and then to feel that you can wear the reproach of Christ as a chain of gold! This is a great help in the life of a tried child of God. Dear friend, if you are a believer in Christ, give yourself up to God without reserve: say, "I will follow thee, my Lord, through flood or flame. I will follow thee up hill or down dale. I will follow wherever the Lord shall lead the way. I will follow at all cost and hazard." Say this in your soul.

If you do this, you cannot tell what God has in store for you, nor need you give it a consideration. Moses, after all,

Was Not a Loser

by his self-denial. He became King in Jeshurun, and was more than a monarch in the wilderness. He refused to be Pharaoh's son, but in the Book of Exodus God said to him; "See, I have made thee a god to Pharaoh." Egypt's haughty monarch feared his plagues, and entreated his intercession. The Lord made Moses so great, that among those who are born of woman he ranks among the first unto this day. Even in heaven he is remembered; for they sing "the song of Moses the servant of God and of the Lamb." Young man, if you give yourself unto the Lord, you can little guess what He will do with you. What you lose will be a mere trifle compared with what you will gain. As to honor, all honor and glory lie in the service of the Most High.

I am come to this pass, my brethren—whether I sink or whether I swim, I am the Lord's! By His grace I will believe His word and cling to its inspiration, whether the Lord shall roll away my reproach or not. I would say with the three holy children, "Our God whom we serve is able to deliver us from the burning fiery furnace, and He will deliver us out of thine hand, O King. But if not, be it known unto thee, O King, that we will not serve thy gods, nor worship the golden image which thou hast set up." With Job my heart has said: "Though He slay me, yet will I trust in Him." Be this the resolve of each one, for Christ's sake. Amen.

[The prayers of the readers of this journal are requested for the blessing of God upon its Editors, and those whose sermons, articles or labors for Christ are printed in it; and that its circulation may be used by the Holy Spirit for the conversion of many sinners and the quickening of God's people. Dr. Talmage and Mr. Spurgeon especially request prayer every Sunday morning on behalf of their labors.]

GEMS FROM NEW BOOKS.

A WISE MOTHER.*

THE boy was neither her pet nor slave; nor was he her prisoner. She allowed him all proper freedom; gave him opportunity for the exercise and development of his power of will and to have his way. While she compelled him to do things to which he was disinclined for the sake of submission to authority, she allowed him to do things he relished for the sake of his good ambition. While she plied the stimulus of command, even of the rod when necessary, she never failed to use the sugar of inducement with every unpalatable morsel of performance or endurance when she could. She endeavored so to connect good conduct with things relished, and evil things with things disrelished, that he would come to know that virtue and goodness always pay, and vice and badness never. But most of all she sought to fix in him those greatest and best of motives which in their measure are boundless, such as the fear of God, the love of virtue, the desire of happiness, and endless rewards. And this she did so well that his conscience came to such growth that, irrespective of all mere earthly considerations, he could commit no moral offence without feelings of remorse.

Helen's Pearls.

Helen opened the paper her mother gave her and read: To Helen Newton, from her mother. A birthday gift of pearls to be worn by her so long as she shall live: I. Be patient; II. Be truthful; III. Be dutiful and trustworthy; IV. Be kind to all; V. Control your temper; VI. Control your tongue; VII. Be happy by making others so.

Helen was silent, and a shade of soberness gathered on her features. Like most girls at her age, she was coming to prize things according to their cost as well as good appearance; and while not inclined to discontent, or to be unhappy in disappointments, she for a little was chilled in feeling by finding imaginary instead of real pearls before her.

"Well, dear, what do you think of ma's pearls?"

"Ma, I don't really know what to think. Tell me please, how I'm to wear them." This was said in a way that indicated thoughts not specially pleasant in relation to her wearing her mother's gift.

"Would you be delighted, dear, if you could grow up to be a strong, influential, happy, and much-loved woman?"

"Indeed, I would, and, what is more, I mean to."

"Without trying?"

"Oh no! Of course I must try. But it's awful hard to be good, ma. Isn't it?'

"Yes, indeed. We need all the help we can obtain, and even then succeed but poorly at

---

* From "Father Solon: or the Helper Helped," by Rev. De Los Lull, a novel portraying in vivid colors the evil of the Mormon system, and its insidious methods of extending its influence on national and domestic life. 268 pages. Price $1.50. Published by *Wilbur B. Ketcham*, 71 Bible House, New York.

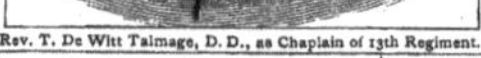

Rev. T. De Witt Talmage, D. D., as Chaplain of 13th Regiment.

Dorothy Introduced to Her Charge.

times. Now it is to assist you to such a life as you desire that mother presents you these pearls. You wish to know how to wear them. I will tell you, Practice, dear, everywhere, always practice them. If, at times, you seem to fail, still keep trying. Even though you think you are getting worse instead of better, still keep trying. Ask God to help you. Don't forget that. We are often sickest when nearest recovery, and often near glorious success when ready to despair. Keep trying, and the time will come when these pearls will be seen in your eyes, on your cheeks, on your lips, in your ways and manners. And these are the pearls none can steal, and which last and shine forever. Will you try to wear these, dear?"

"Yes, ma, I'll try."

Four years from that night, in the same room, at the same hour, on the same lounge, the two were again together. How the girl had grown! She was now sixteen, and advancing to womanhood. Many times, in those four years, her mother had despaired of success. "Either, she has forgotten the pearls," the mother thought; "or she has abandoned all effort to wear them." Hot temper, impatience, impulsiveness, had been among her faults, to which she sometimes yielded, with an abandonment that seemed to say, "There, I don't care! I'll try no more." Then again it was evident that her pearls were in her mind. Never had her mother alluded to them, or questioned her concerning her purposes. But now, when her sixteenth birthday had come, the pearls were where she had wished them to be, and shining more brightly than she dared to hope for.

DOROTHY'S CHARGE.

(See Illustration.)

It was a poor little cottage, old and weather-beaten, but its interior was scrupulously clean, and the garden around it was trimly and neatly kept. Dorothy Winter—or Widow Winter, as her neighbors called her—was not the woman to allow dirt or disorder to exist within her reach. She was a stout, motherly body, of middle age, poor, but with a heart large enough to help all who were in need around her. Money she could not give, but she was the first thought of in the village if sickness, death, or trouble of any kind, came upon a household. Her quiet, ready helpfulness had relieved many a burdened heart of the strain of attending to ordinary duties in a time of sorrow.

Dorothy need not have lived all alone in the poor old cottage. When her husband died, after two years of married life, and frequently since that time, Mr. Nicholls, her former employer, had urged her to return to the service she had quitted to be married. He had known her from boyhood, when, a young immigrant, she first landed in America, and came as a hired girl into his father's family. It was mainly through the blessing of God on her humble efforts, and her prayers, that he was led to look to Christ for salvation; and he often reminded her that he owed her a debt he could never repay. Dorothy, however, preferred to remain in her own home, and all Mr. Nicholls could do was to get her promise that, if she needed money, she would apply to him.

Some years had passed when, one day, to Dorothy's surprise, Mr. Nicholls paid her a visit. "I have come," he said, after he had satisfied her inquiries about his family, "to get help from you, Dorothy."

The good woman looked up in wonder. What help could she render to the wealthy merchant? She smiled in incredulity, but said: "I am sure if I can do anything to oblige you, sir, I shall be only too glad."

"I want you to take charge of a little girl, Dorothy, and see if you can do her any good. She is a particularly hard case; but, poor little thing! it is not all her own fault. Her father and mother have both gone wrong, and she seems bent on going the same sad road, if she is not stopped. Her father was a good hand; he was in my place, and was doing well till he got married. The foolish man lost his heart to a pretty face that belonged to a very bad woman. He began to deteriorate right away. She tempted him to all kinds of evil, and eventually he began stealing to gratify her demands. I forgave him three times, but at last I had to prosecute him, and he is now serving a term of imprisonment. His wretched wife has gone off somewhere, leaving their little daughter behind. I have tried to do something for her, but the child seems to have a taint in her blood. She is perverse, wild, and disobedient. I do not know if she can be saved from ruin, but if any one can do it, *you* can. I want you to see wh[at] you can do. What do you say?"

"God helping me, I will try, sir," said Dorothy. "There is nothing too hard for the Lord[."]

The preliminaries were easily settled, a han[d]some remuneration agreed upon, and next da[y] Mr. Nicholls took the little girl down to the vil[-]lage where Dorothy lived. As they approache[d] the cottage they saw Dorothy outside, broom [in] hand, sweeping away the fallen leaves.

"This is Ellen Smartt, Mrs. Winter. She [has] come to stay awhile with you," said Mr. Nich[-]olls, his hand resting on the child's shoulder.

Dorothy perceived that this was a formal in[-]troduction for the behoof of the little girl, wh[o] stood somewhat sullenly, without raising h[er] eyes to see the person to whom she was intro[-]duced. Dorothy held out her hand to the litt[le] girl in friendly fashion, saying, "You are wel[-]come, my dear; we shall be good friends, I hope[."]

"You are a servant," said the child, glancin[g] at the broom in Dorothy's hand. "I do no[t] shake hands with servants."

Dorothy started as if a snake had stung he[r] and held up her hand, which the child woul[d] not take, as if overcome with amazement. Ev[i]dently a difficult task was before her. "We[ll,] my dear," she said, "never mind shaking hand[s,] but we will try to be friends for all that. W[e] shall both be the happier if we do."

Mr. Nicholls looked on gloomily, still keepin[g] his hand on Ellen's shoulder, but half regre[t]ting, for his old friend's sake, that he had im[-]posed the burden upon her instead of sendin[g] the child to a public institution. Then he o[f]fered his own hand to Dorothy, and gave her a hearty shake as a practical reproof to the chil[d]. "You see what she is," he said, when, havin[g] entered the humble cottage, Ellen had gone t[o] make an exploration of the garden; "are yo[u] still willing to keep her?"

"Oh, yes!" said the good woman, "that['s] only silly pride; very likely her poor misguide[d] mother put that in her mind. God has melte[d] many proud hearts before to-day. I trust in Him[."]

"O woman, great is thy faith!" quoted M[r.] Nicholls, looking at her admiringly. "By al[l] means keep it; you will have need of it all."

The good widow spent a long time in praye[r] that night over the work she had undertake[n.] She took her Bible and read passages from th[e] tory of God's patience with srael in the wilderness, and neditated on the patience of Christ as exemplified in His life nd His dealings with His peo-le. Then again she prayed for he child, and before she retired o rest her heart was full of love nd pity for the poor little waif whose heart was prematurely lled with the evil that God aily bears with in children of irger growth.

Ellen would have been a worse hild than she was if she could ave resisted the love and gen-leness that Dorothy showed to-ard her. She melted day by ay under the benign influence, nd the good woman succeeded, hough not without some diffi-ulty, in getting her morning nd evening to offer a prayer to od, which was formal at first, ut under Dorothy's teaching oon became sincere and earnest. o message or inquiry ever came om the erring mother, for hich Dorothy was thankful. he father wrote at first occa-onally, but after a time regular-and frequently. He was sin-erely penitent, and was glad learn that his child was eing cared for by a Christian oman.

It was less than a year after-ard that Mr. Nicholls paid an-ther visit to the cottage and itnessed the amazing change the child. "How on earth id you succeed?" he asked, in stonishment.

"I have not succeeded," said orothy simply. "It is the Lord's ork, and He knows how to eal with proud and stubborn hearts. Ah me! e have all given Him experience in that work."

A Street Scene in Alexandria, Egypt.

A STREET IN ALEXANDRIA.

(See Illustration.)

IN striking contrast with a street scene in one our western cities is that depicted in the ustration on this page. Its characteristics e those of Oriental life such as we read of in e Bible. In the foreground is the indispensa-e water-carrier bearing a skin filled with water. his is the Oriental "bottle," the mention of hich in Matt. 9: 17 has often puzzled readers ifamiliar with eastern customs. The old and w "bottles," according to our understanding the word, would be of equal strength, and the w wine would be as secure in one as the her; but when the bottles are made of skins, e age of the receptacle is a matter which it is t safe to overlook. In the rear is a lady on ass out for an airing attended by her servant. er features are hidden by a veil which con-als all but her eyes. This custom prevails all rough the East, and is alluded to in Solomon's ng 4: 3 and 6: 7 (Rev. Ver.) "Thy temples e like a piece of pomegranate behind thy il." A woman in Oriental lands appearing in blic without this concealing veil would to is day be regarded as immodest. On the left, an elevation, are two of the traders of the y. Their establishments are of the simplest aracter. A few poles so arranged that a ece of matting can be spread over their heads the hottest part of the day are sufficient to rm a store. They bring their wares in baskets d sit smoking while they wait for customers. The city of Alexandria, of which this street is art, is not the ancient city founded by Alex-der the Great, which was built on the main-d, but the more modern city, which is built on e ancient island of Pharos, now connected by isthmus to the continent. It has 212,000 habitants and is the second city of Egypt. Cairo, the capital, is 112 miles to the southeast of it. It is now in a somewhat dilapidated condition, the Government having as yet failed to repair the damages wrought by the bombardment of the British fleet in 1882, and the ravages of the troops of Arabi Pasha, who made desperate attempts to burn the city.

THE EPOCHS OF A LIFE.

A NEW SERIAL STORY.

By Rev. L. S. Keyser.

(Continued from page 446.)

A Knightly Rescue.

THE next morning Hadley put on his exploration-suit, threw a book-bag over his shoulder, provided himself with pencil and note-book, preparatory to an excursion to the fields and woods.

This time he determined to explore the country west of the town. When he came to the railroad, he followed it northward a short distance, crossing the river that flowed near the town, by a narrow trestle-bridge. The bridge, which was an uncovered one, had no railing or walk for the convenience of foot-passengers. The ties extended about two feet beyond the iron rails on each side. Underneath there was a solid flooring of some kind, so that any one venturing across could not fall below into the river, if he kept between the rails.

"Rather a dangerous bridge to cross," thought Hadley, "especially if a train should come wheeling unexpectedly around the curve at the foot of yonder hill."

Having crossed the bridge he turned an oblique angle to the right, and clambered up the hill from the summit of which he could look down upon the broad valley which lay beneath, with the town nestling among the trees in the foreground and the well-cultivated farms stretching off in the distance toward the south and east. The young man drank in the glorious beauty of the autumnal scene, as he stood for a moment gazing upon it from his elevated position before continuing his walk through the woods in search of interesting specimens of the local fauna and flora. The silence and shade of the forest had a calming influence on Hadley's mind. Scarcely a feathered songster's note was to be heard; the "dim religious light," with the pensive rustling of the leaves in the breeze, produced a more tranquil feeling in the heart of the young man than he had felt for many a day. He was filled with an emotion that was almost worshipful. If it is true generally that "the universe takes its hue and tone and meaning from the inner experience and consciousness of the observer," it is also true that at times the aspect of the world around him exercises a potent influence upon his emotions, stirring him almost involuntarily to worship and reverence. It is difficult for any man, be he theist, atheist, or agnostic, to stand in the sanctuary-shadows of "God's first temples," and not feel that there is, or ought to be, a God.

Unfortunate indeed is the soul-condition of that man who cannot see the suggestions of deeper and diviner meaning in nature than those that appear upon the surface, who cannot see traces of the invisible in the visible. Unhappy, too, is the man whose doubts overwhelm him, who does not know, and yet who has sufficient spiritual earnestness to care to know. How tantalizing to him must be these limits of divinity in nature, that are constantly eluding him!

This was Hadley's mental condition, for whatever other faults may have clung to him, he was earnest. As he sat on a bowlder in the dim solitude of the forest, he seemed at times to hear the divine voice, and then it would again relapse into silence. By his speculations he had eliminated God from nature, and yet what would he not have given to be certain that there is a God! Without Him nature was only a blind force. There was no point upon which the mind could posit itself. There was no significance in all nature's mysterious beauty and mechanism; all her operations were devoid of purpose; her origin and destiny were shrouded in a mystery that appalled the mind. Evidences of design were all around him—in the veined leaves, in the solitary notes of a warbler in the distance — all things proclaimed the divine worker, and at times he felt that he was on the brink of a great discovery; then it would elude him, as the *ignis fatuus* eludes the bewildered traveller, and his mind was left dazed and blinded. Altering Huxley's agnostic paragraph to suit the trend of his thoughts, he said:

"If any man should tell me that there is a God, I should say to him, How do you know it? If he were to say to me, There is no God, I would still be compelled to repeat the question, How do you know *that?* I seem to be," he continued, "surrounded by an all-pervasive personal Presence. But I cannot grasp it. The proof is not absolute. It is shut off from me by an *opaque veil* of mystery. I cannot deny the existence of a personal Creator, neither can I assert it. Yes, Herbert Spencer is right in maintaining that what is beyond the cognition of our senses is unknown and unknowable. I am an agnostic, and must acknowledge my ignorance. Yet it would be a satisfaction to have certainty. It would give some stay to the soul,—if there is such an entity. What are those lines I read from Tennyson's 'In Memoriam' the other day?

'So runs my dream: but what am I?
An infant crying in the night:
An infant crying for the light:
And with no language but a cry.' "

Not a very satisfying doctrine, even to the young Pyrrhonist himself. His agnosticism diminished his enjoyment of nature. Could he have felt a spiritual contact between his soul and the Over-soul, in such a way that there would have been an assurance of personal communion, the world around him would have worn a different aspect. Pity he could not say with the poet:

"Father, thy hand
Hath reared these venerable columns; thou
Didst weave this verdant roof."

Or with the Psalmist:

"In His hand are the deep places of the earth; the strength of the hills is His also. The sea is His and He made it; and His hands formed the dry land. O come, let us worship and bow down: let us kneel before our Lord and Maker."

So pre-occupied was Hadley's mind with these speculations that a little brown-creeper flitted about among the twigs and leaves directly above him, and yet bird-lover as he was, he did not notice it. Presently he brought himself back to consciousness by a vigorous gesture of impatience, which frightened the little bird to a more distant twig. The fluttering feathered form attracted his attention, and he was once more on the alert. With excited pleasure he watched the bird for awhile, and then he renewed his explorations. As long as he occupied himself in active observations of nature, he was conscious of a spring, an exhilaration, of all his energies. It was only when he got into the speculative mood that the mysteries of life and nature oppressed him and filled him with disquietude.

When the noon hour came, he found a spring of clear, cold water, gushing from the foot of a steep, rocky bluff by the bank of the river, and here he sat down to eat the lunch with which he had provided himself. His walk had been so long and vigorous that he ate with hearty relish, and could not remember when he had enjoyed a repast so much; the spot was so sequestered and the rippling of the fountain mingled so melodiously with the wash of the river.

"Why, I could almost love my worst enemy," he exclaimed, springing to his feet. "No one can commune with nature in her calm, pensive moods without becoming a better man. I wonder whether, in spite of all the dogmatism of the theologians to the contrary, nature has not in herself the power to regenerate humanity. It is impossible for me to hate even that despicable divinity student with the rancor I felt toward him last night."

Yes; because nature is the handiwork of God, she possesses some of the morally renewing potencies that belong to her Creator.

On his return late in the afternoon, after he had made an extended tour, he at last stood upon the brow of the hill from which he had viewed the town and valley in the morning. The oblique rays of the western sun wrapped the whole scene in a mellow glow. Unless he cared to walk a mile and a half out of his way to the carriage-road, it was necessary for him to cross the river where he had crossed it earlier in the day. His limbs were tired, and he concluded to follow the more direct route across the bridge.

As Hadley sauntered down the hill, his attention was caught by the figure of a woman moving leisurely along the railway not far from the river and toward it. He stopped in surprise. He could not be mistaken. That lithesome form and graceful carriage would have been recognized by him at a greater distance. It was Miss Winters. His pulses bounded in him, and he involuntarily quickened his pace.

What object had the girl in view in coming to this out-of-the-way place? Ah! it was easy to conjecture. She had a bunch of wild-flowers in her hand and a book under her arm. Evidently she, too, was a lover of nature and outdoor life, and had found a quiet place in which to read, and analyze the flowers which she had gathered.

It was with some misgiving that he saw her start across the bridge. She hesitated a moment before she set her foot upon it; but it was evident that many people crossed it afoot, and of course, it was safe as long as there were no trains, for the ties were close together and, as has been said, the solid flooring underneath made it impossible for the pedestrian to fall through into the stream. The girl seemed to have little fear, although she selected her steps carefully upon the wooden ties.

When Hadley had reached the end of the bridge, she was almost half way across it. He had taken but a few steps upon the structure, when he heard a sound that froze the blood in his veins to cords of ice and almost paralyzed him. It was the whistle of the fast express train as it swept around the curve at the foot of the hill only a short distance away. With quick intuition he saw that he could easily make his escape by springing back from the bridge before the train came up; but as the girl was now just at the centre of the long span, it would probably be impossible for her to reach the other end before she was overtaken by the swiftly rushing engine. It was a moment of terrible suspense. The whistle of the locomotive had attracted the girl's attention, causing her to turn quickly and look back. In a moment she realized the danger. Hadley saw that her face turned white with terror, and for a moment she lost her power of movement. Then she started to run.

Meanwhile the engineer of the train had taken in the appalling situation. A quick succession of piercing sounds from the engine rent the air, and the brakes were immediately put on. But Hadley feared that it would be impossible to stop the train in so short a distance. For a moment he stood undecided, looking alternately at the approaching train and at the moving figure of the girl. But alas! her rapid pace prevented her now from choosing her steps carefully, so that her foot slipped between two of the ties, and she fell. "She is lost!" he cried.

Could he save his own life and allow the girl to perish? Could he rescue her if he tried? If she were beyond the power of human help, why should he throw away his own life in a futile effort to rescue her? These questions flashed with more than telegraphic speed through his mind. Suddenly, like an intuition, a plan by which he might save her, if he could reach her in time, came to him. It would involve a great risk, but he had no time for mental debate. His decision was made.

Then the terrified spectators on the engine saw the young man start forward and run with almost superhuman speed towards the prostrate woman's form. When Hadley reached Miss Winters, he found that she had just wrenched her foot loose from its fastening. As he rushed to her, she glanced up at him with an appealing look, but said not a word.

"Miss Winters, I will save you if I can," said he. "You must submit entirely to me."

Bending down, he lifted her outside of the track and laid her down near the ends of the cross-ties, parallel with the rails.

"Lie down here," he said, authoritatively, "and cling to the ties for your life."

She could not be injured if she remained in that position. He had just succeeded in securing her safety when the train came bearing down almost upon him. He made a quick leap to the ties that hung over the river in mid-air. The swaying motion of the bridge, and the too great momentum with which he had projected himself forward, caused him to lose his equipoise and he swayed outward a moment, and then seeing that he could not regain his balance, he allowed himself to drop from the bridge into the stream nearly twenty feet below.

Miss Winters saw him fall, and in her terror she relaxed her hold upon the ties. The oscillating movement of the bridge caused her to sway outward, and the next moment she too rolled off into the stream below, near her brave rescuer.

Once when Hadley was a lad, he and some of his playmates were bathing in a creek near his country home. By some mishap he got beyond his depth, and would have been drowned had not some of his more dexterous associates swam to him, and piloted him safely to shore. As soon as he had recovered his presence of mind, he formed a resolution to learn to swim, not knowing when a certain amount of aquatic ability would be necessary for the preservation of his life. Having carried out his resolve, he had become a dexterous swimmer.

It was to this acquired skill that he owed his safety and that of Miss Winters when they fell from the trestle-bridge into the river; for there was abundant scope for his dexterity just then. Fortunately both of them had struck the water in a vertical position, so that the harshness of their fall was broken. Divesting himself of coat and boots Hadley swam to the unfortunate girl, who had by this time sunk once, and was just coming again to the surface; and seizing her firmly, he instructed her not to throw her arms about him so as to impede his movements, and then struck out bravely for the shore, allowing the current to bear him and his charge down the stream below the bridge. With admirable presence of mind, the girl permitted him to pilot her through the deep water. In a few minutes he had reached shallow water, and by the time the frightened train-men had stopped the train, and had come to the river-bank, he and his dripping protégée were wading toward the shore.

Miss Winters did not faint or fall helplessly into any one's arms when she was at last deposited on *terra firma*. The only evidence of perturbation was her preternaturally pale face. Her seeming composure contrasted strangely with the terrible experience through which she had just passed. With a faint smile she said to Hadley before the wondering passengers who had hastened to the scene:

"Mr. Madelling, you are a real hero! You have saved my life, at the risk of your own. I have not words to thank you as I ought, but I shall never forget how much I owe you."

"Do not speak of it," said Hadley, bowing and blushing like a girl. "I am thankful I happened to be near enough to see your danger in time to save you. It was quite a chance that any one was there, and I am glad the opportunity of rendering you a service fell to my lot."

"I thank God," said Miss Winters, "that in the moment of peril, the man who did see me was a man so brave as to think less of his own danger than of mine. If you had not come when you did I must have been killed." The color mounted to her cheeks as she looked gratefully and admiringly at her preserver, who simply took the hand she held out to him, and grasped it fervently, without making any reply.

Of course the railroad men and passengers who had gathered around, were loud in praise of Hadley's feat, and eager in their offers of help. A coat and hat were thrust upon him, and a lady insisted on Miss Winters accepting a hat in place of the one now floating down the river. A countryman who had been drawn to the scene by the standing train and the unusual commotion, was despatched to get a carriage, on the arrival of which Hadley and Miss Winters were driven to their homes.

"I hope we shall be friends, Mr. Madelling," said Miss Winters, as they approached her destination; "it was a strange introduction, but I am not likely, for my part, ever to forget it."

"You make too much of it, Miss Winters. Any man in my place, worthy the name of man, would have done as I did. In offering me your friendship, you make me feel that I am much over paid. Believe me, it is a privilege I value very highly. Good-bye," Hadley said, as he saw Miss

Winters safe in her room: "I trust you will suf-er no ill effects from your immersion." Then, e-entering the carriage, he was driven to his own rooms, where he had to give minute explanations to Dane of his drenched condition.

(*To be Continued.*)

THE TABERNACLE.

By Mrs. M. Baxter.

S.S. Lesson for July 29, Exodus 40: 1—16. Golden Text, Rev. 21: 3.

The Human Tabernacle—God Dwelling in Man—The Outer Court of the Body—The Place of Burnt Offering—The Place for the Laver of Cleansing—The Tabernacle of the Church—Fitly Framed Together—The Desire to be Pillars—The Best Parts not Conspicuous—Givers Restrained—The Furnishing and Anointing—The Names on Christ's Heart—Possession Taken—The Essential of Consecration.

"AND I heard a great voice out of heaven, aying Behold, the tabernacle of God is with nen, and He will dwell with them, and they hall be His people, and God Himself shall be with them, and be their God." (Rev. 21: 3.) The tabernacle was to be God's witness that He welt with His people; that He was not like he false Gods of the heathen—afar off. Some eople treat God simply as a referee to be called pon in extreme and unusual emergencies; but hese do not really know Him at all. Others, nd they are God's children, rejoice in His presence sometimes; but at others they would rather eep Him at a distance. But those who live in ommunion with God dwell in God and God in hem. Each child of God may be a little tabernacle with its outer court of the body, its holy lace of the soul, and its Holy of holies in the pirit where God is specially manifest. "What, now ye not that your temple is the temple of he Holy Ghost, which is in you?" (1 Cor. 6: 19.) : is in

The Outer Court

hat we find the altar of burnt offering, "before he door of the tabernacle," for if the body is ot presented "a living sacrifice, holy, acceptable to God, which is our reasonable service" Rom. 12: 1), we cannot become the dwelling-lace of God. On the altar of burnt offering the wards of the sin offering were also offered in he outer court, where Jews and Gentiles alike ad access. God wills that our bodies should e a witness that sin is put away and atoned for. The open countenance which says, "There is herefore now no condemnation to them which e in Christ Jesus." (Rom. 8: 1.) The new song thanksgiving to our God (Ps. 40: 3), the unhesitating step and erect gait of one who has st his burden upon the Lord, the healing of e body as well as the soul with His stripes—l this is in the outer court of the tabernacle, hich answers to the body.

Again, we find the laver in the outer court. he priests must be cleansed there before they n enter into the holy place. "Thou shalt set laver between the tent and the altar of burnt fering." It is in the outer court that greediss, laziness, self-indulgence, etc., are cleansed. nd then within the holy place there stands e table with "the bread of thy God, the ndlestick, for "Ye are the light of the world" Matt. 5: 14), and the altar of incense continual mmunion—all signifying intercourse with od. But within, beyond the veil, there was e ark and the mercy-seat with the glorious ekinah; God filling the Holy of holies with mself, represented by the candlestick in the ly place which yet no eye but that of a priest ight see, and approached by the blood upon e altar, the witness to a whole world that sin s atoned for.

But while the tabernacle is a type of our dies, it is before all things a type of the urch of Christ, the many in one. "For as we ve many members in one body, and all memrs have not the same office, so we, being ny, are

One Body in Christ.

d every one members one of another. (Rom. 12: 4-5.) God ordained that the tabernacle should be moveable, easily erected, and easily taken down, but the parts made so perfectly to fit one into the other that one board, one socket, one pin, one hook, one fillet, one tache, one ring wanting, and it would be imperfect. God would have us not only to fit into Him, but into one another, so that if one member suffer, all the members suffer. (1 Cor. 12: 26). In the erection of the tabernacle, there were parts which formed the frame-work, such as the pillars and boards; there were others, and few of them, which were seen from without, such as the curtains, which were four thicknesses. Many a child of God wants to do some great thing, or to be some great one, prominent before the eyes of all men. Yet only one of the curtains was seen from without, and that the roughest one, of badgers' skins. At the door of the tabernacle, a little part of the other curtains might be seen, but the innermost were for the eye of God and His priests alone. "The King's daughter is all glorious within." (Ps. 45: 13.) Some would willingly be like pillars, but while these were comparatively few in number, the smaller parts were very, very numerous. The pillars and the board were only overlaid with gold, while the sockets, the pins, the rings, the taches, the hooks, and all the little parts which went to make up the unity of the whole were of gold, silver, or brass, which would stand wear or fire, as the overlaid boards and pillars could not. Let us be content, however small our place is, so that we are ministering to the unity of the Church of Christ.

The people were so happy in the giving of their free-will offerings and their free-will service, that they continued to bring offerings every morning, until there was "much more than enough for the service of the work which the Lord commanded to make," and Moses was obliged

To Restrain the People from Bringing!

Bezaleel joined the parts together, and "it became *one* tabernacle," just as in the Church of Christ there is "one Lord, one faith, one baptism"; and it is our privilege and duty to "keep the unity of the Spirit in the bond of peace." (Eph. 4: 3-5.)

On the *first* day of the *first* month, Moses was commanded to erect and furnish the tabernacle. "Seek ye *first* the kingdom of God, and his righteousness." (Matt. 6: 33.) Moses did not seek to improve upon the pattern which God had shewn him; he followed out the plan of God. The ark was placed within the Holy of holies, and covered in with the veil. Then there was the table garnished with the shewbread, in token that we have the privilege to minister to God, and the candlestick placed and lit—type of Christ as the Bread of Life and the Light of the world. And then came the golden altar with its smoke ascending before the veil—a type of Christ's constant intercession for us. The altar of burnt offering and the laver were set up in the outer court, and there Moses took the anointing oil. God had commanded that none should be made like it: "Upon man's flesh it shall not be poured; neither shall ye make any other like it, after the composition of it; it is holy, and it shall be holy unto you." (Ex. 30: 32.) As a type of God the Holy Ghost, the anointing oil was most holy, and everything which had been made by man must be anointed with it in order that the tabernacle might be the dwelling-place of God. "Thou shalt take the anointing oil, and anoint the tabernacle and all that is therein, and shalt hallow it and all the vessels thereof: and it shall be holy." The altar and its vessels, and the laver too, must be sanctified, or set apart, for God by the holy anointing oil. No ceremony, no sacrament, no worship, can be accepted by God except it is anointed by the Holy Ghost. "God is a Spirit, and they that worship Him must worship Him in spirit and in truth." (Rom. 4: 24.) Then Aaron and his sons must be anointed: first washed, then clothed with holy garments, then anointed. Jesus, our great High priest, being baptized, and praying, the heaven was opened, and the Holy Ghost descended in a bodily shape, like a dove upon Him." (Luke 3: 21, 22).

He as Man was Anointed.

When the anointing oil was poured upon Aaron he bore upon his shoulder the signets of onyx stones, graven with the names of the children of Israel, and on his heart he bore the breastplate engraven with the same names. No man saw on the breast of Jesus those precious stones and names engraven, but most surely He bears our names upon His heart, and the government of every one who trusts Him is surely placed upon His shoulders. But Aaron's sons must also be anointed. "He shall see his seed." (Isa. 53: 10.) As Adam begat a son after his likeness, so Christ has a seed after His likeness: "He made us to be a kingdom, priests with His God and Father. (Rev. 50: 6, R. V.) Moses was commanded, "Thou shalt anoint them as thou didst anoint their father, that they may minister unto Me in the priests' office; for their anointing shall surely be an everlasting priesthood throughout their generations." "Thus did Moses, according to all that the Lord commanded him, so did he." Seven times in this chapter it is said that Moses did "as the Lord commanded Moses." It was no hard task to him to carry out the mind of God; it was perfect joy and delight; it was the way of wisdom, whose "ways are ways of pleasantness, and all her paths are peace." (Pro. 3: 17.) "So Moses finished the work." But the chief thing of all had yet to happen. The tabernacle was made, set up, joined together, a glorious type of perfect unity; it was sanctified, but it was yet empty. "Then a cloud covered the tent of the congregation, and the glory of the Lord filled the tabernacle." It was the supreme moment—

God had Taken Possession.

Moses was no longer busily going in and out; his work was done, and he stood outside. "Moses was not able to enter into the tent of the congregation, because the cloud abode thereon, and the glory of the Lord filled the tabernacle." O how many there are who make every provision for a life consecrated to God! they anxiously seek to know His will, and just as earnestly accomplish it when it is known; they offer themselves, with all they are and have, to God; but because they do not go outside, and leave to God what they have given to Him, the cloud of glory does not fill them. Self, with all its energy and zeal, with all its anxiety and care, with all its fear and unrest, must give place before an indwelling God. Self must be without for God to be within. "I want," "I think," "I hope," "I feel," "I can," "I can't," and all the other "*I's*" have to go outside, that what *God* wants, what *He* thinks and plans and purposes, may take the place of self. When God came in He took the entire responsibility; Moses had not the management; God took it all. "When the cloud was taken up from over the tabernacle, the children of Israel went onward in all their journeys; but if the cloud were not taken up, then they journeyed not till the day that it was taken up." "For the cloud of the Lord was upon the tabernacle by day, and fire was on it by night, in the sight of all the house of Israel, throughout all their journeys." God dwelt with them.

CONTENT.

"I have learned in whatsoever state I am, therewith to be content."—PHIL. iv: 11.

HAVE I learned, in whatsoever
State, to be content?
Have I learned this blessed lesson,
By my Master sent,—
And with joyous acquiescence
Do I greet His will,
Even when my own is thwarted,
And my hands lie still?

Surely it is best and sweetest,
Thus to have Him choose,
Even though some work I've taken,
By this choice I lose.
Folded hands need not be idle,—
Fold them but in prayer,
Other souls may toil far better
For God's answer there.

They that reap receive their wages,
Those who work, their crown,
Those who *pray*, throughout the ages
Bring blest answers down:
In "whatever state" abiding
Till the Master call,
They at eventide will find Him
Glorified in all.

What though I can do so little
For my Lord and King,
At His feet I sit and listen,
At His feet I sing.
And whatever my condition,
All in love is meant;
Sing, my soul, thy recognition!
Sing, and be content!

—*Selected.*

J. E. JEWETT, Publisher, 77 Bible House, New York, will furnish the above poem in leaflet form at twenty cents per hundred. *A Sample Packet of 50 leaflets assorted (no two alike), will be sent post-paid, for ten cents.* Postage stamps taken.

Christian Work in Mexico.

Through the reading of the Holy Scriptures translated into Spanish some earnest souls in Mexico have, by God's blessing, been led to a clear knowledge of the Gospel. From their numbers able preachers of the Christian faith in its primitive purity have been raised up, around whom congregations have been gathered from among the humble poor, who have been the first to publicly welcome and defend the pure Gospel in Mexico. The members of these congregations, rich in faith, have worked earnestly and bravely for Christ and His truth among their fellow countrymen in that beautiful Southern portion of North America called Mexico. Schools have been established by them, in which large numbers of bright boys and girls have received a good secular education and have been carefully taught the Christian faith. From the children thus educated faithful Christian workers have been raised up. A Mexican Branch of the Church of Christ, that maintains the faith in its purity and integrity, has been organized among these native Christians in the Republic of Mexico. The members of this Mexican Church of Christ, though gathered mostly from among the poor, are yet doing a most important Christian work. To continue that work, we need to pay a few leading workers small monthly salaries, and also to defray some current expenses. To raise the needed funds we have formed a society with an office at 43 Bible House, New York, U. S., and should be pleased to have many of our fellow Christians join this society by becoming regular contributors to its treasury. We are trying to secure monthly or quarterly contributions to meet the regular monthly expenses of the work. In order to continue and extend the work, we wish to raise four hundred dollars a month, by endeavoring to have four hundred persons each give on an average *one dollar every month* to this object, leaving the donors to give less or more as they may be able and willing.

We earnestly invite all who will, to join us in this systematic effort in behalf of the cause of Christ in Mexico, by becoming monthly subscribers to this fund. We have already regular subscribers whose gifts amount monthly to over eighty dollars, and a growing circle of friends who are forwarding us occasional donations.

This Mexican Church of Christ is a very effective instrumentality through which to do Christian work among the many millions on this Western Hemisphere who speak the Spanish language, comparatively few of whom have ever had a Bible in their hands. A beautiful church building has been secured in the City of Mexico as the centre of the activities of this Mexican Church of Christ. Through the workers connected with that centre more than forty congregations have been gathered from among the poor in different parts of the Republic of Mexico. We have some faithful and able preachers now in the field, but more young men need to be trained for the ministry. Multitudes of Protestant children in Mexico, some of them orphans, need to be educated. We make three requests of you, Christian reader: *first,* that you will, if possible, become a monthly or quarterly subscriber in behalf of this Christian work; *second,* that you will try and induce your friends also to contribute to it; *third,* that you will remember this precious work in Mexico in your prayers.

We most sincerely thank all who are already generously contributing to this Christian work for their timely and generous gifts, and we earnestly invite many others, to unite with us in aiding it by also becoming monthly subscribers in its behalf. Those who may not feel that they can give as much as a dollar a month are earnestly asked to give what they can, whenever they are able—EVERY LITTLE HELPS. Fellow Christian, if you will generously consent to contribute a dollar a month or more or less to the work, will you kindly inform me of the fact? Contributions either large or small can be mailed directly to my address as follows:

BISHOP H. C. RILEY, care of J. P. HEATH,
No. 43 Bible House, New York, U. S.

Vol. XI., No. 30. Office, 63 Bible House, N. Y. THURSDAY, JULY 26, 1888. Annual Subscription, $1.50.

PRESIDENT CLEVELAND.

CONTENTS OF THIS NUMBER.

PORTRAITS AND LIVES OF PRESIDENT CLEVELAND AND GENERAL HARRISON, and PICTURE OF THE WHITE HOUSE.
THE USES OF STRATAGEM. Dr. Talmage's Sermon Last Sunday Morning at the Peekskill Camp.
ANECDOTES RELATED AT EVANGELISTIC MEETINGS.
PROPHETIC EVENTS BETWEEN 1889 and 1891. By William Birch.
Mexican Mothers at School—A Living National Emblem—A Million-Dollar Life Insurance—Infidelity in Utah—Theatre Preaching in Japan—A Hindoo Doctor's Conversion.
SELF-INFLICTED WOUNDS. A New Sermon by C. H. Spurgeon.
PORTRAITS AND LIVES OF LEVI P. MORTON AND ALLEN G. THURMAN.
A ROOM IN THE WHITE HOUSE.
OWEN LITTLE'S VINDICATION. (Illustrated.)
THE EPOCHS OF A LIFE. (Con.)
THE BURNT OFFERING. By Mrs. M. Baxter.

GEN. BENJAMIN HARRISON.

THE RIVAL CANDIDATES FOR THE PRESIDENCY—THE WHITE HOUSE.

THE RIVAL CANDIDATES.

THE great quadrennial struggle between the two political parties for the control of the Government is this time to be waged on questions of principle and policy rather than on personal qualities. That is a decided advantage to the country. The bitter personalities which characterized the campaign of 1884 will never be forgotten, and the social dissension and ill-feeling they evoked have not even yet been allayed. Campaign speakers devoted their eloquence to the denunciation or the defence of the moral character of the candidates, and to a discussion of scandals which were an offence to the public ear. This year there is reason to hope that the speeches will be of a higher order. The voters will have to be instructed. What they need to know in order to make an intelligent decision between the rival candidates is the effect of an economic principle. On the one side is the Republican candidate, who holds that our national prosperity demands for its maintenance and development, that goods imported from foreign countries shall pay certain duties, with the avowed object of raising their price in order that producers of the same articles at home may not be undersold in our own markets by foreign producers who pay low wages. On the other side the Democratic candidate contends that the duties should be abolished in some cases, and lowered in others, in order that the masses of the people may purchase their goods at the lowest price attainable.

That these two platforms open a very wide field for discussion is evident. They affect the interests not only of manufacturers and producers, but of wage-earners and tradesmen, and it will become every citizen to study them carefully before casting his vote. At this crisis his affiliation with his party will be of less importance to him than the right settlement of this question of national policy. A discussion of this momentous question would be out of place in these columns; but from the campaign documents of the rival parties, and from the speeches of the rival statesmen, abundant opportunities will be afforded for gaining information on the subject.

The fact that this struggle will during the next three months be the all-absorbing subject of interest throughout the nation is not to be ignored. THE CHRISTIAN HERALD, therefore, in conformity with its usual custom of dealing with live topics, this week presents its readers with portraits and brief sketches of the lives of the rival candidates. This is done without political bias, and with less apprehension of invidious construction than there would have been had the personality of the men been a more prominent feature of the campaign.

PRESIDENT CLEVELAND.

GROVER CLEVELAND, the Democratic candidate for the Presidency, was born at Caldwell, N. J., on March 18, 1837. He is, therefore now in his fifty-second year. His great-grandfather, Aaron Cleveland, who was a native of Norwich, Conn., was, in 1779, a member of the Legislature. He afterward became a Congregational minister, and died at New Haven in 1815. Richard Cleveland, the father of Grover Cleveland, was born in Norwich in 1804, and was a graduate of Yale College. He taught school in Baltimore, studied theology, spent some months at Princeton, and in 1828 was ordained a Presbyterian clergyman. Grover Cleveland, who was the fifth of nine children, was educated at the public schools of New Jersey, and at an academy in Clinton, Oneida County, N. Y.

At the age of sixteen he became a clerk in the New York Blind Asylum. There he happened to meet a young man who prevailed upon him to seek his fortunes in the West. They started for Cleveland, O. On their way they stopped at Buffalo, N. Y., where young Cleveland paid his respects to his uncle, Mr. Lewis F. Allen. This gentleman was very favorably impressed with the young man, whom he then saw for the first time. As much to dissuade his nephew from the western venture as anything, Mr. Allen told him that he was in need of a clerk, and if he would stop in Buffalo, he should have the situation. The offer was accepted; but after a short time the young man persuaded his uncle to let him study law, and consent was given. He was articled to a law firm in Buffalo, and served them so much to their satisfaction, that they voluntarily paid him a handsome salary. In 1859 Mr. Cleveland was

Admitted to the Bar.

He continued, however, with his employers for four years afterward. He was then appointed Assistant District Attorney for the county of Erie, which position he filled for a period of three years. He was nominated by the Democratic County Convention, in 1865, for District Attorney, to succeed Mr. Torrance, but was defeated at the polls by Lyman K. Bass. Mr. Cleveland then formed a law partnership with the late I. V. Vanderpoel, on the 1st of August, 1866, which was continued until January, 1869. He then became a member of the firm of Laning, Cleveland & Folsom, the late A. P. Laning and the late Oscar Folsom—*whose daughter he married on June 2, 1886*—being his associates. The firm remained in existence until Mr. Cleveland retired therefrom to assume the duties of Sheriff of Erie County, to which office he was chosen at the election in November, 1870. At the expiration of his official term as sheriff, he became a member of the firm of Messrs. Bass, Cleveland & Bissell, with Lyman K. Bass and Wilson S. Bissell as associates. From this Mr. Bass soon retired, owing to ill-health, and the firm became Cleveland & Bissell. In 1881 Mr. Cleveland was elected

Mayor of Buffalo

by an unprecedented majority, running five thousand ahead of his own ticket! The following year he was nominated for the governorship of New York. The disaffection between the stalwart and half-breed sections of the Republican party was then at fever heat, and this election afforded an opportunity for the gratification of revengeful feelings that had been smouldering for some time. Many Republicans voted for the Democratic candidate, and he was elected by the large majority of 192,854.

The Presidency.

Two years later came the Presidential election. The nomination by the Republican Convention of Mr. James G. Blaine was made with the knowledge that it was distasteful to certain Republican leaders; but so strong was the candidate and so enthusiastic were his friends, that it was believed that the opposition to him would be counterbalanced. That conviction very nearly came true—but not quite. Mr. Cleveland did not carry New York by the former enormous majority in 1884, but he did carry it, and it gave him the Presidency. During his administration some of his fiercest opponents have been men of his own party, but there can be no question that in the main the party has been satisfied with him, for his renomination on June 7 last by the Democratic National Convention was made with an enthusiasm and a unanimity almost unprecedented in political history.

GEN. BENJAMIN HARRISON

THE Republican candidate for the Presidency was born at North Bend, Ohio, August 20, 1833, and is therefore fifty-five years of age. Among his ancestors, one especially gained distinction in history. He was hanged for the part he took in helping to deliver Great Britain from the tyranny of King Charles I. In the well known diary of Samuel Pepys, the following passage occurs, under date of October 13, 1660: "I went out to Charing Cross to see Major-General Harrison hanged, drawn and quartered, which was done there; he looked as cheerful as any man could do in that condition. He was presently cut down, and his head and heart shown to the people, at which there was great shouts of joy. It is said that he said that he was sure to come shortly at the right hand of Christ to judge them that now had judged him, and that his wife do expect his coming again. Thus it was my chance to see the King beheaded at Whitehall, and to see the first blood shed in revenge for the King at Charing Cross." General Harrison had signed the warrant for the execution of Charles I., and had been appointed by Oliver Cromwell, to convey the captive king from Windsor to Whitehall, for trial. When, therefore, Charles II. came to the throne, and began to take vengeance for his father's death, Harrison was not overlooked. He died a martyr to his country. The descendants of the patriot of the Commonwealth came to America soon after the hanging at Charing Cross, but the family did not come prominently into view until just before the Revolutionary War.

His Family.

Benjamin Harrison, of Virginia, the great-grand-father of the candidate, was one of the signers of the Declaration of Independence, and was prominent in public affairs from 1774 until his death in 1791, being for four years a member of Congress and three times Governor of Virginia. General William Henry Harrison, his son, served his country almost continuously from 1791 to 1841, both in military and civil positions. He fought the battle of Tippecanoe in 1811, was a member of Congress, a United States Senator from Ohio, and for one month (March 4 to April 4, 1841, when he died), President of the United States. His son, John Scott Harrison, who was a member of Congress from 1853 to 1857, died in 1879, or 1880, at his home in Cincinnati.

The youth of the candidate was a studious one. He acquired the rudiments of education at home, and then went to a private school at Cincinnati to be prepared for college. In 1852 he graduated from Miami University, Oxford, Ohio, fourth in a class of sixteen. He immediately commenced the study of law in the office of Judge Storer. The next year he married the daughter of Rev. J. W. Scott, of Oxford, O., and with the small sum of $1,000, part of which was a legacy from an aunt and part given him by his father, commenced married life at twenty years of age. He shortly afterward removed to Indianapolis, where his painstaking labor soon won him a fair

Practice at the Bar.

A remarkable murder case was left unexpectedly on Harrison's hands about a year after his admission to the bar. The prosecuting attorney was called away, and Harrison had to take charge of the case with only one night for preparation. It was a case of poisoning, and he sat up all night with a physician studying the nature of poisons. The next day his speech showed so complete a command of the subject that he won the case, and Mr. Wallace, the counsel opposed to him, offered him a partnership. This firm continued business until 1860, when Wallace became clerk of the Circuit Court, and Harrison Supreme Court Reporter. It was in that year that Harrison first became prominent in politics. Thomas A. Hendricks was stumping for the Democratic nominee in the Presidential election of 1860, and his friends challenged Harrison to a debate with him. Harrison accepted, and Hendrick's friends exclaimed: "What a headlong fool the young man must be!" But the story goes, that Hendricks was worsted in the battle of logic and appeal, and that the Chairman of the meeting remarked: "I never heard a man skin an opponent as quickly as Ben Harrison did Hendricks that day."

On the Outbreak of the War

Mr. Harrison, at the suggestion of Gov. Morton, recruited a regiment, and, after being a second lieutenant and then captain, he was made colonel of the seventeenth Indiana. After garrison duty in Kentucky and Tennessee, he went into the thick of the fight, and at the battle of Resaca, May 15, 1864, he led the assault, rushed at head of his regiment over to the enemy's lines, and captured both men and guns. For his charge at Resaca he was brevetted brigadier-general. Again, at Peach Tree Creek he was publicly complimented for his bravery.

He continued to do gallant work in the field, and served till the end of the war.

After the war General Harrison was re-elected Supreme Court Reporter, and served till 1868 Then he gave himself up to the law altogether for eight years. He kept out of politics until 1876, when Godlove Orth, the nominee for Governor, having declined the honor, Harrison took it. He made a hot contest, but he was beaten. In 1880 he was rewarded for his services to his party by being elected

United States Senator.

At once he went to the front in that body as a forcible debater. He also took a prominent share in the labors of the Committee on Foreign Relations. In 1887, the Indiana Legislature was Democratic, and Gen. Harrison lost the opportunity of being his own successor. He then retired to private life in Indianapolis.

Gen. Harrison is not an orator in the popular sense of the word, but he is a very forcible speaker. His voice is somewhat shrill, but not unpleasant, and his enunciation is so clear that he is easily understood. In stature, he is under the average size. A massive head, short neck, broad shoulders, rather robust chest, and short legs, make him a noticeable man. He is an active member of the Presbyterian Church, and for several years conducted a Bible-class in the Sunday School.

Gen. Harrison's portrait on the first page, is from a photograph by Messrs. Sherman & McHugh, 11 East 42d Street, New York.

THE WHITE HOUSE.

(*See picture on first page.*)

THE Executive Mansion is on the west side of the city of Washington, and is one mile and a half from the Capitol. It is two stories high, 170 feet long, and 86 feet deep, with a portico on the north supported on eight Ionic columns, and a semicircular colonnade on the south of six Ionic columns. It is of free-stone, and is painted white, from which circumstance it is popularly known as the "White House." The corner-stone was laid in 1792, and the edifice was occupied by President Adams in 1800. It was burned by the British in 1814. In 1815 Congress authorised its restoration, and it was again occupied in 1818. The grounds lie between Fifteenth and Seventeenth Streets, and extend to the Potomac, comprising about 75 acres, of which about 20 are enclosed as the President's private grounds, are handsomely laid out, and contain a fountain.

The mansion is furnished with the magnificence becoming the abode provided by the people for the Chief Executive. The numerous suites of rooms are handsomely decorated, and, in many cases, beautifully frescoed, while oil paintings of great rarity and value adorn the walls. The President and his family occupy the western wing, while the eastern side is mainly devoted to reception rooms and offices, the Great East Room being the principal saloon where the President holds his great receptions. The other saloons are called the Green, Blue, and Red Rooms, after the color of their furniture and fittings.

ANECDOTES RELATED AT RECENT EVANGELISTIC MEETINGS.

Janet's Melancholy Cured.—Mr. Davison, speaking at a revival meeting, said: "On one occasion I was asked to visit an aged woman, who, though a Christian, was a joyless one, and apparently always sunk in the depths of melancholy, unable to find in Christ that precious sense of satisfaction for which every believer yearns. I called upon her and read to her that verse, 'This is My beloved Son in whom I am well pleased.' 'Now,' I said, 'you see that God is well pleased with Christ; is He not sufficient to satisfy you?' Janet looked up with tears in her dim eyes and, clasping her hands, said, 'Yes, from this hour I shall rest satisfied with Christ.' Her melancholy is now a thing of the past, and she looks the picture of contentment."

The Midnight Letter.—An Evangelist Remarks: "I had a very peculiar experience not long ago. Upon retiring to bed one night, though tired, I was unable to sleep, and at last, yielding to an unaccountable and irresistible influence at midnight, I arose, and taking out a sheet of paper, proceeded to write to a friend these words, 'Where, oh where will you spend eternity?' I addressed the letter and laid it aside, and going again to bed soon fell fast asleep, the uneasiness being now entirely removed. I mailed the letter the first thing next morning, and I learned soon afterwards that my friend received it just twenty minutes before he died and was ushered into eternity. Whether he had taken heed to that momentous question I know not for certain, but I believe he did: but it was most assuredly a very special call."

Cause of a Mother's Anxiety.—A Friend relates: "A lady residing in the country, and whose son was about to begin business in a great northern city, visited her clergyman and asked him to pray for her boy, that God might keep him and preserve him from the power of temptation. 'I am not afraid of his falling into sin,' said the lady, 'but what I fear is his getting into a circle of Christians who drink wine.' Christians and wine drinkers? Does it not seem as if there were a contradiction in the very terms? Yet it is too true that in nominally Christian society a young man is often induced for the first time to take wine, and continuing to take it, as he says, in moderation, and what is the frequent result? A lost character, ruined health, and ultimately a drunkard's grave. No wonder the mother felt solicitude for her son!"

How an Early Martyr Died.—Rev. R. F. Horton said: "I recollect reading that when the first missionary went into the country which is now called Prussia, in the tenth century—St. Adelbert—a country which was then quite as heathen as China is to-day, he went barefooted and in a serge gown, and he walked through the streets of the villages, and along the high-roads, and he talked to them all about the love of Christ, and at last, his biographer tells us, he came into the grove of the gods, where the priests rushed out upon him in fury, and clubbed him to death, and he fell down and died, saying, 'Lord Jesus, receive my spirit,' and he fell upon the earth in the form of a crucifix. If we are to call this world to Christ, we must bring before the people the cross of Christ, and we can do that only by ourselves becoming crucified with Him who died for us."

The Memory of "Father David."—Mr. A. T. Swann, of *The Good News* mission vessel, Lake Tanganyika, Central Africa, said: "Moffat is dead, Livingstone is dead, but God liveth and reigneth, and shall reign in spite of all His enemies. He has been at work on all our mission fields. What has He done in Central Africa? Well, He has started by taking to the Great Lake a small boat called *The Morning Star*. Men said we were all fanatics—well, they very often say that when we get enthusiastic over the work of God. But to-day she floats, a living witness to what can be done by men who have got the work of God at their very hearts. I well remember standing at Ujiji, that historic town, and looking at the very spot where Stanley met Livingstone. Why, I felt it was sacred ground, and I thought, 'Well, if that good man was as good as we read he was, he has left some trace behind him.' I said to one gray Arab, a slave-hunter, a man who is the cause of the death of some hundreds of Central African people every year, 'Did you know Dr. David Livingstone? do you remember him?' He said, 'No.' My heart went down. I said, 'Don't you know the man who used to wear the peaked cap, and who had the box of medicine, and who used to go about looking for the rivers and the mountains?' 'Oh!' he said, 'you mean Father David.' That is the impression that a godly life left on one of the blackest men that ever walked Central African ground. And I am proud to think that God has given me the privilege of walking in some of Father David's footsteps."

An Instance of Moral Suicide. A Minister says that "a little time ago a City Missionary was called upon to visit a man who was dying. He read and prayed with him, and strove to comfort the dying man by showing him Christ the only true way of salvation; but all to no effect. At length the poor unhappy man roused himself up and, turning to his visitor, said, 'See here, young man; it is no use your wasting time with me: you can do no good. I know the way of salvation as well as you, and I should like to enter it but I *cannot*; listen to my story. In the year 1860 it was a time of great revival, and I, among others, was urged to give myself to Christ, but I would not. Many times the Holy Spirit renewed His strivings, and I felt constrained to yield, yet I steadfastly set my face against it. From that time God's Spirit left me, and though I *would* come I *cannot*, and I am going into the internal world a lost sinner.' 'God's Spirit will not always strive with man.'"

Standing Like a Daniel.—Mr. Hamilton says: "I remember a young fellow of seventeen years, employed in the office of a professional gentleman, a manager in a fashionable city church, being sent by him to another gentleman, a brother manager, requesting him to take his turn at the collection plate. While the messenger waited his reply, the gentleman offered him a glass of spirits. My young friend, being an abstainer, declined; he next offered him wine, but again getting a refusal, he said, 'Then surely you will take a glass of stout?' But the lad stood firm to his principle. The gentleman, looking slightly disappointed, said, 'Well, I like to see a young man with strict principles.' But it is certainly a strange way to show appreciation by trying to overcome principles which you admire. What can be expected of young men when they see their elders, their leaders in business and religion, not only themselves taking liquor, but urging it upon young men."

An Unexpectedly Bright Sunset.—Mr. Stewart says: "It is wonderful how Christ lights up the dark passages in our life and makes the rough places smooth; even the valley of the shadow of death He irradiates with His smile. I knew a man who had been a drunkard for over twenty years, but at length was brought to Christ, and remained a consistent Christian for seventeen years. During all that time the recollection of his evil days seemed to cast an habitual gloom upon him and constituted a great burden on his mind. This would be the last man one would expect to show a joyous spirit in the face of death, yet I, who was a witness to that death-bed, can testify that a more glorious one I never saw. What a glorious difference came over him before the end! The smile from the Father's face was reflected upon that of the dying man. All the while his mind was perfectly clear, though living in an ecstasy of joy. He quoted with great accuracy long passages of Scripture bearing upon his salvation. Just immediately before the end those who watched were surprised to hear him beginning to sing that beautiful hymn, 'I do believe, I will believe, that Jesus died for me.' Nothing but the veritable presence of the Saviour could have illumined that death-bed and made it glad with the unutterable gladness of heaven."

THE USES OF STRATAGEM.

Dr. Talmage's Sermon to the Thirteenth Regiment of the New York State National Guards, preached at the Camp at Peekskill, N. Y., last Sunday morning, July 22, 1888.

"Then ye shall rise up from the ambush, and seize upon the city." Josh. 8 : 7.

A Thrilling Drama—The Ambuscade Planned—The Night Before the Battle—The General's Anxiety—The Stratagem Successful—I. A Victorious Retreat—A Wise Policy for the Drunkard—A Fatal Spoonful of Brandy—A Flight from Bad Books—The Church's Retreat—Before Persecution—The Retreat in the "Mayflower"—Christ's Retreat from Throne to Manger—The Disturbance in the Tomb—II. The Triumph of the Wicked is Short—The Gambler's Triumph—The Death of Famous Swindlers—III. Ambush for Good—Watching for Opportunities—Stealing a March on the Devil—IV. Importance of the Aim—Point with the Cross—Liberal Christianity—On Which Side are You?

MEN of the Thirteenth Regiment, and their friends here gathered, of all occupations and professions, men of the city and men of the fields, here is a theme fit for all of us.

One Sabbath evening with my family around me, we were talking over the scene of the text. In the wide-open eyes, and the quick interrogations, and the blanched cheeks I realized what

A Thrilling Drama

it was. There is the old city, shorter by name than any other city in the ages, spelled with two letters—A, I.—Ai. Joshua and his men want to take it. How to do it is the question. On a former occasion, in a straightforward, face to face fight, they had been defeated; but now they are going to take it by ambuscade. General Joshua has two divisions in his army—the one division the battle-worn commander will lead himself, the other division he sends off to encamp in an ambush on the west side of the city of Ai. No torches, no lanterns, no sound of heavy battalions but thirty thousand swarthy warriors moving in silence, speaking only in a whisper; no clicking of swords against shields, lest the watchmen of Ai discover it and

The Stratagem

be a failure. If a roystering soldier in the Israelitish army forgets himself, all along the line the word is "Hush!" Joshua takes the other division, the one with which he is to march, and puts it on the north side of the city of Ai, and then spends the night in reconnoitring in the valley. There he is, thinking over the fortunes of the coming day, with something of the feelings of Wellington the night before Waterloo, or of Meade and Lee the night before Gettysburg. There he stands in the night, and says to himself: "Yonder is the division in ambush on the west side of Ai. Here is the division I have under my especial command on the north side of Ai. There is the old city slumbering in its sin. To-morrow will be the battle. Look! the morning already begins to tip the hills. The military officers of Ai look out in the morning very early, and while they do not see the division in ambush, they behold the other division of Joshua, and the cry,

"To Arms! To Arms!"

rings through all the streets of the old town, and every sword, whether hacked and bent or newly welded, is brought out, and all the inhabitants of the city of Ai pour through the gates, an infuriated torrent, and their cry is: "Come, we'll make quick work with Joshua and his troops." No sooner had these people of Ai come out against the troops of Joshua, than Joshua gave such a command as he seldom gave: "Fall back!" Why, they could not believe their own ears! Is Joshua's courage failing him? The retreat is beaten, and the Israelites are flying, throwing blankets and canteens on every side under this worse than Bull Run defeat. And you ought to hear the soldiers of Ai cheer and cheer and cheer. But they huzza too soon. The men lying in ambush are straining their vision to get some signal from Joshua that they may know what time to drop upon the city. Joshua takes his burnished spear, glittering in the sun like a shaft of doom, and points it toward the city; and when the men up yonder in the ambush see it, with hawk-like swoop they drop upon Ai, and without stroke of sword or stab of spear take the city and put it to the torch. So much for the division that was in ambush. How about the division under Joshua's command? No sooner does Joshua stop in the flight than all his men stop with him, and as he wheels they wheel, for in a voice of thunder he cried "Halt!" One strong arm driving back

A Torrent of Flying Troops.

And then, as he points his spear through the golden light toward that fatal city, his troops know that they are to start for it. What a scene it was when the division in ambush which had taken the city marched down against the men of Ai on the one side, and the troops under Joshua doubled up their enemies from the other side, and the men of Ai were caught between these two hurricanes of Israelitish courage, thrust before and behind, stabbed in breast and back, ground between the upper and the nether millstones of God's indignation. Woe to the city of Ai! Cheer for Israel!

Lesson the first: There is such a thing as

Victorious Retreat.

Joshua's falling back was the first chapter in his successful besiegement. And there are times in your life when the best thing you can do is to run. You were once the victim of strong drink. The demijohn and the decanter were your fierce foes. They came down upon you with greater fury than the men of Ai upon the men of Joshua. Your only safety is to get away from them. Your dissipating companions will come around you for your overthrow. Run for your life! Fall back! Fall back from the drinking-saloon! Fall back from the wine-party! Your flight is your advance. Your retreat is your victory. There is a saloon down on the next street that has almost been the ruin of your soul. Then why do you go along that street? Why do you not pass through some other street rather than by the place of your calamity? *A spoonful of brandy* taken for medicinal purposes by a man who twenty years before had been reformed from drunkenness, hurled into inebriety and the grave one of the best friends I ever had. Retreat is victory!

Here is a converted infidel. He is so strong now in his faith in the gospel, he says he can read anything. What are you reading? Bolingbroke? Andrew Jackson Davis's tracts? Tyndall's Glasgow University address? Drop them and run. You will be an infidel before you die, unless you quit that. These men of Ai will be too much for you. Turn your back on the rank and file of unbelief. Fly before they cut you with their swords, and transfix you with their javelins. There are people who have been well-nigh ruined because they risked a foolhardy expedition in the presence of mighty and overwhelming temptations, and the men of Ai made a morning meal of them.

So, also, there is victorious retreat

In the Religious World.

Thousands of times the kingdom of Christ has seemed to fall back. When the blood of the Scotch Covenanters gave a deeper dye to the heather of the Highlands, when the Vaudois of France chose extermination rather than make an unchristian surrender, when, on St. Bartholomew's Day, mounted assassins rode through the streets of Paris, crying, "Kill! Blood-letting is good in August! Kill! Death to the Huguenots! Kill!" When Lady Jane Grey's head rolled from the executioner's block; when Calvin was imprisoned in the castle; when John Knox died for the truth; when John Bunyan lay rotting in Bedford Jail, saying, "If God will help me, and my physical life continues, I will stay here until the moss grows on my eyebrows rather than give up my faith"—the days of retreat for the church were days of victory.

The Pilgrim Fathers Fell Back

from the other side of the sea to Plymouth Rock, but now are marshaling a continent for the Christianization of the world. The Church of Christ falling back from Piedmont, falling back from Rue St. Jacques, falling back from St Denis, falling back from Wurtemburg castles, falling back from the Brussels market-place, yet all the time triumphing. Notwithstanding all the shocking reverses which the Church of Christ suffers, what do we see to-day? Three thousand missionaries of the cross on heathen grounds; sixty thousand ministers of Jesus Christ in this land; at least two hundred millions of Christians on the earth. All nations to-day kindling in a blaze of revival. Falling back, yet advancing until the old Wesleyan hymn will prove true:

> "The lion of Judah shall break the chain,
> And give us the victory again and again!"

But there is a more marked illustration of victorious retreat in the life of our Joshua, the Jesus of the ages. First falling back from an appalling height to an appalling depth, falling from celestial hills to terrestrial valleys,

From Throne to Manger;

yet that did not seem to suffice Him as a retreat. Falling back still further from Bethlehem to Nazareth, from Nazareth to Jerusalem, back from Jerusalem to Golgotha, back from Golgotha to the mausoleum in the rock, back down over the precipices of perdition, until He walked amid the caverns of the eternal captives and drank of the wine of the wrath of Almighty God, amid the Ahabs, and the Jezebels, and the Belshazzars. Oh, men of the pulpit, and men of the pew, Christ's descent from heaven to earth does not measure half the distance! It was from glory to perdition. He descended into hell. All the records of earthly retreat are as nothing compared with this falling back. Santa Anna, with the fragments of his army flying over the plateaux of Mexico, and Napoleon and his army retreating from Moscow into the awful snows of Russia, are not worthy to be mentioned with this retreat, when all the powers of darkness seem to be pursuing Christ as He fell back, until the body of Him who came to do such wonderful things lay pulseless and stripped. Methinks that the city of Ai was not so emptied of its inhabitants when they went to pursue Joshua, as perdition was emptied of devils when they started for the pursuit of Christ, and He fell back and back, down lower, down lower, chasm below chasm, pit below pit, until He seemed to strike the bottom of objurgation and scorn and torture. Oh, the long, loud, jubilant shout of hell at the defeat of the Lord God Almighty!

But let not the powers of darkness rejoice quite so soon. Do you hear that

Disturbance in the Tomb

of Arimathea? I hear the sheet rending! What means that stone hurled down the side of the hill? Who is this coming out? Push him back! the dead must not stalk in this open sunlight. Oh, it is our Joshua. Let him come out. He comes forth and starts for the city. He takes the spear of the Roman guard and points that way. Church militant marches up on one side, and the church triumphant marches down on the other side. And the powers of darkness being caught between these ranks of celestial and terrestrial valor, nothing is left of them save just enough to illustrate the direful overthrow of hell and our Joshua's eternal victory. On His head be all the crowns. In His hands be all the sceptres. At His feet be all the human hearts; and here, Lord, is one of them.

Lesson the second: *The triumph of the wicked is short.* Did you ever see an army in a panic? There is nothing so uncontrollable. If you had stood at Long Bridge, Washington, during the opening of our sad Civil War, you would know what it is to see an army run. And when those men of Ai looked out and saw those men of Joshua in a stampede, they expected easy work. They would scatter them as the equinox the leaves. Oh, the gleeful and jubilant descent of the men of Ai upon the men of Joshua! But their exhilaration was brief, for the tide of battle turned and these quondam conquerors left their miserable carcasses in the wilderness of Bethaven. So it always is. The triumph of the wicked is short. You make $20,000 at the gaming-table. Do you expect to keep it? You will die in the poorhouse. You made a fortune by iniquitous traffic. Do you expect to keep it? Your money will scatter, or it will stay long enough to curse your children after you are dead. Call over the roll of

Bad Men who Prospered

and see how short was their prosperity. For a while like the men of Ai they went from conquest to conquest, but after a while disaster rolled back upon them and they were divided into three parts: misfortune took their property, the grave took their body, and the lost world took their soul. I am always interested in the building of theatres and the building of dissipating saloons. I like to have them built of the best granite and have the rooms made large, and to have the pillars made very firm. God is going to conquer them, and they will be turned into asylums and art galleries and churches. The stores in which fraudulent men do business, the splendid banking institutions where the president and cashier put all their property in their wives' hands and then fail for $200,000—all these institutions are to become the places where honest Christian men do business.

How long will it take your boys to get through your ill-gotten gains? The wicked do not live out half their days. For a while they swagger and strut and make a great splash in the newspapers, but after a while

It all Dwindles Down

into a brief paragraph: "Died suddenly, July 22, 1888, at thirty-five years of age. Relatives and friends of the family are invited to attend the funeral on Wednesday, at 2 o'clock, from his late residence on Madison Square. Interment at Greenwood." Some of them jumped off the docks. Some of them took prussic acid. Some of them fell under the snap of a Derringer pistol. Some of them spent their last days in a lunatic asylum. Where are William Tweed and his associates? Where a Ketcham and Swartwout, absconding swindlers? Where is James Fisk, the libertine, and all the other misdemeanants? The wicked do not live out half their days. Disembogue, O world of darkness! Come up, Hildebrand and Henry II. and Robespierre, and with blistering and blaspheming and ashen lips hiss out; "The triumph of the wicked is short."

Lesson the third: How much may be accomplished by lying

In Ambush for Opportunities.

Are you hypercritical of Joshua's manœuvre? Do you say that it was cheating for him to take that city by ambuscade? Was it wrong for Washington to kindle camp-fires on New Jersey Heights, giving the impression to the opposing force that a great army was encamped there when there was none at all? I answer, if the war was right then Joshua was right in his stratagem. He violated no flag of truce. He broke no treaty, but by a lawful anbuscade captured the city of Ai. Oh that we all knew how to lie in ambush for opportunities to serve God. The best of our opportunities do not lie on the surface, but are secreted; by tact, by stratagem, by Christian ambuscade, you may take almost any castle of sin for Christ. Come up toward men with a regular besiegement of argument and you will be defeated: but just wait until the door of their hearts is set ajar, or they are off their guard, or their severe caution is away from home, and then drop in on them from a Christian ambuscade. There has been many a man up to his chin in scientific portfolios which proved there was no Christ and no divine revelation, his pen a scimetar flung into the heart of theological opponents, who, nevertheless, has been discomfited and captured for God by some little three-year-old child who has got up and put her snowy arms around his sinewy neck, and asked some simple question about God.

Oh, make a flank movement;

Steal a March on the Devil;

cheat that man into Heaven! A five-dollar treatise that will stand all the laws of homiletics may fail to do that which a penny tract of Christian entreaty may accomplish. Oh, for more Christians in ambuscade, not lying in idleness, but waiting for a quick spring, waiting until just the right time comes! Do not talk to a man about the vanity of this world on the day when he has bought something at "twelve," and is going to sell it at "fifteen." But talk to him about the vanity of the world on the day when he has bought something at "fifteen," and is compelled to sell it at "twelve." Do not rub a man's disposition the wrong way. Do not take the imperative mood when the subjunctive mood will do just as well. Do not talk in perfervid style to a phlegmatic nor try to tickle a torrid temperament with an icicle. You can take any man for Christ if you know how to get at him. Do not send word to him that to-morrow at 10 o'clock you propose to open your batteries upon him, but come on him by a skilful, persevering, God-directed ambuscade.

Lesson the fourth: The importance of

Taking Good Aim.

There is Joshua, but how are those people in ambush up yonder to know when they are to drop on the city, and how are these men around Joshua to know when they are to stop their flight and advance? There must be some signal—a signal to stop the one division and to start the other. Joshua with a spear on which were ordinarily hung the colors of battle, points toward the city. He stands in such a conspicuous position, and there is so much of the morning light dripping from that spear-tip, that all around the horizon they see it. It was as much to say: "There is the city. Take it.

God knows and we know that a great deal of Christian attack amounts to nothing simply because we do not take good aim. Nobody knows and we do not know ourselves which point we want to take, when we ought to make up our minds what God will have us to do, and point our spear in that direction and then hurl our body, mind, soul, time, eternity at that

One Target.

In our pulpits and pews and Sunday-schools and prayer-meetings we want to get a reputation for saying pretty things, and so we point our spear toward the flowers: or we want a reputation for saying sublime things, and we point our spear toward the stars; or we want to get a reputation for historical knowledge, and we point our spear toward the past; or we want to get a reputation for great liberality, so we swing our spear all around; while there is the old world, proud, rebellious and armed against all righteousness; and instead of running any further away from its pursuit, we ought to turn around, plant our foot in the strength of the eternal God, lift the old cross and point it in the direction of the world's conquest till the redeemed of earth, marching up from one side and the glorified of heaven marching down from the other side, the last battlement of sin is compelled to swing out the streamers of Emanuel. Oh Church of God, take aim and conquer.

I have heard it said: "Look out for a man who has only one idea; he is irresistible." I say: Look out for the man who has one idea, and that a determination for soul-saving. I believe God would strike me dead if I dared to point the spear in any other direction. Oh, for some of the courage and enthusiasm of Joshua! He flung two armies from the tip of that spear. It is sinful for us to rest, unless it is to get stronger muscle and fresher brain and purer heart for God's work. I feel on my head the hands of Christ in a new ordination. Do you not feel the same omnipotent pressure? There is a work for all of us. Oh, that we might stand up, side by side, and point the spear toward the city! It ought to be taken. It will be taken. Our cities are drifting off toward loose religion, or what is called

"Liberal Christianity,"

which is so liberal that it gives up all the cardinal doctrines of the Bible; so liberal that it surrenders the rectitude of the throne of the Almighty. That is liberality with a vengeance. Let us decide upon the work which we, as Christian men, have to do, and, in the strength of God, go to work and do it.

It is comparatively easy to keep on a parade amid a shower of bouquets and hand-clapping, and the whole street full of enthusiastic huzzas; but it is not so easy to stand up in the day of battle, the face blackened with smoke, the uniform covered with the earth ploughed up by whizzing bullets and bursting shells, half the regiment cut to pieces, and yet the commander crying "Forward, march!" Then it requires old-fashioned valor. My friends, the great trouble of the kingdom of God in this day is the cowards. They do splendidly on a parade day, and at the communion, when they have on their best clothes of Christian profession; but in

The Great Battle of Life,

at the first sharpshooting of scepticism, they dodge, they fall back, they break ranks. We confront the enemy, we open the battle against fraud, and lo! we find on our side a great many people that do not try to pay their debts. And we open the battle against intemperance, and we find on our own side a great many people who drink too much. And we open the battle against profanity, and we find on our own side a great many men who make hard speeches. And we open the battle against infidelity, and lo! we find on our own side a great many men who are not quite sure about the Book of Jonah. And while we ought to be massing our troops, and bringing forth more than the united courage of Austerlitz and Waterloo and Gettysburg, we have to be spending our time in hunting up ambuscades. There are a great many in the Lord's army who would like to go out on a campagn with satin slippers and holding umbrellas over their heads to keep off the heavy dew, and having rations of canvas-back ducks and lemon custards. If they cannot have them they want to go home. They think it is unhealthy among so many bullets!

I believe that the next twelve months will be the most stupendous year that heaven ever saw.

The Nations are Quaking

now with the coming of God. It will be a year of successes for the men of Joshua, but of doom for the men of Ai. You put your ear to the rail-track and you can hear the train coming miles away. So I put my ear to the ground and I hear the thundering on of the lightning train of God's mercies and judgments. The mercy of God is first to be tried upon this nation. It will be preached in the pulpits, in theatres, on the streets, everywhere. People will be invited to accept the mercy of the Gospel, and the story and the song and the prayer will be "mercy." But suppose they do not accept the offer of mercy—what then? Then God will come with His judgments, and the grasshoppers will eat the crops, and the freshets will devastate the valleys, and the defalcations will swallow the money markets, and the fires will burn the cities, and the earth will quake from pole to pole. Year of mercies and of judgments. Year of invitation and of warning. Year of jubilee and of woe.

Which Side are You

going to be on? With the men of Ai or the men of Joshua? Pass over this Sabbath into the ranks of Israel. I would clap my hands at the joy of your coming. You will have a poor chance for this world and the world to come without Jesus. You cannot stand what is to come upon you and upon the world unless you have the pardon and the comfort and the help of Christ. Come over. On this side is your happiness and safety, on the other side is disquietude and despair. Eternal defeat to the men of Ai! Eternal victory to the men of Joshua!

MEXICAN MOTHERS AT SCHOOL.

AN encouraging school work is being done in New Mexico. In a letter to the *Church*, from Mrs. A. M. Granger, who dates from Capulin, that lady says: "Last week, a Mexican came from his ranch with his ten-year-old boy to put him into school. His ranch is twenty-four miles from Capulin. He spent all day in the school-room, and was much pleased with all the exercises, especially the writing. He put him in the school for five years, and said he should come to the Sabbath-school, which he joined last Sunday. He is a man of so much influence among the Mexicans that our people feel much pleased over this accession to the school. I have *four married women pupils* in the school; two of these started last November, the other two since Christmas. One of these is a young woman who lost her little boy last winter, and the other is a young woman who entered the school with a baby in her arms six weeks old. It is now four months old. *The mother and baby have not missed school one day since they started.* She brings two pillows, which she puts in a chair, and it lies there and sleeps most of the time. All these are members of my class in Sabbath-school. One of these entered the school in November. Her husband never came with her to Sabbath-school until last Sunday. He is much older than she is, and I found could talk some English. He took his seat near the organ, and seemed much interested in all our exercises. We always stay after Sabbath-school and sing. He stayed, and was one of the last to leave the church. When he bade me good-by he said he would come next Sunday. Two young girls gave evidence of becoming Christians.

A LIVING NATIONAL EMBLEM.

AN instance of punishment, as lawless as the offence punished, is reported from Chicago. It shows, however, on the part of the wrongdoers, a patriotic veneration for the emblem of freedom which it is much to be wished that the subjects of the King of kings would show when His glory is outraged by His enemies. (Mark 8:38.)

A despatch from Chicago states that on July 5 a well-known Anarchist was seen at the door of a cigar store waving a red handkerchief attached to a cane and shouting "Hurrah for anarchy." Then he began to tear down the Stars and Stripes that decorated the door-post. Half a dozen young Americans in the cigar store heard the insult to the flag. Some dragged Kintz inside, and others brought pots of red, white and blue paint from a neighboring paint store. The Anarchist's face was painted a deep blue, and bespangled with white. His clothing was painted white, and red streaks were daubed on the white background, from his head to his feet. He had three of his tormentors arrested. Justice Lyon rallied the Anarchist in court about seeking the protection of a law in which he disbelieved, but he insisted upon his rights. The boys were dismissed with suspended fines.

A MILLION DOLLAR LIFE INSURANCE.

IN an article on Life Insurance in a Philadelphia daily journal the statement is made that the death of a prominent citizen would call for the payment of a million dollars from certain life insurance companies. It says: The greatest achievement in the history of life insurance has been made by Mr. John Wanamaker, who is now paying premiums on $1,000,000 to twenty-nine different companies. The last policy issued on his life was received by him on Thursday last, and so far as is known, there is no other man in the world whose life is insured for such an enormous amount. There are a number of men in this city who have been trying for years to achieve the point just gained by Mr. Wanamaker, but they have so far failed, although one manufacturer has succeeded in getting policies on his life amounting to $750,000. He is desirous of putting the amount up to a round million. But Mr. Wanamaker is not the only man in this city upon whose life big risks are issued. Two other citizens are insured for $100,000, another is insured for about $150,000, a fifth is insured for one-tenth of a million, and his partner for twice that amount. These facts show that wealthy men do not forget that they must die, and leave their riches behind them. Some of these, as in the case of the million dollar insurer, are Christian men, who do not neglect the higher preparation for the great change; but in too many cases the men who thus recognize the inevitable event, and make provision for it in one way, fail to make that provision which would ensure their own safety. (Luke 12:20, 21.)

INFIDELITY IN UTAH.

IT would appear from the report of a Christian missionary in Utah that there is a growing revolt in the Mormon Church against its tyranny and superstition. Unhappily it is not tending toward Christianity, but to infidelity. The missionary says that he meets with a large number of these infidels, who are unusually strong in argument and opposed to all religious teaching. Their experience has been such that they are apt to hate the very name of religion. Generally, too, the infidel has been a member of a Christian church, and honestly joined the Mormon Church because he thought it was purer, more spiritual, than his own Christian church. When he gives up Mormonism, therefore, he thinks there is nothing left. He has tried all and found them wanting. He thinks the experience of all others in religion is similar to his own, except that they have not found out their mistake yet. With few exceptions, these infidels will not attend our meetings. Occasionally, especially when a new man preaches, the novelty will attract them. They do not object to their children coming to our Sabbath-school or meetings; but if the children tell the parents what they have heard, the parents will do their best to prevent it from having any influence over them.

THEATRE PREACHING IN JAPAN.

AN extended tour in northern Japan has been taken by six missionaries, of whom three were ladies. They traveled in jinrikishas about two hundred and twenty-five miles, being without beds, chairs, and other home comforts, living on the floor, and part of the time on Japanese food, speaking at least once a day on the average, for ten days, to audiences ranging from three to twelve hundred. Most of these preachings were in theatres, which were the only buildings the missionaries could hire large enough for the audiences.

In the course of an account of this tour sent to the *Missionary Herald*, by Mr. Albrecht, who was one of the party, he says: "Wherever we went we met with audiences crowding the largest theatres in the city, listening with Japanese eagerness and responsiveness to three or four speakers each evening. While undoubtedly the better classes of the people are generally not found amongst them, we noticed on this trip more intelligent faces, evidently officials and professional men, than during former visits. In Shibata, we spoke by invitation of two prominent lawyers. In Murakami, the town officials occupied the front seat in the church during the dedication services. In Nagaoka, many of the teachers of the various schools of that city were present. In Kashiwazaki, Buddhism rallied its forces to withstand the first aggression of Protestant Christianity, interrupting the speakers with sounds of jeers and taunts, Buddhist priests vying with each other to hurl ridicule and contempt at them; but as the speakers proceeded undaunted, and were able gradually to gain the attention of the better class of hearers, the interrupters were silenced by their own people, and the truth was pressed home to their conscience.

In Shibata brother Nakai is working most effectively. The brethren there have hired a pleasant room for holding services, and are gaining in power and numbers. By giving lessons in English, Mr. Nakai is gathering twenty-three soldiers of the garrison stationed there, bringing them under the influence of the gospel. One young sergeant, the only one of all that large garrison, was recently baptized, and spends his daily hour of furlough in reading the Bible with a friend *a young merchant who, when he was converted, destroyed all wines and liquors which were a part of his stock in trade.*

A HINDOO DOCTOR'S CONVERSION.

IN January of last year there was living in Dera Ghazi Khan, in the Punjab, a Hindoo doctor named Mir Alam Khan, who was following his profession, when one day a Hindu friend of his said to him, "You should go to Keenjur; you will find something there." Not caring to do this, he consulted some magical books for guidance, and got the following direction: "You must to Keenjur." So to Keenjur he went, and day after day sat in the bazaars, wondering what he was to get there. On February 14 the Rev. T. Bomford and Munshi Talib Masih ("Seeker after Christ") arrived in the place and went to the bazaar to preach. Mir Alam Khan had heard Christian preaching in Dera Ghazi, and had read some Christian books, but now, for the first time, he felt drawn to Christianity, and came to every preaching, and also to the missionary. Mir Alam Khan came at seven next morning to announce his intention of becoming a Christian. That day the missionaries left Keenjur for Mozuffergarh, and arrived there on Friday the 18th. On Saturday the 19th, Mir Alam Khan came in, having walked twenty-four miles. He could not, he said, rest; he must be baptized. He acknowledged sins committed in his past life, and professed his faith in Christ as his Saviour. He was accordingly baptized on Sunday, February 20. His baptism caused no little stir in Dera Ghazi Khan. Since then he has been living with Talib Masih, studying the Bible and working with him. Meeting Talib Masih one day after having not seen him for some months, the Rev. T. Bomford asked how Mir Alam Khan was going on. "Very well," was the answer, "but he is not the man you knew." "What do you mean?" "I never saw any one alter so much through reading the Bible; he is quite a different man." That is good testimony to the reality of the change in him. The latest news is, that one of his friends intends to follow his example, and that his father has asked for a Bible.

LITTLE GIRL WAIFS IN CHINA.

VALUABLE work is being done in China among the despised female children by the devoted missionary ladies who are laboring there. Dr. Mary Gale, who writes to the *Missionary Link* from Shanghai, tells the story of two slave girls whose maladies were treated in the hospital, and who were deeply touched by the kindness they received. "One of them," says Dr. Gale, "is about twelve years of age, and attends the school in the native teacher Mrs. Day's house in the morning, and in the afternoon is a bright little helper in the hospital. You would wonder, to see her anticipate the doctor's wants so quickly, and would smile at her air of authority over the patients. Miss McKechnie made her face perfectly radiant one day by telling an inquisitive invalid that she was our assistant. She is an affectionate child, and never tires of waiting on others. You would certainly praise her amiable disposition, and would not be at all prepared for the change that comes over her on the appearance of her mistress. She will not look at her, and her face is black with scowls, while she grumbles all kinds of hard things about her! But one day she had to go home, and there were agonizing leave-takings, thanks and sobs mingling in a truly distressing chorus. The child was not well, and the bad little thing tore the bandages off, after she got home, would not have the sores dressed, refused to eat, and altogether conducted herself in such a way that the mistress brought her back in despair, and left her. We hope her stay will be permanent, for she will make a good helper for the hospital.

"Another little girl, a poor paralyzed child of eight, was *picked up from the road where she had been left to die*. There was nothing pretty about her, pale faced with prominent teeth, and both limbs helpless. I do not know how many days it was before a smile could be won from her. Only a cowed, frightened look would greet one. But gradually the face brightened and the limbs grew strong, till at length she was walking about well, and full of mischief. She was a little tease, but it made one happy to see the change in her. She became quite a little needlewoman, and plans had been matured for putting her in the school, when the woman who owned her pounced upon her and took her away. Poor little soul! She did not rage like the other, but her face haunts me still as I saw it last, pale, sad, and patient."

PROPHETIC EVENTS BETWEEN 1889 AND 1901.

THE FIRST RESURRECTION.

Mr William Birch's 775th Printed Sunday Sermon, Delivered in Free Trade Hall, Manchester, England, March 11, 1888.

"Blessed and holy is he that hath part in the First Resurrection; on such the second death hath no power, but they shall be priests of God and of Christ, and shall reign with Him a thousand years.

"And I saw the dead, small and great, stand before God; and the books were opened; and another book was opened which is the book of life. And whosoever was not found written in the book of life was cast into the lake of fire.—Revelation 20: 6, 12, and 15.

The Impending Storm of Trouble—The Half-Starved Heathen at Home—The Coming War the Greatest Ever Known—The Rise of the Napoleonic Antichrist Between 1891 and 1893—The First Angel Message—The Red Horse of Anarchic War—The Great Tribulation—The Battle of Armageddon in April, 1901—The Last Week of this Age, April 4 to 11, 1901—Remarkable Personal Experiences.

WE live in critical times. The End of this Age is coming almost within view. In the lifetime of some of us, the First Resurrection will probably take place, and our Lord come again to call His people home.

The evidences around us point to the conclusion that Europe will shortly enter a storm of trouble such as the world has never seen. The competition in trade is at the height of cunning in attempts to climb to wealth; and machinery and inventions are pushing out human labor. Our towns are crowded with half-starved men and women, and it is no fable to say that the majority of the population of Europe are neither comfortably fed nor properly clothed. Many of the laboring population are being *jostled* through life in crowded slums, sunless and godless. It is true that the churches send an occasional lifeboat to pick up a few stragglers, but the great proportion of the population of Europe live without knowledge of the true God, and die as if no man cared for their souls.

Fifteen years ago, I appealed to the churches and to rich men to remember that the poor had both feeling bodies and never-dying souls, but it was said that I was setting class against class, and seeking to turn the world upside down. The neglected classes with anti-Christian socialists at their head will before long, I fear, take the law into their own hands, and our present race of kings and aristocracy be driven from their thrones and palaces, red-republicanism then becoming the ruling force of Europe. Some of you who hear and many who read this statement may laugh at what they consider the foolish idea of an alarmist; but what I have said is clearly foretold in God's written word, and if so will surely come to pass.

Between 1888 and 1891 Daniel's seventh chapter shows that

The Greatest War Ever Known

will burst upon Europe, and its map be wholly changed. More than twenty kingdoms or states that are now lying within the countries of Cæsar's old Roman Empire will be reduced into a *confederacy of ten kingdoms*, prefigured by the Wild-beast with *ten horns* and the Image with *ten toes* in Daniel 2: 31 and 7: 24. France will apparently extend its boundary once more to the river Rhine, so as to include Belgium and the remainder of the left bank of that river within its frontiers. Then Europe west of the Rhine and south of the Danube, together with Britain, will crystallize into the form of *seven* kingdoms, *Britain, France, Spain, Italy, Austria, Greece, Balkan States*, with *three* others, namely, *Turkey* reduced in size, *Syria* made independent, and *Egypt*, amounting altogether to *ten*.*

Subsequently, between 1891 and 1893, we may look for a man of Napoleon name or nature, whom God's Word calls "the Little Horn" and "Antichrist," to become ruler over a little state in Greece or Turkey, and to "wax exceeding great," and become "King of the North" (Syria), and make a seven years' covenant or league with the Jews in Jerusalem from Passover Week (April 21-28), 1894, to Passover Week, 1901, which will lead, among other things, to the restoration of their morning and evening sacrifices several months later, in November, 1894.

When true Christians shall see these phenomenal events come to pass, there will be a great expectation of our Lord's appearance.

The Midnight Cry

will go forth, "Behold, the Bridegroom cometh!" and there will be an extraordinary religious revival, prefigured by ALL the virgins arising, and by the travail of the Christian Church (Matt. 25: 1-10; Rev. 12: 2, 5.)

The Jewish daily sacrifices are indicated in Daniel 8: 14, and 12: 11, 12, to be renewed in Jerusalem 2,345 literal days before this Age ends on the last day of Passover Week, Thursday, April 11, 1901, and therefore to be renewed about November 8, 1894. A future command to rebuild Jerusalem is also to go forth upon the same day, and sixty-nine weeks of literal days afterward (namely, about March 5, 1896, eight years from now) there may be expected, according to Daniel 9: 25, Rev. 14: 4, and 1 Thess. 4: 17, the Coming of Messiah the Prince as a Bridegroom, to raise all "the dead in Christ," and together with them to translate to Himself into the aërial heavens 144,000 living watchful Christians, like Enoch and Elijah, without dying. The heavenly Jerusalem, their future home, descends perhaps at that time into the aërial heavens, as predicted in Rev. 21: 2, although it does not become visible to the earth until just before the Millennium.

"The Lord Himself shall descend from heaven with a shout, with the voice of the archangel, and with the trump of God; and the dead in Christ shall rise first; then (afterward) we which are alive and remain shall be caught up together with them in the clouds, to meet the Lord." (1 Thess. 4: 16, 17; I Corinth. 15: 51, 52; Rev. 12: 5.)

"This same Jesus, which is taken up from you into heaven, shall so come in like manner as ye have seen him go into heaven." (Acts 1: 11.)

"And I looked, and, lo! the Lamb stood on the Mount Zion, and with him an 144,000, having His Father's name written in their foreheads. . . . And they sang, as it were, a new song before the throne . . . These were redeemed from among men, being the FIRST-FRUITS unto God and to the Lamb."

Then after several months of world-wide Gospel preaching, during the First Angel Message and First Seal,

"The Red Horse"

of red-republican war will ride through the earth during the first half of 1897, and the ten kingdoms become Red Republics with the Church of Rome, as ruling chaplain, sitting upon them, and making herself drunk with the blood of faithful Christians, in fulfillment of the prophetic emblem of

The Scarlet Woman

inebriated with the blood of martyrs, seated boastfully upon the Ten-horned Scarlet Wild Beast, in Revelation 17, exclaiming, "I sit a Queen." (Rev. 14: 6; 6: 2, 4; 17.) The Imperial Antichrist will then presently stop the Jewish sacrifices, and set up his own image in Jerusalem and in every town of the Ten Kingdoms as if he were a god, while the ten kings "will give their power and strength to him" during his reign as Emperor for "forty-two months," or three and a half years, from about August, 1897, to January, 1901. Millions of foolish virgins and other Christian converts will, however, flee into the wilderness shortly before those three and a half years, and so escape the martyrdom that will afterwards befall multitudes of subsequent converts everywhere throughout Christendom, who will be beheaded on huge public scaffolds for refusing to worship the Antichrist as their god, or bow down before his image, or receive his mark, 666.* (Dan. 9: 27; Rev. 17: 13; 12: 13.)

Meanwhile famine, pestilence and other plagues and woes of the Seals and Trumpets in Revelation 6 to 11 will everywhere distress mankind. This is

The Great Tribulation

of which our Lord speaks in the twenty-fourth chapter of Matthew. Our Lord may finally be expected in Passover Week, 1901, to raise to life all true Christians who shall have died or been slain since the resurrection, about five years previously, and to take them up to heaven together with all His true people found alive on earth, and then in a few days He will descend with them to destroy Antichrist at the battle of Armageddon. In that battle, the armed men of Europe and of "the whole world" will be gathered to battle at Jerusalem: but a tumult will arise amongst them, hatred and jealousy burst forth, and every man will fight against his comrade. Mounted on horses suddenly blinded, the cavalry soldiers, like mad fiends, will attack their companions as if they were foes, until the battle-field becomes a shambles, and as foretold, "the blood shall come up even unto the horses' bridles by the space of a thousand and six hundred furlongs." The imperial Antichrist together with his chaplain, called in the word of God the false prophet, will be destroyed. (Zech. 14: Ezek. 38; Rev. 14: 20; 19: 19.)

The Jews will then be converted by this personal appearance of their long rejected Messiah, and will go about preaching the gospel to those who are left alive among the nations of the earth, and Christ shall reign for a thousand years, during which He will have "the heathen for his inheritance, and the uttermost parts of the earth for His possession." At the end of that period,

The Periodical Visits of our Lord

will suddenly cease; and the nations released from the restraint of His beneficent government, will again allow themselves to be deceived by Satan, who will be "loosed for a little season," after which Gog and Magog will be gathered to battle against Jerusalem, when fire from God shall devour them. (Rev. 20; Isaiah 66.)

(*To be concluded.*)

* It is not unworthy of observation that the 1882 years insisted by Professor Piazzi Smyth, Astronomer Royal for Scotland, to be indicated by the Great Pyramid of Egypt, to elapse from the Birth of Christ to the commencement of Daniel's Troublous Times—if dated from A. D. 6, which seems from the late Duke of Manchester's "Times of Daniel" to be the true date of Christ's birth, will coincide in its termination with the close of 1888, as the commencement of the Troublous Times. (See "The Pyramid Pointing to 1888-9."—Id.)

* The fact of 666 being found in the requisite dative dedicatory form of *Napoleon* has been long ago pointed out by expositors, thus:

N 50, α 1, π 80, ο 70, λ 30, ε 5, ο 70, ν 50, τ 300, ι 10 = 666.

It is also remarkable that it is contained in nominative *E.* (the initial of *Ernest*) *Boulanger*, who thus may be indicated to be the Initiator of the coming wars that shall form the Ten-kingdomed Confederacy, and the Forerunner who shall prepare the way for the coming Napoleon:

E 5, B 2, ο 70, υ 400, λ 30, α 1, ν 50, γ 3, ε 5, ρ 100 = 666.

CHRISTIAN HERALD AND SIGNS OF OUR TIMES.

OFFICE, 63 BIBLE HOUSE, NEW YORK.

ENTERED AT THE POST-OFFICE AT NEW YORK, N. Y., AS SECOND-CLASS MATTER.

EVERY NUMBER CONTAINS:

The Portrait and Biography of some eminent person.
The Sermon Dr. Talmage preached the last Sunday morning.
An Exposition of Unfulfilled Prophecy.
A Summary of the Events of the Week, Notes of Religious and Temperance Movements, etc.
A Sermon by Rev. C. H. Spurgeon, of London, from advance sheets sent by special arrangement.
Pictures of Missionary Life, etc., and Descriptive Articles.
An instalment of a Serial Story.
An Exposition of the International Sunday-School Lesson, by Mrs. M. Baxter.

ANNUAL SUBSCRIPTION, $1.50.

Remittances by mail should be by bank cheques, Post-office orders, or Express money-orders whenever possible. If currency is sent it should be in a registered letter. Cheques and money-orders should be made payable to THE CHRISTIAN HERALD. Making them payable to individuals often causes delay.

New subscriptions may commence at any time. When subscribers do not indicate their wish, they commence with the first number of the month in which the subscription is received.

PUBLISHER'S NOTICE.

The whole edition of The Christian Herald was mailed last week to subscribers during Tuesday, July 17. The last delivery at the New York Post Office was made at 9.25 P. M.

CURRENT EVENTS.

The Crucial Clause of the Mills' Tariff measure reached a vote on July 16. The action of the Republican National Convention distinctly marked the proposal to put wool on the free list as the one most obnoxious in the bill. The Democrats in the house joined issue on that question, and refused to compromise. The result was that the clause passed the House by a vote of 120 to 102. Only three Democrats voted with the minority. They were Mr. Wilkins and Mr. Foran, of Ohio, and Mr. Sowden, of Pennsylvania. Mr. Randall was absent, through severe illness, or he would doubtless have voted on the same side. The only Republican voting with the Democrats was Mr. Anderson, of Iowa.

An Important Reform in the Telegraphic system is proposed in a bill which was favorably reported to the Senate on July 18. It places the telegraph regulations under the control of the Interstate Commerce Commision, on the same principles as now govern the railroad rates. In its present shape it gives even greater powers to the Commission over the wires than are confided to it over the railroads. It says that rates shall not be unreasonable or exorbitant, though the determination of what is unreasonable and exorbitant, is left with the Commission. It forbids discrimination in rates between similar classes of matter. It permits telegraph companies to give special rates to the Federal, State, and municipal Government. It forbids discrimination between press companies. It also prohibits the present practice of charging higher rates for short distances where there is no competition, than for long ones where there is competition. Whether the "influence" that will be brought to bear upon Congress against the measure will be strong enough to effect its rejection does not yet appear, but it will doubtless be applied vigorously.

The Civil Service Commission Sent its Fourth report to the President on July 17. It is a bulky document of 731 printed pages. It covers not only the statement for the year ended June 30, but gives a résumé of results since the approval of the act in 1883. From this it appears that of every one hundred persons who successfully passed the examination of the commission more than 41 received appointments. It also shows that from July 16, 1883, to July 30, 1887, 33,343 persons were examined for all branches of the service, of which number 11,378, or less than one-half, failed to pass, and 21,965 passed; of these 8,612 received appointments. From January 16, 1883, to January 15, 1885, the number of appointments made to the departments at Washington was 480; from January 16, 1885, to January 15, 1886, 239; from January 16, 1886, to January 15, 1887, 392, and from January 16, 1887, to June 30, 1887, 150, making the total number of appointments to the departments at Washington since the approval of the law 1,266. Of this number 171 were women, the proportion of men to women being more than 6 to 1.

Valuable Suggestions as to the Treatment of criminals were made last week by the National Prison Association, which was in session in Boston. Among other reforms recommended were: The substitution of indeterminate sentences in all cases, even for minor offences, a sentence now almost universal in reform and industrial schools; the extension of this sentence into perpetual confinement for incorrigibles, making it merely restraint without penal features in cases of habitual drunkenness, insanity, or the like; the removal of criminal administration from all connection with politics or popular elections, and the speedy completion of the trial and the prompt execution of the sentence in case of murder or other cases of much popular interest.

The Discovery of Another Dynamite Plot in Chicago startled the country last week. On July 17 information reached the police that arrangements had been made to blow up the houses of the officials who conducted the trial of the Haymarket assassins. The victims were to be Judge Gray, Judge Grinnell, Inspector Bonfield, and Chief of Police Hubbard. The disclosure was made by a member of the anarchist group which had charge of the commission of the revolting crime. The police immediately went to the house of John Hronek, a Bohemian, who was the "number one" of the group, and surrounded it. As he was known to be a desperate man, and was reported to have dangerous explosives always at hand in his house, no attempt was made to raid the building. Soon after daybreak the man came out, and he was surrounded, and, after a desperate resistance, was made prisoner. The police then searched his house and found, in a corner of his bedroom, twelve dynamite cartridges wrapped in brown paper. A further search of the room disclosed, hidden in the bed, a large revolver and a dagger. Then, in almost similar fashion, visits were made at 498 West Twentieth Street, where Frank Chapek was arrested, and to a house in Zion Place, where Frank Chibowa was also captured. In both places arms and explosives were found. Hronek was an intimate friend of Lingg, the convict in the Haymarket affair who committed suicide to avoid hanging. The plans of the conspirators were fully matured, and the murder of the four officials was fixed simultaneously for July 18, the very next day to the one on which the capture was made. The police are now looking for other anarchists, who are known to have dynamite and Winchester rifles in their possession.

The Commission of Judges to Investigate the charges against Mr. Parnell, which were made by the English Attorney-General at the recent action of O'Donnell against the London *Times*, is formally constituted in a bill which has been read a first time in the House of Commons. Very large powers are vested in the commission, and power will be given them, if the bill passes in its present shape, to make a very thorough investigation of Mr. Parnell's relation with the Phœnix Park murderers and the Invincibles. The judges who will constitute the commission, are authorized to enforce the attendance of witnesses, and examine them under oath. The witnesses will be required to give evidence, *even though their evidence may criminate themselves*; but they will not be liable to prosecution on account of their own testimony. Every witness making a full disclosure is to be entitled to a certificate from the commission which will indemnify him if proceedings should be commenced against him at a future time in respect to any matter about which he may be examined in this inquiry. Finally, the commission may send a sub-commission to examine witnesses abroad. It would appear that more ample powers for discovering the truth could not be given, and if Mr. Parnell does not avail himself of the opportunity, his reputation with the English public will suffer.

The Emperor of Germany Set out on his Visit to the Czar on July 14. His departure from Kiel presented a spectacle, splendid beyond anything ever before witnessed on the German seas. The town and harbor were uniquely decorated. The route from the station to the harbor was lined with masts covered with oak leaves and adorned with weapons and banners. Triumphal arches and floral decorations, in which naval designs predominated, entirely transformed the aspect of the old town. The Emperor drove slowly toward the harbor, giving as he went special greetings to the guilds and corporations which lined the streets. The yacht *Hohenzollern*, in which he sailed, arrived at Cronstadt on July 19, accompanied by an imposing squadron of German war vessels. The Czar went out in his yacht to meet the Emperor, the Russian and German fleets pouring out thunderous salutes. The Emperor went on board the Czar's yacht, which then bore the German and Russian imperial standards, and the two monarchs were carried to Peterhof, where the Czarina met them. Banquets and reviews of troops were down on the programme for the next three days, after which the Emperor leaves for Stockholm.

General Boulanger's Condition is Causing anxiety to his friends. The wound in his neck which he received in his duel with Prime Minister Floquet, though not in itself serious, threatens dangerous complications. M. Floquet's rapier was driven into the flesh two inches deep, and passed between the jugular vein and the carotid artery. Had either of the two been cut, Boulanger would have died on the field. His physicians anticipate that if no complications arise he will be well in a week or ten days, though he is not as yet safe from lockjaw, or the less familiar complaint of embolic, caused by clots of blood in the bronchial tubes, or, still rarer, suffocation by hematuria in the respiratory channels. The duel does not appear to have injured the character of either man in the eyes of their respective friends, and M. Floquet has been overwhelmed with congratulations on his prowess. The fact, however, is not creditable to the French people, who, if they had more wisdom, would perceive that there can be little hope for the welfare of the Republic under such leaders.

Speculation About "The White Pasha" who was recently reported to be approaching Khartoum is still unsettled. No white traveller except Stanley is known to be in Africa with a following so large as to impress the native mind with the idea of his being a Pasha. That Stanley, however, should be on the way to Khartoum would indicate so wide a divergence from his route as to imply that he had abandoned his attempt to relieve Emin. The whole affair is shrouded in mystery, which only time can remove. The New York *Herald* has published an interview and a letter on the subject from Sir Richard Burton, the noted African traveller, which simply guess at a solution of the difficulty. He thinks that the white Pasha is Emin himself pressing northward, though he intimates that it would not surprise him to learn that it was *General Gordon*, of whose death he is not assured. If, however, it should turn out to be Stanley, then Stanley is attempting to divert the ivory trade to the Congo from the Zanzibar route. Sir Richard is evidently jealous of Stanley's fame, and, while faintly praising him, attempts to depreciate his ability.

The Rev. W. F. Re Qua writes that he is ılding a camp meeting at South Canadian, dian Territory, from July 17 to 24, for Indians d believing whites. His work in the Terri- ry grows rapidly under his hands, and many plications for teachers who are Christian men ıve come to him. The gospel tent for which : and his good wife have been praying and lieving has been ordered, and is likely to ach them soon. They ask us to thank the nd friends who are contributing to this spe- al purpose, and also to their general work. lso, to say in answer to inquiries, one of hich, from a lady at Rock City, Ill., is anony- ous, that *they have facilities for getting eques cashed*. Any Christian friends who ally feel the responsibility of the Church for ission work among the Indians, and are will- g to help Mr. and Mrs. Re Qua in the self- nying effort they are making to reach those ho are without the knowledge of Christ, may : sure that their gifts will be very thankfully ceived if sent to Rev. W. F. Re Qua, P. O. ox 14, McAlester, Choctaw Nation, Ind. Ter.

The First Anniversary of the Bethesda Mis- on at 29th Street and Eighth Avenue, New ork, was held July 14. A truly valuable work being done by this mission in a locality hich urgently needs it. A year ago Rev. Wil- ım H. Childs and a few Christian friends ımmenced the work in faith by hiring a build- g which had formerly been a Jewish syna- gue. They held evangelistic services, opened Sunday-school, and went around among the ck and destitute, working for Christ. During ıe year about 36,000 persons have been counted the various services on Sunday and week ıys. Over four hundred persons have made a ofession of faith, as the result of God's bless- g on the work, and many are now anxiously eking Christ. The most noteworthy feature the enterprise is that no one connected with receives any salary, the services being carried by voluntary workers. The collections and ınations from friends who know the character the work, nearly covered the expense of rent ıd gas last year. A small balance of $52.66 is ıe to the Treasurer, Rev. Stephen Merritt, o Eighth Ave., New York, to whom donations ay be sent.

New Counterfeit Bills were Circulated in rge quantities in New York last week. They ere of the one-dollar denomination, and the ıgraving was so exquisitely done as to deceive acticed bank-tellers. Several money-brokers ıok them without question, and ordinary citi- ıns were easily victimized. The Government cret service officers in cautioning the public ıout the counterfeits, say that like the five- ıllar spurious bills, they cannot be detected by ıe engraving, which is absolutely perfect, but the paper on which they are printed. It is ıt "fibre paper" and therefore has not the rength of the genuine notes. Religious coun- rfeits have the same characteristic. The out- ard appearance is correct, and often deceives, ıt fibre is lacking and there is no strength in ıem. (II Timothy 3:5.)

A Victim of Mormon Fraud and Tyranny as found fainting in Chicago on July 15. She ıld a pitiful story. She said her name was lizabeth Rutter, and she was a native of North ıields, England. Six years ago her young son as cajoled by some Mormon missionaries there, ıd went with them to Utah, against the wishes his parents. His father heard reports which ndered him uneasy about the boy, and sus- ecting that his letters were intercepted, resolv- l to go to Utah and rescue him. On his ar- val there he found that return was difficult, ıd he remained for a time working for a farm- . He wrote to his wife saying that he would turn as soon as he could, and giving a vivid count of the misery of Utah. The Mormons tercepted his letter, and forged one which ıey sent in its place, urging his wife to come him. She suspected nothing and came. ıortly after her arrival her husband was mur- ered. He had imprudently revealed to a young Mormon his intention to escape, and his wife believes that he lost his life in consequence. The experience she had after his death so hor- rified her that she resolved to brave death rather than remain. She set out from Ogden, and walked the whole distance to Chicago, where, tired, and exhausted for lack of food, she fell fainting in the street. She was taken to the County Hospital, and when sufficiently recov- ered will be sent back to England. If Satan's victims, who are in bondage worse even than that of the Mormons, were similarly determined to escape they might be saved; for they are as- sured of the help of Christ. (Ps. 37:40.)

Buried Relics of Warfare were Exhumed in Broadway, New York, last week. A laborer digging in the trenches of the Phœnix Construc- tion Company, which is laying electrical subway conduits, hit his shovel against a hard sub- stance on July 18, in the excavation at Broad- way and Warren Street. The hard substance turned out to be a six-pound cannon-ball in- crusted with rust. The day before there were found in the same place an empty twelve-pound shell, two twelve-pound balls, two six-pounds shots, a trunnion ring eighteen inches across, and three inches thick, and an English penny. Each piece was thick with rust and hard deposits from the soil. Superintendent Robert R. Bush- wick, who is in charge of the work, thinks there was a fort in ante-Revolutionary times along the present Warren Street line, and these projectiles were part of the stores which were not thought worth removal. The mementoes of past con- flict were a strange spectacle amid the peaceful business surroundings of Broadway. They cal- led to mind the fierce struggle waged for the freedom which we enjoy. The Christian, too, is liable to find in himself, even after Christ has delivered him from his bondage to Satan, traces of his enemy's occupation, in old appetites and desires, which were intended for his destruction. But unlike the British cannon-balls, they are still dangerous and have to be carefully watched against. (Galatians 5:1.)

An Octogenarian's Suicide was Reported in New York on July 16. Some eight years ago a prosperous farmer on Staten Island disposed of his farm and came to live in New York City. He invested a large part of the proceeds of the sale of his farm in setting up his son-in-law in business. The young man was not successful, and the ex-farmer continued making up the de- ficiency until all his property was gone. The son-in-law obtained a situation, and was able to support his family for some time, the father-in- law living with them. But he fell sick, and he and his wife died within a few months of each other. A Methodist church took compassion on the old man, who was now alone and penni- less. They paid his rent for him, and in return he assisted the janitor of the church. That ar- rangement, however, was discontinued after a few months, through the old man's fault. Then he assisted the janitor of some offices in return for board and lodging, but last week he learned that the janitor was about to give up the charge of the offices, and was much depressed in con- sequence. He was *eighty-six years of age*, and was well aware how little chance there was of earning his own living. He said he thought he should starve. On July 17 he was found hang- ing from a beam in his room, quite dead. Bereft of family, and stripped of fortune, it was not surprising that the old man should have become depressed, but he would not have committed his terrible crime if he had trusted in God's promises. (Ps. 34:22.)

A City Belle's Death in a Poorhouse is Re- ported from Oxford, N. Y. A wealthy family in New York City was notified last week of the death of one of its most attractive members. She was a girl of great beauty and most win- some manners. Some years ago, while she was at a boarding-school at Richfield Springs, she made the acquaintance of a young man, far be- neath her in position and education, and mar- ried him. She was ostracized by her family, but ultimately they relented and offered to forgive her and receive her back to her home if she would abandon her husband. She indignantly refused, and the couple, who were in extreme poverty, settled in a little shanty near Oxford. They managed to live by hard and menial labor until a few months ago, when both of them fell ill and were removed to the county poorhouse. The wife's relatives heard of it and went to her. They begged of her to return to her home, em- ploying every inducement to get her to leave her husband and accept the comforts and lux- uries they were ready to lavish upon her. She remaind true to her husband, however, and as the family would not invite him they had to re- turn without her. In the poorhouse the wife stayed, but she grew worse, and on July 15 she died. Whatever her faults may have been it is impossible to withhold admiration for her fidel- ity to the husband she had chosen. Too often the Christian, who has far more reason than she to be faithful, is not proof against the allure- ments of wealth and luxury which Satan holds out to those who forsake their Lord. (Rev. 2:4).

BRIEF NOTES.

Rev. E. P. Roe, the famous novelist, died on Friday last of neuralgia of the heart. He was fifty years of age.

Over forty thousand accessions have been made by pro- fession of faith to the Congregational Churches of the United States during the past two years.

More than one-half the scholarships given at Cornell this year were won by female students. The scholarships were given as prizes for the best records in mathematics, architecture, and botany.

Rev. Dr. George Duffield, an eminent Presbyterian clergyman and hymn writer, died at his residence in Bloomfield, N. J., on Friday, July 6, of heart disease. He was seventy years of age.

Dr. Siverka sailed last week on the *Anchoria* to com- mence operations on his project for colonizing Palestine. He proposes to rebuild Jerusalem, and has no doubt as to funds being furnished for the work.

There are in New York City more than three hundred religious and charitable institutions or societies, whose object it is to help the poor; these institutions receive and distribute annually about $4,000,000.

The first Spanish Juvenile Teetotal Society in the world is the Juvenile Temple, formed last April at Monte Video, South America, by Rev. Geo. Viney, in connection with the Good Templar Order. Its superintendent is Senorita Quano Puente.

The renewal of a liquor dealer's license at Parkersburg, W. Va., was recently granted by the court, but was re- voked after the address of the liquor-dealer's own daughter, who came into court, and in eloquent words protested against the renewal.

At the sixty-fourth anniversary of the American Sun- day-school Union recently held at Springfield, Mass., it was reported that over fifteen hundred new Sunday- schools had been organized last year. Teachers in them, 3,326; scholars in them, 54,129.

Mr. George Muller's visit to New Zealand, writes Mr. Gordon Forlong, has proved a great blessing. His energy and experience have given a wonderful stimulus to all the Christians in Invercargill, Dunedin, Wellington, and Wanganui. He is now in Auckland.

Kojiro Matsaga, one of the graduates of the Yale Law School this year, is a son of the Japanese Minister of Finance, and is of royal blood. He has been in America four years, and speaks English, Latin, and German. He expects to return to Japan two years hence.

Mr. E. P. Telford has been conducting a mission at Mr. Charrington's Assembly Hall, in the East End of London, during the past month. He will shortly return to America by way of Canada, and afterwards to the Australian colonies, on an evangelizing tour.

The effort to crystallize the Societies of Christian En- deavor into a Church union at the recent conference was a failure. The convention pledged the loyalty of its Societies to the particular Churches with which they were connected, and disavowed any intention to break down denominational lines.

The number of slaves set free in Brazil is estimated at over two millions. The Brazilian Legation at Wash- ington has received despatches stating that the public rejoicing was most enthusiastic. The slaves, in the majority of cases, have arranged to work for wages in the employ of their former owners.

A new departure was taken on a recent Sunday by Rev. George T. Dowling, D. D., Pastor of Euclid Bap- tist Church, Cleveland, O., who invited all present who loved the Lord Jesus Christ in sincerity and truth to unite with the Church at the Lord's table. Other Bap- tist ministers who have done this have been called to ac- count for it, but it is thought that no action will be taken in Dr. Dowling's case.

SELF-INFLICTED WOUNDS.

A New Sermon by Pastor C. H. Spurgeon.

"How long wilt thou cut thyself?" Jer. 47 : 5.

A Shocking Oriental Custom—Forbidden of God—I. A Question Asked in Despair—Of Church Members Doing Nothing for Christ—Of Backsliders—Of Men Neglecting Opportunities—Of Lost Souls—II. A Question Asked Hopefully—Of the Bereaved—A Quaker's Question to a Mourner—Of the Rebellious—A Conversation with a Gambler—Of the Jewish Nation—Of Souls Afflicted with Needless Fears—A Grandfather Demented by Despair.

TRAVELLERS in the East tell us that among the most melancholy scenes they witness is the following: Men inflict upon themselves very grievous voluntary wounds, and then exhibit themselves in public. They even disfigure themselves with gashes and cuts in the presence of excited throngs. I am speaking of what has occurred even within the last few years among the Moslems. When some great prophet or emir is coming that way, a certain number of fanatical Mahometans take swords, spears, and other sharp instruments, and gash themselves terribly therewith, cutting their breasts, their faces, their heads, and all parts of their bodies. Frequently they have taken care to dress themselves in white sheets, in order that, as the blood flows copiously from their bodies, it may be the more clearly seen, that they may become the more ghastly spectacles of misery, or the more fully display the religious excitement under which they labor. As everything in the East remains for ever the same, this

Moslem Superstition

carries us back to the olden times whereof we read in the Old Testament, when the priests of Baal, having cried in vain to their idol, cut themselves with lances and with knives. Thus they displayed their inward zeal, and thus, perhaps, they hoped to move the pity of their god. The Lord expressly forbade His people, the Jews, to perpetrate such folly. They were not even to shave the corners of their beards, or to hack their hair, as the Orientals do in the hour of their grief; and then they were further prohibited from injuring their bodies by the command, "Ye shall not make any cuttings in your flesh for the dead, nor print any marks upon you: I am the Lord." (Lev. 19 : 28.) Men in Eastern lands, not only in connection with fanaticism, but in reference to domestic affairs, will cut themselves to express their grief and anguish, or to make other people believe that they are feeling such grief and anguish. We congratulate ourselves that we are free from at least one foolish custom.

I. First, dear friends, I shall ask this question very despairingly: "How long wilt thou cut thyself?"—for

Many are Cutting Themselves

very terribly, and will have to feel the wounds thereof for a long, long time; neither can we induce them to cease therefrom. I allude, first, to some professors of religion who have been church-members for ten, twenty, or more years, and yet have practically done nothing at all for the Saviour. If they were really to awaken to a sense of their neglect, I do not know how long they would be in anguish, or how deep would be their distress: for if Titus mourned that he had lost a day when he had done no good action for twenty-four hours, and he but a heathen, what would happen to a Christian if he were really to see his responsibility before God, and to feel that he has not only lost a day but a year—perhaps many years? Have not some of you well-nigh lost a whole lifetime?

Oh, if I am addressing such—and honestly in the sight of God I fear I am—then how long will you chasten yourselves for your neglect? It must be long before you can forgive yourselves for such wicked indolence. How long will you afflict yourselves to think that you should have suffered time which you can never recall, and opportunities which you will never enjoy again, to go by you wasted? Do I make you feel uncomfortable? I shall thank God if I do; and I shall be happy, indeed, if, instead of cutting yourselves with vain regrets, you lacerate yourselves with my sharp remarks as with spears and knives, and then gird up your loins, and say, "God helping me, there shall never be another wasted year, nay, nor another wasted day!"

The same may be applied, and applied very solemnly, too, to

Those who Backslide

—who, in addition to being useless, are injurious, because their example tends to hinder others from coming to Christ. Oh, if any of you that name the name of Jesus, and have been happy in His service, and have enjoyed high days and holy days in His presence, turn aside, I shall use this lamentation over you. The Lord will bring you back and save you, as I believe; but oh, how long will you cut yourselves? You will feel in after life how grievously you have injured your souls. David's great sin was put away so that he did not die, but he was never the same David as before. The Lord, out of very love to him, chastened him sorely, and pursued him with plague upon plague. His family became his dishonor and his sorrow. He went with broken bones to the grave—a man of sorrows, and acquainted with grief. How grievously he had injured himself! How long he had to cut himself with anguish for that one sin!

What is true of David applies also to others who have in any great measure turned aside. Solomon, in a high degree, hurt himself by his terrible follies. In the New Testament, Peter is a conspicuous example. It is a tradition that whenever Peter heard the cock crow he used to weep; and I do not wonder at it. Alas! if you and I should ever be suffered to fall into grievous sin, it may be all done in ten minutes, but it cannot be got rid of in fifty years. We shall bear the scars of that ten minutes' sin until the Lord shall take us home, and permit us to wake up "without spot, or wrinkle, or any such thing," in the full likeness of our perfect Lord. Oh, my brethren, watch anxiously lest you have to mourn for years over the sin of an instant!

There is one thing which comes after these, and comes in connection with them. If you and I should know that souls have been lost—lost as far as we are concerned—

Through our Neglect,

how long should we cut ourselves on that account? A dear soul said to me yesterday, "My husband died. He had been a sad drunkard, but in his last illness, through the blessing of God upon those who visited him, I trust he found peace. He said he believed in the Lord Jesus, and there is my comfort. But oh, if he had died without finding Christ, I should have been indeed a widow! I know not what could have comforted me." I am grateful that our sister called in her Christian friends, and that, by their efforts and her prayers, she was spared the keenest edge of sorrow. "Surely the bitterness of death is past." But suppose *you* were to lose your son, and that, your son should die in sin which he learned of you; or in sin which you saw in him and never rebuked! Suppose I say, your son should die in his iniquity. Shall I tell you how you will behave yourself when the news comes to you that he is dead? You will get by yourself alone, and cry, like David, "O my son Absalom, my son, my son Absalom! would God I had died for thee, O Absalom, my son, my son!" You can lay your children down upon the bed all stark and cold, and follow them to the tomb, and even sing as you commit their mortal remains to the grave, when you know that they die in hope; but if they perish in their sin, guilty, red-handed, unforgiven, what will you say to yourselves?

A Tradesman's Self Reproach.

These are solemn things, but there is deep truth in them, and they ought to be considered by all of you who profess to be Christians. I knew one who used to have a man calling upon him in the way of business, and bringing certain articles which he bought across the counter. This tradesman said one day to himself, "I have dealt with that man for nine or ten years, and we have scarcely passed the time of day. He has brou in his work, and I have paid him across counter, but I have never tried to do him good. Surely this cannot be right. Provide has put him in my way, and I ought at least have asked him whether he is saved in Chri Well, the next time the man came, our g brother's spirit failed him, and he did not to begin a religious conversation. The m never came again, but a boy brought in the n lot of goods. "How is this?" said the sh keeper. "Father is dead," said the boy. friend, the shopkeeper, said to me, "I co never forgive myself. I could not stay in shop that day. I felt that I was guilty of t man's blood. But I had not thought of it fore. How can I ever clear myself from guilty fact that, when I did think of it, ungracious timidity prevented me from openi my mouth." My own dear friends do not bri upon yourselves such cutting regrets!

Eternal Regret.

One other most solemn use may be ma of this question: God grant that it m never be so, but if any one of you should die his sins, how long will you regret it, think yo It looks dreadfully possible that some of you w perish for ever, since you have so often been e treated to come to Christ, and have never com O souls, how long—how long will you grie and mourn when it shall come to this? Accor ing to my reading of that book—and I wou gladly read it otherwise if I did not feel th truth and honesty forbid me to do so—your lo your anguish will be for ever. For ever you w cut yourselves. For ever will you lament th when the opportunity was so near you, y put it away from you, and when Christ w ready to receive you, you would not be r ceived, but committed eternal suicide.

II. There I leave this very painful use of t text, to try and use it at greater length in happier sort, by way of consolation and hopef comfort to those who will, we trust, be soo brought to receive the Lord Jesus. "How lo wilt thou cut thyself?" I shall ask this que tion hopefully, trusting that in many the sorrow is nearing its end. This text may very profitably and prudently applied *to tho who have been bereaved*, and who, being bereave sorrow, and sorrow to excess. I hope that am not about to say a harsh word, but I woul deal faithfully with

Rebellious Repining.

"Jesus wept," and he that does not weep whe he loses a dear one must be something less tha a man, and unworthy to be called a Christia But there is such a thing as carrying to a extreme our sorrow for those we lose, till becomes rebellion against God. You rememb the Quaker saying to the lady who was wearin very deep double mourning years after one her children had died, "Madam, hast thou no forgiven God yet?" And there is truth abou that remark; some do not forgive God for wha He has done. Their sorrow amounts to this—that they have a quarrel with God over His di pensations. "How can He be good and hav taken away my mother?" said one to me "How can God be good and have taken awa my child?" cried another.

There is a want of faith, a want of reverence a want of love, a want of many sweet and plac graces, in such mourning as that; and, withou dwelling long upon it, I beg to put that que tion to any mourner here who is mourning wit the ungodly sorrowing of the heathen—as there were no hope. "How long wilt thou cu thyself?" Is not thy child in Jesus' bosom Has not thy friend gone among the angels, t join the sweet singers of God? Put awa thy disputing and murmuring, and either, lik Aaron, hold thy peace, or better still, like Job, bless the name of the Lord, and rejoice in th God.

But now, turning to quite another character, I would use the same expression for another purpose. There are some persons with whom God is dealing in great love, and yet they are rebellious. They persevere in known sin, ɔugh the evil way has become exceedingly to them. They seem as if they would over red-hot ploughshares to hell. I have wn some who have found the pleasures h once delighted them to become a nuise, a trouble, a pain, a disgust, and a weari-; and yet they continue in their unprofit- course. They are following a wild course fe, and they are losing money at it, and they likely to lose much more. They are plung- down. What are they thinking of? "How wilt thou cut thyself?" Already they have with great disasters and misfortunes; they meet with many more. When the dogs are hunting, they run in packs. The plagues Egypt are ten at least, and every one who s the Pharaoh may expect the full number.

A Gambler's Hope.

ɔke some time ago with the son of a very y man. He seemed to be an infidel out-t, and had taken to horse-racing, and the My inmost soul was grieved concerning : I could have wept. As he talked very ely, and mild words were lost on him, I said im, "Keep as many race-horses as you can, go in for gambling most heartily, for thus sooner you will lose all your money. Some ligals never come back to the Father's e until they sink as low as the pig's trough, that is probably the way for you. When get a hungry belly, I trust you will come e." He knows what my warning meant, I fear he intends to make it true. The way ansgressors is hard; and it is a mercy when comes so hard that they are resolved to it for another and a better way. Is this pening to anybody here? "How long wilt cut thyself?" Have you not had enough e consequences of your folly? Have you played the fool long enough? "How long thou cut thyself?" might use this expression even to

The Jewish Nation

I. Ah, God, through what seas of trouble they had to swim since the day when they "His blood be on us, and on our chil-"! Alas, the story of Israel is enough to e one's blood turn to ice within his veins! will they not come back? Will they not e back? Must they be hunted in Germany, hounded in Russia? Shame on the coun- that dare do such things! But must it be God grant that they may no longer pro- their Holy One to indignation against n! How long will they cut themselves? still these great evils happen to them ac-ing to the eternal counsels of the God of aham, Isaac, and Jacob, because of their elief. When they turn to the Messiah, their y shall return also, and the crown where- God crowned His people shall again be upon their head, and their ancient city shall n be "beautiful for situation, the joy of whole earth." Assuredly, the Lord gave the of Canaan to Abraham and his seed forever; long will they shut themselves out of it? at, now, all this has rather kept me from my design, which is to speak to those dear ds of ours who are afflicting their souls with

Needless Fears.

good can possibly come by a continuance in r unhappy moods; they are cutting them- s quite needlessly. They might at once peace and rest and joy, if they were will- to accept the Lord's gracious way of salva-. You, who are burdened with sin, and are g to get rid of it, but will not come to st for deliverance—I want to ask each one ou, "How long wilt thou cut thyself?" , there are some persons who think that re they can believe in Christ they must un- o a world of torture! Whence do they de- the notion, and what scripture do they t to support it? Find me, if you can, any e where the Lord requires this at your hand at you should be

Dragged About by the Devil—

you should be despairing, that you should be tempted to blaspheme, and all that. I know that some who have come to Christ have endured such misery, but I defy you to prove that it is any part of the gospel, and that we are to preach up such an experience as a necessary preface to believing in Christ. The case is far otherwise. Hear me, and be not obstinately wedded to your wretchedness. You are a sinner: you cannot question that fact. Christ Jesus came into the world to save sinners. If you trust him—you are saved. This, in brief, is the glad tidings of salvation. This is

The Gospel Way.

Who has required at your hands that you should despond?

"Oh," said one to me, "I cannot think that the way can be so plain, for my grandfather was so miserable for years that they had to put him into a lunatic asylum, before he found the Saviour." You smile, but the good woman who told me this was in terrible earnest. I cannot help quoting what she said, for it was the natural and outspoken form of an error which lurks in thousands of minds. I believe that many think they must be driven near to madness, or they will not be able to come to Christ. But what benefit could this despair possibly be to you? If the gospel were, 'Doubt and be saved," I would bid you doubt. And if it were, "Despair and be saved," I would preach up despair to you with all my might, though it might go a little against the grain. But it is not so written. The scripture is, "Believe: trust: confide: rely. Trust in Jesus—and you are saved."

A sick man is dying, and the physician says, "Here is medicine that will restore you: will you take it?" The dying man answers, "Sir, I believe in your medicine, but I will not take it till I feel better." If that man dies, who murders him? Shall the physician be blamed? Surely not. On his own head his death must lie. And recollect that it will be as certainly your ruin to refuse Christ because you want to be better, as it will be to refuse Him from any other reason. Any reason which leads you to reject the Lord Jesus is a bad one. One man refuses Christ because he hates Him, and he blasphemes Him; another refuses Him because he thinks that he must be a little better; there may be a difference in the motive, but the result will amount to the same thing. Take heed, I pray you, lest through your pride in refusing to receive the gospel just now, and just as you are, you should put it away from you till you get where there will be no gospel preaching, and no invitations to Christ, and you are cast away for ever.

Now let me ask you this question: *what good have you got by all this up till now?* O you, good sir, who always mean to have Christ by-and-by, how much farther have you got after all your good intentions and painful waitings? You used to sit in that pew, twelve, fifteen, twenty years ago, mayhap; and even then you had hopeful resolves. Are you any nearer Christ now than you were then? Say, does the preaching affect you any more than it did in those bygone days? "No" say you, "not so much." This is

A Dangerous Symptom:

what does it mean? Has the preacher changed? I will take my share of the blame. I grow older, I know. Perhaps I get more stupid too; but still, when I sat yesterday to see the converts coming to join the church, I saw them till I had not physical power to see any more, for God had brought so many to come and tell me that I had led them to the Saviour. Therefore I think that there cannot be much difference in my preaching. It must be *you* that are getting hard! I fear you are getting chilled into indifference, and I pray that the deadly process may go no further.

Would to God that you, my dear hearers, would leave all things else, and just come and cast yourselves on Jesus! If you will not, I must again persecute each one of you with this inquiry, "How long wilt thou cut thyself?" How long must you go on with your piteous prayers, and get no answer? Must you have more tears, more groans, more cries, more despairs, more regrets, more broken vows? How long will you cut yourselves with these vain attempts to be your own Saviour? How long? How long? God end it ere you cross the portal of this house of prayer, and go down those stone steps, which will again conduct you to the level of a careless world! Stop here till you have yielded yourself to Jesus. I beseech you not to go home a stranger to eternal life. The Lord grant that you may now throw yourself into the arms of Jesus, for His dear name's sake!

GEMS FROM NEW BOOKS.

THE REVIVAL IN GERMANY.*

THE remarkable wave of evangelical revival that has passed over Germany during the past few years, presents a very hopeful feature in the hold it has taken on the younger generation. In 1883 twelve Christian young men met in Berlin, and Herr von Schlümbach said, "Could we not organize a Young Men's Christian Association, as they have in England and America? We shall want men and money, but let us go to Him who can give us both." So these twelve disciples formed themselves into a Christian Association, which now numbers about a thousand members, and is doing excellent work in that great city. Similar associations have been formed in other towns in Germany, one of the most earnest and successful being at Cöthen, near Halle, which began with six members, and has now over a hundred. There they have erected a building of their own, and to assist in defraying the cost of this undertaking, Herr Pastor Westphal, of Cothen, secured the co-operation of eighteen of the ablest evangelical preachers in producing a volume of sermons, to be published on behalf of their "Evangelisches Vareinshaus," and do good work for the Master at the same time. Thus this volume came into existence.

Tholuck's Heroic Work.

These meditations on our Lord's sufferings have a special value in showing what the ordinary teaching in the evangelical pulpits of Germany is at the present day. The gospel is preached with fullness, with power, in all simplicity and faithfulness, and the Cross is the standard round which the soldiers of Christ are rallying. The influence of Strauss has been dead for many years in Germany, and the last nail driven into the coffin of the Tübinger theology. The life of Dr. August Tholuck affords an interesting illustration of this change. When appointed professor of theology in the University of Halle, in 1826, a protest was entered by all the professors, including such men as Gesenius, and the whole of the students except five (the only ones who believed in the divinity of Christ), the sole ground of their opposition being Tholuck's evangelical belief. The Government refused the prayer of the petition, but Perthes wrote of the young professor: "His adversaries are bold and cunning. A baptism of fire awaits him at Halle." So it proved; but in 1870 what did we find? Evangelical belief in the ascendency, and all Halle *en fête* for three days, to do honor to Professor Tholuck, whose Christian teaching largely wrought this revolution in the religious thought of the country. On the occasion of this jubilee, the universities poured congratulations and honors upon him; Court Preacher Hoffman brought him the salutations of the Ecclesiastical Council; the Emperor William conferred on him the Order of the Red Eagle. When, in 1878, the noble and sainted teacher was taken away, all Protestant Germany realized that a Prince had fallen in Israel.

The reaction against rationalism was not entirely owing to Tholuck's influence, but he was one of the greatest teachers that God ever raised up in a time of spiritual darkness, and

* From "The Voice from the Cross" a series of sermons on our Lord's Passion, by eminent living preachers in Germany, including Rev. Drs. Ahlfeld, Baur, Bayer, Conard, Faber, Frommel, Gerote, Hahnelt, Hansen, Kogel, etc., with biographical sketches; edited and translated by William Macintosh, M. A., F. S. S. 265 pages. Published by *Scribner & Welford*, 743 Broadway, New York.

Levi P. Morton, of New York.

East Room in White House. (*See page 467.*)

Allen G. Thurman, of Ohio.

did a work the results of which we see to-day in the Protestant pulpits of Germany. "I have had but one passion," said he, "and that is Christ, and Christ alone. Every one out of Christ I look upon as a fortress which I must storm and win."

How National Ruin Comes.

"Away with the Man, and release unto us Barabbas!" Where this cry is heard, where Christ is driven from heart and home, from country and nation, then that day it becomes darker, and they seek in vain for healing and salvation. Away with Him! This was proposed in France at the end of the last century. We will destroy and reform all things without Thee; we will be left alone with our reason. Leave our houses, our councils, our schools—away with Thee! Then we ourselves shall rule! "Your will be done"' said the Lord; and the world of existing states fell into ruins! "Away with this man, and release unto us Barabbas!" Away with all that is holy and noble, Divine and Christian. In our own nation also, we heard this cry from the depths, by many thousands of voices. We hear it now again from a neighboring country. God has warned us in good time: the wild waters are assuaged; the cries have become fainter.

MR. LEVI P. MORTON,

Republican Candidate for Vice-President.

THE Republican nominee for the Vice-Presidency, is the well-known New York banker, of the firm of Morton, Bliss & Co. He is sixty-four years of age, having been born at Shoreham, Vt., May 16, 1824. His father was Rev. Daniel O. Morton, a Congregational minister, and a lineal descendant of George Morton, one of the Puritan Fathers, who came to this country from England in 1623. The boy received only a common-school education, and early began business life as a dry-goods clerk, in Concord, N. H. He commenced business on his own account in that town in 1845, but four years later removed to Boston, and afterward to New York. In the last named city the firm became financially involved, and compromised with its creditors at fifty cents on the dollar. Some years afterward each of these creditors received from Mr. Morton an invitation to dinner, and each man found on his plate an envelope containing the amount he had lost, with interest. At that time Mr. Morton had commenced business as a banker, and was prospering. His partner in New York was Mr. George Bliss, and in London, Sir John Rose. The firm materially aided the United States Government in funding the Public Debt, and in resuming specie payments.

Mr. Morton did not enter political life until 1876, when he ran for Congress, but was defeated. Two years later he was again a candidate, and was elected. He took a prominent part in the discussion of financial questions, and rendered valuable service, independent of party, to the nation at large in that department. On the accession of President Garfield, Mr. Morton was made Minister to France, and while there, hammered the first rivet in the Statue of Liberty, presented by French citizens to the city of New York. On his retirement from Paris, he was highly complimented by the French Government and the American colony there. As is well known, Mr. Morton has made many munificent charitable gifts, one of the most conspicuous of which being a quarter of the cost of freighting the *Constellation* with corn for the starving poor of Ireland in 1880.

EX-SENATOR ALLEN G. THURMAN,

Democratic Candidate for Vice-President.

THE Democratic nominee for the Vice-Presideney needs no introduction to American readers. He has been so long in political life and has been so outspoken in his opinions, that he is among the best known of our statesmen. He is now in his seventy-fifth year, having been born November 13, 1813, at Lynchburg, Va. The family removed to Chillicothe, O., in 1819, where the boy was sent to the Academy. At the same time he gained a thorough knowledge of French from a little playmate, who with her father, a French refugee, were hospitably received in the Thurman home. After leaving the Academy, the boy studied law for three years in the office of his uncle, William Allen. Subsequently he became private Secretary to Governor Lucas. He continued his law studies, however, and in 1835 was admitted to the Bar.

Mr. Thurman's introduction to political life occured in 1844, when, without his knowledge, he was nominated for Congress and was elected. At the close of his term he was offered a renomination, but declined it and returned to his law practice. In 1851 he was elected to his second public office—that of Judge of the Supreme Court of Ohio, which he filled for four years, the last two as Chief Justice. He again declined renomination and returned to the Bar. His decisions as Chief Justice had added so much to his fame that his services commanded high fees, and for the first time in his life Mr. Thurman found himself with a competent income.

In 1867 Mr. Thurman ran against Mr. Rutherford B. Hayes for Governor of Ohio, but was defeated. A Democratic Legislature was however elected which sent Mr. Thurman to the United States Senate, and he was re-elected at the end of his term, serving till March, 1881, when John Sherman succeeded him. He w
member of the Electoral Commission of 187

OWEN LITTLE'S VINDICATION.

(*See Illustration on page 477.*)

"THERE is a chance for you now, my bo
said Mr. Little, a hard-working farmer.

"What is it, father?" Owen asked.

"Your uncle Hadleigh has offered to take
into his store," said Mr. Little. "If you
have, it will be the making of you. With
son of his own to take to the business, you mi
drop into a good thing there if he takes a fa
to you. But he's a smart man, and he'll take
fancy to you unless you work well and h
your wits about you. That's so, isn't, mothe

Mrs. Little nodded her confirmation and
not trust herself to speak. She knew t
Owen would be on the way to fortune with
brother and that he would never do any g
on the farm; but she did not like to lose
boy. Besides, he had recently shown a conc
about his soul, and to send him away from
Christian influence into the home of her brot
who was a worldly man, engrossed in busin
involved a danger she shuddered to think of

Two weeks later Owen was in Mr. Hadleig
store being initiated into the rudiments of
grocery business. All but one of the ot
clerks lived out-of-doors, and he, a young n
named Norris, conceived a dislike for Ov
from the first as an interloper who by reaso
his relationship to Mr. Hadleigh would be lik
to become a favorite.

The first few months of Owen's life in his
cle's home passed uneventfully. Owen tried
utmost to learn his duties, but mistakes wo
necessarily arise from his inexperience,
these Norris made the most of in his reports.
Hadleigh, too, disliked the boy. She was
judiced against religion, and at once percei
that Owen was "infected" with it. Worse
she saw that Clarice liked her cousin, and o
heard her talking with him about relig
Owen had given his heart to the Saviour,
was earnestly endeavoring to win his
sin for Him. She was seeking Christ he
with that concern that is never unrewarded.

There was trouble, however, in the st
Norris reported that small articles were mis
from the reserve stock, which was under Ow
care in the basement. Mr. Hadleigh could
suspect his nephew of theft, but he knew
boy was poor, and the loss made him une
Owen was questioned, but could throw no li
on the matter. He became utterly misera
for the goods continued to disappear, and
uncle must think him wanting in care, if
did not suspect him of dishonesty. What wo

'ather say if his uncle ld dismiss him in dis- :! Owen mourned and :d, and redoubled his :nce.

iile this anxiety was him, Owen was sud- thrown upon a sick- As the youngest hand ie store, he was under orders of the older s, and Norris especially a delight in setting hard and disagreeable s, and was captious t the way in which they discharged. One day is ordered him to carry id into the basement. 1 promptly lifted it on houlder, and prepared scend the ladder, which rom a trap-door in the of the store to the rground regions. In his tience, or through spite, is accompanied an in- ion to "step lively," a touch to the load. It out a slight touch, but ficed to disturb Owen's ibrium, and he fell the basement, with his oubled under him.

ien the bone broken by ill was set, and the boy what more comfortable, gh in great pain and weakness, Clarice softly into the room, and watched him moment with tears in her eyes. He look- white and suffering; and to think it d happen through the carelessness and idness of another! Presently Owen open- s eyes. "Is that you, Clarice?"

es; how are you now?" she asked.

in't it a good thing I was saved in time?" oice was feeble, though the tone was glad.

aved in time?" questioned Clarice.

es, I mean saved before this happened. iee, I could not have thought about these s while I was in such pain—at least it l have made me feel worse. Now the pain outside; my heart is happy. Jesus comes ays to me, 'My peace I give unto you.'"

rice knelt down by the side of the bed, oftly stroked the boy's hair back from his ead. He seemed to like the caressing on, for he did not move till she said softly, m glad that I know something of that , too, Owen, and it was through your lips blessing came to me." A sunny smile d over the white face as he said. "It was all the pain to know that, Clarice. God ound us both now. Would you mind read- me a little? My head is so bad; I think uld comfort me, and give me something to of while I am alone in the night."

rice opened Owen's Bible, and softly read 'salm that so many, young and old, have their souls on in times of joy and sor- "The Lord is my Shepherd; I shall not ." Quietly and slowly, without any com- she read the Psalm through, and then, g the boy was exhausted, went noiselessly f the room to seek some refreshment for

at same night, Mr. Hadleigh visited his ew in his room and, though cold and un- athizing, was more friendly toward him he had been since the robberies commenc- He remained some time with him, and then nded to his office at the back of his store that the safe was locked and all in order. was his usual custom before retiring to but this night he was later than usual ow- his visit to Owen. He glanced around ras about to leave, when his quick ear de- l a noise in the basement. He moved in his slippered feet to the head of the ladder and there stooping down he discovered how his goods, were being abstracted. Norris was down there filling his pockets with bottles of perfume and other portable articles, intending the next day to "finish Owen's business" in the store, as the boy, being now laid aside, there would be an excuse for a thorough examination of his department and the loss could be clearly proved.

About an hour later, Mr. Hadleigh, having handed Norris over to the police, paid another visit to the sick boy. No doctor nor doctor's medicine could have done so much for the sufferer as did that visit. Clarice found him the next morning radiant with joy, and together they thanked God, who knoweth how to deliver them that trust in Him.

Owen Little's Comforter.

THE EPOCHS OF A LIFE.

A NEW SERIAL STORY.

By Rev. L. S. Keyser.

(Continued from page 463.)

A New Light.

THE news of the adventure spread rapidly through the college, and Hadley found that he was regarded as a veritable hero. One and another congratulated him on his brilliant feat, and praised his courage and presence of mind. The only note of depreciation came from his rival, Duneman, who hinted that these stories of rescue were always exaggerated after the event, and probably there was not so much heroism in this as was made to appear. Hadley was inclined, at first, to believe Duneman's ill-natured remark, which was reported to him, sprang from his academic rivalry, but when, a day or two afterward, he saw Duneman speak to Miss Winters, and accompanying her from the college to her rooms, he suspected that it was another kind of rivalry which was stirring his enemy.

Certain it was that Duneman could be regarded in no other light, for his animosity against Madelling was displayed whenever an opportunity occurred, and he frequently made an opportunity when one was not provided. If, as he would have had it supposed, he was concerned for the religious welfare of his fellow-students and was apprehensive of the mischievous effects of Hadley's sceptical opinions on their minds, it seemed strange that he should so often endeavor to provoke him to their utterance. It appeared that he was rather desirous to force Hadley to go on record as an infidel and to have him well known in the college in that light. It might be that he wished him to be ostracized, or it might be that he hoped to gain some glory for himself, as the champion of religion, or there might be other reasons. However, that might be, he always endeavored to give any subject under consideration a religious turn, and then to wait expectantly for Hadley's rejoinder, to which he would make a reply pointed with personal insult.

One of these altercations occurred on the following Friday evening, at the Athenæum Society, and at its conclusion Hadley came away exasperated at the man's persistent persecution, and angry with himself for having been moved by him to a display of anger. He had not walked many yards when he overtook Belle Havelock. There was no one who would be more likely to sympathize with him in his present mood, and he joined her willingly in her walk. He told her what had occurred at the Society and marked the contemptuous expression which sat on her fine features as she listened.

"You should put an end to this," she said, "by boldly avowing your opinions and declaring war upon superstition. Mr. Duneman's aggressive personal campaign against you relieves you of responsibility. No man can be blamed for defending himself against unprovoked attack."

That was Hadley's own impulse in his irritated state of mind, and under Miss Havelock's influence he almost resolved upon taking her advice. He was held back, however, by a consideration he did not care to avow to her. He had an intuition that in declaring himself he would prejudice Miss Winters against him, and he was reluctant to lose the position in her good opinion which he flattered himself that he had attained. Miss Havelock would undoubtedly have treated such a restraining influence with scorn had he confessed it. Besides, he would have felt some delicacy about introducing Miss Winters' name in the conversation, his own having been so publicly associated with hers in the college and in the local papers by his saving her life, and it was strange, too, that Belle did not speak of the rescue at this first meeting after the occurrence. Acquaintances with whom he was not nearly as intimate as he was with her had overwhelmed him with congratulations; but Belle, who must have known of it, did not even allude to it. Her silence mystified him.

On returning to his rooms, Hadley found Dane as much irritated as himself by the affair at the Athenæum. He, too, perceived the personal animosity of Duneman's persistent attacks, and was as eager as Belle Havelock was to have Hadley declare open war. It seemed as if circumstances were also conspiring to bring about such a result, for on the following Sunday morning fresh fuel was added to the fire. The two young men had agreed to go to a somewhat celebrated Sunday-school connected with one of the churches. They were at once recognized as college students and were taken to the Bible-class.

A man of some intelligence was the teacher of the class. The young men, being strangers, listened quietly, to the remarks made upon the lesson. Several questions of a non-committal character were addressed to them, and they answered them in a non-committal way. Presently a point of some interest was raised. A member of the class, perhaps more acute than the rest, remarked:

"The sceptic would not accept that doctrine."

In an instant the young men were all attention. They were anxious to learn how the teacher would vindicate the Scripture against an objection. To their disappointment, not to say disgust, he replied dognatically:

"He would have to accept it, for it is a plain statement of the Word of God."

"Ah, yes, that is true enough," replied the first speaker, "but the sceptic would dispute your premises; he would deny the authority of the Bible, and to quote it to him as an argument would only be a begging of the question. How would you answer him in that case?"

"I would have nothing whatever to do with him," retorted the teacher, curtly, with a defiant glitter in his eye. "I wouldn't stop to talk to a man who denies the authority of God's Word."

"Yes, but he will not admit that the Bible is the Word of God," persisted the other speaker.

"I tell you, I shouldn't bother with a caviler at the Bible. Any man who has gotten to such a degraded level as to deny the Word of the Almighty is not worth my time or attention."

"What! would you not try to explain."

"No; I should explain nothing," replied the teacher. "He is not honest in his infidelity, and I should dismiss him forthwith, without ceremony. The Bible says that we are not to cast our pearls before swine."

This was too much for Hadley, who was naturally of a quick and impetous temper, and he could not restrain himself. His face became hot and crimson with anger, and his eyes snapped with defiance.

"That proves, sir, that you are—an insufferable bigot!" he burst out, in a voice tense with suppressed wrath.

In a moment every eye was bent upon Hadley's flushed face. Some of the members of the class were evidently shocked, while it was just as obvious that others sympathized with his indignant outburst; the face of the teacher twitched painfully. There was anger in his voice as he said authoritively:

"Young man, remember that you are in God's house, and it is not to be desecrated by such—such vile language; and remember that this is *my* class and no such impertinence can be allowed here."

"Then I shall leave it, and never enter this nest of bigots again!" retorted Hadley, and grasping his hat, he walked haughtily out of the door, with his inseparable companion, George Dane, close at his heels.

"What a hot-headed Boanerges you are!" exclaimed Dane as the two young men were clear of the churchyard. "Will you never learn to control yourself? There was no reason for telling that fellow what you thought of him."

"I could not help it," said Hadley. "His supercilious air and the dogmatic tone of his teaching were simply unbearable. Why cannot believers understand that unbelief is not necessarily perversity? The very essence of this man's belief is the right to think for himself. Two or three centuries ago he would have been required to believe the superstitions of the Roman Catholic Church, and if he had answered 'I cannot,' he would have been denounced as a heretic and most likely would have been burned. He would have been loud then in favor of the right of private judgment, yet now he says men who exercise it are on a degraded level. We are on the same line as all Protestants; we only go one step further. They claim the right to believe or reject any doctrine outside the Bible, we contend that the Bible also shall be tested. There is no difference in principle."

"That is so," said Dane. "If I were convinced that the Bible was issued by the Creator of the world, I, for one, would accept it in bulk, and be guided by it; a man would be wicked as well as foolish to do otherwise. But while we have no proof that it is issued by Him, we must ascertain whether the claims made for it are substantiated. When Christians refuse to argue that, and object to an examination, what are we to infer? I should say they are aware that it will not bear critical examination."

"That is the only logical conclusion, and such talk as that of the teacher to-day inclines me to suspicion at once. After that, one is disposed to examine it in a hostile spirit, while before one would have given it an impartial hearing."

The remainder of the day the young men spent in the rooms, deep in the study of a recently published attack on the doctrine of the inspiration of the Bible. In the evening Dane went to church alone, and Hadley went to call on Miss Havelock by previous arrangement. Dane was the first to return, and he waited somewhat impatiently for his room-mate. At length Hadley came in, looking dull and gloomy.

"Hadley, my boy," he said, "you have missed a treat. I wish you had been with me. I have actually heard a sermon that has done me good."

"A sermon!" exclaimed Hadley. "How could a sermon do you good? Perhaps it sent you to sleep, and that did you good; I cannot imagine a sermon benefiting you in any other way."

"Not at all, sir; it was a kindly and sympathetic talk for the benefit of honest doubters. The preacher is obviously a man of ability and culture, and, more than all, he is endued with a large and generous nature. It was strange, almost phenomenal, to hear a pulpit man talk as he did. He told us that he had little commiseration for the frivolous niggler at religion, but for the 'honest doubter' he had the deepest sympathy, the highest respect, and the most glowing hope. Yes, sir, these are his very words."

"Honest doubter!" echoed Hadley, in genuine astonishment. "Did he concede that there are such specimens in the market? Well, that is the most liberal concession I ever heard from the lips of a preacher. I shall be interested to know what such a wonderful man had to say."

"I will only give you a few of the leading thoughts. He had something to say about the lack of information among many opposers of religion, although he said everything in a very kind spirit."

"Did he not say," broke in Hadley at this point, "that these young men are immoral, vile, conceited, big-headed and pig-headed?"

"No, sir; he used no epithets, I assure you. He spoke as if he loved the sceptic, and had a message of incalculable importance for him, and his only comment upon the mental inability of the young men to whom he referred was that they had not yet had time to give the difficulties that thorough examination which they deserved. His tone was uniformly kind."

"Excellent! A noble spirit!" exclaimed Hadley, with animation. "And you say the preacher really used the words 'honest doubters'?"

"Oh yes! and meant it, too. And he read the church members a sound lecture on the evil they were doing in abusing sceptics, instead of treating them kindly, and showing them the open door of truth."

The surprise and pleasure with which Hadley heard this report were visible in the expressions playing over his features. "But how did he ever come to understandsour feelings so well?" he asked.

"Oh, his analytical skill is easily accounted for," observed George. "After he had modestly excused himself for making several personal allusions, he described his own life of unbelief in a few terse and graphic sentences. He said that he had traversed the arid waste-lands of doubt, pursuing one iris-tinted bubble after another, until, disappointed and heart-sick, he had turned to the fertile fields of religion; and he could therefore speak upon the subject with some degree of authority."

"Is it possible," queried Hadley, "th person can go through all this experience yet become a believer? I do not unders Did he point out a way by which one escape from this 'arid land of doubt,' a calls it?"

"He did," replied George. "He said was only one door of escape from the labyr and only two ways to the door—one direct one indirect. The indirect, a difficult and cuitous path, was through investigation—a of works *on both sides* of the question. H us hard there, for he said he had found sceptics generally read works on one side That, you must admit, is our case precisely

Hadley glanced up at their library and a ted that it was so. "Did he suggest any works on the side of the Bible?" he asked

"Yes; he said he wanted to avoid all ap ance of acting the pedagogue, but for the fit of any sceptics who might be in the aud he would name some books that might be ful. Not to say anything of such old and known works as Bishop Butler's, Wi Paley's, Bishop Home's, and Archbi Whateley's, which are still valuable, but what outgrown by modern discoveries desired to call special attention to ' ern Doubt and Christian Belief,' a that it would do any inquirer after truth to read; Professor Fisher's 'Supernatural O of Christianity"; Rawlinson's 'Historical dences'; and Dr. Schaff on 'The Perso Christ.' He also said that the man wh perplexed by the modern scientific objectio the Bible would find a recent little work e led 'The Ages before Moses' very hel These were all the works he thought it n sary to mention, although he had to omit invaluable works from his brief catalogue. investigator would soon discover them a prosecuted his inquiries."

"And did he maintain that any sceptic travelled the route he mapped out would 'the undiscovered country' at last?"

"He said that he believes it would effe willingness on the part of the doubter to *the direct path* to the door which *he* had f infallible."

"What was that?" asked Hadley, anxio

"Well," said George, in a subdued voice, told us that there is only one way to find truth beyond a doubt, and that is—*on knees*."

An expression of blank surprise passed Hadley's countenance, then a cloud gathere his brow, which was succeeded by a scor curl of his lip and an angry gleam in his At first he was too much taken aback to sp but presently he broke out into a dry, mechar laugh, and said:

"Ha! ha! Dane; it was the old story of mountain in labor, then, after all. And that the contemptible mouse then? The comm place chatter of the whole tribe! Well it is disappointing. I thought this man must ha guiding light, but if that is the conclusion, it is an *ignis fatuus* for certain. How is a to pray if he is not sure there is a God to him? He reverses the natural process of duct."

"Yes; it seems so to me now. In listeni him, however, one could not but think tha man was honest. It was as if, having mad own escape, he was telling some prisoner he did it. Not attempting to explain or ju but simply to narrate. I tell you it was touching. I should like you to hear him."

"I will," said Hadley. "We will go Sunday night. If he has any real light to this miserable man will be thankful for it."

(*To be Continued.*)

THE BURNT OFFERING.

S. S. Lesson for Aug. 5, Levit. 1 : 1-9. Golden Text, Isa. 53 : 6.

eshadowings of the Great Atonement—Only the erfect Acceptable—Must be Voluntary—The lace of Offering—Identification Required—Substitution Implied—The Manner of Sacrificing—he Offerer Himself to Kill—The Perpetual Fire A Type of the Holy Ghost—The Meat Offer g a Type of Christ—Sharers with God—Sta - hanksgivings Not Acceptable—The Sin and respass Offerings—Their Lesson of the Holiss of God.

ALL we, like sheep, have gone astray; we e turned every one to his own way; the Lord h laid on Him the iniquity of us all." (Isa. 6.) All the sacrifices under the law of Moses shadow the great coming sacrifice of Christ, one great Offering for a world's sin. The nt offering is the most perfect of them all. It is great type of Christ, the perfect Man, a Subute for imperfect fallen humanity.

he highest form of the burnt offering was "of herd." "If his offering be a burnt sacrifice he herd, let him offer a male without blem-" "Ye shall offer at your own will a male hout blemish ..... But whatsoever hath a mish, that shall he not offer; for it shall not acceptable for you ..... it shall be

Perfect to be Accepted."

v. 22 : 19-21.) It was the complaint of God ough Malachi, the last prophet under the old pensation, "If ye offer the blind for sacrifice, t not evil? And if ye offer the lame, and the k, is it not evil? Offer it now unto thy govor: will he be pleased with thee, or accept persons? saith the Lord of hosts." (Mal. 8.) There was nothing perfect in humanity en sin had entered in, and so Jesus, the sin-'s Friend, came down from heaven and took on Him our flesh, that we might have an offer- to bring to God, which should be perfect, it it might be accepted. All praise and honor His great name of Love!

"He shall offer it of his own voluntary will." st as God will accept nothing that is imper-t, so He will accept nothing that is unwilling, by constraint. God complains of those who of God's service, "What a weariness it is?" al. 1 : 13), and of such as grudge the little ney and the little time which they may give the service of the Lord, "With their mouth ey show much love, but their heart goeth af- their covetousness." (Ezek. 33 : 31.) Their art is not in what they do. When we think the mass of outward professors who attend r churches and chapels, and of how many ongst them take credit to themselves for eir piety, all of which is an imperfect and erefore unacceptable offering—Oh, how awful the thought of the moment when they shall undeceived, and shall find that all the outrd religion they have had, everything which s not really touched God, dealt with God, and en founded on the perfect sacrifice of Christ, ll be at fault in the great day of account! nd then, even among believers, every penny udged, every hour of time given unwillingly the service of God, although offered, has not ally been accepted by Him! "God is a Spirit. d they that worship Him must worship Him spirit and in truth." (John 4 : 24.) The burnt fering must be offered only in one place, "at e door of the tabernacle of the congregation fore the Lord."

"And he shall put his hand upon the head of e burnt offering; and it shall be accepted for m to make atonement for him." This was in der that the man who offered might be

Identified,

r made one with the offering; that it might e accepted as though it were himself, and dealt ith as he acknowledged he should be dealt ith. There is no room for personal merit here. We are accepted of God and forgiven our sins, ot because of what *we* are, but because of what hrist is; our prayers are heard, and our offergs accepted as though prayed and offered by Him, the perfect One. Because He died for us, we, as identified with Him, are treated by God as though *we* had died for our sins, and so *we* are "crucified with Christ" by being identified with Him, we are made to sit with Him in heavenly places. (Eph. 2 : 6.) But if we are offering the sacrifice of some little zeal or love or energy, or anything else that we possess, except as identified with Him, and making part of Him, we are detracting from the value and the glory of Jesus, and setting up, in a measure, on our own account. It must be of our own voluntary will, and not because we are driven to it by sheer necessity, that we thus identify ourselves with Him.

Once the identification complete, then the bullock must be killed before the Lord, and the blood—which is the life thereof—must be sprinkled round about the altar. It is the blood which maketh an atonement for the soul (Lev. 17 : 2). The man who offers must kill the bullock and "flay the burnt offering, and cut it into his pieces." And the sons of Aaron, the priest, must put fire on the altar, lay the wood in order, and cover the pieces of the sacrifice in order upon the wood; and, last of all, the inwards, the type of the will and the affections, must be burnt upon the altar, and all consumed with the Holy fire of God. Thus Jesus' members were consumed, used up for God, and thus His will and heart's affections all served their true purpose, and the savor of His sacrifice is ever going up to God, and cementing the unity between God and man, which He has brought about. It is only as identified with Him, only as washed by His blood, and as members of His body, that we are in a position to present our "bodies a living sacrifice," and to yield our members as "instruments of righteousness unto God." The burnt offering was to be offered morning and evening, perpetual burnt offering. And it becomes us continually, daily, and more than daily, to remember with thanksgiving how our blessed and perfect Sacrifice has brought nigh unto God all who will identify themselves with Him.

The burnt offering was so called "because of the burning upon the altar all night unto the morning. . . . And the fire upon the altar shall be burning in it.

It Shall not be Put Out,

and the priest shall burn wood on it every morning, and lay the burnt offering in order upon it. . . . The fire shall ever be burning upon the altar; it shall never go out." (Lev. 6: 9, 13.) That altar fire came down from heaven; it was a type of the Holy Ghost. The very identification of ourselves with Christ may become a mere dry, dead doctrine, but for the Holy Ghost, the Spirit of burning, who consumes and reduces to ashes all that is of man, that the perpetual communion with God may be kept up. There is always something more to be consumed. A perfectly renounced will has daily occasion to be consumed as the tests and trials of the day go on. The members and affections really given over to God have daily opportunities of yielding, and of being in new circumstances reduced to ashes, as the unbroken communion with God, the undying fire in the soul, burns on.

But Jesus is also *the meat offering*. This was a bloodless sacrifice, and consisted of the food used to sustain life—a beautiful type of Jesus as "the Bread of Life." A portion of this was offered upon the altar, and the remainder was the daily food of Aaron and his sons. God had His portion. It was a beautiful type of what we have in fellowship with God. Through our dear Lord we have not only peace *with* God through our Lord Jesus Christ, but "the peace *of* God which passeth all understanding."

We Share with God.

Not only have we joy in God, but Jesus says, "that *My* joy may remain in you, and that your joy may be full." (John 15 : 2.) We share His wisdom and His power. "Unto them which are called, both Jews and Greeks, Christ the power of God, and the wisdom of God." Blessed, glorious provision! And Christ is the Peace Offering—the offering of one who is at peace with God, and in full communion. This may be either "for thanksgiving," or "a voluntary vow," and typifies the outflow of a heart full of love to God. If it is "for thanksgiving," it must be eaten the same day on which it is offered. Stale thanksgivings are not acceptable. (Lev. 7: 15.) If it be for a voluntary vow, it may be eaten the day of the offering, or the next day, but not on the third day, which is always the type of resurrection. No resurrection vows for God; they must be fresh, and accounts well paid up. "Pay that thou hast vowed."

There is another class of offering: *the sin and the trespass offerings*. Those we have already mentioned are offerings "of a sweet savor"; no such thing is said of these. They are the provision for sin. "If a soul shall sin through ignorance (a wilful sin is not even contemplated!) against any of the commandments of the Lord, concerning things which ought not to be done, and shall do against any of them, . . . then let him bring, for his sin which he hath sinned, a young bullock without blemish unto the Lord for a sin offering. The bullock was to be slain at the door of the tabernacle by the man who offered; he was to lay his hand upon its head in token of his identification with it; but this was not to be "of his own voluntary will," but by the will of God, who hates sin. The priest was to take the blood, and sprinkle it seven times before the Lord, before the veil of the sanctuary, and to put some of the blood upon the horns of the altar of sweet incense, lest God's communion with His people should be interrupted by the sin. All the blood was to be poured out at the altar of burnt offering, and then the whole bullock burned without the camp where the ashes are poured out. Only the inwards, type of the will and affections, are to be burned upon the altar—"A broken and a contrite heart, O God, Thou wilt not despise," but the members are not accepted by God; they are cast out, because God hates sin, and removes it away as far as the east is from the west. The sin offering and the trespass offering are wonderful types of how God can forgive and cleanse from sin, but, at the same time, they teach us how God hates the sin itself, how He is "of purer eyes than to behold evil," and cannot "look on iniquity." (Hos. 1: 13) The sin offering was not to be eaten. "No sin offering whereof any of the blood is brought into the tabernacle of the congregation to reconcile withal in the holy place, shall be eaten; it shall be burnt in the fire." (Lev. 6: 30.) Yet the trespass offering was to be eaten. The sin offering met the actual breaking of a commandment, the trespass offering met the sins of omission. God would have us, like Paul, exercise ourselves to have a conscience void of offence toward God and toward man. It is food for the priests of God when His children have a delicate conscience, and cannot tolerate the breath of sin upon them; nothing so helps religious teachers as tender consciences in themselves and others.

LANTERN LIGHTS.

"Let your light so shine before men, that they may see your good works and glorify your Father which is in heaven."—MATT. v., 16.

"The man who carries a lantern in a dark night may have friends all about him, walking safely by its rays and he be not defrauded. So, he who bears the God-given light of hope within his breast, may help on many others in this world's darkness, not to his own loss but to their precious gain."—Henry Ward Beecher.

Let your light shine out, O Christian,
Do not fear to let the ray
Send a gleam of dazzling brightness
Through the darkness of the way.
Lantern-like 'twill pierce the shadows,
Golden circles round you throw,
Chase the gloom from off the pathway,
Help you, as you onward go.

And though the distance may be short,
That the trembling beam may thread,
Yet 'twill light the step before thee,—
Just the step you need to tread.
And tho' small the space illumined,
Yet, within its kindly glow,
Many a friend it may encircle,
And to him the pathway show.

Your own path will be the brighter
That you helped your friends in this;
Guided them into the shining
Of the Sun of Righteousness;
Led the way to God's own city,
Where, with all the darkness riven,
You shall, with your friends rejoicing,
Come within the gates of Heaven.

"Lantern lights" amid the darkness,—
Homely simile,—and yet,
It may teach us all a lesson
Which 'twere well ne'er to forget.
Suns nor stars, in this world shining,
Beacon lights we may not be;
Make us, loving Saviour, useful,
Humble "lantern lights" for Thee.

—*Carrie E. Hall.*

J. E. JEWETT, Publisher, 77 Bible House, New York, will furnish the above poem in leaflet form at twenty cents per hundred. *A Sample Packet* of 50 leaflets assorted (no two alike), will be sent post-paid, for ten cents. Postage stamps taken.

Christian Work in Mexico.

Through the reading of the Holy Scriptures translated into Spanish some earnest souls in Mexico have, by God's blessing, been led to a clear knowledge of the Gospel. From their numbers able preachers of the Christian faith in its primitive purity have been raised up, around whom congregations have been gathered from among the humble poor, who have been the first to publicly welcome and defend the pure Gospel in Mexico. The members of these congregations, rich in faith, have worked earnestly and bravely for Christ and His truth among their fellow countrymen in that beautiful Southern portion of North America called Mexico. Schools have been established by them, in which large numbers of bright boys and girls have received a good secular education and have been carefully taught the Christian faith. From the children thus educated faithful Christian workers have been raised up. A Mexican Branch of the Church of Christ, that maintains the faith in its purity and integrity, has been organized among these native Christians in the Republic of Mexico. The members of this Mexican Church of Christ, though gathered mostly from among the poor, are yet doing a most important Christian work. To continue that work, we need to pay a few leading workers small monthly salaries, and also to defray some current expenses. To raise the needed funds we have formed a society with an office at 43 Bible House, New York, U. S., and should be pleased to have many of our fellow Christians join this society by becoming regular contributors to its treasury. We are trying to secure monthly or quarterly contributions to meet the regular monthly expenses of the work. In order to continue and extend the work, we wish to raise four hundred dollars a month, by endeavoring to have four hundred persons each give on an average *one dollar every month* to this object, leaving the donors to give less or more as they may be able and willing.

We earnestly invite all who will, to join us in this systematic effort in behalf of the cause of Christ in Mexico, by becoming monthly subscribers to this fund. We have already regular subscribers whose gifts amount monthly to over eighty dollars, and a growing circle of friends who are forwarding us occasional donations.

This Mexican Church of Christ is a very effective instrumentality through which to do Christian work among the many millions on this Western Hemisphere who speak the Spanish language, comparatively few of whom have ever had a Bible in their hands. A beautiful church building has been secured in the City of Mexico as the centre of the activities of this Mexican Church of Christ. Through the workers connected with that centre more than forty congregations have been gathered from among the poor in different parts of the Republic of Mexico. We have some faithful and able preachers now in the field, but more young men need to be trained for the ministry. Multitudes of Protestant children in Mexico, some of them orphans, need to be educated. We make three requests of you, Christian reader: *first*, that you will, if possible, become a monthly or quarterly subscriber in behalf of this Christian work; *second*, that you will try and induce your friends also to contribute to it; *third*, that you will remember this precious work in Mexico in your prayers.

We most sincerely thank all who are already generously contributing to this Christian work for their timely and generous gifts, and we earnestly invite many others, to unite with us in aiding it by also becoming monthly subscribers in its behalf. Those who may not feel that they can give as much as a dollar a month are earnestly asked to give what they can, whenever they are able—EVERY LITTLE HELPS. Fellow Christian, if you will generously consent to contribute a dollar a month or more or less to the work, will you kindly inform me of the fact? Contributions either large or small can be mailed directly to my address as follows:

BISHOP H. C. RILEY, care of J. P. HEATH,
No. 43 Bible House, New York, U. S.

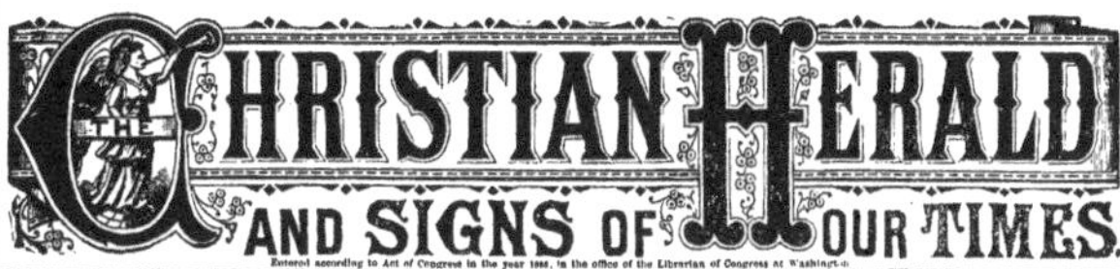

Entered according to Act of Congress in the year 1888, in the office of the Librarian of Congress at Washington.

Vol. XI., No. 31. Office, 63 Bible House, N. Y. THURSDAY, AUGUST 2, 1888. Annual Subscription, $1.50.

CONTENTS OF THIS NUMBER.

THE PAN-PRESBYTERIAN COUNCIL: PORTRAITS AND LIVES OF REVS. DR. LANG; DR. SAPHIR, AND PRINCIPALS DYKES AND McVICAR.
MARTYRS OF EVERY-DAY LIFE. Dr. Talmage's Sermon at Lakeside, Ohio, Last Sunday Morning.
ANECDOTES RELATED AT RECENT EVANGELISTIC MEETINGS.
PROPHETIC EVENTS BETWEEN 1889 and 1891. By Rev. William Birch. (Concluded.)
Mr. Arnot's Adventure with a Lion—New Chinese Temple in New York—An Enemy's Prayer in the War—An Idolatrous Wife Thwarted—Conversions Through Contact—Miss Whately's Cairo Schools.
PORTRAIT AND LIFE OF THE LATE REV. E. P. ROE, Author of "Barriers Burned Away," etc.
THE LAWYER'S COMMISSION. (With Illustration.)
THE CHARGE OF THE ANGEL. A New Sermon by Rev. C. H. Spurgeon.
Gems from New Books: An Outcast Blind Girl—A Drunkard's Wife—Dr. Guthrie Repulsed.
EXPLAINING THE POPE'S RESCRIPT IN KILDARE CHURCH. (With Illustration.
THE EPOCHS OF A LIFE. A New Serial Story by Rev. L. S. Keyser. (Continued.)
THE DAY OF ATONEMENT. By Mrs. M. Baxter.

REV. DR. MARSHALL LANG, OF THE BARONY CHURCH, GLASGOW.

PROFESSOR OSWALD DYKES, QUEEN'S SQUARE COLLEGE, LONDON.

REV. DR. ADOLPH SAPHIR, PRESBYTERIAN CHURCH, BELGRAVIA.

REV. PROFESSOR MACVICAR, PRESBYTERIAN COLLEGE, MONTREAL.

FOUR OF THE PROMINENT SPEAKERS AT THE RECENT PAN-PRESBYTERIAN COUNCIL.

THE PAN PRESBYTERIAN COUNCIL.

THIS year has been remarkable for the number of the religious councils which have been convened for earnest consultation on the best methods of conducting the aggressive campaign of the Church against the kingdom of Satan in the world. The Quadrennial Conference of the Methodist Episcopal Church in New York was followed by the International Missionary Conference in London, by the Pan Presbyterian Council, and by the gathering of the bishops of the Protestant Episcopal Church. A notable feature of all these assemblies has been the spirit of brotherhood which has characterized them. The eminent men who have met together, while retaining their denominational lines and preferences, have manifested a desire rather to diminish than to magnify the denominational differences which separate them from evangelicals of other denominations. The activity and intensity displayed, and the objects at which they have aimed, are in the direction of winning souls at home and in heathen lands, from the bondage of Satan to the Liberty of Christ. The speakers have been urging their ministerial brethren to aim at making Christians rather than proselytes. Other religious bodies than that to which they belong have been spoken of rather as friendly rivals in the campaign of light against darkness, than as antagonists. This has been a most encouraging feature of the meetings, and is an augury of success. It leads us to hope that in

The Short Time that Now Remains

before the coming of Christ, for the work of gathering out of the world of a people for Him will be a period unprecedented since apostolic days for harmonious, vigorous, and successful soul-winning. This activity is precisely what students of prophecy have long expected to be developed at this time, as the gospel must be proclaimed as a witness throughout the whole earth before the final consummation. Never were there so many missionaries at work as now; never so many volunteers to go out to heathen lands; and never so much money subscribed for the prosecution of missionary work. Godly men, who do not look for the speedy advent of the Lord, are stirred up to work by the love of souls, while those who have read correctly the signs of the times, are animated by still stronger motives for earnest labor, being convinced that the day is far spent, and the opportunity for gospel work is drawing to a close.

Prominent among the assemblies of the season is the fourth triennial Pan Presbyterian Council, comprising representatives of Presbyterian churches all over the world, which sat in London from July 2 to July 12. The delegates numbered three hundred, and represented twenty millions of members and adherents in different parts of the globe. Among the speakers, besides Dr. Dykes, who preached the opening sermon, were Pastor Monod, Rev. M. Pressensé, and Pastor Bersier, of Paris; Dr. Drummond, Dr. Dods, and Dr. Lang, of Glasgow; and besides representatives from Ireland and England and Wales, there were from America and Canada, Rev. Dr. Cavan, of Toronto; Dr. Drury and Dr. Schaff, of New York; Dr. Pierson and Dr. Cravan, of Philadelphia; Dr. Hoge, of Richmond; Dr. McVicar, of Montreal; Dr. Apple, Dr. Gill, Dr. Worden, Dr. Junkin, and others. From among the eminent leaders we select four—Dr. McVicar, Rev. Dr. Marshall Lang, Rev. Dr. Adolph Saphir, and Dr. Oswald Dykes—as fairly representative of this grand assembly, for illustration, and their portraits appear on the first page.

REV. J. MARSHALL LANG, D. D.

THE Barony Church of Glasgow, Scotland, has become almost like the cathedral of Presbyterianism since the late Norman McLeod rendered it famous throughout the world by his powerful preaching, his magnetic character, and his magnificent power of organizing its people for Christian work. His successor is Rev. John Marshall Lang who led the discussion of "The Social Tendencies of the Age," which was one of the earliest questions before the Pan Presbyterian Council. He was born in Lanarkshire in 1834, so that he is now fifty-four years old. He was taught at home by tutors before going to the High School of Glasgow, from which he passed to the University, becoming

An Undergraduate at Thirteen

years of age. Young as he was, he won an honorable place for himself there by his talents and industry. He had already decided what his life-work should be; he, too, would be a minister of the gospel. The Church required at that time an eight years' curriculum of all who sought to occupy her pulpits: four in the University and four in the Divinity Hall. Mr. Lang passed through such a curriculum, with credit to himself and gratification to his friends. He was licensed in 1855, and immediately afterwards was called to assist Dr. Clark in the ministerial and pastoral charge of Dunoon and Kilmun churches.

In May of the following year he was presented by the Town Council of Aberdeen to the care of the East Church in that city. The work was arduous and responsible, but he threw himself heartily into his new duties. The strain was, however, too great to be borne long. The minister's health threatened to give way. He was shut up to one of two alternatives: he must either do less, or remove to another sphere of service. He chose the latter and went to Fyvie, a parish which was distant some miles from Aberdeen, and which had a population of only 4,000. He spent in it six happy and useful years, following those methods which had made his father a model country minister.

His Fame Travelled to Glasgow,

and he was asked to undertake the oversight of a new church there. He consented. The building was ready, but the congregation had to be gathered. He set himself to the task of gathering one; and in the course of two years the membership rose from nothing to upwards of 700. Circumstances subsequently induced him to remove to a church in the fashionable suburb of Morningside, Edinburgh, which was soon filled with an appreciative audience.

When in Morningside he was sent in 1873 on a deputation to the General Assembly of the Presbyterian Churches of the United States. He was received with open arms. Welcomed at first for the sake of the Church he represented, he was soon loved and respected for his own sake. His addresses roused great enthusiasm, and the tact with which he discharged the duties which fell to his lot won the admiration of his brethren on this side of the Atlantic. While in Albany, he heard of

The Death of Dr. Norman Macleod.

He and his companions mourned the fall of a "prince in Israel." Speculation was rife at once as to who would be the successor of the departed leader. It fell to the lot of Dr. Lang. The appointment was vested in the hands of the Queen, who, in compliance with the expressed desire of the Barony Church, appointed Dr. Lang. He has now been fifteen years in the Barony Church, and the glory of that centre of truth is not dimmed, nor is its activity abated.

DR. OSWALD DYKES.

THE responsible office of Principal of the Presbyterian College in London is ably filled by Dr. Dykes, whose portrait is second of the four on the first page. Dr. Dykes is also a Scotchman, having been born in Renfrewshire some fifty-five years ago. His preliminary training was received at the Academy of Dumfries, whence he proceeded to Edinburgh University, where he graduated in Arts in 1853. Thence he proceeded to Germany, where he studied for about three years. In 1858, having been licensed by the Free Church, the young Scottish student became an ordained pastor at East Kilbride, where he ministered in the Gospel to an admiring flock for three years. His gifts soon gained for him a more important sphere, and he accepted a call in 1861 to be the colleague of one of Scotland's most famous ecclesiastics, Dr. Candlish, of

Free St. George's Church, Edinburgh.

This was a centre of influence that might satisfy the most ambitious, but his health broke down and, in obedience to the mandate of his physicians, Dr. Dykes laid aside his work, and took a voyage to Australia. During his absence, Dr. James Hamilton died, leaving vacant the pulpit of the church at Regent Square, London, the scene of the labors of Edward Irving. On his return Dr. Dykes accepted the pastorate, and commenced his work in October, 1869, and has continued it with brilliant success, until this year, when he became Principal of the Presbyterian College.

The English Presbyterian Church owes a deep debt of gratitude to the minister of Regent Square. His rare pulpit powers, and his clear-headed wisdom as an ecclesiastical legislator have been a tower of strength to the denomination. His uniform Christian courtesy, and the nobility of his character, have rendered him universally beloved. He was Moderator of the Synod in 1876, which merged him into the United Church, and to his tact the happy termination of the union negotiations was largely due.

Dr. Dykes was chosen in April last, to fill the Moderator's Chair this year, which involved his prominence as representative of the Synod, at the Pan-Presbyterian Council. He preached the opening sermon on July 3, in his old pulpit in Regent Square Church, to a crowded and interested audience. On English platforms, and in English pulpits, Dr. Dykes is a less familiar personage than some other Presbyterian ministers. This is owing to his retiring disposition and to the fact that his health has never been sufficiently robust to permit of his taking much outside duty. In the Presbytery and Synod his voice is often heard, and his weighty words always command respect. His discourses are singularly polished and scholarly. Some of them have been published, notably his sermons on the life of Abraham, The Ten Commandments and The Sermon on the Mount.

REV. DR. ADOLPH SAPHIR.

THIS distinguished writer and preacher, whose name is well known throughout evangelical Christendom, is of Jewish parentage. He was born at Pesth, in Hungary, about fifty-seven years ago. Through God's blessing on the efforts of the late Dr. Schwartz, of the Continental Mission, Dr. Saphir's father and his entire family renounced Judaism, and publicly confessed their change of convictions in the ordinance of Christian baptism. Adolph was a boy of twelve years old at this time, but with him the baptismal rite was no mere ceremony, for, as his subsequent history has amply proved, it prefigured the consecration of all his powers to the service of his Redeemer.

As a youth he was a student at one of the Gymnasia of Berlin, and afterwards proceeded to Glasgow University, where he graduated in 1852. Resolving to devote himself to the Gospel ministry, he proceeded to the Divinity Hall of the Presbyterian College, Edinburgh. Upon being licensed to preach by the Presbytery of Belfast, in 1854, he did not immediately proceed to a settled pastorate, but took the position of

A Jewish Missionary at Hamburgh,

and this formed an excellent preparation for the duties awaiting him as a minister. It was at this early period of his ministerial career that he began to employ pen as well as voice in the service of his Master. A series of tracts written in German, and intended to influence the Jewish mind, was written and published. These tracts have been translated into English, Dutch, Hebrew, and the Jewish-German dialect, and have been extensively circulated. They struck the same national keynote as we find thirty years later in the writings of another illustrious convert from Judaism to Christianity, Rabinowitz, and probably prepared the way for him.

At the end of two years, in 1857, he received a call to become minister of a Presbyterian church, at South Shields, and in this sphere of work he continued for five years, when, in 1862, he removed to Greenwich, where his ministry proved very useful, and attracted the notice and excited the interest of Christians generally throughout London. He gathered a large and an attached congregation, and the building was twice enlarged for their accomodation. While at Greenwich he preached the sermons since published in the volumes entitled, "The Lord's Prayer," "Christ and the Scriptures," "Lectures on the Hebrews," etc.

His references to His own people Israel are always honest, tender, and dignified. He holds that, for a period, namely during the Times of the Gentiles, Israel was to be rejected, the kingdom to be taken from them until they shall say, "Blessed is He that cometh in the name of the Lord," until Jesus restore unto Israel the kingdom, and the inscription written over His Cross shall be fulfilled in the sight of all the nations. That the interval between Christ's first and Second Coming was a period for the most part ignored by the Old Testament prophets, who beheld two mountain tops, between which in reality many and long valleys and plains interposed, in such close proximity that they describe them as if they were one, though between them lay the period during which from among the Gentiles the Church, the Bride of Christ, would be gathered.

At the end of twelve years Dr. Saphir removed from Greenwich to a church at Notting Hill, in the western district of London, and thence recently to Belgrave Square, in an adjacent district, where he still labors.

REV. D. H. McVICAR, D. D., LL. D.

THE fourth of the portraits on the first page is that of the esteemed Principal of the Presbyterian College of Montreal. Dr. McVicar is now fifty-three years of age, having been born near Campbelltown, Cantyre, Scotland, in 1835. His parents emigrated to Canada while he was yet quite a boy, and settled near Chatham, Ont. His early education was conducted by a private tutor, and he subsequently pursued his studies with diligence and distinction at the Toronto Academy and University. Having successfully passed his theological course in Knox College, for two years he taught classics and other subjects in a private school in Toronto. In 1859 he was licensed to preach the gospel by the Toronto Presbytery. Immediately afterward he was offered pastoral charges in Collingwood, Erin, Bradford, Toronto, and Guelph. He accepted a unanimous call to Knox Church, in the last-named city. He remained here only a year, but during that time fifty-two members were added to the church, and its work in every direction greatly stimulated. His eminent pulpit qualifications had already become widely known and appreciated, and in the autumn of 1860 he received a call from Free Church, Montreal, as

Successor to Dr. Donald Frazer.

This congregation was then, and is still, one of the leading and most influential in Canada. He accepted the call, and was inducted into his new charge on January 30, 1861. During his pastorate, which lasted for nearly eight years, the congregation attained a very high state of efficiency; the membership almost doubled, and great home missionary zeal was manifested in the founding of several district Sabbath-schools, two of which have since developed into self-supporting and influential city congregations. His Bible-class was one of the largest and most successful in the country, bearing most unmistakable testimony to his teaching ability. In 1868 he was

Appointed Professor of Divinity

in the Presbyterian College, Montreal. The work entrusted to him was in reality the founding of the institution which existed then only in its charter. It had no buildings, no library, no endowment, and only five or six students, who met for instruction in the basement of Erskine Church. For four years he was only professor, and conducted classes in all departments of the theological curriculum, being aided by occasional lecturers. Now the Seminary has extensive and costly buildings, a large and valuable library, a staff of four professors, and four lecturers, with more than seventy students in attendance, and it has sent out over one hundred fully equipped ministers and missionaries.

Dr. McVicar has taken deep interest in

French Evangelization.

By overture to the Presbytery of Montreal and the Assembly, he originated the work of training French and English-speaking missionaries and ministers, and organized the Presbyterian French work which has been so successful. He served for many years on the Protestant Board of School Commissioners, Montreal, and his services in this connection have been invaluable to the cause of education—a fact to which the Canadian press has borne repeated testimony. Among his numerous admirable educational works his two arithmetics, primary and advanced, are standard text-books.

In 1876 and 1884 he delivered courses of lectures on Applied Logic, and in 1878 a course on Ethics, before the Ladies' Educational Association at Montreal. During the session of 1871 he was a lecturer on Logic in McGill University. In 1870 he received the degree of LL.D., from the University of which he is a Fellow. In 1881 he was chosen

Moderator of the General Assembly

of the Presbyterian Church in Canada, the duties of which office he discharged with firmness, courtesy, and judgment. In the same year he received the diploma of membership of the Athénée Oriental of Paris; and two years later his *Alma Mater* conferred upon him the degree of D.D. He was appointed a delegate to each of the three great Presbyterian Councils which met in Edinburgh in 1877, in Philadelphia in 1880, and in Belfast, in 1884

ANECDOTES RELATED AT RECENT EVANGELISTIC MEETINGS.

Prayers in Bed.—The Rev. Mr. McCaul Remarks: "I recollect being very tired one night when I was a boy, and after battling between right and wrong for a few moments, I went into bed without saying my usual prayer, meaning to do so in bed; but I soon found that that would not do. I felt as if the words I spoke did not rise higher than the ceiling. I accordingly got up out of bed, and kneeling, I prayed to God more earnestly than I had hitherto done, and joyfully I went to sleep that night, knowing that God's blessing rested upon me. We are not forbidden to have sweet fellowship with God at all times and in all places, but it is a perilous proceeding to postpone your regular time of prayer until you are in bed."

How the Missionary's Head was Saved.—Mr. Swann said: "Coming to the Zambesi River, a distance of 1,400 miles, I saw an old chief, gray-headed, and he said to me, 'You cannot go down the river.' Well, I felt very much annoyed with the old man at the time. I was hurrying up to spend my Christmas at home with my old father and mother. He said, 'Well if you go down that river you will lose your head.' Well, I thought I had better lose Christmas. He stopped me for over three weeks, and this was the reason: He said to me, 'It shall never be said that Ramo Ku Kang let a white man go to his death.' Ramo Ku Kang—who is he? None other than one of the little Makoloko boys who followed Livingstone in his travels through the great continent. So that I can be thankful to God that ever Livingstone went to Central Africa, or perhaps I should have lost my head if he had not gone."

The Greatest Blasphemer in the Prison. Richard Weaver said: "One day I was visiting the Callon prison, and as I was leaving, the governor, pointing to a particular cell, said, 'In there, there is the greatest blasphemer we have ever had within these walls?' I went in immediately and saluted the wretched woman with, 'God bless you, my dear sister! Do you know that God loves you?' 'No,' she replied, 'it is untrue; God does not love me.' 'You are mistaken, God loves the sinner and has sent His Son to die in proof of it.' I then prayed with her, leaving her visibly affected. Next day, when I again visited the prison, I got a letter from that woman, saying she had left her old life, and had accepted Christ, and asking me to speak to the other women in the prison of Jesus, and plead with them to come to Him, and to assure them that none need despair since she had been saved. Nor had she over-estimated the influence her conversion would have on the others, for as soon as they heard that she was saved, they exclaimed, 'If there be mercy for her there is certainly mercy for us also!' God is not willing that even the greatest sinner should perish, but that all should have everlasting life."

Alive in the Hearse.—Pastor Joshua Denovan relates that "Some years ago, in Scotland, a woman was condemned for crime and publicly executed. After being pronounced dead by the proper authorities—dead to the law and the world—her body was handed over to her relatives, put in a hearse, and over a pretty rough country road, driven a good many miles to her native village. The dismal cortége having arrived at its destination, the mourners opened the door of the hearse to take out their unfortunate relative's corpse, when, judge of their surprise at finding her sitting up, alive! She had only been partially strangled, and the rough jolting of the hearse had shaken her blood into motion again. But mark, in law she was dead, and her crime could not be legally punished again. Such is the relation of believers in Christ to the law. They were crucified with Him, and live again in Him."

"God is Not Dead." A Christian Worker relates: "Not long ago a poor Christian woman lay dying. She did not fear to die, but her chief cause of anxiety as she lay there, feeling herself getting weaker and weaker, as she drew nearer eternity, was her husband, who, until then, had proved himself a drunkard, and consequently a most careless husband and father, and now her last prayer was for him. A short time after her death the man's little child said to him, 'Father, I want to say my prayers.' 'Oh, never mind that now,' was the reply, 'mother is dead and you do not need to say your prayers any more.' 'But father,' said the dear child, as he turned his face towards him, 'God is not dead.' The words went straight to the hard heart of the man; they seemed to be spoken by the dead mother through her child. God used them to the conversion of this inebriate, and he rejoiced in a living God as his Father, and a living Christ as his Saviour. 'God is not dead.' Christians as well as unconverted people often require to be reminded of this fundamental truth."

Colporteurs Roughly Handled.—Rev. W. Burgess, of the Deccan, India, remarked: "Our catechist was very roughly handled about the year 1883 for preaching in one of the suburbs of Hyderabad. He was violently laid hold of and hurried into the city, and then thrust into prison. He was detained there until midnight, and only when, during a questioning he was put through, he happened to say he belonged to Mr. Burgess's mission, was he set at liberty, and glad he was to get away, for Hyderabad police are strange hands to fall into. They are never very scrupulous as to their treatment of their victims. Colporteur Joseph, out in Kurinaghur the furthest advanced outpost, was very much less gently handled by the Rohillas. They took his books, tore them all to pieces, and then they began to prick him with the sharp points of their knives. He was stripped and beaten with more than 'forty stripes save one.' His hands were tied together, and he was pegged down to the ground in a kneeling posture, and kept there till weariness and fatigue left him with barely strength enough to crawl back to headquarters. Joseph's nerves were fearfully perturbed, and he is now at his post selling his books again and proclaiming the gospel of peace and good-will to men."

MARTYRS OF EVERY DAY LIFE.

Dr. Talmage's Sermon, Preached at Lakeside, O., Last Sunday Morning, July 29, 1888.

"Thou therefore endure hardness." II Timothy 2: 3.

The Heroes of History—Chiefly Slaughterers—A Scroll of Heroes Overlooked—I. Heroes of the Sick Room—Sickness a Test of Character—II. Heroes of Toil—The Patient Seamstress—The Real Battlefields of Life—III. Heroes of the Home—The Exasperating Wife—Women Who Make Men Drunkards—Neglected Wives—A Fifty Years' Martyrdom—The Funeral of the Drunkard's Wife—Her Throne in Heaven—IV. The Heroes of Christian Charity—The Poor Who Help the Poor—Heroes Whom God Knows—A Tombstone in Melrose Abbey—A Brave Little Scotch Heroine—The Murder of the Edinburgh Carrier—Coronation Day in Heaven.

HISTORIANS are not slow to acknowledge the merits of great military chieftains. We have the full-length portraits of the Cromwells, the Washingtons, the Napoleons, and the Wellingtons of the world. History is not written in black ink, but with red ink of human blood. The gods of human ambition do not drink from bowls made out of silver or gold, or precious stones, but out of the bleached skulls of the fallen. But I am now to unroll before you

A Scroll of Heroes

that the world has never acknowledged; those who faced no guns, blew no bugle-blast, conquered no cities, chained no captives to their chariot-wheels, and yet, in the great day of eternity, will stand higher than those whose names startled the nations; and seraph, and rapt spirit, and archangel will tell their deeds to a listening universe. I mean the heroes of common, every-day life.

In this roll, in the first place, I find all the

Heroes of the Sick Room.

When Satan had failed to overcome Job, he said to God: "Put forth Thy hand and touch his bones and his flesh, and he will curse Thee to Thy face." Satan had found out what we have all found out, that sickness is *the greatest test of one's character*. A man who can stand that can stand anything. To be shut in a room as fast as though it were a Bastile. To be so nervous you cannot endure the tap of a child's foot. To have luxuriant fruit, which tempts the appetite of the robust and healthy, excites our loathing and disgust when it first appears on the platter. To have the rapier of pain strike through the side, or across the temples, like a razor, or to put the foot into a vice, or throw the whole body into a blaze of fever. Yet there have been men and women, but more women than men, who have cheerfully endured this hardness. Through years of exhausting rheumatisms and excruciating neuralgias they have gone, and through bodily distresses that rasped the nerves, and tore the muscles, and paled the cheeks and stooped the shoulders. By the dim

Light of the Sick-Room

taper they saw on their wall the picture of that land where the inhabitants are never sick. Through the dead silence of the night they heard the chorus of the angels. The cancer ate away her life from week to week and day to day, and she became weaker and weaker, and every "good-night" was feebler than the "good-night" before—yet never sad. The children looked up into her face and saw suffering transformed into a heavenly smile. Those who suffered on the battle-field, amid shot and shell, were not so much heroes and heroines as those who, in the field-hospital and in the asylum, had fevers which no ice could cool, and no surgery cure. No shout of a comrade to cheer them, but numbness and aching and homesickness—yet willing to suffer, confident in God, hopeful of heaven. Heroes of rheumatism. Heroes of neuralgia. Heroes of spinal complaint. Heroes of sick-headache. Heroes of lifelong invalidism. Heroes and heroines! They shall reign for ever and ever. Hark! I catch just one note of the eternal anthem: "There shall be no more pain!" Bless God for that!

In this roll I also find the *heroes of toil*, who do their work uncomplainingly. It is comparatively easy to lead a regiment into battle, when you know that the whole nation will applaud the victory: it is comparatively easy to doctor the sick when you know that your skill will be appreciated by a large company of friends and relatives; it is comparatively easy to address an audience when, in the gleaming eyes and the flushed cheeks you know that your sentiments are adopted; but to do sewing, where you expect that the employer will come and thrust his thumb through the work, to show how imperfect it is, or to have the whole garment thrown back on you, to be done over again; to build a wall, and know there will be no one to say you did it well, but only a swearing employer howling across the scaffold: to

Work Until Your Eyes are Dim,

and your back aches, and your heart faints, and to know that if you stop before night your children will starve. Ah! the sword has not slain so many as the needle. The great battle-fields of our last war were not Gettysburg and Shiloh and South Mountain. The great battle-fields of the last war were in the arsenals, and in the shops, and in the attics, where women made army jackets for a sixpence. They toiled on until they died. They had no funeral eulogium, but, in the name of my God, this day, I enroll their names among those of whom the world was not worthy. Heroes of the needle! Heroes of the sewing-machine! Heroes of the attic! Heroes of the cellar! Heroes and heroines! Bless God for them!

In this roll I also find the *heroes who have uncomplainingly endured domestic injustices*. There are men who, for their toil and anxiety, have no sympathy in their homes. Exhausting application to business gets them a livelihood, but an unfrugal wife scatters it. He is fretted at from the moment he enters the door until he comes out of it. The exasperations of business life, augmented by

The Exasperations of Domestic Life.

Such men are laughed at, but they have a heart-breaking trouble and they would have long ago gone into appalling dissipation but for the grace of God. Society to-day is strewn with the wrecks of men, who, under the north-east storm of domestic infelicity have been driven on the rocks. There are tens of thousands of drunkards in this country to-day, made such by their wives. *That is not poetry. That is prose.*

But the wrong is generally in the opposite direction. You would not have to go far to find a wife whose life is a perpetual martyrdom. Something heavier than a stroke of the fist; unkind words, staggering home at midnight and constant maltreatment which have left her only a wreck of what she was on that day when in the midst of a brilliant assemblage the vows were taken, and full organ played the wedding march, and the carriage rolled away with the benediction of the people. What was the burning of Latimer and Ridley at the stake compared with this? Those men soon became unconscious in the fire, but here is

A Fifty Years' Martyrdom,

a fifty years' putting to death, yet uncomplaining. No bitter words when the rollicking companions at two o'clock in the morning pitch the husband dead drunk into the front entry. No bitter words when wiping from the swollen brow the blood struck out in a midnight carousal. Bending over the battered and bruised form of him, who, when he took her from her father's home, promised love, and kindness, and protection, yet nothing but sympathy, and prayers and forgiveness before they are asked for. No bitter words when the family Bible goes for rum, and the pawnbroker's shop gets the last decent dress. Some day, desiring to evoke the story of her sorrows, you say: "Well, how are you getting along now?" and rallying her trembling voice, and quieting her quivering lip, she says: "Pretty well, I thank you, pretty well." She never will tell you. In the delirium of her last sickness she may tell all the secrets of her lifetime, but she will not tell that. Not until the books of eternity are opened on the thrones of judgment will ever be known what she has suffered. Oh! ye who are twisting a garland for the victor, put it on that pale brow.

When she is dead the neighbors will beg linen to make her a shroud, and she will be carried out in a plain box with no silver plate to tell her years, for she has lived a thousand years of trial and anguish. The gamblers and swindlers who destroyed her husband will not come to the funeral. One carriage will be enough for that funeral—one carriage to carry the orphans and the two Christian woman who presided over the obsequies. But there is a flash, and the opening of a celestial door, and a shout: "Lift up your head, ye everlasting gate, and let her come in!" And Christ will step forth and say: "Come in! ye suffered with me on earth, be glorified with me in heaven." What is the highest throne in heaven? You say: "The throne of the Lord God Almighty and the Lamb." No doubt about it. What is the next highest throne in heaven? While I speak it seems to me that it will be the throne of the drunkard's wife, if she with cheerful patience endured all her earthly torture. Heroes and heroines! I find also in this roll the

Heroes of Christian Charity.

We all admire the George Peabodys and the James Lenoxes of the earth, who give tens and hundreds of thousands of dollars to good objects. But I am speaking this morning of those who, out of their pinched poverty, help others—of such men as those Christian missionaries at the West, who proclaim Christ to the people, one of them, writing to the secretary in New York, saying: "I thank you for that $25. Until yesterday we have had no meat in our house for three months. We have suffered terribly. My children have no shoes this winter." And of those people who have only a half loaf of bread, but give a piece of it to others who are hungrier; and of those who have only a scuttle of coal, but help others to fuel, and of those who have only a dollar in their pocket, and give twenty-five cents to somebody else; and of that father who wears a shabby coat, and of that mother who wears a faded dress, that their children may be well apparelled. You call them paupers, or ragamuffins, or emigrants. I call them heroes and heroines. You and I may not know where they live, or what their name is.

God Knows,

and they have more angels hovering over them than you and I have, and they will have a higher seat in heaven. They may have only a cup of cold water to give a poor traveler, or may have only picked a splinter from under the nail of a child's finger, or have put only two mites into the treasury, but the Lord knows them. Considering what they had, they did more than we have ever done, and their faded dress will become a white robe, and the small room will be an eternal mansion, and the old hat will be a coronet of victory, and all the applause of earth and all the shouting of heaven will be drowned out when God rises up to give his reward to those humble workers in his kingdom, and to say to them: "Well done, good and faithful servant."

You have all seen or heard of the ruin of Melrose Abbey. I suppose in some respects it is the most exquisite ruin on earth. And yet, looking at it I was not so impressed—you may set it down to bad taste—but I was not so deeply stirred as I was at a tombstone at the foot of that abbey—the tombstone placed by Walter Scott over the grave of an old man who had served him for a good many years in his house—the inscription most significant, and I defy any man to stand there and read it without tears coming into his eyes—the epitaph: "Well done, good and faithful servant." Oh! when our work is over, will it be found that because of anything we have done for God, or the church, or suffering humanity, that such an inscription is appropriate for us? God grant it!

Who are those who were bravest and deserved

the greatest monument—Lord Claverhouse and his burly soldiers, or *John Brown the Edinburgh carrier*, and his wife! Mr. Atkins, the persecuted minister of Jesus Christ, in Scotland, was secreted by John Brown and his wife, and Claverhouse rode up one day with his armed men and shouted in front of the house.

John Brown's Little Girl

came out. He said to her: "Well, miss, is Mr. Atkins here?" She made no answer, for she could not betray the minister of the Gospel. "Ha!" Claverhouse said, "then you are a chip of the old block, are you? I have something in my pocket for you. It is a nosegay. Some people call it a thumbscrew, but I call it a nosegay." And he got off his horse, and he put it on the little girl's hand, and began to turn it until the bones cracked, and she cried. He said: "Don't cry, don't cry; this isn't a thumbscrew; this is a nosegay." And they heard the child's cry, and the father and mother came out, and Claverhouse said: "Ha!" it seems that you three have laid your holy heads together, determined to die like all the rest of your hypocritical, canting, snivelling crew; rather than give up good Mr. Atkins, pious Mr. Atkins, you would die. I have a telescope with me that will improve your vision;" and he pulled out a pistol. "Now," he said, "you old pragmatic, lest you should catch cold in this cold morning of Scotland, and for the honor and safety of the king, to say nothing of the glory of God and the good of our souls, I will proceed simply and in the neatest and most expeditious style possible, to blow your brains out."

John Brown Fell Upon His Knees,

and began to pray. "Ah!" said Claverhouse, "look out, if you are going to pray; steer clear of the king, the council, and Richard Cameron."

"O Lord," said John Brown, "since it seems to be Thy will that I should leave this world for a world where I can love Thee better and serve Thee more, I put this poor widow-woman and these helpless, fatherless children into Thy hands. We have been together in peace a good while, but now we must look forth to a better meeting in heaven; and as for these poor creatures, blindfolded and infatuated, that stand before me, convert them before it be too late; and may they who have sat in judgment in this lonely place, on this blessed morning, upon me, a poor, defenceless fellow-creature, may they in the last judgment find that mercy which they have refused to me, Thy most unworthy, but faithful servant. Amen."

He rose up, and said: "Isabel, the hour has come of which I spoke to you on the morning when I proposed hand and heart to you; and are you willing now, for the love of God, to let me die?" She put her arms around him, and said: "The Lord gave, and the Lord hath taken away. Blessed be the name of the Lord!" "Stop that snivelling," said Claverhouse. "I have had enough of it.

Soldiers do Your Work.

Take aim! Fire!" and the head of John Brown was scattered on the ground. While the wife was gathering up in her apron the fragments of her husband's head—gathering them up for burial—Claverhouse looked into her face and said: "Now, my good woman, how do you feel now about your bonnie man?" "Oh!" she said, "I always thought weel of him; he has been very good to me; I had no reason for thinking anything but weel of him, and I think better of him now." O what a grand thing it will be in the Last Day to see God pick out His heroes and heroines. Who are those paupers of eternity trudging off from the gates of heaven? Who are they? The Lord Claverhouses and the Herods and those who had sceptres, and crowns, and thrones, but they lived for their own aggrandizement, and they broke the heart of nations. Heroes of earth, but paupers in eternity. I beat the drums of their eternal despair. Woe! woe! woe!

But there is great excitement in heaven. Why those long processions? Why the booming of that great bell in the tower? It is

Coronation Day in Heaven.

Who are those rising on the thrones, with crowns of eternal royalty? They must have been great people on the earth, world-renowned people. No. They taught in a ragged school. Taught in a ragged school! Is that all? That is all. Who are those souls waving sceptres of eternal dominion? Why they are little children who waited on invalid mothers. That all? That is all. She was called "Little Mary" on earth. She is an empress now. Who are that great multitude on the highest thrones of heaven? Who are they? Why they fed the hungry, they clothed the naked, they healed the sick, they comforted the heart-broken. They never found any rest until they put their head down on the pillow of the sepulchre. God watched them. God laughed defiance at the enemies who put their heels hard down on these His dear children; and one day the Lord struck His hand so hard on His thigh that the omnipotent sword rattled in the buckler, as He said: "I am their God, and no weapon formed against them shall prosper." What harm can the world do you when the Lord Almighty with unsheathed sword fights for you? I preach this sermon for comfort. Go home to the place just where God has put you, to

Play the Hero

or the heroine. Do not envy any man his money, or his applause, or his social position. Do not envy any woman her wardrobe, or her exquisite appearance. Be the hero or the heroine. If there be no flour in the house, and you do not know where your children are to get bread, listen, and you will hear something tapping against the window-pane. Go to the window, and you will find it is the beak of a raven, and open the window, and there will fly in the messenger that fed Elijah. Do you think that the God who grows the cotton of the South will let you freeze for lack of clotes? Do you think that the God who allowed the disciples on Sabbath morning to go into the grain-field, and then take the grain and rub it in their hands and eat—do you think God will let you starve? Did you ever hear the experience of that old man: "I have been young, and now am old, yet have I never seen the righteous forsaken, or his seed begging bread?" Get up out of your discouragement, O! troubled soul, O! sewing woman, O! man kicked and cuffed by unjust employers, O! ye who are hard beset in the battle of life, and know not which way to turn, O! you bereft one, O! you sick one with complaints you have told to no one, come and get the comfort of this subject. Listen to our great Captain's cheer: "To him that overcometh will I give to eat of the fruit of the tree of life which is in the midst of the Paradise of God."

THE LATE REV. E. P. ROE.

(See Portrait on page 492.)

GENUINE sorrow was caused last week in many homes on both sides the Atlantic by the anouncement of the death of this popular writer. Mr. Roe's stories were read everywhere, and so healthful and pure was their character that many Christian men who object to novel-reading on principle, made an exception in favor of his works and encouraged their children to read them. His death therefore is felt as a personal bereavement by many thousands of persons who had grown to love the man who taught them sound moral lessons in so entertaining a way. It appears that Mr. Roe finished the last chapters of his new novel, "Miss Lou," on the night of July 18, and spent the following day among the flowers and shrubs which were his favorite hobby at his beautiful home at Cornwall-on-the-Hudson. In the early evening he gathered his family and some visitors in his spacious library, where he read to them selections from his favorite author Nathaniel Hawthorne. While thus engaged he suddenly clasped his hands over his heart and exclaimed, "Oh that pain again; I shall have to stop." With a smile he excused himself, and retiring to his bed-room, sent for his physician. After an hour of agonizing pain he passed away. He had been seized with neuralgia of the heart, of which he had suffered a slight attack while visiting Charleston, S. C., in September, 1886, soon after the earthquake.

Edward Payson Roe was fifty years of age, having been born at New Windsor, N. Y., on the 7th of March, 1838. When scarcely twenty years of age he entered Williams College to study for the ministry. He graduated from there in 1860, and spent the next year at Auburn Theological Seminary, after which he entered the Presbyterian ministry. In 1862 he was appointed chaplain of the Second New York regiment, known as the "Harris Light Cavalry," and he remained in the field until the close of the war. In 1864 he took part in the raid of Richmond, which was led by Colonel Ulric Dahlgren, son of Admiral Dahlgren, and in which Colonel Dahlgren was killed. Mr. Roe had a narrow escape in the fight on the banks of the James River. Later, President Lincoln appointed him chaplain of the hospitals at Fortress Monroe, Virginia. After the war closed Mr. Roe accepted a call from the Presbyterian Church at Highland Falls, N. Y., within a mile of West Point.

How Mr. Roe was led to quit the ministry for authorship he has himself told in his preface to "*Without a Home.*" He was deeply impressed by the burning of Chicago, in 1871, and visited the city to look upon the smoking ruins. As he stood among them, the idea of a story shaped itself in his mind. He said that it grew as naturally as a plant on his farm. It was not intended for publication, but on reading the opening chapters to a friend, he was so strongly advised to publish it that he yielded, and it was printed under the title of "*Barriers Burned Away.*" Its remarkable success encouraged him to write another story, which should decide whether he should devote his future wholly to literary work. That story was "*The Opening of a Chestnut Burr,*" and it unmistakably settled the question Mr. Roe sent it out to ask. Its success was phenomenal, and Mr. Roe then settled at Cornwall where he established a fruit farm and nursery, such as he describes in his well-known work "Driven Back to Eden," and devoted himself industriously to weaving healthful stories. They were eagerly sought and read, and they issued regularly and rapidly from his pen. They came in about this order: "The Opening of a Chestnut Burr," "What Can She Do?" "Near to Nature's Heart," "From Jest to Earnest," "A Knight of the Nineteenth Century," "A Face Illumined," "A Day of Fate," "Without a Home," "His Sombre Rivals," "A Young Girl's Wooing," "An Original Belle," "Driven Back to Eden," "Nature's Serial Story," "He Fell in Love with His Wife," and "Success with Small Fruits." Many of Mr. Roe's books have been published in England, and have been translated into French and German. It is said that the aggregate circulation of his works has reached more than a million copies.

Mr. Roe was personally one of the most popular of men. Tall and soldierly in bearing, of commanding presence, slightly bald and wearing a fine full beard, his was a well-known figure in the neighborhood. Exceedingly courteous and hospitable, he delighted in filling his house with guests, especially with men of his own craft, to whom he was generous to a fault. He worked hard, studying scenes for his stories in cottage homes, the slums of cities, the police-courts, in stores and factories, and wherever he could find the people engaged in ordinary work, and he spared no pains in making his sketches true to the life. Mr. Roe leaves a widow and five children.

AN ADVENTURE WITH A LION.

IN a recent letter from Katanga, Mr. Arnot writes: "I returned last week from a three weeks' tour on foot, which I enjoyed exceedingly, in spite of the long grass and marsh-wading. Besides Dick and other lads who accompanied me, I got a professional hunter to join the party, so as to relieve me of the extra fatigue of hunting. The first villages we reached were those of Mirambo, a little way beyond Kagoma's, on the Lukurrwe River. We rested there one day, and then went down the river, making for a company of Ba-na-lunda villages. At this spot we had quite a remarkable adventture with a lion, which, but for the protecting care of our God, would have ended more seriously. All night we were kept awake more or less by three lions serenading us, and the lads had enough to do to keep their bivouac fires burning. I, however, got a good night's rest. Next morning, when passing through a clump of long reedy grass, I heard distinctly in front the low angry growl of a lion. The man who was in front stopped, saying it was a buffalo, and asked for my gun that he might shoot it. I urged him to move on, and tried to prevent the three lads from stopping, but it was too late to avoid the brute's charge. He made straight at the hindmost lad, who was carrying my mat and blanket. I ran back and succeeded in intercepting him, so that he fell short in his spring, a few feet from his intended victim, and before my very face, too near indeed for shooting with a rifle, and I had no spear. The man and the three lads dropped the things, and were off like deers, leaving me and my royal friend alone in the reed thicket face to face. He was raging like a maniac, and would fain have sprung on me, but seemed to lack the nerve. I held him hard between my eyes, and slowly cocked my rifle, lifting it to my shoulder for a steady aim, when he suddenly gave in, his huge tail dropped, and drawing his teeth under his lips he made off. The lad whose life I thus saved belongs to Bihé, and I overheard a young Bihean say to his fellows he would 'go anywhere with such a white man, who would throw his own body between a lion and a black lad of no account.'"

THE NEW CHINESE TEMPLE IN NEW YORK.

THE fact that there is idol worship in the Empire City, will doubtless excite astonishment. It is not the worship of the dollar, which is also a sad fact, but of an actual hideous heathen idol. It is set up at 10 Pell Street, in the Chinese quarter. Last month, the Chinese began looking around for a house for Joss, a new idol imported direct from China, the only deity of his peculiar sanctity east of San Francisco. In Pell Street they found an old warehouse which they hired, and since then they have been busy cleaning and decorating it. The renovation has now been completed and Joss installed.

"The house of Joss is reached," says a reporter, "by a narrow but neatly oil-clothed flight of stairs. The temple is what might be termed rococo in decoration, there being colors numbering more than the raindrop ever thought of. Oil cloth covers the floor, and from the ceiling hang elaborately-carved lanterns, *prayer sheets*, offerings of indestructible nature, one of them being, it is said, a bag of chewing gum. Ranged around the walls are teak stools, also beautifully carved, and separated from each other by small tables, resembling pedestals, also profusely decorated. The windows are half hidden with lace curtains, and the south wind blows directly across the temple into the spreading nostrils of the mighty Joss. Before him are ranged the utensils of his worship. Upon silver standards are the emblems of his power, conspicuously ugly being the dragon. Big bouquets of paper flowers, which are upheld by silver holders and pink candles, half burned, stand on either side. Small receptacles between the insignia of power hold prayer sticks and bits of paper which are sacred to the devil, mainly because the worshippers believe that when strewn they cause his Satanic Majesty so much bother in picking them up that he loses sight of his original object. These implements of worship are upon a richly-carved table, covered with an embroidered cloth. At the rear of the temple is a kitchen where worshippers of a charitable turn of mind deposit chickens for Joss. All of the inauguration day a pot of tea and cups stood on a table to the left of Joss, and all those who came were served. From sunrise until midnight there was a constant stream of Chinamen going to and from the temple, but no more were in it at once than could be comfortably seated.

Here is a sphere in which Christians longing to go out as missionaries to China, may acquire experience. It is a reproach to the Christians of the city that men should be living among us practicing the rites of idolatry.

AN ENEMY'S PRAYER IN THE WAR.

IN illustrating the fact that enemies may find a common ground for reconciliation, the Rev. Moses D. Hoge, D.D., of Richmond, Va., related the following incident at a meeting of the Pan-Presbyterian Council: "A Federal officer was mortally wounded in one of the battle fields near Virginia. As he lay upon the ground, far from his comrades, and conscious that his end was near, while the scattered soldiers of the Confederate army went swiftly by, he called to an infantry man who was passing, to stop, and asked if he would offer a prayer for him. The man replied, 'I am sorry I can't comply with your request; I have never learnt to pray for myself.' But he did what he could; he moved the officer into the shade, put something under his head, gave him some water out of his canteen, then hurried on. Presently a dismounted cavalryman, who had lost his horse, came up. The officer called him and made the same request. 'Won't you stop and make a prayer for me?' The trooper kneeled down at the side of the dying man and commenced a prayer, but as he uttered one tender petition after another, the officer used the little strength that remained in him in creeping closer and closer, until he placed both arms around the neck of the petitioner, and when the last words of the prayer were said, he was lying dead on the bosom of his late antagonist in battle, but in the final moment one with him in the bonds of the Gospel, a brother in Jesus, united in love for evermore. Yes, the Gospel is the great reconciler."

AM IDOLATROUS WIFE THWARTED.

IN a letter from Fenchow-Fu in China to the *Missionary Herald* Mr. Thompson describes the result of a matrimonial struggle in which, unlike those in American homes, the wife was not victorious. It appears that two men, father and son, who had been under the instruction of the missionaries for some time, desired baptism. Before granting their request the missionaries asked if they had idols in their homes. On being answered in the affirmative they were told that the idols must be destroyed before the men could be baptized. They agreed, and invited the missionaries to come and see it done. On arriving at the house, however, the wife of the senior convert made so strenuous an opposition to the destruction of the idols that it was postponed. What occurred afterwards Mr. Thompson does not state—probably could only guess—but the next day he was again sent for. Htsi, the senior convert, then informed him that his wife "did not rule" in his house, and he was going to make an end of the idols. "Htsi himself began the work of destruction," says Mr. Thompson. "Three of the idols were of brass and three of clay, and these were so broken that no two of the pieces could be put together again. Three valuable tablets were first split into pieces, and then burned, along with two paper gods that had been worshipped for a long time. *The burning was done in the court before the front door.* Only one or two outsiders had the courage to witness the spectacle. All the neighbors kept religiously within doors. Still we could not but feel that that burning, with the destruction of the images, was the best sermon that has ever been preached in Fenchow-Fu. It has greatly cheered our hearts. God has said, 'The idols shall be utterly abolished;' and now that we are beginning to witnes the fulfilment of that promise we thank Him and take courage. There was a full chapel on Sunday to witness the baptisms. Htsi testified before them all that he had destroyed his idols, and was now worshipping the true and living God."

CONVERSIONS THROUGH CONTACT.

THE virtue that lies in a touch was recently impressed on an audience by the Rev. A. T. Pierson, D. D., of Philadelphia, who related a number of incidents in proof. He said: One who had been released from prison was told that he would find in Lord Shaftesbury a sympathizing friend and helper. The ex-convict went to the earl for advice, and he became from that hour a new man. He entered into business, and by and by became a prosperous man in the midst of the city; supporting his family, attending upon the ordinances of religion, and leading in many Christian activities in the Church to which he belonged. A friend inquired how all this great change had come about. His reply was, "I owe it all to Lord Shaftesbury. I forgot what he said to me, but I do remember one thing. He put his hand on my shoulder and said, '*John, by the grace of God, we will make a man of you yet.*' It was the touch that did it!" Here is a man on this platform, whose name is eminent in the Presbyterian Church (Dr. Blaikie). He told me to-day that on a certain occasion, when he was attending one of Richard Weaver's meetings, he was asked to go into the inquiry-room and speak a few words to seven young men who sat there waiting for counsel; and that years afterwards, a young man on his dying bed sent for him. "You don't remember me," said the young man, "but I remember you. In that inquiry-room you put your hand on my shoulder and your arm round my neck, and to that I owe the fact that I came to Jesus as I was." We want contact; not kid glove contact either, for the kid glove is a non-conductor. It does not conduct, but hinders, sympathy. You have got to go down among the people, be one with the people, and be identified with the people. In the City of Philadelphia there stands a church attended by two hundred people, largely composed of the working classes. Mr. Wanamaker, doing business on as large a scale as, perhaps, any man in the United States of America, comes in among those poor people, and you would never know that he owns a dollar, or that he conducts a business so colossal. He is one of them in counsel, and one of them in action, and you could find no distinction between him and them in airs of superiority. A man in Cincinnati built a mission chapel for the poor, and he could not get anyone to go into it. One would have supposed that written over the door were the words: "This is for the poor." Then he took sittings in it for himself and family, and from that hour its success was assured.

MISS WHATELY'S CAIRO SCHOOLS.

THE value of the work to which Miss Whately has devoted her life, as well as the urgent need there is for its extention among the degraded people of Egypt, is shown in the following extract from a recent statement she has made:

"Twenty-six years ago, when I first visited Egypt, there was scarcely any educational provision for the boys, and none at all for the girls. The lower classes of the people are now what they were then, very ignorant, and live in squalor and wretchedness. *The lot of the women* is a sad one: wherever there are Mohammedans there are slaves, and among the women in that portion of the community there is little or no happiness. I once heard a woman say, 'When we are dead we turn to dust, and are finished—finished—finished.' The importance of the school as a nursery cannot be exaggerated. The schoolmaster has declared that of the boys brought up under his tuition not one had, so far as he could find, taken more than one wife. This shows a great breaking away from the iniquities of Mohammedanism. The majority of the boys gladly learn English and French; the girls, who do not stay at school so long, are only taught to read and write well in the vernacular.

"But firstly, secondly, and thirdly, all are instructed in the Scriptures. The children are very charming, but yet we cannot leave the poor women out of account. They come to the Medical Mission, and while they wait for treatment by Dr. Azoury, we read to them the Bible in Arabic. In the course of a year we have five or six thousand patients. Many Mohammedans know the truth, but are afraid to declare themselves; trodden down so long, the Egyptian people have but little courage left. Nevertheless, a great change is being effected in a quiet way. There are about 600 children in attendance at the schools, although the accommodation is only sufficient for about 400."

PROPHETIC EVENTS BETWEEN 1889 AND 1901.

THE FIRST RESURRECTION.

Mr. William Birch's 775th Printed Sunday Sermon, Delivered in Free Trade Hall, Manchester, England, March 11, 1888.

(*Continued from page 471.*)

THE Second Resurrection is the next event, and includes the resurrection of all the unrighteous dead since the Creation, and probably also of the righteous who have died during the Millennium. The great white throne will appear, and all of them, both small and great, will stand before God, to be judged according to their works. "And whosoever was not found written in the Book of Life was cast into the lake of fire." "This is the second death." "And I saw a new heaven and a new earth, for the first heaven and the first earth were passed away, and there was no more sea." (Rev. 21: 1.)

The First Resurrection is described in Rev. 20: 4-6, as being *completed after* Antichrist's three and a half years' reign by the *resurrection* of His martyrs, and of all the "blessed and holy" who have died up to that time, as well as by the *Harvest Translation* of the "great multitude of *all* living Christians, "both great and small," just before Antichrist's destruction, when "the Marriage of the Lamb is come" (compare Rev. 7: 9-14; 11: 18; 14: 15; 19: 7.) All this may be expected in Passover Week, 1901.

But this *first resurrection commences* about five years earlier (probably about the first week of March, 1896) with the resurrection of all saints who have died up to that time and their ascension to meet Christ "in the air" at the *first stage* of His Second Advent together with 144,000 living *watchful* Christians—the Wise Virgins—who shall be caught up in this *First-fruits Translation* without seeing death. The other *unwatchful* Christian, numbering some *millions*, who are denoted by the five foolish virgins, will be left behind upon this earth for about *five* years, including the three and a half years of "great tribulation," during which they will be hidden in a wilderness, and then they together with further converts throughout Christendom—constituting the *Harvest*—will be caught up to heaven in the *Harvest Translation*, just before the Marriage of the Lamb, and a few days afterwards Christ descends upon the Mount of Olives at the battle of Armageddon on the last day of Passover-Week, 1901, and terminates this Gentile Age, and begins the Millennial Age of 1000 years. (See Rev. 19: 7; 7: 17; 14: 16; 20. Matt. 24: 31; 25: 1-10.)

Passover Week* (April 4-11), 1901, is

* Lindo's Jewish Calendar for 64 years, from 1838 to 1902, is the standard almanac of the Jews, and gives the first and last days of Passover Week as follows:—1889, April 16 to 23—1890, April 5 to 12—1891, April 23 to 30—1892, April 12 to 19—1893, April 1 to 8—1894, April 21 to 28—1895, April 9 to 16—1896, March 29 to April 5—1897, April 17 to 24—1898, April 7 to 14—1899, March 26 to April 2—1900, April 14 to 21—1901, April 4 to 11—1902, April 22 to 29. This last, in 1902, may be expected to be the First Passover Week in the Millennium of 1000 years, as foretold in Ezekiel 45: 21.

The Last Week of this Age

because it is 2345 years (2300 with 45) distant from Passover Week, B. C. 446, when Artaxerxes gave the command to Nehemiah to rebuild Jerusalem, exactly 69 Weeks or 483 years before Messiah was "cut off" in a Passover Week (Dan. 8: 14; 9: 25); and also because it is forty-five years distant from the Crimean War Treaty of Peace, ratified on the last day of Passover Week, 1856, which thus, at the end of Daniel's 2300 years, "cleansed the sanctuary" of the Holy Land from Mahomedan laws of murderous intolerance, which were then repealed (the forty-five years being the excess of the 1335 years in Dan. 12: 11, 12, over and above the last 1290 years of the 2300.) No doubt some may reply, "Of that day and hour knoweth no man, not even the angels, neither the Son"; but those words of our Lord applied only to the time when they were uttered; they cannot mean that neither our Lord nor His people should ever know the time of the End. Surely, Christ knew that day when He inspired John to write the Book of Revelation. And, again, until Messiah was "cut off" or "made a covenant" (*karath*) at the *end* of the 483 years in a Passover Week, it could not be known that therefore those 483 years and also the 2300 years (from which the 483 were "determined" or "divided off" as its first section) necessarily *began* in a Passover Week, and that consequently the 2300 years must end in Passover Week, 1856, and that, therefore, likewise the additional forty-five years must end in Passover Week, 1901. (Dan. 8: 14; 9: 24-5; 12; 11, 12).

You have, perhaps, seen a picture in the Art Gallery, in the outer hall of the Assize Court—the aged father leans upon his stick; the venerable mother sits by his side, her face covered with her handkerchief. Two little children stand at their knee, and close by is a young woman who leans against the wall in an agony of grief too deep for tears. Through the half-open door of the court of justice you see a young man being tried at the criminal bar, and these people—his father and mother, and his wife and children—are

Waiting to Hear the Verdict.

My friend, if you stand before God to be judged at the last day, unwashed in the blood of Christ, we who have preached the gospel and solemnly warned you, will also be present, waiting to *hear the verdict*; and our hearts will be sad because we know what the sentence will be—"condemned already"; for to be judged by your works means that there is not the ghost of a chance of your salvation. If you die an unpardoned sinner, you will have to stand before God to be judged and be cast into the lake of fire. *It is a personal matter.* You cannot appoint some one to go instead; you must yourself stand before God to be judged.

Have you ever stood at the death-bed of an unpardoned sinner? A young man, who had been often warned, but who had given himself wholly to pleasure and rejected Christ, exclaimed, "I'm lost, I know! Well, all I can say is, I am sorry!—very sorry!" They were his last words. Another seemed to have a vision, and cried, "Oh! I see the pearly gate of heaven opened to me. Oh! what a glorious sight." Then he suddenly shrieked, "Oh! I am lost! I am lost! I am lost! They have shut the gate; I am too late!" They were his last words.

Another man had been convinced of his sin and warned not to resist the Holy Spirit's strivings, but he went away saying, "Oh, bother that Spirit, let me have some gin instead!" When he was dying, it was noon, but the man said, "It is getting dark; wind up the blind." Then raising himself he cried, "It is getting dark—darker—dark"—when he fell back dead.

My unpardoned friends, the Holy Spirit has striven with many of you, and you will be unable to have quiet rest, either night or day, until you have decided either to be saved or damned. If you make up your mind to reject Christ, the devil may give peace of mind until you are on your death-bed, but even the devil cannot then stifle your conscience, and your horror will be more terrible than any bodily pain. The sting which hurts men when they die is unpardoned sin. Are you ready to die? I once asked this question at a religious meeting, when an objector replied that we were donkeys if we were always thinking of being prepared to die; but with the written word of God before me, telling us to be "ready," it it evident that God wants us to be always prepared for death or for the advent of Christ, and always sure of salvation.

"Nothing is worth a thought beneath,
But how I may escape the death
That never, never dies!"

It is a blessed fact that God wishes you to have part in the first resurrection. The gospel of the pardon of sin is to be preached to every creature, therefore to you. Christ died for sinners, therefore for you. The word of God is clear that you may be saved, and now!

My Remarkable Experience this Week.

This week I have twice passed through the fear of death, and I do not know the reason why, excepting as a means of instruction to you, under similar circumstances. On each occasion I felt that I was about to die, although at the time I was, and am now, in perfect health and strength. The first time was last Sunday night, March 4, or rather about 2 A. M. on Monday morning, March 5, after writing out my Sunday evening sermon for publication as usual. I had retired to rest, and was at once falling into a sound sleep. Suddenly I awoke, without any bodily pain or oppression, but with a strong feeling that the hand of death was on me. For a moment I was awe-struck, but the next moment felt a blessed peace, which brought tears to my eyes as I said within myself, "Glory be to God; I am resting on the precious blood"; and calmly awaited for the last stroke. Then a voice sounded, "*Not now, but be always ready!*"

The second time was last night (Saturday, March 10th). Suddenly I awoke, as if some one had touched me, and the voice sounded within,

"Are You Ready?"

But I found myself without any feeling of peace. In a state of sudden alarm I got up, and began to walk about the room in a struggle against the angel of death. I said, "Oh, where is the peace which is promised to the adopted children of God?" And, not finding peace, I examined my foundation for the hope of salvation. I prayed, "Hast Thou not said that all manner of sin shall be forgiven unto men? I know that I believe Thy dear Son died for my sins; and Thy word says that whosoever doth so believe, shall not perish. Therefore, according to Thy word, all my sins are forgiven, and my soul is saved." The feeling of death, however, still clutched me—no pain or convulsion of body; it was the feeling of the soul. The fear of death was with me; but having God's word for it that I was a saved sinner, I quietly trusted His word, and, leaning against a chair, calmly waited for the visit of death. Then the inward voice again exclaimed, "*Not this time, but be always ready!*"

Dear friends, if death comes, the question is not so much whether we have any *feelings* of peace or not; let us just trust our souls to Christ, and rest on God's word that "His blood cleanses us from all sin." (1 John 1: 8.)

Some of you, likewise, may be awoke in a similar manner; and, if so, how will it be with your soul? Will you struggle like a truant boy dragged before his master? Ah, no; be at rest. Trust, and be sure that our Lord's precious blood was really shed to make atonement for your guilty soul; and while you trust your soul to what God says about that blood, as you trust your body on a ladder, you shall not be afraid.

CHRISTIAN HERALD AND SIGNS OF OUR TIMES.

OFFICE, 63 BIBLE HOUSE, NEW YORK.

ENTERED AT THE POST-OFFICE AT NEW YORK, N. Y., AS SECOND-CLASS MATTER.

EVERY NUMBER CONTAINS:

The Portrait and Biography of some eminent person.
The Sermon Dr. Talmage preached the last Sunday morning.
An Exposition of Unfulfilled Prophecy.
A Summary of the Events of the Week, Notes of Religious and Temperance Movements, etc.
A Sermon by Rev. C. H. Spurgeon, of London, from advance sheets sent by special arrangement.
Pictures of Missionary Life, etc., and Descriptive Articles.
An Instalment of a Serial Story.
An Exposition of the International Sunday-School Lesson, by Mrs. M. Baxter.

ANNUAL SUBSCRIPTION, $1.50.

Remittances by mail should be by bank cheques, Post-office orders, or Express money-orders whenever possible. If currency is sent it should be in a registered letter. Cheques and money-orders should be made payable to THE CHRISTIAN HERALD. Making them payable to individuals often causes delay.

New subscriptions may commence at any time. When subscribers do not indicate their wish, they commence with the first number of the month in which the subscription is received.

PUBLISHER'S NOTICE.

The whole edition of The Christian Herald was mailed last week to subscribers during Tuesday, July 24. The last delivery at the New York Post Office was made at 9.30 P. M.

CURRENT EVENTS.

The Conference Between the Two Chambers of Congress on the River and Harbor Bill has ended with a practical victory for the Senate. The bill as finally agreed to, calls for the expenditure of $22,277,116, which is an increase of $2,374,333 since it first passed the House jurisdiction. Most of the schemes for the purchase and improvement of canals in various parts of the country, have been stricken out, but there are provisions for the surveys and location of several local canals. The amount appropriated is the largest ever made in a River and Harbor Bill.

The Work of the Immigration Commission was commenced in New York, on July 23, and the Commissioners have visited the Italian quarter to see for themselves the condition of the immigrants. About sixty witnesses have been subpœnaed, among whom are several agents of the immigration companies. It appears from the report issued by the bureau of statistics that the immigrants received during the year ended June 30 last were 539,818 against 483,116 in the previous year. The immigration from England and Wales exceeded that from Ireland by nearly 10,000, in addition to which over 24,000 immigrants came from Scotland. The total from the British Islands was 180,766, against 150,783 the previous year. From Germany there were 107,624, a slight increase. From Norway and Sweden the number rose from 58,741 to 72,915, and that from Italy increased from 47,524 to 51,075. There was only a very slight increase in immigrants from Hungary and Bohemia, the number for each year being a little below 20,000.

The Republican Senators have Accepted the challenge of the Democrats, and have decided to produce a tariff bill of their own, as a substitute for the Mills bill. At a meeting held last Thursday night, at the house of Senator Evarts, it was found that the Republican Senators were practically unanimous as to the necessity for that course, though it is well known that Mr. Blaine is strongly opposed to it. The outlines of the bill were discussed, and there was little difference of opinion on that matter. The skeleton bill, which has been prepared by Senator Allison, was examined. Its provisions have been kept secret pending the decision of the sub committee, but its leading principles were disclosed. The wool and woollen duties will remain as in the present law, except that worsted will be raised. Steel rails will be cut down to $14—they are now $17—and the Mills bill cuts them down to $11. Sugar and rice are to be cut down fifty per cent.; there will be a general reduction in chemicals, glass, pottery. The tobacco tax is put down in the bill for repeal, and alcohol for the arts is to be made free. Hoop iron, cotton and hay ties are raised, also tin plate. Altogether the bill is expected to reduce the revenue by about seventy-five millions, and to be so framed that no home industry will be affected. As the Mills bill passed the House by a majority of only thirteen there is a possibility of the Republican substitute being accepted there. The discussion is expected to protract the session until October.

The Prospects of the Nicaragua Canal are declared to be excellent by Sub-Chief Engineer Peary, who arrived last week in New York, from the Isthmus. Mr. Peary brings the records and final results of the survey, which was finished early in July. The men speak in high terms of the climate and conditions of life in Nicaragua, and say that no obstacle to the work of constructing the canal will be found in them. A slight change of route has been made which reduces the length of canal in excavation and yet gives increased extent of free navigation. Mr. Peary adds the information that the latest surveys in the Tola Basin, on the western division, decrease the length of canal in excavation by about half a mile, leaving the actual canalization less than thirty miles in all. Mr. Peary left San Juan del Sur on July 7, and spent four days on the Panama Isthmus examining the canal work there. Work is going on on certain sections of the canal, but it is not of a kind nor extent to secure its completion in six years.

Another Dynamiter was Captured in Chicago on July 25. The police regard him as still more valuable than the other three arrested the previous week. He is Rudolph Sevic, a Bohemian gunsmith. Within a year he has purchased fifty-five pounds of dynamite, all of which, it is believed, he has used in bombs. A few of these explosives have been found by the police. They contain about one pound of dynamite, and it is therefore concluded that the other fifty-four pounds are now scattered among the Anarchist groups in the shape of bombs. The missiles are vastly better made and more destructive than that used at the Haymarket massacre. They consist of a zinc tube, five inches long and two and a half inches in diameter. Enclosed is a second and smaller tube, one inch in diameter, which holds the dynamite. The inch and a half space between that and the outer tube is filled with pebbles, nails, broken glass, etc., and a fulminating cap is attached to one end, while the other is hermetically sealed. Such a bomb, if thrown into a crowd, is capable of destroying a hundred persons. Sevic was not charged with participation in the plot to kill the judges and police inspectors, but simply, under the new dynamite act, with handling dynamite illegaly. There will be no difficulty in obtaining a conviction on that charge.

Emperor William's Visit to the Czar Came to an end July 24. The visit was a succession of festivities, reviews, and pageants. The Emperor intended to leave two days earlier. St. Petersburg Court circles think that the prolongation of his stay, together with the courteous and cordial nature of the interviews between the two Emperors, although no direct political allusions were made, indicates a resumption of amity between Russia and Germany, tending to a general European peace. Leading diplomatists believe that no tangible outcome will result from the visit, but that the two Emperors simply desire to remove misunderstandings between the two countries. On Thursday the Emperor arrived at Stockholm, where he was cordially received by the King of Sweden and the Crown Prince, who went out with the Swedish squadron to meet him. The King and the Prince went on board the German Imperial yacht, and saluted the young Emperor with kisses. A great crowd assembled to witness the disembarkation, and cheered heartily as the two monarchs drove to the castle. The Emperor appeared delighted with his reception. King Oscar, in toasting the Emperor at the banquet given in his honor, said that his most cherished recollection was the friendship extended to him by the late Emperor William I. The King thanked the Emperor for this visit, and expressed the hope that God would grant him a long and glorious reign. The Emperor's next visit was to the King of Denmark, at Copenhagen.

Mr. and Mrs. Gladstone Celebrated their golden wedding on July 25. Testimonials in the shape of letters, telegrams and presents poured in upon them by hundreds. A reception was tendered to the couple at the residence of Earl Spencer, and they were presented with portraits of themselves, and also with three large silver cups, and an address signed by a hundred and fifty members of Parliament. Lord Granville made the speech of presentation. Mr. Gladstone, replying to the congratulatory address, wished to indorse all that the address contained with reference to his wife. It would be difficult, he said, to give an adequate idea of the domestic happiness of his married life. With regard to the allusions to himself, he felt that they were too flattering. His conduct had been often criticised, sometimes, perhaps, unjustly, but he thought that on the whole, the criticising had been more to his benefit than the reverse. He could fairly say that he was hardly able to recall an incident in his public life that was in any way painful to recollect. He will be seventy-nine years old in December next.

French Journalists Predict International complications as a result of the round of visits the Emperor of Germany is paying to the Courts of Europe. A series of articles in two prominent Paris journals affirm that the French Republic, and the danger with which it menaces monarchy in Europe, are the real subjects of the Imperial interviews. An effort was made to convince the Czar that France, is a perpetual breeding house of revolution, and is, with her hopes of revenge, a constant danger to the peace of Europe; that the only way to put an end to this is to compel France to disband the greater portion of her army and maintain only her colonial troops and gendarmerie, and to renounce solemnly and definitely all hope of regaining Alsace and Lorraine. In an interview with a French statesman on the subject he is reported to have said: "France will disarm on these conditions and on no others:—First, that Germany give back Alsace-Lorriane, and second, that all European Powers also disarm."

The Commission for the Trial of the Charges against Mr. Parnell has been named. Mr. W. H. Smith, the Government leader in the House of Commons, stated on July 23 that the Government would not be doing justice to the accused if it did not give them the completest chance to clear themselves. He had confidence in the proposed tribunal. It rested with the House to say how complete the powers of the commission ought to be. Sir James Hannen would be the president and Justices Day and Smith would be the other members of the commission. Mr. Gladstone, however, is less warm in his approval of the selection. He said, he was not prepared to give that unqualified confidence to the commission which Mr. Smith appeared to entertain. It was in the power of the Government to make a better selection of commissioners—a selection which would have commanded warm acclamations from everybody. The Government ought to make definite charges against definite persons. The committee of the Parnellite party has drafted a series of amendments to the bill. The leading amendment instructs the commission to inquire how the *Times* obtained its alleged information. Another amendment requires that the names of the "other" persons referred to in the bill shall be stated.

Evangelists or Christian Workers Desiring opies of the CHRISTIAN HERALD for distribuion at camp meetings or other religious gatherngs, will receive parcels of back numbers free of harge by writing, stating number required, to he Manager, 63 Bible House, New York

Encouraging News from Cuba is Kindly sent s by a correspondent who has later informaion of religious work in the island than that ublished in our issue of June 21. The moveient, which commenced under the labors of Ir. A. J. Diaz, who was converted about two ears ago and immediately began laboring for 'hrist in Cuba, is extending rapidly. He has ow been obliged to hire a theatre with a seatg capacity of four thousand for his Sunday ervices, no other building being large enough hold the numbers that come. About twelve undred persons have made a profession of ith and received Christian baptism since he mmenced preaching. The Roman Catholic ishop of Havana has denounced Diaz from e Cathedral pulpit, and has had his photoaph publicly burned. The Bishop has also lemnly warned his flock against attending the eatre services, and has threatened with exmmunication any who bury their dead in the rotestant cemetery. All of which advertises e work Diaz is carrying on, and stimulates iblic interest in it.

The Unexpected Result of Threatening a idge is reported in a despatch from Barbourlle, Ky. It states that suspicion has been rife r some time that liquor was being sold in conlerable quantity at Harlan, which is a Prohibin district. County Judge Lewis used every fort to discover who the vendors were, but thout much success. A few days ago several ominent grocerymen were arrested on the pposition of being engaged in the liquor busis. The trial failed to show any proof, hower, and the parties were discharged. The arsts aroused the resentment of those arrested, d that evening, as Judge Lewis rode out of wn, he was stopped by one of the accused n, who, with loaded revolver, was in the act shooting the Judge off his horse, when the apon was caught by a bystander. Judge wis, undismayed, rode back, and, assembling ose whom he knew to be enemies of the isky ring, proceeded to search the place iere the obnoxious liquor was thought to be. veral stores were entered, and barrels, kegs d bottles in profusion hustled into the street, ere the Judge coolly proceeded to knock ngs and heads out with an axe, turning the itents into the street, while his comrades, out twenty in number, stood guard with their inchesters.

Twelve Years of Silence Between Husband d wife have been maintained by a couple in icago. A daily journal of that city states, it sixteen years ago, an Englishman came ere and obtained work in the Union stockds. He had a pretty and attractive wife, who med much attached to him, but four years er his settlement in Chicago he had a quarrel h her, and made a vow that he would never ak to her again. The couple continued to in the same house, but occupying separate ms, for twelve years, without a word passing ween them. The wife continued doing her sehold duties, and the husband put money for her use every week. He would send her ssages by a child, but, if she attempted to ak to him, a threatening scowl on his face nced her. Two weeks ago he fell ill of hoid fever. His wife cared for him, gave medicine, and performed all the offices of sick-chamber. He never spoke to her, and epted her attention in the same silence he observed for twelve years. On July 20 the sician in attendance said the man had but a hours to live. Then the wife burst into rs, and the dying man with open eyes watchber. With a sudden impulse of a love that survived the years of cruel treatment, she ew her arms around her husband's neck, ed him fondly, and begged him to speak to her once, to break, before he died, the silence of a dozen years. He repulsed her, and turning to the doctor, spoke to him, but would not address his wife. She made no further effort to soften him, and that night he died. Few men are capable of cherishing resentment for so many years, but too many forget the limit imposed in the Apostolic injunction (Eph. 4:26) and the solemn warning Christ gave to men who refuse to forgive (Matt. 6:15.)

A Strangely Inhuman Act is Reported from Madison, Wis. It is stated that four weeks ago three small children belonging to a family living in a lonely cottage on the outskirts of the city were stricken with diphtheria. The mother was scared almost out of her wits when the doctor told her what the disease was. She said she had heard that an adult taking the disease from a child was sure to die. A day or two later it was learned that both parents had abandoned the premises and left the helpless children, who subsequently died, alone and without any attendance whatever. The neighbors went to the mother and endeavored to make her return to her children, but she answered that *her life was dearer to her than theirs.* She also refused to allow her husband to return, because she thought too much of him. The local papers say that the people of the town are greatly excited over the matter, and the parents may be made to suffer for their shocking conduct. Maternal love is frequently used to illustrate the love of God for men, but this incident shows that there are cases in which maternal love is not so strong as love of life. The whole world must have been lost if the love of Jesus had not borne that test. (Isa. 49:15.)

Five Dollars for the Renunciation of a Name was paid and accepted in Newark, N. J., a few days ago. The parties to the bargain were a father and son. The father has always borne a good character, but the son has been in disgrace continually. Recently the youth was charged by his employer with a theft of two dollars, but was told that he might escape prosecution if he would refund the money. He applied to his mother, who advanced him the two dollars to save him from prison, but instead of using it for that purpose he spent it in liquor. When the father heard of the affair his patience was at an end. He had an interview with his son in a private room, and asked him what he would take for his right, title, and interest in the family name. The young man said he would sell for five dollars. The father called in four neighbors to witness the transaction, and paid his son the money. The son signed a legal document acknowledging the receipt of the five dollars and pledging himself never again to use his surname, and to renounce all claim on the family. Apart from considerations of filial duty the son made a bad bargain in a pecuniary sense, as the father is a man of some property. He seemed, however, quite satisfied to dispose of his expectations for the small sum of money in hand. Everyone calls him foolish, but the majority of men act in the same way toward God. They prefer the pleasures of sin in this life to the Fatherhood of God and the certainty of unending bliss after death. (Heb. 12: 16, 17.)

A Providential Escape from a Horrible death was granted to a party of lumbermen in Canada last week. A press despatch from Ottawa says that the men were working on the Perley and Pattees timber limits on Bouchere River, when bush fires started simultaneously at four points of the compass, a short distance from the camp where they were at work. The flames swept down upon the men, who were not aware of their perilous situation until the fire was almost upon them, and all means of escape shut off. They were forced to retreat from the lumber depot in which all their provisions, stock, and implements were stored, only to see it doomed by the fiery element which was fast overtaking them. Men who probably never prayed before fell upon their knees and asked to be saved from the dreadful fate that seemed inevitable. Their prayers were answered; as the last ray of hope of deliverance had vanished a black cloud was seen rapidly gathering in the West, and in a short time a heavy storm passed over the burning district in which the men were imprisoned, deadening the fire sufficiently to enable them to escape. A number of the men were suffering from the intense heat they had endured. These men did not know of their danger until the fire was almost upon them, or they would not have waited to see it before making their escape. Unhappily when sinners are warned of the fire of God's indignation they are too often unmoved, and when they wait until the fire is upon them prayer cannot avail. (II Chron. 36: 16.)

An Interesting Lawsuit is to be Tried at the next term of the United States District Court in Massachusetts. It is brought by a widow against a well-known firm of Boston stockbrokers, to recover the value of over sixty thousand dollars worth of stocks and bonds which were left to her by her late husband. It appears that the papers were in the custody of her son, a young man who was bitten by the stock-speculating mania. Though he was not of age at the time, he speculated with his own fortune of forty thousand dollars and lost the bulk of it. He then carried to his brokers some of his mother's stocks, and finally the whole of them. He was as unsuccessful with her property as he had been with his own, and her fortune also disappeared. As she had not given her consent to the disposal of her stocks, she contends that she is entitled to recover their value from the brokers who were the medium her son employed in his disastrous transactions. There would apparently be more justice in calling upon her son for restitution, as he was the custodian of the deeds, and was the culpable party in their abstraction; but as he has lost his own fortune it would be useless to press him. He must, however, if he has filial feeling, bitterly deplore his faithlessness and must suffer agonies of remorse. Similarly, faithlessness is exhibited by men who ignore the fact that their time, talents, and opportunities are the Lord's, intrusted to them to use in His service. (Peter 1:17.)

BRIEF NOTES.

The Reformed Presbyterian Church Synod, at its recent session, directed the local sessions to prosecute, according to church discipline, members who advertise in Sunday newspapers.

During the past nine months 1,155 young men have professed-conversion in the various Young Men's Christian Associations of the State of Illinois, and 410 have united with evangelical churches.

Judge White, of Pittsburgh, Penn., gives it as his deliberate opinion from thirteen years' experience in the criminal court, that there are far more evils resulting from the use of beer than from whiskey.

The International Bible Convention at Asbury Park, N. J., last week was largely attended. Dr. L. W. Munhall, who conducted it, made an earnest address on Divine Healing. Dr. W. W. Clark gave a chart illustration of Gospel scenes. Prof. and Mrs. Towner conducted the services of song.

At the State Sunday-school Convention of Pennsylvania at Williams Grove, nearly 10,000 Sunday-school workers were present. An interesting feature was the presence of several hundred Indian boys and girls from the Government Indian Training School in Carlisle, who delivered speeches and sang songs.

Mr. Moody's Church on La Salle Avenue, Chicago, was struck by lightning during the afternoon service on July 22. The congregation was alarmed, but was tranquillized by the appeal of the pastor, Rev. Charles F. Goss. An examination proved that the damage done was confined to the steeple, and the service proceeded.

The unhappy division in the Elsey Memorial Faith-Cure Chapel on Jersey City Heights will, it is believed, be overruled to more extended Gospel work in the neighborhood. Mr. Phillips, the pastor dismissed by the proprietors, is beginning mission work among the poor, and a new pastor, possibly the Rev. E. W. Oakes, will be secured for the Elsey Chapel.

The National Temperance camp meeting being held this week at Ocean Grove, N. J., promises to be of unusual interest. Among those taking an active part in the proceedings are President Stokes of the Ocean Grove Camp Meeting Association; Gen. Clinton B. Fisk, Dr. Steele, Miss Julia Coleman; Rollo Kirk, the Michigan chalk talker; George W. Bain, of Kentucky; and F. C. Iglehart, of Newark.

THE CHARGE OF THE ANGEL.

A New Sermon, by Pastor C. H. Spurgeon.

"The angel of the Lord by night opened the prison doors, and brought them forth, and said, Go, stand and speak in the temple to the people all the words of this life."—Act. 5 : 19, 20.

The Apostles Persecuted by the Sadducees—God's Answer to them—The Best Antidote—The Apostles to Preach the Gospel to the People—I. The Agents Employed—Men not Angels—An Honor to Manhood—A Delight to Jesus—King Edward III. and the Black Prince—II. Their Duty to Preach to the People—Not to Classes—The Rich and the Poor both Welcome—A Significant Difference in the Reformations—III. The Message Described—Its Seven Points—IV. The Whole Message to be Given.

The second persecution of the Church, in which all the apostles were put into the common prison, was mainly brought about by the sect of the Sadducees. These, as you know, were the Broad School, the liberals, the advanced thinkers, the modern-thought people of the day. If you want a bitter sneer, a biting sarcasm, or a cruel action, I commend you to these large-minded gentlemen. They are liberal to everybody, except to those who hold the truth; and for those they have a reserve of

Concentrated Bitterness

which far excels wormwood and gall. They are so liberal to their brother errorists that they have no tolerance to spare for evangelicals. We are expressly told that "the high priest, and all they that were with him (which is the sect of the Sadducees), were filled with indignation."

To them the only answer which God gave was spoken by His angel: "Go, stand and speak in the temple to the people all the words of this life." Argument will be lost upon them; go on with your preaching. They have lost the faculty of believing: go and

Speak to the People.

They are so given over to their doubts, that it is like rolling the stone of Sisyphus to persuade them to faith. They are so eaten up with objections, that to attempt to answer all the questions they raise would be as vain as the labor of filling a bottomless tub. Go on with your preaching, you apostles; but address yourselves mainly to the people. Extend as widely as possible the range of the truth, and thus answer the opposition of its adversaries. It is better to evangelize than to controvert. The preaching of the word of life is the best antidote to the doctrine of death.

Clearly enough, if they had known it, and had been capable of seeing it, these blind Sadducees were answered at every point when the apostles were brought out of prison and bore witness to their Lord. Here was the creed of the Sadducees: they said that "there was no resurrection, neither angel nor spirit," but these apostles stood up and witnessed to the resurrection of Jesus Christ from the dead. What did they make of that? An angel had come down from heaven and had brought these apostles out of prison. Then there were angels. As these apostles were set free while the sentries remained standing before the doors, and those doors were afterwards found fastened, if there were no spirit, assuredly materialism had acted in a singular fashion. Every item of their negative creed had been made to fall like Dagon before the ark. *The Lord always arranges Red Seas for Pharaohs.* All that the apostles had to do was to go on with their preaching, and this they did; for "daily in the temple, and in every house, they ceased not to teach and preach Jesus."

I. In reviewing the whole story which we read just now, from the seventeenth verse to the end of the chapter, my first thought is that

The Agents Employed

for spreading the gospel are men, and not angels. The angel of the Lord opened the prison door and set free the preachers, but might not be a preacher himself. He might give the ministers their charge, but he had no charge to preach himself. This divine choice of human instrumentality puts honor upon manhood. Those redeemed by the blood of Christ are men, and their redemption from sin by power is to be instrumentally accomplished by men. The great fight which began in the garden of Eden is to be waged by men even to the end. The conquest of the revolted world is to be achieved by men under the leadership of the all-glorious Son of Man. Ye see your calling, brethren. I pray you, every one, to preach the gospel in your vocation; but specially would I plead for zeal with those whose very vocation it is to preach.

My dear hearers, you may be yourselves grateful that this ministry is committed to men, because it is a condescension to human weakness. Imperfect as human ministers are, we are better preachers to you than angels could be. We know your sins, your sorrows, your struggles. We know the roughness of the road you traverse; for we, too, came in at the wicket-gate, and have floundered in the Slough of Despond, and scrambled up the Hill Difficulty. We can have compassion and give

Direction Learned by Experience.

I suppose an angel would command a very large congregation for a time; but, after a while, you would feel that there was something alien and distant about the manner of his teaching. You would be awed rather than comforted. A being altogether superior to yourself would before long drive you to cry for your old minister again, with lips of clay and heart of love. You would prefer our feeble pleadings to the more glorious, but less brotherly, address from an angel from heaven. Somebody once said that it proved the divinity of our holy religion that it survived ministers; and there was a good deal of truth in the remark. How I have wondered that this congregation has survived me! and I think we may wonder that as a whole the gospel survives its advocates. We are poor tools. I do not refer to you, brethren, from America, but I mean all of us in England, and specially myself. We are poor tools after all; and if God uses us to save sinners and sanctify saints, He must certainly have all the glory of it.

I cannot help adding that the employment of men as soul-winners gives a tender joy to the heart of Jesus. It pleases the Lord Jesus Christ that God should use men; for He Himself is a man. The Lord Jesus must take great pleasure in the attempts of His servants to seek and to save souls; for they are learning to be sheperds like Himself. When our

King, Edward III.,

heard that the Black Prince was having a hard battle with the French, he smiled to think that his son was in a place where he could show his valour. When he was entreated to send off reinforcements, he refused; for he wished his son to have the undivided honors of the day. The Lord Jesus, the Captain of our salvation, puts some of His chosen into places of great peril, and He does not seem to send them all the help they could desire, in order that they may prove their faith and consecration, and thus earn their spurs. He takes a brotherly pleasure in the courage and faith which He Himself has wrought in them. The father in the parable was glad when his prodigal son was found; but he would have been gladder still had a brother found him.

All these are good reasons why the Lord should employ men, and women to spread the gospel rather than cherubim and seraphim. Dear friends, do you not think that the

Angels Must Often Wonder

at us? When they see men eager upon politics and negligent of souls, are they not astonished? Do they never say, "We wish the great Lord would let us go and speak to perishing souls. We would speak with all our hearts." Do they not sometimes say to one another, "What are these men at? Do they disdain their high calling? God has given to them the great privilege of preaching and teaching His holy word, but they do not care to do it. They speak as if they were half asleep. Where is their zeal for God, their love to men, their earnestness for Christ?" Brethren, these holy spirits must feel ashamed of us!

So have I spoken to you who are men. As for thee, O angel of God, thou hast opened the prison doors and set free the men of God; but thou must now go back to Him that sent thee. Bright spirit, I dare not offer thee my pulpit. Feeble as I am, I must do the preaching. Oh that thy Lord and mine may help me, and enable me to make full proof of my ministry. Farewell, angel of God, go thy way!

II. Secondly, these men are

To Teach the People.

The manner of their teaching is hinted at. They are to do it promptly, yea, immediately. "Go," says the angel, "go. Do not linger here. Go at once." I should have been tempted to linger a little, just to find out how the angel released the prisoners. He had opened the doors, so we are told, but yet they were found closed and fastened when the officers came, and the sentries had not left their posts. Here is a mystery; I should like to clear it up. Are there not many such mysteries? But the command is pressing and peremptory: "Go, speak to the people." "Let me tarry; one does not see angels every day. Let me stay."

Dear fellow-worker, we perhaps are tempted to study very deeply into the mysterious points which do not minister to profit; let us, then, hear the angel say. "Go, speak to the people." Let us keep our thoughts to that gospel which we are sent to preach. "The words of this life" will furnish ample scope for all our powers; let us not wander into endless debates, which are rather for curiosity than salvation, and tend rather to gratify our taste than accomplish our life-purpose.

The First and Chief Business

of the man of God is, "Go speak to the people." It is clear from the text that they were to take a conspicuous place and speak boldly. "Go, stand in the temple." Go where the Sanhendrim holds its sittings, where the high priest and his Sadducean comrades are on the watch. Let not the danger hinder you. Go where all can see you; stand up and stand out. Wherever the people are, there let your voices be heard. Be there perseveringly, taking your stand, and keeping it till removed by force. Brethren, it is not ours to hide in holes and in corners; our gospel is like the sun, whose line has gone out through all the earth.

The persons for whom this preaching is designed, are mentioned. "Speak unto the people." "Unto the people," that does not mean the poor to the exclusion of the rich, nor the many to the exclusion of the few. The expression is most comprehensive, and embraces both

The Masses and the Classes.

If we take the word "people" in its popular sense, it has a lesson to all who teach the word. To obey the text, we must "Go and speak to the people." They need it; are they not perishing for lack of knowledge? The gospel is adapted to their needs and capacities—it is simple, suitable, seasonable, saving. The people will receive it. If the poor have the gospel preached to them, they will hear it. God inclines the hearts of the multitude to hearken. We read of Jesus, that "all the people were very attentive to hear Him." Moreover, the people retain the truth when they receive it. Note the fact in history: the Reformation in Spain was among the nobility, and it was the same in Italy, and the work soon subsided. In England the common people received the truth from Wycliffe, and it never died out. If you want to burn a haystack, you would set it alight at the bottom; and if you want a whole nation to feel the power of the gospel, it must first be received by laborers and artisans. We are glad to see the noble, the great, the rich, the cultured dedicated to our Lord; but, after all, our chief hope lies among the people.

III. This Message is Described:

"Speak to the people all the words of this life." Our teaching, if we are true to Christ, will be not only a doctrine, but a life. The high priests conceived that they preached doctrine; for he said, "Ye have filled Jerusalem with your doc ne." Yet it may as truly be called life as th. The Christian religion is like Christ— , truth, and life. We have to preach "words life"; truth which brings life, feeds life, and fects life. We are to preach all the great ths which concern eternal life.

What are the "words of this life"? If I had give a short list of them, I should say, the t word of this life is "*Jesus Christ*"; for in forty-second verse we read, "They ceased to teach and preach Jesus Christ": Jesus the words of eternal life. We preach his ity, his manhood, his offices, his sacrificial th, his resurrection, and everything about . We preach Christ crucified, and if we did , we should not speak the words of life. The t word to use would be "*atonement*." There o preaching "the words of this life" except preach the sacrificial death of the Son of d. The apostles boldly spoke of our Lord's th, for they said to the council, "Whom ye and hanged on a tree." "The words of life" are not preached to the people where

The Cross is in the Background.

next word would be "*resurrection*." is they preached very fully, saying, "Him h God raised from the dead." If the resurtion were more fully preached at this time, I sanguine that it would be a powerful means conversion. Nor could the apostles forget *generation*." They would echo their Lord's ds, "Ye must be born again." Then comes *ith*." What a word is this! "Without h it is impossible to please God." "By grace are saved through faith." He who does not ach justification by faith, has not begun to ch "the words of this life." The sixth out seven words is "*indwelling*." The Holy rit comes into the heart, and abides there, king sanctification within, and producing ness without. Then comes the doctrine of *eternal life:* that the life given by the Holy rit never dies. "The water that I shall give , shall be in him a well of water, springing nto everlasting life."

hus have I very roughly told you what you to preach.

/. But now, fourthly, the whole of the di- message must be delivered. "Stand in the ple, and speak unto the people *all* the words his life." Dear brethren, it is

Forbidden us to Omit

part of the gospel. I am very glad it is; if were permitted, we should sometimes k the unpopular parts of it. Yet surely it ould be very *dangerous* to omit any part of gospel, would it not? It would be like a sician giving a prescription to a dispenser, the dispenser omitting one of the ingreds. He might kill the patient by the omis. The worst results follow the keeping of any doctrine: we may not see those re-, but they will follow. Possibly only the generation will fully display the mischief e by a truth concealed or denied. It would dangerous experiment for us to make.

is a thousand mercies that we are not left ick and choose, for this would involve us sponsibilities too weighty to be borne.

It is Too Responsible a Business.

ould not the liberty be injurious to us? ld it not encourage pride? Would not this tly dishonor God? Would it not suggest God's gospel is full of superfluities and ex-ences, and needs our wisdom to make it ct? Should we not conclude that the Lord not so wise as ourselves if he needed our tance to adapt His gospel to the occasion? ou not think it would open a very easy way nother gospel? If we might omit, we might add; and I feel sure we should very soon a great deal which would neutralize and yze that of the gospel which remained. If lt at liberty to leave out something, we ld naturally omit that which is offensive, away would go the tooth and edge of the el. That which is offencive in the gospel t that which is effective. It is not left to e are to preach "all the words of this life."

Have we done so? That is the question. Have we knowingly concealed anything? "Well," says one, "I have not preached *all* the words of this life *to the people*, but I have preached them to a choice company." But you are told to preach them *all to the people*. The doctrine of reserve must not be tolerated among Protestants. We must not make that philosophical division which is expressed in those two ugly words

Esoteric and Exoteric.

This is abolished by the command to preach to the people "*all* the words of this life." At the present moment there is a great tendency to be obscure upon the true and proper Deity of Christ. I enjoyed the commencement of the prayer just offered by *our dear friend Dr. John Hall*. I enjoyed the whole of it, but I was greatly touched by his lowly adoration of our divine Lord. The Broad men will say that Jesus is divine, but they do not mean that He is God; they speak of His divinity, but they reject His Godhead. This is juggling with words. I hate deceptive phrases. We believe in the Godhead of Jesus, and worship Him as God.

The work of the Holy Ghost is left too much in the rear by many preachers. Have we not heard of late that certain children do not need to be converted, that the divine life is in them at their birth? Have they not preached education rather than regeneration, evolution rather than conversion? This is not speaking "all the words of this life." It is telling out

"Old Wives' Fables."

If there be any other point of truth which is kept back, let us bring it the more forward. Let us insist doubly upon that which others neglect. It needs that the whole gospel be brought before the people, that they may know it, and feel its power. It will involve you in strife and struggle if you resolve on delivering an all-around gospel; but fear not, the Lord will help you, even He who says to you by His angel, "Go, stand and speak in the temple to the people all the words of this life."

I have done when I have asked what we are doing about this? We who are God's people, what are we doing in this matter? Some of us are preaching; are we preaching the whole gospel? Has any doctrine been withheld? Let us bring forth things new and old, and keep back nothing. Let us put every stone into the arch, lest our building come to nothing. Have we also preached these truths as words of life? Have we felt the life in them?

But, beloved, are there not some of you who

Never Tell Anybody

"the words of this life?" In such a congregation ought it to be possible to put your finger upon a single regenerated man or woman who has never for a whole lifetime spoken to another about the things of God? Are such persons regenerated? I will not come round and mark you; but, alas! some of you have never even confessed your faith in Christ. If you have not obeyed that important command for yourselves, you are not likely to have done much for the souls of others. But having joined the church of God, are any of you satisfied to be silent?

Could not some of you do more than you are doing? Are there not young men who might preach in a street-corner or at a cottage-meeting? Some of our evangelistic societies flag for want of preachers. It ought not to be the case. What are you at? If you could not preach to men and women, could you not

Teach the Children?

What are you at? You confess that you are not your own, but bought with a price by the Lord Jesus; why, then, do you not serve Him? *I have succeeded to a large degree in routing some of you out;* I miss you on Sunday evenings, and a good miss too, since I know where you are, and that you are out serving God. You take your meal in the morning, and then you feed others in the after part of the day. The Lord bless you in it. You were not created to sit in these pews and listen to me; there is something better for a man than to be a hearer only.

I charge every Christian man and woman here to listen to what I am about to say. Though I am no angel, I repeat in the name of the Lord Jesus the command of the heavenly messenger: Go, stand out boldly, and speak unto the people all the words of this life; and may God bless you! Amen.

GEMS FROM NEW BOOKS.

AN OUTCAST BLIND GIRL.*

"About three years since," says Mrs. Knowles, in her diary, "a young girl, a Roman Catholic, who was then a pupil at the Institution for the Blind, was brought to my notice. She became deeply interested in the Bible, and afterward embraced the Protestant faith, and since that time has continued firm in her belief and practice. She remained at the Institution until the end of the term, which expired in June. It was now necessary for her to seek another home. She was taken to the house of a relative, who insisted on her going to confession. This she refused, and was on this account rendered homeless. It was a source of great anxiety to know how to provide for her. The girl was sincere, evidently willing, 'not only to believe in Christ, but also to suffer for His sake.' Her case was stated to some ladies who felt an interest in her, and although they could not give her a home, they kindly assisted in paying her board; other friends to whom the case was made known did the same, and she is now learning a trade by which we hope she will soon earn enough for her own support. Her employer speaks well of her, and considers her very industrious."

The Drunkard's Wife.

"Some time ago I visited a woman whose husband had beaten her till she was almost helpless. She told me about his coming to her with a knife, and expected he would have taken her life. She asked me to engage in prayer with her. He sat by, apparently unmoved. When I was leaving, he asked me to forgive him. I told him it was not me he must ask; he must go to God for forgiveness. It was distressing to see the poor wife, as she asked me what she must do, as she had no friend on earth but me. I then spoke to the husband; he said he was very sorry he had acted so badly, and would *drink no more*. I intend getting him to sign the pledge, which he says he will do. The evil of intemperance meet us in so many ways, we often feel discouraged, and yet at times a case occurs which bids us *work on* and hope on. The man mentioned above, from that time continued to refrain from drink, and has treated his wife well ever since. She wept with gratitude as she told me, a few evenings since, that he came in and handed her all his money as he had received it for work, never having opened it. She could never forget the day when I came in and found almost everything in the room broken to pieces, and his promise which he faithfully made to me that he would *try and do right*."

Dr. Guthrie Repulsed.

I have read somewhere the story of Dr. Guthrie, when he was first called to the metropolis of Edinburgh. Of their filling his pockets with tracts, and with all the ardor of his noble heart, commenced his great work. He ascended the creaking stairs of a high building in the old town, and knocking at the door, an elderly woman made her appearance, whereupon he offered her a tract. Looking earnestly upon him, and in a loud, shrill voice, she exclaimed, pathetically, "Deed, sir, I dinna want yeer tracts, I weed thank ye for a loaf of breed." Ah! he thought to himself, here is a case of destitution, and excusing himself, he hurried down stairs, and going to the baker, he ordered bread; and to the butcher, he ordered beef; and to the grocer, he ordered some English breakfast tea and sugar, a few dainties, and a cart of coal, and requested them to be sent at once to the woman

* From "Gathering Jewels," a memoir of Mr. and Mrs. James Knowles, by Rev. Duncan McNeil Young. Mrs. Knowles in her later years was a missionary in New York City, and these items are extracts from the diary she kept of her work among the poor. 382 pages. Published by *William Knowles*, 104 East Thirteenth Street, New York.

The Late Rev. E. P. Roe. (*See page 485.*)

Father Murphy Explaining the Pope's Bull to His Congregation.

in want. Calling a few days afterward, he found her comfortably seated with a neighbor, around a cheerful hearthstone, drinking their newly-made tea. When she opened the door, she enthusiastically exclaimed, "Come awa, noo, Doctor, I am ready to hear you on the subject o' religion." Our departed sister also recognized the necessity of attending to the temporal as well as the spiritual wants of her parishioners simultaneously. "*After relieving their wants*, I tried to lead them to Christ."

A Gift of Fifty Dollars.

I remember once, during the same year in which the circumstances we are now commenting on transpired, of calling upon a friend, a broker, in Wall Street, of this city, and after some general conversation about Christian work, he called me into his rear office, and said:

"How are you getting along financially?"

"Well," I said, "I am able to keep my head above water."

"Ah!" he replied, "I have been watching you in your work, and want to make you a present of fifty dollars for your immediate wants."

I looked upon him with astonishment, and exclaimed:

"How is it, my friend, you can be so kind to me, as I am a comparative stranger to you?"

"Well," he said "I believe you are doing the Lord's work, and I feel that all the money belongs unto Him, and I am only His steward."

EXPLAINING THE POPE'S RESCRIPT.

(*See Illustration.*)

ONE of the most difficult duties the Irish Roman Catholic priests have had to do of late years, was that of explaining and impressing upon their flocks the Bull or Rescript of the Pope, condemning boycotting and "the Plan of Campaign." The priests had sanctioned both, and had encouraged their people to use these methods of warfare against obnoxious landlords and officials. It was, therefore, a most painful and humiliating task to read the Pope's condemnation from the altar, and exhort as they were required to do, their people to obey. The illustration herewith depicts the scene in the church at Kildare when Father Murphy read the Rescript, the effect of which is seen in the astonished faces of the congregation.

What the priest had to do was to convince his hearers that an Italian priest, far away in Rome, Italy, shut up in his magnificent palace of the Vatican, and surrounded with luxuries, knew all about their condition, and how they ought to act in their difficult circumstances. Happily for the priests they were not without guidance. Their bishops traced a line of argument which might be expected to operate on the devout and the brainless who might reasonably be expected to form the majority of the congregation. The bishops observed: "So far from intending by this decree to injure our national movement, it was the hope and purpose of his holiness to remove those things which he judged might, in the long run, be obstacles to its advancement and ultimate success. We must warn our people against the use of any hasty or irreverent language with reference to the Sovereign Pontiff, or to any of the sacred congregation through which he usually issues his decrees to the faithful. While expressing our deep and lasting gratitude to the leaders of the National movement for the signal services they have rendered to religion and the country, we deem it our duty at the same time to remind them and our flocks, as we most emphatically do, that the Roman Pontiff has an inalienable and divine right to speak with authority on all questions appertaining to faith and morals."

The feeling of the people, however, may be inferred from a resolution passed at a meeting of the citizens of Dublin, by which the meeting "cordially endorses and adopts in their integrity the resolutions of the Irish Catholic members of Parliament with reference to the Circular of the Holy Office of the Inquisition, and respectfully declines to recognize any right in the Holy See to interfere with the Irish people in the management of Irish politics.

THE LAWYER'S COMMISSION.

(*See Illustration on page 493.*)

"WHAT a pity it is that men cannot foresee the time of their death," said Mr. Hanson, a middle-aged lawyer to his partner one morning as the two sat looking over their mail. "It is enough to make poor Raynor turn in his grave if he could know the way his money is going, and the trouble there will be about it."

"The young one is going the pace, I suppose; I have seen him here pretty often."

"Yes, and he is coming again this morning. Here is his letter; he wants more money. He has the most expensive collection of vices he could get hold of. Horse-racing, cards and worse are among them. I do not know what the end will be. The worst of it is that poor Raynor was so procrastinating, and went off so suddenly that people whom he loved and helped will have to suffer. That would not have been if he had known that he would die so soon. He meant to have destroyed several notes; but he never did it, and they stand there perfectly valid claims that young Charles will want to press. It is a disagreeable business all around. I shall have some painful work to do, I am afraid."

"You cannot help that. You are simply the agent. When Raynor made you executor he should have given you more power. I wonder, knowing his son's character he did not put the whole thing in trust."

The lawyer went off to court, and his partner, Mr. Hanson, went to examine the ledger, and to turn over the papers in a tin box, in preparation for the coming interview. He expected a painful struggle with the young heir, and was not disappointed. Mr. Charles Raynor duly arrived, punctual when the receipt of money was concerned, though punctuality was not one of his virtues.

"Rather a heavy draw this time, Mr. Hanson," he said, as he seated himself languidly in the client's chair, and surveyed the lawyer through his eye-glass. "I have had a run of shocking luck this week, and it will take five thousand to put me right. Luck is a fickle jade; I suppose she will visit me again soon, I have not seen her for some time. If you have no rents or dividends in, we shall have to see what we can sell."

"A bad time this for selling, Mr. Raynor," said the lawyer. "Prices are sure to rise. It is a pity to sell while the market is so low. Would it not be possible to wait a few weeks? Several dividends will be in then."

"Oh, no! these are debts of honor. They cannot be held over. What securities are there available? You have never given me a detailed list. Of course I know the lump sum, but I should like to know how it is made up."

"I have had the list prepared," said the lawyer, opening his drawer and producing a paper. "I should tell you that it contains several notes for money loaned by your late father, which he did not wish to be collected. They were advanced to old friends and men whom he helped in difficulties, and he intended to destroy the notes, but never did so."

"Lucky for me he did not," said the young man; "I should have been so much the poorer. Let me see the list."

The lawyer passed it to him, and Mr. Raynor ran quickly over it. "Ah!" he said, "here is the identical sum, note on demand from Edward Goff, $5,000. He is our man. Write and call it in."

"It will ruin him, Mr. Raynor. Your father set him up in business with that money. He has always paid the interest regularly, and he had your father's promise that, so long as he did that, he would not be asked for the principal."

"Was that promise in writing?" asked the young man, quickly.

"No; it was merely verbal, but it was quite clear."

"Then tell him he must pay up. I do not mean to carry on this philanthropic business; can't afford it, you know."

"It is not a question of affording, Mr. Raynor. You could not get a better return for your money, however it was invested, and I think it is safe."

"Invested! No. Don't I tell you I am going to pay it away immediately?"

"Excuse me, Mr. Raynor, as an old friend of your father—he used to take my advice—begging you not to call in this money. This Goff will have to realize every stick he has to pay it and his large family will be in want. They have nothing but their business to depend upon. I am sure your father would be grieved to have the man ruined."

"It is a comfort, then, that he does not know, or at any rate cannot prevent it. Goff should look around for some other confiding old gentleman to come to the rescue. You see I am pressed myself. Tell the man so. You can say there is a sudden and unexpected demand you know—very sorry, but unavoidable. You will know how to put it. And you had better give all those other fellows notice that their debts must be paid. I shall be sure to need the money some day."

"I need scarcely remind you that if you reduce your capital your income will suffer."

"Oh, there is plenty yet. Besides, after a time, I shall slow up. I have been kept close so long that I must have a fling for a year or two. I must go now. I'm glad we have arranged this account. Get the money and send it to me as quickly as you can." So saying the young man sauntered out of the office, humming an operatic air as he went.

Mr. Hanson sat motionless for some minutes. He was a kind-hearted man, and had taken a personal pleasure in executing his dead friend's generous projects. This was a grievous commission, and he was reluctant to execute it. He pictured to himself the consternation of the debtor, and the misery of his family when the application reached the home. The young heir, however, had treated his protest so flippantly that there was not the slightest hope of avoiding the trouble. He wrote the letter, and, with a deep sigh, sent it to the mail.

The lawyer's prognostication was fully verified when poor Goff read the letter. He was stunned by the blow, and would have been utterly prostrated had not his wife, a pious woman, reminded him of God's promises and joined him in prayer for deliverance. They consulted together, and decided on Goff making a personal appeal to Mr. Raynor. His journey was a doleful one, and though he spent the time in silent prayer, the burden was not lifted when he entered Mr. Hanson's office.

"I feared it would ruin you," said the lawyer, when he had heard Goff's story. "Have you no friend who will help you? you might as easily move a mountain as to touch the heart of this young scapegrace."

"None, if he insists it must all go"; and the poor fellow's lip quivered as he thought of his wife and children.

"You are a pious man, Goff; have you prayed about it?"

The Lawyer's Interview With the Heir.

"Yes," said Goff," and my wife believes we shall come out right; but my faith fails me."—

"I have prayed for you," said the lawyer solemnly, "and I am impressed with the idea that I can do more, and ought to do it. I have not the money, but, perhaps, my credit is good for that much. Come with me to the bank and let us see."

An hour or two later Goff was speeding homeward with a heart relieved. Mr. Hanson had borrowed the money on his own security, and had become his creditor instead of the heartless young profligate.

"I expect my partner will blame me," said Mr. Hanson, as he sat in his office and reflected on the transaction, but I have the satisfaction of having obeyed the Divine precept: "Do good, and lend hoping for nothing again." It was like a direct command from God to help the man, and I am glad I did it."

THE EPOCHS OF A LIFE.

A NEW SERIAL STORY.

By Rev. L. S. Keyser.

(Continued from page 478.)

An Admission.

NOTWITHSTANDING Hadley's contempt for the advice given by Mr. Mardont in his sermon, as reported by Dane, and though believing the preacher to be illogical in recommending sceptics to pray, the young man accompanied his friend next Sunday night to Mr. Mardont's church. From his first appearance the preacher favorably impressed his critical hearer. The absence of self-consciousness and all trace of what Hadley called "cant," prepared him to give respectful attention to what he might have to say. The preacher's presence, too, was prepossessing. A man of some thirty years of age with a broad, scholarly brow, strong, well-chiselled mouth and chin, and clear, bright eyes, he was in the vigor of manhood and had the look of being a physical and mental athlete.

His opening sentences were in a sense apologetic. The fact that the majority of persons composing church audiences did not need to be convinced of the Divine origin and inspiration of the Bible was, he intimated, a sufficient reason for preachers dealing in their sermons with more advanced religious truth, which their hearers needed to learn, and treating the existence of God and the authenticity of the Bible as rudimentary truths already firmly established in their minds. Nevertheless, for the sake of some who had intellectual difficulties in accepting those truths, he had decided to go again over the beaten path and cite the evidences in their favor.

It was his opinion that sceptics were often unwisely and unkindly treated by Christians. Honest doubters seeking for truth, who might be won by patience and gentleness, where repelled when they described their difficulties, if Christians meet them acerbity, blamed them for doubting and treated them as moral lepers. The hearts of many sceptics were like ice that will melt in the sunshine of kindness and love, while some believers regarded those hearts as rocks needing to be blasted with dynamite. To some extent doubtless sceptics had provoked such treatment by a kindred disposition. They affected a superior air, as if the fact of their having these doubts were a proof of their having a more vigorous and acute intellect than that of the believer, and were apt to speak superciliously of the devout Christian as an ignorant dupe or a narrow-minded bigot far beneath them in mental calibre. They forgot that great philosophers have believed in the Bible, and that an institution which had been a blessing to the world and the comfort and stay of thousands in all ages and all lands, deserved serious and respectful examination and is not a fit subject for ridicule and invective. Men who spend their time in quibbling and lampooning Christianity simply advertised their own lack of mental and moral penetration.

"That's rather a bitter dose," commented Hadley, mentally.

"Who was Christ, the founder of our religion?" asked the preacher in animated tones. "Was He a base, designing character? Was He a man of puerile mind? What is the testimony of the most intelligent sceptics to the character of Jesus of Nazareth? A number of scholarly investigators have been to the pains of collecting these tributes, and I shall ask the privilege of giving extracts from a few of them."

Here the preacher quoted brief extracts from a number of sceptical and rationalistic writers, who have spoken in terms of the highest eulogy of Christ, and the system of religion which was founded by Him. Among these were Rousseau, Gœthe, Friederick Strauss, Ernest Renan, Lecky, John Stuart Mill, and Theodore Parker. He also cited a brilliant passage from Thomas Carlyle. It is unnecessary to transcribe these quotations here, as they are familiar to all who are acquainted with theological literature; but to the young sceptics they were a revelation.

"These encomiums are not cited to prove Christianity divine," the minister went on, "but only to show you that thoughtful and scholarly men do not make it the object of mockery, but of profound regard. I assure you that nothing is ever gained by derisory speech. The sceptic will only make those who believe the Scripture impatient with his diatribes, and they will probably regard him as incorrigible. Christians and honest doubters should not occupy a belligerent attitude toward one another, but while there should be no temporizing with error, the olive-branch of peace should be taken in the hand of the opposing forces, and all bad blood should be eliminated."

The sermon was replete with sage advice, and as the young sceptics returned to their room many words of praise were upon their lips. Usually on their way from church services they indulged in vigorous criticism or scornful ridicule, but this evening they had listened to a man who could sympathize with their doubts and unrest, and so they were for once disarmed of all hostility.

"We should feel very little antipathy toward Christians if they were all as large-orbed and well-poised as that man is," remarked Dane. "I could easily forgive their belief of the Scriptures, if are sincere, but their unreasoning narrowness and dogmatic airs are harder to forgive."

"That's so," Hadley responded; "but we are guilty of exhibiting the same spirit that we condemn in them, as the preacher told us this evening. We have invited their angry assaults by our ridicule. If an institution that we revered were held up to derision I suppose that it would touch us also into a lurid flame, and no doubt there is still a good deal of human nature about these Christians, even if they do profess to be 'new creatures.' But what a difference there is in the disposition of this preacher and that of the porcupine-like Bible-class teacher who bristled up so last Sunday morning! There seem to be two kinds of temper among Christians. I wonder whether both are in consonance with the religion they teach. If so, it must be a hotchpotch of contradictory maxims."

"I rather think," said Dane, after a reflective pause, "that the disposition shown by the preacher to-night is the one that is congruous with the teaching of the Bible, as far as I understand it. But I suppose there is an underlying cause for the ungenerous temper exhibited by the Sunday-school man. He has perhaps never been perplexed with doubts, as you and I are, and as Mr. Mardont evidently was at one time. That the Bible is true, has doubtless been 'a foregone conclusion' with him, and it is probably as difficult for him to sympathize with us as it is for us to sympathize with him."

"You are bound to defend that bigoted fellow," said Hadley, with some impatience. "For my part, I do not believe that any man who pretends to be an instructor to others has any right to be so narrow. He ought to broaden out his mental horizon."

By this time the young men had reached their room, and Hadley was just about to resume his criticism on the object of his dislike, when there was a knock at the door, and upon opening it, to his surprise he was confronted by the very man whom he held in contempt. After a few cold courtesies, the young students offered their unwelcome guest a chair, wondering what his errand might be.

"I have come," he began, in embarrassed tones, "to apologize to you, my young friends, for the ungenerous words I spoke to you last Sabbath morning."

The young men glanced at each other in amazement. This was rather an unexpected turn in the situation they were discussing. They could not find their voices to reply, and therefore after a moment of silence, during which the man made a visible effort to control himself, he resumed:

"At the time I spoke to you as I did, I supposed that my theory of the attitude of sceptics toward religion was the correct one. I have never been troubled, myself, with doubts of the divine authority of the Bible, and could only attribute opposition to it to perversity and badness of heart; but I have been at Mr. Mardont's church to-night, at which I heard his second discourse on infidelity, and—"

"Ah! did you hear his sermon this evening?" interrupted Hadley, finding his voice at last.

"Yes, sir; I have just come from the church. Well, the sermon opened my eyes, so that I see that I was wrong, and I have therefore come to apologize. The religion I profess, and I hope possess, will allow me to do no less than make an acknowledgment of my mistake. Young gentlemen," said the man, rising and extending his hand, "will you accept my apology?"

"By making an apology for our bad conduct," exclaimed Hadley, with some emotion, as he grasped the man's proffered hand.

"And as for me, I beg pardon for following my chum's bad example," said Dane, also shaking the man's hand; "and I cannot refrain from saying that I believe our first impressions of your character were entirely erroneous."

"Thank you, thank you," said the man gratefully, while a tear glittered on his bearded cheek. "Good-night, my young friends. If I can do you any good—" But he could say no more, and having taken them again warmly by the hand, he left the room.

The young men looked at each other in silence for a few moments, and then broke out into merry laughter, in which there was no feeling of gloating triumph, but only an emotion of genuine pleasure in noble deed.

"Well Hadley, what do you think of a religion that will make a man do that?" queried George, when his risibles were again under control.

"Ahem! I confess, in the vernacular of the politicians, that I—am—on—the fence!"

"But you do not mean to remain there I suppose?" said Dane. "For my own part, I want this question settled once for all. I thought it was settled for me, but Mr. Mardont has convinced me that I was too hasty. I believe we have accepted the evidence against the book too easily. Every defendant has a right to a hearing in his own defence. What do you say to a hearing right away?"

"Agreed!" said Hadley. "Let us see what some champion of the Bible has to say." He turned, as he spoke, to the shelves of their joint library, and glanced along the rows of books, Dane looking over his shoulder. The collection was somewhat large, but a few minutes brought them both to the same discovery. There was not a single book in their possession in defence of Christianity! They burst simultaneously into laughter.

"Well," said Dane, "Mr. Mardont was right; we are not fit to be judges in this matter: we have prejudged the case. We must remedy that in common fairness."

"Yes; still we have the Bible itself" said Hadley. "Let us look into the book itself for to-night, for an initial step."

That was a wise suggestion had it been executed wisely, but there are unwise ways of examining the Sacred Book, and one of these is the captious and fragmentary way. In pursuing other lines of research, men usually proceed methodically; but when they are about to seek for light on religious themes, how desultory and illogical their methods often are!

The young investigator opened the Bible at random, as if it were a work of bric-à-brac with no logical connection among its constituent parts. It happened that the Bible fell open at one of the imprecatory Psalms. He read aloud the first few verses, in which David rehearses the persecutions which he had suffered at the hands of his adversaries, closing with the sentence: "But I give myself unto prayer."

"Well, he bore his afflictions with becoming fortitude," commented Dane, with a pleased smile. "It is good so far."

Then followed the next verse: "Set thou a wicked man over him, and let Satan stand at his right hand."

"What is that?" asked George, musingly, leaning forward as he spoke.

Hadley read the verse again.

"I do not understand it," said Dane, "Does the writer ask God to deliver his enemy over to satanic powers?"

"It seems so; but let me read farther." Then Hadley resumed his reading: "When he shall be judged, let him be condemned, and let his prayer become sin."

"Good Heavens!" exclaimed George; "wh a sacrilegious prayer!"

"Let his days be few," the reading continu "and let another takes his office. Let his c dren be fatherless, and his wife a widow. Let children be continually vagabonds, and beg; them seek their bread also out of their deso places."

"The vindictive brute!" muttered Dane, w compressed lips. "The idea of invoking t imprecations of Heaven upon a man's proge for sins with which they had nothing to do!"

"It is pure fiendish malignity," said Hadl "and there is more and worse. 'Let there none to extend mercy unto him; neither there be any to favor his fatherless children; the iniquity of his fathers be remembered wi the Lord; and let not the sin of his mother blotted out.' Did you ever come across su inhuman ferocity. The man seems positive diabolic in his malice. I'll read no more of it

"No; shut it up," said Dane; "it is a repu sive exhibition of what malignity human natu can produce."

"If Duneman feeds on this nourishment, it not surprising that he has developed into th vicious, savage creature he is. This may accou for it."

"What an anomaly it is that Mr. Mardo should be another development of the sam teaching!" said Dane. "It produces very diffe ent effects in him. And what puzzles me mo than anything else is that the sentiments yo have been reading are so utterly out of conso nance with the principles elsewhere enunciate in the Bible; for Christ told His disciples t love their enemies, and He Himself, when H was on the cross, prayed for His murderer How can these disparities be reconciled?"

"They cannot be," declared Hadley, bluntly "Evidently the extolled Book is a medley o contradictions. How people of any intelligen can accept this hotchpotch as the revelation o God is more than I can understand. It make me mad to think of it."

"And this is the outcome of our investiga tions, which were begun in such a sanguin mood," said George, in disgust. "I am bitterl disappointed."

"Well, I shall do no more burrowing in th bogs of superstition to-night. I do not want t have a tilt with a spectre in my sleep, and think it time to dismiss these harassing ques tions. I'm going to bed." And he retired, an was soon "snoring the snore of the weary."

And thus these impetuous young logician leaped precipitately to a conclusion, withou mature consideration, without attempting t understand the character of the writer o the Psalm, or the circumstances in which i was written, and, above all, without readin the Psalm through to the end. Had they pro ceeded farther in their perusal, they would hav discovered the reason that these penalties wer called down upon David's enemy. It was no a vindictive prayer, but rather a prophecy of th evil that would inevitably befall one who wa implacable and obdurate in sin, who "remem bered not to show mercy, but persecuted th poor and needy man," and who, "clothed him self with cursing as with a garment." The pun ishment was condign, the justice of God's la falling upon the head of the inexorable foe o righteousness and mercy. All this they migh have discovered, had they been less impatien and more thorough in their investigations a they would have been with the works of a secu lar author Yet the majority of sceptics and infi dels treat the Book in the same superficia way, and call their desultory reading of it "a *study*" of the Bible!

(*To be Continued.*)

The Seeking Saviour and Other Themes. by the late Dr. Mackay, of Hull. This work has been publishe since Dr. Mackay's death, but the greater part was ready fo publication when he died, and to that has been added th striking discourse which he delivered the last time he entere the pulpit, and a few manuscri ts found among his papers 347 pages, cloth cover; Price 75 cents, including postag For sale at this office, 63 Bible House, New York.

THE DAY OF ATONEMENT.

By Mrs. M. Baxter.

S. Lesson for August 12, Levit. 16 : 1-22. Golden Text, Heb. 9: 22.

be Meaning of the Day—The Strange Fire on the Altar—The Way of Access to God Blocked by Sin—Symbolism of the Offerings—The Priest also Needing Atonement—The Two Goats—Two Sacrifices Needed—The Dead and the Living—No Forgiveness Without Confession—Confession to Men not Sufficient—The Great Sin-Bearer—Consecration Symbolized in Burnt Offering.

"ALMOST all things are by the law purged ith blood, and without shedding of blood is o remission." (Heb. 9: 22.) Nothing but the ood of Jesus cleanses from all sin. It is only hen the conscience is satisfied because *God* is itisfied that there is any real sense of freedom om sin. The day of atonement, with all its remonies, is full of teaching about God's atred of sin, and the fullness of the atonement f Jesus. There had been sin in the priesthood -Nadab and Abihu, the sons of Aaron, had been uilty of the sin of offering strange fire upon the tar. The fire which came from heaven was to e always burning there, but they had kindled re of their own. Oh how often evangelists and inisters seek to kindle

Their Own Fire

istead of waiting for the fire from heaven—the ue Holy Ghost—who alone can make souls ive which were "dead in trespasses and sins." o amount of human energy or human enthuasm can kindle God's fire; it always comes om heaven. It is blasphemy to attempt an nitation or a creation of God the Holy Ghost. s well might we seek to produce a Saviour—od the Son—as to produce God the Holy host by human energy. The fire of the Lord ıme forth, and consumed the men who offered range fire. (Lev. 10: 1, 2.) The cousins of the ain men were called to come and carry their mains "from before the sanctuary out of the amp." But their own brothers were not allowd to uncover their heads, or rend their garents, or show any sign of mourning. As priests God, they must take part with God before nsidering father, mother, brother or sister Matt. 10: 37); "for the anointing oil of the ord is upon you." (Lev. 10: 6, 7.) It was on is occasion that God commanded every priest God to abstain from wine or strong drink, that ye may put difference between holy and holy, and between unclean and clean, and at ye may teach."

"And the Lord spake unto Moses after the ath of the two sons of Aaron . . . . Speak to Aaron, thy brother, that he come not at times into the holy place within the vail; at he die not; for I will appear in the cloud on the mercy-seat." The direct and contin-l access to God had been blocked up by sin, d sin in the priesthood." *Thus* shall Aaron me into the holy place: with a young bullock r a sin offering, and a ram for a burnt offering. ese must be the

Acknowledgment of Sin.

ıen Aaron must be clothed, his flesh must be vered. When Jesus died upon the cross, He s uncovered, for He was holy; there was no in Him. Aaron's sin offering was to make nement for himself and his house; Jesus, r High Priest, needed no sacrifice, for He ew no sin. "For such an High Priest beme us who is holy, harmless, undefiled, sepae from sinners, and made higher than the avens; who needeth not daily as those high ests, to offer up sacrifice, first for his own s, and then for the people's; for this He did ce when He offered up Himself." (Heb. 7: 27.) After offering for himself, Aaron must sent two kids of the goats at the door of the ernacle, and he must cast lots upon them, ne lot for the Lord, and the other lot for scape-goat." One must be offered for a sin ering, and the other, the scape-goat "shall be sented alive before the Lord, to make an nement with him, and to let him go for a pe-goat into the wilderness." Aaron must slay "the bullock of the sin-offering which is for himself." It was God's provision that none of the Jewish priesthood should have occasion to arrogate to themselves any holiness beyond the holy calling, and the holy functions which were entrusted to them. In themselves they were but sinners, needing atonement as much as any sinners in Israel. When he had slain the bullock, in token that every sinner, though he be a priest, has slain Jesus by his sins, he must take a censer full of burning coals from off the altar (God's fire), and his hands full of sweet incense, a token of the praise which God accepts when it is offered in the spirit. The sweet incense must be beaten small, like the praise which enters into the detail of God's love and goodness to us; and this he may bring within the veil, into the immediate presence of God. "And he shall put the incense upon the fire before the Lord, that the cloud of the incense may cover the mercy-seat that is upon the testimony, that he die not. And he shall take of the blood of the bullock, and sprinkle it with his finger upon the mercy-seat eastward; and before the mercy-seat shall he sprinkle of the blood with his finger seven times." "The soul that sinneth it shall die," (Ezek. 18: 4.) The blood poured out is a proof of

Life Sacrificed.

God cannot clear the guilty, cannot ignore sin, but He can accept of an atonement. The blood of Jesus "speaketh better things than that of Abel." (Heb. 12:24.) Having thus established his own communion with God, the priest must bring the people's sin offering. He can do nothing for the people unless he is right himself. The blood of the ram, the people's offering, must also be sprinkled upon and before the mercy seat. "And he shall make an atonement for the holy place, because of the uncleanness of the children of Israel, and because of their transgressions in all their sins: and so shall he do for the tabernacle of the congregation that [dwelleth] among them in the midst of their uncleanness." All must be atoned for, all cleansed with blood. And God would have no witness, all this must be done entirely alone with Him. "There shall be no man in the tabernacle." Then straight from this transaction he must go out to the altar of burnt offering, "and make an atonement for it, ... and cleanse it, and hallow it from the uncleanness of the children of Israel." "Without shedding of blood is no remission."

"And when he hath made an end of reconciling the holy place, and the tabernacle of the congregation, and the tabernacle of the congregation and the altar, he shall bring the live goat: and Aaron shall lay both his hands upon the head of the live goat, and confess over him all the iniquities of the children of Israel, and all their transgressions in all their sins, putting them upon the head of the goat, and shall send him away by the hand of a fit man into the wilderness: And the goat shall bear upon him all their iniquities into a land not inhabited; and he shall let go the goat in the wilderness." To represent Jesus, who is a propitiation for our sins, needs two sacrifices—the one dead, for He has died for us; the other living, for "He ever liveth to make intercession for us" (Heb. 7:25); while the blood of the sin offering speaks before the mercy-seat, Aaron confesses the sins of the people over the head of the live goat. "If we confess our sins, He is faithful and just to forgive us our sins, and to cleanse us from all iniquity." (1 John 1; 9.) There is no forgiveness without confession of sin, and certainly no cleansing. "Whoso covereth his sins shall not prosper; but he that confesseth and forsaketh them shall have mercy." (Prov. 28: 13.) "I said, I will confess my transgressions unto the Lord, and thou forgavest the iniquity of my sin." (Ps. 32: 5.) But the sin must be confessed

Over the Head of the Goat.

There are some, such as Balaam and Judas, who confess their sins, but not unto the Lord. Balaam said "I have sinned" to an angel, but he did not say it to God. (Num. 22: 34.) Saul confessed to Samuel, and asked his forgiveness, but he did not deal personally with God (1 Sam. 15: 30), and Judas confessed only to the chief priests, to receive in return the heartless, taunting reply, "What is that to us? see thou to that." (Matt. 27: 3, 4.) There are people who seem to take a pleasure in spinning out the story of their sins with no sense of shame or contrition, but apparently to excite the interest of the hearers. Oh, how awful must such things be in the sight of a holy God, who has made the real confession of sin by the sinner to be a confession with our hands upon the devoted head of Jesus, identifying ourselves with Him who, though He "knew no sin," was made sin for us, . . . that we might be made the righteousness of God in Him. (II Cor. 5: 21.) "And the goat shall bear upon him all their iniquities." "The Lord hath laid on Him the iniquity of us all." (Isa. 43: 6.) God does not want us to bear the burden of the sins which Jesus died for. "Cast thy burden upon the Lord" (Ps. 55: 22) —even the burden of thy sin. Reconciled, because atoned for, and cleansed by His blood. He wants us to "rejoice in the Lord alway," to be glad in what *He* is, and in what He has done for us. "He will turn again, He will have compassion upon us, he will subdue our iniquities: and Thou wilt cast all their sins into the depths of the sea." (Mic. 7: 19.) "As far as the east is from the west, so far hath He removed our transgressions from us." (Ps. 103: 12.) "In those days, and at that time, saith the Lord, the iniquity of Israel shall be sought for, and there shall be none, and the sins of Judah, and they shall not be found: for I will pardon them whom I reserve."

After Aaron had made confession of the people's sins, which he must have heard first from their own lips, he must put off his holy garments, leaving them in the holy place, must wash his flesh in water, and then must put on his altar garments, and offer the burnt offering in token that the people now cleansed yielded themselves in the burnt offering wholly unto God. But the man who let go the scapegoat must also wash his clothes and bathe his flesh in water, and afterward come into the camp. All which had to do with sin must be put out of sight—

Done Away With

altogether. How hateful then must it be to God to have details of sin told from mouth to mouth, or read in the papers, or made into novels! How depraved is the taste, how far from God the mind, which dwells upon these things! God's Word, speaking of one class of sin, says, "But fornication, and all uncleanness or covetousness, let it not be once named among you as becometh saints: neither filthiness nor foolish talking; nor jesting, which are not convenient, but rather giving of thanks." (Eph. 5: 3, 4.) The day of atonement was observed once a year. But Christ our High Priest has made atonement once for all. Let us continually remember, and live in the power of His atoning work.

CONSECRATION.

E. W. BROWN.

Now ye have consecrated yourselves unto the Lord, come near and bring sacrifices and thank offerings into the house of the Lord.—II. CHRON. xxix: 31.

Are you willing, wholly willing,
  Just the little things to do,
Caring more to please the Master,
  Than for what men say of you?

Are you sure you are not able
  Just a falt'ring prayer to raise,
Choosing not *your* will and pleasure,
  If your Saviour it will praise?

Do you feel no obligation
  To acknowledge Christ in you?
Have you never asked in earnest,
  "Lord, what wilt Thou have *me* do?"

You have asked, and He has shown you,
  But your shrinking heart cried "No!
It is true, I asked for service,
  But,—*this* way I cannot go!"

While you *choose*, you are not willing;
  Consecration yieldeth all!
Consecration means obedience
  To the Spirit's every call:—

Meaneth dying, meaneth living,
  (Death of self and life in God.)
Meaneth work, or patient waiting,
  Or submission 'neath the rod!

Meaneth such a full surrender,
  We shall never dare to ask
Why God gives our faith such testing,
  Or assigns so hard a task.

We are here to be perfected;—
  Only Christ our needs can see:
Rarest gems bear hardest grinding,
  God's own workmanship are we!

He loves harmony, not discord,
  And what ever may befall,
Life's grand Psalm He is perfecting;
  Let us praise Him for it all.

J. E. JEWETT, Publisher, 77 Bible House, New York, will furnish the above poem in leaflet form at twenty cents per hundred. *A Sample Packet* of 50 leaflets assorted (no two alike), will be sent post-paid, for 10 cts., or 100 for 20 cts. Postage stamps taken.

Christian Work in Mexico.

Through the reading of the Holy Scriptures translated into Spanish some earnest souls in Mexico have, by God's blessing, been led to a clear knowledge of the Gospel. From their numbers able preachers of the Christian faith in its primitive purity have been raised up, around whom congregations have been gathered from among the humble poor, who have been the first to publicly welcome and defend the pure Gospel in Mexico. The members of these congregations, rich in faith, have worked earnestly and bravely for Christ and His truth among their fellow countrymen in that beautiful Southern portion of North America called Mexico. Schools have been established by them, in which large numbers of bright boys and girls have received a good secular education and have been carefully taught the Christian faith. From the children thus educated faithful Christian workers have been raised up. A Mexican Branch of the Church of Christ, that maintains the faith in its purity and integrity, has been organized among these native Christians in the Republic of Mexico. The members of this Mexican Church of Christ, though gathered mostly from among the poor, are yet doing a most important Christian work. To continue that work, we need to pay a few leading workers small monthly salaries, and also to defray some current expenses. To raise the needed funds we have formed a society with an office at 43 Bible House, New York, U. S., and should be pleased to have many of our fellow Christians join this society by becoming regular contributors to its treasury. We are trying to secure monthly or quarterly contributions to meet the regular monthly expenses of the work. In order to continue and extend the work, we wish to raise four hundred dollars a month, by endeavoring to have four hundred persons each give on an average *one dollar every month* to this object, leaving the donors to give less or more as they may be able and willing.

We earnestly invite all who will, to join us in this systematic effort in behalf of the cause of Christ in Mexico, by becoming monthly subscribers to this fund. We have already regular subscribers whose gifts amount monthly to over eighty dollars, and a growing circle of friends who are forwarding us occasional donations.

This Mexican Church of Christ is a very effective instrumentality through which to do Christian work among the many millions on this Western Hemisphere who speak the Spanish language, comparatively few of whom have ever had a Bible in their hands. A beautiful church building has been secured in the City of Mexico as the centre of the activities of this Mexican Church of Christ. Through the workers connected with that centre more than forty congregations have been gathered from among the poor in different parts of the Republic of Mexico. We have some faithful and able preachers now in the field, but more young men need to be trained for the ministry. Multitudes of Protestant children in Mexico, some of them orphans, need to be educated. We make three requests of you, Christian reader: *first*, that you will, if possible, become a monthly or quarterly subscriber in behalf of this Christian work; *second*, that you will try and induce your friends also to contribute to it; *third*, that you will remember this precious work in Mexico in your prayers.

We most sincerely thank all who are already generously contributing to this Christian work for their timely and generous gifts, and we earnestly invite many others, to unite with us in aiding it by also becoming monthly subscribers in its behalf. Those who may not feel that they can give as much as a dollar a month are earnestly asked to give what they can, whenever they are able—EVERY LITTLE HELPS. Fellow Christian, if you will generously consent to contribute a dollar a month or more or less to the work, will you kindly inform me of the fact? Contributions either large or small can be mailed directly to my address as follows:

BISHOP H. C. RILEY, care of J. P. HEATH,
No. 43 Bible House, New York, U. S.

THE CHRISTIAN HERALD AND SIGNS OF OUR TIMES.

Vol. XI., No. 32. Office, 63 Bible House, N. Y. THURSDAY, AUGUST 9, 1888. Annual Subscription, $1.50.

CONTENTS OF THIS NUMBER.

PORTRAITS OF THIRTEEN OF THE ARCHBISHOPS AND BISHOPS OF THE PROTESTANT EPISCOPAL CHURCH AT THE PAN-ANGLICAN CONFERENCE.
ORTHODOXY NOT OBSOLETE. Dr. Talmage's Sermon at Chautauqua Last Sunday Morning.
DIAGRAM OF THE FOUR PROPHETIC EPOCHS.
The Limit to a Sheikh's Power—An Invitation from Persecutors—Mr. Aitken Among the Santhals—A Sign-board Destroyed—An Offending Lamp—An Operation Averted—A Dumb Man's Testimony.
PALESTINE AND THE JEWS. By Dr. Wild.
PORTRAIT AND LIFE OF JOSEPH RABINOWITZ.
HOW TO BE SAVED FROM SIN. A New Sermon by Rev. C. H. Spurgeon.
CONVERSION OF A SMYRNA JEW. (With Illus.)
MAUD FEATHERSTONE'S LETTER. (With Illus.)
THE EPOCHS OF A LIFE. A New Serial Story by Rev. L. S. Keyser. (Continued.)
FEAST OF TABERNACLES. By Mrs. M. Baxter.

MOST REV. G. HILLS, D.D.,
Metropolitan of Columbia.

RT. REV. F. F. GOE, D.D.,
Bishop of Melbourne.

RT. REV. C. W. SANDFORD, D.D.,
Bishop of Gibraltar.

RT. REV. C. A. SMYTHIES, D.D.,
Bishop of Central Africa.

MOST REV. W. W. JONES, D.D.,
Bishop of Capetown and Metropolitan.

RT. HON. AND MOST REV. W. THOMSON, D.D.,
Archbishop of York.

MOST REV. H. W. JERMYN, D.D.,
Bishop of Brechin and Primus of Scotland.

RT. HON. AND MOST REV. LORD PLUNKET, D.D.,
Archbishop of Dublin.

MOST REV. A. BARRY, D.D.,
Bishop of Sydney and Metropolitan.

MOST REV. J. MEDLEY, D.D.,
Bishop of Fredericton Metropolitan of Canada.

RT. REV. E. BICKERSTETH, D.D.,
Bishop of Japan.

RT. REV. L. G. MYLNE, D.D.,
Bishop of Bombay.

The Pan-Anglican Conference—The Archbishop of Canterbury and Twelve Prominent Members.

THE CONFERENCE OF BISHOPS

Of The Protestant Episcopal Church.

FOLLOWING the representatives of the Presbyterian Church who took part in the Pan-Presbyterian Council, whose portraits appeared in this journal last week, we this week give portraits of the representatives of the Protestant Episcopal Church who with many others of eminence were gathered in a great conference in London. The Archbishop of Canterbury issued a general invitation to the bishops of the Church some time ago, and on July 3 one hundred and forty one met in response to his invitation. They came from all quarters of the world.

The American Bishops

were: the Bishops of Minnesota, New York, Western New York, Tennessee, Maine, Missouri, Oregon, Albany, Pennsylvania, Central Pennsylvania, Arkansas, North and South Dakota, Massachusetts, North Carolina, Colorado, Milwaukee, New Jersey, Northern New Jersey, Chicago, Iowa, Quincy, Springfield, Michigan, New Mexico, Washington, Miss., Pittsburg, Mississippi, Indiana, and Maryland. Those *from Canada* were the Bishops of Fredericton, Ontario, Quebec, Newfoundland, Toronto, Huron, Qu'Appelle, Niagara, Saskatchewan, and Nova Scotia.

This was the third of these Pan Anglican Conferences.

The First Conference,

which was held in 1867, *originated in a suggestion from the United States.* Dr. Sumner, who in 1851 was Archbishop of Canterbury, sent in that year an invitation to Dr. Hopkins, then Bishop of Vermont, and at that time Presiding Bishop, to share in the third jubilee of the venerable Society for the Propagation of the Gospel in Foreign Parts. Bishop Hopkins replied that the time had now come to meet in the "good old fashion of synodical action. How natural (he added) and how reasonable would it seem, 'in a time of controversy and division,' that there should be a council of all the bishops in communion with your Grace; and would not such an assemblage exhibit the most solemn and, under God, the most influential aspect of strength and unity in maintaining the true Gospel? It is my own firm belief that such a measure would be productive of immense advantage, and would exercise a moral influence far beyond that of any secular legislation." The time however, had not come then, and such were the conflicting opinions of the prelates, and so burning were the questions which would inevitably arise, that wider division was more probable as a result of Conference than unity.

Sixteen years later many and important changes had occurred in the Episcopal bench in England and America, and the time was deemed favorable for the meeting of a conference. The preliminaries were settled, and on February 22, 1867, the invitation was issued by the Archbishop of Canterbury to all the bishops in communion with the Church of England—Dr. Colenso alone excepted—to meet on September 24 and the three following days at Lambeth palace. The objects of the conference were specified to "unite together in the highest acts of the Church's worship" and in "brotherly consultation; to consider together many practical questions, the settlement of which would tend to the advancement of the kingdom of our Lord and Master, Jesus Christ; and to the maintenance of greater union in the missionary work, and to increased intercommunion among ourselves." When the conference met only seventy-eight of the two hundred and more Bishops of the Anglican Communion were present, but the debates were vigorous and their influence healthful. "*The American Bishops,*" said Dr. Wilberforce, Bishop of Oxford, "*won golden opinions.*"

The Second Conference

was held in 1878. Dr. Tait was at that time Archbishop of Canterbury. He had an interview in 1874 with Dr. Kerfoot, Bishop of Pittsburg, who passed through London on his way home from attending the Old Catholic Conference at Bonn. The effect of the first Pan-Anglican conference was considered at that interview, and Dr. Kerfoot was strongly in favor of the summoning of a second. Dr. Tait requested his American brother to consult with the American Bishops on the subject, and he complied at the next General Convention. The result was a request to the Archbishop of Canterbury, signed by forty-three of the forty-six Bishops at the convention, that he would summon a second conference. The Archbishop acceded, and sent a cordial invitation to the American Bishops, personally by his son, Rev. Crawford Tait. The conference commenced its sittings July 2, 1878. One hundred Bishops were in attendance, of whom nineteen came from America.

The results of the Conference were more practical and definite than those of its predecessor. Committees were appointed to consider specific subjects, and their reports were presented and discussed by the whole Conference. The final decisions were embodied in an official letter signed by the Archbishop as its President. The Reports dealt with a wide range of subjects, including the best means of maintaing union among the Anglican churches, the establishment of ecclesiastical tribunals, the relations of missionary Bishops and missionaries; and the adaptation of the Book of Common Prayer to the needs of native congregations in heathen lands was, among other things, recommended.

The Third Conference

assembled on the third of last month. Though its results are not yet publicly known, the Bishops having sat with closed doors, the subjects discussed show that the high dignitaries of the Church turned their attention to matters of practical moment, and were solicitous for the union and advancement of the Church in the work of evangelization. They included: "Definite Teaching of the Faith to Various Classes, and the Means Thereto;" "The Anglican Communion in Relation to the Eastern Churches, to the Scandinavian and other Reformed Churches, to the Old Catholics, and others;" "Polygamy of Heathen Converts—Divorce;" "Authoritative Standards of Doctrine and Worship;" "Mutual Relations of Dioceses and Branches of the Anglican Communion;" "The Church's Practical Work in Relation to Intemperance, Purity, Emigration, and Socialism."

A Cordial Welcome

to the Bishops from America and other lands was extended by the Archbishop of Canterbury, at a solemn public service on June 30 in Canterbury Cathedral. They were received at a prefatory luncheon, spread in the crypt of the old Abbey of St. Augustine's Missionary College. The proceedings were informal, but there was a grace and dignity about the speeches of the Archbishop and his episcopal brethren. Dr. Whipple, the beloved Bishop of Minnesota, replying on behalf of the "sister or daughter Church of America," said: "There is no branch of the Anglican Church which has more reason for devout thanksgiving and gratitude than the Church in Canada and the United States. Wherever she is known she is loved, and thousands are looking to her to-day as the Church of the reclamation." Then followed the service in the Cathedral, which was of a most imposing character.

The *Te Deum* having been sung, the Archbishop of Canterbury (Dr. Benson) sitting between the two wings of the historical marble throne called St. Augustine's Chair, delivered a brief address, in the course of which he said, "Brethren, most dear and to me most reverend, few privileges of my office can surpass that which, though unworthy, I exercise to-day. It is to bid you welcome in the name of the Lord." Evening service followed the Archbishop's address. The final hymn was "The Church's one foundation," and such hearty congregational singing as it evoked has rarely echoed through the aisles of the cathedral. Atthe end of the service the Bishops were entertained at the Deanery, and returned to London in readiness for the sessions of the following week.

THE THIRTEEN PORTRAITS.

Dr. Benson, Archbishop of Canterbury.

EDWARD WHITE BENSON, the Archbishop of Canterbury, whose portrait occupies the centre of the group on the first page, is the son of E. W. Benson, Esq., of Birmingham, England. He was born in 1829, and is now fifty-nine years of age. He was educated at King Edward School, in his native town, and at Trinity College, Cambridge, of which he was successively Scholar and Fellow, and where he graduated B. A. in 1852, with much distinction; M. A. in 1855; B. D. in 1862; D. D. in 1867, receiving also the honorary degree of D. C. L. from Oxford in 1884. He was for some years an assistant master in Rugby School, and he held the Head Mastership of Wellington College from its opening in 1852 to 1872, when he was appointed a Canon Residentiary and Chancellor of Lincoln Cathedral. He was Select Preacher to the University of Cambridge in 1864, 1871, 1875, 1876, 1879, and 1882; and to the University of Oxford, 1875-76; Hon. Chaplain to the Queen in 1873; and Chaplain in Ordinary, 1875-76. In December, 1876, he was nominated by the Crown, on the recommendation of the Earl of Beaconsfield, to the newly founded Bishopric of Truro, and he received episcopal consecration in St. Paul's Cathedral, on April 25, 1877. In December, 1882, he was appointed to the Archbishopric of Canterbury in succession to Dr. Tait.

Dr. Hills, Bishop of Columbia.

GEORGE HILLS is the son of the late Rear-Admiral George Hills, and was born at Eyethorn, Kent, in 1816, so that he is now seventy-two years of age. He was educated at Durham University, where he graduated M. A. in 1838, and took the degree of D. D. in 1858. His ordination as priest took place in 1829. He was incumbent of St. Mary's, Leeds, in 1846; vicar of Great Yarmouth in 1848; and appointed honorary Canon of Norwich Cathedral in 1850. He was consecrated first Bishop of British Columbia, North America, in the year 1859.

Dr. Goe, Bishop of Melbourne.

FIELD FLOWERS GOE is the son of the late Mr. F. F. Goe, solicitor, and was born at Louth, Lincolnshire, in 1832, so that he is now fifty-six years old. He was a pupil of King Edward Grammar School in his native town, and after studying law for a time went to Oxford University in 1854, graduating M. A. in 1857. He was ordained in 1858 to the Curacy of Christ Church, Hull, and in the same year succeeded the Rev. J. King as incumbent of that church. In 1873 he was appointed to the Rectory of Sunderland; four years later he was appointed to the Rectory of St. George's, Bloomsbury. In 1884 he was Select Preacher to the University of Cambridge; and in 1886 was selected by Lord Salisbury to fill the Bishopric of Melbourne, Australia, vacated by the translation of Dr. Moorhouse to the see of Manchester.

Dr. Sandford, Bishop of Gibraltar.

CHARLES WALDEGRAVE SANDFORD is the son of the late Archdeacon Sandford. He is sixty years of age, having been born in Kent, in 1828. He received his academical education at Oxford, was several years Senior Censor of Christ Church, became Commissary of the Archbishop of Canterbury in 1869, and Rector of Bishopsbourne, Kent, in 1870. On the resignation of Bishop Harris, he was nominated to the see of Gibraltar, and was consecrated at Oxford, on February 1, 1874. The work of his diocese has been most successful.

Dr. Smythies, Bishop of Central Africa.

CHARLES ALAN SMYTHIES is about sixty years of age, and is an East Anglian by birth and descent. Having successfully passed through his College curriculum at Oxford University, he was ordained in 1871, and in 1883 consecrated Lord Bishop of Central Africa. The diocese comprises an area possibly of 8,000,000 square miles, with a population roughly guessed as 100,000,000. It comprises the Congo Valley, the Great Lakes, Equatorial Africa proper, and the whole of the native states north of the Zambesi.

Dr. Jones, Bishop of Capetown.

William West Jones is a graduate of Oxford University, and was consecrated to the see in 1874. He is about 55 years of age. Capetown is the capital of Cape Colony, South Africa, and is the centre of an extensive region, which includes Port Elizabeth, Grahamstown, Kimberley, the seat of the diamond trade; and within easy reach of Bechuanaland, the Orange Free State, Basutoland, and Natal, which together with the Atlantic on the west, the Orange River on the north, and the Indian Ocean on the south, constitute the boundaries of the Colony.

Dr. Thomson, Archbishop of York.

William Thomson was born at Whitehaven, Cumberland, on February 11, 1819, and is now 69 years old. He was educated at Shrewsbury School and at Queen's College, Oxford, of which he was successively Scholar, Fellow, Tutor, and Provost. He was ordained priest in 1843, and after four years experience of parochial labor at Guildford and at Cuddesdon, he became tutor of His College. On the translation of Dr. Baring to Durham, Dr. Thomson was on the recommendation of Lord Palmerston, appointed to the vacant see of Gloucester and Bristol in December, 1861. On the death of Archbishop Sumner, Dr. Longley was translated to Canterbury, and the archiepiscopal see of York thus becoming vacant in November, 1862, the appointment was conferred on Dr. Thomson.

Dr. Jermyn, Bishop of Brechin,

Hugh Willoughby Jermyn, Bishop of Brechin, and Primus of Scotland, was born in 1820, and received his education at Trinity Hall, Cambridge University, where he took his B. A. in 1841, M. A. in 1847, and D. D. in 1872. Having been ordained priest by the Bishop of London in 1846, he eventually accepted an appointment in the West Indies, and was made Archdeacon of St. Christopher. Returning to England he became Rector of Nettlecombe, Somerset, in 1858, and in 1871 was appointed Bishop of Colombo, being consecrated in the chapel of Lambeth Palace on October 28, of that year. He resigned this See early in 1875, but in January, 1876, he was installed Bishop of Brechin. In September, 1886, he was elected Primus of the Episcopal Church of Scotland, in succession to the late Bishop Eden.

Dr. Lord Plunket, of Dublin.

William Conyngham Plunket, Protestant Archbishop of Dublin, is the eldest son of the third Lord Plunket. He was born in 1828, being now sixty years old, and succeeded to the title on the death of his father in 1871. He was educated in Trinity College, Dublin. He was chaplain to his uncle, the late Bishop of Tuam, from 1857 to 1864, during which period he was Rector of Kilmoylan and Commoner; Treasurer, and subsequently Precentor of St. Patrick's Cathedral from 1864 to 1876; and Bishop of Meath from 1876 to 1884. On the resignation of Archbishop Trench, in 1884, Lord Plunket was elected Archbishop of Dublin.

Dr. Barry, Bishop of Sydney.

Alfred Barry is the second son of the late eminent architect, Sir Charles Barry. He was born in London in 1826; and is, therefore, now sixty-two years old. Proceeding from King's College, London, to Trinity College, Cambridge, he graduated B. A. with considerable distinction, obtaining a fellowship in 1848. He was ordained in 1850, and was Sub-Warden of Trinity College, Glenalmond, from 1851 to 1854, and held from 1854 to 1862 the Head Mastership of the Grammar School at Leeds, which he raised to a very high position by his energy and ability; and in 1862 he was appointed to the Principalship of Cheltenham College. In 1868 he became Principal of King's College, London; in 1869 Examining Chaplain to the Bishop of Bath and Wells; in 1871 a Canon of Worcester; and in 1881 Canon of Westminster. In 1883 he was consecrated Primate of Australia, Metropolitan of New South Wales, and Bishop of Sydney.

Dr. Medley, Bishop of Fredericton.

John Medley, Bishop of Fredericton and Metropolitan of Canada, was born in 1804, being now eighty-four years of age. He was educated at Wadham College, Oxford University, where he graduated B. A., in honors, in 1826, and M. A. in 1830. He was for several years after his ordination vicar of St. Thomas's, Exeter, and Prebendary of that Cathedral, and so long ago as 1845 was consecrated first Bishop of Fredericton. His diocese includes the entire province of New Brunswick, a province of the Dominion of Canada, and has an area of 27,322 square miles, of which Fredericton is the capital, and the chief commercial city St. John. The population is about 322,000.

Dr. Bickersteth, Bishop of Japan.

The name of Bickersteth is well known in the English Church of past generations, and is represented to-day abounding in every good word and work by Dr. Edward Bickersteth, Dean of Lichfield, and Dr. Edward Henry Bickersteth, Bishop of Exeter. Another Dr. Edward Bickersteth is the present Bishop of Japan, whose portrait is given on our front page. He is about fifty years old, and was ordained priest in 1874 by the Bishop of London, and consecrated missionary-bishop of the English Church in Japan in 1886.

Dr. Mylne, Bishop of Bombay.

Louis Charles Mylne, the Bishop of Bombay, is the son of Major Charles David Mylne, of the Hon. East India Company's service, and was born in Paris in 1843, being now therefore forty-five years of age. He received his early education at Merchiston Castle School, Edinburgh, at the University of St. Andrews, and at Corpus Christi College, Oxford University, where he graduated B. A., first-class in Classics, in 1866; M. A. in 1870; and D. D. in 1876. He was curate of North Moreton, Berkshire, from 1866 to 1870, and senior Tutor of Keble College, Oxford, from 1870 to 1876. He was appointed Bishop of Bombay in succession to the late Rev. Dr. Douglas, and was consecrated in St. Paul's Cathedral, London.

ANECDOTES RELATED AT RECENT EVANGELISTIC MEETINGS.

The Big Prize to be Won.—The Rev. Mr. Gullan says: "Some time ago, one of my two little girls came to me and said, 'Father, there is an examination coming on; a big prize is to be given, and I mean to have it if it be at all possible.' 'Very well, my child,' I said, 'try your best, and I think there is every chance of your succeeding if you enter in that spirit.' My other daughter also brought me the news of the approaching examination. She entered my study, and in the most lachrymose tones, said, 'Father, there is a terrible examination coming on; a large money prize is to be given. I should like to have it very much, but I know there is not any chance; I could never manage it.' 'No,' I replied. 'I am quite sure there is not, especially if you try in that way.' Similarly, when Christians set out to live the sinless life, if they say, 'I know that I cannot do it; I shall be sure to stumble,' then that man is sure to fulfil his fear; but if he start with the firm resolution to succeed, then in God's strength he will go further towards the attaining of his goal."

A Signalman's Story. "**A Couple of Years** ago I was drinking with a lot of railway men, abusing my wife, neglecting my home, and going right to ruin. Again and again the railway missionary and some of my Christian mates tried to get me to come and hear the gospel. But not for me; I liked best when off duty to lean over the bar of a saloon. One Sunday evening, two years ago, I heard some men singing. I was rather fond of singing. I stopped to listen, and soon I saw it was some of my mates. I wanted to bolt, but they caught sight of me, and one of them came and took hold of my arm. 'You wait a bit and hear us sing, and hear what we've got to say.' I did, and rather liked it, so that I was there my next Sunday off duty. That night I followed them to the tent and went home mighty angry, for it seemed they talked just about me. However, I went away. I began to see I was a sinner, and then that Christ was a Saviour. The end of it was, I cried for mercy, and now I know my sins are forgiven. Oh, its made a rare difference at home—the wife can tell you that."

Increasing the Sunday-School.—The Rev. Mr. Gunn remarks: "When, as a student, I was connected with the North Leith Parish Church, our Sunday-school was 200 strong, but the minister thought it could be largely increased if some proper means were taken to do it. So he proposed to a dear friend of mine, who was also studying for the ministry, and myself, that we should begin a systematic canvass of the district. This we did, taking the whole district street by street, and door by door. When we got through the parish, the school had increased in number from 200 to 600, and many of them were led to accept Jesus as their Saviour. Yes, one of the best ways of raising the standard of morality is to get at the children early, ere they have learned the terrible power of sin and been tainted by it. It is better to prevent a child from becoming a drunkard or a thief, than to rescue him after he is steeped in iniquity."

A Mistaken Sunday-school Teacher.—I knew a Sunday-school teacher who was constantly getting discouraged regarding his work, and sending in his resignation, saying he was unfitted to be a teacher. We persuaded him more than once to stay on, but ultimately he went to Edinburgh, and for years we heard nothing more of him. A long time afterward, a missionary, one of our most prominent Christian workers, asked me where this gentleman had gone, as he had been his Sunday-school teacher, and he would like to see him, that he might tell him what a great help his Sunday-school teaching had been to him, and how it was in his class he had received the first impetus toward the mission field. We never know all the good that, with God's blessing, may come from our efforts. We should never be discouraged, but, scattering the gospel seed in faith and hope, leave the harvest to be ripened in due course by the Great Husbandman who "gives the increase."

A King's Apostacy and Assassination.—Mr. Hamilton relates: "It is told of King Henry IV. of France, that when he was only king of Navarre, Protestantism had not a more vigorous upholder. But, when his cousin, the king of France, died, and he prepared to fight for his right to the French throne, he showed himself no true follower of Christ, but a follower of the mammon of this unrighteous world. When some French nobles sought an audience, and promised him their support, which would tend to secure him the throne, if he abjured the reformed doctrine, his reply was, 'The kingdom of France is well worth a mass.' And he actually gave up his Protestant faith for an earthly crown. Yet look at his tragic end—assassinated by the emissary of Popery for which he had given up Protestantism. How unlike Moses, who gave up the prospect of the throne of Egypt, choosing rather to suffer affliction with the people of God than enjoy the pleasures of sin for a season."

A Heroic Spanish Prince.—"One of the Bigoted kings of Spain authorized the Jesuits to destroy the heretics wherever they were found, and of whatever rank. Accordingly, peasants, priests, and nobles were dragged to the Inquisition, and thence to the stake. Yet still Protestantism lived. At length it was whispered that one of the king's sons was tainted with the hated heresy. How could the most Catholic king expect a blessing when in his own family he nourished a viper. It was urged upon him that, as a Roman Catholic king, he must make an example of even his own son. At length the king gave way, and his son was handed over to the Inquisitorial tyrants. In spite of torture, persuasion, and threats, the son stood firm. As a prince, he was permitted the choice of his mode of death. At his own request, he was put into a warm bath and there had his veins opened. He chose to suffer martyrdom with the servants of God rather than purchase safety at the expense of betraying his Divine Saviour."

ORTHODOXY NOT OBSOLETE.

Dr. Talmage's Sermon Preached at Chautauqua, N. Y., Last Sunday Morning, August 5, 1888.

"Ask for the old paths, where is the good way, and walk therein and ye shall find rest for your souls." Jer. 6: 16.

Ministers in a Fog—An Authoritative Declaration on Inspiration—The Bible Stands Intact—Inspired Throughout—Mistakes of Copyists Unimportant—Freedom for Religious Thought—The Road to Atheism—The Splendors of Orthodoxy—Its Missionaries—Sure Foundation for a Church—Theodore Parker's Ephemeral Work—The Certitudes of Orthodoxy—As to Origin and Destiny—Believing the Bible in Spots—The Two Destinies—Belief in Eternal Perdition Essential—Glorious Orthodox Death-Beds—Isabella Graham's Will.

A GREAT London fog has come down upon some of the ministers and some of the churches in the shape of what is called "advanced thought" in Biblical interpretation. All of them, and without any exception, deny the full inspiration of the Bible. Genesis is an allegory, and there are many myths in the Bible, and they philosophize and guess and reason and evolute until they land in *a great continent of mud*, from which, I fear, for all eternity they will not be able to extricate themselves.

The Bible is not only divinely inspired, but it is divinely protected in its present shape. You could as easily, without detection, take from the writings of Shakespeare, "Hamlet," and institute in place thereof Alexander Smith's drama, as at any time during the last fifteen hundred years a man could have made any important change in the Bible without immediate detection. If there had been an element of weakness, or of deception, or of disintegration, the Book would long ago have fallen to pieces. If there had been one loose brick or cracked casement in this castellated truth, surely the bombardment of eight centuries would have discovered and broken through that imperfection. The fact that

The Bible Stands Intact.

notwithstanding all the furious assaults on all sides upon it, is proof to me that it is a miracle, and every miracle is of God. "But," says some one, "while we admit the Bible is of God, it has not been understood until our time." My answer is, that if the Bible be a letter from God, our Father, to man, His child, is it not strange that that letter should have been written in such a way that it should allow seventy generations to pass away and be buried before the letter could be understood? That would be a very bright father who should write a letter for the guidance and intelligence of his children, not understandable until a thousand years after they were buried and forgotten! While as the years roll on other beauties and excellencies will unfold from the Scriptures, that the Bible is such a dead failure that all the Christian scholars for eighteen hundred years were deceived in regard to vast reaches of its meaning, is a demand upon my credulity so great that if I found myself at all disposed to yield to it I should to-morrow morning apply at some insane asylum as unfit to go alone. Who make this precious group of

Advanced Thinkers

to whom God has made especial revelation in our time of that which He tried to make known thousands of years ago and failed to make intelligible? Are they so distinguished for unworldliness, piety, and scholarship that it is to be expected that they would have been chosen to fix up the defective work of Moses and Isaiah and Paul and Christ? Is it at all possible? I wonder on what mountain these modern exegetes were transfigured! I wonder what star pointed down to their birthplace! Was it the North star, or the evening star, or the Dipper? As they came through and descended to our world did Mars blush or Saturn lose one of its rings? When I find these modern wiseacres attempting to improve upon the work of the Almighty, and to interlard it with their wisdom, and to suggest prophetic and apostolic errata, I am filled with a disgust insufferable. Advanced thought, which proposes to tell the Lord what He ought to have said thousands of years ago, and would have said if He had been as wise as His nineteenth century critics! All this comes of living away back in the eternities instead of 1888. I have two wonders in regard to these men. The first one is, how the Lord got along without them before they were born. The second wonder is how the Lord will get along without them after they are dead.

"But," say some, "do you really think the Scriptures are

Inspired Throughout?"

Yes, either as history or as guidance. Gibbon and Josephus and Prescott record in their histories a great many things they did not approve of. When George Bancroft puts upon his brilliant historical page the account of an Indian massacre, does he approve of that massacre? There are scores of thing in the Bible which neither God nor inspired men sanctioned. Either as history or as guidance the entire Bible was inspired of God. "But," says some one, "don't you think that the copyists might have made mistakes in transferring the divine words from one manuscript to another? Yes, no doubt there were such mistakes; but they no more affect the meaning of the Scriptures than the misspelling of a word or the ungrammatical structure of a sentence in a last will and testament affect the validity or the meaning of that will. All the

Mistakes Made by the Copyists

in the Scriptures, do not amount to any more importance than the difference between your spelling in a document the word forty, fourty for forty. This book is the last will and testament of God to our lost world, and it bequeaths everything in the right way, although human hands may have damaged the grammar or made unjustifiable interpolation.

These men who pride themselves in our day on being advanced thinkers in Biblical interpretation, will all of them end in atheism, if they live long enough, and I declare here, to-day, they are doing more in the different denominations of Christians, and throughout the world, for damaging Christianity and hindering the cause of the world's betterment, than five thousand Robert Ingersolls could do. That man who stands inside a castle is far more dangerous, if he be an enemy, than five thousand enemies outside the castle. Robert G. Ingersoll assails the castle from the outside. These men who pretend to be advanced thinkers in all the denominations, are fighting the truth from the inside, and trying to shove back the bolts and swing open the gates.

Now, I am in favor of the greatest

Freedom of Religious Thought

and discussion. I would have as much liberty for heterodoxy as for orthodoxy. If I should change my theories of religion I should preach them out and out, but not in the building where I am accustomed to preach, for that was erected by people who believe in an entire Bible, and it would be dishonest for me to promulgate sentiments different from those for which that building was put up. When we enter any denomination as ministers of religion, we take a solemn vow that we will preach the sentiments of that denomination. If we change our theories, as we have a right to change them, then there is a world several thousand miles in circumference, and there are hundreds of halls and hundreds of academies of music where we can ventilate our sentiments.

I remember that in all our cities, in time of political agitation, there are the Republican headquarters and the Democratic headquarters. Suppose I should go into one of these headquarters, pretending to be in sympathy with their work, at the same time electioneering for the opposite party! I would soon find that the centrifugal force was greater than the centripetal. Now, if a man enters a denomination of Christians, taking a solemn oath, as we all do, that we will promulgate the theories of that denomination, and then the man shall proclaim some other theory, he has broken his oath, and is an out-and-out perjurer. Nevertheless, I declare for largest liberty in religious discussion. I would no more have the attempt to rear a monument to Thomas Paine interfered with than I would have interfered with the lifting of the splendid monument to Washington. Largest liberty for the body, largest liberty for the mind, largest liberty for the soul!

Now, I want to show you, as a matter of advocacy for what I believe to be right, the splendors of orthodoxy. Many have supposed that its disciples are people of flat skulls, and no reading, and behind the age, and the victims of gullibility. I shall show you that the word orthodoxy stands for the greatest splendors outside of heaven.

Behold the Splendors

of its achievements. All the missionaries of the Gospel the world round are the men who believe in an entire Bible. Call the roll of all the missionaries who are to-day enduring sacrifices in the ends of the earth for the cause of religion and the world's betterment, and they all believe in an entire Bible. Just as soon as a missionary begins to doubt whether there ever was a Garden of Eden, or whether there is any such thing as future punishment, he comes right home from Beyrout or Madras, and goes into the insurance business! All the missionary societies this day are officered by orthodox men, and are supported by orthodox churches.

Orthodoxy, beginning with the Sandwich Islands, has captured vast regions of barbarism for civilization, while heterodoxy has to capture the first square inch. Blatant for many years in Great Britain and the United States, and strutting about with a peacockian braggadocio, it has yet to capture the first continent, the first State, the first township, the first ward, the first space of ground as big as you could cover with the small end of a sharp pin. Ninety-nine out of every hundred of the Protestant churches of America were built by people who believed in an entire Bible. The pulpit now may preach some other gospel, but it is *a heterodox gun on an orthodox carriage.*

The Foundation of all the Churches

that are of very great use in this world to-day were laid by men who believed the Bible from lid to lid, and if I cannot take it in that way I will not take it at all; just as if I received a letter that pretended to come from a friend, and part of it was his and part somebody else's, and the other part somebody else's, and it was a sort of literary mongrelism, I would throw the garbled sheets into the waste basket. No church of very great influence to-day but was built by those who believed in an entire Bible. Neither will a church last long built on a part of the Bible. You have noticed, I suppose, that as soon as a man begins to give up the Bible he is apt to preach in some hall, and he has an audience while he lives, and when he dies the church dies. If I thought that my church in Brooklyn was built on a quarter of a Bible, or a half a Bible, or three-quarters of a Bible, or ninety-nine one-hundredths of a Bible, I would expect it to die when I die; but when I know it is

Built on the Entire Word

of God, I know it will last two hundred years after you and I sleep the last sleep. Oh, the splendors of an orthodoxy, which with ten thousand hands and ten thousand pulpits and ten thousand Christian churches, is trying to save the world! In Music Hall, Boston, for many years stood *Theodore Parker*, battling orthodoxy, giving it, as some supposed at that time, its death wound. He was the most fascinating man I ever heard, or ever expect to hear, and I came out from hearing him thinking, in my boyhood way, "Well, that's the death of the Church." On that same street, and not far from being opposite, stood Park Congregational Church, called by its enemies, "*Hell-fire Corner.*" Theodore Parker died, and his church died with him; or, if it is in existence, it is so small you cannot see it with the naked eye. Park Congregational Church still stands on

"Hell-fire Corner," thundering away the magnificent truths of this glorious orthodoxy just as though Theodore Parker had never lived. All that Boston or Brooklyn or New York or the world ever got that is worth having came through the wide aqueduct of orthodoxy from the throne of God.

Behold the *splendors of character* built up by orthodoxy! Who had the greatest intellect the world ever knew? Paul. In physical stature, insignificant; in mind, head, and shoulders, above all the giants of the age.

Orthodox from Scalp to Heel.

Who was the greatest poet the ages ever saw; acknowledged to be so both by infidels and Christians? John Milton—seeing more without eyes than anybody else ever saw with eyes. Orthodox from scalp to heel. Who was the greatest reformer the world has ever seen; so acknowledged by infidels as well as Christians? Martin Luther. Orthodox from scalp to heel.

Then look at the certitudes. Oh, man! believing in an entire Bible, where did you come from? Answer: I descended from a perfect parentage in Paradise, and Jehovah breathed into my nostrils the breath of life. I am a son of God!" Oh, man! believing in a half-and-half Bible, *believing the Bible in spots*, where did you come from? Answer: "It is all uncertain; in my ancestral line, away back, there was an orang-outang, and a tadpole, and a polywog, and it took millions of years to get me evoluted." Oh, man! believing in a Bible in spots,

Where are You Going To,

when you quit this world? Answer: "Going into a great to be, so on into the great somewhere, and then I shall pass through on to the great anywhere, and I shall probably arrive in the nowhere." That is where I thought you would fetch up. Oh, man! believing in an entire Bible, and believing with all your heart, where are you going to when you leave this world? Answer: "I am going to my Father's house; I am going into the companionship of my loved ones who have gone before; I am going to leave all my sins, and I am going to be with God, and like God forever and forever." Oh, the glorious certitudes of orthodoxy!

Behold the splendors of orthodoxy in its announcement of two destinies—palace and penitentiary. Palace, with gates on all sides, through which all may enter and live on celestial luxuries world without end, and all for the knocking and the asking. A palace grander than if all the Alhambras, and the Versailles, and the Windsor Castles, and the Winter Gardens, and the imperial abodes of all the earth were heaved up into one architectural glory. At the other end of the universe, a penitentiary, where men who want their sins can have them. Would it be fair that you and I should have our choice of Christ and the palace, and other men be denied their choice of sin and eternal degradation?

Palace and Penitentiary!

The first of no use unless you have the last. Brooklyn and New York would be better places to live in, with Raymond Street Jail, and the Tombs, and Sing Sing, and all the small-pox hospitals emptied on them, than heaven would be if there were no hell. Palace and penitentiary! If I see a man with a full bowl of sin, and he thirsts for it, and his whole nature craves it, and he takes hold with both hands and presses that bowl to his lips, and then presses it hard between his teeth, and the draught begins to pour its sweetness down his throat, shall we snatch away the bowl, and jerk the man up to the gate of heaven, and push him in if he does not want to go, and sit down and sing psalms forever? No! God has made you and me so completely free that *we need not go to heaven unless we prefer it*. Not more free to soar than free to sink.

Nearly all the heterodox people I know believe all are coming out at the same destiny; without regard to faith or character we are all coming out at the shining gate. There they are, all in glory together. Thomas Paine and George Whitefield, Jezebel and Mary Lyon, Nero and Charles Wesley, Charles Guiteau and James A. Garfield, John Wilkes Booth and Abraham Lincoln—all in glory together! All the innocent men, women, and children who were massacred, side by side with their murderers! If we are all coming out at the same destiny, without regard to character, then it is true. I turn away from such a debauched heaven. Against that cauldron of piety and blasphemy, philanthropy and assassination, self-sacrifice and beastliness, I place the two destinies of the Bible forever, and forever, and forever apart.

Behold also the splendors of the Christian *orthodox death-beds*. Those who deny the Bible, or deny any part of it, never die well. They either go out in darkness or they go out in silence portentous. You may gather up all the biographies that have come forth since the art of printing was invented, and I challenge you to show me a triumphant death of a man who rejected the Scriptures, or rejected any part of them. Here I make

A Great Wide Avenue.

On the one I put the death-beds of those who believed in an entire Bible. On the other side of that avenue I put the death-beds of those who rejected part of the Bible, or rejected all of the Bible. Now, take my arm and let us pass through this dividing avenue. Look off upon the right side. Here are the death-beds on the right side of this avenue. "Victory through our Lord Jesus Christ!" "Free grace!" "Glory, glory!" "I am sweeping through the gates washed in the blood of the Lamb!" "The chariots are coming!" "I mount, I fly!" "Wings, wings!" "They are coming for me!" "Peace, be still!" Alfred Cookman's death-bed, Richard Cecil's death-bed, Commodore Foote's death-bed. Your father's death-bed, your mother's death-bed, your sister's death-bed, your child's death-bed. Ten thousand radiant death-beds of those who believed an entire Bible.

Now, take my arm and let us go through that avenue, and look off upon the other side. No smile of hope! No shout of triumph! No face supernaturally illumined! Those who reject any part of the Bible never die well. No beckoning for angels to come. No listening for the celestial escort. Without any exception they go out of the world because they are pushed out; while on the other hand the list of those who believed in an entire Bible, and have gone out of the world in triumph, is a list so long it seems interminable. Oh, is not that a splendid influence, this orthodoxy, which makes that which must otherwise be the most dreadful hour of life—the last hour—positively paradisaical?

Young men, old men, middle-aged men,

Take Sides in this Contest

between orthodoxy and heterodoxy. "Ask for the old paths, walk therein, and ye shall find rest for your souls." But you follow this crusade against any part of the Bible—first of all you will give up Genesis, which is as true as Matthew; then you will give up all the historical parts of the Bible; then after a while you will give up the miracles; then you will find it convenient to give up the Ten Commandments; and then you will wake up in a fountainless, rockless, treeless desert swept of everlasting sirocco. If you are laughed at you can afford to be laughed at for standing by the Bible, just as God has given it to you and miraculously preserved it.

Do not jump overboard from the stanch old *Great Eastern* of old-fashioned orthodoxy until there is something ready to take you up stronger than the fantastic yawl which has painted on the side *Advanced Thought*, and which leaks at the prow, and leaks at the stern, and has a steel pen for one oar, and a glib tongue for the other oar, and now tips over this way and then tips over that way, until you do not know whether the passengers will land in the breakers of despair, or on the sinking sand of infidelity.

I am in full sympathy with the advancements of our time, but this world will never advance a single inch beyond this old Bible. God was just as capable of dictating the truth to the prophets and apostles as He is capable of dictating the truth to these modern apostles and prophets. God has not learned anything in a thousand years. He knew just as much when

He Gave the First Dictation

as He does now, giving the last dictation, if He is giving any dictation at all. So I will stick to the old paths. Naturally a sceptic, and preferring new things to old, I never so much as to-day felt the truth of the entire Bible, especially as I see into what spectacular imbecility men rush when they try to chop up the Scriptures with the meat-axe of their own preferences, now calling upon philosophy, now calling on the Church, now calling on God, now calling on the devil. I prefer the thick, warm robe of the old religion—old as God—the robe which has kept so many warm amid the cold pilgrimage of this life, and amid the chills of death. The old robe rather than the thin, uncertain gauze offered us by these wiseacres who believe the Bible in spots.

On July 27, 1814, at seventy-two years of age, expired Isabella Graham. She was the most useful woman of her day amid the poor and sick, at the head of the orphan asylums, and Magdalen asylums, and an angel of mercy in hospital and reformatory. Dr. Mason, one of the mightiest men of his day, said at her funeral that she was mentally and spiritually the most wonderfully endowed person he had ever met. She was an impersonation of the most orthodox orthodoxy. As a sublime peroration to my sermon, I give

An Extract from her Will

and testament, showing how one who believes in an entire Bible may make a glorious exit. "My children and my grandchildren I leave to my covenant God, the God who hath fed me all my life with the bread that perisheth, and the bread that never perisheth, who has been a Father to my fatherless children, and a husband to their widowed mother thus far. And now receiving my Redeemer's testimony, I set to my seal that God is true; and believing the record of John that God hath given to me eternal life. I also believe that He will perfect what concerns me, support and carry me safely through death, and present me to His Father, complete in His own righteousness, without spot or wrinkle. Into the hands of this redeeming God, Father, Son, and Holy Ghost I commit my redeemed spirit.—ISABELLA GRAHAM."

Let me die the death of the righteous, and let my last end be like hers. "Glory be to the Father, and to the Son, and to the Holy Ghost; as it was in the beginning, is now and ever shall be, world without end. Amen and Amen!"

A CONSECRATED SON.

"Is it not a great trial to you to part with your eldest son?" said a missionary secretary to gentleman who had come to London to take leave of his son, who was to embark the next day for a foreign land. "Yes," was the answer, "it is a great trial, but I have been expecting it for a long time. The day my son was born," he continued, "I attended a missionary meeting, and was greatly impressed with what I heard. When I went home I took the baby out of the bed, and holding it in my arms, I said to my wife, Will you give this boy to the missions?' 'Yes,' she replied, 'I will.' From that time I have been expecting he would go, though he never knew the circumstances till he offered himself for a missionary."

A DUMB MAN'S TESTIMONY.

A MOST remarkable incident is reported in the *Indian Witness*. It states that among the converts at a mission station was a man curiously afflicted. He could hear and read, but could not speak. His intelligence, however, could not be doubted. In the course of time this poor man was proposed for baptism. The pastor and brethren hesitated, feeling that it was impossible to gain from his speechless mouth any adequate proof that he had the knowledge requisite for church membership, or that he was not acting with duplicity. He was brought before the church, however, and the minister asked him this question: "What is the ground of your belief that there is salvation for you in Jesus Christ?" The others looked at one another in dismay; this question seemed impossible of answer from a dumb man. But he, on hearing it, instantly arose and proceeded to answer by significant signs. First, he put his hands upon his breast with an expression of loathing, to indicate his own sense of sin; then he stepped forward and looked down, as if beholding a deep and awful pit, from which again he shrank back with a look of terror; but presently drawing near again, he looked and seemed to see something just beyond; then he made the sign of the cross! Jesus was there! And now again he looked into the pit and smiled, as that he saw his own sins cast in there! At last he looked up and pointed to heaven with a smile of ecstasy. Jesus had died for his sins, and was risen forever to make intercession for him!

AN INVITATION FROM PERSECUTORS.

A TRIP to Ordoo, on the Black Sea, was recently taken by Dr. Constantine, who has charge of the American Board's mission at Smyrna. In a letter to the *Missionary Herald*, describing his tour, he says: "The church and school committee of the district of Saint Nicholas sent me a written invitation, asking that I should preach in their schoolhouse. Yet these men were the leaders, awhile ago, *in stoning one of the brethren*, determined to drive him away from the place. The next day, Saturday, the whole committee appeared, and it was decided that a preaching service should be held every evening in the week, while the day should be free for visitors and inquirers. During the thirteen days spent there, I had eighteen services, and addressed one meeting for women, besides paying visits and meeting inquirers. On one occasion I had as many as thirty or forty inquirers in my room. The interest was marked from the outset; people came in great crowds, and from great distances; the women were largely represented, and the attention was intense. We had gatherings of from two to five hundred people, and once had from one hundred and fifty to two hundred women present. Wherever there was a group in the market, the services were the topic of conversation."

MR. AITKEN AMONG THE SANTHALS.

A RECENT letter from Mr. B. Aitken who is preaching the gospel in India, at his own charges, describes a visit he recently paid to Santhalistan, where it appears that other mission work beside that of Mr. Haegert is being done and that is being blest with success. Mr. Aitken accompanied one of the native preachers in his journey through the villages, and saw the character of the work. He says: "I spent a day with him at his own station, and afterward went preaching with him and two catechists or elders, to five villages. He was a humble man, ignorant of English, *with bare feet*, and very simply dressed, but a grand evangelist. On a terribly hot day we walked from 8 o'clock in the morning till 1 in the afternoon, and I could not but admire the steadfast purpose with which he pursued his preaching. We would enter a village, when the pastor would ask for seats, and several *charpais* would be brought out of the huts, and placed in the shade of a tree. When we were seated, the pastor would deliberately undo his hymn-book from his *kummerbund* and begin to sing. This brought a crowd of men, women, and children, and dogs around us, and then the preaching was done—earnest, faithful pleading, carried on in the spirit of our Lord, whether the people mocked, objected, or approved. Although the day was awfully hot, and more trudging through fields and lanes remained to be done, the pastor showed no disposition to scamp his work, but patiently spoke on till scoffers were quieted and the serious were satisfied."

A SIGN-BOARD DESTROYED.

IN a letter from Yokohama, Japan, to the *Missionary Link*, Mrs. Pierson relates how the establishment of a mission led to a nefarious business being abandoned. She says that, having recently opened a school in an immoral locality, one of the "singing girls" applied for admission, and as her character was not then known she was admitted. Subsequently the managers learned what she was and for the sake of the other girls attending the school, it was necessary to exclude her. Mrs. Pierson, however, was much drawn to her and visited her in her home. She says: I found the family to consist of father, mother and grandmother, all of whom the poor girl undoubtedly supports. They did not seem to care to hear the message of our King, proclaiming pardon to the penitent through faith in His precious blood; but whether they would or not, we delivered it, and rented a room in the neighborhood for one evening in the week, where we are holding meetings. The man in whose house they are held is a stranger to us, and we know little of his past or present circumstances. We learned recently that he was engaged in *a nefarious business*. I was led to speak most plainly and unreservedly of the great sin and terrible penalty of unhallowed traffic in immortal souls. The man was converted, *destroyed his sign-board*, which I had not seen, as it was always taken down the evening we are there, and gave up his business. We are praying that some other means of support for his wife and children may be opened to him.

AN OPERATION AVERTED.

THE remarkable healing of a tumor, in answer to prayer, when eminent physicians and specialists pronounced it incurable by any other means than a dangerous operation, is described in this month's number of *Thy Healer*.* It appears that a Mrs. Houldey, of Gloucester, England, was afflicted with an abdominal tumor, which became so critical that she was taken to the City Infirmary for treatment. She was there for over two months without relief, and was then advised to go to an institution in Birmingham to have a noted specialist remove the tumor by the knife. The poor woman was at that time so weak that she could not stand, and had to be lifted in and out of bed by two nurses. She naturally shrank from the operation, and wrote to Bethshan. The following is her own account of what followed: "As I did not feel led to go through the operation, I made it a matter of prayer, and asked the Lord what I was to do, and I wrote to Bethshan three weeks ago. On the following Thursday I was examined by another surgeon, and he said that the sooner I was under the surgeon's hand the better, as the tumor was very much larger. I asked the doctor to allow me to go home for a few days, and I was permitted to go for a fortnight, but they would much rather I stayed in. I had mentioned to nurse that I was going to trust God to heal me, but they seemed to think it would be a thing impossible. Praise God; nothing is impossible to him that believeth. I must now add that, after I came home—from the Thursday till the Sunday night—I was in dreadful pain. I even went so far as to get the young woman that is with me to get up at twelve o'clock on the Sunday night to get some hot salt to see if I could get easier; but just as she was about to get it I got easier, and said: 'Never mind, now, the pain is better,' and from that time I have had no pain to speak of, and from last Wednesday I have felt quite healed. I was anointed for healing on the Thursday. On the Saturday I got up, and on the Sunday I came down, and have been down ever since, and have helped in the household duties, and in washing and nursing baby. I could not do anything before—not even lift the baby, but now, praise God, I am healed and in better health than I have been for eight years. Praise God, I can say I am perfectly whole."

* *Thy Healer and Faith Witness*, a monthly Magazine, edited by Mrs. M. Baxter, contains original articles on Holiness and Healing, Authentic Testimonies of Divine Healing, and Items of Intelligence from Heathen Lands where Missionaries are laboring in faith, soliciting no help from man, but relying solely on God for support. Annual Subscription, 75 cents, may be sent to the Manager of CHRISTIAN HERALD, 63 Bible House, New York.

THE LIMIT TO A SHEIKH'S POWER.

IN a report from the American Board's Mission in Syria a case of persecution is reported with a significant comment. Some time ago three Moslem men asked permission to attend the evening services at one of the mission stations. They had become interested in Christianity by means of a Bible possessed by one of their number. They were cordially invited to attend all the meetings. They came regularly for three months. They appeared very attentive, and made occasional visits to the missionaries to talk about religion, and to ask for explanation of Bible texts. When they ceased coming, a native teacher met one of them, and asked him why he and his friends did not come to the meetings any more. He replied that they had been summoned before their sheikh, and imprisoned for two weeks. Then they were required to give bonds for a large sum that they would never attend the meetings, never visit the missionaries at their homes, never talk on the Protestant religion with any one. This they promised faithfully to do. They were told to go and sin no more. "And remember," said the sheikh, "if you violate this agreement, I will collect these bonds, and you will be imprisoned for life." The men added, "They can prevent us from attending your meetings, and from talking with you on religion, but *they cannot stop us from thinking*."

AN OFFENDING LAMP.

TWO missionaries in Mexico have been called to account in court for an illumination, with the result that the curiosity of the people has been excited, and larger audiences secured. The story is told in the course of Mr. Wright's report to the *Missionary Herald*. He says: "One day Mr. Case and I made an illumination, a simple frame covered with cloth, on which was printed an announcement of the services, and, with a candle placed inside, this was hung over the door. The words were 'Evangelical Service' on one side, and 'Entrance Free' on the other. It attracted a great deal of attention, and within half an hour a policeman came with an order that it be removed. Our audience had already been attracted, so we complied with good grace. Later we were both summoned to appear before the mayor of the place. We went, glad of the opportunity to talk of our work. He expressed surprise that we had dared to put up such a notice without first asking his permission. We begged his pardon, explaining that we had done the same thing both in Parral and Chihuahua without thought of previous notice. He explained that he feared it would excite opposition, perhaps a mob, which with his small police force he would be unable to quell.

Mr. Case embraced the opportunity, as did Peter before the council, to preach a good gospel sermon to the mayor, explaining the object of our meetings. I asked him in what consisted the offence. He said that it was in the letters or words on the sign. I asked if there would be any objection to placing over the door such a light without the words, to light up the entrance. He replied that there would be none whatever. With that we were quite content, although we well knew that there was no law against the full notice. But we expressed ourselves as much pleased with this result, and thanked him for this permission, and were dismissed. We took the offending letters off, put on new cloth, put up the light the next night, and it now attracts a great deal more attention than before. People ask what those words were and why they were taken away. Sunday evening at the communion service there were over one hundred present, in the room and at the door, and all were as attentive and quiet as can be imagined."

PALESTINE AND THE JEWS.

By Rev. Joseph Wild, D. D., of Toronto.

Palestine, its Glories and Advantages—An Emigration Fever—How the Jew Himself Regards the Question—The Custom at the Close of the Feast of the Passover—Jewish History, a Proof of the Existence of Providence—Rest at Last.

A STRIKING passage in reference to the Jews occurs in Isaiah 10 : 23 : "For the Lord of hosts shall make a consumption even determined in the midst of all the land." By the phrase, "in the midst of all the land," we understand all the world in general. At the appointed time, which will be, I presume, in a few years, a fine fever with respect to the return of certain people to Palestine, will possess all men—a fever that will spread itself out in all parts of the world. It is determined upon already in the counsel of the Divine mind. A perfect mania will possess the nations, and the general topic of conversation in a very few years from to-day will be

Palestine and its Advantages.

This emigration fever will rage most violently among the Jews; then it will take hold of other races and nations; for the prophet Isaiah assures us that God will gather others to Him besides the literal seed of Judah and of Israel. The exertions of the Church, the forces of the nations, are hastening on the preparatory conditions of this great consumption. Very soon Jerusalem will become pre-eminent. Salem will stand once more, lifting her head from the dust, and standing with majesty among the nations of the earth, she will again be the glory of all lands. Many men are ready to ask how this consumption will be brought about, and because they are not now interested in any great degree, they rather doubt the matter. Neither their doubts, nor anything, any difficulties that they can see in their mind just now, will stand in the way of Him who reigns in the heavens, who will, in His own good time, bring His own purposes to pass.

It is often very difficult beforehand to say by what means God is going to produce certain things, what means He will adopt to bring about certain events. The great point for us all to settle is, Is this thing to take place? The signs of the times seem, I think, in some degree, to forecast this great event. Think of the beautiful imagery of the Saviour, "Ye see the fig-tree putting forth its leaves, and ye know that summer is nigh." So, also, when certain things are fulfilled, do we know that other things must come to pass. The signs of the times indicate very clearly that *the period of this consumption is*

Not Very Far Distant.

The method and enthusiasm attending upon such a work we may form an idea of by looking in our own times, and, in times past, at similar movements. Twenty years ago no man could have predicted the enthusiasm that rages through Canada touching Manitoba. There was not a man who had prescience enough to see that that part of the Dominion would take possession of homes, of hearts, of minds, of interests, from one end of the Dominion to the other. The land was thought to be barren, the climate uncongenial, and no one would suppose that he could leave the fair fields and the lakes of the province of Ontario and go to that far-off land. But we see how soon a rage is created, how soon a consumption can be started. Now this is an evidence of what can be done if men can only get up an excitement or fever upon any point. You crowd out reason, and men become subject to the law of impulse, and follow out the line of that interest.

You may ask, Do the Jews take any knowledge of this? The Jews throughout the world are getting keenly alive to this question; their papers are now discussing it, and a great change is taking place in the Jewish mind on these points. The London *Standard* remarks, "It is interesting to notice the way in which the Jews, scattered throughout the world, are beginning to turn their eyes toward their own land. Palestine is not altogether a place to please a capitalist, but yet even such keen financiers as the Jews are busy buying it up. The *Jewish Chronicle* reckons now some 18,000 Jewish brethren in Jerusalem alone. It is said they are not a desirable population to maintain, yet $300,000, is sent to help these people maintain themselves.

The Occupation of Palestine

by a people who have retained an indestructibility as a race, while they have learned a complete cosmopolitan character during these eighteen centuries—a nation at once European in education and Asiatic origin—would be by no means a bad arrangement. It might not be impolitic on the part of the European Powers to assist in placing so influential a people in so important a position, and would solve what, before many years, will be the vexed question among the nations—namely, the territory of Syria." Now, you might ask one of the Jewish brotherhood in Toronto here, and probably he would not know as much about it as I do, because he is not as much interested in the prophecies as I am. He is interested in doing business; he knows his own line of thought remarkably well, but he does not know the line of thought that runs in this direction. A man's eye is keen in the direction his interest lies.

Some time ago the *Hebrew Observer* had an article, which asked: "Is there no other destiny for Palestine but to remain a desert? Syria will soon be the *entrepot* between the East and the West, and the old trade will revive. Old cities will revive, and new ones will be built; the old time will come back, and the steam-car will run in the track of the caravan. Syria will be a place of trade; but the people who are pre-eminently the traders of the world, will they be there when the coming change takes place? The country wants capital and population. The Jew can give it both."

Do you know what the Jews do now at the close of the Feast of the Passover, and have done for the last 1800 years? At the close of that solemn day's services they take each other by the hand and say, "Good-by;

We Meet at Jerusalem

next year." They did so here in Toronto last year, and will do so again next year. They will as surely meet in Jerusalem some year as they have carried out the idea. They say, "Good-by; we meet in Jerusalem next year;" and they will say it *until they do*. Ah, brethren of Judah, some of your children, I believe, will live to realize this long-expected blessing. The outlines of history are fast filling in, and you will ere long be placed in your own land, with the accumulated experience of centuries to guide you to duty and labor.

How Will This Be Brought About?

It *will* be brought about, as was the great deliverance in the land of Egypt; it will be brought about by God's own purpose. "For thus saith the Lord, It shall come to pass that they shall say no more, the Lord God which brought us up out of the land of Egypt, but, The Lord God liveth which brought us from all countries whithersoever He had scattered us, and placed us in our own land"—that is, they will forget about the deliverance from Egypt, and say, "The Lord God which brought us from all countries," etc. And the latter will be as true as the first; and when will it be? God has determined this great consummation, and it *must* take place. Are the Jews to be always outcasts, wandering over the earth? And yet all their sufferings may be traced to this—they prayed the prayer, "*His blood be upon us and upon our children.*" Oh, that they had a clasp on their mouths when they asked that for their children! But it has been upon them, has it not? If you, free-thinker, if you, man that disbelieves the Bible, if you want *a proof of an answered prayer*, the bloody lines and tracks down the centuries tell you that one prayer, at least in God's Word has been terribly answered.

What is it God said? That they should be wanderers, without national life, without government or king, until He should return them to their own land. And this has been true for 1800 years anyway. Has not it? Do you not see that what He has been telling you about them is true? And He says there is to be a great consumption in the land. That is true also. There is to be a great consumption, in the providence of God, and they are to be gathered together. They will be persecuted, until they say in their sorrow:

"Let Us Go into Our Own Land."

We shall be glad to see them go, my brethren, to that land which is theirs of right. We may argue as we will, but I am myself under the impression that the time is now near for the call to go forth, as the cry is said to have run like an electric shock through the French when Bonaparte gave out his first proclamation: "Frenchmen, come home!" And so God will cause those wandering ones to come home, and they will hear the call and return in peace to their ancient land.

THE FOUR EPOCHS.

DIAGRAM OF CONJECTURAL LENGTH of each of the Four Epochs or Intervals which have yet to elapse during the ensuing Six Years between the present month of June, 1888, and April 21, 1894.

FIRST EPOCH of Continuance of the existing general European Peace onward from the present month of June, 1888.	Certainly no longer than *two years* until about the middle of 1890, but more likely to be not longer than *one year*, until near the middle of 1889. We may be thankful if even the rest of 1888 passes without a European war.
SECOND EPOCH of the Greatest European War ever known, which will end with changing the existing 23 kingdoms of Cæsar's Roman Empire into 10 Confederated Kingdoms ruled by ten Kings as foretold in Daniel 7, 24; 2, 41.	Most likely not shorter than *eighteen months*, nor longer than *three years*, and beginning in 1889 more probably than in 1890, and ending in 1891, or less probably in 1892.
THIRD EPOCH of ensuing interval of peace from the Confederacy of the Ten Kings until the rise of Napoleon as an Eleventh Little Horn or King in or near Macedonia.	This interval may be expected to be scarcely less than several months, not longer than about a year, and probably in 1891 or 1892.
FOURTH EPOCH of Napoleon's earlier career, from his first rise as a Little Hellenic King, and his "waxing great toward the South and the East and Pleasant Land," until he becomes King of Syria and makes a seven years' covenant with the Jews on Passover Day, April 21, 1894.	Napoleon's initial exploits included in this Epoch would seem to occupy at least *eighteen months*, and, therefore, as they culminate in April 21, 1894, to commence not later than the latter part of 1892, but they might occupy as long a time as two or two and a-half years, and therefore begin toward the close of 1891, or the early part of 1892.

We pass out of the present "unchronological" interval into the "chronological" interval of the first seven years upon April 21, 1894—after which the sacrifices are renewed on November 8, 1894, and the Resurrection and the Translation of the 144,000 watchful living Christians is on March 5, 1896, and Antichrist's 1,260 days begin on August 15, 1897, and the end of this age is on April 11, 1901.

CHRISTIAN HERALD AND SIGNS OF OUR TIMES.

OFFICE, 63 BIBLE HOUSE, NEW YORK.
ENTERED AT THE POST-OFFICE AT NEW YORK, N. Y., AS SECOND-CLASS MATTER.

EVERY NUMBER CONTAINS:

The Portrait and Biography of some eminent person.
The Sermon Dr. Talmage preached the last Sunday morning.
An Exposition of Unfulfilled Prophecy.
A Summary of the Events of the Week, Notes of Religious and Temperance Movements, etc.
A Sermon by Rev. C. H. Spurgeon, of London, from advance sheets sent by special arrangement.
Pictures of Missionary Life, etc., and Descriptive Articles.
An instalment of a Serial Story.
An Exposition of the International Sunday-School Lesson, by Mrs. M. Baxter.

ANNUAL SUBSCRIPTION, $1.50.

Remittances by mail should be by bank cheques, Post-office orders, or Express money-orders whenever possible. If currency is sent it should be in a registered letter. Cheques and money-orders should be made payable to THE CHRISTIAN HERALD. Making them payable to individuals often causes delay.

New subscriptions may commence at any time. When subscribers do not indicate their wish, they commence with the first number of the month in which the subscription is received.

PUBLISHER'S NOTICE.

The whole edition of The Christian Herald was mailed last week to subscribers during Tuesday, July 31. The last delivery at the New York Post Office was made at 9.00 P. M.

CURRENT EVENTS.

The Sudden Death of General Philip Sheridan on Sunday night, took the country by surprise. The reports of his condition, especially those since his removal to Nonquitt, Mass., encouraged the hope that the General was on his way to recovery The nature of his disease, however, must have led his physicians to expect that the end would be sudden, though it might be delayed for some months, or even years. No alarming symptoms appear to have been observed on the day of his death. About nine o'clock in the evening the General's brother, Colonel Sheridan, bade him good-night, and went to his hotel. Half an hour later the dreaded signs of heart failure manifested themselves, and the physicians who were with the patient administered the remedies which had relieved him in previous attacks. But this time they failed. The illustrious soldier sank into unconsciousness, and at twenty minutes past ten he died. He was fifty-seven years of age.

The Effort to Defeat the Organization of trusts by legislation appears likely to be defeated. The House Committee appointed to deal with the subject has submitted a partial report, not having had sufficient time to thoroughly investigate the system of operations. The committee, however, has discovered that the legislation proposed will not touch the trusts under their present system. All such legislation is directed against combinations to fix the price or regulate the production of articles of merchandise or commerce; whereas the trustees do not fix prices or regulate production, and the several corporations absorbed are not in combination with each other. The effect of the trusts, however, is evidently to curtail production and so to raise prices, though the trustees have craftily avoided the appearance of regulating either. The companies agrees with each other as to production, and all the trustees do, is to receive and distribute dividends on the stock surrendered. It will, therefore, be necessary to revise the bills submitted, so as to meet these subtle tactics.

The Committee on Pauper Immigration, now pursuing its inquiries in New York, made a discovery last week which shows that it is not from Italy only that undesirable immigrants come. A witness informed the committee that there was a society at Munich, Germany, that bent its energies to sending discharged convicts to this country. This society had branches in different parts of Germany. The reports of the society for the years 1883 and 1884 were among the records of the State Department. They showed that in 1883 the society had assisted twenty-seven discharged criminals to emigrate to the United States. In the following year the society and its branches had assisted thirty discharged criminals to come here. Criminals had been sent back from this country, and had been returned by way of England. This society assisted none but discharged criminals to emigrate, and those it assisted were generally of the most vicious kind. Every emigrant of this sort landed in America with $25 in his pocket. A general feeling is now growing that the time has arrived for restricting immigration from all countries, and especially that funds must be provided for maintaining a vigilant watch at European ports against the export of criminals.

The System of Private Letter-Boxes which has long been an aid to fraud and immorality, has at length been denounced in Congress. The Committee on Post Offices last week favorably reported a bill for the suppression of the evil. In New York and other large cities small stores have been doing a considerable business by the rental of these private letter-boxes. Persons carrying on a clandestine correspondence, and others engaged in fraudulent advertising are able to hire a box in a store for fifty cents a month. Their mail is deposited there instead of being taken to their residences by the carrier or placed in the family box at the Post Office. A great deal of swindling has been carried on through this medium, and many homes have been wrecked by the facilities afforded by private letter-boxes. It may be hoped that Congress will find time to pass the bill now reported, which prohibits the delivery of mail matter outside the usual Post Office channels.

The Famous Struggle between a Plain Farmer and a great corporation which has attracted public attention throughout the country, has passed the ordeal of the Interior Department with gratifying results. Guilford Miller is to keep the farm which the Northern Pacific Railroad Company endeavored to wrest from him, so far as the Department has the power to confirm his title. Secretary Vilas issued his decision on Thursday last. He holds that Miller's quarter section was not included in the lands withdrawn from settlement, on account of the first provisional location of the route of the road, which was the only one allowed by law. It was, however, within the limits from which the company could choose its indemnity lands, but the final location of the road left the section open for settlement when Miller took possession in 1878. Finally, assuming the company's contention as to the lands withdrawn from settlement to be correct, it is held that it had no right to include this land in its selections for indemnity for lands lost within the granted limits. If this decision is sustained, the country may congratulate itself that for once a greedy monopoly has been foiled. It is stated that over two thousand homesteads depended on this decision.

The Sioux Indians Appear Unalterably Opposed to the treaty submitted to them by the United States Government. At the conference on Thursday last, at Standing Rock Agency, the speeches of the chiefs clearly showed that no progress had been made by the Commissioners in removing the objections of the tribe. The Commissioners, however, profess to feel hopeful of success. The object of the treaty is to acquire, by the payment of one million dollars, eleven million acres of the twenty-five million assigned to the tribe in Dakota. The lands are to be sold to actual settlers at fifty cents an acre, and the proceeds invested for the benefit of the Sioux. The tribe is to give up its hunting habits and to settle on farms to be selected individually. The objections of the Indians are, first, that they do not want to sign any treaty, because the Government has never kept faith with them, but has always cheated and defrauded them; second, they do not wish to part with their lands; and third, that if they did, the compensation offered is ridiculously inadequate. The only consideration that appears to weigh with them is that the whites are resolved on having the lands anyway, and it may be better to accept the million dollars than to fight and be compelled to surrender the lands without any compensation.

Another Change in the Rule of Bulgaria appears to be imminent. Prince Ferdinand, it is stated by well-informed press correspondents, is to be removed from the throne by diplomatic means. The Emperor of Germany and the Czar of Russia agreed upon that step at their recent interview. The Emperor of Germany adheres to the policy of Prince Bismarck, which is opposed to interference in Bulgarian affairs, but being desirous of removing the Balkan question from European disquieting elements, he has promised to support Russia in demanding Ferdinand's deposition. That Austria will take up arms in defence of her protégé, is deemed improbable and, therefore, Ferdinand's expulsion is regarded as settled. Various petty princes are mentioned as his probable successors. Among them the Duke of Cumberland, whose claims on Hanover Germany might thus liquidate. Prince Waldemar, a son of the King of Denmark, is also mentioned. He is a brother of the King of Greece, and a brother-in-law of the Czar and of the Prince of Wales.

Alarming Rumors Respecting Mr. H. M. Stanley continue to be received. But little credence is given to them, though it is an ominous fact that, though they differ in detail, their general tenor is alike gloomy. They all represent him as deserted by the bulk of his followers, and in imminent danger of massacre. A despatch from Zanzibar, dated August 1, said that reports which had filtered from tribe to tribe were in circulation there that Stanley was denuded of men and supplies, and hemmed in between the Naboda country and the Albert Nyanza. Other reports were to the effect that Stanley, after several conflicts with the Matongora and Mino tribes, had been compelled to divert his course in an unknown direction. Deserters from Tippu Tib's caravan testify to his willingness to assist Major Barttelot, but they say that, owing to the rumors regarding Stanley's fate, he had the greatest difficulty in obtaining men willing to penetrate into the interior. A letter has also been received from Mr. Jamison, the naturalist, from Kasongo, on the Congo River, stating that he is making preparations to leave with Major Barttelot, Tippu Tib, and 900 men, to search for Henry M. Stanley. He says all the Europeans in the expedition are well. That information implies that Tippoo Tib is re-establishing his supremacy over the Arab tribes, and is still faithful to Stanley.

The Commission to Investigate the Charges of the London *Times* against Mr. Parnell and his party was the subject of debate all last week in the British House of Commons. The Parnellites presented a number of amendments with the object of limiting the scope of the inquiry, and making more specific the questions to be considered by the Commission, but they were all rejected by the vote of the majority of the House. The Government has excited prejudice and suspicion as to its impartiality by admitting that its leader in the Commons had a long interview with Mr. Walter, the proprietor of the *Times*, on the very day that an important change was made in the bill appointing the Commission. Mr. Parnell reiterates his statement that the letters purporting to be written by him, and published in the *Times* are forgeries, and he promises to bring clear proof of his assertion. A member of the Government said, however, that the letters were not the charges but only evidence of the charges against Mr. Parnell. He admitted that the letters were extremely important, and said that without doubt the Commission would early inquire into their authenticity.

Mr. Moody's Bible Conference, at Northfield, commenced on August 1. The attendance is larger than ever before. Mr. Sankey, assisted by Mr. and Mrs. Stebbins, has charge of the musical arrangements, and among the speakers are Rev. J. Hudson Taylor, of the China Inland Mission, Rev. George Needham, Dr. E. W. Faunce, Rev. W. W. Clarke, and other well known ministers. Marquand Hall has been turned into a hotel, principally for ladies. Its beautifully appointed chapel, with large open fireplaces at either end, serves as a dining-room, where the young lady students, with their bright, cheery manners and very evident desire to make every one as happy as possible, assist in making a most ideal place for physical refreshment. East Hall, a building used almost exclusively for a dormitory in term time, is now an abode for the gentlemen, with a restaurant on the lower floor. Other cottages on the grounds are filled with sleeping-arrangements, and the occupants can go to either Marquand or East Halls for meals. Besides these there are the white tents on the lawn, which, at present, are occupied chiefly by young men, mostly members of the Mt. Hermon school for boys.

A Delay in Performing an Operation has proved fatal to an injured man in New York. Three weeks ago a laborer was engaged in lifting stone in the cellar of a building on the Bowery. One of the stones slipped from his grasp and fell on the little finger of his left hand, crushing it badly. He went to the Chambers Street Hospital for treatment, and was told that the finger would have to be amputated. The man strongly objected to the operation, but after a few days of suffering, returned and had a part of the finger cut off. His suffering did not abate, and, after two days more, he went into a hospital and had the whole of the finger taken off. The surgeons were then of opinion that the operation had been delayed too long. So it proved. The man began to complain of stiffness of the neck, which rapidly grew worse, and in spite of repeated doses of chloral hydrate, lockjaw set in, and on July 29 he died. The surgeons insist that if he had consented to the operation immediately after the injury, he would have lived. Similar reluctance to undergo a painful ordeal has often involved a still more terrible result. A sinner who clings to his sin, and tries to get the better of it by degrees, instead of abandoning it once for all, trusting in Christ for strength, generally protracts his suffering and loses his soul. (Matt. 5:30.)

A Man Buried for a Week in a Well was rescued on July 28, at Omaha, Neb. While digging the well the sand caved in, and the man would have been smothered but for some boards under which he took refuge. It was at first supposed that he must be dead, and the coroner and undertaker were summoned. Digging was commenced to extricate the body. The operation caused the boards above him to sink in a threatening manner, and the man, fearing they would give way, attracted the attention of the diggers and notified them of his being alive. They easily perceived the danger to him of continuing their efforts, and therefore suspended the attempt to reach him directly, and commenced to tunnel toward him. After working two days and nights they succeeded in getting a tube to his place of confinement, which was fifty-eight feet below the surface of the earth. Through this tube small quantities of nourishing food were passed to him to sustain life. He was then able to communicate with his rescuers, and warned them that the slightest motion would bring down the sand upon him. A long box, open at both ends, and large enough to admit the man's body was made and pushed through the cutting toward him. Through this a rope was passed, which the man tied around him under the arms. He then crept into the box and was drawn through it into the tunnel, and so after being immured for seven days, he once more saw the light of the sun. The excitement in the neighborhood was intense, and the man was overwhelmed with congratulations when he was delivered. In his case, unlike that of the rescue of sinners through Christ, there were no discussions about free will and predestination. When the rope was passed to him he attached himself to it and was saved. The sinner sometimes fails to perceive that his faith serves the same purpose of availing himself of Christ's finished work. (Rom. 5:2.)

The Troubles of a German Immigrant were indignantly described in a New York court last week. When the German steamer arrived at her dock on Tuesday, a stalwart young German pushed through the crowd and made his way to the steamer's side. He closely scanned the passengers, and at length his eyes rested on a pretty woman, whom he clasped in his arms with demonstrations of joy and love. A few hours afterwards, however, he applied for her arrest, and the next day appeared in court to give evidence against her. He said that they were betrothed in the Fatherland, and he came to America to earn money to be married, leaving the woman behind. He sent her small sums from time to time to help support her, and finally, when he had a home well furnished for her reception, he sent her money to pay her passage out, and begged her to come. He calculated by which steamer she could come, and went to meet her. To his amazement she came accompanied by her husband, to whom she had been married more than a year and whose passage had been paid with the money he had sent her from time to time for her support. He wanted her imprisoned for obtaining money by false pretences. The woman's perfidy was disgraceful, but even it was not so wicked as is that of some who profess to belong to Christ, yet are married to the world and spend their lives in its pleasures and pursuits. (II Pet. 2:20.)

An Offence Against Good Form is Charged against the wife of the President. As it is mentioned by a Republican journal which applauds Mrs. Cleveland's conduct, there is no reason to doubt its veracity. It appears that among the guests at the White House last winter, was a young lady who had been a school-friend of the hostess. Personally charming, she delighted all the assemblies by her skill as a pianist, and her wonderful singing. Aristocratic society in Washington was completely taken captive by her, and hoped that her visit would be prolonged. But a rumor began to circulate that the young lady was poor, and had to earn her own livelihood. It was confirmed when she accepted the position of musical instructress in a seminary in Washington. Then aristocratic society was shocked, but it went into convulsions when Mrs. Cleveland continued to receive her old friend, and actually went driving with her. Her conduct has been condemned by ladies whose husbands and fathers belong respectively to each of the political parties. It is stated that several consultations have been held to devise some means of convincing Mrs. Cleveland that "so daring an outrage on good form" as associating with a person who has to earn her own bread will not be tolerated by the ladies of Washington. It may be hoped that they will not succeed. They should try to overcome their objections, otherwise even Heaven itself would not be a happy place to them. In the court of the King of kings, the poor of this world have a place of honor. (1 Sam. 2:8.)

The Title and Rank of a Russian Princess was recently declined by a young Canadian lady. The romantic story is told by a journal of Cleveland, O., in which city an interview between her and her suitor occurred on July 28. Two years ago, while traveling in north Germany, the young lady, who comes from Chatham, Ont., and her companions, were detained by snow-drifts in a small country village. They could not speak the dialect of the village, and would have been much embarrassed but for the help of a Russian gentleman, who spoke English fluently, and interpreted for them. He became quite intimate with the Canadians, and finally asked permission to visit them, as he intended coming to America. He gave them his address in Russia, and references to persons of the highest rank. He said that he was a noble of high rank, distantly related to the imperial family, was commander of a Russian brigade, a member of the Czar's personal staff, and was enormously wealthy. He seemed particularly anxious that his social and financial position should be investigated. On meeting the lady at Cleveland last month, he at once renewed the acquaintance, and made her an offer of marriage. To his astonishment, he was rejected. It is stated that inquiries had been made by the lady's family, at the noble's suggestion, which fully confirmed his statements as to his rank and wealth, but they extended further, and elicited the information that his moral character was bad, and this secured his rejection. Probably his astonishment arose from an opinion that his rank and wealth were sufficient qualifications, and that moral leprosy was of no importance. A similar mistake is made by many who expect to be received into heaven when they die. Outward qualifications and large benefactions will avail nothing without regeneration and imputed holiness. (Matt. 7:22, 23.)

BRIEF NOTES.

The National Temperance Hospital of Chicago, founded two years ago, has treated successfully seven hundred patients without alcohol.

Dr. Cullis's Faith Training College will open for its fourteenth annual course of lectures on October 1, at Beacon Hill Church, Boston, Mass.

Mr. Charles Herald has been conducting services in Bethesda Chapel, Brooklyn, N. Y. The mission is in connection with the Central Congregational Church, of which Dr. Behrends is pastor. Much good has been done.

About seventy delegates from American Young Men's Christian Associations have sailed for Stockholm, Sweden, to attend the World's Conference, commencing August 15.

The revival services conducted by Rev. Thomas Harrison in the Old John Street Methodist Church closed on Thursday last. Three thousand persons have made a profession of faith.

It is reported from Batavia that the Governor-General of the Dutch possessions in the East has prohibited the importation of all spirituous liquors into the Dutch portion of New Guinea.

A sporting man said, after hearing Ingersoll's recent oration in New York, "It's a spicy thing to laugh at for an hour, but not a very cheering doctrine to have around when there is a funeral in the house."

In Philadelphia a home for Baptist ministers is nearly ready for occupation. Deacon George Nugent, of the Second Baptist Church of Germantown, Philadelphia, left by will over $250,000 to found such a home.

A volcanic eruption at Bandaisan, fifty leagues from Yokohama, has destroyed several villages and killed 1,000 persons, including 100 visitors at the Thermal Springs. A fresh crater has formed and the eruption has not yet ceased.

The New York Y. M. C. A. has opened a Savings-Fund for the use of its members. It has proved a very helpful agency in enabling the subscribers to save small sums at frequent intervals. Since March 26 $559.60 has been received on deposit.

Merton Smith has been conducting services every night during the past month in the large gospel tent on State and Twenty-third streets, Chicago, under the Evangelization Society. The opening sermon was given by Rt. Rev. Charles Edward Cheney, D. D.

Recent advices report great progress in missionary work in some parts of China. Mr. Stanley Smith, of the China Inland Mission, reports 210 baptisms in central China at one time, and another missionary reports that he preaches to audiences, sometimes numbering 4,000.

A camp-meeting is to be held at Wilmington, Mass., September 6–16, under the direction of Rev. William A. Thurston. The following preachers and evangelists among others are expected to assist in the services: Rev. William McDonald, Rev. J. W. Hamilton, D. D., Rev. E. R. Thorndike, Rev. A. McLean.

The Young Men's Christian Association in Toronto is doing a good work. A tent has been built at Little York, a suburb, to be used as a reading-room and for gospel meetings. A great number of railway employees are connected with the works there, whom it is hoped the tent work will reach.

A time of danger for American missionaries in Corea is reported in the Shanghai journals. It seems that a Chinaman started the report that American missionaries had bought native children and killed them, using their bodies for medicine. Aid was asked and received from the foreign men-of-war in the harbor, but not until several natives had been decapitated by the mob.

HOW TO BE SAVED FROM SIN,

A New Sermon, by Pastor C. H. Spurgeon.

"Stand in awe, and sin not: commune with your own heart upon your bed, and be still. Selah. Offer the sacrifices of righteousness, and put your trust in the Lord."—Psalm 4: 4, 5.

David's Refuge in Persecution—His Four Directions to Sinners—I. Stand in Awe—Ours a Flippant Age—Reasons for Awe—A Soldier's Swoon—II. Thoughtful Self-Examination—The Subject—The Method—Bells Heard in the Night—III. A Right Approach to God—By Confession—Through Christ—IV. Exercise Faith—The Surest of all Sin-Killers—Attended with a New Nature—Christ's Hospital—The Coming Glory.

DAVID was surrounded with many wicked and cruel enemies. They touched him in a tender place when they mocked his religion, and so turned his glory into shame. They invented all kinds of lies against him; but the worst of all was that they said, "There is no help for him in God." As much as to say, "God hath cast him off; therefore, let men cast him off. He that is forsaken of the Lord is not fit to sit upon the throne of Israel; let us set up Absalom in his place." This was malice indeed.

David first made his appeal to God in prayer. Herein he showed his wisdom. You can drive a better bnsiness at the mercy-seat than in the world's jangling markets. You will get more

Relief from the Lord

than from ungodly men. To enter into debate is never so profitable as to enter into devotion. Carry not your complaint into the lower courts, but go at once to the Court of King's Bench, where the Judge of all presides. Copy David, and David's Lord, who in the days of his flesh with strong crying and tears poured out his soul before the Father.

After David had prayed, he expostulated with his adversaries. The first showed his sonship towards God, the second his brotherliness towards men. There is nothing of bitterness in the words I have read to you: they have a kindly voice in them. If his foes had been at all reasonable, they would have listened to his pleadings; but it is to be feared they were otherwise minded. He urges them to cease from sin, and he teaches them the way to do so. In four sentences he helps them to escape from their evil ways, and to become better men. Upon these four precepts I would speak this morning as the Holy Spirit shall give me utterance, trusting, hoping, believing that many who desire a better life may find it while I speak. Here are four stepping-stones across the filthy slough of sin; may you mark them well, and step from one to the other by the help of God's Spirit, till you reach the other shore, and stand on safe and clean ground!

I. First, *feel reverent awe:* "Stand in awe." It might be translated, "Tremble, and sin not." Awe is not a common emotion now. This is

A Flippant Age.

Men are rather triflers than tremblers. If there be any doctrine which has peculiar weight and solemnity about it, they try to pare it down to less terrible proportions. Sin is not exceeding sinful to them, nor its punishment exceeding terrible. They would not have us know the terrors of the Lord, though by these very terrors we persuade men. But true religion must have a savor of awe about it: "My heart standeth in awe of Thy word," is the expression of one that knows God, and is reconciled to Him. Let me say, then, to you who have been thoughtless and careless about your souls until now—we earnestly desire you to consider these words: "Stand in awe."

Remember, there is a God: whatever you may desire, or others may declare, there is a God who is everywhere present, at all times. He has seen all your evil ways, and heard all your hard speeches. No night is so dark as to hide from His eye; no chamber so retired as to shut Him out. He has even read your thoughts and imaginations. He notes all, and forgets nothing. Remember, that this God, who is everywhere and sees everything, is your Judge. He is pure and holy, and cannot bear iniquity. He is angry with the wicked every day, and will surely visit them for their transgressions. Every sinful act shall have its recompense of reward. Do not doubt it. The world is all in a tangle now, but there will be a day when the Lord will draw out a straight thread for each man.

Stand in awe of God because he is infinitely good. To me personally, some little time ago, the Lord drew very near in a most special and memorable providence. As I saw the hand of the Lord stretched out so marvellously, I felt my very flesh creep, not with alarm, but with a joyful awe of One who could work so tenderly and condescendingly for His tried servant. I knew that He was God by His marvellously gracions care over me, and nearness to my soul in adversity. God has dealt with me very graciously. Oh, His great goodness! A sense of it is overwhelming. We fear and tremble for all the goodness which the Lord makes to pass before us. Think of sin forgiven, of righteousness imputed, of spiritual life imparted, of that life preserved, supplied, nurtured. Think of providence with all mindful foresight, and abounding supplies. The love of God should make us reverent as angels, and humble as penitents. If the impudence of pride might dare to insult justice, yet it should scorn to injure love.

A Soldier's Swoon.

My dear hearers, stand in awe in reference to *a future state.* You do not doubt the truth which the Holy Spirit has revealed, that when you die you will not cease to be. There will be a resurrection of the dead, both of the just and of the unjust; "for we must all appear before before the judgment-seat of Christ." Oh, that all persons would remember this wherever they go! I have heard of a soldier—I think he was employed in the survey of Palestine—who was in the valley of Jehoshaphat, outside Jerusalem, and some one remarked that it was reported by some that this valley would be the scene of the last judgment, and in that place the multitudes would be gathered. The soldier, hearing this, said, "What a crowd there will be! I shall be there, and I will sit on this stone." He sat down to realize the scene, and his imagination acted so powerfully that he seemed to himself to be among the throng, and to behold the great white throne. He was seen to swoon, and fall to the ground. Do you wonder? If any one of us could, in our inmost souls, behold that scene, should we not be overcome? I wish I could so speak this morning that some of you would picture that last tremendons day, for which all others were made.

O my dear hearers, do not forget that you have to live in a future state, and that you will see Him who died upon the cross, seated on the throne, in that day when all nations shall be gathered before Him, and He shall divide them, the one from the other, as the shepherd divideth the sheep from the goats. May the thought of the eternal reward also rest on your minds! Hear ye, even now, that word of the King to the righteous—"Come, ye blessed of my father, inherit the kingdom prepared for you from the foundation of the world." Hear, also, that dread sentence to those on His left hand, "Depart from Me, ye cursed, into everlasting fire, prepared for the devil and his angels." Oh, think of these things, and "stand in awe, and sin not!"

II. In the second place, David admonished the ungodly to practice

Thoughtful Self-Examination.

"Commune with your heart upon your bed, and be still. I am not trying, my dear hearer, to preach a sermon this morning, but I am longing to take you by the hand, and to lead you in the right way. I pray the Holy Spirit to make you willing to follow my gentle guidance. My dear friend, you are now asked to *think about yourself*—"commune with your own heart." When once men choose the way of evil, they run in it with their eyes shut. They do not wish to consider; it is easier to go blindly on. They will think about their worldly concerns, their profits and losses, their pleasures and amusements; but they refuse seriously to consider their condition before God. O my friend, think of what you are, and where you are, what you have done, what you are doing, what it will all lead to! Are you such a fool that you will not consider? *Then put on the cap and bells,* and wear motley, and take to

Your Proper Trade.

Especially think of the state of your heart. This is the vital point. Are you right with God? Do you serve your Maker? Have you truly repented of former sin? Have you fled to Christ as your refuge? Have you been born again? Are you the subject of sanctifying grace? "Commune with your own heart" upon these essential points. He that would have his face clean must look in a glass to see his spots; and he that would have his heart clean must gaze into the looking glass of God's Word, that he may discover his secret faults.

I commend this text most heartily to your immediate practice. If you are unsaved—think rather than sleep. The tendency of most men with regard to eternal things is to go to sleep, and let matters drift: I pray you do not so. I dare not let you take your rest while all is wrong with you. Sleep, if you like, in a house that is on a blaze; sleep, if you like, in a ship that is settling down, and rapidly sinking; but I charge you, do not sleep while you are an unforgiven man, and your soul is nearing the eternal woe.

I beseech you, give yourselves space for thought, before thought becomes the worm of eternal misery to you. Remember, before you hear that voice from heaven which spoke to the rich man in hell, and said to him, "Son, remember." Ye slaves of fashion and frivolity, think I pray you! Ye serfs of daily money-grubbing rest a while, and hear what God the Lord shall speak to you! You can hardly hear the great bell of St. Paul's when the traffic is thundering around, but it sounds solemnly in the stillness of night. We who live in the more remote suburbs hear Big Ben of Westminister at night but we seldom note it amid the stir and noise of the day. Do give an opportunity for the eternal voices to pierce the clamors of the hour. Do for God's sake, and for your own soul's sake, hear what wisdom teaches concerning everlasting things!

III. Very briefly, let us note that David gives a third piece of advice, which in essence means

Approach God Aright.

"Offer the sacrifices of righteousness." Now, I do not quite know what David himself may have intended by it, but this is how I interpret it. Come to God; come to God in His own way; come as Israel came to the tabernacle in the wilderness, bringing their sacrifices with them.

When they brought their sacrifices, the first thing they did was to lay their hand on the victim, and make a confession of sin. Come, then, with broken and contrite hearts unto the Lord. "The sacrifices of God are a broken spirit." Own your shortcomings and transgressions. Do not cloak or excuse your sins. Get to your chamber, and tell the Lord what you have done. Pour out your hearts before Him, turn them upside down, as it were, and let all flow out, even to the dregs. Confess your pride and unbelief, your Sabbath-breaking, your dishonesty, your falsehcod, your disobedience to parents, your every breach of divine law; whatsoever you have done amiss, confess it before Him, and thus go to Him in the only way in which He can receive you, even as sinners owning your guilt.

Go also to the Lord with gracious desires to be rid of sin. Entreat reconciliation, saying, "I would no longer be what I have been. I throw down the weapons of my rebellion, I pluck out the plumes of my pride; O Lord, I stand before Thee, guilty, and I pray Thee forgive me, and then rid me of the tyrant evils which now rule me so terribly! Oh, that I may sin no more! If I have been a drunkard, help me from this day to relinquish the intoxicating cup; if I have been a swearer, wash out my mouth; may

:eforth, speak nothing but that which will cceptable to Thee! If I have been unchaste, nse my mind, that I may keep my body !" In this way come to God with contrite ts. How much do I long that you may r nigh to God with true repentance and ty resolves to conquer sin!

ie main thing, however, is to bring unto Lord the offering which He has divinely ointed and provided. You know what that There is one sacrifice of righteousness with-which you cannot be accepted. Come to by faith in Jesus Christ, plead the precious d of atonement, and say, "My Lord for His sake who died upon the tree, receive Thy derer, and now be pleased to grant me that ntance and remission of sins which He is ted to give." If you come through Christ, will never be cast out. The Father will re-e any sinner that pleads the name of Jesus; Jesus is willing that you should plead His e. He died on purpose to be the propitia-for our sins: God grant that you may pt Him as such!

/. I must now close with the fourth point, ch is, in some respects, the most important:

Exercise Faith.

'hen holy awe and thoughtful self-communion ied us to seek the Lord, then we are prepared he great precept which follows. It is the com-d of the gospel in its Old Testament form: it your trust in the Lord." First, trust Him 'illing to receive you, to forgive you, to ac-. you, and to bless you. Especially trust in Lord as He reveals Himself in the person of Son Jesus Christ. In Him you see love ten out in capital letters. "Put your trust he Lord" as having provided the one sacri-for sin, whereby He has put away for ever he sins of those who believe in Him. God ist, and the justifier of him that believeth. eve that the precious blood can make you ter than snow, scarlet sinner as you are. ne with that daring trust which ventures all n the bare promise of a faithful God. Say, will go in unto the King, and if I perish, I sh." If you do not trust in Christ, you must ost; therefore come and

Try the Divine Way.

rust in the Lord, next, that by the work of Holy Spirit He can renew you. The glori-Lord, who made the world out of nothing, make something out of you yet. If you are en to anger, the Holy Spirit can make you n and loving. If you have been defiled with urity, He can make you pure in heart. If have been grovelling, He can elevate you. ay be addressing a forlorn man, who thinks t nothing can be made of him. I tell you, have no idea what God can do with you. can put heavenly treasure in earthen vessels. can set you at last among the heavenly choris-, that your voice, sweeter than that of angels, y be heard amongst their symphonies.

ly closing theme is this—it has been asserted certain of the modern school that we preach salvation by a simple intellectual operation alvation by merely believing a certain doc-ial statement. This is their way of stating, mis-stating, justification by faith, which we assuredly preach, and preach most distinctly l confidently. We are not responsible for ir caricatures of our teaching, but we would moved thereby to be more and more explicit. far as faith is an intellectual operation, it is iple enough; but simple faith is no trifle. e is a simple element, but it has a measure-s power. Connected with faith there are ces of the mightiest kind for influencing racter and purifying life.

Faith is the Surest of all Sin-Killers;

fact, its tendency is to extirpate sin. The ral and spiritual change which accompanies h, and grows out of it, is of the most remark-e kind. Faith's work in the soul is some-ng to be wondered at, and to be admired to eternity. For, mark, when a man believes he Lord Jesus Christ, when he believes that us so died for him that he is effectually re-deemed, when he believes that the Lord Jesus has cleansed him, and that he is saved, the result upon his heart and life cannot be com-monplace. So divine a persuasion operates upon his whole nature. He is filled with ador-ing gratitude, and that gratitude breeds an intense love, which fervent love sets itself to work for the glory of God by

The Purification

of the soul from sin. "My Jesus died because of my sin," says the pardoned sinner, "therefore no sin shall abide in my heart. Away, O sin! Away, for ever." Some favorite sin cries, "Let me lodge within thee," but he cries, "It cannot be, for I love Jesus." Sin slew our Saviour; how can we be on friendly terms with it? We hate it with perfect hatred. Sin pleadeth, "Is it not a little one?" But the grateful heart sees great evil in a little sin, since the great Father abhors all iniquity. Nothing creates more indignation and revenge against sin than a grateful sense of "free grace and dying love." Surely this is no mean help toward moral purification.

Faith feels that she cannot buy the transient joys of earth at the cost of an immortal soul. Faith destroys the power of temptation. When Satan says, "You are in trouble, and here is an easy way of escape: only do a little wrong, and you will get a great good." "No," says faith,

It is God's Business

to get me out of my trouble, and I will not go to the devil for His aid." "Ah!" says Satan, "everybody else does so!" Faith answers, "I have to do with nobody but God, and that which is right." Moreover, faith is always at-tended with a new nature. That is a point never to be forgotten. No man has faith in God of a true kind unless he has been born again. Faith in God is one of the first indica-tions of regeneration. Now, if you have a new and holy nature, you are no longer moved tow-ard sinful objects as you were before. The things that you once loved you now hate, and, therefore, you will not run after them. You can hardly understand it, but so it is, that your thoughts and tastes are totally changed. You long for that very holiness which once it was irksome to hear of, and you loathe those very pursuits which were once your delights. When the Lord renews us it is not half done; it is a total and radical change.

If there were no work of the Holy Spirit con-nected with faith, and if faith were nothing more than human assent to truth, we might be blameworthy for preaching salvation through it; but since faith leads the van in the graces of the Spirit of God, and turns the rudder of the soul, we are more and more concerned to place faith where God places it, and we say without hesita-tion, "Believe on the Lord Jesus Christ, and thou shalt be saved." Remember you will thus be saved from the power of sin, and from the practice of sin, by being saved from the love of sin. Our Lord

Jesus Has Opened a Hospital,

and into it He receives all manner of sick folk: yet He does not receive them that they may continue sick, but that He may heal them, and make them whole.

If by believing in Christ Jesus you receive a change of nature, and live a different life, and stand at the last day accepted in the Beloved, what bliss it will be! What joy will be yours when Jesus comes, when His smile shall light up the universe, and when He shall acknowl-edge you before the angels of God! You were with Him in His humiliation; you shall be with Him in His exaltation; you loved Him and served Him here below; you shall sit upon His throne, and reign with Him for ever and ever. Ah! then, whatever little you may have suffered for His sake will be as nothing in com-parison with the exceeding weight of glory. Whatever struggling of heart and pain of soul you felt in escaping from the sin which enthrall-ed you will be your joy when the result is seen in your eternal perfection. The bliss of behold-ing the face of our Beloved will be heaven enough for us. Even now I feel eager to quit this feeble body at the bare thought of being with the Bridegroom of my soul.

"Mine eyes shall see Him in that day,
The God that died for me;
And all my rising bones shall say,
Lord, who is like to thee?"

May you and I behold our Redeemer when He shall stand in the latter day upon the earth!

[The prayers of the readers of this journal are requested for the blessing of God upon its Editors, and those whose sermons, articles or labors for Christ are printed in it; and that its circulation may be used by the Holy Spirit for the conversion of many sinners and the quickening of God's peo-ple. Dr. Talmage and Mr. Spurgeon especially request prayer every Sunday morning on behalf of their labors.]

GEMS FROM NEW BOOKS.

ASCENDING A MOUNTAIN IN MEXICO.*

NINE miles below the city of Zacatecas the railroad begins to rise, by a triumph of magni-ficent engineering, up a grade of one hundred and seventy-five feet to the mile, making on the passage some of the most abrupt curves conceiv-able. It recalled the old Colorado cañons, only that here we went around the hill-side instead of plunging over precipices and bridging gorges with trestles. The powerful engine panted like some hard-pressed animal, and the train of heavy cars dragged wearily up after it. We forgot fatigue, forgot fear, forgot—what is harder to forget then either—supper, and crowded the narrow platforms with an excite-ment almost painful. At last, with one mighty final effort, we turned the last sharp mountain spur, and with the Bufa rising high on the left, its enormous crest of rock above like the dorsal fin of some fossile monster, with a glow of red gold over all the western sky and the evening star shining palely in the east, we rested on the crest on the hill above the dark, little, sleeping town, with only three faint points of light to indicate its location, or give any sign of life.

An Answer Through a Grating.

"Barter and the obtaining of gold for Spain," which was all that Cortes and the Spaniards asked, when they landed in Mexico, have left a stamp upon the country which one generation of comparatively tranquil independence cannot be expected to efface. A traveller who passed through Mexico mny years ago, saw a face peering out of a window upon a vista of won-derful beauty. Whether prisoner or recluse he knew not, but said, through the grating: "How beautiful!" "*Transeuntibus*" (to those who pass by) was the laconic answer. So has it has been with Mexico. Beautiful to those who robbed her, beautiful to the tourist, her real condition is one which depresses her own people, whose poverty, ignorance, and loneli-ness, make them the most pitiable, as they are certainly the most kindly and polite people on this continent.

The Houses of the Poor.

The very poor live within four walls of dried mud on a floor of the same material. Any-where upon this a fire of mesquite faggots may be kindled, to cook the universal tortilla, which forms almost the sole food of a large class. A few crockery utensils for cooking and eating, a hand-brush for sweeping, some water-jars and baskets, perhaps a bundle of maguey fibres for a bed, and the furniture is complete. The za-rape is a cloak by day and a covering by night; the smoke flies out of open door or four-paned window, as it listeth; the floor is at once chair and table; and that is all—or rather it is not all; for with it stay patience, kindness, and content, three graces hard to account for with such meagre plenishing.

The Homes of the Rich

are on a magnificent scale of luxury. An arched driveway leads from the street to the central

* From Mexico: Picturesque, Political, Progressive. By Mary Elisabeth Blake and Margaret F. Sullivan. 228 Pages. Published by *Charles T. Dillingham*, 718 and 720 Broadway, New York.

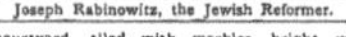
Joseph Rabinowitz, the Jewish Reformer.

A Missionary's Visit to an Invalid Jew in Smyrna.

courtyard, tiled with marbles, bright with flowers, statues, and splashing fountains, surrounded by all the appliances which wealth can suggest to indolence. Around this inner pleasaunce the house rises in a series of light arched galleries resting on carved pillars, communicating by broad outer stairways of stone, and opening into every room by windows and doors of plain or stained glass. Vines and hanging plants cover the low stone balustrades; and inside the broad dimly lighted salons and chambers, whatever luxurious taste can bring to aid comfort is lavishly supplied. A host of servants divide among them those more personal services which our rigid aristocrats prefer to render themselves, and a clap of the hands brings instantly a swift and silent attendant. Below, under the arches, on the ground floor, horses stand in their open stalls; there are carriages, store-rooms, and servants' quarters; so that when the great gates leading to the street are closed, all the elements of luxurious living are complete within.

JOSEPH RABINOWITZ.

(See Portrait.)

A REMARKABLE movement among the Jews of eastern Europe has recently attracted general attention. The leader of it is Joseph Rabinowitz, a Jew of considerable learning and strong national enthusiasm. He has gathered around him a large number of sincere Jewish converts, to whom he preaches Jesus as the Messiah, and the hope of Israel. The account of his own conversion is remarkable. It appears to have been through the direct influence of the Holy Spirit, without the intervention of human instrumentality.

He was born at Regina, in Bessarabia, in 1837, and was brought up by his grandfather, a learned Rabbi, and himself the son of a Rabbi. The old man was at great pains to instruct the boy thoroughly in the Talmud, and was so proud of his progress that he used to take him to the chief of the Chasidim, to which sect he belonged, that his proficiency might be admired. When Joseph was only ten years of age, he was sent to Orgieff, where he distinguished himself as a diligent and successful student of the Talmud. As he grew older, however, the youth separated himself from the orthodox Jews and joined the Reformers. At eighteen he married and commenced business, but two years later he lost the whole of his stock in trade by a fire. Thereupon he commenced the study of law, and settled at Kischeneff. In 1882 he paid a visit to Palestine, and was deeply moved by the spectacle of the desolation of Jerusalem. He read and re-read the closing chapters of Jewish history, and as he did so the passage, "They mocked the messengers of God, and misused His prophets until the wrath of the Lord arose against His people, till there was no remedy" (II Chron. 36: 16.), gave him cause for thought. It was then that, under the guidance of the Holy Spirit, he was led to see that in their rejection of Jesus of Nazareth the Jews filled up the cup of their iniquities, and brought upon themselves the judgments of God. He returned home full of this new light, devoted himself to the study of the New Testament, and soon began to preach. His followers continue to practice the rite of circumcision, keep the feasts, but have ceased to look for the promised Messiah, acknowledging Jesus as "Him of whom Moses and the prophets did write."

A VISIT TO A SMYRNA JEW.

(See Illustration.)

THE Rev. J. M. Eppstein, one of the agents of the Society for Promoting Christianity among the Jews, and who is stationed at Smyrna, the seat of one of the seven churches mentioned in the Book of Revelation, thus writes: "One of my casual inquirers was taken ill, and I at once set out to see him, to administer medicine to his body and the means of spiritual healing to his soul. I was amply rewarded for my trouble by the hearty welcome I received from him and his wife. It required a good deal of caution and tact to make the necessary inquiries after my friend, for the simple fact of my visiting him was quite enough to throw suspicion on him, and expose him to persecution and suffering. I could do it with a better grace on my next visit, as I stated to those from whom I sought the information that Mr. S. was very unwell, and that I wished to examine him in my medical capacity.

"I found him seriously ill, and in very low spirits. His wife, to show her gratitude to me, hospitably left the room to make a cup of coffee, and that gave us an opportunity of speaking together about the Saviour. He showed me the copy of the New Testament which I had given him, and assured me that it gave him great pleasure and comfort, although there were several things in it which he could not quite understand. I offered to explain to him some of his difficulties, but he said that his opportunities were limited, as his wife was violently opposed to the Christian religion. She retu with the coffee while we were talking, and w my friend still held the Testament in his h As she was deeply grateful to me for the p cal benefit her husband had received thr me, I took the opportunity to speak to h the Great Physician, and she did not resen remarks. Since then my friend has compl recovered, and both he and his wife are am my most promising inquirers, and neither, I lieve, is far from the Kingdom of God."

MAUD FEATHERSTONE'S LETTER

(See Illustration on page 509.)

"HERE is a letter for you, Maud," said a of quiet demeanor and plain attire, as she her sister in the hall of an aristocratic man Maud herself was in dress and manner an e opposite of her sober, sedate, elder sister. contrast between the two Misses Featherst which was always remarkable, could not been more conspicuous than it was as they s thus together in the hall near upon midn Marion had still upon her the quiet, tranqu that her watch by the bedside of a sick ser had produced, while Maud, though tired an evening's gaiety, had the sparkling eyes flushed cheeks which tell of a period of ex ment not yet subdued. Maud took the le gave a cry of pleasure as she recognized handwriting, and turned into a luxuri furnished room to devour the contents of missive.

Many a time had letters in that firm, m line caligraphy filled the gay maiden's with joy. She was proud of her lover, w talents and learning were fast winning for distinction in a career which might ultim place him in the Senate, if not in the W House itself. Gerald Cameron was a man w many women had admired, and Maud Fea stone's delight in winning him was enha by the thought of the envy with which he umph had filled her rivals. And he was d voted lover, too, whose attentions were con and unwearied. The expression on her fa she took the letter from its envelope, and b to read it, not having even the patience to herself, was one of unalloyed pleasure.

A few moments later she had thrown the ter to the floor, and flinging herself on an o man was weeping bitterly. Her sister Ma found her so half an hour afterward, her fr shaking with sobs, and her hands cold trembling. Any one who saw her then co have recognized the beauty of an hour …ead it," was all she … in response to her …ympathetic inquir…ing as she spoke to …hed letter at her …rion picked up the …nd read the com…on which had so her sister.

…bly Gerald Cameron …mething, when he …, of the shock it …roduce. He had a …uty to perform, and …red to do it tender… first words were of love such as he …n made, but they …ipered by a reserve in his letters, which … sentences explain… strange, wonderful …ce had come to him …ad changed himself whole future since wrote to his be… His most intimate … fellow student at had recently re… from a European …d was a changed Gay and frivolous …e set out, he had …ck an earnest Chris…tent on devoting his time, fortune, that he had to the of Christ, and was a theological sem…reparing himself for in a heathen land. was the first of his …nds he had sought …aded with for Christ. …is friend's influence and later on his own …, Gerald had been seek salvation, and …v rejoicing in Christ. He had renounced …ld, with its gaieties and pleasures, and …v no ambition but to spend and be spent …ord's service. His affection for Maud …iminished; he was anxious that she, too, share in the joy and happiness which …nsformed him, but he was aware how …t he was now from the man to whom … given her troth, and, therefore, he could …d her bound by her promise.

…s a delicate, manly letter, and Marion, who …y experience what that joy was which …e writer's heart as he wrote, loved him …words. He was her brother now—more …ther than marriage with her sister could …ade him. Oh that the conversion of her …or which she had longed and prayed, …ow be achieved through the influence of … whom she loved!

…r Maud," she said, throwing her arms …her sister's neck, "why do you weep? …is more lovable now than ever."

…, to you, perhaps; but not to me. I hate …sitively hate him, for his stupidity. Only …k of what he is giving up! Think of … might be! and now, I suppose, he will …acher in some little poking church; or, … get killed and eaten by savages. Of … shall give him up. I am not going to …ny life like that. It is positively fanati… should not dream of marrying him now. …rite and tell him so this very night, and …ake care to make him know that I des…n."

…s useless to plead with her. Her antipa…religion was strengthened by the thought …ad robbed her of her lover; and though, …ks and months afterward, Marion sought …eans to win her to Christ, she utterly failed. Eventually she made what was considered a brilliant marriage, and drained the cup of pleasure to the dregs. Some two years after that, Gerald Cameron, then the faithful pastor of a Christian church, sought and won the affection of Marion, and Maud cynically declared them thoroughly suited to each other. She continued to despise them and their work until trouble came upon her. Deserted and disgraced, cast out by worldly society, she sought a refuge with them, and found that, like their Master, they were prepared to welcome the repentant sinner.

Maud Featherstone Reads Her Letter.

THE EPOCHS OF A LIFE.

A NEW SERIAL STORY.

By Rev. L. S. Keyser.

(Continued from page 494.)

A Jealous Woman.

AN engagement Hadley Madelling had made to take Belle Havelock to a literary lecture in Chapel Hall fell due on the Tuesday after that sermon of Mr. Mardont's. The fascination which the highly cultured girl exercised over him was very potent that night. The su'ject of the lecture was not connected with religion, and therefore there was an absence on her face, and in her manner of the cynical spirit which the mention of religion always brought there, and which repelled Hadley and counteracted her attraction of him. He thought he had never seen her look so beautiful, so intelligent, and so brilliant as on that evening.

In accompanying her to her home after the lecture Hadley spoke of the subject which was uppermost in his mind. He told her of the sermon he had heard, and of the result of the effort he and Dane had made to follow Mr. Mardont's advice. A sneering, contemptuous smile curled Belle's lips as she listened.

"I have been through all that," she said, as they reached her door. "I have studied several books of so-called Christian evidences, and I have read the Bible more perhaps than many believers, but I have not been convinced. Will you come in? I can show you how my line of investigation has run, and we can dip into these books together for an hour."

Hadley readily consented, and Belle took down first one book and then another from the well-filled shelves. "See," she said, opening a popular treatise in defence of Christianity, "this author begins by asserting that one of the chief causes of infidelity is *want of knowledge*, or as the author puts it, varying his phraseology, *lack of information*. You see, he begins by insulting the sceptic, and so I flung the book aside, and have never looked into it since. But the Bible must stand on its own merits. What does it signify if it is bolstered up by a huge pyramid of 'historical evidences,' if it does not bear the impress of the divine mind upon its ethical teachings? Now, there are certain men held up in Scripture as models for imitation. Abraham is called 'the friend of God,' but we cannot forget the falsehoods that he told in Egypt, or his harsh treatment of Hagar and her son in sending them out into the wilderness. The Bible teaches that Jacob was arbitrarily chosen to fulfill God's purposes, while he hated Esau, and was one of the most selfish, calculating and perfidious plotters of history. David is especially extolled. Have you ever read the dying requests of this so-called "sweet singer of Israel?"

"I do not remember, although I know something about his vindictive spirit from reading the imprecatory Psalms," replied Hadley.

"His dying anathemas are entirely in keeping with the impression that you have received from his writings. Look," she said, taking down a well-worn Bible from the bookcase, and turning the leaves rapidly, "here are David's instructions to Solomon, his successor on the throne. Solomon is enjoined to take vengeance on his father's enemies. David from motives of policy had forgiven them, but Joab's hoar hair is not to go down to the grave in peace. Shimei who had David's pledge that he would not kill him, is to be brought down to the grave in blood. And Solomon executed both behests. Look at the laws of Moses. Venial faults, mere errors, if committed against the priests or the temple are punished with death, while vile crimes can be expiated by an offering."

"That is what puzzles me. The Bible is held up as the rule and standard of morality, yet cruel wars of extermination, immorality, slavery, and polygamy are mentioned there with approval, tacit or explicit, and men who practice them in these days can quote passages in their defence."

"True, and what is needed now," said Belle, "is that some man of logical and forensic abilities undertake to expose the false ethical teachings of this book, and strike the fetters from the minds of the uninformed and priest-ridden." And she bent her flashing eyes upon him with a look of expectancy.

It was not difficult for him to interpret the significance of her words and looks. "And you think that I ought to be the one to begin the work of emancipation?" he remarked.

"I do," she answered.

"As soon as an opportunity affords—"

"Create an opportunity."

"In a few weeks an oration will be expected of me in Chapel Hall on Saturday morning, and then—"

"Will be the opportune time."

"Yes."

"Will you take advantage of it?" she asked, her eyes full of interrogation points.

"I will see."

A shadow of disappointment flew across her face like a cloud at his evasive answer; but she said: "I shall anxiously wait for the time."

He walked home in a deeply meditative mood. This girl exercised a commanding influence over his intellect. She had the faculty of placing every objection to the Bible in a strong, electric light, so to speak, and under the new impetus she had given him he now felt that he had gained sufficient courage to make the long-projected assault on the Bible.

Then his thoughts reverted again to the strange and heterogeneous emotions that the girl had aroused in him. While she had been steadily gaining a more potent influence over his intellect, her power over his conjugal affections was becoming more and more minimized. It was only when he thought of Miss Winters that his pulses tingled with an emotion at once passionate and tender, and her name could not be mentioned in his hearing without causing an uncomfortable flow of color to his face. Yet he was somewhat in a quandary. His attentions to Belle Havelock had revealed to him the fact that she was taking a deep personal interest in him, which was of a more potent quality than mere pleasure in intellectual affiliation. Although he was not endowed with a superabundant amount of vanity, this conclusion was forced upon him, and if it were true he disliked to cease his attentions to her and transfer them to another. What reason could he give for a sudden cessation of his calls at the Havelock residence? For awhile he oscillated between two lines of conduct, not knowing to which of the girls he should pay his addresses.

Yet, with his customary decision of character, he finally decided to seek the society of Miss Winters, and cultivate her acquaintance, and at the same time he might perhaps occasionally visit Belle for intellectual stimulus and social pleasure without compromising himself. He had purposely refrained from making an appointment with the latter for Sunday evening, because he wished to be free to call upon Miss Winters if he should conclude that it was desirable to do so. When he reached his room that evening his resolution was formed.

In order to make an appointment with Miss Winters for the coming Sabbath evening the young student had recourse to one of the social customs of the college. The next day he said to his room-mate: "George, you have been introduced to Miss Winters, have you not?"

"Certainly; you introduced me yourself, old Forgetfulness."

"Oh, yes, I remember. Will you carry a note to her for me this afternoon?"

"Of course I will. I shall gladly be your Mercury."

Hadley seated himself at his writing-desk, and after destroying a number of sheets of note-paper, he at last had his brief missive complete. It was a simple communication, asking courteously for the pleasure of accompanying her to church on the following Sunday evening, if his proposition did not conflict with any other engagements which she might have made.

George took the note and hurried to the house in which the young lady roomed. When the door was opened he inquired for Miss Winters, who was immediately sent for, and appeared the next moment in the hall-way. After interchanging the usual civilities he handed her the note, which Hadley had intrusted to him, and said:

"I am requested to remain for a reply."

"Please step in," she said, with a smile, as she took the missive.

He was shown into the parlor, where he remained while the young lady retired to her own room to read the letter and pen an answer. When she came back he noticed that there was a pleased flush, which reminded him of a summer sunset, upon her cheeks, and a smile wreathed her lips, and he leaped instinctively to the conclusion that her response to Hadley's epistle was a favorable one. "No wonder," he thought, "that Hadley admires this beautiful girl!"

Never before had she appeared so fascinating to George's eyes as she did then, in her light evening dress. He was loathe to leave immediately, feeling that it would be delightful to have an half-hour's conversation with so charming a girl; but, as he was acting in the capacity of a messenger for another, he feared that it would be straining the rules of social decorum to linger. After exchanging a few commonplaces with her, he bowed himself out of the room, and reluctantly took his departure.

Young Madelling was waiting his friend's return in a state of nervous anxiety. His hand trembled visibly as he took the small, rose-tinted envelope from George. With breathless haste his eye scanned the neat, brief lines, and, when he had read the missive through, a sigh of relief escaped his lips. A heavy burden of suspense was lifted from his mind.

"Why, Hadley," said Dane, after a respectful pause, "you were actually pale! I hope that your anxiety is allayed."

"Yes, the note is entirely satisfactory," replied Hadley, with a smile.

"I congratulate you," said George, warmly. "You have reason to feel elated, Hadley, for you will appear with the most beautiful and clever girl in the college or town. Let me tell you confidentially, that if you had not made me your Mercury this afternoon, I should have been tempted to make an appointment with the bright being myself."

"Ah! you will be my rival yet, I fear," returned Hadley, with a rather mechanical attempt at hilarity.

Had Belle Havelock known of that invitation and its acceptance, she would have better understood a question that was puzzling her. She could easily perceive that Hadley admired her, and was susceptible to her charms. He had given clearer proof of it on that Tuesday evening than at any previous interview. Yet he had not suggested any future meeting. Why had he not proposed taking her to hear Mr. Mardont next Sunday evening, as he seemed so much interested in the preacher, and as her experience of the college customs told her would have been a natural thing for a young man to do, who had spent the evening in so intimate and personal a conversation as they had enjoyed?

Still, why should she care about what he did or did not do? She sat down to think the matter out. Was this young Madelling becoming more to her than other young men had been whom she had known? She examined herself, and she had to acknowledge that he had stirred depths in her being that no one had ever touched before. Mere intellectual affinity was not sufficient to explain the emotion his presence and words aroused. Was this love? Belle's cheeks flushed as the thought rose in her mind, and her heart beat quickly. If this was really love, was it reciprocated? No word or sign could she recollect that encouraged any such hope. The survey of their past intercourse brought her to the point from which she started: Why had he not proposed to take her to church the next Sunday night? Perhaps he intended to do so, and would write her before Sunday. And with that thought to support her, Belle went to bed and to sleep.

Each day brought its disappointment, for no letter of invitation came. Belle could no[t un]derstand it, and there was growing up in [her] mind a feeling of resentment at the app[arent] slight. True, she had no claim on the young [man], but the discovery she had made of her own re[gard] for him would be, to one so proud and hau[ghty] as she, a humiliation, if it was not retu[rned]. No one knew of it; but *she* knew, and her [self-]respect would be hurt, which was really a bitter humiliation to one so independent a[nd] careless about the opinions of other people [as] to have them despise her. With her own [con]science approving her she could have met [scorn] and ridicule with contempt, but to know [that] she had given love where it was not apprec[iated] nor sought would be an unutterable shame [and] would make her loathe herself. She gre[w al]most fierce as she thought of it, and th[ough] she could never stoop to woo, she resolved [that] such power as she knew she had, should b[e put] forth to the utmost to bring Hadley to he[r feet] as a lover. No other result could save her [from] self-reproach.

Not until Sunday morning dawned di[d she] abandon hope of receiving an invitation fo[r the] evening. None came, but she must see H[adley]. Perhaps he wished to go with Dane to [the] church, as they had gone together last [week]. He would surely be going, and she decided [that] she would go too, if only to solve her do[ubts]. Accordingly as the hour for service approa[ched] she dressed, and walked alone to the Ma[in] Street church, taking her seat in the rear [of the] auditorium a few moments after the mi[nister] had entered the pulpit. The audience wa[s] gathering rapidly, and soon all the pews, e[xcept] a few at the side of the pulpit, were occu[pied]. With an anxious eye Belle watched every arrival.

What was it that caused her to start, and turn pale, as if her heart had refused to [send] the vitalizing fluid to her face? A young c[ouple] were just walking up the aisle, brushing a[lmost] against her, and almost instinctively her vigilant eye recognized them. They were [Had]ley Madelling and Miss Winters, the g[irl he] had saved on the railroad bridge. She had [been] pointed out to Belle a few days before. [The] couple were conducted to one of the pe[ws at] the right of the pulpit, so that they sat [facing] the main body of the audience at right a[ngles]. Their position gave Belle a good opportun[ity to] watch them. Her quick eye detected tha[t self-]consciousness about Hadley's manner whi[ch in]dicated more plainly than words tha[t his] thoughts were upon the fair girl by his [side]. There was a deference, almost a tenderne[ss, in] the way he saw her comfortably seated, [that] told Belle all too plainly that she was, f[or the] time at least, forgotten; and her heart [sank] within her with an agony that she had [never] known before.

Here, then, was the explanation of Ha[dley's] apparent neglect of her. Even on the pr[evious] Tuesday evening, he must have had th[is ap]pointment with Miss Winters in view, and [that] was the reason he had not spoken about [calling] again at the Havelock residence. Belle [saw] through it all. After the first pang, which [was] one of genuine grief, another feeling suc[ceed]ed. It was that of jealously, fierce and v[indic]tive. She could not submit tamely to [the] thought of a rival in the young man's [affec]tions; for in this light she regarded [Miss] Winters. She did not believe that H[adley Madel]ling would seek the society of a young [lady] for mere social enjoyment. He was [too] busy with his studies to spend his time i[n that] way, and therefore she believed that an[y one] who would be able to lure the industrious [stu]dent from his college work, must have a[roused] his interest to an unwonted degree.

Although the services were of an unu[sually] interesting character that evening, holdin[g the] audience with spell-bound attention, the [burn]ing thoughts fell unheeded upon Belle H[ave]lock's preoccupied mind. With the eyes o[f a fal]con she watched the changing expressions o[f the] faces of Hadley Madelling and his compa[nion].

the close of the services, she stood for a oments intently watching the young couple ad engrossed her attention all the evening. noted the young man's polite and almost r attention to his companion's comfort. ach act, each look, penetrated her heart . dagger. She hurried from the church s she reached her own room, flung herself r couch, and gave way to a flood of passion- eeping.

(To be Continued.)

THE FEAST OF TABERNACLES.

By Mrs. M. Baxter.

Lesson for August 19, Levit. 23:33—44. Golden Text, Ps. 118:15.

Holidays under the Theocracy—Distinctly igious—The Passover Commemorative of t Deliverance—Pentecost a Recognition of ine Faithfulness—Tabernacles Commemora- of Nomadic National Life—Suspension of La- —Type of Indwelling of God—Manner of ping the Feast—A Great Increase of Offerings he Peculiar Temporary Shelter—The Eighth of the Feast Made Memorable, John 7:37— Feast to be Kept in the Millennium.

:he rule of God over His people Israel, was no distinction made between political piritual; the government was immediately irectly under the control of God, and His nd word were sought in all particulars. it came to pass that the seasons of the vere not marked by Easter, Whitsuntide, st and Christmas public holidays, but by special feasts unto the Lord. The Pass- which was the first and was celebrated in pring, the beginning of the Jewish year, commemorate God's deliverance of His e from the land of Egypt and from the of bondage. This was calculated to stir gratitude of His people's hearts and fill with thankful joy. Would that our ob- ice of Good Friday and Easter Day were an universal thanksgiving of saved souls ghout the land for redemption through ood of the Lamb! The second feast is erfully significant; it is

The Feast of Pentecost;

the offering of the first fruits, not memo- ke the Passover. It is a type of how a soul, after being forgiven, and washed in ood of Jesus, is now in a position to give hing to God which He can accept. "Ye eat neither bread, nor parched corn, nor ears, until the self-same day that ye have ht an offering unto your God. (Lev. 23: Seek ye *first* the kingdom of God and His ousness" (Matt. 6:33). It is our glorious ge under the gospel to present our bodies e are) a living sacrifice to God (Rom. 12: d to count all that we have, not our own, is. The Pentecost was to be seven sab- after the Passover. Seven is the perfect er: here are seven sevens; we never en- lly into the rest of God until it is a settled r that all we are and all we have is God's, willed and disposed of by Him. So long have a voice about ourselves and our rty, except as faithful stewards for Him, y, jealousy, coveteousness, etc., find an door in our hearts. But when all is yielded m, He puts His own Sentinel, the Holy , to guard our hearts and our thoughts. cost was the time when the Holy Ghost iven. He cannot take possession of an un- dered heart.

r the offering of the first fruits the harvest land was reaped, the first fruits, being to God, sanctified the work; it was to be under His eye, in His name, to manifest manner of God ruled over them, and what r of rule His was. Therefore, "when ye he harvest of your land, thou shalt not a clean riddance of the corners of thy when thou reapest, neither shalt thou every gleaning of thy harvest; thou shalt them unto the poor, and to the stranger; he Lord your God." sweating system here; no monopoly of y large shops starving out the small trades- men; no oppression of man by man; the fear of God and His law, "Thou shalt love thy neighbor as thyself," governed trade transactions, and not the love of money, the "golden calf" of guilty Christendom in these days.

In the seventh month another feast was to be observed. It is called the feast of tabernacles, but also "the feast of ingathering." (Ex. 23:16; 34:22.) It was commanded concerning all the feasts of the Lord that no servile work was to be done, but on the Sabbath

No Work,

and on the day of atonement, which preceded the feast of tabernacles, "no manner of work." The day of atonement, as we have seen, prefigured the work of Christ upon the cross; no work of man can add to that one work of God. "Not by works of righteousness which we have done, but according to His mercy He saved us by the washing of regeneration." (Tit. 3:4.) "And whatsoever soul it be that doeth any work in that same day, the same soul will I destroy from among His people." What shall I *do?* What must I *do?* is ever the sinner's cry, and the cry of the doubting Christian. Appreciate, receive, rest on what God has done, for "this is the work of God, that ye believe on Him whom He hath sent." (John 6:29.) What, then, have we nothing to do? Yes, again and again we are taught to "keep His commandments."

As the Passover is a type of salvation, and Pentecost of consecration and sanctification, so the feast of tabernacles is

A Type of God's Indwelling.

The first fruits have been offered by a reconciled people and accepted by God, who is well pleased, the harvest has been gathered, the fruits of the earth are garnered; it is time to rest. It calls us to look forward to the fulfilment of the prophecy, "Behold, the tabernacle of God is with men, and He will dwell with them, and they shall be His people, and God Himself shall be with them and be their God. And God shall wipe away all tears from their eyes; and there shall be no more death, neither sorrow nor crying, neither shall there be any more pain; for the former things are passed away." (Rev. 21:3, 4.) But this is future, and God wills even now to dwell in man: "I will dwell in them and walk in them." (II Cor. 6:16.) "He that dwelleth in love dwelleth in God, and God in him." (I John 4:16.) "I in them and Thou in Me that they may be made perfect in One, that the world may believe that Thou has sent Me." (John 17:23.)

On the very first day of the seventh month, ten days before the day of atonement, the people were to have a holy convocation, accompanied with blowing of trumpets (Num. 29:1); this was peculiar of the feast of tabernacles. Although the solemn day of atonement was to follow, yet they would commence with praise and with joy. There was also a peculiarity in the offerings which celebrated the feast of tabernacles. On the fifteenth day of the seventh month they were to offer thirteen young bullocks, two rams, and fourteen lambs, for a burnt offering, and each day of the seven days the bullocks were to be decreased by one; on the second day twelve young bullocks; on the third day eleven, and so on, while the two rams and the fourteen lambs were to continue each day the same. The bullock was the highest type of the burnt offering. The bullock was strong to labor and implied a fuller and more complete surrender. But on the seventh day seven bullocks (the perfect number) were to be offered. Never less than a perfect offering, i. e., our all. On the eighth day, the type of resurrection, but one, the type of the perfect sacrifice of Jesus, which cannot be added to. (Num. 29:12–36.) Each of the burnt offerings must be supplemented with meat and drink offerings, all mingled with oil (the Holy Spirit), the wine of the drink offerings poured out, not drunk. These were the portion of the priests.

But besides all these offerings, there was another peculiarity of the feast of tabernacles. The people were to bear witness before the world that they were pilgrims and strangers. "Ye shall take for the first day the boughs of goodly trees, branches of palm-trees, and the boughs of thick trees, and willows of the brook; and ye shall rejoice before the Lord your God seven days. . . . Ye shall dwell in booths seven days: that your generations may know that I made the children of Israel to dwell in booths when I brought them out of the land of Egypt; I am the Lord your God." Jesus is coming; our hearts say, come quickly, and we watch for the signs of His appearing. He exhorts us, "Let your loins be girded about, and your lights burning, and ye yourselves like unto men which wait for your Lord." (Luke 12:35, 36.) Not like men who take root on earth, but whose citizenship is in heaven. If we

Live upon the Watch

for God's marching orders—whether to another sphere on earth, India, China, Africa, or to some dark village in our own land, or whether away to heaven—our root is not deep in things present. As pilgrims and strangers it is our privilege to live in hourly gratitude for all the comforts and privileges we have, but to be ready to leave them at an hour's notice, if God wills. Oh, how much of sorrow would be spared if we held all we have on earth as subject to be taken away at any time, and, therefore, not to be reckoned on. If we reckon on a certain income, it may soon become uncertain; if we count on a situation we are holding, we may soon have to leave it; nothing on earth is sure—but the living God changes not. We may be pilgrims and strangers upon earth, having no certain dwelling-place, but if we dwell in God we have a house built upon the rock, and no storm or tempest can make it fall.

The feast of tabernacles points us to the millenial glory. When the Lord shall have come and taken away His people, when He permits the great tribulation, with all its attendant horrors, to sweep away "the third part of men" (Rev. 11:15), when the winepress of the wrath of God shall have been trodden after the harvest has been gathered, (Rev. 14:14–20)—then Christ shall reign with His people upon the earth, and there shall be again a yearly observance of the feast of tabernacles. "And it shall come to pass, that every one that is left of all the nations which came against Jerusalem, shall even go up from year to year to worship the King, the Lord of hosts, and to keep the feast of tabernacles. And it shall be that whoso will not come up of all the families of the earth unto Jerusalem to worship the King, the Lord of hosts, even upon them shall be no rain" (Zech.: 14: 16, 17.) Then the feast of tabernacles will have its glorious fulfilment; then the Lord will dwell with men and probably visibly appear on earth. And then there will be no longer the distinction between secular and spiritual. In that day shall there be upon the bells of the horses,

Holiness Unto the Lord.

And the pots in the Lord's house (the most common things) shall be like bowls before the altars. Yea; every pot in Jerusalem and in Judah shall be holiness unto the Lord of Hosts; and all they that sacrifice shall come and take of them, and settle thereon." Oh, how things will be reversed! Holiness popular! Holiness recognized! Holiness universal! and Christ reigning! Lord, hasten the time. No wonder that then there shall be no more the Canaanite (the trader) in the house of the Lord; no more preaching for the sake of gain.

COMMUNION;

OR,

"A LITTLE TALK WITH JESUS."

A LITTLE talk with Jesus,—
How it smoothes the rugged road!
How it seems to help me onward,
When I faint beneath my load!
When my heart is crushed with sorrow,
And mine eyes with tears are dim,
There's naught can yield me comfort
Like a little talk with Him.

I tell Him I am weary,
And I fain would be at rest,
That I'm daily, hourly, longing
For a home upon His breast;
And He answers me so sweetly,
In tones of tend'rest love,—
"I am coming soon to take thee
To My happy home above."

Ah, this is what I'm wanting—
His lovely face to see,
And, I'm not afraid to say it,
I know He's wanting me!
He gave His life a ransom
To make me all His own,
And He can't forget His promise
To me, His purchased one.

I know the way is dreary
To yonder far-off clime,
But a little talk with Jesus
Will while away the time;
And yet the more I know Him,
And all His grace explore,
It only sets me longing
To know Him more and more.

I cannot live without Him,
Nor would I if I could;
He is my daily portion,
My medicine and my food.
He's altogether lovely,
None can with Him compare—
The chief among ten thousand,
The fairest of the fair.

I often feel impatient,
And mourn His long delay,—
I never can be settled
While He remains away;
But we shall not long be parted,
For I know He'll quickly come,
And we shall dwell together
In that *happy, happy* home.

So I'll wait a little longer,
Till His appointed time,
And glory in the knowledge
That such a hope is mine.
Then in my Father's dwelling,
Where "many mansions" be,
I'll sweetly talk with Jesus,
And He shall talk with me.

J. E. JEWETT, Publisher, 77 Bible House, New York, will furnish the above poem in leaflet form at twenty cents per hundred. *A Sample Packet* of 50 leaflets assorted (no two alike), will be sent post-paid, for 10 cts., or 100 for 20 cts. Postage stamps taken.

For Mental Depression

Use Horsford's Acid Phosphate.

DR. L. C. S. TURNER, Colfax, Ia., says: "I am very much pleased with it in mental depression from gastric troubles."

"The Gods give no great good without labor," is an old proverb, and a true one; the hardest labor is not always that which is best paid, however. To those in search of light, pleasant and profitable employment, we say write to B. F. Johnson & Co., Publishers, Richmond, Va.

Only One Cent.

Readers of the CHRISTIAN HERALD have undoubtedly seen the large advertisement of a prominent Soap manufacturing firm which appeared in our July 12 issue. A good many will wonder how any one in this grasping age is willing to give so much for so little money.

"How do you like your bargain" was asked of a well-known lawyer a few days ago.

"Like it? Why, man, how can I help but like it. The laundress says 'Sweet Home" is the best soap she has ever used. Think of it. Enough soap to last a year, toilet soap enough to start a drug store, and presents for the lady of the house, seven children, two servant girls and the hired man;" and he passed down the street whistling "Sweet Home."

It will only cost a cent for a postal card to send your name and address to J. D. Larkin & Co., Buffalo, N. Y. The great bargain box will then be delivered at your door, and if in thirty days, you are not pleased with the goods in every way, you need not feel under any obligation to keep the case, but it will be called for and taken away free of all expense to you.

WANTED INFORMATION OF WILLIAM Reynolds, an orphan boy, age about 19. Adopted from the Chicago Home of the Friendless in 1880. Any one having knowledge of his whereabouts will confer a great favor on his sister, Lizzie, by addressing MRS. S. G. CLEVELAND, City Missionary, care of Y. M. C. A., Chicago, Ills.

HAND-BOOK FOR WORKERS. A Manual of Bible Texts and Reading for use in Christian Work. 147 pages; flexible leather 25 cents. **PEARL OF DAYS**, an illustrated monthly devoted to the interests of the Christian Sabbath. $1.00 a year. Sample copy 10 cents. Our new catalogue of books, banners, etc., free on application. Wilbur B. Ketcham, Publisher and Bookseller, 71 Bible House, New York.

AGENTS WANTED to sell "The Child's Bible." Introduction by Bishop J. H. Vincent, D.D. The best selling book handled by agents. Recommended by all clergymen. Address Cassell & Co., B.B.S.D., 104 and 106 Fourth Ave., New York; 40 Dearborn St., Chicago, Ill.

Christian Work in Mexico.

Through the reading of the Holy Scriptures translated into Spanish some earnest souls in Mexico have, by God's blessing, been led to a clear knowledge of the Gospel. From their numbers able preachers of the Christian faith in its primitive purity have been raised up, around whom congregations have been gathered from among the humble poor, who have been the first to publicly welcome and defend the pure Gospel in Mexico. The members of these congregations, rich in faith, have worked earnestly and bravely for Christ and His truth among their fellow countrymen in that beautiful Southern portion of North America called Mexico. Schools have been established by them, in which large numbers of bright boys and girls have received a good secular education and have been carefully taught the Christian faith. From the children thus educated faithful Christian workers have been raised up. A Mexican Branch of the Church of Christ, that maintains the faith in its purity and integrity, has been organized among these native Christians in the Republic of Mexico. The members of this Mexican Church of Christ, though gathered mostly from among the poor, are yet doing a most important Christian work. To continue that work, we need to pay a few leading workers small monthly salaries, and also to defray some current expenses. To raise the needed funds we have formed a society with an office at 43 Bible House, New York, U. S., and should be pleased to have many of our fellow Christians join this society by becoming regular contributors to its treasury. We are trying to secure monthly or quarterly contributions to meet the regular monthly expenses of the work. In order to continue and extend the work, we wish to raise four hundred dollars a month, by endeavoring to have four hundred persons each give on an average *one dollar every month* to this object, leaving the donors to give less or more as they may be able and willing.

We earnestly invite all who will, to join us in this systematic effort in behalf of the cause of Christ in Mexico, by becoming monthly subscribers to this fund. We have already regular subscribers whose gifts amount monthly to over eighty dollars, and a growing circle of friends who are forwarding us occasional donations.

This Mexican Church of Christ is a very effective instrumentality through which to do Christian work among the many millions on this Western Hemisphere who speak the Spanish language, comparatively few of whom have ever had a Bible in their hands. A beautiful church building has been secured in the City of Mexico as the centre of the activities of this Mexican Church of Christ. Through the workers connected with that centre more than forty congregations have been gathered from among the poor in different parts of the Republic of Mexico. We have some faithful and able preachers now in the field, but more young men need to be trained for the ministry. Multitudes of Protestant children in Mexico, some of them orphans, need to be educated. We make three requests of you, Christian reader: *first*, that you will, if possible, become a monthly or quarterly subscriber in behalf of this Christian work; *second*, that you will try and induce your friends also to contribute to it; *third*, that you will remember this precious work in Mexico in your prayers.

We most sincerely thank all who are already generously contributing to this Christian work for their timely and generous gifts, and we earnestly invite many others, to unite with us in aiding it by also becoming monthly subscribers in its behalf. Those who may not feel that they can give as much as a dollar a month are earnestly asked to give what they can, whenever they are able—EVERY LITTLE HELPS. Fellow Christian, if you will generously consent to contribute a dollar a month or more or less to the work, will you kindly inform me of the fact? Contributions either large or small can be mailed directly to my address as follows:

BISHOP H. C. RILEY, care of J. P. HEATH,
No. 43 Bible House, New York, U. S.

Best Steel Wire GALVANIZED. WOVEN WI[illegible] FENCING Wire [illegible] Selvage McMULLEN'S 80c. to $2 per rod. All sizes and widths. Sold by us or any dealer in this line of goods. FREIGHT PAID. Information free. Write The McMULLEN WOVEN WIRE FENCE CO. N. Market and Ontario Sts., Chicago, Ill

WANTED FOR CASH! POSTAGE STAMPS OLD U. S. and Confederate used prior to 1865 These old stamps will bring fine prices IF LEFT UPON THE ORIGINAL ENVELOPE and in GOOD condition. Some stamps bring as much as $25.00 each. Send stamp for circulars describing kinds wanted. Best references furnished if desired. Address G. M. BASTABLE, Catlett, Va.

TEAS *LADIES* Send at once for our new terms. THE GREAT AMERICAN TEA CO., 31 and 33 Vesey St., New York, N. Y.

NIECE'S India Ink Portraits.

Portraiture in India Ink is certainly the most beautiful process of producing the human face in monochrome,—black and white as more commonly termed.

The skill, artistic taste and care required to produce India Ink Portraits have prevented them from becoming more widely known, and their beauties have only been enjoyed by the wealthier classes of our large cities.

We have recently perfected an ingenious process whereby we secure the most beautiful effects with India Ink with much less labor than heretofore.

Resplendent in rich shadows full of detail, cool gray half tints, and pure, silvery lights, they possess such a beautiful life-like appearance that to introduce color in them would seem superfluous.

Avoiding the two outrageous extremes so commonly practised, viz., deceptive cheapness and fancy high prices, we give our customers the finest results, at very moderate prices.

Our special feature in India Ink is a Life Size Portrait framed in a Carved Oak Frame, steel lining and white Torchon Mat, or Florentine Bronze Frame and Torchon Mat, boxed complete for $20.00.

One-half the amount must accompany order when goods are to be sent C.O.D.

Complete satisfaction is assured or money returned.

Send best photo or other small picture with particulars to NIECE, 15 and 73 Bible House, New York.

$75.00 to $250.00 A MONTH can be made working for us. Agents preferred who can furnish a horse and give their whole time to the business. Spare moments may be profitably employed also. A few vacancies in towns and cities. B. F. Johnson & Co., Pub's, 1009 Main St., Richmond, Va.

POCKET SERIES OF

By JAMES WILLIAM KIMB

ALL PRINTED NEATLY ON TINT

8 pp. *10 cents per dozen. 50 cents per 100.*

3001 Effectual Prayer.
3002 Only Believe.
3003 Wanting Jesus for a Friend.
3004 Save My Soul.
3005 Science and Religion.
3006 An Opportunity.
3007 How to Read the Bible.

12 pp. *10 cents per dozen. 75 cents per 100.*

3020 How Shall I Pray?
3021 Giving.

Helps to Peace Series. 16 pp. *10 cents per dozen. 75 cents per 100.*

3030 Peace in Believing.
3031 Yes or No.
3032 Christ the Living Bread.
3033 The Sufferings of Christ.
3034 The Comforter.
3035 Sanctification.
3036 Have You Found God?
3037 Seeing Jesus.
3038 Finding God Real.
3039 The Living Sacrifice.
3040 A Word to the Sorrowing.

Two Page Tract Ca

5 cts. per Doz., 25 cts. per H

How are You to be Saved?
I Expect to Pass Through this Life but
The Greatest Wonder—Great Things.
Who is Right?—Judgment to Come.
If I Die To-night where Shall I Spend
Lost.—What is Lost?
Two Roads—Two Gates.
Is your Soul Saved?
Please Don't Swear.

Some of the above are printed on th side only, and can be used, by stampi notices on the back, for advertising Re Send a two-cent stamp for Samples quantities.

ALABASTER BOX

Four pages on heavy card-board, one cents per dozen.

Four Page Tracts

5 cts. per Doz., 30 cts. per H

301 A Little Pilgrim.
302 Conversations with Christ.
303 Communion.
304 Put in "I," "My," "Me."
305 Coming.

You can order as many of each as des ing please order by number when giver you time and is more convenient for us.

CHOICE LEAFLET

I have over 100 choice one and two-pa send a SAMPLE PACKET of 50 assorted— post-paid for 10 cents, or 100 for 20 c stamps taken.

Special prices for large quantities given on application. Address

J. E. JEWETT, Publisher and
77 Bible House, New York

1,000 Agents Wanted to Se Dop es National Hand Book **American Progre** S. O. HAVEN, LL.D., & othe **1492 to date. Six Vo in One.** A non-partisan r erence Cyclopedia, of History, Biograph Politics, for School, Home and Office. pages, $2. E. E. TREAT, Pub. 771

THE BRYANT SCHOOL, 23 *miles from N. Y., overlooking L.* Incorporated Academy for Boys *sical, Commercial. Military organ... unte of U. S. M. A. (West Point). Buil and general equipment unsurpassed.* Geo. Bruce Cortelyo

PRICE $160 **UNIVERSITY FROM $160** SOLD DIRECT TO FA the enormous... home before you... six years. Marchal & Smith Piano Co., 235 E.

IF YOU WANT AN "OXFORD" TEACHER'S OR BAGSTER BIBLE send for complete Bible Catalogue givi tion of styles, sample of type, and price, J. E. JEWETT, Publisher and 77 Bible House, New York

SEATTLE The largest City in Territory. Population mercial center of Country. Coal, Iron, Timber and Lands. Send for full information of CHAS. H. **SE-AT-TLE.** Seattle,

Entered according to Act of Congress in the year 188, in the office of the Librarian of Congress at Washington.

Vol. XI., No. 33. Office, 63 Bible House, N. Y. THURSDAY, AUGUST 16, 1888. Annual Subscription, $1.50.

CONTENTS OF THIS NUMBER:

THE PAN-PRESBYTERIAN COUNCIL—PORTRAITS OF FIVE FREE CHURCH LEADERS.
QUEER CHRISTIANS. Dr. Talmage's Sermon in Georgia last Sunday Morning.
PROPHETIC EVENTS BETWEEN 1889 and 1891. THE COMING OF THE BRIDEGROOM.
THE BIBLE CONFERENCE AT NORTHFIELD.
REV. W. F. RE QUA'S INDIAN MISSION
REMARKABLE DIVINE HEALING IN JAPAN.
PORTRAIT AND LIFE OF THE LATE GEN. PHILIP H. SHERIDAN.
PICTURE OF A MISSIONARY'S ENCOUNTER WITH A WOLF.
PETER'S RESTORATION. A New Sermon by Rev. C. H. Spurgeon.
Gems from New Books: Washington's Prayer in a Hut.
A FATAL INTERVIEW. (With Illustration.)
THE EPOCHS OF A LIFE. A New Serial Story by Rev. L. S. Keyser. (Continued.)
PILLAR OF CLOUD AND FIRE. By Mrs. Baxter.

Speakers at the Pan-Presbyterian Council—1. Dr. D. Fraser—2. Principal Brown—3. Dr. S. Paterson—4. Principal Cairns—5. Dr. T. Davidson.

DR. DONALD FRASER.

The portraits and lives of four of the prominent speakers at the recent Pan-Presbyterian Conference, which appeared in this journal on August 2, are this week supplemented by five of their brethren of the Free Church, whose standing among Presbyterians, and whose work in the cause of Christian religion at large, demand and receive world-wide recognition. In the first of the five, Dr. Donald Fraser, America has a kind of proprietary interest, as he received his early scholastic and theological training at Knox College, Toronto, and was for nine years a popular preacher in Montreal.

Dr. Fraser is a native of Scotland, and is sixty-two years of age, having been born at Inverness in 1826. His father having settled in the Dominion, the future preacher received, as we have said, his early training in Toronto. He was licensed to preach in 1851, when he accepted a call from Cote Street Church, Montreal, where he was ordained. Throwing himself with characteristic energy and whole-heartedness into his pastoral work, he soon became widely known as an efficient and influential preacher and platform speaker.

In 1860 an urgent call from the Free Church in Aberdeen, Scotland, reached him, which special circumstances led him to accept. He labored there for eleven years with signal and growing success, entering with ardor into the revival work which at the time was stirring all Scotland. He often preached to thousands of attentive hearers in the open air, and was instrumental in leading many of them to the acceptance of Christ. The congregation under his more especial care greatly increased and prospered; the church building was enlarged, and a much-needed Mission Church was erected through his untiring exertions.

In 1870 he was honored by a call from London, and became pastor of the Marylebone Presbyterian Congregation, as *successor to Dr. William Chalmers*. There the most affluent of blessings has rested upon him and his fervid ministry. From the first the capacious church was crowded in every part, and it had to be rebuilt on a considerably larger scale. At present it is *the largest church building in England connected with the Presbyterian Church*, and has the largest congregation and membership. In addition to his pastorial work, Dr. Fraser is one of the Hon. Secretaries of the Evangelical Alliance, and is a vice-president of the British and Foreign Bible Society.

Dr. Fraser is a voluminous author. He has written many articles in reviews and magazines, and several books. His chief work, however, is entitled "Synoptical Lectures on the Books of Holy Scripture," in two volumes. This work is now in its fourth edition, and is well known and highly prized in America as well as in England. With this may be mentioned "Metaphors in the Gospels," and "Speeches of the Holy Apostles." Dr. Fraser rejoices to be of the number of those who are looking for the Speedy Personal Pre-millennial Coming of Christ.

REV. PRINCIPAL BROWN.

The Principal of the Free Church College, Aberdeen, Dr. David Brown, was born in that city in 1803, and has, therefore, now attained the venerable age of eighty-five years. His father was twice chief magistrate of the city, and the family was one of much influence in the locality. David received a very careful educational and religious training at home, and was then sent for the usual course of literary study to the local grammar school, proceeding thence, in due course, to the University, where he took his Master of Arts degree in 1821.

He was designated for the ministry, and his own inclination harmonizing with the wishes of his parents and friends, he began the prescribed course of Divinity. Unhappily, however, through the too eager study of German rationalistic theology, and too close association with a learned sceptical friend, his views of Bible truth became so unsettled that he seriously contemplated abandoning his intention of entering the Christian ministry. His life, for some months, was unhappy, and his future prospects uncertain. At length he went to Edinburgh, where he remained for six months, during which time his doubts were removed, and he returned to Aberdeen to resume his studies. His sceptical friend also overcame his doubts, and was afterwards known to the world as Rev. Dr. Duncan, Professor of Oriental languages, New College, Edinburgh.

Mr. Brown was licensed to preach by the Presbytery of the Church of Scotland in 1826, but continued a course of private study till 1830, when he became assistant to the *Rev. Edward Irving*, and remained in this capacity for two years. He then became colleague of the parish minister of Dumburton, whence in 1835 he removed to a small rural charge in Banffshire, and in this place he was ordained in 1836.

The disruption of the Church of Scotland, which occurred in 1843, severed the relation of Mr. Brown with his church, for he threw in his lot with his brethren who felt it their duty to quit their manses and establish the Free Church. At the close of the year he was appointed minister of Free St. James's, Glasgow, and it was while he was in this sphere of labor that he wrote his book on the Second Advent of Christ. In 1857 he was appointed Professor of Divinity in the Free Church College, Aberdeen, and in 1876, he became Principal of his college. In 1885 he was unanimously elected Moderator of the General Assembly, a position which he most efficiently filled; and in 1886 he resigned his Professor's chair, after thirty years of honorable and arduous service; but he still retains the office of Principal much to the satisfaction of the Church of which he is so distinguished a representative. His "Commentary on the Gospels" has had a large circulation, not only in Great Britain, but also in the Colonies and the United States. Dr. Brown was one of the courageous and learned men who undertook the work of revising the New Testament in 1870. In common with his fellow laborers in that work he labored earnestly and conscientiously to give the Church a correct and reliable translation of the Word of God, and has received, instead of the gratitude to which he was entitled, the obloquy of men whose prejudices are greater than their regard for truth and accuracy.

DR. H. SINCLAIR PATERSON.

The most active and valiant champion of Rev. C. H. Spurgeon in that minister's recent trouble with his brethren in the Baptist Union was Dr. Hugh Sinclair Paterson, who frequently preaches for the famous pastor in the Metropolitan Tabernacle, when illness renders Mr. Spurgeon unable to occupy his usual place. Dr. Paterson wields a powerful pen, and has no mercy for any preacher who does not hold by the orthodox creed. He also is a Scotchman. He was born at Campbelltown, Argyllshire, in 1832, and is consequently fifty-six years of age. He received his early education at the Grammar School of his native place, and so marked was his success, the result of patient, untiring industry, that when he was only twelve years old, he received the gold medal for classics and mathematics from the Duke of Argyll. Thence he proceeded to the University of Glasgow, passed through the usual curriculum for five sessions, and won for himself a position of considerable distinction, gaining, before he was twenty-one, the second place for the Blackstone Gold Medal, a prize most eagerly desired by the students.

When his literary course was ended, he underwent a theological course at Edinburgh for four years. In 1849, with the intention of becoming a foreign medical missionary, he studied medicine for five years, and took his M. D. degree. But suffering from rheumatic fever, which he has had no fewer than five times in his life, he was unwillingly compelled to abandon the prospect of foreign mission-work, and, entering the Free Presbyterian Church, he was ordained in 1854, as minister of Free St. Mark's, Glasgow. His success there was remarkable, especially among the intelligent artisans.

At the time of the Moody and Sankey revival movement in Scotland, he labored so strenuously that his health failed, and a change of sphere was strongly recommended. By a coincidence, a call came to him at that time from a Free church in London, which he accepted, and he has since labored successfully in the British metropolis. Dr. Paterson has published several valuable works, some in exposition and some in defence of orthodoxy; and also some excellent lectures delivered to the London Young Men's Christian Association, entitled "Studies in Life." "I like," he said, on one occasion, when speaking of his own work, "to have a definite subject before my mind, and endeavor to get the exact sense of the Scripture, and to found on that such lessons as may be most suitable. I have always been accustomed to do this. When in Glasgow, I had many engineers among my people, and that mode of preaching was relished by them." Dr. Paterson's language is precise and clear; there is no straining after rhetorical effect; he is almost conversational in style, yet can be very emphatic on occasions, when he considers emphasis to be necessary. His point is to aim at a clear, instructive "talk," as he himself expresses it, and to teach and suggest thought, rather than to amuse his hearers.

PRINCIPAL CAIRNS.

To Christian readers in the United States the venerable scholar whose portrait accompanies that of his Free Church brethren on the first page is best known through his famous work on "Unbelief in the Eighteenth Century," published by *Messrs. Harper and Brothers*, New York. To his own countrymen, however, Principal Cairns is held in quite as high honor as a preacher. He is a native of Berwickshire, where he was born in 1820, so that he is now sixty-eight years old. He was little more than a boy when he became a student at Edinburgh University, but speedily made his mark there, far out-distancing all his competitors of a similar age. Metaphysics had a peculiar fascination for him, the result in great measure of the lectures of Sir William Hamilton, who then occupied the chair of Logic and Metaphysics. Young Cairns gained the highest place in the class, and, what he esteemed of greater value, the cordial personal friendship of the gifted Professor himself. An anecdote is related of how, after his conversion to Christ, the former student wrote Sir William a tender and respectful, yet courteous letter about his soul's welfare. He never received an answer; but after the brilliant teacher's death, the letter was found most scrupulously preserved among his private papers.

Vacation times were always eagerly anticipated by young Cairns with delight, and employed to the utmost advantage. "They gave him time," he said, "to grow both mentally and spiritually." Book in hand, and wrapped in a plaid, he would go among the sheep on the hills of his native district, and as he wandered to and fro, would read and think and pray. It was an excellent preparation for the work of his life for which his Heavenly Father had designed him.

Having completed his theological curriculum in 1843-44 in the United Secession Hall with marked distinction, he spent nearly a year in Germany, for the purpose of equipping himself yet more thoroughly to become an expounder and teacher of the truths of Holy Scripture. His fixed ambition now was to enter the ministry. His ordination took place on August 6, 1845, when he was appointed minister of the United Secession Congregation, Golden Square, Berwick-on-Tweed. Signs of prosperity were soon apparent. A heavy outstanding debt on the church was cleared off, and the rapidly increasing numbers attending Mr. Cairns's ministry made it necessary to erect a much larger structure, and this, too, when it was completed, was also regularly filled to its utmost capacity.

The minister's reputation became so brilliant

that it seemed a wrong to the church that he should be preaching in so obscure a corner of the country, and the calls he received to other spheres of labor were so many, that it was recognized as a kind of joke in a vacant congregation that Mr. Cairns should be called first. But he turned a deaf ear to all such invitations, happy in having won the love and attention of his people, which he retained to the end. In 1867, however, a call came to him which he recognized as imperative, but in accepting it he resolved on cleaving to his church, and so doing double duty. He was appointed Professor of Apologetics in the Theological Hall of the United Presbyterian Church. For some years he combined pulpit and educational work, but in 1876 he was finally driven by the double burden to choose the one of most value to the church at large, and he resigned his pastorate. In 1879 he became principal of his college.

DR. J. THAIN DAVIDSON.

THE name of "*the Young Men's Bishop*" has been won by the eminent preacher, lecturer, and author, whose portrait is fifth of the group on the first page. He believes in young men, because a young man converted and set to work is the most valuable acquisition he can lay at the feet of his Master. Dr. Davidson has won many such trophies, not only by his preaching in his own land, but by his books in this country and Canada. (*Messrs. A. C. Armstrong & Co.*, of New York, are his publishers on this side of the Atlantic.) His "Talks with Young Men," "Forewarned—Forearmed," and "The City Youth." are the best books a father can put into the hands of his son, and they have been abundantly blessed.

Dr. Davidson is fifty-eight years of age. He was born in 1833, in the manse of a Presbyterian minister near Dundee, but when the boy was ten years old, he was initiated into a life of faith by his father quitting pulpit and home for conscience sake. The lad gave early indications of piety and ministerial capacity; he was therefore prepared for college, and sent to Edinburgh University. His first charge was as assistant pastor at Free St. Mary's, in Edinburgh, and his next, at Maryton, in Forfarshire. His next charge was at Salford, Manchester, where he remained for three years, and then he accepted, in 1863, a call to a church at Colebrook Row, Islington, the northern district of London, where he still continues. In 1872 Dr. Thain Davidson was elected Moderator of the English Synod, the highest official position in the Presbyterian Church.

Islington is a sphere of Christian service that might satisfy the most ambitious and energetic of men, especially if he is an enthusiastic and patriotic Scotchman. It has often been described as *a little Scotland*, from the fact that so many of the young Northerners, who come in considerable numbers to push their fortunes in London, reside within its borders. With a quick and sympathetic eye to the situation and its exceptional opportunities, the pastor of the Colebrook Church laid himself out to catch this very class of the Islington community, and his success has been phenomenal. He commenced a series of Sunday afternoon services for young men in a large hall, which have been continued with the most blessed results for over twenty years. Dr. Davidson has been assisted in this work by preachers of all denominations, including bishops of the Protestant-Episcopal Church and Christian laymen.

In company with Rev. Newman Hall, Dr. Monro Gibson, the late Rev. William Fraser, of Brighton, and other clerical brethren, Dr. Davidson paid a three months' visit to Egypt and Palestine in 1886. He found much stimulus and benefit from the interesting journey, and doubtless his congregation has reaped the fruits of his observation. Having devoted considerable attention to the study of popular science, he has given in his own church and in other places a series of astronomical discourses, which have been much appreciated by young men.

ANECDOTES RELATED AT RECENT EVANGELISTIC MEETINGS.

A Nail in a Sure Place.—The Rev. William Ross observed: "A ship which for many years had done useful service, at last became old and rotten. In this condition it was painted up and made to look good and strong, and sent to sea for the last time. When about half of its voyage was accomplished she sprang a leak. The leak was found, and they proceeded to nail planks on to the leaking part; but such was the state of her timbers, that whenever a nail was driven in she seemed to spring a fresh leak. Under such circumstances work was hopeless, and nothing could save the ship. But the Bible says that the words of God are like *nails in a sure place;* where they are put in they *hold;* if we nail ourselves to Christ with a text of Scripture, with one of His blessed promises, then we are safe: the nails of God hold fast."

An Aged Pilgrim's Victory.—A Christian worker related: "A minister was visiting an aged man who for many years had been stricken with paralysis, and was now approaching the river of death. The minister wanted to know how he felt in prospect of the grim change which was imminent, and asked the aged pilgrim if he were at all afraid. The invalid could not speak, so the minister handed him a pencil and a piece of paper. With trembling hand the old man attempted to write, but failed. A second attempt only produced a few illegible scratches. Then a sudden gleam of light overspread his dying features, as for a third time seizing the pencil he began painfully to print in Roman characters the one word, 'Victory.' 'Ah,' said the minister, 'I know the text you mean. "Thanks be unto God, who giveth us the victory, through our Lord Jesus Christ."' The dying man smiled, and nodded his head. He was meeting death, thanking God for the victory He had given him over self, the flesh, the devil, and even death itself."

A Flag for Christ.—A Few Years ago a Converted Sikh lay dying at Amritsar, in the Punjaub, India. Before he passed triumphantly into the glory he expressed his desire to put up a flag for Christ, and left some money for the purpose. To-day a flag waves in the breeze above the houses of that city, bearing simply the words, "For Christ," in bold letters on a scarlet ground. "That bright flag seemed to us," says a missionary, "a monument of the grace and mercy of God, who could transform an idolater into a saint: and also a glad prophecy of the future when all nations shall own the sovereignty of our coming King. Below in the city the Hindoos bow before their idols; the Mohammedans perform their religious rites, not acknowledging the Saviour, and in ignorance of His love; and within a short distance the Golden Temple of the Sikhs shines and glitters in the sunlight. But still the flag floats calmly above it all, a reminder of the glorious fact that Christ shall reign and all His enemies be put beneath His feet."

An Infidel Don Juan Saved.—Mrs. Emily Lopez Rodriguez relates: "The recent conversion of Don Juan Salvador Borras has given us great joy. Having lost his parents when young, he was placed by his guardian as a boarder in the Royal Academy in Madrid, where he studied as a civil engineer. Like many other students he had imbibed infidel views, and was utterly indifferent on religious subjects. Don Juan, on seeing the reality of the Lord's work here, had his infidelity shaken, but when personally appealed to about his soul's salvation he would invariably put the subject off, urging that he had never consciously injured anyone nor done anything particularly wrong. One Sunday last month the pastor preached a very earnest sermon on the words, 'You must be born again.' At the close we had personal conversation with Don Juan on the subject, but still there was no conviction of sin. The following day we wrote out some texts for him under the heads of 'What is sin?' 'The sinner and the Saviour!' with earnest prayer for blessing. The Word proved 'quick and powerful,' for soon after Don Juan came to tell us the joyful news that 'Those texts have taken away the veil from before my eyes.' In earnest but broken prayer he accepted Christ as his Saviour, and dedicated his life to His service. He is very anxious, and so are we, for the conversion of his young wife, Dona Rosa. The influence of a Christian home in this country is of great importance."

A "Poor Lost Lassie" Found.—Mr. W. B. Dunn related: "Some time ago I was speaking in Edinburgh, and in the course of my remarks I said that the Saviour who saved me could save any sinner within reach of my voice if he would but come to Him. At the close of the address, as I was walking through the audience, a fine-looking young woman seated at the end of one of the pews, touched me on the shoulder, and asked if I could speak with her for a moment. I replied 'Yes,' and when we had moved a little aside she said, 'Towards the end of your address you said that Christ could save from the very brink of hell, and I wish to know if it be strictly true?' 'Yes,' I answered, "He is able to save to the uttermost."' Then with eyes overflowing she told me her sad story. She had left her home in Glasgow, and had gone to Edinburgh, where she had plunged into sin. With a heart full of sorrow for the lost one, I sat down by her side, and pointed her to Jesus, the friend of sinners, and soon I had the joy of seeing her, like Mary of old, sitting at the feet of her Saviour, and committing herself to His keeping. On the following night she was again at our meeting, and when I spoke to her, she said, 'You are from Glasgow, Mr. Dunn; when you go back will you call upon my father and mother, and tell them that God has found and saved their poor lost lassie?' Yes, thank God, He saves the lost. He is the Saviour we need."

Wonderful Deliverances.—A Sailor Said: "If ever a man had reason to thank God for frequent deliverances from imminent danger, I am that man, though even these repeated perils and warnings did not bring me to Christ. While in India, working on a railway line, I was caught between two trucks and almost smashed to death. I was taken to the hospital, and for three days was insensible. However, I recovered, and my first request was for brandy. This the doctor absolutely refused, saying it would kill me, but after he left the hospital the chief gave me brandy until my brain was aflame. For days I again lay unconscious, and when I did come to myself I could not bear to be alone with my thoughts. God was awakening my conscience and calling me to Him, but still I would not come. When I was able I left the place and became a sailor on board a steamboat. One day I was sent aloft to scrape the mast, and when shifting from one part to the other, I missed my hold, and fell into the Pacific. For some cause there was great delay in bringing the ship to, and then they seemed to think that they had steamed too far from the spot to do any good, and calmly pursued their voyage, leaving me to the mercy of the waters. I paddled to keep myself afloat for a time, when my hand struck a plank that had been thrown overboard. To this I clung, with the despair of a drowning man to his only hope of rescue, for two days. The third morning rose, and cold and weary I was almost tempted to let go. I saw the sun overhead, I saw it as it neared the horizon, then all was blank. The next thing I knew was my hands being chafed by some good-hearted sailors. So God in His mercy had again rescued me, yet even then I did not thank God as I ought. The vessel came into port and I went ashore. I heard singing at the corner of a street there; God arrested me, and I left that place trusting in Christ and a saved man."

QUEER CHRISTIANS.

Dr. Talmage's Sermon Preached near Atlanta, Ga., last Sunday Morning, August 12, 1888.

"And he was angry and would not go in." Luke 15:28.

A Neglected Character in the Parable—The Father afflicted with Both his Sons—The Unnatural Senior—Reproves his Father—His Descendants Still Around—I. The Self-Satisfied Man—Cheated by a Perfect Man—Two Kinds of Higher Life Christians—The True Higher Life—II. Christians Sceptical of Genuine Conversion—Why Prodigals Do not Come Home—Icebergs in their Way—Sinners who are Welcomed—One-Cent Contributors—An Inebriate in the Tabernacle—A Ruined Glasgow Merchant—III. Envious and Jealous Christians—A French General Dismounted—IV. Pouting Christians.

"Is the elder son of the parable so unsympathetic and so cold that he is not worthy of recognition? The fact is that we ministers pursue the younger son. You can hear the flapping of his rags in many a sermonic breeze, and the cranching of the pods for which he was an unsuccessful contestant. I confess that for a long time I was unable to train the camera obscura upon the elder son of the parable. I never could get a negative for a photograph. There was not enough light in the gallery, or the chemicals were poor, or the sitter moved in the picture. But now I think I have him. Not a side-face, or a three-quarters, or the mere bust, but

A Full-Length Portrait,

as he appears to me. The father in the parable of the prodigal had nothing to brag of in his two sons. The one was a rake, and the other a churl. I find nothing admirable in the dissoluteness of the one, and I find nothing attractive in the acrid sobriety of the other. The one goes down over the larboard side, and the other goes down over the starboard side; but they both go down.

From the window of the old homestead bursts the minstrelsy. The floor quakes with the feet of the rustics, whose dance is always vigorous and resounding. The neighbors have heard of the return of the younger son from his wanderings, and they have gathered together. The house is full of congratulators. I suppose the tables are loaded with luxuries. Not only the one kind of meat mentioned, but its concomitants. "Clap!" go the cymbals, "thrum!" go the harps, "click!" go the chalices, up and down go the feet inside, while outside is a most sorry spectacle. The senior son stands at the corner of the house.

A Frigid Phlegmatic.

He has just come in from the fields in very substantial apparel. Seeing some wild exhilarations around the old mansion, he asks of a servant passing by with a goatskin of wine on his shoulder what all the fuss is about. One would have thought that, on hearing that his younger brother had got back, he would have gone into the house and rejoiced, and if he were not conscientiously opposed to dancing, that he would have joined in *the Oriental schottische*. No. There he stands. His brow lowers. His lip curls with contempt. He stamps the ground with indignation. He sees nothing at all to attract. The odors of the feast coming out on the air do not sharpen his appetite. The lively music does not put any spring into his step. He is in a terrible pout. He criticises the expense, the injustice, and the morals of the entertainment.

The father rushes out bareheaded, and coaxes him to come in. He will not go in. He scolds the father. He goes into a pasquinade against the younger brother, and he makes the most uncomely scene. He says, "Father, you put a premium on vagabondism. I stayed at home and worked on the farm. You never made a party for me; you didn't so much as kill a kid; that wouldn't have cost half as much as a calf; but the scapegrace went off in fine clothes, and he comes back not fit to be seen, and what a time you make over him! He breaks your heart, and you pay him for it. That calf to which we have been giving extra feed during all these weeks wouldn't be so fat and sleek if I had known to what use you were going to put it! That vagabond deserves to be cowhided instead of banqueted. Veal is too good for him!" That evening, while the younger son sat telling his father about his adventures, and asking about what had occurred on the place since his departure, the senior brother goes to bed disgusted, and slams the door after him.

That Senior Brother Still Lives.

You can see him any Sunday, any day of the week. At a meeting of ministers in Germany some one asked the question, "Who is that elder son?" and Krummacher answered, "I know him; I saw him yesterday." And when they insisted upon knowing whom he meant, he said, "Myself; when I saw the account of the conversion of a most obnoxious man, I was irritated."

First, this senior brother of the text stands for *the self-congratulatory, self-satisfied, self-worshipful man*. With the same breath in which he vituperates against his younger brother he utters a panegyric for himself. The self-righteous man of my text, like every other self-righteous man, was full of faults. He was an ingrate, for he did not appreciate the home blessings which he had all those years. He was disobedient, for when the father told him to come in he stayed out. He was a liar, for he said that the recreant son had devoured his father's living, when the father, so far from being reduced to penury, had a homestead left, had instruments of music, had jewels, had a mansion, and instead of being a pauper, was a prince. This senior brother, with so many faults of his own, was merciless in his criticism of the younger brother.

The Only Perfect People

that I have ever known were utterly obnoxious. I was never so badly cheated in all my life as by a perfect man. He got so far up in his devotions that he was clear up above all the rules of common honesty. These men that go about prowling among prayer-meetings, and in places of business, telling how good they are—look out for them; keep your hand on your pocket-book! I have noticed that just in proportion as a man gets good he gets humble. The deep Mississippi does not make as much noise as a brawling mountain rivulet. There has been many a store that had more goods in the show-window than inside on the shelves.

This self-righteous man of the text stood at the corner of the house hugging himself in admiration. We hear a great deal in our day about the higher life. Now, there are *two kinds of higher-life men*. The one are admirable, and the other are most repulsive. The one kind of higher-life man is very lenient in his criticism of others, does not bore prayer-meetings to death with long harangues, does not talk a great deal about himself, but much about Christ and heaven, gets kindlier and more gentle and more useful, until one day his soul spreads a wing, and he flies away to eternal rest, and everybody mourns his departure. The other higher-life man goes around with a Bible conspicuously under his arm, goes from church to church, a sort of general evangelist, is

A Nuisance

to his own pastor when he is at home, and a nuisance to other pastors when he is away from home; runs up to some man who is counting out a roll of bank-bills, or running up a difficult line of figures, and asks him how his soul is; makes religion a dose of ipecacuanha; standing in a religious meeting making an address, he has a patronizing way, as though ordinary Christians were clear away down below him, so he had to talk at the top of his voice in order to make them hear, but at the same time encouraging them to hope on, that by climbing many years they may after a while come up within sight of the place where he now stands! I tell you plainly that a roaring, roystering, bouncing sinner is not so repulsive to me as that higher-life malformation. The former may repent; the latter never gets over his pharisaism. The younger brother of the parable came back, but the senior brother stands outside entirely oblivious of his own delinquencies and deficits, pronouncing his own eulogium. Oh, how much easier it is to blame others than to blame ourselves! Adam blamed Eve, Eve blamed the serpent, the serpent blamed the devil, the senior brother blamed the younger brother, and none of them blamed themselves.

Incredulous Christians.

Again, the senior brother of my text stands for all those who are faithless about the reformation of the dissipated and the dissolute. In the very tones of his voice you can hear the fact that he has no faith that the reformation of the younger son is genuine. His entire manner seems to say, "That boy has come back for more money. He got a third of the property; now he has come back for another third. He will never be contented to stay on the farm. He will fall away. I would go in too and rejoice with the others if I thought this thing was genuine; but it is a sham. That boy is a confirmed inebriate and debauchee." Alas! my friends, for the incredulity in the Church of Christ in regard to the reclamation of the recreant. You say a man has been a strong drinker. I say, "Yes, but he has reformed." "Oh," you say with a lugubrious face, "I hope you are not mistaken, I hope you are not mistaken." You say, "Don't rejoice too much over his conversion, for soon he will be unconverted, I fear. Don't make too big a party for that returned prodigal, or strike the timbrel too loud; and if you kill a calf, kill the one that is on the common, and not the one that has been luxuriating in the paddock." That is the reason

Why More Prodigals Do Not Come Home

to their father's house. It is the rank infidelity in the church of God on this subject. There is not a house on the streets of heaven that has not in it a prodigal that has returned and stayed home. There could be unrolled before you a scroll of a hundred thousand names—the names of prodigals who came back, for ever reformed. Who was John Bunyan? A returned prodigal. Who was Richard Baxter? A returned prodigal. Who was George Whitefield, the thunderer? A returned prodigal. And I could go out in all directions in this audience and find on either side those who, once far astray for many years, have been faithful, and their eternal salvation is as sure as though they had been ten years in heaven. And yet, some of you have not enough faith in their return.

You do not know how to shake hands with a prodigal. You do not know how to pray for him. You do not know how to greet him. He wants to sail in the warm gulf-stream of Christian sympathy. You are

The Iceberg Against Which he Strikes

and shivers. You say he has been a prodigal. I know it. But you are the sour, unresponsive, censorious, saturnine, cranky, elder brother, and if you are going to heaven one would think some people would be tempted to go to perdition to get away from you. The hunters say that if a deer be shot the other deer shove him out of their company, and the general rule is away with the man who has been wounded with sin. Now, I say, the more bones a man has broken the more need he has of a hospital, and that the more a man has been bruised and cut with sin, the more need he has to be carried into human and divine sympathy. But for such men there is not much room in this world—the men who want to come back after wandering. Plenty of room for elegant sinners, sinners in velvet and satin and lace, for sinners high-salaried, for kid-gloved and patent leather sinners, for sinners fixed up by hair-dresser, pomatumed and lavendered and cologned and frizzled and crimped and "banged" sinners—plenty of room. Such we meet elegantly at the door of our churches, and we invite them into the best seats with Chesterfieldian gallantries; we usher them into the house of God, and put soft ottomans under their feet, and put a gilt-edged prayer-book in their hand, and pass the contribution box before them with an air of apology, while they, the generous souls! take out the exquis

portemonnaie, and open it, and with diamonded-finger push down beyond the ten-dollar gold pieces and delicately pick out as an expression of gratitude their offering to the Lord of one cent. For such sinners, plenty of room, plenty of room. But for

The Man Who Has Been Drinking

until his coat is threadbare and his face is erysipelased, and his wife's wedding-dress is in the pawnbroker's shop, and his children, instead of being in school, are out begging broken bread at the basement-doors of the city—the man, body, mind, and soul on fire with the flames that have leaped from the scathing, scorching, blasting, consuming cup which the drunkard takes, trembling, and agonized, and affrighted, and presses to his parched lip, and his cracked tongue, and his shrieking yet immortal spirit—no room.

Oh, if this younger son of the parable had not gone so far off, if he had not dropped so low in wassail, the protest would not have been so severe; but going clear over the precipice as the younger son did, the elder son is angry and will not go in.

Oh, be not so hard in your criticism of the fallen, lest thou thyself also be tempted. A stranger, one Sunday, staggered up and down the aisles of my church,

Disturbing the Service,

until the service had to stop, until he was taken from the room. He was a minister of the Gospel of Jesus Christ of a sister denomination. That man had preached the Gospel, that man had broken the bread of the Holy Communion for the people. From what a height to what a depth! Oh, I was glad there was no smiling in the room when that man was taken out, his poor wife following him with his hat in her hand and his coat on her arm. It was as solemn to me as two funerals—the funeral of the body and the funeral of the soul. Beware, lest thou also be tempted.

An invalid went to South America for his health, and one day sat sunning himself on the beach, when he saw something crawling up the beach, wriggling towards him, and he was affrighted. He thought it was a wild beast, or reptile, and he took his pistol from his pocket. When he saw it was not a wild beast. It was a man, an immortal man, a man made in God's own image; and the poor wretch crawled up to the feet of the invalid and asked for strong drink, and the invalid took his wine flask from his pocket and gave the poor wretch something to drink, and then under the stimulus he rose and gave his history. He had been

A Merchant in Glasgow,

Scotland. He had gone down under the power of strong drink until he was so reduced in poverty, that he was lying in a boat just off the beach. "Why," said the invalid, "I knew a merchant in Glasgow once," a merchant by such and such a name, and the poor wretch straightened up and said, "I am that man." "Let him that thinketh he standeth take heed lest he fall."

Again, I remark that the senior brother of my text stands for *the spirit of envy and jealousy*. The senior brother thought that all the honor they did to the returned brother was a wrong to him. He said, "I have stayed at home, and I ought to have had the ring, and I ought to have had the banquet, and I ought to have had the garlands." Alas, for this spirit of envy and jealousy coming down through the ages! Cain and Abel, Esau and Jacob, Saul and David, Haman and Mordecai, Othello and Iago, Orlando and Angelica, Caligula and Torquatus, Cæsar and Pompey, Columbus and the Spanish courtiers, Cambyses, and the brother he slew because he was a better marksman, Dionysius and Philoxenius, whom he slew because he was a better singer. Jealousy among painters: Closterman and Geoffrey Kneller, Hudson and Reynolds. Francis, anxious to see a picture of Raphael, Raphael sends him a picture. Francis, seeing it, falls in a fit of jealousy, from which he dies. Jealousy among authors: How seldom contemporaries speak of each other. Xenophon and Plato, living at the same time; but from their writings you never would suppose they heard of each other.

Religious Jealousies:

The Mahommedans praying for rain during a drought, no rain coming. Then the Christians begin to pray for rain, and the rain comes. Then the Mahommedans met together to account for this; and they resolved that God was so well pleased with their prayers, He kept the drought on, so as to keep them praying; but that the Christians began to pray, and the Lord was so disgusted with their prayers that He sent rain right away, so He would not hear any more of their supplications. Oh, this accursed spirit of envy and jealousy! Let us stamp it out from all our hearts.

A wrestler was so envious of Theogenes, the prince of wrestlers, that he could not be consoled in any way; and after Theogenes died, and a statue was lifted to him in a public place, his envious antagonist went out every night and wrestled with the statue, until one night he threw it, and it fell on him and crushed him to death. So jealousy is not only absurd, but it is killing to the body, and it is killing to the soul. How seldom it is you find one merchant speaking well of a merchant in the same line of business! How seldom it is you hear of a physician speaking well of a physician on the same block! Oh, my friends, the world is large enough for all of us. Let us rejoice at the success of others. The next best thing to owning a garden ourselves, is to look over the fence and admire the flowers. The next best thing to riding in fine equipage, is to stand on the street and admire the prancing span. The next best thing to having a banquet given to ourselves, is having a banquet given to our prodigal brother that has come home to his father's house.

Besides that, if we do not get as much honor and as much attention as others, we ought to congratulate ourselves on what we escape in the way of assault.

The French General,

riding on horseback at the head of his troops, heard a soldier complain and say, "It is very easy for the general to command us forward, while he rides and we walk." Then the general dismounted and compelled the complaining soldier to get on the horse. Coming through a ravine, a bullet from a sharpshooter struck the rider, and he fell dead. Then the general said, "How much safer it is to walk than to ride!"

Once more I have to tell you that this senior brother of my text stands for *the pouting Christian*. While there is so much congratulation within doors, the hero of my text stands outside, the corners of his mouth drawn down, looking as he felt—miserable. I am glad his lugubrious physiognomy did not spoil the festivity within. How many pouting Christians there are in our day—Christians who do not like the music of our churches, Christians who do not like the hilarities of the young—pouting, pouting, pouting at society, pouting at the fashions, pouting at the newspapers, pouting at the church, pouting at the government, pouting at the high heaven! Their spleen is too large, their liver does not work, their digestion is broken down. There are two cruets in their castor always sure to be well supplied—

Vinegar and Red Pepper!

Oh, come away from that mood. Stir a little saccharine into your disposition. While you avoid the dissoluteness of the younger son, avoid also the irascibility and the petulance, and the pouting spirit of the elder son, and imitate the father, who had embraces for the returning prodigal, and coaxing words for the splenetic malcontent.

Ah! the face of this pouting elder son is put before us in order that we might better see the radiant and forgiving face of the father. Contrasts are mighty. The artist in sketching the field of Waterloo, years after the battle, put *a dove in the mouth of the cannon*. Raphael, in one of his cartoons, beside the face of a wretch put the face of a happy and innocent child. And so the sour face of this irascible and disgusted elder brother is brought out, in order that in the contrast we may better understand the forgiving and the radiant face of God. That is the meaning of it—that God is ready to take back anybody that is sorry, to take him clear back, to take him back forever, and forever, and forever, to take him back with a loving hug, to put a kiss on his parched lip, a ring on his bloated hand, an easy shoe on his chafed foot, a garland on his bleeding temples, and heaven in his soul. Oh, I fall flat on that mercy! Come, my brother, and let us get down into the dust, resolved never to rise until the Father's forgiving hand shall lift us.

Oh, What a God we Have!

Bring your doxologies. Come, earth and heaven, and join in the worship! Cry aloud! Lift the palm branches! Do you not feel the Father's arm around your neck? Do you not feel the warm breath of your Father against your cheek? Surrender, younger son! Surrender elder son! Surrender, all! Oh, go in to-day and sit down at the banquet. Take a slice of the fatted calf, and afterward, when you are seated, with one hand in the hand of the returned brother, and the other hand in the hand of the rejoicing father, let your heart beat time to the clapping of the cymbal and the mellow voice of the flute. "It is meet that we should make merry, and be glad: for this thy brother was dead, and is alive again; and was lost, and is found."

AN ENCOUNTER WITH A WOLF.

(*See Illustration on page 524.*)

A STARTLING encounter with a wolf occurred in broad daylight during a missionary's journey in southern Russia recently. The Rev. M. Walkenberg, who is laboring among the Jews in that region, set out from Jassy for a town distant about three hours' ride, and located on the river Pruth, which constitutes the boundary between Moldavia and Russian Bessarabia. Accompanying him was a colporteur of the Bible Society, who went in the hope of selling some Christian books in the Hebrew character to the Jews who trade on the frontier. The roads were almost impassable with the unmelted snow, and when the conveyance in which they travelled arrived at the foot of a steep hill, the ascent appeared so difficult that both men alighted to relieve the horses. They toiled up the hill and at the top waited for the vehicle. They could hear the driver below encouraging the horses by his queer cries, and judged that he was about fifty yards below them. As they were waiting and talking they were alarmed by seeing a wolf emerge from the forest and approach them. That they were in some danger was obvious, for reports were in circulation of travellers having been attacked and injured, and in some cases killed, in these very regions by the wolves, whom the unusually severe winter had made bold. They had no weapon but that of "All-prayer," which Bunyan's pilgrim used. That, however, sufficed; for the wolf, after eyeing them hungrily, turned tail and trotted leisurely back to the forest, leaving the two Christian men to thank God for their preservation.

MRS. M. BAXTER'S WORKS.

THE following works by Mrs. M. Baxter, and others, may be had from the office of THE CHRISTIAN HERALD, 63 Bible House, New York:

"Words for Daily Life," "Practical Lessons," "Life Lessons," "Leaves from Genesis," "Trials and Teachings of Paul." By Mrs. M. Baxter. Each, paper, 25 cts.; cloth, 35 cts. "Record of International Conference on Divine Healing. London," 15; Paper, 25 cts. "Living Word in the Gospel of St. John." Paper, 25 cts.; cloth, 50 cts. "God's Prophets." Paper 35 cts.; cloth 50 cts. "Lessons from St. Matthew's Gospel." Paper, 35 cts.; cloth 50 cts. "Teachings from St. Mark's Gospel." Paper, 35 cts.; cloth, 50 cts. "Sunday-School Lessons, 1877 and 78." By Mrs. M. Baxter. Each, cloth, 50 cts.

Any of Mrs. M. Baxter's tracts in the following list may also be had at *one cent each* or ten cents the dozen: "If it be Thy Will," "Does Sickness Sanctify?" "Casting All Your Care," Two cents each or twenty cents the dozen, "God's Purpose in Sickness," "The Great Physician," "Job's Sickness," "God's Side of Prayer," "Pastor Rein."

WONDERFUL HEALING IN JAPAN.

A LETTER from Tokio, Japan, published by Dr. Cullis in his *Times of Refreshing*, describes one of the most remarkable instances of Divine power, exercised in answer to believing prayer, that has been recorded in modern times. In the course of his letter, the writer, Joseph Cosand, says: "On January 4, a shoemaker in Tokio, who had attended our meetings, brought a deaf and dumb boy, who had been so afflicted from his birth, and asked us to pray for him, that he might receive his hearing, and become able to hear the gospel. We promised to do so, and they went home; but the next night only a young man from the family came back to the meeting. He said the shoemaker had lost his faith, and had returned to his idol worship, and that, though Jesus performed miracles when on earth, He was not here now, and we did not know that He was alive, and it was, therefore, impossible for the boy to be healed.

"Upon hearing this, we felt condemned for not having the boy kneel down with us the night before in the face of the meeting, and publicly ask God to heal him, thereby showing that we had faith in Him. Our feeling of shame was so great that my wife and I, in company with two of our Christians, went to their house at 10 o'clock at night, and asked permission to pray for the boy's healing. The shoemaker at first resisted, but finally consented that he would bring the boy to the meeting the next evening.

"They brought him, according to promise, the next evening, and at the close of the meeting we announced that such a boy was present, and why he had been brought. Then I asked them to bring him forward, where all the Christians could kneel down with him. About ten prayers were then offered, occupying one hour, but he could not hear.

"All were invited to come back the next evening at five o'clock, and pray until six o'clock for him, at which time the usual meeting would begin. This was done, with about as many vocal prayers as before, after which the meeting went on perhaps until 7:30 o'clock, when it was discovered that our prayers were answered, for *the deaf and dumb was no longer deaf*; he could hear the speaker in the far part of the house from him. It created almost a panic among his relatives and friends. He is not the shoemaker's son, but word had been sent to his parents and they were both present. They went home with him, and at ten o'clock, less than three hours from the time he first heard distinctly, they returned with him to show us that he had begun to lisp the vocal sounds said to him.

"It is now the tenth day since, and he is learning as fast as could be expected. The family gave us their two idols, which we sent to the Association at Philadelphia, where any one can see them. There are many witnesses who can testify to the truth of the above. The *Tokio Christian* published an account of the healing."

MR. MOODY'S BIBLE CONFERENCE.

THE interest manifested in the Conference at Northfield increases day by day. The *Rev. J. Hudson Taylor*, of the China Inland Mission who is taking a prominent part in the meetings, referred in one of his addresses to the work of the college students in China. He said that he had seen them in their labors, and they were filled with the Spirit, and were rejoicing in having left home and friends and fortune for Christ. "There is such a thing as spiritual barter. Paul knew this and counted all things, the good as well as the bad, as loss that he might know Christ. If you would be filled with the Spirit you must be emptied of sin. Let sin out of your hearts and the Spirit of God will come in. Two bodies cannot occupy the same space; no more can the Spirit and sin dwell in the heart at the same time. Let sin out and the Spirit will come in. I find that men's faces brighten when they have made room for Christ."

Evangelist Yatman wished to plead for India, but was so impressed with the need of work among the young men of America that he must place that work first. "Out of every hundred young men, seventy-five never darken a church door. If you wish to see the evidences of sin, go with me to Baltimore. A mother raised a beautiful boy. He became a murderer, not with the knife, but of his mother's heart. She had worried over that boy till she was dying. Her last request was to see her boy. She asked him in her dying breath to give up drink. He promised his mother never to touch another drop, but hell had hold of his appetite, and he went in where his mother lay dead with his liquor and drank damnation to his soul and body. We need to reach our boys. It makes my blood tingle. We want to work for America."

Dr. Chester, of South India, was astonished to find on returning to this country after twenty years' labor in India, that there were people here who thought mission work a failure. The promise "Lo, I am with you alway" was to missionary Christians. Every one should be doing something for the Evangelization of the world. What greater service can we give than ourselves? We should give our dearest objects, our own children, to the cause of Christ. "It grieves me to see parents, from selfish motives, keeping back their children, who are willing to go. Some say there are heathen in this country, but in Dindigal, where I am, it is as if there was one missionary to the whole of Philadelphia. Every church that is able should have a missionary in the field."

Mr. D. L. Moody, in expounding the thirteenth chapter of 1 Corinthians said: "This chapter is the highest peak that Paul ever reached. Without love a man might as well blow a trumpet or sound a tea-bell in his pulpit on Sunday morning. A man may be a good doctor, and not love his patients; a good lawyer, and not love his clients; a good geologist and not love the science; but he cannot be a good Christian without love. Love is greater than prophecy, greater than faith. If a man is unsound in the faith we cut his ecclesiastical head off, but he may be unsound in love or patience, and he was still regarded as a good Christian. What we need is a baptism of love. Love makes gifts acceptable before God. Love will keep a mother up night after night, waiting for her wandering boy. Love does away with that spirit of envy and jealousy which is the greatest obstacle in the Christian life. It is a sign that we are growing in love when Christ becomes larger and we smaller in our own estimation. We are to keep ourselves in the love of God by doing more for him every day."

Among the later arrivals at the Conference are Rev. E. P. Hammond, Father Chiniquy, and Miss Vassilka Stefanora, from Bulgaria.

REV. W. F. RE QUA'S INDIAN WORK.

IN a letter from this faith missionary, who is laboring in the Indian territory and whose support hitherto has mainly come from readers of this journal whom God has moved to contribute, he describes the camp-meeting to which we referred in a former number. He praises God that many souls were converted both whites and Indians, some of whom had travelled twenty miles to attend the meeting. Mr. Re Qua goes on to say: "We camped out, of course, but the people were very kind to us in bringing to our tent plenty to eat.

"The chief of the Creek Indians, who is a fine looking, intelligent full-blood Indian, was at the meeting, and urged that we come among his people to hold meetings, and we have arranged after a *few days'* rest at home, to go and spend two weeks out among the Creeks, about seventy-five miles from here. We shall go by wagon, and then shall go on out west among some other tribes. How we do desire all the dear, kind readers of THE CHRISTIAN HERALD to pray that we may see many of the red-faces brought to Jesus! Some have come, but we want so much of the *power of the Holy Spirit* to arouse their *stoical natures*, convicting and impelling the people toward Christ, that scores will come to surrender and find pardon. I wish you could have seen my wife in these meetings, speaking and laboring for the people. She says sure we have a work out here, and the Lord has shown her that it is He who has led us hither, and gives us grace to remain and work among them.

"The Indians do love music so much, and can be drawn by it and held by it so well, that I cannot give up asking the Lord to send us a good *portable chest organ*, and I somehow feel that, as the Lord has so blessedly provided us with a team, wagon, and a harness, that He will send us the organ soon for the mission. Time would fail us to tell how good the Lord has been to us. There are now 114 names on our "*Providence memorandum-book*," who have contributed toward our Indian mission, and about all of these are subscribers of the "C. H.", for whom we pray that the Lord will abundantly reward and bless them for their kindness, and who have written us that they felt as they learned of our work, that the Lord prompted them to help us prosecute the work. Oh what encouraging words have come to us to hold on; they were praying for us, and they felt the Lord has led us out into this work and He would see us through. This, of course, we have always believed, even when we have passed through trying times, not knowing just how we were coming out for means; but, bless God! when we have gone and asked the Lord to send us means, directly it has come. It's true, we have received nowhere as much as when we were in the pastorate, but the Lord has gloriously provided for our needs.

"I can't tell you how the Lord has touched our hearts to pray for means for Christian Manual Training Orphanage, into which we may gather Indian orphan boys and girls of every tribe into such a home, and fit them to care for themselves in life and some to return to their tribes as teachers and missionaries, and we believe the Lord will yet—if He has not already—touch some man or woman's heart or move more than one perhaps and incline him or her to furnish the means to erect such an orphanage.

"If there are any who would like to send us at once lithograph cuts illustrating Bible lessons we shall be glad of them, and can use them effectually in our work among the Indians. Also as some write us to know how they can remit to us, I would like them to know that drafts, cheques, by express or registered letter we consider safe, and a cheque or draft the traders will cash for us. Four persons who sent us contributions said they *did not wish to be known* or to receive any receipt, but we should like them to know that we received their money safely, if you would mention it in THE CHRISTIAN HERALD. We are setting out again to visit the tribes and hope your readers will pray earnestly for the Holy Spirit to go with us and bless the Word to the people."

A COUNT IN LIVERY.

A TITLED bell-boy waits on the guests of a Chicago hotel. About two years ago a young man of aristocratic appearance, and speaking English with a foreign accent, applied to the manager of the hotel for employment. As he was urgent and was evidently in extreme poverty, he was taken on as a bell-boy, and was quite willing to accept that office. He was attentive to his duties and polite to the guests, and soon became a favorite in the hotel. He was reticent about his past history, but his distinguished bearing and courtly manners won him the sobriquet of "Count." Recently a clue to his identity was obtained, and as ridiculous reports were circulated about him, the young man told his story. He is the grandson of the Marquis Sainte-Croix, who was some years ago French ambassador at St. Petersburg. He was born in Odessa, and was educated there. His liberal notions led to his affiliation with one of the insurrectionary societies, and he was implicated in a plot which was discovered. The youth made his escape, for he was aware that not even his aristocratic French connection could have saved him from condign punishment had been caught. Besides, his relations were disgusted with him for mixing himself up in seditious plots, and were not disposed to shield him. He, too, had conceived a dislike for monarchy and aristocracy. America attracted him, and he came here to make his fortune. It was not quite so easy as he expected, and he wandered around until his funds were exhausted, unable to obtain employment. It is his intention now to read law as soon as he has saved enough money to support him. Meanwhile the guests at the hotel have the gratification of being waited upon by the scion of an ancient and noble house. It may be hoped that the young man, though he has abjured his titles and cut himself off from his aristocratic family, will be led to aspire to a higher order of nobility, and in becoming a son of the King of kings, have a title to an eternal inheritance. (1 Peter 1:3, 4.)

PROPHETIC EVENTS BETWEEN 1889 AND 1901.

"BEHOLD, THE BRIDEGROOM COMETH."

Mr. William Birch's 776th Printed Sunday Sermon, delivered in Free Trade Hall, Manchester, March 18, 1888.

"And at midnight there was a cry made, Behold, the Bridegroom cometh." Matt. 25:6.

The Scriptural View of Human Progress—The Events at the End of the Age—The Time Disclosed—The Image of Nebuchadnezzar's Vision—The Setting Up of the Everlasting Kingdom—The Constitution of a Decem Regal Confederacy—The Seven Years' Covenant With the Jews—The Confederacy to Adopt Communism—The Romish Church Persecuting Again—A Kaiser Chosen by Plebiscite.

IT is supposed by many that the world will become better, like a progressive growth, one generation improving on the previous one; but the written word of God does not give us any hope of mankind becoming universally godly before our Lord appears again, nor can we hope for the conversion of the Jews as a people until Christ once more stands on Mount Olivet as the glorious King of kings, but, at the same time, still bearing the marks of the nails in His hands and feet. Scripture chiefly foretells

Very Remarkable Incidents

that shall occur in the earth. For one thing, it shows that our Lord Jesus shall come again in the clouds, and draw up to Himself the resurrected bodies of departed saints; secondly, those Christians who are living and watching for Him shall be suddenly changed and also caught up. The number of Christians so changed will only be 144,000 persons; and about five years afterwards, our Lord's angels shall come to remove to heaven the remaining Christians who are left behind, together with new converts, and the faithful ones who meanwhile have died. And then in like manner as He ascended, our Lord Jesus shall descend and stand upon Mount Olivet near Jerusalem, when He will begin the one thousand years of His kingdom on the earth. (Rev. 14:4, 15; 19:20.)

Does God give us any idea of the *time* when the End of this Age shall come? He does. May the Holy Spirit open our understanding so that we may see what He means and not be overtaken unawares!

The ancient king Nebuchadnezzar had a vision, which is recorded in Daniel's second chapter, of the Gentile empires of Babylon, Persia, Greece, and Rome, prefigured as a metallic Image of a man, whose head was gold, the breast and arms of silver, the loins brass, the legs iron, and the feet partly of iron and clay. A miraculous stone struck the toes, shattering the entire Image, and the stone then grew bigger until like a mountain it filled the earth. Our Lord Jesus is that Miraculous Stone, who in due time will abolish the present national governments of mankind and establish His personal reign for a thousand years.

The prophet Daniel states that the

Ten Toes of the Image

mean ten kings who are to divide among themselves the original territory of the Roman empire, the whole of which is represented by the two iron legs of the Image, namely, *Britain* separated from Ireland—and all *Europe* west of the Rhine and south of the Danube and the Carpathian mountains—and all the north coast of *Africa*, with *Asia Minor*, *Palestine*, and *Syria*, up to the river Euphrates on the frontiers of Persia.

In Dan. 2:44 it is said that "in the days of these ten kings shall the God of heaven set up a kingdom that shall never be destroyed." It is clear, therefore, that the twenty-three kingdoms now established within the boundaries already named shall be transformed into ten nations. These ten will apparently be, (1) France, (2) Britain, (3) Spain and Portugal united, (4) Italy, (5) Austria, (6) Slavonic States—Roumania, Bulgaria, and Servia, &c.—(7) Greece, (8) Turkey, (9) Syria, and (10) Egypt. As the ten toes are partly *clay* and partly *iron*, it shows that the ten nations will be *democratic-monarchic*; and it is remarkable that the spirit of democracy, that is, the desire for government by the people for the people, through presidents or sovereigns elected by universal suffrage or plebiscites, instead of by hereditary kings and aristocrats, is now spreading on every hand.

Daniel speaks also of the four Gentile empires, already referred to under the forms of *wild beasts* rising up one after another, namely, a lion, a bear, a four-headed leopard, and a ten-horned wild beast, the latter meaning the territories of Cæsar's Roman empire just the same as the two iron legs of the Image.

Daniel's prophecies show us that the *time* of the international

Wars and Civil Commotions,

which are essential in order to change the twenty-three kingdoms into ten, will be between 1888–1891, because the confederacy of ten nations is to be formed by about ten years before the End of this Age, which Daniel shows to be in Passover Week in 1901, at the end of 2345 years from the command to rebuild Jerusalem, in Passover Week, B. C. 445, as stated in Nehemiah 2, and Daniel 8:14; 9:25; 12:11, 12. Hence between this year 1888 and 1891, France will recover her territory up to the Rhine, and Britain will be drawn into a great European war, and Ireland, taking advantage of the opportunity, will obtain Home Rule, and become practically independent of England. When it is remembered that about one-fourth of the British army consists of Irish Romanists, and that there are many thousands of the same nationality and religion in each of our large towns, it will be seen that if, at a time of European war and bad trade, they join with the socialists and the thousands of discontented, the consequences to Britain may be most disastrous.

As a nation we have forgotten God, and merit His indignation. One among many of our national sins is the widespread disregard of the injunction to "keep holy the Sabbath-day," and the use of it by many as a day of pleasure or business or dissipation, instead of a day for the worship of God. Notice the fashionable dinners and amusements of the rich, and the irreligious pleasures of many of the poor on that sacred day; together with no inconsiderable number of the "cultured classes" looking upon the written word of God as uninspired, and upon the Judgment Day as a superstition. I fear, therefore, that the English people have a dreadful rod in pickle waiting for them, and that bad trade at home and grievous disasters abroad are within measurable distance ahead. Throughout all Europe there is coming a "time of trouble such as never was since there was a nation even to that same time." (Daniel 12:1.)

When the allied ten nations have been formed within the territories of the Roman Empire, there will arise, some time near 1892, an eleventh little horn, or

King of Napoleon Name

or nature, as monarch over some little State, such as Macedonia for instance, inside the present Turkish Empire. He will then "wax exceeding great toward the South, and toward the East, and toward the pleasant land" (Palestine), and by dint of flatteries climb into power as "King of the North," or Syria, by 1894, (as predicted in Daniel 7:24; 8:9; 11:21, 40). Forthwith he will make a covenant or league for seven years with the Jews—presumably from Passover Week, 1894, to Passover Week, 1901—giving them the right of free worship in Jerusalem, where they will build a temple and offer morning and evening sacrifices as in ancient times, according to Daniel 8:14; 9:27—probably about November 8, 1894, exactly 2,345 literal days before the Last Day of this Age, which is shown by Daniel's dates to be Thursday, April 11, the last day of Passover Week in 1901.* This Syrian King will then wage three wars against the King of the South (Egypt), and in the second war be hindered by the ships of Kittim; but in about two years and a half after the signing of the covenant with the Jews, he will conquer Egypt; and after heading a red republican revolution in Europe, he will become its Military Dictator, about April, 1897. (Daniel 11:25, 29, 40; Rev. 17:3, 13.)

A Communistic Republic.

At this point of time, which will be about three years after the Jewish covenant, the ten Roman nations will be formed into a red-republican and Roman Catholic confederacy, as stated in Revelation 17:3: "I saw a woman arrayed in scarlet, sit upon a scarlet-colored beast, full of names of blasphemy, having seven heads and ten horns," meaning that the Church of Rome will adopt the doctrines of Communism and Socialism, and will regain her temporal power, and seated upon her seven-hilled city (for the "seven heads are seven mountains," verses 9 and 18), she will inspire the nations of the earth to obey her. Then, as stated in Rev. 17:6, she will slay the Christians who refuse to bow down to her, and will boastfully say, "I sit a queen, and am no widow, and shall see no sorrow." (Rev. 18:7.) It is obvious that as the scarlet woman is represented as sitting upon the beast with ten horns, namely, the ten nations already enumerated, that she will, by that time, have incorporated with herself the Greek Church and Mahometanism. God's Word calls her the "Mother of harlots and Abominations of the earth" (Rev. 17:5); in fact, she will have universal ecclesiastical dominion (Rev. 17:1, 15).

The first form of the Ten-kingdomed Confederacy, about 1891, will have been purely *monarchical* and *liberal*, but this second or *scarlet* form in 1897 will be *Red-republican* and *Ultramontane*. Then the third form of the confederacy of the ten nations in the latter part of 1897 will be *Democratic-Imperial*—that of the

Antichrist Elected by a Plebiscite

as Emperor over the ten kings of the ten nations. The Pope will then be his obsequious servant, and looking upon him as a God, shall command the world to worship him under pain of death. This shall last three and a half years until our Lord descends on Olivet. (Rev. 17:13.)

(To be Concluded.)

* Passover Week (April 4-11), 1901, is regarded as the Last Week of this Age, because it is 2,345 years distant from Passover Week, B. C. 445, when Artaxerxes gave the command to Nehemiah to rebuild Jerusalem, exactly sixty-nine weeks or 483 years before Messiah was "cut off" in a Passover Week (Daniel 8:14; 9:25), and also because it is forty-five years distant from the Crimean War Treaty of Peace, ratified on the last day of Passover Week, 1856, which "cleansed the Sanctuary" of the Holy Land, at the end of Daniel's 2,300 years, from Mahomedan laws of murderous intolerance, which were then repealed (the forty-five years being the 1,335 minus the 1,290 years in Daniel 12:11, 12).

CHRISTIAN HERALD AND SIGNS OF OUR TIMES.

OFFICE, 63 BIBLE HOUSE, NEW YORK.

ENTERED AT THE POST-OFFICE AT NEW YORK, N. Y., AS SECOND-CLASS MATTER.

EVERY NUMBER CONTAINS:

The Portrait and Biography of some eminent person.
The Sermon Dr. Talmage preached the last Sunday morning.
An Exposition of Unfulfilled Prophecy.
A Summary of the Events of the Week, Notes of Religious and Temperance Movements, etc.
A Sermon by Rev. C. H. Spurgeon, of London, from advance sheets sent by special arrangement.
Pictures of Missionary Life, etc., and Descriptive Articles.
An instalment of a Serial Story.
An Exposition of the International Sunday-School Lesson, by Mrs. M. Baxter.

ANNUAL SUBSCRIPTION, $1.50.

Remittances by mail should be by bank cheques, Post-office orders, or Express money-orders whenever possible. If currency is sent it should be in a registered letter. Cheques and money-orders should be made payable to THE CHRISTIAN HERALD. Making them payable to individuals often causes delay.

New subscriptions may commence at any time. When subscribers do not indicate their wish, they commence with the first number of the month in which the subscription is received.

PUBLISHER'S NOTICE.

The whole edition of The Christian Herald was mailed last week to subscribers during Tuesday, Aug. 7. The last delivery at the New York Post Office was made at 11.36 P. M.

CURRENT EVENTS.

The Funeral of General Philip H. Sheridan took place on Saturday last, at Arlington, the family having expressed a preference for the Washington cemetery over the Soldier's Home, which was at first proposed. The spot selected for the grave is near the mansion on the hillside that slopes eastward. Standing on the spot chosen as his resting-place one can see Washington City spread out before him in front, right, and left. Georgetown is at the extreme right, and the Potomac and Analostan Island, the bridges, and the Virginia and Maryland shores are included in the broad scene. Behind the spot where Sheridan's grave was dug lie the bodies of some 12,000 Union soldiers, the men who died in camp along the Potomac, the slain at Bull Run and in the Wilderness. In compliance with the wishes of the dead General, the funeral was as private as was possible in the case of so distinguished a man. The body was taken from Nonquitt on Wednesday, under the charge of General Schofield. It was placed in St. Matthew's Roman Catholic Church, in Washington, where it was watched by a local guard of honor until the ceremony of interment.

A Stringent Anti-Chinese Immigration Bill was passed by the Senate on August 8. It absolutely prohibits the entrance into the United States of any Chinaman except officials, teachers, students, merchants, or travelers for pleasure or curiosity, and not even those unless they shall first obtain the permission of the Chinese Government, and hold a certificate establishing their personal identity, to be made out by the diplomatic representative or consul of the United States in the country from which the person named therein comes. The bill also prohibits the return to this country of any Chinaman who may have acquired residence here and afterward visited China, unless he has a lawful wife, child or parent in the United States, or property therein of the value of one thousand dollars, or debts of like amount due him and pending settlement.

General Clinton B. Fisk, and Dr. John A. Brooks, formally accepted their respective nominations by the Prohibition party for the Presidency and Vice-Presidency on August 6. General Fisk in his letter describes his poignant regret at severing his connection with the Republican party, but adds: "Every day since then has shown yet more clearly the logic of my course, and the truth of my conclusions. In Michigan, in Texas, in Tennessee and Oregon, so-called non-partisan efforts to establish prohibition have failed through partisan necessity, born of liquor elements in old party composition. In Iowa, Rhode Island, and Maine the laws have been shamelessly defied for like reason. The entire trend of things these last four years has proved hopeless, the broader range of prohibition effect through non-partisan means, and equally futile, as a final consummation, the narrower methods of local option and high license, while from the Supreme Court itself has come with startling emphasis a declaration so nationalizing this reform that it can never be made of local or State limitation again. No lines of territorial wish or will can hereafter bear the liquor traffic and its fearful brood, while by national policy that traffic is recognized as legitimate, and while under that policy the National Government derives revenue therefrom." Dr. Brooks is equally emphatic, and while endorsing the protection policy of the Republican platform, says: "A proper protection of American labor and the infant industries of our country may and does commend itself to the majority of our people, but of infinitely more importance is the protection of our homes. To this end your platform subordinates all other questions."

Startling Disclosures are being Made to the Committee on Immigration which is pursuing its inquiries in New York. Witnesses testified last week, giving names and dates, that, in spite of the contract labor law, prominent manufacturers import large numbers of men through recognized agents. In one case the witness heard an employer give the order to a Russian agent for a specified number of Poles, who were then in Europe, and who were duly brought over, and set to work, American laborers being discharged to make room for them. In the shirt industry, hands had been brought from Europe under contract, who have displaced the women and girls formerly employed. The women still employed have had their wages reduced from eight dollars a week to four dollars, and find it difficult to get work at that rate. It is a curious and significant fact that the firms most active in thus evading the law are among the most strenuous advocates in New York of high tariff, and are loud in their protestation against reduction, urging the plea that it would reduce the wages of the American workingman. As a case in point, it was stated that the West Shore Railroad, of which Mr. Chauncey Depew is President, recently imported fifteen hundred Italians, who were engaged at lower wages than American laborers received.

Mr. James G. Blaine Received a Royal Welcome in New York on his arrival from England last week. One huge demonstration in his honor preceded his arrival. The steamer by which he came was due on Wednesday, and it was arranged that he should review a monstre procession of Republican clubs, trade organizations, and deputations from several States. The vessel was delayed, however, by an accident to her machinery, and did not reach New York until Friday. Mr. Blaine was, therefore, unable to witness the ovation intended for him. The parade took place on Thursday night, in his absence; but the enthusiasm displayed was clearly evoked by the expectation of his presence. The familiar campaign cry of 1884, "Blaine, Blaine, James G. Blaine," was raised at intervals all along the line, and a large portrait of the statesman, which occupied the place on the reviewing stand that it was hoped that he would have filled in person, was saluted with ringing cheers by each detachment as it passed. It was such a procession as New York has rarely seen. Starting soon after eight in the evening, it had not entirely passed the stand before midnight. The vessel was sighted early the following morning, and a special steamer, laden with personal and political friends, was sent down the bay to meet him at Quarantine, and bring him to the city. On his landing, his enthusiastic admirers wanted to take the horses from his carriage and drag it to his hotel; but Mr. Blaine would not allow it. An immense throng, however, accompanied him, and in the evening he was serenaded, and an address of welcome presented to him. In reply, he made a speech to a vast audience in the open air. Such a reception to a private citizen is unprecedented, and must have been deeply gratifying to Mr. Blaine.

The International Medical Congress, which has devoted all its sessions to the subject of tuberculosis, has come to the conclusion almost unanimously that consumption is a contagious disease, and may be transmitted from animals to human beings, by means of infected food, drink, or air. It is the opinion of these experts that many cases of consumption are derived from tuberculous cows, through the agency of milk, or from tuberculous beef cattle through the agency of half-cooked meat. Consequently the delegates to the congress point out that danger from these sources may be avoided by boiling milk and cooking meat thoroughly.

The Appearance of the Red Flag on the streets of Paris caused a disturbance on August 8. The trouble arose over the funeral of General Eudes, the ex-communist, who dropped dead while addressing a body of strikers on August 5. Fifty thousand persons gathered in the streets adjacent to the house of the deceased, and thousands lined the route to the cemetery, along which cavalry was stationed. The other troops belonging to the Paris garrison were held within their barracks in readiness for any emergency. Traffic in the streets through which the cortège passed was suspended and the stores were closed. Among those who attended the funeral were Henry Rochefort and Louise Michel. Many flowers and wreaths were placed upon the coffin. When the procession reached the Boulevard Voltaire, three red flags were unfurled. A commissary of police attempted to seize one, when some one in the crowd fired a revolver at him, but the bullet went wide of its mark. The gendarmes then took a hand in protecting the police: they used the butt-end of their muskets, and after a short fight arrested twenty-four of the anarchists and captured the three flags. The procession went on to the cemetery shouting, "Vive la Commune!" "Vive la Revolution!"

An Incisive Speech by the British Premier was made on August 10, in the House of Lords, on the Parnell Investigation Bill, which having passed the Commons, was introduced in the upper house. In explaining the character and object of the unusual mode of inquiry, Lord Salisbury said that in recent years the agitation in Ireland had gone on two parallel lines. One party professed to act constitutionally, and to a certain extent had so acted; the other party was connected with crime, violence, intimidation, mutilation and murder, which means were used to intimidate constitutional opponents, and to force from England the concession of a change which England was not prepared to grant. These organizations had been professedly apart, but they worked for the same ends; they had the same friends and enemies, and injured the same persons. An impression had naturally arisen that they were really not so far apart as they seemed to be, and that there was complicity or connection between them. The charges of complicity with crime had not driven the Parnellites to the courts, but they had demanded an investigation by a Committee of the House of Commons, which did not appear to be a competent tribunal. The Government therefore had appointed a Commission of judges which would close these controversies. It was not well that members of the House of Commons should be accused, in the most solemn manner, of having tampered with murder. The truth should be known, whatever might be the issue. The Government was convinced that it had done good service in driving from the arena of political discussion this foul and scandalous controversy.

Evangelists or Christian Workers Desiring copies of THE CHRISTIAN HERALD for distribution at camp meetings or other religious gatherings, will receive parcels of back numbers free of charge by writing, stating number required, to the manager, 63 Bible House, New York.

Contributions to the Fund for Supplying colored ministers in the South with this journal have been received since our last acknowledgment to the amount of $11. They are from Prairie City, Ia., $1; Walcot, Va., $1; Boston, Mass., $1; Woodhaven, N. Y., $2; West Newbury, Vt., $3; A Friend, $2; San Francisco, Cal.,

We have now on hand the names of over one hundred and twenty colored ministers who are anxiously desiring to receive the paper through this fund. Many of them, who have received it in the past, speak in most grateful terms of the valuable service it has been the means of rendering to them and their congregations. They earnestly pray that it may be continued another year. All we can do is to lay their request before our readers, trusting that the need so pathetically urged may be met.

Deeply Interesting Lectures on Spain, Mexico, Central and South America, illustrated by stereopticon views have been delivered by Bishop H. C. Riley in Ascension Chapel, New York, and in other places in the city and neighborhood during the past few weeks. Pastors of churches who desire to interest their people in this important sphere of labor, would find no better mode of enlightening them as to its needs and capacities than by inviting the Bishop to deliver one of his lectures in their churches. His address is 43 Bible House, New York.

Four Years of Painful Travel have been undergone by a negro in Georgia. The Macon *Telegraph* states that an aged negro was found on August 7, on the Houston Road, near Gilesville, who was suffering severely, and was put into a wagon and taken to the Roff Home. He said that he belonged to Macon, but had settled at Jacksonville. There he fell into misfortune, lost his toes by frost-bite and became paralyzed. He had an irrepressible longing to get back to his old home in Macon, but having no money he determined to make the journey by crawling on his hands and knees. He travelled in this painful manner by unfrequented roads, only going near human habitations to beg for food. His strength and condition would not permit him to cover more than a quarter of a mile a day, and, crawling over the ground as he did, he was often compelled to remain off the road for days and weeks by reason of rain and severe weather. He lived on what was given him, and sometimes, being a great distance between villages, he suffered much for both water and food. It was four years since he left Jacksonville, and he had had no ride until that which took him to the Roff Home. The man's perseverance through such obstacles is truly wonderful. Christians travelling through life to their heavenly home often have need of such patience and perseverance as the old negro exercised. Though the way may seem hard to them their welcome is assured, especially if, like him, they journey on their knees. (Zech. 13:9.)

A Curious Reason for Confession and Restitution was given by a thief in the Tombs Police Court, New York, on August 7. Among the prisoners brought up before the justice on that day was a youth about eighteen years old, against whom there were no witnesses. He told the justice that his mother was dead and that she had been a good mother to him, bringing him up honestly and warning him against evil doing. They lived in Philadelphia, but after her death he came to New York, where he fell into bad ways. On August 4, he was in West Street and noticed a lady waiting an opportunity to cross the street, which was crowded by vehicles. Her attention being concentrated on the passing drays and cars, he went behind her and succeeded in stealing her watch. She did not notice her loss, and he got away unobserved. He pawned the watch and meant to have a good time with the money, but on going out that night he saw a shadowy form follow him in a menacing manner. He looked at it over his shoulder and recognized his dead mother. He tried to shake off her pursuit by running, by going into crowded thoroughfares, and by drinking; but, wherever he went, the shadowy form followed, and when he went home it stood by his bed, terrifying him. He suffered the torture for two days and then, being unable to bear it longer, he went to the police, made a confession and gave up the pawn-ticket and what money was left. Then he said the spectre left him, and the night in his cell was the first night he had slept since his crime. The spectre was, of course, the product of his conscience and his imagination, but to him doubtless it was very real. Better informed rogues would have seen no spectres, but if they could see the vengeance of God which really does follow them, they would be quite as much alarmed as the young man was by his superstitious idea. (Prov. 11:21.)

A Whole Family Perished in a Tenement house fire in New York, last week. A man and his wife and daughter and mother-in-law occupied the highest floor in a crowded building on Fifty-sixth Street, which the driver of an ash-cart discovered was on fire, as he passed in the night. He ran to the nearest alarm box and sent out a call for an engine, and then returned to the burning house to assist in rescuing the inmates. There was the usual confusion for some time, and as the stairs were burning, there was considerable difficulty in getting the people out, which had to be done through the fire escapes. It was supposed that all were saved, but when the firemen climbed on the roof to "wash down" they found the four bodies of the family on the top floor all dead. In the hurry and confusion they had been forgotten by the other tenants. They had evidently been asleep in bed, and not being warned, slept on until it was too late to escape. Doubtless their fellow-tenants reproach themselves now for their neglect, but their responsibility is but slight compared with that of Christian men who see their acquaintances in danger of the far worse calamity of perishing eternally, and make no effort to arouse them. (Ezek. 33:8.)

An Utterly Friendless Lady Died at Nyack, N. Y., two weeks ago. She was a teacher for seventeen years in the New York Juvenile Asylum. Her situation was peculiar. Her parents emigrated to this country from England shortly after her birth, and settled in New York. Some family affairs occurred while she was still a child which necessitated the return of both father and mother to the old country. As the child was delicate and the parents were obliged to go in the steerage, they were anxious to leave her in this country, especially as they intended to return almost immediately. A kind clergyman readily undertook the care of her during their absence, and they gratefully accepted his offer, feeling sure that they were leaving her in good hands. A disaster occurred to the vessel by which they sailed, and both father and mother were drowned. The clergyman continued to support the child, and when she grew old enough obtained for her the position in the Nyack Asylum, which she held until her death. She always believed that she had many relatives in England, but she was too young when her parents left to remember their names or anything about them; and, though she lived to be forty years old she never heard tidings of any of them. The loneliness of her life was apparent at her funeral, in the unusual absence of mourning relatives. That fact, however, would not distress her then, if it had done so in her life. The only question of any concern to her would be whether, through faith in Christ, she had become a child of God, and a member of His family. (Rev. 21:27.)

An Adventure with a Bear is Described in a despatch from Round Island, in the St. Lawrence River. It states that, on August 6, a citizen of Rochester, N. Y., accompanied by a friend, started on a pedestrian trip across the island. They took no guns, as no reports of bears or other wild animals being on the island had reached them. About half the journey had been accomplished, when they struck some rough ground, and had to make their way over rocks, fallen trees, and thick underbrush. They were sitting down on a fallen tree to rest, when they heard a heavy tread and the breaking of branches behind them; and, looking around, they were terrified at seeing a big black bear approaching. The Rochester man ran to the nearest tree, which he climbed as nimbly as a boy, while his companion ran off at the top of his speed. The bear came to the foot of the tree, and made an attempt to climb it, but failed, as it was very thin. He gave a low, fierce growl, and sat down at the foot, as if to starve the man out. Half an hour passed, the man comforting himself with the hope that his companion would get the farmers to come with guns to his assistance. Another hour passed, and the man was still in the tree, when it occurred to him that he had a revolver in his pocket. It was not large enough to kill the bear, but it might scare him away. He drew it and fired. The bear received a painful flesh wound, and rose, shaking himself savagely. One more shot finished the business, for at the second wound he started off at a run, and disappeared in the woods. Glad as the man was at his deliverance, he blamed himself for his folly in not thinking of his weapon before. That is the case with many Christians when they are beset by the enemy of souls. They have a weapon which Satan dreads, but they neglect to use it. (Eph. 6:16–18.)

BRIEF NOTES.

Out of seventy-five Protestant Episcopal churches and chapels in New York City, forty-four are absolutely and unconditionally free.

The Russian Government has issued an edict forbidding Jews who have migrated from the central provinces of Russia to distil or sell spirituous liquors in the provinces of Turkestan.

At a discussion of the subject of Christianity *vs.* Poverty, held in London recently, Dr. Newman Hall estimated that $350,000 is spent for intoxicants in London every Saturday and Sunday.

Christobal Colon, a young man in the Spanish Department of the New York Life Insurance Company, is said to be the only surviving descendant in a straight line from Christopher Columbus.

The Rev. George Duffield, who died at Bloomfield, N. J., a few days ago, was the author of the familiar hymn, "Stand up, stand up for Jesus," and the father of the late Rev. S. W. Duffield, the hymnologist.

The Moravians report for the past year 29,283 communicants in their mission fields, with a total of 83,052 persons under the care of their missionaries. The total receipts were $95,345. There is a deficiency of upward of $5,000.

Judge T. K. Wilson, of the San Francisco Superior Court, was asked recently what percentage of divorces were caused by intemperance. He promptly replied, "seventy-five per cent." During the year 1887, 399 citizens of that city obtained divorces.

The corner-stone of the Presbyterian Hospital of Chicago, was laid last month with appropriate ceremonies. The new hospital building is to be constructed from an endowment of $100,000 provided for in the will of Daniel A. Jones, who died about three years ago.

A summary of the statistics of the Christian churches of the United States shows that there are now 138,885 churches, 94,457 ministers, and 19,790,323 members in this country. The net gains for the past year were, 6,434 churches, 4,505 ministers, and 774,861 communicants.

Rev. E. W. Oakes is rejoicing in signal marks of God's blessing in his work at Manchester, N. H. His church being free, having no pew rents or assessments, the neglected classes in the city have flocked to it, and hundreds of them have made profession of their faith in Christ.

The Young Men's Christian Association of Cincinnati have begun the erection of a new and elegant hall, the cost of which will be $150,000. This will be the centennial gift, in memory of the organization of the northwestern Territory, of this Association to the cause of Christianity.

Very successful revival services are being held at Lynn, Mass., in a large tent. The number attending is unprecedented in summer services in that city. Messrs. McLean and Willis, who conduct the meetings, are much encouraged also by the number who have ascribed their conversion to God's blessing on these services.

The *Jewish Chronicle* intimates that the Jews, stimulated by the example of the Pan-Anglican Synod, are meditating the propriety of summoning a Pan-Judaic Synod. The subjects suggested for discussion are the limits of Scripture inspiration, the attitude of the Synagogue toward the latest teachings of geology and biology, the restoration of the Jewish sacrifices, and even the more profoundly important question of the Messiah.

PETER'S RESTORATION.

A New Sermon by Pastor C. H. Spurgeon.

"And immediately, while he yet spake, the cock crew. And the Lord turned, and looked upon Peter. And Peter remembered the word of the Lord, how He had said unto him, Before the cock crow, thou shalt deny Me thrice. And Peter went out and wept bitterly."—Luke 22:60-62.

A Deplorable Sin—What Led up to It—The Fruit of Presumption and Self-Confidence—A Happy Conjunction—I. The Lord Looking upon Peter—His Thoughtful Love—Condescension—Divine Power—Christ-like Christians Looking After Backsliders—II. The Look—Refreshed Peter's Memory—Penetrated his Heart—Peter Must Have Been Looking at Jesus—III. Peter After the Look—His Awakening—His Foolhardiness Vanished—Ashamed to be Ashamed.

PETER had terribly fallen. He had denied his Master, denied Him repeatedly, denied Him with oaths, denied Him in His presence, while his Master was being smitten and falsely charged; denied Him, though he was an apostle; denied Him, though he had declared that should all men forsake Him, yet would he never be offended. It was a sad, sad sin. Remember

What Led up to It.

It was, first, Peter's presumption and self-confidence. He reckoned that he could never stumble, and for that very reason he speedily fell. A haughty spirit goes before a fall! Oh, that we might look to the roots of bitter flowers, and destroy them! If presumption is flourishing in the soil of our hearts to-day, we shall soon see the evil fruit which will come of it. Reliance upon our firmness of character, depth of experience, clearness of insight, or matureness in grace, will, in the end, land us in disgrace and failure. *We must either deny ourselves, or we shall deny our Lord;* if we cleave to self-confidence, we shall not cleave to Him.

Immediately, Peter's denial was owing to cowardice. The brave Peter, in the presence of a maid was ashamed; he could not bear to be pointed out as a follower of the Galilean. He did not know what might follow upon it; but he saw his Lord without a friend, and felt that it was a lost cause, and he did not care to avow it. Only to think that Peter, under temporary discouragement, should play the coward! Yet cowardice treads upon the heels of boasting; he that thinks he can fight the world, will be

The First Man to Run Away.

I desire in this discourse to speak chiefly of Peter's restoration. Peter was down; but he was soon up again. One writer says the story should rather be called Peter's restoration than Peter's fall. His fall was soon over: he was like a little child learning to walk, scarcely down before his mother has him up again. It was not a continuance in a sin, like that of David, who remained for months without repentance; but it was the quick speech of a man carried away by sudden temptation, and it was followed by a speedy repentance. Upon his restoration we are going to meditate.

It was brought about by two outward means. I like to think of the singular combination: the crowing of the cock, and a look from the Lord. When I come to preach to you, it almost makes me smile to think that God should save a soul through me. I may find a fit image of myself in the poor cock. Mine is poor crowing. But as the Master's look went with the cock's crowing, so, I trust, it will go with my feeble preaching. The next time you also go out to try and win a soul for Jesus, say to yourself, "I cannot do it: I cannot melt a hard, rebellious heart; but yet the Lord may use me; and if there come

A Happy Conjunction

of my feeble words with my Lord's potent look, then the heart will dissolve in streams of repentance." Crow away, poor bird: if Jesus looks whilst thou art crowing, thou wilt not crow in vain; but Peter's heart will break. The two things are joined together, and let no man put them asunder—the commonplace instrumentality and the divine Worker. Christ has all the glory, and all the more glory because He works by humble means. I trust that there will be this morning a conjunction of the weakness of the preacher with the strength of the Holy Spirit; so that stony hearts may be broken and God glorified.

I. First, let us look at the Lord, who looked upon Peter. Can you picture Him in the hall, up yonder steps, before the high priest and the council? Peter is down below, in the area of the house, warming his hands at the fire. Can you see the Lord Jesus turning round and fixing His eyes intently upon His erring disciple?

What See You in that Look?

I see in that look, first, that which makes me exclaim: What thoughtful love! Jesus is bound, He is accused, He has just been smitten on the face, but His thought is of wandering Peter. You want all your wits about you when you are before cruel judges, and are called upon to answer false charges; you are the more tried when there is no man to stand by you, or bear witness on your behalf; it is natural, at such an hour that all your thoughts should be engaged with your own cares and sorrows. It would have been no reproach had the thoughts of our Lord been concentrated on His personal sufferings; and all the less so because these were for the sake of others. But our blessed Master is thinking of Peter, and His heart is going out toward His unworthy disciple. Blessed be His dear name; Jesus always has an eye for His people, whether He be in His shame or in His glory.

I exclaim, next, What a boundless condescension! If our Lord's eye had wandered that day upon "that other disciple" that was known to the high priest, or if He had even looked upon some of the servants of the house, we should not have been so astonished; but

When Jesus Turns.

it is to look upon Peter, the man from whom we should naturally have turned away our faces after his wretched conduct. He had acted most shamefully and cruelly, and yet the Master's eye sought him out in boundless pity! If there is a man here who feels himself to be near akin to the devil, I pray the Lord to look first at him.

But then, again, what tender wisdom do I see here! "The Lord turned, and looked upon Peter." He knew best what to do: He did not speak to him, but looked upon him. How wisely doth Christ always choose the way of expressing His affection, and working our good! If He had spoken to Peter then, the mob would have assailed Him, or at least the ribald crowd would have remarked upon the sorrow of the Master and the treachery of the disciple: our gracious Lord will never needlessly expose the faults of His chosen. Our Saviour employed the most prudent, the most comprehensive, the most useful method of speaking to the heart of His erring follower. He looked volumes into him. His glance was

A Divine Hieroglyphic

full of unutterable meanings, which it conveyed in a more clear and vivid way than words could have done. As I think of that look, I am compelled to cry out: What divine power is here! Why, dear friends, this look worked wonders! I sometimes preach with all my soul to Peter, and, alas! he likes my sermon and forgets it. I have known Peter read a good book full of most powerful pleading, and when he has read it through he has shut it up and gone to sleep. I remember my Peter when he lost his wife, and one would have thought it would have touched him, and it did, with some natural feeling; yet he did not return to the Lord, whom he had forsaken, but continued in his backsliding. See, then, how our Lord can do with a look what we cannot do with a sermon, what the most powerfull writer cannot do with hundreds of pages, and what affliction cannot do with even its heaviest stroke. The Lord looked, and Peter wept bitterly.

Let me beg you to note what sacred teaching is here. The teaching is of practical value, and should be at once carried out by the followers of Jesus. You, dear friend, are a Christian man or a Christian woman; you have been kept by divine grace, from anything like disgraceful sin. Thank God it is so. I dare say, if you look within, you will find much to be ashamed of; but yet you have been kept from presumptuous and open sins. Alas! one who was once a friend of yours has disgraced himself: he was a little while ago a member of the church, but he has shamefully turned aside. You cannot excuse his sin; on the contrary, you are forced to feel great indignation against his folly, his untruthfulness, his wickedness. He has caused the enemies of the Lord to blaspheme, and has done awful mischief to the cause of righteousness. Now I know what will be suggested to you. You will be

Inclined to Cut His Acquaintance,

to disown him altogether, and scarcely to look at him if you meet him in the street. This is the manner of men, but not the manner of Jesus. I charge you, act not in so un-Christlike a manner. The Lord turned, and looked on Peter; will not His servants look on him? You are not perfect like your Lord; you are only a poor sinful creature like your fallen brother. What! are you too proud to look at the fallen one? Will you not give him a helping hand? Will you not try to bring him back? The worst thing you can do with a backslider is to let him keep on sliding back. Your duty should be your pleasure, and your duty is to "restore such an one in the spirit of meekness, remembering thyself also, lest thou also be tempted."

One more lesson: observe what heavenly comfort is here: "The Lord turned and looked upon Peter;" yes, Jesus looks upon sinners still. The doctrine of God's omniscience is far oftener set forth in a hard way than in a cheering way. Have you never heard a sermon from "Thou God seest me," of which the pith was, "Therefore tremble, and be afraid"? That is hardly fair to the text; for when Hagar cried, "Thou, God, seest me," it was because the Lord had interposed to help her, when she had fled from her mistress. It was comfort to her that there she also had looked after Him that had looked upon her. There is a dark side to "Thou, God, seest me"; but it is not half so dark as it would be if God did not see us. It is true, O sinner, that God has seen your sin, and all the aggravations of it; but it is also true that as He sees your ruin, your misery, your sadness, He has compassion on you. He sees your sin that He may remove it, and make you clean in His sight. As the Lord looked upon Peter, so He looks upon you. He has not turned His back on you; He has not averted the gaze of His pity.

II. Now let us go on to the second point and

Look into the Look

which the Lord gave to Peter. That look was, first of all, a marvellous refreshment to Peter's memory: "The Lord turned, and looked upon Peter." What a sight it must have been for Peter! Our dear Master's face was that night all red from the bloody sweat. He must have appeared emaciated in body, His eyes weary with want of sleep, and His whole countenance the vision of grief. If ever a picture of the Man of Sorrows could have been drawn, it should have been taken at that moment when the Lord turned and looked upon Peter. By torchlight and the flickering flame of the fire in the court of the hall of Caiaphas, Peter saw a vision which would never fade from his mind. He saw the man whom he loved as he had never seen Him before. Though the lineaments of that reverend face were distained with blood, yet Peter could tell that it was the selfsame Lord with whom he had enjoyed three years of intimate intercourse and tender unveiling. All this must in a moment have flashed upon poor Peter's mind; and I do not wonder that in the recollection of it all he went out and wept bitterly.

Next, that turning of the Master was a special reminder of His warning words. Jesus did not say it in words, but He did more than say it by His look. "Ah, Peter, did I not tell you it would be so? You said, 'Though all men shall be offended because of thee, yet will I never be

ded.' Did I not tell thee that before cock-
ing thou wouldst deny Me thrice?" No
ke was uttered; and yet the tender eye of
Lord had revealed to Peter his own extreme
and his Master's superior wisdom.
hat do you think that look chiefly said?
hought about it, as I turned it over, was
when the Lord looked upon Peter, though
d refresh his memory, and make an appeal
s conscience, yet there was still more evi-
ly a glorious manifestation of love. Judg-
what would break my heart the soonest if I
thus denied my Master, it seems to me that
ould be most affected by His saying to me,
d yet I love thee still." Love is

The Great Heart-Breaker.

utable love is that divine hammer which
ks the rock in pieces. I love to believe that
Lord will bring His wanderers back. O ye
are anxious to return to Him, let this cheer
"Yet doth He devise means, that His ban-
d be not expelled from Him."
gain: this look penetrated Peter's inmost
t. It is not every look that we receive that
s very deep. I look with eyes of deep affec-
at men from this pulpit, and I perceive that
y know my meaning; but they soon shake
ff. But our Saviour has an eye to which
joints and marrow are visible. He looks
the secret chambers of the soul; for His
k is a sunbeam, and bears its own light with
lighting up the dark places of our nature by
own radiance. Peter could not help feeling,
he was pricked in the heart by the arrow of
rist's glance. How many persons are affect
by religion only in the head! It does not
ect their heart and life. I am grieved when I
r of some of you, who are regular hearers, and
e pleasure in my preaching, and yet, after
ny years, you are not a bit better. Oh that
y Lord would give such a glance at you this
rning as should dart light into you, and
use you to see yourself, and to see Him, and
en the tears would fill your eyes!
One fact may not escape our notice: our
rd's look at Peter was a revival of all Peter's
oking unto Jesus. The Lord's look upon
ter took effect because Peter was looking to
e Lord. Do you catch it? If the Lord had
rned and looked on Peter, and Peter's back
d been turned on the Lord, that look would
t have reached Peter, nor affected him.

The Eyes Met

produce the desired result. Notwithstanding
l Peter's wanderings, he was anxious about
s Lord, and therefore looked to see what was
one with Him. Even while he warmed his
nds at the fire, he kept looking into the inner
ll. His eyes were constantly looking in the
rection of the Lord Jesus. While he wander-
about among the maids and serving-men,
d got talking to them, fool that he was, yet
ill he would perpetually steal a glance that
y to see how it fared with the man he loved.
e had not given up the habit of looking to
s Lord. If he had not still, in a measure,
oked to his Master, how would the look
Jesus have been observed by him? It is
rough the eye that looks to Jesus that Jesus
oks, and lets fresh light and hope into the
ul. Oh that you who have this lingering faith
the Lord may now receive a look from Him,
hich shall work in you a bitter, salutary, sav-
g repentance, without which you can never
restored!
This look was altogether between the Lord
d Peter. Nobody knew that the Lord looked
Peter, except Peter and his Lord. That
ace which saves a soul is not a noisy thing;
ither is it visible to any but the receiver.
his morning, if the grace of God comes to any
e of you in power, it will be unperceived by
ose who sit on either side of you in the pew:
ey will hear the same words, but of the divine
eration which accompanies them they will
ow nothing; the eye of the Lord will not
eak to them as it is speaking to the awakened
e. Do you know anything of the secret love-
ok of the Lord Jesus?

III. Now I must go to my third point: Let us look at Peter after the Lord had looked at him. What is Peter doing? When the Lord looked on Peter

The First Thing Peter Did

was to feel awakened. Peter's mind had been sleeping. He had forgotten his Lord's Deity, and thus he had, in thought, denied his Lord. He was off the lines, and was in a sleepy state. He was what Paul calls "bewitched," and under the influence of a spiritual soporific, administered by Satan. The Lord's look brought him to his better self, and aroused all the spiritual life which had been dormant in him: "Peter remembered," and he was restored.

The next effect was, it took away all Peter's foolhardiness from him. Peter had made his way into the high priests' hall, but now he made his way out of it. He had not felt in any danger though in the worst of company. What did he care for the girl that kept the door? Surely he was too much of a man to mind her remarks. What did he care for the men that were round the fire? They were rough fellows; but he had been a fisherman, and quite able to cope with the priests' bailiffs. But now the brag is gone out of him. No sooner had Jesus looked upon him than Peter declined all further risks.

All Peter's daring vanished; he turned his back on maids and men, and went out into the darkness of the night. We do not hear of his coming near the cross; in fact, we hear no more of him till the Resurrection morning, for Peter was sensible enough to feel that he

Could Not Trust Himself

any more. He immediately placed himself in the background till his Lord summoned him to the front. I wish that some religious professors whose lives have been questionable, had grace enough to do the same. When I see a man who has sinned grievously, pushing himself speedily to the front, I cannot believe that he has a due sense of the evil he has wrought, or of his own unfitness to be in the place of peril. Above all, shun the place where you have fallen. Do not linger in it for a moment. Go out, even though you leave the comfortable fire behind you. Better be in the cold than stay where your soul is in danger. Till Peter had received from the Lord's own mouth abundant assurance of his restoration to his office, by the threefold charge to feed the sheep and lambs, we do not find him again in the forefront.

That look of Christ also opened the sluices of Peter's heart: he went out, and wept bitterly. There was gall in the tears he wept, for they were the washings of his bitter sorrow. Dear friends, if we have sinned with Peter, God grant us grace to weep with Peter. Many will think of Peter's wandering who forget Peter's weeping. Sin, even though it be forgiven, is a bitter thing; even though Christ may look away your despair, he will not look away your penitence. "He went out and wept bitterly." Oh, how he chided himself! He remembered it all his life, and could never hear a cock crow without feeling the water in his eyes.

And now, to conclude, it made Peter, as long as he lived,

Ashamed to be Ashamed.

Peter was never ashamed after this. Who was it that stood up at Pentecost and preached? Was it not Peter? Was he not always foremost in testifying to his Lord and Master? I trust that if any of us have been falling back, and especially if we have wandered into sin, we may get such a restoration from the Lord Himself, that we may become better Christians ever afterwards. I do not want you to break a bone, I pray God you never may; but if you ever do, may the heavenly Surgeon so set it that it may become thicker and stronger than before. Courage was the bone in Peter which snapped; but when it was set, it became the strongest bone in his nature, and never broke again. When the Lord sets the bones of His people, they never break any more—He does His work so effectually. The man who has erred by anger becomes meek and gentle. The man who has erred by drink, quits the deadly cup, and loathes it. The man who has sinned by shame, becomes the bravest of the company.

Oh, Lord Jesus, I have tried to preach Thee this morning, but I cannot look with Thine eye. Thou must look on erring ones Thyself. Look, Saviour! Look, sinner! "There is life in a look AT the crucified One," because there is life in a look *from* the crucified One. May Jesus look, and the sinner look! Amen.

GEMS FROM NEW BOOKS.

WASHINGTON'S PRAYER IN A HUT.*

"I REMEMBER an incident," said Wilson, "that will give you some idea of the heart George Washington had in his bosom. I suppose Colonel Harmar has told you something of the sufferings of our men during the winter we lay at Valley Forge. It was a terrible season. It is hard to give even a faint idea of it in words; but you may imagine a party of men with ragged clothes and no shoes, huddled around a fire in a log hut; the snow about two feet deep on the ground, and the wind driving fierce and bitter through the chinks of the rude hovel. Many of the men had their feet frost-bitten, and there were no remedies to be had. The sentinels suffered terribly, and looked more like ghosts than men as they paced up and down before the lines of huts.

"Washington saw how the men were situated, and I really believe his heart bled for them. He would write to Congress of the state of affairs, and entreat that body to procure supplies; but you see Congress had not the power to comply. All it could do was to call on the States, and await the action of their assemblies.

"Washington's headquarters were near the camp, and he often came over to see the poor fellows, and try to soothe and comfort them; and, I tell you, the men loved that man as if he had been their father, and would rather have died with him than have lived in luxury with the red-coat general.

"In the next hut to the one in which I messed an old friend named Josiah Jones lay sick. He was lying on a scant straw-bed, with nothing but rags to cover him. He had been sick for several days, but wouldn't go under the doctor's hands, as he always said it was like going into battle certain of being killed. One day, when we had no notion of anything of the kind, Josiah called out to us as we sat talking near his hut, that he was dying, and wanted us to pray for him. We were all anxious to do anything we could for the man, for we loved him as a brother; but as for praying we did not exactly know how to go about it. To get clear of that duty I ran to obtain for the poor fellow a drink of water to moisten his parched lips.

"While the rest were standing about, not knowing what to do, some one heard the voice of General Washington in the next hut, where he was comforting some poor wretches who had their feet frozen. Directly he came to our door, and one of the men went and told him the state of things. Now, you see, a commander-in-chief would have been justified in being angry that the regulations for the sick had been disobeyed, and have turned away; but he was a nobler kind of man. He entered the hut and went up to poor Josiah, and asked him how he was. Josiah told him that he felt as if he were dying, and wanted some one to pray for him.

"Washington saw that a doctor could do the man no good, and he knelt on the ground by him and prayed. We all knelt down, too; we couldn't help it. An old comrade was dying away from his home and friends, and there was our general kneeling by him, with his face turned toward heaven, looking, as I thought, like an angel's.

"Well, he prayed to his Heavenly Father for mercy on the dying man's soul, to pardon his sins, and to take him to Himself; and then prayed for us all. Before the prayer was con-

* From "Noble Deeds of Our Fathers," Revised and Adapted from Henry C. Watson. (Illustrated) One of the "Classics for Home and School." 157 pages. Price by mail 35 cents. Published by *Lee & Shepard*, Boston, Mass.

The Late General Philip H. Sheridan.

Missionaries in Russia Followed by a Wolf. (See page 517.)

cluded, Josiah's spirit had fled. Washington felt the brow of the poor fellow, and seeing that his life was out, gave the men directions how to dispose of the body, and then left us to visit other parts of the camp."

"Praying at the death-bed of a private!" mused Smith, aloud. "Well, I might have conjectured what he would do in such a case, from what I saw of him. I wonder if history ever spoke of a greater man!"

THE LATE GEN. P. H. SHERIDAN.

(*See Portrait.*)

FEW soldiers of this generation have had a more brilliant career than the distinguished general who died on August 5, and whose portrait we now publish. In the records of the war, his name is conspicuous not only as a strategist, but as a man of marvellous personal courage, and of almost romantic heroism. With no prestige, no aristocratic or official influence, to help him, he rose from the humblest origin to be commander in-chief of the army of the United States, and to have the unanimous consent of his countrymen to his eminent fitness for that exalted position, and in the whole army there was not a soldier who did not speak lovingly and admiringly of "*Little Phil.*" His reputation was one of which the whole country was proud, and even his enemies whom he met on the battle-field held him in the highest esteem.

Philip H. Sheridan was born in Somerset, O., on March 6, 1831, so that he was but little more than fifty-seven years old when he died. His parents were Irish, and had come to America only three years before his birth. He was sent out to earn his living in a dry-goods store when he was thirteen years of age. He served four years in that station, and then at last succeeded in getting what he had long desired, a nomination to West Point. He graduated in July 1853, and was appointed immediately in the army with the brevet rank of second lieutenant of Infantry.

When the war broke out he was serving as Captain of the Thirteenth Regiment of United States Infantry, but his superior ability had already been recognized, and he was appointed Quartermaster to Gen. Halleck in the Mississippi campaign of 1862. His qualities as an inspiring leader on the battle-field marked him out for rapid promotion, and before that campaign ended he was made Colonel of the Second Michigan Volunteer Cavalry. After the memorable engagement at Booneville, Gen. Rosecrans reported his "fearless gallantry" and recommended him for further promotion. President Lincoln thereupon made him Brigadier-General of Volunteers. His career after that was one of glorious activity and usefulness to the Union cause. He led the advance in Kentucky at the head of the Eleventh Division, took part in the battle of Perryville, and was in the subsequent notable march to the relief of Nashville. He was assigned to the command of the Army of the Cumberland, and with his division did brilliant service in the Tennessee campaign, particularly at the battle of Murfreesboro', his splendid work at the latter engagement securing him promotion to the rank of Major-General. He was a conspicuous figure in the actions in and about Cold Harbor, and on August 4 was put in command of the Army of the Shenandoah.

It was in October, 1864, that he made the famous ride on his war horse to Winchester that was the subject of Thomas Buchanan Read's familiar and stirring war poem, "Sheridan's Ride." He dashed into the panic-stricken ranks of Union soldiers who were fleeing from General Early. His presence acted like magic in restoring the hope and spirits of the fugitives. They rallied around the gallant little commander, and he charged upon Early's force, who hadn't dreamt of his coming to the front, and drove them back in disorder. He had splendidly turned a sorry rout into a notable victory. The feat won him the familiar title of "The Hero of Winchester," and the new honor of an appointment of Brigadier-General in the regular army, and the special thanks of Congress.

From Feburary 27, to March, 1865, he made a great raid from Winchester to Petersburg. He was in the Richmond campaign from March 25 to April 9. On April 1 he defeated the Confederates at Five Forks, which battle compelled the abandonment of Petersburg and Richmond by the enemy. He gallantly led the pursuit of the Confederate commander, General Lee, and was present when the latter capitulated on April 9.

After the war he held several important and responsible positions, and finally on the retirement of General W. T. Sherman in Feburary, 1884, he was made Commander-in-Chief of the United States Armies, which position he held when he died. The illness which resulted in his death commenced on May 12, last, when he had a severe attack of heart failure, which was succeeded by others. He rallied with difficulty, and his removal to a more bracing air was said to be the only chance of saving his life. On June 30 he was pronounced able to travel, and he was conveyed in a Government steamer Nonquitt, Mass., where for two or three week he seemed to improve. On Sunday, August however, he was again seized with an attack heart failure and in less than an hour afterwar he breathed his last. The General leaves widow and four children—three girls, and a bo who is only seven years old.

A FATAL INTERVIEW OVERHEARD.

(*See Illustration on page 525.*)

"SAY, cook, why don't Master Reginald eve come to prayers?" asked the parlor-maid at th rectory, addressing her fellow-domestic as th two returned to the kitchen after attendin family worship in the library.

"I don't know," responded the cook; "yo had better ask him, if you are curious."

The parlor-maid laughed and made a grimace "You'd like to be by when I did it, wouldn' you? My! how he'd flare up. I fancy I see him and that French wife of his jabbering to him i her gibberish. She's a spit-fire, she is. I believ there's trouble coming for the poor old doctor and if there is she's the cause of it. I never like her from the first time I set eyes upon her."

"Well," said the cook, "you had better se your eyes on your work, now; that's more you concern than Master Reginald and his wife. H didn't marry to please you."

"That's so, and, I guess, not to please hi father either. If he's going to be a clergyman and have his father's church when the old ma gives up or dies, as we've all expected, he'd ha done a deal better to marry a good America girl. There's plenty around better looking tha this French woman, and more fit for a parson' wife. I can't understand her talk, but I kno it's bad by the look of her eyes. And she don' come to prayers any more'n he does. I wonde the Doctor don't speak about it!"

"You leave Dr. Turner to attend to his ow affairs," said the cook.

"I don't think much of his management; els how came Master Reginald to marry a woma like that! Whered' he pick her up?"

"I presume, he met her in Europe," said th cook, whose taciturnity never could resist persistent attacks. "He was always teasing hi father to let him go to a German college. H used to be always joking about ours. He use to tell a story about a monkey being made D. D I guess that was only his fun, but he made hi father own up that one preacher as was made Doctor didn't know a word of Latin or Greek or Hebrew. Once he got punished for guying one of the boss preachers as stopped here. He asked him who wrote Ecclesiastes. The preacher said 'Solomon,' and Reginald burst out laughing. He didn't laugh though when his father was through with him."

"And his father let him go to Germany?"

"Yes, he went. He got through his college there in two years. His father was mighty proud when the papers came, saying how well his Regy had done. I guess he made the Germans open their eyes. They didn't have any idea what Americans could do before. They are slow out there. The Doctor expected Reginald would come home right off; but he didn't. He wanted to look around a bit, and his father was so pleased with him that he sent him a lot of money to go about with. Pretty near all he'd saved, I guess. The Doctor got kind of restless and fidgety about his stopping over there so long, but he didn't say much. At last about a month back he stopped me as I was going down-stairs, and says he, 'Master Reginald's coming home, and he's going to bring his wife with him.' That's all he said, and I didn't ask him anything more about it; but I guess he didn't know himself about the marriage till that morning."

"He'll wish yet he'd *never* heard of it," opined the parlor maid.

"Mebbe, mebbe," assented the cook. "It'll be a cruel shame, though, for he's been just wrapped up in his boy these ever so many years. There, be quiet, she is in the library now talking to the doctor."

The two girls stopped speaking and listened. Through the open window of a room overhead two voices could be heard distinctly in the kitchen. The one high pitched, almost shrill, speaking rapidly with a foreign accent, and the other lower in tone, but sonorous, with which they were familiar—the voice of good old Dr. Turner, whose character and labors had won him the respect not only of that household but of the whole neighborhood, where he had been a Christian pastor nearly forty years.

"It is best that you know," said the shrill voice. "My faith! why, has not Reginald you told for himself? He has not the courage of his opinions. He a priest! No, never will that be. He will be lawyer, doctor, what you will; but a priest—oh, never! He is disillusioned of religion. If he did preach I would laugh! Ah, that would be droll!"

"I cannot believe it." The words came slowly and hesitantly in the good clergyman's voice. "My son cannot have abandoned his faith. Madam, you are jesting with me. It is a painful subject for frivolity."

"Jest? Oh no, it is not I who jest. It is the truth that from you he has too long concealed. He comes not to your devotions, you perceive. Why is that? He believes not one word of your book; then he will not teach. That is right, is it not so? In Paris he was on the opposite, and he spoke grandly, and the people laughed and shouted. I heard them. You should get him to make his speeches for you to hear. Oh, he is a mocker. It is like Voltaire. He was infidel when he came from Germany, but in Paris he grew bold. Oh, he is grand, I adore him. I knew not he had a father so serious."

A deep groan was the only reply. There was silence for a few moments, and then a sudden movement. A minute later the door of the upper room was flung open and a loud, piercing call was heard. The two girls ran up from the kitchen and at the head of the stairs met the daughter-in-law of their employer, coming out of the library. "See," she said, "your master is sick, he faints, get water, get—send for the physician. My faith! but he is pallid."

The girls pushed past her into the room, and there lay the clergyman in his usual chair, his head thrown back and his hands hanging limp over the arms. "Go and fetch Master Reginald," said the cook. "He is out walking," replied the wife; "go summon the physician, as I say to you."

But the clergyman was beyond the help of man. "Apoplexy" was the cause assigned on the medical certificate for his death, and his congregation mourned for him as a friend whose place none could fill. When inquisition is made for blood in the Great Assize not all who are held guilty of murder will be men whose hands have done violence. Many a useful life has been shortened, many a hoary head has been hastened to the grave, by sorrow and shame over the apostacy and misconduct of beloved children.

Dr. Turner's Fatal Interview.

THE EPOCHS OF A LIFE.

A NEW SERIAL STORY.

By Rev. L. S. Keyser.

(*Continued from page 511.*)

Plotting.

A GIRL of Belle Havelock's spirit was little likely to exhaust her passion in tears. Those she shed on her return from Mr. Mardont's church were quickly dried. They were the natural effect of feminine weakness, which for the moment could not be overcome. They were by no means an acceptance of defeat. The discovery that she had a rival for the love for which her heart yearned, provoked her, piqued her, irritated her, but did not dismay her. She was sure that the acquaintance between Hadley and Miss Winters could not have reached an advanced stage, and she did not doubt but that with a little tact it might be interrupted.

"Ah!" she said, in an angry whisper, shaking a minatory finger at a mental image in the darkness, "you may be very crafty, Miss Winters, but it is possible to out-general you; and though I should not be capable of putting myself in front of an express-train to win a man's attentions, you will find that you have a rival in Belle Havelock who will be equal to the emergency. Wrong? Who can draw a distinction between right and wrong in a Godless world like this?"

Her atheism soothed her conscience, which had momentarily been aroused into rebellion against a resort to unfair tactics for attaining her ends. It must have been past midnight when she retired. Even then she could not sleep, but tossed restlessly on her bed, revolving one plan after another in her mind; and when morning dawned, although she had not mapped out as yet a definite line of action, she had fully determined to allure Hadley Madelling from her rival, by fair means or foul, and with this purpose in mind she awaited further developments that might help her in her projects.

Nor was she obliged to wait long. A number of the young men and ladies of the best musical talent in the college and town were making extensive preparations to present a popular cantata before a public audience in Chapel Hall. On account of her rich contralto voice Belle had been chosen to take an important part in the musical performance. When she went to the first rehearsal on the following Tuesday evening she found that Miss Winters, who had an excellent soprano voice, and Mr. Duneman, who sang tenor, were also to take part. Belle had met the latter on several occasions, and had succeeded, to her own satisfaction, in gauging his mental and moral qualities.

While the different parts of the cantata were being assigned, Belle was furtively watching Miss Winters, and in doing so she made an important discovery. She noticed that Duneman was constantly hovering about that lady, and his eyes were frequently bent upon her with an admiration he made no attempt to conceal. It was evident to the watchful Belle that the young man was in love. If so, here was an ally whose natural interest it was to aid her in detaching Hadley from Miss Winters. That his aid could be enlisted, Belle did not doubt, nor did she doubt as to its extent. She fully believed from her estimate of his character that he would be utterly unscrupulous about the use of any means that might accomplish an end on which he had set his heart. His jealousy, dexterously aroused, would stifle any protests of honor or conscience and render him a fit instrument for her use.

An opportunity for opening negotiations for an alliance occurred before rehearsal was over. The cantata called for several duets by the leading tenor and alto voices which were somewhat difficult of rendition. It was, therefore, quite natural for Belle to suggest to Duneman, after they had been singing together several times, that a private rehearsal of their parts would be advisable. Duneman assented, and accepted her invitation to come to her home on the following Saturday evening for the purpose.

Revolving in her own mind during the next few days various schemes for effecting her purpose, she more than once felt compunctions of conscience, and a mental effort was necessary to silence them. All things, she reflected, were the result of an evolution without God, and consequently all ethical distinctions were but the figments of a morbid fancy. She herself was only borne along unresistingly on the wave of this great law, which took all moral responsibility out of her hands. Furthermore, she had recourse to a casuistical mode of argument by which she justified her purpose. Miss Winters, she reasoned, was a bigoted Christian girl, and hence her mental attitude was not at one with that of Mr. Madelling. They would therefore not be congenial. It would be a misalliance, and would entail unhappiness upon them both. It was entirely different with herself and Mr. Madelling. Their views on religion and all other important questions were in complete harmony. Yes, if there was any basis for moral distinctions, it was right for her to prevent an unhappy conjugal union. One cannot allow himself to be governed by sentiment alone in marital affairs, she argued, but reason must be the arbiter, and those who are wise will study the laws of intellectual affinity. Hadley's admiration of Miss Winters was only a momentary passion; but still, in his blindness and infatuation, he might succumb to her blandishments, and thus blight his whole life. Belle would therefore save him from such a sad alliance even if she had to resort to strategy to do so.

Of course, the sophistry of this mode of reasoning was obvious to her, but she resolutely closed her eyes to it, and proceeded to mature her plans.

Saturday evening brought Mr. Duneman to her door. When she looked into his eyes she was fully convinced that she could mould him to her purposes.

"His religion is not an inch deep," she thought, "but his selfishness and egotism are unfathomable."

They rehearsed their parts in the cantata with considerable enthusiasm, for the divinity student had an inordinate ambition to distinguish himself as a vocal artist, and he was well aware that his tenor voice was one of unusually fine *timbre*. After the rehearsal, as they sat talking, Belle dexterously turned the conversation to the students of the college. One after another ran the gauntlet of their criticism, until presently she remarked, with well-feigned nonchalance:

"What do you think of Miss Winters's singing?"

A slight flush came to the young man's face at the sudden mention of the name, but he answered, quietly:

"I think hers is the best soprano voice engaged in the cantata. Did you notice how quiet all the performers became as she sang her solos? And yet it was her first practice. You will not think me guilty of flattery if I say that she holds the same place in the soprano that you hold in the contralto."

Belle blushed slightly, and was not displeased with the compliment paid her.

"I fancy that is the highest praise you could give me," she said, significantly. "I am inclined to think Miss Winters is perfect in your eyes. Oh! do not blush; there is no shame in loving so beautiful and accomplished a girl. I detected your secret at the rehearsal, and I thought then how well suited you were to each other."

"Pray do not speak of it, Miss Havelock; your intuitions have certainly surprised my secret, but I think no one else has discovered it. Still, as I am not engaged to Miss Winters I should be sorry to have the matter talked of in the college. It would be embarrassing for both Miss Winters and me. I admit that you are right as to my own feelings, and that extent of confidence must give me ground for making an appeal to you for reticence."

"Oh, your confidence is quite safe with me, and I most sincerely wish you success in your suit. I think she would make an ideal minister's wife. You intend being a minister, do you not?"

"Yes, that is my ambition, and as you say, Miss Winters is eminently fitted to aid me in that high vocation. Still, it was not that utilitarian motive that drew me to Miss Winters. Do you believe in love at first sight? But why do I ask? It is not fair to a comparative stranger to inflict personal experiences upon her."

"Oh, do not apologize, Mr. Duneman, my sex, you know, is always interested in love affairs. You may confide in me. Besides, I might be able to do you a service of value to you."

"How so?"

"By putting you on your guard. I have reason to think that you have a rival. Perhaps I ought not to speak of it, but I do not like to see a good match thwarted, and besides, I feel quite an interest in your wooing."

"A rival!" exclaimed Duneman, starting and turning pale. "Are you sure? Who can it be?"

"Do you forget that Mr. Madelling saved Miss Winters's life at some personal risk some time ago? Is it not possible that he may be disposed to develop love out of her natural gratitude for the service? I saw them together at the Madison Street Church last Sunday night, and I should judge, from their manner toward each other, that Mr. Madelling has made good use of his advantage. Remember, a girl must feel some obligation to a man who risks his life to save hers."

"Ah! I should have no fear of Madelling. His principles would make him ineligible. Do you know that he is a blatant infidel? A sincere Christian girl like Miss Winters might endure his company for an evening out of gratitude for the service he is supposed to have rendered her, but as a lover, she would never think of him for a moment."

"Perhaps she does not know of his infidelity. Young men are generally shrewd enough to avoid subjects which would be unpleasant to their friends."

"She must know; she shall know! I will warn her."

"That is just a man's way!" said Miss Havelock. "Why, Miss Winters would naturally think you were aspersing your rival's character from interested motives. Now, a woman would go to work in a very different way. She would let the disclosure come from some other lips—his own for instance."

"You are right; why, Miss Havelock, you are a most excellent mentor. Your advice is a treasure. I shall take it with pleasure. There will be no difficulty about it. Madelling's temper is most explosive. If he has sufficient provocation, he will put himself on record beyond the possibility of mistake. I have tried to force him into speaking plainly and publicly on the subject, but not with all the pressure I could bring to bear. Now I will set to work in earnest."

"If you succeed you will do Miss Winters a service, and advance your own interests at the same time; but how will you do it?"

"I have an oration to deliver next Saturday morning, and I will throw hot shot into the infidel camp. It is my duty to fight my Master's enemies, and I shall do it without fear or reservation."

"You are a brave man" said Belle repressing a feeling of disgust at the sanctimonious disguise cast over the man's real object. "I hope you will succeed. If you do arouse Mr. Madelling to come out in his true colors, and yet that fails to set Miss Winters against him, come to me and we will consider what else can be done to prevent this most incongruous match."

"I will, I will!" said Duneman. "You are a true friend. I can never tell you how much I am obliged to you for your counsel."

"Wait until you are married," said Belle, with a smile. Duneman laughed and blushed as he rose and bade her good-night. "I wonder if he thinks that he deceives me," said Belle, giving a sigh of relief when the door closed on her visitor. "I suppose to a certain extent he deceives himself. But what a hollow-hearted hypocrite he is! How any one who has much to do with Christians can believe in the elevating influence of religion, is more than I can understand." Possibly if any one had been there to hear her, she might have been reminded that human nature without religion was also a sorry spectacle, and if an example were necessary Belle herself could furnish it.

A common subject of remark during the following week among the students in the college, was the blunders that Duneman made in his recitations. It seemed as if he had made no preparation for them of any kind, and there was some speculation as to the cause.

On Saturday morning the problem received an unexpected solution; for it was then seen that other matters had been engrossing his attention during the week. A larger audience than usual had gathered in Chapel Hall to hear the speeches of the young aspirants for oratorical honors. Hadley had been mistaken in supposing that his opportunity would come that day. As it happened, the class to which he belonged would not "exhibit" until the next morning devoted to these exercises, which would be in three weeks.

The students were allowed to choose their subjects *ad libitum*, and usually the title of an oration was not announced until the speaker himself made it known. It was thought best by the Faculty to allow a large measure of liberty among the young men and women in the expression of their sentiments, and thus far no evil results had come from this policy. True, many of the effusions were ridiculously crude and puerile, but as many of the performers were mere novices in public speaking, they were laughed at good-humoredly and their blunders readily excused. However, some of the addresses delivered by the older and better-trained students would, in the opinion of the students, have done credit to a public lecture-platform or to the halls of legislation.

"Let me see," said Dane; "I believe that Duneman belongs to the class that exhibits to-day, doesn't he?"

"Of course he does!" Hadley replied. "I wonder what kind of stuff he will pour into our ears."

"Something sufficiently diluted, I'll wager." And then suddenly changing the topic he added, "Ah! I see that Miss Havelock is here."

And George pointed her out to his friend. She appeared nervous and impatient, having the air of one who was waiting in anxious expectancy for an important event.

There were usually two speakers from each of the four college classes. The representatives of all the lower classes and one of the seniors had spoken, leaving Duneman for the last. As he stepped to the platform, all eyes were bent upon him, and, according to the custom of the Grand Central College, he was soundly applauded while he made his bow. It must not be thought, because his mental endowment was inferior to that of some of his classmates, that he was an intellectual imbecile. He had considerable power of mental grasp, and his abilities, though not remarkable, shone out more conspicuously perhaps in his public speeches than anywhere else.

More than that, his voice was pleasant and well modulated, his gesticulations were graceful, and in the unfolding of a theme he showed not a little logical skill. Another characteristic feature of his public addresses, which was in his favor before an audience, was his faculty of putting a thought in a strategic light, or in a startling and unexpected manner, with a dash of histrionic art, so that his hearers were frequently thrilled by surprises that moved them to applause. Add to this a large amount of self-confidence, concealed under a mask of well-feigned modesty, and the portrait of Mr. Duneman, as he appeared upon the platform, is as complete as necessary.

The announcement of his theme caused a movement of surprise in the audience, especially among those who were inclined to be sceptical. His opening sentence vibrated in clear, modulated tones through the hall:

"The theme which I have chosen for my discussion to-day is, 'The Moral Laxity of Unbelievers.'"

The eyes of the Professors, who occupied seats upon the platform in the rear of the speakers, were bent curiously upon Duneman, and an involuntary rustle in the audience bore witness to the sensation the announcement had produced. Belle Havelock cast a stealthy glance toward the seat where Madelling, with Jane, was sitting, and noticed that his face flushed, and that he made an uneasy movement as if under nervous excitement. Then an angry scowl came to his brow and a fierce gleam shot from his eyes. As Belle noticed these symptoms of perturbation, she settled herself in her seat in full expectation of an explosive interruption of the orator, which would make a sensation in the college that would never be forgotten.

(*To be Continued.*)

THE PILLAR OF CLOUD AND FIRE.

By Mrs. M. Baxter.

S. S. Lesson for August 26. Numbers 9: 15-23. Golden Text, Ps. 43: 3.

The Tabernacle Hidden—The Presence of God in the Human Tabernacle—Shade and Illumination—Guidance Granted to Those who Depend Upon It—The Voice of the Spirit Recognized and Obeyed—Hurry and Dilatoriness both to be Avoided—The Responsibility of every Movement with God—Every Need Provided for—Patience Demanded—The Desert Experience a Necessary Preparation.

After Moses had completed the Tabernacle—carrying out, in its erection and furnishing, the exact plan of God—both the outside and the inside were filled with glory by the manifest Presence of God. "A cloud covered the tent of the congregation" (the glory was *without*), "and the glory of the Lord filled the tabernacle" *within*," . . . The cloud of the Lord was upon the tabernacle by day, and fire was upon it by night, in the sight of all the house of Israel throughout all their journeys." (Ex. 40: 34, 38.) The tabernacle was hidden, covered, clothed with the cloud of glory. As God fills His church, the church becomes more hidden. When the child of God is built up into Him, he himself becomes hidden, that the glory may be seen. But the glory of God which is seen upon him is only the index of the glory within. The very purpose of the tabernacle was that God's people should have a witness to His dwelling among them. All the beauty of the tabernacle itself was for the eye of God, the presence of God for the eye of man. The presence of God was not an occasional or an intermittent thing. "On the day that the tabernacle was reared up, the cloud covered the tabernacle," namely, the tent of the testimony; "and at even there was upon the tabernacle, as it were, the appearance of fire, until the morning."

So it Was Alway.

The cloud covered it by day, and the appearance of fire by night. The heat of an earthly sun was tempered by day, and the warmth of a divine fire was kindled by night. The presence of God was a shadow from the heat, but also a glowing light in the darkness. While the heathen around saw in their gods only something to terrify, the presence of God among His people was love and mercy: His glory is His goodness. It is the experience of many Christians that the conscious presence of God with them is an intermittent thing; one day they may bask in its glory, the next day they may think that God has forsaken them. Those who rest in the continued consciousness of the presence of God know also what His guidance is. But, like Moses, they have gone outside the tabernacle of their being, and given up the possession of it to God. They dwell in Him, and He dwells in them. Their home, their citizenship, their claim, is in God; they are heirs of God, that His home, His portion, His inheritance may be in them. And this is not a mere doctrine, but a glorious, precious reality.

"And when the cloud was taken up from the tabernacle, then, after that the children of Israel journeyed"; if God moved, they moved with Him. "And in the place where the cloud abode, there the children of Israel pitched their tents." Where God abode that was the place for them. Oh, how many Christians trust to their own judgment or that of friends, or, it may be, to the way in which circumstances turn, to guide them, instead of waiting for the direct guidance of God! He never guides contrary to His written word, but very often His guidance is contrary to our judgment. We need to be very still in order to perceive when the cloud is taken up. If we are living in habitual communion with God, there will be a quiet consciousness that

"He is Here,"

a kind of sense how really He is at hand, so really within, to undertake anything which is put to Him; that it is just as though a visible person were there; it is a reality, not a dream or an imagination, that He is there. When the cloud lifts, there is a consciousness that something is on the move; God's plan for us may not be developed, but there is a sense that some change is at hand. Then is the time to prove whether, in very deed, our will is given up to the Lord. Philip went down to Samaria, and there was so blest that "the people with one accord gave heed unto the things which Philip spake, hearing and seeing the miracles which he did. . . . and there was great joy in that city." (Acts 8: 6-8.) Philip's human judgment might have led him to think that he was indispensable in the place where he had been so used of God: but the cloud was lifted. God called him to go away into the desert. He did not begin to wonder whether, indeed, it was God who had spoken to him, or whether it was his own idea. The voice of the Holy Ghost was known well by the first disciples; "he arose and went." When the cloud lifts,

However Strange it May Seem

to us, we have not to weigh the bearings of the question, but simply to obey. God's directions are clear enough, but we are so little versed in the language of the Holy Ghost that often we do not recognize what He says to us. It is very true that the subject of divine guidance is one which Satan has terribly caricatured. Some have thought they were guided by God into all kinds of extravagances and vagaries, and also into error and sin. The guidance of God is unlike all other—it never exalts man; it keeps him under the cover of the cloud of His presence.

To be always and surely led of God, we need to believe that He wishes to guide us, and really wants us to know His will; perplexity and conflict always come from doubt or from self-will. Some of us have a high value for time, and cannot bear to see the moments wasted, and our temptation is to be in a hurry; but if we would be guided by God, we must learn to trust Him with the use of time; what He can afford, who is the universal Proprietor, *we* can afford also. "When the cloud tarried long upon the tabernacle many days, then the children of Israel kept the charge of the Lord, and journeyed not." Every step we take without waiting for the Lord's direction, we have to retrace. Jonah had to return to Nineveh when he ran away from God, and Peter had to see God heal the ear of Malchus, which he, in his rash zeal, had cut off.

"So it was when the cloud abode from even unto the morning, and that the cloud was taken up in the morning, then they journeyed: whether it was by day or by night that the cloud was taken up, they journeyed." There was no question as to whether it was convenient or not, whether family circumstances were suitable, or whether they were in health to travel. If God was indeed the Father of His people, all this responsibility belonged to Him. He had already shown His wondrous providence in making a way through the sea. With such a Pioneer, capable of such road-making, overcoming such difficulties, how could they fear any way by which He should lead them? He had rained down bread from heaven, and continued to do so daily. He made the spring of water which He brought forth from the stony rock accompany them all along their journey; how could they fear starvation? He had promised them that He would take sickness from the midst of them (Ex. 23: 25), and the record of their journeyings was this: "He brought them forth also with silver and gold, and there was not one feeble person among their tribes." (Ps. 105: 37.) How, then, could they anticipate sickness? He cared for their very clothing, so that Moses could remind them, "Thy raiment waxed not old upon thee, neither did thy foot swell these forty years." (Deut. 8: 4.) How could they, with their eye upon such a God, fear any step which He might lead them to take?

Most of the fear which believers have of the direct leading of God, arises from the fact that they are not living in the presence of an indwelling God. Christ does not dwell in their hearts by faith (Eph. 3: 17), the mystery which hath been hid from ages and generations, but now is made manifest to God's saints. . . . "Christ in you the hope of glory" (Col. 1: 26, 27), may be held by them as a doctrine, but it is not a living experience, which transcends all the other realities of life. If the tabernacle of their being were filled with the glory of an indwelling God, so near as to dwell within them, they would be sufficiently acquainted with Him to trust Him implicitly, and then there would be

No Mischance

to the making known of His will. God would, however, teach us to be attentive to His directions. The ark of the covenant over which the glory rested, was carried before the people on their journeys. "When ye see the ark of the covenant of the Lord your God, and the priests and the Levites bearing it, then ye shall remove from your place (when the ark is gone away, then the place which was God's place before, becomes *our* place till we follow Him), and go after it. Yet there shall be a space between you and it, about two thousand cubits by measure [about six-tenths, or rather more than half a mile]: come not near unto it, that ye may know the way by which ye must go." (Josh. 3: 3, 4.) There must be a space sufficient for the people to observe the turns which were taken by the priests who carried the ark. God wants us to observe His movements in our lands, our churches, our families, our own souls, that we may learn His ways.

Perhaps there is nothing in which we are exercised so much as in patience by depending upon the Lord for His direction. Oh, let us never forget that we are no more masters of our moments than of anything else; this is God's property; if He holds us back from any course, let us trust His infallible wisdom and true economy of time. Whether it was two days, or a month, or a year that the cloud tarried upon the tabernacle, the children of Israel abode in their tents and journeyed not. What? When God had called them to take possession of the promised land? Was it not a loss of time? Did it not seem most tantalizing? He who had "prepared for them a city," was preparing them for an eternal land of promise, and He sacrificed the lesser good for the greater. Obedience, patience, and trust in God were

Of far more Importance

to them than the milk and honey of the land of Canaan. Therefore, it was only when the cloud was taken up that they journeyed. It needs as much faith *not* to move sometimes as to move at others. "At the commandment of the Lord they rested in their tents, and at the commandment of the Lord they journeyed: they kept the charge of the Lord at the commandment of the Lord by the hand of Moses."

THE MASTER'S QUESTIONS.

"If any man serve Me, let him follow Me: and where I am, there shall also My servants be: if any man serve Me, him will My Father honor."—JOHN xii. 26.

Have ye looked for sheep in the desert,
  For those who have missed their way?
Have ye been in the wild waste places,
  Where the lost and wandering stray?
Have ye trodden the lonely highway,
  The foul and the darksome street?
It may be ye'd see in the gloaming
  The print of My wounded feet.

Have ye folded home to your bosom
  The trembling neglected lamb,
And taught to the little lost one
  The sound of the Shepherd's name?
Have ye searched for the poor and needy,
  With no clothing, no home, no bread?
The Son of Man was among them—
  He had no where to lay His head.

Have ye carried the living water,
  To the parched and thirsty soul?
Have ye said to the sick and wounded,
  "Christ Jesus makes thee whole?"
Have ye told My fainting children
  Of the strength of the Father's hand?
Have ye guided the tottering footsteps
  To the shore of the "golden land?"

Have ye stood by the sad and weary,
  To smooth the pillow of death,
To comfort the sorrow-stricken,
  And strengthen the feeble faith?
And have ye felt, when the glory
  Has streamed through the open door
And flitted across the shadows,
  That I had been there before?

Have ye wept with the broken-hearted
  In their agony of woe?
Ye might hear Me whispering beside you,
  "'Tis the pathway I often go!"
My brethren, My friends, My disciples,
  Can ye dare to follow Me?
Then, wherever the Master dwelleth,
  There shall the servant be!

—*Selected.*

J. E. JEWETT, Publisher, 77 Bible House, New York, will furnish the above poem in leaflet form at twenty cents per hundred. *A Sample Packet* of 50 leaflets assorted (no two alike), will be sent post-paid, for 10 cts., or 100 for 20 cts. Postage stamps taken.

Christian Work in Mexico.

Through the reading of the Holy Scriptures translated into Spanish some earnest souls in Mexico have, by God's blessing, been led to a clear knowledge of the Gospel. From their numbers able preachers of the Christian faith in its primitive purity have been raised up, around whom congregations have been gathered from among the humble poor, who have been the first to publicly welcome and defend the pure Gospel in Mexico. The members of these congregations, rich in faith, have worked earnestly and bravely for Christ and His truth among their fellow countrymen in that beautiful Southern portion of North America called Mexico. Schools have been established by them, in which large numbers of bright boys and girls have received a good secular education and have been carefully taught the Christian faith. From the children thus educated faithful Christian workers have been raised up. A Mexican Branch of the Church of Christ, that maintains the faith in its purity and integrity, has been organized among these native Christians in the Republic of Mexico. The members of this Mexican Church of Christ, though gathered mostly from among the poor, are yet doing a most important Christian work. To continue that work, we need to pay a few leading workers small monthly salaries, and also to defray some current expenses. To raise the needed funds we have formed a society with an office at 43 Bible House, New York, U. S., and should be pleased to have many of our fellow Christians join this society by becoming regular contributors to its treasury. We are trying to secure monthly or quarterly contributions to meet the regular monthly expenses of the work. In order to continue and extend the work, we wish to raise four hundred dollars a month, by endeavoring to have four hundred persons each give on an average *one dollar every month* to this object, leaving the donors to give less or more as they may be able and willing.

We earnestly invite all who will, to join us in this systematic effort in behalf of the cause of Christ in Mexico, by becoming monthly subscribers to this fund. We have already regular subscribers whose gifts amount monthly to over eighty dollars, and a growing circle of friends who are forwarding us occasional donations.

This Mexican Church of Christ is a very effective instrumentality through which to do Christian work among the many millions on this Western Hemisphere who speak the Spanish language, comparatively few of whom have ever had a Bible in their hands. A beautiful church building has been secured in the City of Mexico as the centre of the activities of this Mexican Church of Christ. Through the workers connected with that centre more than forty congregations have been gathered from among the poor in different parts of the Republic of Mexico. We have some faithful and able preachers now in the field, but more young men need to be trained for the ministry. Multitudes of Protestant children in Mexico, some of them orphans, need to be educated. We make three requests of you, Christian reader: *first*, that you will, if possible, become a monthly or quarterly subscriber in behalf of this Christian work; *second*, that you will try and induce your friends also to contribute to it; *third*, that you will remember this precious work in Mexico in your prayers.

We most sincerely thank all who are already generously contributing to this Christian work for their timely and generous gifts, and we earnestly invite many others, to unite with us in aiding it by also becoming monthly subscribers in its behalf. Those who may not feel that they can give as much as a dollar a month are earnestly asked to give what they can, whenever they are able—EVERY LITTLE HELPS. Fellow Christian, if you will generously consent to contribute a dollar a month or more or less to the work, will you kindly inform me of the fact? Contributions either large or small can be mailed directly to my address as follows:

BISHOP H. C. RILEY, care of J. P. HEATH,
No. 43 Bible House, New York, U. S.

Entered according to Act of Congress in the year 1888, in the office of the Librarian of Congress at Washington.

Vol. XI., No. 34. Office, 63 Bible House. N. Y. THURSDAY, AUGUST 23, 1888. Annual Subscription, $1.50.

CONTENTS OF THIS NUMBER.

PORTRAIT AND LIFE OF GEN. CLINTON B. FISK, PROHIBITION CANDIDATE FOR THE PRESIDENCY.
TROUBLE ON BOTH SIDES. A Vacation Sermon by Dr. Talmage.
ANECDOTES RELATED AT RECENT EVANGELISTIC MEETINGS.
PROPHETIC EVENTS BETWEEN 1889 and 1891.
THE COMING OF THE BRIDEGROOM.
THE BIBLE CONFERENCE AT NORTHFIELD: Addresses of Mr. Moody and Father Chiniquy.
THE TERCENTENARY OF THE DEFEAT OF THE SPANISH ARMADA. (With Illustration.)
PETER AFTER HIS RESTORATION. A New Sermon by Rev. C. H. Spurgeon.
Gems from New Books: A Beatific Vision, etc.
PORTRAIT AND LIFE OF DR. BROOKS, Prohibition Candidate for the Vice-Presidency.
A Wife's Premonition—A Little Outcast Leper—An Old Jewish Rabbi Learning—A Long Search for a Wife—Prayer in a Cyclone—Gospel Work in Rome—A Thief's Restitution.
MRS. BRETTELL'S GRANDDAUGHTER. (Illust.)
THE EPOCHS OF A LIFE. A New Serial Story by Rev. L. S. Keyser. (Continued.)
THE SPIES SENT INTO CANAAN. By Mrs. M. Baxter.

GENERAL CLINTON B. FISK, Prohibition Candidate for the Presidency—Scenes in His Life.

GENERAL CLINTON B. FISK.

The Prohibition Candidate for the Presidency.

The Birney Boy—His Prophecy Fulfilled—Born in a Distillery—His Father's Character—A Sermon in Payment for Horse-Shoes—Father's Removal to Michigan, and Death—Purchase of a Board for a Writing Copy—Apprenticeship to a Deacon—Two Days' Hoeing for a Book—Conversion—Sent to a College—His Marriage—Successful Business Life—A Child's Momentous Question—War Experiences—A Teamster's Profanity—A Soldier's Tears—Commissioner of Freedmen's Bureau—Fisk University—Later Years.

THE obloquy and scorn of both political parties, which must inevitably be endured by the man who accepts the position of standard-bearer of the Prohibition party in the National campaign, will this year fall upon a man who in his boyhood had some experience of the consequences of representing an unpopular cause. Nearly half a century ago a little town in Michigan was in the ferment of political excitement. Not only every *man* but every *boy* was expected to declare his preference for Harrison or Van Buren. One lad, however, a poor boy, only twelve years old, the son of a widow, had the audacity to declare that he was neither for Harrison nor Van Buren, but for James G. Birney. Nor was he disposed to make any secret of his political faith. The other boys belonged to old parties with campaign funds, and therefore had no difficulty in getting neat little banners. The widow's son was not so fortunate, but he was not to be beaten on that account. A few cents were earned by the manufacture and sale of molasses candy, and they were invested in a yard of muslin; a little axle grease served for paint, his mother's broom lost its handle to make a staff (which cost him a flogging), and the boy was equipped with a banner bearing the legend

"Birney and Lemoyne."

The little fellow had the courage to show it, too, in the rival camps, and to endure the juvenile molestation it provoked. He even took it into a Democratic meeting, and displayed it in front of the speakers' platform. "*See here, boy, go away with your dirty rag*," said one of the orators. In no way disconcerted, the Birney boy retorted, "*This dirty rag will swallow up all other banners some day.*" The Birney boy who thus prophesied was Clinton B. Fisk. Twenty years afterward, when the cause symbolized by the dirty rag was triumphant, and the same orator was then singing its praises, Fisk had the gratification of reminding him of the prophecy.

The widow's son was not a native of Clinton. He was born on December 8, 1828, at a little place in western New York, then known as Clapp's Corners, and now as Greigsville—so that he is now in his sixtieth year. It is a curious coincidence that the Prohibition candidate was

Born in an Old Distillery.

His father was a blacksmith, the youngest of *a family of sixteen children*, a hardworking but somewhat eccentric man, who, hoping to better his circumstances, removed from the old location of the family, at Killingly, Conn., to Clapp's Corners. He settled in a small cottage, but, subsequently, as his business grew, and the building used as a distillery became vacant, he removed into it, and there his fifth son, Clinton Bowen Fisk, was born. The blacksmith is said, by people who remember him, to have been neither a temperance man nor a church-goer. He seldom or never heard preaching. But there was one droll exception. A Baptist minister from York drew up one day at the blacksmith's shop, and asked the cost of shoeing his horse all round. "Preach me a sermon right there on that horse-block," said the blacksmith, "and I'll do the job and not charge you a cent." The preacher agreed, the horse was shod, and the minister, nothing loth, mounted the horse-block and solemnly and deliberately gave out his text, divided his subject, and preached a regular sermon, as if in church. (*See Illustration, No.* 1.)

Education Under Difficulties.

Business prospects in Clapp's Corners proved less encouraging than was expected, and the blacksmith determined on moving farther West. He set out for Lenawee County, Mich., to a village named Clinton, after Governor De Witt Clinton, after whom, also, Fisk had named his boy. Clinton henceforward was the family home. The blacksmith prospered, bought land, and built a house, but did not long enjoy it. He sickened and died in 1832, leaving his widow to bring up her six boys, the youngest a mere babe. Mrs. Fisk was a woman of energy and decision. She settled four of her boys among the farmers of the neighborhood, and, keeping Clinton and his younger brother with her, opened a boarding-house. The chance of obtaining an education seemed to little Clinton very small, and the little boy was very anxious about that. He had learned to read, but he wanted to write well. Seeing one day, outside the village store, a box addressed to the proprietors by some New York clerk, the lad went into the store and tried to buy the box, but that purchase being beyond his means, he bargained for the board on which the writing was. The price was named, the venders agreed to take pay in eggs, and to give credit, and the boy marched off with his prize. He had no slate, but his mother's hearthstone was broad and smooth, and on that, by the light of the fire, he copied the characters over and over again, until he could write the style easily and well. (*See Illustration No.* 2.)

Natural Grit

was in the boy, and he could not fail to get on, but his opportunities were necessarily limited. The mother hoped to keep him with her, but he, too, had to go. When he was nine years old a good deacon agreed to take him and keep him until he was twenty-one. The boy was to do general work on the farm; was to have three months' schooling in each of the next four years, and, when he was of age, to receive $200 in cash, a horse, saddle, and bridle, and two suits of clothes. The mother wept, but she consented, and next day the boy went to the deacon's farm. There the deacon's hearthstone was put in requisition, and Clinton wrote and read in his spare moments, which were all too few. Books, too, were scarce. The first he ever bought was a mutilated copy of Shakespeare, and *the price he paid for it was to hoe the vender's corn for two days.* Later, and by similar means, he acquired the "Pilgrim's Progress," "Paradise Lost," and a "Columbian Orator."

A Momentous Event

occurred before he had been a year at the deacon's home. The Rev. Robert Powell, a Baptist missionary, was holding revival meetings in a school-house about two miles west. Clinton went after his day's work was done. The text was: "Come unto Me all ye that labor and are heavy laden, and I will give you rest." (Matt. 11: 28.) The poor, weary lad appreciated the words, and the talk that followed. He was interested, impressed, converted, and a few Sundays afterward Elder Powell baptized him in the river Raisin. A sturdy little Baptist he proved, too, well-grounded in the pros and cons of the immersion doctrine, though he afterward identified himself with the Methodists.

The bargain with the deacon was dissolved the next year by mutual consent. Clinton's little brother died, and his mother coveted her youngest surviving boy. Terms were arranged and the boy returned to his beloved mother.

Important Changes

in Clinton Fisk's life came during the next few years, which must be briefly summarized here. In 1841 Mrs. Fisk became the wife of a wealthy farmer at Spring Harbor. Clinton's opportunity was come at last, for the step-father was kind to him and sent him to Albion Seminary. There, among his fellow students, was the pretty bright-eyed girl who has been his wife now nearly forty years. He fell in love with Jeannette A. Crippen at once, and soon learned that she loved him well enough to wait for the time when he could make her his wife. His college course was interrupted at the end of 1844 by the death of his step-father. He then taught school in Bridgewater for a term. His mother, a little later, made another marriage, her third husband being our old acquaintance Elder Powell, who immersed Clinton in the Raisin. The youth could now return to Albion, but was prevented by an affection of the eyes, the result of his youthful exercises on the hearthstone, where the fitful light and the heat of the logs had injured his sight. He therefore accepted a position as clerk in a store in Manchester, Mich., where he displayed an unexpected capacity for business. There was, however, a powerful loadstone, drawing him elsewhere, in the person of Miss Crippen. Her father was in business at Coldwater, Mich., and thither Clinton Fisk went in 1848, ostensibly to visit his old college mate, her brother. Mr. Crippen, Sen., doubtless understood the affair, and being pleased with the young man, the firm was extended so as to include Clinton B. Fisk and his own son J. B. Crippen. The arrangement proved eminently successful; Clinton was a first-class business man and the most active and energetic member of the firm. Nothing now stood in the way of his marriage, and on February 20, 1850, the ceremony took place.

A Child's Question

was the occasion of the next vital change in Clinton Fisk's life. He had thrown himself into business pursuits with his characteristic ardor after his marriage, pushing the business, opening branches, buying property, establishing a bank, but neglecting his soul's concerns. Gradually he had ceased to think of religion and had given up prayer. One night, about four years after his marriage, his wife being occupied, his little three year-old daughter came and knelt at his knee to say her evening prayer (*See Illustration No.* 3). It was a trying experience to the young father, especially when Mary prayed, "God bless Papa and Mamma." It was still worse when rising to kiss him good-night, the child asked: "Papa, why don't *you* pray?" He made some light answer, and went off to the bank to balance the accounts. But he was deeply moved. When he returned home, and he and his wife were alone, he said: "Did you hear the question Mary asked me?" "Yes, Clinton, I heard it," said Mrs. Fisk. "Well, Jenny, I've been thinking it all over, and I've made up my mind, that with God's help we'll have the prayer there ought to be in this household hereafter. If you'll hand me the Bible we'll begin now." They did so; the family altar was reared, and never since, either in sunshine or in storm has it been taken down.

The panic of 1857 caught the young firm, as it caught so many others, unprepared. The bank and the business were swept before it, but creditors were settled with honorably, dollar for dollar. Fisk was terribly shaken by the anxiety and harass through which he had passed, and was for a time in broken health; but under his wife's loving care he speedily rallied and accepted an offer by an insurance company to be its agent in the West, with headquarters at St. Louis. The activity and travel suited him and diverted his mind. He recovered his old energy and did a profitable business for the company. He entered upon it in 1858, and continned it until all such work was suspended by

The Outbreak of War.

Fisk had taken a deep interest in the questions which had this issue, and he was among the first in Missouri to undertake the raising of a regiment, of which he was made colonel. While the regiment was forming, Fisk had religious services conducted in the Fair-grounds, and at the last one before marching, his old friend, Dr. Robert Nelson, officiated. Dr. Nelson took a practical view of the situation, warning the regiment against various sins which army life tended to induce. One of them was that of profane swearing. He told a story of a commodore who insisted that swearing was his department, and that no one else should swear on board his ship. "Now," said Dr. Nelson, "I want you to agree that Colonel Fisk shall do all the swearing for the Thirty-third Regiment. As many of you as will enter into this contract, stand up." Every man rose, and the covenant was made.

A Teamster's Profanity

subsequently recalled the incident. The men had been very careful to observe the contract, but one day, when General Fisk's command lay at Helena, after the Yazoo expedition, the General heard some fearful curses in the woods. He went to a bluff and looked over. There was a teamster with six mules who, coming through the wood, had snagged on a tree and broke the wagon-pole. The teamster's exasperation burst the contract, and he poured out maledictions on the Confederacy, the wood, the mules, and everything around. General Fisk walked back and sat down. By and by, soberly leading his six mules, along came the teamster. (*See illustration No. 4.*) Saluting him kindly, the General said: "John, didn't I hear some one swearing dreadfully over there a while ago? Who was it?" "That was me, sir," the man replied. "But," said General Fisk, "don't you remember the covenant made up at the Benton Barracks, between you and me and the others of the regiment, that I was to do all the swearing for the Thirty-third Missouri during the war?" "Oh, yes," the man answered promptly, "I remember that; but you were not there to do it, and *it had to be done then.*"

General Fisk was as amused at this reply as he had been pained by the occasion for it, and gave it over to his staff. It gained wide currency, and afterward, through all the Mississippi region, whenever a teamster was heard cursing, some one would suggest that he wait till General Fisk came along to have the job.

A Soldier's Letter.

Shut away from all mail communication, during the six weeks that the Yazoo expedition lasted, when General Fisk returned to Helena all his men were eager for home news, and besieged the post-office tent at once. After receiving his own postal budget, with its precious letters from wife and children, and pastor and Sunday-school, General Fisk sat down on a log near his headquarters tent to peruse them. Presently an old soldier who did not recognize General Fisk came along and said, "Say, will you read my letter for me?" General Fisk turned and looked at him, and then reached out his hand, into which the letter was placed. In a straggling, downhill fashion, it was addressed to "John Shearer, Helena, Ark." "But can't you read it yourself, John?" the general asked. "No," the man answered, half ashamed. "Then I will, of course," said the General.

The letter was from his wife, and General Fisk read it through, slowly, aloud. It spoke of the crops, and the harvest, and all the little affairs of home—" mentioning even Susy's new dress," and then it went on with a bit of wholesome reminder like this: "Now, John, I want you to remember the promise you made, as you were leaving me and the children, that you would be a good man." And as the General read on, big tears began to run down John's cheeks, until finally he raised the sleeve of his blue blouse and wiped them away. (*See Illustration No 5.*) "Well, John," asked the General, finally, "have you been the good man you promised to be?" Then with more tears came a sad story of drunkenness, and gambling, and sinful speech, until the General's heart ached. Disclosing his identity at last, somewhat to the man's confusion, General Fisk talked with him as a brother, and won his pledge of renewed consecration and a better life. John Shearer came to all the brigade prayer-meetings after that, a changed man.

After the War

General Fisk, who had gone through that long period without leave of absence, and without being off duty, taking his full share of the fighting, desired to return to his family and begin some kind of business that would make some provision for them. He was needed, however, for work that few could do so well as he. He was made assistant commissioner of the Freedmen's Bureau, and assigned to the States of Kentucky and Tennessee. The difficulties of his task were enormous, for the freedmen were prejudiced against their old work, and against their former owners.

The spirit in which he entered upon his task may be inferred from an address he issued to the freedmen, in the course of which he gave this advice as to "your old master": "He has had a hard time of it, during the war, as well as yourselves. His wealth has melted away like wax before the fire. His near relatives, and in many cases his sons, have died on the field of battle, or have been crippled for life. . . . You must think of these things, and think kindly of your old master. You have grown up with him, it may be, on the same plantations. Do not fall out now, but join your interests if you can, and live and die together."

Fisk University

was the direct outcome of the General's efforts on behalf of the freedmen. He recognized at the outset that an education must be placed within their reach. At first *the Scriptures and the Spelling book* covered the ground within his reach. He opened a school for freedmen in January, 1866, in a Government building west of Chattanooga depot. The charge of it was given to the American Missionary Association, but Gen. Fisk's purse and credit were its mainstay. As the school grew, its course of studies extended and it became Fisk University. The work was wonderfully successful, but its demands for money were awful. One of its crises was grandly met. A band of the students who took the title of the Fisk Jubilee Singers, went on a tour through Great Britain, where Mr. Gladstone, Mr. Bright, Rev. C. H. Spurgeon, Dr. Parker and other prominent men approving their object, recommended them to the public, and attended their concerts. By their efforts a clear profit of $100,000 was realized for the University.

General Fisk was finally mustered out of military service September 1, 1886. At President Grant's urgent request, however, he was for a time drawn into Government service. He was induced to make an attempt to do for the Indians something of the same kind of labor that he had done for the freedmen. The establishment of the Indian schools at Hampton, Va., Carlisle, Pa., etc., were largely due to his efforts. That part of his life's work, important as it was, cannot be described here. General Fisk's later years have been passed in the railroad business, though his interest in Sunday-schools,

Philanthropic and Temperance

work, has occupied much of his time. He clung to the Republican party until 1884, but in that year the reception Miss Frances E. Willard and other Prohibition advocates met with at the Chicago Convention, convinced him that the gigantic evil of the liquor traffic could not be grappled with through that party. He was also convinced that by legislation alone could it be successfully dealt with, and he therefore joined hands with the Prohibition party. He ran in 1886 as Prohibition candidate for Governor of New Jersey, and his personal popularity attracted an unexpectedly large vote. The manner in which he conducted the campaign attracted the attention of the whole country, and rendered his nomination for the Presidency inevitable. On May 31 last, the Prohibition National Convention, at Indianapolis, nominated him by acclamation. For Vice-President, its candidate is Rev. John A. Brooks, D. D., of Missouri, whose portrait is *on page* 540 of this number.

The sketch of General Fisk's life given here is necessarily imperfect and fragmentary. We have endeavored to give such incidents as would throw light on the grand character of the man, but much more is needed to fully describe a life so full of activity as his. We would strongly recommend our readers to read the life of General Fisk, by Alphonso A. Hopkins, in a volume containing also the life of Dr. Brooks, price $1.00, published by *Messrs. Funk & Wagnalls*, Astor Place, New York, to whose courtesy in supplying us with advanced sheets of the work we are indebted for the materials for this sketch.

ANECDOTES RELATED AT RECENT EVANGELISTIC MEETINGS.

A Man Sells Himself as a Slave.—"Sometimes native Christians develop remarkable zeal. In connection with the Baptist Missionary Society a native assistant became so interested in a number of his countrymen about to emigrate to Demerara, that he began earnestly their instruction. Having no money to pay his passage, he sold his person as a coolie, or slave, in order that he might have the privilege of accompanying them upon their voyage and preaching the gospel. When they reached their destination he gave them his spiritual ministrations, and at the same time diligently worked out his ransom and redeemed himself. He was so successful that he established a church of some two hundred members, who out of their deep poverty had so abounded in their liberality that they have not only sustained themselves, but they are sustaining a chapel and a missionary in their native city of Canton. I think that was an act of zeal worthy to be compared with any event upon our missionary annals."

A Gipsy-Boy's Death-Bed.—Mr. John Barnsley, said: "I read the other day a simple and touching story. A company of gipsies had encamped near a large town. A good lady, doing her Master's work, asked permission to enter one of the vans, and, after some delay, she was allowed to do so. She found inside a poor boy lying upon a wretched bed, and evidently at the very point of death. She spoke to him kindly, but received no answer. Then, stooping down, she whispered in his ear the old verse, '*God so loved the world that He gave His only begotten Son, that whoever believeth in Him should not perish, but have everlasting life.*' There was no reply. A second time she repeated it, and a second time there was no answer; a third time, kneeling down, she whispered in his ear the same verse, and then the eyes, already glazing in death opened, the thin white lips moved, and the answer slowly came, '*Nobody never told me this before, but thank Him kindly for it.*' What a rebuke there was in these words! At this very moment there are myriads of men, women, and little children for whom Christ died, and whom He loves as much as He loves you and me, who, if they could hear the verse, which has helped so many, 'God so loved the world,' would say, 'Nobody never told me this before.'"

A Cannibal Island Converted.—Rev. J. Jones, of Maré, South Seas, said: "The island of Maré is one of the Loyalty Group. Mr. Cray and myself landed there as two young missionaries thirty-four years ago last October. The bulk of the people were then cannibals and savages of the fiercest description. The tribes determined, when they found that the chief of the converted people had resolved no more to fight, to see whether they could not destroy Christianity from the island, and they attacked us. The chief sent a message to me to say that he was coming down, and that he would cook my wife and me in his ovens for his men, and my little children he would not take so much trouble with, but would throw them upon the fire, and roast them as he did his yams. Now, we did not intend to run away from our work, but we wished to act prudently, and to retire to some little island on the west, and await the storm blowing over. Although the angry cannibals came within sight of our premises, and attacked the village, and killed five of the people, God so disposed their hearts and so ordered events that they retired to a distant district. Then our Christian people took courage, and went forward to preach to them the Gospel of peace, and the chief who had threatened our lives said: 'I have heard what you have said in days gone by, when I heard you preach the Gospel. I have heard of Pharaoh—how he hardened his heart against God, and perished, and now I begin to fear the word of God. Go back and tell the missionary that I will never attack him again, or any of his people.' Subsequently this chief and all his people embraced Christianity."

TROUBLE ON BOTH SIDES.

A Vacation Sermon by Dr. Talmage.

"There was a sharp rock on the one side, and a sharp rock on the other side." 1 Sam. 14:4.

A Wonderful Conflict—Two Famous Rocks—The Ascent Between Them—Dangers on Right and Left—Crises of Simultaneous Misfortune—I. Health and Fortune Failing Together—What a Good Wife May Do—The Nerves Shattered by Financial Embarrassment—What the Man so Beset Should Do—Greater Faith May Come by It—II. Trouble at Home and Abroad—The Objurgations of Milton and Luther—The Persecuted and Maligned Man's Case—Complicated by Unhappiness at Home—Clerical Declaration not Sufficient to Unite a Couple—Wesley's Wife—III. Bereavement and Poverty for a Woman—The Widow's Heights of Promise—IV. A Wasted Life and a Dark Eternity.

THE cruel army of the Philistines must be taken and scattered. There is just one man, accompanied by his bodyguard, to do that thing. Jonathan is the hero of the scene. I know that David cracked the skull of the giant with a few pebbles well slung, and that three hundred Gideonites scattered ten thousand Amalekites by the crash of broken crockery; but here is a more wonderful conflict. Yonder are the Philistines on the rocks. Here is Jonathan with his bodyguard in the valley. On the one side is a rock called Bozez; on the other side is a rock called Seneh. These two were as famous in olden times, as in modern times are Plymouth Rock and Gibraltar. They were precipitous, unscalable, and sharp. Between these two rocks Jonathan must make his ascent. The day comes for

The Scaling of the Height.

Jonathan, on his hands and feet, begins the ascent. With strain and slip and bruise, I suppose, but still on and up, first goes Jonathan, and then goes his bodyguard. Bozez on one side, Seneh on the other. After a sharp tug, and push, and clinging, I see the head of Jonathan above the hole in the mountain; and there is a challenge, and a fight, and a *supernatural consternation*. These two men, Jonathan and his bodyguard, drive back and drive down the Philistines over the rocks, and open a campaign which demolishes the enemies of Israel. I suppose that the overhanging and overshadowing rocks on either side did not balk or dishearten Jonathan or his bodyguard, but only roused and filled them with enthusiasm as they went up. "There was a sharp rock on the one side, and a sharp rock on the other side."

My friends, you have been, or are now, some of you, in this crisis of the text. If a man meets one trouble he can go through with it. He gathers all his energies, concentrates them upon one point, and in the strength of God, or by his own natural determination, goes through it. But the man who has trouble to the right of him, and trouble to the left of him, is to be pitied. Did either trouble come along, he might endure it, but two troubles, two disasters, two overshadowing misfortunes, are Bozez and Seneh. God pity him! "There is a sharp rock on the one side, and a sharp rock on the other side."

In this crisis of the text is that man whose

Fortune and Health Fail

him at the same time. Nine-tenths of all our merchants capsize in business before they come to forty-five years of age. There is some collision in commercial circles, and they stop payment. It seems as if every man must put his name on the back of a note before he learns what a fool a man is who risks all his own property on the prospect that some man will tell the truth. It seems as if a man must have a large amount of unsalable goods on his own shelf before he learns how much easier it is to buy than to sell. It seems as if every man must be completely burned out before he learns the importance of always keeping fully insured. It seems as if every man must be wrecked in a financial tempest before he learns to keep things snug in case of a sudden euroclydon.

When the calamity does come, it is awful. The man goes home in despair, and he tells his family "We'll have to go to the poor-house." He takes a dolorous view of everything. It seems as if he never could rise. But a little time passes, and he says: "Why, I am not so badly off after all; I have my family left."

Before the Lord turned Adam out of Paradise, he gave him Eve, so that when he lost Paradise he could stand it. Permit one who has never read but a few novels in all his life, and who has not a great deal of romance in his composition, to say, that if, when a man's fortunes fail, he has a good wife—

A Good Christian Wife—

he ought not to be despondent. "Oh," you say, "that only increases the embarrassment, since you have her also to take care of." You are an ingrate, for the woman as often supports the man as the man supports the woman. The man may bring all the dollars, but the woman generally brings the courage and the faith in God.

Well, this man of whom I am speaking, looks around, and he finds his family is left, and he rallies, and the light comes to his eyes, and the smile to his face, and the courage to his heart. In two years he is quite over it. He makes his financial calamity the first chapter in a new era of prosperity. He met that one trouble—conquered it. He sat down for a little while under the grim shadow of the rock Bozez; yet he soon rose, and began, like Jonathan, to climb. But how often it is that physical ailment comes with financial embarrassment. When the fortune failed it broke the man's spirit. His nerves were shattered. His brain was stunned. I can show you hundreds of men in New York whose fortune and health failed at the same time. They came prematurely to the staff. Their hand trembled with incipient paralysis. They never saw a well day since the hour when they called their creditors together for a compromise. If such men are impatient, and peculiar, and irritable, excuse them. They had two troubles; either one of which they could have met successfully. If,

When the Health Went,

the fortune had been retained, it would not have been so bad. The man could have bought the very best medical advice, and he could have had the very best attendance, and long lines of carriages would have stopped at the front door to enquire as to his welfare. But poverty on the one side, and sickness on the other, are Bozez and Seneh, and they interlock their shadows, and drop them upon the poor man's way. God help him! "There is a sharp rock on the one side, and a sharp rock on the other side."

Now, what is such a man to do? In the name of Almighty God, I will tell him what to do. *Do as Jonathan did*—climb; climb up into the sunlight of God's favor and consolation. I can go through the churches, and show you men who lost fortune and health at the same time, and yet who sing all day and dream of heaven all night. If you have any idea that sound digestion, and steady nerves, and clear eyesight, and good hearing, and plenty of friends, are necessary to make a man happy, you have miscalculated. I suppose that these overhanging rocks only made Jonathan scramble the harder and the faster to get up and out into the sunlight; and this combined shadow of invalidism and financial embarrassment has often sent a man up the quicker into the sunlight of God's favor and the noonday of His glorious promises.

It is a difficult thing for a man to feel his dependence upon God when he has ten thousand dollars in the bank, and fifty thousand dollars in Government securities, and a block of stores and three ships. "Well," the man says to himself, "it is silly for me to pray, 'Give me this day my daily bread,' when my pantry is full, and the canals from the west are crowded with bread stuffs destined for my storehouses." Oh, my friends, if the combined misfortunes and disasters of life have made you climb up into the arms of a sympathetic and compassionate God, through all eternity you will bless Him that in this world "there was a sharp rock on the one side, and a sharp rock on the other side."

Trouble at Home and Abroad.

Again, that man is in the crisis of the text who has home troubles and outside persecution at the same time. The world treats a man well just as long as it pays best to treat him well. As long as it can manufacture success out of his bone and brain and muscle, it favors him. The world fattens the horse it wants to drive. But let a man see it his duty to cross the track of the world, then every bush is full of horns and tusks thrust at him. They will belittle him. They will caricature him. They will call his generosity self-aggrandizement, and his piety sanctimoniousness. The very worst persecution will some time come upon him from those who profess to be Christians.

John Milton—great and good John Milton—so forgot himself as to pray, in so many words, that his enemies might be eternally thrown down into the darkest and deepest gulf of hell, and be the undermost and most dejected, and the lowest down vassals of perdition! And Martin Luther so far forgot himself as to say, in regard to his theological opponents: "Put them in whatever sauce you please, roasted, or fried, or baked, or stewed, or boiled, or hashed, they are nothing but asses!" Ah, my friends, if John Milton or Martin Luther could come down to such scurrility, what may you not expect from less elevated opponents? Now, sometimes

The World takes after Them;

the newspapers take after them; public opinion takes after them; and the unfortunate man is lied about until all the dictionary of Billingsgate is exhausted on him. You often see a man whom you know to be good and pure and honest, set upon by the world, and mauled by whole communities, while vicious men take on a supercilious air in condemnation of him; as though Lord Jeffreys should write an essay on gentleness, or Henry VIII. talk about purity, or *Herod take to blessing little children*.

Now, a certain amount of persecution rouses a man's defiance, stirs his blood for magnificent battle, and makes him fifty times more a man than he would have been without the persecution. So it was with the great reformer when he said: "I will not be put down; I will be heard." And so it was with Millard, the preacher, in the time of Louis XI. When Louis XI. sent word to him that unless he stopped preaching in that style, he would throw him into the river, he replied: "Tell the king that I will reach heaven sooner by water than he will reach it by fast horses." A certain amount of

Persecution is a Tonic

and inspiration, but too much of it, and too long continued, becomes the rock Bozez, throwing a dark shadow over a man's life. What is he to do then? Go home, you say. Good advice, that. That is just the place for a man to go when the world abuses him. Go home. Blessed be God for our quiet and sympathetic homes. But there is many a man who has the reputation of having a home when he has none. Through unthinkingness or precipitation, there are many matches made that ought never to have been made. An officiating priest cannot alone unite a couple. The Lord Almighty must proclaim banns. There is many home in which there is no sympathy, and no happiness, and no good cheer. *The clamor of the battle* may not have been heard outside, but God knows, notwithstanding all the playing of the "Wedding March," and all the odor of the orange-blossoms, and the benediction of the officiating pastor, there has been no marriage.

Sometimes men have awakened to find on one side of them the rock of persecution, and on the other side

The Rock of Domestic Infelicity.

What shall such an one do? Do as Jonathan did—climb. Get up the heights of God's consolation, from which we may look down in triumph upon outside persecution and home trouble. While good and great John Wesley was being silenced by the magistrates, and having his name written on the board-fences of London in doggerel, at that very time his wife was making him as miserable as she could—acting as though she were possessed by the devil, as I suppose she was; never doing him a kindness until the day she ran away, so that he wrote in his diary these words: "I did not forsake her; I have not dismissed her; I will not recall her." Planting one foot, John Wesley did, upon outside persecution, and the other foot on home trouble, he climbed up into the heights of Christian joy, and after preaching forty thousand sermons, and travelling two hundred and seventy thousand miles, reached the heights of heaven, though in this world he had it hard enough—"a sharp rock on the one side, and a sharp rock on the other."

The Widow's Struggle.

Again, that woman stands in the crisis of the text who has bereavement and a struggle for a livelihood at the same time. Without mentioning names, I speak from observation. Ah, it is a hard thing for a woman to make an honest living, even when her heart is not troubled, and she has a fair cheek, and the magnetism of an exquisite presence. But now the husband, or the father, is dead. The expenses of the obsequies have absorbed all that was left in the savings bank; and wan and wasted with weeping and watching, she goes forth—a grave, a hearse, a coffin behind her—to contend for her existence and the existence of her children. When I see such a battle as that open, I shut my eyes on the ghastliness of the spectacle. Men sit with embroidered slippers and write heartless essays about women's wages; but that question is made up of tears and blood, and there is more blood than tears. Oh, give women free access to all the realms where she can get a livelihood, from the telegraph office to the pulpit. Let men's wages be cut down before hers are cut down. Men have iron in their souls, and can stand it.

Make the Way Free to Her

of the broken heart. May God put into my hand the cold, bitter cup of privation, and give me nothing but a windowless hut for shelter for many years, rather than that after I am dead there should go out from my home into the pitiless world a woman's arm to fight the Gettysburg, the Austerlitz, the Waterloo of life, for bread. And yet, how many women there are seated between the rock of bereavement on the one side, and the rock of destitution on the other! Bozez and Seneh interlocking their shadow and dropping them upon her miserable way. "There is a sharp rock on the one side, and a sharp rock on the other side."

What are such to do? Somehow, let them climb up into the heights of the glorious promise: "Leave thy fatherless children; I will preserve them alive, and let thy widows trust in Me." Or get up into the heights of that other glorious promise: "The Lord preserveth the stranger and relieveth the widow and the fatherless." Oh! ye sewing women, on starving wages. Oh! ye widows, turned out from the once beautiful home. Oh! ye female teachers, kept on niggardly stipend. Oh! ye despairing women, seeking in vain for work, wandering along the docks, and thinking to throw yourself into the river last night. Oh! ye women of weak nerves, and aching sides, and short breath, and broken heart, you need something more than human sympathy; you need the sympathy of God. Climb up into His arms. He knows it all, and He loves you more than father or mother, or husband ever could or ever did; and, instead of sitting down, wringing your hands in despair, you had better begin to climb. There are heights of consolation for you, though now "there is a sharp rock on one side, and a sharp rock on the other side."

Ruin in Life and Eternity.

Again, that man is in the crisis of the text who has a wasted life on the one side, and an unilluminated eternity on the other. Though a man may all his life have cultured deliberation and self-poise, if he gets into that position, all his self-possession is gone. There are all the wrong thoughts of his existence, all the wrong deeds, all the wrong words—strata above strata, granitic, ponderous, overshadowing. That rock I call Bozez. On the other side are all the retributions of the future, the thrones of judgment, the eternal ages, angry with his long defiance. That rock I call Seneh. Between these two rocks Lord Byron perished, and Alcibiades perished, and Herod perished, and ten thousand times ten thousand have perished.

Oh! man immortal, man redeemed, man blood-bought, climb up out of those shadows. Climb up by the way of the Cross. Have your wasted life forgiven; have your eternal life secured. This morning just take one look to the past, and see what it has been, and take one look to the future and see what it threatens to be. You can afford to lose your health, you can afford to lose your property, you can afford to lose your reputation; but you cannot afford to lose your soul. That bright, gleaming, glorious, precious, eternal possession you must carry aloft in the day when the earth burns up and the heavens burst.

You see from my subject that when a man goes into the safety and peace of the Gospel, he does not demean himself. There is nothing in religion that leads to meanness or unmanliness. The Gospel of Jesus Christ only asks you to climb as Jonathan did—

Climb Toward God,

climb toward heaven, climb into the sunshine of God's favor. To become a Christian is not to go meanly down: it is to come gloriously up—up into the communion of saints; up into the peace that passeth all understanding; up into the companionship of angels. He lives up; he dies up.

Oh, then, accept the wholesale invitation which I make this morning to all the people! Come up from between your invalidism and financial embarrassments. Come up from between your bereavements and your destitution. Come up from between a wasted life and an unillumined eternity. Like Jonathan, climb with all your might, instead of sitting down to wring your hands in the shadow and in the darkness—"a sharp rock on the one side, and a sharp rock on the other side."

AT MR. MOODY'S BIBLE CONFERENCE.

The closing session of the Bible Conference at Northfield, Mass., on August 10, showed no decline of interest, no weariness, but rather increased eagerness to hear all that the eminent men present had to say. The venerable *Father Chiniquy*, who has suffered so much to spread the light of the true gospel among the benighted members of the Church of Rome, of which he was a priest for a quarter of a century, was the first speaker on Friday. In the course of his address, he said:

"I do not come here to speak against the Catholics; I would prefer to die a thousand times rather than say aught against them. I have been bruised and have bled to give them the true gospel of Christ. I preach against the errors of the Catholic Church, but I do not hate the Catholics. When men are in a ship, and see it is going to be wrecked, they cry out to be saved. I was crossing the sea of life in a royal ship. Everything about it was magnificent. The sails were made of cloth of gold, and it was filled with precious things. One day I went to the bottom of the ship, and found that it was rotten. As we were passing a rock, I jumped from that ship upon the rock, which was Christ Jesus. You Protestants know nothing about the Roman Catholics. You have created a Catholic in your imagination, but he is not the true one. Because the Catholic Church is a Christian church, you do nothing to convert them. The Catholic Church is an idolatrous church, and their idolatry is of a more diabolical kind than that of any heathen nation. When I was a priest I was as religious and as faithful as I could be. I was worshipping a Christ, and was doing everything to show my adoration for Him. What was that Christ? It was an idol. I was cruelly deceived."

"The priest must take a solemn oath not to interpret the Bible according to common sense and common intelligence, but according to the rules and principles laid down by the Pope and Cardinals of the Church of Rome. Thus the Catholics have a Bible, but they cannot follow it. God has sent the Roman Catholics among you, because you have the true gospel and can teach them the truth. See that you heed the admonition. The hierarchy of the Church have sworn to destroy your land and your cities and your liberty. I was one of the members of a Catholic council when it was determined that not a single American Protestant should have any position under the Government from president down to a city policeman, if Roman Catholic influence could prevent the appointment. They have already determined that your sons shall attend the colleges of the Jesuits and your daughters the schools of the nuns. They have the power over the Board of Education in New York and in Chicago, and it is high time the American people were waking up to save their country. And how can it be done? Not by attacking the Catholics in the Catholic Church, but by converting them."

Mr. D. L. Moody

gave an address on the Acts of the Apostles, the value of which book he thought was too much overlooked by preachers and teachers. He regarded the Acts as the gospel of the Holy Ghost. "The receiving of the Holy Ghost was the book of Acts in a nutshell. The other gospels tell us what Christ did in the body. Acts tell us what He did in His glorified state. It might better be called the Acts of a glorified and exalted Christ. Christ's real work did not begin till after His death. The four other gospels are four currents that sweep into one grand stream in the Acts of the Apostles. Let us take up the ten sermons preached in this book. Five were preached by Peter, one by Stephen, and four by Paul, nine by apostles and one by a layman. If you will read them carefully you will notice that they preached of the death of Christ. They had been witnesses of His death, and told what they had seen and heard. What this world wants is more witnesses for Christ. After Peter got the power of the Holy Ghost he began to preach. I don't think he had preached five minutes before the Holy Ghost broke up the sermon, for the people began to cry out, 'What shall we do to be saved?'

The council told these men not to preach in the name of Christ. What a wily old devil it was to put that into the heads of the council. I might preach with all the eloquence of Demosthenes, and the newspapers might applaud, but let me preach in the name of Christ, and all the hounds of hell will be let loose upon me.

"In the third sermon, the Holy Ghost tells them what to say. They might have studied five years and they could not have given such an answer as that, for the answer came from the throne of God. In the fourth sermon, they filled Jerusalem with their doctrines. People talk about obstacles. Was there ever a darker city to preach in than Jerusalem? Christ had been crucified there by the Jews. Yet were these apostles His witnesses in that wicked city. Witnesses in our courts don't have to be theologians or college-bred men, so you can be witnesses for Christ if you can't write a sermon. The fifth sermon is the longest one in the Bible, except the Sermon on the Mount. Stephen preached it.

"The sixth is the first sermon to the Gentiles. We are especially interested in this, to see what doctrine Peter preached to the Gentiles. He preached the death and resurrection of Christ, and the Holy Spirit put His seal upon it. The eighth sermon was the first sermon preached by Paul, and it was the same old doctrine. Paul preached it to those educated Athenians, and it was just as effectual to save them. In the ninth sermon Paul preached before the mob in Jerusalem, and in the tenth he pleaded before Agrippa, not for his life and his liberty, but that Agrippa might accept Christ."

A WIFE'S PREMONITION.

THE editor of *Words and Weapons* relates a remarkable instance which came under his own notice, of a wife's premonition of her husband's danger. He says: "At a union prayer-meeting held in a New Jersey village not long since, some cultured ladies were very much troubled by the prayer of a woman who seemed greatly concerned for her husband. Her manner, tones and words combined to give the idea of extravagant emotion, so that not only the ladies referred to, but a number of others in the congregation, seemed to feel that the proprieties were considerably disregarded. Among other seemingly wild expressions, this woman made use of the words, '*Oh I fear he is losing his last chance!*' The next week these ladies met a gentlemen who had attended the meeting and to whom they had criticised the prayer. They said that they wanted to retract their statements, and that they would never again be guilty of what might prove to be rash and inconsiderate words concerning the prayer of any brother or sister, for the previous day the man whose wife had felt that he was 'losing his last chance' had taken his own life, and was now about to be carried to the hopeless grave of a suicide."

A LITTLE OUTCAST LEPER.

A VERY pathetic incident is mentioned by Miss Lathrop, who is laboring in India, in the course of a letter to the *Missionary Link*. She says: "While singing in a house in the Mohammedan quarter of the village, I noticed a little girl standing outside, and trying to join. I motioned her to sit down, but she shook her head and turned partly away. A woman, sitting close by, said to me. 'She is sick; look at her hands.' Involuntarily I did so, and before she had time hurriedly to cover them with her cloth, I saw she had *the fatal marks of leprosy*. I hope she did not know I saw her hands, as I looked quickly up to her face—such a sad, sweet face as it was. I asked her if she wished to learn, and she said she very much wished it, but her brother forbade her going to school, and had promised to teach her at home, in the evening. The teacher says she often comes, and *sits while the others learn*, and in this way she is getting the words of the hymns, and, I hope, the Bible verses. Finding her mother peeping at me through the purdah next door, I stopped and spoke with her. She told me the child was often too ill to go out of the house, but when she could, she loved to go and sit by the school. She said if she could get the permission of the husband and brother, the missionary might read and sing with them. I saw two young women peeping over her shoulder, and I hope we may be allowed to visit there. I am sure, as you read of this afflicted little one, you will join us in praying that the words of the Lord Jesus may come to be her stay and comfort."

AN OLD JEWISH RABBI LEARNING.

THE Rev. B. Z. Friedmann, who is laboring among the Jews of Safed, writes: "Among the Jewish visitors who have come to me for religious conversation is an old Rabbi, with whom I spent a long time, listening to the confession of his belief in Christ. He received a New Testament from Mr. Oczeret, and has been carefully reading it. What astonishes me most is that his faith in Christ has not in the least shaken his attachment to Jewish law and customs. It was with great difficulty I could persuade him to believe that I am not scrupulous in cosher or trephah [the clean or unclean food in the ceremonial law]. The truth of the Gospel has been forced upon his conviction by reading the simple narrative of the Holy Gospels, without his realizing the true liberty of the Gospel of Christ. The next week his wife called upon me at the dépôt, telling me that her husband was ill and wished me to visit him. I went at once, and found him in bed, suffering great pain. I had some friendly conversation with him and several neighbors who were present. These gradually left, and I was left alone with the patient. 'I was thinking,' he then said, 'about the words in Kedushah for the Sabbath.' (The hymn of the Seraphim, Isaiah 6:3, appointed for the congregation to sing on the Sabbath, the words being 'And *He will redeem us the second time*.') This phrase, he thought, must refer to the first and second coming of the Messiah, the truth of which is commonly denied by the Synagogue at large. 'There are many prophecies in Scripture,' I said, 'by which two comings of Christ, first to suffer and atone for the sins of all who believe in Him, and again the second time to reign and judge the world, can be easily proved.' When I saw, however, that he was inclined to think his own explanation the true one, I did not wish to discourage him further. In his room he showed me three New Testaments. The Epistle to the Hebrews he generally carries about with him. He is much disturbed by visitors, but when alone reads the New Testament, especially the Gospel of St. John. He needs, of course, still much enlightenment. May the Lord grant him more light, and bring him to a saving knowledge of Christ our Redeemer!"

A LONG SEARCH FOR A WIFE.

TEN thousand miles of travel for a wife has been cheerfully undergone by a young man in Chicago. Some three or four years ago he was living in Nottingham, England, where he fell in love with an extremely pretty girl, seventeen years of age. He believed that his affection was reciprocated, and a day was set for their marriage. But the girl was very vacillating, and a short time before the wedding-day, she ran away to America. The young man followed, found her in New York, and forgave her. She was again willing to be married, but again changed her mind, and before the young man's arrangements for the marriage was completed, she secretly slipped on board a steamer and returned to England. Her lover, still bent on making her his wife, followed, went to Nottingham, but found that she had left that town. He spent some weeks in searching for her in England, and at length discovered that she had gone to Paris. He traced her from that city through a long continental wandering, which at last led him back to Nottingham, where he caught her, and she consented to be married on condition that they should go at once to America. The lover gave his promise, and the ceremony at last took place. They came to New York, but, after a few weeks, removed to Chicago, where they settled down. Last week the young husband, after only six months of married life, reported to the Chicago police that his wife was missing, and asked them to assist him in searching for her. He said she had already involved him in ten thousand miles of travel, but he was ready to tramp ten thousand more, if necessary. Few men would have thought a woman so wayward and inconstant, worthy of any mere trouble, and we naturally infer the ardor and intensity of his love by his readiness to undertake another search. What, then, must be the love of God for His people, whose sins and unfaithfulness have been a continual trial of it? (Nehemiah 9:16, 17.)

PRAYER IN A CYCLONE.

IN the course of some reminiscences of his recent voyages the Rev. Henry Varley mentions the following incident: "We were voyaging to Melbourne. The day had been close and sultry, and the rapidly falling glass indicated a coming storm. One short hour and we were driving before the tempest, which lashed the sea into foam and fury. 'The tail end of *an Indian cyclone*,' our commander whispered, as I stood watching the stowing of the canvas. Great seas struck us, and literally filled the main deck from end to end. 'There, sir,' said our gallant captain, 'all has been done that can be done; she must take her chance now.' All the officers were on deck, and I quietly said to Captain Black, 'We might go down to your cabin and have some special prayer.' 'Good,' was his reply. We descended to the quiet sanctum, where often we had read the Word together and met for prayer. Ten minutes had scarcely elapsed when our words were no longer audible. This was caused by a downpour of hail, such as I never remember to have seen or heard. For wellnigh a half an hour the air was charged with a rain of bullets, which covered the decks and buried myriads of ice-balls in the surging foam of the angry sea. Nothing could have been more timely, no intervention more appropriate or effectual. The effect upon the raging billows was simply wonderful. They were beaten back and down, until their turbulence had given place to comparative rest. Truly our experience comprised the necessity, prayer, Divine intervention, and natural law, amidst the fierce and circling eddies of the Indian Ocean."

GOSPEL WORK IN ROME.

IN a letter from the Rev. James Wall, who is laboring under the shadow of the Pope's palace in Rome, the following among other incidents are cited as illustrations of the progress of the gospel in the city: A respectable woman received a Gospel in one of the streets of Rome. She was employed in making the embroidery which the Canons of St. Peter's use. One of the priests she served, seeing the Gospel in her house, took it away as a pestilential book, and threatened to take the work elsewhere. The Gospel made considerable impression on the woman's mind, and she longed to know the truth. Occasionally, disguised as a servant, she went to an evangelical meeting, and at last made the acquaintance of our Bible-woman, who brought her to worship. She soon accepted, and confessed the Saviour. She is excommunicated, but is happy in the Saviour.

A man passing before one of our halls received a Gospel, and, taking it home, gave it to his boy, a child of ten years. The child read it, and went through Rome in search of the place where the book was sold. That place was shut, but a boy of whom he inquired directed him to come to our Sunday-school, which he did the next morning. He is now one of our most regular attendants, not only at the school, but at all the meetings during the week. He often comes to our house, and has brought his mother and elder brother. The mother is delighted at the change in the child.

Several days since I was cited by the inspector of police in this parish, and asked to give information respecting a man who had in his possession a Bible and a number of tracts. As the man was poor, and had said he had received the books from us, the inspector wanted to hear me. I said I was surprised that the possession of evangelical books by anyone in Rome should be a ground of suspicion, and that if such was the case the authorities would have enough to do, since in the past year we had distributed, perhaps, 20.000 Scriptures and portions, and nearly a hundred thousand tracts, and that shortly we hoped there would not be a house in Rome without a copy. The inspector smiled, and said, "*I have it myself, and have read it for years.*"

A THIEF'S RESTITUTION.

THE following incident is published by Rev. Henry Varley: A clerk in a wholesale dry goods house in London some years ago left his employment to study for the ministry in Rev. C. H. Spurgeon's Pastor's College. He is now the well-known Rev. B. Sawday, the successful pastor of Vernon Chapel, near King's Cross, London. When he was in the dry goods house a silver watch was stolen from his bedroom, and no trace could be discovered of the missing property. Ten years passed away. Mr. Sawday had given himself to the work of the ministry, and was preaching in Vernon Chapel. One Sunday morning he preached a startling discourse upon Repentance and Restitution. His words evidently made a deep impression upon his hearers. During the ensuing week a young man came up to Mr. Sawday requesting an interview. Mr. Sawday, who was walking quickly to catch a train, said, "Walk with me," and in his usual friendly way linked his arm in the inquirer's on the way to the station. In a few words, the young man said, "It was I who stole your watch, some years since, at Messrs. Hitchcock's." "What did you do that for?" said Mr. Sawday, hardly knowing what to say. "I am very sorry, and I am deeply anxious to settle the matter. Here, I'll give you £10 to square it. I was passing your chapel last Sunday, and I saw your name; I thought I would go in and hear you, and your sermon broke me all to pieces; I have been wretched and miserable ever since." "Thank God!" said Mr. Sawday. "No," he added, "I cannot take £10; the watch was only worth £4; I'll take that; but I'm far more anxious that you should confess your sin to God, and obtain His pardon and grace." "That," said the man, "I have sought, and obtained."

PROPHETIC EVENTS BETWEEN 1889 AND 1901.

"BEHOLD THE BRIDEGROOM COMETH."

Mr. William Birch's 776th Printed Sunday Sermon, delivered in Free Trade Hall, Manchester, March 18, 1888.

(Continued from page 519.)

"And at midnight there was a cry made, Behold, the Bridegroom cometh." Matt. 25 : 6.

The Rapture in the Second Year of the Covenant—Simultaneous Resurrection of the Justified—The New Celestial Bodies—The Heaps of Clothes Left—Antichrist's Work After the Rapture—To Subdue Three of the Confederated Nations—Submission of the other Six—His World-wide Dominion—America also to be Part—His Vast Army—Drawn from all Nations—Jerusalem Besieged—Sudden Appearance of Christ—Panic in Antichrist's Army.

NEARLY two years after the signing the seven years' term of the Jewish Covenant, the Lord Jesus shall suddenly appear in the clouds, but His presence will be felt only by the Christians who, like the five Wise Virgins, are ready and watching for Him. Though there may be several millions of Christians, yet only 144 000 of them will

Be Ready to Ascend

in the air to be with the Lord. We read in Daniel 9 : 25, "From the going forth of the commandment, to restore and build Jerusalem UNTO Messiah the Prince shall be seven weeks and threescore and two weeks" (Dan. 9 : 25), or sixty-nine weeks. A future Commandment to restore and rebuild Jerusalem will go forth at the same time as when the Jewish sacrifices shall be restored in a rebuilt temple at Jerusalem, about November 8, 1894: and in sixty-nine weeks afterward, namely about March 5, 1896, our Lord may be expected to come as a Bridegroom to call His waiting disciples to His side.

At the same time "the dead in Christ shall rise first," that is, all the saints who have died since the world began shall be raised. This is called the Resurrection of the Just; in other words, those who are justified through the precious blood of Christ shed in their stead. But only the 144,000 living saints, who believe in the speedy personal coming of Christ, and are watching for Him, will be caught up in this first ascension of Christians to heaven. As steel is drawn to the magnet, so the saints will be drawn to Christ; and in the twinkling of an eye, it will be done. He who raised His crucified body to life is able to raise us in

New Celestial Bodies

to the skies. Glory to God, these bodies of flesh and blood, of dishonor and corruption, of weakness and pain, will be transfigured and transformed into bodies of immortality, incorruption, and glory; we shall be changed. In a moment, by a miracle, our bodies will be made into heavenly celestial bodies. The moment the drawing power of our Lord is felt by our waiting souls, we shall see Him, and when we see Him be made like Him, in spirit, soul, and body. And when we meet our fellow-Christians in the air, we shall see that every face and every form is heavenly and divine.

It may be without noise, only those who are called hearing the trumpet's sound. The world at large and our companions will know that the Lord has taken us only by our absence. "In that night, two shall be in one bed; the one shall be taken, and the other left. Two shall be in the field; the one shall be taken, and the other left." (Luke 17: 34.) In some places, the Lord will come at midnight when His people have gone to bed, no doubt praying, "Lord, if thou comest while I sleep, awake me and call me to Thyself." But in other parts of the earth at that precise moment, it may be morning, afternoon, or evening, when people will be at their daily labor, or resting after work; but exactly at the same moment all over the earth, the waiting disciples, in the twinkling of an eye, will suddenly receive a celestial body and be caught up to meet the Lord in the air (1 Thess. 4 : 16; Rev. 14 : 4.)

When our Lord rose from the dead, He did not need the napkin or grave-clothes, but wrapping them up, He left them in the tomb. So we

Shall not Need Our Coats

and dresses, but may leave behind here and there little heaps of clothes—visible proofs of the ascension of the translated ones who will then be before the throne of God, "dressed in robes of everlasting wear." Many Christians left on the earth will afterwards fly into a wilderness.

After this *Frstfruits* Translation of the 144,000, business and political affairs will proceed on the earth as usual.

The King of Syria

will cast covetous eyes on Egypt, seek to obtain control of the Suez Canal; but though the ships of Kittim (probably meaning Britian) shall hinder him, he will eventually take possession of Egypt, and having previously overcome three of the ten nations (Dan. 7 : 24), the remaining six will submit to his victorious arms, and acknowledge him as their Head. He will break his covenant with the Jews, and stop the morning and evening sacrifice. About this time he will receive a frightful wound and be slain, but by a miracle Satan will raise him from death, and on the supposition that this miraculous man is divine, the Pope and the ungodly world will worship him. In God's Word he is called the Antichrist, the Man of Sin, the Wilful King, and the wild beast. (Rev. 13 : 3-18; 17 : 8; Zech. 11 : 17; Dan. 11.)

Having overcome the Jews and other nations, his navy being the combined fleets of Europe, he will rule the world,

Including America,

and in his pride, believing himself to be more than a man, he will sit upon a throne in the temple of Jerusalem, surrounded by the representatives of every ruling nation under heaven, probably being considered by most of the Jews as the Messiah; and the Pope of Rome, called the false prophet, his obedient friend, will say, "It is the voice of a God," when the princely assembly will fall down and worship him. But many Christians will escape into a wilderness and be hidden there during his three and a half years. Those 1,260 days from August, 1897, to January 1901, will be the time of great tribulation, for the Wilful King and the Pope will seek out the faithful Christians, and if they refuse to receive the mark of the beast on their forehead or hand, he will order them to be beheaded. There will be

A Huge Scaffold Erected

in every town of Europe. Two sackcloth-robed witnesses, like Elijah and John the Baptist, will go about to preach the gospel, and will be slain at the end of the 1,260 days, but God will raise them from the dead, and take them up to heaven in the sight of thousands of people in the city looking upon their dead bodies.

Some of the Jews will then turn from their idolatry of the False Christ, and look for the Messiah (Rev. 12, 6:13; 11.) In due time the Antichrist will receive tidings of the approach of the kings of the East, supposed to be the lost ten tribes, guided by Scripture prophecies of the Coming of Messiah, to meet Him at the Mount of Olives. Antichrist shall then make a stupendous effort, once for all, to conquer the Jews, and his army will surround Jerusalem in a compass of two hundred miles, with the view of driving them in and putting them to death. He will meet with some success. His vast army will number

Millions of Soldiers

of all nations, and Jerusalem and the Holy Land will be taken, and the houses rifled, and the women ravished. (Zechariah 14, 2.) Then the Jews shall lift up their despairing cry to God. The whole earth shall be stained with the blood of faithful Christians, the slaughter of whom will continue in every country on the earth, and there will be such a time of tribulation as mankind has never known. Then in that terrible day, our Lord's angels shall gather the harvest of faithful Christians who are alive, together with 144,000 converted Jews (quite distinct from the 144,000 Christians translated five years earlier), and take them to heaven without dying.

The same day, the LORD JESUS will appear, standing upon the Mount of Olives, which shall suddenly cleave in two, and thus make a great valley through which the tens of thousands of Jews who cannot escape from the invading army shall flee from death and find safety. Then when they see the Christ whom their fathers pierced on the cross, they shall be converted. The same day,

A Tumult will Arise

in the vast army of Antichrist—the horses will suddenly become blind, the soldiers mad, and every man will attack his comrade as an enemy, only a remnant escaping. The battle-field, extending two hundred miles on three sides around Jerusalem, the Mount of Olives being the other side, will be like a shambles, and in the valleys the blood will form lakes of blood up to the horses' bridles. It will take the converted Jews seven months to bury the dead, and for seven years the muskets, wheels, carts, tents, and other things on that battle-field will keep them in firewood. On the day of the battle, Antichrist and the false prophet will be seized and cast alive into a lake of fire burning with brimstone. (Rev. 19, 20; Ezekiel 39; Zech. 14.)

Then the converted Jews, being the only Christians left on the earth, will go up and down to instruct the nations, and our Lord Jesus will begin His personal reign of a thousand years.

The Celestial City in the Air,

to which all God's people have been taken, shall then be let down within sight of the earth, and in the blue vault of the sky, the people then alive, as the earth revolves, will be able through their telescopes to see through the transparent golden pavement of the celestial city and observe some of the glory of that blessed place, while our Lord's saved ones will come down periodically to assist Him in His reign on the earth for a thousand years, during which time Satan shall be so securely fastened that he cannot deceive the nations. The desert shall blossom as a rose, and the nations learn war no more. (Rev. 21.)

It seems like a dream; but as it is revealed in God's Word as a fact shortly to come to pass, I earnestly exhort you, one and all, to be ready. Remember that many of us believe the Lord may call His waiting people home within eight years from now; and I hope that every one of you, dear friends, will be of that heavenly company who shall meet the Lord Jesus in the air.

CHRISTIAN HERALD AND SIGNS OF OUR TIMES.

OFFICE, 63 BIBLE HOUSE, NEW YORK.

ENTERED AT THE POST-OFFICE AT NEW YORK, N. Y., AS SECOND-CLASS MATTER.

EVERY NUMBER CONTAINS:

The Portrait and Biography of some eminent person.
The Sermon Dr. Talmage preached the last Sunday morning.
An Exposition of Unfulfilled Prophecy.
A Summary of the Events of the Week, Notes of Religious and Temperance Movements, etc.
A Sermon by Rev. C. H. Spurgeon, of London, from advance sheets sent by special arrangement.
Pictures of Missionary Life, etc., and Descriptive Articles.
An instalment of a Serial Story.
An Exposition of the International Sunday-School Lesson, by Mrs. M. Baxter.

ANNUAL SUBSCRIPTION, $1.50.

Remittances by mail should be by bank cheques, Post-office orders, or Express money-orders whenever possible. If currency is sent it should be in a registered letter. Cheques and money-orders should be made payable to The Christian Herald. Making them payable to individuals often causes delay.

New subscriptions may commence at any time. When subscribers do not indicate their wish, they commence with the first number of the month in which the subscription is received.

PUBLISHER'S NOTICE.

The whole edition of The Christian Herald was mailed last week to subscribers during Tuesday, Aug. 14. The last delivery at the New York Post Office was made at 11.30 P. M.

CURRENT EVENTS.

Yellow Fever was Declared to be Epidemic at Jacksonville, Fla., on August 10, by the President of the State Board of Health. Energetic measures have been taken to stamp out the disease. Tar fires were lighted in the streets, and lime was scattered so freely that the city looked as if there had been a snow-storm. The theory that concussion of the air was fatal to the fever germs was tried by firing salvos of artillery at the battery at intervals, day and night. Dr. Echemendia, a skilful Cuban physician of experience, was appointed to manage the disinfection arrangements, and authority was given him *to burn any building* he might deem it advisable to destroy. A refugee camp was opened at Boulogne, twenty miles west of the city, and a competent physician placed in charge. There was, however, a more hopeful feeling prevalent toward the end of the week, and the tide of migration was checked.

The News of the Appalling Marine Disaster which reached New York on Thursday last, sent a thrill of horror through the whole community. It was brought by the captain and a handful of the passengers and crew of the steamship *Geiser*, which left New York for Copenhagen on Saturday, August 11. She had reached Sable Island, off the Nova Scotia coast, in safety, but on Tuesday morning, August 14, she was run into by her sister ship, the *Thingvalla*, and sunk. The collision occurred shortly before 4 o'clock in the morning, when a heavy rain was falling, and a mist hung over the sea. The *Geiser* was in charge of the first officer, the captain having gone to lie down on the sofa in the stateroom. About half-past three the lights of a large steamer were seen, and two whistles were blown, to indicate the course the *Geiser* was taking. A few minutes later the steamer crashed into the *Geiser's* side, cutting through amidships almost half across the ship. A panic immediately ensued. The sailors lowered two boats, but did it so clumsily that both were rendered useless. The two life-rafts on board were entangled in the rigging, and they and the other boats went down with the ship. The rent in the *Geiser's* side was so huge that, although she had water-tight bulkheads, she settled and sank stern-foremost in seven minutes after the fatal blow was struck. She had on board 93 passengers, and crew of 56, in all, 149 lives. Of these, only 31 were saved—14 passengers and 17 of the crew. All the other 118 were drowned, or crushed to death in their berths by the prow of the colliding steamer. The *Thingvalla*, which did the mischief, was a smaller boat than the *Geiser*. Her prow was crushed in by the collision, and but for the rapid closing of the forward bulkhead, she, too, must have sunk. As it was, she was so much crippled that her passengers, and those rescued from the *Geiser*, were transferred to a passing steamer, and carried to New York. She was on her way from Copenhagen to New York, but after the catastrophe she headed for Halifax, N. S., which was only 180 miles away, and arrived there on Friday. One of the sailors saved was in his berth on the *Geiser* when the collision occurred; but he clung to the prow of the *Thingvalla*, and when that vessel backed away, climbed upon her deck. The other thirty were picked up by the *Thingvalla's* boats as they swam or floated on pieces of wreckage.

Still another Political Party with a National ticket was put in the field last week. The American party assembled in national convention in Washington, D. C., on August 14. It adopted a platform and nominated Mr. James L. Curtis, of New York, its candidate for the presidency. The platform is of the type of the old Know-nothing party. Among other things it favors the total abolition of the naturalization laws, demands that no criminals, paupers, or insane persons shall be allowed to immigrate, and that in order to become an emigrant to the United States a man must satisfy the Consul at the port from which he wishes to sail that he does not come under the prohibited classes, and must pay a per capita tax to the Consul before sailing. It declares in favor of prohibiting immigration of all persons not in sympathy with the Government of the United States; against alien ownership of land; in favor of free technical schools for American children, and in favor of the expenditure of the surplus for the building of fortifications and naval vessels.

The Tariff Bill which the Republican Senators are preparing as a substitute for the Mills Bill, will, according to their own calculation, reduce the revenue by eighty million dollars. Its details have not been disclosed, but the New York *Tribune*, which ought to be well informed on the subject, declares that the bill will make a cut of fifty per cent. in sugar and will do away with the entire Internal Revenue tax on tobacco and spirits used in the manufactures and the arts. The duty on lumber is to remain as now, and the wool question, which has given more trouble to the committee than any other, is settled in "a way satisfactory to both growers and manufacturers." A report to the full committee is expected to be made during this week.

An Important Legal Decision Which Should have a salutary influence was rendered last week by Judge Wallace, of the United States Circuit Court. Its effect is to hold stock-brokers responsible in cases of bank failures, when they have received bank property in payment of personal accounts of the officers of the bank. The question arose out of the failure of the Albion Bank. The president of the bank speculated with the bank's funds through a firm of brokers, and the ultimate consequence was the wreck of the bank through his default. The decision of Judge Wallace sustains a verdict by which the brokers are compelled to refund the money of the bank which they received from the president in payment of his personal obligations. It is not suspected that the brokers had any intention of defrauding the bank, but their receiving property which they must have known belonged to the bank and not personally to the president of it rendered them liable. If this decision is sustained, there will probably be less speculation with bank funds, and the safety of these institutions will be proportionately increased.

The World's Conference of Young Men's Christian Associations assembled in Stockholm, the capital of Sweden, on August 15. The convention was formally opened in a brief address by Count Bernstorff, of Berlin, President of the convention held four years ago in Berlin. Dr. von Scheele was elected President, and Mr. George Williams, of London, Count Bernstorff, of Berlin, and Mr. Lucian Warner, of New York, Vice-Presidents. The following Americans were appointed members of committees: Business Committee — Mr. Robert Orr, of Pittsburg; Resolutions and Credentials Committee — Mr. Thomas K. Cree, of New York, Chairman; and Mr. Robert McBurney, of New York. Brief reports were made of the work in America by Mr. Richard C. Morse, of New York; for France by Mr. Van der Beken, of Paris; for Great Britain by Mr. Hind Smith, of London; and for Germany by Mr. Phildius, of Berlin. Four hundred delegates are in attendance, of whom 200 are English-speaking, and some sixty are from America. Among the American delegates are Messrs. Morse, Cree, Wishard, and Olandt, secretaries of the International Committee; Mr. Hall, State Secretary of New York; Mr. McBurney, Secretary, New York City; Mr. McConaughby, Secretary, Philadelphia; and Mr. Orr, Secretary, Pittsburg.

The British Parliament has Adjourned, after an unusually long session. Besides Irish affairs, which have been a source of embarrassment, only two measures of importance have been carried. They are Mr. Goschen's scheme for the reduction of the interest on the public debt, and the bill changing the system of county and municipal government. The former appears to be a valuable measure, and has been approved by the country. England was paying more interest on her public debt than her credit entitled her to pay, and the Chancellor of the Exchequer has remedied the waste. Of the other bill, approval is withheld until a practical test comes. The prospect is that, as it is an innovation and touches the privileges and dignities of a class extremely sensitive to change, there will be some dissatisfaction with it.

Labor Troubles in France are Causing Uneasiness. A deputation of navvies made an indignant protest on August 14, against the attitude of the Government, to M. Floquet, the Prime Minister. They declared that the masters would have complied with their demands, if the Government and police had not supported the employers. M. Floquet reminded the delegation that although the Republic allowed workmen to discuss the conditions of labor, it did not allow them the right to impede labor. The Government would protect workers against all violence. It had closed the Labor Exchange in order to put an end to the culpable provocations which the strikers had been guilty of. A number of unemployed workmen entered the shipbuilders' yards at Calais on the same day for the purpose of inducing the men at work therein to go on strike. They *carried a red flag* and acted in a disorderly manner. Troops were called, and dispersed the rioters.

A Speech by the Emperor of Germany, Displaying martial spirit, was made on August 16 at Frankfort-on-the-Oder, where he unveiled a statue of the late Prince Frederick Charles. After eulogizing the prince, he went on to say: "This is a serious time. Emperor William I., Prince Frederick Charles and other great military commanders and helpers in the creation of the empire, are no more, though they will continue to live in the memory of the German people forever. Just as the people of Brandenburg, with their iron strength and unwearied activity, wrest a livelihood from the sterile soil, so the Third Army Corps wrested victory from the enemy. The deeds which the Third Army Corps achieved they owe to the prince. There can be no question as to the surrender of what has thus been gained. Our eighteen army corps, our forty-six millions of people, ought rather to be left on the battle-field than to permit one stone of what has been gained to be taken." The young Emperor, in enumerating the sacrifices which should be made rather than surrender the conquests, appears, from the cable report, to have omitted to express his own readiness to be "left on the battle-field."

The Rev. C. H. Spurgeon's Attitude toward his brother ministers of the Baptist Union was described in a letter published last week, of which the cable brings a brief summary. Mr. Spurgeon says: "I have incurred much odium, yet I am not discouraged. Though I seem to have spoken in vain, I trust there is yet enough love for sound doctrine among Baptists to prevent these errors having unlimited sway." "These errors" are, of course, those which Mr. Spurgeon denounced in the recent Downgrade controversy. Mr. Spurgeon insists that his withdrawal from the Union does not imply any change in his doctrinal standing as a Baptist.

A Pathetic Complaint was Made by a Child in Hoboken, N. J., on August 16. She and her sister were found wandering in the streets, near the City Hall, about midnight, and were taken care of by the police. The two children, who appeared to be respectively about eight and ten years old, stated that their mother was dead, and their father had placed them in a children's Home. He paid for their maintenance for some time, but he had ceased to pay, and was gone away to some distant place. The managers of the Home would keep them no longer, and they were sent in charge of a woman to the Juvenile Asylum in Jersey City, but they were refused admittance there. The woman then left them in the streets. They set out to walk to Hoboken where they formerly lived, but when they arrived they found the house they used to live in empty, and they did not know where to go. The elder child cried bitterly when they were taken to the police station. She said, "*No one cares for us now.*" No child in a Christian country should have cause to make such a complaint. It may be hoped that they will fall into the hands of some Christian people, from whom they may learn not only that there is human kindness for them, but that God is their Almighty Friend and Protector. (Matt. 18 : 10.)

The Extraordinary Candor of a Wife has led to a divorce suit in Chicago. On August 14, a well-known wealthy citizen petitioned the court to set him free from his wife. He testified that they had been married twenty-one years, but during that time, on various pretexts, his wife had been absent from his home over fifteen years. She had travelled through all the States and in Europe, and he, believing the reasons she gave him were valid, had supplied her liberally with money. He had lived in boarding-houses during her long absences. Finally his patience was exhausted, and he insisted on her staying at home. He purchased a beautiful home, furnished it, and presented her with the deeds. Then she complained that she was so far from her mother and sisters, who were poor. The indulgent husband, to gratify her, bought them a home in the neighborhood, and made a settlement upon them. The wife then being divested of every shadow of excuse for absenting herself, told him frankly that she liked to have his money, but did not like him, and would never live with him. That statement decided him, and he at once began suit for divorce. His course is perfectly natural, and the wife cannot complain of his refusing to bestow his wealth on a woman who does not love him, nor care for his society. God's people have often been guilty of similar ingratitude toward Him, accepting His bounties, yet turning their backs upon Him and His laws. (Jer. 2 : 31.)

A Blind Veteran's Account of What He could see, astonished some visitors at an exhibition in New York, last week. He went with his granddaughter to a cyclorama representing the battle of Gettysburg, and sat down while she described to him the features of the picture in detail. She had described to him in her own way the hand-to-hand conflict at the stone fence where the Pennsylvania veterans met the charge of the Southerners, when he asked, "Is there a grove of trees?" "Yes, grandpa. It seems to be full of men, but the smoke is so thick you cannot see them." "Oh, I can see them," he replied. It was then noticed by several people who were listening to him that he was blind. The little girl said: "Oh, no, grandpa; you can't see them." "Yes, I can," he answered. "I can see them very well, and the broken cannon too. That was the last thing I ever saw on earth. There was a caisson exploded there just this side of that fence, and it was then I lost my eyesight, and I have never got the picture of it out of my head." It is a pity that the terrible picture could not be replaced by that scene which was witnessed a few days ago at Gettysburg, when the veterans on both sides met on the scene of the dreadful conflict and clasped hands in amity. Though the blind man doubtless heard of it, he could not realize it as he did the other scene. It is sometimes so with the sinner under conviction. The terrors of Sinai are very clear to him, but he is unable to see his interest in that other scene on Calvary which would give him peace and joy. (Heb. 12 : 18-24.)

A Sixty-Dollar Coffin for a Dog and a Two-hundred dollar lot in Woodlawn Cemetery were provided by a wealthy lady in New York last week. On August 15, an undertaker applied to the Health Department for a burial permit for Cosey Bell, and presented a regular doctor's certificate of death. The permit was being drawn out in due form, when the undertaker explained that the deceased was a dog. He was then informed that no permit was necessary. The application excited the curiosity of a reporter, who paid a visit to the bereaved household. He found the dead dog lying in a satin-lined coffin, which had cost sixty dollars, and learned that a lot had been secured in Woodlawn Cemetery at a cost of two hundred dollars for its interment. The dog's owner was weeping bitterly over the casket, and that evening, clad in mourning, she followed it to the grave. Probably this expenditure and grief are signs of care and affection which were lavished upon the dog during his life. As the place of household pet is now vacant, it may be hoped that some Christian friend of the lady will suggest to her that she fill it with some poor, neglected orphan child. In doing so, she may not only save a human being from a life of sin and shame, but may enjoy the blessing of God which is promised to those who have pity on the poor. (Prov. 19 : 17.)

A Search for Diamonds in a Dust-Heap is being industriously prosecuted in San Francisco. It appears that a few weeks ago, a lady took her departure from that city to spend a month in a summer resort. She left behind her in the charge of her daughter a diamond brooch and several other ornaments containing diamonds, worth altogether over six thousand dollars. The daughter became a prey to fears of burglars and took the housemaid into her confidence. The two, after consultation, decided on concealing the precious gems in the family dust barrel, where they thought that the burglars, if they came, would not dream of looking for them. But unfortunately they did not acquaint the cook with their intention. On the following Saturday morning, the daughter, on going as usual to the ash-barrel, to remove the diamonds to the casket which they occupied during the day, found the barrel empty, the cook having handed it over to the scavenger, to be dumped into his cart. The diamonds had therefore gone with the city refuse to the public dump. A search was immediately commenced, but not a jewel could be found. Subsequently it was learned that an Italian ash-picker had sold a diamond brooch to a jeweller for ten dollars, and that ornament was recovered; but no trace has, as yet, been found of the other gems. Further search will probably be futile, but if search is made among the human refuse of any of our great cities there will be found many a precious jewel which would adorn Christ's crown in the day when He makes up His jewels. (Mal. 3 : 17.)

A Mournful Parting in a New York Police Court occurred on August 15. A policeman brought before the justice a man and woman whom he had found the previous night fighting for the possession of a pretty little girl six years old. They were a divorced husband and wife, and the husband complained that the wife would not give up the child. He submitted to the justice his divorce papers, regularly signed, giving him the custody of his little daughter. Then ensued a painful scene. The mother admitted that the divorce had been granted because of her own wrong-doing, but she pleaded with tears that she might keep her child. She flung herself on her knees and besought the justice not to separate them. The little girl, too, added her entreaties. She was crying and kissing her mother, and she said, "I won't—I won't leave mamma. I won't go with him." The justice was visibly affected, but he said he had no power to interfere with the decision of the Divorce Court. The man was legally entitled to the custody of the child. The woman groaned, and clung to her convulsively. The little girl was, at last, wrested from her grasp by physical force, and was carried, screaming, out of court, leaving her mother almost demented with grief on the floor. If the woman had not repented of her sin before, she did so then, when it was too late. Only the one hope is left to her that after a few years she and her child may be reunited. How precious would that hope be to those who die in their sins when they see themselves separated, on the day of final account, from their beloved ones who go into everlasting happiness. (Matt. 25 : 46.)

BRIEF NOTES.

Rev. Sam Jones has been conducting a large camp-meeting at Warrensburg, Mo.

Bishop Harris, of Michigan, who attended the Pan-Anglican Synod, has been stricken with paralysis in England.

In many churches of different denominations the Christian Endeavor Society has maintained the weekly church prayer-meeting through the summer vacation.

The annual Convention of the National Woman's Christian Temperance Union will be held in this city in the Metropolitan Opera-House, commencing October 19, and continuing four days.

The statement of a contemporary that Rev. C. H. Spurgeon is sick and unable to preach is incorrect. Mr. Spurgeon has recovered, and since the beginning of July has been preaching regularly.

By the will of the late Margaret R. Smith, of Philadelphia, who died in Norway recently, the Presbyterian Board of Home Missions has received $20,000, and the Board of Foreign Missions $10,000.

An English journal states that a prayer-meeting is held weekly in the precincts of the House of Commons. Several prominent and influential members of the House are among those who attend regularly and take part in the exercises.

Rev. David Smith, who opened the recent General Conference of the African Methodist Episcopal Church with prayer, is said to be the oldest preacher in the world. He is 104 years of age, and has been a professing Christian ninety years.

The North Pacific Mission Institute, in Hawaii, has just held its graduating exercises. Eleven young men have completed the four years' course of instruction there under the care of Rev. C. M. Hyde, D. D. Many of them are already called to pastorates of native churches.

The centennial anniversary of the birth of Adoniram Judson, the famous Baptist missionary, was celebrated at Malden, Mass., his birthplace, Thursday, August 9. The celebration was held under the auspices of the Baptist church in Malden, whose walls bear an inscription in honor of his memory.

The American Reformation Society has commenced a series of services in the People's Church, on Columbia Avenue, Boston, the object of which is announced to be "the evangelization of Roman Catholics, and the preservation of our national and constitutional liberties and institutions."

The wealthy Hebrews of the Mt. Sinai congregation, New York, assembled on August 3 in their recently purchased edifice formerly belonging to St. James Episcopal Church, and were about to dedicate the building, when word was received from Chief Rabbi Joseph, that as two crosses remained upon the church the ceremony must be postponed. The existence of the crosses had been overlooked.

Mr. Ben Hogan delivered temperance addresses in Harlem, N. Y., on Tuesday, Thursday, and Saturday of last week. He has engaged to continue these addresses those three evenings of each week through the next two months, in New York and the neighborhood. On the other evenings of the week he is at liberty, and would be glad of opportunities to engage in evangelistic work. Applications, if sent to this office, will be forwarded.

PETER AFTER HIS RESTORATION.

A New Sermon by Pastor C. H. Spurgeon.

"When thou art converted strengthen thy brethren." Luke 22:32.

Satan at Prayer—Received an Answer—Reasons for Special Temptation—Remarkable Discipline—Preparing for Remarkable Service—Christ Praying for His Tried Disciple—Peter's Restoration Assured—What the Backslider has to Do—I. His Duty—He Staggers his Brethren—Should Strengthen Them—II. His Qualification for the Work—Knows the Bitterness of Denying his Master—Knows the Weakness of the Flesh—And the Joy of Restoration—III. His Reward—Will Derive Benefit Himself—A Comfort—A Prayer Between Fighting Women.

PETER was to be sifted, so our Lord warned him; and Satan was to operate with the sieve. Satan had an intense desire to destroy Peter—indeed, he would like to destroy all the chosen of God—and therefore he desired to sift him as wheat, in the hope that he would be blown away with the husks and the chaff. "Satan hath desired to have you": it would be a satisfaction to him to have a believer in his power. He was anxious to get Peter into his clutches, to give him as tremendous a shaking as he could manage. If Satan knows, as he no doubt does, concerning any one believer that he cannot quite destroy him, then he is especially anxious to worry him. If he cannot devour the chosen, he would at least defile them: if he cannot ruin their souls, he would break their quiet. As the Revised Version puts it, Satan even asks God to have them, that he may sift them as wheat. This is a curious statement, for it seems from it that

The Devil Can Pray;

and that his petition may be granted him. The margin has it, "Satan hath obtained you by asking." The Lord may grant the request of the devil himself, and yet He would not prove thereby that He had any love towards him. The Lord's wisdom may grant Satan's desire, and in the very act overthrow his evil power. Let us not then stake our faith in the Lord's love upon His giving us the precise answer we desire, for what He gives to Satan He may see fit to deny to those whom He loves, and He may do so because He loves them. We are not bound to know God's reasons for what He does or permits. It is sometimes sinful to inquire into those reasons. What the Lord does is right; let that be enough for us who are His children. But we can see sometimes a reason why the saints should be sifted as wheat; for it appertains unto wheat to be sifted, because it is wheat. Sifting brings a desirable result with it: it is for the saints' good that they should be tried. Satan has often done us a good turn when he has meant to do us a bad one. After all, he is only

A Scullion in God's Kitchen

to clean His vessels; and some some of them have received special scouring by means of his harsh temptation. God also may find a reason for allowing His saints to be tempted of Satan, and that reason may have more relation to others than to themselves. They may have to be tested *for other people's good*. The testing of their faith is "more precious than that of gold that perisheth, though it be tried with fire," and part of its preciousness is its usefulness. The child of God under temptation, behaving himself grandly, will become a standing example to those who are around him. "Ye have heard of the patience of Job"; but ye never would have heard of the patience of Job if Satan had not sifted him. Let us accept remarkable discipline if thereby we are qualified for remarkable service. If by the roughness of our own road we are trained to conduct the Lord's sheep along their difficult pathway to the pastures on the hill-tops of glory, let us rejoice in every difficulty of the way. If apostles, and men like Peter, had to be put into Satan's sieve while they were being trained for work, we may not hope to escape.

Observe, dear friends, what came before the sifting and went with the sifting. Note well that blessed "but." "*But I have prayed for thee.*" Jesus, that Master in the art of prayer, that mighty Pleader who is our Advocate above, assures us that He has already prayed for us. "I have have prayed for thee," means—Before the temptation I have prayed for thee. I foresaw all the danger in which thou wouldst be placed, and concerning that danger I have exercised My function as High Priest and Intercessor. "I have prayed for thee." What a divine comfort is this to any who are passing through deep waters! Blessed be God! Satan may have his sieve, but as long as Jesus wears His breastplate we shall not be destroyed by Satan's tossings.

Notice that the object of the prayer of our Lord was "that thy faith fail not." He knows

Where the Vital Point Lies,

and there He holds the shield. As long as the Christian's faith is safe, the Christian's self is safe. Faith is the standard-bearer in every spiritual conflict; and if the standard-bearer fall, then it is an evil day: therefore our Lord prays that the standard-bearer may never fail to hold up his banner in the midst of the fray: "I have prayed for thee, that thy faith fail not." If faith fails, everything fails: courage fails, patience fails, hope fails, love fails, joy fails. Faith is the root-grace; and if this be not in order, then the leafage of the soul, which shows itself in the form of other graces, will soon begin to wither. "I have prayed for thee that thy faith fail not."

Learn a lesson from this, my brother—that you take care to commend your faith unto your God. Do not begin to doubt because you are tempted: that is to lay bare your breast. Do not doubt because you are attacked: that is to loosen your harness. Believe still. "I had fainted," said David, "unless I had believed." It must be one thing or the other with us; believing, or fainting: which shall it be? "Above all, taking the shield of faith." Not only taking it so that it may cover all, but making this the vital point of holy carefulness. Watch thou in all things, but specially guard thy faith. If thou be careful about one thing more than another, above all be careful of thy faith. "I have prayed for thee, that thy faith fail not." Our Saviour's pleading goes to the point, and thus it teaches us where to direct our own desires and our own prayers. He asks for us far more wisely than we shall ever learn to ask for ourselves: let us copy His petitions.

Therefore it follows because of Christ's prayer that, though Peter may be very badly put to it, yet he shall be recovered, for Christ speaks of

An Assured Fact

—"*when* thou art converted." As much as to say—when thou comest back to thy old life and thy old faith, then exercise thyself usefully for thy Lord. He speaks of Peter's restoration as if it were quite sure to be. And is it not quite sure to be? If Jesus, the Beloved of the Father, prays for His people, shall He not win His suit with God? He will win it! He will uplift Peter from among the siftings where Satan has thrown him. We are sure He will, for in prospect thereof, He sets him a loving and suitable task: "When thou art converted, strengthen thy brethren."

Now, beloved friends, I may be addressing a number of persons who believe on the Lord Jesus Christ as Peter did, but they have fallen into a bad state and need a new conversion. I am very sorry for you, but I am by no means staggered at the sight of you, for you belong to a numerous class. When sitting to see inquirers I am constantly stumbling on backsliders, who come back very sincerely and very truly, and feel right pleased to find a Christian home again. I meet with many who have been outside in the world, some of them, for years, attending the house of God very irregularly, and seldom or never enjoying the light of God's countenance. They have wandered so that none can tell whether they are the Lord's or not, except the Lord Himself, and He always knoweth them that are His. I bear happy witness that the Lord brings His own back again. Though the Lord's sheep stray, yet the Good Shepherd finds them. Though the Lord's children go int[o] the far country, yet they each one in due tim[e] say, "I will arise and go to my Father." It is no[t] every prodigal that returns, but only the prodigal *son*. In due time the son returns to th[e] Father's house.

It may be, some of you have wandered int[o] error. May you be brought back very speedily and if you are, we are going to say to you now "Strengthen your brethren." Perhaps you hav[e] been neglectful. I find that many who wer[e] good Christian people in the country, always a[t] the house of prayer, and walking near to God will come up to this wicked London to live, an[d] the change is a serious injury to them. The[y] get lost to Christian society, and by degree[s] they become deteriorated by the ungodliness o[f] this modern Sodom. Nobody in the stree[t] wherein they live ever goes to a place of worshi[p] and they do not know anybody at the chapel, o[r] at the church, and so they give up going t[o] public worship, and fall into the ways an[d] habits of the world. They are not happy You will not make an expert sinner now, for

Your Hand is Out of It.

Once converted, you must be a child of God, o[r] nothing. You are ruined for this world; and i[n] the world to come is not yours, where are you The devil himself will not like you long; yo[u] are not of his sort. There is something abou[t] you that will not suit Satan any more tha[n] Jonah suited the whale. The whale was quit[e] as glad to part with Jonah as Jonah was to b[e] set free from the whale. I see arrangement[s] for your coming home again. A deceived hea[rt] has turned you aside, but in love to your so[ul] the Lord has made you aware of it, and your cr[y] is, "I will go and return to my first husband for then was it better with me than now. These are tokens by which I am assured th[at] the Lord will bring His own back. I rest confi[-] dent that He will turn them, and they shall [be] turned; and I am going to talk to backslide[rs] about what they are to do when they do co[me] back again.

I. First, it is his duty. He has gone astra[y] and he has been brought back; what better c[an] he do than to strengthen his brethren? He w[...]

Help to Undo the Evil

which he has wrought. Peter must have sta[g-]gered his brethren. Some of them must ha[ve] been quite frightened at him. John soon loo[k-]ed after him, but then they were not all John[s.] Full of love, John soon hunted up Peter; b[ut] the others must have felt that he was a me[re] reed shaken by the wind. It must have stagg[er-]ed the faith of the weaker sort to see that Pet[er] who had been such a leader among them, w[as] among the first to deny his Lord. Therefo[re] Peter, you must build what you have thro[wn] down, and bind up what you have torn! Go a[nd] talk to these people again, and tell them how fo[ol-]ish and weak you were. Warn them not to imit[ate] your example. You must henceforth be m[ore] bold than anybody else, that you may in so[me] measure undo the mischief which you have do[ne.]

Now, do think of this, any of you who ha[ve] been cold towards the Lord. You have was[ted] months, and even years, in backsliding. Try to cover lost ground. It will be almost impossi[ble] for you to do it, but do at least make a seri[ous] attempt. If anybody has been staggered by y[our] backsliding, look after him, and try to bring [him] back, and strengthen him. Ask his pardon, beg him to recover the strength of which [you] helped to rob him. This is

The Least You Can Do.

If almighty love has drawn you back again a[fter] sad wanderings, lay yourself out with all y[our] heart to do good to those who may have b[een] harmed by your sad turnings aside. Am I ask[ing] more of you than simple justice demands?

Besides, how can you better express your g[rat-]itude to God than by seeking to strengt[hen] your weak brethren when you have b[een] strengthened yourself? Those of you whom [the] Good Shepherd has restored should hav[e a] quick eye for all the sickly ones of the fl[ock] and watch over these with a sympathetic c[...]

u should say, "This is the field which I shall to cultivate. Because in my spiritual sick- s the Lord has been pleased to deal so gra- usly with me, I would therefore lay myself out cherish others who are diseased in soul."

Still in the Family.

3y the way, the very wording of the text seems suggest the duty: we are to strengthen our rethren." We must do so in order that we y manifest brotherly love, and thus prove our iship towards God. Oh, what a blessed thing s when we come back to God, and feel that are still in the family! To have a question out your position in the heavenly family is a y painful thing, and should not be endured : moment if it be in our power to solve the ıbt. But if the Lord has brought you back His child, you now know that you belong to family, and it will be suggested at once to ı to do something for *the brethren*. Natural- you will look around to see whether there be child of God to whom you can show favor his Father's sake. You have injured all by ır backsliding; and hence it is your duty, en restored to the family, to benefit them all special consecration and double earnestness. it be your delight, as well as your duty, to ngthen your brethren.

I. Now, secondly, he has a qualification for it. is Peter is the man who, when he is brought k again, can strengthen his brethren. He strengthen them by telling them of

The Bitterness of Denying

Master. He went out and wept bitterly. s one thing to weep; it is another thing to ep bitterly. There are sweet tears, as well as tears; but oh, what weeping a sin costs a ld of God! I recollect a minister speaking y unguardedly: he said that the child of God t nothing by sin except his comfort; and I ught, "Oh, dear me! And is that nothing? hat nothing?" It is such a loss of comfort t, if that were all, it would be the most aw- thing in the world. The more God loves ı, and the more you love God, the more ex- ısive will you find it to sin. Now Peter, be- se he could tell of the bitterness of back- ing, was the man to go and speak to anyone was about to backslide, and say, 'Do not my brother; for it will cost you dear.'"

gain, Peter was the man to tell another of weakness of the flesh, for he could say to ı, "Do not trust to yourself. Do not talk out never going aside. Remember how I ked about it.

I Used to Be Very Lofty

my talk and feelings, but I had to come vn; I felt so sure that I loved my Lord and ster, that I put great confidence in myself, I could not think that I should ever wander m Him. But see, see how I fell! I denied n thrice ere the time called cock-crowing." us, you see, Peter was wonderfully qualified, having known the bitterness of sin, and by ling the weakness of his own flesh, to go l strengthen others in these important nts.

And could not Peter fully describe *the joy of toration?* "Oh," he would say, "do not oder. There is no good in it. Do not go ay from Jesus. There is no profit to be found re. Come back to Him: there is such peace, h rest with Him. Never, never go away in." Peter ever afterwards in his epistles— l we are sure that it must have been the ne in his spoken ministry—would testify to love and goodness of Christ, and urge the nts to steadfastness in the faith. I would ap- l to any child of God here whether he ever ned anything by going away from Christ. ser, closer, closer, this is the way to spiritual alth. To follow afar off, and live at a distance m Christ, even if it does not make your soul perish, yet it will wither up your joys, and ke you feel an unhappy man, an unhappy man. Therefore, all those who have tried it uld bear their witness, and put their experi- e into the scale as they thus strengthen ir brethren.

III. And lastly, the restored believer should strengthen his brethren, because it will be

A Benefit to Himself.

He will derive great personal benefit from endeavoring to cherish and assist the weak ones in the family of God. Brother, do this continually and heartily, for thus you will be made to see your own weakness. You will see it in those whom you succor. I think that a true minister is often excited to better work by what he sees of weakness in his people, because he says to himself, "Am I feeding this flock well?" Perhaps he thinks to himself, "If I had properly tended them they would not have shown all these weaknesses"; and then he will begin to blame his own ministry, and look to his own heart, and that is a good thing for us all. We very seldom, I think, blame ourselves too much, and it is a benefit to us to see our own failings in others.

But what a comfort it must have been to Peter to have such a charge committed to him! It is a grand proof of our being fully restored to the divine heart, when the Lord entrusts us with work to do for His own dear children. If you and I are made the means of strengthening our brethren, what a comfort it will be to our hearts! I know that it is not the highest form of comfort, for Jesus would say of it, "Rejoice not in this, but rather rejoice that your names are written in heaven"; but still to a loving child of God it is no mean consolation to find that God is using him. I know, for my own part, that when I go to see our friends who are ill, and near to die, it is a supreme consolation to see how calm they always are, without any exception; yes, and how joyful they generally are—how triumphant in the departing hour! Then I say to myself, "Yes, my Master has owned my ministry." So you see that it is a benefit to a man to strengthen his brethren, because it becomes a comfort to his own soul.

And, brethren, whenever any of you lay yourselves out to strengthen weak Christians, as I pray you may, you will get benefit from what you do in the holy effort. Suppose you pray with them. With regard to those who are strangers to divine things, there will often occur opportunities in which you have put them under an obligation, or they have come to you in trouble to ask advice, and then you may boldly say, "Do not let us part till we have prayed." We used to have

An Old Member

of this church who used to pray in very extraordinary places. Two women were fighting, and he knelt down between them to pray, and they gave over fighting directly. Before a door, when there has been a noise in the house, he has begun to pray. He was better than a policeman, for his prayer awed the most obstinate. They could not understand it: they thought it a strange thing, and they did not care to put themselves into direct opposition to the man of God. There is a wonderful power in prayer to bless ourselves, beside the blessings that it will bring upon others. Pray with the weak ones, and you will not be a weak one yourself.

And again, suppose that in trying to strengthen these weak ones, you begin to

Quote Scripture

to them—quote a promise to them—this will bless you. Some of you do not know which promise to quote. You do not even know where to find it in the Word. But if you are in the habit of studying Scripture with a view to strengthening the weak, you will understand it in the best way, for you will get it in a practical form and shape. You will have the Bible at your fingers' ends. Moreover, one of these days the text that you looked out for old Mary will suit yourself. How often have we paid Paul with that which we meant to give Peter! We have ourselves fed on the milk we prepared for the babes. Sometimes what we have laid up for another comes in handy for ourselves.

Now, I have said all this to you that have wandered and come back, and I want to say it right home to you. May the Holy Spirit speak to your inmost souls. You know who you are, and how far all this applies to you. The Lord bless you. But, dear friends,

If You Have Not Wandered,

if the Lord has kept you these twenty years close to Him, and given you the light of His countenance all that time, then I think that you and I, and any of us of that sort, ought to strengthen our brethren still more. Oh, what we owe to sovereign grace! To be kept from wandering—what a blessing is that! Let us feel that instead of having a small debt to pay, we have a greater debt to acknowledge. Let us wake up to strengthen our brethren. Amen.

GEMS FROM NEW BOOKS.

A BEATIFIC VISION.*

A FRIEND of mine lay dying not many months ago. His voice was clear and strong almost to the very latest syllable. Then the light of the eyes went out, and the hands dropped, and the head drooped, and we said one to another, "He is gone." Suddenly the head turned upon the pillow, the hands moved, and light was in the eyes again. Surprise, wonder, adoration, rapture, wave on wave, rolled across that pallid face. It was the beatific vision. Now I know the meaning of that text, "I shall be satisfied, when I awake, with Thy likeness."

The Living Voice.

A Bible in every human habitation is something well worth trying to achieve. But I can tell you of something better still. It is Christ Himself in any one of the humblest of His disciples casting His shadow on the wall. Breathing men, not breathless books, must carry salvation round the globe. Despise not the little tract. "Come to Jesus," written by a London clergyman, has been the means of saving many souls. But there is nothing to rival the human voice. What would Peter the Hermit have accomplished had he stayed in his monastery, and from that retreat had issued a printed call to arms, even though he had showered Europe with his circulars? Who cares for circulars? But when that fiery little monk, lean, swarthy, keen-eyed, eloquent, bare-headed, bare-footed, girded about the loins with a heavy cord, and mounted on his mule, undertook the tour of Europe, preaching the first crusade, with tears and groans, smiting his breast, kissing his crucifix, passionately invoking the vengeance of God and man on the ruthless Saracen, all Europe sprang madly to its feet and hurled itself steel clad upon the Orient. So of the gospel now and always. It must be in the blood like iron, in the eye like fire, in the voice like a trumpet call. It must be preached: preached by men who have had it preached to them; preached to sinners by men who have sinned themselves; by dying men to dying men.

The One Book.

The story told of the burning of the famous library of Alexandria by order of the Caliph Omar is probably apocryphal. But what the Caliph is reported to have written to Amru, his general commanding in Egypt, has a grand moral. "If those books contradicted the Koran, they were false and ought to be destroyed; if they agreed with the Koran, they were superfluous and might well be spared." One book was enough for Mohammedans. So when Sir Walter Scott lay dying, he said to his son-in-law one day, "Lockhart, read to me." "What book shall it be?" said Lockhart. "Why do you ask? there is but one," said Scott.

Now if this book itself were in danger of being destroyed, and I might have only one chapter out of it, I rather think it would be the fourteenth chapter of John's gospel. Probably no single chapter is read so much. We read it to ourselves when we are all alone, on the land,

* From "Eternal Atonement," by Roswell Dwight Hitchcock, D. D., LL. D., late President and Professor of Church History in the Union Theological Seminary. This book contains nineteen brief sermons, selected, since Dr. Hitchcock's death, from about thirty, which were overlooked when he destroyed his manuscripts, or were saved intentionally for future use. 306 pages, with portrait. Price $1.50. Published by *Charles Scribner's Sons*, 743 Broadway, New York.

Dr. John A. Brooks, of Kansas City, Mo.

Knighting the Captains After the Defeat of the Spanish Armada, July, 1588.

on the sea, in the solitudes of nature, in the solitudes of personal experience. We read it at the communion table, catching the very tones which made such music nearly nineteen hundred years ago. We read it to the dying, and they are soothed. We read it over the dead, and thank God that they are safe. These are sacred and tender offices. But we narrow the chapter when only such offices are thought of. It was the speaker himself who was about to die. His hearers were about to be launched into the life-long service. Their feet were on the threshold of a ministry whose first and whose last necessity was absolute child-like faith.

REV. JOHN A. BROOKS, D. D.

THE Prohibition nomination for the Vice-Presidency could have gone to no man more worthy of the honor, nor better fitted for the labor of the campaign, than to John Anderson Brooks, the pastor of the Church of the Disciples in Kansas City, Mo. His piety, his manliness, and his self-sacrificing spirit are well known in the Prohibition party, and it has honored itself in honoring him.

Dr. Brooks is fifty-two years of age, having been born in Mason County, Kentucky, in 1836. His father was comparatively poor, having undertaken the support of his wife's widowed mother and her three daughters, besides his own family. In addition to this he gave much of his time which he might have devoted to his business as a planter to preaching the gospel in the villages near his home. The boy had not many school advantages, but he made up for the lack of those by home study, often reading far into the night after a day's hard labor with his father's negroes in the tobacco-field. His evident love of study, and his bright intellectual promise led his father to send him to Bethany College, where he labored so diligently that he graduated with honors at the end of three years. This was in 1856, when he was twenty years old.

Brooks intended to be a lawyer, but just at the end of his college course he was converted under the preaching of Alexander Campbell, and resolved to devote the remainder of his life to his Master's service. He commenced his ministerial labors at a protracted meeting in his native county, where he was so much blessed that his services were called for all around. Finally, while he was holding meetings at Flemingsburg the church there invited him to become its pastor. He accepted on condition that he should have time for the work of a revivalist. His ministry there was a wonderful success, and during its course a college was built for the education of ministers, of which Dr. Brooks became President. During the war Dr. Brooks was active in promoting the good, physical and spiritual, of the wounded on both sides.

The Temperance crusade early enlisted his sympathies and active service. He joined Murphy in his movement, but soon saw reason to separate from him, and labor independently, where his unselfish spirit could have free play. With a few others he called a convention at Sedalia, Mo., which assembled on July 4, 1880, and organized the Prohibition State Alliance, of which Dr. Brooks was made first President. Since then his efforts to have a Prohibition amendment submitted to the people have been unceasing. He was nominated for Governor of Missouri in 1884, and during the campaign had a memorable controversy with Senator Vest. He polled 10,500 votes by the admission of his opponents, who had charge of the ballot-boxes. His nomination by the Indianapolis Convention for Vice-President has given unqualified satisfaction throughout the party.

A NOTABLE TERCENTENARY.

(See Illustration.)

ON July 19 last, the English people celebrated with considerable enthusiasm the three hundredth anniversary of one of the most notable deliverances in the history of their country. In July, 1588, Philip, King of Spain, Portugal, the Netherlands, and part of Italy, despatched the Armada, which under the blessing of the Pope, was to oust Queen Elizabeth from her throne, seat Philip there in her stead, and restore England to her former condition of subordination to papal rule. The story has been often told of the scattering of that magnificient and powerful fleet. After suffering severely by the storm, it was attacked with consummate skill and courage by Lord Howard, who was in command of the English fleet, which was much smaller in number and power. He succeeded in beating the Armada in detail, carefully avoiding engaging its main body in pitched battle, and by sending fire ships among them, drove the remnant in terror from English waters. Our illustration represents the rewarding of the three captains whose bravery had most materially contributed to the victory. The sailors had received gifts of money, but the three captains were to be knighted. They were Captains Hawkins, Frobisher, and Drake. By Queen Elizabeth's command, they were taken on the *Ark Royal*, and there Lord Howa[rd per-] formed the ceremony of laying the sw[ord on] their shoulders, bidding them rise, knigh[ts.]

MRS. BRETTELL'S GRANDDAUGH[TER.]

(See Illustration on page 541.)

A COSY old-fashioned mansion was [the house in] which the widow Brettell lived. Its roo[ms were] small and its ceilings low; but no new[er resi-]dence, however magnificent, would have [pleased] her so well as that. There she had com[e as a] bride more than forty years before; th[ere her] only daughter had been born, grown u[p, and] been married; there her husband had die[d;] and her old help—almost as old as herself—[had be-]fore occupied the house.

"Sadie," said Mrs. Brettell, one m[orning,] "what is to be done about little Ethel? [Do you] think we could manage a child now?"

"Bless your dear heart, ma'am, yes, [was the] reply; "why not? Such a sweet little cr[eature,] too, and all alone in the world! Why, in[deed,] and manage her better than her own fat[her and] mother, as wouldn't have had the heart [to say] her nay, whatever she wanted."

Little Ethel was the four-year-old c[hild of] Mrs. Brettell's daughter, and the proble[m sud-]denly developed arose from her being [left an] orphan by a railroad catastrophe, in whic[h her] father and mother had perished.

So it was settled, and little Ethel was b[rought] to the home in which her mother, befo[re her,] had grown up. Sadie's notion about [the ad-]vantages of such a training were not, h[owever,] fully realized. Still, the child grew up a [bright,] loving, and loveable, possibly thought[ful be-]yond her years, and rather more sedat[e than] were most of her girl friends. At sevent[een she] was still more the idol of her two aged p[rotect-]ors than she had been when, as "little [Ethel,"] she came into their quiet lives. To the w[idow's] heart she was unspeakably dearer, for Et[hel had] been brought to the Saviour, and he[r] young faith was a joy to her grandmoth[er, who] had herself been converted late in life.

Only one cause for anxiety, in regard [to Ethel,] pressed upon Mrs. Brettell's mind, and [recent] circumstances intensified it. She wa[s anxious to] make some provision for Ethel. True, [Ethel] might marry, and she had already had o[ne offer] from the son of a farmer in the neighbo[rhood,] but young Manton, the suitor in questi[on, was] dull and stupid; and, moreover, was n[ot only] not a Christian, but had shown signs of sities. He jected. widow meddlong over problem of fortune, length, dazy reports of housands in a day by speculators, her lawadvice, and ked on the speculation. nd was the one in such The widow ll her little and was becalled upon ake good of the marher brokers. nvolved bor, which was bomination. was no alive, however, home was aged, and Manton, the of Ethel's d suitor, beher creditor, lebt was a y one, and how, now Ethel was ng her edu-, Mrs. Bretuld not save ng out of her income, as she used to do. she borrowed, she agreed to pay at the two years; but when the time came, the was not at command. She had to write Manton, asking the favor of an exten- In reply, her creditor came in person. idow heard of his arrival with a sinking

It seemed to her that God had deserted She had prayed for success on her specu-, and her prayer had not been answered; e had prayed that she might be able to the appointed time, and that, too, had en granted.

u ain't able to pay, you say, marm," said anton. "Well, I've got a little scheme ose that'll suit you, I guess. That boy o' reglar sweet on your granddaughter. ouldn't have anything to say to him, but on't know their own minds always. Now want to propose is this. We'll let them ched, and you just pay the interest of this tle sum to them and the principal when ready. It'll be a little income to start nd I'll make it up enough."

u are very much mistaken Mr. Manton," e widow, "in thinking such a plan would me. Nothing would tempt me to enter- It's like selling the girl."

at's nonsense," was the reply. "Your a good home and a husband fit for any nd you get time with the mortgage. I call od bargain."

ould not consent to such a marriage on ms," said the widow, firmly.

hen I'll foreclose," said the farmer, putting nds on the arms of the chair and leaning d as if to spring on his interlocutor. "So n get ready to turn out."

hat moment Ethel entered the room with n letter in her hand, and a young man ed her. She knew something of the nature grandmother's relations with Mr. Manton r money embarrassment, though of course g of the farmer's good bargain. The news ned in the letter, she rightly judged, would rtinent to the interview, and therefore t hesitated to break in upon it. She came around to her grandmother's chair and held the letter for her to see, while her companion stared contemptuously at the farmer. Mrs. Brettell took her spectacles out of their case to read the letter, saying as she did so to the man arrested in his menacing attitude, "If that is the only condition you have to propose you must do as you will."

Mrs. Brettell's Interview with Her Creditor.

Turning to the letter, however, she saw at a glance that the consequences she dreaded were averted. Ethel was already a heiress in her own right. Some land belonging to her deceased father, hitherto regarded as worthless, had suddenly become of great value, and the girl was rich. Ethel's companion was her late father's lawyer, who had come to give all necessary information. God had answered the widow's prayers, as He so often does, not in the way expected, but fully and bountifully. It was a joy to Ethel to repay some of her grandmother's kindness by relieving her of her creditor with some of her own wealth, and Mrs. Brettell was relieved of her anxiety about Ethel's future, which was now so abundantly provided for.

THE EPOCHS OF A LIFE.

A NEW SERIAL STORY.

By Rev. L. S. Keyser.

(Continued from page 527.)

The Campaign Opened.

THE opening words of Duneman's oration showed considerable sagacity. He desired first of all to put his audience into a good humor and thus elicit their sympathy. After he had arrested their attention, he ventured upon several mild and facetious thrusts at infidelity, and seemed to be much gratified with the vociferous merriment which they evoked from his hearers. Satisfied that he was carrying the audience with him, he proceeded to the main part of the discussion with more self-assurance. Straightening himself up to his full height, he began, at first adroitly, and then more boldly, to hurl thunderbolts of scorn and sarcasm and insinuative logic into the camp of unbelievers. What he said was true enough, but even truth in the hands of an insincere man has a distorted aspect. The spirit of hatred and malignity which animated him was revealed beneath the armor of the champion of truth, showing that he was prepared "to fight the Lord's battle with the devil's weapons."

"What has been the tendency of unbelief in all ages and countries?" he cried. "Look at its black record. It cuts the nerve of all moral restraint, it opens the flood-gates of iniquity, allowing it to pour its foul deluge upon all community and individual life. If a young man would have all his moral instincts destroyed, his conscience anæsthetized so that it utters no admonitory cry at the approach of sin, let him throw away the religion in which he was reared, and espouse the cause of infidelity. By a sure and gradual process his moral principles will be undermined, and he will lose his sense of right and wrong. Even now we have among us those who deny the validity of all moral distinctions, asserting that sin is only an accident or lapse."

As he said this he turned toward the seat occupied by the young sceptics, his eyes gleaming upon them like burnished metal.

"What can we expect from men whose thinking is controlled by vicious and degrading theories—men who have so depleted and stultified the higher rational faculties of their souls that all sense of moral responsibility is lost? What must be the result upon their individual lives? Can you repose confidence in a man who denies the existence of God, the authority of the Bible, and throws off all moral obligations? God save our country from the withering blight of atheism!"

There was an audible "amen" from one of the Professors in his rear. The speaker accepted the ejaculation as sanction of his utterance, and proceeded with more vigor than before.

"There is abundant evidence in the history of unbelief of the effect that negation of God has upon moral principle and character. You have only to examine the teachings and lives of the men whom our modern sceptics venerate—the saints of the devil's calendar—to perceive the moral degradation which is the natural product of unbelief. A few examples, fairly representative, will suffice here. *Hobbes* was a prominent rejecter of Christianity. The standard of his morality may be inferred from the fact that he held a man blameless who, being a Christian, might deny his faith when being examined before a magistrate. *Lord Bolingbroke*, another noted unbeliever, taught that morality was only the principle of self-love in action, and that even avarice and sensuality might be lawfully gratified, if they could be safely gratified. He believed that man was only a superior animal, whose chief end in life was the gratification of the appetites and desires of the flesh. *Hume*, the most celebrated of English infidels, has left behind him a 'private correspondence' full of teaching so base and sensual that I could not describe it before an audience of decent persons. *Gibbon*, the author of 'The Decline and Fall,' was more decent; but his portrait, sketched by his own hand, shows him to be utterly heartless and grossly selfish, servile of the rich and contemptuous of the poor. *Voltaire* was as notorious for his gross immorality as for his infidelity, and a man whose character was stained by all kinds of baseness, perfidy, and lechery. *Rousseau* was a horrible example of dishonesty, perjury, and profligacy. *Tom Paine*, a miserable inebriate. *Blount* was a man of passions so uncontrolled that he committed suicide in his chagrin when disappointed of their gratification.

"The list might be indefinitely extended. These are only a few of the most prominent of the leaders of the last century in the war against religion, but their followers were like them, and are they not sufficient to prove the truth of my assertion, that infidelity saps the foundations of national, social and individual purity?"

"Yes, yes!" was shouted by an excited listener from the audience; which exclamation was followed by a perfect stampede of applause.

"Are not these facts sufficient to fasten suspicion upon the moral character of any man who advocates the principles of Free Thought, and seeks to undermine public confidence in religion?" the speaker questioned, bending forward with flushed face and glowing eyes.

The insult was too great to be borne with equanimity. Hadley would have sprung to his feet had not his friend, who was more self-restrained, held him down to his seat with desperate energy, while he whispered: "Your turn will come before long, Hadley; for goodness' sake, keep quiet!"

A pair of flashing eyes across the aisle also noted Hadley's excited movement. They were the eyes of Belle Havelock, and a feeling of exultation filled her bosom "At last his blood is stirred," she thought. "What a crushing retort he will make when his opportunity comes! How this callow declaimer will get castigated! Well, that will be a double blessing. It will give an impetus to Free Thought in the college, and it will put an end to this miserable infatuation with Miss Winters. If he speaks as he feels now, she will have no more to say to him." Then she gave her attention again to Duneman's speech.

"In juxtaposition with the champions of infidelity, I place representative champions of Christianity. What a contrast of life and character! Paul, Chrysostom, Luther, Knox, Whately, Payson! Can any one find a blemish on their characters? And yet these, and thousands of noble men of God, trace the purity and uprightness of their lives to the regenerating and sanctifying influences of the Gospel under whose standard they marched to victory over the forces of sin. The religion of Christ revitalizes, strengthens, binds together, and sustains the moral energies of the human soul; whereas, infidelity in all its forms, devitalizes, benumbs, and disorganizes the higher nature with which God has endowed the human family."

Very various were the effects produced upon the audience by the speech. "A fine oration," said one. "That man will make a grand preacher." "What a merciless exposure of infidelity!" said another; "it ought to put some of our young friends on their guard." "Very smart," said a third, "but to me it did not sound true. I should say Duneman could speak just as well on the other side if it suited his purpose. He spoke like a hired advocate, not like a man arguing from conviction." "Did you ever hear so malignant an effusion!" said a young man inclined to Free Thought; "how bitter the fellow is. I suppose his facts are right, he would hardly dare to misstate them, but I doubt his fairness, I would not be surprised to find that he has exaggerated. He would never convince me; he seemed more anxious to denounce than convince." As for Madelling and Dane, they were certain that Duneman's object was to ostracize them in the college, and to create a prejudice against them personally, as men whom it was dangerous if not dishonorable to know.

Hadley stood in the hall quietly observant of the reception accorded to Duneman by his acquaintances. While many pressed around him to congratulate him, the manner of two persons particularly impressed him. They were Miss Winters and Miss Havelock. The former looked at the orator with her usual kindly smile, but her manner was cool, and her congratulations by no means effusive. Belle Havelock, on the other hand, who might have been expected to feel hurt by so savage an attack on her principles, greeted Duneman warmly, and seemed to be praising and complimenting him. "What does she mean?" Hadley asked himself. "Surely she cannot approve of such an outrageous exhibition of spleen! There is some mystery about it. I must call on that young lady, and find out what part she is playing."

He was still brooding over the mystery when he returned to his rooms, and he found Dane as much mystified as himself. "Well, I will ask her to explain," said Hadley; "she must have some motive," and accordingly that evening he presented himself at the Havelock mansion. Belle met him with so hearty a welcome, and was so evidently delighted to receive him, that he dismissed on the instant a passing thought that she had abandoned her attitude of opposition to religion, and had been won over by Duneman's eloquence. After a conversation on commonplace topics, Hadley introduced the subject of his visit.

"I noticed you were at Chapel Hall this morning. What did you think of Mr. Duneman's effusion?"

"I was disgusted," said Belle shamelessly; "I thought it displayed a lack of good breeding, and was a gratuitous insult to some of his fellow-students. Those innuendoes were meant for you, I presume. Well, I shall hope to hear you give him the castigation he deserves. It was a most unjustifiable and unmanly attack!"

"Why, then, did you congratulate him so warmly?" asked Hadley with some sharpness.

Belle was evidently taken aback. She had no idea that her reception of Duneman had been witnessed by her visitor. She was confused by the direct question, and hesitated in replying. At last she said: "Oh, that was only his rhetorical genius that I praised, but, Mr. Madelling, I was really pleased that he had made the attack, for now at last you will be spurred to aggressive action. You seemed to need a stimulus, and Mr. Duneman certainly furnished that."

Naturally unsuspecting in his disposition Hadley accepted the explanation, and declared his purpose of picking up the gauntlet his rival had thrown down, and Belle dexterously fanned the flame of his angry passion.

"Do you not see, Mr. Madelling," she said, "what was implied in those innuendoes? It is obvious that his address was a personal thrust at you. He wanted to stigmatize you, and create suspicion against you in the college. Certainly you did not fail to notice the manner in which he turned to you when he said, 'Can you trust a man's moral purposes if he denies the existence of God and rejects the Bible?'"

"Yes, his directness was unmistakable, the insolent hypocrite!" muttered Hadley.

"You ought to exonerate yourself from the false accusation," continued Belle, "and prove that it is not a larger liberty of thought, but a superstitious reverence for defunct dogmas, that depletes man's moral nature. You ought not to delay your reply. Seize your opportunity, Mr. Madelling! Strike while the iron is hot," she concluded, in urgent tones.

During the weeks that followed, Hadley devoted almost every moment that he could spare from his regular studies to the preparation of his speech. Not only did he ransack the Bible for disparities, but he also read carefully every book that would throw light upon his theme. Having filled his mind with the subject, he proceeded to systematize his data, and with pen in hand the theme was unfolded in a terse, logical, and climactic address that he knew would startle his audience, and, as he hoped, convince them.

As the example of torpedo-like assault had bee set by Duneman, Hadley was not loathe to fo low it, and therefore his manuscript was embe lished with cutting retorts, which were mo the outgrowth of passion than of reason.

Meanwhile, Miss Winters was the recipie of his polite attentions. But as he was extrem ly wary in her company, he successfully pilote their conversation away from theologic themes, so that there was no conflict of wor between them. Whether she knew of his ho tility to religion or not, he was not aware; b she had had ample opportunity to make the di covery, if she was sufficiently interested in h spiritual welfare to make inquiries.

Yet he was not altogether left in doubt as her moral earnestness, and it must be said, to h credit, that he respected her more highly c account of her solicitude than if she had bee indifferent as to her beliefs. One Sunday evenir he proposed, half jestingly, that they rema away from church, because he thought it wou be pleasanter to talk on literary topics.

"No, Mr. Madelling," she replied, with a glo in her eyes that he had never seen there pr viously, "I think it is not only a duty to go the house of God, but also a privilege. Tl Bible tells us that we should not forsake the a sembling of ourselves together, as the mann of some is. Since I have enlisted in the service Christ, I have determined not to miss an o portunity of attending church. Besides, o presence there will encourage others to go, a in that way they may be induced to accept t truth."

"Oh, certainly, certainly," he began, apol getically, "if you wish to go, I would not pe suade you to stay at home. I merely thoug that, perhaps, an examination of some good l erary or scientific work would be just as prof able."

Hadley was just a little nettled by her wor for they seemed to imply a rebuke. The g was, perhaps, quick-witted enough to divi the unpleasant feeling, and therefore said:

"Thank you for being so considerate. B we have plenty of science and literature eve day of the week in our college work, and I li to devote Sunday to the cultivation of my rel ious faculties. Is not that philosophical?" s subjoined, smiling.

"Oh—yes—yes," he conceded, rather relu antly. But he made a mental reservation, whi was, "Providing there are such faculties in c psychological make-up."

"Really, Mr. Madelling," she continued, am anxious that you go to church. Mr. M dont's sermons are so germane to—to—all needs, that I hope they will do you—us all great deal of good."

Like the dew that distills from heaven her words fall on his ears. It is to be fear however, that his anxiety for her personal gard was more potent with him than her ma fest concern for his salvation. Unable to und stand the solicitude of the earnest Christian every individual, he was inclined to think t her interest in his welfare was the index c feeling in her heart similar to that which mo himself.

More than these few words she had not v tured to say. She seemed as anxious as him to avoid every provocative to controversy. deed, she had said frankly, one evening: am by nature averse to verbal disputes. G seldom comes from them. I do not allow own attitude to be misunderstood; I am alw ready to avow my faith, and I would defend if attacked, to the best of my ability, but I r er seek controversy. There are better way influencing opponents than by argument."

(*To be Continued.*)

THE SPIES SENT INTO CANAAN.

By Mrs. M. Baxter.

Lesson for Sept. 2, Num. 13: 17-33. Golden Text, Num. 13: 30.

Exploration Suggested by the People — A mmon Disposition—Not Content With God's idance — Human Light Sought — Rejecting uths if There Has Been no Experience of em—God's Condescension to Human Infirm -Men of Faith Would Have Believed With-t Exploring—Discovering Difficulties — The vo Reports — From Different Standpoints — ar Where There is no Faith.

IE thought of sending spies into the land of ian, who should explore, and then give a re- of the land, seems, in the first instance, to originated with the people, and not with . Moses, in recapitulating the history of children of Israel in their wilderness jour-, says, "We came to Kadeshbarnea. And d unto you, Ye are come unto the moun- of the Amorites, which the Lord our God give us. Behold, the Lord thy God doth he land before thee; go up and possess it, ie Lord God of thy fathers hath said unto ; fear not, neither be discouraged. And ame near unto me, every one of you, and . We will send men before us, and they shall ch us out the land, and bring us word again hat way we must go up, and into what s we shall come." (Deut. 1: 19-22.) What, , would they not give credence to the Word ie Lord unless it was supported by the tes-ny of some human witness? Did they k the God who led them through the sea mpetent to guide them into Canaan? Alas he evil heart of unbelief, which requires that very Word of God Himself shall be support-y some further proof than its own witness self, which is

God's Own Signature!

yet, how common it is for God's children idge the Word of God by their own expe-ce, and so to explain it away until its force st. Some explain away the miracles of our because in their own experience they have wn nothing of the supernatural, they have yet been born again, have not "passed from h unto life." Some who are saved so far as now the new birth, yet experience that sin dwelleth in them is mightier than their will forts to control it. Selfishness, pride, temper, ot untruth, impurity, and dishonesty, have some measure of power over them, and they ot believe that the old man can be put off his deeds, the body of sin be destroyed, or cease its dominion over them (Col. 3:9; . 6:6, 14), until some spy has gone up into land and comes back to tell that God keeps word. And even then, they will doubt the rience which has been told them, and catch ny straw which may prove an excuse for n if they do not go up and possess the lands. this suspicion of God? Oh, is it not be-e so few of His people form a deep and ing acquaintance with Him? Is it not that reat a part of many lives, even amongst children, is lived in semi-independence of ? Are not the business and social habits of y Christians formed by assimilating them to e of the religious professions around them, out asking, "Is this God's way for me?" thus God becomes to them more a Referee mes of emergency, or a distant Sovereign to m periodical homage is offered, than an in-lling, ever present, and Almighty Friend. few trust the Lord as Provider in times of l, or as Healer in times of sickness, yet they give Him His place will find, with David, if the Lord is their shepherd, they shall not t, and like the same David, that if He e Lord that healeth thee, He "Healeth all diseases." (Ex. 15: 26; Ps. 103: 3.) t God is so tender that

He Meets Us Where We Are.

people could not trust His word without spies, and so in His wonderful long-suffer-He came down to their weakness. He or-ed that these spies should be representative men, each of them rulers, and twelve in number, that each tribe might be represented. Moses himself sided with the people, and said, "And the saying pleased me well, and I took twelve men of you, one of a tribe." (Deut. 1: 23.) It seems strange that Moses should not have encouraged the people to

Trust the Bare Word

of God. The land of Canaan was the Land of Promise. Every believer may and ought to be at home in the promises of God, not only knowing them intellectually, but counting on them, and staking all upon the truth and faithfulness of Him who has spoken them. The spies are very like people who try experiments with the promises of God. After all, their journey was to be one of discovery. "Moses sent them out to spy out the land of Canaan, and said unto them, Get you up this way southward, and go up into the mountain; and see the *land*, what it is." But God had already spoken of Canaan as "a good land and a large . . . . a land flowing with milk and honey." (Ex. 3: 8.) What need, then, to go and search whether God had told the truth?

They were to see whether the people that dwelled therein were "strong or weak, few or many." But God had already declared, "I will send My fear before thee, and will destroy all the people to whom thou shalt come; and I will make all thine enemies turn their backs unto thee." (Ex. 23: 27.)

With Such a Promise,

what mattered it how strong or how many soever were the inhabitants of the land? The spies were to search what cities they dwelt in, "whether in tents or in strongholds." But with the promise behind them, "I will send hornets before thee, which shall drive out the Hivite, the Canaanite, and the Hittite from before thee," would it not have been better for them, and more to the glory of God, if they had rested on His Word, and left their unknown enemies to His conquering hand? The only visible witness which they could bring back was a specimen of the fruit of the lands. It required two of them to carry one cluster of grapes on a pole between them, so wondrously fertile was the land. We may toil all night and take nothing, but the right side of the ship is the Land of Promise—there grow the giant grapes, there is found a multitude of fish. When we look away from our resources to God's, then five loaves can feed five thousand, and water can spring out of the solid rock. God's promises when received by faith, exceed all our expectations; He always does abundantly above all we can ask or think.

The spies were forty days searching the land, just the same length of time that Moses was in the mountain alone with God, both the first and second time. Moses came down with His face shining, for he had been looking on what God was and what God said. The spies had been looking on what man was: they had spent forty days in

Exploring Their Difficulties,

a most unprofitable occupation! When they gave in their report to Moses, they said, "We came unto the land whither thou sendest us, and surely it floweth with milk and honey; and this is the fruit of it. Nevertheless (if they had been content to trust the living God, there would have been no nevertheless) the people be strong that dwell in the land, and the cities are walled and very great; and, moreover, we saw the children of Anak there." These children of Anak are always to be found where they are looked for, and they are a real power. The spies were not exaggerating the greatness of their difficulties; their mistake was in going after them, and so being led to measure them with their own powerlessness instead of waiting until God took the initiative and revealed them at the same time as He made known His power in destroying them. Oh how many a child of God is kept in bondage to some sin of appetite or temper, because he has been exploring in his family history the fortresses of the foe, has learned how this tendency has descended to him through generations of his forefathers, instead of looking at the right hand of the Most High, and His written Word, "Sin shall not have dominion over you, for ye are not under the law but under grace"! (Rom. 6: 14.) How many a missionary has explored the difficulties of caste in India, ancestral worship in China, polygamy in Africa, and his heart has sunk within him! and still more where the opium trade and the liquor traffic, carried on by professedly Christian people, stand in his way, he has seen before him, like the spies, insuperable difficulties. Two of the spies who accompanied the other ten saw

With Other Eyes.

The cities indeed were great and the walls were strong; the sons of Anak were giants indeed—but against them all these men of faith measured the almightiness of God, and said, "Let us go up at once and possess it, for we are well able to overcome it." With God on our side, God fighting our battles, God pledged by promise to overthrow them, how shall we fear? Shall our hereditary tendencies of mind and body prevail against God? Shall the unbelief or indifference of our families prevail against God? Shall the drink traffic, the opium trade, caste or anything else prove mightier than God? Let us not explore the difficulties, but explore the height and depth and length and breadth of the love and power of our mighty God. The ten spies contradicted Caleb, and said, "We be not able to go up against the people, for

They are Stronger Than We."

They told no lie, but they left God out of their reckoning. What! were God's promises all to go for nothing, and to be counted as sounding brass or a tinkling cymbal, because the odds against *themselves* were so great? Was God nothing, God nobody, that He should be thus ignored? that God whose bread from heaven was falling daily around their tents? did they count Him out of their reckoning? "O fools and slow of heart to believe." "They brought up an evil report of the land which they had searched unto the children of Israel." The exploration of their difficulties had not answered, themselves were disheartened, and they encouraged others in unbelief. They said, "The land through which we have gone to search, it is a land that eateth up the inhabitants thereof: and all the men that we saw in it are men of great stature." The more we look at our difficulties, the more we talk of them, the more eloquently we describe them, the greater they grow. Many people expect that if they exercise faith in a promise of God which they have not been awake to until now, all difficulties will vanish. But it is not so. There are sons of Anak in every corner of the Land of Promise, and it is only by looking unto Jesus that they are overcome. The spies said, "Then *we* saw the giants, the sons of Anak, which come of the giants, and we were in our own sight as grasshoppers, and so we were in their sight." *David* said, "I have set the Lord (not the sons of Anak) always before me; because He is at my right hand, I shall not be moved." (Ps. 16: 8.) Let this be our confidence also.

"CASTING ALL YOUR CARE UPON HIM." 1 PETER v. 7.

What! all our burdens—every little trial—
The cares that seem so very, very small?
We know that heavy griefs He soothes and lightens,
But does He note, and will He carry all?

When at our waking, everything seems dreary,
And all day long our spirits are at strife
With little, never ending, ever changing
Annoyances that fill the thread of life;

And when we do our best, yet fail of pleasing,
And they to whom our very lives are given,
So little comprehend, so little heed us—
Do these things touch the heart of Christ in heaven?

And may we tell Him all things, nor offend Him?
Will He not weary of our ceaseless 'plaint?
And does He care to have us bring before Him
Our every need with child-like unconstraint?

Oh, yes! Thou never yet hadst any trial,
However trivial it has seemed to be,
That did not hold the sympathy of Jesus,
And bind His heart still closer unto thee.

Well, God loves patience! Souls that dwell in stillness,
Doing the little things, or resting quite,
May just as perfectly fulfil their mission,
Be just as useful in the Father's sight,

As they who grapple with some giant evil,
Clearing a path that every eye might see!
Our Saviour cares for cheerful acquiescence,
Rather than for a busy ministry.

And yet He does love service, where 'tis given
By grateful love that clothes itself in deed;
But work that's done beneath the scourge of duty,
Be sure to such He gives but little heed.

Then seek to please Him, whatso'er He bids thee!
Whether to do—to suffer—to lie still!
'Twill matter little by what path He led us,
If in it all we sought to do His will.

J. E. JEWETT, Publisher, 77 Bible House, New York, will furnish the above poem in leaflet form at twenty cents per hundred. A Sample Packet of 50 leaflets assorted (no two alike), will be sent post-paid, for 10 cts., or 100 for 20 cts. Postage stamps taken.

Christian Work in Mexico.

Through the reading of the Holy Scriptures translated into Spanish some earnest souls in Mexico have, by God's blessing, been led to a clear knowledge of the Gospel. From their numbers able preachers of the Christian faith in its primitive purity have been raised up, around whom congregations have been gathered from among the humble poor, who have been the first to publicly welcome and defend the pure Gospel in Mexico. The members of these congregations, rich in faith, have worked earnestly and bravely for Christ and His truth among their fellow countrymen in that beautiful Southern portion of North America called Mexico. Schools have been established by them, in which large numbers of bright boys and girls have received a good secular education and have been carefully taught the Christian faith. From the children thus educated faithful Christian workers have been raised up. A Mexican Branch of the Church of Christ, that maintains the faith in its purity and integrity, has been organized among these native Christians in the Republic of Mexico. The members of this Mexican Church of Christ, though gathered mostly from among the poor, are yet doing a most important Christian work. To continue that work, we need to pay a few leading workers small monthly salaries, and also to defray some current expenses. To raise the needed funds we have formed a society with an office at 43 Bible House, New York, U. S., and should be pleased to have many of our fellow Christians join this society by becoming regular contributors to its treasury. We are trying to secure monthly or quarterly contributions to meet the regular monthly expenses of the work. In order to continue and extend the work, we wish to raise four hundred dollars a month, by endeavoring to have four hundred persons each give on an average *one dollar every month* to this object, leaving the donors to give less or more as they may be able and willing.

We earnestly invite all who will to join us in this systematic effort in behalf of the cause of Christ in Mexico, by becoming monthly subscribers to this fund. We have already regular subscribers whose gifts amount monthly to over eighty dollars, and a growing circle of friends who are forwarding us occasional donations.

This Mexican Church of Christ is a very effective instrumentality through which to do Christian work among the many millions on this Western Hemisphere who speak the Spanish language, comparatively few of whom have ever had a Bible in their hands. A beautiful church building has been secured in the City of Mexico as the centre of the activities of this Mexican Church of Christ. Through the workers connected with that centre more than forty congregations have been gathered from among the poor in different parts of the Republic of Mexico. We have some faithful and able preachers now in the field, but more young men need to be trained for the ministry. Multitudes of Protestant children in Mexico, some of them orphans, need to be educated. We make three requests of you, Christian reader: *first*, that you will, if possible, become a monthly or quarterly subscriber in behalf of this Christian work; *second*, that you will try and induce your friends also to contribute to it; *third*, that you will remember this precious work in Mexico in your prayers.

We most sincerely thank all who are already generously contributing to this Christian work for their timely and generous gifts, and we earnestly invite many others, to unite with us in aiding it by also becoming monthly subscribers in its behalf. Those who may not feel that they can give as much as a dollar a month are earnestly asked to give what they can; whenever they are able—EVERY LITTLE HELPS. Fellow Christian, if you will generously consent to contribute a dollar a month or more or less to the work, will you kindly inform me of the fact? Contributions either large or small can be mailed directly to my address as follows:

BISHOP H. C. RILEY, care of J. P. HEATH,
No. 43 Bible House, New York, U. S.

THE CHRISTIAN HERALD AND SIGNS OF OUR TIMES

Entered according to Act of Congress in the year 1888, in the office of the Librarian of Congress at Washington.

Vol. XI., No. 35. Office, 63 Bible House. N. Y. THURSDAY, AUGUST 30, 1888. Annual Subscription, $1.50.

CONTENTS OF THIS NUMBER.

PORTRAIT OF THE LATE MR. CLARENCE S. LINDSAY, AND PICTURE OF A SCENE AT THE DIAMOND DIGGINGS IN AFRICA.
THE EVENTFUL EPOCH. A Vacation Sermon by Dr. Talmage.
INCIDENTS OF MISSION WORK IN AFRICA.
AFTER THE MILLENNIUM. By John Storie.
Church Founded by a Hermit—A Father's Profanity Overcome—The Romance of Missions—A Mute Testimony in China—A Cry of Alarm from India.
THE LETTER-CARRIER'S STORY. (Illust.)
THE RULE OF THE RACE. A New Sermon by Rev. C. H. Spurgeon.
ANECDOTES RELATED AT RECENT EVANGELISTIC MEETINGS.
Gems from New Books: The Harrison Regicide, etc.
PORTRAIT OF COUNT VON WALDERSEE, the Successor of Von Moltke.
PICTURE OF SLAVES BEARING IVORY TO TANGIERS.
THE EPOCHS OF A LIFE. A New Serial Story by Rev. L. S. Keyser. (Continued.)
THE UNBELIEF OF THE PEOPLE. By Mrs. M. Baxter.

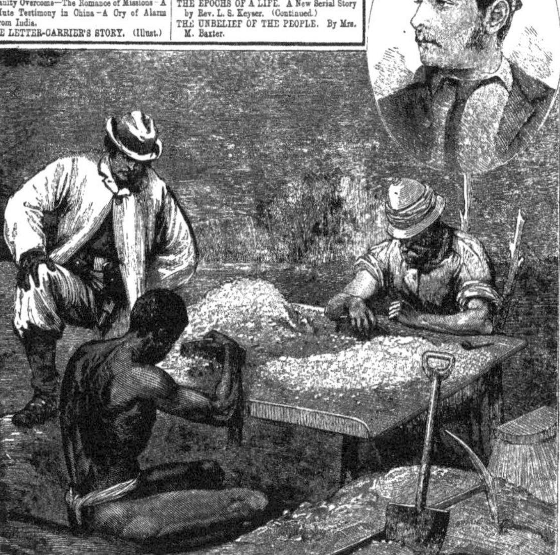

AT THE SORTING TABLE IN THE SOUTH-AFRICAN DIAMOND DIGGINGS.

The Late Clarence S. Lindsay, Killed in the Recent Fire in the De Beers Diamond Mine in S. Africa.

THE LATE CLARENCE S. LINDSAY.

THE untimely death of this gentleman among those who perished at the disastrous conflagration at the De Beers Diamond Mine, near Kimberley, in South Africa, on July 11, has excited deep regret in the English mining districts, where he was widely known and highly esteemed. He was the son of Mr. James Lindsay, an official in the civil service at Sunderland, and was twenty-eight years of age. Having been educated for the profession of mining engineer, he was first employed at the Marsden Colliery, where he distinguished himself in some remarkable operations; and about 1883 he was appointed by Sir Charles Mark Palmer, manager of the Ilsworth Colliery.

While occupying that position he performed a feat of courage and daring which gave him a national reputation. There was an explosion in the mine in 1885, and young Lindsay with a couple of miners descended into the mine to rescue the workmen. Both his companions succumbed to the after-damp. Lindsay found some *rusty nails*, the chewing of which counteracted the poisonous gas he had inhaled, and thus saved his life. In a half unconscious condition he dragged his companions a considerable distance through the workings at the risk of his life. His efforts to save them were futile, but that he should make those efforts in a condition so full of peril proved the heroism of the man.

Mr. Lindsay could not, at the time of his death, have been more than a full week at the mine, since he had not long arrived in South Africa, being appointed manager of four great diamond mines, of which the De Beers is one. As proof of the estimation in which he was held by the profession, on the occasion of the visit of the Institute of the Mining and Mechanical Engineers to Newcastle he was appointed to inspect and report upon the various methods of ventilation in mines in Great Britain and on the European continent.

THE FIRE IN THE DIAMOND MINE AT KIMBERLEY, SOUTH AFRICA.

AN appalling calamity occurred on July 11 at the famous diamond mines in South Africa, by which more than two hundred lives were lost. There are four of these mines within the borders of Cape Colony, which have recently been amalgamated under one management. They are known as the Griqualand, East and West, the Kimberley, and the De Beers mines.

On the evening of July 11 a general alarm was caused around the De Beers mine by the sudden ringing of the fire-alarm bell, indicating that there was fire in the mine. Soon a large crowd, consisting of thousands of people—men, women, and children, of every grade and nationality—assembled at the edge of the mine. They had not been there long when the rumor began to circulate that there were more than

Six Hundred Souls Entombed

in the mine, and that there were no means of exit for them. It is needless to dwell on the heartrending scenes that followed such a rumor. They can be well imagined when it is known that there were wives and mothers whose husbands and children had just descended into the mine.

The first intimation of the accident was given between the hours of six and seven in the evening, when the night shift of workmen was relieving the day shift. There are two shafts, which have lately been constructed for the better underground working, known as No. 1 and No. 2 shafts. These are incline shafts, and No. 1 leads to the 500-foot level. From these again, other vertical shafts lead to greater depths. One known as the Friggens shaft leads to the 700-foot level. It was in this shaft that the fire first broke out, but in an incredibly short space of time it spread to the main shaft.

The First Horror

was caused by the breaking of the rope of the skip which was employed in hauling up the men of the day shift. Several men had rushed to this skip to be hauled up, as soon as they saw signs of danger, and the engineer at the mouth of the shaft at once proceeded to haul, but the heat of the fire burnt the ropes and precipitated the skip with its occupants to the bottom of the shaft, where they must have been crushed to death or have died by suffocation if they escaped death by burning.

It was daybreak before any organized attempt could be made to proceed to the rescue or assistance of the miners.

The Rescue Party

gained an entrance to the mine through an opening to a long-disused passage, and worked with a will until they had reached the natives and white men confined in the tunnels. They found the foot of the main shaft piled up with the bodies of natives who had evidently fallen on the top of each other as they rushed to get out of the mine. In other places, where ladders were placed to gain a higher level from a lower, many natives were found hanging on these ladders, with their hands firmly grasping the ropes as if in the last death struggle they had laid hold of them as their only hope of safety. The explorers also came upon some white men, whom they rescued and brought to the surface, where they were received by their friends, and the crowd anxiously awaiting them with a welcome cheer and shouts of joy.

Providentially, a fresh breeze was blowing all day, which caused a strong draught in the tunnels and shafts. Had it been otherwise there would have been no hope of any being saved alive. As it was, the exploring party brought back word that there were piles of dead bodies of natives lying in the mine, and that they recognized the bodies of many white men, some of them lying peacefully, as if they had died without a struggle, and others looking as if they had made desperate efforts to escape.

All day long the toilers worked, and before nightfall they had succeeded in recovering about 408 natives alive, and forty-seven white men. As the natives working in the mine must all pass through a searching-house, it was no difficult matter to obtain the number who had gone down for the night. The number of white men was ascertained to be about sixty-seven. Of these forty-seven were rescued. The remaining twenty, in addition to about two hundred natives, were given up as dead. Among the dead was the young manager, Mr. Lindsay. He was comparatively unacquainted with the course of the workings. When he saw the first indications of danger, he at once prepared to descend to help in the work of rescue. Already the skip was full of brave men, intent on risking their lives for the rescue of their comrades, but Mr. Lindsay ordered one of the men who was going into the skip to retire, while he took his place to meet, as it proved, his doom, for after the descent of the cage he was not again heard of.

Many stories are told of daring and heroic courage on the part both of the Europeans and of the natives. One white man could have escaped, but he returned to try to save his comrades, and was suffocated in the attempt. A native also, who had formerly been distinguished in the Caffre wars, took up and carried his master, who was exhausted and in a fainting condition, to a place of safety. The natives generally showed great coolness. About $100,000 of damage has been done to the mine.

THE DIAMOND DIGGINGS

are situated, for the most part, in the Valley of the Vaal River, to the northeast of the Orange River Free State, but within the boundary of the Cape Colony. The land is intersected by long stony ridges, called Kopjes by the Dutch Boers, which consist of large fragments of rock thrown together, and covered with a deep ferruginous gravel. In this gravel, which fills the interstices between the loose rocks, the precious gems are found. The manner of working is simple enough. The miners remove the loose blocks of stone, which are cast aside; then take up the gravel, and sift it thoroughly, either in a dry state or with abundance of water, i sieve rocked by a cradle. When the peb have been thus separated from the sand, t are cleansed and placed upon the sorting-t (*as shown in the illustration on our frontispie*) and are most carefully examined, to find diamonds that may lie in the heap. The re is often disappointing, but sometimes the gers are richly rewarded for their toils drudgery by the discovery of a glittering p Much of the work is done by natives, who, b almost naked, have no pockets in which to c ceal the precious gems which otherwise t might be tempted to purloin.

The Diamond fields have been the cause

Political Trouble.

It was in 1835 that the Dutch families in C Colony, becoming dissatisfied with British ru sent out from among themselves a sturdy ba chiefly of young men, across the Orange Riv to found the Orange Free State. The Briti made no objection to their going, and doubtle expected that the natives, who enormously o numbered them, would soon kill them or dri them back. Quite unexpectedly, however, t Dutch got on tolerably well with their nat neighbors, and, in spite of quarrels now a again over stolen cattle, succeeded in maintai ing their position. Then the British, regardi them as the Queen's subjects still, endeavor to impose the British rule over them, but we stubbornly resisted. In 1852 it was finally dec ed to abandon the attempt, and the indepe dence of the Orange Free State was recogniz the Orange River to be the boundary of t British possessions. This treaty was renew in 1869, after a rupture caused by an appeal the Basutos to the British for protecti against the encroachments of the Boers.

The Discovery of Diamonds

was made soon after the treaty of 1869 was ra fied. The diamond field was north of the ange River, and, therefore, outside British t ritory, but neither was it technically in the te tory of the Orange Free State. It was in la held by a Griqua chief named Waterboer, w in former troubles, had been an ally of the B ish. The Boers treated his claim contemptuo ly and took possession of the magnificent pr Waterboer then appealed to his former all the British, who, with like cupidity to that the Boers, went to his aid. Finally, they to possession of the diamond fields, gave a li more than one-tenth to Waterboer, and kept remainder, Lord Kimberley giving his name the new territory.

Fresh trouble arose out of this proceedi England had just arranged to unite her So African colony under a parliament, as in Can and Australia, and she intended the diam field to be a possession of the colony. B large proportion of the voters were of Du origin, fathers of families whose sons brothers had gone out in 1835 to found Orange Free State. They were much m friendly to the Free State than to Great B ain. Accordingly, when the parliament of Cape Colony assembled, it was found that members declined the gift of the diamond fie or would accept it only on condition that Orange Free State declared itself satisfied w the arrangement. They bluntly said that English Government had pledged itself in two treaties of 1852 and 1869 not to inter beyond the Orange River, and if the Gove ment chose to break its treaties through cu ity, it must keep the spoil itself; they on t part would not be party to the iniquity. E nent men among the English who had res for justice and righteousness, made rem strances to their Government, and finally Brand, the President of the Orange Free St went to London to plead its cause. He succe ed so far as to obtain from the English Treas $450,000, as compensation.

Another attempt was subsequently made bring the Orange Free State under British d ination, by annexing the Transvaal, which was expected would ultimately bring the F into confederation. The terrible war followed in 1880, with the disaster of ba Hill, and the death of Sir George Col- prang from this scheme. Valuable as the diamonds is, its acquisition has been pur- d at a deplorable cost of money, life, and cter.

ISSION WORK IN SOUTH AFRICA.

E Paris Evangelical Society sent to the tos in 1833 three missionaries, Messrs. Rol- Lemue, and Besseux. On their arrival at Cape, they were welcomed by a few descend- of the French Huguenots, who had emi- d there after the revocation of the Edict of es. They settled at Mosega, but had hard- gun work when Moselkatse, the chief of Matabeles, and the terror of the country, them an order to appear before him. Know- hat he fully intended to murder them, they from the district, and subsequent fiendish of the Matabeles proved that they were ent in doing so. Ultimately, the fugitives d a refuge near Litaku, which they named to, where they labored until Providence ed the way for labor among the Basutos.

Oxen in Exchange for a Man of Prayer.

circumstances that led to the beginning of work among the Basutos of South Africa peculiar. A raid had been made upon them heir enemies, the Korannas and Griquas, many of their cattle had been driven off. e of them, in their extreme destitution, ed the marauders, being resolved to retake of their property or die in the attempt. heir great surprise, they found among the s to which their enemies belonged, men were touched by a recital of their woes, who treated them with generosity. One ese, who had previously been in contact the missionaries, told the Basuto chief the Christian religion alone could give e and prosperity to his people. The chief ediately expressed to this man an earnest e for missionaries; and some time after- , fearing that he had forgotten the matter, him some oxen with the naive request that ould procure him "in exchange a man of er." Providentially Messrs. Casalis and ousset had arrived about this time, and eeded without delay to Basutoland.

Chief Moshesh

the greatest and wisest of the chiefs of the Ba- s. He was remarkable for his patience, tact, ness, and firmness. He found his people ered, oppressed, overrun by their enemies, apparently destined to extinction. For s the country had been desolated by tribal and stained with the blood of cannibal or- The peace-loving Basutos had been the of every invader. But Moshesh, without ing any long-continued or sanguinary wars, aged to restore order and peace, and make nation one of the most powerful and respect- n South Africa. He, his uncles, and his were all converted through God's blessing he labors of the missionaries. He died in ch, 1870, in perfect peace.

The Conversion of Libe,

uncle of Moshesh, and called the "Father of Basutos, was very remarkable. He was an man nearly eighty years of age. For a long e he bitterly hated the missionaries. He d, however, to influence his nephew Mo- sh against them, though he earnestly endea- d to persuade him to expel them. Finally, he could not get the missionaries driven y, he removed his own residence from their ghborhood, in order that he might be out of ring of their singing and preaching. So ch did their visits enrage him, that they were ength obliged to leave him alone. Imagine ir astonishment, then, when one day a mes- ger from the old man arrived at the station ing: "Behold Libe prays and begs you to go pray with him!" It was true! The old eftain was found at prayer, eagerly desiring ruction, and shortly afterward, at his own re- st, was publicly baptized.

ANECDOTES RELATED AT RECENT EVANGELISTIC MEETINGS.

Taking a Public Stand for Christ.—"Soon after my conversion," said a speaker, "I was helping at an open-air meeting near a saloon in which I was well known. I went forward and took my place beside the minister. Soon the bar-tender came to his door to look at the proceedings. It was not long before he recognized me, and turning, he called to his wife to come out and see me. I could stand that, but when it came to the close, and I was asked to offer prayer in the hearing of that man who had so lately seen me helplessly intoxicated, I felt very nervous. For a few moments I went through intense agony, the perspiration was running down my face, and my limbs almost gave way under me, but through the grace of God I was enabled in His strength to publicly show on whose side I had taken my stand. Then the minister linked his arm in mine, and took me home with him. What joy I had after that first public avowal of my faith! It seemed to be another and very strong band binding me to Christ, and such always is open confession of Christ."

Smashing the Whisky Bottle.—A Member of the Mizpah Band testifies: "Some years ago I was well known as a hard drinker. Not content with six days to indulge my depraved appetite, I generally brought home a supply on Saturday night to last me until Monday morning. One Saturday night I had brought home the usual allowance, and after placing it on the table fell asleep. Next morning when I awoke with an aching head, I found my little girl in the room. Motioning towards the bottle on the table, I said, 'Annie, will you hand me that over?' Annie did not move, but with eyes swimming in tears she said, 'Oh, father, I cannot. Don't you know I am a member of the Band of Hope?' And coming nearer, she laid her hand on my shoulder, and said, 'And, father, if you would give up the drink how happy we should all be!' 'Ah, I replied, 'if I only could I would gladly do so.' 'But you can do it, father,' persisted the child. 'Jesus says He will help you if you will trust Him.' With these words she left the room, and rising from my bed I dashed the whisky bottle in pieces, and kneeling I asked God to forgive the past, and to receive me for Christ's sake. He did so, and still keeps me."

Mother and Daughter at the "Penitent form."—Richard Weaver says: "Not long ago I was preaching in a meeting where the front form got the name of the 'penitent form,' to which, at the close of the address, we invited all who were weary of sinning, and willing to come to Christ. Scarcely was the invitation given when a young woman in the body of the hall rose and made her way to the form; she was quickly followed by an aged woman. Those two knelt humbly before God, and soon it was evident that the Holy Spirit was striving with them, for the young woman in a short time rose to her feet, and with a shout of 'Praise God!' gave evidence that the Lord had saved her. Nor was the elder woman long behind, and soon both were praising God. So great had been their anxiety about their salvation, that they had not looked at each other, but now that anxiety had given way to joyful confidence, they had more leisure to regard one another. At the first look there was an exclamation of joyous surprise, and the next instant they were in each other's arms. They had recognized in each other, the one a long lost daughter, and the other a forsaken mother, whom she had not seen for nine years."

A Mistake of Two Rum-sellers.—Mr. Dunn, evangelist, remarks: "Another evangelist and myself had been working for some time in a district in the south of Scotland, and the Lord had greatly blessed our efforts. But the work was telling upon our bodily health, and we went for a day's rest to Melrose, returning the same night. When we entered the railway-station there were two very fine-looking and apparently wealthy old gentlemen walking up and down the platform. They appeared to take a great interest in us. When we had taken our seats, and the train was just about to move, one said to the other, 'There are those two fellows gone at last. We are well rid of them now.' Hurriedly I took down the window, and thrusting out my head said, 'No, gentlemen, you are mistaken; we shall be back to-night, and have our meeting as usual.' When we got back I asked the booking-clerk who these gentlemen were. 'What!' he exclaimed in surprise, 'have you been so long in the town and yet do not know who those two gentlemen are? They are the leading saloon-keepers of the town.' These are the people who wish to keep back the Gospel. They fear lest the people learn to do right and give up the intoxicating cup and accept Christ."

A Variety Theatre Singer's Conversion.—A member of the Mizpah band testifies: "For fifteen years I earned my livelihood by singing in a variety theatre. About two years ago, having an interval of two weeks between the end of one engagement and the beginning of the next, I thought I could not do better than have a big spree, so came to this city for the purpose. But, thank God, that spree has never come off yet. I was wandering about, at the wrong end of the town, looking for a certain theatre, and not knowing the city well, my search was in vain. But I heard a song. I stopped and listened. In the open air a band of men were singing: 'I will sing of my Redeemer, and His wondrous love to me.' I waited until they were done, and then followed them into the meeting. There I heard of Jesus, about whom my mother had taught me. I went away deeply impressed, and during all that week was very anxious about my soul. The Holy Spirit strove to bring me to Christ, but I thought if I gave myself to Christ, I should require to give up my profession, my only means of gaining a living. I asked God to guide me. I then opened my Bible and read, 'Seek ye first the kingdom of God and His righteousness.' There and then I sought the kingdom of God, and giving myself to Christ, He has kept His promise, and given me all things which I require."

A Prodigal's Father Softened.—An Evangelist said: "While I was preaching in a well-known chapel in London, I noticed a young man, seated in one of the pews, every now and then brush a tear from his eye. As soon as I could I spoke to him. 'Can God save me?' he excitedly asked. 'Yes, He can,' I answered. We knelt, and at once he gave himself to the Saviour. In the chapel a gentlemen recognized the unfortunate youth, and kindly offered to take him home, but on the way they had to pass the prodigal's old home. The young man thought he would like to ask his father's forgiveness, so, though trembling with fear and shame he knocked at the door. We requested the servant to ask the gentleman to speak for a moment. He came, and the young man dropping on his knees said, 'God has forgiven me, will you forgive me?' The father at first seemed petrified, but recovering himself, bade his son begone, as he would never forgive him. We had just arrived at the friend's house, and were striving to comfort him, when we were surprised by a knock at the door. It was a servant who had followed us with a cab to convey the young master home. That night at family worship, as the father prayed, 'Forgive our trespasses as we forgive them who trespass against us,' his daughter interrupted him with 'No, father, you cannot pray that, for you know you have not forgiven my brother.' The old man saw he was acting in an un-Christlike spirit, and sent off at once for his son, knowing that he could not hope for God's favor until he had forgiven him."

THE EVENTFUL EPOCH.

A Vacation Sermon by Dr. Talmage.

"I will show wonders in the heavens and in the earth." Joel 2 : 30.

A Momentous Time—A Period of Disaster—An Epileptic Earth—Disasters Volcanic—A Series of Earthquakes—Disasters Cyclonic—A Cyclone at Sea—Disasters Oceanic—The Roll of the Lost—Disasters Epidemic—An Era of Blessing—Of Longevity—Rapid Travel—Blessing of Quick Information—Of Gospel Proclamation—A Falsehood on its Travels—Wonders of Self-Sacrifice—The Track and the Engineer—Relics of Peter the Great—The Incoming Fleet.

Our eyes dilate and our heart quickens its pulsation as we read of events in the third century, the sixth century, the eighth century, the fourteenth century; but there are more far-reaching events crowded into the nineteenth century than into any other, and the last quarter bids fair to eclipse the preceding three quarters. We read in the daily newspapers of events announced in one paragraph and without any especial emphasis—of events which a Herodotus, a Josephus, a Xenophon, a Gibbon would have taken whole chapters or whole volumes to elaborate. Looking out upon our time, we must cry out in the words of the text: "Wonders in the heaven and in the earth."

A Period of Disaster.

I propose to show you that the time in which we live is wonderful for disaster and wonderful for blessing, for there must be lights and shades in this picture as in all others. Need I argue this day that our time is wonderful for disaster? Our world has had a rough time since by the hand of God it was bowled out into space. It is an *epileptic earth*. Convulsion after convulsion. Frosts pounding it with sledge hammer of iceberg, and fires melting it with furnaces seven hundred times heated. It is a wonder to me it has lasted so long. Meteors shooting by on this side and grazing it, and meteors shooting by on the other side and grazing it, none of them slowing up for safety. Whole fleets and navies and argosies and flotillas of worlds sweeping all about us. Our earth like a fishing smack off the banks of Newfoundland, while the *Gallia* and the *Bothnia* and the *Arizona* and the *Great Eastern* rush by. Beside that our world has by sin been damaged in its eternal machinery, and ever and anon the furnaces have burst, and the walking-beams of the mountains have broken, and the islands have shipped a sea, and the great hulk of the world has been jarred with accidents that ever and anon threatened immediate demolition. But it seems to me as if our century were specially characterized by

Disasters Volcanic,

cyclonic, oceanic, epidemic. I say volcanic, because an earthquake is only a volcano hushed up. When Stromboli and Cotopaxi and Vesuvius stop breathing, let the foundations of the earth beware. Seven thousand earthquakes in two centuries recorded in the catalogue of the British Association! Trajan, the emperor, goes to ancient Antioch, and amid the splendors of his reception is met by an earthquake that nearly destroys the emperor's life. Lisbon, fair and beautiful, at 1 o'clock on the first of November, 1755, in six minutes 60,000 have perished, and Voltaire writes of them: "For that region it was the last judgment, nothing wanting but a trumpet!" Europe and America feeling the throb; fifteen hundred chimneys in Boston partly or fully destroyed.

But the disasters of other centuries have had their counterpart in our own. In 1812, Caraccas was caught in the grip of the earthquake; in 1822, in Chili, 100,000 square miles of land by volcanic force upheaved to four and seven feet of permanent elevation; in 1854, Japan felt the geological agony; Naples shaken in 1857; Mexico in 1858; Medosa, the capital of the Argentine Republic, 1861; Manilla terrorized in 1863; the Hawaiian Islands by such force uplifted and let down in 1871; Nevada shaken in 1871; Antioch in 1872; California in 1872; San Salvador in 1873; Ischia in 1883; Charleston in 1886.

But look at the cyclonic, the disasters cyclonic. At the mouth of the Ganges are three islands—the Hattiah, the Sundeep and the Dakin Shabazpore. In the midnight of October, 1877, on all those three islands the cry was: "The waters, the waters!" A cyclone arose and rolled the sea over those three islands, and of a population of 340,000, 215,000 were drowned. Only those saved who had climbed to the top of the highest trees. *Did you ever see a cyclone?* No. Then I pray God you may never see one. I saw one on the ocean, and it swept us eight hundred miles back from our course, and for thirty-six hours during the cyclone and after it we expected every moment to go to the bottom. They told us before we retired at nine o'clock that the barometer had fallen, but at eleven o'clock at night we were awakened with the shock of the waves. All the lights out. Crash! went all the lifeboats. Waters rushing through the skylights down into the cabin and down on the furnaces until they hissed and smoked in the deluge.

Seven Hundred People Praying,

blaspheming, shrieking. Our great ship poised a moment on the top of a mountain of phosphorescent fire, and then plunged down, down, down, until it seemed as if she never would again be righted. Ah! you never want to see a cyclone at sea. But a few weeks ago, I was in Minnesota, where there was one of those cyclones on land that swept the city of Rochester from its foundations, and took dwelling-houses, barns, men, women, children, horses, cattle, and tossed them into indiscriminate ruin, and lifted a rail-train and dashed it down, a mightier hand than that of the engineer on the air-brake. Cyclone in Kansas, within a few months; cyclone in Missouri, cyclone in Wisconsin, cyclone in Illinois, cyclone in Iowa. Satan, prince of the power of the air, never made such a cyclonic disturbance as he has in our day. And am I not right in saying that one of the characteristics of the time is disaster cyclonic?

Disasters Oceanic.

But look at the disasters oceanic. Shall I call the roll of the dead shipping? Ye monsters of the deep, answer when I call your names. *Ville de Havre! The Schiller! City of Boston! The Melville! The President! The Cimbria! The Oregon!* But why should I go on calling the roll when none of them answer, and the roll is as long as the white scroll of the Atlantic surf at Cape Hatteras breakers. If the oceanic cables could report all the scattered life and all the bleached bones that they rub against in the depths of the ocean, what a message of pathos and tragedy for both beaches! In one week eighty fishermen perished off the coast of Newfoundland, and whole fleets of them off the coast of England. God help the poor fellows at sea, and give high seats in heaven to the Grace Darlings and the Ida Lewises and the life-boatmen around Goodwin's Sands and the Skerries!

The sea, now owning three-fourths of the earth, proposes to capture the other fourth, and is bombarding the land all around the earth. The moving of our hotels at Brighton Beach backward from where they once stood, a type of what is going on all around the world and on every coast. The Dead Sea rolls to-day where ancient cities stood. Pillars of temples that stood on hills, geologists find now three-quarters under the water, or altogether submerged. The sea having wrecked so many merchantmen and flotillas, wants to wreck the continents, and hence disasters oceanic.

Disasters Epidemic.

Look at the disasters epidemic. I speak not of the plague in the fourth century that ravaged Europe; and in Moscow and the Neapolitan dominions and Marseilles wrought such terror in the eighteenth century; but I look at the yellow fevers, and the choleras, and the diphtherias, and the scarlet fevers, and the typhoids of our own time. Hear the wailing of Memphsis and Shreveport, and New Orleans, and Savannah, of the last two decades. From Hurdwar, India, where every twelfth year three million devotees congregate, the caravans brought cholera, and that one disease slew 18,000 eighteen days in Bossorah. Twelve thous in one summer slain by it in India, and twe five thousand in Egypt. Disasters epiden Some of the finest monuments in Greenw and Laurel Hill, and Mount Auburn are to tors who died battling with Southern epiden

An Era of Blessing.

But now I turn the leaf in my subject, a plant the white lilies and the palm-tree a the nightshade and the myrtle. This age more characterized by wonders of disaster t by wonders of blessing. Blessing of longev The average of human life rapidly increas Forty years now worth four hundred years o A short time ago I came from Manitoba to N York in three days and three nights. In o times it would have taken three months. other words, three days and three ni now are worth three months of other days. average of human life is practically greater than when Noah lived his 950 years, and Me saleh lived his 969 years. Blessing of int gence. The Salmon P. Chases and the Abra Lincolns and the Henry Wilsons of the co time will not be required to learn to read pine-knot lights, or seated on shoemak bench, nor will the Fergusons have to s astronomy while watching the cattle. Kn edge rolls its tides along every poor man's d and his children may go down and bath them. If the philosophers of the last cen were called up to recite in a class with our b at the Polytechnic, or our girls at the Pac those old philosophers would be sent dow the foot of the class because they failed to swer the questions! Free libraries in all important towns and cities of the land. torical alcoves, and poetic shelves, and maga tables for all that desire to walk through t or sit down at them.

Quick Information.

Blessings of quick information; newspa falling all around us thick as leaves in a Sep ber equinoctial. News three days old rancid stale. We see the whole world twice a d through the newspaper at the breakfast-t and through the newspaper at the tea-t with an "extra" here and there between.

Blessing of *Gospel proclamation*. Do you know that nearly all the missionary soc have been born in this century? and near the Bible societies, and nearly all the philanthropic movements? A secretary o of the denominations said to me one d Dakota: "You were wrong when you said denomination averaged a new church every of the year; they established nine in one w so you are far within the truth." A clerg of our own denomination said: "I have been out establishing five mission stations tell you Christianity is on the march, while

Infidelity is Dwindling

into the imbecility that was demonstrated long ago at Rochester, N. Y., where after blowing of the trumpets and the gatheri all the clans there assembled a small gro semi-idiots to denounce the Christian rel and eulogize one of their dead patrons, a tine, arrested in New York and Boston and again for scattering obscene literat that dead man the patron saint of the movement. While Infidelity is thus dwindlin dropping down into imbecility and indec the wheel of Christianity is making about a sand revolutions in a minute. All the cop Shakespeare and Tennyson and Disraeli a any ten of the most popular writers of the less in number than the copies of the Bibl ing out from our printing-presses. Two ago, in six weeks, more than two million c of the New Testament purchased—not away, but purchased, because the world have it.

More Christian men in high official pos to-day in Great Britain and in the United S than ever before. Stop that falsehood through the newspapers—I have seen

:y—that the judges of the Supreme Court e United States are all infidels except Judge By personal acquaintance I know three em to be old-fashioned evangelical Chris- sitting at the holy sacrament of our Lord ; Christ, and I suppose that the majority of 'are stanch believers in our Christian relig- And then hear *the dying words of Judge* ;, a man who had been Attorney-General e United States, and who had been Secre- of the United States, no stronger lawyer of entury than Judge Black—dying, his aged kneeling by his side, and he uttering that me and tender prayer: "O Lord God, from n I derived my existence and in whom I always trusted, take my spirit to Thyself et Thy richest blessing come down upon lary!" The most popular book to-day is lible, and the mightiest institution is the ch, and the greatest name among the na- , and most honored, is the name of Jesus.

Wonders of Self-Sacrifice.

rgyman told me in the northwest on one / visits, that for six years he was a mission- t the extreme north, living 400 miles from st-office, and sometimes he slept out of in winter, the thermometer sixty and six- e degrees below zero, wrapped in rabbit woven together. I said: "Is it possible? lo not mean sixty and sixty-five degrees *be-* ero?" He said: "I do, and I was happy." or Christ. Where is there any other being will rally such enthusiasm? Mothers sew- heir fingers off to educate their boys for the el ministry. For nine years no luxury on able until the course through grammar ol and college and theological seminary be leted. Poor widow putting her mite into ord's treasury, the face of emperor or presi- impressed upon the coin not so conspicu- s the blood with which she earned it. Mil- of good men and women, but more women men, to whom Christ is everything. Christ and Christ last, and Christ forever.

ıy, this age is not so characterized by in- on and scientific exploration as it is by el proclamation. You can get no idea of less you can ring all the church bells in one e, and sound all the organs in one diapa- and gather all the congregations of Chris- om in one *Gloria in Excelsis*. Mighty camp- ings, mighty Ocean Groves, Mighty Chau- as, Mighty conventions of Christian work- Mighty General Assemblies of the Presby- n Church, Mighty Conferences of the odist Church, Mighty Associations of the ist Church, Mighty conventions of the copal Church. I think before long the investments will not be in railroad stock estern Union, but in trumpets and cymbals estal decorations, for we are

On the Eve of Victories

and world-uplifting. There may be many of hard work yet before the consumma- but the signs are to me so encouraging I would not be unbelieving if I saw the of the apocalyptic angel spread for its last phal flight in this day's sunset; or if to- ow morning the ocean cables should thrill ith the news that Christ the Lord had ted on Mount Olivet or Mount Calvary to aim universal dominion.

, you dead churches, wake up! Throw back hutters of stiff ecclesiasticism and let the of the spring morning come in. Morning e land. Morning for the sea. Morning of cipation. Morning of light and love and . Morning of a day in which there shall chains to break, no sorrows to assuage, espotism to shatter, no woes to compas- te. Oh, Christ, descend! Scarred temple, the crown! Bruised hand, take the scep- Wounded foot, step the throne! "Thine kingdom!"

ese things I say because I want you to be . I want you to be watching all these ers unrolling from the heavens and the . God has classified them, whether calam- or blessing. The divine purposes are harnessed in traces that cannot break, and in girths that cannot slip, and in buckles that cannot loosen, and are driven by reins they must answer. I preach no fatalism. A swarthy engineer at one of the depots in Dakota, said: "When will you get

On the Locomotive

and take a ride with us?" "Well," I said, "now, if it suits you." So I got on one side the locomotive and a Methodist minister, who was also invited, got on the other side, and between us were the engineer and the stoker. The train started. The engineer had his hand on the agitated pulse of the great engine. The stoker shoveled in the coal and shut the door with a loud clang. A vast plain swept under us and the hills swept by, and that great monster on which we rode trembled and bounded and snorted and raged as it hurled us on. I said to the Methodist minister on the other side the locomotive: "My brother, why should Presbyterians and Methodists quarrel about the decrees and free agency? You see that track, that firm track, that iron track; that is the decree. You see this engineer's arm; that is free agency. How beautifully they work together! They are going to take us through. We could not do without the track, and we could not do without the engineer."

So I rejoice day by day. Work for us all to do, and we may turn the crank of the Christian machinery this way or that, for we are free agents: but there is

The Track Laid

so long ago no one remembers it; laid by the hand of Almighty God in sockets that no terrestrial or Satanic pressure can ever affect. And along that track the car of the world's redemption will roll and roll to the Grand Central Depot of the Millennium. I have no anxiety about the track. I am only afraid that for our indolence God will discharge us and get some other stoker and some other engineer. The train is going through, with us or without us. So, my brethren, watch all the events that are going by. If things seem to turn out right, give wings to your joy. If things seem to go wrong, throw out the anchor of faith and hold fast.

There is a house in London where

Peter the Great,

Czar of Russia, lived a while when he was moving through the land *incognito*, and in workman's dress, that he might learn the wants of the people. A stranger was visiting at that house recently, and saw in a dark attic an old box, and he said to the owner of the house: "What's in that box?" The owner said: "I don't know; that box was there when I got the house, and it was there when my father got it; we haven't had any curiosity to look at it; I guess there's nothing in it." "Well," said the stranger, "I'll give you two pounds for it." "Well, done." The two pounds are paid, and recently the contents of that box were sold to the Czar of Russia for fifty thousand dollars. In it, the lathing-machine of Peter the Great, his private letters and documents of value beyond all monetary consideration. And here are events that seem very insignificant and unimportant, but they encase treasures of divine providence and eternities of meaning which after a while God will demonstrate before the ages as being of stupendous value. As near as I can tell, from what I see, there must be a God somewhere about.

God at the Helm.

When Titans play quoits they pitch mountains; but who owns these gigantic forces you have been reading about the last few years? Whose hand is on the throttle-valve of the volcanoes? Whose foot suddenly planted on the footstool makes the continents quiver? God! God! He looketh upon the mountains and they tremble. He toucheth the hills and they smoke. God! God! I must be at peace with Him. Through the Lord Jesus Christ this God is mine and He is yours. I put the earthquake that shook Palestine at the crucifixion against all the down-rockings of the centuries. This God on our side, we may challenge all the centuries of time and all the cycles of eternity.

The Incoming Fleet.

A short time ago I was at Fire Island, Long Island, and I went up in the cupola from which they telegraph to New York the approach of vessels hours before they come into port. There is an opening in the wall, and the operator puts his telescope through that opening, and looks out and sees vessels far out at sea. While I was talking with him, he went up and looked out. He said: "We are expecting the *Arizona* tonight." I said: "Is it possible you know all those vessels? do you know them as you know a man's face?" He said: "Yes, I never make a mistake; before I can see the hulks, I know them all by the masts · I know them all, I have watched them so long." Oh, what a grand thing it is to have ships telegraphed and heralded long before they come into port, that friends may come down to the wharf and welcome their long-absent loved ones. So to-day, we take our stand in the watch-tower, and we look off through the glass of inspiration or providence, we look off and see a whole fleet of ships coming in. That is *the ship of peace*, flag with one star of Bethlehem floating above the top-gallants. That is *the ship of the Church*, mark of salt wave high up on the smoke-stack, showing she has had rough weather, but the Captain of salvation commands her, and all is well with her.

The Ship of Heaven,

mightiest craft ever launched, millions of passengers, waiting for millions more, prophets and apostles and martyrs in the cabin, conquerors at the foot of the mast, while from the rigging hands are waving this way as though they knew us, and we wave back again, for they are ours; they went out from our own households. Ours! Hail, Hail! Put off the black and put on the white. Stop tolling the funeral bell and ring the wedding anthem. Shut up the hearse and take the chariot. Now, it comes around the great headland. Soon she will strike the wharf and we will go aboard her. Tears for ships going out. Laughter for ships coming in. Now she touches the wharf. Throw on the planks. Block not up that gangway with embracing long-lost friends, for you will have eternity of reunion. Stand back and give way until other millions come on. Farewell to sin. Farewell to struggle. Farewell to sickness. Farewell to death. All aboard for heaven!

A CHURCH ON A FARM.

In the course of a journey in Asia Minor, which Dr. Constantine, of Smyrna, describes in a letter to the *Missionary Herald*, he came upon a little gathering of Christians upon a farm, who in spite of persecution and without the help of a clergyman had remained true to their faith. He says: "The work began ten years ago through a colporteur, and three years ago the converted few were anathematized and cast out of the old church by their bishop. They were stoned and terribly abused by their fellow-townsmen, yet they not only held their own, but steadily increased. There are now seventy-five souls who have accepted the gospel, including the children. They have services on Sunday, a Sunday-school, a prayer-meeting during the week, a day-school, and a women's meeting. In winter they meet in a silkworm shed, and in the summer out-of-doors.

"The driver of the buffalo-cart that brought me to the village, while going through a ravine struck up 'What a Friend we have in Jesus!' in Greek, and when I asked him if Jesus was his friend, he pulled out of his bosom a copy of the whole Bible; and yet the teacher of this people is a farmer and the preacher is a shepherd. While there I examined for the communion four men and ten women; among them was a tall man who had been the terror of the village; he was a thief, a drunkard, and a cruel husband; he would tie his poor wife's hands, and then beat her unmercifully. Yet that little woman became converted, and through faith brought her wild husband to Christ. Both of these united with church on that day."

A CHURCH FOUNDED BY A HERMIT.

AN interesting story of the founding of a church in Africa is told by the biographer of the late Bishop Hannington. He says: "Some time ago a native servant of the pioneer evangelist, Rehmann, ran away from the Mission station of Rabai, Africa, under somewhat peculiar circumstances. He was a Christian, and, as the event proves, a sincere one. But—his temper was not always under control. In a fit of passion he struck his wife; the blow was fatal, and he fled. With the guilt of blood upon him he sought the discipline of solitude. He became a hermit. He lived 'for some time in great obscurity and absolute solitude.' He did not relapse into savagery. On the contrary, he seems to have lived a life spent chiefly in the study of the Gospel of St. Luke, his sole possession when he left the station. It happened, upon a certain day, that a man of Godoma, gathering wood in the forest, chanced upon the hermit reading a book. The encounter was alarming to both; but presently the man recognized in the forlorn student an old acquaintance, and called him by name—Abe Ngoa. After this the two had several interviews. The man of Godoma was curious to know what was the nature of the book which had so engrossed the other's attention. Abe Ngoa offered to teach him to read its pages. A comrade soon joined them; and the two persuaded the man of letters to leave his retreat and to return with them to the village as their instructor. He proved to be no ordinary tutor. His mind was saturated with the spirit of the book which he had so long pondered over. He imparted his knowledge with such fervor of faith, that eleven persons renounced their heathen 'customs,' and made it known that they had 'joined the book.'

"It was in 1874 that three men came into Frere Town from this obscure village of Godoma, to ask for baptism. A native catechist was sent to the village, and was warmly welcomed by the inquirers, over thirty in number. This body of thirty-four catechumens, so strangely found in an unknown village of a wild district, and far removed from all outside influence of any kind, had been gathered together solely and entirely by the teaching of one man, himself but half taught, and the possessor of but a single copy of the Gospels, but whose faith had been intensified by his long solitude in the wilderness, and by his continued pondering over the words which brought him a release from his sense of guilt.

"The first baptism took place on August 22, 1875, and about two months later a very important convert was won in the person of Abe Sidi, the head-man of the village. This Abe Sidi was a remarkable man, well fitted to be a leader, and who could not fail to influence others strongly. This man at once assumed the leadership and direction of the new Christian settlement, and became a zealous propagandist of the faith. Under his directions a church was built, and the community was regularly organized.

"From this time this 'independent, self-supporting, and simple, native Church continued to increase rapidly. In 1880 the opposition of the surrounding chiefs became rather pronounced, as more and more of the people declared against the old fetish 'customs.' The medicine men began to be aggressive. There were threats of burning down the church and village, and even of shooting or poisoning Abe Sidi himself. For this and other reasons it seems to have been decided that Abe Sidi should leave a strong community at Godoma, and himself lead off a 'swarm' to seek a new settlement farther north. He found a good site at Fulladoyo, which is an island on the river Voi. There he built his church and erected his grass huts, and there a considerable Christian population soon gathered around him, as they had done at Godoma.

"For three years this little independent self-governed community of African Bible Christians held their own against threats and persecutions. At last, reports spread that the slave-traders had prevailed to destroy the Christian settlement, and that Abe Sidi was a prisoner. Then came worse news; he is said to have died 'a horrible death' at the hands of the Mohammedan slave-holders. His settlement is destroyed, his people are scattered. It is the story of John the Baptist over again. The wicked seem to prevail, the godly man seems to perish. It is but seeming. The foundation-stones of the City of Peace are often cemented with blood."

A FATHER'S PROFANITY OVERCOME.

VICTORY over the habit of profane swearing, which is one of the most difficult to achieve, has come to a man in Kansas through the guidance of his little child. A journal of that State reports that a young man who was much given before his marriage, to the utterance of blasphemous ejaculations, and whose ordinary conversation was interlarded with oaths, was married a few years ago. Under the influence of his wife he made strong efforts to overcome the habit, but without much success, though he was ashamed of it, and restrained himself in her presence.

One morning, standing before the mirror shaving, the razor slipped, inflicting a slight wound. True to his fixed habit, he ejaculated the single word, "God!" and was not a little amazed and chagrined to see reflected in the mirror the pretty picture of his three-year-old daughter, as laying her doll hastily down, she sprang from her seat on the floor, exclaiming eagerly, and looking expectantly about the room, "Is Dod here?"

Pale and ashamed, and at a loss for a better answer, he simply said, "Why?"

"'Cause I thought He was, when I heard you speak to Him!"

Then, noticing the sober look on his face, as he gazed down into the innocent, radiant face, she patted him lovingly on the hand, exclaiming assuringly; "Call Him again, papa, and I dess He'll surely come!"

Catching the wondering child up in his arms, he knelt down, and for the first time in his life implored of God forgiveness for the past and help for his future, thanking Him in fervent spirit that He had not "surely come" before, in answer to some of his awful blasphemies.

A MUTE TESTIMONY IN CHINA.

A BROTHER of Mr. Studd, the young collegian who is now a missionary in China, thus writes of his experience during a tour in the country: "About a year ago I started, with my brother and Mr. Orr Ewing, to go inland from Tien-tsin. We travelled first by boat for three or four days, until we came to a large city called Pau-ting Fu, and there we found American missionaries, who helped us on our way. Then we went overland, and for ten days we travelled on. Occasionally we met at an inn, or on the roadside, a man who had heard something about the foreigners' doctrine, but there was no missionary, no one in the ten days' journey to tell of the Lord Jesus Christ and His salvation; and yet the people were ready enough to hear. If one only sat down at a tea-shop on the roadside, there would at once be a crowd. Well, we were travelling along through the country, a sixteen days' journey, and there was only one station where there was a missionary; and yet we were passing through villages every two or three miles, and we went across a plain every day with, perhaps, three or four large walled cities. One felt oppressed with the multitude of people there—millions to whom the gospel had never yet been taken. And that is in a part of China which is, I suppose, as well supplied with missionaries as any other part. After sixteen days' journey we arrived at a station called T'ai-yuen, and there it was my privilege to be present at a service.

"It may be that we appear fools in the eyes of the Chinamen, especially at first, when we can only say two or three words. I have been through a little of that experience myself, because I did not learn the language at all; but still I used to enjoy going out into the streets night after night, with one of the friends who was preaching, and taking a banner or scroll, with the fundamental truths of Christianity, or a text, upon it, perhaps to be laughed at, and asked questions which I could not answer, because I could not understand. One felt that even to *stand there mute as a witness for the Lord Jesus* was an unspeakable privilege. I well remember one morning sitting on the city wall at T'ai-yuen. I was reading by myself, and a young Chinaman came up. He watched me for some time, and then he came closer, and seemed very friendly. I longed to be able to talk to him and tell him about Jesus. I asked the Lord that He would give me some little word to say, and He brought to my memory some words that I had heard preached in the streets the day before. I could point to the mission-house, and tell him of the meetings, and ask him whether he would not come. My heart felt that I would have given anything to preach the gospel to that man. And there are millions who would listen; it needs people to go and tell them."

THE ROMANCE OF MISSIONS.

IN the course of an address delivered by the Rev. A. J. Gordon, D. D., of Boston, Mass., before an English audience, he graphically sketched the result of individual effort in the case of certain well-known missionaries, which he called the romance of missions. He described the marvellous outbreak of Christian faith among the Karen tribes, through one of the slave converts of Dr. Adoniram Judson's co-laborer, Mr. Boardman. In three years' time that slave was instrumental in leading to Christ 2,500 souls who were admitted into the Church by baptism. From that seed wonderful fruits have grown. The Karens have recently built a memorial hall to celebrate the jubilee of their missions, and for that purpose they raised among themselves 15,000 dollars. In contributing annually to the funds of the American Baptist Mission, the Karens come next in amount to the wealthy States of Massachusetts and New York. Another case of missionary success, even more wonderful, is that of *the Telegu Mission*, the story of which is now pretty well known. The first missionary to that part of India, said Dr. Gordon, is still living. The other day he celebrated his eightieth birthday in America, and his great desire is to be sent back to his loved field at Ongole. For thirty years he toiled on there without success. Then came the story of the young American engineer, Mr. Clough, who went to the Telegu—called "The Lone Star" Mission. The time of famine came, and the young engineer undertook the construction of a canal as relief works. He employed batches of 4,000 or 5,000 at a time, preaching the gospel to them in the evenings. Then, after a while he took on a fresh batch of laborers, and dealt with them in the same way. Almost the only thing he could preach in the language was John 3: 16, but that was enough for God to work upon, in fructifying the seed sown during many years. In the result 10,000 people made public profession of Christ *in one year*, and after being fully tested.

A CRY OF ALARM FROM INDIA.

THE terrible plague of drunkenness is menacing India. Hitherto, both the Mohammedans and the high caste Hindoos have been preserved from it by the commands of their religion, but now the *Indian Witness* says: "Strong drink is raging furiously in India. The unimpeachable testimony of Christian officials places the fact beyond question. The moral, social, and *religious inundation* of India by this liquor deluge, which is hardly less destructive than the Noachian, seems probable. The Mahommedan smiles when you ask him why his co-religionists drink; the three Napali castes, forbidden by their shastras to drink, are now slain by the excise system; while liquor-shops in Darjeeling are mostly kept by Brahmans! If caste is brushed aside by this awful tide, what can withstand its rage? 'For every native the mission is ncing for good,' says the Rev. Mr. Turnbull, e drink traffic is influencing ten for evil.' iere is only one evil which can destroy the 'er of the body, the power of the spirit, and power of the spirit at one fell stroke, and t,' says an English bishop, 'is the evil ef- ed by strong drink.' As a speaker at Dar- ing said, 'Our drink traffic commences with ging up a sign, "Wines and spirits sold here," ends by hanging up a man on the gallows.' it does not end there, and will not end le the flames of perdition continue to burn."

AFTER THE MILLENNIUM.

By John Storie, F. R. S. T.

or. 15: 24-28; Col. 1: 16-20; Rev. 20: 21, 22.

: Final Subjugation of all Authority—To be xecuted by Christ—The Seven-Sealed Com- ission—Part Executed at the Second Advent— wo Enemies Still Remaining — Satan and eath—Satan Works a Second Fall—Dire Mis- hief to Follow—Final and Supreme Assault on e Deity—Satan Struck Down Red-handed— eath the Last Enemy—The End of its Reign.

VE are taught in these passages the Divine pose in respect to this fallen world; that it been selected as the field on which is to be ght out to its close the great spiritual con- of the universe; that on it shall be put rn "all rule, and all authority, and all pow- that is arrayed against the majesty and ninion of the Godhead; that the Second son of the Divine Trinity has accepted the nmission to this end; that He has been in- ;ed, as the Son of Man, with the power ded for its complete execution; that He is fulfil here on this earth all that righteous- s demands for the expiating and arresting human sin; that He is to preside here in gment, and to reign here as King till He has dued and restrained rebellion, and "put un- His feet" all the enemies of the Godhead; t He is to deliver up to the Father

A World Redeemed;

ce rescued and immortal; creation in all its illen Principalities and Powers re-establish- and reconciled: and that, this done, and fidence and peace restored throughout the verse, *all* will then be received into *immedi-* and eternal union with the Godhead; and l will thenceforth be "*all in all.*"

Vhen the Lord Christ, as the Son of Man, eived from the Father's hand that seven- ed roll (Rev 5: 1-7), it conveyed to Him world as its Redeemer, and invested Him n the authority and power to enter on its iplete possession; to deliver it from that dage in which it had been so long enslaved; to rescue God's people, the living and the d, from the malign influence of Satanic ver. We see how the Son of Man descending he Glory and Majesty of His Epiphany, will down "the rule, the authority, and the ver" of the Antichrist and the false Prophet; end this troubled dispensation by binding an in the prison of the abyss. One part of ist's commission thus fulfilled, but

Two Enemies will then Remain

God and man—the Devil or Satan and Death. ore the end can come, He is to put these two mies beneath His feet; and end their power ever.

t the period we are now considering, the gdom of the Son of Man is established here, Satanic Tempter imprisoned, and the Spirit God poured out on all flesh. The earth is ding again its rich primeval harvests; the ons have known what it is to live in a world God would have it, free from war and want; n grief and pain, and under the pious and teous rule of the Great King and His risen ts; a life like that of Adam in Paradise. this is destined to be invaded by a second ptation and

A Second Fall;

ll in which not one man, but nations, perish. l by whose agency is to be wrought this nd wreck? By the same, that old Serpent's, e Devil and Satan," who had before and through its ages of sin and sorrow deceived the world. "When the thousand years are finish- ed, He shall be loosed again out of His prison. (Rev. 20: 7.) He is to be once more free. In this period of His long imprisonment He shall have the time and the opportunity to look back over His blighted and wretched past; and will He come forth taught by the experience of that past; saddened and subdued by the conscious- ness of past wrong; convinced of the madness of renewed defiance; and prepared to enter, as modern spiritists are teaching, on a wiser and nobler career? No! "He shall go forth" un- changed and unchangeable, fired with only madder passion, "to lead astray the nations which are in the four corners of the earth, Gog and Magog"; and exciting in them a spirit of malignant hostility against the favored nation and its king. "He will gather them together to the war, the number of them as the sand of the sea;" and lead them on to

This Last Assault

on the Son of Man and His cause. They cover with their armies the whole breadth of the Land of Israel, and, breathing extermination, "they compass with a beseiging host the camp* of the saints and the Beloved City." (Ver. 9.) As to these invading nations, it is ruin. "Fire comes down out of heaven to destroy them." In this last act of impiety they perish, and remain among the dead for judgment. But the Devil, He who leads them in this last rebellion, what of Him? "He is cast into the Lake of fire and brimstone; where the Beast and the false Prophet already are." Ver. 10; Matt. 25: 41.)

But why—if it be fore-known that this will be His immediate action and this

Dire Mischief is to Follow

—why is He to be let loose again by the Son of Man? What can justify this act of his liberation? We are told that there is not only a reason for it, but a divine necessity. "When the thousand years are fulfilled He *must* be loosed for a little season." (Ver. 3.) The statement is absolute. "He *must* be." This last loosing of man's tempt- er and man's destroyer is declared to be an act of mediatorial administration, in which the Son of Man is under the control of a divine decision. It is not only to be permitted, but is, at this last stage of the Divine judgment, inevitable; and if for some great end or ends judged to be essen- tial and inevitable, then certainly for these two:

First. That there may be, before the closing of Christ's intermediation, one last dreadful manifestation of sin; one last example in the face of creation of its blinding, corroding, mad- dening, merciless power; of that ineradicable and unrestrainable force in which it may rise when it reigns within the will of one to whom a nature has been given, intelligent and free.

The Infatuating Impulse

of a single malignant passion in a strong, intel- ligent agent, bent on resistance to the Eternal Law of right, free to act, and conscious of abil- ity to act its purpose out, is known only to God. We do not yet know the daring defiance to which this may reach, nor does creation know it—its aim the deposing of the Godhead. But in this, the last act of the fallen Archangel, the demonstration is complete. Transgression is then to be seen by men and angels in its finish, its crisis, and its close; its last act the foulest and the maddest; and its gain, perdition.

And *second*, It "must be" in order to the vindication of Eternal righteousness. This mighty Being has chosen deliberately to fall from his fidelity to God, and to spend the life and powers God-given in resisting and degrad- ing that Law which lives and reigns within the Godhead, and binds the Creator and intelligent universe in one. He has chosen to be, through these long troubled ages, the instigator of trans- gression, disorder, and ruin; false and the fath- er of lies; deceiving men and angels; instigat- ing hatred and murder; destroying the bodies and souls of unnumbered men; all this amid divine forbearance. But is the long-suffering of heaven never to end? Yes! It is to end, and to end now that he is seen using this last hour of granted liberty to assault the camp of the saints of God, and head the nations to their destruction. In justice to those who might live on in fear to fall his victims; in justice to those who have been the wondering and anxious wit- nesses of his long license and his unavenged misdeeds; in mercy to a creation that has suf- fered in confusion and danger so long, the de- cisive hour has come to stop his career, and to stop it for-ever. He is

Struck Down Red-handed

by the Son of Man, into the Lake of Fire; and heaven and earth set free. He inspired men of light and leading to teach that though men live and die here unsaved, they may yet find a place of repentance. He has found none. He gave currency to the lie that there is no Hell. He believes it now, that everlasting fire has been prepared for him and his angels. Damna- tion he has long set at defiance; its sentence is now resting on his head. He has spread far and wide the doctrine that annihilation is the doom of the lost; he is himself to live on for ever; in prison for ever; in torment for ever; Satanic for ever. This his end! he is put down by the Son of Man. "It *must* be."

One enemy still remains,

The Last Enemy,

death. That, too, is to be put down by the Son of Man. "After this," John writes, "I saw a great White Throne, and Him that sat on it; and I saw the dead, the great and the small, standing before the Throne, . . . and the sea gave up the dead that were in it;* and Death and Hades gave up the dead which were in them"—that is, Death gave up its hold on the bodies, and Hades its hold on the souls of men. "And they were judged every one according to their works. And Death and Hades were cast into the Lake of Fire. This is death the second. And if any was not found written in the Book of Life, he was cast into the Lake of Fire." (20: 11-13.)† Thus is brought to pass the end of death; not in its extinction; not in the de- struction of its power, but the end of its reign here. While death was under the power of Satan, it reigned over all flesh. But in that dread Day of judgment it is to be severed from his control by the Son of Man; restrained for ever from acting on this regenerate earth; and shut up by Him in the Lake of Fire, there to hold in its grasp the lost and the condemned. This is death as it shall be; death in its new and eter- nal form; *Death the Second.*

Thus is to end the conflict and the victory of the Son of Man; not in annihilating the Anti- christ, the Devil, the dead, or death, or Hades (a breath of the Almighty might do that), but in putting down all rule and authority and pow- er that has lifted head or hand against heaven; and in ending for ever within the scope of this world both the will and power of transgression.

* The exact meaning of this word is to my mind by no means clear. Scott and Liddel give it: "A drawing up in battle order; a body so drawn up; then, a camp; a fortified place."

* Not only those who from time to time have found a grave in it, but more especially the bodies of that whole gen- eration which perished in the flood; and it may be the fallen angels who had led the daughters of Adam astray. (Comp. Jude 5: 6.)

† This is the final resurrection and final judgment. These are the dead who have lived and died in all ages since the fall of Adam, the millions who have not shared in the first resurrection and have not been with the Lord in glory during the Parousia and the millennial age.

CHRISTIAN HERALD AND SIGNS OF OUR TIMES.
OFFICE, 63 BIBLE HOUSE, NEW YORK.
ENTERED AT THE POST-OFFICE AT NEW YORK, N. Y., AS SECOND-CLASS MATTER.

EVERY NUMBER CONTAINS:

The Portrait and Biography of some eminent person.
The Sermon Dr. Talmage preached the last Sunday morning.
An Exposition of Unfulfilled Prophecy.
A Summary of the Events of the Week, Notes of Religious and Temperance Movements, etc.
A Sermon by Rev. C. H. Spurgeon, of London, from advance sheets sent by special arrangement.
Pictures of Missionary Life, etc., and Descriptive Articles.
An instalment of a Serial Story.
An Exposition of the International Sunday-School Lesson, by Mrs. M. Baxter.

ANNUAL SUBSCRIPTION, $1.50.

New subscriptions may commence at any time. When subscribers do not indicate their wish, they commence with the first number of the month in which the subscription is received.

Remittances by Mail should be by Post-office money order, bank cheques, or drafts or express money order, whenever possible, and should always be made payable to THE CHRISTIAN HERALD. Letters containing money sent in this way need not be registered, as when lost, duplicates can always be obtained.

If a Postal Note or currency is sent, it should always be in a registered letter. Letters can be registered at any office. Subscribers sending money of this kind, and not registering, do it at their own risk.

Change of Address. Name of Post Office and State, of both old and new address, should always be given in case of removal, as without the previous address it is impossible to find the name on our list.

PUBLISHER'S NOTICE.

The whole edition of The Christian Herald was mailed last week to subscribers during Tuesday, Aug. 21. The last delivery at the New York Post Office was made at 11.40 P. M.

CURRENT EVENTS.

The Rejection of the Fisheries Treaty with Great Britain and Canada was carried in the Senate on August 21, by the strict party vote of 30 to 27. It has been evident throughout the long debate that the Senators were determined, for political reasons, that the treaty should not be ratified. That the treaty was defective, was generally admitted, even by Democrats, but had it been perfect it would have had no chance of ratification by the Republican Senate. That fact was proven by the reception given to an amendment moved by Senator Gibson, of Louisiana, who, foreseeing the rejection of the treaty, proposed that it be referred to a committee who should point out its defects and suggest such improvements as would render it acceptable to the Senate. This proposal was also rejected by a strict party vote. The Senate, evidently, did not wish the question settled, at any rate by a Democratic administration. The treaty was therefore rejected, and the subject must remain in abeyance until after the Presidential election. There is a possibility that then, when political capital cannot be made out of it, another effort will be made to arrive at an amicable settlement with Canada of the question.

The Project of Retaliation upon Canada was revived in a message sent by President Cleveland to Congress on Thursday last. The rejection of the treaty leaves the fishery question in an anomalous condition, and disputes are likely to arise in which the claims of American fishermen will be disregarded by the Canadian authorities. The President, therefore, asked Congress to grant him power to suspend certain laws which operate in favor of Canada. He appears to think that it may not be necessary to use such power, but the fact of his having it might exercise a deterrent influence on Canada. The Canadian authorities would be less likely to take severe measures with American fishermen if they knew that their doing so would provoke the President to exercise the power granted to him. The laws which the President wishes to have the power to suspend, are those permitting the transportation of goods through the United States to and from Canada without the payment of duties. When the St. Lawrence River is closed in winter it is a convenience to Canada to have goods from Europe landed at United States ports and sent by rail to Canada, and to have her exports sent in the same way. During the past six years goods worth $270,000,000 have been so sent without the payment of duty. This right or privilege the President now asks Congress to give him the power to withhold. It was doubtless suggested by the fact that a prominent subject of dispute in the negotiation of the treaty was the desire American fishermen expressed to send their catch home by Canadian railroads. Another form of retaliation is connected with canal traffic. At present the boats of both countries pay the same tolls, but the President states that Canadian boats, though paying the same tolls as United States boats, are repaid a portion of the tolls paid. He now proposes to exercise similar discrimination on American canals in favor of American vessels. This mode of dealing with the question may be good politics, but it is undignified, and unworthy of two great Christian nations.

The Cyclonic Storm which Traversed the United States from New Orleans to New York, on Tuesday, August 21, was of extraordinary violence, and caused serious loss of life and property. Its centre travelled from New Orleans to Louisville, Ky., at the rate of twenty-three miles an hour; but from that point its speed increased to fifty-two miles an hour. As it passed over Maryland it cut a clean path fifty feet wide, for several miles, tearing up and destroying buildings, trees, and shipping. In the village of Still Pond, it overthrew a factory, *killing eleven persons* and injuring six others severely. At Wilmington, Del., one man was killed, and about a score seriously injured. At Pittsburg, Penn., bridges were swept away and four persons drowned. In New York, the furious downpour of rain by which it was accompanied, caused barrels of lime to slack in unfinished buildings, and led to four disastrous fires. Many buildings were injured and much property was washed away.

The Yellow Fever Epidemic at Jacksonville, Fla., developed with alarming rapidity last week. The first notable rise in the daily bulletins occurred on Wednesday, when nine new cases were reported, and this was followed by Thursday's report of sixteen new cases, and two deaths. It is believed that the sudden rise in the rate is in part due to the greater promptitude of the physicians in reporting cases, but the disease is unquestionably spreading. This fact is now clearly recognized by the authorities, and greater care in enforcing isolation and quarantine is being taken. The physicians, also, are becoming more systematic in their management of the sick and convalescent. The general cleaning up of the city is still going on. Lime is again to be sprinkled everywhere. The whitewash gang is giving every tree trunk, post, hydrant, curbing, and sidewalk edge another thick coat of lime, to which some of the chloride of mercury will be added. Congress has appropriated $200,000 to aid State or municipal Boards of Health in establishing efficient quarantine and sanitary precautions.

Another Fatal Marine Disaster Occurred on August 22 off the San Francisco coast. The steamer *City of Chester* set out from San Francisco at half-past nine o'clock in the morning, bound for Eureka, on the northern coast of California. When near Fort Point she ran into a fog and began sounding her fog-horn. In a few moments it was answered by another fog-horn, and the *City of Chester* signalled to the approaching vessel to pass on the left side. Her signal must have been misunderstood, for in less than a minute the huge prow of the other steamer crashed into her side, cutting her almost in half. The colliding vessel proved to be the *Oceanic*, from Hong Kong. Some of the *City of Chester's* passengers and crew climbed upon the *Oceanic* before she backed out of the chasm her prow had made, and were saved. Others ran to the boats and cut them adrift, and others, again, seized life-preservers and jumped over into the sea. The *Oceanic* also promptly lowered her boats to rescue the floating human beings. All were saved who managed to keep afloat, but some were below the decks of the *City of Chester*, and had not time to get out. The vessel sank in five minutes, and at least thirteen persons sank with her. This catastrophe, like that of the *Thingvalla*, emphasizes the need for a better system of signalling in a fog.

The Earthquakes and Volcanic Eruptions in Japan are more fully described in the mails received last week than in the previous telegraphic reports. It appears that on July 15, about 8 o'clock in the morning, there was a terrific volcanic eruption on Mount Bandai, in the province of Inawashiro, one of the northern and hilly provinces. Over five hundred people were buried alive and over one thousand wounded. This eruption was preceded by three severe shocks of earthquake. The third shock had scarcely passed, when Mount Bandai was seen to have lost its head, and an immense black cloud hung over the mountain and the sky. In another second the cloud was broken up into fragments and began to fall in minute lava and ashes, soon covering the ground six inches deep. At the same moment two streams of boiling mud, presumably burned stones and rocks, were thrown up from the fiery peak, which filled up valleys in the vicinity, and newly formed many a hill over them. The area of ground thus covered with the boiling mud is now roughly estimated at fifteen miles square, burying everything underneath, including nearly every living thing. The estimate of deaths at five hundred is a mere guess on the part of the authorities.

The African Slave Trade, to which the Attention of Europe is being called by M. Lavigerie, appears to be largely the result of ignorance as well as of cupidity. M. de Brazza, the explorer, stated, in an interview published in the New York *Herald*, that he once bought forty slaves, and kept them for some months under the care of kind overseers. Then he set them at liberty, and supplied them with huts and tools in the hope that they would settle down to agriculture, but they ran away, returned to their old homes, and were re-enslaved. Subsequently he bought *three hundred men for ten cents each*, and conducted them to the coast, where they worked for two years. There they saw that a ball of rubber, which cost practically nothing in their woods, would sell for more than a slave cost. When they returned to their tribe, they told what they had seen, and the tribe, instead of selling their able-bodied men as slaves, set them to work carrying rubber to the coast. Slave dealing, M. de Brazza states, has wholly disappeared among that tribe. He argues that education and enlightenment would do more to annihilate the slave trade than soldiers. The tribes themselves connived at the traffic, or it could not be carried on.

General Boulanger has Gained a Political triumph in the French elections. He was last week at the head of the poll in three separate districts. He was triumphantly elected by the Department of the Somme, and in the Departments of the Nord and the Charente Inférieure he received more votes than any of his rivals, though not the majority of all the votes cast, which under the French constitution is required for election. His aggregate majority in the three Departments was 101,894, in a total vote of 678,700. The fact that in spite of his failure as a legislator, and in spite of the ridiculous figure he made in his recent duel, he should receive so large a support at the polls, receives a significant explanation in Parisian journals. It is stated that Legitimists, Royalists, and Bonapartists have combined to support him under the belief that he is an enemy to the Republic, and that in his popularity and ambition are the surest means of overthrowing it. It is confidently believed that a popular vote, like Louis Napoleon's plebiscites, would make Boulanger the ruler of France.

The Right Rev. Samuel S. Harris, Bishop of the Protestant Episcopal Diocese of Michigan, died in London on August 21. As mentioned in our last week's edition, he was stricken with paralysis at a service in Winchester Cathedral. The Bishop was only forty-seven years of age, having been born in Alabama in 1841. His early manhood was spent in the study of the law, but he practiced for only a few months before the war broke out. He enlisted in an Alabama regiment, and before the close of the war he had risen to the rank of colonel. He opened an office in New York in 1866, but soon afterward quitted the profession to study theology. He was ordained in 1869, and was elected Bishop of Quincey, Ill., in 1878. At the urgent request of his church in Chicago, he declined the office, but the following year he was again elected, this time by the Diocese of Michigan, and that call he felt it his duty to accept.

A Letter from the Rev. C. H. Spurgeon was received last week by Dr. William Stewart, of Winchester, Ky., in acknowledgment of the resolutions of sympathy and confidence recently adopted by the General Association at Eminence, Ky. In the course of his letter Mr. Spurgeon says: "I must beg you to thank all the kind friends who have thought upon me in the day of trouble, and have so generously sympathized with me. The letter was a note of good cheer, and the resolution stirs my soul as a clarion blast arouses a warrior. I feel that I must live a noble life to deserve such Christian love. I am none the less a Baptist because I leave the Baptist Union, but I think I am all the more a Baptist of the old style. I am, at least, one with you all. I feel that I am spiritually a member of an International Baptist Union, a part of which is in Kentucky. God bless that portion of a great whole! Of personal affliction I have lately had a varied store, but none too much. My beloved wife, though a great invalid, is spared to me, and the joy of having her alive is a very great mitigation of the pain of having her ill. The Lord has so enriched me by pain and sorrow that I cannot wish to be spared a measure of it. It has brought me nothing but good. It has brought me the precious spices of your brotherly sympathy, and in its sweet odor I am very happy this day. The Lord reward you all for this great deed of kindness. Peace be to your churches. Success to your ministers. Bliss to all your hearts."

A Snake at a Camp Meeting Caused Some excitement at Asbury Park, N. J., on August 19. About noon on that day the gospel tent was crowded with colored people, and a prayer was being offered by an earnest preacher, when a piercing shriek rang through the meeting, and a woman, jumping on a chair, pointed to the straw in the aisle. All eyes were directed to the spot, but nothing could be seen that could account for the woman's terror. She declared, however, that she had seen a big black snake crawling toward the platform. Search was made for it, but without success. The service was resumed, but in a few minutes there was a chorus of screams from the front. A huge snake emerged from the straw close to the platform. The women ran, but one of the preachers jumping off the platform, set his foot vigorously on the snake's head, while others trampled its body flat. It would be well if Satan, of whom the serpent is a type, always met with so vigorous a resistance when he comes, as he often does, into religious assemblies. Unhappily his motions are generally too subtle for recognition, and he succeeds in distracting thought, encouraging procrastination and deadening the soul to divine influence. (II Cor. 11: 3.)

A Dismayed Bridegroom Fled from Virginia City, Nev., to California recently. A newspaper of that city states that some time ago a clerk twenty-three years of age, in a grocery house, entered into correspondence with a Chicago lady whom he heard of through a matrimonial agency. She represented that she was owner of considerable real estate, and was of amiable disposition. Her photograph which she sent to him was of a woman about thirty, with blond hair and handsome features. It was the last she had had taken, she said, but did not say how long a time had elapsed since she sat for it. The clerk having ascertained that the real estate was genuine, promptly proposed marriage, and when the lady accepted him, he was highly elated, and was congratulated on his good fortune, by his friends. The marriage was to take place at Virginia City, two weeks ago. On the day before that fixed for the ceremony, the bridegroom went to meet his bride at the depot. To his amazement he met a lady fully sixty years of age, whose hair was snowy white and whose features were wrinkled with age. Concealing his disappointment as well as he could, he conducted her to the rooms engaged for her in the hotel, and then excusing himself for a brief absence on business, he hurried to the depot, and took the first train for California. The lady, on hearing of his departure, rightly concluded that he did not intend to return, and took her departure for Chicago. She must have been prepared for the clerk's disappointment at her appearance, but may have supposed that he would overlook that for the sake of her property. It is well for the Church, which is Christ's bride, that she need have no such apprehension, though she is both poor and disfigured by sins and shortcomings. When she meets the Bridegroom she will be transformed, and be perfect in beauty. (Eph. 5:27.)

Detailed Preparations for a Funeral were made fifteen years ago by a citizen of Mobile, Ala., who died August 15. The deceased was a man of singular habits. Fifteen years ago he purchased a red cedar log, which he had taken to a saw-mill and sawed into plank; then he went to the shop of a cabinetmaker, had his measure taken, and gave directions for the manufacture of a coffin of the red cedar planks. The casket when finished was regarded as a fine piece of workmanship. The owner then had it taken to an undertaker's place, where it was trimmed according to his taste. The coffin was then taken to his bedroom, and has ever since occupied a place against the wall at the head of his bead. After his death on Wednesday, it was taken down, and on being examined was found to contain a complete suit of clothing and underwear, to be used in laying out his body. He was buried in this coffin on August 16. The Mobile journal which records these facts, does not say whether the deceased was a Christian man. The natural inference, from the fact that he had contemplated his death, and had made preparation for it, would be that he did not neglect the most important preparation of all—that of securing through Christ a place in heaven. Unhappily the inference is not always a safe one. Too often men make every preparation for death but that. (Prov. 19:20.)

Six Days of Lonely Suffering on a Mountain were endured by a traveller in Colorado recently. He started out from Breckenridge, Col., on August 10, to cross the Silver Plume by the Argentine Pass. He reached the top of the range at about dark. He missed the road at a very dangerous place, and followed an abandoned trail. Missing his footing on a broken bridge, he was precipitated to the bottom of the gulley, a distance of twenty-five feet. The poor fellow broke one arm and both legs in his fall. In this condition the unfortunate traveller remained on the mountain for a period of six days and six nights, suffering untold torture, with no food or drink. He cried for help, but no succor came until the sixth day, when a traveller happened to cross the range and found the helpless man yet conscious. After giving the sufferer a drink of water, the rescuer at once went for assistance, a distance of fifteen miles, and upon his return he found the suffering man still alive. He was carried to a carriage and placed upon a comfortable cushion, and taken back to Breckenridge, but before reaching that place he died. Such work as that rescuer did for the helpless traveller needs to be done for many, quite as helpless, who have fallen upon the mountains of sin. The Christian worker who seeks such, has more hope to encourage him because none ever perish who are led by him to Christ. (Matt. 28: 18–20.)

Twenty-five Dollars were Paid for a Pen-knife on August 12 under peculiar circumstances. A lady residing at Ashland, Ky., was notified by the postmaster that a registered letter was awaiting her at the post-office. On opening it she was surprised to find enclosed twenty-five dollars, and a note explaining the remittance. The writer said: "You will doubtless be surprised in receiving the contents of this letter. When your father lived in Clarksburg, O., and sold goods, I was a boy. I took a pen-knife from his store and never paid for it. I feel it my duty to compensate some one of the family for it. I have learned that you are his youngest child. Hence send you $25." It is now over fifty years since the lady's father was in business at Clarksburg, so it would appear that the thief's conscience has operated after half a century. He has now gone beyond the Levitical law, which required that in making restitution to the person wronged, or his kinsman, a fifth of the value should be added to the principal. (Num 5:7.) It may be hoped that the repentant thief has also remembered that his sin was a sin against God, for which even restitution to man will not atone, but which can be blotted out through faith in Christ. (Zech. 13: 1.)

BRIEF NOTES.

The King of Sweden entertained the delegates to the Conference of Young Men's Christian Associations at luncheon on August 20.

An aged Christian Burmese lady, who was baptized by Dr. Adoniram Judson, has given three thousand rupees (about $1,500) to the Judson Memorial Church building fund.

The priests of the Roman Catholic Church of the Holy Family in Chicago have notified parents that any child attending the public schools of the city will not be prepared for first communion.

It is believed that fully five hundred persons were converted at the Sing Sing Camp Meeting, which closed on August 19. Rev. Thomas Harrison and other preachers addressed audiences of eight thousand persons.

Rev. A. B. Simpson announces that the annual convention of the Gospel Tabernacle Church in New York will be held October 1 to 8. As the Tabernacle has been sold recently, the place of meeting has not been fixed.

An effort to build a Free Will Baptist Church is being made by our friends of Concord, Ky. They need a little outside help, and their cause is strongly endorsed by well-known men. Contributions may be sent to Mr. W. H. Cox, Concord, Ky.

The corporation of Holy Trinity Church, New York, has appealed to the United States Supreme Court against the decision of Judge Wallace, condemning it to a fine for importing a rector (Rev. E. Walpole Warren) from England, in violation of the contract labor law.

At the late meeting of the Moody Bible Society, in Northfield, Mass., ninety persons pledged themselves to foreign mission work, twenty of them having formed a band for missionary work since the school opened. Several expect to begin work in the foreign field this year.

The centennial of the Friends' Meeting House at Plainfield, N. J., was celebrated on August 20. The Society was organized in 1721, but the meeting-house was not built until 1788. Among the members who attended the celebration on Sunday was Miss Catherine R. Laing, who is ninety-two years old.

The anarchist, Johann Most, in his examination before the Congressional Immigration Committee made the statement that the laws of this country were as stringent against socialism as those of any other land, and that in these days there was no difference between monarchies and republics. If European journals will publish his statement, perhaps, some of his brethren contemplating emigration will stay in Europe.

Dr. George T. Dowling, pastor of the Euclid Avenue Baptist Church, Columbus, O., has resigned his pastorate. As mentioned in a recent number of this journal he invited all in the congregation who loved the Lord Jesus Christ to join with the church in celebrating the Lord's Supper. The comments upon this action by his brethren have led him to retire from the denomination. After a season of rest he will recommence preaching, probably among the Congregationalists.

Evangelists or Christian Workers Desiring copies of THE CHRISTIAN HERALD for distribution at camp meetings or other religious gatherings, will receive parcels of back numbers free of charge by writing, stating number required, to the manager, 63 Bible House, New York.

THE RULE OF THE RACE.

A New Sermon by Pastor C. H. Spurgeon.

"Let us run with patience the race that is set before us, looking unto Jesus the author and finisher of our faith; who for the joy that was set before Him endured the cross, despising the shame, and is set down at the right hand of the throne of God." Heb. 12 : 1, 2.

The Foot-Race in the Olympic Games—The Celestial Spectators—The Weights to be Laid Aside—A Competition Between Ploughmen—All Eyes to be on Jesus—I. As the Author of Faith—On What He has Wrought—II. As the Finisher of Faith—As a Rewarder of the Victors—What to Look Away From—III. As the Pattern of Faith—In Motive—In Endurance—A Man Stung to Death by Wasps—IV. As the Goal of Faith—Getting Nearer to Him.

THE apostle saith, "Let us run." He has in his mind's eye the Olympic games, where all the different tribes of Greece were gathered together in general assembly to display the prowess of the race. Among the athletic exercises were foot-races. The apostle makes this foot-race an illustration of the Christian life. We must run with patience along the appointed course if we would win the prize of our high calling.

Before we start, with a wave of the hand the apostle directs us to

The Spectators

who throng the sides of the course. There were always such at those races: each city and state yielded its contingent, and the assembled throng watched, with eager eye the efforts of those who strove for the mastery. Those who look down upon us from yonder heavens are described as "so great a cloud of witnesses." These compass us about. Thousands upon thousands who have run this race before us, and have attained their crowns, behold us from their heavenly seats, and mark how we behave ourselves. This race is worth running, for the eyes of "the nations of them which are saved" are fixed upon us. This is no hole-and-corner business, this running for the great prize. Angels and principalities and powers, and hosts redeemed by blood, have mustered to behold the glorious spectacle of men agonizing for holiness, and putting forth their utmost strength to copy the Lord Jesus. Ye that are men, now run for it!

Our apostle, anxious that we should so run that we may obtain, points to certain

Burdens and Impediments

which he foresees will hinder us, and he says, "Let us lay aside every weight." Note how he includes himself, so that his warning may not sound like upbraiding. We cannot win if we are weighted; the pace will have to be very swift, and we cannot get to it, or keep it up, if we have weights to carry. Unloaded, we shall find the race taxing all our powers; but weighted, we shall be doomed to failure. Oh, to lay aside all carking care, fretfulness, ambition, anger, greed, and selfish desire! These were never worth the labor they have cost us; but now that we have become running-men, we *must* have done with them.

Still attentively considering us, the apostle notes that even when the weights are laid aside, there is a garment about us which will assuredly twist about our feet, and throw us down.

Sin, as Well as Care,

must be laid aside. It doth easily beset us, and therefore we must be more careful to be rid of it. Our original sin, our natural tendencies, our constitutional infirmities—these must be laid aside as garments unsuitable for men who are running the heavenly race. We cannot win heaven and wear sin. Heaven is for the holy: "there shall in no wise enter into it anything that defileth." Darling sins must go first; these as they are most loved, will have the most power to hinder. Every kind of sin must be watched against, and struggled against, and mastered. "Sin shall not have dominion over you." We hope to see all our tendencies to sin killed and buried—buried so deep that not even a bone of a sin shall be left above ground. This will be heaven to us.

Do I not hear you say, "May God help us"? This must be a tough race which requires such stripping as this. If every weight of care must be laid aside, and every rag of sin, who is sufficient for these things? We are compelled even before we take a step in the running, to bow the knee, and cry unto the strong for strength. We dare not retreat from the contest; but how can we begin a struggle for which

We are so Unfitted?

Who will help us? To whom shall we look? Does not all this very admirably introduce the verse which is specially my text—"Looking unto Jesus, the author and finisher of our faith"?

But the apostle has not quite done with us, for he warns us to remember the rules of the course in these words, "Let us run with patience the race that is set before us." You are not to run anyhow, or anywhere: you must keep the appointed course, or you might as well stand still. The way of God's command, the way of obedience, the way of humble trustfulness, the spiritual way, the way of the life given from above—this, and no other way will do, for this is the race set before you! Do you shrink? Does the way seem too mysterious, too contrary to the flesh, too trying? All this adds to the force of the precept—"Looking unto Jesus." Because the way itself and the rules of the running are such as your nature will fight against, therefore look the more earnestly to the great Captain of your salvation.

In a race a great point is the way in which a man keeps his eyes. I have read of

A Competition Between Ploughmen

who were set to plough for a prize. The most of them made very crooked work of it. After they had ended, one of the judges said, "Young man, where did you look while you were ploughing?" "I kept my eyes well on the plough handles, sir, and saw what I had to hold." "Yes," the judge said, "and your plough went in and out, and the furrow is all crooks." He asked the next ploughman, "And where did you look?" "Well, sir," he answered, "I looked at my furrow; I kept my eye always on the furrow that I was making. I thought that I should make it straight that way." "But you did not," answered the judge; "you were all over the place." To the next he said, "What did you look at?" "Well, sir," he said, "I looked between the two horses to a tree that stood in the hedge at the other end of the field, right in front of me." Now that man went straight, because he had a fixed mark to guide him. This helps us to appreciate the wisdon of the text, "Looking unto Jesus." Run: run straight: you cannot run straight except you keep your eye on one who is always the same.

I. First, then, we are to look to Jesus as

The Author of Faith.

The beginning of faith is "Looking unto Jesus." Let us consider this. We have to look to Jesus, first, by trusting in that which He has wrought for us. It is described in these words—"Who for the joy that was set before Him endured the cross, despising the shame." Jesus has endured the suffering and shame which were due to us. O soul, thou canst never start on the road to heaven unless thou dost look to Him who "endured the cross" on thy behalf! Thy sin will make thee to endure the wrath of God forever, unless thou dost look to Him who bore our sins in His own body on the tree. Thou must get a faith's view of the Lamb of God, which taketh away the sin of the world, or else thou hast not even begun the heavenward race.

Dost thou look upon thine own righteousness with pleasure? This is an ill start for thee, thy back is on the prize. "As many as are of the works of the law are under the curse." Dost thou look to thy frames and feelings? Thou wilt make a bad start with these, for they will guide thee into a fog, in which thou wilt lose the track. Look thou to Jesus, the suffering Saviour. He by His bearing the cross, has removed thy heaviest weights, and by His death has destroyed thine entangling sin. He can renew thy nature by His resurrection power, and save thee from the dominion of sin by His glorious reign. If thou lookest alone to Him, thou startest well; but not else.

But then, dear friends, we also begin looking unto Jesus, because of what He has wrought in us. I would remind you who are a good way on in the course of those first eager paces with which you started heavenward. Did you not begin with looking unto Jesus? As you have received Christ Jesus the Lord, so continue in Him. The Lord Jesus first called us out of darkness into His marvellous light. Did He not give us pardon at our setting out? It was by looking to Him that the great load of sin fell from off our conscience. With pardon of sin came a great loathing of sin; washed in the precious blood, we could not wantonly repeat the stains. Our earliest repentance and its fruits came from "looking unto Jesus."

Have I any here this morning who are about to start for heaven? Mind that you start aright. I pray you, do not fall into any delusion. Do not imagine that your life will avail you anything, however good and moral it may have been, unless you begin by looking unto Jesus. Mr. Bunyan, in his "Pilgrim's Progress," frequently speaks of those who tumbled over the wall, or came in by other irregular ways; but they all missed the end. As they came in without Christ, so they went out without hope. One who came near to the celestial city, who had not come in at the gate, was made to know that there is a back way to hell, even from the gate of heaven. You must begin with looking unto Jesus, or you will end with a fearful looking for judgment. Doth not Jesus say, "I am the beginning"? Would you set up another beginning?

II. But now, secondly, we must look to Jesus as

The Finisher of Faith.

As Jesus is at the commencement of the course, starting the runners, so He is at the end of the course, the rewarder of those who endure to the end. Those who would win in the great race must keep their eyes upon Him all along the course, even till they reach the winning-post.

Jesus has sat down; He takes His rest because He has completed His work. Here on earth He was filled with shame, but yonder in glory He is full of honor, for He is set down "at the right hand of God." Here He was bound, and led captive; there He is King of kings and Lord of lords, for He sits at the right hand of the throne of God. Here on earth we see His manhood, born in a manger, living in poverty, dying the ignominious death of the cross; there we adore His divine glory, for He is "at the right hand of the throne of God." Think of your Saviour as your God, clothed with all power and authority. Surely this should urge you to quicken your pace, and never to become weary or faint. You began by looking to Him as a sufferer, persevere by looking to Him as a victor.

Looking unto Jesus, you will get many a direction; for, as He sits at the winning-post, His very presence indicates the way. If our eyes are up to Him, as the eyes of a servant to her mistress, we shall run well. "Be ye not as the horse, or as the mule, which have no understanding, whose mouth must be held in with bit and bridle"; but say with David, "Thou shalt guide me with thine eye."

A Look from the Eye

of Jesus is enough for a saint; and if you, my hearer, are indeed "looking unto Jesus," you will avoid crooks and turns, and will take the shortest road to holiness and eternal glory. Consider Him who endured such contradiction of sinners against Himself, and you will not grow weary, neither will you miss your way.

When the race is over, Jesus will appear as the finisher of faith by coming forward to crown you with His own right hand. Yes, His hand shall award the prize, and His lips shall say, "Well done, good and faithful servant." Jesus Himself will admit the faithful to the place which He has gone to prepare for them. Wherefore be of good courage and run! Jesus at the end of the race will enthrone us with Himself.

I invite you, taking the sense of the word "looking" which I have already hinted at, to rn over in your mind these things. Look ay from all self-denials, difficulties, labors, fferings, temptations, and persecutions; and qually look away from all pleasures, profits, nd preferments, and look to Jesus, who has on the race Himself, and now helps you in the ace, and holds out the crown at the end of it. oes Jesus lean forward as if He would crown e even now? Then I will quicken my pace to ome to Him. Does the Holy Spirit help my nfirmities? Then will I run in His strength.

III. Let us next consider our Lord Jesus as

The Pattern of Faith.

Run, as Jesus ran, and look to Him as you run, hat you may run like Him. How did our Lord ursue His course? You will see this if you rst note His motive: "Who for the joy that vas set before Him." Jesus had a motive in all hat He did. Men do not do much if they act from nere feeling, and have no underlying design. ndeed, a life without an object must be a frivolous, useless life. Jesus had before Him the reat joy of glorifying the Father in the salvation of His chosen. For this He lived, for this He died: it was a joy to Him to think of accomplishing this object. Beloved, if you want o run your race aright, it must be for the glory of God, and in the hope of the salvation of your fellow-men. These two things, blended into one, must be your joy. Oh that this motive ook possession of our entire being!

Wherein are we to imitate Jesus? First, we re to copy His endurance. He

"Endured the Cross."

Ours is a trifling cross compared with that which pressed Him down; but He endured it. He took it up willingly, and carried it patiently. He never rebelled against it, and never relinquished it. He bore the cross till the cross bore Him, and then He bore death upon it. He could say, "It is finished." Brethren, let us do the same. Are you persecuted, are you poor, are you sick?—take up the appointed cross. Do not try to escape trouble: the followers of the Crucified must be familiar with the cross.

Imitate your Lord in His magnanimity. He endured the cross, "despising the shame." Shame is a cruel thing to many hearts. Our Lord shows us how to treat it. See, He puts His shoulder under the cross, but He sets His foot upon the shame. He endures the one, but He despises the other. What! Shall His disciples make much of that which He despised? Are you such gentlemen, that none may come between the wind and your nobility? I wonder when I hear some people say, "I cannot stand being laughed at." Does laughter break bones? "But ridicule is very sharp!" Is it? Do the wounds bleed? "Well," cries one, "a keen sarcasm from a wit stings you!" Does it? Have you no cures for such bites? Some of us have been like Marcus Arethusa, who was

Stung to Death by Wasps;

and yet we are none the worse, but rather are we all the better, for there remains no place whereon a new sting can operate. Oh, that some of you, who are so tender, could have thicker skins in this respect! I heard of a prayer the other day which I did not quite like at first, but there is something in it after all. The good man said, "Lord, if our hearts are hard, make them soft; but if our hearts are too soft, make them hard." I know what he meant, and I think I can pray that last prayer for some of my friends who are so delicate that a sneer would kill them. Shut your ears and run, despising the shame.

Our Saviour is to be imitated in His perseverance. For the joy that was set before Him He endured the cross, despising the shame, and "is set down." He never stopped running till He could sit down at the right hand of the throne of God; and that is the only place where you may sit down. My brother, Satan puts before you a comfortable arm-chair, and he says: "Take thine ease." No, no; run till you can sit down at the right hand of the throne of God. There are many dainty little arbors all along the Hill Difficulty, with settles and tables; and men, if they get into them, are very apt to fall asleep, and lose their roll of comfortable assurance: therefore, pass these arbors by. The only running that will save is persevering running. From starting-point to winning-post there must be no pausing. We must practice daily obedience, daily holiness, daily service. An off-and-on religion is a false religion. We must keep to the running till God gives us rest.

IV. Lastly, our text sets before us Jesus as

The Goal of Faith.

We are to run "looking unto Jesus" as the end we should aim at. We go towards our Lord every step that we take. True faith neither goes away from Christ Jesus, nor takes a roundabout road to Jesus, nor so much as dreams of going beyond Jesus. We have wise men about us nowadays who are going a long way beyond the gospel. The old faith which inspired apostles, enabled the glorious army of martyrs to lay down their lives, and produced the noblest of human characters in past ages, is not good enough for the superfine sophists of these days. This boastful nineteenth century demands a new God, a new Christ, a new heaven, a new hell, a new gospel, and everything else new except a new heart. But we, brethren, are not going to run in that direction. We run toward Christ.

Let us run toward Jesus, that we may grow more like Him. It is one of the virtues of Jesus that He transforms into His own image those who look at Him. He photographs Himself upon all sensitive hearts. There are no looking-glasses that I know of which improve the looker's eye; but this mirror of God, as you look into it, enlightens your eyes and beautifies your character. As you see Christ you become Christians. Oh, beloved, our lives would not be so faulty, so wrinkled, so uncomely, if our eye were more completely taken up with beholding the transcendent charms of the Lovely One!

Run, that you may come

Nearer to Jesus.

Seek after more near and dear fellowship with Him. He is not far away from us. He is absent as to His corporeal frame, but He is with us in spirit. He comes very close to us at times, when He finds us fit for the joy. We can never forget the golden moments and the hallowed places wherein He has manifested Himself unto us as He doth not unto the world. There are hours when our head is on the bosom of Christ. There are times when we sit at His feet and hear His words, and, looking up, behold His beauty, and are ravished therewith. Run towards Him till you are nearer to Him in communion than up to now you have been. This is worth running for; but you will not have it without running.

Keep on looking and running till you are with Him. Oh, I talk to you now about being with Him, but how soon this may be realized in the most literal sense! During my ministry in this place it has occurred two or three times, that when the service has ended, dear friends have essayed to go to their homes, but they have died in this House of Prayer. What must it be to go from this congregation to the assembly above? We do not know how near to Jesus on the throne we may now be. The sea-fog is around our vessel. Could we see before us, the white cliffs of our native shore are almost within touch. Think not that we are far out at sea. Within the next week, perhaps, some of us will see the King in His beauty. We may spend next Sunday in heaven! Does anybody shrink from such a prospect? No; each heir of heaven says "Amen; so let it be."

Formerly when great ships went to the Indies, the passengers would for a while toast the friends they had left behind. But when they were in the Indian Ocean they begun to drink the health of friends ahead. Though comparatively young, I have many, many friends who are in the land beyond, to which I am making my way. I salute the glorified. Some of the dearest and best people that ever lived were members of this church, but they are now safely landed on the celestial shore. They are waiting and watching for us. We are coming, brethren! We will be with you soon. Best of all, our Lord is there. Once crowned with thorns, His head is now radiant with the diadem of universal dominion. He will come to welcome us on that blessed shore. Hasten, oh, time! Be like a seraph with six wings, and bear us swiftly to that golden strand where we shall see the face of Him we love, and shall be

"Far from this world of grief and sin,
With God eternally shut in."

GEMS FROM NEW BOOKS.

HARRISON THE REGICIDE.*

THERE was in the first half of the sixteenth century a Thomas Harrison, known as Harrison the Cromwellian. It is thought that he began life as a vender of beef in the open market, and he might have continued such indefinitely in his native England but for the quarrel between Charles I. and Parliament. Macaulay has made it unnecessary to speak at length of the points involved in that dispute. Briefly stated, the King claimed certain privileges by prerogative right. Parliament denied the claim, and protested against it in the name of the people of England. Theretofore there had been English kings and barons; then for the first time an English people was distinctly heard of. The dispute was waged through a long term of years. Parliaments came and went at the royal pleasure. At last one assembled to stay. In the meantime battles had been fought, and war grew into a normal condition of the country, finally involving Cromwell and his Roundhead battalions. With reputation born of hard fighting and much praying, not to speak of a skilful use of scriptural phrases, illustrative of sincere religious convictions, up, one of many, rose Thomas Harrison. Swapping his butcher's apron for a martial cloak, he at length appeared a lieutenant-general, beloved by the companies, and trusted by Cromwell. Nor were his talents of exclusive application to the field. One great day he was found in his seat, a member of the Parliament court in session for the trial of Charles I. There is an historical picture of the assemblage in ruffs and broad-brimmed, steeple-crowned hats, sitting solemn as ghosts, with the King over against them, face to face. A company of ghosts would have been doubtlessly of pleasanter aspect and sweeter effect to the monarch's troubled soul. Lieutenant-General Harrison was amongst them. Though now unrecognizable, we know he was there because of his signature; in a hand clear, legible, almost as bold as John Hancock's on an instrument of yet greater celebrity, may be read below the death-warrant which was the final resolution of the high court. Opposite it is his seal in red wax, on which, singularly enough, is stamped an eagle, winged like the bird on our silver dollar.

The staunchness of the man was subsequently tested. Upon the return of the Royalists to power, like other regicides, he might have fled to America, and found refuge in its impenetrable woods; that, however, was not his way. He remained at home, was seized, summarily convicted, and executed. Pepys was an eyewitness of the execution, and saw the heart of the Roundhead Lieutenant-General borne round as evidence that the son of the King had come to his own again.

Captain Harrison's Marriage.

When Fort Washington was established at Cincinnati William Henry Harrison was stationed there. Duty called the gallant captain to North Bend, and he became a guest at the Symmes residence. It was not long until he succumbed to the black eyes of Miss Anna. She was at that time twenty years of age, small, graceful, intelligent, and by general agreement beautiful. He was twenty-two years of age, with a reputation well established as a gallant soldier. The two were mutually pleased with each other,

* From the "Life of General Ben. Harrison," by Lew Wallace, author of "Ben Hur," dealing with the Record of the Republican Candidate as a Lawyer, Soldier, and Politician. 348 pages, with Portraits and Illustrations. Published by *Hubbard Brothers*, Philadelphia, Chicago, and Kansas City.

Count Von Waldersee, Successor of Von Moltke.

March of African Slaves Bearing Ivory to Tangiers.

and an engagement followed, which could hardly fail to be satisfactory to the father. The Judge, in fact, consented to the marriage; but hearing some slanderous reports of the captain, he afterwards withdrew his consent. The lovers were in nowise daunted. They resolved to proceed with their engagement. November 29, 1795, the day appointed for the wedding, arrived. Judge Symmes, thinking the affair off or declining to be present, rode to Cincinnati, leaving the coast clear.

In the presence of the young lady's stepmother and many guests the ceremony was performed by Dr. Stephen Wood, a Justice of the Peace. The company assembled to witness the marriage of Captain Harrison and Miss Anna Symmes would astonish polite circles of to-day. They arrived on horseback, each man carrying a rifle, a powder-horn, and a pouch lined with patching and bullets. Travelling through narrow paths cut through thickets of blackberry and alder bushes and undergrowth of every variety, every step taken might be into an ambush of Indians. They moved in the mood, and ready for instant combat. A wife, coming with her husband, rode behind him. When they dismounted at the door, as it was winter, ten to one he wore buckskin for coat and breeches, and a coonskin cap, while she was gay with plaided linsey-woolsey of her own weaving, cutting, and sewing; her head was protected from the wind by a cotton handkerchief. The wedding-cake was of New England doughnuts. Such was in all probability the general ensemble of the wedding.

The bride may have had an outfit of better material. So recently from the East, she may have had a veil, a silk frock, and French slippers. The bridegroom, of course, wore his captain's uniform, glittering with bullet buttons of burnished brass, and high boots becoming an aide in favor with his chief, the redoubtable Anthony Wayne, whom the Indians were accustomed to describe as "the warrior who never slept." Taken altogether, the wedding celebrated at Judge Symmes's house that November day, 1795, cannot be cited as a proof of aristocratic pretension on the part of the high contracting parties.

Some time afterward Judge Symmes met his son-in-law; the occasion was a dinner-party given by General Wilkinson to General Wayne.

"Well, sir," the Judge said, in a bad humor, "I understand you have married Anna."

"Yes, sir," Harrison answered.

"How do you expect to support her?"

"By my sword and my own right arm," was the reply.

The Judge was pleased, became reconciled, and in true romantic form happily concluded the affair by giving the couple his blessing.

COUNT VON WALDERSEE.

(See Portrait.)

A CABLEGRAM from Berlin, last week, announced the retirement of General Von Moltke from the office of Chief of the General Staff of the German Army, and the appointment of General Von Waldersee as his successor. The significance of this news is fully appreciated in France, where it is regarded as a triumph of the war party, with whom the new Emperor appears to have cast his lot.

Count Von Waldersee is fifty-six years of age, having been born at Potsdam in 1832. He entered the army as second lieutenant in the artillery at the age of eighteen. He served with distinction in the Schleswig-Holstein campaigns, the Austro-German war, and commanded the Hanoverian Uhlans in the war with France. He became a brigadier-general in 1875, and in 1882 was made Quartermaster-General.

The promotion of Count Von Waldersee to the post of chief director of the most powerful military machine in the world has special interest for Americans, in the fact that his wife is a native of this country. She was born in 1838 in New York, where her father was a wholesale grocer. After his death she went with her mother and sisters on a visit to Europe, where she made the acquaintance of the Prince of Schleswig-Holstein, who, after the loss of his Duchies, took the Austrian title of Count Von Noer. He was very much her senior, but he fell in love with her and married her. Two months afterward he died, and his widow went to Vienna. There she met Count Von Waldersee, whom, in 1866, she married. One of her sisters is married to Baron Wachter, who is in the diplomatic service of the King of Wurtemberg.

THE AFRICAN SLAVE TRADE.

(See Illustration.)

A STARTLING narrative is given by M. Lavigerie, who was mainly instrumental in establishing the French Missionary Society known as the White Fathers. He is endeavoring to arouse public opinion throughout Europe to the horrors of the slave trade in Africa. He states that at the present time fully half a million human beings are yearly kidnapped in the interior, and are made to traverse the barren deserts to be sold as slaves at the coast. Nearly two-thirds of the number perish of fatigue and hardship on the way. The ivory hunters are, he states, the most inhuman of these kidnappers. They collect men, women, and children in the peaceful villages, load them with ivory, and, tying them together, as shown in the illustration, drive them, day by day, over their long journey. M. Lavigerie says, that in the last letter he had received from his missionaries, dated in March last, they stated that convoys of slaves were daily passing their station to Tangiers. M. Lavigerie believes that a small band of resolute Europeans could suppress this horrible traffic.

THE LETTER-CARRIER'S STORY.

(See Illustration on page 557.)

"WHAT a cruel, heartless creature," said an old bachelor, who was one of a group of men sitting chatting on the piazza of a hotel in the Adirondacks one summer afternoon. They had just been discussing a recent scandal about a wife who had deserted her home and children, leaving a babe dangerously sick. "I tell you," he continued, "women have no hearts! They have not the nobility necessary to sacrifice their ease and comfort for the sake of any one else."

"What do you say to that, father?" said another of the group, addressing a venerable man, not far short of eighty years of age.

"Say?" replied the veteran; "why, I say I don't believe it; and what's more, I know it ain't so.

There was a general laugh at the old man's vigorous speech, and his son, who joined in it, said, by way of apology, "Father is a great believer in the fair sex. He thinks women are better than men on the whole."

"Why, of course I do, and they are, I know. Now see here, sir," turning to the bachelor, "you said women would not sacrifice themselves for others. Now I'll tell you of a thing that occurred in my own experience that proves you wrong. You must know that when I was in the old country I was a letter-carrier, what they call a postman there. Well, I knew most everybody on my route, and among them was a family named Spencer. They lived in a fine house, with a large garden around it. The mother was dead, but there were three young ladies, fine, tall, lovely girls, who kept house for their father. I used to take particular notice of the letters I took to them, because I expected such handsome girls would be having love-letters, sure."

"Didn't read them, I hope?" queried the bachelor.

"Not I, sir; I've always been an honorable man all through. What I mean by particular notice is that I reckon myself a judge of handwriting, and when I see the kind of address on a letter I can pretty well guess the kind of man that wrote it. Well, there used to come letters for Miss Mabel, the youngest of the three, addressed in a bold, dashing hand, that I made up my mind were love-letters. I formed my opinion of the man who wrote them, and I was not altogether satisfied. The flourishes about the name, and the general character of the writing, made me think he was kind of vain and weak-minded."

"You ought to have stopped the correspondence if you did not approve of him," said the bachelor.

"Don't you be in a hurry, young man," said the ex-letter-carrier: "I'm coming to the point that concerns *you*, right away. Well, the letters stopped coming, and I looked around; for, I said to myself, he's come to see her; and I was right. I saw him one day, and I looked him over. He was pretty much what I had thought, conceited and priggish-like, I considered. Well, to make a long story short, he used her badly. The story leaked out, and went all around the village. I felt so mad at him myself that, though he was a good thirty years younger than I, he would have felt the weight of my fist if I could have had the chance. He was a young surgeon, we heard, and a regular bad, fast man he turned out; though he'd managed to keep that a secret from Miss Mabel. It seems he thought foreign air would suit him; and just then the war between the French and Germans broke out, so he volunteered to go with the hospital service. We heard all about it afterward. He wrote just one letter, to bid Miss Mabel good-bye, and it seems she answered it.

The Letter-Carrier's Momentous Missive.

"After that there were no letters for two or three months, but one morning we got a letter from the seat of war. The postmaster showed it me. It was addressed to him, and inside was a letter directed to 'Mabel, writer of a letter to Surgeon Fielding.' 'That's for Miss Mabel Spencer, sure,' says I; and he said, 'I think so, too; take it and see.' I did, and saw her in the garden before ever I got up to the house; and she came running to meet me, for she must have seen in my face as I had a letter. I was afraid of giving her a shock, and so I just pulled out the letter and pretended I wasn't quite sure about it. While I was squinting at it through my spectacles, she came close up and looked over my shoulder. 'That's for me; it's all right,' she said, and took it out of my hand.

"Well, sir, that letter was from another surgeon at the wars, and it was to tell her that her lover had been hurt, and needed some one to take him away and nurse him. Miss Mabel's letter had been found in his pockets, and that was how they came to write to her. Now, what did that girl do? Why, she talked her old father into letting her go right into that hurly-burly and nurse that fellow who had used her so badly. She forgot all his wickedness, and she went, and she saved his life, after everybody thought he'd die. There ain't many men would have left their home and gone out to tend a man as had served them a scurvy trick. But she did, and she not only saved his life, but she saved his soul. When she brought him back, looking more like a ghost than a living man, all his wickedness was gone out of him. They are married now, and he has quit all his bad ways, and is a changed character. Saved, sir, by a woman's love and self-sacrifice!

"That's only one case. I could tell you of others, not so striking, but just as convincing. I don't deny there's some bad women, like her you've been talking of, but if you want real goodness, go to a genuine Christian woman, and if you get her love, she'll die for you if it's necessary."

THE EPOCHS OF A LIFE.

A NEW SERIAL STORY.

By Rev. L. S. Keyser.

(*Continued from page 542.*)

At Bay.

THE campaign on which Belle Havelock had entered did not languish under her management. She meditated upon it day and night, and concentrated all her woman's skill and ingenuity on the arrangement of plans for detaching young Madelling from Miss Winters and attaching him to herself. Among other manœuvres which her fertile brain devised, was one which proved successful in arousing an irritated feeling in Hadley's mind against Miss Winters. At one of the casual interviews, which none knew so well as Belle how to bring about, she rallied Duneman on his apathy as a lover, and asked him how it happened that he was so seldom Miss Winters' escort at the various social gatherings, while Mr. Madelling was so often at her side. "Why do you not ask her, for instance, to go with you to Professor Parker's lecture next Tuesday night? It is very improbable that Mr. Madelling has asked her."

"I will, I will," said Duneman enthusiastically. "It never occurred to me to forestall him in that way. Thank you, for suggesting it. How kind and thoughtful you are!"

Thus it happened that, when on Sunday evening Hadley asked permission to accompany Miss Winters to the lecture on Tuesday, he learned, to his mortification, that she was already provided with an escort. He was perfectly well aware of the customs of the college, which allowed a young lady to accept invitations of the kind, and, indeed, discouraged her from confining such favors to any one young man, unless he were her acknowledged lover; yet his egotism was hurt. He would have liked Miss Winters to refuse all such offers out of regard for him, though he had no claim upon her. Very foolishly and weakly he showed temper about it, and when on Tuesday he saw Miss Winters enter the hall with Duneman, he set her down as a flirt, and felt scarcely less bitter toward her than toward the man who had forestalled him. His irritation was increased still more by seeing his rival at church with her on Sunday evening. Duneman was evidently supplanting him, and Miss Winters, apparently, was content that he should do so. Though neither could be charged with any offence against politeness or the social customs of the college, Hadley was deeply mortified, and his indignation was stirred against them both, and still more against the religion both professed. He settled down to the preparation of his forthcoming speech in a fierce frame of mind, smarting under the sting of personal resentment. Thus Belle's stratagem was successful at all points, and the breach it had effected between Hadley and Miss Winters would probably be widened by the utterance of opinions, which consideration for her feelings might otherwise have restrained.

Saturday morning came at last, bringing a large assemblage of students and town people into Chapel Hall. As it was conceded that Hadley was the best speaker of the day, he was reserved for the last. All the other addresses were delivered, and then the name of H. C. Madelling was announced by Dr. Hartridge.

The young man made his way with firm, elastic steps to the platform, received with a courteous acknowledgment the clamorous ovation accorded him as an honored student of the college and a gifted speaker, and then, in clear, resonant tones, he announced his theme: "The False Ethics of the Hebrew Writings."

There was not a tremor in the tones of the speaker as he began his address. However much he may have hesitated beforehand to antagonize the current thinking of the college, now that he stood before his audience, looking into their expectant faces, and receiving their expressions of applause, all the misgivings which he had felt were dispelled, and his clarion tones rung with a clear, confident emphasis through the large hall.

As he uttered the first few words, which, though moderate in tone, were unmistakable in their bearing, he caught the eye of Belle Havelock, and the expression of confident expectation that played over her features acted as an exhilarant upon his mind, and lifted him, as it were, above himself. Turning to another part of the audience, he saw that Duneman's face was pale with anger and nervous dread, and this fact nerved Hadley to still bolder utterance. During his entire address, however, he avoided looking in the direction of Madeline Winters, who, as it happened, was seated at one side of the hall to his left and a little in his rear. Could he have seen her blanched, agitated face, his heart must have failed him, but as he did not see her, he was able to keep on resolutely in the course which he had mapped for himself.

Only a brief *résumé* of his address need be

given, and that only to throw light on the questions that trouble the sceptic and on the motives that actuate him to rabid speech. His oration showed a good deal of conceit, and considerable knowledge, though of a superficial character. He maintained that the moral sense is innate in man, being written in his consciousness, and that, therefore, morality exists apart from the Bible, and is independent of it. At this point he took occasion to deal several sharp blows at men who had the presumption to say that the Hebrew Scriptures were the sole custodians of ethical truth; perhaps he did not know that there is not a Christian scholar in the land who would make such a preposterous claim, for intelligent Christians candidly admit that there are many gleamings of moral truth in pagan literature, and that "God has not left Himself without a witness in any nation." But the young sceptic, having set up his man of straw, put forth as much effort to "floor" him as if he had been an actual antagonist, instead of a phantasm of his own imagination.

In the next place he undertook to show that the Bible is not a good moral teacher, because many of its most lauded characters were guilty of heinous offences, as if the mistakes of these men were not reprobated, either explicitly or tacitly, in the Bible. In this connection he fired a return shot at Duneman, who had pointed out the "moral laxity of unbelievers." Hadley maintained that believers were often as lax in their morals as unbelievers, and, in doing so, he painted the obliquities of some of the patriarchs in such bold, irreverent colors that there was an uneasy movement among the Faculty; and some of the students thought at one time that Dr. Hartridge was on the point of interrupting the speaker; but the Doctor settled down into his chair again, and Hadley was allowed to go on.

The doctrine of eternal rewards and punishments, especially the penalty that attaches to unbelief, was made the object of the most bitter invective. "As if a man could help what he believes!" Hadley exclaimed, scornfully. And yet the poor man inconsistently continued to ridicule Christians for their belief in the tenets of religion! Growing bolder as he proceeded, he contended that the doctrine of vicarious righteousness through Christ is immoral in its tendencies, affording an excuse for sin. "No man can go to heaven on borrowed capital," vibrated through the hall. "There is no way of entrance into the holy city, except by the gate of intrinsic moral worth." His argument struck at the very root of the atonement, and to reverent minds it sounded shockingly sacrilegious.

A look of pain came to the face of Dr. Hartridge as these statements were made. It was evident that he had not suspected the presence of so ultra a type of infidelity in the college, and dreaded the influence of Hadley's speech on the students.

It is unnecessary to give further details of Hadley's argument. The main facts have been revamped in various ways by opponents of the Bible from time immemorial, and have as often been answered by Christian apologists. So long had the young sceptic repressed his sentiments, and so frequently had he been goaded to anger by Duneman's insults, that it seemed all the pent-up bitterness of his nature had at last found a valve of escape, making him almost reckless in his utterances. One or two of his closing paragraphs will show the *animus* of his address:

"These statements are neither defiant nor aggressive, but are simply made in self-defence, and in defence of my colleagues in this venerable institution of learning. I should not have ventured to point out the immoralities of Biblical characters and believers in the Bible, had not an unprovoked assault been made a few weeks ago from this platform, reflecting on the personal honor of those who question certain current forms of belief. It is evident that the design of the speech was to cast odium on the advocates of freedom of thought in the college, and to destroy confidence in their honesty and moral character. The speaker luxuriated in the faults and foibles of those whom he was pleased to call 'representative infidels,' and no doubt he enjoyed the banquet that he had prepared for his delectation, as he seems to have vulture-like proclivities; but there were others who did not look upon his effusion with such fond favor."

Stretching himself up to his full height, and raising his voice to its fullest compass, while his face became flushed with excitement, Hadley said: "Leaving myself out of the category altogether, I will say that there are unbelievers in this college whose characters are above reproach, and I defy any calumniator to point to a single deed in their lives that would smirch the proudest name. Their whole course has been marked by manliness and honest endeavor. If their assailants were as free from dishonesty, it would be better for the cause of Christianity. Our opponent, in making an inventory of the immoralities of infidels, forgot to mention the crimes of those who venerate the Bible. I suppose," Hadley said, putting an ictus of withering sarcasm into his tones, "that the speaker's native modesty prevented him from making an allusion of so personal a character as would have been involved in retailing the vices of those like-minded with himself."

When the speaker had finished his peroration, in which there was more florid oratory than thought, he was greeted with a volley of applause from a large number of the students, although it was obvious that sentiment was divided as to the merits and wisdom of the address. Among those who were pained by Hadley's bold utterances was Dr. Hartridge, the President of the college. It had been his custom to dismiss the audience as soon as the last speech was delivered, but to-day he thought fit to depart from the usual order, and so he rose, and asked the indulgence of the audience for a few minutes. He meant no discourtesy, he said, to the speaker who had just addressed them, for all knew that he was one of the most gifted and respected students of the college; but still the President could not help but say that he was pained beyond measure to see so talented a young man expending his God-given powers in assailing the religion that had been a blessing to the world, and had built nearly all our institutions of learning, of which the Grand Central College was an example.

As to the partial apology that had been made for the moral offences of unbelievers by setting opposite them the sins of believers, the Doctor begged his young friends to remember that the latter were in direct conflict with the plain teachings of the Scripture, while the obliquities of infidels were, as a rule, in accord with the philosophies they advocated.

"I was sorry," the President went on, "to hear our young friend indulge in raillery against the doctrine of vicarious righteousness. Pray remember that the righteousness of God, which is given us in Christ, is a perfect righteousness, while our own is at best but fragmentary, because we are sinners against the divine law. The righteousness of Christ is *imparted* as well as *imputed* to us; it is *given*, not *loaned*, and is therefore our own intrinsic possession. In regard to the doctrine of eternal retribution, which seems so repugnant to the speaker, I have only this question to ask and then I am done: Can a man ever come nearer God if he is persistently going further from Him?"

The President was about to dismiss the audience, when there was a movement in the locality of the Senior class, and George Dane rose and requested the privilege of saying a word. As there were loud calls in every part of the hall for Dane to be heard, the Doctor thought it best to grant his request. Dane's voice quavered with excitement and his breath came almost in gasps as he began:

"Doctor, I am in favor of fair play. The speech to which we have just listened was made in self-defence, as my colleague has said. It was in answer to the tirade made against unbelievers three weeks ago. The young men in the college who are in favor of freedom of thought (and there are many such) had to be exonerated from those malicious misrepresentations. Now, sir, when the enemy of free-thought made his address, in spite of its unmanly calumnies, it was allowed to go unchallenged; but no sooner is my friend's oration delivered than it is publicly put into the crucible of analysis, and an attempt is made to refute its arguments and destroy their moral force. In the name of common fairness, I ask, Doctor, whether this is right?"

Loud applause greeted this speech, but the President stood calm and composed while it lasted, and when it had subsided, he explained: "The Grand Central College is, in the best sense of the term, a Christian institution, having been founded by Christian energy and endowed with the money of Christian people, and it would be an anomaly to allow such sentiments as those just uttered to stand for an hour unrepudiated, opposed as they are to the principles by which the college has been established."

It was an unheard of piece of effrontery for a student to "talk back" to the President, but George had gone too far and was too excited to retreat, and so he retorted, sarcastically: "Are we to understand that the Grand Central College is committed, now and forever, to the advocacy of certain pet dogmas, whether true or false?"

"Christianity having been proven true so often, both by experience and historical evidence, I should say that the college *is* committed to the advancement of truth," replied the Doctor, a little grimly.

"My friend's address this morning has proven that it is a debatable question whether Christianity is true or not, and men of broad intelligence will allow it an untrammeled discussion," returned George, in a great, patronizing way.

His conceit was a little amusing to the President, who replied, good-naturedly: "The self-confidence of some young men is unbounded."

"The dogmatism of some older men is—unfounded!" muttered George, speaking so low, however, that he could be heard only by those who sat near him; and then he took his seat with a flushed face.

"I can readily see," continued the President, "why our young friends should think that they have been unfairly treated, and I will say that some of the strictures made against unbelievers three weeks ago seemed to me a little ungenerous; but not knowing that there was any personal feeling at the root of the address, or that there was scepticism of so positive a type in the college, I thought it unnecessary to add an explanation. But it is a little different when religion itself is attacked. You touch a man in a sensitive and vital part of his being when you assail his religious principles, for they are as dear and sacred to him as his life. A speaker might pass criticism on many things without stirring your antagonism, but if he were to speak disrespectfully of your mother or your sister, how quickly you would leap to their defence! And that is the feeling that is aroused in a man when the religion he loves has suffered an attack."

"The President forgets that our principles are 'dear and sacred' to us, too," said Hadley to George, when the young men had reached their room.

As was to be expected, sentiment in the college was greatly divided as to the course pursued by the young free-thinkers, their friends maintaining that they had done the college a service by opening the eyes of the blind and credulous, while others were shocked at the temerity of mere neophytes in learning making so violent an assault on sacred institutions.

Thus the theological warfare raged, becoming hotter and fiercer, and expanding into wider proportions, as the time passed. Never had the college been in a greater ferment of excitement, even when fraternity politics, or class-rivalry were at their height. The President and Faculty did what they could to stem the tide of unbelief, but only partially succeeded.

(*To be Continued.*)

THE UNBELIEF OF THE PEOPLE.

By Mrs. M. Baxter.

S. S. Lesson for September 9, Num. 14: 1-10. Golden Text, Heb. 3: 19.

God's Promises and Past Deliverances Forgotten – A Common Failing – Difficulties not Fully Committed to God—The Night of Weeping—Propose to Return to Bondage – An Utterance of Faith—The Enemies of Faith—A Dread of Treading Alone a New Path—The People menaced with Destruction—Successful Intercession of Moses—National Sins Punished in Time—Perversity Produced by Remorse.

"THEY could not enter in because of unbelief." (Heb. 3: 19.) Such is the apostle Paul's declaration regarding the children of Israel at the time of the spies. The whole multitude leant to the testimony of man, and set aside the promises of God and the testimony of the faithful two who stood true to Him! Would that this were an uncommon thing! But oh how few there are who *endure* as seeing Him who is invisible! The whole of Psalm 78 is devoted to God's complaint of His people's unbelief. "They believed not God, and trusted not in His salvation. . . believed not for all His wondrous works . . . their heart was not right with Him, neither were they steadfast in His covenant . . . They turned back, and tempted God, and limited the Holy One of Israel." (Ps. 78: 22, 32, 37, 41.) But how many of us do the same thing! How many there are who put a burden or perplexity into the hands of God, and then, instead of being filled with calm confidence, go over the difficulties again and again, as though they expected God to do nothing!

Talking over Difficulties,

or thinking over them, or even continuing to pray over them when we might be trusting the promises—all this savors of unbelief.

"The congregation lifted up their voice and cried; and the people wept that night." What was the matter? Had God withdrawn His promises? Had He left His people? Was there anything fresh in the situation? No; but the people had been looking at their difficulties instead of looking at God, and they had been overcome, and in heart they did not think God was able to do as He had promised. Yet they did not directly find fault with God, but with His servants. They murmured against Moses and Aaron, and said, "Would God we had died in the land of Egypt! or would God we had died in this wilderness! And wherefore hath the Lord brought us into this land to fall by the sword, that our wives and our children should be a prey?" Poor, senseless people! No enemy was near them; they were no longer slaves, but children cared for by the most loving of Fathers; they were miraculously fed and clothed, and the very presence of God was with them; yet, because they did not see on the instant the fulfillment of God's promises, they let them go for nothing! They even contemplated returning to Egypt, and consulted one with another. "Let us make a captain, and let us return into Egypt." Is it possible that they had so soon forgotten the burdens which oppressed them there, and the plagues and wonders which God had brought upon the Egyptians for their deliverance? Were they so childish that the present moment—in which they had

No Real Trouble

at all, but only an apprehension of trouble which might possibly overtake them in case God broke His word—was sufficient to wipe out of their hearts every grateful remembrance of the past? It was a sad moment for Moses and Aaron, but they knew God, and did not attempt to take things into their own hands, they "fell on their faces before all the assembly of the congregation of the children of Israel"; and this was not in token that they were crushed by them, but that they sought their God.

Then Joshua and Caleb once again bore their testimony for God. They rent their clothes, for their hearts were stirred within them, and "they spake unto all the company of the children of Israel, saying, the land which we passed through to search it is an exceeding good land. If the Lord delight in us, then He will bring us into this land, and give it us." The ten spies never mentioned the name of the Lord at all, but only the circumstances; Joshua and Caleb could not forget their God; they saw the land, they saw the people, but only in their relation to God. Where God is a living reality, there unbelief cannot exist. "Only rebel not ye against the Lord," they said, "neither fear ye the people of the land; for they are bread for us; their defence is departed from them, and the Lord is with us; fear them not." This is the utterance of faith.

What are the enemies which keep us from appropriating as our own any of the promises of God? Is there the fear that other and older Christians will not go with us? How many there are who say, "If such and such a thing were right, surely such a holy man as Mr. So and So would preach it." Perhaps no man lived a much holier life than the prophet Elijah, yet if Elisha had obeyed him rather than the direct command which he had received from God, he would have lost the blessing which he craved, "a double portion of thy spirit." (II Kings 2: 9.) Is the difficulty that your past experience contradicts the promise of God? But God can make a new thing in the earth; Peter's past experience of water was that it would bear no solid weight, but he treated the "Come" of Jesus as superior to his past experience, and, in the power of that word, he walked upon the water. Elijah had no experience of resurrection, and in all the past history of the world it had not been told, but from the deep acquaintance with God which he had formed at the brook Cherith, he knew he dared to ask it, and he found as he had trusted, that God was above death; and the widow's son lived again. (I Kings 17: 21-23.) To these men of old, difficulties, yea, impossibilities, were

Bread for Them

a very nourishment of their faith, in calling out the resources of the living God. They saw that the defence of all enemies and all difficulties was departed from them; the Lord was with them, and this answered every purpose. In His presence they knew no fear. When God's two champions spoke thus to the people, they commenced persecution, and bade stone them with stones: and just then the Lord appeared upon the scene. Nebuchadnezzar's fiery furnace, the den of lions, the stones which sped Stephen up to heaven, did not shut God out: in the furnace, in the lions' den, and standing within an opened heaven, ready to receive Stephen, there was the Son of God. Once again Moses was put to the test, and God for the second time offered to destroy the people, and to make of him a great nation. But Moses was not to be overcome, and he reasoned with God, how this would be to play into the hands of the Egyptians, and that the glorious witness of the cloudy and the fiery pillar would go for nothing. "Now if Thou shalt kill all this people as one man, then the nations which have heard the fame of Thee will speak, saying, Because the Lord was not able to bring this people into the land which He sware unto them, therefore He hath slain them in the wilderness. And now, I beseech Thee, let the power of my Lord be great... pardon, I beseech thee, the iniquity of this people, according unto the greatness of Thy mercy, and as Thou hast forgiven this people from Egypt, even until now— Let thy power be great in mercy, not in wrath." Again the Lord allowed Himself to be conquered by Moses, for Moses had appealed to His very name and character; there was no resisting him. "The Lord said, I have pardoned according to thy word; but—but as truly as I live, all the earth shall be filled with the glory of the Lord."

God must be Justified

for His glory's sake. He decreed that the men who had ten times (Ex. 14:11; 15:24: 16:2; 17:2; 32:1; Lev. 10:1-2; Num. 11:1-4; 12:2; 14:1, 2,) tempted Him, or disbelieved Him, should die in the Wilderness, and never see the Promised Land. "But My servant Caleb, because he had another spirit with him, and hath followed Me fully, him will I bring into the land whereinto he went; and his seed shall possess it." And God enlarged His judgment upon the people, and declared that the children whom the people said should be a prey, "them will I bring in, and they shall know the land which ye have despised. But as for you, your carcasses, they shall fall in this wilderness. And your children shall wander in the wilderness forty years... After the numbers of the days in which ye searched the land, even forty days, each day for a year, shall ye bear your iniquities, and ye shall know My breach of promise." It has been well said that nations have no hereafter, as such, in another world, and therefore national sins must be punished in time. The sin of the spies was adopted by the congregation, and made their own, and thus, as a people, they must suffer. The guilt of England in forcing the opium trade on China by the last war, when the authorities of that heathen land protested against it, the millions of souls and bodies ruined by it—this iniquity will have to be punished—

England Must Suffer.

The iniquity of forcing the liquor traffic on India, so that the revenue was doubled in one year, but at the cost of numbers of natives demoralized and ruined—this must be punished; and then the horrible system of licensed vice which has, thank God, been put a stop to—these things must meet with retribution. "When the land sinneth against Me, by trespassing grievously, then will I stretch out Mine hand upon it... and will cut off man and beast from it. Though these three men, Noah, Daniel, and Job, were in it, they should deliver but their own souls by their righteousness saith the Lord.

The Lord having pronounced His judgment upon the nation, next dealt with individual sinners: the ten spies died by the plague before the Lord." But Joshua and Caleb were spared. When Moses told the people God's severe message of judgment, and that the ten spies were dead, they "mourned greatly." But it was a mourning more of remorse than of repentance; they were less sorry for their sin than for its consequences. Instead of yielding themselves now fully up to the Lord, "they rose up early in the morning, and got them up into the top of the mountain, saying, Lo, we be here, and will go up unto the place which the Lord hath promised: for we have sinned." But they were as wilful in going forward now, as they had been in hanging back before. "Moses said, Wherefore now do ye transgress the commandment of the Lord? but it shall not prosper. Go not up, for the Lord is not among you; that ye be not smitten before your enemies." Let us never forget that when we have fallen into error, we cannot restore ourselves; we can confess and yield up ourselves afresh, but we can never make up for lost time, but as the Lord undertakes and leads us. Moses said, "Because ye are turned away from the Lord, therefore the Lord will not be with you." But they presumed to go up unto the hill-top; nevertheless the ark of the covenant of the Lord and Moses departed not out of the camp. What could they do without the ark of the Lord? their enemies came down 'and smote them,' and discomfited them, even unto Hormah."

Thoughts Between the Lines.

BY O. F. IRELAND.

"Jesus, lover of my soul,"
Who on the cross such love displayed,
"Let me to Thy bosom fly,"
There I cannot be dismayed;
"While the nearer waters roll,"
Alone I cannot breast the wave;
"While the tempest still is high,"
Thy protecting arm can save.

"Hide me, O my Saviour, hide!"
Blessed thought, to hide in Thee
"Till the storm of life is past,"
And from dangers we are free,
"Safe into the haven guide,"
Haven of eternal rest;
"O receive my soul at last,"
There to be forever blest!

"Other refuge have I none,"
And none other is complete:
"Hangs my helpless soul on Thee,"
Here it finds a safe retreat,
"Leave, O leave me not alone,"
In this wild and lonely place:
"Still support and comfort me"
With Thy rich, abounding grace.

"All my trust on Thee is stayed,"
Thy rich promises are sure;
"All my help from Thee I bring,"
All Thy gifts are rich and pure.
"Cover my defenceless head"
With Thy benedictions mild;
"With the shadow of Thy wing"
Overspread Thy trusting child!

"Plenteous grace with Thee is found:"
None may want who trust in Thee;
"Grace to cover all my sin"
Thou wilt not withhold from me.
"Let the healing streams abound,"
Flooding now my waiting soul;
"Make and keep me pure within,"
Pure and every whit made whole.

"Thou of life the fountain art,"
Coming from the Father's throne;
"Freely let me take of Thee,"
That I Thy righteousness may own,
"Spring Thou up within my heart,"
Blessing all my future days;
"Rise to all eternity,"
And I'll sing Thy endless praise.

J. E. JEWETT, Publisher, 77 Bible House, New York, will furnish the above poem in leaflet form at twenty cents per hundred. *A Sample Packet* of 50 leaflets assorted (no two alike), will be sent post-paid, for 10 cts., or 100 for 20 cts. Postage stamps taken.

To Our Fellow Christians

Who Are Forwarding Contributions in Aid of Christian Work in Mexico.

Bishop Riley requests me to inform the kind friends who are generously contributing in aid of Christian work in Mexico that we have now over one hundred monthly subscribers who are forwarding contributions every month in its behalf. Bishop Riley sends to all who are contributing in aid of the work in Mexico his most sincere thanks for their timely gifts.

As there are no doubt many who would be glad to contribute something monthly in behalf of the cause of Christ in Mexico, but who feel that they cannot afford to give as much as one dollar a month, we venture the suggestion, that when possible *the friends of the work should try and collect small contributions from such* and forward the same with their own contributions to Bishop Riley, 43 Bible House, New York. For example, some friend of the work who is now forwarding one dollar a month, might induce ten others, to each give ten cents a month, and collect and forward the same with his own contribution. Another who now contributes one dollar a month, might induce four others, to each give one cent a day, or thirty-one cents a month, and collect and forward the same with his own contribution monthly. Still a third who now contributes a dollar a month might induce two friends, to each give fifty cents a month, and collect and forward the same regularly with his own contribution.

If this plan could be adopted generally among the more than one hundred regular monthly subscribers to the work, we might soon be able to report to our friends that we had over two hundred dollars a month contributed regularly in behalf of the work in Mexico.

We remind our friends that to continue the work in Mexico effectively we most pressingly need a regular monthly income, as we have to meet a regular monthly expense.

A most precious Christian work has been commenced in Mexico, and we are doing what we can to continue it, by raising an income in its behalf. We earnestly appeal to our fellow Christians to aid us in this effort. There are one hundred and thirteen millions who speak the English language, and seventy-five millions who speak the Spanish or Portuguese languages. Among those who speak the English language, there are multitudes who know and love the pure gospel, and are doing what they can for the Master. Among those who speak the Spanish or the Portuguese languages, there are a few who know and love the pure gospel, and are faithfully working for our dear Master. Our Spanish-American society is working hard to raise an income to aid in building up a strong centre of Christian work in Mexico. The influence of that work has already extended into Spain and Cuba, and we trust will yet extend into South America. Fellow Christians, think of seventy-five millions who speak the Spanish or Portuguese languages, millions and millions, and millions of whom, have never had a Bible in their hands!!! Help us! help us! to do Christian work in their midst.

Bishop Riley has been instrumental in having more than one hundred thousand copies of the Bible or New Testament circulated in Mexico. Many hundreds of children have been educated in Christian schools established by him. More than forty congregations have been gathered in the Republic of Mexico through his efforts. He has secured two magnificent stone churches in the City of Mexico where the Gospel has been preached for years. He has trained up a noble band of able preachers of the pure gospel. He has given nineteen years of his life and his fortune to aid in building up this great work, and he now appeals to his fellow Christians to contribute the monthly income needed to continue it effectively.

Dear friends, will you not only continue to contribute to this good work yourselves, but also encourage others to do the same. Some may not be able to contribute monthly but could do so occasionally. Occasional gifts are most thankfully received. Pray for the work, and that many may be moved to befriend it.

With best Christian wishes, I am, your brother in Christ,

A. D. MAINE.

ol. XI., No. 36. Office, 63 Bible House, N. Y. THURSDAY, SEPTEMBER 6, 1888. Annual Subscription, $1.50.

CONTENTS OF THIS NUMBER.

PORTRAITS AND LIVES OF THE REV. THOMAS, AND THE LATE MRS. WAKEFIELD, Missionaries in East Africa.
PLASTERS THAT WILL NOT STICK. A Vacation Sermon by Dr. Talmage.
ANECDOTES RELATED AT RECENT EVANGELISTIC MEETINGS.
THE PROPHETIC DAY—Aug. 14-15.
The Juggernaut Festival Last Month—The Healing of a Chicago Clergyman—A Cheerful Missionary—A Chinese Demoniac—Italiau Newspaper Enterprise, etc.
THE WICKED AT CHRIST'S COMING. By. Rev. Henry Varley.
THE LORD'S SUPPER: A REMEMBRANCE. A New Sermon by C. H. Spurgeon.
Gems from New Books: A Praying General, etc.
PORTRAIT OF THE NEW CHIEF-JUSTICE FULLER.
PICTURE OF THE PANIC AMONG ELEPHANTS AT THE BAVARIAN CENTENNIAL.
A PROVIDENTIAL ESCAPE. (With Illustration.)
THE EPOCHS OF A LIFE. A New Serial Story by Rev. L. S. Keyser. (Continued.)
THE SMITTEN ROOK. By Mrs. M. Baxter.

AN EAST AFRICAN MISSION HOUSE.

A GROUP OF NATIVE GALLAS CHRISTIANS OF RIBE.

A FAMILY OF HEATHEN NATIVE GALLAS OF RIBE.

IN THE SLAVE MARKET, ZANZIBAR.

REV. THOMAS, AND THE LATE MRS. WAKEFIELD, Formerly Missionaries in East Africa—Scenes in the Sphere of their Work.

REV. THOMAS WAKEFIELD.

President of the Methodist Free Churches.

Born in 1836 - Apprenticed to a Printer in 1852—Converted at Nantwich—Enters the Ministry in 1858—Becomes a Missionary to Africa in 1861 Arrival at Zanzibar in 1862—Struggles and Successes at Ribé—Visits the Galla Country in 1865—Returns Home in 1868—Further Service and Sorrow in East Africa—Another Visit Home in 1882—Founds the Galla Mission in 1883—Home Labors—Elected President.

THE Free Methodist denomination in England has made a wise and welcome innovation in placing in its seat of honor this year a minister whose laurels have been won in heathen lands. This step is the more gratifying because there has been a tendency in the past on the part of the churches of all denominations to regard missionaries as in a sense inferior in rank to the preacher at home. We are glad to notice that the Congregationalists have also entertained the same project, though the Rev. Griffith John, the eminent missionary in China, who was the missionary suggested for the chairmanship of the Union, declines the honor on account of the urgency of his work in China.

The newly elected Free Methodist President, Rev. Thomas Wakefield, was born at Derby, Eng., on June 23, 1836, so that he has now passed his fifty-second year. When he was only three years old the family removed to the city of Chester, where his mother died in 1886, at the age of ninety-two years. As a child he was affectionate and thoughtful, as well as diligent in reading every book he could lay his hands on. Full of fun and frolic as a boy, he has carried a sparkling cheerfulness with him all through life, which has no doubt brightened him in long seasons of darkness and depression. In 1852 he was apprenticed to a printer in Nantwich. While resident in this ancient town he was converted to God, and began to preach the gospel. In the early part of 1858 he entered the ministry of the United Methodist Free Churches, and was appointed to the Bodmin Circuit. After the Assembly of 1860 he removed to the Helston Circuit, until he was led in the year following to offer himself for the work of

The New Mission in East Africa.

The establishment of this mission was greeted throughout the whole of the connexion with immense enthusiasm, and deep interest has ever since surrounded the history of it. The first missionary party consisted of Dr. Krapf (the German missionary pioneer), two other Germans, and the Revs. T. Wakefield and J. Woolner. They arrived at Zanzibar after a tedious and perilous voyage in January 1862. In time they proceeded to Mombasa, and then to Ribé, where the mission was established. Dr. Krapf and the Germans soon left the mission and returned to Europe. Mr. Woolner was prostrated by fever, and in a few weeks had to be brought back to Europe with a shattered constitution. Left alone in a strange land, and repeatedly prostrated by African fever, Mr. Wakefield yet struggled on to establish the mission, and to erect the buildings which were necessary.

The heroic servant of Christ was at length gladdened by the arrival in April, 1863, of the brave and self-denying Rev. Charles New, and in the spring of the following year by the lamented Edmund Butterworth. Then came a long hard struggle with many discouragements, brightened now and then with promise of success, some of the heathen desiring to give themselves to God. Mr. Wakefield made an interesting

Journey to the Galla Country

in 1865, an account of which was published under the title of "Footprints in Eastern Africa." In the following year, accompanied by Mr. New, he visited another part of the Galla country with a view to obtain consent to open a mission there; but the time had not yet come, and the missionaries returned to Ribé to plod on and hope for brighter days.

In October, 1868, Mr. Wakefield visited England to recruit his health, remaining till the spring of 1870, and doing work of immense service to the churches as a missionary deputation. His descriptions of missionary life and labors were received with intense interest by the audiences which assembled. Then, accompanied by Mrs. Wakefield and the Rev. W. Yates, he returned to East Africa. Mr. Yates was compelled to return home through illness, and his solitude was still more sadly intensified by the illness and death of his beloved wife. This was followed in a few months by the death of Mr. New on his return from Chagga. Mr. Wakefield's health became so shattered that he quite expected his own grave would be added to those already made. However, it pleased God to restore him to health, and he gave himself with fresh zeal to the carrying out of the work.

In 1882, after another visit to England, and another spell of deputation work, his residence was fixed at Jomvu, and he again visited the Galla country, and at length fulfilled the long-cherished hope of the Free Churches in the

Establishment of the Galla Mission.

It was in December, 1885, that this mission was taken charge of by Rev. J Houghton (*whose portrait and life appeared in this journal on January 27, 1887*) and his wife. They took up their quarters at Golbanti; but only a few weeks later the dreaded Masai warriors suddenly appeared in the neighborhood, burned down a number of huts, took away cattle, and killed between forty and fifty of the Gallas, among whom were four Christians. On May 3, 1886, the Masai warriors speared to death both Mr. Houghton and his devoted wife: but the gospel standard had been planted, and though the hands that bore it were laid in the grave, it has not fallen. The cause has won many triumphs, and the good work is satisfactorily progressing.

For many years Mr. Wakefield devoted himself to the translation of portions of the Holy Scriptures and Christian hymns into the languages and dialects of eastern Africa, so that he has produced a literature which will no doubt do much in the near future for the evangelization of those regions.

In May, 1887, Mr. Wakefield again returned to his native land in broken health, and with the probability that for a long time, at least, he would not be able to return to Africa, where in

The Labor of Twenty-Six Years

he had toiled for the uplifting of the degraded races of that land, and the spread of the gospel in the dark places, which are full of the habitations of cruelty. Amid dangers in travel over sea and land, in perils from disease, and the yet more treacherous conduct of the natives and others, with death striking down one after another of his co-laborers and loved ones, through long periods of solitude occasioned by these sad bereavements, he stood with unflinching courage and devotion to his post, carrying on the work with a steadfast perseverance which has resulted in the establishment of a Christian church in that portion of the Dark Continent.

He settled in Leeds, and, with an improvement in health, engaged in deputation work. At the Louth Assembly last year Mr. Wakefield was nominated for the chair, the nomination being received with acclamation; but on account doubtless of his want of acquaintance with home affairs, he withdrew from the nomination, but was afterwards elected a member of the Missionary Committee. This manifestation of enthusiasm virtually assured his election as President at the Assembly this year.

THE LATE MRS. WAKEFIELD.

Born in 1844—Takes Charge of a School—Interest in Christian Work—Goes to Birmingham in 1864—Accepts an Offer of Marriage from Rev. J. Mitchil, a Missionary in Ceylon—Aids in a Revival—Death of Mr. Mitchil—Life at Woolwich—First Meeting with Mr. Wakefield—Marriage—Sets Sail for Africa in 1870—Visits the Zanzibar Slave-Market—Mission Labors—Death of a Son in 1873—Illness, Farewell Interview with Native Christians, and Death.

MRS. REBECCA WAKEFIELD (*née* Brewin), for nearly four years the wife and efficient helpmeet of her husband, now the President of the Methodist Free Church Conference, was born at Mountsorrel, England, on August 19, 1844, and died on July 16, 1873, in the twenty-ninth year of her age, at Ribé, in eastern Africa. Her childhood was a very sunny one, until her good father's death in 1857. In the spring of 1861 she took charge of a young ladies' school in her native village, and there she continued her duties as principal for three years. On Sundays she taught in the Sunday-school, and engaged in tract distribution. From a child she was greatly interested in mission work; and the salvation of the heathen was at all times very near her heart.

In November, 1862, Rebecca was called to follow her mother to the grave. This great trial fell very heavily upon her. The school was kept on for eighteen months afterwards, during which period she lived with her aunt, in whom she found a mother's watchful care and tender affection. In the summer of 1864 a lady in Birmingham, a cousin of her mother, and in delicate health, strongly desired Miss Brewin's companionship, and offered her a quiet, comfortable home. She acceded to the proposal, and her connection with the Mountsorrel school terminated.

One morning, a few days after the closing of her school-life, an event occurred which for a time changed the current of her thoughts in reference to her own future, and promised also to change the whole course of her life. It was the receipt of a letter, just as she was leaving her aunt's with a party of friends to spend a day in Bradgate Park. She did not open the letter until the rendezvous was reached. Standing under a tree, and hidden by its friendly trunk from the remainder of the company, she breaks the seal. It is closely written on very thin paper, and the envelope bears a foreign stamp. There is a somewhat troubled, tearful smile upon the beautiful countenance that is bending over it, for it contains

An Offer of Marriage

from the Rev. John Mitchil, a friend of her earlier years, and who was at this time the Principal of the Educational Department of the Missionary College at Jaffna, Ceylon. The offer was ultimately accepted.

In August, 1865, Asiatic cholera was raging around the mission-house at Jaffna. The Rev. John Mitchil assiduously devoted himself to relieving the bodily and spiritual necessities of the many helpless natives stricken by

The Dreadful Pestilence,

when suddenly it seized him in its relentless grasp, and on November 6 he lay down upon his couch in the study of the mission-house to die. His last audible words were, "I am going to Jesus," and on the evening of November 7 he sank peacefully away. The tidings reached England on December 14, and filled with anguish the heart of the expectant bride; but she cast her sorrow upon the Saviour, and found needed consolation and efficient support in Him.

Miss Brewin removed to London in August, 1867, where she joined the Beresford Street Church, Woolwich, which was under her brother's care, and identified herself with its various organizations and agencies, and God richly blessed her work, both to her own heart and to the hearts of others. In the spring of 1869 she attended the "May Meetings" in London. The annual gathering of the United Methodist Free Churches Missions was especially interesting to

er, on account of the presence on the platform f Exeter Hall of one of the earliest of the east African missionaries, Rev. Thomas Wakefield, whom ie now saw for the first time. During the sitng of the Annual Assembly in Sunderland, in uly and August of the same year, Mr. Wakefield offered her marriage, and was accepted.

Her Marriage

ook place on December 2, 1869, at Louth, Linolnshire. On February 24, 1870, Mr. and Mrs. Vakefield set sail from Gravesend, together ith the Rev. W. Yates, and Dado, a negro boy hom Mr. Wakefield had rescued from slavery ist prior to his visit to England. On June 2 nchor was dropped in the harbor of Zanzibar.

One evening Mr. Wakefield took his wife to e the well-known slave-market in this place, nd the sight filled her with wonder and sorrow. he writes: "I could scarcely believe my own yes as we threaded our way among the crowds f buyers and sellers of human flesh and lood. The poor creatures offered for sale ood in rows here and there; and were marked n the forehead by a daub of yellow paint, to istinguish them. They were of all ages, from wo years and upward; aye, and less than that, or a mother with a baby in her arms or strapped t her back, gypsy fashion, were frequently ofred in one lot. Several auctioneers were busy ushing their way among the crowd, dragging y the wrist the wretched victim they were sellg, and shouting at the top of their voices the ighest bid that had yet been reached, while e buyers felt the arms of the poor slave as she as hurried past them. I had read of slavearkets before, but never thought that I should yself be a witness of the horrid doings and ainful sights of these still existing places of affic. (*See Illustration No. 4.*)

It was not, however, until the following Janary that Mr. and Mrs. Wakefield removed to

Their Home at Ribe.

hey proceeded by way of Mombasa, about 120 iles; then for about twelve miles in a small oat up a creek and river, and finally, overland or six miles, to the Mission station at Ribé, here, excepting occasional changes between hat place and Mombasa, they remained till the ay of Mrs. Wakefield's death. (Specimens of e Ribé are depicted in the *Illustration, No. 2.*)

Into the details of missionary life it is not ossible here to enter. Sunshine and sorrow lternated with Mr. and Mrs. Wakefield, as they o in all households, and not less in missionry households than in others. At length, owever, just after a son was born to them (a aughter had been given them in December, 870), the mother was smitten by disease, with hich she bravely battled for six weeks, at the nd of which time she succumbed. But before er own departure her little son died. This as on July 12, 1873. What remains of this orrowful day's history is best told in Mr. Wakeeld's own words: "In the evening, when

The Babe's Coffin

as ready, I brought it into the bedroom, and aid little Bertie in it. I got Mrs. Wakefield up ith great difficulty, and dressed her, and she at upon the edge of the bed. Her tender, otherly love wanted to do something in assistng me with the preparations, and she made everal efforts; but her right arm, for some time aralyzed by rheumatism, was now utterly powrless. After laying Bertie in his last narrow ed, my wife took a last look at her babe, and carried him into the next room. When I reurned to her she put something into my hand nd told me to lay it in the coffin, on Bertie's reast. It was a few African wild-flowers, and he sight touched my heart. What her feelings ere at that time I cannot tell; she did not reep; one more calm and subdued I never saw.

A Pathetic Interview

ook place on July 16, when the natives residing n the station, Gallas, Wanika, and Wasawahili, ere admitted to a last look at their beloved lying friend. As they stood by her bedside, Ar. Wakefield reminded them of how much she ad undergone for their sakes; of her leaving home; of the long and tempestuous voyage across the ocean; of her trials at Zanzibar; of the rough passage to Mombasa; of the discomforts of the house there; of her successive attacks of fever at Ribé, and of her great sufferings in other respects. "All this," he continued "has been bravely, and without a murmur, endured for your sakes. For you who are standing around her dying bed, she has sacrificed comfort, health, friends, brother, home, and all that is bright and joyous, and borne the burden and heat of a fever-stricken country. She can no longer speak to you: but if she could do so, she would even now tell you to love Jesus, to give yourselves to Him, to live for heaven, and follow her to the rest to which she is going."

After this address the people retired. Soon after sunset that evening it became evident that the last conflict was at hand, and at ten minutes after 7 o'clock, with her right hand firmly clasped by those of her husband, Mrs. Wakefield calmly drew her last breath, and, with a sweet smile, indicative of her joyous confidence, passed away from her work on earth to her reward in heaven.

ANECDOTES RELATED AT RECENT EVANGELISTIC MEETINGS.

Fatal Fall from a Scaffold.—Mr. Hamilton observes: "A young man had been out to his work in the morning, and coming home, had breakfasted with his wife and children, and then returned to his work at the building upon which he was employed. To reach the place at which he was working he had to climb up to a scaffolding. He reached the scaffolding in safety, but when about to pass from one part of it to another, he trod upon a plank imperfectly attached, and in a moment was precipitated to the ground. His fellow-workmen rushed to the spot, and strove to bring him to consciousness, but it was of no avail. In a few minutes all was over. The man had gone to give an account to God of the deeds done in this life. In the face of such a calamity no one thought of resuming work that day. The men might have been seen in groups of threes and fours talking over the sad occurence, and the general burden of their talk was, 'It was so sudden!' May not your call and mine be as sudden? 'Prepare to meet thy God.'"

From the Hospital to Heaven.—Mr. Hogg says: "I knew a little boy who was converted at a children's meeting, and what a joyous little fellow he was! I think I hear him now singing his favorite hymn, 'Shall we gather at the river?' He left home when nineteen years of age and joined the Seventy-first Regiment, with which he went out to Egypt and at the battle of Tel-el-Kebir he was wounded in both legs. After the battle he was removed to the hospital, where his shattered limbs were amputated, but he did not long survive the operation. A lady was visiting the hospital, and as she walked along between the beds she was surprised to hear one of the wounded men singing. It was this soldier repeating his favorite hymn. He had no fear at the approach of death. The lady promised to send a message to his parents. She left the hospital and telegraphed to them, telling them of their son's condition. She returned to the dying soldier's bedside, but ere she got back he had gone to be with Christ. His last words were, 'Though I walk through the valley of the shadow of death, I will fear no evil, for Thou art with me, Thy rod and Thy staff they comfort me.'"

His Last Drunken Spree.—A Seaman Related: "I thank God that He takes a man when he is 'down in his luck,' as we say, when the devil has been paying him his wages. I had just returned from a fifteen months' voyage, and had over $300 in my pocket. I arrived at a port in the west of England, and at once set out for a spree. I do not know how I got on, but one night I found myself lying in an out of the way corner in a Glasgow street, with dirty, ragged clothes on, and only a few pennies in my pocket; this in only a few days after my return. I got up and spent the remaining money on beer. Then I began to wander aimlessly about; I had not even the heart to look for a ship. As I walked along I came upon an open-air Gospel meeting. I stopped and listened to the singing; if I had had a penny in my pocket I do not believe I should have done so. While there a gentleman came up to me, and, placing his hand upon my shoulder, kindly said, 'My man, you seem a bit downcast.' 'Not more so than usual,' was my surly response. Taking no notice of this, he continued, 'Come along into our meeting, and spend an hour.' 'I would rather not,' I replied. Seeing I was determined to be contrary he left me. The singers went into the hall; I went in and listened. They sang beautifully. I was sitting as near the door as possible, but there the Holy Spirit met me and led me to Christ, who saved me, and, bless His name, has kept me ever since."

Willie Joins Jane and Effie.—Mr. McFarlane remarks: "I was lately visiting a lady, who, when telling me of the death of one of her children, said: 'Formerly I did not believe all that I heard about children and their faith in Christ. But since my little boy, eight years of age, has died, I could believe anything. When he was taken ill at first we did not send for a doctor. As he lay in bed one day, he said to me, 'I want to go with Jane and Effie to be with Jesus.' 'But they are both dead,' I answered. 'Yes, but they are with Jesus, and I am going to Him, too,' he replied. And he would speak so fondly and familiarly about Jesus, all the while he was not supposed to be seriously ill. At length his father, becoming alarmed with the boy's serious talk, unwisely said to him, 'Now Willie, you must not speak like that; you know if you die we shall have to put you in a big hole, and leave you there.' The dear little fellow just looked up into his father's face, and, with a smile, said, 'I am not afraid; for soon God will send an angel, who will say, "Willie, arise," and I shall get up.' At last he fell asleep in Jesus, leaving a bright testimonial behind."

Native Preachers Clubbed to Death.—Rev. J. Jones said: "I remember that on one occasion, when I asked who would go to a certain tribe, there were two men, named Wagidro and Motace; and Wagidro said, 'I will go,' and Motace followed, and said, 'I will go with him.' Others offered themselves, and thus the whole tribes were supplied, and the preachers went forth on the Monday morning. That day the savages prepared to attack them, and as these two men went forth they heard the report that they were to be killed. But they had often heard such reports as that, and they said, 'It matters not. We have given ourselves to work for the Lord Jesus Christ, and we shall go, even if we die'; and they went forth. On their way they met another tribe, who endeavored to dissuade them from proceeding, on account of the danger; but, not listening to them, they suddenly came into a district where there was a stretch of forest, and there they met some armed men. The old man was leading in front, having a stick of sugar-cane for his walking-stick. With calm demeanor he stood and said: 'What is this? Are you come to kill us, as we have heard?' The calmness of the question seemed to paralyze them, and as the calm was stealing over them there came a shout from one behind. That was the rallying cry, and in a moment the calm was dispelled. Their eyes glared, the clubs were uplifted, and the savages fell upon the two men, and killed them on the spot. But let me tell you that that man who shouted that cry afterward accepted Christ, and became a deacon of the church. After about ten years of weary waiting, and of toil and danger and labor, the whole of these tribes became converted."

PLASTERS THAT WILL NOT STICK.

A Vacation Sermon by Dr. Talmage.

"Miserable comforters are ye all." Job. 16:2.

The Fair World Ruined by Sin—A Predominance of Thorns—Consequent Need of Comforters—Persons Incompetent to Console—I. Very Voluble People—Tearing the Bandages off a Wound—II. Worldly Philosophers—An Instrument of Many Strings—Edmund Burke's Emotion Over a Horse—The Blessed Relief of Tears—III. The Hypochondriac—IV. People Who Have Had no Trouble—The Mystery of a Broken Heart—Suggestions to Comforters—God Sends Trouble in Love—To Increase Usefulness—Iron in the Furnace—Trouble a Revelation—Future Reconstruction Assured—A Preparation for Glory—A Light in a Chamber of Death.

THE man of Uz had a great many trials—the loss of his family, the loss of his property, the loss of his health; but the most exasperating thing that came upon him was the tantalizing talk of those who ought to have sympathized with him. Looking around upon them, and weighing what they had said, he utters the words of my text.

Why did God let sin come into the world? It is a question I often hear discussed, but never satisfactorily answered.

God Made the World Fair

and beautiful at the start. If our first parents had not sinned in Eden, they might have gone out of that garden, and found fifty paradises all around the earth—Europe, Asia, Africa, North and South America so many flower-gardens, or orchards of fruit redolent and luscious. I suppose that when God poured out the Gihon and the Hiddekel, he poured out, at the same time, the Hudson and the Susquehanna; the whole earth was very fair and beautiful to look upon. Why did it not stay so? God had the power to keep back sin and woe. Why did He not keep them back? Why not every cloud a roseate, and every step a joy, and every sound music, and all the ages a long jubilee of sinless men and sinless women? God can make a rose as easily as He can make a thorn. Why, then,

The Predominance of Thorns?

He can make good, fair, ripe fruit as well as gnarled and sour fruit. Why so much, then, that is gnarled and sour? He can make men robust in health. Why, then, are there so many invalids? Why not have for our whole race perpetual leisure, instead of this tug and toil and tussle for a livelihood? I will tell you why God let sin come into the world—when I get on the other side of the River of Death. That is the place where such questions will be answered, and such mysteries solved. He who this side that river attempts to answer the question, only illustrates his own ignorance and incompetency. All I know is one great fact, and that is, that a herd of woes have come in upon us, tramping down everything fair and beautiful. A sword at the gate of Eden, and a sword at every gate. More people under the ground than on it. The graveyards in vast majority. The six thousand winters have made more scars than the six thousand summers can cover up. Trouble has taken the tender heart of this world in its two rough hands, and pinched it until

The Nations Wail

with the agony. If all the mounds of graveyards that have been lifted were put side by side, you might step on them and on nothing else, going all around the world, and around again, and around again. These are the facts. And now I have to say that, in a world like this, the grandest occupation is that of giving condolence. This holy science of imparting comfort to the troubled we ought all of us to study. There are many of you who could look around upon some of your very best friends who wish you well and are very intelligent, and yet be able truthfully to say to them in your days of trouble, "Miserable comforters are ye all!"

I remark, in the first place, that very

Voluble People

are incompetent for the work of giving comfort. Bildad and Eliphaz had the gift of language, and with their words almost bothered Job's life out. Alas for these voluble people that go among the houses of the afflicted, and talk, and talk, and talk, and talk! They rehearse their own sorrows, and then they tell the poor sufferers that they feel badly now, but they will feel worse after a while. Silence! Do you expect, with a thin court-plaster of words, to heal a wound deep as the soul? Step very gently around about a broken heart. Talk very softly around those whom God has bereft. Then go your way. Deep sympathy has not mcuh to say. A firm grasp of the hand, a compassionate look, just one word that means as much as a whole dictionary, and you have given, perhaps, all the comfort that a soul needs.

A man has a terrible wound in his arm. The surgeon comes and binds it up. "Now," he says, "carry that arm in a sling, and be very careful of it. Let no one touch it." But the neighbors have heard of the accident, and they come in, and they say, "Let us see it." And

The Bandage is Pulled Off,

and this one and that one must feel it, and see how much it is swollen; and there is irritation and inflammation and exasperation, where there ought to be healing and cooling. The surgeon comes in and says, "What does all this mean? You have no business to touch those bandages. That wound will never heal unless you let it alone." So there are souls broken down in sorrow. What they most want is rest, or very careful and gentle treatment; but the neighbors have heard of the bereavement or of the loss, and they come in to sympathize, and they say, "Show us now the wound. What were his last words? Rehearse now the whole scene. How did you feel when you found you were an orphan?" Tearing off the bandages here, and pulling them off there, leaving a ghastly wound that the balm of God's grace had already begun to heal. Oh, let no loquacious people, with ever-rattling tongues, go into the homes of the distressed!

Again I remark, that all those persons are incompetent to give any kind of comfort who act as

Worldly Philosophers.

They come in and say, "Why, this is what you ought to have expected. The laws of nature must have their way;" and then they get eloquent over something they have seen in post-mortem examinations. Now, away with all human philosophy at such a time! What difference does it make to that father and mother what disease their son died of? He is dead, and it makes no difference whether the trouble was in the epigastric or hypogastric region. If the philosopher be of the stoical school he will come and say, "You ought to control your feelings. You must not cry so. You must cultivate a cooler temperament. You must have self-reliance, self-government, self-control"; an iceberg reproving a hyacinth for having a drop of dew in its eye.

A violinist has his instrument, and he sweeps his fingers across the strings, now evoking strains of joy, and now strains of sadness. He cannot play all the tunes on one string. The human soul is an instrument of a thousand strings, and all sorts of emotions were made to play on it. Now an anthem, now a dirge. It is no evidence of weakness when one is overcome of sorrow. Edmund Burke was found in the pasture-field with his arms around a horse's neck, caressing him, and some one said, "Why, the great man has lost his mind!" No; that horse belonged to his son who had recently died, and his great heart broke over the grief. It is no sign of weakness that men are overcome of their sorrows. *Thank God for*

The Relief of Tears.

Have you never been in deep trouble when you could not weep, and you would have given anything for a good cry? David did well when he mourned for Absalom, Abraham did well when he bemoaned Sarah, Christ did well when he wept for Lazarus; and the last man I want to see come anywhere near me when I have any kind of trouble, is a worldly philosopher.

Again I remark, that those persons are incompetent for the work of comfort-bearing who have nothing but cant to offer. There are those who have the idea that you must groan over the distressed and afflicted. There are times in grief when one cheerful face dawning upon a man's soul is worth a thousand dollars to him. Do not whine over the afflicted. Take the promises of the gospel, and utter them in a manly tone. Do not be afraid to smile, if you feel like it. Do not drive any more hearses through that poor soul. Do not tell him the trouble was foreordained; it will not be any comfort to know it was a million years coming. If you want to find splints for a broken bone, do not take cast-iron. Do not tell them it is God's justice that weighs out grief. They want now to hear of God's tender mercy. In other words, do not give them aqua fortis when they need valerian.

Again I remark, that those persons are poor comforters who have

Never Had any Trouble

themselves. A larkspur can not lecture on the nature of a snow-flake—it never saw a snow-flake; and those people who have always lived in the summer of prosperity cannot talk to those who are frozen in disaster. God keeps aged people in the world, I think, for this very work of sympathy. They have been through all these trials. They know all that which irritates and all that which soothes. If there are men and women here who have old people in the house, or near at hand, so that they can easily reach them, I congratulate them. Some of us have had trials in life, and although we have had many friends around about us, we have wished that father and mother were still alive, that we might go and tell them. Perhaps they could not say much, but it would have been such a comfort to have them around. These aged ones, who have been all through the trials of life, know how to give condolence. Cherish them; let them lean on your arm—these aged people. If when you speak to them they cannot hear just what you say the first time, and you have to say it a second time, when you say it the second time do not say it sharply. If you do, you will be sorry for it on the day when you take the last look and brush back the silvery locks from the wrinkled brow just before they screw the lid on. Blessed be God for the old people. They may not have so much strength to go around, but they are God's appointed ministers of comfort to a broken heart.

People who have not had trial themselves cannot give comfort to others. They may talk very beautifully, and they may give you a great deal of poetic sentiment; but while poetry is perfume that smells sweet, it makes a very poor salve. If you have a grave in your pathway, and somebody comes and covers it all over with flowers, it is a grave yet. Those who have not had grief themselves know not

The Mystery of a Broken Heart.

They know not the meaning of childlessness, and the having no one to put to bed at night, or the standing in a room where every book and picture and door is full of memories—the door mat where she sat, the cup out of which she drank, the place where she stood at the door and clapped her hands, the odd figures that she scribbled, the blocks she built into a house. Ah no; you must have trouble yourself before you can comfort trouble in others. But come, all ye who have been bereft, and ye who have been comforted in your sorrows, and stand around these afflicted souls, and say to them, "I had that very sorrow myself. God comforted me, and He will comfort you"; and that will go right to the spot. In other words, to comfort others we must have faith in God, practical experience, and good, sound common sense.

But there are three or four considerations that I will bring this morning to those who are sorrowful and distressed, and that we can always bring to them knowing that they will effect a cure. And the first consideration is that

God Sends Our Troubles

in love. I often hear people in their troubles say "Why, I wonder what God has against me!

ey seem to think God has some grudge inst them because trouble and misfortune e come. Oh no. Do you not remember t passage of Scripture, "Whom the Lord eth He chasteneth"? A child comes in with ery bad splinter in its hand, and you try to ract it. It is a very painful operation. The ld draws back from you, but you persist. u take the child with a

Gentle but Firm

sp; for although there may be pain in the splinter must come out. And it is e that dictates it, and makes you persist. friends, I really think that nearly all our rows in this world are only the hand of r Father extracting some thorn. If all these rows were sent by enemies, I would say, arm urselves against them; and, as in tropical mes, when a tiger comes down from the ountains and carries off a child from the vil- e, the neighbors band together and go into e forest and hunt the monster, so I would e you, if I thought these misfortunes were nt by an enemy, go out and battle against em. But no; they come from a Father so nd, so loving, so gentle, that the prophet, eaking of His tenderness and mercy, drops e idea of a father, and says, "As one whom s mother comforteth, so will I comfort you."

Again I remark, there is comfort in the ought that God, by all this process, is going

To Make You Useful.

Do you know that those who accomplish the ost for God and heaven have all been under e harrow? Show me a man that has done any- ing for Christ in this day, in a public or pri- te place, who has had no trouble, and whose th has been smooth. Ah, no!

I once went through an axe-factory, and I w them take the bars of iron and thrust them to the terrible furnaces. Then besweated orkmen with long tongs stirred the blaze. hen they brought out a bar of iron and put it to a crushing-machine, and then they put it etween jaws that bit it in twain. Then they ut it on an anvil, and there were great ham- ers swung by machinery—each one a half- n in weight—that went thump! thump! thump! that iron could have spoken, it would have id, "Why all this beating? Why must I be ounded any more than any other iron?" The orkmen would have said, "We want to make xes out of you, keen, sharp axes—axes with hich to hew down the forest, and build the ip, and erect houses, and carry on a thousand nterprises of civilization. That's the reason e pound you." Now, God puts a soul into

The Furnace of Trial,

nd then it is brought out and run through the rushing-machine, and then it comes down on e anvil, and upon it blow after blow, blow fter blow, and the soul cries out, "O Lord, hat does all this mean?" God says, "I want make something very useful out of you. You hall be something to hew with, and something build with. It is a practical process through hich I am putting you." Yes, my Christian iends, we want more tools in the Church of od. Not more wedges to split with; we have nough of these. Not more bores with which drill; we have too many bores. What we ally want is keen, sharp, well-tempered axes, nd if there be any other way of making them han in the hot furnace, and on the hard anvil, nd under the heavy hammer, I do not know hat it is. Remember that if God brings any ind of chastisement upon you, it is only to ake you useful. Do not sit down discouraged, nd say, "I have no more reason for living; I ish I were dead!" Oh, there never was so much eason for your living as now! By this ordeal ou have been consecrated a priest of the Most igh God. Go out and do your whole work for he Master.

There is comfort in the thought that all our

Troubles are a Revelation.

Have you ever thought of it in that connection? The man who has never been through chastise- ent is ignorant about a thousand things in his soul he ought to know. For instance, here is a man who prides himself on his cheerfulness of character. He has no patience with anybody who is depressed in spirits. Oh, it is easy for him to be cheerful, with his fine house, his filled wardrobe, and well-strung instruments of music, and tapestried parlor, and plenty of money in the bank waiting for some permanent investment. It is easy for him to be cheerful. But suppose his fortune goes to pieces, and his house goes down under the sheriff's hammer, and the banks will not have anything to do with his paper! Suppose those people who were once elegantly entertained at his table get so short-sighted that they cannot recognize him upon the street! How then?

Is it Easy to be Cheerful?

It is easy to be cheerful in the home, after the day's work is done, and the gas is turned on, and the house is full of romping little ones. But suppose the piano is shut because the fingers that played on it will no more touch the keys, and the childish voice that asked so many questions will ask no more. Then is it so easy? When a man wakes up and finds that his resources are all gone, he begins to rebel, and he says, "God is hard; God is outrageous. He had no business to do this to me!" My friends, those of us who have been through trouble know what a sinful and rebellious heart we have, and how much God has to put up with, and how much we need pardon. It is only in the light of a flaming furnace that we can learn our own weakness and our own lack of moral resource.

There is also a great deal of comfort in the fact that there will be a family

Reconstruction in a Better Place.

From Scotland or England or Ireland a child emigrates to this country. It is very hard parting, but he comes, after a while writing home as to what a good land it is. Another brother comes, a sister comes, and another, and after a while the mother comes, and after a while the father comes, and now they are all here, and they have a time of great congratulation and a very pleasant reunion. Well, it is just so with our families: they are emigrating to a better land. Now, one goes out. Oh, how hard it is to part with him! Another goes. Oh, how hard it is to part with her! And another, and another, and we ourselves will after a while go over, and then we will be together. Oh, what a reunion! Do you believe that? "Yes," you say. You do not! You do not believe it as you believe other things. If you did, why, it would take nine-tenths of your trouble off your heart!

The fact is, heaven to many of us is a great fog. It is away off somewhere, filled with an uncertain and indefinite population. That is the kind of heaven that many of us dream about; but it is the most tremendous fact in all the universe—this heaven of the gospel. Our departed friends are not afloat. The residence in which you live is not so real as the residence in which they stay. You are afloat, you who do not know in the morning what will happen before night. They are housed and safe forever. Do not, therefore, pity your departed friends who have died in Christ. They do not need any of your pity. You might as well send a letter of condolence to Queen Victoria on her obscurity, or to the Rothschilds on their poverty, as to pity those who have won the palm. Do not say of those who are departed, "Poor child!" "Poor father!" "Poor mother!" They are not poor. You are poor—you whose homes have been shattered—not they. You do not dwell much with your families in this world. All day long you are off to business. Will it not be pleasant

When You Can be Together

all the while? If you have had four children, and one is gone, and anybody asks how many children you have, do not be so infidel as to say three. Say four—one in heaven. Do not think that the grave is unfriendly. You go into your room and dress for some grand entertainment, and you come forth beautifully appareled; and the grave is only the place where we go to dress for the glorious Resurrection, and we will come out radiant, radiant, mortality having become immortality. Oh, how much condolence there is in this thought!

I expect to see my kindred in heaven; I expect to see them as certainly as I expect to go home to-day. Ay, I shall most certainly see them. Eight or ten will come up from the graveyard back of Somerville; and one will come up from the mountains back of Amoy, China; and another will come up from the sea off Cape Hatteras; and thirty will come up from Greenwood; and I shall know them better than I ever knew them here. And your friends—they may be across the sea, but the trumpet that sounds here will sound there. You will come up on just the same day. Some morning you have overslept yourself, and you open your eyes and see that the sun is high in the heavens, and you say, "I have overslept, and I must be up and off." So you will open your eyes on the morning of the Resurrection, in the full blaze of God's light, and you will say, "I must be up and away." Oh yes, you will come up, and there will be a re-union, a reconstruction of your family. I like what Halburton—I think it was good old Mr. Halburton—said in his last moments: "I thank God that I ever lived, and that I have a father in heaven, and a mother in heaven, and brothers in heaven, and sisters in heaven, and I am now going up to see them."

I remark, once more: our troubles are

Preparative for Glory.

What a transition it was for Paul—from the slippery deck of a foundering ship to the calm presence of Jesus! What a transition it was for Latimer—from the stake to a throne! What a transition it was for Robert Hall—from insanity to glory! What a transition it was for Richard Baxter—from the dropsy to the "saint's everlasting rest"! And what a transition it will be for you—from a world of sorrow to a world of joy! John Holland, when he was dying, said, "What means this brightness in the room? Have you lighted the candles?" "No," they replied, "we have not lighted any candles." Then said he, "Welcome, heaven!" the light already beaming upon his pillow. O ye who are persecuted in this world! your enemies will get off the track after a while, and all will speak well of you among the thrones. Ho! ye who are sick now, no medicines to take there. One breath of the eternal hills will thrill you with immortal vigor. And ye who are lonesome now, there will be a thousand

Spirits to Welcome You

into their companionship. O ye bereft souls! there will be no grave-digger's spade that will cleave the side of that hill, and there will be no dirge wailing from that temple. The river of God, deep as the joy of heaven, will roll on between banks odorous with balm, and over depths bright with jewels, and under skies roseate with gladness, argosies of light going down the stream to the stroke of glittering oar and the song of angels! Not one sigh in the wind; not one tear mingling with the waters!

"There shall I bathe my weary soul
In seas of heavenly rest,
And not a wave of trouble roll
Across my peaceful breast."

THE WICKED AT CHRIST'S COMING.

By Rev. Henry Varley.

The Distinction Made—The Moral Characteristics of the Age—The World Unconverted at Christ's Coming—The Thousand Years in the Prison House—Paul's Vision—Heresy in the Last Days.

"WHERE shall the ungodly and the sinner appear?" The distinction is between the righteous and the ungodly, the saved and the sinner. It is asked, Where shall they appear? That is—at the Lord's return. He distinctly says His coming shall be "as a snare to all them that dwell on the face of the whole earth." And again, "The Lord Jesus shall be revealed from heaven with His mighty angels, in flaming fire, taking vengeance on them that know not God, and that obey not the gospel of our Lord Jesus Christ." If any feel a doubt as to the moral characteristics which belong to this age of the end, these passages may set your mind at rest. Observe He is

To Come in Flaming Fire,

taking vengeance—He would not so come if the moral condition of things did not demand it. If the large proportion of people were prepared for His coming, then such a manifestation of His wrath would be altogether out of place. Then, again, we are told that when He comes the kings of the earth and other great men are to call to the mountains and rocks, "Fall on us, and hide us from the face of Him that sitteth on the throne, and from the wrath of the Lamb." Is that a picture of a world brought to Christ by the preaching of the gospel? Do you not see the truth clearly emphasized that the world-rulers shall be in opposition to God, and shall be dashed to pieces at the coming of Christ? And, indeed, do we not see a foreshadowing of that state of things in the frightful condition of Europe to-day? Fourteen or fifteen million armed men; science lending her mighty aid in the perfection of the forces of destruction. The only key to unlock the wards of this lock is the Coming of Christ.

And when He *does* come, where will you, my unconverted friends, appear? The materialistic

Scepticism of the Age

in which we live laughs these things to scorn, but "If any man love not the Lord Jesus Christ, let him be anathema maranatha"; let him be accursed at the coming of the Lord. Note also in Eph. 5:5, "This ye know, that no whoremonger, nor unclean person, nor covetous man, who is an idolater, hath any inheritance in the kingdom of Christ and of God." That kingdom comprehends, I believe, the thousand years of blessing. "The wicked," it is written, "lived not again till the thousand years are finished." Without question, that immortal personality of yours will, O unconverted hearer! at the coming of the Lord, enter the abode of condemned spirits, the prison house, as Isaiah calls it, till the thousand years are past, and then comes the fulfilling of judgment. When these years are over and eternal ages dawn, your doom is described by the great King Himself in these awful words, "The fearful, and unbelieving, and the abominable, and murderers, and whoremongers, and sorcerers, and idolaters, and all liars, shall have their part in the lake which burneth with fire and brimstone: which is the second death."

Such is the testimony of Scripture, and if we are asked "Where shall the ungodly and the sinner appear?" we can only reply—in perdition with unblest spirits. After that thousand years of remand—for it is judicially a remand until the trial at the great white throne—then

Judgment and Doom.

Do you wonder that men of old, realizing this, wept over their congregations? Do you wonder that Paul says, "I ceased not to warn every one night and day with tears?" Do you marvel he calls God to record "How greatly I long after you all in the mind and heart of Jesus Christ?" Paul knew the future of the unsaved, he had seen God, for he tells us of being translated into Paradise—very likely (as you will find by comparing Acts 14:19, 20 with II Cor. 12:2) when his body was lying stoned apparently to death outside the city of Lystra.

I remember dear Henry Bewley saying to me at Dublin: "What do you think was the power that moved Paul?" I replied, "The love of Christ." "Yes, that constrained him, but I will tell you what I think—when caught up to Paradise he saw the King in His beauty; from that moment he was dead to the world." Now, while you and I cannot expect to see God with the outward eye, we may have such a view of Him by faith, which is a whole second sense to us—that we may henceforth live as we have never yet done.

I trust my testimony may lead many who are believers to come out and be separate, looking heedfully to the times in which we live.

These are Appalling Times.

Think of the laxity in love and truth among professing Christians, and thank God that beloved ministers are standing out for God's truth and against error on every hand. Away with teachers who make light of the atonement: away with all principles that profess to seek a righteousness in man! Seek the righteousness of God, which is by faith; and when He comes this poor disordered earth shall become as the garden of the Lord.

Man's government is wellnigh at an end; the sand-glass of time is running out. He is coming whose right is to reign; the Lamb of God, whose blood fell around the precincts of the Cross of Calvary. He is coming again in power and great glory to bring this reprobate earth into the beneficence of His government, and into harmony with the mind of God. Then shall be fulfilled the first prayer that came from His blessed lips, that prayer He has taught us to pray: "Thy Kingdom come: Thy will be done on earth as it is in Heaven." That prayer of faith shall shortly be accomplished as surely as He lives. Meanwhile, let us occupy till He comes.

THE PROPHETIC DAY—AUGUST 14-15.

By Rev. M. Baxter.

SEVERAL years ago Dr. Bright, in his "Coming of the Antichrist" who, he believes, will be a Napoleon, predicted that August 15, being both the Bonapartist Fête Day and the Feast of the Assumption of the Virgin Mary, would probably be a very notable date in the future career of the Antichrist.

Strange to relate, when in March 1887, it was discovered that the Last Day of Passover Week, April 11, 1901, will be the End of this Age, as being 2,345 years distant from the "Command to rebuild Jerusalem" (Dan. 8:14; 9:25; 12:11, 12; Nehem. 2), it then appears that *the first day of Antichrist's reign for 1,260 days will actually be August* 15, 1897, because that day is exactly 1,335 days previous to April 11, 1901. (Daniel 12:12.)

On Wednesday, August 15, this year, the Bonapartists held their annual fête as usual. Imperialist masses were celebrated in several churches, artificial violets were worn by the faithful, and Platonic addresses were signed and sent to Prince Victor Napoleon. Since the death of the Prince Imperial deprived them of a rallying-point, the Bonapartists have been split up into rival factions. Prince Napoleon is an exile in Switzerland, and Prince Victor, his recalcitrant son, has sought refuge in Belgium. Both aspire to the purple; Prince Victor is the favorite. His partisans are the more numerous, influential, and perhaps the more noisy—witness the diatribes of his leading advocate, Paul de Cassagnac.

The 15th of August is also a great religious and social fête. The day remains, in spite of revolution, what it has been for centuries—one of the highest festivals of the Roman Catholic Church, that on which the assumption of the Holy Virgin is commemorated. This event was duly observed this year in France by pompous services in the churches. Formerly processions took place outside the sacred edifices, but they are now forbidden save in the country villages. The procession was instituted by Louis XIII. as a thanksgiving to the Virgin Mary for the birth of a son, which he attributed to her divine intercession. Although shorn of this outward splendor the festival attracts as many of the faithful as ever. The churches were well attended, despite the fact that a goodly portion of the regular congregations were at the seaside. Evidently atheistical teachings have not yet done much harm to the Catholic Church in Paris. So much for the religious side of the date.

Its social character is equally interesting. The French, as most people, do not keep birthdays like other nations, but the days of the saints after whom they are christened. August 15 is the Sainte Marie, and as nearly every family has a Mary in it, it is easy to see the amount of feasting that must attend every Mary's birthday throughout the country. From early morn people were seen hurrying to and fro in all directions, with nosegays and pots of flowers in their hands, *en route* to all their female relatives whose fête it is. Gifts of all kinds were made, but the great majority choose flowers, the sale of which, during August 15, is something fabulous. Perhaps this is one of the prettiest observances to be met with anywhere. It is not costly, and everybody can share in it. Old as well as young receive these floral offerings of affection, and sad indeed is any Mary in France who is forgotten or neglected.

THE JUGGERNAUT FESTIVAL.

THE ceremony of the migration of Juggernaut, the Indian deity, takes place still at this season of the year. The *Indian Witness* thus speaks of the spectacle as it is now witnessed: "Juggernaut, seated on his car of state, is dragged from his own house to that of his father-in-law, Radhabullub, and after a stay of eight days returns with his bride and is dragged back to his own quarters, where he lives in connubial bliss till next year. *Playing at dolls* we might call it, but the festival attracts thousands to Comillah from the outlying districts. Among the crowds who begin to pour in a week beforehand, there are Hindoos and Mahommedans, hill men and women, Tipperahs, Kukis, and a few Lushais, with their picturesque costumes and Mongolian cast of features, easily distinguishable among the crowd. On the day the car is to be dragged, the crowds assemble in their thousands round it; a strong force of police preserves the peace; the District Superintendent is also out, and as much order as can be expected is observed.

"The car itself is a trumpery affair, constructed almost entirely of bamboos, three stories high. Tinsel, red cloth, and other ornaments are lavishly laid on wherever they can be induced to stick, and the whole is daubed over with red paint in barbarous profusion. The musicians are seated on the top story, which is roofed in with a pyramid roof, exactly like a huge red extinguisher, with a flag at the apex. The instruments they play are drums, clarionets, flutes, and brass gongs. The gentlemen on the gongs are particularly energetic, and have several solos allotted to them. Offerings of fruits and flowers are placed before the god. Those who cannot get near enough to place them at his feet throw them about at each other, and it simply rains pineapples, plantains, chunks of plantain-tree, and over-ripe melons.

"The Prime Minister of Hill Tipperah arrives, seated on a richly caparisoned elephant, followed by his suite, also on elephants. The *tamasha* then begins. The shouting grows louder and louder, the people, worked up to the highest pitch of religious frenzy, fight and dance and behave like lunatics. The procession of elephants goes seven times round the car, when at a given signal from the head priest—who, as master of the ceremonies, stands and waves his baton from the second story, while two men with *daos* stand by ready to cut the ropes, should any fanatic wish to throw himself under the wheel—and the car is started. The musicians put their instruments to the severest tests, and the gongs are heard even above the shouts and ells of the multitude. Every one tries either to ouch the car or to drag the ropes; it being aid down that all who are so fortunate as to do o, will have an exceptionally good time during he next life.

"With innumerable halts, the car at last reaches ts destination—a quarter of a mile from starting-point. Here it is housed, and the crowds isperse. Dancing, singing, and festivities of ll sorts are the order of the day for a week.

"There is not quite so much enthusiasm in Calcutta as at Comillah, but the thousands who ather there, and the frenzy which many of the evotees develop on the occasion, are still marvellous. To see native gentlemen, who hold igh and trusted positions in commercial and ivil life, half naked before the little car, singing nd gesticulating in the most intense manner is ot an edifying sight. The old flames burst out gain under these weird enchantments, and the oor ignorant ones are ready to fall beneath the ar as their ancestors did, but these would-be artyrs have a very wholesome dread of an fficer's whip, and a very light stroke of it dispels every desire for suicide."

ITALIAN NEWSPAPER ENTERPRISE.

A VOLUNTEER service to gospel work, which God may bless, though it proceeds from secular motives, has been undertaken in Milan by Signor Sonzogno, the proprietor of the leading daily newspaper, the *Secolo*, who has commenced the ssue of a popular edition of the Bible in halfpenny numbers. The paper and type are to be xcellent, and about one fifth of each page is ext, and the rest notes and illustrations. The heapness of the book is such as to bring it within the reach of all. Signor Sonzogno undertakes this work not in the interest of religion, but apparently as a commercial venture, yet believing that the Bible tends to promote iberty. In his paper, the *Secolo*, he uses the ollowing remarkable words: "There is one book which gathers up the poetry and the cience of humanity, and that book is the Bible, and with this book no other work in any literature can be compared. It is a book that Newton read continually, that Cromwell carried at his saddle, and that Voltaire kept always on his study-table. It is a book that believers and unbelievers should alike study, and that ought to be found in every house. The text will be that of Martini, translated from the Vulgate, and care will be taken to insure accuracy." This edition cannot be hindered by the Church of Rome. It cannot be said that it is circulated by Protestants or by foreigners, and it will be a reach of the new penal code to interfere with he liberty of publication. There surely is hope or Italy in this enterprise. Fifty thousand copies of the first number were sold in one week. It is on all the news-stands, and sells at one cent.

A CHEERFUL MISSIONARY.

A GRAPHIC picture of missionary work in Japan is given in a letter from the Rev. J. P. Hearst, who writes to the *Church* from Osaka. The extract here given is especially worthy of note on account of the light it sheds on the character of the writer. Few men when pelted with mud would have seen in it grounds for thankfulness, but Mr. Hearst gratefully acknowledges *that there were no stones in it*. He says: 'We have a very hopeful mission. It is true that evangelistic work, in which most of us are engaged, is not so pleasant in many respects as school work either in the academic or theological department. We cannot have things as systematic as our friends the teachers have, nor have we as many opportunties of study, as we are constantly preaching to simple-minded people, and a great deal of time is necessarily spent away from home; and then the small steamers and *jinrikishas*—not the most comfortable means of travelling ever invented—are not friendly to books. But still we have our encouragements as well as our discomforts. It is always a pleasure to preach the gospel to large and appreciative audiences, and if we do now and then get a few curses or a little mud, yet for my own part I am glad to say that I have never yet had stones thrown with my mud, an experience which some of my friends have met. Usually our audiences are wonderfully patient. They will sit through three hours' preaching without any disturbance except it be an occasional howl of no! no! We do not mind that very much, as we are sure most of the company are glad to hear. Wherever one goes, there are always good audiences, and I do not hesitate to say that while some places are more hopeful than others, there is no place where one may not begin work with full expectation of some immediate fruit from his labor.

LABOR-SAVING IN CHINA.

A PRACTICAL lesson in labor-saving appliances and the advantages of Western methods in a time of emergency was recently given in China, much to the astonishment of the natives. It is much to be wished that some among them who are laboriously striving, by good works and offerings to impotent idols, to work out their salvation might go to Western missionaries, who also would be able to show them "a more excellent way." (Rom. 8: 3.)

"The awful devastation in the province of Honan, China, caused by the overflow of the Yellow River, has apparently been the means," says a missionary of the American Board, "of bringing more enlightenment to the people of the province than could probably have been secured in any other way in so short a time. A Chinese paper gives an account of the way in which the repairs in the breach in the river-banks have been conducted. At first long lines of workmen were formed, with baskets and wheelbarrows, bringing earth a distance, in some cases, of several miles. This process was desperately slow, whereas great haste was necessary. Moreover, the quarrels among the workmen were so frequent that, shocking as it was to Chinese prejudices, a portable railroad was obtained. Officials and laborers watched with unbounded delight the operations of the new and swift method of carrying the earth. So great was the necessity for haste that work was kept up day and night; and working with candles was difficult and so unsatisfactory that soon an electric-lighting machine with twenty-five lights was set up. It was found to be a great saving of expense as well as a great help to the work. People came in large numbers from all the surrounding country to look upon the new light and see the railroad, and were profoundly impressed with the value of foreign inventions."

A CHICAGO CLERGYMAN HEALED.

THE recent remarkable recovery of the Rev. Dr. John Williamson, of Chicago, from a disorder usually both painful and tedious, is reported by the Rev. A. B. Simpson in his *Christian Alliance*. Dr. Williamson, who has been pastor of the First Methodist Episcopal Church, the Wabash Avenue and the Michigan Avenue churches, described his cure at a meeting of Methodist ministers, after which he was interviewed by a reporter.

"Mine was an uræmic ailment," he said; "my liver was also affected, and I was in a bad way generally. I know also that I was overworked, and sometimes felt that perhaps, I might never be able to do regular work in my pulpit again. I consulted some of the best physicians in Chicago, and they advised me to rest. I did not want to give up my labors, but I am enough of a physician to know that nature will assert itself. *I am a graduate of Rush Medical College*, though I have never practiced. Thus it was I went to God. I prayed as I had never prayed before, and I felt that I was in close and perfect communion with Him. I cannot describe it. I told God all my troubles, and received assurances that everything would be well. My plan of action was to lay down three rules, if they can so be called—prayer to God, cessation from work, and to take more physical exercise. I understood, of course, that rest and exercise would not effect the complete cure wished for."

"What is the difference, Doctor, between your prayers at this time and those previously?" was asked.

"*I had something definite to ask for*; that was all," he replied. "*I wanted to be cured*," he added, with a smile. "The trouble with too many people is, that when they pray they don't know what they want. I knew exactly what I wanted, and got it."

"How soon after your prayer to God did you realize that you had been answered?"

"Almost immediately. I have been able to work right along, with the exception of a short time when I was at Bay View. I took a rest there in the summer, and spent my days in rowing and praying to God. While I have no regular charge now, I fill the pulpit of some brother nearly every Sunday, and have other labors in addition, so that I cannot say that I am not busy."

"Have you any idea, Doctor, what might have been the result had you depended on ordinary physical treatment, and taken the year's rest the physicians recommended?"

"I simply would have lost a year's work, and probably not felt so well as I do now. In fact, I might not have recovered at all, though I do not assert this. But my recovery has been wonderful in this, that I did not follow the advice of my physicians, and I took no medicines. My cure is the direct result of divine healing, and so I have been free to proclaim."

A CHINESE DEMONIAC.

AN appeal for help was recently made to a missionary in China, who, if the afflicted man correctly diagnosed his own case, was authorized to give him relief. (Mark 16: 17.) The Rev. W. P. Chalfant, Presbyterian missionary at Tsinan-fu, says in a letter to the *Church*: "I had a curious experience at the inn at which I was stopping, which, by the way, belongs to the Christian Fang. A man 'possessed with a devil' came into the inn and fell down before Mr. Fang, beseeching him to help him. They called me out to see him. I found him sitting in a chair, trembling from head to foot, and with tears streaming down his face. He was about fifty years of age, and rather small of stature. His face bore an expression of intense nervous apprehension. He said that he had been afflicted by this devil for more than ten years. The paroxysms came on suddenly, sometimes in the middle of the night. He described with excited vividness how the devil would begin by trying to 'scoop out his eyes,' and then would give him a succession of sharp pricks in different parts of his body, and would end by 'whispering in his ear' that he should 'go and strike that man!' 'Take this club and run up and down the street.' He said that he could not sleep, and had no appetite; in short, he presented the appearance of a nervous wreck. He besought me to go out to his house and drive away the demon. I must say I felt somewhat embarrassed. I tried to calm him by telling him that I thought he was merely troubled with a nervous disease, but I soon saw that I was hopelessly in the minority, even my own helper politely hinting that, with all deference to western rationalism, he thought that there actually was a devil in the man. Finally I was compelled to go with Mr. Fang and the helper to the unfortunate man's cottage just outside the village. We sat down in the humble abode and spoke a few comforting words, directing the attention of the family to Him who once cast out demons in a land 'not so very far from China.' I then called upon the helper to pray. I could hardly suppress a smile as he began, 'O Lord, we are not sure whether this man is really possessed of the devil or not, but if it be so, then, Lord, drive it out,' etc. By the time we had finished the man was considerably calmer."

CHRISTIAN HERALD AND SIGNS OF OUR TIMES.

OFFICE, 63 BIBLE HOUSE, NEW YORK.

ENTERED AT THE POST-OFFICE AT NEW YORK, N. Y., AS SECOND-CLASS MATTER.

EVERY NUMBER CONTAINS:

The Portrait and Biography of some eminent person.
The Sermon Dr. Talmage preached the last Sunday morning.
An Exposition of Unfulfilled Prophecy.
A Summary of the Events of the Week, Notes of Religious and Temperance Movements, etc.
A Sermon by Rev. C. H. Spurgeon, of London, from advance sheets sent by special arrangement.
Pictures of Missionary Life, etc., and Descriptive Articles.
An instalment of a Serial Story.
An Exposition of the International Sunday-School Lesson, by Mrs. M. Baxter.

PUBLISHER'S NOTICE.

THE whole edition of THE CHRISTIAN HERALD was mailed last week to subscribers during Tuesday, August 28. The last delivery at the New York Post-office was made at 11:55 P. M. It is unnecessary to continue these notices, as those made here for three months past show that the variation in the time of mailing is one of minutes only. Subscribers may be assured that the paper is invariably mailed on the Tuesday of each week, and they may therefore calculate when it ought to reach them. When it is late, complaint should be made to the local postmaster. If it should not come at all, notice should be sent to this office, so that if there is any error in the address, it may be rectified immediately; and if there is no error, the case will be reported to the Postmaster-General.

CURRENT EVENTS.

The House Committee on Foreign Affairs has responded to the President's request for power to deal with the Fishery question by retaliation. It has framed a bill granting both the requests he made. Its first section gives him authority to suspend in whole or in part the transportation across United States territory, in bond and without payment of duties, of merchandise imported into or exported from Canada through United States ports. The second section authorizes the President, whenever there is discrimination against American vessels in the use of the Welland, St. Lawrence River, and Chambly canals, to impose a toll on Canadian vessels for the use of the Sault Ste. Marie and St. Clair Flats canals, or to prohibit their use to such vessels. In both cases the exercise of this authority is left to the discretion of the President, and it is understood that he will not use it if the Canadian Government yields the points in dispute.

The New York State Republican Convention which assembled at Saratoga on August 28, had a duty to perform of momentous concern to the party. The selection of a State ticket for New York at an election in which the vote of the State will probably decide the Presidential contest, was a responsible undertaking, the import of which was fully realized both within and without the State. The convention, however, consented to register the decision previously made by Ex-Senator Platt and the other three managers of the party. Ex-Senator Warner Miller was nominated by acclamation for Governor, and Col. S. V. R. Cruger for Lieutenant-Governor. The comments made by the Republican daily journals indicate that the result does not satisfy the party in New York City, but it is accepted as the only basis on which the dissensions of the past twelve years could be held in abeyance for a time. Mr. Miller profits by the internal jealousies now, as he did when he gained a seat in the United States Senate. The platform adopted by the convention is the result of a similar compromise, and must have cost the committee which framed it enormous labor. The High License plank, which Warner Miller insisted on incorporating, was adopted, though many influential liquor-dealers were among the delegates. It declares that the Republican party unequivocally condemns the course of Governor Hill in obstructing, by his vetoes, acts for increasing the fees for licenses, by which a larger share of the cost of government might be levied on the liquor traffic, and approves the efforts of the Republicans in the last Legislature upon the liquor question, especially on passing the act, nullified by such Executive action, to restrict that traffic by charges which would lift some of the burdens of taxation caused by the liquor traffic from the home and farm; and expresses the belief that such charges should be advanced by standards similar to those successfully enforced in other States under Republican control. Though this plank is not sufficiently outspoken to satisfy the temperance element in the party, it is an offence to the liquor interest.

The Settlement of a Colony of Mormons in Wyoming Territory is reported. It is stated by the Salt Lake *Herald* that four hundred Mormon families have gone into the southwestern part of the Territory and taken homesteads there. The *Herald* copies from a Wyoming paper the prediction that the census-takers in 1890 will find in the western part of the Territory Mormons enough to control the county elections. It is well known that thousands of Mormons have settled in Idaho, and it is stated by political managers there that one-fourth of the men of voting age in the Territory are Mormons. There are colonies also in Colorado and Arizona. In Nevada the number of Mormon settlers is so large that the Salt Lake *Herald* declares it would not be difficult for them to gain control of the government of the State if they make an organized effort to do so.

The Yellow Fever Scourge at Jacksonville, Fla., continued its terrible ravages all through last week. On Wednesday the number of new cases rose to thirty-three, and four deaths for the twenty-four hours. On Thursday the new cases were twenty-three, and the deaths three; but the ominous feature was noticed that the new cases were scattered over the city, instead of being confined to any one district. On Friday the new cases were again twenty-three, and the deaths four. On Thursday the official bulletin gave the total number of cases to that date as 188. Of those, twenty-six had died, thirty-four had recovered, and the remainder were still under treatment. About a thousand people left the city during the first four days of the week, at the suggestion of the executive committee, who believe that in depopulating the city as far as possible, the most effectual way of fighting the scourge is to be found. All who are willing to go are sent to Camp Perry. No fugitives are allowed to go beyond Way Cross. This order, issued by Surgeon-General Hamilton, is causing much indignation, and will increase the distress already existing, as many women and children were being sent out to the mountain districts of Georgia, and other places impregnable to yellow fever. At the close of last week business was almost entirely suspended, only a few grocery stores remaining open. The clergy remain bravely at their posts, and the Protestant Episcopal Bishop, who was away on vacation, promptly returned when he heard of the outbreak of the fever.

The Tension between France and Italy, which two weeks ago assumed a menacing aspect, has been relieved by the prudence, or forbearance, of the French Government. It was caused by Italy taking possession of a strip of land on the African coast of the Red Sea, including Massowah and the town of Zulla, a seaport south of Massowah. The Italian Government duly notified the European powers that the Italian flag has been hoisted, and that a protectorate has been proclaimed, in compliance with the demands of the local sheiks. M. Goblet, French Minister of Foreign Affairs, then sent a note to the French representatives abroad in reference to the announcement, entering a protest against the annexation, as a violation of Italian pledges. The French newspapers also claim that Zulla was ceded to France, under a treaty signed by Abyssinia. The situation was further complicated by an ostentatious visit of Signor Crispi, the Italian Premier, to Berlin, which had the appearance of an intimation to France that Italy was under German protection. After the publication of a series of inflammatory articles in the newspapers of France and Germany, the French Government relieved the strain last week by the publication of a despatch to the Italian Court, stating that France desires to avoid entering upon irritating polemics, and does not care to prolong the debate; but it is impossible to avoid recalling the fact that a French Consulate, sanctioned by the Porte, was established at Massowah twenty-five years before the date of the Italian occupation.

A Plan for the Settlement of the Bulgarian question is said to be under the consideration of the Powers interested in its solution. The fact that it emanates from Russia renders its acceptance probable, especially as it conciliates England and Austria, which are the opponents of the Russian policy in the Balkans, and also would be regarded favorably for other reasons by Germany. The proposal is to place the Duke of Cumberland on the Bulgarian throne. The Duke is a cousin of Queen Victoria, and he is also a claimant to the throne of Hanover, and has pressed his claims against the Berlin Government with a pertinacity which will render his elevation to the throne of Bulgaria a relief to Bismarck. It is rumored that the Czar proposes not only to amalgamate Bulgaria with the Ottoman province known as Eastern Roumelia, but to annex also a section of Macedonia, thus giving the new kingdom access to the Ægean. Turkey would thus be cut off from land communication with Albania and her possessions west of Salonica, most of which would naturally fall to Austria. Italy would be placated by a small strip of the Dalmatian seacoast, which Austria would probably surrender to balance the acquisition of so large a slice of territory. The sufferer, as in every new rearrangement of the European map, would be Turkey, which is too helpless to resist. This extensive project is at present merely a matter of rumor, but it is clearly on the lines of prophecy.

Another Nihilist Plot to Assassinate the Czar is reported from St. Petersburg. The *Gaulois* publishes despatches from that city stating that only a timely discovery prevented the present Czar dying a similar death to that of his father. The quarters occupied by the conspirators, which were near the imperial palace, were raided by the police, who captured twelve men and three women. They also secured a number of bombs. Since this raid, several other arrests are said to have been made.

The German Socialists have Won a Victory at the polls. They succeeded on August 30 in electing Herr Liebknecht, their candidate for the Reichstag, in the sixth district of Berlin. He received 26,067 votes in a total of 41,791. The successful candidate is known as one of the most prominent men of his party, a friend and disciple of the late Karl Marx, and at present the ablest expounder of socialism in Germany. The district which elected him is a densely populated one, its inhabitants chiefly consisting of storekeepers and workingmen. Hasenclever, who formerly represented it, was also a socialist, but he became incurably insane, hence the necessity for the election of last week. Liebknecht's election was vigorously opposed by the Government. The man himself was personally obnoxious to the Court party, as he bore a musket in the rising of 1848. The election was carried chiefly by the efforts of the wives and daughters of the socialists, who canvassed actively for Liebknecht from house to house, and succeeded better than any man could have done in disseminating socialistic literature in violation of the law.

Contributions to the Fund for Supplying colored ministers in the South with this journal have been received, since our last acknowledgment, to the amount of $9. They are from Kansasville, Wis., $5; Fort Edward, N. Y., $2; Titusville, Penn., $2. On behalf of the nine ministers whose names we are thus enabled to place on our list, we heartily thank the friends who have sent these contributions. We earnestly pray that still more money for the same object may be sent. Patriotic Christians who are concerned about the welfare of the colored race will easily perceive that this is an excellent method of helping them through their pastors. Many of these have no commentary nor theological work, and they sadly need just such help in their studies as THE CHRISTIAN HERALD supplies. We have over a hundred applications from colored clergymen now waiting. Every dollar not only helps one minister directly, but the whole congregation to whom he ministers.

The Imprisoned Boston Clergyman, the Rev. W. F. Davis, is to be released to-morrow, September 7. He has served about ten months of the year in the Charles Street Jail, to which he was sentenced for preaching on the Common. As he has a time allowance of thirty-six days for good behavior, the authorities have no right to hold him longer. Mr. Davis, after his release, will remain a week with his family in Boston, then visit friends in Providence, and will probably preach at Olneyville, where at one time he was settled as a pastor. Later, he will preach in Connecticut.

An Ingenious Device for Photographing thieves has been constructed by an inventor in Connecticut. In describing it recently to a reporter of a local journal, he said: "I propose to have it fixed in the vaults of banks to protect them from burglars. I have a camera connected with a flash-light, the camera placed in a position where it would command in the field of the lens a space of ten feet square or more in front of the door of the vault, and have the other apparatus so arranged that as soon as tampering with the vault door was attempted the whole would be placed in operation. My plan would of course include retaining the burglar alarm connecting with police headquarters. As soon as the burglars had begun operations the police would be alarmed, and at the same instant a picture of the men would be made by the camera and flash-light combined, so that even if the men escaped the police, they would leave behind them evidence which would very probably eventually result in their detection." Even so ingenious a device might fail if the burglars were not at the moment in the field of the camera, but all wrongdoers may be sure that they leave evidence behind them of which God takes cognizance, and which, unless they obtain pardon through Christ, must bring down upon them everlasting punishment. We are explicitly told that He "setteth a print on the heels of our feet." (Job. 13:27.)

Two Tramps Were Caught in Burning Oil during a stolen ride on the Pennsylvania Railroad on August 27. A long freight train, while proceeding from Devon to Stratford, parted into two sections owing to the breaking of a coupling. There was a considerable space between the two at the top of an incline, but the rear section continued moving slowly until it began to descend, when its speed became accelerated, and it passed down the declivity at a fearful rate. At the foot, it crashed into the forward section with terrific force. The last car of the forward section was laden with grain, and the first car of the rear section with cans of oil. The concussion exploded the oil, and in a minute the grain was on fire and burning fiercely. While the train-hands were congratulating themselves that no one happened to be on those cars two fearful shrieks rent the air, and two men, their clothes blazing, sprang out of the wrecked grain car. The flames were speedily extinguished, but the men were both badly burned, and one of them will die. They were tramps, who had crawled into the grain car before the train started to steal a ride. It doubtless seemed to them then a very comfortable place in which to travel, and they must have been amazed when it turned out to be the most fatal place on the train. Similar amazement will one day come upon some who have entered the church for the sake of its comfort and respectability, but having no right to be there will be cast into the fire prepared, not for men, but for Satan and his angels. (Matt. 25:41.)

A Spacious House Floating on Long Island Sound caused some astonishment to people on shore on August 30. Inside the house the family appeared to be pursuing their ordinary course of life. At one of the windows a young lady sat rocking herself and reading. The servants were cooking in the kitchen, and even the household cat was comfortably sleeping on the rail of the piazza. The house rested on two immense scows, securely lashed together, and three puffing tugboats in front dragged it along. It appears that the house formerly stood on one of the hills at Stratford, Conn., but the owner desired to remove to Bridgeport, so had his house brought bodily to the shore of the Housatonic River, where it was lifted on the scows and towed down the river into the Sound to the Bridgeport Harbor. A site had been prepared for it, and on its arrival, work was at once commenced on the removal of the house from the water to its final resting-place. A party of friends accompanied the owner and his family on the novel voyage, and had a merry time on board as the strange craft floated to its destination. It would be well if the families who are unconcernedly floating down the stream of time toward their eternal destination had a similar reason for unconcern. Unhappily many of them, unlike this family, have not troubled themselves about the end of their voyage, and have not accepted the offer God makes to them of an everlasting habitation. (1 Tim. 6:19.)

A Disappointed Immigrant Committed Suicide in New York on August 30. As the sun was setting that evening, a pale, wan-faced man, about thirty years of age, was walking on the pier at the foot of Fifth Street. He was shabbily dressed, and his depressed expression of countenance attracted the notice of the passers-by. Suddenly he threw off his coat and plunged into the river. It was impossible to rescue him, for the tide carried him under the crowd of boats around the pier. It was not until the tide turned that his body was recovered. In his coat-pocket was a letter addressed to his wife, in Germany, which had not been mailed, probably because he had not money to buy a postage-stamp. In the letter he told his wife that he was bitterly disappointed with this country. He had not been able to obtain work in several weeks, and was not only unable to send the money he had promised, to bring her over, but had not money to buy food for himself. He had been fourteen weeks in America, and they had been weeks of such hardship that he expressed an ardent wish that he could get enough money to pay for a passage back to Germany. Hardships and trials come to those who undertake the pilgrimage to the heavenly country, but they have no such desire. They are supported and sustained on their way, and we are expressly told that, though they might have opportunity to return to the country whence they came out, they journey on to the city God has prepared for them. (Heb. 11:15, 16.)

A Bride and Bridegroom Separated, Bewailed their condition last week in New York. A reporter observing a crowd in Forsyth Street, made inquiries as to its cause, and found that a wedding-party had been summarily dispersed by an indignant woman. On going into one of the houses he found a young man locked up in an upper room, who complained bitterly that his mother had rushed him in-doors, driven away the wife whom he had just married, and locked him in his bedroom. Down-stairs, the mother, in a state of wild excitement, declared that her son should never have his wife, that she was not good enough for him, that the marriage should be dissolved, and otherwise manifesting her displeasure. On the other side the street the reporter discovered the bride, hiding in the rear of a house, in terror at the threats of her mother-in-law, whose shrill voice could be distinctly heard denouncing her. She was weeping over the loss of her young husband, and protesting against the cruelty of the separation. Public sympathy was evidently with the young people and against the vixenish mother-in-law, but no active interference was made with her arrangements. She was clearly a woman with whom it was dangerous to meddle, and as she had overawed her son, there seemed no probability of connubial bliss at present. If, however, the young people are true to each other they must eventually be reunited, as no one has a legal right to keep them separate. In the union between Christ and His church, of which marriage is a type, separation is also impossible, though Satan uses various agencies and exhausts all his arts in trying to effect it. We have apostolic assurance that even death, which dissolves all other ties, only consummates that one. (Rom. 8:38, 39.)

BRIEF NOTES.

There are about fifty-four thousand men in the penitentiaries of the United States, and about five thousand women.

The National Association of Methodist Local Preachers holds its next annual convention in Columbus, Ohio, September 15-18.

Rev. D. L. Moody and Mr. Sankey were at Greenfield, Mass., on August 26. The Second Presbyterian Church, in which the meetings were held, was crowded.

An important conference on Jewish missions will be held in the Hebrew Christian Church (Rev. Jacob Freshman's), 17 St. Mark's Place, N. Y., October 30 and 31.

New York State has $60,000,000 invested in prisons, asylums, hospitals, and almshouses. New York City alone has 10,000 dram-shops to help provide the inmates.

Mr. J. H. Kellogg, of Troy, N. Y., has given $1,000 to the National W. C. T. U., to be used in prosecuting its work. This is the largest single contribution ever received by the society.

Philadelphia calls attention to the fact that she has now 675 churches to New York's 432, Chicago's 371, and Brooklyn's 300. These 675 churches represent 46 different denominations.

Dr. Dowkontt, Director of Medical Missions in New York, announces that nine young Norwegian missionaries, who have had a medical and a theological training, are about to leave for South Africa and Madagascar.

The Twenty-first Convention of the General Council of the Evangelical Lutheran Church in North America will be held in St. John's Church, Minneapolis, Minn., Rev. G. H. Trabert, pastor, commencing on Thursday, September 13, at 10 o'clock A. M.

A Dutch missionary in Africa bought a negro boy, two years old, who was deaf and dumb, for six pounds of salt. But for the interposition of the missionary, the child would have been put to death on account of his infirmity. He is now a pupil in an institution for deaf mutes at Maestricht.

Dr. L. W. Munhall took part on August 24 in the dedication of a lay college at Crescent Beach, Mass. The Institution is founded to give Christian young men who have "a good English education, three years of academic and religious education, to prepare them for evangelical work or as assistants to pastors."

The Presiding Bishop of the Protestant Episcopal Church is about to celebrate his jubilee. It was on September 2, 1838, that John Williams was ordained a deacon in Christ Church, Middletown, Conn., by Bishop Brownell, whom he has since succeeded both as Bishop of Connecticut and as Presiding Bishop.

By the will of Isaac N. Phelps, the millionaire banker of New York city, the American Bible Society will get $5,000; the American Home Mission Society, $10,000; the American Tract Society, $5,000; the American Board of Commissioners for Foreign Missions, $10,000; and other philanthropic organizations smaller ones.

A Russian physician declares that subcutaneous injections of strychnine are an infallible cure for drunkenness. The patient, he claims, will after a treatment of eight days loathe the taste and smell of intoxicating liquor. The dose is one grain in 200 drops of water, and five drops of the solution injected every twenty-four hours.

Senor Vila, of Malaga, Spain, has been sentenced to two years' imprisonment, merely because he had been faithful and courageous enough to protest against the degrading form of image worship which prevailed so largely throughout his native land. His protest was a reply to a violent attack by a Romish priest upon the Reformed Church.

THE LOR ./'S SUPPER: A REMEMBRANCE.

A New Sermon by Pastor C. H. Spurgeon.

"This do in remembrance of Me." Luke 22 : 19.

The Comma:.d Precise—Peter Astonished at the Mass—I. The Main Object of the Lord's Supper—Personal Remembrance—As a Saviour—As Soon to Come—II. The Mode—The Mass a Puerility—The Apostles at St. Paul's Cathedral—Especially a Remembrance of His Death—Of the New Covenant—III. The Result—Most Inviting—Increases Strength—Restores Backsliders—No Perfect Church—The Place for Ending Quarrels.

"THIS do"—that is, take bread, give thanks, break it, and eat it—take the cup, filled with the fruit of the vine, give thanks, and drink ye all of it. *"This do." Take care that you do just what Jesus did;* no more, and no less. This act was done at a table where they had been eating the Passover. This act was performed at a common meal, and was not a sacrifice, nor a celebration, nor a function, nor anything more than a significant eating of bread and drinking of wine after a devout fashion. This do, then. As often as ye break the bread, and as often as ye drink of the cup, remember the Lord Jesus. It is this that we are to do, and not something else, which may be supposed to grow out of it.

Alas, how sadly have men forgotten this! The plain supper has not been a grand enough display. To break bread, and to drink wine, have not seemed to them to be sufficiently solemn, or sufficiently gorgeous, and so they have added all kinds of rites and institutions. That which was only a table, they have made into an altar, and that which was a supper and nothing more, they have changed into a celebration. They do not *this*, but they do something else which they have devised. Imagine Paul or

Peter Attending Mass,

and observing the various genuflexions—the movings to and fro, the liftings up, and the stoopings down, and all the various operations of the Roman priesthood, too many to describe! Paul would pluck Peter by the sleeve, and say: "Our Master did nothing like this when He took bread and gave thanks and brake it." Peter would reply, "Very different this from the guest-chamber at Jerusalem!" And Paul would add, "Ay, indeed, my brother, very different this from the time when the first believers met together, and brake bread, and drank of the cup in common, in remembrance of their Lord."

Whatever other communities may do, be it ours, my brethren, to stand fast by "*This* do in remembrance of Me." "*This*," simply "this," and nothing more, and nothing less; bread, not a wafer; fruit of the vine, not the concoction of chemistry inflamed with fiery spirit. We use this fruit of the vine in a cup, and that cup not reserved, but partaken of by all. We have before us bread, and that not worshipped, as at the elevation of the host, but broken and eaten. The Lord and His disciples sat at a table and ate: it was a feast, and not a sacrifice; they reclined, and did not kneel. So would we do, because He said, "*This* do," and not something else.

Seeing that this is a feast of remembrance, let us ask ourselves a question—

Do We Know the Lord?

"This do in remembrance of Me." If you know nothing of a person; if you have had no acquaintance with him, you cannot remember him. Like a two-edged sword, this simple statement of truth sweeps through this audience, and divides it in twain. Whether or not I may come to the Lord's table must depend upon whether I know the Lord Jesus, or do not know Him. If I am a stranger to Him, I may not come, for I may only come to remember Him, and I cannot come to remember Him if I do not know Him; so that it were a profanation of this blessed institution for any man to draw near to the table who does not know Christ already. O sirs, this is no saving ordinance: it was never meant to be; its intent relates only to those who are saved. To know Jesus Christ is eternal life; and you may not come without that knowledge.

If any of you dream that your participation, in your last moments, in what is called "the sacrament" will save you, you are under a deep delusion. *You may as well trust to the incantations of a witch* as to the performance of any ceremony whatever, by whomsoever, in order to convey salvation to you. Salvation is by faith in Jesus Christ; and that is not wrought by the corporeal act of swallowing bread and wine. Ye must be born again; and that is not effected by material substances, however consecrated; it is the work of the Holy Spirit. Until you have believed in Jesus, and so know Him, and know His power within you, and have come to personal dealings with Him, instead of getting a blessing from the ordinance, you would eat and drink condemnation to yourselves, not discerning the Lord's body. You are not capable of discerning that body if you have no faith. Let every man examine himself as to his knowledge of our Lord, and so let him eat of this bread and drink of this cup. If you do not know Him you cannot remember Him, and therefore, hands off from the tokens of remembrance.

I. My first point shall be, that

The Main Object

of the Lord's supper is evidently that we should remember Christ by it. Notice this particularly. It is not that you should call to mind a doctrine, though I would not have you ignorant or unmindful of any truth which the Spirit of God has revealed; neither is it that you should be mindful of a precept, though, beloved, I would have you careful that in all things you do your Saviour's will. But the pith and the essence of your business at His table is, "This do in remembrance *of Me*," that is, of Himself—of His own blessed person. Think not of Him as an abstraction! Dream not of Him as a mere idea! Do not merely contemplate Him as a historical personage who was once before men, and has now passed from off the canvas of history, as Confucius, Zoroaster, or the like. No; He ever liveth, and abideth an actual, ever-energetic force and

Power among Men of Every Age.

And if we do this, we shall remember Him, first, with gratitude as our Saviour. If I have aught of hope, I owe it all to Thee, incarnate God, Son of the Highest, and Son of Mary, too. Thy love, Thy life, Thy death, Thy resurrection, Thy power at the right hand of God—these must be the pillars of my hope, if hope I have at all. Remember Jesus Himself, I pray you, and think neither of pardon, nor of justification, nor of sanctification apart from Him.

You must remember Him, next, with profound reverence as your living example—your living and reigning Lord. Know ye not that as many of you as have been washed in His blood are henceforth God's servants, even as He was? You are not to do your own will, but His will who has redeemed you. His example is to you the embodiment of the Lord's will. It is yours, then, to remember the Lord Jesus that you may follow Him. In sickness, recollect Him in His patience. When you are persecuted, recollect Him in His gentleness. In holy service, remember Him with His burning zeal. In your times of solitude, remember Him and His midnight prayers; and when you are in public, and have to bear witness, remember Him and His lion-like declarations of the gospel. Remember Him so that He becomes your pattern, and you are the reproduction of Himself, and so the best memorial of Him Remember Him, again, as

Soon to Come.

Perhaps while yet these lips are feebly fashioning halting words concerning wondrous mysteries, the trumpet may ring out above all earthly sounds. Even on this Sabbath night we may be called to behold the cloud upon which the Son of Man has come! He said long ago, "Behold, I come quickly." He has been coming in haste ever since, and He must be drawing very near. Now, this is what we are always to remember, for His coming will be the manifestation of His people as well as of Himself. His coming will witness the reward of His saints as well as His own reward. Then shall He shine forth; and with Him "the righteous shall shine forth as the sun in the kingdom of their Father."

Alas, we too much forget Him in all these aspects! I fear that we more easily forget than remember; and yet the remembrance of one so dear should be natural to us. How often we act as if we had not the living Christ to run to! We fret as if Jesus were still lying in the sepulchre. We act as if we were going to live here for ever, and did not expect our Lord to come and take us away to be with Him. We act as if we had no Master but our own wanton will. We act despairingly as if we had no Shepherd to take care of us, and no Saviour who had redeemed us with His precious blood. Come, brethren, this will never do. It is dishonorable to our Lord, and disgraceful to ourselves. You see the reason why the supper should have been instituted; our treacherous memories require it.

II. And now I take a second point. I want to show you all that

The Mode

which our Lord has ordained of helping our memories is in itself exceedingly striking. It could not be more so. If I stood opposite to an altar garnished with paper roses and other childish things, and if I were to try and perform, before you all, some of these prettinesses which are considered sacred by the followers of Rome, I should want a long time to explain it all to you; and when I had done my best, you would not be able to make head or tail of it. I have stood and watched the Catholic priest at the altar with the earnest desire to see if there was anything to be learned, and I could not learn anything. I could not make out what the ornamental person was at. I think I have read as much as most people about such things; but it does seem to me that if the behavior of the priest at the mass be a symbol, it is a very dark one: if it is intended to teach the people, they need to know a great deal before they can learn anything from it. Surely to find anything in the mass, the devout must bring it with them, for there is nothing there. But if you take the cloth from yonder table, you will see before you simply bread and wine; and when you see us celebrate the ordinance, you will notice that we do nought but break the bread and eat it, and pass round the wine-cup and drink therefrom. All that is done is

Extremely Simple;

and the Saviour seemed to wish for that simplicity, because He was Himself a very simple, unaffected, plain man. Only fancy some of His disciples rising from the dead and stepping into—well—St. Paul's cathedral, which is called Protestant, but is about as Popish as it very well can be! Supposing they walked in there—James and John together—the two sons of Zebedee. Perhaps, stopping before some of the pretty things, James would wonderingly ask, "John, where have we got?" And John would say, "We are in a chamber of imagery, a temple of idols. Our Lord Jesus would not be happy here." "Why," says James, "*it is Paul's church! fetch him in.*" Surely when Paul came in, and looked at all those images and decorations, he would say, "Here I see another gospel, which is not another; but there be some that trouble you, and would pervert the gospel of Christ."

We are getting to have the idolatries of Rome set up in the churches called national; and this is not done by those called, outwardly and honestly, Romanists, but by those who are really so in their hearts, and yet wear the Protestant name. The Lord Jesus Christ was just

A Simple Peasant at Galilee,

and the dress he wore was analogous to our common smock-frock, a garment "without seam, woven from the top throughout." There was not a bit of stateliness or affectation about Him; and in all that He ordained you cannot find one single pompous ceremony. Where did He make the sign of the cross, or set forth sponsors? His followers gathered for worship and sang hymns in His praise, but where were their "thurifers," d their "crucifers"? Where are all these ings in the Scriptures? They are inventions later and darker days, but Jesus knew noth- g of them; neither did His apostles, and those ho followed them, know anything of such rub- sh. It was all plain telling out of the dear ve of God to men, and of how men should ve one another, and love Jesus as their Sav- ur; and that was all. Our Lord instituted is simple supper as the memorial of a plain, mple, honest Saviour, who had no gaudy tricks priestcraft about Him, but was simply a man mong men.

But, next, our Lord's Supper was intended to e very frequent. "This do ye, as oft as ye rink it, in remembrance of Me." He has laid own no rule as to when we shall break bread; ut the custom was certainly to break it on the rst day of the week, and I think oftener, for it eems to me that they broke bread from house o house. It was not a ceremony that required minister or a priest. When believers were to- ether they broke bread in memory of Christ— ny two or three of them—and so they remem- ered Him. It is most delightful, when travel- ng, to remember Christ in your own room, here two or three brethren meet together. I now of nothing more sweet or more instructive han this divine ordinance, which grows more mpressive the oftener you attend to it. It ought o be frequent.

But to come a little closer to the table. I ant you to notice that when our Lord bids us emember Himself—"This do in remembrance f *Me*"—He gives us an ordinance which brings efore us His death. He Himself regarded

His Death as the Very Centre,

eart, and soul of what He would fix on our emories. Therefore those who say that His xample is everything, or His teaching is every- hing, do greatly err; for when we remember Him, the first thing to remember is, "He hath edeemed us to God by His blood." "Redeemer" s the name to which our memories must most enaciously cling. His blood, His redemption, His atonement, His substitutionary sacrifice, are lways to be kept to the front. "We preach Christ crucified," and you believe in Christ rucified. The reason of our success under God in this house of prayer is, that we have al- ways preached Christ as the atoning sacrifice, he sinner's substitute; and whosoever shall reach this boldly, clearly, and thoroughly, put- ing it as the crown of the gospel system, shall nd God bless his word.

Next, notice another thing: this festival re- minds us of the covenant of grace. Our Lord esus Christ, while He bade us remember Him- elf, said of the cup, "This cup is *the new coven- nt* in My blood." That is the word. Read testament," if you prefer it; but I feel sure ou are nearer the sense when you read "the ew *covenant* in My blood." What, then? When I am to remember Jesus Himself, I am o take the cup which is the token of the cov- nant. As we take that cup, we do own and ccept joyfully our interest in that covenant which was made with Christ, which is establish- d on the sure foundation of His perfect obedi- nce. Behold the blood of the everlasting ovenant!

III. Now, lastly, the object for which we are o come, namely, to

Remember Christ,

one which is in itself most inviting. Let me how you what I mean. There is one here who ries, "I have forgotten my Saviour. I did love Him. I hope my love has not quite gone, but seem to be very chill and cold. Alas? I have orgotten my Lord." Where should you go to ave that love revived and refreshed? Should ou not come where you will be helped to re- member Him? He says, "This do in remem- rance of Me." You say that you have forgot- en your Lord. Come, and remember Him gain. Do not stay away, but come with all the more eagerness. Remember Him as you did at irst, when you came laden with guilt, and full of fears, and when you just cast yourself upon your Lord, and found peace. Come, and rest in Him over again.

"Oh, but I feel so weak." Yes, but when a little child is very weak, there is still one thing which it can surely do: it can remember its mother. Memory is often quickened by our need: it is well when our sense of weakness makes us remember where our great strength lieth. Remember, then, the Lord, who is your strength and your song, for He also hath be- come your salvation. Now, you poor little weak ones, where are you? How gladly would I help you; but what better help can you desire than that which your Lord sets before you in these dear memorials of His death?

No Perfect Church.

There is one more thing I am going to say, and I feel half ashamed to say it. Some pro- fessedly Christian people urge that they cannot come to the table because there are certain per- sons there who, in their judgment, should not be allowed to come. Is the Lord's table to be a judgment-seat, whereat we are to revise the verdict of the church? "I cannot," said one to me, "join a church, because I cannot find one that is perfect." No, I said; and if you do not join a church till you find a perfect one, you must wait till you get to heaven; and, besides, my dear friend, if you ever find a perfect church they will not take *you* in; for I am sure they would not be perfect any longer if they did. One sickly sheep would then have passed into the fold. So it is idle for you to be looking out for perfection.

"But there is a person at communion who acted inconsistently." That is highly probable; and *he may be wearing your coat*, and looking out of your eyes. If you know of any case of open sin, let the elders of the church be inform- ed, and it will be dealt with tenderly and firmly. In so large a church as this there may be cases of evil living not known to the overseers of the flock; but we invite the co-operation of all in maintaining the purity of the entire body, and we trust that we have it. But now, really, what have you to do with the faults of others, when you are remembering Christ Jesus? Sure- ly this is the most unseasonable time for harsh judgments; or, indeed, for any judgments. I know many a brother with whom I could not agree in certain points, but I agree with him in remembering the Lord Jesus. I could not work with him in all things; but if he wants to re- member Jesus, I am sure I will join him in *that*. It will do him good, and it will do me good, to think of Jesus. That dear name is so sweet to me that I will remember Jesus with the poorest, meanest, and most imperfect of mortals.

A precious Christ He is, not only to have saved me, but tens of thousands of His saints everywhere: for there are

People of His in all Churches,

even in the churches that are most full of error. Shall I then set myself up for a judge, and say, "No, I will not remember my Lord, because one of the brethren does not behave properly"? What would you say to your child if he said, "Father, I shall not come to see you on your birth- day; I shall not join with the rest of the family in the usual festival"? Why not? "Because my brother is not what he ought to be; and till he mends his ways, I shall not keep your birth- day." Your father would say, "My dear son, is that any reason why you should not remember *me*? Surely I am not to blame for what your brother does. Come to the feast, and think of me." So do I say to you, if you have any per- sonal angers and differences, do not smother them, but end them. Do not come to the table till you have got rid of them, for you have no right to come; but end all wrath at once. Get rid of every ugly feeling you have toward every- body in the world, and love all believers in Christ for Christ's sake, and then come to this table, and you will find it help you to remember your Master as you shall join with others who remember Him. I think I may say that you will not be likely to see anybody at the table worse than yourself. So come along, and let not pride keep you back. May God's infinite mercy bless the Lord's Supper to the Lord's people!

And as for those that cannot come and re- member Him, because they do not know Him, may they go home and seek Him; and if they seek Him, He will reveal Himself to them. If you desire Christ, Christ desires you. If you have a spark of love to Him, He has a furnace full of love to you; and if you want to come to Him and trust Him to save you, come and wel- come. The Lord bless you, for His name's sake! Amen.

[The prayers of the readers of this journal are requested for the blessing of God upon its Editors, and those whose sermons, articles or labors for Christ are printed in it; and that its circulation may be used by the Holy Spirit for the conversion of many sinners and the quickening of God's peo- ple. Dr. Talmage and Mr. Spurgeon especially request prayer every Sunday morning on behalf of their labors.]

GEMS FROM NEW BOOKS.

A PRAYING HERO.*

GEN. MORGAN, the hero of so many fields, professed religion and united himself with the Presbyterian Church in Winchester, Va., under the pastoral care of the Rev. Dr. Hill, who preached in that house some forty years. His last days were passed in that town; and while sinking to the grave, he related to his minister the experience of his soul. "People thought," said he, "that Daniel Morgan never prayed; people said that old Morgan never was afraid. People did not know." He then proceeded to relate in his blunt manner, among other things, that the night they stormed Quebec, while wait- ing in the darkness and storm with his men paraded for the word to advance, he felt un- happy. The enterprise appeared more than perilous; it seemed to him that nothing less than a miracle could bring them off safe from an encounter at such an amazing disadvantage.

He stepped aside, and kneeling down by a can- non, most fervently prayed that God would be his shield and defence, for nothing less than an almighty arm could protect him. He continued on his knees till the word passed along the line. He fully believed that his safety during that night of peril was due to the interposition of God.

Again, he said about the battle of the Cow- pens, which covered him with glory as a leader and a soldier, he had felt afraid to fight Tarle- ton, whose numerous army was flushed with success, and that he retreated as long as he could, until his men complained, and he could go no further. Drawing up his army in three lines on the hillside, contemplating the scene, in the distance the glitter of the advancing en- emy, he trembled for the fate of the day. Going to the woods in the rear, he kneeled in an old tree-top, and poured out a prayer to God for his army, for himself, and for his country. With relieved spirits he returned to the lines, and in his rough manner cheered them for the fight. As he passed along they answered him bravely. The terrible carnage that followed the deadly aim of his lines decided the victory. In a few moments Tarleton fled.

"Ah!" said he, 'people said old Morgan never feared, they thought Morgan never pray- ed. They did not know. Old Morgan was oft- en miserably afraid.' And if he had not been in the circumstances of crushing responsibility in which he was placed, how could he have been brave?

A Heroine of the Revolution.

When New York and Rhode Island were in the possession of the British armies, and the Jerseys, overrun by their victorious generals, op- posed but a feeble resistance to their over- whelming power, Lord Cornwallis, commanding a large division of their troops stationed at Bordentown, addressing Mrs. Borden, who re-

* From "The Boston Tea Party and other Stories of the Revolution." By Henry C. Watson. 292 pages. Illustrated. Price, by mail, 35 cents. Published by *Lee & Shepard*, Boston, Mass.

Chief-Justice Fuller, of the U. S. Supreme Court.

Panic-Stricken Elephants at the Bavarian Centennial.

sided on her estate in a mansion of superior elegance, demanded in an authoritative tone, "Where, Madame, is your rebel husband? Where is your rebel son?"

"Doing their duty to their country, under the orders of General Washington," was the prompt reply.

"We are well apprised," rejoined the English officer, "of the influence you exercise over the political creed of your family, and that to them your opinion is law. Be wise then in time, and while mercy is tendered to you, fail not to accept it. Bid them quit the standard of rebellion, and cordially unite with us in bringing his Majesty's deluded subjects to submission, and a proper sense of their errors and ingratitude to the best of kings. Your property will then be protected and remain without injury in your possession. But should you hesitate to profit by our clemency, the wasting of your estate and the destruction of your mansion will inevitably follow."

"Begin, then, the havoc which you threaten," replied the heroic lady; "the sight of my house in flames would be a joy to me, for I have seen enough of you to know that you never injure what it is possible for you to keep and enjoy. The application of the torch would I know be the signal for your departure, and I should consider the retreat of the spoiler an ample compensation for the loss of my property."

The house was burned, and the whole property consigned to waste and desolation. But, as had been foreseen, the perpetrator of the ruthless deed retreated to return no more.

CHIEF-JUSTICE FULLER.

(*See Portrait.*)

THE office of Chief-Justice of the United States Supreme Court, the highest judicial position in the country, is now filled, after the mature consideration of the Senate, by the lawyer whose portrait appears on this page. When the eminent Chief-Justice Waite died it was expected that the President would have promoted one of the Justices to the vacant post, and filled the lower position from the Bar; but in the exercise of his discretion he selected Melville Weston Fuller, of Illinois, for the Chief-Justiceship, and as both the Republican Senators from Illinois approved of the nomination, the Senate after some delay confirmed it.

The new Chief-Justice was born at Augusta, Me., on February 11, 1833. He is therefore in his fifty-sixth year. He studied at Bowdoin, from which institution he graduated in 1853. He studied law at Bangor and Harvard, and began his practice in Augusta. Though successful there, and prominent in municipal affairs, he removed to Chicago, where he at once sprang into prominence in legal and political circles. In 1862 his personal popularity placed him at the head of the poll in a Republican district for a seat in the Legislature. He rendered distinguished service there in constitutional questions, and though a strong party man, took a broad view of public measures.

In person Mr. Fuller is short of stature and slight of form. His hair and mustache are now silvery, but his face is singularly youthful and handsome. He has been twice married, the second time in 1866. He has five daughters and one son; and the family is said by Illinois society to be one so remarkable for geniality and vivacity as to be sure of winning its way to popularity in the Capital

PANIC-STRICKEN ELEPHANTS.

(*See Illustration.*)

THE stories of Oriental magnificence which came across the Atlantic from Munich, in Bavaria, at the time of the death of the demented King, are almost paralleled by recent accounts of a wonderful festival in the same city. It was held to celebrate the centennial anniversary of the birth of King Ludwig I. The decorations and illuminations made the city like fairyland, and a wonderful procession, in which the celebration culminated, is described as magnificent beyond conception. A prominent feature of it was the triumphal cars, which were designed by Munich artists. One of the most singular of these was the car bearing *the golden cradle of King Ludwig I.*, heralded by one hundred singing children in white, mounted, and escorted by a number of blooming maidens draped in the elegant attire of the time of Louis XVI.

Another very striking adjunct of the procession was the representation of mechanical art with a monstrous dragon covered with many-colored scales, and ejecting smoke and steam from its mouth. This was the cause of a catastrophe that marred the peaceful course of the day's pageantry. Eight elephants—some recently arrived from Ceylon—marched with their keepers in the Oriental department. In doubling back in the Ludwig Strasse, these elephants unfortunately came opposite the steam-dragon, and taking alarm, broke their chain bindings, and, under the impulse of terror, dashed through the panic-stricken crowd. The animals backed into the Wittelsbacker Platz, rushed down the Brienner Strasse, on to the Hof Theatre, and to the Mint, upsetting people and cabs, breaking through doors, and dashing into all manner of strange places. One boy of sixteen was seized by the trunk of an elephant, and hurled into the river Isar with no further injury. At length, about 5 o'clock, most of the beasts, having been got into a cellar, were secured. As it was, thirteen persons were seriously injured and four are dead.

A PROVIDENTIAL ESCAPE.

(*See Illustration on Page 573.*)

"IT'S going to be a real lovely day for the picnic, Ada. Ain't you glad you'll breathe sea-air instead of sweltering in that factory? I've been dreaming about it all night. Do get up and look at the sky!"

"Don't worry so, Rachel; there's no need to get up. What's the use of being so excited about it? I guess I'll enjoy it without going crazy over it. And it wasn't the sea-air you were dreaming about, Rachel Ellis. Much you'd care about the sea-air if it wasn't that Edgar Milverton was going!"

A conscious laugh from Rachel confirmed her sister's imputation, and led to her adding:

"You are fairly gone on that man, Rachel. I cannot make you out. I wish to goodness you'd have nothing more to do with him. He don't belong to us, any way. I'd sooner by half marry a good, industrious, sensible young fellow in the factory than a man like that Milverton. You've never been to Sunday-school since you took up with him, nor to church at night. You know what we promised mother before she died. Say, Rachel, give him up, I know you'll repent it if you don't."

"I couldn't, Ada; it would kill me. I know it sounds crazy, but I'd die for him!"

"Has he ever asked you to marry him? Tell me that, Rachel Ellis!"

"No; not exactly," in a hesitating voice, "but he means it; and I think he'll say it straight out to-day."

"He'd better, if he means business. If he does not pretty soon, I'll ask him myself. I'm not going to stand by and see my sister fooled, and her heart broken by a lazy good-for-nothing. I've a good mind to speak to him this very morning, before we start."

"Oh! don't do that, Ada; now you must leave that to me. I'll tell him to-day how you feel about it, and I know he'll speak straight and honorably. He's sure to want to go away from the others when we get to the beach, and I'll take the opportunity. I will, indeed. Now you won't speak to him, will you Ada?"

"Well, I don't want to interfere."

Rachel had her own reasons for wishing to bring her admirer to a decisive attitude, and she therefore lost no time, when the party of factory-hands reached the beach, in going away at his desire for a stroll over the rocks. Her sister Ada saw them go, and most devoutly hoped at Rachel would keep her romise.

"Guess that fellow has illed Rachel and eaten er," said one of the party Ada, about two hours ter. Look at the conceited llow sitting on that rock noking! He wasn't too oud to come with us, but 's too proud to join in e games."

"I don't like him," said da. "Where is Rachel? she does not come soon, I go and ask him where e is, though I hate to eak to him."

"Oh, there's no need to go him, he'll soon be here. The de is coming in, and that ck where he is sitting will under water by and by."

Ada ran away to join in e games and make the st of the opportunity, very re with her and her companions of enjoying themlves. She cast uneasy ances now and again in e direction of the rock here Milverton sat, and at st saw him rise and stroll ward the sandy beach, ough to a point distant om that where the games ere in progress.

"What's the matter yoner?" she asked, presently, one of her friends. "What e they all running to look ? Let us go and see."

They hurried off, and skirtg a rock which shut out eir view of the object, whatver it was, that interested the throng of gazers, ame among them. Milverton also had joined e crowd, and stood looking, with his hands in is pockets, in the languid, nonchalant style abitual with him. One glance sufficed to arouse da to agonizing distress. Rachel was standg on a low rock, the waves all around her, and reatening to overwhelm her. She turned round and faced Milverton. "What do you ean by standing idle there?" she cried. "Don't ou see she will be drowned? You led her out ere. If you have any manliness in you, go nd save her."

"I cannot swim," he said. "I could not save er. I did not know she was there; she left me n hour ago."

"Are you going to let her perish, you hound?" hrieked Ada.

"I cannot save her; I should only be drowned yself," he said.

A fisherman laid a hand on Milverton's shouler. "There's a line of rocks out there where ou could wade to her. The place is only half mile away. If I was young and strong like ou, I'd run for it. It's just there where you e the foam on top of the water."

Milverton shook his head. He was not of a eroic mould. Happily, however, help was approaching the imperilled girl. A man was strikg out boldly for the rock, and others were ushing a boat down from the place whence he tarted, to follow him. The swimmer was soon t the rock on which Rachel stood, and as a ave struck her and floated her off, the watchrs saw him catch her and support her in the ater. A few minutes later the boat reached hem, and, with a sigh of relief, Ada saw rescuer nd rescued lifted on board.

"Well," said Ada, when Rachel's clothes ere dried, and they were sitting together under hospitable roof, waiting for the time fixed for he departure of their friends, "I should think ou'll have no more to do with that Milverton. e wouldn't have cared if you'd been drowned."

A Sister's Fruitless Appeal for Help.

"No, Ada, I won't. I found him out before the water came. It was just as you said; he is a wicked man. He spoke heartlessly to me, and I sat down to cry. I suppose I fainted, for the next thing I knew the water was all around me, and I was almost drowned."

"Well," said Ada, "it was almost worth the fright, Rachel, to have you saved from that man. He was causing you to forget God. You'd have made a bad bargain if you'd lost your soul in gaining a husband."

THE EPOCHS OF A LIFE.

A NEW SERIAL STORY.

By Rev. L. S. Keyser.

(Continued from page 558.)

Artful Intrigue.

The Saturday morning on which Hadley elivered his famous speech, formed an epoch in the spiritual history of our two young exponents of infidelity. Both had publicly avowed their sentiments, so that their reasons for concealment were now removed, and they therefore became bold in their arraignments of Christianity. At every favorable opportunity, in private conversation and public address, they made known their principles. Vulcan himself could not have forged more fiery thunderbolts than those hurled by the young iconoclasts at sacred institutions. They were only made more acrimonious by the severe scourgings they received from their fellow-students, many of whom, though not professing Christians, had the intelligence to perceive the weakness of their arguments, and the courage to tell the young men that arrogance and conceit were poor equipment for a campaign against religion. Unhappily, the attitude which Madelling and Dane had taken was so openly hostile that even the real Christians in the college felt reluctance in manifesting a friendly interest in their spiritual welfare, and could do nothing for them but pray in private that God would open their eyes to the truth.

Among those who listened to Hadley not one was more elated than Belle Havelock. The gleam in her eye and the exultant smile on her lips evidenced her delight. The speech went beyond her expectations in its directness and positiveness. During its delivery she slyly watched the face of Miss Winters. That young lady was evidently deeply agitated. As Hadley uttered some of his most daring sentences she became pale and flushed by turns. There was no anger, no cynicism on her countenance, but every expression was indicative of profound distress and inexpressible pain.

As Belle watched the varying expressions on the face of her rival, she believed that her plan for alienating Miss Winters from Hadley Madelling had been successful. Little did Belle know of the motives that actuate the life of a true Christian. The very fact that Hadley was so blindly confident in advocating error would be an irresistible incentive, to a girl like Madeline Winters, to try to bring him under her influence, and point him to the way of escape from his perplexities. But to this overpowering motive Belle had no key.

Her surprise and consternation were therefore beyond all description when, a few evenings afterward, she met Mr. Madelling and Miss Winters walking together along the street, engaged so earnestly in conversation that they did not notice her as she passed them. The moon revealed a face that was almost lurid with the fires of jealousy and hatred, as Belle turned and looked after the pre-occupied couple. She felt that it was base to act the spy upon them, but the impulse was irresistible, and so she turned and followed them at some distance, and saw, to her agony, that Hadley entered the house with Miss Winters. Belle passed the house, and saw through the open blinds that the young couple were seated together in the parlor, still engrossed in an earnest colloquy.

The agitated girl put her hand to her heart a moment, and then passed on beyond the house several blocks. Presently she retraced her steps, and though she despised herself for her prying espionage, she halted a few minutes, and looked into the parlor through the window. Hadley had risen, and she could see by his animated gestures that he was speaking very earnestly, while Miss Winters sat before him with blanched cheeks and appealing eyes. Presently she put her handkerchief to her face, and Belle knew that she was weeping. Then the agitated spectator of the scene saw the young man whom she loved step up to her rival, and tenderly take her hand.

Poor Belle could endure no more. She almost sprang from the spot to which she had been riveted for a few minutes, and made her way home with fluttering, uncertain steps. Once in her room, she abandoned herself to a wild paroxysm of despair.

So well had the girl schooled herself that it was not long before she overcame her emotions, and then she set her wits to work to thwart Miss Winters in her attempt to win young Madelling; for Belle believed that this was her rival's ulterior purpose. During the night the girl's plans were laid. She was ready to do anything that would bring to her side and under her influence the object of her passionate love,

Her scheme required an ally, and she felt convinced that Duneman, if skilfully handled, would not hesitate to enter into the conspiracy. The next evening saw him at her door, and a few minutes later closeted with her in earnest conversation.

"How strange it is," said Miss Havelock, after a few commonplace remarks, "that Miss Winters should still continue her intimacy with Mr. Madelling! I should have thought that his exhibition last Saturday would have erased his name from her list of friends."

"I think it must have done so," said Duneman. "No good Christian girl would associate with so avowed an enemy to Christianity as he showed himself to be. I think he has ruined his character in that quarter beyond recovery."

"Yes; that would be a logical conclusion, yet facts are against it. Mr. Madelling had a friendly conversation with Miss Winters only last evening, and she gave him a very cordial welcome at her home."

"You amaze me!" said Duneman; "you are surely misinformed."

"Oh no! I am not. I have the evidence of my own eyesight." And Belle told him what she had witnessed, with a fullness of detail that made Duneman writhe with jealous rage. She knew by her own experience how, by a few dexterous touches, to fan the flame until his sluggish nature was thoroughly aroused to the required pitch of intensity. She ended with the abrupt question, "Well, what do you mean to do?"

"I do not know," he said, "I am too surprised and agitated to form any plan. But I am resolved that he shall not win this good girl without a struggle. It would be monstrous. She would be miserable all her life allied to such a man. Any scheme would be justifiable which would put an end to her infatuation, and save her from her own folly and his wiles."

That was the point to which Belle desired to bring him. When a man declares that the end justifies the means, he is not likely to be troubled with scruples in his choice of means.

"I have had nearly twenty-fours hours start of you in considering this matter," said Belle; "and I have thought out a plan which is a little complicated, but which promises success. If you approve I will aid you in carrying it out."

Belle drew her chair nearer to that occupied by Duneman, and in tones slightly suppressed, but with increased intensity, laid before him the details of her scheme. He listened intently, and before he quitted her home had not only approved it, but pledged himself to aid in its execution.

The next morning, when the early train left the Bromfield depot Belle Havelock was one of the passengers. Some time after dark the following evening she found herself at the station in the town of Banesville, the village near Hadley's home, in the academy of which he and George Dane had pursued their preparatory studies. Having found accommodations at a small and quiet hotel, she retired early, and slept soundly until the next morning's sun shone into her window.

Then she began in earnest to carry out her machinations. Her winsome ways and fascinating beauty abetted all her plans. By deft inquiries she extracted from the garrulous landlady a large amount of information concerning the village and surrounding country. It was soon evident that this woman, who was versed in all the local gossip, was the very tool she needed for her purposes.

It was early winter, approaching the holiday season, and there had been a considerable snowfall during the night, which wrapped the earth in a winding-sheet of glowing white. While Belle was listening to a long story, told with much voluble circumlocution and many tiresome parentheses by the landlady, she heard the jingle of sleigh-bells upon the street.

"What a delightful day for a sleighride!" exclaimed Belle in delight. "I have a few days to spend here on business, and if you will go with me, Mrs. Dossing, I will hire a sleigh for a drive into the country. I would like to see the neighborhood, and as you seem to be acquainted with everybody, you could give me a great deal of useful information."

Her hostess was only too glad to assent to the proposition, especially as it would not subject her to expense, and therefore as soon as the mid-day meal was over, the sleigh was driven to the door of the hotel, and the two strangely assorted companions, warmly robed, were starting out on their post-prandial drive.

"By the way," said Belle, with an assumed carelessness, "were you acquainted with a young man by the name of Madelling, who lives—"

"Hadley Madelling?" exclaimed Mrs. Dossing. "Guess I ought to know him; he used to take his meals here when he went to the academy. He is smart! He's at college now."

"Do you know where his mother lives?"

"Guess I do! I'm acquainted all through this neighborhood for ten miles around, and if you want to go anywhere I can give you the history of every family—"

"Suppose we drive out to the place where Mr. Madelling's mother lives. I have met the gentleman several times, and his character and brilliant talents interest me."

"All right. Turn the horse down this street."

They drove rapidly until they had reached the open country. Belle studied the topography of the country with close scrutiny, so as to familiarize herself with its changing scenery. While her eye was thus busily engaged, her ears were also on the alert for all the information that came from the lips of her talkative companion, taking special pains to learn the names of all the families in the neighborhood.

"We will soon be there now—at Hadley Madelling's home," said Mrs. Dossing. As they emerged from an oak forest at the top of a small, sloping hill, the landlady exclaimed, "There it is!"

A neat cottage by the wayside, surrounded by pines and hemlocks and fruit trees, greeted Belle's sight and made her pulse flutter with excitement. While passing the house, an elderly lady, doubtless attracted by the jingling of sleigh-bells, stepped to the window and looked out.

"That's Hadley's mother," the landlady informed her.

After that Belle adroitly encouraged her companion to speak more fully of Hadley's early life, and was pleased to learn that he bore a good reputation, albeit "he was such an infidel," as the landlady vouchsafed. In this way she managed to glean many interesting biographical facts concerning the young man in whom she was engrossed, all of which were valuable accessories to her schemes.

Following the curvatures of the wood a mile further, they came in sight of a large well-built house, embowered among the snow-laden trees at the foot of a long, steep hill. It was the residence of a wealthy farmer.

"This is where Mr. Richardson lives," said Belle's companion. By the by, he has a very handsome daughter, that Hadley Madelling was once interested in when he was around here in these parts; so they say, anyway. Of course, he was very young then, and since he has gone to college I guess he has forgotten her, and I guess she has forgotten him too, for she has a regular beau now from Wilmot, a town about ten miles from here. She is a real beauty, and pretty well educated, too."

"Richardson, did you say? What's her Christian name?" queried Belle, with an interest she could scarcely disguise.

"Mabel Lettie," answered the other.

During the remainder of the drive Belle was comparatively silent, but very attentive to her communicative friend's rattling talk. On their return, she again drove past Hadley's home, making more observations.

That night a light might have been seen burning in her room until long past midnight, and could one have entered the apartment unperceived, it would have been seen that she was bending over a desk engaged in writing. It might have been noticed, further, that she wrote in a disguised hand, although the chirography was delicately feminine. One sheet after another was filled, and then torn up before she was satisfied with her efforts. At last she folded her letter and enclosed it in an envelope, on which she wrote in the same disguised hand the address, "Mr. Hadley C. Madelling, Bromfield, I——." Having carefully locked it in her portmanteau she retired.

Early the next morning she found her way to the post-office and asked the postmaster, who, she saw, was a young man, for a stamp, which she fastened upon the envelope. The office, like the village, was a small one, and, as Belle had hoped would be the case, the postmaster put the postmark of the office upon the wrapper as soon as she handed it to him, and then threw it into the letter-box with other mail matter. Belle had made a feint to turn away, but reappeared a moment later at the stamp-window.

"If you please," she said, pretending considerable uneasiness, "I have forgotten to put something of importance into that letter. Will you allow me to take it again?"

"Certainly," said the postmaster, courteously; for the face at the window was of that order of beauty to make a susceptible country postmaster forget the regulations which Uncle Sam has framed for the conduct of his employees. The letter was put back into her hand. With a winsome smile and a polite "Thank you," she took it and hurried back to her room. Her design had been to get the printed impression of the Banesville post-office upon the envelope, and when this was accomplished she locked it up carefully, and it never went back into the hands of the gentlemanly postmaster.

In the afternoon she ordered a sleigh and drove out alone into the same locality which she had visited the day before, her chief design being to make herself more familiar with the neighborhood of Hadley's home. After driving along several roads, each of which afforded her a new view of the place, she turned in the direction of the house belonging to Mr. Richardson. It might prove an invaluable acquisition to her plans if she could see the girl whom her hostess had called Mabel.

When she had driven up before the house, she sprang nimbly from the sleigh, tied her horse at the hitching-post, and in a moment was ringing the bell at the front door. An elderly lady answered the summons.

"Excuse my troubling you," said Belle, courteously, "I am a stranger in this neighborhood and I am chilled with a long drive. Would you kindly allow me to warm myself and inquire the way to Banesville?"

She was welcomed into the warm sitting-room with cordial hospitality. A young lady was sitting in the room, doing some crochet work, and Belle knew instinctively that it was Mabel Richardson. She was a beautiful girl, with her gray, expressive eyes and jet black hair and brows.

Belle chatted on good-humoredly about the weather, the neighborhood, and the people for a few minutes and then receiving directions as to her way, drove off with many thanks. On her road she called again on the courteous postmaster.

"If any mail should come to this office for *Mabel R. Richerson*, will you be kind enough to forward it to Bromfield, I——?" she said.

"Ah! is Miss Richardson going away?" inquired the postmaster, inclined to prolong his conversation with the beautiful girl before him.

"Oh, you mistake," corrected Belle. "I believe there is a Miss Richardson in this neighborhood, and it is very vexing that there should be such a close similarity in the names. It might cause confusion if there were a less intelligent postmaster, but I am sure you will take care that there is no mistake. If you will give me a slip of paper I will write my name, and then it will be quite clear. There, you see, Mabel R. Richerson, not Mabel L. Richardson."

aid Belle, with a sweet smile, as she handed ack the paper.

Belle returned to the hotel and prepared for eparture on the next train. "It has been so leasant," she said to the friendly landlady in aking leave, "and you have been so kind, that shall surely come to you when I am in this eighborhood again; and if I should be in need f information for business purposes about any f your people you will not mind my writing to sk you? I know I can rely on what you say."

The landlady was profuse in her promises to blige, and Belle was soon speeding back home ith a heart elated by the success of her visit.

(*To be Continued.*)

THE SMITTEN ROCK.

By Mrs. M. Baxter.

. S. Lesson for September 16, Num. 20:1-13. Golden Text, 1 Cor. 10:4.

he Thirst of the Desert—The Complaint of the People—Proved Their Lack of Faith—Moses Reproached for the Trouble—The Appeal to the Lord—Commanded to Speak to the Rock—The Patience of Moses Exhausted—His Denunciation of the People as Rebels—Justified but not Enjoined—Assumption of Personal Authority—The Punishment—The Failures of God's People.

THE children of Israel, in the course of their ourneys, came into the desert of Zin, and bode in Kadesh. One of the condemned generation which listened to the evil report of the pies was Miriam, Moses' sister, and God's word as fulfilled in her case, for she died here in he wilderness. Now a trial of no light order vertook the people: "There was no water for he congregation." From a human point of iew, madness and death stared them in the ace; and if they had been unacquainted with od, we should not have wondered that "They athered themselves together against Moses, nd against Aaron. And the people chode with loses, and spake, saying, Would God we had ied when our own brethren died before the ord." But had they had no experience of od's providing care, that they should thus ig-ore the God who made them, and turn in such

Senseless Anger

gainst a man who was a creature like themelves? Alas, when men are angry, they do not nd can not reason. An angry man is always a ool. Once the Lord had sweetened the bitter aters for them when they thirsted (Ex. 15:23-5), and once He had brought water out of the ock. Were these things to be forgotten in the rgency of the present need! Oh, how often ave we been like them, and under some fresh ressure have forgotten God's past wonders of ove and faithful answers to prayer! When the eople were in Rephidius, there had been no ater for them to drink, and they had then eproached Moses, and murmured against him, aying, "Give us water, that we may drink. . . Vherefore is this that thou hast brought us up ut of Egypt, to kill us and our children and ur cattle with thirst?" The need was a real ne, indeed. But instead of looking upon it as

An Opportunity to Trust the Lord,

ho had done so much for them, they thought hemselves badly used, and visited their anger pon Moses, just as though he had imposed pon them in bringing them out of Egypt. No hought of gratitude for his devotedness possessed them: they counted him as a traitor nd an enemy. He had sacrificed all for them, nd they imputed to him the worst of motives. t was enough to arouse the indignation of loses. But he dwelt too much in the presence f God to be moved as another man would be. lis instinct and his habit was to take everyhing as it arose to God. He "cried unto the ord, saying, What shall I do unto this people? hey be almost ready to stone me. And the ord said unto Moses, Go on before the people, nd take with thee of the elders of Israel; and hy rod wherewith thou smotest the river, take thine hand and go: behold, I will stand before hee there upon the rock in Horeb; and thou shalt smite the rock, and there shall come water out of it, that the people may drink. And Moses did so in the sight of the elders of Israel. And yet these very elders and this very people were acting now as though no such intervention of God had ever taken place, and as though the living God among them counted for nothing at all.

Now, in Kadesh their murmurings were yet louder and more bitter than at Rephidim, and they reproached Moses and Aaron, saying, "Wherefore have ye made us to come up out of Egypt, to bring us into this evil place? It is no place of seed, or of figs, or of vines, or of pomegranates; neither is there any water to drink." They well knew, if they had reflected for a moment, that had it not been for their unbelief, when the spies brought up their report of the land, they would have been now possessors of the promised land, which was the place of seed and figs and pomegranates. *They* were hindering Moses and Aaron from going up into the land; it was neither God nor Moses and Aaron who hindered them. Their own stubbornness, wilfulness, and unbelief were the cause of all their present misery. Yet Moses speaks no reproach; the people were in sore need, and Moses and Aaron did not argue with people who were half mad with anger and suffering. They "went from the presence of the assembly unto the door of the tabernacle of the congregation, and they did what the people ought to have done, "they fell upon their faces": And the glory of God, who was only waiting to be called upon, appeared to them. "And the Lord spake unto Moses, saying, Take the rod and gather thou the assembly together, thou and Aaron thy brother,

Speak Ye Unto the Rock

before their eyes; and it shall give forth his water, and thou shalt bring forth to them water out of the rock: *so* shalt thou give the congregation and their beasts drink." At Rephidim Moses was to smite the rock, now he was but to *speak* to it. But Moses, for the first and only time in his life, added to and changed the command of his God. Moses was the meekest man upon the face of the earth (Num. 12:3), but this once the people "provoked his spirit, so that he spake unadvisedly with his lips." (Ps. 106:33.) True, "He took the rod from before the Lord, as He commanded him," but in the heat of his spirit, stirred up to indignation that a second time the people should accuse both God and him so falsely, he said, "Hear now, ye rebels; must *we* fetch you water out of this rock? And Moses lifted up his hand, and with his rod he smote the rock twice." Was this sin? There are many, and among them are some dear children of God, who would say of an ebullition of temper such as this that it was only righteous indignation. But God counted it sin, and for this sin Moses lost the promised land! God forbid that we should

Lower God's Standard of Sin!

Perhaps there are few children of God who do not sometimes know the temptation to anger, heat of spirit, and indignation when under sore provocation. There are few who are not tempted to retaliate, and to yield to such a temptation is sin, and this sin in a religious teacher, a leader such as Moses, is a thousand-fold more guilty than is one to whom God has not committed so much. Thank God, there is no need to yield to the temptation; the power of God is enough to keep us under any temptation. We are "kept by the power of God through faith" (1 Pet. 1:5), and if we fall it is because we do not believe and yield ourselves fully up to God. A fall always comes from considering ourselves, or relying upon ourselves. Moses' habitual meekness was not sufficient to keep him at this time: his past wondrous communing with God for forty days and nights on two several occasions had no power to keep him now: he was guilty of disobedience and of unbelief. True, the water came out abundantly, and the congregation were relieved from their terrible pressure of need. But God in very faithfulness could not suffer the sin of Moses and Aaron to pass unnoticed and unpunished. He said to them, "Because ye believed Me not to sanctify Me in the eyes of the children of Israel, therefore ye shall not bring this congregation into the land which I have given them."

Some may argue, "Was not this a severe punishment for so small a sin as a moment's anger and disobedience? Was there, after all, so much difference between speaking to the rock and smiting the rock?" Yes; much more was involved than is seen at first sight. It is not for man to

Improve Upon the Plan of God;

and Moses, in his anger, had gone so far as attempt to do this. The people had already seen how God could bring water out of the rock when Moses smote it with his rod, the very rod which he had lifted up in Egypt, when such wonders followed, and they may have imagined that God could do nothing without Moses' rod. God makes use of every emergency in which we are placed to teach us something new about Himself, and they were to learn just now the power of His word, apart from any outward means, and that the water would flow in response to the message of God through Moses, just as much as through the striking of the rock. Moses' fit of anger had intercepted the lesson of God on its way to the people; he had failed to sanctify God before them, and he had come under their spirit instead of under the Spirit of God. God forgive us if we excuse ourselves when we fail to sanctify God in the eyes of our children and those who surround us. Oh how often have we too smitten the Rock of Ages when God would have had us only speak to the Rock, Christ Jesus, and surely the living water would have flowed out to us.

There is no doubt that Moses and Aaron were under the pressure of thirst equally with the people, and the temptation to irritability is tenfold greater when under physical suffering or extreme weakness, which makes the nerves unstrung, than at any other time. Oh what need, then, in our moments of weakness to commit our way very specially to the Lord, that He may hold us up! It is very striking how many of God's truest and holiest servants mentioned in Scripture met with some failure. Abraham failed in truthfulness, Moses in temper, Aaron fell into idolatry, David into impurity, Asa into unbelief, etc. Even Peter fell into dissimulation, and Paul called the high priest "Thou whited wall!" and said to the Galatians, "I would they were even cut off which trouble you!" God thus teaches us that no man is perfect in himself, and it is His grace which keeps as well as saves us.

BY-AND-BY.

By Mrs. Helen E. Brown.

By-and-by all will be over,
  All the earthly care and pain:
Every wearying endeavor
  After worldly good and gain,
Discord sharp, and tribulations
  Which like fire our spirits try,
All the tears and all the sighing
  Will be over by-and-by.

By-and-by will come the victory,
  Satan bruised beneath our feet;
Sin no more shall sting and wound us,
  We no more temptations meet;
Weapons of defence and warfare
  Conquerors need no longer ply;
We may lay aside the armor
  In the triumph, by-and-by.

By-and-by will shine the glory
  All about us and within,
When in heaven we join the anthem
  To the blood that makes us clean.
Oh, the long, the blissful rapture
  Of the bride, the bridegroom nigh!
When in joy supreme, eternal,
  We are with Him by-and-by!

By-and-by! Why heed the present?
  Though the shadows thickly fall;
Be the anguish ne'er so bitter,
  Be the pleasures ne'er so small,
An eternal weight of glory
  Afterward shall satisfy;
We can bear life's worst and longest
  With the watchword, By-and-by.

J. E. Jewett, Publisher, 77 Bible House, New York, will furnish the above poem in leaflet form at twenty cents per hundred. *A Sample Packet* of 50 leaflets assorted (no two alike), will be sent post-paid, for 10 cts., or 100 for 20 cts. Postage stamps taken.

"There is a divinity that shapes our ends,
Rough hew them as we may."

No close observer of human affairs can gainsay the poet as above quoted. The close observer aforesaid must have noted, however, that there are many persons who seem to think that their ends will be shaped without any "rough hewing" on their part. How much nobler is it for young men to strike boldly out to build well their own characters under God's guidance. To all who aspire to do a good work and do it well, we say write to B. F. Johnson & Co., Publishers, 1,009 Main St., Richmond, Va., who will give you helpful suggestions.

The latest and best imperial Photographs of **Dr. Talmage** and **Rev. C. H. Spurgeon,** with their fac-simile autograph, and also imperial photograph of **Rev. Henry Ward Beecher,** can be obtained from J. E. Jewett, 77 Bible House, New York. Sent postpaid for twenty-five cents each. Postage stamps taken.

MEXICO

Contributions in aid of Christian work in Mexico are most pressingly needed; and can be mailed to the address of

BISHOP H. C. RILEY,
Care of J. P. HEATH,
43 Bible House, New York.

To our Christian Friends:

As there is a regular monthly expense in connection with the work a regular monthly income is needed to meet that expense. We, therefore, specially ask for regular monthly contributions in its behalf. If many will each send a little every month, or quarter, or whenever they can, it will do great good. *Remember, every little helps.*

H. Chauncey Riley.

To Our Fellow Christians

Who Are Forwarding Contributions in Aid of Christian Work in Mexico.

Bishop Riley requests me to inform the kind friends who are generously contributing in aid of Christian work in Mexico, that we have now over one hundred monthly subscribers who are forwarding contributions every month in its behalf. Bishop Riley sends to all who are contributing in aid of the work in Mexico his most sincere thanks for their timely gifts.

As there are, no doubt, many who would be glad to contribute something monthly in behalf of the cause of Christ in Mexico, but who feel that they cannot afford to give as much as one dollar a month, we venture the suggestion, that when possible *the friends of the work should try and collect small contributions from such* and forward the same with their own contributions to Bishop Riley, 43 Bible House, New York. For example, some friend of the work who is now forwarding one dollar a month, might induce ten others, to each give ten cents a month, and collect and forward the same with his own contribution. Another who now contributes one dollar a month, might induce four others to each give one cent a day, or thirty-one cents a month, and collect and forward the same with his own contribution monthly. Still a third who now contributes a dollar a month might induce two friends, to each give fifty cents a month, and collect and forward the same regularly with his own contribution.

If this plan could be adopted generally among the more than one hundred regular monthly subscribers to the work, we might soon be able to report to our friends that we had over two hundred dollars a month contributed regularly in behalf of the work in Mexico.

We remind our friends that to continue the work in Mexico effectively we most pressingly need a regular monthly income, as we have to meet a regular monthly expense.

A most precious Christian work has been commenced in Mexico, and we are doing what we can to continue it, by raising an income in its behalf. We earnestly appeal to our fellow Christians to aid us in this effort. There are one hundred and thirteen millions who speak the English language, and seventy-five millions who speak the Spanish or Portuguese languages. Among those who speak the English language, there are multitudes who know and love the pure gospel, and are doing what they can for the Master. Among those who speak the Spanish or the Portuguese languages, there are a few who know and love the pure gospel, and are faithfully working for our dear Master. Our Spanish-American society is working hard to raise an income to aid in building up a strong centre of Christian work in Mexico. The influence of that work has already extended into Spain and Cuba, and, we trust, will yet extend into South America. Fellow Christians, think of seventy-five millions who speak the Spanish or Portuguese languages, millions and millions, and millions of whom have never had a Bible in their hands!!! Help us! help us! to do Christian work in their midst.

Bishop Riley has been instrumental in having more than one hundred thousand copies of the Bible or New Testament circulated in Mexico. Many hundreds of children have been educated in Christian schools established by him. More than forty congregations have been gathered in the Republic of Mexico through his efforts. He has secured two magnificent stone churches in the City of Mexico where the Gospel has been preached for years. He has trained up a noble band of able preachers of the pure gospel. He has given nineteen years of his life and his fortune to aid in building up this great work, and he now appeals to his fellow Christians to contribute the monthly income needed to continue it effectively.

Dear friends, will you not only continue to contribute to this good work yourselves, but also encourage others to do the same. Some may not be able to contribute monthly but could do so occasionally. Occasional gifts are most thankfully received. Pray for the work, and that many may be moved to befriend it.

With best Chsistian wishes, I am, your brother in Christ,

A. D. MAINE.

THE CHRISTIAN HERALD AND SIGNS OF OUR TIMES.

Entered according to Act of Congress in the year 1888, in the office of the Librarian of Congress at Washington.

Vol. XI., No. 37. Office, 63 Bible House. N. Y. THURSDAY, SEPTEMBER 13, 1888. Annual Subscription, $1.50.

CONTENTS OF THIS NUMBER.

PORTRAIT AND LIFE OF MR. THOMAS A. EDISON, the Electrician and Inventor.
THE DEER HUNT. Dr. Talmage's Sermon last Sunday Morning.
ANECDOTES RELATED AT RECENT EVANGELISTIC MEETINGS.
THE SLAYING OF THE WITNESSES.
PICTURE OF TWO PATAGONIAN INDIANS.
JOHN BARTON'S BIBLE READING. (Illust'd.)
A Blind Buddhist in Japan—An Inquiry from a Car-Window—Preaching in Persian Shops—A Six Years' Wedding Tour—A Royal Reception at Stockholm—A Criminal Trial in Africa.
ANTICHRIST'S BROKEN TREATY. By Rev. John Storie.
SOWN AMONG THORNS. A New Sermon by Rev. C. H. Spurgeon.
Gems from New Books: A King's Answer to a Proselyter—The Massacre at Toulouse, etc.
PORTRAIT OF REV. THOMAS CHAMPNESS.
HOW LAND WAS BOUGHT IN SPAIN.
THE EPOCHS OF A LIFE. (Continued.)
THE DEATH OF MOSES. By Mrs. M. Baxter.

R. THOMAS A. EDISON—REGISTERING A CONCERT ON THE PHONOGRAPH—LISTENING TO A REPRODUCTION BY THE PHONOGRAPH.

MR. THOMAS A. EDISON.

The Electrician.

A Curious Entertainment—Listening to Automatic Voices—A Visit to Menlo Park—Wonderful Inventions—Mr. Edison's Early Years—A Newspaper Printed on a Train—Disastrous Chemical Experiments—The Turning-Point—The Invention of the Ticker—His Brilliant Success—Domestic Life—His Rapid Courtship—An Interesting Experiment at a Concert.

A REMARKABLE evening's entertainment was given on August 14 by an American gentleman in London to a party of astonished friends. He informed his guests that Mr. Thomas A. Edison would be the speaker of the evening, and though Mr. Edison was at home, in New Jersey, three thousand miles away, the promise was duly kept. The mystery was explained when the host, Col. Gouraud, produced Mr. Edison's famous invention, the Phonograph, the sensitive plates of which had been subjected, two weeks before, to the concussion of Mr. Edison's voice. He had talked and sung into the Phonograph for a whole evening, and the wonderful instrument had not only accurately registered every word and sound, but, after two weeks and a long voyage, reproduced them distinctly, to the amazement of the company. First of all

The Wonderful Phonograph

gave utterance to a speech by Mr. Edison in his exact tone of voice, in which he dwelt upon his first visit to England, eighteen years ago, and then devoted himself to a humorous criticism of English politics and climate. He then proceeded to amaze the company by reciting "Bingen on the Rhine," and winding up with a most extraordinary whistling spasm. Then he sang a funeral march, and without waiting gave "Mary had a little lamb." He told funny stories, and, in fact, conducted quite a variety entertainment all by himself.

The company were then invited to talk to Mr. Edison. The wax cylinders received, first, ringing cheers, which were given as an expression of gratitude for his novel entertainment, then each member made a little speech into the phonograph, and afterward some, who were of a musical turn, sang into it, others whistled. The machine was then packed up and sent back to America, where Mr. Edison would be able to extract from it the kind words and humorous felicitations of his friends in their own tones of voice and expression.

A Visit To Menlo Park,

the home of Mr. Edison, is thus described by a press correspondent: After an hour's ride from New York, on the Pennsylvania road, the train stops at Menlo Park—no ancestral domain, with its grand oaks and towering beeches, but a new-looking suburban hamlet, the country home of a few New York business men. One of the villas to the right of the station is Professor Edison's house, and to the left, across a wide meadow, on rising ground, is a long two-storied wooden building, painted white, with a piazza at one end. This is the laboratory of

The Magician of the 19th Century,

as his countrymen love to call him. At night-time light streams from every window, and the whirr of machinery in motion breaks the illusion of the country quiet. The visitor passes up the dark stairs, and enters a long, well-lighted room, fitted at intervals with all kinds of strange-looking apparatus. The walls are lined with shelves containing bottles filled with chemicals, and the whole place smells like a photographer's studio. About a dozen plain-looking mechanics are engaged, apparently, in conducting some chemical experiments. One of them is bending thoughtfully over a number of lamps. He is a slight man, about forty-one years of age, with a mass of dark hair, already streaked with gray, which hangs tumbled and unkempt over his forehead. His features are large and prominent, and but for the wrinkles into which they are knit, he looks quite youthful. The hands are stained with acids, and his shabby clothes are of common make. He glanced at the letter of introduction I presented. The dull-looking gray eyes brightened, and he came back, as it were, from some far-off region of thought, into which he had wandered, with a cordial smile of welcome. It was Edison himself.

The Great Inventor of the Age.

Here was the great genius at home. You walk with him round the laboratory, and see jumbled together like so much lumber some of his most wonderful inventions. Here is the Phonograph, *which registers by slight indentations on a disc of tinfoil the most delicate intonations of the human voice*. Here, too, is the projected Aerophone, a giant two-hundred-and-fifty voice power, which might have belonged to Virgil's fabled Cyclops. This wonderful instrument acts by fluttering the valves of a steam jet, which carries the tones of the voice to the limit of its capacity, and is designed to lift up its mighty tones from lighthouses and ships at sea.

Near the Aerophone are lying the *disjecta membra* of what looks like a great speaking-trumpet, and two ear-trumpets. This is the Megaphone. By its help, two persons can converse at a distance of four miles, but the instrument has an unhappy trick, at present, of gathering up all intermediate sounds. Thus, two lovers, separated by distance, might find their fond vows intermingled with the amorous croaking of the frogs in an intervening pond. Here is a talking-box, and a bird to fly a thousand feet, mere playful excrescences of inventive genius. Here, too, is a new system of telegraph printing, by which the sender of a message can transmit his own handwriting. The writing is in white ink, which rises in strong relief on the paper. These are only specimens of his inventions, noticed at random as one walks round Edison's laboratory.

The History of the Man Himself,

apart from the marvellously developed faculty which makes him stand out an unique figure among the crowd of every-day inventors, is commonplace enough. Thomas Alva Edison was born in 1847, of humble parentage—Dutch on the father's side—at Milan, Erie Co., Ohio. His mother, though born in Massachusetts, was the daughter of Scotch parents. At her knee he received his education, or rather such education as he had acquired previous to the age of twelve, when he began the battle of life. No other member of the family has shown any signs of remarkable talent. The boy himself was one of those shy, studious little fellows who shrink from the ruder play of their companions. At ten he was reading Hume's "England," Gibbon's "Rome," and the "Penny Encyclopædia." At twelve he began to earn his living as a train-boy on the Grand Trunk Railroad of Canada and Central Michigan, and combined with a legitimate business in the daily news, a trade in apples, pea-nuts, and figs. But young as he was, the boy began to show promise of the metal of which he was made, and gave

Promise of his Brilliant Future.

An old baggage-car was given up to him to store his wares. By making friends with some of the printers of the *Detroit Free Press*, into which town his train ran, he managed to buy some founts of old type, and started the *Grand Trunk Herald*, a weekly sheet, edited and printed by himself on the cars, the contributors being all railway hands. It had the honor of being the only newspaper in the world printed on a railway train. The young train-boy combined the study of chemistry with the pursuit of journalism, but a little bottle of phosphorus happened to break and ignite one day, and set the baggage-van in flames, and came near burning the train; whereupon the irate conductor hurled chemicals, printing-press, and all out of the car, and gave the editor of the *Grand Trunk Herald* a good thrashing, which unfortunate circumstance led to the suspension of that journal.

Then it was that Edison struck the groove in which he was to win fame. Telegraphy attracted his attention. He fitted up the basement of his father's house with telegraph wires, using in the batteries stove-pipe wire, old bowls and zinc, which friendly companions obtained clandestinely from under their domestic kitchen-stoves, and retailed to him at three cents a pound. His passion for reading still continued unabated. He conceived the strange boyish notion of reading all through the Detroit Free Library, and actually succeeded in wading through fifteen feet in a line, including such books as Newton's "Principia," and Burton's "Anatomy of Melancholy." The accident, however, of his saving a telegraph operator's child from an approaching train, at Detroit, was

The Turning-Point in His Career,

which definitely started him on the track of his great inventions. The grateful father taught him telegraphy. His history during the next four years was still one of apparent failure. His erratic disposition was calling him irresistibly to one new pursuit after another; and he was constantly being dismissed from his situations for neglect of duty, till, having been successively employed at Port Huron, at various places in Michigan, and in Canada, and at Indianapolis, Cincinnati, and Boston, somewhere about 1868 he reached New York. Here a happy circumstance occurred to him. He repaired the indicator of the Gold and Stock Company, and invented an automatic printer of stock quotations, familiarly known as "*the ticker*," in use to this day, and on the manufacture of which he at one time employed a force of 300 men; and so indefatigable was he in his labors that at one time his corps of assistants were busy upon no less than forty-five different inventions. The Western Union Telegraph Company became his patrons, and from that moment his success has been rapid and unbroken. It was here that he invented what is known as the quadruplex system, the transmission of four simultaneous messages by one wire through the division of the electric current, and he talks hopefully of sextuplex. He has spent about $500,000 in the last few years in experiments, but his income from his inventions is enormous. The Western Union Company paid him $100,000 for the carbon telephone, and as much again for the quadruplex system. He is the owner of over a hundred patents of inventions, and he is said to receive a royalty of $500 a week for the exhibition of the phonograph alone.

Edison's domestic life is tinged with the color of his ruling passion, telegraphy. His wife was a lady telegraph-operator, whose soft and nimble fingers attracted the shy student's attention as she worked at one of his instruments, and the following is

The Story of the Courtship,

and is thoroughly characteristic of the man. One day when standing behind the chair of one of his female *employees*, Miss May Stillwell, that young lady suddenly turned round and exclaimed, "Mr. Edison, I can always tell when you are behind me or near me." "How do you account for that?" mechanically asked Mr. Edison, still absorbed in his work. "I don't know, I am sure," she answered; "but I seem to feel when you are near me." "Miss Stillwell," said Mr. Edison, looking the lady in the face, "I've been thinking considerably of you of late, and if you are willing to have me I'd like to marry you." "You astonish me!" exclaimed Miss Stillwell. "I—I never—" "I know you never thought would be your wooer," interrupted Mr. Edison; "but think over my proposal, Miss Stillwell, and talk it over with your mother." Then he added in the same off-hand, business-like way, as though he might be experimenting upon a new mode of courtship, "Let me know as early as possible, as, if you consent to marry me, and your mother is willing, we can be married next Tuesday." This was the extent of Mr. Edison's courtship. The lady laid the abrupt proposal before her mother, and next day informed her lover of the maternal consent. "That's all right," said Mr. Edison, in reply; "we will be married a week from to-day." And so they were. The two were married in a week and a day from the beginning of Mr. Edison's novel and precipitate courtship. For once, also, the old adage of "ma ed in haste" proved false, as the union was in very sense thoroughly happy. *Two of his little nes*, who climb on his knees when he comes ome from work, are named *Dot* and *Dash*, after he letters of the telegraphic alphabet.

A Notable Experiment

ith the Phonograph is the subject of the pper illustration on the first page. It was used ith a large trumpet-like attachment at a grand oncert. The instrument was fixed in the gal-ry opposite the orchestra, when Handel's "Is-ael in Egypt" was sung by four thousand voices. he entrancing strains were fully caught and egistered, and, after the concert, were clearly eproduced. The plates or phonograms are in he possession of Mr. Edison, and will doubtless e a source of gratification to musical parties.

HOW LAND WAS BOUGHT IN SPAIN.

MRS. EMILY LOPEZ RODRIGUEZ, whose heroic ork for Christ in Spain is widely known, sends his narrative to THE CHRISTIAN HERALD:

"There is urgent need for a Gospel Hall in he busy market town of Figueras. A friend, tely travelling in Italy, most kindly wrote tell-g us to buy the land at once, adding, 'I will over the cost.' Pastor Rodriguez lost not a oment in trying to secure it, but the lawyer ould not credit the assurance that the money ould shortly be sent, and refused to draw up he necessary document. The landlady, how-ver, agreed to wait a couple of weeks. The omanists at once seized the opportunity. eputations from the Societies of St. Vincent e Paul and the Holy Cross, headed by the ector of St. Peter's, the largest church here, alled on the landlady, and urged that she must, n no account, be guilty of selling land for a rotestant capilla! At the same time, they laid own the money, $2,000, for the site, and also 3,000 to purchase a house and garden adjoin-g, thus effectually shutting the Protestants ut on each side. All we could do was to unite prayer that the Lord would undertake for us, nd for the honor of His cause. The triumph f the enemies of the truth seemed complete. ut, contrary to all expectations, a far better te was immediately offered for sale. It is tuated in a principal street in a central part of he town, having also the great advantage that commands a back street, by which many who, ke Nicodemus, lack courage may be able to nter the hall unobserved. Our only difficulty as that the price, came to $1,250 more than e had in hand. This we laid before the ord in prayer, and He graciously answered by clining the hearts of His servants to come to he rescue. In addition to a former liberal do-ation of $500, a friend sent $1,000, and another ost kindly sent $250. Thus the *exact sum* eeded arrived *just in time* for the purchase to e made, which called forth our most heartfelt raise. All that now remains for us to do is to uild the *first permanent* Gospel Hall in the rovince of Gerona. Since writing the above, e have heard, on reliable authority, that a riest belonging to a church quite near to our ew site, said, 'I would gladly have given $5,000 o have prevented the Protestants buying that lot of land.' Last Sunday night as we were re-urning from the service, a man was seen hang-g about our house, armed with two long nives, and was fortunately arrested by the ivic guards. We thank God for what we be-eve to have been a narrow escape."

NEW AND ENLARGED EDITION—1888.

An Illustrated Work on the Unfulfilled rophecies of the Bible, by the Rev. M. Baxter, entitled, Forty Coming Wonders," may be had from the office of HE CHRISTIAN HERALD, 63 Bible House, New York, by mitting 75 cents. It is a book of 528 pages, is handsomely ound in cloth, and contains fifty full-page pictures and dia-rams representing the scenes described in the prophecies of aniel and in the book of the Revelation. It also contains a ésumé of the opinions of other expositors, and extracts arefully collated from the works of all the most eminent riters on prophecy from the earliest ages of the Christian ra down to those of recent date. It thus forms the most seful and complete guide the student can have on entering he study of that portion of the Word of God.

ANECDOTES RELATED AT RECENT EVANGELISTIC MEETINGS.

Bengali Schoolboys to the Rescue. The Rev. A. Jewson, the Baptist missionary of Commilla, India, says: "In March, 1886, I went into a district where there is no missionary. A million of people are there without a Christian teacher or minister. I preached at a large agricultural show as it was getting dark. Crowds of people, almost all young Mussulmans, stood in front of me, and presently those behind gave a lurch and rushed upon me. With the utmost difficulty I kept my feet. I knew it was no good expostulating, so I was pleasant with them and kept my temper; but it was hard work to keep my feet. I looked away, and saw the Bengali police; but they did not come to me, and I thought it was better to trust in God than in the Bengali police. The field was covered with great ant-hills, and it was with the utmost difficulty that I could keep standing, as I was pushed down between those ant-hills, wondering at what moment I should be trampled down by that crowd of roughs. But suddenly I heard a cry, and I saw a lot of Bengali schoolboys striking out from the shoulder, and that great crowd of Mussulman roughs cleaved in twain, and I was rescued.

An Astonished Missionary.—Rev. Mr. Haffendeu says: "I know an American missionary who was sent to Burmah thirty years ago to make inquiries about the languages. He himself spoke Burmese, and travelled up the country for many hundred miles. One night he encamped near a small village. Here he heard prayer going on in Burmese. He listened, and to his utter astonishment heard, not the name of Buddha, or that of any idol, but the name of our Lord Jesus Christ. He was the more surprised, for he knew that no missionary or white man had ever been to that part of the world, and so he went into the village and began to make inquiries. He found out that the headman of the village had some years previously been down to another village some miles distant, and had bought an article of food wrapped up in Burmese-printed paper, which happened to be one single chapter of the Word of God, with a piece torn out of the corner. He read it, and having himself sought to put sin away, he found that Saviour which is the Son of God, and who he found was able to cleanse from sin. He now called his friends together, and read that piece of the Word of God to them, and induced them to put away their idols. And when this missionary found them, they had been for six years praying to Christ as the Saviour of sinners. Thus is the blessing of God upon our work of spreading abroad simply and solely the Truth as in Jesus Christ."

Tourists Overtaken by the Tide.—Mr. Thomson said: "Two young fellows were travelling in the north of Scotland, and in the course of their sight-seeing took a walk along the beach to view the beautiful scenery. They walked thoughtlessly on, admiring their surroundings, but never casting a glance upon the fast-approaching waters until they were startled by a man on the rocks above them shouting: 'Young men, the tide is coming in, and the only road from the shore is almost covered.' The young men stopped and looked about them. From where they were they could not see the imminence of their peril. For a moment they wavered, then continued their walk. Again the man shouted a warning to them, but they took no notice of it. Soon, however, seeing the tide getting nearer and nearer, they began to be alarmed, and turned back. They tried to find a road up the cliff, but there was none. They rushed quickly along the beach, thinking to escape by the way they had come, but the road was covered. In despair they tried to climb the face of the rock, but it was too steep. The water rose higher and higher until it reached their necks, then covered them. There was a brief convulsive struggle, and then they were gone. They did not know that that warning voice was their last opportunity or they would gladly have hearkened to it. Sinners, too, if they knew this would be the last time salvation would be offered to them, would eagerly accept it. To neglect the warning is to run great risk of being lost for ever."

"Still in the Same Box."—An Evangelist said: "I was holding meetings in a country place some time ago, and one day when on the way to visit some friends, I saw before me a man to whom I had often seriously spoken at the meetings, but who would never decide, who was always trying to believe, and trying to do his best, as he said. Overtaking him, I asked, 'Are you still in the same box, my friend?' 'Still in the same place, sir,' he rejoined. I then said to him: 'You are like a man who has tumbled into deep water, and, being unable to swim, is struggling about, but whose efforts only serve to make him weaker. Out from the shore comes a strong swimmer, and when near the struggling man he stops and shouts, "Cease your struggles, shut your mouth, and put your hands down. Trust me, and I will save you." The man hears, and knows his only chance is to obey. He does so. The swimmer approaches, helps, and soon both are in safety. This is what Christ wants us to do—to cease our struggles, our own feeble efforts, and trust Him.' Then, lifting his eyes to mine, and taking hold of my hand, he said, simply, 'I see it now; I can trust my Saviour.'"

A Priest was Converted Through the Confessional recently, as related in *Evangelical Christendom*. "An anxious penitent in a Spanish town confessed to a priest that she had been to a Protestant service. He questioned her closely, for his curiosity was greatly excited. She gave him a full account, and acknowledged that a great impression had been made on her mind. The impression communicated itself to him, and shortly after he requested his own sister to go to the nearest place where Protestants assembled, to listen, as with *his ears*, and under his responsibility, and to bring him full details of everything. Reluctantly she did so, but faithfully reported all. The priest was convinced that there were truths of which he was ignorant, entered into communication with the pastor, appointed a secret place for a prolonged interview, and found immediate peace in the finished work of Jesus. The secluded place in which he labors allows him comparative freedom of action; he preaches Jesus; all his parishioners have the New Testament; the children learn more of Christ than of ceremonies; and confessions are stopped short, and belief in the full satisfaction wrought by the Lord Jesus is substituted for penance."

How the Lieutenant Lost His Life.—The Rev. Mr. Hamilton related: "A ship was crossing the Bay of Biscay one dark night, when the cry arose, 'A man overboard!' In a moment the lieutenant of the watch leaped into the water and swam to the rescue. The boats were lowered with all speed, and anxiously the men looked around to see who was missing. It was soon discovered that the captain of the foretop was not at his post. A death-like silence reigned on board. Suddenly a voice from the masthead shouted, 'I hear them.' And presently the dip of the oars became audible to all. The commander seized his trumpet and inquired, 'Have you got them both?' 'Yes, sir,' was the reply. And a grateful murmur of 'Thank God!' went through the company. But soon they were busy with the rescuer and the rescued. The seaman was sensible, and as he was helped on deck he said, 'Noble fellow; I had gone down, but he dived for me and saved my life.' But what of the officer? He had saved his fellow-creature's life, but died in doing so. The grief of that rescued sailor over the death of his savior was overwhelming. He treasured up every word that he had ever spoken to him, and determined to live as much as possible after the character of the man who had died for him, and who was a true Christian. So the sinner when he is saved resolves to live no longer unto himself, but unto Christ who died for him."

THE DEER HUNT.

Dr. Talmage's Sermon Preached Last Sunday Morning, September 9, 1888.

"As the hart panteth after the water brooks." Ps. 42: 1.

Allusions to the Deer in the Bible—A Talk with a Hunter in the Adirondacks—The Race to the Lake—People Pursued by the Hounds of Trouble—The Mistake of Fighting Them—A Wounded Dog—Antler Against Tooth—Shedding the Horns—The Finer the Stag, the Hotter the Pursuit—The Hounds Kept by Sin and Trouble—A Chain of Three Letters—King Nimrod's Three Vases—A Christian Woman in an Earthquake—A Lost Insane Man Rescued and Restored.

DAVID, who must some time have seen a deer hunt, points us here to a hunted stag making for the water. The fascinating animal, called in my text the hart, is the same animal that in sacred and profane literature is called the stag, the roebuck, the hind, the gazelle, the reindeer. In central Syria in Bible times there were whole pasture fields of them, as Solomon suggests when he says: "I charge you by the hinds of the field." Their antlers jutted from the long grass as they lay down. No hunter who has been long in "John Brown's track" will wonder that in the Bible they were classed among clean animals, for the dews, the showers, the lakes, washed them as clean as the sky. When Jacob, the patriarch, longed for venison, Esau shot and brought home a roebuck. Isaiah compares the sprightliness of the restored cripple of millennial times to the long and quick jump of the stag, saying: "The lame shall leap as the hart." Solomon expressed his disgust at a hunter who, having shot a deer, is too lazy to cook it, saying: "The slothful man roasteth not that which he took in hunting." But one day David, while far from the home from which he had been driven, and sitting near the door of a lonely cave where he had lodged, and on the banks of a pond or river, hears a pack of

Hounds in Swift Pursuit.

Because of the previous silence of the forest the clangor startles him, and he says to himself: "I wonder what those dogs are after!" Then there is a crackling in the brushwood, and the loud breathing of some rushing wonder of the woods, and the antlers of a deer rend the leaves of the thicket, and by an instinct which all hunters recognize, plunges into a pond or lake or river to cool its thirst, and at the same time by its capacity for swifter and longer swimming, to get away from the foaming harriers.

David says to himself: "Aha, that is myself! Saul after me, Absalom after me, enemies without number after me; I am chased, their bloody muzzles at my heels, barking at my good name, barking after my body, barking after my soul. Oh, the hounds, the hounds! But look there," says David, "that reindeer has splashed into the water. It puts its hot lips and nostrils into the cool wave that washes the lathered flanks, and it swims away from the fiery canines, and it is free at last. Oh, that I might find in the deep, wide lake of God's mercy and consolation escape from my pursuers! Oh, for the waters of life and rescue! As the hart panteth after the water brooks, so panteth my soul after Thee, O God."

I have just come from the Adirondacks, and the breath of the balsam and spruce and pine is still on me. The Adirondacks are now populous with hunters, and

The Deer Are Being Slain

by the score. Talking a few days ago with a hunter, I thought I would like to see whether my text was accurate in its allusion, and as I heard the dogs baying a little way off, and supposed they were on the track of a deer, I said to the hunter in rough corduroy: "Do the deer always make for the water when they are pursued?" He said: "Oh yes, Mister; you see they are a hot and thirsty animal, and they know where the water is, and when they hear danger in the distance, they lift their antlers and snuff the breeze and start for Racquet or Loon or Saranac; and we get into our cedar shell boat or stand by the 'runway' with rifle loaded ready to blaze away."

My friends, that is one reason why I like the Bible so much—its allusions are so true to nature. Its partridges are real partridges, its ostriches real ostriches, and its reindeer real reindeer. I do not wonder that

This Antlered Glory

of the text makes the hunter's eye sparkle, and his cheek glow, and his respiration quicken. To say nothing of its usefulness, although it is the most useful of all game, its flesh delicious, its skin turned into human apparel; its sinews fashioned into bow-strings; its antlers putting handles on cutlery, and the shavings of its horns, used as a restorative, taken from the name of the hart and called hartshorn. But putting aside its usefulness, this enchanting creature seems made out of gracefulness and elasticity. What an eye, with a liquid brightness as if gathered up from a hundred lakes of sunset! The horns, a coronal branching into every possible curve, and after it seems done, advancing into other projections of exquisiteness, a tree of polished bone, uplifted in pride, or swung down for awful combat. It is velocity embodied. Timidity impersonated. The enchantment of the woods. Eye lustrous in life and pathetic in death. The splendid animal a complete rhythm of muscle and bone and color and attitude and locomotion, whether couched in the grass among the shadows, or a living bolt shot through the forest, or turning at bay to attack the hounds, or rearing for its last fall under the buckshot of the trapper.

It is a splendid appearance, that the painter's pencil fails to sketch, and only a hunter's dream on a pillow of hemlock at the foot of St. Regis is able to picture. When, twenty miles from any settlement, it comes down at eventide to the lake's edge, to drink among the lily-pads, and, with its sharp-edged hoof, shatters the crystal of Long Lake, it is very picturesque. But only when, after miles of pursuit, with heaving sides and lolling tongue and eyes swimming in death, the stag leaps from the cliff into Upper Saranac, can you realize how much David had suffered from his troubles, and how much he wanted God when he expressed himself in the words: "As the hart panteth after the water brooks, so panteth my soul after Thee, O God."

The Hounds of Trouble.

Well now, let all those who have coming after them the lean hounds of poverty, or the black hounds of persecution, or the spotted hounds of vicissitude, or the pale hounds of death, or who are in anywise pursued, fly to the wide, deep, glorious lake of divine solace and rescue. The most of the men and women whom I happen to know, at different times, if not now, have had trouble after them, sharp-muzzled troubles, swift troubles, all-devouring troubles. Many of you have made the mistake of

Trying to Fight Them.

Somebody meanly attacked you, and you attacked them; they depreciated you, and you depreciated them; or they overreached you in a bargain, and you tried, in Wall Street parlance, to get a corner on them; or you have had a bereavement, and instead of being submissive, you are fighting that bereavement; you charge on the doctors who have failed to effect a cure; or you charge on the carelessness of the railroad company through which the accident occurred; or you are a chronic invalid, and you fret and worry and scold, and wonder why you cannot be well like other people, and you angrily charge on the neuralgia or the laryngitis or the ague or the sick-headache. The fact is, you are a deer at bay. Instead of running to the waters of divine consolation, and slaking your thirst, and cooling your body and soul in the good cheer of the gospel, and swimming away into the mighty deeps of God's love, you are fighting a whole kennel of harriers.

A few days ago I saw in the Adirondacks a dog lying across the road, and he seemed unable to get up, and I said to some hunters: "What is the matter with that dog?" They answered:

"A Deer Hurt Him."

And I saw he had a great swollen paw and a battered head, showing where the antlers struck him. And the probability is that some of you might give a mighty clip to your pursuers; you might damage their business, you might worry them into ill-health, you might hurt them as much as they have hurt you; but, after all, it is not worth while. You only have hurt a hound. Better be off for the Upper Saranac, into which the mountains of God's eternal strength look down and moor their shadows. As for your physical disorders, *the worst strychnine you can take* is fretfulness, and the best medicine is religion. I know people who were only a little disordered, yet have fretted themselves into complete valetudinarianism, while others put their trust in God, and came up from the very shadow of death, and have lived comfortably twenty-five years with only one lung. A man with one lung, but God with him, is better off than a Godless man with two lungs. Some of you have been for a long time sailing around Cape Fear, when you ought to have been sailing around Cape Good Hope. Do not turn back, but go ahead. The deer will accomplish more with its swift feet than with its horns. I saw

Whole Chains of Lakes

in the Adirondacks, and from one height you can see thirty; and there are said to be over eight hundred in the great wilderness. So near are they to each other that your mountain guide picks up and carries the boat from lake to lake, the small distance between them for that reason called a "carry." And the realm of God's Word is one long chain of bright, refreshing lakes; each promise a lake, a very short carry between them, and though for ages the pursued have been drinking out of them, they are full, up to the top of the green banks; and the same David describes them, and they seem so near together that in three different places he speaks of them as a continuous river, saying: "There is a river the streams whereof shall make glad the city of God"; "Thou shalt make them drink of the rivers of Thy pleasures"; "Thou greatly enrichest it with the river of God, which is full of water."

But many of you have turned your back on that supply, and confront your trouble, and you are soured with your circumstances, and you are fighting society, and you are fighting a pursuing world; and troubles, instead of driving you into the cool lake of heavenly comfort, have made you stop and turn round and lower your head, and it is simply

Antler Against Tooth.

I do not blame you. Probably under the same circumstances I would have done worse. But you are all wrong. You need to do as the reindeer does in February and March—it sheds its horns. The Rabbinical writers allude to this resignation of antlers by the stag when they say of a man who ventures his money in risky enterprises, he has hung it on the stag's horns; and a proverb in the far East tells a man who has foolishly lost his fortune, to go and find where the deer shed his horns. My brother, quit the antagonism of your circumstances, quit misanthropy, quit complaint, quit pitching into your pursuers, be as wise as, next spring, will be the deer of the Adirondacks. Shed your horns!

But very many of you who are wronged of the world—and if in any assembly between Sandy Hook, New York, and Golden Gate, San Francisco, it were asked that all those that had been sometimes badly treated should raise both their hands, and full response should be made, there would be twice as many hands lifted as persons present—I say many of you would declare: "We have always done the best we could and tried to be useful, and why we become

The Victims of Malignment,

or invalidism, or mishap, is inscrutable." Why, do you not know that the finer a deer, and the more elegant its proportions, and the more beautiful its bearing, the more anxious the hunters and the hounds are to capture it? Had that roebuck a ragged fur, and broken hoofs, and an obliterated eye, and a limping gait, the hunters would have said, "Pshaw! don't let us waste our ammunition on a sick deer." And the hounds would have given a few sniffs of the track, and then darted off in another direction for better game. But when they see a deer with antlers lifted in mighty challenge to earth and sky, and the sleek hide looks as if it had been smoothed by invisible hands, and the fat sides enclose the richest pasture that could be nibbled from the bank of rills so clear they seem to have dropped out of heaven, and the stamp of its foot defies the jack-shooting lantern and the rifle, the horn and the hound, that deer they will have if they must needs break their neck in the rapids. So if there were no noble stuff in your make-up, if you were *a bifurcated nothing*, if you were a forlorn failure, you would be allowed to go undisturbed; but the fact that the whole pack is in full cry after you is proof positive that

You Are Splendid Game

and worth capturing. Therefore sarcasm draws on you its "finest bead." Therefore the world goes gunning for you with its best Maynard breach-loader. Highest compliment is it to your talent, or your virtue, or your usefulness. You will be assailed in proportion to your great achievements. The best and the mightiest being the world ever saw had set after Him all the hounds, terrestrial and diabolic, and they lapped His blood after the Calvarean massacre. The world paid nothing to its Redeemer but a bramble and a cross. Many who have done their best to make the world better have had such a rough time of it that all their pleasure is in anticipation of the next world, and they would, if they could, express their own feelings in the words of the Baroness of Nairn, at the close of her long life:

"Would you be young again?
So would not I;
One tear of memory given
Onward I'll hie;
Life's dark wave forded o'er,
All but at rest on shore,
Say, would you plunge once more,
With home so nigh?

"If you might, would you now,
Retrace your way?
Wander through stormy wilds,
Faint and astray?
Night's gloomy watches fled,
Morning all beaming red,
Hope's smile around us shed,
Heavenward, away!"

Yes; for some people in this world there seems no let up. They are pursued from youth to manhood, and from manhood into old age. Very distinguished are Lord Stafford's hounds, and the Earl of Yarborough's hounds, and the Duke of Rutland's hounds; and Queen Victoria pays eight thousand five hundred dollars per year to her Master of Buckhounds. But all of them put together do not equal in number or speed, or power to hunt down the great kennel of hounds of which Sin and Trouble are owner and master.

But what is a relief for all those pursuits of trouble and annoyance and pain and bereavement? My text gives it to you in a word of three letters, but each letter is a chariot if you would triumph, or a throne if you want to be crowned, or a lake if you would slake your thirst—yea,

A Chain of Three Letters

—G-o-d, the One for whom David longed, and the One whom David found. You might as well meet a stag which, after its sixth mile of running at the topmost speen through thicket and gorge, and with the breath of the dogs on its heels, has come in full sight of Scroon Lake, and tried to cool its projecting and blistered tongue with a drop of dew from a blade of grass, as to attempt to satisfy an immortal soul, when flying from trouble and sin, with anything less deep and high and broad and immense and infinite and eternal than God. His comfort, why, it embosoms all distress. His arm, it wrenches off all bondage; His hand, it wipes away all tears. His Christly atonement, it makes us all right with the past, and all right with the future, and all right with God, all right with man, and all right forever.

King Nimrod's Three Vases.

Lamartine tells us that King Nimrod said to his three sons: "Here are three vases, and one is of clay, another of amber, and another of gold. Choose now which you will have." The eldest son, having the first choice, chose the vase of gold, on which was written the word "Empire," and when opened, it was found to contain human blood. The second son, making the next choice, chose the vase of amber, inscribed with the word "Glory," and when opened, it contained the ashes of those who were once called great. The third son took the vase of clay, and opening it, found it empty, but on the bottom of it was inscribed the name of God. King Nimrod asked his courtiers which vase they thought weighed the most. The avaricious men of his court said the vase of gold. The poets said the one of amber. But the wisest men said the empty vase, because one letter of the name of God outweighed a universe.

For Him I thirst: for His grace I beg; on His promise I build my all. Without Him I cannot be happy. I have tried the world, and it does well enough as far as it goes, but it is too uncertain a world, too evanescent a world. I am not a prejudiced witness. I have nothing against this world. I have been

One of The Most Fortunate,

or, to use a more Christian word, one of the most blessed of men, blessed in my parents, blessed in the place of my nativity, blessed in my health, blessed in my field of work, blessed in my natural temperament, blessed in my family, blessed in my opportunities, blessed in a comfortable livlihood, blessed in the hope that my soul will go to Heaven through the pardoning mercy of God, and my body, unless it be lost at sea or cremated in some conflagration, will lie down in the gardens of Greenwood among my kindred and friends, some already gone, and others to come after me. Life to many has been a disappointment, but to me it has been a pleasant surprise, and yet I declare that if I did not feel that God was now my friend and ever present help, I should be wretched and terror-struck. But I want more of Him. I have thought over this text and preached this sermon to myself until with all the aroused energies of my body, mind, and soul, I can cry out: "As the hart panteth after the water brooks, so panteth my soul after Thee, O God."

Through Jesus Christ make this God your God, and

You Can Withstand Anything,

and everything, and that which affrights others will inspire you. As in time of earthquake, when an old Christian woman was asked whether she was scared, answered: "No, I am glad that *I have a God who can shake the world*," or as in a financial panic, when a Christian merchant was asked if he did not fear he would break, answered: "Yes I shall break when the fiftieth Psalm breaks in the fifteenth verse: 'Call upon me in the day of trouble; I will deliver thee, and thou shalt glorify me.'" O Christian men and women, pursued of annoyauces and exasperations, remember that this hunt, whether a still hunt or a hunt in full cry, will soon be over. If ever a whelp looks ashamed and ready to slink out of sight it is when in the Adirondacks a deer by one long, tremendous plunge into Big Tupper Lake gets away from him. The disappointed canine swims in a little way but, defeated, swims out again, and cringes with humiliated yawn at the feet of his master. And how abashed and ashamed will all your earthly troubles be when you have dashed into the river from under the throne of God, and the heights and depths of heaven are between you and your pursuers.

We are told in Revelations 22d and 15th: "Without are dogs," by which I conclude there is a whole kennel of hounds outside the gate of heaven, or, as when a master goes in a door, his dog lies on the steps waiting for him to come out, so the troubles of this life may follow us to the shining door, but they cannot get in. "Without are dogs!" I have seen dogs, and owned dogs, that I would not be chagrined to see in the heavenly city. Some of the

Grand Old Watch-Dogs

who are the constabulary of the homes in solitary places, and for years have been the only protection of wife and child; some of the shepherd dogs that drive back the wolves and bark away the flocks from going too near the precipice; and some of the dogs whose neck and paw Landseer, the painter, has made immortal, would not find me shutting them out from the gate of shining pearl. Some of those old St. Bernard dogs that have lifted perishing travellers out of the Alpine snow; the dog that John Brown, the Scotch essayist, saw ready to spring at the surgeon lest, in removing the cancer, he too much hurt the poor woman whom the dog felt bound to protect; and dogs that we caressed in our childhood days, or that in later time laid down on the rug in seeming sympathy when our homes were desolated. I say, if some soul entering heaven should happen to leave the gate ajar, and these faithful creatures should quietly walk in, it would not at all disturb my heaven. But all those human or brutal hounds that have chased and torn and lacerated the the world; yea, all that now bite or worry or tear to pieces, shall be prohibited. "Without are dogs!" No place there for harsh critics or backbiters, or despoilers of the reputation of others! Down with you to the kennels of darkness and despair! The hart has reached

The Eternal Water Brooks,

and the panting of the long chase is quieted in still pastures, and "there shall be nothing to hunt or destroy in all God's holy mount." Oh, when some of you get there, it will be like what a hunter tells of when he was pushing his canoe far up north in the winter, and amid the ice-floes, and a hundred miles, as he thought, from any other human beings: He was startled one day as he heard a stepping on the ice, and he cocked the rifle ready to meet anything that came near. He found a man, barefooted and insane from long exposure, approaching him. Taking him into his canoe, and kindling fires to warm him, he restored him, and found out where he had lived, and took him to his home, and found all

The Village in Great Excitement.

A hundred men were searching for this lost man, and his family and friends rushed out to meet him; and as had been agreed at his first appearance, bells were rung, and guns were discharged, and banquets spread, aud the rescuer loaded with presents. Well, when some of you step out of this wilderness, where you have been chilled and torn, and sometimes lost amid the icebergs, into the warm greetings of all the villages of the glorified, and your friends rush out to give you welcoming kiss, the news that there is another soul forever saved, will call the caterers of heaven to spread the banquet, and the bell-men to lay hold of the rope in the tower, and while the chalices click at the feast, and the bells clang from the towers, it will be a scene so uplifting, I pray God I may be there to take part in the celestial merriment. And now do you not think the prayer in Solomon's Song, where he compared Christ to a reindeer coming down in the night to pasture on the plains, would make an exquisitely appropriate peroration to my sermon: "Until the day break and the shadows flee away, be thou like a roe or a young hart upon the mountains of Bether"?

A BLIND BUDDHIST IN JAPAN.

IN a letter from Dr. H. Loomis, who is laboring at Yokohama, Japan, to the *Interior*, he mentions the following interesting incident of spiritual vision resulting from the cure of natural blindness: "In the town of Fugioka lives a man sixty four years of age, named Machida Totaro. He has long been afflicted with a weakness in his eyes, and went from place to place and to various doctors and priests for some remedy. But his efforts were of no avail, and he become almost totally blind. Then he heard that there was a skilful foreign physician living in Tokyo, by the name of Whitney, and he went to him for relief. After careful treatment for awhile his sight was partially restored, and he was greatly rejoiced and thankful for the services that had been rendered. Hitherto, he had been a firm believer in the Buddhist religion. But this kindness on the part of a Christian doctor so touched his heart that he quite changed his views, and was very ready to hear about the Christian belief. After some instruction from the doctor and others, he made a full confession of his faith in Christ as his Saviour, and received baptism from the Rev. Mr. Fuwa. So there has come to him a double healing, and he can now truly say with a double meaning, 'Whereas I was once blind, now I can see.'"

A wonderful work among prisoners in Japan, is also reported by Dr. Loomis. He says: "The pastor of the church at Shidzuoka has been visiting the prison and holding services for the benefit of the inmates. The result has been a most marked change in the mind and conduct of many of the prisoners. About fifty copies of the New Testament have been purchased by them, and several have united with the church upon their release from confinement. The officers are much interested, and are also studying the Bible. A Christian has been for some time employed as a teacher of morals in Kobe prison. As the result of his work, he reports the conversion of some of the most hardened criminals. These men have been released, and are now living honest and industrious lives."

A ROYAL RECEPTION AT STOCKHOLM.

AN interesting letter has been kindly sent to us by the secretary of the International Committee of Young Men's Christian Associations, which he has received from a delegate to the recent Conference in Stockholm. In addition to the reports we have already published, the writer supplies the following details of the reception tendered to the Conference by the royal family of Sweden: The King was absent in Berlin at the opening of the Conference, but as the delegates were sitting at dinner a telegram was read from him expressing his regrets that he could not be present to enjoy the benefits of the Convention and participate in the deliberations and invoking the benediction of the Holy Spirit on the Convention. The contents of the telegram were announced in English, French, German, and Swedish. The health of the King was then drunk (in water) and the national hymns of Sweden, Great Britain, and America were then sung. Mr. Morse, of New York, then proposed the health of the Queen. The King and Queen and his Royal Highness the Crown Prince have exhibited much interest in the preparatory arrangements for the Conference. It was held in Stockholm at the personal solicitation of the King, and both he and the Crown Prince made liberal subscriptions for the expenses of it.

On Monday, August 19, the delegates left the city by special boat for a lunch, on special invitation, with the Crown Prince at the Royal Palace at Drottningholm. The palace and royal garden were thrown open to the visitors. The Crown Prince, in the absence of the King, who is in Germany, and the Queen, who is in Norway, presided, and welcomed the delegates. A very pleasant afternoon was spent, and the party returned to the city by boat at 4 o'clock.

The Convention has been a very successful one, and everybody, from the King and Queen and royal family down to the servants in the hotels, has done everything to make it a success and to provide for the comfort of the delegates. The King makes a liberal contribution annually to the Y. M. C. A., and the court chaplains, the chamberlains, cabinet officers, and other prominent men are in sympathy with it. The Queen is an earnest Christian woman, the King's sister is president of a home for cripples and the orphan asylum; home for old men, home for old ladies and other benevolent institutions have the support of the Royal Family.

A SIX YEARS' WEDDING TOUR.

THE guests at a wedding solemnized in Buffalo, N. Y., in 1882, were amused at an invitation given on the wedding cards. It stated that the bride and groom would be at their home in Sacramento, Cal., on May 10, 1888, *six years from date*, and would be pleased to receive their friends. They were going on a bridal tour around the world, and they set out immediately after the marriage ceremony. The San Francisco papers in announcing their return, say: "There is scarcely a spot of interest on the globe that they have not visited. Children were born to them *en route*—twin boys in St. Petersburg; a girl in China, and another boy in Brazil. The journey cost them $75,000. The remarkable fact, however, which astonished the invited guests, was that the bridal couple returned punctually on the day specified, though so much had intervened that might have delayed them. There will be far greater astonishment among unwatchful Christians in a few years, when they hear that the Bridegroom has come, as He said He would (Matt. 24: 44), and those that were ready have gone in with Him to the marriage.

A CRIMINAL TRIAL IN AFRICA.

A BARBAROUS method of deciding the guilt or innocence of suspected persons in Africa is described by Dr. George D. Dowkontt, the director of the Medical Missionary Society of New York, in his *Medical Missionary Record*. He states that two missionaries, Messrs. Henry and M'Intyre, on two occasions, witnessed the cruel and absurd practice of testing guilt by drinking mwavi. The chief suspected some among his people of crime, among them one of his wives, and he wanted to find out who was guilty. The chief "resolved to settle the matter by making all the men and some women of his own and some surrounding villages drink mwavi. His plan was to bring so many to his village at one time, and, placing them in a circle, make them drink the poison in public. If they lived, they were held to be guiltless; if they died, no one seemed to care much. This scene occurred on the meadow on the edge of which our tent was pitched. After the people were assembled, a fantastic figure, dressed up with a head-dress of feathers, danced about the circle for a time. The poison, which is the bark of the sassy-tree, was then beaten with a rude mortar and pestle, and, being put into water, was drunk by the suspected, who came up by twos for this purpose, and then ran off to vomit or die. This was given to about two hundred and fifty people the first time, and to more than a hundred the second time. One of the head-men said that the poison was made weak, yet each time one person died, and on previous occasions six died.

AN INQUIRY FROM A CAR WINDOW.

WHEN there is only a moment's opportunity for a friend to ask a question and receive a reply, the information sought is sure to be that which the questioner deems most important. The following incident, which is related in the *Watchword*, suggests the thought that a time is coming when there will be but one question that will be really worth asking in respect to our friends: A dear brother of the writer, living in New York, was recently on a train which was just leaving the station. By the side of it, on the next track, was another train, which was about starting in the opposite direction. A man near my brother suddenly jumped to his feet, opened the window, and hurriedly called, "John!" A man at an open window in the other train, instantly recognized his friend, and quickly responded, "William!" A hearty grasp of hands, and the short, solemn inquiry came ringing from William:

"John, have ye kept the faith?"

"Aye, by the help of God, I have."

The cars moved away, a smile of pleasure on the face of each, and they saw each other no more. Was it strange that a thrill of Christian sympathy took possession of my brother's heart, as he at once took a seat by the side of William, who had hitherto been a stranger, but now was known to him as a Christian brother?

Not, "Have you made money?" "Have you made a great name for yourself?" but, "Have you kept the faith?" What stronger evidence of conversion could have been given, than in the question and answer which came from these two travelers to eternity?

Happy the man who can give a right answer to this important question, and who at the end of life, and in the day of judgment, can say with Paul, "*I have kept the faith*."

THE HEALING OF A CRIPPLE.

AT a recent meeting at Bethshan, Miss Stone related a remarkable experience, which Mrs. Baxter publishes in *Thy Healer*.* Miss Stone, who said that she had travelled over a hundred miles to give her testimony to the Lord's power to heal, as manifested in her experience, said: "Twenty-six years ago an accident was permitted to befall me, and I was made a helpless cripple. I came, or rather was brought, up to London to see if anything could be done for me, for I had two bones dislocated. Two others came up with me. Dr. Hutton (the late well-known bone-setter) put the bones in their places, but there was no hope for me. I went back home to *lie on my bed for twenty-three years*. Then a sister told me how she had given her sickness and everything else to the Lord, and the Spirit revealed to me, as He had never done before, the meaning of Matt. 8: 16, 17: "And He cast out the spirits with His word, and healed all that were sick; that it might be fulfilled which was spoken of by Esaias the prophet, saying, Himself took our infirmities, and bare our sicknesses." I believed that He had taken my infirmities as well as my sins, and He raised me up three years ago, and I have been able to walk since then, and have not had to lie in bed one day, nor be awake one night."

PREACHING IN PERSIAN SHOPS.

AN account of a tour through a few Persian villages, is sent by Rev. S. G. Wilson, of Tabriz, to the *Church*. In the course of his narrative he says: "When we came to Boshminch, I went into the bazaars. After a few words of greeting, a trader invited me to sit down in his open shop, the floor of which is about three feet above-ground, and on the front of which his merchandise is exhibited. A crowd gathered around, drawn to see a new thing. The gospel words and narrative attracted them; the claims put forth for Christ drew out lively repartee, and a shower of questions which led over a large range of the topics at issue between Christianity and Islam. Only a few showed a bigoted spirit, while the majority listened to the exaltation of Christ as the divine Redeemer and Judge of all, perhaps smiling at the idea of their becoming converts. After some conversation and reading, a spirit of opposition arose, and on the morrow they tried to persuade our host to oust us, as defiling to his house. Poor man! In the morning his milk was spilt, and in the evening one of his cows died. 'The curse of heaven,' will be the popular verdict. When I next went out into the street I thought to moderate pub-

* *Thy Healer and Faith Witness*, a monthly Magazine, edited by Mrs. M. Baxter, contains original articles on Holiness and Healing, Authentic Testimonies of Divine Healing, and Items of Intelligence from Heathen Lands where missionaries are laboring in faith, soliciting no help from man, but relying solely on God for support. Annual Subscription, 75 cents, may be sent to Manager of CHRISTIAN HERALD, 63 Bible House, New York.

c feeling by talking on a subject about which e could all agree, namely, repentance; and narated the parable of the Prodigal Son. Before finished, a man stuffed his fingers into his ears nd went away, saying that it was defiling to lisen to me. His ground of offence was, that I ad mentioned 'swine,' and said the father mbraced the boy who had been feeding them.

"At the next place we had a good reception, nd a fine opportunity for work in the house of soldier. Having been to Teheran, and under he drill of European officers, he, like his class, as somewhat liberalized. In the course of conersation he asked me if I knew of *dog-worshipers*. I told him I had heard of fire-worshippers, nd even snake-worshippers, but not of dogorshippers. He said he had seen some in Teeran. I asked him who. He said there were eople in the capital who fed dogs at their own able, washed and clothed them, took them in heir laps, and in their carriages to ride. Were hey not dog-worshippers? This misconception f the lap-dog craze, while ludicrous in itself, hows how the common people conceive that all ustoms have a bearing on religion."

ANTICHRIST'S BROKEN TREATY.

By Rev. John Storie.*

Antichrist Conciliating the Jews—Undertakes to Protect Them—Encourages Them to Rebuild he Temple—The Treaty Ruptured—Their Deady Enemy—His Death and Resurrection—The Tribulation of the 1260 Days.

WHEN the last awful week [Daniel's final seven years; Dan. 9:24] of Time begins, the Jews return and seek to rebuild their Temple. It is hen that the Antichrist rises into power. It is hen that the Messiah is in *Parousia* in these errestrial heavens. It is then that the events of judgment, in the Book of the Revelation will be consummated. Before these closing years begin, many of the Jews will, it would appear, have been gathered back, still in unbelief but in expectation, to the land of their fathers.

"The Prince, the Coming One," the Antichrist who is to be, stands forward in His earliest policy as the advocate of religious freedom,

The Protector of the Persecuted

and oppressed; and, seeking to attach the Jewish race, with their vast resources of wealth and their immense influence over the moving nations, as allies in the confederacy he is forming, is willing to sustain the attitude of their patron and their friend. They accept His protection, and enter into a *seven years' league or covenant* with Him, during which He is to protect them in their land, their city, and their worship. They then complete the temple and revive its ritual—the sacrifice and oblation—in the impious spirit foretold in Isaiah 28:14 and 66. With this predicted event is renewed the broken succession of the Seventy weeks; and now too, commence the last eventful seven years of this dispensation; the last septenary of Daniel's prophecy.

Thus will these Jews act in covenant with the Man of Sin; corrupted by his flatteries—Dan. 11:32—deluded and defiant, for the first half of this last septenary; and then, "in the middle of the week."

They Hear the First Knell

of the approaching tribulation. He breaks the covenant; turns against them; marches into their land; interdicts their worship: "causes the sacrifices and oblations to cease." And then commences his own "consummate impiety and transgression," when opposing and exalting himself above all that is called God, or that is worshipped, "he seats himself in the very temple" they have reared, "showing himself that he is God," and demanding worship. That temple is at last made the central seat and shrine of impious "abominations." (Dan. 9:27; 2 Thess. 11:4; Rev. 13:8, 12.)

The last words in the prophecy are brief. "And upon the wing of Abomination shall be the Desolator." (ver. 27.) Here, "the Desolator" is evidently this King—the Man of Sin—become the persecutor and oppressor. Next, the term "Abomination" as the common term in Hebrew for a false god or his idolatrous image, like Milcom or Chemish or Moloch. Here it may designate the Man of Sin, his image, his worship (Rev. 13: 14, 15), and again, "the wing" is apparently some pinnacle or summit of

The Profaned Temple.

To this the Lord's words of warning apply; "When ye therefore shall see the Abomination of Desolation spoken of by Daniel, the prophet, stand in the Holy Place..... then let them which be in Judea flee to the mountain," (Matthew 24:15, 16.) There may be some mysterious descent on the temple's wing, so calculated and arranged as to present the Man of Sin to the assembled Jews as in the predicted advent of their Messiah: "And the Lord whom ye seek shall *suddenly* come to His temple; even the Messenger of the covenant whom ye delight in." (Mal. 3: 1.) However that be, this impious and defiant profanation will be permitted to go on till it reach "the consummation"; and the persecution of those of the Jews who refuse to receive his mark, will proceed, till "that which has been determined" in the Divine Decree is in its full measure "poured upon the desolate."

We have here, too, a new and startling fact in the manifestation of the Man of Sin:

His Death and Resurrection.

"And I saw one of his heads as having been slain to death; and his death-stroke was healed; and the whole earth, or land, wondered after the Beast." (Ver. 3.) That Head is still the seventh. After reigning for a time as king; after breaking the covenant with Israel; and it may be immediately before Satan's expulsion from the heavens; He had fallen assassinated or slain in battle. Men had seen Him stabbed by a sword. They had seen His body lie slain and dead. But now He lives, raised or risen from the dead; reanimate by the power of Satan, to occupy the Satanic throne, and consummate the "mystery of iniquity." The death wound is there, on His body; visible, tangible, as were the wounded hands and side of Jesus. "The whole world wondered" as they heard of the miracle or gazed on Him, captivated, entranced. All men begin to render.

Homage to the Dragon,

in whose power this glorious Head of Empire has come (ver. 4), and they worship the Man of Sin, saying "Who is like Him" in knowledge, in magnificence, in spiritual power? This is He who has conquered death! This is He who is bringing life and immortality to men! Who is like to this glorious and deathless King? Who, in heaven or earth, "is able to make war with Him," the universal, invincible Lord. (Ver. 4.) And to Him "there was given a mouth (the lion's mouth), speaking great things," in the way of revelation and promise, for the advance of manhood to a diviner eminence; and "blaspheming the name of God and His tabernacle, and them that are in His tabernacle with Him" (ver. 6); that is the Lord, Christ, and those already with Him in that heavenly pavilion—the risen and raptured saints who, in the morn of His advent, had been taken up, and are now with their Lord. (Matt. 24:39, 41; 1 Thess. 4:17. Rev. 4:2-8.) "And it was given him to make war on the *saints*, and to overcome them"; not in their faith and fidelity, for many of them, if not all, remain steadfast. But

The Great Tribulation is Come;

and the "unwise virgins," and those who have not been "ready" to rise and join the Lord will, almost equally with those of Judah, have now to pass, living or dying, through its persecution and its agony; for the mighty and merciless sway of this dread king is to extend "over every tribe, and people, and tongue, and nation." (ver. 7). This is given Him by Satan, and by Jehovah's fiat permitted; "and all who are dwelling on the earth shall worship him" as the present and incarnate deity; and be compelled to worship (ver. 15, 27); all except those "whose names are written in the Book of Life of the Lamb." (ver. 8). And so shall be completed the apostacy from God and His Christ.

Here, again, the duration of this period of oppression and blasphemy is determined. It is to last "forty and two months" (ver. 5); that is, 1,260 days. It begins in the middle of the last septenary—the last of the seventy weeks revealed to Daniel—when the Man of Sin breaks his covenant with the Jewish nation; and it terminates with the Epiphany of the Lord. (Rev. 19: 20.)

*From an article entitled "The Final Seven Years," in *The Prophetic News* for August; price six cents by mail. On sale at this office, 63 Bible House, New York.

THE SLAYING OF THE WITNESSES.

By the Rev. Dr. John Snodgrass.

THE persecution of the Albigensis and Waldenses, and the cruel martyrdom of those two holy men, John Huss and Jerome, of Prague, was not the last persecution of the Church by Antichrist, which the prophecy of the Slaying of the Witnesses (Rev. 11: 3-10) plainly supposes it to have been. The same objection in Rev. 11: 3-13 holds against any subsequent period of the Church's sufferings that has yet occurred, whether at the Reformation, the Parisian massacre, the revocation of the Edict of Nantes, or any other.

As this prophecy, then, remains to be fulfilled in the future sufferings of the Church from the hand of Antichrist, it confirms the opinion of those men who have thought that his power and tyranny will then prevail; that the true church will suffer much from his implacable enmity, and religion be brought to a very low ebb. It must, indeed, be acknowledged that appearances, at present, are against this opinion. Popery's dominion seems greatly declined, and the progress of knowledge threatens speedy destruction. We learn from experience, however, that appearances are not to be built upon. Worldly power may forcibly obstruct the progress of knowledge, and unforeseen events revive the influence of the Romanists of Rome.

After many awful judgments poured out upon them, we shall still see them.

Under the Sixth Vial,

uniting with the dragon, and gathering together, by their influence, the kings of the earth, and of the whole world, to fight in his cause. This shows what great power Romanists shall have immediately before their total overthrow. About that time, then, probably we may look for the slaying of the Witnesses, as described in this prophecy; for we know it shall be a time of great difficulty and danger to the saints. Therefore our Lord saith, "Behold, I come as a thief: blessed is he that watcheth."

The third angel in Rev. 14: 9 will probably appear soon after the second angel who cries, "Babylon is fallen"; for then the judgments upon the Romish Antichrist will hasten on apace. But his voice will be chiefly heard from the time of the drying-up of the great river Euphrates till the battle of Armageddon. During that period, every possible artifice will be employed in the support of the last interests of tyranny and superstition; and the enmity and cruelty of Antichrist against the people of God will again break forth. This will be a trying time to Christians. Every seductive allurement, and every terrifying menace, shall be made use of, to gain their compliance with the iniquitous system, which at the same time shall be colored over with every sophistical recommendation. It was therefore necessary that an antidote should be provided against so great a danger. This is done by the voice of the third angel, who in the clear accomplishment of prophecy, and in the awful appearances of Providence against these enemies of God, will solemnly and loudly proclaim the guilt and danger of all who stand in connection with them.

CHRISTIAN HERALD AND SIGNS OF OUR TIMES

OFFICE, 63 BIBLE HOUSE, NEW YORK.

ENTERED AT THE POST-OFFICE AT NEW YORK, N. Y., AS SECOND-CLASS MATTER.

EVERY NUMBER CONTAINS:

The Portrait and Biography of some eminent person.
The Sermon Dr. Talmage preached the last Sunday morning.
An Exposition of Unfulfilled Prophecy.
A Summary of the Events of the Week. Notes of Religious and Temperance Movements, etc.
A Sermon by Rev. C. H. Spurgeon, of London, from advance sheets sent by special arrangement.
Pictures of Missionary Life, etc., and Descriptive Articles.
An instalment of a Serial Story.
An Exposition of the International Sunday-School Lesson, by Mrs. M. Baxter.

ANNUAL SUBSCRIPTION, $1.50.

New Subscriptions can commence at any time. When no date is mentioned, we begin it with the issue of the week in which the subscription is received.

Remittances by Mail should be by Post-office money order, bank cheque, draft, or express money order, whenever possible, and should always be made payable to THE CHRISTIAN HERALD. Letters containing money sent in this way need not be registered, as when lost, duplicates can always be obtained.

If a Postal Note or currency is sent, it should always be in a registered letter. Letters can be registered at any office. Subscribers sending money of this kind, and not registering, do it at their own risk.

Change of Address. Name of Post-office and State, of both old and new address, should always be given in case of removal, as without the previous address it is impossible to find the name on our list.

CURRENT EVENTS.

The Rumored Rejection by China of the New treaty led to the prompt passage last week by Congress of a rigid exclusion bill. Official notice of the failure of the treaty had not been received, but Congress acted on its own responsibility. There are, it appears, some twelve thousand Chinamen now in China who are entitled to return to this country under the old treaty, as they hold certificates granted by our courts of their previous residence here. A suspicion is prevalent that those certificates are sold in China to men sufficiently resembling the original holders in personal appearance, to escape detection. The bill passed by Congress, therefore, prohibits the issue of any more certificates by the courts, and absolutely prohibits the landing of any more Chinamen, except such as have a family in this country, or property here of specified value. This is in effect to dishonor the certificates legally issued by our own courts, on the faith of which Chinamen visited their own country. If the bill should become law by the signature of the President, it will give the Chinese a very unfavorable idea of our national morality. Some measure for the detection of illegal transfer of certificates would have been legitimate, but to prohibit a Chinaman landing after guaranteeing him permission to do so is a dishonorable violation of our engagements.

The Restriction of Immigration Which is now advocated by both the political parties, is the object of a bill in course of preparation by Representative Oates, of Alabama, who acts under the request of the select Committee on Immigration. The bill, as at present drawn, has not yet been endorsed by the Committee, but Mr. Oates intimates that in the event of its rejection, he will offer it in the House as an individual expression of opinion. It provides that the entire inspection of immigrants shall be placed in the hands of the Treasury Department instead of, as now, partly in the hands of Federal and State authorities. This, he believes, will lead to more efficient and responsible supervision. A substantial head tax, which Mr. Oates thinks should be fifty dollars at least, should be exacted from the steamship companies to discourage the importation of paupers. Intending immigrants are to be required to inform American Consuls six months before leaving home, and on their arrival in this country will have to make affidavit that they have not been assisted by National or municipal authorities; that they are not under contract; have not been convicted of felony nor taken from poorhouses. Part of the head tax is to be set apart for hospitals and such buildings as may be required to shelter immigrants detained for examination. The bill will also prescribe a punishment for steamship companies who violate its provisions.

The Liquor Dealer's Convention which Assembled at Buffalo, N. Y., on September 4, made an emphatic protest against high license. The Convention declared: "That we are opposed to that attempt to regulate which seeks by high license to discriminate between the rich and the poor, or against one locality. We are willing to pay a reasonable license that yields such a revenue to the State as our industry can bear with justice to them engaged in it, but are opposed to the effort to grind such enormous sums from one branch of business as will drive responsible men from the trade and destroy our property." The ridiculous feature of the resolution is that high license does not drive responsible men out of the trade, but is expressly devised to exclude all but responsible men from it, though it does not succeed in doing that. The resolution was a surprise to people who believe that liquor dealers, as a rule, do not object to high license. It was probably passed in deference to the wish of large brewers who hold mortgages on small saloons, and who find that high license will render their traffic less profitable. Even they are not wise, in their generation, or they would see that high license is a bulwark between them and prohibition.

The Reports from Jacksonville, Fla., Grew more gloomy last week. The worst record was that of Friday, when the number of new cases reached seventy. On Wednesday it was decided by the Association to issue an appeal for help. The committee accordingly sent out a statement that the epidemic had reached a stage at which the funds were insufficient to meet the demand, and as business was entirely suspended, outside help was necessary. Mr. James M. Schumacher, the President of the First National Bank, was appointed treasurer for the fund, and authorized to receive subscriptions. A census of the city has been taken, showing that there are now 13,757 persons still there. Of these, the number without means is 8,995. The project of temporarily depopulating the city has not yet been executed, though the citizens are especially anxious to have the women and children sent away. The Surgeon-General, however, remains firm in prohibiting the exodus, fearing the infection of other localities. A refugee camp in now being constructed on land purchased for the purpose on the Florida Railway line, seven miles away, as Camp Perry is almost useless owing to the damp character of the land. The accommodation and management of the camp are also defective. All reports speak in the highest terms of the heroism of the physicians and clergymen, who are doing their duty nobly. Dr. W. L. Baldwin, one of the most prominent of the physicians, has fallen a victim to the fever, and his death is deeply regretted. It is remarked by attentive observers, that while the disease attacks all races and all classes, those who are the least likely to recover from it are those addicted to strong drink.

A Destructive Hurricane Passed over the island of Cuba on September 4, doing much damage to property and causing the loss of many lives. In Sagua alone fifty persons perished. The loss of life in Havana was not so severe, but the pecuniary loss is overwhelming. A telegram from that city says: "Ruin and destruction mark the path of the storm throughout the city; not a street but bears evidence of the force of the hurricane. All the principal cafés, places of amusement, and public buildings were more or less damaged. In all the parks and boulevards extending from La Punta to Calzada del Monte, and also in the plazas del Cristo, Armas, Tacon, and Infanta, immense trees were uprooted, in some instances their huge trunks being carried several blocks by the force of the wind. Signs, shutters, and débris of every description were piled in the streets, blocking traffic. To add to the horror of the scene nearly all the street lamps were destroyed, leaving the city in total darkness throughout the night." The northern streets were all inundated. The chief loss of life occurred in the harbor, which, though landlocked, was beaten by huge waves. Some of the shipping was sunk, and some beaten to pieces against the wharves. The telegraph wires are down, so that reports from other districts had not been received in Havana, but it is feared that the devastation is general throughout the island.

Extracts from the Private Journals of the late Emperor William, of Germany, were published last week by order of his grandson, the present Emperor. The documents show a meek, humble, religious spirit, in sharp contrast with the undignified swagger of the young Kaiser. In one of them, written in 1878, after his recovery from the wounds inflicted by the assassin, Nobiling, the aged monarch wrote: "I must submit to the will of God, who permits all this to happen. At the same time let His grace and mercy predominate, for not only did He spare my life, but healed me in such a way that I could once more fulfil the duties of my post. Specially I offer my warmest thanks to my consort for the love and sympathy she gave me, notwithstanding her own sufferings; then to my daughter, who tended me with filial affection, and to all the members of my family. And whence comes this sympathy? Whence but from the Almighty, who willed it that I should be so circumstanced in this world that His grace, which watched over me, should settle upon all around me. Men have been willing to overlook my weaknesses and mistakes, but may He, who knows them, be to me afterward a merciful Judge in cases where I have not respected the doctrines and precepts of the only begotten Son of our heavenly Father. Lord, thy will be done on earth as it is in heaven."

The Warlike Disposition of the German Emperor was displayed last week in a thorough review of several army corps. The Emperor had two sham-fights conducted in one day for his delectation. His energy and the profound interest he manifested in the manœuvres recalled the traditions of his favorite model, his predecessor, Frederick the Great. One of the sham-fights took place at a village ten miles west of the city of Posen. In this, two regiments of foot and one of hussars had to defend the village against an enemy of equal strength advancing from the south. The latter, after cleverly turning their right flank, compelled the defenders to retreat. Other reviews and sham-fights are ordered for this week. A notable feature of them will be the first introduction of the telephone to connect the outposts with headquarters. The telephone to be used consists of a wooden box containing dry elements the composition of which is a secret. It is fastened by a broad belt to a soldier, who carries it wherever it is wanted.

The Mysterious White Pasha who is Reported to be at the head of a large native army in the Soudan is not yet identified. All kinds of conjectures are hazarded about him. Some assert that it is Stanley, others believe that Emin Pasha has made his escape from Wadelai, and others, again, believe that the White Pasha is General Gordon, whose death in Khartoum they think may have been falsely reported. The mystery deepens as the improbabilities of either of the three leading a force against the Mahdi are considered. It appears certain, however, that the White Pasha, whoever he may be, is an able general, and has a powerful force under his command. A despatch from Suakim, dated August 31, states that the Mahdi has sent out three expeditions to annihilate his approaching foe, and that each one has been repulsed.

A Horrible Parody on a Christian Institu-on is reported from Chicago. The correspond-t in that city of the New York *Herald*, states at the anarchists and socialists have estab-hed Sunday-schools for the propagation of eir doctrines, and for instruction in socialistic arfare. He says that those in charge of the asses where instruction is given, are careful as who are admitted, and an outsider will find an impossibility to gain an entrance. These hools have not been organized more than a onth, but the attendence upon them is al-ady large, and constantly upon the increase. is estimated by Grottkau and others inter-ted that 25,000 people will soon be enrolled these schools, including children. Of those w attendants many are *children not more than 2 years of age.*

Doubtful Amusements Have Long Been Rec-gnized as a prominent cause of the alienation young people from the churches. Pastors ho are concerned about the growth of the evil ll be glad to learn that a remedy which has en extensively tried has proved remarkably ccessful. General testimony from pastors in our States, who have organized Christian ndeavor Societies in connection with their urches, is to the effect that the Societies have ven the young people so much earnest aggres-ve work to do for Christ, that not only has eir leisure time been occupied, but they have nceived a distaste for worldly amusements. The result of their labors," says one pastor, have been no less a blessing to the church an their own increased spirituality.

A Baroness was Married to a New York ergyman in Hanover on September 3. The cable ings the news that a wedding was solemnized tween the Rev. G. F. W. Busse, pastor of St. ike's Lutheran Church, in Forty-second Street, ew York, and Baroness Agnes Harlessem, ughter of Counsellor Rudolf Harlessem. Jus-ce Harlessem's family is one of the oldest in anover, and can be traced back to the ninth ntury. Mr. Busse has been pastor of St. Luke's urch for fourteen years. About three months o he went abroad for recreation, expecting to turn in October. At the time of his depart-e, it is said, he had no idea of being married, ough the Harlessem family have long been nong his friends. The Baroness is twenty-ne years old, and is said to be both beautiful d charming. Mr. Busse is expected to arrive th his bride from Antwerp on September 18. nong European aristocrats it is possible that e Baroness will be regarded as having married neath her rank. The time is coming, how-er, when the world's ideas of nobility will un-rgo a radical change. Those whom God has ade kings will be known as such. (Rev. 5 : 10.)

A Remarkable Family Reunion Took Place Minnesota on September 2. Twenty-seven ars ago a young man was living with his pa-nts in Missouri. He married shortly before e war broke out, but being an eager politi-n, he left his home and entered the Union my. His parents became unpopular in the ality on account of their northern principles, d they found it advisable to leave suddenly. ey wandered about for some time, but finally tled on a lonely farm some ten miles from tonville, Minn. The soldier's wife stayed hind, in Missouri, but she died about six onths afterward, in giving birth to a daughter. some way a false report came that the soldier d been killed. The babe was adopted by a nily who moved West, and when the soldier urned from the war, he could find no trace his parents or his child. He had no funds r making an extended personal search, but er obtaining employment in Philadelphia, he nt letters of inquiry to all the old friends of e family. They were widely scattered, and ost of his letters went to the dead-letter office. e gave up the search until a month ago, when heard that the daughter, whom he had never en, was married, and living in a Wisconsin wn. He immediately set out to visit her; d, by an extraordinary coincidence, in pass-ing through Minneapolis, discovered the where-abouts of his parents. The joy of the parents on seeing their son and granddaughter after twenty-seven years may be imagined. An anal-ogous coincidence occurs with every man at his conversion. He not only finds God to be his loving Father, but he realizes that he has many brethren. (1 John 3 : 14)

The Subsidence of the Earth in a District of Pennsylvania has caused a serious loss to some families living there. A despatch from Wilkesbarre states that a big cave-in occurred over the abandoned workings of the old Waddel mine at Pittston on August 29. The surface, which covers an area of five acres, went down about two feet. It was covered with gardens, which disappeared entirely from view. That morning the owners were congratulating them-selves on their good crops. Now all their labor is lost. Several houses were nearly wrecked, and the new Lehigh Valley Railroad bridge was damaged. In some places the gaps in the earth's surface are large enough to admit a man's body. That is the fate of much of human labor. Those who toil for an earthly reward are often disap-pointed. If it does not pass out of their hands, they have to leave it when death summons them. Happily, Christ has told us of labor the reward of which is sure and everlasting. (Luke 12 : 33.)

A Dog's Curious Vocation is Described in a Boston journal. It states that in a family, well known to the editor, is a small boy, not more than five years old, who has an inveterate habit of straying away. He is a sturdy, stout-legged little fellow of great courage and enterprise, but his father and mother have been put to a good deal of anxiety on his account. Sometimes he is found by the railroad, and again in a cer-tain pasture where he enjoys the congenial society of several young colts, but it is always a matter of doubt where he will be discovered. Recently, however, the family have acquired a sagacious dog, recommended for the purpose, who hunts up Sammy with unerring accuracy. Whenever Sammy is missing, his mother shows his jacket to the dog and tells him to find the boy, whereupon the animal sets off with his nose to the ground, the hired man or somebody else follows, and in due time the young vagabond is brought to bay. In God's family upon earth are many afflicted with a similar habit of straying away. It is a matter for joy and thankfulness that very often hounds of trial and affliction follow them and drive them back to God re-pentant. (Ps. 119 : 67.)

A New Ship was Sold for Ten Dollars by the Government recently. Before the close of the war the construction of a large wooden frigate was commenced. She was built of well-seasoned oak, *and over a quarter of a million dollars* were spent upon her. The preparations for launching her were completed, even to the finishing of her boilers and engines, which were all ready to be shipped and set up in the vessel. When launched she was to be called the *New York*, and her tonnage would be slightly larger than the Chicago. When the era of steel ves-sels set in, work was suspended on the frigate, and she has remained unfinished on the stocks in the navy-yard for nearly a quarter of a century. A large sum would still be required to finish her, and then she would be comparatively worthless against a hostile power with steel cruisers. It was therefore decided by the Navy Department to spend no more money on her, and to break her up. It was found, however, that the wood was so hard, and her timbers so securely bolted to-gether, that it would be a work of difficulty. Finally she was offered for sale to contractors who would break her up. The price asked by the Government was more than any contractor would pay, and it was lowered until the ship has finally been sold for ten dollars. He would have been a bold man who would have predicted twenty-five years ago that the magnificent ship, which had cost a quarter of a million, so well proportioned and so strongly made, would be sold for ten dollars before ever she touched water. So it has been, however, and we are told in the Bible that much human work, now highly valued, will one day shrink to even less value when it is tried by the supreme test that God will apply. (1 Cor. 3: 13–15.)

An Inebriate's Gratitude has been Signally displayed by a western immigrant. Six years ago temperance meetings were being held at Erie, Penn. Among the men who came for-ward to sign the pledge was one who had much difficulty in staggering across the platform and writing his name. The man had once been prosperous, but he had got through all his prop-erty, had been cast out by his family, and was clothed in filthy rags. Still, there was one man who believed in him, and that man not only en-couraged him to sign the pledge, and inspired him with the belief that he could keep it, but lent him two hundred dollars to go West. For-tune favored the immigrant, who was a man of good business capacity. He began to prosper, soon repaid the loan, and went on accumulating a fortune. Two weeks ago he died in Kansas City, Mo., leaving in city lots, western lands, and railroad stocks in Albuquerque, New Mexico, about $150,000 worth of property. By his will, recorded on August 29, the bulk of this sum, after the payment of a few small legacies, is left to the man who stood by him in his degrada-tion, and helped him to recover himself. The Church of Christ would not now have to restrict her missionary and other evangelistic enter-prises for lack of funds if all who, through her instrumentality, have been rescued were similarly mindful of their obligations. (Phil. 19.)

BRIEF NOTES.

Sunday marriages are null and void in Pennsylvania.

Two boys, one six, the other seven years old, were recently taken to the Receiving Hospital, San Francisco, drunk and incapable.

Bishop Taylor, of Africa, recently raised $5,000 for mission work after preaching a sermon one hour and fifty-five minutes long at Ocean Grove.

Rev. J. C. Lamphier, who has conducted the Fulton Street Daily Prayer-Meeting for more than a quarter of a century, entered upon his eightieth year on September 3.

John Currie, the self-educated evangelist, after a series of meetings at Leadville went to Cheyenne, where the meetings were well attended, and good results followed.

The seventy-ninth annual meeting of the American Board of Commissioners for Foreign Missions will be held in Cleveland, Ohio, beginning on October 2, 1888.

A new church at Talus, in South Africa, has adopted the regulation: "No member of this church shall drink the white man's grog nor native beer, nor touch it with his lips."

An effort is being made by the Rev. Constantine Stauder to build a Home for the "Italian Young Men's Christian Association," and for the "Italian Young Women's Christian Association," of New York.

The Central Union Mission of Washington, D. C., is doing valuable and successful work in reaching the dissipated, the vicious, and criminal classes of the city. They are holding forty meetings a week.

George W. Cable, in a recent address, emphasized in strong words mission work among the colored people of the South. He said, "Right here at our doors is the greediest people of education and the gospel there is on the face of the earth."

The death of Mrs. Harriet Beecher-Stowe, author of "Uncle Tom's Cabin," was hourly expected through last week. She was attacked two weeks ago by congestion of the brain, and did not recover consciousness. She was seventy-six years of age last June.

It is proposed to hold a world's Sunday-school convention in London next June. If this convention is held it will be made up of delegates from all parts of the world, and a ship will be chartered which will take three hundred delegates to London from this country alone.

The Presbyterian General Assembly enjoined the presbyteries to "take such steps as to them appear wisest, to discourage and put a stop to such riding on Sunday trains and steamboats by church members, and by ministers of the gospel in going and returning from appointments, as cannot be justified on the grounds of necessity or mercy."

The pastors of six churches in California, five of whom are resident in San Francisco, have recently each received a letter in which was enclosed from an unknown donor a check for $5,000, amounting to $30,000 in all, to be used according to the custodians' judgment for the benefit of the church. The benefactor is a resident of San Francisco, is sick, and wished to disposed of his fortune before his death.

SOWN AMONG THORNS.

A New Sermon by Pastor C. H. Spurgeon.

"And some fell among thorns; and the thorns sprung up, and choked them." Matt. 13:7.

"He also that received seed among the thorns is he that heareth the word; and the care of this world, and the deceitfulness of riches, choke the word, and he becometh unfruitful." Matt. 13:22.

Preaching Wasted without Conversions—The Difference in the Ground—I. The Seed—The Same in each Case—Received with Pleasure—Accepted—The seed Living and Growing—II. The Thorns—Natural to the Soil—Established in It—Rob the Seed of Nutriment—Four Specified Thorns—A Preacher Neglecting his Duties to Catch Butterflies—III. The Result—The Seed Choked—A Pie-vender's Answer—Badly Washed Christians—A Showman's Indifference—The Use of the Thorns.

WHEN that which comes of his sowing is unfruitful, the sower's work is wasted: he has spent his strength for nought. Without fruit the sower's work would even seem to be insane; for he takes good wheat, throws it away, and lores it in the ground. Preaching is the idlest of occupations if the word be not adapted to enter the heart and produce good results. O my hearers, if you are not converted, I waste time and energy in standing here! Men might well think it madness that one whole day in the week should be given up to hearing speeches: madness, indeed, it would be if nothing came of it to conscience and heart. If you do not bring forth fruit unto holiness, and the end is not everlasting life, I should be better employed in breaking stones on the roadside than in preaching to you.

Fruit-bearing Made the Difference

appear in the various soils upon which the sower scattered seed. You would not so certainly have known the quality if you had not seen the failure or success of the seed. We do not know your hearts till we see your bearing toward the gospel. If it produces in you holiness and love to God and man, then we know that there is good soil in you: but if you are merely promising people, but not performing people, then we know that the ground of your heart is hard, or stony, or thorny. The word of the Lord tries the heart and reins of the children of men, and in this it is as the fire which distinguishes between metal and dross. O my dear hearers, you undergo a test to-day! Peradventure you will be judging the preacher, but a greater than the preacher will be judging you. For the Word itself shall judge you.

What fruit have you borne hitherto from all your hearing? May I venture to put the question to each one of you very pointedly? Some of you have been hearers from your childhood—are you any the better? What long lists of sermons you must have heard by now! Count over your Sundays; how many they have been! Think of the good men now in heaven, to whom you once listened! Remember the tears that were drawn from you by their discourses! If you are not saved yet, will you ever be saved? At this time I will only deal with one class of you. I will not speak to those of you who hear the Word, and retain none of it because of the hardness of your hearts; such are the wayside hearers. Neither will I address myself to those who receive the truth with sudden enthusiasm, and as readily quit it when trial befalls them; such are the rocky-ground hearers. But I will deal with those of you who hear the Word attentively, and, in a sense, receive it into your hearts and understandings, so that the seed grows, though fruit never comes to perfection.

I. First, a little about

The Seed.

Remember, first, that it was the same seed in every case. Yonder it has brought forth thirty-fold; it was the same seed which was lost upon you. In a still better case, the seed has brought forth a hundred-fold; it was precisely the same corn with which your field has been sown. The sower went to his master's granary for all his seed; how is it that in your case it is all lost? They heard no more than you have heard, but how much better they treated it than you have done! I want you to consider this. How covered with briars and thorns must your mind be that the gospel which converted your sister or friend never touched you! Though you may be nominally a believer in the Word of God, it has never so affected you as to make you gracious and holy. You are still a hearer only. How is this? The fault is not in the seed, for it is the same which has been so useful to others.

Those described in my text were not only hearers, but in a measure they accepted the good Word. The seed fell not only on this ground, but into it, so that

It Began to Grow.

Of you it is true that you do not refuse the gospel, or raise disputes concerning it. I am glad that you have no difficulties about the inspiration of Scripture, or the Deity of our Lord, or the fact of His atonement. You do not befog yourself with "modern thought," but you avow your belief in the old, old gospel. So far, so good; but what shall I make of the strange fact that your acceptance of the truth has no effect upon you? It is a very lamentable case, is it not, that a man should believe the gospel to be true, and yet should live as if it were a lie? If it be the truth, why do you not yield obedience to it?

The seed sown among thorns lived and continued to grow. And in many men's minds the gospel of divine truth is growing after a fashion: they understand it better, can defend it more valorously, and speak of it more fluently. Moreover, it does influence them in some form and degree, for gross vices are forsaken. They are *decent imitations of believers:* you can see the shape of an ear: the stalk has struggled up through the thorns until you can see its head, and are led to expect corn. But go to that apparent wheat-ear, and feel it: there are the sheaths, but there is nothing in them; you have all the makings of an ear of wheat, but it will

Yield no Grain.

I would speak to those before me who, perhaps, have been baptized, and are members of the church; I want to ask of them a question or two. Do you not think that there is a great deal of empty profession nowadays? Do you not think that many have a name to live and are dead? "Yes," say you, "I know a neighbor whom I judge to be in that condition." May not another neighbor judge the same of you? Would it not be well to raise the question about yourself? Have you really believed in the Lord Jesus? Are you truly converted from sin and self? Turn that sharp eye of yours homeward for a while. Examine your own actions, and judge your condition by them. A thorough examination will do the healthy no harm, and it may bless the sick. "Lord, let me know the worst of my case!" is one of my frequent prayers.

II. But now I would speak a little about

The Thorns.

They are by Matthew described as "the care of this world, and the deceitfulness of riches." Luke adds, "and pleasures of this life"; and Mark still further mentions, "the lusts of other things." I suppose that the sower did not see any thorns when he threw the handful of corn: they had all been cut down level with the surface. He probably hoped that it was all good ground, and therefore he sowed it, little suspecting that the thorns were in possession.

Note well that thorns are natural to the soil. Evil things are easy things: for they are natural to our fallen nature. Right things are rare flowers that need cultivation. If any of you are being injured by the cares of the world and the deceitfulness of riches, I am not astonished; it is natural that it should be so. Therefore, be on your guard against these mischiefs. I pray you say to yourself, "Come, there is something in this man's talk. He is very slow and dull, but still there is something in what he says. I may, after all, be tolerating those thorns in my heart which will kill the good seed, for I am of like passions and infirmities with other men." I beseech you look to yourselves, that you be not deceived at the last.

The thorns were already established in th soil. They were not only the natural inhab tants of the soil, but

They were Rooted and Fixed

in it. Our sins within us claim the freehold c our faculties, and they will not give it up if the can help it. They will not give way to the Hol Spirit, or to the new life, or to the influences c divine grace, without a desperate struggle. Th roots of sin run through and through our natur grasp it with wonderful force, and keep up the grasp with marvellous tenacity. Sin has en clasped our nature as a boa-constrictor encircl its victim; and when it has maintained its hol for twenty, forty, or sixty years, I hope you a not so foolish as to think that holy things wi easily get the mastery. Our evil nature is rad cally conservative, and it will endeavor to crus out every attempt at a revolution by which th grace of God should reign through righteou ness. Wherefore, watch and pray, lest tempt tion choke that which is good in you. Watc earnestly, for grace is *a tender plant in a forei soil,* in an uncongenial clime; while sin is in own element, and is strongly rooted in the so

The thorns sucked away all the nutrime from the wheat, and it was starved; for there only a certain quantity of nourishment in t soil, and if the thorns have it, the wheat mu go without it. There is only a certain amou of thought and energy in a man; and the world gets it, Christ cannot have it. our thoughts run upon care and pleasure, th cannot be eager about true religion; is not th clear? That is the way in which those thor served the wheat;

They Starved It

by devouring its food, and they choked it keeping off the air and sun; and the poor thi became shrivelled and weak, and quite unable produce the grain which the sower expected it. So it is with many professing Christia They are at first worldly, but not so ve worldly. They are fairly religious, though no means too zealous. They seek the pleasu of the world, but by no means quite so much others we could name. But very soon t thorns grow, and it becomes doubtful whi will win, sin or grace, the world or Christ. T masters there cannot be; and in this case i specially impossible, since neither of the c tending powers will brook a rival. Sin h sprung from a royal though evil stock, and if be in the heart it will struggle for the thro So it came to pass that the tares, being tol ated, choked the good seed.

Let me describe these thorns a little. P ting together Matthew, Mark, and Luke we f that there were

Four Sorts of Thorns.

The first is called "*The care of this worl* This assuredly comes to the poor; they are to grow anxious and mistrustful about tempo things. "What shall we eat? What shall drink? Wherewithal shall we be clothe This trinity of doleful questions much affl many. But anxiety comes to rich people al Care dwells with wealth as well as with pove "How shall I get more? How shall I lay it How shall I still increase it?"—and so on.

There were others who felt "*the deceitful of riches.*" Our Lord does not say "riche but "the deceitfulness of riches." The things grow together: riches are evermore ceitful. They deceive people in the getting them, for they judge matters very unfairly w a prospect of gain is before them. The jin of the charming guinea, or of "the almig dollar," makes a world of difference to the when it is hearing a case. Men cannot aff to lose by integrity, and so they take the dou ful way, and either sail near the wind, or spe late till it amounts to gambling. They wo not endure the idea of such conduct, were not that the hope of gain deceives them. line of conduct ought never to be ruled by g or loss. Do right, if the heavens fall. Do wrong, even though a kingdom should be reward.

Riches are very deceitful when they are ned, for they breed in men many vices which y do not themselves suspect. One man is se-proud, but he thinks he is humble. ere is apt to grow up in the mind an idolatry this world and its treasures. "I don't love ney," says one. "You know it is not ney that is the root of all evil, but the love it." Just so; but are you sure that you do love it? Your thoughts run a good deal er it. You hug it rather closely, and you d it hard to part with it. I will not use you; but I would have you awake to the t that riches worm themselves into a man's rt before he is well aware of it.

Luke tells us of

Another Kind of Weed,

mely, "*the pleasures of this life.*" I am sure se thorns play a dreadful part nowadays. I e nothing to say against recreation in its per place. Certain forms of recreation are dful and useful; but it is a wretched thing en amusement becomes a vocation. Amuse-nt should be used to do us good, "like a dicine"; it must never be used as the food the man. From early morning till late at ht some spend their time in a round of fri-ities, or else their very work is simply carried to furnish them funds for their pleasures. is is vicious. Many have had all holy thoughts d gracious resolutions stamped out by per-ual trifling.

Mark adds, "*and the lusts of other things.*" ill not enumerate all those other things; but things except the things of Christ and of the ther are "other things." One person is emi-ntly scientific, and he will do well if his sci-ce is used for holy purposes; but it can be d to choke the seed. I met with a clergy-n many years ago who was going a long dis-ce to find a new beetle. He was

A Great Entomologist,

d I did not blame him for his study of it, to a thoughtful man entomology may yield ny profitable lessons. But if he *neglected his eaching to catch insects*, then I do not wonder at a parishioner should wish that the beetles uld nibble his old sermons, for they were very le. The seed is choked in our souls whenever rist is not our all in all. You see my drift: it what it may—gain, glory, study, pleasure all these may be briers that choke the seed. My dear friend, Dr. Taylor, of New York, eaks of some Christians nowadays as having a utterfly Christianity." When time and ength and thought and talent are all spent on mere amusement, what else are men and men but mere butterflies? "Society" is just mass of idle people, keeping each other in untenance. Oh, dear hearers, surely we did t come into this world to play away our days! do not think we came into this world either slave ourselves to death, or to rust away in iness. We have come here as a man enters to the porch, that he may afterwards enter the use. This life is the doorway to the palace heaven. Pass through it in such style that u may enter before the King with holy joy. you give your minds and thoughts to these sing things, be they what they may, you ll ruin your souls, for the seed cannot grow.

III. So I close in the last place by noticing

The Result.

e seed was unfruitful. These briers and thorns uld not pull the seed up, or throw it away: it mained where it was; but they choked it. So may be that your business, your cares, your asures, have not torn up your religion by the ots—it is there still, such as it is. But these ings suffocate your better feelings. What an ount of choked religion we have around us! may be alive: I do not know whether it is or t; but it looks very black in the face. God ve you from having your religion choked!

I have already told you it was drained of all sustenance. Look at many Christians; I ll them Christians, for they call themselves . A boy in the streets, selling mince-pies, pt crying, "Hot mince-pies!" A person bought one of them, and found it quite cold. "Boy," said he, "why did you call these pies hot?" "*That's the name they go by, sir,*" said the boy. So there are plenty of people that are called Christians, but they are not Christians—that's the name they go by; but all the substance is drained out of them by other matters. You see the shape of a Christian, the make of a Christian, and some of the talk of a Christian, but the fruit of a Christian is not there. That is the result of the choking by the thorns of care, riches, pleasure, and

Worldliness in General.

What life there was in the wheat was very sickly. Let me remind certain persons that their spiritual life is growing weak at this time. Morning prayer this morning, how long did it take? Do not grow red in the face. I will say no more about it. You are not coming out to-night, are you? Half a Sunday is enough worship for you. Would you not like to live in some country place, where you did not need to go to a place of worship even once? Such people never seem to bathe in their religion, but they give themselves a wetting with the end of the towel; thus they try to look decent, but they are not inwardly cleansed.

When it comes to defending the gospel, where do you see it in this age? I hoped that many would be found among Baptists who would care for the truth; but now I come to the conclusion that it is with many as with

The Showman,

when asked which was Wellington and which was Buonaparte: "Whichever you please, my little dears. Pay your money, and take your choice!" Free will or free grace, human merit or Christ's atonement, it does not matter now. New theology or old theology, human speculation or divine revelation—who minds? What do they care whether God's truth stands or the devil's lies? I am weary of these drivellers! The thorns have choked the seed in the pulpits and in the churches, as well as in individuals.

Thank God we have some brethren here whose prayers could unlock the windows of heaven or shut them up! but it is not so with many. Go to the prayer-meetings of most of the churches. What poor things! Of course I find in country places that many drop the prayer-meeting during hay-time and harvest. In London they do not drop

The Prayer-Meetings

in summer, because they are too small to need dropping; they take up the fragment of a prayer-meeting and mend with it the worn-out lecture, so that it becomes neither lecture nor prayer-meeting. How can we expect a blessing when we are too lazy to ask for it? Is it not evidence of a dying religion when, to cover their carelessness about meeting for prayer, we even hear ministers doubting the value of prayer-meetings, and calling them "religious expedients"?

I would put it to you, my dear hearer, Have you been fruitful? Have you been fruitful with your wealth? Have you been fruitful with your talent? Have you been fruitful with your time? What are you doing for Jesus now? Salvation is not by doings, you are saved by grace; but if you are so saved, prove it by your devoted lives. Consecrate yourself anew this day wholly to your Master's service. You are not your own, but bought with a price; and if you would not be like these thorn-choked seeds, live while you live, with all-consuming zeal. Still, there is

A Use for Thorns.

What is that use? First, if you have thorns about you to-day, make a child's use of them. What does a child do? If he gets a thorn in his finger, he looks at it and cries. How it smarts! Then he runs off to his mother. That is one of the sweet uses of his adversity—it admits him to his mother at once. She might say, "What are you coming in for? Run about the garden." But he cries, "Please, mother, I've got a thorn in my finger." This is quite enough argument to secure him the best attention of the queen of the house. See how tenderly she takes out the little dagger! Let your cares drive you to God. I shall not mind if you have many of them, if each one leads to you to prayer.

May we meet in heaven! Oh, may we all meet in heaven! What a congregation I have addressed this morning! I feel overawed as I look at you. From the ends of the earth have many of you come. The Lord bless you! Strangers are here in vast numbers, for the most of our regular hearers are at the seaside. I may never see you again on earth. May we all meet in heaven, where thorns will never grow! May we be gathered by the angels in that day when the Lord shall say, "Gather the wheat into my barn!" Amen. So let it be.

GEMS FROM NEW BOOKS.

THE HUGUENOT MASSACRE AT TOULOUSE.*

JEAN ESTIENNE DURANTI, the first President of the Parliament at Toulouse, warmly advocated the persecution of the Huguenots, and took an active part in extending the massacre that began on St. Bartholomew's Day [August 24, 1572] to the city of Toulouse. Soon after the tidings came of the murderous work done at the capital, the unfortunate Protestants at Toulouse were thrown into the various convents and jails of the city. A few weeks later they were transferred to the Conciergerie, or prison, attached to the Parliament House. Some days passed, and the command was brought by Delpeuch and Madron, special messengers from Paris, that if the massacre had not yet been consummated, it should be at once put into execution.

The judges of Parliament were convened to deliberate with the "Capitouls" of the city respecting the course which was to be pursued. The majority of the members present drew back in horror from the proposal to perpetrate so foul a crime as that to which they were invited. Some were outspoken in favor of clemency. Others, more timid, shrugged their shoulders and kept their eyes upon the ground. But Duranti knew no compunction. Rising, he exclaimed to his more tolerant colleagues: "You will do what you please, and say what may seem good to you. As for myself, I am going to execute, in the King's name, what my charge and my duty require of me." Abruptly leaving the company, he at once issued the necessary orders.

How well he was obeyed appeared on the morrow, when two unworthy scholars of the University, with a following of seven or eight wretches of the like sanguinary type, forced their way into the Conciergerie, armed with cutlasses and axes. Summoned one by one into their presence, the prisoners were successively butchered at the foot of the stairs, to the number of three hundred or more. Surely Duranti was a follower of Holy Mother Church, whose exploits might well earn for him immunity from suspicion of disloyalty.

Henry's Answer to a Proselyter.

The Duke of Epernon, one of the principal minions of King Henry of Valois, took occasion to visit the court of King Henry of Navarre with the intention of inducing him to abjure Protestantism, and separate himself from the Huguenots. But the Duke's arguments availed nothing. The king had not yet forgotten his mother's instructions, and could not at present be persuaded to barter his convictions against temporal advantages. It was so that, a year before, he had met the solicitations of his cousin, the young Archbishop of Rouen, when that stripling—the prelate was not yet twenty-one years of age—requested him to change his religion in order to win favor with the nobles. "Tell those who make such proposals, my cousin," said he, "that religion—should they chance to know what religion is—is not stripped off like a shirt; for it has its home in the heart, and, thank God, is so deeply impressed upon

* From "The Huguenots and Henry of Navarre." By Henry M. Baird, Professor of History in the University of the City of New York. Two volumes. Published by *Charles Scribner's Sons*, 743 Broadway, New York.

Rev. Thomas Champness.

John Barton's New Work.

mine that it is as little in my power to rid myself of it as it was at the beginning to enter upon it, this grace being of God alone, and coming from no other source. Believe me, cousin, the course of your life will teach you that the only true plan is to commit one's self to God, who guides all things, and who never punishes anything more severely than He does the abuse of the name of religion."

REV. THOMAS CHAMPNESS.

(See Portrait.)

A REMARKABLE work has been done in neglected districts in England by the earnest preacher and laborer whose portrait appears on this page. He has collected a band of young men, who devote themselves to open-air preaching, receiving no payment therefor but board and clothing. They now number twenty, but Mr. Champness hopes soon to have a hundred of them engaged in this self-denying labor for Christ. His own method, which is adopted by his young men, is to go out alone into the rural districts, to fairs or agricultural gatherings, or into the lowest streets in towns. He carries with him a few large pictures of Bible scenes, and a dark-lantern with which he illuminates the pictures at night. The exhibition of the pictures soon attracts a crowd, and then Mr. Champness begins to explain them, ending with an earnest exhortation, a hymn, and a prayer. It is astonishing how many souls have been won for Christ by these services, which have been held now for nine years past.

Mr. Champness has two brothers, both of whom are successful Methodist preachers. They are the sons of a workingman, who was induced by the keeper of a boarding-house to attend the services conducted by Dr. Osborne when, in his young days, he was first stirring the people by his marvellous eloquence. The man was converted, and now his three sons are preaching the gospel. Thomas was, in his youth, strongly drawn to foreign mission work. He offered himself to the Missionary Society, was accepted and sent out to western Africa. There he labored for six years, until his health was utterly broken down by that fatal climate, and further service there became impossible for him. One after another of his fellow-laborers there succumbed, and Champness sorrowfully buried them all. He continued the work alone until he too was stricken with the fever. He lay for some time so near the brink of the grave that he heard his attendants say, "He is gone!" He had just strength enough to murmur, "Not yet; I cannot leave the work. I must get better." He recovered, but could do no more work there. He returned home, and, after a short period of pastoral labor, commenced the enterprise above described.

JOHN BARTON'S BIBLE READING.

(See Illustration on this Page.)

"WHERE'S Lucy?" asked Mr. Dale, a prosperous farmer, as he came in hot and tired from the harvest-field and met his wife on the threshold of his home.

"She went out half an hour ago," said Mrs. Dale; "did you not meet her? I thought she went to look for you."

"Guess she went to look for John Barton," said the farmer.

"Well, I suppose you do not mind that," was the reply. "John is a steady fellow, and a sensible. Good family too, I guess. If he buys a farm near us, I should like that of all things. I cannot bear the thought of Lucy marrying and going a long way off."

"No, no, Lucy might do worse. It is astonishing how quick he is picking up farming ways, for a young fellow who was never on a farm till he came here. And that was a smart idea of his to come and work for a year or two on a farm before he bought land for himself. He's got a pretty good sum of his own too. No, I presume Lucy could not do better. Think there's anything in it?"

"Oh, I guess so. Lucy has not said anything, but she's brightened up wonderfully since Barton came. More like her old self. I haven't seen her so smiling and cheerful since—"

Mrs. Dale stopped sharply. She was entering on forbidden ground. Her husband knew what she was about to say, and his frown would have been translated into words if she finished her sentence. The fact was that there was a skeleton in the Dale household. The farmer's only son, Robert, was a scape-grace. He early showed a disinclination for farm life, and persuaded his father to get him employment in a city bank. There, in a moment of temptation, he borrowed some of the bank's funds, intending to replace them, but was detected before he could do so. The farmer was convinced of his guilt; he reimbursed the bank, but he cast his son off, and refused to ever see him again. Three years afterward, Robert, miserable, penniless, and repentant, came home and begged for fc giveness, but Mr. Dale, whose pride in his u stained name had been cruelly abased, dro him ignominiously from his doors, and when I wife and daughter pleaded for the boy, he ster ly forbade them ever mentioning his nar again. Since that time, Lucy, who tende loved her brother, had been sorrowful a gloomy, and had gone about the old farm wi a tearful face until the recent arrival of Jo Barton, the embryo farmer, whose cheerful fa and ways made her smile again.

Mr. Dale was right in his conjecture abo Lucy's object in going out. She did go to s John Barton. Not that she would have adm ted the fact under any circumstances. S wanted to go out, and perhaps she might s Mr. Barton. She found him hard at work i wagon, but not so busy that he did not see h

"Why, Mr. Barton, you are working as if the manner born," said Lucy. "Don't you fi it more fatiguing than you did preparing for examination at college?"

"Yes, it tires one more, but this work su me better; I never felt so strong and healt as I do now. I am very glad to see you to-d Miss Lucy. I have some news for you if y will wait for me to give it you." John Bar vaulted over the wagon's side, and came arou to where Lucy was standing. "I want you," said "to come around to my rooms to-nig There is some one there who is longing see you."

"Not Robert! Oh, is it Robert?" said Lu "There is no one else who could long to see m

Barton looked at her very much as if th might be such a longing in some one else, he only said: "Yes; it is Robert. I found utterly despairing around the farm last nig and I spoke to him. In fact, I took him ho with me, and he is there now. He came make another appeal to his father, but whe came to the point his courage failed."

"Oh, thank you, Mr. Barton," said L "God will reward you for your kindness. sure I will come without fail."

"And when you come I will go and ha talk with Mr. Dale myself while you are chee your brother. I will try to soften his heart.

John Barton kept his word. When he Lucy wrapped in her brother's arms, he hu away to the farm, leaving them together. Dale was sorry Lucy was out, and worried a it she said Lucy was only gone to a friend, and would be back pres-y. John was quite willing to re-n, and as it was Mr. Dale's custom ave family prayer early in the ing. John joined in the devotion. Shall I read for you, Mr. Dale?" sked.

Do, do!" said the farmer. "My are not as good as they used to Lucy reads when she is at home." hn took the Bible and opened the fifteenth chapter of Luke's el. He was a cultivated reader, the inimitable parable of the digal Son seemed to the assem- family never so pathetic as it from his lips. Mrs. Dale wept ntly, and once or twice the far-'s lips quivered. His prayer was rt, for he could scarcely control voice. At its conclusion, when and Mr. and Mrs. Dale were left e, John spoke. He said he had ouble favor to ask. He wanted mission to ask Lucy to be his , and he wanted Mr. Dale to for- his son. The former was readily nted, but the latter needed some ding. The Bible reading, how-r, had prepared the way, and an hour from the time that it read, Mr. Dale was on his way the side of his prospective son-aw, prepared to welcome the digal with open arms.

HE PATAGONIAN INDIANS.

(See Illustration)

THE Indian tribes found in the reme south of South America, ugh known as Patagonians, do themselves recognize that name. was given to them by the Span-ds, in allusion to the large foot-ps the Spaniards noticed in the before they saw the men who made them. The Indian name Tehuelche, or Tsonecas. This in refers to the whole race, and re are many subdivisions, the ef one being between the Indians the North and South. The north- Tehuelches occupy the district ween the Cordilleras and the , from the river Chupat northward to the Negro. The southern branch is mainly lo-ed south of the Rio Santa Cruz, reaching as as Punta Arenas. A third branch is found ween the Rio Negro and the Chupat. They called the Pampas Indians. A fourth tribe, om the Tehuelches call the Chennas, have ir headquarters at Las Manzanas. They are s erratic than the other three tribes, and own cks of sheep and herds of cattle. The num-r of the four tribes is now believed to be little re than three thousand, the introduction of eign rum having caused an appalling mortal- among them.

Physically the Tehuelches are magnificent ecimens of humanity. The men are generally feet four inches in stature, and the women erage but little less than six feet. They are et of foot, and have an amazing power of durance. They have been known to bear, thout apparent inconvenience, prolonged ab-sence from food, and to continue their march th no relaxation of speed for several days with-t nourishment of any kind. Their uniform ter garment is a loose and not ungraceful antle of guanaco-skin, worn with the hairy le in, and painted on the other side with gro-sque devices in various colors. Unlike other uth American Indians, they do not worship e sun, though they salute the new moon with a ecies of adoration. It was to these Tehuelches, Patagonians, that Captain Allen Gardiner hose portrait appeared in this journal on May) was endeavoring to carry the gospel message hen he went on his last and fatal journey. His death led to the organization of the South American Missionary Society, which has been successful, through God's blessing, in winning some of the Indians to the gospel, and encouraging reports are sent of future prospects.

Two Tehuelche Indians of Patagonia.

THE EPOCHS OF A LIFE.

A NEW SERIAL STORY.

By Rev. L. S. Keyser.

(Continued from page 575.)

A Pathetic Protest.

AN interview with Mr. Duneman was Belle Havelock's first business after her return from Banesville. The fire of jealousy which rendered him an apt instrument for her wicked purposes had not diminished in her absence.

"I cannot understand Miss Winters," he said. "She seems infatuated with that fellow."

"Yes," said Belle, "you use the right word; it is an infatuation and nothing else. It is very sad, for if she marries him she will be miserable all her life. In fact, it is an infatuation on both sides. Mr. Madelling would be miserable too. She is no fit wife for him. They are like two children who do not know what is good for themselves. Any one who separates them will do them a friendly service. It ought to be done for their own sakes."

"That is my own feeling," said Duneman. "I do not particularly care whether Madelling is miserable or not—the mischief he is working in the college deserves punishment—but I should be truly sorry if Miss Winters ruined her life, and I would do almost anything to save her. What success have you had with the scheme you mentioned to me?"

"The very best, and your part in it is one that will not strain your conscience unduly when you consider how good the object is that you are seeking to achieve. This is the letter. You see it is addressed to Mr. Madelling, stamp duly cancelled, and the stamp of the office upon it. Now all you have to do is to get it into Miss Winters's hands in such a way as will lead her to think that her precious admirer has received it here and dropped it; and that some good friend of hers has sent it to her to open her eyes to Madelling's duplicity."

"Very likely Miss Winters will just look at the address, and when she sees Madelling's name upon it will hand it to him without reading it."

"That you can prevent by enclosing it in an anonymous letter explaining that the enclosure vitally concerns her," said Belle. "If you word it shrewdly you may depend on a woman's curiosity for her reading it."

"I do not see how I could write such a letter without telling a lie in it, and I would not do that."

Belle looked at him in amazement. The whole scheme was a falsehood, and here was her confederate straining at swallowing this morsel. Her mental comment was: "You poor shallow hypocrite! This is truly straining at a gnat and swallowing a camel." But she was too prudent to expose the man to himself. "Look," she said, "there is no need to tell a direct falsehood," and drawing the paper to her she rapidly wrote a short note. "There is no lie there. You are not responsible for the construction Miss Winters puts upon it. If you write some such note as that the work will be done, and Mr. Madelling will have some difficulty in making any more engagements with Miss Winters."

Duneman took the note and read it critically. "Yes," he said, "I could write that with a clear conscience. There is nothing there but what is true, and it will accomplish the purpose."

That night, however, as he sat, pen in hand before his desk, he had a struggle with his better self. His conscience reproached him, and he felt inclined to withdraw from the scheme. "Suppose I do"—he said to himself. The vista, the hypothesis opened before him was not agreeable. He saw the girl he loved engaged to his rival, marrying him, being hurt day by day by his cruel scoffs at her religion; perhaps being herself drawn into infidelity. It was too horrible! If by practicing this little deception upon her he could save her from such a fate, ought he not to do it? So Jacob may have reasoned when he deceived his blind father. So many a man has reasoned on the brink of crime, justifying himself in wrong-doing by the purity of his motive. It is a most successful device of the evil one, that has entrapped many, and only those are safe from its seductions who are determined to do right at any cost and leave the issue with God. Duneman was not one of those. The letter was written in carefully disguised handwriting, the letter Miss Haverlock had given him was enclosed, and the packet placed in the post-office to do its work.

Then Duneman breathed more freely. He felt assured that when Miss Winters read the contents of that envelope she must sever her acquaintance with his rival. He was still at a loss, however, to understand how his former scheme had miscarried. How was it possible for so genuine a Christian girl as Madeline Winters to feel any pleasure in the society of so pronounced an infidel as Madelling?

The fact was, that it was precisely because she was so true a follower of Christ that she felt so strong an interest in the young man. The address to which she had listened that Saturday morning had shocked and pained her inexpressibly. Hadley's words spoken in so emphatic a manner from a public platform had pierced her soul like the thrust of a dagger. Little had she imagined that her generous friend, who had succored her from danger at the risk of his own life, would be capable of making so acrimonious an attack upon a holy cause. The religion of Christ had been so potent an influence for good in her life, had so often strengthened her against temptation, and had so comforted her in sorrow, that Hadley's utterances shocked and appalled her. For awhile she felt herself repelled by him. A bad heart only, it seemed to her, could be the armory of such weapons as those which he was wielding. Perhaps Duneman had been right in his strictures upon the moral character of unbelievers, although at the time she had thought them unnecessarily severe. Perhaps it was true that those who reject Christianity have so deadened conscience and despoiled their higher nature, as to render them incapable of discerning and appreciating moral beauty, so that they have become like certain characters portrayed by the prophet, who call light darkness, and darkness light.

Yet it occurred to her that young Madelling had always in all her interviews with him shown himself honorable and magnanimous, and even now, as she listened to him, her quick mind noted the fact that he made no attack on morality. In fact his attack on the Bible was based on the mistaken view that it did not inculcate true morality of the highest standard. If such a man could be convinced of his error, could be brought to see that there is no moral standard so high as that of the Bible, then he would surely become the defender, not the assailant, of God's Word. Surely such a man was worth saving, and she determined to do her best to give him proper guidance. True, she felt unequal to the task, as far as her own strength was concerned, but there was One who could baptize the simplest word with divine efficiency.

The young man's arguments did not disturb her. With her, religion was a matter of experience, and no argument could dislodge her faith. She knew that religion was true, for she had tasted and seen that the Lord is good.

When she next met Mr. Madelling, she smiled upon him so kindly that he was greatly conciliated toward her, and even felt encouraged to approach her again and seek her society. It so happened a few days later that he was walking out one evening for relaxation after a hard day's study, and as he passed the post-office, he met Miss Winters on her way to her room. As she appeared friendly, he joined her, and they walked slowly along the dimly lighted street.

It was on this occasion that they passed Belle Havelock without noticing her. The reason of their pre-occupation was not far to seek. With gentle approach Miss Winters led the conversation to Hadley's speech. After entering the parlor the subject was resumed, and they were so engrossed in the discussion that they did not notice that the blind was still open.

Hadley, as might have been expected, stood on the defensive, and soon became so earnest that he denounced the Bible with great vehemence. Miss Winters had not wished to arouse him, but a word that she had said caused his impetuosity to get the better of him. It distressed the girl so much to hear him denounce in such bitter terms the religion she loved, that, notwithstanding her utmost efforts to control her emotions, she burst into tears.

The young man was touched, and immediately became penitent. Tenderly taking her hand, he begged her pardon for his harsh and ungenerous expressions. It was this scene that had been witnessed by Belle Havelock.

"Is it possible that religion means so much to you, Miss Winters?" he said, in astonishment. "I do not understand it."

"No, you do not know, Mr. Madelling," she said, smiling through her tears, "how terribly your words sound to one who has experienced the love of Christ."

"Please explain," he said, more mystified than ever.

"Let me illustrate," she rejoined. "Do you love and revere your mother?"

"I have the best of mothers," he responded, with some feeling.

"Suppose some one were to ridicule or abuse her?"

"I see that I am getting myself into a trap, but I will answer honestly: I should make him swallow his words, if I could."

"Ah! it would not only hurt you, but would stir your wrath. Well, it is with a still deeper feeling of filial reverence that we regard God when He has adopted us into His family, and has put the Spirit into our hearts; and do you not see how it must pain us if His Word is held up to contumely?"

"Did you feel so while I was speaking the other morning?" questioned Hadley, in quavering tones.

"I will tell you honestly, Mr. Madelling, that I could not have felt so painfully agitated if you had abused my own parents," she replied, feelingly. "I speak plainly, and assure you that I know whereof I affirm. Christ has done so much for me; He has expunged so much evil from my nature, has put so much love and light into my poor, riven life; His grace and promises have so often comforted me in sorrow, especially in bereavement—that my heart turns sick when I hear His Word derided."

"Great heavens!" exclaimed Hadley, in dismay. "I never heard any one speak as you do. Is it possible that religion, which has always seemed to me so fanciful, is a *real* power in your life? And have I been trampling so recklessly on your feelings? Why—I—I never supposed any one—. Yes, I remember now, my mother used to burst into tears when I assailed religion. You are like her. But I cannot understand you. I have never felt as you do, Miss Winters. I feel so bitter against religion, against the Bible, against God."

"I understand your feelings," she answered, kindly. "At one time in my life I was full of rebellion too, and chafed against the things that eluded my understanding and seemingly obstructed my pathway."

She hesitated, at which he asked, eagerly, "And how did you become so wonderfully changed?"

"The process was very simple. When I went to God humbly in prayer, He changed my nature, old things passed away, and all things became new, and His Spirit bore witness with my spirit that I belonged to His family. Pray do not think that this is mere cant; it is actual reality. After that experience the bitter feeling was gone, and a devout love for God took its place."

The young sceptic looked at her incredulously. He could not believe that the solution of the great problems of life was to be attained in that way. It would have been just as reasonable, in his opinion, to pray that God should solve a problem for him in Differential Calculus, or translate a stubborn Greek idiom. It was also incomprehensible to him that an intelligent girl like Miss Winters should resort to what seemed to him a puerile and illogical method of gaining light on any subject. Yet he could not disprove her assertions.

"Perhaps you are right," he said meditatively, "but it seems to me that it is a matter of temperament to a great extent. Some are more inclined to be religious than others."

"That may all be, for it does appear that there are persons who are almost naturally Christian; but none are so disinclined to spirituality that they cannot receive the assurance of which I have spoken, if they will use the proper means to secure it. I speak from experience when I say that I was inclined to be sceptical, to take nothing on trust. Yet this experience came to me. It is for all. It is for *you*, Mr Madelling," she added, in a voice of deep solicitude.

"Would you have me smother all my doubts and believe the Bible per force?" he queried, a little petulantly.

"Not by any means. That cannot be done. It is against the laws of mental action; it is a psychological impossibility to force belief. No one can believe without evidence. But you can open your heart to Christ, waiving all prejudice, and then He will enter and dispel all your unbelief and doubt. I hope that you will do this soon."

"I am willing to do anything reasonable for the sake of truth."

"Are you—perfectly?"

"Do you doubt it?"

"If you are," she replied, "I can say to you what Christ said to a young man who came to Him, 'Thou are not far from the kingdom of God!'"

"Do you really expect me to become a Christian?" he questioned, doubtfully.

"I do."

"And you care?" he ventured.

"More than I can tell."

"Why should you be so anxious about my welfare?"

"Because all those who make religion a real factor of their lives, are solicitous for the conversion of others."

Hadley was disappointed with her rejoinder. He was only one among many, then, for whose salvation she was concerned. He had hoped that her personal regard was the secret spring of her anxiety for him; but her remark had put him on a par with the whole circle of her acquaintances. He himself had little solicitude for those for whom he did not entertain a personal liking, and he "measured others by his own yardstick." For a few moments, while these reflections were passing through his mind, he had averted his face from her, and was looking abstractedly at the key-board of the piano. When he turned to her, he found that her eyes were bent anxiously upon him. So suddenly had he looked at her, that she flushed slightly, and her eyes dropped before his earnest gaze. What did it mean? Did she care for him after all, in a twofold way? The thought gave him a momentary thrill of rapture. How he loved this fair, winsome girl! He felt then how incomplete his life would be without her.

"My thoughts have been wandering away from the theme which we have been discussing," he remarked.

"Into forbidden paths?" she said, *naïvely*.

"I hope not, Miss Winters," he answered, looking her full in the face. A brief silence followed. "I hope not," he repeated. "I was thinking of—*you*."

"A very dull and unprofitable subject for a reverie," she said, laughing; but a rose bloomed on both cheeks.

"Very interesting to me."

Again her eyes fell, and she did not answer.

"Miss Winters," he said, rising and coming toward her.

"Mr. Madelling," she said, rising also, "let me advise you not to indulge in reveries. Or, perhaps, I should rather speak for myself than advise you. I am obliged to refrain from building castles in the air, and any other occupation that would divert my thoughts from my studies. Our time at college is so short, and our opportunities for acquiring knowledge so limited, that I resolutely put away from me thoughts of any subject that might engross my attention. Just now, too, when the examinations are so close upon us, and our work so difficult, it is more than usually important to have my mind free for work. So as it is getting late I shall say good-night."

Hadley smiled. He perfectly understood the kindness and delicacy which interposed, so gently, to prevent his making a premature and ill-considered declaration, and he had the good sense to perceive that he would gain rather han lose ground in her esteem by deferring he question upon his lips until a better oppor- unity. Pressing her hand gently, and with a ook of affectionate regard, the meaning of which he could understand, he took his leave.

(*To be Continued.*)

DEATH AND BURIAL OF MOSES.

By Mrs. M. Baxter.

. S. Lesson for September 23, Deut. 3:4. Golden Text, Prov. 4:18.

he Last Two Months of the Wilderness—A Figurative Day—A Significant Intervention of God for the Protection of Women—The Last Day of Moses' Life—God Calling Him—His Natural Powers in Full Vigor—No Disease—The Function of Ancient Physicians—A Fitting End to a Consecrated Life—His Last Words—His Miraculous Survey of Canaan—A Glorious Dying Hour—God's Epitaph on Moses.

THE journeys of the children of Israel in the vilderness were drawing to a close. Forty years hey had wandered as a punishment for their nbelief at the time of the spies. It was in the leventh month of the fortieth year that they nade their last encampment by the Red Sea Deut. 1:3), and now their marching orders vere, "Straight forward, into the land." It was t this time, during the last two months of his ife, that Moses recapitulated the law of God, nd commanded the children of Israel to set up reat stones, "and plaster them with plaster," nd "write upon them all the words of this law." (Deut. 27:1-3.) It is somewhat difficult to understand the exact chronology of these last two nonths. Again and again we read of "this day," which, if we take it literally, would lead s to think that the whole book of Deuteronomy comprised but one day. For instance, "Thou rt to pass over Jordan *this day*" (Deut. 9:1); "*This day* will I begin to put the dread of thee and the fear of thee upon the nations that are under the whole heaven" (Deut. 2:25); "Thou hast avouched *this day* the Lord to be thy God." (Deut. 26:17.) This cannot mean one literal day of twenty-four hours, because the people mourned for Moses thirty days out of this two months before they crossed over Jordan. It probably means this period of time which ended their wilderness journeys before they entered the promised land.

It is not quite clear when the account of Moses' last day on earth began; but, if not earlier, it certainly begins in the thirty-first chapter of Deuteronomy, but probably in the twenty-ninth. The people were encamped at this time "in the plains of Moab, by Jordan, near Jericho." Here it was that God taught Moses the extent of the land of their inheritance, singled out those who should divide it, and appointed the portions of the Levites, and the cities of refuge, and recognized the claim of the daughters of Zelophehad to hold property. Thus one of the latest interventions of God in the government of this people before entering on their possession, was an action for *the protection of women.* (Num. 33:50-56; 34 and 35.)

Moses' Last Day

had come. It was no day of sickness, surrounded with medical appliances, doctors, nurses, and anxious friends; it was a day of steady service from morning till evening. He said to the people, "I am an hundred and twenty years old this day; I can no more go out and come in." Did he mean that he had fallen lame, or that his muscular strength had waned? Did he mean that his hand was palsied and his back was bent with age? No; God Himself tells us that "his eye was not dim, nor his natural force abated." Why, then, could he no more go out or come in? Why, because the Lord was calling him to another service, from time to eternity, from earth to heaven. "The Lord hath said unto me, Thou shalt not go over this Jordan." Moses was as willing to depart as to remain; during his long life, ever since his deep acquaintance with God, he had "*endured* as seeing Him who is invisible." (Heb. 11:27.) The light of eternity and the presence of God were not transient things with him, they were the atmosphere which he breathed.

Moses' last birthday, his last day on earth, was characteristic of the man; with the announcement of his own departure, he told the people that the Lord their God should go over before them, and destroy the nations before them, and that Joshua should be their leader; as much as to say, "My going will be no loss to you; the Lord will provide." He next called Joshua and constituted him leader "in the sight of all Israel," charging him to "be strong and of a good courage," because the Lord would go before him. He would not leave nor forsake him. He next wrote the law in such a compass that it might be contained in the ark, and carried with them into the land "for a witness against thee." (Deut. 31:1-26.) Probably he simply completed on this day the work of transcription, on which he had been long engaged. He next held communion with God, and the Lord showed him how the people would lapse into idolatry, and then inspired him to compose and write the song contained in the chapter 32, "that this song may be a witness for Me against the children of Israel." (Ch. 31:16-21.) Moses

Wrote This Song the Same Day,

and taught it to the children of Israel." Was this all which took place on this remarkable dying day? No; "The Lord spake unto Moses *that self-same day*, saying, Get thee up into this mountain Abarim, unto Mount Nebo, which is in the land of Moab, that is over against Jericho: behold the land of Canaan, which I give unto the children of Israel for a possession: And die in the mount whither thou goest up, and be gathered to thy people; as Aaron, thy brother died in Mount Hor, and was gathered unto his people." What, climb a mountain to die! And at the age of a hundred and twenty, and after a tremendous day's work! Yes, the tabernacle of Moses' flesh had not to be taken down pin by pin, and curtain by curtain—a blind eye, a deaf ear, a lame leg, as the first preliminary warnings, and then all manner of diseases. We do not read of his having a vestige of disease or infirmity of any kind. When a man dies, everyone asks, "What did he die of?" as though no man had ever died without sickness or accident. The patriarchs never seem to have died of sickness. "Abraham gave up the ghost, and died in a good old age, an old man, and full of years, and was gathered to his people." (Gen. 25:8) Isaac gave up the ghost, and died, and was gathered unto his people." (Gen. 25:29.) "When Jacob had made an end of commanding his sons, he gathered up his feet into the bed, and yielded up the ghost, and was gathered unto his people." (Gen. 19:33.) Only after death were the physicians called in, not to lengthen out his life by all kinds of human contrivances—but to embalm his body, that he might be buried in the land promised to his fathers, and so express in his burial his faith in God. "These all died in faith" (Heb. 11:13), and their way home was not a forced march; they "gave up the ghost."

God's announcement to Moses that he was to die that day seems to have come to him like any other command; no doctor was called to help him to ward off death for a few hours, no lawyers to make a hurried will. Moses lived a life in which nothing that happened could be an interference: so long as God had His way, Moses had his, for his will was one with God's. To some who do not lean on the Lord for strength, it might appear impossible that after this full day's work he could do anything else.

His Last Words,

like the last words of his coming Master, were words of blessing, and as tribe after tribe passed before him, he uttered a blessing always prophetical of the future of that tribe. At last, his long day's work was at an end, and without a shade of weariness, with fresh and easy motion, keeping step with God as he ascended, Moses went up the mountain before the sun went down, to see the land of Canaan, and then go home! The Lord was his guide, the Lord Himself shewed him the land he must not enter. How he could take in the whole panorama is difficult to understand, but Moses was not nearsighted, and his eyes were in no way dim. It is not impossible that God gave him more than natural sight to view that land of promise. He had lost his right to a possession there because of his unbelief, but it was more to the heart of Moses that *his people* should have possession than that *he* should, and most surely he will hold possession in "a city which hath foundations, whose Builder and Maker is God." (Heb. 11:10.) God said to him, "This is the land which I sware unto Abraham, unto Isaac, and unto Jacob, saying, I will give it unto thy seed; I have caused thee to see it with thine eyes, but thou shalt not go over thither." To a certain extent under judgment, but still in communion with God, suffering the loss of an earthly possession, but in full title to "an inheritance incorruptible, undefiled, and that fadeth not away," it was

A Glorious Dying Hour

when all was over; not the struggling for breath, the last injection, the last morsel of food, but the last commands and directions to the people of God, the last song of praise, the last blessing upon those he was leaving, the last mountain ascent alone with God, the last look at the promised land; there was nothing left to be done but to die. How did death get hold of this vigorous, hale, old man? God willed it, this was all, and Moses willed with God. "So Moses, the servant of the Lord, died thus in the land of Moab,

According to the Word of the Lord."

Of Moses' funeral, and Moses' tomb, no one knows but God. He allowed no human hand to place His servant in the grave; "He buried him." No tears moistened his grave; no sad procession carried him. It was Moses' joy to die when God willed it, it was God's joy to receive him home. The children of Israel wept down in the plain, and mourned for Moses thirty days. It was a glorious and enviable death to die, with none other present than the Lord, and to have nothing to do but to die! Why should there be so few deaths like that of Moses, in full health and vigor, but just called home because God wills it? Is it not because so few live in His presence continually? Moses' service was not interrupted by sickness or death. When Jesus was transfigured, Moses appeared, testifying to the death which He should accomplish. He testified of God. "There is no one like unto the God of Jeshuron who rideth on the heavens in thy help" (Deut. 33:26), and God testified of him, "There arose not a prophet since in Israel like unto Moses, whom the Lord knew face to face." "When Moses was gone into the tabernacle of the congregation to speak with [God], then he heard the voice of One speaking unto him from off the mercy-seat that was upon the ark of testimony, from between the two cherubim, and He spake unto him." (Num. 7:39.) Such direct intercourse is not mentioned between God and any other man. "And in all the signs and the wonders which the Lord sent him to do in the land of Egypt to Pharaoh, and to all his servants, and to all his land, and to all that mighty land, and in all the great terror which Moses shewed in the sight of all Israel." Such is God's epitaph of Moses.

IF WE KNEW.

If we knew when walking thoughtless
Through the crowded, noisy way,
That some pearl of wondrous whiteness
Close beside our pathway lay;
We would pause when now we hasten,
We would often look around,
Lest our careless feet should trample
Some rare jewel in the ground.

If we knew what forms were fainting
For the shade that we should fling,
If we knew what lips were parching
For the water we should bring,
We would haste with eager footsteps,
We would work with willing hands,
Bearing cups of cooling water,
Planting rows of shading palms.

If we knew when friends around us
Closely press to say, "Good bye,"
Which among the lips that kiss us,
First should 'neath the daisy lie;
We would clasp our arms around them,
Looking on them through our tears;
Tender words of love eternal
We would whisper in their ears.

If we knew what lives were darkened
By some thoughtless word of ours,
Which had ever lain among them
Like the frost among the flowers;
Oh! with what sincere repentings,
With what anguish of regret,
While our eyes were overflowing,
Would we cry—*forgive,—forget!*

If we knew—alas, and do we
Ever care or seek to know,
Whether bitter herbs or roses
In our neighbor's gardens grow?
God forgive us, lest hereafter,
Our hearts break to hear Him say,
"Careless child I never knew you,
From my presence flee away."

—*Selected.*

J. E. Jewett, Publisher, 77 Bible House, New York, will furnish the above poem in leaflet form at twenty cents per hundred. *A Sample Packet* of 50 leaflets assorted (no two alike), will be sent post-paid, for 10 cts., or 100 for 20 cts. Postage stamps taken.

MEXICO

Contributions in aid of Christian work in Mexico are most pressingly needed, and can be mailed to the address of

BISHOP H. C. RILEY,
Care of J. P. HEATH,
43 Bible House, New York.

To our Christian Friends:

As there is a regular monthly expense in connection with the work a regular monthly income is needed to meet that expense. We, therefore, specially ask for regular monthly contributions in its behalf. If many will each send a little every month, or quarter, or whenever they can, it will do great good. *Remember, every little helps.*

H. Chauncey Riley.

To Our Fellow Christians

Who Are Forwarding Contributions in Aid of Christian Work in Mexico.

Bishop Riley requests me to inform the kind friends who are generously contributing in aid of Christian work in Mexico, that we have now over one hundred monthly subscribers who are forwarding contributions every month in its behalf. Bishop Riley sends to all who are contributing in aid of the work in Mexico his most sincere thanks for their timely gifts.

As there are, no doubt, many who would be glad to contribute something monthly in behalf of the cause of Christ in Mexico, but who feel that they cannot afford to give as much as one dollar a month, we venture the suggestion, that when possible *the friends of the work should try and collect small contributions from such* and forward the same with their own contributions to Bishop Riley, 43 Bible House, New York. For example, some friend of the work who is now forwarding one dollar a month, might induce ten others, to each give ten cents a month, and collect and forward the same with his own contribution. Another who now contributes one dollar a month, might induce four others to each give one cent a day, or thirty-one cents a month, and collect and forward the same with his own contribution monthly. Still a third who now contributes a dollar a month might induce two friends, to each give fifty cents a month, and collect and forward the same regularly with his own contribution.

If this plan could be adopted generally among the more than one hundred regular monthly subscribers to the work, we might soon be able to report to our friends that we had over two hundred dollars a month contributed regularly in behalf of the work in Mexico.

We remind our friends that to continue the work in Mexico effectively we most pressingly need a regular monthly income, as we have to meet a regular monthly expense.

A most precious Christian work has been commenced in Mexico, and we are doing what we can to continue it, by raising an income in its behalf. We earnestly appeal to our fellow Christians to aid us in this effort. There are one hundred and thirteen millions who speak the English language, and seventy-five millions who speak the Spanish or Portuguese languages. Among those who speak the English language, there are multitudes who know and love the pure gospel, and are doing what they can for the Master. Among those who speak the Spanish or the Portuguese languages, there are a few who know and love the pure gospel, and are faithfully working for our dear Master. Our Spanish-American society is working hard to raise an income to aid in building up a strong centre of Christian work in Mexico. The influence of that work has already extended into Spain and Cuba, and, we trust, will yet extend into South America. Fellow Christians, think of seventy-five millions who speak the Spanish or Portuguese languages, millions and millions, and, millions of whom have never had a Bible in their hands!!! Help us! help us! to do Christian work in their midst."

Bishop Riley has been instrumental in having more than one hundred thousand copies of the Bible or New Testament circulated in Mexico. Many hundreds of children have been educated in Christian schools established by him. More than forty congregations have been gathered in the Republic of Mexico through his efforts. He has secured two magnificent stone churches in the City of Mexico where the Gospel has been preached for years. He has trained up a noble band of able preachers of the pure gospel. He has given nineteen years of his life and his fortune to aid in building up this great work, and he now appeals to his fellow Christians to contribute the monthly income needed to continue it effectively.

Dear friends, will you not only continue to contribute to this good work yourselves, but also encourage others to do the same. Some may not be able to contribute monthly but could do so occasionally. Occasional gifts are most thankfully received. Pray for the work, and that many may be moved to befriend it.

With best Christian wishes, I am, your brother in Christ,

A. D. MAINE.

Entered according to Act of Congress in the year 1888, in the office of the Librarian of Congress at Washington

Vol. XI., No. 38. Office, 63 Bible House. N. Y. THURSDAY, SEPTEMBER 20, 1888. Price, 3 Cents. Annual Subscription, $1.50.

CONTENTS OF THIS NUMBER.

ORTRAITS AND LIVES OF FIVE LEADERS OF THE BIBLE CHRISTIAN CHURCH.
HE CHAIN OF INFLUENCES. Dr. Talmage's Sermon Last Sunday Morning.
NECDOTES RELATED AT RECENT EVANGELISTIC MEETINGS.
ROPHETIC CHRONOLOGY. By G.H.Pember, M.A.
STRIKING CONVERSIONS AT WESLEY GROVE CAMP MEETING.
An Offering to God Accepted—A Wicked Plot Defeated—Chinese Idols Destroyed—Preaching Before Images—A Buddhist Parable.
PICTURE OF A NICHE IN THE ANCIENT WALL OF JERUSALEM.
THE MINER'S SECRET (with Illustration).
THE PERSONAL REVELATION. A New Sermon by Rev. C. H. Spurgeon.
Gems from New Books: Toltec Marriages, etc.
PORTRAIT AND LIFE OF DR. SAMUEL A. CROWTHER, P. E. Bishop of the Niger.
THE EPOCHS OF A LIFE. A New Serial Story by Rev. L. S. Keyser (Continued).
SELFISHNESS. By Mrs. M. Baxter.

THE LEADERS OF THE BIBLE CHRISTIAN CHURCH.

1. The Late Rev. James Thorne—2. Rev. F. W. Bourne—3. Rev. John Keen, D. D., the President—4. Rev. W. H. Tickell—5. Mr. F. T. Gammon.

THE BIBLE CHRISTIAN CHURCH.

THE origin of the denomination of Bible Christians, five leaders of which appear by portrait on the first page, was in the Wesleyan Methodist Church. In 1815 a local preacher in England, named William O'Bryan, was wonderfully successful in evangelistic work. He went into neglected districts, preaching the gospel where he could. Sometimes he preached in the open air, at other times in barns or cottages, but always the Holy Spirit honored his labors, and souls were converted. There were no Methodist churches in the villages where he labored, but O'Bryan gathered the converts together into societies, intending to have them incorporated in the Wesleyan Methodist communion to which he belonged. But a difficulty arose. Mr. O'Bryan being a married man, was ineligible for entrance into the Methodist ministry. The societies he had formed desired to retain his services as their pastor, and if they entered the Methodist body they must have a regular minister, and must bid farewell to O'Bryan. They preferred to remain outside the connection and keep their chosen preacher. They therefore formed a separate denomination and called themselves Bible Christians. They now have churches in all parts of the globe, and are remarkable for their energy and aggressive work. Their statistics are: 245 itinerant preachers, 1,854 local preachers, 830 church buildings, 139 preaching stations, 30,168 full members, 739 members on trial, 548 juvenile members, 9,012 Sunday-school teachers, and 51,038 scholars.

THE LATE REV. JAMES THORNE.

THE preacher whose portrait is in the centre of the group on the first page, was one of the earliest converts of William O'Bryan. He was born on September 21, 1795, and died on January 2, 1872, at the age of seventy-seven. There was a strong Puritan strand in his family line, and his father was remarkable for his stalwart piety. He was a hospitable man, and his house, in a secluded district of Devonshire, England, was always open to any Methodist preacher who might pass that way. In August, 1815, William O'Bryan held meetings in his native village. James attended, and was converted. He was twenty years old at that time, and his natural ardor led him to desire most earnestly to preach the gospel. He commenced in his father's house to a gathering of the neighbors, and later was appointed a regular local preacher like O'Bryan. When his spiritual father came out of the Wesleyan Methodist connection James Thorne followed, and became an itinerant preacher.

The itinerant ministry, in those years, was one of hardships and privations, but the young preacher did not shrink from it on this account. He devoted all the powers of body and mind to the work, toiling from early morning till late at night, and as riding was impossible, sometimes he was found walking nearly all night to reach his appointments. He labored like an apostle, and had an apostle's reward in seeing conversions at nearly every service he held. In August, 1819, at Launceston, where the first Bible Christian Conference took place, he was chosen secretary, and from that time forward, for half a century, he attended these annual gatherings of the brethren, and took the most prominent part in the proceedings. He had the distinguished privilege of being five times chosen President of the Conference. In 1837 he signed the temperance pledge, and became a most effective temperance lecturer. Through his efforts a few years later, in 1841, a Connexional school was established in his native town, Shebbear, which has since developed into a college.

His labors continued with a vigor which astonished all who witnessed them. Travelling continually, preaching in churches, barns, cottages, and the open air, the man's zeal seemed inexhaustible. Even after he had passed the age of threescore, and had been preaching forty years, he could not be persuaded to curtail his efforts. On December, 31, 1871, when he was over seventy-six years of age, he insisted on attending a watch-night service, and speaking for his Master. It was his last address. He was seized with paralysis that night, and two days later he passed from labor to reward.

THE REV. F. W. BOURNE.

IF the Bible Christians had an archbishop, the Rev. F. W. Bourne would be the unanimous choice of the connection. He is practically at the head of the denomination no matter who is chairman of the Conference. He is well known and highly respected in this country, which he visited in 1881. He is now fifty-eight years of age, having been born July 25, 1830, at Woodchurch, England. He received an excellent education at the local school, where he was conspicuous by his devotion to study and his brilliant talents.

At the age of fifteen he attended a revival conducted at the Bible Christian Church at Tenterden, where he was then residing. He was deeply impressed, and after a severe experience, passed from death into life. Almost insensibly his giving his testimony for Christ in the meetings passed into religious addresses, and those into sermons. God blessed them, and by the time he was eighteen years of age he was preaching every Sunday, and churches were eagerly seeking his services. He tells one amusing anecdote of this period of his life. He went to a country church that was very much crowded, the fact that the preacher was only eighteen, and yet so famous, having drawn a large congregation, and he could scarcely get in. He was pushing his way in as best he could, when one of the Elders of the chapel took hold of him in a very unceremonious way, and said, "What do you mean by pushing like that; do you not see there is no room?" He replied very quietly, "I suppose there will be nothing going on till I do get in." The Elder then said, "You bean't the preacher, be you?" And he said, "Yes, I be," and the Elder then graciously helped him forward.

Mr. Bourne occupied several of the most important stations of the Conference until 1869, when it was decided to give him functions of an episcopal character, and also to make him editor of the printed organ of the connection. From that time he resided in London, and visited the various churches as need arose. He has been twice president of the Conference, and has held other important and responsible offices. In 1881 he made a tour of the United States, Canada, Australia, and New Zealand, visiting the Bible Christian Churches, giving them counsel and stirring them up to greater zeal. Mr. Bourne has also found time to write several books. One of them, entitled, "The King's Son: a Memoir of Billy Bray," has found its way all over the world, and has been blessed to the conversion of many souls. Some time ago its sales had passed the 200,000 line. Mr. Bourne retains his natural and spiritual vigor, and is the right hand of the denomination.

THE REV. JOHN O. KEEN, D. D.

THE present president of the Conference of the Bible Christians is Dr. Keen, whose published works have won for him university recognition in the title of Doctor of Divinity. Dr. Keen, though only forty-two years of age, has been preaching for twenty-six years. His parents were members of the Bible Christian body, and his earliest impressions were received in a Bible Christian Sabbath-school. He was admitted into the church in 1860, when he was only fourteen years of age, and by the time he was sixteen he began to preach in cottages, and to fill engagements on emergencies. He continued this activity for over three years with so much success that he was urged to offer himself for the regular ministry. He was accepted, was put through a searching examination on account of his youth, and passed successfully. In 1865 he was regularly appointed, and at once became pastor of a church in Devonshire. He proved one of the most popular preachers in the denomination; the churches he presided over increased in numbers, and became active in aggressive labor.

Dr. Keen has published several pamphlets, and a volume of sermons remarkable for freshness and force, under the title, "On the King's Business," which has passed through several editions; also another volume similar in character and size, called "Suggestive Thoughts for Busy Workers"; and an exceedingly clever sketch, entitled "Parson Jacques"; he is also an occasional contributor to various English and Colonial magazines.

THE REV. WILLIAM H. TICKELL.

THE fourth of the group of portraits on the first page is that of a man who has trodden in his Master's footsteps as a friend of publicans and sinners. Mr. Tickell, in 1880, was appointed to the charge of a church in the poorest and most degraded section of London, familiarly known as "The New Cut." He set to work immediately to evangelize that hardest of all districts of the country. Church services were but a part of the agency he employed. He perceived that one of the chief sources of the misery which surrounded, was drunkenness, and he organized a Temperance Society to contend with it. A Fresh-air Excursion Fund, a Sick Benefit Society, and Benevolent Societies for the benefit of men and women were established, and the church became a centre of beneficent work. The poor, the miserable, the sick, blessed the church and its pastor. Men who had scoffed at religion were grateful when some good lady from the Bible Christian Church visited their sick wives and took care of the home and the children. Women who never went to church, rejoiced when their husbands quitted drinking under the influence of Mr. Tickell's Temperance Society. The church grew rapidly, not so much in wealth as in number and spirituality. It begged that Mr. Tickell's term might be renewed again and again, and the Conference, recognizing the value of his labors in the locality, consented. He is still there, and his labors are increasingly blessed.

Mr. Tickell is now forty-one years of age, having been born March 19, 1847. As in so many cases in which men become useful or famous, he had *a remarkable providential escape* from death in boyhood. When nine years of age he was playing with some companions near his home, when one of the walls of a house fell, and buried him in the ruins. He was taken out for dead, but consciousness being restored, it was found that his most severe injury was a mangled leg. This entailed confinement to bed and couch for six months, and it was during this lengthened period of enforced abstinence from exercise of all kinds that he first developed that passion for reading which has characterized the whole of his after life. As an instance of his love of books at this early age, it may be noted that he committed to memory the whole of the "Pilgrim's Progress."

His conversion occurred in 1867, when he was twenty years of age. He was then living in a town where there was no Bible Christian Church, so he joined the Methodist New Connection, but so strongly was he drawn to the church of his father and his own boyhood that he removed to Bodmin to be in that communion. He was ordained in 1874, and before settling in his present London Church of the New Cut, he labored successfully in several large p[illegible] churches.

MR. FREDERICK T. GAMMON

OUR fifth portrait is that of a layman, but one whose activities have done much for the advancement of the Bible Christian Church. His father, the Rev. John Gammon, [illegible] one of the most highly respected ministers [illegible] nomination. He was born in Somerse[illegible] 1849, and educated at the denominatior[illegible] lege at Shebbear, where he was greatly respected. He left college at an early age and went to London to seek his fortune. He entered the employ of a well-known firm of publishers, and s found so capable and so trustworthy, that ter a time they gave him the management of department, and eventually he became the le acting partner of the firm.

The first office he took in Christian work was connection with a Bible Christian Sunday-hool, where he accepted an invitation to do me secretarial work, but after a time he be-me superintendent, and so well has he per-rmed his duties that the school is now one the most prosperous and best regulated in ondon. His worth as a Christian worker has en thoroughly appreciated by the pastors nder whom he has labored, as well as by his llow-members. The Missionary Society has ceived his warmest support, and he has infused s own spirit into the school, so that a regular nnual contribution of a large sum is always re-ived from the school. The denomination ave recently undertaken a China Mission, and e has shown his sympathy with the movement y becoming the largest contributor to its funds.

In addition to the work at his own school, Ir. Gammon undertook the secretaryship of e South London Auxiliary of the Sunday-chool Union, and has thrice been elected Presi-ent, which position he now holds. His inter-st in religious movements is deep and broad, nd at the same time practical. The hardships nd privations which Bible Christian ministers ncountered in the early years of the denomina-on, showed him the difficulties that ministers ave been called upon to undergo, and have hus given him considerable sympathy with hese hardworking and underpaid brethren.

BUDDHA'S PARABLE.

THE following extract, from a recently pub-ished work, is significant just now when an ffort is being made to propagate Buddhism in ur great cities. This extract shows that though uch an effort may succeed with some people, it an have no hope of success among any who are amiliar with the Bible:

"Two of the most famous of Buddha's parables trikingly resemble in more than one feature hose of the Sower and the Prodigal Son in the ospel. In the prodigal son, out of many weari-ome details comes the image of the father full f compassion for the son, who, after leaving im has fallen into abject misery, while the ather is living in wealth and plenty. He be-noans himself in a piteous manner that he, now ld, broken down and ready to die, cannot find is son to make him the sharer of his goods; hen, without knowing it the son comes back o the threshold of his father's palace, in vile aiment, and hoping for nothing but the pau-er's portion. His father, who has recognized im, cries out in his joy: 'Lo, I have found im who is to inherit all that is mine. I thought f none but him. And now he is come of his wn accord, and I am old and bent.' The rec-nciliation does not take place immediately, owever. The father wishes to prove the wan-erer, and so he sets him to the most menial asks, that of sweeping up the refuse. At ength after twenty years of this hard service, he father clasps him in his arms. 'Thou art ny son,' he exclaims, 'and all that I have is hine.' But the son still stays outside the alace feeling his poverty. This is a sure proof hat the ordeal is no longer needed. The father alls together all his relations, and pointing to he beggar, says: 'This man is my beloved son. [illegible] who begat him. For fifty years he dis- [illegible] from this town. Far and wide have I [illegible] king him; I came back here, and lo I ave found him. He is my son and I am his ather. All this wealth is his.' The son falls t his father's feet, saying: 'Here am I then in ossession of all these treasures!'"

[illegible]king Saviour and Other Themes. by [illegible] Mackay, of Hull. This work has been published [illegible] Mackay's death, but the greater part was ready for ublication when he died, and to that has been added the triking discourse which he delivered the last time he entered he pulpit, and a few manuscripts found among his papers 47 pages, cloth cover; Price 75 cents, including postage, For sale at this office, 63 Bible House, New York.

ANECDOTES RELATED AT RECENT EVANGELISTIC MEETINGS.

"When One Door Shuts, Another Opens."—"It is told of Whitefield that, on one occasion, he was speaking to a large congregation in the open air. His text was 'And the door was shut.' He impressively repeated his text several times. Two young men who stood in the crowd seemed to think the repetition superfluous, and one remarked to the other, 'Well, what matter if the door be shut. When one door shuts, another door opens.' The preacher seemed intuitively to know what was said, and thus continued: 'Some may say, What matter if one door be shut! another door will open. Yes, that is true. If the door of heaven is shut against you, the door of hell will open. If you are shut out of heaven, you must enter hell.' These solemn words went to the hearts of the young men, and at the end of the meeting they stayed to speak to the preacher, and, through God's grace, he was instrumental in bringing them both to Christ."

Charlie's Confession of Christ.—The Rev. Mr. Gullan remarks: "I know a little boy named Charlie, and on one occasion when I met him at his grandmother's home I asked, 'Charlie, do you love Jesus?' 'Yes, I do,' was the prompt reply. 'How long have you loved Him?' I inquired. 'For two years,' he said. 'Are you quite sure you have loved Him all that time?' I queried. 'Quite sure,' replied the little fellow confidently. 'If I were to ask your mother if she knew that you had been a Christian for two years, do you think that she would be surprised to hear it?' I next asked. 'No,' was the reply, 'I think she would know.' Soon afterward I saw his mother, and asked her if she knew that Charlie had been a Christian for two years. And this was her answer: 'Yes, I do know that he is a true Christian, and, I confidently believe, would die for Him if necessary to do so.' Yes; it was quite true: not only did the boy testify with his mouth, but his life also bore testimony for his Saviour."

Over the Parapet into the River.—"A Few years ago two gentlemen met. One was an energetic Christian worker, and the other, one of the world's respectable people. As they were together the latter said, 'Well, I do not know how you stand it all—Monday, a prayer-meeting; Tuesday, a prayer-meeting; Wednesday, Thursday, Friday, and Saturday all the same. And on Sunday, what a day you have at it from morning to night! It must be the hardest working day you have. I would not make such a fuss about religion, and you will see that I shall be all right at the end. When I come to my death-bed I will make three words do it all. God is ready to save at any time. Soon afterward, that man met his death, but he had neither time nor presence of mind to say the three words on which he had built his hope, 'Lord, save me,' that were necessary to his salvation. He was driving in his carriage, and on an incline that led down to a river; the horses became restless, and rushed down the hill. The driver was unable to stop or guide them, and on they rushed. The bridge was before them, but it was narrow; they swerved, and half leaping, half tumbling, over the low parapet, they fell into the river, dragging the carriage and its helpless occupant with them. He only uttered one exclamation, and that was an oath. With that on his lips he was ushered into eternity."

A Forger's Sad Story.—A Clergyman Says; "There were two friends like David and Jonathan; they had been born in neighboring houses, had played together, gone to school together, and commenced life at one time, in the same office. At first both seemed to prosper alike, but when a certain height was reached one seemed to draw rapidly ahead. A few years passed, and one was the proprietor of a large business, while the other made no progress. But the prosperous merchant remembered his old companion, and invited him to become his general manager at a liberal salary. For years all went well, but one day a discovery was made—a forgery had been committed. It was traced to the manager. His employer called him in, and said: 'John, you know about this forgery. You did it. It is no use denying it.' 'I am not going to deny it. I did do it,' was the painful reply. 'Well, John, I am not going to prosecute *you*, but you cannot be here any longer.' The man at once rose, and taking one last look round, left the place. No more was heard of him until years afterward, when a little girl called at the house of the now wealthy merchant, and asked him to come and see John. The gentleman went, and there on a bed of straw lay his former friend, who feebly held out his hand, imploring forgiveness. With tears in his eyes, his former employer bent down and grasped his hand, saying, 'I do forgive you, John. 'Ah,' replied the dying man, 'I knew you would; but why did you send me away? I would have served you like a dog if you had only let me.' Christ's is no half forgiveness. When the repentant backslider returns, he, like Peter, is taken back into favor.

The Destroyer of His Comrade.—A Minister observes: "After one of our battles in the East a clergyman visited the military hospital in which our wounded lay. As he went from bed to bed whispering words of holy comfort and inquiry, he came to one bed in which lay a seriously wounded man. 'Can I help you by reading to or writing for you?' said the servant of God, kindly. 'No,' was the gruff reply. 'Can I do nothing for you?' inquired the minister, still lingering by his side. Here the man, raising himself on his elbow, glared into his visitor's eyes as he asked, 'Can you *undo?* I shall be glad of your help if you can *undo!*' By this time he had sunk back on his pillow, but he continued, 'When I joined the army first my chum was a Christian, a fellow who walked straight, and read his Bible, and I used to try to laugh him out of it, until at last he got ashamed of his religion. Not even then did I leave him alone. I took him to my haunts of vice until he was as evil as myself. All that was well enough as long as we were both well, but one day he marched into the battle never to return; he was shot by my side, and the one half-uttered word that escaped his lips as he fell helpless was an oath. How that oath cut me to the heart! That man is lost, sir, and it is through me. Tell me now, can you undo the past?' It is an awful thing to have on the conscience, that through our influence or example some soul has been turned away from God."

The Leisure Hour the Devil's Opportunity.— A Christian worker narrated: "In the town where I spent the first twenty years of my life the railway station was eighteen miles away. Into that town there ran an omnibus, over a lovely road, with gentlemen's mansions occasionally to the right and left of the road, and sometimes you would find a flaring pair of gates standing at the entrance to a gentleman's house; so that fresh young horses in that 'bus would start opposite the white gates. So the coachman, two or three hundred yards before getting up to the gates, would crack his whip and talk Welsh to the horses with the most marvellous effect. They pranced, and they danced, and they galloped past; the frisky member of the team had no time to think about the white gate, and went on peacefully and caused no trouble. Then, if you asked the driver why all this hubbub, 'Well,' the old man would say, 'you see that member of the team there; he is rather frisky and young, and on one or two occasions he has given me some trouble; and in order to put him past the white gate, I have just been shouting and cracking my whip, and getting up a tremendous noise so as to give him something to think on, and then he will pass the gate by harmlessly.' Now, the difficulty with the millions of our land is to give them something profitable to think on; some help to rush past the white gate of temptation—'something to think on.' Oh that My people were wise,' says God, 'that they would consider their latter end.' But the devil doesn't like us to think."

THE CHAIN OF INFLUENCES.

Dr. Talmage's Sermon last Sunday Morning, September 16, 1888.

"Make a chain." Ezek. 7:23.

Bible Associations of the Chain—Adornment and Captivity—The Power of a Congeries of Links—The Chain of the Cradle—A Cradle Floating on the Ohio—The Links of the Chain—Prayer, Teaching, Example—The Chain that Pulls the Young from Evil—The Weak Link—The Collapse of a Chain Bridge in France—The Chain of Companionship—The Levelling Influence of Association—The Chain of Captivity—Directions for the Downward Road—The Chain Finished—Trying to Get Loose—A Power that can Break any Chain—The Demand of the King of Sparta—A World in Chains.

AT school and in college, in announcing the mechanical powers, we glorified the lever, the pulley, the inclined plane, the screw, the axle and the wheel, but my text calls us to study the philosophy of the chain. These links of metal, one with another, attracted the old Bible authors, and we hear the chain rattle, and see its coil all the way through from Genesis to Revelation, flashing as an adornment, or restraining as in captivity, or holding in conjunction as in case of machinery.

The Chain in the Bible.

To do him honor, Pharaoh hung a chain of gold about the neck of Joseph, and Belshazzar one about the neck of Daniel. The high priest had on his breast-plate two chains of gold. On the camels' necks, as the Ishmaelites drove up to Gideon, jingled chains of gold. The Bible refers to the Church as having such glittering adornments, saying: "Thy neck is comely with chains of gold." On the other hand, a chain means captivity. David, the psalmist, exults that power had been given over his enemies "to bind their kings with chains." The old missionary apostle cries out: "For the hope of Israel, I am bound with this chain." In the prison where Peter is incarcerated, you hear one day a great crash at the falling off of his chains. St. John saw an angel come down from heaven to manacle the powers of darkness, and having "a great chain in his hand," and the fallen angels are represented as "reserved in everlasting chains," while in my text for the arrest and limitation of the iniquity of his time, Ezekiel thunders out: "Make a chain!"

What I wish to impress upon myself and upon you is the strength, in right and wrong directions, of consecutive forces, the superior power of a chain of influences above one influence, the great advantage of

A Congeries of Links

above one link; and in all family government, and in all effort to rescue others, and in all attempt to stop iniquity, take the suggestion of my text and make a chain!

That which contains the greatest importance, that which encloses the most tremendous opportunities, that which of earthly things is most watched by other worlds, that which has beating against its two sides all the eternities, is the cradle. The grave is nothing in importance compared with it, for that is only a gully that we step across in a second, but the cradle has within it a new eternity, just born and never to cease. When three or four years ago the Ohio River overflowed its banks, and the wild freshets swept down with them harvests and cities, one day was found floating on the bosom of the waters

A Cradle with a Child in it

all unhurt, wrapped up snug and warm, and its blue eyes looking into the blue of the open heavens. It was mentioned as something extraordinary. But every cradle is, with its young passenger, floating on the swift currents of the centuries, deep calling to deep, Ohios and St. Lawrences and Mississippis of influence bearing it onward. Now what shall be done with this new life recently launched? Teach him an evening prayer? That is important, but not enough. Hear him as soon as he can recite some gospel hymn or catechism? That is important, but not enough. Every Sabbath afternoon read him a Bible story? That is important, but not enough. Once in a while a lesson, once in a while a prayer, once in a while a restraining influence? All these are important, but not enough. Each one of these influences is only a link, and it will not hold him in the tremendous emergencies of life. Let it be constant instruction, constant prayer, constant application of good influences, a long line of consecutive impressions, reaching from his first year to his fifth, and from his fifth year to his tenth, and from his tenth year to his twentieth. "Make a chain!"

Spasmodic education, paroxysmal discipline, occasional fidelity, amount to nothing. You can as easily hold an anchor by one link as hold a child to the right by isolated and

Intermittent Faithfulness.

The example must connect with the instruction. The conversation must combine with the actions. The week-day consistency must conjoin with the Sunday worship. Have family prayers, by all means; but be petulant and inconsistent and unreasonable in your household, and your family prayers will be a blasphemous farce. So great in our times are the temptations of young men to dissipation, and young women to social follies, that it is most important that the first eighteen years of their life be charged with a religious power that will hold them when they get out of the harbor of home into the stormy ocean of active life. There is such a thing as impressing children so powerfully with good, that sixty years will have no more power to efface it than sixty minutes.

What a rough time that young man has in doing wrong, carefully nurtured as he was! His father and mother have been dead for years, or over in Scotland, or England, or Ireland; but they have stood in the doorway of every dram-shop that he entered, and under the chandelier of every house of dissipation, saying: "My son, this is no place for you. Have you forgotten the old folks? Don't you recognize these wrinkles, and this stoop in the shoulder, and this tremulous hand? Go home, my boy, go home! By the God to whom we consecrated you, by the cradle in which we rocked you, by the grass-grown graves in the old country churchyard, by the heaven where we hope yet to meet you, go home! Go home, my boy, go home!" And some Sunday you will be surprised to find that young man suddenly asking for the prayers of the church. Some Sunday you will see him at the sacrament, and perhaps drinking from the same kind of chalice that the old folks drank out of years ago when they commemorated the sufferings of the Lord. Yes, my lad, you do not have such fun in sin as you seem to have. I know

What Spoils Your Fun.

You cannot shake off the influences of those prayers long ago offered, or of those kind admonitions. You cannot make them go away, and you feel like saying: "Father, what are you doing here? Mother, why do you bother me with suggestions of those olden times?" But they will not go away. They will push you back from your evil paths, though they have to come down from their shining homes in heaven and stand in the very gates of hell, and their backs scorched of the fiery blast, and with their hand on your shoulder, and their breath on your brow, and their eyes looking straight into yours, they will say: "We have come to take you home, oh, son of many anxieties!" At last that young man turns, through the consecutive influences of a pious parentage, who out of fidelities innumerable made a chain. That is

The Chain that Pulls

mightily this morning on five hundred of you. You may be too proud to shed a tear, and you may, to convince others of your imperturbability, smile to your friend beside you; but there is not so much power in an Alpine avalanche after it has slipped for a thousand feet, and having struck a lower cliff, is taking its second bound for fifteen hundred feet more of plunge, as there is power in the chain that pulls you this moment toward God and Christ and Heaven. Oh, the almighty pull of the long chain of early gracious influences!

But all people between thirty and forty years of age, yes, between forty and fifty—aye, between fifty and sixty years—and all septuagenarians as well, need a surrounding conjunction of good influences. In Sing Sing, Auburn, Moyamensing, and all the other great prisons, are men and women who went wrong in mid-life and old age. We need around us a cordon of good influences. We forget to apply the well-known rule that a chain is no stronger than

Its Weakest Link.

If the chain be made up of a thousand links, and nine hundred and ninety-nine are strong, but one is weak, the chain will be in danger of breaking at that one weak link. We may be strong in a thousand excellences and yet have one weakness which endangers us. That is the reason that we sometimes see men distinguished for a whole round of virtues collapse and go down. The weak link in the otherwise stout chain gave way under the pressure.

The first chain bridge was built in Scotland. Walter Scott tells how the French imitated it in a bridge across the river Seine. But there was one weak point in that chain bridge. There was a middle bolt that was of poor material, but they did not know how much depended on that middle bolt of the chain bridge. On the opening day a procession started, led on by the builder of the bridge: and, when the mighty weight of the procession was fairly on it, the bridge broke and precipitated the multitudes. The bridge was all right except in that middle bolt. So the bridge of character may be made up of mighty links strong enough to hold a mountain, but if there be one weak spot, that one point unlooked-after may be the destruction of everything. And what multitudes have gone down for all time and all eternity because in the chain bridge of their character there was lacking a strong middle bolt! He had

But one Fault,

and that was avarice; hence, forgery. He had but one fault, and that was a burning thirst for intoxicants; hence, his fatal debauch. She had but one fault, and that an inordinate fondness for dress; and hence, her own and her husband's bankruptcy. She had but one fault, and that a quick temper; hence, the disgraceful outburst. What we all want is to have put around us a strong chain of good influences. Christian association is a link. Good literature is a link. Church membership is a link. Habit of prayer is a link. Scripture research is a link. Faith in God is a link. Put together all these influences. Make a chain!

Most excellent is it for us to get into company better than ourselves. If we are given to telling vile stories, let us put ourselves among those who will not abide such utterances. If we are stingy, let us put ourselves among the charitable. If we are morose, let us put ourselves among the good-natured. If we are given to tittle-tattle, let us put ourselves among those who speak no ill of their neighbors. If we are despondent, let us put ourselves among those who make the best of things. If evil is contagious, I am glad to say that *good is also catching*. People go up into the hill-country for physical health; so if you would be strong in your soul, get yourself up off the lowlands into the altitudes of

High Moral Association.

For many of the circumstances of our life we are not responsible. For our parentage we are not responsible. For the place of our nativity, not responsible; for our features, our stature, our color, not responsible; for the family relation in which we were born, for our natural tastes, for our mental character, not responsible. But we are responsible for the associates that we choose and the moral influences under which we put ourselves. Character seeks an equilibrium. A B is a good man. Y Z is a bad man. Let them now voluntarily choose each other's society, A B will lose a part of his goodness and Y Z a part of his badness, and they will gradually approach each other in character and will finally stand on the same level. One of the old painters refused to look at poor pictures because he said it damaged his style.

A musician cannot afford to dwell among discords, nor can a writer afford to peruse books of inferior style, nor an architect walk out among disproportioned structures. And no man or woman was ever so good as to be able to afford to choose evil associations. Therefore, I said, have it a rule of your life to go among those better than yourselves. Cannot find them? Then what a pink of perfection you must be! When was your character completed? What a misfortune for the saintly and angelic of heaven that they are not enjoying the improving influence of your society! Ah, if you cannot find those better than yourself, it is because you are ignorant of yourself. Woe unto you, Scribes and Pharisees, hypocrites!

The Chain of Captivity.

But, as I remarked in the opening, in sacred and in all styles of literature a chain means not only adornment and royalty of nature, but sometimes captivity. And I suppose there are those in that sense deliberately and persistently making a chain. Now here is a young man of good physical health, good manners, and good education. How shall he put together enough links to make *a chain for the down-hill road?* I will give him some directions.

First, let him smoke. If he cannot stand cigars, let him try cigarettes. I think cigarettes will help him on this road a little more rapidly, because the doctors say there is more poison in them, and so he will be helped along faster; and I have the more confidence in proposing this because about fifty of the first young men of Brooklyn during the last year were, according to the doctors' reports, killed by cigarettes.

Let him drink light wines first, or ale or lager, and gradually he will be able to take something stronger, and as all styles of strong drink are more and more adulterated, his progress will be facilitated. With the old-time drinks a man seldom got delirium tremens before thirty or forty years of age; now he can get the madness by the time he is eighteen.

Let him play cards, enough money put up always to add interest to the game. If the father and mother will play with him, that will help by the way of countenancing the habit. And it will be such a pleasant thing to think over in the day of judgment, when the parents give account for the elevated manner in which they have reared their children.

Every pleasant Sunday afternoon *take a carriage ride*, and stop at the hotels on either side the road for Sabbath refreshments. Do not let the old-fogy prejudices against Sabbath-breaking dominate you. Have a membership in some club, where libertines go and tell about their victorious sins, and laugh as loud as any of them in derision of those who belong to the same sex as your sister and mother. Pitch your Bible overboard as old-fashioned and fit only for women and children. Read all the magazine articles that put Christianity at disadvantage, and go to hear all the lectures that malign Christ, who, they say, instead of being the Mighty One He pretended to be, was an impostor and the implanter of a great delusion. Go, at first out of curiosity, to see all the houses of dissipation, and then go because you have felt the thrall of their fascination. Getting along splendidly now!

The Chain Finished.

Let me see what further can I suggest in that direction. Become more defiant of all decency, more loud-mouthed in your atheism, more thoroughly alcoholized, and instead of the small stakes that will do well enough for games of chance in a ladies' parlor, put up something worthy, put up more, put up all you have. Well done! You have succeeded. You have made a chain—the tobacco habit one link, the rum habit one link, the impure club another link, infidelity another link, Sabbath desecration another link, uncleanness another link, and altogether they make a chain. And so there is a chain on your hand, and a chain on your foot, and a chain on your tongue, and a chain on your eye, and a chain on your brain, and a chain on your property, and

A Chain on your Soul.

Some day you wake up and you say: "I am tired of this, and I am going to get loose from this shackle." You pound away with the hammer of good resolution, but cannot break the thrall. Your friends join you in a conspiracy of help, but fall exhausted in the unavailing attempt. Now you begin, and with the writhing of a Laocoön, to try to break away, and the muscles are distended, and the great beads of perspiration dot your forehead, and with the concentered energies of body, mind, and soul you attempt to get loose, but have only made the chain sink deeper. All the devils that encamp in the wine-flask and the rum-jug and the decanter—for each one has a devil of its own—come out and sit around you and chatter.

In some midnight you spring from your couch and cry: "I am fast! O God, let me loose! O ye powers of darkness, let me loose! Father and mother and brothers and sisters, help me to get loose!" And you turn your prayer to blasphemy, and then your blasphemy into prayer, and to all the din and uproar there is played an accompaniment—not an accompaniment by key and pedal, but the accompaniment is rattle, and the rattle is that of a chain.

But I take a step higher, and tell you there is

A Power that can Break any Chain

—chain of body, chain of mind, chain of soul. The fetters that the hammer of the gospel have broken off, if piled together, would make a mountain. The captives whom Christ has set free, if stood side by side, would make an army. Quicker than a ship-chandler's furnace ever melted a cable, quicker than the bayonets of revolution pried open the Bastile, you may be liberated, and made a free son or a free daughter of God. You have only to choose between serfdom and emancipation, between a chain and a coronet, between Satan and God. Make up your mind, and make it up quick.

When the King of Sparta had crossed the Hellespont, and was about to march through Thrace, he sent word to the people in the different regions, asking them whether he should march through their countries as a friend or an enemy. "By all means as a friend," answered most of the regions; but the King of Macedon replied, "I will take time to consider it." "Then," said the King of Sparta, "let him consider it; but meantime we march — we march!" So Christ, our King, gives us our choice between His friendship and His frown, and many of us have long been considering what we had better do; but meantime He marches on, and our

Opportunities are Marching by.

And we shall be the loving subjects of his reign, or the victims of our own obduracy. So, I urge you to precipitancy rather than slow deliberation, and I write all over your soul the words of Christ I saw inscribed on the monument of Princess Elizabeth, in the Isle of Wight, the words to which her index-finger pointed in the open Bible when she was found dead in her bed, "Come unto Me, all ye who are weary and heavy laden, and I will give you rest."

Is there a drunkard here? You may, by the Saviour's grace, have that fire of thirst utterly extinguished. Is there a defrauder here? You may be made a saint. Is there a libertine here? You may be made as pure as the light. When a minister, in an outdoor meeting in Scotland, was eulogizing goodness, there were hanging around the edge of the audience some of the most depraved men and women, and the minister said nothing about mercy for prodigals. And a depraved woman cried out, "Your rope is not long enough for the like of us." Blessed be God, our gospel can fathom the deepest depths, and reach to farthest wanderings, and here is a rope that is long enough to rescue the worst: "Whosoever will."

But why take extreme cases, when we all have been or are now the captives of sin and death? And we may, through

The Great Emancipator,

drop our shackles and take a throne. You have looked at your hand and arm only as being useful now, and a curious piece of anatomy, but there is something about your hand and arm that makes me think they are an undeveloped wing. And if you would know what possibilities are suggested by that, ask the eagle, that has looked close into the eye of the noonday sun; or ask the albatross, that has struck its claw into the black locks of the tempest; or ask the condor that this morning is descending to the highest peak of Chimborazo. Your right hand and arm and your left hand and arm, two undeveloped wings, ready for the empyrean.

"Rise, my soul, and stretch thy wing,
Thy better portion trace."

There have been chains famous in the world's history, such as the chain which fastened the prisoner of Chillon to the pillar—into the staple of which I have thrust my hand—on the isolated rock of the Lake of Geneva; such as the chain which the Russian exile clanks on his way to the mines of Siberia. Aye, there have been races in chains, and there has been

A World in Chains;

but, thank God, the last one of them shall be broken, and, under the liberating power of the omnipotent Gospel, the shackles shall fall from the last neck and the last arm and the last foot. But these shattered fetters shall all be gathered up again from the dungeons and the workhouses and the mines and the rivers and the fields, and they shall again be welded and again strung link to link, and polished and transformed until this world, which has wandered off and been a recreant world and a lost world, shall by that chain be lifted and hung to the throne of God, no longer the iron chain of oppression, but the golden chain of redeeming love. There let this old ransomed world swing forever! Roll on, ye years, roll on, ye days, and hasten the glorious consummation!

THE WALLS OF JERUSALEM.

(*See Illustration on Page 602.*)

VISITORS to Jerusalem are generally disappointed by the comparatively modern character of its buildings, and still more by the fact that its chief religious edifices are devoted to Mohammedan worship. But few parts of the ancient city remain. Among those few is the fragment of the old wall depicted in the illustration. Mr. Laurence Oliphant states in his recently published work that "it is without doubt the oldest existing remains in Jerusalem, and formed part of the ramparts of the city." He believes its date to be the time of David.

The same author, who has spent many years in Jerusalem and other parts of Palestine, and who visited the city recently, was surprised to find a remarkable impression prevalent among the Jews who arrived there on pilgrimage, as well as among the settled population. He says that though he met and talked with Jews "of all nationalities and sects which, as a rule, hold each other in abhorrence, it is singular that they all have one view in common, or, rather, perhaps it should be said that they all seem to labor under one impression or presentiment, and that is, that before very long the Holy City will undergo a change of some sort." His descriptions of these conversations show that the expectation varies with the nationality of the person. Many expect annexation by either Russia or England, but all are feverishly inspired, as never before, with the idea that important changes are imminent which will in some way tend to the restoration of Jewish nationality. Thus not only are Jews of all nations vaguely expecting change, but Christians who, like Daniel, "understand by books the number of the years" (Dan. 9:2), are convinced that shortly, in about six years, the Jews under the protection of the Napoleonic Antichrist will return in large numbers to Jerusalem and commence the rebuilding of the city and the Temple.

STRIKING SCENES AT A CAMP-MEETING.

MANY striking conversions occurred at the recent camp-meeting at Wesley Grove, Orange County, N. Y., after the sermon which the Rev. Thomas Harrison preached, on "the Baptism of Fire." The Rev. John Boyd, who assisted in the personal work at the conclusion of the service, thus describes the most notable cases:

"**An Aged Mother,**

apparently near seventy years old, came to the altar in great distress, after listening to Mr. Harrison's sermon. 'Are you willing to give your heart to God?' said the brother to whom she spoke. 'I am,' said the aged woman, her eyes filled with tears. 'Then He accepts you now: do you believe it?' The Holy Spirit was working in her soul, and in a moment, with changed and glad countenance, she replied: 'I do give Him my heart, and I know He now saves me.' She rose to her feet, and told the friends standing by that her precious son, before he died, some time ago, had had a vision of heaven, with its gates of pearl, and shining walls, and the crystal throne, and hosts of glorious angels, and the sight was so resplendent that he seemed afterward unfit for earth, and a few days later he passed away. He earnestly desired to write what he had seen, but was unable to do so. When he died he had not even begun the book, which, could he have written it, would have been truly marvellous. 'Mother,' he said, shortly before he died, 'meet me in heaven. You are not a Christian now, but come to Jesus, and He will willingly save you.' The aged mother had been troubled in her soul from that moment, and found her way to Wesley Grove, where the seeking Saviour revealed Himself to her heart, and she went home rejoicing with joy unspeakable and full of glory.

"**Seven Young Ladies**

went forward, after the same sermon by Mr. Harrison, and found Christ for the first time. The more intelligent of the seven, who was a school-teacher, was the last and most difficult to direct and help—she was so fearful, should she obtain forgiveness, lest she might lose it; and Satan troubled on this line so much that there seemed little hope of her salvation. But the patient brother who assisted at the altar-service, kept looking to the Lord, that He might break the chain and set the captive at liberty; and the glad moment of her rescue at last came, and she exulted in her new-found Friend and Saviour.

"**A Burden Removed.**

"A lady who lives at Newburgh-on-the-Hudson, has been for many years a devoted and pious Christian lady, but for some time past had a burden on her heart, of which she could not speak to her nearest friend. She had no conception of how, if, indeed, she ever, in this world could obtain relief; but the Holy Spirit applied the sermon of Mr. Harrison to her soul, and suddenly she found herself deprived of her strength, and fell prostrate to the ground. She remained in this state for about thirty minutes, when suddenly she cried, 'Glory to God! glory to Jesus! O Lord and Master, how my soul loves Thee! Thou blessed and glorious Saviour, Thou Christ of my soul, praise be to Thy sweet name forever!' And rising to her feet, her face was seen to be lit up with divine sunshine, and she told the assembled thousands that the burden was gone from her heart, and the Lord had made her indescribably happy. The transformation in her face was indeed wonderful. It was now beautiful, indicating a heart relieved and filled with the love of God and the blessed influence of the Holy Spirit.

"**A Long-Sought Possession.**

"A similar case of direct operation of the Holy Spirit's power occurred on Sunday, August 19, in an Evangelical church in New York City. The regular pastor was absent, and the minister who supplied his pulpit preached an earnest sermon on the assurance of salvation given to those who believe. After the service an aged lady, whose name and family are well known in Christian and philanthropic circles in New York, went up to the platform and said to the preacher, clasping her hands, while the tears ran down her cheeks: 'O sir, is it possible for me to get that assurance of which you have been speaking? That is exactly what I want. I have been a member of —— church for many years, but I have never had that witness of the Spirit that you have described.' 'Well Madam,' said the preacher, 'you know that it is there for you. You have only to take it by faith. Wait a moment, and we will pray that you may have the blessing.'

"The preacher beckoned two or three ladies, earnest members of the church, and two of the officers, who knelt down and joined the preacher and the lady in earnest pleading to God to reveal Himself by His Holy Spirit in the aged lady's heart. Her tears were still falling, and her expressive features showed how thoroughly in earnest she was. Addressing her, the preacher said: 'You know the Lord wants your heart, sister.' 'I do,' said she, with much feeling. 'He asks you for it now.' 'I know it,' said she. 'Are you willing, here and now, to give your heart to Him?' 'Why, yes, indeed I am,' was the quick and earnest response. 'Do you now give it to Him?' 'I do, most surely,' with much earnestness. 'Well, now, dear sister, does He accept it?' Before she could answer, the glory and salvation of God rushed into her soul, and her face was radiant with indescribable joy. She was overcome for a moment by the sudden rapture, but soon she rose from her knees crying, 'O glory to God, He has saved me! O Lord, I thank Thee, I thank Thee! I thought I was a Christian from my girlhood, but never until now, have I had the sure and certain witness of the Spirit. I have it now. Glory to God! Bless His Holy name!' She went away from that church with a new light on her face as clearly perceptible as the light that sparkled from the diamonds which glistened on her fingers and among her garments. God had filled her soul with joy unspeakable, and her face reflected His glory."

CHINESE IDOLS DESTROYED.

IN a letter recently received from a lady missionary of the China Island Mission, she says: "Mr. Chang *brought his idols to be destroyed* with those the old man in Yang's family had given us. After prayers we took them into the yard, and they were shivered to atoms. To our great joy, Mr. Yang stepped up and asked and gave *the first blow to his*, after which we all helped in turn. Those who have had the same experience will know something of our feelings as, for the first time, we saw the men smashing their false gods. Those who have not, can have no idea of the intense joy that welled up in our hearts, remembering the promise—'The idols shall be utterly abolished.' I am trusting to see the day when there shall not be one left in Hiao-i. That morning we found that Yang's old uncle had been smoking opium, and that his wife was in the habit of doing the same; we told them that this bad habit must also be given up, and they at once agreed to do so. They are both seventy-eight years old."

AN OFFERING TO GOD ACCEPTED.

A STRONG, healthy man recently gave the following testimony at Bethshan, as reported in *Thy Healer*:* "Fourteen years ago I was given up by doctors to die of consumption. I had three sisters who died at the ages of twenty-one, twenty-two, and twenty-six, of consumption. I was then taking an active part in open-air work, and the verdict was that unless I gave it all up I must die. I had been plastered and medicined, and all other things. One night I said: 'O Lord, if you will heal my body, and give me a pair of sound lungs, you shall have my body, and you shall have the good of it while I live.' I then and there, fourteen years ago, gave my body to the Lord. Then I said to my mother: 'I have done now with medicine and doctors for ever, by the grace of God.' She began to cry over me. She was afraid, for she had seen what the girls had gone through. I said: 'I have done now, and am going to the open air to preach Christ.' I then laid by the medicines and the plasters, and for fourteen years, excepting fourteen weeks in which I suffered from exhaustion through overwork, I have been in perfect health. I am a living proof that Jesus Christ is a living Saviour, and that His power is equal to all emergencies."

* *Thy Healer and Faith Witness*, a monthly Magazine, edited by Mrs. M. Baxter, contains original articles on Holiness and Healing, Authentic Testimonies of Divine Healing, and Items of Intelligence from Heathen Lands where missionaries are laboring in faith, soliciting no help from man, but relying solely on God for support. Annual Subscription, 75 cents, may be sent to Manager of CHRISTIAN HERALD, 63 Bible House, New York.

A WICKED PLOT DEFEATED.

A LADY missionary, who is laboring in India in connection with the Church Missionary Society, reports the following incident which occurred this spring, as an illustration of the hostility of the high-caste Hindoos to Christian converts: "One of our converts is a woman of a very respectable class of Hindoos. Her husband had deserted her, and left her to the care of her parents. Coming to the Mission Hospital one day as a patient, she heard for the first time the story of Jesus and His redeeming love which so impressed and moved her, that she could not rest until she had become His follower by public baptism. Her parents, on learning what she had done, became angry and at once separated her from all companionship with them. Henceforth she had to live in a miserable outhouse alone with her child, being made to feel on every possible occasion, she was now a thing unlovable, untouchable, and unclean.

"All this she bore bravely, so long as her boy was permitted to share her isolation with her. But alas! the dreaded trial soon came. The child, her 'ankh ki putli' (pupil of the eye) as the natives so expressively call their children, was forcibly taken from her, lest he too should become, like his mother—a castaway. He was then sent to his father, who, in spite of his desertion of his wife, was considered by the woman's parents to be a better guardian of the boy's spiritual interests than his unhappy mother. But the poor creature's troubles were not to end here. A female relative, having heard of what —— had done, instantly sent word that the parents should poison her, and thus rid the family of a living disgrace. At the same time she remarked that if there should be any difficulty about it, —— might be sent on a visit to her. The parents not daring to do as was proposed, the female relative, a morose creature and hitherto no particular friend to ——, took the trouble to travel some hundreds of miles to see ——, and for the only time in her life showed excessive kindness to her newly made Christian relation, pressing her repeatedly to accompany her back to her home. Happily we heard of this spider-like attention to the innocent fly, and at once warned our young convert who, not suspecting the purpose for which she was invited, was most eager to go. The female relative soon after was obliged to leave. And thus the poor hunted soul escaped by the providence of God from the fatal net of the fowler."

A SERMON BEFORE IMAGES.

DURING a tour in Northern Mexico, which Mr. Crawford, of Hermosillo, describes in a letter to the *Missionary Herald*, he stopped at a village up the Sonora River, where, he says: "We held a meeting and the room was full. My Bible was lying upon the only table in the room, and it a family shrine, or at least used as such, for there was the large clay image of the Virgin, adorned and crowned with gaudy dress and tinsel crown. I opened the Bible at Exodus 20 and talked to them for over half an hour upon the second and fourth commandments. Though I spoke of images, I took no notice nor made any allusion to the one at my back, close to the Bible from which I was reading. I dismissed them, but they sat still. It was then 9:30 P. M.

then explained to them the simple practice nd usages of the gospel, but yet they made no ove to go; so I took the hymn-book and sang everal hymns alone. It was after 10 P. M. when hey arose one by one, several requesting me to old a meeting the next night. After all were one, the owner of the house, sitting with me t the table with the image upon it, expressed he hope that we might come there and hold ervices, and when he learned that I had a wife nd children he offered his house to us to live n and hold services. He was very kind, and harged nothing for his hospitality. When we ished to retire he provided me with a mat, hich I laid down in the driveway to the corral, here it would be cool."

PROPHETIC CHRONOLOGY.

By G. H. Pember, M. A.*

he Suspension of Prophetic Time—Lasts During Israel's Subjection or Exclusion From Palestine—A Key to an Apparent Contradiction—The Ninety-three Years Missing From the Old Testament Record—Made Up of Five Periods of Suspension—The Line of Gentile Prophecy Unbroken From Nebuchadnezzar to Antichrist—The Resumption of Israel's Record Explained to Daniel—The People to Return Under Antichrist—The Last of the Seventy Heptads.

INSPIRED writers sometimes use a mystical hronology in dealing with the times of Israel hich is based on a very simple principle. Israel nce brought out of Egypt should have been he people of God for ever without any intermission. But they provoked Him by their dolatries, so that He repeatedly "sold them" nto the hands of their enemies. And whenever He did so,

The Theocracy Was Suspended,

and the time of their servitude was not reckoned in the mystic chronology.

A remarkable illustration of this fact is connected with the prophecy of the Seventy Weeks. There the whole time from the Lord's rejection as King by the daughter of Zion to the still future day on which Antichrist will make his covenant with the Jews, is omitted from the calculation, because it is the *Lo-ammi*-period, during which no Israelites of any tribe can be nationally recognized as the people of God.

Another instructive instance occurs in the Book of Kings (1 Kings 6:1), where we are told that Solomon began to build the Temple in the fourth year of his reign, and "in the four hundred and eightieth year after the children of Israel were come out of Egypt."

But if we turn to the thirteenth chapter of "Acts" we shall meet with a very different computation. For there Paul speaks of the Israelites as having passed forty years in the wilderness, four hundred and fifty under the judges, and forty under Saul. (Acts 13:18–21.) If to these five hundred and thirty years we add the forty during which David was king (1 Kings 2:11), and the three of Solomon's reign which had gone by before he commenced his great work, we see that Paul reckons five hundred and seventy-three years between the Exodus and the building of the Temple. Here, then, is

An Apparent Discrepancy

of no small magnitude. For the same period contains—

According to Paul	573	years.
And according to the Book of Kings	480	"
So that the difference is	93	"

Now some chronologists defend Paul's calculation, some that of the Book of Kings: but, for aught they say, the result is in either case equally disastrous, since one of the two inspired writers is always shown to be wrong. If, however, we apply the principle stated above, the discrepancy vanishes, and it appears that neither the author of the Book of Kings nor Paul is mistaken; but that the former is reckoning by the mystical and the latter by the ordinary chronology. Nor is there any difficulty in demonstrating the fact.

During the period in question the only instances of God's formal, though temporary, rejection of His people occur in the Book of Judges. And turning to that book we find that He sold them to Chushan-rishathaim, king of Mesopotamia, for eight years; to Eglon, king of Moab, for eighteen; to Jabin, king of Canaan, for twenty; to the Midianites, for seven; and to the Philistines, for forty.

There is also mention of an oppression by the Ammonites lasting eighteen years; but this was contemporaneous with that of the Philistines (Judges 10:7), and may, therefore, be omitted from our calculation.

The times, then, during which their enemies ruled over the Israelites, and the theocracy was, consequently, suspended, were as follows:

Cushan-rishathaim	8	years.
Eglon	18	"
Jabin	20	"
The Midianites	7	"
The Philistines	40	"
	93	"

Thus the sum of the times of servitude is ninety-three years, which, as we have just seen, is the exact difference between the lengths assigned to the period from the Exodus to the Temple in the "Acts" and the Book of Kings.

This instance unquestionably demonstrates the principle of the mystic chronology as applied to the history of Israel. And, among other lessons, it warns us to beware of finding mistakes in the Scriptures. If a discrepancy so utterly hopeless, to all appearance, as that which we have been considering is made to vanish in a moment by the discovery and application of one of the Divine laws, should we not unhesitatingly attribute other difficulties which we may encounter to our own ignorance of the clue rather than to error in the revelation of God?

The whole line of

Gentile Prophecy,

flows in an unbroken stream from Nebuchadnezzar to the last great head of the Fourth Empire. And we are now in the clay-iron times of the feet of the image, and the world is soon to see the revival of the Roman Empire under the form of ten confederate kingdoms, the brief but memorable course of which will be cut short by the fall of the stone from the mountain—that is, by the descent of the Lord Jesus from the height of His power.

But while earth was bending to the sway of the Babylonian monarch, or shuddering beneath the tread of Persian myriads; while men were wondering at the lightning-rapidity and irresistible bravery of the legions of Alexander, or saluting Cæsar as Lord of the world and a present deity; when the crown was placed on the brow of Charlemagne, and the majesty of Rome again hovered over Europe; while the Eastern Empire was being destroyed by Moslem hordes; or while the armies of Napoleon were spreading like a prairie-fire over the surface of Christendom—what, during these long times of commotion and change, was the counsel of God in regard to the Jew? Had He cast away His people? God forbid! He had not cast away His people whom He foreknew.

Through all the turmoil of Gentile times His purpose concerning Israel has remained sure. And although the children of Abraham have long been a nation scattered and peeled, a nation meeted out and trodden down, whose land invaders, like overflowing rivers, have spoiled; yet when the iniquity of the Gentiles is full, and God's patience with them exhausted, Israel shall come into remembrance and be again gathered. Great Babylon shall fall, and Jerusalem shall arise and shine as the true city of the great King, and the joy of the whole earth.

The Key to the Future

of Israel is to be found in the ninth chapter of Daniel. If we understand that portion of God's Word, our difficulty with the remainder of Hebrew prophecy will be greatly diminished, and we shall easily see how to arrange other predictions each in its own place.

Nor is this all. The closing verses of the chapter, by marking out the times of God's dealings with the Jews, instruct us also in regard to the position of the Church in the grand progress of his purposes; and show us that, although her members will hereafter reign with Christ, she, nevertheless, at present occupies a mere parenthesis in the world-history. The Church has indeed a glorious destiny; but her calling is heavenly, while the Israelites shall be the Kings of the Earth. Since, therefore, prophecy mainly refers to earth, the Israelite has by far the greatest share of it.

The Lord has given but two continuous prophecies of the Church, while the prophetic Scriptures abound with details of the time when He will resume His covenant relations with Israel.

This was the outline of God's dealings with the Jews, as it was revealed to Daniel; For four hundred and eighty-three years, commencing with the decree of Artaxerxes, March 14, 445 B. C. His Spirit strives with them in their own land, and at the close of that appointed time, Messiah the Prince appears, and they reject Him. He comes unto His own, and His own receive Him not. Then He also rejects them, and casts them out to endure the curse uttered by Moses.

Anon they will return, and place themselves under the protection of the last head of the Fourth Gentile Empire. And when He makes His covenant with them, then man, the world, and Satan know that *but seven short years remain* for the indulgence of unbridled sin. At that time the great body of the nation will be in unbelief, and will, therefore, share in the madness of the world, and wonder after and worship the Beast. And of the small number who do fear Jehovah, few, if any will know the Lord Jesus as the Lamb of God, however they may recognize Him as their Messiah and King; for, according to Zechariah, neither the house of David, nor the inhabitants of Jerusalem, will find out the fountain that is opened for sin and for uncleanness, until they have actually beheld the face of Him whom they pierced. That

They Will Rebuild the Temple,

is implied in the eighth and ninth chapters of Daniel, and so it is also in the sixty-sixth of Isaiah. But the latter passage reveals to us the spirit in which the restored exiles will undertake the work, and the Lord's indignant rejection of that which is done by proud and self-willed sinners, who choose their own ways, and know nothing of the broken and contrite heart in which alone He delights.

At the same time there is a recognition of some few who will tremble at the word of the Lord, and whose brethren will hate them and cast them out for His name's sake, while they hypocritically say: "Let the Lord be glorified." These afflicted ones are strengthened for their brief trial by the significant words, "But He shall appear to your joy, and they shall be ashamed."

When the Temple has been thus erected by the unsuspecting Jews, all will be ready for the fearful scenes which are to close the dispensation, and which are especially foretold in the sermon on the Mount of Olives, and in some of the chapters of the Apocalypse.

* From the third edition of his invaluable work entitled "The Great Prophecies Concerning the Jews, the Gentiles, and the Church of God." It is written in a most popular and eloquent style, and describes the impending fulfilment of Revelation and Daniel, and is illustrated by a colored chart. 458 pages. For sale at this office, 63 Bible House, New York. Price, including postage, $1.

CHRISTIAN HERALD AND SIGNS OF OUR TIMES.

OFFICE, 63 BIBLE HOUSE, NEW YORK.

ENTERED AT THE POST-OFFICE AT NEW YORK, N. Y., AS SECOND-CLASS MATTER.

The thanks of the Publishers of "The Christian Herald" are cordially tendered to subscribers who are endeavoring to extend the sphere of its usefulness by sending it to their friends, to clergymen, and others to whom its contents may prove useful. In order to facilitate and multiply such efforts as far as possible, a concession in price will be made. Any person wishing to introduce "The Christian Herald" where it may do good, may send

TWENTY-FIVE CENTS

to the Manager, 63 Bible House, New York, for which sum the paper will be mailed from date until the end of the year 1888, to any address in the United States or Canada. A similar offer in former years has been much blessed. Persons have written to this office expressing their thankfulness that the paper, thus introduced to them through the kindness of some friend, has been the means of good to their own souls, or has helped them in their labors for the salvation of others. The Publishers prayerfully hope that a like result may attend the effort this year.

CURRENT EVENTS.

The New York State Democratic Convention at Buffalo, on September 12, renominated David B. Hill for Governor. The nomination was made by acclamation, and was zealously pressed by influential members of the party. Unusual interest centres about this nomination. It was made in defiance of those Republicans who have been supporting Mr. Cleveland, and who are pledged to support him again this year. They, with a section of the Democrats, held a large meeting recently in New York City, to protest against the nomination, and warned the forthcoming convention that if Hill were nominated they would not vote for him. The Governor, however, has the enthusiastic support of the powerful liquor interest, which he earned by his veto of the High License bill. He has also the support of the older Democrats, who have no sympathy with the new civil-service system. Henry George, and several other prominent men, are as strongly opposed to him. They declare that they will vote the Democratic ticket for President, and the Republican ticket for Governor. The result will be worthy of analysis, as it will throw light on that much-disputed question—the value of the Mugwump vote.

Both Mr. Cleveland and Gen. Harrison have issued their letters of acceptance. It is clear that in both cases the candidates have made an effort to voice the platform of their respective parties, and to the critical reader it would seem that in each case an effort was needed. Mr. Cleveland apparently desires to conciliate the Randall wing of his party, while Gen. Harrison is anxious to secure the support of those western Republicans who are not so strongly protectionist as the eastern section of the party. Thus the two candidates approach each other more nearly than might have been expected of the leaders in so gigantic a struggle. Mr. Cleveland says: "We have entered upon *no crusade of free trade.* The reform we seek to inaugurate is predicated upon the utmost care for established industries and enterprises, and a jealous regard for the interests of American labor." Gen. Harrison, writing on the same subject, says; "We do not offer a fixed schedule, but a principle. *We will revise the schedule and modify rates,* but always with an intelligent provision as to the effect upon domestic production and the wages of our working-people." This in both letters appears to mean revision and reduction of duties, with special regard for the interests of labor. The American workman, who has not lost faith in the promises and pledges of candidates for his vote, will therefore be under no apprehension in either case, as both candidates promise that his interests shall be carefully guarded. One feature of Gen. Harrison's letter should not be overlooked. He declares himself an enemy of "trusts," which he stigmatizes as "abuses," and thinks that they should be dealt with by legislative authority. This is important, because Mr. Blaine's recent utterance on the same subject led many persons to believe that the Republican programme did not include hostile action against the trusts.

The Election in Maine Last Week did not afford the decisive indications expected of it as to the result of the Presidential contest. The average Republican plurality of September elections in Maine in the years in which the Republicans carried the State since 1868 has been, according to the New York *Tribune*, 18,228. Last week it was 18,495. In 1884 it was 19,851, and in 1886, 12,850. Comparing the party votes last week with the votes of the September election of 1884, the latest Presidential year, it appears that the Republican vote has increased by 1,824, and the Democratic vote has increased by 3,038. As the vote for the Presidency in the State is generally much heavier than in a State election, it is evident that neither party has much material on which to base an estimate. The Prohibition vote was 2,971, which is slightly less than in 1886, when it was 3,872. In 1884 it was 1,190.

The Death of the Famous Astronomer, Richard A. Proctor, caused a sensation in New York on September 12. Mr. Proctor died of yellow fever in a city hospital. He arrived from his home in Marion County, Florida, which is eighty miles from Jacksonville, on September 10. There was no case of yellow fever anywhere near his residence, but he had to travel through the infected district to reach New York. On his arrival he complained to the hotel-keeper of lassitude and fatigue, and as he came from Florida it was deemed advisable to have medical advice. The physician first summoned, on examining the patient suspected yellow fever, and called in two other physicians for consultation. His opinion was confirmed, and Mr. Proctor was removed to a hospital. The disease made rapid progress, and he died in less than twenty-four hours. The health authorities took prompt measures to prevent the spread of the infection. The entire contents of the room he had occupied at the hotel, were immediately removed and burned, and other preventive measures taken. Mr. Proctor was only fifty-one years of age. He was on his way to England for a lecture tour, his passage having been taken on a steamer which left New York on Sept. 15.

The State of Affairs at Jacksonville, Fla., throughout last week was one of increased depression. The plague continued to seize new victims, and the daily record of deaths grew heavier. On Wednesday the new cases were reported to be fifty-nine for the previous twenty-four hours. On Tuesday there were twelve deaths, the heaviest death-list for any day since the outbreak. The physicians and nurses are completely worn out, but others have heroically gone from various points to their relief. The most welcome of these volunteers was Dr. L. A. Bryan, who arrived from Houston, Tex., on September 13. He was one of the heroes of the Memphis epidemic ten years ago, and probably knows more about yellow fever than any physician in the country. A refugee train was at last permitted to leave the city on September 12. It carried about 320 persons. They were taken to Hendersonville, N. C., where they were to be detained in quarantine for ten days before proceeding to their respective destinations. A remarkable feature of the city in its affliction is the almost total cessation of liquor drinking. The warning of the physicians has had its effect the people. Several bar-rooms have closed tirely, and in those that are still open custom are rare.

Destructive Floods are Reported from Mico, with serious loss of life. The entire cas coast has suffered severely. Advices from zaba state that all the rivers and creeks in vicinity have overflowed their banks. M houses have been thrown down, and sev lives have been lost. All the streams on road from the city of Mexico to Vera Cruz risen, stopping traffic. Medellin was compl ly under water and abandoned, the inhabita having fled to the hills. The Alvarado railr is fully one meter under water, and in so parts even three meters. The inhabitants Janapa, Medellin, Soledad, and Boca del are in a pitiable condition, and are without necessaries of life. The crops near the Cata and Janapa rivers and their tributaries are to ly lost. At the Paso Solis de Soledad ra over twenty thousand animals were drown

Ominous News from Africa was Received September 13. Reports from the Congo Ri stated that intelligence had come from the pedition sent to find and relieve Mr. H. Stanley, that Major Barttelot, the leader of expedition, had been murdered by his carri His companion, Jamieson, was reported to be Stanley Falls, organizing a new expedition. many false reports of disaster to white explor circulate among the natives that there is s hope that this news may not be true. Ma Barttelot's expedition left Yambuga, on t Aruwimi River, in the spring, for Emin Pash station at Wadelai, with the 500 loads of goo for Emin which Stanley was compelled to lea behind him. Major Barttelot is the offic whom Stanley left in charge of his camp Yambuga a year ago last June. He was to fo low Stanley with the rest of the goods as soo as a sufficient number of carriers were obtaine Tippu Tib was unable for many months to fu nish the carriers he had promised. Finall Tippu Tib and Mr. Jamieson, one of Stanley officers, raised a force of carriers, and a no from Jamieson, dated April 15, this year, sa that Major Barttelot and he were preparing leave Yambuga for Wadelai with Tippu Tib a 900 men. A later despatch announced that t expedition had started. The carriers were, f the most part, natives recruited from Kasong the home of Tippu Tib.

A Remarkable Marriage Took Place Turin, Italy, on September 11. The daugh of Prince Jerome Napoleon and the Princ Clotilde, sister of the King of Italy, was marri to the Duke of Aosta, who is the brother of Princess Clotilde, and therefore the uncle of bride. The union, strange as it appears, is dee ed perfectly legitimate by Roman Catholics, the Pope granted his approval of it. The bri groom is forty-three years old, and the bri twenty-two. The Duke was made King Spain in 1870. He was popular for a short ti but in 1873 the discontent of the Spaniards w his rule culminated in plots against his life, a he therefore abdicated and returned to It It is not impossible that he may succeed brother, King Humbert, on the Italian thro as the King's only son is in precarious hea The Duke of Aosta is the next heir.

The Emperor of Germany is to Visit Rome October. A difficult question of royal etique has arisen out of his proposed trip. The Po whom the Emperor is especially desirous of c ciliating, on account of his influence o German Catholics, haughtily refuses to rec nize the King of Italy, who will be the Emp or's host during his visit to the Italian cap Hence there was a necessity for delicate di matic negotiations to soothe the sensibilitie the Pope. An effort has been made to ind the Emperor to visit the Pope before going the King's palace, but this is said to have b unsuccessful. Both the spiritual and temp potentate are reported to be making g efforts to render the visit a memorable one.

The Offence of Preaching on the Common of Boston, Mass., has been expiated, and the offender, the Rev. W. F. Davis, having served his sentence of a year's imprisonment, with the usual deduction to which he was entitled by good behavior, has been set at liberty. Several carriages containing his friends went to meet him at the jail, and he received a warm welcome. A Boston journal reports that Mr. Davis preached to a large audience on the Sunday after his release. He spoke for an hour with much earnestness and seemingly unimpaired vigor. He declared that God had called him to the especial work of preaching Christ, and that he meant to persist in preaching the gospel to common people on common ground. His experience in jail he had found profitable, in that it had given him sympathy with and access to the people most in need of help. The city of Boston, in his opinion, is ruled by the rum-sellers and the Jesuits. Mr. Davis's counsel is reported to have secured a permit for his client, who will therefore not be molested hereafter by the police. He is said to have taken this step without the knowledge or consent of Mr. Davis.

The Opposition of the Roman Catholic Priests of Boston to the public schools, and their recent announcement that children attending them will not be prepared for their "first communion," has stirred up the Protestants of the city to united action. At a meeting of the Evangelical Alliance, held on September 10, it was resolved: "that the State should at once resume the entire control of public education, and make attendance compulsory upon all children of school age and good health, except those who attend such private schools as are under the approval of the State; and we hereby petition the General Court to enact laws that shall secure this result; and we call upon all citizens, irrespective of partisan relations, to unite in maintaining the public schools."

A Blind Man's Skill in Distinguishing Bank-notes was mentioned in the obituary notice of a well-known restaurant keeper of Paterson, N. J., last week. When he was a young man he was working at his trade as a machinist, and met with an accident which resulted in the loss of a leg. He started a restaurant. In a few years he became blind in one eye from cataract, and had numerous operations performed by Dr. Agnew and others. They were of no avail, and soon the disease extended to the other eye and he became totally blind. He possessed the faculty of making change as well as a man with his sight. Not only coins, but bank-bills could be distinguished by him. He never failed to recognize the denomination, except when the Government issued a new form, which would confuse him for a day or two. He said that each denomination had a distinct feeling about it that made it immediately distinguishable. He officiated for many years as cashier of his restaurant, and was never known to make a mistake. Astonishing as this faculty was in ordinary affairs, it is by no means uncommon in spiritual concerns. Many who are utterly blind to spiritual realities are unsurpassed in their power of accurately appraising earthly values. (1 Cor. 2: 14.)

A Romantic Legacy was paid Last Week to a widow in Brooklyn, N. Y. It appears that in 1863, the widow, then a girl of nineteen, was living with her father in Pennsylvania, not far from the field of Gettysburg. Her two brothers were privates in the Union army, and both fought in the celebrated three-days' struggle. One was killed, and the other, when wounded, was carried into his father's house, which had been converted into a hospital, and in which the girl herself was a most indefatigable nurse. Among the other inmates was a young Confederate officer, who had his left arm shot off. He recovered under the girl's care, and impressed her father so favorably that he agreed to be responsible for his parole. When the war closed, the young officer found himself in love, but the girl refused him. She said she could never bring herself to accept an officer of the army under whose bullets her beloved brother had fallen. He begged a lock of her hair as a memento, and returned to the South. The girl came north, married, and settled in Brooklyn. Her husband died last year and she opened a boarding-house. Nothing more was heard of the Confederate officer until last week, when the widow received a letter from a New Orleans lawyer, stating that the officer was dead and had left her $5,000. In the letter was a gold locket containing the lock of hair she had given him a quarter of a century ago. The officer must have kept track of her all those years without her knowledge. The widow was much surprised by the handsome bequest. In the day of final reward, similar surprise will be felt by many, whose deeds of love and kindness are then divinely acknowledged. (Matt. 25: 37-40.)

A Defective Rope Led to the Death of Two men and a woman in Ohio recently. A press despatch from Steubenville, O., states that a farmer near that town was, with his son's assistance, digging a well, hoisting the earth and stone with a windlass and big bucket. When one load was near the surface the rope broke, and the bucket fell ten feet upon the son, who was in the well. The father got help, and was lowered into the well, where he found the young man insensible. He tied the rope to his body, and the neighbors drew it out, and lowered the rope for the father; but as they drew him up, the rope again broke, and he fell to the bottom, breaking his neck and dying instantly. By the time the dead body of the father was brought out the son had died. The wife and mother was so shocked at the death of her husband and son, that she died in a few hours. It seems extraordinary that men who were about to depend on the strength of a rope should have neglected to thoroughly examine it before venturing their lives; yet men with eternal life at stake are found trusting to good works, religious profession, and other vain hopes of salvation, when an examination of them in the light of God's Word would reveal their frailty. (Acts 4: 12.)

Two Five-Thousand-Dollar Coffins are in process of construction in Boston, Mass. The Boston *Budget* states that a local manufacturer is executing an order for two caskets for a customer, who shows a princely disregard of outlay. They are intended for the use of himself and his wife when they die, and each will cost $5,000. They are made of mahogany, seven inches thick, carved in bold relief with the most elaborate designs. All of these are in some manner emblematic of death. On the panel a spider—itself symbolic of the grim destroyer—has caught the fly at last in a web delicately executed. In another place a griffin's claw supports a human skull, from a fracture in which a lizard is crawling. Still another panel shows an owl in the act of capturing a mouse, and so on, the intention being to express the idea that death comes soon or late to every living thing. On the top of each coffin is carved a coat-of-arms, and every available inch of the interior is beautified by the cutting tools. Inside of each of these superb caskets is swung a silken hammock for the eventual reception of a body, and a mausoleum to cost $150,000 is to be erected to contain them. It would appear that this couple intend that their bodies shall be splendidly housed after death, whatever may then be the condition of their souls. Happily, the place in which the soul will abide through eternity is not determined by wealth. The eternal mansions are open to the rich and poor without money and without price, and more of the poor than of the rich will inherit them. (Mark 10: 23.)

A Narrow Escape From a Rattlesnake Oc-curred to a Brooklyn, N. Y., girl two weeks ago in the Catskills. The reptiles have been unusually numerous and bold in that locality this year, and at the beginning of this month reports were circulated in the boarding-houses about Overlook Mountain, of a very large rattler having been seen in the woods on the mountain. A party was organized to go out and kill it, and several ladies insisted on going with the men. When a few black snakes were found, however, most of the ladies lost their courage, and returned home. A few went on, including a young lady from Brooklyn, who laughed at the idea of danger. As she had a persistent habit of wandering off on solitary rambles, she was warned against straying from the party on this occasion. But she slipped away after a time, and her absence was not noticed until a sharp scream, and then a second fainter one, alarmed the party. Rushing to the spot whence the cries proceeded, an enormous rattlesnake was seen already coiled, and about to spring on the prostrate body of the girl, who had swooned and was lying on the ground. A heavy blow from a stout cane crippled the snake, but it showed fight still, and there was considerable difficulty in killing it. When the girl recovered consciousness she insisted that the snake had bitten her, but she had not been injured. Unhappily, young people who disregard the warnings given them against going into moral danger seldom so escape. More frequently they are ruined, body and soul. (Prov. 28: 26.)

BRIEF NOTES.

A Baptist church in Louisville, Ky., reports an accession of ten members from the Church of Rome during the past three months.

Chancellor Horsman, of the Archdiocese of Philadelphia, says there are in that city 182,000 Romanists, and in the archdiocese 400,000.

Judge Ney, of Iowa, has decided that under the prohibitory liquor law of that State it is unlawful for a man to manufacture cider for use in his own family.

The eight theological seminaries of the Presbyterian Church had, last year, 607 students. The average cost for the education of each of these students was $453.

Rev. B. Fay Mills, the evangelist, is holding services near his home. In October he goes to Philadelphia for united services on the invitation of fifteen churches.

Senator Blair estimates that there are at least ten millions of people in the United States who are in favor of the abolition of the liquor traffic by national legislation.

The Boston Young Men's Christian Association are co-operating in gospel tent work, in that city, under the direction of G. S. Avery and Myron D. Fuller. The former is the evangelist.

Rev. Henry E. Benoit, of the Methodist Church, who has been appointed to missionary work among the four hundred thousand French residents in New England, proposes to itinerate with a tent.

An offer of $5,000 a year to play base-ball has been made to Mr. Stagg, of the last graduating class of Yale University. He has refused it to enter upon theological studies in preparation for the ministry.

The Day of Prayer designated by the officers of the World's and the National W. C. T. Unions is October 14. It is earnestly requested that on that day ministers will preach on the temperance question.

The Woman's Christian Temperance Union of New Hampshire are making arrangements to open a home for intemperate women. The State Legislature has granted the sum of $5,000 to start the work.

Though printers and publishers of books complain that their business is dull beyond precedent, the Bible Society issued during the month of August 63,457 volumes, which make 389,851 issued since April.

Rev. Louis R. Scudder, M. D., has sailed with Mrs. Scudder on the *Furnessia* for Glasgow, on their way to join the Arcot Mission. The Students' Missionary Association has pledged itself for their support in the field.

Rev. John T. Vine, Baptist evangelist, has commenced his fall and winter special services in the First Baptist Church at Gouverneur, N. Y. Mr. Vine may be addressed at 238 West Fifty-first Street, New York City.

Arrangements are in progress for establishing a California Congregational Colony, in a very delightful and salubrious locality, which shall be a place of resort as well as residence, and an educational centre, with a church.

The treasurer of the American Board of Commissioners of Foreign Missions states that the receipts for the eleven months of the fiscal year amount to $479,757, against $397,562 for the same period of the previous year.

At the Cincinnati annual Methodist Episcopal Conference, in session in Jamestown, O., Dr. I. C. Iliff, in charge of the Methodist Mission in Utah, said that, notwithstanding reports given out by the press in general, polygamy is on a decline in Utah, owing to the vigorous enforcement of the Edmunds law.

Mr. John Currie, the self-educated evangelist, has gone to Leadville, Col., with Mr. Peter Bilhorn, the gospel singer, to hold services among the miners. Mr. Bilhorn's hymn-book entitled "Crowning Glory," which contains his solos and songs is having a large sale. The profits go to the support of a People's Mission in Chicago.

THE PERSONAL REVELATION.

A New Sermon, by Pastor C. H. Spurgeon.

"Flesh and blood hath not revealed it unto thee, but my Father which is in heaven." Matt. 16: 17.

The Test Question—A Distinction Between the World and Disciples—Wrong Judgments—May be Respectful—Are Unblessed—The Knowledge the Disciples had of Jesus—I. Different from that of the World—Solemn and Personal—Definite—Permanent—II. Revealed in a Special Way—Reasoning Useless—Teaching Fails—Regeneration Necessary—Purity Essential—III. Its Peculiar Marks—Full of Certainty—Attended with Sacred Operations—Abides Forever—IV. Secures Peculiar Privileges.

THIS is one of the earliest places in the New Testament in which we find any mention of the church. Jesus says, in verse eighteen, "I will build my church." It is very significant that our Lord should connect with the church the right idea of Himself. In our text we have the test question which must be put to every one who is to be admitted into the assembly of the Lord—"Whom say ye that I am?" The first question to be put to one who would join the church is, "What thinkest thou of Jesus?" You cannot be right in the rest unless you think rightly of Him. If you do not begin aright with Jesus, the Christ, the Son of the living God, you will not go on aright, and your joining of any visible church will be a mistake which will be injurious both to yourself and the church. Beloved, let it be with you first Christ, then the church.

In putting the question about Himself, our Lord made a distinction between

Two Classes of Persons,

who are named as "men," and as His disciples. He inquired, "Whom do *men* say that I, the Son of man, am?" These "men" formed their judgment of Christ according to flesh and blood; they went upon the ground of carnal reasoning; or else they followed current opinion. They went upon natural, and not upon spiritual, grounds; they discerned nothing of spiritual things: their judgment was that of flesh and blood. What conclusion did they arrive at while guided by flesh and blood?

The conclusions were *diverse:* "Some say thou art John the Baptist; some, Elias; and others, Jeremias, or one of the prophets." Error is multiform; truth is one. A thousand lies will live together, and tolerate each other, especially at this time, when errorists are all crying out, "Cast in thy lot with us; let us all have one purse." The results to-day of the judgments of men about Christ are very many; but they agree in this, that they contradict the one and only truth. To-day, some say, "He is a good man," others say, "Nay, but He deceiveth the people." Some say that He is divine, though not actually God; others, that He has become God, though He was not always so; and a third company think Him a divine man. Some agree that His teachings were admirable for the occasions on which He delivered them, but that they are somewhat stale in this advanced age; while others ridicule His teachings as altogether impracticable. The doctrines of flesh and blood concerning Jesus are various.

The Judgments of Men

here recorded are respectful to our Lord Jesus. It is usual nowadays to speak very respectfully of Him—if there can be any respectfulness in words which deny His Godhead. To-day they rend the seamless vesture of the Crucified. They retain His example, and profess to value it; but His sacrifice they fling aside as a rag of superstition. They dare to deny His miracles while they applaud His precepts: they will have nothing to do with the doctrine of the cross; but with the self-denial of the cross they affect to be enamored. Our Lord will not thus be divided. Those who take not a whole Christ take not Christ at all.

Whether the conclusions of flesh and blood are respectful to Jesus or not, they are every one of them wrong. In the favorable summary here given, not one conjecture of men is correct. Jesus was not John the Baptist, nor Elias, nor Jeremias, nor one of the prophets. Assuredly He was not Beelzebub. Men did not know what Jesus was. They neither knew Him, nor His Father. The character of Jesus is much too hard a nut for philosophic teeth to crack.

The conclusions of flesh and blood are unblessed. No blessing attached to any of the various notions which men hold concerning the Son of man; but that judgment which came by revelation from the Father made Simon Peter blessed, and our Lord beheld and declared the blessing. Gazing at Jesus as if He were John the Baptist, or Elias, brought no blessing with it; and if Jesus be not known by the revelation of the Holy Ghost, He is not known as a well-spring of blessedness to the soul. If you know no more of Christ than the world knows, than the learned know, than the philosophical know, you have not found the blessing. If you know no more of Christ than you have found out for yourselves, even by reading the Word of God, unaided by the Father, you are not blessed. If you know no more of Jesus than flesh and blood has revealed to you, it has brought you no more blessing than the conjectures of their age brought to the Pharisees and Sadducees, who remained an adulterous and unbelieving generation.

The Disciples' Knowledge.

There was a handful of people in the world in the Saviour's day who were known as His disciples. To them He put the question, "Whom say ye that I am?" They were disciples, that is, learners; they were not so much "thoughtful men," as the cant phrase now is, as learners. They received what He imparted to them; His "Verily, verily," being to them *better than reasoning*. As disciples, they were also *servants*—they learned obedience. They knew Jesus by following in His steps. Put these two things together, learners and servants, and you will see how different they were from the men of the world. Judge ye, dear hearers, to which you belong, whether ye are "men," boasting of your intellect, guided by "flesh and blood," or whether ye are "His disciples," who judge after the Spirit, and are taught of the Father.

I. Our first observation is this—the knowledge of the disciples of Jesus

Differs From That of the World.

It is more serious, more thoughtful, more personal. Men of the world said, "We do not know who Jesus may be. He is a very remarkable person: He disturbs the quiet of the age, and He is certainly out of His element among us. We do not know who He may be, and we do not particularly care." Herod came to the hasty conclusion that John the Baptist was risen from the dead. Others said, "It is very likely Elijah, who was to appear before the coming of the Messiah." A third party, hearing of His sorrows, thought that He might be Jeremiah *redivivus*. He might be some other prophet, but it did not matter which. The disciples had arrived at their conclusion solemnly, thoughtfully, carefully, each one for himself; and when the Saviour said to them, "Whom say ye that I am?" they would any one of them have spoken, only they had fallen into the habit of making Peter the foreman and mouthpiece of the twelve, and so he spake first, and said, very properly and positively, "Thou art the Christ, the Son of the living God."

To my mind these words have a tone of deep solemnity. Evidently the man means what he says, values the truth he speaks, and attaches deep importance to it. The replies of the world were flippant and frothy; but the answer of the apostles was devout and deliberate, for they judged the subject to be one of the highest importance. Now, beloved, what do you think of Jesus? Is His name a weighty matter with you? Has He washed you in His blood? Have you taken Him to be your all in all? Personally, for yourself, have you done this, and done it with care and deliberation? Will you repeat your choice this morning? Well, then, in this you are what a disciple should be.'

In the next place, the disciples' knowledge

Is More Definite,

more clear, more assured. If you had asked the outsiders about Jesus, they would have said, "Well, perhaps He is John the Baptist, or perhaps He is Jeremias"; but their notions were all in the clouds: they could not make Him out. But to the disciples Jesus was known, and His personality was distinct. They knew enough to say for certain, "Thou art the Christ, the Son of the living God." I will not enlarge upon this, but come to the close grips with you. Do you believe in Jesus by an inward discernment of Him? Is He to you, clearly and distinctly, the Son of man and the Son of God? Is He to you, definitely, your Saviour, whom God hath set forth to be the propitiation for your sins? Is He your surety, substitute, and sacrifice? Beware of a misty religion! Beware of that which is without form, for it is sure to be void!

Thirdly, this knowledge of the disciples was unanimous. Outside the circle Jesus was a dozen things; inside the circle He was only one—"Thou art the Christ, the Son of the living God." Beloved, men sometimes talk to us of the divisions in the Christian church, and it is a pity there should be even the semblance of a division there; but I am bold to say that there is no real division in the true church of Jesus Christ. Those who are really taught of the Father believe one doctrine concerning Jesus.

Furthermore, the true disciples' knowledge of Christ differs from that of men in that

It is Permanent.

The verdict of men concerning the Lord Jesus is changeable as the wind. In one age, Jesus was hounded down as the Nazarene, the blasphemer. By-and-by men would set up His statue in the Pantheon among the gods. In one age, His teachings were held to be deeply philosophical, and the gnostics began to mystify them at a great rate: at another period they were denounced as visionary, or ridiculed as absurd. They say well of Him one day, they speak ill of Him another day: what matters it what they say? He needs no honor from them, and He fears not their dishonor. Unless they will believe in Him as Lord and Saviour, it is of no importance what they think of Him.

Once more, the knowledge which disciples have of Christ differs from that of the world, in that it is more influential. The world is not influenced by believing on Jesus as John the Baptist; but we are greatly influenced by believing that He is the Son of God. This takes possession of our heart, our head, our eye, our hand, our foot, our body, our soul, and our spirit. This Son of God is Lord over us. He sits supreme upon the throne of our hearts, and our lives show that He rules and governs our thoughts. Is it not so? This is no inert opinion but a living, active principle. I leave these things with you that you may search yourselves and see whether you belong to the mass outside guessing and blundering; or whether you are of the inner circle, who are taught of the Father.

II. Secondly, and this is a very important point: The knowledge of Christ possessed by true disciples is

Received in a Special Way.

"Flesh and blood hath not revealed it unto thee." Beloved, if we know the Saviour aright we have not learned it alone by the instruction of other men. Peter had heard others speak but he did not know Jesus as the Christ till the Father revealed Him. Paul tells us concerning the gospel, that he neither received it of man neither was he taught it, but he received it by the revelation of Jesus Christ. I grant you that God uses men to instruct us; but all the prophets and apostles could not teach us Christ if the Father did not reveal the Son in us.

Nor had Peter found out the nature and glory of the Lord Jesus by his own reasonings. These were the flesh and blood by which Jesus is never made out. No doubt, as he read the Old Testament, he said—"This prophecy and that are fulfilled in Jesus"; but, even that would not have sufficed to make Jesus known to him as ırist and God. The Father, who sent Jesus us, must also make Jesus known to each one us, or we shall remain in ignorance of Him. an cannot by searching find out God, nay, not en God in Christ Jesus. Peter came to the nclusion that Jesus was the Son of the living ɔd, because the Father in heaven made him see and know that it must be so.

Can you follow me experimentally in this? as the Father revealed Christ to you by a birth you? You can never know the Father till you come a son; you can never know the Son till u are yourself a son.

A Spiritual Faculty

ıst be created in us, by which we are enabled perceive the Son of God. "That which is rn of the flesh is flesh," and nothing more, d flesh cannot discern spiritual things. "That ıich is born of the Spirit is spirit," and spirit ɔne can enter into the spiritual world, and derstand spiritual things. "Ye must be born ain." You must be begotten again of the .ther; otherwise Jesus Christ will be as little own to you as the light of the sun is known dead men.

Moreover, the Father must also purify us. As have already heard, "the pure in heart shall God." It is only when the Father by the ɔly Spirit purifies the mental eye, by cleansing e heart and life, that we are able to underınd and perceive the true nature, work, and ices of the Lord Jesus Christ. Regeneration ıst be followed up by sanctification if we ɔuld obtain edification in the things of Christ. Without holiness no man shall see the Lord": may have the Lord set before him, but he nnot see Him without holiness; he may hear out Jesus, he may read about Jesus, but he unot see him as Christ and God unless his .ture is sanctified.

Let me refresh the memories of God's people. ave there not been times with you when e Son of God has been revealed in you with ɪwer? Certain of these occasions have hapːned when you were in trouble: you found no st till you thought of Jesus, your Lord and ɔd, and then your peace was like a river. The ɔrm raged till you saw Jesus walking on the e waves, and bidding them be still; and then ıu said, "Truly this is the Son of God." At nes my heart has been so full of joy that I uld hardly have endured more. Jesus has ɛen heaven within my heart. In standing one, contending for the faith, I have enjoyed sweet content in the sole fellowship of my ɔrd. In His presence, anxieties and fears ıve fled away, and questions have been solved ıce for all in a peaceful sense of infinite love.

III. Thirdly, this knowledge has

Its Own Peculiar Marks.

First, it has this mark—it comes with an inllible certainty to the heart. If you read of ːsus in books, or hear of Him from ministers, is well; but if the Father reveals Him to you, is infinitely better; for then no shadow of ıspicion rests upon the testimony. The witːss of God cannot be questioned. Men must ɔt wonder that we grow indignant when the orious truths concerning our Lord are quesoned; for to our hearts they are not in the reon of things to be disputed. There is conructive blasphemy in discussing those facts ɔncerning the Son of God which the Father ıs revealed to us. When such questions do oss our minds, they are exceedingly painful to ı, and we chase them out as thieves which dee the temple of the Lord; but when the ather is revealing Jesus as the Christ, the inuders do not come near; they could not. here is no doubting when the Father is witːssing to the heart.

"Oh," saith one, "but the Father has never ɔoken to me in that way." I am sorry for you. sk Him to do so. I am glad that you confess ɔur want of such an experience; but it is a ɪry serious want. The Lord must deal with ɔu; His Spirit must come into contact with ɔur spirit: there must be an inward illuminaon by the Holy Ghost, or else you will never be truly blessed. It was not only what Peter knew, but the way in which he came to know it, which made Peter blessed. Truth thus revealed comes with a force far transcending the arguments of pure reason.

In the next place, this knowledge has this peculiar mark: that it is attended with sacred operations. When the Father reveals Christ to a man, He at the same time

Reveals the Man

to himself. This discovery of the sin and ruin of self leads on to humiliation, contrition, repentance, and renewal. The man is moved to desire holiness, to long to be like Jesus; and this is a blessed fruit of knowing Jesus. All manner of holy and blessed work goes on in the heart at the time when Jesus becomes known: faith, hope, love, patience, zeal, and joy in the Holy Ghost come with a discovery of Jesus.

There is this one more mark about it, that this conviction of the Godhead and glory of Christ abides for ever. The man who has obtained his religion from other people may have it taken away by other people; but he who has received it from the Father, holds it by a tenure which cannot be broken. That which we have learned from the Father will never be unlearned. Nothing can erase what the Holy Spirit has engraved. Beloved, I beseech you beware of a home-made religion, cobbled on your own lapstone. Equally beware of a religion which is a sort of patchwork, made up by the kind contributions of Christian friends; and none of it your own. Jesus stood and cried, "If any man thirst, *let him come unto Me*, and drink." There is no safe religion in the world but that which comes through a personal application to Jesus, and a reception of Him for yourself. Get the better part by sitting at the feet of Jesus, and it will never be taken from you; but religion which does not come by a personal revelation is a mere mirage—there is no reality about it, and it will disappear like a dream of the night.

IV. Lastly, this knowledge

Secures Peculiar Privileges

to its possessor. What saith the Lord Jesus? "Blessed art thou, Simon, Bar-jona: for flesh and blood hath not revealed it unto thee, but My Father, which is in heaven." How was he blessed? Simon Peter was blessed, first, because *he had eternal life*. How do we know? Our Saviour said "This is life eternal, that they might know Thee the only true God, and Jesus Christ, whom Thou hast sent." "This *is* life eternal": if you know Jesus as sent of God, you have eteral life. The knowledge of Him is life eternal. You read about Julius Cæsar, Mark Antony, and the like; but you certainly do not know them. You cannot know them. You know about them in proportion to your scholarship, but you do not know them as living persons, or as sent of God to you. They are dead and gone long ago, and to you they never had an existence or a mission. With regard to the Lord Jesus Christ, you not only know a great deal about Him, but I trust you know HIM. Is He a friend, a brother to you? This is life eternal.

He that knows Christ is in a favored position wherever he is. In every condition he is blessed. You are very ill—you are

Blessed in Being Ill.

You are prospering in the world—if you know Christ, your prosperity is blessed. Do you lament that you are going down in the world? Mourn not, for your adversity is blessed. You are very simple-minded, and have not much education. Never mind, you are blessed if you know Christ; His knowledge is the most excellent of the sciences. Are you well-instructed? Rejoice not in all knowledge, but glory in this one thing, that thou knowest Jesus, and art blessed. Does the world curse thee? Fret not. Does the devil snuff at thee? Tremble not, but resist him. Jesus says thou art blessed, and I wot that he whom Christ blesses is blessed, and none shall reverse the word.

Do not suppose, my hearers, that you will find out the Lord Christ by your own wit and wisdom. Young man, do not say, "I will be a student, I will by my own ability discover this Son of man." Remember that Jesus can only be seen by His own light. Only Godhead can teach as Godhead. Christ is a book in which no man can read except Christ Himself shall spell the words to him. Jesus is His own interpreter. He is the door, but He is also the key. He is to be seen, but He supplies the light in which He is to be seen. Jesus came forth from God, and the power to know Jesus also comes forth from God, so that all comes from God; and unto God let us return it, adoring Father, Son, and Holy Spirit, one God for ever.

[The prayers of the readers of this journal are requested for the blessing of God upon its Editors, and those whose sermons, articles or labors for Christ are printed in it; and that its circulation may be used by the Holy Spirit for the conversion of many sinners and the quickening of God's people. Dr. Talmage and Mr. Spurgeon especially request prayer every Sunday morning on behalf of their labors.]

GEMS FROM NEW BOOKS.

TOLTEC MARRIAGES.*

MARRIAGE among the Toltecs was celebrated with ceremonies it may interest the reader to know something about. On this occasion friends and relations were invited, the walls of the best apartment were adorned with pretty devices made with flowers and evergreens, whilst every table and bracket was covered with them. The bridegroom occupied a seat to the right, *the bride sat on the floor* to the left of the hearth, which stood in the middle of the room, where a bright fire was burning. Then the "marriage-maker," as he was called, stood up and addressed the young people, reminding them of their mutual duties in the life they were about to enter, and at the termination of his speech they were *given new cloaks*, and received the good wishes and congratulations of their friends, who, as they came up, threw each in turn some perfume on the hearth. Now the bride and bridegroom were crowned with chaplets of flowers, and the day was wound up with dances, music, and refreshments. There was also a religious ceremony similar to this in all respects, in which a priest officiated; when instead of cloaks they put on costly dresses with *a skeleton* head embroidered on them, and thus attired, the new married couple were accompanied to their home and left to themselves.

Counsel to a Toltec Bride.

A Toltec maiden about to enter married life was admonished with great tenderness by her father to preserve great simplicity in her manners and conversation. "Speak calmly," said he; "do not raise your voice very high, nor speak very low, but in a moderate tone. Neither mince when you speak, nor when you salute; nor speak through your nose; but let your words be proper and your voice gentle. In walking, see that you behave becomingly, neither going with haste nor too slowly. Walk through the streets quietly; do not look hither or thither, nor turn your head to look at this and that. See likewise that you paint neither your face nor your lips in order to look well, since this is a mark of vile and unmodest women. But that your husband may take pleasure in you, wash yourself and wear nothing but clean clothes. This was the course and manner of your ancestors. In this world it is necessary to live with prudence and circumspection. See that you guard yourself carefully and free from stain."

The Sculptures on Chapultepec.

Duran tells how Montezuma had himself and his first minister sculptured. Feeling that his end was drawing near, he summoned the doughty warrior, Tlacael, who for three reigns had shown his valor on the field of battle, and his wisdom in council: "Brother Tlacael," said the monarch, "it would be well that our names and persons should be graven on the rock of Chapultepec, and thus pass to posterity."

* From the Ancient Cities of the New World, by Désiré Charnay. 514 Pages, Illustrated. Published by *Harper & Brothers*, Franklin Square, New York.

Dr. Crowther, P. E. Bishop of the Niger.

The Miner's Reverie.

Tlacael answered, "Your wish, most noble king, shall be instantly obeyed." And calling together the most renowned sculptors, Tlacael communicated to them the royal command. In a few days, two bas-reliefs were executed, so striking in resemblance and so exquisite in workmanship, as to surprise Montezuma.

The Building of Campeche.

"Campeche," says the brilliant Charnay, "was built on the site of an Indian city, and visited by Antonio Cordova in his first expedition (1517). 'The natives', he says, 'were friendly, and took us to extensive buildings which had in them idols and sanctuaries. These edifices were built of lime and sand. On the walls were enormous serpents, and near them, paintings representing their idols, round a kind of altar stained with drops of blood still quite fresh.' The Spaniards sailed away, and did not settle at Campeche until 1541. In process of time Campeche became the most flourishing city of the peninsula, and was plundered several times by French and English privateers. Campeche with its tortuous suburbs, its drawbridges, its unsymmetrical high buildings, is the least eastern looking place in Mexico."

REV. SAMUEL A. CROWTHER, D. D.

(*See Portrait.*)

THE Protestant Episcopal Bishop of the Niger region in Africa, whose portrait is here given, has had a more eventful life than any bishop of his communion. His biography opens in the little town of Oshogun, in the Yoruba country of western Africa. He was then known as Adjai. When he was eleven years old, a slave raid led by the Eyo Mohammedans desolated the town. Many of the men were killed, Adjai's father among the number. The women and children, and such of the men as had been made prisoners, were made up into gangs, tied together by the neck and marched away. In the partition that followed, Adjai and one sister fell to the lot of one chief and his mother and a second sister to another chief. After a short time the chief bartered Adjai for a horse, and he was afterward sold again and again. Sometimes he was bought with money, but more frequently was thrown in, in a bargain for tobacco or rum. His last sale was to a Portuguese slave-dealer, who put him and a large number of others on board ship at Lagos. The vessel was captured before she had been twenty-four hours at sea by an English ship. The prize was taken to Sjerra Leone and the captives set at liberty. Adjai was then little more than twelve years old. The date of the ship's arrival was June 17, 1822, so that he must be now about seventy-eight years old.

The boy was placed under the care of Christian missionaries at Bathurst, where he speedily became a favorite. He was intelligent and alert and took kindly to learning. His diligence soon placed him at the head of the two hundred boys then under the care of the missionaries. He learned to read the New Testament and gave evidence of a change of heart. In 1825, three years after his landing, he made profession of faith in Christ and was baptized by the name of Samuel Adjai Crowther. So encouraging was his progress in learning that he was sent to an institution at Fourah Bay, established for the training of evangelists. In 1842, at his earnest request, he was detailed for missionary work on the Niger by the Church Missionary Society. A preliminary course of study was deemed advisable, and he was sent to England for a term of instruction in the Society's Training College.

In December, 1843, he returned and commenced his missionary labors in his native country of Yoruba Land. He had not been there three weeks before *he found his mother*, whom he had not seen for twenty-one years. She had been ransomed from slavery in her old age, and had returned to her native country. She told her missionary son where his sisters were, and he succeeded in ransoming them both. His mission was a decided success. He worked assiduously at his headquarters at Abbeokuta, and made periodical mission journeys up the Niger, planting stations and establishing native teachers. In 1857 he and his wife visited England, to report progress and describe his work. He was invited to Windsor Castle, and there had an audience with the Queen, who expressed her deep interest in him and his labors. What was of more utility, he also succeeded in arousing the interest of persons willing to help him practically by their gifts for the support of his stations, and for the publication of a dictionary of the Yoruba language, and translations of books which he had prepared.

The Protestant Episcopal Church in 1864 decided to make the Niger region a bishopric, and, to facilitate ordinations, Samuel Crowther was made its first bishop, and the degree of D was conferred upon him. He was consecr in Canterbury Cathedral on June 29, 1864. has labored earnestly since that time, with most encouraging results. At the recent Anglican Council Bishop Crowther was ent, and was received with marked cordiali

THE MINER'S SECRET.

(*See Illustration.*)

"THAT is not one of your regular hands, I pose," said an evangelist who had descend coal-mine in company with the superinten to distribute tracts and have a few words of ious talk with the men. He directed the su intendent's attention, as he spoke, to a who, having finished his mid-day meal, had f into a reverie with his pick in his hand.

"Oh yes, he has taken employment regular miner. One of the new men. Bee work about two weeks. He don't look as if been brought up to it, does he? I cannot him out. When he came to ask for wo thought he wanted a clerk's place, but he not. He wanted to do regular work below I took him on. His hands look as if he handled a pen more than a pick."

"I should like to have a talk with that m the evangelist said. "What is his name?"

"Tom Ward he calls himself."

The room in which, that night, the ev list found the man who had excited his int differed in no respect from those occupie the other miners in the village. The man hi though he was washed and shaved, wa dressed in broadcloth, as was the custom of men in the district who were addicted to ough ablutions. He wore the commones roughest clothes obtainable. His face ha sad, burdened expression which it had earlier in the day. But it was thoughtfu the evangelist thought, bore the marks ture. After apologizing for a visit that to a man might appear an intrusion, he said

"I am deeply concerned, my friend, your soul. When I saw you this morning strongly moved about you, and I could n until I had asked you if all is well betwee and God."

"That is very kind of you," said the "I assure you I sincerely appreciate your m Still, there are reasons why I prefer not swer your question. It would lead to discu

would be pain-
me, and could
› beneficial

evangelist
l earnestly with
n, but ineffect-
Respectfully
mly he refused
rawn into con-
m. "May I offer
prayer?" the
Christian asked,
.h.
tainly," said the

knelt down,
: evangelist
earnestly that
uld reveal Him-
re as the loving
willing to re-
ll who come to
ı faith, willing
ive, to restore,
the burden of
ary and heavy
ınd to comfort
tressed. When
from his knees
l out his hand
trange compan-
d said, "Good
, my brother;
od bless you in
special need,
er it may be."
y," said the
"I will speak
' With a strong
ıe mastered his
ı and said:
is no need
ıto details; and
I have not sufficient self-command. My
a very sad and shameful one. I have
Christian. More than that, I have been
her of the gospel. But there was a taint
lood. I knew my danger, and for years
n the watch against it. I thought at last
was eradicated, and I grew less vigilant.
oment of fierce temptation I fell into
s sin, and brought scandal on the name
st. The world pounced upon my fall
de it the occasion for jeering at religion
gious professors. The mischief was ap-
and it can never be undone, for I was
I wanted to bury myself beyond the
ity of discovery. I would like to have
n the very face of God if that were pos-
I came here. It was better than sui-
nd perhaps I might be able, by teaching
ınce, and by kind words and acts, to do
ng for these poor workers around me. I
ot atone for the mischief I have done. I
deceive myself about that, but I still
kind, and would serve them if I could
the short time I am likely to live. Now
ow my case, and will understand why
no hope of salvation for me."
I do not understand that, and I could
it it while the case of the Apostle Peter
on record. There *is* hope for you, and
ll receive you through Christ if you go to
His blood cleanseth from all sin.'"
miner shook his head; but the evangel-
inued pleading and arguing. At last the
aid, "Leave me now; I must think. I
e alone. I will see you again."
next day a brief note came to the evan-
It simply said: "Come to me again to-
I have found peace!" Very joyfully he
e appointment, but the miner was not
He waited some time, until the hurrying
ed people through the streets attracted
ntion. Inquiring the cause, he heard
ere had been an explosion in the pit.
distress, he made his way to the scene of
and was soon engaged in giving comfort to the afflicted women. He turned as a cry was raised, and saw that a dead body had been brought up from the pit. He bent over it and saw that it was the body of the man whom only a few hours before he had been instrumental in leading back to God.

A Fragment of the Ancient Wall of Jerusalem.

THE EPOCHS OF A LIFE.

A NEW SERIAL STORY.

By Rev. L. S. Keyser.

(Continued from page 591.)

The Tender Mercies of the Wicked.

As Hadley entered the recitation-room of one of the professors the next morning, his tutor took him to one side, saying that he wished to have a few words apart with him. The substance of his communication was, that the temperance people of Dundee, a village about five miles distant, had asked him to send them a good speaker to address them on the following Saturday evening in the Town Hall. As Hadley's temperance principles were well known, the professor decided to send him, if he would consent to go.

"My horse and sleigh are at your service," said the professor, "as you will have to go overland. You can take a friend with you, if you wish. I hope that you will not decline, sir."

Hadley had a temperance speech already prepared, which he had delivered in Banesville during one of his vacations, and he knew that he could soon revise it, and so he gave his consent.

While Hadley was taking his seat in the class after the interview with his professor, his eye fell upon the fair face of Miss Winters, and almost involuntarily the resolution formed itself in his mind to take her with him to the place in which he was to speak. The professor had said that a friend might accompany him. It was not long before he took steps to translate his resolve into a reality. While the class was passing down the stairs, from one recitation-room to another, he sought Miss Winters' side, and briefly stating the circumstances, he told her that he should be pleased to have her accompany him; to which she gave a ready assent.

All arrangements having been made, he set himself to work on the revision of his speech. It is uncertain whether the prospect of making the address, or the expectation of having a long drive with Miss Winters, filled him with the greater anxiety. He determined, for her sake as well as his own, that he would make the occasion a crowning triumph.

At last Saturday evening was approaching. The lecture was to begin at half-past 7. At 6 o'clock he was driving briskly, with jingling bells, toward the house in which Miss Winters roomed. In a moment she was at his side, and he felt that she had never looked so lovely as she did that evening, wrapped in her soft furs, while the sharp wintry air caused her cheeks to glow with the unmistakable hue of health.

The road wound about through the deep, flexuous valleys, and over hills of considerable altitude. As is apt to be the case with a speaker shortly before he is to deliver an address, Hadley was unusually taciturn on the way to the town: his mind, naturally enough, was divided between Miss Winters and his speech; and their conversation was, therefore, inclined to go by fits and starts, although it was none the less interesting on that account.

At a few minutes before the time for the lecture to begin, they drove up to the hall. Miss Winters was conducted to a seat, and Hadley was hurried by the chairman of the association to the ante-room, where he threw off his overcoat and gloves, and sat down for a few moments to draw breath and compose himself. Then he was conducted to the stage, and was greeted by a large audience.

Suffice it to say, that the speech was a marked success, even surpassing the expectations of the young orator himself. More than once was he greeted with vociferous cheers as he broke out into an impromptu burst of eloquence. Miss Winters was gratified with the firm stand he took against the hydra-headed evil he was denouncing; and especially when she saw that he put his argument on high humanitarian grounds. More than ever was she confirmed in her belief that, notwithstanding his hostility to religion, he was still actuated by high principles; and then she thought, if all his powers, all his philanthropic impulses, could be harnessed into the service of Christ, how useful he might be to his fellow-men. There was no doubt that Miss Winters was more prepossessed in the young man's favor than ever, as she listened.

His peroration was greeted with a storm of applause that shook the hall; and after many hearty congratulations from those who came to the platform to take his hand, he made his way to his sleigh, and was soon driving rapidly out of town with Miss Winters by his side.

The moon had risen, and her light falling upon the glistening snow, converted the night almost into day. How the girl's cheeks glowed in the mellow lunar light! Never before had her conversation been so bright and sparkling.

Hadley had not thought her capable of so much vivacity, and more than that, she referred to themes that proved her the possessor of a fund of knowledge that surprised him.

When they had left the town several miles in their rear, Hadley slackened the speed of his horse, concluding to allow the animal to walk the remainder of the way.

Miss Winters had said very little about his speech, for she was not given to profuse complimenting; but at last, when there was a lull in the conversation, she said:

"That was a magnificent address, Mr. Madelling. The argument was masterly and the earnestness almost electrifying."

"Miss Winters, that is a high encomium."

"But it is not extravagant," she declared. "I was much pleased with the stand you took for high principle. Nothing in your speech did me more good than your positive endorsement of the Pauline principle of abstaining from intoxicants for the sake of a weak and stumbling brother. That is putting the matter on high humanitarian ground."

"Ah! you thought," remarked Hadley, laughing, "that because I do not accept the Bible as Christians do, I am blind to everything good in it. In that way many persons misunderstand my position. I accept everything good and true, from whatever source it is derived. In short, I am an eclectic philosopher," he concluded, with a smile.

"That would all be very well if you recognized the true Source and Author of all good, which would give system and organic unity to your philosophy." Hesitating a moment, she added: "The Bible says that Christ 'is the light that lighteth every man that cometh into the world.'"

"You do not mean that He is the author of all the good there is in every system of religion and philosophy, do you?"

"That is my meaning in a nutshell," she said.

"I cannot see it so."

"Oh, I do not wish to argue the question; I only want you to look at the subject from that point of view. It is almost too bright a night to discuss abstruse theological questions;" and she settled comfortably in the seat of the sleigh.

"So it is—bright and romantic," he returned. "I am glad that you liked my speech this evening better than the one you heard me deliver in Chapel Hall not long ago."

"Yes, it was better in every respect. If you continue to improve, your prospects in life are very bright."

"My prospects in life!" echoed Hadley; then a pre-view of his future came before him in vivid relief, like a procession of pictures passing through a stereopticon, and as every new scene appeared, there was a bright being at his side. It was the girl who was with him now. But what if she should not be there! What if he should be compelled to make that long and tiresome journey alone, without the dear girl who held his happiness in her hands! A thrill of horror ran through his frame, and he could not endure to contemplate the picture of aridness painted upon the canvas of his fancy. He looked around at her furtively, and their eyes met in a glance that spoke more than the most voluble speech. Words came to his lips that would not be hushed.

"My prospects in life depend upon a very important circumstance," he ventured to say.

There was a moment of silence, broken only by the tinkling of the sleighbells and the creaking of the crisp snow under the runners.

"Oh, of course, we never can safely predict the future, for we do not know what contingencies await us," she remarked, thinking a trite utterance less embarrassing than silence.

"You misunderstand me," Hadley said, quickly. "I do not refer to those casualties over which we have no control. Miss Winters," he added, fervently, "my happiness in life depends very much on one person."

"That must be a very important individual," said the girl, with a rather perfunctory laugh.

"Will you allow me to say something very philosophical?" asked Hadley. "It is not very abstruse, however. This is what I wish to say: A man's life is very incomplete—indeed, it is scarcely half a life—unless it is complemented by the life of the woman he—loves."

The blood mounted to her cheeks. What could she say? With a carefully constrained voice, she remarked: "That certainly is a very recondite observation, but it seems to me that experience is necessary to test and verify its truth, and you—" the ingenuous girl stopped and blushed. It was evident that she was no adept at fencing, so transparent and truthful was her nature.

"Ah! there are some truths that one knows by intuition, and this is one of them," said Hadley, categorically. "But let us have done with circumlocution. It is better to be open and frank. It is not necessary for me to make a declaration of my feelings toward you, my dear—oh, if I dared to call you Madeline! You certainly must have drawn the correct inference from my words and actions since I have met you. It is not in my nature to conceal the emotions that stir me, unless there is sufficient reason for doing so. Yet, though you know it already, I must tell you plainly, my dear Madeline, that I love you." And he took her hand in his.

The blood rushed to her cheeks and as suddenly left them, rendering her face almost as white as the surrounding snow. Evidently very strong emotions had been stirred by Hadley's words, and were contending for the mastery. She would have spoken; but speech failed her. Hadley saw how deeply she was moved, and interpreting her silence in his favor, he continued:

"I have loved you from the first time I saw you, and my love has grown continuously ever since. I believe I could make you happy. I assure you it would be my most earnest endeavor to do so; and as for me, with you by my side, and your sweet influence inspiring me, I feel that I should be strong for labor and for good. We are made for each other. Say Madeline, will you not speak the word that will fill my heart with joy and hope?"

For a moment she was silent, but, at last, slowly and tremulously, her silvery voice sounding to his ear like the notes of an Æolian harp, she said: "I cannot—I must not answer you now. I must have time to think. My heart bids me give you the answer you wish. I admit that. But I distrust it."

"Oh listen to its voice, dear Madeline," said Hadley, eagerly. "It is a safe, a true counsellor. It is nature's voice, the great mother bids you unite your destiny with mine. It would be wrong to resist nature's pleadings."

"I am not sure of that," said Miss Winters. "Sometimes duty requires us to resist. The pleasant and the joyous are not always the right. I am sure you realize how momentous to us both is the question you ask. You would not have me decide on impulse. I must have time to think, I must consult my parents, and—why should I conceal it from you?—I must seek divine guidance."

Hadley, in spite of his softened mood, could not restrain a contemptuous smile, and Madeline saw it, in the moonlight, flit across his face. She shuddered, and if he could have known it, he did his cause real harm in that instant. "I would not hurry you against your own wish, my dear girl," he said. "But do remember how keen is my anxiety. Suspense will consume me. Think of it, and end it as quickly as you can. Will you send me the answer to-morrow?"

"I promise you to send it within a week," she said, and with that delay Hadley saw that he must content himself. But he had the assurance that her heart was with him, and he drew her more closely to his side.

All too soon the drive ended, and Hadley stopped before the gate at which he was to part with his companion. When she stood upon the sidewalk, he said, as he took her hands and pressed them between his own:

"Madeline, I shall await your answer with an anxiety I cannot describe. Remember, my existence will be riven and wretched if your re[illegible] is unfavorable. But forgive me: it is unma[illegible] to appeal to your sympathy. Let your affectio[illegible] decide, and I shall abide by the result."

Then he lifted her hands tenderly, alm[illegible] reverently, to his lips and kissed them with p[illegible]sionate fervor, and saying good-night, he leap[illegible] into the sleigh and drove rapidly away.

Madeline entered her room, and throw[illegible] herself into a chair, abandoned herself to ple[illegible]ant thought. Serious questions must co[illegible] soon, but just now it was impossible to thi[illegible] of anything but that this gifted and attract[illegible] young man really loved her and wanted her [illegible] be his wife. She had spoken truly when [illegible] said her heart bade her accept him. She kn[illegible] that she loved him, and what true-hearted [illegible] could not but rejoice that her love was recip[illegible]cated! But—

Madeline would not think of buts to-nig[illegible] The black cloud on the horizon, the grim shad[illegible] of Hadley's infidelity, of his unconcealed op[illegible]sition to religion, cast its shadow on her, [illegible] she would not be depressed by it now. [illegible] loved her, and her heart beat with joy. [illegible] would not put away from her the cup of hap[illegible]ness proffered to her, and the very thought [illegible] she might be compelled by her conscience [illegible] do so, made her clutch it the more convulsiv[illegible] now before it became forbidden nectar to [illegible] She thought of Hadley at his best, and [illegible] heart yearned over him and exulted in his d[illegible]laration of his love.

Her reverie was broken after a few minu[illegible] by the sight of a letter lying on her desk, wh[illegible] had escaped her notice on entering her roo[illegible] She looked at it now, and its bulk and the [illegible] known character of the handwriting excited [illegible] curiosity. She opened it and saw within a lett[illegible] addressed in a delicate feminine hand to Had[illegible] Madelling. She turned again to the outer [illegible]velope, thinking there must be some mista[illegible] But no, it was clearly for her, addressed in m[illegible]culine characters, name and address correc[illegible] and in full. Then she looked at the paper [illegible] which the inner letter was wrapped, and th[illegible] was the explanation!

It was very brief, and in the same writing [illegible] that on the outer envelope. The writer sim[illegible] said: "A well wisher of Miss Winters, who kn[illegible] something of her life and her associates, [illegible] been concerned by seeing her in company [illegible]casionally with a young man of whom she [illegible] know but little, or she would avoid him. [illegible] writer has a horror of young men who deli[illegible]ately amuse themselves by flirting and win[illegible] the affections of young ladies, only to trifle [illegible] them. The enclosed letter tells its own s[illegible] of a confiding girl placing her trust in one [illegible] as Miss Winters must be aware, is acting a[illegible] no such girl were in existence. It fell into [illegible] writer's hands by a curious circumstance, a[illegible] sent to Miss Winters in the hope that it [illegible] save her from life-long misery, by revealin[illegible] her the duplicity of the young man whom sh[illegible] honoring by her favor. Miss Winters may [illegible]member the missive handed to Cæsar on [illegible] fatal Ides of March, and avail herself of the [illegible]formation now fortunately at her service."

What woman would not have read the enc[illegible]ure? The letter had been changed but l[illegible] from the rough draft Belle Havelock had ske[illegible]ed. Duneman had used almost her exact wo[illegible] and Belle had known how to excite the curi[illegible] of one of her own sex. Madeline took up [illegible] letter addressed to Hadley Madelling, and l[illegible]ed at it critically. It bore the post-office st[illegible] of Banesville, his home; and its writer, if [illegible] handwriting was evidence, must be a woma[illegible] culture. The end of the envelope was torn [illegible] and as she drew the letter from it, Made[illegible] thought it had the worn look of a paper [illegible] had been read and re-read and carried ar[illegible] for some time in a man's pocket. Hadley [illegible] probably dropped it somewhere, and it [illegible] been found by some one who knew them b[illegible] She drew her chair to the light, and opened [illegible] sheet to see what his correspondent had to [illegible]

(*To be Continued.*)

SELFISHNESS.

By Mrs. M. Baxter.*

S. Lesson for September 30. Golden Text II Cor. 5: 15.

Apostolic Verdict on the Human Race—Selfishss Condemned by God's Word—Prompts Comtition in Home Evangelism and Neglects Forgn Fields—Christ's Life a Witness Against lfishness—His Teaching Against It—In the rmon on the Mount—In the Parables—A Sunbt Photograph of Men—The Unselfishness of e Consecrated Christian—Person, Time, and oney Given Up.

TAKE heed, and beware of covetousness. a man's life consisteth not in the abundance he things which he possesseth." (Luke 12:

Both the life and teaching of our Lord e eminently directed against the almost unial sin of selfishness. "All seek their own," e apostle's summary of mankind in general. so little is selfishness seen to be a sin that world absolutely admires it; "Men will se thee when thou doest well to thyself." 49: 18.) Business, politics, family and solife, are governed chiefly by the motive, hat shall I get by it?" Even in the educaof children this debasing motive governs nts, "How shall I best educate my daughto secure rich husbands?" or, "How shall I educate my sons to get on in the world?" h is the real motive.

Selfishness Governs Even Religion.

of the world will profess just as much ren as they think will forward their own insts, give just as much in charity as will save r reputation, thus making the world, and , *and God* revolve round them, as though ything and everybody existed for them. numbers of converted people seek in ren their own joy or comfort more than the y of God. Now the whole tone of God's rd is directed to subvert this tendency in ian nature. The law of God is against it. ou shalt love the Lord thy God with *all* heart" leaves self no longer as the heart's re, but makes God first. "Thou shalt love neighbor as thyself," gives self only an equal e with others. If every converted man and ian loved God with all their heart, and their bhor as themselves, the number of missions and the receipts of missionary societies ld be so large, that in a few years the diffiy would be to find a part of the earth which not evangelized.

lfishness governs churches and missions. no uncommon thing, when a good work is g in a place, for some other society to come set up another close to it, for the very pur. of injuring the work of God, instead of go. into fields which are unworked, and are cry. out for laborers. India, China, Africa, are g out for workers; if we banded together sent out one-half, and the best half, of those ave at home, it would be a benefit to the hen, and would make those at home to with greater diligence, and to be more ap. iated. The church at Jerusalem would ably have settled down in the enjoyment of knowledge of God, if He had not, through oldness of Stephen, permitted persecution eak out—then "they that were scattered ad went everywhere preaching the Word." s 8: 4.) Must we wait until persecution ks out before we are unselfish enough to he claims of the heathen upon us? Alas,

Politics are Governed by Selfishness.

e consideration of a Government is not al-, "What is best for the people governed?" "How may the revenue be increased?" and we find England guilty of forcing opium the Chinese, until hundreds of thousands he people have been ruined in soul and and family by the accursed drug; and berless wives and daughters have been sold a life of shame by their husbands and fathers, because the revenue of England gained some millions by this diabolical traffic! Political selfishness is murderous in its results. The same pleas of the need of revenue is supposed to justify the awful forcing of the liquor traffic on the formerly sober Hindoos, and the buying and selling of Hindoo girls for purposes of sin, because, as a nation, England is determined to have money at any cost. God turn her from her guilty national selfishness!

Jesus came on earth, not only to save us from our sins by giving Himself a ransom for many, but also to be in His own life a witness against selfishness. "Christ pleased not Himself." (Rom. 15: 3). He never went hither or thither for His own pleasure; He did always those things which pleased God. (John 8: 29.) We never hear of Jesus saying, "I don't like this," or "I don't like that," or "I don't want to go here or there." He never considered Himself, but only His Father. In His birth He was unselfish, ranking amongst the poor. In His childhood He was unselfish, subject to His parents, although the Son of God. In the temple He was unselfish, for, while He was Himself the source of all knowledge, He heard the doctors, and asked questions, and, when His parents questioned Him as to why He had tarried behind in Jerusalem, He urged no selfish plea, but said: "Wist ye not that I *must* be about my Father's business?" (Luke 2: 49.) In His ministry we see that self-consideration had no place: He sought no ease; He would not receive honor from men; even when wearied with His journey, He found His refreshment in seeking the salvation of a woman who had rudely repulsed His request for a drop of water! Self-pity, retaliation, and all other marks of selfishness were as far from Jesus as darkness is from light. Even in Gethsemane, while dripping with the bloody sweat, He excused His disciples for sleeping. On the cross He thought of His enemies, and prayed for them, and in dying He commended His mother to His disciple.

There Was No Selfishness in Jesus.

In His teaching we see how continuously He exposes, and warns against selfishness. The main gist of the sermon on the mount is: "Be unselfish." The blessing is given not to the greedy and grasping, but the "poor in spirit," the "mourners," the "meek," the "peacemakers," etc. If we are "the light," or "the salt of the earth," it is for the good of others. No gift can be accepted on the altar while our brother has aught against us; and the summing up of Christ's edition of the law is: "I say unto you, That ye resist not evil." If any man smites thee, don't resist; takes away thy coat, don't resist; compels thee to go a mile, don't resist; asks of thee, don't resist. "*Love* your enemies," that you may do something more than the publicans, who only love those that love them. Don't seek credit for what you give, or how you pray, or when you fast. Don't be anxious about eating and drinking and clothing. You are here on earth as witnesses that you do not need to be devoted to your own interests like the ungodly. "Your Heavenly Father knoweth that ye have need of all these things."

Parables Directed Against Selfishness.

In His parables Jesus teaches the same lessons. He who sowed seed in stony places lost all through selfishness. He could not stand "persecution because of the Word." The seed among the thorns was fruitless because of selfish cares and selfish gains. The merchantman hid his treasure instead of letting others participate. The unmerciful servant forfeited his very forgiveness through his selfish dealing with his fellow-servant. The laborers who agreed with the householder for a penny a day, reaped the reward of their selfish bargaining, and saw that those who would trust the householder without looking after their own interests got the better of them. The friends who were invited to the marriage feast "made light of it," because they gave preference to their own selfish interests. The rich man who was perplexed what to do with his riches, was suddenly called into the presence of God to give an account of his useless, selfish life. The prodigal son went away from his aged father in heartless self-seeking, and it was only when he had reaped what he had sown that he turned back to his father's house. The elder brother had no heart for the wanderer when he did return, because he thought in his selfish heart that his younger brother was treated better than he. The unjust steward sacrificed his master's interests to his own, as many professed Christians do now by

Discounting the Claims of God.

The rich man, "who was clothed in purple and fine linen, and fared sumptuously every day," found his way to hell, not because he had broken the commandments by thieving, killing, committing adultery, breaking the Sabbath, or worshipping idols, but because he had lived a selfish life. Instead of loving God with all his heart, and his neighbor as himself, he had loved himself with all his heart, and his neighbor a very great deal less than himself. And this respectable kind of rich man is to be found in every town and city of our land, perhaps of most lands; he is a very ordinary character on earth, but no man will ever meet him in heaven. Christ "died for us, that they which live should *not* henceforth live unto themselves, but unto Him which died for them, and rose again."

Of the ten lepers, nine were too selfish even to turn back and give glory to God for their healing. The unjust judge, who no doubt would serve the rich whose houses he might visit with the greatest alacrity, would not avenge a poor widow whom nobody knew or cared about, until, by her continued coming, she wearied him. The Pharisee carried his selfishness into his very prayers, and his religion consisted of exalting himself and despising others. The servant to whom the one pound was committed, selfishly hid it away where it was of no use to his lord or his fellow-men. This is how God sees men! This is no exaggeration; it is

A Sunlight Photograph of Man,

shewing him up as he is. It is the purpose of God to overturn this selfishness, and to conform us to the image of His Son. But He wants us to be fellow-workers with Him by recognizing this sin on which He lays His holy finger, and by trusting Him to cleanse, and conquer it. In the early days of the primitive church, when the Holy Ghost filled every believer, it was wonderfully absent from the disciples. It is an intense relief to turn from the exposure of selfishness in our Lord's parables to that simple description. "And the multitude of them that believed were of one heart and of one soul; neither said any of them that aught of the things which he possessed was his own; but they had all things common." (Acts 4: 32, 33.) Many look upon this as a utopian idea, but it is a Holy Ghost fact. Men have lived who refused to own their possessions; true Levites, who had no inheritance among their brethren, because the Lord was their part and their inheritance! Christ is the only cure for selfishness. When Christ fills a heart, it ceases to be selfish—every earthly possession, every moment of time, every opportunity, is only valued as it serves the purpose of Christ's Kingdom. Then, it is no longer the question, "What do I like? What would suit me? Which is the most convenient to me? But, What is best to please Jesus? This becomes the ruling principle of our lives, and then, as regards giving, it is never the residue which goes to the work of God—He gets the first and best of all, and we come in, like the sons and daughters of Aaron, to have our share with Him; all His, but we are blest in our partnership with Him. Infidelity, superstition, and all Satan's fortifications could never stand against an unselfish church.

---

*rs. Baxter sends this article as a suggestion to teachers schools in which the choice of a subject for Septemis optional. The International Lesson is either a Reof the Quarter's Lessons—Temperance: Deut. 21: 18-, Missionary Work: 1 Thess. 1: 1-10.

AS A LITTLE CHILD.

"Except ye become as little children ye cannot enter the kingdom of heaven."

"As a little child, as a little child!
 Then how can I enter in?
I am scarred, and hardened, and soul defiled,
 With traces of sorrow and sin.
Can I turn backward the tide of years
 And wake my dead youth at will?"
"Nay, but thou canst, with thy grief and thy fears,
 Creep into My arms and be still."

"I know that the lambs in the heavenly fold
 Are sheltered and kept in Thy heart;
But I—I am old, and the gray from the gold
 Has bidden all brightness depart.
The gladness of youth, the faith and the truth,
 Lie withered or shrouded in dust."
"Thou'rt emptied at length of thy treacherous strength;
 Creep into My arms now—and trust."

"Is it true? can I share with the little ones there
 A child's happy rest on Thy breast?"
"Aye, the tenderest care will answer thy prayer,
 My love is for thee as the rest,
It will quiet thy fears, will wipe away tears—
 Thy murmurs shall soften to psalms,
Thy sorrows shall seem but a feverish dream,
 In the rest—in the rest in My arms.

"Thus tenderly held, the heart that rebelled,
 Shall cling to my hand, though it smite;
Shall find in My rod the love of its God,
 My statutes its songs in the night,
And whiter than snow shall the stained life grow,
 'Neath the touch of the love undefiled,
And the throngs of forgiven at the portals of heaven,
 Shall welcome one more little child."

—*Mary Lowe Dickinson.*

J. E. JEWETT, Publisher, 77 Bible House, New York, will furnish the above poem in leaflet form at twenty cents per hundred. *A Sample Packet* of 10 leaflets assorted (no two alike) will be sent post-paid, for 10 cts., or 100 for 20 cts. Postage stamps taken.

MEXICO

Contributions in aid of Christian work in Mexico are most pressingly needed, and can be mailed to the address of

BISHOP H. C. RILEY,
Care of J. P. HEATH,
43 Bible House, New York.

TO OUR CHRISTIAN FRIENDS:

As there is a regular monthly expense in connection with the work a regular monthly income is needed to meet that expense. We, therefore, specially ask for regular monthly contributions in its behalf. If many will each send a little every month, or quarter, or whenever they can, it will do great good. *Remember, every little helps.*

H. CHAUNCEY RILEY.

To Our Fellow Christians

Who Are Forwarding Contributions in Aid of Christian Work in Mexico.

Bishop Riley requests me to inform the kind friends who are generously contributing in aid of Christian work in Mexico, that we have now over one hundred monthly subscribers who are forwarding contributions every month in its behalf. Bishop Riley sends to all who are contributing in aid of the work in Mexico his most sincere thanks for their timely gifts.

As there are, no doubt, many who would be glad to contribute something monthly in behalf of the cause of Christ in Mexico, but who feel that they cannot afford to give as much as one dollar a month, we venture the suggestion, that when possible *the friends of the work should try and collect small contributions from such* and forward the same with their own contributions to Bishop Riley, 43 Bible House, New York. For example, some friend of the work who is now forwarding one dollar a month, might induce ten others, to each give ten cents a month, and collect and forward the same with his own contribution. Another who now contributes one dollar a month, might induce four others to each give one cent a day, or thirty-one cents a month, and collect and forward the same with his own contribution monthly. Still a third who now contributes a dollar a month might induce two friends, to each give fifty cents a month, and collect and forward the same regularly with his own contribution.

If this plan could be adopted generally among the more than one hundred regular monthly subscribers to the work, we might soon be able to report to our friends that we had over two hundred dollars a month contributed regularly in behalf of the work in Mexico.

We remind our friends that to continue the work in Mexico effectively we most pressingly need a regular monthly income, as we have to meet a regular monthly expense.

A most precious Christian work has been commenced in Mexico, and we are doing what we can to continue it, by raising an income in its behalf. We earnestly appeal to our fellow Christians to aid us in this effort. There are one hundred and thirteen millions who speak the English language, and seventy-five millions who speak the Spanish or Portuguese languages. Among those who speak the English language, there are multitudes who know and love the pure gospel, and are doing what they can for the Master. Among those who speak the Spanish or the Portuguese languages, there are a few who know and love the pure gospel, and are faithfully working for our dear Master. Our Spanish-American society is working hard to raise an income to aid in building up a strong centre of Christian work in Mexico. The influence of that work has already extended into Spain and Cuba, and, we trust, will yet extend into South America. Fellow Christians, think of seventy-five millions who speak the Spanish or Portuguese languages, millions and millions, and millions of whom have never had a Bible in their hands!!! Help us! help us! to do Christian work in their midst.

Bishop Riley has been instrumental in having more than one hundred thousand copies of the Bible or New Testament circulated in Mexico. Many hundreds of children have been educated in Christian schools established by him. More than forty congregations have been gathered in the Republic of Mexico through his efforts. He has secured two magnificent stone churches in the City of Mexico where the Gospel has been preached for years. He has trained up a noble band of able preachers of the pure gospel. He has gi[illegible] nineteen years of his life and his fortune to aid in building up th[illegible] great work, and he now appeals to his fellow Christians to contrib[illegible] th[illegible] monthly income needed to continue it effectively

Dear friends, will you not only contin[illegible] to contribute to this good work yourselves, but also encourage others [illegible] do the same. Some may not be able to contribute monthly but c[illegible] do so occasionally. Occasional gifts are most thankfully received. [illegible] ay for the work, and that many may be moved to befriend it.

With best Chsistian wishes, I [illegible] your brother in Christ,

A. D. MAINE.

Vol. XI., No. 39. Office, 63 Bible House, N. Y. THURSDAY, SEPTEMBER 27, 1888. Price, 3 Cents. Annual Subscription, $1.50.

CONTENTS OF THIS NUMBER.

[P]ICTURE OF THE FATAL STEAMSHIP COLLISION OFF SABLE ISLAND.
[S]UPERFLUITIES A HINDERANCE. Dr. Talmage's Sermon last Sunday Morning.
[A]NECDOTES RELATED AT RECENT EVANGELISTIC MEETINGS.
[D]ANIEL'S VISION OF FOUR WILD BEASTS.
NOTABLE CONVERSIONS IN NEW YORK.
A RESCUE FROM THE STREETS.
A Remarkable Service in Madagascar, etc.
Gems from New Books: A Girl's Picture.—The Poison-Oak.—A Slave's Prayer.
PORTRAITS AND LIVES OF PROF. HENRY DRUMMOND AND THE LATE DR. MACKENZIE AND PROF. RICHARD A. PROCTOR.
CROSSING THE JORDAN. A New Sermon by Rev. C. H. Spurgeon.
EDWARD WILSON'S RESTORATION (With Illustration).
THE EPOCHS OF A LIFE. A New Serial Story by Rev. L. S. Keyser (Continued).
THE COMMISSION OF JOSHUA. By Mrs. M. Baxter.

The Fatal Collision Between the Thingvalla and the Geiser, off Sable Island, N. S.

THE FATAL STEAMSHIP COLLISION
OF THE "THINGVALLA" AND THE "GEISER."

THE terrible maritime disaster, briefly reported in a previous number of this journal, and which is now portrayed in the picture on the first page, will long be sadly memorable in many a home on both sides of the Atlantic. It is now learned that when the *Geiser* sank under the terrible blow from the prow of the *Thingvalla*, no less than 118 persons lost their lives.

The *Geiser* was an iron screw-steamer of 2,831 gross tons, built at Copenhagen in 1881; and the *Thingvalla*, an iron screw-steamer of 2,524 gross tons, built at Copenhagen in 1874. Both steamers belong to the Thingvalla line, are owned in Copenhagen, and run between that port and New York. The *Thingvalla* was on her voyage from Copenhagen to New York, while the *Geiser* was proceeding eastward. The *Geiser* had ninety-three passengers and fifty-six crew, out of whom seventy-nine of the passengers and thirty-nine of the crew were drowned—one hundred and eighteen in all. She left New York for Copenhagen, Christiana, and Stettin on Saturday morning, August 11, and the vessel was off Sandy Hook by noon that day. The weather was fine, and by nightfall the vessel was hull down and speeding toward her destination.

Captain Muller did not leave the bridge for rest until Monday evening at eleven o'clock. The weather was at that time fair. Second Officer Jergensen was left in charge of the bridge, with instructions, the captain said, to wake him at twelve o'clock if nothing occurred in the meantime. This was done, and the captain, saying that at four he would take a sounding, went to sleep again. He knew no more, until he was awakened by

The Crash of the Collision,

a little before daybreak. It was during one of the dark moments before dawn that the two steamers approached each other, unknown to the officers on the bridges. The collision was only a matter of a few moments. The vessels were not running at full speed, but it did not need an experienced eye to tell what the crash would result in. The officers gave hurried orders, and the *Geiser's* helm was forced hard to starboard, and the *Thingvalla's* to port, while the engines were promptly reversed. It was afterward discovered that had these orders been reversed, the collision would not have occurred. If the *Geiser* had not reversed her engines, she would have shot safely across the *Thingvalla's* bows, while if the *Thingvalla's* helm had not been turned to port she would have just grazed the *Geiser's* side. This fact shows that there is urgent need for a better code of signals being adopted. The alarm had barely been given to the officers below, and they were not fairly awake, and nearly all the passengers and many of the crew were still fast asleep, when the prow of the *Thingvalla*,

Towering High Above Her Sister Ship,

plunged into the starboard side of the *Geiser* with a terrific crash and a tremendous shock. The scenes that followed no pen can describe. There was a momentary stillness, and then the hoarse cries of men, mingled with the agonizing screams of women and the wails of children, were heard distinctly above the roaring wind. The inter-locked vessels separated in a few minutes, and the rift of light which betokened the breaking of day disclosed in a measure the damage done. In both steamers there was a huge hole. That of the *Geiser* was large enough to drive three elephants through abreast. It extended from below the water-line clean to the bulwarks and half-way across the beam. The forward cabin had been smashed like a paper-box, and it is believed that on board the *Geiser* a score or more

Sleeping Passengers were Killed Outright,

or battered into insensibility. The bow of the *Thingvalla* was broken some distance below the deck, and torn open to the water-line, making a gap not less than 25 feet square. It made her bow look in the early morning light like the stern of a vessel with the rudder gone, and a big block of the hull chopped away. When the *Thingvalla's* bow was withdrawn by the reverse action of the wheel, one of the officers of the *Geiser* was discovered clinging to the chains.

Captain Moller, of the "Geiser,"

did his best to control the crew and clear away the life-boats and other life-saving apparatus, but there was so much excitement that he was only partly successful. The life-raft was launched, and there was a scramble to get to it. Many men leaped into the sea to reach it, and a few women and children were lowered to it in safety. There was such a rush for the life-boats that the seamen were hampered in their work, and in two cases at least the davits were broken at one end, and the boats became suspended and useless. A large number of the frantic persons had the presence of mind to find life-belts and put them on before jumping overboard. To the survivors and those on board the *Thingvalla* it seemed barely five minutes after the collision that the *Geiser* settled; and after rocking to and fro like a cradle, disappeared like a chip in the vortex of the Niagara whirlpool. The life-raft, with its human freight and many persons struggling in the water, was engulfed. The raft came to the surface, but there was no one on it.

Captain Moller was lying on a sofa when the alarm was given, and ran up on the bridge with his trousers in his hand. "I saw at once (he says) that the *Geiser* would go down, and shouted to the men on deck, 'Call all hands and get out the boats!' We instantly sent up rockets and burned lights. The first life-boat on the starboard side was launched. The man in charge, after lowering the tackle, lost his hold of the line, and her stern fell in the water, and she filled. The second boat was lowered, but the people were afraid to leap into her, as she was some feet away from the ship's side. I shouted to the men who were amidships to get the women and children into the boats first, and

My Crew Behaved Admirably,

keeping cool and collected, while the wildest excitement prevailed among the terrified passengers. They came rushing up the companion-ladders pell-mell. I shouted to them to bring up life-belts, which were stowed in racks down the centre of the steerage, and could be picked up by any one with ease, even in the greatest hurry. They, however, were too much excited. There were over 700 of these belts in the ship, all within reach of the passengers. When I saw that they did not avail themselves of the belts, I threw down on the deck to them six life-belts kept on the bridge for the safety of the officers. The steamer settled very fast. I climbed on the bridge-rail and stood there. The ship gave a plunge, and I felt her go from under me like the whirlpool created by the displacement of the water. I felt myself drawn down by the suction, and was whirled round in the eddy, but did not lose consciousness. I was fully a minute under water, and when I came to the surface there were numbers of people and a large quantity of wreckage floating. I swam about for thirty-five minutes, when I was picked up by one of the *Thingvalla's* boats."

The Third Officer of the "Geiser,"

Jorgin D. Petersen, who was the officer on the watch when the terrible accident took place, tells a story. He says: "I had just come upon my watch on the bridge when the collision occurred. No sooner had I gone on the bridge when the crash came. I ran down on deck and tried to assist in making clear the first boat I came to. As soon as the boat got down to the water it capsized. Almost as soon as the collision occurred, the captain, who had been below in his berth, was on the bridge and in command. After the first boat capsized I went to assist the second boat to get clear of the vessel. Before I got to the boat a number of boatmen and passengers were trying to get it off. This also capsized when it got to the water. I ran forward on the deck and found some assistant engineers and firemen trying to get away the life-raft. At this moment the vessel began to sink with terrible rapidity, and the people were jumping overboard. There was nothing to stay on the steamer for now, and I jumped overboard, too. When I came to the surface there was no trace of the *Geiser*. I swam to an upturned boat, and after I had been clinging to it a little while, I heard some one shouting out. The semi-darkness prevented me from seeing who it was. I thought I recognized the captain's voice, and grabbed a life-belt. I threw it to him. He missed it. I grabbed another, and he missed this, too. He caught the third one, and then, with the aid of two oars that I found floating on the water, I assisted him to the upturned boat, and we all clung to it. As soon as the *Thingvalla* pulled out of the collision she began to assist in saving life. One of her boats came to us, but the captain said:

"No; Save Everybody Else First."

The captain was the last man to leave the sinking ship. He stayed upon the bridge until the ship went down, and when it did he went down with it. We were finally picked up by the *Thingvalla*. I should say that five, six, or seven minutes elapsed between the time of the collision and the time I jumped into the water.

The Officers of the "Thingvalla"

after all the struggling creatures who were in sight had been picked up, and the condition of their own boat had been ascertained, ran up signals of distress, for they found that it would be hazardous, with their original load of 455 passengers, and with thirty-one persons from the *Geiser*, to make for port. At last

They Were Sighted by the "Wieland,"

The work of removing the passengers then began, and some hours were necessary to accomplish the task; as not only had the rescued people from the *Geiser* to be taken off, but, by the desire of the captain of the *Thingvalla*, the passengers of that vessel had also to be conveyed to New York. His ship's disabled condition, he said, made it dangerous for him to attempt to reach port with them. The *Wieland* had 113 cabin and 455 steerage passengers of her own, bound for New York from Hamburg, but Captain Albers, without hesitation, agreed to receive from the *Thingvalla* her 455 passengers, as well as fourteen passengers and seventeen sailors of the *Geiser*, bringing the *Wieland's* passenger list up to 1,054. The *Thingvalla* then slowly, and in momentary danger of sinking, turned around stern foremost to avoid the rush of water into the hole in her bows, and made for Halifax, N. S., where she arrived the next day. In an interview with a reporter,

Captain Laub, of the "Thingvalla"

said: "Everything went well, until shortly after 4 o'clock on Tuesday morning. I was in bed. The second officer relieved the first officer at 4 o'clock and was in charge of the ship. Fifteen or twenty minutes past 4 o'clock I awakened by hearing him shout, 'Port the helm!' At the same moment I heard the signal ring, 'Reverse engines.' I jumped out of my birth and rushed on deck in my night-clothes. Just as I arrived there, a tremendous crash took place which made the *Thingvalla* quiver like a leaf in an autumn storm. We had cut a big steamer almost in two, striking her fair amidships. Our bow was under her mainmast.

"My first duty was to my own ship and passengers. I ran aft, ordered the boats to be ready for launching, and quieted my passengers as far as I could. Then I went forward to ascertain what damages we had sustained. Minutes seem like hours at such a crisis, and then again, half an hour seems to be but a minute. Therefore I cannot give you the exact time that elapsed during that thrilling time, but before I got on the bridge from ordering the boats ready the *Thingvalla*, whose engines were now going at full speed astern, had torn herself clear of the huge monster which hung on her bow. The lights on both steamers were burning and there was no fog. The day was just breaking and rain was falling.

"When I got on the bridge, after ordering the boats launched, I found there the second fficer of the ship with which we had collided, nd then I learned that she was our sister ship, he *Geiser*, of the same line. Our bows had cut nto his stateroom, and as we tore out of the ole he climbed up our anchor chains and umped aboard. Our crew and passengers behaved well under the trying circumstances.

"No human tongue can describe the scene when the *Gieser* went down. The last two mintes before that ill-fated vessel was swallowed p in the sea would baffle the imagination of Rider Haggard. It was a hundred times worse han the most thrilling romances of the sea that have ever read. The wild shouts from the illated people on the *Geiser* were deafening, and wail of despair rang out upon the morning ir that made my hair stand on end, and almost roze the blood in my veins. I can hear the mad hrieks of the drowning even now. This cry of renzy from a hundred and fifty strong men and rail women lasted two minutes.

An Appalling Silence.

"Then an appalling silence prevailed. The ilence was more awful than the never to be forotten two minutes, if that were possible. The *Geiser* had been swallowed up. The suction of he vortex she created had engulfed everything ithin reach. Some of the crew say she broke n two before she foundered, but I doubt this. I hink many of the passengers were mangled and illed in their berths and probably never knew hat struck them. Others, who were swept or umped overboard, were drawn down by the uction of the sinking vessel, became entangled ith the wreckage, and never rose to the surface.

"Many of those who were picked up were ound clinging to the keels of the *Geiser's* capized boats. Others were floating on pieces of reck. As soon as the *Geiser* sank, our three oats were out and picked up all that could be een floating—some thirty-one. These were aken on board, and the boats cruised around or two hours thereafter, but could find nothing ut the body of a woman, a steerage passenger, mong the débris.

"Some of the survivors had thrilling escapes. he third engineer had his arm broken during he collision. With the first and second engieers he got on a life-raft. Strange to say, the isabled man was saved, and the other two were rowned."

The boatswain of the *Geiser* caught hold of a oat when he came up. He helped the doctor nd two passengers upon the upturned boat, nd then feeling something clutch his ankle, nd fearing sharks, he jerked up his leg. It was *woman's hand* clutching his ankle, but the oor creature let go and sank. The boatswain dded that he still felt those fingers clutching im. Two people hung on to his oilcloth coat, ut one let go, and was lost.

Most of those on board the *Geiser* were northestern farmers in well-to-do circumstances, ho, having formerly emigrated from Germany America, were returning to visit their native nd; some, it is said, intending to pay a visit the Copenhagen Exhibition.

A Strange Premonition.

The wife of Martin Seehuns, of Chicago, was e of the passengers in the ill-fated steamship *Geiser*. Mr. Seehuns burst into tears when the d news of his bereavement was made known him by a reporter. He was anxious to learn e particulars, and with tears still in his eyes ld the dramatic story which follows: "We re married five years ago at Christiana, Norway, her home," he said. "My wife's father is Lutheran minister of that city. Eight days ter the wedding we started for Chicago. She as going to visit her home for the first time nce then. She had a premonition that she ould not reach home, and talked of waiting til the next steamer. I insisted that she ould go on this to avoid the fall storms. I sh I had not. I dreamed last night the vesl she was on had sunk. She was the best immer in the Christiana Natatorium, but I n't glean much hope from that, for a woman the ocean waves is but a feather.

ANECDOTES RELATED AT RECENT EVANGELISTIC MEETINGS.

Hearing Restored in Answer to Prayer.—Mr. D. Forbes related at a gospel service: "I knew a young lady who was very unwell, and to the grief of herself and her friends it was found that her illness was affecting her hearing, and at length she became entirely deaf. A Christian gentleman, fearing that she might die without again having the salvation of Christ pressed upon her, felt himself moved to wrestle with God that she might have her hearing restored. He prayed earnestly by the sick-bed for that object, then sat down to wait an answer. About fifteen minutes afterwards she asked that friend to tell her about Christ. 'You can hear, then?' he said, turning to her. She replied, 'Yes.' Her sense of hearing continued for three months, when she fell asleep in Jesus; for during that time she had used the sense that God had restored to drink in the precious truths of His salvation. Such is the power of God in answer to believing prayer."

Mother "as Bad as Maggie."—The Rev. Mr. Gullan says: "On one occasion I visited a young girl who had been converted to Christ at one of our meetings. Speaking to her mother of her I said, 'Do you see any difference in Maggie since her conversion?' 'Yes, indeed I do, sir,' she replied. 'She is not half so careful of me now. She used never to leave the house until it was neat and clean, and now she is not so careful as to how she leaves it; she must be out to this meeting and that meeting; I would rather have Maggie as she used to be.' Thus she prejudiced her mother against religion. Some time afterwards the mother also gave her heart to Jesus, and when next I visited her I inquired, 'Is Maggie improved now?' She looked up with a smile as she answered, 'I am just about the same as Maggie now. I find myself not so precise and fidgety as to how I leave things, that I may go and hear more of my dear Saviour's love.' Both made a mistake. They could have served God just as well cleaning the house as out at a gospel meeting. Probably the neighbors, seeing the untidy, dirty house, would be inclined to blame religion for it."

The Drowning Sailor's Cry.—A Christian sailor thus testifies: "The immediate cause of my conversion to Christ was a story I heard when by seeming accident I wandered into a Gospel meeting. It was an old sea-captain who was speaking, and he was relating the sad death of one who had served under him on board ship. The man was known to be the most reckless and wicked of the whole crew. No danger was too great for him to face, though the least prepared to meet God. A great storm overtook the vessel; for a time she battled bravely with the elements, but soon it became evident that she would sink. Their only hope was in the boats. This seaman got into one to assist in its being lowered, but through some accident it was not lowered properly, and the man precipitated into the seething sea, which was far too rough to admit of rescue being possible, or even attempted. They saw him strike out manfully for a few strokes, then, as the waves overwhelmed him, he threw up his hands and cried aloud, so as to be heard by all on board, 'Lord, save me for Jesus' sake.' That story took great hold of me, and by God's grace, it was the means of causing me also to come to Christ."

John's "Hurrah for Jesus!"—Mr. Fergueson relates: "There is a converted fisherman in the north of Scotland formerly known by the name of 'Drunken John,' and well he deserved the name. At night he was generally to be found in the saloon, from which he emerged at closing-time to reel home to his wretched dwelling and miserable wife. One night he left the saloon earlier than usual, and as he wandered homeward he came upon a large and well-lighted building. He stepped inside, and found himself in an evangelistic meeting. He mechanically sat down, and during the address he fell asleep. He awoke quite sober, and rose to go out; but a gentleman stopped him and conversed with him, the result being that before he left the place he had professed to accept Christ. The first words he said, when he arrived home, were, 'Wife, I am converted.' 'Drunk as usual,' she quietly remarked. 'Oh, Mary; if you do not believe it, come, let us pray, and thank God for His goodness.' His wife approached, and knelt beside her husband. But though he could swear, he could not pray. He knelt there for some time, unable to utter one word. At last, jumping to his feet and throwing his bonnet in the air, he exclaimed, 'Hurrah for Jesus!' That was his prayer, and God would understand it."

A Doctor's Appalling Condition.—"In 1874 I met a doctor who was in great concern about his soul, but he determined to shake off the impression. Passing down a street in the city one day, he suddenly came upon an open-air evangelistic meeting. He stopped and listened; a workingman was speaking, and though the tone of voice was not cultured, nor the speaker eloquent, the words were the words of God, and went home with power. Until that time he had not believed in conversion, but now he saw there was a real turning to God and trusting in Him, followed by an inward assurance of salvation. As the doctor himself has said: 'I would not tell any one what my thoughts were at that time. I felt the Holy Spirit working in me, but I refused to surrender, and resolved to put Christ from me!' In 1880 I again met this same gentleman. Talking of our former acquaintanceship and of his anxiety about his soul, I asked him if he had now found peace in Christ. 'No,' he replied, 'I have not. Often have I wished I could get the same impressions that I had many years ago, but they never returned. Then everything was so clear, and the road so open, but now the way seems shut, and I know it is too late. The day of mercy has passed for me. That was my last chance, and it is gone.' That man still lives, not able to give himself to Christ."

The Text at the Railway Station.—"A few years ago a young gentleman in London found himself suddenly put into possession of a large fortune, which like a prodigal he straightway began to waste in riotous living. He entered into all kinds of sin and dissipation, and not content with destroying his own soul, he set himself to ruin another. He had a female companion, upon whom in his generous moods he lavished all she could desire. One day, when he was from home he felt a desire for her company, and at once sent word for her to come to him. Obedient to his command, she at once set out, but when she arrived at the railway station, she found the train was not due for a few minutes. Walking into the waiting-room she carelessly glanced round, and on the wall she saw the text, 'God so loved the world,' etc. It was like a flash of light from the glory land right into her hard, wicked heart, revealing the love of God to her lost and degraded soul. Straight to the bookstall she went and demanded a Bible. Being asked what kind, she replied, 'It does not matter so long as it has that text, "God so loved the world," etc., in it.' The stall-keeper, who knew Christ himself, handed her a Bible, and carefully marked the text. All the way in the train she read eagerly, the Holy Spirit applying the word, and before she had completed her journey she had found forgiveness in Jesus Christ. 'O, Captain,' she cried, when she met him, 'I am saved! God has shown me His great love, and now our old life of sin must cease.' He offered her great wealth if she would but stay with him. 'No,' she answered, 'I will never meet you again until it is before the Great White Throne of Christ.' That lady is now one of the brightest Christian workers in London."

SUPERFLUITIES A HINDERANCE.

Dr. Talmage's Sermon, Preached last Sunday Morning, September 23, 1888.

"A man of great stature, whose fingers and toes were four and twenty, six on each hand, and six on each foot: and he also was the son of a giant. But when he defied Israel, Jonathan the son of Shimea, David's brother, slew him." 1 Chron. 20:6, 7.

Modern Instances of Superabundant Extremities—Neither Stature nor Digits Saved the Giant—The Work Done by Ordinary People—The Swamp Angel and the Peacemaker—The Value of Common Lawyers and Physicians—Superfluous Wealth—A King who Became a Porter—Financial Obesity—Peter Cooper's Remedy—Paulo-Post Future Benevolence—The Magnificent Ordinary Equipment—Gospel Handshaking—The Wonders of the Foot—Where to Walk—Three Women in Rivalry.

MALFORMATION photographed, and for what reason? Did not this passage slip in by mistake into the sacred Scriptures, as sometimes a paragraph utterly obnoxious to the editor gets into his newspaper during his absence? Is not this Scriptural errata? No, no; there is nothing haphazard about the Bible. This passage of Scripture was as certainly intended to be put in the Bible as the passage, "In the beginning God created the heavens and the earth," or, "God so loved the world that He gave His only begotten Son."

And I select it for my text to-day because it is charged with practical and tremendous meaning. By the people of God the Philistines had been conquered, with the exception of a few giants. The race of giants is mostly extinct, I am glad to say. There is

No Use for Giants Now

except to enlarge the income of museums. But there were many of them in olden times. Goliath was, according to the Bible, eleven feet, four and a half inches high. Or, if you do not believe the Bible, the famous Pliny, a secular writer, declares that at Crete, by an earthquake, a monument was broken open, discovering the remains of a giant forty-six cubits long, or sixty-nine feet high. So, whether you prefer sacred or profane history, you must come to the conclusion that there were in those times cases of human altitude monstrous and appalling.

David had smashed the skull of one of these giants, but there were other giants that the Davidean wars had not yet subdued, and one of them stands in my text. He was not only of alpine stature, but had a surplus of digits. To the ordinary fingers was annexed an additional finger, and the foot had also a superfluous addendum. He had twenty-four terminations to hands and feet, where others have twenty. It was not the only instance of the kind. Tavernier, the learned writer, says that the Emperor of Java had a son endowed with the same number of extremities. Volcatius, the poet, had six fingers on each hand. Maupertuis in his celebrated letters, speaks of two families near Berlin, similarly equipped of hand and foot. All of which I can believe, for I have seen two cases of the same physical superabundance. But this giant of the text is in battle, and as David, the dwarf warrior, had despatched one giant, the brother of David slays this monster of my text, and there he lies after the battle in Gath,

A Dead Giant.

His stature did not save him, and his superfluous appendices of hand and foot did not save him. The probability was that in the battle his sixth finger on his hand made him clumsy in the use of his weapon, and his sixth toe crippled his gait. Behold the prostrate and malformed giant of the text: "A man great of stature, whose fingers and toes were four and twenty, six on each hand, and six on each foot: and he also was the son of a giant. But when he defied Israel, Jonathan, the son of Shimea, David's brother, slew him."

Behold how superfluities are a hinderance rather than a help! In all the battle at Gath that day there was not a man with ordinary hand and ordinary foot and ordinary stature that was not better off than this physical curiosity of my text. As physical size is apt to run in families, the probability is that this brother of David, who did the work, was of an abbreviated stature. A dwarf on the right side is stronger than a giant on the wrong side, and all the body and mind and estate and opportunity that you cannot use for God and the betterment of the world is a sixth finger and a sixth toe, and a terrific hinderance. The most of the good done in the world, and the most of

Those who Win the Battles

for the right, are ordinary people. Count the fingers of their right hand, and they have just five, no more and no less. One Doctor Duff among missionaries, but three thousand missionaries that would tell you they have only common endowment. One Florence Nightingale to nurse the sick in conspicuous places, but ten thousand women who are just as good nurses, though never heard of. The Swamp Angel was a big gun that during the war made a big noise, but muskets of ordinary calibre and shells of ordinary heft did the execution. President Tyler and his Cabinet go down the Potomac one day to experiment with the Peacemaker, a great iron gun that was to affright with its thunder foreign navies. The gunner touches it off, and it explodes, and leaves Cabinet Ministers dead on the deck, while at that time, all up and down our coasts, were cannon of ordinary bore, able to be the defence of the nation, and ready at the first touch to waken to duty. The curse of the world is big guns. After the politicians, who have made all the noise, go home hoarse from angry discussion on the evening of the first Monday in November, the next day the people, with the silent ballots, will settle everything, and settle it right; a million of the white slips of paper they drop making about as much noise as the fall of an apple-blossom.

Clear back in the country to-day there are mothers in plain apron, and shoes fashioned on a rough last by the shoemaker at the end of the lane, rocking babies that are to be the Martin Luthers and the Faradays and the Edisons and the Bismarcks and the Gladstones and the Washingtons and the George Whitefields of the future. The longer I live, the more

I Like Common Folks.

They do the world's work, bearing the world's burdens, weeping the world's sympathies, carrying the world's consolation. Among lawyers, we see rise up a Rufus Choate, or a William Wirt, or a Samuel L. Southand, but society would go to pieces to-morrow if there were not thousands of common lawyers to see that men and women get their rights. A Valentine Mott or a Willard Parker rises up eminent in the medical profession, but what an unlimited sweep would pneumonia and diphtheria and scarlet fever have in the world if it were not for ten thousand common doctors. The old physician in his gig, rolling up the lane of the farm-house, or riding on horseback, his medicines in the saddle-bags, arriving on the ninth day of the fever, and coming in to take hold of the pulse of the patient, while the family, pale with anxiety, are looking on and waiting for his decision in regard to the patient, and hearing him say, "Thank God, I have mastered the case; he is getting well!" excites in me an admiration quite equal to the mention of the names of the great metropolitan doctors, Pancoast or Gross or Joseph C. Hutchinson of the past, or the illustrious living men of the present.

Yet what do we see in all departments? People not satisfied with ordinary spheres of work and ordinary duties. Instead of trying to see what they can do with a hand of five fingers, they want six. Instead of usual endowment of twenty manual and pedal addenda, they want twenty-four. A certain amount of money for livelihood, and for the supply of those whom we leave behind us after we have departed this life, is important, for we have the best authority for saying, "He that provideth not for his own, and especially those of his own household, is worse than an infidel"; but the large and fabulous sums for which many struggle, if obtained, would be a hinderance rather than an advantage. The anxieties and annoyances of those whose

Estates have Become Plethoric

can only be told by those who possess them. It will be a good thing when, through your industry and public prosperities, you can own the house in which you live. But suppose you own fifty houses, and you have all those rents to collect, and all those tenants to please. Suppose you have branched out in business successes until in almost every direction you have investments. The fire-bell rings at night, you rush up-stairs to look out of the window, to see if it is any of your mills. Epidemic of crime comes, and there are embezzlements and abscondings in all directions, and you wonder whether any of your book-keepers will prove recreant. A panic strikes the financial world, and you are like a hen under a sky full of hawks, and trying with anxious cluck to get your overgrown chickens safely under wing. After a certain stage of success has been reached, you have to trust so many important things to others that you are apt to become the prey of others, and you are swindled and defrauded, and the anxiety you had on your brow when you were earning your first thousand dollars is not equal to the anxiety on your brow now that you have won your three hundred thousand.

The trouble with such a one is he is spread out like the unfortunate one in my text. You have more fingers and toes than you know what to do with. Twenty were useful, twenty-four is a hindering superfluity. Disraeli says that

A King of Poland

abdicated his throne and joined the people, and became a porter to carry burdens. And some one asked him why he did so, and he replied "Upon my honor, gentlemen, the load which I quit was by far heavier than the one you see me carry. The weightiest is but a straw, when compared to that world under which I labored. I have slept more in four nights than I have during all my reign. I begin to live and to b[e] a king myself. Elect whom you choose. A[s] for me, I am so well it would be madness to return to court."

"Well," says somebody, "such overloaded persons ought to be pitied, for their worriments are real, and their insomnia and their nervou[s] prostration are genuine." I reply that the[y] could get rid of the bothersome surplus by giving it away. If a man has more houses than he can carry without vexation, let him drop a fe[w] of them. If his estate is so great he cann[ot] manage it without getting nervous dyspeps[ia] from having too much, let him divide up wi[th] those who have nervous dyspepsia because the[y] cannot get enough. No! they guard their sixth finger with more care than they did the original five. They go limping with what they c[all] gout, and know not that, like the giant of m[y] text, they are lamed by a superfluous toe. A fe[w] of them by charities bleed themselves of thi[s]

Financial Obesity

and monetary plethora, but many of the[m] hang on to the hindering superfluity till deat[h] and then, as they are compelled to give the mon[ey] up anyhow, in their last will and testament th[ey] generously give some of it to the Lord, expe[ct]ing, no doubt, that He will feel very much obl[ig]ed to them. Thank God that once in a wh[ile] we have a Peter Cooper, who, owning an inter[est] in the iron works at Trenton, said to Mr. L[...]ter: "I do not feel quite easy about the amo[unt] we are making. Working under one of c[...] patents, we have a monopoly which seems to [...] something wrong. Everybody has to come [to] us for it, and we are making money too fa[st]." So they reduced the price, and this while [the] philanthropist was building Cooper Institu[te,] which mothers a hundred institutes of kindn[ess] and mercy all over the land. But the world [...] to wait five thousand eight hundred years [...] Peter Cooper!

I am glad for the benevolent institutions t[hat] get a legacy from men who during their [...] were as stingy as death, but who in their last [...] and testament bestowed money on hospitals issionary societies; but for such testators I ave no respect. They would have taken every ent of it with them if they could, and bought p half of heaven and let it out at ruinous rent, r loaned the money to celestial citizens at two er cent. a month, and got a corner on harps nd trumpets. They lived in this world fifty or ixty years in the presence of appalling suffering nd want, and made no effort for their relief. 'he charities of such people are in

"Paulo-Post Future" Tense,

nd they are going to do them. The probabil-ty is that if such a one in his last will by a do-ation to benevolent societies tries to atone for is lifetime close-fistedness, the heirs-at-law will ry to break the will by proving that the old ian was senile or crazy, and the expense of the itigation will about leave in the lawyers' hands 'hat was meant for the American Bible Society.) ye overweighted, successful business men, 'hether this sermon reach your ear or your yes, let me say that if you are prostrated with nxieties about keeping or investing these tre-iendons fortunes, I can tell you how you can o more to get your health back and your spir-s raised than by drinking gallons of bad-tast-ng water at Saratoga, Homburg, or Carlsbad—ive to God, humanity, and the Bible ten per ent. of all your income, and it will make a new ian of you, and from restless walking of the loor at night you shall have eight hours sleep, 'ithout the help of bromide of potassium, and rom no appetite you will hardly be able to wait our regular meals, and your wan cheek will fill p, and when you die the blessings of those who ut for you would have perished will bloom all ver your grave.

Perhaps some of you will take this advice, but he most of you will not. And you will try to ure your swollen hand by getting on it more ingers, and your rheumatic foot by getting on t more toes, and there will be a sigh of relief 'hen you are gone out of the world; and when ver your remains the minister recites the words: 'Blessed are the dead who die in the Lord," ersons who have keen appreciation of the ludi-rous will hardly be able to keep their faces traight. But whether in that direction my 'ords do good, or not, I am anxious that all 'ho have only

Ordinary Equipment

e thankful for what they have and rightly em-loy it. I think you all have, figuratively as well s literally, fingers enough. Do not long for indering superfluities. Standing in the pres-nce of this fallen giant of my text, and in this ost-mortem examination of him, let us learn ow much better off we are with just the usual and, the usual foot. You have thanked God or a thousand things, but I warrant you never hanked Him for those two implements of work nd locomotion, that no one but the Infinite nd Omnipotent God could have ever planned r made—the hand and the foot. Only that sol-lier or that mechanic who in a battle, or through nachinery, has lost them knows anything about heir value, and only the Christian scientist can ave any appreciation of what divine master-pieces they are.

Sir Charles Bell, the English surgeon, on the attle-field of Waterloo, while engaged in ampu-ations of the wounded, was so impressed with he wondrous construction of the human hand hat when the Earl of Bridgewater gave forty housand dollars for essays on the wisdom and oodness of God, and eight books were written, Sir Charles Bell wrote his entire book on the wisdom and goodness of God as displayed in he human hand. The twenty-seven bones in and and wrist with cartilages and ligaments nd phalanges of the fingers all made just ready o knit, to sew, to build up, to pull down, to weave, to write, to plow, to pound, to wheel, to attle, to give friendly salutation. The tips of its fingers are so many telegraph offices by rea-son of their sensitiveness of touch. The bridg-s, the tunnels, the cities of the whole earth are

The Victories of the Hand.

The hands are not dumb, but often speak as distinctly as the lips. With our hands we in-vite, we repel, we invoke, we entreat, we wring them in grief, or clap them in joy, or spread them abroad in benediction. The malformation of the giant's hand in the text glorifies the usual hand. Fashioned of God more exquisitely and wondrously than any human mechanicism that was ever contrived, I charge you use it for God, and the lifting of the world out of its moral pre-dicament. Employ it in the sublime work of *gospel handshaking*. You can see the hand is just made for that. Four fingers just set right to touch your neighbor's hand on one side, and your thumb set so as to clench it on the other side. By all its bones and joints and muscles and cartilages and ligaments the voice of na-ture joins with the voice of God commanding you to shake hands. The custom is as old as the Bible, anyhow. Jehu said to Jehonadab: "Is thine heart right as my heart is with thine heart? If it be, give me thine hand." When hands join in Christian salutation a gospel elec-tricity thrills across the palm from heart to heart, and from the shoulder of one to the shoulder of the other.

Shake Hands all Around.

With the timid and for their encouragement, shake hands. With the troubled and in warm-hearted sympathy, shake hands. With the young man just entering business, and dis-couraged at the small sales and the large ex-penses, shake hands. With the child who is new from God and started on unending jour-ney, for which he needs to gather great supply of strength, and who can hardly reach up to you now, because you are so much taller, shake hands. Across cradles and dying beds and graves, shake hands. With your enemies, who have done all to defame and hurt you, but whom you can afford to forgive, shake hands. At the door of churches where people come in, and at the door of churches where people go out, shake hands. Let pulpit shake hands with pew, and Sabbath-day shake hands with week-day, and earth shake hands with heaven. Oh the strange, the mighty, the undefined, the mysterious, the eternal power of an honest handshaking! The difference between these times and the millennial times is that now some shake hands, but then all will shake hands, throne and foot-stool, across seas na-tion with nation, God and man, church mili-tant and church triumphant.

Yea; the malformation of this fallen giant's foot glorifies

The Ordinary Foot,

for which I fear you have never once thanked God. The twenty-six bones of the foot are the admiration of the anatomist. The arch of the foot fashioned with a grace and a poise that Trajan's arch at Beneventum, or Constantine's arch at Rome, or Arch of Triumph at the end of Champs Elysées could not equal. Those arches stand where they were planted, but this arch of the foot is an adjustable arch, a yield-ing arch, a flying arch, and ready for move-ments innumerable. The human foot so fash-ioned as to enable man to stand upright as no other creature, and leave the hand that would otherwise have to help in balancing the body free for anything it chooses. The foot of the camel fashioned for the sand, the foot of the bird fashioned for the tree-branch, the foot of the hind fashioned for the slippery rock, the foot of the lion fashioned to rend its prey, the foot of the horse fashioned for the solid earth, but the foot of man made to cross the desert, or climb the tree, or scale the cliff, or walk the earth, or go anywhere he needs to go. With that divine triumph of anatomy in your possession

Where do You Walk?

In what path of righteousness or what path of sin have you set it down? Where have you left the mark of your footsteps? Amid the pet-rifactions in the rocks have been found the mark of the feet of birds and beasts of thou-sands of years ago. And God can trace out all the footsteps of your lifetime, and those you made fifty years ago are as plain as those made in the last soft weather, all of them petrified for the Judgment day. Oh, the foot! Give me the autobiography of your foot from the time you stepped out of the cradle until to-day, and I will tell your exact character now and what are your prospects for the world to come.

That there might be no doubt about the fact that both these pieces of divine mechanism, hand and foot, belong to Christ's service, both hands of Christ and both feet of Christ were spiked on the cross. Right through the arch of both His feet to the hollow of His instep went the iron of torture, and from the palm of His hand to the back of it, and there is not a muscle or nerve or bone among the twenty-seven bones of hand and wrist, or among the twenty-six bones of the foot, but it belongs to Him now and forever.

That is the most beautiful foot that goes about paths of greatest usefulness, and that the most beautiful hand that does the most to help others. I was reading of

Three Women in Rivalry

about the appearance of the hand. And the one reddened her hand with berries, and said the beautiful tinge made hers the most beauti-ful. And another put her hand in the mountain brook, and said, as the waters dripped off, that her hand was the most beautiful. And another plucked flowers off the bank, and under the bloom contended that her hand was the most attractive. Then a poor old woman appeared, and looking up in her decrepitude asked for alms. And a woman who had not taken part in the rivalry gave her alms. And all the women resolved to leave to this beggar the question as to which of all the hands present was the most attractive, and she said: "The most beautiful of them all is the one that gave relief to my necessities," and as she so said her wrinkles and rags and her decrepitude and her body disap-peared, and in place thereof stood the Christ, who long ago said: "Inasmuch as ye did it to one of the least of these, ye did it to Me!" and who to purchase the service of our hand and foot here on earth or in resurrection state, had His own hand and foot lacerated.

DR. KENNETH MACKENZIE.

(See Portrait on Page 620.)

THE young missionary physician whose por-trait appears on this page died at Tientsin, China, on April 1, this year at the age of thirty-eight years. He was chief of the medical staff in the Missionary Hospital at that place, and was as highly distinguished for his faith and mis-sionary zeal as for his surgical skill. He was one of the brilliant band of university men for whom the foreign mission cause is indebted under God to the labors of Mr. D. L. Moody. He heard the great evangelist in 1873, just as he was completing his studies in Edinburgh, for the medical profession, and was converted. He passed his university examinations in Edinburgh and London with honor, receiving his diploma, and then, instead of entering on a lucrative practice, offered himself as medical missionary.

His first work was done at Hankow, in con-nection with the Rev. Griffith John, whom he accompanied on some of his long journeys of preaching and healing. After four years there, he was called to Tientsin, where he remained until he died. A crisis occurred soon after Dr. Mackenzie's arrival, and a meeting of the medi-cal staff was called to pray for help. Scarcely had the meeting broken up when a request for a foreign doctor came from the Viceroy, whose wife had been given up for death by native phy-sicians. Dr. Mackenzie and Dr. Irwin treated her so successfully that she was completely re-stored to health, and the Viceroy in his gratitude undertook to defray regularly all the expenses of the hospital. After that the hospital work prospered and extended, and Dr. Mackenzie labored in it heart and soul. Early this year, however, he contracted a severe cold, which de-veloped into pneumonia, and on April 1 he died, deeply regretted by all who knew him.

NOTABLE CONVERSIONS IN NEW YORK.

THE following incidents are related by Rev. John Boyd, who assisted in the personal work of the revival services during the recent visit of Rev. Thomas Harrison:

"I'm Coming, Mother."

One evening during the West Side meetings, a young man who came to the church was thrown, after the sermon, into a state of deep concern about his soul by the power of the Spirit. He lost his strength, his body becoming rigid and immovable as a statue, he was carried to a pew and laid down on the cushion by some of the officers of the church. After remaining in that apparently unconscious condition for about thirty minutes, he gradually opened his eyes, and gazing upward with rapt face, he said in a low, earnest, pathetic tone, "I'm coming, mother, I'm coming, mother." It appears that his mother, when on her death-bed, a year or so ago, called him and his brother to her bedside, imploring them to come to the Saviour and meet her in heaven. The other brother had been converted at Mr. Harrison's meeting the previous night, and when he went home with his glad heart and shining face, his testimony was believed, and the subject of these remarks came to the Central M. E. Church, where a vision of heaven, of the faithful mother and of the Lord Jesus Christ, resulted in his conviction, repentance, and salvation.

A Politician's Experience.

On Sunday afternoon, August 26, Mr. Harrison preached from text "*What shall it profit a man if he gain the whole world and lose his own soul?*" The sermon was delivered with unusual convincing and convicting power. At the close, the ordinary invitation was given to sinners who wished to seek the Lord, to come to the altar. Several persons responded promptly, among whom was a gentleman of unusual intelligence, about sixty years of age. He came from the outer edge of the great congregation, deliberately walking down the central aisle. Every eye was fixed upon him. He knelt at the altar, in the straw, in front of the platform.

One of the workers from New York approached him and asked if he was there to seek God and the pardon of his sins. With great deliberation he replied, "I am." "To comply with the conditions you must give your heart to God, as He says to you. 'Son, give me thy heart.' Will you do that?" "I will; I think *I understand the theory* of salvation, but *I want to realize the experience.*" "The first condition is that you give your heart to God. Having done that, He accepts it, and it is therefore His. Your next step is to accept the Lord Jesus Christ as your personal Saviour, and trust Him to save you now. Will you do that?" "I will." "Do you now trust Him?" After a long pause, he replied, "I do." "Jesus says: 'Whosoever cometh unto me I will in no wise cast out,' and on that word you are authorized to believe He receives and pardons you. Can you trust His word to save you now?" "I can." "Do you?" "I do." "Then He saves you. Are you conscious of that fact?" "I am." "Then He saves you now." "He does." "How do you know it?" "I am inwardly conscious of it." "Then praise Him, and go from here saying: 'I am the Lord's, and Jesus is my Saviour.' Now stand on your feet, thus witnessing that you are saved," which he did with beaming face.

At the 6:30 P. M. meeting he was introduced to the audience by the Presiding Elder, as Mr. Downing, ex-District-Attorney of Queens Co., and was requested to address the audience. He said: "I came to Mount Tabor on Saturday for recreation, with no thought of serious matters. I am past sixty years of age, and had many times been impressed with the thought that it was my duty to become a Christian, but had as often put it off. Under the searching sermon of this afternoon I felt that the time had arrived for decisive action, and I presented myself at this bench, seeking the pardon of my sins, and here God, for Christ's sake, has forgiven and accepted me. My past life has been wasted. My great regret is that I did not sooner take this step; and just here let me appeal to you in this audience who like myself may be putting off this important matter, to settle it this very night."

While the speaker was thus addressing the great audience, the marvellous change in the expression of his face was manifest to all. In the afternoon it was sad and gloomy, *now* it was illumined with Divine light.

Mr. Downing was District-Attorney of Queens Co., New York, for six successive terms.

A BACKSLIDER RESTORED.

IN a letter to Dr. Cullis, published in his *Times of Refreshing*, a Christian worker, writing from San Buena Ventura on July 16, says: While I am waiting in the depot here, I will try to write you a few lines. I have to wait nearly three hours. I came this morning to try to find a young man who left Santa Barbara yesterday morning in a very discouraged condition; he was converted three weeks ago and has had a most blessed experience, so triumphant and joyous; but on Saturday his employer abused him, and he was overcome with temper, and then the devil tried to tell him that the Lord had not been faithful to him or He would have kept him from anger, and he got terribly mixed up and left. He did not feel like seeing any of us, but I could not give him up, so I followed him, trusting the Lord to guide me to him, and He did. I met him on the street corner with some young men, and he was surprised to see me. I told him what I was here for, and he gladly went with me to the seashore, where we could have a quiet place for conversation and prayer; and he has returned in sweet trustfulness to the dear Lord, and is to return with me this evening. Do you wonder that I rode thirty miles this morning to find him, lest the adversary should get control of him?

A RESCUE FROM THE STREETS.

A remarkable instance of the power of God working through means apparently insignificant, is related among the reminiscences of the work under the late Dr. Stephen H. Tyng, Sr., when at St. George's, New York. A little, deformed girl, a sufferer from spinal complaint, was converted, and earnestly desired to do something for Christ. In her condition, poor, weak, and suffering, it seemed impossible, but the girl was in earnest about it, and she prayed and thought anxiously. At last she made an effort. She had a few tracts, and going into a side-street, near her home, she planted herself near a house which was given up to vice, and was frequented by notorious women of the more wealthy class.

Presently one of these women, beautiful and richly dressed, emerged and passed the spot where the deformed girl stood. Instantly with an earnest word a tract was placed in her hand. The handsome woman glanced at it, then at the poor, twisted, ill-clad girl, and her face flushed with anger. Some previous annoyance, or possibly the influence of liquor, rendered her less able to control herself, or her womanly feeling must have kept her from cruelty to one so weak and helpless. She raised her hand and struck the girl in the face, felling her to the ground, and then went on her way. It was a brutal act, but the poor girl thought of her Saviour's suffering and patience, and she was glad to suffer in His cause. She remained at her post until a late hour, giving away her tracts to all who came from that haunt of vice.

Night after night the little deformed creature was at her post praying silently for God's blessing, and giving her tracts to all who would accept them. Especially was she anxious that the woman who had struck her should have one, and whenever she saw her, the poor girl with gentle pleading face would hold out the silent messenger of the gospel. It was always rejected with derision, until one night under some unaccountable influence, possibly some reminiscence of other days, or under the direct power of the Holy Spirit, the woman yielded, and the persistent girl was rewarded by the acceptance of the tract; attached to it was an invitation to some gospel services Dr. Tyng was then holding. The woman asked the girl to show her where the services were held. She gladly did so, and the two strange companions, the one lovely in person and splendid in attire, but with her soul dwarfed and hideous by sin; and the other wretched and misshapen of body, but with her soul all-glorious by Christ's transforming power, went into the house of God together.

The vicious woman was that night in the strangely softened, sensitive condition into which such women sometimes fall in the reaction inevitable to artificial excitement, and in her receptive state the Spirit of God carried the gospel message with power to her heart. She went to the preacher at the close of the service and told her story, anxious that she, like the woman who was a sinner in the gospel story, might sit at Jesus' feet. She was assured of acceptance by the Saviour, and was soon rejoicing in the consciousness of pardon. A lady present offered her employment in her own household, and that night took her to her home, where she remained an efficient and faithful help.

A member of the family fell sick, and this rescued woman was installed as nurse. An astonishing gentleness and tenderness and patience, so markedly in contrast with her disposition before her conversion, had characterized her, and it was this which led to her being selected for attendance in the chamber of sickness. During that illness, the woman showed so remarkable an aptitude for the duties that all about her perceived that she had found her place in life. She was a born nurse, patient, vigilant, intelligent; and soon, under training, she became experienced.

During the terrible epidemic of yellow fever in Memphis, Tenn., among the records of heroic self-sacrifice there was one of a nurse from New York who had volunteered for duty. Her labors were incessant, her conduct fearless, her words of Christian appeal effective, and she was called an angel by the poor sufferers in that time of sickness and death, many of whom under her guidance were led to Christ. Her identity was disclosed under sad circumstances. Worn down by long labor and watching, she was seized with the fever, and from the first symptoms it was evident that one so exhausted could not recover. The dying woman so blessed in her labor, so gentle in her ministrations, so successful in alleviating pain and winning souls, was the vicious woman who years ago, in New York, had struck the deformed child for offering her a tract, and had been transformed by the grace of God. Her death is described by those who witnessed it, as one of the most joyful and triumphant that had been seen in the whole course of that awful scourge.

A NOTABLE SERVICE IN MADAGASCAR.

ON March 28 there was observed in the Memorial Church at Antananarivo, the thirty-ninth anniversary of the event which the church was built to commemorate. The large building was crowded to excess, the services lasting from three to four hours. The story relating to the early martyrdoms on the 28th of March, 1849, was rehearsed; how that on that day four Christians were burned alive, and fourteen were hurled from the summit of the precipice on which the Memorial Church is built. Many of the older Christians, including relatives of the martyrs, were seated on the platform and took part in the services. This commemoration of the faith and zeal of the early Christians will, it is believed, help much in stimulating the spiritual life of the present generation of the Malagasy. Various reports are sent of large meetings which have recently been held in different parts of Madagascar, indicating a quickened spiritual life on the part of the people. Yet in some sections of the great island the people are still unsupplied with missionaries, and are constantly calling for them. A native pastor said to a visiting missionary not long since: "We look across to yonder road [the main road from Antananarivo],and when we see a palanquin we have exclaimed for many a long year, 'The missionary has come at last!' But no." Pointing to his hair, he said: "When my hair was yet black and my teeth were sound, we were always looking out for the missionary, and now you see I am a gray-haired old man and many of my teeth are gone, and yet no missionary." But these people, though their longing is not gratified, still hold fast to their Christian faith, and are doing what they can to evangelize their neighbors.

DANIEL'S VISION OF THE FOUR WILD BEASTS.

By Rev. E. Guers.*

Their Rise—The Spirit of Their Rule—The Fourth Empire Founded—Its Reconstruction in a New Form—Its Ten Component Parts—Its Extent—The Little Horn Paramount—Identity With the Beast—Persecutes All Saints—His Malignity Concentrated on the Jews—His Judgment and Destruction.

THE four beasts rise from the "great sea," the name that Scripture gives to the Mediterranean, that sea entirely surrounded by countries composing the prophetical earth. The 2d chapter of Daniel characterizes the power with which the four empires would be invested; the seventh describes the use they would make of it; it represents

The Spirit of Their Rule,

and also marks the cause of their ruin. Four wild beasts! Admirably just emblem! for the empires they describe, the Chaldean, Persian, Grecian, and Roman, would make the same use of the power delegated to them that a wild beast makes of his strength. Woe to the people of God under their rule!

The Chaldean, the Persian, and the Grecian have accomplished their time as empires (seven or eight centuries), but their life has not ended with their rule; their existence as nations must be prolonged indefinitely (ver. 12): "until a time, and an epoch," translates Perret; Osterwald translates, "during a certain time"; the original does not necessarily imply a precise and determined duration.

The Fourth Empire

is that which particularly concerns prophecy: the first three, if I may so use the term, are only present to introduce it. The Roman Empire founded by Augustus Cæsar included in its first form the inheritance of the empires which had preceded it. It continued their part and absorbed them. The emblem of chapter 2d, the statue, could hardly by its nature express what was wanted; but that of the seventh chapter expresses it admirably; in the fourth wild beast we find something of the three first—the lion, the bear, and the leopard (*Comp.* Dan. 7 with Rev. 13: 2.)

The fourth empire still exists in a prophetic point of view. At the beginning of this empire the Messiah appeared in the world. He will again return to earth to destroy it, and to re-establish in its place His glorious reign. The Roman Empire has crucified the Son of God, persecuted the Church, destroyed Jerusalem, dispersed Israel among the nations, but it has not terminated its career. Re-established under an entirely new form,

The Ten Kingdoms Reunited

under one chief, it will again make war against Christ, thus filling up the measure of its iniquities. The blasphemies and the persecutions of its last chief, the little horn, his judgment and his destruction, followed by the universal reign of the Messiah, such are the special subjects of the vision before us; it is the history of royalty, not of priesthood; of secular power concentrated at the end in the hands of a great blasphemer, and not of ecclesiastical power which God has delegated to none; this is the future, not the past of imperial Rome.

It is easy to convince ourselves of this. In truth

The Ten Horns of the Fourth Beast

have the same signification as the ten toes of the statue: they represent ten kingdoms; but as these kingdoms have not yet existed in the emblem of the statue, neither have they existed in that of the fourth beast. They are yet to come. It is a form which the empire, once compact, now broken in pieces, shall assume as soon as it is reconstructed. As in general this vision carries us on to that moment, the time of the last trial and last deliverance of the people of God; Israel has then returned to his own land, and the restored empire justifies in every point the emblem under which it here appears.

That which proves better than anything that the emblem of the ten horns is not yet verified, is the duration assigned to the reign of the little horn. This reign will be terrible, but by a merciful compensation, its duration—at least that of the blasphematory and persecuting period, its last period—will be very short, for it will only be three and a half ordinary years; so soon as these three and a half years shall have elapsed, the beast will be judged, and the Millennium will commence. Prophecy could not explain more clearly that the fourth empire will be re-established towards the end of the present economy, and re-established for a very short time, and for a very odious work. Besides, this confirms the parallel passages (Rev. 13, etc.). To those persons whom

This Future Reconstruction

of the Roman Empire surprises, we simply say, if, as we believe, it is written in the Word of God, it certainly will be accomplished, despite all improbabilities, and even all the impossibilities, our minds are pleased to see; and which of us dare say what may not take place in these days of rapid and wonderful changes, which astonish the wisest? Integrally restored at the decline of the nations, but divided then into ten kingdoms, the Roman monarchy, such as Augustus Cæsar founded it, will recover its ancient limits from the Euphrates to the Rhine, from the Atlas to the Danube, embracing thus in *its vast circumference* all the states and present kingdoms of Europe, Asia, and Africa whose shores are washed by the Mediterranean Sea, and uniting them under one rule.

Interrogated further, our vision of chapter 7 will explain itself best to us at the same time that it gives us sufficient glimpses of

The Political Future

of the re-established empire. Cast your eyes on that little horn which raises itself from among the ten horns (a horn is generally the emblem of power) concentrated in one individual (ver. 17 and 23). See how it rules over the ten others, and how it gives its distinctive character to the beast! It is all, it does all; it identifies itself with the beast, who is only its instrument; and in a measure it absorbs it, and, at the same time, little horn and beast, it can say, "*La bête c'est moi*" (Dan 7; Rev. 17 and 19); the ten horns it afterwards reduces to seven are completely subject to it.

Let us here beware, for what we have before us is not a beast, or a little horn (at this time they are one) who perishes after having lived a certain time, and ten horns which survive it; no, it is a beast or little horn, and ten horns which exist simultaneously. Let us not alter the emblem. It does not show us ten kingdoms which spring from the Roman beast and survive it, as the barbarous kingdoms of the Middle Ages issued formerly from the western part of the empire, and divided its spoils amongst themselves; on the contrary, they are ten kings, existing at the same time as the beast, and who give him their power (Dan. 7; Rev. 17:12, 13) This surely has not yet been seen, but it will certainly be seen in the empire, once it is restored. Such is precisely the entirely new form under which it will present itself to us. Then empires and kingdoms, beasts and horns, emperor and kings, will exist simultaneously according to our emblem. The spectacle which the Roman Empire will offer at that time will be

A Vast Confederation of States

united under one common head (the little horn is always identified with the beast), under an imperial chief who will represent monarchy, who will in some manner sum it up in person, who will rule it as one man, and will be able to say, "*La monarchie, c'est moi.*" Contemporaneous history has several times presented to us an anticipated image in the reign of a celebrated emperor. Not only will the Roman beast and the ten horns, the supreme dictator and the ten kings, afterwards reduced to seven, exist together during the same period, but will perish under the same direct, immediate, unexpected, and terrible judgment of God.

The Blasphemous Horn.

We have said that the little horn gives to the Roman beast its distinctive character. It is also principally on this horn that the gaze of the prophet Daniel is fixed, stupefied no doubt, as at a later period was he of Patmos (Rev. 17) at the sight of so much insolence and rebellion in man against his Creator. Clothed with dictatorial power, this little horn pronounces blasphemous words against heaven; he persecutes the saints, and presumes "to change times and laws." Times of feasts is the sense in the original, the feast days, the Levitical feasts returning at regular seasons, the Passover for example, Pentecost, and the Feast of Tabernacles. Here, then, we are

On Jewish Ground.

No doubt the little horn is then persecuting all the saints, it persecutes them throughout the empire, in Christendom as well as in Judea; but Palestine is especially the theatre of his tyrannical oppression. The children of Israel, at this time, have returned to their own land; their temple has been rebuilt in restored Jerusalem, their worship has recommenced there. The little horn carries on with rage his work of blasphemy and persecution during one thousand two hundred and sixty days. Then the Ancient of Days sits on His throne. The books are opened, and the judgment held. Remark here, God does not judge the dead, but the pagan nations, the people of the fourth empire, divided into ten kingdoms under Antichrist.

He Judges the Roman Beast,

the little horn, who perishes for having openly set himself up against God, against His word, His people, and His authority. The blow of Divine vengeance falls on the fourth beast, as it fell on the feet of the statue. God strikes it also in the same manner, that is to say, directly, immediately, and without employing any providential means. He consumes it utterly by the fire of His wrath. He simply took away the empire from the three preceding beasts, and left them life for a period His word does not determine, but He strikes this beast with a destroying judgment.

With the fourth beast, and in it, perishes all that remained of the three that preceded it, for in a certain manner these will revive in the Roman beast: this is why prophecy represents it as having in it something of the lion, the bear, and the leopard. (Rev. 13:2.) As soon as the fourth beast is judged, God takes back the power confided for a time to the Gentiles, and invests it solemnly in the Son of Man and the saints. Not long ago Antichrist wore ten crowns (Dan. 7; Rev. 13), now all the diadems of this world adorn the glorious brow of Christ (Rev. 19: 12); the sovereignty of the world is given to the Son of Man. The vision of the seventh chapter has then the same end, the same final results as that of the second chapter. They both terminate in the Millennium.

* From his article in *The Prophetic News* for September; price six cents by mail. On sale at this office, 63 Bible House, New York.

CHRISTIAN HERALD AND SIGNS OF OUR TIMES.

OFFICE, 63 BIBLE HOUSE, NEW YORK.

ENTERED AT THE POST-OFFICE AT NEW YORK, N. Y., AS SECOND-CLASS MATTER.

EVERY NUMBER CONTAINS:

The Portrait and Biography of some eminent person.
The Sermon Dr. Talmage preached the last Sunday morning.
An Exposition of Unfulfilled Prophecy.
A Summary of the Events of the Week, Notes of Religious and Temperance Movements, etc.
A Sermon by Rev. C. H. Spurgeon, of London, from advance sheets sent by special arrangement.
Pictures of Missionary Life, etc., and Descriptive Articles.
An instalment of a Serial Story.
An Exposition of the International Sunday-School Lesson, by Mrs. M. Baxter.

ANNUAL SUBSCRIPTION, $1.50.

Single Copies, Price Three Cents, may be obtained by order of any Newsdealer.

NOTICE.

A concession in price will be made to subscribers desiring to introduce **THE CHRISTIAN HERALD** to ministers, evangelists, or personal friends. It will be mailed regularly every week to any address in the United States or Canada, from September 20 to the end of the year 1888, for twenty-five cents. Address The Manager, 63 Bible House, New York.

CURRENT EVENTS.

An Attempt was Made in the Senate Last week to withdraw from the hasty action recently taken on the Chinese immigrant question. The fact that China had not decided to reject the treaty, having been communicated to the Senate by the President, completely changed the situation. If the Chinese Government ratified the treaty there would, it was admitted, be no need of legislation. Besides which, the enactment of a law while the treaty was under consideration appeared undignified. A motion to reconsider the vote was therefore made, but on Sept. 17, it was rejected by a vote of twenty to twenty-one. The majority was composed of fifteen Republicans and six Democrats; the minority, of fourteen Democrats and six Republicans. Among the latter were Senators Edmunds, Evarts, and Sherman. It is remarkable that three Republican statesmen so prominent and influential as they, should have failed to carry their colleagues with them, on a question so vitally affecting the national honor.

The Assessment of Federal Office-Holders for campaign purposes, which has always been a sore subject with the party which happened to be in opposition, will this year be watched more jealously than usual, on account of the pledges Mr. Cleveland gave during the campaign of 1884. In order that office-holders may have a perfect knowledge of their position, the National Civil Service Reform League is about to issue a circular addressed to all the more important departments and offices, explaining clearly and explicitly what may and what may not be done under the civil-service law. The action is wise, but the League is doubtless aware that the assessment will be levied and paid as usual, and will simply supply the office-holder with a standard by which to judge himself and the conduct of his party.

The Relations Between the United States and Great Britain and Canada were the subject of an important speech made by Senator Sherman on September 18. The Senator, who took a prominent part in securing the rejection of the treaty, moved that during the recess the Foreign Affairs Committee inquire into the subject, and report at the next session the best way to promote *friendly commercial and political intercourse* between these Governments; that the Committee have power to sit during the recess, and its expenses be paid out of the public purse. Mr. Sherman contended that the retaliation proposed in the President's message does not concern the fisheries, and transcends in importance the grievances undertaken to be redressed by it. He said that the time had come when the people of the United States and of Canada should take a broader view of their relations to each other than had been hitherto practicable. The whole history of the two countries had been a continuous warning that they could not remain at peace with each other except by political as well as commercial union. But the way to union was not by unfriendly legislation, but by friendly overtures. Still more plainly, he said, no greater good could be accomplished than by a wise and peaceful policy to unite Canada and the United States *under one common government*, carefully preserving to each its own local autonomy. This is a much larger question than that of the Fisheries, and probably there has been no time when Canada was less disposed to regard the project favorably. In the meantime Mr. Sherman, who doubtless in this case represents his colleagues, is opposed to granting the President the retaliatory power he has asked for.

The Effort to Induce the Sioux to Assent to the sale of part of their lands has evidently been closely watched by the Government and the people. Charges have been freely made that the Commissioners have tried, through the agencies and the police, to force the Indians to agree. A protest was made in the House against such a proceeding, and the attention of the Secretary of the Interior was called to the conduct of the Commission. Mr. Vilas has, it is now reported, matured a plan for obtaining an expression of the real views of the Indians, and particularly of the objections of those of them who do not like the plan proposed. This plan is said to involve a visit of Sioux chiefs to Washington, where it is thought that away from tribal influence the chiefs may be brought to see that the Government proposal is advantageous to the Indians, and may consent to its realization.

Over a Thousand Deaths were Caused by the cyclone in Cuba on September 4 mentioned in these columns two weeks ago. The facts were not fully ascertained until last week, owing to the utter destruction of the telegraphic system. A Havana journal says: "At Cardenas alone property was destroyed or damaged to the extent of $1,000,000, and the deaths amounted to over one hundred. The vortex of the cyclone entered the island near Sagua, crossing between Havana and Batabano, and through Consolacion del Sur, leaving Cuba for Vera Cruz. A peculiarity of this cyclone was its southward tendency. At the port of Batabano nine sailors were drowned by the foundering of the Spanish gunboat *Lealtad*. Trees were torn up, roofs torn off, and the violence of the hurricane was great. The schooner *Suarez*, which had made the port the previous day, was completely wrecked, and several of the crew were lost. The Captain-General of the island organized a board of relief and placed $20,000 at its disposal.

The Increased Number of Yellow Fever victims at Jacksonville, Fla., last week, which resulted from the unfavorable weather, has called out the sympathy and practical beneficence of the country. Besides the large gifts from various cities, Mr. Edmunds proposed and the Senate adopted a resolution, appropriating $100,000 for the relief of the stricken city. There is evidently urgent need for this and for all the private gifts that can be obtained; for not only has hospital work on an extensive scale to be carried on, but food must be distributed to large numbers, whom the total suspension of business has thrown out of employment. Tuesday was the worst day in the history of the epidemic. The number of new cases rose to 156, and the deaths to twenty. This is an appalling record, when it is remembered that the city is more than half depopulated. On Wednesday there were 130 new cases and fourteen deaths. On Thursday, 131 new cases and fifteen deaths. On that day the numbers given out showed that since the outbreak of the scourge there had been 1,464 persons seized with the disease, and a total of 185 deaths. This is about thirteen per cent., which is worse than in some former visitations, but not so bad as at Memphis, in 1879, where the rate reached thirty-two per cent. The Red Cross Society, with Miss Clara Barton at its head, is doing its utmost for the relief of the sufferers, and many physicians have heroically gone to the relief of the city doctors, who are quite worn out. An ominous feature was the extent in the affected area last week. Gainesville, Fernandina, and Ocala each had cases, and there was a panic which promised to scatter the seeds of disease still more widely. At Decatur, Ala., also, suspicious cases were reported, and large numbers of people fled. Four cases were detected at Jackson, Miss. They were all residents who have not been out of the city for months. On the news reaching other southern cities, the quarantine against Jacksonville was extended to Jackson.

The Commission to Try the Charges Against Mr. Parnell and other Irish leaders held a preliminary meeting on September 17. Its main business was to formulate an issue between the *Times* and the Nationalists. The judges insisted on having direct charges and specifications made. After considerable wrangling between counsel, the articles in the *Times* on "Parnellism and Crime" were put in, and the shorthand notes of the counsel in the O'Donnell trial. These were taken as the charges to be investigated. Application was made, on behalf of Mr. Parnell, for an order compelling the *Times* to produce the letters which it boasted of having, connecting Mr. Parnell with the Phœnix Park murders. The lawyers representing the newspaper, firmly resisted the application, as the *Times* was pledged to keep the source of its information secret. It is hinted that the information was obtained from traitors in the Nationalist camp, whose lives would be in peril if their identity were disclosed. The judges took time to consider the question of what documents it would be right to require the *Times* to produce. They granted an order for the production of the bank-books of the League. The Commission then adjourned to October 22.

Confirmation of the Report of the Murder of Major Barttelot has been received. He was shot on July 19 by his Manyema carriers. The head Arab and his men thereupon ran off to Stanley Falls, where Jamieson was making arrangements with Tippoo Tib for the organization of an expedition. The news of the murder of Major Barttelot has given rise to speculation regarding the fate of Henry M. Stanley himself. The London newspapers are unanimously of the opinion that Major Barttelot was betrayed by Tippoo Tib, who organized the native portion of the expedition, and the question is asked, "Why may not Stanley have been also the victim of his treachery?" The opinion of explorers is, however, less hostile to Tippoo Tib, and they incline to attribute Major Barttelot's death to his own recklessness in the choice of carriers. Tippoo Tib conceived a dislike to the Major, and showed a disposition to hinder instead of facilitating him. It would appear that Major Barttelot himself determined to have Manyema carriers, though warned that they were treacherous. On Friday news was received in Brussels that Prof. Jamieson, who was about to lead an expedition in search of Stanley, had died suddenly of African fever at Bangalas, on the Congo, on August 17.

The Seceders from the Liberal Party in England were in consultation in Bradford, last week. Especial prominence was given to Mr. Chamberlain, who appears to have succeeded in superseding Lord Hartington in the leadership. Mr. Chamberlain hailed the union of the Unionists with the Conservatives as the coming national party. He said he did not see why Irishmen should not have local government, though experience showed that, whether in Dublin, New York, or Boston, Irish government was always inefficient and corrupt. Once he had thought that the Liberals would reunite upon a feasible policy, but now the schism in the party was widening daily. The alliance between the Liberal Unionists and Tories depended upon placing principles above party interests.

Contributions to the Fund For Supplying colored ministers in the South with THE CHRISTIAN HERALD have been received since our last acknowledgement to the amount of $10. They are from Warren, N. H., $5; Mt. Jackson, Va., $1; Parsons, Kan, $2; Bachelor, Mich., $1; Elliott, Iowa, $1. We sincerely thank our friends who have thus responded to our appeal on behalf of these ministers. We are now enabled to add ten more names to the list. It would give us great pleasure to add many more. If those ministers who have so pathetically presented their claims and write so strongly of the benefits they have derived from it in the past, will pray in faith, God will surely incline the hearts of His people to give them the help they need for their work.

An Important Religious Concession has Been obtained from Turkey by Mr. Straus, the United States Minister to the Porte. Mr. Straus, who is now about to return to Constantinople from his visit to Washington, made an argument to the Sultan, shortly before coming home, in support of the application of the American Bible Society, for permission to print New Testament and Biblical tracts in the Turkish language. The privilege had been denied by the Minister of Public Instruction. Word has been received that the desired permission has now been granted by the Porte, and the American Bible Society has already formally expressed its thanks to Minister Straus. The British Bible Society and similar organizations of other countries will unquestionably receive the same courtesy at the hands of the Porte, and Mr. Straus will be entitled to their thanks.

A Death from the Prick of a Pin is Re-ported from Lancaster, Penn. Among the fifteen hundred persons who attended the funeral of Mennonite Bishop Heer, on August 29, was a gentleman who married the granddaughter of the Bishop. He noticed a pimple on one of his fingers while listening to the funeral sermon, and he pricked it with a pin. Before the funeral was over he became so ill that he had to be taken home. His hand and arm were swollen to twice their natural size by the time he reached there. The swelling spread over his entire body, and he died on September 3, in great agony. He was only thirty-three years old, but he had, through his own efforts, acquired a large fortune, and by hard study had become a classical scholar. It appeared a very trivial cause to produce so fatal a result, but the man's blood must have been in a condition to render contact with the pin poisonous. It is so with some indulgences. Many a man has been ruined for time and eternity by a glass of intoxicating liquor which another might have drunk without harm, but which in him raised a demon he was powerless to subdue. (Rom. 14:2, 13.)

A Mysterious Bequest has Been Made to a young mechanic of New Haven, Conn., as reported in a press despatch from that city. It states that four years ago the mechanic, who was then a cook on board a vessel belonging to Messrs. Staples & Philips, of Taunton, Mass., was at Newport for a day, waiting for the boat to sail. As he walked on the sands, he saw a young lady fall out of a rowboat about fifty yards from shore. Though the water was very rough, the young man swam out to her rescue, and brought her safely to land, though he came near losing his life in doing so. An elderly gentleman who was on the beach when the rescued girl was brought in, said he was her father, and overwhelmed the young man who had saved her with thanks, gave him a thousand dollars, and took his name and address, that he might further recompence him. The old man stipulated, however, that his own name should be kept a secret. Two weeks ago the young man received a request from a firm of lawyers in New York that he would call at their office. He did so, and was informed that his aged Newport acquaintance was dead, and had left him fifteen thousand dollars, on certain conditions, which were disclosed after the legatee had given his promise never to reveal them. The young man took time for consideration, and now states that he shall not accept the legacy on the conditions attached. His decision surprises those who esteem money as the greatest good. In this life men are apt to think a man foolish who will not sacrifice his principles when it is necessary, to make a fortune. In the next life it will be found that those who made the sacrifice were the fools. (Mark 8:36.)

A Fatal Fortune was Inherited Recently by a business man, in Boston. He carried on a lucrative plumbing business, and employed a dozen men. He was noted for his industry, frugality, and close attention to business. Six months ago, through the death of a relative, he unexpectedly came into possession of a fortune. The money completely turned his head. He became careless, idle, and dissipated. Finally, he left Boston with a large sum of money in his pocket, and let no one know whither he was going. Search was made for him, but he was not found. The police were notified, and they made inquiries in that and other cities, but without success. On September 15, news of him was received from Philadelphia. He had been found on a stoop in a back street, early that morning, with a bullet-hole in his head. He was still conscious, and tried to conceal the fact that he had intentionally shot himself. Later, however, when informed that he had but a few hours to live, he told his story. He said that since leaving Boston, he had been drinking continually, and squandering his money. When at last he sobered up in Philadelphia, he had not a cent in his possession. He was so overcome with remorse that he shot himself there and then. But for the sudden acquisition of wealth he might now have been living and happy. This is not the first time by many that the riches for which so many pine and toil have proved a fatal possession. (1 Tim. 6:9.)

An Inventor has been Disappointed in the results of many years of thought and labor. On September 14 a curious vessel, which attracted considerable attention among shipowners and sailors, was moored in the East River at the foot of Gouveneur Street, New York. It was guaranteed by the inventor to be non-sinkable. Its main feature, is that the fore and aft compartments are air-tight, and are fitted with valves to admit or eject water for ballast. These can be regulated by the captain at will, so as to render the vessel, whether laden or empty of freight, just the right height above water. Many visited the craft and took much interest in the ingenious contrivances of its construction. The next morning, however, it was nowhere to be seen. It had sunk in the night and lay on the river's bed. Wreckers were summoned and the craft was raised. It was then found that the valves connecting one of the ballast compartments with the water were out of order and had filled the compartment during the night. The weight being all on one side, the craft had capsized and gone to the bottom. Happily none of the crew had proved their confidence in the invention by remaining on board all night, or some lives might have been lost. It is much to be wished that the devices which moral and spiritual philosophers have invented for the development and salvation of mankind similarly involved no fatalities when they fail. Many souls have been lost by putting faith in human guarantees—papal and others—rather than in God's way of Salvation. (Eccles. 7:29.)

Imprisonment in a Bank Safe for Fifteen hours nearly proved fatal to a young man in Philadelphia, last week. On September 17, several young people were in a vault under the Keystone National Bank, on Chestnut Street, looking at the huge safes constructed for the safe keeping of bullion and valuable property. One of the young men entered a safe, which was as large as a moderate-sized room. Immediately a companion playfully swung to the huge door, and the spring-latch caught. There was then a general alarm, for none of the party could open the door. The bank officials were summoned, but they could do nothing, for the safe was under repairs and there was no knob on the outside to withdraw the bolts. A number of workmen labored with bars and chisels to pry the door open, but succeeded only in getting it open about an inch. This, however, admitted some air, and it was considered safe to leave the young man in his strange prison for the night. An expert from the safe-maker's was telegraphed for, and at 8 o'clock next morning he arrived, and with a pair of long pliers he managed to draw the bolts and release the prisoner. The young man was badly frightened, but not much the worse. He said he suffered considerably, until the one-inch aperture gave him some fresh air. The joy of the young man who had thoughtlessly closed the door was as great, when release came, as that of the victim. He had found, as many do who get others into difficulties, that it is easier to do mischief than to undo it. There are some cases in which the evil is irretrievable, but God will avenge the victim's misery on the wrongdoer. (Prov. 28:10.)

BRIEF NOTES.

The Fulton Street Daily Prayer-Meeting celebrated its thirty-first anniversary on Monday last.

Philip Phillips, the Singing Pilgrim, has gone to Europe. He will hold services in England during the next few months.

By the will of the late Henry Winkley, of Philadelphia, who died August 9, the Young Men's Christian Association in that city receives $20,000.

The bicentenary of the death of John Bunyan has been celebrated at Bedford, and many Americans joined in a pilgrimage to his tomb in Bunhill Fields, London.

Cardinal Lavigerie has obtained the consent of the King of the Belgians to make use of an armed force to stop slave caravans passing between Stanley Falls and Lake Tanganyika.

Major Whittle, of Chicago, has set out for an evangelistic tour in Ireland. He goes first to Belfast. The profound Irish prejudice against England gives an American a peculiar advantage over an English evangelist.

Mr. H. W. Brown, the evangelist, is holding meetings in Plainwell, Mich., this month, and will spend his time in that State till November, when he goes to Leavenworth, Kan., spending the rest of the winter in that State.

Mr. Henry Varley has just held some most successful services at Torquay. On Sunday, September 9, he commenced a series of meetings in the Victoria Hall, Sunderland. He and his family will sail for Australia, October 4, where he expects to remain a few years.

A Presbyterian contemporary states that over fifty Presbyterian ministers in the United States and Canada were at one time Roman Catholic priests. Quite a number of converted priests are now Methodist ministers and members of the Protestant Episcopal Church.

At the recent camp-meeting at Douglas, Mass., a man who rose to ask for prayers, and was converted, gave evidence of his sincerity by confessing that he had recently escaped from the penitentiary, and by going and surrendering himself to serve out his term.

Miss Florence Nightingale, the famous hospital nurse, is now a confirmed invalid, and is a patient at St. Thomas Hospital, London. Her services during the Crimean War injured her spine, and she has never recovered from the effects. She is sixty-nine years old.

One of the measures adopted by the World's Convention of Young Men's Christian Associations in Stockholm was the employment of a college secretary to visit all the institutions of learning in heathen lands, and then organize branches of the associations among the students. Mr. L. D. Wishard, of New York, was appointed.

The Mormon "Apostle," George Q. Cannon, has surrendered himself to the United States Marshal. Cannon was a former delegate to Congress from Utah, and virtual head of the Mormon church for years. He pleaded guilty to two indictments of having too many wives, and was sentenced to seventy-five days' imprisonment, and a fine of $200 on the first indictment, and to one hundred days' imprisonment and $250 fine on the second.

Col. Robert Ingersoll, the notorious infidel, who has until this year been a prominent speaker in the Presidential canvass, will not be invited to speak in New York State this year. The Republican candidate for Governor is firmly opposed to availing himself of his services. In Minnesota, where he was to speak, there is also a protest. The Christian public of St. Paul has notified the Republican Committee that he will not be welcome to them.

CROSSING THE JORDAN.

A New Sermon by Pastor C. H. Spurgeon.

"Then Joshua commanded the officers of the people, saying, Pass through the host, and command the people, saying, Prepare you victuals; for within three days ye shall pass over this Jordan, to go in to possess the land, which the Lord your God giveth you to possess it." Josh. 1:10, 11.

A Marvellous Event—An Established Type of Christian Death—A Lady's Sudden Death—The Notice Given to the Israelites—I. Its Tenor—Preparation Ordered—The Proper Food—Purification Needed—Safety Assured—Possession Promised—II. The Sequel of the Notice—Special Faith Imparted—Guidance Afforded—Dying Before Christ Comes—A Christian's Needless Fears—The Quick Passage—A Memorial Set Up—Preaching in Heaven.

THE story of the passage of the Jordan might instructively be used in many ways. It was a very wonderful event. It occurred on the tenth day of the first month, on the same day of the year as the passage of the Red Sea. Of that glorious miracle it was the fortieth anniversary, and you may very properly join the dividing of the Red Sea to that of the Jordan, for so the Holy Spirit has done in the one hundred and fourteenth Psalm: "The sea saw it, and fled: Jordan was driven back."

I am going to use the passage of the Jordan as our forefathers employed it, as a type of

Our Passage Out of this World

into the place appointed for our rest. Canaan is only measurably a type of that better land, for the Canaanite was still in the land, and Israel had to fight many a battle to obtain possession of the country. In our more perfect Canaan there are no enemies to encounter, no sins to struggle with, and no powers of darkness to conquer. Still, I think the type, if imperfect, has been so long established in the Christian church, and has yielded so much of edification to godly people, that I may safely use it.

The Israelites, before they crossed the Jordan, had notice given them. The officers went through the host with the message, "Prepare you victuals; for within three days ye shall pass over this Jordan." The Lord often favors His people with notice that the time of their departure is at hand. Mr. Bunyan describes the pilgrims as tarrying on the shore of that river which parted them from the celestial country until a post came to one and another, announcing that the silver cord must be loosed and the golden bowl be broken. Father Honest, and Mr. Ready-to-halt, and Christian, and the rest of them, received each one a call from the hill-country, and passed over the black water to the golden strand, where the shining ones stood to meet them. A few Sunday evenings ago, when I was unable to preach to you, my beloved and esteemed friend, Mr. Newman Hall, most generously occupied this pulpit, and his sermon touched upon heaven and the joyous entrance of the saints into the immortal state. One of our sisters was greatly rejoiced by that sermon. She went home, and in going into her bedroom she fell down and entered in a second into rest. Possibly that sermon was to her a stray note from the harps of angels to call her home. We, too, may have such

A Speedy Summons;

or we may have months of waiting. What matters? Let the angelic convoy appear when our best Beloved shall see fit: it shall be no question of preference with us whether the Master shall call us to-day, to-morrow, or in twenty years. When God's children have their candle lighted for them, and they know that it is *time to go up-stairs*, they feel glad to end their pilgrimage, and rest in Jesus. We are all of us much nearer home than we think. It will be greatly wise to talk with our last hours, and to anticipate that time when the message shall come, "Within three days ye shall pass over this Jordan."

I. First, observe

The Tenor of the Notice.

Notice that there are three leading words in it: "prepare," "pass over," "possess." "Prepare you victuals; for within three days ye shall pass over this Jordan, to go in to possess the land." The first word that came to them was, "Prepare." Be in journeying order. The soldier carries his rations with him when he has to make a quick march: "Prepare you victuals." Children of God, be ready to go from this world. Let not your roots strike deep into this earthly soil, for you must in due time be transplanted; and the more root-hold you get to this world, the worse it will be for you. Hold everything with a loose hand. The soldier in a foreign land must not settle down, and begin to gather surroundings about him which would naturalize him in the country.

He is an Alien,

tarrying till his prince shall call him back to the home country. You cannot be in exile long. Keep in marching order; be prepared at a moment's notice to start on your way.

But inasmuch as He said, "Prepare you victuals," did he not mean, "Begin to feed on food of that sort upon which you are henceforth to live"? I wish that professing Christians were more cautious about what they feed on. I am afraid that some professors, if they hear a sermon, are satisfied, whatever the sort may be. They do not care what the doctrine may be, if a clever man talks prettily, and gratifies their ear. Some people can eat sawdust, and make a meal of shadows. I could almost wish it were true of them, that they could drink any deadly thing, and it should not hurt them; for assuredly they do drink very deadly things when they go to the tavern of modern thought. But I would say to you this morning, feed on Christ, feed on spiritual food, feed on the pure truth of God's Word, and feed your souls on nothing else.

But then he said also, "Sanctify yourselves." If we knew we were

To Die in Three Days,

should we not wish to put our hearts, our thoughts, our families, into a better state? I remember a sister, by no means superstitious, who, when she came to die, was very earnest that all her linen, and everything about her body, should be white and clean; and I somewhat sympathized in her feeling, because I knew that it was only the outward expression of her inward desire to be purely arrayed as to her spirit. Since we may die suddenly, let us purify ourselves of all filthiness of the flesh and of the spirit. Let us pray our Lord to wash us again; and, as our dear brother prayed just now, "may the dust of our last day's march be taken from our feet!"

The next word was, "Pass over this Jordan." They were not called to linger on the brink, nor to sit with their feet in the stream, but to cross over it. Israel had been forty years in the wilderness, and surely that was long enough. Some of you have been fifty, sixty, seventy, perhaps eighty years in the desert; but when the summons shall come, you will have no more marchings over the burning sand, and no more fear of the fiery serpents and scorpions. "Within three days ye shall pass over this Jordan" will put an end to the wilderness trampings. He liveth long that liveth well. He who hath served his God with all his heart will not wish to linger a moment after his life-work is done. You are not called to linger on the bed of sickness for ages, but to pass over to your rest.

Our text reads like a promise—"Within three days ye *shall* pass over this Jordan." Some of them might have said, "How?" They saw no apparent means—no bridge, no pontoons, no ferry-boat. Ah! but says Joshua, "Within three days ye shall pass over this Jordan"; and

The Word was True.

Do you say, "I do not see how I am to be helped to die?" The Lord will give dying grace in dying moments. He comes in when the need is pressing. Those who have wrestled earnestly in life shall march off triumphantly in death. It is yours to obey, it is His to provide. Sometimes you are so foolish as to try your hand at providing, and then you neglect the obeying, and as a consequence you fail both in the providing and the obeying. Mind your own business, and the Lord will perform His word.

Somebody might have said, "We cannot pass over Jordan, for the torrent is furious, and the river is unusually swollen." In the spring, at the time of barley harvest, Jordan overflows all its banks, and becomes a river which only the very strongest of David's heroes could ford. So some child of God might say, "But

My Prospect

in dying is darker than that of any other believer. I shall suffer more pain, more depression, more poverty; and thus to me Jordan overfloweth all its banks." Yes, yes; but still you shall go over it, for the Lord hath said it, and none of His words shall fail. You shall cross the swollen torrent, and smile at your own fears.

The third word was '*possess*.' They were to pass the river to possess the land which God had given them. We possess nothing here. Those goods which we think we possess melt away like an icicle from a hot hand. But we have on the other side of Jordan treasures worth owning. There was in Palestine a portion of land for each man of Israel: so is there in heaven a heritage appointed for each one of the Lord's people. You have to go over Jordan, but you are not going away from home, you are returning to your Father's house. You are not going to a land of toil and poverty, sorrow and death; you are going to be for ever with the Lord, where no evil can reach you. If, then, the message should come to your ear to-day, "Within three days thou shalt pass over this Jordan," say to yourself, "It is well, for I shall behold the face of Him I love, and meet with those who are redeemed by His blood."

II. I want you now to observe

The Sequel of the Notice,

or what followed upon the summons. I shall try to show what will follow to you who are in Christ. When you receive your notice to depart, what will happen to you? The first thing that happened to Israel was this: a singular faith was bestowed. I can hardly believe that the people under Joshua were the children of those unbelieving Jews whose carcases fell in the wilderness; for throughout the early chapters of Joshua it is recorded that they believed Joshua, whatever he said to them. He had strange and strong things to utter, but they did not doubt or demur. What pleases me most is that when he spoke to the Reubenites, and told them what they had to do, they said, "Whosoever he be that doth rebel against thy commandment, and will not hearken unto thy words in all that thou commandest him, he shall be put to death: *only be strong and of a good courage*."

Think of that! They took upon themselves to encourage Joshua, saying,

"Only be Strong

and of a good courage." They admonished the bravest of captains—even they who were but of the rank and file. Some of God's very poor and tried people are occasionally so full of faith and courage that they try to cheer up their minister. I like to see them thus returning the compliment, for it shows that they are in a happy condition themselves. I do not know what change death itself makes in the soul; but I believe that a little before death a wonderful advance is often made by the believer. The man of God matures at a marvellous rate; even as these Israelites, who had been so prone to murmur, were now filled with a unanimity of faith which is perfectly amazing. May God thus brace up our faith when the time comes!

Next, note that the people had with them

A Conquering Leader.

Joshua was at their head, to encourage and direct them. When you and I shall pass over Jordan we shall have Jesus with us. If our Joshua should seem to leave us, it will be on the flowery hill-side, or in the gardens of delight; but He will not even appear to do so when the dark waters flow at our feet, and we are called upon to pass through the stream. Blessed be our Lord Jesus Christ, He never forgets His own. He is always with us, but He is most clearly so when our last trouble is upon us. He is gone away into the hill-country, to make ready the house where hall shortly be at home; but He will surely e again, and receive us unto Himself, that re He is, there we may be also. Therefore, ot afraid, for Jesus is with you.

ut what next? The Israelites had a clear ance afforded them. Read the fourth verse e third chapter. The ark of the covenant he Lord went before them, and a distance set between them and the priests bearing rk, so that they might show reverence to it, might clearly see it as their guide. Thus Joshua to them, "When ye see the ark of covenant of the Lord your God, and the sts the Levites bearing it, then ye shall re- e from your place, and go after it. Yet e shall be a space between you and it, about thousand cubits by measure: come not unto it, that ye may know the way by which ust go: for ye have not passed this way tofore."

ou have been through many experiences, but ie will be a new one. You have traversed ain roads more than once or twice, but

This Road is New to You,

can only be trodden once. Once for all, you t cross this Jordan, therefore the divine ence shall go before you, and show you the . The Lord will surely direct your steps. not begin saying to youself, "What shall I n sickness?" You will be guided by Him bore our sorrows and infirmities. Some dren of God are always delighted at the idea Christ may come, and that they shall er die. I would be delighted if the Lord ld come at once; but as to dying or not dy- I do not care a jot. I think that of the two, ight be preferable to die, because those who will have a kind of fellowship with Christ in death which will not be experienced by se who never sleep in the tomb. They that alive and remain till

His Coming

miss the privilege of passing through the b as the Saviour did, though even they must changed. Brethren, we traverse a road which known the feet of the Crucified. Where uld the dying members rest but with their ng Head?

lor did the forerunner quit the scene, for the ine presence remained. The priests went on they came to the river-bed, and descended hollow, going on the very centre of it. There y stopped till all the host had passed over. ur after hour the priests remained with the y burden on their shoulders: they stood firm dry ground in the midst of Jordan. Jesus go before you as your great High Priest, r propitiation and your covenant; and He abide with you in the last solemn article il you are safe landed on the shore of the d of promise.

n consequence of the priests going down into river, the stream was dried up. Suppose, en you die, the Jordan should turn out to be

No River at All.

at if you should go over dry-shod? Why uld it not be so? It has often been the case h the Lord's chosen. Many make a joyful t. A sister used to be much troubled about ng; she knew where she was going, but she aded the passage. She died in her sleep, l in all probability never knew when she sed from the one state to the other till she nd herself among the angels. Death is a 's prick to many.

hen notice, the people were very quick in ssing. Death is short work. According to tenth verse of the fourth chapter, we read: and the people hasted and passed over." ey did not hurry because they were afraid; they hasted because they were many, and uld fain be over before the sun went down. course it would take a considerable time h so vast a number to cross; but they were moving on in an orderly and rapid manner. er all, what is the act of death? "What!" s one, "is there not a terrible amount of n connected with death?" I answer—No! a life that has the pain; death is the finis of all pain. You blame death for a disease of which he is the cure. You imagine a thing called death, which does not really exist. In the twinkling of an eye we shall be up and away!

> "One gentle sigh, the fetter breaks;
> We scarce can say, 'He's gone,'
> Before the ransomed spirit takes
> Its mansion near the throne."

Therefore, because you will haste to pass over, you need not be alarmed at so short a trial, which will actually turn out to be no trial at all.

We read in the ninth verse of the fourth chapter, that the Israelites in traversing the Jordan left a memorial behind. Before they had quite passed out of the river-bed, a number of chosen men looked out twelve of the great masses of rock which lay in the botton of the river, and piled them on end upon each other, to remain as a perpetual memorial that Israel had been there. You also will bear your testimony in departing: you will set up your memorial for your children after you, and they shall say, "Our father died in sure and certain hope of being with Jesus." Perhaps some unconverted ones will be saved, after you are dead and gone, by your last testimony. Even if your death-bed should not be so bright as some, even its clouds may not be without their effect.

A Fearful Death Blessed.

A holy man had prayed much for his boys and girls, but never saw them converted, and this, with the troubles which grew out of their waywardness, made his last hours to be sadly clouded. For this cause he was sorely troubled, for he feared that it would confirm his sons in their unbelief. But mark how the Lord wrought! They buried their father, and when they were met together, the eldest son turned to his brothers and remarked upon the sorrows which had weighed down their father at the last. "Brothers," said he, "if our father, who was so good a man, was so troubled in death, what will become of us when we die?" This most reasonable remark was the means of the conversion of the brothers. I would like to die in the dark, if it would bring all my people to the Saviour.

One thing more: they also raised a memorial on the other shore. Twelve men took from the river twelve stones, and bore them on their shoulders before the ark. Can you not see them with their loads, and the ark coming up after them from the river-bed? They piled these twelve stones upon each other in Canaan. You and I, when we get to heaven, shall take our memorials with us, and pile them up. We will make known to angels and principalities and powers the manifold wisdom and goodness of God to us in life and death. I hope to begin to preach before long, not to this little congregation of six thousand, but to countless multitudes of the redeemed in heaven. Myriads of

Angels will Come to Hear

how God helped a sinner to declare his love. You will stand with your groups about you, and shining ones will linger to hear of your salvation, your trials, your joys, and your achievements, or, rather, of what the Lord has wrought for you and by you; and so God will be glorified, and the other side of Jordan will be adorned with memorials to the grace of God.

You will have to turn this subject over in your meditations: I have only been able to give you the rough outline of a sermon. Read the whole narrative, and may God bless it to you!

But, dear friends, *suppose you are not the people of God.* You will have to die, all the same. One of these times

You Will Have to Pass

over the torrent. What a different lot will be yours! You will have to leave your possessions behind. A sage said to a worldling, when he looked over his beautiful gardens, "These are the things that make it hard to die." You will have to leave everything which you call your own here; and you have no possessions over yonder. You have no Joshua to be your leader, no priest to be your forerunner, no God in covenant to hold the ground for you: you have, in fact, nothing to overcome the bitterness of death. The water-floods will carry you away. Dare you to take the dreadful plunge? Mark how the black current rushes down to that dreadful sea of death! Are you resolved to be swept down to that place of desolation? The Lord have mercy upon you before you are drifted into the abode of the accursed! "Believe in the Lord Jesus Christ, and thou shalt be saved; for he that believeth and is baptized, shall be saved." So saith the Lord Jesus.

GEMS FROM NEW BOOKS.

A GIRL'S PICTURE.*

THERE is not one whom God does not seek to arouse to a consciousness of higher things, and some are feeling unsatisfied because they have them not. They sit with hearts empty as she sat in a picture I saw lately, entitled, "Love's Labor Lost." A beautiful young girl, whose childhood is swiftly passing away, sits clasping her knees as she gazes with the strange far-away look of one lost in thought. The puppets and pleasures that have contented her till now can satisfy her no longer. The basket of toys is untouched, the efforts of the girl-attendants to amuse her are unheeded; the singers and musicians entering the room do not receive a single glance, and the pet fawn is wondering that no caress is given to her now. The girl has been aroused to something more—higher and better—than these, and if you have had an inward awakening nothing will satisfy you but Christ, for in the flush of your girlhood or in the dignity of your womanhood, He still says, "If any one thirst, let him come unto Me and drink. Whosoever drinketh of the water that I shall give him shall never thirst."

Instruction From a Novice.

It is said that Hannibal, one of the ablest generals of ancient or modern times, once heard an address delivered upon the art of war, and was asked afterward what he thought of it. With his usual rugged abruptness he replied, "Well, I've heard many an old poltroon, but I never heard such a poltroon as this, for he is talking about war when he knows nothing about it." That is the spirit in which counsels would naturally be received from one whom Paul calls a novice (1 Tim. 3:6); but when they come from one who has lived near God, and done brave and successful service, the wise man will listen and obey with reverence and promptitude.

The Poison-Oak.

In Colorado there grows a shrub known popularly as the Poison-Oak, which is regarded with horror by the inhabitants. Some people are completely prostrated by merely breathing near it, and a scratch from one of its prickly leaves will produce boils or sores which are extremely difficult to cure; though others, curiously enough, seem uninjured by it; just as I have known some stricken down by erysipelas, who have merely sat in a room where arnica and water stood unperceived in a saucer, while others may freely apply it as a healing lotion. We do not know why the virus is harmful to one and harmless to another, and none of our scientists are able to explain the secret or to foretell, without experiment, who will be harmed and who will not. But the fact is unquestionable; and in the higher sphere the phenomenon repeat itself in the observed influence of a sceptical tone in society, which leaves one unscathed, but prostrates another under the bane of infidelity. Yet out of this, good will come, however little we foresee it, just as from the fatal poison-oak is gained the *Rhus toxicodendron*, which, used aright, has cured many a hurt and sprain. Watching against the insidious influence of unbelief, let us hold fast our confidence, as the apostles did who dared to speak with authority, and to this end let us put up their prayer, "Lord, increase our faith!"

A Slave's Prayer.

Many a heathen slave-owner has been rebuked

* From Paul's "Ideal Church and People." A popular commentary, with a series of forty sermonettes on the First Epistle to Timothy. By Rev. Alfred Rowland, LL. B. Pp. 287. Price $1.50. Published by *E. B. Treat*, 771 Broadway, New York.

Prof. Henry Drummond.

The Late Prof. Richard Proctor.

The Late Dr. Mackenzie. (*See page 613.*)

by the saintly lives of Christian slaves, and probably the hearts of many were touched through the prayers of those they despised. We have read of a slave who was caught praying by her master, and cruelly beaten for her pains. Stripped and tied fast to the post, as the blood-stained whip ceased for a moment to fall on her quivering flesh, she was asked if she would give over praying. "No, massa, never," was the answer; "I will serve you, but I must serve God." Again the lashes rained down on her bleeding back; but when once more they ceased, the voice of the follower of Jesus was heard praying, "O Lord, forgive poor massa, and bress him!" Suddenly the whip fell from his hand; stricken with the finger of God, he broke down in penitence. The prayer was answered—the godless master was saved through the faithfulness of the slave he had despised. We may be sure that more than one such convert was rejoiced over by angels centuries ago, in homes where Paul's message was heeded.

PROF. HENRY DRUMMOND.

THE author of "Natural Law in the Spiritual World" is by this time well known to American Christians. His extensive tour this year has made him personally acquainted with many whose study of his famous work had prepared them to meet a remarkable man. His earnestness, his intensity and directness, as well as the close friendly relation in which he stands to Mr. D. L. Moody, assured for him a cordial welcome from Christian workers in all the cities he has visited.

Professor Drummond is about forty years of age. He is a Scotchman, and was educated at a school in Stirling and at Edinburgh University. He also took a course of study at Tubingen, in Germany. He devoted himself with ardor to the study of natural science, and became so famous for his profound knowledge of it that in 1878 he was appointed lecturer, and afterward professor, of the subject in Free Church College, Glasgow. His reputation became world-wide in 1883, when he planned and executed a geological and botanical survey in Central Africa.

Professor Drummond, in 1873, became a conspicuous figure in religious circles by a remarkable address he delivered before the New College Theological Society on Spiritual Diagnosis. In that address he contended that an indispensable part of a successful minister's work was individual dealing with souls; that in a few minutes' conversation with a young man the discovery might be made of his individual need, and the proper teaching applied, while the preacher who limited his efforts to the pulpit might never reach that particular soul. The address caused a deep impression on the religious public, and led to good results. In the same year, Messrs. Moody and Sankey visited Scotland, and Mr. Moody was introduced to young Drummond. The evangelist at once recognized his value, and invited him to accompany him in his evangelistic tour to work among the hearers. Professor Drummond accepted, and he and Mr. Moody have ever since been warmly attached friends.

PROF. RICHARD A. PROCTOR.

THE eminent astronomer whose death from yellow fever in New York on September 12 was briefly mentioned in these columns last week, was well known in most of our large cities. He had a remarkable genius for presenting scientific facts in popular language, and for arousing an interest in science in persons indisposed to dry study. In 1873, and again in 1875, he made a lecture-tour through the United States, speaking on Astronomy before large audiences, imparting information in a most brilliant and entertaining manner, and encouraging young people to pursue the study for themselves. Another tie binding him to this country was made in 1881 when he married Miss Sallie D. Crowley, of St. Joseph, Mo. For some time afterward he resided in that city, and contemplated making it his permanent home. Later, however, he paid a visit to Florida, where he was enthusiastically received, and an offer was made him by the State to build an observatory for his use. This offer he accepted, and in April of last year he removed to Oaklands, near Orange Lake, Fla., where he finally fixed his abode.

Richard A. Proctor was born in England on March 23, 1837. He was, therefore, only fifty-one years old when he died. As a boy he was a most indefatigable student, and by the time he was fourteen he had worked his way to the head of a large academy over boys considerably older than himself. He hoped then to have gone to college, but an expensive lawsuit which followed the death of his father, about that time, prevented his widowed mother giving him that privilege. Young Proctor obtained employment in a bank, but after three years in that occupation his mother inherited a small fortune. The young man then had his wish, and was received as a student at St. John's College, Cambridge, from which institution he graduated in 1860, when he was twenty-three years old.

Public attention was first attracted to his remarkable astronomical knowledge in 1863, when he published an essay on Double Stars. This was followed by a more ambitious work on Saturn and its System. Since that time his life has been full of work. His popular lectures alone would have kept most men busy, but Mr. Proctor was an enthusiast in his study, and he wanted all the world to share in its delights. He produced book after book, and each received a warm welcome. Among his best-known works are: The "Gnomonic Star Atlas," "Constellation Seasons," "Sun Views of the Earth," "Half Hours with the Telescope," "Half-Hours with the Stars," "Other Worlds than Ours," and "Myths and Marvels of Astronomy."

EDWARD WILSON'S RESTORATION.

(*See Illustration on page 621.*)

IN the inner office of a large wholesale business house a merchant was busy balancing the day's accounts, assisted by his nephew, who acted as his confidential clerk. There was no more upright or conscientious man among the merchants of that city than Mr. Armstrong. A Christian man, too, whose religion did not end in church membership. Edward and Lucy Wilson were two orphans, the children of Mr. Armstrong's sister, whose death had been the most severe affliction the merchant had known. Lucy was just completing her education at a college, and Edward was now his uncle's trusted clerk.

Before the balancing was quite completed, Mr. Armstrong was called into the outer office. Returning quickly, he said to his nephew, "Go on as far as you can, Edward, and then wait for me. The cashier of the bank wishes to see me. I expect I shall not be long away."

The young man started and turned pale, but he hid his confusion by stooping to pick up some papers he had let fall in his agitation, and his uncle hurried away. Scarcely was Mr. Armstrong clear of the premises when Edward put on his hat and went out. He turned into a broker's office on the same block and called one of the clerks, a showily dressed young man, a few year older than himself.

"The game is up," Edward whispered; "my uncle has just been sent for to the bank."

"How much is the cheque for?" asked his friend.

"Two hundred and fifty," said Edward. "You had one hundred, you know, and I wanted one hundred and fifty for my own affair."

"Have you paid it all away?"

"No; but I promised to do so to-night."

"Well, that's lucky. I wish it had been more but get away with that. I know old Armstrong. He'll never forgive; and he's such a conscientious kind of man, with his notions about his duty to society, that he is likely enough to have you arrested. If you take my advice you wil ke the next train west, and de yourself till you can find me new opening."

"I must see my sister first," id Edward. "I could not go ithout wishing her good-e. How I wish I had never ritten my uncle's name to at cheque! It was your ult, but I ought to have own better than to yield you."

"That plea won't help you uch, if Armstrong cuts up ugh. You'd better get away ow, and lose no time about ur sister. You can write her."

Edward hurried away, sor-w and shame burdening his eart. He was resolved to e his sister, in spite of his iend's advice. He knew of a or boarding-house within ght of the college where she as, and he went there. He ecured a room, from the win-ow of which he could see the oor by which all the students ame out, and he placed him-elf there to watch for Lucy. He was afraid to go to the ollege and ask for her, as he had been accustomed to do. Scarcely an hour had passed before he was startled by seeing his uncle enter that door. He drew back carefully out of sight, but still watching intently for the merchant's reappearance. His gaze being fixed on the door, he did not see that Lucy herself was passing on the opposite side of the street, nor did he notice her until she also went into the college.

Lucy Wilson's Interview with Her Uncle.

A few minutes later he saw Lucy at an open window, talking earnestly with Mr. Armstrong. The merchant had evidently told her the shameful story, and Lucy was pleading with him. Though Edward had no hope of her success, he knew he could have no better advocate. Presently the merchant came out, and then Edward, after watching him carefully out of sight, sent a note over to Lucy, asking her to come to him. In a few minutes she was at his side.

"Oh, Edward," she said, "what have you done?"

Tears were in her eyes and in her voice, and her brother's eyes fell before her reproachful gaze. He told her his wretched story, not attempting to defend himself, but clearly showing how he had been led into crime by his bad acquaintances. "I am going away, Lucy; but I could not go without seeing you. I am broken-hearted. I wish I had died before doing such a wicked thing."

Lucy looked at him keenly, and saw that he was not exaggerating. "Are you really sorry, Edward?" she asked.

"Sorry!" he said; "that is no name for it; I hate, I loathe myself."

'Then," said Lucy. "I can promise you forgiveness. Only a few minutes ago our uncle went away from me. He thought you would come to me, and he commissioned me to tell you that if you were really repentant he would forgive you for his sister's—our mother's—sake. Oh, Edward! it was a shame to wrong so good a man."

"Lucy! Lucy! is it true?" asked Edward, almost beside himself with joy.

"Yes, it is quite true; I could scarcely believe it myself; but he promised with his own lips, and I will go with you now to him, if you will come, and we will thank him together."

Edward felt that the meeting with his uncle would be less painful with his sister, and he accordingly accepted her offer. They went together, and he was overcome by his uncle's magnanimity. "It is for your mother's sake," said Mr. Armstrong. Years afterward, when Edward was seeking salvation, and he was told that God, for Christ's sake, would pardon him and receive him as a son, Mr. Armstrong's words recurred to his mind, and he had no difficulty in understanding the way of salvation.

THE EPOCHS OF A LIFE.

A NEW SERIAL STORY.

By Rev. L. S. Keyser.

(*Continued from page 606.*)

Duped.

THE reading of the letter which Belle Havelock had concocted and Duneman had sent, was to Madeline Winters a double revelation. It convinced her that Hadley Madelling was a deceiver, and it also revealed to her the depth of affection she had unconsciously conceived for him. She suffered bitterly, and after a first amazed perusal she flung herself on her bed and wept bitterly. Then she rose as if after a nightmare, and read it a second time.

The letter was signed Mabel R. Richerson, and purported to be a reply to one received from Madelling. The writer thanked him for his frequent, long, and brilliant letters, expressed her pride in his college triumphs, in the manner of one whose personal interest was natural only toward a lover, and then openly referred to their betrothal as to an event of long standing. She gave him news of the neighborhood with accurate and minute local coloring, and dwelt on the pleasure with which she looked forward to his vacation, when they could resume their old walks and blissful companionship. The real sting of the letter which rankled in Madeline's breast was in the concluding paragraph, in which the writer admitted that when Madelling went to the college her jealous disposition made her tremble, lest his love should be transferred to some fellow-student, and she rejoiced that he was still true to her, in spite of the pursuit of the girl, whose eagerness to secure him had put his life and her own in peril on the railroad bridge. "I agree with you, dear Hadley," she wrote, "as to the indelicacy of her placing herself in your way and following you in your rambles, and as to her recent ruses; but I have perfect confidence in your fidelity, and I am sure you will not be caught by her blandishments."

And this was the man, thought Madeline, who had been making love to her only a few hours ago! What must he have written to this Mabel Richerson to elicit such a reply as this? So he thought she had been pursuing him, and he had thought her indelicate and had expressed that opinion to this girl! Self-reproach, indignation, chagrin, had their way for a time, and even Belle Havelock herself must have been moved to pity, could she have seen how her plot had tortured the innocent girl.

What should she do? The spirit of that "wisdom which is from above, which is first pure, then peaceable, gentle, and easy to be entreated," had so long ruled her life that even now its voice could not be hushed. Did not the Scripture in many places deprecate a harsh and precipitant judgment? She would not condemn Hadley rashly. There might be some blunder. Perhaps, he could explain. At any rate, she would hold her verdict in abeyance for a few days until she had investigated the mystery that hung over him. Since Hadley had made a proposal of marriage to her, she felt that she was justified in taking such steps as would either disprove or confirm his guilt. As an initiative to her investigations she determined to write to the author of the letter which she had just read. Although it was past midnight, she seated herself at her writing-desk and penned the following brief missive:

"DEAR MISS RICHERSON: Word has come to me that you and Mr. H. C. Madelling have been engaged for a number of years, and that this relation still exists between you. You will greatly oblige a friend if you will write me whether these rumors are true or not. Rest assured that any confidence you may repose in me shall not be betrayed. Your friend.

"MADELINE WINTERS."

There was no strategy in this Christian girl. It seemed to her that a direct appeal to Mr. Madelling's *fiancée*, if that was the relation in which Miss Richerson stood to him, would be the surest avenue to the truth. Little could the unsuspecting girl imagine that the same brain which had devised the plot had also foreseen that this test would be applied, and had provided for it. Madeline's letter on its arrival at Banesville recalled to the accommodating postmaster his fascinating visitor, and he at once fulfilled his promise of forwarding it to her.' Belle Havelock smiled triumphantly when she received it, and promptly penned a suitable reply, and sent it to her friend, the hostess of the Banesville hotel, to be mailed from the Banesville post-office to Miss Winters.

Another test which Madeline devised was an indirect examination of Madelling himself. She resolved to find out as delicately as she could from him something about this Miss Richerson at the first opportunity.

The following day, which was Sunday, was one of the most trying of her life. A dull headache distressed her, but it was nothing compared to the anguish of her heart. One who had not schooled herself to faithfulness in the performance of religious duty would have found an excuse for remaining away from church at such a time; but Madeline felt that the atmosphere of worship might soothe her grief, and, of course, she must obey the voice of duty. It was difficult to concentrate her mind on the services, for she seemed like one in a dream.

When Hadley saw that morning in church how pale she was, he was almost frightened. Had her long drive made her ill? He was filled with vague misgivings, and could scarcely wait for the long hours of Sabbath afternoon to drag themselves away, until the time should come to call upon the girl and conduct her to the evening services, as he had arranged to do.

The death-like pallor was still on her face when she met him at the door, but to all his anxious inquiries she replied truthfully—it was impossible for her to prevaricate—that she had received news through the mail when she came home on the previous evening that had made her very sad. Some time she would perhaps tell him what it was, but for the present he must rest content with this indefinite explanation. Hadley saw that it was useless to press her further.

Her religious principles were sorely put to the test that night. How could she go with another woman's betrothed husband to church? Yet she did not dare to decline to go with him, and go herself, as he was not yet proven to be a mere adventurer. To stay at home was contrary to her principles. At last she gained the victory over herself, and they went to the services. As she listened to Mr. Mardont's earnest words, she was glad that she had come, for she felt that the sermon was a special message to her requirements, and her agony was somewhat alleviated. She could trust God, even if man proved treacherous.

It was when they sat together in the parlor that evening that the opportunity came to obtain more light on the disclosures that distressed her. With an adroitness that was alien to her natural disposition, she led him to speak of his past life and old home. Then she made some inquiries about his neighbors. Her dismay can better be imagined than described when he mentioned the name of Richardson first of all in the catalogue he gave of his old home-friends.

"That is quite a familiar name to me," she said, presently. "Did Mr. Richerson have any—children—young people—in his family?" And she looked at him with a glow in her eyes that she could not hide.

Neither of them noticed the difference in syllabication which they used in pronouncing the name. Her eyes gleamed so, as she looked at him, that he flushed—a perfectly natural consequence when it is remembered that he loved her with the whole power of his affection; but she immediately construed it into an evidence of guilt.

"Yes, he had a daughter, whose name was Mabel," Hadley answered.

Madeline's heart sank. "As she lived so near your home, I suppose you were schoolmates?"

"Oh yes, we were thrown together a great deal," he answered, in a straightforward way. "Mabel was a pretty girl, and I can remember that in my boyish way I admired her, and she seemed to reciprocate my esteem for her."

All this seemed confirmatory of the information contained in the letter. His additional remark seemed to be another witness subpœnaed against him.

"Mabel was quite an intelligent girl, too," he continued. "In fact, she graduated from the Banesville Academy at the same time I did. She is a good composer, and writes a very creditable essay and a delightful letter."

There was no room to doubt his guilt. She "writes a delightful letter." How would he know this if he had not had some epistolary communication with her? As the evidences of his duplicity accumulated, the girl's lips became ashen.

"Miss Winters, you are not well," said Hadley, with deep concern. "It is not right for me to detain you any longer, though I am loath to leave you so soon. If you need my services at any time, I am at your command. Have I not at least a partial right to help you? But what am I saying? I know that you are not ready to answer me this evening." And there was an imploring expression in his eye.

"No," she replied, with quivering lips; "you must give me a few days yet. Good-night."

The days passed wearily for Madeline. One evening, toward the latter part of the week, a letter came to her through the mail, bearing on the envelope the Banesville post-mark, and written in the same hand in which the one that had criminated young Madelling had been written. In the seclusion of her room she opened the letter and read:

"MY DEAR MISS WINTERS: Your letter of inquiry just received. It becomes me to speak modestly of my relations with Mr. Madelling; but as you seem to be kindly disposed, I do not mind telling you that we are engaged. Almost four years ago the plight was made, before he went to college, and it has never been broken. In my happiness I feel the impulse to write more; but I must remember that what is pure felicity to me may seem mere sentimentality to others. Hoping that my answer is satisfactory, I remain, Your friend,

"MABEL R. RICHERSON."

The last item of proof needed to fasten guilt upon Hadley Madelling was now obtained, and Madeline's resolution was quickly made. That very day she sat down and penned him a note, and sent it to the post-office. It contained her answer to the important proposal he had made nearly a week prior.

When Hadley Madelling said with perfect simplicity that Mabel Richardson was a delightful letter-writer, he little imagined the effect his words would have upon the girl to whom he spoke. Had he had the faintest suspicion of the plot that was thickening around him, he would have quickly added that a friend of his had kept up a correspondence with Mabel for some time, and had allowed him to read several of her tersely written letters. Madeline's last words depressed him. That warmth of manner that had characterized her treatment of him on the evening before was now absent, and he became fearful lest her answer would be unfavorable.

Nor was his anxiety allayed when he saw that her dejected mood continued through the week. In the class-rooms she scarcely seemed herself. More than once was she so preoccupied with her own thoughts that she did not notice the questions addressed to her by the professor until they were repeated. All this boded ill for his love-suit, he feared.

On Saturday afternoon George Dane returned from the office with a letter for Hadley. At once the latter recognized Miss Winters's chirography on the envelope. Why had she written? He could not conjecture. Leaning against his book-case, he opened and read the following letter:

"MR. H. C. MADELLING: There are some things that it is less embarrassing to say by letter than by word. My answer to the important proposal you made a few days ago is of that character. After mature consideration I find that, for various reasons which I cannot explain, I am forced to give you a negative reply. Pray let our lives run henceforth in separate channels, as it would only stir bitter memories and regrets for us to meet as we have done in the past. Should you be tempted to seek an explanation, I beseech you not to yield to the temptation.

"Your friend,

"MADELINE WINTERS."

A heavy groan broke from the young man as he read the letter, and he almost reeled to the floor, while his face became as white as the winding-sheet of snow that enwrapped the earth. It seemed as if an avalanche of crushed hopes had suddenly been hurled upon his soul.

"What is it, what is it, Hadley?" cried George, springing forward to support his stricken friend. "Hadley, what has happened? You are as pale as death!"

"Miss Winters has —" began Hadley. And then, unable to say more, he put his arms about George's neck and leaned his head heavily upon his shoulder, groaning aloud, with a nameless, unutterable agony, while his whole frame trembled like a breeze-shaken leaf. George gently conducted him to a chair and seated him in it.

"Brace up, old fellow!" he said, trying to speak cheerily. "Don't give way in this style. Show that you are a brave man, as you are. Oh, don't give up so!" cried George, taking the pale face of his room-mate between his hands and holding up his head. "O Hadley, I almost wish I could pray for you! Such grief needs an omnipotent support."

"Pray!" muttered Hadley, somewhat aroused by his friend's earnest entreaties. "Don't talk to me about prayer, or God, or angel, or heaven. I cannot believe in them now. To-day and henceforth I am an avowed, an uncompromising, atheist. What have I done that my life should be crushed in this fashion? I tell you this world is ruled by caprice. There is no good in life. It is full of blighted hopes and disappointments, and it cannot be that it is directed by a God of love."

Such is invariably the effect of affliction upon those who are "without hope and without God in the world." While it purifies and sweetens and mellows the life of the true believer, it drives the sceptic into deeper hostility against God and the moral order of things.

The disappointed young man was also exposed to another peril. An atheist may have moral principles, but they lack a unifying bond; they lie separate and unconnected in his being, without sufficient adherence to constitute a consistent code of life. Hence one by one these principles are easily dissevered and cast aside. That such was the result in Hadley's case was brought to light later in the day.

Until evening George remained with him in his room, doing his utmost to soothe and assuage his anguish. When night came some duty called George away for an hour, and when he returned he found that his friend had gone. He waited an hour in great uneasiness, not knowing to what rashness Hadley might be driven in his desperation, and was on the point of going in search of him, when he heard an uncertain foot-fall upon the stairway. It did not sound like his friend's quick, firm step, and George was wondering who it might be. In a few moments the door was thrown violently open, and on the threshold stood Hadley Madelling, with flushed face and blood-shot eyes, the very embodiment of inebriety. Then he started reeling across the room. George sprang to him to save him from falling, and recognized the fumes of liquor on the staggering man's breath.

It was with the greatest difficulty that George restrained his intoxicated friend from becoming hilarious, and thus attracting attention to his disgraceful condition. Carefully bolting the door, George applied himself to the unpleasant task of curbing Hadley's imbecile merriment. His troubles were evidently drowned for the moment, and he could even ridicule his infatuation. He would talk and declaim, raising his voice in his efforts to keep his pompous words from running into each other. At last George managed to get him undressed and into bed, where he fell into the heavy sleep of the drunken, to wake next morning with a head splitting from his first debauch, and a spirit burdened with sorrow and shame. It was not difficult for Dane to extract a promise then from Hadley that he would never again touch a drop of intoxicating liquor. The promise was given and faithfully kept.

(To be Continued.)

THE COMMISSION OF JOSHUA.

By Mrs. M. Baxter.

S. Lesson for October 7, Josh. 1: 1-9. Golden Text, Eph. 6: 14.

hua's Antecedents—His Call—Moses' Petition for a Divinely Appointed Successor—Joshua's Training—The Marvellous School of Intimacy with Moses—The Law Giving Place to the Deliverer—Personal Entrance Upon the Land Necessary—The Promise Reiterated—The Secret of Power—The Self-Immolation of the Leaders—The Treble Strength Imparted.

THE name Joshua is the same as Jesus; it eans Saviour or Deliverer. We first hear of shua as the general in command when the malekites were smitten (Ex. 17: 23), and terwards as Moses' minister when he went up to the mount of God. (Ex. 24: 13.) We are not ld that Joshua was with him during the wonrous forty days and forty nights of his communing with God in the mountain, but when he me down again, Joshua accompanied him. robably he had remained in some lower part the mountain, ready for the descent of Moses, d had, therefore, neither knowledge of nor rt in the idolatry of the golden calf. (Ex. 32: .) Joshua was one of the two spies who testied faithfully for God when their ten companns "brought up an evil report of the land," d they survived the forty years' wandering in e wilderness (Num. 14: 6, 30, 38), according the promise of God.

The Call of Joshua

mentioned in the course of Moses' rehearsal the dealings of God with His people. "The ord was angry with me for your sakes, saying, hou also shalt not go in thither [unto the and]. But Joshua, the Son of Nun, which andeth before thee, he shall go in thither: ncourage him; for he shall cause Israel to inerit it." (Deut. 1: 37, 38.) But there is a earer and more definite account of it in the ook of Numbers. God had commanded Moses get up into Mount Abarim, to view the land f Israel before he was gathered to his people as is brother Aaron was gathered; because, on ccount of this unbelief at the water of Meribah, either he nor Aaron was permitted an entance into the land of Canaan. And Moses id not plead for longer life, nor did he ask God turn from His purpose, as he had done when od spoke of destroying His people. Moses' etition was characteristic of his whole life—he as in every sense a living sacrifice for the peole—"Let the Lord, the God of the spirits of ll flesh," he said, "set a man over the congreation, which may go out before them, and hich may go in before them, and which may ad them out, and which may bring them in; hat the congregation of the Lord be not as heep which have no shepherd." (Num. 27: 16, 7.) Oh that spiritual teachers now were like loses! He asked nothing, desired nothing, for imself; like Paul, like the Lord Himself, he id down his life daily for the brethren.

"And the Lord said unto Moses, Take thee oshua the son of Nun, a man in whom is the pirit, and lay thine hand upon him; and set im before Eleazar the priest, and before all he congregation; and give him a charge in heir sight. And thou shalt put some of thine onor upon him, that all the congregation of he children of Israel may be obedient. And e shall stand before Eleazar the priest, who hall ask counsel for him after the judgment of Urim before the Lord: at his word shall they o out, and at his word they shall come in, both e and all the children of Israel with him, even ll the congregation." And then Moses laid ands on him in public, before all the congregaion, and "gave him a charge." Thus was oshua called to his work. There was nothing ysterious or secret about it, all the congregaion knew as well as Joshua himself what God equired of him.

Joshua's Training.

His forty years of service as Moses' minister ust have been the best school possible for the esponsible life he was to live. He had learned f Moses, to carry everything to God, and to prove how truly God understood all that was trusted to Him. He had learned to trust God not only with his own concerns, but with those of others. It was a marvellous school; perhaps no other man ever had such a training. God commanded Moses to "encourage him" (Deut. 1: 36), and to bid him "be strong and of a good courage," because God would be with him. (Deut. 31: 23.) These latter were probably the last words Moses ever uttered to Joshua, and they were his life's motto. But Joshua had had the advantage of seeing what it meant for God to be with a man. He had seen how God could, for the fulfilling of His Word to His people, alter the course of things in nature—make a path through the sea, rain bread from heaven, make the rock give water, hold Moses in life forty days and forty nights without any food, and he knew that "I will be with thee" meant that nothing was impossible.

That wondrous day of Moses' death was over; it was a kind of summing up of his whole marvellous life; and now God speaks directly to Joshua. "Now after the death of Moses, the servant of the Lord, it came to pass that the Lord spake unto Joshua the son of Nun, Moses' minister, saying, Moses My servant is dead; now, therefore, arise, go over this Jordan, thou and all this people, unto the land which I do give to them, even to the children of Israel. Every place that the sole of your foot shall tread upon,

That have I given You,

as I said unto Moses." This is a wonderful type of the life of conquest and victory to which God calls us. Unless Moses (the law) is dead, we have no power to arise and take possession. While we are under the spirit of bondage, "*I must* do this," "I *ought* to do the other," "*God expects* such and such things of me," and our spirit frets under the constant pressure to attempt impossibilities, and we have no power to arise and take possession of the land. But when Joshua takes the place of Moses, then victory takes the place of bondage, the groanings cease, for "the battle is the Lord's," and what we cannot do, He undertakes to do for us, and in us. Oh what a relief it is to know that Christ in us is the fulfilling of the law, that, as He takes possession of us, He sets up His own law in our hearts, and writes it there, making it come natural to our new or Christ-nature to do, and to love the will of God, which our own nature so rebels against! There are those who struggled with their own wills, or affections, or desires, and vainly attempted to control them, but when the whole conflict was handed over to Jesus, how surely He undertook and conquered! Now instead of the sad "I wish I could, but I can't," there is the joyous song, "Jesus saves me now; Jesus prevails"; and the experience whenever I put down my foot upon the promises of my God, then I claim and *have* possession. But as the foot must touch the soil, stand on it, and let it bear our weight, so with every promise of God. "We which have believed do enter into rest" (Heb. 4: 3); we are not afraid to rest our weight on to the promises of God, to step out upon them as Peter stepped out upon the water. Joshua and the children of Israel

Could not Claim the Land by Proxy,

they could not receive possession by word of mouth; they must come into personal contact with it, they must have to do with the land, that it might be theirs. And we too must have to do with God, in every promise, for soul or body, in order that He may fulfil that promise to us.

This promise made to Joshua, had before been made to Moses, and God reiterates to Joshua what He had told Moses of the extent of the land. And then, repeating to Joshua His promise made to Moses (Deut. 7: 24), "Thus shall not any man be able to stand before thee all the days of thy life," He adds, "As I was with Moses, so I will be with thee: I will not fail thee, nor forsake thee."

But would it not be presumptuous for an ordinary Christian to take such promises to himself? Were not Moses and Joshua, Elijah and Daniel, etc., extraordinary men? James tells us that Elijah at least was "a man of like passions as we are." (James 5: 17.) Moses did not esteem himself anything remarkable. That which made their lives so wonderful, was that they were small enough in their own eyes to give God room to work. It was not they who were wonderful; it was He: and if we were less conceited and self-sufficient, He would work mightily in our lives too. It stands to reason that if God is really on our side in any single thing, man counts for nothing, and cannot stand before us. What is man to God, any way? But I will not fail thee, nor forsake thee" is no promise that faith shall not be tried; Joshua's faith was sorely tried again and again. It was no pledge that, come what may, Joshua should be kept involuntarily from ever doing wrong. He was

As Liable to Sin as any other Man,

but ready to his hand, at every moment, was the Almighty God as his Strength and his guarantee of victory. If he acted independently of God, he would fail, despite all his past experience, and so it proved at Ai, and in the affair of the Gideonites. If he was humble enough to seek and act upon God's direction, all would go well; so it proved with him, and so it will ever prove with us.

"Be strong and of a good courage." When God says, "Be strong," He creates the strength of His Word. A naturally timid man to whom God says, "Be strong," can be as strong and stronger than one who is naturally courageous, so that we need never be discouraged or brought to a stand-still because of what *we* are. The question is always, "What can God make of me?"

In these connections Joshua was told to "be strong and of a good courage." First in connection with his vocation as regarded the people, "Unto this people shalt thou divide for an inheritance the land which I sware unto their fathers to give them." Secondly in connection with his vocation as regarded God, "That thou mayest observe to do according to all the law, which Moses My servant commanded thee." Thirdly, because of God's provision for sustaining him. "The Lord thy God is with thee whithersoever thou goest." In the first place, Joshua could not stand alone—as leader of the people, he must lead or mislead them; hesitation or wavering on his part might turn them aside from the Lord, as had been the cases with regard to Aaron and the golden calf. But God knew that it would need courage to keep the law; and so it does to this day, especially in points which have been overlooked by the church of Christ for years. To stand with God against the world is an easy thing, but to stand with God against the misconceptions of dearly loved and honored Christian teachers requires a courage which nothing can give but the consciousness that the Lord is with us. It is clearly the mind of God that His Word shall be the main teaching and matter of His workers. "This book of the law shall not depart out of thy mouth; but thou shalt meditate therein day and night, that thou mayest observe to do according to all that is therein." Let us take the last words home to our hearts. "Have not I commanded thee? Be strong and of a good courage; be not afraid, neither be thou dismayed; for the Lord thy God is with thee whithersoever thou goest."

TRUST.

I cannot see with my short human sight,
Why God should lead this way or that for me;
I only know He saith: "Child, follow me;"
But I can trust.

I know not why my path should be at times
So straightly hedged, so strangely barred before;
I only know God *could* keep wide the door;
But I can trust.

I find no answer, often, when beset
With questions fierce and subtle on my way,
And often have but strength to faintly pray;
But I can trust.

I often wonder, as with trembling hand
I cast the seed along the furrowed ground,
If ripened fruit for God will there be found;
But I can trust.

I cannot know why suddenly the storm
Should rage so fiercely round me in its wrath,
But this I know, God watches all my path;
And I can trust.

I may not draw aside the mystic veil
That hides the unknown future from my sight,
Nor know if for me waits the dark or light;
But I can trust.

I have no power to look across the tide,
To know, while here, the land beyond the river;
But this I *know*, I shall be God's forever!
So I can trust.

J. E. Jewett, Publisher, 77 Bible House, New York, will furnish the above poem in leaflet form at twenty cents per hundred. *A Sample Packet* of 50 leaflets assorted (no two alike), will be sent post-paid, for 10 cts., or 100 for 20 cts. Postage stamps taken.

For Nervous Debility
Use Horsford's Acid Phosphate.

Dr. A. M. Bilby, Mitchell, Dak., says: "I have used it in a number of cases of nervous debility, with very good results."

Young men who need business experience, and at the same time to increase their cash on hand, will find it greatly to their interest to confer with B. F. Johnson & Co., Richmond, Va.

BEAUTIFUL WINTER FLOWERS.

For only 10cts. we will send free by mail 3 *Elegant New Bulbs* for winter blooming, or 7, all different, for 30 cts. Every one is a gem of rare beauty and sure to bloom well in small pots during winter. When ordering ask for our Fall Catalogue of *Bulbs* (Free) with directions for culture, &c., if you do not already possess it.

OUR FALL CATALOGUE

Of **Hardy Bulbs** and **Plants** for winter and early spring blooming, is now ready, and is the most elegant and complete catalogue of the sort ever issued in the world. In it is offered, with directions for culture, the best Hyacinths, Tulips, Crocus, Narcissus, Lilies, Calochortus, Ornithogalum, Iris, Fritelia, Freesias, Alliums, and a score of other new and rare winter and spring blooming Bulbs, besides many new and rare Fruits, including the Ever-bearing Tree Blackberry and Raspberry. This catalogue will be sent free to any who send us an order, or who will send one after receiving it. Among the special offers it contains are 12 Crocus for 15c., 12 Double or Single Tulips for 40c., 12 Hyacinths for 75c., the Great Chinese Sacred Lily, 15c., 30 beautiful winter blooming Bulbs, $1.00, &c. Any one can have gay flowers in the house during winter, or in the garden as soon as snow melts, at small cost. Our Catalogue tells all about them. Address

JOHN LEWIS CHILDS, Floral Park, N.Y.

AGENTS—Our **Christmas Books** (selling from 50 cents to $3.50) will pay you a larger profit than any other's the next three months. One agent made a profit last year of $84.20 in two weeks; one reports an average profit of $7.00 a day from September till Christmas. All time not necessary. CASSELL & CO., B.B.S.D., 104 & 106 Fourth Ave., New York. 40 Dearborn St., Chicago.

MEXICO

Contributions in aid of Christian work in Mexico are most pressingly needed, and can be mailed to the address of
BISHOP H. C. RILEY,
Care of J. P. HEATH
43 Bible House, New York.

UNIVERSITY ORGANS.—They Lead the World.—$35 to $500. Sold Direct to Families. No Middlemen. Solid Walnut-5 Octaves-Double Couplers. Guaranteed for Six Years and sent, with Stool and Book, for trial in your own home before you buy. Established 1859. **$35** MARCHAL & SMITH, 235 East 21st Street, New York.

In all the world there is but one sure cure for the **OPIUM** Habit. The Dr. J. L. Stephens Remedy never fails, and no other treatment ever cures. We have cured more than 10,000 cases. No other treatment ever cured one case. NO PAY TILL CURED. Remember this, and write to the J. L. Stephens Co., Lebanon, Ohio.

AGENTS WANTED to sell "The Child's Bible." Introduction by Bishop J. H. Vincent, D.D. The best selling book handled by agents. Recommended by all clergymen. Address Cassell & Co., B.B.S.D., 104 and 106 Fourth Ave., New York; 40 Dearborn St., Chicago, Ill.

$75.00 to $250.00 A MONTH can be made working for us. Agents preferred who can furnish a horse and give their whole time to the business. Spare moments may be profitably employed also. A few vacancies in towns and cities. B. F. Johnson & Co., Pub's, 1009 Main St., Richmond, Va.

TEAS *LADIES* Send at once for our new terms. THE GREAT AMERICAN TEA CO., 31 and 33 Vesey St., New York, N. Y.

BOOK AGENTS WANTE
MY STORY OF THE W
By Mary A. Liverm

Her own narrative of "Four Years' Personal ... ence as Field and Hospital Nurse." It ... Womanly or "Heavenly" side of the War, its L... Shadows "as a woman saw them." Bright, Pure, ... full of "laughter and tears," of thrilling interest ... pathos, it sells at sight to all. Splendid Steel-P... famous old Battle-Flags, richly colored in exact ... The "booming" book for Men and Women Agents. ... $200 a month made. Distance no hindr... we Pay Freights and give Extra Terms. Write for ...
A. D. WORTHINGTON & CO., Hartford,

For Gas
BAILEY'S COMPOUND light-spreading Silver-Plated CORRUGATED GLASS **REFLECTORS** A wonderful invention for Lighting Churches, Halls, etc. Handsome designs. Satisfaction guaranteed. Catalogue and price list free.
Bailey Reflector Co. 113 Wood st. Pittsburgh, Pa.

WANTED at once, a representativ... or Woman, in every ... until Dec. 25th. Libera... All time not necessary. Give references.
R. H. Woodward & Co., Baltimor...

FEATHERS. The finest live white geese ... ers in the country, 75 cts. ... Hair Mattresses made over for $2.50. H. PICK... 11 Nassau Street, Brooklyn, New York.

1,000 Agents Wanted to Sell 10... Copies National Hand Book of
American Progress,
E. O. Haven, LL.D., & others. 1492 to date. Six Vols. in One. A non-partisan reference Cyclopædia, of History, Biography, Stati... Politics, for School, Home and Office. Illustrate... pages, $2. E. B. TREAT, Pub. 771 B'wa...

PRINTING Book of Type, 5c. Amateur Printers' Guide Book, 15c. **PRESS...** CIRCULAR JOSEPH WAT... 19 Murray St...
Samples of Scrap Pictures and Cards, 10cents.

THE MARCH OF PROGRESS!
OUR LATEST IMPROVEMEN

"Competition is the life of trade," and if you have not seen our improved $3 ... made for the Fall trade of 1888, you cannot imagine how lively trade is, or how ha... competitors have to work to keep within sight of us.

Ask your retailer for the James Means' $3 Shoe, or the James Means' $4 Shoe, according to your ne...

Positively none genuine unless having our name and price stamped plainly on the ... Your retailer will supply you with shoes so stamped if you insist upon his doing so; if you ... insist, some retailers will coax you into buying inferior shoes upon which they make a larger ...

JAMES MEANS' $3 SHOE,
UNEXCELLED IN STYLE, UNEQUALLED IN DURABILITY AND PERFECTION OF FIT
JAMES MEANS' $4 SHOE
CANNOT FAIL TO SATISFY THE MOST FASTIDIOUS.

Such has been the recent progress in our branch of industry that we are no... to affirm that the James Means' $4 Shoe is in every respect equal to the ... which only a few years ago were retailed at eight or ten dollars. If you will tr... pair you will be convinced that we do not exaggerate.

Ours are the original $3 and $4 Shoes, and those who imitate our ... of business are unable to compete with us in quality of factory products ...

In our lines we are the largest manufacturers in the United States ...

Shoes from our celebrated factory are sold by ... wide-awake retailers in all parts of the co...

We will place them easily within your reach ... state or territory, if you will invest one ce... postal card and write to us, men... this paper.

Ask also for the James Means' $2 Shoe for Boys.

JAMES MEANS & CO.,
41 Lincoln Street, - - Boston, Mass.

THE CHRISTIAN HERALD AND SIGNS OF OUR TIMES.

Vol. XI., No. 40. Office, 63 Bible House, N. Y. THURSDAY, OCTOBER 4, 1888. Price, 3 Cents. Annual Subscription, $1.50.

CONTENTS OF THIS NUMBER.

THE BICENTENARY OF JOHN BUNYAN'S DEATH—HIS PORTRAIT AND LIFE.
THE NEBULAR EQUIPAGE. Dr. Talmage's Sermon Last Sunday Morning.
ANECDOTES RELATED AT RECENT EVANGELISTIC MEETINGS.
A DEMONIAC AT A CAMP-MEETING.
THE ANGEL'S MESSAGE TO DANIEL. By G. H. Pember, M. A.
PORTRAIT OF MR. W. JENNINGS DEMOREST.
THE CONQUERING WEAPON. A New Sermon by Pastor C. H. Spurgeon.
Gems from New Books: Home of the Tarantula, etc.
Rev. W. F. ReQua's Work Among the Indians—Mr. Muller in New Zealand—A Buddhist's Idols.
PICTURE OF THE NEW MEMORIAL OVER JOHN BUNYAN'S TOMB.
AN ARTIST'S DIFFICULTY. (With Illustration.)
THE EPOCHS OF A LIFE. A New Serial Story by Rev. L. S. Keyser. (Continued.)
CROSSING THE JORDAN. By Mrs. M. Baxter.

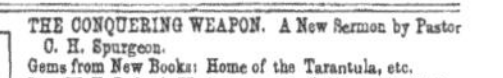

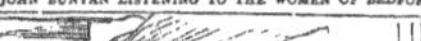

JOHN BUNYAN LISTENING TO THE WOMEN OF BEDFORD.

BUNYAN'S WIFE INDUCING HIM TO READ

JOHN BUNYAN, THE AUTHOR OF "THE PILGRIM'S PROGRESS"—SCENES IN HIS LIFE.

JOHN BUNYAN.

Author of the "Pilgrim's Progress."

His Bicentenary this Year—The Influence of the Puritans—Bunyan's Birth and Early Life—His Childhood's Dreams—Military Service—Early Marriage—Recklessness and Profanity—An Impressive Sermon—A Struggle on a Sunday Ball-ground—Meeting With the Pious Women—Conversion—Begins to Preach—Arrested and Committed to Prison—Twelve Years in Jail—The "Pilgrim's Progress" Written in His Cell—His Release—Last Journey and Death.

AMONG the anniversaries recently celebrated, not one had larger claim on the religious world than that which has just taken place of the Bicentenary of the Death of John Bunyan. What the English-speaking race owes, here and the world over, to the author of the "Pilgrim's Progress" can never be estimated. It is the fashion of modern culture to sneer at Puritanism, but the philosophers who despise it have to admit that their schools have never produced any book which has so won the admiration of cultured and uneducated alike, and held it for so long a period as the work of the Puritan tinker. Moreover, it has also to be admitted that the Puritanism was not concealed in the book, but was the very essence of it. The "Pilgrim's Progress" is in every home to this day; the children read it and love it before they understand its theology; the experienced Christian finds new beauties in it as he goes on his own pilgrimage, and even the cultured unbeliever is overcome with admiration as he recognizes in it the one perfect allegory in the language, a masterpiece of genius in a line in which so many have ventured and failed. We are in danger of forgetting

What America Owes to Puritanism,

while men are holding it up to public scorn and are idolizing the toleration which Puritanism was too conscientious to give, and which in our day is becoming only another name for religious indifference. It may be well, therefore, if this celebration of the Bunyan bicentenary leads us to look back two centuries and see what manner of man this was whose book has lived and kept its hold on the people, while works of his learned contemporaries have sunk into oblivion.

John Bunyan was born in the year 1628, at Elstow, a village about a mile from Bedford, England, and died in 1688, shortly before the landing of England's greatest king, William III. In his wonderful autobiography, entitled "Grace Abounding to the Chief of Sinners," Bunyan tells us that he was the son of a *very* poor man. "My father's house," he says, "being of that rank that is meanest and most despised of all the families in the land." But the lowly parents of John Bunyan had the advantage of living near an excellent free school, established by a philanthropist, where their boy was taught to read and write, which was all the instruction he ever received. Bunyan has left us

A Description of his Childhood,

which shows us that even at an early age his imagination was unusually strong and active, and was deeply saturated with the Puritan doctrines, then gaining a hold over the poorer classes in England, and reaching higher into the ranks of the more thoughtful of the aristocracy. He was haunted by dreams and visions, in which evil spirits in monstrous forms appeared to him, threatening to drag him to the pit; or the day of judgment, with its flaming heavens and trump of terror seemed come; or Tophet disclosed its jaws beside him, belching out horrors, while a circle of fire began to close around him; and at nine or ten years of age grave and troubled thoughts beyond his years agitated and perplexed him. He represents himself as a wicked child, but there is no evidence that his propensities were worse than might be expected in a child in his circumstances. Still there is no doubt that he was a bold, reckless boy; the wilfulness of his character being apparently left without restraint, save the occasional whispers by which conscience stirred his apprehensions and appealed to his fears. "Yea," he says, "I was also then so overcome with despair of life and heaven, that I often wished either that there had been no hell, or that I had been a devil, supposing that they were only tormentors; that if it must needs be that I went thither, I might rather be a tormentor than be tormented myself."

He Became a Tinker,

like his father, when his brief school-days were over, and there is evidence that he was an adept in the trade. From mending the pots and kettles of the neighbors, he must have advanced to a larger business, if we may judge from the list of articles which he made over to his wife some years later, when in danger of arrest for preaching. It is certain, however, that for some five or six years he made little progress in financial position, but worked in his father's shop at the ordinary labor. It was an exciting time. The civil wars between King Charles I. and his Parliament were raging, and England was rent asunder by religious and political divisions of the most stirring nature. Bunyan, though only seventeen years old, was drawn for the army. So little importance did he attach to any event outside of religion, that he omits to tell us on which side he was enrolled. Incidental allusions, however, conclusively show that it was on the King's side that he was called to serve. All that is known of his military life is that he was present at the siege of Leicester in 1645. It is probable that it was while he was in the army that he gathered illustrations for his "Holy War," finding in Cavalier troops and Roundhead officers models for the mystic warriors who figure in the annals of beleaguered Mansoul. The troop in which he served was evidently soon disbanded, and Bunyan returned to his tinker's work at Elstow much as he had left it. He was fond of athletic sports, and seems to have been a jovial, reckless youth, addicted to profane language, but never drunken or unchaste.

His Early Marriage,

which occurred soon after his return, was probably not opposed by his friends, who may have thought it would steady him. The girl whom he chose was a poor orphan, whose deceased parents had been "counted godly." She was as poor as himself, *her only dowry being two books.* "This woman and I," Bunyan writes, "though we came together as poor as poor might be, not having so much household stuff as a dish or spoon betwixt us both, yet this she had for her part, 'The Plain Man's Pathway to Heaven,' and 'The Practice of Piety,' which her father had left her when he died." These books proved to be treasures above all price to the poor tinker. Moreover, his wife was a devout Churchwoman, and she led her boy-husband, then only nineteen, from the Sunday games on Elstow Green to the parish church, to which she was in the habit of going morning and evening; and when the evening service was concluded, the youthful pair would return to their humble cottage and read together until darkness closed, and obliged them to shut the volume.

But the strong imagination and eager unsatisfied intellect of Bunyan yearned for some greater excitement than the calm, reverent services of the Church of England. He went back to the village green to join in the Sunday games of ball, and was not sensible of the evil and danger of sin. One Sunday the clergyman preached

A Sermon on Sabbath-Breaking,

which greatly impressed his singular parishioner, who says he was set "thinking and believing that he made that sermon on purpose to show me my evil doing, and so went home with a great burden on my spirit." Having partaken, however, of his Sunday dinner, the impression wore off, and he joined the revellers on the village green with accustomed energy and delight. "The same day, as I was in the midst of *a game of tip-cat,*" he says, "and having struck it one blow, just as I was about to strike it a second time a voice did suddenly dart from heaven into my soul," which uttered the words that come to every thoughtful man of every creed at some time in his life, and which place before him the alternative from which he cannot escape: "Wilt thou leave thy sins and go to heaven, or

Have Thy Sins and go to Hell?"

"At this I was put to an exceeding maze; wherefore, leaving my cat upon the ground, I looked up to heaven, and was *as if I had*, with the eyes of my understanding, *seen the Lord Jesus looking down upon me*, and as if He did severely threaten me with some grievous punishment." The effect of this singular experience was a fit of despair, as "it was now too late for me to look after heaven, for Christ would not forgive me nor pardon my transgression"; and he resolved that as he *must* be lost, to enjoy at least the present as far as it was possible. He returned desperately to his sport again, and from that day relapsed into the sins he had for a time abandoned, using habitually such profane and blasphemous language, that a woman, "though she was a very loose and ungodly wretch," actually reproved him for it, saying that his words made her tremble, and that he would ruin all the youths in the village. He was struck with a conviction of his fearful wickedness, and turned away silent and ashamed. From that day he strove hard to break himself of his sinful habit, and tried to speak without oaths and curses.

One day he met with a pious man who "talked pleasantly" to him "of the Scriptures and of religion." He procured a Bible, but read only the historical books, avoiding, as was natural, the Epistles of Paul. He set the Commandments before him as his way to heaven, and for a year lived a reformed life externally. He was looked upon as a prodigy of piety. His neighbors, who had been shocked by his daring wickedness, were much pleased with the change, and Bunyan, ever eager for the sympathy of others, rejoiced greatly in their esteem and commendations; yet was inwardly conscious that they were not fully deserved; "for," he writes, "had I then died, my state had been fearful."

Four Pious Women

whom, while engaged in his work in a street in Bedford, Bunyan overheard talking of religion, were the first means used of God to put the young man in the way of salvation. The women were sitting knitting and spinning at the door in the sun, and talking about the things of God. (*See Illustration on first page.*) "Being now willing to hear their discourse," he relates, "I drew near, for I was now *a brisk talker* in matters of religion; but they were far above my reach. Their talk was about a new birth, the work of God in their hearts, as also how they were convinced of their miserable state by nature. They talked how God had visited their souls with His love in the Lord Jesus, and with what words and promises they had been refreshed, comforted, and supported against the temptations of the devil. They also discoursed of their own wretchedness of heart, and of their unbelief; and did condemn, slight, and abhor their own righteousness as filthy and insufficient to do them any good.

Full of the new train of thought which the conversation of these pious women had awakened, Bunyan sought their company again and again; he told them of his condition, and was by them introduced to their pastor, John Gifford, a Baptist preacher, and who in all probability is the Evangelist in the "Pilgrim's Progress." At this time he underwent severe spiritual trials and fiery temptations, but the record is too long and too elaborate to be given here. A detailed account of them is given in his "Grace Abounding," and "The Jerusalem Sinner Saved." At length he lighted on a tattered copy of Luther's "Commentary on the Galatians," which afforded him great support and comfort. It seemed to him, he said, as if it had been written out of his own heart; and he ever afterwards prized the work of the Reformer next to the Bible itself. A vivid scene (depicted in illustration No. 2) flashes out upon us in his autobiography. It is that of Bunyan and his wife in conversation about an expression like a revelation from heaven. "Wife," said c, " is there such a Scripture as, 'I must go to esus?' She replied, "I cannot tell;" therebre Bunyan stood musing, to see if he could emember it. In the course of a few minutes, e recalled what is written in the twelfth chapr of Hebrews: "Ye are come to Mount Zion . . to God, the Judge of all, and to the spirits f just men made perfect, and *to Jesus the Meditor of the New Testament*, and to the blood of prinkling." Then with joy he told his wife, Oh now I know, I know!" He writes, "That ight was a good night to me; I have had but ew better. All my former darkness had fled way, and the blessed things of heaven were set n my view."

Being now able to confess Christ as his Savour, he was baptized by Mr. Gifford, and enolled in the membership of the church. This ook place in the same year as that in which Dliver Cromwell became Lord Protector, 1653, Bunyan himself being about twenty-five years of age. Two years afterwards he was

Chosen to Become a Preacher

and attained marvellons popularity. His friend Charles Doe says: "When Mr. Bunyan preached in London, if there were but one day's notice given, there would be more people come together to hear him preach than the meetinghouse would hold. I have been to hear him preach to about 1,200 at a morning-lecture by seven o'clock on a working-day, in the dark winter time. I also computed about 3,000 that came to hear him one Lord's day at London, at a town's-end meeting-house (in Southwark) so that half had to go back again for want of room, and himself at a back door had to be pulled almost over the people to to his pulpit."

A heavy grief fell on Bunyan in the year 1658. He lost his beloved wife, who left four young children to his care. Some little time afterwards he gave them a stepmother as well chosen as his first wife had been. The restoration of Charles II., after Cromwell's death, brought trouble on Bunyan and his fellow-Nonconformists. They were forbidden to meet for Divine worship, or for preaching, under pain of being stripped of their property, consigned to a gaol, and doomed to all kinds of indignities. Preachers were exposed to especial danger. At length, on November 12, 1660, only five months after the Restoration, Bunyan became one of the sufferers. He was about to preach at Samsell, a hamlet near Harlington, Bedfordshire, when he was interrupted and

Arrested for Preaching

by a constable. (*See Illustration No. 3.*) He was not taken by surprise. He had had timely warning of his danger, but had disdained to shrink from that which he considered his duty, from fear of death or imprisonment. The next day he was committed to Bedford gaol by Mr. Justice Wingate, where he lay like a captive eagle for *twelve long years.*

Bunyan's wife made most persevering efforts to obtain her husband's liberation. She appealed to the House of Lords, to the Judges of Assize, and to the excellent Chief Justice Hale himself, who gave her his pity, but as Bunyan would not give his promise to abstain from preaching if released, even Hale could do nothing for him, and probably thought that he was better in prison than running the risk of getting transported for open defiance of the King. In the "den," as he called the cell of Bedford gaol, Bunyan wrote the first part of

"The Pilgrim's Progress,"

the most delightful of the prison books that have been the gift of sanctified captive genius to the world. It is worth noticing, and is certainly very remarkable, that the visions which haunted Bunyan's mind during his thraldom were of a brighter character than those which had belonged to his free, wandering life. The quiet of the gaol seems to have disciplined and calmed his imagination. Still his sufferings were considerable.

His Release

from prison came in the year 1672, and was due not to the King's sympathy, but his desire to relieve the Roman Catholics of their disabilities. He could not show favor to them alone of the numerous sects which were opposed to the Church of England. He, therefore, had to make common cause with the Roman Catholics and other denominations. Bunyan consequently was released with other preachers of divers sects, and at once recommenced his work. We learn from Doe's narrative that he became pastor of the congregation in Bedford shortly before his liberation from gaol. "The pastor of the Bedford congregation died, and, after some years, vacancy, John Bunyan, though a prisoner, was by the Church called to the pastoral office, December 12, 1671," and by the connivance of the local authorities he had been let out of prison to preach, returning to his cell at night. The remainder of his life was passed in happy and uneventful labor for the Master.

During the last year of his life, Bunyan is said to have published six volumes of his writings (he was the author of no fewer than *sixty* different works), and, at length, worn out with sufferings, premature age, and abundant labors, the day of his dissolution drew near. His last act was a labor of Christian love. A young gentleman, a neighbor of his, having, in some way or other, offended his father, who was dying, was much troubled in mind on that account, and also because he had learned that it was his father's intention to disinherit him. He, therefore, earnestly desired Mr. Bunyan to go and plead with his offended parent, and prepare his mind to receive and forgive him. He readily undertook the mission; and so, riding to Reading, he there used such pressing arguments that the father was mollified, and was soon completely reconciled to his son. Proceeding from Reading to London on horseback, he was overtaken by a heavy shower of rain, and was wet through. On arriving at the house of his friend, Mr. Strudwick, a grocer on Snow Hill, he felt ill and depressed. He had only strength to preach once. Two days later he was seized with fever, and in ten days he was dead. His last words were, "Take me, for I come to Thee."

ANECDOTES RELATED AT RECENT EVANGELISTIC MEETINGS.

An Aged Man's Dying Testimony. — Mr. Stewart remarks: "I was recently at the deathbed of an old man, who was so weak that he could not even raise his head, yet he wanted to leave his testimony for Christ. Making a very feeble sign with his hand which I knew meant to come near to him, I did so. I bent my ear close to his mouth, and he whispered to me, 'Tell everyone that it is only, trust Jesus. If it had been required that I must do anything to save myself, I should not have been able to do it, but I can trust Jesus, and am saved. Blessed be His name!' After this simple testimony he passed away with a smile upon his lips."

Working Inside a Cylinder.—"In the Construction of a railway bridge over the Forth, a number of cylinders were being sunk in sections, the one on top of the other. Sometimes they did not fit, and in that case a composition, consisting mostly of iron turnings, was filled in, and this being wetted it expanded and filled the crevices. A number of the cylinders were up, and most of the work had been done by one man. One dull, hazy day, heavy with oppressive heat, this man, who was engaged as usual, was observed to become overpowered with some mysterious influence. A companion descended by a windlass to help him, and managed to prop him up in the bucket; and soon he was pulled into the fresh air, where he quickly recovered. But his deliverer was in turn overpowered, and, falling back into a pool at the bottom of the cylinder, was drowned. One of the engineers descended to examine, first putting a rope about his body. It was well he did so, for he, too, was rendered insensible. There was no actively injurious gas at the foot of the cylinder, but the composition in its rapid oxidation took the greater part of the oxygen from the air, and left only that part which cannot support life. Does this not illustrate how the careless Christian, who would not go where there is active sin, but too often goes heedlessly where the name of God is never mentioned, where there is no continual current of grace to sustain the soul, falls, becomes insensible, and unless some higher power takes hold of him, he is lost for ever?"

A Drunken Pugilist Won. — An Open-Air evangelist said: "At one of the tent meetings there was a man who entered rather the worse for drink. As he behaved ill the preacher had him ejected. He retired to the neighboring saloon and told how he had been treated at the tent. A man well known in all that district as a pugilist and a very great drunkard was present and heard the first man's complaints. 'I will go up to the tent myself,' said he, 'and see whether he'll turn *me* out.' He went in, fully intending to create a disturbance; but he was interested by what he heard and waited to hear more. He listened with ever-increasing interest and wonder to the end of the meeting, having no longer any desire to make a disturbance. He came again the next night, and it was soon clear that the Holy Spirit was working in his heart. He never missed a meeting; he gave up the drink; he yielded his heart to the Lord. It was impossible that such a remarkable work of grace should not become known. It was notorious in the district, and many people came from miles round to hear a man whose preaching had changed even such a fellow as the pugilist."

The Preaching He Couldn't Stand.—The same devoted worker observes: "At Draycott a man who had been a great drinker came to the meeting, as he said, 'to see what an evangelist was like.' He attended for a few nights, and then said to a friend at the close of one of the services, 'I sha'n't come again; I can't stand this preaching. It's too straight for me.' He kept away some nights, and then he was with us once more. This night he resisted the pleadings of God's grace no longer, but yielded himself to Christ. 'And now,' said he, 'I must sign the pledge.' The following Sunday I was visiting a few sick people, and found myself near this man's house. I thought I would take the opportunity to call on him. As I entered I found all the family gathered around him reading the Bible. I expressed my pleasure at finding him thus employed. 'Ah!' said he, 'I am a new man now, and I am going to have new rules in my house. I used to spend my Sunday afternoon in drink. Now I must spend it in a better way.' It has been my pleasure to see him twice since that time, and I have had the joy of seeing that he is adorning the doctrine which he professes."

A Deadly Opiate of Satan's.—Mr. Ross said; "I had a friend who was very much interested in the use and abuse of opium. In order to judge more correctly of its nature he frequently experimented upon himself. I remember on one occasion he took an overdose, which nearly proved fatal. His friends saw the danger in which he was, and at once procured a doctor, who, after examining his patient, shook his head and said, 'No, I fear he will not live; but the only chance is for two of you to take him by the arms and drag him up and down the room the whole night, and if he can be kept awake until morning, by that time the influence of the drug will to a great extent have passed off.' His friends only needed the hint, and throughout all that long night they relieved each other at their work of mercy, but never for one minute letting their half-conscious patient be at rest. As the daylight began to creep in at the window, they were rewarded by their friend being restored to them. How many sinners seem to have fallen asleep under that devilish opiate, 'Go thy ways for this time; when I have a convenient season I will call for thee.' It seems to lull them to sleep, and the longer they sleep the more difficult it is to awaken them. Let us who are their friends give them no rest until we have brought them from under the influence of that falsely soothing and soul-losing delusion."

THE NEBULAR EQUIPAGE.

Dr. Talmage's Sermon Preached Last Sunday Morning, September 30, 1888.

"Who maketh the clouds His chariot." Ps. 104 : 3.

Man Encouraged to Look Up—The Grandeur of Cloudland—A Favorite Bible Simile—The Ancient Chariot—The Cloud Monsters—Modern Royal Chariots—God's Morning-Cloud Chariot—Light Giving—His Evening-Cloud Chariot—Its Call to Prayer—The Black Night Cloud Chariot—Never Turns Aside—What It Has Crushed—Halted by Prayer—Its Two Wheels of Justice and Mercy—The King Himself Drives—A Captain's Prayer on Lake Erie—Notable Historical Deliverances—Clouds that Touch the Earth—Momentous Cloud Rides—The Judgment Chariot.

BRUTES are constructed so as to look down. Those earthly creatures that have wings, when they rise from the earth still look down, and the eagle searches for mice in the grass, and the raven for carcasses in the field. Man alone is made to look up. To induce him to look up, God makes the sky a picture-gallery, a Dusseldorf, a Louvre, a Luxembourg, a Vatican, that eclipses all that German or French or Italian art ever accomplished. But God has failed to attract the attention of most of us by

The Scenery of the Sky.

We go into raptures over flowers in the soil, but have little or no appreciation of the "morning-glories" that bloom on the wall of the sky at sunrise, or the dahlias in the clouds at sunset. We are in ecstasies over a gobelin tapestry or a bridal veil of rare fabric, or a snowbank of exquisite curve, but see not at all, or see without emotion, the bridal veils of mist that cover the face of the Catskills, or the swaying upholstery around the couch of the dying day, or the snowbanks of vapor piled up in the heavens.

My text bids us lift our chin three or four inches and open the two telescopes which under the forehead are put on swivel easily turned upward, and see that the clouds are not merely uninteresting signs of wet or dry weather, but that they are embroidered canopies of shade, that they are the conservatories of the sky, that they are thrones of pomp, that they are crystalline bars, that they are paintings in water color, that they are the angels of the mist, that they are great cathedrals of light with broad aisles for angelic feet to walk through and bow at altars of amber and alabaster, that they are the mothers of the dew, that they are ladders for ascending and descending glories, Cotopaxis of belching flame, Niagaras of color, that they are the masterpieces of the Lord God Almighty. The clouds are

A Favorite Bible Simile,

and the sacred writers have made much use of them. After the Deluge God hung on a cloud in concentric bands the colors of the spectrum, saying: "I do set my bow in the cloud." As a mountain is sometimes entirely hidden by the vapors, so, says God, "I have blotted out as a thick cloud thy transgressions." David measures the divine goodness, and found it so high he apostrophized: "Thy faithfulness reacheth unto the clouds." As sometimes there are thousands of fleeces of vapor scurrying across the heavens, so, says Isaiah, will be the converts in the millennium "as clouds and as doves." As in the wet season no sooner does the sky clear than there comes another obscuration, so, says Solomon, one ache or ailment of old folks has no more than gone than another pain comes "as clouds return after the rain."

A column of illumined cloud led the Israelites across the wilderness. In the book of Job, Elihu, watching the clouds, could not understand why they did not fall, or why they did not all roll together, the laws of evaporation and condensation then not being understood, and he cries out: "Dost thou know the balancing of the clouds?" When I read my text it suggests to me that the clouds are the Creator's equipage, and their whirling masses are the wheels, and the tongue of the cloud is the pole of the celestial vehicle, and the winds are the harnessed steeds, and God is the Royal occupant and driver "who maketh the clouds His chariot."

To understand the Psalmist's meaning in the text, you must know that the chariot of old was sometimes a sculptured brilliancy, made out of ivory, sometimes of solid silver, and rolled on two wheels, which were fastened to the axle by stout pins, and the awful defeat of Œnomaus by Pelops was caused by the fact that a traitorous charioteer had inserted a linch-pin of wax instead of a linch-pin of iron. All of the six hundred chariots of Pharaoh lost their linch-pins in the Red Sea, for the Bible says: "The Lord took off their wheels." Look at the long flash of Solomon's fourteen hundred chariots, and the thirty thousand chariots of the Philistines.

If you have ever visited the buildings where a king or queen keeps the

Coaches of State,

as I have, you know that kings and queens have great varieties of turnout. The keeper tells you: "This is the state carriage, and used only on great occasions." "This is the coronation carriage, and in it the king rode on the day he took the throne." "In this the queen went to open Parliament." "This is the coach in which the Czar and the Sultan rode on the occasion of their visit." All costly and tessellated and enriched and emblazoned are they, and when the driver takes the reins of the ten white horses in his hands, and amid mounted troops, and bands in full force sounding the national air, the splendor starts, and rolls on under arches entwined with banners, and amid the huzza of hundreds of thousands of spectators, the scene is memorable. But my text puts all such occasions into insignificance, as it represents the King of the Universe coming to the door of His palace, and the gilded vapors of the heavens rolling up to His feet, and He, stepping in and taking the reins of the galloping winds in His hand, starts in triumphal ride under the arches of sapphire, and over the atmospheric highways of opal and chrysolite, the clouds His chariot.

My hearers, do not think that God belittles Himself when He takes such conveyance. Do you know that the clouds are among the most

Wondrous and Majestic Things

in the whole universe? Do you know that they are flying lakes and rivers and oceans? God waved His hand over them and said: "Come up higher!" and they obeyed the mandate. That cloud, instead of being, as it seems, a small gathering of vapor a few yards wide and high, is really seven or eight miles across, and is a mountain, from its base to its top, fifteen thousand feet, eighteen thousand feet, twenty thousand feet, and cut through with ravines five thousand feet deep. No, David did not make a fragile or unworthy representation of God in the text, when he spoke of the clouds as His chariot. But as I suggested in the case of an earthly king, He has His morning-cloud chariot and His evening-cloud chariot — the cloud chariot in which He rode down to Sinai to open the law, and the cloud chariot in which He rode down to Tabor to honor the gospel, and the cloud chariot in which He will come to judgment. When He rides out in

His Morning Chariot

at this season, about 6 o'clock, he puts golden coronets on the dome of cities, and silvers the rivers, and out of the dew makes a diamond ring for the fingers of every grass blade, and bids good cheer to invalids who in the night said: "Would God it were morning!" From this morning-cloud chariot He distributes light—light for the earth and light for the heavens, light for the land and light for the sea, great bars of it, great wreathes of it, great columns of it, a world full of it. Hail Him in worship as every morning He drives out in His chariot of morning cloud, and cry with David: "My voice shalt thou hear in the morning, in the morning will I direct my prayer unto thee and look up." I rejoice in these Scripture ejaculations: "Joy cometh in the morning." "My soul waiteth for thee more than they that watch for the morning." "If I take the wing of the morning." "The eyelids of the morning." "The morning cometh." "Who is she that looketh forth as the morning." "His going forth is prepared as the morning." "As the morning spread on the mountains." "That thou shouldest visit him every morning." What a mighty thing the King throws from His chariot when He throws us the morning! Yea; He has

His Evening-Cloud Chariot.

It is made out of the saffron and the gold and the purple and the orange and the vermilion and upshot flame of the sunset. That is the place where the splendors that have marched through the day, having ended the procession, throw down their torches and set the heavens on fire. That is the only hour of the day when the atmosphere is clear enough to let us see the wall of the heavenly city with its twelve manner of precious stones, from foundation of jasper to middle strata of sardius and on up to the coping of amethyst. At that hour, without any of Elisha's supernatural vision, we see horses of fire, and chariots of fire, and banners of fire, and ships of fire, and cities of fire, seas of fire, and it seems as if the last conflagration had begun and there is a world on fire. When God makes these clouds His chariot let us all kneel. Another day past, what have we done with it? Another day dead, and this is its gorgeous catafalque. Now is the time for what David called the "evening sacrifice," or Daniel called the "evening oblation."

Oh! oh! what a chariot made out of evening cloud! Have you hung over the taffrail on the ocean and seen this cloudy vehicle roll over the pavements of a calm summer sea, the wheels dripping with the magnificence? Have you from the top of Ben Lomond or the Cordilleras or the Berkshire hills seen the day pillowed for the night, and yet had no aspiration of praise and homage? Oh, what a rich God we have that He can put on one evening sky pictures that excel Michael Angelo's "Last Judgment," and Ghirlandjo's "Adoration of the Magi," and whole galleries of Madonnas, and for only an hour, and then throw them away, and the next evening put on the same sky something that excels all that the Raphaels and the Titians and the Rembrandts and the Corregios and the Leonardo da Vincis ever executed, and then draw a curtain of mist over them never again to be exhibited! How rich God must be to have a new chariot of clouds every evening!

But the Bible tells us that our King also has

His Black Chariot.

"Clouds and darkness," we are told, "are round about him." That chariot is cloven out of night, and that night is trouble. When He rides forth in that black chariot, pestilence and earthquake and famine and hurricane and woe attend Him. Then let the earth tremble. Then let nations pray. Again and again He has ridden forth in that chariot of black clouds, across England and France and Italy and Russia and America, and over all nations. That which men took for the sound of cannonading at Sebastopol, at Sedan, at Gettysburg, at Tel-el-Kebir, at Bunker Hill, were only the rumblings of the black chariot of the Almighty. Aye, it is the chariot of *storm-cloud armed with thunder-bolts*, and neither man nor angel nor devil nor earth nor hell nor heaven can resist Him. On those boulevards of blue,

This Chariot Never Turns

out for anything. Aye, no one else drives there. Under one wheel of that chariot, Babylon was crushed, and Baalbeck fell dead, and the Roman Empire was prostrated, and Atlantis, a whole continent that once connected Europe with America, sank clear out of sight, so that the longest anchor of ocean steamer cannot touch the top of its highest mountains. The throne of the Cæsars was less than a pebble under the right wheel of this chariot, and the Austrian despotism less than a snowflake under the left wheel. And over destroyed worlds on worlds that chariot has rolled without a jar or jolt. This black chariot of war-cloud rolled up to the northwest of Europe in 1812, and four hundred thousand men marched to take Moscow, but that chariot of clouds rolled back, and only twenty-five thousand out of the four hundred thousand troops lived to return. No great snow-storm like that had ever before or has ever since visited Russia.

Aye, the chariot of the Lord is irresistible. There is only one thing that can halt or turn any of His chariots, and that is prayer. Again and again it has stopped it, wheeled it around, and the chariot of black clouds, under that sunlited human breath, has blossomed into such brightness and color that men and angels had to veil their faces from its brightness. Mark you, the ancient chariot which David uses as a symbol in my text had only two wheels, and that was that they might turn quickly, two wheels taking less than half the time to turn than four wheels would have taken. And our Lord's chariot has only two wheels, and that means instant reversal, and instant help, and instant deliverance. While the combined forces of the universe in battle array could not stop His black chariot a second, or diverge it an inch, the driver of that chariot says: "Call upon me in the day of trouble and I will deliver thee." "While they are yet speaking, I will hear."

Two-wheeled Chariot,

one wheel justice, and the other wheel mercy. Aye, they are swift wheels. A cloud, whether it belongs to the cirrhus, the clouds that float the highest; or belongs to the stratus, the central ranges; or to the cumulus, the lowest ranges—seems to move slowly along the sky if it moves at all. But many of the clouds go at a speed that a vestibule-limited lightning express train would seem lethargic, so swift is the chariot of our God; yea, swifter than the storm, swifter than the light. Yet a child ten years old has been known to reach up, and with the hand of prayer take the coursers of that chariot by the bit and slow it up, or stop it, or turn it aside or turn it back. The boy Samuel stopped it. Elijah stopped it. Hezekiah stopped it. Daniel stopped it. Joshua stopped it. Esther stopped it. Ruth stopped it. Hannah stopped it. Mary stopped it. My father stopped it. My mother stopped it. My sister stopped it. We have in our Sabbath-schools children who again and again and again have stopped it.

Notice that these old-time chariots, which my text uses for symbol, had what we would call a high dash-board at the front, but were open behind. And the king would stand at the dash-board and drive with his own hands. And I am glad that He, whose chariot the clouds are,

Drives Himself.

He does not let natural law drive, for natural law is deaf. He does not let fate drive, for fate is merciless. But our Father King drives Himself, and He puts His loving hand on the reins of the flying coursers, and He has a loving ear open to the cry of all who want to catch His attention. Oh, I am so glad that my Father drives, and never drives too fast, and never drives too slow, and never drives off the precipice, and that He controls by a bit that never breaks the wildest and most raging circumstances. I heard of a ship captain who put out with his vessel with a large number of passengers from Buffalo on Lake Erie, very early in the season and while there was much ice. When they were well out, the captain saw, to his horror, that the ice was closing in on him from all sides, and he saw no way out from destruction and death. He called into the cabin the passengers and all the crew that could be spared from their posts and told them that the ship must be lost unless God interposed, and although he was not a Christian man, he said: "Let us pray," and they all knelt,

Asking God to Come

for their deliverance. They went back to the deck, and the man at the wheel shouted: "All right, cap'n, it's blowing nor' by nor'west, now." While the prayer was going on in the cabin the wind changed and blew the ice out of the way. The mate asked: "Shall I put on more sail, cap'n?" "No!" responded the captain. "Don't touch her. Some one else is managing this ship." Oh, men and women, shut in all sides by ay troubles and misfortunes, in earnest prayer put all your affairs in the hands of God. You will come out all right. Some one else is

Managing the Ship!

It did not merely happen so that when Leyden was besieged, and the Duke of Alva felt sure of his triumph, suddenly the wind turned, and the swollen waters compelled him to stop the siege, and the city was saved. God that night drove along the coast of the Netherlands in a black chariot of storm-cloud. It did not merely happen so that Luther rose from the place where he was sitting just in time to keep from being crushed by a stone that the instant after fell on the very spot. Had he not escaped where would have been the Reformation? It did not merely happen so that Columbus was saved from drowning by an oar that was floating on the waters. Otherwise, who would have unveiled America? It did not merely happen so that when George Washington was in Brooklyn a great fog settled down over all the place where this church stands, and over all this end of Long Island, and that under that fog he and his army escaped from the clutches of Generals Howe and Clinton. In a chariot of mist and cloud the God of American Independence rode along here.

On that pillow of consolation I put down my head to sleep at night. On that solid foundation I build when I see this nation in political paroxysm every four years, not because they care two cents about whether it is high tariff, or low tariff, or no tariff at all, but only whether the Democrats or the Republicans shall have the salaried offices. Yea, when European nations are holding their breath, wondering whether Russia or Germany will launch a war that will incarnadine a continent, I fall back on the

Faith that my Father Drives.

Yea, I cast this as an anchor, and plant this as a column of strength, and lift this as a telescope, and build this as a fortress, and propose without any perturbation to launch upon an unknown future triumphant in the fact that my Father drives. Yes, He drives very near. I know that many of the clouds you see in summer are far off, the basis of some of them five miles above the earth. High on the highest peaks of the Andes, travellers have seen clouds far higher than where they were standing. Gay Lussac, after he had risen in a balloon twenty-three thousand feet, saw clouds above him.

But there are clouds that touch the earth and discharge their rain; and though the clouds out of which God's chariot is made may sometimes be far away, often they are close by, and they touch our shoulders, and our homes, and they touch us all over. I have read of

Two Rides that the Lord Took

in two different chariots of clouds, and of another that He will take. One day, in a chariot of clouds that were a mingling of fog and smoke and fire, God drove down to the top of a terrible crag fifteen hundred feet high, now called Jebel-Musa, then called Mount Sinai, and He stepped out of His chariot among the split shelvings of rock. The mountain shook as with an ague, and there were ten volleys of thunder, each of the ten emphasizing a tremendous "Thou shalt," or "Thou shalt not." Then the Lord resumed His chariot of cloud and drove up the hills of heaven. They were dark and portentous clouds that made that chariot at the giving of the law. But one day He took another ride, and this time down to Mount Tabor; the clouds out of which His chariot was made, bright clouds, roseate clouds, illumined clouds, and music rained from all of them, and the music was a mingling of carol and chant and triumphal march: "This is My beloved Son, in whom I am well pleased." Transfiguration chariot!

"Oh," say hundreds of you, "I wish I could have seen those chariots—the black one that brought the Lord to Jebel-Musa, at the giving of the law, and the white one that brought Him down to Tabor!" Never mind, you will see something grander than that, and it will be a mightier mingling of the sombre and the radiant, and the pomp of it will be such that the chariots in which Trajan and Diocletian and Zenobia and Cæsar and Alexander and all the conquerors of all the ages rode will be unworthy of mention; and what stirs me the most is, that when He comes in that chariot of cloud and goes back, He will ask you and me to ride with Him both ways. How do I know that

The Judgment Chariot

will be made out of clouds? Revelation i: 7: "Behold He cometh with clouds." Oh, He will not then ride through the heavens alone as He does now. He is going to bring along with Him escort of ten full regiments. Inspiration says: "Behold the Lord cometh with ten thousand of His saints." But these figures simply mean that there will be a great throng. And as we shall probably, through the atonement of Christ, be in heaven before that, I hope that we can come down in that escort of chariot. Christ in the centre chariot, but chariots before Him to clear the way, and chariots behind Him, and chariots on either side of Him. Perhaps the prophets and patriarchs of the old dispensation may ride ahead, each one charioted—Abraham and Moses and Ezekiel and David and Joshua, who foretold His first coming. On either side of *the central chariot* apostles and martyrs, who, in the same or approximate centuries suffered for Him—Paul, Stephen and Ignatius and Polycarp and Justin Martyr, and multitudes who went up in chariots of fire, now coming in chariot of cloud, while in the rear of the central chariot shall be the multitudes of later days and of our own time, who have tried to serve the Lord—ourselves, I hope, among them. "Behold the Lord cometh, with ten thousand of His saints."

Yes, although all unworthy of such companionship, we want to come with Him on that day to see the last of this old world which was once our residence. Coming through the skies, myriads of chariots rolling on and rolling down. By that time

How Changed this World will Be!

Its deserts all flowers, its rocks all mossed and lichened, its poor-houses all palaces, its sorrows all joys, its sins all virtues, and in the same pasture-field lion and calf, and on the same perch hawk and dove. Now the chariots of cloud strike the earth, filling all the valleys and covering all the mountain-sides, and halting in all the cemeteries and graveyards, and over the waters deep, where the dead sleep in coral sarcophagus. A loud blast of the Resurrection trumpet is given, and the bodies of the dead rise and join the spirits from which they have long been separated. Then Christ our King, rising in the centre chariot of cloud, with his scarred hands waves the signal, and the chariots wheel and come into line for glorious ascent. Drive on! Drive up! Chariots of cloud ahead of the King, chariots of cloud on either side of the King, chariots of clouds following the King. Upward and apast starry hosts and through immensities, and across infinitudes, higher, higher, higher, unto the gates, the shining gates. Lift up your heads, ye Everlasting Gates! for Him who maketh the clouds His chariot, and who, through uplifting grace, invites us to mount and ride with Him!

The Prophetic News and Israel's Watchman (London), edited by the Rev. M. Baxter, may be had from the office of this journal, 63 Bible House, New York; price six cents, including postage. Annual subscription, seventy cents. The following articles, among others, are contained in the number for September:

The Nineteenth Century in the Light of Prophecy.
The Signs of the Coming of the Son of Man.
A Sermon on Christ's Second Coming.
Daniel's Seventh Chapter: The Four Wild Beasts.
Only One Abomination of Desolation.
The Fulfilment of Prophecy. By Frederick S. Gervis.
The Children of Light. By H. Marriott.
The Millennium Far from a Perfect State.
Graven Images: What the Bible Says About Them.
The Seven Trumpets Explained in Their past Year-day Historical Fulfilment.
Passing Events Viewed from a Prophetic Standpoint.

A DEMONIAC AT A CAMP-MEETING.

AN incident which, we believe, has never been published, was recently described in a New York pulpit by a clergyman who witnessed it. He states that, five years ago, he attended a camp-meeting about forty miles west of Chicago. An unusual solemnity pervaded the assembly, and the preachers were filled with the Spirit and with power. One sermon especially moved the crowd which listened to it. The preacher was a young man of remarkable mental gifts, whose handsome features and ready wit had once made him a favorite in worldly society.

After the service a large number of anxious seekers after salvation gathered near the platform, and the preacher went from one to another, answering questions and quoting God's promises to the repentant sinner. He came to one lady, richly dressed and of singularly attractive countenance. She whispered something to him, and the servant of God started back in horror, as if a snake had darted upon him. "Madam," he said, "God will surely send you to perdition!" and then he moved quickly away. The lady was a Norwegian, who a short time before had connected herself with a Methodist congregation in Chicago. The preacher's sermon had been lost upon her, but his appearance had kindled in her wicked heart lustful passions, to which she had long been a slave. The preacher's solemn reply to her abominable suggestion made her quail, and she rose and hurriedly left the meeting.

Shortly before the gathering separated, the woman returned, her face a never-to-be-forgotten embodiment of terror. It was ghastly in its pallor, and in the strange, unearthly light, that blazed in her staring eyeballs.

"What Was it He Said?"

she cried. "Oh, it is true! Hell yawns to receive me! I am lost! lost!" Kind Christian ladies gathered around the agitated woman, and attempted to make her understand that God's mercy in Christ was unbounded, and that the blood of Jesus cleansed from all sin. But the woman's agony was not relieved. Her cries continued, and, as if the very powers of the evil one already held her, she shook with appalling distress. One and another of the preachers came, and realized that in such a case human speech was vain. Only God Himself could relieve the agony of conviction which His Spirit had awakened. All knelt in prayer, the horror-stricken woman in the centre of a circle of pleading Christians. It was about 7 o'clock in the evening, and the scene drew a crowd of sympathetic spectators. Not for long, however. The horror of the struggle sent them away, overcome. It was as if Satan himself held possession of the woman and refused to depart. Spasmodically, as though struggling against a power trying to compel silence, she uttered

Fearful Confessions

and self-accusations. She said that she was a woman living on vice, that she was an inmate of a well-known disorderly house in Chicago. Her prey had been men of high character, and she had frequented churches to get acquainted with them, had fascinated them, got them in her power, and then blackmailed them. Was it possible such a sin could be forgiven? But there was worse. Some awful crime struggled for confession. A terrible conflict was going on. The woman's face was distorted, and perspiration and tears rendered her comely features repulsive as she knelt on the ground, now almost prostrate, now raising herself and sitting back on her heels and bending wild, distracted eyes on those who were telling her of Christ and pardon. "I must tell!" she cried, in agony. Then the faces of all around her were blanched as she told how that she had a child, that it became an intolerable burden to her, and how, finally, she and another woman had taken the babe to the lake one night and had drowned it. She bent forward as she revealed her awful secret, her eyes fixed on the ground. More than four hours had passed since she first knelt there, and her mental suffering had been so fierce and protracted that strong men had broken down in witnessing it, and it seemed as if the woman must die in the struggle. It was

A Strange, Weird Scene.

All around nature lay calm, beautiful, peaceful in the still midnight of the country. There was a dark background of forest trees, and away, undulating under the placid light of the moon, the wide plain clad in summer verdure. But there was no corresponding calm in the group of anxious, sympathizing, compassionate men and women, watching the conflict of the human being who, so long the slave and instrument of Satan, working his will, ever bringing new and noble victims to his prison-house, was struggling to break from his power, and to serve him no more. The spectators thought of that scene in the gospels (Mark 9 : 26), when the spirit rent the demoniac sore, "and he was as one dead, insomuch that many said he is dead."

Piercing screams rent the air after the woman had uttered the last appalling confession. She declared that she saw the abode of the lost open before her, that Satan was dragging her down to torment there, and besought those near her to hold, to save her. Their powerlessness seemed to be borne in upon her mind, and looking up to the deep summer sky above her, she cried out in piteous entreaty:

"O Jesus, Save Me!"

It was scarcely a human face that she raised to heaven. The agony of the conflict, the fierce passion with which it had been waged within her, had distorted her features until the countenance was tigerish, almost devilish, in its ferocity and desperation. Only for a minute was that face seen. As when the Master said to the storm-tossed sea, "Peace be still, and there was a great calm," so over that upturned face came a heavenly peace. The passion, the terror, the despair, faded out of it, and in their place came the sweetest, softest, most placid expression of rest in Christ. The conflict, which had continued from 7 o'clock until after midnight, was at an end. The victory was won. Satan was cast out, and his poor victim, weak and exhausted, but full of joy unspeakable, was resting in the arms of her Deliverer.

Among the successful Christian workers in Chicago, there is not one now so much used of God in rescuing the fallen and despairing, as the woman thus delivered on that camp-meeting ground five years ago. In the haunts of vice, in the prisons, and in the dens of infamy of the city, she points men and women to Christ and tells them of His power to deliver. "Her sins, which were many, are forgiven, and she loves much."

REV. W. F. RE QUA'S WORK.

IN an encouraging, cheerful letter about his work, received last week, Mr. Re Qua informs us that he has received an invitation from a chief of the Sac and Fox Indians to visit the tribe and hold meetings. The Indian who forwarded the invitation said that if the time could be fixed, word would be sent to all scattered members of the tribe, and a large number would gladly attend. This is a door unexpectedly opened to Mr. Re Qua of which he will not be slow to avail bimself.

At the time of writing, he and his devoted wife were setting out in their wagon, with tent and baggage, to hold meetings sixty miles away. The call there stated that no missionaries had been there, and that the prospect of good meetings was bright. Mr. Re Qua earnestly desires the prayers of our readers that these meetings may be blessed of God to the the conversion of many benighted souls.

Consecrated Corn

is one of the sources from which this self-denying missionary and his wife derive help in their home in the Indian Territory. They live from day to day with no regular income; but God, in whom they trust, alone knows their needs, and has hitherto never suffered them to want. Among the cheering letters which have reached them is one from a good brother at Eau Claire, Wis., who says that he earnestly desires the spread of the gospel among the Indians, who, living in the midst of a Christian nation, ought not now to be in a condition of heathenism. As he cannot himself preach the gospel to them he feels it his duty to help those who are doing so. He has, therefore, set apart a field of corn, the produce of which will be always devoted to the support of Mr. Re Qua's work. He authorizes the missionary also to purchase on the installment plan the portable organ of which he has been so long in need, and promises to remit the payments regularly. This is an encouragement to the missionary in his work. Hardship and toil he expected when he entered upon it, and he has found them in abundance; but God has raised him up many friends whose gifts and sympathy have greatly helped him. His address is, Rev. W. F. Re Qua, McAlister, Ind. Ter.

MR. GEORGE MULLER IN NEW ZEALAND.

A PRIVATE letter from Auckland, dated July 16, 1888, gives incidentally intelligence of the movements of this venerable servant of God, now *eighty-three years old*. In the course of his letter the writer says: "Since I last wrote we have had a long visit from dear Mr. Müller. The Lord's people generally have benefited much from his ministrations. He was particularly happy in the choice of his subjects; this has tended greatly to confirm the tottering faith of some in Auckland, especially on points like 'the larger hope,' 'conditional immortality,' and other forms of error, which have been rife here of late. He spoke out also in no uncertain sound upon the doctrine of 'the higher Christian life,' which you will remember had been taken up so enthusiastically by some here. Mr. Müller put it upon a firm Scriptural basis, but I do not know if he reached that particular section of the community. At his meetings in the City Hall every school of thought was represented. One could see Jews, sceptics, and, indeed, all classes of the people, both religious and irreligious. A prominent Christian gentleman told me how greatly he had benefited, and how deeply grateful he was to dear Mr. Müller for his help. Our mutual friend, Rev. ——, also got a lift, although he was away from Auckland the greater part of the time. Mr. Müller is now in Sydney, and proceeds thence *via* Melbourne and Colombo to Burmah."

AN AGED BUDDHIST'S IDOLS.

IN a recent letter from Miss Reuter, of the China Inland Mission, who is stationed at Hon-chau, she relates the following story of the conversion of an aged Buddhist: An elderly gentleman, named Ce'ien, has been several times to the open-air meetings, and listened very attentively. Yesterday he really gave testimony before the people, telling them how true this our doctrine was. This morning he came to see the native pastor Hsi, because he wanted to believe in Jesus, who would save him from hell. He wished to see us, so Pastor Hsi led him in. He told us his story. He has been in six provinces of China, has heard the gospel doctrine in Shanghai, T'ai-yuen and P'ing-yang. Being in business in Shan-tung, he had heard the doctrine there also. In Tung-chau he fell ill with fever, when some Christians saved his life, which he could never forget. When we came to Hon-chau his hope was to hear of the doctrine, but outsiders prevented him, saying he was an old man and we young, and also that we did not receive poor people. Well, we began some out-door meetings, and he attended them. As Mr. Hsi, spoke, he said, his words sank deep into my heart. He has come again and again, and got so convinced of the truth that he dared not put up idols on New Year's Day. He had been a zealous worshipper of Buddha for eighteen years. I asked him what his opinion was about the worship of idols, if it was a sin. He said, I know they are all false, and whenever you like to come to my home we will take them all down. I want to walk in the light. He is fifty-eight years of age.

He has told that his wife's hands were very much swollen one day, since he became a Chris tian, and that he taught her to pray, and they both together asked God to heal her, and that she was healed. He himself was unwell, and could not sleep, but, after praying, he was all right. Some women came in, and, after some conversation, he took down his paper idols and his ancestral tablets, and burned them. As we were talking, he said, I have got something more here, and lifting a door to a shrine, I saw two dressed dolls sitting inside. That's my father and my mother, he said; I will bring them also and burn them! I had to promise the women to come again and teach them more. As we knelt to pray, the old man asked God to help him to break off his opium-smoking, and forgive him his sins. Leaving his house, we were almost forced into another, so anxious were the people to learn of Christ.

THE ANGEL'S MESSAGE TO DANIEL.

By Geo. H. Pember, M. A.*

A Crisis in Jewish History—Daniel's Perplexity—His Recourse to Prayer and Fasting—An Angel Sent to Explain—He Reveals the Period of Testing—Sixty-nine Weeks of Years—Then the Prince to Appear—The Exact Fulfilment—Prophetic Time Suspended—The Seventieth Week Yet Future.

In the fourth year of the reign of Jehoiakim, just before Nebuchadnezzar came to Jerusalem for the first time, God foretold the impending trouble by the mouth of Jeremiah, and also set His limit to it. Judah should be a desolation, and should serve the king of Babylon seventy years; at the close of which time Babylon should be punished, and the land of the Chaldeans destroyed. (Jer. 25: 8-14.) The prophet did not, however, add anything respecting the restoration of his countrymen.

But shortly after the departure of the second band of captives—Jehoiachin and those who were taken with him—the false prophet Hananiah declared that within the space of two years the Lord would break the yoke of Nebuchadnezzar from off the neck of all nations, and bring back to Jerusalem the vessels of the Lord's house which had been carried away to Babylon. (Jer. 28: 10-17.) The same strain was taken up among the captives by Ahab, the son of Kolaiah, and Zedekiah, the son of Maaseiah: the hope of the exiles was raised, and many of them contemplated an immediate return to Judea.

But this was forbidden by a letter from Jeremiah, who directed them to settle in Babylonia, since God would have them to do so until the end of the seventy years, and would then visit them, and permit them to return to their own country. (Jer. 29: 4-14.) Apparently the people obeyed and remained where they were.

At last, however, the empire of the Chaldeans fell, and in the first year of the reign of Darius the Mede, Daniel, who had been promoted to the place of prime minister, became perplexed and anxious, probably from

A Twofold Cause.

He had carefully studied the prophecies of Jeremiah, and found that permission had been given to return to Jerusalem within two years from that time; for it was then about the sixty-ninth year of the captivity. Yet when he considered the disposition of his people, he saw that their exile had not led them back to God, that they were not chastened and humbled by affliction, and were, therefore, by no means in a condition to receive mercy at the hand of the Lord.

And again, he was well aware that there would be a gathering of all Israel from the nations among which they had been scattered, when the Messiah would rule over them in their own country; and he seems to have looked upon this grand restoration as identical with the return at the end of the Seventy Years. Hence a great perplexity; for he knew by former revelations that four Gentile empires must run their course before the sovereignty could be transferred to Israel. And as yet only one of these had fallen; there were still three to fulfil their destiny, and the last of them must pass through three phases; while for all these great events there remained but a little more than one year!

Such seems to have been Daniel's perplexity, and he was quite unable to solve the enigma. His procedure was, however, characteristic. The difficulty in regard to the empires he left, not doubting that God would find a way to accomplish His own purpose; but remembering that, in the terrible prediction of Moses respecting the captivity (Levit. 26: 40-46), confession is mentioned as that which will cause the Lord to return to His people, he set his face unto the Lord God, to seek by prayer and supplication, with fasting and sackcloth and ashes, and made humble confession for himself and his people, earnestly entreating the Lord to turn away His anger and fury from them and from Jerusalem.

An answer was speedily vouchsafed to the prophet. While he was yet speaking, his prayer was interrupted by a gentle touch, and looking round, he saw the man Gabriel, who had interpreted his previous vision, again standing near him. This heavenly messenger had been despatched from the Throne to assure the greatly beloved one that his petition had been heard, and should ultimately be granted. Thus the prayer of the prophet opened a channel of blessing and called forth

The Great Revelation

of the Seventy Weeks, upon which all other prophecy appears to hinge, and without a clear knowledge of which it seems vain to attempt to understand anything.

The meaning of the angel seems to be—The seventy years of probation will not suffice; nay, after them must come seven times seventy other years. The passage is literally "seventy sevens." The word week is retained because we have no exact equivalent for the Hebrew original, which signifies a period of seven, but does not decide whether the seven are hours, days, months, years, or any other measure of time. That point must always be determined by the context; and in the present passage periods of seven *years* each are doubtless intended, because Daniel's mind is dwelling on the years of Jeremiah.

The four hundred and ninety years of God's pleading with His people were to produce six results: (1) To shut up the transgression; (2) To seal up sins; (3) To cover iniquity; (4) To bring in everlasting righteousness; (5) To seal up vision and prophet; (6) To anoint a Holy of Holies. Such, then, will be the results of God's dealing with the Jews, at the close of the Four Hundred and Ninety Years.

The appointed time for

The Commencement

of these four hundred and ninety years would be the going forth of a command to restore and build Jerusalem. From this date until the appearance of an Anointed One, who should also be a Prince—that is a Royal Priest—Seven weeks, and sixty and two weeks were to elapse; or in other words, there should be forty-nine and four hundred and thirty-four or four hundred and eighty-three years between the edict and the coming of Messiah as a Prince.

The Anointed One, who should also be a Prince can be none other than the Lord Jesus. But at what period of our Lord's life can He be said to have presented Himself as Priest and King? Not at His birth: for He was then only known as the carpenter's son. Not during the greater part of His ministry: for, although He was anointed by the Spirit, and quickly revealed Himself as the great Priest by teaching the people, by cleansing lepers, and by forgiving sins, He, nevertheless, would not put Himself forward as King. On the contrary, He forbade His disciples to disclose His real nature; and when the crowd, excited to enthusiasm by His wonderous words and works, would have set the crown upon His head, He refused.

But at His entry into Jerusalem, four days before His death, His manner changed, and He suffered the whole multitude which followed Him to break forth into the cry;—"Blessed be the King that cometh in the name of the Lord." And when the Pharisees urged Him to rebuke His disciples, He replied;—"I tell you that, if these should hold their peace, the stones would immediately cry out." In other words, He chose at that time to have Himself openly proclaimed King, and Matthew informs us that He did so to fulfil the prophecy of Zechariah: "Tell ye the daughter of Zion, Behold, thy King cometh unto thee, meek, and sitting upon an ass, and a colt the foal of an ass." This prophecy reveals the significance of the event, and shows us that the day indicated was that of the appearing of Messiah as the Prince.

Thus, then, the commencing-point of the Four Hundred and Ninety Years was the promulgation of the edict in the month of Nisan of the twentieth year of the reign of Artaxerxes Longimanus; and the Four Hundred and Eighty-third Year ended on the tenth day of the month Nisan, when Christ entered Jerusalem as the King of the daughter of Zion. Both starting-point and goal are so clearly indicated in Scripture that, as believers, we have no need to trouble ourselves with the uncertainties of human computation, but may at once assume that the interval was exactly four hundred and eighty-three years.

At this point it seems there is a gap separating the sixty-ninth from

The Seventieth Week—

the Four Hundred and Eighty-third Year from the last Seven. For God had given up the sinful nation which rejected His Son: His covenant was suspended, so that they were no longer His people: and, consequently, the course of the Four Hundred and Ninety Years had ceased to run on.

We thus find that there has now been for more than eighteen hundred years an entire cessation of God's dealing with the Jews as a nation. A great gap extends from Messiah the Prince to the false prince that shall come; from the good Shepherd, Whom the flock abhorred and rejected, to the idol shepherd, whom the majority of them will follow to their own destruction; from Him Who came in His Father's name, to that other, who shall come in his own name.

And during the interval between the true Messiah and the false, Hebrew prophecy is almost entirely in abeyance, and there remain in present operation only one or two fearful utterances which stretch, as it were, here and there across the whole width of the chasm. The knowledge of this fact is indispensable to a right understanding of prophecy; for events connected with the two great but now widely separated eras are often mentioned together, even in the same sentence. Nor is there any confusion in such an arrangement: for had the Jews received Christ at His first coming, John the Baptist would have been Elijah to them, the last Seven Years would have followed immediately, and then the kingdom would have been restored to Israel. But the unbelief of the Jews separated those things which might have been joined together, and, consequently, the marvellous events of the last Week have not yet begun to take place.

* From the third edition of his invaluable work entitled "The Great Prophecies Concerning the Jews, the Gentiles, and the Church of God." It is written in a most popular and eloquent style, and describes the impending fulfilment of Revelation and Daniel, and is illustrated by a colored chart. 458 pages. For sale at this office, 63 Bible House, New York. Price, including postage, $1.

OFFICE, 63 BIBLE HOUSE, NEW YORK.
Entered at the Post-Office at New York, N. Y., as Second-Class Matter.

EVERY NUMBER CONTAINS:

The Portrait and Biography of some eminent person.
The Sermon Dr. Talmage preached the last Sunday morning.
An Exposition of Unfulfilled Prophecy.
A Summary of the Events of the Week. Notes of Religious and Temperance Movements, etc.
A Sermon by Rev. C. H. Spurgeon, of London, from advance sheets sent by special arrangement.
Pictures of Missionary Life, etc., and Descriptive Articles.
An instalment of a Serial Story.
An Exposition of the International Sunday-School Lesson, by Mrs. M. Baxter.

ANNUAL SUBSCRIPTION, $1.50.

Single Copies, Price Three Cents, may be obtained by order of any Newsdealer.

NOTICE.

A concession in price will be made to subscribers desiring to introduce THE CHRISTIAN HERALD to ministers, evangelists, or personal friends. It will be mailed regularly every week to any address in the United States or Canada, from September 20 to the end of the year 1888, for twenty-five cents. Address The Manager, 63 Bible House, New York.

CURRENT EVENTS.

The Senate Substitute for the Mills Tariff Bill has at length been reported by the sub-committee to the full committee on Finance. Mr. Allison, Mr. Aldrich, and Mr. Jones of Nevada, are credited with having done the bulk of the work upon it. The reduction which its provisions would effect is estimated at sixty-five millions. The additions to the free list are principally chemicals, with a few raw materials, such as manila, sisal grass, and jute. The largest item of the total reduction is fifty per cent. in the sugar duties. Next to this, and nearly as large an amount, is due to an entire repeal of the tobacco tax. The Republicans, however, are not united on this provision of the bill, and if it is not changed in committee, an effort to modify it will be made in the Senate. A number of Senators believe that cigars, cigarettes, and cheroots should not be left untaxed. The sub-committee itself is not certain that the whole tobacco tax should be repealed, although it is so provided in the bill as it stands. The next largest item of reduction is from $5,000,000 to $6,000,000, taken off by putting alcohol for use in the fine arts on the free list. The duty on higher grades of wool is increased one cent per pound. That on tin plates, which it was expected would be raised, has not been changed. The bill may undergo changes before it reaches the Senate, as an effort is to be made to have it perfectly satisfactory to every Republican Senator before it is reported, in order to avoid discussion in the Senate. At present it would not have the cordial support of the whole party.

A Slight Improvement in the Reports from the yellow fever district was noted last week. There was but little decrease in the figures from Jacksonville, Fla., each day, but the cases were of a milder type, and a more hopeful feeling was said to prevail. Each day, however, there were more than a hundred new cases, and on Tuesday the number reached 143. There were only four deaths on that day however, and the highest number on any day of the week was ten. The reports at the close of the week showed that about 2,500 cases in all had been under treatment, and the total number of deaths under 250. Liberal contributions flow into the city from all quarters. They are distributed with as much care as possible, but it is found that many families who really need help do not get it, through their reluctance to push their way through a greedy crowd which besieges the relief bureau. Reporters describe the city as greatly changed. Business is suspended, and an intense stillness prevails, as if it were a city of the dead. The Marine Hospital corps has gone to the relief of the local physicians by taking charge of the principal hospital, and several army surgeons have volunteered for service there. The panic at Decatur, Ala., and Jackson, Miss., has considerably abated, though large numbers quitted the city and have not returned. No new cases are reported in either place. At Ocala, Gainesville, and Fernandina the sick are recovering, and the new cases are of a mild type.

The Nomination of Mr. John H. Oberly as Commissioner of Indian Affairs was sent to the Senate last week by the President. Mr. Oberly held the office of Superintendent of Indian Schools before entering the Civil Service Commission, and it is reported that his experience led him to take a deep personal interest in the solution of the Indian problem. His nomination will, therefore, be personally gratifying to himself, as it will give him opportunities for applying principles to the Indian difficulty which thought and experience have led him to adopt. What these principles are the public do not know, but we may sincerely hope that he will be wisely guided. The Indians have suffered so long from mismanagement, and blunders of many kinds, that a truly intelligent and just policy is sorely needed by the much-injured race. Mr. Oberly's place on the Civil Service Commission will not easily be filled. The man needed for it should be in hearty sympathy with the law, with faith in its usefulness. Such a man it will be difficult to find in the ranks of the class from among which office-holders are usually chosen.

A Decisive Lesson to Mormon Agents was administered last week by the Collector of the Port, in New York. The steamship *Wisconsin*, which arrived on September 25, had among her passengers fifteen little girls, whose ages ranged from four to twelve years, who were in charge of two Mormon elders. They had no money, and only two of them had friends in this country. In that case the friend was a grandmother, and there was no evidence that she was able to support them. Beside the little girls were a man and his wife, with two sons of weak intellect, and two girls. The man had thirty-one dollars in all, and was fifty-five years of age. They were all going through to Utah, and admitted that they did not know who defrayed the expenses of their passage to this country. The superintendent communicated the facts to the Collector, who promptly ordered the owners of the *Wisconsin* to take the whole party back to England. It may be hoped that the lesson will not be lost upon the Mormons, who of late have grown bold and reckless in evading the law.

The Publication of Extracts from the Diary of the late Emperor of Germany has caused much excitement in the Empire and throughout Europe. Prince Bismarck declares the extracts inaccurate, and has asked the Emperor's permission to prosecute the firm which published them. There are, however, many circumstances which tend to prove the extracts authentic. It is believed that they were given to the press by Baron Roggenbach, the Baden statesman, who was an intimate friend of the late Emperor and was frequently with him during his illness at San Remo. One of the important disclosures made in the diary is the Emperor Frederick's assertion that during the negotiations at Versailles it was proposed to proclaim as King of France Leopold II., King of the Belgians. M. Thiers said he would favor the scheme if it implied a union of Belgium and France. The diary does not state the reason for the abandonment of the proposal, but the French people will accurately surmise that Prince Bismarck's project to create a Franco-Belgian monarchy implied the disruption of France into several States, and the acquisition by Belgium of the northern provinces. Many interesting incidents are related which throw light on the late Emperor's personal character. Among them is a conversation with a French colonel, a prisoner, who had said, "We have lost everything." Frederick replied: "You are wrong in saying that. You have not lost everything; having fought like brave soldiers, you have not lost your honor." It would appear from the diary that the Emperor, had he lived, would have kept his pledges to the Liberals, who consented to let the unification of Germany take precedence over the development of constitutional liberty.

Marshal Bazaine, the Famous French General died in Madrid on September 23. The general was in exile. During the Franco German war of 1870, he took refuge in Metz, where he was surrounded by the German forces under Prince Frederick Charles. After a siege of seven weeks he surrendered with 180,000 men. His countrymen not unreasonably thought that with a little courage and skill Bazaine might, with so large a force, and with so impregnable a fortress as Metz for his base, have fought his way through. After the conclusion of peace, he was charged with treason, tried by court-martial and condemned to death. President MacMahon commuted the sentence to twenty years' imprisonment. After a few months confinement the general succeeded in making his escape. He went to England, and subsequently to Spain, where he spent the last four years of his life. Bazaine was seventy-seven years of age. It was he who conducted the French expedition to Mexico, and placed Maximilian on the throne.

Turkey and Greece are Disturbed Over a fishery difficulty resembling the Canadian trouble. Turkey has seized a vessel which was fishing for sponges in the Ægean Sea under the Greek flag. Greece promptly demanded reparation, which Turkey has refused. Now Greece has ordered her fleet to get up a hostile demonstration among the islands where the Greek flag had been insulted, and to seize upon the first opportunity of capturing something worth taking. The Greek navy is no powerful fleet, but the fact of the little nation so boldly bidding defiance to Turkey, leads European diplomats to infer that she has the promise of help from Germany, if affairs reach a crisis.

Anxiety About the Fate of Mr. Henry M. Stanley continues unabated. Some slight encouragement to hope for his safety is however afforded by Farran, who was formerly Mr. Stanley's interpreter. He returned to Europe last week, and he confirms the rumors of Major Barttelot's imperious disposition, which may have led to his murder. This it may be hoped was really the cause, as, if he died through the treachery of Tippoo Tib, it is probable that the same treachery may have been fatal to Stanley. Farran left Aruwhimi on account of illness, three days before Major Barttelot started on his fatal journey. He tells many stories of Barttelot's hot temper and the brutality shown by him to the natives, and says he expected that Barttelot would be killed. Stanley, he says, insisted upon the natives being kindly treated. The acts of brutality began soon after Stanley left. Farran believes that Stanley reached Emin Pasha, but he admits that the anxiety felt concerning the explorer is justified. Tippoo Tib, he says, hated Barttelot and, therefore, obstructed the progress of the expedition. King Leopold will send Lieutenant Becker to the Congo to organize a strong expedition to search for Stanley.

A Remarkable Illustration of the Evils of the sweating system has come to light in England. In the course of the Parliamentary inquiry into the causes of pauperism, it was disclosed that even the contractors who supply the Queen and her household are guilty of grinding the faces of their employes. It was shown that the magnificent embroidery of her Majesty's carriage cushions had been worked by a cripple, living in a garret and paid barely sufficient to keep off starvation.

The Rev. A. B. Simpson Announces that the (th annual Convention for Christian Truth, ife, and Work, and Divine Healing will be eld October 7 to 15, in Standard Hall, on roadway and Forty-second Street, New York. he first sessions will be given to teachings con- ected with spiritual life, followed on Thursday id Friday by the subject of Divine Healing. aturday and the closing Sabbath will be de- oted to the great theme of practical consecra- on, with special reference to Christian Work id Missions. The last Monday forenoon will e spent in parting greetings and testimonies. he subject of the Lord's Coming will be also illy presented. Several missionaries are ex- ected to go out from this meeting to Africa, idia, and China. Delegates and others intend- ig to attend the Convention may obtain par- culars as to board, etc., by communicating ith Rev. A. E. Funk, No. 254 West Fifty-fifth treet, New York. The Rev. A. B. Simpson's ongregation will occupy Standard Hall on Sun- ays until the new church building on Eighth venue and Forty-fourth Street is ready for use. is to cost, including site, $178,000, and will in- ude a College Home and a new Berachah Home.

The Government Indian Training-School at arlisle, Pa., has sent out this year about venty-five children who have spent five or iore years at this institution. They were sent their homes, though many would have pre- rred to remain in the East. Some went to Iontana, some to Idaho, others to Arizona, 'ew Mexico, Indian Territory, Nebraska, and akota, representing fifteen different Indian gencies. This party of Indian youth is be- eved by the teachers to be the brightest rowd of boys and girls ever sent out by this hool. So much confidence was placed in iem that they were allowed to return to their Vestern homes without an escort, something ever before done in the history of the school. he party consisted of thirty-five large boys, x small ones, and twenty-one girls.

Prize Suits for Convicts have been Introduc- d in the Michigan State Penitentiary. A new 'arden took charge of the Institution a few ionths ago, and had the convicts clad in the ideous striped clothing used in New York and ther States. The object of the regulation was identify the convicts about the prison, and make them to conspicuous that if they escap- d they would be easily recognized and recap- ired. The change was bitterly resented by the onvicts, but they were obliged to submit. lecently, however, they prepared and presented petition to the prison authorities, proposing a ew system of merit. They asked that any ian who signed a written pledge of good be- avior, promising to obey the prison regula ions in letter and spirit, and kept his pledge or six months, should be entitled to wear the ld plain gray suit until he forfeited it by mis- onduct. Their petition was granted, and the hange in the behavior of the prisoners has een very marked. About eighty per cent. of ie convicts signed the pledge, and are earnestly ying to win the right to wear the coveted suits. lappily for the sinner, he does not have to go rough such a period of probation before he is othed with the robe of Christ's righteousness. le obtains that, not by merit, but by the free ift of God, and with it the power of the new fe. (Rom. 4:4, 5.)

A Method of Exterminating Yellow Fever icrobes is said to have been discovered by Mr. dison, the electrician. A New York daily urnal states that during the past three weeks ir. Edison has given his exclusive attention to periments suggested by the terrible visitation Jacksonville, Fla. His object was to discover me cheap and effective way of lowering the mperature of an infected house to a degree in hich the microbe could not live, and also at ie same time to get rid of the moisture which evelops the microbe. He stated to a reporter e results he has reached. He found that gaso- ie causes an evaporation that destroys the ater in vegetable and organic matter, and the microbe must belong to one of the two kingdoms. Caustic soda has the same effect on wet earth. Rhigolene he found effective in reducing the temperature. Mr. Edison states that on applying rhigoline to a coat in a temperature of eighty-two degrees, it fell to twenty-three degrees in fifteen minutes. The cost of the three articles is less than a cent a pound. Mr. Edison thinks that by coating a house with gosoline, or, in extreme cases, with rhigoline, it would be perfectly disinfected, and that the passage of the microbes would be stopped by sprinkling all roads with caustic soda used in a street sprinkler. A small town like Decatur, Ala., could be disinfected by this process for less than $5,000. The principle on which the remedy is based is that the deadly microbes cannot exist where there is neither heat nor moisture. By eliminating these, the germs could have no power. It is so in the spiritual world. When the soul is completely given up to God, and self utterly dead, temptation and sin lose their power, and perish of inanition. (1 John 5: 18.)

A Baby was Carried off by an Eagle in Kansas on September 22. A farmer living near the Cimarron River went to work in the morning, leaving his babe aged two months in charge of a little girl. When he returned for the mid-day meal, he found the girl in a distracted state, crying bitterly. She said that she took the babe into the garden, and having to return to the house for a minute, she left it there. As she was returning she heard a cry, and saw "the child flying away." The farmer knew at once that an eagle had visited his home and carried away his child. He sent around to his neighbors, and a search party was organized. In about an hour the discharge of a gun attracted attention to one point. The searchers hurried thither and found one of the party struggling with a large eagle, which he was trying to kill with the butt-end of his gun, while the bird was using wings and talons vigorously. The eagle was soon lamed by the new-comers and fluttered away to a bush. It was followed and the child was found there; but it was dead and horribly lacerated. The catastrophe will doubtless lead to dwellers in that locality being careful not to expose their children to that peril. It is much to be wished that such watchfulness resulted from the attacks of the great enemy of souls. Parents who see the children of others become his prey, often neglect the only means of protecting their own offspring. (Prov. 22: 6.)

A Bridal Trip in a Balloon was Taken by a young couple at Providence, R. I., on September 27. The State fair was being held in the Narragansett Park grounds, and an immense concourse of people were present. In the course of the afternoon the news that a wedding was about to take place drew the throng to a spot where a large balloon was tethered. The crowd found the bride and bridegroom in the basket attached to the balloon, and the Rev. E. D. Hall, a Methodist minister, was present to conduct the marriage ceremony. After the words were spoken which made the couple man and wife, the guy ropes were cast off and the balloon rose rapidly and sailed away, the bride and bridegroom waving their farewells to their friends below. Nothing more was seen of them there that day, but at Easton, Mass., about six o'clock a very different scene was witnessed. In a cedar swamp near that place the balloon was being driven by the wind, dragging with it through mud and water the car containing the bridal party. It was carried nearly two miles, the occupants being obliged to cling to the ropes above the basket to keep themselves out of the mud. It was eventually stopped by some spectators, who seized a rope flung out from the balloon, and twisted it around a tree. The eccentricity recently displayed by so many young people in choosing the surroundings of the marriage ceremony implies a lack of appreciation of the solemnity of the occasion, which is confirmed by the records of the divorce courts. This couple especially, may learn from their experience that any exaltation they may attain at the wedding festivities is but temporary. They must return to the miry ways of the earth, when they will need something above them to cling to, to save them from defilement. It may be hoped that they will then be preserved by the only effectual support. (James 1: 27.)

A Hungarian's Application for Naturalization was refused in Philadelphia last week. He presented himself in Judge Arnold's Court of Common Pleas, and presented his first papers, declaring his intentions. Testimony was given as to his having been in the country the prescribed time, and the applicant satisfactorily answered the questions put to him. The clerk was about to administer the oath of allegiance, when the applicant requested to be allowed to affirm. The judge asked on what ground he objected to take the oath, and the man said that he was an atheist, he "did not believe in a Deity of any kind." "Then I will not naturalize you," said the judge, who was at the moment signing the papers, and stopped abruptly. "We do not want infidels in this country," he continued; "we have more than enough of your kind already." The man retired discomfited, blasphemously expressing his disappointment and disgust. Unless he repents, and is pardoned through Christ, there will come another time when citizenship will be refused him. He will not be an infidel then, for he will have ocular proof that God is; but there will be no place in heaven for him. (Rev. 21: 8.)

BRIEF NOTES.

The Rev. Sam Small is running as candidate on the Prohibition ticket for State Senator from Atlanta, Ga.

The two Episcopal dioceses in Ohio will hold special conventions October 16, for the purpose of electing assistant bishops.

Bishop W. X. Ninde and Bishop Hurst, of the Methodist-Episcopal Church, are among the advocates of the Prohibition National Ticket this year.

A computation of the statistics of the internal revenue department shows that the people of this country spend annually more than $800,000,000 for liquor.

The Rhode Island Annual Convention on Divine Healing will be held in Providence on October 22. The meetings will convene in Rev. C. Ryder's Mission Hall.

A gift of $10,000 has been made by Mrs. M. A. Crocker, of San Francisco, to the Young Women's Christian Association of that city, as a nucleus for a building fund.

Remarkably successful revival services are being held at Wellington, Kan., by Rev. H. H. Wells, D. D., formerly evangelist of the Presbyterian Synod of Missouri.

Dr. Wm. M. Taylor, of the Broadway Tabernacle, New York has been elected President of the American Missionary Association, to succeed ex-Governor Washburn.

An Icelandic Lutheran Church has been organized in Winnipeg, Manitoba, and a building erected at a cost of $4,000. Winnipeg has two thousand citizens of Icelandic nationality.

A whole village in Brazil has accepted the Gospel, says a Chicago contemporary, through the instrumentality of a young business man, who invited a missionary to that place.

Mr. Harold Brown, of Newport, R. I., has just given $100,000 for the missionary work in the Episcopal Church. It will be used for the endowment of the missionary episcopate of the church.

In one of the cities of Massachusetts, recently, a middle-aged woman was borne to her last resting-place by four pall-bearers, each of whom she had been the means of rescuing from the clutch of strong drink.

The Synod of the Reformed Presbyterian Church has decided by a vote of 93 to 24 that the ordination of a woman as deacon is in harmony with the New Testament and the constitution of the Apostolic Church.

The success of the publication in Milan of an Italian translation of the Bible in one-cent numbers, has suggested to Ramon Molinas, of Barcelona, the issue of a Spanish translation in the same cheap form. The circulation of the Italian edition is now fifty thousand.

The China Inland Mission, in its annual report for the past year, sets down the number of its stations at 64 in fifteen provinces, with 65 out-stations, 110 chapels, 294 missionaries, 132 helpers, and 2,105 communicants. The number of persons baptized last year was 551. There are 66 organized churches.

The locust plague in Algeria is growing more serious. Sixty thousand laborers and 2,000 soldiers have been utterly unable to keep back the living tide, and the destructive "crickets" blacken the land from Setif to the borders of Tunis. They spread over a surface of about seventy miles, and advanced in black battalions several miles in breadth. The country is completely devastated.

THE CONQUERING WEAPON.

A New Sermon by Pastor C. H. Spurgeon.

"And they overcame him by the blood of the Lamb, and by the word of their testimony; and they loved not their lives unto the death." Rev. 12:11.

The Characteristics of Satan—His Malignant Power—A Formidable Opponent—Yet Has Been Overcome—I. What Weapon was Used—The Blood of the Lamb Signifying Christ's Death—And Substitution—II. How to Use It—Not for Ornament—Not to Quiet Conscience—To Subdue Sin—The Battle-field in the Heavenlies—The Accuser Vanquished—The Way of Access to God Opened—The Battle-field on Earth—Power to Move Men—The Need of the Time.

Wherever evil appears, it is to be fought with by the children of God in the name of Jesus, and in the power of the Holy Ghost. When evil appeared in an angel, straightway there was war in heaven. Evil in mortal men is to be striven against by all regenerate men. If sin comes to us in the form of an angel of light, we must still war with it. If it comes with all manner of deceivableness of unrighteousness, we must not parley for a single moment, but begin the battle forthwith, if indeed we belong to the armies of the Lord. Evil is at its very worst in Satan himself: with him we fight. He is no mean adversary. The evil spirits which are under his control are, any one of them, terrible foes; but when Satan himself personally attacks a Christian, any one of us will be hard put to it.

When this dragon blocks our road, we shall need heavenly aid to force our passage.

A Pitched Battle with Apollyon

may not often occur; but when it does, you will know it painfully: you will record it in your diary as one of the darkest days you have ever lived; and you will eternally praise your God, when you overcome him. Satan is *the* enemy, the enemy of enemies. That prayer of our Lord's, which we usually render, "Deliver us from evil," has the special significance of "Deliver us from the evil one"; because he is the chief embodiment of evil, and in him evil is intensified, and has come to its highest strength.

In this chapter the devil is called the "great red dragon." He is great in capacity, intelligence, energy, and experience. Whether or not he was the chief of all angels before he fell I do not know. Some have thought that he was such, and that when he heard that a man was to sit upon the throne of God, out of very jealousy he rebelled against the Most High. This also is conjecture. But we do know that he was and is an exceedingly great spirit as compared with us. He is a being great in evil: the prince of darkness, having the power of death. Satan is

A Mysterious Personage

though he is not a mythical one. We can never doubt his existence if we have once come into conflict with him; yet he is to us all the more real because so mysterious. As a dragon he is full of cunning and ferocity. In him force is allied with craft; and if he cannot achieve his purpose at once by power, he waits his time. He deludes, he deceives; in fact, he is said to deceive the whole world. To this cunning he adds great speed, so that he is quick to assail at any moment, darting down upon us like a hawk upon a poor chick. He is not everywhere present; but it is hard to say where he is not. He cannot be omnipresent; but yet, by that majestic craft of his, he so manages his armies of fallen ones that, like a great general, he superintends the whole field of battle, and seems present at every point. No door can shut him out, no height of piety can rise beyond his reach. He meets us in all our weaknesses, and assails us from every point of the compass. He comes upon us unaware, and gives us wounds which are not easily healed.

But yet, dear friends, powerful as this infernal spirit certainly must be, his power is defeated when we are resolved never to be at peace with him. According to the text it is said of the saints, "They overcame him." We are never to rest until it is said of us also, "They overcame him." He is a foeman worthy of your steel. Our text brings before us a very important subject for consideration: *What is the conquering weapon?* With what sword did they fight who have overcome the great red dragon? Listen! "They overcame him by the blood of the Lamb." Secondly, *how do we use that weapon?* We do as they did who overcame "by the word of their testimony."

I. First, what is this conquering weapon?

They Overcame Him

by "the blood of the Lamb." The blood of the Lamb signifies, first, the death of the Son of God. The sufferings of Jesus Christ might be set forth by some other figure, but His death on the cross requires the mention of blood. Our Lord was not only bruised and smitten, but He was put to death. That death was the grand fact which is set forth by the words "the blood of the Lamb." The moderns cry, "Why not preach more about His life, and less about His death?" I reply, Preach His life as much as you will, but never apart from His death: for it is by His blood that we are redeemed. "We preach Christ." Complete the sentence. "We preach Christ *crucified*," says the apostle. Ah, yes! there is the point. It is the death of the Son of God which is the conquering weapon. Had He not poured forth His soul unto death, even to the death of the cross—had He not been numbered with the transgressors, and put to a death of shame—we should have had no weapon with which to overcome the dragon prince.

Next, by "the blood of the Lamb" we understand our Lord's death as a substitutionary sacrifice. Let us be very clear here. It is not said that they overcame the arch-enemy by the blood of Jesus, or the blood of Christ, but by the blood *of the Lamb;* and the words are expressly chosen because, under the figure of a lamb we have set before us a sacrifice. The blood of Jesus Christ, shed because of His courage for the truth, or out of pure philanthropy, or out of self-denial, conveys no special gospel to men, and has no peculiar power about it. Truly it is an example worthy to beget martyrs; but it is not the way of salvation for guilty men. You must make it known that "the chastisement of our peace was upon Him," and that "the Lord hath laid on Him the iniquity of us all," or you have not declared the meaning of the blood. Here is

The Hope of Men.

Furthermore, I understand by the expression, "The blood of the Lamb," that our Lord's death was effective in taking away of sin. When John the Baptist first pointed to Jesus, he said, "Behold the Lamb of God, which taketh away the sin of the world." Our Lord Jesus has actually taken away sin by His death. Beloved, we are sure that He had offered an acceptable and effectual propitiation when He said, "It is finished." Christ crucified, Christ the sacrifice for sin, Christ the effectual redeemer of men, we will proclaim everywhere, and thus put to rout the powers of darkness.

II. I have shown you the sword; I now come in the second place, to speak to the question,

How do we Use It?

"They overcame him by the blood of the Lamb." When a man gets a sword, you cannot be quite certain how he will use it. A gentleman has purchased a very expensive sword with a golden hilt and an elaborate scabbard; he hangs it up in his hall, and exhibits it to his friends. Occasionally he draws it out from the sheath, and he says, "Feel how keen is the edge!" The precious blood of Jesus is not meant for us merely to admire and exhibit. We must not be content to talk about it, and extol it, and do nothing with it; but we are to use it in the great crusade against unholiness and unrighteousness, till it is said of us, "They overcame him by the blood of the Lamb." This precious blood is to be used for overcoming; and consequently for holy warfare. We dishonor it if we do not use it to that end.

Some, I fear, use the precious blood of Christ only as a quietus to their consciences. They say to themselves, "He made atonement for sin, therefore let me take my rest." This is doing a grievous wrong to the great sacrifice. A man who wants the blood of Jesus for nothing but the mean and selfish reason that, after having been forgiven through it he may say, "Soul, take thine ease: eat, drink, and be merry: hear sermons, enjoy the hope of eternal felicity, and do nothing"—such a man blasphemes the precious blood, and makes it an unholy thing. We are to use the glorious mystery of atoning blood as our chief means of overcoming sin and Satan: its power is for holiness. Oh, my brothers, to some of us atonement by blood is our battle-axe and weapon of war, by which we conquer in our struggle for purity and godliness—a struggle in which we have continued now these many years. By the atoning blood we withstand corruption within and temptation without. This is that weapon which nothing can resist.

The Battle-field.

Let me show you your battle-field. First, you are to regard Satan this day as being already literally and truly overcome through the death of the Lord Jesus. Satan is already a vanquished enemy. By faith grasp your Lord's victory as your own, since He triumphed in your nature and on your behalf. The victory was the victory of all who are in Christ. He is the representative seed of the woman, and you who are of that seed and are in Christ actually and experimentally, you then and there overcame the devil by the blood of the Lamb. Can you get a hold of this truth? Come, my soul, thou hast conquered Satan by thy Lord's victory! Wilt thou not be brave enough to fight a vanquished foe, and trample down the enemy whom thy Lord has already thrust down? Thou needst not be afraid, but say, "Thanks be to God which giveth us the victory through our Lord Jesus Christ."

This day I would have you overcome Satan in the heavenlies in another sense: you must

Overcome Him as the Accuser.

At times you hear in your heart a voice arousing memory and startling conscience; a voice which seems in heaven to be a remembrance of your guilt. Hark to that deep, croaking voice boding evil! Satan is urging before the throne of justice all your former sins. Things which you had forgotten he cunningly revives. *He knows your secret sins, for he had a hand in most of them.* He knows the resistance which you offered to the gospel, and the way in which you stifled conscience. He knows the sins of darkness, the crimes of the inner chambers of imagery. Since you have been a Christian he has marked your wickedness, and asked, in fierce sarcastic tones, "Is this a child of God?"

The foul fiend tells out the wanderings of our hearts, the deadness of our desires in prayer, the filthy thoughts that dropped into our mind when we have been at worship. Alas! we have to confess that we have even tolerated doubts as to eternal verities, and suspicions of the love and faithfulness of God. When the accuser is about his evil business, he does not have to look far for matter of accusation, nor for facts to support it. Do these accusations stagger you? Now is your opportunity for overcoming through the blood of the Lamb. When the accuser has said his say, and aggravated all your transgressions, be not ashamed to step forward and say, "But I have an advocate as well as an accuser. O Jesus, my Saviour, speak for me!" When He speaks, what does He plead but His own blood? "For all these sins I have made atonement," says He; "all these iniquities were laid on Me in the day of the Lord's anger, and have taken them away." Where is the accuser now? That dragon voice is silenced by the blood of the Lamb.

Still further, the believer will have need to overcome the enemy in the heavenly places in reference to access to God. It may happen that when we are most intent upon communing with God, the adversary hinders us. You seem

Shut Out From God,

and the enemy triumphs over you. You feel very near the world, and very near the flesh, and very near the devil: but you mourn your mise distance from God. You are like a child canhot reach his father's door because a k dog barks at him from the door. What is ay of access? If the foul fiend will not e out of the way.

Can We Force Our Passage?

hat weapon can we drive away the adverso as to come to God? Is it not written we are made nigh by the blood? Is there a new and living way consecrated for us? e we not boldness to enter into the holiest ne blood of Jesus? The dog of hell knows dread name which makes him lie down: we confront him with the authority, and ially with the atonement of the Lamb of He will rage and rave all the more if we Moses to him; for he derives his power our breaches of the law, and we cannot ce him unless we bring to him the Lord has kept the law, and made it honorable. ou must first overcome in the heavenly es before the throne; and when you have thus triumphant with God in prayer, you have grace to go forth to service and to deevil among your fellow-men. How often I personally found that the battle must be fought above!

We Must Overcome

rder to service. Satan would hinder our getsupplies of grace wherewith to overcome ; but with the blood-mark on our foot we go anywhere; with the blood-mark on our d we dare take anything. Having access confidence, we also take with freedom tsoever we need, and thus we are provided nst all necessities, and armed against all asts through the atoning sacrifice. This is the ntain of supply, and the shield of security. Ve overcome the great enemy by laying hold n the all-sufficiency of God, when we really the power of the precious blood of Christ. s, being victorious in the heavenlies, we e down to the pulpit or to the Sundayool class made strong in the Lord and in the ver of His might. Spiritual power of a holy d rests upon us to overcome the spiritual ver of an evil kind which is exerted by Satan, world, and the flesh. The Lord scatters the ver of the enemy, and breaks the spell which ds men captive. Through the blood of the nb we become masters of the situation, and weakest among us is able to work wonders. t is time that I now showed you how this e fight is carried on *on earth*. Amongst n in these

Lower Places of Conflict

its overcome through the blood of the Lamb their testimony to that blood. Every believer o bear witness to the atoning sacrifice and power to save. He is to tell out the doctrine; is to emphasize it by earnest faith in it; and is to support it and prove it by his experience he effect of it. You cannot all speak from pulpit, but you can all speak for Jesus as portunity is given you. You can bear witness he power of the blood of Jesus in your own l. If you do this, you will overcome men in ny ways. First, you will arouse them out of thy. This age is more indifferent to true gion than almost any other. It is alive ugh to error, but to the old faith it turns a f ear. Yet I have noticed persons captivated the truth of substitution, who would not en to anything else. Try that story when ention flags. It has a fascination about it. e marvellous history of the Son of God, who ed His enemies, and died for them—this will est them.

Ve also overcome men in this way, by softenrebellious hearts. Men stand out against law of God, and defy the vengeance of God; the love of God in Christ Jesus disarms m. The Holy Spirit causes men to yield ough the softening influence of the cross. bleeding Saviour makes men throw down ir weapons of rebellion. "If He loves me " they say, "I cannot do other than love Him return." We overcome men's obduracy by blood, shed for the remission of sins.

How wonderfully this same blood of the Lamb overcomes despair. Have you never seen a man shut up in the iron cage? It has been my painful duty to talk with several of such prisoners. I have seen the captive shake the iron bars, but he could not break them, or break from them. He has implored us to set him free by some means; but we have been powerless. Glory be to God, the blood is a universal solvent, and it has dissolved the iron-bars of despair, until the poor captive conscience has been able to escape. How sweet for the desponding to sing—

"I do believe, I will believe,
That Jesus died for me!"

Believing *that*, all doubts and fears and despairs fly away, and the man is at ease.

There is nothing, indeed, dear friends, which the blood of the Lamb will not overcome; for

It Overcomes Vice,

and every form of *sin*. The world is foul with evil, like a stable which has long been the lair of filthy creatures. What can cleanse it? What but this matchless stream? Satan makes sin seem pleasurable, but the cross reveals its bitterness. If Jesus died because of sin, men begin to see that sin must be a murderous thing. Even when sin was but imputed to the Saviour, it made Him pour out His soul unto death; it must, then, be a hideous evil to those who are actually and personally guilty of it. If God's rod made Christ sweat great drops of blood, what will His axe do when He executes the capital sentiment upon impenitent men! Yes, we overcome the deadly sweetness and pleasurableness of sin by the blood of the Lamb.

Consecrated Energy.

But I must close with this. It is not merely by testimony that we use this potent truth. We must support that testimony by our zeal and energy. We need concentrated, consecrated energy; for it is written, "They loved not their lives unto the death." We shall not overcome Satan if we are fine gentlemen, fond of ease and honor. As long as Christian people must needs enjoy the world, the devil will suffer little at their hands. They that overcame the world in the old days were humble men and women, generally poor, always despised, who were never ashamed of Christ, who only lived to tell of His love, and died by tens of thousands rather than cease to bear testimony to the blood of the Lamb. They overcame by their heroism; their intense devotion to the cause secured the victory. Their lives to them were as nothing when compared with the honor of their Lord.

Brethren, if we are to win great victories we must have greater courage. Some of you hardly dare speak about the blood of Christ in any but the most godly company; and scarcely there. You are very retiring. You love yourselves too much to get into trouble through your religion. Surely you cannot be of that noble band that love not their own lives unto the death! Many dare not hold the old doctrine nowadays because they would be thought narrow and bigoted, and this would be too galling. They call us old fools. It is very likely we are; but we are not ashamed to be

Fools for Christ's Sake,

and the truth's sake. We believe in the blood of the Lamb, despite the discoveries of science. We shall never give up the doctrine of atoning sacrifice to please modern culture. Oh to be at a white heat! Oh to flame with zeal for Jesus! O my brethren, hold you to the old faith, and say, "As for the respect of men, I can readily forfeit it; but as for the truth of God, that I can never give up" This is the day for men to be men; for, alas! the most are soft, molluscous creatures. Now we need backbones as well as heads. To believe the truth concerning the Lamb of God, and truly to believe it, this is the essential of an overcoming life. Oh for courage, constancy, fixedness, self-denial, willingness to be made nothing of for Christ! God give us to be faithful witnesses to the blood of the Lamb in the midst of this ungodly world!

As for those of you who are not saved, does not this subject give you a hint? Your hope lies in the blood of the Lamb. The atoning sacrifice, which is our glory, is your salvation. Trust in Him whom God has set forth to be the propitiation for sin. Begin with this, and you are saved. Every good and holy thing which goes with salvation will follow after; but now, this morning, I pray you accept a present salvation through the blood of the Lamb. "He that believeth in Him hath everlasting life."

GEMS FROM NEW BOOKS.

THE HOME OF THE TARANTULA.*

TARANTULAS live in warm countries, and the further south we go the larger and more poisonous we find them. Our small spiders only use their poison to kill their prey; but the large ones of the Tropics will strike people as well as insects with their fangs, which sting severely, and sometimes even cause the victim's death. So the tarantulas are to be feared, and we may be glad the huge creature is not a neighbor of ours. But if they are dangerous and horribly ugly too, with their eight great hairy legs, often long enough to cover a dinner-plate when spread out, they certainly are interesting creatures. Those that live in the warmer parts of our own country are not nearly so large or deadly, and if you ever see one of their houses you will almost forget the owner of it was a little goblin you would not have cared to call upon when at home.

This is the way the tarantula makes a home: instead of spinning an ordinary web, she first digs a tunnel straight into the ground; and when it is large enough, lines it with a web so smooth and soft that it feels like the finest silk. Here is a comfortable home, but you may be sure the spider has no intention of leaving it open for the public to walk in; no, indeed, she must have a front door. So she makes a nice little round door out of earth and sticky web, lines the under side with silk, and fits it exactly to the hole, fastening it with the neatest little hinge, made also of web. Nothing can be prettier than one of these silk-lined tunnels, with the closely fitting door, that opens and shuts so easily. The spider lives inside this comfortable dwelling, which is several inches deep; and if any one tries to pull her front door open, she will hold it down from inside with all her might. What is more wonderful, she will sometimes make a branch tunnel, opening into the first by another little door, and run in there if she does not succeed in keeping intruders out of her main hall.

As the outside of the front-door is rough, and possibly covered with turf, nobody would know, when it is closed, that the spider's house is anywhere near, as the ground looks the same all about; but sometimes it may be found wide open. It is then that the spider ventures forth; and opening her door, which she ties back by a few threads, lest it fall shut again by its own weight, she spins a web all around the mouth of the hole, and goes in again. She does not go in far, but just stands on the threshold waiting for prey, and catches the moths and night-beetles that blunder into the net; just as our own more familiar spiders in the grass spin their webs and dart at their prey from the tunnels they have made. But before morning the tarantula clears away the web and the remains of her supper, that no trace of it shall linger in the neighborhood and betray her whereabouts, and going into her house again, shuts the door and enjoys the seclusion of her safe silk-lined walls.

The Katydid's Music.

Where do they keep their instruments? Look at the hard plates on the katydid's wing covers, close to the body, and behold the secret of its noisy disputes. Did you never see one of these little green-coated creatures, that fill the August evenings with their never-ending discussions?

* From "Little People," by Stella Louise Hook. An excellent little work for young folks, introducing them to the world of natural wonders lying around them, and showing the wonderful wisdom of God in the construction of the tiny bodies of insects in the meadows, woods, and waters. 233 pages, with illustrations. Price $1.50. Published by *Charles Scribner's Sons*, 745 Broadway, New York.

Mr. W. Jennings Demorest.

The New Memorial Over John Bunyan's Grave.

You have often heard them, for they are by no means rare; yet they look so much like the green leaves behind which they hide, that it is not strange you have often passed very near them without seeing them.

The katydid is a slender insect, with a soft, green body, long green legs, large thin wing-covers, that look like leaves, and two very long thread-like feelers. He lives a happy life up in the branches, or in some sheltering vine, protected by the cool leaves, stepping from twig to twig on his long legs, and sometimes spreading his green wings to fly into the shady depths of another tree, when he is tired of the first. All day he rests in the shade of broad leaves that rustle in the summer-breeze, with the birds for neighbors and, perhaps, a few squirrels; but there are not many enemies to molest him, and he passes the long August day peacefully in his cool green tent. Then when darkness falls and the moths come out, katydid comes out too, and begins to assert his opinion. I say *his*, for Mrs. Katydid never joins in her lord's arguments. She has no plates on her wings, and whether she has any opinion as to whether katy did it or not, she has no voice in the matter.

MR. W. JENNINGS DEMOREST.

THE reception tendered on September 24, by the leaders of the Prohibition party in New York, to Mr. Demorest on his return from Europe, was an unequivocal expression of the esteem in which he is held by the large body of his fellow-citizens, who are laboring, according to their lights, for the suppression of the most formidable foe of our national welfare.

Mr. Demorest is a native of New York City. He was born June 10, 1822, and is therefore now sixty-six years of age. His parents were well-known members of the Methodist-Episcopal Church, and it was his own earnest desire to become a minister of that church. Circumstances, however, prevented the young man realizing his cherished wish, and he reluctantly, but with a distinct recognition of duty, entered into business pursuits. His success was phenomenal. He showed a remarkable inventive genius, combined with rare business sagacity. He succeeded in applying electricity as a motor to the sewing machine, and took out a large number of patents for inventions, which gave employment to a large number of hands. Successful purchases of real estate and the founding of several popular trade journals further added to his wealth, until now Mr. Demorest is possessed of a large fortune.

The acquisition of money, however, by no means monopolized Mr. Demorest's time and attention. Various philanthropic enterprises enlisted his sympathy, and to these he devoted money and labor. At one time he was one of the visitors of the Society for the Improvement of the Condition of the Poor, was President of the State Temperance Society, a Manager of the National Temperance Society, and also one of the trustees of the Hospital for Women. For many years he was an active teacher in the Sabbath-school, and was a member of the choir in the old Tabernacle Church on Broadway. But it has been to the Prohibition cause that Mr. Demorest has devoted his chief attention of late years. He became so thoroughly absorbed in its interests, that he turned the management of his business over to his sons, in order to give to Prohibition all his time and energies. He has also been a large contributor to the funds. It was mainly through his munificence that Prohibition speakers were able to visit the South and expound the principles of the movement. In 1885 Mr. Demorest was nominated for Lieut.-Governor of New York, and ran nearly a thousand votes ahead of his ticket.

JOHN BUNYAN'S TOMB.

(See Illustration.)

THE body of the great Puritan preacher and writer, whose portrait and life appear on other pages of this journal, was, like his Master, laid, after his death, in another man's tomb. When seized with the fatal illness which resulted from his long ride in the rain in his journey as a peacemaker, he was at the house of a friend in London. This friend was Mr. John Strudwick, a prosperous grocer belonging to the Baptist community, and a great admirer of Bunyan. When the illness terminated fatally, Mr. Strudwick appears to have extended his hospitality permanently to the body of his dead friend. Bunyan was buried in Mr. Strudwick's tomb in "the Dissenter's Burial Ground" of Bunhill fields. Twelve other persons were subsequently interred in the same grave, whose names were inscribed on the headstone, with this brief record of Bunyan: "Mr. John Bunyan, Author of the 'Pilgrim's Progress.' Ob. August, 1688. Æt. 60." As time passed the inscription grew almost undecipherable, and it was several times refreshed. Latterly, however, the headstone itself was falling into decay, and it was also felt that some more worthy monument of the great writer ought to be raised to his memory. A movement was organized to raise funds for the purpose, and the result is the beautiful memorial represented in the illustration. On the top is a recumbent figure of Bunyan; at the foot is a tablet bearing the original inscription, and on the sides two bas-reliefs, the one representing Christian toiling up the with his burden on his back, and the ot Christian with his burden rolling off at the si of the cross.

AN ARTIST'S DIFFICULTY.

(See Illustration on page 637.)

A CITY clergyman was walking slowly thro a lovely country district one summer morni when, having climbed a little knoll shaded w trees, he sat down to rest. He was evider recovering from illness, for his tall frame shrunken, his steps slow and uncertain, and face intensely pale. He drew in, with evid relish, long breaths of the clear, pure air, so freshing to one whose past few years had b spent in ministering to the spiritual health c people living for the greater part in rear te ments and noisome courts.

As the clergyman mused, he became c scious of a new feature in the landscape. W he sat down to rest, not a human being wa sight, but now there was a girlish figure c fortably settled on a grassy bank, with an art pad and a paint box before her. Sketching not going on very briskly, for now and ag the pencil ceased its motion, and the girl lost in thought. Might not here be an op tunity for service? the clergyman asked hims At any rate he would see. He was soon at girl's side, chatting sociably with her, and f ing her frank and open in manner. She nai admitted that she ought not to be spending morning as she was doing. She had prom her elder sister to take a class in a mis school for the morning; but the children w troublesome, teaching was irksome, and temptation to go out in the lovely summer and sketch was irresistible. "I find," she with a sigh, "that to be good and do one's d is much more difficult for me than it seem be with other people."

"You are fond of sketching, I suppos asked the clergyman.

"Yes; there is nothing I like so much."

"Yet you do not appear to have made m progress this morning," glancing at the pad

"No; and that is a strange thing that zles me. Violet is responsible for a wasted m ing. I did no good in the school, and I done no good here. I suppose my consci reproaches me. I cannot give my mind to sketch as I generally do. Perhaps I am laz

"No," said the clergyman, "I think not. other reason is the more natural explana The consciousness of neglected duty is very to rob our usual enjoyments of their grati tion. If you had taught the class, and have come out to sketch, you would prob

The Young Artist's Sketching Interrupted.

e enjoyed it more n usual."

Then you think I being punished for lect of duty."

Oh, I would not that. It is only a ural law that works all. After a time, ou were to make a ctice of neglecting y, you would ex- ience no discom- . Conscience is very pertinacious. seldom continues trouble any one does not listen t."

But that would be ery bad state to into, would it ?"

he clergyman led sadly. "I can ik of none more ible," he said.

But how is one to right when one s so much not to it? Now, my sis- Violet seems to by doing disagree- things. I believe takes pleasure teaching those y, noisy children, I have known to be quite happy in staying away from the st pleasure expedition to nurse some poor, old woman who had no claim upon her. I not understand it; I know I could never by such things. I might bring myself to do a penance, but I should never like it."

Ah!" said the clergyman," that is no new iculty. It has puzzled wise people since the ld began. The best men have always been ng to learn how to make the higher nature reme over the lower. We all have the two ures, and the lower never will take its sub- inate place without a struggle. It is more ce and brutal, and generally stronger. Some e tried letting it have its way, and pacifying higher nature for deposing it, by penances money payments, but that is a cowardly out of the difficulty. Some of the great then philosophers did better, but their success not great. The only real solution that ever eeded was given by a poor Oriental peas- very much despised in his day, and very h misunderstood; but he had the secret. taught that happiness was not to be sought n end; that self, with all its desires and joys, t be ignored, annihilated in fact, and that the right and the good and the true would upreme, and all lower pleasures would be- e tasteless."

But would not that be very difficult?" ask- he girl, sadly.

Yes, he recognized that, and met that dif- ty with a remedy. There is a power that s for righteousness, he declared, and that r may be had by those who desire its help. an ally on the right side in the conflict. In it fights the battle alone, if the person who alled in its help is only faithful in alle- e to it."

Oh, I wish I had it!" said the girl, "I am eak, and I am always trying to be good, failing."

That is all that you need at the outset, my d. You will find other needs as you go on; the sincere desire is the first thing. The er is the Holy Spirit. Read your New Tes- ent, and you will find that Jesus distinctly rts that God gives the Holy Spirit to those ask Him."

I will ask Him," said the girl.

Do; your nature will be transformed. It is the secret of the grandest lives the world has ever seen, and when you have proved it, tell it to all you know."

THE EPOCHS OF A LIFE.

A NEW SERIAL STORY.

By Rev. L. S. Keyser.

(Continued from page 622.)

Joyless Days.

During the remainder of the session Hadley's studies were carried on in a rather desultory and perfunctory manner, and it was only by virtue of his superior native ability that he was able to maintain his position at the head of the class. He had comparatively little zest for his work, and still less exultation in his triumphs.

Every day he met Miss Winters, but he never spoke to her. With careful studiousness he ignored her, although at times he glanced at her stealthily, and was surprised and pained at the pallor of her beautiful face.

No change came in that session. The short spring vacation had come and gone, and Hadley and George had entered upon their last session of college life. The spring opened gloriously, bringing with it its resurrection of life and beauty. Under the magic wand of the opening season some of Hadley's old physical exhilaration was returning, and almost every Saturday found him making long expeditions into the country, collecting data in regard to the local fauna and flora. In many of these excursions he was accompanied by his friend Dane. He also found in Belle Havelock a ready sympathizer with all his naturalistic researches. Very often she rendered him invaluable assistance in classifying the results of a day's collection, frequently astonishing him with her extensive knowledge of science.

Madeline Winters held steadily on her course, gaining one trophy after another in the college. Her leisure time was spent in self-improvement and in works of love in the town. A class of half-grown boys were becoming civilized under her wise and prayerful instruction at the Sabbath-school; and on Sabbath afternoons she was frequently seen in the houses of the poor, carrying light and cheer wherever she went. Very seldom did she appear in society with a male escort. Occasionally she would, by kindly sufferance, allow Duneman to accompany her to a lecture, but he made little progress in his suit, even though he had the field all to himself.

The season was advancing, as was evidenced by the increased warmth of the weather and the thickening foliage of orchard, grove, and forest, and nearly all the spring songsters had come back on their annual migratory visit, and were making the woods and fields vocal with their carols.

The prospect was so inviting to a half-dozen young men of the Senior class, who had a special predilection for out-door life, that a scheme was set on foot to make an excursion to a lovely spot several miles from town. The half-dozen young men referred to were members of the same fraternity, and included Hadley and George. Indeed, they were the main instigators of the plan. Each young gallant was to find a young lady to accompany him, the young ladies being expected to furnish the edibles for the picnic dinner on the grounds. A double team and a large carryall, with a driver, were to be hired for the occasion.

George Dane had so studiously avoided feminine society during his stay in college that he was sorely puzzled as to whom he should choose for a partner. A number of young ladies were suggested, but none of them passed muster. At last he said to Hadley, confidentially:

"There is only one girl whose society would be agreeable to me on the excursion."

"And who is she?" questioned Hadley.

"Miss Madeline Winters," returned George bluntly. And then seeing an expression of rigidity on Hadley's features, he added, reassuringly: "Oh, you needn't be jealous, my dear fellow. Neither she nor any other girl has been playing havoc with my affections, but I admire her for her mental gifts, and believe that her company would be more agreeable than any other. You will not ask her, shall you?"

"Not at all," replied Hadley. "I have already engaged the company of Belle Havelock." Then a rueful look came into Hadley's face. "Ask Miss Winters to go with us by all means; she will make an excellent foil, with her sweet, serious ways, to our gay crowd."

Accordingly a note was sent to Miss Winters, and in a short time an answer came accepting with thanks George's proposal, and the occasion was anticipated by Hadley with mingled dread and tremulous delight.

When the appointed gala-day arrived, the large open spring wagon, drawn by four horses, was filled with gay excursionists. Miss Winters was the last young lady to ascend the steps of the vehicle. As she appeared at the gate, accompanied by George Dane, a warm flush was visible on her fair oval cheeks, and it deepened in intensity when she had seated herself, and saw Miss Havelock by the side of young Madelling.

Soon the gayly caparisoned steeds had trotted out of town. The freedom of the country relaxed all the latent gayety of the picnicers. Their road wound like a broad white band along the flexures of the valleys, and about the steep hill-sides, every turn bringing new surprises to nature's loving eyes. In an occasional lull of the conversation and laughter, Hadley caught the roundelays of the grass-finch, or the cheery whistle of the oriole, and he resolved that when they reached the picnic-grounds, he would steal away from his companions awhile, for the purpose of making observations on the bird life of the locality.

As the excursionists were passing a cottage, a woman drew a bucket of water from a well below the house, and lifting the vessel to her head, she carried it with perfect ease up the hill. The performance was watched so intently by all that there was a brief pause of complete silence, and then Miss Winters remarked:

"How Oriental that appears! It reminds one of a real Bible scene."

"It is very like the pictures I used to see in the old family Bible when I was a small boy," answered George.

As the conversation was of a general character, Belle Havelock interlarded laughingly: "That was a good while ago, wasn't it, Mr. Dane? I fancy that you do not see many such pictures nowadays"; and there was a mocking smile on her face.

"I do not catch—I do not understand you," said George, looking a little puzzled.

"Obtuse!" laughed Hadley. "She means that you do not look into the Bible as often as you did once."

"Thank you for sharpening my dull faculties," George replied. "Your surmise is correct, Miss Havelock. I do not look into the old Book as often as I did in the days of my innocence."

"In the days of your crudeness and gullibility, you mean," said Belle, with a touch of sarcasm. "You have outgrown these defunct traditions and have come out into a wider field of thought."

"That is rather severe," put in Hadley.

"Not more so than such superstitions deserve," maintained Belle.

"I am inclined to think," said Madeline, in tones that were modulated with kindness, "that the childlike receptive spirit is the more healthful. No matter how much we grow, we are learners still, and we learn more the more docile we are."

"But we learn to discriminate between truth and error," said Belle. "The simple child who believes a ghost story, and in consequence is afraid to go to bed in the dark, pays the penalty of the credulous, childlike spirit. As he grows older he has more sense than to believe in ghosts, and if he has courage too, he refuses to believe in miracles. He fails to see in the Bible, evidence of Divine authorship."

"Yes, some do!" said Madeline, stirred up to polemical attitude by the attack of a sceptic of her own sex; "but the Book itself forewarned us that it would be so. 'The natural man receiveth not the things of the Spirit of God; for they are foolishness unto him: neither can he know them, because they are spiritually discerned.'"

"Oh," said Belle, smiling, "you must not beg the question. That is too much the habit of believers. When the credibility of the Bible is in dispute, a quotation from its pages is not decisive, as it might be in a Methodist class-meeting."

"I did not quote the passage as a proof of inspiration," said Madeline, "I quoted it simply to show that the Bible foresaw such objections as yours, and explained their cause."

"A very inadequate explanation," Belle replied. "It is the part of reason to examine statements before it accepts them. The majority of Christians remind me of what I saw in an orchard near my old country home: a "yellow-hammer—more elegantly called the golden-winged woodpecker—had made a nest in the hollow hole of an apple-tree. I went to see the bird-domicile almost every day while the young birds were feathering, and whenever I made a slight noise about the tree, a half-dozen mouths in the nest were thrown open like little caves, ready to receive whatever was dropped into them, while an incessant chirping for more was kept up. Christians put me in mind of those callow young birds. They open their mouths and shut their eyes, and gulp down unquestioningly everything that their religious teachers see fit to pour down their throats." As this simile was delivered, a suppressed titter went around the wagon.

"Poor little birds!" exclaimed Miss Winters, compassionately, after a pause; "if they *hadn't* opened their mouths they would have starved to death."

For a moment there was dead silence until the company caught the point, and then a vociferous outburst of merriment, accompanied by a vigorous clapping of hands, ensued, while cries of "Good! good!" were interspersed. Belle joined as heartily as possible in the laugh against herself, but she felt piqued at the thrust in this fencing of words. During the remainder of the drive, no more theological discussions were obtruded into the conversation.

In a cool, umbrageous retreat on the bank of the river the young people spread the dinner, and a merry meal it was, with light persiflage and unrestrained hilarity. When the repast was finished, while the company was engaged in a post-prandial chat, Belle Havelock, feeling a desire to be even with Miss Winters for the defeat she had experienced earlier in the day, threw a pebble into the river, accompanying the action with the remark:

"I believe, Mr. Madelling, that you once took an unceremonious bath in this river several miles from here."

Every one in the company was silent for a moment. Madeline blushed painfully. Then Hadley broke the awkward silence by saying: "Yes, I performed an aquatic feat; but it was an involuntary undertaking."

"Oh, you were forced into it, were you?" said Belle, with a deep purpose. "Suppose one of us were to fall—*accidently or on purpose*—into the river to-day, do you suppose that you would have the gallantry to plunge into the awful tide and bring us out?" asked Belle, a little melodramatically.

"My heroism might fail; it would not be safe to put it to the test *too* often," said Hadley.

The girl for whom Belle's shaft was intended turned to George Dane and began to converse with him for the purpose of masking her wounded feelings. The jesting words that had fallen from Hadley's lips, though innocent enough in themselves, acquired a deep significance when collated with the letter that had been put into her hands a few months before. The conviction forced itself upon her that Hadley had intended to insult her by his remark, and her enjoyment for the rest of the day was destroyed.

The party soon separated into smaller groups, each treating the occasion in characteristic style. Hadley felt piqued at Belle for obtruding a disagreeable subject upon the company, especially in Madeline's presence, and in order to calm himself, he obeyed an impulse to stroll away into the woods that crowned a rocky bluff up the river a short distance. Obviously he had escaped unobserved. For an hour he was deeply engrossed in watching the performances of a rare warbler and a winter wren as they flitted among the twigs, and in noting the exquisite quality of their songs. Fearing that his prolonged absence might be regarded as an incivility, he started to retrace his steps. Near the edge of the woods, a pine-finch, whistling in a low bush, attracted his attention. As he had not yet secured a specimen of this species for his ornithological collection, he drew his pocket-rifle and brought down the gay vocalist. Its fall was followed by a cry of alarm from some one beyond the bush into which he had discharged the shot. Much excited, Hadley sprang forward, and stood face to face with Miss Winters. Her countenance was pale and bore a frightened expression.

"For mercy's sake! tell me, Miss Winters—have I hurt you?" gasped Hadley.

"Do not be alarmed," she said calmly. "Several of the shots whizzed close to me, but non[e] of them hit me."

"What if I had shot you! Oh, horror! [I] can't bear to think of it!"

"But you did not," said the girl, reassuringl[y], "and so you need not distress yourself on ac[-]count of an imaginary catastrophe."

"You and I seem to be fated to—to—mee[t] under peculiar circumstances," he burst out.

"I suppose you will think that I followed yo[u] purposely to-day, as you seem to think I di[d] the time you saved my life," she said, blushin[g] crimson.

He opened his eyes in amazement, as sh[e] spoke. The real force of her words was lo[st] upon him, not knowing anything of the circum[-]stances that motived them, and he looked a[t] her in a dazed way.

"Miss Winters, I protest that I never though[t] of such a thing. It is an unjust, an uncharitab[le] imputation," he said angrily.

"Your conversation with Miss Havelock a[n] hour ago seemed to imply as much."

"Oh, Miss Winters," cried Hadley, "I neve[r] dreamed that you would place that constructio[n] on our words. Nothing was farther from m[y] thoughts, I assure you. It was an unpleasan[t] theme to introduce, and I was vexed and morti[-]fied over it. In fact, I felt so piqued that I le[ft] the company awhile to regain my composure."

"That is just the reason I am here," sai[d] Madeline, the tears starting to her eyes.

"Why, you have been crying," exclaime[d] Hadley. "Did it wound you so deeply? Wel[l,] I am very sorry, but I hope that you will n[ot] blame me for it."

Impulsively he stepped closer to her, and [a] feeling of inexpressible tenderness filled h[is] heart. The two stood on the rocky heigh[t] looking into each other's eyes. At last he spok[e] impetuously.

"Why did I meet you here? It has opene[d] the old wound afresh, though it was never hea[l-]ed. You have forbidden me to seek an expla[n-]ation of my rejection, and yet your dear fac[e] whenever I see it, drives me to desperation."

She held up her hand imploringly.

"You do not wish me to speak, I see," [he] said, bitterly. "So be it, then. I must te[ar] your image from my heart, but I curse the de[s-]tiny that has crushed every hope of my life."

"You should not be so irreverent," she sai[d].

"What can I do but curse it?" he broke o[ut] desperately. "When there is nothing but bli[nd] caprice to rule the world, there is nothing [to] revere."

"How can you speak so?" she said, in distre[s-]sed tones. "It is appalling to hear your athe[is-]tic utterances. Do you not see that there is [no] community of feeling on the subject of rel[ig-]ion between us? Your words make me ve[ry] unhappy."

"Ah!" he muttered, a new light breaki[ng] upon him. "It is this religious supersti[tion] that has raised a barrier between you and [me.] It has brought me nothing but sorrow."

"It is your opposition to it that brings [so] much grief into your life."

"Miss Winters," he said, imploringly, "I w[ill] do anything but sacrifice principle to win y[our] love, if you—"

"No, no, do not say any more. It is best [to] drop the subject now." Then a moment[ary] pang of jealousy prompted her to say: "Y[ou] have another claim upon you, too. You [are] not dependent upon me for your joy. Le[t us] go back to the party."

"Madeline," Hadley began excitedly, thi[nk-]ing that she referred to Belle Havelock, [and] having no clue to the Mabel Richerson epis[ode] which really was the basis of Madeline's [re-]proach, "I swear to you that no other—"

Madeline's upraised hand checked what [he] imagined would be a perjury, and the oppo[rtu-]nity for explanation was lost. Hadley shrug[ged] his shoulders and obeyed the admonitio[n to] silence, and quietly the two descended the [hill] and joined their companions.

(*To be Continued*).

CROSSING THE JORDAN.

By Mrs. M. Baxter.

. S. Lesson for October 14, Josh. 3:5-17. Golden Text, Isa. 43:2.

he Welcome Warning—The Wilderness to be Exchanged for a Home—The Work Required of the Cis-Jordanic Tribes—Unselfishness Expected—Work for the Church Before Resting—Spies Sent Out—The Three Days of Waiting—The Last Instructions—Sanctification Ordered—The People's Part—They Were to Follow the Ark—The Covenant a Pledge of Safety—The Procession Over the Bed of the River.

PREPARED by the direct command and prom-ıes of God, Joshua took up his vocation, and ommanded the officers of the people, whom loses had set over thousands, hundreds, fifties, nd tens (Ex. 18:25), to give orders to the peo-le that they should prepare provision, for in ıree days' time they were to pass over Jordan.)h what joy must the message have brought ıem! Not one of the whole company had ever nown a home, with its joys and comforts. ome had left Egypt as little children, and thers had been born in the wilderness, and new only a wilderness life. And the two dults, Joshua and Caleb, who had grown up in he land of Egypt, had known only slavery, not home, there. And now they were going home, very family was to have a dwelling-place.

Their Long Wanderings Were to End in Rest.

lut there must be no selfishness among the peo-le. The Reubenites, Gadites, and half the tribe f Manasseh had chosen their portion on the ·ilderness side of Jordan. But Joshua reminded hem that they were bound to pass on before heir brethren armed, leaving only their wives nd children in the land of their possession un-ıl the Lord had given their brethren rest as He ad given them. Even in the Old Testament, he lesson of unselfishness is taught; how much ıore is it our privilege, who live under the New 'estament, to seek the salvation of others, and ot to settle down upon our lees until India, hina, Africa, and the heathen in our own land re evangelized! "He that gathereth not with le, scattereth abroad. (Matt. 12:30.) These ibes acknowledged their obligation and the uthority of Joshua, and promised to obey, say-g. "All that thou commandest us we will do, ıd whithersoever thou sendest us we will go. ccording as we hearkened unto Moses in all ings, so will we hearken unto thee: only the ord thy God be with thee, as he was with oses, . . . only be strong and of a good cour-e." It is a very usual thing that when the rulers teachers of a people are changed, there is a eat deal of ill feeling, jealousy, and prejudice. he new man is criticised and compared with his edecessor to his disadvantage, and received ith coldness and distrust. But here is a man llowing another, and that man such a man as ever lived before, and yet his successor is re-lived without any ill feeling! Why? Because shua trusted God, and God upheld Joshua. he report of two men whom he sent as spies to richo was this, "Truly the Lord hath delivered to our hands all the land; for even all the in-bitants of the country do faint because of us." ow different from the report of the ten spies! There seem to have been two periods of three ys, one spent in making preparation, while e spies were in the land of Canaan, and an-her later, when the people were encamped by rdan. "Joshua rose

Early in the Morning."

did Abraham twice when he had important ings to do—to cast out the bondwoman, and sacrifice his Isaac on the altar. (Gen. 21:14; :3.) Jesus was wont to rise up early, some-nes "a great while before day," that He ght commune with His Father. Few days days which tell much for God when there s been no early hour of taking counsel with m. "Joshua rose early in the morning; and ey removed from Shittim, and came to Jor-n, he and all the children of Israel, and lged there before they passed over." They uld see the land now every moment, just across the river, and what they saw was theirs, assured to them by the covenant promises of God. How long the three days must have seemed while they waited there! "And it came to pass after three days, that the officers went through the host, and they commanded the people" to pay attention to the ark of God, and to the priests which bore it, that they might follow in its track. But they must leave a space between it and them, that they might all see the direction which it took. From this we learn that the guidance which God gives us requires constant attention to Him. "For ye have not gone this way heretofore." It was indeed a new way; they were leaving behind for ever the old wilderness way of treading perpetually over the same ground, and they were going to pass on to continuous victory and assured possession. Many and many a child of God spends a lifetime in the wilderness, always trying, striving, struggling, to serve God, and to overcome sin and self; which results either in a hardened conscience and self-righteous spirit, or in a state of chronic depression. What is wrong? Simply this: that instead of entering into the land, accepting the true and gracious promises of God, and rejoicing in Him who gives us the victory and leads us into our possessions, these poor souls are still in the wilderness, attempting, by their own efforts, to do what can only be done by the hand of the Most High.

What man ever delivered himself from self? What man ever made himself humble, or produced in himself faith in the living God? It takes divine power to do these things, and when our Joshua (Jesus) leads us out of efforts into the blessed land of God's promises, and we claim them as ours, it is

Rest Indeed,

not inaction, not idleness, not supineness, but rest in the midst of labor, in the midst of sorrow, and in the midst of temptation, because God undertakes for all. "Joshua said unto the people, Sanctify yourselves; for to-morrow the Lord will do wonders among you." This was Joshua's testimony to God. It is our part to sanctify ourselves when we have first been sanctified by God. Before the law was given, Moses sanctified the people. (Ex. 19:10.) God says of His people now: "But ye are washed, but ye are sanctified, but ye are justified." (1 Cor. 6:11.) The Corinthians were "sanctified in Christ Jesus." (1 Cor. 1:1.) Peter wrote to those who were "elect . . . through sanctification of the Spirit." (1 Pet. 1:2.) Yet these very Corinthians are taught to cleanse themselves "from all filthiness of the flesh and spirit" (II Cor. 7:1), and this same Peter says, "Be ye holy, for I am holy." (1 Pet. 1:16.) Surely, here it meant a thorough abandonment to God, in preparation for the wonders God would work. Had there been such a sanctifying of themselves in the synagogues at Nazareth, it would not have been said, "And He did not many mighty works there because of their unbelief."

Then Joshua commanded the priests, "and they took up the ark of the covenant, and went before the people. And the Lord said unto Joshua, This day will I begin to magnify thee in the sight of all Israel, that they may know that, as I was with Moses, so I will be with thee." God would never glorify Joshua to make him great in his own eyes, for that would have been to do him an incalculable injury. His greatness consisted in God's making common cause with him, and making him a worker together with Him (II Cor. 6:1), a chosen vessel to respond to the heart of God, understand and carry out His counsels, and be His interpreter.

What a Vocation!

And some who are called to a life such as this turn from its wondrous glory to live for the world and self! God directed Joshua to command the priests who bore the ark of the covenant of the Lord, when they came to the brink of Jordan that they should stand still in Jordan. And immediately afterwards Joshua speaks his first word direct to the people themselves. "Come hither, and hear the words of the Lord your God." One cannot but think of the "Come" of Jesus, so different from the thunders of the law. And Joshua was speaking no words of his own; he gave God's authority for what he said: "Hereby ye shall know that the living God is among you, and that He will without fail drive out from before you the Canaanites, etc. . . Behold the ark of the covenant of the Lord of all the earth passeth over before you into Jordan." That is to say, "Before a man of you can be drowned, the ark of God's covenant must be drowned; where He goes, you may go. Oh, it is

No Venture to Follow God.

Let us be only sure that our God is on before, and, whether it is into a fiery furnace, or to walk upon the waters of Genesaret, or inside a prison cell, or whether to work all day with those who despise God, we are perfectly safe with Him. But if we venture any step, even from room to room, in our own house, without Him, we are in danger. If we enter into a conversation, write a letter, make a purchase, or commence a work of any kind without the Lord's companionship, we are in danger.

"And it shall come to pass, as soon as the soles of the feet of the priests that bear the ark of the Lord, the Lord of all the earth, shall rest in the waters of Jordan, that the waters of Jordan shall be cut off from the waters that come down from above, and they shall stand upon an heap." Before God could work a miracle, the priests must take a step of faith; they must stand bearing the ark of the covenant in the very waters of the swollen river. ("For Jordan overfloweth all his banks all the time of harvest," the snows of Mount Lebanon melt in May and June, the harvest months in Palestine, and thus the river is swollen at that time). As kings and priests unto God, we who believe have the privilege of bearing the ark of the covenant of the Lord. Jordan means judgment, and it is our vocation to carry the promises of God right into the place where judgment overflows. Not only where our sins and shortcomings condemn us, but right out among the heathen who "sit in darkness in the shadow of death," may we carry the ark of the covenant, and most surely the moral and social judgment which lies upon heathen countries shall give way before the Word of the living God. It is for the leaders of the people to prove first that God is faithful. As the people moved forward with their little ones, their cattle, and their baggage-wagons, every man and woman in Israel would look up, and see the wondrous sight of the ever-increasing heap of water which came down from the source of the Jordan and then, on the other hand, the dry bed of the stream as the nether waters failed, and every one would acknowledge that

The Hand of a Present God

had done this. The long procession passed through the bed of the river, and, as they slowly filed through, in their tribes and families, every one had to pass by the ark of the covenant of the Lord, and see in it God's guarantee of safety. Some think it a most dangerous proceeding to trust their spiritual state and health, without anxiety and without fear, into the hands of the living God, and they think they are taking too easy a way; but the ark of the covenant, the promise of God, is the warrant we have for entering into rest, and ceasing from our own works "as God did from His." But He will find us plenty of good work to do, which He hath "prepared for us to walk in." if we will only cease from the runnning uncertainly and the fighting as them that beat the air (1 Cor. 9:26), which has hindered God and lost our own time. He will not fail us. His word is true. "The priests that bore the ark of the covenant of the Lord stood firm on dry ground in the midst of Jordan, and all the Israelites passed over on dry ground, until all the people were passed clean over Jordan."

"SOME TIME."

MRS. MAY RILEY SMITH.

Some time, when all life's lessons have been learned,
And sun and stars forevermore have set,
The things which our weak judgment here has spurned—
The things o'er which we grieved with lashes wet—
Will flash before us out of life's dark night,
As stars shine most in deeper tints of blue;
And we shall see how all God's plans were right,
And how what seemed reproof was love most true.

And we shall see, that, while we frown and sigh,
God's plans go on as best for you and me;
How, when we called He heeded not our cry,
Because His wisdom to the end could see:
And e'en as prudent parents disallow
Too much of sweet to craving babyhood,
So God, perhaps, is keeping from us now
Life's sweetest things, because it seemeth good,

And if, some time, commingled with life's wine,
We find the wormwood, and rebel and shrink,
Be sure a wiser hand than yours or mine
Pours out this potion for our lips to drink;
And if some friend we love is lying low,
Where human kisses cannot reach his face
Oh! do not blame the loving Father so,
But bear your sorrow with obedient grace.

And you shall shortly know that lengthened breath
Is not the sweetest gift God sends His friend,
And that sometimes the sable pall of death
Conceals the fairest boon His love can send.
If we could push ajar the gates of life,
And stand within, and all God's working's see,
We could interpret all this doubt and strife,
And for each mystery could find a key.

But not to-day. Then be content, poor heart!
God's plans, like lilies pure and white, unfold;
We must not tear the close-shut leaves apart;
Time will reveal the calyxes of gold.
And if, through patient toil we reach the land
Where tired feet, with sandals loosed, may rest,
When we shall clearly know and understand,
I think that we shall say that "God knew best."

J. E. JEWETT, Publisher, 77 Bible House, New York, will furnish the above poem in leaflet form at twenty cents per hundred. *A Sample Packet* of 50 leaflets assorted (no two alike), will be sent post-paid, for 10 cts., or 100 for 20 cts. Postage stamps taken.

PRINCIPAL CHURCH BUILDING OF THE
MEXICAN CHURCH OF OUR LORD JESUS CHRIST,
CITY OF MEXICO.

MEXICO

Contributions in aid of Christian work in Mexico are most pressingly needed, and can be mailed to the address of

BISHOP H. C. RILEY,
Care of J. P. HEATH,
43 Bible House, New York.

To our Christian Friends:

As there is a regular monthly expense in connection with the work a regular monthly income is needed to meet that expense. We, therefore, specially ask for regular monthly contributions in its behalf. If many will each send a little every month, or quarter, or whenever they can, it will do great good. *Remember, every little helps.*

H. Chauncey Riley.

Vol. XI., No. 41. Office, 63 Bible House, N. Y. THURSDAY, OCTOBER 11, 1888. Price, 3 Cents. Annual Subscription, $1.50.

CONTENTS OF THIS NUMBER.

PORTRAIT AND LIFE OF RAMON BETANCOURT AND PICTURE OF THE FAMOUS PERUVIAN RAILROAD BRIDGE.
THE THREE GREATEST THINGS TO DO. Dr. Talmage's Sermon Last Sunday Morning.
THE SPANISH-SPEAKING NATIONS. By Bishop H. C. Riley.
ANECDOTES RELATED AT RECENT EVANGELISTIC MEETINGS.
THE FIRST RESURRECTION. By J. Urquhart.
CURRENT EVENTS: The Republican Tariff Bill Introduced—The Yellow Fever Epidemic—Disasters on the Lakes—European Notes—An Explorer's Opinion about Stanley—A Ninety Thousand Dollar Lawsuit—A Fierce Struggle with a Dog—A Photograph of a Shadow.
ALL AT IT. A New Sermon by Rev. C. H. Spurgeon.
A NIGHT AT THE FLORENCE MISSION.
THE NEW JERUSALEM. By the late P. H. Gosse.
A Deformed Child Cured—An Octogenarian's Conversion—A Consecrated Ten-Dollar Bill—A Despairing Wife.
Gems from New Books: The Magnetic Smile—Girls Dead at Heart—What a Lady Is, etc.
PICTURE OF MR. WILLIAM NOBLE'S SATURDAY NIGHT DEMONSTRATION.
A CASE FOR PATIENCE. (With Illustration.)
THE EPOCHS OF A LIFE. A New Serial Story by Rev. L. S. Keyser. (Continued.)
THE STONES OF MEMORIAL. By Mrs. M. Baxter.

The Late Ramon Betancourt, The Cuban Evangelist—The Railroad Bridge in the Andes. (*See page* 652.)

RAMON BETANCOURT.

The Converted Cuban Desperado.

Precocious Diabolism—An Atrocity on a Horse—Attempted Murder—Flight and Sea Life—A Notorious Desperado—Takes Refuge in New York—A Pugilistic Victory—Stanger Religious Association—Hears of Spanish Evangelistic Services at Trinity Chapel—Plot to Kill the Preacher—His Conversion—Becomes an Evangelist—Set Upon by a Mexican Mob—An Indian Girl's Heroism—His Death.

ONE of the most remarkable instances in modern times of the power of God's grace to change the heart of the persecutor, and, as in the case of Saul of Tarsus, to use him for the promotion of the persecuted cause, is that of the devoted man who died recently in Brooklyn, N. Y., and whose portrait appears on the preceding page. A few years ago, Ramon Betancourt made his appearance in New York. He was a Cuban, but he had no home there or elsewhere, when he drifted to the great metropolis. The man had been

A Desperado From His Youth.

One incident which occurred when he was only twelve years old has been related to us, which reveals a depth of cruelty inconceivable in so young a child. He deliberately tortured and mutilated a horse with such fiendish atrocity that the details are too horrible for publication. The poor animal had to be killed to put it out of its agony. The punishment meeted out to him for this offence, instead of subduing his evil proclivities, stirred his passions to a murderous pitch. He was determined to revenge himself on the owner of the horse, who had caused his punishment. The young scamp actually set fire to the man's dwelling, fully expecting and intending that his enemy would be burned to death—a result very nearly achieved.

He found it conducive to his safety to absent himself from the locality after that feat, and during the next few years he led

A Wild Life,

at first on shipboard, and afterward in the towns of Spanish America. There were few vices, if any, to which he was not addicted. Gambling and drinking when he had money, burglary and highway robbery when he had none, occupied his time. He was always the first to scent the development of the frequent revolutions in Spanish America, and to make his way to the locality, that he might be ready to take a share in the robbery and bloodshed which might be expected. His bull-dog courage, his powerful frame, and his uncontrolled ferocity made him the terror of any community he visited. The man must fight, and he took a demon's delight in offering taunts and provocations to the biggest and strongest man around, to exasperate him to fighting pitch, when Betancourt would prove himself the king of the company by administering punishment that would prevent any other man disputing his supremacy.

In New York,

on his arrival, he avoided prominence for a time. Recent troubles, in which he had been a leader, might involve extradition. For some weeks, therefore, Betancourt's presence in the city was not known, save to a few of the gambling fraternity. Even self-imposed retraint, however, could not be long maintained. Betancourt heard of a powerful Spanish-American, whose prowess and physical strength were vaunted in the Spanish colony of New York. Betancourt could not rest until he had fought that man. He succeeded at length, and his rival's prowess was sung no more.

It was a curious fact—one of those strange anomalies that human nature so often develops—that this desperate man was

An Enthusiastic Roman Catholic.

Throughout his mad career he had somehow managed to maintain his adherence to his Church. How any kind of religious feeling could find soil in a nature so thoroughly given up to Satan, and so bent on deeds of violence, can scarcely be conceived. It is a fact, however, that wherever he might go, Betancourt sought out a Roman Catholic church, and scrupulously attended the services. At this time, Bishop Riley was holding services, and preaching in Spanish, in Trinity Chapel, near Madison Square. Betancourt heard of the services, and the fact of their being in his native language aroused his interest. He made inquiries about them, and found that they were Protestant services. The clergyman conducting them was, he was given to understand, undermining the power of the Roman Catholic Church, and was at the head of a movement for spreading the heretical Protestant faith in Mexico. Betancourt's ire was kindled. The two strong passions of his nature were stirred: to kill the enemy of his Church, and at the same time to make the American metropolis ring with

A Deed of Unparalleled Daring,

seemed to him an achievement after his own heart. He made a reconnoissance of the building in the week, and thought out a plan of operations. By sitting near the middle aisle, he could move quietly from his seat, spring upon the preacher, kill him, and escape by a side door conveniently near the preacher's platform, before any of the audience could stop him. He exulted in the scheme, planned every minute detail, and purchased a long dagger-knife, good for cutting or stabbing, for the instrument.

Armed with this formidable weapon, Betancourt presented himself at the service and took the seat he had selected. All unconscious of his danger, Dr. Riley opened the service. Doubtless, led by the Holy Spirit, who knoweth all hearts, the Bishop chose for his subject the Conversion of Saul of Tarsus. He dwelt on the earnestness of the man, on his unquestionable sincerity, and on his perfectly assured conviction that his deeds of cruelty were not only justifiable, but meritorious. Taking the reverse side of the picture, Dr. Riley sketched the character of the persecuted people; described their gentleness, their love for each other and the world, their joy and happiness in their faith, which they longed to have others share, and pointed out how Saul's malignity was based on a misconception of their character and aims. Then came the picture of the revelation from Heaven to Saul on his way to Damascus; the persecutor's amazement at discovering that he had been wrong all along, and had been resisting God instead of serving Him.

Betancourt listened intently. He kept deferring the time for the execution of his plot. He even began to hesitate about carrying it out. The preacher seemed gentle, kindly, lovable, not by any means the fierce assailant of the Catholic Church. Rather, he seemed anxious for the good of humanity in general, and of Catholics in particular, desiring them to enter into an experience of higher happiness than they had attained. Finally, the preacher seemed, to Betancourt, to have an insight into his own heart. "The worst man in the audience," Dr. Riley declared, "no matter what his past, no matter what villany he might have in his heart at that moment, would receive a welcome from the loving Saviour if he applied for it. He who forgave Saul of Tarsus waited still with outstretched arms to receive any repentant sinner who sought Him."

Betancourt sat the sermon through, and at its close went to Dr. Riley and asked him if he could have a Spanish Testament. He received one, came again and again to the services, and at last became like a child in gentleness and humility, seeking the Saviour with all his heart. Before making a profession of his faith, he told the foregoing story, and showed the murderous weapon he had carried under his vest the first time he came to the service.

Anxiety for Work

soon manifested itself. He collected, by sheer personal influence, all his rough gambling friends in New York, almost forced them to meet, and then sent for Dr. Riley to come and preach to them. Soon he felt that he must go to Mexico. He went with little argumentative force, little theological knowledge, but with the story of his own conversion, to tell the people of the change in his own heart and life and to invite them to Christ. God blessed his work, and he was instrumental in many conversions. The chief difficulty, almost the only one, that Dr. Riley had with him was in restraining him in the bounds of prudence. He insisted on going to preach at places where certain death must have befallen him at the hands of the fanatical people. Once he evaded Dr. Riley's vigilance and went into a country district to preach. There he was set upon by a mob, who tried to stone him to death. As he lay

Wounded and Bleeding

on the ground, and stones were being brought to crush out his flickering life, a little Indian girl about twelve years old, who had heard him preach, flung herself upon him, and with her frail form protected his head from his assassins. (The portrait of this child, who became an inmate of one of Bishop Riley's schools, appeared last year in this journal, September 1, page 556.) Betancourt was carried away by some Protestant friends, and his wounds were dressed. He recovered, but the injuries he received accelerated a disease from which he was suffering, and compelled his retirement from active work. He returned to New York to end his days. A few weeks ago he passed away, rejoicing in Christ.

Our readers are aware of the interest which THE CHRISTIAN HERALD has taken in the noble, self-sacrificing endeavors of Bishop Riley to spread the knowledge of the Gospel in Mexico. It cannot do better service in presenting the claims of that enterprise on the Christians of the United States than by printing the following article:

THE SPANISH-SPEAKING NATIONS.

By Bishop H. C. Riley.

THERE are one hundred and thirteen millions (113,000,000) who speak English. There are seventy-five millions (75,000,000) who speak the Spanish or Portuguese languages. Among those who speak the English tongue there are multitudes who know and love the gospel. Among those who speak the Spanish or Portuguese there are, comparatively, only a few who know and love the gospel in its purity. There are

Seventeen Distinct Nationalities,

where the Spanish language is spoken, namely, the Kingdom of Spain, and sixteen Spanish-American Republics. Nine of these Spanish-American Republics are in South America, five in Central America, and the remaining two are the West Indian Republic of Santo Domingo, and the Republic of Mexico. The Jews having been expelled from Spain in 1492, many of their number found their way from Europe to the Holy Land, carrying the Spanish language with them, and their descendants have continued to speak that language to this day, so that Spanish is generally spoken in Jerusalem.

Spain's former possessions in North and South America emancipated themselves from the political rule of the mother country, and became independant republics. Several of these Spanish-American nations have promulgated liberal constitutions, and decreed liberty of worship throughout their domains. There is now

Liberty of Worship

in Cuba, Mexico, and a large portion of Central and South America. These liberal movements in Mexico and South America have deeply influenced Spain. Many of the more educated in Spain, Mexico, and in other portions of the vast Spanish-American field, have, to a greater or less degree, separated themselves from the Roman Catholic Church. In the midst of those thus separated in Spain and Spanish-America, a few native Christians, who through the reading of the Holy Scriptures have learned to know and love the pure gospel, have gathered small congregations and faithfully preached the gospel in its purity. Several of these congregations in Spain have been gathered into a general church organization, so that there is now

A Native Spanish Church,

that maintains the faith in its purity and integrity in the ancient kingdom of Spain. In the Republic of Mexico, also, some congregations of ive Christians, in whose midst the pure gos- has been faithfully preached for years, have en gathered into a Mexican church organiza- n, so that there are native churches, both in ain and in Mexico, that maintain the Chris- n faith in its primitive purity and integrity. ese faithful Spanish and Mexican churches ve, through their authorities, entered into of- al communion with one another, and are no- working to extend the knowledge of the th among their fellow-countrymen. Schools ve been established by these churches in ain and in Mexico, where hundreds of bright ys and girls have been carefully educated. me persons of much ability and power are to found among their clergy and leading laity.

Most of those connected with these Christian mmunions in Spain and in Mexico have been thered from among the humble poor, who ve been the first to welcome and defend the re gospel in their native lands. To assist their ding workers with the funds needed to ena- them to continue effectively their Christian bors, the gifts of the faithful in other lands are st pressingly needed. To aid in collecting e needed funds,

A Society has Been Organized,

th an office at 43 Bible House, New York, ere contributions can be sent, addressed to shop Riley, care of J. P. Heath. The society asking many to each give something monthly behalf of the work in Mexico.

There are many facts of deep interest con- cted with this work in Spain and Mexico. bly, faithfully, and bravely has that work been essed forward by native Christians, in spite great difficulties. God is with them, guiding d blessing their Christian labors. Many once nk in idolatry have been won through their strumentality to the truth, and have after- rds become

Faithful Preachers

the pure gospel. Some former Roman Cath- c ecclesiastics, both in Spain and in Mexico, ve, through the reading of the Holy Scriptures, rned to distinguish between the faith in its rity and the idolatry of Rome, and then by eir faithful labors have greatly aided in engthening these scriptural communions in ain and Mexico.

Among those who have taken part in this rnest Christian work the names of Manuel guas and J. Babtista Cabrera, both of them mer Roman Catholic ecclesiastics, are great- respected. Manuel Aguas (*whose portrait d life appeared in this journal on April 7, 7*) did a noble work in Mexico, as first Bishop- ct of the Mexican Church of our Lord Jesus rist. He died some years since, rejoicing in Saviour; but the influence of his noble work ll lives in that neighboring land.

J. B. Cabrera is now (in 1888) the first Bishop- ct of the Spanish church of which we have oken, and, by God's blessing, is doing a grand rk in Spain. We trust that the blessed in- ence of this Christian work in Spain and exico, may yet extend into the vast continent South America.

Please remember, that the Spanish language now spoken from Jerusalem to the Straits of gellan, near Cape Horn, in South America. the Spanish race with its growing influence be induced to espouse the cause of a pure th, and to place themselves on the side of an en Bible, and the truth in its primitive purity, ey will become most noble allies in the Chris- n crusade to extend the knowledge of the spel throughout the world. Some who were ce embittered opponents of those who are aching the pure gospel in Spanish, have erwards learned to love the same gospel, and preach it themselves.

Already thirty-seven persons connected with Mexican Church of our Lord Jesus Christ ve died the martyr's death in Mexico for their ristian faith and labors—murdered by the atical Romanists.

The Romanists in Mexico, who have not hes- ted to stain their hands with Christian blood, in their fanatical efforts to check the progress of the pure gospel in that Republic, have not been slow to use other means to try to gain their object. Efforts have often been made to starve our workers into silence, by trying to take away their means of livelihood. Our leading workers in Mexico, like a little army in a hostile field, need to be supplied from a friendly base of supplies. As this Mexican Christian communion has been gathered from among the humble poor, its leading workers have to look abroad for the aid needed to continue that work effectively. We earnestly ask our Christian friends to aid this precious Christian work in Mexico, by generously contributing in its behalf. Fellow-Christians, please remember that *every little helps*, and that you can *mail* your contributions in aid of this precious Christian work at any time directly to the following address:

Bishop H. C. RILEY, Care J. P. Heath, Esq., 43 Bible House, New York.

ANECDOTES RELATED AT RECENT EVANGELISTIC MEETINGS.

The German Baron's Æolian Harp.—Mr. Campbell remarks: "There was an old baron in Germany who had a series of wires stretched from the pinnacles of two towers in his castle. Often he would sit in his favorite seat and listen to the wind as it sighed through the wires, causing them to play like a harp. Sometimes the tone would be soft and low, then as the wind rose so did the music, until when a storm came the tone was wild and terrific, an orchestra worthy of the wind. God Himself is the Great Musician, producing in the soul sometimes softest, sweetest notes of love, and other times filling it with alarm because of the deep roar and mighty tumults of stormy trials and tempestuous griefs when 'deep calleth unto deep.'"

A Discharged Soldier's Arrest.—Mr. Lakin says: "I once saw a policeman roughly seize hold of a fine-looking man who was standing at a street corner, and tell him he was arrested as a deserter. The man, when he heard the charge, instead of continuing to struggle, quickly drew from his pocket a piece of paper, and handed it to the policeman, saying, 'What do you say to that?' It was the man's discharge from the army. He had been a soldier, but was one no longer. The policeman could only beg his pardon, and release him. Satan makes many saints miserable by reminding them of their former sins, and telling them that such sins cannot be forgiven, that they are still soldiers in his army. Let them not be dismayed, but pull out their discharge, upon which is written, 'Thy sins, which are many, are all forgiven thee.' The law cannot arrest you, and you may go on your way rejoicing."

A Disgraced Merchant Prince.—"There Resided in Venice a merchant prince who, at first respected and beloved by all who knew him, had fallen under the fell influence of drink, which had dragged him lower and lower, until he was a constant source of disgrace to his two sons, who tried every means to reform him. They got his friends to reason with him, and spiritual men to advise him, but to no avail. At last they determined to make one last supreme effort to save their father. He had invited a large company to spend the evening with him in drinking. His sons being aware of this, went into the dining-room before the company arrived, and with a stick of phosphorus wrote upon the wall, in large-sized letters, in Italian, 'Prepare to meet thy God.'" The company arrived, and soon were in deep carousal; one by one they dropped under the table, or hung limply over the arm of their chairs. Time went on, the candles went out, the room became dark, and the words written with the phosphorous stood out distinctly. The host moved in his chair, and opened his eyes, which at once fell on the letters of fire. He gazed in astonishment. In a moment the sinfulness of his life appeared to him, and thinking he was about to die, he cried for mercy, pleaded with God for forgiveness, and asked to be kept from the power of strong drink; and he bore testimony years afterwards, that from that moment his chains dropped from him, and he was a free man. God uses many strange instrumentalities by which to call His children to Himself, and if we will not come by gentle wooing He sometimes leads us by fear of judgment."

A Full Forgiveness Granted.—Mr. H Thorne says: "I remember when I was in London, a man came to me at the end of one of my meetings and said, 'I am so glad I came in here to-night, for I feel that now I have *some* of my sins forgiven.' 'Some of them?' I repeated, in surprise. 'My dear fellow, do you think God deals with the sinner in that way, and forgives some of his sins and not others?' 'I thought so,' said the man. 'No, there is no such thing as half-and-half salvation,' I replied. 'If God would allow us to give up the most of our heart to Him and keep just one little corner with our favorite sins to ourselves, there would be many more professing Christians, but He must have the whole heart or none.' At my request we knelt, and there that man pleaded with God to forgive *all* his sins for Jesus' sake, and to take full control of his heart. As we rose to our feet he held out his hand to me saying, with a bright look, 'God has forgiven *all* my sins.' It is gloriously true: 'If we confess our sins He is faithful and just to forgive us our sins and cleanse us from all unrighteousness.'"

A Rum-seller Asks to Take the Pledge.—Mr. Ralston remarks: "Not long ago, a well-dressed man came in to a meeting I was conducting and asked to have the pledge given to him. Some of us spoke to him, and found out that he was a seller of strong drink, but that which at the beginning had been his *servant*, to bring gold to his coffers, had assumed the *mastery*, and he was now the abject slave of intemperance, and it was to free himself from its thraldom that he wished to pledge himself to abstain. We pressed him to give up the traffic altogether. He replied that he would only be too glad to do so, but he had nothing else to which he could turn his hand. Then he added, very significantly, 'I have prayed God to smash up the whole trade, but while it lasts I cannot give it up.' Of course under the circumstances we refused to give him the pledge, and he went away disappointed. Oh, that such a trade, that ruins all with whom it comes in contact, should be legalized and allowed to flourish in a professedly Christian land—a trade which, while it brings money to its seller, so disgusts him that he is almost ready to give it up to escape from it."

Solemn Scenes during an Earthquake.—"Coming across the Atlantic Ocean lately, I met on board ship a young man from Charleston. He had been there when the earthquake took place a few years ago, and referring to the visitation he said, 'I never saw such a time as that. There were people everywhere on bended knees crying to God for mercy. When they felt the earth upheave, and saw the buildings tumble, they thought the end of the world had come. Years ago I left my mother in Scotland, and I never bent my knee to God until the earthquake came. Men who were gambling when the shock came dropped the cards from their hands, and some went away to pray. Men and women in the ballroom stopped in the midst of a wild dance, and hurriedly excusing themselves, went home to pray.' That was a time of great awakening. The people felt in the mighty throes of nature the hand of an Almighty God. And that young man was not the only one by hundreds who date conversion to Christ from that place and time. But why wait for the arrival of a great danger before you seek mercy? Without time even to offer a prayer you may be cut off. Come just now, when all is calm and you have time, so that in the hour of danger you may rest secure on Christ your Saviour."

THE THREE GREATEST THINGS TO DO.

Dr. Talmage's Sermon Preached Last Sunday Morning, October 7, 1888.

"The people that do know their God, shall be strong and do exploits." Dan. 11: 32.

The Deliverance of the Jews from Antiochus Epiphanes—Opportunities Rare for Earning Distinction—Three Great Exploits Possible—I. How a Man may be Saved—From a Felon's Life—From Bankruptcy—II. Opportunities to Save Women—A Girl's Lost Money Replaced—Men who Prey on Needy Women—A Woman in a New York Store—What a Woman is—How Women may be Helped—A Wealthy Man's Daughter Converted—III. Opportunities to Save a Child—A Mother's Estimate of a Child's Value—Where to Get the Strength for Exploits—A Brother Saved from a Shipwreck.

Antiochus Epiphanes, the old sinner, came down three times with his army to desolate the Jews, advancing one time with a hundred and two trained elephants swinging their trunks this way and that, and sixty-two thousand infantry, and six thousand cavalry troops, and they were driven back. Then, the second time, he advanced with seventy thousand armed men, and had been again defeated. But the third time he laid successful siege until the navy of Rome came in with the flash of their long banks of oars and demanded that the siege be lifted. And Antiochus Epiphanes said he wanted time to consult with his friends about it, and Popilius, one of the Roman embassadors, took a staff and made a circle on the ground around Antiochus Epiphanes, and compelled him to decide before he came out of that circle; whereupon he lifted the siege. Some of the Jews had submitted to the invader, but some of them resisted valorously, as did Eleazer when he had swine's flesh forced into his mouth, spit it out, although he knew he must die for it, and did die for it; and others, as my text says, did exploits.

An exploit I would define to be a heroic act, a brave feat, a great achievement. "Well," you say, "I admire such things, but there is no chance for me; mine is a sort of

A Hum-drum Life.

If I had an Antiochus Epiphanes to fight, I also could do exploits." You are right, so far as great wars are concerned. There will probably be no opportunity to distinguish yourself in battle. The most of the brigadier-generals of this country would never have been heard of had it not been for the war. General Grant would have remained in the useful work of tanning hides at Galena, and Stonewall Jackson would have continued the quiet college professor in Virginia. And whatever military talents you have will probably lie dormant forever.

Neither will you probably become a great inventor. Nineteen hundred and ninety-nine out of every two thousand inventions found in the Patent Office at Washington never yielded their authors enough money to pay for the expenses of securing the patent. So you will probably never be a Morse or an Edison or a Humphrey Davy or an Eli Whitney. There is not much probability that you will be the one out of the hundred that achieves extraordinary success in commercial or legal or medical or literary spheres. What then? Can you have no opportunity to do exploits? I am going to show that there are

Three Opportunities Open

that are grand, thrilling, far-reaching, stupendous, and overwhelming. They are before you now. In one, if not all three of them, you may do exploits. The three greatest things on earth to do are to save a man, or save a woman, or save a child.

During the course of his life, almost every man gets into an exigency, is caught between two fires, is ground between two millstones, sits on the edge of some precipice, or in some other way comes near demolition. It may be a financial or a moral or a domestic or a social or a political exigency. You sometimes see it

In Court Rooms.

A young man has got into bad company and he has offended the law, and he is arraigned. All blushing and confused, he is in the presence of judge and jury and lawyers. He can be sent right on in the wrong direction. He is feeling disgraced, and he is almost desperate. Let the District-Attorney overhaul him as though he were an old offender; let the ablest attorneys at the bar refuse to say a word for him, because he cannot afford a considerable fee; let the judge give no opportunity for presenting the mitigating circumstances, hurry up the case, and hustle him up to Auburn or Sing Sing. If he live seventy years, for seventy years he will be a criminal, and each decade of his life will be blacker than its predecessor. In the interregnums of prison life he can get no work, and he is glad to break a window-glass, or blow up a safe, or play the highwayman, so as to get back again within the walls where he can get something to eat, and hide himself from the gaze of the world.

Why don't his father come and help him? His father is dead. Why don't his mother come and help him? She is dead. Where are all the ameliorating and salutary influences of society? They do not touch him. Why did not some one long ago in the case understand that there was an opportunity for the exploit which would be famous in heaven a quadrillion of years after the earth has become scattered ashes in the last whirlwind? Why did not the District-Attorney take that young man into his private office and say: "My son, I see that you are the victim of circumstances. This is your first crime. You are sorry. I will bring the person you wronged into your presence, and you will apologize and make all the reparation you can, and I will give you another chance." Or that young man is presented in the court room, and

He has no Friends

present, and the judge says: "Who is your counsel?" And he answers: "I have none." And the judge says: "Who will take this young man's case?" And there is a dead halt, and no one offers, and after a while the judge turns to some attorney, who never had a good case in all his life, and never will, and whose advocacy would be enough to secure the condemnation of innocence itself. And the professional incompetent crawls up beside the prisoner, helplessness to rescue despair, when there ought to be a struggle among all the best men of the profession as to who should have the honor of trying to help that unfortunate. How much would such an attorney have received as his fee for such an advocacy? Nothing in dollars, but much every way in a happy consciousness that would make his own life brighter, and his own dying pillow sweeter, and his own heaven happier—the consciousness that he had saved a man!

So there are commercial exigencies. A very late spring obliterates the demand for spring overcoats and spring hats and spring apparel of all sorts. Hundreds of thousands of people say: "It seems we are going to have no spring, and we shall go straight out of winter into warm weather, and we can get along without the usual spring attire." Or there is no autumn weather, the heat plunging into the cold, and the usual clothing which is a compromise between summer and winter is not required. It makes a difference in the sale of millions and millions of dollars of goods, and some over-sanguine young merchant is caught with a vast amount of unsalable goods that never will be salable again, except at prices ruinously reduced.

That Young Merchant

with a somewhat limited capital is in a predicament. What shall the old merchants do as they see that young man in this awful crisis? Rub their hands and laugh and say: "Good for him. He might have known better. When he has been in business as long as we have, he will not load his shelves in that way. Ha! Ha! He will burst up before long. He had no business to open his store so near to ours anyhow." Sheriff's sale! Red flag in the window: "How much is bid for these out-of-the-fashion spring overcoats and spring hats, or fall clothing out of date? What do I hear in the way of a bid?" "Four dollars." "Absurd; I cannot take that bid of four dollars apiece. Why, these coats when first put upon the market were offered a fifteen dollars each, and now I am offered onl four dollars. Is that all? Five dollars, do I hear Going at that! Gone at five dollars," and h takes the whole lot.

The young merchant goes home that nigh and says to his wife: "Well, Mary, we will hav to move out of this house and sell our piano That old merchant that has had an evil eye on me ever since I started has bought out all that clothing, and he will have it rejuvenated, and next year put it on the market as new, while w will do well if we keep out of the poor-house.

The Young Man, Broken-spirited,

goes to hard drinking. The young wife with her baby goes to her father's house, and not only is his store wiped out, but his home, his morals, and his prospects for two worlds—this and the next. And devils make a banquet of fire and fill their cups of gall, and drink deep to the health of the old merchant who swallowed up the young merchant who got stuck on spring goods and went down. That is one way, *and some of you have tried it.*

But there is another way. That young merchant who found that he had miscalculated in laying in too many goods of one kind, and been flung of the unusual season, is standing behind the counter, feeling very blue, and biting his finger-nails, or looking over his account-books, which read darker and worse every time he looks at them, and thinks how his young wife will have to be put in a plainer house than she ever expected to live in, or go to a third-rate boarding-house where they have tough liver and sour bread five mornings out of the seven. An old merchant comes in and says: "Well, Joe, this has been a hard season for young merchants, and this prolonged cool weather has put many in the doldrums, and I have been thinking o you a good deal of late, for just after I started in business I once got into the same scrape. Now if there is

Anything I can do to Help

you out I will gladly do it. Better just pu those goods out of sight for the present, an next season we will plan something about them. I will help you to some goods that you can se for me on commission, and I will go down t one of the wholesale houses and tell them tha I know you and will back you up, and if yo want a few dollars to bridge over the present, can let you have them. Be as economical you can, keep a stiff upper lip, and rememb that you have two friends, God and mysel Good morning!" The old merchant goes aw and the young man goes behind his desk, an the tears roll down his cheeks. It is the fir time he has cried. Disaster made him mad everything, and mad at man and mad at Go But this kindness melts him, and the tears see to relieve his brain, and his spirits rise from t below zero to eighty in the shade, and he com out of the crisis.

About three years after, this young mercha goes into the old merchant's store and say "Well, my old friend, I was this morning thin ing over what you did for me three years ag You helped me out of an awful crisis in my co mercial history. I learned wisdom, and prosp ity has come, and the pallor has gone out of wife's cheeks, and the roses that were th when I courted her in her father's house ha bloomed again, and my business is splendid, a I thought I ought to let you know that y saved a man!" In a short time after, the merchant who had been a good while shaky his limbs and had poor spells, is called to le the world, and one morning after he had re the twenty-third Psalm about "The Lord is Shepherd," he closes his eyes on this world, a an angel who had been for many years appoi ed to watch the old man's dwelling, cries upw the news that the patriarch's spirit is about cending. And the twelve angels who keep twelve gates of heaven, unite in crying down this approaching spirit of the old man; "C in and welcome, for it has been told all c these Celestial lands that *you saved a man.*"

There sometimes come exigencies in the life a woman. One morning about two years ago saw in the newspaper that there was a young oman in New York, whose pocketbook con- ining thirty-seven dollars and thirty-three nts had been stolen, and she had been left ithout a farthing at the beginning of winter, a strange city, and no work. And although e was a stranger, I did not allow the 9 o'clock ail to leave the lamp-post on our corner, with- t carrying the thirty-seven dollars and thirty- ree cents; and the case was proved genuine. ow I have read all Shakspere's tragedies, and l Victor Hugo's tragedies, and all Alexander mith's tragedies, but I never read a tragedy ore thrilling than that case, and similar cases the hundreds and thousands in all our large ties; young women

Without Money and Without Home

nd without work in these great maelstroms of etropolitan life. When such a case comes nder your observation, how do you treat it? Get out of my way, we have no room in our stablishment for any more hands. I don't be- eve in women anyway, they are a lazy, idle, orthless set. John, please show this person ut of the door." Or do you compliment her ersonal appearance, and say things to her which if any man said to your sister or daughter ou would kill him on the spot? That is one ay, and it is tried every day in these large ities, and many of those who advertise for emale hands in factories, and for governesses in amilies, have proved themselves *unfit to be in ny place outside of hell.*

But there is another way, and I saw it the ther day in the Methodist Book Concern in New York, where a young woman applied for ork and the gentleman in tone and manner aid in substance: "My daughter, we employ omen here, but I do not know of any vacant lace in our department. You had better inquire t such and such a place, and I hope you will be uccessful in getting something to do." The mbarrassed and humiliated woman seemed to give way to Christian confidence. She started ut with a hopeful look that I think must have von for her a place in which to earn her bread. rather think that considerate and Christian entleman saved a woman. New York and Brooklyn ground up last year about thirty thou- and young women, and would like to grind up bout as many this year. Out of all that long rocession of women who march on with no ope for this world or the next, battered and ruised and scoffed at, and flung off the preci- ice, not one but might have been saved for ome and God and heaven. But good men and ood women are not in that kind of business. Alas for that poor thing! nothing but the thread f that sewing-girl's needle held her, and the hread broke.

I have heard men tell in public discourse what man is; but what is a woman? Until some ne shall give a better definition, I will tell you

What a Woman Is.

Direct from God, a sacred and delicate gift, with ffections so great that no measuring line short f that of the infinite God can tell their bound. 'ashioned to refine and soothe and lift and radiate home and society and the world. Of uch value that no one can appreciate it, unless is mother lived long enough to let him under- tand it, or who in some great crisis of life, hen all else failed him, had a wife to reinforce im with a faith in God that nothing could dis- urb. Speak out, ye cradles, and tell of the eet that rocked you and the anxious faces that overed over you! Speak out, ye nurseries of ll Christendom, and ye homes, whether deso- ate or still in full bloom with the faces of wife, other, and daughter, and help me to define hat woman is.

But as geographers tell us that the depths f the sea correspond with the heights of the ountains, I have to tell you that good woman- ood is not higher up than bad womanhood is eep down. The grander the palace, the more wful the conflagration that destroys it. The grande the steamer *Oregon*, the more terrible her going down just off the coast. Now I should not wonder if you trembled a little with a sense of responsibility when I say that there is hardly a person in this house but may have

An Opportunity to Save a Woman.

It may in your case be done by good advice, or by financial help, or by trying to bring to bear some one of a thousand Christian influences. You would not have to go far. If, for instance, you know among your acquaintances a young woman who is apt to appear on the streets about the hour when gentlemen return from business, and you find her responding to the smile of entire strangers, hogs that lift their hat, go to her and plainly tell her that nearly all the destroyed womanhood of the world be- gan the downward path with that very behavior.

Or if, for instance, you find a woman in finan- cial distress and breaking down in health and spirits trying to support her children, now that her husband is dead or an invalid, doing that very important and honorable work, but which is little appreciated, keeping a boarding-house, where all the guests, according as they pay small board, or propose, without paying any board at all, to decamp, are critical of everything and hard to please, busy yourselves in trying to get her more patrons, and tell her of divine sym- pathy. Yea, if you see a woman favored of fortune and with all kindly surroundings, find- ing in the hollow flatteries of the world her chief regalement, living for herself and for time as if there were no eternity, strive to bring her into the kingdom of God, as did the other day a Sabbath-school teacher, who was the means of

The Conversion of the Daughter

of a man of immense wealth, and the daughter resolved to join the church, and she went home and said: "Father, I am going to join the church and I want you to come." "Oh, no," he said, "I never go to church." "Well," said the daughter, "if I were going to be married, would you not go to see me married?" And he said: "Oh, yes." "Well," said she, "this is of more importance than that." So he went, and has gone ever since, and loves to go. I do not know but that faithful Sabbath-school teacher not only saved a women, but saved a man. There may be in this audience, gathered from all parts of the world, the most cosmopolitan assembly in all the earth, there may be a man whose be- havior toward womanhood has been perfidious. Repent! Stand up, thou masterpiece of sin and death, that I may charge you! As far as pos- sible, make reparation. Do not boast that you have her in your power and that she cannot help herself. When that fine collar and cravat and that elegant suit of clothes comes off and your uncovered soul stands before God, you will be better off if you save that woman.

There is another exploit you can do, and that is

To Save a Child.

A child does not seem to amount to much. It is nearly a year old before it can walk at all. For the first year and a half it cannot speak a word. For the first ten years it would starve if it had to earn its own food. For the first fifteen years its opinion on any subject is absolutely valueless. And then there are so many of them. My! what lots of children! And some people have contempt for children. They are good for nothing but to wear out the carpets and break things and keep you awake nights crying. Well, your estimate of a child is quite different from that mother's estimate who lost her child this summer. They took it to the salt air of the sea- shore and to the tonic air of the mountains, but no help came, and the brief paragraph of its life is ended. Suppose that life could be re- stored by purchase, how much would that be- reaved mother give? She would take all the jewels from her fingers and neck and bureau and put them down. And if told that that was not enough, she would take her house and make over the deed for it, and if that were not enough, she would call in all her investments, and put down all her mortgages and bonds, and if told that were not enough, she would say: "I have made over all my property, and if I can have that child back I will now pledge that I will toil with my own hands and carry with my own shoulders in any kind of hard work, and live in a cellar and die in a garret. Only give me back that lost darling!" I am glad that there are those who know something of

The Value of a Child.

Its possibilities are tremendous. What will those hands yet do? Where will those feet yet walk? Toward what destiny will that never-dy- ing soul betake itself? Shall those lips be the throne of blasphemy or benediction? Come, chronologists, and calculate the decades on de- cades, the centuries on centuries, of its lifetime. Oh, to save a child! Am I not right in putting that among the great exploits?

But what are you going to do with those children who are worse off than if their father or mother had died the day they were born? There are tens of thousands of such. Their parentage was against them. Their name is against them. The structure of their skulls against them. Their nerves and muscles con- taminated by the inebriety or dissoluteness of their parents; they are practically at their birth laid out on a plank in the middle of the Atlantic Ocean, in an equinoctial gale, and told to make for shore. What to do with them is the ques- tion often asked. There is another question quite as pertinent, and that is, what are they go- ing to do with us? They will, ten or eleven years from now, have as many votes as the same number of well-born children, and they will hand this land over to anarchy and political damna- tion just as sure as we neglect them. Suppose we each one of us save a boy or save a girl. You can do it. Will you? I will.

How Shall We Get Ready

for one or all of these three exploits? We shall make a dead failure if in our own strength we try to save a man or woman or child. But my text suggests where we are to get equipment. "The people that do know their God shall be strong, and do exploits." We must know Him through Jesus Christ in our own salvation and then we shall have His help in the salvation of others. And while you are saving strangers you may save some of your own kin. You think your brothers and sisters and children and grandchil- dren all safe, but they are not dead, and no one is safe till he is dead. On the English coast there was

A Wild Storm, and a Wreck

in the offing, and the cry was: "Man the life- boat!" But Harry, the usual leader of the sail- or's crew, was not to be found, and they went without him, and brought back all the ship- wrecked people but one. By this time, Harry, the leader of the crew, appeared and said: "Why did you leave that one?" The answer was: "He could not help himself at all, and we could not get him into the boat." "Man the lifeboat!" shouted Harry, "and we will go for that one." "No," said his aged mother, standing by, "you must not go. I lost your father in a storm like this, and your brother Will went off six years ago, and I have not heard a word from Will since he left, and I don't know where he is, poor Will, and I cannot let you also go, for I am old and dependent on you." His reply was: "Mother, I must go and save that one man, and if I am lost, God will take care of you in your old days."

The lifeboat put out, and after an awful strug- gle with the sea, they picked the poor fellow out of the rigging just in time to save his life, and started for the shore. And as they came within speaking distance, Harry cried out: "We saved him, and tell mother it was brother Will." Oh, yes, my friends, let us start out to save some one for time and for eternity, some man, some woman, some child. And who knows but it may, directly or indirectly, be the salvation of one of our own kindred, and that will be an ex- ploit worthy of celebration when the world itself is shipwrecked, and the sun has gone out like a spark from a smitten anvil, and all the stars are dead!

A NIGHT AT FLORENCE MISSION.

THE work carried on at the famous institution in Bleecker Street, New York, has grown rapidly since the founder of it, Mr. Crittenden, consecrated the whole of his time and property to the Lord's service after the death of his beloved wife. On a recent evening, many valuable testimonies were given, from among which we select the following:

A Betrayed English Woman.

Much interest was felt in the testimony of a person who had just returned from England. On the voyage out, one of her fellow-passengers had confided in her, and told her so much of the Florence Mission and what she owed to it, that she determined to come and see it when she returned to New York, and to encourage the workers by reporting what she had seen and heard. She said that her fellow-passenger was a young lady of education and refinement. She was living in a happy home in England, when she was fascinated by a man, who betrayed her, and had persuaded her to escape disgrace among her friends by eloping with him to America. She fell ill in New York, her companion deserted her, and she was taken to a hospital. There she was visited by a lady who had been rescued and converted at the Florence Mission. The sick girl was very near death, and believing she could never recover, was induced to give herself to Christ. But to the astonishment of all, she recovered, and her Florence Mission friend took her to Bleecker Street, where she stayed some time, helping in the work and giving her testimony for Jesus. She wrote to her home, and learned that a welcome awaited her. She immediately set out for England repentant, but rejoicing. The lady who was her fellow-passenger, and who told the story last week, said that none were so active in Christian work on board as this rescued girl.

A Young Hebrew

gave a remarkable testimony for Christ. He said he was twenty-one years of age. One evening, when passing the Florence Mission, the sound of music and singing attracted him. He was passionately fond of music, and he entered the building to see what was going on. He sat down and listened. The Holy Spirit blessed the testimonies he heard and the appeals made, and he was deeply moved. Mrs. Lily Van Dun, who has been a most earnest worker at the mission, noticed his emotion, and seating herself near him, she told him of Jesus of Nazareth, and urged him to become a Christian. She prayed with him, and finding that there were strong obstacles to his conversion not to be easily overcome, she gained his promise to come again to the mission. He came, and finally admitted that his Jewish father was bitterly opposed to Christianity, and he dreaded the effect of his becoming a Christian. Soon afterward he was stricken with illness, and sent a note to the mission, asking for Mrs. Van Dun to visit him. She went, and had the joy of leading him to Christ. Standing up in the mission the other night, he spoke of his recovery from his sickness, declared himself on the Lord's side, and pledged himself to labor in the cause of his Saviour at any cost to himself and his fortune.

Two Rescued Girls

next told their story. It appeared that two wealthy New York men had found them given to frivolity, fond of dress, and disposed to flirtation, but otherwise virtuous, though without religious principle. They were dazzled by the brilliant promises of luxury, of jewels and magnificent dresses, which they might have by living with the men in New York, and at length yielded to their solicitation. To do the men justice, the promises had been kept. Money had been lavished upon them without stint. They had enjoyed every luxury that money could buy, and pleasure of all kinds had been afforded them. A carriage and ponies were provided for their use, and costly jewels were given to them. Florence Mission workers, however, heard of them, and visited them. They were led to see the awful iniquity of the life they were leading, and were brought to seek Christ for mercy. They quitted their luxurious home, gave up the wages of sin, renounced the gay clothing and the rich jewels that had been given to them, and declared their resolve to live henceforward for Christ, whatever of hardship or poverty it might involve.

AN OCTOGENARIAN'S CONVERSION.

AN interesting letter to the *Church* from the Rev. Hunter Corbett, D. D., who is laboring at So An in China, contains the following striking instance of filial love winning a soul for Christ: At one of our little churches in the country it was my privilege last month to baptize a widow eighty-three years of age. Ten years ago her youngest son became an earnest Christian, and has been growing in wisdom and grace continually. From the first this son has been deeply concerned for his mother's salvation. He not only prayed for her daily, but often asked the Christians to join him in prayer, and go with him to his home and plead with his mother. Her constant reply was, she was too old to learn a new religion. She would neither study nor come to the church, although only a few footsteps from her door. Last autumn she seemed to awaken as from a dream. She wondered what made the difference between her younger son and her two older ones, who many years ago went to Manchuria, and since then had done nothing for her support, but had repeatedly sent for their younger brother and wished him to desert her. She argued if it is Christianity which makes her son and his wife, also an earnest Christian, willing to labor diligently for her support, and show her every kindness in their power, then this truth must be priceless, even if there is no reward hereafter. She resolved to begin a new life. Since then she has been studying and praying with child-like faith and humility. The clear evidence she gave of having grasped the truth, and a fixed purpose to trust only in Jesus for salvation, filled every heart with joy. Her very features spoke of inward peace and joy. The careworn and anxious face of former years was so changed that even her heathen neighbors were filled with wonder. Her daughter, a bright and gifted woman, was baptized at the same time on profession of faith.

A CONSECRATED TEN-DOLLAR BILL.

A CLERGYMAN in New York who recently called at the office of this journal, has a ten-dollar bill with remarkable associations. It was given to him in Vesey Street on July 28 last to use in the Lord's work. Eight years ago, in the same place, he met an old friend whom he had not seen for many years, not, in fact, since they were young men enjoying themselves, not in the most profitable way, in New York. They had been employed in business houses in the city, but the clergyman's friend had inherited a considerable sum of money, and had given up his situation to attend to the investment of his fortune. When they met in 1880, they naturally inquired of each other as to the results of the years which had elapsed since they separated. The man who had inherited the fortune said that he had bought property, but had given too much for it. Other losses had compelled him to mortgage it heavily. It had stood unoccupied for some time, the interest on the mortgage was in arrears, and foreclosure was threatened. He could not sell the property, he had no funds, and was intensely miserable. He had been trying to get work but had failed. He had been promised employment in the shops of the Erie road, but on applying, one boss had sent him to another, until he was wearied out, and had come away disgusted. So despairing was he that, coming over the ferry that morning, he was strongly tempted to throw himself overboard.

The clergyman then related his history during the past years. He told how he had been brought to God and used in His service. Then, encouraging his friend, he said: "You must give yourself to Jesus—you and your wife. Do not think of the awful crime of suicide. Go to God for mercy, and all will come right." A time was appointed for special prayer together, and eventually both the man and his wife we saved. Prayer was offered about the mon trouble also. On the same night, a messeng came to the despairing man, requesting him call again at the Erie shops. He did so, and w taken on at five dollars a day to start with, a his immediate wants were thus relieved. T property, however, was still in danger of for closure, and prayer was offered about th When the two friends met in Vesey Street, la July, the man joyfully produced a roll of bil "The value of that property is going up fast he said. "I have sold one lot, and I am comi out right." He initialled one ten-dollar b and handed it to his friend. "That is part the first-fruits," he said. "I want to give it the Lord. He sent it in answer to prayer. I ow it all to Him."

A DEFORMED CHILD CURED.

IN an interesting report from Rev. G. Morri which Mrs. M. Baxter publishes in *Thy Healer*, is the following account of the recovery of little child from one of the most painful and di tressing maladies that can afflict a human being I went down to the country ten months ago there was in the house where I was staying, dear little one three years old, who suffered wit a curved spine—it was a sort of half-circle. Th poor little thing could only stand a little whi leaning against her mother's knee. The moth told me she was getting worse, and the loc physician said she must be kept lying down, an an instrument made for her which she mu wear. That seemed painful to me in the pre ence of the Lord; but I had not confidence the that the mother would be able to join me in re ceiving the blessing from the Lord. I prayed the Lord, and asked Him what to do. Then told her what I had in my mind, and said: " you can be present with faith in the Lord th He will do the work, I would much prefer yo should be present." She said she wished to b present. I said to her—for a day was not im portant—"I should much prefer if you woul bring that child to me to-morrow morning, an meantime I will lay myself in an attitude prayer before the Lord." Well, she brought th child. I, however, put both my hands roun the dear child's back, with her clothes on, an the next morning, at the same hour, the lit thing walked up two flights of stairs, and la Monday-week that little creature walked up me at Speldhurst—a distance of about two mil —and back again. She is a beautiful witness f the Lord. She knows it is Jesus who healed he

A DESPAIRING WIFE.

THE miseries that result from child marria in India are never realized fully, save by the u happy victims. One of these, evidently a we educated girl, reveals some of the horrors in sorrowful letter published in the *Indian Wi ness* of Calcutta. She says: "If you, sir, searc Hindoo society, you will find thousands of gi situated as I am. Parents, as you and yo readers know, have the arrangement of ma riages. The chief contracting parties have n a word to say in the matter: unhappiness is n unfrequently the result. The powers plac in the hands of parents are often abused. It all very well to say that these natural guardia of young people will so arrange for their futu as to secure for them the largest amount happiness possible in a world full of sorro change, and suffering. But people who arg in this way, forget that human nature is wea and human motives are operated on by ma injurious causes. Greed of gold is the chi source whence flow unhappy marriages. Ta my case: I was sold by my avaricious paren and ill-educated brothers, for 100 rupees [abo

* *Thy Healer and Faith Witness*, a monthly Magazi edited by Mrs. M. Baxter, contains original articles Holiness and Healing, Authentic Testimonies of Div Healing, and Items of Intelligence from Heathen La where missionaries are laboring in faith, soliciting no b from man, but relying solely on God for support. Ann Subscription, 75 cents, may be sent to Manager of CHR TIAN HERALD, 63 Bible House, New York.

o]—a paltry sum, indeed—to a miserable retch whose disease makes him a loathsome)ject. I shrink from his very touch. His esence is irksome to me. I am often filled :th thoughts of self-destruction. If I may not me day rid myself of the burden of life by sting myself into some friendly tank or well. some of my equally unfortunate sisters do, y life must be weariness and a burden."

THE FIRST RESURRECTION.

By Rev. John Urquhart

WHAT is the Scripture doctrine regarding the st Resurrection? The meaning of the words :ev. 20 : 4–6) is unmistakable. It is that the esurrection of all the dead is not simultaneous. iere are favored ones who will rise first. These ll reign with Christ for a thousand years, and ien the thousand years close, the rest of the ad will be raised, the present mode of life upon e earth will be brought to an end, and there ll be a new heaven and a new earth (Rev. 21 :

But, explicit as these statements are, the ctrine is so startling that we naturally inquire iether there is anything to show that they are

To be Taken Literally.

there anything said elsewhere in Scripture rerding the first Resurrection? We have a simi- representation in Dan. 7 : 27: "And the ngdom and the dominion, and the greatness the kingdom under the whole heaven, shall given to the people of the saints of the Most gh: His kingdom is an everlasting kingdom, d all dominions shall serve and obey Him." id the book closes with a promise which apars to give to Daniel, himself, this very hope the first Resurrection: "Go thou thy way till e end be: for thou shalt rest, and shalt stand thy lot at the end of the days." (12 : 13.)

There are references to the same truth in sevl passages of the New Testament. Paul says in 'hess. 4 : 16, 17, that "the dead in Christ shall e first: then we who are alive and remain ill be caught up together with them in the uds, to meet the Lord in the air: so shall we r be with the Lord." The Resurrection of e dead in Christ is here spoken of as

An Event by Itself,

d as taking place while the earthly life of the tions still continues. In 1 Cor. 15 : 23, 24, the surrection is described as having three stages epochs: "But every man in his own order: rist the firstfruits; afterward they that are rist's at His coming. Then cometh the end, en He shall have delivered up the kingdom God, even the Father."

There is the resurrection of Christ, who, with erfect and complete humanity, with a body well as a spirit redeemed from death and the ive, has passed into the presence of God, the stfruits of that mighty harvest which will yet reaped from the fields of sin and death. That he first stage. The second is the resurrecn of those that are Christ's at His coming. e third is what the Scripture names "the l," that is, the end of Christ's mediatorial rk, and of the period of grace—the time of last resurrection and of the eternal judgnt, and the kingdom is given up to God.

We have another reference to the same hope Phil. 3 : 11. The Apostle explains the purse of his unceasing endeavor to reach still her heights in Christian life. He states it in se words, "If by any means I might attain to the Resurrection of the dead." What does mean? No man, bad or good, will be able escape the Resurrection, and if there is no arate and anterior resurrection of the Christ-, the Apostle's words are pointless. But if understand him to look onward to his first urrection from the dead, everything is clear. desires to make sure of his being one with rist now, that he may be one with Christ then. Let us ask now, what is

The Glory Reserved

those who will in this way be claimed by the n Redeemer as His own? They will share triumph. They will not be mere spectators His glory: they will be participators in it. "I saw thrones," says the Apostle, "and they sat upon them." "The kingdom and dominion, and the greatness of the kingdom under the whole heaven, shall be given to the people of the saints of the Most High." (Dan. 7 : 27.) Who may tell the glory of that dominion, which is after the image of Christ's? What earthly dominion equals His now? Which, of all that men have ever known, has been so founded on the heart's deepest affections, which has so grasped the inmost thought, so swayed the deepest purposes, so purged the desire and imagination, and so moulded anew the soul of man? What beauties and noblenesses and glories have risen up in man's life under the rule of Jesus! What divine peace, what God-like joy and splendor have revealed His presence in the human heart!

And if all this has marked His sway during this period of waiting, what shall we say of it when the kingdom is made His in very truth, and the earth is indeed the Lord's? What shall it be when hearts are His as they have never been His yet, when every opposing power has been swept away, when God's will and not man's shall be accomplished everywhere, when the earth shall be the place of fullness and joy God meant it to be, and every life shall attain to His ideal? If we could conceive and express the glory of that reign, we should be able to say what our glory will be. Incredible as it may appear, this is the future for us. We shall reign with Him, and hold the earth for God.

THE NEW JERUSALEM.

By P. H. Gosse.

Its Descent—Magnitude, Boundaries, and Inhabitants—Its Foundations—The Light of the City—The Gateways in the Walls—Intercommunication between Heaven and Earth.

IN Revelation 21 we read of a heavenly city, 16,000 furlongs, *i.e.*, 1,500 square miles, which is to descend from God out of heaven, into our atmosphere at the Second Advent of Christ, and to be suspended over the earthly Jerusalem. No doubt the sudden coming into sight, from heavenly space, of a glittering object, unknown to astronomers, self-luminous, above the brightness of the sun, steadily approaching, till it enters our atmosphere, and comes into close proximity to this globe,

Transcends all Human Experience,

and defies all natural philosophy. But the epoch is an epoch of miracle: the Almighty God is henceforth visibly interposing; and is not bound by natural laws, which He made, and which He can interrupt, or counteract, at His pleasure. The suspension of a non-rotating cubic mass, 1,500 miles every way, in our atmosphere or near it, composed of such materials as gold and gems, and inhabited by millions of human beings, in bodies, however ethereal, would surely so augment and throw out of bearing, the specific gravity of the earth, so alter its relations to the sun, to the moon, even to all the other planets, as to be inconceivable and impossible! Nay; I dare not say so. What compensations the "Upholder of all things" (Col. 1 : 17; Heb. 1 : 3) may make for the anticipated disturbances, I cannot conjecture. My business is with His Word. "Hath He spoken, and shall He not make it good?" I am sure He will; though how, I do not know.

What is described is a City, an aggregation of human dwellings; with walls, and gates, and

One Broad Street

(*plateia*), through which a river runs. How the many mansions are arranged *inter se* is not told; but the whole forms a perfect cube of 12,000 stadia in length and breadth and height. Suspended, with its centre over Jerusalem, its boundaries will reach to the shore of the Euxine northward; to Nubia and the middle of Arabia southward; to the Caspian and the Persian Gulf eastward; to Greece and the Sahara westward. If we consider London as covering 100 square miles, and containing 4,000,000 inhabitants (or a million to twenty-five square miles), then this Heavenly City, including 900,000 square miles, would contain 36,000,000,000; supposing it only a plane surface, like London; but immensely more as a cube. So that there will be plenty of room for

"The Redeemed to Walk There!"

I suppose this cube to face the earth cornerwise; to consist, indeed, of two pyramids, placed base to base, of which the upper will be the city-proper, and the lower will consist of twelve glorious foundations. These foundations are the most remarkable feature in the whole material structure; and they form its distinctive character; "the City that hath the foundations."

Each of these twelve foundations is one vast slab of precious stone; what we know only in minute atoms! but, even so, the most costly objects that earth produces. Each a slab of ninety miles in thickness, diminishing, in succession from 1,500 miles square (the first) to an inverted square pyramid of 150 miles' base (the twelfth). Imagine such immense slabs of jasper (probably diamond), sapphire, emerald, laid one over another, yet suffering no diminution of translucency; for *the whole* is said to be "clear as crystal." Imagine the light of the blazing Glory of God flashing down from the Throne, through these gemmeous foundations; the combined effect of the various hues producing an

Unimaginably Beautiful Radiance

to the beholders on earth; while all around there appear broad edges of diverse color, where each slab, in the increasing pyramid, overlaps its successor! To secure this extraordinary magnificence in the eyes of Israel below, is no doubt the object of this pyramidal arrangement of slabs, and of the suspension above the earth.

We know that, after the Resurrection, "they that be wise shall shine as the brightness of the firmament; and they that turn many to righteousness as the stars" (Dan. 12 : 3); that, when the Lord Jesus was transfigured "His face did shine as the sun, and His raiment was white as the light" (Matt. 17 : 2); and that, when He arrested Saul at Damascus, "a light from heaven, *above* the brightness of the sun at midday" (Acts 26 : 13) shone. Above all, "the Glory of God doth lighten this City, and the Lamb is the lamp thereof." What inconceivable intensity of brightness, then, will pervade every part of this pyramidal City, and flame down, softened and tinted by the clear but colored media, on the Sanctuary in the earthly Jerusalem, and worshippers beneath! The wall is pierced by

Three Gateways on Each Side,

which, as they are never closed, must be considered as magnificent portals to the main broad-streets, each surmounted by an enormous globe of purest pearly lustre and iridescence, inscribed with a name of one of the Tribes of Israel. These gates are 350 miles apart; and so, consequently, are the great broad-streets: so that we may suppose myriads of subordinate streets, sudividing the area of the City. And, besides these, other streets and terraces, rising on beauteous arches and on pillars, mansion above mansion, tier above tier, even to the very summit of the vast pyramid.

What is the use of these open gates? No stranger will ever be admitted there: nor will the perfected Bride ever be augmented. Yet some intercommunication between the heavenly and the earthly seems implied. The glory and honor of the nations, and of their kings are brought to (*eis*) it; and this is said in connection with the ever-open gates. And the leaves of the Tree of Life are transmitted to the nations, till death is wholly done away. Perhaps there may be a grand stairway, like that of Jacob's vision, leading from every pearly portal to the earth below. And as an angel is stationed at each, these may still be ministering spirits to redeemed men of the earthly family.

CHRISTIAN HERALD AND SIGNS OF OUR TIMES.
O[illegible] FICE, 63 BIBLE HOUSE, NEW YORK.
ENTERED AT THE POST-OFFICE AT NEW YORK, N. Y., AS SECOND-CLASS MATTER.

EVERY NUMBER CONTAINS:
The Portrait and Biography of some eminent person.
The Sermon Dr. Talmage preached the last Sunday morning.
An Exposition of Unfulfilled Prophecy.
A Summary of the Events of the Week, Notes of Religious and Temperance Movements, etc.
A Sermon by Rev. C. H. Spurgeon, of London, from advance sheets sent by special arrangement.
Pictures of Missionary Life, etc., and Descriptive Articles.
An Instalment of a Serial Story.
An Exposition of the International Sunday-School Lesson, by Mrs. M. Baxter.

ANNUAL SUBSCRIPTION, $1.50.
Single Copies, Price Three Cents, may be obtained by order of any Newsdealer.

NOTICE.

A concession in price will be made to subscribers desiring to introduce THE CHRISTIAN HERALD to ministers, evangelists, or personal friends. It will be mailed regularly every week to any address in the United States or Canada, from September 20 to the end of the year 1888, for twenty-five cents. Address The Manager, 63 Bible House, New York.

CURRENT EVENTS.

The President's Message Accompanying his signature of the Chinese exclusion bill, which was sent to Congress, on October 1, was doubtless an effort to place the legislative act in its most favorable aspect, for the benefit of other peoples as well as our own. Some such effort was evidently necessary, though the President must have found it somewhat difficult. His defence of the measure, and of his own part in ratifying it, is based on the contention that so long as the Chinese Government had not decided whether to accept or reject the treaty, the bill was to be regarded as merely a machinery, designed to give effect to the treaty and as contingent on its acceptance. But so soon as China rejected the treaty it became a defensive law, necessary to give this country the protection which was the object sought under the treaty. Mr. Cleveland holds that China had of her own free will proposed to establish a system of strict prohibition of the departure of her laborers for the United States, including such as had once been here and returned home. But the control of her Government over their movements was not complete, and it was recognized that the only effective exclusion must operate upon this side of the Pacific. It is also suggested that this mode of solving the difficulty will be more acceptable to the Chinese Government than the ratification of the treaty, as it relieves that Government of responsibility and saves it from complications with other nations.

The Republican Tariff Bill was Presented to the Senate on October 3. It is now claimed that it would effect a total reduction of nearly seventy-four millions, which is only some three millions less than the total reached by the Mills bill, for which it is offered as a substitute. It differs, however, from that measure in the method of effecting the reduction. While Mr. Mills placed raw wool on the free list, the Republican bill raises the duty on that article by a cent a pound. On the other hand, it sweeps away the sugar duties, now yielding $27,759,783, the tax on tobacco, of $24,371,460, and proposes to abolish the revenue on alcohol used in the arts, now producing about $7,000,000. The additions to the free list are estimated at $6,428,095, and the changes in the schedules generally, effect a reduction of $8,109,654. It must be remembered that in both measures the exact effect of a change in the revenue can only be accurately gauged in cases of *total* abolition, as it is likely that when the duty on any article is only decreased, the decrease may stimulate consumption, and so the total revenue from the duty at the lower rate may be as large as that from the higher rate. Those Democratic journals which represent the Randall wing of the party are urging Democrats to accept the new bill, pass it as the only practical solution of the problem, and send it to the President before the election in November. If the advice were to be taken, it would be one of the most remarkable and momentous political surprises in our history.

A Curious Interpretation of the Civil Service reform law appears to have been made by Gen. S. V. Benet, and it is not surprising that his political opponents brought it last week before Congress. Gen. Benet came to the conclusion that the object of the new law was to effect an equal division of the offices between the two political parties, and, therefore, that it was necessary, the Republicans having been so long in power, that now in employing or discharging employés of any or all grades in the Government arsenals and armories, other things being equal and qualifications satisfactory, Democrats be favored. This rule, as Gen. Benet was careful to explain, was intented to apply "*to women and children* as well as to men." The civil service commission is endeavoring to secure the application of the rules to the arsenals and armories. If it succeeds, the military officials will, like their civil brethren, discover that the law was not designed to discriminate between Democratic and Republican women and children, but simply and exclusively between efficient and non-efficient applicants for employment.

Distressing Reports of Disasters on the Lakes were received on October 2. On Lake Huron a wild storm raged throughout the night. One fatality was peculiarly sad. A steamtug which was towing six heavily laden barges, made her way with immense difficulty to the harbor of refuge at Sand Beach, but, just as she entered, the tow-line broke, and the six barges drifted out helplessly before the gale. On one of the barges were six men and a woman, and learning the fact, the life-saving crew went to their rescue. They succeeded in taking all the seven off the barge just as it was going to pieces. As it was impossible to return to the harbor in the storm and darkness, the brave fellows put their boat before the wind, and rowed unsiringly the whole night through. About seven o'clock they sighted Port Sanilac, and steered their craft for that point. As they rounded the headland a tremendous wave struck the boat and capsized it. The life-saving crew and two of the men from the barge succeeded in swimming ashore, but the other four men and the woman were drowned. From other points news comes of wreck, but it is hoped no other lives were lost.

A Welcome Report of Abatement in the Yellow fever mortality was sent out from Jacksonville, Fla., last week. On Tuesday the gratifying record was made for the first time in many weeks, of no death from the scourge in the preceding twenty-four hours. On Thursday there was only one death. On that day, the figures for the entire epidemic stood at a total of 2,971 cases, and 271 deaths. The number of new cases each day of the week ranged from 75 to 100, but it was observed that they developed in houses previously infected. From this fact the encouraging inference was drawn that the infection was no longer in the air, but was localized. There is no reason, unhappily, at present, for any relaxation of the benevolent efforts for the relief of the sufferers. Now, and probably for a long time to come, many families must depend on outside benevolence. Both the families who stayed in the city, and those who went to the camps and, in some cases, even to the woods for refuge, have exhausted their resources, and will require help to enable them to live until business begins to resume its wonted course. There is ground for thankfulness that though the epidemic has been very severe, the proportion of deaths has been smaller than in some former visitations. This is doubtless due to the heroic fidelity to duty displayed by physicians, nurses, and kind Christian helpers. Among the interesting facts mentioned in connection with the scourge is the efficacy of a *very simple remedy*. It is stated that the eating of bananas, or the drinking of a decoction of them, frequently produces most beneficial results, especially in the earlier stage of the seizure.

An Extraordinary Series of Brutal Murders has appalled London. During a few weeks past seven women, belonging to the most vicious and degraded class in the city, have been put to death. All the crimes have evidently been committed by the same person. The murderer appears to act with no motive of robbery. He cuts his victim's throat and then horribly mutilates the body, taking away with him one and the same organ from the intestines. His work shows signs of a familiar acquaintance with the anatomy of the human body. A surgeon stated, however, at the inquest of one of the victims, that such knowledge might be possessed by a butcher, and was not necessarily proof that the criminal was a surgeon. The police are absolutely at fault, and though two murders were committed in the heart of London on Sept. 30, no clue to the murderer has been obtained.

The Publication of the Extracts from Emperor Frederick's diary continues to be a prominent subject of discussion throughout Europe. The proprietors of the journal in which they were published, being threatened with prosecution for contumacy, have informed the Government who it was that furnished them with the extracts. They stated that they had received them from Professor Geffcken, of Hamburg, who enjoyed the confidence of the late Emperor. Dr. Geffcken lived in London several years—as he had previously in Berlin—in the capacity of Hanseatic Minister Resident. He is a frequent contributor to English magazines on German politics. He was arrested at Hamburg on September 30. Hamburg being a free city, extradition proceedings were necessary, and his case has been remitted to the Supreme Court at Leipsic. Bismarck has developed a strong animosity against Geffcken, who he not unnaturally regards as an enemy to his fame, as the German people have learned from the diary that Bismarck had far less to do with achieving German unity than was popularly supposed. Still more bitter does he feel toward the late Emperor's widow, whom he unjustly suspects of prompting the publication.

In the Prevalent Anxiety as to Mr. H. M. Stanley, the interview with Lieut. Mason Schufeldt, of the U. S. Navy, published last week, affords welcome encouragement. Lieut. Schufeldt has been twice down the East African coast, three times to China, and twice around the world in opposite directions. He crossed Madagascar in 1884–5 with 500 men, only 15 finishing the journey, and escaped across the Mozambique Channel in an open boat. When asked his opinion of Stanley's present whereabouts, he said he was convinced that "the explorer may be following the Aruwimi River in the hope, as many travellers suppose, that the river has its rise in one of the great chain of African lakes; or he may have crossed that river and be travelling north to reach Wadelai. He had with him sufficient stores for a long isolation from outside aid. Generally speaking, the African races themselves are neither belligerent nor treacherous. Only when incited by some outside influence, the promises of reward on the part of the slave-dealers, or their threats, do they show marked hostility to the pure European. It is the terrible slave-trade, stretching its innumerable arms over the whole interior, that renders travel through the Continent so extremely hazardous to the foreigner. The Akka country in which Stanley is now supposed to be, is inhabited by a peaceful race, and unless they have been incited by the persuasions or threats of the slave-traders, I do not see any reason to believe that Stanley has met with a violent death."

Very Liberal Terms are Offered to any Person canvassing for subscriptions to THE CHRISTIAN HERALD. Sample copies will be sent, postage paid, on application from any one desiring to undertake the work. Ministers and others will find it easy to obtain subscriptions. Send postal card for terms, and state number of sample copies required. Address The Manager, 63 Bible House, New York.

Contributions to the Fund for Supplying Colored ministers in the South with this journal have been received since our last acknowledgement to the amount of $8. They are from: Seward, Me., $5; Orwigsburg, Pa., $1; Woodhaven, L. I., $2. One of the preachers who has been receiving THE CHRISTIAN HERALD during the past year through this fund, wrote last week: "I have been greatly blessed in reading its pages. I do hope it will be continued another year." Similar testimonies in large numbers come in. We earnestly pray that, the need being so urgent, and the preachers so anxious to have the benefit of the sermons and religious comment which the paper contains, God will incline His people to supply their wants.

Mission Potatoes Shipped to New York Last week were a practical proof of what children may do for a good cause. The consignment consisted of twelve sacks of potatoes, holding three bushels each. They were shipped to the Five Points Mission, from Richmond Hill, L. I. They were the yield of the Mission field, cultivated by the Sunday-school of the Union Congregational Church of that village. The children heard the cry for potatoes that went up from Five Points last fall, and decided upon this practical plan of charity in the hope that it might be generally followed. Police Inspector Steers, who knew of the scheme, and who used to do patrol duty at the Five Points in its worst days, sent a barrel of seed potatoes to the school. His two bushels and a half have grown to thirty-six bushels, and the yield would have been larger but for the fact that new ground had to be broken for the mission field.

Litigation Involving Ninety Thousand Dollars was initiated last week in New York. The defendants are ten Ferry and Railroad Companies. Last May the Legislature passed a law requiring every such company to post notices outside of each ferry house and on each boat, in plain view of passengers, stating the rates of ferriage. In case of any company posting a false list, or neglecting to comply with the law, it was to be subject to a fine of fifty dollars for each and every day of such neglect, and any person might collect the penalty by suing for it in the courts. A curious fact is that no notice of the law was sent to the Ferry Companies, and ten of them have neglected to comply with the law. Suit has been accordingly commenced by an enterprising citizen, and the Sheriff last week served each company with a notice. If the full penalty is enforced in each case, the total sum will be ninety thousand dollars. The fault of the Companies does not appear to have been one of defiance of law, but either ignorance of it or neglect. Evidently it is not safe for any citizen to be ignorant of the enactments of the Legislature of his State. Still more essential is it for every one to carefully study God's law, which is revealed in His Word. That study must lead to self-condemnation, but, also, to the discovery of the way provided for reconciliation with God. (Ps. 19:7-9.)

A Fierce Fight with a Dog over a Corpse Occurred in Salem, Mass., on October 1. In a house at South Salem Point, a well-to-do bachelor lived alone with a huge Newfoundland dog, who was his constant companion. For some unexplained cause the man grew much depressed, and finally committed suicide. He was missed from his usual haunts, and on Monday of last week the police visited his house, to find out what had become of him. There they found his dead body, guarded by his faithful dog. He growled as they approached his dead master, but was at length coaxed into allowing them to endeavor to resuscitate the man. When they discovered that he was really dead, they proceeded to remove the body, but the dog resisted. He bit two of the policemen severely, and stood over the body, his eyes burning and his teeth exposed, ready to attack the next who touched his dead master. The policemen retreated, and the dog fell to licking the dead face, and otherwise showing his love. It was clear that the body could not be removed while the dog lived, and, therefore, the policemen sadly and reluctantly shot the animal. Even after several wounds were inflicted, the dog still held his post, and not until he was quite dead did the men dare to touch the body. That a dog should manifest fidelity, even to the death, teaches a lesson to Christians, whom greed of gain or love of social distinction is often sufficient to tempt to forsake their Master. (Isa. 1:3, 4.)

A Mistake as to a Honey Tree Caused Disappointment and terror to a farm-laborer near Hanover, Penn., recently. While at work near a wood, he heard a sound like bees humming, and finally located it in a hollow tree near by. Although he could see no bees going into or coming out of the tree, he was satisfied that he had found a honey tree, and he went to work at once to cut down the tree and secure the honey. Every stroke of his axe on the tree set the humming and buzzing going with renewed vigor. He had but a few inches to cut into the tree before the hollow place was reached. The axe had barely penetrated to the hollow, making a hole two or three inches in diameter, when he was horrified by the sight of the head of a huge rattlesnake protruding. The snake squirmed out of the hole, and before the man had recovered from his astonishment, other snakes followed, until the ground seemed alive with the venomous reptiles. The buzzing which the man had supposed was made by a swarm of wild bees was the noise made by the combined rattling of the snakes. They had evidently found the hollow tree a cosey place for them to winter in, and had settled themselves there with the coming of frosty nights. Unhappily, an analagous mistake is often made by young people about the pleasures of the world. They expect to get the honey of life from them, but they find trouble which is worse to deal with than serpents. (Prov 5:3, 4.)

A Man Unconsciously Took a Photograph of his own shadow in Oregon recently. An Oregon journal states that an amateur photographer, who accompanied the recent expedition to Crater Lake, taking views of charming bits of scenery, accomplished one thing which he did not look for—the photographing of his own shadow. He stood on Vidæ Cliff, 2,000 feet high, and had the camera pointed at the lake in the distance. Between the camera and its object, and about sixty feet away, was another cliff, which is shown in the photograph. The upper portion of it is of a light photographic color, while the lower part is jet black, and looks as if it had been painted with a brush. It is just above the jet-black streak that the shadow appears. The form of a man in the act of removing the cap of the camera to expose the plate is clearly shown. It was 5 o'clock in the evening when the photographer took the picture, and the sun was setting behind the romantic hills and cliffs. The permanent registration of so simple an act must be an object of interest to the operator, but how terrible would it be to many men to see accurately limned all the actions of their lives! Such a record exists in every case in which it has not been expunged by the cleansing blood of Christ. (Rev. 20:12.)

A Lover's Persistency under Discouragement has been rewarded in Boston, Mass. A journal of that city, in announcing a recent marriage, gives a suggestive account of the circumstances which led to it. It states that some years ago, the young man began paying attentions to the lady, but they were not cordially received. He continued calling upon her, however, and at length visited her regularly every Sunday evening. She did not wish to appear rude or inhospitable, but she was intensely weary of his visits, and in a polite and courteous manner tried to let him see the fact. But he was deaf to all hints, ignored all her slights, treated her coldness with unfailing good-humor, and regularly presented himself as sure as the day came round. At last she could bear it no longer, and as hints were lost upon him, she wrote him explicitly requesting him in future to discontinue his Sunday visits. To her amazement, he presented himself on the very night of receiving her letter, coolly observing that he had no objection to changing his day. His composure and evident determination not to be dismissed were too much for the lady's resolution. She doubted whether it was possible to shake him off, and ultimately yielded to his pleadings and married him. It is a pity that similar persistence is not more frequently displayed by those who are seeking for union with the Saviour. It never fails of success, and Jesus explicitly commended it. (Matt. 15:22-28.)

Fire was Kindled by the Aid of Ice in a hotel at Washington, D. C., a few days ago. The Washington *Star* says that a group of smokers were chatting in the garden of one of the principal hotels when a gentleman, who had taken a fresh cigar, asked his companions for a match. None of them had the article, but one of them suggested that a lump of ice might be used to light the cigar. There was a general laugh at the suggestion, but the man was in earnest. After being jeered at, and made the butt of witticisms for some time, he quietly proceeded to prove his suggestion feasible. Taking a piece of clear ice about an inch thick from the water-cooler, he whittled the edges, and then held it between the palms of his hands until it took the shape of a convex disc or burning-glass. Holding it where it caught the sun's rays, he focussed them on the end of a cigar, and triumphantly held it out fully lighted for the inspection of the company. Many a cold, blighting affliction, from which nothing but sorrow seemed likely to come, has been similarly the medium of new fire to the Christian's faith and love by transmitting into his heart the beams of the Sun of Righteousness. (Heb. 12:11.)

BRIEF NOTES.

Mr. W. F. Bischoffe and Mr. Alfred Hart, are holding evangelistic meetings at Midland, Mich.

Dr. L. W. Munhall has been conducting a two weeks' series of meetings at the Y. M. C. A., Detroit, Mich.

A daily afternoon prayer-meeting has been established at the Plymouth Church, Minneapolis. Dr. Thwing is the pastor.

The next course of Crozer Lectures in Philadelphia will be delivered by Dr. Maclaren, the famous Baptist preacher, of Manchester, England.

The Rev. J. Edgar Johnson, whose theatre services in Philadelphia have been so signally blessed, reopens this month in the Continental Theatre.

Miss Clara Barton, President of the Red Cross Society, besides her personal labor, has given $1,000 out of her own pocket to the yellow fever sufferers.

The English Government has recently communicated with the Government of Canada, desiring information regarding the working of the restrictive laws there.

Mr. Petter, one of the founders of the great publishing house of Cassell, Petter & Galpin, has just died in England, at the age of 65. He was an earnest Christian.

The National Prison Association asks us to remind our readers that the day appointed as Prison Sunday, for special prayer for our criminal population, is October 21.

The Gospel Wagon workers in Washington, D. C., have had a most successful summer campaign. Multitudes in the neglected parts of the city have heard the Gospel gladly, and many have united with churches.

Mr. I. Ferris Lockwood will address the American Institute on November 1, on Force in its Relation to Theism. Meetings of the Institute will be held in its rooms, 4 Winthrop Place, New York, on the first Thursday of each month from now until June.

A persecution of Prohibitionists has been commenced in Merrimac, Wis. John E. Nosum, Chairman of the Prohibition party there, has had the front wheels of his carriage removed and thrown into the river. His barn, filled with hay and grain, was fired by incendiaries and burned to the ground. The loss was $2,000.

The National Woman's Christian Temperance Union will hold its fifteenth Annual Meeting October 19 to 23, in the Metropolitan Opera House, New York. Mrs. Mary T. Burt and Gen. Clinton B. Fisk will welcome the delegates. Among the speakers will be Bishop Fallows, Mrs. Mary A. Livermore, Miss Frances E. Willard, Mrs. Mary A. Woodbridge, etc.

The Brooklyn Sunday-school teachers' classes will be held weekly through the winter. Dr. Meredith will expound the International lesson weekly at the Tompkins Avenue Congregational Church every Tuesday evening, and Mrs. Ostrander at the Y. M. C. A. building every Saturday afternoon at 3 o'clock for the primary teachers. In the same building, at 4.30 o'clock, ministers of various denominations will take their turn a month each.

ALL AT IT.

A New Sermon by Pastor CH.S purgeon.

"Therefore they that were scattered abroad went everywhere preaching the word. Then Philip went down to the city of Samaria, and preached Christ unto them." Acts 8: 4, 5.

"Then Philip opened his mouth, and began at the same scripture, and preached unto him Jesus." Acts 8: 35.

A Necessity for the Scatt-ring of the Church—Persecution Sometimes Used to Effect It—The Object of the Scattering—I. The Universality of the Work of Evangelizing—The Apostles at Home—A Soldiers' Battle—A Fatal Military Policy—No Professional Distinctions—No Professional Exceptions—No Exclusion on Account of Sex—II. The Naturalness of It—Their Obligation Compelled—Their Spiritual Health Prompted—The Nearness of Christ's Coming—III. A Joyful Work—IV. The Supremacy of the Work—V. Its Specialty.

"THEY that were scattered abroad went everywhere preaching the word." God intended that His church should be scattered over the world. Jerusalem was at first the central point of Christianity. The church there was highly favored with its twelve apostles and a multitude of minor lights; and the tendency would have been to keep the centre strong. I have often heard the argument, "Do not have too many out-stations; keep up a strong central force." But God's plan was that the holy force should be distributed: the holy seed must be sown. To do this the Lord made use of

The Rough Hand

of persecution. The disciples could not stay in Jerusalem: Saul made them run for their lives, or, if they did not, he shut them up in prison; and prisons in those days were so foul and noisome as to be the vestibules of the grave. One went this way, and one went the other way; and the faithful were scattered.

In every church where there is really the power of the Spirit of God, the Lord will cause it to be spread abroad, more or less. Just now we have little of that form of persecution which drives men from home. But godly people are scattered through the necessity of earning a livelihood. Sometimes we regret that certain young men should have to go to a distance; but should we regret it? We lament that certain families must migrate to the colonies. Does not the Lord by this means sow the good seed widely? The Lord's design is not the scattering in itself, but scattering for a purpose. He intended that, being scattered, the saints of Jerusalem should go everywhere preaching the Word. Upon this I am going to speak at this time.

I. I shall call your attention, first, to

The Universality of the Work

of evangelizing—of course I mean its universality among believers. "They that were scattered abroad went everywhere preaching the Word." They; that is, all the scattered. There does not appear to have been any exception. You thought it would have read, "Then the apostles went everywhere preaching the Word. They were just the people who did not go at all; for the twelve remained at headquarters as yet; but the rest went everywhere preaching the Word. Generals may have to stand still in the centre of the battle to direct the forces; but in this battle all the common soldiers marched to the fight. This was to be a soldiers' battle; and of that sort all the battles of the Cross ought to be.

Observe then, first, that in this there were no professional distinctions. We have among ourselves a distinction between ministers and others. But you are all to minister. There are many ministries of one form and another; and though God gives to His church apostles, teachers, pastors, evangelists, and the like, yet not by way of setting up a professional caste of men, who are to do the work for God while others sit still. I have aforetime used the following parable: In olden times a certain host had conquered wherever they went forward in one mass. But it came to pass that they thought themselves so exceeding strong that they said, "Let not every man go to war. Let us choose a few, and make this few into a select standing army." They picked out their champions, and sent them to the war. These continued the conflict with difficulty; many of them fell in the fight. No provinces were added to the kingdom, and things were at a standstill. They had followed a fatal policy. The true method was for the whole of them to march to battle. This is

The True and Only Policy

of Christianity—all Christian soldiers of the Cross, and all on active service. Every converted man is to teach what he knows; all those who have drunk of the living water are to become fountains out of which shall flow rivers of living water. We shall never get back to the grand old times of conquest until we get back to the old method of "all at it."

Observe, next, that there were no professional exceptions. Philip is mentioned as going down to Samaria to preach; but Philip was originally set apart to attend to the distribution of the alms of the church. It is good for every man to attend to his own special office; but where that office ceases to be needful, let him get to that work which is common and constant. The time had come when there was no need for the deacon to sit in the vestry, for the poor people were all scattered. What does the deacon do? As the work to which he was appointed has come to an end, he keeps to the work for which every Christian is appointed, and he proclaims the gospel of Jesus Christ. No one of us, then, can be exempted from the work of spreading the gospel because we have some other work.

Observe that there were no educational or literary exceptions. It is thought nowadays that a man must not try to proclaim the gospel unless he has had a good education. To try and preach Christ, and yet to commit grammatical blunders, is looked upon as a grave offence. People are mightily offended at the idea of the gospel being properly preached by an uneducated man. This I believe to be a very injurious mistake. There is nothing whatsoever in the whole compass of Scripture to excuse any mouth from speaking for Jesus when the heart is really acquainted with His salvation. Has the gospel ever been spread to any extent by men of high literary power? Look through the whole line of history, and see if it is so. Have the men of splendid eloquence been remarkable for winning souls? I could quote names that stand first in the roll of oratory, which are low down in the roll of soul-winners.

Those Whom God has Most Honored

have been men who, whatever their gifts, have consecrated them to God; and have earnestly declared the great truths of God's Word. Men who have been terribly in earnest, and have faithfully described man's ruin by sin, and God's remedy of grace—men who have warned sinners to escape from the wrath to come by believing in the Lord Jesus—these have been useful. If they had great gifts, they were no detriment to them; if they had few talents, this did not disqualify them. It has pleased God to use the base things of this world, and things that are despised, for the accomplishment of His great purposes of love. I say, then, to you, my dear friend, who unhappily may be lacking in education, do not therefore stay your testimony to our Lord. Rescue the perishing. What if you are not a great theologian? If you understand the plan of salvation you are sufficiently instructed to be a good witness for your Lord. Oh, that the Holy Spirit may make you such!

As there were no exceptions on account of educational defects, so were there

No Exclusions

on account of sex. Men and women were to spread abroad the knowledge of Jesus. We read that, "As for Saul, he made havoc of the church, entering into every house, and haling men *and women* committed them to prison. Therefore they that were scattered abroad" (and these must have been men *and women*) "went everywhere preaching the Word." There are many ways in which women can fittingly proclaim the Word of the Lord, and in some of these they can proclaim it more efficiently than men. There are minds that will be attracted by the tender, plaintive, winning manner in which the sister in Christ expresses herself. A Christian mother! What a minister is she to her family! You see, dear friends, how the Lord gave to all His people the holy work of making Jesus known to men. How well they carried it out! Within a hundred years after the death of our Lord, His name had been made known to all the known world. But I do not know how many years it will take to make Christ known at the rate of our present movement.

II. Secondly, having asked you to notice the universality of the work, will you please to notice

The Naturalness of It.

That word "therefore," at the commencement of the fourth verse, says a great deal to me. "Therefore they that were scattered abroad went everywhere preaching the word"—as if it followed, as a sort of natural consequence, that being scattered they went everywhere preaching the Word. They that were scattered might have said, "Clearly our duty is to hold our tongues; we have got into great trouble at Jerusalem because we preached Christ. We must now look to our own safety, and the comfort of our families; and in these foreign countries we had better live godly lives, and go to heaven on the sly, but we need not again expose ourselves to the dangers of persecution." They did not thus argue. It is not said, "Therefore they that were scattered abroad slunk away, and held their tongues." No, they never thought of that.

We do find that they even said, "This gospel of ours is evidently not in accord with

The Spirit of the Age.

The Scribes and Pharisees all differ largely from us, and we must endeavor to win them by altering our tone." They did not dream of cutting off the angles of truth, nor of inserting pleasant fragments of popular thought to please the powers that be; but they set forth "the Word" in its pure simplicity, and the Cross of Christ, which is an offence to so many. They never said, "The old gospel did very well when Jesus was here; but, you see, He has gone, and circumstances alter cases, and alter gospels, and we had better adapt our teaching to the period." They did not so, because of the fear of the Lord. They did not endeavor to mend the gospel, but they went everywhere proclaiming it. They preached the Word as they received it; they set forth the kingdom as their King had revealed it. Ah, dear friends! if you are true to the Lord Jesus Christ you have to spread the gospel somehow, and it must be the old, old gospel.

The principal reason for their constant proclamation of Jesus was, that they were in a fine state of spiritual health. They went everywhere preaching the Word when scattered abroad, because they had told it out when at home. You will never make a missionary of the person who does no good at home. If you do not seek souls in your own street, you will not do so in Hindostan. If you are of no use in Whitechapel, you will be of no use on the Congo. He that will not serve the Lord in the Sunday-school, at home, will not win children to Christ in China. Distance lends no real enchantment to Christian service. You who do nothing now are not fit for the war, for you are in sad health. The Lord give you spiritual health and vigor, and then you will want no pressing, but you will cry at once, "Here am I; send me!" O my friends, go at once to your families, to your workshops, and declare the name of Jesus!

Surely also the times must have urged them onward, to go with hurried step as messengers for Christ; for Jerusalem was soon to be destroyed. This made them quick in their movements, that the last warning might come to all their countrymen. You know what the times are now! I am no prophet; but as we read, week by week, the appalling crimes that are chronicled by the press, if ever Christian men should be in earnest they should be in earnest now. *All the signs of the times arouse us to look for the coming ur Lord.* No token tends to quiet us, but all awaken us. We must work at double quick e; and if any one among us has done nothing ll, it is time for him, as a good servant, to rk and to watch, "for in such an hour as he nks not, the Son of man cometh."

II. Thirdly, carefully notice

The Joyfulness of the Work.

hey were scattered abroad"; but as "they nt everywhere preaching the Word," the amity became a blessing. Their work took sting out of their banishment. The house- e had to leave her comfortable little home, d tramp to a strange country; the man of siness had to sell his stock, and quit his posi- n. Those were hard times, beyond question. ncy that happening to us! What distress uld spread over this congregation if you had run for your lives! But then they said to emselves "It is all right; for as we live to read abroad the knowledge of Jesus, we shall this wherever we go. Our flight shall be a ssion." This changed the aspect of affairs. ar friends, if your heart is set on a purpose, d there comes a crash which spoils your com- t, you hardly lament it if it subserves your ief design in life. If you are possessed with idea that you, as a Christian, must live only serve Christ, and to win souls, then anything ich happens, however painful, will be wel- med if it places you in a better position for ur holy life work. That is the better place in ich you can serve the Lord better.

Moreover, as they told the story, and it made eir own hearts glow with holy fire, their irits were refreshed, and their souls made d. Jesus seemed still to be near them: yes, was with them. They found the surest medy for their grief in His sacred fellowship: y, the grief itself became gladness. If you nt to get rid of low spirits, preach the gospel. take Christ's yoke is to find rest unto your uls. If you are in the very dust, go and tell a ary one of salvation by Jesus: you will thus ise yourself, even if your message be rejected.

IV. Notice, fourthly,

The Supremacy of This Work.

They that were scattered abroad went every- ere preaching the Word." I suppose they did mething for a living. I do not know what eir handicrafts might be; but each one had a lling, and followed it industriously. We are t told what they did. It is incidentally men- ned, further on in history, that the apostle ul made tents: but you never read anywhere the Bible that Paul went everywhere tent aking. He did make tents, but that was not s vocation; his business was to save souls. I onder how many Christian people here could ve their biographies condensed into this line, He lived to make Christ known." Might it t be said of one, he lived to open a shop, and en to open a second? or of another, he lived save a good deal of money, and take shares limited liability companies? or of a third, he ed to paint a great picture? or of a fourth, he s best known for his genial hospitality? Of any a minister it might be said—he lived to each splendid sermons, and to gain credit for e oratory. What of all these? If it can be ld of a man, "He lived to glorify Christ," en his life is a life. Every Christian man ight so to live. Oh that my memorial might : He preached Christ crucified"!

We note the supremacy of this work, not on- because it swallowed up all their trades, but

It Obliterated all Trace of Caste.

hilip is a Jew, but he goes to Samaria. Philip, what made you go to Samaria? Jews ave no dealings with Samaritans." Brethren, hen it comes to preaching Christ we have ealings with everybody—Jews, Turks, infidels, annibals. The Jew goes to Samaria for Christ, nd the Samaritans accept the Messiah of the ews. Anon Philip is called down south to urney along a desert way, and there he meets Ethiopian, probably a black man. Ah well! hite men were not particularly anxious for the ompany of Ethiopians, but Philip gets up into his chariot, and rides with him. *Black and white make a fine mixture when the book of the prophet Isaiah lies between them.*

What is more, we shall not only be willing to work for the poor and fallen, but we shall work with them. You, a person of taste and culture, will join hands with the illiterate worker, and while you are half amused at his blunders, you will be charmed by his zeal. You will not despise him, but you may even feel humbled as you see how, with less knowledge than yourself, he often shows more spiritual wisdom and energy. You will take a brotherly pride in such a man. Caste is gone when Christ is come.

See, also, the supremacy of their purpose in the fact that they were willing to be at the beck and call of the Holy Spirit, and

To Go Anywhere.

Philip was getting on splendidly at Samaria, and the church grew under his care. Surely he ought to stop there; he is evidently the man for the place! But he does not stop there. Philip has a call, not to a larger church, but to the road through the desert, and away he goes to talk to one person. The genuine soul-winner has his inward directions, and he follows the guidance of the Spirit of God. Here, there, anywhere he goes, where the hope of conversions tempts him.

Note yet one thing more: the supremacy of this work was seen in the fact that these good people were quite willing to subside. Philip has done a great work at Samaria, but he sends for the apostles Peter and John to come down from Jerusalem. Some few earnest workers have been impatient of discipline, but the best of them are the most orderly people in the world. Some brethren are just as ready to obey church authority as if they were the least of all saints, instead of being the most successful of the brotherhood. It is not well when our Philips are too big to work in connection with the mother-church. I have never found them so. The idle are troublesome; the laborious are loving. Blessed is that man who knows how to subside. Oh, that there were thousands of workers of this kind willing to come to the front, and lead the way, and just as willing to step aside, if thereby the cause might advance!

V. Thus have I brought this matter before you, and I shall now beg you to observe

The Specialty of this Work.

I have shown you its universality, its naturalness, its joyfulness, and its supremacy; and now we will dwell upon its speciality. Philip is set before us as a specimen of those who were scattered abroad. A sample shows the whole. What did Philip make prominent? "Philip went down to the city of Samaria, and preached *Christ* unto them." That is all he had to preach, he preached the Messiah, the Anointed One, the Christ. But when Philip had to instruct an educated nobleman, did he dwell on the same subject as that which he brought before common Samaritans? Read the thirty-fifth verse. "Then Philip opened his mouth and began at the same scripture, and preached unto him *Jesus*." Here we have the same subject as before: to the Samaritans Christ, to the Ethiopian Jesus. See, then, what we have to do.

This is the old, old story. It is a very simple story, but the telling of it will save the people. Keep to that gospel. Many have lost faith in it. It is hoped that people will now be saved by new socialistic arrangements, by moral precepts, by amusements, by societies, and what not. Let the church of God be glad when anything is done which helps temperance, purity, freedom, and so forth; but *her* one business is to preach Christ. Stick to this, my brethren. If we will each one speak for our Lord, we shall see results that will perfectly astound us. If, during the next few months, this church would fully wake up, and if every member would feel, "I have something to do, and I must do it," we should then see a glorious harvest. If you will go after people at their houses, and give them your own personal testimony in loving earnestness, the Holy Spirit will bless you. Oh, may God arouse us to this! If the Lord will fill you with His Spirit, the opening of yonder front doors and your going out will be like the bursting of a bomb-shell in London. If you are all in earnest, your existence will be like the shining of the sun in the heavens. Oh, how I long that God may be glorified! For His truth's sake I have been "abundantly filled with reproach"; but I would gladly accept a seven-fold baptism of it so that His kingdom would come. May the Lord make bare His holy arm in the eyes of all the people! Amen, and Amen.

GEMS FROM NEW BOOKS.

THE MAGNETIC SMILE.*

IT is related in the life of the celebrated mathematician, William Hutton, that a respectable looking country-woman called upon him one day, anxious to speak with him. She told him, with an air of secrecy, that her husband behaved unkindly to her, and sought other company, frequently passing his evenings from home, which made her feel extremely unhappy; and knowing Mr. Hutton to be a wise man, she thought he might be able to tell her how she should manage to cure her husband. The case was a common one, and he thought he could prescribe for it without losing his reputation for wisdom. "The remedy is a simple one," said he, "but I have never known it fail. *Always greet your husband with a smile.*" The woman expressed her thanks, dropped a curtesy, and went away. A few months afterward she waited on Mr. Hutton with a couple of fine fowls, which she begged him to accept. She told him, while tears of joy and gratitude glistened in her eyes, that she had followed his advice, and her husband was cured. He no longer sought the company of others, but treated her with constant love and kindness.

Girls Dead at Heart.

A physician lately remarked: "There is no study in human nature so difficult to me as a certain class of young-girls. I spent a part of this summer with two specimens of this class. They had the usual amount of capacity for observing, understanding, and feeling. They had been educated at much cost to their parents; both were constant attendants at church. I saw nothing in their faces or bearing to show that they were imbecile. Their mother was an invalid nearing the grave. Nothing could be more touching than the patient, appealing gaze with which her eyes followed them, watching for some sign of affection; but they had eyes and thoughts for nothing but some gowns they were making. They were used to her love, to her illness—even to the thought of her death. I walked out with them through a great forest, under the solemn stars. They saw no beauty, no sublimity in them; they chatted incessantly of the new trimming on their bonnets. They were used to the meaning of the trees and stars. The only things, apparently, to which they were not used, were the changes in ribbons, puffs, and flounces. I went to church with them, and listened to the great *Te Deum* which has come down to us through the ages, and has lifted the hearts of countless worshippers to God. They nudged each other, while they sang it, to look at a beaded cloak in the next pew. We physicians now test the temperature of a patient's body, and if we find it below a certain degree, know that death is already in the heart. When I find so low a degree in the words, thoughts, and actions of a human body, I begin to fear that the soul within is dead beyond recall."

What a Lady is.

The word "lady" is derived from the Saxon word "*hlaf*," a loaf, and "*digan*," to serve, and means literally one who serves or dispenses bread to the family; as "Lord" means the supplier of bread. The two words reflect an arrange-

* From "The Five Talents of Woman," a book for Girls and Women, by the Author of "How to be Happy, Though Married." This book is full of sound, practical advice to our sisters, married and single, on culture, behavior, home-influence, nursing the sick, study, recreation, etc. An excellent book to give to a daughter who wishes to be something more than a useless ornament in the world. 301 pages; price $1.25. Published by *Charles Scribner's Sons*, 745 Broadway, New York.

Mr. William Noble's Saturday Night Demonstration in London.

ment of the Almighty which cannot be ignored by even the most advanced confounder of the respective duties of the sexes. The natural, healthy state of things is for the husband to supply the bread and other kinds of food, and for the wife to serve them out to the family in the most healthful and economical way possible. A young man was practical, and was making love on that basis. The girl was a little that way herself. "Can you cook?" he inquired. "Can you supply the food to be cooked?" she asked, in reply. It was a match.

Curing a Husband's Temper.

Lavater, the famous physiognomist, made the following entry in his journal: "The servant was sweeping my study, and overturned a bottle of ink which was standing on a shelf. She was much terrified. I called out, harshly, 'What a stupid creature you are! Have I not told you to be careful?' My wife, slowly and timidly, followed me up-stairs. Instead of being ashamed, my anger broke out anew. I took no notice of her, and ran to the table, lamenting and moaning as if the most important writings had been spoiled, though in reality the ink had touched nothing but a blank sheet and some blotting paper. The servant watched an opportunity to steal away, and my wife approached me with loving gentleness. 'My *dear* husband!' said she. I stared at her with vexation in my looks. She entranced me; I wanted to get out of her way. Her face rested on my cheek for a few moments. At last, with unspeakable tenderness, she said, 'You will hurt your health, my dear!' I now began to be ashamed; I was silent, and at last, began to weep. 'What a miserable slave to my temper I am,' I said. 'I cannot rid myself of the dominion of that sinful passion.' My wife replied, 'Consider, my dear, how many days and weeks pass away without your being overcome by anger. *Let us pray together.*' I knelt down beside her; and she prayed so maturely, so fervently, and so much to the purpose, that I thanked God sincerely for my wife."

MR. WILLIAM NOBLE IN LONDON.

(*See Illustration.*)

THE many friends of Mr. Noble in this and other lands to which this journal goes, will be glad to have news of his work. The accompanying illustration will give them some idea of the scenes in which he is moving. It represents a Saturday-night demonstration as witnessed a few weeks ago by an American visitor.

It appears that it is Mr. Noble's custom on Saturday night when the streets are thronged with street peddlers' trucks, and workingmen spending their money (not always in the best way), to set out for a march round the district, accompanied by brass and drum-and-fife bands, with banners. Already this forward movement has created quite a stir in the district, and as the procession proceeds through the various streets, the greatest interest is exhibited. One special feature is the holding of open-air meetings *en route*. When a favorable spot is reached a halt is made, and a meeting held. On this way some half-dozen meetings are held during the evening, in order to reach the people in each section. The workers distribute themselves along the line of route, and spread literature amongst the people, and invite them to the various meetings which are held in Hoxton Hall on Sunday, and during the week.

An eye-witness, who accompanied Mr. Noble on a recent Saturday, thus writes: "The procession was led by a strong brass band, which at six o'clock set out from the Hall for a two hours' march. It passed right through streets of tenement houses, streets that were almost alleys, and into drowsy, dowdy-looking squares, where meetings were held. The earnest attention and absence of hostile remarks or opposition amongst the people listening was simply remarkable. There are certainly some factors of success which the Hoxton workers carry with them."

THE MOUNTAIN RAILROAD BRIDGE

(*See Illustration on first page.*)

To persons in the habit of thinking of South America as outside the borders of civilization, the picture of the stupendous engineering work on the first page will come as a revelation. The bridge is in the heart of the Andes, in Peru, and it is part of a railroad stretching right to the Pacific coast. Formerly the traveller was invited to cross from peak to peak on foot upon hanging bridges, which bent beneath his tread, and to which even the wind would give a lateral motion. Now he is carried up and across the dizzy heights on a railroad which is acknowledged to be the most daring engineering exploit in the world. The bridge depicted in the illustration is the crown and prodigy of the whole. Mr. Henry Meigs, who built it, is the well-known Californian contractor, whose commercial failure in that State some years ago was the cause of widespread suffering. He went to South America after the disaster, and there in the construction of this and other works amassed an immense fortune. He returned to California and though legally released from his debts, he sought out his creditors and paid nearly all of them in full with interest.

A CASE FOR PATIENCE.

(*See Illustration on page 653.*)

A FIELD of ripe wheat, surrounded by hedges the banks of which are glowing with beautiful wild-flowers, does not greatly impress people who live where they see it every fall; but it is a glorious sight to the dwellers in a city, weary of the hot pavement, the dirty stones of the roadways, and the smells of the gutters. Such were Mrs. Carleton and her daughter Julia, who were boarding for a few weeks at a farm-house, only two hours ride from the city. The locality was chosen for the convenience of Mr. Carleton whose business required his presence every day and Mrs. Carleton declared that the country would be unendurable if her husband could not spend his evenings with her.

"Mamma, dear, you look weary," Julia said one morning when, after her late breakfast Mrs. Carleton had tried a little embroidery, a little novel-reading, a little letter-writing, and finally, had thrown herself discontentedly on a garden seat on the piazza. "Do come with me around the next field; there are the loveliest flowers growing on the banks."

"What inexhaustible energy you have, Julia!" said the mother, listlessly. "Well, I cannot stay here the *whole* time, and there is *nothing* to amuse one. Yes, I will go; it will pass the time."

"I will see if Minnie can go with us," said Julia, and she ran around to the rear of the house, where she knew she would find the farmer's daughter, who was glad to act as guide, or do anything else for the beautiful, brilliant city girl. Minnie returned with her, and the three strolled around the field gathering the little floral gems. A delicate, melodious warble attracted Julia's attention presently, and she must needs clamber over the fence to catch a sight of the feathered songster. Minnie was arranging a bouquet for Mrs. Carleton, when the latter made an angry, impatient exclamation, and gave a nervous clutch to her skirts.

"That wretched brier! Look at it, how it clings!" and she tugged at her dress, in the lower flounce of which the brier was entangled.

Minnie dropped her flowers immediately

move the offending thorn, t not until a sound sugges-e of rending told of the schief that it would take urs to remedy.

"Wait a moment, mamma," id Julia; "Minnie will soon ve you clear."

Mrs. Carleton looked rue-lly at the rents, and asked r daughter to remind her get papa to take the lace the city next morning for pairs. In the evening Mr. arleton was duly instructed, e wreck was exhibited to m, and he was told where must be taken, and when e work ought to be finished.

"You must be making quite n explorer of your mamma, ulia," he said that night, as e and his daughter walked ut by moonlight while Mrs. arleton dozed over her novel. She must get an exploring it for the country, or all er pretty dresses will be ined."

"Oh no, papa," said Julia, we have not explored at all eyond sight of the house. bramble caught mamma's ress in the next field, and he tugged at it before Min-ie could disentangle it."

Mr. Carlton was silent a ew minutes. Then he said uietly, as if to himself, Patience is a great virtue. My daughter will find great eed of it in her life," and he father laid his hands ffectionately on the girl's houlder. "The world is full of briers—entanglements of one kind and an-other, that cannot be escaped. Those who walk heedlessly get in contact with more of hem than do others; but the most careful sel-dom wholly escape."

"Do you mean sins, papa?" Julia asked.

"Not just now, my dear, though the principle applies to them too. A person, through pure kindness, may become entangled in enterprises and associated with other persons, and so be led nto difficulties and inconsistencies. Sometimes the discovery comes that one has been acting under a misconception of character or circum-stances, and one is caught in the disagreeable po-sition of either going on in the hope of saving reputation or of turning back and acknowledg-ing errors, which is a painful thing to do. I have known men allied in business partnership, when a good, honest man has been held re-sponsible for wicked conduct, which his partner had carried on in the name of the firm. I have known, too, a pure Christian girl discover be-fore her marriage that her lover was godless, and had been pretending to be religious to help his suit. She has had to choose between keep-ing her promise to be married, or breaking it at the risk of being called a coquette, and the certainty of suffering to herself and general em-barrassment."

"What ought one do in such cases, papa?"

"There are difficulties about laying down rules applicable to cases which vary in important details. Of course, severance is the main duty. We must not be partakers—you know the pas-sage. But it is the manner of separation which is so distressing, and I have known the manner of doing it to be very injurious. There is one thing that has impressed me very much in a few cases in which I have been concerned. It seemed to me, at first, to be a coincidence, but I am beginning to think it is a law. I practice it, and recommend it. In a case of that kind, I lay it fully before God in prayer and determine to wait for light. And do you know, Julia, in every case in my experience I have never had to take action at all. God Himself has settled the whole thing and extricated me completely."

Mrs. Carleton's Patience Exhausted.

THE EPOCHS OF A LIFE.

A NEW SERIAL STORY.

By Rev. L. S. Keyser.

(Continued from page 638.)

Farewell to College.

THE remainder of Hadley's college days were days of dull pain. The best antidote to his troubles was the society of Belle Havelock. With a pertinacity and devotion worthy of a better girl, she gave herself up to the work of cheering and trying to win his affections. Piqued as she was by the knowledge that Hadley preferred Miss Winters to herself, still she swallowed her humiliation, and never allowed her devotion to him to flag for a single moment. She was always in sympathy with the disappointments and vic-tories of his academical life; she read the books in which he was interested, and investigated the problems that perplexed him, so that he fell into the habit of exchanging many con-fidences with her. The web of sympathy was binding them daily into a nearer intimacy. When a spell of the "blues" attacked him, he was in-variably seen making his way to the Havelock mansion, where he always received a cordial welcome.

There were times too when a consideration which would have been decisive with some men occurred to Hadley's mind. Though he was one of the most unworldly of men, he could not have visited so much at Belle Havelock's home with-out perceiving that her husband, whoever he might be, would have the advantage of a good start in life. How many years of drudgery that would save him in his ambitious career! How it would relieve him of the carking care that fills the mind, and prevents it climbing upward!

The final examination of the Senior class was over, and the honors were distributed. Accord-ing to general expectations, the first honor was awarded to Hadley Madelling, and the second had to be shared equally between George Dane and Madeline Winters.

It is not necessary to de-scribe the manner in which the interim until Commence-ment was spent. At last it was past, and that culminat-ing period in the career of every young collegian had come all too soon—Com-mencement Day. The per-sons whose college careers we have watched acquitted themselves brilliantly in the delivery of their graduating speeches, as was to be ex-pected of those whose whole course had been distinguish-ed with honorable success. All the meetings incident to the week of Commencement in a thriving college had been held, and the sad, sad morning of separation from class-mates and teachers had dawned.

Before making his way to the depot, Hadley had gone to say good-bye to Belle at her home. The girl's face indicated that this parting meant more to her than words could tell. As for Hadley, he was sorry to leave her, for she had been a con-genial and sympathetic friend to him, and, except in matters of religion, had always given him sage counsel.

"Miss Havelock," he said, sadly, "I feel this parting very much; you have been a kind and helpful friend to me."

The tears started to the girl's eyes, and she sobbed with a grief she could not repress. Dry-ing her tears after awhile, and trying to control her feelings, she answered:

"You must excuse my weakness, Mr. Madel-ling. We have been together so much that it is natural for us to regret parting. I was just thinking what a strange compound life is. Our paths have run parallel for a while, and now they must diverge, and we shall become almost like strangers. Yes, I will tell you candidly that these separations from—from—old friends are very sad to me, and I shall miss you sorely—more than I can tell."

"I hope that we shall not become like stran-gers," he broke out, impulsively. Then he check-ed himself. He looked at her, and she seemed more beautiful than ever, with her tearful eyes and pale lips. Why not put his destiny in her hands? He could not hope to win Miss Win-ters, and this girl was more congenial in some respects than her rival in his affections. Then he looked about him at the richly furnished room. Here was every evidence of refinement and affluence, which were the very portals to the life he coveted. He had almost risen with the intention of taking her hand and asking her to be more than a friend to him, when an incident, apparently trifling in itself, occurred, which caused him to alter his resolution.

A butterfly had come into the room through an open door, and was fluttering to and fro from window to window, moving up and down the smooth panes of glass, in a vain endeavor to escape from its imprisonment.

"Ah!" thought Hadley, "how much easier it was for that golden insect to get into the room than it is to get out! Perhaps that is symbolical of the fate of the man who marries one woman while he loves another."

The time for his departure had come. Rising, he tenderly took her hand in his and looked into her eyes. She met his gaze at first with a firm look, but turned away to hide her tears.

"Good-bye, Belle, good-bye," he said, in fervent tones. "Will you permit me to write to you occasionally?"

As well as she could she consented to the proposed correspondence, and then returning the pressure of his grasp, she whispered, "Good-bye," and turned from him with a heart-broken sob. Had not the young man put the reins upon his sympathies, he would have clasped her in his arms and asked of her the boon she would have been only too ready to grant. Grasping his valise, he walked hastily from the room, and from temptation, and hurried toward the depot.

"After all my—my efforts to win him, he went away without telling me that he loved me!" cried the wretched girl he had left, flinging herself into a chair and giving herself up to a delirium of disappointment.

When Hadley reached the depot, it still lacked some minutes of train-time. Miss Winters, whose train left a few hours later, had come to say good-bye to her friends, and was standing apart from the remaing groups of students, as if lost in thought. The young man was sorely puzzled whether he should approach her or not. What a different emotion she aroused in him from that which he had felt for Belle. That was sympathy, this was love. Their parting would perhaps be final. Could he go away without bidding her good-bye, without one clasp of the hand? His pulses almost stood still. A cold dew broke out on his forehead. It was impossible to resist the impulse.

Miss Winters was looking at him, too, and not unkindly, he thought. He stepped up to her and extended his hand, into which she softly laid hers, looking him in the eyes. By an irresistible impulse he retained her hand in a firm pressure. It had been the furthest from his intentions to refer to their past unhappy relations, but suddenly his great disappointment came back upon him like an avalanche as he stood holding her hand, and a bitter accusation broke from his lips.

"Miss Winters," he said, in a husky whisper, "I never knew what agony meant until you—brought it upon me."

The girl trembled like a leaf before a tempest, her lips became white, and it was some moments before she could reply.

"Those are bitter words," she said, reproachfully. "Do you suppose that I caused you this sorrow purposely or capriciously? Do you think that I took the course I did without sufficient reason for doing so? Oh, Mr. Madelling, your grief is no more poignant than my own. I, too, can say that I was a stranger to anguish until I met—until within the last year." She halted, fearing that she had overstepped the bounds of propriety.

"Do you mean what you say?" he asked, looking at her earnestly, while a ray of hope broke into his mind. "Why do you cast me off, then? Miss Winters—Madeline—"

They stood facing each other, regardless of all their surroundings, forgetting the existence of any one but themselves. His persistency in professing his attachment to her disarmed her for a moment of her suspicions of his duplicity. It seemed impossible that this intense, earnest, honest face before her was only the mask of a hypocrite and adventurer. A feeling that there might have been some mistake crossed her mind. Then she thought of that terrible letter which first caused her to suspect him, and the evidences of his prior engagement appeared so conclusive that she again became distrustful. Another girl's life would be blighted if she should win the young man's affections. Mabel Richerson had a prior claim upon him. She had loved him longer than Madeline had. It would be wrong to decoy him from her. Madeline therefore replied, with inexpressible sadness.

"I think it best that we say no more about this distressing subject. We cannot change the unalterable. Providence has not designed that we should be more than friends."

"Is your decision irrevocable?" he groaned. Seeing that she was resolute, he continued: "Madeline, a cruel, relentless destiny keeps us apart. I cannot believe that a kind, benevolent Father has anything to do with our hopeless sorrow. But if you cannot be my wife, Madeline," he whispered, "I swear that I still love you, and I shall always love you—love you, and only you. Forgive me for giving expression to my hopeless passion; but it affords me relief to tell you at last of my undying love for you. Good-bye, Madeline!"

She said good-bye; and, in spite of herself, his protestations of love sounded like music to her heart. Again it seemed impossible that this man was the mendacious character she had suspected him to be. A feeling of uncertainty took possession of her. Shall she speak out boldly and tell him about the letter, so derogatory to his character, which had been placed in her hands? But it was too late—he had turned away.

Just then a poor blind man, led by a small boy, came upon the platform, begging for a few pennies. A pitiful expression was upon his face, which evoked Madeline's sympathy. Some of the young men turned away from the beggar, others laughed at him, and others tried their wits upon him. Madeline noticed that Duneman wheeled on his heel with a sneer. By and by the blind man approached Hadley.

"Boys, it's a downright shame to treat a poor man like this," Madeline heard him say. And he took from his pocket a number of pieces of silver and laid them upon the man's open palm, saying as he did so, "Chip in, boys, and help the poor man."

The generous act, performed at a time when his own heart was aching, touched Miss Winters's breast as nothing else in all her intercourse with the young man had done, for it indicated a nature full of kindly impulses. The example set by the honor-man of the college was speedily followed by his fellow-students, and the blind man received a sufficient amount to make his heart glad for many a day. He overwhelmed his benefactors with expressions of gratitude.

Hadley's impulsive generosity increased the uncertainty in Madeline Winters's mind. It could not be possible, she thought, that such a man should be guilty of a base deception. What a terrible mistake it would be if her suspicions of him were groundless after all! She almost started toward him to set her uncertainty at rest forever, by asking whether he was bound to another woman; but it was too late: the train just then wheeled into the depot, and there was a rush for the coaches; for, as it was probable that they would be crowded, everyone was anxious to secure a seat. Hadley leaped aboard the train, found a seat, and then leaned from the car-window not far from where Miss Winters stood. He saw Duneman bidding her good-bye, but he did not fail to notice the comparative coldness with which she returned his fervent farewill.

Then the train began its smooth, gliding movement out of the depot. Among all the voices that shouted, "Madelling, good-bye!" Hadley had ears for but one clear, silvery voice, which cried, "Good-bye, Mr. Madelling!" with a cadence of sadness. Among all the waving handkerchiefs, as he looked back, he saw but one. Madeline Winters! Oh, perverse fate! Could it be possible that he should never meet her again? A nameless terror rent his heart, rushing over it like the wild surges of a storm-tossed sea, pressing the tears into his eyes and many broken groans from his lips.

During his stay at home, Hadley was gloomy and listless. While he rejoiced at the meeting of old friends, and while his academical honors were a source of self-gratulation to him, yet his disappointed love weighed heavily upon his heart, making his life dark and hopeless; so that he was no longer the companionable young man that he once had been.

If he wished to accomplish anything in life, it would not do, as he saw plainly, to spend time in repining, and he therefore resolved to seek relief in work, which, he felt, would be a much wiser course than to abandon himself to misanthropic melancholy. Accordingly through the recommendations of his professors in his *alma mater*, seconded by the efforts of a relative, he secured an honorable and lucrative position in the public schools of a large inland city in a State farther west.

After a rest of about three months, he bade good-bye to his mother and the friends about his old home, and went to the scene of his new activities. He entered upon his work with all the zest his crushed and disappointed life could command.

In the city whose schools he had entered, an uncle of Hadley was the pastor of a flourishing church, at the services of which the young agnostic was a frequent attendant, more out of respect for his beloved relative than on account of any interest in the religious exercises. It had been the all-absorbing desire of his uncle that Hadley should enter the ministry, especially since the young man had manifested a desire to educate himself; but Hadley had lightly cast aside all these earnest exhortations with evasive excuses. Once, however, a short time prior to his graduation, he declared to his uncle the actual reason of his disinclination to enter the sacred office. His uncle had said:

"Hadley, if you will consent to study for the ministry, I will secure the funds necessary for your education," and a wistful expression was in the old man's eye.

Hadley laughed, at first half-evasively, and then replied, in serious tones: "My dear uncle, I thank you heartily for your interest in me; but I cannot accept your well-meant offer, because I do not and can not believe the Bible as you do, and I never could preach what I do not believe. That would be hypocrisy. As far as the funds you speak of are concerned, I need them and could put them to good use, but I cannot accept them upon the conditions you make."

"That settles it, then," said his uncle sadly, for he could not conceal his disappointment in his nephew. Then he added: "There is a way by which you might be convinced of the divine authenticity of the Bible."

But Hadley turned away, unwilling to hear more on a subject that was so distasteful to him. Yet the faithful old pastor had never relinquished hope of his nephew's conversion, and during the years that intervened he had at intervals referred in one way and another to the subject that lay upon his heart, and thus had kept it before the young man's mind. Perhaps Mr. Bidder's chief design in securing Hadley a situation in the schools of the city, was to bring him more directly under his influence, and if so, he was surely making use of the Christian strategy recommended by the Apostle Paul.

Many a sermon, after Hadley's entrance into the city, no doubt received a peculiar coloring from the fact that Mr. Bidder expected his nephew to be in his congregation. The young man was often in the preacher's mind as he sat in his study, preparing his discourses for the ensuing Sabbath, and although there was no open arraignment of infidelity in any of his sermons, there were much positive proving and vindicating of the claims of Christianity.

The efforts were well meant, but they had no success. Hadley liked his uncle, respected his earnestness, was grateful for his affection, but he entertained a very slight opinion of his mental calibre. "If he knew more, he would believe less," was his silent comment after listening to the good old man's sermons. True, the preacher was not a scholar; his opportunities had been small, and the Bible almost his only well-read book. Doubt of that he could never have had, or the proofs he cited would not have satisfied him. And he, too, begged and prayed and pleaded as if unbelief and doubt were sins perversely cherished, instead of iron barriers between the soul and faith. His uncle misunderstood him, and Hadley grew less and less regular in attendance on his ministry.

(*To be Continued.*)

THE STONES OF MEMORIAL.

By Mrs. M. Baxter.

S. S. Lesson for October 21. Josh. 4:10-24, Golden Text, Josh. 4:22.

The Holy Spirit as a Remembrancer—The Common Tendency to Remember Personal Suffering and Wrong—The Believer's Trials Associated with the Memory of Mercies—The Command as to the Twelve Stones—A National Memorial—Answers Provided for Children's Questions—Memorials in the Household—Memorials of Answered Prayers—The Passage Through Judgment—The Ark of the Covenant Accompanies the Believer in his Trial—The Rites of the Changed Life.

"Bless the Lord, O my soul, and all that is within me, bless His holy name. Bless the Lord, O my soul, and forget not all His benefits." (Ps. 103:1.) It is part of the office of the Holy Ghost to bring to our remembrance all things whatsoever Jesus has said to us (John 14:26); and because He testifies of Christ, it is His office to remind us of all things which God has done for us. While self dominates our life, our memory is apt to be filled with all those things in the past through which we have suffered, or been wounded, or injured, and the remembrance of God's mercies is at a discount. How many people will remember every sickness which they have ever suffered, and with marvellous volubility they will describe all their symptoms, just as though they were passing through them to-day. Or they will recount some wrong which they have suffered at the hands of some fellow-creature, with all the feelings of bitterness which were aroused by it at the time, and up to this very day all is as vivid and distinct in their memories as though it were now happening. They

Pity Themselves To-day

for what happened forty years ago; they feel resentful to-day for what occurred when they were yet young. Because self is their very life, all its wrongs and all its sorrows and all its wounds are a present reality to them. But these same people fail to remember "all His benefits." Not seeing the hand of God, but only that of man, or of circumstances, in what happens from day to day, they do not recognize at the time, and they cannot remember afterwards, what God has done for them.

Oh, how different with the child of God, who has recognized His hand in everything! "I will mention the loving kindnesses of the Lord, and the praises of the Lord according to all that the Lord hath bestowed on us." (Isa. 63:7.) The memory of the just is his memory of God; the memory of the sinner and of the selfish believer is his memory of that which touches himself. The child of faith remembers all the way which the Lord has led him, to humble him, and to prove him, and to know what was in his heart (Deut. 8:2), while the child of self remembers all the injuries, taunts, disappointments, losses, mortifications, and sufferings of his life. The child of faith, who gives his God credit for having a good intent in all that befalls him, has an eye open to, and a memory stored with, God's mercies. It is most noticeable how often God exhorts His people of old to remember His goodness toward them. In speaking of all God's past dealings with the people, Moses says, "Only take heed to thyself, and keep thy soul diligently, lest thou forget the things which thine eyes have seen, and lest they depart from thy heart all the days of thy life; but teach them, thy sons and thy sons' sons." "Thou shalt well remember what the Lord thy God did unto Pharaoh, and unto all Egypt." "Thou shalt remember that thou wast a bondman in the land of Egypt, and the Lord thy God redeemed thee." "That thou mayest remember the day when thou camest forth out of the land of Egypt all the days of thy life." (Deut. 4:9; 7:18; 15:15; 16:3.) David delighted to call the goodness of God to remembrance. "Remember His marvellous works that He hath done, His wonders, and the judgments of His mouth. . . . be ye mindful always of His covenant." (1 Chron. 16:12, 15.) "Forget not all His benefits" was his exhortation to his own soul. When he was tempted, as many have been, to depression, and to the sinful thought that God had forsaken him, he found that the remembrance of God's goodness brought him back into the sunshine. "I said, this is my infirmity, but I will remember the years of the right hand of the Most High. I will remember the works of the Lord: surely I will remember the wonders of old." (Ps. 77:10-17.)

It is no wonder, then, that when the children of Israel passed through the Jordan, God made special provision that His marvellous interposition on their behalf should be remembered. "When all the people clean passed over Jordan, the Lord spake unto Joshua, saying, Take you twelve men out of the people—out of every tribe a man—and command ye them, saying, Take you hence out of the midst of Jordan, out of the place where the priest's feet stood firm, twelve stones, and ye shall carry them over with you, and leave them in the lodging-place, where ye shall lodge this night." It was not one man, nor two, who were charged to remember the passage of the Jordan, it was a national deliverance, and only

A National Remembrance

of it could be an adequate acknowledgment to God. For national sins there must be national humiliation and confession; for national mercies there must be national thanksgiving; and where such a national recognition of God is wanting, most surely national judgment will follow. "Then Joshua called the twelve men whom he had prepared (see Ch. 3:12) of the children of Israel, out of every tribe a man," and he gave them commandment to do as God had said, and added, "That this may be a sign among you, that when your children ask in time to come, saying, What mean ye by these stones? then ye shall answer them that the waters of Jordan were cut off before the ark of the covenant of the Lord; when it passed over Jordan, the waters of Jordan were cut off; and these stones shall be a memorial unto the children of Israel forever." Again and again we read in the Old Testament how God makes provision that the questions which naturally arise in the mind of a child shall be answered. But children do not ask questions about things which they never hear spoken of, or of which they see no sign. If parents are not occupied with the things of God, and if they neglect to teach them diligently unto their children, and to talk of them when they sit in their home, and when they walk by the way, and when they lie down, and when they rise up (Deut. 6:7), the probability will be that the children also will show no interest in the things of God. God would have our lives to be full of stones of memorial. In some houses we meet with memorials of travel, in some of family greatness, in some of the learning of the inhabitants, in some of the terrible way in which life is frittered away. But in some houses

Everything Speaks of Answered Prayer.

You take up an album, every photograph has a story; it is a stone of memorial; every little trifle, worth nothing in itself, is the gift of some soul which has found Jesus, or a memorial of some signal answer to prayer. God loves to see these memorials in the houses of His children. But there were also memorial stones for none but the eye of God to see—neither priests nor elders touched these; Joshua alone had to do with them; he set up twelve stones in the midst of Jordan, in the place where the feet of the priests which bare the ark of the covenant stood, "and they are there unto this day." Christ has His own unseen memorial of His death and suffering for us. Deep in the judgment which He bare for our sins, He has His memorial, the Jordan flows over it, no man sees it, but only the eye of Him who made His soul an offering for sin. But He keeps this memorial before God "unto this day."

While God spoke to Joshua, and Joshua to the people, the priests, bearing the ark of the covenant, stood still in Jordan, "and the people hasted and passed over"; the ark still stayed back the waters. The laws of nature were not suspended by some temporary strain. Until the Word of the Lord bid them return, they would continue to be held back in that piled up heap from which not so much as a drop of spray fell upon God's people! What a picture! Jordan means judgment. In Christ, the ark of the covenant,

We May Go Through

judgment unhurt, untouched. He was crucified, He bore our sentence, and so He stays back judgment from us; precious, glorious Redeemer! And again, as He dwells in our hearts by faith, He brings us to judge of ourselves and of circumstances with Him, and to go with Him into the Jordan which flows between us and the old wilderness of struggle, and between us and the old world life of Egypt. In Him we see fear and anxiety and self, in all its forms, judged as much as drunkenness, theft, impurity, and other outward sins; but in the very Jordan, in the very judgment, as soon as we are conscious of the sin, and judge it, we have the Deliverer discovering to us the sin, that He may deliver us.

It was "when all the people were then passed over" Jordan, and not till then, "that the ark of God passed over, and the priests, in the presence of the people." Then it was that "the Lord spake unto Joshua, saying, Command the priests that bear the ark of the testimony, that they come up out of Jordan." He did so, and they began to move, but the waters remained until they had reached the shore. Then the pile of water began to flow down, and, little by little, it disappeared, and "the waters of Jordan returned unto their place, and flowed over all his banks as they did before." God will never command any of His children to walk in an impossible path without sending the ark of the covenant with them. "When He putteth forth His own sheep, He goeth before them, and the sheep follow Him." (John 10:4.) We need not inquire whether such and such a path is possible. All we need to know is this—Is it the will of God? All the rest is His responsibility.

Whenever a Man Honors God, God Honors Him.

Joshua set up the twelve memorial stones in Gilgal, commanding the people to tell their children how the Lord dried up the waters of Jordan before them as He had dried up the Red Sea, "that all the people of the earth may know the hand of the Lord, that it is mighty; that ye might fear the Lord your God for ever." Thus Joshua magnified God. "*On that day* the Lord magnified Joshua in the sight of all Israel; and they feared him as they feared Moses, all the days of his life." It was in Gilgal that the children of Israel who had been born in the wilderness were circumcised, and then brought into outward covenant with God. Under the Christian dispensation we are baptized, not circumcised. A circumcised Jew must *do* the law, and live by it. But baptism buries us, and it is no longer "*Do*," but "*Believe*" for salvation, not "Do, and thou shalt live," but, "Do the will of God because thou dost live." Another remarkable circumstance happened to them. They kept the passover four days after they passed over Jordan, and from that time the manna ceased, and they began to "eat of the old corn of the land . . . . the fruit of the land of Canaan"—the fruit of the Land of Promise, the fruit of the promises of God! Oh how blessed it is! He eats of it who continually takes God at His Word, and reckons that He cannot fail to accomplish what He has spoken; the Word *does* profit him because it is mixed with faith in him that hears it. (See Heb. 4:2.)

CHRIST'S LOVE.

There's a song of praise in my heart to-day,
And a gladness no words can tell,
As I think of the love that is holding me,
That never can change or fail.
Other love may grow cold, as the years roll by,
Other friends may forgetful be,
But Jesus never forgets His own
Through the years of eternity.

That love everlasting what tongue can express?
What heart can its strength understand?
A love that can reach to the depths of sin,
And seat us at His right hand.
He hath borne our sorrows, He hath known our griefs,
He hath suffered with us below;
And now from His throne He in pity looks down
To comfort all human woe.

Sorrows may gather about my path,
Kind friends may be borne from my side,
But the arms everlasting around me fold,
And still I in peace abide.
He hath promised me strength for the stormy days,
As well as for those that are bright—
He hath bidden me rest in His loving care
In the darkness as well as the light.

My footsteps may falter along the path,
And I may lie down to rest;
But nothing can sever me from His love—
In life or in death I am blest—
For He knoweth each grave where His loved ones sleep,
They are safe in His tender care;
And though I may pass through death's gloomy vale,
His love will surround me there.

As the living plant to the sunlight turns,
Unconscious of all beside,
So my heart would forget all its earth-born joys
In the love of the Crucified.
Oh, I cannot be satisfied until I shall see
The light of His beautiful face,
And hear the sweet welcome He hath for me—
Forgiven and saved by grace!

J. E. JEWETT, Publisher, 77 Bible House, New York, will furnish the above poem in leaflet form at twenty cents per hundred. *A Sample Packet of 50 leaflets* assorted (no two alike), will be sent post-paid, for 10 cts., or 100 for 20 cts. Postage stamps taken.

MEXICO

Contributions in aid of Christian work in Mexico are most pressingly needed, and can be mailed to the address of
BISHOP H. C. RILEY,
Care of J. P. HEATH,
43 Bible House, New York.

To our Christian Friends:

As there is a regular monthly expense in connection with the work a regular monthly income is needed to meet that expense. We, therefore, specially ask for regular monthly contributions in its behalf. If many will each send a little every month, or quarter, or whenever they can, it will do great good. *Remember, every little helps.*

H. CHAUNCEY RILEY.

Christian Work in Mexico.

Through the reading of the Holy Scriptures translated into Spanish some earnest souls in Mexico have, by God's blessing, been led to a clear knowledge of the Gospel. From their numbers able preachers of the Christian faith in its primitive purity have been raised up, around whom congregations have been gathered from among the humble poor, who have been the first to publicly welcome and defend the pure Gospel in Mexico. The members of these congregations, rich in faith, have worked earnestly and bravely for Christ and His truth among their fellow countrymen in that beautiful Southern portion of North America called Mexico. Schools have been established by them, in which large numbers of bright boys and girls have received a good secular education and have been carefully taught the Christian faith. From the children thus Branch of the Church of our Lord Jesus Christ, that maintains the faith in its purity and integrity, has been organized among these native Christians in the Republic of Mexico. The members of this Mexican Church of our Lord Jesus Christ, though gathered mostly from among the poor, are yet doing a most important Christian work. To continue that work, we need to pay a few leading workers small monthly salaries and also to defray some current expenses. To help to raise the needed funds two societies have been formed—one with an executive committee of ladies and the other with an executive committee of gentlemen—and we earnestly invite our fellow Christians to aid the work by contributing in its behalf. We are trying to secure monthly or quarterly contributions to meet the regular monthly expenses of the work. In order to continue and extend the work, we wish to raise seven hundred dollars a month by endeavoring to have seven hundred persons to each give on an average *one dollar every month* for this object, some giving more than a dollar a month and others giving less as they may be able and willing.

We earnestly invite all who will, to join us in this systematic effort in behalf of the cause of Christ in Mexico, by becoming monthly subscribers to this fund. We already have regular subscribers whose gifts amount monthly to over one hundred dollars, and a growing circle of friends who are forwarding us occasional donations.

This Mexican Church of our Lord Jesus Christ is a very effective instrumentality through which to do Christian work among the many millions on this Western Hemisphere who speak the Spanish language, comparatively few of whom have ever had a Bible in their hands. A beautiful church-building has been secured in the City of Mexico as the centre of the activities of this Mexican Church of our Lord Jesus Christ. Through the workers connected with that centre more than forty congregations have been gathered from among the poor in different parts of the Republic of Mexico. We have some faithful and able preachers now in the field, but more young men need to be trained for the ministry. Multitudes of Protestant children in Mexico, some of them orphans, need to be educated. We make three requests of you, Christian reader: *first*, that you will, if possible, become a monthly or quarterly subscriber in behalf of this Christian work; *second*, that you will try and induce your friends to also contribute to it; *third*, that you will remember this precious work in Mexico in your prayers.

We most sincerely thank all who are already generously contributing to this Christian work for their timely and generous gifts, and we earnestly invite many others, to unite with us in aiding it by also becoming monthly subscribers in its behalf. Those who may not feel that they can give as much as a dollar a month are earnestly asked to give what they can, whenever they are able—EVERY LITTLE HELPS. Fellow Christian, if you will generously consent to contribute a dollar a month or more or less to the work, will you kindly inform me of the fact? Contributions either large or small can be mailed directly to my address as follows:

BISHOP H. C. RILEY, care of J. P. HEATH,
No. 43 Bible House, New York, U. S.

Vol. XI., No. 42. Office, 63 Bible House, N. Y. THURSDAY, OCTOBER 18, 1888. Price, 3 Cents. Annual Subscription, $1.50.

CONTENTS OF THIS NUMBER.

THE OPENING OF THE EXHIBITION AT MELBOURNE, AUSTRALIA, AND PORTRAITS OF THE PRESIDENT AND ARCHITECT.
THE EPIDEMIC OF SUICIDE. Dr. Talmage's Sermon Last Sunday Morning.
ANECDOTES RELATED AT RECENT EVANGELISTIC MEETINGS.
PROPHECY IN THE PENTATEUCH.
PORTRAIT OF DR. DWIGHT, PRESIDENT OF YALE COLLEGE.
A PHYSICIAN'S RESTORATION. (With Illust.)
A Japanese Murderer Forgiven—The Berachah Mission—Women Ransomed with Ivory—A Religion Collector—An Editor's Revenge—An Anxious Night in China.
CONVERSIONS AT SING SING CAMP-MEETING.
MILITARISM A PROPHETIC SIGN.
FURTHER AFIELD. A New Sermon by Rev. C. H. Spurgeon.
Gems from New Books: A Little Girl's Inquiry. A Hawaiian Mother's Lesson—A Child's Penetration.
PICTURE OF THE CATHEDRAL MOUNTAINS IN THE YOSEMITE.
THE EPOCHS OF A LIFE. A New Serial Story by Rev. L. S. Keyser. (Continued.)
THE FALL OF JERICHO. By Mrs. M. Baxter.

SIR JAMES MACBAIN, PRESIDENT OF EXHIBITION. READING THE QUEEN'S TELEGRAM. MR. G. R. JOHNSON, THE BUILDING ARCHITECT.

Opening of Melbourne Exhibition—Procession of the Governors of Australia up the Grand Avenue of Nations.

THE INTERNATIONAL EXHIBITION IN MELBOURNE, AUSTRALIA.

THE position occupied by the United States in the International Exhibition with which Melbourne is celebrating the centenary of New South Wales, will render welcome to our readers the pictures on the preceding page, representing the inaugural ceremony, with portraits of Sir James MacBain, the President of the Exhibition, and Mr. G. R. Johnson, the architect of the building. The immense labor involved in the undertaking is readily realized among ourselves, past experience being a guide. The Australians have spared neither time nor labor in making it a success. They have been aided by a Royal Commission in the Mother Country, over which the Prince of Wales presided, and which has made arrangements for exhibits from that and other countries. Apart from Great Britain and the Colonies, the countries officially represented are the United States, Germany, France, Austria-Hungary, Belgium, while Sweden and Norway, Turkey, Italy Spain, China, Japan, and Madagascar are privately exhibiting.

The Exhibition Buildings

occupy a picturesque sight in Carlton Gardens, and the area they cover is thirty-five and a half acres. The front of the building proper faces the south, and it has a very imposing effect upon the visitor. The architecture is a compromise between the French and Italian orders. The frontage of the main building runs 500 feet, and the main entrance is a vast archway between pavilion-crowned towers. The main hall is surmounted by a dome 220 feet in height, with a broad terrace and gold-crowned pavilion. The latter is a prominent object, and in the sunlight can be distinguished many miles down the bay. The Exhibition is intersected from north to south by the "Grand Avenue of Nations." In this Grand Avenue, a quarter of a mile long, passing down it from the north end, are the entrances to the courts, respectively, on the right hand side, of the United States of America, Germany, Austro-Hungary, Belgium, France, and Great Britain; on the left hand side, those of Canada, New Zealand, Queensland, South Australia, the large Court of Victoria, Tasmania, and New South Wales. Under the dome which covers the intersection of the Eastern and Western Avenues with the Grand Avenue of Nations is the entrance to the south end, where are the great hall, the fernery, the State reception-rooms, and the offices of the Exhibition Commissioners, with galleries, courts, and various departments specially ornamental or attractive.

Here, in the east gallery of the nave, above the concert-hall, is the German Trophy, which represents Germania congratulating Australia on the attainment of her centenary; and in the south gallery is the statue of Victory, which is a gift from the Germans to Victoria. The British, French, German, Belgian, and Victorian Art Galleries are in the balconies on the north and south sides of the nave, in this part of the buildings. Proceeding thence up the Grand Avenue of Nations, and passing the Courts of Great Britain and France on one hand, New South Wales and Victoria on the other, and several foreign and colonial courts, the visitor, approaching the north end, reaches that of Germany, and the United States Court next it. The entrance to the German Court is through an immense arch hung with rich draperies, which leads directly into a saloon filled with pianos, and these are continually being played.

The United States Court

is distinguished by the stars painted on columns, and by the name in large gold letters under the sidelights; its front is occupied by Singer's sewing machines, and Edison's phonographs attract much curiosity. In the machinery annex, at the north end, Great Britain, America, and Germany divide the space between them; the collection of British machinery is said to be the most important ever brought together. There is not very much ground outside the buildings, or anything worthy of note except two portable railways, and the inevitable "switch-back," now a popular amusement at all Exhibitions. As a well-furnished and well-ordered show of leading arts and industries European, American, and Australian, and of Colonial products, the Melbourne Exhibition is complete. Though occupying less space than the Philadelphian and Paris Exhibition buildings, the great edifice in which a world's civilization is displayed in Melbourne, is one of the most marked illustrations of the vast resources of the colony which is now doing its share in the celebration of the Australian centenary.

The Opening Ceremony,

which took place on August 1, was in all respects a red-letter day in the local history, and citizens of Melbourne, which is the capital city of Victoria, turned out to do honor to the great occasion. The Governor of the colony, Sir Henry Brougham Loch, accompanied by Lady Loch, performed the ceremony. Invited guests, to the number of seven thousand, were present. Among them were viceregal parties from the other Australian colonies; military, naval, Church, and State dignitaries; judges of the supreme courts, and a host of the political rank-and-file. From early morning the points of vantage along which the procession of governors, with their escorts, were to pass, were covered with people; and towards noon, looking from the top of Collins Street, there were in sight over 150,000 well-dressed, prosperous-looking witnesses to Melbourne's greatness. Altogether, it is estimated that between 400,000 *and* 500,000 *people* turned out. From the far north of Queensland and the northern territory, from New South Wales, Tasmania, New Zealand, and from other lands, crowds had gathered.

The Whole Line of the Route,

from Government House to the Exhibition building, was kept by military and naval guards, and as the viceregal parties passed along the streets, escorted by the local cavalry and mounted rifle corps, the people cheered enthusiastically. Guns were fired, announcing their departure from Government House, and the processions of fire-brigades and trade unionists and friendly societies were formed, and marched up from Spencer Street to the Exhibition grounds. In the procession there were over 14,000 members of friendly societies, with bands playing. The whole affair afforded

A Spectacle Not Easily Forgotten.

From every house flags fluttered, and people cheered and waved hats and handkerchiefs; thirty bands marched at regular intervals between the various societies, and the rich banners of the Orders, borne on vast lorries drawn by magnificent teams of horses, seemed to fill the music-burdened air with light and joyousness. The day was cold, and a little rain fell, but the enthusiasm of the great concourse of people was not to be damped, and as the various governors and other high officials descended from their carriages, there arose a vast roar of cheers which went echoing along the black line down and away to Prince's Bridge. Then the Exhibition gates were opened, and at the doors of the Grand Avenue of Nations a procession was formed, which marched into the great hall. Never before in Australia has such an array been seen. First were borne the royal colors, followed by the naval and military officers, British and foreign; then the Ceremonial Committee, the civic authorities, the judges, the executive commissioners, the Crown Ministers from the other colonies, the Speakers of the Australian Parliaments, and the governors of the various colonies, all of whom were cheered. As

The Magnificent Procession

moved slowly up the Grand Avenue of Nations, the national anthems of America, Germany, Austria, and France were played by bands stationed in each of the courts named, and when the Grand Hall was reached, the British national anthem was sung, Mr. F. H. Cowen conducting. There the distinguished guests mounted a dais which had been erected in the great hall, and within view of the spectators in every part of the main building. In the western nave was the orchestra and a chorus, eight hundred strong, the lady singers all dressed in white, some with blue and others with cardinal sashes across their breasts. Over 30,000 people were assembled, and yet all was as quiet and orderly as could be desired. Looking up from the Avenue of Nations to the dais, the scene was one of grand impressiveness. Over the brilliant groups of statesmen, soldiers, governors, and dignitaries of the Church and Bench and the ladies, a great statue of Victory extending a wreath seemed as though about to crown, not the conquerors of men and the shedders of blood in the cause of kingly or national ambition, but the subduers of a great wilderness, the bearers of the flag of peace, the pioneers of civilization in a land which a hundred years ago was known only as a great dark land inshore, and which has grown from a community of rough pioneers into one of the commercial centres of the world.

At this stage of the ceremonies came the solution of a problem which had been a source of much perplexity and somewhat embittered controversy. The commissioners had very properly decided that the inauguration should include a prayer, but the question arose as to who should say the prayer. It was urged on the one hand that the Bishop of the English Church should officiate, as Victoria is part of the British Empire; on the other hand it was said that the head of the Roman Catholic Church, being an Archbishop, was entitled to precedence; another person asked why should not the Moderator of the Presbyterian Assembly be asked to pray. The controversy waxed warm, but ultimately it was decided that Sir James MacBain should read a prayer, which was to be written by the Anglican bishop and approved of by the heads of the other denominations. This was done, and it is a remarkable illustration of the fact that the three sects, though so antagonistic in operation, easily find a common ground when they come before the Mercy Seat to present their wants and praises. This was

The Prayer:

"Almighty God, the Father of all the families of the earth, who hast made of one blood all nations of men, and hast determined the times before appointed, and the bounds of their habitation, we humbly pray Thee to bless and hallow this our undertaking. The heaven, even the heavens, are Thine, but the earth hast Thou given to the children of men. And as Thou didst at the first bid them to multiply and replenish the earth, and subdue it, we give Thee hearty thanks that in Thy gracious Providence Thou didst guide our fathers to this exceeding good land—a land flowing with milk and honey—and hast so prospered us that the little one has become a thousand, and the small one a strong nation.

"And inasmuch as all knowledge of the resources of nature cometh from Thee, and all the skill of man is Thy gift, we thank Thee for the discoveries and applications of science whereby we are enabled to meet together in this place from distant regions of the globe. O Lord! our God, we acknowledge that all the treasure of human industry and art cometh from Thy hand, and is all Thine own. We humbly lay it at Thy feet, beseeching Thee to grant that it may advance the interests of trade and commerce, that it may encourage useful learning, and promote unity, peace, and concord throughout the world. Hasten the time, we pray Thee, when men shall not learn war any more; and when the nations shall only provoke one another to such good works as will ennoble and benefit mankind.

"And now, O Gracious God! as we have begun this enterprise in dependence on Thy goodness, and with prayer for Thy blessing, so we entreat Thee to look favorably upon it even to the end. Protect this building, and those who shall assemble within its walls, from all harm and accident. Let no disaster befall the precious stores contained in it. Let not the hope of its promoters be disappointed. But establish Thou, O God! the work of our hands upon us; yea, he work of our hands establish Thou it. And o Thee will we ascribe all praise and glory, in he name of our Lord and Saviour Jesus Christ. Amen."

The prayer having been said, the "Old Hun-redth" was sung by the choir, and the grand old hymn of praise could scarcely have been heard to better advantage. It had a very marked effect on the vast audience, some strong men being moved to tears as the great tones filled the building, awakening memories sacred, beautiful, and full of grace, after which Mr. Cowen's "Hymn of Thanksgiving" was most effectively rendered.

The Conclusion of the Ceremony

came when a gold master-key to all locks in the building was handed to the governor, who thereupon gave the signal for hoisting the national colors, and, amid the thunders of the guns from the batteries and the ships in the harbor, declared the exhibition open. 'A telegram was loyally despatched to Queen Victoria, announcing the event, and subsequently (as shown in the illustration between the portaits on the first page) the Governor read to the assembled people their monarch's condescending reply, congratulating them on the success which had already been achieved, and wishing them greater prosperity in the future.

AN ANXIOUS NIGHT IN CHINA.

In a letter to the *China Inland Mission* Miss Miles, who is one of the missionaries of the society now laboring at Ta-ning, says: "We have had our first communion service at Taning. I am sure our Father must have rejoiced to see the little band lately reclaimed from heathenism, remembering the death of the Lord Jesus. There were eleven, besides us foreigners. Yesterday, Miss Scott and I went outside the city and burnt three idol shrines in one house Our hearts were full as we sang, 'Praise God, from whom all blessings flow,' and watched the hideous things burn to ashes. 'Thanks be unto God, who always leadeth us in triumph'—we can thankfully say that we are being led in triumph in Ta-ning. Last Friday at midnight an ox was sacrificed at the city temple in honor of Confucius, and all the scholars were expected to assemble and join in the idolatrous rites. For some weeks back we have had two bright young students coming to hear the gospel, and one of them destroyed the idols in his house. They told us they did not mean to go to the sacrifice; would we pray for them? They were quite prepared to be beaten, knowing how much the Mandarin here dislikes foreigners, and all who have to do with them. After going to bed, I lay awake thinking of these two men, and asking God to protect them; several crackers had been fired off, and soon a great bang sounded, and re-echoed through the hills. A few minutes after, these two men who were in the kitchen with our servants, sang 'Onward go,' and then after prayer, they all sang again, this time 'Follow, follow, I will follow Jesus.' Since then, we have heard that the Mandarin is afraid to ill-treat them on account of higher authorities."

ANECDOTES RELATED AT RECENT EVANGELISTIC MEETINGS.

Memorable Ride Across a Bridge.—The Rev. M. McCaul observes: "I once rode with a gentleman over a bridge in Canada. As we were passing across, he suddenly stopped, and turning toward me, exclaimed, 'Man, this is an awful place! Some years ago I was coming over this bridge with a farmer and his wife, and when in the very middle, the horse took fright and swerved, throwing the man and woman clean over the bridge. Down, down they sank, until crash they came upon yon rock, and were mutilated almost beyond recognition. Do you know,' he continued, 'I never pass this place without remembering that fearful moment—a moment in which I felt very near to God, and standing helpless before Him. I offered my heartfelt thanks for deliverance. From that moment I was a converted man.' There is nothing like danger for making one feel his need of Christ, and it is only when in great peril that men truly feel their own insignificance and His power."

Objecting to Close Quarters.—The Same Minister observes: "A few nights ago I was visiting a family in which both the husband and wife had been in the habit formerly of coming to our Gospel meeting, but for a considerable time had not put in an appearance. Talking to the woman, I seriously asked her why she had stopped attending our meeting. 'Well, sir,' she replied, 'I did not like the way your workers, as you call them, do at your meeting. They will never let one go to the meeting, and rise quietly and go home again; they must run after one, and *ask if your soul is saved*.' 'And what is better,' I answered, 'than to say your soul *is* at peace with God, if it be so, and if not, to set about securing the blessing?' 'Ah! that is true enough,' was the reply; 'but if you say your soul is not saved, they will not let you go till they try to persuade you to come to Christ, and though I mean to do so some day, I am not going to do it just yet.' Many people, like this woman, object to being personally dealt with at a meeting. You may speak to them, according to their idea, about almost anything except salvation."

They All Had "A Bit of the Pig."—The Rev. Mr. Pugh says: "An Irishman was one day apprehended on a charge of stealing a pig. He was brought up for trial, but it was noticed that as soon as he had scrutinized the features of the twelve jurymen who were trying his case, that a look of comfortable contentment settled upon his face. The case proceeded. The lawyers pleaded for and against him. The case was beginning to look very bad for the man, yet still he maintained the same complacent look. All the evidence was finished; the jury retired, but soon returned. Amidst profound silence the question was asked, 'Guilty or not guilty?' And to the surprise of all but the prisoner, the answer was given, 'Not guilty.' The prisoner was dismissed. One of his friends meeting him outside shortly afterwards, said, 'Well, Pat, I was surprised. However did they let you off?' 'As soon as I saw the jury,' replied Pat, I knew I was all right, for every one of them had a bit of the pig.' I think this story illustrates to some extent why we cannot get any truly efficient restrictive measure passed in reference to the drink traffic. Too many of the members of our legislatures have a hand in it themselves. They have all had a bit of the pig."

"Call Him Victor, Frank."—Mr. Holness says: A friend of mine told me the following incident, he having visited the lady mentioned: Mrs. W. was a young wife and mother; her babe was but seven days old when she was called upon to leave this world. For a month prior to her departure, her confidence in Christ had been unshaken, and she knew whom she had believed. But a short time before her death the tempter came, and tried to undermine her faith and trust in Jesus. He suggested to her money, dress, pleasure, health, etc., and promised her all these things if she would give up her Saviour. It was a terrible conflict; she was young, and there was much on earth that she could cling to. A profuse perspiration bedewed her, and her heart throbbed painfully with the agony of the strife. But she conquered; by the grace of God she was victorious. She steadfastly refused all the overtures of Satan, and the cloud passed away from her heart, and left her rejoicing in the radiance of her Saviour's love. And now she asked the nurse to fetch her baby. It was brought to her. She kissed the child, then turning to her husband, said, "Frank, call him Victor, for I have just obtained the victory through the blood." And then she passed peacefully into the presence of her Lord. Happy mother, thus to be able to surrender all for Jesus, and find in Him her all in all.

A Prodigal Caught at the Corner.—One of the band of workers says: "About seven years ago I wandered away from my parents, and came to this great city, going about the streets singing the songs of sin for the devil, obtaining a coin here and there. One Sunday night, about four years ago, I came out of one of those saloons on the Dials and heard a band of open-air workers singing at the corner. I stopped and listened, and the words uttered struck me to the heart. They were saying that perhaps some of us in the crowd had praying mothers. I knew I had a praying mother away down in the country. After the speaking they sang another hymn, and it was, 'Where is my wandering boy to-night?' I had a look at myself and thought, 'Can it be possible that my mother loves me still? No, there is no one cares for me.' And at the close of the open-air meeting the friends invited us to go into the Mission Hall, and something seemed to say, 'Go in.' But I said, 'No, I will not go in to-night with these people, I will go the other way.' I walked along Earl Street, but as I went I thought, 'Can I get in without those people seeing me?' I came back and crept inside, as I thought, unnoticed. At the close of the meeting they had a prayer-meeting, and Miss Ling came down the room and asked me, 'Do you love the Lord?' This led to further conversation, but it was three weeks before I could quite make up my mind to accept Christ, and I thought then it was time I found something better to do than sing in the streets."

A Sceptic's Dying Confession.—I Witnessed a young man's conversion who was a sceptic for some years of his short life, but who found out the falseness of all human reasonings before he died. While he lived I saw but little of him, but when he was dying he sent for me to come and see him. I went to his bedroom with his father; and as I gazed upon his face, I was startled for a moment to see the ravages of disease. He was far gone in consumption; his eyes were bright, his cheeks flushed, and his voice was low. I took his hand and sat by his side. He held my hand for some time, and then said: "It has been all dark with me, all dark, but it is brighter now. I think I see the light. I found out last night that I was a vile sinner." Then I saw the tears gather in his eyes and roll down his poor thin cheeks. And, looking at me, he added, "I want to tell you about my life. I've been a sceptic." He was only twenty-one! His friends set him up, and as his voice was very faint I bent close to him, and he began: "I had a good education, but I got to be sceptical. I began to pick the Bible to pieces; and when a young man begins to do that, you know there are many things he cannot understand; and I was young." He paused a moment, then continued, "Now I want you to explain to me fully and clearly the birth of Christ." Lifting a silent prayer to God, I turned to Luke 1, and read a few verses; then spoke to him of sin and the necessity of atonement; At last he had his feet upon the Rock. He had been to God about his sins before I saw him. I knelt and thanked God for His mercy to him; and left him trusting in the Saviour. He went from the night of scepticism into the morning of faith. He found happiness and peace in gazing with believing eyes on the Christ of God.

THE EPIDEMIC OF SUICIDE.

Dr. Talmage's Sermon Preached last Sunday Morning, October 14, 1888.

"He drew out his sword and would have killed himself, supposing that the prisoners had been fled. But Paul cried with a loud voice, saying, Do thyself no harm." Acts 16 : 26, 27.

The Sheriff's Dismay—His Anticipation of Disgrace—Resolves to Avoid it by Suicide—Historical Suicides—A Common Modern Crime—The Worst of Crimes—Napoleon's Attempt—Demented Suicides—Hugh Miller's Overtaxed Brain—William Cowper Saved—The Suicide's Place After Death—How God Regards the Crime—The Rogues' Picture-Gallery—The Cause of the Present Epidemic—Infidel Teaching of Annihilation—Appendices to a Bad Book—How to Meet Temptation—The Sorrowless World.

HERE is a would-be suicide arrested in his deadly attempt. He was a sheriff, and according to the Roman law, a bailiff himself must suffer the punishment due an escaped prisoner; and if the prisoner breaking jail was sentenced to be endungeoned for three or four years, then the sheriff must be endungeoned for three or four years; and if the prisoner breaking jail was to have suffered capital punishment, then the sheriff must suffer capital punishment. The sheriff had received especial charge to keep a sharp lookout for Paul and Silas. The government had not had confidence in bolts and bars to keep safe these two clergymen, about whom there seemed to be something

Strange and Supernatural.

Sure enough, by miraculous power, they are free, and the sheriff, waking out of a sound sleep, and supposing these ministers have run away, and knowing that they were to die for preaching Christ, and realizing that he must therefore die, rather than go under the executioner's axe on the morrow and suffer public disgrace, resolves to precipitate his own decease. But before the sharp, keen, glittering dagger of the sheriff could strike his heart, one of the unloosened prisoners arrests the blade by the command: "Do thyself no harm."

In Olden Time,

and where Christianity had not interfered with it, suicide was considered honorable and a sign of courage. Demosthenes poisoned himself when told that Alexander's ambassador had demanded the surrender of the Athenian orators. Isocrates killed himself rather than surrender to Philip of Macedon. Cato, rather than submit to Julius Cæsar, took his own life, and after three times his wounds had been dressed tore them open and perished. Mithridates killed himself rather than submit to Pompey, the conqueror. Hannibal destroyed his life by poison from his ring, considering life unbearable. Lycurgus a suicide, Brutus a suicide. After the disaster of Moscow, Napoleon always carried with him a preparation of opium, and one night his servant heard the ex-emperor arise, put something in a glass and drink it, and soon after the groans aroused all the attendants, and it was only through utmost medical skill he was resuscitated from the stupor of the opiate. Times have changed, and yet

The American Conscience

needs to be toned up on the subject of suicide. Have you seen a paper in the last month that did not announce the passage out of life by one's own behest? Defaulters, alarmed at the idea of exposure, quit life precipitately. Men losing large fortunes go out of the world because they cannot endure earthly existence. Frustrated affection, domestic infelicity, dyspeptic impatience, anger, remorse, envy, jealousy, destitution, misanthropy, are considered sufficient causes for absconding from this life by Paris-green, by laudanum, by belladonna, by Othello's dagger, by halter, by leap from the abutment of a bridge, by fire-arms. More cases of *felo de se* in the last two years than any two years of the world's existence, and more in the last month than in any twelve months. The evil is more and more spreading.

A pulpit not long ago expressed some doubt as to whether there was really anything wrong about quitting this life when it became disagreeable, and there are found in respectable circles people apologetic for the crime which Paul in the text arrested. I shall show you before I get through that suicide is

The Worst of all Crimes,

and I shall lift a warning unmistakable. But in the early part of this sermon I wish to admit that some of the best Christians that have ever lived have committed self-destruction, but always in dementia, and not responsible. I have no more doubt about their eternal felicity than I have of the Christian who dies in his bed in the delirium of typhoid fever. While the shock of the catastrophe is very great, I charge all those who have had Christian friends under cerebral aberration step off the boundaries of this life, to have no doubt about their happiness. The dear Lord took them right out of their dazed and frenzied state into perfect safety. How Christ feels toward the insane, you may know from the kind way He treated the demoniac of Gadara and the child lunatic, and the potency with which He hushed tempests either of sea or brain.

Hugh Miller's Suicide.

Scotland, the land prolific of intellectual giants, had none grander than *Hugh Miller*. Great for science and great for God. He came of the best Highland blood, and was a descendant of Donald Roy, a man eminent for piety and the rare gift of second-sight. His attainments, climbing up as he did from the quarry and the wall of the stonemason, drew forth the astonished admiration of Buckland and Murchison, the scientists, and Dr. Chalmers, the theologian, and held universities spellbound while he told them the story of what he had seen of God in the old red sandstone.

That man did more than any being that ever lived to show that the God of the hills is the God of the Bible, and he struck his tuning-fork on the rocks of Cromarty until he brought geology and theology accordant in divine worship. His two books, entitled "Footprints of the Creator" and the "Testimony of the Rocks," proclaimed the banns of an everlasting marriage between genuine science and revelation. On this latter book he toiled day and night, through love of nature and love of God, until he could not sleep, and his brain gave way, and he was found dead with a revolver by his side, the cruel instrument having had two bullets—one for him and the other for the gunsmith, who at the coroner's inquest was examining it and fell dead. Have you any doubt of the beatification of Hugh Miller, after his hot brain had ceased throbbing that winter night in his study at Portobello? Among the mightiest of earth, among the mightiest of heaven.

William Cowper's Escape.

No one doubted the piety of William Cowper, the author of those three great hymns, "Oh, for a closer walk with God," "What various hindrances we meet," "There is a fountain filled with blood"; William Cowper, who shares with Isaac Watts and Charles Wesley the chief honors of Christian hymnology. In hypochondria he resolved to take his own life, and rode to the river Thames, but found a man seated on some goods at the very point from which he expected to spring, and rode back to his home, and that night threw himself upon his own knife, but the blade broke; and then he hanged himself to the ceiling, but the rope parted. No wonder that when God mercifully delivered him from that awful dementia he sat down and wrote that other hymn just as memorable:

> "God moves in a mysterious way
> His wonders to perform;
> He plants His footsteps in the sea,
> And rides upon the storm.
>
> "Blind unbelief is sure to err
> And scan His work in vain;
> God is His own interpreter,
> And He will make it plain."

While we make this merciful and righteous allowance in regard to those who were plunged into mental incoherence, I declare that that man who in the use of his reason, by his own act, snaps the bond between his body and his soul, goes straight into perdition. Shall I prove it? Revelation 21 : 8: "Murderers shall have their part in the lake which burneth with fire and brimstone." Revelation 22 : 15; "Without are dogs and sorcerers and whoremongers and murderers." You do not believe the New Testament? Then, perhaps, you believe the Ten Commandments: "Thou shalt not kill." Do you say all these passages refer to the taking of the life of others? Then I ask you if you are not as responsible for your own life as for the life of others. God gave you a special trust in your life. He made you

The Custodian of Your Life,

as He made you the custodian of no other life. He gave you as weapons with which to defend it two arms to strike back assailants, two eyes to watch for invasion, and a natural love of life which ought ever to be on the alert. Assassination of others is a mild crime compared with the assassination of yourself, because in the latter case it is treachery to an especial trust, it is the surrender of a castle you were especially appointed to keep, it is treason to a natural law, and it is treason to God added to ordinary murder.

To show how God in the Bible looked upon this crime, I point you to

The Rogues' Picture-Gallery

in some parts of the Bible, the pictures of the people who have committed this unnatural crime. Here is the headless trunk of Saul on the walls of Bathshan. Here is the man who chased little David—ten feet in stature chasing four. Here is the man who consulted a clairvoyant, Witch of Endor. Here is a man who, whipped in battle, instead of surrendering his sword with dignity, as many a man has done, asks his servant to slay him; and when the servant declined, then the giant plants the hilt of his sword in the earth, the sharp point sticking upward, and he throws his body on it and expires, the coward, the suicide. Here is Ahitophel, the Machiavelli of olden times, betraying his best friend David in order that he may become prime minister of Absalom, and joining that fellow in his attempt at parricide. Not getting what he wanted by change of politics, he takes a short-cut out of a disgraced life into the suicide's eternity. There he is, the ingrate!

Here is Abimelech, practically a suicide. He is with an army, bombarding a tower, when a woman in the tower takes a grindstone from its place and drops it upon his head, and with what life he has left in his cracked skull he commands his armor-bearer: "Draw thy sword and slay me, lest men say a woman slew me." There is his post-mortem photograph in the book of Samuel. But

The Hero of This Group

is Judas Iscariot. Dr. Donne says he was a martyr, and we have in our day apologists for him. And what wonder, in this day when we have a book revealing Aaron Burr as a pattern of virtue, and in this day when we uncover a statue of Georges Sand as the benefactress of literature, and in this day when there are betrayals of Christ on the part of some of His pretended apostles—a betrayal so black it makes the infamy of Judas Iscariot white! Yet this man by his own hand hung up for the execration of all the ages, Judas Iscariot.

All the good men and women of the Bible left to God the decision of their earthly terminus, and they could have said with Job, who had a right to commit suicide if any man ever had—what with his destroyed property, and his body all aflame with insufferable carbuncles, and everything gone from his home except the chief curse of it, a pestiferous wife, and four garrulous people pelting him with comfortless talk while he sits on a heap of ashes scratching his scabs with a piece of broken pottery, yet crying out in triumph: "All the days of my appointed time will I wait till my change come."

Notwithstanding the Bible is against this evil and the aversion which it creates by the loathsome and ghastly spectacle of those who have hurled themselves out of life, and notwithstanding Christianity is against it, and the arguments and the useful lives and the illustrious deaths of its disciples, it is a fact alarmingly patent that suicide is on the increase.

What is the Cause?

I charge upon infidelity and agnosticism this whole thing. If there be no hereafter, or if that hereafter be blissful without reference to how we live and how we die, why not move back the folding-doors between this world and the next? And when our existence here becomes troublesome, why not pass right over into Elysium? Put this down among your most solemn reflections, and consider it after you go to your homes: there has never been a case of suicide where the operator was not either demented, and therefore irresponsible, or an infidel. I challenge all the ages, and I challenge the whole universe. There never has been a case of self-destruction while in full appreciation of his immortality and of the fact that that immortality would be glorious or wretched according as he accepted Jesus Christ or rejected Him.

You say it is a business trouble, or you say it is electrical currents, or it is this, or it is that, or it is the other thing. Why not go clear back, my friend, and acknowledge that in every case it is the abdication of reason or

The Teaching of Infidelity,

which practically says: "If you don't like this life get out of it, and you will land either in annihilation, where there are no notes to pay, no persecutions to suffer, no gout to torment, or you will land where there will be everything glorious and nothing to pay for it"? Infidelity always has been apologetic for self-immolation. After Tom Paine's "Age of Reason" was published and widely read, there was a marked increase of self-slaughter.

A man in London heard Mr. Owen deliver his infidel lecture on socialism, and went home, sat down, and wrote these words: "Jesus Christ is one of the weakest characters in history, and the Bible is the greatest possible deception," and then shot himself. David Hume wrote these words: "It would be no crime for me to divert the Nile or the Danube from its natural bed. Where, then, can be the crime in my diverting a few drops of blood from their ordinary channel?" And having written the essay, he loaned it to a friend, the friend read it, wrote a letter of thanks and admiration, and shot himself. Appendix to the same book.

Rousseau, Voltaire, Gibbon, Montaigne, were apologetic for self-immolation.

Infidelity Puts Up No Bar

to people's rushing out from this world into the next. They teach us it does not make any difference how you live here or go out of this world: you will land either in an oblivious nowhere or a glorious somewhere. And infidelity holds the upper end of the rope for the suicide, and aims the pistol with which a man blows his brains out, and mixes the strychnine for the last swallow. If infidelity could carry the day and persuade the majority of people in this country that it does not make any difference how you go out of the world you will land safely, the Hudson and the East rivers would be so full of corpses the ferry-boats would be impeded in their progress, and the crack of a suicide's pistol would be no more alarming than the rumble of a street-car.

I have sometimes heard it discussed whether the great dramatist was a Christian or not. I do not know, but I know that he considered appreciation of a future existence the mightiest hindrance to self-destruction:

"For who could bear the whips and scorns of time,
The oppressor's wrong, the proud man's contumely,
The pangs of despis'd love, the law's delay,
The insolence of office, and the spurns
That patient merit of the unworthy takes,
When he himself might his quietus make
With a bare bodkin? Who would fardels bear,
To grunt and sweat under a weary life,
But that the dread of something after death—
The undiscovered country, from whose bourne
No traveller returns—puzzles the will?"

Would God that the coroners would be brave in rendering the right verdict, and when in a case of irresponsibility they say: "While this man was demented he took his life"; in the other case say: "Having read infidel books and attended infidel lectures, which obliterated from this man's mind all appreciation of future retribution, he committed self-slaughter!"

Ah! Infidelity, stand up and take thy sentence! In the presence of God, angels and men,

Stand Up, Thou Monster,

thy lip blasted with blasphemy, thy cheek scarred with lust, thy breath foul with the corruption of the ages! Stand up, Satyr, filthy goat, buzzard of the nations, leper of the centuries! Stand up, thou monster, Infidelity! Part man, part panther, part reptile, part dragon, stand up and take thy sentence! Thy hands red with the blood in which thou hast washed, thy feet crimson with the human gore through which thou hast waded, stand up and take thy sentence! Down with thee to the pit, and sup on the sobs and groans of families thou hast blasted, and roll on the bed of knives which thou hast sharpened for others, and let thy music be the everlasting miserere of those whom thou hast damned! I brand the forehead of Infidelity with all the crimes of self-immolation for the last century on the part of those who had their reason.

My friends, if ever your life through its abrasions and its molestations should seem to be unbearable, and you are tempted to quit it by your own behest, do not consider yourself as worse than others. Christ Himself was tempted to cast Himself from the roof of the Temple; but as He resisted, so resist ye. Christ came to medicine all our wounds. In your trouble I prescribe life instead of death. People who have had it, worse than you will ever have it, have gone songful on the way. Remember that

God Keeps the Chronology

of your life with as much precision as He keeps the chronology of nations, your death as well as your cradle. Why was it that at midnight, just at midnight, the destroying angel struck the blow that set the Israelites free from bondage? The four hundred and thirty years were up at twelve o'clock that night. The four hundred and thirty years were not up at eleven, and one o'clock would have been tardy and too late. The four hundred and thirty years were up at twelve o'clock, ane the destroying angel struck the blow, and Israel was free. And God knows just the hour when it is time to lead you up from earthly bondage. By His grace make not the worst of things, but the best of them. If you must take the pills, do not chew them. Your everlasting rewards will accord with your earthly perturbations, just as Caius gave to Agrippa a chain of gold as heavy as had been a chain of iron. For the asking—and I do not know to whom I speak in this august assemblage, but the word may be especially appropriate—for your asking, you may have the same grace that was given to the Italian martyr, Algerius, who, down in the darkest of dungeons, dated his letter from "the delectable orchard of the Leonine prison." And remember that this brief

Life is Surrounded by a Rim,

a very thin but very important rim, and close up to that rim is a great eternity, and you had better keep out of it until God breaks that rim and separates this from that. To get rid of the sorrows of earth, do not rush into greater sorrows. To get rid of a swarm of summer insects, leap not into a jungle of Bengal tigers.

There is a sorrowless world, and it is so radiant that the noonday sun is only the lowest doorstep, and the aurora that lights up our northern heavens, confounding astronomers as to what it can be, is the waving of the banners of the procession come to take the conquerors home from church militant to church triumphant, and you and I have ten thousand reasons for wanting to go there, but we will never get there either by self-immolation or impenitency. All our sins slain by the Christ who came to do that thing, we want to go in at just the time divinely arranged, and from a couch divinely spread, and then the clang of the sepulchral gates behind us will be overpowered by the clang of the opening of the solid pearl before us. O God, whatever others may choose, give me a Christian's life, a Christian's death, a Christian's burial, a Christian's immortality!

THE CHRISTIAN CONVENTION.

The fifth annual gathering at the Rev. A. B. Simpson's church, in New York, of Christian friends from all parts of the country who believe in and practice Divine Healing, commenced on Sunday, October 7. The church being just now without a home, pending the erection of their new commodious building, the hospitality of the Central Baptist Church, in Forty-second Street, was accepted, and at all the meetings the house was well filled.

Three meetings were held each day, the subjects being Christ our Saviour, Christ our Sanctifier, Christ our Healer, and Christ our Coming Lord. The addresses were more lengthy than on previous occasions, but no sign of weariness could be detected in the large gatherings. Prominent among the speakers were Dr. Wilson, of St. George's Church, Dr. John Cookman, Rev. E. W. Oakes, who is doing a grand work at Manchester, N. H., Rev. Dr. Peck, Miss Carrie F. Judd, of Buffalo, N. Y., and Miss Mattie Gordon, of Nashville, Tenn.

One of the most interesting meetings was that of Friday afternoon, when several testimonies of Divine Healing were given. One of these was from Miss Mattie Gordon, who related her experience in a voice singularly soft and melodious. She had been in weak health from a child, but five years ago she became a confirmed invalid, and was confined for six months to her bed. Several doctors were consulted about her, but they did not agree in their diagnosis, though the results of their various modes of treatment were alike, in their failure to cure her. During this long illness she gave her heart to the Saviour, and dwelt much on His love and power. Expecting a speedy release from her suffering, to go to be with Him in glory, her mind became more and more detached from the things of the world and concentrated on Christ and His life and work. She read much, prayed much, and her meditations brought her near to the Saviour.

At length the thought occurred to her that the word of Jesus must be as efficacious now as when He was upon earth. She had trusted her soul to Him, could she not trust her body? The thought of His working a miraculous cure for her seemed impious at first, but, as she meditated upon it, the trust seemed logical and well founded. She began to pray for healing, but always begging that if she was wrong in doing so she might be forgiven. Finally, after a long struggle with doubt and temptation, she was enabled to triumph, and solemnly put herself physically as she had previously done spiritually into the Lord's hands. Immediately new strength passed into her body. She rose, astonished her family by going down-stairs unassisted, and the very next day was taking her full share of household duties in perfect health.

Another remarkable case among those described was that of Mr. W. J. Fenton, of Toronto, Canada. He said that on November 13, 1886, he was seized with a severe attack of *congestion of the brain*. He fell unconscious in his own house, and it was believed by his physician that he was suffering from apoplexy. After remaining in bed for a week, or more, he managed to struggle to his office, but the pain in his head was so violent that he could scarcely sign his name, and was so dizzy that he had difficulty in walking at all. He was advised to spend a few weeks in New York. On his way he had another attack. While in New York he called on Mr. Simpson, whom he had known in Canada, was anointed, and was perfectly cured. Since that time his testimony has been the means of convincing a sceptic that God is, and is the Rewarder of those who seek Him, and also of leading to the Divine Healing of a lady afflicted with heart disease, who is now whole.

A JAPANESE MURDERER FORGIVEN.

AN affecting scene in Japan, which occurred recently, is reported in the *Spirit of Missions*. It states that a few months ago a native pastor was celebrating the Lord's Supper in one of the Christian churches of the island empire. He was a relative of a man who, about twenty-five years ago, conceived the idea that for his country to open her gates to Occidental civilization would be a benefit and blessing, and with the prophetic foresight of a practical patriot and statesman, dared publicly to advocate the abandonment of the exclusive policy hitherto pursued by his nation. For such advocacy he became so obnoxious to his countrymen that it was resolved to put an end to his influence by putting an end to his life. On a great festival day, when Japanese came from all quarters to do honor to the gods of the kingdom, three bands prepared to waylay him. He escaped the first, but fell into the hands of the second and perished. At the recent service, the native pastor referred to his relative, who was the first modern martyr to his country's advancement. In the congregation an old man arose and begged to be heard. He said, "I am one of those who murdered that man, twenty-five years ago, and I want to confess my part in that crime." The young pastor said, "By all the ancient customs of Japan, I am bound to avenge that blood-feud by plunging my dagger into the throat of the man who was the murderer of my relative. But Christ's blood reconciles all blood-feuds, and in Christ's Name I wish to extend to this brother the right hand of fellowship." The men who witnessed the scene knew what would have happened but for the grace of God, and praised Him as the two men clasped hands.

THE BERACHAH MISSION.

AN astonishing report of work done, and the blessing of God upon it, comes from the Berachah mission, a picture of which, with the portraits of Mr. and Mrs. Henry Naylor, its founders, appeared in this journal on August 4, 1887. In addition to making efforts to reach the depraved characters who are to be found in the streets surrounding the mission building, special efforts have been directed to the salvation of sailors, railroad men, horse-car men, policemen, firemen, and others. During the past year a wonderful blessing has rested upon the work. One English seaman, who was converted at the mission, has gone back to his native country, and has opened a mission in Hull for the benefit of sailors, and is working earnestly and successfully among them.

The Work Ashore and Afloat,

during the past twelve months has been far-reaching in its influence. Sailors who have been blessed have brought their shipmates to the mission, and no less than 3,335 have been counted at the various services. Besides this, permission has been obtained from captains to hold services on ships in the harbor, and 1,521 vessels were visited and successful meetings held. The sea work is growing fast, and many Christian mothers in far away lands are blessing God that, through God's blessing on the work of the Berachah mission, their wandering sons have been brought into Christ's kingdom. The number of sailors alone who have made confession of Christ at the services is 306. Street services are also held when the weather permits. Four hundred of these were held during the past twelve months, and it was no uncommon occurrence to have gatherings of from three to four hundred at a time. In these cases tracts were freely distributed, and invitations to the mission scattered among the people. No less than 34,887 Bibles, Testaments, and Scripture portions were given away to families without them, and unable to purchase. An industrial school and a free medical mission have also been established, which are thoroughly appreciated in the neighborhood.

The whole expense of building and supporting the mission has been gladly defrayed by Mr. and Mrs. Henry Naylor, who feel joy and thankfulness in the success which is attending their labors. They are about to establish a library of religious works, for the benefit of the sailors and others who frequent the reading-room. They wish to make it as extensive and complete as possible, and, therefore, will gladly welcome any gifts made for this object. They may be addressed to Mr. Ernest W. Blandy, superintendent of the mission, 463 West Thirty-second Street, New York. Both Mr. Blandy and his wife have had considerable experience in mission work and street services, and Mr. and Mrs. Naylor are glad to have secured their assistance in the work. The prospects for the coming season are, therefore, exceedingly bright, and all the workers are looking in faith to God for a continued outpouring of His Spirit, without which they are conscious all labor would be vain.

CONVERSIONS AT SING SING.

THE recent camp-meeting at Sing Sing, N. Y., will long be memorable to all who attended it. Among the preachers were Revs. Thomas Harrison, Gallaway, Merritt, Wardle, Mrs. Van Cott, and two earnest members of the Society of Friends, Mr. Updegraff and Dr. Dugan Clark.

Seven Conversions

in a family of ten persons occurred after one of the night meetings, which had been addressed by the two Quaker brethren. The mother of the family and her youngest daughter had previously given their hearts to God. All the family, except one boy who was away at school, were however present at the meeting. The aged father had been a despiser of the Truth all his life, and the younger members of the family had resisted all appeals to seek Christ. At this night-meeting the father's heart was touched, and he went up to the seat in front of the platform, overcome with anxiety. His children were moved by the Holy Spirit also, and all the six, one after another, made their way to their father's side. The Rev. Mr. Couch gave them his whole attention, talking with them, quoting the promises, and praying earnestly. The scene was a very solemn one, the moon gleaming through the over-hanging foliage, and the silence of the still summer night broken by no sound but that of supplication. Sympathizing people stood and watched it, moved away and came again, drawn by the strange spectacle of a whole family together seeking entrance to the kingdom. It continued until near midnight, when a cry of praise and exultation was raised, and the throng of sympathetic spectators joined with the family in joyful thanks to God that all were saved.

A Wholesale Tea Merchant

from New York City was another to whom the camp-meeting will never cease to be a memorable place. He suffered long under deep conviction of sin. The light was long in penetrating a soul long sunk in carlessness and indifference. When, at last, it broke upon him, he uttered a cry of intense joy and remained kneeling, with his eyes closed. "Open your eyes, brother, and stand upon your feet," said the preacher who had been talking and praying with him. "Nay," said he, "I can see a thousand times better with my eyes closed. *I see Jesus!* Glorious, precious Saviour! How my soul loves Thee! Glory, glory to God in the Highest!"

WOMEN RANSOMED WITH IVORY.

WHEN the report was published that Major Barttelot had been murdered by Manyema carriers while on his way to find and relieve Mr. H. M. Stanley, the news was imperfectly understood by ordinary readers. But a letter from Mr. Graham Wilmot-Brooke, who recently returned from Stanley Pool, throws a ghastly light on the intelligence in its description of Manyema character. He says that the Manyemas are cannibals. When they can obtain a supply of guns and powder, they set off on a slave raid, feasting on the men they kill, and growing rich on the ransom of the female captives.

"Eye-witnesses, both English and Arab," says Mr. Brooke, "have assured me that it is a common thing, which they themselves have seen on passing through the Manyema camps, to see human hands and feet sticking out of their cooking-pots. To these men the Arabs issue fire-arms, and send them off to catch the human beings, with whom the ivory must be bought. Off go the man-eaters, with shouting and yelling and great jubilation. What follows is now too well known. The raid is over, the first unexpected volley usually rendering further opposition hopeless, the dead are cooked and eaten, the village is nothing but smouldering embers, the women and children are hurried off as prisoners to the Zanzibari camps, with rich stores of plunder, goats and fowls and plantains, and native canoes, and native furniture, far more than covering the cost of the raid. And now 'trade' begins. In a few days the unfortunate husbands and parents of the prisoners come out of the bush; they know what is wanted; they have to ransom their relatives with ivory, and, the price having been agreed upon, the poor creatures go off and collect it. When at last they have scraped it all together the prisoners are returned, and the remnants of a once populous town go off to find a new refuge.

"The Zanzibaris have an object in giving back the prisoners when the ransom is paid; they will do duty again. Hardly have the wretched fugitives settled down again, built some huts, and begun to plant, than the Manyemas sweep down on them afresh, and the whole process is gone through again, as the residents at Aruwimi camp can testify."

A RELIGION COLLECTOR.

IN a report from China published in the *Missionary Herald*, Mr. Smith, of Pang Chuang, gives this account of a Chinese lady who is now one of his most active helpers in his work: "She is a Shantung woman, though this, her present home, is in Chihli, sixty-five miles away. She learned to read when she was a girl. She has the true spirit of a Bible-woman, and has been the life of the movement there. She was the victim of severe persecution till last winter, being beaten every time she went to a meeting, to which she was obliged to go altogether by stealth. Her husband was very curious to know what it was that made her at once so obstinate and so much better behaved at home than before, and at length asked her. He was led through her earnestness to become an inquirer and was baptized at Pao-ting-fu last winter. He had previously told her that it was *no business of hers to 'collect religion' for the family*, and that if there was anything of that to be done he was the one to do it. This little band have a small sum laid by, with which they are hoping to get a little chapel at an out-station, and we are helping them a little with funds."

EDITORIAL COALS OF FIRE.

AN editor's revenge on his enemy is de scribed in the *Constitution*, of Atlanta, Ga. I states that some years ago the editor of a Ne York daily journal made the acquaintance of wealthy and fashionable man about town. Th two, after a period of friendly relations, had violent quarrel. The editor, believing himse deeply wronged, contented himself with igno ing his enemy, but the latter took a mor aggressive course. He availed himself of ever opportunity of annoying and injuring the ed tor, and finally gave him such provocation tha a duel was fought. The combat was stoppe before either was injured, but the two parted i bitter enmity. Soon afterward the editor wa relieved by hearing that his enemy had quitte New York. He heard nothing more of hi until recently, when among his press despatche was one stating that his enemy had been arres ed in a distant city for trying to shoot a police man, and that he had lost all his property. Th despatch also stated that the bail was fixed a $5,000, and had been procured with difficulty as it was feared that the man would make h escape to avoid the long term of imprisonmer o which he would surely be sentenced. The ditor was deeply moved. Before the day was ver he telegraphed his agent in that city to ive the bondsmen the five thousand dollars or which they were liable, and to notify the riminal that he might fly without entailing oss on his friends. The man was completely vercome by his enemy's magnanimity, and he urried to New York to express his gratitude. Though he has escaped punishment for his ffence, his life shows that he is in danger of ternal punishment. It is much to be wished hat he might learn that in that case, too, One f whom he is still an enemy has paid the dread orfeit for him, and waits for him to avail himelf of the sacrifice. (Rom. 5: 8.)

PROPHECY IN THE PENTATEUCH.

By Rev. W. J. Erdman, D. D.

THERE are certain expressions in these five ooks of the Bible which involve the Personal nd Pre-millennial Coming of Christ; their fulllment demands a time or

A Dispensation Still Future

o us. Especially in Genesis are found the seeds nd beginnings and typical forms of all the fulilments and consummations of the great Mesianic future, revealed in the Apocalypse.

In Genesis 3: 15 is the germ and mysterious utline of all prophecy concerning the enmity nd conflict of the two seeds whose representaives have been in all ages, but whose final personal manifestations are only two, and to appear n a time, a crisis toward which the race is rapidy moving. This crisis is coincident with the eturn of our Lord.

In Genesis 3: 24 is evidently implied a guarding, but much more a keeping and preserving of the tree of life; and yet later scriptures tell when and by whom the way to it shall e opened again, and

Eve's Great Primal Hope,

Gen. 4: 1, of a Restorer of a paradise lost, at ast after weary, waiting centuries, fulfilled.

In Genesis 5 : 24 is found the brief note ouching a man who by thousands of years anicipated the highest form of redemption; that waiting such as shall be alive at our Lord's eturn. Such translation even possible then, 17. 2; 35: 13. In the light of typical and prophetic criptures it is evident Enoch lived in the beinning of the crisis of the world before the Flood. His prophecy in Jude is of the Coming n judgment and as preceded by a translation.

In Genesis 5: 29 comes before us the man who assed through that crisis. His deliverance was arthly, that of Enoch heavenly; one vertical, he other horizontal; the one corresponding to he rapture, the other to the apocalypse in udgment; one of heavenly calling, the other arthly, yet both the men of God. He too was ooked upon as the bringer of the promised rest, he remover of the curse; but the greater than Noah is yet to come; and before He comes and hen He comes the corruption and the judgment of the world shall be as in the days of Noah, Gen. 6: 5–8. In Genesis 12: 1; 22: 18,

The Seven-fold Promise

o Abraham and his seed contains the most agnificent hope ever known among men, and he secret consequently of all the contentions nd crafty plottings in the patriarchal families. And the promise of land and heirship of the orld still belong to Him, the Seed of Abraham, ho once came to His own possessions and His wn people received Him not, but who in due ime will come again, to be acknowledged as eir and Lord at last.

In Genesis 14: 8, is seen the priest king like nto Him who shall sit a priest upon his throne, ossessor of heaven and earth, Abraham's seed nd Abraham's priest. In Genesis 49: 10 all he promises of Genesis concentrate and culinate concerning the Shiloh, the Prince of Peace, the Lion of the tribe of Judah, unto hom the gathering of the peoples shall be.

In Exodus 3: 14, 15; 6: 2, 3 is given the great emorial name to be forever attached to the verlasting covenant as the pledge of all fulfilments, and these as seen in Genesis lie in the great Messianic age to come.

In Numbers 24: 7–9 is foreseen the King and kingdom to be exalted. In 24: 16–24 is outlined the whole course of human history until Messiah comes again.

In Deuteronomy 18: 15–19, is foretold the great Prophet who would speak with authority, who once came and spoke on earth, who is still speaking from heaven, and who is coming again to judge them who obey not His gospel. (Acts 3: 22, 23.) In Deuteronomy 32: 1–43 we have the "compendious outline and the common

"Key to all Prophecy"

(Delitzsch). It is the mould of Jewish and Gentile history; it confirms (32: 8, 9) Israel as the head and heart of the human family; it foresees Israel's apostasies to Gentile idols and Israel's punishments by Gentile hands; it declares the unchanging mercy of God according to the promises made to the fathers, and announces the judgments in turn to come upon the proud, self-deifying Gentile oppressors and usurpers, who after all were only Jehovah's hammers, and saws and axes and scourges; and finally through Israel's deliverance and blessings as the people of God and of the Messiah, the Rock and Stone of Israel, all the blessings foretold in Eden, all afterward promised to Noah, to Shem, to Eber, to Abraham, shall come upon all the nations.

To conclude, we find then in the Pentateuch touching the

Personal and Pre-Millennial

coming of the Lord the very teachings of the later and fuller scriptures of the prophets and apostles, even the Prophet, the Priest, and the King yet to come; and accordingly the final bruising of Satan, the restoration of the tree of life, and both as preceded by the momentous preparatory events of the millennial day; the Enoch-like rapture of the Church, and the Noah-like deliverance of Israel (Isa. 26: 20), the restoration of Israel to imperial pre-eminence over a consolidated world of nations under Messiah, the Lion of the tribe of Judah, the Star out of Jacob; the fulfilments of the promise to Abraham and his seed as the heir of the world (Rom. 4: 13); and the Melchizedek priesthood of a harmonized heaven and earth when in the name of Jesus as Lord over all every knee shall bow and every tongue shall sing to the glory of God the Father. (Phil. 2: 9–11.)

MILITARISM A PROPHETIC SIGN.

By the Rev. E. J. Hytche.

OUR Lord, in answer to the question of His disciples (Matt. 24: 3–8), "What shall be the sign of Thy coming? and of the end of the age," or dispensation, pre-reported some physical as well as moral and social signs which would indicate its proximity. Amongst the political signs were these (5: 6, 7). "Ye shall hear of wars, and *rumors* of wars: for nation shall rise against nation, and kingdom against kingdom. All these are the *beginning* of sorrows."

What Have We Seen?

In 1870–71 there was a life-and-death struggle between France and Germany, whereby Alsace and Lorraine were torn from France, and which as a fatal legacy has sown the seeds of that *future war of revenge in which Germany will doubtless be defeated by France.*

Far indeed, unhappily, from there being any signs of universal peace, the *whole* of Europe is so disturbed by "rumors of wars," that, as predicted (Luke 21: 26) all thinking "men's hearts are failing them for fear, and for looking after those things which are coming on this earth." The mechanical and chemical forces of the world, in fact, appear to be concentrated on forging such weapons of destruction as render a modern battle-field a veritable Aceldama. Nor is this all; for as conscription is the rule throughout Europe—England *for the present* excepted—the manhood of Europe is taken from the plough and the loom, in order to fit it to wade in human gore. Yes, every man (Cant. 3: 8) "hath his sword on his thigh, because of fear in the night" of this dispensation.

I have said that never in the chequered history of this world have there been such

Gigantic Armies

as during these, the closing years of this nineteenth century. For example, Russia has no less than 750,000 soldiers on the peace-footing, whilst in the event of its declaring that war which every statesman expects sooner or later, it can count upon upwards of 5,000,000 armed men. France, too, has already 2,000,000 enrolled in its army, and is increasing its forces every year with the view of reclaiming the two provinces forcibly annexed by Germany in 1871. Austria and Italy have each about 2,000,000 of soldiers; and England, including its Indian army, has about 500,000.

According to the *Révue Générale de l'Etat major*, than which there is no better authority as to military statistics, the European armies on the war-footing have increased since 1869 from 6,918,000 men to 16,000,000. Under the new military laws, actually existing or proposed, it estimates that the European war-footing will soon be 19,000,000 armed men. As might be supposed, the cost of these armaments annually is enormous, for about $750,000,000 are expended on the military and navies.

Painful, however, as are these facts, they only verify the truths of predictions uttered two thousand five hundred years ago. Hence it is that at a period when so much scorn is thrown upon the prophecies of the Old Testament, respecting the latter days, we see its

Truths Vindicated

even in these our days. For example, Joel was instructed by the Holy Spirit to write (3: 9–14): "Proclaim ye this among the *Gentiles*—prepare war; wake up the mighty men; let all the men of war draw near; let them come up: Beat your ploughshares into swords and your pruninghooks into spears." In response to this proclamation of war, we learn that there will be "multitudes in the valley of Jehoshaphat."

Prominent among these armed men will be

The Wild Hordes of Central Asia.

Hence we read (Jeremiah 51: 27, 28), "Blow the trumpet among the Gentiles; prepare the Gentiles against her [revived Babylon]; call together the kingdoms of Ararat, Minni, and Ashchenaz: cause the horses to come up as the rough caterpillars: prepare against her the Gentiles, with the kings of all the Medes, the captains thereof, and all the rulers thereof." As Russia is already dominant in Central Asia, and is incorporating one wild tribe after another in its dominions, we cannot but infer that it will necessarily become their leader in the last invasion of the Holy Land by Gog—the then autocrat of Russia. Hence we read that among the many nations which will accompany him in this invasion will be (Ezek. 38: 1–9) *Persia*. So vast will be his forces that he will (5: 9) "ascend like a storm, and be like a cloud to cover the land, he and all his armies, and the many peoples with him."

Looking, then, at the present military forces of Christendom alone, and the vast increase in their number every year—Prussia alone having added to its standing army no less than 70,000 this very year—we can see how literally true is the prophetic forecast of these last days. And thus the Old Testament is so vindicated by what is now passing around us, that it can only be a Satanic delusion, that any man can doubt for a moment its frightful picture of the fast coming national woes.

[*It will be seen from the above remarks that already preparations are far advanced for the fearful conflict, which the study of prophecy leads us to believe will break out during the ensuing eighteen months, and involve all the nations of Europe.*—ED.]

CHRISTIAN HERALD AND SIGNS OF OUR TIMES.

OFFICE, 63 BIBLE HOUSE, NEW YORK.

ENTERED AT THE POST-OFFICE AT NEW YORK, N. Y., AS SECOND-CLASS MATTER.

EVERY NUMBER CONTAINS:

The Portrait and Biography of some eminent person.
The Sermon Dr. Talmage preached the last Sunday morning.
An Exposition of Unfulfilled Prophecy.
A Summary of the Events of the Week, Notes of Religious and Temperance Movements, etc.
A Sermon by Rev. C. H. Spurgeon, of London, from advance sheets sent by special arrangement.
Pictures of Missionary Life, etc., and Descriptive Articles.
An instalment of a Serial Story.
An Exposition of the International Sunday-School Lesson, by Mrs. M. Baxter.

ANNUAL SUBSCRIPTION, $1.50.
Single Copies, Price Three Cents, may be obtained by order of any Newsdealer.

CURRENT EVENTS.

Congress Disposed of the Last Obstacle to an adjournment, except the tariff bill, on October 10, when the House agreed to the conference report on the Deficiency Appropriation Bill. It is probable, therefore, that this week will see the end of the session. Members are anxious to get away to their own States to take part in the campaign, and so many have already gone, that it is difficult to maintain a quorum. The only important legislative event of the week was the presentation in the Senate of a report from the select committee appointed to investigate the operations of the Civil-Service law. Senator Hale presented it, and the Senate ordered it to be printed. As might be expected, it is a severe arraignment of the Administration for its unfaithfulness to the cause of civil-service reform. The President cannot complain of the investigation, *if it has been done fairly*, because a large number of independent voters supported him four years ago on that and no other ground. His opponents, therefore, were justified in exposing any infractions of his pledges, if they could find them, and active politicians of either party may be trusted not to miss the opportunity in such a case. The report is a bulky document of fifty pages, and is very unequivocal in tone. It charges that "the letter of the law has been repeatedly evaded, and its spirit uniformly violated," and that, too, with the connivance of the President or members of the Cabinet. It deals mainly with the civil service in New York, Pennsylvania, Maryland, and Indiana, and charges "active partisanship," removal of Union soldiers, appointments of drunken and incapable clerks, and the assessment of office-holders. Unless some friend of the Administration with access to materials compiles an exhaustive and convincing document in reply, the President will find very few of George William Curtis's league voting for him again next month.

The Alarming Labor Struggle which Developed in Chicago last week caused general apprehension throughout that city. The employees on the North-side cable-road, some five hundred in number, went on strike October 6. The company of which Mr. C. T. Yerkes is president promptly secured drivers and conductors to operate the road with horses instead of by cable. The new men had to be protected by the police, and the strikers, though evidently dangerous, abstained from violence, but embarrassed the new men by placing obstructions on the tracks, kindling bonfires there, and upsetting bricks, etc., in the way. As Mr. Yerkes is president also of the West-side lines, the two thousand men employed there showed their sympathy with their fellow-workmen on October 9 by going on strike. The West-side men made no complaint on their own account as to hours or pay, but notified the company that they should hold out until the demands of the North-side men were granted. On that day there were several fights, and the police had to use their batons in the charges on the strikers. There were few cars run, and the public used any vehicle available, or walked. On October 10, two officers of the company, who rode out in front of a car, were set upon by a howling mob, throwing stones and threatening them with death. Both officers, and the police protecting them, used their revolvers to save their lives. On Thursday the trouble increased. Cars were smashed, rails torn up, dynamite cartridges laid on the tracks, and severe fighting in many places. The police are apprehensive of a still further extension of the trouble by the accession of sympathizers from other trades, and fear that, unless the company yields, there will be much bloodshed.

Though Slightly Better News Comes from Jacksonville, Fla., the scourge is evidently still rampant, and death, sickness, and destitution are afflicting the community. The daily record of deaths last week varied from nine to two, and of new cases from ninety-three to thirty-three. On October 10 *a bride was seized* with the dreaded premonitory chill while receiving the congratulations of her friends at the conclusion of the wedding ceremony. She received prompt medical attention, and it is believed that she will recover. The frost is anxiously looked for. One encouraging item of news received a glad welcome in the city on Tuesday. It was contained in a letter from Surgeon-General Hamilton to Dr. Porter, informing him of the intention of the Government to establish a public disinfection house in the city and asking for suggestions in regard to it. The hopes of the people were raised by the news. They have been longing for the time when the stores would be again opened and labor would be resumed. It has been dreary work living on charity, and the hardships of the camps have been very severe. With the disinfection house established, there will be a prospect of better things, and those outside the city can return. Last week the relief committee fed 10,688 persons daily.

The Appalling Railroad Disaster on the Lehigh Valley road at Mud Run, near White Haven, Penn., on October 10, directs public attention to the conduct of railroad companies in employing engineers unfit for their duties. The annual convention of Father Mathew societies was being held at Hazleton, and so large was the crowd of visitors from Luzerne and Lackawanna counties that seven long trains were required to carry them, and these were crowded to the doors. The journey there was made safely, but in returning in the evening, shortly after 5 o'clock, the sixth train had reached Mud Run, and was standing on the track when the seventh train ran into it. The heavy engine ploughed its way into the crowded car, telescoping it with the next car, and throwing the third car up on its forward end, and then its boiler burst. The horrors of the scene are beyond description. One hundred and forty men, women, and children scalded, crushed, and mangled, every one in the three cars more or less hurt, and groups of relatives and friends around watching the awful carnage, but unable to extricate the wounded. Axes were found at length, but it was terrible work cutting through the walls of the telescoped cars, and the cries of the wounded warned the workers of the danger of incautious blows in the darkness. When the work was done, *fifty-seven dead bodies* were taken out of the wreck, twenty-five badly injured persons were sent to hospital, and a crowd of the less seriously hurt went to their homes. The engineer of the seventh train escaped with a sprained ancle, and it is he of whom public opinion demands an explanation of the catastrophe. The red danger signals were burning, and could be seen nearly a mile away, and it is stated that a flagman with a red lamp was sent back from the sixth train as an additional precaution to stop the seventh. How it was that the signals were unheeded is a mystery. Whether the engineer was asleep, or intoxicated, or was not looking ahead, is not disclosed, but strict inquiry will doubtless be made.

The Growing Tendency in England Toward federation found expression on October 10 in a speech by Lord Rosebery, Mr. Gladstone's ex-Secretary of State. Speaking in Leeds on the Canadian Fishery difficulty, Lord Rosebery advocated the appointment of a non-political Foreign Secretary, who should speak with the united voice of the English people, without distinction of party. He said that England's colonial policy was becoming more and more involved with her foreign policy, and that if she wished to retain her colonies she must admit them to a larger share in promoting the influence of England in foreign affairs. In connection with this idea comes a statement that in the fall of 1885 a well-known Gladstonian ecclesiastic laid before Mr. Gladstone a plan for electing National Parliaments at London, Dublin, Carnarvon, and Edinburgh. Mr. Gladstone asked if the Scotch would accept it. "Perhaps not the Scotch members," replied the ecclesiastic, "but certainly the Scotch people." Mr. Gladstone's reply was that the Irish question demanded settlement before the larger question of federation.

The French Government has Issued a Decree regulating the proceedings of foreign visitors to that country. The Paris correspondent of the New York *Herald* states that in a total population of 37,930,759 there were, two years ago, not less than 1,126,531 foreigners in the country. It is therefore fair to assume that for every thirty Frenchmen, France to-day counts at least one resident stranger enjoying all the advantages of citizenship without any corresponding share of its burdens or responsibilities, and this proportion is increasing with extraordinary rapidity. French authorities regard this state of things with dissatisfaction, as the mass of these strangers show little disposition to identify themselves with the country. A decree has therefore been promulgated, requiring all resident foreigners to give an account of themselves to the Prefect of Police. It is aimed at the vast influx of the lowest strata of society from all nations, who are gradually making France an asylum for the thieves, vagabonds, and outcasts of other countries. Moreover, most of these foreign tramps come from two nations which France most hates—Germany and Italy. American visitors will be required to make only a formal registration.

Dr. Mackenzie's Vindication of His Treatment of the late Emperor Frederick was given out last week for publication. The British *Medical Journal* gives long extracts from it, in which the Doctor says that he was not deceived in his patient's real condition, of which there was ample proof. The German doctors made this charge, knowing it to be false, in order to prejudice Frederick against his British adviser. At the beginning of October, 1887, Dr. Bergmann admitted that Dr. Mackenzie's course was correct. The visit of Frederick to England was arranged before Dr. Mackenzie was summoned. Dr. Mackenzie does not hesitate to say that the death blow was given to the Emperor on April 12, when a false passage made by Dr. Bergmann's tube caused extensive suppuration around the trachea, which steadily drained away the Emperor's remaining strength and shortened his life at least ten months. Except when the false passage was made and Dr. Bergmann thrust his finger into the wound, the Emperor never suffered actual pain.

A Disastrous Inundation in China is Reported in advices by a steamer which arrived in San Francisco on October 8. The chief scene of devastation is in the Province of Moukden, about three hundred and fifty miles northeast of Pekin, where the overflow caused the death of hundreds of the natives, the utter annihilation of very many homes, the destruction of crops, and the prospect of a general famine for the coming winter. The whole of the new embankment of the Yellow River, at Chang Chou, begun last autumn, and carried on at a cost equal to over $9,000,000, has been completely swept away by the flood. Of the eight thousand lineal feet of river wall which has been completed, not one inch remains, and the waters are pouring unchecked through the immense gap into Honan. From eight hundred to one thousand laborers, who were on the bank, were swept away and drowned.

The McAll Mission in Paris has Just Acquired room for its work in the Rue St Antoine which as a remarkable history. On the site of the gar- n of the palace of a Queen Blanche, about one undred years ago a ballroom was built, called the al de la Reine Blanche. It was largely frequent- d by artists and their models, and was thus used ll the year 1844. Then it was, for a few years, rned into a billiard-room, to be re-opened as dancing-saloon, under the name of the Salle ivoli, of a lower kind than before. It was then ed three or four times a week, especially on undays, and the worst class of society frequent- d it. It was also a meeting-place for the anar- hists. More than once has Louise Michel made er passionate appeals from its platform. In ct, the hall had about as bad a name as could e for low society and for tumultuous political atherings. It is a fine building, well arranged, nd will seat, with the galleries, 800 people.

An English Convert to Prohibition has Re- ently been made. The editor of a prominent eligious journal, who has heretofore advocated igh license, local option, and other ineffectual emedies for the liquor curse, paid a visit to this ountry a month ago. On his return he prompt- y ran up the Prohibition colors in the following ditorial paragraph: "At first sight Local Option eems more reasonable, more feasible, more prac- cal than Prohibition. It even seems more fair to hose who do not think as we do. But the more e think, the more evident is it that the drink raffic is an offense against God and man. No egislative act could do so much good by pre- enting so much evil as the absolute prohibition f this pernicious trade. But it is constantly aid that Parliament can do nothing until pub- c opinion is educated up to it. How, then, ill public opinion be the more speedily educat- d? By such devices as Local Option on the one and, or High License on the other; or by af- rming the principle that the traffic is evil, and emanding its prohibition? Surely by the lat- er. We shoot higher, aiming at the stars."

The Discovery of Pearls in Kentucky is An- nounced in the Louisville *Courier-Journal*. It tates that the attention of State Geologist Proctor was recently called to some peculiarly eautiful stones found by some boys in the imestone regions of the State, and he immedi- tely pronounced them to be pearls of singular urity. He has now taken hold of the work, nd is laboring to have the resource developed or its full worth. The pearls have been found n no less than twelve counties. They are of reat value to jewelers, who can utilize to great dvantage all the pearls of shape and size they et. Some of the stones are very beautiful when ouched up by the jeweler. Hundreds of beau- iful stones have no doubt been found by the oys along the banks, who, after keeping them or a few days as a "pretty thing," would throw hem away ignorant of what they had found. But Mr. Proctor's report will show them the rue worth of these pearls, and more systematic earches will be made. It would be well if the Church of Christ were similarly awakened to the rue value of jewels which, in the shape of hu- man souls, are lying around neglected, but which, if won for Christ, would add to the glory of His crown. (Mal. 3:17.)

An Unguarded Valuable Gem Outside a eweller's store on Broadway, New York, attract- d public attention recently. Some time ago, he jeweller, who had found a ready sale for olished blocks of petrified wood, heard that arge pieces of it were being found at Chalce- lony Park, Arizona. A member of the firm went ut to secure specimens, and soon after his arri- al notified his partners that he had succeeded n purchasing the very largest piece that had ver been found. He sent it on to New York, nd it was deposited on the sidewalk in front of he store, where it remained for several days. Customers, who had been accustomed to the ight of pieces about the size of a silver dollar, were amazed by this gigantic specimen, which was a cube measuring over thirty-three inches ach way, and *weighed two tons*. The polished surface showed a beautiful blending of yellow and black, with some tints resembling those of the red wood of the big California trees. It was so hard that two hundred blocks of marble could be cut up while one block of the agitized wood was cut. The gem belongs to the class known as chalcedony. It is believed that there is in existence no gem to equal it in size or beauty, but the time is now near at hand when that and all other precious stones will be eclip- sed as men see descending out of heaven the city which John saw in prophetic vision, the wall of which rested on twelve jewels the third of which was a chalcedony. (Rev. 21:19.)

A Cruel Execution for Witchcraft took Place recently in California. Ranchers who have been in the eastern part of St. Bernardino Coun- ty, state that during the past two months the Indians of the Mojave tribe have suffered from an epidemic which has carried off many of their bravest men. They slaughtered dogs and bur- ros to appease the wrath of the Great Spirit, but without avail. Finally a council was held, which resolved on offering a human sacrifice. Believing that the epidemic was produced by "the black art," they caught a male pigeon and his mate, and administered to both a de- coction of herbs. The male flew away, but the female fluttered and fell to the ground. The in- ference the red men drew was that the guilty person was a squaw, and they drove their women past the dying bird, while the medicine-men watched. As the women went by, a young squaw stepped out of the rank and attempted to pick up the bird. Her act was deemed proof that she was the woman guilty of witchcraft. She was seized, dragged to the council-place, and burned to death. The Indians expect that the sacrifice of the squaw will propitiate the Great Spirit, and the scourge will be stayed. If, as is stated, the disease is malignant typhoid fever, their removal to another district was the reme- dy needed, not the death of the squaw. Chris- tian teachers must be sadly needed among them to teach them that cruel sacrifices cannot rem- edy physical evils, and that for their great spir- itual malady of sin, one Sacrifice has been offer- ed for the sins of the whole world. (Rom. 3:25.)

The Strange Reconciliation of Two Rival suitors is described in the *Americus Republican*. It states that in a southwestern town two young men had been warm friends from child- hood. They were almost like brothers. Nothing occurred to disturb their friendship until the advent of a very beautiful girl, with whom both fell in love. They soon hated each other more intensely than they had formerly loved. They never met but they reviled and cursed each oth- er. At length words were spoken that could have but one result. They agreed to have a duel in the woods, and the time and place were arranged. One of the duelists passed a restless, miserable time before the hour fixed. His wretchedness would not let him eat or sleep. He was at the appointed place long before the time, and sat down to wait for his enemy. It was a hot afternoon in August, and the man, wearied out, fell asleep. He was awakened by the report of a pistol, and, looking up, he saw his rival standing near him, with his smoking weapon in his hand. At his feet was a large, venomous snake writhing in death agony. "John," said the awakened man, "you have saved my life, let us be friends. I give the girl up to you." "No," said the other, "when I saw that snake about to strike you, I found I loved you still, and I, too, give up the girl. Let us be friends." They shook hands and returned to- gether. A reconciliation so romantic is not often recorded, but many cases occur in which one who is rescued from the power of Satan, who is called the old serpent, finds hate climi- nated from his heart, and makes peace with his enemies. (1 John 3:14-16.)

A Mother's Intense Devotion to a Wicked son has achieved his release from prison in Baltimore, Md. Four years ago a young man, the son of an eminent physician in New York State, wound up a long series of disgraceful performances by the commission of a murder. He had gone on an excursion of sinful pleasure to Baltimore, where, in the midst of a drunken orgie, he slew one of his companions in sin. He was arrested and tried. His mother visited him in prison, engaged the best lawyers for his de- fence, and made prodigious exertions to save his life and liberty. Largely through her efforts his neck was saved from the noose, but he was sentenced to a long term of imprisonment. The mother continued her labors in his behalf, and has ever since been untiring in her efforts to get him a pardon. She hunted out the members of the jury that convicted her son, and obtained the signatures of ten of them to a petition to the Governor for his release. She pleaded with the judge who tried the case, and with the State's attorney, and by her persistent pleading won their signatures to her petition. She even gained the intercession of Governor Hill, of New York. Then she presented it to Governor Jackson, and begged as a mother for her son's liberty. On July 19, the Governor yielded, and to her intense joy, her four years of labor were crowned with success, and she returned to her home in triumph, taking her son with her. Not one of the men who signed the petition, nor the Governor who granted it, has a particle of sympathy for the son, who is said to be utterly worthless, but they yielded to the mother's im- portunities for her sake. It is so that the sinner obtains his pardon, not for his own merits, but because of what Jesus has done and suffered on his behalf. (1 John 2:12.)

BRIEF NOTES.

Rev. George C. Needham passed through New York last week on his way to Ireland, to commence an evan- gelistic tour.

The Rev. Dr. Spear has resigned the position of treasurer of Madison University, after having held it for twenty-five years.

More than three hundred delegates attended the recent Conference of the Young People's Christian Endeavor Societies of New York State in Elmira.

A revival has been going on simultaneously in different parts of Japan. It is estimated that as a result the in- crease of membership in the churches of Tokio cannot be much less than a thousand.

The Mormons are acquiring large tracts of land in Mexico by quiet purchase from private parties. The purchases have been made in agricultural lands in the valley of the Casas Grande River.

At the last meeting of the American Institute of Chris- tian Philosophy, the Rev. John C. Clyde, D. D., of Bloomsbury, New Jersey, read a paper entitled "The Christian Temper and Scientific Thought."

Tobacco is to be shut out at the Chambersburg, Pa., academy. No boy will be admitted who uses it in any way. It is prohibited to day and boarding pupils alike on the ground that it injures mind and health.

The General Conference of the Evangelical Alliance will meet in Montreal from the 22d to the 25th of Octo- ber. Its sessions will be held in the Crescent Street and the American Presbyterian churches of that city.

Both of Mr. Moody's Northfield schools are obliged to refuse entrance to an army of applicants for whom there is no room. The Mount Hermon school for boys has 318 students, and there are 300 girls at the Northfield Seminary.

The third annual convention of Christians interested in Christian work among the unevangelized classes in the cities and towns of America, will be held in the Taber- nacle M. E. Church, Detroit, Mich., for six days, No- vember 15 to 20, inclusive.

A correspondent writes to the Norwich *Bulletin*: "Permit me to say that there is no town in Connecticut without a church in which regular Sunday services are maintained. There is only one town (Beacon Falls) in which there is not a Congregational church."

In an address delivered by the Rev. D. A. Reed, in Springfield, Mass., at a reception upon his return from a European trip, Mr. Reed said that he found in the Scandinavian countries, Norway and Sweden, that the people had a peculiar reverence for the Gospel. The churches were all very large, having a seating capacity of between 3,000 and 4,000. There were 100,000 Con- gregationalists and 15,000 Methodists in Stockholm.

FURTHER AFIELD.

A New Sermon by Pastor C. H. Spurgeon.

"Then Paul and Barnabas waxed bold, and said, It was necessary that the Word of God should first have been spoken to you; but seeing ye put it from you, and judge yourselves unworthy of everlasting life, lo, we turn to the Gentiles," etc. Acts 13 : 46–48.

Paul's Message Ill-Received—I. Rejection of Christ a Solemn Business—It was so for the Jewish Nation—Many Rejecters Now—Do Not Believe in the Resurrection—Reject the Evidence of Honest Men—Spots of Royal Blood on a Prayer-Book—An Experience with the Phonograph—II. The Rejection Led to a More Extended Effort—Are Example for the Church of To-day—III. Encouraged by the Fromise of God IV.—And by Speedy Success.

DEAR friends: Last Sabbath morning I tried to stir you up to sacred activity. I heard from many that they felt thoroughly aroused, and I know of some who at once commenced to speak for Christ. I wish I could hope that your whole company kept step together in this. If what is said on Sabbath were really carried out, what splendid advances we should make! But if not, it is as though a commanding officer spoke to his troop, and the men did not march according to orders. However, I am thankful for what was done, and for the many of you who did keep step together in an earnest march to conquer the powers of sin by making known the gospel of Jesus Christ. "They that were scattered abroad went everywhere preaching the Word," and I hope that you, as you scattered to your various abodes, did go everywhere teaching the Word of God

According to Your Capacity.

If so, you have already come far enough to have met with individuals upon whom your warnings and invitations have been spent in vain.

I thought it would be well for us this morning to go with Paul to Antioch, in Pisidia, and just see how he was treated there, and what he did when he met with an ill reception from the Jews, that we might not be discouraged if our message has been refused, but that we might be instructed by the example of Paul and Barnabas as to what we should do; and be comforted by the success which their perseverance achieved. The Jews of Antioch, after having heard Paul with considerable attention, made up their minds to refuse Jesus, the Son of David, and not to accept Him as their Messiah and Saviour.

I. Our first point for consideration will be that the rejection of Christ is

A Very Solemn Business.

It has been a very solemn business for the Jewish nation. The history of the Jews since their rejection of our Lord may be written in blood and tears. No Gentile should read it without ten thousand blushes, for they have been evil entreated by all the nations, though through them the greatest blessing that ever came to men has come to us. Never should we forget that our Redeemer is of the seed of Israel. Yet, when the chosen people rejected Jesus deliberately, from that day a history of woe and sorrow began, which has gone on even to this day. Oh, that they had received the Messiah! I shall not attempt to picture what would have been their history if they had accepted the Son of David as their Lord. I am bound to talk about a people nearer home, about some here present, who have refused the Saviour. Perhaps they will say, at the very outset, "We have not done so; we will receive Him one day." Yes, but you refuse Him *now*. If you do not now believe in Him, you have up till now rejected Him.

This you have done as they did at Antioch, against the evidence of honest men. They doubted whether Christ had really risen from the dead, although His resurrection was attested by hundreds of true witnesses. My unconverted hearer, if you do not believe in the Lord Jesus Christ, and in the work which was crowned by His rising from the dead, you set aside the witness of apostles, saints, and martyrs. The number of martyrs has been very great from that day till now, but you set aside the testimony borne by their lives and death. You also impute foolishness or deceit to your dearest friends, some of whom are with God, and who died in the faith, exhorting you to believe in Jesus Christ. Indeed, you make all of us who preach the gospel to be liars; and we are not so; neither do you think so badly of us when we speak in every-day life. We shall not be gainers by your conversion, nor losers by your ruin; but we love you, and therefore pray you to believe those necessary truths without which you can never enter the kingdom of heaven.

These people next did violence to Christ Himself and His precious blood. It does seem amazing to those of us who love Jesus and worship Him that any should reject Him. He comes so tenderly, so meekly, the Lamb of God! All that He does is so generous, so self-denying, that we marvel that you refuse Him. "He taketh away the sin of the world"; why does the world despise Him? What has He done that you should refuse to become His disciples and accept His salvation? Do you not know that you do despite to His blood? To me there is a great sanctity about the blood of man. I saw last Wednesday the prayer-book which Bishop Juxon held in his hand as he stood by the side of Charles I. on the scaffold at Whitehall. There are two

Spots of Blood on the Page

wherein he was reading the prayers as the axe fell upon the monarch's neck. *I have no reverence for Charles I.*, but I have reverence for drops of blood. I looked at them, and they were no theme of jest for me: the blood of a man is sacred. But what shall I say of the blood of the Son of God! God Himself, incarnate, in some mysterious manner taking into union with Himself our humanity, and then shedding His blood to redeem us! What is to be said of this? Look with reverence upon that precious blood.

These people had to do despite to all the marvels which lie wrapped up in the gospel. To us, my dear hearers, who believe in Jesus, the gospel is the most wonderful thing that can ever be. The more we know of it, the more astounded we are at it. It is a compound of divine and infinite things. When we study it, we go from wonder to wonder. Here we behold the heart of God, and hear the voice of His infinite tenderness, His infallible wisdom, His stern justice, and His supreme beneficence. How can all this be rejected by you? Surely, you do not know what is in the gospel, or you would hearken to its every tone. I sat yesterday with *two tubes in my ears* to listen to sounds that came from revolving cylinders of wax. I heard music, though I knew that no instrument was near. It was music which had been caught up months before, and now was ringing out as clearly and distinctly in my ears as it could have done had I been present at its first sound. I

Heard Mr. Edison Speak:

he repeated a childish ditty; and when he had finished, be called upon his friends to repeat it with him; and I heard many American voices joining in that repetition. That wax cylinder was present when these sounds were made, and now it talked it all out in my ear. Then I heard Mr. Edison at work in his laboratory: he was driving nails, and working on metal, and doing all sorts of things, and calling for this and that with that American tone which made one know his nationality. I sat and listened, and I felt lost in the mystery. But what of all this? What can these instruments convey to us? But oh, to sit and listen to the gospel when your ears are really opened! Then you hear God Himself at work; you hear Jesus speak: you hear His voice in suffering and in glory, and you rise up and say, "I never thought to have heard such strange things! Where have I been, to be so long deaf to this? I pray you, do not despise it. Be not such dull, driven cattle that, when God has set before you what angels desire to look into, you close your eyes to such glories, and pay attention to the miserable trifles of time and sense.

This rejection of the gospel of Christ is the more grievous because it is a decided act of the will. When a man refuses to be saved, it is his own act and deed. Nothing in Scripture will support us in throwing the blame elsewhere. The devil himself cannot refuse Christ for a man; he must do *that* for himself. *Only yourself can bolt the door* against yourself. There is a will in man, and it

Is a Sadly Perverse Will,

so that the Saviour said of it, "Ye will not come to Me, that ye might have life." The not coming of which the Lord complains is a direct act of the man's own will. You choose to sin; you choose to remain uncleansed from guilt; you choose to abide under the wrath of God. You have deliberately chosen to be without Christ for years; and therein you are choosing your own destruction. This is a fearful thing.

Notice! We have here the rejection of Christ regarded as a man's own verdict upon himself. No man can claim a fairer jury than to let his own faculties sit in judgment upon himself. Listen! "Ye judge yourselves unworthy of everlasting life." This, then, is your own verdict, you who refuse the gospel. In looking the whole thing up and down, you have felt hither to that you were not the men to believe in Christ, you were not the women to be saved. You felt rather that you were the kind of people who should spend your zeal in attending the theatre or the dance. You felt that you best answered the end of your being when you did your daily labor, or opened your shop and saved a little money; but that you were not called upon to think of more high and heavenly things. You judged yourselves worthy to live a temporary life, and then, like beasts, to die and be no more; but an eternal destiny of glory and immortality you have not judged yourselves worthy to obtain. Remember, this is your own verdict upon yourself. If you deliberately prefer sin to Christ, and let go pardon, everlasting life, and heaven, who is to blame? Will you not curse yourselves to all eternity? and will not this be hell?

There stands the case; they put everlasting life from them, and judged themselves unworthy of it. What an unhappy state of things! It is too painful for me. I cannot speak longer upon it; I must hasten to my second point.

II. This rejection of Christ by some led to

A More Extended Effort.

When Paul and Barnabas found that their message was rejected, what did they do? They met the Jews with this bold sentence: "Seeing ye put it from you, and judge yourselves unworthy of everlasting life, lo, we turn to the Gentiles." In consequence of the ill manners of the Jews, they did not turn away from their work. It never entered their minds to give up their ministry because it did not succeed among these Jews. They did not say, "Lo, we turn away from preaching Jesus: we will speak no more in the name of the Lord." Neither, my brethren, may we speak thus. I know the heart grows sick when tender testimony is rejected. The constant reiteration of the same gospel, to ears that will not hear, becomes wearisome work. It needs great faith to go on from day to day ploughing a rock. Oh, shall we always have to cry to you in vain! Will you always be so perverse? Yet we dare not cease to plead with you. We cannot give you up. We overcome the suggestion of our weariness, "I will speak no more in the name of the Lord." For love of you the gospel is as fire in our bones, and we cannot cease to warn every man, and

Plead with Every Man for Jesus.

Instead of turning from the work, these holy men addressed themselves to those who had been somewhat neglected: "Lo, we turn to the Gentiles." Beloved, if you have been mainly laboring with the children of godly parents, and these refuse, turn you to the slum children. If you have tried to bless respectable people, and they remain unsaved, try those who are not respectable. That, I believe, is the Lord's mind toward the church of to-day. Let her break up sh soil, and she will have richer harvests. her open new mines, and she shall find rare hes. We too often preach within a little cir- where the message of life has already been ected scores of times. Let us not spend all time in knocking at doors from which we e been repulsed; let us try elsewhere. Dur- this new week, and throughout the rest of lives, let us

Seek After the Neglected,

utterly irreligious, the worldly and profane. rt not: I mean just what I say. Let the in- el and the superstitious be the object of our yers; let the frivolous and worldly be spoken h. This seems to me to be the parallel of ul's conduct when he turned to the Gentiles. There is this happy, and yet unhappy, circum- nce to urge us on—the outsiders are by far larger number. What were the Jews in mber as compared with the Gentiles? If you rk for Christ among those who are in our re- ious circles, and fail to win them, the field is world, and the larger part of that field has ver been touched as yet. We have labored London; but if London counts itself un- rthy of eternal life, let us think of Calcutta, nton, and the Congo. If these near ones will reward our endeavors, let us be of enter- sing spirit, and do as traders do, who, when y find no market at home, strike out new es. This is precisely what the text teaches us.

III. Thirdly, please notice that this enlarge- nt of effort was

Encouraged by the Promise

God. "For so hath the Lord commanded saying, I have set thee to be a light of the ntiles, that thou shouldest be for salvation to the ends of the earth." Let us notice s: God has set Jesus to be a light, and a ht He must be. God's appointment is no pty thing. No man thinks of setting up a ht if nobody will ever see it; and if God has pointed Christ to be a light, depend upon it me are to see that light. But all men are nd by nature. So, as the Lord has set Jesus be a light, you may be sure that He means to en blind eyes.

Our Lord is set to enlighten every class. The w no longer has a monopoly of the light of aven. God has not appointed His Son to ve a few dozen people who go to a particular eting-house. He has set Him to be a light the nations, and He means He shall be so. tis encourages us to labor among all classes. sus is a fit light for the upper ten thousand, d some of them shall rejoice in that light: He equally set to be a light to the teeming mil- ns, and they shall rejoice in Him, too.

The great Father has set Christ Jesus to be alvation unto the ends of the earth." So, en, if any are further off than others, they are ecially included. If any seem so far gone at they stand on the verge of creation, out of e reach of civilization and charity—these are e people whom Jesus is set to save. He can re to both ends of the earth, and all that lies between. To the most debauched, depraved, unken, and desperate, Jesus is set to be salva- on. From that poverty which has been ought on by vice, and that degradation which the consequence of sin, Jesus can uplift man- od. Where even the image of manhood seems literated, and the brute reigns supreme, the rd Jesus can set the superscription of God. the lost, Jesus is set to be a Saviour. The umphs of the gospel at the first were largely ong the lowest of the low. Slaves and out- sts embraced Christianity, and rose to holi- ss. It was by such that the Lord overthrew e idols of Greece and Rome. The Lord can rk such wonders again, and He will.

IV. Observe that this effort was

Encouraged by Speedy Success:

And when the Gentiles heard this, they were ad, and glorified the Word of the Lord: and many as were ordained to eternal life believ- . And the Word of the Lord was published roughout all the region."

First, the Gentiles were glad. We little guess with what joy the message of mercy would be received by those who had never yet heard it. Go, and see what it will do. How I should like a congregation of people who have never heard of Jesus Christ before! I should expect to have a blazing time of it, like the man who set light to a straw-stack, and found that he had a world of fire before him in no time. To hear of salvation by the blood of Jesus for the first time must be a sensation indeed! As for many of my hearers, they have heard of Jesus so long that the topic is stale. I feel you will never accept the Saviour, but will die in your sins. Those who have never heard of Jesus at all, often hear the gospel with great interest, and believe unto eternal life.

The Gentiles accepted the Word. They did not sit down and cavil and raise questions, and so forth; but it is written, "they were glad, and glorified the Word of the Lord." This is more than many ministers do. Look at our divines now! What are they doing? They are not glorifying the Word of God, but taking the glory from it. According to some of them the Word of God in His Book is full of blunders: how much less trustworthy must it be as it is preached! The

Shepherds are Now Destroying

the pastures. Holy Scripture, according to them, is not infallible. The sure word of testimony is no longer sure, according to modern ideas. With these I have no fellowship. O my soul, come not thou into their secret! Let us loathe such dishonoring of the Word of God. Let us get far away from all pretense of communion with these enemies of our faith.

Get among the poor, the lowly, the sinful. Tell them the glad news of pardon bought with blood. I warrant you they will not turn critics, and cavil and find fault; but they will, many of them, believe unto eternal life. The man who has grown accustomed to luxuries is

The Man who turns His Meat Over,

and picks off a bit here, and a bit there; for this is too fat, and that is too gristly. Bring in the poor wretches who are half-starved. Fetch in a company of laborers who have been waiting all day at the docks, and have found no work, and in consequence have received no wage. Set them down to a joint of meat. They find no fault: they never dream of such a thing. If the meat had been a little coarse, it would not have mattered to them; their need is too great for them to be dainty. Oh, for a host of hungry souls! How pleasant to feed them! How different from the task of persuading the satiated Pharisees to partake of the gospel!

I wish specially to speak to any here present who are not familiar with the gospel. I speak to rank outsiders, to people who know nothing of these things. "Believe on the Lord Jesus Christ, and thou shalt be saved"—

Saved at Once.

"But I never go to a place of worship." I mean exactly you, my friend. "But I have been a swearer." I am thinking of the blasphemer. "But I have been an awful drunkard." To you I speak this gospel. "Alas!" cries one, "I shrink from your eye. I crept in here this morning, but I am a daughter of shame." I say to you, even to you—"This is a faithful saying, and worthy of all acceptation, that Christ Jesus came into the world to save sinners." You are aimed at in the mission of Jesus. Trust Him, and you are saved. "But I have been violent against the gospel." You are the very man that I am specially looking for. I prayed for you before I came to this place; for I prayed that Saul of Tarsus might this day become Paul the apostle. I long to win, by this sermon, some outrageous enemy of God, that he may become a fervent friend of Jesus.

Oh, for a batch of great saints made out of great sinners! Oh, that your energy, now used to fight against God, may be subdued by sovereign grace, and employed in defending and spreading the gospel of Jesus! Shall it be so, my friend? Oh, that some woman that is a sinner, would come and wash our Lord's feet with tears, and wipe them with the hairs of her head! Come, you with long hair, unbind your tresses, and honor them by this service. If they have been a net in which to entangle precious lives, make them a towel for your Saviour's feet. Come, sinners, come to Him who loves you! Bring them, O Lord! Hear us, O Jehovah, as we entreat Thee to save them by the blood of Thy well-beloved Son! Hear us now, we beseech Thee, and save myriads! Amen.

GEMS FROM NEW BOOKS.

A LITTLE GIRL'S INQUIRY.*

"Papa, are you going to say anything to-day that I can understand?" asked a little girl of her father—a Massachusetts pastor—as he was setting out for church on a Sabbath morning. This tender appeal touched the loving father's heart, and he could not answer his daughter nay; he could not say to his child that she must sit in penance through all the long service, with never a word designed for her instruction or cheer. So, as he preached he said, "And now, children, I will say something to you about this." At once the face of every child in that audience brightened. Sleepy little ones started up; tired ones took fresh heart. Looking, first at the minister, then at each other, then back to him. They were all eagerness for his message, as though now there was something else for them than to nod and ache and yawn, uncared for; and although the pastor's following sentences to them were few and simple, doubtless many felt as did the child who pleaded for this attention, when, on her return at noon, she said, contentedly, "Papa, I understood all that you said this morning." Dear children! who wouldn't do as much as this for them in every sermon? They are gratified so easily.

A Child's Penetration.

Riding along a country road, on the borders of his parish, a Connecticut clergyman stopped to speak to a boy whom he saw there. After asking the boy's name, he attempted a little pastoral catechizing, after this sort: "Do you know who made you, boy?" "Yes, sir, God made me." "Where is God?" "In heaven, sir." "Isn't God anywhere else?" "I didn't know that He was, sir." "Well, my boy, God is not only in heaven, but He is everywhere else at the same time; and He can see you always, wherever you are." That was a new thought to that boy. It impressed him as a new thought. Pointing to a close-faced, heavy stone wall, near which he stood, the boy said, inquiringly: "Can God see through that stone wall?" "Yes, indeed," answered the pastor, "God can see through that wall. God can *go* through that wall." "*Go!*" responded the boy, instantly. "*Go!* I don't see how God can go at all, if He is everywhere to begin with!" "Ah!" said that pastor to me, as he told the story, "that boy had made the truth of God's omniscience more really his own, in those two minutes, than I had made it mine in the thirty years of my ministry." And it was because he was a child, that that boy received the truth of God as a child. To the minister, God's omniscience was a doctrine; to the child, it was a reality.

A Hawaiian Mother's Lesson.

I heard the Rev. Dr. Titus Coan, the veteran missionary to the Sandwich Islands, tell of seeing the native mothers among the Christian Hawaiians bring their infants in arms up to the church contribution-box and practice them there in giving money into the Lord's treasury. The mother would put a piece of money into the child's hand. With the instinct of nature—not of grace—the child's fingers would close tightly over the money, and hold it fast. Then the mother would take the child's arm by the wrist, and hold the little hand over the contribution-box, and with gentle firmness would shake the

* From "The Sunday-School: Its Origin, Mission, Methods, and Auxiliaries." By Dr. H. Clay Trumbull. An exhaustive treatise on the institution, and the duties of the teacher, superintendent, and pastor with regard to it, showing what it may do, if efficiently worked for the Church of Christ. 415 pages; Price $1.50. Published by *John D. Wattles*, Philadelphia.

Dr. Dwight, President of Yale College.

The Physician's Welcome Home.

hand until the grasp on the money was loosened, and the coin dropped into the box. The mother's loving smile and words of approval were the child's reward for its submissiveness, and the frequent repetition of this process brought the child to a certain enjoyment of winning his mother's commendation in this way, and of performing an act to which he was urged. Thus it was that before the child was able to go alone, he was in the habit of bearing a part in missionary giving; and by the whole course of his training, of which this was a portion, he found the blessing of being a giver in behalf of the Lord's cause.

A Connecticut Pastor's Need.

He was in conference with several of his ministerial brethren over a proposal to invite a well-known evangelist to labor in their immediate field. He expressed a readiness to co-operate in any such effort to promote the religious welfare of the community. "Well," said one of the ministers, "I hope the evangelist will come; for even if the time is not quite ripe for him, he may be the means of bringing in a few additions to our church-membership." "Oh, that's not what I'm hoping for," said this pastor, earnestly; "it is not any more members that I want, but it's improvement in those I have. Why, I would refuse an offer to-day of two hundred more of the average sort now in my church. But if an evangelist can stir up a few of those I have, and bring them up to a fair standard of Christian activity, I'll hold up both hands for his coming, and will sit up nights to pray for him."

DR. TIMOTHY DWIGHT,

President of Yale College.

THE eminent professor who is now President of Yale is the grandson of the famous scholar of that name who held the Presidency of the same institution from 1795 to 1817. His father, James Dwight, was a merchant living at Norwich, Conn., where the future president was born November 16, 1828. He is, therefore now nearly sixty years of age. He entered Yale College in 1845, and graduated with high honors four years afterward. He then spent two years in studying in the Divinity school, at the expiration of which he was chosen tutor in the college, and continued his work in that capacity until 1855, when he resigned. In the following year he went to Europe and spent two years in the universities of Germany, returning to America in 1858. His college promptly elected him to the chair of Sacred Literature and New Testament Greek in the Theological Seminary. This chair he filled for twenty-eight years, until his recent elevation to the Presidency of the college.

President Dwight is eminently qualified, by his personal and social gifts as much as by his profound learning, for the efficient discharge of the duties of his high position. He has the quality popularly known as magnetism, attaching to himself professors and students alike. His home in New Haven has always been known for its generous atmosphere. No man in Yale entertains so much as Professor Dwight. At the annual Commencement of the college his house is continually packed, and on every night of the week there is some reunion or other afoot there, and never one event under his roof has had dullness in it. This social home life brought into a sort of official relation to the college will largely affect Yale society. Fathers and mothers will have less anxiety about the well-being of their sons during the critical period of their college career, while Dr. Dwight has the oversight of the college.

A PHYSICIAN'S RESTORATION.

(*See Illustration on this page.*)

IT was a dark, chill winter's day and the sky seemed heavy with a coming fall of snow. On the streets were very few pedestrians, and such as there were hurried with quick steps toward their destination, anxious to escape the bitter wind that blew as if it had come direct from the region of eternal ice and snow. Poor half-clothed beggars shivered under their rags at the street corners, and seeing no prospect of alms, went in quest of lodging for the night.

Noticeable in the throng of pedestrians was the figure of a man walking with a firm, erect bearing toward the outskirts of the city. He could not have been much over thirty years of age, but his face was bronzed with exposure, and there were marks upon it of thought and care. He walked rapidly until he came to a large house surrounded by a garden, and bearing on its outer gate the name of Dr. Sedgwick. He turned in there with the manner of a man well acquainted with the place, and mounting the stoop he rang the bell. When the door was opened he inquired, "Is Mrs. Reade at home?" and receiving an affirmative answer he entered and bade the help tell Mrs. Reade that "a friend wished to see her."

After a few minutes waiting in a room which seemed familiar to the visitor, a lady entered, her face, of almost childish beauty, wearing a look of innocent wonder. She stood for a m ment regarding her visitor with intense earne ness, and then with a cry of joy nestled in outstretched arms, exclaiming, "My husban my darling husband!"

This was the moment to which John Rea had looked forward for more than two lo years during which he had been separated fr his young wife. As she held him off at arn length to note the changes time and travel h produced in the bronzed, bearded face before h he saw the look of love in her eyes, and on more clasped her to his breast in joyful gladne Then she wanted to hear an account of his ventures and unexpected return, but before could give it, the door was thrown open a John Reade was overwhelmed with hearty gre ings from a group of delighted friends. Sedgwick, who was Mrs. Reade's father, h been driving with another daughter and friends, and returning had heard of his son-law's arrival and rushed at once to the ro where he was, to give him cordial welcome.

"I am delighted to see you, Reade," said Sedgwick, grasping with both hands Reade's tended palm; "you are just in time for a re lar round of entertainments and New Ye parties; you will have quite a public ovati coming in like this as if you were an angel fly among us without a word of preparation."

"I think quiet and rest would be the great blessings to me just now," said Reade.

"Oh! you will soon overcome all that; now to dinner, and then let us know someth of your adventures."

The joyful family were soon seated at a w spread board, and an hour later gathered arou a roaring log fire to listen to the travell story. Dr. Reade was an ambitious man, w having devoted himself to the study of chem try and medicine, had accepted an appointm which involved frequent and prolonged abse from home. He did this to increase his o knowledge as well as to gain for himself a pu reputation. Dr. Sedgwick was proud of his s in-law, and had approved of his course, and w true fatherly kindness consoled his daugh Emily for her husband's absence. His story he told it that night, thrilled every auditor. was a narrative of danger and of hair-brea escapes from death by drowning, from w beasts, and by savage hands. At its conclus Dr. Sedgwick proposed that they should all u in offering thanks to God for His preserv

The Cathedral Mountain in the Yosemite, California.

over one so dearly d.

know you do not pathize with me, ," said Dr. Sedg-, "but let me have own way to-night." was an allusion to Reade's well-known elity. He had during his college course ied the works of dillac, and had led to doubt the ence of the soul, had abandoned his in God Himself. y were the efforts Sedgwick had made onvince his son-in-but they had al-failed.

the astonishment ll, however, Dr. He replied, when his er-in-law made the osal, "I will join very heartily in the cise. My heart is ged and I will tell how it came about." peared that during ourney he had visa hospital where n aged man who, e suffering from an rable disease, had fearfully crushed mangled in a railroad accident. Reade had r witnessed suffering such as the old man ured from his injuries and his disease. He cted to find him overwhelmed, but instead, aw him, even in the paroxysms of his agony, ly looking forward to release, and confident e belief that his soul would be carried into presence of his glorified Saviour. The soul uninjured, and while the body was racked tortured, the man himself seemed to rise e his frame. Reade saw him die, and heard last triumphant words, and he came away that death-bed a believer in the immortal-of the soul and the truths of revelation. had answered prayer, and the student who resisted Dr. Sedgwick's arguments was come by the spectacle of a Christian's h-bed.

THE CATHEDRAL MOUNTAIN.

HE wonderful pile of rocky heights depicted e illustration on this page, has from each a sufficiently striking resemblance to a edral to justify the name given to it. It is of the most prominent objects in the Yo-ite Valley, in California. The Government acted wisely in reserving so grand and pic-sque a district for a national park. It is e eight miles long, and about one mile wide. ugh properly called a valley, its surface is thousand feet above the level of the sea, e the hills that tower around it rise from thousand to six thousand feet above the of the valley. The Cathedral rocks are t 2,660 feet high, while in the rear rises the ary peak called the Sentinel Rock, 4,500 high.

e valley itself is richly wooded, and the r Merced, with its tributaries, flows through dding to the wonder and exquisite beauty of scene by numerous waterfalls. Geologists hazarded many theories to account for the ous depression. It is, however, now gener-believed to have been caused suddenly by arthquake or sinking of the earth's crust, not, as was formerly believed, by the action ashing water. Another theory is that the e was once a lake, which was gradually filled o its present level by huge masses of rock ng into it from the heights above. It was until 1851 that anything was known of this most beautiful of earth's glorious scenes. The miners in the Sierras organized an expedition in that year to punish the marauding Indians, and traced them to this retreat. Its grandeur at once impressed them, and by 1856 tourists had made acquaintance with the spot, and the first hotel was erected.

THE EPOCHS OF A LIFE.

A NEW SERIAL STORY.

By Rev. L. S. Keyser.

(Continued from page 654.)

Surprises.

It happened one day, as Hadley was glancing languidly over the column of church announcements in one of the daily papers of the city, that his attention was arrested by the statement that Mr. Hanson, the pastor of one of the churches, would preach the next Sabbath morning on "The Sin of Unbelief." The announcement stirred him into a belligerent posture at once. "The idea that unbelief is a sin!" he muttered, contemptuously. Howbeit, the hostility he felt was the very stimulus he needed to make him resolve to attend the services.

As he entered the church the next Sabbath morning, he was surprised to find that the preacher was still a young man, perhaps a few years Hadley's senior. It was a strong, handsome face, with features well-chiseled, and expressive of the kindliest sympathies, that appeared before the sceptical visitor as the clergyman rose to begin the service; and in spite of Hadley's previous feelings of antipathy, he was favorably impressed by the preacher's appearance and the clear, firm ring of his voice. There was no affectation, no pomposity, no assumption of superiority, in his bearing, but he was perfectly natural, and free from all appearance of a desire to display his abilities. Yet a few sentences indicated the educated Christian man.

After the preliminary exercises, which were very simple, were over, the preacher announced that his text would be found in John 3:18: "But he that believeth not is condemned already, because he hath not believed on the name of the only begotten Son of God."

The preacher's line of argument was simple but cogent. He dwelt on the responsibility involved by the claims of God's word. If it is a Divine revelation, it must be a sin to reject it. It is, therefore, a duty on the part of any man disposed to doubt, to take every means at his command to find out whether its claims are substantiated before he rejects it—a duty he neglects at his peril.

So far Hadley agreed, and his conscience acquitted him. He had not rejected the Bible lightly or hastily. Had he not studied and thought and shrunk from unbelief until it was forced upon him by the power of reason? Yes, he admitted that, *if* the Bible was God's word, rejection would be sin, but he believed that it was not, and he had taken all means to find out before arriving at that conclusion. But what was the preacher saying now?

"Let not the sceptic think that he has exhansted all the means at his command, if he has not used humble, earnest prayer to God for enlightenment. What means can be so effectual as to ask his Maker to enlighten the reason that Maker has endowed him with? It is a logical method, and experience justifies it. Many have by that road found conviction and assurance after trying in vain every other road." The preacher then gave a striking account of his own deliverance from scepticism through prayer, and affectionately pressed on his hearers the remedy which had saved him.

Hadley was startled by the unexpected turn in the argument, and he listened intently as the preacher cited John Bunyan, Thomas Chalmers, Dr. Tholuck, George Müller, and others, who by the same path had come to the light.

At the conclusion of the service Hadley, who had been ushered to a seat in the front of the church and was impeded in leaving by the crowd in front of him, heard himself addressed by name, and turning, found his hand grasped by the preacher, who said: "Mr. Madelling, I am glad to see you in my congregation to-day. Ah!" noting the wonder in Hadley's face, "you are surprised at my knowing you. I am interested in young men; it does not seem long since I was young myself. When I heard of your appointment in the schools here, I was curious about you, and a friend pointed you out to me in the street. That is how I came to recognize you this morning."

"You did not know that I should be here, or I should think that you were personal in your sermon, Mr. Hanson."

"Ah! is it possible? But that often happens. We are guided unconsciously in the selection of a subject, and do not know until afterward that there was a special purpose in it. But, really, have you been troubled with these doubts? I know what a rough, toilsome road that is to travel alone. Give me your address, and let me call on you and have a talk on the subject. Perhaps my experience may help you."

Hadley willingly gave it, and with a friendly pressure of the hand the two parted. That afternoon after turning over many books listlessly, Hadley fell into a reverie.

It had been many months since he had been in so humble and tractable a mood, and so ready to welcome religious teaching. With more alacrity than usual he made his way to the church of which his uncle was pastor; and never had a sermon from the old man's lips seemed so replete with the eloquence of relevant and cogent truth. It was far different from the argumentative discourse to which he had listened in the morning, but it was full of appeal, comfort, and loving admonition. "The dove that flew out over the illimitable waters of the Deluge found no rest for the sole of her foot until she flew to the window of the ark, and was taken beneath its shelter by the hand of the patriarch. So the soul that is tossed in the tempest of sin and doubt can only find rest in the ark of redemption built by the bleeding hands of the Saviour." It was the same doctrine that he had heard in the morning.

"It is inexplicable," he said to himself, "that these two men, who are so different in mental traits, should teach doctrines so perfectly accordant, and in the same day prescribe the same antidote for doubt."

Although the following day was one of ceaseless questionings, yet it was the brightest day he had spent for many months. When his work in the school-room was done, he decided to take a walk into the suburbs of the city for relaxation. With an interest ever on the alert when he came into contact with nature, he wandered far beyond the limits of the town, along the wooded banks of the clear river, gathering many data of interest and value, and it was almost dusk when he again returned to the outskirts of the city. The street-car was just ready to leave the park, which was a resort outside the city limits, when the pedestrian arrived at that locality. Swinging himself into the car, he scarcely looked about him to see who his fellow-passengers were as he seated himself.

He was just in the act of drawing a magazine from his pocket for the purpose of finishing an article in which he had become interested, when he almost bounded to his feet in astonishment; for directly opposite him his eyes fell upon a familiar face. He rose impulsively and spoke: "Miss Winters, surely! This is indeed a surprise. I almost wonder whether I can be dreaming. You are quite the last person I should have thought myself likely to meet."

"Ah! you did not know that I was living in this city," said Miss Winters, a warm flush coming to her cheeks.

"No, I did not. It certainly was not your home while you were at college."

"That is true; but soon after I left Bromfield my father moved to this place for business reasons, and so you find us domiciled here. Our home is at 318 Franklin Street."

The expression, "Fate is determined to make our paths cross, for better or for worse," had almost broken from his lips; but he remembered that the eyes of his fellow-passengers were upon him, and their ears were eagerly devouring every word of the conversation, and he therefore said, as he reseated himself: "It is a strange coincidence that we should be living again in the same town; but—but it will give us an opportunity to review the old college days."

"Yes," she responded, in evident embarrassment, for she was startled at the significance of making a retrospect of the past. Then she said, more composedly: "But I knew some time ago that you were employed in the schools here. I saw the notice of it in the town papers."

"Why did you not — why have I not met you before, then?" he asked. He despised himself the next moment for asking the awkward question. But the girl was equal to the emergency.

"In a city of this size," she answered, "a person may not meet his acquaintances for a long time. I have seen you several times on the street, but was not near enough to you to speak."

The conversation was an embarrassing one, in view of the relations that had previously existed between them, and Hadley was glad when the car had reached the street where he would leave it. Making her a courteous bow, he stepped from the car, and hurried to his room.

His mind was hurtled hither and thither by conflicting currents of emotion. Whether agony or joy preponderated, he could not tell. His meeting with the girl had revived all the old anguish, but there was also a feeling of ecstasy in being near her, and being able to look occasionally into her sweet face and deep blue eyes. So in spite of the awful quavering of his heart, he trembled and thrilled with pleasure. Perhaps — oh, enrapturing thought! — by meeting her again and again, he might eventually overcome the barriers that stood in the way of their union.

A few days afterward, Mr. Hanson paid his promised visit, and Hadley welcomed him with a pleasure he never expected to feel in greeting a minister of the gospel. With excellent tact the visitor easily fell into a chat about the books which lined the walls of the room in which they sat. The silent, eloquent friends of the young man were a good index to his character, and Mr. Hanson moved from shelf to shelf, uttering short, acute comments, which showed his intimate acquaintance with Hadley's favorite authors. There was a cheerfulness, an enthusiasm, about the man, very refreshing at a time when most cultured men of Hadley's acquaintance wore a bored, wearied air, and affected a pessimism of spirit depressing to an ardent nature. On Hadley remarking upon it, Mr. Hanson said, with a smile:

"Oh yes, I am hopeful of the future, and I think a great deal of the gloom now fashionable is due to bad digestion, and still more of it to wounded vanity. When a man is waiting for all the world to bow down at the shrine of his genius, and discovers that the world is occupied with other matters, and has little time to humor his egotism, he begins to feel that he is badly treated, that the world is steeped in selfishness, and is unable to appreciate his superior qualities of mind, and then he gets to berating the world as a great big sensuous, grovelling, self-centred clown. He looks at the world through a glass that has been colored by his own wounded vanity. Let any man imagine himself to be the hub of the universe, and he will soon discover that the universe is not endowed with the centripetal qualities necessary to meet his requirements. There is plenty of wickedness and stupidity in the world, but to sit down and mourn helplessly over the sad fact, is imbecile to the last degree, especially when there is a way by which a man may become jubilant and hopeful in spite of it."

"Have you learned the secret of happiness in a dismal world like this, Mr. Hanson?" questioned Hadley, in tones that evinced his surprise and interest. "If so, perhaps you may allow others the benefit of your discovery."

"There was a time when I was inclined to take a despondent view of life, but since my doubts took wing, religion has brought brightness and joy into my life. It has wrought a change in my nature, and consequently I look at the world with different eyes. In short, it has converted me from despondent pessimism into a hopeful optimism."

"I do not understand how religion could produce a change like that."

"Well, if it were possible to be assured of the truth of religion, so that the evidences were indisputable, would not that fact have a quieting and exhilarating effect upon a man's mind?"

"It certainly would," conceded Hadley.

"Let me say, friend Madelling, that it is possible to get just such an experience of the truth."

"Ah! you mean by the method which you recommended in your sermon last Sunday."

"Yes, and I would urge that course upon you."

"Mr. Hanson, I will tell you candidly that there are difficulties in the way that seem to me insuperable. It appears to me that the plan you recommend, carries upon the face of it its own condemnation. It seems so illogical, so inconsequential. How can an appeal to supernatural powers bring about a solution of a man's intellectual difficulties with the Bible? There are the historical discrepancies; will Heaven vouchsafe an explanation of these, and thus save us the trouble of investigating them?"

"No," replied the clergyman, readily; "those are matters for intellectual research, and God allows plenty of play for man's mental powers in the study of His Word. However, it is a debatable question whether there are historical discrepancies, or any other, in the Bible; and it would be unwise for a man to stake his everlasting welfare upon that assumption."

This remark stirred Hadley into a somewhat aggressive frame of mind. "Do you mean to say that there are no disparities in the Bible? They are certainly very palpable."

"Yes, I know to what you refer," replied Hanson, kindly; "and I sympathize with you in your perplexities; but if you were assured by the testimony of the Spirit of God that the Bible is His Word, would you not feel then that some explanation of these discrepancies is possible, and would you not, therefore, investigate them in a more sympathetic and less hostile spirit? Such an assurance is possible. You perceive that the sincere inquirer may be certified of the truth of the Bible without understanding all the difficulties, just as he breathes the air about him without understanding all the mysteries of respiration or meteorology."

"Possibly, though I cannot conceive of the process. It seems to me more manly and rational to grapple with such problems than to look for a revelation."

"Were there any professors in the college you studied at, Mr. Madelling?"

"Certainly," said Hadley, laughing. "There would not have been much benefit in the institution without the professors."

"And you did not think it unmanly or igno ble, when you encountered difficult problems, to receive their help and suggestions?"

"Oh, certainly not! Why should I? Th expectation of getting help attracted me there."

"Now, Madelling," said Mr. Hanson, "wh not deal so with these problems? You expec to get the truth by research. You admit tha there are many difficulties in the way. How lon will it require to clear them all up? It will b a long and toilsome process, and may end ur satisfactorily. There ought to be a shorter an surer route to the land of truth, especially whe we remember the importance of the questio at issue. A man might die before his arduou task of investigation was completed. There i as there should be, a sure and direct route."

"Your positiveness is infectious, but I co fess that the whole subject is shrouded in my tery to me."

"Yes, I know how you feel. Once you thoug that the land of truth was just before you, ar all you needed to do was to step in and posse the land. So you began your journey hopefull But soon disillusion came, and your bright oas turned out to be a deceptive mirage, ever rece ing from you in the distance, and to-day you a in greater aridness than when you began yo investigations. Am I not right?"

"I am surprised, sir, at the accuracy wi which you have described my mental life," r joined Hadley. "I confess, candidly, that n disappointments have made an agnostic of m

"Are you not ready, then, to try the panac for doubt which I have recommended?" ask Hanson, anxiously.

The young man hesitated. "Not yet, n yet," he said. "I will think about it. You m not expect too much of me so soon. I do n feel ready just yet to resort to heroic measure

"Perhaps you are right," Hanson repli "But allow me to remind you that there is da ger in delay. There is special danger that y will lose your interest in religion, and subs into indifference, which would be a more pe ous state of mind than your present one."

"I shall come to your church occasionally, a that will keep the subject fresh in my mind.'

"I hope that you will also call upon me my study," answered Hanson, rising.

The two men shook hands cordially, w mutual expressions of pleasure in having each other.

(To be Continued.)

THE FALL OF JERICHO.

By Mrs. M. Baxter.

. S. Lesson for October 28, Josh. 6: 1-16. Golden Text, Heb. 11: 30.

›shua Learning—Spiritual Progress More Important than Work—The Captain of the Lord's Host—Joshua's Submission to Him—The True and the False Power—How to Know the One from the other—Self Satisfaction Never the Work of the Spirit—Fatal Ignorance—Degrees of Guilt and Punishment—The Faith that Implies Possession—The Destruction of the City—Rahab the Inn-Keeper Alone Spared.

"By faith the walls of Jericho fell down after ›ey had been compassed about for seven days." ›eb. 11: 30.) Such is the pithy, comprehen›ve version given by the Holy Ghost in the ›ew Testament. The spies had described the ›ties of the Canaanites as "great, and fenced › to heaven." (Deut. 1: 28. R. V.) Jericho was ›e of these. Before, however, the Lord sent ›shua forward to take the city, He taught ›m one of the most important lessons he ever ›arned. God will never sacrifice

The Education of His Children

›r the sake of the work they do. He could do › which He wants done independently of us if ›e would, and in so far as the work we do is a ›nderance to our spiritual progress, we shall find ›od thwarting us on all sides. Often and often ›e work is obliged to stop for the sake of the ›orker, or the conversion of the child has to be ›layed for the sake of the mother, that she may ›arn lessons of faith which she could learn in › other way.

Joshua had led the children of Israel over ›rdan, Moses was no longer missed; the people ›w that God was with Joshua, and the cele›ation of the Passover after the universal cir›mcision which had taken place, must have ›eatly confirmed them in their covenant rela›onship to God. All was going well; they ›ent forth to conquer and to possess. "And it ›me to pass, when Joshua was by Jericho, that › lifted up his eyes and looked, and, behold, ›ere stood a man over against him with his ›ord drawn in his hand." What should ›shua do in such a case? What did Moses ›ways do? Did he not invariably inquire of ›e Lord? True, God had said to Joshua, There shall not any man be able to stand be›re thee all the days of thy life"; but He had ›lded, "As I was with Moses, so I will be with ›ee; I will not fail thee, nor forsake thee." ›osh. 1: 5.) Neither Moses nor Joshua were › act on their own responsibility. Joshua took ›r granted that it was his vocation to conquer ›d overcome the Stranger. Oh, how often we ›ke things for granted, and when God has been ›eatly blessing us, how often are we tempted to › right on, without stopping to get God's mind › every tiny detail of our lives! How often we ›rget that it is not our own lives we are living, ›t that God has chosen us for Jesus to repeat ›is life in us, and that we can no more divine ›is mind about this or that without asking ›im and receiving His answer, than if we were ›converted. We cannot, must not, dare not, be

Independent of Him

›r a single moment. Joshua, without a mo›ent's hesitation, addressed the Stranger as ›ough he alone were marshal of Israel's hosts. ›Art thou for us or for our enemies?" Oh, how ›hamed he must have been, how small in his ›vn eyes, when the answer was, "Nay: but as ›ptain of the host of the Lord am I now ›me." Joshua's heart was right, he only want› to know the right thing in order to do it: he ›ell on his face to the earth, and did worship, ›d said unto him, what saith my Lord unto ›is servant?" In an instant he fell back before ›od, and took the second place. Until we ›arn this lesson, God cannot do much with us. ›ow many there are who seek a baptism of ›wer, and what they long for is something ›hich will make them remarkable people, not ›at witness of the Holy Ghost with them which ›ll enable them to show that God is a wonder› God. They want men to feel the power of *their* words, of *their* holiness; in fact, they want something which shall be a satisfaction to themselves, something which really ministers to their spiritual pride. They want the power of the Holy Ghost, but that they may use it in their own way, and too often the devil simulates the power of the Spirit, and just fills these Christians with that which their hearts desire—intense self-satisfaction, a power of utterance, often power in healing too, and very remarkably with visions and dreams. But how shall we know the true from the false? By this—the Spirit of God never glorifies man, but always testifies of Jesus, glorifies Him. The first command of the Captain of the Lord's host, who is none other than Jesus "the Captain of our salvation," was, "Loose thy shoe from off thy foot, for the place whereon thou standest is holy." Now things were in order;

God was in Command

and Joshua was only second in command; God was responsible for victory, and Joshua was only responsible to trust and to obey. When we come to this point, where we let the management of our souls and bodies and all we are and have so pass into God's hands that we see Him responsible for all, a wonderful, deep peace, "which passeth all understanding," drives anxiety and worry out of our lives. How can anything go wrong which God has undertaken? how, if we have no will but God's will, can anything be wrong to us? "And Joshua did so."

The people were now in the plains of Jericho. A terror had seized upon the inhabitants; the siege of the city was strict. Orders were given by the authorities that no one should leave the city on any pretext. All traffic, all trade outside the city, was stopped. Poor doomed people! they knew not God, and they must perish! And so must the heathen, Chinese, and Hindus, the natives of Africa, and all the people who know not God. True, their doom will not be so terrible as that of those who have heard of Christ and wilfully rejected Him, but they cannot have their part with those who are saved by the blood of the Lamb. Now that God had prepared Joshua for the work, He says to him, "See, I *have given* into thine hand Jericho, and the king thereof, and the mighty men of valor." Are we to reckon as ours that which we have not in hand, which we cannot feel or touch or see? Has Joshua to act as though Jericho already were theirs, or as though he hoped it was? God was in command, and He gave orders that the priests bearing the ark, and the people following, should compass the city for seven days, and the priests should blow the rams' horns. What for? In token that the city was theirs. But the walls were standing, the gates were closed, the armed men were within, waiting to sally forth and discomfit the children of Israel? Did not God know this? Surely yes. Dear reader, you have put into God's hand some great need of yours. He has shed light upon a promise in His Word which assures that very thing to you. All things whatsoever ye pray and ask for,

Believe that ye Have Received Them,

and ye shall have them." (Mark 11: 24, R.V.) How do we act if we believe we have received money because the cheque or the postal order is in our hands? Do we not write a thankful acknowledgment at once, although we do not see the coin? Joshua did as God commanded him. There was nothing in the "march past" of this wilderness-born people to awe the people of Jericho, and perhaps some of them may have recovered in a measure from their terror, and strongly criticised the generalship and the military tactics of Joshua. We have to count the cost if we put the Lord in command, for His way of working reflects no honor upon man in the eyes of the world. It is only as seen on the side of heaven that faith in God is appreciated. Had Joshua not learned to take the second place, he might have fretted and chafed in spirit at the apparent loss of time and waste of strength and of shoe-leather, but he knew God well enough to trust Him. Again, his pride might have been mortified at cutting such a grotesque figure in the eyes of the people of Jericho. But God was responsible, and He was training all this time to good account in teaching them to obey and trust Him.

At last, the supreme moment had arrived. Seven days the Lord had succeeded in keeping people's hands off the work He was about to do, and the seventh day they had at His command compassed the city seven times, and were still contented, although no break had been made in the walls, and there was no apparent sign of victory. Then came the command, "Shout; for

The Lord Hath Given You the City!"

The people shouted by faith in His promise, and, with a roar as of thunder, the walls cracked all round the city, and fell, not in a confused mass, but flat, making a roadway right into the city, so that every man north, south, east, or west could enter from the very point where he stood! And, in very deed, no man was able to stand before them; the poor heathen people who would not know God, although His eternal power and Godhead may be clearly seen in His works (Rom. 1: 20), these also glorified not as God the Maker of all the things which they saw around them, and therefore were without excuse, fell before the sword of God's people. Some way they had had their chance of salvation, they had fallen into awful sins, which their very nature condemned, and now they must perish for ever. God commanded that everything that had life should be slain, and everything which could be destroyed by fire should be destroyed, but all the silver and gold and vessels—all which could abide the fire (Num. 31: 23)—was to be devoted to the Lord, and put into His treasury. God must always have the first-fruits; this was the first city taken in the promised land, and no man in Israel was to be enriched by its spoils, for this would be sacrilege, and God would show by its utter destruction His anger against the fearful sins of the Canaanites (Deut. 18: 10-12).

One command and one reservation was made. God commanded, "Ye, in any wise keep yourselves from the accursed (or devoted) thing," that is "Do not take for yourselves

That Which is God's Portion,

"Lest when ye have devoted it ye take of the devoted thing: so should ye make the camp of Israel accursed, and trouble it." It is the trouble of the Church of Christ that Christians live unto themselves.

The reservation was in the case of Rahab the harlot. She had been a wicked woman, but when she heard of God and of God's people, she took sides with God, and hid the spies because they belonged to God, and she had faith to trust the promise that this her house should be spared when the city was destroyed. And God took the matter in hand. He meets the first turning of a sinner towards Him, the first putting forth of faith or confidence in Him.

The city was burned; no man, woman, child, animal, or substance of any kind, except the devoted thing, was spared. Nothing was left but God's portion: this is His will for each of His children. "But Rahab the harlot, and her father's household, and all that she had, did Joshua save alive." So faithful is God to His Word. "And Joshua charged them with an oath at that time, saying, Cursed be the man before the Lord that riseth up and buildeth this city Jericho: with the loss of his first born shall he lay the foundation thereof, and with the loss of his youngest son shall he set up the gates of it!" (R. V.) One man was found wicked enough and daring enough to challenge God to fulfil His Word, and, surely enough, his eldest and youngest were sacrificed to his wilful disobedience. (1 Kings 16: 34.)

A CALL TO THE WEARY.

BY R. M. OFFORD.

Come, ye weary, do not tarry,
Bring to Jesus all your grief;
Why your burden longer carry
Since he offers sure relief?
Heavy-laden, sin distrest,
Come to Jesus Christ and rest.

Have you tried all worldly pleasure,
Sounded all the depths of sin,
Found no joy in earth's best treasure,
Seek you other joy to win?
Come to Jesus, He imparts
Lasting joy to joyless hearts.

On His lips is no upbraiding,
Though from God thou far hast strayed,
Though thy life's brief light is fading,
Sad the record thou hast made,
Come and welcome, do not wait,
Late it is, yet not too late.

Vile and most unworthy feeling,
'Twas for such His life He gave;
Bring thy wounded heart for healing,
If not lost how could He save?
Hast thou sinned beyond compare?
Greater need His grace to share.

J. E. JEWETT, Publisher, 77 Bible House, New York, will furnish the above poem in leaflet form at twenty cents per hundred. *A Sample Packet* of 50 leaflets assorted (no two alike), will be sent post-paid, for 10 cts., or 100 for 20 cts. Postage stamps taken.

MEXICO

Contributions in aid of Christian work in Mexico are most pressingly needed, and can be mailed to the address of

BISHOP H. C. RILEY,
Care of J. P. HEATH,
43 Bible House, New York.

TO OUR CHRISTIAN FRIENDS:

As there is a regular monthly expense in connection with the work a regular monthly income is needed to meet that expense. We, therefore, specially ask for regular monthly contributions in its behalf. If many will each send a little every month, or quarter, or whenever they can, it will do great good. *Remember, every little helps.*

H. CHAUNCEY RILEY.

This Journal contains every week a Portrait and Biography of some eminent person; a new Sermon by the Rev. C. H. SPURGEON, of London, and the Rev. Dr. TALMAGE'S latest Sunday morning Sermon; also always a Prophetic Article, and a Summary of Current Events, as well as Stories, Anecdotes, etc.

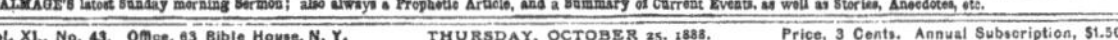
Vol. XI., No. 43. Office, 63 Bible House, N. Y. THURSDAY, OCTOBER 25, 1888. Price, 3 Cents. Annual Subscription, $1.50.

CONTENTS OF THIS NUMBER.

ORTRAIT AND LIFE OF DR. MOORHOUSE, BISHOP OF MANCHESTER, AND PICTURE OF MANCHESTER CATHEDRAL.
EVEN IN THE BIBLE. Dr. Talmage's Sermon Last Sunday Morning.
NECDOTES RELATED AT RECENT EVANGELISTIC MEETINGS.
HE GREAT ELOHI'S TRIUMPH IN TURKEY.
NCIDENTS OF THE REVIVAL IN JANE ST. M. E. CHURCH, NEW YORK.
URRENT EVENTS: Congressional Notes—The Presidential Campaign—Emperor William in Rome—The New Map of Europe—A Widower's Embarrassment—A Service Disturbed by a Cat.
HE EARTH'S FUTURE METROPOLIS.
CONSOLATION FROM RESURRECTION. A New Sermon by Rev. C. H. Spurgeon.
Gems from New Books: Louisa Alcott's Childhood—Personal Hardships Retold in her Books, etc.
PORTRAIT OF LORD STANLEY, the New Governor-General of Canada.
PICTURE OF MR. EDISON TESTING HIS PHONOGRAPH.
An Infidel Judge Converted—A Brooklyn Pastor's Healing—How the Gospel Fails in India—A Persian Nobleman's Gratitude—A Dutiful Son Blessed.
THE FISHERMAN'S LITTLE FRIEND. (With Illustration.)
THE EPOCHS OF A LIFE. A New Serial Story by Rev. L. S. Keyser. (Continued.
DEFEAT AT AI. By Mrs. M. Baxter.

THE RT. REV. JAMES MOORHOUSE, D. D., Bishop of Manchester—Manchester Cathedral.

THE RIGHT REV. JAMES MOORHOUSE.

P. E. Bishop of Manchester, Eng.

Education and Clerical Training—His Life Work—An Apology for Flight—Autobiographical Incidents—A Struggle with Poverty—Voluntary Resignation of Income—A Bishop's Life in Australia—A Hurricane in a Forest—Sexagenarian Reasons for Leaving Australia—Not to be Trusted with Money—A Gift he Could Not Use—A Husband's Tribute—A Witty Rejoinder—Reproof to the Press—A Bishop Pumping Water for Starving Cattle—The Questions of the Day.

THE bishop who this year has had the honor of welcoming the Congress of his Church, and whose portrait, with a picture of his cathedral, appears on the first page, is a man whose qualifications for his responsible duties have been tested and proved in two hemispheres. He was formerly Bishop of Melbourne, Australia, and is now Bishop of Manchester, England.

James Moorhouse was born in Sheffield, in the year 1826, and is sixty-two years of age. His parentage was essentially a North of England one, which means something different in degree, both in personal characteristics and in training, from Southern English than the difference in latitude suggests. His father was the senior partner of a large firm of Sheffield cutlers (Messrs. Moorhouse, Rushforth & Steele), while his mother, formerly a Miss Jane Frances Bowman, of Whitehaven, came of an old Cumberland family. Young Moorhouse received his early

Educational Training

at the Sheffield Collegiate School, and in course of time proceeded to Cambridge, where he entered as an alumnus of St. John's College. He graduated B. A. (Senior Optime) in 1853, and received his M. A. degree in 1860. Ordained deacon in the former year by the Bishop of Ely, he was curate at St. Neot's until 1856, when he removed to Sheffield, and remained until 1859, having meanwhile been ordained priest. After that he held a pastoral charge at Hornsey. In 1861 he received preferment to the vicarage of St. John's, Fitzroy Square, London, and here he remained till 1867. In that year he was presented to the vicarage of Paddington, and was made rural dean. He was Hulsean Lecturer at Cambridge in 1865; Warburtonian Lecturer in 1874; and was appointed chaplain in ordinary to the Queen, and prebendary of Caddington Major in St. Paul's Cathedral in 1875. On the resignation of the bishopric of Melbourne by Dr. Perry, in 1876, he was appointed to the diocese, and his University conferred upon him the degree of D. D. There he remained for ten years, his work being characterized by much vigor and enthusiasm. In 1886, the death of the lamented Dr. Frazer having rendered vacant the See of Manchester, it was given to Dr. Moorhouse.

That is the bare record of facts, but the Bishop, when leaving Australia two years ago, found so much surprise and regret manifested in his diocese, and so many testimonies of esteem showered upon him, that he felt it incumbent upon him, at a public meeting, to give, as he said,

An Apology,

not for his life, but for his flight. As his speech on that occasion was largely autobiographical, some extracts from it will serve to clothe the skeleton of facts above given. The Bishop said: "Early in my life I found it very necessary to establish for myself some rule about possible promotion, and after some consideration I adopted this principle: I determined never to seek preferment; never to ask any man to give me or get me a place; but I thought that if work were offered to me of a larger and more important kind than that in which I was engaged, I would accept it without regard to consequences. I have always followed that principle to its results. Sometimes the following of it brought me what people call worse fortune, and sometimes it brought me what they call better fortune. For instance, it was worse fortune, as the world counts fortune, when I accepted the living of St. John's, Fitzroy Square—a living containing 22,000 people, nearly all poor, without a parsonage, without a penny of income, with only the four bare walls of the church. For six whole years my connection with that parish was

A Struggle With Poverty,

but though the ship very often scraped the rock, yet it never altogether foundered, even in the midst of those storms. Again, when I came to you it was not to better my fortune. I was receiving in a London parish the same sum of money which you promised me if I came to work amongst you. But in that rich London parish I had very light responsibilities. I came, nevertheless, following out my principle, for the work offered to me here was larger and more important than that in which I was engaged. [The population of the bishop's Australian diocese was 606,000 souls, scattered over an area of 45,000 square miles.] When I settled down amongst you I found that the sum of $1,500 of my yearly income was taken from a fund which might be devoted to the maintenance of the poor clergy, and I immediately resigned that sum of money, because I wanted you to give me only what was secured in trust for the Bishop of Melbourne, and what you could not divert to any other purpose. Therefore, you see that by my own act I

Made Myself Poorer

by $1,500 a year when I settled in Victoria. Now I think that is proof enough that I have followed my principle, not only to good fortune but to bad fortune; and if it is sufficient proof, I hope you will believe me when I say that I accepted the offer of the See of Manchester because I thought I should be consistently following out the principle that had always regulated my action in the case of offered preferment. I thought, and I think, that in the present circumstances the See of Manchester offers a more important and influential field of labor than even that in which I was engaged. When you remember the terrible crisis in which the Church stands at home, and when you remember the population of Manchester, and the weighty factor it must be in the national life, you will easily guess the reasons which led me to that conclusion. What I feared in the diocese of Melbourne was the failure of physical strength in

The Hardships

of visitations in a diocese larger than half England and Wales, with roads that are mere tracks through its forests, and with a population necessitating more and more of hard visitation as it scattered itself more widely over the land. I never was afraid of the mental strain in Melbourne. I was only afraid of the bodily strain in visitations, and it was for that reason that I wanted the diocese divided, that I might have mental work to do here rather than physical work out in the open country. Now I know that I shall not find any of that physical strain when I go to Manchester. 'Physical strain?' you may ask, 'what are you talking about?' Well, you are not likely to understand it, because you have not experienced it; but I may tell you that in the short tour I have just completed, I began with three tremendous thunder-storms, that being in an open buggy, I got wet to the skin, and then I had to encounter

A Hurricane

among the lofty forest trees, with the boughs crashing down around me, any one of which, if it struck me, would have killed me on the spot. The latter was peril, not hardship, and I do not think I ever cared for peril. But there was this hardship, aggravated by unavoidable hard living and unavoidable hard shaking. Ladies and gentlemen, when I say this, I am not charging any one with neglect. The people of this diocese, and especially the people in the country, have given me hospitality in the most generous way. But as one advances in years, getting wet to the skin brings on twinges of rheumatism and the like; and eating good wholesome food which is not well cooked is not conducive to health when the digestion is delicate. That is the kind of trouble I was always facing. I know the work in the diocese of Manchester will require great effort both of brain and heart, but it will not impose upon me such hardships as I have described. Therefore I believed that I should be able to work for a longer period in the Church of God if I changed the place of my labors. That, to a man of my temper and my habits, is an unspeakable profit and pleasure."

Not Trusted with Money.

From the time it became known that he had accepted of the See of Manchester it was determined that leave should be taken of him in a manner worthy of the man and his nine years of work. One feature was that of the gift of a sum of money. At the public meeting at which this was inaugurated, one of the speakers suggested that the money should be given to the Bishop with the distinct understanding that it should be appropriated to none but personal uses; for, added he, "*the Bishop cannot be trusted with money*. If we give him money without this limitation he will leave it in the Colony for some Church purpose." This was a noble testimony to the unselfishness of his character, and not more noble than true.

A Husband's Tribute.

One of the Bishop brightest speeches was the one he made to the ladies of the colony, who, before the embarkation, presented Mrs. Moorhouse with a diamond necklace. The Bishop said: "I beg to thank you for the token of kindness which you have just bestowed upon my wife. If you will let me say so, I am very glad your benevolence took the especial shape it did; for had you given her a clock, a service of plate, or anything of that kind, I should have had the use of it in common with her. But, ladies, you are well aware *I cannot wear a diamond necklace*. Therefore, it is quite clear that the gift is a personal gift, and all I can do is to look upon it with pride, and fancy—if it be a fancy—that the light of Australian love shines from its brilliants.

"You are very right in saying that my wife has been a constant companion to me. She has been, but I do not think she deserves quite as much credit for that part of her work as for some other parts. I do not mean that she likes to go with her husband, for that goes without saying, but she likes travelling; and I believe if I could look back through her genealogy I should discover somewhere a trace of Gipsy or Arab blood. [She was the daughter of Dr. Sale, who was rector of the church in which Dr. Moorhouse served, when a young man, as curate.] She bore the fatigues of my journeys bravely, and faced whatever dangers there were undauntedly. *She undauntedly faced the bush*, and it proved a great comfort to me that she should go, for her presence lightened half the burden of my visitations, not only in relieving the discomforts incidental to travelling, but also in helping me with her ready sympathy with country clergymen and country people.

A Witty Reply

to a warning which was given to him on going to Australia, also evidenced the Bishop's freedom from vanity and his love for his fellows. He was entertained on his arrival by one of the Australasian governors, who told him that in Victoria he must expect every man to consider himself just as good as he was, and a good deal better. "If that be so," replied the Bishop, "*I shall meet with a good many men of the same opinion as myself*." "Oh," said the Governor, "in that case, when you start you will be sure to get on." Bishop Moorhouse then said that he had been used to that kind of feeling; he had been born in a democratic community, brought up in one, and afterward ministered in one, and that he had great sympathy with democracy. It is no doubt to this trait in the character of the new ruler of the See of Manchester that he owes his success, for he has always possessed the faculty of placing himself *en rapport* with men, both collectively and individually.

A Reply for the American Press

was given to a reporter by the Bishop on his arrival in his new diocese, when he was questioned about some of his reported eccentricities. "You gentlemen of the Press," said the Bishop, "did me an injustice once. Australia is overrun with rabbits, and I was actually asked a one time to frame a prayer to Almighty God that these animals might be smitten with sterility. Of course, on the grounds of consistency, I refused to do anything of the kind. To my surprise, some time afterward I received a copy of the *Glasgow Herald*, in which it was stated that I had prepared and framed a prayer in which a desire was set forth that the rabbits might be rendered for the future barren, and accompanying this paper was an American publication, which quoted the story, and added point to it by the heading, 'An Eccentric Bishop.' As a matter of fact, I had taken the very opposite course, and the Melbourne representative of the *Glasgow Herald*, knowing the error into which his paper had fallen, asked, and obtained, my consent to contradict it." At the same interview the reporter said: "Since your appointment, my Lord, we have heard many stories about you—of your declining to prepare a form of prayer for rain because the people would not irrigate their country, and of *your pumping water yourself to slake the thirst of dying cattle*, and so on." "Oh, yes, they are quite true," said the Bishop, laughing at the repetition of these stories. "I took my own line in Melbourne and acted accordingly. The people approved and disapproved, but in spite of some objections to the course I pursued, in general the people approved of it."

True Christian Socialism,

which is the great need of the Church in these times when the hearts of the poor are sore and agitators are laboring to inflame them to hate the rich, who squander in luxuries money that would save many from dying of starvation, was the subject of a ringing utterance by the Bishop on a recent occasion, and it applies as much to the Church in this country as that across the Atlantic. The Bishop said: Why should he love his neighbor as himself? He looked at many of his neighbors, and found that they were ignorant and vicious, that they were unlawful in their lives, coarse in their manners, disagreeable and disgusting to a refined taste. *Why was he to take the rough, uncultured, vicious vagabonds of the street to his heart* and love them as himself? Would they be good enough to tell him that? It was because they were Christians, because the Lord Jesus loved them all and came to die for them all. That was the sanction, that was the basis, that was the justification, of his obedience to the law of the second table. If they did not teach their children that, they *took away the basis of all morality*.

Dr. Moorhouse is not a prolific writer. A series of four sermons preached before the University of Cambridge, and entitled "Nature and Revelation," was his first publication, and he has also published his Hulsean lectures in 1865, under the title of "Our Lord Jesus Christ the Subject of Growth in Wisdom," his sermons on "Jacob" before the University of Cambridge in 1870, and "The Expectation of Christ."

THE CATHEDRAL.

MANCHESTER cathedral, of which a picture appears on the first page, dates back as a parish and collegiate church nearly five hundred years, and has undergone many alterations and had many additions. As completed, it has a choir and nave, both with aisles from end to end; and chantry chapels form, as it were, additional aisles, also very nearly from end to end: a projecting lady chapel on the east; a semi-octagonal chapter-house on the south side of the choir; and a south porch and a noble tower on the west. The church measures 220 feet from east to west, and 112 feet from north to south. In elevation it consists of arcades with a lofty clere-story; the whole is built in a highly ornate Perpendicular style, and the plan is full of interest and variety.

ANECDOTES RELATED AT RECENT EVANGELISTIC MEETINGS.

A Quarrel with the Mistress.—Mr. McKeith relates: "At one of our meetings the wife of a working-man brought in a girl, sixteen years of age, whom she had seen standing in the street without any apparent object. She had gone up and spoken to her, and found out the cause of her present forlorn condition. She was a country girl, and had recently come as a servant to a respectable family in the city, but she had a quarrel with her mistress, whom she had left at once, and had since then been wandering about the streets. She was taken to an institution and kept there, while inquiries were made, and when it was found that her story was true, a situation was found for her, where she is giving every satisfaction. But during the time she was in the institution, she was shown the way to Jesus, and when she left it she was rejoicing in her Saviour. What a noble work it is for women to rescue their sisters, fallen, or in danger of falling, from the dreadful fate which threatens them. How many a sinner, just on the brink halting between right and wrong, may be turned toward Jesus and saved, by the timely kind word or action of a worker for Christ."

"That Pipe and Baccy."—Mr. Jameson remarks: "Among many cases of good which I have recently seen are the cases of three men who were drunken, dissipated, and low. We influenced them by our open-air singing and preaching. They gave up the intoxicating cup at once. Little by little they learnt what were the claims of God upon their lives, and as the claims of God were brought to bear upon them they were prepared at any price to fulfil them. I shall never forget one of them coming to me one day, perhaps about four months after his conversion, and he said: 'I am in trouble, sir; may I walk home with you this morning after the service?' I said, 'Most decidedly.' We walked along. 'What is your trouble?' said I. 'Ah,' he said, 'I have been troubled about that pipe and baccy. I want you to buy me every week a shilling's-worth of tracts, and the money that was wasted in smoke I will spend in buying tracts to distribute for my blessed Master.' Every week for eighteen months that man has religiously spent his shilling a week, and you will find him every Sabbath day distributing tracts which he buys himself for the glory of God."

The "Star" on an Orphan's Brow.—Mr. Thorne observed: "A lady and gentleman were on a visit to Paris, and one day, while passing through the streets, they came upon a poor girl who was crying bitterly. They stopped and spoke to her, and discovered that she had neither home nor parents. As the lady and gentleman had no children of their own, they took this poor girl and adopted her, bringing her up as their own daughter. When the child was educated, it was found that she had a wonderful taste for music, in which she became so proficient, that people came from great distances to see and hear her. After one of her recitals a gentleman who was acquainted with the story of her life, asked her benefactor, 'How was it you adopted her?' He replied, 'When I first met her in the Paris streets, and looked at her, I saw that there was the star, the true mark of genius, on her brow, therefore I adopted her, and you see she has not disappointed me.' Yes, though she was poor and starving, she had what the gentleman called the star of genius on her brow. Similarly the sinner saved by grace, and adopted into God's family, though poor and toiling through this life, has the star of Divine sonship on his brow."

A Typical Story of Wrong and Ruin.—Mr. Napier reports: "As illustrating the difficulties of our evangelistic work on account of one-room life, we instance the case of a young woman about eighteen years of age, who waited in the inquiry-room after the free breakfast, on a bitterly cold morning last spring. She was scantily clad, and her bleared eyes and thin figure told the tale of weak health and incipient consumption; while to make her more pitiable still, she held in her arms a little child, which looked even more sickly and miserable than its mother. She was spoken to by our workers, to whom she told her sad story of wrong and ruin, and said that she was now earning her livelihood by singing in the streets. On visiting the room in which she lived, it was found to be occupied by about a dozen persons. Three or four men, three or four women, a number of children, and a dead child. We tried to induce her to come to us—at least to be fed—but after a few visits she disappeared, and we learned she was apprehended for cruelty to her child in exposing it to the inclemency of the weather while singing in the streets. She was sent to prison, and while there her child died, and the mother, after her release, again appeared at our breakfast, but only once or twice, falling away again into that old, hopeless condition with which it is so difficult to deal."

A Strange Means of Locomotion.—Mr. George Hatton says: "On Sunday evening, April 8, at the close of a children's service, I made my way to the mission chapel. It was a very wet night, and the street being entirely deserted, brought prominently to my notice a costermonger's hand-barrow standing directly in front of the entrance to the chapel. After the meeting I was about to start on my homeward journey, leaving the vehicle to its fate, when to my astonishment I saw a man, poorly clad, come out of the chapel and place himself between the handles of the barrow. Immediately behind him came a woman assisting a deformed cripple. The first-comer helped the cripple on to the barrow, and having made him as comfortable as he could under the circumstances, yoked himself to the vehicle, and amid the pouring rain trotted off with his human load. As this curious turn-out appeared to be going the same way as myself, I thought I should like to see how far it had to go before reaching its destination; so I quickened my pace and kept it in sight for a considerable distance, but upon reaching High Holborn, the road being clear of traffic, the man in the shafts proceeded at such a quick run that the barrow and its freight disappeared from my view near Red Lion Street. What a lesson, thought I, to those in health and strength who enjoy the luxuries of life, plenty to eat and drink and good warm clothing, and yet find some paltry excuse to stay away from the house of God."

Capture of a Desperado.—There is a Story told of one of the French towns, which was lighted by lamps hung on ropes, which stretched from one side of the street to the other. Their light was very imperfect, and in the partial darkness thefts, murders, and many other crimes were too often committed. The perpetrators were frequently caught, but there was one who spread terror, by the boldness and success of his crimes, whom the officers had never been able to capture. His face was well known, and though he was rigorously searched for, the place of his retreat remained unknown. A special day of rejoicing came upon the whole country. That town among others prepared to hold a fête. There was to be a grand procession, followed by illuminations. Everyone was anxious to see it; even the robber heard of it, and felt a longing to view what was to be seen. He crept from his lair and took his place among the crowd. Rough, unkempt, and savage-looking, he soon attracted general attention. Who was that strange-looking man? He was brought under the notice of the authorities, who recognized in him the robber who had so long eluded justice. He was apprehended, tried, and condemned. He was comparatively safe as long as he lurked in darkness, but as soon as he was exposed to the light of day, people saw his true colors and dealt with him accordingly. Many people think that they can safely sin in darkness and never be discovered. But there cometh a time when there shall be no shirking the eye of justice; when the light of God's righteousness will blaze down upon the unforgiven sinner and show him as he is.

SEVEN IN THE BIBLE.

Dr. Talmage's Sermon Preached last Sunday Morning, October 21, 1888.

"God blessed the seventh day." Genesis 2:3.

The Mathematics of the Bible—Remarkable Biblical Associations of the Number Seven—The Number in Nature—I. The Seven Candlesticks—Light-Bearers Not Lights—Churches to be Beautiful—Christ Not to be Put in a Kitchen—Christless Churches—Degradation of St. Sophia—II. The Seven Stars—The Ministers of the Churches—A Captain's Dying Words—The Stars and the Comets—III. The Seven Seals—The Folly of Consulting Spiritualists and Soothsayers—IV. The Seven Thunders—Evils to be Thundered Down—Fraudulent Commerce—Drunkenness—Atheism—Social Impurity—Awaiting Omnipotent Thunder—The Seven Precious Stones.

THE mathematics of the Bible is noticeable: the geometry and the arithmetic: the square in Ezekiel: the circle spoken of in Isaiah: the curve alluded to in Job: the rule of fractions mentioned in Daniel: the rule of loss and gain in Mark, where Christ asks the people to cipher out by that rule what it would "profit a man if he gain the whole world and lose his soul." But there is one mathematical figure that is

Crowned Above All Others

in the Bible: it is the numeral seven, which the Arabians got from India, and all following ages have taken from the Arabians. It stands between the figure six and the figure eight. In the Bible all the other numerals bow to it. Over three hundred times is it mentioned in the Scriptures, either alone or compounded with other words. In Genesis the week is rounded into seven days, and I use my text because there this numeral is for the first time introduced in a journey which halts not until in the close of the Book of Revelations its monument is built into the wall of heaven in chrysolite, which, in the strata of precious stones, is the seventh.

A Curious Recurrence.

In the Bible we find that Jacob had to serve seven years to get Rachel, but she was well worth it: and, foretelling the years of prosperity and famine in Pharaoh's time, the seven fat oxen were eaten up of the seven lean oxen: and wisdom is said to be built on seven pillars: and the ark was left with the Philistines seven years: and Naaman, for the cure of his leprosy, plunged in the Jordan seven times: the dead child, when Elisha breathed into its mouth, signalled its arrival back into consciousness by sneezing seven times: to the house that Ezekiel saw in vision, there were seven steps: the walls of Jericho, before they fell down, were compassed seven days: Zachariah describes a stone with seven eyes: to cleanse a leprous house, the door must be sprinkled with pigeons' blood seven times: in Caanan were overthrown seven nations: on one occasion Christ cast out seven devils: on a mountain He fed a multitude of people with seven loaves, the fragments left filling seven baskets: and the closing passages of the Bible are magnificent and overwhelming with the imagery made up of seven churches, seven stars, seven candlesticks, seven seals, seven angels, and seven heads, and seven crowns and seven horns, and seven spirits, and seven vials, and seven plagues, and seven thunders.

Yea, the numeral seven seems

A Favorite with the Divine Mind

outside as well as inside the Bible, for are there not seven prismatic colors? And when God with the rainbow wrote the comforting thought that the world would never have another deluge, He wrote it on the scroll of the sky in ink of seven colors. He grouped into the Pleiades seven stars. Rome, the capital of the world, sat on seven hills. When God would make the most intelligent thing on earth, the human countenance, He fashioned it with seven features—the two ears, the two eyes, the two nostrils, and the mouth. Yea, our body lasts only seven years, and we gradually shed it for another body after another seven years, and so on, for we are, as to our bodies, septennial animals. So the numeral seven ranges through nature and through revelation. It is the number of perfection, and so I use it while I speak of the seven candlesticks, the seven stars, the seven seals, and the seven thunders.

The Seven Candlesticks

were and are the churches. Mark you, the churches never were, and never can be, candles. They are only candlesticks. They are not the light, but they are to hold the light. A room in the night might have in it five hundred candlesticks, and yet you could not see your hand before your face. The only use of a candlestick, and the only use of a church, is to hold up the light. You see it is a dark world, the night of sin, the night of trouble, the night of superstition, the night of persecution, the night of poverty, the night of sickness, the night of death; aye, about fifty nights have interlocked their shadows. The whole race goes stumbling over prostrated hopes and fallen fortunes and empty flour-barrels and desolated cradles and deathbeds. Oh, how much we have

Use for All the Seven

candlesticks, with lights blazing from the top of each one of them! Light of pardon for all sin! Light of comfort for all trouble! Light of encouragement for all despondency! Light of eternal riches for all poverty! Light of rescue for all persecution! Light of reunion for all the bereft! Light of heaven for all the dying! And that light is Christ, who is the Light that shall yet irradiate the hemispheres.

But, mark you, when I say churches are not candles, but candlesticks, I cast no slur on candlesticks. I believe in beautiful candlesticks. The candlesticks that God ordered for the ancient tabernacle were something exquisite. They were a dream of beauty carved out of loveliness. They were made of hammered gold, stood in a foot of gold, and had six branches of gold blooming all along in six lilies of gold each, and lips of gold, from which the candles lifted their holy fire. And the best houses in any city ought to be the churches—the best built, the best ventilated, the best swept, the best windowed, and the best chandeliered. Log-cabins may do in neighborhoods where most of the people live in log-cabins; but let there be palatial churches for regions where many of the people live in palaces. Do not have a better place for yourself than for your Lord and King. Do not live in a parlor and put your

Christ in a Kitchen.

These seven candlesticks of which I speak were not made out of pewter or iron; they were golden candlesticks, and gold is not only a valuable but a bright metal. Have everything about your church bright—your ushers with smiling faces, your music jubilant, your hand-shaking cordial, your entire service attractive. Many people feel that in church they must look dull, in order to be reverential, and many whose faces in other kinds of assemblage show all the different phases of emotion, have in church no more expression than the back wheel of a hearse. Brighten up and be responsive. If you feel like weeping, weep. If you feel like smiling, smile. If you feel indignant at some wrong assailed from the pulpit, frown. Do not leave your naturalness and resiliency home because it is Sunday morning. If as officers of a church you meet people at the church-door with a black look, and have the music black, and the minister in black preach a black sermon, and from invocation to benediction have the impression black, few will come; and those who do come will wish they had not come at all.

Golden candlesticks! Scour up the six lilies on each branch, and know that the more lovely and bright they are, the more fit they are to hold the light. But a Christless light is a damage to the world rather than a good. Cromwell stabled his cavalry horses in St. Paul's Cathedral, and many now use the church as a place in which to stable worldliness. A worldly church is

A Candlestick Without the Candle,

and it had its prototype in St. Sophia, in Constantinople, built to the glory of God by Constantine, but transformed to base uses by Mohammed the Second. Built out of colored marble; a cupola with twenty-four windows soaring to the height of 180 feet; the ceiling one great bewilderment of mosaic; galleries supported by eight columns of porphyry and sixty-seven columns of green jasper; nine bronze doors with alto-relievo work, fascinating to the eye of any artist; vases and vestments encrusted with all manner of precious stones. Four walls on fire with indescribable splendor. Though labor was cheap, the building cost one million five hundred thousand dollars. Ecclesiastical structure, almost supernatural in pomp and majesty. But Mohammedanism tore down from the walls of that building all the saintly and Christly images, and high up in the dome the figure of the cross was rubbed out that the crescent of the barbarous Turk might be substituted.

A great church, but no Christ! A gorgeous candlestick, but no candle! Ten thousand such churches would not give the world as much light as one home-made tallow candle by which last night some grandmother in the eighties put on her spectacles and read the Psalms of David in large type. Up with the churches, by all means! Hundreds of them, thousands of them, and the more the better. But let each one be a blaze of heavenly light, making the world brighter and brighter, till the last shadow has disappeared, and the last of the suffering children of God shall have reached the land where they have no need of candlestick or "of candle, neither light of the sun, for the Lord God giveth them light, and they shall reign forever and ever."

Turn now in your Bible to

The Seven Stars.

We are distinctly told that they are the ministers of religion. Some are large stars, some of them small stars, some of them sweep a wide circuit and some of them a small circuit, but so far as they are genuine they get their light from the great central sun around whom they make revolution. Let each one keep in his own sphere. Ministers of religion should never clash. But in all the centuries of the Christian church some of these stars have been hunting an Edward Irving or a Horace Bushnell or an Albert Barnes; and the stars that were in pursuit of the other stars lost their own orbit, and some of them could never again find it. Alas for the heresy hunters! The best way to destroy error is to preach the truth. The best way to scatter darkness is to strike a light. There is in immensity room enough for all the stars, and in the church room enough for all the ministers. The ministers who give up righteousness and the truth will get punishment enough anyhow, for they are "the wandering stars for whom is reserved the blackness of darkness for ever."

I should like, as a minister, when I am dying, to be able truthfully to say what a captain of the English army, fallen at the head of his column and dying on the Egyptian battle-field said to General Wolseley, who came to condole with him: "I led them straight; didn't I lead them straight, General?" God has put us ministers as captains in this battle-field of truth against error. Great at last will be our chagrin if we fall leading the people the wrong way; but great will be our gladness if, when the battle is over, we can hand our sword back to our great Commander, saying: "Lord Jesus! We led the people straight; didn't we lead them straight?" Those ministers who go off at a tangent and preach some other gospel are

Not Stars, but Comets,

and they flash across the heavens a little while and make people stare, and throw down a few meteoric stones, and then go out of sight if not out of existence. Oh, brethren in the ministry, let us remember that God calls us stars, and our business is to shine and to keep our own sphere, and then when we get done trying to light up the darkness of this world, we will wheel into higher spheres, and in us shall be fulfilled the promise "they that turn many to righteousness shall shine as the stars forever."

Ah, the ministers are not all Pecksniffs and canting hypocrites, as some would have you think! Forgive me, if having in your presence at other times glorified the medical profession and the legal profession and the literary profession —I glorify my own. I have seen them in their homes and heard them in their pulpits, and a grander array of men never breathed, and the Bible figure is not strained when it calls them stars; and whole constellations of glorious ministers have already taken their places on high, where they shine even brighter than they shone on earth; Edward N. Kirk, of the Congregational Church; Stephen H. Tyng, of the Episcopal Church, Matthew Simpson, of the Methodist Church; John Dowling, of the Baptist Church; Samuel K. Talmage, of the Presbyterian Church; Dr. DeWitt, of the Reformed Church; John Chambers, of the Independent Church; and there I stop, for it so happens that I have mentioned the seven stars of the seven churches.

I pass on to another Bible seven, and they are

The Seven Seals.

St. John in vision saw a scroll with seven seals, and he heard an angel cry: "Who is worthy to loose the seals thereof?" Take eight or ten sheets of foolscap paper, paste them together and roll them into a scroll, and have the scroll at seven different places sealed with sealing wax. You unroll the scroll till you come to one of these seals, and then you can go no further until you break that seal; then unroll again until you come to another seal, and you can go on no further until you break that seal; then you go on until all the seven seals are broken, and the contents of the entire scroll are revealed. Now, that scroll with seven seals held by the angel was the prophecy of what was to come on the earth: it meant that the knowledge of the future was with God, and no man and no angel was worthy to open it; but the Bible says Christ opened it and broke all the seven seals.

He broke the first seal and unrolled the scroll, and there was a painting of a white horse, and that meant prosperity and triumph for the Roman Empire, and so it really came to pass that for ninety years virtuous emperors succeeded each other—Nerva, Trajan, and Antoninus. Christ in the vision broke the second seal and unrolled again, and their was a painting of a red horse, and that meant bloodshed, and so it really came to pass, and the next ninety years were red with assassinations and wars. Then Christ broke the third seal and unrolled it, and there was a painting of a black horse, which in all literature means famine, oppression, and taxation; and so it really came to pass. Christ went on until He broke all the seven seals and opened all the scroll. Well, the future of all of us is a sealed scroll, and I am glad that no one but Christ can open it.

Don't go to Some Spiritualist

or soothsayer or fortune-teller to find out what is going to happen to yourself, or your family, or your friends. Wait till Christ breaks the seal to find out whether in your own personal life or the life of the nation or the life of the world it is going to be the white horse of prosperity or the red horse of war or the black horse of famine. You will soon enough see him paw and hear him neigh. Take care of the present, and the future will take care of itself. If a man live seventy years, his biography is in a scroll having at least seven seals: and let him not during the first ten years of his life try to look into the twenties, nor the twenties into the thirties, nor the thirties into the forties, nor the forties into the fifties, nor the fifties into the sixties, nor the sixties into the seventies. From the way the years have got the habit of racing along, I guess you will not have to wait a great while before all the seals of the future are broken.

I would not give two cents to know how long I am going to live, or in what day of what year the world is going to be demolished. I would rather give a thousand dollars not to know. Suppose some one could break the next seal in the scroll of your personal history, and should tell you that on the 4th of July, 1890, you were to die—the summer after next; how much would you be good for between this and that? It would from now until then be a prolonged funeral. You would be counting the months and the days, and your family and friends would be counting them; and next 4th of July you would rub your hands together and whine—"One year from to-day I am to go. Dear me! I wish no one had told me so long before. I wish that necromancer had not broken the seal of the future." And meeting some undertaker, you would say: "I hope you will keep yourself free for an engagement the 4th of July, 1890. That day you will be needed at my house. To save time, you might as well take my measure now, five feet, eleven inches." I am glad that Christ dropped a thick veil over the hour of our demise.

There is another mighty seven of the Bible, viz.,

The Seven Thunders.

What those thunders meant we are not told, and there has been much guessing about them; but they are to come, we are told, before the end of all things, and the world cannot get along without them. Thunder is the speech of lightning. There are *evils in our world which must be thundered down*, and which will require at least seven volleys to prostrate them. We are all doing nice, delicate, soft-handed work, in churches and reformatory institutions, against the evils of the world, and much of it amounts to a teaspoon dipping out the Atlantic Ocean, or a clam-shell digging away at a mountain, or a tack hammer smiting the Gibraltar. What is needed is thunder-bolts, and at least seven of them. There is the long line of *fraudulent commerical establishments;* every stone in the foundation, and every brick in the wall, and every nail in the rafter made out of dishonesty; skeletons of poorly paid sewing girls' arms in every beam of that establishment; human nerves worked into every figure of that embroidery; blood in the deep dye of that proffered upholstery; billions of dollars of

Accumulated Fraud

entrenched in massive storehouses, and stock companies manipulated by unscrupulous men, until the monopoly is defiant of all earth and heaven. How shall the evil be overcome? By treatises on the maxim: Honesty is the best policy? Or by soft repetition of the golden rule that we must do to others as we would have them do to us?" No, it will not be done that way. What is needed, and will come, is the seven thunders.

There is *drunkenness* backed up by a capital mightier than in any other business. Intoxicating liquors enough in this country to float a navy. Good grain to the amount of 67,950,000 bushels annually destroyed to make the deadly liquid. Breweries, distilleries, gin shops, rum palaces, liquor associations, our nation spending annually seven hundred and forty millions of dollars for rum, resulting in bankruptcy, disease, pauperism, filth, assassination, death, illimitable woe. What will stop them? High license? No. Prohibition laws? No. Churches? No. Moral suasion? No. Thunderbolts will do it; nothing else will. Seven thunders!

Yonder are intrenched

Infidelity and Atheism

with their magazines of literature scoffing at our Christianity: their Hoe printing-presses busy day and night. There are their blasphemeing apostles, their drunken Tom Paines and libertine Voltaires of the present as well as the past, reinforced by all the powers of darkness from highest demon to lowest imp. What will extirpate those monsters of infidelity and atheism? Thunderbolts! The seven thunders!

For *the impurities of the world* empalaced as well as cellared, epauletted as well as ragged, enthroned as well as ditched: for corrupt legislation which at times makes our State and National capitals a hemispheric stench: for superstitions that keep whole nations in squalor century after century, their Juggernauts crushing, their knives lacerating, their waters drowning, their pyres burning, the seven thunders!

Oh, men and women, disheartened at the bad way things often go, hear you not a rumbling down the sky of heavy artillery, coming in on our side, the seven thunders of the Almighty? Don't let us try to wield them ourselves; they are too heavy and to fiery for us to handle; but God can and God will; and when all mercy has failed and all milder means are exhausted, then judgment will begin. Thunderbolts? Depend upon it, that what is not done under the flash of the seven candlesticks will be done by the trampling of the seven thunders.

But I leave this imperial and multipotent numeral seven, where the Bible leaves it, imbedded in the finest wall that was ever built, or will be constructed, the wall of heaven. It is

The Seven Strata

of precious stones that make up that wall. After naming six of the precious stones in that wall, the Bible cries out—"the seventh chrysolite!" The chrysolite is an exquisite green, and in that seventh layer of the heavenly wall shall be preserved forever the dominant color of the earth we once inhabited. I have sometimes been saddened at the thought that this world, according to Science and Revelation, is to be blotted out of existence, for it is such a beautiful world. But here in this layer of the heavenly wall, where the numeral seven is to be embedded, this strata of green is to be photographed, and embalmed and perpetuated, the color of the grass that covers the earth, the color of the foliage that fills the forest, the color of the deep sea. One glance at that green chrysolite, a million years after this planet has been extinguished, will bring to mind just how it looked in summer and spring, and we will say to those who were born blind on earth, and never saw at all in this world, after they have obtained full eyesight in heaven: "If you would know how the earth appeared in June and August, look at that seventh layer of the heavenly wall, the green of the chrysolite."

And while we stand there and talk, spirit with spirit, that old color of the earth which had more sway than all the other colors put together, will bring back to us our earthly experiences, and noticing that this green chrysolite is the seventh layer of

Christalized Magnificence

we may bethink ourselves of the domination of that numeral seven over all other numerals and thank God that in the dark earth we left behind us we so long enjoyed the light of the seven golden candlesticks, and were all of us permitted to shine among the seven stars of more or less magnitude, and that all the seven seals of the mysterious future have been broken wide open for us by a loving Christ, and that the seven thunders having done their work have ceased reverberation, and that the numeral seven, which did such tremendous work in the history of nations on earth, has been given such a high place in that Niagara of colors, the wall of heaven, "the first foundation of which is jasper; the second, sapphire; the third, a chalcedony; the fourth, emerald; the fifth, sardonyx; the sixth, sardius; the seventh, chrysolite."

"When shall these eyes thy heaven-built walls
And pearly gates behold;
Thy bulwarks with salvation strong,
And streets of shining gold?

"HOW THE GOSPEL FAILS."

The report that the Gospel fails in India and other lands where missionaries have gone has been extensively circulated. The following, however, which is a cutting from the *Indian Witness*, published in Calcutta, does not confirm the report: The *Dnyanodaya* describes the results of an hour's reading in three current newspapers as follows. Baptisms: a prominent priest in Jaffna, a Brahman student in Tinnevelly, a Brahmo preacher in Faizabad, a Brahman *munshi* at Asansole, a veteran school-master near Calcutta, 160 persons at Budaon, five of whom were Mahommedans, eleven Hindus at Simla, 134 adults in the Scotch Mission at Darjeeling, 365 persons added to thirty-six churches in Madura Mission; a Hindu teacher in Nepal sends word to the King of Nepaul that his predecessor told him Christ was the true *Guru*, and he is now proclaiming Jesus to his followers. This is the way the Gospel *fails* in India.

AN INFIDEL JUDGE CONVERTED.

THE following incident related by Mr. D. L. Moody appears in Dr. Cullis's *Times of Refreshing*: I knew an old judge who had gone through all the honors of his locality, but was an infidel. Pressed by his Christian wife, I approached him; but it was no use, and I left him, saying, "Judge, I am no match for you now, but when you are converted, will you please let me know?" He laughed, but promised to do so. A year and a half later, great was my surprise when, being in the same town, the old judge came to me and announced his conversion. His narrative of how it happened was as follows: One evening his wife had gone to church, and he was all alone, when he commenced to think, "Suppose my wife is right?" Then he commenced to think that the world could not have made itself, and must have been created by a God, and he said, "Why don't you ask that God to teach you, judge?" He did so, and from that moment things appeared to him in a different light. But still he did not want a mediator, and wished to communicate with the heavenly Father direct; and he felt burdened. Then, falling on his knees, he exclaimed: "For Christ's sake, deliver me from this burden!" The burden was taken off, and from that moment he was a Christian, after his wife had prayed twenty years.

A DUTIFUL SON BLESSED.

AN incident of blessing following a Christian father's death is related by Rev. M. Phillips, of South India, who says: "I went last month on a tour through Tripatore. Large crowds listened daily to our preaching. Some years ago a Sudra farmer in one of the out-of-the-way villages was baptized under the name of Israel. At first his wife and family gave him a great deal of trouble, refusing to associate with him for fear of defilement, and his wife even declined to give him food. He gradually overcame these difficulties, but his family seemed as far as ever from Christianity. When camping last month within seven miles of Israel's village, a young man came to the tent and said he was Israel's eldest son. 'Well, come and sit down,' I said, 'I am very glad to see you.' He sat down, and told me that last year his father died. I replied, 'Your father was a good man, and he is now in heaven with Jesus.' 'Yes,' he said, 'I believe that. When my father was very ill, and could not read the Bible, he asked me to read to him.' 'And did you?' 'Yes, I read to him every day, and he seemed always better after I read to him.' 'What did you read?' 'I read the Psalms and the Gospels. My father was very fond of the Psalms and the Gospels.' 'When he died, did you burn the body like a heathen?' 'No; we had a grave dug for him in the field, and we buried him as a Christian.' 'I suppose there was no Christian present to read the Scriptures and pray?' 'No; but I read Psalm 23 after the body was lowered to the grave.' I said, 'I am very glad to hear that. How did you have the courage to do it?' 'Well, I felt that it was right, and that it was in accordance with the wish of the departed, and so God gave me courage. And not only that, but I am determined to become a Christian, too, and die like my father.' 'What about your wife?' 'She is quite willing to be baptized.' 'Do you want to be baptized now?' 'No; I will wait till you come again, for I want my brothers and their families to be baptized at the same time.'"

A PERSIAN NOBLEMAN'S GRATITUDE.

THE value of medical missionary work in overcoming the prejudices of the heathen is illustrated in a letter recently received by Dr. George D. Dowkontt. It refers to the work of Dr. Cochran, the eminent medical missionary in Persia. "On his way to a distant village," says the writer, "Dr. Cochran unwittingly passed the door of a nobleman whose son, a young man, he had saved from death. The grateful man saw the Doctor, however, and running out, begged him to alight and be his guest, wishing to get up a great supper for him. Being told that he was on his way to see a sick person and could not stop, he said, 'At least come in long enough to drink a cup of tea with me,' and this he did. This man had opposed our teachers being sent to his village to preach or to teach, and showed his hatred to Christianity. Now he has asked for one of our teachers to be *settled* in his village (He Soy) to teach 'my Christian subjects'; but he takes his Mohammedan friends, and goes *himself* to listen and ask him to read and explain the Bible to him and his companions. When his Mohammedan acquaintances express their astonishment at the change in him, he replies, 'I did not *know* these men till I went to the hospital where the Doctor took care of my son. They are good people, and now I shall have their preachers to teach in my village. Other cases there are of Mohammedans having been changed outwardly from the influence of the physician and our helpers in the hospital, but this will suffice. Nothing arrests their attention like surgery, and causes them to exclaim, 'Surely we have never seen the like!' In this department the blessing of God has been particularly apparent. In more than forty cases of lithotomy *not one* has been *lost!* This I say to the glory of God's mercy, for thereby, as in other lines of surgery, the success attending operations has given the highest classes confidence in the missionaries as 'Just and true men, doing good to all, and only good.'"

Dr. Dowkontt has now sixty Christian young men in training for the foreign mission field. They are gaining experience in free dispensaries, and in the homes of the poor, in New York and Brooklyn. The cost of the work for last year was $9,000. It is a work of faith. Contributions toward it may be sent to Dr. George D. Dowkontt, 118 East 45th Street, New York.

A BROOKLYN PASTOR'S HEALING.

AT the recent Christian convention in New York, the Rev. H. C. McBride, pastor of a Methodist Episcopal Church in Brooklyn, gave a vivid account of his recovery after a quarter of a century of suffering. He said: "I was converted at seventeen and began to preach at eighteen in the school-house on my father's farm in western Pennsylvania. Until within a year I have been a great sufferer from a difficulty that baffled the skill of physicians. When I was fourteen years old I was trying with some boys to see who could dive furthest in the mill-pond. While I was under the water, holding my breath, *a stitch took me at the base of my brain*, and since that time my suffering has been very great, not so much during the day-time as at night, so that I have been thought pretty well, though not very rugged. But I usually lay propped up in bed, frequently without closing my eyes all night.

"I went to many physicians, but received only temporary relief. This went on for twenty-five years. None but God, my wife, and myself know what I suffered. Often after passing such a night I have preached three times on Sunday. God has been very good to me. I have never had a charge where, by His blessing, there were not from fifty to a hundred and fifty converted.

Last winter I was suffering as usual; my wife, who had come to believe in Divine healing, wanted me to give up all remedies and trust the Lord entirely, but I was not quite able to do so. I said to a dear sister who was talking to me about it, "It seems to me God thinks it is necessary for me to suffer to keep me humble." "Brother McBride," said she, "if you keep under the blood of Jesus, won't that be enough to keep you humble?" It was an argument that could not well be answered. I finally went forward with forty-seven others in my own church to be annointed in the name of the Lord, and have taken no remedies since; I have gone through severe testings; I thought I should die on the night after, but I stepped out on the promises, and I will stand there though the heavens fall. I have been learning the Word on this subject since then, and fight the devil with it, many a time, when he has tried to keep me awake since, I have given him some word of the Lord, and have gone to sleep as quietly as a baby. I have never had such peace in soul and body as now."

INCIDENTS OF THE REVIVAL

AT JANE ST. M. E. CHURCH, NEW YORK.

THE revival commenced under the labors of the Rev. Thomas Harrison has been continued under Mr. Yatman, and during this month under Dr. George D. Watson, formerly of Indianapolis, and the author of "White Robes," "Live Coals," "Fruit of Canaan," etc., etc. It is the intention of the Rev. Stephen Merritt, the pastor of the church, to secure the services of some earnest evangelist for a month at a time, all through the winter, that the work which has been so much blessed may go on.

A Reunited Family.

A Christian worker, connected with the church, reports a most delightful restoration of domestic happiness in connection with the revival. At one of the services she noticed a dissipated man standing up to ask the prayers of God's people for himself. The man's evident intelligence and refinement impressed her, though they were almost effaced by the brutalizing influence of liquor. She spoke to him, and learned his story. He said, that not long ago he was in good circumstances, with a flourishing business, and devotedly attached to his wife and children. He was accustomed to go on occasional "sprees," at long intervals, much to the grief of his wife. Gradually they became more frequent, until he became an habitual drunkard, and his wife and children were terrified when they heard his step. Finally, after many futile attempts to reform and many broken promises of amendment, the woman, who was an earnest Christian, was driven to seek a home for herself and children elsewhere.

The man had strayed into the revival service, heard of the power of God to change the heart and life, knew that it was just what he needed, and humbly, but anxiously, sought it in prayer. "The pledge is of no use to me," said the man, with pathetic conviction; "I have signed it already several times. *It is the power I want*—the power that holds. Can I get that? Is it too late?" He was assured that God would give him the power if he sought in faith. He was evidently sincere, and before he left the church he received the assurance of acceptance, and went out to live his new life.

The Christian worker who had spoken to him and been the means of leading him to Christ, sought out the wife and told her what had occurred. The faith of the woman manifested itself immediately. If she had been told that her husband had signed the pledge, she would have felt little joy; but this was a different matter. Instantly she was eager for reconciliation. Knowing by happy experience the power of grace, she felt secure for her husband's reformation, and authorized her visitor to invite the husband to her home. He went, was joyfully welcomed, and the whole family thanked God together. Since then, the husband, with his elder son, who is also a seeker after God, have been in regular attendance at the services, and the light in both their faces is evidence of the light that has come into their home.

A Momentous Eight Minutes.

At one of the services an engineer was present and listened intently. He was deeply moved. As the evangelist passed through the meeting afterward, the engineer caught him by the arm and said to him, in a voice shaking with excitement: "Is it possible to be saved in eight minutes?" "Certainly; why not?" was the reply. "I am the locomotive engineer of the New York and Troy Express," he said, "and I have but eight minutes before I must leave to catch my train." The evangelist conducted him to the altar, where several Christian friends were engaged in praying with anxious souls. The engineer knelt and prayed earnestly for salvation, and others prayed with him. In his anxiety he took no note of the lapse of time, but when he rose to his feet to testify of the joy that had come into his heart, the evangelist, looking at his watch, said, "You are in time to catch your train." There is good reason to believe that in those few minutes a change took place which will be felt throughout eternity.

THE GREAT ELCHI'S TRIUMPH.

THE Great Elchi was a name popularly bestowed in Turkey on the late Lord Stratford de Redcliffe, who, when he was the Right Honorable Stratford Canning, was British Minister at Constantinople. The name was a recognition of the extraordinary influence he had acquired over the Sultan and his wonderful skill as a diplomatist. To the student of prophecy his career, as unfolded in his recently published biography, is noteworthy from the fact that during his term of office, and largely through his efforts, the Sultan was led to grant the two important Reforms which progressively promoted the "cleansing of the Jewish Sanctuary" of the Holy Land at the ending of the 2,300 years of Daniel 8: 14. *First*, on Nisan 1 (March 21) 1844—being 2,300 years from Ezra's Reforms on Nisan 1 B. C. 457, and *secondly*, on Nisan 22 (April 27) 1756, at the ratifying of the Crimean War Treaty of Peace—being 2,300 years from Nehemiah's Reforms begun on Nisan 22, B. C. 445 in Nehemiah 2; Daniel's forty-five years in Daniel 12: 11, 12—the excess of the 1,335 beyond the 1,290—extend from that Treaty on Nisan 22, 1856, to Nisan 22 (April 11) 1901 as the End of this Age.

The following is an extract from the 32d chapter of his life, which relates to the Turkish "Charter of Reform," granted in 1856:—Lord Stratford de Redcliffe's negotiations in connection with the peace after the Crimean War, had one great point, viz., to confirm, corroborate, and, so to speak, codify, all the reforms which had been wrung from the Sultan of Turkey since the decree of Gulhane in 1838. The Elchi was busy with the former of these two points before the opening of the negotiations at Paris, in the spring of 1856. It was important that the details should be settled by the Sultan himself, before Russia had the opportunity of putting in her oar. To effect this, the ambassador set to work with all his might, and the result was the crown of all his many efforts for the regeneration of Turkey,

The Famous Hatti-Humayun

of February 21, 1856 (afterward recorded as part of the Treaty of Paris on April 27, 1856, ending the Crimean War.) In this imperial proclamation the Sultan announced his desire of renewing and enlarging the numerous improvements which had been introduced into his institutions with a view to making them worthy of the place which his empire held among civilized nations; he was anxious, he said, to assure the happiness of his people, "who, in my sight, are all equal, and equally dear to me"; and with this object he first confirmed the former guarantees of the Hatti Sheriff of Gulhane to all his subjects, without distinction of class or religion, for their security in person, property, and honor; and at the same time renewed all the privileges and spiritual immunities granted *ab antiquo* and subsequently to Christian and other non-Mussulman communities established in Turkey. The proclamation went on to enumerate various

Ecclesiastical Privileges,

guaranteed the free exercise of its religious rites and the control of its sacred and educational buildings to each and every sect; and announced in bold terms that: Every distinction or designation tending to make any class whatever of the subjects of my Empire inferior to another class on account of their religion, language, or race, shall be forever effaced . . . As all forms of religion are and shall be freely professed in my dominions, no subject of my Empire shall be hindered in the exercise of the religion which he professes, nor shall in any way be annoyed on that account. No one shall be compelled to change his religion.

The eligibility of all Turkish subjects, without distinction, to public offices; their admission to the civil and military schools; the abolition of the system of farming the taxes; and various other reforms tending to the repression of corruption, extortion, and malversation, and the equal encouragement of good citizenship without prejudice of class or creed, were all promised in this great charter.

Lord Stratford's hand is traceable in every line; these were his reforms, either already carried, or pressed upon the Porte; this was

The Culminating Moment

in Lord Stratford's reforming career, and the seal to all his labors on behalf of just and equal Government in Turkey. It was a signal triumph to have extorted such a programme of reform from a Mahommedan sovereign, in face of the hostility of the vast majority of his Moslem subjects, despite the opposition of most of the men in office, and notwithstanding the indifference, if not contempt, manifested by the European Powers for all dreams of Turkish regeneration. Lord Stratford himself was astonished: "Considering that of the five persons who joined me," he wrote, "in drawing up the Charter, two were Mohammedans, two Roman Catholics, and one a member of the Greek Church, its acceptance was *little short of a miracle*. I confess that I had no previous expectation whatever of overcoming the prejudices of such colleagues in negotiation, and particularly of those who professed the Mussulman belief." No one but Lord Stratford could have won such a victory. The Hatti-Humayun was indeed part of the Treaty of Paris of April 27, 1856, ending the Crimean War. It was recognized in Article IX.

THE EARTH'S FUTURE METROPOLIS.

[THE following is the substance of a remarkable interview with Dr. H. P. Mendes, the well-known Jewish Rabbi, which is printed in the *Jewish Chronicle*. It will be seen that the learned Rabbi fully expects the restoration of Jewish nationality, and fully realizes the blessings to result from it to his own race and the world. He is mistaken, however, in supposing that centuries may elapse before that restoration is achieved, not having taken into account the power of Antichrist, under whose protection it will take place.]

"The subject of restoration is one not clearly understood. It is as distinctly a prophecy of the Bible as our expatriation and dispersion, which has come to pass. Apart from patriotic or Jewish sentiment, let us look over it for a moment from a common-sense standpoint.

"First, is the land of Palestine desirable? The answer is, most emphatically, it is

A Desirable Land.

Its fertility was proverbial, and the soil, after its centuries of rest, must, from a farmer's standpoint, be fully recovered. Apart from Bible sources, where it is constantly called 'a land flowing with milk and honey,' or 'the land is exceeding good' (Num. 14: 7), or 'a good land whose stones are iron and out of whose hills thou mayest dig copper'—apart from these and other such Biblical sources, we find in Josephus, Strabo, Hecateus, and Tacitus statements as to the large population it sustained.

We must draw a distinction between Palestine and the Promised Land, which we regard as our inheritance. The former was from about latitude 31 deg. 7 min. to latitude 33 deg. 15 min., or about one hundred and fifty miles in length. The latter is from about latitude 29 deg. 31 min. to latitude 37 degrees, or *upwards of five hundred miles*. The breadth of the former was, as can be seen by a glance at any ordinary map, but very few miles. The breadth of the latter is from the Nile longitude 30 deg. 2 min. west, or the 'River of Egypt,' as the Bible calls it (Gen. 15: 28, &c.), to the Euphrates, longitude 48 deg. 26 min., or more than eleven hundred miles.

"Now, as for its geographical position as

A Trade Centre.

Imagine Canada and the United States with 826,000,000, which is the given population of Asia. Imagine South America with 307,400,000, which is the given population of Europe. And the millions of Africa, estimated at 206,000,000. Imagine next that Central America has the milder climate of Palestine; that the supply and demand between North and South America, with all these millions of people with wants to be supplied, passes through, as it must, when North and South America will be connected by rail. Would not Central America offer brilliant promises for business purposes?

"Just so is Palestine. Railroad communications between Africa and Asia, and through Asia to Europe, and *vice versa*, must pass through our promised land. The connecting line, already talked of as the Euphrates Valley road, to connect the European system of railways with India and the further East, will also roll trade into the confines of our land. And when this comes to pass, strange to say, history will only be repeating itself. For in the days of Solomon, as Dean Milman so aptly points out, the five great caravan and trading lines of the ancient world converged in Palestine, and hence it was that in his days the national prosperity was so great that they used to say 'silver was in Jerusalem as stones, and cedars as the sycamore-trees that are in the vale, for abundance' (1 Kings 10: 27).

"A common idea is that the doctrine of our restoration means that all Hebrews must go back to Palestine. Our great prophet, however, seems to distinctly indicate that

All Will Not Return,

but that some will stay and engage in prosperous business among Gentile nations. Thus, 'And their seed shall be known among the Gentiles, and their offspring among the people: all that see them shall acknowledge them, that they are the seed which the Lord hath blessed' (Isa. 61: 9). Or again, 'I will take you one of a city and two of a family, and I will bring you to Zion' (Jer. 3: 14). However, as soon as business possibilities are visible you will see that the Hebrews will be ready enough to return to Palestine.

"Every Day Brings Us Nearer.

Long years doubtless have to pass first. Even centuries perhaps. At any rate, events at this moment seem to indicate that only decades and not centuries are destined to slide away before our restoration becomes a fact. Notice the strained attention at times in connection with the Eastern question—often enough it is brought up. Rational common sense has already suggested that the only way to calm the jealousies of the Great Powers as to Syria, which all of them want, is to make it a neutral state; then give it in charge of the Jews, who are peaceful and able to develop business posibilities."

"But do not let it be at all imagined that Palestine is desired by us simply because it gives us a national home. We desire it on account of

What Things it Involves.

To briefly state these I would say—First, the establishment of *a respected court of arbitration* for the settlement of international and such like disputes, thus causing war to cease (Isa. 2: 4); second, an evidencing of a religionizing religion, if I may coin a phrase. I mean a religion which shall not be a conventionality, so that no more shall we see how these Christians do *not* love one another, or how orthodox Jews are oft most unorthodox and reformed Jews sadly need reforming. *Verbum sap*. For the expectation of a better moral tone in the world see Isa. 11: 10, or Jer. 31. 34.

"In short, to sum up what we mean by our restoration to Palestine, we mean the institution of universal peace and universal brotherhood. Universal happiness must naturally follow. This will be not simply a consolation for the Jews, or the consolation of Zion, so long bereaved of her children. It will be the consolation of the world after all the sobbing and shrieking which history's page records of each and every nation."

CHRISTIAN HERALD AND SIGNS OF OUR TIMES.

OFFICE, 63 BIBLE HOUSE, NEW YORK.

TERMS AND INSTRUCTIONS.

Published Weekly. Subscription price in the United States, Canada, and Mexico, $1.50 a year; $1 eight months; 75 cents six months; sent two months on trial for 25 cents, postage free; in Europe and in all countries in the Postal Union, 50 cents extra postage; subscriptions always payable in advance. Single copies, price 3 cents. Any newsdealer will furnish the paper weekly when ordered.

New Subscriptions can commence at any time. When no date is mentioned, we begin it with the issue of the week in which the subscription is received.

Remittances by Mail should be by Post-office money order, bank cheque, draft, or express money order, whenever possible, and should always be made payable to THE CHRISTIAN HERALD. Letters containing money sent in this way need not be registered, as when lost, duplicates can always be obtained.

If a Postal Note or currency is sent, it should always be in a registered letter. Letters can be registered at any office. Subscribers sending money of this kind, and not registering, do it at their own risk.

Change of Address. Name of Post-office and State, of both old and new address, should always be given in case of removal, as without the previous address it is impossible to find the name on our list.

CURRENT EVENTS.

Both Houses of Congress Agreed, by a Joint resolution on October 18, to adjourn indefinitely on October 20. The proposal originated in the Senate, and some capital was made by the Democrats in the House out of the readiness of the Senators to adjourn without passing the substitute for the Mills tariff bill. There was, however, no possibility of passing it, or even of debating it with the thoroughness so momentous a question demanded, as in neither house was there a quorum during the week. The prevalent feeling, however, which doubtless prompted the decision of the Senate, was that voiced by Senator Brown, who suggested that the verdict of the people at the polls next month would settle what sort of a tariff-bill should be passed, and he could see no use in remaining there to talk on that subject. It has been the longest session of Congress on record, and probably one of the most barren.

An Important Factor in the Approaching Presidential election is the curious situation in New York. It forms an instructive illustration of the selfishness of spirit which seems inseparable from politics in State and city. It is notorious that many politicians are indifferent to national questions, but are deeply concerned, for obvious reasons, in city or State government or misgovernment. When, therefore, it happens that there is a hard fight over the election to the mayoralty to be decided on the same day as the election of a President of the United States, an opportunity for deals is presented, which is sure to be extensively used. It is easy for bosses of particular districts in New York City to effect an exchange of votes, on the principle of barter, which may have a mighty influence on national prosperity for the next four years. Instead of voting the straight tickets of their respective parties, they can vote, and cause their hundreds of henchmen to vote, a composite ticket bearing the names of the candidates of one party for the national offices and the candidates of the opposite party for State and city offices. There are this year exceptional inducements to do this. The Democratic candidate for governor is obnoxious to an influential section of the Democratic party, which would prefer seeing, in the State executive mansion, even Warner Miller to David B. Hill. Again, the prospect of another term under Mayor Hewitt is sufficient to make any strong Democrat prepared to scratch the ticket, if he can get some party compensation from the Republicans that will soothe the thing which he calls his conscience. Thus, if the present situation holds over November 6, and New York gives, as is almost certain, the casting vote in the Electoral College, that vote will be determined, not by the respective merits of Cleveland and Harrison, not by the question of the tariff, but by the question of who shall give away contracts, and put his friends into office in New York. Were it not that the Christian has a strong and abiding confidence that God controls and guides the destinies of this nation, the situation would fill him with disgust and despair.

The Settlement of the Strike of the Chicago car drivers and conductors proved a difficult undertaking, and caused much angry feeling on both sides. Mr. Yerkes, the President of the Company, directed his efforts to separating the West Side men, who had no grievance, from their brethren or the North Side. Several conferences were held, in which, at length, one of the West Side men plainly said that there was an apprehension that if Mr. Yerkes succeeded in lowering wages on the North Side, he would require the West Side men to accept the same terms. Mr. Yerkes then volunteered to maintain the present rate for five years, whatever might be the issue of the North Side struggle, and to discharge none of the strikers if the men went back to work at once. The men accepted those terms and resumed their places on the cars. To the North Side men, after some pressure and a resort to arbitration, the offer of six per cent. advance of wages was conceded. The strike was declared at an end, but when the strikers found that the new men were to be retained, and consequently there would not be so many trips per man per day, the dissatisfaction broke out afresh, and there was some fighting, in which several of the new men were injured. No new strike was, however, declared, and as Mr. Yerkes has promised to transfer the new men, as speedily as possible, to other roads, it is hoped that the trouble is over for the present.

The Reduction in the Death Rate from Yellow fever at Jacksonville, Fla., last week, and also in the number of new cases, affords reason to hope that the end of the epidemic is near at hand. Thursday passed over with only one death and twenty-nine new cases, which was the lowest figure of the preceding week. The list given out on that day placed the total number of cases since the outbreak of the epidemic at 3,692, and the deaths at 322. There is considerable uncertainty about the work of disinfection and destruction of property. It appears probable that the work will not be done with the thoroughness essential to future security, unless the owners of property regarded as infected are compensated for its loss. It was expected that the Government would bear the cost of compensation, but there is doubt of this, and there is reason to fear that some property may be spared which safety requires destroyed.

The Visit of the Emperor of Germany to Rome has been the occasion of unprecedented festivities and magnificent ceremonies. The King of Italy has spared no pains to entertain his exalted guest in a manner worthy of Italian traditions. The Colosseum and the Forum were illuminated in his honor. A naval and a military review were held and a new ironclad launched. An excursion was made to Naples, where the excitement of the populace exceeded any demonstration made since Garibaldi's entrance into the city in 1860. Fifty brass bands accompanied the imperial carriage, and 120,000 persons assembled to give the visitor a characteristic Neapolitan welcome. A visit was paid to Pompeii, and the excavations were examined. The workmen duly "discovered" several beautiful vases while the Emperor was present and gave them to him as souvenirs of his visit. The most significant event of the trip, however, was the call the young Emperor made upon the Pope. In order not to hurt Papal sensitiveness the Emperor set out for the Vatican from the German Embassy, not from the Royal palace, and in a carriage of his own instead of using the one placed at his disposal by the King. The Pope received him with impressive courtesy, and the two potentates were closeted together in private conversation for some time. It is more than eight hundred years since a pope and an Emperor of Germany met before this. It was in 1077, when Henry IV. did penance in the snow at the feet of Hildebrand at Canossa.

A Crisis in French National Affairs Appears likely to be developed by the scheme proposed by the Cabinet for the revision of the Constitution. M. Floquet, the Premier, introduced it on October 15. He contended that the present Constitution, which was adopted in 1875, was never regarded by Republicans as more than temporary, and that the time had arrived for making a permanent system. The Republic, he said in explaining his scheme, would remain. Its existence was beyond discussion, since it was the issue of universal suffrage. The revision was aimed against royalist plots, and *plots for the creation of dictators;* a remark intended for the benefit of General Boulanger and his friends. M. Floquet remarked that the bill proposed to grant the Ministers a legal period during which they should remain in power. They would thus be less preoccupied by votes of the Chambers, and have some chance of showing what stuff they were made of. At the same time the Chambers would always possess the right to impeach Ministers. President Carnot is reported to be resolutely opposed to this scheme of the Cabinet.

The Irish Situation was Rendered More difficult of settlement last week, by acrimonious utterances on both sides. On October 18, Mr. Balfour, who is Secretary for Ireland and the nephew of the Premier, was entertained at Manchester by a local political organization, and was subsequently fêted by deserting Liberals, who vied with their political rivals in doing honor to the Conservative statesman. They congratulated him upon "his patient courage in dealing with the Parnellites." In replying to the address Mr Balfour charged the English followers of Mr. Gladstone with sharing the guilt of the Parnellites in supporting politics by crime. On the other side Mr. Michael Davitt sent in a letter to the *Times*, in which he says that the Irish will not accept the scheme proposed by the liberals for the Government of Ireland unless an Irish Parliament is allowed to solve the land question and fix the compensation to be paid to the landlords.

Prince Bismarck's New Map of Europe Was a revelation made last week by the New York *Herald*, but whether it was based on reliable information does not appear. Its intrinsic probability, however, has gained credence for it in many quarters. The following are its main features: The impending death of the King of Holland, the last male descendant of William the Silent, and the consequences that it involves, have been thoroughly discussed at Berlin, St. Petersburg, and Vienna. The eventual annexation of the delta of the Rhine, including Holland, Luxemburg, and part of Belgium, by Germany is already tacitly assented to by Russia and by Austria. Holland's colonies go, of course, with Holland herself. Even the boundary line is already clearly defined. In consideration of their acquiescence Russia and Austria are of course to have adequate compensation. Russia is to have a perfectly free hand to take, whenever she chooses, Constantinople, the eastern half of the Balkan Peninsula, and all she can grasp in central Asia, Persia, and India. Austria is to have the western half of the Balkan Peninsula and Salonica. Prince Bismarck's secret is to isolate England; to unite Russian and German fleets against England, while Russia strikes at India; to keep France in check by giving her a slice of Belgium; to work with the Dutch colonies and newly acquired German coaling-stations in the Indian Ocean and Pacific, as a basis to oust England from her present colonial supremacy.

Christian Workers Throughout the United States and Canada, have been invited to attend a conference next month at Detroit, Mich., and the request is made that the widest publicity be given to the invitation at this early date, to allow of all who can attend, making arrangements to do so. The convention is called by the Committee of Christian Workers in the United States and Canada. Pastors, missionaries in cities and towns, superintendent of city evangelization socities, workers in missions, evangelists, theological students, Y. M. C. A. secretaries, business men, Christian women, and all others especially interested in aggressive Christian effort, are invited to be present as delegates without further notice. The convention will meet in the Tabernacle M. E. Church, Detroit, Mich., November 15-20. The purpose is mutual acquaintance and conference of workers, discussion of practical themes and methods of work, and prayer for God's blessing upon the workers in their efforts "to seek and save the lost" in America. The names of all who expect to attend should be sent immediately to John C Collins, Secretary, New Haven, Conn., in order that delegates' certificates may be sent for use in securing reduced railroad rates, and other necessary arrangements made.

An Important Convention Commenced its sessions in New York on Friday last. It was the fifteenth annual convention of the National Woman's Christian Temperance Union. The meetings were held in the Metropolitan Opera-House, and attracted an immense concourse of outsiders besides the delegates of the Union. Every State was represented in the Convention, over three hundred and fifty elected and duly certified ladies being present as delegates. A prayer-meeting lasting one hour preceded the opening of the convention. It was conducted by Mrs. S. M. J. Henry, of Illinois, presiding officer of the Evangelistic Board of the National W. C. T. U. The convention was then called to order by Miss Frances E. Willard, the president. In the evening addresses of welcome by Mrs. Henry T. Burt, the president of the W. C. T. U. of New York, and by Gen. Clinton B. Fisk, were well delivered. Mrs. Mary A. Livermore, of Massachusetts, responded. A delicate question has to be decided by this convention. An attempt is to be made to exclude from the Union certain ladies, notably Mrs. J. Ellen Foster, of Iowa, for supporting the Republican candidate for the Presidency of the United States, instead of the Prohibition candidate. A very strong feeling has been developed on both sides by the question, and it is feared that a large secession from the Union may result.

A Wife's Last Request is Causing her Widowed husband considerable trouble in New York. The wife died suddenly, of hemorrhage, three weeks ago, at Fort Riley, Kan. Her husband, who is a commercial traveller, was away from home at the time. When he heard of his bereavement he was much distressed, and hurried home immediately. He was about making arrangements for her funeral, when a neighbor, who had been with the lady when she died, came to him and said that his wife made it her last request that he would bury her beside her dead mother. The husband felt a melancholy pleasure in complying with her wish, but he had no idea where her mother was buried, nor where her home was. He knew, however, that it was somewhere in the East, so he had the body embalmed, and brought it to New York, and inserted personal advertisements in the daily journals asking for information. His ignorance of his wife's family is remarkable; but he says that he first met her in the West, where she was travelling for her health. He fell in love with her, persuaded her to marry him, and afterward was so much occupied with home and business matters, that he made no inquiries about his wife's family or her antecedents: hence his present embarrassment. It is strange that one, who evidently cherished loving recollections of her mother, should not have spoken to her husband more about her, and her childhood home. Unhappily we are too familiar with such reticence in religious matters. Some Christians so seldom speak of their Heavenly Father that few know that they are His children. (Matt. 10: 32.)

Two Trains Were Wrecked and Eight Men killed and twenty-four injured on the Lehigh Valley Railroad, on October 16, owing to a flagman's failure to signal the rear train. A Lehigh gravel train, to which was attached a car containing a number of railroad employees, was being switched to a siding to allow the Pennsylvania Railroad fast freight to pass. There was some delay in making the passage to the siding, and a flagman was sent back to stop the Pennsylvania train. Whether he took the wrong road, or did not go far enough back, was not known, but the train came on at full speed and dashed into the cars of the gravel train, which had not reached the siding. Among these was the car containing the railroad men. Both trains were wrecked, with the loss of life and limb above-mentioned. The most vexatious part of the catastrophe was that provision should have been made to prevent it and some awful blunder should have thwarted the precaution. It will be so in the more terrible loss of souls. The atonement which Christ has made would suffice for the salvation of the whole world, but comparatively few will benefit by it. Some, there is reason to fear, will perish through the negligence or mistakes of those who are appointed to watch for souls. (Ezekiel 33: 7, 8.)

A Cat at a Religious Service Caused Some excitement in Philadelphia recently. The *Telegraph* of that city says that during the Sunday afternoon service in the Masonic Home, Germantown, the proceedings went on as usual until the first hymn was sung, when the piteous wailing of a cat was heard, and the persons present looked at one another in amused surprise. No cat was to be seen, and when the hymn was over the mewing ceased. It commenced again, however, during the reading of the Scriptures and was much more noticeable then. Several persons searched around for the miserable creature, but failed to find it, until the organist opened a door in the side of the organ, when the cat jumped out, and made a wild rush through the building for the door. It was much emaciated, and is believed to have been in the organ since it was used on the previous Sunday. Possibly curiosity or the hope of getting food had tempted the animal into the building. Similar motives have sometimes led human beings into churches, and like the cat, they have been disappointed. Happily, however, some who have been so led have through the influence of the Holy Spirit found a satisfaction which mere amusement, or the gain for which they came, could never have afforded them. (Rom. 10: 20.)

A Young Man's Hair Turned White Through terror in the Catskills recently. A local journal says that on the northern point of Samsonville, High Point, is a rocky slide of slate, about 1,500 feet in length, as smooth as polished marble, and inclined at an angle of about 55 degrees. At the base is a yawning chasm, fifty feet in depth. While a young man, who was spending his vacation in the mountains, was amusing himself by casting huge boulders down the slide so as to see them bounce to the opposite side of the chasm and fall with a crash into the yawning abyss, he lost his balance, and away he went down the steep. What passed through his mind in his rapid flight, he will never be able to state clearly, but his clothes bore unmistakable evidence of what friction will do. As he was about to topple in the yawning abyss below, he caught a firm hold of a young cedar, and clung for his life. As he hung suspended in mid-air, a party of young ladies appeared on the cliff. They heard the voice of the young man and saw his queer predicament. Shouting to him to retain his grip on the tree they ran for help, and soon the young man was rescued by the aid of ropes. When the reporter saw him, his hair had turned white. Probably the young man's experience will make him more cautious about venturing in dangerous places in future. There are still more fatal inclines which he will also do well to avoid. Numbers who go for amusement near the downward path, which leads to perdition, have lost their balance and have not been able to take hold of Christ, who alone can save them. (Prov. 4: 14, 15.)

A Bridegroom was Near Being Left Behind on his wedding trip a few days ago. The marriage had taken place at Union City, Conn., and the newly married couple at once boarded a train for Philadelphia. At Waterbury the train was side-tracked to allow the up-train to pass. The bride boarded the train, while the groom stood with grip-sack in hand watching the up-train. The down-train started for Bridgeport and had proceeded several rods, when the bride rushed to the brakeman at the rear and exclaimed: "Oh, stop the train; that's my husband, and we have only been married about ten minutes." The brakeman looked up the track, and saw a man running towards them, took pity on the bride, pulled the bell-rope and stopped the train. It is much to be hoped for his wife's sake and his own, that this fatal habit of procrastination will not characterize him through life, or there may be some misfortunes come of it that his wife cannot remedy. Especially would it be deplorable if, on that decisive day when so many separations will take place, his wife should be caught up, and he be left behind. Her intercession would be futile then. (Matt. 24: 40.)

BRIEF NOTES.

Mr. George Bancroft, the eminent historian, recently celebrated his eighty-third birthday at his cottage, at Newport, Mass.

The Rev. Sam Jones has been preaching at Cartersville, Ga., and at McMinnville, Tullahoma, and Sparta, Tenn. He has now commenced services in Nashville.

Mr. D. L. Moody commenced his work on the Pacific slope with three services in San Francisco. He then went to Portland, Oregon, and will return to San Francisco later in the year.

The Church Unity Society of Chicago has issued a request to ministers of all denominations, to make the unity of the churches of Christ the subject of sermons and prayers next Sunday.

Remarkable success is attending the evangelistic tour of the State of Illinois by Allen Folger. In all the sixteen years of his labors, there has never been so much eagerness to listen to the gospel.

There has been a water famine in Jerusalem. Nine hundred children in Jewish homes died during the summer for lack of plenty of pure water. Money contributions to a water-fund are being sent by London Jews.

A new mission for Frenchmen in New York was opened on Sunday, October 14, at No. 58 West Third Street, near South Fifth Avenue, the Rev. Paul Desjardins, pastor, under the auspices of the New York City Church Missionary Society, and there was a large attendance.

A convention of branches of the Evangelical Alliance in New York State will be held at Syracuse, N. Y., November 20-22. Pastors from towns in which no branch is yet organized are invited. It is intended at this convention to perfect arrangements for a permanent State organization of the Alliance.

A notable celebration in Berlin was held on October 8. A large convention of Sunday-school officers and teachers assembled to commemorate the introduction into Germany of the American Sunday-school system thirty-five years ago. Rev. W. Reinhard, minister of the Prussian National Church, was appointed travelling agent.

A wonderful blessing has attended the labors of Rev. R. G. Pearson, of the Cumberland Presbyterian Church, in evangelistic services in North Carolina. At Winston and Salem there was a widespread movement. The revival was preceded by a Union Prayer-meeting, in which the Moravian, Methodist, Baptist, Episcopal, Methodist-Protestant, and Presbyterian churches participated.

The Rev. B. Fay Mills is now conducting revival services in Philadelphia, and expects to remain there nearly all the year. At Deckertown and Middletown, N. Y., his labors have been followed by large accessions to the churches. In the latter town the services were held in the First Presbyterian, Second Presbyterian, Congregational, Methodist, and Baptist churches alternately.

The following statistics of the Baptist Denomination in the United States were presented at the recent conference. There are 1,281 Baptist associations in the United States, 31,891 churches, 20,497 ministers, 158,373 baptisms last year, 23,228 restorations, 26,403 deaths. The associations have a membership of 2,917,315. There are 15,447 Sunday-schools and 1,126,405 pupils. The value of the church property is $48,568,686.

CONSOLATION FROM RESURRECTION.

A New Sermon By Pastor C. H. Spurgeon.

"I will ransom them from the power of the grave; I will redeem them from death; O death, I will be thy plagues; O grave, I will be thy destruction; repentance shall be hid from mine eyes."—Hosea 13:14.

A Rock of Mercy in a Sea of Wrath—I. A Fact Used as a Figure—A Special Resurrection for Believers—From Among the Dead—Through Redemption—By Divine Power—Death Abolished at the Resurrection—II. Implies Deliverance out of Troubles—The Passover Lamb Supplied both Blood and Food—III. Resurrection from Death and Sin—IV. From Other Forms of Death—The National Death of the Jews—The Spiritual Death of the Church—Individual Churches—The Depressed Child of God—A Man Imbedded in Snow.

This verse stands in the midst of a long line of threatenings. Like a rock of mercy, it rises in the midst of a sea of wrath. Hence many critics have felt bound to see in it a continuation of threatening. I am quite content to accept the united authority of the Authorized and the Revised Versions, and to believe that the mind of the Holy Spirit is fairly expressed in the grand old Bible of our fathers. I regard our text as a promise overflowing with delight.

While it does stand as a rock apart, this gracious word is far from being the only one in the book of the prophet Hosea.

In the Torrent Bed

of this prophet's denunciations we find dust of the gold of promise. Hosea, in his style, is jerky and abrupt: he says exactly what you do not think he is going to say. The Holy Spirit, speaking through him, interjects promises in the midst of threatenings, in wrath remembering mercy. If any should think that this passage is exceptional, let them read the rest of Hosea's prophecy.

Israel was coming to its very worst. The people were to be carried to Babylon, and thence to be scattered to the ends of the earth. Yet the Lord, in His great love, lets them know that this was not to be a final and entire destruction. He would not utterly cast away the people whom He did foreknow, nor allow death to hold them in bondage for ever. He would open their graves, and bring them out, and make them to know Jehovah. Therefore, he drops in this word of promise when it was least expected.

I. I shall ask you this morning, to consider

The Fact

which is here used as a figure. The Resurrection of the dead is here employed as a figure of that which the Lord was about to do for His people. At one time salvation from sin is called a creation, and creation is a fact; here it is a Resurrection from the dead, and that also is sure to be accomplished in due time: we have the first-fruits of it already.

Brethren, there will be *a special Resurrection* for those who are in Christ Jesus. "There shall be a Resurrection of the dead, both of the just and unjust." But for the members of the body of Christ there is a Resurrection from among the dead. These are the many that sleep in the dust of the earth who shall awake to everlasting life. (Dan. 12:2.) That which is sown in weakness shall be raised in power; that which is covered with dishonor by the very fact of death and decay shall be raised in splendor, made like unto the glorious body of Christ. This is no poetic fiction, but a literal matter of fact, even as was the Resurrection of the Lord Jesus. We hear our Redeemer say, "Thy brother shall rise again," and we accept it literally. Our dear ones whom we have laid in the grave shall come again from the land of the enemy. Concerning ourselves, also, we believe, as we just sang—

"Sweet truth to me,
I shall arise,
And with these eyes
My Saviour see."

We accept the doctrine of the Resurrection of the dead as the revelation of Christianity. The immortality of the soul was seen before the appearing of our Lord in a dim and cloudy manner; but the Resurrection of the dead was not discoverable by the light of nature, and when it was at first preached, men called the preacher a "babbler"; they could not understand that such a thing could be. The philosophy of human nature rejected the Resurrection, and rejects it still. Only by the revelation of Christ do we know that the dead shall rise again.

This Resurrection is connected with redemption: "I will ransom them from the power of the grave." A ransom is the paying of a price for something. There was

A Price Paid for Us,

to deliver us from the death which is the desert of sin. You know who paid it, and how He paid it. Remember how He opened wide His hands, and poured forth more than gold; remember how His side was digged by the spear, that the deep mines of his life-wealth might be emptied out for us. Jesus our Lord has paid the ransom price. Now are we "waiting for the adoption, to wit, the redemption of our body." (Rom. 8:23.) Regeneration has liberated the soul, and Resurrection will do the like for the body before long. The grave holds the bones of the saints as with the grasp of an iron hand; but the redemption of our Lord Jesus will open the giant fist and set the prisoners free. Glory be to God for the sure hope of resurrection! No mass of stone, nor superincumbent clay, shall keep down these bodies of ours when our Saviour's angels shall "their golden trumpets sound."

This, according to our text, is wrought entirely by divine power. It must be so; for how could the dead contribute to their own lives? How can bodies which have been dissolved in the sepulchre reconstruct themselves? But all things are possible to the Creator. We have heard many objections raised to the doctrine of the Resurrection. Let them object as long as they please. Grant us a God, and

Nothing is Impossible,

or even difficult to Him. By the risen Christ we shall be raised again from the dead. We shall sing hallelujahs to Him that was slain. He by death has destroyed death, and by His Resurrection has torn away the gates of the grave. This is our Lord's doings, and we adore Him because of it.

Observe next, that by the Resurrection death itself is transformed, and totally overcome. Satan gloated over the mischief which he had wrought by death; but lo, it is through death that Jesus has destroyed him, and delivered His people. God makes His

Dying People to be Like the Sun,

which never seems so large as when it sets. All the glories of mid-day are eclipsed by the marvels of sunset. Watch the west! See how the clouds are mountains of gold, and anon the skies are seas of fire. All the tapestries of heaven are hung out to welcome the returning hero of the day to his rest beyond the western sea. So does the dying saint light up his dying chamber with heavenly splendor as he sets upon this world to shine in another. Thus the Lord plagues death, leaving the monster powerless to harm or even terrify the believer.

To close this first subject—this Resurrection will abolish death and every possibility of it in the future. I notice that certain persons, in their anxiety to suck the meaning out of the word "everlasting," so as to avoid everlasting punishment, have questioned the everlasting nature of heaven. They have even gone the length of hinting that they are not quite clear that if believers get to heaven they will always remain there. Yes, and this is what it comes to. Nothing is safe from these revolutionists. They would tear away every covenant blessing from the children of God in their zeal to make the punishment of sin a trifle. But it is not so. Jesus has said: "Because I live, ye shall live also." So long as God is God, His children, partakers of the divine nature, must live for ever, and be for ever blessed. Raised from the dead, and taken up to Christ's right hand, we shall henceforth fear no second death.

II. In the second place, in these words lies an encouragement to look for

Deliverance Out of Great Troubles.

The encouragement comes in this way: God, that will surely raise His people from the dead by His own power, can and will as surely raise them from every kind of trouble and apparent destruction. If there can be any comparison of case with omnipotence, it must be easier to raise Job from his dunghill than to raise Job from his grave. If God, therefore, shall restore us from the sepulchre, He can certainly restore us from sickness, from poverty, from slander, from depression of spirit, from despair. That is clear; who shall doubt it? When the Lord puts us into the furnace, it is to refine us; and as soon as the dross is consumed, He will bring forth the pure gold. He puts us under chastisement for our profit; and when that profit is seen, He will break the rod. We may assuredly expect that He who bringeth up dead bodies from the grave, will bring His distressed people up from their troubles, when those troubles have wrought their lasting good.

And now, to come to the text, we must traverse the same ground again: this deliverance comes through redemption. He that died for you, lives for you, and cares for you. You shall be supplied not only with grace and glory, but with food and raiment. "Thy bread shall be given thee; thy waters shall be sure." Oh, rest in the Lord; especially confide in the redemption of Jesus. Let the precious blood speak peace to you; for if He has bought your soul, He has bought all that goes with it, and all that is needed for this life as well as the next. As well our temporal as our eternal concerns come under the protection of the blood. The Paschal lamb, whose sprinkled blood shielded the house wherein the Israelite was sheltered, also became food for his journey. He who provides heaven will provide all necessaries on the road thither

This deliverance will also be God's work. What aid does He need in rescuing His servants? Oh, learn to wait only upon the Lord! Do not think that I am talking mere words. No; trust in God must be real and practical, and it must be simple and unmixed. "My soul, wait thou only upon God; for my expectation is from Him." Oh, how sweet it is to rest

On God's Bare Arm!

Long have I known what it is to trust in God, and at the same time to repose on the help of many friends; but now I know what it is to rest in Him unmoved when forsaken by many. I cling to that dear arm, and find it all the help I need. And now I will henceforth abide in my confidence in that lone arm; and should deserters all return, and ten thousand friends rally to my side, I will not spare them a particle of my reliance, but still cry, "My soul, wait thou only upon God!"

When the Lord delivers His people, His work is singularly complete, for He triumphantly turns evil into good. He will enrich you by your impoverishment; He will make you strong out of weakness; He will give you health by means of sickness; and fullness by emptying you. Does the adversary threaten to destroy you? You shall be more than a conqueror. Are you led away in bonds? You shall lead your captivity captive. Those who seek your ruin will unconsciously be doing the best thing that could be done for you. That which seemed to be the death and burial of your hope shall be the overthrow of your fears.

The Lord will do this so completely that He will make you sing concerning it. We shall before long look back upon all our afflictions with gladness, and bless the Lord for them as for our chiefest blessings. We may yet feel like that great saint who, when he recovered from sickness, cried, "Take me back to my sick-bed again, for there have I enjoyed such fellowship with Christ as I never knew before." We may yet have to say, as certain saints of the Church of Scotland said, "Oh, that we were meeting among the moors and the hills once more; for never had the bride of Christ such fellowship with the Bridegroom as when she met Him in secret places!" The Lord knoweth how to lift us high by that which cast us low, and to make psalms for our stringed instruments out of the dirges which drowned our music. The God of the Resurrection has delivered, doth deliver, and will deliver His people.

III. Time fails me, and, therefore, I must hurry on, else I had loved to linger and expand. See here a declaration that God will save

From Death in Sin.

He that will raise our bodies from the grave will, according to His everlasting covenant, raise His chosen from their death in sin. This must be so. If the Lord did not raise His people's souls from their death in sin, a resurrection of their bodies would be a curse rather than a blessing. Resurrection will be no boon to those who die unregenerate. My hearers, you will all rise from the grave; but I fear that some of you will rise to shame and everlasting contempt. This regeneration must come to all of you, if you are to be partakers of the glory of Christ hereafter. Ye must be quickened, though ye were dead in trespasses and sins. That fact suggests a question to each—have you received the divine life?

If you are indeed made alive unto God, you will agree with me that this resurrection comes to us entirely through redemption. There is no quickening a dead soul, except by the process here described: "I will ransom them from the power of the grave; I will redeem them from death." Beloved, life only came to you when you received Christ, your Redeemer. Well do I remember when I first looked unto Him, and lived!

The Life and the Look Came Together.

There is no receiving eternal life apart from believing in Him who is the life. There is no life except by looking unto Jesus. In Him we died unto sin, in Him we were redeemed from death and the curse, and in Him we live for ever. Our resurrection from spiritual death is always connected with the precious blood once shed for many for the remission of sins.

This work once done is an abiding work. I point to the seal at the bottom of the text. "Repentance shall be hid from mine eyes." God resolves that they shall live, for He has redeemed them, and His redemption price is too precious to be wasted. He has ransomed them from the grave, and they shall never return to their grim prison-house again. Man's work is superficial, and, therefore, soon disappears. All that nature spins, nature unravels: all that is woven in the loom of human excitement will be rent to pieces by the hand of time and trial; but surely I know that what God doeth He doth for ever, and it standeth fast without a change. Oh, that He would this morning come and quicken dead souls!

IV. What little time you can yet afford me, I will use in stating that here we have an assurance that the Lord can deliver from

Any Other Form of Death.

The Jews: as an organized nationality, they are dead. They are a people scattered and divided under the whole heaven. Truly might they say, as in the prophet Ezekiel, "Our bones are dried, and our hope is lost: we are cut off from our parts." We have no instance in history of a nation dying and coming to life again. Assyria, Babylon, these had their day, and they failed and passed away. Where are they now? Can these empires live again? Persia, Greece, Rome, these vast dominions, died morally, and then they ceased to be a living power. Can they ever be restored? Impossible! But because her God liveth, Israel can never die. Israel will be a nation yet again, and a glorious one. Restored to her own land, and rejoicing in her own Messiah, who is "the glory of His people Israel," it shall be seen that the Lord hath not cast off His people.

In the next place, suppose the *church at large* should decline to a spiritual death—and I am sure it does so just now—what then? The faults which are now so apparent may only be the beginning of worse evils. Brethren are prophesying that the Jesuits will ruin us, and others that Rationalism will eat out the heart of the Church. I think both these sets of prophets have a good deal to say for themselves;

The Signs of the Times

are much with them. But suppose error should become rampant in all our churches, as it may; suppose those who bear testimony should grow fewer, and their voices should be less and less regarded, as they may be; suppose at last the true Church of Christ should scarcely be discoverable, and that men should bury it, and dance a saraband upon its grave, and say, "We have done with these believers in atonement. We have done with these troublesome evangelical doctrines." What then? The truth will rise again. The gospel will burst her sepulchre.

Some of you perhaps from the country may happen to belong to churches which have come near to death's door. That which is true of the church at large is true of any individual church. Have faith in God. He can trim the expiring lamp. They talk about shutting the doors of the chapel. Has it come to that? Prayer-meetings—are they given up? Gospel preaching—have you almost forgotten the joyful sound? The Sunday-school—has that become a farce? Does everything seem dead? Cry to the living God. Do not say to yourself, "Can these dry bones live?" They can, if the living God intervenes. God, who made Ezekiel see the dry bones stand up as a great army, can make you see it yet. Be of good confidence. "When the Lord shall build up Zion He will appear in glory."

Suppose I am now speaking to *some child of God*, who says, "I can believe all this; but, alas! I feel dead myself." We do sometimes faint, and are full of fears, and cry, "Will the Lord cast off for ever? and will He be favorable no more?" We trust we do really love the Lord; but we get very dull at times. We feel as if we could not pray; there is no singing in us; and we feel as if we could not feel. At times we are so dull and stupid that we cannot think ourselves to be enlightened of the Lord at all. For my own part, "I am more brutish than any man" at times, in my own esteem. Be our case as it may, let not faith waver because feeling changes.

When You are down in the Dumps,

remember that as the Lord will raise your dead body, He can certainly revive your fainting heart. Trust in Him to restore your soul. A man, finding himself *imbedded in the snow*, discovered, to his horror, that he could not move his feet, for they were frozen; nor his hands, for they were stiff with cold. He would have given himself up, therefore, as certainly doomed to die, but he found that he could speak, and here was hope. His tongue was not frozen, so he began to call aloud; and he did not call long before helpers came and dug him out, and thawed him back to life. If you cannot do anything else, my dear friend, do cry aloud. Cry, "O God, help me! Quicken thou me, O Lord."

Do any of you say, "Well, I never get into so sad a state. I am always lively?" I am very glad to hear it, if it be true. But I have heard that the statues in St. Paul's Cathedral are never afflicted with rheumatism; and the reason is because they have no life. I am just a little afraid that you also may have no changes and no fears, because you have no spiritual life. God knows whether it is so or not. Look to it. I would sooner have the rheumatism, and be alive, than be without pain, and be a statue.

Hope for the Unconverted.

Lastly, let us have that same hope about our unconverted friends. Let us begin by knowing what they are, and what is their condition. Do not say, "I hope my boy will be saved, because I do not see much evil in him." Your boy is as spiritually dead by nature as anybody else's boy. "That which is born of the flesh is flesh"; and however good your flesh may be, it is only flesh, and only flesh has come of it. I beg you to regard every soul that is not begotten unto God as being dead in sin, else you will not go to the bottom of things, and you will not go the right way to work. Next, go to the Lord and Giver of life, and say, "Lord I cannot make this dear child live; I cannot bring my unconverted husband to Thee. I will do all I can by teaching, persuasion, and example; but O my Lord, I look to Thee to give the spark of divine life." Go to God with your anxiety for dead souls, and cry, "Lord quicken them!" In dependence upon the Spirit of God, preach the gospel, which is the vehicle of divine life, and you shall see them live. Have faith about those who are laid on your heart. God grant your faith a full and speedy reward, for Jesus' sake! Amen.

[The prayers of the readers of this journal are requested for the blessing of God upon its Editors, and those whose sermons, articles or labors for Christ are printed in it; and that its circulation may be used by the Holy Spirit for the conversion of many sinners and the quickening of God's people. Dr. Talmage and Mr. Spurgeon especially request prayer every Sunday morning on behalf of their labors.]

GEMS FROM NEW BOOKS.

LOUISA MAY ALCOTT.*

It was on the 29th of November, in the good year 1832, when a dear little baby girl came into a sweet and beautiful home in the pleasant suburb of Germantown, near the great City of Brotherly Love, or Philadelphia. Very welcome was the dear baby, for she came to loving, true hearts: to a father who was noble and good, and felt reverence for every child; to a mother whose great, generous heart was ready to hold all in its loving embrace; and to a little sister who was full of delight in the baby. This baby was Louisa Alcott, the children's friend. A picturesque house it was, and it is still standing, though the little town has grown into a great one, and is not so country-like and pretty as it was then. Her father taught a school in Philadelphia, and the little ones grew and throve under their mother's watchful eye.

Her Education.

At this time Mr. Alcott kept that school in the Masonic Temple which has become so famous through the account Miss Peabody has given of it. Some things in the school at Plumfield are taken from this model, but not much, for this was only a day school, and I don't think the teacher thought quite so much of making the children's bodies strong and giving them a jolly time as Mr. Bhaer did. But he did encourage them to talk and express all their earnest thoughts. "It was a school of thirty children, mostly boys under ten years of age; well disposed, good-natured, overflowing with animal spirits, and all but intoxicated with play." Louisa never went to this school, but the children had very good times at home. She went later to a smaller school kept by her father in the home at Beach Street, Boston. In fact, Louisa went to school very little, and learned all she knew from her father and mother, and the bright intelligent people they always had about them. She went a little while once or twice to a child's school, and a few weeks to a district school, but her education was very varied and irregular. But the children were taught by their father in the pleasantest way at home. For two hours in the morning they were either in his study or on some shady seat in the garden under his care. He taught them much by writing, and they each kept a journal of their work and their lives. They wrote down words and their meanings, and often made drawings to illustrate them. The father sometimes made pictures of the houses in which they were staying, or the landscapes they loved, and I have seen in one of the journals a sketch of himself, with the little Elizabeth in his lap.

Early Hardships.

I want you children to realize how fully Miss Alcott had known almost all she has described in "Little Women" and her other books. She knew the bitterness of poverty, when even the

*From "Louisa May Alcott, the Children's Friend," a memorial volume by Mrs. Ednah D. Cheney. Illustrated by Miss L. B. Comins, with two views of Miss Alcott's home and burial place, and a colored frontispiece representing Miss Alcott reading, from a volume of "Little Women," to children of various nationalities. Price $1. Published by *L. Prang & Co.*, Boston, Mass.

Lord Stanley, Governor-General of Canada.

Mr. Edison Listening to the Phonograph's Reproduced Concert.

daily food, if not scanty, was simple in quality and sweetened by no luxuries. All that she has told you of the struggles of young girls, turning their dresses and painting their shoes, and carrying a torn glove in the hand, and every little petty misery of the toilet, she has not only seen but known. All the sacrifices made by one sister or friend to help another were felt or observed by her, and all the tender, wise rebukes from father and mother were treasured up in her memory. Scarcely an adventure in her stories but is painted from life, altered in time or place, but still revealing some real person.

Her Secret.

Out of their hard trials, borne with love and courage, but felt just as keenly as other girls feel them, as out of a dark mine she has drawn the gold and silver and precious jewels with which she has brightened the lives of so many children and hard-working girls; for nothing helps us like knowing that others have suffered as we have and conquered as we may. What was the secret of her power to do this? It was that her heart was full of love and faith and courage. She was never ashamed of the poverty or hardships she had been through, but was proud that she could do whatever work was necessary for herself or her family, and she was full of loving thought for everybody else, and longing to help them in the trials she knew so well herself.

BARON STANLEY,

Governor-General of Canada.

THE present representative of monarchy in Canada, in succession to the Marquis of Lansdowne, is a member of the family of the Stanleys whose head is Earl of Derby. He is the second son of the late Earl of Derby, who was three times Prime Minister of England, and whose parliamentary ability won him the name of "the Rupert of Debate." The Governor-General may yet inherit the title and estates of the Earl of Derby, as his elder brother, the present Earl, has no son who can succeed him.

Frederick Arthur, Lord Stanley of Preston, was born in 1841, and after the completion of his education entered the army. The brief period of seven years sufficed to satisfy his military ardor, and in 1865 he quitted the Grenadier Guards for a political career. He was elected to Parliament as a Conservative by the town of Preston, in Lancashire, and subsequently was honored by an election by the northern section of the county. In 1868 he was appointed to an office under the Government as one of the Lords of the Admiralty. In 1874 he was made Financial Secretary of the War Office, and in 1878 he entered the Cabinet as Secretary of War. He retired from office with his party in 1880, but in 1885, the Conservatives being in the ascendant, he was made Secretary of the Colonies. Lord Stanley now receives one of the most coveted prizes in the gift of the British Government.

THE NEW PHONOGRAPH.

(*See Illustration.*)

A PORTRAIT of Mr. Thomas A. Edison, and a picture of his phonograph receiving the strains of music at a concert, appeared in this journal on September 13. We are now enabled to give a picture of Mr. Edison seated in his laboratory at Menlo Park, listening to the reproduction of the record.

When the first phonograph was invented, some years since, it was generally felt that, though the machine as then constructed was no better than a toy, and reproduced vocal sounds in the unnatural tones of a parrot, it was the germ of an important discovery which Mr. Edison in time might develop into a successful reproducer of the human voice. This in great measure he has done. He has replaced the tinfoil recorder by a ring of more durable material, which can be removed and transmitted through rhe mails. The ring is placed upon a cylinder, which is slowly revolved by means of a battery. The sender of a message speaks through a tube, the modulations of his or her voice being accurately impressed upon the ring. When the recipient wishes to hear the phonogram, he places it in the same position on his reproducing cylinder, which revolves as before, and he listens to the words of his correspondent through tubes which, having connection with a battery, he applies to his ears. Both the receiving and reproducing phonographic instruments have been privately exhibited in England by Colonel Gouraud.

Among the guests who accepted invitations to inspect the instrument was *the Rev. C. H. Spurgeon*, whose sermons appear every week in this journal. In the course of his sermon on the following morning he thus referred to the phonograph: "I sat yesterday with *two tubes in my ears* to listen to sounds that came from revolving cylinders of wax. I heard music, though I knew that no instrument was near. It was music which had been caught up months before, and now was ringing out as clearly and distinctly in my ears as it could have done had I been present at its first sound. I heard Mr. Edison speak: he repeated a childish ditty; and when he had finished, he called upon his friends to repeat it with him; and I heard many American voices joining in that repetition. That wax cylinder was present when these sounds w made, and now it talked it all out. I sat and tened, and I felt lost in the mystery. But w of all this? What can these instruments c vey to us? But oh, to sit and listen to the g pel when your ears are really opened! T you hear God Himself at work; you hear Je speak: you hear His voice in suffering and glory, and you rise up and say, 'I never thou to have heard such strange things!'"

THE FISHERMAN'S LITTLE FRIENI

(*See Illustration on page 685.*)

"HERE again, my little man!" said a stalw fisherman to a bright, intelligent boy, whom had seen day by day playing about the roc sometimes with his sisters, but more frequen alone. "You must be fond of the briny."

"Oh yes," said the child, with that readin to make acquaintance with strangers wh characterizes all American children. "We not have the sea at my home. I never sav in all my life till this summer."

"Maybe you'd like to go out with me in boat some fine day, if your mamma wouldn't scared? You'd know more about the sea if y were out on it."

"That's just what I want," said the child. asked mamma to let me have one of the bo out yonder. I am sure I could row. But sh worrisome, you know, and she laughed at and wouldn't think of it."

"Well, tell your mamma that a man who g out fishing every night of his life will take y if she is willing."

"Oh! I'll ask her, you may depend. H you always been a fisherman?

"Most ever since I could walk. I went w father when I was a little un, and got to h him as soon as I could, till I could go it alon

"Did you ever try to walk on the sea?" as the boy, looking up in his new friend's face.

The fisherman burst out laughing. "N he said, "I often swim *in* it; I guess I s never try to walk *on* it, unless I am drunk crazy. What made you think of that?"

"Something my papa told us when we w at home. I'll tell it you: I remember all ab it, because he showed us a picture of it."

"Well," said the fisherman, "I'll put you this rock and then we'll be more on a level conversational purposes, and you can tell your story without cricking your neck." T boy was lifted up, and the tall fisherman st by his side.

"Well," said the boy, "papa said that th was a boat went out one night for fishing o ind it was driven about by wind, and the men were d. And they were out all : In the morning, before it quite light, they saw some walking on the sea toward , and they thought it was ok."

:xactly what I should have ght, myself," put the rman.

h! but it wasn't. When ot close He spoke to them old them who He was, and do you think it was? Why, s Jesus!"

and He was alive, and walk-n the water?"

h yes! But then, you Jesus could do anything. there was something else. of the men in the boat—ame was Peter—thought ould like to do it, too, so sked Jesus if he might. Jesus said 'Yes.' So Peter out of the boat and he ed, too. And he walked ight while he looked at , but he looked off once he saw the big waves roll-and the wind was blowing , and he got scared and away down he went."

Drowned, I guess."

No, he called out to Jesus, Jesus put His hand out and him up till they got to the and they both got in."

'hat's a wonderful story," the man. "No, I never anything like that, and expect to."

But it's quite true," said the . "It's in the Bible. I have book of fairy stories ever nderful, but *they* ain't true, says. What's in the Bible ough, and this story is ere. Papa read it to us, after he had told out it."

've got a Bible," said the fisherman; "it my mother's, but I never read that in it. is, I ain't read it as I'd ought to. Never good at reading, somehow. But I'll look it It's wonderful."

Papa said it was put there to teach every-when they were in trouble to call out to —pray, you know—and He would help like He did Peter. I say my prayer every . You do, too, I suppose."

Well, no, I can't say I do. I know I ought My mother trained me to, but somehow dropped out of it. More shame for me."

Well, you should. Papa says God does so for us, it would be real mean not to thank even if we don't ask Him to do anything ."

guess that's so."

There's my mamma," said the boy, looking nd. "I'll run and ask her now if I may go you. It's a good time, because she don't I'm big enough to take care of myself. she can see you now, and she can't say you ot big enough."

e boy ran off and soon returned with his er, to whom he introduced his new friend. rged his request. It was granted, and that, many a sail did the two strangely as-d companions have together. The boy's e stories, about Jesus hushing the tempest, ssage of the Israelites through the sea, other incidents which he told, as being na-ly interesting to a seafaring man, strongly ssed the fisherman. He wanted to see the boy's stories really were, and remem-g his mother's reverence for the Bible, he d up the Book and read for himself.

ew weeks later, the boy's father came down to fetch his family home, and the boy could not rest until he, too, was introduced to the fisherman. The latter, by that time, was in an inquiring, receptive state, and the earnest Christian father had the joy of leading him to Christ.

The Fisherman Hears a Wonderful Story.

THE EPOCHS OF A LIFE.

A NEW SERIAL STORY.

By Rev. L. S. Keyser.

(Continued from page 670.)

A Congenial Companion.

THE next Sunday morning Hadley listened with rapt attention to a sermon by Mr. Hanson on the reasonableness of faith, which still further dissipated the prejudices that he had entertained against religion.

When, a few days afterwards, he called upon the minister in his study, Hadley's bias against clergymen as a contracted and uncultured class of men received a still further shock. He was surprised at the large and choice collection of works in Mr. Hanson's library—critical commentaries on the Scripture, theological and apologetic works, the best works on philosophy, books of reference in several different languages, the best literature and poetry, and also, much to Hadley's amazement, a shelf full of the productions of the leading sceptical writers of the past and present.

Mr. Hanson noticed his visitor's look of pleased surprise, and led him from shelf to shelf, while he discoursed on the merits of the principal writers.

"I did not suppose," remarked Hadley, "that a minister required such extensive apparatus for his work."

"A preacher of the Gospel cannot know too much," replied Hanson. "No knowledge comes amiss to him, if he knows how to use it. We come in contact with all classes of persons, with the learned and the unlearned, and if we can adapt ourselves to all, we may, as Paul says, win some. Of course, it would be unpardonable pedantry for a preacher to make a display of his knowledge in the pulpit, but still, when there is a real demand for the discussion of difficult questions, he ought to be equal to the exigency. It is, however, in his intercourse with scholarly people that his culture is most needed, if he wishes to win them to Christ. It gives him so much greater purchase power."

"I have heard sermons that did not give evidence of a library like this at the back of them."

"There are ignorant preachers as well as ignorant lawyers and physicians," interposed the minister. "Sometimes uneducated preachers do a great deal of good. It depends upon whether they are well-balanced men or not, and whether they know that their intellectual resources are limited."

Hadley mused awhile. "I have a difficulty that I wish you would explain," he said. "I never could understand how an educated man can believe the Bible to be the Word of God, when it seems to me so preposterous."

"Ha! ha! you think that it is a book for the illiterate only, do you? Let me divulge the secret to you. An educated man accepts the Bible for the same reason that an uneducated man does: *because he has been born from above.*"

The young sceptic was silent. Somehow every difficulty seemed to find a solution in the supernatural, which, though an unknown quantity to him, was very real to believers. Mr. Hanson noted the young man's thoughtful silence and felt sure that the grain of seed would be better left to grow in its own way without further attention. The talk drifted off into literature and local topics. An incidental allusion to lonely bachelor evenings led Hadley to ask: "Are you, also, a bachelor, Mr. Hanson?"

"Yes, sir, so far, that is my condition," replied Hanson, blushing.

"That is not saying that your 'emotional life' is still in an undisturbed state," suggested Hadley, with a laugh.

The clergyman turned crimson, which indicated to Hadley that he had driven a shaft into a sensitive spot of his friend's heart. "I am not good at fencing on that delicate theme," he said. "Good-day, sir; I hope that you will come often."

As Hadley walked away, he felt convinced that his clerical friend was not heart-whole.

"He is the most intelligent and able parson I ever met," mused Hadley on his return toward his room. "He has accumulated a vast fund of knowledge, and it does not seem to be composed of *disjecta membra*, either, but appears to be well systematized and assimilated. Yes, it is remarkable for a *parson*. I wonder whether he is an exception—a *rara avis*. Now, he venerates the Bible. Certainly that is a strong endorsement of the old Book. At any rate, I like him immensely and believe that he is perfectly honest. He elucidated some of the questions that have been perplexing me very satisfactorily; I shall avail myself of the opportunity of seeing him often."

A few steps farther brought another train of thought. "Judging from his appearance, he must be about five years my senior—yes, he is fully thirty. His blush betrayed him, when I spoke of his being in love. I wonder who the object of his choice might be."

The reflection that his friend had fallen a victim to Cupid's wiles, reminded Hadley of the perturbed state of his own affections, and caused him to say to himself: "She told me that she lives at 318 Franklin Street. I am like a poor moth fluttering about a candle, but I cannot resist the temptation to see her home."

Turning to his left he soon reached Franklin Street, which he followed, carefully scanning the numbers on the houses as he passed. His heart fluttered into his throat when he reached the looked-for residence. It was a pleasant home, the house being larger than those near it, which indicated that its owner was in comfortable circumstances, although not affluent. Tall elms, maples, and willows, relieved by green, sighing pines, surrounded the house, while a closely shaven lawn and beds of late autumn flowers showed that careful hands and an artistic taste might be found within. All these signs of æsthetic culture suggested Madeline to Hadley. They were like her. Her taste would bring all her environments into harmony with her characteristic love of the beautiful and good. A cat-bird among the trees was filling the air about the place with his vibratory melody.

Ah! what was that? There was the flash of a woman's dress as some one issued from a side door. The pulsations in the hot temples of the young man might have almost been counted, so intense was his excitement, as the girl's figure stepped carefully and lightly across the lawn beneath the trees, while she looked up toward the place whence the bird-song was emanating. Evidently she had been attracted by the bird's raptured strains. After standing in a listening attitude for a few moments, she sat in a rustic seat that stood by the bole of an elm-tree.

Hadley had recognized her at once. Her lithe form and graceful carriage were indelibly stamped upon his memory, for how often had his eye surreptitiously followed her as she went down the walks of the campus in the old-college days! She was the same girl she had been then, except that she was a little paler, as if some sorrow had left its traces on her life.

In his absorption Hadley had slackened his pace, and was treading so quietly upon the cement walk that his steps were scarcely audible; so that the girl did not perceive him until he had come directly opposite the place in which she was sitting, which was a few rods from the street. When she saw him, the tell-tale blood flowed to her cheeks. "It is always embarrassing for her to meet me after what has happened between us," reflected Hadley, when he saw the flush on her face. He lifted his hat and bowed, which she acknowledged with her characteristic gracefulness.

"Ah, you are listening to the song of *Mimus Carolinensis*, are you?" asked Hadley.

"You mean the cat-bird, do you?" she answered. "I had forgotten his scientific name. Yes, I have been listening to him; he is an exquisite vocalist."

"I am glad that you are a lover of our feathered contemporaries."

"I learned to care for them through—you—at college; you know that you were always directing the attention of your fellow-students to the birds."

Oh! she remembered his idiosyncrasies, did she? Why should any peculiar propensity that he had shown at college impress itself upon her memory? Did she care? He felt an almost ungovernable impulse to decrease the lineal distance between them by stepping across the lawn and taking the seat by her side. But he feared that it would be too bold to do so uninvited. He hoped that she would say, "Can't you come in awhile?" as she had said so often in the happy days before his ill-fated proposal; but the girl was evidently restrained, by some reason best known to herself, from making the wished-for overture, and he therefore felt that the only course open was to pursue his way.

Saying, "Ah! you remember my scientific hobby, I see. Well, I have not worn it out yet," he lifted his hat and resumed his walk.

"She does not care to have an interview with me," he said to himself, bitterly. "The conclusion is self-evident. Our relations are still unchanged. I am still the rejected suitor who is to keep at a distance from her. My fate is a hard one to bear. What have I done to deserve it?"

And again the old rebellion, the old chafing under affliction, rose in his heart, almost causing him to call down imprecations upon his seemingly inimical destiny. The old questioning, the old ground of complaint, was gone over again.

"Why must I carry this eidolon of a hopeless love on my heart? My life is a parody on the doctrine of a kind overruling Providence—a travesty on the Christian conception of God as a 'Father.' I wonder what solution Hanson would give of these harrowing problems! I shall draw him out on this matter when I meet him again."

A little more than a week later—it was a pleasant Saturday morning of Indian summer—Hadley heard a firm, elastic step on the stairway, and the next moment there was a knock at the door of his room. On opening it, "Why, Mr. Hanson, you are out early; come in," broke from his lips.

The clergyman was dressed for a walk, and under his arm he was carrying several books and pamphlets, among them the hand-Bible which Hadley had seen upon his writing-desk a few days before.

"I hope that my unseasonable visit is not unwelcome," he began, without taking the chair which Hadley had offered him. "The fact is, I am going to take a jaunt along the river today, for a little recreation, and as I was passing your room, the thought struck me that you might perhaps be willing to join me. What do you say, Mr. Madelling?"

"I shall be delighted," replied Hadley, in his heartiest style. "I was just wondering how I should pass the day, as in my present mood books are a little dull. May your shadow never grow less for your thoughtfulness in inviting me to go with you," he added, gratefully.

Presently the two friends were walking along the street toward the suburbs of the city. Little had the young sceptic thought, a few months prior to that morning, that he would ever entertain so warm a feeling of friendship for a member of the profession which he had despised so long. He had often called clergymen "pensioners on the public bounty," and once when he saw a group of divinity students he had derisively called them "a flock of charity birds." And yet here he was walking arm-in-arm with a "parson." But the secret of it was, as Hadley well knew, that there was no clerical stiffness, no repellant sanctimoniousness about the minister with whom he was conversing. Indeed, so completely had Hanson thrown off all professional airs, that Hadley almost forgot that he was in the company of a man who was to stand in the pulpit on the following day.

The pedestrians made their way across a bridge that spanned the river at the outskirts of the town, and then, leaving the highway, they turned to their left and followed the curvature of the river to a grove of beeches and maples, where the ground was carpeted with a green lawn-like sod, that came up everywhere flush with the stream. It was a beautiful dreamy day, such as is known only to Indian summer.

For awhile the young men carried on their conversation in a rather desultory fashion, the sights and sounds of the natural world claiming a large share of their attention. The season, the falling leaves, all the aspects of nature, served to recall to Hadley's mind some of the episodes of his past life. It was on a day like this, a year ago, that he had succored Madeline Winters from a terrible death. It seemed to him, now, that he had saved her only to blight his own happiness. These reflections filled him with profound melancholy, and it was natural that his pensive mood should give color to his remarks.

"What a medley of joy and pain existence is!" he observed, sadly. "To-day the sparrows are singing their *Jubilate;* to-morrow, some casualty may change it into a dirge."

"Ah, you are low-spirited to-day," remarked his friend.

"Yes; I suppose it is because 'the melancholy days have come, the saddest of the year.'"

"I think not altogether, if you will allow so blunt a contradiction," said Hanson.

"Do you think that our surroundings have nothing to do with our moods?"

"Somewhat, no doubt," answered Hanson, sententiously, and then continued: "But more frequently our pensiveness is the outgrowth of some unsatisfied longing of the soul, some craving, some disappointment."

Hadley looked at his friend in wonder. What had this acute analyst of the human heart divined. "Are you gifted with a second sight?" he asked.

"Human experience is pretty much the same the world over," Hanson said, philosophically; "and when I take a leaf out of my own biography and read it carefully, I have found the key that unlocks the secrets of almost every heart; and so I say that disappointment in ambition, or love, or fond desire has more to do with our melancholy moods than our external environments have, unless, of course, our environments are extraordinary."

Hadley looked at his friend in surprise, and wondered whether a bitter disappointment had ever cast its shadow upon his path.

"I have been wishing to have a talk with you about the ills of life," he said, at length. "There is the great problem of human sin and suffering—how do you explain it? And especially, how do you reconcile it with the doctrine of the fatherhood of God?"

"That is a mystery of which no complete explanation has ever been found. Many have tried with unsatisfactory results. The best answer is that which the Bible gives."

"Your usual treasury of wisdom," said Hadley.

"Yes, that is so," replied the clergyman, simply. "In this case, we learn that sorrow has its uses and brings its blessings. Among others, moral discipline and clearer spiritual light." Then, seeing Hadley smile incredulously, Mr. Hanson added, "You, too, recognize the difficulty of the problem of sorrow and suffering; what light does agnosticism throw upon it?"

"None at all: it is a great mystery."

"And you have not the consolatory hope we cherish that what we know not now, we shall know hereafter," said Mr. Hanson, sadly. "But let us continue our walk."

"This has been a most delightful ramble to me," said Mr. Hanson, as in the shades of evening they re-entered the city. "I am indebted to you for more bird-lore than I could have thought it possible to gain in one day. Come to my church to-morrow and give me an opportunity to repay the obligation."

They were turning a corner as Mr. Hanson spoke, and Hadley started as he observed Madeline Winters only a few paces ahead and coming toward them. He was also surprised by that strange, subtle, inexplicable perception that his companion was also agitated. He was still more surprised when, raising his own hat in courteous greeting, he saw Mr. Hanson do the like, uttering her name, as he did so, in his singularly sweet, musical tone. Hadley's curiosity was aroused. "Ah," he said, "you know Miss Winters?"

"Oh, yes; she is a member of my congregation. I formed her acquaintance about three months ago, when she first came to this city. But I am surprised to find that you are acquainted with her."

"Why, she was a class-mate of mine at college; we graduated the same time."

"Is that so?" said Hanson, turning a penetrating look upon Hadley, as if he meant to rea his secret. Then he said: "She seems to be a noble girl."

They parted soon, each taking his own course. Hadley was ill at ease. "So he knows Miss Winters, and she is a member of his congregation! Why should that fact cause him to blush so when he met her? I wonder—well, I can't say that I am glad that he is acquainted with her. Of all men he—"

The sentence was left unfinished.

(To be continued.)

DEFEAT AT AI.

By Mrs. M. Baxter.

S. S. Lesson for November 4. Josh. 8:1-12. Golden Text, Ps. 119:36.

Sin Injurious to the Sinner's Surroundings as well as to the Sinner—Joshua Acts on his own Responsibility—Relies on the Report of the Spies—Small Spiritual Foes not to be Despised—May be Difficult to Overcome—Light Obtained through Humiliation and Prayer—Death may be Spiritual Deliverance—A Lesson on the Heinousness of Sin—Tainting all the Belongings—Purification Followed by Victory.

While God deals with the people and carries out His own purposes, He does not forget the education of Joshua. In spite of His command (Josh. 6:18, 19), the children of Israel did commit a trespass in the devoted thing. The deed of one man who was disobedient, and who took for his own that which was devoted to the Lord, was sufficient to trouble and hinder the progress of the whole camp of Israel. We cannot too fully learn the lesson that "none of us liveth to himself, and no man dieth to himself." (Rom. 14:7.) Our surroundings are affected by us more than we are aware. Without our speaking a word or doing a single thing which we imagine may affect other people, our very atmosphere, our very tenor of life, affects all with whom we come in contact. Probably Achan, when he appropriated the spoils from Jericho, thought that he alone was running the risk of God's displeasure. But "the anger of the Lord was kindled against (not Achan only, but) the children of Israel.

In an atmosphere of failure it is much easier to fail. Joshua, who had trusted God at the Jordan, yielded the supremacy to the Captain of the Lord's hosts, and acted second in all the steps of faith in the fall of Jericho, now acts

Without Waiting God's Instructions.

He sends men from Jericho to spy out the land. This is simply his own idea, a prudential manœuvre. Very naturally, the men who are sent return and give counsel, and God was ignored in the matter from first to last. But God did not, therefore, give up the generalship of Israel's hosts. Praise Him. He is wonderfully long-suffering; but He must teach a lesson both to Joshua and to the people. The spies discovered that Ai was but a small place, with few inhabitants, and they thought it was bad economy for all Israel to go up against it. Oh, if we saw the relative position of things, we should not forget that the smallest foe is as difficult to conquer as the greatest, without God. Only three thousand men went up against Ai, and they were discomfited, lost thirty-six of their number, and were smitten and driven back by their enemies. Was God fulfilling His promise, "There shall not any man be able to stand before thee!" If God's promise fails at one time, may it not also fail at another time? Oh, how many ask this question! Joshua at last did the right thing—he went to God, and fell upon his face before the ark of the Lord until the evening; and not he alone, but also the elders of Israel. In any case, he did not charge God with blame, or say that God makes exceptions, and that it cannot always be His will to fulfil His promises. He humbled himself before God, and took a listening attitude. Then God could speak. He cried, "Alas, O Lord God, wherefore hast Thou at all brought this people over Jordan, to deliver us into the hands of the Amorites, to cause us to perish? Would that we had been content, and dwelt beyond Jordan! O Lord, what shall I say, after that Israel hath turned their backs before their enemies!" And then he suggested that utter defeat must follow, and continued, "What wilt Thou do for Thy great name?" and God at once told him the reason of defeat, "Get thee up; wherefore art thou thus fallen upon thy face?"

Israel Hath Sinned.

Therefore the children of Israel cannot stand before their enemies, they turn their backs before their enemies, because they are become accursed. I will not be with you any more, except ye destroy the devoted thing from among you." (R. V.) And He goes on to tell Joshua in detail just how to deal with the matter. Many of us who take counsel with God, have not patience to get the details clear; we are too ready to go ahead at our own pace, and do not wait to keep step with God all the time. But Joshua, although he made mistakes, and was far from being perfect in his walk with God, was always ready to be instructed; he had an ear to hear God at all times.

He returned from the presence of the Lord with a distinct light upon the situation. "God is light, and in Him is no darkness at all." (1 John 1:5.) He went to proclaim among the people, "Sanctify yourselves against to-morrow; for thus saith the Lord, the God of Israel, there is a devoted thing in the midst of thee, O Israel; thou canst not stand before thine enemies until ye take away the devoted thing from among you." And then he announced that a solemn investigation would be made upon the morrow, tribe by tribe, family by family, man by man; "And it shall be that he that is taken with the devoted thing shall be burnt with fire, he and all that he hath: because he hath transgressed the covenant of the Lord, and because he hath wrought folly in Israel." "So Joshua

Rose up Early in the Morning."

Nothing which the Lord commanded him was wrong in the eyes of Joshua; as soon as he knew the will of God, he hastened to do it. God loves this spirit. When a man calculates how much it will cost him to do the will of God, what people may think of it, what he may suffer in his own heart, etc., etc., he does not rise up early to do God's will. Many of the saints of old were early risers, and these were ready doers of the will of God. But was it not hastening Achan to his destruction? Let us look at it in another light. Was it not hastening the time when the devil's hold of Achan's soul should cease? It may be that it was with him as with him who is mentioned in 1 Cor. 5:5, that he should be delivered to Satan for the destruction of the flesh, that the spirit might be saved in the day of the Lord Jesus. God loves souls more than any of us do: He may see that it is a kinder thing to let a man who has sinned, have the chance to confess his sin, and then to let him die, rather than live a longer life on earth. "God *is* Love"; and though we may not understand all His ways, let us at least trust Him.

When the time of trial arrived, the tribe of Judah and the family of Zerak were taken. It was coming near to Achan; how he must have trembled! At last, Achan was taken. It was no use to deny; by God's own test he had been singled out as the guilty one. Joshua said to him, "My son, give, I pray thee, glory to the Lord, the God of Israel, and

Make Confession

unto Him; and tell me now what thou hast done; hide it not from me." Confession meant execution of the most terrible kind; denial was impossible. But oh, there was mercy in this bringing of the truth home to the sinner—anything is better than letting a sin lie on the sinner's conscience. "Achan answered Joshua, and said, Of a truth, I have sinned against the Lord, the God of Israel, and thus and thus have I done: when I saw among the spoil a goodly Babylonish mantle, and two hundred shekels of silver, and a wedge of gold of fifty shekels weight, then I coveted them, and took them; and, behold, they are hid in the earth in the midst of my tent, and the silver under it." Joshua sent to Achan's tent to verify his story, and, sure enough, it was as he had said. Would there be now forgiveness? No; the law could not forgive, the camp must be cleansed, and Achan must die. But how much more blessed must have been his death than if the unconfessed sin had gone before him to judgment; there was shame, there was anguish, in his death, but very probably we shall find Achan among the saved through the merits of a Saviour. Perhaps the most awful part of his doom was that his family was involved in it. Each of them had taken part in the sin because they had not made it known, and therefore they too must suffer. But oh, if he had not sinned, Israel might have been victorious, and his family as well as himself might have lived! One of the awful features of the present day is the making light of sin, and arguing that sins of temper, because inherited, are a misfortune instead of a sin, while sin itself has been inherited from our first parents. God shows us in this history how awful sin is in itself and in its consequences.

It was a solemn funeral procession which wended its way to the valley of Achor, Achan

Followed by his Sin,

"the mantle, the silver, and the wedges of gold—and then by his sons and his daughters (probably his wife was not living), then by his oxen, asses, sheep—the poor, innocent animals were tainted by belonging to a master who had sinned against the Lord; his very tent was contaminated, for it had harbored the devoted thing. All must perish with him. They arrive; Joshua says, "Why hast thou troubled us? The Lord shall trouble thee this day." Then all Israel who were present to witness God's judgment upon the offender, stoned them with stones, and burned them with fire, and a great heap of stones, such as we call a "cairn," was raised over the ashes to remind Israel in all ages of God's judgment against sin.

"And the Lord turned from the fierceness of His anger." The wrong was put right, and God resumed command again. His first words to Joshua were, "Fear not." It had appeared, as though there were everything to cause him to fear. But when we are in touch with God, keeping step with Him, we have nothing to fear. "Fear not, . . . *take all the people of war* with thee, and arise, go up to Ai; see, I have given into thine hand the king of Ai, and his people, and his city, and his land." God's thoughts are not as our thoughts. God would have every man in Israel concerned in taking possession of the city which He gave them. They would obtain nothing by their own efforts anyway, whether by many or by few. But God did not repeat Himself, and make Ai another Jericho. God can do with or without military tactics. In this case He would employ them, and so directed Joshua to set an ambush against the city. He directed five thousand men to lie in ambush on the west of the city, while he with the remainder of his army made an attack from the north, and then made a feint of flying, as before, until Ai was emptied to pursue them; then the ambush arose, fired the city, and then destroyed all the inhabitants. Thus God redeemed His honor, and the honor of His people, as soon as they were right with Him, and the disgrace of their defeat was wiped away. Here Israel might take the spoil and the cattle, for God had received His first-fruits in Jericho.

CHISEL-WORK.

'Tis the Master who holds the mallet,
And day by day
He is clipping whatever environs
The form away;
Which, under His skillful cutting,
He means shall be
Wrought silently out to beauty
Of such degree
Of faultless and full perfection,
That angel eyes
Shall look on the finished labor
With new surprise,
That even His boundless patience
Could grave His own
Features upon such fractured
And stubborn stone.

'Tis the Master who holds the chisel,
He knows just where
Its edge should be driven sharpest,
To fashion there
The semblance that He is carving;
Nor will He let
One delicate stroke too many,
Or few, be set
On forehead or cheek, where only
He sees how all
Is tending—and where the hardest
The blow should fall,
Which crumbles away whatever
superfluous line
Would hinder His hand from making
The work Divine.

With tools of Thy choosing, Master,
I pray Thee then,
Strike just as Thou wilt, as often,
And where, and when,
The vehement stroke is needed;
I will not mind
If only Thy clipping chisel
Shall leave behind
Such marks of Thy wonderous working
And loving skill,
When discipline's hand are over,
Have all sufficed
To mould me into the likeness
And form of Christ.

J. E. JEWETT, Publisher, 77 Bible House, New York, will furnish the above poem in leaflet form at twenty cents per hundred. *A Sample Packet of 50 leaflets assorted (no two alike), will be sent post-paid, for 10 cts., or 100 for 20 cts.* Postage stamps taken.

For Tired Brain

Use Horsford's Acid Phosphate.

Dr. O. C. STOUT, Syracuse, N. Y., says: "I gave it to one patient who was unable to transact the most ordinary business, because his brain was 'tired and confused' upon the least mental exertion. Immediate benefit, and ultimate recovery followed."

"The best thing yet!" That is the way a young man put it who made arrangements to work for B. F. Johnson & Co., Publishers, of Richmond, Va. You can get further information by dropping them a card.

The latest and best imperial Photographs of **Dr. Talmage** and **Rev. C. H. Spurgeon**, with their fac-simile autograph, and also imperial photograph of **Rev. Henry Ward Beecher**, can be obtained from J. E. Jewett, 77 Bible House, New York. Sent postpaid for twenty-five cents each. Postage stamps taken.

MEXICO

Contributions in aid of Christian work in Mexico are most pressingly needed, and can be mailed to the address of

BISHOP H. C. RILEY,
Care of J. P. HEATH,
43 Bible House, New York.

To our CHRISTIAN FRIENDS:

As there is a regular monthly expense in connection with the work a regular monthly income is needed to meet that expense. We, therefore, specially ask for regular monthly contributions in its behalf. If many will each send a little every month, or quarter, or whenever they can, it will do great good. *Remember, every little helps.*

H. CHAUNCEY RILEY.

WHAT EVERYONE WANTS.

Work for All. Large Profits to Agents. An illustrated card picture of the **Twenty-Third Psalm** in delicate colorings, and heavy gold border. The central picture is the **Shepherd** leading His flock. **Everyone likes it.** Single copies 10cts.; three for 25cts.; eight for $1.00. Lower prices for larger orders. Wm. P. Breck & Co., 59 John St., New York.

FEATHERS. The finest live white geese feathers in the country, 75 cts. per lb. Hair Mattresses made over for $2.50. Feathers cleansed & renovated. Pickford, 11 Nassau St., Brooklyn, N.Y.

ALONE WITH GOD:

STUDIES AND MEDITATIONS OF A SICK-ROOM.

By Rev. JOSEPH CROSS, D. D., LL. D.

READ THIS REVIEW.

"In singularly sweet and chaste language he gives expression to the thoughts which one who has long walked with God finds refreshing in hours of solitude. A strange, soothing, solemnizing influence comes over the spirit almost unconsciously as one reads these meditations, as if one were in the very presence of God. They breathe a spirit of simple, trusting faith, full of intelligence, as of one who says, 'I know in whom I have believed.' The section on 'The Christian surrendering his will,' and that on 'The Christian drawing nearer to Christ,' are especially beautiful. We can imagine no book of modern time more fitted for the sick-room or one more adapted to the condition of the Christian sufferer nearing the grave. It speaks of peace, of resignation, of acquiescence in the divine will, a calm loving trustfulness which few in the heyday of health and strength ever attain."—*The Christian Herald.*

SPECIAL OFFER.

Copies of this popular book, containing 324 pages, bound in rich cloth, will be mailed, postpaid, for $1, or copies with full gilt edges for $1.25. Send early and secure a copy of this excellent book.

THOMAS WHITTAKER, Pub'r,
2 and 3 Bible House, New York.

Ladies American Housekeeping. A Ladies' Home Journal. "The Best Ladies' Magazine Published." Full 30 pages with a handsome colored cover each month. Complete on all Home Subjects, COOKING, KITCHEN and DINING ROOM, HOME DECORATION, ART, FASHIONS, FANCY WORK, HINTS TO MOTHERS, HOME READING, BRIC-A-BRAC, Etc. Illustrated Serials by our best Authors. WOMEN'S WAR RECOLLECTIONS is a New feature for a Ladies' Journal. Our Fashion Notes, prepared specially for us, give latest styles of Dress, Millinery, valuable suggestions for Amateurs. To anyone who will BEFORE JANUARY 15th, 1890, send us 50 CTS. to pay for one year's subscription to AMERICAN HOUSEKEEPING, we will send free, THE EVERY-DAY COOK BOOK, an Octavo Volume of nearly 400 pages—best tried receipts on Cooking, Pickling, Preserving, Etc., a complete Home Encyclopedia of practical receipts of all kinds, well bound in illuminated cover. This offer is made to increase American Housekeeping in New Homes. SEND 50 CENTS FOR THE PAPER FOR ONE YEAR, and get the COOK BOOK (Price $1.00) FREE.

$1.00 COOK BOOK FREE

American Housekeeping, Chicago, Ill.

BUNYAN'S PILGRIM'S PROGRESS AND THE HOLY WAR.

A New Large Type Edition, Illustrated, with Marginal Notes and References,

printed from new plates, and beautifully bound in rich English muslin, with beveled edges and gilt back and side. This is the complete edition of the Pilgrim's Progress, The Holy War, and a Memoir of John Bunyan, all bound in one volume of over 700 pages. Price, $1.50, sent postpaid to any address on receipt of price.

J. E. JEWETT, 77 Bible House, N. Y.

For Gas — BAILEY'S COMPOUND Light-spreading Silver-Plated CORRUGATED-GLASS REFLECTORS. A wonderful invention for Lighting Churches, Halls, etc. Handsome designs. Satisfaction guaranteed. Catalogue and price list free. **Bailey Reflector Co.** 113 Wood st. Pittsburgh, Pa. — For Oil

ILLUSTRATIVE GATHERINGS

for Preachers and Teachers. A Manual of Anecdotes, Facts, Figures, Proverbs, Quotations, &c., &c., adapted for Christian teaching. By Rev. G. S. Bowes. Two series, 12 mo. muslin, each $1.25. "For variety, pertinency and availability it is decidedly superior to anything we have seen."—*Biblical Repository.* Sent to any address free on receipt of above price. PERKINPINE & HIGGINS, [illegible] Arch St., Philadelphia, Pa.

$75.00 to [illegible] **A MONTH** can be made working for us. Agents preferred who can furnish a horse and give their whole time to the business. Spare moments may be profitably employed also. A few vacancies in towns and cities. B. F. Johnson & Co., Pub's, 1009 Main St., Richmond, Va.

AGENTS WANTED to sell "The Child's Bible." Introduction by Bishop J. H. Vincent, D.D. The best selling book handled by agents. Recommended by all clergymen. Address Cassell & Co., B.B.S.D., 104 and 106 Fourth Ave., New York; 40 Dearborn St., Chicago, Ill.

MORE MEN WANTED for local and traveling Salesmen. Good Pay. Address E. B. RICHARDSON & CO., Nurserymen, Geneva, N. Y.

THE Non-such Professor

in his Meridian Splendor; by the Rev. William Secker. 16mo, ... $1 25

"It is a mine of sparkling gems."—*Presb. Observer.*

"A sheaf of golden grain, ripened by grace, and sweet with the flavor of rare simplicity and holy wisdom."—*N. Y. Observer.*

GOSPEL SERMONS, by Dr. McCosh, $1 50

THE CREDENTIALS OF SCIENCE, by Prof. Cooke, ... 1 75

THE HEATH IN THE WILDERNESS, by Dr. Richard Newton. With Memoir and Portrait. 1 50

TWO GIRLS ABROAD, by Nellie M. Carter, ... 1 00

FROM FLAX TO LINEN, by Mrs. Conklin, ... 1 50

ROBERT CARTER & BROTHERS,
530 Broadway, New York.

Any of the above sent by mail, postage prepaid on receipt of price.

WEIGHTS AND WINGS

By CHARLES F. DEEMS, D.D., LL.D.,

President of the American Institute of Christian Philosophy, Editor of "Christian Thought," Author of "The Home Altar," "What Now?" etc.

Square, 12 mo., cloth, 272 pp., $1.00

A book which will, by virtue of its practical import, command universal attention. It is full of brief, but sharp-arrowed articles on themes of the most practical import. It contains subjects and hints, full of fire and fervor, that are designed to make church members, true and tried co-operators with their pastors. The power of church members would be strengthened mightily by heeding the hints of this delightful book. Christian pastors will find it abundantly suggestive.

"Forty-five short talks, all founded on texts of the Bible, that members of a congregation are always to the pastor either weights or wings. The author gives excellent rules to be followed by all who profess and call themselves Christians."—*Publisher's Weekly.*

"A very handsome volume, whose contents are well worthy of the faultless dress in which the publisher has sent them forth. No professing Christian who reads it thoughtfully can remain in doubt as to whether his Church membership is a help or hindrance to his pastor—a 'weight or wing'—as he prosecutes his laborious and painfully responsible mission. The whole tendency of the book is to improve the relations of communicants to their pastors; and it would be remunerative to the latter to urge its circulation. There is a freshness and force about the forty-five chapters."—*Southern Christian Advocate.*

"The topics are all practical and thoroughly evangelical and full of genuine interest to the Christian ambitious for a more vigorous piety."—*National Baptist.*

"A series of bright and suggestive brief essays upon Christian duties, by one well and favorably known. The title tells the drift and aim of the volume, which is to urge Christians to lay aside every weight and to mount up with wings in the race upon which we enter at our conversion. Bright, kindly, and stimulating to more vigorous effort, and to more entire devotion of life, the book will attract readers, and cannot fail to benefit those who heed its counsels."—*Episcopal Recorder.*

J. E. JEWETT, Publisher,
77 Bible House, New York.

New Musical Instrument.

10lbs. Boxed. **AUTO-ORGAN** 22 Reeds.

Plays Sacred Music, Popular Airs, Operas, etc. Especially adapted for the family circle. Catalogue of 312 pieces. **AGENTS WANTED** in every town. large commission, best selling musical instrument. For special terms to Agents and descriptive Catalogue address L. A. BARBER & CO., Groton, N. Y.

BAGSTER Comprehensive Teachers' Bibles. With New Helps, New Concordance, Indexed Atlas and Polyglot References, ... Sold by all booksellers, etc. JAMES POTT & CO., 14 & 16 Astor Place, New York, Agents.

UNIVERSITY ORGANS.— They Lead the World. Sold Direct to Families. No Middlemen. Solid Walnut—5 Octaves—Double Couplers. Guaranteed for Six Years and sent, with Stool and Book, for TRIAL IN YOUR OWN HOME BEFORE YOU BUY. ESTABLISHED 1859. **$35** MARCHAL & SMITH, 235 East 21st Street, New York.

TEAS *LADIES* Send at once for our new terms. THE GREAT AMERICAN TEA CO., 31 and 33 Vesey St., New York, N. Y.

A HOME SOLACE — ESTEY ORGAN — A DEVOTIONAL HELPER

Estey Organ Co. BRATTLEBORO VT. ILLUSTRATED CATALOGUE SENT FREE

NEW ENLARGED EDITION.

Encouragements to Faith

207 Pages. Cloth. Price 75 Cents

The Rev. ANDREW MURRAY, in his popular "Abide in Christ," has mentioned this book specially to be recommended for young, weak, doubting Christians.

Here is a warm hand and a loving heart to you, in the name of the Lord, from one who has doubts, and would gladly help you to break away from them. This book has greatly helped many Christians to a stronger faith in the blessed Lord Jesus. I earnestly hope that many more may be benefited by it."—*Preface.*

"This volume by J. W. Kimball, seems to be just such a one as a Christian would desire to put in the hands of any young man or woman troubled with doubts concerning the religious life. It has reference to the experience of the soul rather than the intellect, and is in fact, a tender, confidential exhortation, finding its motive in love to cultivate faith in God."—*Advertiser.*

Sent, post-paid, on receipt of price.

J. E. JEWETT, 77 Bible House, New York.

Agents Wanted for ... Pertaining ... sons, Pla... Things, w... Bible St... Concert ... Prayer-M... Topics, etc. In... by J. H... cent, D... pages. By mail, $2. Immensely popular. Al... new book, **HOW IN THE CLOUD,** ... of Comfort, etc., by **200** Best Authors, $1... **WOMEN'S HAND-BOOK. $2.** Just ... A lady wanted in every town ... duce it. **Quick Sales. Big Pay.** Ad... **E. B. TREAT,** Publisher, 771 Broadw...

PRINTING Book of Type, 6c, Amateur Printers' Guide Book, 15c. **PRESS** CIRCUL... JOSEPH WA... 19 Murray ... Samples of Scrap Pictures and Cards, 10 ...

"Demonology or Spiritual... Ancient and Modern."—"An effective weapon, sword of fire."—"Only unanswerable work ... subject."—Startling disclosures.—History ... data.—Scores saved already. Whole com... re-sound. Every family, preacher and christian needs one. 310 pp. 12mo, cloth. Price reduc... Sent by mail, postpaid, on receipt of price. **J. E. JEWETT,** 77 Bible House, New...

THE DEAF HEAR *The New England Medical Month...* —"WALES' INVI... SOUND DISC for ... by practical demonstra... ranks all other devic... age! Concentrating the ... waves on the drum head ... sibilities are indeed very ... For sale only by the ... H. A. WALES, Bridgeport...

In all the world there is but one sure cure for the **OPIUM** Habit. The Dr. J. L. ... Remedy never fa... other treatment ev... We have cured more than 10,000 cases. No other ... ever cured one case. NO PAY TILL CURED. ... this, and write to the J. L. Stephens Co., Leban...

ALL BOOKS at Wholesale to members ... Book Buyer... *Membership free.* AGENTS WANTED ... members. Send 2c. stamp for catalogue and ... tion to R. H. Woodward & Co., Baltim...

New Catalogue. Now ...

BEFORE YOU BUY ANY BOOKS FOR ...

SUNDAY-SCHOOL LIBRA...

Send to me for a full Catalogue of the cheap... best Sunday-School Books ever offered, and ... **SPECIAL OFFER TO SUNDAY-SCH...** Satisfaction guaranteed or money refunded. **J. E. JEWETT,** Publisher and Bookseller, 77 Bible House, New York.

Vol. XI., No. 44. Office, 63 Bible House, N. Y. THURSDAY, NOVEMBER 1, 1888. Price, 3 Cents. Annual Subscription, $1.50.

CONTENTS OF THIS NUMBER.

PORTRAIT OF THE LATE MAJOR BARTTELOT, THE LIEUTENANT OF MR. H. M. STANLEY

THE DIVINE MISSION OF PICTURES. Dr. Talmage' Sermon Last Sunday Morning.

ANECDOTES RELATED AT RECENT EVANGELISTIC MEETINGS.

NOTES OF THE RECENT PROPHETIC CONFERENCE IN EDINBURGH.

Ladies Learning in Japan—The Effect of a Kiss in a Prison—Mr. Arnot in Africa—A Cure for Insomnia—A Drunkard's Promise.

NO COMPROMISE. A New Sermon by Rev. C. H. Spurgeon.

THE LONDON PROPHETIC CONVENTION.

Gems from New Books: An Answer to Peter—A Daring Life-Boat Captain.

PICTURE OF A SCENE ON THE BANKS OF THE SUSQUEHANNA.

PORTRAIT OF HON. ROBERT B. ROOSEVELT, U. S. Minister to the Hague.

ELLA'S PICTURE. (With Illustration.)

THE EPOCHS OF A LIFE. A New Serial Story by Rev. L. S. Keyser. (Continued.)

CALEB'S INHERITANCE. By Mrs. M. Baxter.

The Late Major EDMUND W. BARTTELOT, Murdered on the Congo—Sketches in the Congo Country.

MAJOR EDMUND M. BARTTELOT.

Mr. H. M. Stanley's Murdered Lieutenant.

MENTION has already been made in our news columns, of the death of Major Barttelot, who was murdered in Africa, as he was setting out for the relief of Mr. H. M. Stanley. We are now enabled to give on the first page of this issue, his portrait and a few illustrations connected with the district he was in when he died.

When Stanley was setting out for the relief of Emin Pasha, whose portrait and life appeared in this journal on March 24, 1887, he chose as his chief lieutenant, Major Barttelot, an officer in the British Army, who had seen active service in Egypt and Afghanistan. The major was a man of good family, courageous, energetic, and reputed shrewdness. He was born in 1859, and was, therefore, under thirty years old when he died. He accompanied Stanley to Africa in January 1887, and was

Left at Yambuya

village near the Aruwhimi Falls, which was the most advanced station on Stanley's route. Here he remained in charge of supplies and ammunition, while Mr. Stanley pressed on, with such loads as he had bearers to carry, toward Wadelai, where he expected to meet Emin. He carried with him considerable ammunition of which Emin represented himself in need, and expected either to assist him in maintaining his position, or to help him in effecting a retreat, but in any case to relieve his immediate wants. Major Barttelot, was to await orders from Stanley or upon obtaining bearers, to proceed after Stanley.

The Leave Taking

of the two brave men at Yambuya, was their final parting. The letter in which Mr. Stanley conferred the command on his trusted associate and friend, has a melancholy interest in the circumstances of the present report. Mr. Stanley, after a warm tribute to the personal qualities of his subordinate, proceeded to give him the most minute instructions for the fortification of the camp, and for the organization of a troop to defend it. For himself, he said, his course would be true east, or by magnetic compass east-by-south. "Certain marches that we may take," said Stanley, "may not exactly lead us in the direction aimed at; nevertheless in the south-western corner of Lake Albert, near or at Kavalli, that is our destination."

For a weary year Major Barttelot waited and watched at his post, and when, in April last, reports began to arrive, through deserters, that disaster had befallen Mr. Stanley and that the explorer was reduced to serious straits, he determined to organise a great expedition for the purpose of following his chief's track, and, if possible, of taking him relief. Major Barttelot accordingly, with the help of Tippoo Tib, the Governor of Stanley Falls, organized a party of some six hundred men, including two white men, Mr. Jameson, and Mr. Bonny, and over one hundred trained and armed Zanzibaris. In Major Barttelot's last report he speaks highly of the head Arab, Muni Somai. But sinister reports of the characteristics of the Manyemas had reached him. Sir Francis de Winton writes that "the Manyema are a tribe considerably to the South, from which, no doubt, Tippoo Tib obtained a supply or porters or carriers to fulfil the contract he entered into with Mr. Stanley. They are a wild tribe, and attempted Livingstone's life on more than one occasion, when he was between Tanganyike and Nyangwe."

It would appear that there were endless delays in getting Tippoo Tib, the Arab trader, whom Stanley had made governor of the region, to fulfil his contract by providing Barttelot with seven hundred carriers. That may have been due to a prejudice excited against Tippoo Tib himself by his alliance with the Europeans. In any case, whether Tippoo Tib could not or would not furnish the carriers promptly, he did not, and Barttelot after waiting a year, had to start with a smaller number of inferior men. He was doubtless, prompted to accept the compromise by the reports of Mr. Stanley's extremity, which continued to reach him, and which have not yet been contradicted. Barttelot left Yambuya Village in April of this year. He proceeded on Stanley's tracks and had reached a place stated to be about thirty-nine days journey from Yambuya by July 19. There

He Was Killed.

It seems, from the reports received of the catastrophe, that Barttelot had been much annoyed by Manyemas practising singing and drumming early in the morning and in the evening, and threatened to stop the practice. On July 19, early in the morning, in spite of Bonny's efforts to dissuade him, he proceeded alone to the drummer's tent. Shortly afterward a shot was heard, and Bonny, running out, found the camp in a state of excitement and heard shouts of "The white man is dead!" Barttelot's body was found lying before the drummer's tent. His breast had been pierced by a bullet and his clothes were burned by gunpowder.

Jameson, who was with the advance guard, heard of Barttelot's death the next day and immediately returned, but the natives had already dispersed, after stealing the stores. Jameson then proceeded to Stanley Falls, leaving Bonny in charge of Camp Aruwhimi. The murderer was discovered and was sent to Stanley Falls, where he was hanged. Mr. Jameson was seized with fever on his journey, and he, too, is dead.

The account represents Tippoo Tib as being grieved at the death of Barttelot. He said he would have given half his fortune to prevent the murder. He also said that both he and the officers at the Falls had often warned Barttelot against the danger of using harshness toward the natives. Tippoo Tib, the telegram goes on to say, with Baert, a Belgian, has started on a four months' expedition for the purpose of exploring the country south of Kassongo and establishing stations therein. He has also sent parties of men to the north, in the hope of hearing some news of Stanley. It is, however, reregarded as impossible to organize another relief expedition, unless the Government sends a large and carefully officered force, which even then would have to encounter gigantic obstacles, and would have to depend on native assistance, which is evidently untrustworthy in the extreme.

INCIDENTS OF THE EXPEDITION.

YAMBUYA, which was the weary waiting-place of Major Barttelot and his company for over a year, was visited by Mr. Stanley in 1883. He appears to have formed a bad opinion of its inhabitants. In his work on the Congo (published by Messrs. Harper & Brothers), he says: "On the left bank of the river were seen a number of villages, all the huts of which seemed to be of the sharp, conical form [*as seen in illustration No. 6 on first page*]. We formed a camp about two miles below the rapids [*shown in illustrations Nos. 3 and 10*] on the right bank, at sight of which, the natives of the villages across made a terrible racket with their drums. Yumbila [Mr. Stanley's guide] was urged to try to start a conversation, the effect of which was that the drumming was silenced, and for nearly an hour the creatures kept bawling across the river, one to another, puerile information relative to bananas and goats. Yumbila, always hungry, clamored to the aborigines to bring food to sell for beads. The natives as loudly denied that they possessed any. We went across in the whale-boat next morning to attempt to obtain the good-will of the natives of Yambuya, but after an hour's effort we were compelled to desist. I fear that they were such consummate actors that not much reliance can be placed on any information given to us, since while they gave us numerous names of places, they never mentioned, for instance, that their own village was Yambuya, but declared it to be Ngondé.

A reporter who accompanied the expedition sends sketches of three specimens of the Bahulu, Wasongolo tribe [*reproduced in panel No. 4 of first page*], who must have been by no means agreeable companions for a long sojourn in camp. He also sends a portrait of a woman of Aruwimi Falls [*panel No. 8*]. The hut in which the correspondent lived is depicted in *panel No. 7*. The curious receptacles in *panel No. 9* are palm-oil pots, which show that the aborigines have some knowledge of pottery, and also are not without taste in matters of graceful form. To make the miseries of the expedition worse the same correspondent reports

A Revolting Discovery,

which was made by some of its members, and which confirmed a suspicion long held by African travellers. He says that the practice of cannibalism is common among the tribes. Mr. Stanley himself had not been altogether explicit in his evidence one way or the other, although the alleged Soko or chimpanzee skulls which he sent to Professor Huxley, as his readers will remember, turned out to be human. Whatever they were, the natives of the village where Stanley found them, confessed they had eaten the bodies, which they called "*Wajimi meat.*" It is only quite recently that the truth has come out. Stanley suspected it. He offered large rewards for a specimen of a "Soko," alive or dead. He saw plenty of skulls of the creature, but could procure no other evidence. This was at a village above Stanley Falls. It is now pretty well understood that these trophies must have been the remains of human beings. Cannibalism exists in the great basin of the Congo, on sundry of its tributaries, and was *active in the neighborhood of the camp at Aruwhimi.*

On Sunday, February 26, 1888, he says: "I went this morning to Nassibu's Camp, which is situated about an hour's march from our camp on the Falls (Aruwhimi). He received me with much ceremony, and, at my request, drummed to the natives, who were in two clearings at the back of his camp. A number came, and went through the usual demonstrations of surprise at seeing a white man. Among them were about a dozen young women, with pleasing countenances. I selected a man as a model for myself, but it was very difficult to induce him to stand still while I sketched him.

"Almost the first man I saw was carrying four

Lumps of Human Flesh

(with the skin on) on a stick, and through Fida I found they had killed a man this morning and had divided the flesh. She took me over to a house where some half-dozen men were squatting, and showed me more meat on sticks in front of a fire; it was frizzling and the yellow fat was dripping from it, whilst all around was a strong odor which reminded me of the smell given out by grilled elephant meat. It was not yet the general meal-time, they told me, but one or two of the natives cut off pieces of the frizzling flesh and ate it and laughed at Majuta, who, being disgusted, held his nose and backed into the bush. I spoke with the natives through Fida, and they told me from what parts the meat was cut. One tall, sturdy native was quietly leaning against a tree and picking off pieces of flesh from a thigh bone, with relish. Other dainty joints were grilling at the fire.

The Dreary Waiting

is awful—waiting for what never comes! Day after day passes; we see no fresh faces, we hear no news. Many of our men are daily growing thinner and weaker, and are dying off. Poor wretches! they lie out in the sun, on the dusty ground, most of them with only a narrow strip of dirty loin-cloth; and all the livelong day they stare into vacancy, and at night gaze at a bit of fire. It was a pitiable sight, a few days ago to see an emaciated skeleton crawl, with the aid of a stick, after a corpse that was being carried on a pole for interment. He staggered along, poor chap, and squatted down alongside the newly-made grave and watched the proceedings with large, round, sunken eyes, knowing that it would only be a matter of a few days and he himself would be a dead man. He told me in a husky voice, 'Amekwa rapiki angu' (he was my friend). Another poor fellow is a mass of bones, yet persists in doing his work, and every evening staggers into camp. He has been told to lay up, and that his manioc shall be provided for him, but he refuses, and in replying to my sympathetic remark that he was very thin, he said, 'Yes, only a short time more, master.' Death is written in his face, and just as plainly in the faces of many others in this camp. Almost as many lives, I fear, will be lost in this philanthropic mission as there are lives of Emin Bey's people to save."

The Unknown Difficulties

which Mr. Stanley must have encountered are sufficiently demonstrated by the known difficulties which have beset his followers in a region which had become familiar to them, and under the express cognisance of Stanley's Arab ally Tippoo Tib. If this gentleman and his officers have been so remiss in the fulfilment of their undertakings, almost within easy reach of settled Congo stations, what may have happened to Stanley in the wilderness, is full of painful possibilities. Major Barttelot lost his life in endeavoring to organize a party to follow his leader. Mr. Jameson has succumbed to fever, probably induced by anxiety and worry in the same direction. The obstacles in the path of an advance towards Wadelai must be enormous. The dangers, while they have in some respects been reduced by the Arab alliance, have in other ways been increased by it. The Arabs harass the natives, and plunder them of ivory and slaves. The natives everywhere seek reprisals on the Arabs; it must be a difficult thing for the native mind to discriminate between Stanley's people and their Arab allies.

The Slave Trade,

the suppression of which it was hoped Mr. Stanley's mission might help to promote, is, it appears, still flourishing and increasing. In addition to the reports which come from Europe carried there by missionaries and explorers, the members of Major Bartelot's company send appalling details of scenes of slaughter which they witnessed, ending in the carrying off of large bands of captives into slavery. The question has frequently been raised as to the destination of these wretched beings, since the chief ports are now in the hands of European powers. A daily journal of New York has been investigating the subject, and it asserts that the majority of them are actually worked to death in Africa itself, the frightful mortality requiring a continually fresh supply. The Arabs and the native chiefs, who encourage their crimes, now absorb the greater part of the new supplies of slaves. The Arabs employ many thousands of these slaves in cultivating the large plantations they have started for three hundred miles along the Congo, between that river and Lake Tanganyika, and the lake and the Indian Ocean.

They no longer engage Zanzibar porters to carry their trade goods into the country and their ivory to the sea, but great slave caravans, often numbering over a thousand souls, now perform these services. While many native chiefs are associated with the Arabs in the business of slave catching, many others gladly exchange their ivory for slaves; and by far the larger part of the field labor and the household drudgery is now performed by slaves.

Within the past two years, the British having relaxed their vigilance in guarding the coast, there has been a partial revival of the export trade. The number of slaves who have been smuggled into Arabia has been insignificant, but of late there has been a large increase of the traffic between the east coast and Madagascar.

A few years ago, when the east coast export slave trade was almost unimpeded, it was easy to see what became of the unfortunates who were driven from the far interior to the sea. Consul Holmwood said that in 1874 1,000 slaves a month passed through the port of Mombasa alone. Captain Elton confirmed these figures, and added that in that year 30,000 slaves were exported from the various ports controlled by the Sultan of Zanzibar. There is reason to hope that the agitation of the question now going on in Europe, may stir up public opinion and lead to pressure being brought to bear on European governments to make them more vigilant to at least prevent the export of slaves.

ANECDOTES RELATED AT RECENT EVANGELISTIC MEETINGS.

A Christian at a Fair.—Mr. Hamilton says: "A Christian once met a friend at a fair, and somehow he felt it impressed upon his mind that he should speak to him about his soul, but thinking that a fair, with all its noise and bustle, was a most unsuitable place for the purpose, he put it off to a more convenient season. What must have been his feelings when he heard that his friend, returning that night from the fair, had been thrown from his horse and killed. He had the warning that might have saved him, and he neglected to give it. If God puts the sinner in your way, my Christian friend, it is your duty to speak to him at that instant; you know not but that the next moment he may be beyond the reach of your ministrations forever."

Refusing to Sing a Lie.—Mr. W. A. Campbell observes: "One of my dearest friends was brought to Christ while singing the hymn beginning, 'Just as I am, without one plea.' He had sung the first two verses right through, but when he came to the end of the third verse, 'Because Thy promise I believe, oh Lamb of God, I come.' He stopped short. 'No,' he said, 'I cannot sing *that*. It is not true. I will not sing a lie. I have *not* believed His promise.' The singing went on. 'Just as I am, Thy love unknown, has broken every barrier down.' In a moment the great love of God came before his eyes. He felt his heart fill with love and gratitude to Him who had given His Son for poor sinners; and there and then he joined in, and sung with truth from his heart, 'Now to be Thine, yea Thine alone, O Lamb of God, I come.' We can make our hymns prayers; we can accept Christ in singing a metrical hymn just as truly as by getting down upon our knees."

Suddenly Called Away.—An Evangelist Relates: "There was a young lad in a warehouse in which I am engaged, who left his work quite well at six o'clock one evening, and went home and had his tea as usual. Afterwards he joined the family circle, and seemed in the same condition of health and spirits as usual. About half-past eight he fell ill, and at nine he was dead. In the Sunday-school of which I am superintendent, a young fellow went the other week from the school, and did not feel altogether well. On Monday morning he was not yet all right, and about ten o'clock set out to see a friend who lived not a stone's throw from his own home. He arrived there, and when entering the room, seemed rather weak. He seated himself, and asked the lady for a glass of water. The lady brought it herself, and as he took it he said, 'I am dying; I know it, I feel it.' The lady at once sent for his mother, and when she arrived it was scarcely half-past ten, not half an hour since her son had left her, and now she stood by his dead body. Oh, young men, count not on the morrow. Take Christ now while you have the opportunity. Christ is holding out His hands in tenderest pity to you, asking you to accept Himself. Will you do so?"

The Twine Under the Thumb-nail. — A minister relates: "A few months after my ordination, I was invited to spend an evening at the house of a parishioner. Among the company was an old gentleman named Mr Ford. When we had tea the most of us gathered round the table, and began to speak about various passages of Holy Scripture. But I was grieved to see, while the majority of the company was thus profitably employed, this old man, seated on the sofa with a number of young ladies around him, engaged in a conversation of a decidedly frivolous and flippant nature. A few days afterward, meeting my rector casually in the street, he asked me if I had heard that Mr. Ford was very ill. While he had been engaged in his office, tying a parcel, the twine had slipped under his thumb-nail and forced it up. Inflamation had set in, which rapidly extended to the hand, and then to the arm, so that great fears were entertained for his life. I hastened to his house, and was immediately shown into the sick-room. As he recognized me he faintly said, 'Ah, it is you, sir; I did not expect to meet you this way.' I sat down and read the Gospel to him, and after a few words of conversation and prayer, left him. He was too weak even to listen. In a few hours that man was in the presence of God. Oh, how he would regret, whether saved or lost, the time he had given to frivolous conduct, to the prejudice of his own salvation and that of others whose attention he diverted from the things of God."

The One Afraid of the Other. — Mr. Climie relates: "I remember two girls, who lived near a place in which I was preaching. One of their friends had been converted, and she often tried to persuade them to come to the meetings, but they refused; they feared if they came they would be converted, and they did not want that. By-and-bye, however, one of the girls who was only on a visit to the other, had to return to her own home; and they both thought they would go to the meeting just for once; there could not be much danger in that. They went. The earnest words of the speaker that night were directed by the Holy Spirit straight to the hearts of both, but neither would show what was in her heart for fear her companion might laugh. Next day, the friends parted, and the one now left in freedom came back to our meeting, and gave her heart to Jesus. About a week afterward the new convert was surprised to see her friend walk into her house. She had not been able to obtain an hour's peace since she left her, and had come back to try and find the Saviour. Her friend brought her to the meeting, when I had the privilege of pointing her to Christ, whom she gladly embraced."

Maggie's Message to her Father.—Mr. Stewart remarks: "A little girl, whose mother was dead, was obliged to live alone with her father, a confirmed drunkard. When the man was in his sober senses, there could not be a kinder or more indulgent father, and often in his fits of remorse he would call his little daughter to him and, looking into her face, the image of her dead mother, he would say, 'Maggie, you have a bad father.' But Maggie always interrupted him with, 'No, father, *you* are not bad, it is *the drink* that is bad. Oh, father dear, if you would give up the drink we should be so happy!' Little Maggie fell ill. For weeks she lay upon her bed, her life slowly ebbing away. Her father saw how ill she was, and knew that soon he would lose his child, but still he could not resist spending his earnings in the saloon. As the father stood by the bed one evening, she slipped her wan hand into his own, and said, 'Father, you might stay with me just for this one night!' He promised. The girl fell asleep with her hand still clasped in his. The time went on. A knock was heard at the door. It was two of the man's companions, who had come for him, and in a few moments he was gone. The girl awoke, asked for her father, and was told by a kind neighbor who was in the room, that he was out, but she would send for him. 'No,' was the reply, 'he is too late to see me die; but tell him not to be too late in coming to Jesus.' Soon afterward the drunkard reeled home. As he entered the room, one glance sobered him; he saw that his child was dead. Her last message was given him. He had not complied with her first request that night, but he would with her last; and he did come to Jesus. Her death was the birth of her father's soul."

The Prophetic News and Israel's Watchman (London), edited by the Rev. M. Baxter, may be had from the office of this journal, 63 Bible House, New York; price six cents, including postage. Annual subscription, seventy cents. The following articles, among others, are contained in the number for October:

The Nineteenth Century in the Light of Prophecy.
The Kingdom of Christ as Predicted by Daniel.
The literal Return of the Jews. By Dr. Kellogg.
The Morning Star, the Sun of Righteousness, and the Everlasting Light. By the Rev. Canon Faussett.
The Rapture of the Saints, and the New Jerusalem.
The Scarlet Woman or the Church of Rome.
Rev. M. Baxter's Prophetic Lectures.
Railways and Prophecy. By W. Appleford.
The Seven Trumpets Explained.
Passing Events Viewed from a Prophetic Standpoint.

THE DIVINE MISSION OF PICTURES.

Dr. Talmage's Sermon Preached Last Sunday Morning, October 28, 1888.

"The day of the Lord of Hosts shall be . . . upon all pleasant pictures." Isa. 2 : 12, 16.

God Scrutinizing Pictures—The Art Sometimes Degraded—The Bad Pictures of Pompeii—A Worse Crater than Vesuvius—Other Arts Bedraggled—Pictures in the Family Bible—Famous Pictures of Bible Scenes—Benefits from Dore's Bible Illustrations—Vandalism in Pictures—A Painter's Itemized Bill—The Sufferings of Poverty-Stricken Artists—Picture-Galleries Needed for the Cities—An Opportunity for Millionaires—Cardinal Mazarin's Last Walk—A Warning to Parents—Pictures Suggesting Immorality—A Universal Language—Christ's Sermons Were Picture-Galleries—A Picture on the Wall of a Cell—The Blind Man at the Cyclorama.

PICTURES are by some relegated to the realm of the trivial, accidental, sentimental, or worldly, but my text shows that God scrutinizes pictures, and whether they are good or bad, whether used for right or wrong purposes, is a matter of Divine observation and arraignment.

The divine mission of pictures is my subject.

That the artist's pencil and the engraver's knife have sometimes been made subservient to the kingdom of the bad is frankly admitted. After the ashes and scoria were removed from Herculaneum and Pompeii, the walls of those cities discovered to the explorers a

Degradation in Art

which cannot be exaggerated. Satan and all his imps have always wanted the fingering of the easel; they would rather have possession of that than the art of printing, for types are not so potent and quick for evil as pictures. The powers of darkness think they have gained a triumph, and they have, when in some respectable parlor or public art gallery they can hang a canvas embarrassing to the good but fascinating to the evil.

It is not in a spirit of prudery, but backed up by God's eternal truth, when I say that you have no right to hang in your art rooms or your dwelling-houses that which would be offensive to good people if the figures pictured were alive in your parlor and the guests of your household. A picture that you have to hang in a somewhat secluded place, or that in a public hall you cannot with a group of friends deliberately stand before and discuss, ought to have a knife stabbed into it at the top and cut clear through to the bottom, and a stout finger thrust in on the right side ripping clear through to the left. Pliny the elder lost his life by going near enough to see the inside of Vesuvius, and *the further you can stand off from the burning crater of sin the better*. Never till the books of the Last Day are opened shall we know what has been the dire harvest of evil pictorials and unbecoming art galleries. Despoil a man's imagination and he becomes a moral carcass. The show-windows of English and American cities, in which the low theatres have sometimes hung long lines of brazen actors and actresses in style insulting to all propriety, have made

A Broad Path to Death

for multitudes of people. But so have all the other arts been at times suborned of evil. How has music been bedraggled? Is there any place so low down in dissoluteness that into it, has not been carried David's harp, and Handel's organ, and Gottschalk's piano, and Ole Bull's violin? and the flute, which though named after so insignificant a thing as the Sicilian eel, which has seven spots on the side like flute holes, yet for thousands of years has had an exalted mission? Architecture, born in the heart of Him who made the worlds, under its arches and across its floors, what bacchanalian revelries have been enacted! It is not against any of these arts that they have been so led into captivity!

What a poor world this would be if it were not for what my text calls "pleasant pictures"! I refer to your memory and mine when I ask if your knowledge of the Holy Scriptures has not been mightily augmented by the woodcuts or engravings in the old family Bible, which father and mother read out of, and laid on the table in the old homestead when you were boys and girls. The Bible scenes which we all carry in our minds were not gotten from the Bible typology, but from the

Bible Pictures.

To prove the truth of it in my own case, the other day I took up the old family Bible, which I inherited. Sure enough, what I have carried in my mind of Jacob's ladder was exactly the Bible engraving of Jacob's ladder; and so with Samson carrying off the gates of Gaza; Elisha restoring the Shunamite's son; the massacre of the innocents; Christ blessing little children; the Crucifixion, and the Last Judgment. My idea of all these is that of the old Bible engravings which I scanned before I could read a word. That is true with nine-tenths of you. If I could swing open the door of your foreheads I would find that you are walking picture-galleries. The great intelligence abroad about the Bible did not come from the general reading of the book, for the majority of the people read it but little, if they read it at all; but

All the Sacred Scenes

have been put before the great masses, and not printer's ink, but the pictorial art, must have the credit of the achievement. First, painter's pencil for the favored few, and then engravers' plate or woodcut for millions on millions!

What overwhelming commentary on the Bible, what reinforcement for patriarchs, prophets, apostles, and Christ, what distribution of Scriptural knowledge of all nations, in the paintings and engravings therefrom of Holman Hunt's "Christ in the Temple"; Paul Veronese's "Magdalen Washing the Feet of Christ"; Raphael's "Michael the Archangel"; Albert Durer's "Dragon of the Apocalypse"; Michael Angelo's "Plague of the Fiery Serpents"; Tintoret's "Flight into Egypt"; Rubens' "Descent from the Cross"; Leonardo Da Vinci's "Last Supper"; Claude's "Queen of Sheba"; Bellini's "Madonna at Milan"; Orcagna's "Last Judgment"; and hundreds of miles of pictures, if they were put in line, illustrating, displaying, dramatizing, irradiating Bible truths until the Scriptures are not to-day so much on paper as on canvas, not so much in ink as in all the colors of the spectrum. In 1833, forth from Strasburg, Germany, there came a child that was to eclipse in speed and boldness and grandeur anything and everything that the world had seen since the first color appeared on the sky at the creation,

Paul Gustav Dore.

At eleven years of age he published marvellous lithographs of his own. Saying nothing of what he did for Milton's "Paradise Lost," emblazoning it on the attention of the world, he takes up the Book of Books, the monarch of literature, the Bible, and in his pictures "The Creation of Light," "The Trial of Abraham's Faith," "The Burial of Sarah," "Joseph Sold by his Brethren," "The Brazen Serpent," "Boaz and Ruth," "David and Goliath," "The Transfiguration," "The Marriage in Cana," "Babylon Fallen," and two hundred and five Scriptural scenes in all, with a boldness and a grasp and almost supernatural afflatus that make the heart throb and the brain reel and the tears start and the cheeks blanch and the entire nature quake with the tremendous things of God and eternity and the dead. I actually staggered down the steps of the London Art Gallery, under the power of Doré's "Christ Leaving the Praetorium." Profess you to be a Christian man or woman, and see no divine mission in art, and acknowledge you no obligation either in thanks to God or man?

It is no more the word of God when put before us in printer's ink, than by skilful laying on of colors, or designs on metal through incision or corrosion. What a lesson in morals was presented by Hogarth, the painter, in his two pictures, "The Rake's Progress," and "The Miser's Feast," and by Thomas Cole's engravings of the "Voyage of Human Life," and the "Course of Empire," and by Turner's "Slave Ship." God in art! Christ in art! Patriarchs, prophets and apostles in art! Angels in art! Heaven in art!

Neglected Painters.

The world and the church ought to come to the higher appreciation of the divine mission of pictures, yet the authors of them have generally been left to semi-starvation. West, the great painter toiled in unappreciation till, being a great skater, while on the ice he formed the acquaintance of General Howe, of the English army, and through coming to admire West as a skater, who gradually came to appreciate as much that which he accomplished by his hand as by his heel. Poussin, the mighty painter, was pursued, and had nothing with which to defend himself against the mob but the artist's portfolio, which he held over his head to keep off the stones hurled at him. The pictures of Richard Wilson, of England, were sold for fabulous sums of money after his death, but the living painter was glad to get for his "Alcyone" a piece of Stilton cheese.

From 1640 to 1643 there were 4,600 pictures wilfully destroyed. In the reign of Queen Elizabeth it was the habit of some people to spend much of their time in knocking pictures to pieces. In the reign of Charles the First it was ordered by Parliament that all pictures of Christ be burnt. Painters were so badly treated and humiliated in the beginning of the eighteenth century that they were lowered clear down out of the sublimity of their art, and obliged to give accounts of what they did with their colors, as

A Painter's Bill

which came to publication in Scotland in 1707 indicated. The painter had been touching up some old pictures in the church, and he sends in this itemized bill to the vestry: "To filling up a chink in the Red Sea and repairing the damages to Pharaoh's hosts"; "to a new pair of hands for Daniel in the Lion's den, and a new set of teeth for the lioness"; "to repairing Nebuchadnezzar's beard"; "to giving a blush to the cheek of Eve on presenting the apple to Adam"; "to making a bridle for the Good Samaritan's horse, and mending one of his legs"; "to putting on a new handle on Moses' basket, and fitting bulrushes, and adding more fuel to the fire in Nebuchadnezzar's furnace." So painters were humiliated clear down below the majesty of their art. The oldest picture in England, a portrait of Chaucer, though now of great value, was picked out of a lumber garret. Great were the trials of Quentin Matsys, who toiled on from blacksmith's anvil till, as a painter, he won wide recognition. The first missionaries to Mexico made the fatal mistake of destroying pictures, for the loss of which art and religion must ever lament. But why go so far back when in this year of our Lord, 1888, and within twelve years of the twentieth century, to be a painter, except in rare exceptions, means

Poverty and Neglect?

poorly fed, poorly clad, poorly housed, because poorly appreciated! When I hear a man is a painter, I have two feelings—one of admiration for the greatness of his soul, and the other of commiseration for the needs of his body.

But so it has been in all departments of noble work. Some of the mightiest have been hardly bestead. Oliver Goldsmith had such a big patch on the coat over his left breast that when he went anywhere he kept his hat in his hand closely pressed over the patch. The world-renowned Bishop Asbury had a salary of $64 a year. Painters are not the only ones who have endured the lack of appreciation. Let men of wealth take under their patronage the suffering men of art. They lift no complaint; they make no strike for higher wages. But with a keenness of nervous organization which almost always characterizes genius, these artists suffer more than any one, but God, can realize. There needs to be a concerted effort for the

Suffering Artists of America,

not sentimental discourse about what we owe to artists, but contracts that will give them a livelihood; for I am in full sympathy with the Christian farmer who was very busy gathering his fall apples, and some one asked him to pray for a poor family, the father of which had broken his leg, and the busy farmer said: "I cannot stop now to pray, but you can go down into the cellar and get some corned beef and butter and eggs and potatoes; that is all I can do now." Artists may wish for our prayers, but they also want practical help from men who can give them work. You have heard scores of sermons for all other kinds of suffering men and women, but I think this is the first sermon ever preached that made a plea for the suffering men and women of American art. Their work is more true to nature and life than any of the masterpieces that have become immortal on the other side of the sea, but it is the fashion of Americans to mention foreign artists, and to know little or nothing about our own Copley, and Allston, and Inman, and Greenough, and Kensett. Let the affluent fling out of their windows and into the back yard valueless daubs on canvas, and call in these splendid but unrewarded men, and tell them to adorn your walls, not only with that which shall please the taste, but enlarge the mind, and improve the morals, and save the souls of those who gaze upon them.

Brooklyn, and all other American cities,

Need Great Galleries

of art, not only open annually for a few days on exhibition, but which shall stand open all the year round, and from early morning until ten o'clock at night, and free to all who would come.

What a preparation for the wear and tear of the day a five minutes' look in the morning at some picture that will open a door into some larger realm than that in which our population daily drudge! Or what a good thing the half hour of artistic opportunity on the way home in the evening, from exhaustion that demands recuperation for mind and soul as well as body! Who will do for Brooklyn, or the city where you live, what W. W. Corcoran did for Washington, and what I am told John Wannamaker, by the donation of a famous picture, is going to do for Philadelphia? Men of wealth, if you are too modest to build and endow such a place during your lifetime, why not go to your iron safe and take out your last will and testament, and make a codicil that shall build for the city of your residence a throne for American art? Take some of that money that would otherwise spoil your children, and build an art gallery that shall associate your name forever, not only with the great masters of painting, who are gone, but with the great masters who are trying to live; and also win the admiration and love of tens of thousands of people, who, unable to have fine pictures of their own, would be advantaged.

Build Your Own Monuments,

and not leave it to the whim of others. Some of the best people sleeping in Greenwood have no monuments at all, or some crumbling stones that in a few years will let the rain wash out name and epitaph; while some men, whose death was the abatement of a nuisance, have a pile of polished Aberdeen high enough for a king, and eulogium enough to embarrass a seraph. Oh, man of large wealth, instead of leaving to the whim of others your monumental commemoration and epitaphology, to be looked at when people are going to and fro at the burial of others, build right down in the heart of our great city, or the city where you live, an immense free reading-room, or a free musical conservatory, or a free art gallery, the niches for sculpture, and the walls abloom with the rise and fall of nations, and lessons of courage for the disheartened, and rest for the weary, and life for the dead; and in the future you will be wielding influences in this world for good.

How much better than white marble, that chills you if you put your hand on it when you touch it in the cemetery, would be a monument in colors, in beaming eyes, in living possession, in splendors which under the chandelier would be glowing and warm, and looked at by strolling groups with catalogue in hand on the January night when the necropolis where the body sleeps is all snowed under. The tower of David was hung with one thousand dented shields of battle; but you, oh man of wealth, may have a grander tower named after you, one that shall be hung not with the symbols of carnage, but with the victories of that art which was so long ago recognized in my text as "pleasant pictures." Oh, the power of pictures! I cannot deride, as some have done, Cardinal Mazarin, who, when told that he must die, took his last walk through the art gallery of his palace, saying: "Must I quit all this? Look at that Titian! Look at that Correggio! Look at that deluge of Caracci! Farewell, dear pictures!"

As the day of the Lord of Hosts, according to this text, will scrutinize the pictures, I implore all parents to see that in their households they have neither in book or newspaper or on canvas anything that will deprave. Pictures are no longer the exclusive possession of the affluent. There is not a respectable home in these cities that has not specimens of woodcut or steel engraving, if not of painting, and your whole family will feel the moral uplifting or depression. Have nothing on your wall or in books that will familiarize the young with scenes of cruelty or wassail; have only those sketches made by artists in elevated moods, and none of those scenes that seem the product of artistic delirium tremens. Pictures are

A Universal Language.

The human race is divided into almost as many languages as there are nations, but the pictures may speak to people of all tongues. Volapuk many have hoped, with little reason, would become a world-wide language; but the pictorial is always a world-wide language, and printers' types have no emphasis compared with it. We say that children are fond of pictures; but notice any man when he takes up a book, and you will see that the first thing that he looks at is the pictures. Have only those in your house that appeal to the better nature. One engraving has sometimes decided an eternal destiny. Under the title of fine arts there have come here from France a class of pictures which elaborate argument has tried to prove irreproachable. They would disgrace a bar-room, and they need to be confiscated. Your children will carry the pictures of their father's house with them clear on to the grave, and, passing that marble pillar, will take them through eternity.

Futhermore, let all reformers, and all Sabbath-school teachers, and all Christian workers realize that, if they would be effective for good, they must make pictures, if not by chalk on blackboards, or kinder-garten designs, or by pencil on canvas, then by words. Arguments are soon forgotten; but pictures, whether in language or in colors, are what produce strongest effects. Christ was always telling what a thing was like, and His sermon on the Mount was

A Great Picture-Gallery,

beginning with a sketch of a "city on a hill that cannot be hid," and ending with a tempest beating against two houses, one on the rock and the other on the sand. The parable of the prodigal son, a picture; parable of the sower, who went forth to sow, a picture; parable of the unmerciful servant, a picture; parable of the ten virgins, a picture; parable of the talents, a picture. *The world wants pictures*, and the appetite begins with the child, who consents to go early to bed if the mother will sit beside him and rehearse a story, which is only a picture. When we see how much has been accomplished in secular directions by pictures—Shakespeare's tragedies, a picture; Victor Hugo's writings, all pictures; John Ruskin's and Tennyson's and Longfellow's works, all pictures—why not enlist, as far as possible, for our churches and schools and reformatory work and evangelistic endeavor, the power of thought that can be put into word pictures, if not pictures in color? Yea, why not all young men draw for themselves on paper, with pen or pencil, their coming career, of virtue if they prefer that, of vice if they prefer that. After making the picture, put it on the wall, or paste it on the fly leaf of some favorite book, that you may have it before you. I read the other day of a man who had been executed for murder, and the jailor found afterward a picture made on the wall of the cell by the assassin's own hand,

A Picture of a Flight of Stairs.

On the lowest step he had written: "Disobedience of parents"; on the second: "Sabbath breaking"; on the third: "Drunkenness and gambling"; on the fourth: "Murder"; and on the fifth and top step: "A gallows." If that man had made that picture before he took the first step, he never would have taken any of them! Oh, man, make another picture, a bright picture, an evangelical picture, and I will help you make it! I suggest *six steps for this flight* of stairs. On the first step write the words: "A nature changed by the Holy Ghost and washed in the blood of the Lamb"; on the second step: "Industry and good companionship"; on the third step: "A Christian home with a family altar;" on the fourth step: "Ever widening usefulness"; on the fifth step: "A glorious departure from this world"; on the sixth step: "Heaven! heaven! heaven!" Write it three times, and let the letters of the one word be made up of banners, the second of coronets, and the third of thrones! Promise me that you will do that, and I will promise to meet you on the sixth step, if the Lord will through His pardoning grace bring me there too.

And here I am going to say a word of cheer to people who have never had a word of consolation on that subject. There are men and women in this world by hundred of thousands, and some of them are here to-day, who have a fine natural taste, and yet all their lives that taste has been suppressed, for they must support their households, and bread and schooling for their children are of more importance than pictures. Though fond of music, they are compelled to live amid discord; and though fond of architecture, they dwell in clumsy abodes, and though appreciative of all that engravings and paintings can do, they are in perpetual deprivation. You are going, after you get on the sixth step of that stairs just spoken of, to find yourselves in

The Royal Gallery of the Universe,

the concentered splendors of all worlds before your transported vision. In some way all the thrilling scenes through which we and the Church of God have passed in our earthly state will be pictured or brought to mind. At the Cyclorama of Gettysburg, which we had in Brooklyn, one day a blind man, who lost his sight in that battle, was with his child heard talking while standing before that picture. The blind man said to the daughter: "Are there at the right of the picture some regiments marching up a hill?" "Yes," she said. "Well," said the blind man, "is there a general on horseback leading them on?" "Yes," she said. "Well, is there rushing down on these men a cavalry charge?" "Yes," was the reply. "And do there seem to be many dying and dead?" "Yes," was the answer. "Well, now, do you see a shell from the woods bursting near the wheel of a cannon?" "Yes," she said. "Stop right there!" said the blind man. "That is the last thing I ever saw on earth! What a time it was, Jenny, when I lost my eye-sight!" But when you, who have found life a hard battle, a very Gettysburg, shall stand in the Royal Gallery of Heaven, and with your new vision begin to see and understand that which in your earthly blindness you could not see at all, you will point out to your celestial comrades, perhaps to your own dear children who have gone before, the scenes of the earthly conflicts in which you participated, saying: "There from that hill of prosperity I was driven back; in that valley of humiliation I was wounded. There I lost my eye-sight. That was the way the world looked when I last saw it. But what a grand thing to get celestial vision, and stand here before the cyclorama of all worlds while the Rider on the white horse goes on "conquring and to conquer," the moon under His feet and the stars of heaven for His tiara!

LADIES LEARNING IN JAPAN.

THE Apostolic example of becoming all things to all men, in order to save some, is being followed and blessed in Japan. The lady missionaries there have opened an educational institute for the higher class ladies, who in learning to play on the organ, and to do fancy work are brought under Christian influence. Miss Bull, who writes to the *Spirit of Missions* from Osaka, Japan, says: "There is nothing in the laws or customs of Japan to keep a man true to his wife. He may even cast her off for another, turn her out of his house, keeping any property she may have brought him; there is no redress for her. Many of the higher class women, whose husbands have more means and opportunity for dissipation usually, and who have themselves learned no means of livelihood, as their sisters of the humbler classes have, hang or drown themselves, or live an unhappy life in a divided household, often made like a 'hell on earth,' as Mr. Mori strongly expressed it, by the abuse of the parents of the alienated husband, if they are a part of the family. Until recently these ladies received very little education aside from the training how to gracefully and deliberately make a 'ceremonial tea,' and other things of that kind. Any real work would have been beneath their station and would have brought discredit on the family. When I realized how little there had been to occupy brain and hand of these unfortunate ladies I wondered that Japan is not full of insane women.

"The *Fujiu Gaku Shiu Kwai* (literally, the Ladies' Educational Society) was founded with the hope to meet some of these cases. It is more than a school, for it provides not only for the daughters, but for the mothers, who have been so despised for their ignorance and helplessness. They may join the English classes, or even those in Japanese or Chinese, without being considered out of place; or they may learn to play on the cabinet organ, fancy work, foreign cooking and sewing. Mr. Mori said it could not be expected that the elder ladies would learn a great deal, but what they do learn will serve to make their lives brighter, and there is always the hope that the Christian influence which is predominant in the work of the *Kwai*, may turn them to the Source of life and light. One has already made public profession of her faith in Jesus."

A CURE FOR INSOMNIA.

A REMARKABLE instance of the removal through faith and prayer of the distressing trouble of sleeplessness, complicated by catarrh and other maladies, is cited in a recently published work entitled "A Cloud of Witnesses," edited by Rev. A. B. Simpson. It is that of Rev. F. C. A. Jones, Baptist pastor of Newark, N. J. Mr. Jones says:

"For ten years I have been anything but strong. For six years or more, because of much affliction, I have been a great sufferer; troubled with sleeplessness and nervousness, I was scarcely in a healthy condition for work. On entering the ministry, a few months over three years ago, I did so with great weakness of body and much restlessness of mind. The cares of a city pastorate did nothing to make me better, and by carrying what I should have laid on our Lord, I broke down. For three months I did not preach. With the nervous prostration, heart disease developed, and it seemed as though my work was at an end. A long rest partially restored me, and I was enabled to resume my work. But my heart gave me great trouble. After preaching I would be exhausted; the heating of my heart, the pain in my head and limbs, would make me unfit for work for nearly two days. Added to this, catarrh and sleeplessness, made it difficult for me to do much else than regard myself.

"This condition lasted until August, 1886. For six months or so I had been seeking in the Word for the truth concerning the indwelling of the Holy Spirit. In that month the Lord made known to me as I never realized before, the glorious truth of Christ in us the hope of glory. In the light of this I saw the possibility of Divine healing. At once I searched the Scriptures, and visited the Gospel Tabernacle, in order to see and hear. After a month's study, I was convinced—not by reason, but by the Word—that in the atonement there was healing for the body as well as cleansing for the soul. But while convinced, I could not accept. Then the Holy Spirit revealed myself to me in all my sinful weakness. At the feet of Jesus I confessed my unbelief. Graciously He gave me His faith. From that moment I cast aside medicine, of which I had a stock on hand. Catarrh medicine, tonics, medicine for the heart, etc., etc. No more medicines for me!

"For a short time I experienced much relief and was very happy. Then came trouble. So long as I could trust secretly all was safe, especially if I happened to be mistaken. To avow my position was very much of a test of faith. This had to be done, however. On October 22, 1886, I obeyed the Word of God. All that day, up to the moment of confession, Satan beset my way with difficulties. During the anointing I had the assurance of healing then and there. The same evening, before reaching home, the catarrh had left me, and the next morning I could feel the air passing through the nasel passages as I had not felt in several years. Nervousness departed, and a sleepless night is now a very rare occurrence."

THE EFFECT OF A KISS.

THE transforming influence of a child's kiss on a desperate convict, is described in the *Issue*. It states, that in a prison in New Bedford, Mass., is a convict known as Jim, who is up for a life sentence. Until last spring he was regarded as a desperate, dangerous man, ready for rebellion at any hour. He planned a general outbreak, but was "given away" by one of his co-conspirators. He plotted a general mutiny or rebellion, and was again betrayed. He then kept his own counsel. While never refusing to obey orders, he obeyed them like a man who only needed backing to make him refuse to. One day in June a party of strangers came to the institution, among them were two ladies with small children. The guide took one of the children on his arm, and the other walked until the party began climbing stairs. Jim was working near by, sulky and morose as ever, when the guide said to him:

"Jim, won't you help this little girl up-stairs?"

The convict hesitated, a scowl on his face, and the little girl held out her hands, and said:

"If you will, I guess I'll kiss you."

His scowl vanished in an instant, and he lifted the child as tenderly as a father. Half-way upstairs she kissed him. At the head of the stairs she said:

"Now, you've got to kiss me, too."

He blushed like a woman, looked into her innocent face, and then kissed her cheek, and before he reached the foot of the stairs again, *the man had tears in his eyes*. Ever since that day he has been a changed man, and no one in the place gives less trouble.

MR. ARNOT IN AFRICA.

THE many friends of Mr. F. S. Arnot in this country, will be glad to read an account he recently gave of the exploration in South Africa, from which he has just returned. He said: It was his intention to reach, if possible, a part of the country very little known, but believed to be high and healthy. With this object he crossed from Natal through the Transvaal and the Kalahari Desert to the Zambesi, intending, if practicable, to proceed from thence northward into the centre of Africa. Most of this part of the journey was performed in a wagon drawn by bullocks, and the chief difficulty was the extreme scarcity of water from the Transvaal frontier, to Lake Ngami, stages of ten or fifteen days being performed without any water except what was carried by the party. Mr. Arnot did not find the Boers unfriendly to himself. He described them as an intensely religious people, high Calvinists, and convinced that they are the chosen people, the modern Israel, and that the natives are Philistines, with no rights which they are not at liberty to override. Mr. Arnot had provided himself with a good stock of Dutch Bibles, and the Boers, though ignorant and narrow, appear to have some good qualities, so that he had little difficulty in making his way.

In the neighborhood of Lake Ngami, Mr. Arnot found a number of outcast natives, separated from their tribe owing to some quarrel, and in imminent danger of starvation. On reaching the Zambesi he appealed for them to the chief, and got them readmitted amongst their fellows of the Barota tribe. For similar acts of kindness he frequently was rewarded, when in difficulties, by the assistance of the benefited persons. Unable to proceed direct north from the Zambesi, Mr. Arnot joined himself to a Portuguese trader he came across, and reached Loando, on the West Coast. From Loando, Mr. Arnot determined to make another search for a high and healthy country, where European missionaries could live. He started about due east, and, keeping nearly on the watershed between the Congo and Zambesi basins, he reached and crossed the Lualaba river.

As a rule he was kindly received by the native chiefs, though having to shake hands in one evening with all a chief's relations, including five hundred wives and other relatives in proportion, must have been a trying ordeal. It appears that women are allowed to become chiefs in Central Africa, and one female chief was most useful in checking the warlike propensities of a diminutive nephew, also a powerful chief, who seemed bent on becoming an African Napoleon. The Lualaba, which is really the upper stream of the Congo, was first discovered by Livingston during his last and fatal journey, and on the east side of that river Mr. Arnot lived some time and founded a mission.

A DRUNKARD'S PROMISE.

A REMARKABLE incident is reported from an evangelistic service on the West side of New York. A poor woman entered the hall accompanied by a miserable-looking man, who had evidently led a dissipated life. He was her husband, and his appearance at the meeting was the result of a promise made by him on a bed of sickness. His drinking habits had undermined a strong constitution, and at length utterly prostrated him in an illness which it seemed must end fatally. His wife, a true heart-consecrated Christian, waited upon her stricken husband with patient devotion, keeping things together about the home by means only such as she know how to use. Her chief concern, however, was about her husband's spiritual state in view of his apparently near approach to the grave. The man professed to be a Roman Catholic, but she knew that even in that profession he was not sincere. His life was a godless one, and his rare attendance at the Roman Catholic church was a mere perfunctory custom of his early education. She pleaded with him earnestly but vainly, to repent and believe in Jesus alone for salvation. Once, when he seemed near death, she did gain a promise from him that if God mercifully raised him up, he would go with her just once to the mission. God did spare his life, and the man kept his promise. He sat stolidly through the early part of the service, but as the evangelist spoke, pleading with the unsaved, the man melted. Great tears filled his eyes and rolled down his cheeks. At the close, his wife, who had been watching him, persuaded him to go to the front and speak with the Christian men and women, who were there conversing with seekers. He went and knelt down while prayer was offered. Before the close of the meeting the man rose and said: "Friends, I never expected to stand here. I have heard about religion all my life, but now I have got it—" striking his breast—"I have got it here. I never knew what it really was, till now. I had no notion that Jesus could make me so happy. I quit all my bad ways and bad companions without a struggle. From this time Jesus is my only Master, for He is my Saviour." His poor wife, her eyes beaming with joy, watched him as he spoke and as he went out with her, she looked as if that moment was the happiest she had ever known.

PROPHETIC CONVENTION IN EDINBURGH.

A THREE Days' Second Advent Convention was held in the Free Assembly Hall, Edinburgh, on October 9, 10, and 11. Among those who took part in it were—Rev. A. Bonar, D. D., Professor Alexander Simpson, M. D., Rev. H. Sinclair Paterson, M. D.; the Rev. H. Grattan Guinness, and many other eminent students of prophecy.

Dr. Andrew A. Bonar, of Glasgow, in the course of his remarks referred to Joshua 6 : 26, and described its exact fulfilment 550 years afterward, in 1 Kings 16 : 34, as an illustration of

Minute Literal Fulfilment

where we might not have quite expected it; and then proceeded to take up the subject under three divisions. There was (1) the land and people of Israel. How exactly what had been predicted of them had all come to pass. In quoting Isaiah 6 : 11, "cities without inhabitant," he called attention to the fact that above 300 sites of ancient cities and towns in Palestine had been ascertained, all of them now heaps of ruins. There was (2) the fulfilment of prophecies concerning the first coming of Christ. He showed how to the letter all was fulfilled that had been foretold regarding the Baptist, the Forerunner, in Isaiah 40 : 3-5. We might have been content to find "the wilderness" in which the "Voice" was to be heard, signifying the land silent and desolate in respect of spiritual life; but no, it was literally "In *the wilderness* of Judea," as the evangelists carefully recorded.

The prediction of Christ's entry into Jerusalem in triumph was, Zechariah 9 : 9, to be marked by His steed being "an ass, and the foal of an ass," and this was

Fulfilled to the Letter

(Matt. 21 : 2). These were some samples of literality; but when we look up the predictions of Christ's suffering, we find "the wagging of the head" by those that passed by the cross, "the piercing of hands and feet," "the vestures" (seamless coat) disposed of by lot exactly as Psalm 22 foretold. Dr. Bonar's third head was the bearing of all this on unfulfilled prophecies regarding the coming of the Lord. He read the first verses, 1 to 9, of Zechariah 14. Following out the principle of literality, he drew attention to the narrative of the Lord's coming given by the prophet. The Lord comes down to earth. "His feet stand on the Mount of Olives," that spot so fragrant with holy memories, "which is before Jerusalem, on the east"—the spot where He took farewell of His eleven.

He will Come to Rejoice

over Jerusalem now, not to weep. He will sweep away His and their enemies as easily as He did Pharaoh, or the Amorites in the "day of battle," and then ascend to His throne "King over all the earth."

Rev. Dr. Elder Cumming said: For twenty years he was an Evangelical minister, without being able to see the truth about the speedy pre-millennial advent. It seemed such a difficult and obscure subject he hardly knew where to get light. But in a time of great sorrow God sent him to the Bible to ask about it, and after one little step had been taken, he then began to find that, instead of being obscure and difficult, a few verses here and there, teaching about it, he was overwhelmed

In Every Part of the Bible,

and especially in those portions that had been but a concealed book before by the marvellous clearness and fullness with which God was setting this truth forth. There had been no Millennium up to now. It was clear that the Lord was not to return in the midst of a Millennium, and it was not possible to insert any Millennium between the present time and the Lord's return. He proceeded to quote numerous portions of Scripture in support of his contentions. He argued that no man could preach from the text "Watch and pray" if he was a believer in the doctrine that a period of a thousand years had yet to elapse before Christ's Second Advent.

The Rev. Canon Faussel, D. D., said it was to be seen that there would be a virtual

Relapse into Pagan Apostacy,

before Christ comes, and at His Advent, saints living and dead must be raised again and transfigured in a moment, and sleeping saints awakened. The topic was calculated to enable them to realise their unity in Christ, overleaping the barriers of denominational distinction. The time of Jesus' coming was fast approaching. There would be the presence of angels at His second coming. At every turn in Jesus' history angels were present. As to the question whether the Lord's coming would precede or succeed the millennium, he was of opinion that the Lord would come before the millennium, for the very purpose of introducing it.

The Rev. Dr. Norman Macleod next addressed the meeting, remarking that their premillennial view of the doctrine of the second coming of Christ had been held by him for twenty years.

Mr. E. Malcolm, of Burnfoot, said what a very great and glorious subject was the subject of the conference.

The Hope of the Church.

She hath waited long her absent Lord to see, and was it not in accordance with the Lord's will, and in agreement with all Scripture, that she should continue so doing. But they knew sometime of the hindrances, and so the purpose of this conference is to enable His people to realize a little more the Second Coming, and to love it more, to watch more, to be more ready for His coming, to wait for Him, to look for Him. Many things might happen before the Lord comes again. Nevertheless, the coming of the Lord was a great fact in Scripture, a great fact in prophecy, a mighty event held out to their acceptation; and while they were prepared for His appearing, looking for it, they were prepared for whatever might come before it.

PROPHETIC CONFERENCE IN LONDON.

AN interesting Prophetic Conference has just been held in London. Amongst the speakers were Revs. Charles Graham, John Wilkinson, W. Frith, and Mr. Henry Varley.

Hon. Carteret Hill, D. C. L., made some remarks on the increasing propagation of communistic and socialistic principles, which are utterly destructive of human society and government, and subversive of the constituted order of things. These can only be attributed to Satanic agency. Again, look at the vast multitudes of armed men—10,000,000 said to be under arms in Europe. Think of the perfecting of machinery and appliances for the destruction of human life. Is it not preparing the way for the "God of forces"? Observe also the spread of the Satanic spirit of reckless lawlessness. These things should deepen in our minds the expectation of Christ's speedy appearing. Let us be found earnestly praying He would "shortly accomplish the number of His elect, and hasten His kingdom."

Mr. G. H. Pember, M. A., speaking on

The Two Heads of Evil

in Revelation 17, said: Here we have presented to us two great forms of evil—the woman and the beast. Two forms of evil which, though naturally antagonistic to each other, can readily combine, like Pilate and Herod, against the Lord Jesus Christ. What are we to understand by these two? Generally speaking, the two great directions in which human corruption flows. When men begin to be in fear about themselves and to feel their helplessness in view of unseen forces, they turn to some form of religion which seems to offer to them supernatural protection. Then, when fears subside, they begin to drift into unbelief, and at last into the mere worship of humanity. These are the two points of evil between which the natural human mind oscillates—superstition and infidelity—never by any accident going to the true faith. In Rev. 17, we have the culmination of these two movements. Notice first the woman—a woman is used in Scripture as symbol of an ecclesiastical system. We have three great

Symbolic Women

—the two "brides," the two elections of God, and the "harlot," Satan's counterfeit church. And this woman has her name written, "Mystery, Babylon the Great." By that name we understand she is that fallen apostate religion begun in the earliest years of the earth's history, and coming down ever since, spreading over the world and now centred in the Roman Catholic Church. Its history is a very remarkable one, and has only been revealed of late years through the opening up of the long-hidden ruins of Babylon and Nineveh. It is a system formed among the Turanian tribes in the earliest period of the world's history in opposition to God, and taught men by fallen angels, the Nephilim doubtless. From that time its existence can be traced throughout entire history. Its centre was for ages at Babylon; on the destruction of that city it was removed to Pergamos, "where Satan's seat is," and later still to Rome. The chief distinguishing mark of the system is

The Satanic Trinity

—father, mother, and child; and this woman worship can be observed in Theosophism, Buddhism, Positivism, as well as Romanism, and in the later day Anglicanism. Venus in Pagan Rome, Diana in Greece, Isis in Egypt, the Virgin Mary in Papal Rome, are one and the same under changed names. The secret history of the events of the reign of Constantine show fully how the Babylonian mystery settled in Rome and became the inspiring spirit of the Roman Church. Then persecution ceased, for Satan had gained his object by corruption from within. And not only does history clearly show that Rome is Mystery Babylon, but many of her dogmas and practices are directly derived from Paganism—as, for example, monks, shaven crowns, the wafer bread, the "Eastward position," the meaning of which is clear from Ezek. 8 : 16.

Then the second great form of evil in the chapter is the beast. From Dan. 7 we learn that the four beasts are four "world-powers." But when the Revelation is given, three of these—Babylon, Persia, and Greece—have passed away, and the beast is the Roman Empire—the body politic being represented by the beast, the emperor or ruler by the head. There is also a shade of meaning whereby "horn" represents things or powers subordinate to the emperor. Now the seven heads have two interpretations, each literal; one as regards the woman, "seven mountains" marking her seat as Rome; and seven kings, five of whom are fallen, indicating a violent death. These probably were Julius Cæsar, Tiberius, Claudius, Caligula, and Nero. The sixth, who then was, is Domitian, who reigned when John wrote. The seventh, who was yet to come, there is reason to believe

Is Napoleon I.

Then, finally, there is an eighth; but before his appearing, or at all events before his full power is displayed, the Lord Jesus Christ shall return to call away His own or some of them. But observe, the indications are that the Lord Jesus appears when the Roman empire is in a state of democracy. And of the alliance of the harlot church with democracy we can see manifest signs all around us. The priests are making a bold bid for popular power. Soon, however, the world-power shall get tired of her. The Antichrist shall strip her and rend her, shall claim to himself the worship of God, and then shall sudden destruction overtake him from the presence of the Lord. "Seeing, therefore, brethren, we look for such things, what manner of persons ought we to be in all holy conversation and godliness?"

CHRISTIAN HERALD AND SIGNS OF OUR TIMES.

OFFICE, 63 BIBLE HOUSE, NEW YORK.

ENTERED AT THE POST-OFFICE AT NEW YORK, N. Y., AS SECOND-CLASS MATTER.

EVERY NUMBER CONTAINS:

The Portrait and Biography of some eminent person.
The Sermon Dr. Talmage preached the last Sunday morning.
An Exposition of Unfulfilled Prophecy.
A Summary of the Events of the Week, Notes of Religious and Temperance Movements, etc.
A Sermon by Rev. C. H. Spurgeon, of London, from advance sheets sent by special arrangement.
Pictures of Missionary Life, etc., and Descriptive Articles.
An instalment of a Serial Story.
An Exposition of the International Sunday-School Lesson, by Mrs. M. Baxter.

ANNUAL SUBSCRIPTION, $1.50.

Single Copies, Price Three Cents, may be obtained by order of any Newsdealer.

CURRENT EVENTS.

The Session of Congress which Closed on October 20, though the longest on record since the foundation of the Government, was not prolific in legislation. The leading correspondent of the New York press thus summarizes its work: The record shows that 15,252 bills were introduced in the two houses, of which 3,644 were put in by the 76 Senators and 11,608 by the 325 Representatives. There were also introduced 231 joint resolutions in the House and 116 in the Senate, a total of 347 joint resolutions, and a grand total of 15,599 measures requiring the consent of both branches of Congress to become laws. Out of this vast mass of proposed legislation the various committees reported in 5,919 cases. The record of measures approved by the President, and thus put upon the statute-books, has not yet been made up, but they aggregate about 1,200. Of these a little over 800 are private measures. And a little less than 400 are public acts. About 14,400 measures therefore, were introduced only to be buried in calendars of business so long that they cannot be cleared off in the short session which begins in December. Some of these measures which have failed to be finally acted upon by the Senate and the House are the Tariff bill, the Retaliation bill, the International Copyright bill, several measures to prevent the formation and operation of trade combinations or "trusts," the bill to incorporate the Nicaraguan Canal, and the bills for the admission as States of Dakota, Washington, and other Territories.

An Indiscreet Letter from the British Minister at Washington was an unpleasant feature developed in the Presidential campaign last week. Lord Sackville received a letter from a person in California, representing himself as a person of British birth, naturalized in this country, asking his advice about the way he should vote next week. With innocence rare in an experienced diplomatist, Lord Sackville fell into the trap. Without directly advising his correspondent to vote any particular ticket, he intimated his own preferences so clearly that no one could misunderstand them. The letter was marked "Private," but it was promptly published, and is being made use of as political capital. The matter has been discussed by the President and his Cabinet, but it is believed that no steps to have the Minister recalled will be taken, although the President has been urged to initiate them. The British press almost unanimously condemns the indiscretion.

Mayor Hewitt, of New York, is Little Likely to present himself at a temperance meeting after his experience of October 19, at the Convention of the National Woman's Christian Temperance Union. He had the effrontery, after advocating the opening of beer gardens and wine shops on Sunday, to appear at the Convention and make a speech. He said to the delegates: "The law must be responsive to public opinion and not in advance of it. Therefore, when you come to raise a standard for us, I care not how high it is, it must be raised by education, which will surely be followed by legislation." Referring to the Brewers' Convention, the Mayor said he had told them that he stood as the executor of the law. If the law was oppressive or behind public opinion they might remedy it. It was always *dangerous to be in advance of public opinion*, but he commended the efforts of the Women's Union toward amendment, and would be in favor of a much higher license than prevails at present in this State. The castigation he received from General Fisk, who boldly declared for "No Compromise" and denounced the Godless tendencies of the Mayor's ideas, and the witty rejoinder of Mrs. Mary A. Livermore, must have moderated the man's inordinate conceit. Happily for him, neither of the speakers was acquainted with his record as Mayor, or they would doubtless have convinced him that he was in no danger of being "in advance of public opinion."

Public Confession of Fraud was Made in New York last week by a notorious spiritualist. Mrs. Margaret Fox Kane, who is the original "Maggie Fox," appeared before a large audience, in which were many spiritualists, and declared that her part in the spiritualistic manifestations which first brought spiritualism before the public, was fraudulent from beginning to end. She said: "That I have been mainly instrumental in perpetrating the fraud of Spiritualism upon a too confiding public many of you already know. It is the greatest sorrow of my life. It is a late day now, but I am prepared to tell the truth, the whole truth, and nothing but the truth. I hope God will forgive me, and those who are silly enough to believe in Spiritualism." She then showed the audience how by legerdemain and the clever touch of a sounding-board with her foot, she had been able to produce the rappings and other phenomena, which have helped to fill our lunatic asylums and work so much other mischief.

The Difficulty in the National Woman's Christian Temperance Union was solved without the apprehended secession. The Convention, on October 24, formally adopted the following resolution: "*Resolved*, That we reaffirm our allegiance to that party which makes its dominant issue the suppression of the liquor traffic, declares its belief in Almighty God as the source of all power in government, defends the sanctity of the Sabbath, recognizes equal suffrage and equal wages for women, demands the abolition of polygamy and uniform laws governing marriages and divorce, and aims to remove sectional differences, promote national unity, and insure the best welfare of our land." The following resolution was presented, but not acted upon, as it would practically read Mrs. Foster out of the Union: "*Resolved*, That it is the sense of the National Woman's Christian Temperance Union that no member should speak from the public platform to antagonize our policy toward the party to which our influence is pledged, and that any member thus antagonizing our policy is hereby declared disloyal to our organization." Miss Frances E. Willard was re-elected president by an overwhelming majority.

The Interview Between the Emperor William of Germany and the Pope appears to have been unsatisfactory on both sides. The European correspondent of the New York *Herald* states that authentic advices from Rome, which are accepted as accurate, by both official and Catholic circles, assert that the Pope forced from the Emperor William a declaration that Germany could not encourage Papal aspirations without endangering the present friendly relations with the Italian Government. From a member of the imperial attendants it became known that the Emperor William, while telling King Humbert how the Pope had insisted upon talking on the question of Rome, said: "I had to destroy his illusions, and it was done effectually." On the other side the Italian correspondent of an English journal reports *an interview with the Pope* himself, who said to him: "That the Emperor came to Rome, was not at our request, nor was his object in coming favorable to us, but rather to those who are against us, to those who for ten years past have practically compelled me to restrict myself to this palace, from which I cannot issue. My dignity forbids me to do so. Of our religious orders which have been expelled from Germany three have been authorized to return—the Franciscans, the Dominicans, and the Benedictines. We are in negotiation about the withdrawal of prohibitions affecting our educational orders, but there is great difficulty in this. The German Government desires to keep in its own hands the exclusive instruction of Catholic children. To this I cannot consent."

An Appalling Railroad Disaster is Reported from Italy. Ten cars of a railroad train filled with excursionists returning from the Naples fêtes were crushed by a landslide made up of 200,000 cubic metres of rock and earth. There were over four hundred passengers on the train. The scene that followed the disaster was horrible. Seventy injured passengers and ninety corpses have been taken from the wreck, and there are still two cars buried beneath the rock. It is certain, therefore, that the list of the dead will be increased. Several headless and armless corpses were found in the neighboring river. A mother, who had been driven mad by the catastrophe, refused to release from her embrace her two dead children. A young priest was buried for two hours, and when extricated it was found that his hair had turned white. An entire family, consisting of six persons, was killed.

The Political Situation in France Gives rise to uneasiness. While the President and his Premier are not in accord on the vital issues of the present conflict, Gen. Boulanger has rallied in opposition to the Government a personal following, curiously made up of Bonapartists, Monarchists, and Communists. All three appear to recognize in the General the one man in France capable of overthrowing the Republic. That is what they agree in wishing done, though they do not agree as to the government to follow the Republic. An intelligent observer in Paris writes: "General Boulanger has more powerful support accorded to him than any one man in France since the time of the Prince-President, Louis Napoleon. The communists—and there are 400,000 of them in Paris alone—believe that when the General has broken down legal barriers, they will be able to rush in and revive the Commune. The Bonapartists and royalists hope to turn him into a voluntary or involuntary General Monk. General Boulanger gains power every day, and people begin to believe that a timely appeal to the nation direct can alone save France from another revolution on the centenary of the first."

The Commission Appointed to Investigate the charges, by the London *Times*, of the complicity with crime of Mr. Parnell and other Irish members of Parliament, held daily sittings last week in London. The Attorney-General occupied each day with the presentation of the case against the Irish leaders and no evidence was taken. From the counsel's speech it appears that some of the charges were based on revelations made by a former clerk of the Land League, who has given the *Times* sundry documents, including a letter which shows that the League was paying the medical expenses of some of the men who were shot by the police in moonlighting affrays. It is also stated that evidence will be given to show that the knives used in murdering Lord Frederick Cavendish and Mr. T. Burke in Phœnix Park on May 6, 1882, were purchased by a member of the Irish Parliamentary party. One admission of the counsel for the *Times*, however, indicated a surprising weakness in his case. He acknowledged that some of the letters on which the journal had at first relied were now discovered to be forgeries. This admission will doubtless be used by the Parnell lawyers to discredit the whole of the incriminating letters, as a journal once deceived might be deceived in all.

Contributions to the Fund for Supplying Colored ministers in the South with this journal have been received since our last acknowledgment to the amount of $13.50. They are from Barrington, N. S., Can., 50c., Washington, D. C., $1; Lancaster, Penn., $5; Montreal, Can., $2; Norwood Park, Ill., $5. These gifts are very welcome. They enable us to supply the need of some of the pastors who are pleading and praying to God for the continuance of the help this journal has afforded them. One pastor in North Carolina, wrote us a few days ago: "THE CHRISTIAN HERALD, sent to me for twelve months past in Christian kindness, has been a great teacher to me. But for it, many passages of Scripture would have continued dark to my mind. To part with the paper now would be a sore loss."

A Remarkable Service in a Penitentiary was held on Sunday, October 21. Thirty-two members of the Order of the King's Daughters went to Blackwell's Island, New York, where they held a service of song in the workhouse chapel. Superintendent Stocking received the young women, and told the assembled prisoners who they were, and why they wore the little silver crosses and purple ribbons "In His Name." The members then sang a number of hymns, during which many of the prisoners were softened to tears. A few earnest words of kindness and gospel invitation were spoken, and then the men and women were asked to sign a pledge not to drink liquors. There were thirty-two King's Daughters, and Superintendent Stocking called for two pledges for each one of the band. Fifty men, and twenty-five women signed the pledges. Five King's Tens were represented in yesterday's delegation, and all are members of the Lexington Ave. Baptist Church.

The Impossibility of Disinfecting a Ship Which has once had yellow fever on board is asserted in a Washington journal. It states that when once the microbe obtains a lodging in the timbers of a vessel, no known process can eject it. "You might," said a naval officer to the reporter, "take such a ship and thoroughly clean her, steam all the woodwork if you chose, and then lay her during an entire winter in a cold climate, and then during the following summer go within range of the yellow fever country, and cases would soon develop on board. An illustration of the strange fact is found in the experience with the *Jamestown*, now the training ship at Baltimore. On one of her trips yellow fever appeared on board, and several deaths followed. Subsequently the vessel was thoroughly renovated and extensively repaired. Her woodwork was steamed. Then she remained in northern harbors for several winters. She was finally ordered South again, and before she reached the fever district, a case of yellow fever developed, and the man died. It is true that once a fever ship, always a fever ship." Happily it is not so with the human being who has been infected with the dread malady of sin. Efforts at self-reformation fail because the germs of evil remain in the heart, but when through faith in Christ the man gets a new heart, he becomes a new creature, and temptation finds nothing in him. (1 John 5:18.)

A Cradle Has Been Turned Into a Coffin at the request of a lady living at Wallingford, Conn. Many years ago the lady, who is now seventy-four years of age, conceived the strange fancy of having the cradle in which she was rocked as a baby made over into a coffin in which her body should lie when she was dead. The cradle had been carefully preserved, and was in her own possession. It was of the large, old-fashioned kind, curiously carved in solid cherry-wood, and contained sufficient material for the purpose. She spoke to an undertaker about the work, but he ridiculed the idea, and there were then no indications of the article being pressingly needed. She still cherished the project, however, and as she passed the line of threescore years and ten, she became urgent about its being carried out. A month ago she became sick, and then she was so uneasy about it that her friends determined to gratify her whim at any cost. The cradle was sent to a coffin manufactory, and it has been duly metamorphosed into a handsome casket, and sent to the eccentric old lady's home, to be ready for her when it is needed. It may be hoped that her concern at the approach of death is not limited to the domicile of her body. Her fancy for thus associating the beginning of life with its close will be more intelligently gratified if she has confided the keeping of her soul to God who gave it. (Eccles. 12:7.)

A Mother's Heroism is Described in a Despatch from Yonkers, N. J. It states that on October 24, a lady of that town was sitting in her dining-room with her two-year-old child, working by the light of a kerosene lamp. She had occasion to leave the room for a minute, and during her absence the child overturned the lamp. The child's cry of terror reached the mother's ears and she ran back quickly. The lamp lay shattered on the floor and the burning oil spreading over the carpet. In her eagerness to rescue her child, the mother tripped and fell upon the blazing oil, which saturated her dress. Though her clothing was instantly all ablaze, she reached out for her child and succeeded in placing him safely in his crib. Then she rushed from the room and down into the street. Here she fell flat on her face in the midst of a horrified crowd. Several men wrapped their coats about the lady, but the flames were not extinguished until she had been terribly burned. In the meantime her husband had come and was rushing off for medical aid, when his wife cried out to him not to trouble about her, but to save the child. He ran up-stairs and found the child safe in his crib and brought him down, and then, and not before, would the mother permit him to attend to her own injuries. These were so severe that her recovery is doubtful. When that child grows up and hears of what his mother endured for his preservation, he will be a monster if his heart is not filled with love and reverence for her. Yet men hear the story of Gethsemane and Calvary and learn what Christ endured to save them, and are unmoved! (1 Pet. 1: 18, 19.)

A Wedding in a Tree is Reported to have taken place in Connecticut two weeks ago. A press despatch from Norwich states that a party of young people was entertained at a farm-house near that city. Among them were two lovers who were engaged to be married. During the evening, however, a quarrel occurred which grew serious, and finally the young lady declared that she would never speak to her lover again. The minister of the church with which both the young people were connected, was present, and, noticing the angry looks of the two, endeavored to act as a peacemaker, but failed. On the way home, after the entertainment, he brought the estranged couple together and renewed his effort. While they were walking through the fields a loud bellow startled them, and, looking back, they saw a Texan steer standing in a threatening attitude at the corner of the pasture. Instantly the animal rushed toward the party, and the young man and the minister had only just time to help the girl to climb a tree and get up themselves, before the furious beast was at its foot. The steer appeared determined that they should not escape, and they were in too much fear to make an attempt while he stood on guard below. As time passed it occurred to the minister that the time was propitious for the object he had at heart, and he again urged the two to forgive each other. He found the young lady more amenable to his arguments then, and she consented to forgive and forget. But the young man was sceptical about the permanence of her mood, and he would not be reconciled unless she consented to be married then and there. After some natural reluctance, she agreed, and the minister pronounced the words that made them man and wife. Soon afterward a passing wagon was hailed, and the trio were released from their unpleasant position. Though their refuge in the tree enabled them to escape one danger, and their marriage put an end to their estrangement for that time, other dangers and trials will come. It may be hoped that then they will find a refuge in Christ, and be made one in Him. (Eph. 2:13, 14.)

A Bungling Chemist's Valuable Discovery was the subject of discussion at Cornell University on October 17. A scientist announced that an amateur chemist in New England has discovered a cheap method of dissolving zinc by combining it with hydrogen and producing a solution called zinc water. This liquid, if applied to certain woods, notably whitewood, makes it absolutely fire-proof, and at a low cost. The learned men present fully appreciated the importance of this achievement, and one of them declared it one of the most important chemical discoveries of the age, and one that will surely revolutionize fire insurance, as well as immensely decrease the loss by fire. The invention is kept secret for the present. Only one foreigner — Sir Lyon Playfair, the English scientist — knows of it. He corroborates all that is claimed for the invention, and says that the inventor is *a bungling chemist*, but that he has a faculty of blundering into the choicest secrets in Nature's laboratory. As soon as patents are perfected and capital interested, zinc water will become an article of commerce. So it will be found in the day of Judgment. Men of whom the learned and cultured have spoken with contempt will be found to have learned the choicest of God's lessons, and to have secured the blessing which alone makes life worth living. (Matt. 11: 25.)

BRIEF NOTES.

The bicentennial of the Baptist churches of New Jersey will be celebrated October 30, at Middletown.

Deerfield, Mass., Congregational Church celebrated its two hundredth anniversary on October 17.

Rev. Dr. Colgate was consecrated Episcopal Bishop of Delaware in St. John's Church, Wilmington, Del., on the 18th inst.

There are now 637 Indian boys and girls at the Carlisle School, and the Apaches constitute the largest element of any one tribe.

At the recent Convention of the Protestant-Episcopal Church, Southern Diocese of Ohio, the Rev. Dr. Vincent, of Pittsburg, was elected Bishop of the Diocese.

The London Young Women's Christian Association has more than one hundred and forty branches scattered throughout London, and of these nearly forty are institutes, homes, or restaurants.

A new and commodious building, known as "The Christian Institute," has been dedicated in Toronto. It was erected by William Gooderham, Esq., and is intended to be a home for Bible study.

Of the 174 Presbyterian churches in the Synod of the Pacific, 54 have pastors, 96 stated supplies, and 24 are vacant. There are no vacancies in Los Angeles Presbytery, and only two in Benicia.

The Evangelical Alliance has addressed a letter of inquiry to candidates for legislative and executive positions in New York, as to their attitude toward the religious training of children in public institutions.

The report of the Seventh Annual Convention of the United Societies of Christian Endeavor, just issued, shows that there are now over five thousand of these societies, with an aggregate of over 300,000 members.

From March 1 to September 1, the missionaries of the American Sunday-school Union in the Northwest established 434 new Sunday-schools, and aided 943 old schools, where 5,022 teachers are now giving Bible instruction to 50,238 scholars.

Bishop Whipple has cabled Rev. James Dobbin, of Fairbault, that he has obtained in England a gift of $50,000 for Shattuck School, Minnesota, its designation being for the building of a new wing to the new Shumway Hall, to serve as a dining-room.

Messrs. Hunter and Crossley, the well-known evangelists, have just closed a series of meetings at Oakville, Ont., at which Methodists and Presbyterians united; 347 persons declared themselves as seekers. After spending a few days at Windsor, the evangelists will commence operations at Winnipeg.

Mr. D. L. Moody, in reply to a San Francisco reporter who asked him if he did not find Californians less enthusiastic than citizens of other States, said: "No, I do not think they are less enthusiastic, but there is certainly a greater amount of scepticism here than in the East. In the Southern States the people make very enthusiastic religious converts. In New England and the Middle States they are colder, but they are perfectly willing to accept religious teachings. Out here they are sceptical."

NO COMPROMISE.

A New Sermon by Pastor C. H. Spurgeon.

"And the servant said unto him, Peradventure the woman will not be willing to follow me unto this land: must I needs bring thy son again unto the land from whence thou camest? And Abraham said unto him, Beware thou that thou bring not my son thither again." etc. (Genesis 24: 5–8.)

The Instructive Allegory—I. The Servant's Weighty Errand—His Master's Heart Set Upon It—Difficulty of Finding a Wife Worthy of Isaac—No Exertion to be Spared—II. A Reasonable Fear—The Woman Might Not Believe—Might not Love One Whom She had not Seen—Migh not Like a Pilgrim Life—III. The Servant's Suggestion—Should Isaac be Taken to Her—The Suggestion of the Hour—The Drift of the Times—IV. The Proposal Repudiated—Numbers not the First Consideration—Confidence that the Wife Would be Found—The Power of the Gospel—V. The Absolution of the Servant.

GENESIS is both the book of beginnings and the book of dispensations. You know what use Paul makes of Sarah and Hagar, of Esau and Jacob, and the like. Genesis is, all through, a book instructing the reader in the dispensations of God towards man. Paul saith, in a certain place, "which things are an allegory," by which he did not mean that they were not literal facts, but that, being literal facts, they might also be used instructively as an allegory. So may I say of this chapter. It records what actually was said and done; but at the same time, it bears within it

Allegorical Instruction,

with regard to heavenly things. The true minister of Christ is like this Eleazar of Damascus: he is sent to find a wife for his Master's Son. His great desire is, that many shall be presented unto Christ in the day of His appearing, as the bride, the Lamb's wife.

The faithful servant of Abraham, before he started, communed with his master; and this is a lesson to us, who go on our Lord's errands. Let us, before we engage in actual service, see the Master's face, talk with Him, and tell to Him any difficulties which occur to our minds. Before we get to work, let us know what we are at, and on what footing we stand. Let us hear from our Lord's own mouth what He expects us to do, and how far He will help us in the doing of it. Abraham's servant spoke and acted as one who felt bound to do exactly what his master bade him, and to say what his master told him; hence his one anxiety was to know the essence and measure of his commission. During his converse with his master he mentioned one little point about which there might be a hitch; and his master soon removed the difficulty from his mind. It is about that hitch, which has occurred lately on a very large scale, and has upset a good many of my Master's servants, that I am going to speak this morning.

I. Beginning our sermon, we will ask you, first to think of

The Servant's Weighty Errand.

It was a joyful errand: the bells of marriage around him. The marriage of the heir should be a joyful event. It was an honorable thing for the servant to be entrusted with the finding of a wife for his master's son. Yet it was every way a most responsible business, by no means easy of accomplishment. Blunders might very readily occur before he was aware of it; and he needed to have all his wits about him, and something more than his wits, too, for so delicate a matter.

The work this man undertook was a business upon which his master's heart was set. Abraham himself was old, and well stricken in years; and he very naturally wished to see the promise beginning to be fulfilled, that in Isaac should his seed be called. Therefore, with great anxiety, which is indicated by his making his servant swear an oath of a most solemn kind, he gave him the commission to go to the old family abode in Mesopotamia, and seek for Isaac a bride from thence. Although that family was not all that could be desired, yet it was the best he knew of; and as some heavenly light lingered there, he hoped to find in that place the best wife for his son. The business was, however, a serious one which he committed to his servant. My brethren, this is nothing compared with the weight which hangs on the true minister of Christ. All the Great Father's heart is set on giving to Christ a church which shall be His beloved for ever. Oh, for grace to carry out this commission!

This message was weighty because of the person for whom the spouse was sought. Isaac was

An Extraordinary Personage;

indeed, to the servant he was unique. He was a man born according to promise, not after the flesh, but by the power of God; and you know how in Christ, and in all that are one with Christ, the life comes by the promise and the power of God, and springeth not of man. Isaac was himself the fulfilment of promise, and the heir of the promise. Infinitely glorious is our Lord Jesus as the Son of man! Who shall declare His generation? Where shall be found a helpmeet for Him? Isaac had been sacrificed. Abraham in spirit had offered up his son; and you know who He is of whom we preach, and for whom we preach, even Jesus, who has laid down His life a sacrifice for sinners. How shall we find men and women who can worthily recompense love so amazing, so divine, as that of Him who died the death of the cross?

Said I not truly that it was a joyful but a weighty errand when you think what she must be to whom his master's son should be espoused? She must, at least, be willing and beautiful. In the day of God's power hearts are made willing. There can be no marriage to Jesus without a heart of love. Where shall we find this willing heart? Only where the grace of God has wrought it. The Spirit of God implants a love which is of heavenly origin, and renews the heart by a regeneration from above; and then we seek to be one with Jesus, but not till then.

Think what she will become who is married to Isaac? She is to be his delight; his loving friend and companion.

She is to be Partner

of his wealth; and specially is she to be a partaker in the great covenant promise, which was peculiarly entailed upon Abraham and his family. When a sinner comes to Christ, what does Christ make of him? Ah, dear friends! it is a very small business in the esteem of some to preach the gospel; and yet, if God is with us, ours is more than angels' service. In a humble way you are telling of Jesus to your boys and girls in your classes; and some will despise you as "only Sunday-school teachers"; but your work has a spiritual weight about it unknown to conclaves of senators, and absent from the counsels of emperors. Upon what you say, death, and hell, and worlds unknown are hanging.

In carrying out his commission, this servant must spare no exertion. It would be required of him to journey to a great distance, having a general indication of direction, but not knowing the way. When he reached the place, he must exercise great common sense, and at the same time a trustful dependence upon the goodness and wisdom of God. It would be a wonder of wonders if he ever met the chosen woman, and only the Lord could bring it to pass. We should have cried, "Who is sufficient for these things?" but we see that the Lord Jehovah made him sufficient, and his mission was happily carried out. How can we put ourselves into the right position to win sinners for Jesus?

II. Secondly, I would have you consider

The Reasonable Fear

which is mentioned. Abraham's servant said, "Peradventure the woman will not be willing to follow me unto this land." This is a very serious, grave, and common difficulty. If the woman be not willing, nothing can be done; force and fraud are out of the question; there must be a true will, or there can be no marriage in this instance. Here was the difficulty: here was a will to be dealt with. Ah, my brethren! this is our difficulty still. Let me describe this difficulty in detail as it appeared to the servant, and appears to us.

She may not believe my report, or be impressed by it. When I come to her, and tell her that I am sent by Abraham, she may look me in the face, and say, "There be many deceivers nowadays." If I tell her that my master's son is surpassingly beautiful and rich, and that he would fain take her to himself, she may answer, "Strange tales and romances are common in these days: but the prudent do not quit their homes." Brethren in our case this is a sad fact. Here is a heavenly marriage, and right royal nuptials placed within your reach; but with a sneer you turn aside, and prefer the witcheries of sin.

There was another difficulty: she was expected to feel a love to one she had never seen. She had only newly heard that there was such a person as Isaac, but yet she must love him enough to leave her kindred, and go to a distant land. This could only be because she recognized the will of Jehovah in the matter. Ah, my dear hearers, all that we tell you is concerning things not seen as yet; and here is our difficulty. Unless God the Holy Ghost shall work a miracle of grace upon your hearts, you will not be persuaded by us to quit your old associations, and join yourselves to our beloved Lord. And yet, if you did come to Him, and love Him, He would more than content you; for you would find in Him rest unto your souls, and a peace which passeth all understanding.

Abraham's servant may have thought:

She May Refuse

to make so great a change as to quit Mesopotamia for Canaan. She had been born and bred away there in a settled country, and all her associations were with her father's house; and to marry Isaac she must tear herself away. So, too, you cannot have Jesus and have the world too: you must break with sin to be joined to Jesus. You must come away from the licentious world, the fashionable world, the scientific world, and from the (so-called) religious world. If you become a Christian, you must quit old habits, old motives, old ambitions, old pleasures, old boasts, old modes of thought. There must come to you as great a change as if you had died, and were made over again.

Moreover, it might be a great difficulty to Rebekah, if she had had any difficulties at all, to think that she must henceforth lead a pilgrim life. She would quit house and farm for tent and gipsy life. Abraham and Isaac found no city to dwell in, but wandered from place to place, dwelling alone, sojourners with God. Rebekah might have said, "That will not do for me.

I Cannot Outlaw Myself.

I cannot quit the comforts of a settled abode to ramble over the fields wherever the flocks may require me to roam." It does not strike the most of mankind that it would be a good thing to be in the world, and yet not to be of it. They are no strangers in the world, they long to be admitted more fully into its "society." They are not aliens here with their treasures in heaven, they long to have a good round sum on earth, and find their heaven in enjoying it themselves, and enriching their families. Earthworms as they are, the earth contents them. If any man becomes unworldly, and makes spiritual things his one object, they despise him as a dreamy enthusiast. Yet the spiritual is, after all, the only real: the material is in deepest truth the visionary and unsubstantial.

So you see our difficulty. Many disbelieve altogether, and others cavil and object. A greater number will not even listen to our story; and of those who do listen, most are careless, and others dally with it, and postpone consideration. Alas! we speak to unwilling ears.

III. In the third place, I would enlarge upon

His Very Natural Suggestion.

This prudent steward said, "Peradventure the woman will not be willing to follow me unto this land: Must I needs bring thy son again unto the land from whence thou camest?" If she will not come to Isaac, shall Isaac go down to her? This is the suggestion of the present hour; if the world will not come to Jesus, shall Jesus tone down His teachings to the world other words, if the world will not rise to the urch, shall not the church go down to the orld? Instead of bidding men to be convert-, and come out from among sinners, and be parate from them, let us join with the ungodly orld, enter into union with it, and pervade it th our influence by allowing it to influence us. The deceitful adulteration of doctrine is at-nded by a falsification of experience. Men e now told that they were born good, or were ade so by their infant baptism, and so that eat sentence, "Ye must be born again," is de-ved of its force.

Repentance is Ignored,

ith is a drug in the market compared with honest doubt;" mourning for sin and commun-n with God are dispensed with, to make way r entertainments, and socialism, and politics varying shades. Be fashionable, and think th those who profess to be scientific—this is e first and great commandment of the modern hool; and the second is like unto it—do not singular, but be as worldly as your neighbors. us is Isaac going down into Padan-aram; us is the church going down to the world. Men seem to say, It is of no use going on in e old way, fetching out one here and an-her there from the great mass. We want quicker way. To wait till people are born ain, and become followers of Christ, is a long ocess: let us abolish the separation between e regenerate and unregenerate. Come into e church, all of you, converted or uncon-rted. You have good wishes and good reso-tions; that will do: don't trouble about more. is true you do not believe the gospel, but ither do we. You believe something or other. ome along; if you do not believe anything, no atter; your "honest doubt" is better by far an faith. "But," say you, "nobody talks so." ossibly they do not use the same words, but is is the real meaning; this is

The Drift of the Times.

an justify the broadest statement I have made the action or by the speech of certain minis-rs, who are treacherously betraying our holy ligion under pretence of adapting it to this ogressive age. The new plan is to assimilate e church to the world, and so include a larger ea within its bounds. By semi-dramatic per-rmances they make houses of prayer to approx-ate to the theatre; they turn their services o musical displays, and their sermons into litical harangues or philosophical essays. Is not so that the Lord's-day is becoming more d more a day of recreation or of idleness, and e Lord's house either a joss-house full of idols, a political club, where there is more enthusi-m for a party than zeal for God? This, then, the proposal. In order to win the world, the rd Jesus must conform Himself, His people, d His Word to the world. I will not dwell y longer on so loathsome a proposal.

IV. Notice his master's outspoken, believing

Repudiation of the Proposal.

e says, shortly and sharply, "*Beware thou that u bring not my son thither again.*" The Lord us Christ heads that grand emigration party ich has come right out from the world. Ad-essing His disciples, He says, "Ye are not of e world, even as I am not of the world." We not of the world by birth, not of the world life, not of the world in object, not of the rld in spirit, not of the world in any respect atever. Jesus, and those who are in Him, stitute a new race. The proposal to go back the world is abhorrent to our best instincts: deadly to our noblest life. A voice from ven cries, "Bring not my son thither again." esides, dear friends, no good can come of try-to conform to the world. Suppose the ser-t's policy could have been adopted, and Isaac gone down to Nahor's house, what would e been the motive? The test of separation wholesome, and by no means ought it to be itted. She is a poor wife who would not e a journey to reach her husband. And all converts that the church will ever make by ening down its doctrine, and by becoming worldly, will not be worth one bad farthing a gross. When we get them, the next question will be, "How can we get rid of them?" They would be of no earthly use to us. Why is there such spiritual death to-day?

Why is False Doctrine so Rampant

in the churches? It is because we have ungodly people in the church and in the ministry. Eagerness for numbers, and especially eagerness to include respectable people, has adulterated many churches, and made them lax in doctrine and practice, and fond of silly amusements. These are the people who despise a prayer-meeting, but rush to see "living waxworks" in their schoolrooms. God save us from converts who are made by lowering the standard.

Besides, Abraham felt that there could be no reason for taking Isaac down there, for the Lord would assuredly find him a wife. Abraham said, "He shall send His angel before thee, and thou shalt take a wife unto my son from thence." Are you afraid that preaching the gospel will not win souls? Are you despondent as to success in God's way? Is this why you pine for clever oratory? Is this why you must have music and architecture and flowers and millinery? After all, is it by might and by power, and not by the Spirit of God? It is even so in the opinion of many.

Brethren beloved, there are many things which I might allow to other worshippers which I have denied myself in conducting the worship of this congregation. I have long worked out before your very eyes the experiment of the unaided attractiveness of the gospel of Jesus. Our service is severely plain. No man ever comes hither to gratify his eye with art, or his ear with music. I have set before you, these many years, nothing but Christ crucified and the simplicity of the gospel; yet where will you find such a crowd as this gathered together this morning? Where will you find such a multitude as this meeting, Sabbath after Sabbath, for five-and-thirty years? There is no need to go down to Egypt for help. To invite the devil to help Christ is shameful.

V. And now, fifthly, observe His righteous

Absolution of His Servant.

"If the woman will not be willing to follow thee, then thou shalt be clear from this my oath: only bring not my son thither again." When we lie a-dying, if we have faithfully preached the gospel, our conscience will not accuse us for having kept closely to it: we shall not mourn that we did not play the fool or the politician in order to increase our congregation. Oh, no! our Master will give us full absolution, even if few be gathered in, so long as we have been true to Him. "If the woman will not be willing to follow thee, then thou shalt be clear from this my oath; only bring not my son thither again." *Do not try the dodges which debase religion.* Keep to the simple gospel; and if the people are not converted by it, you will be clear. Results are in God's hands. If that dear child in your class is not converted, yet if you have set before him the gospel of Jesus Christ with loving, prayerful earnestness, you shall not be without your reward. If I preach from my very soul the grand truth that faith in the Lord Jesus Christ will save my hearers, and if I persuade and entreat them to believe in Jesus unto eternal life; if they will not do so, their blood will lie upon their own heads. When I go back to my Master, if I have faithfully told out His message of free grace and dying love, I shall be clear. I have preached God's truth, so far as I know it, and I have not been ashamed of its peculiarities. That I might not stultify my testimony, I have cut myself clear of those who err from the faith, and even from those who associate with them. What more can I do to be honest with you? If, after all, men will not have Christ and His gospel, it is their own concern.

If Rebekah had Not Come

to Isaac she would have lost her place in the holy line. My beloved hearer, will you have Jesus Christ or not? He has come into the world to save sinners, and He casts out none. Will you accept Him? Will you trust Him? "He that believeth and is baptized shall be saved." Will you believe Him? Will you be baptized into His name? If so, salvation is yours; but if not, He Himself hath said it, "He that believeth not shall be damned." Oh, do not expose yourselves to that damnation! Or, if you are set upon it; then, when the great white throne shall be seen in yonder skies, and the day of wrath has come, do me the justice to acknowledge that I bade you flee to Jesus, and that I did not amuse you with novel theories. Clear me in that day of all complicity with the novel inventions of deluded men. As for my Lord, I pray of Him grace to be faithful to the end, both to His truth and to your souls. Amen.

GEMS FROM NEW BOOKS.

AN ANSWER TO PETER.*

"One night, a few years ago," says Dr. J. M. King, "in one of my pastorates of New York, there came to my home a very degraded man, who said to me, 'Come, come quickly; there is a woman dying over here that wants counsel of a priest.' When I rose and went with him it was to one of the most degraded sections of the city, where fallen women congregate. When I reached the place I found that couriers had been sent in different directions, and a Presbyterian clergyman, and a Roman Catholic priest were already by the side of the dying woman. As I entered the room the priest said, 'We have been talking to her. You talk to her now.' After putting a few simple, direct questions to the dying soul, I said to her, 'Believe on the Lord Jesus Christ and you shall be saved.' Almost in a moment there came into her face a transfigured look. But in the hour and article of death, which came in about thirty minutes after I entered the room, the power of her early education asserted itself over her, and she thought she could not die in safety without the last ministrations of the Church of Rome. She called for extreme unction. But the priest saw that she was dying, and whatever was to be done had to be done quickly. He said to her, 'Do you believe that the blood of Jesus Christ saves you?' 'Oh, yes!' she said, 'I believe it.' 'Then,' said he, 'never mind about extreme unction. When you get up to the gates of glory and meet Peter, and he asks you what is your title of admission, look him in the face and say, 'The blood of Jesus Christ cleanseth me from all sin.' He will understand you, and he will let you in.'"

A Daring Lifeboat Captain.

At the back of one of our capes, four years ago this very day, about 10 o'clock in the morning, the signal-gun was heard. The captain of the lifeboat sounded his trumpet, and his men rushed to the boat. Three times they pushed her out into the surf and three times she came back. The fourth time they were successful. They rowed out in the snowstorm, but found the sea so rough that it was with great danger that they could board. There were eight men on the wreck. Thrice the men in the lifeboat rowed around the wreck. One of the men said, "Captain, what shall we do?" The captain said, "At the next sea I shall put the boat on the wreck, then every man of you save a man." "But," it was asked, "what will become of the other man? there are eight of them." The captain replied, "God will take care of him." At the next sea he put the boat on the raft (for the wreck had become a raft), and every man pulled a man into the boat, and the eighth man jumped in after them. They rowed through the breakers to the shore. They put them into the humane house and carefully nursed them. At 4 o'clock in the afternoon a rocket went up just about on the same shoal, and the captain said, "Men, there is another wreck out there; we can't see it, but there are men perishing." The men went to work once more, took the boat down to the surf, and four times the boat was

* From "Co-operation in Christian Work," being some of the addresses delivered at the Conference of the Evangelical Alliance in Washington, D. C., in December, 1887. Pp. 157. Price, in cloth 60 cents; in paper covers, 30 cents. Published by *The Baker & Taylor Company*, 740 Broadway, New York.

The Hon. Robert B. Roosevelt

Scene on the Banks of the Susquehanna.

driven back. Then the men, straightened up and said, "Captain, back of those hills are our wives and children; if we go again they may be widows and fatherless to-morrow." "Yes," said the captain, "I understand that, but those men out there have wives and children, and if we do not go, there will be other widows and fatherless children!" He sprang into his boat, and they went out again and saved fifteen, men, and brought them on shore, and watched them through the night. The next morning the wives and children came from back of the hills, and telegrams went all over New England, announcing what these men had done; and there came back telegrams from the Governors of two of our States, sending their congratulations to those brave men for saving citizens of their States. *We* have been hearing the signal-gun by day; *we* have been seeing the rocket by night. The Church is the lifeboat, and the only one that has come down from glory; and wherever the signal-gun is heard, if a man here and a man there will respond to it, each will save his man, and in a few years we shall hear no more about the perils; the signal-gun will be silent, there will be no more rockets, and but one strain: "All hail the power of Jesus name!"

MR. ROBERT B. ROOSEVELT.

THE appointment of Mr. Roosevelt as Minister-resident at the Hague has been generally recognized as one peculiarly appropriate, and one which might have been made with as much propriety by a Republican as by a Democratic Administration. Though Mr. Roosevelt has generally acted with the Democrats, his record has been chiefly one of active hostility to corruption and misgovernment; and he has been always ready to attack plunderers, whether they had foisted themselves on one party or the other. It is, however, by his descent and personal predilections that he has the strongest qualifications for the post. His ancestors were among the Dutch settlers who, some two centuries ago, founded the Empire City, and his historical studies have made him an ardent admirer of the nation to which he has now gone as Minister for the United States. In his person the Dutch people will have an opportunity of seeing the effect of transatlantic influences on Dutch character.

Mr. Roosevelt was born in New York in 1829. He is therefore now fifty-nine years of age. He studied at Harvard and entered the legal profession. He was, however, independent of professional income, and was soon so strongly attracted to the political arena that he abandoned his lucrative practice to devote himself exclusively to politics and literature. In 1868, in conjunction with Charles G. Halpine, he edited the New York *Citizen*. He also published several books on the culture and catching of fish, a subject in which he was an acknowledged master. He was made a member of the Fish Commission, and in 1881 became its president. During Tweed's reign of fraud in New York, Mr. Roosevelt was active in uniting the best elements of the two parties in opposition to the unscrupulous dictator. He assisted in the organization of the Citizens Association, which ultimately succeeded in freeing the city of Tweed's rapacity. He also served in the Forty-second Congress, and there, too, he distinguished himself by thwarting the designs of a dishonest ring. Mr. Roosevelt consequently has the best wishes of his fellow-citizens of both parties.

ON THE BANKS OF THE SUSQUEHANNA.

(See Illustration.)

ONE of the many charming scenes to be met with by the lover of nature on the banks of the Susquehanna is depicted in the illustration on this page. Probably that river, in its long and tortuous course, from its rise in Lake Otsego, New York, to its mouth in Chesapeake Bay, at Havre de Grace, presents more of these beautiful pictures than any other river on earth. Its length is about five hundred miles, and in its course receives many tributaries, notably its western branch, which is itself a noble stream some two hundred miles long. The country through which it passes is classic ground to all American readers. James Fenimore Cooper has made it familiar to every schoolboy by his wonderfully graphic descriptions, and the scenes of most of his stories can still be recognized by the admiring traveller. To the American patriot one spot which the river waters will always be sacred ground. It is that of the famous Vale of Wyoming, where, on July 3, 1778, the massacre of the patriots occurred at the hands of Major Butler, of infamous memory.

ELLA'S PICTURE.

(See Illustration.)

"I HAVE been a traveller in many lands," said an old man, who, captured by his four grandchildren, bright girls, just budding into womanhood, yielded to their demand for some story of his own life; "I have seen many sights, and looked on many of the most lovely pictures that the
most famous artists have produced, but n
memory has held none so clearly as one I sa
in my youth, and which I sketched myself afte
ward. It was that of a young girl leaning again
a rustic seat in an old country garden, her ey
bent on some needlework on which her finge
were busy, and her head framed on a backgrou
of leaves and flowers. I have that rough sket
still, and some day I will show it to you."

"Oh! that won't do at all," said the gir
"we must see it now to help us understan
Tell us where it is; we will get it."

"Ah! I do not keep it where heedless finge
might meddle with it, but if you insist on seei
it, I will get it, as I suppose I shall have to
sooner or later."

"Oh yes, we insist, came in a musical chor

The old gentleman rose with a sigh, and w
assumed reluctance crossed the room to an
cabinet, from an inner drawer of which he
tracted a paper yellow with age. "Handle
carefully, girls," he said; "it would not sell
much among the picture-dealers, but I se
high value upon it, as most artists do on th
own productions."

The girls took the picture, and looked at
curiously. As their grandfather had said,
artistic merits were not remarkable, but
youthful hands had evidently worked lovin
upon it, striving, probably vainly, to endow
face and form with some of the charms of
image cherished in his memory. It was eas
see, from the exquisite oval of the face, the d
cately chiselled mouth, and the long eyelas
that the girl must have been very beautiful;
a type of beauty, too, that would make a d
impression on a youth of ardent, though
nature.

"Now tell us about her, grandpapa," said
girls. "Fancy grandpapa having a romanc
his life, and keeping it a secret all these ye
Did she die? Did she marry some one e
How was it you did not win her?" Gra
mamma was still living, and the girls were
that the lined and furrowed face, and the to
less mouth, now fallen in, sweet as it was i
venerable cheerfulness, was not the face ske
ed on the paper.

"Well," said the old gentleman, "you m
let me tell my story in my own way, and
your questions afterward. As I told you, I
that face just as I sketched it, but I did
sketch it at the time, you may be sure. I sa
through a gap in the foliage, and as I kne
might never see it again, I did not take my

during the few minutes I dared stay. The fact ıat it was through love of girl that I was leaving home and native land. were neighbors, and, it ıs to me, we had been ers from childhood. I t think, though, that I r how much I loved her she was lost to me. We to be married after I graduated, and had set- down to the law. But ı I went to college I had nuch money and too lit- principle to do well. ies of my habits and ıe of life reached Ella's e before I was through ge, and her father be- uneasy. She was his daughter, and it was likely that he would ıst such a treasure to orthless, dissolute spend- t."

You are not talking about self, are you, Grand-?" asked one of his tors.

Oh yes, my dear, that was d so it would have been ie end of the chapter but he grace of God. But to n with my story: Ella ed to believe anything ıst me, and I suppose I oo sure of her love to be ehensive. When I went e, however, and there d no longer be any doubt t my *weakness*, as I called my *wickedness*, as Ella's r called it, I soon real- the consequences. I was bidden the house, and herself told me plainly I must think no more er. I was stunned by the blow. Could believe it; pleaded, struggled, entreated, but o purpose. Then I made up my mind to t her, but found it impossible. Worse still, ıld not conquer the evil habits that had ght my trouble upon me, and I lost hope I found that even if I did conquer them, ather would have no faith in the perma- e of my reformation, and, therefore, would refuse his consent to our marriage. And was with him. There was no wavering t her. So, at last, I could bear it no longer, went away. I had some money that I was ing to establish myself and furnish a home. just then a little fortune from an aunt ped in, so I set off for Europe in about the niest frame of mind you can imagine. But ery day of my departure I sneaked down to home and peered about for a parting ose of her. That was the time when I saw s I tried to draw her in that sketch. I did the ship, when I was feeling miserable gh to throw myself overboard."

e old gentleman stopped and sighed ly. "I need not tell you," he went on, the next three years were spent. Vain gles after a better life, helpless sinking back degradation, that was the summary of it. money dwindled. I went from one Euro- capital to another, finding no help, but y of temptation. I became hopeless at and had resolved that when my last dollar spent I would commit suicide. That was ime when God laid hold of me. I was just worst, but, somehow, I had the courage to ve that this time it would not end in fail- I had an inward strength that I had never before—and I knew from Whom it came. ld me, and I recovered my physical and al power with a rapidity that surprised myself. I obtained work, studied hard, and at the end of a year I was a new man. I knew I was safe, for never once had the Power in which I trusted failed me.

"Then I wrote to Ella and her father. I concealed nothing, told the miserable story in its true details, and how I had come to believe myself safe. I asked for nothing. I told them as friends who would be glad to know. That was all. Well, I heard nothing for a long time, and I began to think I had no hope of Ella after all. I used to sit in my Paris lodging and look at that picture, trying to read into the face some expression of pity and love, until my heart would sink at the thought of what I had lost. At last, news came. Ella's father had been making inquiries. It was hard that he did not trust to my word, but I could not blame him. He wrote that if I would come home and lead an honorable, decent life for two years, he would reconsider his resolution. You may be sure I lost no time about doing that, and I went through my probation to his satisfaction. Ella and I were married, and so ends my story."

"But how was it; did she die?" asked the girls.

"Oh no, Ella is living yet. Ah, you did not think it! That is Ella's portrait, and she is your grandmamma! Changed, yes, a little older, may be, but just the same to me."

Ella's Picture.

THE EPOCHS OF A LIFE.

A NEW SERIAL STORY.

By Rev. L. E. Keyser.

(Continued from page 687.)

Delicate Ground.

THE intimacy between Hadley Madelling and his ministerial friend, Mr. Hanson, grew rapidly, and each seemed to esteem the other more highly with closer acquaintance. Both were ardent lovers of nature, and enthusiastic pedestrians. Their walks were enlivened with discussions in which each found in the other a foeman worthy of his steel.

One delightful evening Hadley came upon his friend in the street, and easily persuaded him to enjoy a moonlight excursion. Before they were clear of the city Hadley caught sight of a figure on the opposite side of the street which caused the blood to mount to his forehead. His step quickened involuntarily, and his hands clenched, for in that figure he knew his college rival and personal foe, Harrison Duneman.

"What is it?" asked Mr. Hanson, as if his companion had spoken.

"Look at that man!" said Hadley, almost fiercely; "he was a classmate of mine at college. He is a divinity student now. I tell you, sir, that man's meanness and contemptible tricks confirmed my belief that Christianity has no healthful, ennobling power over a man's moral nature." And Hadley proceeded to sketch Duneman as he knew him.

"It would not have surprised you nearly so much, you would not have thought the man nearly so vile, if he had made no profession of religion?"

"No, that was just it; making the profession, yet being so mean and vile."

"What a tribute you unconsciously pay to religion!" said Mr. Hanson. "You see, you expect a higher morality from Christians than from other men. The standard is higher; you perceive that the man is not living up to it. You imply that he is a hypocrite; that he probably does not possess the religion he boasts of. Well, that hypothesis relieves religion of the responsibility for him. If he has none, it cannot influence him. Honestly, now, if he lived up to the standard he professes, would he not be a better man?"

"Of course," said Hadley.

"Then, you see, you honor the creed in condemning the man."

"Still, you exculpate religion only by hypothesis. *Probably*, you say, he has no religion. How can we tell? I, as an outsider, find a man professing religion and living a contemptible life. Now, I am justified in contending that his creed has not elevated him, and, I should say, cannot elevate him."

"There are many whom that creed does elevate. You must have known such. A physician who administers morphia in doses that cannot fail to produce sleep, would, if he found his patient sleepless, refuse to believe that the medicine had been taken, whatever that patient might say to the contrary. When I find a man living an ignoble, unscrupulous life, his profession counts with me very little, because I *know* that 'he that hath this hope purifieth himself.' He has not the hope—the faith—or he would not be what he is. When you experience that faith you will know it, too."

"But there are cases of men of high Christian character, even preachers, who have committed most disgraceful immoralities." And Hadley mentioned one instance which at that time was making a grave public scandal. "His religion did not preserve him," he said.

"No," said Mr. Hanson, "but your psychology may explain it on charitable principles.

Have you never known what sudden and overwhelming temptation was? Has it in no instance led you to do something inconsistent with the principles that ordinarily govern your life? I, on a theological plane, would say that the remains of the old Adam continue in the human system after conversion, held down and restrained, but still there. Now, if the jailor relax his vigilance for a moment, and the captives burst their bonds and run riot; if then, instead of calling for help, he struggles alone and is overpowered, what then? You blame the man, you pity him, you regret his folly, but you do not utterly execrate him, nor would it be inconceivable that the man should afterward, bitterly deploring his sin and his weakness, become more faithful and vigilant than other men who have not so fallen."

"I see your point," said Hadley, "but who, then, is safe?"

"No one who trusts in himself. Even to the disciples Christ said, 'Watch and pray,' and they learned by most sad experience what cowardice they were capable of when they neglected their duty. But to come back to our original question: you must admit that an infidel who is guilty of sin is not inconsistent with his principles."

"Mr. Hanson," exclaimed Hadley, hotly, "do you mean to arraign—"

"Excuse me," said Mr. Hanson, "the remark was not personal; what I meant was, that the infidel has no help, no restraining influence, but that of his own manhood, and we are sadly conscious how little that can do."

Hadley was silent: the shaft went home, and he could not but admit that the clergyman was right. They were in the city again by this time, and they were separating, when Hadley said. "When shall I see you again? Friday night?"

"No, I am going to the lecture: you will go, too, shall you not?"

"Oh, yes; I had forgotten it." And the two friends bade each other good night, and Hadley went to his room to meditate on the talk of the evening.

On the following Friday he was early at the lecture, and was wishing that Mr. Hanson would come and occupy a vacant seat next to his own, when he saw the clergyman enter; and saw, too, to his dismay, that he was escorting Miss Winters. What the lecturer said, what the applause was about, what so interested the audience after the lecture was over, Hadley never knew. To his mental consciousness only two persons were present besides himself, and in his storm-tossed soul a fiercer tempest raged than any he had ever known. The time came afterward when a more reasonable, equitable spirit asserted itself; but while that meeting continued, blind, unreasoning passion rent his breast. Was the man whom he had learned to love, to revere, to implicitly trust, about to rob him of the only treasure that the world held for him? Was the hope of winning that girl, which, to his amazement, he found to be still strong within him, to be snatched from him by the hand he had grasped in friendship? At that moment he actually hated Hanson! The smooth, dexterous, religious preacher was the most formidable rival he could have. He was just the man Miss Winters would naturally admire. Yet how cruel it was! It was inhuman on Hanson's part to so desolate his life! Yet how was Hanson to know what Madeline was to him? And was it not natural that his friend, so mentally like himself, should be similarly vulnerable to the darts that had pierced his own heart? And so the inward struggle went on, his lower nature tortured by hatred of his rival, his better nature bidding him admit that he had no claim upon Madeline which it was Hanson's duty to respect.

After he left the building, after he had reached his room, he was no nearer calm. He was ashamed of his state of mind; he recognized the injustice of his animosity toward Mr. Hanson, but he was powerless to suppress it. It must be concealed, however. It was so childish, so unreasonable, that to acknowledge it must provoke Hanson's contempt. But he must have time to fight it down, and till then he must avoid his rival. He could not meet him as a friend; he was ashamed to meet him as an enemy. But it was not so easy to avoid him.

Mr. Hanson was strongly drawn toward Hadley, and he longed, with the true fervor of Christ's ambassador, to win the brilliant sceptic for his Master. He was amazed, when meeting Madelling on the street and greeting him warmly, to get no response but a curt, formal bow. Still more surprised was he, when calling upon him, to be told in Hadley's frigid tones that he was engaged—was busy. The clergyman vainly tried to imagine what offence he could have given, and failing to remember any, determined to insist on the explanation that no honorable gentleman could refuse to give to another. Accordingly, seeing Hadley one day walking ahead of him on the street, he followed, and as they reached a retired spot, he thrust his hand within the young man's arm, and said, in his kindest tones:

"Madelling, you are offended; I have wounded you unconsciously in some way. But I cannot afford to have you cherish resentment. Let us be manly about it. Come home with me and tell me my fault. You will not find me slow to apologize, or to make amends. Friendships, such as ours has been, are too rare in life to lose them lightly."

What could Hadley say? This man was too noble, too manly, to be treated petulantly. He was ashamed of his anger, and was completely overcome by the frank cordiality of the clergyman. "I am afraid it can do no good, Hanson," he said, "but you are entitled to an explanation. Yes, I will come."

"Now what is it?" said Mr. Hanson when they were seated in his study. "Consider beforehand that whatever I have done to annoy you has been done unwittingly, and in so far as I am wrong my apology shall be ample."

"You have done no wrong, my dear sir," Hadley broke out, impetuously. "You have not offended me, but you have wounded me deeply and I have not had time to recover. It is I who have to apologize for discourtesy, and I do so humbly. I am fearfully weak in this thing, and I must have time to get back fortitude."

"But what is it, Madelling? I must know. I can surely undo the mischief."

"I fear you cannot, and I am ashamed to tell you the cause."

"False pride and false shame, my friend," said Hanson, laying his hand on the young man's shoulder. "Tell me frankly. There is no trouble but is made the easier to bear by confidence."

"I will tell you, Mr. Hanson, though I may lose your respect by doing so, as I have lost my own by self knowledge. I am jealous, madly, violently, unreasonably jealous. I have long loved Madeline Winters, and you—you—" The tears would come. It was of no use struggling, and Hadley covered his face with his hands, and his whole frame shook with emotion.

Mr. Hanson's face grew ashy pale. A great lump was in his throat, and his hand nervously clutched the edge of the desk near him, as he stood silently looking down on the agitated man. Gradually the sobs ceased, and Hadley, recovering control of his voice, said: "Miss Winters and I were classmates in college. We were thrown into each other's society. For a time she seemed to be pleased with my attentions, and when I confessed my love to her one evening, she almost gave her consent to be my wife, only asking for a little time in which to consult her parents, and I could not help but believe that she cared for me; but for some inexplicable reason she wrote me a week later that our relations must cease altogether. I have tried to banish her from my mind, but when I met her a few weeks ago in this place, all my old love revived again, and—and—forgive me this sentimental outburst. I have no claim upon her. You have a right to win her if you can."

Something very like a frown overcast Hanson's brow as he listened to this confession; but if there was a rising feeling of jealousy in his heart, the traitor was quickly ejected.

"You have made an honest acknowledgment, and I respect you for it, and sympathize with your trouble," he said, in more measured tones than usual. "Now, Madelling, there ought to be a perfect understanding between us, or we cannot hope to do each other good, and a necessary antecedent to that is an honest confession on my part. About five months ago Miss Winters came to this place, just after she had left college. I met her, and received her by letter into my church. From the first she stirred my affections as no other woman had ever done, and I sought her society; but though I confess that I am attached to her, I have never made her a declaration of love. I acknowledge that I have been thinking of it; but if you have any claim—"

"Dear Hanson, your generosity overwhelms me," interrupted Hadley. "Words cannot describe what I have suffered on Miss Winters's account, but still I am only a rejected lover. Yet, Hanson," he broke out, passionately, "she almost told me that she loved me, that I had the first claim upon her affections. Oh why did she reject me?"

Mr. Hanson's voice shook a little as he spoke, but his words were honest and manly. He said, "Madelling, this is a fierce trial for us both. Each heart knoweth its own bitterness; let us help each other. We must be friends in spite of this untoward affair. I will tell you what I propose. I will put aside my suit for a time; you shall have an open field for a reasonable period. See Miss Winters, talk with her, and when you think the time propitious try to ascertain why she rejected you, and satisfy yourself whether there is any hope for you. When you have done so, come and tell me. In the meantime you must trust to my honor. I must visit at her home, I must continue pastoral relations, but I will make no effort to win her love. But if you tell me that there is no hope for you, then I am free to try. I will wait for that."

"That is nobly magnanimous," said Madelling, "more than I could have believed possible. I honor you for it, however it may end."

"Then you agree, and we are to be friends?"

"Certainly, and on my side conduct worthy of your nobility."

"Then," said the clergyman, "since this matter is so important to both of us, so that our lives may be greatly affected by the issue, and as we do not know which of us may have to suffer, but one surely, I feel that it would be wise to consult One who has promised direction in every difficulty. We ought to ask Him to help us to do right and keep every evil passion under control. What do you say, Madelling? Shall we kneel down and pray about it?"

"I cannot pray," said Hadley in broken tones; "but I will kneel with you while you pray."

Full of unfaltering trust was the prayer that went up, in low, tremulous tones, to a throne of grace from the clergyman's lips. Hanson was a man of strong faith in the providential dealings of God in the personal affairs of men. Whatever might be the issue of the matter which he placed under divine advisement, he knew that in the hands of God it would have no end but good to the one who lost as to the one who won. The sceptic who knelt with him had long rejected the doctrine of God's immanence and interest in the lives of men, maintaining that all things were controlled by inflexible law; but as he listened to his friend's earnest prayer, he felt that in some mysterious way there was a Presence near him that was more than human, and he rose from his knees soothed and uplifted. The two men grasped each other's hands warmly and vowed that, whatever should be the issue of their unhappy and involuntary rivalry, they would be loyal in their friendship to each other.

"Come to me," said Hanson, "and tell me frankly if you think that I am not keeping faith h you. Let no suspicion, no doubt, dwell a nent in your mind. Make yourself quite of your position, do not hurry matters to a cipitate conclusion on my account; but when know, then mercifully end my suspense hout delay."

I will," said Hadley, "I promise all, and I or you the more for my own self-knowledge of t your magnanimity must be costing you."

he two men grasped hands, and both knew t their friendship was one that might cost er of them pangs of bitter suffering, but could g neither humiliation nor self-reproach.

(*To be Continued.*)

CALEB'S INHERITANCE.

By Mrs. M. Baxter.

. Lesson for November 11. Josh. 14:5-15.
Golden Text, Ps. 37:3.

eb's Faith and Courage—His Report as a Spy -Confidence Resting on Experience—The Unlaimed Land—Belonging to the Nation, but ot Occupied—The Believer's Unclaimed Priviges—A Healed Woman Scorned—The Heart's houghts Revealed—The Trodden Land Possessed—The Octogenarian's Unabated Force—ellowship Perfected.

TRUST in the Lord, and do good: so shalt u dwell in the land, and verily thou shalt be " (Ps. 37:3.) Thank God, this word of d's, written some three thousand years ago, worn well; and, far from being worn out, it s true to-day, and as fresh and as reliable, as en it was first spoken. Caleb, the son of hunneh, was a child of faith. Through ck and thin, through good report and evil ort, in the wilderness or in the land, he trustn the Lord and did good. He always took d's side of the question, whatever it was.

Ve first hear of Caleb as one of the spies sent by Moses to search out the land of Canaan. ile the fearful, tremulous hearts of the ten s gave them an eye for everything but God, I they saw all things large but the Almighty, eb, whose eye was focussed by faith,

Saw God

ve all, through all, and in all. When the rful spies eloquently described the strength the inhabitants, the impregnability of the tresses, the prevalence of men of gigantic ture, Caleb saw only the promises of God l His faithfulness. He saw the God whom hing daunted, who was never at a loss, who ot His reservoirs in the solid rock, His granin the heavens, and who could engineer a d roadway in the depth of the sea when need of His children required it. In full w of such a God, he had said, "Let us go up once, and possess it; for we are well able to rcome it." This was trusting in the Lord. was Caleb and Joshua who were bold enough, en the matter came to a complete uprising of angry, disappointed people, and Moses and ron were on their faces before God, to take d's side, at the risk of their lives. The people e beside themselves with anger; they looked on Moses and Aaron as deceivers, and Caleb l Joshua, who took God's side, were looked on as traitors, and they were about to stone m to death when they rendered their fearless timony, "The land which we passed through search it, is an exceeding good land. If the rd delight in us, then He will bring us into s land, and give it us; a land which floweth h milk and honey. Only rebel not ye against Lord, neither fear ye the people of the d; for they are bread for us; their defence leparted from them, and the Lord is with us r them not."

Caleb's Strong Point

s, "The Lord is with us." This was trusting the Lord. While we reckon upon our talents, r circumstances, our influence, our experience, prospects, our friends, or anything else but d, we are but weak. All these things change. t when we reckon upon the Lord of hosts t He is with us, we are safe. "When I am ak, then am I strong." (II Cor. 12:10.) The rd can change any circumstance, alter any spect, add or take away any talent, destroy any influence, reverse any experience, turn any friend to foe. It is a vain thing to rely upon anything but the living God.

Caleb was obliged to suffer through the unbelief of the people. He, as well as they, must wander forty years in the wilderness; but it was like Joseph's prison to him, for the Lord was with him, and the time of his wilderness journeyings worked no wear upon his physical frame. God made it the same to him as though that forty years of his life never had been. Joshua had divided out the land of Canaan among the tribes according to the command of the Lord. "As the Lord commanded Moses, so the children of Israel did, and they divided the land." But there was yet

"Very Much Land to be Possessed"

(Josh. 13:1); land which God had given, but which the children of Israel had not claimed. Oh, is not this so with His children now? How many of God's promises lie fallen for want of His people claiming them, how few there are who dare to step out upon the Word of God beyond the miserable boundary line of church conventionalism, and oh, how many stigmatize those who trust in the living God as ignorant and wicked fanatics. At a certain meeting, a dear child of God who had been healed, bore testimony to what God had done for her, and the lady sitting next drew away from her, saying, "Oh how dreadful! have you been healed?" just as though she was infected by a kind of leprosy!

Then the children of Judah came unto Joshua in Gilgal: and Caleb the son of Jephunneh the Kenezite said unto him: Thou knowest the thing that the Lord said unto Moses the servant of God, concerning me and thee in Kadesh-barnea. Forty years old was I when Moses the servant of the Lord sent me from Kadesh-barnea to espy out the land; and I brought him word again as it was in mine heart." Oh what a tale this tells of what was in the heart of the other ten spies! It is when we are put to a test of our faith that we know, and other people know, what is in our hearts. "Nevertheless, my brethren that went up with me made the heart of the people melt; but I wholly followed the Lord my God. And Moses sware on that day, saying, "Surely the land whereon thy feet have trodden shall be thine inheritance and thy children's for ever, because thou hast wholly followed the Lord thy God." No doubt Caleb was attending to two separate promises of God by Moses. First, "My servant Caleb, because he had another spirit with him, and hath followed Me fully, him will I bring into the land whither he went; and his seed shall possess it" (Num. 14:24); and secondly, the general promise, made to all the people, "Every place whereon the soles of your feet shall tread, shall be yours." (Deut 11:24.) Joshua knew God well enough to be sure that it was His joy and pleasure to fulfil His Word whenever that word should be claimed of the faith of His children. And now, behold, the Lord hath kept me alive, as He said, these forty and five years, even since the Lord spake this word unto Moses, while the children of Israel wandered in the wilderness (it was no mere wandering to Caleb, for God was with him); and now, lo, I am this day four score and five years old. As yet I am

As Strong this Day

as I was in the day that Moses sent me: as my strength was then, even so is my strength now for war, both to go out and to come in." God had so cared for His people, that their raiment waxed not old, neither did their foot swell during the forty years (Deut. 8:4); but here was a miracle more wonderful still—forty five years of a man's life had passed away, and because he had been true to God, and had not merited the judgment of the wilderness wandering, God had not allowed the wear of time to tell upon his bodily frame in all that period! Oh what a God we have, so strictly, impartially just! "Now therefore give me this mountain, whereof the Lord spake in that day; for thou heardest in that day how the Amakins were there, and that the cities were great and fenced: if so, He the Lord will be with me (or perhaps more correctly, "If the Lord is with me), then I shall be able to drive them out as the Lord said." Grand old man! He did not say, "Consider my age, and give me something easy, a place where there will be no great difficulties." He looked at the mountain, and all the climbing it entailed; he looked at the giants, and all the force needed to drive them out; and then he looked at the almightiness of

God Against All,

and said in his heart, "God is equal to it." Oh for more heroic souls, oh for more of those who rejoice when difficulties come, as the storm petrel is at home in the wild raging wind and roll of the thunder! We have too many faint-hearted drawing-room, feather bed, Christians, who, alas, in time of temptation fall away."

God loves the daring of faith. "Joshua blessed him, and gave unto Caleb, the son of Jephunneh, Hebron for an inheritance." Hebron means fellowship; and fellowship with God cuts us off from the world. It is like a mountain lifting us into another atmosphere. But he who will have real fellowship with God must be willing to renounce all which is not of God: fellowship is sharing with God, and it means leaving all which we cannot share with God. It was a choice inheritance which fell to the lot of Caleb, but the enemies to be driven out were stronger than in almost any other part of the land. Oh how distraction, the being occupied with trifles, hinders real fellowship with God! Oh how the fear of offending some friend, or of losing ground with some Christian, hinders fellowship with God! How, above all else, some wronged and wounded feeling hinders fellowship! Hebron became Caleb's inheritance *before* he

Drove Out the Giants.

Let us taste the fellowship with God and His Son Jesus Christ, which is our inheritance, and then we can tolerate the giants no longer. "Caleb drove thence the three sons of Anak, Sheshui and Ahiman and Talman." (Josh. 15:14.) Having done this, he offered his daughter Achsah to wife to whoever should unite Kirjah sepher (the city of the book). If we have fellowship with God, we must have His Word opened to us. Othniel, the son of Kenaz, took the city of the book, and Achsah became his wife. But one thing more was wanting: her father had given her a south land, the sun shone on that side of the mountain; but she wanted springs of water, and urged her request on her father. No fellowship with God is sustained, even by His Word, without the living water of His Spirit. "And he gave her the upper springs, and the nether springs." Thus is fellowship perfected.

BEYOND.

Beyond life's toils and cares,
Its hopes and joy, its weariness and sorrow,
Its sleepless nights, its days of smiles and tears,
One bright, unending morrow.

Beyond time's troubled stream,
Beyond the chilling waves of death's dark river,
Beyond life's lowering clouds and fitful gleams,
Its dark realities and brighter dreams,
A beautiful forever.

No aching hearts are there,
No tear-dimmed eye, no form by sickness wasted,
No cheek grown pale through penury or care,
No spirits crushed beneath the woes they bear,
No sighs for bliss untasted.

No sad farewell is heard,
No lonely wail for loving ones departed,
No dark remorse is there o'er memories stirred,
No smile of scorn, no harsh or cruel word
To grieve the broken-hearted.

No long, dark night is there,
No light from sun or silvery moon is given,
But Christ, the Lamb of God, all bright and fair,
Illumes the city with effulgence rare,
The glorious light of Heaven!

No mortal eye hath seen
The glories of that land beyond the river,
Its crystal lakes, its fields of living green,
Its fadeless flowers and the unchanging sheen
Around the throne forever.

Man hath not heard the song
Of rapturous praise within the shining portal;
No heart of man hath dreamed what joys belong
To that redeemed and happy blood-washed throng,
All glorious and immortal.

—*Selected.*

J. E. Jewett, Publisher, 77 Bible House, New York, will furnish the above poem in leaflet form at twenty cents per hundred. *A Sample Packet* of 50 leaflets assorted (no two alike) will be sent post-paid, for 10 cts., or 100 for 20 cts. Postage stamps taken.

THE CHRISTIAN HERALD AND SIGNS OF OUR TIMES.

Entered according to Act of Congress in the year 1888, in the office of the Librarian of Congress at Washington.

This Journal contains every week a Portrait and Biography of some eminent person; a new Sermon by the Rev. C. H. SPURGEON, of London, and the Rev. Dr. TALMAGE'S latest Sunday morning Sermon; also always a Prophetic Article, and a Summary of Current Events, as well as Stories, Anecdotes, etc.

Vol. XI., No. 45. Office, 63 Bible House. N. Y. THURSDAY, NOVEMBER 8, 1888. Price, 3 Cents. Annual Subscription, $1.50.

CONTENTS OF THIS NUMBER.

PORTRAITS OF DRS. FAIRBAIRN, DALE, AND ALLON, AND PICTURE OF A SCENE IN NOTTINGHAM.
DANGER FOR THE BALLOT-BOX. Dr. Talmage's Sermon Last Sunday Morning.
ANECDOTES RELATED AT RECENT EVANGELISTIC MEETINGS.
THE MESSAGE OF THE PROPHETS. By Rev. Albert Erdman, D. D.
The Conversion of a Tough—The Anti-Slavery Crusade—Transformed Temples in Japan—A Visit to King Mwanga—Among Chinese Immigrants.
PORTRAIT OF REV. ALFRED C. WHITE, of Amesbury, Mass.
PICTURE OF THE BOULDER CANYON, COL.
A LIFELONG OCCUPATION. A New Sermon by Rev. C. H. Spurgeon.
Gems from New Books: The Childhood of Agassiz—Franklin's First Compositions.
AN UNPROMISING GUEST. (With Illustration.)
THE EPOCHS OF A LIFE. A New Serial Story by Rev. L. S. Keyser. (Continued.)
HELPING ONE ANOTHER. By Mrs. M. Baxter.

THE REV. A. M FAIRBAIRN, D.D. — THE REV. DR. R. W. DALE. — THE REV. HENRY ALLON, D.D.

THREE CONGREGATIONAL LEADERS—THE MARKET-PLACE, NOTTINGHAM, ENGLAND.

CONGREGATIONALISTS IN COUNCIL.

HAVING already published portraits and notices of the councils of other denominations in Great Britain, THE CHRISTIAN HERALD this week gives three portraits of leading Congregationalists, with a picture of a scene in Nottingham, the town in which the annual council of the denomination has just been held. Over one thousand ministers and delegates attended the meetings, representing churches in all districts of the United Kingdom. Among the subjects discussed was that of Education in Elementary Schools, Nonconformity in the University of Oxford, Total Abstinence, and special questions relating to the progress of Congregationalism generally. The addresses were fully as able as those which have been delivered at former assemblies of this body, showing that there has been no deterioration in the learning or culture of its ministers. It evidently still maintains the position it has so long held at the head of all the denominations in England dissenting from the Established Church, for learning, intellectual capacity, and moral power. The three ministers whose portraits appear on the preceding page are the recognized leaders of the denomination.

THE REV. A. M. FAIRBAIRN, D. D.

THE long cherished desire of the Congregationalists to have a college of their own in the ancient seat of learning at Oxford is now at last to be realized. The recognition for which they have so long contended as a right, the protests they have so continuously reiterated against the monopoly, by the Protestant-Episcopal Church of England, of the higher educational advantages, the strenuous labors of generations of great thinkers, to educate the people up to the point at which the obstacles in the way of nonconformity must be swept away, have in this year of grace been crowned with success. Oxford will now see in the heart of the ecclesiastical city a noble institution rear its head, sheltering a body of professors and students whose principles have been the abhorrence of archbishops and bishops and dons of the dominant church. It is no slight tribute of honor that his brethren have paid to Dr. Fairbairn in calling him to preside over the new institution, and exercise the functions which must at the outset require extraordinary tact, discretion, and administrative ability.

Dr. A. M. Fairbairn was born near Edinburgh in 1838, so that he is now fifty years of age. He received his school and university education in his native city, and his theological training at Glasgow. He afterwards studied at Berlin, where in philosophy he had Trendelenburg as his teacher, and in theology Hengstenburg and Dorner. His first pastoral charge was a small church of the Evangelical Union at Bathgate, in West Lothian, Scotland. From thence he accepted a pastorate at Aberdeen, and on leaving that city in 1877 to take the principalship of Airedale Congregational College, he received from his fellow-townsmen a handsome and valuable testimonial as an expression of their recognition of his high character as "a thinker, a scholar, a gifted Christian teacher, and a public-spirited citizen." There he remained until called to Oxford to take the new position of President of Mansfield College in that ancient and renowned city.

As Muir Lecturer on the Science of Religion in Edinburgh University, a post in which Dr. Fairbairn won a high position as

A Ripe Scholar and Profound Thinker,

and these are still his acknowledged characteristics. In 1883 the Congregational Union elected him to the presidential chair, from which he delivered two addresses remarkable for originality and ability. He is the author of several valuable works, amongst which may be mentioned "The City of God," "Studies on the Philosophy of Religion," "Studies on the Life of Christ," and lectures to workingmen on "Religion in History and the Life of To-day." He has also since 1870 been a frequent contributor to the *Contemporary Review*. In recognition of his scholarship and ability, and as an expression of good-will to Mansfield College, the University of Oxford has conferred on him the degree of M. A. His D. D. is from Edinburgh.

It is well known that, although according to the principles of Congregational Independency each church is at liberty to elect to the pastorate any person whom the members may chose, with or without college training or ordination, Congregationalists as a body have always been strenuous advocates for an educated ministry, and have taken care to make adequate provision to secure it in their academies and colleges. Their latest enterprise in this direction, the founding of

Mansfield College,

Oxford, is without doubt one of the most remarkable movements recorded in their history; certainly it is the most important educational undertaking attempted by Nonconformists since the passing of the notorious Act of Uniformity. The building will be a truly noble structure of white stone, and is expected to be completed about the end of the present year or the early part of the next. The endowments of the new College will be those that belonged to Spring Hill College, Birmingham, for that institution is to be sold, and the net yearly income of the endowments is to be appropriated to Mansfield by order of the Charity Commissioners.

The trustees have been fortunate in securing the Rev. Dr. Fairbairn to be the first Principal of Mansfield College. He has had a training in philosophy and theology such as few men have been favored with, and has given evidence of ability of the highest order, together with sound evangelical doctrine.

THE REV. R. W. DALE, D. D.

AMERICA has a kind of partnership in this most talented as well as most cultured of English Congregational ministers. The title which distinguishes him, and which the educational institutions of his own land refrained from conferring upon him on account of his Nonconformity, came to him from Yale College. It was conferred on him in 1877, as a small token of recognition of the benefits which he rendered to the college in a series of lectures, which at its request, he came here to deliver. The learning, the original thought, the strong logical power, the brilliant eloquence of the man, captivated the college, while his vigorous affection for our republican form of government, which at some cost of social distinction he has not concealed in his own land, endeared him alike to young and old in our famous institution.

Robert William Dale is nearly fifty-nine years of age. He was born in London on December 1, 1829. His career at school was remarkable. The boy seemed to have an inexhaustible capacity for hard work, and his abilities were far beyond those of the majority of boys of his own age. At the conclusion of his school life, the necessity of earning a livelihood precluded him for a time from college training. He, therefore, being resolved to push his way forward in the acquisition of knowledge, obtained a situation as assistant teacher in a school and devoted his nights to hard study. Subsequently he became principal of a school established by a Congregational church, and there his remarkable gifts attracted the attention of pastor and people. They were deeply impressed with the power of the man, and learning that he desired to consecrate his life to ministerial work, they decided to defray his expenses at college. He was sent to Spring Hill College at Birmingham, and there soon proved the wisdom of their decision. He remained in the college the full curriculum of six years, and, as a result of his characteristic application and assiduity, in the year 1853 he *graduated* M. A. at the University of London, with which Spring Hill was affiliated, carrying off the gold medal in the department of Philosophy and Political Economy. Among his tutors at Spring Hill College was Henry Rogers, author of the famous work entitled "The Eclipse of Faith." The marked affection of the venerable tutor for his brilliant pupil, Dale, was heartily reciprocated, and to this day the latter acknowledges his lasting obligations to his mas ter with almost juvenile warmth.

Another remarkable friend of Mr Dale' youth was a good man renowned in the worl of Evangelical Nonconformity, and whose prais yet lingers with grateful fragrance in all th churches as the author of "The Anxious In quirer Directed,"

John Angell James,

who for more than fifty years was the belove and eminently successful pastor of Carr's Lan Chapel, Birmingham; and no sooner had Dr Dale completed his University career and th college course of special and technical study, i 1853, than he was unanimously appointed hi colleague; and eventually, in 1859, on the deat of Mr. James, succeeded to the full charge o that well-known place of worship.

Dr. Dale presents to everyone he meets th appearance of a happy, hearty man, and com bines in no ordinary measure the Laureate' desiderata of manhood, "heart, head, hand. His daily practice and his theory of Christia life constitute a perfect harmony. His soul i in his work. He is a strong admirer of Mr Moody, and took a prominent part in the cam paign of Messrs. Moody and Sankey at Bir mingham, in 1875.

When the pressure of Dr. Dale's pastoral an political duties is considered, the tale of hi *literary labors* appears immense. They includ a "Life of John Angell James," a volume o "Week Day Sermons," "The Atonement," whic ran through seven editions in four years, "Lec tures on Preaching," "Discourses on Specia Occasions," "The Ten Commandments," "Lec tures on the Epistle to the Hebrews," an "Essa on Lacordaire," "A Reply to Mr. Matthew Ar nold's Attack on Puritanism," &c. Besides con tributing to the *British quarterly*, the *Fortnigh ly*, the *Contemporary*, and the *Nineteenth Cen tury*, he has acted as joint editor of the *Eclecti Review*, and for several years as editor of th *Congregationalist*, an organ of his denominatio Tolerance, ability, honesty, and earnestne characterize all his productions. He is an arde politician, and is one of the most effectiv platform speakers in Great Britain. In 1869 h was honored by his brethren in being chosen the highest office in their gift—the Chairma ship of the Congregational Union.

Dr. Dale has travelled extensively. He ha visited Egypt, the Sinaitic Peninsula, and Pa estine, has made long journeys in this countr sojourning in most of our chief cities, and th spring he returned from a long visit to Australi The chief daily journal of Birmingham, t town to which he has given all his minister life in spite of repeated attempts to attract hi to other places, remarked on his return fro Australia: "The whole town will be glad th Dr. Dale is at home again. Birmingham never quite Birmingham without him. T strenuous vigor of his intellect, the tenacity his grasp of great principles, his fiery thorou ness in every labor to which he sets his ha and his sturdy and inflexible morality are, are happy to think, typical of the highest a best life of the town he loves and has served well. All will read of his success with deli He has returned with the sense that the hi desires which animated his journey to Austr have been achieved beyond his utmost hope

THE REV. HENRY ALLON, D. D.

THE veteran minister, whose influence am his brethren in London has been steadily gr ing for over forty years, is a Yorkshireman birth. He is now seventy years of age, ha been born at Welton, near Hull, in 1828. father was a godly merchant, under whose i ence the son was early brought to Christ, an consecrate his life to the Christian minis After graduating from Cheshunt College in he accepted an invitation to become co-pa of a church in Islington, the northern dist of London. His sermons soon attracted pu attention, and drew visitors from all parts of metropolis. Sermons were seldom publishe those days, but those of the young preacher ngton were too powerful and valuable to be , and when a publisher secured the privilege rinting them, they had a wide circulation.

1852 Mr. Lewis, the senior pastor of the rch, died, and Dr. Allon assumed the entire torate at the unanimous request of the church. attracted around him a band of earnest kers, who made the church the centre of a e-reaching circle of Christian influence. Possing in a rare degree the quality known among selves as magnetism, he inspires his young with his own spirit of devotion to the cause Christ, and is perpetually finding new chan for their labors. The problem of reaching masses of non-churchgoers has been the one reme subject of consideration, both of pastor people, of late years, and the Islington rch has organized and operated a most effit means of dealing with it.

r. Allon was elected chairman of the Congational Union in 1864, and devoted his adsses on the occasion to an attempt to refute teachings of Ernest Renan and Bishop Co-o. He has travelled in Palestine and Egypt, has paid one visit to America. Like Dr. e, he derives his degree of Doctor of Divinity n Yale College. Among his published works, most widely known is a volume entitled, ne Vision of God, and Other Sermons."

THE TOWN OF NOTTINGHAM.

(See picture on first page.)

HE town of Nottingham, in which the Congational Council has just been held, has, with uburbs and neighboring industrial villages, pulation of a hundred and twenty thousand, is one of the most important towns in the lish Midlands. It is a place of much note nglish history. It is in possession of agree- suburban places of recreation. The public len, styled the Arboretum, on the north side, stefully laid out; beyond it lie the Church etery, portions of forest-land called "Robin od's Chace," and "the Coppices," with St. e's Well. In the rock that overhangs the n, not far from the Castle, are the hewn- caverns which have got the name of "The ists' Holes," from having been occupied as nits' cells in the Middle Ages, but which are eved to be of much more ancient origin.

he town has produced a far more than averproportion of notable persons, who have incted and delighted mankind, and done good heir day and generation. Among a crowd names more or less familiar, are the poet ry Kirk White, Thomas and Paul Sandby, ert Wakefield, Samuel Ayscough, Dr. Mar- Hall, Rev. Joseph Gilbert, and T. Peet, produced "Poor Robin's Almanack" for years. Among other celebrities are Wil- and Mary Howitt; Bailey, the author of stus"; J. C. Wright, the translator of the an poet, Dante; and Spencer T. Hall. avid, King of Scotland, was imprisoned e in 1346; and the place of confinement ad- ed a Speaker of the House of Commons, a Lord Mayor and Sheriffs of London, who punished for denying the absoluteness of al prerogative in the fourteenth century. It at Nottingham, in 1485, that Richard III. ered his army for the Battle of Bosworth; ottingham, in 1642, that Charles I. raised tandard in the Civil War against the Eng- Parliament. The modern Nottingham le in 1831 was burnt down by a mob of reckrioters during the Reform Bill Agitation, has since been rebuilt, and is now a Fine Museum. *The great market-place, shown e picture on the first page*, is a triangular of nearly six acres, with wooden colons in front of some of the shops, and has a edly old-fashioned air; at one end is the ange Hall, a handsome building, and near e three old parish churches, St. Mary's St. r's, and St. Nicholas', which claim prece- e over a dozen or twenty others of more t date. Nottingham is considered to be of the most religious towns in the United dom, and excellent work is done in it for t by all the churches.

ANECDOTES RELATED AT RECENT EVANGELISTIC MEETINGS.

Turning the World Upside Down. The Rev. Newman Hall said at a recent meeting: "There was an old story of a preacher in Yorkshire who, when preaching on the text, 'They that turned the world upside down have come hither also,' said, in the Yorkshire dialect, 'Ma friends, I shall treat this subject in four divisions. First, the world at first was made right up'rds. Second, devil coom and turn he upsie doon. Third, the world ha' got to be set right agin. Fourth, we are the chaps to set it right.' They should all believe that the world would be set right, and that God in His condescension and mercy had given them the privilege and duty of doing it."

Sixpence for Whiskey.—"This Last Winter a poor workingman noticed a woman singing in the street on a very cold day; he took compassion on her, and stepping over to her, he put an ill-spared sixpence into her hand, and passed on. As he walked down the street his heart was sore for the poor woman, and he looked back to see if she were still there, but what was his surprise to see her entering the nearest saloon. He had not many sixpences to spare, even in charity, and certainly none for drink. He turned, and went right into the saloon after her. The whiskey was being handed to her, and the sixpence lay on the counter to pay for it. Reaching forward his hand, he picked up the money, saying, 'This is mine; I did not give it to you for that purpose,' and putting it into his pocket, he walked out of the shop."

Rev. Edward Irving's Message.—Mr. Arthur remarked: "It is told of that great, good man, Edward Irving, that on one occasion when visiting a hospital, he was brought to the bed of a man who was dying. They knew that soon he must go, and that he was not prepared to meet his God. Irving spoke to him, but he was not heard, the patient was too weak. As a last effort, the Gospel messenger put his mouth close to the ear of the dying man and said, loudly and distinctly three times, these three words, 'God loves you.' Irving then left, but when he next visited that hospital he received the glad tidings that not only was his message heard and understood, but it had found its way into the heart of the dying man and enabled him, at the eleventh hour, to see Christ's great love for him in dying for his sins, and to accept Jesus as his Saviour. He died three days after Irving's visit, trusting in Christ."

"Eureka! Eureka!"—Mr. Climie Relates: "There was a young man once in one of Dr. Moxey's meetings who was very anxious about his soul. The good doctor heard of it, and sitting down by the young fellow, said, 'Do you want to come to Christ?' 'Yes, I do,' was the earnest reply. 'Have you prayed?' 'Yes, I have been praying for the last half hour,' was the sad reply. 'And have you not got saved?' the doctor inquired, tenderly. The young man shook his head. 'Well, look at this text,' said Dr. Moxey, "Him that cometh unto Me I will in no wise cast out." Now, have you come?' 'I have.' 'Then that is all. He says He will not cast you out; and I advise you to stay in Him.' That is all that any sinner has to do—to come to Christ and stay there, keeping close to Him and confessing Him. In a moment, the young man leaped to his feet and laughed aloud, and with tears streaming down his face, exclaimed, 'I have got it! I see it, sir. Oh, how wonderful, how glorious, it is! Praise the Lord!' From that hour to this he has gone on his way rejoicing."

The Danger of Procrastination.—Mr. Linnell said: "A short time ago I knew a young man, the finest and strongest young fellow in the whole village. One night he felt drawn to our meeting in the school-house. He came to the place, and even pressed his face to the outside of the window and looked in, but he would not enter, and did not see the need of being converted when he was young and strong; when the days of sickness and old age came, he would seek Christ. On the Thursday following I was visiting an old woman, and on the road I heard a number of people talking together very excitedly. 'What is wrong?' I asked, and I was told that this young man had died suddenly. I hastened to the place where they said he was lying, and there he lay with his head pillowed on a bundle of rushes. He had died of heart disease without two seconds' warning. He who had put off seeking Christ, until he should be sick, or aged, had in the hey-day of his strength been cut off without the least warning, and ushered before God the Judge to answer for the deeds done in the body. One young man, as he looked at his dead companion, said, 'Oh, if it had been I who was thus unexpectedly called away, where should I now have been?' He knew too well where. God used that thought as the lever to turn his heart towards Him. That young man never rested until he had found Christ, and was able to say that for him sudden death would be sudden glory."

An Artist's Model.—Mr. John Climie Observed: "An artist, who was engaged on a great work, required for a model a very ragged and forsaken-looking boy. After searching for some time in vain, he at length met the very thing in a poor little waif on the street. Going up to him, he gave him his address, and said, 'If you come to me to-morrow, at such an hour, just as you are in all your rags, your face unwashed, and your hair uncombed, I will give you so much money.' The boy thought this a rare opportunity, and promised to come. Next day some one knocked at the gentleman's door; he opened it himself, and there stood what could scarcely be recognized as the boy of yesterday. The face washed, the hair combed, and the rags sewn up a bit. 'Who are you?' demanded the gentleman. 'I am the boy you spoke to yesterday.' 'No, you are not; the boy I spoke to was to come just as he was, poor, ragged, and miserable-looking, not like you. If you are, indeed, the same boy, you have not obeyed me. I can have nothing to do with you.' So it is with the sinner. God says, 'Come just as you are, with all your sins and imperfections upon you;' but the sinner thinks he will wait until he is better, and he draws the rags of his own righteousness closer about him. It is no use. Off they must come. God will not recognize you unless you come as a sinner, trusting in Christ only."

An Unforgiving Spirit Hindering Salvation.—At the Christian Institute Mr. Campbell said: "One evening, when I was addressing a meeting I noticed an old lady, who seemed to be very much impressed with the address. I spoke to her, and at once she told me she was extremely anxious to come to Christ. She was a Sunday-school teacher, and attended church, yet she knew she was not saved. I wondered what it could be that was standing between this woman and Christ, for she was plainly very anxious. Could it be a sin? With a quick, short prayer for help, I turned to the lady and asked, 'Is it that there is one whom you will not forgive?' At once her head sunk on her bosom. Though she made no reply, it was plain that that was the obstacle. 'No,' I continued, 'there can be no salvation for you until you give up hating your neighbor, and God will give you strength to do so if you ask for it. He says, "If ye forgive not men their trespasses, neither will your Heavenly Father forgive those who trespass against Him."' She left that night without coming to Christ, but a few nights afterwards I saw her, her face radiant; she had forgiven her enemy, and God had forgiven her. There are many people who would be very glad to come to Christ, if they could only do so and retain their sins, but there must be an unconditional surrender. All must be given up."

DANGER FOR THE BALLOT-BOX.

Dr. Talmage's Sermon Preached Last Sunday Morning, November 4, 1888.

"Two cubits and a half was the length of it, and a cubit and a half the breadth of it, and a cubit and a half the height of it." Ex. 37:1.

The Ark of the Covenant—The Ballot-Box the American Ark—Its Power and Its Protection—The Foes of the Ballot-Box—I. Ignorance—An Anomaly—Compulsory Education a Necessity—Make Ignorance Criminal—II. Spurious Voting—Modern Uzzas—III. Intimidation—An Indignant Judge—IV. Bribery—Bribes of Money and Office—A National Disgrace—V. Defamation of Character—Illustrious Victims—VI. The Rowdy and Drunken Caucus—Property Qualification no Remedy—A Soldier and a Hair-Dresser—The Prayer Mightier than the Vote—The Manifest Destiny of the Union.

LOOK at it—the sacred chest of the ancients. It was about five feet long, three feet wide, and three feet high. It was within and out of pure gold. On the top of it stood two angels facing each other with outspread wings. In that sacred box was the law, and there were in it a great many precious stones. With that box went the fate of the nation. Carried in front of the host, the waters of the Jordan parted. Divinely charged, costly,

Precious, Momentous Box!

No unholy hands might lay hold of it. It was called the ark of the covenant. But you will understand it was a box, the most precious box of the ages. Where is it now? Gone forever. Not a crypt of church or museum of the world has a fragment of it. But is not this nation God's chosen people? Have we not passed through the Red Sea? Have we not been led with a pillar of fire by night? Has this nation no ark of the covenant? Yes, the ballot-box, the sacred chest of the nation, the Ark of the American covenant. In it is the law, in it is the divine and the human will, in it is the fate of the nation. Carried in front of our host again and again, the waters of national trouble have parted. Mighty ark of the covenant, the American ballot-box! It is

A Very Old Box.

In Athens, long before the art of printing, the people dropped pebbles into it to give expression to their sentiments. After that, beans were dropped into it—a white bean for the affirmative, a black bean for the negative. After that, when they wished to vote a man out of citizenship they would write his name upon a shell and drop that into the box. O'Connell and Grote and Cobden and Macaulay and Gladstone fought great battles in the introduction of the ballot-boxes in England, and to-day it is one of the fastnesses of that nation. It is

One of the Corner-Stones

of our government. It is older than the Constitution. In it is our national safety. Tell me what will be the fate of the American ballot-box, the ark of the American covenant, and I will tell you what will be the fate of this nation. Give the people once a year, or once in four years, an opportunity to express their political sentiments, and you practically avoid insurrection and revolution. Either give them the ballot, or they will take the sword. Without the ballot-box there can be no free republican institutions. Milton visiting in Italy noticed that on the sides of Vesuvius gardeners and farmers were at work while the volcano was in eruption, and he asked them if they were safe. "Yes," said the farmers and the gardeners, "it is safe: all the danger is before the eruption; then comes earthquake and terror, but just as soon as the volcano begins to pour forth lava we all feel at rest." It is the suppression of political sentiment, the suppression of public opinion, that makes moral earthquake and national earthquake. Let public opinion pour forth, and that gives satisfaction, and that gives peace, and that gives permanency to good government. And yet, though the ballot-box is the sacred chest and the ark of the American covenant, you know as well as I know it has its sworn antagonists, and I purpose this morning, in God's name and as a Christian patriot, to set before you the names of some of the sworn enemies of this sacred chest, the ark of the American covenant, the ballot-box.

The Foes of the Ballot-Box.

First, I remark, *ignorance is a mighty foe.* Other things being equal, the more intelligence a man has the better he is qualified to exercise the right of suffrage. You have been ten, fifteen, twenty, thirty years studying American institutions, you have canvassed all the great questions about tariff and home rule, and all the educational questions, and everything in American politics you are well acquainted with. You consider yourself competent to cast a vote in November, and you are competent. You will take your position in the line of electors, you will wait for your turn to come, the judge of election will announce your name, you will cast your vote and pass out. Well done.

But right behind you there will come a man who cannot spell the name of comptroller or attorney or mayor. He cannot write, or if he can write he uses a small "I" for the personal pronoun. He could not tell on which side of the Alleghany Mountains Ohio is. Educated canary birds know more than he. He will cast his vote, and it will balance your vote. His

Ignorance is Mighty

as your intelligence. That is not right. All men of fair mind will acknowledge that that is not right. Until a man can read the Declaration of Independence and the Constitution of the United States, and calculate the interest on the American debt, and know the difference between a republican form of government and a monarchy or a despotism, he is unfit to exercise the right of suffrage at any ballot-box between Key West and Alaska.

In 1872, in England, there were 2,600,000 children who ought to have been in school. There were only 1,333,000, in other words about fifty per cent., and of the fifty per cent. not more than five per cent. got anything worthy the name of an education. Now, take that foreign ignorance and add it to our American ignorance, and there will be in November thousands and thousands of people who are no more qualified to exercise the right of suffrage than to lecture on astronomy. *How are these things to be corrected?* By laws of

Compulsory Education

well executed. I go in for a law which, after giving fair warning for a few years, shall *make ignorance a crime.* There is no excuse for ignorance on these subjects in this land, where the common schools make knowledge as free as the fresh air of heaven. I would have a board of examination seated beside the officers of registration, and let them decide whether the men who come up to vote have any capacity to be monarchs in a land where we are all monarchs. One of the most awful foes of the American ballot-box to-day is popular ignorance. Educate the people, give them an opportunity to know and understand what they do. If they will not take the education, deny them the vote.

Another powerful enemy of the ark of the American covenant, the ballot-box, is

Spurious Voting.

In 1880, in Brooklyn, there were a thousand names recorded of persons who had no residence here, and if there were a thousand attempted fraudulent votes in the best city on the continent, what may we expect in cities not so fortunate? What a grand thing is the law of registration! Without it elections in this country would be a farce. There must be a scrutiny on this subject. The law must have keenest twist for the neck of repeaters. Something more than slight fine and short imprisonment. It is an attempt at the assassination of the republic, when a man attempts to put in a spurious vote. In olden times, when men laid unholy hands on the ark of the covenant they dropped down dead. Witness Uzzah. And when men attempt to put unholy hands on the American ballot-box, the ark of the American covenant, they deserve extermination.

Another powerful foe of this sacred chest

Intimidation.

Corporations sometimes demand that t[illegible] employees vote in this and that way. It is [illegible] fully done. It is not positively in so m[illegible] words demanded, but the employee understa[illegible] he will be frozen out of the establishment unl[illegible] he votes as the firm do. So you can go i[illegible] villages where there are establishments w[illegible] hundreds and thousands of employees, and h[illegible] ing found out the politics of the head men [illegible] the factory, you can tell which way the elect[illegible] is going. Now, that is damnable! If in [illegible] precinct in the United States a man cannot v[illegible] as he pleases, there is something awfully wro[illegible]

How do you treat that employee who vo[illegible] differently from what you do? Oh, you say [illegible] do not interfere with his right of suffrage. [illegible] you call him into your private office, and [illegible] find fault with his work, and after a while [illegible] tell him there is an uncle, or an aunt, or a ni[illegible] or a nephew that must have that position. [illegible] do not say it is because he voted this or t[illegible] way, but he knows and God knows it is. If t[illegible] man has given to you in hard work an equi[illegible] lent for the wages you pay him, you have [illegible] right to ask anything else of him. He sold [illegible] his work; he did not sell you his political [illegible] religious principles. But you know as well a[illegible] do there is sometimes on that sacred chest, [illegible] ark of the American covenant, a shadow c[illegible] porate or monopolistic.

I do not wonder at the vehemence of L[illegible] Chief-Justice Holt, of England, when he sa[illegible] "Let the people vote fairly. Interference w[illegible] a man's vote is in behalf of this or that pa[illegible] I give you notice that if an offender against [illegible] law comes before me, I will charge the jury [illegible] make him pay well for it." No shadow, plu[illegible] cratic or mobocratic or capitalistic. Every m[illegible] voting in his own way—God and his own c[illegible] science the only dictator.

Another powerful foe of that sacred ch[illegible] the ark of the American covenant, is

Bribery.

You know something of the hundreds of th[illegible] sands of dollars that were expended to c[illegible] Indiana in 1880. You know something of [illegible] vast sums of money expended in Brooklyn [illegible] New York in other years to carry electi[illegible] And there will be more money used in bri[illegible] this autumn's election than in any previ[illegible] election. It is often the case that a man is n[illegible] inated for office with reference to his capa[illegible] to provide money for the elections, or with [illegible] erence to his capacity to command money f[illegible] others. You know the names of men who [illegible] at different times gone into the Gubernat[illegible] chair or Congressional office, buying their [illegible] all through. I tell you no news. Your patri[illegible] heart has been pained again and again with[illegible]

Very often it is not money that bribes, b[illegible] is office. "You make me President, and [illegible] make you a Cabinet officer; you make me G[illegible] ernor, and I'll make you Surveyor-General; [illegible] make me Mayor, and I'll put you on the W[illegible] Board; you give me position, and I'll give [illegible] position." That is the form of bribe often [illegible] often in these great cities. I do not say [illegible] in our city, but you know again and a[illegible] throughout the land these have been the f[illegible] of bribe offered. So it is often the case tha[illegible] the time a man comes to an office to w[illegible] he has been elected, he is from the c[illegible] of head to the sole of foot mortgaged [illegible] pledges, and the man who goes to Albany [illegible] Washington to get an office is applying [illegible] some position which was given away [illegible] months before the election. Two long line[illegible] worm fence, one worm fence reaching to Al[illegible] and the other to Washington, and there [illegible] great many citizens astride the fence, and [illegible] are equally poised, and they are waiting t[illegible] on which side there is most emolument, an[illegible] this side they get down. But bribery kicks [illegible] ways. It kicks the man that offers it, and [illegible] man that takes it. Bribery to-day you wil[illegible] mit to be one of the mightiest foes of the A[illegible] ican ballot-box.

\nother great enemy of that sacred chest is

Defamation of Character,

n you find out from the newspapers, when ɔ men are running for office, which is the ɩt? How often in the autumnal elections the ɔd man is denounced and the bad man apnded, so that you can come sometimes to just opinion as to who is the best man, and ıre are hundreds and thousands of electors o go up to vote so utterly befogged they ow not what they do. Is not that a fearful ɩuence to be brought upon the ballot-box of s country? It has been so ever since the ındation of this government.

'homas Paine writes Washington a letter, and olishes it, saying: "Treacherous in all private endship and a hypocrite in public morals, the rld will be puzzled to know whether we had .ter call you an apostate or an impostor, and ether you abandoned good morals, or never d any." That is Thomas Paine's opinion of orge Washington. John Quincy Adams dered that he was solaced in regard to the .ndals and the anathemas inflicted upon him the fact that his father, John Adams, had to go ough the same process, and John Quincy ams declared he really thought in that sent election there were men who gave their .ire time to

Manufacturing Falsehood

regard to him. Martin Van Buren was always torialized as a rat. Thomas H. Benton and ıos Kendall were always pictorialized as rob-'s with battering-rams breaking in the door the United States Bank. On the day on ich Thomas Jefferson was inaugurated Presiıt of the United States, March 4, 1801, the lowing appeared in the *Sentinel*, of Boston: Monumental inscription. Yesterday expired, eply regretted by millions of grateful Ameriıs, and by all good men, the Federal Admin-ration of the Government of the United States, .mated by Washington, Adams, Hamilton, ox, Pickering, McHenry, Marshall, and Stod-d; aged twelve years. Its death was occaned by the secret arts and open violence of eign and domestic demagogues. As one bute of gratitude in these times this monunt to the talents and services of the deceased raised by the *Sentinel*." Under such defaman as that Thomas Jefferson went into office. father told me that when Andrew Jackson s running for President of the United States, whole land was flooded with coffin hands—pictures of six dead men, in allusion to six deserters whom Andrew Jackson had d shot, and all the pictorials of those times resented Jackson as taking his office from hand of the devil. I saw at Put-in-Bay, io, in a museum,

A Prominent Paper of 1844,

ich spoke of Henry Clay as a gambler, a liber-e, and a murderer; and the manner in which was defamed, and the outrages which were ped upon him, may be well guessed from Mr. y's eulogy of his native State, Kentucky. He d: "When I seemed to be assailed by all the t of the world, she interposed her broad and penetrable shield, repelled the poisoned shafts t were aimed for my destruction, and vindied my good name from every malignant and ounded aspersion." Defamation! It is the se of the American ballot-box. Just as soon n the great cities a man is put up for office is made the target. The fact that he is up is *ma facie* evidence that he must be brought vn. His public life and his private life are utinized, and all the electric lights are turned How often it is that men have gone down ler such things. In every autumnal election air is filled with carrion crows scenting cares. Caw! Caw! Caw! There are newsers in the United States that in the great umnal elections take wild license for liberty. ey are filled with calumny. The editorial colns of such papers reek with it; their columns stuffed with it. There are newspapers in United States which in the great popular tions breakfast and dine and sup on indecency. They wallow in it. Swine like the mire. They give more for one quill full of it than a whole hogshead of decent product. There are in these great autumnal elections men sitting in editorial chairs who write with a quill, not plucked from the stupid goose or the sublime eagle, but from a turkey buzzard! Ghouls! Ghouls! They tip the city sewer into their editorial inkstands. Defamation of character is one of the curses of the American ballot-box to-day. In your great Presidential elections who can tell from what he reads who is the man he ought to vote for? Bad men sometimes applauded, good men denounced.

Another powerful foe of the sacred chest, the ark of the American covenant, the ballot-box, is

The Rowdy and Drunken Caucus.

The ballot-box does not give any choice to a man when the nominations are made in the back part of a groggery. When the elector comes up he has to choose between two evils. In some of the cities men have come to the ballot-box to vote, and have found the nominees such a scaly, greasy, and stenchful crew they had no choice. You say, vote for somebody outside. Then they throw away their vote. Christian men of New York and Brooklyn, honorable men, patriotic men, go and take possession of the caucuses. First having saturated your pocket-handkerchief with cologne or some other disinfectant, go down to the caucus and take possession of it in the name of the Lord God Almighty and the American people, though after you come back you should have to hang your hat and coat in the back yard for ventilation.

In some of the States politics have got so low that the nominees no more need good morals than they do a bath-tub. Snatch the ballot-box from such men. Where is the David who will go forth and bring the ark of the covenant back from Kirjath-jearim? Do you not think politics have got to a pretty low ebb in our day when a Tweed could be sent to the Legislature of New York, and a John Morrissey, the prince of gamblers, could be sent to Congress?

How are These Things to be Remedied?

Some say by a property qualification. They say that after a man gets a certain amount of property—a certain amount of real estate—he is financially interested in good government, and he becomes cautious and conservative. I reply, a property qualification would shut off from the ballot-box a great many of the best men in this land. Literary men are almost always poor. A pen is a good implement to make the world better, but it is a very poor implement to get a livelihood ordinarily. I have known scores of literary men who never owned a foot of ground, and never will own a foot of ground until they get under it. Professors of colleges, teachers of schools, editors of newspapers, ministers of religion, qualified in every possible way to vote, yet no worldly success. There has been many a man who has not had a house on earth who will have a mansion in heaven.

There are many who through accidents of fortune have come to great success while they are profound in their stupidity, as profound in their stupidity as a man of large fortune with whom I was crossing the ocean, who told me he was going to see the dykes of Scotland! When a member of my family asked a lady on her return from Europe if she had seen Mont Blanc, she replied: "Well, really, I don't know; is that in Europe?" Ignorance by the square foot. Property qualification will not do. The only way these evils will be eradicated will be by more thorough legal defence of the ballot-box, and a more thorough moralization and Christianization of the people. That ark of the covenant was carried into captivity to Kirjath-jearim, but one day the people hooked oxen to a cart, and they put this ark on the cart, and the cart was taken to Jerusalem—the ark of the covenant coming with the shouting and thanksgiving of the people. And though the American ballot-box, the ark of the American covenant, our sacred chest, has been carried again and again into captivity by fraud and iniquity, and spurious voting, I believe it will be brought back yet by prayer and by Christian consecration, and will be set down in the midst of the temple of Christian patriotism. Whose responsibility? Yours and mine.

A Poor Soldier

went to a hairdresser in London. He wanted to get back to the army. He had overrun his furlough, and he wanted some help to get back in quick transit. The money was given to the poor soldier, who said to the man who had offered the kindness: "I have nothing to give you in return but this little worn-out recipe for making blacking." He gave it, not thinking there was any value in it especially, and the man who took it did not suppose there was any special value in it; but it yielded the man who took it $2,500,000, and was the foundation of one of the greatest estates in England. And that little vote, that insignificant vote which you take out of your pocket—insignificant in your sight and insignificant in the sight of others—may start an influence that will last all through the progress of this Government.

I charge you, then, as American citizens, to

Remember Your Responsibility

on the first Tuesday of November. It will begin early, the snow-storm of suffrages. It will snow all day—snow on until noon, snow on until night. The flakes will fall in every town and village and neighborhood, the white flakes. The octogenarian will come up, his hand trembling, and with spectacled eye he will scrutinize the vote and drop it and pass on. The young man who has been waiting for his time will come up, and proudly and blushingly deposit his first vote and pass on. The capitalist will come up with bediamonded finger, and the laborer with hard fist, and the one vote will be as good as the other. Snow-storm of suffrages, and then these white flakes will be gathered together and compacted into an avalanche that will slide down in expression of the will of the people. Stand out of the way of it! In the awful sweep of this white avalanche let political fraud go down a thousand feet under.

You have not only a vote, you have a prayer. The prayer may be mightier than the vote. Oh, as citizens of this beautiful city, and of this State, and of this nation, let us do our whole duty. We cannot live under any other form of government than that which God has given.

The Stars On Our Flag

are not the stars of a thickening night, but the stars sprinkled amid the bars of morning cloud. We are going to have one government on this entire continent. Let the despotisms of Aisa keep their feet off the Pacific coast, and let the tyrannies of Europe keep their feet off the Atlantic coast. We are going to have one government. Mexico will follow Texas into the Union, and Christianity and civilization will stand side by side in the halls of the Montezumas. And if not in our day, then in the day of our children, Yucatan and Central America will come in dominion, while on the north Canada will be ours, not by conquest—oh, no, American and English swords may never clash blades—but we will woo our fair neighbor of the North, and then England will say to Canada: "You are old enough for the marriage day," and then, turning, will say: "Giant of the West, go take your bride." And then from Baffin's Bay to the Caribbean there will be one government under one flag, with one destiny—a free, undisputed, Christianized American continent. God save the city of Brooklyn! God save the commonwealth of New York!

GOD SAVE THE UNION!

TRANSFORMED TEMPLES IN JAPAN.

INTERESTING news of buildings erected for idolatry being used for the worship of God is sent to the *Church* by Rev. H. Loomis, who is laboring at Yokohama, in Japan. He states that at a recent prayer-meeting in that city, an intelligent looking man named Okabe, about thirty years old, presented himself and asked permission to give an account of a work he had himself initiated in his own town in the distant province of Shinshin. Consent was given, and Okabe told his story with much modesty. He said that he was a member of the Liberal party, and first heard the gospel at Uyeda and Komore, which are about twelve miles distant from his home. As soon as he became acquainted with the teachings of Christ he felt their truth and tried to follow in the right way, and began to teach this religion to the children and people of the village. He had some skill as a teacher, and became popular in the village. Soon he was cheered by the conversion of eight persons, and a missionary was sent for to baptize them.

Without any regular preaching the work grew, and after some time an elder of one of the churches went to assist in teaching and preaching as best he could. More were soon gathered in until in the spring of last year a church was organized, and Okabe was chosen the elder. Such was the confidence in him and in his work that when a place was required for Sunday and other services it was suggested that *the village temple was unoccupied* and not used, and that could be taken for that purpose. So it was cleared out, and has been converted into a Christian place of worship.

Hearing of what had been done at Kasugawa, some people in a neighboring town asked to have the same preacher come and use their temple in like manner. And so without a word of opposition these buildings, erected for the worship of idols, have become the means of spreading the knowledge of the true God and Christ the Saviour of the world.

Okabe is full of love for the Master and the Master's work, and reports that twenty-four have been baptized, and ten more are applicants.

THE CONVERSION OF A TOUGH.

THE police and prison wardens of New York have given the name of "tough" to men so debased and brutalized that punishment seems to have no effect upon them. That even men of this class may be moved by divine influence is proved by the following incident, which is related by Rev. A. T. Pierson in his work, "Evangelistic Work in Principle and Practice."

"No man was so vile or so vicious that Jerry McAuley despaired of him. 'Rowdy Brown' was one of the toughs—a large, strong, bold fellow, who united the brutality of a savage with the ferocity of a wild beast. Passing a man who was seated on the forecastle of a Liverpool packet quietly reading his Bible, Brown, in pure malice, kicked him so violently in the mouth as to knock out his teeth; and this ruffian had killed men while in California. Hearing of the conversion of one of his sailor-mates at the Water Street Mission, New York, he swore that he would go down there, and if that fellow should get up to talk, he would force open his jaws and empty a bottle of whiskey down his throat. He went with his bottle. But there was a Power there on whose resistance to his devilish plot he had not counted. While waiting for his time to come, he became strangely moved himself; a new sensation, a violent trembling, overmastered him. He could not even flee; the crowd was too dense, and his strength was gone. By the time his old chum was giving his testimony, 'Rowdy Brown' was ready to faint; and when, at the close of the testimonies, inquirers were invited to come forward, he startled the whole company by dropping on his knees and crying, 'Pray for me!' The excitement was intense. He yelled and groaned for mercy, while his awakened conscience rocked and racked even his huge frame. Two nights of tempest passed before he heard the voice that speaks the soul into calm. But when he did get peace, he leaped from bed at midnight, and roused the whole house with his shouts of praise. 'Rowdy Brown' no sooner found Christ than he found work for Christ. In his intense passion to save men he would actually pick up bodily and carry some sailor to the Mission, and set down the astonished man on the anxious-seat, and then plead and pray with him till the heat of his own ardor and fervor melted him into submission to Christ."

THE ANTI-SLAVERY CRUSADE.

MENTION was made in a recent number of this journal of the attempt made by Cardinal Lavigerie to arouse public opinion throughout Europe to the atrocities of the slave raids in Africa. It appears that practical measures are now being devised to suppress the awful traffic. Mr. Allen, secretary to the Anti-Slavery Society, has had an interview with Cardinal Lavigerie, and heard the latest details from his lips as to the progress of the new Crusade. The Cardinal observed that it was with much pain that he found a certain clique of French and Belgian journals were systematically misrepresenting his mission, and calling it merely a blind to oppose Mahomedanism; and he considered that such attacks might be traced to the existence of a party whom he must designate the *ligue des negriers*, or persons interested in the continuance of the slave trade. In answer to the question as to whether the Cardinal had drawn up any plan of action for the suppression of the traffic in human beings, provided that men and money were forthcoming, he replied that, both in France and Belgium, the enlistment of volunteers and a subscription-list have commenced, but that nothing will definitely be decided upon for a few weeks. Meantime he wished to state, very emphatically, that he had no intention of instituting a war against the Arabs. By placing a steamer, and that not necessarily a large one, on each of the great lakes, the transit of slaves across those inland seas might be, if not entirely stopped, greatly retarded. He would also plant a few European stations in the country between the lakes, for the observation of the trade, and its possible prevention. The disarmment of the Arabs, and of the natives whom they employ to assist them in their raids, might become practicable if steps were taken to restrict the importation of arms and ammunition into central and eastern Africa. Mr. Allen assured the Cardinal of the warmest support upon this last suggestion of the English Anti-Slavery Society, and undertook to urge upon the British Government to endeavor to obtain a concensus of the European Powers, not only to devise some measure to limit the importation of murderous weapons into Africa, but also of the appalling quantities of cheap and pernicious alcohol which is now pouring in, in such enormous volumes, and is working disastrous effects upon the native races.

AN INTERVIEW WITH KING MWANGA.

MR. GORDON, who is a nephew of Bishop Hannington, the Christian martyr, who was murdered in October, 1885, by Mwanga, King of Uganda, is now in the territory of the murderer of his uncle, laboring for Christ. An assistant has been sent to him in the person of Mr. Walker who sends an interesting account of his first reception by the bloodthirsty King. He says: "Before Bishop Parker [Bishop Hannington's successor, whose portrait and life appeared in this journal on June 7] died, it had been arranged that I should come on here to keep Gordon company, and to show the King that we were quite ready to come and to believe in his good feeling toward us; also to show him that he had nothing to fear from white men. He had sent a messenger, saying that he wanted another white man to come, and mentioned my name, inviting me. On the following Tuesday we arrived. The King's messenger went on to tell of my arrival, and the next morning, early, I set off. On the way I met the King's messenger, who took me to a native house and asked me to wait till he had fetched my things. The King had given a chief the order to carry up all my goods. While waiting, we put the chair together that I had brought as a present for the King. It was a 'chairman's chair,' high back, stuffed and covered with crimson leather. The water had rather spoilt the seat, discoloring the leather in places; we also brought a good-sized piece of carpet as a present for the King. At 7.30 A. M. we set off for the Court.

"At last, after passing through several doors in high reed fences, we came to the Court-house itself. A bodyguard was drawn up in front of it. Gordon made me go first. As I stepped over the raised door-step all in the Court stood up—the Arabs, the chiefs, and the King himself. I walked up the centre aisle towards the King, and in my ignorance went up far too near to him. Gordon hurried after me and touched me on the shoulder; I stopped. The King placed his hand on his breast and bowed towards us; we acknowledged the salute in the same way. Then the King and the chiefs sat down, and we, passing behind the first row, walked up to the wall against which the throne was placed, and took our seats on camp stools some ten feet to the King's right hand. The Court was full of people, and all along the walls were ranged soldiers with guns pointed towards the door. The King spoke kindly to us, made several remarks upon my personal appearance, and decreed that I was not such a good-looking man as Gordon. He asked if I had come in the place of the Bishop. Of course, Gordon, who did all the talking, and told me what was being said, assured him that I had not come in any sense as the Bishop's representative. He then asked if I was a smith or carpenter. Gordon assured him I was neither, but like himself simply a teacher. He seemed pleased and satisfied.

"From the description others have given of King Mwanga, you may know that he looks twenty-three or so, has a weak-looking mouth, and rather a silly sort of laugh and smile; he raises his eyebrows very high, and twitches them in surprise, or in giving assent to a statement. He looked a young, frivolous sort of man, very weak and easily led; passionate, and if provoked, petulant. He looks as if he would be easily frightened, and possessed of very little courage or self-control.

"Such a reception Gordon thinks has never been given to any one before. The Arabs, who came to see us to-day, say they never saw the King of Buganda stand up to receive a guest on any former occasion. They think we are in great favor now, but we do not hang on prince's favor or put any confidence in man."

AMONG CHINESE IMMIGRANTS.

AT a missionary meeting held two weeks ago in Chicago, Mrs. J. M. Condit, who has labored for sixteen years as a missionary among the Chinese in Los Angeles, Cal., told the history of a cup which she brought as a gift to the Presbyterian Board. She said that the night before leaving Los Angeles the little Chinese church held a communion service and not only the twenty-seven church-members living in the city, but the eighteen who came from the country and cannot attend regularly were present. Afterwards one of the members brought to her their two large cups, which, as they have no communion-set, had been used by them in celebrating the Lord's Supper, and begged her to accept them as a gift. She finally agreed to do so on condition that she might present them to the board at 1334 Chestnut Street, and to the presbyterian society with which she has been so long connected. The second cup was shattered, however, before she could deliver it. Replying to one who asked if the Chinese in this country seemed much devoted to their heathen worship, she said that they do not go much to their temples, and the fact that life here so soon destroys their faith in idolatry, makes the duty of giving them the true religion the more imperative. One of her bearers was reminded of her own experience in a joss-house, when in response to question whether or not he would sell her ...e of the incense sticks, the priest replied. ...o, our god would be angry if we should sell ...m to you," adding in a stage whisper, "but ...may steal some." She told him *her* God ...ade that.

THE MESSAGE OF THE PROPHETS.

BY REV. ALBERT ERDMAN, D. D.*

...Subject Pre-eminent—The Millenial Period ...Blessing—What it Comprehends—Must Sure...be After the Second Advent—The Sixteen Ac...ording Voices—Joel's Key-note—The Evangel...al Declarations of Isaiah—A Significant Fact ...Amos—The Fall of Silence—The Silence ...roken by John—The Message Summarized.

...HE Old Testament, especially the prophecies, ...ak of a glorious period of blessedness and ...versal peace under the dominion of Messiah ...King, and if that is not the personal and pre-...lennial coming of the Lord Jesus Christ, then ...rds fail to express the idea. Israel's expecta-...n of that blessed period began in the reign of ...omon, when the kingdom of Israel was at its ...hest earthly glory. It was then that the ...phets began to speak of a more glorious time ...come, and of one greater than Solomon, him-...f a son of David, who should sit upon the ...one of David for ever and ever. That is

The Wonder of the Old Testament.

...hen, when you come to the New Testament, ...l find you are standing in the light of much the glory prophesied for Jesus as coming to ...eem sinners from the power of sin and Sa-..., you learn something more glorious yet to ...ne, even Jesus as King of kings and Lord of ...ds in His eternal glory.

...ut what is comprehended in

This Millennial Period,

..."times of restitution" which holy men of ...d spake of from the foundation of the world? ...omprehends the appearing and the glory of ...great God and Saviour Jesus Christ to ac-...nplish the restoration of all things, the resur-...tion by Him of His departed saints, and the ...ture of His living saints to take part in His ...minion over the living nations; the overthrow ...expulsion of all forms of evil from the earth; ...binding of him who was the source of evil; ...repentance and restoration of Israel in honor ...holiness to their own land; the outpouring ...the Spirit on all flesh that should be spared ...m God's judgments sent upon the earth; the ...ewal of the earth to more than its original ...uty as the blessed home of the race; and, ...lly, at the close of this millennial period, the ...urrection, judgment, and condemnation of ...wicked dead, the casting of Satan into his ...n place of punishment, the abolition, last of ...of death, and then the eternal years of God ...r all, blessed for ever. That is comprehend-...in the phrase, the times of restitution, the ...lennial period, the coming of Messiah. Such ...he uniform testimony of the prophets who ...tified beforehand the sufferings of Christ and ...glories to follow.

...rom Isaiah to Malachi there were sixteen ...y men from God who spake as they were ...ved by the Holy Ghost concerning these ...ngs. They sometimes appeared together, at ...er times at intervals, during a period of near-...oo years. Of

These Sixteen Prophets

...re is a three-fold classification. First, the ...phets down to the seventy years exile, viz.: ...iah, Jeremiah, Hosea, Joel, Amos, Obadiah, ...ah, Micah, Nahum, Habakkuk, and Zepha-...h. Second, those who prophesied during ...Babylonish captivity, viz.: Jeremiah, who ...tinued his ministry a few years into the cap-...ity, Ezekiel and Daniel. Third, the prophets ...of the restoration, Haggai, Zechariah, and Malachi. Some of these prophets belonged to the Northern Kingdom, some to the Southern.

The turning-point in the history of Judah and Israel came when the prophets of Jehovah were rejected and ignored, and the prophets and priests of Baal were honored instead, and it was then that a change occurred from spoken to written prophecy. As soon as the days began to degenerate, then began the writing down of the utterances of Jehovah, through the mouth and pen of those writers inspired of God, indicating, as has been pointed out by another, two things: first, the withdrawal of Jehovah's presence from His people; second, a delay, longer or shorter, in the fulfilment of the Divine purposes concerning Messiah and His Kingdom. Joel and Jonah were acknowledged to be the oldest of the written prophecies, Jonah probably the oldest as to his public ministry, but as his written prophecy was not given until later in his life, Joel probably came first.

In the book of *Jonah*, if it was the earliest of the prophetic books, you find this significant fact, that the Lord makes known the underlying truth in all revelation, and the whole purposes of God, viz.: that God is not the God of the Jews only, but also of the Gentiles, and that grace and mercy are to be proclaimed to the Gentile nations as well, and in the name of Him of whom Jonah himself was but a type.

Then *Joel* came and struck

The Key-Note

for all who followed him. His prophetic vision embraced the future down to the establishment of the millennial kingdom, when Jehovah shall have returned to Israel again in Mount Zion. Joel 3:9–21. There you have the substance of all Old Testament prophecy, and it is that glorious declaration that appears again in the eschatological discourses of Jesus and in the Apocalypse of John. It is in Joel you meet for the first time the phrase, "to bring again the captivity," etc.

Turning to *Isaiah* the evangelical prophet, his prophecy is a vision concerning Judah and Jerusalem.

The Main Subjects

of his prophecy are these: Israel's future in the millennial glory, with Jerusalem as the metropolitan city of the redeemed earth, the judgment of the nations and their blessings afterward in subordination to Judah and Jerusalem, and all in connection with the coming and kingdom of Messiah the Christ, and it is to be observed that Christ and the apostles quoted this prophet more frequently than any other. The first twelve chapters have to do with the destruction of the Assyrian, the great northern power and political enemy of Israel, followed by the deliverance of earth from the curse, with the full redemption of Israel, and Christ the Messiah standing as an ensign to the people, to whom, as the centre of rest and of glory, all should gather. (Isa. 11: 10.) In this section occurred that magnificent promise of the coming King and kingdom, "Unto us a Son is born, etc." There was no possibility of denying the literalness of part of this prophecy and it follows that there could be no reason for denying the literalness of the other part. (Isa. 24: 21-23: 25: 7-9.)

Three things certainly are proven by these two prophets, viz., *first*, that Jehovah Jesus will come again in glory as He once came in weakness and suffering, personally and visibly. *Second*. There is no hope for Israel, and no fullest blessing for the nations until this Jehovah Jesus shall come. *Third*. There will be

No Millennium Before Christ Comes

in person to bring it in. Meanwhile, the church, like the forerunner of the Messiah, of whom Isaiah spoke so definitely, is to proclaim the glad tidings, and make ready the way for the coming of the Lord. That gives us the distinction again between Israel and the church, between the past dispensation, the present, and the coming dispensation. The church is the antitype of John the Baptist, proclaiming the glad tidings of the coming One in glory, making ready the way of the Lord, and when He comes He will take up the line of prophecy, and fulfil that which was written.

Jeremiah, like John the Baptist, was ordained a prophet unto the Lord before His birth. Two of his prophecies (23: 5 6, and 33: 14-17) were exceedingly definite and distinct concerning the personal coming of the Lord Jesus Christ. *Hosea*, whose name meant salvation, or deliverance, prophesied in the long and brilliant reign of Jeroboam the second, in the northern kingdom. It was true he bewailed the apostacy, and in most tender and affectionate terms rebuked the people for their sins, but all through his prophecy of lament and rebuke there runs the blessed promise of hope and glory to come, of spiritual and of national recovery, of the time when Jehovah should return to his own again. (Take specially ch. 3: 4, 5.)

Amos, contemporary with Isaiah and Hosea, spoke of Judah and Jerusalem, and of the Gentile nations. His great Messianic prophecy had

A Significant Fact

connected with it; it is the one which James at the first council in Jerusalem quoted as giving the Divine order of events. (Amos 9: 8-15, compared with Acts 15: 14-17.) If we had no other comment in the New Testament on prophecy than that, it would be sufficient. Amos tells us of the dispersion of Israel, sifted among the nations as corn is sifted, and yet not a grain is to be lost, and then of a glorious time of recovery, a planting of them again in their own land. Amos knew only of the dispersion of Israel, and then of the gathering again, but when they turned over to the New Testament then came in this present dispensation, as James tells us. He said, first it was God's purpose to gather out a people for His name from all the nations, Jew and Gentile, and after this—after the gathering of the church out from among the nations—after this He would return (quoting from Amos) and build the tabernacle of David.

The other prophets filled out and confirmed these things. I have not touched the great prophets, Ezekiel and Daniel, and those after the restoration, Haggai, Zechariah, and Malachi. You are perhaps more familiar with them than with some of the smaller ones, but you see how constantly and increasingly, and with more definiteness, came out this line of revelation, of suffering and glory. There was an unfolding

Until the Silence Fell

in Malachi's day. For 400 years the heavens were brass over the earth, no voice broke the stillness, no words came to comfort the hearts of men. Then suddenly the stillness was broken, the brazen heavens parted and filled with light, and there came the words, "peace on earth, good-will to men," and the revelation of a Saviour, Jesus the Son of David, according to the promise made to the virgin mother, "He shall be great, and the Lord God shall give unto Him the throne of His father David, and He shall rule over the house of Jacob forever, and of His kingdom there shall be no end."

In conclusion, you find in these prophets, *who* is to come, *when* He is to come, *why* He is to come, *how* He is to come. You find the characteristics of the kingdom: it is to be universal over all nations, in righteousness; in it Israel is to have the first place among the nations; it is to be administered by one of the seed of Abraham, and of the family of David: and it is to be the kingdom of Messias the Christ, the ideal Prophet, Priest and King. Your hearts must therefore certainly yield to the blessed influence and teaching of the prophetic Word if you believe that God is a God who has a purpose to accomplish, and who will assuredly accomplish that which He has spoken. All lines run forward and gather together, and are consummated in glory in the person and the coming and the kingdom of our Lord and Saviour Jesus Christ.

---

*An address delivered at the Believers' Meeting for Bible ...y, at Niagara, Ont. Published, with other addresses by ...nent preachers, in a pamphlet of 131 pages, under the ...of "Conference Hill Studies," by *The Willard Tract ...sitory*, Toronto, Canada. For sale, price 50 cents, by J. E. Jewett, 77 Bible House, New York.

CHRISTIAN HERALD AND SIGNS OF OUR TIMES.

OFFICE, 63 BIBLE HOUSE, NEW YORK.

TERMS AND INSTRUCTIONS.

Published Weekly. Subscription price in the United States, Canada, and Mexico, $1.50 a year; $1 eight months; 75 cents six months; sent two months on trial for 25 cents, postage free; in Europe and in all countries in the Postal Union, 50 cents extra postage; subscriptions always payable in advance. Single copies, price 3 cents. Any newsdealer will furnish the paper weekly when ordered.

New Subscriptions can commence at any time. When no date is mentioned, we begin it with the issue of the week in which the subscription is received.

Remittances by Mail should be by Post-office money order, bank cheque, draft, or express money order, whenever possible, and should always be made payable to THE CHRISTIAN HERALD. Letters containing money sent in this way need not be registered, as when lost, duplicates can always be obtained.

If a Postal Note or currency is sent, it should always be in a registered letter. Letters can be registered at any office. Subscribers sending money of this kind, and not registering, do it at their own risk.

Change of Address. Name of Post-office and State, of both old and new address, should always be given in case of removal, as without the previous address it is impossible to find the name on our list.

CURRENT EVENTS.

The President's Proclamation Appointing Thanksgiving Day for November 29 was issued last Thursday. In the course of it the President says: "On that day let all our people suspend their ordinary work and occupations, and in their accustomed places of worship, with prayer and songs of praise, render thanks to God for all His mercies, for the abundant harvests which have rewarded the toil of the husbandman during the year that has passed, and for the rich rewards that have followed the labors of our people in their shops and their marts of trade and traffic. Let us give thanks for peace, and for social order and contentment within our borders, and for our advancement in all that adds to national greatness. And, mindful of the afflictive dispensation with which a portion of our land has been visited, let us, while we humble ourselves before the power of God, acknowledge His mercy in setting bounds to the deadly march of pestilence, and let our hearts be chastened by sympathy with our fellow-countrymen who have suffered and who mourn."

The Statement Issued by the Treasury Department on November 1 showed a reduction of debt, less cash in the Treasury, of only $4,585,619, which is only a little over one-half of the average monthly decrease from the opening of the fiscal year to October 1. The ordinary expenses during the month have, however, owing to the completion of the appropriation bills by Congress, been unusually large, passing $17,000,000; over $3,000,000 more than in October of last year has been paid out in pensions, and there has been expended $4,518,457 in premiums on lands purchased.

The Blunder of the British Minister at Washington, mentioned in these columns last week, has involved his dismissal from his post. A brief note from Mr. Secretary Bayard was sent to him on October 30, informing him that, for reasons which had been fully stated to his home Government, his continuance in his present official position was no longer acceptable to this Government, and would consequently be detrimental to the relations between the two countries. Further recognition of him as the accredited representative of Great Britain was therefore declined. The next day a statement of the case, which had been drawn up by Mr. Bayard for submission to the President, was given to the press. It contained the further information that our Minister in London had formally requested the recall of Lord Sackville. As the British Government did not recall him with the promptitude expected by our Administration, his dismissal by the President followed. There are precedents for Mr. Cleveland's action, but it is generally felt that a more dignified and honorable course would have been to wait a longer time for the British Government to take action. The abrupt dismissal has the appearance of haste and impatience too puerile to befit the head of a great nation. This is the more to be regretted because the results of Lord Sackville's blunder—if any result could come from it—would be damaging to Mr. Cleveland's personal interests, rather than to those of the Government of the United States. His dismissal is doubtless good politics, but it is poor statesmanship.

The Remarkable Origin of the Yellow Fever epidemic in Jacksonville, Fla., was described in an address recently given by Surgeon-General Hamilton, at Norfolk, Va., before the Virginia State Medical Society. He stated that the epidemic had been traced back to the Key West epidemic of last year, the germs having been carried to Tampa in some blankets purchased by Italians in the infected city. The Key West scourge was introduced from Havana by a family who kept a restaurant there, and when they emigrated to Key West brought their effects over in a tramp ship, as regular steamers would not carry bedding and clothes from that city, where the yellow fever was known to be prevalent. There was neither government nor local quarantine at Key West at that time, and the goods were landed without opposition. The whole of the restaurant keeper's family died of the fever, and the disease became epidemic, and this year has been carried with such melancholy results to Jacksonville. Dr. Hamilton strongly urged a change in the laws which should give the Washington government power to control quarantine in all our ports and along the entire coast.

The Startling Discovery That the Murderous Italian society of the Mafia has an organization in New York has been made. An Italian was slaughtered with a knife recently, while standing at the doors of Cooper Union, and as the body had upon it, when found, a quantity of valuable property, it was clear that the object of the murder was not robbery. The police, in investigating the case, found that the deceased was a member of the Mafia, and the mystery was at once explained. When the two Sicilies were united with Italy a determined effort was made to break up the Mafia, which at that time had its agents in every public office, in every business, and even in the palace itself, and which terrorized the community by its audacious murders. Many of its members fled to this country, and it appears, that they have organized the society here. There are 40,000 Italians in New York, and it therefore becomes a serious question how many of them are controlled by the order. The character of the Mafia in Italy leads to the apprehension that not only may Italians be assassinated in obedience to its mandates, but a judge or a policeman or any official who made himself obnoxious to the society might be doomed to death.

The Proceedings of the Parnell Commission have been the prominent topic of interest in Great Britain during the past week. The chief witness was Captain O'Shea, who up to 1886 was an intimate friend of Mr. Parnell, but in that year quarrelled with him on private grounds, and is now evidently strongly hostile to him. His evidence went far to substantiate the charges that the *Times* has made against Mr. Parnell, of his associating with murderers and conniving at outrages. O'Shea said that he heard Parnell promise that if the Government would settle the arrears-of-rent question satisfactorily he would advise tenants to pay their rents, and would denounce outrages, resistance to the law, and all kinds of intimidation. O'Shea asked Mr. Parnell if he was sure he was able to carry out his guarantee to suppress outrages, and Mr. Parnell *gave him assurance that he had the power*. In a subsequent interview with Mr. Parnell he had warned that gentleman that Sheridan was a murderer and a concocter of murders, and the police could not allow him to remain in the country. Mr. Parnell replied that he did not communicate with Sheridan personally, but knew some one who did. Another important item of evidence was given by the witness. It is alleged that the letters purporting to be written by Mr. Parnell, which the *Times* has published, are forgeries. They were submitted to O'Shea, and he said, emphatically, "That is Parnell's writing." He added that he had received numerous letters from Mr. Parnell, of about the same date as the letter referred to, and could not mistake the writing. The evidence caused a sensation in court, which was not diminished by the witness's known hostility to Mr. Parnell.

The Coming Changes in the Constitution of the French Republic promise to give rise to a fierce struggle. The Paris correspondent of the New York *Herald*, who has made a canvass of the leaders of all sections of the political parties, declares that the outcome of it all is the conviction that what the advanced republicans want is to revert to a sort of Directory, a government by committees, without either President or Cabinet or Senate; everything else to be left to the chapter of accidents, while the Constitution will be thrown into the melting-pot, thus to prepare the way for another Napoleon, a new man of December. It is now conceded by all parties that there is a certain amount of political logic underlying Boulanger's formless, incoherent imagination, and that his revision scheme, vague and featureless as it is, exactly reflects the tendencies of the hour, and points out a path for France; meanwhile the Government is bidding for the support of the lowest class of the community by its change in the system of taxation. The proposed income-tax creates quite a fever of excitement among foreigners and all who have an income of over $400 a year, but the great masses of the people, peasantry and workmen, are all in favor of it. It is to win popularity among these classes, who are very important in case of a plébiscite or a general election, that the Premier proposes the bill. There is an uneasy feeling prevalent that France is on the eve of momentous changes, which may issue in an Empire or a Red Republic.

A Sharp Reproof to the German Press Was administered last week by the young Emperor in addressing a municipal deputation in Berlin. Referring to his journeys, on the success of which the deputation had congratulated him, the Emperor said: "I cannot but give expression to a very painful reminiscence of my journey. While I have devoted health and strength to securing the peace and welfare of the Fatherland, and thus of the capital also, by creating ties of friendship, the daily press of the capital has given publicity to and spoken about the affairs of my family in a manner which a private individual would never tolerate. I am not only painfully impressed by this, but my displeasure has been aroused. I wish, above all, that the continuous citing of the name of my departed father shall cease. It most deeply injures my feelings as his son, and it is in the highest degree unbecoming." None of the members ventured to make any remark upon the Emperor's unexpected reproaches. Even if etiquette had allowed it, they were too much amazed to respond. The Emperor spoke in a quiet tone, which was utterly devoid of anger, but his words and manner left the impression that he felt acutely the attacks that had been made.

Direct News of Mr. H. M. Stanley Arrived at Zanzibar on Friday last. A party of Arabs stated that they came upon the explorers' rear guard in November, 1887, at a point west of Albert Nyanza. They did not see Stanley himself. He was two days' march ahead. He had been ill, but was then in good health. He had changed his course from northeast to north, in the hope of avoiding marshes, and intended, when sufficiently far north, to travel due east to Wadelai, and expected to arrive there in January, 1889. The expedition had been obliged to cut its way through forests, in which they could not advance faster than one mile a day. There had been fighting with hostile tribes, but the expedition still numbered 250 men.

Notice to Missionaries in Africa Has Been sent by the British Government of intended hostilities, and they have been advised to quit the eastern coast. The London *Times* announces that the Universities Mission to Central Africa has been officially informed that, in view of the active operations projected by the Government against the slave-traders on the Zanzibar coast, it is desirable that all Europeans be immediately withdrawn from stations on the mainland. The Universities Mission, which was started in 1859 by a society formed in the universities of Oxford, Cambridge, Dublin, and Durham, has a larger number of stations on the mainland back of the Zanzibar coast than any other missionary society. Besides its stations at Mombasa, Mogila, Uruba, Newala, Mkwera, Numange, and Matakai, from fifty to three hundred miles distant from Zanzibar, it has several stations on the east coast of Lake Nyassa, at one of which a fight with Arab slavers recently occurred. When active operations are begun against slave-traders, the country will very likely be untenable, for a while, for one hundred and fifty white men engaged at about thirty missionary stations. How hostilities would affect the twelve or fifteen mission stations supported by the London and Church Missionary Societies, and the Algerian Fathers in the Victoria Nyanza and Tanganyika regions, cannot yet be foretold.

The Imminent Peril of Six Hundred Seamen was described to President Cleveland on October 30, and an appeal made to him for government assistance. It appears that early in September last the whalers in the Arctic were having a very poor time. None of them had any catch, and they became desperate. Thirteen vessels pushed farther north and became caught in the pack ice. News of their distress was brought to San Francisco by a whaler which escaped, and an earnest appeal for assistance was made. The captain states that unless prompt relief is sent scarcely one man of the six hundred on board the thirteen ships can be saved. The only opportunity that the frozen vessels have to get away is the possibility of wind springing up, that they may push off and beat the ice on its drift to the west. It will take a good strong breeze to do this, but usually the first wind of winter comes in the shape of a howling arctic storm, and this makes the chances still worse. The crews have neither food nor clothing enough to stand a prolonged stay in the arctic regions, so that if they escape being crushed they may starve to death. The President has directed the Navy Department to send a relief vessel if possible without delay. The helpless condition of the poor imperilled men is a type of what our whole world was when sin entered it. There was no hope of self deliverance, but God in His infinite love and compassion took pity upon it and Christ came for its rescue. Sad is it that so few of the lost avail themselves of love so great! (Rom. 5: 12, 18.)

The Value of a Husband was Assessed by a Boston court, on October 27, at thirty thousand dollars. It appears that, some years ago, a wealthy doctor became impressed with the talents of a girl, who, he believed possessed a remarkable voice and talents, which under careful training would make her a brilliant star of the operatic stage. He caused her to be well educated at his own expense, and subsequently sent her to Europe for training under the most famous masters of music and the histrionic art. He expended very large sums in perfecting her education for her career, and the girl, who was exceedingly ambitious, appeared likely to justify the hopes entertained of her success. Just as she was about to appear in a play expressly written for her, at the expense of the doctor who had befriended her, and who also provided further sums for her equipment, she accepted an offer of marriage and renounced the stage. The doctor's disappointment and chagrin were intense. He declared that he would have his revenge. Accordingly by a series of letters to the husband he succeeded in prejudicing him against his wife to so serious an extent that, before the honeymoon was over, the husband separated from her and eventually obtained a divorce. The lady sued the doctor for compensation for the loss of her husband and the Superior Court has awarded her $30,000. As the husband was affluent, the damages are not considered excessive, especially as the lady claims that in exposing the secrets of her past life, the doctor maliciously designed to alienate the affections of her husband, to whom she was deeply attached. Happily for the church, the bride of Christ, no attempt to deprive her of His love can succeed. Though "the accuser of the saints" can point to her faults and imperfections and unfaithfulness, Christ's love for her can never be alienated. (Rom. 8: 38, 39.)

A Life Was Saved by a Present of Flowers in Jacksonville, Fla., on October 11. A local journal says that on that day a beautiful girl drove out to the fever camp at Sand Hills, and gave to a physician a magnificent bouquet of flowers, requesting him to give it to one of his patients, a young man then in a critical stage of the disease. The doctor asked if he should say who it was that brought them. The young lady, blushing deeply, replied, "Never mind the name; just give them to him." "It's strange how some things will help along a sick man," said the doctor. "There was this fellow in a bad fix with the fever, and as soon as I told him that a young lady, who refused to give her name, had sent him these flowers, which she had brought out herself to the Sand Hills, the patient smiled, and began to mend from that very minute, and now is out of danger." Doubtless the young patient recognized in the flowers a message of reconciliation and love, and was not the first man who has felt new physical life and recuperating energy spring out of reciprocated love. Something like this has often been the means of restoring a lost soul. When a man, degraded and outcast, realizes, for the first time, that God loves him, he takes new hope and enters into newness of life. (Rom. 5: 8.)

A Lady Made Blind Through Vanity is Bemoaning her sad condition in her home in Evansville, Ind. A journal of that city says that about a year ago a girl of rare beauty became the acknowledged belle of the city. "A pair of large, liquid blue eyes set off a face that would put any picture to shame, and her form was simply perfect. The young lady was highly educated, and possessed all the qualities that go to make up a society belle. Her parents are well-to-do, and she has wanted for nothing since she was old enough to prattle. But she had one fault, and that fault has proved her undoing. It is called vanity. She fairly worshipped her own eyes, and did everything in her power to make them more beautiful than they were. She used numerous drugs before she found what she wanted. This last drug made her eyes sparkle like diamonds, and she used it to such an extent that her right eye began to shrivel. This brought her to her senses, and the family physician was called in. But he came too late, and informed the poor girl that she must lose one of her eyes sure, and probably both. The right eye was taken out some time ago, and she has lost all sight in the left, and will be blind for life." Though it is rare that vanity leads to so direct and manifest a calamity as this, it has often led to spiritual blindness, which has more disastrous results. (Rom. 1: 21.)

A Claim by a Supposed Dead Man Was presented in the Surrogate's Court, New York, on October 29. Twenty years ago a wealthy merchant died, leaving his estate in equal shares to his three children. Four years previously his second son had left home to travel in Africa and India, and nothing had been heard of him since. His share of his father's estate was carefully invested, and the proceeds were added yearly to the principal. Thirteen years passed, and still no tidings came. As there was then a strong presumption that the man was dead, application was made to the court for permission to divide his estate. The judge, concluding that seventeen years' silence was satisfactory evidence of death, made the required order granting letters of administration on his estate, as in the case of a dead man. A few weeks ago the lost brother returned after twenty-four years of wandering and sojourn in unfrequented regions of Asia and Africa. Learning what had been done with his share of his father's property, he took meaures to establish his identity, and last week applied to have set aside the decree of the Surrogate adjudicating him a dead man, and to recover his share of the estate. As his presence in court was an incontestable proof of his being alive, he had no difficulty in getting his claim as heir acknowledged. With the heirs of God the claim rests on exactly opposite grounds. It is to those who are dead to the world, in Christ, that the heritage is awarded. (II Tim. 2: 11, 12.)

BRIEF NOTES.

Dr. Pentecost's visit to Scotland is being owned of God to the quickening of the churches.

Rev. H. W. Brown has closed his services at Plainwell, amid tokens of blessing. He went to Allegan, Mich.

The various Woman's Boards of Missions connected with the American Board brought into the treasury the past year, $152,510.

Rev. W. Humpstone and Mr. Paquett have been conducting revival work at Meredeth, N. Y., and there has been a very hopeful result.

At Evangelist Taft's services at New Salem, Mass., twenty-five persons made public confession of Christ, eight of them being heads of families.

The statistics of Moravian missions, for last year, show that there are 127 stations and out-stations, 288 missionary agents, and 29,707 communicants.

Messrs. E. C. Avis and W. H. Clagell will continue to labor in California during the winter. Their meetings at Casadena, Cal., were much blessed.

The twenty-third annual season of prayer for Young Men and Young Men's Christian Associations will begin as usual, on November 11, and continue one week.

The Presbyterian Church at Elkhart, Ind., has undertaken the entire support of a missionary to the heathen. One half the sum required is given by one member.

Rev. E. P. Hammond will attend the Christian Workers' Convention in Detroit, November 15 to 20, and it is expected arrangements will be made for a children's meeting each day.

The annual convention of the Inter-Seminary Missionary Alliance recently held at Boston resulted in the consecration of seven volunteers for the foreign field and nine others for the home work.

Mr. John Guy Vassar died on Friday, October 26, at Poughkeepsie, after a year's sickness, in his seventy-eighth year. He was the brother of Matthew Vassar, and nephew of the founder of the college.

Rev. Dr. John A. Broadus has been invited to deliver the sermon at Princeton on the Day of Prayer for colleges in January. He also delivers, this year, the Lyman Beecher course of lectures to the Yale Seminary.

Philip Phillips, "the singing pilgrim," as he is familiarly called, is once more making a visit to England, and purposes spending the remainder of 1888 in the north of England and Scotland. Early in 1889 he will hold services in and about London.

The Hoffman chapel in connection with the General Theological Seminary, New York, was consecrated by Bishops Potter and Williams on November 1. Its total cost was over $200,000. The chapel is a memorial of Mrs. Samuel V. Hoffman, the mother of the Dean.

The annual report of the McAll Mission shows the receipts for the past year from all sources to have been $77,000. Great Britain contributed $34,000; the United States, $25,000; France and Switzerland, $15,000; Canada, $1,000; and Australia, $200. Fourteen new stations were opened, making a total of 113.

Dr. Munhall and Prof. Towner expect to begin a series of meetings next week in Davenport, Iowa. Dr. Munhall's meetings at Clifton Springs, N. Y., were very successful. Prof. Towner has been assisting Mr. S. M. Sayford, in the college at Hamilton, N. Y., where many of the young people were led to the Saviour.

The gift of a million dollars to the American Missionary Association has been made by Mr. Daniel Hand, of Clinton, Conn. It is to be used in the States in which slavery was recognized in 1861. The money is to be invested, and the income used in educating colored students, no one student to receive more than $100 a year. It seems that a scholarship in Hampton Institute, Va., for $70 a year.

A LIFE-LONG OCCUPATION.

A New Sermon by Pastor C. H. Spurgeon.

"By Him, therefore, let us offer the sacrifice of praise to God continually; that is, the fruit of our lips giving thanks to His name." Heb. 13:15.

Priestly Functions Under the New Dispensation—I. The Believer's Sacrifice—Presented Through Jesus—Offered Continually—The Sacrifice of Praise—Living Praise—Spoken Praise—Should be Real and Spontaneous—II. The Substance of the Sacrifice—Faith—Gratitude—III. The Exercise Commended—Helps in Other Duties—A Means of Usefulness—IV. To be Immediately Commenced—The Altar to be Used.

IT is instructive to notice where this verse stands. The connection is a golden setting to the gem of the text. Here we have a description of the believer's position before God. He has done with all carnal ordinances, and has no interest in the ceremonies of the Mosaic law. Brethren, as believers in Jesus, who is the substance of the outward types, we have, henceforth, nothing to do with altars of gold or of stone: our worship is spiritual, and our altar spiritual.

"We rear no altar, Christ has died;
We deck no priestly shrine."

What then? Are we to offer no sacrifice? Very far from it. We are called upon to offer to God a continual sacrifice. Instead of presenting in the morning and the evening a sacrifice of lambs, and on certain holy days bringing bullocks and sheep to be slain, we are to present to God continually the sacrifice of praise. Having done with the outward, we now give ourselves entirely to the inward and to the spiritual. Do you see your calling, brethren?

Moreover, the believer is now, if he is where he ought to be, like his Master,

"Without The Camp."

"Let us go forth, therefore, unto Him without the camp, bearing His reproach." What then? If we are without the camp, have we nothing to do? Are we cut off from God as well as from men? Shall we fume and fret because we are not of the world? On the contrary, let us the more ardently pursue higher objects, and yield up our disentangled spirits to the praise and glory of God.

Do we come under contempt, as the Master did? Is it so that we are "bearing His reproach"? Shall we sit down in despair? Shall we be crushed beneath this burden? Nay, verily; while we lose honor ourselves, we will ascribe honor to our God. We will count it all joy that we are counted worthy to be reproached for Christ's sake. Let us now praise God continually. Let the fruit of our lips be a still bolder confession of His name. Let us more and more earnestly make known His glory and His grace.

You see, then, brethren, that the text is rather an unexpected one in its connection; but when properly viewed it is the fittest that could be. The more we are made to feel that we are strangers in a strange land, the more should we addict ourselves to the praises of God, with whom we sojourn. Crucified to the world, and the world crucified to us, let us spend and be spent in the praises of Him who is our joy.

I. First, concerning a believer, let me describe

The Believer's Sacrifice.

"By Him therefore." See, at the very threshold of all offering of sacrifice to God we begin with Christ. We cannot go a step without Jesus. Without a Mediator we can make no advance to God. Apart from Christ there is no acceptable prayer, no pleasing sacrifice of any sort. "By Him therefore"—we cannot move a lip acceptably without Him who suffered without the gate. The great High Priest of our profession meets us at the sanctuary door, and we place all our sacrifices into His hands, that He may present them for us. You do not wish it to be otherwise, I am quite sure. If you could do anything without Him, you would feel afraid to do it. Be thankful that at the beginning of your holy service your eyes are turned towards your Lord. You are to offer continual sacrifice, looking unto Jesus.

Next, observe that this sacrifice is to be presented continually. "By Him, therefore, let us offer the sacrifice of praise to God *continually*." Attentively treasure up that word. It will not do for you to say, "We have been exhorted to praise God on the Sabbath-day." No, I have not exhorted you to such occasional duty; "continually," says the text, and that means seven days in a week. I would not have you say, "He means that we are to praise God in the morning when we awake, and in the evening before we fall asleep." Do that, my brethren, unfailingly; but that is not what I have to set before you. "Let us offer the sacrifice of praise to God *continually*"—"*continually*," that is to say, without ceasing. Bless the Lord at all times. Not alone in your secret chamber, which is redolent with the perfume of your communion with God; but yonder in the field, and there in the street, ay, and in the hurry and noise of the Exchange, offer the sacrifice of praise to God. You cannot always be speaking His praise, but you can always be living His praise.

The apostle tells us what the sacrifice is—

The Sacrifice of Praise.

Praise, that is, heart-worship, or adoration. Adoration is the grandest form of earthly service. We ascribe unto Jehovah, the one living and true God, all honor and glory. When we see His works, when we hear His Word, when we taste His grace, when we mark His providence, when we think upon His name, our spirit bows in the lowliest reverence before Him, and magnifies Him as the all-glorious Lord. Let us abide continually in the spirit of adoration, for this is praise in its purest form.

Praise is heart-trust and heart-content with God. Trust is adoration applied to practical purposes. Let us go into the world trusting God, believing that He orders all things well, resolving to do everything as He commands, for neither His character, nor His decrees, nor His commandments are grievous to us. Let us praise Him by being perfectly

Satisfied With Anything

and everything He does or appoints. Let us take a hallowed delight in Him, and in all that concerns Him. Let Him be to us "God, our exceeding joy." Do you know what it is to delight yourselves in God? Then, in that continual satisfaction, offer Him continual praise.

Praise is heart-enjoyment; the indulgence of gratitude and wonder. The Lord has done so much for me that I must praise Him, or feel as if I had a fire shut up within me. I may speak for many of you, for you also are saying, "He has done great things for us." Your obligations rise above you as high as the heavens above the earth. The vessel of your soul has foundered in this sea of love, and gone down fifty fathoms deep in it. High over its masthead the main ocean of eternal mercy is rolling with its immeasurable billows of grace. You are swallowed up in the fathomless abyss of infinite love. You are absorbed in adoring wonder and affection.

The text evidently deals with spoken praise —"Let us offer the sacrifice of praise to God continually; that is, the fruit of our lips giving thanks to His name"; or, as the Revised Version has it, "the fruit of lips which make confession to His name." So, then, we are to *utter* the praises of God, and it is

Not Sufficient to Feel

adoring emotions. The priesthood of believers requires them to praise God with their lips. Should we not sing a great deal more than we do? Psalms and hymns and spiritual songs should abound in our homes. Some few godly men whom I have known have gone about the fields and along the roads humming sacred songs continually. These are the troubadours and minstrels of our King. Hear how the ungodly world pours out its mirth! Ofttimes their song is so silly as to be utterly devoid of meaning. Are they not ashamed? Then let us not be ashamed. Children of God, sing the songs of Zion, and be joyful before your King.

But if we cannot sing so well or so constantly as we would desire, let us talk. We cannot say that we cannot talk. Perhaps some might be better if they could not talk quite so much. As we can certainly talk continually, let us continually offer to God the sacrifice of praise, by speaking well of His name. Many whom you judge to be irreligious would be greatly interested if you were to

Relate to Them the Story

of God's love to you. But if they are not interested, you are not responsible for that; only tell it as often as you have opportunity. We charge you, as Jesus did the healed man, "Go home to thy friends, and tell them how great things the Lord hath done for thee."

"Well," saith one, "I cannot force myself to praise." I do not want you to force yourself to it: this praise is to be natural. It is called the fruit of the lips. These lips of ours must produce fruit. Our words are leaves: how soon they wither! The praise of God is the fruit which can be stored up and presented to the Lord. Fruit is a natural product: it grows without force, the free outcome of the plant. So let praise grow out of your lips at its own sweet will. Let it be as natural to you, as regenerated men and women, to praise God as it seems to be natural to profane men to blaspheme the sacred name.

Consecrated Wealth.

This praise is to be sincere and real. The next verse tells us we are to do good and communicate, and joins this with praise to God. Many will give God a cataract of words, but scarce a drop of true gratitude in the form of substance consecrated. When I am pressed with many cares about the Lord's work, I often wish that some of my brethren would be a little more mindful of its pecuniary needs. I should be much relieved if those who can spare it would help different portions of our home service. It should be the joy of a Christian to use his substance in his Master's service. When we are in a right state of heart we do not want anybody to call upon us to extract a subscription from from us, but we go and ask, "Is there anything that wants help?" Is any part of the Lord's business in need just now? The great works, such as the Orphanage and College, are provided for; but I often sigh as I see lesser agencies left without help, not because friends would not aid if they were pressed to do so, but because there is not a ready mind to look out for opportunities. This practical praising of the Lord is the life-office of the believer. See ye to it.

II. We will, for a few minutes, examine

The Substance of this Sacrifice.

To praise God continually will need *a childlike faith in Him*. You must believe His word, or you will not praise His name. Doubt snaps the harp-strings. Question mars all melody. Trust Him, lean on Him, enjoy Him—you will never praise Him else. Unbelief is the deadly enemy of praise. Faith must lead you into personal communion with the Lord. It is to Him that the praise is offered, and not to our fellow-men. You must have, also, an overflowing content, a real joy in Him. Dear brothers and sisters, be sure that you do not lose your joy. If you ever lose the joy of religion, you will lose the power of religion. Do not be satisfied to be a miserable believer.

To praise God continually, you need to cultivate perpetual gratitude, and surely it cannot be hard to do that! Remember, every misery averted is a mercy bestowed; every sin forgiven is a favor granted; every duty performed is also a grace received. The people of God have an inexhaustible treasury of

Good Things Provided

for them by the infinite God, and for all this they should praise Him. I pray you, be not only a little grateful, but overflow with it. Let your praises be like the waters of fountains which are abundantly supplied. Let the stream leap up to heaven in bursts of enthusiasm; let it fall to earth again in showers of beneficence; let it fill the basin of your daily life, and run over into the lives of others, and thence again in a cataract of glittering joy let it still descend.

In order to this praise you will need a deep and ardent admiration of the Lord God. Admire ıe Father—think much of His love; acquaint ɔurself with His perfections. Admire the Son [God, the altogether lovely One; and as you ıark His gentleness, self-denial, love, and grace, ıffer your heart to be wholly enamoured of ˈim. Admire the patience and condescension [the Holy Ghost that he should visit you, and well in you, and bear with you. It cannot be ifficult to the sanctified and instructed heart to : filled with a great admiration of the Lord od. This is the raw material of praise.

III. I have been very brief upon that point ecause I want, in the third place, to commend iis blessed exercise. "Offer the sacrifice of raise," because in so doing you will answer

The End of Your Being.

very creature is happiest when it is doing what is made for. Christians are made to glorify od; and we are never in our element till we e praising Him. The happiest moments you ave ever spent were those in which you lost ght of everything inferior, and bowed before :hovah's throne with reverent joy and praise.

Praise God again, because it is His due. hould Jehovah be left unpraised? Praise is ıe quit-rent which He asks of us for the enjoy- ent of all things; shall we be slow to pay? Vill a man rob God? When it is such a happy ork to give Him His due, shall we deny it? . blesses us to bless the Lord. Shall we stint od in the measure of His glory? He does not .int us in His goodness. Come, my brother, ıy sister, if you have become sorrowful of late, ıake off your gloom, and awake all your instru- ıents of music to praise the Lord! Let not ıurmuring and complaining be so much as ıentioned among saints.

Praise Him, dear brethren, continually, for it ill help you in everything else. A man full of raise is ready for all

Other Holy Exercises.

Whenever you go forth to any service, even ıough it be nothing better than taking down ıe shutters, and waiting behind the counter, ɔu will do it all the better for being in the ɔirit of praise and gratitude. If you are a do- ıestic servant, and can praise God continually, ɔu will be a comfort in the house; and if you re a master, and are surrounded with the roubles of life, if your heart is always blessing ıe Lord, you will keep up your spirits, and you ill not be sharp and ill-tempered with those round you. Come, brethren, this is both meat ıd medicine—this praising the Lord.

Brethren, let us praise God because it will be means of usefulness. I believe that a life spent God's praise would in itself be a missionary fe. That matronly sister who never delivered sermon, nor even a lecture, in all her days, has ved a quiet, happy, useful, loving life, and her ımily have learned from her to trust the Lord. ven when she shall have passed away, they ill feel her influence, for she was

The Angel of the House.

eing dead, she yet will speak to them. A raiseful heart is eloquent for God. Mere verb- ge, what is it but as autumn leaves, which will consumed in smothering smoke? But praise golden fruit, to be presented in baskets of lver unto the dresser of the vineyard.

To close this commendation, remember that iis will fit you for heaven. Our hymn expresses frequent aspiration—

> "I would begin the music here,
> And so my soul should rise."

ɔu can begin the music here—begin the halle- jahs of glory by praising God here below. hink of how you will praise Him when you see is face, and never, never sin. Exceedingly agnify the Lord even now, and rehearse the usic of the skies. In glory you may rise to a gher key, but let the song be the same even ere. Praise Him! Praise Him! Praise Him ore and more! Rise on rounds of praise up ıe ladder of His glory, till you reach the top, ıd are with Him to praise Him better than er before. Oh that our lives may not be oken, but may be all of a piece: one psalm r ever rising into the eternal hallelujahs!

IV. I have brought you thus far, and so I come to the closing point, which is, let us

Commence at Once.

What does the text say? It says, "Let *us* offer the sacrifice of praise continually." The apostle does not say, "By-and-by get to this work, when you are able to give up business, and have retired to the country, or when you are near to die"; but now, at once, he says, "Let *us* offer the sacrifice of praise."

Listen! Who is speaking? Whose voice do I hear? Ah! I know; it is the apostle Paul. He says, "Let us offer the sacrifice of praise!" Where are you, Paul? His voice sounds from within a low place. I believe he is shut up in a dungeon. Lift up your hand, O venerable Paul! I can hear the clanking of a fetter. Yes; Paul cries, "Let *us* offer the sacrifice of praise. I, Paul the aged, in prison in Rome, wish you to join with me in a sacrifice of praise to God." Amen. We will do so. O Paul, we are not in prison, and we are not all aged, and none of us are galled with fetters on our wrists; but we can join heartily with you in praising God this morning; and we do so.

The apostle has put us rather in a fix: he compels us to offer sacrifice. Did you notice what he said in the tenth verse? He says, "We have an altar." It is

Not a Material Altar,

but a spiritual one; yet "we have an altar." May the priests of the old law offer sacrifice on it? Answer, "Whereof they have no right to eat that serve the tabernacle." They ate of the sacrifices laid on the altars of the old law, but they have no right here. Those who keep to ritualistic performances and outward ceremonials have no right here. Yet we have an altar. Brothers and sisters, can we imagine that this altar is given us of the Lord to be never used? Is no sacrifice to be presented on the best of altars? "We have an altar." What then? "Let us offer the sacrifice of praise to God continually." Do you not see the force of the argument? Practically obey it.

Beside the altar we have a High Priest. There is the Lord Jesus Christ, dressed in His robes of glory and beauty, standing within the veil at this moment, ready to present our offerings. Shall He stand there, and have nothing to do? What would you think of our great High Priest waiting at the altar, with nothing to present which His redeemed had brought to God? No, "by Him therefore let us offer the sacrifice of praise to God continually." Bring hither abundantly, ye people of God, your praises, your prayers, your thank-offerings, and present them to the Ever-blessed!

Yonder in the distance, seen dimly, perhaps, but yet not doubtfully, behold "a city that hath foundations, whose builder and maker is God." White-robed, the purified are singing to their golden harps, and you will soon be there. When a few more days or years are passed, you will be among the glorified. A crown and a harp are reserved for you. Will you not begin to praise God, and glorify Him for the heaven which is in store for you? With these two sights so wonderfully contrasted—

The Passion and the Paradise—

Jesus in His humiliation and Jesus in His glory; and yourself a sharer in both these wondrous scenes—surely if you do not begin to offer the perpetual sacrifice of thanksgivings and praise unto God, you must be something harder than a stone. God grant us to commence this day those praises which shall never be suspended throughout eternity!

Oh, that you who have never praised God before would begin now! Alas! some of you have no Christ to praise, and no Saviour to bless. Yet you need not so abide. By faith you may lay hold upon Jesus, and He then becomes yours. Trust Him and He will justify your trust. Rest in the Lord, and the Lord is your rest. When you have trusted, then waste no time, but at once commence the business for which you were created, and redeemed, and called. Fill the censer with the sweet spices of gratitude and love, and lay on the burning coals of earnestness and fervency. Then, when praise begins to rise from you like pillars of smoke, swing the censer to and fro in the presence of the Most High, and more and more laud, bless, and magnify the Lord that liveth forever. Let your heart dance at the sound of His name, and let your lips show forth His salvation. The Lord anoint you this day to the priesthood of praise, for Christ's sake! Amen.

GEMS FROM NEW BOOKS.

THE BOYHOOD OF AGASSIZ.*

AGASSIZ was born at Motier, in Switzerland, in 1807, exactly one hundred years after the birth of Linnæus, and his early life very closely resembled that of the illustrious child of the North. Like Linnæus, his childhood was passed in a quiet country parsonage situated on the borders of a lake, and embracing a view of a region of such picturesque beauty that it could not fail to impress itself on the mind of the child.

The home-life of the parsonage was very simple, and the children of the family were early taught to regard only those things as valuable which were independent of wealth, and their childish pleasures were all such as could be found in any of the unpretentious little homes that surrounded them.

Unlike many of the great naturalists, who only took up their special work late in life, Agassiz may be said to have begun his life-work in his early childhood, though he himself was unconscious of it. For, like Linnæus and Cuvier, his first impressions of nature were received from the games and employments of his country home; and in his boyish taste for collecting nests, eggs, birds, and pet animals, and in the little aquarium, supplied with specimens from the lake, could be traced the small beginnings of his scientific career. Thus the love of nature and the finding out of her secrets began with the boy's first consciousness; and in all of his out-of-door sports he was laying up stores of valuable information. To him, as to all country children, the different seasons of the year brought each its offering of gifts and laid them at his feet; and from the first spring blossom to the fall of the snow all nature seemed a harmonious whole, and the wide earth but a treasure-house where one might gather largess at his will. As the years passed, Agassiz learned more and more of the great forces which linked him with the world of nature around him, and began to understand the sympathy which the genuine naturalist feels for all forms of life.

Besides these lessons, learned in the fields and woods and by the shores of the lake, where nature herself was the teacher, Agassiz had a few simple tasks out of books, his father and mother being his teachers, and up to his tenth year he received no instruction outside of his home. But a boy so intelligent and observing as Agassiz could not fail to learn many things not included in his daily hours of study; and the home-life of Motier, which was in many respects very primitive, furnished the boy many a self-imposed but not the less instructive task. From the shoemaker, who came twice a year to fit the family out with shoes, the boy learned how to make a tiny pair of shoes for his sister's doll; from the tailor who was a guest in the house while making the spring and winter outfits, he learned to fashion a suit of clothes, and when the cooper arrived to put the barrels and hogsheads in order for the vintage, he found an apt pupil in the boy, to whom nothing seemed uninteresting and who gained in these childish amusements much of that training of the eye and hand which were invaluable to him later on, when dexterity and delicacy of touch were so necessary to his scientific pursuits.

Franklin's First Compositions.

The news of the capture of a notorious pirate, known as Blackbeard, set the imagination of Franklin aflame, and he at once set about the

* From "Children's Stories of the Great Scientists." By Henrietta Christian Wright. 350 pages, with Portraits and Illustrations. Price $1.25. Published by *Charles Scribner's Sons*, 745 Broadway, New York.

The Rev. Alfred C. White.

The Convalescent Street-Waif.

composition of a poem of which Blackbeard was the hero, and in which he gave his fancy great freedom, and mixed up bold metaphors and bad rhymes to an appalling degree. This production, together with another one celebrating a shipwreck, which had just occurred, was printed and sold about the streets of Boston by the young author, who was immensely flattered at seeing his verses so eagerly seized by the public, and conceived the idea of leaving the printing-office and turning poet. But on being assured by his father that "poets were generally beggars," he gave up the idea of distinguishing himself in poetry and turned his attention to prose. As was his habit, he set himself to the matter with all the seriousness of his nature. Although this work seemed at the time, to his family, but the pastime of a restless boy, yet it bore fruit long afterward, when the force and purity of Franklin's style, both in speaking and writing, were of incalculable value not only to himself but to his country.

This course of study, together with the advantage he received from the conversations carried on in his brother's shop, in which all the important questions of the day were discussed, led in time to another attempt at authorship, but this time Franklin acted in secret, from fear of ridicule, and slipped his manuscript under the office-door, where it was found the next morning by his brother, who read it aloud to his friends, all unconscious that the author stood by, trembling with suspense lest the verdict should be unfavorable. But the paper was well received, and printed in the newspaper which was published at the office, and from this time Franklin made several contributions to the same paper before the author was found out.

REV. ALFRED C. WHITE,

The Ex-Drummer-Boy.

FEW pastors have so novel an experience to look back upon as the Rev. Alfred Corydon White, of Amesbury, Mass. He was born at Newark, O., on November 15, 1852, and is, therefore, now thirty-six years of age. He comes of a family with an illustrious record in Congregationalism. Its pedigree is traced back to John White, a stalwart Puritan settler, who was one of the first body of selectmen of Cambridge, Mass. Since John White's time the family has furnished no less than *fifty ministers* to the Congregational denomination, and more than thirty of them were alumni of Yale College.

The boy, Alfred, was under nine years of age when the war broke out; but he had learned to play the drum with a skill beyond his years, and when his father enlisted in the Union army, Alfred pleaded hard, and at last successfully, to go with him as a drummer-boy. He took his turn in beating calls and standing on guard at outpost, and would have taken part in still more active duty had not affection for him interfered for his protection, much to the boy's disgust. He was especially anxious to witness the battle of Shiloh, but his father, the lieutenant, who knew of his desire, had so little confidence in mild measures that he actually had the boy tied up in an ambulance and sent to the rear. He fell ill at last of a sickness brought on by exposure, and in 1865 he was discharged.

His education was then resumed, and after passing through school and college he determined to consecrate his life to the ministry. He graduated in Divinity in 1880, and settled at Amesbury. He has occupied several pulpits since then, but has now returned to his first sphere, much to the delight of his people. Mr. White is still a member of the G. A. R.

AN UNPROMISING GUEST.

(*See Illustration on this page.*)

"WHAT are you doing there? What is it you want?" The questions were addressed to a miserable lad crouching in the corner of a gateway by Mr. Milner, a merchant, who, after a late political meeting, was returning home, and proceeding to open the gate which admitted him to the garden surrounding his mansion, noticed the boy shrinking in the darkness.

"I'm a-going," said the lad, hoarsely; "I ain't doing no harm. I only wanted to rest a bit. I'm kinder dizzy."

"Where do you live?" asked Mr. Milner, kindly, laying his hand on the boy's head, which he noticed was burning hot. "You ought not to be out this time of night."

The boy rose, but was scarcely able to keep his feet, and leaned his shoulder against the pillar of the gateway, while a hollow cough convulsed his frame. "I haven't any home," the lad said when he had recovered his breath. "Father and mother both dead. I've been selling papers, but I got awful wet last week, and I ain't been able to do anything; I'm coughing all the time, and I can't jump on the cars. The money's all gone, so I can't go to the Home to-night. I'll have to sleep out somewhere. But I wa'n't doing any harm. I'm going."

The merchant looked at the poor, shaking boy in deep pity. A boy of his own, rather younger than this, had been in that feverish condition two years ago, and Mr. Milner had surrounded him with every care, and had secured the best medical skill for him, but the boy drooped and died, and the father felt as if his own heart had died too when he laid him in the grave. "Inasmuch as ye have done it to one of the least of these"—said Mr. Milner to himself. Then to the boy, who was shuffling away with feeble and uncertain steps, "Here, I'll give you a night's lodging; come in with me." He had at first thought of putting a quarter in the boy's hand so that he might go to the Home he had spoken of, and a year ago that is what he would have done; but latterly new ideas of his duties as a follower of Jesus of Nazareth had entered his mind. They had found expression at first in sympathetic treatment of his employees, but the circle had widened, as such circles must, under the laws of our nature, and now he recognized his neighbors in men and women outside his immediate neighborhood. Here was a sad case of suffering, appealing to a conscience that told him that the gift of a quarter did not meet his duty in the case. He put his hand on the boy's shoulder, and guided him through the garden to the door of his house.

Happily for the boy, and for Mr. Milner, too, for that matter, there was no need of any of the diplomacy which some husbands would have had to exercise in bringing into the household after midnight so undesirable a guest. He could count on the ready sympathy of his wife. "*In His name,*" was all he said in presenting the miserable object. Mrs. Milner understood. It might have been difficult to see Christ in the boy who was, to them, His representative, but by their welcome Christ could be seen in them.

Simple remedies were administered for the night, and the boy was taken to a room which, after his hardships, seemed the height of luxury. He was too sick and weary to feel or express gratitude, and was too ignorant to conjecture the motive that influenced his kind entertainers. Nor could he say much when in the morning Mr. Milner went to his bedside.. The boy was evidently very sick.

"You have saved the boy's life, Mr. Milner," said the physician who was called in, after he had seen the boy and prescribed. "I do not know whether you have done him or the country much kindness. These street-waifs are not a very hopeful lot; but we'll hope you have not saved this one to be a prey for the hangman."

"Oh, no, I hope not, but I suppose there is a measure of responsibility even in saving life."

"Strange, sentimental kind of people, those Milners," said the doctor, speaking to his wife, of the case. "A touch of fanaticism about them, but I do not know if a little more of the same kind of fanaticism would not be a good thing for the world."

The doctor would have been still more surprised if he had looked in at the Milner home later in the day. He would have seen his patient, carefully wrapped up, sitting in a cosy arm-chair, while Mrs. Milner waited upon him, brought him delicious cooling drinks, and spoke to him so kindly that he had looked at her in amazement.

"Let us do something for him," she said to her husband, when he returned in the evening. "He has told me his story, and I am sorry for him. He has not a relative in the world, so far as he knows, and as he says, 'it isn't easy to be good in that kind of life.' I believe there is good in the boy; shall we try to develop it?"

Mr. Milner was similarly impressed on talking with the boy, and as recovery from his sickness came, he asked him if he would not like to have an education. The eagerness of the answer convinced the merchant that the project would be successful. It was put in execution, and the rapidity with which he acquired knowledge, and the intelligence he displayed, won the increased regard of his benefactors. Mrs. Milner was right in believing that there was good in him, and the sense of her kindness was a potent factor in developing that good. A mutual love sprang up between them, and as the years passed, and their adopted son became the pride and joy of their home, the Milners almost felt that in taking the poor, miserable waif into their house that dark night they had been entertaining an angel unawares.

Boulder Canyon, Colorado.

BOULDER CANYON, COLORADO.

(See Illustration.)

AMONG the most beautiful of the canyons of Colorado, Boulder Canyon bears the palm. It is near the little mining town of Boulder, and is the pride of all that locality. It is seventeen miles in length, and the mountain walls rise precipitously along its sides, in some places to the height of three thousand feet. A stream rushes down its centre, which is crossed in several places by the wagon road. Its chief point of difference from other canyons is, that while preserving almost unrivalled features of rugged grandeur there is an entire absence of gloom. The roadside is decked with flowers in the summer season, and the eye is refreshed by an almost infinite variety of rock and dell and verdant foliage. The canyon is a favorite health resort for the people of Denver, and those who have benefited by its salubrious air stoutly maintain that it surpasses in life-giving properties the atmosphere of all other resorts, and that for grandeur of scenery it is better worth visiting than any European mountain country, or even than our own Niagara Falls and the Yosemite valley.

Colorado is peculiarly rich in these scenes of imposing natural beauty. Besides Grand Canyon, and Clear Creek Canyon, in the former of which the river runs for miles through walls of granite in some places seven thousand feet high, it possesses the wonderful little park known as "The Garden of the Gods," a level place about five hundred acres in extent, shut in by huge mountains on the north, east, and west. The entrance to the garden is through a narrow defile, called the Beautiful Gate, at which are the famous high rocks of red and white sandstone, said to be the most beautiful in the world. The Gate and the Garden together constitute one of the most lovely scenes on the continent.

THE EPOCHS OF A LIFE.

A NEW SERIAL STORY.

By Rev. L. S. Keyser.

(Continued from page 703.)

New Light.

THE compact between Mr. Hanson and his friend was faithfully kept on both sides. Hadley met Madeline Winters several times, and found her each time more genial and friendly. His hopes rose, and when she invited him to call upon her, he gladly accepted the invitation. He was received by her parents with marked cordiality, and he conceived a sincere respect for their sterling Christian character. Though Madeline always took care to avoid being alone with him, and he had therefore no opportunity of renewing his suit, he could not but realize that he was growing in her favor, and began to entertain sanguine hopes of yet making her his wife. True, he frequently met his old rival Duneman on the street, and was aware that he often visited the Winters; but it was not the rivalry of Duneman that he feared. He had a strong conviction that the really formidable obstacle to be dreaded was the love that Mr. Hanson felt for the girl. Still, he had a free field, and he was pleased to see that Madeline and her parents treated him as a welcome guest and a respected friend. Suddenly, however, the manner of all changed toward him. A marked coldness was perceptible, and while no definite act of unhospitality or estrangement could be named, the sensitive young man became disagreeably aware that his visits were no longer desired. He pondered in much disquietude over the change, but was unable to fathom the mystery.

The fact was, that a detrimental revelation had come, both to Madeline and her parents. To the latter, Duneman, becoming aware of Hadley's relations with the family, imparted the information that young Madelling was a blatant infidel, and had made himself notorious at college by his antipathy to Christianity.

With Madeline, herself a different influence was working. Observing that Hadley was making no preparations for marriage, and that in his conversation there was no hint of any love engagement, but rather every indication that regard for herself was the one and only sentimental feeling in his heart, she began to question in her own mind the fact of his engagement to the Mabel R. Richerson, which had been the cause of her rejection of him. Finally, as she found her love for the young man increasing with his renewed acquaintance, she determined to write to the lady again and ascertain the present situation of affairs. A courteous note was written and sent. But Belle Havelock had taken care to maintain her acquaintance with the Banesville neighborhood, and therefore Madeline's letter was forwarded to her. She answered it in the name of Mabel R. Richerson, suggesting with some asperity that Madeline was taking rather too strong an interest in her affairs, but unequivocally stating that her engagement with Mr. Madelling continued, and a marriage would not be long delayed. She also sent a hint to Duneman, which was promptly acted upon. He incidentally mentioned to Madeline that he had heard that Madelling was to be married in the spring. The information, so clearly corroborating the letter, revived all the painful repugnance to the duplicity of her suitor, and she could not refrain from manifesting a coldness toward him, which, being shown at the same time as that of her parents, constituted a double mystery to Hadley.

The key to one half of the mystery was, however, supplied through the kindness of Mr. Hanson, to whom Hadley had poured out the story of his sorrow. The good clergyman, true to his exalted idea of his friendship for his rival, made it his business to discover the cause of the alienation of Madeline's parents from young Madelling. Incidentally introducing his name in a conversation with them, he saw the start of repugnance which followed in both. A few words of esteem for the young man unlocked their reserve. Mr. Winters said that he knew Madelling, but did not esteem him. Information had reached his ears that he was a blasphemous infidel of the most dangerous character, unfit as an acquaintance for Christian men and unfit to be received in a Christian home. "Had I known his character earlier," Mr. Winters added, "he certainly would not have been received here."

"I think," replied Mr. Hanson, "that it is only just to form our estimate of character on our own knowledge. Personally I have seen a great deal of Mr. Madelling, and I am convinced that he is an earnest and sincere seeker after truth. Believing that, I would rather cultivate his acquaintance than avoid him, I may be able to help him to the right side of the slough. In fact, I think I have been enabled to do him some good. We may do injustice and much wrong, Mr. Winters, by giving too ready a credence to persons who may be misinformed."

"Oh, there is no doubt in this case," said Mr. Winters; "my informant was a college mate of his. Mr. Duneman, in fact. A very worthy young man. He told me of Madelling's violent speeches against the Bible in college, which he had heard himself. He answered them, and in doing so made himself the butt of ridicule and scorn in the college. We must range ourselves on the right side in such a conflict, Mr. Hanson. The enemies of my Lord are no friends of mine."

"That is right, Mr. Winters," said Mr. Hanson, "but if a man is fighting my Lord under a mistake, as Saul the persecutor thought he was doing God service in persecuting the church, and the man is open to conviction, I conceive that the best service I can render to my Lord, will be to convince him of his mistake and disarm his hostility. I firmly believe that Madelling, once convinced, would become a valuable advocate of the truth."

"I wish you success," said Mr. Winters, "but I have little hope, and should have no hope of *my* succeeding in such an effort."

It was impossible for Mr. Hanson to conceal from Hadley the information he had gained. He thought it best to tell him frankly, and to advise him to absent himself for a time from the Winters' home. The fact of Duneman's officious meddling raised a storm in Hadley's nature so violent as to alarm Mr. Hanson. He was amazed that a young man, apparently so well balanced, should be so agitated. Never had he seen written on any face, passion so intense, rage so uncontrollable. A volley of invective poured from his lips, mingled with threats of violence, and then he turned and abruptly quitted his friend's study, where their interview had taken place.

"He will recover his equanimity better in solitude," said the minister to himself, as he restrained his impulse to follow. "He will have too much sense to carry out his threats." And the minister settled down to his desk for work. But somehow he could not keep his thoughts on his task; they would revert to Madelling with a pertinacity in which Mr. Hanson at last recognized a call for action. Rising, he took his hat and made his way to his friend's home. There he learned that the young man had returned, but had gone out again almost immediately. "I think he had some bad news," said his informant; "he seemed mighty queer. Looked dazed like and savage."

With an instinct which, afterward, seemed to the minister providential, he took the path which led to an unfrequented district that was one of Hadley's favorite haunts. It should have been a moonlight night, but storm-clouds now and again obscured the luminary for a quarter of an hour or more at a time. He had walked some distance, when in one of the dark intervals he heard voices. One was hoarse with passion, and the other seemed pleading for mercy. He hurried on, and just then the moon, emerging from behind the cloud, showed him the two figures in a lonely path a little way ahead. Madelling had his enemy grasped by the throat and his clenched right hand was raised menacingly. A few steps more and Mr. Hanson had grasped the upraised arm and compelled his friend to let go that deadly grip on his antagonist's throat.

"Madelling, for shame!" Hanson exclaimed. "A man of your calibre and standing to stoop to violence! Let him alone, I insist. Tell the man what you demand of him and let him go. It is not for such as you to play the part of the savage barbarian."

But Duneman had not waited to be told what Hadley required of him. No sooner was his throat released from that fierce grip than he took to his heels and was soon out of sight.

"Come with me," said Hanson, quietly laying his hand on his friend's arm and leading him back toward home. His very touch had a tranquillizing influence, and as Hadley's arm ceased to throb with the passion that had overpowered him, Hanson continued: "A wrong was never set right by violence yet. You lower, you degrade yourself by resorting to such measures. Be a man and keep the brute in your nature in subjection."

When they reached Hadley's home the young man put his arms about the minister's neck, and in tones that quavered in unison with the trembling of his body, he said:

"Hanson, how shall I ever thank you for the service you have done me this evening? I believe that you have saved me from committing a terrible crime and from disgrace. Oh, I was so crazed with anger that I had lost all control of myself. Oh Heaven! I did not know that I had such a ferocious demon in me."

"Ah! we should never act under an impulse of passion," said Hanson. "We are sure to have reason to rue it if we do."

"What if I had—I believe I should have killed him if you had not interfered. Hanson, you are my good genius. What a wicked, despicable wretch I am! I do not believe that there is any hope for me."

"Come, Madelling, don't give up to despair."

"I never felt that I needed God's mercy as much as I do now. Oh, my—my sins! my wicked, depraved nature! I feel a mountain of guilt, like an Alp, weighing me down."

"I assure you that there is mercy for you if you repent."

"No, no, there is none!"

"'He that asketh receiveth.' 'The blood of Jesus Christ cleanseth from all sin,'" quoted Hanson, feelingly.

The desperate man looked up at his companion in a bewildered way, as these words of Scripture fell from his lips, and presently, as a gleam of light came into his face, he said: "Hanson, you prayed the other evening for me. Do you think you—could—pray—now?"

"With all my heart, sir," and they fell upon their knees, while the clergyman wove into his supplication all the rich promises of God's Word for the penitent. It was a solemn scene, and the words were devout and earnest.

When they arose from their knees the cloud had been partially dissipated from Hadley's face, and taking his friend's hand, he said, with deep emotion: "Hanson, I feel that the forces of evil within me are too strong for me to cope with alone. I must have help from some source, or I am lost. It is the evil principle in my nature that overcomes me. If there is help, as you say, to be had from a supernatural source, I want it."

"Thank God!" said the minister, in fervent tones. "If you feel your need of God, He will help and save you. Go to Christ. In Him you will find strength for your weakness. I leave you with Him. Good-night."

It was far into the night when the clergyman reached his room. He flung himself on his knees and prayed earnestly. The soul he so anxiously sought to win for his Master was passing through its ordeal, and he pleaded, with the whole force of his nature, that God would bring it into the light. It was strange how the clergyman, who had dealt with so many anxious souls in his time, yearned for this one as he had never done for one before. Oh that in that storm-tossed spirit the words of the Master might ring, compelling peace and trust! Long did the good man plead, and gradually an assurance of acceptance came into his mind. He felt that already God had answered his prayer. Almost instantly a sense of what such a change might involve for himself crossed his mind. Hadley converted, a brilliant soldier of the Cross, would not his own love for Madeline be doomed to desolation? It was a suggestion of the evil one, though Hanson knew it was only too true. For a few moments he struggled with the thought. Then he came forth a conqueror through Christ's power. Self-sacrifice, self-immolation—that had been his law for so many years. It triumphed now. Perish all his hopes of the love he had hoped to win, if that were to be the price of his friend's felicity. It was a fierce crisis, but as the man emerged from it victorious in the strength of God, he was a greater man than he had ever been. Unscathed by the flames of the furnace, he could tell those who looked to him for help and guidance that God was sufficient for these things.

He had need of this strength during the next few days. In a large church there are many calls on a minister for sympathy and help in moments of dire affliction. One especially distressing case called, the next day, for Hanson's help. It was that of a Christian family overwhelmed with sorrow over the sudden death of the eldest daughter, a young lady of twenty years, singularly beautiful in person and remarkably noble and lovable of character. Her father and mother, though of ripe Christian character, were utterly prostrated by the unexpected blow, and were wrapped in that dense darkness in which God sometimes permits His children to be enveloped. Mr. Hanson knew how severe would be their affliction. He knew, too, that light would surely penetrate the darkness, and there would be a rare manifestation of the Divine power to assuage the crushing anguish of bereavement. He was anxious that Madelling should witness it, feeling that such a scene must convince him of the reality of God's love and power. On his way to the afflicted household he called for Hadley, and persuaded him to accompany him.

The scene was even more harrowing than the clergyman had anticipated. Even Hadley felt tears of sympathy rise to his eyes as he saw the bereaved parents weeping over the beautiful, lifeless body of their beloved daughter. What power could pour balm into hearts so crushed? What hope could restore peace to souls so riven? He listened as Mr. Hanson spoke, and knelt with him as he prayed. He saw the cloud lift! He saw the light come into the tear-stained faces! He heard the father's trembling lips pronounce the words, "Thy will be done. The burden is gone! My daughter is with God." He heard the mother stifle her sobs and say, "It is the Lord; let Him do what seemeth Him good!" And as they left the bereaved home they heard the father and mother joining in words of love and praise to God for His promises of reunion which would be fulfilled.

Hanson took his companion's arm as they walked up the street from the mysterious scene. For a time each was busy with his own reflections. Presently Hadley said: "What was it, Hanson?"

"It was God," answered Hanson, devoutly.

They walked on in silence for half a block, and then Hanson, feeling that it was now time to send a pointed shaft to the joint in his sceptical friend's armor, said: "Madelling, what would your agnosticism have done for those afflicted parents?"

A shiver passed through Hadley's frame as he responded: "It would have been tested—and found wanting. I frankly acknowledge it. Oh, what a helpless, inane, and inadequate philosophy it is!"

"I am glad that you see it in its true light. Renounce it, my friend," urged Hanson. "It will always leave you in the lurch."

"I can't throw it off myself; it enthralls me."

"I know that; but who gave relief to the poor woman whom we have just left?"

Hadley did not answer, and his comrade, pointing upward toward heaven, added: "Your help must come from the same Source. Good-night."

At the funeral services, which Hadley attended, he listened with irrepressible tears to the impassioned eloquence of the minister as he spoke of the comforts of the Gospel in the crucial exigencies of life, and of the glory of the life to come. Hadley walked away from the house of mourning wrapped in deep thought. "What can mollify the griefs of life like the Christian religion!" he acknowledged to himself. All the petty objections which he had so often raised against the Bible—its apparent discrepancies, its verbal errors, its seeming disagreements with scientific teaching—melted away like morning mist before the sun, when compared with its beneficent, comforting, invigorating influence upon the susceptible heart and life. There must be, he reasoned, some rational explanation of these ostensible errors, for so salutary an influence could not emanate from a medley of blunders and impostures. Once he had heard a preacher, whose enthusiasm ran riot with his reason, aver: "If Christianity is a delusion, it is a blessed, a glorious delusion!" But Hadley felt that if it blessed and regenerated humanity, it could not be an hallucination, for only the truth could operate so beneficently. Thus, it will be seen that his "thoughts were set to a higher key" than ever before in his quest for the truth.

(*To be Continued.*)

HELPING ONE ANOTHER.

By Mrs. M. Baxter.

S. S. Lesson for November 18, Josh. 21:43-45, and Josh. 23. Golden Text, Gal 6:2.

The Promise Fulfilled After Four Centuries—The Blessing Delayed by Unbelief—The Faithfulness of the Two and a Half Tribes—Their Engagements Fulfilled—Helpfulness Enjoined Under Moses—The Poverty of the Present Day—Might be Relieved out of the Superabundance of the Rich—Jealousy Among Christian Workers—Tale-bearing Especially Prohibited—Christ's Own Rule—What Unity has Done in Revival Work—A Misunderstanding.

"AND the Lord gave unto Israel all the land which He swear to give unto their fathers." Thus was fulfilled His promises to Abraham. (Gen. 12:7; 13:15; 15:13-21); to Isaac (Gen. 26:3, 4); and to Jacob (Gen. 28:4; 13, 14.) "And they possessed it and dwelt therein." Four hundred years and more had passed away since God's first promise to Abraham, yet sure as Himself, the word of the Lord came to pass. Why was it thus delayed? No doubt the unbelief of Jacob was one great hindrance, and also the want of consecration in him and in his sons; then, also, the idolatry of the children of Israel in Egypt of which Joshua speaks, "The gods which your fathers served on the other side of the flood, *in Egypt*" (Josh. 24:14); and finally, their unbelief, when the spies brought up an evil report of the land. The hindrance and the fulfilment of God's promises never come from Him, but always from us. He does not tantalize His children, and hold out hopes only to disappoint them, but He seeks to bring us into such a relation to Him that shall fit us to have the blessings He provides, without being injured by them.

"And the Lord gave them rest round about, according to all that He swear unto their fathers: and there stood not a man of all their enemies before them; the Lord delivered all their enemies into their hand." Thus He fulfilled His word. (Ex. 23:27-31; Deut. 7:24; 28:7; Josh. 1:5.) "There failed not aught of any good thing which the Lord had spoken unto the house of Israel;

All Came to Pass."

What an encouragement to trust our God and the word which He has spoken! About four hundred and fifty years had passed by, but God remembered every promise, and proved Himself the Faithful and the True.

"Then Joshua called the Reubenites and the Gadites and the half tribe of Manasseh," who had chosen their portion on the wilderness side of the Jordan, and who had left there their tents and families, their herds and flocks, while they had gone forward to help their brethren take possession of their inheritance (Num. 32:1-33), and he gave them an official release from their service. He said: "Ye have kept all that Moses, the servant of the Lord, commanded you, and have obeyed my voice in all that I commanded you; ye have not left your brethren these many days unto this day, but have kept the charge of the commandments of the Lord your God. And now the Lord your God hath given rest unto your brethren, as He promised them; therefore, now return ye, and get you unto your tents, and unto the land of your possession, which Moses, the servant of the Lord, gave you on the other side Jordan." God loves brotherly love; "Thou shalt love thy neighbor as thyself" is His own summing up of the second table of the commandments. Provision was made again and again under the Old Testament for the exercise of brotherly love. God's people were to open the hand wide to their brother, their poor and needy, in their land. (Deut. 15:11.) Again, with regard to property, "Thou shalt not see thy brother's ox or his sheep go astray, and hide thyself from them; thou shalt in any case bring them again unto thy brother. And if thy brother be not nigh unto thee, or if thou know him not, then thou shalt bring it unto thine own house; and it shall be with thee until thy brother seek after it, and thou shall restore it to him again." God would have us

Take Pains to Help One Another

without considering whether any personal benefit shall accrue to us. (Deut. 22:1-3.) They were not to reap the corners of their fields, nor gather the gleanings of the harvest or of their vineyards. God commanded, "Thou shalt leave them for the poor and stranger; I am the Lord." (Lev. 19:9, 10.) But oh, how unlike to these commands is the spirit of business in the present day! The grasping spirit of the age says, "Every man for himself; I must look after my own interest, although hundreds suffer." The problem of how to find work for the unemployed, and how to feed those who have no work, becomes daily more terrible. And yet the waste in the houses in the West End of London would go far, if economized, to provide capital which would enable bands of men to reclaim and cultivate the waste lands on our moors, etc. But selfishness governs the rich, and selfishness governs the poor, and the spirit of mutual help is wanting. The saddest thing of all is, to see among professing Christians so much of the spirit of jealousy rather than of love and mutual helpfulness. How often in a mission, when one evangelist succeeds another, the one who is going away makes everything as difficult as he can for the one who is coming, that it may not be said that he succeeded better than he. What a denial to the whole spirit of Christ this is! We have this morning received a letter from an evangelist of experience, who is about to be succeeded by two young men, of far less experience and much younger than he, but the letter breathes the most earnest spirit of prayer that God may help them far more than he has been blest, and he has asked that he may introduce them, and make their way easy.

God Multiply Men Like Him!

God says, "Thou shalt not go up and down as a talebearer among thy people; neither shalt thou stand against the blood of thy neighbor: I am the Lord." Thus in the Old Testament, as well as in the New, where malice and evil speaking are so often condemned (Prov. 6:19; 10:32; 12:18; Eph. 4:31; 1 Pet. 4:4; James 4:11), we see how God abhors unkind, gossipping words. He adds, "Thou shalt not hate thy brother in thine heart: thou shalt in any wise rebuke thy brother, and not suffer sin upon him." Alas! it is far more common to hear a man speak of one who has done wrong behind his back; but God shows that brotherly love rebukes him to his face, because a loving heart is as jealous of sin on his brother's soul as on his own. "Thou shalt not avenge nor bear any grudge against the children of thy people, but thou shalt love thy neighbor as thyself; I am the Lord." (Lev. 19:16, 17.) Let us add to this, as the summing up of all the teaching of our blessed Lord, and his peerless example, these, His own words, "A new commandment I give unto you, that ye love one another

As I Have Loved You,

that ye also love one another." (John 13:34.) He would have us bear one another's burdens, make life easy to one another, consider one another, that we may represent our God, and shed light and joy around us. A believer who increases the burden of another by his selfish desire for sympathy, is doing the work of the enemy on earth. God is unselfish, and He calls us to be like Him.

God has so ordered it that we should be members one of another (Num. 12:5), necessary to one another, "that there should be no action in the body; but that the members should have the same care one for another" (1 Cor. 12:20-26). The whole body is "fitly joined together and compacted by that which every joint supplieth according to the effectual working in the measure of every part" (Eph. 4; 16); just in the measure in which we work together and help one another, the cause of Christ makes progress: just in the measure in which we are selfish, the cause of Christ is hindered. When Mr. Moody first came to England, very little good was done. At the beginning of his second visit, when God so marvellously used him, there was no great promise; but when a few ministers and others met together in Sunderland to pray for blessing and to work with him, God began to manifest Himself. In Newcastle the spirit of unity grew and the blessing grew; in Edinburgh it was still more marked; and in Glasgow it became almost the exception for a minister to hold aloof from the blessed work of God which was done when Messrs. Moody and Sankey were there. God set His seal on the spirit of unity which prevailed. It was this which gave power to the work in the wonderful meetings held in the Agricultural Hall, the Haymarket Theatre, and other places in London. It has been the spirit of unity which God has owned at Mildmay, and which shone out so prominently in the Centenary of Missions.

When Joshua sent away the Reubenites, Gadites, and half tribe of Manasseh, he blessed them. They are blessed who are helpers one of another; there is a joy in doing anything for another which we never get in serving ourselves.

A Misunderstanding.

Their first act when they came into their inheritance was to build "an altar by Jordan," a great altar to see to. "This aroused the suspicion of their brethren, and their first hasty judgment was to go to war with them as traitors to the cause of God. But they first sent Eleazar the high priest and an elder from each tribe to remonstrate with them. They did not say hard things against them behind their backs, but said, "Thus saith the whole congregation of the Lord, What trespass is this that ye have committed against the God of Israel, to turn away this day from following the Lord, in that ye have builded you an altar, that ye might rebel this day against the Lord?" And then, with force and eloquence, they urged upon their brethren that what they did affected the whole congregation, and cited the sin of Achan as a case in point. Then the Reubenites, Gadites, and half tribe of Manasseh replied, not in anger, that they were misjudged, but they called on God, the God of gods, to witness that their altar was not built in rebellion, or in transgression against the Lord; that it was not as an altar for offerings, but as a memorial to the trans-Jordan tribes, that they had as much part in God as their brethren had; also to be a memorial to their children in time to come. The explanation was accepted, and instead of war there was mutual love established and confirmed between the tribes. Oh that every misunderstanding ended thus without bitterness, without enmity! If men would be open and straightforward with one another, and patient enough to consider the other side of a question, how often a dispute might be healed and God glorified in His children!

"MY HAND, DEAR LORD, IN THINE."

My hand, dear Lord, in Thine!
However dark the way,
A light within will ever shine,
A beam of day.
While on in faith I press,
My soul Thou dost illume,
And I am full of happiness,
Nor mind the gloom.

My hand, dear Lord, in Thine!
What though the way seem rough?
If I may feel the touch divine,
It is enough,
Onward, o'er hill and dale,
My journey I'll pursue,
Until Thou dost remove the veil,
And heaven I view.

My hand, dear Lord, in Thine!
What though the way seem long?
My weary soul will not repine,
But sing a song,
My rest I'll find in Thee,
In holy work my joy,
And prayer and praise shall ever be
My sweet employ.

My hand, dear Lord, in Thine!
I'll never let Thee go;
Nor wilt Thou e'er my soul resign
To endless woe.
Thy hold will be on me,
Amid the din and strife,
Until I wake to share with Thee
Immortal life.

J. E. JEWETT, Publisher, 77 Bible House, New York, will furnish the above poem in leaflet form at twenty cents per hundred. *A Sample Packet* of 50 leaflets assorted (no two alike), will be sent post-paid, for 10 cts., or 100 for 20 cts. Postage stamps taken.

Canon Farrar's New Book,

Everyday Christian Life;

Or, Sermons by the Way.

BY FREDERICK W. FARRAR, D. D.

12mo, cloth. Price $1.25.

In this volume the distinguished author has collected twenty of his best sermons, all of which treat of themes in the Christian daily life. They are free from controversy and touch only subjects which have wide and deep interest to every reader. The charming eloquence and searching thought of Canon Farrar pervades every page of the book and makes it one above many to read and own.

⁂Copies sent, post-paid, on receipt of price, $1.25.

THOMAS WHITTAKER,
2 and 3 Bible House, New York.

MEXICO

Contributions in aid of Christian work in Mexico are most pressingly needed, and can be mailed to the address of

BISHOP H. C. RILEY,
Care of J. P. HEATH,
43 Bible House, New York.

To our Christian Friends:

As there is a regular monthly expense in connection with the work a regular monthly income is needed to meet that expense. We, therefore, specially ask for regular monthly contributions in its behalf. If many will each send a little every month, or quarter, or whenever they can, it will do great good. *Remember, every little helps.*

H. Chauncey Riley.

This Journal contains every week a Portrait and Biography of some eminent person; a new Sermon by the Rev. C. H. SPURGEON, of London, and the Rev. Dr. TALMAGE'S latest Sunday morning Sermon; also always a Prophetic Article, and a Summary of Current Events as well as Stories, Anecdotes etc.

Vol. XI., No. 46. Office, 63 Bible House. N. Y. THURSDAY, NOVEMBER 15, 1888. Price, 3 Cents. Annual Subscription, $1.50.

CONTENTS OF THIS NUMBER.

PORTRAIT AND LIFE OF "BILLY" BRAY.
SATAN ON HIS TRAVELS. Dr. Talmage's Sermon Last Sunday Morning.
THE RESURRECTION; THE FIRST.
A Romish Festival in New Mexico—Progress in Japan—A Demented Christian Comforted—A Turk's Faith—Saved through a Dream, etc.
IRON CHARIOTS. A New Sermon by Rev. C. H. Spurgeon.
PORTRAIT OF MRS. HARRISON, WIFE OF THE PRESIDENT-ELECT.
PICTURE OF A STREET IN SAN FRANCISCO.
BERTIE HOPE'S FRIEND. (With Illustration.)
THE EPOCHS OF A LIFE. (Continued.)
THE COVENANT RENEWED. By Mrs. Baxter.

"BILLY" BRAY, THE MINER WHO BECAME AN EVANGELIST—SCENES IN HIS LIFE

"BILLY" BRAY.

The Miner and "the King's Son."

Born in 1794—Parentage and Early Life—Narrow Escapes—The Crisis—Prays for Mercy—Conversion—Begins to Work for Christ—Visit to a Dying Saint—Chapel Building—A Horse that "Wouldn't Draw Anything"—Taking a Tithe of Fish—Clothed from the Lord's Wardrobe—The Eccentricity of Bray's Genius—Last Days, Illness, and Death on May 22, 1868.

THE frequent references in the sermons by Rev. C. H. Spurgeon, published in this journal from week to week, to "Billy" Bray will render some account of his remarkable life welcome to our readers.

The same grace which transformed a persecuting Saul of Tarsus into the renowned Apostle of the Gentiles, and John Bunyan, the blasphemous tinker of Bedford, into one of the Saviour's most famous preachers and confessors, changed also "Billy" Bray, *whose portrait is given on the preceding page*, formerly a drunken and lascivious miner, into a loving and consistent disciple of the Son of God. He was born at Twelveheads, near Truro, Cornwall, England, on June 1, 1794, and died on May 25, 1868, at the age of seventy-four. The house in which he was born and died (*shown in panel No. 1*) stood in a village which then consisted of only a few thatched cottages, inhabited by "tinners," but which had its humble Methodist chapel, where his paternal grandfather worshipped, and which he had helped to build. "Billy's" father was also a most pious man, but he died while his children were very young. They then went to live with their grandfather; and with him "Billy" remained until he was seventeen years old, when he went to Devonshire, where, far removed from pious example and instruction, he lived a bad life. His

Drunken Frolics

were many, which he could not recall without deep shame and sorrow; but his soul was stained with viler sins than any that have been mentioned. His gratitude was ever most enthusiastic, because, as he oftentimes said, the Lord had saved him from "the lowest hell." "The Lord was good to me," he frequently remarked, "when I was the servant of the devil, or I should have been utterly lost"; and he felt he must praise the Lord for His goodness. His hair-breadth escapes from danger, though he was such a wicked man, made an impression on his heart at the time, and a deeper impression afterwards. "Once," he tells us, "I was working underground, and I heard a rent overhead; I ran out, and, I think, forty tons fell down where I had been working but a few minutes before."

Turned Away From the Mine

at which he worked for being insolent to the "captain," he removed to another part of Devonshire, and, as if to seal his own ruin for ever, went to live at a beer shop. We may hear his own narrative again: "There, with other drunkards, I drank all night long. But I had a sore head and a sick stomach, and, worse than all, horrors of mind that no tongue can tell. I used to dread to go to sleep for fear of waking up in hell; and though I had made many promises to the Lord to be better, I was soon as bad, or worse, than ever. After being absent from my native county seven years, I returned a *drunkard*." His conscience tormented him by day, and dreams terrified him by night.

The Crisis of His Life,

however, was near at hand. Bunyan's "Visions of Heaven and Hell," came into his hands, and he began to read it. From that time, November, 1823, he had a strong desire to be a better man.

He had married some time before; his wife had been converted when young, but had gone back from the right way before marriage. The remembrance of what she had enjoyed was very sweet, and yet very bitter. She told her husband that "no tongue could tell what they enjoy who serve the Lord." "Why don't you begin again," was his pertinent retort; adding, "for then I may begin, too." He was ashamed to fall on his knees before his wife, "for the devil had such a hold on him," but he knew it was his duty to pray for mercy. He went to bed as usual, one night, without bending his knees in prayer; but about three o'clock he awoke, and thinking that if he waited until his wife was converted he might never be saved, he jumped out of bed and got

On His Knees for the First Time,

and forty years afterwards he could joyfully declare that he had never once since been ashamed to pray. His decision, once formed, was unalterable, "and I found," he said, "that the more I prayed the more I wanted to pray." The whole forenoon was spent in supplication.

On the first pay-day that he came home sober for many years, his wife, he says, "was greatly surprised, and asked, 'How is it you are come home so early to-night?' and she had for answer, 'You will never see me drunk again by the help of the Lord.' And she has never since. Praise the Lord He can cure drunkards. That same night I went up-stairs, and prayed till we went to bed. The next day I did not go to work; I took the Bible and Wesley's Hymn-book, went up-stairs, and read and prayed all day. Sometimes I read the Bible, sometimes the hymn-book, and then I cried to the Lord for mercy. When Sunday morning came it was very wet; the 'Bible Christians' had a class-meeting a mile from our house; I went to the place, but because it was wet none came." This had an unfavorable effect on his mind. Billy returned home, and alone with God, with the Bible and the hymn-book as his companions, he spent all the day in reading and prayer. (*See panel No. 2 on first page.*)

Prayer in the Mine.

Monday forenoon was spent in the same manner. In the afternoon he had to go to the mine, but "all the while I was working I was crying to the Lord for mercy." His state moved his fellow-workmen to pity. He "*was not like Billy Bray*," they said. No relief came, and he went home, "asking for mercy all the way." It was then eleven o'clock at night, but the first thing he did was to go up-stairs and fall upon his knees, and entreat God to have mercy upon him. After awhile he went to bed, but not to sleep. All the forenoon of the next day he spent in crying for mercy. That day passed, and nearly the whole night he spent upon his knees. On the next day he had "almost laid hold of the blessing"; but the time came for him when he must go to the mine. The devil

Strongly Tempted

him while at his work that he would never find mercy: "but I said to him, '*Thou art a liar, devil*,' and as soon as I said so I felt the weight gone from my mind, and I could praise the Lord, but not with that liberty I could afterwards. So I called to my comrades, 'I am not so happy as some, but sooner than I would go back to sin again, I would be burned to death.'" That night he again repaired to his chamber. Beautifully simple and touching are his own words: "I said to the Lord, 'Thou hast said. *They that ask shall receive, they that seek shall find, and to them that knock the door shall be opened*, and I have faith to believe it.' In an instant the Lord made me so happy that I cannot express what I felt. I shouted for joy. I praised God with my whole heart for what He had done for a poor sinner like me; for I could say, The Lord hath pardoned all my sins. I was a new man altogether! I told all I met what the Lord had done for my soul. Some of my companions said I was mad; and others that they should get me back next pay-day. They said I was a *mad*-man, but they meant I was a *glad*-man, and, glory be to God! I have been glad ever since."

He Began to Preach

about a year after his conversion, while continuing his work in the mine. Towards the end of 1824 his name was put on the Local Preacher's Plan, and his labors were much blessed in the conversion of souls. The worldly as much as the pious, the rich and the poor, aged and young, flocked to hear him, and he retained his popularity to the last. As the Rev. Mark Guy Pearse says: "From one end of Cornwall to another no name is more familiar than that of Billy Bray. On Sundays, when one met crowds of strangers making for the little white-washed chapel that was perched up amongst the granite boulders, or when one found the quiet 'church town' thronged by the well-dressed people, the usual explanation was that Billy Bray was going to preach. (*See Illustration No 4.*) If you had overtaken Billy on the way, you could not have been long in doubt as to who he was—a little, spare, wiry man, whose dress of orthodox black, and the white tie, indicated the preacher—and with the first suspicion that this was Billy Bray there would quickly come enough to confirm it. If you gave him half a chance, there would certainly be a straightforward question about your soul, in pointed, pithy words. And if the answer was what it should be, the lanes would ring with his shout of happy thanksgiving."

In the neighborhood of Billy's home there were "many wicked people, and chapels were few." His mother gave him a small piece of land, and on this he

Resolved to Build a Chapel,

which was to be called Bethel. He himself took away the hedge, and dug out the foundation. The Lord helped Billy to go on with the work he had begun, though he was often confronted by difficulty and had to face opposition. By-and-bye timber was wanted for the door and windows. A mine had lately stopped work: and the timber was being sold off. A sufficient quantity was purchased, but a horse and cart were wanted to bring it "home to the dear Lord's house." "One of our neighbors had a horse," says Bray, "but he said it would not draw anything. I asked him to lend it to me. I put it into the cart and brought the timber home. (*See Illustration No. 3.*) I never saw a better horse in my life; I did not touch it with whip or stick, though we had steep hills to come over. When I took back the mare and told my neighbor, 'I never saw a better mare,' he said, 'I never saw such a thing; she will not draw with anyone else.' At length the chapel was finished, and many souls were converted in it. Several other houses of worship were erected through Bray's devotion to the work of extending the knowledge of Christ.

He Went on a Begging Tour

to obtain money to build a chapel at Gwennap. He went to St. Ives, and tried to find out a good man named Bryant. "St Ives," says Bray, "was a small place about the year 1838. Friend Bryant told me that I had come at a very poor time, for there was but little fish caught that year; and some of the people were almost wanting bread. 'It was poor time,' I said, 'with Peter when the Lord told him to let down the net on the other side of the ship.' We went up to the Wesleyan chapel, and we had a good meeting. We prayed to the dear Lord to send some fish, and He did. After the meeting was over, we went into a coffee-house to get a little refreshment; then we began our meeting, and continued it till midnight, praying to the Lord to send in the fish. As we came out of the meeting to go to our lodging, there were the poor women with the pilchards on their plates, and the fish were shining in the moonlight. The women were smiling, the moon was smiling, and we were smiling; and no wonder, for the dear Lord put bread on many shelves that night, and blessed many families. We asked the women what fish was taken, and they told us that many boats had taken 10,000, and some 20,000. Again the next day there were, if I mistake not, 8,000 casks taken. Some of the fishermen said to me, 'Now, you shall have some money for your chapel; and if you will get a boat and come out we will give you some fish.' A friend with me, a carpenter, a bit used to the sea, got a boat and rowed me to the place where the boats were. They looked 'pretty,' for they were shining and leaping about, and the fishermen dipped up the fish, and threw them into our boat *ee Illustration No.* 5). I thought of the urch-ministers, who took their tithe of the rn: but I took mine of the fish. When we me to land, the carpenter 'toid' up the fish to e people that bought them, and I took the oney, which amounted to the grand sum of irty-four dollars."

Bray was Very Poor

ıen he was converted (a workingman who is drunkard must be very poor); a low-priced stian jacket was his best, and he said that was tter than he deserved; but false shame did ıt stop him from going out on the Sunday to ırn his fellow-men to "flee from the wrath to me." At the request of a servant girl, an unıown Quaker friend gave him a coat and waistat, "which suited me," he said, "as if they :re made for me; and they served me for years." In 1867, being then in his seventy-fourth year, continued to be in "labors more abundant." ıs eye had a merry twinkle, his countenance open and benevolent expression, his voice a eerful and pleasant ring even unto the last. e took long journeys, held frequent services, d regular times for fasting and prayer—praise ther than prayer, especially at the last—and tnessed glorious victories even unto the end. is visits to the sick seemed more numerous en than before. The

Infirmities of Age

ıd come upon him, but his ruling passion had ıdergone no change, his spiritual ardor sufred no abatement. One of his last entries in e diary which forms the basis of his biography, ade as late as February 10, 1868, was, "In the orning, after I had breakfast, bad as I was, I ought I would go to see some friends; and ter calling on some of them, I went home. ut I had hard work to get home, I was so ill; ıd my breath was short."

Only a little time before he had been at Newn and Crantock, laboring among the Wesleyıs. There was a revival in progress in the tter place, and in a revival Bray was always home. He returned home pale and exhausted. e left it but once afterwards, when he went to skeard to see his children. He got much orse, and appeared like a man in the last stage consumption. On one occasion he sent for medical man, and when he arrived he said: Now, doctor, I have sent for you because they ll me you are an honest man, and will tell the ople the truth about their state." After the ctor had examined him, Bray said: "Well, ctor, how is it?" "You are going to die." ily shouted, "Glory! glory be to God!

I Shall Soon be in Heaven."

e then added in a low tone, and in his own culiar way, "When I get up there, shall I give em your compliments, doctor, and tell them u will be coming, too?" "This," the doctor ys, "made a wonderful and permanent impresn upon me." (*See Illustration No.* 6.) In his lictions he was visited by persons of all deminations, who liberally contributed to his pport. On Friday, May 22, 1868, he came wn-stairs for the last time. To one of his old ends, a few hours before his death, who asked he had any fear of death, or of being lost, he d, "What, me fear death! me lost! Why, Saviour conquered death! If I were to go wn to hell, I would shout glory! glory! to my ssed Jesus, until I made the bottomless pit g again, and the miserable old Satan would . 'Billy, Billy, this is no place for thee: thee back!' Then up to heaven I should go, outing glory! glory! praise the Lord!" A little er he said, "Glory!" which was his last word, d in a little time he died. He was blessing d praising the Lord all the day, so that heavwas not to him very different to earth. Glory his experience had begun below; he enjoyed nderful foretastes of the fullness and fruition confidently expected to enjoy in heaven ove. He took his departure on Monday, May 1868, having reached the age of seventy-four rs within a few days. His remains were erred at Baldhu Church, where they await joyous resurrection to eternal life.

ANECDOTES RELATED AT RECENT EVANGELISTIC MEETINGS.

"Lord, Save That Big Drunkard!"—A worker at the St. Giles' Mission testifies: "Although I turned a deaf ear to a wife's petitions, I could not help hearing her sing hymns upon her sick-bed. Many a time have I threatened to throw the Bible into the fire, telling her I would have none of that in my house. But one night I came in here, sneaking and creeping behind the door thinking to escape observation. Now I am very tall, and after I had been in a short time I heard our sister in prayer say, 'Oh, Lord, save that big drunkard!' Now drunkenness was my besetting sin, and there being no other big man in the room I could not but think she was referring to me. The Spirit of God seemed to come into my heart and subdue it. I cried unto the Lord and asked Him, for Jesus Christ's sake, to take away from me the craving for drink. Bless God, He has done it for me."

The Pool of Blood.—"An Evangelist, in speaking of the Passover, told his hearers that none but those who were sprinkled with the blood of Christ were saved. A few days afterwards a woman came to him and said, 'When I was a girl I had a most vivid dream. I thought I was alone with my father and mother, yet separated from them by a pool of blood. I tried to get over to them, but was unable. Then my father said, solemnly, "No, you can never be with us unless you are sprinkled with the blood." That dream had faded from my memory, but when you spoke of the blood of Christ, and how none could be saved without it, the remembrance of that dream came upon me. I saw how I could never hope to join my dear parents, unless I came to Christ and was washed in His blood.' The servant of God spoke earnestly to the anxious one, with the result that she left his presence rejoicing in Christ."

"An Uncommonly Curious Thing."—An avowedly unbelieving officer confessed: "When the bullets have been whizzing past my ears, and the shells bursting on every hand, and my comrades have been falling on my right hand and on my left hand, it is an uncommonly curious thing, but *at such times I always begin to pray.* I am not a praying man—I do not profess to pray—but always when I have been in danger of that sort, and think that I might possibly die very soon, I *instinctively begin to pray.*" Multitudes of infidels have been converted to God, and with hardly an exception have testified that their infidelity was a sham and that along with it all there were secret misgivings and doubts, and fears that all was not well. As one infidel said, after having run the round of doubt and unbelief, until at last he confessed his faith in Christ, "I never found anything before to rest upon that would not shake when the wind blew."

Prayer Instead of the "Highland Fling."—A Christian worker remarks: "On one occasion William Burns was preaching in the north of Scotland, and the scene of his effort for Christ was a graveyard. There was a young man in the neighborhood who thought he would like to hear Burns preach. He told his companions that he proposed going. 'Oh,' said one friend, 'if you go to hear him preach, you are sure to be converted.' 'I do not think that is at all likely,' was the reply. They bantered each other for awhile, and at length the one bet the other that he would go and hear Burns preach, and then dance the Highland fling and play the pipes on the village green upon his return. He set out to hear the preacher, but as he got nearer the place of meeting he began to be more and more afraid that, perhaps, after all he might be converted. So to make sure he resolved not to go to the meeting, but to remain at a short distance from it. He stationed himself on the outside of the graveyard, where he could see but not hear. He stood thinking how strange it was to see a man stand up before a crowd and wave his hand, and gesticulate, and yet hear no sound. But once the speaker suddenly raised his voice to a higher pitch than usual, and the young man heard these words, 'Awake, thou that sleepest, and arise from the dead, and Christ will give you life.' These words went into the unwilling listener's ears, and then into his heart. He saw himself asleep and dead in sin. He hastened home, not to dance the Highland fling on the green, but to shut himself in his own room, and there seek and obtain mercy."

A Word in Season.—A Retired Naval Officer was travelling by rail in Lancashire. When the train stopped at some station, a number of cattle dealers and drovers entered the carriage. They were all excited, and it was soon evident that one of the company was being made a laughing-stock by the rest, and at last he was irritated, and uttered some oaths. The officer put his hand on his shoulder, and said, "Sir, you must not swear." The man looked at him, and said, "And pray, who made you, sir, conductor over this carriage?" "No one," replied the officer; "but I am your friend, and you will say so before night." "Indeed I won't," retorted the angry man; "there's many a bad one that goes to meetings." "Too true," replied the officer, "but there's never a swearer that goes to heaven." This caused a deep thought, and little more was said; but when the train stopped, the man, much softened, took the officer by the hand, and with real feeling said, "I don't like ye the less for what ye said to me."

Zeal Misunderstood.—An Evangelist Quoted the following from Mr. Moody: "A man who declared he thought I was doing more harm than good by speaking to everybody about Christ, told me I had seriously offended one of his friends by speaking to him in the street about his soul. Well, it happened in this way. I had not spoken to anyone that day, and on my way home I was on the look-out, and saw a man leaning against a lamp-post, looking very lonesome. Thinking he might be a stranger, I just stepped up to him and said, 'My friend, are you a Christian?' on which he turned round, and looking on me with a scowl, he cursed me, and said it was not my business. And that was why his friend told me he thought I was doing more harm than good, and setting men against religion instead of making them converts. My answer was that I was sorry if it was so; but the fault was from the head and not from the heart. 'Well,' said my friend, 'I believe you are in earnest; but you have too much zeal. What is zeal without knowledge?' 'Well,' I replied, 'I would rather have zeal without knowledge than knowledge without zeal.' Well, months rolled away, and one Sunday morning, about daybreak—a bitter, cold, winter's morning—I heard a rap at my door. 'Who's there?' I said. 'It's a stranger,' answered a voice which I did not recognize. 'What do you want?' 'I want you to talk to me about my soul.' I got up and let in the stranger, wan and pale. 'Do you remember, sir,' he said, 'meeting a man under a lamp-post, three months ago, about ten o'clock at night?' 'Yes,' said I, 'I do.' 'Well,' said he, 'I am that man. I have had no peace since that night. I could not sleep at all, and I thought I would come to you and ask you what I must do;' and so I talked to him and showed him the way to Jesus, and before he left the Son of Righteousness shone into his dark heart, and he went away rejoicing in Christ as his Saviour."

SATAN ON HIS TRAVELS.

Dr. Talmage's Sermon Preached last Sunday Morning, November 11, 1888.

"And the Lord said unto Satan: Whence comest thou? Then Satan answered the Lord and said: From going to and fro in the earth, and from walking up and down in it." Job 1:7.

Satan Among the Angels—A Monster of Many Names—Demonology Certain—Special Demons for Nations and Individuals—Satan a Supervisor-General—His Attack on the World—The Garden and the Talking Serpent—Satan's Travels Still in Progress—Routes he is Apt to Take—In the Atmosphere—Through Domestic Life—The Marriage Ring Played With—Satan in the Factories—A Talk with the Boss—His Suggestions to Workmen—In Mercantile Houses—Despoiling Souls—His Doom Predicted—The Army of Growing Christians—What Every One Needs.

In 1672 was printed the largest book ever published, namely, two huge volumes of near five thousand pages in small type, the author Joseph Caryl. It was a commentary on this Book of Job. When it took a year for the journey from England to India, the son of the author of this commentary started for India, leaving his father writing on his book, and was gone for years, and when he came back to England, still found his father writing on it. I never saw the commentary, but I do not wonder at its size, because there is no end to

The Interest of the Book of Job.

I am not surprised that Goethe, the unbeliever, took from this wonderful book the opening of his drama "Faust," and the Mephistopheles of the great German was only the Satan of Job. It seems that one day in heaven God was on His throne, and angels and messengers came to report on their missions. But while these good spirits were making their reports, a ghastly, grizzly, hideous monster from some miry, sulphurous, filthy world, came into the palace without wiping his feet, and God asked him where and how he had been occupying himself, and this

Greatest Scoundrel of the Universe

made reply with blazing effrontery, and instead of acknowledging any of the mischief he had been doing, said he had been an earthly pedestrian, and had lived a sort of circumambulatory, peripatetic life. "And the Lord said unto Satan: Whence comest thou? Then Satan answered the Lord, and said: From going to and fro in the earth, and from walking up and down in it."

This monster of my text has a great variety of names. You know that notorious villains are apt to take a variety of names. Arraigned in Paris for burglary, a man will give one name; arrested in San Francisco for arson, he will give another name; imprisoned at Montreal for murder, he will give another. So this creature

Has Many Names.

He is called in sacred and profane literature Abaddon, Apollyon, Ahrimanes, Zaniel, Asmodeus the revenging devil, Beelzebub the sovereign of devils, Lucifer the brilliant devil, Diabolus the despairing devil, Mammon the money devil, Pluto the fiery devil, Baal the military devil, Meresin the plaguing devil. He is called the father of lies, and has for his children and grandchildren and great-grandchildren all falsehoods, deceptions, frauds, swindles, slanders, back-bitings, and subterfuges. All men of good sense, whether enlightened by the Bible or in heathendom, have noticed that there are baleful and maleficent influences abroad, that have not their origin in the human race, and

Demonology is Certain

as angelology. The sword of Paracelsus was thought to have had a demon in the hilt, and there is now a demon in every sword hilt. The ancients supposed the air was filled with sylphs and satyrs and sirens and gnomes and vampires. Two or three hundred years ago a demonographer gave the names of ambassadors of evil which he thought Satan sent to different countries: Mammon, ambassador to England; Belphegor, ambassador to France; Martinet, ambassador to Switzerland; Rimmon, ambassador to Russia; Thannia, ambassador to Spain; Hutgin, ambassador to Italy, and that there was a princess of devils by the name of Proserpine. But that that was mere guesswork of mythology or superstition has been made clear by divine revelation. We find that there is somewhere a monarch of all wickedness. He is

The Supervisor of all Mischief,

and what he cannot do himself he delegates others to do, and as each one of our race is supposed to have a guardian good angel, I have no doubt that every human being has a besieging, malignant spirit nagging his footsteps, and trying to make him think wrong and act wrong, an especial devil, a devil of fraud, or a devil of avarice, or a devil of uncleanness, or a devil of poor health, and as in my text the spirits are represented as reporting to the Lord, so I have no doubt the evil spirits report to Satan. "And the Lord said unto Satan, Whence comest thou? Then Satan answered the Lord and said: From going to and fro in the earth, and from walking up and down in it." Satan began

His Attack on this World

long before Adam and Eve were created. While *I believe the Bible record that the world was fitted up for man's residence in one week*, I believe also the geological record that the world was previously for hundreds of thousands of years going through great changes. The lumber for the house that was to be built in a week for our first parents may have been hauled to the spot a million years before. This Prince of the Power of the Air has been trying for all that million years to demolish and use up this world. The record is on the rocks. He tried to drown it with universal waters. He tried to burn it up with universal fires. Then he tried to freeze it into ruin, and covered it with universal glacier. And for ages he kept this world, before our first parents occupied it, in paroxysms. Yea, after the famous Bible week, the world had been fitted into a Paradise for the home of our sinless ancestors, Satan comes into the Garden of Eden, and through the gate of foliage, not upright in posture, but crawls in under the bushes a snake, and having despoiled our first parents, goes to work to ruin Paradise, and does the work so thoroughly that one who recently visited the site of

The Ancient Garden,

between the rivers Tigris and Euphrates, says the place is a desert; not a flower, and the ground so poor that nothing but some date-trees grow there, and the miserable villagers from near by are not so well covered up with their rags as Adam and Eve were covered up with their innocence. So you see the Father of lies for once told the truth when the Lord said unto him: Whence comest thou? and Satan answered and said: "From going to and fro in the earth, and from walking up and down in it."

In my text we have Satan on his travels, and I am going to tell you some of the

Routes He is Apt to Take.

On his way down from the palace where he reported himself in answer to the question: Whence comest thou? the first range of mischief he may be expected to take is the air. It was not a witticism or a slip of the pen when Paul, in his letter to the Ephesians, called Satan the "Prince of the Power of the Air." I think it means that Satan works through conditions of the atmosphere. The west wind is full of angels, the east wind is full of devils. Satan has power in the upper air where highest clouds float, and power over the lower air which we breathe; and as we breathe nineteen times a minute, and take in three hundred and fifty cubic feet of air in every twenty-four hours, and much of this air affects the arterial circulation, you see what opportunities the Prince of the Air has of contaminating and despoiling and demoralizing a man. Through atmospheric influence he clouds the disposition, and rasps the nerves, and covers the best of people with *religious despondency*, as in the case of Edward Payson and William Cowper, and that beloved apostle of Evangelism, James W. Alexander. His great delight is to have the air of churches vitiated, and in that way dulls the preacher and stupefies the people, and sees to it that the atmosphere of not more than one out of a hundred churches is fit to breathe, and whole congregations, Sabbath by Sabbath, are asphyxiated. Yes, he is worthy of the title St. Paul gave him: "Prince of the Power of the Air."

Another route he is apt to take is

Through Domestic Life.

There is no greater sport for him than conjugal quarrel. It does not make any difference how long the marriage ring has been on the finger of the left hand, he will try to pull off the signet. He says to the husband: "What a plain wif you have compared with what she once was! Don't you see that the color has gone out o her cheek, and there are several wrinkles abou her temples, and a sprinkling of frost on he locks? Besides that, you have advanced i intelligence, while she has stood still or gon back. How hard it is that you should be chaine to such dullness and imbecility!" Then h turns and says to the wife: "That man neglect you; you have a right to be jealous. He like his cigar and his club, and anything and everything better than you. Why not get a divorce? Marriage is only a civil contract anyhow, and not a divine alliance. Let me have that ring. It means nothing, and you might as well give it to me." *The ring is handed over* to Satan, and he tosses it up and down, like a plaything, over the mouth of perdition, and says: "I will hand it back, only let me have it a little while." And he keeps tossing that ring, with all its sacred memories, higher up and further out, tossing and catching, tossing and catching it until one day you clutch for it, crying: "Give me back my ring!" but lo, it has dropped into the yawning gulf, and you suddenly find who has been pitching and catching the ring, and you cry out "Whence comest thou?" and he answers "From going to and fro in the domestic life of the city, and from walking up and down in it that is all."

There are thousands of marriage relation strained almost to the breaking, and I commend to all men and women who are restless in the present marriage state that they *resume the old-time courtship*, and take as much pains to make themselves agreeable as they did five or ten or twent years ago, before the wedding march announce to the flushed and fluttering crowd that th bride and groom were coming. According t the statistics of Professor Dikes, in one yea in moral New Hampshire there were 24 divorces; in temperate Maine, 478 divorces; good old Massachusetts, 600 divorces, and in th New England of "steady habits," 2,113. In on county of Illinois 830 divorce suits were begu in one year, and in many places it seems as if new arrangement had been made of the com mandments, and instead of ten there were onl nine, the seventh commandment having bee left out. When you see how many husband and wives are parted by law, and know of many who would like to dissolve conjugal par nership, do you not come to the conclusion th Satan is engaged in mighty industries?

Another route that Satan is apt to take in h active travels, is

The Factories

and other establishments where capital sits the office or counting-room and a good ma hands of laborers are busy among wheels a spindles and fabrics. On this visit he will fi step into the manufacturer's office, and find the owner and proprietor of the great establi ment all alone with his correspondence and account-books, says to him: 'You are not m ing as much money as you ought. You furn all the brains. Were it not for your enterp this establishment would not be in existe These men and women in your employ are very common mould. Their appetite is coar and they do not need the luxuries you requ Their comfort and happiness are of very li importance. Put them down on the very ver of starvation and take all the profits into yo own possession, and if they do not like it t them to go where they can do better." Havi ıne his work in the counting-room, Satan ɛps right out

Among the Workmen.

e says; "You work too many hours and you your work better than it needs to be done. ɔu are serving a bloated bondholder anyhow. e has no right to have any more than you .ve. Why should he ride and you walk? Why ould he have tenderloin steak and you salt ırk? Capital is the enemy of labor. Let labor the sworn foe of capital. Why don't you rike and bring him to terms? Wait until he is a large order to fill by contract, and then he nnot help himself. Go altogether, without a oment's warning, and tell him you are going stop. If he has more resources than you know , and persists in going on and getting new en, give them a volley of brickbats or put a tle dynamite in his office and blow him and s factory all up with the same explosion." *ɔok out there on the night sky!* Great fire mewhere. What is it? The night is cold and ıtan has made a big bonfire of that factory to ırm himself by. The capitalist has lost heavily, ıd the workmen and their families are without ead and clothing. "Whence comest thou, ıtan?" "From going to and fro among employers and employees, and from walking up and ıwn among them. Ha! Ha! I was the only ıe who made anything out of that strike. What fire and smoke! Ha! Ha! I like smoke."

Another route Satan is apt to take in his tive travels is through the

Mercantile Establishments.

e steps in and says to the clerks: "How much lary do you get? Is that all? Why, you can't e on that! You have a right to enough for ivelihood. A few quarters out of the money-awer will never be missed, or here and there a remnant of goods you could take home withıt being found out. Or you could change those count-books a little, and you could make that ¡ure eight a nought and that figure five a ree, and if you do not feel exactly right about ıing that you can some day pay it back, which ıu can do perfectly easy. Don't feel like running the risk? Well, then you can't go to the eatre, and you can't go on that round with the ıys, and you will have to wear that plain coat, ıereas you could have your overcoat fur lined, d take board at a tip-top place, and walk amid ush and tapestries positively Oriental. While u are making up your mind I will just go rough the different parts of this great comɛrcial establishment and try every one from the ɛalthy firm down to the errand boys."

The Result of That Satanic Visit

that one of the partners has drawn so much t of the concern that the whole business is ippled, and a bright and promising boy is sent ıme to his mother in disgrace, and a young ın is in jail for embezzlement. Three lives ined and three eternities. Whence comest ou, Satan? "From going to and fro among ɛrcantile houses, and from walking up and wn among them. I like to ruin splendid felws and blast parental hopes, and of all the uors that I ever tasted, fill my glass with a ɛwing of agonizing tears. Come! let us click gether the rims of our glasses and drink to overthrow of the fifty thousand young men uined last year! Huzzah!" *Satan would ıher have one young man than twenty old ones.* he would win the septuagenarians and the ɔgenarians, he could do but little harm with ɛm. But he says: "Give me a young man, ɛcially if he be bright and generous and ɛial." He sees that young men have, for good bad, been the mightiest influence in this rld. Hernando Cortes conquered Mexico at rty-two. Gustavus Adolphus became imɪrtal in history so early that he died at thirtyht. Raphael, the most famous of painters, d at thirty-seven. William Pitt was Prime nister of England at twenty-four. Jesus rist completed His earthly life at thirty-three. ɪe years in a young man's life are of more wer for good or evil than the last fifteen of old man's life. So Satan is especial greedy for young men, and in going to and fro in the earth he has especial temptation for them.

Another route that Satan on his active travels is apt to take is for the

Despoiling of Souls.

It does not pay him merely to destroy the bodies of men and women. Those bodies would soon be gone anyhow; but great treasures are involved in this Satanic excursion. On this route he meets a man who is aroused by something he has seen in the Bible, and Satan says: "Now I can settle all that; the Bible is an imposition; it has been deluding the world for centuries; do not let it delude you. It has no more authority than the Koran of the Mohammedan, or the Shaster of the Hindoo, or the Zenda-Vesta of the Persian." He meets another man who is hastening towards the kingdom of God, and says: "Why all this precipitation? Religion is right, but any time within the next ten years will be soon enough for you. A man with a stout chest like yours, and such muscular development, need not be bothering himself about the next world." But Satan says nothing to him about the fact that the professor who gave his whole life to the study of health, and could lift more pounds than any American, died at about forty, and that another learned man, who proved conclusively that if we observed all the laws of health we need never die, expired before he got his book on that subject published. Satan meets another man who has gone through a long course of profligacy and is beginning to pray for forgiveness, and Satan says to the man:

"You Are Too Late;

the Lord will not help such a wretch as you; you might as well brace up and fight your own way through." And so with a spite and an acuteness and a velocity that have been gaining for six thousand years, he ranges up and down, baffling, disappointing, defeating, afflicting, destroying the human race. Through his own hand or delegated infernalism he has pursued and hurt us all, and cursed every heart, and cursed every home, and cursed every nation, and cursed every continent. He has instigated every war. He has rejoiced in every pestilence. He has started every groan. He has pressed out every sigh. He has hurled every shipwreck, Lazarettoes, insane asylums, commercial panics, plagues, destroying angels, continental earthquakes, and world-wide disasters are to him a perfect glee. Can you look upon the Communism and the Mormonism and the Mohammedanism and the wide sweep of drunkenness and fraud and libertinism, the Franco-German War and Crimean War, the North and South United States war, and rivers of blood flowing across continents of misery into oceans of wretchedness, without realizing the power of the Evil One, who reported to the Lord Almighty, and when asked, Whence comest thou? answered, "From going to and fro in the earth, and from going up and down in it."

But, blessed be God! I may substitute anthem for requiem, and Hallelujah Chorus for the Dead March in Saul. The New Testament says: "The Son of God was manifested, that He might destroy the works of the devil." It prophesied that an angel would come down from heaven with key and chain and incarcerate and shut up the old dragon. It says that Christ came to "destroy him that had the power of death—that is, the devil." And from the way Christ drove the devil out of those possessed by him until he was glad to hide under the bristles of the swine of Gadara, and from other violent ejectments, we know that there is in existence a power a million-fold

Mightier Than the Diabolic.

The old lion of death shall go down under the stroke and roar of the "Lion of Judah's tribe." Yea, my text shows that Satan was compelled to report to the Almighty and give account of himself. When God said to him: "Whence comest thou?" he was forced to answer. What means that Scripture which says that Christ shall bruise the serpent's head? If you have ever killed a snake, the passage ought to be plain to you. You see, this old serpent, the devil, has crawled across the nations, poisoning whole generations and leaving its trail on everything; but after a while it will be cornered, and hissing and writhing in rage, and with crest lifted and forked tongue shot out, it will make final attack on Christ, and Christ will advance upon it, and lifting His omnipotent foot, that foot strong enough to crush a world, lifting that foot right over the head of the reptile, will put down His heel with a crushing power that shall leave the monster bleeding and mashed, never to hiss again, or bite again, or shake his old rattle again. Thank God, he has already

Received a Stunning Blow.

Hear you not the rumbling of the Christian printing-presses and the whirling of the Gospel chariot wheel? As many souls have been added to the Christian church in the last eighty years as in the previous eighteen centuries, and that is a ratio of increase acclamatory with gladness. The kingdom is coming, and I am so sure of it that I do not propose to fret and worry. The sharp attacks of infidelity and sin are a good sign that especial blessing is coming in showers over the earth. Flies bite sharp just before rain.

If we do not see the full consummation, our children will see it. In the time of the French Revolution a great procession of boys carried through the street a banner with the inscription: "Tremble, tyrants; we shall grow up!" Though we may fail to do our duty, there is a rising generation being gospelized, and coming by the hundreds of thousands from our Sabbath-schools and Christian homes, who might properly have on their banners: "Tremble, ye powers of darkness and sin; for we are growing up!" We may not amount to much in ourselves, but if we put ourselves in the right place we can do great exploits. Two put under two make only four; but placed beside two make twenty-two.

What You and I Most Need

is power to drive back this Apollyon, this Asmodeus, this Ahrimanes, from our heart and lives. And we can do it, not by our own strength, but by divine power afforded, for here is a passage emblazoned with encouragement which says: "Resist the devil and he will flee from you." Remember it is no sin at all to be tempted. The best and the mightiest have been tempted. Milton describes a toad squat at the ear of Eve. The sin is in surrendering. Do not feel so secure in yourself as to think you cannot be overthrown. How do you account for the fact that there are so many old men in Sing Sing and Auburn and the other penitentiaries, serving out their protracted sentences for frauds. The clock in the steeple of old Trinity Church striking the hours did not remind the recreant Wall-streeter of the passage of time that would soon bring exposure and doom to him. The explanation is that Mephistopheles, Apollyon, Satan, got in his work at that time. The man was not naturally bad. He was as good as any of you are, but Satan, with whole battalions of infernals, swooped upon him unawares.

Look out for the wiles of the devil, not only those of you who are young, but the middle-aged and the old. Outside of God

You Are Not Safe

a moment. But yield not to disheartenment. If we put our trust in God, our best days are yet to come—days of victory, days of song, days of heaven—and the best days of the cause of righteousness in all the earth are yet to come. As the ten thousand men of Xenophon's army, when they came to the top of Mount Theches and saw the waters on which they were to sail to their homes, the soldiers with clapping hands and waving banners all together shouted: "The sea, the sea!" So we to-day in our march toward our heavenly home come up to the top of the mountain of holy anticipation, and look off upon oceans of light, and oceans of glory, and oceans of joy; and thrilled as we have never been thrilled before, we clap our hands and wave our gospel ensigns, and cry one to another, and shout up to the responding and re-echoing heavens: "The sea, the sea!"

A ROMISH FESTIVAL IN NEW MEXICO.

A STRIKING illustration of the fact of the near affinity between Romanism and heathenism, which Mr. G. H. Pember has repeatedly mentioned in the columns of this journal, is given in a letter which is sent to the *Spirit of Missions* by Rev. James Fraser, a missionary in New Mexico. He says: "As we were journeying through the Mora region we came to a small country church, which was surrounded by small heaps of split pine wood. This was the preparation for a feast to be held in that village in honor of the guardian saint of that town and locality. Within a quarter of a mile of the church we met the parish priest making his way to the village, who is always the leader in these scenes, kept in honor of these wooden saints.

"At dusk the heaps of pine wood (about fifty to eighty in number, for we counted fully twenty on each side of the church, omitting the ends) are lighted, and when they are blazing in good form the priest, dressed in his robes, sallies forth from the church, with the patron saint of the place in his arms, to lead the people in procession round the church by the light of these fires. The priest now sings and hugs the saint, thanking it for the blessings it bestowed on the village during the year, while the people in crowds follow the priest, whooping and shouting and firing guns at a most boisterous rate; indicating, one would think, the orgies of pure heathenism rather than anything that could pass under the name of a Christian feast. And heathenism doubtless it is. Those of us who have seen the dances of the Indians of Arizona and New Mexico are fully persuaded that these wild scenes (the so-called feasts of the Romanists of this land) have been borrowed, in great part, from the heathenism of the Indians."

PROGRESS IN JAPAN.

IN a recent letter from Dr. H. Loomis, who is laboring in Japan, he gives the following summary of Christian progress in that land: In the town of Fugioka there lives a man, sixty-four years of age, named Machida Totaro. He has long been afflicted with a weakness in his eyes. He went from place to place, and to various doctors and priests, for some remedy, but his efforts were of no avail, and he became almost totally blind. Then he heard that there was a skilful foreign physician living in Tokyo, by the name of Whitney, and he went to him for relief. After careful treatment for a while, his sight was partially restored, and he was greatly rejoiced and thankful for the services that had been rendered. He was very ready to hear the Gospel; and, after some instruction from the doctor and others, he made confession of his faith in Christ.

On the Island of Yesso is a large portion of country that was formerly uninhabited. It having been proposed to occupy the land by means of colonization, a Daimio at Nagoya sent about twenty men each year to a spot called Yakumomura. In this way the village has grown to consist of about one hundred houses. The people in general were much attached to their old ways, and have little thought or desire to make any special change either in their temporal or spiritual condition. But one of their number favored Christianity, and invited Rev. Mr. Nakasu, of Sapporo, to come and teach them. The invitation was accepted; and so great was the encouragement that a second series of meetings was held. In December last four men were baptized. Fifteen more have applied for baptism, and have been taken on trial.

The pastor of the church at Shidzuoka has been visiting the prison and holding services for the benefit of the inmates. The result has been a most marked change in the minds and conduct of many of the prisoners. Several have united with the church upon their release from confinement. A Christian has been employed for some time as a teacher of morals in the Kobe prison. He reports the conversion of some of the most hardened criminals. These men have been released, and are now living honest and industrious lives. The Governor of Nagasaki has applied to the missionaries in that city to conduct services in the prison for the benefit of the inmates. It seems to be more and more understood by all, and especially the officials, that Christianity is one of the best and most important factors in the reformation of the criminal class.

A TURK'S FAITH.

MR. DEWEY, a missionary of the American Board in Eastern Turkey, sends to the *Missionary Herald* a translation of an interesting letter which he recently received from a native pastor at Midyat. In the course of it is the following passage: "One who was accustomed to drink *arak* and play cards in the coffee-houses, a man reckoned not upright. Twelve days ago there was religious talk between him and Melki, son of Shemas Jurjis. The brother Melki spoke to him of faith in Christ, that it is free, and was repeating to him the saying that to him that worketh not, but believeth on Him that justifieth the ungodly, his faith is counted for righteousness. On this very saying he reflected a little, and then in a loud voice said: 'I believe! I am saved, and have full hope in the salvation of Jesus.' And so he clung to this word with a strong hand, and to whomever would talk with him he would say, 'I believe in Jesus, and am saved.' And for this there rose upon him persecution from the priests, and his own family, and all the Syrian community, but he grows strong in his thought, and says to them, 'If ye believe not thus, ye have not salvation.' And according to what we have seen in this person, our opinion is that God has wrought in him a wonderful work, and now he is joyful in what he has gained, and ceases not from attendance at church. There is from him a great impression upon the Syrians, as they see a marvellous thing found in him, and so another has become persuaded with him, and now they both continue in attendance at church."

SAVED THROUGH A DREAM.

NEAR Elderfeldt, in Germany, there lived two Christian men, very intimate, one of whom led a very worldly life. The husband was taken ill, and on his death-bed drew a promise from his friend that he would visit his wife, pray for her, and lose no opportunity of recommending to her the grace of God as revealed in the person and work of Jesus Christ. This the friend readily engaged to do; and, upon the husband's death, which happened shortly after, he visited the widow, and as long as her grief lasted, his visits were well received. Time passed on, but as the wound began to heal, his visits became more and more irksome to the lady, until at last she told him that unless he would speak of something more pleasant, he might as well stay away altogether. Hurt, but not offended, he discontinued his visits, but not his prayers. After a while, however, he forgot her entirely.

Two years had rolled by, when awakening suddenly in the night, he felt unhappy and depressed; and, among other things, he thought of his friend, and then of the wife, and with much sorrow of heart he prayed the Lord that his sin of negligence in forgetting to pray for her, and allowing himself to be hindered from carrying out his promise, might not be the cause of a precious soul being lost. He rose early in the morning, and though he had eight miles to walk, by six o'clock he was at the chateau where the widow resided. He rang the bell. "Can I see madam?"

The servant looked strangely at him, and went away. In a few moments she returned. "You can see madam; she has been longing to see you; *she is dying!*" He went up, and to his surprise and happiness, found her full of joy and peace in believing. She stretched out her hand to him, and said: "Ah, sir! I have found a Saviour just such as I need."

He begged her to repeat the circumstances of her conversion. She said she felt able. The night before, when she fell asleep, she was much disturbed, and had the following dream: a carriage, she thought, drove up to the house; the footman jumped down, threw open the door, and told her that she was invited to the wedding of the king's son; but she must be very quick in dressing as he could not wait. She ran to her wardrobe to find her best dress, but when she put it over her head, it fell around her in dust and ashes. A second and a third met the same fate. The footman cried out: "Make haste, or we must go." Her servant jumped into the carriage, the door slammed, and as she heard the wheels roll away, she sank on her bed in an agony of mortified shame. How long she lay she knew not, but she was roused by a voice whispering in her ear: "There is no robe that will cover you but the robe of the righteousness of Jesus Christ."

She awoke and found it a dream; but though the vision was gone, the reality of her solemn position, as having to do with the living God, was fully before her. She cried to Him, and before the day dawned had found salvation through the blood of a crucified Saviour. A few hours after she fell asleep in Christ.

A DEMENTED CHRISTIAN COMFORTED.

A BEAUTIFUL incident, which a contemporary vouches for as within the editor's knowledge, is an illustration of the fact that the divine message shall not fall to the ground void, but is mighty beyond our comprehension through His power. A lady was summoned to the bedside of a friend, the mother of a family, and whose mental faculties had become deranged. "What could I say or do?" she said. "All was wild excitement. My heart wept over her, yet I had no power to calm her or do her good. But I felt for her so deeply that I could not leave her without one whisper of comfort. I bent above her and said softly, 'Underneath are the everlasting Arms!' It seemed as though she glanced up at the words—hers was a Christian life—but she showed no sign of comprehension and, I left her, believing my whisper unheard." But hours after that delirium there came a lucid interval, and in that period of quiet what were the words that the invalid spoke? "*Underneath are the everlasting Arms!*" Amid all the strange fancies of the restless brain, that one text of heavenly calm had been victorious and reached to heart and memory.

A LADY HEALED OF STRICTURE.

AMONG the remarkable records of the Berachah Home, published by the Rev. A. B. Simpson in his *Cloud of Witnesses*, is the testimony of Mrs. Langley. She says: It was thirteen years ago last April since I had the first operation performed on me for stricture. Since then I have had nine others, and the torture I endured no one knows but God. I was treated by some of the best doctors in Boston and New York, and *pronounced incurable* by all. I never knew one moment's relief from pain. In the summer of 1885 I had an abscess in my head, and the suffering was so terrible I would have taken my life if I could. After trying everything, one night I threw down a poultice just brought me, and began to pray. I spent the greater part of the night in prayer, and gradually the pain left me and I was well. It left me deaf; but I took that to the Lord; and my hearing was restored.

In telling a friend of this, she said: "Don't you think if you had faith, God would cure the stricture?" and told me of a case at Berachah. I thought about it for some time, and then wrote to Mr. Simpson. One of the deaconesses answered, telling me to be sure it was God's will, then I would have a sure foundation, and gave me passages of Scripture to convince me that it was taught in the Word.

I went to see Mr. Simpson. He talked with me perhaps ten minutes, and gave me *The Gospel of Healing* to read. While I sat there I felt a strange, sweet, quiet spirit steal over me. I cannot describe it, but, praise God, it has never left me. I was in a hurry now to get home to ead the book. I had read perhaps an hour, hen I took my pencil and wrote: "Tuesday, ecember 8.—I accept the dear Lord as my hysician." I went to my room and gave myself ntirely to the Lord, as well as I knew how, and had the evidence that I was accepted and ealed. Praise the Lord! I knew it for a fact. n all the past year I have not once had to lie own from pain. I never knew it was possible o enjoy such peace and rest this side of heaven.

THE RESURRECTION: THE FIRST.

By Rev. A. C. Tris, of Howard, Kan.

The Links of a Golden Chain—Erroneous Ideas of Resurrection—It is Not Regeneration—Not a Succession of Human Types—A Literal Rising Again—The First Drama—The Doctrine it Teaches—Consistent with Other Biblical Teaching—1. The Personality of Satan—2. To Rule the World Through His Vicegerent, Antichrist—3. To be Invincible to Human Opposition—4. To be Overthrown by Christ—The Second Drama—The Resurrection Scene—Reasons for a Literal Interpretation—An Essential Resurrection—The Dominion of the Risen Saints.

THE book of the Revelation stands in close onnection with redeeming love, and with the hole history of redeeming love, shown and accomplished on earth; and is a part of that golden chain, beautifully linked together as a perfect unit, not only as a whole, but even perfect n every part, commencing with the First Adam n the Paradise, and ending its closing link with he Second Adam reigning on the restored arth. The great theme of the whole Bible is he fall and the restitution of a fallen race, and he restoration of a sin-cursed earth, to a place f glory, of which it shall be said, "Thy God eigneth."

But, lest the old Scotchwoman's criticism of er minister's discourse should apply, "He was o long laying the cloth, that I feared the diner would never be served," it is time to consider our subject in question, and to contemplate n a few remarks the *first six verses of the twentieth chapter of the Revelations.*

"And I saw . . . . and I saw . . . . This is he first resurrection. Blessed and holy is He hat hath part in the first resurrection, ... nd they shall reign with Him a thousand years."

The great question about these verses is:

What is Meant

ith the word resurrection? Some say it means egeneration; others say it means a succession of en who shall have the spirit and the virtues of ne martyrs of former ages; and yet others say means a literal "rising again," an "upstanding" (Greek) of the bodies of martyrs and saints ho did live in former times.

A cursive examination of those three different xplanations may be very profitable, and direct ur thoughts to a closer study of this grand subect under consideration, *Regeneration.* That he above quoted verses do not mean a regenertion, or a spiritual resurrection (as some would ave it), is evident to every one who, with an nbiassed mind, considers the whole scope of hose mentioned verses. Regeneration, or spiritl resurrection belongs especially to the spiritual art of a human being, and not to his material corporeal part. The text speaks of actions, d of a state to which not every converted generated person can come, or may come, amely: "*To be beheaded,* and *to reign as kings.*" cannot be called fair and just to spiritualize e word in the same verses and not the follow g words; and, indeed, we are at a loss to spirualize the words: "And I saw the souls of em that were

'Beheaded' for the Witness

Jesus, and for the word of God," and to apy them to Regeneration, or spiritual resurrecon. The very word in the text "*pelekizo,*" anslated "beheaded," means in the original nguage, "To cut away with an axe," and is und only *once* in the Bible, signifying the very strument by which the martyrs were beheaded, en the corporeal execution took place; there not one precedent in the whole word of God hich gives us the slightest direction to take at word for Regeneration.

Another obstacle in the time and the extent of the period of which here is spoken. Regeneration has existed longer than a thousand years. It commenced with Adam, and will not end until the last elect shall be gathered into the fold of God.

It is also a fact that Scripture never uses the word "upstanding, rising again," for regeneration, or spiritual resurrection; it always is used for resurrection of the body, the whole man.

It is not a succession of men. We maintain also that the above mentioned verses cannot mean, and do not mean, "a succession of men who will exhibit the spirit and the virtues of the martyrs of former ages." To spiritualize or allegorize those verses must lead us to a labyrinth from which not one can extricate himself. A succession of men and of living generations can never constitute a body of men who were beheaded in former times, and can never represent a multitude

Who Shall Live and Reign

with Christ a thousand years, a period not allowable to any man in this Dispensation. The Hierarchy of Rome, and the Popes, as representatives of Christ, do not claim to reign, and to rule *with* Christ; they only pretend to govern the Church *for* Christ.

The Greek preposition "*meta,*" used in the text in a genitive case, is very strong, and signifies that the object or objects spoken of are in the midst of them (Liddell and Scotts); thus to live and to reign as kings with Christ must mean that Christ is there, and the theory of spiritualizing the text cannot be sustained.

Then, it would not be fair to say that the first verses of the chapter speak of a personal Satan, and that they ought to be understood literally, and to claim that the following verses should be spiritualized. We advocate fair dealing. If the first verses are literal, then the following verses must be literal; and if the last verses must be spiritualized, the consequence must follow that the whole chapter must be spiritualized, and the first verses must mean, also, a succession of evil men, who are incarcerated; and a personal Devil, and a resurrection, or any resurrection, must become a myth—a fictitious or fanciful narrative.

To argue that this vision means: "a succession of men who will exhibit the spirit and the virtues of the martyrs of the former ages" is

Inconsistent With The Period

of the Millennial age. In that period not any person shall be able to exhibit the spirit and the virtues of martyrs whose heads were severed with an axe, and who had suffered an ignominious death when Antichrist did reign, for the very reason that "persecution" never more will raise its head in the Millennial period. "The beast and its image, and the false prophet, were already cast alive into the lake of fire burning with brimstone" (Rev. 19:20), and "Satan was already bound for a thousand years" (Rev. 20:2); also Antichrist shall have no more existence in the Millennial period (II Thes. 2:8): "And then shall that lawless one be revealed, whom the Lord shall consume with the spirit of His mouth, and shall destroy with the brightness of His coming."

In conclusion, on this head, we say: that it makes the Scripture of none effect—yea, ridiculous—to assign to a body or generation of men called the successors of martyrs, and to place them on thrones, such an honor as to make them the kings of the Millennium, and that without having experienced any of the sufferings of those former saints. It is to give a reward inconsistent with the very peculiar character of the word of the Bible. (Matt. 19:28; Acts. 14:22; 2 Thes. 1:5; Rom. 8:17; 2 Tim. 2:12; Rev. 7:14, and Rev. 17:6.)

Literal Rising Again.

Others say, How readest thou? and in accordance with the words of the text, they believe and advocate a literal rising again, a corporeal Resurrection, an upstanding of the martyrs and of the witnesses of Christ, called in the Greek: "The upstanding, the First."

The first of these wondrous dramas is set before us in the first three verses of the eleventh vision of the Revelation, commencing with: "And I saw" . . . . and ending with: "and after that he must be loosed a little season." Teach every lover of truth the following doctrine, found in almost every part of the Bible:

1. That there is a personal devil, the great adversary to Christ and His kingdom, the old serpent known to Eve, called the prince of darkness and the god of this world.

2. That this personal devil is also called: "The great red dragon, who not only deceiveth the whole world" (Rev. 12:1-9), but who with his deputy, "Antichrist," shall be the ruler of

The Roman Earth,

"having seven heads, and ten horns, and seven crowns upon his head, and his tail drew the third part of the stars."

3. That the combined force of Satan, and of the nations, and of the kings of the nations (Ps. 2:1) shall be so great that not any human power or authority (*neither all the churches combined,* shall have any power to resist and to check the encroachments of Satan and of the Antichrist. No person on earth shall be found able and willing to make war with Satan. Only One shall undertake that stupendous work, namely, the Lord Jesus Christ, who is the Lion of the tribe of Judah; the Root of David (Rev. 5:1-10); He shall accomplish that work. (II Thess. 2:8-10; Rom. 16:20.)

4. That it pictures out the manner of Christ's action in subduing the power of the Dragon—not gradually, not by gentle means and persuasion, not by education or reformatory enactments, but with the arm of Omnipotence, as Jehovah Jesus. It is mentioned in the text: That the key of the abyss is in His hand or (in the hand of the Angel), that a great chain "*alusis*" is *over* his hand, signifying in the Greek language "a power which cannot be unloosed" (except by proper authority), and also the place of confinement is pointed out as a locality—namely, "the abyss," the bottomless pit—a place at all times feared as a punishment by the fallen spirits (Luke 8:31); and that place will be safely kept, as we read of the grave of Jesus (Matt. 27:66), a seal was put upon it. The New Verson has it: "and sealed it over Him," so the Dutch translation (1636) and Dr. R. Young; and not, that a seal was put upon Satan: "and set a seal upon him," as it is in the Authorized Version. That abyss shall be guarded in such a way that Satan and his angels shall have no opportunity "to deceive the nations till the thousand years shall be ended. Mark, also, that the abyss and the lake of fire are *two* different places, both mentioned in this chapter, verses 3 and 10. By this act of Christ

The Earth Will be Restored

to her first primitive state of being, freed from the rule of Satan, and of evil spirits, and this will be the first step in the great "restitution of all things." (Acts 3:21.) The first Paradise lost is here united with Paradise regained and restored; "The seed of the woman will bruise the head of the old serpent" (Gen. 3:15), and shut his prison's door (Rev. 20:3) upon that deceiver of the nations, and thereby a reign of peace shall be inaugurated, which was only known in the garden of Eden before man transgressed against His Maker. (Gen. 1:28; Gen. 49:10; Ps. 72:2; Isa. 11:6-8.)

(*To be Concluded next week.*)

CHRISTIAN HERALD AND SIGNS OF OUR TIMES.
OFFICE, 63 BIBLE HOUSE, NEW YORK.

TERMS AND INSTRUCTIONS.

Published Weekly. Subscription price in the United States, Canada, and Mexico, $1.50 a year; $1 eight months; 75 cents six months; sent two months on trial for 25 cents, postage free; in Europe and in all countries in the Postal Union, 50 cents extra postage; subscriptions always payable in advance. Single copies, price 3 cents. Any newsdealer will furnish the paper weekly when ordered.

New Subscriptions can commence at any time. When no date is mentioned, we begin it with the issue of the week in which the subscription is received.

Remittances by Mail should be by Post-office money order, bank cheque, draft, or express money order, whenever possible, and should always be made payable to THE CHRISTIAN HERALD. Letters containing money sent in this way need not be registered, as when lost, duplicates can always be obtained.

If a Postal Note or currency is sent, it should always be in a registered letter. Letters can be registered at any office. Subscribers sending money of this kind, and not registering, do it at their own risk.

Change of Address. Name of Post-office and State, of both old and new address, should always be given in case of removal, as without the previous address it is impossible to find the name on our list.

CURRENT EVENTS.

The Result of the Presidential Election has been the all-absorbing topic of discussion during the week throughout the land. The decisive Republican victory has not occasioned much surprise to those who watched the campaign in the doubtful States, especially in New York. There the Republicans were united and enthusiastic, while the Democrats were quarrelling among themselves over local issues, and were discouraged by the apprehensions of manufacturers and merchants as to the effect of the reductions in the tariff which might be expected to result from Democratic success. It is a significant fact, which justifies the opinion expressed in these columns on October 25, that New York State gave a plurality of about 18,000 to the *Democratic* candidate for Governor, and a plurality of about 13,000 to the *Republican* candidate for President. This may not have been the result of "deals," as the tariff would affect one vote and not the other, but the difference is so enormous that it is impossible altogether to avoid suspicion. The corrected returns from all the States have not been issued at the time of writing, but it would appear that General Harrison carried the following States: California, Colorado, Illinois, Indiana, Iowa, Kansas, Maine, Massachusetts, Michigan, Minnesota, Nebraska, Nevada, New Hampshire, New York, Ohio, Oregon, Pennsylvania, Rhode Island, Vermont, West Virginia, and Wisconsin. If later returns confirm these figures General Harrison will have 239 votes in the Electoral College against 162 for Mr. Cleveland. Democrats naturally feel sore over this defeat, but are generally taking it in good part, acquiescing in an unequivocal verdict which cannot be disputed. New York, though a Democratic city, has her peculiar consolation in the change, which the election has effected. in the City Hall. Mayor Hewitt, who accepted a renomination although he was aware that his candidacy would divide his party and might imperil the National ticket, was, like Samson, himself overwhelmed in the ruin he probably helped to bring about. New York has therefore the prospect of wishing him, in a few weeks, a long and glad good-bye.

The Change in the Balance of Parties in the House of the Fifty-first Congress, which, according to present returns, the election has effected, will have results as momentous to the country as the change in the Presidency. Various estimates have been made of the relative strength of the parties in the House, but the most moderate concedes a working majority to the Republicans, which the Committee on Elections will probably increase. According to this report, which may be accepted as the least sanguine, the Republicans have gained 23 Congressmen, and lost 11, and there will therefore be 166 Republicans in the House, and 159 Democrats. Local influences may have had something to do with the result in a few cases, but substantially it must be accepted as the answer of the people to the tariff question. The Republican principle of a protective tariff for protection's sake is evidently approved, with all it involves. The Republican majority in the Senate will also be increased by two if not three. In Ohio and West Virginia the party is now strong enough in the Legislature to elect a Republican Senator in place of the Democrat, whose term expires next March, and there is a possibility of Delaware doing so too. Thus, if the relations of General Harrison with his party are harmonious, his nominations, and any treaties he may negotiate will receive favorable consideration.

The Prohibition Vote, Though Largely a matter of estimate at present, was undoubtedly a large increase on that of 1884. The *Voice* claims that more than double the number of votes were cast for Fisk and Brooks than were cast for St. John and Daniel. The only losses it admits are in Massachusetts and Vermont. It says: "The gains are heavy, almost without exception, and in some cases are unexpectedly heavy. Thus California increases her St. John vote from 2,960 to 12,000 or 15,000; Minnesota, from 4,684 to 18,000 or 20,000; Indiana, from 3,028 to an aggregate variously estimated at from 12,000 to 18,000; New York increased her vote from 24,000 to about 30,000. The total vote of all the States for the Prohibition candidates is expected to aggregate nearly 350,000." The vote for St. John in 1884 was 150,626. Doubtless the gains would have been far larger had there been any prospect of victory, but in so close a contest between the old parties, many voters, whose sympathies are with Prohibition, were reluctant to throw away their votes.

An Interesting Ceremony Took Place at Augusta, Ga., on November 8. The great national exposition which has been arranged with so much labor and energy was opened by Governor Gordon. The exposition building has a floor space of seven acres, and is 900 feet long by 100 feet wide, with three cross sections respectively 200, 300, and 400 feet deep. Besides space for exhibits it accommodates 15,000 visitors, and has over two miles of frontage in aisles. The Hon. James C. Black, of Augusta, delivered the inaugural oration. In the course of it he called attention to the rapid progress the State has made during recent years. He said the property of Georgia had increased in the last ten years $103,000,000, exclusive of railroad property, while railroad property had increased $20,000,000, or 212 per cent. The property owned by colored people, he said, was in round numbers $10,000,000, an increase in ten years of eighty-five per cent. In the factories the aggregate of wages paid annually now amounted to $1,000,000. At the conclusion of the inaugural ceremonies the wife of the Governor pressed an electric button, which set all the machinery in the building in motion.

Several Important Political Speeches were made in Birmingham, England, by Mr. Gladstone last week. His reception in that town was remarkable for its enthusiasm. Its political leaders are John Bright and Joseph Chamberlain, who, from being Mr. Gladstone's warmest friends, have become his most relentless foes. The people of the town, however, appear still true to him. In the course of one of his speeches Mr. Gladstone said that all efforts to solve *the fisheries question* with the United States had been egregious failures. The Liberals did not wish to increase the difficulty of settling the matter in dispute, but they were desirous that, by *a judicious choice of persons* [evidently referring to the blunder made by the English Government in sending Mr. Chamberlain here to negotiate], and the suggestion of measures, the question should be settled in a manner tending to draw both countries into closer relations. The Sackville incident, he said, was extremely unfortunate. It had resulted in the infliction of a serious slight and disparagement upon England. He hoped the matter was susceptible of satisfactory explanation. The incident ought to serve to moderate a little the spirit of vaunting and bragging which is in vogue among Tories.

The Czar of Russia Has Had a Narrow escape from death by a railroad accident. While travelling in southern Russia, his chief-of-staff ordered the engineer of the Czar's train to increase speed. The man protested, and pointed out the danger of high speed on a track so faulty. The chief insisted, and shortly afterward the whole train left the track and was cast in ruins. The Czar and Czarina were much shaken and slightly bruised. The flooring of the saloon carriage occupied by the Czar and Czarina collapsed, and the occupants were thrown upon the track. The Grand Duchess Olga and the Grand Duke Michael were in the next car, and were thrown upon the track and covered with débris. They were rescued unhurt. As the disaster occurred, a servant was handing the Czar a cup of coffee. The Czar's dog, which was standing near his master, was killed. Nearly every member of the imperial suite received contusions. Twenty-one attendants were killed and thirty-seven were seriously injured.

United European Action Against the African slave trade has been arranged. On November 6 Lord Saulsbury informed the House of Lords that Germany had invited England to co-operate with her in the work of preventing more effectively the exportation of slaves from and the importation of arms to East Africa. England had promised to aid in the work, as it was in accordance with her traditional policy. The proposed measures would be effected by a naval and not a military force. France had also agreed to render assistance, and would send a man-of-war to co-operate with the German and English vessels in a blockade against slave and arm-bearing vessels. The vessels forming the blockade would have the right to search vessels under any flag.

The Evidence in the Parnell Investigation last week, was directed to proving that outrage and lawless acts uniformly followed the organization in any part of Ireland of a branch of the League. Several witnesses testified that Land League hare hunts were organized over land belonging to persons who offended the League for the purpose of damaging their crops. Police testimony from Loughrea, Athenry, and other places in Ireland showed that prior to the founding of League branches in those districts they were comparatively free from crime, and that after League meetings there was much turbulence, often culminating in outrages. It was testified that five murders quickly followed the founding of the Loughrea branch, including the killing of Sergeant Linton, who, witnesses averred, was shot for giving evidence.

General Boulanger's Power and Popularity in France is beginning to seriously disturb the equanimity of both journalists and statesmen. A few extracts from the daily journals, all published on the same day, were cabled here last week, which show how general is the apprehension aroused as to his influence on the future of France. The *Débats* says: "We are sorry for it, but we are obliged to record that Boulanger is now the man of the future"; while the *Temps* adds, "Boulanger now completely overshadows the Comte de Paris and Prince Victor." The *Figaro* says Boulangism is the new epidemic which will eventually kill the Republic. M. Ranc, in the *Matin*, says "Boulanger day by day steadily gains power. Everything turns to his advantage." Other remarks of similar tenor were made by other journals, all of which implied that the General is recognized by all parties as the enemy of the Republic, and the one man likely to overthrow it.

The Serial Story by the Rev. L. S. Keyser, of Elkhart, Ind., published in this journal two years ago, is being published in book form by Messrs. Anson D. F. Randolph & Company, of New York. Its title will be, "The Only Way Out," and its price one dollar. During its publication in this journal in serial form, it was greatly blessed. We have learned with sincere thankfulness that several students in colleges, who were either pronounced sceptics, or were drifting into scepticism, were brought, by the blessing of God on that story, to the feet of Christ, and we earnestly pray that a still greater blessing may attend its publication in book form. Mr. Keyser has had much experience in dealing with scepticism, and in his story he portrayed the difficulties of sceptics with rare skill, and pointed the doubter to the sure way out of the slough with Christian fidelity. The story, as it appeared in these columns, has been carefully revised, and, we understand, has been improved in many respects. Any reader having friends afflicted with doubt, may do them service by placing a copy in their hands.

The Death of the Rev. Dr. Van Meter, in Rome, Italy, is announced. Dr. Van Meter was well known in New York. During his recent visit to this city, he called several times at the office of this journal and described to the editor his plans for an extension of his work in Italy. He was then looking well and strong, and seemed likely to spend many more years in the Master's service. Dr. Van Meter was a native of Kentucky and was sixty-eight years of age. He was one of the organizers of the Howard Mission in New York for the care of destitute children, and superintended it for twenty-five years. He then commenced evangelistic work in Italy, making Rome his headquarters. He set up a printing-press in an old building once used by the Inquisition for torturing Christians, and printed the first copies of the New Testament in Italian. In recent years, he has been doing evangelistic work, and has been largely engaged in the distribution of Bibles through Italy.

A Novel Investigation Brought a Young man from Montana to New York last week. He presented himself on November 5 at Police Headquarters, and said he wanted help to *discover his own identity*, and was prepared to pay for it. He said that from the best he knew he was found a waif, in the streets of New York, twenty-three years ago, and was cared for on Randall's Island for two years. Then, at the age of five, or thereabouts, he was sent West. He arrived in his new home labelled Dexter Roosevelt. He prospered as he grew up, and is now a boss truckman, well off, and with a home of his own. But he is not happy unless he finds out who he is, or at least how he came by the name of Roosevelt. He suspects that somehow he is connected with the old Knickerbocker family of that name. The police records gave him no information. He went to the Department of Charities and Correction to continue his search. His desire is very natural, but a still more momentous question concerns him. His success in his present investigation can but promote his temporal interests, while his condition for all eternity depends upon the question whether his name is inscribed in the Book of Life. (Rev. 20 : 15.)

Every Port Closed Against Storm-Beaten voyagers is a melancholy report that comes from Jacksonville, Fla. It states that eight persons, among whom were two small children, decided, during the height of the yellow fever epidemic, to fly from the city rather than any longer to risk seizure by the dread scourge. One of the number owned property on Lake Worth, and that place was fixed upon as the destination. Together they built two boats, launched and loaded them in Hogan's Creek, at the Adams Street bridge, and started, against the advice of their friends, willing to face the unknown dangers of an ocean voyage in two small boats, whose seaworthiness had never been tried. After their departure from Jacksonville, they were first heard of as trying to land at Mayport. This they were not permitted to do, so they crossed the bar and went safely to Lake Worth; but by the time they had reached that place a rigid quarantine had been established, and they turned back after trying in vain to make a landing. They were compelled to return, and again made the perilous voyage in safety back to St. Augustine. From there, after being driven away, they sailed for Fernandina, where they tried to land, but with no better success. That night a terrific storm arose, and about midnight it was blowing almost a hurricane. The whole party was beyond a doubt drowned, as they have not been heard from since. Sometimes sinners awakened to the danger of continuing in sin meet with an analogous experience in trying to save themselves. Those only find safety who abandon all hope of self-deliverance and accept the refuge provided in Christ. (Hos. 13 : 4.)

A Young Lady's Repudiation of Hypocritical pretense is described in some recently published reminiscences of President Lincoln. The lady, a beautiful daughter of Virginia, was anxious to visit her brother, a Confederate soldier, then a prisoner in the North. She had some influence with a powerful official near the President, and through him was promised an interview with Mr. Lincoln. "But you must be very careful," said her friend, who knew her impulsive disposition, "not to let a word escape you which can betray your Southern sympathies." They were ushered into the presence of Mr. Lincoln, and the object for which they had come was stated. The tall, grave man bent down to the little maiden, and, looking searchingly into her face, said: "You are loyal, of course?" Her bright eyes flashed. She hesitated a moment, and then, with a face eloquent with emotion and honest as his own, she replied: "Yes, loyal to the heart's core—to Virginia!" Mr. Lincoln kept his intent gaze upon her for a moment longer, and then went to his desk, wrote a line or two, and handed her the paper. With a bow, the interview terminated. Once outside, the extreme vexation of her friend found vent in reproachful words. "Now you have done it!" he said. "Didn't I warn you to be very careful? You have only yourself to blame." Miss N. made no reply, but opened the paper. It contained these words: "Pass Miss N.; she is an honest girl and can be trusted." Unhappily, the followers of Christ are not always so brave in acknowledging their allegiance when some worldly advantage is to be gained by concealing it. They too often forget the consequence of cowardice. (Mark 8 : 38.)

A Marriage at a Funeral Took Place in Brooklyn, N. Y., last week. The friends of a well-known business man, recently deceased, were present in large numbers at his house on the day of his funeral to testify their respect for their dead friend. The officiating clergyman was called out of the room before the commencement of the funeral service and remained some time in consultation with the family. When he returned he was accompanied by the youngest daughter of the dead merchant and her lover. They took their places beside the coffin, and the minister joined them in marriage. "This," he said, "is done in compliance with the wishes of the deceased." Inquiry of the family elicited the explanation of the strange ceremony. It appears that the father had set his heart on the marriage, but his daughter continually deferred it. This was not because she did not love her suitor, but from reluctance to enter the marriage state until she was older. Her father, however extracted from her a solemn promise that she would marry the young man, and that the marriage should surely take place in his presence. With the promise he contented himself, reminding his daughter from time to time that if he should be taken ill the wedding must be hurried on, that she might fulfil her promise. But he was seized with apoplexy and died in a few minutes. Then the daughter reproached herself for her procrastination, and could keep her promise, only in the letter, by being married in the room where her father's dead body lay. She grieved that her father had missed the joy the fulfilment of his wish would have afforded him. How often is it that the children of godly parents mourn, in entering into union with Christ, that they have postponed the union too long to gladden the hearts of those who had so long prayed and labored for it! (Prov. 23: 24, 25.)

The Detection of a Murderer in Colorado furnishes clear proof that punishment alone has no reformatory influence on some natures. A convict was recently released from the penitentiary under a law passed by the Colorado legislature, making twenty-five years the maximum limit of imprisonment. The convict had been sentenced to a life term for murder and robbery. No sooner did he regain his liberty under the new law than he went to Pueblo and induced a well-to-do citizen to start with him in a wagon for a mining camp in the mountains. The convict was found a day or two later without his companion, and the police, suspecting that he had stolen the team, arrested him. On examining the wagon, blood stains were found upon it, and the same stains were upon an axe which was found under the seat. Search was made along the road, and the mutilated body of the convict's companion was found in Beaver Creek. In the convict's pocket was the dead man's pocket-book with $238 in it. The crime was almost the exact counterpart of the one for which the convict had suffered his long term of imprisonment. It is so with all forms of sin. Punishment does not eradicate evil from the heart. The only hope for the sinner and for the sinful world is in the remedy God offers through Christ in a new heart changed by the Holy Spirit. (Ezek. 11: 19, 20.)

BRIEF NOTES.

Mrs. Mary Lowe Dickenson, the founder of the order of "The King's Daughters," has been elected to a chair in the University at Denver, and will accept it.

Mr. George Dorsey, of Frankfort, Ky., has been conducting evangelistic services at Stanford, Ky., which have been followed by a widespread awakening.

Cedar Rapids is the first city in Iowa to erect a Y. M. C. A. building. Its corner-stone was laid recently with appropriate ceremonies by Rev. James Marshall, D. D.

The donations to the yellow fever sufferers in Florida to November 1 amount to $309,577.99, and there is a net balance of $101,721.82. About $20,000 is needed.

Nine lady missionaries sailed from New York for India on November 4. They went out under the auspices of the Women's Missionary Society of the M. E. Church.

Dr. Robert Young, author of the *Analytical Bible Concordance*, and numerous other Biblical and Oriental works, died October 4, at his residence in Edinburgh, Scotland, after a protracted and painful illness.

Rev. Wesley Smith, of Sharpsburg, died on October 28, at Pittsburg, at the age of eighty-three years. He was born in Ireland, and was the son of a Methodist minister who was licensed to preach by John Wesley.

The seventh annual Convention of the Woman's Home Missionary Society has just been held in Boston, with a large attendance of delegates from all parts of the country. Mrs. R. B. Hayes, of Fremont, Ohio, presided.

Major Whittle's evangelistic tour in Ireland is being much blessed. He is holding services in churches, factories, and in the Y. M. C. A. halls. Calls are being pressed upon him from the North and South of Ireland.

The number of students in Princeton Theological Seminary is one hundred and seventy-five, a decided increase on last year. Of these, fifty-five are in the senior class. Forty-three Princeton students attended the Inter-Seminary Missionary Alliance in Boston, and many will give themselves to Foreign Mission work.

Dr. G. W. Smith, President of Trinity College, Hartford, was unanimously elected Assistant-Bishop of the Protestant-Episcopal Diocese of Ohio on November 1, at a special convention held in St. Paul's Church, Cleveland. The election was rendered necessary by the continued illness of Bishop Bedell, who is in Europe.

A remarkable revival work in Wisconsin has grown out of the labors of Mr. Weiss, a student of Yale College, who began holding services at Jackson, Davis Corners, and Big Spring. The continued interest has been so strongly manifested that Mr. Weiss has been constrained to remain, and will not resume his studies for a year.

By the will of the late John Guy Vassar, Vassar College will receive $130,000; the Vassar Brothers' Hospital, $25,000 and a maintenance-fund of $200,000; the Home for Aged Men, $70,000 and valuable real estate; a fund is established for the building of an orphan asylum in Poughkeepsie, and many bequests are made to churches and benevolent and religious institutions.

IRON CHARIOTS.

A New Sermon by Pastor C. H. Spurgeon.

"For thou shalt drive out the Canaanites, though they have irou chariots, and though they be strong." Joshua 17; 18.

Canaan Not a Perfect Type of Heaven—The Canaanites of Sin—I. Enemies to be Rooted Out—Sin Always to be Treated as an Enemy—The Difference Between Sheep and Swine—Christ Cannot be Had While Sin is Retained—Even One Sin Enslaves—The Power of the Chariots Exaggerated—Some Sins Hard to Kill—Constitutional Proclivities—II. Sin Can be Driven Out—Proved by Past Conquests—By the Success of Others—III. The Royal Word.

WHEN the children of Israel had come to Canaan, and by God's good care had entered into the land that flowed with milk and honey, they were not immediately at rest, for the Canaanites were there—there in possession, there in strong cities, which seemed to be walled up to heaven; and they had to drive out these Canaanites before they could possibly possess the country. In fact, this was the reason why they were sent there. The Canaanites had been outlawed of God. They had been guilty of such horrible offences that He had adjudged their race to destruction. It was necessary for the purity of the world that ancient races which had become so horribly depraved should be removed from it, and the Israelites were brought to the land, as the Lord's executioners, to smite the Canaanites and exterminate them.

You will see, then, dear friends, that Canaan is hardly a full type of heaven. It may be used so in a modified sense; but it is a far better emblem of that state and condition of soul in which a man is found when he has become a believer, and, by believing, has entered into rest, but not into an absolutely perfect deliverance from sin. He has come to take possession of the covenant heritage, but finds

The Canaanites of Sin

and evil still in the land, both in the form of original sin within, and of temptation from without. Before he can fully enjoy his privileges he must drive out his sins. No doubt many young Christians think that when they are converted the warfare is all over. No, the battle has just begun. You have not come to the winning-post: you have only come to the starting-point. You have entered upon the land in which you will have to fight and wrestle and weep and pray until you get the victory. That victory will be yours, but you will have to agonize to obtain it. He that has brought you into this condition will not fail you nor forsake you; but, at the same time, not without strong contentions and earnest strivings will you be able to win your inheritance. Be not deluded with the idea that you may sit down at your ease, for the very reverse will happen to the true heir of heaven.

Our text is a war-speech to the tribes of Manasseh and Ephraim. Joshua said to them; "Thou art a great people, and hast great power: thou shalt not have one lot only." But he told them that, while he gave them two lots, they would have to drive out those who were then in possession: "Thou shalt drive out the Canaanites, though they have iron chariots, and though they be strong." May the Holy Spirit inspirit us for our life struggles by the meditation!

I. Our first reflection shall be—

We Must Drive Them Out.

It is a command from God—"Thou shalt drive out the Canaanites." Every sin has to be slaughtered. Not a single sin is to be tolerated. Off with their heads! Drive the sword into their hearts! They are all to die. Not one of them may be spared. The whole race is to be exterminated, and so buried that not a bone of them can be found. Here is a labor worthy of all the valor of faith and the power of love.

They must all be driven out, for *every sin is our enemy*. I hope we have no enemies in this world among our fellow-men. It takes two to make a quarrel; and if we will not contend, there can be no contention. We are neither to give nor to take offence; but if it be possible, as much as lieth in us we are to live peaceably with all men. I trust that we have forgiven everybody who has ever harmed us, and would desire to be forgiven by all against whom we have done anything wrong. But every sin, every evil, of every shape is our true enemy, against which we are to wrestle to the bitter end. You cannot say to any sin, "You may dwell in my heart and be my friend." It cannot be your friend: evil is our natural and necessary enemy, and we must treat it as such. One of

The Marks of a Child of God

is that, although he sins, he does not love sin. He may fall into sin, but he is like a sheep which, if it tumbles into the mud, is quickly up again, for it hates the mire. The sow wallows where the sheep is distressed. Now, we are not the swine that love the slough, though we are as sheep that sometimes slip with their feet. Would to God that we never did slip! While you hate sin, sin hates you. It will do you all the hurt it can; it will never be satisfied with the mischief that it has wrought you. It will try to lead you farther and farther into danger, so as to bring you down to hell. Sin would utterly destroy you if it could, and it certainly could and would if the grace of God did not prevent. Proclaim, then,

A Ceaseless Warfare

against all sin. So long as there remains sin in our heart, or in our life, or in the world, it is to be fought against to death.

Again, we should contend against all these Canaanites, and drive them out, for sin is our Lord's most cruel enemy. Jesus abhors all evil, and evil in every shape persecuted Him. All sorts of sins He bore in His own body on the tree. From our sins, all of which were laid upon Him, came the lashings of His back. From our sins came the bloody sweat that covered Him from head to foot. From our sins came the crown of thorns, the nails, the spear, the vinegar and gall, and the dread death of agony. Sin—oh, how our Lord loathes it! In putting it away from us He drank of that cup from which, for a moment, He started, saying, "If it be possible, let this cup pass from me!"

Remember, brethren, we cannot have Christ and have any one sin reigning in our hearts. We come to Christ as sinners, but when we receive Christ we hear Him say, "Sin shall not have dominion over you." Sin may look into our nature, as it does, with

Its Tempting Witcheries.

Sin may ride through our nature, as it does, trampling down all that is good. Sin may lurk in our nature, as it does, ready to plot against the King of kings; but it cannot reign in our nature, for it has come under another sovereignty: Christ is on the throne. Thou mayest have Christ and quit thy sin; but thou canst not not have Christ and hug thy sin. Christ shall help thee to slay thy sin; but if thou sayest, "No, but I will indulge this evil," even though thou addest, "Is it not a little one?" thou wilt perish in thine iniquity.

Suppose that one of our missionaries were to come back from India, and say, "I have achieved a great marvel among the natives. All through one of the districts I went and preached, and wrought wonders. I found them worshipping gods made of the mud of the Ganges. I showed them the folly of it, and they broke their mud-gods to pieces. And some of them had wooden gods, and I induced them to burn them all. But there were some beautiful gods—gods of marble, and of gold, and of silver, and I had not the heart to meddle with them, for they were so artistic, so valuable, and so venerable. Why, one of them had eyes of diamond; and another had about his wrist a bracelet of rubies." Alas, Mr. Missionary! we see no reason for congratulation. So you left the people

Worshipping Precious Gods,

did you? What good have you done? None whatever. It is evidently as evil an idolatry to worship a god of gold as it is to worship a god of mud. Now, if we come among you, and so deal with vice and improve the education and morals of the masses that we elevate the people, what have we done if we end there? We have taken away one set of sins, but have left others. Sins of all sorts must go when grace takes possession of the soul. Bring out the golden calf! This costly idol must be ground to powder, and strewed upon the water. The golden calf is as detestable before the Lord as the most beggarly gods of wood. One form of enmity to God is as obnoxious to His law as another.

Sin in Satin

is as great a rebel as sin in rags. You may wash sin in eau-de-cologne, but it smells no sweeter.

Remember, also, dear friends, that a man cannot be free from sin if he is the servant of even one sin. Here is a man who has a long chain on his leg—a chain of fifty links. Now, suppose that I come in as a liberator, and take away forty-nine links, but still leave the iron fastened to the pillar, and his leg in the one link which is within the iron ring, what benefit have I brought him? How much good have I done? The man is still a captive. As long as a man is held a captive by a single vice, no matter how small it is, he is still in bondage to iniquity. If any one sin binds him, masters him, he is not the Lord's free man. He is still a slave in the worst form of slavery: he is under the dominion of evil. Hence, you see, I spoke not too largely when I said, "Down with all!"

There are certain sins that, when we begin to war with them, we very soon overcome. These Israelites, when they were up in the mountains, and in the woods, soon got at the hill-country Canaanites and destroyed them; but down in the plain, where there was plenty of room for horses and chariots, the Israelites were puzzled what to do; for some of these Canaanites had chariots of iron, which had scythes fixed to the axles, and when they drove into the ranks of an army they mowed down the people as a reaping machine cuts down the standing corn. For a while this seems to have staggered the Israelites altogether; it was a terrible business to think about, and fear exaggerated

The Power of the Chariots.

Dread made them powerless till they plucked up courage; and when they once plucked up courage, they found that these chariots were not nearly so terrible as they were supposed to be. There were ways of managing and mastering them, if Israel would but trust in God and play the man. When a man is converted by divine grace, certain sins are readily overcome: they fly away at once, never to return. I hardly recollect, after talking with thousands of converts, hearing any brother say that he found it difficult to give up swearing. I have often heard people express their wonder that though they had never for years used a single sentence without an oath, yet from the moment of their conversion no profane word ever escaped their lips. Swearing is a kind of Canaanite that is soon settled off—driven out and slain. So it is with many other forms of evil. We get our sword at their throats quickly, and by God's grace we are clean rid of all temptation to return to them. Such sins, though once powerful, are left dead on the field of battle.

Hard to Overcome.

But certain other sins are much tougher to deal with. They mean fight, and some of them seem to have as many lives as a cat. There is no killing them. When you think that you have slain them, they are up and at you again. They may be said to have chariots of iron. These sins are sometimes those which have gained their power—their chariots of iron—through *long habit*. Did you never catch yourselves with a snatch of an old song coming to your memory when you have been in prayer? When you have drawn very near to God, have you not been suddenly startled with the recollection of a filthy thing into which you once plunged? Terrible is the power of habit which has long held sway. It is not easy to uproot the oak of many years' growth. These habits make chariots of iron, into which your sins mount, and they become terrible enemies to our holy desires and fervent resolves.

Some sins get their chariots of iron from being

Congenial to Our Constitution.

ertain brethren and sisters are sadly quick-empered; and as long as ever they live, they ill have to be on their guard against growing uddenly angry, and speaking unadvisedly with eir lips. They are quick and sensitive, and is might not in itself be a serious evil; but hen sin wields that quickness and sensitive-ess, evil comes of it. How many a sincere hild of God has had to go for years groaning, with broken bones, because of the quickness f his temper! As for these constitutional sins, ou must not excuse them. I beseech you, ark what I say about this; for many are ruin-d by supposing that their constitutional faults e hardly faults at all, but unavoidable acci-ents. You must not say of any sin, "I cannot elp it." You have to help it. You must not y, "Oh, but it is natural to me!" I know that is natural—that is the very reason why you ave to be doubly on your guard against it. verything that is of nature—ay, and of your llen nature when it is at its best—has to be ut under the feet of Christ, that grace may ign over every form of evil.

Perhaps one of the things that is worst of all a Christian is that certain sins are

Supposed to be Irresistible.

t is a pernicious error. "These chariots of iron," e Israelites said, "it is of no use to try to con-end with them." So they gave up the plains the Canaanites. It is a sad calamity when a hristian person says, "I can keep straight in verything except *that*. Do not touch me there. ou must allow me a great deal of latitude in at direction. Please make large allowances r my peculiar constitution." All such plead-ng is mischievous. Listen to me, my sister. *I* ill make allowances for you; but, I beseech ou, do not make any allowance for yourself. y brother, I implore you, do not take out a cense to sin. If I make a kind excuse for you sympathy with your weakness, being a man ke yourself, it is one thing; but for you to ake an allowance for yourself will be most in-urious to your soul. You have to overcome nd destroy the sin for which you claim tolera-ion. Mark that! You must not—you dare ot—allow any sin to master you; and if you now that it does overpower you, do not there-re claim that you may indulge it, but draw an ference of the opposite sort: because it has astered you, concentrate your entire strength pon its utter destruction.

II. I now turn to the second head. I have id that we must drive them out. Secondly,

They Can be Driven Out.

do not say that we can drive them out, but I y that they can be driven out. It will be a reat miracle, but let us believe in it; for other reat wonders have been wrought. Note first at *you and I have been raised from the dead.* s it not so? "You hath he quickened, who ere dead in trespasses and sins." If a dead an has been raised, then anything can be one with the man who is now made alive.

He that could raise Lazarus from the dead, an cause his grave-clothes to be unbound, can ise him beyond his imperfections and infirmi-es, can make him perfect in every good work do His will. It can be done. The raising om the dead is the evidence that it can be done.

In the next place, you have already conquered any sins. Look at the heaps of Canaanites at you have killed. Begin at the beginning, here God began with you in the work of grace your soul; is there not a wonderful difference etween what you were then and what you are ow? Were there not sins entrenched in your ature like the Canaanites in their walled cities? ut Jericho fell flat to the ground. Hosts upon osts of unbeliefs and iniquities dwelt within our daily life, but you have driven them out. y God's grace you have resisted temptation, nd escaped from lusts, and risen above doubts. ou have hitherto overcome through the blood f the Lamb. Be strong and very courageous, r the Lord of Hosts Himself is at your side.

Have you not seen other Christians conquer? Oh, let your memory charge you now with breth-ren and sisters in whom you saw great infirmi-ties and sins at the commencement of their spir-itual career; but how they have grown! How they have vanquished inbred sin! The tears come into my eyes when I think of certain mem-bers of this church—some in heaven and some still among us. I remember what they used to be, and what they are now, and I can hardly be-lieve that they are the same persons. Fierce temper has been tamed, strong passions have been bound, black melancholy has been chased away. What God has done for them He can do for you.

Beloved, we have been talking about what can be done and what can not be done. Have we thought about it? We are

Dealing with the Almighty;

and with Him we know all things are possi-ble. I think I see the battle now going on: the enemy seems to prevail, and the timid hearts of the soldiers of the Cross sink within them. Lis-ten! You have not yet drawn upon your re-serves. Do you not know that within call there is eternal power and Godhead waiting to help you in your struggle against all evil? Call up your reserves! Intreat your great ally to send reinforcements in this hour of need. Beseech the Lord to give you more grace; and as you have received life at His hands, pray that you may receive it yet more abundantly.

III. And then we close with our third head:

They Shall be Driven Out.

They must be driven out; they can be driven out; they shall be driven out. That is a speech for a monarch. "Must" is for the king, and "shall" is for the King of kings. Well, well, we venture to say it, because we only give the echo of His sovereign tones. This is what Christ died for. He loved the church, and gave Him-self for it, that He might sanctify and cleanse it by the washing of water by the Word, that He might present it unto Himself a glorious church, not having spot or wrinkle, or any such thing; but that it should be holy, and without blemish. Christ died to save His people, not from some of their sins, but from all their sins. His precious blood cleanseth from all sin.

Brethren, this is what Christ lives for. Up in heaven He pleads for us, and "He is able to save them to the uttermost that come unto God by Him, seeing He ever liveth to make intercession for them." The desire of His heart is that we may be kept from sin. "Holy Father, keep them through thy Word." He pleads that, though Satan may desire to have them and sift them as wheat, they still may be pre-served. This is what the Holy Spirit is given for. He is not given to come into our hearts and com-fort us *in* our sins, but to deliver us from all evil, and to comfort us in Christ Jesus. He quickens, He directs, He helps, He illuminates; He does a thousand things; but, chiefly, He sanctifies us. O brothers and sisters, let us never from this time forth write out a pass for any sin to come and go in our hearts. We will have no licensed sin, no place in which evil may find a lodging. We will not have a spare bed for iniquity, nor give it house-room, even in the barn or the outhouse.

This is the very object of the gospel which we preach to you; and we have preached in vain un-less you are striving against sin. Ours is

A Holy Gospel,

and if it does not make you and me holy it has done nothing for you. If you and I are unholy, we stab religion in its vital parts and murder our profession. When we make up our minds that we will allow any sin within us, we do to that extent deny to Christ the travail of His soul. Nothing grieves the Spirit of God like unholiness; and nothing pleases Christ like seeing His disciples walking in His footsteps.

May the mighty grace of God, without which you can do nothing, help you to keep your sword out of its sheath, driving at the very heart of sin with your utmost strength, until the last sin shall lie dead at the feet of Christ, and you shall be perfectly happy because He has made you perfectly holy. There is no fear of your stop-ping here upon this sin-defiled earth if you have once reached the point of perfectness. This is a poor world for the completely sanctified. God does not leave His ripe wheat out in the fields too long; He takes the sheaves home to His barn when they are quite ready. We shall soon be with Him where He is when we are made like Him. The Lord grant it, for Jesus' sake!

[The prayers of the readers of this journal are requested for the blessing of God upon its Editors, and those whose sermons, articles or labors for Christ are printed in it; and that its circulation may be used by the Holy Spirit for the conversion of many sinners and the quickening of God's peo-ple. Dr. Talmage and Mr. Spurgeon especially request prayer every Sunday morning on behalf of their labors.]

GEMS FROM NEW BOOKS.

HEREDITY IN DRUNKENNESS.*

THE most startling problem connected with intemperance is that not only does it affect the health, morals, and intelligence of the offspring of its votaries, but they also inherit the fatal tendency, and feel a craving for the very bever-ages which have acted as poison on their sys-tem from the commencement of their being. Some instances may be given. Mr. J—— was an habitual drunkard; his wife also had a stomach complaint for which she took spirits: her med-icine was never neglected. Both died confirm-ed drunkards, and *all the children did so like-wise.* They said, "We can't help it; we inherit a strong love for rum or gin." One bound him-self by a heavy penalty, but after some months' abstinence, broke out, saying that the craving was actual torture and he could not help himself.

Mr. B—— and his wife were scarcely ever sober: the lady died early of delirium-tremens, but the husband lived long in spite of his ten-dencies. Out of a large family of children only one escaped the taint: the eldest son, an in-veterate drunkard, committed suicide: and all the others came to an untimely end. The only daughter was on one occasion brought home by the police in a state of intoxication: the shock was too great for the old man, and he did not long survive it.

Four Generations.

The history of four generations of a family, sketched by M. Morel, is instructive. It includes father, son, grandson, and greatgrandson.

1st generation: The father was an habitual drunkard, and was killed in a rum-shop brawl.

2d generation: The son inherited his father's habits, which gave rise to attacks of mania, ter-minating in paralysis and death.

3d generation: The grandson was strictly sober, but was full of hypochondriacal and imaginary fears of persecutions, &c., and had homicidal tendencies.

4th generation: The fourth in descent had very limited intelligence, and had an attack of madness when sixteen years old, terminating in stupidity nearly amounting to idiocy. With him, probably, the race becomes extinct. And thus we perceive the persistence of the taint, in the fact that a generation of absolute temper-ance will not avert the fatal issue.

All moral qualities are transmissible from par-ent to child, with this important addition: that in the case of vicious tendencies or habits the simple practice of the parent becomes the pas-sion, the mania, the all but irresistible impulse, of the child. Even when the very identical vice is not inherited, a morbid organization is the result, which shows itself in some allied morbid tendency or some serious physical lesion. These inheritances, normal or abnormal, are not al-ways immediate from the parents, or even in a direct line, but they miss one or more genera-tions, and sometimes have appeared only in

* From "The Physician's Problems," by Charles Elam, M.D., a work dealing with physiological questions from a moral standpoint, showing how sinful habits affect families and the whole community. 400 pages; price 50 cents; Published by *Lee & Shepard*, Boston, Mass., and 718 Broadway, New York.

Mrs. Benjamin Harrison, of Indiana.

Bertie Hope Hears Distressing News.

collateral branches, as an uncle or grand-uncle, &c. The reason for this is that a man does not inherit all the qualities of his father or mother: and of those which he does inherit, only some are developed, while others remain latent and are probably developed in a brother or sister. But his son may in turn inherit the same faculties, with this difference; that those which were but latent or potential in the father are fully manifested in him; and so he comes to resemble not his own father or mother so much as his uncle or aunt or some more distant relative still descended from one common stock.

The Two Coleridges,

father and son, exemplify the fact that a diminution of the power of the will is the most constant phenomenon attendant both upon drinking and opium-eating. The elder was an opium-eater, and writes of himself that not only in reference to this sensual indulgence, but in all the relations of life, his will was utterly powerless. Hartley Coleridge inherited his father's necessity for the stimulant, and with it his weakness of volition. Even when young his brother thus writes of him: "A certain infirmity of will had already shown itself. His sensibility was intense, and he had not wherewithal to control it. He could not open a letter without trembling. He shrank from mental pain; he was beyond measure impatient of constraint."

MRS. BENJAMIN HARRISON.

THE future mistress of the White House, whose portrait appears on this page, is the same age as her husband, the President-elect, having been born in 1833. She is the daughter of the Rev. William H. Scott, who was formerly a Professor at Miami University, where he had as students under him Benjamin Harrison and many other men who have since risen to distinction. Her father has ceased preaching, and now holds a position in the Pension Office.

She was married to Mr. Harrison in her teens. The couple have a son, Russell, who is a leading citizen and ranchman, residing at Bismarck, Dakota. While a notable housekeeper, Mrs. Harrison moves in the most refined society, and is a woman of attainments. She reads much, and is devoted to decorative art. For an amateur she is unusually skilled as a painter of flowers in water-colors, while her china painting would not discredit a professional artist. Her conversation is brilliant, and her hospitalities celebrated.

Mrs. Harrison has regular features, bright, dark eyes, and abundant dark hair. Her figure is short and somewhat stout. She dresses well, which means becomingly, and, of course, without being a slave to the caprices of fashion.

BERTIE HOPE'S FRIEND.

(See Illustration.)

ARE there demoniacs in our day, as there were in the days of Jesus? The question has often been asked, and many have answered without hesitation in the negative. On others, however, a painful experience has forced the opposite conclusion. Such a man was Bertie Hope, a man whose appearance was old beyond his years, his hair whitened, and his brow furrowed before middle life, with mental anguish.

At the age of nineteen, he had become infatuated with a girl of remarkable personal beauty, whom he married. Before the honeymoon was over, he discovered that he had made a fatal mistake. His wife was vain and frivolous, and, worse than all, with gigantic evil propensities. In spite of all his efforts for her good she had grown worse year by year, became a confirmed drunkard, and at last gave him cause that would justify him, under Christ's law, in obtaining a divorce. He had not availed himself of it, because, being a man singularly free from selfish impulses, he pitied his wife, and saw in the influence which his uniform kindness and tenderness had gained, even over *her* degraded nature, a power that alone stood between her and utter ruin. That knowledge decided him, and he went on living a life of sacrifice, arguing, entreating, controlling her. But what a death in life it was! The life of an eagle chained to a putrefying corpse.

Thirteen long, weary years of sorrowful burden-bearing passed. He removed to a strange city, where none of his friends could discover the misery of his lot, and lived alone with his burden, working hard for a livelihood, having abandoned the country in which he might have won money easily. The moral strength of the man was unabated, for he was supported by a strong faith in God, and by the consciousness that he was doing his duty in a manly, conscientious spirit. But how he yearned for sympathy! One word of gentle pity would have been like water on a parched land.

It was at the end of those thirteen years of withering blight that a great change came in Bertie Hope's heart. One day riding in a horse-car he was strangely impressed with a pair of singularly deep, soft, brown eyes opposite to him. Not unnaturally his experience had produced in him a dislike of feminine society. He had shunned it. But those eyes magnetized him, drew him as none had ever done before. He wondered at their strange influence, but could not explain it. After he had quitted the car they haunted him with a weird attraction, as if calling him to mutual helpfulness.

Strangely enough, a few days later, in a different part of the city, he saw those eyes again. The lady to whom they belonged was plainly but tastefully dressed, and there was about her an air of refinement perceptible to Hope's cultured taste. Accidentally he was able to render her some slight service, and she thanked him in a voice so soft and melodious that it seemed the echo of some angelic harp. In a conversation which followed, he found that her name was Helen Frost, and that she was a daily governess in a family living not far from his own home. The strange natural attraction which we feel without being able to understand, drew the two together, and they found in each other's conversation a singular charm.

One day Miss Frost, whom Hope met hurrying homeward through a pitiless rain without an umbrella, accepted the shelter he offered her. He found her much agitated. The sufferings of the yellow fever patients had touched her gentle heart, and she was trying to get permission to go South and be a nurse to them. "Ah, the brave girl!" said Hope to himself; "she is just the woman to lay down her life for others." To her he said, "There are opportunities for all of us near at hand of doing work as noble and perhaps more beneficent than in a fever hospital." A few more words were spoken between them on the help men and women might render in daily life; and then, for the first time since his burden fell upon his shoulders, Hope broke silence and told his story. He saw tears of pity rise in those wondrous eyes, and he heard her say, in that clear, soft voice of hers, "You have acted bravely, nobly; go on, the burden may be heavy, but God, who has given you strength so far, will help you to the end. Keep up a brave heart."

His voice was broken as he answered, "Thank you; I think I can *now*." As Hope returned to his desolate home that night—it was one of those terrible nights when his wife's outbreak defied even his power of control—he said, as he thought of Helen's tender words, "God in heaven bless her for her sweet compassion!" New heart, new light, had come into his life with her sympathy, and he was a stronger, more valiant ıan under his heavy urden.

The family in which Ielen Frost was emloyed soon afterward emoved to their sumner home, a few miles way, and during their bsence, by her permision, Hope rode out nd spent an hour with er. Poor fellow! havıg drunk once of the elicious draught of ympathy, his lips cravd more of it with pasionate desire. It reeved his despair, it ave him just the suport he needed to keep im true and faithful his weary duty.

His visits had been w and brief, and he as just thinking, one ay of especial woe, hat he would ride own to see her, when letter, the first he ad ever received from er, came to him hrough the mails, begıng him to come at nce. He mounted his orse without delay, nd as he approached he house in which Ielen's employer livd, he saw Helen and er young charges setıng out for their usual walk. Hope at once ismounted and walked by her side.

"I sent for you," said Helen, in a voice of eep emotion, "because I have to tell you painul news. My employer has spoken to me of our visits. He knows you by reputation, and e insists that, as you are married, your visits ompromise my character, and, in short, that hey must be discontinued, or I must leave his ervice. I cannot see that it is just, or that there s wrong in our friendship, but I know little of he world, and I presume that he judges accordıg to the rules of society. I suppose it must be rrong, though I cannot see it. At any rate, I ıust obey."

Argument, entreaty, were useless. Hope pent an hour in trying to move her resolution, ut failed. It was the consciousness of her own istress at being compromised which conquered im. How could he be such an ingrate, he sked himself, as to repay her kindness by ausing her a moment's uneasiness? The preious light which had cheered his solitude must e extinguished at the behest of the conventionlism of society, and the pure, inspiriting, eleating influence which had blessed and helped im for a few months must be given up. He ade her good-bye, and turned back to plod his eary way through the arid desert of his life, a oubly discouraged man, his new-found joy torn rom his soul by the mandate of a society which new nothing of his sorrow nor of his need.

MONTGOMERY ST., SAN FRANCISCO.

(See Illustration.)

Montgomery Street, San Francisco, Cal.

THE sketch on this page represents the street which has been called the Broadway of San Francisco. It has not the width nor the imposıng buildings of New York's famous thoroughare, but when the visitor passing through it emembers that in 1840 the whole city had not a population of more than five hundred, and was in fact a mere fishing village, he is surprised o find it has become so fine a place as it is. The city is situated on the northern end of a peninsula thirty miles long and about six wide. It slopes toward the east, facing the bay, which s from thirty to forty miles long, and from seven o twelve miles wide. The bay is entered from the Pacific by the Golden Gate, a strait five miles long and a mile wide. Lofty hills line the northern shore of the strait, and when a vessel emerges from this gate she enters one of the most beautiful bays in the world, affording safe anchorage for ships of any size.

The present population of the city is about a quarter of a million, and Oakland, its suburb, itself a beautiful city on the other side of the bay, has a population of 35,000 more.

THE EPOCHS OF A LIFE.

A NEW SERIAL STORY.

By Rev. L. S. Keyser.

(Continued from page 719.)

The Dawn.

ONE day Hadley received a note from Hanson inviting him to accompany him in several pastoral calls on the following Saturday afternoon. "I believe" the letter said, "that you, as a sincere inquirer after truth, may on these visits receive help in your quest, of a practical kind that you could not get in any other way."

Hadley willingly accepted, and on the appointed day actually found himself in the position which but a few months ago would have seemed to him impossibly grotesque, of going from house to house with a Christian minister.

When Hadley found that Mr. Hanson was directing his steps toward the poorest district of the city, he opined that their visits would be largely of a charitable nature, as he was aware that the season was an exceptionally trying one, and they were going to the localities where the inhabitants were of the class who were most liable to suffer by the prevalent distress.

"I should think," he said, "that the company of a millionaire would be useful to you in such a district as this. The families here must be more in need of physical than spiritual help."

"I do not know that," said Hanson; "my vocation is the spiritual. I have faith in the efficacy of the remedies I administer in all cases. Of course I am aware of the good that money can do, but I never give it. I take note of cases of genuine distress, and I bring them to the notice of certain persons who trust me, and are liberal givers. But they give personally to those I recommend. The money never passes through my hands. People know the remedy I dispense, and they look for no other. I do not deny that a part of my income goes in charity, but others apply it for me, and they are careful not to disclose me as the giver."

Their first visit was to an uncarpeted rear room, in an upper story of a crowded tenement house. The scarcity of furniture and the presence of a bed in the room showed that it was the sole domicile of the whole family, of mother and father and two children. A boy of tender years lay dangerously ill on the bed, and Hadley, looking at the wan face, was convinced that there was little if any hope of his recovery. The bright welcome his companion received showed him that Hanson was no stranger there. His words of gentle sympathy and earnest prayer had a manifest effect on the little sufferer and the anxious family; and as the two visitors quitted the room Hadley saw that, badly as money might be needed there, no sum could have given the comfort and joy that Hanson's visit had imparted.

From house to house they went, Hanson leaving everywhere behind him a higher realization of God's love, a more cheerful patience under affliction, and a stronger fa.th in God's providential care. The teaching he gave—if such words of friendly, delicate sympathy and direction as he spoke could be called teaching—was varied according to the nature of the person whom he visited, and to the peculiar circumstances of the trial. He gave close attention to the story imparted to him, and then, in a few earnest words, or by a brief prayer, turned the attention of the troubled one to God as the Source of genuine help and guidance. The end was always the same, though the paths to it varied.

At last Mr. Hanson said: "We will make only one more call, and that will be an agreeable change, for there is no trouble there. It will do you good. You can hear for yourself what religion can effect as a moral power. He turned Hadley into a store, and made his way to a desk where a middle-aged man was busily engaged. A warm greeting took place between the business man and the minister, and then Hanson said: "Mr. Gains, this friend of mine has some intellectual difficulties about religion. You know by experience how hard it is to surmount them, and others that grow out of them. You have had over a year's trial of religion; I wish you would tell him how you find it work."

"Certainly, sir; mine is a case that ought to have weight, thank God! It is a very strong one. I was first a sceptic, then an infidel, then a blasphemer, then a drunkard and a libertine. Circumstances I need not fully describe made me desirous of reforming. The most urgent was that I was ruining myself as a business man, and there was a very strong probability, if I did not reform quickly, that I and my family would have to seek shelter in an almshouse. Well, sir, I tried; and I prided myself on my strength of character, so I thought that, though the struggle might be hard, it must end in victory. But the chains were too strong. I failed so miserably and so often that finally I gave up in despair, and regarded myself as irretrievably lost. Well sir, your friend, Mr. Hanson, got hold of me. He put new hope into me, persuaded me at last to make one more effort for emancipation, and promised me invincible Power. I went by his directions; I sought the Power he spoke of, and, sir, I became a new man. I put aside my doubts in my extremity, and took the thing for granted.

"I soon knew that my doubts were baseless. Why, I *knew*, I *felt*, that God is. A man don't question his own sensations. All the arguments in the world are powerless to a man who can say, I *know*. And I *did* know. The change was inexplicable on any ground but one. Here was I, with all my pride of moral power, a beaten and defeated man, the slave of sensual appetites, which held me bound in spite of my desperate struggles; and now I was victor! I was free! I was sober, chaste, and decorous of speech, and have been so ever since. What did it? It was the power of God! If all the world should tell me otherwise, it would make no difference. It was not in the power of man to deliver me. Neither this man (touching his own breast) nor any other. It was God! Now, sir, if you have any doubts and difficulties about God; if you do not think there is a God; or, if you think there is a God, but that He don't trouble Himself about His creatures, just you do as I did. Just try for yourself. Get hold of His love and His help, and no man on earth, no fiend from under the earth, will ever be able to shake your faith again. That is my advice to you, sir; and it comes from a man that knows."

"Is not this an isolated and very exceptional case, Hanson?" inquired Hadley, when they were again upon the street.

"No, sir; I know of many such instances of reformation through the power of the Gospel in this city," returned Hanson.

"Well, let us say no more about it now," said Hadley. "I want to go to my room and think."

And he walked away, lost in a deep reverie. He had now reached that juncture in his spiritual experience when nearly all his quasi-scientific and philosophical objections to the Bible were overcome or forgotten. It was the comforting, hope-inspiring, and especially the morally elevating character of Christianity, that made so strong a case in its favor with Hadley. "The appeal to life" made an impression upon him that deepened the more he reflected upon it.

While these events were transpiring, Hadley had frequently met his uncle, the Rev. Mr. Bidder, and had attended services at his church at least once every Sabbath. The old man had occasionally broached the subject of religion to him, but had as yet received very little encouragement. However, on the night after his last interview with Hanson, the sceptic's thoughts turned to his uncle, to whom he resolved to go for further light on the momentous questions that were agitating him. He was particularly desirous of learning whether Mr. Bidder's advice would comport with that of his younger contemporary, Mr. Hanson.

The next evening found Hadley in his uncle's parlor. The conversation had become a little desultory, when Mr. Bidder said, with a tentative purpose; "I have just witnessed a scene that was very distressing indeed."

"What was it?" asked Hadley.

"In the eastern part of the city there was a young man who, through the influence of a number of scoffers at religion, had imbibed anti-Christian sentiments, and had become quite bitter against the Bible, speaking derisively of it whenever an opportunity afforded. Having come from a consumptive family, it was soon apparent that he had inherited that fatal disease. His health gradually failed. Soon it became evident that the disease was approaching its last stages, and he knew that death was staring him in the face. Then he became alarmed as to his spiritual condition. He felt that he was not prepared to die, and his mental agony was very great. For whom do you suppose he sent to give him help and direction at that trying time? His infidel friends?" asked Mr. Bidder, bending earnestly toward his nephew.

"I—I suppose not," replied Hadley, his temples throbbing.

"You are correct. He despatched a messenger for a Christian clergyman—"

"That is, yourself," suggested Hadley.

"Yes, he sent for me, and also requested several of his Christian friends to come to his bedside and pray with him. I went, and—I will not describe the scene in detail—he prayed to God to forgive all his opposition to His Word, and save his soul from death. After a violent struggle—for he seemed to think for a time that there was no hope for him—a change was wrought and he received an assurance of salvation. Now, Hadley, the significant and startling fact is that he renounced his infidelity, and could not tolerate the thought of going into eternity with it. To-day we buried him."

"Tell me, uncle," said Hadley, with some agitation, "whether you ministers have many such experiences?"

"They are of quite frequent occurrence. I have known, in my own pastoral experience, of many unbelievers who repented of their infidelity before they died. Sometimes, however, their utterances were only cries of despair, and they died without hope."

"Are not their minds usually delirious, or very much weakened by disease?"

"My dear Hadley, that is where you make a mistake. My experience is this: as a rule, when infidels or impenitent sinners lose possession of their rational faculties through disease, they die without giving evidence of repentance or fear; but if the nature of the malady is such as to leave the mind clear and rational, they almost invariably want to be reconciled to God before they die, and are often filled with the most awful apprehensions."

For a brief interval Hadley was silent. Then he thought of the object of his visit—to learn what panacea his uncle would prescribe for unbelief.

"Well, uncle," he said, at length, "suppose a man is troubled with scepticism, and feels dissatisfied with it, and wants to get rid of it if he can, what specific would you recommend?"

"I should tell him to go right to God in the name of Christ with his perplexities and ask for light. 'If any of you lack wisdom, let him ask of God,'" replied his uncle, without a moment's hesitation.

"Are all Christians moulded after the same Procrustean model? or are they all in complicity for the purpose of duping the world? That is precisely what Mr. Mardont, Miss Winters, and Mr. Hanson have prescribed as the remedy for doubt. This ceaseless iteration would become monotonous if the question were not so grave."

Hadley did not say this aloud, but the thoughts passed rapidly through his mind. It was true that all his Christian advisers, instead of counselling him to read, investigate, philosophize, counselled him to pray. Of course, they did not disparage intellectual research, but they made it of secondary importance.

"Is that the only solvent for doubt? Why is there not some other antidote?" asked Hadley, with an intonation of mingled solicitude and impatience in his voice.

"One reason is this: we are all sinners—and the unbeliever must also be put into the same category—and we cannot receive forgiveness or help without confessing our transgressions to the One against whom they were committed. Another is, we are alienated from the life of God, and in order to get back to Him we must turn about in our course. And still another is, salvation is a *moral* revolution of character, and not merely a change of intellectual conviction, and therefore it can only take place when the sinner renounces his sins, and turns to the true source of help."

A few days later Mr. Bidder came to Hadley's room, and conversed with him for an hour in a friendly manner, but for some reason he avoided the subject of religion. The fact is, he had so often spoken to Hadley on the subject that he was afraid of creating revulsion in the young man's mind. As he stepped to the door at the close of their interview, the old man turned and said, with feeling:

"Hadley, I want you."

The young man understood the meaning of the remark, but replied, rather lightly: "Well, I do not know how you will be able to accomplish what you wish."

"I shall ask the Lord Himself to bring you," returned Mr. Bidder, with a smile of love and tenderness. "I am doing so—day and night"; and the old veteran of the Cross, leaving the arrow to find a vulnerable point in the young man's heart, kindly bade him good-night.

And the shaft was well directed. The old minister aimed better than he knew, for his last remark found a joint in the young sceptic's armor that had not been penetrated before.

"Is it possible that the dear old man is so concerned for my welfare that he is praying for me both night and day? What does it mean? And Hanson is praying for me too. What can induce them to be so solicitous? There is something in the religion of Christ that I cannot fathom. The results of my intellectual investigations have been few and unsatisfactory, and it is only right and reasonable that I should try the plan recommended by my best friends. But—not to-night, not to-night."

The disposition to procrastinate this important step was strong with Hadley, as it is with human kind in general. The concatenation of providential events, however, was leading him nearer and nearer the supreme crisis of his life, when his destiny was to be decided. A few days later the report reached his ears through a member of Mr. Bidder's congregation that a prayer-meeting had recently developed so much in interest that the old minister was encouraged to continue the services for several successive evenings. As soon as Hadley heard of it a thrill passed through him.

"I am going to the meetings," was his firm resolution. My agnosticism has left me in inky darkness; it has dried up every fountain in my soul and has robbed me of all comfort; it has been proven insufficient to solve the problems of existence; and I should be imbecile if I did not endeavor to find light elsewhere, especially when a sure door to the truth is pointed out by men like my uncle and Mr. Hanson."

When evening came—it was Friday—he made his way to the church. The audience was not large, as the meetings had not yet attracted general attention. Hadley was glad of this fact, for he disliked ostentation in matters that were so sacred and perplexing to him.

The young man had formed another resolution, which was that he would seek the truth in Christ in the manner that had been recommended to him. There was no excitement about it. It was his all-consuming desire for the truth and for rest to his tossed soul that brought this decision. Although his doubts were not dispelled, he felt less antipathy toward religion and its professors than he had formerly felt; and, moreover, his friends had persistently told him, until the oft recurring statement had become almost monotonous, that none but God could administer the solvent for doubt.

When he had taken his seat in a pew near the pulpit, he noticed that Mr. Bidder looked toward him with a bright smile of welcome, and Hadley fancied that a tear was glittering in the old man's eye. It sent a thrill to his own heart.

"What an interest the hoary saint takes in my welfare!" he thought. "Why should any one care what becomes of my soul? I am utterly worthless and miserable." He really felt so, and was all the more vulnerable as the garment of intellectual conceit and arrogance dropped from him.

(*To be Continued.*)

THE COVENANT RENEWED.

By Mrs. M. Baxter.

S. S. Lesson for November 25., Josh. 24: 14-28; Golden Text, Josh. 24: 24.

Joshua's Approaching Departure—His Address to the Representatives of the People—The Recognition of God in Politics Still Needed—The Condition of Full Inheritance—Courage Shown in Obedience—Enemies Expelled Only on Observance of the Conditions—Joshua's Testimony to God's Faithfulness—Reminds the People of their Calling and Leading—Consecration Required—Prompt Decision Demanded—Negative Consecration Insufficient—How to be Kept Faithful.

MOSES had served his own generation, and now Joshua, too, had completed his mission. A long time after God had given rest unto Israel from all their enemies round about them, Joshua waxed old and "came into days" (margin). Joshua, like the patriarchs who were before him, did not struggle against the intimations which God gave him that his course was nearly run, but, with all the quiet dignity of one who understood and entered into the mind and will of God, he made preparations for his departure. He called for all Israel, as represented by their elders, their heads, their judges, and their officers, and reminded them of what the Lord had done to the nations of Canaan because of them, adding, "For the Lord your God is He that hath fought for you." Imagine in our day the ruler of a nation recognizing God in politics as Joshua did on this occasion! Oh, it would be a grand day for any country if God were once more put in His true place by the governments and rulers of the earth. In Joshua's speech he shows how, although he has divided the land to them by lot, yet there are nations which remain in their inheritance, that God, on His part, will surely drive them out, but they, on their part, must fulfil certain conditions. First, they must be courageous, not in fighting against their foes, but in observing to do the commandments of God in the law of Moses.

It Takes More Courage

to obey God in the midst of an unbelieving world than to fight a battle! Then they were not to mingle with the Canaanitish nations, not so much as to name their gods; still less to swear by them, serve them, or bow down to them. Oh how this teaches us that even conversation about that which is wrong in God's sight is, in itself, offensive to Him! Then they were not to intermarry with these nations. He showed them that it was only on condition that they obeyed the Lord their God that He would continue to drive out those nations. If the people of God did mingle with them, then these inhabitants of the land should be snares and traps to them, and scourges in their sides, and thorns in their eyes, until they should perish from off the good land which the Lord had given them. God's promise to us is, "Sin shall not have dominion over you, for ye are not under the law, but under grace." Thank God, the promise is ours, the land is our possession, yet, from time to time, we come across inhabitants of the land, of the existence of many of whom we knew nothing. We cannot drive them out, but God can and will if we come into His terms. These are, not to mention their names, not to serve,

Never to Excuse a Sin,

or what some are pleased to call an infirmity, but to count on God's most sure promise to drive it out from before us.

Then Joshua added, "Behold, *this day* I am going the way of all the earth"—probably this was his last day on earth—"and ye know in all your hearts and in all your souls that not one thing hath failed of all the good things which the Lord your God spake concerning you; all are come to pass unto you, and not one thing hath failed thereof." And he took occasion to show them that, as all good things promised by God had come to pass, just as surely all evil things which He had threatened should also come to pass. In the religion of the present day there is an attempt to make God a God of love, utterly without righteousness or justice. Numbers of professedly Christian people believe that God will do all the good things He had said, while they hold that He is incapable of carrying out His word in just judgment to the sinner. If God ignores sin, He becomes a party to it. If God breaks His word of solemn threatening, how can we be sure of His promises of "an inheritance incorruptible, undefiled, and that fadeth not away, reserved in heaven for you who are kept by the power of God through faith unto salvation"? (1 Pet. 1: 4, 5.) God, who cannot lie, has said, "As all good things are come upon you which the Lord your God promised you, so shall the Lord bring upon you all evil things . . . when ye have transgressed the covenant of the Lord your God."

And Joshua gathered all the tribes of Israel to Shechem, and there the representatives of the people "presented themselves before God." Oh, when a nation bows before God, then God blesses that nation! In

The State of Israel

at that time no political question could be settled without a direct reference to God. Joshua then brought before them, as a message from God, a summary of their national history, not going into the same detail as Moses did in the book of Deuteronomy, but going much farther back—even to the time of Abraham's call from idolatry—showing how he had called him and had overruled in the subsequent history of his family, how He brought their fathers out of Egypt, how He drove out the Amorites from before them, and how He had turned Balaam's intended curse into a blessing, how He had driven out the nations which possessed the land, and also the two kings of the Amorites. He reminds them "it was not with *thy* sword, nor with *thy* bow." And then he adds, "And I have given you a land for which ye did not labor, and cities which ye built not, and ye dwell in them; of the vineyards, olive-yards, which ye planted not, do ye eat." And on this message from God Joshua grounded his exhortation. "Now, therefore, fear the Lord, and serve Him." There are many people

In a Great Trouble About Sanctification,

and they do not know quite how to begin to consecrate themselves. Here we have a sample: begin with the joyful, thankful remembrance of all God's mercies in the past, and then consider what is a becoming return to make to such a God. Old Testament consecration was to love God with all the heart and soul and mind and strength; New Testament consecration is to present our bodies "a living sacrifice, holy, acceptable unto God, which is our reasonable service" (Rom. 12:1); anything less would be utterly unreasonable and unbecoming. Part of the consecration which God called for by Joshua was, "Put away the gods which your fathers served on the other side of the flood, and in Egypt, and serve the Lord." It is a terrible revelation of the perversity and wickedness of the human heart that annoyed this people—miraculously delivered from Egypt, miraculously brought through the sea, miraculously led, brought through the Jordan, and by the power of God alone made masters of the land—that even now idols were found amongst them, and that after all He had done their hearts were

Not Fully Satisfied With God.

Consecration, *i. e.*, yielding all to God, comes spontaneously from those who appreciate Him, and where hearts are won over to Him by the consideration of His loving kindness. Joshua then put the matter very strongly before the people, "If it seem evil to you to serve the Lord, choose ye this day whom ye will serve"—let there be no mistake about it; take your choice and do it openly—"but as for me and my house, we will serve the Lord." Some people are content to serve the Lord themselves, but have no concern as to whether their children, servants, workmen or women, &c., serve the Lord. Joshua would have all his household with him. "As for me *and my house*, we will serve the Lord." The people answered, "God forbid that we should forsake the Lord to serve other gods." Perhaps up to this time some of them had attempted to serve the Lord, but at the same time to serve some of the gods of the nations, that they might have an easier time of it with the heathen, and might not seem so peculiar, and might not have anything to suffer for their adherence to God. Oh how many there are who try to live with one foot in the kingdom of God and one foot in the world, leading unsaved people to believe that Christ cannot satisfy a heart, and thus misrepresenting the God who has done so much for them! The people recognized their obligations to God in all which He had done for them, and said, "Therefore will we also serve the Lord;"

Joshua then represented to the people how powerless they were to serve the Lord: "Ye cannot serve the Lord; for He is an holy God; He is a jealous God; He will not forgive your transgressions nor your sins." Joshua was speaking as the representative of the law; under the law there is no mercy, but, thank God, "Christ is the end of the law for righteousness to every-one that believeth." (Rom. 10:4.) We have no more power in ourselves to fulfil the law or serve our God than had His people of old, "but unto them which are called, both Jews and Greeks, Christ (is) the Power of God and the wisdom of God." (1 Cor. 1:24.) And the people said unto Joshua, Nay; but we will serve the Lord. And Joshua said unto the people "Ye are witnesses against yourselves that ye have chosen you the Lord, to serve Him." And they said, "We are witnesses." But God wants more than words. There must be earnest deeds as well as words; "Now, therefore, put away, said he, the strange gods which are among you, and

Incline Your Heart

or yield your heart unto the Lord God of Israel." Here are two things to do—first, to put away all which is enmity against God; and, secondly, to cultivate a listening heart for His mind and will. Some are satisfied with renouncing novels, and other modern idols. But, after all, this is only negative, only clearing the ground of weeds. The great work is that which follows—unhindered communion with God. No amount of giving up or of consecration on our part can produce communion with God. This must always come from the Holy Ghost. But He always teaches a listening heart, a heart inclined or bent down to attend to the will of God. The people, led on, no doubt, by some who really took in the import of what they said, declared, "The Lord our God will we serve, and His voice will we obey." Oh how soon did many of them fall away!

"So Joshua made a covenant with the people that day, and set them a statute and an ordinance in Shechem." His manner of doing this was to put the decision of the people in writing. But all possible solemnity, and all the contrivances of man put together, cannot keep either ourselves or others

Faithful to the Lord.

None but the Spirit of God can avail. "So Joshua let the people depart every man unto his inheritance." His work was now done, and it was time for him to go home. "And it came to pass after these things, that Joshua the son of Nun, the servant of the Lord, died, being an hundred and ten years old." He had lived for his vocation; there is no record all through his life of self-seeking; he had led the children of Israel on to victory, but always reminded them that the Lord had fought for them, and that the credit of no victory belonged to him or to them. To the last he kept the place God gave him under the captain of the host of the Lord. No mention of sickness is made in connection with his death, and if this renewal of the covenant was on his dying day, it manifests some little resemblance to the last day of Moses. Joshua was buried in the border of his inheritance. Was the covenant kept? "Israel served the Lord all the days of Joshua, and all the days of the elders that outlived Joshua, and which had known all the works of the Lord, that He had done for Israel." And then? Alas! the historical and prophetical books of the Bible are full of the history of their declension, and of the breaking of their covenant.

I AM HIS AND HE IS MINE.

"I am my Beloved's and my Beloved is mine."—Cant. vi. 3.

"Loved with everlasting love,
Led by grace that love to know!
Spirit, breathing from above,
Thou hast taught me it is so.
Oh, this full and perfect peace!
Oh, this transport all divine!
In a love which cannot cease,
I am His and He is mine.

"Heaven above is softer blue,
Earth around is sweeter green;
Something lives in every hue
Christless eyes have never seen;
Birds with gladder songs o'erflow,
Flowers with deeper beauty shine,
Since I know, as now I know,
I am His and He is mine.

"Things that once caused wild alarm
Cannot now disturb my rest,
Closed in everlasting arms,
Pillowed on His loving breast.
Oh, to lie forever here,
Care, and doubt, and self resign!
While He whispers in my ear,
I am His and He is mine.

"His forever, only His!
Who the Lord and me can part?
Ah, with what a rest of bliss
Christ can fill the loving heart!
Heaven and earth may fade and flee,
First-born light in gloom decline;
But while God and I shall be,
I am His and He is mine."

—*Selected.*

J. E. JEWETT, Publisher, 77 Bible House, New York, will furnish the above poem in leaflet form at twenty cents per hundred. A *Sample Packet* of 60 leaflets assorted (no two alike), will be sent post-paid, for 10 cts., or 100 for 20 cts. Postage stamps taken.

To Our Fellow Christians

Who Are Forwarding Contributions in Aid of Christian Work in Mexico.

Bishop Riley requests me to inform the kind friends who are generously contributing in aid of Christian work in Mexico, that we have now over one hundred monthly subscribers who are forwarding contributions in its behalf. Bishop Riley sends to all who are contributing in aid of the work in Mexico his most sincere thanks for their timely gifts.

As there are, no doubt, many who would be glad to contribute something monthly in behalf of the cause of Christ in Mexico, but who feel that they cannot afford to give as much as one dollar a month, we venture the suggestion, that when possible *the friends of the work should try and collect small contributions from such* and forward the same with their own contributions to Bishop Riley, 43 Bible House, New York. For example, some friend of the work who is now forwarding one dollar a month, might induce ten others, to each give ten cents a month, and collect and forward the same with his own contribution. Another who now contributes one dollar a month, might induce four others to each give one cent a day, or thirty-one cents a month, and collect and forward the same with his own contribution monthly. Still a third who now contributes a dollar a month might induce two friends, to each give fifty cents a month, and collect and forward the same regularly with his own contribution.

If this plan could be adopted generally among the more than one hundred regular monthly subscribers to the work, we might soon be able to report to our friends that we had over two hundred dollars a month contributed regularly in behalf of the work in Mexico.

We remind our friends that to continue the work in Mexico effectively we most pressingly need a regular monthly income, as we have to meet a regular monthly expense.

A most precious Christian work has been commenced in Mexico, and we are doing what we can to continue it, by raising an income in its behalf. We earnestly appeal to our fellow Christians to aid us in this effort. There are one hundred and thirteen millions who speak the English language, and seventy-five millions who speak the Spanish or Portuguese languages. Among those who speak the English language, there are multitudes who know and love the pure gospel, and are doing what they can for the Master. Among those who speak the Spanish or the Portuguese languages, there are a few who know and love the pure gospel, and are faithfully working for our dear Master. Our Spanish-American society is working hard to raise an income to aid in building up a strong centre of Christian work in Mexico. The influence of that work has already extended into Spain and Cuba, and, we trust, will yet extend into South America. Fellow Christians, think of seventy-five millions who speak the Spanish or Portuguese languages, millions and millions, and millions of whom have never had a Bible in their hands!!! Help us! help us! to do Christian work in their midst.

Bishop Riley has been instrumental in having more than one hundred thousand copies of the Bible or New Testament circulated in Mexico. Many hundreds of children have been educated in Christian schools established by him. He has helped to prepare choice gospel hymns and an able evangelical literature in the Spanish language. More than forty congregations have been gathered in the Republic of Mexico through his efforts. He has secured two magnificent stone churches in the City of Mexico where the gospel has been preached for years. He has trained up a noble band of able preachers of the pure gospel. He has given nineteen years of his life to aid in building up this great work, and he appeals to his fellow Christians to contribute the monthly income needed to continue it effectively.

Dear friends, will you not only continue to contribute to this good work yourselves, but also encourage others to do the same. Some may not be able to contribute monthly but could do so occasionally. Occasional gifts are most thankfully received. Pray for this work, and that many may be moved to befriend it.

With best Christian wishes, I am you brother in Christ,

A. D. MAINE.

Entered according to Act of Congress in the year 1888, in the office of the Librarian of Congress at Washington.

This Journal contains every week a Portrait and Biography of some eminent person; a new Sermon by the Rev. C. H. SPURGEON, of London, and the Rev. Dr. TALMAGE'S latest Sunday morning Sermon; also always a Prophetic Article, and a Summary of Current Events as well as Stories, Anecdotes etc.

Vol. XI., No. 47. Office, 63 Bible House. N. Y. THURSDAY, NOVEMBER 22, 1888. Price, 3 Cents. Annual Subscription, $1.50.

REV. J. BURNHAM.

CONTENTS OF THIS NUMBER.

PORTRAITS OF REVS. J. BURNHAM AND J. J. KENDON, EVANGELISTS AMONG THE HOP-PICKERS.
REWARDS FOR THE DULL. Dr. Talmage's Sermon Last Sunday Morning.
THE RESURRECTION: THE FIRST. By Rev. A. C. Tris. (Concluded.)
A Persian Robe of Honor—An Inebriate Under Treatment—A Wife Lent to a Dispensary—A Preacher Confused, etc.
THE LORD'S RETURN IMMINENT. By Dr. L. W. Munhall.
A PARADOX. A New Sermon by Rev. C. H. Spurgeon.
Gems from New Books: A Futile Occupation—A Foreigner's Changed Opinion, etc.
PORTRAIT OF MRS. CHAMBERLAIN
A MOMENTOUS EXCURSION. (With Illustration.)
PICTURE OF THE PEAK OF INSPIRATION IN THE YOSEMITE VALLEY.
THE EPOCHS OF A LIFE. (Continued.)
ISRAEL UNDER JUDGES. By Mrs. M. Baxter.

REV. J. J. KENDON.

EVANGELISTS AMONG THE HOP-PICKERS—SCENES IN THE HOP-GARDENS.

THE REV. J. BURNHAM:

Rev. C. H. Spurgeon's Singing Evangelist.

Born in 1849—Early Devotion to Music—Leaves Home at the Age of Seventeen—Influence of His Mother's Love—Becomes Organist of a Priory—Removal to Devonshire, and Conversion—Arrives in London in 1871—Enters Mr. Spurgeon's College in 1873—Subsequent Work.

THE Rev. John Burnham, of the Pastors' College Society of Evangelists, whose Services of Song have become famous, was born at Cranbrook, England, in 1849, and is, therefore, thirty-nine years of age. When only a few months old, his father, who carried on the business of a clothier and outfitter, removed to Marden, in the same county, and there, amid pleasant rural surroundings, he spent his boyhood. He was sent to the local school for his education, but at the early age of thirteen he joined his father in the business. From his earliest days he was delighted and impressed by sweet music. While other boys were playing with tops and marbles, he was seldom without a music-book in his hand. "I had no instruction," he said; "I owe all I know of music to my own unaided efforts." At the age of eight he entered

The Choir of the Parish Church;

at twelve he played the organ during the absence of the organist for his summer holiday; and in the following year, the post falling vacant, it was offered to him, and accepted. Both his parents were members of the Protestant Episcopal Church, but he paid frequent visits to the Congregational church at Marden. This being contrary to his father's wishes, he ceased to attend the place, but went to the Congregational church in another village. As he was engaged at Marden Church morning and afternoon, of course it was only in the evening that he could gratify this wish. When he was seventeen, a disagreement with his father caused him to leave home and commence the battle of life on his own account. After two years' absence his father invited him to return home, and though he did not accept the invitation, he and his father were reconciled. "During my two years' absence," he says, "my father, I am sorry to say, forbade me to enter home or write; but

I Was Very Fond of My Mother,

and secretly kept up a monthly letter to her through a friend in the place. My struggles she knew little of. Indeed, on two occasions, when I knew she would be anxious at the non-appearance of the usual letter, it was my last penny that bought the postage-stamp which carried to her the intelligence, 'Doing very comfortably!' Cast thus early on the cold world, I believe I should have sunk in sin among godless companions, but for my mother's love and influence, which followed me, and was doubtless a salutary check upon me."

He now went to Godstone, in Surrey, and there it was for the first time that he began really to turn his musical knowledge to account in a monetary sense. He soon discovered that the High Church people were likely to be most remunerative to him, and therefore to them he looked for professional employment. Hence early in 1869 he accepted an engagement as

Organist at a Priory

—another name for monastery—at Cosham, near Portsmouth, presided over by Father Nugee, who is now the Superior of St. Albans's Priory, in London. However, his stay here was not long, owing to the severe restrictions imposed upon him. He removed to London, where, still working at his business as outfitter, he joined the voluntary surpliced choir at St. Mary-the-Less, Lambeth, where Canon Gregory was vicar. "At that time," he says, "I was High Church to the backbone." It was at this period that he removed to Modbury, South Devon. There, to his great disappointment and annoyance, he found himself in the employ of the senior deacon of the Baptist Chapel, of which the Rev. A. English was the minister. Referring to this experience, he says: "I shall never forget the first Sunday morning after my arrival. As we all sat at breakfast, my master's wife said, 'Of course, Mr. Burnham, you will go to chapel with us?' 'No,' I replied; 'I am a Churchman.' 'Just as you please, but we would rather, of course, that there should be no divisions, and that all the household should worship together.' 'Very well, then,' I said, 'I'll go.' I did go—and I never went to church afterwards. I was very much struck with the simplicity which characterized the service, after the ceremonial to which I had been for so long used. And the two passages of Scripture I heard appealed strongly to my judgment—'The poor have the gospel preached to them,' and 'The common people heard Him gladly.' At dinner-time some one asked me, 'How did you like the service?' 'Pretty middling,' was my reply; but I liked it well enough to go again without being asked. Three or four weeks after that I listened to a sermon from the text, 'What shall it profit a man if he gain the whole world and lose his soul?' This sermon seemed to have special reference to me, for I had bartered away my talent for money." In fact, the Holy Spirit so applied the word of truth that young Burnham was filled with concern about his soul, and he knew not what to do. It was

The Crisis of His Life.

It afterwards transpired that a young lady in the same establishment, as well as six or seven other persons in the town, were similarly impressed by this sermon. A week or two later a party of the good deacon's business assistants went for an excursion to a seaside place near by, and here the young lady referred to had a narrow escape from a watery grave. In this the hand of God was so plainly seen, that Mr. Burnham, and others in the party, accepted Christ before they returned home. This was the commencement of a most gracious revival of religion in the church, and on October 9, 1869, the young man and eight others were immersed on a public profession of their faith in Christ.

Mr. Burnham at once commenced to work for Christ. The judicious counsels of Mr. English, his minister, and the prayerful perusal of "The Memoirs of Harlan Page," opened his eyes to the usefulness of

A Pen Consecrated to Christ,

and he determined never to close a letter without "a word for Jesus," and many interesting cases of blessing have resulted from his correspondence for Christ. On his conversion he soon recognized as never before the evils of the common drinking customs, and the barrier they form to Christian service, and he at once espoused the cause of total abstinence. He has ever since taken a keen and active interest in the temperance movement. Soon after he joined the church, too, he started a psalmody class in a neighboring village. This very soon grew into a considerable Bible class. In 1871 he removed to London and united himself with the Baptist church, of which the pastor was the Rev. Philip Gast. He then commenced to preach in the open air; but before long he felt the strain was too great for him, and his physician insisted that either business or public religious work should be given up. He gave up business, and made successful application to be

Admitted to the Pastors' College.

This was in January, 1873, and he remained under Mr. Spurgeon's tuition until November, 1874, when he became the minister of the Baptist church at Fivehead, Somerset. There he spent three happy, useful years, but through a complete breakdown in his health he was compelled to resign. "However," he says, "my naturally restless disposition constrained me to get to work, and I commenced visiting the brethren in isolated places, and holding services among them. This work was blessed beyond my most sanguine hopes, and, coming to the ears of Mr. Spurgeon, I was asked at the next College conference to continue in it. After a fortnight's consideration I decided to accept this work, and from that time I have gone on preaching and singing in all parts of the country."

For some years past Mr. Burnham has conducted annually missions among the hop pickers, in connection with the Rev. J. J. Kendon—*whose portrait is also given on our front page*—and his success in that sphere has been very encouraging. He has compiled and published no fewer than thirty-seven Services of Sacred Song, all of which have had a very large circulation. His solo singing is very attractive, and the bright, natural way in which he conducts his evangelistic missions wins the hearts of all, and is blessed by God to the conversion of many.

THE REV. J. J. KENDON,

The Hoppers' Evangelist.

Early Labors—How He Came to Visit Goudhurst—The Good Work Done There—Privations of a Life of Faith—Mr. Spurgeon's Estimate of It—Mr. Kendon's Boarding-Schools.

THE Rev. Joseph J. Kendon, *whose portrait accompanies that of Mr. Burnham on the first page*, is about sixty years of age. Emphatically a man of the people, he has through a long series of years lived and labored for the welfare of the people, first in a crowded district in the East of London, and then in a hop-growing district of Kent, of which Goudhurst is the centre. Mr. Kendon was brought to accept Christ in his boyhood, and he was at once deeply impressed with a yearning desire to bring souls to the Saviour. In June, 1861, he visited Goudhurst for the benefit of his health, which had become seriously impaired by exhaustive evangelistic labors and domestic sorrow, and there he has remained ever since, where God has made him

A Blessing to the Villages Around.

At the time when Mr. Kendon was led in the providence of God to commence his work in Kent, he found, he says, "the people very dark and very destitute in spiritual things." A farmer lent him an "oast-house," or hop-drying kiln, which became his mission house for the first three years, and he devoted himself in real earnest to a simple Gospel ministry and pastoral visitation and cottage meetings. The congregation was of the very poorest class. From the first there was a spirit of hearing amongst the people, and in course of time the chapel and school buildings were erected, which are now in use, and in 1864 a church of believers formed, and five or six mission stations in neighboring centres established. It was a work commenced and carried on in simple and absolute dependence on God. Mr. Kendon writes of these early years: "How often, when we have been brought to our last penny, and have not known how to provide for our little ones, have we been enabled to go to our heavenly Father and tell Him all our wants in confidence; and in His own time and way He has graciously sent the needed help." This is

True Christian Heroism.

The Rev. C. H. Spurgeon says: "The story of Mr. Kendon's labors at Goudhurst is exceedingly full of interest, and is an instance of how a determined, zealous man may, under the Divine blessing, surmount difficulties and make the influence of the Gospel to be felt in an agricultural district with few to help."

The hop-harvest in Kent has lent itself to the pencil of the artist, and perhaps no rural scene can rival it when "the leaves are turning yellow or kindling into red," and among the troops of hoppers Mr. Kendon and his colleagues have done a marvellous work. Every season it is his privilege to command quite a small army of Christian workers, who compass the whole hop-district around Goudhurst. What results have been accomplished only "the Day will declare." Each year some of the hoppers have gone home to tell what great things the Lord has done for them; souls have been saved, backsliders restored, and many a slave to drink rescued. The expenses of the work are considerable, but funds are sent by friends to whom the value of the mission is known. For some years Mr. Kendon has conducted boarding-schools for boys and girls, and the results have been of the most encouraging character. In his schools he has sought to realize the ideal of a Christian home, and this department of his many-sided ministry has also not been without spiritual results.

EVANGELISTS AMONG HOP-PICKERS.

EVERY year, when the hops in the gardens are ripe, there is a migration of thousands of East-end Londoners to the hop-gardens of Kent and Sussex, and trains full of men, women, and children, all anxious to exchange the crowded alleys and lanes of Spitfields, Whitechapel, and West Ham for the broad, open expanses in the beautiful districts of Orpington, Bromley, and Maidstone, are despatched from the city termini of the railways. Doctors who labor amongst the poor in the parts of London from which these hop-pickers are mainly drawn, say that the effect of this yearly trip is magical upon those who go, saving hundreds of lives.

There was a time when the picking of hops brought with it into the peaceful villages where the gardens are situated a terrible increase of crime. Those were the days when farmers could, without infringing the law, lodge in one common barn the laborers of both sexes who thus temporarily came into the district; when travelling vendors of drink were permitted to debauch the people with horrible liquor; and neither police nor philanthropist gave evidence of caring what became of the hop-picking throng. But, happily, all that is changed now; a sanitary inspector, policemen, and last, but by no means least, Christian Workers, who, by their

Kindly Sympathy,

have thrown a strong humanizing influence over the motley crowds in the hop-gardens, have so altered the state of affairs that crime is scarcely heard of, drunkenness is unfrequent, and the magistrates of the two counties find their work but little increased by the sudden influx of these immigrant thousands. They gain health and strength, money to help them through the winter months, and an acquaintance with Nature, which cannot fail to exercise a good effect upon at least a large proportion of them. About 50,000 hop-pickers are busily employed, and the Revs. J. Burnham and J. J. Kendon are enabled to do great service for Christ. The hop-gardens are visited during the day, words of gospel truth are spoken to the people from bin to bin, tracts are distributed, and short services are held in the camps during the dinner-hour. Open-air services are held every evening on the village green: and in this way many of the poor people hear more of the gospel, and feel more of its power during the hopping season, than they do all the rest of the year. There are also "Hop-pickers' Bible Readings," and "Hop-pickers' Sunday-schools," besides help in the shape of clothing, soup, medical aid, etc.

Living accommodation for so large a number of persons is still a difficulty not completely solved, but great advances have been made on past times. Long low sheds are built, and in many instances provided with fire-places or ovens, and divided off into partitions. Plenty of straw is provided, and to many city laborers this is luxurious sleeping-quarters, after the cold stones of Trafalgar Square or the arches near the river. The comfort of others who are not thus favored depends on their own ingenuity. Straw, poles, and hurdles are furnished, and each builds his own house.

The Process of Hop-Gathering,

which is *illustrated on the first page*, is very interesting. The vine is first cut near the ground, by an instrument which has a knife-blade on one side and a stout hook on the other; the pole, with the vine still on it, is then pulled up and laid across the bin, over a sheet of canvas placed on a frame so as to form a hollow receptacle, somewhat like the bed in a cradle, and here a dozen hands are quickly busied in plucking the hops, which fall into the bin, adding to the previous collection. The leaves and flowers are torn off by one or two parting strokes, and the pole is laid aside for future use. This process is repeated all day long, as fast as the pickers can deal with the plants cut down and laid before them, and, when the bin is filled with hops, containing perhaps twenty bushels, it is lifted and emptied, and they are carried away to the kiln, to be dried by a furnace-fire.

ANECDOTES RELATED AT RECENT EVANGELISTIC MEETINGS.

A Most Welcome Discovery.—A Servant of Christ remarks: "A poor man came to me one day, and said, 'Minister, I want to be saved, I do.' 'Well, just tell that to the Master,' I replied. 'But I am such a poor, weak, sinful sinner, that I do not think He would have anything to do with me,' he replied. 'Just tell Jesus that, too,' I said. We went and sat down together. He prayed to God, telling Him just what He had told me, and as he did so, I whispered, 'Jesus says, "Him that cometh unto Me, I will in no wise cast out."' All at once his countenance brightened; he turned to me, and exclaimed: 'Bless the Lord! I am saved now, and I know it.' If we tell God our wants, and trust in Him who shed His blood for us, we may rest assured that He will hear our prayers."

Pinned to the Wall by Satan.—An Evangelist says: "Dr. Andrew Bonar tells that on one occasion he preached upon the unpardonable sin, and before the end of the week he had five of his congregation calling upon him, each saying, 'Oh, doctor, I am sure I have committed that unpardonable sin.' Once when preaching myself on the same subject, there came to me the next day a foreman from one of the large works in the vicinity, who said, 'Oh, sir, I have thought for some time that I was a Christian, but now I have great fear that I have committed that unpardonable sin. Did you ever know one who had the same idea?' 'That I did,' was the reply. 'The devil has often pinned me to the wall with the same thought, but I knew that if I could come to Christ I had not committed it, for, whosoever cometh to Him He will in no wise cast out.' But if we feel any anxiety to come to Christ it is by His Holy Spirit that we are thus invited, and God will not turn away His invited guests."

An Effectual Antidote to Misery.—The Rev. J. Linnell relates: "I was preaching in a tent, when one of the workers came to me and said there was a man outside who would not speak to any of them, but was particularly anxious to see me. I went out and invited him to come into the tent, and soon we entered into conversation. He told me that if it were not for the thought of what was to be in the hereafter, he would have done with this life at once, for he was utterly helpless, and had not any money to pay for food or lodging. I saw from the man's miserable appearance that he spoke the truth, and I put a coin into his hand. This little act of kindness seemed to raise his spirits. He talked more freely: then I noticed that he had a Scotch accent. 'Did you come from Scotland?' I asked. 'Yes, from Glasgow,' he replied. We then spoke of the city, and of James Morrison Street Hall, which he had often attended, and of the precious teaching he had got there. Before he left the tent he had come to Christ and received life, instead of seeking death at his own hand."

Saved from Gambling.—A Man Speaking of the goodness of the Lord towards him, says that so completely was he addicted to gambling, that from the 1st of October to the 13th of February in the following year, he never slept in a bed. He used to go to the club at night and play cards until five o'clock the next morning, then enter a saloon and spend some time there. On one occasion he was at a ball, and so intoxicated did he get that for two days he did not know what he was doing. His friends became so disgusted with his conduct that they discarded him, and to the present time, although he has been reformed for years, they will not even see him. One night he found himself not very far from the Earl Street Hall, and one of the friends spoke to him, and asked him to come in; they got into conversation, and on being asked to give his heart to the Lord, he answered, "No, I have gone so far I am never going to alter." One night going into Coventry Street he thought of the words of the friend who had spoken to him, and something made him think he would like to go round and see what sort of a place this Mission Hall was; he came in, thinking he would not be noticed, and was spoken to. So impressed was he at what was said to him, that the next night he felt impelled to walk round the same way, and although he got behind the door to keep out of sight, he was again found out, and so mightily did the words spoken seem to strike him that he received Christ, and went away rejoicing."

Photographing a Drunken Husband.—Mr. Cruickshank observes: "There was a woman whose husband was in the habit of drinking very heavily. One night he came home, as he too often did, helplessly drunk, and reeled into a chair and fell asleep. As his wife looked at him, and saw how miserable he appeared, she thought that if he could only see himself in that state he would never touch drink again. This thought took firm hold of her mind. She had a friend, a photographer. If she could get him to come and photograph her husband, just as he lay there, it might have a good effect. She slipped out of the house, and soon returned with her friend, who brought his camera with him, and in a short time the inebriated husband was photographed. A few days afterwards the *carte* came home. The woman first looked at it, and then handed it to her husband. 'Is that anyone I know?' he inquired. 'Yes,' was all his wife said. Another look, and then he asked, 'Is that myself?' 'Yes, that is you,' the woman quietly replied. He took a long look, and then exclaimed, as he turned away to hide his emotion, 'By the help of God I will never touch strong drink again!' He had been shown his true state while under the power of sin, and came to Jesus to be cleansed by Him."

Good Result of a Soldiers' Quarrel.—Mr. Hamilton remarks: "A friend of mine was, on a public holiday, visiting one of the famous historic castles of Scotland, and was shown over the place by a sergeant, one of the guardians. The soldier was a fine, hearty specimen of middle-aged manhood, and did not in the least object to speak of his travels and exploits, and, among other things, he told how he became a total abstainer. 'It was,' he said, 'when we were stationed at Malta. We had comparatively little to do, and, consequently, we passed much of our time at the canteen, and between the bad quality of the liquor and the heat of the sun, the liquor often flew to the drinker's head, and for the time completely maddened him, making the most peaceable man ready to fight with his friend on the slightest pretext. One afternoon I sat drinking with two Maltese: we got into an argument. They would not give in. I lost my temper, and insulted them most grossly. They leaped to their feet, and drawing their knives rushed upon me, and I would have fared badly if some of my comrades had not interfered. The excitement and danger completely sobered me; I saw that the Maltese had been right, and I entirely wrong; and all through that accursed drink. I determined to seek out those men and apologize, and never again while there to let a drop of liquor pass my lips. After my apology the men became very friendly. When we left Malta, I looked back and saw how much good total abstinence had done me, and resolved that I would never again touch strong drink.' Yes, no matter in what country we find it, strong drink is doing the same diabolical work, taking away all manhood, and implanting a fiendish passion that would destroy all with whom it comes in contact."

REWARDS FOR THE DULL.

Dr. Talmage's Sermon, Preached last Sunday Morning, November 18, 1888.

"Unto one he gave five talents, to another two, and to another one; to every man according to his several ability." Matt. 25 : 15.

The Capital Intrusted to the Servants—Faithfulness Expected—I. Becoming a Christian Implies Service—A Voluntary Service—No Drudgery in It—II. Different Qualifications Given to Different People—Ruinous Comparisons—How Solomon's Temple was Built—Every Man Marked for his Place—III. Grace Meant to be Accumulative—Children's Growing Fortunes—IV. Inferiority of Gifts No Excuse for Indolence—Work for Men of One Talent—V. A Day of Settlement Coming—The Awful Aggregate—VI. Degrees of Celestial Happiness to be Graduated.

MANY of the parables of Jesus Christ were more graphic in the times in which He lived than they are now, because circumstances have so much changed. In olden times, when a man wanted to wreak a grudge upon his neighbor, after the farmer had scattered the seed-wheat over the field, and was expecting the harvest, his enemy would go across the same field with a sack full of the seed of darnel-grass, scattering that seed all over the field, and, of course, it would sprout up and spoil the whole crop; and it was to that Christ referred in the parable when He spoke of the tares being sown among the wheat. In this land our farms are fenced off, and the wolves have been driven to the mountains, and we cannot fully understand the meaning of the parable in regard to the shepherd and the lost sheep. But the parable from which I speak to-day is founded on

Something We All Understand.

It is built on money, and that means the same in Jerusalem as in New York. It means the same to the serf as to the czar, and to the Chinese coolie as to the emperor. Whether it is made out of bone or brass or iron or copper or gold or silver, it speaks all languages without a stammer. The parable of the text runs in this wise: The owner of a large estate was about to leave home, and he had some money that he wished properly invested; and so he called together his servants and said: "I am going away now, and I wish you would take this money and put it to the very best possible use; and when I come back return to me the interest." To one man he gave $9,400, to others he gave lesser sums of money; to the least he gave $1,880. He left home and was gone for years, and then returned. On his arrival he was anxious to know about his worldly affairs, and he called his servants together to report. "Let me know," said he

"What You Have Been Doing

with my property since I have been gone." The man who had received the $9,400 came up and said: "I invested that money. I got good interest for it. I have in other ways rightly employed it; and here are $18,800. You see I have doubled what you gave me." "That's very good," said the owner of the estate; "that's grandly done. I admire your faithfulness and industry. I shall reward you. Well done—well done." Other servants came up with smaller accumulations. After a while, I see a man dragging himself along, with his head hanging. I know, from the way he comes in, that he is

A Lazy Fellow.

He comes up to the owner of the estate, and says: "Here are those $1,880." "What!" says the owner of the property, "haven't you made it accumulate anything?" "Nothing—nothing." "Why, what have you been about all these years?" "Oh, I was afraid that if I invested it I might somehow lose it. There are your $1,880." Many a man started out with only a crown in his pocket, and achieved a fortune; but this fellow of my text, with $1,880, has gained not a farthing. Instead of confessing his indolence, he goes to work to berate his master—for indolence is most always impudent and impertinent. Of course he loses his place, and is discharged from the service.

The owner who went out into a far country is Jesus Christ going from earth to heaven. The servants spoken of in the text are members of the Church. The talents are our different qualifications of usefulness given in different proportions to different people. The coming back of the owner is the Lord Jesus returning at the Judgment to make final settlement. The raising of some of these men to be rulers over five or two cities is the exaltation of the righteous at the last day, while the casting out of the idler is the expulsion of all those who have misimproved their privileges.

Learn first, from this subject, that becoming a Christian is merely

Going Out to Service.

If you have any romantic idea about becoming a Christian, I want now to scatter the romance. If you enter into the kingdom of God, it will be going into plain, practical, honest, continuous, persistent Christian work. I know there are a great many people who have fantastic and romantic notions about this Christian life, but he who serves God with all the energies of body, mind, and soul is a worthy servant, and he who does not is an unworthy servant. When the war-trumpet sounds, all the Lord's soldiers must march, however deep the snow may be, or however fearful the odds against them. Under our Government we may have colonels and captains and generals in time of peace, but in the Church of God there is no peace until the last great victory shall have been achieved. But it is

A Voluntary Service.

People are not brought into it as slaves were dragged from Africa. A young man goes to an artisan, and says: "Sir, I want to learn your trade. I by this indenture yield myself to your care and service for the next four or five or seven years. I want you to be my master, and I want to be your servant." Just so, if we come into the kingdom of God at all, we must come, saying to Christ: "Be Thou my Master. I take Thy service for time and for eternity. I choose it." It is a voluntary service. There is no drudgery in it. In our worldly callings, sometimes our nerves get worn out, and our head aches, and our physical faculties break down; but in this service of the Lord Jesus, the harder a man works the better he likes it, and a man in this audience who has been for forty years serving God enjoys the employment better than when he first entered it. The grandest honor that can ever be bestowed upon you is to have Christ say to you on the last day: "Well done, good and faithful servant!"

Learn also from this parable that

Different Qualifications

are given to different people. The teacher lifts a blackboard, and he draws a diagram, in order that by that diagram he may impress the mind of the pupil with the truth that he has been uttering. And all the truths of this Bible are drawn out in the natural world as in a great diagram. Here is an acre of ground that has ten talents. Under a little culture, it yields twenty bushels of wheat to the acre. Here is another piece of ground that has only one talent. You may plow it, and harrow it, and culture it year after year, but it yields a mere pittance. So here is a man with ten talents in the way of getting good and doing good. He soon, under Christian culture, yields great harvests of faith and good work. Here is another man who seems to have only one talent, and you may put upon him the greatest spiritual culture, but he yields but little of the fruits of righteousness. You are to understand that there are different qualifications for different individuals. There is a great deal of

Ruinous Comparison

when a man says: "Oh, if I only had that man's faith, or that man's money, or that man's eloquence, how I would serve God!" Better take the faculty that God has given you and employ it in the right way. The rabbis used to say, that before the stone and timber were brought to Jerusalem for the Temple, every stone and piece of timber was marked; so that before they started for Jerusalem the architects knew in what place that particular piece of timber or stone should fit. And so I have to tell you we are *all marked for some one place in the great temple* of the Lord, and do not let us complain saying: "I would like to be the foundation stone, or the cap-stone." Let us go into the very place where God intends us to be, and be satisfied with the position. Your talent may be in personal appearance; your talent may be in large worldly estate; your talent may be in high social position; your talent may be in a swift pen or eloquent tongue; but whatever be the talent, it has been given only for one purpose—practical use.

You sometimes find a man in the community of whom you say: "He has no talent at all," and yet that man may have a hundred talents. His one hundred talents may be shown in the item of endurance. Poverty comes, and he endures it; persecution comes, and he endures it; sickness comes, and he endures it. Before men and angels he is a specimen of Christian patience, and he is really illustrating the power of Christ's Gospel, and is doing as much for the Church, and more for the Church, than many more positively active. If you have one talent, use that; if you have ten talents, use them, satisfied with the fact that we all have different qualifications, and that the Lord decides whether we shall have one or whether we shall have ten.

I learn also from this parable that the grace of God was

Intended to be Accumulative.

When God plants an acorn, He means an oak; and when He plants a small amount of grace in the heart, He intends it to be growthful, and enlarge until it overshadows the whole nature. There are parents who, at the birth of each child, lay aside a certain amount of money, investing it, expecting, by accumulation and by compound interest, that by the time the child shall come to mid-life this small amount of money will be a fortune, showing how a small amount of money will roll up into a vast accumulation. Well, God sets aside a certain amount of grace for each one of His spiritual children at his birth, and it is to go on, and, as by compound interest, accumulate, until it shall become an eternal fortune. Can it be possible that you have been acquainted with the Lord Jesus for ten, twenty, thirty years, and that you do not love Him more now than you ever did before? Can it be that you have been cultured in the Lord's vineyard, and that Christ finds on you nothing but sour grapes? You may depend upon it, if you do not use the talent that God gave you, it will dwindle. The rill that breaks from the hillside will either widen into a river or dry up. The brightest day started in the dim twilight. The strongest Christian man was once a weak Christian. Take the one talent, and make it two; take five, and make them ten; take ten and make them twenty. The grace of God was intended to be very accumulative.

Again: I learn that inferiority of gifts is

No Excuse for Indolence.

This man, with the smallest amount of money, came growling into the presence of the owner of the estate, as much as to say: "If you had given me $9,400 I would have brought $18,800 as well as this other man. You gave me only $1,880, and I hardly thought it was worth while to use it at all. So I hid it in a napkin, and it produced no result. It's because you didn't give me enough." But inferiority of faculties is no excuse for indolence. Let me say to the man who has the least qualifications, by the grace of God he may be made almost omnipotent. The merchant whose cargoes come out from every island of the sea, and who, by one stroke of the pen, can change the whole face of American commerce, has not so much power as you may have before God in earnest, faithful, and continuous prayer. You say you have no faculty. Do you not understand that you might this afternoon go into your place of prayer and kneel before God, and bring down upon your soul, and the souls of others, a blessing so vast that it would take eternal ages to compute it? "Oh," you say, "I haven't fleetness of speech.

can't talk well. I can't utter what I want to y." My brother, can you not quote one passge of Scripture? Then, take that one passage Scripture; carry it with you everywhere; uote it under all proper circumstances. With iat one passage of Scripture you may harvest thousand souls for God. I am glad that the hief work of the Church is being done by the

Men of One Talent.

nce in a while, when a great fortress is to be ken, God will bring out a great field-piece nd rake all with the fiery hail of destruction. ut common muskets do most of the hard fightg. It took only one Joshua, and the thousands common troops under him, to drive down e walls o. cities, and, under wrathful strokes, make nations fly like sparks from the anvil. only took one Luther for Germany, one winglius for Switzerland, one John Knox for cotland, one Calvin for France, and one John Vesley for England. Dorcas as certainly has mission to serve as Paul has a mission to reach. The two mites dropped by the widow nto the poor-box will be as much applauded as e endowment of a college, which gets a man's ame into the newspapers. The man who indled the fire under the burnt-offering in the ncient temple had a duty as imperative as that f the high priest, in magnificent robes, walking nto the Holy of Holies under the cloud of Jeovah's presence. Yes, the men with one talent re to save the world, or it will never be saved t all. The men with five or ten talents are ompted to toil chiefly for themselves, to build p their own great name, and work for their own ggrandizement, and do nothing for the alleviion of the world's woes. The cedar of Lebanon anding on the mountain seems to hand down e storms out of the heavens to the earth, but bears no fruit, while some dwarf pear-tree has more fruit on its branches than it can carry. etter to have one talent and put it to full use han five hundred wickedly neglected.

My subject teaches me that there is coming

A Day of Solemn Settlement.

When the old farmer of the text got home, he mmediately called all the servants about him, nd said: "Here is the little account I have een keeping. I want to see your account, nd we will first compare them; and I'll pay you hat I owe you, and you'll pay me what you we me. Let us have a settlement." The day ill come when the Lord Jesus Christ will appear, and will say to you: "What have you been oing with my property? What have you been oing with my faculties? What have you been oing with what I gave you for accumulative urposes?" There will be no escape from that ettlement. Sometimes you cannot get a settleent with a man, especially if he owes you. He ostpones and procrastinates, and says: "I'll see ou next week," or "I'll see you next month.' he fact is he does not want to settle. But hen the great day comes of which I am speakg, there will be no escape. We will have to ce all the bills.

I have sometimes been amazed to see how an ccountant will run up or down a long line of gures. If I see ten or fifteen figures in a line, nd I attempt to add them up, and I add them wo or three times, I make them different each me. But I have admired the way an accountnt will take a long line of figures, and without single mistake, and with great celerity, anounce the aggregate. Now, in the last great ettlement, there will be a correct account preented. God has kept a long line of sins, a long ne of broken Sabbaths, a long line of profane ords, a long line of discarded sacraments, a ng line of misimproved privileges. They will ll be added up, and before angels and devils nd men

The Aggregate Will be Announced.

h, that will be the great day of settlement! I ave to ask the question: "Am I ready for it?" is of more importance to me to answer that uestion in regard to myself than in regard to ou; and it is of more importance for you to nswer it in regard to yourself than in regard to me. Every man for himself in that day. Every woman for herself in that day. "If thou be wise, thou shalt be wise for thyself; if thou scornest, thou alone shalt bear it." We are apt to speak of the last day as an occasion of vociferation—a great demonstration of power and pomp; but there will be on that day, I think, a few moments of entire silence. I think a tremendous, an overwhelming silence; I think it will be such a silence as the earth never heard. It will be at the moment when all nations are listening for their doom.

I learn also from this parable of the text that in heaven our degrees of

Happiness Will be Graduated

according to our degrees of usefulness on earth. Several of the commentators agree in making this parable the same one as in Luke, where one man was made ruler over five cities, and another made ruler over two cities. Would it be fair and right that the professed Christian man who has lived very near the line between the world and the Church—the man who has often compromised his Christian character—the man who has never spoken out for God—the man who has never been known as a Christian only on communion-days—the man whose great struggle has been to see how much of the world he could get and yet win heaven—is it right to suppose that that man will have as grand and glorious a seat in heaven as the man who gave all his energies of body, mind, and soul to the service of God? The dying thief entered heaven, but not with the same startling acclaim as that which greeted Paul, who had gone under scorchings, and across dungeons, and through maltreatments into the kingdom of glory. One star differs from another star in glory, and they who toil mightily for Christ on earth shall have a far greater reward than those who have rendered only half a service.

Some of you are hastening on toward the reward of the righteous. I want to cheer you up at the thought that there will be some kind of a

Reward Waiting for You.

There are Christian people in this house who are very near heaven. This week some of you may pass out into the light of the unsetting sun. I saw a blind man going along the road with his staff, and he kept pounding the earth and then stamping with his foot. I said to him: "What do you do that for?" "Oh," he said, "I can tell by the sound of the ground when I am near a dwelling." And some of you can tell by the sound of your earthly pathway that you are coming near to your father's house. I congratulate you. Oh, weather-beaten voyagers, the storms are driving you into the harbor! Just as when you were looking for a friend, you came up to the gate of his house, and you were talking with the servant, when your friend hoisted the window and shouted: "Come in! come in!" Just so, when you come to the gate of the future world, and you are talking with Death, the black porter at the gate, methinks Christ will hoist the window and say: "Come in! come in! I will make thee ruler over ten cities." In anticipation of that land I do not wonder that Augustus Toplady, the author of "Rock of Ages," declared in his last moment: "I have nothing more to pray for; God has given me everything. Surely no man can live on earth after the glories I have witnessed." Oh, my brothers and sisters, how sweet it will be, after the long wilderness march, to get home. That was a bright moment for the tired dove in the time of the Deluge, when it found its way into the window of the ark.

MRS. CHAMBERLAIN.

(See Portrait on page 745.)

THE marriage in Washington, D. C., on Thursday last, of Miss Mary Endicott, daughter of the Secretary of War, to Mr. Joseph Chamberlain, the English politician, adds another name to the long list of those of American ladies who, during the past few years, have left our shores to occupy conspicuous positions on the other side of the Atlantic. Mr. Chamberlain deserves our congratulations. His mission to this country at the beginning of the year, as special commissioner to arrange the Fishery Dispute, was not a success, but his private and personal diplomacy appears to have prospered better. It seem that he met Miss Endicott at one of the Cabinet receptions, became acquainted with her, and persuaded her to become his wife.

The young lady is twenty-six years of age, and is a native of Salem, Mass. Her position on the other side will give her full scope for the talent and tact she is said to possess. Social success counts for a great deal in English politics, and if she can make the Chamberlain receptions attractive, she will give social prestige to a party sadly in need of prestige of some kind. Her husband and Lord Hartington are the leaders of the party which we, in this country, would call "*mugwumps*," and, as Lord Hartington is unmarried, the social side of the party will be under Mrs. Chamberlain's management. Like the Mugwumps here, Mr. Chamberlain and his friends are not loved by the party they have left, nor the party they are now aiding. The Liberals charge upon them their long exclusion from office, and the Tories are opposed to them on every political principle except the one of refusing Home Rule to Ireland. In this uncomfortable position the influence of a charming American lady may perhaps have a helpful influence.

Though it is impossible to foresee the issue of the present curious political situation in England, it is by no means improbable that the young lady, as Mrs. Chamberlain, may yet see as much of official life in the land of her adoption as she has seem, as Miss Endicott, in the land of her birth. Mr. Chamberlain has boundless ambition and no little ability. Until he deserted Mr. Gladstone, he was regarded as the natural successor of that statesman; Lord Hartington, who would occupy that position, will have to quit the House of Commons for the House of Lords whenever the Duke of Devonshire, his aged father, dies. At present the Liberal party would not accept Mr. Chamberlain as its leader, if Mr. Gladstone should die; but if a reconciliation can be effected between the Liberals and Mugwumps, it is safe to predict that Mr. Chamberlain would hold high office in the Government.

This is the third time that Mr. Chamberlain has been married. After the death of his first wife, he married her cousin, only to be a second time bereaved. In both instances his grief was so intense that he had to retire for a time from public life. He is fifty-two years of age and is very wealthy. His fortune is derived from a partnership in the firm of Nettlefold & Chamberlain, screwmakers, which he inherited from his father. It may be hoped that this and the other social ties of the same kind between the prominent families in the two countries may serve to draw the two nations into more friendly relations, and that the prejudice fomented during the recent campaign may be allayed. Mrs. Chamberlain, for her part, will have no difficulty in inspiring her husband with a friendly feeling toward the United States, as he is already an ardent admirer of a Republican form of government, and has incurred some odium in his own land by publicly averring that royalty is an expensive and useless encumbrance with which Great Britain might advantageously dispense.

A WIFE LENT TO THE MISSIONARIES.

In a letter from Dr. Elizabeth Reifsnyder, who is laboring as a medical missionary in China, to the *Missionary Link*, she mentions the valuable assistance she receives in her work from a girl whose husband has been induced to lend her to the Christian ladies. She says: "There came to the hospital a young girl of sixteen years, upon whose face and neck we operated. The result was most satisfactory. As soon as this girl was able to be about, she became most helpful, and our good matron said if she could have her for help, she would much prefer her to an older person, since she was willing, young, quick in her movements, and most kind to the patients. The girl remained with us several months, no one coming to see her, or inquire after her, and finally we concluded to see what could be done for her. She was engaged to be married, but had no relatives whatever. It seems she was secured for a daughter-in-law when quite small, for the sum of thirty dollars. Finding her so bright, useful, and anxious to remain with us, we called the husband, and asked him if he would agree to her remaining two years with us. She would go to our school in the morning, help in the Dispensary in the afternoons, and assist in the wards early in the mornings and nights, being taught at the same time to sew and be useful. He agreed, and we have her with us, a bright, helpful girl."

A PERSIAN ROBE OF HONOR.

A letter from Dr. G. W. Holmes, who is laboring as a medical missionary at Tabriz, which is published in the *Church*, shows that the Oriental custom mentioned in Esther (6:10) and other parts of Scripture, of clothing favored subjects with robes of honor, still exists, and it has recently been conferred on a Christian missionary. It seems that Dr. Holmes, after some hesitation, has accepted the position offered him as physician-in-chief to the heir-apparent to the Persian throne. The Crown Prince had requested that he should delay his departure for America, and in the meantime the Ameer, the Governor-General, who is spoken of as able and powerful, was supposed to be fatally sick, and Dr. Holmes was called to take the entire charge of the case. To the surprise of all the Ameer recovered. Subsequently the infant daughter of the Crown Prince was restored to health, the case being put in charge of the same physician. Dr. Holmes received public thanks and *a robe of honor*. In his present position there are no restrictions upon his engaging in Christian work. Already he has had frequent and earnest discussions with the Crown Prince upon the comparative claims of Christianity and Islam, and the gospel has been faithfully presented to the Prince. Another happy circumstance is the desire of the Governor-General that his household shall receive instruction from the ladies of the mission in various feminine accomplishments, his carriage being sent regularly for the teachers. Aside from the direct influence which these missionaries may exert, it will be made clear in the eyes of all that they are not to be regarded with suspicion. Their motives and aims will be so understood that the prejudice against them must yield.

AN INEBRIATE UNDER TREATMENT.

How thoroughly the principle of Divine Healing enters into every difficulty in life, when it is once adopted, is seen in a letter from the Transvaal, in Africa, which Mrs. M. Baxter publishes in this month's *Thy Healer*.* It appears that there are five families there, who have all taken Christ as their Healer, and go to Him in all their sickness. A. Rosher, the head of one of these families, writing to Mrs. Baxter, says: "About two weeks ago we prayed in faith for a brother sinner, who came into a large inheritance from his father, who died about a year ago, and left him and an only sister about 50,000 shares in the best gold properties. This worldly-lucky man is, or was, so addicted to drink that he lost all self-respect (he was from a highly respected English family). Well, he chose to place himself under me, to bring him off the drink, not expecting such treatment as he received. First night I allowed him his own way with his bottle of whiskey, and prayed for him. The next evening was an appointed meeting night, when five of us laid on hands, and each successively prayed—prayed God to take away the craving and save him from drink and from sin, and make him a useful member of society. We prayed the prayer of faith, believing we were heard. The next day, after noon, he left my house, still with the craving for drink; but now all is over, and he is released from the craving, hating himself for his misconduct."

A PREACHER CONFUSED.

An incident published by Dr. Charles Cullis in his *Times of Refreshing* shows how God uses the apparent failures of His servants for His own wise purposes. A clergyman, in the course of his reminiscences, says: "One Sunday morning I preached to a crowded congregation, chiefly composed of the principal inhabitants of the neighborhood. I was just engaged in giving my audience a picturesque description of a sunset on the Sea of Galilee, when all of a sudden, owing to the close atmosphere, a little girl fell into a fainting fit. The disturbance which it created, though only short and comparatively insignificant, yet so much put me out that I became altogether confused. The rest of my sermon all at once vanished from my memory. I could not recollect one word of it. In my perplexity I cried to God for help. While looking down on my Bible, which was lying open before me, my eye fell upon the words 'all flesh is as grass,' etc. (1 Pet. 1: 24, 25.) Yielding as it were to an instinctive impulse, I read it to my hearers, and began preaching from it an improvised sermon, just as it came up in my heart. And here, having lost *my oratorical flower-basket*, I could not help laying bare the truths of God's word in all their simplicity and startling reality. Connecting the text with my previous description, I called the glory of man a setting sun, but which was never to rise again. I spoke of the utter vanity of everything human, of the certainty of the destruction of this world, and of our everlasting condemnation if we were to die in the midst of our sins.

"Walking home with my wife, after the service, I was in a desponding mood and quite ashamed of myself, 'for the people *must* have noticed my confusion,' I said; 'and what a gossip will it be all over the place that the minister broke down in the middle of his sermon!

"We had scarcely got home, however, when a lady desired to speak to me. The impression which her appearance made upon me was not very agreeable. She was gaudily dressed, and carried a flourish of trinkets, lace, and finery which created a most unfavorable impression.

"'Sir,' she said, while her lip quivered, 'could you permit me to speak to you in confidence?'

"'Certainly, ma'am.'

"'I am a lost woman,' she said, while tears burst from her eyes; 'but you, sir, can perhaps tell me whether there is still salvation for me who have so long lived a careless life.'

"She then briefly told me her history. She was a person held in high esteem in the society in which she moved. But she was living without God and without Christ in the world, and was entirely given up to pleasure and love of dress and display. Church she seldom or never visited. The places which she frequented were the theatre and the ball-room. But on this Sunday morning, having gone out for a walk, her attention was struck by the singing which reached her ears from my church. The thought occurred to her that she might as well step in and sit down among the congregation. But here she found she had come just in time to learn what the glory of man was. My sermon went like a two-edged sword through her heart. She saw that with all her beauty, she was but a withering flower, dead, lost, helpless, and hopeless. And she now besought me to tell her more about that Saviour whom I had spoken of as the only one who was able to save from ruin.

"I need not tell you," the minister continues, "how gladly I told her of Christ. Her eyes were opened to the glory of His sin-atoning love as well as to the beauty of His holiness. It was not long before she became a Christian."

A WEEPING SUPPLIANT IN A CHURCH.

A few weeks ago a young lady entered an Episcopal church in New York, in the evening, and knelt in prayer. She soon lost consciousness of her surroundings, and became absorbed in communion with God. Evidently she was in trouble, for her tears began to flow freely, and occasionally a stifled sob shook her frame. No one noticed her except an elderly lady, who, passing near her, observed her emotion, and, with true Christian sympathy, was moved to learn the cause of her suffering. Presently the girl rose from her knees, and was about to leave the building, when the aged lady accosted her. Gentle words and a manner of kind friendliness drew the girl's story from her.

It appeared that she was a pious English girl, who, years ago, in her own land, was well educated by her Christian mother. The girl lived near to Christ, and ardently longed to spend her life in His service. The claims of the unconverted lay heavily upon her heart, and she determined to give herself to the work of God among the poor. The mother sympathized with her desire, and sent her to be trained for the field of labor. Shortly afterward, however, the mother's health failed, and the daughter, recognizing the call of God to home duty, gave up for the time the preparation for her chosen work, and went home to nurse her mother. The malady was a long and trying one. For eleven years the girl waited upon the invalid, attending to her wants and fulfilling a daughter's duties with filial affection. At last death removed the mother, and the girl was left alone in the world. Peculiar circumstances brought her to America, and three years ago she landed in New York.

Her first effort was to obtain work of a missionary kind in the city. But she was friendless and unknown, and, her small stock of money rapidly dwindling, she was soon brought to the point when neither her ardent longing for distinctively religious work nor her educational accomplishments could stand in the way of her accepting menial employment, which was the only employment she could obtain. She went into domestic service, and soon became a valued household help. Her opportunities for recreation were few and short. In one of them she went to the Young Women's Christian Association, where she was treated kindly, but where, just then, there were no openings for giving her the kind of work she was longing for. The poor girl grieved sadly, most of all because her hope of spending her life in Christ's service seemed doomed to disappointment. Her distress on the night when she entered the church was almost too great for her to bear, and she sought peace and support in the way God has appointed. Her new acquaintance encouraged and cheered her, exhorting her to keep fast her faith in God, trusting Him to open the way to usefulness.

Two days later the girl received a letter, bidding her go to the Young Women's Christian Association, where news of importance was awaiting her. She went. The news was, that the people of Grace Church were about opening a mission in a neglected part of the city, and needed some earnest, devoted Christian lady, of education, kindness, and tact, to take charge of it. She would be expected to look after the women of the neighborhood, hold mothers' meetings, and in various ways help her poor sisters to realize that in the religion of Jesus was the secret of a happy, useful life. The girl's

* *Thy Healer and Faith Witness*, a monthly Magazine edited by Mrs. M. Baxter, contains original articles on Holiness and Healing, Authentic Testimonies of Divine Healing, and Items of Intelligence from Heathen Lands where missionaries are laboring in faith, soliciting no help from man, but relying solely on God for support. Annual Subscription, 75 cents, may be sent to Manager of CHRISTIAN HERALD, 63 Bible House, New York.

ged acquaintance in the church had happened o hear of this opening casually, while conversing with a Christian friend on the very next day fter her interview with the girl in the church, and at once recommended her, feeling sure that God had thus provided an answer to that tearful prayer. The girl was at once engaged, and she is now happy and wonderfully successful in congenial Christian work.

THE RESURRECTION: THE FIRST.

By Rev. A. C. Tris, of Howard, Kan.

(Continued from page 727.)

The second drama is the Resurrection scene and vision: "And I saw thrones, and they sat upon them, and judgment," krima, "was given unto them." . . . Here we meet with new things, and with new actors; and, most singularly, with actors of whom it is said "that *they lived* and *reigned with Christ the thousand years,*" and are marked out as the first-fruits of the great Resurrection army, and the Spirit of God pronounces it, "This is the first Resurrection." The first rising again, "The upstanding, the first." (Dr. R. Young.)

What means this Resurrection scene? We answer: After grave reflection, since long time, we have come to the conclusion that it means

An Essential Resurrection,

a real and a new upstanding of arisen bodies out of the grave, and a re-appearing of blessed spirits, or souls, formerly separated from but now again united with their own bodies, raised from the dust, visiting the scenes of their former earthly careers, now elevated to the highest offices of being priests of God and of Christ, and reigning with Him a thousand years, and, as the Greek has it, "reigning as kings." And to prove our statement, we adduce and offer the following facts:

1. Because, that if this vision must be spiritualized, then we have to acknowledge "a Hierarchy" in the church, and we ought to follow the example given by the Vatican, to have Cardinals and ecclesiastical princes in the Church of Christ.

2. Because we maintain that the objection which is commonly made that this is spoken of "souls" and not of "persons," seems to us a more convincing argument than anything else. It constates the fact that this Hebraism, "souls" taking the best part of man for the whole man, is a proof of the genuineness of this part of the Bible, and that it is a Jewish production which connects the Old Testament with the New Testament, and with the Revelation of Jesus Christ *as one unit*. Let us pay due attention, that we find the same word "souls" meaning living beings, persons, in the O. T. in Gen. 12: 4; Exod. 12: 4, and in *thirty* different places, and in the N. T. in Acts 7: 14; 27: 37; Rev. 18: 13, and in many other places: In Acts 27: 37 is said: "And we were in all in the ship two hundred three score and sixteen *souls*. . . . And so it came to pass that they escaped all safe to land," and in 1 Peter 3: 20: "While the ark was in preparing wherein few, that is eight *souls*, were saved by water."

3. Because the souls mentioned as constituting the rising resurrection are put in opposition to others, who are called

"The Rest of the Dead,"

that word "*loipos*" signifying the *remaining* of the dead ones, makes them, as having been once one whole, and now being only *a remnant* which was not allowed yet, to rise to such a high distinction or state as those who had arisen from the dead.

4. Because it is a prerogative of the saints in their glorified state to be judges. In 1 Cor. 6: 2 the apostle declares: "Do you not know that the saints shall judge the world. Know ye not that we shall judge angels?" This judging does not mean that the saints shall be only counsellors; it means the very act of judging and condemning. Evil and Satan cannot be reformed, neither can innate evil be removed by gentle advice or counsel. That stage shall then have been passed, evil must be rebuked, and Satan must be put down (1 Cor. 15: 24), and that shall be "the great honor which the saints shall have" in the Millennial age. (Ps. 149: 9.)

In conclusion, it is the promise which the Lord Jesus did promise to the Church of Thyatira (Rev. 2: 26, 27): "And he that overcometh and keepeth my works unto the end, to him will I give power over the nations; and he shall rule them with a rod of iron"; that rule, being a part of the glory of the resurrected saints, is vouchsafed to them: "They must rule with Christ on the earth," and how can it be otherwise? The redeemed must be reinstated in all the prerogatives, and in higher privileges than ever Adam did possess. The redeemed arisen saints bearing the image of the Son of God (Rom. 8: 29; 1 Cor. 15: 40), must have

Dominion Over the Earth,

and over the lower animal creation (Gen. 1: 28), and the words (Ps. 8: 5. Heb. 2: 7: 10), must be fulfilled. Man, who was made a little lower than Elohim, "Thou hast crowned him with glory and honor."

Indeed the doxology will be chanted during the ages to come (Rev. 5: 9-10). "Thou hast redeemed us to God by Thy blood, out of every kindred and tongue and people and nation, and hast made us unto our God kings and priests, and we shall reign on the earth." "Blessing and honor and glory and power be unto Him that sitteth upon the throne, and unto the Lamb, for ever and ever." *Amen.*

THE LORD'S RETURN IMMINENT.

By L. W. Munhall, M. D.*

Difference Between Two Schools of Prophetic Students—The Lord's Command—Passages Explicable Only in One Way—An Injunction Useless on any Other Ground—Errors Foreseen—A Duty Enjoined.

THE word Millennium is of Latin derivation. *Mille*, a thousand, and *annus*, a year. It is applied to the one thousand years mentioned in Rev., 20th chapter, during which Satan is bound in the bottomless pit, and righteousness and peace will prevail throughout the earth. The pre-millennialist believes that Christ will come before this period; the post-millennialists believe He will come after.

We are not left in ignorance as to

The Attitude of the Church

during the time of her Lord's absence. The parable of the ten virgins (Matt. 25: 1-13) indicates, very clearly, that she should believe His return to be imminent. Is not the bride taught to have her lamps trimmed and burning, and commanded to "Watch, therefore, for ye know neither the day nor the hour wherein the Son of man cometh." In Luke 12: 35-40 we find the following: "Let your loins be girded about, and your lights burning, and ye yourselves like unto men that wait for their Lord, when He will return from the wedding, that when He cometh and knocketh, they may open unto Him immediately. Blessed are those servants whom the Lord, when He cometh, shall find watching . . . . And if He shall come in the second watch, or come in the third watch, and find them so, blessed are those servants. And this know, that if the good man of the house had known what hour the thief would come, he would have watched, and not have suffered his house to be broken through. Be ye therefore ready also, for the Son of man cometh at an hour when ye think not."

In Mark 13: 34-37 we find the case put in this fashion: "For the Son of man is as a man taking a far journey, who left his house, and gave authority to his servants, and to every man his work, and commanded the porter to watch;

Watch Ye Therefore

(for ye know not when the Master of the house cometh, at even, or at midnight, or at the cock-crowing, or in the morning), lest, coming suddenly, he find you sleeping. And what I say unto you, I say unto all. Watch!" In Matt. 24: 42, 44 we find the case thus stated: "Watch, therefore, for ye know not what hour your Lord doth come. . . . . Therefore be ye also ready, for in such an hour as ye think not the Son of man cometh." In 1 Thes. 5: 6—"Therefore let us not sleep, as do others, but let us watch and be sober."

What is the significance of these Scriptures if it is not that the Lord may come at any moment? The Lord said we "know neither the day nor hour." If the millennium were to begin to-day, I would know it; and I would then know the Lord will be here one thousand years hence. Is it possible that the thrilling and appalling events mentioned in Rev. 20: 1-4, as introductory to the millennium, could transpire without our knowledge of it? I trow not. If the post-millennialists are right, then I know the Lord will not come for more than a thousand years yet, and consequently not in my day. How could I be induced to watch for an event that I know will not take place in my time? What sense would there be in telling me to watch, as the Word of God does over and over again, for an event that I know is more than one thousand years in the future? God does not thus treat His children.

Our post-millennial brethren seek to turn

The Force of this Injunction

to watch, so often repeated, by saying, "Have not more than eighteen hundred years rolled by since the Lord spake these words? and yet He has not come." This is tantamount to saying that His word of promise is not good, because of His delay; or, that it was necessary for Him to return immediately, in order that His promise, "I will come again," might be good. If the lapse of eighteen hundred years invalidates the promise, why not eighteen days? No: the lapse of eighteen hundred years, nor eighteen million centuries, would not make it impossible that the Lord may come at any moment. The promise is sure, and the passing of these eighteen centuries has only brought us so much nearer the glorious event. With the Father are the times and the seasons; and "one day is with the Lord as a thousand years, and a thousand years as one day." (II Peter 3: 8.) The Lord knew what some would say on this point, and so He speaks these words, that they do well to prayerfully contemplate:

"But and if that evil servant shall say in his heart, My Lord delayeth His coming; and shall begin to smite *his* fellow-servants, and to eat and drink with the drunken, the lord of that servant shall come in a day when he looketh not for *him*, and in an hour that he is not aware of, and shall cut him asunder, and appoint *him* his portion with the hypocrites: there shall be weeping and gnashing of teeth." (Matt. 24: 48.)

"Knowing this first, that there shall come in the last days scoffers, walking after their own lusts, and saying, Where is the promise of His coming? for since the fathers fell asleep, all things continue as *they were* from the beginning of the creation." (II Peter 3: 3, 4.)

A post-millennial friend of mine once said to me: "You are watching for the Lord's return. I am not. You will be disappointed. I will not be, because He will not come in our day." I replied: There is another point at which we differ; viz., I am doing just what God commands us to do, and you are living in known and persistent disregard of the explicit command of God.

* From his work entitled "The Lord's Return." Published by *Fleming H. Revell*, 148 Madison St., Chicago, Ill.

CHRISTIAN HERALD AND SIGNS OF OUR TIMES.

OFFICE, 63 BIBLE HOUSE, NEW YORK.

TERMS AND INSTRUCTIONS.

Published Weekly. Subscription price in the United States, Canada, and Mexico, $1.50 a year; $1 eight months; 75 cents six months; sent two months on trial for 25 cents, postage free; in Europe and in all countries in the Postal Union, 50 cents extra postage; subscriptions always payable in advance. Single copies, price 3 cents. Any newsdealer will furnish the paper weekly when ordered.

New Subscriptions can commence at any time. When no date is mentioned, we begin it with the issue of the week in which the subscription is received.

Remittances by Mail should be by Post-office money order, bank cheque, draft, or express money order, whenever possible, and should always be made payable to THE CHRISTIAN HERALD. Letters containing money sent in this way need not be registered, as when lost, duplicates can always be obtained.

If a Postal Note or currency is sent, it should always be in a registered letter. Letters can be registered at any office. Subscribers sending money of this kind, and not registering, do it at their own risk.

Change of Address. Name of Post-office and State, of both old and new address, should always be given in case of removal, as without the previous address it is impossible to find the name on our list.

CURRENT EVENTS.

Important Changes in the Postal Rates are suggested by the Third Assistant Postmaster-General in his annual report issued last week. One of them is, that if one-cent postage should be adopted, letters of the matter now included in the third and fourth classes—that is, general printed matter and merchandise—be included in one class at the rate of one cent for two ounces. The proposition to reduce the letter rate from two cents for one ounce to one cent for two ounces would not, he believes, be so serious a loss to the Department as appears at first sight. The majority of the letters would be of about the same weight as now, while the number would doubtless increase. The number of letters mailed during the fiscal year just closed was 1,769,800,000.

The Suggestion that Congress Should Force upon the Sioux, by a legislative act, the bargain the tribe has rejected should not find favor. The Sioux were asked to dispose of one-half of the great Dakota Reservation. They did not, it appears, absolutely refuse to sell, but demanded better terms than those offered. It is now proposed to take the land summarily, giving its owners whatever price Congress may deem fit. It appears that a bill will be introduced for this purpose at the coming session. That way of dealing with the red men, no doubt, has precedents, yet it would make rather a sharp contrast with the professions of desire to recognize Indian rights and Indian liberty to sell or keep the land with which the original project was broached. The element of consent would disappear as completely as the supposition that when the Government has once pledged itself to make a certain reservation the property of the Indians forever, this pledge can be relied upon. No doubt it would be for the interest of the red men, as it is of the white, to open the Sioux Reservation, but what would be dishonest in dealing with white men, would be equally dishonest in dealing with red men. It may be hoped that this fact will not be forgotten.

The Mining Disaster in Kansas on November 10 was one of the most fatal of recent years. It occurred in the Santa Fe Mine, in the village of Frontenac. The company operating the mine had an unusual press of business and had taken on a number of extra men. They had 164 men in the pit on the morning of the catastrophe. Two explosions of fire-damp were heard, and pieces of slate and large logs of wood were thrown out of the shaft. What must have occurred was soon realized by those above, and when the shaft was cleared sufficiently to allow the cage to descend the worst fears were realized. Dead bodies lay around everywhere, buried under huge pieces of rock. The choke-damp drove away the rescuers for a time, but the cage was lowered, and some of the wounded crawled upon it and were brought up. The fans were got to work and the rescuers again descended. Their first efforts were directed to the wounded, and nine men were brought up. Then the dead bodies at the bottom of the shaft were taken out. There were thirty-seven there, and in the farther workings more were found. The air was too foul that day for an extended search, but it was clear that all in the mine must be dead. The scene above was heartrending. Women with babes in their arms clustered around the cage each time it came up, shrieking and groaning. One went utterly demented. There is scarcely a house in the village that has not suffered at least one bereavement. In one there is a girl who lost father, brother, and lover in the catastrophe. It is supposed that at least sixty men must have perished.

A Steamship Collision between the Umbria of the Cunard line and the *Iberia* of Marseilles, France, occurred on November 10 off Long Island. The Cunarder left New York for Queenstown, at 10:45 A. M., and passed Sandy Hook safely. A dense fog prevailed shortly afterward, and her engines were slowed down. Almost immediately a whistle was heard, and a big steamer loomed up in the fog. Apparently the two vessels were too near when they sighted to avert a disaster. The *Umbria* crashed into the *Iberia's* side, carrying away her stern. The *Umbria's* captain stopped his vessel and sent to see what injury had been done. It was thought that the *Iberia* would float, and her captain asked to be towed back to port. Later, however, her bulkheads gave way under the strain, and as towing would be dangerous, her captain and his crew of thirty men were taken on board the *Umbria* and brought back to New York. The *Umbria* was but little injured, and after a short delay for repairs, started again on her voyage. Providentially no lives were lost.

The Position and Progress of Civil-Service reform formed the subject of an address delivered in New York, on November 16, by Mr. Dorman B. Eaton, ex-chairman of the National Civil-Service Commission. He said that 5,000 clerks in the departments at Washington were made subject to the civil-service rules. When the law first went into operation all of the important custom houses were embraced, with their 3,000 employees. The number of offices thus taken away from public patronage was 15,000. Before the close of President Arthur's term, 7,000 applicants were examined and over 2,000 of them put in office. They were a better class than had occupied the same places before, and a great improvement in the management of the departments resulted. The present number of offices under the law is now a little over 16,000. There are 100,000 offices which Mr. Eaton thought would ultimately come under its operation. He said that civil-service reform was a non-partisan movement; that it was aimed against methods practiced by both parties; and the bill establishing the commission was passed only because public sentiment demanded it, and not because the party representatives in Congress desired it.

A Significant Expression of Ministerial Opinion, on the subject of Home Rule for Ireland, was made in London on November 14. A large number of Nonconformist clergymen of Ireland, who, as a rule, are strongly Liberal, signed an address which was presented at a meeting in London to Lord Salisbury and Lord Hartington by the Moderator of the Presbyterian Assembly. The clergymen strongly deprecated the project of Home Rule, and Lord Hartington showed that he appreciated the significance of their attitude by saying that, although Mr. Gladstone had attacked the Unionists, he failed to answer their contention that Irish Nonconformists were better able to judge the question than their English brethren who supported Mr. Gladstone. Neither of the two parties in Ireland could be trusted to govern the whole. To leave the weaker section at the mercy of their hereditary opponents would be disgraceful. Lord Salisbury declared that he looked with terror at the insanity which had seized English statesmen. They were told to trust to the generous instincts of Irishmen. But revolutionaries always pushed the weak aside, and the Parnellites would not be thrust aside by the sudden appearance of refined, scruplous, and honorable statesmen.

The Parnell Commission was Occupied During the whole of last week in listening to evidence proving that outrages had been committed in Ireland. This fact has never been doubted, and it appears somewhat irrelevant to the question at issue, which is whether Mr. Parnell and other Irish members of Parliament had any connection with the outrages, or controlled the men who committed them. The President of the commission, on November 14, called the attention of the lawyers to this point and said the commission would form an opinion upon whether persons against whom charges were made could be connected with outrages by the mere proof that outrages were committed. They would be unworthy of the position in which they were placed, if they were not able to keep their minds in a state of equilibrium upon this point. He hoped, however, that it would be found possible to curtail the amount of evidence of this kind. The Parnellites have made an appeal for funds. The daily expenses of the trial are enormous, and the League treasury will soon be exhausted.

The Joint Effort of Germany and England for the suppression of the slave trade in Africa is to be directed to the prevention of the export trade in human flesh. In the official correspondence between the two Governments, published last week, Prince Bismarck recognized the existence of the evil in the interior, but said he believed that a military expedition would fail. It appeared to be desirable to confine their joint action at first to a maritime blockade. Portugal must be pressed to forbid the exportation of munitions from her colonies in the vicinity of Zanzibar. Lord Salisbury thought that the extension of French influence in Madagascar and Comoro had stimulated the slave trade. The French, he said, were as anxious as other nations to destroy the traffic, but their naval force there was very small. He had complained of the refusal of the French to allow a search to be made of suspected vessels sailing under their flag, and France had now agreed to permit such search to be made—not in all cases, but as an incident of the blockade. In conclusion he said that the blockade would be strictly limited to the two objects indicated.

The Republicans of France are Excited Over a Royalist gathering held on November 11, at Romans, at which the chiefs of the party and many titled persons were present. Monsignor Cabrieres, a well-known Royalist prelate, preached to the assembly. In concluding his address, he said: "France is agitated and nervous. Her impressionable nature impels her with astonishing facility to rush to whatever side promises her a saviour. Her nerves are now as excited as they have been at any time within the century." Other indications of a movement are noted, and the *Temps* and other journals call attention to the speech made by Baron de Breteuil, as an indication of the abdication of the Monarchists in favor of Boulanger.

The Mysterious White Pacha, Whose Movements in Africa have caused much curiosity, is again reported in action. A cable despatch, coming by way of Cairo, states that the White Pacha has fought a battle in the Bahr-el-Ghazel region, with disastrous results to the dervishes. As the date of this engagement is not given, no definite conclusions can be drawn from the report. It would seem, however, to disprove the claim of Captain Van Gele, that he himself, and not Stanley, or any other, was the "White Pacha." Captain Van Gele returned to Europe from the Congo country about the middle of September. If he was not the mysterious white man, the probability that it was Stanley is strengthened.

Contributions to the Fund for Supplying colored ministers in the South with this journal, have been received since our last acknowledgement to the amount of $6. They are from: East Orange, N. J., $1; Morganville, N. Y., $1; Stamford, Conn., $1; South Manchester, Conn., $3. We have still many names of colored ministers on hand who have written, testifying of the benefits they have derived from studying THE CHRISTIAN HERALD during the past year, and gratefully acknowledging the help it has been to them in their work. Any Christian reader having the interest of the colored race at heart, could find no better way of benefiting the race at small cost than by contributing to this fund. In helping the preachers, the congregations are helped, too.

The Death of Dr. Summers, the Well-known medical missionary in Africa, is the sad news in a letter we have received from his friend and helper Dr. George D. Dowkontt, the Director of the Medical Missionary Association in New York. Dr. Summers has been laboring in Africa since 1885. He came to New York in 1879, and studied medicine under Dr. Dowkontt, for the purpose of fitting himself for the foreign mission field. After passing his examination, and receiving his M. D. diploma, he set out for Africa. He spent a short time at Loanda, and then proceeded to Melange, where he remained a year. His work there was much blessed, and after it was fully established he wrote to Dr. Dowkontt for some one to succeed him, and started on a six months' journey of one thousand miles to the further side of the Congo. In December, 1886, he was at Luluaburg, on the Kasai River, and was making that place a centre of missionary tours. The cause and date of his death are as yet unknown. A portrait and life of him will be published in this journal soon.

A Hindoo's Ashes are to be Scattered on the sea by a passenger on the Cunard steamship *Umbria*, which sailed from New York on November 10. A short time ago a Hindoo named Gorinda Row Sattay came on a visit to this country from Sholapore, India. Sattay, as he was familiarly called, was a finely educated man, and had arranged to remain in New York and teach Sanskrit. The rigors of this climate were, however, particularly severe upon his delicate frame during the early weeks of autumn, and two weeks ago he died. Sattay's dying wish was to be cremated after death, and while he laid no injunction upon the friends about him regarding his ashes, his well-known national opposition to burial caused them to plan another disposition of them. The ashes were accordingly taken out on the Cunard steamer *Umbria* by the President of the Aryan Theosophical Society, who will scatter them over the waters of the Atlantic Ocean on the voyage to Liverpool. Precisely what doctrine underlies this disposition of the dead body is not stated, but it can make no difference to the man himself. God is able, even in this case, to reunite soul and body on the day when a final account must be given of the life they lived together in the world. (Rev. 20:13.)

A Suit to Recover Brains has Been Com-menced in San Francisco. The *Chronicle* of that city states that papers have been served on the Coroner, requiring him to show cause why the brain of an executed murderer should not be given to the father and mother of the deceased. It appears that after the execution the question of insanity, which was raised at the trial, still excited the interest of specialists in brain disorders, and an application was made to the Coroner for permission to dissect the head of the murderer. The Coroner granted the request, and the brain was removed for examination. The body was given to the parents, but on their discovery that the brain was missing, they entered a replevin suit, claiming that they had a right to the whole of the body of their dead son. Their grievance is only a sentimental one, but it is stated that they will press it to the utmost extent the law will allow. Though they do not set a money value on the strange property for which they are to contend with the Coroner, they apparently regard it as valuable. They make a mistake that is very common. Comparatively few realize the true relative values of the body and the soul. The body is pampered and its desires gratified at the cost of money and daily toil, while the soul with its momentous interests is neglected. (Matt. 6:25.)

A Silent Wedding Ceremony was Performed in Brooklyn, N. Y., on November 14. A large assemblage of guests was gathered in a handsome residence of that city in the evening, and a reporter who noticed the festivity inquired the cause. He was informed that the daughter of the owner was to be married, and as the ceremony would be a novel one he might go in and witness it. At the appointed hour he saw the bride, handsomely attired in lavender moire, stand up with the groom, a young sculptor of New York, before the clergyman, whom he recognized as Dr. Gallaudet. Not a word was spoken, but the interest which was manifested by the company showed that the ceremony was in progress. Then the reporter perceived that the young couple were deaf mutes, and that they were attending to questions put to them by Dr. Gallaudet's rapid fingers, and answering them in the same manner. Among the witnesses were several members of Dr. Gallaudet's Deaf Mute Club, who intelligently followed the questions and responses of the ceremony. At the conclusion the couple were declared man and wife, and were congratulated in the usual fashion. An unintelligent observer might have attached little moment to the gestures of the clergyman and the young man and woman, but their subsequent lives would show him that, to them, the ceremony meant union. It should be so with every one who by faith enters into union with Christ. The union may not be noticed, or not be understood, by outsiders, but its effects should be seen in a changed life. (II Cor. 5:17.)

An Electrified Meat Market in New Haven, Conn., caused some excitement a few days ago. Through some disarrangement of the electric light wires the market suddenly became charged with electricity. The salesman laying his hand on a big cleaver received a shock that set him howling with pain. A man who was taking some oysters from a basket which rested against a water-pipe, dropped them with a cry. Another man was told to bring the carcase of a lamb from a hook at the back of the stand, but when he put his shoulder under it and threw his arms around it he received a shock which threw him to the floor. A woman came along and stopped to examine the cabbages in a barrel at the door, but the first she picked up set her screaming and groaning with the prickling sensation which passed from her hands through her body. Not until a lineman, who was sent for, readjusted the wires could any article in the market be touched without receiving a shock more or less violent, according to its nature and position. The surprise of the people was the greater because it came from familiar objects, which had not, before, produced painful sensations. An analogous experience is in the memory of every true Christian. After his conversion the world and all things in his life are changed to him. Pursuits and amusements which, before, yielded him pleasure, would shock his conscience and give him positive pain. But, unlike the experience in the market, the changed condition is not in them but in him. (II Cor. 5:17.)

A Twenty-five Years' Search for a Missing brother was rewarded with success last week, though the triumph was marred by melancholy circumstances. Every year since the close of the war the War Department has received a letter from a lady, inquiring if anything had been heard of her brother, who enlisted in a Massachusetts regiment, and disappeared at the battle of Spottsylvania. Each year a reply in the negative was sent. It seems that the young man was a favorite in his company, and when he was missed after the battle, his comrades made every effort to find his body, believing that he must have been shot. They could find no trace of him. They then raised a flag of truce, and looked for him among the dead in the enemy's lines, but he was not there. Afterward a fruitless search was made for him in the Southern prisons. Since that time his sister has never heard a word from him; but she persisted in the belief that he was alive, and never relaxed her efforts to find him. Last week the police found an insane man wandering in the streets of Boston, and held him while inquiries were made for his friends. The lady heard of it, and went to see him. She found that he was her brother, but he was too demented to recognize her. He had been shot in the head in the battle, and had been insane for a quarter of a century. While his sister had been searching for him, he had been confined in various lunatic asylums, and in the intervals had wandered about in different States. Christian workers, who are seeking souls for the Master, are engaged in a search for their lost brothers who are crazed by the madness of sin. But, happily, when they are recovered, they are delivered from their malady. (Luke 15:17, 18.)

BRIEF NOTES.

Mr. Yaroo M. Neesan, the Persian student who has been preparing in New York for missionary work in his native country, and whose portrait and life appeared in this journal on December 23, 1886, was ordained by Bishop Potter on November 5.

Mr. Ben Hogan, the converted pugilist, has had large meetings at Tarport, Pa. The Methodist church, in which they were held, was crowded each night to the doors by a most attentive congregation. Local journals describe the work as very successful.

Gifts amounting to over eighty thousand dollars are announced by the president and trustees of Princeton College. Of this sum $50,000 has been contributed by Mrs. Susan D. Brown, which is to go toward the erection of a new dormitory, which is much needed.

Rev. S. Gascoigne, Fort Simcoe, Washington Territory, asks readers of this journal who do not keep their copies for binding, to send them to him when they are done with. Many Indians in his Sunday-schools can read, but have no books or papers, nor money to buy them.

Rev. H. C. Yatman's services in Galveston, Texas, are stated by a correspondent to have aroused a remarkable movement there. Such crowds have attended, and so deep an interest has been manifested, as to astonish the citizens and encourage the hope of permanent results.

Rev. John Drake, an English evangelist, who is visiting this country, would like to engage in evangelistic work while he is here. His terms are his expenses and a free-will offering. His address is P. O. Box 198, Norwich, Chenango Co., N. Y.

There are now 191 Societies of Christian Endeavor in New Jersey, with a membership of over ten thousand, representing eight denominations. The societies are found in 65 Presbyterian churches, 53 Baptist, 24 Reformed (Dutch), 20 Methodist, 14 Congregational, 1 Episcopal, 1 Christian, and 1 Union.

Major George A. Hilton has commenced an evangelistic tour in the Pacific States, which we trust will be much blessed. His appointments are as follows: Laramie, Wyoming Ter., November 21–25; Evanston, November 29 to December 2; Tacoma, Washington Ter., December 7–12; Seattle, December 15–23.

At the November meeting of the Board of Managers of the American Bible Society, grants of books were made to various correspondents in the United States and foreign lands; the aggregate value being about $8,762. The issues from the Bible House during October were 83,011 copies; issues since April 1, 545,457 copies.

Mr. Ferdinand Schiverea has been holding meetings at Owen Sound, Ont., Canada. The Presbyterian and Methodist churches united in the work, and over two hundred persons publicly professed faith as the result of God's blessing on his preaching. From that place he went to London, Ont., where preparations were made for ensuring a large attendance at his meetings.

Mr. C. S. Mason, who has been until this month State Secretary of the Young Men's Christian Associations in California, has resigned to undertake evangelistic work, chiefly among young men. The State Association reluctantly accepted his resignation, and passed a resolution heartily commending him in his new sphere, and praying for a blessing on his labors. His address for this month will be, Young Men's Christian Association, Albany, N. Y. Afterward, 232 Sutter St., San Francisco.

A PARADOX.

A New Sermon by Pastor C. H. Spurgeon.

"When I am weak, then am I strong." II Cor. 12 : 10.

A Significant Experience—One Common to All—I. The Terms of the Paradox Reversed—Strong Men Finding Themselves Weak—Strong to Win Heaven by Good Works—Strong to Turn to God at Any Time—Christians Strong in Knowledge—In Experience—In Wisdom and Prudence—II. The Weak Finding Themselves Strong—Must be Consciously Weak—Contritely Weak—Will Have Firm Standing-Ground—Has a Commission to Support Him—Is Driven to his God.

THE expression is paradoxical, and seems somewhat singular; yet it was the experience of the apostle Paul, a man of calm spirit, by no means fanciful, a wise man, and far removed from a fanatic. It was the experience of one who was led of the Spirit of God, and therefore it was a gracious experience: the experience of one who was a father in Israel, who could safely bid us be imitators of him, even as he imitated the Lord Jesus Christ; and therefore it was a safe experience. If we are weak, so was Paul; and if, like him, we are strong in our weakness, we shall be in the best of company. If the same things be seen in us which were wrought in the apostle of the Gentiles, we may join with him in glorying in infirmities, because the power of Christ doth rest upon us, and we may count ourselves happy that with such a saint we can cry, "When I am weak, then am I strong."

I. Perhaps I can expound the text best if I first turn it

The Other Way Up,

and use it as a warning. *When I am strong, then am I weak.* Perhaps, while thinking of the text thus turned inside out, we shall be getting light upon it to be used when we view it with the right side outwards, and see that *when we are weak, then we are strong.* I am quite sure that some people think themselves very strong, and are not so. Their proud consciousness of fancied strength is the indication of a terrible weakness. We have among us certain persons who think that they can do all that is needful for their own salvation whenever they please to do so. They can perform all sorts of good works, or at least quite enough to carry them to heaven. Their first idea is that they are to be saved by their own doings; and they really expect to be so saved. They may admit that they have a few faults and flaws in their character; but these are so trifling as to be hardly worth mentioning, and God Almighty is too merciful to be very particular. Their lives have been excellent, their tempers amiable, their manners courteous, their spirit generous, and they quite believe that by keeping on at the same pace they will win the prize; if they do not, who will? Ah, my friend, there is

No Going to Heaven that Way

—by self and the works of self! Your error is a common one, but it is fatal. I have seen many epitaphs of persons, placed by the mistaken kindness of friends upon their tombstones, which I felt sure would have been sufficient to shut them out of heaven if they had been true. These departed worthies do not appear to have been sinners at all; their virtues were superlative, their faults non-existent. I wonder how they would behave themselves in heaven, if they were really admitted there! All the rest are singing, "We have washed our robes, and made them white in the blood of the Lamb"; but these needed no washing, and so they would be likely to strike up a little song by themselves, and sing, "Our robes never needed washing; we kept them white as snow." What a discord that would create in the music of the skies!

No, my strong and virtuous hearer, you are under a grave delusion. There is a great similarity between your talk and the talk of that religious individual who went up to the temple in our Saviour's days, and, standing before the thrice-holy God, dared to say, "God, I thank Thee that I am not as other men are." He was not justified that day, nor will you be. A poor tax-gatherer, despised by himself, and an off-cast from his own people, stood in the temple at the same time, and all that he dared to say was, "God be merciful to me a sinner." This unworthy sinner went to his house justified, while the other worthy person was not accepted. If you think yourselves strong enough to procure heaven by your own efforts, you are ignorantly insulting the cross of Christ, for you seem to insinuate that your virtues can avail you without Jesus.

Listen to me a moment, and quit your

Fancied Strength:

you, my dear hearer, cannot keep the law of God, for you have already broken it. How can you preserve a crystal vase entire when you have already dashed it to atoms? You must now be saved by the merits and the strength of another, or not at all; for your own merit is out of the question, through past failure. That strength of yours, upon which you dote so much, is perfect weakness. May the Lord show you this, and make you faint at heart on that account; for then you shall be strong, with real and saving strength! Now your imaginary strength is making you really weak, and that boasted merit of yours is shutting you out from true righteousness. He that is strong in the notion of merit is weak even to utter folly before the God of truth.

"Yes," we hear you reply, "there is a gospel way of salvation. We know that there is, for you preach it continually. You tell us that men must repent, and believe the gospel; that they must be renewed in the spirit of their minds, and must both overcome sin, and follow after holiness." Yes, I do say all that; but what do you say to it? Is it really so that you find here a

Ground for Your Own Strength?

Do you say, "I feel that I can repent whenever I please, and believe in Jesus when I choose"? Ah! then I must assure you that when you are strong in that way, you are weak. I never yet knew anybody repent who gloried in his power to repent; I never yet knew a man heart-broken for sin who boasted that he could break his own heart when and where he pleased. "What!" cries one, "surely I can believe in Jesus Christ when I please!" I have not denied that statement, have I? But I tell you that your notion of power to believe is your weakness; and I would rather by half hear you cry, with deep solemnity, "Oh that God would give me faith! Lord, help my unbelief!"

So far I have spoken by way of warning to unconverted people. I desire now to say a word to those who profess to be Christians, and, let us hope, are so; but they are, in a measure, erring in the same way as those to whom I have spoken. They are remarkably strong: at least, in their own esteem

They Are Very Samsons,

although others fear that the Philistines will capture them. By this token may they know their own weakness—even by this, that they think themselves strong.

First, many are wonderfully strong as to knowledge. They know almost everything. If in any department they are a little short, they make up for it by knowing so much more in another direction. If they are too narrow here, they overlap there. They are knowing men, and need no man to tell them so. They are not children, but quite able to think for themselves. They are not credulous, but amazingly clear-headed and cultured. I have noticed that these fine gentlemen have been the first to deny the faith, and to fall into all manner of heresies. Do you wonder? Those who are so very sure are always the most uncertain. O brethren, when we are very wise in our own esteem, we are bordering upon fools, even if we have not already entered into that company. When we tremblingly sit at Jesus' feet, to learn everything fresh, and fresh from Him; when we shudder at anything that questions His Deity, or lowers His sacrifice; when we shut up a book and cast it from us, because we feel that it pollutes us with unbelief—then are we wise and strong.

Again, I have noticed some professed Christian people wonderfully

Strong Through Experience.

Their experience has been very extensive, and the knowledge it has brought them they consider to be specially profound, and, consequently, they are not afraid of temptation, for they feel that they are too wise to be entrapped. They can go just so far, and then stop, for they are fitted with *the patent brakes of prudence.* They are such good mountain climbers that they can stand on the edge of the precipice, and look over, and even hang over, without fear of their ever being giddy and falling over. Of course they would not advise other people to go quite so far as they may safely go; but then, what is temptation to other men is no temptation to them. Their vessel is so tight and trim, and they understand navigation so perfectly, that they rather like a tempest than not, just to show how well their vessel can behave in a storm. Ah me! When you next read the list of wrecks, you may expect to see the name of their ship among the castaways. *Old birds may not be caught with chaff, but they can be shot with a gun.* No one is out of danger, and no one is more in danger than the man who is carnally secure. Those who feel that their experience, be it what it may, only teaches them that the farther they can keep from temptation the better, these are in a better state.

Let us note another point. I have known certain Christians who thought themselves

Strong in Wisdom

and prudence. They have been gifted with clear insight and a measure of shrewdness, and have, therefore, felt that their judgment on most subjects was that of an umpire. If we were called upon to select a man who, as to his life as a whole, perpetrated the greatest folly, we should mention Solomon. Yet he was the wisest of men. Yes, the cream of wisdom, when curdled, makes the worst of folly. Then, brethren, whenever we feel sure of our own superior intelligence, let us suspect ourselves of weakness.

Further, dear friends, we shall often find that our strength will lie in patience—in extreme weakness which yields itself up to the will of God without the power or will to murmur.

> "And when it seems no chance nor change
> From grief can set me free,
> Hope finds its strength in helplessness,
> And, patient, wait on thee."

I am sure that in reference to power, either to do or to suffer rightly, we are not strong when we compliment ourselves upon our ability; and we are strong when, under a sense of absolute inability, we depend wholly upon God. That sermon preached in the glory of our oratory turned out to be mere husks for swine; while that discourse which we delivered in weakness, with a humble hope that God would use it, proved to be royal meat for the Lord's chosen. That work which you performed in the vigor of your unquestioned talent came to nothing, while that quiet act which you washed with your tears, and perfumed with your prayers, will live, and yield you sheaves.

Creature Strength

brings forth nothing at all which has life in it: only the seed which the Creator puts into the hand of our weakness will produce a harvest.

So it is in bearing as well as acting. If we say concerning sickness, "I shall never be impatient. I can bear it like a Stoic," what of that? You will then have done no more than many have done before you, with no great gain to themselves or to others. But if, bowing your head before the Lord, you wait His sovereign will, and say, "Lord, help me! If thy left hand shall smite me, let thy right hand sustain me. I am willing to drink this bitter cup, saying, 'Not as I will, but as thou wilt.' Lord, help me!"—you shall bear up triumphantly, and come out of the furnace refined, to the praise and the glory of your God. When you fancy that you are strong to suffer, you will fail; but in conscious weakness you will be enabled to play the man.

II. Now, let us take our text the right way upwards. "When I am weak, then am I strong." "When" and "then" are

The Two Pivots

of the text—the hinges upon which it turns. "*When* I am weak." What does that mean? It means when the believer is consciously weak, when he painfully feels, and distinctly recognizes, that he is weak, then he is strong. In truth, we are always weak, whether we know it or not; but when we not only believe this to be the fact, but see it to be the fact—then it is that we are strong. When it is forced home upon us, that we are less than nothing and vanity—when our very soul echoes and re-echoes that word, "Without me ye can do nothing"—then it is that we are strong.

We are strong when we are contritely weak. When we confess that much of our weakness is our fault—a weakness which we ought to have overcome—even then we have in that weakness a real strength. The sort of weakness that makes a man say, "I cannot be any stronger, I am doing my best," is not strength, but folly; but that weakness which makes you lament your failures and deplore your shortcomings, has in it a holy stimulus and force. When you can neither repent, nor believe, nor love as you wish to do, you are repenting, believing, and loving with a strength which is more true than apparent. It is the will with which we act which is the strength of the action; and when the will is so powerful that it makes us mourn because we cannot find how to perform its bidding, then are we strong according to the divine measurement of strength. Contrite weakness is

Spiritual Strength.

When a man is thoroughly weak—not only partially, but altogether weak—then is he strong. When, apart from the Lord Jesus Christ, he is utter weakness, and nothing more, then it is that he is strong. Let me persuade you to make a full confession of weakness to the Lord. Say, "Lord, I cannot do what I ought to do; I cannot do what I want to do; I cannot do what I used to do; I cannot do what other people do; I cannot do what I mean to do; I cannot do what I am sure I shall do; I cannot do what I feel impelled to do; and over this sinful weakness I mourn." Then add, "Lord, I long to serve thee perfectly, yet I cannot do it. Unless thou help, me I can do nothing aright." Brother, you are strong while you plead in that fashion. You can do all things through Christ who strengtheneth you; and he will strengthen you, now that you are emptied of self. How true it is, "When I am weak, then am I strong"!

I have brought out the "when." Now lend me your ears and hearts just for a minute, while I bring out the "then." "*Then* am I strong." When is that? Why, a man is strong when he is consciously weak, because now he has reached the truth. He really is weak; and if he does not know that he is so, he is under the influence of a falsehood. Now, a lie is weakness.

Lying Strength

is all fluff and foam; a mere appearance, a mockery, a delusion. Nothing hinders from getting the reality like contentment with a mere appearance. The true heart is heartily sick of shows and shams, and it cries, "Lord, help me to get rid of these shadows! Help me to come at the truth! Help me to deal with realities!" When you are made to feel your utter weakness you are on sure ground of truth—unpleasant truth, no doubt, yet sure truth. Therefore, a man becomes strong when he is consciously weak, because he is on the truth, and is not being flattered by false hopes.

Next, he will be strong, because he will only go with a commission to support him. He will not be eager to run without being sent. He says within himself, when he proposes a service to himself, "No, I am too weak to undertake anything of my own head." He will wait for a call. This is not the kind of man that will climb up into a pulpit, and from a dizzy brain pour out nonsense. He will not crave to lead, for he feels that he needs much help even to follow. He feels himself too weak to set up for a master in Israel. This is not the kind of man that will venture into argument with sceptics for the fun or for the glory of the thing. Oh, no; he is too weak for that. He says, "If I am called to defend the faith, I will do it in God's strength, hoping that it will be given me in the same hour what I shall speak. If I am called to preach I will preach, and nobody shall stop me; for the Lord will be with my mouth. But, you see, until the man is conscious of his own weakness, he will run without being sent; and there is nobody so weak as that man.

The man who is consciously weak is strong, next, because of the holy caution that he will be sure to use. He will be on his guard, because he does not feel able to cope with adversaries. He will ask for a convoy for his little barque, for he is aware of pirates. If this weak man has to pass through the Valley of the Shadow of Death, depend upon it he will carry in his hand the weapon of All-prayer, like a drawn sword. The man that has strength goes hurrying on over hedge and ditch, and soon comes into mischief; but the consciously weak pilgrim keeps to the high-road, and travels carefully; and he is strong.

Moreover, when a man is weak, then is he strong, because he is sure to pray, and

Prayer is Power.

The man who laments his weakness is sure to cry to the strong for strength. The more his weakness presses on him, the more will he pray. While he can do without his God, he will do without his God; but when his own weakness becomes utter and entire, and he is ready to perish, then he turns unto his Lord, and is made strong. The utterly weak cry out unto God as nobody else does. He is too weak to play at praying: he groans, he sighs he weeps. In his abject weakness he prevails, as Jacob did. The weaker a man is in himself, the stronger he is in prayer, if he makes use of his weakness as an appealing argument: "Lord, if I were strong, Thou mightest leave me. Do not leave me, for I am weakness itself! I am the feeblest child in all Thy family; leave me not, neither forsake me. If Thou leavest any, leave not Thy poor dying infant, that can hardly wail out its griefs." Weakness, as a plea with God in prayer, becomes a source of strength.

When we are weak we are strong, again, because then we are driven away from self to God. All strength is in God, and it is well to come to the one solitary storehouse and source of might. There is no power apart from God. As long as you and I look to the creature, we are looking to a cracked, broken cistern that holds no water; but when we know that it is broken, and that there is not a drop of water in it, then we hasten to the great fountain and well-head. While we rest in any measure upon self, or the creature, we are standing with one foot on the sand; but when we get right away from human nature, because we are too weak to have the least reliance upon self whatever, then we have both feet on the rock; and this is safe standing.

Last of all, dear friends, I believe that, when a man is weak, he becomes strong to a large extent, because *his weakness compels him to concentrate all his faculties.* A sense of weakness brings out all the

Forces of a Resolute Spirit,

and leads him to call in all the energy within his reach. Many a poor, weak brother, who says all the little that he knows, gives forth more instruction than the learned divine who only favors his people with a small portion of his vast stores. When a man, in serving God, spends himself to the last farthing, he will often far more enrich his hearers than the man of ten talents who uses his resources with a prudent parsimony. Dear brother, it will often be a good thing for you to feel, "Now, God helping me, I must do my very utmost this time. I have so little ability that every faculty within me must be wide awake, and serve God at its best." Thus your weakness will arouse you and set you on fire, and by the blessing of God it will be the means of gaining you strength.

Very well, then, let us pick up our tools and go to our work rejoicing, feeling—Well, I may be weaker, or I may be stronger in myself, but my strength is in my God. If I should ever become stronger, then I must pray for a deeper sense of weakness, lest I become weak through my strength. And if I should ever become weaker than I am, then I must hope and believe that I am really becoming stronger in the Lord. Whether I am weak or strong, what matters it? He who never fails and never changes, will perfect His strength in my weakness, and this is glory to me. Amen.

GEMS FROM NEW BOOKS.

A FUTILE OCCUPATION.*

WELL do I remember that singular character, Professor John Wilson, of Edinburgh—"Christopher North," he was generally called. He was passionately fond of angling. One day, after fishing for hours in a loch in Selkirkshire, without getting anything, being watched all the time by a shepherd and his dog, he was turning despondently away, when the shepherd said, "Ye'll not have killed many trout, sir?" "No, I have had no sport at all; not a nibble." "I dare say no," said the other, "for it's well known there never was a trout in that loch from the beginning of creation." But *the man who is seeking success and satisfaction in the world is pursuing as hopeless a game.*

A Foreigner's Changed Opinion.

Set your face determinedly against all underhand dealing. Have nothing to do with shuffling or shams of any kind. Do your own part to purify the market-place, and to make the commerce of our land such as Heaven can smile upon it. Detest the gospel of shoddy. Hate all trickery, imposition, and evasion. In the smallest trifles act as under the eye of God. Plant your foot firmly on the line of stern principle, and dare the devil himself to persuade you to cross that line. Even as regards this world, dishonesty is the worst policy. It means, in the end, death to your peace, death to your comfort, death to your interests, and death to your soul. Only two days ago I heard of a young man who had business transactions with a foreign merchant, and was asked, some time since, to send out certain packages of goods marked of a less weight than they actually were, the object being to evade the payment of a heavy import duty. Many a young fellow would have smiled and done it. The friend I am speaking of telegraphed, "I cannot, and won't do it." "Very well," replied the foreigner; "there are plenty of others who will, and our business connection is at an end." This meant a heavy loss to the conscientious youth. Since then the foreign merchant has written him as follows: "Enclosed is a draft for ——, which please put to my credit. I am sending my son to you to learn your way of business. There is nobody in whom I have so much confidence as I have in you. Will you take him into your office, and make him the sort of man that you are yourself?"

General Gordon's Heroic Act.

The men who in any trade or occupation have risen to the top of the tree have been men who, to use President Lincoln's favorite expression, "kept pegging away," and were never in the habit of shelving their own work upon other persons. There is a proverb I used to meet with in Turkey, which advises you never to do to-day what can be put off till to-morrow, and never to do yourself what you can get another to do for you. I hope you will go as much as possible in the teeth of such degrading counsel. The advice General Gordon gave is incomparably more worthy your acceptance. The occasion I allude to was the first day on which fire was opened at Sebastopol from the twenty-one-gun battery, and when the sand-bags forming one of the embrasures caught fire. A corporal and a sapper

* From "Sure to Succeed," by J. Thain Davidson, D. D., a book full of sound advice to young men, showing that the most successful life in the world without Christ is only failure. Pp. 289. Price $1.25. Published by *A. C. Armstrong & Son*, 714 Broadway, New York.

Mrs. Chamberlain, nee Endicott (*See page 741*).

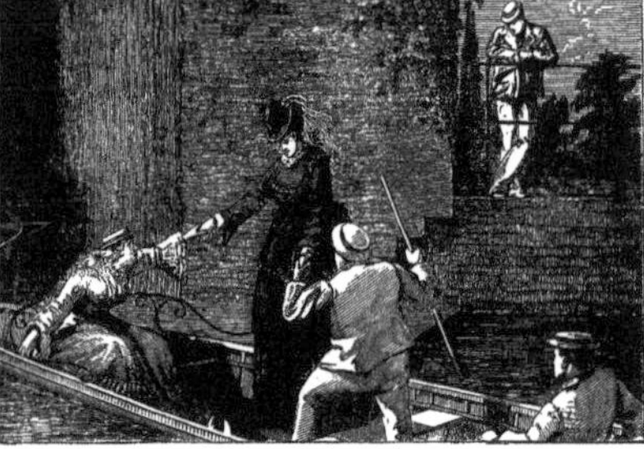

A Momentous Boating Excursion.

of the engineers were told off to repair the damage. The corporal ordered his companion to mount the embrasure, undertaking himself to hand up the fresh bags to him. The firing was heavy at the time, and the sapper demurred to this arrangement, suggesting that the corporal should get up, and that he would do the handing-up business. There was a bit of a wrangle over it. General Gordon, hearing the dispute, came to the spot, mounted the pile of bags himself, and whilst a storm of bullets swept around him, coolly performed the task. Thereupon he quietly descended, and looking sternly at the corporal, said, "Never order a man to do a thing you are afraid to do yourself."

A Foundling's Crest.

About three hundred and fifty years ago there might have been seen trudging along a country lane, not a hundred miles from London, a weary, anxious-looking woman with an infant in her arms. After a while she stood still beside a gate that opened into a field, and, looking keenly on every side to be sure that no one was near, she wrapped the little one in her shawl, laid it down gently under a hedge, and, turning into the lane again, presently vanished out of sight. An hour or two later there chanced to pass down that lane a merry school-boy on his way to a neighboring farm. It was in the warm spring-time, when the hedge-rows were gay with primroses and the insects were fluttering amongst the grass; and as the light-hearted youth scampered whistling along, he thought he heard the loud chirp of a grasshopper, so he bounded over the hedge, and stooped down to catch it, when lo! there lay before him a baby smiling in its innocence! Delighting in his discovery, he took it up in his arms and ran home joyfully with the prize. His mother, a humble farmer's wife, was too kind-hearted to refuse to admit the foundling; and, though she had children of her own, resolved to keep the little stranger, whose life had in all likelihood, been saved through the chirp of a grasshopper.

You know the rest of the story. Years passed, and the infant grew up to be a man, and the man became one of the richest and most influential merchants of the city of London. God blessed all he took in hand, and he rose to be the most noted man in the city. As an expression of gratitude to the metropolis to which he owed so much, he founded the Royal Exchange, and when the building was completed, Sir Thomas Gresham (for it is to him that I refer) placed upon the topmost pinnacle a figure of a grasshopper, in stone, as a memento of the incident that saved his life; and there you may see it preaching to all around a lesson not unlike that which St. Paul uttered eighteen centuries ago, when he declared to the proud men of Corinth that God had chosen the weak and contemptible things of the world to serve some of His grandest purposes.

AN EVENTFUL EXCURSION.

(*See Illustration.*)

"AH, Percy, you are going for a row, I see," said a lady who, with her daughter, was strolling along a path bordering one of our most beautiful rivers.

"Yes, Madam," said the young man addressed, a handsome man of about twenty-five years, who had recently left college and commenced practice as a physician in the neighborhood. "I was coming," he continued, "to your house in the hope of persuading you and Miss Folkestone to accompanying me."

"You are very kind, Percy," said Mrs. Folkestone, "but we have accepted the invitation of the Wynters to join them in an excursion, and we are just on our way to their boat-house."

The reply pained the young doctor, deeply. He was seriously in love with Connie Folkestone, and had earnestly pleaded with her widowed mother for permission to make her his wife. Connie herself would have accepted him, but she would never marry without her mother's consent, nor would she give any promise that might bring her in conflict with her mother's somewhat despotic nature. The widow had not refused him, but had not given him a definite answer, and Percy Collins believed that she was anxious to secure for her daughter a more wealthy husband than he. She was ambitious, he knew, and he feared that she would not be over scrupulous as to the character of a suitor, provided he possessed the fortune she desired her daughter to enjoy. But he worked hard, was growing in popularity, and believed that in a short time he would have such an income as would give him favor in the mother's eyes. Lately, the young Wynters had appeared rather frequently at the widow's cottage, and Percy, who knew them well as fast young men amply endowed with wealth, feared that if either asked Mrs. Folkestone for permission to win Connie's affections, she would give her consent. One of them appeared at this moment, and with a patronizing nod to the young doctor, and an elaborate greeting of the widow and her daughter, walked on with the latter, while Mrs. Folkestone followed with Dr. Collins.

"Pardon me, Mrs. Folkestone," said Collins; "it is not my habit to speak disparagingly of anyone, but I think that if you knew the character of those young men you would not consider them suitable companions for Connie."

"Ah! you are jealous, Percy; you do them an injustice. They appear to me excellent young men. A little wild, perhaps, but they will settle down as they grow older. I know what you are thinking of, but you know you are poor, and it is my duty to consider Connie's future."

"That is the very consideration I would press, dear Mrs. Folkestone," said Percy; "her future cannot be made happy by money only. No refined Christian girl, such as Connie is, could be happy married to a man leading a life such as both these young Wynters are living."

"I am not sure that Connie would be happy with you. She has her dear father's notions about religion, I know, but I think they are antiquated and narrow. A gay, cheerful husband, with the means to gratify her natural tastes, is what I should prefer for Connie; she is inclined to be morbid on that subject, and you would encourage her. But here we are at the boathouse, so I must wish you good-bye."

Percy Collins looked down very sadly from the little wharf at the gay party in the boat as Mrs. Folkestone stepped nervously in, assisted by her daughter and Mr. Alfred Wynter. He saw them push off, and then walked moodily away, oppressed by the thought that the girl he loved was in danger of being sacrificed for money. He was in no mood for boating after that, and walked away to the top of a hill overlooking the river, where he flung himself disconsolately on the grass and gazed after the boat as it glided out of sight.

How long he lay there he never knew; but it must have been two or three hours, for looking up from his reverie he noticed that the sun was near its setting, and he rose hurriedly to return home. As he did so he looked up the river, and there he saw the Wynters' boat returning. He was turning away when he was struck by its erratic movements. The young men were pulling very clumsily, with no regard to time, and Alfred especially, who was pulling stroke, was endangering the safety of the party by his awkward attempts to feather—so awkward that they would have disgraced a novice.

An instant, and a shrill scream reached his ear. Alfred's oar was deep in the water and he could not withdraw it. The boat lurched heavily to that side, and Mrs. Folkestone, springing to her feet in alarm, lost her balance and fell; her weight sufficed to overturn the light craft, and in a moment the whole party were struggling in the water. Happily, the boat had not filled, but turned completely over and floated keel uppermost, and the two ladies were clinging to it while the young men were swimming for the shore.

Quick as thought Percy Collins bounded to the edge of the stream and ran like a deer to a place where a light outrigger was moored. He soon had her detached, and was pulling swiftly for the spot where the ladies were still clinging to the wrecked boat. He was just in time to reach them, as Mrs. Folkestone, fainting from fright and exhaustion, released her grasp and sank. He managed to take her on board, and then rescued the girl he loved. He pulled hard for the shore, where he was able to find shelter and restoratives for the ladies, and then returned to look for the young men. The younger had reached the bank, but Alfred was not to be seen, and it was not for many hours that his dead body was recovered.

It was from Mrs. Folkestone's lips that Percy heard the history of the affair. He learned that both ladies noticed soon after entering the boat that the young men were excited with wine, and just before returning they produced champagne, which was offered to the ladies and declined, but of which Alfred and his brother partook freely. That accounted for the awkward pulling and for the disaster. Mrs. Folkestone's gratitude to Percy for saving her own life and that of her daughter was boundless, and profiting by the check her ambition had received, he had no difficulty in extracting from her the promise so long withheld.

The Peak of Inspiration in the Yosemite Vall?y.

THE PEAK OF INSPIRATION.

ONE of the most remarkable objects in the Yosemite Valley is the gigantic rock to which has been given the name of The Peak of Inspiration. It stands at the entrance of the Valley, and is the point from which the best view of the grandeur of that wonderful ravine can be obtained. Baron Hübner thus describes the scene which burst upon him when, climbing the western slope of the Sierras on his mustang and travelling through forests of redwood, cedar, and pine, he reached the verge of the precipice of the Peak: "In front of us, on the opposite side of the Yosemite, one single immense block of square granite, with a flattened summit and perpendicular flanks, rises out of the valley beneath. The Mexicans gave it the name of *El Capitan*. [It is 3,300 feet above the valley, and almost perpendicular.] Further on toward the northeast, on both sides of the abyss, rise smooth vertical walls of rock, diversified here and there by peaks and domes with narrow aerial terraces, out of which spring gigantic firs. The horizon is bounded by a complete wall of granite, higher than the mountains which surround the valley, and of which the top appears perfectly straight. This is the highest ridge of the Sierra Nevada." Winding down from the peak into the valley the traveller is astonished, at almost every step, with some new view of surpassing beauty. One of these is the Bridal Fall, which makes but two springs in a leap of over nine hundred feet from the west side of Cathedral Rock. This is again surpassed by the Yosemite Fall, which 'as three leaps, the first of which is 1.600 feet.

THE EPOCHS OF A LIFE.

A NEW SERIAL STORY.

By Rev. L. S. Keyser.

(*Continued from page 734.*)

A Conflict.

No words could have made a stronger appeal to that weary, storm-tossed heart than those Mr. Bidder chose for the subject of his brief address: "Come unto Me, all ye that labor and are heavy laden, and I will give you rest." There was no eloquence, no rhetorical skill, in the old man's appeal. He had a treasure to offer that the world with all its resources could not give. A treasure for which aching hearts are pining, and all he attempted to do was to set out clearly where and how it might be obtained. How men were to come, to Whom they were to come, to whom the invitation was sent, and the boon Christ promised—those were the four points touched, and there was in all a clear note ringing, struck on the harp-string of an aged Christian's heart, which had itself basked in the sunshine and sweet calm of that delicious rest.

The effect was electrifying. Hadley, whose face had been bent downward during the address, looked up as the last words were spoken, saw the reverent, triumphant, confident affection which shone in the venerable face, and his own countenance reflected the expression. Rest—perfect peace—what to him were all other things that the world counts precious, compared with that? It was being offered to him here by one who had long enjoyed it, and as Hadley listened he was convinced that it was genuine, and was conscious that his perturbed feelings were becoming strangely tranquillized. His eyes and those of his uncle met, and tears were in both. "May the peace of God *which passeth all understanding*"—began the clergyman in solemn benediction, and Hadley, as he bowed his head, uttered a reverent "Amen."

"Any person present who is conscious that he has not the rest and peace of which I have been speaking," said Mr. Bidder, "but who is also conscious of his need of them and desires to possess them, may be helped in his quest by the prayers of Christian believers. We will gladly talk and pray with any such, if they will remain. Are there any here? Please answer by rising."

One after another rose in various parts of the house, and among them was the once arrogant, scornful unbeliever, Hadley Madelling.

He remained to the more private meeting afterward as invited, and when Mr. Bidder suggested that each of the seekers should state the difficulties that were troubling him and keeping him from accepting the invitation of Christ, and one after another had spoken, Hadley rose. His voice could not be steadied for a moment, but it recovered its clear tone, and he said:

"My friends, for a number of years my attitude toward religion has been a hostile one. I have not only doubted the Bible, but have openly opposed it, thinking it a gigantic fraud and imposture. But I confess to you frankly that my life of scepticism has been an unsatisfactory one—more like an arid, drouth-stricken desert than anything else to which I can compare it, and the startling fact is, the longer I traverse it the more arid does it become. Its total luadequacy to meet the wants of my life appalls me. I started out on a voyage of independent research, but my quest has thus far resulted in nothing but failure. I am tired of *the arid life of unbelief*. I cannot say that I am convinced of the truth of the Christian religion, but if it is true, as Christian people maintain, I want to know it, and I therefore ask you to help and instruct me, for I am blind and ignorant in spiritual matters."

A thrill of joy passed through every heart as the talented young teacher made this honest confession and humbly asked for direction, and all knelt, while Mr. Bidder and his friends pleaded with God to reveal Himself to the souls of the seekers and to guide them into all truth.

His uncle came and knelt by Hadley's side, and presently asked him if light had come.

"It seems that all the doubts I ever entertained have been gathered into one mass and hurled upon me," replied Hadley. "I cannot believe in God, or Christ, or the Bible, or prayer, and even if there is a God, I cannot believe that He will forgive all my arrogant opposition to Him. Will you pray for me?"

The old clergyman, with his arm tenderly clasped about his nephew, prayed fervently for him, for the gift of faith, for the banishment of doubt, for the illumination of the Spirit, until Hadley's heart became so unburdened that he rose to his feet saying:

"It is wonderful, wonderful! Let me go home now, and think it over."

"Before you leave," said his uncle, "allow me to give you a word of counsel and encouragement. When you get to your room, please read the fifty-first Psalm and the fifteenth chapter of Luke, and go to God in prayer."

The young sceptic took the hands of the Christian workers who grouped about him, thanked them for their interest in his welfare, and then hurried to his lodgings to carry out the instructions of his faithful counsellor. As he read the story of the prodigal son, it seemed to scintillate with new meanings. He found it especially pertinent to his own needs, and, when he gave it its proper spiritual exegesis, it appeared to be a veritable biography of his own life of unbelief: the departure of the wayward son from his father's house, his career in the land afar off, his feeding upon the husks, and his final resolution to return to his father, all these were but symbolical representations of Hadley's own experience. Then he wondered whether God would receive him, as the father in the parable received and welcomed his returning son.

He remembered that his uncle had advised him to go to God in prayer. Kneeling by his bedside, he tried to lift up his heart to God, but the feeling that he was mocking at divine things overcame him and choked his utterance, so that he could not say a word but "Lord, have mercy!"

He spent a restless night, and when morning came it seemed to him that the darkness of Erebus could not have been deeper and more impenetrable than the darkness that enveloped his soul, and had he been tormented by the fabled daughters of night, he could not have been more miserable. Some light came to him through the reading of the Scriptures, but to his astonishment he found that he was a great deal more conversant with Greek mythology than with the sacred Book that he had been criticising and deriding so long, and this fact added to his torture.

Not knowing where to find the hope-inspiring and consolatory portions of God's Word, he dipped into it here and there at random, and, as it happened, his eye fell upon a number of comminatory passages: "Woe unto the wicked; it shall be ill with him"; "The wages of sin is death"; "The soul that sinneth, it shall die"; "Your iniquities have separated between you and your God, and your sins have hid His face from you, that He will not hear."

All these verses seemed like so many death-sentences to his hopes of pardon. As a matter of fact, he, like many others who think themselves capable of criticising Holy Writ, found that he did not know how to use it effectually or apply it to his own needs.

All the morning, like Ixion on his wheel, he was kept revolving around and around, until his head was dizzy and his heart was sick, but with all his circular movement there was apparently no progress. After dinner he said to himself: "Perhaps Hanson could help me," and he grasped his hat and hurried to the latter's room.

"I am in trouble," he said, without circumlocution. And then he told Hanson of his public committal the evening before. The clergyman grasped his hand warmly, and as he spoke his lips quivered with joy.

"The most courageous and manly step that you have ever taken, my dear Madelling," he said. "And now tell me about your perplexities."

Hadley complied, giving as accurate a description as he could of the spiritual throes through which he had recently passed.

"Let us go at once to the law and the testimony," said Hanson, when the recital was concluded. And taking up his hand-Bible, he turned the leaves with perfect familiarity, reading the selections that were most relevant to his sceptical friend's spiritual condition. Many of the promises of God were read and explained, and it was shown that God had made all the initial overtures, and had been waiting, with outstretched arms, for the penitent sinner to accept them.

"Ah! if I could only believe in the existence of God!" said Hadley.

"Your difficulty is fundamental, I see," returned Hanson. "You seem to have gone to the very depths of unbelief. But God will reveal Himself to the agnostic as well as to any other sinner who comes to Him."

"Why does He not do so, then, in my case?" questioned Hadley.

"You must ask Him earnestly, and if He does not grant your request immediately, you must show your sincerity and earnestness by continuing to ask; and you must remember, too, that it is for wise reasons that He withholds the coveted blessing for a while."

"I cannot get hold of it; there is something, I know not what, that opposes me continually; I seem to be groping in the dark, and the door that opens into the light is bolted against me," moaned Hadley.

"Suppose you were in a dungeon as dark as your spiritual state seems to be now, and you suspected that I was on the outside and could extricate you from your imprisonment, would you not cry, 'Hanson, are you there? If you are, will you not open the door?'"

"Yes—oh, is it so simple? I see—but if there is a God I have insulted Him so arrogantly that I am ashamed to call upon Him now; it seems like mockery."

"'Though your sins be as scarlet, I will make them white as snow,'" quoted Hanson; and the verse that Hadley had thought so hackneyed and threadbare now gleamed with a new radiance. "Paul," continued Hanson, "was once an unbeliever, a vehement persecutor of the church of Christ, and yet he was accepted when he prayed."

"Paul? Ah—yes—Paul was once a rejector of Christ."

"You are near to the kingdom of God," said Hanson, with a radiant face. "Before you go, let me read you an excerpt from a prayer by a great English preacher, for I think that it will do you good." Opening the volume, Hanson read as follows:

"Almighty God, we bless Thee that Thou hast sent Thy Son to our broken-heartedness, our mourning, our unutterable distress and fear. Thou didst not send Him to our greatness and power, but to our littleness and weakness and utter insufficiency. The Son of Man is come to seek and to save that which was lost—we bless Thee for this, for in that word 'lost' we find our state. All we like sheep have gone astray."

"I feel that there is more in that prayer than I can comprehend," said Hadley, when the book was closed.

"It will become a reality to you bye and bye," returned Hanson, encouragingly.

It is not necessary to follow the young inquirer step by step through all his checkered and oscillating experience. For the confirmed unbeliever the birth-throes of the new life are usually more or less excruciating.

The evening's service still brought him more light. The following day, which was Sabbath, was an epochal day in his life. There was a joy in his heart that was altogether new to him; he felt a reverence for God's house that he had never felt before. Yet there was an unsteadiness in his emotional life that gave him constant solicitude; he felt that his hold upon God was still tremulous and uncertain; at any time he feared that the divine light—for he could call it by no other name—might be extinguished, and leave him again in Cimmerian darkness.

On Sabbath evening, which he spent in his uncle's church, he listened with rapturous joy to the discourse; but, strange to say, no sooner had he stepped from the church into the night, than his whole being was wrapped in the blackness of darkness, and all his old unbelief returned with redoubled power. He groaned aloud in his agony. His mind was filled with the most blasphemous thoughts, and rebellion ran riot in his heart.

It was a remarkable psychological experience, and perhaps it is impossible to account wholly for it. After much thought, he said to himself:

"I feel that I can believe in a God, a God of nature, of providence, of love; but Christ—I cannot believe in Him as the Messiah; He is a stumbling-block to me."

For a few hours he found some relief and satisfaction in his Christless theism; but the relief was only temporary. That night and the following day were memorable for their bald, unmitigated misery. Christless theism did not meet the wants of his being. Yet he decided to attend the service on Monday evening. He went, but derived little help from his uncle's remarks. His friend Hanson was present, and with his aged brother minister spoke to Hadley after the service.

"I am sorry to say," he said, in answer to their questions, "that all my unbelief has returned in an aggravated form. I have prayed so earnestly and continuously for light, that it seems to me that if there were such a God as some passages of the Bible describe, He would have granted my prayer. I seem to be dealing with the God of the Hebrews rather than with the God of the New Testament. Majesty and power and justice I perceive, but mercy, tenderness, and love seem to be denied me."

Mr. Bidder's face showed his disappointment, but he could only urge Hadley to continue his prayers, and assure him that in all his long experience he had never known a persevering, praying soul to fail in the end to obtain light. Mr. Hanson linked his arm in that of his friend and walked home with him. As they left the building together, Hanson said:

"I think your present condition may be a result of your past scepticism. I doubt if you will ever reach the light and truth by intellectual process. You may attain a Christless theism which would benefit you little. It is in Jesus the Incarnate Word, the Unspeakable Gift, the Vicarious Sacrifice, the Risen Mediator, that your hope lies. Accept Him as your Saviour, just as the poor ignorant rustic takes Him and trusts in Him, and peace will come first, and mental light and spiritual penetration later."

Hadley was silent, perplexed, but he knew that his friend was advising him to reverse the process he had hitherto been following. No more was said then until the two reached Hadley's lodging, when with an earnest "God bless you" the clergyman left him.

Hadley entered his room with an aching, despairing heart and a countenance overcast with gloom. On his table lay a letter which had arrived during his absence. He took it up mechanically and saw that it was from Belle Havelock, and was quite a bulky epistle. His correspondence with her since he left college had been kept up according to promise. Its matter was chiefly concerning Hadley's work, affairs at the college, a little gossip occasionally, and a considerable amount of interchange of opinion on literary, scientific, and theological themes, and thus sometimes their epistles were swollen to large proportions. But that which Belle desired above all to see in Hadley's letters she never found there. Love was a theme that he studiously avoided. Once away from the immediate presence of her magnetizing attractions, her hold upon his affectionate nature was relaxed, and his interest in her was merely that which grew out of their intellectual affinity. When the subject of religion was alluded to, Hadley found that her enmity had lost none of its venom.

The brilliant, cynical girl was as anxious as ever that Hadley should take a bold public stand as a speaker and writer against religion. Fame, power, and posthumous glory would be his, she told him, if he took up a crusade against superstition, and his name would be enrolled on the glorious roll of those whom the world honors as its deliverers. Let him go through the land proclaiming liberty to the captives, and opening the eyes that priestcraft had blinded.

How far was Hadley from all that now! The very sight of her familar writing shocked him. He could not bear to read her letter now. Bye and bye, when this terrible anxiety was over, he would read it, and tell her all that had occurred, whether it served her for a jest or not. Little would it matter then, to him, whether she despised him or not. He took the letter and put it unopened into his desk.

(*To be Continued.*)

ISRAEL UNDER JUDGES.

By Mrs. M. Baxter.

S. S. Lesson for December 2. Judges 2:11-23. Golden Text, Heb. 3:12.

Tribute Preferred to Obedience—Content Instead of Energy in Christian Work—Idleness a Preparation for Temptation—God's Gentle Expostulation—Voluntary Exposure to Temptation Always Perilous—A Generation Uninstructed in God's Dealings—Attracted by an Easy Religion—Abandoned to Spoilers—Externals Powerless to Convert—God Educating His People.

As the death of Moses was the signal for an advance, so was the death of Joshua. After his death "the children of Israel asked the Lord, saying, Who shall go up for us against the Canaanites first, to fight against them?" The Lord specified Judah; and then Judah and Simeon agreed to help one another in driving out the Canaanites from their possessions; and God was signally with them, and they were daunted by nothing but the inhabitants of the valley, "because they had chariots of iron." (Judges 1:19.) If they had counted God as more powerful than the chariots of iron, they might have conquered. But the people were contented with their possessions; they had no great objection to the occupation of the Canaanites. "And it came to pass, when Israel was strong, that they put the Canaanites to tribute, and did not utterly drive them out." They thought only of what suited them, and failed to ascertain the mind of the Lord. Oh, how like this is to

Some Christian Workers!

They have a little settled work, a certain number of meetings in the week, a comfortable little home, and a fair salary; they have the respect of the people, and a work in which they have, from time to time, tokens of blessing; what more can they want? But is this the thought of God, when He says, "Go *out* quickly into the streets and lanes of the city, ... into the highways and hedges, compel them to come in, that My house may be filled?" (Luke 14:21-23.) Surely this implies that a Christian worker after God's own heart, should put himself or herself out of the way to win souls. How many are contented with the little good they do, and, strong in their own self-esteem, they fail to follow the Spirit when He urges them to launch out into new fields of labor!

Idleness is a good soil for Satan's temptations; the people soon fell into idolatry. "An angel of the Lord came up from Gilgal to Bochim, and said, I have made you to go up out of Egypt, and have brought you unto the land which I sware unto your fathers; and I said, *I* will never break My covenant with you. And *ye* shall make no league with the inhabitants of this land; ye shall throw down their altars; but ye have not obeyed My voice:

Why Have Ye Done This?"

It was a tender expostulation. God would fain have dealt gently with them, but their sin compelled Him to fall back upon His own word of warning. "Wherefore I also said, I will not drive them out before you; but they shall be as thorns in your sides, and their gods shall be a snare unto you." We cannot put ourselves in the way of temptation without suffering for it. We may go anywhere, when sent of God, and all the influences around us cannot hurt us; but when we go unsent into danger, the influences around us are stronger than we. Pharaoh's court did not injure Joseph, and neither Nebuchadnezzar's court nor that of Darius injured Daniel, for they were for God. But Lot was a loser by his contact with Sodom, and Balaam lost his soul by considering Balak before God and His people. Both these went into danger to serve themselves. Every book we read, every conversation we hold, if it is unguarded by God, may be a snare to us; we are liable to come under the power of anything and everything, if God does not keep us. Oh, how needful, then, to do His will, and drive out, in His name, all the inhabitants of the land, *i. e.*, of our hearts, and never, in any degree, put his enemies to tribute. Perhaps making excuses for sin, and calling it by a less severe name, is the most common way of doing this. When the people heard this message of God they wept, and called on the name of the Lord, and for a time all went well.

But "all that generation were gathered unto their fathers, and then arose another generation after them which knew not the Lord, nor yet the works which He had done for Israel." But how about their parents? Was their life not a life of continual dealing with God in little things? Did these children of the men who crossed the Jordan on dry land never hear the story from them? Was it not the favorite theme among them, as they grew old and feeble, that they had known the manna in the wilderness, had drunk the water from the solid rock, and had seen the walls of Jericho fall down, and the sun stand still in the heavens when Israel fought against the ten Canaanitish kings? God had commanded that His words should be taught diligently unto their children. (Deut. 6:7; 11:19.) Asaph says, "We will not hide them from their children, showing to the generation to come the praises of the Lord, and His strength, and His wonderful works that he hath done. For He established a testimony in Jacob, and appointed a law in Israel, which He commanded our fathers that they should make them known to their children. . . . . that they might set their hope in God." and "not be as their fathers—a stubborn and rebellious generation." (Ps. 78:4-8.) Was it that the fathers did not teach their children, or was it that the children wilfully rejected the teaching of their fathers? We know not. But oh, how we need a prayerful spirit, and the direct guidance of God, in our dealings with our children!

The children of Israel did evil in the sight of the Lord, and served Baalim, and

They Forsook the Lord God of their Fathers,

which brought them out of the land of Egypt, and followed other gods, of the gods of the people that were round about them, and bowed themselves unto them, and provoked the Lord to anger." Oh, how easy it is to succumb to the influence of those whom we see and speak with every day! What love there was in the will of God, that all the inhabitants of the land should be driven out! People around them, who were as gifted and as educated as they, served Baalim, and it was such an easy religion it did not condemn worldliness and lust and passion; they could hold such a religion, and do their own will all the time; other people could be satisfied with this religion, why should not they? It was so inconvenient to have a religion which made them so peculiar, and which led other people to think them such children; how could it matter what religion they had, so that they were only consistent? No doubt some such reasonings were the sops they threw to their own consciences to quiet them, and meanwhile they justified the heathen in their utter ungodliness, and hardened their own hearts against God. The highest thought of many men is, "What religion will suit *me?*" whereas, the true question is, "What does God, who created me, require of me, His creature? God had prophesied this declension of the people to Moses on his dying day.

Now the anger of the Lord was hot against Israel, He delivered them into the hands of spoilers that spoiled them, as He had declared (Deut. 28:48), and "into the hands of their enemies round about," as prophesied (Deut. 28:25; Lev. 26:17), "so that they could not any longer stand before their enemies." Whithersoever they went out, the hand of the Lord was against them for evil, as the Lord had said (Dent. 28:20), and as the Lord had sworn unto them; and they were greatly distressed." Thank God, He would not let them perish unheard. They had sinned with a high hand against Him, but there is no retaliation in God when He punishes; it is "for our profit, that we might be partakers of His holiness." (Heb. 12:10.) In wrath He remembered mercy. (Hab. 3:2.) "Nevertheless, the Lord raised up judges, which delivered them out of the hand of them which spoiled them." But neither wrath nor mercy availed, "Yet they would not hearken unto their judges."

Nothing External

can change the heart of man. Like the demoniac who was possessed of two thousand demons, the heart of man breaks all the fetters and chains which bind it. Nothing but the blood of Christ to cleanse, and the indwelling of Christ by the Holy Ghost to keep Him, will ever make man other than he is; there may be restraining influences, but the old Adam is the old Adam still. "When the Lord raised them up judges, then the Lord was with the judge, and delivered them out of the hand of their enemies all the days of the judge: for it repented the Lord because of their groanings by reason of them that oppressed them and vexed them." They came for the time under a better influence; there was a passing revival, but after all they were dealing with God second hand, and there was no fundamental change in them. As soon as the judge died, back they were again in their idolatry. Thank God, our Judge and Deliverer "ever liveth to make intercession for us" (Heb. 7:25); and He has said, Because I live, ye shall live also. (John 14:19.) Thank God, we are "saved by His life" (Rom. 5:10), and not by any change in our own nature. God had made ample provision for the people to continue faithful to Him. The pillar of cloud and of fire still abode over the tabernacle, to manifest that God still dwelt among His people; He still spoke by the Urim and Thummim; it only needed that the people should seek unto Him. But the majority of them, while rejoicing in all the gifts which he had bestowed upon them, and luxuriating in the milk and honey and rich products of the land, bore no testimony of gratitude to the God who had dealt so lovingly with them. Corruption increased in the land; each generation became worse than that which preceded it. "They ceased not from

Their Own Doings

nor from their stubborn way." 'Their *own* doings'—this was at the root of the evil. God had destined them to be *His* people, to live for Him, and bear witness of Him. They despised this vocation, which angels would have wished, and which the only begotten Son of God accepted in after years; they made light of it, and lived as though they were their own. Thus God's anger waxed hot against them, and He declared that He would no longer "drive out any from before them of the nations which Joshua left when he died"; that He might prove Israel, whether they would keep the way of the Lord or not.

When God cannot do the best thing for us because of our unbelief, He will do the next best. His thought was to drive out the nations from before Israel, and to leave them in undisputed possession of the land, as a light and blessing to the surrounding nations. When, however, He found their tendency to mix with and follow the example of these nations, He gave them their way, until they became a burden to them, and thorns in their sides. Often the truest punishment of a wilful child is to let him take his own way, and bear the consequences; this was God's plan. But during this time, some true servants of God came out of the midst of the confusion and evil which abounded. Othniel served God and his country, and the Spirit of the Lord was upon him. Then the prophetess Deborah arose, and stirred up Barak, at the time when Jabin, King of Canaan, oppressed Israel, and a great deliverance was wrought. It is often in the time of great distress and trouble that God brings out His derelict servants. He never ceases to carry on the education of His children, and the very defection of the many proves the instrument of God to purify the few who stand on God's side amid surrounding unbelief.

GLADNESS.

Oh why should I be glad? Within my heart
 Is sin and folly found.
Within I find no reason for this joy
 No safe and proper ground.
I look away from self. To look within is madness,
O Lord make me, I cry, to hear Thy joy, Thy gladness.

I've done no work, nothing to give me joy,
 I've found no place of rest
In what I've done. In works of my poor hand,
 Not even in my best.
Yet, Thou my Lord, hast made me glad through work Divine,
And Thine own word assures me now that Thine is mine.

Thy work! how great! how wonderful! how free!
 How far beyond compare!
The cross, the curse, the death of Christ for me,
 Oh love! how pure! how rare!
And though I cannot tell out all that Thou hast done,
I praise in silence for my stubborn heart is won.

"The Lord hath done great things for us; we're glad"
 And glad we ought to be.
He took my place. He paid my debt so great,
 And gave His Heaven to me.
He'll come for me. He tells me so in His sweet word.
Then all eternity I'll gaze upon my Lord.

And He is glad. When Lazarus died He said:
 "I was not there: I'm glad
For your sakes." God will now be glorified
 In view of all that's sad.
He raised the dead. He spread His gladness all around.
He's glad. He says there's joy in Heaven o'er lost ones found.

Sydney, Australia. —REV. G. B. GREIG.

J. E. JEWETT, Publisher, 77 Bible House, New York, will furnish the above poem in leaflet form at twenty cents per hundred. *A Sample Packet* of 50 leaflets assorted (no two alike), will be sent post-paid, for 10 cts., or 100 for 20 cts. Postage stamps taken.

MEXICO

Contributions in aid of Christian work in Mexico are most pressingly needed, and can be mailed to the address of
BISHOP H. C. RILEY,
Care of J. P. HEATH,
43 Bible House, New York.

To our Christian Friends:

As there is a regular monthly expense in connection with the work a regular monthly income is needed to meet that expense. We, therefore, specially ask for regular monthly contributions in its behalf. If many will each send a little every month, or quarter, or whenever they can, it will do great good. *Remember, every little helps.*

H. Chauncey Riley.

Entered according to Act of Congress in the year 1888, in the office of the Librarian of Congress at Washington.

This Journal contains every week a Portrait and Biography of some eminent person; a new Sermon by the Rev. C. H. SPURGEON, of London, and the Rev. Dr. TALMAGE'S latest Sunday morning Sermon; also always a Prophetic Article, and a Summary of Current Events as well as Stories, Anecdotes etc.

Vol. XL., No. 48. Office, 63 Bible House. N. Y. THURSDAY, NOVEMBER 29, 1888. Price, 3 Cents. Annual Subscription, $1.50.

CONTENTS OF THIS NUMBER.

PORTRAIT AND LIFE OF THE LATE DR. WILLIAM R. SUMMERS, AMERICAN MEDICAL MISSIONARY IN CENTRAL AFRICA.
AN OBNOXIOUS DIET. Dr. Talmage's Sermon Last Sunday.
ANECDOTES RELATED AT RECENT EVANGELISTIC MEETINGS.
THE COMING OF THE LORD. By the late Dean Alford.
ROUGHING IT IN INDIAN TERRITORY.
A Deserted Chinese City—Saved from the Grave—Woman's Work in India—Chinese Retribution.
JESUS SET AT NOUGHT. A New Sermon by Rev. C. H. Spurgeon.
APPROACHING RENEWAL OF JEWISH SACRIFICES AT JERUSALEM. By Rev. M. Baxter.
Gems from New Books: Queen Elizabeth's Last Days—The Prince's Fall—A King Reproved.
PORTRAIT AND LIFE OF DANIEL HAND, the Octogenarian Philanthropist.
PICTURE OF THE INTERIOR OF THE TRAINING INSTITUTE AT DELHI.
MRS. MULLINS'S TEXT. (With Illustration.)
THE EPOCHS OF A LIFE. (Concluded.)
GIDEON'S ARMY. By Mrs. M. Baxter.

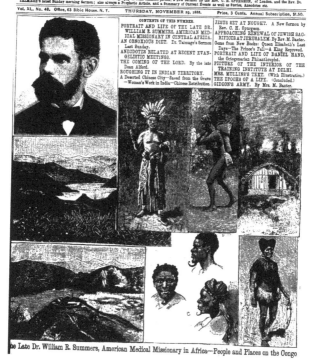

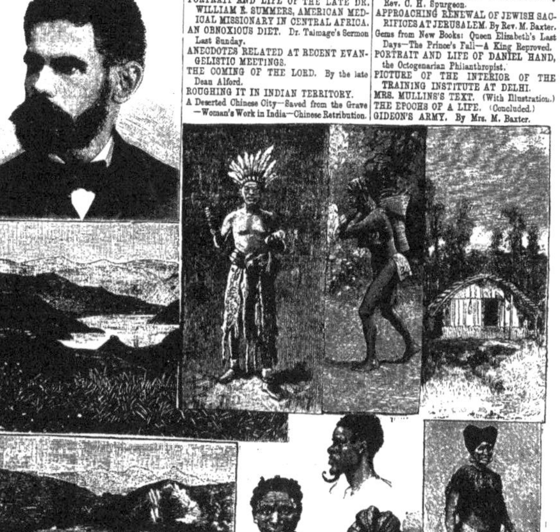

he Late Dr. William R. Summers, American Medical Missionary in Africa—People and Places on the Congo

THE LATE DR. WILLIAM R. SUMMERS.

Medical Missionary in Africa from New York.

The Christian Hero—His Work and His Reward—Early Life of Summers—A Restless and Roving Youth—Joins a Circus—Becomes a Conjuror—His Mother's Conversion—Remarkable Instance of the Power of Prayer—The Young Man Driven to his Knees—The Prodigal's Return—His Equipment Sacrificed—Comes to New York—Admitted to College—Develops Brilliant Intellectual Power—Decides to Become a Medical Missionary—Hardships and Triumph—Goes out with Bishop Taylor—His Letters and Death.

ANOTHER valuable life has been laid down on the altar of sacrifice in Africa! One more noble, heroic soldier of the Cross has fallen on the field in the struggle to win the Dark Continent for Christ! Life after life has been spent in that service, and freely given up that the glorious news of salvation might be carried through the unknown regions of that vast continent. Neither riches, nor power, nor fame could come of the labor. Toil, hardship, exposure to pestilential miasma, and danger from fierce savages, who know not what they do—those are what confront the missionary as he enters upon his work. And his reward? Well, there is no reward, as the world estimates rewards. He expects to die a premature death, to leave the world without seeing the victory, to perish probably in some forest or dreary swamp, without one sight of wife or sister or brother to soothe his dying hour, and to lie in an unknown grave. His predecessors have done so, and the very names of some of them are already forgotten. He has but gone to fill for a brief time the gap where they fell, until he too, falls, and another comes to take up the standard his dying hands shall drop, and carry it forward one stage nearer victory. Grand, valiant, self-sacrificing fellows! The world calls them fanatics, smiles contemptuously at their neglect of the main chance, buries itself again in its ledgers, and prostrates itself in worship of the golden calf. The worldling makes his million, lives to old age in luxury, dies in his marble palace, and is buried with pomp: the visionary is cut off in his youth or middle age, dies poor and unnoticed; but he has labored for a Master who never forgets His servants, and the day is coming when from that African swamp his dead body shall rise and stand among those who will shine as stars forever and ever.

His Early Life

gave little promise of the sublime height of martyrdom which Dr. Summers attained. He was born on April 28, 1855, in the Island of Guernsey. He was, therefore, only thirty-three years of age when he died. Some five years ago, when the writer met him in New York, where he was preparing for his work as a medical missionary in Africa, there was about the man an earnest, consecrated, devoted air, which impressed even a stranger with the heroism of the man; but that had come only with the experience of a few years. In his boyhood he was singularly restless and unmanageable. His mother was not a Christian, but her mother was, and she endeavored to lead her little grandson to Christ. Not successfully, however. He had been apprenticed as a boy of fourteen to a job printer, but tired of the occupation. He wanted to see life, and managed to make his way to London, where his agility and dexterous smartness secured him employment in Hengler's circus. A little later, he came in contact with the notorious Dr. Slade, the actual conjurer, but pretended spiritualist. Summers became an adept in the art, and soon surpassed his employer in his tricks of legerdemain. Every consecutive night for four months he exhibited with Slade in the Rotunda in Dublin, and drew large audiences.

His Conversion

was the result of one of those wonderful interpositions of Divine power which should encourage every Christian to unceasing, earnest prayer. In 1876, while he was wandering around, amusing and outwitting the public, and leading a careless, frivolous life, his mother was seized with serious illness. Her physician was the good Dr. George D. Dowkontt, now the devoted and indefatigable head of the International Medical Missionary Society in New York. The Doctor, while ministering to her physical need, did not miss the opportunity to speak of the Great Healer. The woman was deeply moved, became seriously concerned about her state, and at length Dr. Dowkontt had the joy of seeing her saved through Christ. Her first concern, after her own conversion, was about her wandering boy, whose eternal interests she had neglected. She prayed for him constantly, and to Dr. Dowkontt, and other Christian friends, her reiterated request was, "Pray for the conversion of my poor Will." She was so earnest about it that individual and united prayer was offered for him repeatedly.

Young Summers was many miles away engaged in his conjuring performances. He was twenty-two years of age at that time, and was utterly destitute of any inclination toward religion. His own account, given afterward to his friend Dr. Dowkontt, was, that one night, as he was about to retire to rest, he found himself upon his knees. The attitude was a surprise to himself, for prayer had long since ceased to be a habit with him. "Why, Will," he said to himself, "what are you doing, old fellow? You don't believe in anything of this sort: get up, what a fool you are!" Still the young fellow knelt, held down, as it seemed to him, by a power stronger than his own will. It seemed as if he would not be released till he did pray. But he could remember no prayer. There was a little hymn, however, that his memory still held from his childhood's days. So he said it through: "Now I lay me down to sleep," etc., and then he rose and turned into bed. He could not sleep. The Spirit of God was dealing with him in answer to those prayers offered far away. He lost his interest in his occupation, in his pleasures and companions, began to seek earnestly for Christ, and finally the prodigal found his way to home and mother. There he gave himself wholly to God.

Quit of the Old Life

was the determination he took, and he made his surrender final by a decisive act. His conjuring apparatus, which he had taken home with him, had cost him five hundred dollars, and was of an unusually complete character. He gathered it all together one night, and took it to a junk shop, and sold it for what the dealer would give, which was two dollars and fifty cents. The next day he set out to look for work at his old employment as a compositor. Work of that kind was not easy to obtain near home, and after drifting around for some time he made his way to the United States.

Landing in New York

in September, 1879. Dr. Dowkontt had preceded him, and he gave the young man a cordial welcome. In his search for work he went to Philadelphia, and there began to attend and assist in the meetings of the Salvation Army. They made him a captain, and set him to work at Atlantic City. He proved a very successful worker, but longed for better training and more efficient service. He happened while at Atlantic City to meet with a student from Pennington Seminary, N. J., and by his advice wrote to the Principal of that institution, Dr. Thomas Hanlon, stating his desire for Christian work, his need of education, and his poverty. Dr. Hanlon's heart was drawn toward the young man, and after an interview he was admitted, and set steadily to work. He developed a remarkable and unexpected aptitude for study, and though he was necessarily placed at the bottom of the classes, he worked his way to the head and came out with the first place in the honor-roll.

His Call to Missionary Work

took place while he was in the seminary. Writing to Dr. Dowkontt in December, 1881, he said that he had been led to analyze his abilities and powers, and he had been brought to the conclusion that he could serve God best as a missionary. He even indicated Central Africa as the field to which his mind was drawn. But he said that he had found that the best missionaries for such a field were earnest Christian physicians, and therefore he was anxious to get a medical education. The Medical Missionary Society was then scarcely established, and Dr. Dowkontt could give him little financial help, but the young honor man accepted willingly the post of janitor in the new dispensary at a salary of six dollars a week, and availed himself of every opportunity to become acquainted with the nature of drugs and the practice of medicine. He even slept on the premises that he might save money for a college course, and give a portion of his nights to the study of medical books. After a course of study under Dr. Dowkontt, he succeeded in obtaining a scholarship in the University Medical College of New York, and so assiduously did he labor that in March, 1884, he passed his final examination, and was awarded his coveted prize, the M. D. diploma.

An Introduction to Bishop Taylor

was secured through Dr. Hanlon and that great organizer soon perceived that a genuine prize had fallen into his hands. Dr. Summers had studied every book he could obtain on Africa, and was just the man William Taylor needed for his new enterprise. Dr. Summers was ordained on October 21, 1884, and, accompanied by Mr. Heli Chatelain, a young Swiss student, set sail the next day in the steerage of the *Aurania*. They travelled first to Berlin, where, under Lieutenant Weissman, the eminent German explorer, they gained some knowledge of the dialects of the tribes in Central Africa. On January 7, 1885, they sailed with Bishop Taylor for Africa. Arriving in Liberia, the Bishop remained there to meet his party, who were to sail a month later. Dr. Summers and his companion, Chatelain, went on to Loanda, where they arrived in the middle of the following month. After reconnoitring in Loanda, making friends, and securing a house for the expected party of missionaries, Dr. Summers set out alone for the interior, accomplishing a journey of 400 miles to Melange, and returned to the coast, having opened up the way for the various stations since located there.

The Work in Africa

now commenced in earnest. Dr. Summers remained at Melange about one year, healing, teaching, and preaching the gospel. During this time he so won the hearts of the people by his kindness and medical skill that they were terribly grieved when they first heard of his intended departure from them, on a journey of over one thousand miles to the further side of the Congo. He considered, however, that the work might safely be left, as another missionary would arrive shortly, and he was anxious to press on farther inland, to the point at which, as he believed, missionary operations ought to find their centre. He at length succeeded in tearing himself away, and the people loaded him with gifts, provided him with carriers and the necessaries for his journey. Thus equipped, Dr. Summers set out on his perilous expedition amid tears and good wishes. After a terrible journey of six months, during which the Doctor's life was often saved as by miracle, he reached Luluaburg, on the Kassai River, in safety in December, 1886. Here he remained, busy attending to the needs of the people, many of whose lives he saved, and trying to teach them the "Way of life." With a view of doing this more completely he was busy preparing a grammar and vocabulary of their language.

His Letters from Luluaburg

were full of interesting details of his journey thither and his work after his arrival. In the first, dated August 31, 1887, he reported himself in good health; in the second, dated January 3, 1888, he said he was just recovering from a five weeks' illness, in which he had suffered from pleurisy, septic fever, and an ill-defined but painful lung disease.

"On most of the way from Malange to Kassai," said Dr. Summers, "the country is wild and the population meagre. We suffered from hunger, the people not having food for themselves—as at best they plant but little more than they expect to consume. To the east of the Kassai everything changed for the better. The country was, for the most part, park-like; cut up from three to five times each day's journey by deep-cut and swift-flowing streams; no swamps; hills covered with the oil-palm and dotted with pretty and regularly built towns. I am continually beset by chiefs, who

Ask for Missionaries

and teachers. Every chief wants one. In some places I have had difficulty in leaving the towns, *the chiefs crying, and begging me to remain.* At one place, near the source of the Mwansangomma River, the chief covered himself with pemba, and came crying for me to remain.

"Another chief, Mwamba Mputto, was, with his people, overjoyed at my arrival. He begged me to stay, said he wanted his people to become like white men, that he 'had been expecting me for a long time,' etc. I said that I could not possibly remain, as I must first await the steamer, and that then I would perhaps come back, or some one else would probably come. The chief cried like a child, and said he was sure the white man would come at some time, and that he 'had built a house' for the purpose; that it would be in perfect readiness in a few days. This is

A Case of Faith

in a heathen, but does not speak half of the wonderful desire that the people are continuously expressing for the missionary and teacher. It seems to me that God is preparing a people here for the reception of the Gospel on a grand scale, and that these Bashilange will help to solve the problem of evangelization of great stretches of this part of Central Africa.

"The chances of years of service on the part of missionaries are perhaps better here than in any part of Africa. The climate I consider decidedly healthy. There is but little fever, and that not of a bad character, being generally simple intermittent. Swampy land is scarce. Food is very abundant.

"I have to praise God for many wonderful blessings and providential deliverances. I find that 'the great loving heart of Jesus' is just as near as (if not nearer than) it was in Europe or America; and His 'Lo, I am with you always' tones down all annoyances, makes loneliness companionable, and converts despondency into lively hope."

His Death,

as we stated last week, has been briefly announced to Dr. Dowkontt, without particulars as to date, place, or cause. There is, however, reason to believe, from the intimation given in the letter referred to above that he must have died of consumption developed by exposure and hardship. While we grieve for his loss, we have no fear for his work. Some brave, consecrated, young man will take that up and carry it forward. God is raising up young men all around ready to give their lives to this grand enterprise. Dr. Dowkontt has several such men now in training who are studying medicine, and until they can go out to Africa, are healing, and preaching the gospel, among the poor of New York. He could have many more, had he only the funds necessary for their support while they study. Any help that can be given to the earnest, self-sacrificing man who is thus recruiting for the army of the Lord will be well rendered. *His address is, Dr. George D. Dowkontt, 118 East 45th Street, New York.*

The Illustrations

on the first page are of figures and scenes which must have been among the last on which the eyes of Dr. Summers rested. The scene under the portrait is the Lake Vivi, the two figures to the right are a man and woman of the Congo country, drawn from life by an artist in the Stanley expedition; the picture on the right of them is of a house of the better class at Undunga. The lower panels commencing on the left represents a view from the Station at Isanghila, types of heads of the natives of Mabunga, and a Banyala woman.

ANECDOTES RELATED AT RECENT EVANGELISTIC MEETINGS.

Living with a Cobra.—Rev. T. Heelis, of Dowlaishwarum, India, writes: "I am living in my boat, and with me a cobra has been living for some days: I saw part of its body, some days ago, and suspected that it was of that class, but as one of my men said that it must be of a harmless species, I did not trouble about it, thinking that I would put my foot on its head when I had an opportunity. Yesterday one of the men, in taking firewood from the stern, found the cast-off slough of the snake, and pronounced it to be that of a cobra. I half filled the boat with water, but the snake must have escaped, as it could not be found anywhere. Before getting to sleep last night I was very sensitive to sound, but did not dream that a cobra was on the table, head erect, hood extended, and looking at me with its wicked little eyes. Persuading myself that the snake was venomless, calmed my fears, but such false peace would have been valueless if I had been bitten by the reptile. The Lord in His infinite mercy preserved me."

An Irish Steward's Mother-Wit.—A Minister says: "A steward was one day engaged in cleaning the silver-plate used in the cabin. He did not notice that he was standing in a very dangerons position until, the vessel giving a lurch, he was almost thrown overboard; and, in order to save himself, he had to let the piece of plate he was polishing go, and it fell overboard. He was in great distress, knowing that the captain would be very angry; but, being an Irishman, he resolved to put the best face on it possible, and, summoning his mother-wit to his aid, he went to the captain, who, observing his rueful face, said: 'Well, Terry, what's wrong?' 'Captain, sir,' said the steward, 'is a thing lost when you know where it is?' 'No, Terry; why do you ask such a stupid question?' the captain asked. 'Then, sir, the silver plate is not lost; it is at the bottom of the sea.' The captain knew he would never see it again; but some Christians think that though God has cast their sins into the depths of the sea, they may, at any moment, again confront and condemn them. We who know where they are, remember them; but, thank God, if He has pardoned them, they will never again appear against us."

The King's Highway and the Moor.—A Highland boy who lived in a very quiet out-of-the-way spot, was on one occasion sent to the nearest village, a good distance over the hills, to get some medicine from the doctor. The lad had never been there before, but he had often heard his father and mother speak of the village and the different ways to it. For in that place was the district church, to which they went every third Sabbath, the minister of that district having three churches, and speaking in each of them by turn. From this cotter's home there were two ways, both of which led to the village. One a broad, undefined way over the moors, and the other the highway, well enclosed, and kept in order, and upon which were the milestones. Before setting out on his errand the boy asked his father which of the ways he should take. '*Take the highway* my son, for in it you cannot go astray,' was his father's reply. Similarly there is before every one in this world two ways, one the broad waste that leads to destruction, and the other the narrow, well kept, king's highway, wherein pilgrims cannot go astray, and along which we find many milestones, all showing we are still keeping in the way."

A Whisky Bottle in the Death-Bed.—"There was a woman who came to this hall, and I am sure if I have spoken to her once I have spoken to her scores of times about her soul! and yet she did not come to Christ. Sometimes I went away rejoicing, thinking that she had nearly, if not already, come to Christ. At other times I would come away sad, to think that all our efforts had been in vain. Friends of the supposed convert came from a distance and thanked God for the work that was going on, but I replied, 'Yes, I can thank God for the great work that He is doing here, and for many other things, but I do not think I can yet thank Him for that woman's conversion.' 'Why?' they inquired, in surprise. 'Because I can never believe in conversion when I constantly smell strong drink in her breath.' And circumstances but too soon and too fully justified my suspicions. She was taken ill and died. A Christian worker visiting her found in the room in which she had died a number of whisky bottles, mostly empty, but some in various stages of fullness, stuffed into every conceivable corner, and one bottle was actually in the bed in which she died. Like a legion of devils, they had devoured the poor woman's body and soul, and the love of drink had kept her from accepting Christ."

The Austrians Unexpectedly Routed.—Mr. Hamilton relates: "It is related of Napoleon I., that when opposing the Austrians in Italy, he sent one of his generals, Descroix, away upon a certain expedition, and not long afterwards found himself obliged to fight the whole Austrian army. The French fought long and bravely, but everything was against them, and they were obliged to retreat. The Austrians were elated; their general retired to his tent to send a glowing account of his victory to Vienna; but while so engaged he was surprised to hear firing, and, rushing out, found his own army retreating before the lately conquered French. How was it? Descroix had, when on the march, heard the furious firing of the cannon, and knowing that Napoleon was much the weaker, had without waiting for orders marched his men back again, and arrived in time to find his general retreating from the field. As they approached each other, Napoleon said, 'We have lost one battle, but there is time yet to-day to win another.' And turning his men, he again attacked the Austrians, and completely routed them. Some people seem to think if they be once beaten there is no hope for them; but if Satan once beat you, try again. Christ is never out of reach of your prayer, and the instant it strikes His ear He will hasten to your rescue."

A Collier's Last Revel.—Mr. Climie Said: "I was once preaching among the colliers, and the Lord was blessing my efforts in their midst; but there was one young fellow in whom I felt a special interest, and longed to bring him to Christ. I remember meeting him on one occasion, and asked him to come to Christ, and to come to the meeting, where he would hear more about Him; but he would not come. New Year's Day approached; he must get his bottle filled with whisky, like the other fellows. He said he was going to keep New Year's Day; but that day got hold of him, and held him until his pockets were empty and his head sore. When he came to himself he saw his error, and resolved to accept Christ. At the next meeting I saw him in the front seat. At the close, when I went up to him and placed my hand upon his shoulder, he was shaking like a leaf. 'What do you think, James; would it not be good to have a word of prayer?' I asked. He willingly knelt with me, and after I had led in prayer, he also prayed, 'O Lord, send light from heaven into my poor, dark heart!' Dropping again upon his knees, he clasped his hands, and exclaimed, 'O Lord, Thy Book says, "Whosoever"; I come to Thee as one of the whosoevers. Lord, take me; I give myself to Thee!' He left that meeting a new man, trusting in Christ, who has kept him from that day to this."

The Prophetic News and Israel's Watchman (London), edited by the Rev. M. Baxter, may be had from the office of this journal, 63 Bible House, New York; price six cents, including postage. Annual subscription, seventy cents. The following articles, among others, are contained in the number for November:

Things Coming on the Earth. By late P. H. Gosse, F.R.S.
Some of the Causes of the Coming Apostacy.
A Jewish View of the Restoration to Palestine.
Edinburgh Convention on the Second Advent of Christ.
Eccleston Hall Conference in London.
Crisis, Catastrophe, and Revolution. By Rev. H. Varley.
Railways and Prophecy. By W. Appleford.
Times and Seasons. By G. W. Houghton.
The Lord's Second Coming. By the late Dean Alford.
Passing Events Viewed from a Prophetic Standpoint.

AN OBNOXIOUS DIET.

Dr. Talmage's Sermon, preached last Sunday, November 25, 1888.

"And these are they which ye shall have in abomination among the fowls: . . . the owl, the vulture, and the bat. . . . These also shall be unclean unto you among the creeping things that creep upon the earth: . . . the chameleon and the snail." Lev. 11: 13-30.

The Moral Nature Affected by Food—A Missionary's Experience Among Indians—Spiritual Reasons for Dietary Laws—Creatures Excluded from the Table on Account of their Habits—Symbolic of Qualities to be Excluded from the Soul—I. The Owl—Gloom Out of Place in the Christian—A Girl's Spoonful of Sunshine—II. The Vulture—Scandal not Christian Food—Gossips Working for Satan—III. The Bat—Double Lives—Between Earth and Air—The Choice of Lives—IV. The Chameleon—Variable Creeds—An Infidel's Dying Daughter—V. The Snail—Sluggishness Hateful in Religion.

THE Bible offers every possible variety of theme, of argument, and of illustration. We care not much in what kind of a pitcher the water of life is brought, if it is only the clear, pure water. God gave the ancients a list of the animals that they might eat, and a list of animals that they might not eat. These people lived in a hot climate, and certain forms of animal food corrupted their blood, and disposed them to scrofulous disorders, depraved their appetites, and bemeaned their souls. A man's food, when he has the means and opportunity of selecting it, suggests his moral nature. The reason the wild Indian is as cruel as the lion is because he has food that gives him the blood of the lion. A missionary among the Indians says that, by changing his style of food to correspond with theirs, his temperament was entirely changed. There are certain

Forms of Food

that have a tendency to affect the moral nature. Many a Christian is trying to do by prayer that which cannot be done except through corrected diet. For instance, he who uses swine's flesh for constant diet will be diseased in body and polluted of soul—all his liturgies and catechisms notwithstanding. The Gadarene swine were possessed of the devil, and ran down a steep place into the sea, and all the swine ever since seem to have been similarly possessed. In Leviticus, God struck this meat off the table of His people, and placed before them a bill of fare at once healthful, nutritious, and generous.

But, higher than this physical reason, there was a spiritual reason why God chose certain forms of food for the ancients. God gave a peculiar diet to his people, not only because he wanted them to be distinguished from the surrounding nations, but because certain birds and animals, by reason of their habits, have been

Suggestive of Moral Qualities.

By the list of things from which they were to abstain, God wished to prejudice their minds against certain evils; and, in the list of lawful things given, he wished to suggest certain forms of good. When God solemnly forbade His people to eat the owl, the vulture, the bat, the chameleon, and the snail, He meant to drive out of His people all the sins that were thus emblemized.

I take the suggestion of the text, and say that one of the first unclean things the Christian needs to drive out of his soul is

The Owl.

The owl is the melancholy bird of night. It hatches out whole broods of superstitions. It is doleful and hideous. When it sings, it sings through its nose. It loves the gloom of night better than the brightness of the day. Who has not slept in the cabin near the woods, and been awakened in the night by the dismal "too-hoo" of the owl? Melancholy is the owl that is perched in many a Christian soul. It is an unclean bird, and needs to be driven away. A man whose sins are pardoned, and who is on the road to heaven, has no right to be gloomy. He says: "I have so many doubts." That is because "you are lazy." Go actively to work in Christ's cause, and your doubts will vanish. You say: "I have lost my property"; but I reply: "You have infinite treasures laid up in heaven." You say: "I am weak and sickly, and going to die." Then be congratulated that you are so near eternal health and perpetual gladness. Catch a few morning larks for your soul, and stone this owl off your premises.

As a little girl was eating, the sun dashed upon her spoon, and she cried: "Oh, mamma, I have swallowed

A Spoonful of Sunshine!"

Would God that we might all indulge in the same beverage! Cheerfulness—it makes the homeliest face handsome; it makes the hardest mattress soft; it runs the loom that weaves buttercups and rainbows and auroras. God made the grass black? No: that would be too sombre. God made the grass red? No: that would be too gaudy. God made the grass green, that by this parable all the world might be led to a subdued cheerfulness. Read your Bible in the sunshine. Remember that your physical health is closely allied to your spiritual. The heart and the liver are only a few inches apart, and what affects one affects the other. A historian records that by the sound of great laughter in Rome, Hannibal's assaulting army was frightened away in retreat. And there is in the great outbursting joy of a Christian soul that which can drive back any infernal besiegement. Rats love dark closets, and Satan loves to burrow in a gloomy soul. "Rejoice in the Lord, O ye righteous! and again I say, rejoice!"

Hoist the window of your soul in this the 12 o'clock of your spiritual night. Put the gun to your shoulder, and aim at the black jungle from which the hooting comes, pull the trigger, and drop that croaking, loathsome, hideous owl of religious melancholy into the bushes.

Again: taking the suggestion of the text,

Drive out the Vulture

from your soul. God would not allow the Jews to eat it. It lives on carcases; it fattens among the dead; with leaden wing it circles about battle-fields. Wilson, the American ornithologist, counted two hundred and thirty-seven vultures around one carcase. If crossing the desert when there is no sign of wing in the air a camel perish out of the caravan, immediately the air begins to darken with vultures. There are many professed Christians who have a vulture in their souls. They prey upon the character and feelings of others. A doubtful reputation is a banquet for them. Some rival in trade or profession falls, and the vulture puts out its head. These people revel in the details of a man's ruin. They say: "I told you so!" They rush into some store and say: "Have you heard the news? Just as I expected! Our neighbor has gone all to pieces! Good for him!"

That professedly Christian woman, having heard of the wrong-doing of some sister in the church, instead of hiding the sin with a mantle of charity, peddles it all along the streets. She takes the afternoon to make her long-neglected calls. She

Tells the Story Ten Times

before sundown, and every time tells it larger. She rushes into the parlors to tell it, and into the nursery to tell it, and into the kitchens to tell it. She says: "Would you have thought it! Well, I always said there was something wrong about her. Why, I should not speak to her if I saw her in the street. Is it not horrible? But better not say anything about it, because there may be some mistake. I do not want my name involved in the matter. I guess I will just go over and ask them at No. 263 whether they have heard it. Guess it must be so, for Mary Ann says that her husband saw a man who heard from his business partner that his blind old grandmother had seen something that looked very suspicious!"

The most loathsome, miserable, God-forsaken wretch on earth is a gossip. I can tell her on the street, though I have never seen her before. She walks fast, and has her bonnet-strings loose, for she has not had time to tie them since she heard that last scandal. She looks both ways as she passes, hoping to see new evidences of depravity in the windows. I think that when Satan has a job so infinitely mean that in all the pit *he cannot find a devil mean enough* to do it, and all bribes and threats have failed to get one willing for the infernal crusade, he says to one of his sergeants: "Go up to Brooklyn, and in such a street, on such a corner, get

That Gossipping Woman,

and she will be glad to do it." And sure enough, like a hungry fish, she takes the hook in her mouth, and Satan slackens the line, and lets her run out farther and farther, until after a while he says: "It is time to haul in that line," and with a few strong pulls he brings her to the beach of fire. What do you say? That she was a member of the church? I cannot help that. When Satan goes a-fishing, *he does not care what school the fish belongs to,* whether it is a Presbyterian mackerel or an Episcopalian salmon. Amidst the thunder-crash of Sinai God said: "Thou shalt not bear false witness against thy neighbor." And in Leviticus He says: "Thou shalt not go up and down as a tale-bearer."

Take not into your ear that scum of hell that people call tittle-tattle. Whosoever willingly listens to a slander is equally guilty with the one who tells it, and an old writer says they ought both to be hung, the one by the tongue and the other by the ear. Do not smile upon such a spaniel, lest, like a pleased dog, he puts his dirty paw upon you. Throw back the shutter of your soul, oh Christian men and women! and see if there be within you a vulture with filthy talons and cruel beak. Let not this unclean thing roost in your soul, for my text says: "Ye shall hold in abomination the vulture."

Again: taking the suggestion of the text,

Drive Out the Bat

from your soul. No wonder God set this bird among the unclean. It is an offence to every one. Let it fly into the window of a summer night, and all the hands, young and old, are against it. It is half bird, half mouse. It seems made partly to walk and partly to fly, and does neither well, and becomes an emblem of those Christians who try to cling to earth and heaven at the same time. They want to walk on earth in worldliness, and yet fly toward heaven in spirituality; and their soul, between feet and wings, is constantly perplexed. Oh, my brethren, be one thing or the other! Choose the world, if you prefer it, and see how many dollars you can win, and how much applause you can gain, and how large a business you can establish, and how grand a house you can build, and how fast a span of horses you can drive. You may be prospered until you can fail for five hundred thousand dollars, instead of having the disgrace of failing for only ten thousand; as some unenterprising people do. It is quite a reward to be able for ten or twenty years to be called one of

The Solid Men of Brooklyn

or Boston; and then, to make your fortune last as long as possible, we will give you a splendid funeral, and you shall have twenty-five carriages following you, with somebody in the most of them, and your coffin shall have silver handles on the sides, and we will mourn for you in splendid pocket-handkerchiefs bound with crape, and with bombazine twenty full yards long trailing half across the parlor, so that all the company may stand upon it, and we will write our letters for the next six months on paper edged with black. But, my friends, your worldly fortunes will not last. I will buy out now all that you will be worth in worldly estate seventy-five years from now. I have the money in my pocket with which to do it. Here it is! Two cents! It is a large sum to offer for all you will possess at the close of seventy-five years. Choose the world, if you want to; but if not, then choose heaven. That estate lies partly on this side of the river, but mostly on the other. It is ever accumulating. The prospect of it makes one independent of earthly misfortunes; so that Rogers, the martyr, slept so soundly the night before his burning, that they violently shook him in order to get him awake in time for the execution; and Paul exults at the thought of the "joy unspeakable and full of glory." Oh,

Choose Earth or Heaven!

Make up your mind whether you will walk in earthly joys, or fly with heavenly expectations. Be not a bat, fit neither to walk nor fly, having just enough of heaven to spoil the world, and so much of the world as to spoil heaven. Christ says that your present condition nauseates Him to positive sickness: "Because thou art neither cold nor hot, I will spew thee out of My mouth!" In the ruins of Pompeii there was found a petrified woman, who, instead of trying to fly from the destroyed city, had spent her time in gathering up her jewels. She saved neither her life nor her jewels. There are multitudes making the same mistake. In trying to get earth and heaven, they lose both. "Ye cannot serve God and Mammon." Be one thing or the other. Tread the earth like a lion, or mount the air like the eagle; for my text says: "Ye shall have in abomination among the fowls the bat."

Again: taking the suggestion of the text,

Drive out the Chameleon

from your soul. There is some difference among good men as to the name of this creeping thing which God pronounced unclean, but I shall take the opinion which seems best suited to my purpose. The chameleon is a reptile, chiefly known by its changeableness of color, taking the color of the thing next to it, sometimes brown, sometimes red, and sometimes gray, but always the color of its surroundings, a type of that class of Christians who are now one thing in religious faith, and now another, just to suit circumstances, always taking their color of religious belief from the man they are talking to. They go to one place, and are first-rate Unitarians. "Jesus was a good man, but nothing more." They go to Princeton, and they are Trinitarians, almost willing to die for the divinity of Jesus. Among the Universalists they refuse the idea of future punishment; and, going among those of opposite belief, announce that there is a hell with a gusto that makes you think they are glad of it. Drive out that unclean chameleon from your soul. Do not be ever changing the color of your faith. My friends, Liberal Christianity, falsely so-called,

Believes in Nothing.

God is anything you want to make Him. The Bible to be believed, in so far as you like it. Heaven a grand mixing up of Neros and Pauls. The man who dies by suicide in his right mind in 1888, beating into glory by ten years the Christian man who dies a Christian death in 1898—the suicide proving himself wiser than the Christian. Oh, my friends, let us try to believe in something! An infidel was called to the bedside of his daughter. The daughter said: "Father, which shall I believe, you or mother? Mother took the religion of Christ, and died in its embrace. You say that religion is a humbug. Now I am going to die, and I am very much perplexed; shall I believe you, or take the belief of my mother?" The father said: "Choose for yourself." She said: "No; I am too weak to choose for myself; I want you to choose for me." "Well," said the father, after much hesitation and embarrassment: "Mary, I think you had better take the religion of your mother." The time will come when we shall have to believe something. We can not afford to be

On the Fence in Religion.

Truth and error are set opposite to each other. The one is infinitely right, and the other infinitely wrong. In the Judgment-day we must give an account of what we believed as well as for what we acted. The difference between believing truth and believing error is the difference between paradise and perdition. I beg you, in the light of the Bible, and on your knees before God, to form your religious opinion and then stick to it, though business companions scoff, and wits caricature, and the air crackles with the fires of martyrdom. Surely truths in behalf of which Christ died, and angels of God trooped forth, and the whole universe is marshaled, are worth living for and worth dying for. Amidst the most unclean things is this ever-changing chameleon of religious theory. Away with the reptile! God abhors it with an all-consuming abhorrence.

Once more: taking the suggestion of the text,

Drive out the Snail

from your soul. God has declared it unclean. It is an animal to be found everywhere between the coldest north and the hottest south. There are fifteen hundred species of the snail. They have no backbone, and they are so slow that their movement is almost imperceptible. You see a snail in one place to-day; go to-morrow and you will find it has advanced only a few inches. It becomes an emblem of that large class of Christian people who go to work with a slowness and sluggishness that is wonderful. They are stopped by every little obstacle, because, like the snail, they have no backbone. Others mount up on eagle's wings, but they go at a snail's pace.

Oh child of God, arouse! We have apotheosized Prudence and Caution long enough. Prudence is a beautiful grace, but of all the family of Christian graces I like her the least, for she has so often been

Married to Laziness.

Sloth, and Stupidity. We have a million idlers in the Lord's vineyard, who pride themselves on their prudence. "Be prudent," said the disciples to Christ, "and stay away from Jerusalem"; but He went. "Be prudent," said Paul's friends, "and look out for what you say to Felix"; but he thundered away until the ruler's knees knocked together. In the eyes of the world, the most imprudent men that ever lived were Martin Luther, and John Oldcastle, and Wesley, and Knox. My opinion is, that the most imprudent and reckless thing is to stand still. It is well to hear our Commander's voice when he says "Halt!" but quite as important to hear it when he says "Forward!" This Gospel ship, made to plough the sea at fifteen knots an hour, is not making three. Sometimes it is most prudent to ride your horse slowly, and pick out the way for his feet, and not strike him with the spurs; but when a band of Shoshone Indians are after you in full tilt, the most prudent thing for you to do is to plunge in the rowels and put your horse to a full run, shouting "Go 'long!" until the Rocky Mountains echo it. The foes of God are pursuing us. The world, the flesh, and the devil are after us; and our wisest course is to go ahead at swiftest speed.

When the Church of God gets to advancing too fast, it will be time enough to use caution. No need of putting on the brakes while going up-hill. Do not let us sit down waiting for something "to turn up," but go ahead in the name of God, and turn it up.

The Great Danger to the Church

now is not sensation, but stagnation. Oh that the Lord God would send a host of aroused and consecrated men to set the Church on fire, and to turn the world upside down. Let us go to work and catch the last snail in our souls. With Divine vehemence let us stamp its life out: for my text declares: "These also shall be unclean to you among the creeping things that creep upon the earth; the chameleon and the snail."

I have thus tried to prejudice these Christian men and women against gloominess, and slander, and half-and-half experiences, and changeableness, and sloth. Our opportunities for getting better are being rapidly swallowed up in the remorseless past. This moment may we drive out all the unclean things from our souls —the vulture, and the bat, and the owl, and the chameleon, and the snail; and in place thereof bring in the Lamb of God, and the Dove of the Spirit! The case is urgent. Arouse! before it be eternally too late! "Whatsoever thy hand findeth to do, do it!"

TRAINING INSTITUTION, DELHI.

See Illustration on page 765.

THE Rev. R. F. Guyton, the veteran Baptist missionary at Delhi, India, says: "The photograph (*from which the picture on page 215 is engraved*) was taken on Christmas Day, 1887. Our gathering on that day is always of great interest, not only to ourselves, but also to all the brethren connected with the Mission. They are scattered very widely during the year, and rejoice to come together at the close to greet those who are joined with them in faith and labor. Some came nearly forty miles to join in the day's service of thanksgiving. The engraving shows a part—somewhat less than a third—of the congregation met on Christmas morning. Among them are some of our most trusted native helpers.

"Others are there who are not so well known, because they are younger men, but who have already greatly helped us, and who will yet, we trust, help us still more devotedly. Saul David, our native doctor and excellent helper, Silas Paul, John of Sabzi Mandi, Yaqûb, Joseph, Paul, and many others. On the right of the picture are a few women, wives of our native Christians, Bible women, and girls of the boarding-school. Two of these are now studying medicine in Lahore.

"The room in which they are met is the Lower Hall of the Native Training Institution. The training classes are held in the rooms above. This hall is now regularly used as the native chapel, where services are held on Sunday and Friday. On this occasion it was adorned by flags and banners made by ladies of the Mission. One of the banners is seen on the centre pillar, bearing the text, 'Grace for grace.' Others which you do not see have the texts 'From strength to strength,' 'From glory to glory,' &c., &c. Around the upper bands of the pillars are painted other texts, and along the line of the arches are painted the 103d and 24th Psalms, and about thirty pictures.

THE RESULT OF A RUINED BUSINESS.

A YOUNG man named Ah-song, who is assisting the missionaries at Shao-hing, in China, recently told a remarkable story to Miss Carpenter. She says: "It is several years since he was converted, and his life has since then been singularly consistent and devoted. At morning and evening prayers it was most cheering to see how thoroughly he enjoyed God's precious Word. One evening, as we got up from our knees, Ah-song said, 'I have proved that God has been good to me.' When I asked how he had proved it, he answered, 'Soon after I became a Christian, my business failed. I was willing to starve myself, but could not help being troubled about my mother. She with all my other friends said if I would but give up the foreign religion the trade would be good again. I knew that Jesus was my Saviour, and I could not give Him up. At last I was obliged to close the shop, and go home to my own village. But I soon found my needs supplied. When I had the opportunity of preaching the gospel to my relations I did so, and very soon was rejoiced to hear that my mother had accepted Jesus; in a short time two other relations were converted, and an old lady who was living in the next house. This old lady was taken ill soon after I went to live in the village, and said it was all owing to my having become a Christian, but I told her what Jesus had done for me, and that He was only waiting to save and bless her too, if she would but believe in Him. A few Sundays after she had a sedan-chair brought, and was carried from her bed to the chapel where I was preaching. The following Sunday she also went, and took a young woman with her. Soon she found my words were true, and Jesus became as precious to her as He was to me.' This old lady is now one of the brightest witnesses in the place. Ah-song ended by saying, 'If God had not made my business to fail, I should not have gone to live near my relations, and they would not have heard the gospel. It is worth hundreds of dollars to me to know that they are now rejoicing in Jesus as their Saviour.'"

ROUGHING IT IN INDIAN TERRITORY.

A Night's Combat with Mosquitoes—Twenty-five Miles from Shelter at Midnight—Remarkable Discovery of an Abandoned Bedstead—a Loan of Bed and Pillows—Sickness in an Indian Cabin—Filth and Vermin—An Indian School-House Built—An Appeal for Teachers—Welcome Gifts.

A FEW incidents from a letter recently received from Mrs. Re Qua, who, as our readers are aware, is with her husband, the Rev. W. F. Re Qua, working for Christ among the Indians in the Indian Territory, will give some idea of the kind of life such labor involves. That two Christian persons should give up a comfortable home, an assured income, and the society of their friends, to go out to preach Christ, braving hardships and depending for support on God alone, is an evidence of what faith in God and love for souls can do in a consecrated heart.

Mrs. Re Qua says: "During the latter part of the summer and fall we have travelled many, many miles, over the roughest kind of roads, sleeping sometimes in our small tent, and sometimes in less comfortable quarters. Once riding till after dark, going to an appointment for meeting, we camped in our wagon in what soon proved to be the headquarters of an army of hostile and bloodthirsty mosquitoes. They assailed every available square inch of epidermis in multitudes; their size, by the light of our lantern, showing three times that of the ordinary *domestic* grade; and spite of our all-night's defensive vigilance, we carried numerous marks of their cruel stings for days. Little Beatrice suffered more than we did.

"Again, deceived in the length and badness of a road, we found ourselves, after travelling forty miles (the utmost limit for our ponies and ourselves), at 9 o'clock in the evening, twenty-five miles from a resting-place, and without any provision for the night. We tried to get shelter in a wayside cabin, but were refused. Then, driving under a cluster of trees a short distance from the road, we resigned ourselves to spending a chilly night in a buggy, when lo! we spied a bedstead some one had made and left under the trees, and close by, a man was camped in a wagon with his wife. They became aware of our situation, and brought out from their store a *feather-bed, pillows,* and two or three *comforters,* saying they had plenty without them. How thankful we were for *this bed spread in the wilderness!*

"Two weeks ago we spent a day among the Indian families several miles from here; their log-cabins are all without windows, and are comfortless in the extreme; though I suppose they please their occupants much better than they would people accustomed to homes so different in every way. In one of these huts a poor woman held a young infant in her arms, whose little purple limbs she ineffectually tried to cover with its scanty rags. Near by, in front of a corn-shed, upon a rude bench, lay a very sick woman. The ground was covered with filth and vermin indescribable, and was overrun with the usual number of dogs and pigs. In the midst of which a little rough table was spread with the inevitable greasy black pork and corn-meal cake, the staple diet of these forest dwellers, but repulsive to the last degree to one accustomed to other fare. Some little girls grinned a perpetual welcome to us, while a half-grown boy made himself conspicuous in a single scanty garment. Our business was to minister, which we did in the wisest way we knew.

"One week ago we rode out eight or ten miles to hold a service among the Indians. We found quite a large number collected; the women, mostly barefoot, in ill-made calico dresses, and red bandana kerchiefs twisted, not ungracefully, around their heads. At this place Mr. Re Qua has induced them to build a log school-house, and they are now adding another log building for the residence of a teacher. The teacher, a young lady from N. Y. State, who is spending a few weeks with us, waiting the completion of her home and the arrival of her clothing, etc., accompanied us that day. After the service, perhaps a dozen Indian women consulted together; then one of them, who could speak a little English, came to the teacher, and said, 'Me can't read, me want learn.' I said, 'Do the other women want to learn too?' She answered, 'Yes, all.' We told them all to come, and they should be taught, not only to read, but many other things. They went away very happy. It is surprising how few, even of the civilized (?) Choctaws, can read, write, or speak English. Of course, one occasionally meets an educated Indian, generally a girl who has been sent to the States for an education. These are sufficient to prove that there is ground for believing that these people are capable of profiting by an education; but at present the condition of the bulk of the Indians we have seen is deplorable."

Our two heroic friends have been cheered by many *gifts from the readers* of this journal. Mr. Re Qua asks us to acknowledge here those he received during the month of September last. They are: Mrs. O. Greenleaf, Ill., $2; "A Friend," Conn., $5; Mr. L. Leach, Ia., 50c.; "An S. S.," per Dr. Speicher, Ia., $6; Mr. C. W. D. Jones, Ill., $2. Mr. Re Qua's address is McAlister, Ind. Ter.

A DESERTED CHINESE CITY.

IN an extended tour in the Island of Hainan, China, Dr. C. C. Jerimiassen, a Presbyterian missionary, came upon a suggestive spectacle. In a letter to the *Church* he thus describes it: "Sang hoe Kang is the harbor port of the city of Sang hoe, which is about two miles inland. The harbor is very small, only capable of holding eight or ten junks. It is a great resort for fishermen. During certain seasons of the year they come with their families and put up straw houses on the sandy beach, while they salt and dry their fish, which is taken away by junks to all parts of the mainland. When I arrived there was quite a large straw village, containing not less than sixty or seventy houses. We left at once for the city. Sang hoe is a district city, and has the best-preserved wall of any of the cities I entered, but the city itself might almost be said to have ceased to exist. It reminds me very much of Jerusalem, of which it was said there should not be 'left one stone upon another.' All that is now left of the city is about fifty houses toward the south and east gates, whilst all the remaining part is in ruins. It is said to have been a very prosperous city until fifteen or twenty years ago, since which time it has gradually fallen away, until nothing but a heap of ruins remains. Even the civil and military heads of the district live in hired houses, and all that is to be seen of their yamens is a heap of brick, and the large granite pillars with inscriptions which still stand as a kind of tombstone to remind coming generations of what has been. A new city has lately been built a few miles off, where new residences have been prepared for the civil and military heads, but ghosts or evil spirits are said to have taken possession of the houses; so, of course, there is no room for the officials, who are constantly left out in the cold."

SAVED FROM THE GRAVE.

A SALESMAN in a dry-goods house in New York was dangerously sick. The agony from which he suffered grew so excruciating that he could not doubt that death was upon him. He summoned a lawyer and had a simple will drawn up and signed. Then, calling his landlady, he gave directions for his funeral and the disposal of a few personal belongings. Everything was now arranged, and the man saw, as he believed, the last person leave the room whom he would ever see in this world. The remaining hours—or it might be only minutes—of his life should be spent in communion with God. He felt that he had done with the world completely, and whatever time was left was consecrated to God. He composed himself to think and pray, but to his astonishment, after a short time the intense agony left him. As he cast off all hope of life, cut himself loose from the world, and counted himself as one already dead, new life and vigor entered his frame. Whether he was in or out of the body he could not tell; but this he knew, that the most glorious ecstatic realization of the Divine presence filled his soul, and there was in his body an abundant energy and vitality. At length he began te realize that a wondrous change must have taken place akin to the miraculous. He was awed as Jacob was at Bethel (Gen. 28:16), when he said, "Surely God was in this place and I knew it not." But he felt that his was a purchased, a consecrated life, not his own henceforth. He entered the ministry, and is now being used of God in the conversion of many souls.

WOMAN'S WORK IN INDIA.

THIRTY-FIVE schools are now established in Cawnpore and its environs under the superintendence of lady missionaries. Miss Ward, who is engaged in this work, writes in a letter to the *Missionary Link* a most encouraging account of the progress and prospects of the enterprise. She says: "In one of our Brahmin homes a Hindu priestess is learning to read. One day the missionary was giving a Bible lesson, and the children about were making some noise. The priestess said, 'Be quiet and listen; few speak such words to us as how Christ left Heaven, and suffered for us. How much He must have loved us, and yet we love Him so little, and forget so often about Him. I want to come and listen all day to such words.' Yes it is the Christ-love that draws humanity to Him. These instances help us, and give us faith to go on with our work.

"I was examining lately one of the schools, and I was pleased with it as I heard the recitation of Bible verses, and the ready answers to the questions in a simple catechism. You will be glad to know that truths are stored up in the minds of the children, ready to be taken into the hearts by the Holy Spirit, at some future time, how or when we may not know till we meet on the other shore. Three of the girls read with me from a translation of 'Bible Stories,' a chapter on the history of Joseph, and were much interested. I questioned them on the preceding lessons, and found they had a good knowledge of them. These girls have read two of the Gospels, and can now read the Bible understandingly. I always feel a great step is taken when this is done, for then the pupil can search for herself, if she will. In one school taught by a Mahommedan woman the children are improving. I visited them a few days ago, and saw her sitting on the mat, with her little group around her. Most of the schools have native teachers, but are closely superintended by ourselves."

CHINESE RETRIBUTION.

THE Chinese, it appears, have a habit of ascribing calamities to the direct judgment of Heaven, to an extent which renders many lives miserable. Mr. W. A. Douthwaite, of Che-foo, says: "A man about twenty-five years old, a native of a town forty miles from Chee-foo, was brought to the hospital suffering from dropsy, and the symptoms were so urgent that we decided to tap him without delay. When we saw him at midnight, ten hours after the operation, he was progressing favorably, but at daylight he foolishly arose from bed, took off the bandages, and walked out into the yard. The consequence was that he died in a few hours. His brother was sent for, and, of course, charged us with having killed him. After the body had been taken home, we learned the following particulars concerning this unhappy youth. A week or too previous to our making his acquaintance he had quarrelled with his mother, and had spoken insultingly to her. Shortly after this dropsy set in. This, his friends assured him, was a judgment of heaven upon him for his unfilial conduct. His mother was taken ill at the same time, and he was charged with being the cause of her sickness. She, however, recovered, while he became worse, and, as a *dernier ressort,* he was carried to the hospital at Chee-foo.

When it became known at home that he was dead, his relatives turned on his mother, and accused her of having caused his death by provoking him to anger. The poor woman was so utterly bowed down with grief, and so cruelly persecuted and taunted by her neighbors, that when the body of her son was taken home, she returned to her room and committed suicide. Then, of course, the relatives accused each other of having caused her death. Cases of this kind are of frequent occurrence in China; and very often after two people have quarrelled, one of them will deliberately commit suicide, knowing that the other will be punished for manslaughter, and his family probably ruined."

APPROACHING RENEWAL OF JEWISH SACRIFICES AT JERUSALEM.

By Rev. M. Baxter.

It is generally admitted by numerous expositors of Daniel, Ezekiel, Isaiah, Zechariah, and Revelation, that the Restoration of the Jews to Palestine in the latter days will be, *first* a *partial* Restoration of some of them from political motives, and, while still rejecting Christianity, a few years *before* the Advent of Christ; and, *secondly*, a *full* Restoration of *all* of them *at* and *after* the Advent of Christ at Jerusalem, when the Millennium commences, and when a New Temple will be built, according to the last eight chapters of Ezekiel. But at their *partial earlier* restoration they will erect a different temple of their own design, and offer self-righteous sacrifices in it; and Antichrist, in the midst of the final seven years, will sit in that earlier Temple as the Man of Sin.

The *Rev. J. G. Gregory*, says in his "Earth Eventide" in chapter 3: "When Israel are restored (partially and in unbelief) to their own land, we cannot doubt but that

Their First Act

will be to build their House for worship. Their re-occupation of their own land would be *as nothing* if their Temple, their ritual, and their sacrifices were not present. In fulfilment of the Seventieth Week in Daniel 9:27, 'The Prince shall come,' 'shall confirm a covenant with many for one week, that is, for *seven years:* and in the midst of the week he shall cause the sacrifice and oblation to cease, and for the overspreading of abominations he shall make it desolate, until the consummation.' He will be

The False Messiah

of the Jews and the Antichrist. But after the covenant is made—many Jews resettled in their land under his protection—their Temple and sacrificial rites restored, then presently the covenant is broken, and the sacrifice and oblation caused to cease in the midst of the seven years—*three years and a half* (a "time, times, and a half a time, as predicted in Daniel 7:25; 12:7) will remain for the full display of all the horrors of Antichrist's dominion. Then the Lord shall come and all His saints attending Him, and this Man of Sin shall be consumed.

Numerous other expositors might be quoted who agree that the Jews will re-establish their sacrifices in a rebuilt temple. Among these expositors, Maramensis showed in the *Investigator*, volume 3, page 293, in A. D. 1834, that this renewal of the sacrifices will be 2,345 literal days before the End of this Age. And as it has recently been discovered that the last day of Passover Week, Thursday, April 11, 1901, will be the End of this Age, therefore Thursday, November 8, 1894, being 2,345 days before April 11, 1901, *may be expected to be*

The Day of the Renewal

of the Jewish sacrifices in a rebuilt temple at Jerusalem. Maramensis said: "Now it is evident that the Jews shall, of themselves, return unto their own land and re-establish their own religious worship." With regard to the 2,300 days in Dan. 8:13, 14, the question is asked, "How long shall be the vision concerning the daily sacrifice, and the transgression of desolation, to give both the sanctuary and the host to be trodden under foot?" The answer is: "Unto 2,300 days; then shall the sanctuary be cleansed." The meaning of the question, expressed in other words, seems to be this: How long shall be the period comprising these events? *viz.*, the establishment of the daily sacrifice, the declension of the Jews into apostacy, the consequent desolation of the holy places, and the treading under foot of their sanctuary. The 2,300 days will, therefore, commence with the first administration of the daily sacrifice, and end with the cleansing of the sanctuary.

"The 1,290 days (as well as the 1,260 days—Dan. 12:7, 11) both commence with the setting up of the abomination of desolation. It seems natural to suppose that there must be some relation between the event that marks the close, and that which marks the commencement of any prophetic period. As, therefore, the 1,290 days begin with the taking away of the daily sacrifice and the setting up of the abomination of desolation, they will probably end with the cleansing of the sanctuary from that abomination of desolation, and the re-establishment of the Jewish worship. If so, the 2,300 and 1,290 days have a common termination.

"The last period mentioned is the 1,335 days, which begins simultaneously with the 1,260 and 1,290 days, at the commencement of the unparalleled great tribulation, and of Antichrist's three and a half years of persecuting power, and concludes with a period of blessedness. 'Blessed is he that waiteth and cometh to the 1,335 days.'" (Dan. 12:12.) (Thus Maramensis held that a total period of 2,345 days will elapse from the renewal of the sacrifices, until the full blessedness at the end of the 1,335 days).

THE LORD'S SECOND COMING.

By the Late Rev. Henry Alford, D. D.

It seems very difficult to conceive that the usual course of this world should ever be broken in upon by such an event as the Second Coming of our Lord. It forms one of the most startling contrasts possible to place side by side with the common every-day thoughts of all of us about things around us.

"Yet a little while, and He that shall come will come." This is our belief. But where in our own days, where in days future, can we assign a time when we can realize

The Fact of His Coming?

Shall it be while earth is at peace, amidst the steady labors of the arts, and while man's thoughts are even and undistracted? Shall the merchant on the exchange, the student at his desk, the traveller on his journey, the mother in her family duties, the children in their school or at their play, be startled with the cry of His approach? So seem some places in Holy Scripture to teach us; and yet how difficult to imagine it! What do any of us expect less, than such a surprise in such employments? What seems more unlike God's ways of dealing with man during all these centuries, than that such a sudden crash should break in upon this settled order of things which He has so far established that it is our duty to Him to see it maintained, and to keep its place among ourselves!

Well, but let us then take the other alternative. Shall that day come upon us amidst fierce wars and distresses, when men's passions are let loose, and their thoughts have lost balance? Shall the ears of the wild combatants in the battle-field be pierced by the shout of the archangel rising over the din of their conflict? Shall the lurid glare of burning homes usher in the revelation of the Son of Man with flames of fire? Shall anguish and mourning be already upon mankind before

That Sign Shall Appear in Heaven

at which all the tribes of the earth shall mourn? This, again, seems not inconsistent with the testimony of Scripture in other places. But in that case how difficult to imagine God's faithful people waiting and praying; how must their thoughts be distracted, and their Saviour put out of their sight, by the dire necessities of the time! If the Christian prays against sudden death, if he dreads the passing from perhaps a light jest, or a trifling thought, or a festal moment to the presence of his God, how can we avoid the thought that the Church will then be taken at a disadvantage, when fierce passions are raging even in the bosoms whose law is forgiveness, and the ordinary means of grace are suspended? Again, if we put the alternative as to different times of our ordinary life, we shall find it equally difficult to give reality to our expectations of the Lord's Coming.

Now we know that "that day will come

As a Thief in the Night";

and to some it must, like the thief, come in the night itself. But it is impossible to apply this to all mankind, seeing that night and day share our globe alike; and such a consideration entirely prevents any general application of such a description, or of any description, of men's occupations except on the largest scale, when it shall overtake them. They shall be "eating and drinking, marrying and giving in marriage, buying and selling, planting and building"; these shall be their general employments over the whole earth: on such things shall their thoughts be; but to give any detailed description of the circumstance as applicable to all men is, from the above reason, impossible.

In our daily work it is that we must prepare for Christ's coming: in the occupations of this day, for the account of that day; by living more purely, more truthfully, more charitably: living more in prayer, more in consciousness of God's presence, more in the cleansing power of the Lord's blessed atonement, and by the guidance of His indwelling Spirit.

One thought may perhaps have been in some minds, as they have been reading these lines, and it is this: "Will not the Lord's coming, to most of us, in all probability be the day of our own death? And would it not be more profitable to be preparing us for that, than to warn us of an event which may not come on the earth in our time?" To this question there are

Two Answers,

answers which ought to be ever impressed on a Christian's mind. First, the view of things proposed by the inquirer is not that taken in Holy Scripture, which is the rule and pattern of our teaching. There we do not hear anything of preparation for *death*. I doubt whether one text can be found in which we are exhorted to make such preparation *as such*. But the constant note, the continually recurring exhortation, is to be prepared for the Lord's coming.

Our second answer goes to the reason of the thing, and in fact gives the account and lays open the foundation of the former, namely, He who is prepared for the Lord's coming is necessarliy also prepared for his own death. The greater includes the less. He who so lives, so thinks, so speaks, so works, in his daily life, as to be ready for the sign of the Son of man in heaven, and the voice of the archangel, and the trump of God, will not be found unready when the summons is heard in a more familiar tone in Death, and comes with more previous warning. If he can meet the Lord amidst the flaming heavens and the gathering dead, he will not be loath to obey His call, when its dread reality is tempered with all gentle and kindly alleviation—with the gradual approaches of sickness and infirmity, and the tender solaces of loving friends and watchful attendants.

But, on the other hand, he who has forgotten his Lord's coming, and has simply been careful about readiness for his own dismissal, will ever be too liable in the lesser thing to have neglected care for the greater; and he will also be well-nigh certain to have lowered his standard of attainment and narrowed his sympathies unworthily; in taking thought for himself, to have forgotten the great Body of which he is a member; in minding his own safety, to have forgotten his Lord.

CHRISTIAN HERALD AND SIGNS OF OUR TIMES.

OFFICE, 63 BIBLE HOUSE, NEW YORK.

TERMS AND INSTRUCTIONS.

Published Weekly. Subscription price in the United States, Canada, and Mexico, $1.50 a year; $1 eight months; 75 cents six months; sent two months on trial for 25 cents, postage free; in Europe and in all countries in the Postal Union, 50 cents extra postage; subscriptions always payable in advance. Single copies, price 3 cents. Any newsdealer will furnish the paper weekly when ordered.

New Subscriptions can commence at any time. When no date is mentioned, we begin it with the issue of the week in which the subscription is received.

Remittances by Mail should be by Post-office money order, bank cheque, draft, or express money order, whenever possible, and should always be made payable to THE CHRISTIAN HERALD. Letters containing money sent in this way need not be registered, as when lost, duplicates can always be obtained.

If a Postal Note or currency is sent, it should always be in a registered letter. Letters can be registered at any office. Subscribers sending money of this kind, and not registering, do it at their own risk.

Change of Address. Name of Post-office and State, of both old and new address, should always be given in case of removal, as without the previous address it is impossible to find the name on our list.

CURRENT EVENTS.

In the Observance of this Day as a Day of National Thanksgiving, we not only follow the hallowed customs of our forefathers, but publicly acknowledge the fact that all our mercies, national and individual, are of God. It would be a matter for deep regret if the significance of the observance were ever to be overlooked and the day to degenerate into a mere public holiday. It therefore behooves all Christians to set the example of a religious observance of the day, and to apply it to the purpose for which it is set apart. While in the majority of homes the day will be one of gladness and festivity, the Christian's home will not be made gloomy, but will rather be sanctified and elevated in its joy by the devout recollection that it is from a loving Father that every good and perfect gift has descended. In some homes the day finds the inmates in sadness and grief, but even there the thought of God's love may call forth chastened gratitude for the hope He gives us of a land in which all tears are wiped away. Nor should it be forgotten that one of the best and most practical methods of observing the day is to find out some family on which poverty is pressing; and see to it that the table is well furnished, for this day at least. He who does so will find that his own enjoyment is enhanced by having promoted the enjoyment of others.

An Escape From a Serious National Dispute should be thankfully acknowledged in the present situation of the Presidential vote in West Virginia. The State was at first claimed by the Democrats, then it was positively declared to be Republican, now it is again claimed by the Democrats. Evidently the plurality, to whomsoever it may belong, is small and doubtful. Had the State of New York gone Democratic, the vote of West Virginia would have decided the election. In that case, with so much doubt attached to it, the exciting struggle of 1876 might have, and probably would have, been renewed, with all the lasting acrimony which marked that struggle. Patriots, therefore, who love their country more than party may rejoice on that ground alone that New York went Republican this year.

An Important Rearrangement of Military commands was announced last week. General O. O. Howard, whose portrait and life appeared in this journal on May 31, 1888, has been transferred from the command of the Division of the Pacific to that of the Division of the Atlantic, and General N. A. Miles from Los Angeles to San Francisco, to the command thus vacated by General Howard. The object of the change is to put an end to the double duty hitherto imposed on General Schofield. General Schofield, since the death of General Sheridan, has exercised the command both of the Army and of the Division of the Atlantic, but this was necessarily a temporary arrangement. The officer commanding the army has enough in that relation to occupy his attention, without also carrying the burdens of a division command. The Department of Arizona, in whose administration General Miles has achieved so much credit, and which now passes to a distinguished and veteran officer, Colonel Grierson, is a part of the Division of the Pacific, to the command of which General Miles succeeds.

The Prohibition Vote in the Recent Election appears to have been over-estimated in the statement made here two weeks ago, and then given only as probable. The total vote is now placed, largely on official figures, at 268,505. Gains are recorded in every State but Louisiana, Massachusetts, and Vermont, as compared with the vote of 1884. In each of those States there was a slight loss. In New York State the vote was 30,524, while in 1884 it was 24,999, showing a net Prohibitionist gain of 5,525. The Prohibitionist National Committee, though doubtless disappointed with these figures, yet find in them ground for encouragement. In an address just issued they say, after pointing out the exceptional character of the contest in 1884, when considerable Mugwump support went to the Prohibition ticket: "Eliminating from our St. John vote all who voted the ticket merely as a protest, quite likely the total number would show not more than 100,000 as compared with nearly three times that number who cast their ballots for General Fisk."

The Annual Report of the Treasurer of the United States was issued on Thursday last. It summarizes and condenses the monthly reports of the past year. From this document it appears that during the fiscal year the surplus available for the reduction of the public debt was, in round numbers, $111,000,000—an increase of about $8,000,000 over the previous year. During the year the net Treasury balance increased about $60,000,000, due to an increase of $37,000,000 in the assets, and a diminution of $23,000,000 in the liabilities. The net decrease of the principal of the interest-bearing debt during the year was $75,000,000. Of this amount $51,464,000 in bonds were purchased for the sinking fund; and for the privilege of paying this debt before it was due, the tax-payers gave $8,274,000, a part of which they regain in the cessation of interest. The silver coinage during the year yielded $32,484,000, the bulk of which went into the Treasury vault.

The President-Elect Has Already Had Cause, it appears, to complain of the inundation of applications for appointments. General Harrison, however, is in some measure relieved of a part of the difficulty by the fact that he has not so many offices at his disposal as had his predecessors. During the past few years the scope of the civil-service law has been steadily widened and extended, until now in each of the seven big executive departments, the Agricultural Department, and all their branches, the great mass of the clerical force above the grades of scrubwomen, watchmen, and laborers has been brought within the classified service. The Government Printing-Office is the only establishment still outside of the civil-service rules, and remains so because no practical way of applying the merit system to a thousand or more printers has yet been devised. The practice of transferring clerks, who entered the service under non-competitive rules to offices to which the competitive system now applies, has also been partially checked by the new rule requiring every clerk to serve a year before promotion.

A Statesmanlike and Dignified View of the miserable Sackville incident was taken by Lord Randolph Churchill in a speech delivered in England on November 17. He said there was no doubt that Lord Sackville had been primarily indiscreet, and had made an inexcusable blunder. No fault could be found with the action of the United States Government toward the Minister. The American people were essentially just and proud in their relations with other countries. He deprecated the insulting and menacing articles which had appeared in the English press since Lord Sackville's dismissal. He regarded the attitude taken by Mr. Cleveland after the rejection of the Fisheries treaty by the Senate as an unfortunate one. Mr. Cleveland's action had been rather sharp, but it did not justify the menaces, sneers, and sulks in which the newspapers of England had indulged. A war between England and America, he declared, would be more atrocious and dangerous than any war since God created the earth. He trusted that the Government's policy toward the new Washington administration would be conceived with a view to making the American people England's best allies on all questions, and to producing a durable friendship between the English-speaking races, thus guaranteeing to humanity in turn the blessings of liberty and peace. It may be hoped that Lord Churchill's remarks may exercise a wholesome influence on the newspapers of his party, which seem to have lost their heads over the incident.

The German Reichstag Assembled on No-vember 22, and the session was opened by the Emperor in person. His address on the occasion was marked by the egotism and arrogance which characterizes all his utterances; but was ostensibly of a peaceful tenor. He said that he had undertaken to execute his grandfather's precious legacy with reference to social and political legislation; thus studiously ignoring, according to his unfilial custom, the more enlightened example of his father. He went on to say: "Our relations with all foreign Powers are peaceful. My efforts have been unceasing to strengthen this peace. The alliance with Austria and Italy has no other object. To bring without necessity the miseries even of a victorious war upon Germany, would be incompatible with my Christian faith, and my duties toward the German people. The confidence extended to me and my policy at all courts which I have visited, justifies the hope that I, and my allies and friends, with God's help, will be able to preserve the peace of Europe."

The Grave Indiscretion of a Prominent Irish journalist has involved him in a heavy fine, which has been imposed by the judges composing the Parnell commission. Mr Edward Harrington, the proprietor of the Kerry *Sentinel*, said in that journal that "the judges were showing signs of measles now, although at the opening of the inquiry they had appeared to be spotless. The judges were creatures of the conspiracy entered into by the Government and the *Times*, and were manifestly unable to veil their prejudices." An opportunity was afforded to the offending journalist to apologize, but he nonchalantly replied that he had no statement to make, except that he would accept responsibility for what appeared in his paper. The judges thereupon fined him $2,500.

A Vigorous Attack on the Irish Policy of the British Government was made last week by Mr. Gladstone. The Conservatives proposed to extend the law known as "the Ashbourne Act," which is a law passed in 1885, appropriating $25,000,000 to assist tenants in purchasing the farms they rent. The Government asked the House to make another appropriation of the same amount. Mr. Gladstone, in opposing the grant, moved that in lieu of voting £5,000,000, it is expedient, in view of the lamentable sufferings arising from recent evictions in Ireland, to extend the Land law of 1887 so as to empower the courts to reduce or cancel arrears of rents that are found to be excessive. He said that if the Government had the tenants' welfare earnestly at heart, it they meant to relieve distressed tenants, they would deal with arrears instead of pressing a dangerous measure which provided machinery for preventing a reduction of rent, and which afforded facilities for augmenting rents and multiplying evictions, with all their horrible incidents. The House, however, rejected Mr. Gladstone's amendment by a majority of eighty-four.

Clergymen Desiring to Increase their Income, or to raise money for church purposes, are reminded that THE CHRISTIAN HERALD pays a liberal commission to any person canvassing for subscribers. In several instances recently, quite considerable sums have been realized with ease in this way. Large numbers of Christian persons, whom it is impossible for the publishers to reach, would be pleased to subscribe, if a copy the paper was placed in their hands. The introduction is therefore mutually beneficial. One inadequately paid clergyman has written us that the amount he received in commissions for the year, equalled the amount which he received from his church as salary.

The Blessing that May Follow a Simple Invitation is forcibly illustrated in a statement recently made by the Secretary of the Milwaukee, Wis., Y. M. C. A. He said: "On a recent Saturday evening, a stranger arose at our meeting and said that he had been a dissipated man, and for several days past had been spending much of his time in a gambling saloon; that passing along the street an invitation was handed him, and he found it was a meeting in the Young Men's Christian Association. One of our young men talked with him, and he said he would be at church in the morning. He was there, and said he would be at our afternoon meeting. During that meeting he gave more fully his experience, and said: 'I am going home to Chicago in the morning, and by God's help I will lead a Christian life.' A letter was written that day to the Chicago Secretary, and he was followed up, and two weeks later word came 'that man is all right, and is to be received into —— church, at the next communion.'"

A Wandering Heir is Being Sought by a Firm of New York lawyers. About fifteen years ago a young man named Andrew J. Baker left his home in Tacoma, Washington Territory, to travel. His father was not then in prosperous circumstances, and the young man, besides hoping to make his fortune, was anxious to rid himself of parental control. He has not been heard of by his family since 1881, when he was in Detroit, Mich., in abject poverty. Since his departure, his father made several successful speculations, by which he realized an enormous fortune. He died recently, leaving a will by which his absent son is heir to a large part of his estate. But the young man cannot be found. Advertisements have been inserted in city and country journals, inquiring for him, but without success. It is thought that he must have obtained employment in some obscure place in which New York journals are not taken, or be too poor to get a sight of them. If that is so, the condition of the young man strikingly resembles that of some Christians who, though heirs of God through Christ fail to use the privileges at their disposal, and live in spiritual poverty, neglecting to claim the riches of grace which God is ready to give them. (Rom. 8:32.)

A Judge's Decision in New York Caused poignant distress to a lady and child on November 20. The case before him was an appeal from a mother for the custody of her child. She said that some years ago she was left a widow, with nine children. She was unable to support them, and looked around for kind and well-to-do persons who would relieve her of some of them. She heard of a lady who was willing to adopt a little girl, and the widow agreed to let her have her little daughter Carrie, then six years old. Lately the widow married again, and, her second husband being in prosperous circumstances, she desired to recover her children. The lady who had Carrie, however, declined to part with the child, and the mother thereupon appealed to the court. Both the child and the lady who had adopted her pleaded with the judge against the mother. The child especially begged, with tears, that she might not be given to her mother. The judge, however, had no option in the case. As the mother would not waive her claim, he had to make an order for the restoration of the child. There was a pathetic scene in court when his decision was announced: the lady fainted, and little Carrie hung over her, weeping and kissing the unconscious face, and with her arms about the neck of her adopted mother, piteously entreated that they might not be separated. Finally she had to be removed by force. Happily for those who have become the children of God and received the spirit of adoption, there is no power that can separate them and carry them back to their old life in the world, when they were the children of the wicked one. (Rom. 8: 15, 35.)

Noble Blood was Introduced into a Sufferer's veins in Georgia recently. About two weeks ago a woman residing at Tallulah Falls, Ga., met with a severe accident, in which she lost a large quantity of blood. A physician was sent for, but before he could arrive the vital stream continued to flow, in spite of the efforts of the bystanders to check it. After the physician came, and the hemorrhage was stopped, the patient was in danger of death from exhaustion. She sank continuously, until the physician declared that only transfusion of blood from a healthy person could save her. When this was known, a young French noble, Count Percy N. de Duboyeay, who is staying at Tallulah Falls, offered himself for the purpose. A blood-vessel was opened in his arm, and the life-giving fluid passed through a tube into a corresponding vessel in the arm of the dying woman. The result was astonishing; the patient revived, and the physician predicts that she will recover. If she does, she will owe her life to the nobleman who gave his blood to save her. Though the distinction between noble and plebeian blood is not recognized here as it is in Europe, we can fully appreciate the real nobility of the man who would make the sacrifice for a comparative stranger. It would be well if all who admire it were moved by that far greater sacrifice that the Son of God made when He shed His blood to save sinful men. (Col. 1:20-22.)

A Precaution Caused Disaster in New York on November 21. An automatic fire-alarm signal summoned the firemen, late at night, to a large building on Broadway. The place was let out to several-dry goods firms, each firm occupying an entire floor. When the engines arrived an attempt was made to fight the fire from the stairs, but it was found to be impossible to reach it in that way, as there were long passages between the staircases which used up the hose before getting at the seat of the fire. It was then decided to flood the building from the roof, but, on climbing up by the building next door, the firemen found that the roof of the burning building could not be easily broken up. It seems that the builder had been fearful of its being fired by sparks which might fall upon it if neighboring buildings should be burned. He had therefore taken the precaution of making his roof of solid brick. The firemen spent much valuable time in trying to pry up the bricks, but without avail. The builder had fixed them too securely. Finally they had to go into the next building and break a hole through the party-wall to admit the hose. While these efforts were being made, the fire raged unchecked, and the loss proved five times as great as it would have been if the roof had been an ordinary one. It is so in spiritual matters. In that great fire which the apostle tells us will try all human work, it will be found that those who have trusted in their own devices will suffer loss. (1 Cor. 3: 13, 19.)

A Fatal Wedding Trip was Taken by a young couple in West Virginia last week. On November 20 there was a wedding at St. George, in Tucker County. After the ceremony, the young couple started for a trip in the picturesque region known as the Land of Canaan. They reached Carrack's Ford that night, and the following day set out for the great Falls of the Black Water, crossing by the unfinished bridge of the West Virginia Central Railroad. The only footwalk was a single narrow plank, and when about half-way over, the bride, who had just turned to wave a good-bye to friends on the bank, grew dizzy, lost her balance, and fell from the bridge, with a shriek. Almost before she struck the water her husband sprang after her, and in an instant both had been whirled away in the foaming torrent. Black Water is unusually high, and the current runs at more than fifteen miles an hour, the water being very rough. Several persons saw the accident, and two men launched a boat, which was drawn by ropes into the middle of the stream nearly a quarter of a mile below the bridge. As the husband and wife, clasped in each other's arms, drifted down, they were seized and lifted into the boat. But the husband was dead, and the wife, though restored to life, is likely to lose her reason. When she waved her good-bye to her friends behind her, she doubtless forgot how precarious was her foothold on the narrow pathway. It is so with some who are setting out in the Christian life. The danger of looking back, and the necessity of keeping the eyes fixed on Jesus, are impressed on the young convert by Christ and His apostles. (Luke 9:61, 62.)

BRIEF NOTES.

The Rev. Charles C. Grafton, of Boston, has been elected Bishop of Fond du Lac, Wis.

Mr. Henry Varley and family have arrived safely in Australia. Mr. Varley expects to remain in that country for a few years.

The women of the entire Presbyterian Church North contributed last year for foreign missions, $295,501.03, and to home missions, $226,067.24.

George S. Avery has been secured to conduct special evangelistic meetings among the Massachusetts Young Men's Christian Associations by their State Committee.

The work of the Rev. B. Fay Mills in Philadelphia was largely blessed among young people. Special services were held for them, and the results have been encouraging.

Evangelist Vine has commenced at Jamaica, L. I., a series of meetings, to be held during the winter on Long Island, under the auspices of the L. I. Baptist Association.

At a service recently held for old people by the Rev. Samuel Scoville, at Stamford, Conn., many venerable persons attended. Three of them were over ninety years of age, and six of them over eighty.

There are now in the mission-field 2,400 unmarried ladies, besides probably an equal number of married. In the early days of missions it was not thought a lady could enter the ranks, except as the wife of a missionary.

Evangelist Grace Weiser's meetings at Monson, Mass., were largely attended, and many persons made profession of faith. Among them were several young men of remarkable natural ability. From Monson, Miss Weiser went to Philadelphia.

Dr. L. W. Munhall's work at Davenport, Iowa, is described in the *Morning Democrat*, of that city. It adds: "Never in the history of the city has there been so great a religious awakening as has attended the coming of Dr. Munhall and Professor Towner and wife."

The American Christian Missionary Society, which is auxiliary to the General Board of Missions of the Episcopal Church, held its twenty-ninth annual session in Washington recently. About 250 delegates were present, including many of the bishops of the Church.

In Bartow County, Ga., the results of the Prohibition law are being felt. The last grand jury failed to furnish a single indictment for crime, and the county jail has been without an inmate for months, a condition of things in strong contrast with that preceding the prohibitory amendment. The population of the county is 20,000.

At a meeting lately held in England in connection with the Central African Mission, the collection included a valuable gold ring, and a small parcel was handed to the chairman, which was found to contain a Roman pearl ring, a Roman antique ring, a diamond ring, four ladies' shawl-pins, and other articles, all for the Mission.

A Temperance missionary is employed in Toronto, and during the month of October he visited over two hundred families. Encouraging results have followed the missionary's labors among prisoners. One man who was reclaimed from drunkenness some time ago, has given proof of his reformation by sending a check for $200 to the funds of the mission.

The Executive Committee of the Ramabai Association wish to correct a statement that has lately been made in some papers to the effect that Ramabai had already raised the full sum desired for her school. In all, about $20,000 has been contributed in this country for the Ramabai school-fund, and about $12,000 more will be needed for the erection of a building, on the supposition that the land may be given by friends in India.

JESUS SET AT NOUGHT.

A New Sermon, by Pastor C. H. Spurgeon.

"And Herod, with his men of war, set him at nought." Luke 23 : 11.

A Shameless Business—I. Who is the Most Likely Person to Set Jesus at Nought—Herod at one Time a Glad Hearer of the Word—Had Done Violence to his Conscience—Had Yielded to Bad Companions—II. Herod's Reasons—Christ's Gentleness—His Refusal to Gratify Curiosity—His Royal Claims—III. How Jesus is Set at Nought Now—By Refusal to Consider His Claims—By Attention to Business and Amusements—By Despising the Gospel—His Speedy Coming—IV. What Believers Say of Their Lord.

It is your Lord whom Herod set at nought! Once worshipped of angels and all the heavenly host, He is made nothing of by a ribald regiment. In Himself "the brightness of His Father's glory, and the express image of His person"; but now set at nought by men not worthy of the name. Soon to reassume all His former glory with the Father, and to descend in infinite splendor to judge the earth in righteousness, and reign as King of kings; and yet here He is set at nought! It is a sight of horror and of shame. How could angels bear to see it? This paltry prince and his rough retinue made nothing of Him who is All in all; they treated Him as beneath their contempt. The veriest abjects flouted Him. The meanest soldier in the petty army of a petty princelet made unholy mirth of heaven's high Lord and earth's Redeemer. What a sorrowful and shameless business! May we be helped to sorrow over it!

Herod himself set Him at nought. In this loathsome being I see the most likely person to think nothing of the Lord Jesus. Let me just say a word or two about this member of a detestable family, that I may see whether his like can be found here to-night. I will not give you any history of this Herod. It is not worth while. This "fox" is not worth unearthing. The page of history is stained by the Herodian name. I will give you enough concerning him to help you to answer the question—Are you like him? Have you set Christ at nought?

The Persons Who Do It.

I. This shall be our first inquiry: Who is the most likely person to set our Lord at nought? Herod was a man who had once heard the word of God; yes, he heard it with a measure of attention and apparent benefit. We read: "Herod feared John, knowing that he was a just man, and an holy, and observed him; and when he heard him, he did many things, and heard him gladly." According to the margin, Herod "kept him or saved him"—preserving him from those who would have laid violent hands upon him. But he broke away from his respectful regard of John, and now that Jesus stands before him, his memory of the Baptist does not restrain him from mocking the Baptist's Lord. We often find that the greatest despisers of Christ are those who formerly were hearers and readers of His Word, but have turned from it. Am I talking to any here who, not so many years ago, were regular attendants upon a faithful ministry, but who have grown weary of it, and given it up? It troubles your conscience that you have done so, and now you try to conceal your uneasiness by picking holes in your former minister, and finding fault with the truths which he preached to you. Herod heard John, but he ridiculed Jesus. See to what unconverted hearers may come!

If I look at Herod again, I see in him a man who, after hearing the Word faithfully preached, had distinctly

Done Violence to his Conscience.

He heard John until John came home to him about the woman with whom he was living in an incestuous union. Herodias would have killed John at once; and though Herod did not dare to go so far as that, yet he shut him up in prison. A filthy lust must not be rebuked; Herod imprisons his reprover. The man who could do this was in training for the more daring act of setting the Lord Jesus at nought. First despise the man, and then the Master.

My friend, do you remember that night when you distinctly decided for the devil? Do you recollect when, after having the evil set before you, and seeing it, and counting the cost, you decided to continue in it? Then you turned with bitterness upon the honest reprover whose rebuke you had aforetime endured. Perhaps it was your wife upon whom you turned with anger. What hard words you said to her for the gentle remark she ventured to make! It was an effort for you. You gave conscience an awful wrench; and therefore you put youself into a passion, and talked like an injured man. Or was it your brother? It may be you quitted his society in order to be free from his remarks. Was it your child, or your friend? You could not put them in prison; but you were determined that you would not bear any more of their protests. By all this you have prepared yourself to set the Lord at nought; and we cannot wonder that you do so.

This man also had yielded to sinful companions, and had committed a gross sin as the result of it, for when Herodias danced, and he promised to give her whatsoever she desired, she asked the head of John the Baptist in a charger; and he, not liking to break his word in the presence of the guests, and not willing to stand out against the woman with whom he

Lived in Unhallowed Intercourse,

yielded, and the Baptist's head was taken from his shoulders. Ah, well! you may not have sinned quite in that way; but you, too, once had better thoughts and higher aims. Your companions were too many for you, and drove all good out of you. If there had been a spark of true manhood in you, you would have resisted the suggestion of those enemies in the garb of friends. This is the man that thinks nothing of Christ—the man who thinks so much of drinking and dancing, and of the companions which such things have brought around him. Of course, he does not think anything of Christ, for His ways would take from him these vile associates. Jesus cannot be valued by a man of Herod's sort, who puts so high a value upon the opinion of those who sit at his banquets.

Once more: the man who thinks nothing of Christ is the man that

Means to Go On in Sin,

even as Herod did. The die was cast; his mind was made up for evil. He would be very glad to hear Christ: he has no objection still to go to a place of worship and listen to a preacher. He would be very pleased to see a miracle; he would join in a revival, for he would be glad to enjoy something sensational, but he does not mean to give up the sin in which he lives, nor the company which eggs him on in it. He does not mean to cut off the right hand, and pluck out the right eye. Not he! "It is not at all surprising that such a man should speak evil of Christ. It is as natural to such a man to talk against Christ as for a dog to bark." When a bad fellow once praised Socrates, that philosopher said, "I wonder what I can have been doing amiss, that such a man should speak well of me!" If lustful lips praised the Saviour, one might begin to be afraid; but when they denounce and deride Him, we feel that it is the only homage which vice can pay to purity.

This, then, is the man who sets Jesus at nought. I wonder whether he is here now! Possibly it is a woman who is doing this. Women fall into precisely the same evils as men from their own side of the house, and the same remarks apply to both sexes. You who once were hearers, you who once were impressed, you who did wilful violence to conscience, you who persist in sin, you who are the slaves of evil company, and dare not do right for the life of you, for fear of ridicule—you are the kind of people of whom Herod was a sad specimen: you set Jesus at nought.

His Reason for His Act.

II. Having tried to find out Herod, let us now answer a second question—On what ground did he set our Lord at nought? Herod sets Him up as the butt of his ridicule, and makes nothing of Him. I suppose that part of the reason why he and his men of war made nothing of our Lord was because of His gentleness and patience. Our Lord had no sword, and none of the temper of men who wear weapons. His visage was not like the face of a man of war: it was marred with grief, but not with anger; worn with sorrow, but not with battle. If He had any weapons they were His tears and His almighty love; but these the Herodian ruffians utterly despised. All unarmed He stood before them, and when He was reviled He reviled not again. The Christian religion teaches us to be meek and gentle, to forgive injuries, and even to give up our own rights rather than to inflict wrong. Such precepts savor of cowardice to the blustering world. Non-resistance they cannot hear of. The sweet savor of

Gentle Forbearance,

which the spirit of Jesus breathes into the hearts of His people, is by many held in contempt. They call it cant and hypocrisy, because it is so inconsistent with their ideas of manly conduct.

Furthermore, our Lord was ridiculed by Herod because He refused to gratify his curiosity and amuse his love of sensation. The wicked Herod virtually said to the holy Jesus: "Come, work us a miracle. We hear that thou didst deliver from death: now release Thyself from our hands. Thou canst do all things, so report says of thee—come, do some little thing, that we may see and believe. Work a miracle before us." There stands our Lord, with all power in His hands, but He will not lift a finger for His own deliverance and Herod's amusement. Oh, blessed Jesus! it is the same still—thou wilt not amuse, and therefore men prefer any charlatan to thee.

The Royal Claims of Jesus

excited their scorn. I think I hear the "Aha! aha! aha!" of Herod as he said: "Call *Him* a King? You could find such kings as this in every street in Jerusalem. Talk of a kingdom for Him! Go to the pool of Bethesda, and fetch up some poor wretch who lies waiting there for the moving of the water, and call him a king! King! What hosts are at Thy command? What kingdom dost Thou govern? What laws canst Thou make? Here! put the white robe upon Him. Let Him at least look like a monarch. Yes, that old robe will do! Is He not every inch a King?" Then the soldiery took up the jest! How bitterly, how derisively, did they make His Royalty the football of contempt! Thus to-day the world makes nothing of the royalty of King Jesus. A nominal King He may be, but as a real King they will not have Him. Those who would be in the dust before the meanest princelet have no esteem for Him.

Those, I suppose, were the grounds upon which Herod, and such as Herod, make light of Christ. Poor grounds they are, and such as will fail to justify them before the bar of God.

How He is Set at Nought.

III. Now, dear friends, let us consider. How do men now set our Lord at nought? Herod is dead and buried, and there is no sort of reason why we should not let him rot into oblivion. I therefore speak to you, and try to discover whether you are setting Christ at nought. I fear there are such. Who are they?

Some set him at nought, for *they will not even consider His claims*. "Oh," say they, "we have plenty else to think about besides religion! What is there in it which will fill our pockets? There is nothing at all in it worth a moment's attention." How do they know? They do not know. Nothing in it? God gives His own Son to die for guilty men, and there is nothing in it! The highest thoughts of God are set forth in the person of the Lord Jesus Christ, and you do not think it worth while even to consider what God has therein revealed? Who is to save the man who will not listen when salvation is put before him? Yet the great mass of our fellow citizens are of this kind. In London there are millions who make so little of Christ that they will not even come to hear what His ministers have to say about Him, nor read their Bibles, nor show the least interest in the matter. It many a house in London, Mahomet is practically as much esteemed as Jesus. Ah me!

There are many others who prefer their business to Jesus. They would not mind giving some little attention to the Lord Jesus, but then they are too busy just now. They say that they really cannot afford the time. Oh my busy hearer! you will have to find time to die before long: why not think of that solemn certainty? You are very busy, and yet you find time to eat. Have you no time to feed your soul? You find time to put on your dress; have you no time to dress your souls? You seek out the surgeon when you are ill; have you no time to seek out a Saviour for your soul? Ah! it is not that: you have the time, but you have not the heart.

Others Prefer Amusements

to the Lord Jesus. "Well," says one, "we must have recreation. In my spare time I like a game." I know that. I am not for denying you healthy recreation, but everything should be in order, and I claim first place for Jesus Christ and His salvation. What! is it not worth while to give up a sport to seek Jesus? Do you think a game of cards more important than seeking the pardon of your sin? An evening at the theatre or the music-hall; do you really think so little of Jesus that you can live without Him, and satisfy your mind with these poor things? Can you suffer the paltry amusements of the world to stand before the Lord Jesus? Yet it is so with some of you.

You Will Know Better One Day.

Another sort of persons make nothing of Christ, because they profess to see nothing profound and philosophical in the faith which he has revealed. These are the Greeks, to whom the doctrine of the Cross is foolishness. Oh foolish Greeks! These wise men will not hear some of us because we can be understood of the people. "Anybody can understand you," say they; "you speak after the manner of the crowd, and what you say is simple enough to be clear to the most ignorant. We like something deeper, something too profound to be readily grasped. We are above commonplace people, and need something more intellectual and philosophical." A man of note once said to me, "Why do you keep on preaching to those thousands at Newington? Preach so that the mob will leave you, and the *élite* will support you." To whom I answered, that if one man's soul was of less value than another, his was of the least value who could talk so slightingly of others.

Others make nothing of the Lord because *they confide in themselves*. They think themselves quite good enough without a Saviour. If they are not quite perfect, they believe that they can make themselves so, and be saved without an atoning sacrifice, or a new heart, or union to Christ. They are doing their best, and they make no doubt whatever that they will find their way to heaven as well as others. Do you thus think? You are in grave error. There was a learned Romanist who once ventured to say that if salvation could only be had on terms of free grace, he would not have it. Do you know what happened? Why, he did not have it: that was all. And that is what will happen to you.

Many have no fears concerning the day of His appearing. Whether you believe it or not, Jesus, as your Judge, is at the door. He said, years ago, "Behold, I am

Coming Quickly."

He is still coming, and must soon arrive to commence the last dread session of justice. What matters it how many more years may elapse? They will fly like the wind. The day will come when heaven and earth shall be ablaze. The thick darkness will lower down,

"And, withering from the vault of night,
The stars shall pale their feeble light."

The hour will come when the earth and sky will rock and reel, and pass away, rolled up like a worn-out vesture. Then shall the trumpet ring out exceeding loud and long—"Awake, ye dead, and come to judgment!" How will you endure that voice which shall disturb the stillness of the sepulchre? "Come to judgment! Come to judgment! Come to judgment!" How it will peal forth! None of you will be able to resist the call. From your beds of dust you will start up, amazed, to a terrible awakening. From the sea, from the land, from the teeming cemetery, from the lonely grave, men will rise, and all of them stand before Christ! In that day you will see nothing but the great white throne, and Him that sits upon it. You will be unable to close your eyes, or turn your gaze elsewhere.

IV. But I close with this: What do believers say about their Lord? Herod made nothing of him:

What do we Make of Him?

Well, we say, first, that we mourn and lament that there ever was a time when we ourselves made nothing of the glorious One. It is many years ago with some of us; but we cannot forget it, nor cease to bewail it. There were a certain number of years in our lives in which it was nothing to us that Jesus should die. Oh, my dear hearers, perhaps some of you have been lately converted after forty or fifty or sixty years of sin. Repent with all your hearts that you were Herods so long. Christ has forgiven you; but can you forgive yourselves? No; I think that you still smite on your breast, and say, "Lord, I grieve that ever I lived a moment without acknowledging my Lord—that I ever ate a meal or drew in a breath without bowing before Him." Lord, bury those years in forgetfulness which we spent in forgetfulness of thee!

Next, it is now our grief that any others should set the Lord Jesus at nought. It must be a great grief to any man here if she who lies in his bosom sets the Lord at nought. Dear woman, I know what your daily burden must be if the husband who is so dear to you does not love your Saviour, whom you love with a higher love. What an anguish it is to nourish and bring up children, and see them refuse our Lord! "I have no greater joy than to hear that my children walk in the truth"; and no greater sorrow than to see them running into evil ways. Could we really see the heart of an unregenerate man or woman, it would cause us the utmost distress. It is an awful thing: as awful as hell itself! Out in that street to-night think of the thousands who will be hunting for the precious life. Walk along our crowded thoroughfares, and think of the myriads even of this city who live and die without God, and without hope, making nothing of Jesus, and you will feel a heartbreak which will make life a burden. I could wish that you felt that heartbreak for their sakes, and for Christ's sake.

But then, dear friends, what do we make of Christ ourselves now? Well, that I cannot tell you, except it be in one word

Christ is All.

Herod made nothing of Him; we make everything of Him. Could any of you who love my Lord tell me what you think of Him? I am sure that you would break down in the attempt. For my own part, I always fail in the glad endeavor. If we could give every drop of our blood for Jesus, if we could be burnt at a slow fire for a century for Him, He deserves all our suffering and all our life. Could our zeal no respite know, a whole eternity of service would not adequately set forth what we think of Him.

I close with this practical thought: Sometimes believers show their love and their appreciation of their Master by special acts of homage. Herod, you see, when he made nothing of Him, said, "Here, bring out that glittering white robe of mine, and put it on Him, that we may heap contempt upon Him. He calls Himself a King! Let us pay Him homage!" They mocked Him, and they put the robe upon Him, and then sent Him back to Pilate. Now, I want you to imitate Herod in the opposite direction. Let us resolve that for His sake we will speak well of His name to somebody to whom we have not yet spoken. Herod set Him at nought, but let us set Him on high in our best manner. Set Him at the highest figure that your thought and your imagination can reach. Oh, how would I honor Him! But what am I? What can one person do? Therefore do I summon all things that are to praise the Lord, without whom was not anything made. I charge all living things to adore Him who is the Resurrection and the Life. Let space become one great mouth for song. Let time unceasingly flow with hallelujahs. Let eternity become an orchestra to the praise of Jesus, who was mocked of Herod and his men of war. Glory be to His name! Hallelujah! Hallelujah! Amen.

GEMS FROM NEW BOOKS.

QUEEN ELIZABETH'S LAST DAYS.*

There are few more jarring scenes in English history than the last days of Queen Elizabeth. "As life was passing away," a historian says, "she clung to it with a fierce tenacity. She hunted, she danced, she jested with her young favorites, she coquetted and frolicked and scolded at sixty-seven as she had done at thirty." "The Queen," wrote a courtier, "a few months before her death was never so gallant these many years, nor so set upon jollity." She persisted, in spite of opposition, in her gorgeous progresses from country house to country house. She clung to business as of old, and rated in her usual fashion one "who minded not to give up some matter of account." And then a strange melancholy settled upon her. Her mind gave way, and food and rest became alike distasteful. Clever woman, yet very foolish in not discerning how vain it was to attempt to carry the brisk habits of youth into old age, and most profoundly foolish in not having taken pains to provide for old age the enjoyments appropriate to itself. How differently it has fared with those who have been wise in time and made the best provision for old age! "I have waited for Thy salvation, O my God," says the dying Jacob, relieved and happy to think that the object for which he had waited had come at last. "I am now ready to be offered," says St. Paul, "and the time of my departure is at hand. I have fought the good fight; I have finished my course; I have kept the faith: henceforth there is laid up for me a crown of righteousness, which the Lord, the Righteous Judge, will give me at that day." Which is the better portion—he whose old age is spent in bitter lamentation over the departed joys and brightness of his youth, or he whose sun goes down with the sweetness and serenity of an autumn sunset, but only to rise in a brighter world, and shine forth in the glory of immortal youth?

The Prince's Fall.

A recent writer, when narrating the fall of Cardinal Wolsey, powerfully describes the way of Providence in suffering a career of unexampled wickedness and ambition to go from one degree of prosperity to another, till the moment of doom arrives, when all is shattered by a single blow. "There was long delay, but the hour of reckoning at length arrived. Slowly the hand had crawled along the dial-plate; slowly, as if the end would never come; and wrong was heaped on wrong, and oppression cried, and it seemed as if no ear had heard its voice, till the measure of the wickedness was at length fulfilled. The finger touched the hour, and as the strokes of the great hammer rang out above the nation, in an instant the whole fabric of iniquity was shivered to ruins." This hour had now come to Absalom. He had often been reproved, but had hardened his heart, and was now to be destroyed, and that without remedy.

A King Under Reproof.

When Nathan ended his message (II Sam. 12: 13-25), plainly and strongly though he had spoken, David indicated no irritation, made no complaint against the prophet, but simply and humbly confessed—"I have sinned." It is so common for men to be offended when a servant of God remonstrates with them, and to impute their interference to an unworthy motive, and to

* From "The Expositors' Bible: The Second Book of Samuel." By Professor W. G. Blaikie, D. D., LL. D.; a book of unusual interest, explaining and commenting on the leading events of David's reign in the manner of the modern historian, enabling the reader to realize vividly the life of the warrior king and the condition of his kingdom. Pp. 400; Price $1.50. Published by *A. C. Armstrong & Son*, 714 Broadway, New York.

Mr. Daniel Hand, the Connecticut Philanthropist.

The Training Institute at Delhi, India. (See page 757.)

the desire of some one to hurt and humiliate them, that it is refreshing to find a great king receiving the rebuke of the Lord's servant in a spirit of profound humility and frank confession. Very different was the experience of John the Baptist when he remonstrated with Herod. Very different was the experience of the famous Chrysostom when he rebuked the Emperor and Empress for conduct unworthy of Christians. Very different has been the experience of many a faithful minister in a humbler sphere, when, constrained by a sense of duty, he has gone to some man of influence in his flock, and spoken seriously to him of sins which bring a reproach on the name of Christ. Often it has cost the faithful man days and nights of pain. Girding himself for the duty has been like preparing for martyrdom, and it has been really martyrdom when he has had to bear the long, malignant enmity of the man whom he has rebuked. However vile the conduct of David may have been, it is one thing in his favor, that he receives his rebuke with perfect humility and submission. He makes no attempt to palliate his conduct, either before God or man, but sums up the whole feeling in those expressive words: "I have sinned against the Lord."

MRS. MULLINS'S FRAMED TEXT.

(*See Illustration on page 765.*)

IT had been a long, tiring day in the Mullins household, for Mrs. Mullins was packing up all her home treasures for removal to the new home in the village three miles away. Not that the whole contents of the house would have brought much under the auctioneer's hammer. Treasures they could not properly be called, in the sense of the market, but they were treasures to her, for the home she was leaving had been her home from her birth, and she was glad that when she married she did not have to leave it. Her aged father and mother had welcomed her lover to their household, and had urged that their only remaining daughter should not leave them, but set up her married home in the extension at the side of the cottage. But she had to leave the dear old place now, for John had had what the neighbors called, "a stroke of luck." The squire in the next village had taken a fancy to him, and offered him the position of head-gardener, with a nice roomy cottage to live in. Mrs Mullins, therefore, packed up cheerfully, though she wished the luck could have come to them in the old place. At last everything was piled in the wagon, which John's new employer had lent them; and Mrs. Mullins, putting on her bonnet, prepared to walk by Silas the wagoner's side to the new home.

"What makes you carry the picter for?" Silas asked, when they had walked beside the loaded wagon a short distance. "Put her in the wagon. There's room; she won't be broken."

"Oh, it isn't heavy," said Mrs. Mullins; "I wouldn't feel it was safe if I didn't carry it myself."

"Something extra pretty, is it?" asked Silas.

"Maybe you won't think so," said Mrs. Mullins, taking the cloth off it and holding it up, "but it means a good deal to John and me."

Silas looked at it and read, "Without shedding of blood, there is no remission of sins." He thought silently for a moment and then said, "No, I don't see much in it, that's a fact."

"I guess not," said Mrs. Mullins. "It's like water, or money, or health: when you know the want of it, you know the worth of it—not before. You see, remission means—"

"Oh, I know that," Silas interrupted; "good cause to know. When the old man died, and mother was awful sick, and all the money was gone, I went to the agent to ask time with the rent. Mother couldn't go, so I went. I told him all about it, and he said he'd see the squire, and I was to come again next week. Well, I went, and what do you think the agent said? He said the squire told him the rent was to be remitted. I didn't know what he meant, and I guess I looked a bit mixed. But the agent, he laughed and he said, 'Where did you go to school, Silas? The squire means you have not got to pay it at all. That's better than you asked for. You wanted time to pay, but he's letting you off free.' I guess I won't need to ask anybody again what remission means. It meant bread and meat to us that time. But I don't see the point of the picter, for all that."

"Don't you? Well, it means about the same. You know what happened at our house after the old folks died. John kept all right while they lived, and so did I. Afterward, you know, he went wrong, and I don't say but what I was to blame too. You heard all about it, I guess. It was talked about pretty well. (Silas nodded.) Well, we made up our minds to turn over a fresh leaf, and we did—pretty nearly. The clergyman talked, and one or another had their say, and altogether we pulled around. But we were troubled about the past. Not so much because of people throwing it up at us, but both of us wanted to get religion, and seemed as if what we'd done shut us out. We asked John's uncle about it one day, when he came in to see how we were doing, and he allowed God wouldn't hold it against us if we did right now. We weren't sure though, and its a bad thing to make mistakes in.

"Well, one day there were some meetings b- ing held by a sort of wandering preacher, ar John and I, we went to hear him. He preach about these very words. Said sin couldn't l got rid of by turning over a new leaf. We kne that, because it kept on worrying us. There w only one way ever known, and that was l death; and then he told us how Jesus knew tha and He was so anxious about all of us, and sorry because we had all sinned, and could nev be happy after we were dead, that He agreed die for us. And that was how He came to l crucified, like the clergyman preaches abou And then God remits—wipes out, you kno Well, that was just what we wanted; and had some talk with the preacher, and got it o quite clear and sure, and, I tell you, it made right over new, and took all the load off. Soo after that, when John was over in the city, l saw that very text all framed in a window, ar he went right in and bought it to hang up our house, and this is it."

"You ain't had any more worry?" asked Sil

"No; this holds good always."

"Well I ain't quite clear myself," said Silas.

"Get this, and you will be," said Mrs. Mullin

MR. DANIEL HAND.

The Millionaire Philanthropist.

THE most extreme Socialist could obtain hearing for his onslaughts on "bloated bon holders" if many of our millionaires were infl enced by the principles of Daniel Hand. would be difficult to conceive of an act of pur patriotism than that which, as we recently me tioned in our news columns, he has just pe formed. In placing in the hands of the Ame can Missionary Association a million dollars be used in educating the colored race, he h conferred a benefit on the whole nation. F the ignorance of any class or section involv danger to all other classes.

Daniel Hand is eighty-seven years old, havi been born at Madison, Conn., in 1801. Wh he was seventeen years of age he went Sout and assisted his uncle in a grocery business Augusta, Ga. His uncle eventually made hi his heir. He prospered financially, being of industrious, painstaking disposition. He al took an active part in Christian work, and w for upward of thirty years superintendent of t Sunday-school of the First Presbyterian Chur of Augusta. He subsequently opened a sto at Charleston, S. C., and that too was a succe His abolition principles rendered it unsafe remain in the South during the war. He w in prison for two weeks, but was respectfully a kindly treated. When he was released he hand ısiness over to his chief , Mr. George W. Will- a Southern gentleman :erling integrity, and no receipt for it. At :lose of the war Mr. ams sought out Mr. l, and handed over to the value of the busi- and the profits which ıccrued since Mr. Hand amounting in all to o.ɔo.

. Hand was a widower, :hildless, and he looked nd for some channel in h he could use his prop- for the public good. condition of the colored in the South commend- self to him as an urgent ssity. Ultimately, after ing investigation, he de- ined to devote a million hat purpose, and to e the American Mis- ary Association his al- ers. The terms of his show the sagacity of the . The million dollars is y invested, and each the Association is to d the interest of it in :ating colored children youths, no one individ- to receive more than in one year. As scholar- s can be obtained for $75 a year, Mr. ıd's gift will enable a large number to obtain od education.

Mrs. Mullins's Framed Text.

THE EPOCHS OF A LIFE,

A NEW SERIAL STORY.

By Rev. L. S. Keyser.

(*Continued from page 750.*)

The New Day.

was well for Madelling that he did lay aside e Havelock's letter for perusal at some more rable time. Though it was not the kind of r he supposed, it was of a nature to stir his ions deeply, and arouse an agitation within prejudicial to his spiritual life.

was a curious fact that the same mail carried ter in the same handwriting to Madeline ters. It reached her at the close of a day orry and distress. In the morning she had ived a call from Mr. Duneman, who, after aining some days in his rooms, in fear of a tition of violence at the hands of Madelling, ngth mustered courage to venture out.

glance at the young man showed Madeline he had devoted more care than usual to ersonal appearance, and his manner was so essive as to suggest that his visit was hted with an important purpose. What purpose was, Duneman soon revealed. the circumlocution which he would have in opening an address in college, he describ- s position and prospects, and then formally her an offer of marriage.

ice or twice Madeline tried to interrupt to spare him, if possible, the pain she knew ould have to suffer. But it was useless. man had strong faith in the power of his eloquence. His proposal had been care- prepared to appeal to the strongest points adeline's nature, and he expected much his final words, which, in the character of a ation, depicted in glowing colors the joy happiness she would have as the wife of a ter of the gospel.

deline saw that the whole story must be so she sat still, with all the patience she command, until the end was reached, and man, bending on one knee beside her, tried ssess himself of her hand. No good woman isten unmoved to an avowal of sincere love, if she cannot reciprocate it. It is a treas- ot to be purchased by wealth or labor, and she realizes that it is not to be treated lightly or frivolously. Besides this, Madeline's kind heart shrank from inflicting pain on any one, and in this case especially she dreaded making it more acute than was necessary. Duneman's coarser nature misunderstood this delicate consideration, and failed to perceive the hopelessness of his suit. A girl who could speak so gently and tenderly must surely have, he thought, some regard for him. He continued to plead, and at length told her that if she refused him he should be so overwhelmed by the disappointment that he would have no heart to pursue his studies, and should abandon the ministry. On her would rest the responsibility of destroying his career of usefulness.

"Do not threaten me, Mr. Duneman," she said. "I think if you can be turned from such a career by my refusal—if you have no stronger, higher motives for entering upon it than those that any words of mine can influence—it would be well that you should abandon it. If you are called of God to the work, you dare not disobey; if you are not so called, your engaging in it would be a profanation. In either case my answer is the same. I can never marry you, for I do not love you. That is final."

"It is that infidel ruffian Madelling," he said, an angry flush overspreading his features, "who has prejudiced you against me. You will marry him and be miserable."

"I do not wish to hurt your feelings," said Madeline; "when you are more collected, you will see that your words are ungentlemanly. Do not let us import an irrelevant question into an interview which is painful to us both. Accept my answer for yourself, and let that content you. I assure you that under no circumstances could I give you any other. Now you will go, will you not?"

At last even Duneman, obtuse as he was, perceived that he had no hope, and he went from her presence hot and angry, and with an ardent longing for revenge on the man whom he deemed his successful rival.

Madeline was restless and distraught all through the remainder of the day. She spent some time in solitary self analysis. Duneman was wrong about Madelling. If she had never known Hadley, she would have given Duneman the same answer; but was there in her heart a love for him that steeled it against all others? Madeline wished she could answer in the negative, but she was honest with herself, and could not but admit that, in spite of all, no man but he had won a place in her heart. Yet his engagement to another woman, and his duplicity about it, must separate him from her forever. Well, women had suffered so before. Hard as it would be, she must tear from her heart a love that dishonored her, and must forget him. She wept over it, prayed for strength to do her difficult duty, and then, removing as far as she could the traces of tears from her face, she went about her daily duty with a softened, chastened spirit. Late that night, with Belle Havelock's letter, which she had read and reread, clasped in her hands, she was kneeling by her bedside, thanking and praising God, her face suffused with tears of mingled anguish and joy.

The same night was the supreme epoch of Hadley's life. He lay sleepless upon his bed, trying vainly to overcome the habit of sceptical doubt and attain that state of mind which Jesus so cogently described as that of a little child. Hadley could not reach it, and at last he fell into a troubled sleep. He had a strange dream. He was at college again, and preparing an address against the Bible, which was to be a masterpiece. His ambition was kindled; his determination to deal one crushing, overwhelming blow at the Book, which should once for all annihilate its influence in the college, was absorbing. Yet, with the common experience of dreams, he could not find his notes, could not put his hand on the books of reference he needed, nor even find writing-materials in his study. Suddenly some one was helping him. At one time it seemed to be his old friend, George Dane; at another it was Belle Havelock; again, it was a stranger of great learning and imposing appearance.

His confusion vanished, his books were in order, his notes arranged, and his guide was pointing with unerring finger to this and that powerful passage of anti-Biblical argument. He was elated, triumphant. Now he was dealing with the miracles, and quoting the miracle of the exorcising at Gadara. He turned to put a question to his new mentor, and was struck with amazement and terror. It was no man that had been helping him, but the Spirit of Evil himself. "Am I an amanuensis for the devil?" he cried in his dream. "Depart! In the name of Jesus of Nazareth, depart!" His own cry and his agitation awoke him. He was lying in cold perspiration and trembling from head to foot. In a few minutes he passed from the dazed, confused condition of waking, into full intelligence and a realization that he had been dreaming, and of what.

Was it possible, he thought, that these doubts which had been distressing him and keeping him from peace and faith in Christ were suggested by Satan? It might be so. How weak and helpless was he, then, to contend against so wily and powerful an enemy! Was he a victim doomed to be Satan's prey? The possibility appalled him. He sank on his knees and prayed. Never before had he so felt his own weakness and utter helplessness without God. "O Jesus," he cried, "take me as I am, hold thou me, save me or I perish; I have no hope but in thee!" It was an absolute surrender! an unfaltering confidence in Christ's power and love, and it was followed by such peace and rest, and such a sense of joyful security, as no words could describe.

He returned to his bed and fell into a deep, refreshing slumber. As soon as it was light he was awake, dressed rapidly, read the Bible, and offered a prayer of joy and thanksgiving, and then hurried out to tell Hanson the glorious news. He found the clergyman, early as it was, engrossed at his desk. He looked up as Hadley entered, read on his face the intelligence he came to bring, and springing to his feet he grasped his hand.

"Madelling, my brother," he exclaimed, "you have been born again!"

"Yes, Hanson, nothing short of that, thank God!"

The two men sat down, and Hadley told his story, and then they knelt and offered their united praises to God. As they parted, their hands were clasped in the warm fraternal grip that he alone fully understands who gives his hand to a brother in Christ. As Hadley went through his duties that day, a warm glow of joy and happiness seemed to radiate from his heart throughout his whole being. "'The peace of God,' he murmured once, 'which passeth all understanding.' Yes, that is it; mine now and throughout eternity."

That night he took up Belle Havelock's letter and opened it. It could do no harm now. As Mr. Hanson's business friend had said to him, now he *knew*; it was no longer speculation or opinion or religious views: he *knew*. But what was this? Belle's style had changed. "This letter," she began, "costs me more pain, more shame and humiliation, than any act of my life. I have done you a cruel, bitter wrong and caused suffering to you and another, and I can have no peace nor rest until I have borne the pain of doing what I can to atone for my sin. To Miss Winters I am making a similar confession and I implore both to forgive me if it is possible."

Belle then fell into the narrative style and told a surprising story. It appeared that she had continued attending Mr. Mardont's ministry after Hadley left college, and, recently, that earnest preacher whose sermons had so stirred Hadley had penetrated the armor of agnosticism in which Belle's soul was wrapped. A long, agitating struggle followed, and she had been unable to find peace until she had resolved to make a full and complete confession of a sin that lay heavily on her conscience. She was persuaded that God had forgiven her, and now she wished to confess to the two persons she had wronged, and to beg their pardon.

Then followed a circumstantial and detailed history of the plot which, with Duneman's assistance, she had engineered for Hadley's discomfiture, and with which the reader is already familiar. She assumed responsibility for it all, and dwelt but slightly on Duneman's share in it. In conclusion she said: "May I venture to hope for your forgiveness? It ill becomes me to offer advice to you after such a confession as this, but my experience of the past few days forces me to offer you counsel, which, if you take it, will bring you happiness infinitely greater than the misery I have caused you. It is that you will take all your doubts and difficulties to Christ. Agnosticism and infidelity will bring you, as it has me, nothing but sorrow and disquiet. Do as I have done, and you will find peace. Then you will, perhaps, be able, when you think of me, to say, 'I forgive her.'"

"There is nothing too difficult for the grace of God to accomplish!" said Hadley, when he had read the last sentence of the remarkable communication. "The change in myself is no less extraordinary than that produced in the character of Belle Havelock. Once I should not have been able to forgive her, but now I can."

"But Madeline must have received her letter from Belle by this time."

What possibilities might follow in the wake of that fact! The thought thrilled him. If she loved him, she might still be his own. But the prospect was too transporting to be indulged. He would not allow himself to be too sanguine, lest the disappointment which might follow would blight his life. Since the love of God had taken possession of his heart, he felt that he loved Madeline with a stronger, holier fervor than ever before.

After dark he arranged his toilet, and putting Belle Havelock's letter into his pocket, he walked slowly toward the Winters' residence; his hand was on the door-bell, but his courage almost failed him, and he paused, stood irresolute, glancing up and down the street. Presently, however, he rang the bell lightly.

The door opened, and he was ushered by a servant into the parlor. There was no one in the room, and he sent his card to Madeline.

Presently he heard a light footstep in an adjoining room. His pulses stood still with suspense. The next moment the door was thrown open, and there stood Madeline, radiant and smiling, with the beautiful roses blooming on her cheeks. To the excited lover that smile meant welcome, and those blushes meant—love.

"Madeline, Madeline!" he exclaimed, rising, and stepping forward toward her, as she crossed the room to greet him.

She extended her hand, but he impetuously took both her hands in a warm clasp, and looking at her, he tried to read her secret in her eyes. The ingenuous girl could not conceal her feelings.

"Madeline, have you received a letter from Belle Havelock?" he asked.

"I have."

"And what have you to say—"

"That God is very good to us."

"My darling, you will be mine at last?"

"In heart I have been yours for—for—"

"My dear, dear Madeline!" and he took her unresisting form to his arms, and held her in a long, clinging embrace, while he pressed his lips to her brow and lips.

Then they sat down together and read Belle's letters over again, and many explanations and sweet but delicately embarrassing confessions had to be made. The hours sped happily. When he was ready to take his leave, he said:

"Madeline, dearest, my happiness is more than I deserve, and I can scarcely bear so much felicity."

"Perhaps if we put our strength together we can manage to carry the onerous burden," she said, with sweet naïveté.

"You are the same ingenuous girl I used to know at college."

A few days later he was in the company of his uncle, when the latter said: "Hadley, you believe the Gospel now!"

"With all my heart."

"Will you preach it?"

The question was sprung upon him so suddenly that he was not prepared to answer at once. He paced the floor thoughtfully for a few minutes, and finally said:

"Let me think the matter over for a few days. The vocation is a great and responsible one, and I do not wish to rush into it with undue haste."

"That is right. Think and pray about it."

In a few days he had revolved the subject in his mind thoroughly, and came to his uncle to announce his decision.

"I have come," he said, "to inform you that I have concluded to enter the ministry."

The joy of his uncle was inexpressible. "Thank God!" he said, reverently. "My place will soon be vacated, and now God has raised up a man to fill it when I am gone. But what are your plans?"

"One thing is evident," replied Hadley, positively. "I cannot think of preaching until I have taken a theological course of studies in some good seminary. I have had some literary training, but I am densely ignorant of the Scripture and of theology."

"Your head as well as your heart is in the right place. When will you go?"

"After the holidays. I dislike to resign my position in the schools of this place, but 'necessity is laid upon me; woe is me if I preach not the Gospel.'"

Both Mr. Bidder and Mr. Hanson approved of Hadley's course. But he had still one more task to perform. However, with his characteristic promptness, he went that evening to see Madeline, and when they were alone, he said:

"Madeline, I have decided to enter the ministry. It is right that you should know what my chosen calling in life is to be, and I ask you now whether you are willing to share with me in the toil, sacrifices, and joys of the vocation to which God has called me."

Without a moment's faltering the girl replied, quoting Ruth's resolute words to her mother-in-law: "The Lord do so to me, and more also, if aught but death part thee and me!"

"But, Madeline," he continued, tentatively, "I must go to a seminary for three years before I can make you—my—my—wife."

"Dear Hadley, that is just what I should have advised you to do," she answered smilingly. "The times demand a ministry that is thoroughly trained, and I want you to be as useful as possible in our Master's service. My love has stood a severer test than an absence of a few years for so noble a purpose."

The three years sped rapidly. During Hadley's absence at the theological school, he was informed by Madeline that Hanson had been called to a position of wider usefulness in one of the largest cities in the Middle States, and although he was loath to leave the people with whom he had labored so long, he felt that he ought to obey the call.

A few months before Hadley had completed his theological studies, he was summoned to the city in which his spiritual birth had taken place, to attend the obsequies of his beloved uncle, Mr. Bidder, and before the young man went back to his seminary work, he received a unanimous call to become the deceased clergyman's successor. Thus the veteran's desires had received their accomplishment.

Events must be hurriedly passed over. One evening, six months later, Hadley Madelling and his wife (*née* Madeline Winters) were sitting in the young pastor's study, talking over the vital interests of the work upon which they had entered. Hadley had just returned from an annual meeting of the clergymen of his denomination, which had been held in another part of the State. Presently Madeline said:

"Hadley, I have pleasant news for you."

"Well?" (interrogative inflection.)

"Mr. Hanson is married."

"Married! And who is the bride worthy of such a husband?"

"I do not know her, but I am told she is an excellent, devoted, and cultivated lady, and—not at all wealthy."

"Good! but I have an item of news to match it," said Hadley, gleefully. "Whom do you suppose I met on the train as I was returning from the meeting?"

"I am no expert at guessing."

"Mr. Mardont, the preacher whom we used to admire so much at college."

"Did he give you much news about the dear old place?"

"Column after column. But there was one item of special interest. During our conversation I said: 'I suppose that you know Miss Havelock—Belle Havelock?' 'Oh, yes,' he answered, with a curious smile that I could not interpret. 'Well,' said I, 'she was an admirable girl, but the most bitter infidel, at one time, that I ever met; but I have learned that she has been converted. I wonder how she is succeeding in her Christian life.' 'Very well,' he replied, with the same peculiar smile: 'she is one of the most devoted Christian workers of the town of Bromfield.' 'I am glad to hear it. Is she still unmarried?' I asked. A droll laugh escaped his lips, and then he replied, 'Belle Havelock is now *Mrs. Mardont*.'"

"Madeline laughed gaily as she said, "And she used to despise preachers so!"

"Well, I quizzed Mardont about that, and

s reply was characteristic: 'Belle says frankly at there was a time when she scorned me artily, on account of my profession; but after r conversion, her eyes were opened, and she gan to see—well—*merits*, you know'—he said, th a jocose expression—'that had previously caped her notice, and so her prejudices were ppily overcome.'"

"I am so happy to hear of Belle's conversion," id Madeline, with tears in her eyes. "But ere still remains one of the two sceptics at e college who has not been reclaimed."

"Ah, you mean George Dane. Well, I shall down right away and write to him."

And Hadley seated himself at his desk and nned his friend Dane a long letter. It was st midnight before he had finished it.

THE END.

GIDEON'S ARMY.

By Mrs. M. Baxter.

S. Lesson for Dec. 9, Judges 7: 1-23. Golden Text, Zech. 4: 6.

e Nation Sinning and Suffering—Their Cry Reaching the Ears of God—He Prepares a Deliverer—An Obscure Farmer's Son Selected—The Inspiring Assurance—Made Him the Equal of Moses—His Weak Faith Borne With and Strengthened—Fidelity in the Family Required—The Reformer Unpopular—His Father's Logical Defence—An Army Gathered—Gideon's Dependence on God for Direction—The Test of Courage Applied—The Second Test for the Consecrated—The Night Attack—Panic and Rout—The Source of Gideon's Power.

IT was God who raised up judges to deliver s people: they were not self-made men, nor re they educated in any earthly school. They re needed and called for a special work. Gidn's call was to be a simple, willing instrument, o should show forth, in his life-work, that th which the great apostle of the Gentiles rned in after years: "When I am weak, then I strong." (II Cor. 12: 10.) Israel had sinned, d God delivered them into the hand of Mid- seven years, until the land was spoiled by ese invaders, and the children of Israel could ain neither cattle nor harvest, nor could they safe in their own houses. Industry ceased; d very many tried to drag out a precarious istence in mountain dens and caves. At last ey began to cry unto the Lord, who sent a ophet to tell them of their sins. But that cry netrated the heart of a Father as well as a dge, and God set about preparing a deliverer. ere was nothing in Gideon's antecedents to d to the supposition that he should become military leader. He was but the son of a mer, who farmed his own land, and probably had learned little beyond the tillage of the ound and the care of cattle. He says of himf, "My family is poor in Manasseh, and I am e least in my father's house." Should such a n deliver Israel? But the first word of God His call to him extinguished all his unfitness:

"The Lord is With Thee,

ou mighty man of valor." This made everyng possible to this weak and ordinary man. is put him on a level with Moses and Joshua. d all things became possible to him, because ll things are possible to him that believeth." Even when repeatedly assured by God that was with him, Gideon's faith was so weak t he required a sign that God talked with n; so that it was not the strength of his faith, t the might of the presence of Jehovah with n, which made him victorious. Even when had the sign he asked for, and his offering s accepted, Gideon feared, and God reassured n in saying unto him, "Peace be unto thee: r not; thou shalt not die." When God sent him a mission, in the first place, to overturn the latry in his own house and family, and commanded him to throw down the altar of Baal ich his father had made, and to cut down the ve (or Asherah, a kind of wooden image) that by it, he so feared his father's household and men of the city, that he could not do it by , yet he did it by night. His timidity and orance were not made an excuse for disdience, but a reason for leaning upon the Lord. No weakness or incapacity of any kind is an excuse for neglecting the known will of God.

His Will is Our Power.

When the weakest Christian is true to God in his own family, because he knows God is with him, the Lord will make him a power greater than he knows. Natural power, talents, and education are only useful to God as they are surrendered to Him: natural weakness of character, and want of ability, are only a hindrance to God when they are made an excuse for not obeying Him.

There is no true service of God which does not provoke persecution. The men of Abiezer soon found out that the image of their god was destroyed, and an altar set up unto the Lord in the house of Gideon's father. And, with one consent, they demanded this new-made reformer, that he might be slain. But God has a voice in all which regards His children. "The Lord knoweth how to deliver the godly out of temptations." (II Pet. 2: 9.) He was at no loss as to how Gideon was to be rescued—God works by the most unlikely means; the very father who was the great patron of Baal worship in Abiezer was the instrument chosen of God for his defence. Although Gideon's action had been a direct reproof to his father's idolatry, yet Joash takes up his cause, and says to those who were about him: "Will ye plead for Baal? will ye save him. . . . If he be a god, let him plead for himself, because one hath thrown down his altar." A god who cannot take care of himself is no god for us to worship. Thus Gideon saw the hand of God, the Spirit of God came upon him, he blew a trumpet, and Abiezer, the city which but an hour ago sought his life, "was gathered after him, and he saw himself at the head of an army." Thus in twenty-four hours God had made Gideon what He called him, a "mighty man of valor." He sent messengers to Manasseh, Asher, Zebulun, and Naphtali, "and they came up to meet them." But now, what should *he* do with such an army? Gideon did the wisest thing possible: he went alone with God and secured from Him, through a double sign, the assurance that He would deliver Israel by his hand.

But Gideon never asked God for a plan of campaign, or for any knowledge of what he was to do, beforehand. He counted God equal to the management of the war. The Israelitish army was now pitched by the well of Harod, with the Midianites on their north flank.

The First Direction

given to Gideon was this: "The people that are with thee are too many for Me to give the Midianites into their hands, lest Israel vaunt themselves against Me, saying, "Mine own hand hath saved me." In God's dealings with us, He has always two ends in view: He not only works the deliverance which may be the pressing necessity of the hour, but, at the same time, He regulates our relations to Him, and so carries on our education. Israel had sinned; it was of grace that they were permitted to rally to the standard of the Lord at all, and He would teach them that their deliverance was wholly His doing, and no credit to them any way. The first thinning of the ranks took place when the proclamation was made, "Whosoever is fearful and afraid, let him return." O what a sifting! Out of thirty-two thousand, only ten thousand remained—less than one-third! So it is now; hardly one in three has the courage to trust God. Another test was applied, for God would thin the ranks again. This time it was neither the people who decided, nor yet Gideon, who should be approved.

God Tried Them.

He brought them down to the water, and the greater number (seven hundred) bowed down upon their knees to drink, while three hundred were contented to dip their hands in the water, and drink just so much as should suffice them. These were the chosen ones, the really consecrated—those who do not halt long by the way to drink of earthly waters. Now the army was equipped; there was not a fearful heart among them; there was not one whose personal concerns were put first, before the work of God. And the word of command, the word of deliverance, was once more given to Gideon. "By the three hundred men that lapped will I save you, and deliver the Midianites into thine hand."

Had Gideon been an accomplished warrior, he might have questioned whether he was not mad to go against the host of Midian with such a handful. But Gideon knew that the *Lord* of hosts was with him; how, then, should he fear? Gideon did not sleep that night, but his waking companion was God; and He called him to "arise, and get thee down unto the host, for [He said] I *have* delivered it into thine hand." He obeyed, and with Phurah, his servant, he went near enough to hear one of the Midianites tell a dream to his fellow—how he saw a cake of barley-bread fall on one of the tents and overturn it. And the man made answer: "This is nothing else save the sword of Gideon, the son of Joash, a man of Israel, for into his hand hath God delivered Midian and all his host." When Gideon heard this, he did not hurry back until he had worshipped God.

Time is Never Lost in Worshipping God.

Guided by Him, he returned, aroused all his followers, supplied them with empty pitchers containing lamps, and trumpets, and commanded them, "Look on me, and do likewise." It was a novel equipment; there was nothing which demanded skill, but only faith and obedience. His men were in three companies, and approached the camp from three sides, just when the middle night-watch had been set. Gideon raised the trumpet to his lips, and in an instant, on every side of the camp the sound of the trumpet was heard, but nothing was to be seen. Then, with a loud crash, three hundred pitchers were shivered into atoms, and three hundred lamps lit up the faces of the trumpeters. The sleeping Midianites arose half awake, and seized their swords, and, not knowing friend from foe in the dazzle of the lamps and the intervening darkness, they fell one upon another throughout the host, until, with one general movement, they burst through the children of Israel, and fled.

The news soon got abroad that the Midianites had been routed, and those who had been fearful and afraid, now that they found victory on the side of Israel, arose and helped in the pursuit. Then Gideon sent to Ephraim that they should take the waters before the Midianites, unto Bethbarah and Jordan, so as to cut off their retreat on that side. And the Ephraimites arose, took the waters, and slew two Midianitish princes, Oreb and Zeeb. When the Ephraimites contended with him, it was Gideon's humility which appeased their anger, and he passed on with his unbroken little band of three hundred, faint, yet pursuing, until the Midianites were utterly discomfited.

Thus were the words of the prophet fulfilled: "Not by might, nor by power, but by My Spirit, saith the Lord of hosts." "I *can't*" is a

Poor Excuse for a Christian.

Paul said, "I *can* do all things through Christ, which strengtheneth me." I can be patient through Christ, which strengtheneth me; I can be firm through Christ, which strengtheneth me; I can cease from anxiety through Christ, which strengtheneth me; I can win souls through Christ, which strengtheneth me; yes, I can give up my will through Christ, which strengtheneth me; I can endure injustice through Christ, which strengtheneth me. Gideon's strength lay in his certainty that God was to be depended on, and he was perfectly willing to be put at a disadvantage in numbers if it was part of the plan of God. We see how dependent he was on God all the time, making no move without settling things with God. Oh, how rapidly God develops things as soon as He has his children quite subject to Him, quite ready to His hand! There are no Midianites in the heart, in the family or the Church, in the shop or in the Bible-class, in the business or elsewhere, whom the Lord will not discomfit if we will only take the exact place God gives us as His fellow-workers.

THE CHRISTIAN'S PRAYER.

Let me not die before I've done for Thee
My earthly work, whatever it may be;
Call me not hence with mission unfulfilled,
Let me not leave my space of ground untilled.

Impress this truth upon me, that not one
Can do my portion that I leave undone;
For each one in Thy vineyard hath a spot—
To labor in for life—and weary not.
Then give me strength all faithfully to toil,
Converting barren earth to fruitful soil.

I long to be an instrument of Thine
To gather worshippers unto Thy shrine;
To be the means one human soul to save
From the dark terrors of a hopeless grave.

Yet most I want a spirit of content,
To work where'er Thou'lt wish my labor
spent.
Whether at home or in a stranger clime,
In days of joy, or in sorrow's sterner time.

I want a spirit passive, to be still,
And by Thy power to do Thy holy will;
And when the prayer unto my lips doth rise,—
Before a new home doth my soul surprise,—
"Let me accomplish some great work for
Thee;"
Subdue it, Lord; let my petition be,
"Oh make me useful in this world of Thine
In ways according to Thy will, not mine.
Call me not hence with mission unfulfilled
Let me not leave my space of ground untilled,
Let me not die until I've done for Thee,
My earthly work, whatever it may be."

J. E. Jewett, Publisher, 77 Bible House, New York, will furnish the above poem in leaflet form at twenty cents per hundred. A Sample Packet of 50 leaflets assorted (no two alike), will be sent post-paid, for 10 cts., or 100 for 20 cts. Postage stamps taken.

Horsford's Acid Phosphate.
Beware of Imitations.

"Why should a man whose blood is warm within his veins sit like his grandsire carved in alabaster?" He shouldn't, he should stir around and make something of himself. One of the best ways of doing this is to engage with B. F. Johnson & Co., Publishers, Richmond, Va.

The latest and best imperial Photographs of **Dr. Talmage and Rev. C. H. Spurgeon**, with their fac-simile autograph, and also imperial photograph of **Rev. Henry Ward Beecher**, can be obtained from J. E. Jewett, 77 Bible House, New York. Sent postpaid for twenty-five cents each. Postage stamps taken.

To the Reader.

If you are on the lookout for a particularly excellent religious book for either your own use or for a gift to a friend, we can recommend this one.

AT JESUS' FEET,

A Prayer, Promise and Poem for Every Day in the Year.

(Thoroughly Scriptural and Evangelical.) 18mo, 372 pages, neat cloth binding, gilt top and a silk marker. Price, by mail, $1.25, or five copies sent prepaid for $5.00.

"We believe this class of books have a blessed mission, and we think the reader will find this among the choicest of the many that are sending streams of sunshine through the world."

It makes a very acceptable Christmas Gift or New Year's Present.

THOMAS WHITTAKER,
2 & 3 Bible House, New York.

YANKEE GIRLS IN ZULU LAND.

By Louise Vescelius-Sheldon.

With one hundred photogravure illustrations by G. E. Graves, from original sketches by J. Austen. 1 Vol. illus. extra cloth, gilt top, *with portraits of the Sisters*. 287 pp. $1.25.

"A delightfully piquant book of travels."—Burlington Hawkeye.

"A dainty volume, brim full of fun and frolic and the sparkle of youthful spirits."—The Critic.

"A book worthy to be laid upon the library table of the most fastidious bibliophile or to find a place among the tit-bits of the boudoir."—American Bookmaker.

FOR SALE BY ALL BOOKSELLERS OR BY

Worthington Company, 747 Broadway, N. Y.

Send your name and address for our new descriptive circulars of beautiful ribbon booklets, suitable for Christmas presents. Selling for 15, 20, 25 and 30 cents each. Sample on receipt of price. New catalogue of new and second hand books offered at low prices now ready. Wilbur B. Ketcham, Publisher, 71 Bible House, New York.

BIBLE & LAND. Rev. James B. Converse, $1.00, post-paid. Morristown, Tenn.

"Original." "Eminently timely." "Will shed much light on a most perplexing subject." "Go far to guide public sentiment."

AGENTS WANTED to sell "The Child's Bible." Introduction by Bishop J. H. Vincent, D.D. The best selling book handled by agents. Recommended by all clergymen. Address Cassell & Co., B.E.S.D., 104 and 106 Fourth Ave., New York; 40 Dearborn St., Chicago, Ill.

FELT SHOES AND SLIPPERS.

NOISELESS,
WARM,
DURABLE.

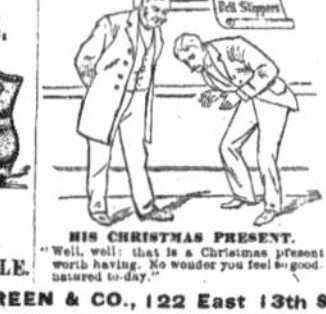

HIS CHRISTMAS PRESENT.
"Well, well! that is a Christmas present worth having. No wonder you feel so good natured to-day."

Perfect Ease and Comfort.

Made in all Styles for Men, Women, and Children.

Prevents Rheumatism and Cold Feet.

Send for Illustrated Price-List.
Mention *Christian Herald.*

DANIEL GREEN & CO., 122 East 13th Street, New York.

Perfection Attained at Last. Only $6 with Music.

The New American **ROLLER ORGAN** is operated similar to the finest French Music Boxes and PLAYS 250 TUNES, from a waltz to a hymn, with perfect tune and time. Gives better satisfaction than a $100 PARLOR ORGAN and ten times more pleasure. This Organ is the perfection of musical instruments and the grandest and most marvellous instrument ever presented to the public. It plays **SACRED MUSIC, MARCHES, WALTZES, POLKAS, JIGS,** Reels, Opera Selections, Popular Songs, Church music, as well as any organ. Nothing grander or combining so many features can be found in French or Swiss Music Boxes, costing $100. **Price Only $6,** in BEAUTIFULLY CARVED CASES with music. Send for one. It will fill you with astonishment and delight. If sent C.O.D. send $2.50 when you order, pay balance when you get organ. Send P.O. order, Registered Letter or by Express. Send all orders for this organ to

WORLD MANUF'G CO., 122 Nassau Street, New York.

MEXICO

Contributions in aid of Christian work in Mexico are most pressingly needed, and can be mailed to the address of

BISHOP H. C. RILEY,
Care of J. P. HEATH,
43 Bible House, New York.

To our Christian Friends:

As there is a regular monthly expense in connection with the work a regular monthly income is needed to meet that expense. We, therefore, specially ask for regular monthly contributions in its behalf. If many will each send a little every month, or quarter, or whenever they can, it will do great good. *Remember, every little helps.*

H. Chauncey Riley.

PENTECOST for 1889.

COMMENTARY on the SUNDAY-SCHOOL LESSONS.

PRICE, 50 CENTS, postpaid; CLOTH, $1.

A. S. BARNES & CO.,
111 and 113 *WILLIAM STREET, NEW YORK.*

PRICE $180.

We Sell DIRECT to FAMILIES By avoiding Agents you save their enormous expenses and profits which double the costs on every first class Piano they sell. PIANOS ORGANS $150 to $1500 $35 to $500. Sent for trial in your own home before you buy. GUARANTEED SIX YEARS. Catalogues free. Marchal & Smith Piano Co., 235 E. 21st St., N.Y.

1700 Temperance Publications.

Books for Sunday-school Libraries, Pamphlets and Tracts upon every phase of the Temperance Question, for all lines of Temperance Work. Catalogues free. Address National Temperance Society, 58 Reade Street, New York.

WANTED

Old U.S. & Confederate postage stamps from 1843 to 1868. Many are very rare and command high prices when on the original letters or envelopes. Send stamp for price lists and circulars, explaining what is wanted. **Semmes & Lambert**, Alexandria, Va. P.O. Box 9.

SEATTLE No blizzards, heavy snows or cyclones. Average winter temperature 43° above zero. Seattle, largest city in Washington Terr'y. Population 35,000. Commercial, educational and financial center of Puget Sound Country. Full information of Queen City **SE-AT-TLE.** CHAS. H. KITTINGER, Seattle, Wash. Territory.

The Gladstone Lamp is the best in the world. Gives a pure, soft, brilliant white light of 85 candle power,—*a marvelous light from ordinary kerosene oil!* Never smokes nor breaks chimneys; no leaks, no smell, no annoyances of any kind, cannot explode. Besides, it gives a clear, white light, 10 to 2 times the size & brilliancy of ordinary lamps. Elegant designs in Brass, Nickel, Gold or Antique Bronze. Send postal card for illustrated price list. Single lamps at *wholesale price*, boxed and sent by express. Get our prices. "*Seeing is believing.*" Address GLADSTONE LAMP CO., 10 East 14th St., New York.

New Catalogue, Now Ready.

BEFORE YOU BUY ANY BOOKS FOR YOUR

SUNDAY-SCHOOL LIBRARY,

Send to me for a full Catalogue of the cheapest and best Sunday-School Books ever offered, and our SPECIAL OFFER TO SUNDAY-SCHOOLS. Satisfaction guaranteed or money refunded.

J. E. JEWETT, Publisher and Bookseller,
77 Bible House, New York.

ON 30 DAYS' TRIAL.

THIS NEW **ELASTIC TRUSS**

Has a Pad different from all others, is cup shape, with Self-adjusting Ball in center, adapts itself to all positions of the body while the ball in the cup presses back the intestines just as a person does with the finger. With light pressure the Hernia is held securely day and night, and a radical cure certain. It is easy, durable and cheap. Sent by mail. Circulars free. EGGLESTON TRUSS CO., Chicago, Ill.

In all the world there is but one sure cure for the **OPIUM** Habit. The Dr. J. L. Stephens Remedy never fails, and no other treatment ever cures. We have cured more than 10,000 cases. No other treatment ever cured one case. NO PAY TILL CURED. Remember this, and write to the J. L. Stephens Co., Lebanon, Ohio.

ALL ABOUT EGGS.

Egg Cookery.

A manual of 80 pages giving 150 ways of cooking and serving eggs by some of the most celebrated French cooks. Compiled by a practical cook of seventeen years' experience. Sent postpaid on receipt of 25 cents.

J. E. JEWETT, Publisher,
77 Bible House, New York.

"Demonology or Spiritualism, Ancient and Modern."—"An effective weapon."—"A sword of fire."—"Only unanswerable work on the subject."—Startling disclosures.—History *facts* and data.—Scores saved already. Whole communities rescued. Every family, preacher and christian worker needs one. 310 pp. 12mo, cloth. Price reduced to $1. Sent by mail, postpaid, on receipt of price. Address **J. E. JEWETT**, 77 Bible House, New York.

$75.00 to $250.00 A MONTH can be made working for us. Agents preferred who can furnish a horse and give their whole time to the business. Spare moments may be profitably employed also. A few vacancies in towns and cities. B. F. Johnson & Co., Pub's, 1009 Main St., Richmond, Va.

FEATHERS. The finest live white geese feathers in the country, 75 cts. per lb. Hair Mattresses made over for $2.50. Feathers steamed and renovated. H. Pickford, 11 Nassau St., Brooklyn, N. Y.

SILKS, SATINS, VELV

Jas. McCreery &

IMPORTERS AND MANUFACTURE

Our Imports and Man tures are confined exclusiv Pure and Reliable Goods. ing the Holiday Season we at very moderate prices, pieces of Plain and No Black Silks from which lect.

Mail orders carefully promptly executed.

Broadway and 11th Stree
New York.

XMAS MUSI

FOR THIS YEAR!

THE ROYAL SON.—A new Service Robert Lowry Intelligent Scripture Selections, with new an inal Songs. The whole exercise is one of gre and beauty.

$4 per 100; 5 Cents each by Ma

ANNUAL No. 19.—Pleasing Carol vorite Authors; supply of Songs for any Sunday School Xmas

$3 per 100; 4 Cents each by Ma

SANTA CLAUS' PRIZE.—The ne Cantata W. H. Doane, will be issued early in Novembe is believed to be one of Dr. D.'s best effor Songs are very bright, the dialogue and plan entertaining. Easily gotten up by any School.

30 Cents each by mail; $25 per 1

WAITING FOR SANTA CLA

(30 cts.) by Dr. Doane. New last year, a popular.

A full Catalogue of our other popular Canta tions and Xmas Music sent on request.

BIGLOW & MAIN, 76 E. Ninth St., New
81 RANDOLPH ST., CHICAGO.

MR. KEYSER'S BOO

THE ONLY WAY O

which attracted so much attention running through the Christian H has now been published in book fo Anson D. F. Randolph & Co., West Twenty-third St., New York. $1.00 Sent by mail postpaid price by them, or by

J. E. JEWETT, Publisher and Books
77 Bible House, New York

IF YOU WANT AN

"OXFORD" TEACHER'S BI

OR

BAGSTER BIBLE,

send for complete Bible Catalogue giving full tion of styles, sample of type, and price, to

J. E. JEWETT, Publisher and Bookse
77 Bible House, New York.

Agents wanted for

Pertaini sons, Ph Things, Bible S Concert Prayer-M Topics, etc. In by J. E cent, pages. By mail, $2. Immensely popular. Al new book, **BOW IN THE CLOUD,** of Comfort, etc., by 200 Best Authors, $1. **WOMEN'S HAND-BOOK.** $2. A lady wanted in every town duce it. **Quick Sales, Big Pay.** Ad **E. B. TREAT,** Publisher, 771 Broadw

PRINTING Book of Type, &c. Amateur Printers' Guide Book, 15c. Samples of Scrap Pictures and Cards, 10 cent **PRESS** CIRCUL JOSEPH WA 19 Murray

TEAS *LADIES* Send at one our new te THE GREAT AMERICAN T 31 and 33 Vesey St., New York

THE CHRISTIAN HERALD AND SIGNS OF OUR TIMES.

Entered according to Act of Congress in the year 1888, in the office of the Librarian of Congress at Washington.

This Journal contains every week a Portrait and Biography of some eminent person: a new Sermon by the Rev. C. H. SPURGEON, of London, and the Rev. Dr. TALMAGE'S latest Sunday morning Sermon; also always a Prophetic Article, and a Summary of Current Events as well as Stories, Anecdotes etc.

Vol. XI., No. 49. Office, 63 Bible House, N. Y. THURSDAY, DECEMBER 6, 1888. Price, 3 Cents. Annual Subscription, $1.50.

CONTENTS OF THIS NUMBER.

PORTRAITS OF THE RT. HON. W. E. GLADSTONE AND SIR W. FOSTER, AND PICTURE OF THE DEMONSTRATION IN BIRMINGHAM.
THE FRAGRANCE OF THE GOSPEL. Dr. Talmage's Sermon Last Sunday Morning.
ANECDOTES RELATED AT RECENT EVANGELISTIC MEETINGS.
THE PREDICTED REVIVAL OF DEMONISM IN THE LAST DAYS. By Rev. H. W. Congdon.
THE PILGRIMS AT LOURDES.
A Centenarian's Awful Reminiscence—A Sufferer from Hernia Healed—A Converted Chinaman's Faith—A Paralytic's Influence.
PICTURE OF THE SOUTH DOME IN THE YOSEMITE.
THE WORD A SWORD. A New Sermon by Rev. C. H. Spurgeon.
Gems from New Books: Degenerate Roman Sons, etc.
PORTRAIT OF MRS. MORTON, Wife of the Vice-President-Elect.
MARY HARCOURT'S REFUGE. (With Illust.)
ESCAPED FROM THE MORMONS—A Life Story.
DEATH OF SAMSON. By Mrs. M. Baxter.

The Rt. Hon. W. E. Gladstone, M. P. and Sir W. Foster, M. P.—The Welcome to the Ex-Premier in the Birmingham Town Hall.

THE RT. HON. W. E. GLADSTONE.

His Recent Ovation in Birmingham—Birth, and Early Life—Enters Parliament—The Protege of Sir Robert Peel—His First Book—Classical Lore—Lord Macaulay's Estimate of Him—Changes his Party—Becomes Premier in 1866—Vicissitudes of Official Life—Personal Affairs.

THE attitude Mr. Gladstone has taken in Irish politics, and his earnest desire to give to Ireland a government similar to that of one of our States, has won for him a large measure of popular approval on this side of the Atlantic. At times his speeches and official acts have been exasperating to the American public, but the Irish policy he has adopted has made him, with as least a large section of our people, the most popular of living English statesmen. It has, however, alienated from him many of his most ardent admirers and supporters in his own country, and especially has aroused against him the opposition of the Evangelical and Protestant members of the community, who fear that if his programme were carried out, the Protestants of Ireland would be crushed by the great Roman Catholic majority. His new departure, therefore, has disunited the great Liberal party, and even in the Liberal strongholds Mr. Gladstone now is only supported by a section of the party. The most remarkable instance is that of Birmingham, which has always been the most stalwart of Liberal towns, but now sends to Parliament the most determined opponents Mr. Gladstone has in the House. It was, therefore, somewhat remarkable that his recent visit to that town should have called forth so much enthusiasm, and it proves that even there his brilliant genius and commanding abilities still exert an influence, and the magic of his eloquence is still felt. As a full narrative of his life was published in these columns some three years ago, it is unnecessary to do more than briefly summarize its leading facts in connection with his portrait, which is given on the preceding page, with the *portrait of Sir W. Foster*, his host in Birmingham, and the picture of the enormous meeting which gathered in the town-hall to give him vociferous welcome.

William Ewart Gladstone was born Dec. 29, 1809. He is, therefore, in his seventy-ninth year.

At the Age of Twelve

(in September, 1821) he was entered at Eton College, where the education at that time was largely confined to classics and Latin and Greek compositions; but there were there with him many scholars who afterward achieved fame in public life. Young Gladstone was a studious boy, and became a sound classical scholar.

He entered Christ Church College, Oxford, as a student in 1829, remaining there until 1831, leaving at Michaelmas in that year with distinguished educational honors—a Double First in Classics and Mathematics. While there he exhibited an almost *superhuman industry*, and a wonderful aptitude for learning, neither of which has in the least abated or become dimmed in his subsequent career; but, on the contrary, they have increased with his years.

After leaving the University of Oxford, he spent a year in a *continental tour*, which period was devoted to the study of men, manners, and things in the various countries of Europe. In 1831 he *entered Parliament* as a Conservative member for Newark. He had been in "the House" but two years when Sir Robert Peel, then Prime Minister, appointed him to the unimportant post of a junior Lordship of the Treasury. In the next year, 1835, he was appointed Under-Secretary for Colonial Affairs. But as Sir Robert Peel's ministry was only four months in office, Mr. Gladstone, with his chief, was soon sitting on the opposition benches.

His First Book.

Relieved of official duties, Mr. Gladstone devoted his leisure to the production of a book, which, at its appearance, created a profound sensation throughout Great Britain. It was entitled, "The State in its Relations with the Church." During the same period of exclusion from office he devoted himself with delight to his classical studies. He was then, and still is, a master of the language and literature of Greece and Rome. He has published Latin sacred verses not appreciably inferior in grace to those of Buchanan or Milton, and as a Homeric student his "Studies of Homer and the Homeric Age" entitles him to a well-earned niche among scholarly critics. Classical study is with him a delightful pleasure, and it is related of him that on one occasion, when his seat in Parliament hung in the balance, and he was the prey of torturing anxiety, he shut himself in his study on the decisive polling-day, and spent the anxious hours in translating Homer. He is credited with having written the most elegant Latin translation of Toplady's hymn, "Rock of Ages," to relieve the weariness of a dull debate, *while sitting on the Government benches* in "the House."

In 1839, when he was becoming prominent in Parliament, Lord Macaulay wrote of him: "He is a young man of unblemished character, and of distinguished Parliamentary talents, *the rising hope of those stern and unbending Tories* who follow reluctantly and mutinously a leader whose experience and eloquence are indispensable to them, but whose cautious temper and moderate opinions they abhor. . . . But we believe we do him no more than justice when we say that his abilities and his demeanor have obtained for him the respect and good-will of all parties." Since that was written, Mr. Gladstone has made rapid strides upward, leaving the quagmire of Toryism far behind him. Now, instead of being the rising hope of the Tories, he is their dread and aversion.

Official Work.

In 1841 Mr. Gladstone came back to office, again under the leadership of Sir Robert Peel, and occupied for two years the subordinate position of Vice-President of the Board of Trade. He then stepped into the office of President of the same department, a position in which his ability began to have weight in the ministerial councils.

When the Government, in 1846, proposed the *Repeal of the Corn Laws, he resigned his seat* for Newark, because the Duke of Newcastle, who owned the borough, and who was his patron, held anti-repeal views. Upon his *re-entering Parliament* for the University of Oxford, he threw the weight of his great debating power into the scale in favor of *University Reform* and the *Removal of Jewish Disabilities.* Up to that time no Jew could occupy a seat in Parliament, or hold any office under the Crown.

Mr. Gladstone had been known as a Conservative, but in 1851 he finally severed himself from the great Conservative party; and in the same year he was called by purely domestic circumstances to Naples. There his humanity was stirred to its very core by the unheard-of brutalities of King Bomba, who had imprisoned twenty thousand of his subjects without trial. His passionate cry for redress sounded throughout the civilized world.

In 1852, when Lord Derby became Prime Minister, Mr. Gladstone declined to join his Ministry; and the Budget, which was propounded by Mr. Disraeli, who was then Chancellor of the Exchequer, was so severely criticized by Mr. Gladstone that Lord Derby's Conservative Ministry was overthrown. Lord Aberdeen then formed a Liberal Government, of which Mr. Gladstone became

Chancellor of the Exchequer,

and in 1853 he made his first great financial speech, bringing forward a Budget. After the dissolution of Lord Aberdeen's Cabinet, in 1853, Mr. Gladstone did not take any prominent part in Parliamentary affairs for several years, but occupied himself a good deal in literary studies. In the Administration of 1859 Mr. Gladstone, as Chancellor of the Exchequer, was instrumental in the repeal of the paper duty, and in negotiating the commercial treaty with France. At the general election of 1865 he was defeated at the University of Oxford, but he was elected for Southwest Lancashire. In the election of 1868, however, he lost his seat after a fierce contest, which excited the most intense interest throughout the country. His victorious opponent was this time Mr. Cross, who became Secretary for the Home Department. This event, however, did not exclude him from Parliament as the electors of *Greenwich* had a few days previously elected him by a large majority. He was subsequently elected by the Mid-Lothian district in Scotland, which he still represents.

When the death of Lord Palmerston took place, in 1866, Mr. Gladstone became

Prime Minister

of England, and brought in a *Reform Bill.* He was, however displaced by Mr. Disraeli's Ministry for two years; but again, in December, 1868, became Prime Minister, and in 1869 the Irish Church Disestablishment Act was passed.

In January, 1874, Mr. Gladstone dissolved Parliament, and at the general election, which ensued, the votes were, for the first time, taken by secret ballot. The result was that 351 Conservative members were elected, and only 302 Liberals. Hence Mr. Gladstone at once *resigned*, and Mr. Disraeli, afterward Lord Beaconsfield, became Prime Minister. In April, 1880, Mr. Gladstone again became Premier, and held office until June, 1885, when he was succeeded by the Marquis of Salisbury. On February 6, 1886, he again resumed office as Premier, but in August of that year the verdict of the country on his Irish policy was against him, and he again gave place to Lord Salisbury.

Private Life.

Mr. Gladstone is an early riser, and when at Hawarden Castle, his country residence, may be seen, shortly after 8 o'clock in the morning, walking down to prayers in the village church, where his son ministers. Early devotion and breakfast over, he gives the remainder of the morning, till the gong sounds for luncheon at 2 o'clock, to work, reading, writing, meditation, or to the performance of arithmetical feats which no Cabinet Minister has ever surpassed, or, in the proper season, to a bout of *tree-felling*, at which he is an expert. After luncheon more reading follows, and in due time he shows himself at dinner, to be "a singularly temperate man in meat and drink."

Although he is the best controller of the *National* Exchequer that England has ever had, and is notoriously by no means a wealthy man, his personal *charities* are almost reckless. In the course of his long walks in the neighborhood of Hawarden *his pockets* have an astonishing knack of emptying themselves, and amusing stories are told of his having had to walk home inconvenient distances of ten and twelve miles in the dark because of his inability to raise so much as a railway fare. As Prime Minister he refused an increase of salary, and it is not generally known that *he has never drawn the pension* to which he is legally entitled since his retirement from office, showing plainly that he has no desire to become rich, or even to increase his comforts, at the nation's expense.

His piety is, in its manifestations, of a humble and unaffected character. Even when Prime Minister of England he has been found in the humblest houses, reading to the sick or dying consolatory passages of Scripture in his own soft, melodious tones.

Mr. Gladstone at Hawarden.

Hawarden Park, in Wales, in the centre of which stands Hawarden Castle, Mr. Gladstone's residence, is one of the finest country-seats in Great Britain. Visitors who arrive at Hawarden for the first time are surprised at the extent of the grounds, and the beauty of the Park. Hawarden Park, with Hawarden Castle, came to Mr. Gladstone with his wife. When Mr. Gladstone married, he had no intention of making his seat in Wales, but finding that Sir Stephen Glynne, his wife's father, was in circumstances which rendered it disadvantageous to the family for him to live in the Castle, Mr. Gladstone bought some of the land, and took up his quarters with his father-in-law in the Castle, which had been temporarily closed. This arrangement lasted for many years, and was attended with none of the disagreeable consequences which so often happen when two generations live under one roof. The two families lived side by side, and nothing could exceed the harmony of the united households. Sir S. Glynne always sat at the head of the table, while Mrs. Gladstone sat at the other end; Mr. Gladstone sat between. This arrangement continued down to the death of Sir Stephen Glynne, and it was rather curious to see a statesman whose name and whose fame were familiar throughout the world, always taking the second place in his own house. But for the somewhat embarrassed circumstances of Sir Stephen Glynne, which led Mr. Gladstone to buy up some of his estate, it was his intention to have bought an estate in Scotland, to which he has always been strongly attached.

The Library at Hawarden

is one of the finest private libraries in the country. It consists of more than 20,000 volumes, and considerable curiosity exists as to what Mr. Gladstone intends to do with this collection of books after his death. Contrary to the usual practice obtaining in magnificent private libraries, Mr. Gladstone allows his books to be lent out to almost any one in the neighbourhood who wishes to read them. At one time this liberty was unlimited; any one could take a book out and keep it an indefinite period, provided that he simply left an acknowledgment of having borrowed the book. This privilege, however, was so much abused by some persons, that a few years ago a rule was laid down limiting the time for which a book might be kept to one month. With that exception, however, the Hawarden library is still the free loan library of the country-side.

Mr. Gladstone's Father.

It is not generally known that if Mr. Gladstone had not been swayed by a very stong sense of filial duty he would never have entered Parliament, his own strong predisposition being to take orders and go into the Church. This desire his father strongly opposed, as he wished him to enter Parliament and serve his country in the Legislature. Mr. Gladstone reluctantly but loyally obeyed. Another incident, which is not generally known, is that it was the same principle of filial obedience which first brought to light that extraordinary aptitude for figures which enables Mr. Gladstone to be far and away the greatest Chancellor of the Exchequer whom England has ever had. When he was at Oxford he wrote home saying that he didn't care for mathematics, and intended to concentrate his attention upon classics. His father wrote back that he heard with much grief his son's decision. He did not think a man was a man unless he knew mathematics. Mr. Gladstone, on receiving this intimation of his father's wishes, abandoned his own plan, and applied himself with his usual concentration to the study of mathematics. Much to his surprise he came out double first. He often said in after life that he had done it to please his father, and that he would never have been Chancellor of the Exchequer had it not been for the bent given to his mind by his compliance with his father's wish that he should pursue mathematical studies.

The Town Hall,

Birmingham, was crowded to excess, when the Liberal leader was presented with an address by the President of the local Liberal Association. Mr. Gladstone, in reply, spoke for an hour and forty minutes, and said he did not intend to retire from public life so long as the Irish Question remained unsolved. Birmingham Town Hall holds between 3,000 and 4,000 people, and has been the scene of many memorable political and religious meetings. Mr. John Bright, M. P., and Mr. Chamberlain, M. P., and other politicians have on various occasions addressed crowded political meetings in it. There have also been large religious meetings held in it in the past by the Rev. Charles Leach on the Sundays of the winter months for some years. The lady evangelist, Miss McLatchie, also addressed large audiences in it a few years ago.

ANECDOTES RELATED AT RECENT EVANGELISTIC MEETINGS.

A Religion That is Moonshine.—"There was a man who, in answer to one who was trying to persuade him to trust Christ, and to rest on His blessed promises, replied, 'What is the use? Your religion is all moonshine.' 'Yes,' said the Christian, 'in one sense that is so. As the moon has no light in herself, but only reflects on the earth the glorious rays of the sun, so we, with no light or goodness of our own, only reflect upon men the glorious light of holiness which comes from the Sun of Righteousness!' Christians would do well to remember that they have no light of their own, and it is only by keeping themselves looking unto Jesus that they can be of use in Christ's work."

Sunset Time in the Alps.—Mr. W. D. Dunn, remarks that "In the evening the Swiss cowherds on the Alps watch the sun go down, and he who is highest, just as the glorious orb sinks, puts his horn to his mouth, and blows a lusty note, giving praise to the Lord. This is at once taken up by a second, a little below, who repeats the shout; then a third follows, until it goes right down the mountain, and throughout the valley —a blast of praise to God. If the churches would similarly unite and with one great shout of praise to the Lord cast aside their petty differences, and, shoulder to shoulder, face the great army of sin and Satan, then Christ's kingdom would progress, and numbers of lost sheep be gathered into the fold."

The Giver Rather than the Gift.—"The Rev. Mr. Hudson Taylor, of the China Inland Mission, tells that at one time at a Christian Convention he met a young lady with whom he was slightly acquainted. With a face radiant with joy, she said to him, 'Oh, Mr. Taylor, I have got it, I have got salvation!' and she proceeded to speak of it, and of her joy and peace. A few days later, he again met the lady, and this time her face showed only too clearly that she had lost her joy. He went away to China, and after laboring there some time, came back, and among the first people he met was that same lady. A smile of gladness and sweet content lighted up her face; she was quite ready to speak, not this time about *it*, but about *Him*. The first time she had only looked at the gift and not at the Donor, and she was resting on her feelings and not solely on her Saviour. God wants His children to rest only in His Son, whom He glorifies, and whom we, if we are to be pleasing to God, must also glorify."

A Memorable Hour of Freedom.—The Rev. Mr. Munro relates: "In the island of Antigua, on the last night of their slavery, the slaves gathered into the churches there to await the hour of legislated emancipation. Many of the whites anticipated a night of riot, as the slaves had not been treated in anything like a generous manner, and it was feared that they might take the first opportunity of wreaking vengeance upon their former taskmasters. Instead, the negroes met in the churches, and, as 12 o'clock approached, knelt in prayer. When the hour chimed, with a shout of joy they rose to their feet and shouted praise to God who had given them their liberty. Then leaving the churches they went towards their homes, leaping and laughing for joy that they were free. Yet they had only escaped from slavery of the body. And there are many free-born men who are groaning under that old taskmaster, Satan, who keeps them in abject slavery chained by their own sins. To such we offer freedom, not in the future, but now."

Mr. Moody and the Modern Athenian.—Mr. Murch says: "One of Mr. Moody's great gatherings was interrupted by a man, crying from the audience, 'Tell us something new! tell us something new!' Mr. Moody stopped instantly in his discourse, and turning to Mr. Sankey, who sat beside him, said, 'Mr. Sankey, will you please sing that grand old hymn, "Tell me the old, old story"?' Mr. Sankey did so, and with wonderful effect. When it was finished, Mr. Moody said to the man who had interrupted, 'You ask me for something new; and I give you the old, old story, ever new.' It was the means of leading him to Christ. How many, like this man, will not accept the simple message of the Gospel; it is too old and simple for them. Like the Athenians of ancient times, who spent their time on the Areopagus, 'in nothing else but either to tell or to hear some new thing' (Acts 17. 21), they must have something new to tickle their intellectual palate. We have nothing but Christ to offer. He is the only sacrifice for sin, and He alone can do helpless sinners good."

Deciding to Become a Child of Satan.—Mr. Hamilton remarks: "A young fellow whom I met at an evangelistic meeting recently, testified thus: 'In 1882 I went to a Gospel meeting in a small town near Glasgow. The minister was speaking of the terrible doom that awaited the sinner, and as I listened, I trembled. I knew he was describing what would be my fate, if I did not repent. The preacher spoke to me afterwards, and urged me to give myself to Christ. I would not then decide, but went home determined to be a Christian soon. Next day I began my Christian career, and that same day I fell into sin several times. Satan whispered, 'You a Christian? You will never be one, you are nothing but a miserable sham!' For three days and nights I was intensely miserable, striving to be a Christian, and continually failing. Then I deliberately decided to become a child of the devil. I mingled with evil company, and was soon rapidly traversing the road to hell. I disgraced myself and ran off to sea, where I continued to serve Satan; and well he paid me. I remember standing on the vessel's side, and wondering whether I should throw myself into the sea or not, and thus end my miserable existence. But just then God whispered to my soul, "After death, the judgment." I was afraid to die. Then it seemed that God showed me His great love for me, and my own wickedness in rejecting His mercy. I turned to Him as my only hope, and resting my weary soul on Him found rest.'"

The Broken Oar and the Safe Anchor.—The Rev. Dr. Kneeland related: "A short time ago a man was rowing on the St. Lawrence River, just above the fatal rapids. Intent upon other things, he absent-mindedly rowed along until he was startled to find that he had drifted into water where the current was strong, and he was being carried swiftly toward the rapids. Putting all thoughts aside but that of his imminent danger, he applied himself to the oars, and straining every muscle, he was able to hold his own, and even to creep up the river. But one of the oars, unable to stand the great strain, snapped close to the blade; and now he was helpless. At first he sat still in despair; but when he noticed an anchor lying in the bow of the boat, hope revived. He was not so far from the shore, he thought, but that he could throw that light anchor on some protruding part of the bank, and so keep himself from being borne down the rapids. He threw the anchor, but it did not reach the shore. Again he threw it with all possible force, but with a like result. A little ahead, there was an island jutting far out into the river; when he was opposite that, he, with an effort that threatened to upset his frail craft, launched the anchor with all his might. It caught in a hollow, and was wedged between two rocks. Will that little chain stand the great strain? Yes, it did; and slowly the man drew himself to the shore, assisted by some people who had gathered, and soon he stood among them safe. As the anchor and chain saved that man, so the Lord Jesus is the only Anchor that can save a sinner when he is carried down in the mad torrent of sin, which threatens to hurl him into eternal darkness."

THE FRAGRANCE OF THE GOSPEL.

Dr. Talmage's Sermon Preached last Sunday Morning, December 2, 1888.

"All thy garments smell of myrrh, and aloes, and cassia, out of the ivory palaces." Ps. 45:8.

The Costly Vestments in the Cathedral of Notre Dame—Christ's Kingly Robes—I. Odorous with Myrrh—One of the First Presents He Had—Its Interminable Perfume—A Type of Christ's Love—II. Odorous with Aloes—Significant of Bitterness—The Bitterness of Scourging, and the Cross—Denied Cradle and Death-bed—III. Odorous with Cassia—Healing and Curative—Unconscious Sufferers—Helpless Sufferers Brought by Friends—IV. The Ivory Palaces—Surpassing Beauty—Dead Children and Christian Friends There—A Mystery for Eternal Study.

AMONG the grand adornments of the city of Paris is the Church of Notre Dame, with its great towers and elaborated rose-windows, and sculpturing of the last Judgment, with the trumpeting angels and rising dead; its battlements of *quatre-foil*; its sacristy, with ribbed ceiling and statues of saints. But there was nothing in all that building which more vividly appealed to my plain republican tastes than the

Costly Vestments

which lay in oaken presses—robes that had been embroidered with gold, and been worn by popes and archbishops on great occasions. There was a robe that had been worn by Pius VII. at the crowning of the first Napoleon. There was also a vestment that had been worn at the baptism of Napoleon II. As our guide opened the oaken presses, and brought out these vestments of fabulous cost, and lifted them up, the fragrance of the pungent aromatics in which they had been preserved, filled the place with a sweetness that was almost oppressive. Nothing that had been done in stone more vividly impressed me than these things that had been done in cloth, and embroidery, and perfume. But to-day I open the drawer of this text, and I look upon *the kingly robes of Christ*, and as I lift them, flashing with eternal jewels, the whole house is filled with the aroma of these garments, which smell of myrrh, and aloes, and cassia, out of the ivory palaces."

In my text

The King Steps Forth.

His robes rustle and blaze as He advances. His pomp and power and glory overmaster the spectator. More brilliant is He than Queen Vashti, moving amid the Persian princes; than Marie Antoinette, on the day when Louis XVI. put upon her the necklace of eight hundred diamonds; than Anne Boleyn, the day when Henry VIII. welcomed her to his palace—all beauty and all pomp forgotten, while we stand in the presence of this imperial glory, King of Zion, King of earth, King of Heaven, King forever! His garments not worn out, not dust-bedraggled; but radiant, and jewelled, and redolent. It seems as if they must have been pressed a hundred years amid the flowers of heaven. The wardrobes from which they have been taken must have been sweet with clusters of camphire, and frankincense, and all manner of precious wood. Do you not inhale the odors? Ay, ay. They "smell of myrrh, and aloes, and cassia, out of the ivory palaces."

Your first curiosity is to know why the robes of Christ are

Odorous With Myrrh.

This was a bright-leafed Abyssinian plant. It was trifoliated. The Greeks, Egyptians, Romans, and Jews bought and sold it at a high price. The first present that was ever given to Christ was a sprig of myrrh thrown on His infantile bed in Bethlehem, and the last gift that Christ ever had was myrrh pressed into the cup of His crucifixion. The natives would take a stone and bruise the tree, and then it would exude a gum that would saturate all the ground beneath. This gum was used for purposes of merchandise, One piece of it, no larger than a chestnut, would whelm a whole room with odors. It was put in closets, in chests, in drawers, in rooms, and its perfume adhered almost interminably to anything that was anywhere near it. So when in my text I read that Christ's garments smell of myrrh, I immediately conclude the exquisite sweetness of Jesus.

I know that to many He is only like any historical person; another John Howard; another pilanthropic Oberlin; another Confucius; a grand subject for a painting; a heroic theme for a poem; a beautiful form for a statue; but to those who have heard His voice, and felt his pardon, and received His benediction, He is music, and light, and warmth, and thrill, and

Eternal Fragrance—

sweet as a friend sticking to you when all else betray; lifting you up while others try to push you down; not so much like morning-glories, that bloom only when the sun is coming up, nor like "four-o'clocks," that bloom only when the sun is going down, but like myrrh, perpetally aromatic—the same morning, noon, and night; yesterday, to-day, forever. It seems as if we cannot wear Him out. We put on Him all our burdens, and afflict Him with all our griefs, and set Him foremost in all our battles; and yet He is ready to lift, and to sympathize, and to help. We have so imposed upon Him that one would think in eternal affront He would quit our soul; and yet to-day He addresses us with the same tenderness, dawns upon us with the same smile, pities us with the same compassion.

There is no name like His for us. It is more imperial than Caesar's, more musical than Beethoven's, more conquering than Charlemagne's, more eloquent than Cicero's. It throbs with all life. It weeps with all pathos. It groans with all pain. It stoops with all condescension. It breathes with all perfume. Who like Jesus to set a broken bone, to pity a homeless orphan, to nurse a sick man, to take a prodigal back without any scolding, to illumine a cemetery all ploughed with graves, to make a queen unto God out of the lost woman, to catch the

Tears of Human Sorrow

in a lachrymatory that shall never be broken? Who has such an eye to see our need, such a lip to kiss away our sorrow, such a hand to snatch us out of the fire, such a foot to trample our enemies, such a heart to embrace all our necessities? I struggle for some metaphor with which to express Him: He is not like the bursting forth of a full orchestra; that is too loud. He is not like the sea when lashed to rage by the tempest; that is too boisterous; He is not like the mountain, its brow wreathed with the lightnings; that is too solitary. Give us a softer type, a gentler comparison. We have seemed to see Him with our eyes, and to hear Him with our ears, and to touch Him with our hands. Oh that to-day He might appear to some other one of our five senses! Ay, the nostril shall discover His presence. He comes upon us like spice gales from Heaven. Yea, His garments smell of lasting and all-pervasive myrrh.

Oh that you all knew His sweetness! how soon you would turn from your novels. If the philosopher leaped out of his bath in a frenzy of joy, and clapped his hands, and rushed through the streets, because he had found the solution of a mathematical problem, how will you feel leaping from the fountain of a Saviour's mercy and pardon, washed clean, and made white as snow, when the question has been solved: "How can my soul be saved?" Naked, frost-bitten, storm-lashed soul, let Jesus this hour throw around thee the "garments that smell of myrrh, and aloes, and cassia, out of the ivory palaces."

Your second curiosity is to know why the robes of Jesus are

Odorous with Aloes.

There is some difference of opinion about where these aloes grow, what is the color of the flower, what is the particular appearance of the herb. Suffice it for you and me to know that aloes mean bitterness the world over, and when Christ comes with garments bearing that particular odor, they suggest to me the bitterness of a Saviour's sufferings. Were there ever such nights as Jesus lived through—nights on the mountains, nights on the sea, nights in the desert? Who ever had such a hard reception as Jesus had? A hostelry the first, an unjust trial in oyer and terminer another, a foul-mouthed, yelling mob the last. Was there a space on His back as wide as your two fingers where He was not whipped? Was there a space on His brow an inch square where He was not cut of the briers? When the spike struck at the instep, did it not go clear through to the hollow of the foot? Oh, long, deep, bitter pilgrimage! Aloes! aloes!

John leaned his head on Christ, but who did Christ lean on? Five thousand men fed by the Saviour; who fed Jesus? The sympathy of a Saviour's heart going out to the leper and the adulteress; but who soothed Christ?

Denied both Cradle and Death-bed,

He had a fit place neither to be born nor to die. A poor babe! A poor lad! A poor young man! Not so much as a taper to cheer his dying hours. Even the candle of the sun snuffed out. Oh, was it not all aloes? All our sins, sorrows, bereavements, losses, and all the agonies of earth and hell picked up as in one cluster and squeezed into one cup, and that pressed to His lips, until the acrid, nauseating, bitter draught was swallowed with a distorted countenance, and a shudder from head to foot, and a gurgling strangulation. Aloes! aloes! Nothing but aloes. All this for Himself? All this to get the fame in the world of being a martyr? All this in a spirit of stubbornness, because he did not like Cæsar? No! no! All this because He wanted to pluck me and you from hell. Because He wanted to raise me and you to heaven. Because we were lost, and He wanted us found. Because we were blind, and He wanted us to see. Because we were serfs, and He wanted us manumitted. Oh, ye in whose cup of life the saccharine has predominated; oh, ye who have had bright and sparkling beverages, how do you feel toward Him who in your stead, and to purchase your disenthrallment, took the aloes, the unsavory aloes, the bitter aloes?

Your third curiosity is to know why these garments of Christ are

Odorous With Cassia.

This was a plant which grew in India and the adjoining islands. You do not care to hear what kind of a flower it had or what kind of a stalk. It is enough for me to tell you that it was used medicinally. In that land and in that age, where they knew but little about pharmacy, cassia was used to arrest many forms of disease. So, when in my text we find Christ coming with garments that smell of cassia, it suggests to me the healing and curative power of the Son of God. "Oh," you say, "now you have a superfluous idea. We are not sick. Why do you want cassia? We are athletic. Our respiration is perfect. Our limbs are lithe, and in these cool days we feel we could bound like the roe." I beg to differ, my brother, from you. None of you can be better in physical health than I am, and yet I must say we are all sick. I have taken the diagnosis of your case, and have examined all the best authorities on the subject, and I have come now to tell you that you are full of wounds and bruises and putrefying sores, which have not been bound up, or mollified.

The Marasmus of Sin

is on us—the palsy the dropsy, the leprosy. The man that is expiring to-night in Fulton street—the allopathic and homeopathic doctors having given him up, and his friends now standing around to take his last words—is no more certainly dying as to his body than you and I are dying unless we have taken the medicine from God's Apothecary. All the leaves of this Bible are only so many prescriptions from the Divine Physician, written, not in Latin, like the prescriptions of earthly physicians, but written in plain English, so that a "man, though a fool, need not err therein." Thank God that the Saviour's garments smell of cassia!

Suppose a man were sick, and there was a phial on his mantel-piece with medicine he knew would cure him, and he refused to take it, what would you say of him? He is a suicide. And what do you say of that man who, sick in sin, has the healing medicine of God's grace offered him, and refuses to take it? If he dies, he is a suicide. People talk as though God took a man and led him out to darkness and death, as though He brought him up to the cliffs and then pushed him off. Oh, no! When a man is lost it is not because God pushes him off; it is because he jumps off. In olden times a suicide was buried at the cross-roads, and the people were accustomed to throw stones upon his grave. So it seems to me there may be in this house a man who is

Destroying His Soul,

and as though the angels of God were here to bury him at the point where the roads of life and death cross each other, throwing upon the grave the broken law and a great pile of misimproved privileges, so that those going by may look at the fearful mound, and learn what a suicide it is when an immortal soul, for which Jesus died puts itself out of the way.

When Christ trod this planet with foot of flesh, the people rushed after Him—people who were sick, and those who, being so sick they could not walk, were brought by their friends. Here I see a mother holding up her little child saying: "Cure this croup, Lord Jesus! Cure this scarlet fever!" And others: Cure this ophthalmia!

Give Ease and Rest

to this spinal distress! Straighten this club-foot!" Christ made every house where He stopped a dispensary. I do not believe that in the nineteen centuries that have gone by since, His heart has got hard. I feel that we can come now with all our wounds of soul and get His benediction. O Jesus! here we are. We want healing. We want sight. We want health. We want life. "The whole need not a physician, but they that are sick." Blessed be God that Jesus Christ comes through this assemblage now, His "garments smelling of myrrh"—that means fragrance; "and aloes"—they mean bitter sacrificial memories; "and cassia"—that means medicine and cure.

According to my text, He comes "out of

The Ivory Palaces."

You know, or if you do not know, I will tell you now, that some of the palaces of olden time were adorned with ivory. Ahab and Solomon had their homes furnished with it. The tusks of African and Asiatic elephants were twisted into all manners of shapes, and there were stairs of ivory, and chairs of ivory, and tables of ivory, and floors of ivory, and pillars of ivory, and windows of ivory, and fountains that dropped into basins of ivory, and rooms that had ceilings of ivory. Oh white and overmastering beauty! Green tree branches sweeping the white curbs. Tapestry trailing the snowy floors. Brackets of light flashing on the lustrous surroundings. Silvery music rippling on the beach of the arches. The mere thought of it almost stuns my brain, and you say:

"Oh if I could only have walked over such floors! If I could have thrown myself in such a chair! If I could have heard the drip and dash of those fountains!" You shall have something better than that if you only let Christ introduce you. From that place He came, and to that place He proposes to transport you, for His "garments smell of myrrh, and aloes, and cassia, out of the ivory palaces."

What a Place Heaven Must Be!

The Tuileries of the French, the Windsor Castle of the English, the Spanish Alhambra, the Russian Kremlin, dungeons compared with it! Not so many castles on either side the Rhine as on both sides of the river of God—the ivory palaces! One for the angels, insufferably bright, winged, fire-eyed, tempest-charioted; one for the martyrs, with blood-red robes from under the altar; one for the King, the steps of His palace the crowns of the church militant; one for the singers, who lead the one hundred and forty and four thousand; one for you ransomed from sin; one for me, plucked from the burning. Oh, the ivory palaces!

To-day it seems to me as if the windows of those palaces were illumined for some great victory, and I look and see, climbing the stairs of ivory, and walking on floors of ivory, and looking from the windows of ivory, some whom we knew and loved on earth. Yes, I know them. There are father and mother, not eighty-two years and seventy-nine years, as when they left us, but blithe and young as when on their marriage day. And there are brothers and sisters, merrier than when we used to romp across the meadows together. The cough gone. The cancer cured. The erysipelas healed. The heart-break over. Oh, how fair they are in the ivory palaces! And your dear little

Children That Went Out From You—

Christ did not let one of them drop as He lifted them. He did not wrench one of them from you. No. They went as from one they loved well to One whom they loved better. If I should take your little child and press its soft face against my rough cheek, I might keep it a little while; but when you, the mother, came along, it would struggle to go with you. And so you stood holding your dying child when Jesus passed by in the room, and the little one sprang out to greet Him. That is all. Your Christian dead did not go down into the dust, and the gravel, and the mud. Though it rained all that funeral day, and the water came up to the wheel's hub as you drove out to the cemetery, it made no difference to them, for they stepped from the home here to the home there, right into the ivory palaces. All is well with them. All is well.

It is not a dead-weight that you lift when you carry a Christian out. Jesus makes the bed up soft with velvet promises, and He says: "Put her down here very gently. Put that head which will never ache again on this pillow of hallelujahs. Send up word that the procession is coming. Ring the bells. Ring! Open your gates, ye ivory palaces!" And so

Your Loved Ones are There.

They are just as certainly there, having died in Christ, as that you are here. There is only one thing more they want. Indeed, there is one thing in heaven they have not got. They want it. What is it? Your company. But oh, my brother, unless you change your tack you cannot reach that harbor. You might as well take the Baltimore and Ohio Railroad, expecting in that direction to reach Toronto, as to go on in the way some of you are going, and yet expect to reach the ivory palaces. Your loved ones are looking out of the windows of heaven now, and yet you seem to turn your back upon them. You do not seem to know the sound of their voices as well as you used to, or to be moved by the sight of their dear faces. Call louder, ye departed ones! Call louder from the ivory palaces!

When I think of that place, and think of my entering it, I feel awkward; I feel as sometimes when I have been exposed to the weather, and my shoes have been bemired, and my coat is soiled, and my hair is disheveled, and I stop in front of some fine residence where I have an errand. I feel not fit

To Go In As I Am

and sit among the guests. So some of us feel about heaven. We need to be washed—we need to be rehabilitated before we go into the ivory palaces. Eternal God, let the surges of Thy pardoning mercy roll over us! I want not only to wash my hands and my feet, but, like some skilled diver, standing on the pier-head, who leaps into the wave and comes up at a far-distant point from where he went in, so I want to go down, and so I want to come up. O Jesus, wash me in the waves of Thy salvation!

And here I ask you to solve a mystery that has been oppressing me for thirty years. I have asked it of doctors of divinity who have been studying theology half a century, and they have given me no satisfactory answer. I have turned over all the books in my library, but got no solution to the question, and to-day I come and ask you for an explanation. By what logic was Christ induced to exchange the ivory palaces of heaven for the crucifixion agonies of earth? I shall take the first thousand million years in heaven to study out that problem; meanwhile and now, taking it as the tenderest,

Mightiest of all Facts

that Christ did come, that He came with spikes in His feet, came with thorns in His brow, came with spears in His heart, to save you and to save me. "God so loved the world that He gave His only begotten Son, that whosoever believeth in Him should not perish, but have everlasting life." O Christ, whelm this audience with Thy compassion! Mow them down like summer grain with the harvesting sickle of Thy grace! Ride through to-day the conqueror, Thy garments smelling "of myrrh, and aloes, and cassia, out of the ivory palaces"!

O sinner, fling everything else away and take Christ! Take Him now—not to-morrow. During the night following this very day, there may be an excitement in your dwelling, and a tremulous pouring out of drops from an unsteady and affrighted hand, and before to-morrow morning your chance may be gone.

STREET WORSHIP IN BOGOTA.

SOME of the difficulties attending the work of Christian missionaries in Bogota may be realized by the following statement, which the Rev. M. E. Caldwell sends to the *Church*: "There is nothing, perhaps, more annoying to Protestants in Bogota than the practice of carrying the 'Host,' or sacred wafer, through the streets. Suddenly you are surprised by hearing the tinkling of bells, and before you know, you have run into a procession carrying the 'Host,' and you presently find the people all around you taking off their hats, many falling on their knees, praying and showing every sign of the greatest reverence. If you stand looking on, without taking off your hat, you will be scowled at as a monster. It will not be strange if you are stoned or knocked down. You will notice in the procession a boy ringing a bell; then a bare-headed priest, dressed in his stately robes, comes walking under a broad red canopy or an umbrella, which an attendant holds over his head. After the priest comes a bare-headed rabble, and all persons within sight of the red canopy are expected to be on their knees, or at least to take off their hats. If you ask what all this means, you will be told that the priest is carrying the sacred wafer to some sick-bed, that the wafer is truly Christ our Lord, His body and blood, and that, therefore, you must worship the Host as it passes by. Sometimes Protestants are greatly annoyed by these processions, and are obliged to enter some house or store, or retrace their steps, to avoid insults or violence.

"Similar to this is the custom of striking the bell in the tower of the cathedral or the principal church of a town or city three times at morning mass, just at the time when the priest within the church elevates the Host. As far as the bell can be heard, the people take off their hats in the streets, and walk or ride bare-headed until the third tap of the bell dies away. They do not, however, cease from their business or conversation. If the great market-square in front of the church should be full of people, at the first sound of the bell off come the hats until the third stroke of the bell.

"When the archbishop walks out, wearing his costly robes, many of the people fall upon their knees and do reverence to the 'most holy father.' He is to the people their king and lord, and his word to them is law and gospel. In short, these poor people are taught to fear man more than God, and to bow down to images and perishable things rather than to worship in spirit and in truth the unseen Jehovah."

Clergymen and Evangelists who will Allow Copies of the CHRISTIAN HERALD to be placed in the seats of churches, or will have them distributed at the doors, will be supplied with assorted parcels of back number if they will write to the Manager, 63 Bible House, New York.

City Missionaries, Christian Workers, and others may obtain miscellaneous back numbers of THE CHRISTIAN HERALD for mission, hospital, and prison work, and for general distribution, at $1 per 100. They will be found most valuable as tracts. Address The Manager, 63 Bible House, New York.

THE PILGRIMS AT LOURDES.

AN interesting description of the scenes at Lourdes, the famous shrine to which the French Roman Catholics go to be healed of their diseases, is given by a journalist who recently visited the place. To one who has witnessed Divine Healing in this country or Europe, it is suggestive of the thought that even the miracles of Moses before Pharaoh were imitated by the magicians with their enchantments. In the course of his letter the journalist says:

"The most interesting class of pilgrims are the humblest peasants who have hoarded up their savings for years perhaps, to come from distant Brittany, Normandy, Flanders, Burgundy, or the Alps. These poor people invariably undertake this long and weary railway trip in the heat and dust of summer, to ask the Virgin for some favor for their own homes, for some sick one who has stayed behind, or for the invalid they have brought on a mattress or in their own strong brawny arms. They only hope that they may be fortunate enough to be able some day to invest the remains of their savings in a small marble slab to record their gratitude for a miraculous cure or a prayer vouchsafed. How many, alas! depart year after year with heavy hearts and lighter purses, and with disappointment on their faces. Such is the faith of these French peasants that, even when thus disappointed, their features will be lit up with a proud satisfaction. Their voices will tremble with emotion when they naïvely relate to their neighbors the miracles that they were told had been accomplished during the very pilgrimage from which they, at least, came back empty-handed and disappointed.

"At Lourdes Station I saw some of the many invalids that are brought to the shrine in the hope that either a miraculous and sudden cure will be obtained by the intercession of the Virgin, or that some relief will be the result of ablutions in the water that issues from the rock close to the spot where Bernadette said that she had received the commands of Notre Dame de Lourdes, in 1858, to call upon the faithful to raise a church on the banks of the Gave. Most of the invalids seemed to be suffering from diseases that deprived them of the use of their legs. They had quite a number of Bath chairs and stretchers on wheels at the station, upon which the sick were laid and taken very comfortably to the carriages, and in some cases to their quarters. When the main body of the pilgrims arrive they bring with them so many invalids that the means of conveyance run short. An association composed of young men, and gentlemen even of the very highest classes, has therefore organized a sort of ambulance service. It is touching to see the sick and the cripples carefully tended and borne on stretchers by old and young men. The relatives of the sufferers who walk behind are profuse in their blessings and thanks for this kindness.

"The invalids are carried in the same way to the church and grotto, and there another association, composed of ladies and young girls of rank and fortune, tends to the wants of the invalids of their own sex. They are carried into the wooden sheds where the water of the famous fountain runs through large baths. The screaming and suffering creatures are lowered, often with great trouble, into the cold, clear water that sometimes has a salutary effect upon the disease or wound. The head of the ladies' association gravely assured me that she had witnessed marvellous results from this water cure, aided by the singular nervous excitement produced in the sufferers by their religious faith, and by the whole scene at this Mecca of Catholic pilgrimages. The priests and the associations for the relief of the pilgrims take care to have always some reliable medical assistance at hand. The physicians, who are all, of course, devout Catholics, now and then give certificates of duly authenticated and attested cures, and most of these documents are drawn up in cautious and guarded language. The inhabitants and clergy of Lourdes say that during almost every great pilgrimage, and always during the national pilgrimage in August, they witness some of these cases of faith and water cure."

A SUFFERER FROM HERNIA HEALED.

ONE of the most remarkable cases of Divine Healing on record is reported by Mrs. Baxter in this month's *Thy Healer*.* It is that of Mrs. Ward, of Southsea, England, who says: "I had suffered internally for *over twenty years*, when the Lord healed me. The internal injury prevented me walking scarcely any distance, and at last I was unable to walk even across my room. During that time I never knew what it was to live without medicine, or wearing a support. However, on December 18, two years ago, or some time before that, after reading *The Christian Herald*, I thought if the Lord could heal others He could heal me; and the Lord Himself showed me I was to trust in Him. I had no human help, and no one to teach me, but was led to trust Him fully. I had been given up by London and local physicians, and was brought near to death's door; so near, that they said mortification must set in, and it was only a matter of a few days. Then I wrote to Miss Sisson, and asked her prayers. After that, however, I became, if possible, much worse, but I still trusted the Lord; and after a long and severe trial of faith I recovered, and I am quite well, so that I can now walk miles, even in a hilly country. Since that time, three years ago next December, I have not taken any medicine, whereas previously it was impossible for me to go without it—it was to me just like my daily food. But the Lord led me to trust Him, and He has kept me without it, for I have not required it. Also, a month after I trusted the Lord with my body, He led me to give up the support I wore; and when the doctor next came, he was astonished to find the internal organs gone back to their right places. Formerly there was such a congestion of the internal parts that I could eat no solid food, and I was kept on Brand's essence; but now I can sit down and eat a hearty dinner.

A CENTENARIAN'S AWFUL REMINISCENCES

ONE of the most remarkable men in France is M. Chevreul, an eminent scientist who has just celebrated his one hundred and third birthday. His strength of body is astonishing at his years, and his mental vigor is not abated at all. His habits are very regular. He rises early and takes a plate of soup. He goes to bed again and sleeps till noon. He then has his breakfast, which consists of two eggs and some minced meat. This repast over, he drives out for two or three hours. On his return he reads scientific and literary works, following with interest the recent proceedings of various scientific bodies, and the accounts given of recent discoveries in many departments of science. At 4 o'clock in the afternoon he takes a bowl of milk with two biscuits. He lies down again for two hours, after which he has another plate of soup and goes to bed for the night.

M. Chevreul still vividly remembers some of the blood-stained episodes of the great Revolution, particularly the war in La Vendée. He was at Nantes during the *Noyades* and *Fusillades* ordered by the blood-thirsty Carrier, President of the Revolutionary Tribunal, who drowned, shot, or decapitated 15,000 persons, and was afterwards justly "guillotined." The guillotine used by Carrier stood before the house where M. Chevreul lived; and the centenarian himself relates that one day he was out near the place of execution when he saw two young ladies—friends of his family—brought up to the guillotine and decapitated. He was almost glued to the spot by the horrible sight, and his terror was increased tenfold when the executioner came up to him, seized him by the body and trailed one of his hands in the blood around the block, saying at the same time, "There! that's a good Republican baptism for you. It will make a fine *sans-culotte* of you, you young rascal!" Young Chevreul was two months ill after this event, and had he been of weaker mould he would have died with fright. M. Chevreul visited the Paris Sanitary Exhibition at the Palace of Industry, a few days ago; arm-in-arm with a friend, he mounted the stairs and walked through the Exhibition.

A CONVERTED CHINAMAN'S FAITH.

AT a recent baptism in South China, the native pastor told a touching story of the steadfastness and unwavering faith of the husband of the woman he had just baptized. It appeared that several years ago he went to Australia, when he came under the influence of Christians, and gave himself to Christ. Not long since he returned with a small fortune, to settle in his native village. Troubles, however, beset him at once; his efforts at farming failed, and he lost much of his money; then a business in which he sunk the remainder failed, and he was left utterly destitute. Then, to add to his troubles, his child fell sick and died, and his wife became very ill. He seemed overwhelmed with troubles, but still his faith did not falter; his friends came about him, urging him to forsake his God, and attributing all his trials to the displeasure of the idols: they brought him incense-sticks, urging him to burn a few of them, but still he was firm, replying to all in the words of Job, "The Lord gave, and the Lord hath taken away." He struggled on like this for some time, his wife only growing worse; then he and Mok, the catechist, agreed to meet together every day to pray for her, and ere long she began slowly to mend. Still, times went very hardly with them, and, in order to procure food enough, the man (Un Yung) journeyed to Canton, to try his fortune there, working as a coolie. He was not long there, however; for Mok, feeling how hard it was for the sick wife to be left alone, called him home, and asked him to become his cook. Here he gets perhaps five or six shillings a month, and his rice, but he is thankful even for this, and his other great mercy. His wife gradually recovered, and more than this, to the great joy of her husband his earnest words and the words of Mok reached her heart, and, by the power of the Holy Ghost, she has become a true believer. Since believing, she has been as active for Christ as she was previously in the service of the gods of the country, and has been paying visits to all the villages around, telling the women what God has done for her.

A PARALYTIC'S INFLUENCE.

THE recently issued report of the Church Missionary Society describes the happy results of the influence of a paralyzed convert in India, one Pundit Mohan Lall Vidyabagish. Mr. Hall says: "The little room in our Christian compound, where he dwells, is filled from day to day with inquirers. There is a strange power of attraction about that couch on which he lies. His bright, happy face (a face never clouded, although suffering is no stranger to him), his telling words, chain men to his side, and those who are induced to visit him once, come again, and again, and again. Whatever may be the case with other Christians, all at least confess this, that this faith in Christ brings deep, abiding peace, and influences his life. Conviction is contagious, and not a few own to the truth of his words, yet fear to rank themselves, once and forever, upon the side of Christ."

A deep heart-work is going on, Mr. Hall believes, in high circles of society. One wealthy gentleman invited him to a sumptuous repast. He writes: "Lingering in the halls and corridors of the spacious house stood a number of Babus, each politely bowing as we passed; and I hoped inwardly that an opportunity to address them might be afforded before our departure. It came in a way least expected. 'Will you come below and pray?' said our host, when the meal

* *Thy Healer and Faith Witness*, a monthly Magazine edited by Mrs. M. Baxter, contains original articles on Holiness and Healing, Authentic Testimonies of Divine Healing, and Items of Intelligence from Heathen Lands where missionaries are laboring in faith, soliciting no help from man, but relying solely on God for support. Annual Subscription, 75 cents, may be sent to Manager of CHRISTIAN HERALD, 63 Bible House, New York.

was wellnigh ended. Ay, that I would, and I thanked God for the request. Descending the stairs and passing through numerous rooms, small and large, we entered the reception-hall, in which stood a large table and a number of empty chairs. One by one, members and friends of the household crept in and took their seats; and there, for an hour, I preached Christ to them. From the earliest prophecy, right through the ages, I tried to trace in the history of the Jews the purposes of God: His justice, His infinite love, His holiness and truth. Then in Christ's birth and life, and works and words, in His death and passion, His glorious resurrection and ascension, I showed how His purposes on behalf of poor ruined man were fulfilled. Then, while I knelt and prayed aloud, they bowed their heads in adoration, and worshipped. Since that day he has visited me several times a week, and I am convinced that he is a Christian."

THE PREDICTED REVIVAL OF DEMONISM IN THE LAST DAYS.

By Rev. H. W. Congdon.

A Judicial Punishment—Spiritualism a Mixture of Fraud and Ancient Sorcery—Prohibited in the Old Testament—Spirits in the New Testament—Their Malign Influence—An Infallible Test—Modern Spiritualism—Partly Fraud—Clairvoyance—Psychology—Wholly Unreliable—Opposed to Revelation—Immoral in its Tendencies—Must be Avoided.

By referring to II Thess. 2:11, it will be seen that the "strong delusion" of the last days will come as a judicial punishment because men "receive not the love of the truth." "Not liking to retain God in their knowledge, God gives them over to a reprobate mind, to do those things which are not convenient" (Rom. 1:28), and so they are taken captive at the will of Satan, in all his snares. A strong delusion certainly is the revival of *demonism* under the modern name of spiritualism. But all there is in it beyond mere fraud and trickery is as old as the Bible itself. It would be well for every one to give heed to the testimony of God's Word concerning it.

In the Old Testament

we find, in the first place, that all commerce between living men and the other world, whether beings of another order or the spirits of departed men, was prohibited under pain of death. See Exod. 22:18; Lev. 19:31; 20:6, 27; Deut. 18:10–14. In addition to those who use the mysterious arts and divination, especial mention is made in these passages of those who "consult with familiar spirits"—demons, and of "necromancers," or those who deal with the dead.

In the next place, Old Testament examples of these sins may be seen in the case of Manasseh (II Kings 21:6; II Chron. 33:6); and in the case of Saul (I Sam. 28:8–21; I Chron. 10:13). From II Kings 23:24, we infer that this

Spiritism was Prevalent

in the time of Israel's apostacy, and was one of the signs of the divine retribution soon to fall upon the nation. In all of these cases the displeasure of God was manifest; and the special judgments which He denounced, as well as the general penalty of death prescribed by the law, all show the estimate which God puts upon such dealings with spirits. And this estimate is still further seen in the prophets: Isa. 8:19; 19:3; Jer. 27:9; 29:8, 9; Micah 3:7; Zech. 10:2. It is evident that God regards with very great disapprobation this whole business of "seeking for the living to the dead," instead of seeking "to the law and to the testimony." There were very great reasons for all this severity. If men believe in Jehovah and love His commandments, they will govern their conduct by His law, instead of running after the "spirits." If being of such a mind as this, they want practical guidance in cases of doubt and perplexity, they will consult the oracles of the living God rather than seek mediums that "peep and mutter," and "whisper out of the dust." And it is only when people have lost their faith in God (at least in a large degree), regard His Revelation as insufficient, and the practical guidance of His providence and Spirit as unsafe, that they will turn away from Him to listen to

Voices From Another World.

And as under the conditions of society in the times of the Old Testament, apostacy meant contamination with all the pollutions of the heathen, God ordained that all dealing with the other world, except through His own oracles, should be punished with death.

In the New Testament, the agency of spirits appears very frequently in the narrative, but generally as the possession of living persons by the unclean spirits of demons. The most casual reader of the Gospels and Acts will remark how numerous these cases are, and that Christ and His apostles recognized fully their demoniacal character. For examples see Matt. 12:22–28: Matt. 8:29; Mark 5:7; Luke 8:28; Acts 16:16. The nature of the request made by the demons of Gadara, is worthy of particular remark—they did not want to be sent into the *abyss* to be "tormented *before the time*." They understood that there is a day appointed in which God will judge both fallen spirits, and wicked men. (II Pet. 2:4.) They knew also that the place of their punishment is the *abyss*—in Hebrew *Abaddon*, in Greek *Apoleia*, in the Revelation of St. John, the *Lake of Fire*—and recognizing Jesus to be the Son of God and Judge of all, they were in terror lest He would consign them at once to this place of torment. Hence their entreaty. In I Tim. 4:4, we have

A Distinct Warning

that these malignant agencies will continue till the end of the present dispensation; and in I John 4:1–3, we have a test which, taken in connection with Isa. 8:20, will enable any one to decide infallibly whether a communication purporting to come from the other world has been sent by God, or proceeds from a fallen spirit. The Word of God will remain forever true, and Jesus Christ, the Son of God, is its Divine interpreter.

And now in this light derived from the Bible let us look at

Modern Spiritualism.

We note the following facts concerning it: By its own acknowledgment *it is necromancy and demononism*. Its whole teaching is directly attributed to communications from spirits, either of dead men or beings of another order. It is thus directly within the prohibitions of the law forbidding intercourse with the spirit world.

It is inseparably mixed up with frauds and delusions. Many persons under its influence are entirely honest, without doubt; but it invites to its ranks all sorts of impostors, from the mere sleight-of-hand trickster to the adept in the mysteries of the black art. Its secret séance, its darkened room, its required attitude of expectancy on the part of the spectator—indeed, all the conditions of the "manifestation"—favor the imposition of fraud upon its innocent victims.

Another element of uncertainty in it is delusions produced by *clairvoyance and mesmerism*. Any one who has studied the subject knows that the human mind possesses certain capacities and undeveloped faculties, not in exercise in our normal condition, in the present state. When they do occasionally come into exercise, we catch glimpses of possibilities to be realized, probably in another state of life. Such is that power, exhibited in the mesmeric trance, of putting the mind into connection with things at a distance, or even into direct communication with the minds of other people, so as to be able to disclose matters entirely hidden from ordinary knowledge. This is called by the name of clairvoyance.

Similar to this is the power sometimes called

Psychology,

by which one person may obtain such complete control over another person's mind as to make all its faculties subject to his dictation. In this condition the subject may experience delusions of mind and hallucinations of sense, and yet be utterly unable to discriminate between the true and the false, all being equally real to him. He will see things that never existed, and hear sounds that never vibrated in the air; or, if there is a slight foundation in fact for these pseudo-phenomena, it is so distorted and exaggerated as to be essentially false as presented to the mind of the confiding dupe. All this is simply mesmerism in one of its many forms.

Now, how much of this there may be in the phenomena of spiritualism at any given time, no one can know except those who work the mechanism of the séance. It is certain that the usual expectancy and

Credulity of the Spectators,

as well as the conditions demanded for the "manifestation," favor the frequent intervention of mesmerism. In all this there is nothing supernatural; but it enables bad men to invoke these mysterious agencies, under the guise of the supernatural, to give credit to their vicious and pernicious teachings.

It is entirely unreliable. The spirits themselves are unseen and unknown, and can be judged of only by their own utterances. They come promiscuously—good, bad, and indifferent—and the hearer must judge between them. Now he listens to one who speaks against the Bible and the Christian religion; directly another comes along to tell him that the Bible is a good book, and the better he knows and practices what is in it the better for himself.

Besides this, the spirits often *personate* others. No one can be certain that the spirit communicating is the one he is alleged to be. When a living person comes to inquire of the spirit of a good dead man, it may be a departed relative—there is no assurance that the spirit responding is the one called for. It may be a wicked spirit or a demon, who is passing himself off in place of the one asked for. And if the facts of mesmerism and clairvoyance teach anything, they teach us that it is impossible for the medium to be so completely *en rapport* with the inquirer as to be able to obtain from his own mind all those facts which appear so supernatural when given in the communications. Now, amid all this uncertainty, the inquirer is thrown back entirely upon his own judgment to discriminate between the true and the false, the good and the bad. No candid spiritualist will deny the facts stated above concerning spirit communications; and on

Its Own Testimony,

spiritualism is utterly unsafe and unreliable, either as a medium for finding the truth, or as a practical guide for the present life and the life to come.

In ancient times it was connected with the pollutions of the heathen. Its tendency in modern times is in the same direction. Its doctrine of "spiritual affinities" invades the sanctities of the domestic relations. It tends to a light estimation of the sanctity of marriage and the relations of the sexes; to induce people to enter upon such relations without the binding obligations of marriage itself; to easily lay aside these obligations when they have once actually been assumed; and finally to end in the communism of free love.

Such is spiritualism. It is a revival of the demonism of ancient times. It is a stupendous delusion, a snare of the devil. The only course for any one to take who would not be captured by it and led astray from eternal life, is to *let it entirely, absolutely alone.*

CHRISTIAN HERALD AND SIGNS OF OUR TIMES.
OFFICE, 63 BIBLE HOUSE, NEW YORK.

TERMS AND INSTRUCTIONS.

Published Weekly. Subscription price in the United States, Canada, and Mexico, $1.50 a year; $1 eight months; 75 cents six months; sent two months on trial for 25 cents, postage free; in Europe and in all countries in the Postal Union, 50 cents extra postage; subscriptions always payable in advance. Single copies, price 3 cents. Any newsdealer will furnish the paper weekly when ordered.

Remittances by Mail should be by Post-office money order, bank cheque, draft, or express money order, whenever possible, and should always be made payable to THE CHRISTIAN HERALD. Letters containing money sent in this way need not be registered, as when lost, duplicates can always be obtained.

If a Postal Note or currency is sent, it should always be in a registered letter. Letters can be registered at any office. Subscribers sending money of this kind, and not registering, do it at their own risk.

Receipts are not sent; the receipt of the paper by a subscriber is a sufficient proof that the remittance has been received. If the paper does not arrive promptly, please advise us, that we may see if the address is correctly entered.

CURRENT EVENTS.

The Postmaster-General Sent His Estimate for appropriations to the Secretary of the Treasury last week. This is for the fiscal year ending June 30, 1890. It is nearly six million dollars larger than the appropriation for the current year. One million is due to the extension of the free delivery system. The balance is made up of small sums incident to the opening of new offices. Mr. Dickinson allows, in his estimate for an expected increase of revenue, of $9,813,482 over the present year. He places it at $62,508,658. The apparent deficiency under these figures will be about $4,500,000.

A Welcome Pledge From the President-Elect is declared to have been given in an interview with a correspondent of the New York *Herald*. The rumor has been extensively circulated in the South, that General Harrison would nominate to Federal offices in that section, carpet-baggers and ignorant colored men; and Southerners understood only too well what that would mean. The correspondent states, in substance, that nothing is further from General Harrison's intention. He is anxious that every representative of the Federal Government in the South shall be a native, and of consideration and influence in the locality in which he will exercise his powers. As a further evidence of this intention the *Herald* quotes part of a letter from the President-elect to a gentleman in South Carolina, which concludes with the remark that "the policies in legislation advised by the Republican party, I believe are wholesome for the whole country, and if those who in their hearts believe with us upon these questions, would act with us, some other questions that give you local concern, would settle themselves." These words may well encourage our friends in the South to avoid the discomfort of indulging in gloomy apprehensions that may never be realized.

The Fifty-first Congress Will Have to Decide the question of the admission of several Territories, which are now preparing for pressing their claims. One important matter should not escape the attention of either the Territories or Congress. The strongest opposition to admission will come from the fear of Mormon power. Congress has had so much difficulty in dealing with polygamy in Utah, in spite of the advantages secured by territorial subordination, that it is little likely to raise to statehood any Territory promising to become a Mormon stronghold. Idaho has realized this, and has passed a law disfranchising the Mormons who control her southern counties; but the law was identical in principle with that which in Nevada has been declared unconstitutional. In Wyoming and Arizona there are large settlements of Mormons. In Wyoming four hundred Mormon families have settled in the last two ears. It will therefore be wise on the part of the Territories seeking admission, to provide beforehand effectual guarantees against Mormon supremacy, or Congress may be apprehensive.

The Necessity for Vigilance and Vigor in respect to the Anarchists, on the part of both legislative and executive departments of the Government, was proved by the evidence given at the trial of Hronek in Chicago on November 28. A detective produced thirty-four sticks of dynamite and eight bombs which were in Hronek's house, and an expert testified that the dynamite was of a more powerful kind than that used in legitimate business. Eight sticks of dynamite and a bomb were found in the house of a companion of Hronek. The police had tested one of the bombs out on the prairie, and it knocked to fragments a shed six feet high and six feet square. The chiefs of the Anarchist gang, it appears, are Bohemians, which fact should put the immigration commissioners on the alert. The general public has little idea how extensive is the extreme Socialist organization, and how desperate and reckless its members are. Unless effective measures to extirpate the evil are taken soon, our national freedom will be assailed by a conspiracy far more formidable than any that could be organized to bring the United States under monarchical government.

The Trouble in the Grand Army Which has developed in the West calls for the friendly offices of comrades in other sections. It will be a grievous misfortune if so valuable an organization should be divided by matters which are not within its province. The seat of the trouble is in Indiana, where the nucleus of a rival order was formed on November 28. It is to be distinctly political, and its leaders allege that they have been driven to its organization by the fact that the Grand Army in that and other States has become a political machine, with political principles opposed to their own. When the idea of the organization of the veterans in the Grand Army was first developed, it was with the purpose of keeping alive the spirit of comradeship and patriotism. As its members were drawn from the ranks of both political parties, the possibility that a majority, belonging to either party, might give a political character to the organization was foreseen, and it was decided that it should take no part whatever in politics. It may be hoped that if this wholesome rule has been infringed in Indiana and elsewhere, and cause given for organizing a rival association, comrades in other States will by friendly protests induce a reform of methods, and secure such a pledge as to the future as will recall the seceders to their old association.

The Federal Courts in Utah are Still Busy with the effort to suppress polygamy in the Territory. The Salt Lake *Herald* publishes the criminal calendar for the November term of court in the First District. The calendar contains fifty-nine cases, in which the defendants are held for violation of the Edmunds act. There are very few prosecutions for direct polygamy, because it is difficult to prove the polygamous marriage. In this list of fifty-nine no one is accused of having committed polygamy, but nearly all of the defendants are to be tried under that section of the act which defines and forbids "unlawful cohabitation." The names of a majority of the accused, indicate that they are immigrants from Norway or Sweden.

The Return of the Refugees from Jacksonville, Fla., who, it is stated, number twenty-three thousand, is prohibited for the present. The committee of the Board of Health has issued an address, warning them of the danger of a too early return, and enjoining patience. The committee say that the Federal Government has empowered Dr. Porter, the surgeon in charge of relief measures, to proceed with the purifying and cleansing process at the expense of the General Government, and he has since been actively, and with as much expedition as consistent with the attainment of the objects in view, perfecting the necessary arrangements. Infected houses and apartments are being opened during the present cold snap, and all means available are being used to prevent a recurrence of the plague. The committee do not ask those anxious to return to wait until the entire work is completed, but at least not to imperil their own lives and impede the work by the premature incoming of outside friends, or subjecting them to danger which may result fatally, and for which they should and will be held responsible, as the guardians of the public health. In conclusion the committee say: "It is impossible to state, as yet, just when we can admit the many who are anxiously waiting to come in, but we ask no long delay, and promise to work with hand and heart, night and day, to its early accomplishment; and we can give assurance that there will be imposed upon our absent friends and neighbors but a few days of delay in addition to that which ordinary prudence requires."

A German Expedition for the Relief of Emin Pacha is being rapidly organized. A committee has been formed, and at its meeting in the Lower House of the Landtag Herr von Bennigsen made an address, in which he pointed out that the interests of the German nation were involved in the East African troubles, and that the proposed expedition would materially conduce to the restoration of German prestige. It was unanimously decided to send Lieutenant Wissmann as soon as possible to lead the first column. Dr. Peters will in the meantime prepare to equip a supporting column, of which he will have the command. Lieutenant Wissmann will wait on the Emperor to resign his commission in the army, and to state his plans for the Emin relief expedition. He expects to be ready to leave Berlin about December 15. The fund subscribed for the expedition amounts to $80,000.

An Ominous Election in France Took Place on November 25. The Department of the Var chose as its representative in the Chamber of Deputies the notorious communist Gen. Cluseret. He was one of the leaders in the horrible days of 1870, when the communists held control of Paris. He was imprisoned afterward at Mazas, but escaped in November, 1871, after which he went to England, thence to this country, and lastly to Switzerland. August 30, 1872, he was sentenced to death, *in contumaciam*, by a Versailles court-martial. The general amnesty granted to the communists enabled him to return to France, where, for the past seven years, he has taken a leading part in radical politics. He is a man of considerable courage and dash, as he proved when, in his younger days, he fought under Fremont and McClellan in our civil war. His election is a significant sign of the trend of affairs in France. The present Government is stated, by well-informed persons in Paris, to be generally despised, and they believe that society is settling itself into the camp of General Boulanger as the only refuge from the dreaded communists.

The British Government Appears to Have failed to please the Irish party in the House of Commons by its plan of advancing $25,000,000 for the relief of Irish tenants. It is denounced as a plan for the relief of landlords, though it may inure to the benefit of the tenants ultimately. The correspondent of a prominent journal thus predicts the result of its operation: The working of this plan will be as follows: First, the Government will buy out the landlord at a figure much above the market value. Then the Government becomes the creditor of the tenant, who has 49 years in which to buy his land on the installment plan. Being his own landlord, the peasant will then have the privilege of paying taxes and dues of every description, including those now borne by the landowner, and which will be added to his yearly purchase money. When increasing hard times shall make it impossible for him to pay, the Government will find itself in the uncomfortable position of evicting the peasant. Several amendments have been proposed by Irish members, but they have been rejected by the House.

The Help Rendered to the Educated Indian by the ladies of the National Indian Association is more valuable than is generally known. At a recent meeting in the parlors of Mrs. William E. Dodge, of New York, Chaplain Frizzelle spoke from actual observation of its benefits. He said that the young Indians were too often sent back to their homes after receiving their education without a cent of money, and found themselves helplessly stranded for want of a little capital. He knew of cases where the Association, in advancing a little money for the purchase of a set of tools, or a horse, or a cow, or a small house, had set despairing graduates on their feet, and made industrious, saving men and women of them. In many cases these loans had been repaid, with interest.

A Deeply Interesting Description of Medical mission work in China was given to medical students in Association Hall, New York, on November 25, by Dr. Boudinet C. Atterbury, who has been laboring in Pekin. He said the medical missionary's first step on entering a new field, was to open a small house and hang over the door the imposing sign, "*Everybody's healing-place.*" At first none came. Then a few coolies took courage enough to venture within; and as they came out alive, and felt better, they soon gave a basis for securing the confidence of others. The Chinese, he said, were extremely superstitious and suspicious, and commonly believe that the medical missionary mixes with his medicine something which will induce them to believe in Christianity. This was one of the greatest annoyances they had to contend with. Another annoyance was, that the Chinaman did not like moderate treatment. He thought that if a small dose would cure a little of his pain, a big dose all at once would settle it. He first found this fact out by learning of a Chinaman who had saved up powders that had been given him from time to time, and taken them all at once. They nearly killed him. The opportunities for usefulness of a medical missionary in China, Dr. Atterbury said, were unlimited.

A Novel Experiment in Locomotion Was made in New York on November 27. Three cars containing sixty-five passengers started from the Fourteenth Street station of the Ninth Avenue Elevated road, and were drawn to Fiftieth Street and back at the rate of twenty miles an hour. The motor used was the new one invented by Mr. Daft, who operated it on the trip. Its power is gained from electricity. The engines generating the electricity were in Fifteenth Street, between Ninth and Tenth avenues. The circuit was completed by means of two wires, one of which connected with a copper rod running along the guard-rail. From this rod the motor gathered the electricity through an electric brush. A low, tension current was used. The motor weighed nine and one-half tons, about half as much as an ordinary Elevated railroad engine. The remarkable feature in the experiment is that there was no power in the motor that drew the train. Its capacity to move and draw its load was picked up as it went along, by contact with the wire by means of the patent brush. The Christian's progress in Divine life is analogous to this principle. The power is not in him, but comes from contact with his Lord, and without that he is powerless for the good of himself and others. (John 15: 5.)

The Ceremony of Hoisting the Stars and stripes from the flagstaff at the Battery, New York, was duly observed on November 25. It was the one hundred and fifth anniversary of the evacuation of the city by the only remaining British garrison in the United States. A company of veterans assembled around the flagstaff at a little before sunrise, to perform the usual commemorative ceremony of running up the national colors. Promptly as the sun rose above the horizon, the flag was run up, and amid the cheers of the assembled spectators, waved proudly in the breeze. A little later, however, the wind rose and soon began to blow a gale. It was too much for the flag, or it was thought to be so by those who had a fatherly interest in the flagstaff, so at noon the stars and stripes were hauled down. Happily for the country, the only significance in the lowering of the standard was the meteorological one suggested by prudence. It is sometimes otherwise, however, in our churches. Much to the regret of pastors and Christian workers, the human citadel from which it was hoped that the great enemy of souls was utterly and permanently ejected, and has hoisted the blood-stained banner of the Cross, lowers it before the storm of ridicule or social ostracism. In that case it is deplorable, because it signifies a return to the thraldom of its oppressor. (II Peter 2: 20, 22.)

A Restoration to Life by a Brother's Kiss is an occurrence described in an Indianapolis journal. It states that a lady residing in Jefferson County, Ohio, now visiting friends in Indianapolis, owes her life to the affection of a twin brother. Some years ago she fell on the threshold of her father's house, in what was supposed at first to be a fainting fit. A physician was summoned, who, after laboring for more than an hour to restore consciousness, pronounced her dead. Preparations were made for the funeral, but the interment was delayed to allow of the attendance of her twin brother, who was at college in a distant city. Though the body had been kept for several days, it was noticed that there were no signs of decomposition. When the brother came, he insisted that she was not dead. He threw himself on the unscious form, took the loved head on his arm, and kissed her passionately. As he did so the bandage around the head fell off, and as the mouth opened he declared that he saw a slight motion of the tongue. A physician was again sent for, and after a long time of alternate hope and despair, the girl struggled back to life. She said that during the five days in which she had lain awaiting burial, she had had moments of consciousness, but was powerless to move or speak. Her brother's touch and kiss were the first things that really aroused her from her trance-like condition. There are some, who have come out of spiritual death into newness of life, who give similar testimony. Not until they knew how Christ loved them, and died for them, did they awake to eternal life. (John 5: 25.)

An Urgent Plea for Mercy is Under the consideration of District-Attorney Burnet of Cincinnati. It has been presented by the friends of a bank president now under indictment for misappropriation of the funds of a National Bank. It is represented that the friends of the indicted man have made full restitution to the bank on his behalf, and that he is sincerely repentant, and has suffered great mental anguish on account of his offence. The District-Attorney, on consultation with Attorney-General Garland, received authority to act on his discretion. He went to the retired New England hamlet where the accused man is staying, awaiting his trial. He found him a hopeless physical wreck, borne down with shame and remorse, scarcely able to recognize his friends, and wholly unable to appear in court and make any defence. The District-Attorney did not announce any decision in the case, but from his sympathy and evident commiseration the unhappy man's friends believe that he will enter what is called a *nolle prosequi* plea, indicating that he is unwilling to press the charge. It is all that he can do. He cannot absolve the culprit, nor reinstate him in public esteem, and the man will still remain a criminal though spared from punishment. It is not so when the sinner goes to God for mercy through Christ. He not only escapes punishment, but his sins are blotted out and he is justified. (I Cor. 6: 11.)

A Temporary Recovery of Sight by an Aged blind lady in Pennsylvania is reported in the Philadelphia *Record*. It states that the wife of a farmer in Montgomery County, who is in her seventy-fifth year, has been totally blind for four years. The affliction caused a great depression of spirits, and the lady prayed earnestly, as her last wish on earth, that she might look once more on the faces of her children and grandchildren. Recently she suffered from a sudden attack of embolism, and for some time was in danger of death. After being four days in bed the crisis passed, and she sank into a refreshing sleep. When she awoke she found herself, to her intense surprise, able to see. She called her husband and begged him to send for the scattered members of the family immediately. He did so, and when they came the aged matron recognized each of them and greeted them affectionately. Neighbors hearing of the strange event, came too, and offered their congratulations. She was glad and thankful, but was not elated. She said that she knew the change was only the temporary one that she had prayed for. So it proved. After two days the light faded, her sight became indistinct, and finally she was again in total darkness. Happily, when the sufferer from spiritual blindness is, through faith and prayer, enabled to see the face of Jesus, and accept salvation through Him, the sight is not temporary, but lasts through eternity. (II Cor. 4: 6, 18.)

BRIEF NOTES.

Mr. D. L. Moody is holding revival meetings at Portland, Ore.

The Rev. Dr. McCosh has promised to deliver a course of lectures to the students of Ohio Wesleyan University.

Rev. Thomas Harrison's labors in Philadelphia are causing as remarkable a movement as they did in New York.

The Supreme Court upholds the law prohibiting the sale of liquors within one mile of the Soldiers' Home at Grand Rapids, Mich.

The Rev. Tan Khe, moderator of the Amory Presbytery, first heard of the gospel in the shop of a village barber who was a Christian.

A colored church society has been organized at Putnam, Conn. The pastor is Thomas Sunrise, a full-blooded Indian of the Oneida tribe.

An Iowa journal reports that since the passing of the Prohibition Amendment in that State the prison population has decreased from 725 to 537.

The Rev. Allan McKay has been commissioned by the Presbyterian Board of Home Missions to take charge of the native church at Fort Wrangell, Alaska.

The Rev. Mr. Kendrick, of Columbus, Ohio, has been elected Missionary Bishop of the Episcopal Church over the jurisdiction of New Mexico and Arizona.

The new Episcopal church at Nice, which has been built principally by the contributions of Mrs. Niven, formerly of New York, is to be consecrated December 13.

Lewis E. Jackson, the energetic Secretary of the New York City Mission and Tract Society, is dead. Few persons outside the Society have any idea of the labor he was enabled to perform.

Of 81,176 arrests made by the police of New York City in 1887, 28,337 were for drunkenness, 4,708 for violation of the excise laws, and 25,638 for crimes attributable to the use of intoxicants.

The Rev. Dr. Willis Lord's death will be news of sadness in many homes in Brooklyn, Philadelphia, and other cities in which his ministrations are gratefully remembered. He was eighty years of age.

A contemporary recommends the phonograph to the use of clergymen. It thinks that, if a clergyman could hear himself preach once in a while, he might notice faults that he would take pains to correct.

Mrs. H. Tudor, of Baltimore W. C. T. U., sends each week to the Maryland Prisoners' Aid Association 400 copies of a *Gospel Letter*, that are distributed in such a way that about 1,200 prisoners can read them. The chaplain speaks hopefully of the results.

The convention of Christian Workers at Detroit spent five days in earnest discussion of evangelistic methods, and in hearing suggestions from experienced evangelists. It is believed that the winter's work will prove much more aggressive as the result of the convention.

The Rev. E. P. Hammond's meetings for children, at Detroit, were much blessed. The evangelists at the convention assisted in the after-meetings, and over two hundred children professed conversion. Mr. Hammond is now holding children's services at Jackson, Mich.

Mr. W. K. Snider, the railway conductor evangelist, preached on a recent Sunday in the Methodist Church, Owen Sound, Canada, to a crowded house. Mr. Snider has become a noted personage, "who runs his trains all the week, and speaks three or four times each Sunday."

The National Sabbath Union of the United States will hold its first convention in Washington, D. C., December 11-13. The themes for discussion are: National Sabbath Reform; Sabbath Laws and Civil Liberty; The Sabbath of our Foreign Population; The Sabbath and the Labor Problem. For further information address the Secretary, Rev. J. H. Knowles, 71 Bible House, New York.

THE WORD A SWORD.

A New Sermon by Pastor C. H. Spurgeon.

"For the word of God is quick, and powerful, and sharper than any two-edged sword, piercing even to the dividing assunder of soul and spirit, and of the joints and marrow, and is a discerner of the thoughts and intents of the heart." Heb. 4 : 12.

Different Interpretations of the Passage—Applies to Christ and the Bible—Men Who Separate the Two—I. The Qualities of the Word—A Quick or Living Word—Alive and Imparting Life—Powerful or Active—Tested by Personal Experience—By Its Power on Others—Cutting—Piercing—Discriminating—II. Lessons from the Qualities—The Book to be Reverenced—Get Life from It—And Power—And Discernment.

THOSE who are fond of a labyrinth of exposition will find a maze, perplexing to the last degree, if they will read the various commentators and expositors upon this verse. This is the question: By the Word of God, are we here to understand the Incarnate Word, the Divine Logos, who was in the beginning with God; or does the passage relate to this inspired Book, and to the Gospel, which is the kernel of it, as it is set forth in the preaching of the truth in the power of the Holy Ghost? It is a happy circumstance if we can see a way to agree with all those who did not themselves agree. But I have been greatly instructed by the mere fact that it should be difficult to know whether in this passage the Holy Ghost is speaking of the Christ of God, or the Book of God. This shows us a great truth, which we might not otherwise have so clearly noted. How much that can be said of the Lord Jesus may be also said of the inspired volume!

This I like to think of, because there are some nowadays who deny every doctrine of revelation, and yet, forsooth, they praise the Christ. The Teacher is spoken of in the most flattering style, and then His teaching is rejected, except so far as it may coincide with the philosophy of the moment. They talk about Jesus, while

The Real Jesus,

namely, His gospel, and His inspired Word, they cast away. I believe I do but correctly describe them when I say that, like Judas, they betray the Son of man with a kiss. They even go so far as to cry up the names of the doctrines, though they use them in a different sense, that they may deceive. They talk of loyalty to Christ, and reverence for the Sermon on the Mount; but they use vain words. I am charged with sowing suspicion. I do sow it, and desire to sow it. Too many Christian people are content to hear anything so long as it is put forth by a clever man, in a taking manner; I want them to try the spirits, whether they be of God, for many false prophets have gone into the world.

Christ and his Word must go together. What is true of the Christ is here predicated both of him and his Word. Behold, this day the everlasting gospel has Christ within it. It is only because Jesus is not dead that the Word becomes living and effectual, "and sharper than any two-edged sword"; for, if you leave Christ out of it, you have left out

Its Vitality and Power.

As I have told you that we will not have Christ without the Word, so neither will we have the Word without Christ. If you leave Christ out of Scripture, you have left out the essential truth which it is written to declare. Ay, if you leave out of it Christ as a Substitute, Christ in His death, you have left out of it all that is living and powerful.

Oh, it is a sad thing to have to stand in any house of prayer and listen to the preaching, and then have to cry, "They have taken away my Lord, and I know not where they have laid Him!" Rest assured that they have laid Him in a tomb. You may be quite certain of that. They have put Him away as a dead thing, and to them He is as good as dead. True believer, you may comfort your heart with this recollection, that He will rise again. He cannot be holden by the bonds of death in any sense; and though His own church should bury Him, and lay the huge lid of the most enormous sarcophagus of heresy upon Him, the Redeemer will rise again, and His truth with Him, and He and His Word will live and reign together for ever.

I. First let me speak concerning

The Qualities of the Word

of God. It is "quick and powerful, and sharper than any two-edged sword." The Word of God is said to be "*quick*." I am sorry the translators have used that word, because it is apt to be mistaken as meaning speedy, and that is not the meaning at all; it means alive, or living. "Quick" is the old English word for alive, and so we read of the "quick and dead." The Word of God is alive. This is a living Book. This is a mystery which only living men, quickened by the Spirit of God, will fully comprehend. Take up any other book except the Bible, and there may be a measure of power in it, but there is not that indescribable vitality in it which breathes, and speaks, and pleads, and conquers in the case of this sacred volume. No other writing has within it a heavenly life whereby it works miracles, and imparts life to its reader.

It is a living and incorruptible seed. It moves, it stirs itself, it lives, it communes with living men as a living Word. Solomon saith concerning it, "When thou goest, it shall lead thee; when thou sleepest, it shall keep thee; and when thou awakest,

It Shall Talk With Thee."

Have you never known what that means? Why, the Book has wrestled with me; the Book has smitten me; the Book has comforted me; the Book has smiled on me; the Book has frowned on me; the Book has clasped my hand; the Book has warmed my heart. The Book weeps with me, and sings with me; it whispers to me, and it preaches to me; it maps my way, and holds up my goings; it was to me the Young Man's Best Companion, and it is still my Morning and Evening Chaplain. It is a live Book; all over alive; from its first chapter to its last word it is full of a strange, mystic vitality, which makes it have pre-eminence over every other writing for every living child of God.

See, my brothers, *our* words, *our* books, our spoken or our printed words by-and-by die out. How many books there are which nobody will ever read now because they are out of date! There are many books that I could read profitably when I was a youth, but they would teach me nothing now. There are also certain religious works which I could read with pleasure during the first ten years of my spiritual life; but I should never think of reading them now, any more than I should think of reading the "a-b ab," and the "b-a ba," of my childhood. Christian experience causes us to outgrow the works which were the class-books of our youth. "The grass withereth, and the flower thereof falleth away: but the word of the Lord

Endureth Forever."

Its vitality is such as it can impart to its readers. Hence, you will often find, when you converse with revelation, that if you yourself are dead when you begin to read, it does not matter; you will be quickened as you peruse it. You need not bring life *to* the Scripture; you shall draw life *from* the Scripture. Oftentimes a single verse has made us start up, as Lazarus came forth at the call of the Lord Jesus. When our soul has been faint, and ready to die, a single word applied to the heart by the Spirit of God has aroused us; for it is a quickening as well as a living Word. Plants unknown in certain regions have suddenly sprung from the soil; the seeds have been wafted on the winds, carried by birds, or washed ashore by the waves of the sea. So vital are seeds that they live and grow wherever they are borne; and even after lying deep in the soil for centuries, when the upturning spade has brought them to the surface, they have germinated at once. Thus is it with the Word of God: it liveth and abideth for ever.

In our text the Word is said to be "*powerful*" or "active." Perhaps "energetic" is the best rendering, or, almost as well, "effectual." Holy Scripture is full of power and energy. Oh the majesty of the Word of God! Have you never noticed, when persons are converted, that they almost always attribute it to some text that was quoted in the sermon? It is God's Word, not our comment on God's Word, which saves souls. The Word of God is

Powerful For All Sacred Ends.

How powerful it is to convince men of sin! We have seen the self-righteous turned inside out by the revealed truth of God. Nothing else could have brought home to them such unpleasant truth, and compelled them to see themselves as in a clear mirror, but the searching Word of God. How powerful it is for conversion! It comes on board a man, and without asking any leave from him, it just puts its hand on the helm, and turns him around in the opposite direction from that in which he was going before; and the man gladly yields to the irresistible force which influences his understanding and rules his will. The Word of God is that by which sin is slain, and grace is born in the heart. It is the light which brings life with it.

How active and energetic it is, when the soul is convinced of sin, in bringing it forth into gospel liberty! We have seen men shut up as in the devil's own dungeon, and we have tried to get them free. We have shaken the bars of iron, but we could not tear them out, so as to set the captives at liberty. But the Word of the Lord is a great breaker of bolts and bars. It not only casts down the strongholds of doubt, but it cuts off the head of Giant Despair. No cell or cellar in Doubting Castle can hold a soul in bondage when the Word of God, which is the master-key, is once put to its true use, and made to throw back bolts of despondency. It is living and energetic for encouragement and enlargement. O beloved, what a wonderful power the Gospel has to bring us comfort! It brought us to Christ at the first, and it still leads us to look to Christ till we grow like Him. God's children are not sanctified by legal methods, but by gracious ones. The Word of God, the Gospel of Christ, is exceedingly powerful in promoting sanctification, and bringing about that whole-hearted consecration which is both our duty and our privilege.

The Word of God, then, is quick and powerful in our own personal experience, and we shall find it to be so if we use it in laboring to bless our fellow-men. Dear brethren, if you seek to do good in this sad world, and want

A Powerful Weapon

to work with, stick to the Gospel, the living Gospel, the old, old Gospel. There is a power in it sufficient to meet the sin and death of human nature. All the thoughts of men, use them as earnestly as you may, will be like tickling Leviathan with a straw. Nothing can get through the scales of this monster but the Word of God. This is a weapon made of sterner stuff than steel, and it will cut through coats of mail. Nothing can resist it. "Where the word of a king is, there is power." About the Gospel, when spoken with the Holy Ghost sent down from heaven, there is the same omnipotence as there was in the Word of God when in the beginning He spoke to the primeval darkness saying, "Let there be light," and there was light.

Next, the apostle tells us that this Word is *cutting*. "Cutting" would be as correct a translation as that of our own version: it is "more cutting than any two-edged sword." I suppose the apostle means by the description "two-edged" that it is all edge. A sword with two edges has no blunt side: it cuts both this way and that. The revelation of God given us in Holy Scripture is edge all over. It is alive in every part, and in every part keen to cut the conscience and wound the heart. Have you never heard of one who heard read, as the lesson for the Sabbath-day, that long chapter of names, wherein it is written that each patriarch lived so many hundred years, "*and he died*"? Thus it ends the notice of the long life of Methuselah with "and he died." The repetition of the words, "and he died," woke the thoughtless hearer to a sense of his mortality, and led to his coming to the Saviour.

Anyhow, any bit of Holy writ is very

Dangerous to Play With,

nd many a man has been wounded by the criptures when he has been idly, or even pro-anely, reading them. Doubters have meant to reak the Word to pieces, and it has broken hem. Yea, fools have taken up portions, and tudied them, on purpose to ridicule them, and hey have been sobered and vanquished by that hich they repeated in sport. There was one who ent to hear Mr. Whitefield—a member of the Hell-fire Club," a desperate fellow. He stood p at the next meeting of his abominable asso-iates, and he delivered Mr. Whitefield's sermon ith wonderful accuracy, imitating his very one and manner. In the middle of his exhor-ation he converted himself, and came to a sud-en pause, sat down broken-hearted, and con-essed the power of the gospel. That club was issolved. That remarkable convert was Mr. Thorpe, of Bristol, whom God so greatly used fterwards in the salvation of others.

There is no sin-killer like the Word of God. Wherever it comes, it comes as a sword, and in-icts death upon evil. Sometimes when we are raying that we may feel

The Power of the Word,

e hardly know what we are praying for. I saw venerable brother the other day, and he said o me: "I remember speaking with you when ou were nineteen or twenty years of age, and never forgot what you said to me. I had been raying with you in the prayer-meeting that God would give us the Holy Ghost to the full, nd you said to me afterwards, 'My dear broth-r, do you know what you asked God for?' I nswered, 'Yes.' But you very solemnly said o me, 'The Holy Ghost is the Spirit of judg-ment and the Spirit of burning, and few are repared for the inward conflict which is meant y these two words.'" My good old friend told me that at the time he did not understand what meant, but thought me a singular youth. "Ah!" said he, "I see it now, but it is only by painful experience that I have come to the full omprehension of it." Yes, when Christ comes, He comes not to send peace on the earth, but sword; and that sword begins at home, in our wn souls—killing, cutting, breaking in pieces.

But I want you to notice, next, that it has a urther quality: *it is piercing*. While it has an dge like a sword, it has also

A Point Like a Rapier.

Piercing even to the dividing asunder of soul nd spirit. The difficulty with some men's earts is to get at them. In fact, there is no piritually penetrating the heart of any natural man except by this piercing instrument, the Word of God. But the rapier of revelation will o through anything. Men may wrap them-elves up in prejudice, but this rapier can find ut the joints of their harness; they may re-olve not to believe, and may feel content in heir self-righteousness, but this piercing wea-on will find its way.

And next, the Word of God is said to be dis-riminating. It divides asunder soul and spirit. Nothing else could do that, for the division is ifficult. In a great many ways writers have ried to describe the difference between soul nd spirit; but I question whether they have ucceeded. No doubt it is very admirable to ay, "the soul is the life of the natural man, nd the spirit the life of the regenerate or spirit-al man." But it is one thing to define and uite another thing to divide. We will not at-empt to solve this metaphysical problem. God's Word comes in, and it shows man the difference etween that which is of the soul, and that hich is of the spirit; that which is of man, and hat which is of God; that which is of grace, nd that which is of nature.

Many times, I do not doubt, dear brothers, ou have found comfort in the discerning power f the Word. Unkind lips have found great ault with you; you have been trying to do hat you could for the Lord, and an enemy has andered you, and then it has been a delight to emember that the Master discerns your motive. Holy Scripture has made you sure of this by the way in which it understood and commended you. He discerns the true object of your heart, and never misinterprets you; and this has in-spired you with a firm resolve to be the faithful servant of so just a Lord. No slander will sur-vive the judgment-seat of Christ.

II. I have been all this while over the first part of the discourse. I have only a minute or two just to show one or two

Lessons We Ought to Gather

from the qualities of the Word of God that I have described. The first is this. Brothers and sisters, *let us greatly reverence the Word of God.* If it be all this, let us read it, study it, prize it, and make it the man of our right hand. And you that are not converted, I do pray you treat the Bible with a holy love and reverence, and read it with the view of finding Christ and His salvation in it. Augustine used to say that the Scriptures are the swaddling-bands of the child Christ Jesus; while you are unrolling the bands I trust you will meet with Him.

Next, dear friends, let us, whenever we feel ourselves dead, and especially in prayer, get close to the Word, for the Word of God is alive. I do not find that gracious men always pray alike. Who could? When you have nothing to say to God, let Him say something to you.

The Best Private Devotion

is half of searching Scripture, in which God speaks to us, and the other half of prayer and praise, in which we speak to God. When thou art dead, turn to that Word which still lives.

Next, whenever we feel weak in our duties, let us go to the Word of God, and the Christ in the Word, for power; and this will be the best of power. The power of our natural abilities, the power of our acquired knowledge, the power of our gathered experience, all these may be vanity, but the power which is in the Word will prove effectual. Get thou up from the cistern of thy failing strength to the fountain of omni-potence; for they that drink here, while the youths shall faint and be weary, and the young men shall utterly fall, shall run, and not be weary, and shall walk, and not faint.

Next, if you need as a minister, or a worker, anything that will cut your hearers to the heart, go to this Book for it. I say this because I have known preachers try to use very cutting words of their own. God save us from that! When our hearts grow hot, and our words are apt to be sharp as a razor, let us remember that the wrath of man worketh not the righteousness of God. Let us not attempt to carry on Christ's War with the weapons of Satan. There is noth-ing so cutting as the Word of God. Keep to that. I believe also that one of the best ways of convincing men of error is, not so much to denounce the error, as to proclaim the truth more clearly. If a stick is very crooked, and you wish to prove that it is so, get a straight one, and quietly lay it down by its side, and when men look they will surely see the differ-ence. The Word of God has a very keen edge about it, and all the cutting words you want you had better borrow therefrom.

Next, if we want to discriminate at any time between the soul and the spirit, and the joints and marrow, let us go to the Word of God for discrimination. We

Need to Use the Word

of God just now on several subjects. There is that matter of holiness, upon which one saith one thing, and another, another. Never mind what they all say; go to the Book, for this is the umpire on all questions. Amidst the controver-sies of the day about a thousand subjects, keep to this Book, and it will guide you unerringly.

And lastly, since this Book is meant to be a discerner or critic of the thoughts and intents of the heart, *let the Book criticise us.* When you have issued a new volume from the press—which you do every day, for every day is a new treatise from the press of life—take it to this great critic, and let the Word of God judge it. If the Word of God approves you, you are approved; if the Word of God disapproves you, you are disapproved. Have friends praised you? They may be your enemies in so doing. Have other observers abused you? They may be wrong or right—let the Book decide. A man of one Book—if that Book is the Bible—is a *man*, for he is a man of God. Cling you to the living Word, and let the gospel of your fathers, let the gospel of the martyrs, let the gospel of the Re-formers, let the gospel of the blood-washed multitude before the throne of God, the gospel of our Lord Jesus Christ, be your gospel, and none but *that*, and it will save you and make you the means of saving others.

GEMS FROM NEW BOOKS.

DEGENERATE ROMAN SONS.*

WHEN the son of Fulvius was found in the conspiracy of Catiline, the displeased father rep-rehended him sharply, saying, "I did not beget you for Catiline, but for your country." This is the language of God to His children: "I gave you not bodies and souls to serve sin with, but to serve Me with." Our bodies were not formed to be the instruments of unrighteous actions, nor our souls the gloomy abode of foul spirits. The Roman censors took such an utter dislike to the debauched son of Africanus, that they refused to let him wear a ring on which his father's likeness was engraven; alleging, "that he who was so unlike the father's person, was unworthy to wear the father's picture." Thus God will never grant any to enjoy the love of Christ in heaven, who are destitute of the like-ness of Christ on earth.

A Present Rejected.

Pharmaces, the son of Mithridates, the King of Pontus, sending a crown to Cæsar at the time he was in rebellion against him, he refused the present, saying, "Let him first lay down his rebellion, and then I will receive his crown." There are many who set a crown of glory on the head of Christ by a good profession; and yet plait a crown of thorns upon His head by an evil conversation. By the words of our mouth we may affect to adore religion; but it is by the works of our lives that we adorn religion.

The Martyr Spirit.

It is reported of Hooper, the martyr, that when he was going to suffer, a certain person addressed him, saying, "O, sir, take care of your-self, for life is sweet and death is bitter." "Ah, I know that," replied he; "but the life to come is full of more sweetness than this mortal life; and the death to come is full of more bitterness than this uncommon death." A man may suf-fer without sinning, but he cannot sin without suffering. When Philip inquired of Demos-thenes, whether he was afraid to lose his head, he answered, "No; for if I do lose it, the Athen-ians will bestow an immortal one upon me." He that loses a base life *for* Christ, shall here-after find a better life *in* Christ.

A Persian Nobleman's Heroism.

It is reported of Hormisdas, a nobleman of Persia, who, being degraded of all his promo-tions because he would not change his profes-sion, that afterward his persecutors restored them all again, and solicited him to deny Christ. But he rent his purple robe, and laid all his honors at the feet of the Emperor, saying, "If you restore me these honors with an intention to make me desert the Saviour, I beg leave to decline accepting them upon such conditions." Good man! he thought, and that justly, too, that Christ without worldly honor, was better than worldly honor without Christ. It is re-corded concerning one of the martyrs, that when he was going to the stake, a nobleman besought him in a compassionate manner to take care of his soul. "So I will," he replied, "for I give my body to be burned, rather than have my soul defiled." How many professors are there who would rather have their sinful self satisfied than crucified!

A Feast Trampled On.

Plato entertaining a few friends at an elegant-ly spread table, Diogenes, the famous cynic

* From "The Nonsuch Professor." By the Rev. William Secker. With an Introduction by the Rev. T. L. Cuyler, D. D. 367 pages. Published by *Robert Carter & Brothers* 530 Broadway, New York.

Mrs. Morton, Wife of the Vice-President Elect.

The South Dome in the Yosemite.

philosopher, coming in at the same time, trampled upon it, saying, "I trample upon the pride of Plato." To whom Plato replied, "Yea, but with greater pride in Diogenes." They are fittest to find fault in whom there is no fault to be found. There is no removing blots from the paper by laying upon them a blurred finger. What do you get by throwing stones at your enemy's windows while you own children look out at the casements? He that blows into a heap of dust is in danger of putting out his own eyes.

Leanness and Victory.

It is said of the Lacedæmonians, who were a poor and homely people, that they offered lean sacrifices to their gods, and that the Athenians, who were a wealthy people, offered fat and costly sacrifices; and yet in their wars the former had always the mastery of the latter. Whereupon they went to the oracle to learn the reason why those should speed worst who gave most. The oracle returned this answer to them: "The Lacedæmonians were a people who *gave their hearts* to their gods; but the Athenians gave only gifts to their gods." Thus a heart without a gift is better than a gift without a heart. Religion is a sacrifice, but the heart is the altar upon which it must be offered. As the body is at the command of the head which rules it, so should the soul be at the command of God, who gives it. For a man to take his body to the service of God, and leave his soul behind him, is as if a person should send his garments stuffed with straw instead of making a personal appearance.

MRS. LEVI P. MORTON.

(See Portrait.)

VICE-PRESIDENT-ELECT MORTON, whose portrait appeared in this journal on July 26, soon after his nomination to the office to which he has now been elected, is said to be the most wealthy man who ever filled the Vice-Presidential chair. Popular rumor, which probably does not exaggerate in this case, places the amount of his fortune at twenty million dollars. He will, therefore, if he so desires, be able to entertain during his term on the most magnificent scale, and his wife, whose portrait we now give, is fully qualified to render those hospitalities as charming as they may be costly.

Mrs. Morton is a lady of dignified presence. She is above the average height, and is graceful of figure. Her countenance is pale, her features are finely formed, and her eyes, which are large and blue, are expressive of the amiability and refinement of her nature. But for her gray hair, Time has dealt kindly with Mrs. Morton. She is the mother of six children, of whom the only boy is dead. The eldest daughter is fourteen years old, and the youngest member of the Morton establishment is a baby. The family belong to the Protestant-Episcopal Church. Mrs. Morton's maiden name was Anna Livingstone Street, and she is a native of Poughkeepsie, N. Y., where her father was a lawyer in practice, and where she was educated. Subsequently her family left Poughkeepsie and made their residence in New York, where Mr. Morton made her acquaintance, and had the good fortune to win her for his wife. Mrs. Morton has been quite a traveller, and is well-read and accomplished. Her musical gifts are said to be unusually developed for an amateur. Washington society is to be congratulated on the acquisition the election has given it at the expense of New York.

THE SOUTH DOME IN THE YOSEMITE.

(See Illustration.)

BELOW the Yosemite Falls, the most conspicuous objects in the landscape are the gigantic rocks to which the names of North and South Domes are given. The South Dome has so far defied all efforts of man to scale it. It rises almost perpendicularly from the plains, and appears to have been split by some convulsion of nature, leaving a sheer surface on one side, with not a foothold nor projecting ridge. The presence of enormous rock avalanches at the foot of the mountain supports this hypothesis, they evidently having remained to this day in the place where they fell. If the side of the mountain had been worn to its present condition by aqueous erosion or any other process, there would probably have been much smaller débris found at its base. The state of the rocks and bowlders which now lie between the Domes and the river Merced, also precludes the idea of their having been subject to the wearing operation of rushing torrents of water.

A recent visitor gives a vivid description of these and other mountains which are in the Yosemite region. He says: "The peculiar and unique feature of the valley seems to me to be the height and boldness of the cliffs, which spring out from the mountain-sides like sentinels to watch and ward over the secrets of the gorge. The brush of the painter, charged with the truest colors and guided by the finest hand and eye, could never do justice to these cliffs."

MARY HARCOURT'S REFUGE.

(See illustration on page 781.)

THE snow was falling heavily, and the roads were heavy and soft. It was bad walking in the country districts, for the snow had filled up the tracks left by the wagons, and it was next to impossible to avoid stepping into them with a suddenness which was not unlikely to cause a fall. Mary Harcourt found this out as she tramped along, shielding her baby as well as she could from the cutting blasts of wind and the driving snow with her cloak.

Mary was going home. That thought was all which kept her moving. She pined for some shelter. At the city boarding-house where she had spent the last six months, she was told that the gentleman who had paid her bills up to three weeks before had not paid anything since. She had better look him up. Poor Mary tried to look him up, but failed. He had left the city, deserting the woman who had loved and trusted him to her shame. How she wished she had never seen him! How she wished herself back in the comfortable situation which her relations with him had caused her to lose! She had to face the hard-hearted boarding-house keeper, and tell her that she was going to look for employment, and to ask for patience with the bill.

"You cannot get employment, and, if you could, you could not attend to it with that baby on your hands," the woman had said. "I cannot afford to go on keeping you. I suppose I'll have to lose the three weeks' board, though it's a heavy loss to me; but I won't go on making bad worse. You must go."

Poor Mary felt the woman was right. It would be impossible to get employment. She must turn out, and it was winter too! Where could she go? A few friends she had in the days before her sin and her trouble, but there were none now to whom she could apply for help or shelter. The thought of suicide crossed her mind, as it has done the minds of so many others similarly circumstanced, but though her moral principles were sapped, and the dread of offending God, which in her girlhood would have preserved her from the temptation, was now gone, her natural timidity and shrinking from pain of any kind stood between her and self-destruction.

The thought of her widowed mother and the home of her childhood came up in her mind. Yes, that was the only hope. Her mother knew nothing of her trouble. Mary could not bring herself to write about it, and she had put the disagreeable duty off so long as she was cared

, as she had always t off everything dis- eeable all through her . The mother was a us woman, rather rn, and in training ry she had been strict, not severe. The poor man dreaded facing with her shameful ry; but what else ld she do? If her own ther would not shelter , to whom could she ? So Mary Harcourt, h empty pockets and breaking heart, was mping through the w, along the heavy ds, mile after mile, to- rd her widowed moth- s home.

t would not do to nk of that coming in- view. Mary drove the ught out of her mind. e needed stimulus, or would sink down by roadside from sheer igue. She told herself t she was going home, d she thought of the amber she had occu- d as a child, and that ught gave her courage d strength to press on. t, when at last she ne near the house, she pped. Courage failed . Between her and comfort for which pined lay the dread- ordeal of telling her ry to her mother. It d to be met, however; d Mary opened the or and went in.

Mrs. Harcourt jumped from her chair in azement as Mary ered. She could not ve been more startled if Mary had been an parition. Her look of astonished inquiry, d her exclamation of "Why, Mary!" was to expected, but not that horror-stricken, almost ce, gaze at the burden Mary carried, which lowed. Evidently the old woman needed no planation. She understood the situation at a nce. The terrified, pleading look Mary bent her mother's face awakened no response, the rn, hard features showed no sign of relent- , and Mary sank down on a chair in sheer ror at her mother's look. A few minutes er, and the woman and child were out again the snow, the former cowering like a beaten g, under the bitter words with which her ther had upbraided her for bringing disgrace the family name.

What are you doing here, my good woman? u will make yourself ill." The words were ken by a clergyman to Mary Harcourt as she shivering under a tree, and with a look of er despair on her face.

I am trying to get courage to kill myself."

Come with me," said the clergyman, briefly. Mary rose, and followed him to his home.

"My love," said the clergyman, when he had n his charge deposited by his kitchen fire, ing almost ravenously the food given to her, d had found his wife in the nursery, "go down the kitchen and find out what is wrong with oman there. A bad case, I fear. Get her to you her story, and then come and tell me at we can do."

That night the clergyman, who had encoun- ed scoffers, infidels, and opponents of all ds in his time, had the most difficult of all encounters in controversy. He had set self to convince a Christian woman, proud of her good name and unblemished character, that forgiveness and Christian charity are duties, no matter what the wrong-doing may have been. He failed miserably until he said, "Well, Mrs. Harcourt, let us pray about it." When they rose from their knees the old woman said, "Bring her back, sir; I see I was wrong. I'll be good to the poor creature, for the dear Lord's sake. God forgive me for my hardness: He has not been like that to me."

Mary Harcourt's Interview With Her Mother.

ESCAPED FROM THE MORMONS.

A Life Story: By Mrs. Stenhouse,

For More than Twenty-five Years the Wife of a Mormon Missionary and Elder.

Early Days.

THE story which I propose to tell is a plain, unexaggerated record of facts which have come immediately under my notice, or which *I have myself personally experienced*. Much that to the reader may seem altogether incredible, would to a Mormon mind appear simply a matter of ordinary every-day occurrence, with which every one in Utah is supposed to be perfectly familiar. The reader must please remember that I am not telling—as so many writers have told in newspaper correspondence and sensational stories—the hasty and incorrect statements and opinions gleaned during a short visit to Salt Lake City, but my own experience—the story of a faith, strange, wild, and terrible it may be, but which was once so intimately enwoven with all my associations that it became a part of my very existence itself; and facts, the too true reality of which there are living witnesses by hundreds, and even thousands, who could attest if only they would.

I was born in the year 1829, in St. Heliers, Jersey. From my earliest recollection I was favorably disposed to religious influences, having been blessed with Christian parents, and surrounded by the sweet and holy influences of a Christian home, and when fourteen years of age I became a member of the Baptist Church, of which my father and mother were members.

My childhood passed away without the occurrence of any events which would be worthy of mention, although, of course, my mind was even then receiving that religious bias which afterwards led me to adopt the faith of the Latter-day Saints. Like most girls in their teens, I had a natural love of dress—a weakness, if such it be, of the sex generally. I was not extravagant, for that I could not be; but thirty years ago members of dissenting churches were more staid in their dress and demeanor, and were less of the world, I think, than they are to-day. In plainness of dress the Methodists and Baptists much resembled the Quakers.

My girlish weakness caused me to be the subject of many a reprimand from older church members, who were rather strict in their views. I mention these apparent trifles, not because I attach any importance to them in themselves, but because similar religious tendencies and similar weaknesses were almost universally found to be the causes which induced men and women to join the Mormon Church. From among Roman Catholics, who place unquestioning confidence in their priesthood, and also from among persons predisposed to infidelity, came few, if any, converts to Mormonism. But it was from the religiously inclined, the Evangelical Protestants of the Old World, that the greater number of proselytes came.

But to return to my story. I was one of the younger members of a large family; and when I thought of the future, I readily saw that if I desired a position in life I should have to make it for myself; and this I resolved to do, it being apparent to us all that our dear father, who had been an invalid for many years, was failing.

An English lady, the wife of a captain in the British army, to whom I had confided my aspirations, proposed, although I was not yet fifteen years of age—to take me with her to France, in the temporary capacity of governess to her children, assuring me, at the same time, that she would advance my interests in every possible way after our arrival. This lady and her husband were as kind to me as my own parents could have been; and soon after our arrival in France they procured for me a situation in one of the best schools in St. Brieux, called the Maison-Martin, where, young as I was, I engaged myself to teach the young ladies fancy needlework and embroidery, as well as to give lessons in English. Some of the elder girls, I soon found, were further advanced in fancy needlework and other matters than I was myself. This, of course, I did not tell them; but to supply my deficiency I spent many a midnight hour in study and in preparing myself to give the advanced instruction which would be required by my pupils on the following day. For some time after I began my work as teacher in that school, I spent the whole of my salary in paying for private lessons to keep me in advance of my pupils. It was for a while a severe task and a strain upon my youthful energies; but I have never since regretted it, as it gave an impulse to my mind that has remained with me through life.

I had not been more than six months in my situation, when the parents of one of the pupils objected to the school retaining a Protestant teacher, and I was consequently given to understand that unless I consented to be instructed, if nothing more, in the Roman Catholic faith, I could not remain in my present position. This was my first experience of that religious intolerance of which I afterwards saw so much. The principal of the establishment, however, being very kindly disposed towards me, advised me to submit, and it was finally agreed that I should be allowed twelve months for instruction and consideration.

During this probationary year I attended mass every morning from 7 to 8 o'clock, and was present at vespers at least three times a week Every Saturday morning I accompanied my pupils to the confessional, where I had to remain from 7 o'clock till noon; after which we returned to breakfast. On Sundays there was the usual morning mass, and after that high mass; and in the afternoon, from 2 to 4, we listened to a sermon. In addition to all these services, at which I was expected to "assist," a very interesting young priest was appointed to attend to the spiritual instruction of the young Protestant, as they called me, after school hours. He saw me frequently, but he was ill-qualified to instruct me in the Catholic faith or to remove my doubts, for he was not himself too happy in the sacerdotal robe. At first he aimed at convincing me that the apostolic priesthood vested in the fishermen of Galilee had descended in unbroken succession in the Church of Rome; but he seemed to me much more inclined for a flirtation than for argument; I thought I could at times discover something of regret on his own part at having taken holy orders, and in after years I heard that he had abandoned his ecclesiastical profession.

To the numerous stories of Catholic oppression and artifice in undermining Protestants and seducing them from their faith, I cannot add my own testimony. Those among whom I lived very naturally desired that I should be instructed in their religion, and join the Church to which they belonged; but their bearing towards me was ever kind and respectful; although when the twelve months of probation had expired, I found myself as much attached to the religion of my childhood as ever, and had in consequence to resign my situation. I had made many warm friends in the school, and none were kinder to me than the principal, who proved her attachment by finding for me a lucrative situation in a wealthy private family.

My new position was a decided advance in social life. The family consisted of husband and wife, two children, the husband's brother, and an elderly uncle. The little girls were, when I first knew them, of the ages of five and seven respectively. The young gentleman alluded to—the husband's brother—had been educated for the Church, but when the proper time came, had refused to take orders; the uncle was a fine old gentleman, a retired general in the French army, and a bachelor. Altogether they formed as happy a domestic circle as I had ever known. The position which I occupied among them was that of governess and English teacher to the two little girls.

My young charges during the first year made rapid progress, which was very gratifying to the family, and secured for me their good-will and interest. Had I been their nearest relative, I could not have received more respect and consideration from them. One member of the circle alone seemed to be entirely indifferent to my presence; this was the brother of Monsieur D. Though I had lived in the same house a year, and had sat at the same table every day, scarcely a word had passed between us beyond a formal salutation.

The young gentleman was very handsome, and when conversing with others his manner was extremely fascinating. I did not believe that I particularly desired his attentions, but his indifference annoyed me—for I had never before been treated with such coldness, and I determined to become as frigid and formal as he could be himself. This formal acquaintanceship continued for two years, and I persuaded myself that I had become altogether indifferent to the presence of my icicle, while at the same time all the other members of the family increased in their manifestations of attachment to me. However, several things occurred during the second year, which puzzled me not a little. Some unknown person availed himself of every opportunity on which presents could be made. I frequently found myself the recipient of anonymous gifts, chiefly flowers.

I naturally felt embarrassed by these delicate attentions, and determined to take Madame D. into my confidence. She, little thinking that the mysterious donor would prove to be her husband's brother, told me not to worry, because I was with friends who loved me.

In time the secret was solved; one little attention led to another, until at the end of three years I found myself the *fiancé* of the wealthy Constant D. Madame D. was opposed to my marriage with her brother-in-law, as she desired that he should marry one of her own wealthy cousins of the old *noblesse* of France. She treated me, notwithstanding, with great kindness, and confined her opposition to persuading me not to listen to her brother's suit; but finding opposition to his wishes ineffectual, she finally consented to our engagement, which took place in the following winter.

I loved the French people, and was pleased with their polite manners, but I was not French in character; and though the prospect before me of an alliance with a wealthy and noble family was certainly pleasant, and I was greatly attached to my *fiancé*, my mind was considerably agitated upon the subject of marriage, as it had before been occupied with religion.

During my sojourn in France I had frequently questioned myself whether I had not done wrong in remaining absent for so many years from my home and from communion with the church of my childhood, and I had always looked forward to the time when I should return to them again. To this occasional self-examination was now added another cause of anxiety, produced by the thought of marriage with a person of a different faith. Marriage, to me, was the all-important event in a woman's life, and some mysterious presentiment seemed to forewarn me that marriage in *my* life was to be more than an ordinary episode—though little did I then dream that it would have a polygamic shaping.

My young ambition alone had led me to France. I had aspired to an honorable social position, and had found both it and also devoted friends. Sometimes I felt that I could not relinquish what I had gained; at other times I yearned for the associations of my childhood, and the guiding-hand of earlier friends. The conflict in my mind was often painful. My early prejudices, and the teachings of those around me, induced me to believe that the Roman Catholic religion was entirely wrong; yet, notwithstanding, while living among Catholics I saw nothing to condemn in their personal lives, but much to the contrary. In fact, Romanism fascinated me, while it utterly failed to convince my judgment.

While laboring under these most conflicting sentiments, I resolved to visit my native land, to consult with my parents about my contemplated marriage; and for that purpose I asked and obtained two months' vacation. During my residence in France, my parents had left St. Heliers, and had gone to Southampton, England. To visit them now, I had to take a sailing vessel from Portrieux to the Isle of Jersey, and thence I could take the steamer to Southampton. Monsieur and Madame D., together with the two little girls, accompanied me in their private carriage to Portrieux, a distance of forty miles, in order to confide me safely to the captain's care. As they wished me "*bon voyage*," and embraced me affectionately, Mons. D. handed me a valuable purse for pocket-money during my absence, and they all exhibited great anxiety for my welfare, saying over and over again *au revoir*, as they entered their carriage to return to their happy home—thereby implying that this was not a final adieu.

It was not necessary for me to stop in Jersey for more than a few hours, but I wanted to revisit the scenes of my childhood's happy days, and to speak again with those whom I had known and loved in early life. At St. Heliers I heard for the first time of the Latter-day Saints, or Mormons, as they were more familiarly called; but I cannot express how perfectly astonished I was when I learned that my father, mother, sisters, and one of my brothers had been converted to the new faith. It was my own brother-in-law who told me this. He himself, with my sister, were "Apostate" Mormons. They had been baptized into the Mormon Church, but became dissatisfied and abandoned it.

The St. Heliers branch of the Latter-day Saints had had a turbulent experience. Their first teachings had been a mixture of Bible texts about the last days, and arguments about the Millennium, the return of the Jews to Palestine, the Resurrection of the dead, and a new revelation, and a new prophet; but the improper conduct of some of the elders had disgusted the people with their doctrines, and the tales of wickedness which I heard were, if true, certainly sufficient to justify them in rejecting such instructors. The more I heard of this strange religion the more I was troubled; yet, as I knew my parents were devoted Christians, I could hardly believe that Mormonism was such a vile delusion and imposture as it had been represented to me, or they would never have accepted it; still it was possible that they had been led astray by the fascinations of a new religion.

In this state of mind I met in the street the wife of the Baptist minister. She greeted me affectionately, and then began at once to warn me against the Latter-day Saints. I inquired what she knew of them; and she replied that personally she knew nothing, but she believed them to be servants of the Evil One, adding, "There is a strange power with them that fascinates the people, and draws them into their meshes in spite of themselves. Let me entreat you not to go near them. Do not trust yourself at one of their meetings, or the delusion will take hold of *you* too."

"I cannot ignore Mormonism in this way," I said, "or pass it by with indifference; for my parents, whom I tenderly love, have been blinded by this delusion, and I can do no less than investigate its teachings thoroughly, and if I find it false, expose its errors, and, if possible, save my father's family from ruin." She was not convinced that this was the wisest course for me to pursue, but I resolved to attend a meeting of the Saints at once and judge for myself. My brother-in-law, when he heard of my intentions, tried to dissuade me, but, finding me determined, finally offered to escort me to the meeting-place.

What I heard on this occasion made a great impression on my mind, and set me thinking as I had never thought before. On returning to my sister's house she asked me what opinion I had now formed of the Latter-day Saints. I replied that I had not yet formed any conclusion, but that what I had heard had given me serious cause for reflection. "Oh," she said, "you have caught the Mormon fever, I see." I felt a disposition to resent this implication, but I was half afraid that, after all, my sister was right.

(*To be Continued.*)

DEATH OF SAMSON.

By Mrs. M. Baxter.

S. S. Lesson for December 16. Jud. 16: 21-31. Golden Text, Job 33: 9.

Samson's Place Among Bible Characters—Angelic Directions for his Mother—Her Sensible Argument—The Spirit Adapting His Operations to the Child Nation—Samson's Infatuation—Contrary to the Law—His Parents Accessories—Development of the Hebrew Hercules—Lion-Slaying the Usual Beginning—The Strange Mixture of Physical Strength and Moral Weakness—A Judge Whose Own Life was Wrong—A Second Infatuation—His Fall and Self-Sacrifice.

THE life of Samson is a puzzle to many of God's children. That one so impure, so rebellious, should be mentioned among the men of faith in Hebrews 11, side by side with Abel, Noah, Abraham, Moses, Joshua, David, and Samuel, shocks many readers of the Bible. But let us not forget that Rahab the harlot has her place there too, not because God would tolerate sin, but because, as soon as she knew of the true God, she put faith in Him, and God reckons "according to that a man hath, and not according to that he hath not." (II Cor. 8: 12.) "For unto whomsoever much is given, of him shall be much required: and to whom men have committed much, of him they will ask the more." (Luke 12: 43.) Samson lived in a time when the law was not enforced: "Every man did that which was right in his own eyes." (Jud. 21: 25.) He was raised up by God as a scourge to the Philistines, not as an example to Israel, and the only thing God commends in him is his faith.

After the death of Jephthah—who was a preacher as well as a warrior, and a true man of God—"the children of

Israel Did Evil Again

in the sight of the Lord; and the Lord delivered them into the hand of the Philistines forty years." God's children cannot sin without incurring the consequences: "Whosoever committeth sin is the servant of sin." (John 8: 34.) Most surely bondage and trouble follow the sins of God's children: He loves us too much to let the path of sin be an easy one. It is very touching to trace how, in the constantly recurring defection of the children of Israel, it was so frequently the Lord, and not the people, who first thought of deliverance.

"There was a certain man of Zorah, of the family of the Danites, whose name was Manoah," and he was the father of Samson. Dan means *judgment*, and it is no accident that Samson came of this tribe. In his own life, judgment followed his sin; and in his life work he executed judgment upon the Philistines. His birth was singular. He was born of godly parents, of a barren mother, who was to act as a Nazarite for his sake, and he was to be a Nazarite from his birth. There is a sweet simplicity in the description of the angel's visit to Manoah's wife, announcing that she should have a son, and afterwards to her husband. Neither of them doubted the angel's word, and Manoah prayed to the Lord for His direction as to how they should "order" the child that should be born. But the angel's answer left no direction concerning the child, but only concerning the mother. Does not God teach mothers that they need first of all to

Follow Him Closely Themselves

and then He will deal with the children? Neither Manoah nor his wife knew that the messenger was an angel of the Lord until, when they had offered a kid with a meat offering, the angel ascended in the flame of the altar. Then Manoah was afraid, but his wife shewed her common sense when she stilled his fears, and said, "If the Lord were pleased to kill us, He would not have received a burnt offering and a meat offering at our hands; neither would He have shewed us all these things." God's word came to pass: "the woman bare a son, and called his name Samson, and the Lord blessed him." No doubt there was some real acquaintance with God which began in early life. "And the Spirit of the Lord began to move him at times in the camp of Dan between Zorah and Eshtaol." In the Old Testament, the Spirit of the Lord came upon men in a way which accorded with the light they had upon the mind of God. The Spirit of the Lord came upon Bezaleel "to devise curious works, in gold, and in silver, and in brass," &c., for the tabernacle. (Ex. 35: 30-34.) He came upon Moses for rule, upon Gideon and Jephthah for war (Jud. 6: 34: 11: 29), and upon Samson He came as strength. Probably his parents had great joy in him. As a child, there was promise of real piety, but as the strength of manhood developed, a strong self-will developed also. Oh, if he had possessed the obedience of his father with his own faith, what a glorious instrument he might have been! He was

Born to Be a Leader,

and was no doubt recognized as such. When he was a young man, he was attracted by a Philistine woman of Timnath. He did not conceal his affection from his parents; there was no attempt to deceive them, and although they objected to the match, Samson prevailed upon them to make overtures for him to her parents. His parents knew that this was directly against the command of God, and yet they lent themselves to do Samson's will! Samson's plea that he should marry this woman was no higher than this, "She pleaseth me well." Is this the motive of a man of God? "Christ pleased not himself." (Rom. 15: 3.) An unequal yoking, oh how it grieves God, and what misery it brings to hearts and homes! But Samson, although he was not a consecrated man, was God's chosen instrument to judge Israel, and all he did must have its effect for good or ill upon the people. God overrules what He cannot bless, and He did so in this instance. "He sought an occasion against the Philistines."

Like David, Samson's first manifestation of strength was in the slaying of a lion, when the Spirit of the Lord came upon him. He afterwards perceived, in passing by, that a swarm of bees had formed a honeycomb within the carcase, and he asked a riddle of the Philistines for a wager—"Out of the eater came forth meat, and out of the strong came forth sweetness." They had found out his weak point, how this man who was so strong by faith in God, was weak in the point where he had sinned in marrying an unbeliver. It was his wife who worried out his secret, and gave the Philistines the advantage over him. This so stirred up his wrath that he slew thirty of them. But his domestic life must be a troubled one, his marriage, which could not be blest of God, was broken by man, and his wife given to another. This was God's message to him personally, and, at the same time, an incentive to revenge himself on God's enemies. He was thoroughly roused, and, single handed, he slew the Philistines "with a great slaughter," and there with the jaw bone of an ass he slew a thousand men. In every emergency he called on God, who worked a miracle for him when he was thirsty, cleaving a hollow place in the jaw bone of the ass, and giving him drink from it.

For twenty years Samson judged Israel, exercising faith in God for feats of strength against the Philistines, while at the same time his own life was wrong. He still was guilty of

Self Pleasing,

and this led him to the terrible sin of fornication. He could not play with fire without being burnt. It is an unsafe thing to play with edge tools. His disregard of God in his affection, led at last to his ruin and death. He had set his heart on another woman, who proved a traitor to him. He loved with a selfish love, because it pleased him, and she turned out to be selfish too. A bribe of the Philistines proved too great a temptation to this unworthy woman, and she set herself to discover wherein his great strength lay. Thus the one he loved became his enemy, and almost his murderess. Delilah had her own way of enticing him to tell her wherein his great strength lay. There could have been nothing remarkable in the muscular development of the man, or it would have been manifest in his build. Samson's strength lay, not in him, but in God, and so long as his relation to God stood fast, he was stronger than other men. His answers to Delilah were but lies—Samson was not only an impure man, but a liar. Oh how far even a child of God can go in sin! Delilah had liers in wait ready to seize Samson when she bound him with green withes and then with new cords, and again wove, at his suggestion, the seven locks of his head with the web; but the same strength which had lifted the gates of Gaza from their hinges, and carried them to the top of a hill, broke the green withes "as a thread of tow is broken when it toucheth the fire," the new ropes were broken from his arms like a thread. The web which being woven, was torn away with the iron pin which held it to the beam, and all the liers in wait, with Delilah herself, were confounded. The wicked woman saw that the large fortune which was to make her a woman of property was receding from her grasp, and that soon Samson would surely be alive to her perfidy. She had no care for him, but she took him

On his Weak Side,

and said to him, "How canst thou say, I love thee, when thine heart is not with me?" Poor Samson! he had wronged God, he had sinned against his own soul; his sin made it easier for Delilah to sin too; he was near a fall; God was leaving him; Delilah was first, God was second. "He told her all his heart," and she saw at once that he had done so. His doom was sealed, but, like many a backslider, he went to sleep, and while he slept, that hair which had never been shaven, and which was the pledge of his Nazarite vow, was shorn off. He was rudely wakened out of his sleep by an alarm which had become familiar, "The Philistines be upon thee, Samson"; and he said, "I will go out as at other times before, and shake myself. And

He Wist Not

that the Lord was departed from him." Oh how often a backslider knows not that the Lord has left him! he preaches as before, but there is no unction; he prays as before, but there is no answer; others perceive, if he does not, that the Lord is not with him. The Philistines blinded and imprisoned Samson, and set him to grind corn like a woman. But tidings reached him that the Philistines were about to have a great feast, and offer a great sacrifice to Dagon their god, because Samson their enemy was delivered into their hands, and Samson conceived a plan which they had not reckoned upon. Samson was sent forth from the prison to make them sport. The house in which the feast was held was crowded with three thousand Philistines, and all their chief dignitaries were there. Samson besought the Lord to strengthen him only once; his life had been one terrible mistake; while he had avenged himself on the Philistines, he had set the worst example of selfishness and sin; he had but one thing to give to God and to his country, and this he gave. Laying hold on the two middle pillars on which the house stood, he once more received strength of God, and "bowed himself with all his might." "Let me die with the Philistines" were his last words. He did die, but with him all the Philistines in that house, "so the dead which he slew at his death were more than they which he slew in his life." And thus it is when we give up ourselves, our self-life, then God's enemies are slain as never before; then His power does great things in a short time.

THE ALTERED MOTTO.

Oh, the bitter shame and sorrow
That a time could ever be,
When I let the Saviour's pity
Plead in vain, and proudly answered:
"All of self, and none of Thee!"

But He found me. I beheld Him
Bleeding on the accursed tree,
Heard him pray: "Forgive them, Father;"
And my wistful heart said faintly:
"Some of self, and some of Thee!"

Day by day His tender mercy,
Healing, helping full and free,
Sweet and strong, and, ah! so patient,
Brought me lower, while I whispered:
"Less of self, and more of Thee!"

Higher than the highest heavens,
Deeper than the deepest sea,
Lord, Thy love at last hath conquered;
Grant me now my soul's desire—
"None of self, and all of Thee!"

—*Theo. Monod.*

J. E. JEWETT, Publisher, 77 Bible House, New York, will furnish the above poem in leaflet form at twenty cents per hundred. *A Sample Packet* of 50 leaflets assorted (no two alike), will be sent post-paid, for 10 cts., or 100 for 20 cts. Postage stamps taken.

THE CHRISTIAN HERALD AND SIGNS OF OUR TIMES.

Entered according to Act of Congress in the year 1888, in the office of the Librarian of Congress at Washington.

This Journal contains every week a Portrait and Biography of some eminent person; a new Sermon by the Rev. C. H. SPURGEON, of London, and the Rev. Dr. TALMAGE'S latest Sunday morning Sermon; also always a Prophetic Article, and a Summary of Current Events as well as Stories, Anecdotes etc.

Vol. XI., No. 50. Office, 63 Bible House. N. Y. THURSDAY, DECEMBER 13. 1888. Price, 3 Cents. Annual Subscription, $1.50.

CONTENTS OF THIS NUMBER.

PORTRAIT AND LIFE OF THE RIGHT REV. BISHOP WHIPPLE, of Minnesota, and Pictures of Four of the Faribault Institutions.
THE COMING OF THE KING'S WAGONS. Dr. Talmage's Sermon last Sunday.
ANECDOTES RELATED AT RECENT EVANGELISTIC MEETINGS.
THE STUDY OF PROPHETIC DATES. By the late Canon Berks.
Chinese Amusing an Idol—A Fatal Struggle on a Bridge—A Deliverance from Disease—A Night in Galilee—Ineffectual Beating, etc.
"ON HIS BREAST." A New Sermon by Rev. C. H. Spurgeon.
Gems from New Books: A City Boarding-House —A Dry Goods Clerk — A Mother's Prayers.
INVIOLABLE COVENANT. By Rev. A. C. Tris.
PORTRAIT OF MRS. MARY HARRISON McKEE, Daughter of the President-Elect.
PICTURE OF A COLPORTEUR IN THE JEWISH QUARTER AT JAFFA.
ROSE BERKLEY'S LIFE. (With Illustration.
ESCAPED FROM THE MORMONS. An Autobiographical Story by Mrs. Stenhouse. (Con.)
RUTH'S CHOICE. By Mrs. M. Baxter.

No. 1. Seabury Divinity School—2. Cathedral of Our Saviour—3. St. Mary's Hall—4. Phelps Cottage.

The RIGHT REV. BISHOP WHIPPLE, of Minnesota—FARIBAULT CATHEDRAL and INSTITUTIONS.

THE RT. REV. H. B. WHIPPLE,

Bishop of Minnesota.

A Bishop's Humorous Reproof—Bishop Whipple's Birth in 1822—Business and Political Life—Called to the Ministry—Unexpectedly Elected Bishop—His Election an Answer to Prayer—Arrival in His Diocese—A Dead Indian Baby—A Visit from Inquiring Indians—The Sioux Massacres—A Crisis Met by Prayer—A Quarter of a Century's Work—The Faribault Institutions.

A HUMOROUS retort, made not long ago by a bishop of some distinction among his episcopal brethren, was a tribute of no slight order to the earnestness and intense devotion of the character of the good and noble man whose portrait appears on the preceding page. The bishop in question was attending a convention, and, in the course of the various meetings which were held, he met Bishop Whipple several times in the corridors of the building. Bishop Whipple, absorbed in his own thoughts and the plans for the benefit of the redskins, whose interests are always the uppermost subject in his mind, passed his Right Reverend brother as if he had been a stranger. At last in one of these encounters the bishop laid hands on Bishop Whipple and good-humoredly took him to task for his lack of courtesy. Bishop Whipple, who would not willingly be discourteous to any man, was profuse in his apologies, and endeavored to remove from his friend's mind any wounded feeling there might be. "Ah!" retorted the Bishop with affected indignation, "*If I had been an Indian, you would not have passed me without speaking.*" And that was true. Whatever lack of attention and cordiality the distinguished and the wealthy may have to complain of at Bishop Whipple's hands, no Indian however ignorant, poor, or degraded, ever failed to reach his heart, or to find a ready ear and hand for his story and his relief. The Bishop is, before all things, the friend of the Indian, the champion of his race and the unwavering advocate of his claims. It is a thankless office now, as it has been any time in the past history of our nation, but it may be said of the grand man who now fills it, as Christ said of the friends of the poor: He will be blessed, for they cannot recompense him; but he "shall be recompensed at the resurrection of the just."

Birth and Early Life.

Henry Benjamin Whipple is now sixty-six years of age, having been born at Adams, Jefferson Co., N. Y., on February 15, 1822. He is the son of John H. and Elizabeth Whipple; his mother's family name was Wager. Ill health prevented the future bishop entering college after being prepared, and he engaged in mercantile business in his native place, and was much interested in political affairs. God had, however, more important work for the young man than money-making or assisting in the election of candidates for political offices, and very soon the Holy Spirit signified to him that he was called of God to the ministry of the Church. He then studied Theology with the Rev. W. D. Wilson, D. D., now a Professor in Cornell University. He was ordained deacon in Trinity Church, Geneva, N. Y., August 17, 1849, and priest in Christ Church, Sackett's Harbor, N. Y., July 16, 1850, both orders being conferred by Bishop De Lancey. He became rector of Zion, Rome, N. Y., which position he held until 1857, when he removed to Chicago, and became rector of the Church of the Holy Communion in that city.

Mr. Whipple found in Chicago an abundance of hard work, and he settled down to it with the vigor and energy characteristic of the man. No man could have been more surprised than he, when, in the midst of his labors, word was brought to him that he had been

Elected Bishop

of the new diocese of Minnesota. At first he did not see his way to accepting. Replying to the clergyman who informed him of his election, he said: "I cannot go. It is a mistake. I am not a scholar, theologian, or preacher. I am not even a graduate of college. I was trained up a merchant. I gave up my business to tell the story of the love of Jesus. I know that I can do that, and I can be a shepherd to the poor; but a bishop I can never be." There was, however, no mistake about the appointment; the election was made in due form, the choice of the clergy being fully confirmed by the laymen and there was also about the election a significance which specially appealed to the piety of such a man as Mr. Whipple. It appeared that the Convention was assembled in session in Chicago, vainly endeavoring to find a suitable man for the new and important diocese. At length, after many ballots, the great body knelt in silent prayer, being unable to agree upon any one. Mr. Whipple's name, scarcely mentioned before, was put in nomination, and he was unanimously chosen. He was consecrated in Richmond, Va., as first Bishop of Minnesota, and at once set out for his new field of labor, late in the fall of 1859, he being then thirty-seven years old.

Since his consecration his life has been one of self-sacrificing labor. Some idea of the

Difficulties He had to Encounter,

and the spirit in which he met them, may be gained from some facts recently given to the public by a writer in *Harper's Weekly*. That authority states that when the Bishop reached Minnesota there were 20,000 Indians in the State. Indian affairs were at their worst estate. The funds so liberally supplied by the Government, were stolen or wasted by the agents. The deadly fire-water flowed freely on all sides. Bad white men had dragged the Indians down to a depth of unparalleled sorrow and depravity. Disease and death held carnival in every village.

"I shall never forget," says the Bishop, "the awful sights which met my eyes at my first visit to the famous Gull Lake Agency. A dead Indian was lying by the roadside; a few miles from the agency I saw bruised and bleeding men suffering from the wounds received in a drunken fight. An Indian mother was scraping the inner bark of the pine-tree, to save her starving babes. The Sioux had suffered less than the Chippewas, but there were then the smouldering fires, which burst forth in the massacre of 1862."

Bishop Whipple says that no work has given him so much pleasure as that among the Indians. He is familiarly known as

The "St. John of the Wilderness,"

and the Indians know him as "*Straight Tongue,*" or the "*Father-who-don't-lie.*" Many whom he first met as painted savages are to-day civilized Christian men, leaders in business and Christian movements of all kinds. In Bishop Whipple's time he has appeared before Congress, before Presidents, and before the highest dignitaries of this and other countries, in the interest of, and to demand justice for, his beloved subjects. Large funds have been placed in his hands from time to time. He has been a member of Indian commissions, and in the pulpit, and through the press, he has fought for the rights of the red men. For over a quarter of a century he has been the most steadfast and persistent of the many people who have enlisted in this cause.

The Bishop's Field

of labor is but little known as yet, even to our own people. Speaking of some of his experiences in a recent sermon he said, "Every friend that I consulted said to me, as a young bishop that had schools to plant, and churches to found, and work to make the heart weary, 'Do not have anything to do with Indian Missions.' I looked up to my Saviour, and I made a vow that, God being my helper, I would never turn my back on the heathen at my door. I found that a visitation of our field required that I drive my horses 3,000 miles every year, and travel from 500 to 1,500 miles every year on foot or in a birch-bark canoe. *I took my blanket with me and slept on the ground.* The first day I came to an Indian village, I saw hung at the door of a wigwam a little bundle, and it was ornamented with bead-work so beautifully, that I turned to my guide and said, 'I would like to buy that:' and he whispered, 'Why, Bishop, that is a dead baby; it is the way the Indians show that a mother has lost her baby.' And then he said that when an Indian mother loses her baby, she wraps together everything that belonged to the baby, and makes a little bundle of it, and ornaments it with bead-work, and carries it wherever she goes, and, if she has anything very nice to eat, the baby's portion is always taken out, and no one of the family can touch it, but a wayfaring man may eat it, and, if not, it is given to the birds. 'Ah!' I said, 'an Indian mother's heart is like the white mother's heart.'"

A Suppliant.

"I sat one day," says the Bishop, "in the door of my study, and some Indians were coming up the road, and one of them knelt at my feet. I said: 'Do not kneel at my feet; I am a man.' He said: 'I do not kneel to worship you, but because my heart is so warm for the man that pitied my people. I live 400 miles from here. I knew that all the Indians to the east had perished. I never looked into the faces of my children that my heart was not sad. My fathers had told me there was a Great Spirit. I have often gone out into the woods and tried to talk to Him. One day, when I thought the sky was made of iron, an Indian came to my wigwam, and he said to me: "I heard a very wonderful story from that white man. He said the Great Spirit loves poor people, that His Son has come into the world, and he has told our people what He did, and how wicked men killed Him, and that he has gone into heaven, and now looks with an eye of pity on anybody in trouble." "I must hear that story," I said. I walked 100 miles to where I heard you were to be, and when I reached there they said you were ill and were going to die. I said, "The Great Spirit will not let him die until I hear the story." And then I asked for the nearest missionary, and I walked 100 miles. I have been with him three moons. I have got the glorious story all in my heart now; it is not dark any longer, but light, and is laughing for very gladness all the while.'"

The Bishop's memories of

The Terrible Sioux Massacre

of 1862 are of painful interest. He regards it as one of the saddest and darkest pages of our history, and had it not been for the civil war, would have attracted the attention of the civilized world, and taken its place in history by the massacre of Delhi, in India. In speaking of the massacre, he says: "The Sioux had been the friends of the white people in our section. For a quarter of a century they had not taken the life of a white man. The wretched Indian system was at its worst. It left red men without government or personal rights of property, and by its almshouse system, was training up savage paupers. In 1858 the Sioux sold us 800,000 acres of land on the north side of their reservation. They did not receive the moneys promised them. They waited four years, and all they received was a few thousand dollars' worth of goods. Meetings were held, and loud murmuring complaints were heard. The civil war was raging furiously, and the Indians began to think, from what they heard, that the South was victorious. The spark had been laid to the train of powder, and it was settled that the whites should be massacred. The terrible deeds followed in rapid succession, and in a short time the country was aroused. Many people were murdered at different points. Captain Marsh led a company against the Indians, was ambuscaded, and twenty-four were shot to death. The acts of heroism on the part of Christian Indians will forever live in the pages of history. Altogether, over 800 innocent people were butchered by the maddened savages, and only the most vigorous measures put an end to the great massacre."

How Bad News was Heard

in those dark days, the bishop recently told. He said: "The times grew worse. Many said, as of old, 'In the morning, Would God it were evening;' and 'in the evening, Would God it were morning.' Our schools and missions were crippled for lack of means. It is a miracle of God's goodness that we did not give up in despair. I only remember once that my heart failed me. One day I sat in my study. The unbidden tears stealing down my cheeks. One of our professors entered the door. I saw in his tell-tale face despair. I sprang to my feet and said, 'Don't tell me, brother; let us kneel in prayer.' We did pray; we arose; without one word, he threw his arms around my neck and kissed me, and went away. That was the nearest to failure in the history of Faribault."

A Quarter of a Century

of work in the Diocese of Minnesota, dating from the arrival of the Bishop, represents a prodigious expenditure of labor. The writer of the article in *Harper's Weekly*, already quoted, thus briefly summarises it: "In the first twenty-five years of his work this good man preached and delivered 6,000 sermons and addresses, confirmned 9,263, baptized 708 infants and 308 adults, celebrated the Holy Communion 978 times, buried 80 persons, performed 72 marriages, ordained 86 deacons and 67 priests, travelled over 50,000 miles on horseback or by carriage, and told the Gospel story to more savages than any other man in the West, if not in the whole country."

The Faribault Institutions,

four of which are illustrated on the first page, formed another branch of the Bishop's work, distinct from that of his labors for the Indians, and demanded effort in itself sufficient alone to exhaust any ordinary man. Our author says that when Bishop Whipple first entered his diocese and fixed his residence at Faribault, the surrounding hills were covered with dense forests. There were no railroads or telegraph lines, the town a mere trading-post. He found in equal numbers the tepees of the Dakotas, the wigwams of the Winnebagoes, and the log-cabins of the first settlers, with a very few small basswood frames. There was not a brick or stone house in the place. What marvellous changes have taken place in a comparatively short space of time!

Shortly before the arrival of Bishop Whipple, the Rev. J. Lloyd Breck and the Rev. S. W. Manney had commenced educational work in the struggling village. The Bishop entered the work with tireless energy. Mr. Breck was the pioneer missionary, and his natural bent was work among the Indians. The new Bishop threw his very soul into his new work in the far Western wilderness. In 1862 the corner-stone was laid of a cathedral for the diocese. A large educational establishment—a hall named after the Rev. Dr. Seabury, first Bishop of the American Church—was begun the same year.

The Whipple Institutes

now include the Seabury Theological School, Shattuck Military Institute, and St. Mary's Hall. The Military School is magnificently equipped, and is named in honor of Dr. George C. Shattuck, of Boston, one of the most liberal benefactors of the Church work in Faribault. On the grounds is a memorial chapel which cost $30,000. It was built in 1872 by Mrs. J. G. Shumway, of Chicago, as a memorial to her daughter. Bishop Whipple met this lady while traveling in Spain, and she became greatly interested in his work. Several years after the death of her first husband she married a Mr. Huntington, of Boston. A few years ago, while traveling in the West, she fell from a coach, receiving injuries which caused her death. She left a bequest of $300,000 to Bishop Whipple—$100,000 to build a memorial hall at Shattuck, $100,000 to endow it, and $100,000 to build a memorial hall for the Seabury School. The first, Shumway Hall, has just been completed, and it is one of the finest school buildings in the West. Work on the second structure, to be called Johnson Hall, in honor of Mrs. Huntington's father, is now under way.

Seabury Divinity School is the theological school of the Episcopal Church. The building is in the mediæval style of architecture, and is very imposing. It is well equipped in every way. Many Indian missionaries have been graduated from it. St. Mary's School is a part of the educational work carried on by the Episcopal Church. It is a seminary of great repute, and occupies a large and very beautiful building. It was opened as a girls' school in the Bishop's own house in 1866, and in 1883 the present buildings were completed. These three institutes are incorporated as the Seabury Mission, and managed by a Board of Trustees. Large sums of money have been contributed from time to time by wealthy Eastern people who have become interested in Bishop Whipple's work.

While loving his own Church, Bishop Whipple has ever maintained a friendly attitude in relation to all who love the Lord Jesus in sincerity and truth; and in his many religious and philanthropic works he has received valuable help from members of various evangelical communions. On the twenty-fifth anniversary of his episcopate the citizens of Faribault gave him a public ovation, and in other ways expressed their high esteem for him. Without respect of party, sect, or nationality, they acknowledged his excellence, and rehearsed his many good qualities.

ANECDOTES RELATED AT RECENT EVANGELISTIC MEETINGS.

The Inscription on the Castle Window.—Mr. W. A. Campbell says: "It is told that on one of the windows of an old German castle, there are scratched with a diamond the following words: 'We live we know not how long. We die we know not when. We go we know not where. And yet we are happy!' How is it possible to be happy with the answers to these three questions still in doubt? But why should they be in doubt, when Christ has come to seek and to save us? And if we but trust Him we shall be able to say, 'He loved us, and gave Himself for us.' And, instead of looking forward to the end of this life as a great leap into the dark, we know we go to be for ever with the Lord."

A Centenarian's Procrastination.—"At 5 o'clock one morning, as I stood in my fisherman's boots and oil-skins, taking a look round me on North Shields pier, I noticed an old woman, and was surprised to notice with what nimbleness she was knitting, though she must, I knew, be very old indeed. Going over to her, I said, 'You appear very old, granny?' 'Yes,' she replied, with a smile, 'I shall be 105 years of age next birthday; and just a few weeks ago I buried my eldest daughter, seventy-five years of age.' 'You have, indeed, lived a long time; and I suppose it is needless to ask you now if you have trusted Christ?' The face that had formerly smiled so sweetly, and the tongue that had been so ready to give an account of her life, became changed in an instant. With a frown on her brow, she muttered, as she turned away, 'There is plenty of time for that yet!' The habit of procrastination had grown and strengthened so much upon that aged woman that she found it almost impossible to realize the pressing urgency of the truth that 'Now is the accepted time, now is the day of salvation.'"

A Sinking Ship and a Drunken Captain.—An evangelist relates: "A friend of mine was on board a vessel crossing the Atlantic. They encountered a great storm, but managed to weather it all right themselves, and two days later they came upon a vessel which had not been so fortunate. It was evident she was sinking, in spite of all that the crew, who stuck manfully to the pumps, could do. Boats were lowered and rowed to the sinking ship, though the sea was still so high that it threatened to swamp the boats. When they got alongside, the sailors began to let themselves down from the ship into the boats. While they were thus engaged, the rescuers were surprised to see the captain of the sinking vessel interfere, and threaten to shoot any sailor who attempted to leave the ship. He was drunk to madness, and had been so ever since the ship had sprung a leak; and not content with making himself drunk, he had actually brought out liquor and offered it to the men, saying they would soon be dead, and they should enjoy themselves while they could. But, to their honor be it said, not one of them took advantage of the opportunity, but stuck to the pumps like men, until at the end of forty-eight hours' hard pumping, and when thoroughly exhausted, they were rescued, including the captain, who was forced into the boat, hugging his liquor case to him, without which he would not move. This proves how far drink will lead its victim. The captain, who should have been the first at duty and the last to leave it, should have cheered and encouraged his men, but he could not keep away from the drink. Drink robbed him of his manhood, and might have been the cause of losing his own life, and the lives of all entrusted to his care."

The Lamp in the Miner's Cap.—"I was driving along a country road near Wishaw, with a minister of that town, when I was surprised to see coming toward us a miner with his little lamp, which he carried in his cap, burning brightly. 'Why is that man carrying that light?' I asked my companion; 'if it were dark I could understand it.' But he could not tell me. By this time the miner had come nearer, and I recognized him as a Christian who had attended our meetings. 'Why have you got that light in your cap?' I shouted. 'I have no light there,' he said, putting up his hand and taking off his cap, and there, sure enough, was his lamp burning. 'Now,' he said, as he blew it out, 'I never knew it was there! I thought I had put it out before I left the mine.' And with a hearty 'God bless you!' we separated. 'Ah!' I thought, as I drove on, 'that illustrates how the children of God should walk in this world—with God's mark upon their forehead, bright and shining, but they themselves walking humbly, unconscious that they are 'letting their light so shine before men, that they may see their good works, and glorify their Father in heaven.'"

Found Dead on the Stairs.—Mr. McLauchlan remarks: "I remember a young man who once came to one of our meetings. I spoke to him about his soul, and urged upon him the necessity of accepting Christ, but he declined. He acknowledged he was a sinner, and that he must come to Christ, some time or other, but not that night. He promised to be at the meeting the next night and settle it: but though some of us waited until it was late, hoping, praying, that he might come, he did not arrive. Next day a worker, who knew where the young man lived, called at his lodgings, and found him—*dead!* He had been a hard drinker, often staying out until early in the morning. The night before his death he had gone out, saying he was going to turn over a new leaf, and become a Christian. But he did not come near us. Next morning he was found lying on his own stairs, dead. He had gone home intoxicated, at a very late hour, and death had overtaken him. He had procrastinated when salvation was pressed upon him, and with what fearful result! With such cases before us, is it any wonder that we press upon you not to risk your salvation?"

Delivered From a Trap.—Mr. Dunn says: "A fellow-worker said to me not long ago, 'Oh, Mr. Dunn, I have had an awful temptation!' He had, before his conversion, been a very great drunkard, and through the agency of my wife, in our own sitting-room, had been brought to Christ. For eighteen months he had led a consistent Christian life, and now, when he had been attacked with this strong temptation, I was the first person to whom he came for comfort. As he was walking in the street the old thirst after strong drink had come upon him with increasing fury; he felt his strength of mind and his faith going, and it seemed as if he must enter the saloon which he was then passing; but just when all appeared lost, the man rallied, and looking up to heaven, gasped a prayer for help. At once strength came. The man was enabled to pass that trap of Satan, and was safe through the help so quickly sent. We bent our knees and thanked God for the temptation that He permitted, and in which His grace proved triumphant. We cannot help being tempted, but we can help falling under temptation. We cannot keep birds from alighting on our heads, but we can prevent them from building their nests there."

THE COMING OF THE KING'S WAGONS.

Dr. Talmage's Sermon, Preached Last Sunday, December 9, 1888.

"And when he saw the wagons which Joseph had sent to carry him, the spirit of Jacob their father revived, and Israel said, It is enough: Joseph, my son, is yet alive." Gen. 45 : 27, 28.

The Glories of the Egyptian Capital—Grandeur, Wealth, and Luxury—Joseph Second in the City—A Contrast with his Former Lot—Famous Men not Ashamed of their Origin—The Wagons Sent for Joseph's Humble Father—Jacob's Departure—Brought into a Palace—The King's Wagons to the Sin-stricken World—Bearing Food and Clothing—Bringing Good News—Joseph-Jesus Still Alive—The Wagons Returning—Bearing Souls to the Palace—The Presence of Jesus Makes Heaven—Reunion with Kindred—A Reminiscence of Boyhood—The Last Journey.

THE Egyptian capital was the focus of the world's wealth. In ships and barges, there had been brought to it from India frankincense and cinnamon and ivory and diamonds; from the North, marble and iron; from Syria, purple and silk; from Greece, some of the finest horses of the world, and some of the most brilliant chariots; and from all the earth that which could best please the eye, and charm the ear, and gratify the taste. There were temples aflame with red sandstone, entered by gateways that were guarded by pillars bewildering with hieroglyphics, and wound with brazen serpents, and adorned with winged creatures—their eyes and beaks and pinions glittering with precious stones. There were marble columns blooming into white flower-buds; there were stone pillars, at the top bursting into the shape of the lotus when in full bloom. Along the

Avenues, Lined with Sphinx

and fane and obelisk, there were princes who came in gorgeously upholstered palanquin, carried by servants in scarlet, or else were drawn by vehicles, the snow-white horses, golden-bitted, and six abreast, dashing at full run. There were fountains from stone-wreathed vases climbing the ladders of the light. You would hear a bolt shove, and a door of brass would open like a flash of the sun. The surrounding gardens were saturated with odors that mounted the terrace, and dripped from the arbors, and burned their incense in the Egyptian noon. On floors of mosaic the glories of Pharaoh were spelled out in letters of porphyry and beryl and flame. There were ornaments twisted from the wood of the tamarisk, embossed with silver breaking into foam. There were footstools made out of a single precious stone. There were beds fashioned out of a crouched lion in bronze. There were chairs spotted with the sleek hide of leopards. There were sofas footed with the claws of wild beasts, and armed with the beaks of birds. As you stand on the level beach of the sea on a summer-day, and look either way, and there are miles of breakers, white with the ocean foam, dashing shoreward; so it seemed as if the sea of the world's pomp and wealth in the Egyptian capital for miles and miles flung itself up into white breakers of marble temple, mausoleum, and obelisk.

This was the place where Joseph, the shepherd boy, was called to stand next to Pharaoh.

What a Contrast

between this scene and his humble starting, and the pit into which his brothers threw him! Yet he was not forgetful of his early home; he was not ashamed of where he came from. The Bishop of Mentz, descended from a wheelwright, covered his house with spokes and hammers and wheels; and the King of Sicily, in honor of his father, who was a potter, refused to drink out of anything but an earthen vessel. So Joseph was not ashamed of his early surroundings, or of his old-time father, or of his brothers. When they came up from the famine-stricken land to get corn from the king's corn-crib, Joseph, instead of chiding them for the way they had maltreated and abused him, sent them back with wagons, which Pharaoh furnished, laden with corn; and old Jacob, the father, in the very same wagons was brought back, that Joseph, the son, might see him, and give him a comfortable home all the rest of his days.

Well, I hear the wagons, the king's wagons, rumbling down in front of the palace. On the outside of the palace, to see the wagons go off, stands Pharaoh in royal robes; and beside him, Prime Minister Joseph, with a chain of gold around his neck, and on his hand a ring, given by Pharaoh to him, so that any time he wanted to stamp the royal seal upon a document, he could do so. Wagon after wagon rolls on down from the palace, laden with corn and meat and changes of raiment, and everything that could help a famine-stricken people. One day I see

Aged Jacob

seated in front of his house. He is possibly thinking of his absent boys (sons, however old they get, are never to a father any more than boys); and while he is seated there, he sees dust arising, and he hears wagons rumbling, and he wonders what is coming now, for the whole land had been smitten with the famine, and was in silence. But, after a while, the wagons have come near enough, and he sees his sons on the wagons, and before they come quite up they shout: "Joseph is yet alive!" The old man faints dead away. I do not wonder at it. The boys tell the story, how that the boy, the long-absent Joseph, has got to be the first man in the Egyptian palace. While they unload the wagons, the wan and wasted creatures in the neighborhood come up and ask for a handful of corn, and they are satisfied.

One day the wagons are brought up, for Jacob, the old father, is about to go to see Joseph in the Egyptian palace. You know it is not a very easy thing to transplant an old tree, and Jacob has hard work to get away from the place where he has lived so long. He bids

Good-bye to the Old Place,

and leaves his blessing with the neighbors, and then his sons steady him, while he, determined to help himself, gets into the wagon, stiff, old, and decrepit. Yonder they go, Jacob and his sons, and their wives, and their children, eighty-two in all, followed by herds and flocks, which the herdsmen drive along. They are going out from famine to luxuriance; they are going from a plain country home to the finest palace under the sun.

Joseph, the Prime Minister, gets into his chariot and drives down to meet the old man. Joseph's charioteer holds up the horses on the one side—the dust-covered wagons of the emigrants stop on the other. Joseph, instead of waiting for his father to come, leaps out of the chariot and jumps into the emigrants' wagon, throws his arms around the old man, and weeps aloud for past memories and present joy. The father, Jacob, can hardly think it is his boy. Why, the smooth brow of childhood has become a wrinkled brow—wrinkled with the cares of state, and the garb of the shepherd-boy has become a robe royally bedizened! But as the old man finds out it is actually Joseph, I see the thin lip quiver against the toothless gum as he cries out: "Now let me die, since I have seen thy face; behold, Joseph is yet alive." The wagons roll up in front of the palace. Help out the grandchildren, nd take them in out of the hot Egyptian sun. aHelp old Jacob out of the wagon. Send word to Pharaoh that the old shepherd has come.

In the Royal Apartment

Pharaoh and Jacob meet—dignity and rusticity—the gracefulness of the court and the plain manners of the field. The king, wanting to make the old countryman at ease, and seeing how white his beard is, and how feeble his step, looks familiarly into his face, and says to the aged man: "How old art thou?" Give the old man a seat. Unload the wagons; drive out the cattle toward the pastures of Goshen. Let the slaves in scarlet kneel and wash the feet of the newly arrived, wiping them on the finest linen of the palace From vases of perfume let the newly arrived be sprinkled and refreshed; let minstrels come in with sandals of crimson, and thrum the harps, and clap the cymbals, and jingle the tambourines, while we sit down, at this great distance of time and space, and learn the lesson of the king's wagons.

My friends, we are in a world by sin famine-struck; but the King is in constant communication with us, His wagons coming and going perpetually; and in the rest of my discourse I will show you what the wagons bring and what they take back.

In the first place, like those that came from the Egyptian palace,

The King's Wagons

now bring us corn and meat, and many changes of raiment. We are apt to think of the fields and the orchards as feeding us; but who makes the flax grow for the linen, and the wheat for the bread, and the wool on the sheep's back? Oh, I wish we could see, through every grain field, by every sheep-fold, under the trees of every orchard, the King's wagons. They drive up three times a day—morning, noon, and night. They bring furs from the Arctic, they bring fruits from the Tropic, they bring bread from the Temperate zone. The King looks out, and he says: "There are twelve hundred millions of people to be fed and clothed. So many pounds of meat, so many barrels of flour, so many yards of cloth and linen and flannel, so many hats, so many socks, so many shoes"; enough for all, save that we who are greedy get more shoes than belong to us, and others go barefooted.

None but a God could feed and clothe the world. None but a king's corn-crib could appease the world's famine. None but a king could tell how many wagons to send, and how heavily to load them, and when they are to start. They are coming over the frozen ground to-day. Do you not hear their rumbling? They will stop at noon at your table. Oh, if for a little while they should cease, hunger would come into the nations, as to Utica when Hamilcar besieged it, and as in Jerusalem when Vespasian surrounded it; and the nations would be hollow-eyed, and fall upon each other in universal cannibalism; and skeleton would drop upon skeleton; and there would be no one to bury the dead; and the earth would be a field of bleached skeletons; and the birds of prey would fall dead, flock after flock, without any carcases to devour; and the earth in silence would wheel around, one great black hearse! All life stopped because the King's wagons are stopped. Oh thank God for bread!

I remark again, that, like those that came from the Egyptian palace, the King's wagons

Bring us Good News.

Jacob had not heard from his boy for a great many years. He never thought of him but with a heart-ache. There was in Jacob's heart a room where lay the corpse of his unburied Joseph; and when the wagons came, the King's wagons, and told him that Joseph was yet alive, he faints dead away. Good news for Jacob! Good news for us! The King's wagons come down and tell us that our Joseph-Jesus is yet alive; that He has forgiven us because we threw him into the pit of suffering and the dungeon of shame. He has risen from thence to stand in a palace. The Bethlehem shepherds were awakened at midnight by the rattling of the wagons that brought the tidings. Our Joseph-Jesus sends us a message of pardon, of life, of heaven; corn for our hunger, raiment for our nakedness.

Joseph-Jesus is yet Alive!

I go to hunt up Jesus. I go to the village of Bethany, and say: "Where does Mary live?" They say: "Yonder Mary lives." I go in. I see where she sat in the sitting-room. I go out where Martha worked in the kitchen, but I find no Jesus. I go into Pilate's court-room, and I find the judges and the police and the prisoner's box, but no Jesus. I go into the Arimathean cemetery; but the door is gone, and the shroud is gone, and Jesus is gone. By faith I look up to the King's palace; and behold I have found him! Joseph-Jesus is still alive! Glorious religion, a religion made not out of death's heads, ınd cross bones, and undertaker's screw-driver, ɔut one bounding with life and sympathy and gladness. Joseph is yet alive!

"I know that my Redeemer lives,
What comfort this sweet sentence gives!
He lives, He lives, who once was dead,
He lives, my ever-living Head!

"He lives to grant me daily breath,
He lives, and I shall conquer death.
He lives my mansion to prepare,
He lives to bring me safely there.

"He lives, all glory to His name;
He lives, my Jesus still the same,
Oh, the sweet joy this sentence gives,
I know that my Redeemer lives!"

The King's wagons will after a while unload, ınd they will turn around, and they will go

Back to the Palace,

ınd I really think that *you and I will go with hem.* The King will not leave us in this famine-truck world. The King has ordered that we ɔe lifted into the wagons, and that we go over nto Goshen, where there shall be pasturage or our largest flock of joy, and then we will drive up to the palace, where there are glories waiting us which will melt the snow of Egyptian marble into forgetfulness.

I think that the King's wagons will take us ıp to see our lost friends. Jacob's chief anticipation was not seeing the Nile, nor of seeing he long colonnades of architectural beauty, nor of seeing the throne-room. There was a focus o all his journeyings, to all his anticipations; ınd that was Joseph. Well, my friends, I do ıot think heaven would be worth much if our brother Jesus was not there. If there were two ıeavens, the one with all the pomp and paraphernalia of an eternal monarchy, but no Christ, ınd the other were a plain heaven, humbly hatched, with a few daisies in the yard, and Christ were there, I would say: "Let the King's wagons take me up to the old farm-house."

If Jesus were not in heaven, there would be ıo music there; there would be but few people here: they would be off

Looking for the Lost Christ,

rying through the universe, "Where is Jesus? where is Jesus?" and after they had found Him, with loving violence they would take Him and bear Him through the gates; and it would be he greatest day known in heaven within the memory of the oldest inhabitant. Jesus never went off from heaven but once, and He was so badly treated on that excursion they will never et Him go again.

Oh, the joy of meeting our brother, Joseph-Jesus!—after we have talked about him for ten or fifty or seventy years, to talk with Him, and o clasp hands with the hero of the ages; not crouching as underlings in His presence, but as Jacob and Joseph hug each other. We will want some new term by which to address Him. On earth we call Him Saviour, or Redeemer, or Friend; but when we throw our arms around Him in everlasting embrace, we will want some new name of endearment. I can think of what we shall do through the long ages of eternity; but what we shall do the first minute I cannot guess. In the first flash of His countenance, in the first rush of our emotions, what we shall do I cannot imagine. Oh, the overwhelming glory of the first sixty seconds in heaven! Methinks we will just stand, and look and look and look.

The king's wagons took Jacob up to see his lost boy, and so I really think that the King's wagons will take us up

To See Our Lost Kindred.

How long is it since Joseph went out of your household? How many years is it now last Christmas, or the 14th of next month? It was a dark night when he died, and a stormy day it was at the burial; and the clouds wept with you, and the winds sighed for the dead. The bell at Greenwood's gate rang only a few moments, but your heart has been tolling, tolling, ever since. You have been under a delusion, like Jacob of old. You have thought that Joseph was dead. You put his name first in the birth-record of the family Bible, and then you put it in the death-record of the family Bible, and you have been deceived. Joseph is yet alive. He is *more alive than you are.* Of all the sixteen thousand millions of children that statisticians say have gone into the future world, there is not one of them dead, and the King's wagons will take you up to see them. You often think how glad you will be to see them. Have you never thought, my brother, my sister,

How Glad They Will be to See You?

Jacob was no more glad to see Joseph than Joseph was to see Jacob. Every time the door in heaven opens, they look to see if it is you coming in. Joseph, once, standing in the palace, burst out crying when he thought of Jacob—afar off. And the heaven of your little ones will not be fairly begun until you get there. All the kindnesses shown them by immortals will not make them forget you. There they are, the radiant throngs that went out from your homes! I throw a kiss to the sweet darlings. They are all well now in the palace. The crippled child has a sound foot now. A little lame child says: "Ma, will I be lame in heaven?" "No, my darling, you won't be lame in heaven." A little sick child says: "Ma, will I be sick in heaven?" "No, my dear, you won't be sick in heaven?" A little blind child says: "Ma, will I be blind in heaven?" "No, my dear, you won't be blind in heaven." They are all well there.

In My Boyhood,

for some time we lived three miles from church, and on stormy days the children staid at home, but father and mother always went to church: that was a habit they had. On those stormy Sabbaths when we staid at home, the absence of our parents seemed very much protracted; for the roads were very bad, and they could not get on very fast. So we would go to the window at 12 o'clock to see if they were coming, and then we would go at half-past 12 to see if they were coming, and at a quarter to 1, and then at 1 o'clock. After a while, Mary, or David, or DeWitt would shout: "The wagon's coming!" and then we would see it winding out of the woods, and over the brook, and through the lane, and up in front of the old farm-house; and then we would rush out, leaving the doors wide open, with many things to tell them, asking them many questions. Well, my dear brethren, I think we are many of us in the King's wagons, and

We are on the Way Home.

The road is very bad, and we get on slowly; but after a while we will come winding out of the woods, and through the brook of death, and up in front of the old heavenly homestead; and our departed kindred, who have been waiting and watching for us, will rush out through the doors and over the lawn, crying: "The wagons are coming! the King's wagons are coming!" Hark! the bell of the City Hall strikes 12. Twelve o'clock on earth, and likewise it is high noon in heaven.

The Last Journey.

Does not the subject of to-day take the gloom out of the thoughts that would otherwise be struck through with midnight? We used to think that when we died we would have to go afoot, sagging down in the mire, and the hounds of terror might get after us, and if we got through into heaven at all, we would come in torn and wounded and bleeding. I remember how my teeth chattered and my knees knocked together when I heard anybody talk about death; but I have come to think that the grave will be the softest bed I ever slept in, and the bottom of my feet will not be wet with the passage of the Jordan. "Them that sleep in Jesus will God bring with Him." I was reading of Robert Southey, who said he wished he could die far away from his friends—like a dog, crawling into a corner and dying unobserved. Those were his words. Be it ours to die on a couch surrounded by loved ones, so that they with us may hear the glad, sweet, jubilant announcement: "The King's wagons are coming!" Hark! I hear them now. Are they coming for you or me?

AN OPPOSER CONVERTED.

The remarkable conversion of a young man so rabidly opposed to Christianity as to become an active member of an "Anti-Christ Society" is described in a letter from a missionary in Ceylon to the *Missionary Herald.* He says: "A remarkable convert was received into our Church on Sunday morning, the 15th instant, on profession of faith. This young man is a native of the island of Velany, belonging to a rigid heathen family, quite abstinent from flesh-eating. He was a leading member of the Anti-Christ Society formed some time ago for printing and circulating tracts against the Christian religion. One day in March last he, in company with some of his comrades, attended a meeting held at Nellore by the Rev. Mr. Grubb, one of the English Church missioners, with a view of disturbing the meeting by putting questions on some subjects. While at the meeting his attention was drawn to the general calmness and stillness of the whole congregation at the time of their worship, and the thought was strongly impressed on his mind that unless God were present there could not be such a scene of solemnity. He remembered at the same time the disorders and irregularities of their own assemblies, when the heathen come together for their religious worship. From that day he began to search after the truth of Christianity, and he is wonderfully convinced of its truth, and has now become a sincere and devoted Christian, in spite of all the entreaties of his friends, to their utter despair and disappointment. In consequence of his conversion, his parents have entirely forsaken him, and he is now in the industrial department of our Training Institution."

A JAPANESE FATHER'S THREATS.

In a recent letter from Yokohama, Japan, to *The Church*, the Rev. H. Loomis says: "A young Christian from Kumamoto recently went to a distant mountain village to become a teacher in the local school. There was living in the same place a young man of about the same age, who had been adopted by the most wealthy person in that region. When he learned that the teacher was a Christian, he would not associate with him at all, and for a considerable time tried to make it as unpleasant for him as he could. But the teacher was not deterred from the path of duty, and in time won the confidence and esteem of the one who had hated and opposed him. Then a warm friendship sprang up between them, and the teacher was able to lead his friend to a belief in and acceptance of Christianity.

"When the father of the young man heard of what had happened, he threatened to disown and cast him out if he did not give up this new and hated religion; but these threats were of no avail, as the son said that the presence of Christ in his heart was of more value than either gold, houses, or lands.

"When the time came for the young man to be baptized, the father was present. Both returned to their home, and by neither word nor act was there any manifestation of opposition. On the contrary, the father seemed to be convinced of his former error, and allowed the son to do as he chose. This young man has been chosen to be the head-man of the village; and when he goes to the Christian services every Sabbath, he takes all his associates and officials with him."

A DELIVERANCE FROM DISEASE.

AN interesting testimony published in this month's *Thy Healer*, edited by Mrs. M. Baxter, comes from Mrs. Brodie, who is well known in Christian circles in America. Speaking at Bethshan recently, she said : "I feel I ought to give a testimony to what the Lord has done for me. About February last I was taken very ill, and for three days suffered much with my lungs. I had serious symptoms, but the mention of them did not pass over my lips, excepting to my God. And when these symptoms appeared—as expectoration, blood-spitting, and night sweats, I thought the Lord wanted me home; and then came the sweet consciousness that He wanted me for Himself, and not for myself; and, though it seemed against my own will, He led me on still to trust in Him for perfect healing, with the result that I have had every one of these symptoms removed by the Lord, and He is my Life and my Love. I mention this, because there are some—and there may be some here—who do not give the Lord credit for being the Life of the body as well as of the soul. My husband, about three weeks ago, said I must be examined before the winter by a medical man, that as I had come from the tropics, he felt that for my own comfort, as well as those dependent on me in my home, I ought to be so examined. I therefore went to Doctor McKilliam, and he said: 'You have not a particle of disease, but you have traces of what you have passed through.' God, however, had delivered me from all disease.

"I have felt that the Lord has been teaching me a very deep lesson in permitting this sickness to come. When He first called me in British Honduras and brought me to Himself, He took away from me all fear of man in witnessing for Him, but the enemy made this sickness an occasion for a new temptation here in England, and the fear of man has come to be fear of refusing man when asked to engage in any Christian work; and so, all through this year, I have been under pressure, accepting invitations, because I did not like to refuse lest I seemed selfish, but God had been teaching me this lesson we have all to learn, that our life is not our own, but is sacredly given to Him."

A NIGHT IN GALILEE.

"I WAS travelling with a friend in Galilee," says a Christian lady, "and as we were riding along, tired and hungry, near the waters of Merom, we longed to find some place where we could rest, and get shelter for the night. There were no villages or houses near, where we might ask for a lodging, so we continued our journey until we came in sight of some black camel's-hair tents, which, we knew, belonged to the Bedouin. These people are very hospitable and kind to travellers, and after having eaten bread with a stranger, consider themselves bound to protect and care for him. So we rode up to the tent-door and asked for the sheik. He came out to welcome us, and sent for his wives to entertain us. Very soon we were surrounded by a crowd of dark figures; carpets were brought out, and we were seated in the middle of the ring of women. The first thing we did was to get some bread from our saddle-bags and invite the chief wife to eat with us. She took a small piece and liked it so much that she asked for more, and in a few minutes our little store of bread had quite disappeared.

"It was a strange, dark place, about thirty feet long, with no furniture but a few mats round the camel's-hair walls. A large wood fire was burning in the centre opposite the door, and our beds were put down behind it. An immense iron pot filled with rice was taken off the fire as we entered; we all sat round on the floor, and dipping our fingers into the unsavory mess, managed to eat a few mouthfuls. Then we talked to the group around of the goodness of our heavenly Father, who not only gives us temporal mercies, but loved us so much that He sent His beloved Son to die for us. The poor, ignorant women could hardly understand, and when we knelt down to pray seemed very much mystified. The sheik informed me that he could pray, and spreading a small carpet on the ground, bowed himself down on hands and knees, repeating over many times: 'There is no God but God, and Mahomet, the prophet of God.' He knew nothing about the God he prayed to, so, as he could read a little, I gave him a Testament, which I told him would teach him about God. Then we gathered the children together, and tried to make them learn a text.

"When all the men had left the tent, we lay down on the mats provided for us, and watched one after another of the tall, black-robed women disappear into the darkness in the corner of the tent. One only remained crouching with her long pipe over the smouldering embers, and every few minutes a man would glide softly in, light his pipe and go out again. Dogs and goats came in and out as they pleased, and evidently thought we had no business to be there from the suspicious way in which they snuffed around us. We lay, unable to sleep very much amid such strange surroundings. Early in the morning before anybody was awake, we crept out of the tent, called our muleteers, saddled our horses, and set off again on our journey to the Sea of Galilee, feeling quite rested after our night among the Bedouin."

INEFFECTUAL BEATING.

ONE of the China Inland Mission workers—Mr. Ballard—who has recently returned from his field of labor for a brief rest, says: "In Chou Siu, some time ago, there was a famine, occasioned by a scarcity of rain. Along with some others, I went and distributed meat to the starving people, and that kindness has borne much fruit in the drawing of the people to hear what we have to say to them about Christ. And now there are in that province from two to three hundred Christians. One of them was a keeper of the temple, who has a position somewhat analogous to the Levites of old. They get so much from the people, and have, besides, a small plot of their own; so, for that man to come to Christ, was to give up his sole means of support. He heard the gospel, accepted Christ, and resolved never again to worship idols. His conversion was soon noised abroad, and as one of the monthly religious festivals was approaching, he was commanded by the Mandarin to be in his place, and worship the gods as usual. He refused to obey this command, and the Mandarin, with the easy-going justice of the Chinese, said: 'Very well, I'll beat you.' He was beaten and sent away, and recommended to think over the matter again. A second time he refused to worship the idols, and a second time he was beaten, then turned out of his office. Now he is preaching Christ throughout the provinces with amazing success."

A FATAL CONFLICT.

A CANINE duel on a bridge was watched with interest on November 22 by a crowd of workmen. On each side of the long skeleton bridge which carries the track of the Greenwood Lake Railroad over the Passaic River, a dog has his home, and the two had a long-standing animosity between them. They were both powerful animals, and the men, who knew of the hatred existing, predicted that if ever they came into close quarters one, if not both, would be killed. On Thursday the two dogs stood at opposite ends of the bridge howling defiance at each other. After some time one of the dogs began to cross, stepping carefully on the ties. The other went to meet him, and they met just at the line where the movable part of the bridge separates on its swivel. As the dogs met and grappled the workmen were preparing to open the swinging draw. The bridge was drawing them apart, but the two brutes were biting viciously, and neither would let go his hold. They held together in their fierce struggle until the opposite corners of the bridge at the final point of contact swung apart, and the two savage creatures fell into the river below and were drowned. Even after they reached the water they could have swum ashore, but it was a duel to the death, and they went down, probably to fight as long as either breathed. Men, who ought to know better, sometimes allow their angry passions to gain so complete a control over them that they and their enemies are destroyed together. In the Christian life especially all anger is forbidden, and it is too often forgotten that its indulgence is an evidence of separation from God. (1 John 4: 20, 21.)

CHINESE AMUSING AN IDOL.

IN May of this year the Rev. A. D. Winchester, who is laboring at Pao-ting-fu, in China, was present at a remarkable religious festival, of which he sends the following description to the *Missionary Herald*:

The occasion was the annual visit of a god whose temple is outside the city, to a goddess whose temple is within the city walls. The festival lasts about three days. First, the god is amused by theatrical performances in front of his own temple. Theatres are built in front of the majority of temples for this purpose, and the most grotesque things are done to please him. Comedies and farces are ludicrously performed by the hired buffoonists, as though they were bound to make the god laugh.

The theatrical performance is followed by small offerings of various kinds, and the burning of large quantities of incense. Speedily the theatricals are resumed, and like the prophets of Baal on Mount Carmel, though they do not *cut* themselves and call, they *play* and call upon their god until completely exhausted and tired nature drops down, unable to make another sound or motion. On the third day is the great procession, when his godship is brought into the city temple. The procession lasted the whole day—from early morn until late in the afternoon. Innumerable bands of music (if the crashing roar produced by the utmost expenditure of physical strength in thumping huge gongs and clashing a multitude of discordant cymbals, the shrill scream of lutes, clarionets, whistles, &c., all in different keys, can be called music) were alternated by troops of players, acrobats, high-stilted pantomimists, knights in tournaments, jugglers, wrestlers, &c. The jugglers did really marvelous things. I have seen a good deal in my younger days, but nothing in acrobatic or juggling feats to compare with these. The remainder of the entertainment part of the procession was farcical and childish. The religious part, which comes last, is a most imposing and specious, but withal an utterably sad, spectacle.

The next scene, though more horrible and repulsive than the others, was, after all, only on a par with them. Thirty or more young men, from fifteen to forty years old, walk painfully slow and with measured tread, stopping at times for a few minutes to get their balance. Each one has his arms extended at right angles from his body, and propped up by a beautifully polished stick reaching from hand to hip. From the fleshy part of each lower arm was suspended, by an iron hook sunk in the flesh, a steel censer full of burning incense. It was a strange, a sad sight! For probably ten consecutive hours these intelligent-looking men bore that torture, with the hope that that would atone for some of their own or their relative's sins, or secure the favor of the god of medicine on behalf of some sick friend, or in fulfilment of a vow conditionally given on the restoration of some loved one to good health.

The day's proceedings were closed by an event more tragic than anything I have mentioned. In front of the temple where the god was visiting was dug a deep, wide pit, into which an immense amount of incense was thrown and fired. There the grand oblation of the day was offered. A poor wretch who was intensely anxious for the recovery of a near relative—some said it was his mother—in order to propitiate the god and save the life of that relative by giving his own, leaped into the flaming pit and was speedily consumed. Of course his "good and glorious deed" was applauded, and his tablet will be worshipped from henceforth by all his relatives. Though more noticeable, was this poor man's sad fate any more hopeless than that of the thousands who here daily cross death's sullen stream, possessed of a like false faith?

THE INVIOLABLE COVENANT.

By Rev. A. C. Tris.

THE very important question may be raised. Why does the 89th Psalm speak of David and his seed, and does not say a word of Abraham and his seed? Is Abraham not higher than David? We answer: Here we find a beautiful symmetrical unit, which is well worthy our attention. The Abrahamic covenant is the first and the highest, and comprehends all the lineal seed of Abraham, "the Jews." It might be called the Magna Charta of Israel's commonwealth. The covenant for David and his seed is

The Royal Charter

of Israel, and included royal prerogatives, supremacy, and world dominion. The first belongs to all Israel, the last exclusively to the rulers of that people. If we desire to see a bright picture of the covenants of Israel blended and drawn into a focus, let us study Luke 2:21-32. There we see Jesus, our Lord, the Son of David, receiving the circumcision as the token of the Abrahamic covenant. Jesus' mother offering a sacrifice of "a pair of turtle doves," paying homage to the Mosaic covenant or law (Lev. 12:2) and then Jesus in the arms of Simeon, who spoke by the Holy Spirit, saying that that child should be "a light to lighten the Gentiles, and the glory of thy people Israel," is the acknowledgment of Israel's superiority and of the Davidic covenant. Mark particularly, first, the dispensation of the Gentiles (the present time, in which we are receiving light from Jesus our Lord); and second, after that, light should follow glory (which is above light), not principally to the nations, but to thy people Israel; the millennial era, and the personal reign of Jesus as the King of Israel in Jerusalem.

We ask your particular attention to those words, *thy throne.* "And

I Have Built Thy Throne,"

says the Lord, and these words are not in the future tense—they speak of a completed work. It is something that *David had already in possession;* thy throne is an earthly throne. David never reigned in heaven, as the Apostle Peter teaches us (Acts 2:34), and as Paul reasons (Acts 13:34-37), and consequently "the sitting of our Lord Jesus Christ at the right hand of the Majesty on high" is quite different from *thy* throne, which is here mentioned. It cannot be said, that our Lord is building a house, is establishing a throne of David in heaven. The apostle in Hebrews 4:14 tells us "That Christ is the great High Priest"; (Heb. 8:2) "A minister of the sanctuary," and in verses 8-12 he speaks of "a new covenant with the house of Israel, and with the house of Judah" in the future time "after those days." We find the same distinction made in Rev. 2:21, and in Matt. 25:31: "To him that overcometh, will I grant to sit with Me in *My throne,* even as I also overcame, and am set down with My Father in *His* throne." "Then shall He sit upon *the throne* of His *glory,* and all nations shall be gathered before Him." Indeed, this is a subject of study, worthy of our attention.

The Time.

It is a sworn declaration (Heb. 6:16-18) made to David. "Even forever, I established thy seed and have built thy throne, to generation and generation." It means of ages and ages to come (II Sam. 7:25). Now the question arises: Was this promise, oath, and covenant ever fulfilled? We say, not in its whole extent. The rule of the Dynasty, or David's house, over *the whole house of Israel,* was not longer than eighty years. It was curtailed in power by the revolt of the ten tribes, and only for three hundred and eighty seven years they were rulers over the house of Judah. Can four centuries be called forever? And now, for nearly two thousand five hundred years the Dynasty of David has not reigned over the Jews. The period of the Asmonean, or Maccabean rule, cannot be called David's Dynasty.

What a Hiatus!

What a period? David's house is set aside, not exterminated (Luke 2:2-4); and his royal descendants, the sons of David, *are in the midst of us* and may be seen in some of the poor, despised, scattered Jews, neglected by many of us Gentile believers. We have no doubt that many of them have a pedigree of royalty, far above that of the reigning Dynasties of Europe or Asia. Those sojourners among us must and will surely return to Canaan, the land of Jehovah, where the graves of the kings can be seen. The promise was made to Abraham and to David *in that land of Canaan,* and there they shall abide foreyermore. (Ezekiel 39:25, 29.)

That covenant of Jehovah cannot be broken, curtailed, or abrogated. The promise is *not made to depend on the perfect obedience of David's house,* dynasty or sons; the very Psalm under consideration declares emphatically (vs. 31-37) —" If his children forsake my law . . . break my statutes . . . I change not . . . I lie not to David; his seed is forever, and *his throne as the sun.* As the witness in the cloud is steadfast."

The people of Israel will return to Canaan and so *the crucified King of the Jews* "will return from heaven (Acts, 1:2, Zech. 14:5) having received His kingdom" (Luke 10:12); will be seen in Jerusalem (Matt. 23:39); will be Priest upon his throne (Zech. 6:13); and this whole Psalm shall then be sung, as the glorious covenant Psalm of the Millennial period.

THE STUDY OF PROPHETIC DATES.

By the Late Canon Berks.

LET us examine the most usual and principal of the objections to the computation of prophetic dates in reference to the Second Advent of Christ, and we shall find them to be shadowy and vain; and that the duty of seeking insight into the seasons God has revealed, will only stand out in fuller and brighter relief.

1. We are often reminded that "*secret things belong unto the Lord our God.*" (Deut. 29:29.) But when these words are perverted into an absolute prohibition to search into the prophecies, the rest of the verse supplies a conclusive answer. "The

Things that are Revealed

belong to us and our children." Surely every part of God's Word is a revelation. To number it among the secret things which are best honored by neglect, is really to fling back the Divine gift in the face of Him who bestows it. He declares solemnly that all inspired Scripture is profitable for us, and that whatever is written therein is written for our learning. Who are we, that we should pretend to be wiser than God, or profess that some of His revealed sayings would have been more wisely kept back from us? as if our neglect were to remedy the alleged unwise communications of the Spirit.

2. The words of our Lord to His apostles have given rise to another scruple: "*It is not for you to know the times or the seasons which the Father hath put in His own power.* (Acts 1:7.) These, however, when searched, are a

Warrant for an Inquiry

into the times and seasons of prophecy. The words are not general, as our version seems to imply, but special. "It is not for you to know *the* times and seasons which the Father hath reserved in His own power." There is here a direct allusion to a text familiar to the apostles, and which explains the true meaning of the answer. Daniel (chapter 12) had heard two angels put the inquiry, "How long shall it be to the end of these wonders?" The Son of God replied, with a solemn oath, that "It shall be for a time and times and half a time, and when he shall have accomplished to scatter the power of the holy people, all these things shall be finished." The prophet then asks for further light, but receives the answer, "The words are closed up and sealed till the time of the end."

The answer, then, of our Lord to His apostles on earth is only the echo of His reply to the prophet in the vision. The event spoken of is clearly the same in both, "the restoration of the kingdom to Israel, and the end of the scattering of the holy people."

The "Times" of Delay

before that event were sealed till the time of the end; until then the Father, by the lips of the covenant angel, had expressly reserved them in His own power. The disciples asked the *time* of that restoration. Our Lord, as if pointing them to the words of Daniel, introduces the very term employed in the vision, "It is not for you to know the *times or the seasons* which the Father hath put in His own power." As if He had said, The "period of which you speak follows certain *times* of predicted delay; and these *times and seasons* have been reserved at present from a complete revelation, until the Father Himself, at the time of the end, shall begin to unseal them."

We have thus a fourfold answer to this objection from Acts 1. 7. First, the words are not *general as to all times,* but refer specially to the *three times and a half* which were to be sealed and closed until a later period. Secondly, they are not general as to Christians in all ages, but relate, with a marked emphasis, to the apostles themselves, and Christians in their day. "Such knowledge," our Lord implies, "may be hereafter given to others, but it is not for you. Another work is assigned you, to found the Church and spread the gospel through the world." It is only when faith begins to decay that

The Father Will Unseal the Times

of that blessed hope, which will be as life from the dead to the unbelieving world. And hence, thirdly, they are a secret assurance that there will be other Christians of a later age to whom these times will be unsealed, as the seventy years of Jeremiah were to Daniel himself, shortly before their close. (Dan. 9:2.) Fourthly, there were other times not reserved which the apostles themselves might know, as the fall of Jerusalem and of the Temple in their own generation from the prophecy in Matt. 24:34.

3. But this leads us to the words of Christ in the prophecy on the mount, which are often viewed as a clear censure on all prophetic inquiries: "*Of that day and that hour knoweth no man, no, not the angels which are in heaven, neither the Son, but the Father*" (Mark 13:32.) How far the spirit of this caution extends may require much spiritual wisdom to determine; but conclusions loosely and rashly drawn from it have nothing to sustain them. First, *the assertion is strictly true only of the time when our Saviour spoke those words:*—for, surely, with regard to the Son of God, *they must have ceased to be true when He was risen and ascended into glory.* Our Lord Himself, since they were uttered, has received in His human nature immeasurable wisdom; and we may infer that His Church also, though in measures infinitely short of His own, will receive from age to age an increase of knowledge. "At the time of the End many shall run to and fro, and knowledge shall be increased." (Daniel 12:2.)

To ascertain our true place in the decrees of Providence, and the prophetic features of the generation in which we live; nay, even to make computations with caution, on *the year when revealed numbers may expire,* are justified by the examples of Scripture, and encouraged and commended by the Spirit of God.

CHRISTIAN HERALD AND SIGNS OF OUR TIMES.

OFFICE, 63 BIBLE HOUSE, NEW YORK.

TERMS AND INSTRUCTIONS.

Published Weekly. Subscription price in the United States, Canada, and Mexico, $1.50 a year; $1 eight months; 75 cents six months; sent two months on trial for 25 cents, postage free; in Europe and in all countries in the Postal Union, 50 cents extra postage; subscriptions always payable in advance. Single copies, price 3 cents. Any newsdealer will furnish the paper weekly when ordered.

Remittances by Mail should be by Post-office money order, bank cheque, draft, or express money order, whenever possible, and should always be made payable to THE CHRISTIAN HERALD. Letters containing money sent in this way need not be registered, as when lost, duplicates can always be obtained.

If a Postal Note or currency is sent, it should always be in a registered letter. Letters can be registered at any office. Subscribers sending money of this kind, and not registering, do it at their own risk.

Receipts are not sent; the receipt of the paper by a subscriber is a sufficient proof that the remittance has been received. If the paper does not arrive promptly, please advise us, that we may see if the address is correctly entered.

CURRENT EVENTS.

The President's Message to Congress on its reassembling on December 3 takes a somewhat sombre view of the future, while admitting the present general prosperity of the nation. Mr. Cleveland is apprehensive that we are menaced with danger from the fact that the poorer classes of our people have just cause of complaint of past legislation. He believes that the policy of Congress has operated so completely in the interest of wealth and capital, that the poor have had little opportunity to rise out of their poverty, and that their opportunities are continually growing smaller. He said: "The existing situation is injurious to the health of our entire body politic. It stifles, in those for whose benefit it is permitted, all patriotic love of country, and substitutes in its place selfish greed and grasping avarice. Devotion to American citizenship for its own sake, and for what it should accomplish as a motive to our nation's advancement, and the happiness of all our people, is displaced by the assumption that the Government, instead of being the embodiment of equality, is but an instrumentality through which especial and individual advantages are to be gained. . . . . . Communism is a hateful thing, and a menace to peace and organized government. But the communism of combined wealth and capital, the outgrowth of overweening cupidity and selfishness, which insidiously undermines the justice and integrity of free institutions, is not less dangerous than the communism of oppressed poverty and toil, which, exasperated by injustice and discontent, attacks with wild disorder the citadel of rule." The President probably does not anticipate that there ever will be communism among the wealthy —there is little prospect of that—but that the combination of the wealthy constituted as great a danger to the nation as communism would among the poor.

The Canadian Fishery Question is the Only important foreign topic discussed by the President in his message. On this he says: "Having essayed, in the discharge of my duty, to procure by negotiation the settlement of a long-standing cause of dispute, and to remove a constant menace to the good relations of the two countries, and continuing to be of opinion that the treaty of February last, which failed to receive the approval of the Senate, did supply 'a satisfactory, practical, and final adjustment, upon a basis honorable and just to both parties of the difficult and vexed question to which it related,' and having subsequently and unavailingly recommended other legislation to Congress, which I hoped would suffice to meet the exigency created by the rejection of the treaty, I now again invoke the earnest and immediate attention of the Congress to the condition of this important question as it now stands before them and the country, and for the settlement of which I am deeply solicitous." A brief defence of his conduct in the Sackville incident, of a not very happy or dignified character, is given by the President, but it will not tend to allay the feeling which that incident aroused.

Dealing With the Details of Administrative operations, the President states that the total sum expended for pensions and administration of the office is over $82,000,000, and forms, he says, twenty-one and one half per cent. of the gross income, and nearly thirty-one per cent. of the total expenditures of the Government. 452,557 persons are now receiving pensions, of whom 806 are of the War of 1812, with 10,787 widows of those who served in that war. Sixteen hundred and sixty pensioners served in the Mexican War, and 5,104 are widows of those who served in that war. The army consists of 2,189 officers and 24,549 enlisted men, and costs $32,000,000. Eleven effective vessels will be added to the navy within the next twelve months, and the ordinary expenses of the Navy Department have been decreased by more than twenty per cent. from the sum expended for the same purposes in the years 1882 and 1884.

The Report of the Secretary of the Treasury shows that the taxes actually collected during the fiscal year ending last June amounted to $379,250,000, and the actual necessary expenses, including $80,000,000 for pensions, were $259,000,000, leaving a surplus of unnecessary taxation of $119,750,000. Of this $46,500,000 was used for the already overpaid sinking fund, and the debt was redeemed and bonds bought with all the rest except $36,500,000. He had a new proposal to make on the subject of the coinage of silver dollars, which has been continued under the mandatory regulation of Congress, until the Government is embarrassed by the accumulation. Mr. Fairchild now suggests that silver purchases shall be temporarily stopped whenever the Treasury owns five millions more than a maximum sum to be fixed by Congress, and that all further coinage shall be stopped at once, the silver purchased being held as bullion.

The Senate Set Promptly to Work on the Tariff Bill on its reassembling, and it is currently reported that if it should be rejected by the House, as is probable, it will be vigorously pressed, practically in its present shape, in the next Congress. All the internal revenue clauses of the bill were voted upon, and all the Democratic amendments were considered, and one of them accepted. There was very little debate—the bill having been exhaustively discussed in committee. Mr. Sherman gave notice that he had grave doubts as to the practicability of releasing from tax alcohol to be used in the arts without promoting great frauds, and that he would submit some amendments to this portion of the bill. This will take place after the committee of the whole has finished its duties, when there will probably be other amendments made.

England is Again Preparing for a Fight in the Soudan. A body of troops has been sent out to aid the Egyptian army in defending Suakim from the assaults of the Arabs. The expedition has called forth an indignant protest from Lord Randolph Churchill, who, since he ceased to be a member of the cabinet, has been a merciless critic of the policy of his former colleagues. Speaking in the House of Commons on December 4, he said that he believed that the Government was going against the advice of high and responsible military authorities. Within a few days a battle would be fought, and probably a desperate one, between British and Egyptian troops and Arab tribes. For what end were a mere handful of British soldiers exposed to the risk of an encounter with the Soudanese? They were a totally inadequate force, and the presence of 4,000 utterly unreliable Egyptians did not remove the danger. Even if success attended the battle it would necessitate larger operations in the interior. He implored the House to prevent renewed slaughter in the Soudan, and to save the lives of the soldiers who were being uselessly sacrificed. The House, however, rejected his advice by a large majority.

The Parnell Commission Examined Several important witnesses last week. Their testimony was, as much of the testimony previously given was not, pertinent to the subject of the inquiry, inasmuch as, if true, it proved that the League paid for the commission of outrages. The chief of these witnesses was a man named O'Connor, who said he had been a member of a secret society calling itself "The Boys." He took part in moonlight expeditions carrying guns and revolvers. Timothy Horan, *secretary of a branch of the League, paid witness and nine others six shillings each on the occasion of one outrage.* He also swore that Timothy Harrington had employed "The Boys" in an election. He instructed them not to kill voters, but only to frighten them greatly and compel them to sign voting papers. Those who refused were coerced and compelled to sign. Mr. Harrington paid the witness $35. All the members of the "inner circle" belonged to the League. Membership in the League was essential to membership in "The Boys." The commission has now adjourned for a month.

The Dreaded Second of December, the Anniversary of several momentous events in French history, passed over this year quietly in Paris. Extensive preparations were made to suppress any disorder that might arise, and at one time there were indications that a procession, organized to decorate the grave of a deputy who died fighting on the street-barricades on December 2, 1851, might commit outrages. The procession, however, was allowed to proceed unmolested, and it spent its strength in shouting "Long live the Republic!" singing the Marseillaise, and in other inoffensive ways. From thirty to forty thousand persons took part in it. Much to the relief of the law-abiding classes, there was no conflict with the mob. The significant feature of the celebration was the evident unpopularity of General Boulanger with the Communists. One of the most frequent cries was, "Down with Boulanger!" and the orator of the day clearly had him in mind when he said, "The democracy, acquiring renewed strength in the example of the glorious dead, is prepared to face Cæsarism, which is raising its head."

A Distinguished Advocate of Woman Suffrage has declared himself in England. In a speech delivered last week in Edinburgh, Lord Salisbury, the English Prime Minister, said he was in favor of woman suffrage, and he hoped the day was not far distant when women would be allowed to vote. He has, however, made no concession in his Irish policy. In the same speech he said, referring to the treatment of Irish political prisoners, that such treatment ought to deter others from following their example, and that so long as such offenders were dangerous to the community, they must be treated like other offenders. He warned the unionists to watch Mr. Gladstone, who, he said, was showing an increasing tendency to accept the extremest views of the separatists. There was growing in Mr. Gladstone's mind a distinct idea of the entire separation of Ireland.

Rumors of the Serious Illness of the Emperor of Germany were current last week. The Emperor's physicians reported that he was suffering from a catarrhal affection and prohibited his going out of doors. Persons usually well informed, however, assert that his illness is a renewal of his periodical ear trouble, which develops at intervals, and is expected ultimately to affect his brain. He employed part of his enforced leisure in elaborating the details of further army and navy reforms. He kept his military cabinet very busy, demanding immediate reports on a variety of questions. The officials of the Cabinet find his incessant activity something too much for them. He keeps them working sometimes night and day, insisting that there be no delay in the reports he demands, his unvarying orders being to reply within twenty-four hours.

Contributions to the Fund for Supplying colored clergymen in the South with this journal have been received since our last acknowledgment to the amount of $15. They are: from China, Me., $1; W. Lebanon, Ind., $1; Lacota, Mich., 50 cents; Independence, Mo., $1; Spokane Falls, Wash. Ter., $1; Lewiston, Penn., $1; Syracuse, N. Y., $3; Starbuck, Wash. Ter., 50 cents; Westford, Penn., $1; Baltimore, Md., $1; Denbigh, Ont., Canada, $4. "During the past twelve months," says one of these clergymen, in a letter received last week, "THE CHRISTIAN HERALD, which was sent to us through the kindness of some good friend subscribing to your fund, has been a shining light in our home, and has been a great help to me in my mission work among our people. They are always very poor, and this year many of them having lost their crops through freshets, they are still less able than ever to pay a preacher. My income is therefore very small, and I cannot afford to pay a subscription, but I shall miss the HERALD terribly." Many such letters come.

A Large Audience was Held Spell-bound in the Fourth Presbyterian Church in 34th Street, New York, on Tuesday December 4, by the deeply interesting lecture of Bishop H. C. Riley, of Mexico. The Bishop's stereopticon views illustrating his journeys in the Holy Land, in Spain, Mexico, and Central America, are of a very superior order, and were watched with intense interest. The views of the Mount of Olives, the Garden of Gethsemane, and the Sea of Tiberias were especially vivid, and enabled the spectator to realize better than before the scenes of the most momentous events in human history. Bishop Riley gave an eloquent and impressive sketch of the work in Mexico, and of the vast possibilities of usefulness which the present condition of that land affords. Ministers of churches could give their people a very high gratification, and might at the same time help to arouse public interest in Bishop Riley's important work, by inviting him to lecture.

The Value of Three Fingers was Assessed last week by the Supreme Court of New York at two thousand dollars. The question was raised by a suit of a young man to recover damages for injuries which he received nine years ago. A little before that time he was employed as an errand boy in the service of a tinware manufacturer. His employer promoted him to work in the factory, and the boy, being ignorant of the machinery used, was injured. His right hand was caught in a belt and carried over the wheels, where it was so hurt that he had to lose three fingers. The employer contended that the injuries resulted from the boy's carelessness and negligence, and that, therefore, there was no ground for a suit for damages. The court decided against him. It held that the boy having been put to work where he was liable to be injured, and having had no instruction as to the nature of his danger, could not be considered negligent, and therefore he had a right to recover damages from the person who had placed him there. The employer was therefore ordered to pay $2,000 as compensation. When parents, anxious to secure worldly advantages for their children, place them in situations of spiritual danger, and they fall into sin, God will not hold them guiltless. But there can be no compensation then. (Lam. 5: 7.)

The Release of an Embezzler From Prison in Salem, Ore., on December 3, led to an affecting scene in the Governor's room. The man's crime had been a very gross breach of trust, with no extenuating circumstances, and it was supposed that he would have to serve out to the very last day the long term of imprisonment to which he had been sentenced. His wife, however, was not daunted by the obstacles in the way of a pardon. She left her home in Washington, D. C., where she was well provided for, and devoted her whole time to intercession with every one whose influence could aid in obtaining her husband's release. No one pitied the criminal, but few could resist the wife's pleading, and ultimately she gained the signatures of so many influential men, and her cause was so strongly endorsed, that the Governor yielded and pardoned her husband. When at last the wife's efforts were crowned with success, the two went to the executive mansion to thank the Governor, and his Excellency, addressing the released man said: "If you ever speak an unkind word to that little woman, you ought to be returned to the place from which you have just been released for the remainder of your natural life. You owe her a debt that can only be repaid by a life of truest devotion." Every one will agree with the Governor. Ingratitude in such a case would be very base. But what shall be said of those who, having been rescued from a far worse fate by the death of Christ, are unmindful of their obligations? (1 Cor. 6: 20.)

The Suicide of a Rejected Lover is Reported from Boston, Mass. A young man in good circumstances in South Boston, about a year ago became engaged to a young lady who lived near him. He loved her passionately, and was overjoyed when she accepted him and promised to become his wife. He set about making preparations for their marriage, and was full of hope as to his future happiness. His friends frequently rallied him on the ardor of his affection, which grew more intense as the time set for the marriage approached. But for some cause, which the report does not disclose, the lady's affection cooled, and three weeks ago she plainly told him that she would never marry him. The lover was heart-broken, and when he found that his rejection was irrevocable he lost all interest in life. Finally, after bearing his disappointment a few days, he resolved to take his own life. He went to a Boston hotel, and deliberately suffocated himself with gas. Various indications about the room in which he died, showed that he had completely lost his reason. He is not the first lover, by thousands, who has so centred his affections on a woman that, when she has disappointed him, life seemed not worth living. No man or woman is in danger of being overcome by any such disappointment who loves God supremely. He changes not, and His love affords a refuge for the mourner that keeps him from despair. (Mal 3: 6.)

A Curious Delusion Came Before a Philadelphia court on December 3, in a charge of assault brought by a lady against a man of respectability and generally blameless character. The lady said that the defendant came to her house and requested an interview with her sister, a middle-aged lady, who was on a visit to her. As her sister had been annoyed before by the same man, she declined allowing him to see her. Then the man became violent, declared that her sister was his wife, and insisted that he had a right to see her. When the refusal was maintained the man became furious, and declaring that no one should keep his wife from him, assaulted the lady and endeavored to make his way to the room where he supposed her sister was. Thereupon a policeman was called in and the intruder was arrested. In court the man persisted in his claim that he was married to the lady whom he went to see, but on being cross-examined he was unable to produce any proof of his assertion. It was shown that he had been ardently attached to the lady from his boyhood, and his infatuation had so affected his mind, as at length to produce the delusion that he was really married to her. Hence his strange behavior at her sister's residence. There is reason to fear that many who now cherish the belief that they are united to Christ by an eternal bond will at last find themselves similarly mistaken. The outward and visible church has many members whose Godless lives prove that they are destitute of the faith and purity which alone can make them part of Christ's bride. (Luke 13: 26, 27.)

Millions of Dollars go to a Waif Rescued by the Children's Society of New York, as the heir of a wealthy citizen. Mr. Gerry, the president of the society, is the authority for the story. He told a reporter that in 1876 an agent of the society was in one of the city police courts when a man and his wife were on trial for drunkenness. It was a very gross case, and when they were sentenced it was shown that they had also maltreated their child, a bright, intelligent looking boy. The officer asked for the custody of the boy, and the judge granted his request. Shortly afterward, while he was in charge of the society, a wealthy gentleman saw him, heard his story, and took an interest in him. He brought his wife to see him, and she too was attracted by the lad. Finally legal papers were drawn up, and the society turned the boy over for adoption to his rich friend. He was sent to school and afterward to college, his progress fully justifying the good opinion of the couple who adopted him. The gentleman is just dead, and he has left his large fortune in equal shares to his wife and adopted son. The latter's share is over two millions, and he will doubtless inherit the other two when the widow dies, as she is passionately fond of him. Doubtless the boy's good fortune will make him the object of envy of other boys; but they may know that a far higher position is open to them all. They may become the adopted sons of the King of kings, and heirs of all things. (Rom. 8, 16, 17).

BRIEF NOTES.

Mr. C. S. Billings is conducting services in Nebraska, with much success. Omaha, Neb., is his permanent address.

The Rev. H. W. Brown is meeting with much success in Indiana. Reports of the meetings at Goshen and Vincennes are very encouraging.

Mr. E. W. Bliss, of Chicago, whose work both in the East and West is well known, proposes to resume evangelistic labor at the beginning of next year.

At the American Institute of Christian Philosophy, on December 6, Professor George M. Powell, of Philadelphia, read a paper on the "Cash Value of Conscience."

The Rev. Alexander Patterson, of Chicago, intends devoting himself entirely to evangelistic work through the winter. His address is, Y. M. C. A., Chicago.

Rev. Justin D. Fulton, D. D., has commenced a course of Sunday afternoon lectures on the errors of Romanism, at Cooper Union, N. Y. They begin at 3 o'clock.

The Berkeley Street Church, Boston, has decided to send Mr. Noyes, at its own expense, as a missionary to Japan, as he has been rejected by the American Board.

The General Mission Committee of the Methodist Church has appropriated $1,200,000 for missions for the coming year. Of this sum $567,000 are for foreign missions.

A Christian Convention on Holiness and Divine Healing will be held at Portland, Me., on December 20. Full particulars may be obtained by addressing Rev. D. W. Lelacheur, Portland, Me.

In Illinois there are now 208 Christian Endeavor societies, with over 12,000 members, nearly half of them having been formed during the year. The largest society is connected with the Warren Avenue Church of Chicago.

Bishop William Taylor sailed from New York for Africa, on the S. S. *Gallia*, on December 1. On the evening of November 30 a farewell meeting was held in Jane Street Church. The Bishop said he had no dread of going back.

The Rev. C. H. Yatman's work at Galveston Tex., will long be gratefully remembered by the clergymen of the city. The Baptist, Presbyterian, and Methodist churches united in the meetings, and all have been blessed themselves, and increased in numbers.

The new edifice of the First Congregational Church of Northampton, Mass., was ruined by fire on November 28. The building cost $65,000, and was insured for $50,000. The parish had the famous Jonathan Edwards as its pastor for twenty-three years. This is the fifth church building erected by the society.

The Sunday-school teachers of New York are deriving great benefit from meeting on Saturday evening to converse on the International Lesson for the next day. Dr. Kittredge conducts the meeting and answers questions. The meeting is held in Madison Avenue Reformed Church at 57th Street at 8 o'clock.

The American Board of Foreign Missions recently received notice of the death of the Rev. Harry Gardiner, who was being trained for mission work in Zululand. Two days later the Board received an application for an appointment from a student in the Pacific Theological Seminary, who expressed a preference for the Zulu field.

The Next Few Weeks will be the best time for canvassing for new subscribers. We are happy to learn that many of our friends are already introducing THE CHRISTIAN HERALD among their friends and neighbors. Any one desiring sample copies *for this purpose*, will be supplied free of cost by writing for them, stating explicitly how many can be advantageously used. Address "The Manager," 63 Bible House, New York.

"ON HIS BREAST."

A New Sermon by Pastor C. H. Spurgeon.

"Now there was leaning on Jesus' bosom one of His disciples, whom Jesus loved," &c. John 13:23-26.

Two Strangely Different Men at the Table—The Place Nearest the Master's Heart—I. Some Disciples Specially Loved—Why Christ Loved John—His Loving Heart—Made him His Executor—Saints Left in Charge Now—II. Their Greatest Honor—Birth Names Dropped by Nobles—John Did not Boast of It—III. Brings Special Privileges—Being Near to Jesus—Receiving Tokens of Endearment—Great Confidence—Great Liberty—A General Injunction.

PICTURE the Lord and His apostles at the holy Supper! A world of interest centres here. Two figures strangely different met in this scene—met, shortly afterwards to part, and never to meet again. To look upon them, they seemed equally disciples of Jesus, and from the position which one of them occupied, as leaning on the Lord's bosom, and the other as the treasurer of the Master's little store, they seemed to be equally trusted and honored followers of the great Lord. You might not have known, by mere sight, which was the better man of the two—John or Judas. Most probably you would have preferred the gentle manners of John; but I should suppose—for our Lord never chose a man to an office unless he had some qualification—you would also have admired the calm prudence of Judas, and his quiet business tact. They sat at the same table, engaged in the same exercises, and looked much the same kind of men. None of us would have guessed that one of them was John the divine, and the other was Judas the devil.

There is something very solemn about this meeting of such strangely different characters in one common act, and in the society of the same divine Lord. John is here; is Judas here? Let the question be started and passed round, "Lord, is it I?" He is the least likely to be the traitor who is

Nearest to His Lord's Heart.

He who occupies such a place as John did is not the betrayer. Oh that we might be fired with a loving ambition to be the disciple whom Jesus loved, leaning on Jesus' bosom! for then, though we ask the question, "Lord, is it I?" it will not linger long upon our hearts; for His love, shed abroad within them, shall answer every question of self-examination, and we shall cry, "Lord, thou knowest all things; thou knowest that I love thee." Let that stand as an introduction. And now our remarks will be very simple.

I. And the first is this—

Some Disciples are Specially Loved

of their Lord. The Lord had a people around Him who were His disciples. Within them He had twelve. Within the twelve He had three. Within the three He had one disciple whom He loved. Probably our Lord's attachment to John was partly a human one; and so far as it was human, though we have known Christ after the flesh, yet now after the flesh know we even Him no more. There may, also, have been such affection in Jesus toward John as there would be in any eminent Christian toward another Christly believer—in any one whom the Lord made to be a leader of His church, toward such and such a member of that church in whom He could see most of the lovely characteristics of Christ. I cannot but think that it was so. But it strikes me that our Lord Jesus loved John in some measure more than the rest, in the entirety of his character, as Jesus Christ, the Son of God as well as the Son of man. He loved all His own then, and He loves all His own now. There is infinite love in the heart of Jesus toward all His people; and if there be any degrees in that love, yet the lowest degree is inconceivably great. The very least member of the divine family may say, "He loved me, and gave Himself for me." He loves us beyond all human expression. We are quite sure of this. Yet that love has this difference about it, that it is more enjoyed by some on earth than by others.

It is clear, as a matter of fact, that the divine love is manifested to some more clearly than to others. My beloved brethren, you must know this to be the case; for there are those among us who walk with God, who enjoy the light of Jehovah's countenance at all times, who if depressed have the art of rolling their burden upon the Lord, and soon are delivered from it. You know them; they are the brethren who feel like singing all the while, for Jesus is their friend, and they rejoice in him. There was one in the Old Testament who was called "a man greatly beloved," and there are

Daniels on Earth.

Christ has among women still his Marys, whom he loves. He loved Martha, too; but still there was a special place for Mary. Jesus has still his Johns, whom he peculiarly loves. There are first as well as last. All may be of Israel, but all the tribes are not Judah, and in Judah all the men are not Davids. Who shall deny that there are degrees in grace? Have we not among us babes, and young men, and fathers? Have we not first the blade, then the ear, and then the full corn in the ear? It is so; and though I will not argue for degrees in glory, and, indeed, deprecate the spirit in which the doctrine of degrees in glory is often set forth, yet we are sure, for we see it with our eyes, that there are degrees of grace, and especially degrees in the enjoyment of the love of Jesus. Amongst those who do really love their Lord, and are really loved by him, one star differeth from another in that love.

Why Was It John

that was "that disciple whom Jesus loved"? Certainly it was not because he was naturally higher in rank than the others, for he was a fisherman, like the most of them; and James was certainly equal in birth, for he was his brother. Our blessed Lord did not love John because of any excess of talent; for albeit that John's Apocalypse and his Gospel are, in some respects, the highest parts of revealed Scripture, being both the simplest and the most mysterious portions of Holy Writ, yet we should not say that John betrayed evidence of so great a mind in itself, naturally, or by education, as Paul had. He had as much talent as his Lord gave him, but there was nothing about him so special that he should for that cause have been loved; and, to dismiss the thought with a word, Jesus never loves men on account of talent. These things are external. Our Lord loved John, specially, for a better reason than that. *Men love those that are like them*, and Jesus, as man, loved John because the processes of grace had developed in John the image of Jesus. John, like his Lord, had much love. He may have lacked some qualities in which Peter, and James, and others excelled, but he towered above them all in love. He was full of tenderness, and therefore his Master at once selected him to be His choicest companion and His dearest friend. You know the way, then, to the heart of Christ. Let your own heart be full of love, and you will know His love. You greatly need, not a great head, but a great heart. You must have, not more knowledge, but more affection; not a higher rank in society, but a higher rank in the power to love Jesus and to love your fellow-men. Less of self, and more of Jesus, and then you shall enjoy more of His love.

This being the case, that John had this loving spirit, and our Lord Jesus Christ loved him more than others, it led on to the fact that John was the recipient of confidences from Christ which others had not. Jesus

Made John His Executor,

and He left him in His will all His earthly possessions. You will say to me, "And pray, what possessions had the Master?" Well, He had one possession of which He was very fond, and He could not die until He had disposed by His last will and testament of that one earthly possession. It was His mother. He loved her, and must care for her; and there passed a little word, a kind of sign, between Him and John at the last moment. Do not think that John would have understood what Jesus meant when He said: "Woman, behold thy son," and, "Son, behold thy mother!" if there had not been a quiet talk about that matter some time before. But Jesus, I doubt not, had told John that the only earthly care He had, as man, was that while He was away slumbering in the grave He would have His mother cared for still, and so He left her in John's charge.

If you love Jesus Christ very much, He will leave something in your charge, depend upon that; and the more you love Him, the more will He trust you with some loving commission which He would not trust with anybody else. I have known Him leave a dear child of His, some dear old saint, for a favored believer to look after, whom He never would have had to look after if Jesus had not said: "I love this dear old saint, and I shall commit him—I shall commit her—to the custody of such a one, because he loves Me, and he will take care of this poor one for My sake." Some of you have nobody to care for. Do you not grieve to think that you lack this token of His special love? As sure as ever there is any intimate love between Jesus and any soul, He trusts that soul with something to be done, to be endured, to be guarded, to be mourned over, or in some way to become a sacred trust.

II. Now, secondly, we note that the beloved ones count this to be

Their Greatest Honor.

This is evidently in the text; for John, who wrote these words, called himself "one of His disciples, whom Jesus loved"; and I think three times besides he speaks of himself as "that disciple whom Jesus loved." He took his name from his Lord's love, which he evidently counted to be his greatest honor. This was John's most notable title. As a servant of the Queen, having distinguished himself in the service of her Majesty, becomes the lord of such and such a town, and he takes the name of the place as a name of honor, so John drops his own birth-given name, as it were, and takes this title instead of it—"that disciple whom Jesus loves."

Now, had John been proud he would have altered the title thus. He would have said, "That disciple who loved Jesus." This would have been true, though not modest. There was, as far as his heart was capable of it, a reciprocity of love between John and Jesus. If Jesus loved him, he loved Jesus; but John never called himself "That disciple who loved Jesus." No, for he felt as if his own love was altogether unworthy of mention in the presence of the love of Jesus.

Then notice also, as if to show us that there was no pride in taking the title, that he does not say, "John was the disciple whom Jesus loved." We gather from other facts that it was John. All the traditions and beliefs of the early church went to testify that it was John. We have not, any of us, any doubt about the fact that it was John. It has, as it were, leaked out; but John nowhere says that he was the man. All that he has said is "That disciple whom Jesus loved"; and thus he makes the love more conspicuous than the person who received it. We know that it must have been John, for many reasons; but still he does not say so. He hides John behind the love of Jesus, which proves that John gloried in the love of Christ, but did not boast of it egotistically.

III. A step farther. This special love

Brings Special Privileges.

It brought to John the first privilege of being very near to Jesus, his Lord. At that supper he was nearest to the place which Jesus occupied. But his position of being nearest was brought about by his being best loved. He was nearest in fellowship because dearest in love. Now, beloved, if you are best loved by Christ, you live nearest to Him. I am sure of it. If you love Him best, and He loves you best, you will be more in prayer than others; you will spend more time alone with Jesus than other Christians do. You will abound in petition and praise. You will read His Word with greater diligence;

you will drink it in with greater delight. You will live for Him, too, with greater consecration. Your whole time will be spent in His company. When you are at your work in the house, or the field, or the shop, you will still be with Him. The dearest must be the nearest. That is the first privilege.

The second was the privilege of using and receiving tokens of endearment. He leaned his head on Jesus' bosom, looking up into His face; and Jesus looked down on him. There was mutual endearment, for Jesus loved him, and

He Loved Jesus.

As for John, it must have been a heaven below to be thus in the bosom of his Lord. He mentions it three times, you see; twice in this passage, and once in the last chapter of his gospel, where there was no necessity for mentioning it. He had such a recollection of his head having once been laid on his Lord's breast, that he must put it in when he is speaking about Peter and himself. He says, "The disciple which also leaned on His breast at supper, and said, Lord, which is he that betrayeth thee?" He must needs repeat the charming fact, for it was such a delight to him. O beloved, we cannot now touch the bosom of Jesus after the flesh, for He is gone up on high; but there are still most sweet endearments of spirit between the Lord Jesus and His loving disciples. I hope very many of you know this choice blessing of living in the immediate enjoyment of your Saviour's love. May you never lose it!

Then is there a third boon, not only of nearness and endearment, but of confidence toward the Lord; for it was a bold thing, surely, for John to lean his head on Christ's bosom. If you can get your very heart into His heart and come closer to Him than even John dared to do—if you carry that coming beyond all previous comings, yet Jesus neither will nor can resent the nearest approaches of any one of His believing people. We lose a great deal of Christ's loving fellowship because we are so formal and distant toward Him. Jesus seeks to reach our hearts, He stoops to our littleness; let us pluck up courage to draw near to Him.

Surely there was a great

Liberty Given to Him,

Some would have said he took a liberty in thus leaning where no head of king or emperor might aspire to rise. He was the most honored of all human beings; but surely he took great liberties. No, he did not, for the Lord Himself gave him access with boldness. Great love has privileges which make her boldest advances no intrusion. Love has the key of all the rooms of the Father's house. Love has the range of Paradise. Love may read the very heart of God. Love may come where she wills, and go unchallenged. John said to our Saviour, "Lord, who is it?" Jesus looked down at him and said, as if He did not want the others to know at all, "He it is to whom I shall give a sop." He had just to watch a little while. He that can most often pray the prayer of faith, he that can see farthest into Christ's mysteries, is the man whose heart loves Jesus best, and whose head lies most in the bosom of his Lord.

Now a step farther, and a very little more, and we have done. This creates

Special Knowledge.

The special privileges of love lead on to a special knowledge of Christ. I do not think that any other evangelist notices Christ's emotion at the supper in the matter of his spirit as John has done. He writes, "When Jesus hath thus said, he was troubled in spirit," and so on. John was so close to the Lord, with his head on his breast, that he could tell, by the heaving of His bosom, that He was troubled. The mind of God is not so revealed to any man now that he can set up to foretell the future like a prophet; but, mark you, the choice ones amongst the saints have intimations of the mind of God about many things. Those who live at court can often foresee the king's movements when others cannot. It is my firm conviction that favored believers have tokens, warnings, and hints from above. Even the choicest spirits may not understand the Lord's meaning all at once; but if any man can read anything of the future, it is he that puts his head where all eyes grow clear, and all hearts become pure, even upon the breast of Jesus.

I have done, when I notice two things. The first is this—that the favored position which John occupied did not screen him from the necessity of asking the question, "Lord, is it I?" There really was no suspicion of him, nor any reason for such suspicion; but his heart was in a right state, and therefore he felt it necessary to say, "Lord, is it I?" as well as any of the rest. And I make this remark because the very persons who do not say, "Lord, is it I?" are those who ought to say it. If you are enjoying more of God's love to-night than ever you did in your life, yet do not profess to have climbed above the need of self-examination, when the question comes, "Art thou really one of His?" do not chase it away, as if it were an impertinence. Entertain the inquiry till you can satisfy it with a sufficient answer. It is not your bold talker that is your true lover after all. There is a confidence which is fatal.

The other remark, with which I finish, is this: That John's nearness to Christ did not authorize him to make answer to his fellow disciples, nor to judge any one of them. Time was when John might have sat in judgment over them. Did he not desire to sit upon a throne judging the twelve tribes of Israel with his brother James? But now that he has his head in his Lord's bosom, he is

Not Anxious to Judge,

but far otherwise. His brethren keep asking, "Lord, is it I?" Peter makes signs to him. John does not presume to make a guess as to the traitor's name, but he softly says, "Lord, who is it?" He asked that question of his Lord; but he did not himself pitch upon Judas. No, he might, perhaps, have laid his suspicions upon someone else who would have been innocent. It was wise to refer the matter to the Lord.

Some say that they live very near to Jesus. It is an evil sign when men speak of their own attainments. These are the people who, in the next breath, begin to condemn others. But this is not after the manner of the beloved John. Some professors affirm that they are going to have a particularly fine place in the glory, all by themselves. I do not quite understand their theory, but I am sure I do not grudge any of my Master's servants any special honor they may desire. I have kept company on earth with such a poor lot of brethren, and I have learned to love them so well, that I would rather abide with them in their inferior heaven than rise with the cream of the cream into the upper places. I like to be with God's people of the poorer class, and of the more struggling and afflicted sort. I like to be with God's people who wrestle hard with sins and doubts and fears. If I get spoken to by my

Very Superior Brethren,

I find that I have very little pleasant fellowship with them, for I know nothing about their wonderful experience of freedom from conflict, and complete deliverance from every evil tendency. I have never won an inch of the way to heaven without fighting for it. I have never lived a day but I have had to sorrow over my imperfections. I sometimes get near to God, but at that time I weep most about my faults and failings. Although I have thus spoken after the manner of men, I do not believe in these superior beings, nor in their superior heaven.

I close by saying—you remember what Jesus said to Peter. Peter was always a little too fast, and he therefore ventured to peer into things which did not concern him, and so he said to Jesus, as he looked at John, "Lord, and what shall this man do?" He did not think badly of brother John; I should have been ashamed of Peter if he had done so. But still he said, "What shall this man do?" Our blessed Lord replied to him, "What is that to thee? Follow thou me." So, when you feel inclined, because you are growing in grace and becoming somebody, to say, "Lord, and what shall this poor member do? And what shall this imperfect brother be? What shall that poor, blundering new convert do?"—remember the words of Jesus: "What is that to thee? Follow thou me." Mind your Master, and mind yourself, and let your brethren stand or fall to their own Lord, as you must. Now, come and lay your head in your Lord's bosom, and never mind Peter. May God bless you, for Christ's sake!

[The prayers of the readers of this journal are requested for the blessing of God upon its Editors, and those whose sermons, articles or labors for Christ are printed in it; and that its circulation may be used by the Holy Spirit for the conversion of many sinners and the quickening of God's people. Dr. Talmage and Mr. Spurgeon especially request prayer every Sunday morning on behalf of their labors.]

GEMS FROM NEW BOOKS.

A CITY BOARDING-HOUSE.*

HERE is a true sketch of one lodging-house. Flats are unknown in the part of the world where it stands, and it is a large house of four floors. On the ground floor is the dining-room, with a bedroom opening off it. A music-master has these rooms, and his piano jangles all day. On the first floor is the drawing-room, which is occupied by two ladies. The stair to the first floor is carpeted, and comparatively well lighted. On the next stair—in the ascent of which it is well to grip the banisters—there is a piece of ragged carpet here and there. Beyond that all is plain wood, which, however, is hidden from you unless you carry a candle. At the top of this stair the new lodger has his room. It looks out on chimney-tops, which is not a disadvantage in this street, where for a view you have to choose between the dingy houses opposite, and a lumpy plain of roofs. The room is of fair size, with a bed on one side and a dilapidated couch on the other. The occupant will have to use the bed as a sofa, for the couch gives way if it leaves the wall. There is a wash-stand flanked by two chairs; an aged easy-chair, which rocks uncomfortably, owing to a caster being missing; and two decaying tables. Nelson is dying at Trafalgar in a flashy frame on the wall. The ceiling is very low, as in nearly all London houses when you come higher than the second floor. There is no gas. The cost of the whole with board is eighteen shillings ($4.50) to thirty shillings ($7.50) weekly, according to the quality of board, and location.

A Dry Goods Clerk.

At first he is expected to "live in"—that is, to make his home on the premises of the firm. He will breakfast, dine, have tea, and sup at the warehouse or shop, and probably sleep on some adjacent premises, where his leisure time must be spent. About 7:30 A. M. every one is expected to have left the dormitory, and to be at the warehouse. In some houses the junior hands will have to use the broom, and sweep off the floor; in almost all they will be expected to dust the goods. This work done, the young man changes his clothes, arranges his toilet, and goes to breakfast. Tea, coffee, and bread and butter are the invariable fare. From 8:30 to noon he follows the usual routine of business life. Few customers have to be served before 11 o'clock, but there are cases to be unpacked, windows to be dressed, goods to be displayed, bales of stuff to be measured, and innumerable duties to be accomplished before the world comes to buy. At noon the first party goes to dinner: in most city houses it goes up to the third, fourth, or fifth floor. In some neighbor-

---

* From "Tempted London," a series of articles reprinted from a religious journal, describing the temptations of the English metropolis, in order to put young men who go up from the country districts on their guard against men and women who would inveigle them into gambling-places and improper resorts. The same kind of temptations assail young people in New York and other large cities of the United States, and therefore the publication of the book on this side may be made useful to them. 288 pages; Price $1.25. Published by *A. C. Armstrong & Son*, 714 Broadway, N. Y.

Mrs. McKee, Daughter of the President-Elect.

A Christian Colporteur in the Jewish Quarter at Jaffa.

hoods it often goes down to the dismal gas-lit cellar, or basement. Beer of a very indifferent quality is put on the table in pitchers for all who choose to drink. After dinner comes most of the buying and selling, and from 12 to 5 are the busiest hours of the day. A quarter of an hour is allowed for tea, after which the day's work is wound up. The place is closed to the public at 6, and except in busy times most of the employees are at liberty to leave about 7, and do what they like with the hours until 11.

A Mother's Prayers Answered.

I have now been five years in London, and well do I remember my first impressions. I had had one situation, and then came into a London warehouse. My father and mother were Christians—good examples to me—but they never warned me of the temptations I should be subjected to. Probably parents think their example sufficient. It is a good thing, example, but not enough. A few words from them would have put me on my guard. I was not then a Christian. The house I went to, I suppose, is like many more in town—contained many men who laughed at virtue, and extolled vice. Such were my associates. For a time I stood my ground, but gradually got accustomed to many objectionable things, did not notice them, and then (although I detested swearing) I did not mind hearing or making a joke about vice. I then met an old school-mate, who was not particularly moral, and we attended several restaurants together. Luckily he gave me the cold shoulder subsequently, and I was thus, perhaps, prevented from going further into dissipation. The chance, as some might call it, was, I am sure, the restraining grace of God in answer to a praying mother. As I look back, I can now see plainly how it was I was not allowed to go my own way; the prayers of a believing mother were answered, and I was converted to Christ a month after her death.

MRS. MARY McKEE.

Daughter of the President-Elect.

THE beautiful and winsome lady whose portrait appears on this page, is to be one of the ladies who will conduct the hospitalities of the White House during the term of General Harrison. She is about twenty-seven years of age, and is married to Mr. J. R. McKee, a wholesale boot and shoe dealer in Indianapolis. She is no stranger in Washington, for when her father was Senator Harrison she made many friends among the young people at the Federal capital, who will be glad to resume their friendly relations with her. Mrs. McKee has two children: Benjamin Harrison McKee, who will be two years old in March next, and Mary Lodge McKee, who will be eight months old.

Mrs. McKee is a well-skilled musician, like her mother, excelling as a performer on the piano. She is a sprightly, interesting woman, and the responsibilities of married life have not taken from her that charming liveliness which made her so popular when she was a belle in Washington.

THE GOSPEL AMONG EASTERN JEWS.

(See Illustration.)

ONE of the most interesting spheres of Christian work is that at Jaffa, and other Eastern cities, where an effort is now being made to bring Jews to see in Jesus of Nazareth the Messiah promised to their fathers. The illustration on this page depicts one branch of this work—that of a colporteur circulating New Testaments and gospel portions among the Jews who frequent that centre of trade. Their work has been much blessed, and though many still live on in wilful and obstinate blindness, others have been drawn, by the majestic life of Jesus, to love and serve Him. Here, also, Bible-women have been greatly blessed among the females of the locality. The senior Bible-woman at Jaffa, a Christian Jewess, is named Hannah. The following incident shows the character of her work. She says: "I was going from house to house, and in a yard I found seven or eight families. A woman came to me, saying, 'Are you a Bible-woman?' I answered, 'Yes.' She said, 'I do not wish you to come into my yard; I will fence it round.' 'But I must come to let you hear the Word,' I said. 'I will shut the door, that you may not come in! I don't want to hear your Book. I belong to the people of God, and do not want to be taught by you,' the woman answered. 'But,' said I, 'the people of God wish to hear His Holy Word, and they read His Book, and love those who read it; but you are contrary to all this; from this it appears that you are a lost sheep of the House of Israel.'

"Then the woman went into her house; but the neighbors called me, saying, 'Come here; if she does not want to hear the Book of God, we do; please read to us.' So I read to them about the lost lamb. Then the woman was much ashamed, and came back to listen very quietly. Some said, 'We know how to pray to God.' I answered, 'It is not enough; we must act as we pray.' Some call me into their houses and gather themselves together to hear the Word of God."

ROSE BERKLEY'S CONSECRATED LIFE.

(See Illustration on page 797.)

WAS that the clatter of a horse's hoofs? The girl who sat listlessly sewing at the foot of a large tree, against which she rested her back, was alert in a moment, and looked eagerly toward the gate which opened from the lane into the park, where she sat. Yes, a horse was trotting down the lane, but it was not the horse she was looking for, and, still more to the purpose, its rider was a good twenty years older than the man whose coming was the one event wanting to make the glorious summer morning perfect bliss to Rose Berkley. An expression of disappointment escaped her lips, and she resumed the work which she was doing for her sister, the clergyman's wife, with whom she was spending the summer. It seemed to Rose a long time that she had waited; the work made little progress and at last dropped unheeded on her lap, as the dark eyes closed, and she slept.

At the time Rose took her seat under the tree, a horseman was riding rapidly some two miles away, with that tree as his destination. It was a familiar road to him, though in former years he had been accustomed to travel half a mile farther upon it than he intended to do this morning. But at that time the object of his journeys had been an hour or two of talk with his brother clergyman, the husband of Rose's sister, a discussion of theological problems, consultation about methods of aggressive Christian work, and always an earnest prayer together for God's blessing on their work for the Master. That was before Rose made her appearance at the parsonage. Since then, and since she had promised to be his wife, Grey had spent less time with his friend, and found his great enjoyment in wandering with Rose through the woods, or, stretched on the velvety turf at her side beneath their favorite tree, in talking to her of his work, his hopes and aspirations. There had never been much love-talk between them, for Grey was too much absorbed in his labors, and too intense in his habits of thought, to have the disposition for uttering the airy nothings which make the staple of the conversation of more shallow lovers. Rose did not understand much of what he said; but she loved him passionately, and with a reverence that had made her for the first time in her life really in earnest in spiritual thought and life. She wanted to be worthy of him, and to be what a wife should be—her husband's confidante and companion.

Grey would have been at the tree long before Rose fell asleep but for a catastrophe, which was one of those mysterious dispensations of Providence that perplex Christians and drive them back to the firm faith which trusts God and loves Him, in spite of events that must wait for eternity to explain. As he was taking a cross-cut over a rising ground to the main road, he saw a carriage approaching at frightful speed. Two ladies were in it, and they had in their terror abandoned the effort to control the excited horses, and were clinging convulsively to each other in helpless despair.

Grey put his horse instantly to a gallop and entered the road a hundred yards ahead of the runaway span. He dismounted and planted himself directly in their way, ready to clutch the reins when they came up. The horses seemed to understand his intention, and swerved as they came to where he stood. He bounded forward, however, and caught the reins, but not so effectually as he had hoped. Hanging to them with all his might, he checked the speed of the horses, but as he was dragged along, he fell, and, before he had brought them completely to a stand, he had been trampled upon and crushed. It was a lonely country road in which the accident had occurred, and before the two ladies could recover their presence of mind and obtain assistance, the brave man who had saved their lives had breathed his last.

For a long time after the news was broken to her, Rose lay hovering between life and death. When, at length, her young strength triumphed over the shock, and it was known that she would live, she would sit silently thinking of her dead lover for hours, and then would fall into fits of weeping, that were the relief to her crushed heart that saved her from losing her reason. It was through her brother-in-law that at last light and spiritual strength came to enable her to live out her life.

"You will see him again," he said. "Would you not like, when you meet him, to tell him that you tried in some measure to do the work he hoped you would have done as his wife? Could you not live among the people whose eternal interests were so near his heart, and cheer their burdened lives and lead them to Christ? Their need is terrible; Grey saw it, and consecrated his life to pointing them to the only remedy. Some one else will come to do it, but he wanted you to do what neither he nor any *man* could do in the homes, with the women and children. You can do that still, and as you work for Christ among those poor darkened souls who are ignorantly rejecting the joy and blessedness that Christ could give them, you will feel that Grey's dearest hopes are being realized."

Rose Berkley's Morning Tryst.

Poor Rose grasped the idea eagerly. It kept her still associated in heart and life with her dear dead love, and as she gradually entered into the life of usefulness to which her brother-in-law pointed her, and saw one and another workingman's home transformed by her gentle teaching and ministrations, and darkened lives brightened by the sweetness and light of the Saviour's love, her own sorrow grew lighter. Her life became a busy one, and in its labors a sweet calm and holy restfulness took the place of bitter and unavailing sorrow.

ESCAPED FROM THE MORMONS.

A Life Story: By Mrs. Stenhouse.

For More than Twenty-five Years the Wife of a Mormon Missionary and Elder.

(*Continued from page 782*).

Under the Spell.

MUCH that I had heard at the Mormon meetings could, I knew, be proved true from Scripture; and the rest seemed to me to be capable of demonstration from the same authority. I resolved, however, to fortify myself against a too easy credulity, and thought that probably if I heard more of these doctrines, I might be able to discover their falsity.

On the following day, the elder who had preached at the meeting, and who, by the way, is one of the present proprietors of the Salt Lake *Herald*, called specially to see me, as he had been intimate with my parents before they left the island. I hardly knew how to be civil to him, though he had done nothing to offend me, nor had he been the cause of my parents entering the Mormon Church; but I disliked him solely on account of the stories which I had heard about the Mormons. Intending only to be kind to me, he told me that on the following day he proposed to take the steamer to Southampton, as he was going to attend a conference of the Saints in London, and that he should be pleased to show me any attentions while crossing the Channel, and would see me safe home. I confess I really felt insulted at a Mormon Elder offering to be my escort; and although my trunks were ready packed for my departure by the same steamer, and Mr. Dunbar knew it, I thanked him politely, but said I would not go by that boat. He tried to persuade me to change my mind, and said that I should have to wait a whole week for another vessel; and at last I told him the abhorrence I felt at the strange things I had heard about the Mormons, and that I should be afraid to travel in the same steamer with him or any of the Mormon Elders, whom I regarded as no better than so many whited sepulchres. He, however, kindly took no offence, for he knew that I had been listening to those who disliked the Saints.

I felt ashamed at having been betrayed into such unladylike rudeness, but, notwithstanding, tried to persuade myself that his civility was, after all, an insult; for I had conceived an intense detestation of every Mormon, on account of the deception which I felt sure had been practiced upon my family. This feeling was not lessened by the consciousness that an impression had been made upon my own mind. The more in accordance with Scripture the teaching of the Elders appeared, the more firmly I believed it must be a powerful delusion. Here, I said, Satan has indeed taken the form of "an angel of light, to deceive, if possible, the very elect."

Elder Dunbar, finding me unyielding, left by the next steamer, and had a pleasant passage across the Channel, and I remained on the island another week. During that interval, my mind was haunted with what I had heard of this "new Gospel dispensation," as it was called. That angels had again descended from heaven to teach man upon earth; that a prophet had been raised up to speak again the mind of the Lord to the children of men; that the Saints were partakers of the gifts of the Spirit, as in the early Christian Church—all these assumed facts took the form of reality, and came back into my mind with greater force every time I strove to drive them away; just as our thoughts do when we desire to sleep, and cannot—our very efforts to dismiss them bring them back with greater force to torment us. We had an unusually bad passage across the Channel, which annoyed me all the more when I remembered my scornful refusal to go in the same boat with Elder Dunbar.

On my arrival in Southampton I soon discovered that my father, mother, and sisters were full of the spirit of Mormonism. They were rejoicing in it, ardently believing that it was "the fulness of the everlasting Gospel," as the Elders styled it; and whatever I might think of the new religion, I was forced to confess that it brought into my father's house peace, love, kindness, and charity, such as were seldom seen in many households of religious people. My sisters were completely changed in their manner of life. They cared nothing for the amusements which girls of their age generally crave and enjoy. Their whole thoughts seemed to be occupied with the church, attending the meetings of the Saints, and employing every leisure hour in preparing comforts for the Elders, who were travelling and preaching without purse and scrip. And in all this they were as happy as children.

Of my parents I might say the same. My dear mother rejoiced in the belief that she had been peculiarly blessed in being privileged to live at a time when "the last dispensation" was revealed; and my father, though an invalid, rejoiced that he had entered into the kingdom by baptism. Such was the condition of my father's house; and who can wonder that, accustomed as I was to listen with respect to the opinions of my parents, I was more than ever troubled about the new religion which they had adopted? The first Sunday morning that I was in England, my parents asked me to accompany them to meeting, and I readily complied, as I wanted to hear more of the strange doctrines which in some mysterious way had made our family so happy, but which in other quarters had provoked such bitter hostility. I know now that this joyousness of heart is not peculiar to new converts to Mormonism, but may be found among the newly converted of every sect which allows the emotional feelings to come into play. To me, however, it was a mystery, but I must confess that the change which had taken place in those nearest and dearest to me, affecting me personally, and being apparently in accordance with the teaching of the Saviour, led me to regard Mormonism with less antipathy. The bright side alone of the new faith was presented to the world abroad; we had yet to go to Utah and witness the effects of Brigham Young's teachings at home before we could know what Mormonism really was.

I shall never forget the trial it was to my pride to enter the dirty, mean-looking room where the Saints assembled at that time. No one would rent a respectable hall to them, and they were glad to obtain the use of any place which was large enough for their meetings. On the present occasion there was a very fair gathering of people, who had come together influenced by the most varied motives. The presiding Elder—I should here remark that the word "Elder" has among the Mormons no reference whatever to age, but is simply a rank in the priesthood — called the meeting to order and read the following hymn:

"The morning breaks, the shadows flee;
Lo! Zion's standard is unfurled!
The dawning of a brighter day
Majestic rises on the world.

The clouds of error disappear
Before the rays of truth Divine;
The glory bursting from afar,
Wide o'er the nations soon shall shine!

The Gentile fullness now comes in,
And Israel's blessings are at hand,
Lo! Judah's remnant, cleansed from sin,
Shall in the promised Canaan stand.

Angels from heaven and truth from earth
Have met, and both have record borne;
Thus Zion's light is bursting forth
To bring her ransom'd children home."

Every word of this hymn had a meaning, peculiar to itself, relating to the distinctive doctrines of the Saints. The congregation sang with an energy and enthusiasm which made the room shake again. Self and the outer world were alike forgotten, and an ecstacy of rapture seemed to possess the souls of all present. Then all kneeled down, and prayer was offered for the Prophet, the apostles, high-priests, "seventies," elders, priests, teachers, and deacons; blessings were invoked upon the Saints, and power to convert the Gentiles; and as the earnest words of supplication left the speaker's lips, the congregation shouted a loud "Amen!" There was no prepared sermon. There never is at a Mormon meeting. The people are taught that the Holy Ghost is "mouth, matter, and wisdom." Whatever the preaching Elder may say is supposed to come directly by inspiration from heaven, and the Saints, listening, as they believe, not to his utterances, but to the words of God Himself, have nothing to do but to hear and obey.

The first speaker on this occasion was a young gentleman of respectable family, who had been recently baptized and ordained. He, too, was from St. Helier's, and I had known him from childhood. His address impressed me very much. He had been a member of the Baptist church, and he related his experience: told how often he had wondered why there were not inspired men to preach the glad tidings of salvation to the world to-day, as there were eighteen centuries ago. He spoke of the joy which he had experienced in being baptized into the Mormon Church, and realizing that he had received the "gift of the Holy Ghost." The simplicity with which he spoke, his evident honesty, and the sacrifice he had made in leaving the respectable Baptists and joining the despised Mormons, were, I thought, so many evidences of his sincerity.

Alas! how little could that young preacher conjecture how different the practical Mormonism in Utah was from the theoretical Mormonism which he had learned to believe in Europe, before polygamy was known among the Saints. A short time afterwards he gave up his business, married an accomplished young lady, and went with her to Salt Lake City. There they were soon utterly disgusted with what they witnessed, apostatized, and set out for England. When they had gone three-fourths of their way back to the Missouri River, *the young man, his wife, child, and another apostate and his wife, were killed* by "Indians"—such, at least, was the report; but dissenting Mormons have always charged their "taking off" to the order of the leaders of the Mormon Church.

But to return to the meeting: The reader must please forgive me if I dwell a little upon the events of that particular morning, for naturally they made a deep impression upon my own mind—it was there that I saw for the first time my husband who was to be. I had heard a good deal about a certain Elder, from my family and from the Saints who visited at our house. They spoke with great enthusiasm of the earnestness with which he preached, of the effect which his addresses produced, and of his confidence in the final triumph of "the kingdom."

At that time—the summer of 1849—although the branch of the Mormon Church in Britain was in a most flourishing condition, there were not in England more than two or three American Elders preaching the faith, for when—two years before the period of which I speak—the Saints left Nauvoo and undertook that most extraordinary exodus across the Plains to the Rocky Mountains, the missionary Elders were all called home, and the work of proselytizing in Europe was left entirely to the native Elders. To direct their labors, there was placed over them an American Elder named Orson Spencer, a graduate of Dartmouth University, a scholar and a gentleman—a man well calculated from his previous Christian education to give an elevated tone to the teachings of the young English missionaries.

Mormonism in England then, had no resemblance to the Mormonism of Utah to-day. The Mormons were then simply an earnest, religious people, in many respects like the Methodists, especially in their missionary zeal and fervor of spirit. The Mormon Church abroad was purely a religious institution, and Mormonism was preached by the Elders as the Gospel of Christianity restored. The Church had no political shaping, nor the remotest antagonism to the civil power. The name of Joseph Smith was seldom spoken, and still more seldom was heard the name of Brigham Young, and then only so far as they had reference of the Church of the Saints.

About eighteen months before I visited Southampton, one of the Mormon missionaries had come into that town, "without purse or scrip." He was quite a young man and almost penniless, but he was rich in faith and overflowing with zeal. He knew no one there; and homeless, and frequently hungry, he continued his labors. Of fasting he knew much, of feasting nothing. He first preached under the branches of a spreading beech-tree in a public park, and when more favored he held forth in a school-room or public hall. He had come to convert the people to Mormonism, or he was going to die among them; and before such zeal and determination, discouragements, of course, soon vanished away.

He troubled the ministers of other dissenting churches when they found him distributing tracts and talking to their people. He was sowing, broadcast, dissatisfaction and discontent wherever he could get any one to listen to him, and thus he drew down upon himself the eloquence of the dissenting pulpits and the derision of the local press. But the more they attacked him the more zealously did he labor, and defied his opponents to public discussion. Mormonism was bold then in Europe—it had no American history to meet in those days. This, and a great deal more, I had heard discussed in glowing language by my relatives and friends; and thus the young missionary—Elder Stenhouse—was, by name, no stranger to me.

It was Elder Stenhouse who now addressed the meeting, and I listened to him with attention. The reader must remember that at that time polygamy was unheard of as a doctrine of the Saints; and the blood-atonement, the doctrine that Adam is God, together with the polytheism and priestly theocracy of after-years, were things undreamed of. The saving love of Christ, the glory and fullness of the everlasting Gospel, the gifts and graces of the Spirit, together with repentance, baptism, and faith, were the points upon which the Mormon teachers touched; and who can wonder that with such topics as these, and fortifying every statement with powerful and numerous texts of Scripture, they should captivate the minds of religiously inclined people? However this may be, I can only confess that, as I listened to Elder Stenhouse's earnest discourse, I felt my antipathy to Mormonism rapidly melting away.

At the close of the service, when he left the platform, he was warmly received by the brethren and sisters—for so the Saints speak of one another—and they came about him to shake hands, or it might be to seize the opportunity of slipping a trifle into his hand to help him in his work. Young and old, the poor and the more wealthy neighbors, mingled together like one happy family. It was, altogether, a most pleasing scene; and, whatever explanation may yet be given of Mormonism in America, one thing I know—the facts of its early history in Europe are among the most pleasant reminiscences of my life.

Elder Stenhouse came up in a familiar and open-hearted way to my mother and sisters, and I was introduced to him as "the other daughter from France." He kindly welcomed me, and when I frankly told him the state of my mind, he made, I must admit, a successful attempt to solve my doubts, and when I left the meeting it was with sentiments towards the Saints and their religion far different from those which I entertained when I entered. The meeting was a memorable era in my life.

(*To be Continued.*)

RUTH'S CHOICE.

By Mrs. M. Baxter.

S. S. Lesson for December 23. Ruth 1:16-22. Golden Text, Ruth 1:16.

Elimelech's Worldly Prudence—Argued a Lack of Faith—Led to his Sons' Marrying Illegally—A Series of Calamities—Naomi's Wise Decision—What Ruth's Choice Appeared to Involve—Prepared for Sacrifices—The Journey of the Two Widows—Ruth's Introduction to her Future Husband—A Significant Greeting—Boaz Blessing Her—The Nearer Kinsman.

THE history of the times of the Judges is one long record of sin and judgment. At this time there was a famine in the land. In most countries a famine is looked upon as an inevitable misfortune, and men do the best they can to save themselves from its consequences. It was with this intention that Elimelech of Bethlehem-Judah took his family and went to sojourn in the land of Moab. A very wise move, some would say; but was God saying nothing through this famine? and had Elimelech no direction from Him how to act? God had declared, "If ye will not hearken unto Me, and will not do all these commandments . . . they shall deliver your bread again by weight: and ye shall eat and not be satisfied." (Lev. 26:14, 26.) And this is His direction to His people: "Trust in the Lord and do good; dwell in the land, and verily thou shalt be fed." (Ps. 37:3.) Elimelech had not confidence enough in God to trust Him. Oh how truly he that findeth or saveth his life shall lose it! (Matt. 10:39.) Elimelech died, and his two sons also. But before their death, Mahlon and Chilion, Elimelech's sons, had married wives of Moab. This was not pleasing to God. (Neh. 13:23-28.) Now only Naomi was left, with her two daughters-in-law.

Ever since the family had left the land of promise, things had gone ill with them; but Naomi now determined to return, and she exhorted her daughters-in-law to return to their own families, and wait until they had another chance of settling in life.

Orpah was quite ready to do this. The life of widowhood was distasteful to her, and, though with regret, she kissed her mother-in-law, and went her way. Naomi then appealed to Ruth, "Behold, thy sister-in-law is gone back unto her people and her gods: return thou after thy sister-in-law."

After Her Gods—

this was the point. Far as the family had fallen in their unbelief in God for temporal supplies, they still worshipped the God of Israel, and no doubt the ready ears and heart of Ruth had drunk in the blessed truth which Naomi had taught them, of the power and love and personal intervention of the God of Israel. She counted the cost. To follow Naomi she must give up all her friends in Moab, she must go out penniless into a strange land, and, humanly speaking, she must sacrifice all her prospects in life. On the other hand, if the God of Israel were indeed the only true God, if He did rain down bread from heaven to satisfy his people's need, if He did make a way in the sea for His people to pass over—what had she to fear in going anywhere with such a God? She made her choice, and said to Naomi as she clung to her, "Entreat me not to leave thee, nor to return from following after thee, for whither thou goest I will go, and where thou lodgest I will lodge. (As though to say, anything that will do for thee, will do for me, so long as God is with us.) Thy people shall be my people, and thy God my God: where thou diest I will die, and there will I be buried; the Lord do so to me, and more also, if aught but death part thee and me." Thy God shall be my God; this was the main point. Homeless or with a home, penniless or not, she would take her part with God and with God's people.

This Was a True Conversion.

Oh how many there are who choose God so far as He ministers to their own will! They like the knowledge of sin forgiven, but they like the praise of men too. They like to indulge themselves in smoking, candies, or novel-reading, dress, ornaments, or in gossip over the tea-table with a neighbor, and yet make use of Christ's salvation to keep a claim on heaven. In fact, they want Christ, and Christ's religion, to minister to their own selfishness, so that they can be selfish with an easy conscience because their past sins are forgiven. But in Ruth's choice there was no selfishness. She was prepared to sacrifice all; her thought was not to get, but to give. She had mastered the true relations between God and man, and she saw that God does not exist for man's sake, but man exists for God. And thus the question with her was, not what it would cost her, and how far it would suit her to follow Naomi: it was the way to serve God; and she renounced forever the life of serving herself. Elimelech set out to serve himself, and loss and death were the consequence. Ruth set out to deny herself, and serve God, and joy and union were the result.

When Naomi saw that she was steadfastly minded, she left off dissuading her. So the two widows journeyed together to Bethlehem.

Absence from the Land of Promise

had worked a great change in Naomi; just such a change as comes upon all who go astray from complete dependence upon God. "I went out full, and the Lord hath brought me home again empty." *I* went out, the *Lord* brought me home; this is the backslider's history.

It was barley-harvest, and a woman of Ruth's character would not degrade herself by living on the charity of others; "Let me now go to the field and glean," was her petition to Naomi. God guided her steps, and she began her work in a field belonging to Boaz, a rich relation of her deceased father-in-law. Her first introduction to her future husband was when he entered the field with his morning greeting to the reapers, "The Lord be with you!" and she heard their response, "The Lord bless thee!" Oh what a revolution it would work in all the factories, shipyards, iron-works, &c., if such a greeting were to take place daily between master and men! How could there be oppression, how could there be strikes, if there were oneness in the Lord? But taking Boaz as the type of the heavenly bridegroom, oh how precious to know that day by day He greets His reapers with His blessing.

Boaz noticed Ruth, and spoke to her, telling her not to go to another field, and to share the refreshments provided for the reapers. Ruth was astonished, and fell on her face and said; "Why have I found grace in thine eyes, that thou takest knowledge of me, seeing I am a stranger?" And Boaz answered: "It hath fully been shewed me all that thou hast done unto thy mother-in-law since the death of thine husband, and now thou hast left thy father and thy mother, and the land of thy nativity, and art come unto a people which thou knewest not.

The Lord Recompense

thy work, and a full reward be given thee of the Lord God of Israel, under whose wings thou art come to trust." Boaz recognized Ruth's true conversion to God, and, for God's sake, shewed kindness to her. She was beginning to reap what she had sown, and to find how faithful God is to them who trust in Him. It is no risk to trust God when we have a promise to go upon. Anxiety in Christians is as much as to say that God is not equal to bear our burdens when they are cast upon Him, and that He does not really care for us, although His Word declares He does. Boaz also provided that Ruth should share the mid-day meal with his laborers, and gave orders that some of the ears should be scattered on purpose for her. The fruit of her day's work, when she had beaten out the wheat, was about an ephah, *i. e.*, about seven and a half gallons of wheat. This would support her mother-in-law and herself for some weeks.

On her return home, Naomi inquired of her where she had gleaned, and when she learned it was on the field belonging to Boaz, she recognized the hand of the Lord, and said, "Blessed be he of the Lord who hath not left off His kindness to the living and to the dead!" And telling Ruth that Boaz was a near kinsman, she advised her to keep fast by his maidens until the end of harvest. So Ruth went on steadily at work, gleaning every day for their support. But the harvest-home came at last, and the gleaning was over. Then it was that Naomi explained to her the law of Israel, how a brother's or next kinsman's, duty was to take the widow of a childless kinsman, to raise up the name of the dead upon his inheritance; and then she directed Ruth to claim her right by the law of Israel. Ruth did so, and Boaz recognized her claim, but at the same time he said, "There is

A Kinsman Nearer

than I." Christ gave Himself for His Church, and gave Himself for it "that He might present it to Himself a glorious Church, not having spot or wrinkle, or any such thing." (Eph. 5:25-27.) Union with Him is "the hope of our calling, the glory of our inheritance, the goal of our life." But before we can be united to Him, it must be found whether there is a kinsman nearer. Is Christ really first with us in everything, or is there a kinsman nearer? Self-interest ruined Elimelech, and self is at the root of many sins. It is self which hinders real abiding union with Jesus. Boaz undertook to deal with the kinsman. None but Christ can deal with self. Boaz sat in the gate of Bethlehem and watched for the kinsman, and there, in the presence of ten of the elders of the city, he stated how Naomi sold a parcel of land belonging to Elimelech; and offered him the first refusal, and the kinsman accepted the offer, and said, "I will redeem it." Then Boaz said, "What day thou buyest the field of the hand of Naomi, thou must buy it also of the hand of Ruth the Moabitess, the wife of the dead, to raise up the name of the dead on his inheritance." And now the kinsman drew back; he was ready to buy the field, to make a good business investment, and "add house to house, and field to field"; but he was not ready to sacrifice his interests for another, and so he replied, "I cannot redeem it

Lest I Mar Mine Own Inheritance;

redeem thou my right thyself, for I cannot redeem it." It was self-interest again. But Boaz did the unselfish thing, and turning to the elders, he called upon them to witness that he bought the land, and with it Ruth the Moabitess, "to raise up the name of the dead upon his inheritance, that the name of the dead be not cut off from among his brethren, and from the gate of his place." The blessing of the elders was their only answer. Thus Boaz took Ruth and married her; and so she, who had left all for God, found Him faithful to her; and God gave her a child, who was the grandfather of David, and the progenitor of Christ.

A CALL TO THE WEARY.

BY R. M. OFFORD.

Come, ye weary, do not tarry,
Bring to Jesus all your grief;
Why your burden longer carry
Since he offers sure relief?
Heavy-laden, sin distrest,
Come to Jesus Christ and rest.

Have you tried all worldly pleasure,
Sounded all the depths of sin,
Found no joy in earth's best treasure,
Seek you other joy to win?
Come to Jesus, He imparts
Lasting joy to joyless hearts.

On His lips is no upbraiding,
Though from God thou far hast strayed,
Though thy life's brief light is fading,
Sad the record thou hast made,
Come and welcome, do not wait,
Late it is, yet not too late.

Vile and most unworthy feeling,
'Twas for such His life He gave;
Bring thy wounded heart for healing,
If not lost how could He save?
Hast thou sinned beyond compare?
Greater need His grace to share.

J. E. JEWETT, Publisher, 77 Bible House, New York, will furnish the above poem in leaflet form at twenty cents per hundred. *A Sample Packet* of 50 leaflets assorted (no two alike), will be sent post-paid, for 10 cts., or 100 for 20 cts. Postage stamps taken.

Horsford's Acid Phosphate,
For Indigestion,
Dyspepsia, and diseases incident thereto.

Have you read the advertisement of B. F. Johnson & Co., Publishers, of Richmond Va., in another column? If not, please do so at once. You may not be specially interested in what they have to say, but if you will call some of your friends' attention who need employment to their advertisement you may confer a life-long favor on them.

The latest and best imperial Photographs of Talmage and **Rev. C. H. Spurgeon,** with their fac-simile autograph, and also imperial photograph of **Rev. Henry Ward Beecher,** can be obtained from J. E. Jewett, 77 Bible House, New York. Sent postpaid for twenty-five cents each. Postage stamps taken.

MEXICO

Contributions in aid of Christian work in Mexico are most pressingly needed, and can be mailed to the address of

BISHOP H. C. RILEY,
Care of J. P. HEATH,
43 Bible House, New York.

To our Christian Friends:

As there is a regular monthly expense in connection with the work a regular monthly income is needed to meet that expense. We, therefore, specially ask for regular monthly contributions in its behalf. If many will each send a little every month, or quarter, or whenever they can, it will do great good. *Remember, every little helps.*

H. Chauncey Riley.

UNIVERSITY PIANOS
PRICE $180
FROM $180 TO $1500.
FINEST PIANOS IN THE WORLD.
SOLD DIRECT TO FAMILIES, saving the enormous expenses of agents. Sent with beautiful cover, stool and book, for trial in your own home before you buy. Guaranteed six years. Send for catalogue to
Marchal & Smith Piano Co., 235 E. 21st St., N. Y.

ILLUSTRATIVE GATHERINGS
for Preachers and Teachers. A Manual of Anecdotes Facts, Figures, Proverbs, Quotations, &c., &c., adapted for Christian teaching. By Rev. G. S. Bowes. Two series, 12 mo. muslin, each $1.25. "For variety, pertinency and availability it is decidedly superior to anything we have seen."—*Evangelical Repository.* Sent to any adress free on receipt of above price.
Perkinpine & Higgins, 914 Arch St., Philadelphia, Pa

$75.00 to $250.00 A MONTH can be made working for us. Agents preferred who can furnish a horse and give their whole time to the business. Spare moments may be profitably employed also. A few vacancies in towns and cities. B. F. Johnson & Co., Pub's, 1009 Main St., Richmond, Va

THE ALFRED DOLGE Felt Shoes AND Slippers.

NOISELESS, WARM, DURABLE.

Prevent Rheumatism, Coldness of the Feet, and Excessive Perspiration.

COMFORT AND EASE.

OLD GENTLEMAN: "Now for a comfortable evening after a busy day. Those felt slippers are real havens of rest to my tired feet."

Send for Catalogue and Price-list.
Mention this Publication.

PERFECT EASE AND COMFORT!
BY USING
Slippers and Shoes
WITH
SOLES AND UPPERS OF ALL-WOOL FELT.

DANIEL GREEN & CO., 122 East 13th Street, New York.

EVERY LADY HER OWN DRESS MAKER.

WOMEN enjoy, above all other things, neat-fitting garments. By the use of Worth's French Taylor System on Dress Cutting, a person of ordinary intelligence can cut and fit any article of dress perfectly without trying the garment on. This system is so plain, and the book of instructions so complete and clear, that a child may cut and fit as perfectly as the most experienced Dress Maker. With the Diagrams and Book of Instructions you know exactly the amount of goods you need. How to fit stout or lean people; how to fit round or hollow shoulders, how to fashion waists, and all the secrets of Dress Making. The extra sleeve pattern is well worth $5 to any woman. Worth's is the only simple and correct system by which a person can measure, cut and fit garments without first learning the trade. Instruction Book Special Sleeve Pattern and System, $10.00.

OUR BIG OFFER On receipt of $1.00, we will send the Worth System of Dress Cutting, Complete Book of Instructions, Sleeve Pattern, and one year's subscription to American Housekeeping. To each of the first 1000 Answers to this advertisement, we will send The Every Day Cook Book, 300 pages, FREE. [Price, $1.00]
Agents Wanted. American Housekeeping.
143 La Salle St., Chicago, Ill.

American Housekeeping.
A Ladies' Home Journal.
Full 50 pages with a handsome colored cover each month. Complete on all home subjects. Cooking Receipts, Kitchen and Dining Room, Household Decoration, Art and Fashion, Fancy Work, Bric-a-Brac, Etc. Well Illustrated. New Serials by our best authors. Women's Recollections of the late War is a New, Novel and very Original feature for a Ladies' Magazine. Entertaining to all, young and old. Our Fashion Notes prepared specially for us, give the latest styles, hints and suggestions to amateurs. Worth to any woman, several times the subscription price. Yearly Subscription, 50 cents.

$10.50 FOR $1.00

We know that the above offer is just as represented, a bargain, and recommend it to our subscribers.

BOOK AGENTS WANTED FOR
MY STORY OF THE WAR
By Mary A. Livermore

Her own narrative of "Four Years' Personal Experience as Field and Hospital Nurse." It portrays the Womanly or "Heavenly" side of the War, its Lights and Shadows "*as a woman saw them.*" Bright, Pure, and Good, full of "*laughter and tears,*" of thrilling interest and touching pathos, it *sells at sight to all.* Splendid Steel-Plates, and famous old Battle-Flags richly colored in *exact fac-simile.* The "*booming*" book for Men and Women Agents. $100 to $200 a month made. Distance no hindrance, for we *Pay Freights and give Extra Terms.* Write for circulars to A. D. WORTHINGTON & CO., Hartford, Conn.

ON 30 DAYS' TRIAL.
THIS NEW ELASTIC TRUSS

Has a Pad different from all others, is cup shape, with Self-adjusting Ball in center, adapts itself to all positions of the body while the ball in the cup presses back the intestines just as a person does with the finger. With light pressure the Hernia is held securely day and night, and a radical cure certain. It is easy, durable and cheap. Sent by mail. Circulars free. EGGLESTON TRUSS CO., Chicago, Ill.

THE DEAF HEAR

The New England Medical Monthly says—"WALES' INVISIBLE SOUND DISC for deafness by practical demonstration ranks all other devices ... age! Concentrating the ... waves on the drum ... sibilities are indeed ..." For sale only by ... inventor H. A. WALES, Bridgeport, Conn.

In all the world there is but one sure cure for the **OPIUM** Habit. The Dr. J. L. Stephens Remedy never fails, and no other treatment ever cures. We have cured more than 10,000 cases. No other treatment ever cured one case. NO PAY TILL CURED. Remember this, and write to the J. L. Stephens Co., Lebanon, Ohio.

SEATTLE The largest City in Washington Territory. Population 20,000. Commercial center of PUGET SOUND Country. Coal, Iron, Timber and Agricultural Lands. Send for full information of Queen City. **SE-AT-TLE.** CHAS. H. KITTINGER, Seattle, Wash. Terr.

TEAS *LADIES* Send at once for our new terms. THE GREAT AMERICAN TEA CO., 31 and 33 Vesey St., New York, N. Y.

FEATHERS. The finest live white geese feathers in the country, 75 cts. per lb. Hair Mattresses made over for $2.50. Feathers cleansed & renovated. Pickford, 11 Nassau St., Brooklyn, N.Y

BLACK SILK WARP.
HENRIETTA CLOTH.

We are now offering an unusual opportunity to buy this favorite weave of Black Goods, from the looms of a world-renowned maker.

We have purchased about 200 pieces, regular made in every respect as to weight, quality and finish, subject only to slight manufacturer's imperfections, and have marked the different grades as follows:

$1.25 per	yard,	regularly	marked		$1.75
[illegible]	"	"	"	"	1.85
1.50	"	"	"	"	2.00
1.75	"	"	"	"	2.50
2.00	"	"	"	"	2.75

These goods may be safely ordered by mail or express.

James McCreery & Co
Broadway, cor. Eleventh St.,
NEW YORK.

New Musical Instrument.
19 lbs. Boxed. **AUTO-ORGAN.** 22 Reeds
Plays Sacred Music, Popular Airs, Operas, etc. Especially adapted for the family circle. Catalogue of 342 pieces. AGENTS WANTED in every town. Large commissions, best selling musical instrument. For special terms to Agents and descriptive Catalogue address L. A. BARBER & CO., Groton, N. Y.

FALL ISSUES—18

STUDIES IN MARK'S GOSPEL. C. S. Robinson, D.D., LL. D. 12mo. 300 pp. $1.25. Paper, 50c.
The author does not follow the beaten ... commentators, but presents in his own happy ... new phases and fresh illustrations of Script... which the reader is instructed and enriched. These "studies" elucidate from week to we... Sunday-school lessons for first half of 1889.

THE LIFE OF ST. PAUL. Rev. Stalker, M. A., with map. 12mo. 183 pp. C...
A new and admirable work on this exh... theme. The author presents the gist of the be... vious writings and his own fresh thoughts clea... concisely. Highly commended for S. S. Teache...

NEWLY ENLISTED. By Rev. Th. L. C... D.D., LL. D. Square. 16mo. Paper, 25c. 50c. Cloth, gilt, 75c.
Counsels for young converts from this prince... pastors. Dedicated to Mr. Moody & compa... "Heart Life."

FROM THE FORECASTLE TO PULPIT. C. J. Jones, D.D. 12mo. 540 pp.
A truly wonderful story—the life of a sailor ... the mast, its rough and strange experiences, h... formation into a faithful Christian minister, an... wonders of grace God wrought through his labo...

JUDGE HAVISHAM'S WILL. I. T... kins author of "Good-Times Girls," etc. 4 cuts. 311 pp. $1.25.
A story that boys will enjoy, illustrating the ... of firm faith under trial. The young hero will ... mired for his sterling manly qualities.

MARGIE AT THE HARBOR-LI... Rev. E. A. Rand. 12mo. 6 cuts. 264 pp.
A sequel to "Her Christmas and Her Easter;" with the same fresh sea-air; stirring and helpfu...

CHANGING PLACES; or How One Climbed Up and Another Slipped D... Miss G. M. Trowbridge, author of "Vict... Last." 12mo. 4 cuts. 217 pp. Cl., 90c.
Full of incidents suggested in the title; mor... hinting to boys how they may succeed in life.

BERNIE'S LIGHT. Minnie E. K... author of "Mrs. Morse's Girls." 12mo. ... 272 pp. Cloth, $1.10.
The charming story of a young girl whose li... kindled at a Mission Sabbath-School and ... cheer to many in dark places.

THE GARMENT OF PRAISE. He... Strong, author of "His Abiding Pres... Monotint booklet. Daintily illustrated, in colors and gold. Large 16mo. 36 pp. ...
An elegant gift and devotional volume, full ... quisite designs in harmony with the inspired ... with which the church in all ages praises God.

THE SEA IS HIS; or, Words of Co... for Sea and Shore. Susan A. Brown. 48 pp. 60c.
In ten colors and gold. Elegant sea and shore ... and sea mosses, on alternate pages with choic... form God's Word and our best poets.

STORIES TOLD BY A DOLL. Mis... Hunter. 4to. 6¼x8¾ in. 89 pp. 60c. Nu... illustrations. Handsome chromo cover. A fasc... book for the nursery, with much quiet humor; ... be a universal favorite and home classic.

CLASSICS FOR THE CLOSET.—N... The Lord's Prayer. Dr. A. Tholuck. 46 pp. Limp cloth, 20c. Evangelical, rich, ... ful.

PICTORIAL WALL-ROLL. 13x20 ... pp., on walnut roller. 75c. A choice full page ... on each page, with a few lines of suggestive expl... Pictures tell a whole story without a word.

APPLES OF GOLD. Four col'd pic... 200 other cuts. 208 pp. 4to. Cl. back, lim... er, 50c.

DEAR OLD STORIES TOLD ... MORE. Quarto. In six parts. Bright c... cover. Each part contains six Bible S... with full-page illustrations, one colore... stout paper cover, 15c; boards, 20c.

FAMILY CHRISTIAN ALMANAC, ... Illustrated. Single copies, 10c.; $1 per ... $7 per 100; $60 per 1,000. A household tre...

AMERICAN TRACT SOCIE...
150 Nassau St., New York; 54 Bromfiel... Boston; 1512 Chestnut St., Philadel... 93 State St., Rochester; 122 Wabash ... Chicago; 735 Market St., San Francis...

Agents Wanted for ... Pertaini... sons, ... Things, ... Bible S... Concert ... Prayer-M... Topics, ... etc. Int... by J. H. ... cent, D... pages. By mail, $2. Immensely popular. Al... new book, **BOW IN THE CLOUD,** ... of Comfort, etc., by 200 Best Authors, $1. **WOMEN'S HAND-BOOK $2.** Just ... A lady wanted in every town ... duce it. **Quick Sales. Big Pay.** Ad... **E. B. TREAT,** Publisher, 771 Broadwa...

PRINTING PRESS Book of Type, &c. Amateur Printers' Guide Book, 15c. CIRCUL... JOSEPH WA... 19 Murray S... Samples of Scrap Pictures and Cards, 10 cents

"*Demonology or Spirituali...*
Ancient and Modern."—"An effective weapon, ... sword of fire."—"Only unanswerable work ... subject."—Startling disclosures.—History ... data.—Scores saved already. Whole comm... re cued. Every family, preacher and christian ... need one. 340 pp. 12mo, cloth. Price reduce... Sent by mail, postpaid, on receipt of price. A... ... 77 Bible House, New ...

AGENTS WANTED to sell "The ... Bible." Introduc... Bishop J. H. Vincent, D.D. The best sellin... handled by agents. Recommended by all cler... Address Cassell & Co., B.B.S.D., 104 and 106 ... Ave., New York; 40 Dearborn St., Chicago, Ill.

MORE MEN WANTED for local ap... ... Sel... Good Pay. Address
E. B. RICHARDSON & CO.,
Nurserymen, Geneva, N...

This Journal contains every week a Portrait and Biography of some eminent person; a new Sermon by the Rev. C. H. SPURGEON, of London, and the Rev. Dr. TALMAGE'S latest Sunday morning Sermon; also always a Prophetic Article, and a Summary of Current Events as well as Stories, Anecdotes etc.

Vol. XI., No. 51. Office, 63 Bible House, N. Y. THURSDAY, DECEMBER 20, 1888. Price, 3 Cents. Annual Subscription, $1.50.

THE EMPRESS OF RUSSIA.

CONTENTS OF THIS NUMBER.

PORTRAITS AND LIVES OF THE CZAR AND CZARINA OF RUSSIA, and Picture of their Recent Railroad Disaster.
LIFTED FROM THE MIRE. Dr. Talmage's Sermon last Sunday Morning.
ANECDOTES RELATED AT RECENT EVANGELISTIC MEETINGS.
LAWLESSNESS AND THE LAWLESS ONE. By Dean Vaughan.
Mr. Re Qua's Work in the Indian Territory—The Interest on Thirty Cents—A Crippled Christian's Testimony—Conversion Through a Vision—A Dead Man's Secret—A Recovery from Spinal Disease—A Chinese Patriarch's Admission.
THE APPROACHING APOSTACY. By James Stephen, M. A.
FIRST GRACE, THEN WORKS. A New Sermom by Rev. C. H. Spurgeon
Gems from New Books: Gibraltar—Its Owners—A Typical Current.
PORTRAIT AND LIFE OF MUNEMITSU MUTSU, Japanese Minister to the U. S.
TWO CHANGED LIVES. (With Illustration.)
PICTURE OF A SCENE IN CHINATOWN, SAN FRANCISCO.
ESCAPED FROM THE MORMONS. An Autobiographical Story by Mrs. Stenhouse. (Con.)
THE SWORD OF THE SPIRIT. By Mrs. M. Baxter.

ALEXANDER III., EMPEROR OF RUSSIA.

HE WRECKED RAILROAD TRAIN FROM WHICH THE CZAR AND HIS FAMILY ESCAPED.

THE CZAR IN A RAILROAD DISASTER.

WITH the tardiness with which Russian news circulates through that empire and eventually reaches the outside world, a full report of the almost miraculous escape of the Czar from a disaster on the railroad on October 29, has arrived to supplement the vague telegraphic account published at the end of last month. It now appears that the Imperial family were returning to the capital from their visit to the Sea of Azov, and when the train by which they travelled reached Borki, in South Russia, it left the tracks at a sharp curve and fell into utter ruins. The dining-saloon car, in which the Czar and Czarina were seated at table at the time, was reduced to fragments, and how they escaped death is marvellous. The

Accounts of Eye-Witnesses

of the disaster have been published. One correspondent says: "The last three carriages were still on the rails, but the fourth was driven sideways, and overhung a steep incline of some forty feet or more. Beyond we saw nothing but a second-class carriage in fragments half-way down the hill, a number of bodies covered up, and broken timbers, planks, and a general wreck on the bankside. On proceeding further we saw the full effect of the disaster. The first carriage beyond the one I have mentioned had disappeared entirely; it was one mass of splinters tossed up in every conceivable direction, and the roof lying crosswise on the crushed woodwork; beyond was another carriage wrecked, but still partly standing, and then were some carriages leaning to the right, some to the left, some completely down, and two next the two engines still apparently little damaged. It was out of the crushed woodwork of the one most completely ruined that three-and-twenty living souls were rescued, with one or two exceptions, almost unbruised. It was the dining-saloon and there their Imperial Majesties, with every child of theirs, save the little Grand Duchess Olga, were seated with the suite at dinner. A sudden shock sent them all down on the floor; a second, and the sides of the carriage were down on them, the roof across the whole; a third, and a dead stop—a terrible silence, broken by the shrieks of the dying and the wounded.

"Those who were there told me there was neither time to think, nor even to feel; their wounds and bruises they discovered afterwards. One gentleman told me he only found that he had lost half his finger an hour later. The Empress was one of the first to extricate herself from the wreck, crying:

'Where is the Emperor

and my children?' The Empress's right hand was badly bruised, and the left slightly cut about, but she went at once to tend the wounded as they were extricated from the wreck. For nearly four hours she sat in the drizzling rain, on that sopping bank, binding up their wounds, or soothing them with words healing as the balm of Gilead. One poor fellow lay there mortally hurt, with his face fearfully scalded, and she sat by him, cooling his face with her handkerchief dipped in water, and the poor fellow died, kissing her hand.

"His Majesty and the Grand Dukes Nicholas and George Alexandrovitch were everywhere lending a helping hand, extricating the wounded and the dead. I heard nothing but blessings showered upon them wherever I went.

"A dog—Kamtchatka, the Czar's favorite hound—was lying at his feet when the accident occurred; a servant was presenting to him a tray with a glass of tea. How near the Czar was to death may be inferred from the fact that both the servant and the dog were killed instantaneously. It was a moment of sudden and appalling horror. Under the feet of the whole Imperial party, seated around the dining-table, the floor sinks, the whole bottom of the carriage disappears. The four walls are crushed together in the sudden smash; the unsupported roof gives way, and is prevented from falling on the heads of the Empress and the august children only *by the powerful arms of the Emperor*, who for several minutes supports it alone above the heads of his family. The little Grand Duchess Olga is thrown out to a distance of 10 sagen (60 feet) down the embankment; the little Grand Duke Michael Alexandrovitch is buried under the ruined carriages so deep that he could hardly be discovered, and then dug out and rescued from under the débris with the greatest difficulty—and both children are perfectly safe and unhurt! The Grand Duke George (the second son) finds himself squeezed between two seats, and at the same moment a heavy iron bar is descending on his head; but a second—just one second—earlier, a heavy brass frame falling on to the same seats, is found vertically dovetailing into the two, leaving a recess just large enough to contain and protect his body; and, meanwhile, Count Tcheremetieff arrests the heavy bar in its fall, which almost tears three fingers off his hand, but George remains uninjured.

The Czar's Injuries.

"In a pouring rain, knee-deep in the cold mud, bleeding from both arms and hands (the bandages were only removed on November 3), and he helping personally to rescue the dying and the wounded for over two hours, his colossal strength doing him goodly service on that day. They tell how he spoke words of consolation to those sufferers still alive, pledging his word to the dying to care for their families as long as they lived.

Some carriages preceded the two engines, which were placed together in the middle of the train. One of the engines, decorated with branches of trees and wreaths of foliage, *is seen in the picture on the front page*, thrown off the rails, with an engine tender behind it. There is no doubt that the rails, which were in bad repair, gave way under the excessive speed at which the train was driven.

THE CZAR AND CZARINA.

Early Days of the Czar—Affiliation with Secret Societies—His Separation on Discovering their Murderous Intentions—Personal Characteristics—Accession to the Throne—Effect of his Marriage—Character of the Czarina—Visits to Copenhagen—Difficulties of Government—Remarkable Answer of a Peasant—The Only Hope for Russia.

THE ruler of the mighty empire of Russia, whose portrait, with that of his wife, appears on the first page, is in his forty-fourth year, having been born March 10, 1845. He is the second son of the late Emperor Alexander II. His elder brother, Nicholas, who was a year and a half older than he, died in April, 1865, and Alexander then became heir to the throne. He became Czar in 1881, on the assassination of his father by the Nihilists on March 14, of that year. Alexander, like some other Crown Princes, allied himself during the lifetime of his father to the most progressive party in politics, and is believed to have coquetted as lately as 1878 with the more advanced Panslavistic organizations, which were acting in concert with, though not openly allied to, the associations formed for the promotion of a revolutionary movement in Russia. Upon more than one occasion the Grand Duke's relations with native patriots of the advanced Panslavistic school are stated to have led to distressing differences between himself and his father, to whom, moreover, his son's avowed antipathy to Germany was particularly painful.

When, however, it became evident, not only to the Imperial family, but to the public, that the chief aim of the Nihilistic conspiracy was the assassination of the Czar, his son, the present Emperor, broke off all connections with every description of secret society in and out of Russia, and identified himself unreservedly with the line of action adopted by his father's advisers for the perpetuation of the Romanoff dynasty.

The Emperor is said to be a strong, determined man, though his nerves have been severely shaken by the continual peril of assassination in which the years of his life since his accession to the throne have been passed. His face has none of that pathetic melancholy peculiar to his father's. His expression is active, keen, and somewhat severe. His manners are quick, decided, and occasionally brusque. He is not quite so tall as other members of his family, being a little under six feet in height, but his frame is large, thickset, and muscular. An American press correspondent who saw him recently, says: "That the Czar has been no carpet soldier is evident from the marks of frost-bites on the third and fourth fingers of his left hand, and *a slight scar on his temple*, where a bullet grazed his head in the Turkish war."

The Coronation

of the Czar did not take place until May 27, 1883. The delay was due to several causes, the chief of which, doubtless, was the activity of the Nihilists, who, finding that the new Czar was utterly alienated by the murder of his father from the progressive associations to which he had been friendly in his younger days, and was firmly opposed to granting a constitution, had resolved to kill him too. The large assemblage of illustrious personages, which would be gathered from all nations to witness the ceremony, would present an opportunity for a wholesale slaughter by dynamite, and time was needed to take the most complete precautions against such an event. The coronation was, however, performed safely, though more than one of the Princes who attended admitted afterward that the day was one of fear and trembling.

The Czar's Habits

show a marked improvement on those of his early days. His marriage was the turning-point in his career, for the good and gentle princess who became his wife exerted so complete an ascendency over him, that he withdrew from his evil associates and devoted himself to studies which were a preparation for the responsible career before him. His study in the Anitchkov Palace is a small room fitted up with maps and globes and well-filled bookcases, in which historical works in all languages predominate. That he is a reader is shown by the pile of newspapers which he collects at the different stations when on a railroad journey to peruse on the road, and he has taken personal interest in the publication of the State correspondence in Russia. The Czar is an early riser, and the labors of his day commence at 9 in the morning. Till 1 o'clock he is occupied in his study receiving the Ministers, who present their weekly or daily reports, and consulting with them over affairs of State.

It is especially significant of the policy of the Czar that while high officials have often a difficulty in obtaining an interview, His Majesty is always accessible to provincial deputations, which are sometimes composed of wild Khirgis, sometimes of swarthy Kalmuks, or skin-clad Samoyedes, and sometimes of illiterate Russian peasants who desire to present a holy picture to their great father and to express their loyalty and devotion to his person. The Emperor receives one and all with a stern dignity, which, though accompanied in most cases by a certain kindness of manner, always leaves the conviction that Alexander III. feels himself an autocrat, and is determined to yield none of his prerogatives, but to impress on all who approach him that they are in the presence of an absolute though kindly master. This species of self-assertion was a trait in the character of the Emperor in his very earliest days.

The Danish Princess,

who is the wife of the Czar, is a daughter of King Christian of Denmark, and the sister of the Princess of Wales, and of the King of Greece. She was originally betrothed to Nicholas, the elder brother of the Czar, but when he died, the Russian statesmen and the late Czar were so anxious to break the succession of German matrimonial alliances which had been continued since the time of the Czar Peter, that they commenced negotiations at once for the transfer of the Princess Dagmar to the new heir to the Imperial throne. The negotiations were successful, and in November 1866, the Princess became the wife of Alexander.

An American gentleman who recently spent some months in St. Petersburg, says: "The Empress is as much liked in Russia as her sister, the Princess of Wales, is in England. The two sisters resemble each other, not only in looks, but in *sweetness of character*. Alexander's domestic life has hitherto been pure and wonderfully happy, and unless something happens to mar this, we may look for a considerable improvement over the period of the late Czar in the ideas of the court on the subject of morals. The Czarina has *five beautiful children*—the eldest, Nicholas, a fine youth of seventeen; the second, George, about fourteen, who bears a striking resemblance to the early pictures of Alexander II., and three much younger ones, Xenia, Michael, and Olga. She has accompanied her husband to all parts of European Russia, and has gained the affection of the people, particularly of the Poles. In the winter, at the Anitchkov Palace, she has *an annual Christmas tree*, but it is not invariably the children of the nobles who are invited, but a number from the most squalid homes in St. Petersburg, recommended by some of the members of the Society for the Relief of Distress, and these are always sent away with a good stock of warm clothing.

Visits to Copenhagen,

the home of the Empress are among the most pleasant recreations of the Imperial couple. There the Czar devotes himself to his family, and lays aside for a time the cares of his vast Empire of more than a hundred million souls. He is popular in the Danish capital, where he and the Princess Dagmar, as she is still fondly called by the Danes, walk about the town together in the most unceremonious manner, and are always ready to take their part in any popular entertainment during the time they stay at her father's court. It also speaks well for him that he is supposed to require no extra amusement there, but to be perfectly happy, leading a simple life with his wife and children.

It is asserted by those who know the Czar, that he is far less averse to granting a constitution than were his predecessors. His difficulty lies chiefly in the determined opposition of the nobles, on whom he would have to rely for the conduct of the Government. They would probably conspire against him on the first intimation of constitutional tendencies; or if they refrained from that course, might give him so half hearted a support as to thwart his intentions. The Government continues a pure despotism: but the hopes of the people are not yet utterly abandoned. Their longing was pathetically expressed by a condemned prisoner to the Czar himself. He was only a peasant, but he had been condemned to death for a share in a conspiracy: "I have the power to pardon you," said the Czar, "and I would do so if I thought you would become a faithful subject." "Sire," said the condemned man, whose name was Michael Bestoujil, "that is *our great misfortune, that the Emperor can do everything, and that there is no law!*"

The only real hope for Russia lies, however, in the fact that now, as never before, efforts are being made to spread the knowledge of the gospel throughout the vast land, and to emancipate the people from the superstitions of the Greek Church. Through the distribution of the Scriptures, and earnest evangelistic efforts on the part of men like Lord Radstock and M. Pashkhoff, there is a quiet growth and deepening of spiritual life, at least in Northern Russia, and an increased attention to the Word of God. Colportage also is being favored with an increasing measure of success. The people are, however, densely ignorant, and there is need for prayer by all who offer the petition "Thy kingdom come," that not only the rulers of that mighty empire (the Emperor and Empress) themselves, may know Christ the King of kings as their Saviour, but that the millions of their subjects may be led into the light of that glorious Gospel which is the true charter of man's highest freedom, and "the power of God unto salvation to every one that believeth."

ANECDOTES RELATED AT RECENT EVANGELISTIC MEETINGS.

Shutting One's Eyes to the Disease.—"When I was preaching once at Motherwell," said Mr. Climie, "a woman came to me and asked if I would speak to her husband about his soul. I promised to do so, and on the following day, as I was going to her house, I met her coming up the street. 'Are you going to see my husband?' she asked. When she heard that I was, she said, 'Well, please do not speak to him about sin.' 'Why not?' I inquired. 'Oh, he can't stand that,' she replied. 'But,' I said, 'I cannot do him any good, nor offer him salvation, unless the man knows and acknowledges that he is a sinner. Christ came not to call the righteous, but sinners to repentance.' Simple though it was, the woman seemed scarcely to understand the plan of salvation herself. She turned with me to the house, and there, not long afterwards, both husband and wife acknowledged themselves sinners, and sought forgiveness at the hand of a loving Father."

A Coolie's Loyalty to Christ.—The Rev. J. Backus writes from Ceylon: "One of our converts, who was employed on an estate managed by a heathen, was known among his comrades to be a Christian. When the manager insisted one day on his going, with other coolies, to the neighbouring heathen temple, the poor man said, 'No, sir, I will not go to worship an idol. I am a Christian, and I worship the only true God.' When the manager threatened to turn him off the estate, he boldly said, 'I would rather beg than worship idols. My bread is not in your hands, but in the hands of Him whom I worship. Although you turn me out, He will never forsake me.' He was immediately turned out, but the Lord has provided for him, and he is doing an exceedingly good business as a trader, and is known far and wide for his unfailing joy, and the earnest desire which constrains him to lead his fellow-men to the Lord Jesus Christ."

Preaching Christ at the Hunters' Campfires.—Mr. Stevenson, of the Bethel Santhal Mission, observes: "The Santhals are demon-worshippers, and are difficult to influence for good. I have often overtaken a man on the road and talked to him of his country and of local traditions; then gliding on to his hope for the future, pointed out to him the striking contrast between the demons whom he worships from fear, and our God who endured pain and died for His followers. Often by this comparison many wandering ones have been brought to Christ. We secure the largest and most attentive audiences at the hunting-parties, while they are around their camp-fires, for often a whole village will assemble, and armed with axes, set out for a grand hunt. While there assembled, we preach the Gospel to them, frequently illustrating what we say by the magic-lantern. Their general excuse for not accepting Christ is, 'I'll become a Christian when my friends become Christians.' None like to take the initiative, so while many may be convinced of sin, few acknowledge Christ as their Saviour, yet often we have had blessed times at those hunt meetings, and Christ has been accepted by some."

Riding Out a Perilous Storm.—Dr. Kneeland said: "A merchant vessel in the Mediterranean Sea was overtaken lately by a great storm. So violent was the tempest that even the oldest sailor confessed that he had never seen such a gale, even in these stormy parts. Before they could make much headway to the nearest port, they found themselves drifted so near the rocks, and the wind and waves so beating them toward the inhospitable shore, that they knew their only hope was to cast anchor; and if it held until the morning, they knew they would be saved. The sailors got the largest and heaviest anchor, with a great massive chain, and threw it overboard. It held only for a moment, then the chain parted, and the helpless ship drifted on. Another and another anchor was cast, but none held, and now they were very near to the rocks. There remained only one anchor—a comparatively small one. This they prepared to let go, praying the while that God would make it hold. One man interrupted, saying, 'What is the use of that little thing? Leave it, and let us ask the forgiveness of our sins, and make peace with God.' But the captain replied, 'Stand by the anchor; I know the man who made the chain; and everything he did was of the best. Every link in that chain can be depended upon.' They let go the anchor, and waited in breathless silence. It caught, and the vessel was enabled to ride out the storm. Christ is the only true Anchor that will enable us to ride out the storms of life. Other anchors there are which men trust, but which, in the time of need, fail them."

The Silver Lining to the Cloud.—Mr. Ralston, the evangelist, observed: "I stood, a little time ago, by the bedside of a Christian worker as he lay dying, and tried to comfort his wife. While speaking to her, she suddenly interrupted me with, 'Do you know, Mr. Ralston, at one time I determined never to go back to your meeting, because you speak as a man who has never known what it is to have any great trouble.' 'How did you come to think so?' I responded. 'Because I have heard you say things that seem to show that life has been very smooth with you,' she said. 'Well, you are mistaken,' I replied; 'I do know what it is to have trouble, but I also know what it is to have a God who takes it all away, and bears it for me.' 'But,' she continued, 'my husband lies there, dying; and here am I, and my five little children, about to be left helpless. Does the future not look black?' 'Do you think that God ever makes a mistake?' I asked. 'Oh, no!' she replied. 'Then all this trouble, no matter what it appears, is for your good, for "All things work together for good to them that love God."' 'Yes,' she replied, 'it must be for my good; but I never looked at it in that way before.' We are so apt to look only at the black side of the cloud, and forget altogether the silver lining, namely, God's loving purpose that He has in view, and which He could not attain without the strokes of what we call affliction."

A Basket With a Baby in It.—Mr. Grey Relates: "A wealthy merchant living in one of the suburbs of New York, coming down-stairs one morning, found a large basket addressed to him. On opening it, to the surprise of himself and his wife, they found in it a little baby. The merchant said, 'We will keep it to-day and tomorrow, then I will take it to such an institution and leave it there.' 'Can we not keep it?' 'Yes; if all the family agree, we will keep it,' her husband answered. All the family did agree, and the waif was formally installed as if she were naturally one of themselves. The child grew, and was sent to school with the others, and on one occasion she quarrelled with a companion there, a little girl belonging to a family who lived in the same street, and who knew all about the adoption and the attendant circumstances. 'And what are you?' said the one; 'nothing but an adopted brat!' She did not know the meaning of these words, but she inquired and found their meaning; then running home, she threw herself into her adopted mother's arms, and gave vent to a great burst of tears. Her mother, astonished at her behavior, asked what was the matter, only to be confronted with the startling question, 'Are you my mother?' 'Yes my child,' was the answer. 'But are you my real, true mother?' persisted the child, still dissatisfied. The lady could not say that she was. Nothing that generous lady or gentleman could do could make that child their natural daughter. But the sinner, when he comes to God, becomes the real, true son of God; and heir by birth, being born of the Holy Spirit into sonship and heirship of God."

LIFTED FROM THE MIRE.

Dr. Talmage's Sermon, Preached Last Sunday, December 16, 1888.

"Though ye have lain among the pots, yet shall ye be as the wings of a dove covered with silver, and her feathers with yellow gold." *Ps.* 68 : 13.

The Israelites among the Brick-kilns—Doves on Egyptian Houses—The Hardest of all Taskmasters—Hume's Admission—Christians Pitied Instead of being Congratulated—I. What Religion can Do for a Man's Heart—Becomes more Cheerful—Laughter that is Hollow—The Memory of a Mother's Last Look—II. Religion Bringing Usefulness—Two Young Men—Three Spectacles—A Dying Student of Providence College—III. What Religion Does for Him in Heaven—Friends Waiting—The Fall of Louis Philippe.

I SUPPOSE you know what the Israelites did down in Egyptian slavery. They made bricks. Amid the utensils of the brick-kiln there were also other utensils of cookery—the kettles, the pots, the pans, with which they prepared their daily food; and when these poor slaves, tired of the day's work, lay down to rest, they lay down among the implements of cookery and the implements of hard work. When they arose in the morning they found their garments covered with the clay and the smoke and the dust, and

Besmirched and Begrimed

with the utensils of cookery. But after a while the Lord broke up that slavery, and He took these poor slaves into a land where they had better garb, bright and clean and beautiful apparel. No more bricks for them to make. Let Pharaoh make his own bricks. When David, in my text, comes to describe the transition of these poor Israelites from their bondage amid the brick-kilns into the glorious emancipation for which God had prepared them, he says: "Though ye have lain among the pots, yet shall ye be as the wings of a dove covered with silver, and her feathers with yellow gold."

Miss Whately, the author of a celebrated book, "Life in Egypt," said she sometimes saw people in the East cooking their food on the tops of houses, and that she had often seen, just before sundown, pigeons and doves, which had, during the heat of the day, been hiding among the kettles and the pans with which the food was prepared, picking up the crumbs that they might find: just about the hour of sunset they would spread their wings and fly heavenward, entirely unsoiled by the region in which they had moved, for the pigeon is a very cleanly bird. And as the pigeons flew away the setting sun would throw silver on their wings and gold on their breasts. So you see it was not a far-fetched simile, or an unnatural comparison, when David in my text says to these emancipated Israelites, and says to all those who are brought out of any kind of trouble into any kind of spiritual joy: "Though ye have lain among the pots, yet shall ye be as the wings of a dove covered with silver, and her feathers with yellow gold."

Sin is the hardest of all taskmasters. Worse than Pharaoh, it keeps us drudging, drudging in

A Most Degrading Service;

but after a while Christ comes, and He says: "Let my people go," and we pass out from among the brick-kilns of sin into the glorious liberty of the Gospel: we put on the clean robes of a Christian profession, and when, at last, we soar away to the warm nest which God has provided for us in heaven, we shall go fairer than a dove, its wings covered with silver, and its feathers covered with yellow gold.

I am going to preach something which some of you do not believe, and that is, that the grandest possible adornment is the religion of Jesus Christ. There are a great many people who suppose that religion is a very different thing from what it really is. The reason men condemn the Bible is because they do not understand the Bible; they have not properly examined it. Dr. Johnson said that Hume told a minister in the bishopric of Durham, that he had never particularly examined the New Testament, yet all his life warring against it. Halley the astronomer, announced his scepticism to Sir Isaac Newton, and Sir Isaac Newton said: "Now, sir, I have examined the subject and you have not; and I am ashamed that you, professing to be a philosopher, consent to condemn a thing you never have examined." And so men reject the religion of Jesus Christ because they really have never investigated it. They think it something undesirable, something that will not work, something Pecksniffian, something hypocritical, something repulsive, when it is so bright and so beautiful you might compare it to chaffinch, you might compare it to a robin-redbreast, you might compare it to a dove, its wings covered with silver, and its feathers with yellow gold.

Wasted Pity.

But how is it if a young man becomes a Christian? All through the club-rooms where he associates, all through the business circles where he is known, there is commiseration. They say: "What a pity that a young man who had such bright prospects should so have been despoiled by those Christians, giving up all his worldly prospects for something which is of no particular present worth!" Here is a young woman who becomes a Christian; her voice, her face, her manners the charm of the drawing-room. Now all through the fashionable circles the whisper goes: "What a pity that such a bright light should have been extinguished, that such a graceful gait should be crippled, that such worldly prospects should be obliterated!" Ah, my friends, it can be shown that religion's ways are ways of pleasantness, and that all her paths are peace; that religion, instead of being dark and doleful and lachrymose and repulsive, is bright and beautiful, fairer than a dove, its wings covered with silver and its feathers with yellow gold.

See, in the first place, what religion will do for a man's heart. I care not how cheerful a man may naturally be before conversion,

Conversion Brings Him Up

to a higher standard of cheerfulness. I do not say he will laugh any louder; I do not say but he may stand back from some forms of hilarity in which he once indulged; but there comes into his soul an immense satisfaction. A young man not a Christian depends upon worldly successes to keep his spirits up. Now he is prospered, now he has a large salary, now he has a beautiful wardrobe, now he has pleasant friends, now he has more money than he knows how to spend; everything goes bright and well with him. But trouble comes—there are many young men in the house this morning who can testify out of their own experience that sometimes to young men trouble does come—his friends are gone, his salary is gone, his health is gone; he goes down, down. He becomes sour, cross, queer, misanthropic, blames the world, blames society, blames the Church, blames everything, rushes perhaps to the intoxicating cup to drown his trouble, but, instead of drowning his trouble, he drowns his body and drowns his soul.

But here is a Christian young man. Trouble comes to him. Does he give up? No! He throws himself back on the resources of heaven. He says: "God is my Father. Out of all these disasters I shall pluck advantage for my soul. All the promises are mine, Christ is mine, Christian companionship is mine, heaven is mine. What though my apparel be worn out? Christ gives me a robe of righteousness. What though my money be gone? I have

A Title Deed to the Whole Universe

in the promise, 'All are yours.' What though my worldly friends fall away? Ministering angels are my bodyguard. What though my fare be poor, and my bread be scant? I sit at the King's banquet!"

Oh, what a poor, shallow stream is worldly enjoyment compared with the deep, broad, overflowing river of God's peace, rolling midway in the Christian heart! Sometimes you have gone out on the iron-bound beach of the sea when there has been a storm on the ocean, and you have seen the waves dash into white foam at your feet. They did not do you any harm. While there, you thought of the chapter written by the Psalmist, and perhaps you recited it to yourself while the storm was making commentary upon the passage: "God is our

Refuge and Strength,

a very present help in time of trouble. Therefore will I not fear, though the earth be removed, and though the mountains be carried into the midst of the sea, though the waters thereof roar and be troubled, though the mountains shake with the swelling thereof." Oh, how independent the religion of Christ makes a man of worldly success and worldly circumstances! Nelson, the night before his last battle, said: "To-morrow I shall win either a peerage, or a grave in Westminster Abbey." And it does not make much difference to the Christian whether he rises or falls in worldly matters: he has everlasting renown anyway. Other plumage may be torn in the blast, but that soul adorned with Christian grace, is fairer than the dove, its wings covered with silver, and its feathers with gold.

You and I have found out that people who pretend to be happy are not always happy. Look at that young man caricaturing the Christian religion, scoffing at everything good, going into roystering drunkenness, dashing the champagne bottle to the floor, rolling the glasses from the bar-room counter, laughing, shouting, stamping the floor. Is he happy? I will go to

His Midnight Pillow.

I will see him turn the gas off. I will ask myself if the pillow on which he sleeps is as soft as the pillow on which that pure young man sleeps. Ah! no. When he opens his eyes in the morning, will the world be as bright to him as to that young man who retired at night saying his prayers, invoking God's blessing upon his own soul and the souls of his comrades, and father and mother and brother and sister far away? No, no! His laughter will ring out from the saloon so that you hear it as you pass by, but it is hollow laughter; in it is the snapping of heart-strings and the rattle of prison gates. Happy! that young man happy?

Let him fill high the bowl; he cannot drown an upbraiding conscience. Let the balls roll through the bowling alley; the deep rumble and the sharp crack cannot overpower the voices of condemnation. Let him whirl in the dance of sin and temptation and death. All the brilliancy of the scene cannot make him forget the last look of his mother as he left home, when she said to him: "Now, my son, you will do right; I am sure you will do right; you will, won't you?" That young man happy? Why, across every night there flit shadows of eternal darkness; there are adders coiled up in every cup; there are vultures of despair striking their iron beak into his heart; there are skeleton fingers of grief pinching at the throat.

I come in amid the clicking of the glasses and under the flashing of the chandeliers, and I cry: "Woe! woe! The way of the ungodly shall perish. There is no peace, saith my God, to the wicked. The way of transgressors is hard." Oh, my friends, there is more joy in one drop of Christian satisfaction than in whole rivers of sinful delight. Other wings may be drenched of the storm and splashed of the tempest, but the dove that comes in through the window of this heavenly ark has wings like the dove covered with silver, and her feathers with yellow gold.

Again I remark, religion is an adornment in the style of usefulness into which it inducts a man. Here are

Two Young Men.

The one has fine culture, exquisite wardrobe, plenty of friends, great worldly success, but he lives for himself. His chief care is for his own comfort. He lives uselessly. He dies unregretted. Here is another young man. His apparel may not be so good, his education may not be so thorough. He lives for others. His happiness is to make others happy. He is as self-denying as that dying soldier falling in the ranks, when he said: "Colonel, there is no need of those boys tiring themselves by carrying me to the hospital; let me die just where

I am." So this young man of whom I speak loves God, wants all the world to love Him, is not ashamed to carry a bundle of clothes up that dark alley to the poor. Which of those young men do you admire the better? The one a sham, the other

A Prince Imperial.

Oh, do you know of anything, my hearer, that is more beautiful than to see a young man start out for Christ? Here is some one falling; he lifts him up. Here is a vagabond boy; he introduces him to a mission school. Here is a family freezing to death; he carries them a scuttle of coal. There are eight hundred millions perishing in midnight heathen darkness; by all possible means he tries to send to them the Gospel. He may be laughed at, and he may be sneered at, and he may be caricatured, but he is not ashamed to go everywhere, saying: "I am not ashamed of the Gospel of Christ. It is the power of God and the wisdom of God unto salvation." Such a young man can go through everything. There is no force on earth or in hell that can resist him. I show you

Three Spectacles.

Spectacle the first: Napoleon passes by with the host that went down with him to Egypt, and up with him through Russia, and crossed the continent on the bleeding heart of which he set his iron heel, and across the quivering flesh of which he went grinding the wheels of his gun-carriages—in his dying moment asking his attendants to put on his military boots for him.

Spectacle the second: Voltaire, bright and learned and witty and eloquent, with tongue and voice and stratagem infernal, warring against God and poisoning whole kingdoms with his infidelity, yet applauded by the clapping hands of thrones and empires and continents—his last words, in delirium supposing Christ standing by the bedside—his last words: "Crush that wretch!"

Spectacle the third: Paul—Paul, insignificant in person, thrust out from all refined association, scourged, spat on, hounded like a wild beast from city to city, yet trying to make the world good and heaven full;

Announcing Resurrection

to those who mourned at the barred gates of the dead; speaking consolations which light up the eyes of widowhood and orphanage and want with glow of certain and eternal release; undaunted before those who could take his life, his cheek flushed with transport, and his eye on heaven; with one hand shaking defiance at all the foes of earth and all the principalities of hell, and with the other hand beckoning messenger angels to come and bear him away, as he says: "I am now ready to be offered, and the time of my departure is at hand; I have fought the good fight, I have finished my course, I have kept the faith; henceforth there is laid up for me a crown of righteousness which the Lord, the righteous Judge, will give me."

Which of the three spectacles do you most admire? When

The Wind of Death

struck the conqueror and the infidel, they were tossed like sea-gulls in a tempest, drenched of the wave and torn of the hurricane, their dismal voices heard through the everlasting storm; but when the wave and the wind of death struck Paul, like an albatross he made a throne of the tempest, and one day floated away into the calm, clear summer of heaven, brighter than the dove, its wings covered with silver, and its feathers with yellow gold. Oh, are you not in love with such a religion—a religion that can do so much for a man while he lives, and so much for a man when he comes to die?

I suppose you may have noticed the contrast between the departure of a Christian and the departure of an infidel. Diodorus, dying in chagrin because he could not compose a joke equal to the joke uttered at the other end of his table: Zeuxis, dying in a fit of laughter at the sketch of an aged woman—a sketch made by his own hand: Mazarin, dying playing cards, his friend holding his hands because he was unable to hold them himself. All that on one side, compared with the departure of the Scotch minister, who said to his friends: "I have no interest as to whether I live or die; if I die, I shall be with the Lord; and if I live, the Lord shall be with me." Or the last words of Washington: "It is well." Or the last words of McIntosh, the learned and the great: "Happy!" Or the last word of Hannah More, the Christian poetess: "Joy!" Or those thousands of Christians who have gone, saying: "Lord Jesus receive my spirit! Come, Lord Jesus, come quickly!" "O death! where is thy sting? O grave! where is thy victory?"

Behold the Contrast.

Behold the charm of the one, behold the darkness of the other. Now, I know it is very popular in this day for young men to think there is something more charming in scepticism than in religion. They are ashamed of the old-fashioned religion of the cross, and they pride themselves on their free-thinking on all these subjects. My young friends, I want to tell you what I know from observation: that while scepticism is a beautiful land at the start, it is the great Sahara Desert at the last.

Years ago *a minister's son* went off from home to college. At college he formed the acquaintance of a young man whom I shall call Ellison. Ellison was an infidel. Ellison scoffed at religion, and the minister's son soon learned from him the infidelity, and when he went home on his vacation broke his father's heart by his denunciations of Christianity. Time passed on and vacation came, and the minister's son went off to spend the vacation, and was on a journey, and came to a hotel. The hotel-keeper said: "I am sorry that to-night I shall have to put you in a room adjoining one where there is a very sick and dying man. I can give you no other accommodation." "Oh," said the young college student and minister's son, "that will make no difference to me except the matter of sympathy with anybody that is suffering." The young man retired to his room, but could not sleep. All night long he heard the groaning of the sick man, or the step of the watchers, and his soul trembled. He thought to himself: "Now, there is only a thin wall between me and a departing spirit. How if Ellison should know how I feel? How if Ellison should find out how my heart flutters? What if Ellison knew

My Scepticism Gave Way?"

He slept not. In the morning, coming down, he said to the hotel-keeper: "How is the sick man?" "Oh," said the hotel-keeper, "he is dead, poor fellow! the doctors told us he could not last through the night." "Well," said the young man, "what was the sick one's name; where is he from?" "Well," said the hotel-keeper, "he is from Providence College." "Providence College! what is his name?" "Ellison." "Ellison!" Oh, how the young man was stunned! It was his old college-mate—dead without any hope.

It was many hours before the young man could leave that hotel. He got on his horse and started homeward, and all the way he heard something saying to him:

"Dead! Lost! Dead!

Lost!" He came to no satisfaction until he entered the Christian life, until he entered the Christian ministry, until he became one of the most eminent missionaries of the Cross, the greatest Baptist missionary the world has ever seen since the days of Paul—no superior to Adoniram Judson. Mighty on earth, mighty in heaven—Adoniram Judson. Which do you like the best, Judson's scepticism or Judson's Christian life, Judson's suffering for Christ's sake, Judson's almost martyrdom? Oh, young man, take your choice between these two kinds of lives. Your own heart tells you this morning the Christian life is more admirable, more peaceful, more comfortable, and more beautiful.

Oh, if religion does so much for a man on earth, what will it do for him in heaven? That is the thought that comes to me now. If a soldier can afford to shout "Huzza!" when he goes into battle, how much more jubilantly he can afford to shout "Huzza!" when

He has Gained the Victory!

If religion is so good a thing to have here, how bright a thing it will be in heaven! I want to see that young man when the glories of heaven have robed and crowned him. I want to hear him sing when all huskiness of earthly colds is gone, and he rises up with the great doxology. I want to know what standard he will carry when marching under arches of pearl in the army of banners. I want to know what company he will keep in a land where they are all kings and queens forever and ever. If I have induced one of you this morning to begin a better life, then I want to know it. I may not in this world clasp hands with you in friendship, I may not hear from your own lips the story of temptation and sorrow, but I will clasp hands with you when the sea is passed and the gates are entered.

That I might woo you to a better life, and that I might show you the glories with which God clothes His dear children in heaven, I wish I could this morning swing back one of the twelve gates, that there might dash upon your ear one shout of the triumph, that there might flame upon your eyes one blaze of the splendor. Oh, when I speak of that good land, you involuntarily think of some one there that you loved—father, mother, brother, sister, or, dear little child garnered already. You want to know what they are doing this morning. I will tell you what they are doing. Singing! You want to know what they wear. I will tell you what they wear. Coronets of triumph! You wonder why oft they look to the gate of the temple, and watch and wait. I will tell you

Why They Watch and Wait

and look to the gate of the temple. For your coming! I shout upward the news to-day, for I am sure some of you will repent and start for heaven: "Oh, ye bright ones before the throne, your earthly friends are coming. Angels, posing mid-air, cry up the name! Gatekeeper of heaven, send forward the tidings! Watchman on the battlements celestial, throw the signal"!

"Oh," you say, "religion I am going to have; it is only a question of time." My brother, I am afraid that you may lose heaven the way Louis Philippe lost his empire. The Parisian mob came around the Tuileries. The National Guard stood in defence of the palace, and the commander said to Louis Philippe: "Shall I fire now? Shall I order the troops to fire? With one volley we can clear the place." "No," said Louis Philippe, "not yet." A few minutes passed on, and then Louis Philippe, seeing the case was hopeless, said to the general: "Now is the time to fire." "No," said the general, "it is too late now; don't you see that the soldiers are exchanging arms with the citizens? It is too late." Down went the throne of Louis Philippe. Away from the earth went the House of Orleans, and all because the king said: "Not yet! not yet!" May God forbid that any of you should adjourn this great subject of religion, and should postpone assailing your spiritual foes until it is too late, too late—you losing a throne in heaven the way that Louis Philippe lost a throne on earth.

"When the Judge descends in might,
Clothed in majesty and light;
When the earth shall quake with fear,
Where, oh where, wilt thou appear?"

IN THE INDIAN TERRITORY.

THE following is an extract from a letter received last week from the Rev. W. F. Re Qua, whose work among the Indians is chiefly supported by the readers of THE CHRISTIAN HERALD: We now have a mission school station opened among the full-blood Indians. With some help, the Indians have built a log-house, and a log school-house adjoining, so the teacher has a place to live. She came from Cohoes, N. Y., out of a good, comfortable home, believing the Lord led her into the work. Her people sent out her house-keeping goods, so she can board herself. Her brother came out, and has taken hold and helped the Indians, with myself, to finish up the buildings for the school purposes. Monday and Tuesday, this week, I helped them move out and settle; both are excellent Christians, and I believe the Lord has a good work for them out here. If I had others like them—devoted and consecrated, to offer themselves to the work—and means to assist the Indians in different parts of the country to build mission schools (log buildings), furnishing flooring, windows, and doors, we might in a year have a number of good working schools. The young lady who takes this mission station has a very kind father, who aids in her support. I am in hopes to furnish you with some good views of scenes in our work—perhaps a picture of the new mission station, and one of a curious cemetery, not far off in the woods, where the Indians inter their dead; each grave being covered with an odd little frame or log structure that looks like a little grotesque hut. I expect to stop in Tahlequah, the capital of the Cherokee Nation, on my return home from Fort Smith, Ark., and hold some meetings there, by urgent request, as I go within twenty-five miles of there, by mail, which distance has to be covered by stage. Then, on reaching home (D. V.), I shall start with tabernacle tent to the Sac and Fox tribe, about 175 miles by wagon. I believe there are more obstacles to contend with in this Territory than in a foreign field; but gradually we are overcoming them.

A CHINESE PATRIARCH'S PLEA.

EVERY one who knows Jesus as the Way, the Truth, and the Life—who has known by experience the truth of His words: "I am the Door: by Me if any man enter in he shall be saved" (John 10: 9.)—must feel an intense desire to respond to a desire expressed by an aged Chinese priest with whom Dr. Jonathan Lees had an interview in a temple. Dr. Lees thus related the incident at a public meeting:

"It is now more than twenty years since I travelled into the interior, a distance of over 1,000 miles, visiting a multitude of places where no foreigners had been before, and preaching in city, markets, town, and village, not only without serious hindrance, but often with the marked intelligent interest of the people. Such journeys have become frequent since, yet it is rarely that one hears of a different experience. Some present may have heard me relate a touching incident I met with on a shorter tour a few years ago. It was near the close of a winter afternoon, and my carter was pushing on to reach our halting-place for the night, when, on passing through a village my eye was suddenly caught by what was evidently an extemporized temple mat-shed. Though pressed for time, curiosity led me to enter. Yes, there was the idol—a large picture hanging at the end opposite to the door, and there was the familiar altar table, with its incensepot, candlesticks, and various offerings, while the sides of the enclosure were made gay with pictures. A few old men were at the moment the only visitors. As I stood there a man came to burn incense and to perform his prostrations. Then we talked. You can imagine it easily enough. They told me that their worship was to secure good crops. I spoke of the great loving Father in heaven who supplies all our wants, and then I spoke of Jesus. Rising to go, they begged me to retell the story, and when at length I must leave, sad at heart that we might almost certainly never meet again on earth, one old, whitehaired patriarch cried out: 'Oh, do stay and teach us. We did not know this was wrong. Our fathers worshipped thus; we cannot find the door.' Those words haunted me for days; they haunt me still."

A CRIPPLED CHRISTIAN'S TESTIMONY.

A YOUNG man having lost both limbs below the knee, while in Satan's service, is now an active Christian in Florida. In a recent letter to a missionary in New York, he says: "I am every day reminded of God's infinite mercy and goodness to me, and can never give Him praise and thanks enough. I have been to Tampa today, and was offered the charge of a property consisting of over 1,000 acres of land and six hundred head of cattle. They said some very kind things about my being trustworthy and capable, and all that, but I do not take any of the praise to myself, for I know it is all *God's* work. What would I be now, if by His mercy I had not been led to learn of the meek and lowly Jesus? I would be a drunkard, and maybe a convict in some prison. He has *saved* me, and I praise Him every day.

"You ask me how I can build a barn (having artificial limbs); I will tell you: 'I left it all with Jesus long ago,' and *He* leads me, and helps me to do everything. It is *Jesus* doing the work. He gives me strength, power, and ability to do what otherwise would be an utter impossibility. So I know it is Jesus who does the work."

THE INTEREST ON THIRTY CENTS.

As a lady missionary in New York was going down Cherry Street by the sailors' boarding-houses a few days ago, a bronzed sailor suddenly confronted her, and said abruptly, but respectfully, "Do you remember giving me thirty cents last March?" The lady did remember. He insisted on paying it back, and afterward accepted an invitation to the meeting for sailors at the Mission. At that meeting he rose and said, "I've got a big heart, but I can't express myself as I ought to. When I was in New York last March I had no place to sleep, and two nights I crawled into an ice-cart, and slept there. But I was very cold and hungry; oh I was *so* down! I was all broken. I didn't know nothing! If help hadn't come, I was going to cut my throat, or jump into the river. But you spoke kind to me, and you prayed for me, and gave me money for lodging; that's worth *thousands* to me! I've been a different man ever since; could not pray much, but I prayed the Lord to make a good fellow out of me. I have prayed every day since that night. We had a heavy storm coming to New York; we thought all would be lost, and I prayed, O my God, let me get back to thank that lady"! Putting a dollar on the table, he said, "You may want to give some other poor fellow a lodging." After kneeling in prayer, in which he joined with genuine earnestness, he extended his great, brawny hand, and the firm grasp corresponded with the hearty "*thank you*," which welled up from his heart. Who can compute the compound interest on the trifle—thirty cents?

A RECOVERY FROM SPINAL DISEASE.

IN a letter recently received by Miss Carrie F. Judd, and published in her *Triumphs of Faith*, the writer says: "In January, 1879, I fell on the ice and injured the upper part of my spine. It would be a long story, if I could tell all that I went through for six years after that. I consulted one doctor after another, but medicine did me no good. Thirty-six blisters were applied at different times, beside many other applications. I suffered dreadfully, and sometimes felt as if my head were being twisted from my body. Most of the time I could not read, and I could not hold my head up for five minutes without supporting it with my hand. I had frequent hemorrhages, and my liver and stomach troubled me all the time. In June, 1883, I was obliged to take to my bed altogether, and could not sit up any for a year. I could not allow any one to remain in my room more than five minutes, and could scarcely endure to hear any one speak. My doctor had told me long before this that he could do nothing more for me. One day I was thinking of my dreadful condition, with no hope of ever being any better, of no use to myself and a great trouble to my dear brother, and I looked up to heaven and said, 'Lord, wilt thou not do something for me? Thou canst make me well if thou wilt,' and the Lord heard and answered. You prayed for me October 30, 1884. My disease was all removed that night. My face changed at once to a healthful color. It was a long time, however, before I was strong enough to work all day or go to church, which is about three-quarters of a mile from where I live, but I knew that I was healed. It was something new here, and people could hardly believe it. The next week after prayer was offered for me, I felt much worse, and could hardly walk for a week, but the Lord took these feelings away, and I have never felt any of my old trouble since."

A DEAD MAN'S SECRET.

A LONG search for hidden treasure has proved successful in Montana. Some thirteen years ago, a Frenchman and his son, a boy of fifteen, were prospecting near Helena. Finally the man, who was old and eccentric, sank a shaft near the summit of Old Bald Mountain. He was ridiculed for seeking gold in a place among the clouds. The Frenchman said nothing, but continued his work. He was extremely secretive, and not even his son knew the result of the labors in which he assisted. It appears, however, that the rock was so rich in gold that the old man cached it in order to prevent his secret leaking out. The boy and he continued working the shaft, the old man carefully concealing the product of their joint work. But one day, in hoisting a load of the precious ore, the rope broke, and the dead weight fell upon the old man, killing him instantly. After the funeral, the son remained two or three months on the place, searching for his father's hidden treasure. He could not find it, and finally abandoned the search for a time, carefully filling in the entrance to the shaft. He remained absent for two years, but at the end of that time he returned with money he had earned, and resumed his search. He took an old miner into his confidence, and together they made a minute examination of the locality. A press despatch from Helena now announces their success. The treasure has been found, and specimens sent to an expert for analysis. There are many sons of pious parents who would do well to exercise as much perseverance in seeking the treasure which made the lives of their parents blessed. That search would be successful and satisfying. (Prov. 2: 4. 5.)

CONVERSION THROUGH A VISION.

AT a recent meeting at the Sailors' Mission in New York, a sailor from Maine, whose honest, frank face was evidence of his sincerity, related the following remarkable experience which led to his conversion:

"I was converted when I was eighteen, but did not intend to be. I went to a Methodist prayer-meeting, and when the invitation was given to those who had a desire for prayer, I raised my hand *just for fun*; they asked all to come forward. I went to the front merely to make fun, but when I knelt the Spirit of the Lord came upon me and took me at my word. I went home and told mother. For two or three weeks I was in great trouble, and could not pray. One night I lay tossing about on my bed, unable to sleep, trying to pray, but having no words. I lay so a long time, and it seemed to me that I was still wide awake when a bright light shone in the dark room. I lay still, awed by the strange light, when soon I distinctly heard the softest, sweetest music, as if angels were singing. I could not account for it, and whether I was sleeping or waking, I cannot say; but to me, it was so real and true that I cannot doubt the fact. Even the words printed themselves on my memory. It was an old Methodist hymn that was sung. As it ceased, the light disappeared. I was surely wide awake then, for I jumped out of bed and fell on my knees, and I could pray then."

The speaker is thirty-three years of age. He dates his conversion from that night when he knelt down after his vision and gave himself to God. His life in the fifteen years that have elapsed since, has been that of a simple, earnest, humble Christian.

THE APPROACHING APOSTACY.

By James Stephens, M. A.

Boastings of Progress—The Scriptural Warning—The Future Gloomy, Not Bright—The Days of Scoffers—Licentious Men—False Security—Apostasy Inevitable—Awful Ending of the Age—Antediluvian Scepticism—Present Indifference—The Practical Issue.

WE are told that we live in the age of progress. Comparisons are often made between the present time and times that are past, greatly to the advantage of the former. It is pointed out how, by means of education and the development of commerce and art and science, we are in far better circumstances than our forefathers were. And this is made a ground of expectation for the future.

Many of these statements, having regard as they have to secular things, we in no way wish to deny or call in question. But secular progress is in nowise identical with spiritual progress; and when Christian men speak as if the progress of this age were an *upward* progress, culminating in a world-wide triumph of Christianity, and the establishment of universal peace and brotherhood, we are obliged to demur, and to point out how contrary is the teaching of God's Word.

First, in II Tim. 3 we read words pointing out what shall be in the last days, clearly setting before us what our age is developing into. Its development is not in an upward direction, or toward universal conversion, but, on the contrary, toward the practice of daring sins. These daring sins will be associated with a form of godliness. There will be profession of God, but practical denial. And the consequent character of the last days will be that they will be perilous. God, whose eye surveys all the future, sees and tells us what our age is advancing to.

But further we find Peter in his Second Epistle writing that there shall come in the last days scoffers; unto this, then, our age is going on. We are not advancing to days of universal conversion, but to

Days of Contempt

for the Word of God. The scoffing will be on the part of those who have heard and who know that Word, and who are acquainted with its teaching on the subject of the second coming of Christ. Such scoffing is quite compatible with the great advances in science. Indeed, in these days, science is not infrequently marked by disregard, even daring disregard, for what God has said. Theories are started and maintained as if they were proved facts—theories which treat with disdain the historic authority of God's Word. Whatever attempts are made to show the reconciliation between revealed religion and science (and let us not undervalue these), yet, none the less really, will the last days be days of scoffing.

Men will walk *after their own lusts*, saying, Where is the promise of His coming? They will walk in wilfulness. They will be a law to themselves, and will put aside the will of God. Liberty will become lawlessness; and scepticism, as to the most definitely foretold fact of the coming of Christ, flaunt itself.

Nor will the scornful scepticism of the Coming be without *some little* show of reasonableness. Century after century passes, and all things continue as they were. There is no appearance or likelihood, they say, of anything supernatural. But they "*wilfully forget*" (II Pet. 3: 5, R. V.) that by the Word of God the heavens were of old, and the earth. They ignore the creative fiat of the Almighty, and they deny the very possibility of *creation*.

Our day, with its teaching of *evolution*, has connected itself with "the last days."

The Days of Scoffing.

That God made everything, "*after its kind*," as His Word affirms, has been denied, and even professing Christian teachers have been carried away in numbers by the evil current. It would almost seem as if in certain cases one would be esteemed to have forfeited his scientific, if not even his intellectual, reputation if he upheld the scriptural doctrine.

But we take a further step. Paul, when writing to the Thessalonians in his Second Epistle, tells us that before the day of the Lord comes the great apostasy will take place. Our age, then, is going on to apostasy, excelling all apostasy that has been known. There have been departures from Christ in different ages, but here we have the grand departure, a departure culminating in the manifestation of him who is called *the* man of sin.

Notwithstanding all progress in secular things, in science, and in art, there remains and grows rebellion against God. The days before the Flood were days of progress in arts (Gen. 4: 21, 22), and days of renown (Gen. 6: 4), but with this secular progress the imagination of men's hearts was evil continually, and the race became spiritually and morally utterly corrupt. And the present days have a likeness to the days before the Flood. With all the glorious increase to the number of Christ's disciples through times of refreshing, yet so far from the world getting converted, the world is in many cases converting and corrupting the Church. And we are going on to days when multitudes will depart from the profession of Christ to the denial of Him. *The* apostasy will take place.

What a fearful issue this is! What a solemn and

Awful Ending of our Age,

with all its boasted civilization and refinement and culture and science and liberty! As we have seen, the age is advancing to the denial of godliness (though the form of godliness be held) to the scoffing at or denial of the Word, and finally to the denial of God Himself, and His only begotten Son. How different this from the thoughts of many, that commerce, education, and art, united with the preaching of the Gospel, will usher in the Millennium!

When our age reaches the fearful crisis that is foretold, then the Lord Jesus Christ must interpose in administrative and punative power. When man became wholly corrupt before the Flood, the Lord interposed in righteous judgment, and when the world becomes again mature in corruption, again there will be interposition in righteous judgment. The revelation of the Lord Jesus, to which His own people expectantly look, will be to others

A Coming of Judgment,

as was the Flood, or as the fire and brimstone which came on Sodom.

In the days of Noah men were living in scepticism of the fact of coming judgment. This is what is suggested by "eating and drinking, marrying and giving in marriage." Notwithstanding the warnings given by Noah during one hundred and twenty years, there was utter unconcern and universal unbelief. Many may have said then, "Where is the threatened flood? all things continue as they were." In any case their manner of life expressed profound indifference to what was foretold. The Flood was at hand, and the world was "wilfully ignorant"; they knew not till it came.

As it was then, so shall it be in the last days. The Lord Jesus has indeed given the plainest warnings, and "He that shall come will come, and will not tarry." With all the warnings, however, men will go on in their wilful course, and in lawlessness, and in mockery And "when they shall say, Peace and safety, then sudden destruction." When the Lord Jesus comes down upon this earth in judgment, His own will be like Noah in the ark. They will be gathered to Himself before the breaking forth of wrath, and after He shall thus have come forth in righteous and administrative power, executing judgment, and have bound Satan, millennial blessings shall crown this earth. What is

The Practical Issue

of all this? The prospect of this age is indeed a dark one; and those who set forth God's Word as to the end of the age may be regarded as gloomy foreboders, men incapable of rightly appreciating the so-called good features of the times, and on these grounds have scant welcome, or even quarter. Such teaching is exceedingly opposed to the views of even Christian men. Still, if God condescends to make known the evil to come, we shall do well to lay it to heart.

LAWLESSNESS AND THE LAWLESS ONE.

From a Sermon by the Late Rev. Dean Vaughan.

ST. PAUL speaks (II Thess. 2 : 3, 7, 8) of a certain particular growth and spirit of evil, which must have full scope and play before the Advent. Nor does he leave us in any uncertainty as to the direction in which we must look for the rise of that state of things which will bring down upon itself God's latest, sorest, and direst judgment. He selects for it a particular name, not one of the common names for sin in Scripture, but a name which he only uses twice or thrice in all his writings, and which has always a very definite and precise meaning. Our English version has somewhat lost sight of the peculiarity. It renders this word in one verse as "*iniquity*," and in the next verse "*the wicked one*"; but in the original the word is substantially the same in both verses—in the one "the mystery of *lawlessness* doth already work"; and, in the other, "then shall the *lawless one* be revealed."

This "*lawlessness*" of the seventh verse passes into the "*lawless one*" of the eighth—"then shall the *lawless one* be revealed"—unveiled or disclosed in all his features of horror and blasphemy—"*whom the Lord shall consume with the spirit of His mouth, and shall destroy with the brightness of His coming.*" St. Paul seems to prepare us for a sort of incarnation of lawlessness; principle, power, or person, sitting, as it were, in the very temple of God, "*showing Himself that He is God,*" and yet, in reality, deriving from the devil all the "*powers and signs of lying wonders*" by which he deludes the unhappy victims who are not fortified and preoccupied by the devout love of the truth.

The important thought for us all is this, that *lawlessness* is the predicted characteristic of the last age, as the time of the end draws on, to be stimulated and exasperated into a terrible virulence. I ask this congregation, Is it not now—is it not abroad on the Continent of Europe, is it not abroad in one integral portion of what we still fondly term "the United Kingdom"? Is it not abroad among ourselves; in the family and the church; in the workshop and in the study; in the literature of a "*science falsely so-called*"; and in the lurking-places of political fanatics, who count not their lives dear if they can but embitter an existence or topple down a throne?

A mystery of *lawlessness* is working everywhere with ingenious industry among the time-honored institutions of society itself. Frightful outbreaks of lawlessness have startled us again and again, until they have almost ceased to startle. We expect them; we look for them. Soon the paper will be flat and dull which records not one of them—assassinations and attempted assassinations of rulers, crowned and uncrowned, despotic, constitutional, or democratic—it matters not. These are but samples and specimens of a system which spares neither high nor low, which strikes not at *oppression*, but strikes at *order*, the determined foe of superiority, by one hair's breadth, of man over man. The owner of the decent home, the wearer of the decent coat, is an offence, an affront, to the evil eye that watches it.

Yes, the reign of *lawlessness* is begun, though a few years may yet intervene before the actual unveiling of the *lawless one*, who is to be destroyed by the personal advent of Christ.

CHRISTIAN HERALD AND SIGNS OF OUR TIMES.
OFFICE, 63 BIBLE HOUSE, NEW YORK.

TERMS AND INSTRUCTIONS.

Published Weekly. Subscription price in the United States, Canada, and Mexico, $1.50 a year; $1 eight months; 75 cents six months; sent two months on trial for 25 cents, postage free; in Europe and in all countries in the Postal Union, 50 cents extra postage; subscriptions always payable in advance. Single copies, price 3 cents. Any newsdealer will furnish the paper weekly when ordered.

Remittances by Mail should be by Post-office money order, bank cheque, draft, or express money order, whenever possible, and should always be made payable to THE CHRISTIAN HERALD. Letters containing money sent in this way need not be registered, as, when lost, duplicates can always be obtained.

If a Postal Note or currency is sent, it should always be in a registered letter. Letters can be registered at any office. Subscribers sending money of this kind, and not registering, do it at their own risk. Postage stamps should never be sent if it is possible to remit in any other way.

Receipts are not sent; the receipt of the paper by a subscriber is a sufficient proof that the remittance has been received. If the paper does not arrive promptly, please advise us, that we may see if the address is correctly entered.

Renewals can be sent any time previous to date of expiry, and the time will be added to that to which the subscriber is already entitled. Some time must always necessarily elapse after receipt of money before the date opposite to the name on label can be changed.

Notice of Expiration of subscription is always sent in addition to the date being given on the address label. When not renewed by date of expiration, the paper is stopped; no notice from the subscriber being required.

CURRENT EVENTS.

There is Still Doubt About the Politics of the next House. The "unofficial list" of members that appears in the Congressional Directory makes out a Republican majority of five, allowing for errors discovered since its preparation. This majority is obtained by listing Evans of Tennessee and two Republicans from West Virginia. It is still the belief of West Virginians that three Democrats will have certificates from that State. If they do, the Republican majority will disappear. If Evans of Tennessee is refused a certificate and it is given to the Republicans, they will number 163 and the Democrats 162. That outlook encourages the Democrats in doubting whether the Republicans can organize the House promptly enough to secure any early tariff legislation.

The Incorporation of the Nicaraguan Canal Company is meeting with unexpected opposition in the House. The bill passed the Senate comparatively unobstructed, but some causes are evidently operating in the House to delay, if not to kill it. As the bill before the House does not commit the United States to any financial responsibility, but simply gives the undertaking national approval and countenance, it has seemed to the public to be a worthy as well as a great enterprise, and as its practicability is assured upon the surveys of eminent and well-known engineers, who have recently made a careful examination of the proposed route, the opposition it is meeting with provokes adverse comment. The plan appears to be to so load it with amendments that the House may grow weary of the discussion and let the bill drop.

Our Dispute With Hayti, to Which the President briefly referred in his message, has reached a stage at which active measures are deemed necessary. The insurgent General Légitime, who is now the actual President of the Haytian Republic, though the dignity has not been formally conferred upon him, having failed to release the American steamer *Haytian Republic*, a naval expedition has been ordered to proceed to Port au Prince to enforce the demand of the United States Government. Admiral Luce was placed in charge of the expedition, which consisted of the *Yantic*, the *Galena*, and the *Richmond*. He was directed to present a formal demand for the release of the American vessel, and, if met with a refusal, to seize her by force of arms and carry her to some neutral ground for restoration to her owners. The *Galena* sailed on December 12, with Admiral Luce on board; but with the usual ill-fortune that seems to attend everything connected with our Navy Department, she had not proceeded many feet from her dock before she stuck ingloriously in the mud, and three powerful tugs were unable to drag the cumberous hulk off. She had to wait several hours for the turn of the tide before she could start on her voyage to uphold the dignity of the United States. After a delay of five hours she floated again, and was towed out of the harbor to meet the danger of a seven days' voyage to Hayti. There will probably be no difficulty in securing the result aimed at without resort to force, General Legitime being too shrewd a man to court a quarrel with the United States while his own position is far from fully established. President Cleveland's contention is that sufficient notice of a blockade had not been given, and that the blockade had not been maintained.

A Curious Joint Resolution on the Canadian question, which will probably arouse angry comment in Canada, was introduced in the House on December 13, by Mr. Butterworth, of Ohio. It authorizes the President "to invite negotiations looking to the assimilation and unity of the people of the Dominion of Canada and the United States under one Government, such unity and assimilation to be based upon the admission of the several provinces of the Dominion, or any one of them, into the Union of States, upon the same terms and equality with the several States now composing the Union, and the assumption by the United States of the indebtedness of the Dominion of Canada or a just proportion thereof, and such other equitable terms as justice to the high contracting parties may demand; and that, with a view to such negotiation, the President invite the appointment of Commissioners by the Government of Great Britain and the Dominion of Canada, to consider the wisdom and expediency of settling and adjusting all controversies and differences which now exist between the two Governments growing out of the fisheries, or otherwise, by such a union and assimilation as is hereinbefore suggested, either as to the whole or any province or several provinces of said Dominion."

The Distressing Fatality at Birmingham, Ala., on December 9 has aroused the interest of the whole country. Various views have been expressed about it, but there can be no question in the mind of the Christian patriot as to the right one. A man charged with brutal and unnatural murders had been arrested and lodged in jail. Public indignation was strongly felt against him, and threats of lynching were freely made. Men of conscience and influence endeavored to discourage the project, but without avail. A mass meeting numbering several thousands assembled on Sunday night and surrounded the prison in which the accused man was confined. Demands were shouted that he should be brought out, but the Sheriff refused. He warned the crowd that he and his men had arms, and would use them in case of an attack. The Sheriff says that the crowd threatened to blow up the jail with dynamite, and at last opened fire upon his men. Thereupon, having notified the crowd that he would fire if they did not withdraw, he gave the order and a volley was poured into the dense mass. Three men were killed on the spot, seven more were mortally wounded, all of whom have since died, and thirty others received wounds more or less serious. Unhappily, some of the men who fell were peaceable citizens who were trying to dissuade the mob from the attack. The sheriff has been arrested for murder, but it may be hoped that when public excitement has subsided the charge will not be pressed. He was engaged in the execution of his duty and was bound to defend his prisoner. It is time now that in a civilized country like this, the trial and execution of criminals should be conducted by the appointed authorities and not by an irresponsible mob.

A Massacre of Missionaries in China Was briefly reported last week by the New York *Herald*. It states that Miss Sophic Preston, of Waitsburg, Washington Territory, who went to China as a missionary two years ago, has been murdered near Canton, and several Europeans with her. There was a general uprising among the natives. The residence of the missionaries in which she lived was attacked at dead of night by several hundred Chinese armed with long spears, knives, and guns, and a number of people were killed. The mob next attacked the residence of some Europeans and slaughtered them without mercy. So far as known, there was no immediate cause for the massacre. Miss Preston was twenty-two years old, and a native of China, where her father was a missionary.

A Papal Rebuff to the Irish People was Administered last week. A telegram from Rome says: A sensation has been caused by the Pope's refusal to bless medals and reliquaries sent to Rome by an Irish priest who intended them for distribution in Ireland. The Pope sternly said:—"I cannot bless them. The people of Ireland are disobedient. They seem to prefer the gospel of Dillon and O'Brien to the Gospel of Jesus Christ." While such words may cause consternation in Ireland, their effect may be beneficial in the end. If the Pope's utterance should alienate the people from him there is more hope for them. They have been kept back from the light of the gospel mainly through their subjection to their priests, and after all, there is no boon that Parliament could grant, or the League achieve, which would be so beneficial to the country as its emancipation from Papal rule.

The Loan of Twenty Million Dollars to Russia by the French people was one of the significant events of the week. There has been considerable friction between the governments of Russia and Germany on financial subjects recently. The persistent efforts of the German press to discredit Russian securities has called forth a diplomatic protest from the Czar, who rightly believes that the Berlin government could stop the newspapers attacking him if they wished. Heretofore, the Russian government has relied mainly upon Berlin financiers for the vast sums needed to cover the annual deficits of the Russian Treasury. The French, however, having manifested their friendship for Russia, it was suggested to the Czar that if he were to offer the new loan of twenty million dollars, which he needs this year, in the French market, he would meet with much better success. He did so, and in one day seventy millions, more than three times his request were subscribed. This will cement the bond of friendship between Russia and France, and frees the former from the financial tutelage of Germany, which was often irksome in the past.

A Report that Mr. H. M. Stanley and Emin Pasha are prisoners in the hands of the Mahdi's troops was circulated last week. It emanated from the London *Standard*, which has had hitherto the most reliable press correspondents in Africa. It states that a letter received at Suakim from Osman Digna, the Mahdist General, contains, it has reason to believe, the news that Emin's troops have mutinied and delivered him, with a white prisoner supposed to be Stanley, to Osman Digna. With his letter, as proofs of the identity of his prisoners, Osman Digna sent several Snider cartridges, which, he alleged, were taken from the white traveller. The Zanzibaris in Stanley's expedition were armed with Snider rifles, but there were none in the possession of the dervishes. He also sends an official letter, which is recognized as one Stanley had in his possession. Osman Digna in his letter expressed a willingness to surrender Emin Pasha and his white companion provided Egypt would agree to abandon Suakim. If this proposal is not accepted, it is believed that both captives will be killed.

The Centenary of the Death of Rev. Charles Wesley, the poet of Methodism, was celebrated by two enthusiastic meetings held last week. On December 14, a union meeting was held in Calvary Baptist Church, New York, and on December 13 at Hanson Place Methodist Episcopal Church, Brooklyn. At the latter a touching letter was read from the octogenarian author of the hymn "My Country, 'tis of Thee," the Rev. Samuel F. Smith. Over 1,200 persons were present, and joined heartily in the singing of Charles Wesley's hymns, led by a choir of forty voices. Addresses eulogizing the Wesleys and expressing appreciation of Methodist labor, were given by clergymen of various denominations. Among them were the Rev. Dr. Cuyler, the Rev. E. P. Thwing, the Rev. Dr. Charles H. Hall, Rector of Holy Trinity Protestant Episcopal Church, and by the Rev. Dr. W. C. P. Rhodes, of Marcy Avenue Baptist Church.

A **Wonderful Movement at Walla Walla** Wash, Ter., appears to have followed Mr. D. L. Moody's services there. Despatches to the Portland *Oregonian* say that never in the history of the city has there been such interest manifested as is now existing. As early as 6 o'clock the streets each side of the Opera House are densely packed with people waiting the opening of the doors. At that time enough people are in waiting to fill a building four times as large. Afternoon meetings are attended by a crowded house, and morning prayer-meetings by almost as many. The excitement with many is unprecedented some hardly stopping long enough to eat their meals. People in going to the meetings almost run. Men holding the hands of women fairly drag them along. The meetings inside are of the usual character of those Mr. Moody conducts. There is no resort to the exciting or sensational, but the work is extraordinary.

A Fatal Perversity Appears to Have Caused the loss of two promising lives at Cornell University on December 12. A number of students were skating, and others were on the bank fixing their skates. Among the latter a student of civil engineering, named Nevins, who while buckling the straps of his skates heard a crash. Looking up, he saw a lady with two children disappear through a hole in the ice. Instantly he plunged into the icy water after her. The students on the bank stretched themselves on the ice, and succeeded in rescuing the two children, who soon rose to the surface. Minutes passed, but young Nevins and the lady whom he went to rescue did not appear. The spectators were surprised, for Nevins was known to be a strong and expert swimmer. Several students dived into the water and one of them at last brought up the body of Mr. Nevins, and afterward the body of the lady was recovered. Both were quite dead. It is believed by all who knew the young man's power as a swimmer, that the lady must have been so terrified as to lose her presence of mind, and by trying to save herself, have thwarted the efforts of her rescuer, who could have saved her had she been passive. There are many awakened souls who might be saved if they would cease their efforts for self-salvation. When they learn that they can never save themselves, and trust only in Christ's power, then deliverance comes. (Rom. 10: 3.)

A Curious Freak of Fashion is Reported in the Fashion columns of the Philadelphia *Record*. It appears that the demand for girls who are skilful in embroidery, recently became so pressing as to attract the attention of a reporter, who visited one of the embroidery establishments that was doing a large business. He found a large number of girls, who were working at full speed and long hours to keep up with the press of orders. Inquiring what was being done, he was informed that "the girls of upper-tendom" have become infected with a craze for having monograms in gold or colored silks embroidered on the instep of their stockings, just at the lowest point exposed by the low shoes worn at balls and parties. In the majority of cases the monogram is composed of the initials of the wearer; but in some cases one of her feet will be decorated with her own initials, and the other with those of the gentleman whose wife she has promised to be. The result will evidently be significant of much. If at the aristocratic gatherings of the season, a young lady, who is engaged, persists, against her lover's wish, in wearing her own monogram on each foot, he will naturally conclude that she is ashamed to acknowledge the bond between them. In such assemblies there are often found persons who have pledged themselves to Christ. When, by their manner and conversation, those about them find no indications of such a pledge, their Lord is dishonored, and He is wounded in the house of His friends. (Zech. 13: 6.)

The Proposal to Tattoo Soldiers is Arousing considerable indignation among officers and men, and many citizens sympathize with them. The proposal emanated from a retired army officer, who, after an experience of forty-five years in the army, asserts that there is no other way to prevent the practice of desertion, which is now more prevalent than ever. He says that deserters come from two classes. One is composed of the men who are too restless to remain long in any pursuit, and the other of men who have entered the army in money or other trouble, and wish to remain only until the trouble is removed. A large proportion of the army comes from these two classes, and desertions are therefore numerous. He suggests that every soldier should be marked with a tattoo mark, which would involve him in the necessity of producing his discharge on being challenged when away from duty, or of being arrested as a deserter. Many enlist in the army of the Prince of Peace from unworthy motives, and afterward desert; and many, too, while retaining the name, neglect the great Captain's orders, and are absent from duty. But there is no need to tattoo soldiers who enlist in that army. The omniscient Lord knows them that are His (II Tim. 2: 19), and in the day of final reward, those who have neglected their duty will be brought to shame. (Matt. 25: 26–28.)

A Lady Locked in an Iron Safe had a Narrow escape from death in Washington, D. C., on December 8. She was engaged in a millinery store on F Street, and late in the evening went into the large safe-vault in the rear of the store to put away some articles of value from the stock. A clerk, who passed shortly afterward, seeing the safe-door open, and not knowing that she was inside, closed the door and turned the knob, thus setting the combination. The young lady's predicament was soon discovered, and caused great excitement from the fact that there was no one present who knew the combination. The question of engaging a safe-burglar was being seriously discussed, when some one suggested sending for the proprietor. That was done, and when he was found he at once came to the store and opened the safe, releasing the young lady from her perilous position. She had been locked in for over an hour, and might have suffocated to death if her release had been delayed much longer. In spiritual matters, persons are sometimes enmeshed through their own imprudence or that of others, and are in danger of disaster for time and eternity. Even the best and wisest advisers are often powerless to deliver them, but in such cases deliverance is sure if, as in the case in which the disciples failed, application is made to the Master. (Mark 9: 17–27.)

A Girl Was Released From Prison to Become a bride in Baltimore, Md., on December 13. She had been captured earlier in the week in a raid on a disorderly house, and was kept in prison to await her trial. In the course of Thursday a young man called on the captain of the police station in which she was confined, and after an interview with him, was permitted to talk to the prisoner. Apparently the result of the conversation was satisfactory, for the young man left in high spirits. He returned later in the day with legal papers authorizing the captain to release the prisoner. He was also accompanied by a dry-goods clerk, who brought several silk dresses, a bonnet, a plush sacque, and a complete set of underclothing. These were sent into the girl's cell, and she arrayed herself in the new attire. While this was being done the young man talked with the captain about his affairs. He said that he was a wealthy stock raiser and was making a big fortune. He was convinced that the girl would make him a good wife, and would abandon her evil ways. As soon as the transformation in the girl's appearance was complete they started for the Justice's room, where they were married, and then set out for the husband's home. Few men would have felt so much confidence in choosing a wife out of a prison, and if there really is good in the girl, she will show her appreciation by her future life. That is what Christ expects of His bride the Church. He found her Satan's captive and released her; clothed her with the robe of His righteousness, and espoused her to Himself. Unfaithfulness in her is therefore a hideous crime. (Rev. 19: 7, 8.)

BRIEF NOTES.

Persons having written original hymns, are invited by Mr. G. Tabor Thompson, 295 Broad Street, Bridgeport, Conn., to send them to him, to set them to music.

The Rev. Dr. Cyrus F. Knight, Rector of St. James' Episcopal Church, Lancaster, Penn., has been elected Bishop of Milwaukee in succession to the late Bishop Wells.

Mr. Philip Phillips, the "Singing Pilgrim," gave his new illustrated song addresses at Mr. C. H. Spurgeon's Metropolitan Tabernacle, London, December 11, 12, and 14.

As the result of a series of lectures delivered by Mr. George Woodford at Victoria, New Brunswick, nearly $2,000 has been raised towards a Rescue Home for women, to be established in that place.

The Rev. C. H. Spurgeon has gone to Mentone to escape the rigors of the English winter. Two of his deacons accompanied him. During his absence his recent evening discourses will be published here.

Rev. S. N. Whiteson, of Raleigh, N. C., dropped dead of heart disease in a railroad station at Midway, Pa., on Monday, December 3. He had preached the day previous in the Baptist church on "Sudden Death."

Ben Hogan has been holding meetings at Olean, N. Y. The Olean *Herald* says that his graphic autobiographical story of his early life and conversion, frankly but cleanly told, chained the attention of an audience that tested the capacity of the large hall.

Dr. L. W. Munhall's services at Davenport, Iowa, closed with a great jubilee-meeting, at which over two thousand persons were present, in the Rink. The mission has been much blessed. On December 9 Dr. Munhall commenced services in Bloomington, Ill.

The Children's Aid Society of New York is anxious to give dinners and gifts of clothing to poor, homeless children for Christmas. Any person willing to aid in the good work is invited to send provisions or clothing or money to the Secretary, Mr. C. L. Brace, 24 St. Mark's Place, N. Y.

The Baptist ministers of Chicago have requested the secular newspapers of the city not to publish the announcements of church services on Sunday; the Congregational and Methodist Episcopal ministers have since made the same request, to mark their disapproval of Sunday issues.

Dr. Pentecost has during the last few weeks been conducting evangelistic meetings in Dublin; two meetings at least were held each day, and much good is believed to have been done. Major Whittle's meetings in Belfast have also been much blest. He is now at Ballymena, Ireland.

At the revival services held by the Rev. B. Fay Mills in Germantown, Philadelphia, between nine hundred and one thousand persons professed conversion, and these have been distributed, by their own expressed choice, among the twelve churches of five denominations which united in the movement.

The conference held in New York recently, to consider the best means of reaching the masses, appointed a committee of twenty-five, representing the churches and missionary societies of the city, "for the careful study and execution of such plans as may seem to them wise for more efficient co-operation in aggressive Christian work, both on the part of the churches and existing missionary organizations."

The Next Few Weeks will be the best time for canvassing for new subscribers. We are happy to learn that many of our friends are already introducing THE CHRISTIAN HERALD among their friends and neighbors. Any one desiring sample copies, *for this purpose*, will be supplied free of cost by writing for them, stating explicitly how many can be advantageously used. Address "The Manager," 63 Bible House, New York.

Mr. Mutsu, Japanese Minister to the U. S.

Serious News Lightly Spoken.

taken by a *coup de main* that is one of the strangest incidents in history. It was the War of the Spanish Succession, waged by half Europe to determine which of two incompetents should occupy the throne of Spain. The English sent a squadron into the Mediterranean, under Sir George Rooke, who, after cruising about and accomplishing little, bethought himself, in order not to return in complete failure, to try his hand on Gibraltar. The place was well fortified with a hundred guns, but inside the walls only a hundred and fifty men, (a man and a half to a gun!) so that it could offer but a brief resistance to a bombardment, and so the Spaniards lost in three days what they spent more than three years in trying to recover, in vain.

MUNEMITSU MUTSU.

Japanese Minister to the U. S.

A SINGULARLY checkered life has been that of the gentleman whom the Japanese Government has sent to represent it in this country. The family to which he belongs is one of the most distinguished in Japan, but while he was still a youth it was proscribed, and the ancestral estates were confiscated. He devoted himself to private study, and soon won a prominent place among the adherents of the Mikado, whose fortunes he followed during the ascendency of the Shogunnite government. His life was frequently in peril, but his valor and prudence always extricated him from his complications. When the Mikado's power was established, Mutsu became one of his chief officers. He represented his government in Germany during the Franco-German War. On his return he was made Finance Minister, and afterward Vice-President of the Senate. His popularity with the Mikado and the people was unbounded, but the vicissitudes of political life had not been exhansted. Mutsu was deprived of offices and dignities, and found it advisable to take a foreign tour. He travelled extensively in Europe and America, making a study of the forms of government and the customs of the various peoples. His reappearance in Japan was greeted with a restoration to the royal favor, and he has now received the most coveted diplomatic post in the Mikado's gift.

Mr. Mutsu is forty-five years of age. He is a close student, a gifted orator, and is the author of several standard works used in the Japanese seats of learning.

TWO CHANGED LIVES.

(See Illustration.)

ON a beautiful moonlight evening two men ran a light rowing boat up on a sandy beach and sat down on a rough log to rest. They had about two miles to go to the little hotel where they proposed to pass the night. Strangely assorted companions they were, but each liked the other for the qualities he did not himself possess. Harry Bennett, the younger of the two, was an easy, good-natured fellow, with a moderate fortune inherited from his father. It was securely invested, and he lived luxuriously as a bachelor on its proceeds, without making any effort to increase his capital. John Hardcastle, his companion, was a hard-working builder, who had risen by sheer labor and frugality to the possession of a small fortune, to which he was adding year by year. He had been coaxed by his friend Bennett, to take a short holiday, and was now beginning it by a row along the coast.

"How beautifully serene everything is here," said Hardcastle. "One forgets, on such an evening as this, that not far away there are busy streets, and men toiling and perspiring in the struggle of life."

"Yes," said Bennett. "I suppose hard-working fellows like you enjoy such a scene. As for me, it seems dull and lifeless. It bores me; but then everything does bore me."

"I cannot conceive of you as being anything but bored," said Hardcastle. "You are such a luxurious fellow. If you tried work you would give it up quickly, for you would have no incentive to brace you up to overcome difficulties. Now I have a wife and a family of little children, and when I meet with an obstacle or something disagreeable, I see on the other side of it my children's bread and butter, and do not mind a little struggling nor a few knocks in trying to get it for them. Men like you, with no one depending on them and anxious only to amuse themselves, are of very little use in the world."

"You speak disparagingly of men like me, and I don't know but you may be right, but there are times in which I think we have the advantage of you. Now as I came down from the city this morning, I saw some men there who were in a good deal of trouble. A bank has burst, and I fancy it means ruin to some folks who will have to go under. I think some of them, if they are unencumbered bachelors, will be glad that they have neither wife nor children."

"What bank is it?" asked Hardcastle. "I make a point when I leave business to leave it altogether, and I never open a newspaper all the while I am away. So I have heard nothing of this bank failure, but I am sorry for the sufferers all the same, though I don't know them."

"It's Rufford's bank," said Bennett, rising as he spoke; and yawning and stretching himself, as if he were bored even by the conversation. But he was startled by the sound of a deep groan, and turning around, saw his companion with his head in his hands, and his body writhing as if in pain. "What's the matter, old fellow?" he asked. "Are you sick?"

"That bank, Harry, is the matter; every cent I have is there, and I paid in a big sum the very day I came down here. Harry, I'm ruined!"

"That is bad," said Harry. "Those rascals who manage these failures ought to be severely punished. But come, now; let us go up to the hotel and get a good night's rest. Things may not look so gloomy in the morning."

Hardcastle arose almost mechanically, and accompanied his friend to the hotel. But he had no expectation of a good night's rest. The proceeds of a life of hard, unremitting toil were swept away, and his wife and children, of whom he was so fond, were penniless.

The next morning Hardcastle was travelling as fast as an express train could take him to his home. His news was soon told. But from his wife he heard no reproaches, no lamentation, no childish repining, such as some women utter over their husband's misfortunes. A sweet, womanly pity filled her eyes, and she said: "My poor, brave husband, how you must be suffering! Let us pray to God for His guidance in our trouble."

For more than two hours the two had been engaged in conversation and prayer, and when at last they left their room and descended to the cosey parlor, in which so many happy hours had been spent, but which now they must prepare to leave, Hardcastle was full of chastened hope, and the bitterness of his trial was past.

As they entered, they heard the sound of some one talking to their children, and the husband at once recognized Bennett's voice. "Ha! Hardcastle," he said, as their entrance was perceived, "you see I have followed you. This husband of yours, madam," he said, turning to Helen, "was delivering a sage lecture to me, before he heard of his losses, on the advantage a married man has over a single one, and I thought I would come over and see how it stood the test. But, seriously, I have other business with you, Hardcastle, besides that. I am not such a brute as to intrude at such a time without good cause. You know what I am, an idle, careless dog, wasting my life, and as you told me last night, not much good in the world. But I have some money, and as you have brains, I thought we might work well together. Now, if you will have me for a partner I am ready to go with you, and we will see whether you can make me of some use in the world."

Hardcastle was too much affected to speak, but he wrung his friend's hand, and for the first time for many a year his eyes filled with tears.

Bennett affected to be in haste, to avoid noticing his emotion, and said he must go away and get some clothes to wear instead of his yachting costume, which in his hurry to follow his friend he had neglected to change; and he would come in again shortly to hear what husband and wife thought of his proposal, after considering it.

When he was gone, Hardcastle and his wife returned to their room, and there poured out their hearts in thankfulness to God, who had heard their prayer before it was uttered, and had made a way of escape for them. There, too, Hardcastle registered a vow in God's strength, which he was enabled to keep, that for the remainder of his life he would acknowledge God in all his ways and look to Him to direct his steps.

CHINATOWN, SAN FRANCISCO.

Every visitor to San Francisco is taken to see the Chinese quarter. He takes a guard with him if he is prudent, for there are characters to be met with there who have little respect for law, and not much for life when money is to be made for taking it. The Chinese have erected but few buildings themselves in the section which they have made their own, but they have adapted the houses they found there to their own customs, and by making balconies, and putting up awnings and lanterns, have transformed the locality into as near an imitation of Chinese towns as they are able. Much has been written by visitors of the horrors they have seen in the gambling dens and opium joints which abound. It is gratifying to learn that of late years the efforts made to suppress these fearful evils have had some success, though there are sufficient still existing to call for earnest Christian effort.

There are over 30,000 Mongolians collected in the comparatively small area, and they herd together in such close propinquity as to make it a mystery how in such foul air, and amid such dirt, life can be sustained. The restaurants of Chinatown, which are numerous, present the most characteristic features of the race, not only as to the viands prepared, but the manner of consuming them. In some of them, however, the American taste and habits have exercised an influence. One gentleman who visited the quarter recently, dined there as an experiment. He says that he had chicken soup with a paste resembling macaroni, a tender chicken sliced through, bones and all, served in a bowl; another bowl of duck; and quail and spinach served in a pewter chafing dish. These were placed on the table, and the diners helped themselves from the common stock with pairs of ebony chopsticks, to such morsels as they might desire.

In San Francisco as everywhere else, the most potent moralizing and reforming influence has been found, not in the severity of the laws, but in the Christian labors of the servants of Christ, notably in the efforts of devoted ladies who have opened Sunday-schools for the Chinese, and have had the blessing of God on their work.

A Scene in Chinatown, San Francisco.

ESCAPED FROM THE MORMONS.

A Life Story: By Mrs. Stenhouse.

For More than Twenty-five Years the Wife of a Mormon Missionary and Elder.

(*Continued from page 798*).

Received into the Church.

In the afternoon I attended a meeting of a still more interesting character. These Sunday-afternoon meetings were held for the purpose of receiving the Sacrament, and the confirmation of those who had been baptized during the week; they were intended exclusively for the Saints, but for certain reasons I was permitted to be present. The meeting was opened with singing and prayer, and then the presiding Elder—Brother Cowdy—arose, and invited all those who had been baptized during the week to come to the front seats. Several ladies and gentlemen came forward, and also three little children. Upon inquiry, I found that children of eight years of age were admitted members of the church by baptism—which is administered by immersion. At that age they are supposed to understand what they are doing; but before that, if of Mormon parents, they are considered members of the church by virtue of the blessing which they received in infancy.

Brother Cowdy—the presiding Elder—then called upon two other Elders to assist him in the confirmation. One of the ladies took off her bonnet, but retained her seat, when all three of the elders placed their hands upon her head, and one of them said: "Martha; by virtue of the authority vested in us, we confirm you a member of the Church of Jesus Christ of Latter-day Saints; and as you have been obedient to the teachings of the Elders, and have gone down into the waters of baptism for the remission of your sins, we confer upon you the gift of the Holy Ghost, that it may abide with you for ever, and be a lamp unto your feet, and a light upon your pathway, leading and guiding you into all truth. This blessing we confirm upon your head, in the name of the Father, and of the Son, and of the Holy Ghost. Amen."

Then, before they took their hands off her head, the presiding Elder asked the other two if they wished to say anything. Whereupon one of them began to invoke a blessing upon the newly confirmed sister. He spoke for some time with extreme earnestness, when suddenly he was seized with a nervous trembling which was quite perceptible, and which evidently betokened intense mental or physical excitement. He began to prophecy great things for this sister in the future, and in solemn and mysterious language proclaimed the wonders which God would perform for her sake. When we consider the excited state of her mind, and—if the statements of psychologists be true—the magnetic currents which were being transmitted from the sensitive nature of the man into the excited brain of the new convert, together with the pressure of half a dozen human hands upon her head, it is not at all astonishing that when the hands were lifted off she should firmly believe that she had been blessed indeed. She had been told that she should receive the gift of the Holy Ghost; and she did not for an instant doubt that her expectations had been realized. Each of the newly baptized went through the same ceremony, and then they all partook of the Sacrament, when, after another hymn, the meeting was closed with prayer.

In the evening I returned, to listen to a lecture upon "the character, spirit, and genius" of the new church, delivered by Elder Stenhouse; and I was captivated by the picture which he drew of the marvellous latter-day work which he affirmed had already begun. The visions of bygone ages were again vouchsafed to men; angels had visibly descended to earth; God had raised up in a mighty way a Prophet, as of old, to preach the dispensation of the last days; gifts of prophecy, healing, and the working of miracles were now, as in the days of the Apostles, witnesses to the power of God. The long-lost tribes of Israel were about to be gathered into the one great fold of Christ; and the fullness of the Gentiles being come, they, too, were to be taken under the care of the Good Shepherd. All were freely invited to come and cast away their sins, ere it was too late; and the fullest offers of pardon, grace, sanctification, and blessing, in this world and in the next, were presented to every repentant soul.

Surely, I thought, these are the self-same doctrines which my mother taught me when I knelt beside her in childhood, and which I have so often heard—only in colder and less persuasive language—urged from the pulpits of those whom I have ever regarded in the light of true disciples of Jesus. Who can wonder that I listened with rapt attention, and that my heart was even then half won to the new faith? The days passed; and as I pondered over these things, it appeared to me that I had at last found that which I had so long earnestly desired and prayed for—a knowledge of that true religion for which the Saviour presented Himself a Holy Sacrifice, and which the Apostles preached at peril of their lives—the *only* faith in which I might find joy and peace in believing.

But why should I dwell upon those moments, soul-absorbing as was their interest to me *then*—sadly-pleasing as is their memory *now?* The reader can see the drift of my thoughts at that time; and I feel sure, although I have but hastily sketched the causes which brought about these great changes in my religious belief and in my life, that he will not hastily accuse me of fickleness and love of change, if he himself has fought the battles of the soul, and has learned, even in a slight measure, to realize the mystery of his inner being. Each day the finger of destiny drew me nearer to the final step.

The young Elder whose words I had listened to with such strange and, to me, momentous results, was intimate with my father's family, and called frequently to see us, and before long he convinced me that it was my duty to test for myself whether the work was of God, or not. In the agitated state of my mind at that time, I could not withstand the earnest appeals which were made to my affections and hopes; and within two weeks after my arrival in England I became formally a member of the Church of Jesus Christ of Latter-day Saints; or, in more popular language—I became a Mormon. The day was fixed for my baptism. Several others were to be baptized at the same time; for scarcely a week passed without quite a number of persons joining the Church. For this purpose we all repaired to a bathhouse on the banks of the Southampton River. This place was not perhaps the most convenient, and it certainly was devoid of the slightest tinge of romance; but it was the only one available to the Saints at that time.

When we were all assembled and had united in singing and prayer, Elder Stenhouse went down into the water first, and then two men went down and were baptized, and came up again. Now came my turn. I was greatly agitated, for I felt all the solemnity of the occasion. I had dressed myself very neatly and purely, for I believed that angel eyes were upon me: I wished to give myself a perfect and acceptable offering to my God, and I was filled with the determination henceforth to devote my whole life to His service. As I went down into the waters of baptism, how thankful I felt that it had been my privilege to hear the Gospel in my youth, for now I could give my heart in all its freshness to the Lord, before it had been chilled by the cold, hard experience of life.

I descended the steps, and Elder Stenhouse came forward and led me out into the water; then, taking both my hands in one of his, he raised his other hand toward heaven, and in a solemn and impressive voice, he said: "*Fanny; by virtue of the authority vested in me, I baptize you for the remission of your sins, in the name of the Father, and of the Son, and of the Holy Ghost. Amen.*"

Then he immersed me in the water; and as I reascended the steps I really felt like another being; all my past was buried in the deep—the waters of baptism had washed away my sins; and a new life lay open before me, in which my footsteps would be guided by the inspired servants of God. All now would be peace and joy within me, for I had obeyed the commands of God, and I doubted not that I should receive the promised blessing, and that now I could indeed go on my way rejoicing. My baptism took place one Saturday afternoon, and the afternoon following I was confirmed a member of the Church. Elder Stenhouse presided at the meeting, and he, with Elder Cowdy and two other Elders, confirmed me. As the "blessing" which I then myself received differs somewhat from the one which I have already given, and as it is a very fair specimen of those effusions, I present it to the readers in full.

Elder Stenhouse, Elder Cowdy, and the two other Elders, placed their hands solemnly upon my head, and Elder Stenhouse said: "Fanny: by virtue of the authority vested in me, I confirm you a member of the Church of Jesus Christ of Latter-day Saints; and inasmuch as you have been obedient to the command of God, through His servants, and have been baptized for the remission of your sins, I say unto you that those sins are remitted. And in the name of God I bless you, and say unto you, that inasmuch as you are faithful and obedient to the teachings of the priesthood, and seek the advancement of the kingdom, there is no good thing that your heart can desire that the Lord will not give unto you. You shall have visions and dreams, and angels shall visit you by day and by night. You shall stand in the Temple of Zion, and administer to the Saints of the Most High God. You shall speak in tongues, and prophecy, and the Lord shall bless you abundantly, both temporally and spiritually. These blessings I seal upon your head, inasmuch as you shall be faithful; and I pray heaven to bless you; and say unto you—*Be thou blessed*, in the name of the Father, and of the Son, and of the Holy Ghost. Amen."

After the meeting, I received the congratulations of all the Saints present, and more particularly those of my own family. My dear mother and father were overjoyed; and I now learned how anxious they had been, and how they had feared that I should return to France and reject the faith of the new dispensation. Altogether we were very happy. Elder Stenhouse and Elder Cowdy returned home with us to tea, and afterwards we all attended the usual evening lecture. In this way was passed one of the happiest days of my life—one which I shall ever remember—and yet that memory will always be mingled with regret that so much love and devotion as I then felt were not enlisted in a better cause.

Thus began a new era in my life. All my former friends and associations were now to be remembered no more; my lot was cast among the Saints; and in the state of my mind at that time, I believed that I should be happy in my new position, and resolved to give evidence of the sincerity of my faith. The untiring energy and restless activity of Elder Stenhouse was ever before our eyes, and inspired all who associated with him with a similar enthusiasm. There were no drones in that hive. The brethren, at a word from him, would roam the country, teaching and preaching in the open air, while the sisters would go from house to house in the city, distributing tracts about the new faith. I caught the enthusiasm of the rest, and was soon in the ranks with the other sisters, as devoted in my endeavors as a young, ambitious heart could be. I was, indeed, like one born again from an old existence into a new life. I felt grateful and happy—I began to dream of the eternal honor which crowns a faithful missionary life; and I soon found an ample field for testing my fitness for that vocation.

At the time of which I speak, the Primitive Methodists in England were doing a great work in the way of converting sinners. Their missionaries were zealous and devoted men, though generally poor and uneducated. They resembled very closely the Mormon Elders in their labors; and, in fact, a very large number of the leading Mormons had been Methodist local preachers, and the greater number of the new-born Saints had come from that denomination with their former teachers, or had followed them soon after. The change from Methodist to Mormon was, in course of time, very strongly marked; but for a considerable period the same, or what seemed the same, influences were at work among the people. Remarkable scenes of excitement were often witnessed at the "love feasts"; and from the "anxious seats," as they were called, might be heard the entreaties of self-accusing souls, frightened by a multitude of sins, crying earnestly, nay, wildly, for grace, mercy, and the Holy Ghost; while many of the supplicants would fail upon the ground, completely overcome by nervous excitement. Then they would have visions, and behold great and unutterable things, receive the forgiveness of their sins, and, coming back to consciousness, believe themselves now to be the children of God, and new creatures, doubting not that they would, ever after, be happy in the Lord. The experience of the Saints at their meetings, when Mormonism was first preached, was exactly similar to this. Into the psychological, moral, or religious causes of these scenes of excitement I cannot here enter; I simply mention facts as they came under my own observation.

The Mormon missionary often came upon whole communities in the rural districts of England where this "good time" was in full operation; and being a man of texts he would follow up the revival, preaching that the spirit of the prophet was subject to the prophet, and not the prophet subject to the spirit. Controversy would arise, and his appeal to Scripture, literally interpreted, was almost invariably triumphant. Even in America, especially in New York and Ohio, the same causes produced the same effects. It was after his mind was excited by a general revival near his native place that Joseph Smith, the founder of Mormonism, received his first religious impression. His followers, even in the early days of the Church and revival meetings, and meetings at which the most extraordinary excitement was manifested—when the Saints fell into ecstatic trances—saw heaven opened, and spake with tongues. But Joseph, shrewd man as he was, albeit "a prophet," when he found too many rival seers were coming into the field, announced by "special revelation" that these too gifted persons were possessed by devils, and their visions and prophesyings must be suppressed. And he did suppress them.

Not long after my own baptism I was present at a meeting of this description in Southampton. It was called a "testimony meeting," and was held in a large upper room situated, if I rightly remember, in Chandos Street. No one from the outside would have supposed that it was the place of assembly of the Saints, for it was generally used for ordinary secular meetings, and I have heard that great objections were at first raised as to the propriety of letting it to the Mormons.

As we entered the door we were saluted by Brother Williams, who expressed great pleasure at seeing us. There was a full attendance of the Saints, and every face wore an expression of peaceful earnestness. A person who has never attended a Mormon meeting can form no idea of the joyous spirit which seemed to animate every one present. I am not, of course, speaking of modern meetings, but of meetings *as they used to be*. Whence and whatever that "spirit" might be which moved the sisters and brethren when they met in early times, I cannot tell; but I, and with me 10,000 Mormons and seceding Mormons in Utah, can testify that *that* spirit no longer visits the Tabernacle services over which Brigham Young presided, or the meetings of the Saints since they adopted the accursed doctrine of polygamy, and forsook the gentle leadings of their first love. Often have I heard Mormons of good standing and high position in the Church lament the "good old times" as they called them, when the outpouring of the Spirit was so abundant, and mourn over the cold, barren services of the present day. But the Elders say it is the fault of the people themselves, and because their own hearts have become cold.

At the Testimony meeting of which I speak, a happy spirit was peculiarly present. An encouraging smile or a kind word greeted me on every side, and, as a newly converted sister, I received the most cordial welcome. The brethren were seated on forms and chairs and any other convenient article which came to hand, while at the further end of the room was Brother Bench, who was to preside, and with him several other leading elders. Brother

Bench gave out a suitable hymn. The whole congregation joined in the singing, and every heart seemed lifted up with devotion. Then another elder rose, and offered a spirit-moving prayer; and then the brother who presided stated that for the time he withdrew his control of the proceedings, and, as the phrase was, he "put the meeting in the hands of the Saints," exhorting them not to let the time pass by unimproved.

(To be Continued.)

THE SWORD OF THE SPIRIT.

By Mrs. M. Baxter.

S. S. Lesson Suggested for December 30, II Tim. 3: 14-17.

Christians who Do not Carry their Bibles Around—Neglecting to Verify Quotations in Church—How to Gain Familiarity with the Bible—Incident of a Disobedient Child—Reminiscence of Christian Work in Germany—The Comprehensiveness of the Book—A Refractory Servant—A Dressmaker Encouraged—Remarkable Conversion of a Soldier.

A SOLDIER without a sword! Such is every Christian who ventures into a religious meeting without his Bible. He is like a seaman without a chart, a traveller without a guide-book, a workman without a tool, an astronomer without a telescope, a surgeon without an instrument. It is astonishing, in numberless congregations, especially those of Nonconformists, to see hardly a Bible in the place, except that which is used by the minister! It is the custom of the Roman Catholic to carry his missal with him to church, and he is not ashamed to carry his books of devotion with him into a horse-car or a railway carriage. The churchman carries his prayer-book and Bible as well as his hymn-book to church; the churchman is

Not Ashamed of His Bible.

The Scotch Presbyterians are seen on the Sunday morning walking to church with their Bibles under their arms or in their hands; and in every religious meeting in Scotland the audience is accustomed to turn to the passages quoted by the preacher, and so to gain by every religious service in the knowledge of the Bible; the Scotchman is not ashamed of his Bible. But among English dissenters, in America, and in the Protestant countries of Europe, the use of the Bible in church is scarcely known. Why should a Lutheran, or Free Church Swiss, an English Wesleyan, Baptist, or Independent, be ashamed to carry and to use his Bible? The consequence is that the greatest ignorance of the Bible prevails; in a Bible-reading we find people looking for Revelations among the Books of Moses, and for the minor prophets among the Epistles! Numbers of men who are members of churches can find a place in a railway guide with the greatest readiness, while it would take them half an hour to discover the locality of one of the sayings of Jeremiah, or some passage in Deuteronomy!

How can I get a knowledge of my Bible? many say. By the simplest process: make use of your Bible whenever you have an opportunity; carry it to church, and, when the Lesson is read, find the place and read after the minister. When he refers to any text in his sermon, find the place, and read it, that you may remember it again. Always bring your Bible to family prayer, and follow the reader; if possible, form the good habit of reading round verse by verse, so that all may take part. Then, when any special thing occurs in your family, say a birth, a marriage, or a death, search in your Bible all which God says about it. If you are in perplexity, search what God says about perplexity; if in fear, what He says about fear; if in want, what He says about His children's needs. If a child is naughty, search what He says about a parent's training.

A Little Boy

of seven years old was one day very naughty; he had been impertinent to his governess, and would not acknowledge his fault. After being kept in bed twelve hours, he at last yielded, and owned himself in the wrong, and then asked his mother to read him from the Bible all the directions which God has given for parents to punish their children. Happily the mother knew her Bible, and was able at once to turn to every passage. But what respect would the child have had for his mother if she had been obliged to confess she did not know these passages?

The Christian's sword exercise consists in knowing how to handle the Bible. Paul writes to Timothy as one who from a child has known the Holy Scriptures. In those days portable Bibles were out of the question; the huge parchment rolls then in use could not be carried from place to place. Timothy must have learned the Holy Scriptures by heart. But how great an advantage we have with pocket Bibles, which we can, and ought to, carry everywhere with us! Some will say, "I find it a distraction to read after the minister, I would rather listen." Suppose a child learning geography thought it a great distraction to be referred to the map! Is it not rather a lazy way of listening when we do not take the trouble to compare Scripture with Scripture, and so take from God and not from the minister the truths which are being taught? Another objection is, "I am so unused to handle my Bible, that I should feel awkward." But every one is awkward in the commencement of anything that is new to him. The writer, when evangelizing in Switzerland and Germany, often held meetings in villages where the Bible was very little known. She carried a certain number of Bibles with her, and lent them to the people who occupied the first rows of seats, and exhorted all the other people to bring their own Bibles to the next meeting. She then gave time, whenever she quoted a passage, for the people to find it. The consequence was that hundreds bought portable Bibles, and began to study them; many souls were brought to Christ; and a large number of weekly Bible-readings were formed among those who had found Jesus.

The apostle Paul says that "all Scripture is given by inspiration of God, and is profitable for doctrine, for reproof, for correction, for instruction in righteousness,

That the Man of God May be Perfect,

throughly furnished unto all good works.(II Tim. 3: 16.) Oh how unfurnished are those who know little of their Bibles! The Bible, not certain parts of it, but the whole Bible, furnishes us with doctrine. A man who thoroughly knows *all* his Bible, cannot well be a hasty man. He will give elbow room to those who do not see just as he sees, because he will see how comprehensive is the Word of God. But at the same time he will be guarded from extravagances and errors, because he will accept nothing which is not clearly stated in the Word. The Bible "is profitable. . . for correction"; not only the correction of our own individual souls, but it decides points between husband and wife, parent and child, master and servant, poor and rich, believer and unbeliever, in such a way that, to a subject mind, really yielded to God, there can be no difficulty in knowing the will of God. A minister one day asked the writer to speak to

A Refractory Servant

of his. The girl was full of her own wrongs, bitter in spirit, and indignant against her employer, and yet to all appearance the fault was her own; she wanted to have everything her own way, and because her employer was a Christian, she thought he ought not to oppose her in anything. The writer prayed the Lord for direction, and then asked the girl to open her Bible at 1 Tim. 6: 1, 2: "Let as many servants as are under the yoke count their own masters worthy of all honor, that the name of God and His doctrine be not blasphemed. And they that have believing masters, let them not despise them, because they are brethren; but rather do them service, because they are faithful and beloved, partakers of the benefits." The poor girl did not know such words existed in the Bible. She at once went to her employer, humbled herself, and did her work as he willed, and cheerfully, because she acknowledged the authority of God.

By handling the Word of God more, things are discovered which we have not noticed before. An earnest Christian dressmaker, who had to support herself and mother, one day mourned that she could not do more spiritual work, when a friend pointed out to her that God's Holy Spirit was not above instructing in the use of the needle. "The Lord hath called by name Bezaleel, . . . and he hath filled him with the Spirit of God . . . all manner of work, of the embroiderer, in blue and in purple, in scarlet and in fine linen etc." (Ex. 35: 30-35.) A cook may feel how much more dignity there is in her work, when she sees that one of God's Levites "had the set office over the things that were made in the pans" (1 Chron. 9: 31.) Gardeners may be encouraged when they know that the Bible speaks of "potters, and those that dwelt among plants and hedges: there they dwelt with the king for his work." (1 Chron. 4: 23.) The mill girls in Lancashire, and in the north of Ireland, may like to hear of "the families of the house of them that wrought fine linen;" (1 Chron. 4: 21.)

If the man of God is to be perfect through his knowledge of the Word of God, how many imperfect Christians there must be! How many unfurnished ones! Surely if the Bible were carried to religious meetings, and there studied, and places marked with pencil to help the memory, the conversation over the dinner or tea table would not be so often on the minister or speaker, but rather on the truth which he had taught, and so the minds of the people would be more exercised upon the Word of God. It is a precious thing to be familiar enough with the text of Scripture to be ready always to give a reason of the hope which is in us in Scripture language. In a testimony meeting, it is most refreshing to hear testimonies

Full of Scripture Quotations

which have become a living and precious reality to the speaker. Nothing has such power with the unawakened, with these sinners, or with sceptics and infidels, as the Word of God itself. They may scoff at it, but God has declared that it is "quick (or living) and powerful, and sharper than any two-edged sword, piercing to the dividing asunder of soul and spirit and of the joints and marrow, and is a discerner of the thoughts and intents of the heart." (Heb. 4: 12.) A soldier had been urged by a Christian worker to turn to the Lord. He met all her entreaties with blaspheming and ridicule. Impelled by the Spirit of God, she said at last one day only these words, "He that, being often reproved, hardeneth his neck, shall suddenly be destroyed, and that without remedy." (Prov. 29: 1.) He went away with a jeering word, but on his way the words rang through his mind again and again with such power that he threw himself upon his knees, and sought and found the Lord.

God's Word partakes of His own Almightiness; how strange that we should prefer our poor powerless words to His! The best of human utterances are but dilutions of the Word of God: undiluted it has wondrous power. If my readers should be stirred up by these words to search the Scriptures, and to make use of their Bible as their daily and hourly hand-book, their constant companion, their indispensable requisite at all times, I shall not have written or prayed in vain. And it is with earnest prayer that these few feeble words are sent forth. "For it is not a vain thing for you, because it is your life." (Deut. 32: 47.) "The words which I speak unto you, they are spirit and they are life."

then half won to the new faith? The days passed; and as I pondered over these things, it appeared to me that I had at last found that which I had so long earnestly desired and prayed for—a knowledge of that true religion for which the Saviour presented Himself a Holy Sacrifice, and which the Apostles preached at peril of their lives—the *only* faith in which I might find joy and peace in believing.

But why should I dwell upon those moments, soul-absorbing as was their interest to me *then*—sadly-pleasing as is their memory *now*? The reader can see the drift of my thoughts at that time; and I feel sure, although I have but hastily sketched the causes which brought about these great changes in my religious belief and in my life, that he will not hastily accuse me of fickleness and love of change, if he himself has fought the battles of the soul, and has learned, even in a slight measure, to realize the mystery of his inner being. Each day the finger of destiny drew me nearer to the final step.

The young Elder whose words I had listened to with such strange and, to me, momentous results, was intimate with my father's family, and called frequently to see us, and before long he convinced me that it was my duty to test for myself whether the work was of God, or not. In the agitated state of my mind at that time, I could not withstand the earnest appeals which were made to my affections and hopes; and within two weeks after my arrival in England I became formally a member of the Church of Jesus Christ of Latter-day Saints; or, in more popular language—I became a Mormon. The day was fixed for my baptism. Several others were to be baptized at the same time; for scarcely a week passed without quite a number of persons joining the Church. For this purpose we all repaired to a bathhouse on the banks of the Southampton River. This place was not perhaps the most convenient, and it certainly was devoid of the slightest tinge of romance; but it was the only one available to the Saints at that time.

When we were all assembled and had united in singing and prayer, Elder Stenhouse went down into the water first, and then two men went down and were baptized, and came up again. Now came my turn. I was greatly agitated, for I felt all the solemnity of the occasion. I had dressed myself very neatly and purely, for I believed that angel eyes were upon me; I wished to give myself a perfect and acceptable offering to my God, and I was filled with the determination henceforth to devote my whole life to His service. As I went down into the waters of baptism, how thankful I felt that it had been my privilege to hear the Gospel in my youth, for now I could give my heart in all its freshness to the Lord, before it had been chilled by the cold, hard experience of life.

I descended the steps, and Elder Stenhouse came forward and led me out into the water; then, taking both my hands in one of his, he raised his other hand toward heaven, and in a solemn and impressive voice, he said: "*Fanny: by virtue of the authority vested in me, I baptize you for the remission of your sins, in the name of the Father, and of the Son, and of the Holy Ghost. Amen.*"

Then he immersed me in the water; and as I reascended the steps I really felt like another being; all my past was buried in the deep—the waters of baptism had washed away my sins; and a new life lay open before me, in which my footsteps would be guided by the inspired servants of God. All now would be peace and joy within me, for I had obeyed the commands of God, and I doubted not that I should receive the promised blessing, and that now I could indeed go on my way rejoicing. My baptism took place one Saturday afternoon, and the afternoon following I was confirmed a member of the Church. Elder Stenhouse presided at the meeting, and he, with Elder Cowdy and two other Elders, confirmed me. As the "blessing" which I then myself received differs somewhat from the one which I have already given, and as it is a very fair specimen of those effusions, I present it to the readers in full.

Elder Stenhouse, Elder Cowdy, and the two other Elders, placed their hands solemnly upon my head, and Elder Stenhouse said: "Fanny: by virtue of the authority vested in me, I confirm you a member of the Church of Jesus Christ of Latter-day Saints; and inasmuch as you have been obedient to the command of God, through His servants, and have been baptized for the remission of your sins, I say unto you that those sins are remitted. And in the name of God I bless you, and say unto you, that inasmuch as you are faithful and obedient to the teachings of the priesthood, and seek the advancement of the kingdom, there is no good thing that your heart can desire that the Lord will not give unto you. You shall have visions and dreams, and angels shall visit you by day and by night. You shall stand in the Temple of Zion, and minister to the Saints of the Most High God. You shall speak in tongues, and prophecy, and the Lord shall bless you abundantly, both temporally and spiritually. These blessings I seal upon your head, inasmuch as you shall be faithful; and I pray heaven to bless you; and say unto you—*Be thou blessed*, in the name of the Father, and of the Son, and of the Holy Ghost. Amen."

After the meeting, I received the congratulations of all the Saints present, and more particularly those of my own family. My dear mother and father were overjoyed; and I now learned how anxious they had been, and how they had feared that I should return to France and reject the faith of the new dispensation. Altogether we were very happy. Elder Stenhouse and Elder Cowdy returned home with us to tea, and afterwards we all attended the usual evening lecture. In this way was passed one of the happiest days of my life—one which I shall ever remember—and yet that memory will always be mingled with regret that so much love and devotion as I then felt were not enlisted in a better cause.

Thus began a new era in my life. All my former friends and associations were now to be remembered no more; my lot was cast among the Saints; and in the state of my mind at that time, I believed that I should be happy in my new position, and resolved to give evidence of the sincerity of my faith. The untiring energy and restless activity of Elder Stenhouse was ever before our eyes, and inspired all who associated with him with a similar enthusiasm. There were no drones in that hive. The brethren, at a word from him, would roam the country, teaching and preaching in the open air, while the sisters would go from house to house in the city, distributing tracts about the new faith. I caught the enthusiasm of the rest, and was soon in the ranks with the other sisters, as devoted in my endeavors as a young, ambitious heart could be. I was, indeed, like one born again from an old existence into a new life. I felt grateful and happy—I began to dream of the eternal honor which crowns a faithful missionary life; and I soon found an ample field for testing my fitness for that vocation.

At the time of which I speak, the Primitive Methodists in England were doing a great work in the way of converting sinners. Their missionaries were zealous and devoted men, though generally poor and uneducated. They resembled very closely the Mormon Elders in their labors; and, in fact, a very large number of the leading Mormons had been Methodist local preachers, and the greater number of the new-born Saints had come from that denomination with their former teachers, or had followed them soon after. The change from Methodist to Mormon was, in course of time, very strongly marked; but for a considerable period the same, or what seemed the same, influences were at work among the people. Remarkable scenes of excitement were often witnessed at the "love feasts"; and from the "anxious seats," as they were called, might be heard the entreaties of self-accusing souls, frightened by a multitude of sins, crying earnestly, nay, wildly, for grace, mercy, and the Holy Ghost; while many of the supplicants would fall upon the ground, completely overcome by nervous excitement. Then they would have visions, and behold great and unutterable things, receive the forgiveness of their sins, and, coming back to consciousness, believe themselves now to be the children of God, and new creatures, doubting not that they would, ever after, be happy in the Lord. The experience of the Saints at their meetings, when Mormonism was first preached, was exactly similar to this. Into the psychological, moral, or religious causes of these scenes of excitement I cannot here enter; I simply mention facts as they came under my own observation.

The Mormon missionary often came upon whole communities in the rural districts of England where this "good time" was in full operation; and being a man of texts he would follow up the revival, preaching that the spirit of the prophet was subject to the prophet, and not the prophet subject to the spirit. Controversy would arise, and his appeal to Scripture, literally interpreted, was almost invariably triumphant. Even in America, especially in New York and Ohio, the same causes produced the same effects. It was after his mind was excited by a general revival near his native place that Joseph Smith, the founder of Mormonism, received his first religious impression. His followers, even in the early days of the Church and revival meetings, and meetings at which the most extraordinary excitement was manifested—when the Saints fell into ecstatic trances—saw heaven opened, and spake with tongues. But Joseph, shrewd man as he was, albeit "a prophet," when he found too many rival seers were coming into the field, announced by "special revelation" that these too gifted persons were possessed by devils, and their visions and prophesyings must be suppressed. And he did suppress them.

Not long after my own baptism I was present at a meeting of this description in Southampton. It was called a "testimony meeting," and was held in a large upper room situated, if I rightly remember, in Chandos Street. No one from the outside would have supposed that it was the place of assembly of the Saints, for it was generally used for ordinary secular meetings, and I have heard that great objections were at first raised as to the propriety of letting it to the Mormons.

As we entered the door we were saluted by Brother Williams, who expressed great pleasure at seeing us. There was a full attendance of the Saints, and every face wore an expression of peaceful earnestness. A person who has never attended a Mormon meeting can form no idea of the joyous spirit which seemed to animate every one present. I am not, of course, speaking of modern meetings, but of meetings *as they used to be*. Whence and whatever that "spirit" might be which moved the sisters and brethren when they met in early times, I cannot tell; but I, and with me 10,000 Mormons and seceding Mormons in Utah, can testify that *that* spirit no longer visits the Tabernacle services over which Brigham Young presided, or the meetings of the Saints since they adopted the accursed doctrine of polygamy, and forsook the gentle leadings of their first love. Often have I heard Mormons of good standing and high position in the Church lament the "good old times" as they called them, when the outpouring of the Spirit was so abundant, and mourn over the cold, barren services of the present day. But the Elders say it is the fault of the people themselves, and because their own hearts have become cold.

At the Testimony meeting of which I speak, a happy spirit was peculiarly present. An encouraging smile or a kind word greeted me on every side, and, as a newly converted sister, I received the most cordial welcome. The brethren were seated on forms and chairs and any other convenient article which came to hand, while at the further end of the room was Brother Bench, who was to preside, and with him several other leading elders. Brother

Bench gave out a suitable hymn. The whole congregation joined in the singing, and every heart seemed lifted up with devotion. Then another elder rose, and offered a spirit-moving prayer; and then the brother who presided stated that for the time he withdrew his control of the proceedings, and, as the phrase was, he "put the meeting in the hands of the Saints," exhorting them not to let the time pass by unimproved.

(*To be Continued.*)

THE SWORD OF THE SPIRIT.

By Mrs. M. Baxter.

S. S. Lesson Suggested for December 30, II Tim. 3: 14-17.

Christians who Do not Carry their Bibles Around—Neglecting to Verify Quotations in Church—How to Gain Familiarity with the Bible—Incident of a Disobedient Child—Reminiscence of Christian Work in Germany—The Comprehensiveness of the Book—A Refractory Servant—A Dressmaker Encouraged—Remarkable Conversion of a Soldier.

A SOLDIER without a sword! Such is every Christian who ventures into a religious meeting without his Bible. He is like a seaman without a chart, a traveller without a guide-book, a workman without a tool, an astronomer without a telescope, a surgeon without an instrument. It is astonishing, in numberless congregations, especially those of Nonconformists, to see hardly a Bible in the place, except that which is used by the minister! It is the custom of the Roman Catholic to carry his missal with him to church, and he is not ashamed to carry his books of devotion with him into a horse-car or a railway carriage. The churchman carries his prayer-book and Bible as well as his hymn-book to church; the churchman is

Not Ashamed of His Bible.

The Scotch Presbyterians are seen on the Sunday morning walking to church with their Bibles under their arms or in their hands; and in every religious meeting in Scotland the audience is accustomed to turn to the passages quoted by the preacher, and so to gain by every religious service in the knowledge of the Bible; the Scotchman is not ashamed of his Bible. But among English dissenters, in America, and in the Protestant countries of Europe, the use of the Bible in church is scarcely known. Why should a Lutheran, or Free Church Swiss, an English Wesleyan, Baptist, or Independent, be ashamed to carry and to use his Bible? The consequence is that the greatest ignorance of the Bible prevails; in a Bible-reading we find people looking for Revelations among the Books of Moses, and for the minor prophets among the Epistles! Numbers of men who are members of churches can find a place in a railway guide with the greatest readiness, while it would take them half an hour to discover the locality of one of the sayings of Jeremiah, or some passage in Deuteronomy!

How can I get a knowledge of my Bible? many say. By the simplest process: make use of your Bible whenever you have an opportunity; carry it to church, and, when the Lesson is read, find the place and read after the minister. When he refers to any text in his sermon, find the place, and read it, that you may remember it again. Always bring your Bible to family prayer, and follow the reader; if possible, form the good habit of reading round verse by verse, so that all may take part. Then, when any special thing occurs in your family, say a birth, a marriage, or a death, search in your Bible all which God says about it. If you are in perplexity, search what God says about perplexity; if in fear, what He says about fear; if in want, what He says about His children's needs. If a child is naughty, search what He says about a parent's training.

A Little Boy

of seven years old was one day very naughty; he had been impertinent to his governess, and would not acknowledge his fault. After being kept in bed twelve hours, he at last yielded, and owned himself in the wrong, and then asked his mother to read him from the Bible all the directions which God has given for parents to punish their children. Happily the mother knew her Bible, and was able at once to turn to every passage. But what respect would the child have had for his mother if she had been obliged to confess she did not know these passages?

The Christian's sword exercise consists in knowing how to handle the Bible. Paul writes to Timothy as one who from a child has known the Holy Scriptures. In those days portable Bibles were out of the question; the huge parchment rolls then in use could not be carried from place to place. Timothy must have learned the Holy Scriptures by heart. But how great an advantage we have with pocket Bibles, which we can, and ought to, carry everywhere with us! Some will say, "I find it a distraction to read after the minister, I would rather listen." Suppose a child learning geography thought it a great distraction to be referred to the map! Is it not rather a lazy way of listening when we do not take the trouble to compare Scripture with Scripture, and so take from God and not from the minister the truths which are being taught? Another objection is, "I am so unused to handle my Bible, that I should feel awkward." But every one is awkward in the commencement of anything that is new to him. The writer, when evangelizing in Switzerland and Germany, often held meetings in villages where the Bible was very little known. She carried a certain number of Bibles with her, and lent them to the people who occupied the first rows of seats, and exhorted all the other people to bring their own Bibles to the next meeting. She then gave time, whenever she quoted a passage, for the people to find it. The consequence was that hundreds bought portable Bibles, and began to study them; many souls were brought to Christ; and a large number of weekly Bible-readings were formed among those who had found Jesus.

The apostle Paul says that "all Scripture is given by inspiration of God, and is profitable for doctrine, for reproof, for correction, for instruction in righteousness,

That the Man of God May be Perfect,

throughly furnished unto all good works. (II Tim. 3: 16.) Oh how unfurnished are those who know little of their Bibles! The Bible, not certain parts of it, but the whole Bible, furnishes us with doctrine. A man who thoroughly knows *all* his Bible, cannot well be a hasty man. He will give elbow room to those who do not see just as he sees, because he will see how comprehensive is the Word of God. But at the same time he will be guarded from extravagances and errors, because he will accept nothing which is not clearly stated in the Word. The Bible "is profitable. . . for correction"; not only the correction of our own individual souls, but it decides points between husband and wife, parent and child, master and servant, poor and rich, believer and unbeliever, in such a way that, to a subject mind, really yielded to God, there can be no difficulty in knowing the will of God. A minister one day asked the writer to speak to

A Refractory Servant

of his. The girl was full of her own wrongs, bitter in spirit, and indignant against her employer, and yet to all appearance the fault was her own; she wanted to have everything her own way, and because her employer was a Christian, she thought he ought not to oppose her in anything. The writer prayed the Lord for direction, and then asked the girl to open her Bible at I Tim. 6: 1, 2: "Let as many servants as are under the yoke count their own masters worthy of all honor, that the name of God and His doctrine be not blasphemed. And they that have believing masters, let them not despise them, because they are brethren; but rather do them service, because they are faithful and beloved, partakers of the benefits." The poor girl did not know such words existed in the Bible. She at once went to her employer, humbled herself, and did her work as he willed, and cheerfully, because she acknowledged the authority of God.

By handling the Word of God more, things are discovered which we have not noticed before. An earnest Christian dressmaker, who had to support herself and mother, one day mourned that she could not do more spiritual work, when a friend pointed out to her that God's Holy Spirit was not above instructing in the use of the needle. "The Lord hath called by name Bezaleel, . . . and he hath filled him with the Spirit of God . . . all manner of work, of the embroiderer, in blue and in purple, in scarlet and in fine linen etc." (Ex. 35: 30-35.) A cook may feel how much more dignity there is in her work, when she sees that one of God's Levites "had the set office over the things that were made in the pans" (I Chron. 9: 31.) Gardeners may be encouraged when they know that the Bible speaks of "potters, and those that dwelt among plants and hedges: there they dwelt with the king for his work." (I Chron. 4: 23.) The mill girls in Lancashire, and in the north of Ireland, may like to hear of "the families of the house of them that wrought fine linen:" (I Chron. 4: 21.)

If the man of God is to be perfect through his knowledge of the Word of God, how many imperfect Christians there must be! How many unfurnished ones! Surely if the Bible were carried to religious meetings, and there studied, and places marked with pencil to help the memory, the conversation over the dinner or tea table would not be so often on the minister or speaker, but rather on the truth which he had taught, and so the minds of the people would be more exercised upon the Word of God. It is a precious thing to be familiar enough with the text of Scripture to be ready always to give a reason of the hope which is in us in Scripture language. In a testimony meeting, it is most refreshing to hear testimonies

Full of Scripture Quotations

which have become a living and precious reality to the speaker. Nothing has such power with the unawakened, with these sinners, or with sceptics and infidels, as the Word of God itself. They may scoff at it, but God has declared that it is "quick (or living) and powerful, and sharper than any two-edged sword, piercing to the dividing asunder of soul and spirit and of the joints and marrow, and is a discerner of the thoughts and intents of the heart." (Heb. 4: 12.) A soldier had been urged by a Christian worker to turn to the Lord. He met all her entreaties with blaspheming and ridicule. Impelled by the Spirit of God, she said at last one day only these words, "He that, being often reproved, hardeneth his neck, shall suddenly be destroyed, and that without remedy." (Prov. 29: 1.) He went away with a jeering word, but on his way the words rang through his mind again and again with such power that he threw himself upon his knees, and sought and found the Lord.

God's Word partakes of His own Almightiness; how strange that we should prefer our poor powerless words to His! The best of human utterances are but dilutions of the Word of God: undiluted it has wondrous power. If my readers should be stirred up by these words to search the Scriptures, and to make use of their Bible as their daily and hourly hand-book, their constant companion, their indispensable requisite at all times, I shall not have written or prayed in vain. And it is with earnest prayer that these few feeble words are sent forth. "For it is not a vain thing for you, because it is your life." (Deut. 32: 47.) "The words which I speak unto you, they are spirit and they are life.

DAILY VICTORY.

"And this is the victory that overcometh the world—even our faith.—I JOHN v. 4.

I want a present, living faith,
That I may prove each day, each hour,
Amid the toils and cares of life,
My precious Saviour's love and power;
I want, amid the petty cares
That daily worry and annoy,
To live by faith so near my God
That life shall be a constant joy.

I want a firm unwavering faith,
That bringeth good from seeming ill;
That e'en amid affliction's blast,
Rejoices in the Father's will;
That when long-cherished hope's denied,
Still sings a "glad triumphant song,"
Knowing that He who reigns on high—
A God of love—can do no wrong.

I want a faith that falters not,
Let skies be bright or tempest beat,
That 'mid earth's joys, and cares, and griefs
Victorious sits at Jesus' feet.
Give me such faith, and then I know
When I shall pass cold Jordan's wave,
The faith that kept me day by day
Will be triumphant o'er the grave.

—*Selected.*

J. E. JEWETT, Publisher, 77 Bible House, New York, will furnish the above poem in leaflet form at twenty cents per hundred. *A Sample Packet* of 60 leaflets assorted (no two alike), will be sent post-paid, for 10 cts., or 100 for 20 cts. Postage stamps taken.

Entered according to Act of Congress in the year 1888, in the office of the Librarian of Congress at Washington.

This Journal contains every week a Portrait and Biography of some eminent person; a new Sermon by the Rev. C. H. SPURGEON, of London, and the Rev. Dr. TALMAGE'S latest Sunday morning Sermon; also always a Prophetic Article, and a Summary of Current Events as well as Stories, Anecdotes etc.

Vol. XI., No. 52. Office, 63 Bible House, N. Y. THURSDAY, DECEMBER 27, 1888. Price, 3 Cents. Annual Subscription, $1.50.

CONTENTS OF THIS NUMBER.

PORTRAIT AND LIFE OF THE RT. HON. JOHN BRIGHT.
A BAD BOIL CURED. Dr. Talmage's Sermon.
ANECDOTES RELATED AT RECENT EVANGELISTIC MEETINGS.
THE USES OF PROPHETIC STUDY.
RETROSPECT OF THE YEAR 1888.
Gems from New Books: Two Little Southerners in the War—Freedom Refused by a Slave, etc.
PORTRAIT OF THE REV. WILLIAM H. SCOTT, D. D., Father-in-Law of President-Elect Harrison.
PICTURE OF A STREET DISCUSSION WITH JEWS IN BRESLAU.
THE TRIAL OF YOUR FAITH. A New Sermon by Rev. C. H. Spurgeon.
PICTURE OF A RESTORED PALACE IN ANCIENT NINEVEH.
THE MISSION OF JOHN THE BAPTIST. By Mrs. M. Baxter.
INDEX TO VOLUME XI.

THE RIGHT HON. JOHN BRIGHT, THE VENERABLE STATESMAN, NOW NEARING DEATH.

THE RT. HON. JOHN BRIGHT.

Born in 1811—Espouses the Temperance Cause in His Youth—His First Public Address—Advocacy of the Claims of the Bible Society—Advancing Culture—First Election Contest in 1843—The Corn Law Agitation—Protest Against the Crimean War in 1853—Defence of the Queen in 1863—Demonstrations in Birmingham in 1883.

THE news cabled early last week that the famous statesman, who has throughout his life been the one steady and faithful friend of the United States in English public life, was lying at the point of death, has recalled to memory his many acts of friendliness to this country, and especially, how, when twenty-seven years ago, English politicians were clamoring for war with America, he alone of men of eminence stood up bravely for peace and conciliation. No man in Europe deserves more thoroughly the sympathy and good-will of our people. We therefore give his portrait, with the following details of his biography.

He was born at Greenbank, Rochdale, on November 16, 1811, and is, therefore, seventy-seven years of age. His father was the late Mr. Jacob Bright, a respected member of the Society of Friends, who by dint of sterling moral worth and business ability succeeded, notwithstanding many disadvantages, in making himself master of a cotton mill near Rochdale. He was thrice married, and had eleven children, all of whom were the offspring of his second wife. She was a woman of no common order, having a clear, well-furnished, and richly gifted mind, and a tender, loving, and Christian heart.

As a youth Mr. Bright was not without practice in public speaking. Before he was out of his teens he was regarded as an orator of considerable promise. At the age of nineteen he became a most earnest

Advocate of the Temperance Cause.

It is stated that, in conjunction with some like-minded gentlemen, he was the first to introduce the subject of organized temperance to his native town in 1830. Meetings followed in neighboring villages, and it was at one of those meetings that Mr. Bright delivered his first public address. On the way to that meeting, we are told that he and his friend Mr. Oliver Ormerod recited to each other their prepared speeches, and it was arranged between them that they were to prompt each other if there was any likelihood of a breakdown. The room was crowded, and Mr. Bright, in beginning his address, was very nervous, but gained confidence as he proceeded, and delivered his maiden speech with effect, and was warmly applauded.

The Bible Society.

Amongst the most noteworthy of the early addresses of Mr. Bright, was one delivered at Rochdale at a meeting of the Bibie Society. The Rev. John Aldis, an honored and distinguished Baptist minister, was staying at a friend's house when John Bright arrived to accompany him to the meeting, which was to be held in the Friends' Meeting House. "Soon," says Mr. Aldis, "a slender, modest young gentleman came, who surprised me by his intelligence and thoughtfulness. I took his arm on the way to the meeting, and I thought he seemed nervous. I think it was his first public speech—at all events in such connection. It was very eloquent and powerful, and carried away the meeting but it was elaborate and *memoriter*. On our way back, as I congratulated him, he said that such efforts cost him too dear, and asked me how I spoke so easily. Years rolled away. I had entirely forgotten the name of the young friend, when the Free Trade Bazaar was held in London. One of those engaged in it, calling on me, asked if I had called on Mr. Bright. I said I had not been able to attend the meetings, and did not personally know him at all. He replied, 'You must, for I heard him say that you gave him his first lesson in the art of public speaking.' I went to a subsequent meeting, and immediately recognized the young friend of 1832."

In 1833 Mr. Bright paid his first visit to the Continent. Passing over from London to Ostend, he visited Ghent, Brussels, Antwerp, Cologne, Frankfort, and Mayence. He sailed down the Rhine to Rotterdam, but was compelled by the prevalence of cholera to return to England. The visit, however, short as it was, was not lost upon his eager and observant mind. Subsequent and more prolonged visits made him the possessor of much that is most valuable in the results of European travel. Already he had decided literary tastes. He revelled in the biographies of illustrious men and in works of history. But above all, the great poets delighted him. Their far-reaching vistas of thought, their mastery of expression, their sense of the sublime and beautiful, their loftiness and tenderness, their sweetness and light, passed into his very nature and became part of his inmost being. Amidst all his other interests, whether of business, literature, or politics, John Bright *never neglected his Bible*, and it has been remarkable how even his political speeches in the House and elsewhere teem with Bible allusions and quotations.

His First Election Contest

took place at Durham in April, 1843, when he was unsuccessful. Four months later the seat was again vacant, and Mr. Bright, nothing daunted by his previous failure, renewed his candidature, and this time gained a decided victory. It was not long before his voice was heard in Parliament. The poor and the helpless were from the first his clients, and there can be no question that the secret of his power lay in the fact that he was utterly unselfish and thoroughly in earnest. The whole heart of John Bright was deeply moved by what he knew of the sufferings of the masses, and he was entirely convinced that the first and paramount duty of Parliament was to abolish the monopoly legalized by the Corn Laws, which was to a great extent the cause of the mischief.

But probably no part of his career was the subject of greater diversity of opinion in England than his attitude during

The Crimean War,

which broke out at the close of the year 1853. There was a strong anti-Russian sentiment in England, amongst almost all classes, and a widespread feeling that Russia would have to be fought sometime if England's supremacy in India was to be maintained, and that there was no time so propitious as that. Almost alone in that great crisis, John Bright stood up to protest against what he held to be an unjustifiable war. His action on the question cost him his seat for Manchester, and made him, for the time, one of the most unpopular men in the country. At the beginning of 1856 Mr. Bright had a severe illness, the result of his public labors, which necessitated a prolonged period of rest and travel. During a subsequent visit to the Continent he had an interview with the Empress of Russia.

Defence of the Queen.

In 1866, at a great meeting in St. James's Hall, London, Mr. Ayrton, M. P., thought fit to remark upon the Queen's infrequent appearance on public occasions, after the death of her husband, and censured her Majesty for not recognizing the people when they gathered in such numbers in front of one of her palaces. Mr. Bright interposed, and repudiated the insinuation. "I am not accustomed," he said, "to stand up in defence of those who are the possessors of crowns. But I could not sit and hear that observation without a sensation of wonder and of pain. I think there has been by many persons a great injustice done to the Queen in reference to her desolate and widowed position. And I venture to say this, that a woman—be she the Queen of a great realm, or the wife of one of your laboring men—who can keep alive in her heart a great sorrow for the lost object of her life and affection is not at all likely to be wanting in a great and generous sympathy with you." Mr. Bright's manly and Christian sympathy was not forgotten in the royal palace. When his own home was darkened by the death of Mrs. Bright in 1878, and expressions of kind condolence poured in upon him from all quarters, there came among the rest a telegram from Queen Victoria, expressing her deep sympathy with him in the hour of his sorrow.

Mr. Bright at Court.

On Mr. Gladstone's accession to power in 1868, Mr. Bright accepted the Presidency of the Board of Trade; and Her Majesty, on learning his acceptance of the post, with queenly courtesy and thoughtful kindness caused it to be intimated to Mr. Bright that any court ceremony which might be opposed to his principles as a Quaker should, in his case, be entirely dispensed with, and that he need not wear the costume of blue and silver, which Cabinet members are expected to wear when they go to the palace.

On being offered Cabinet rank he said he would have preferred to remain in the common rank of the simple citizenship in which he had hitherto lived. He said: "There is a charming story contained in a verse of the Old Testament which has struck me as one of great beauty. Many of you will recollect that the prophet, in journeying to and fro, was very hospitably entertained by what is termed in the Bible

The Shunammite Woman.

In return for the hospitality of his entertainment he wished to make her some amends, and he called her and asked her what there was that he should do for her. 'Shall I speak for thee to the King, or to the Captain of the Host?'—and it has always appeared to me to be a great answer that the Shunammite woman returned. She said, 'I dwell among mine own people.' When the question was put to me whether I would step into the position in which I now find myself, the answer from my heart was the same—*I wish to dwell among mine own people*. Happily the time may have come—I trust it has come—when in this country an honest man may enter the service of the Crown, and at the same time may not feel it in any degree necessary to dissociate himself from his own people."

Since 1857, when he was

Elected by Birmingham

by an overwhelming majority, Mr. Bright has continued to represent that constituency in Parliament. To celebrate their political silver wedding, in 1883, Birmingham did honor to their popular member in a series of fêtes, processions, speeches, etc. On June 11 of that year there was a monstre procession of welcome "extending over a route fully five miles long," and composed chiefly of artisan battalions, who to the blare of numerous brass bands marched with steady tramp amid the fluttering of flags and appropriate banners. On the following day there was a great meeting in Bingley Hall, the audience numbering, at a necessarily rough estimate, over 20,000 people. At this meeting the Rev. Dr. R. W. Dale presented Mr. Bright, in the name and on behalf of Birmingham, with a silver dessert service and portrait, to an accompaniment of the most enthusiastic applause. Throughout the jubilee every class of the community participated in the festivities. The enthusiasm that was kept up throughout the week was as spontaneous as it was generous. The significance of this mighty outburst of popular feeling lay in the character of the great Englishman who raised it. He had fought the battle of the public unselfishly; he had not scrupled to brave unpopularity when it appeared to him that the public were being led in the wrong direction; and he always presented to the world *the white flower of a blameless life*.

"Be just and fear not" is the motto which John Bright adopted in preference to all others, and which he has honestly lived up to at every moment of his life. And it may unquestionably be said of him that his justice and fearlessness have won the respect of the civilized world.

ANECDOTES RELATED AT RECENT EVANGELISTIC MEETINGS.

Jamie the Idiot's Discovery.—A Poor Highland lad in the north was one night converted to Christ, and the next morning, with hands and face well washed and shining, he set out for the meeting which was to be held. His clothes were in tatters, but he was unusually clean. Soon his unwonted appearance attracted the attention of the school children, who flocked after him, shouting, "You're braw this morning, Jamie; you're braw this morning." Turning to them Jamie replied, "Aye, He was braw Himself that morning He rose from the dead." That half idiot, on the night before, had recognized that simply taking God at His word and accepting Christ as his Saviour, he had passed from the deadness of sin into the glorious life of redeemed freedom.

"No Fanatics in Our Church."—The Rev. W. Haslam one day, in the course of conversation with a clergyman, remarked: "You have been praying for an outpouring of the Holy Spirit. Now, if the Holy Spirit did settle on your church, and some of your congregation began to make evident manifestations of it, what would you do?" "Turn them all out," was his quick response, "turn them all out at once; we would not have any fanatics in our church." Such is the attitude of many Christian churches in this day. They pray for what they do not wish, and which, if they did obtain, they would get rid of as quickly as possible. With them Christianity is fast becoming a mere ceremonial. It is not this ceremonialism we would offer sinners, but a living, risen, glorious Saviour, who died for sinners, and rose again.

Extricated from a Slough.—Mr. Thompson said: "I remember the first time that God showed me that I was a sinner—that a good, respectable, church-going young man was nevertheless in God's eyes a sinner. My friends all laughed at me, and said surely I was going crazy; but the Holy Spirit had given me a glimpse of myself in God's looking-glass, and there I saw myself in my true colors. I strove after salvation with all my might, I prayed as I had never prayed before, yet all the time I did not see that God was standing, holding out this salvation for my acceptance. To add to my despondency, my friends told me that I could not be saved for six weeks; for that time at least I would require to repent and humble myself before God; then, perhaps, in His grace, He would lift me out of the slough of despond. But, praise His name, He showed me that it did not take six days to be converted, but that at once, if I came to Him, ceasing from my own struggles after righteousness, and trusting in the finished work of Christ, I might have Him as my Saviour. The work was done. There is no regulation time of repentance, there is no time of penance, during which the sinner tones down the glaringness of his sin. Christ invites the sinner to come to Him, 'now,' just as he is."

A Dress-piece in the Contribution Plate.—A Scotch evangelist said; "In a town in the north of Scotland they had been having missionary services, in which the duty of giving to Foreign Mission schemes was urgently pressed upon the people. The meetings were continued for several nights, and on the last night there was to be a special collection. The address was closed, and the collection plates were being passed round, the people contributing as the Lord enabled them; but when one plate had almost gone its round, it received rather an unusual contribution. A young lady took from underneath her plaid a rather bulky parcel, and handing it to the usher, said, 'I have nothing else but this to offer.' On examination it proved to be a piece of cloth, which the girl had purchased to make a dress, but the stories of the heathen dying without the Gospel had so touched her heart that she determined she must give something. But all her pocket-money was spent; what could she give? Mentally she examined all her possessions. There was the cloth for her new dress; could she give that? It was a struggle to part with it, but she must do something to show her love for Christ, and so that bulky contribution found its way into the collection. It is our duty, if we cannot go ourselves to preach the Gospel of Christ's salvation to the heathen, to help to sustain those who are able and willing to devote their lives to that purpose."

THE USES OF PROPHECY.

By John Urquhart.

Why the Study of Prophecy is Neglected—Predictions of Christ's First Coming Misunderstood—Neglect of Prophecy Involves Unpreparedness for His Second Coming—The Kingdom Will not Come by Evangelization—Necessary as a Testimony—Neither Experience nor Promise of Triumph—The Hope of the Early Church—Signs of Christ's Approach.

MANY persons are quite of the opinion that Revelation either finds a man mad, or makes him mad, and they have what seems to them a wholesome dread of prophetic studies. I have no desire to conceal the difficulties which abound in the pathway of those who explore this domain, or to deny that deplorable mistakes have been often made—mistakes which have brought the study of prophecy into undeserved contempt. But it may be well to ask whether, in putting aside all consideration of these things, we are not robbing ourselves of the very highest power.

The predictions regarding Christ's first coming were obscure enough to the Jews. There was much that they could not reconcile, and we know that they made mistakes. But they, nevertheless, laid hold of a mighty truth, or rather that truth laid hold of them. They

Knew that Christ Would Come,

and each line they read, and each text they studied—no matter how dark it was—deepened that conviction. If they had said: "No man can understand these things fully. They lead to endless theories, and the absurdest dreams," and if, in consequence, they had treated the Prophets as a sealed book, then all that power would have been lost to them. The sense of that mighty destiny would no longer have held them, and separated them from the peoples of the earth.

Are we, then, losing nothing through neglect? We desire that this good, to which we look onward, should make its appeal to us. We have entreated that it might hold us, and separate us for itself. But how can it do so if we turn away from God when He would speak with us regarding it? It would appear as if our Lord, foreseeing the discredit which would be cast upon this branch of Divine teaching, had specially warned us against the danger of neglecting it. This is the only Book of Scripture which has a special

Promise Attached to its Study.

A blessing is to rest upon him that readeth, and upon them that hear. We accomplish the Lord's will, therefore, not by turning away from this book, but by turning to it, however deep our consciousness may be of inability to penetrate its mysteries.

The predictions regarding Jesus, with which the Bible teems, are as yet only half-fulfilled. They speak of His birth, His humiliation, His suffering and atoning death, His victory over the grave, but they do not end there. All His enemies are to be put under His feet. Iniquity is to be judged and cast out. The world is to be covered with the knowledge of God as the waters cover the sea. The prayer which the Lord taught us to offer shall then be fulfilled. God's kingdom will have come: His will shall be done on this sin-stained earth even as it is done in heaven.

Some have imagined that all this is to be accomplished through the preaching of the Gospel. We cannot limit the Spirit's power; but those who indulge this hope should ask themselves on what it is based. If it is entertained on the ground of experience, the past certainly encourages no hope of such a future as the result of evangelization alone. But if the hope is founded upon the promises of Scripture, there are some passages which have surely not been pondered. He who bids us to carry the message of peace to earth's furthest bounds and preach the Gospel to every creature, has told us that it is for "a testimony" to them. Mercy runs before the car of judgment. Before Christ comes to visit for the earth's iniquity, "this Gospel of the kingdom shall be preached in the whole world for a testimony unto all the nations; and then shall the end come." (Matt. 24: 14.) There is

A Note of Warning

there that to the end there will be rejection as well as acceptance of our message. Then we have distinct predictions that in the last days there is trouble in store for the Church, and not triumph. They who hold the strength of the nations will make a final attempt to resist the Divine decree. The thrones of to-day will be swept away forever from the earth which they have so long saturated with blood. Their guilt will mould their punishment. As they have risen in blood, so will they go down in blood.

Man's sin will thus pave the way for God's triumph. The earth, so long and so deeply defiled by sin, shall be made glorious by righteousness. The place where God has been so terribly forgotten shall resound with His unceasing praise. We know how

This Day of the Lord,

in which He shall see, even here upon the earth, of the travail of His soul, and shall be satisfied, was the hope of the early Church. They strengthened one another with the assurance that it was at hand. They looked on to that as the great event in the world's history, and they rejoiced in the conviction that it was nigh—even at the doors. They were not the victims of an amiable and salutary delusion. They knew that much must happen ere then. Paul warned the Thessalonians, in one of the first Epistles which he wrote, that the day of the Lord should not come till the apostasy had taken place, and the man of sin had been revealed.

And yet, though much had to transpire ere the Lord should come, that coming of the Lord, which was the one grand event of the future for which they waited, and which every hour was bringing nearer, that event so overtopped every other that they ever thought and spoke of it as at hand. The mighty mountain, as one has said, though far away in point of space, is ever nigh by reason of its very greatness. Or, say that we are expecting the arrival of a much-loved and long-absent friend. He is to come by a certain way, and on the far distant rising ground we have marked what seems to be his approach. From that moment, distant though he is, there is for us but one event—His coming. There are various nearer objects of the deepest interest for those around us; they have little or none for us, because he is near. The nearer He comes the more absolute is His hold of our heart and mind.

And the Lord comes—the Son of God, who loved us, and gave Himself for us. We have marked His approach:

We Know that He is Nigh.

The Scripture spoke of the apostasy which should precede His coming; *it has taken place*. This book has described the great harlot, whose seat was to be Imperial Rome, the city of the seven hills: *she has appeared*. It speaks of a false prophet, who should also delude the nations of the earth: *he, too, has been manifested*. The Revelation of the Old Testament—the Book of Daniel—predicts that the one Empire of Rome should be broken up into ten kingdoms, and that "in the days of these kings" the kingdom of God should be established. The Roman Empire has been divided, and these ten kingdoms are with us now almost in their completeness. How can we fail to note the Lord's approach? What interest is able to compete with that excited by the thought that the Desire of all nations draws nigh? How can we fail to hear, and to be thrilled by the cry, which was never louder than it is to-day: "Behold the Bridegroom cometh! Go ye forth to meet Him!"

RETROSPECT OF THE YEAR 1888.

ALTHOUGH the close of one year and the beginning of another are not with us, as they were with God's chosen people, associated with momentous events or commemorative of epochal deliverances, the fact that we are passing one more milestone in our national and individual life suggests retrospective consideration. The year which has passed over us since we last stood at the annual dividing line in our journey of life has not left us as we were then. We have moved backward or forward as the days have flown by, and our souls are either stronger and purer, or weaker and more sin-burdened than at the beginning of the year. Numerous opportunities of service have been afforded us; have we used them with the zeal which we promised when we entered the service of the Master? Our national life—has that been higher, more righteous, more in accord with Christian principles, than former years? And have we individually done our part as Christian citizens to make it so? It is well that in passing these annual milestones we sit down for a brief period and look back, so that we may learn the lessons the past may teach, and go forward with chastened souls, taught by experience our own weakness, and clinging more closely to the One and only Source of all strength.

Our Political Life

as a nation, during the year now drawing to a close, has been one of intense struggle and agitation. The decisive stand taken by the President, in December, 1887, on the subject of the tariff, and his insistance that, in extensive reductions of our customs duties, the way would be opened for the removal of dangerous anomalies, and one means of solving difficult political and social problems of the day, placed an issue before the people which, as every one recognized, would be momentous for himself and his party. The Presidential campaign was fought mainly on that issue. Other considerations doubtless had their weight. Many citizens were too busy to give the difficult question an exhaustive study, or they were influenced by party loyalty, or by their position and circumstances, in deciding on which side they should cast their votes; but the public discussion—and that was matter for thankfulness—was devoted, not to personal abuse and private scandal, but to the bearings of a great and momentous question of national policy. We all know how the people decided the question. The Republican party, pledged to the maintenance of protection for home industries, was called back to office, and in March next will resume its grasp on the helm of the ship of state. This is a matter for rejoicing to one half of the nation; the other half bows loyally to the decision, and should pray to the God of nations that the men who will guide the national course during the next four years may themselves be guided of Him.

As is usually the case in years of presidential elections, *Congress* has effected but a small amount of practical work. There has also been a hindrance to progress, in the fact of the Senate being controlled by one party, while the House was controlled by the opposite party. In the tariff debate this was especially conspicuous. The Mills Bill, which passed the House, was scarcely debated in the Senate, and a substitute, which is not yet perfected, was prepared in its place. It is not greatly to the credit of the legislative body that the two branches, while differing so widely on political questions, found little difficulty in agreeing to pass *a River and Harbor Bill* of more than twenty million dollars, a large part of which will, as usual, be devoted to party rather than national advantage. The conflict of parties had a still more disagreeable result in the *Fisheries Dispute* with Canada. There was an evident disposition on the part of Great Britain and Canada to effect a permanent settlement of this vexed question. The treaty effected by the commissioners for the purpose was, however, summarily rejected, when by a more conciliatory policy it might have been so modified as to be mutually satisfactory to both nations. *The dismissal of Lord Sackville*, the British Minister, was another act of a similar character, for which the President was responsible. The Minister's own blunder could not be ignored, but it might wisely have been treated in a more dignified and courteous manner.

The Social Events

of the year have been chiefly of local importance, though it is gratifying to notice the growing disposition of the whole country to sympathize with and aid any section that may be under suffering. This disposition was manifested during the prevalence of *yellow fever* at Jacksonville, Fla., which during the months of August and September made that city a scene of desolation. There were about four thousand seizures, and nearly four hundred persons died. Business was entirely suspended, and private benevolence, assisted by a grant from the Federal Government, were needed by the afflicted people. That help was cheerfully given. *The severity of the weather* was a memorable feature of the early months of the year. In the Northwest a fierce blizzard, especially severe in Dakota, caused the loss of over two hundred lives in February, and in March New York was visited by the most terrible storm within the memory of its citizens. For two days traffic was entirely suspended, communication with other cities was cut off by the destruction of telegraph apparatus, and many persons lost their lives. *Labor troubles*, as usual of late years, caused much distress in several sections. The strike in Pennsylvania of the miners in the Reading collieries threw 30,000 men and boys out of employment, and when the engineers and switchmen on the Burlington Railroad came to their aid by refusing to carry coal mined by the men who had taken the place of the strikers, the area of the trouble was largely increased. Another distressing struggle was that of the car drivers in Chicago, which resulted in conflicts with the police and the loss of several lives.

In Foreign Lands,

notably in *Germany*, the year will be a memorable one. On March 9 died the venerable Emperor William I., whose long life and reign have been one of the most remarkable periods of national history. The aged monarch had lived to see the dream of national unity realized, his home policy, so stubbornly maintained, justified by events, and the historic foes of his country, who were triumphant in his youth, defeated and humiliated in his latter days. William died, and his son Frederick III. succeeded him. During his short reign of three months the world saw signs of the liberal policy which would have guided him had his life been prolonged, and joined with Germany in mourning when on June 15 he passed away. William II., the new Emperor, has shown no disposition to tread in his father's footsteps, but is evidently possessed with the exploded notions of the divine right of kings to which his grandfather was wedded. In *France* the Republic has not strengthened its hold on the country during the year. The utter absence of any statesman of commanding ability has given prominence to the farcial General Boulanger, who by dexterously encouraging the hopes of Imperialists, Royalists, and the middle classes, appears to be gaining a power that menaces the very existence of the Republic, and leads to the impression that a dictatorship like that of the first Napoleon may once more overthrow liberty in France.

In *Great Britain* the affairs of Ireland have again been the most prominent subject of public interest. The operation of the Coercion Law, and the policy of the landlords have caused much suffering among the Irish people, though there has been a marked decrease in the number of agrarian outrages, and less bloodshed than in former years. The deeply interesting inquiry, now being prosecuted, into the conduct of the National League promises to settle the vexed question of its responsibility for crime. Mr. Parnell asked for the Commission, thus challenging inquiry into the charges which the leading English newspaper persistently brought against him and his colleagues, of encouraging crime, hiring and rewarding criminals, and abetting, aiding, and concealing murders and outrages. This inquiry will be closely watched, not only across the Atlantic, but among the friends of Ireland here, who, while sympathizing with the Irish people, have too much respect for law and order to support men against whom charges such as those made by the *Times* can be proved.

Students of prophecy surveying the condition of the whole of Europe, cannot fail to be impressed with the fact that, though the year has been one of general peace, there are below the surface numerous signs that it is like *the hush that precedes the storm*. While there has been no war, while there are no stirring questions out of which war seems likely to arise, every country is making active preparations for war. In Germany, in Russia, in Austria, in Italy, and even in England, military measures, looking to increased strength and efficiency of the armies, are devised and executed. With the prescience which knowledge of international affairs gives to statesmen, they are preparing for the conflict which students of prophecy believe will shortly convulse the world.

The Religious Life

of the year, both at home and across the Atlantic, has been of that awakened character which prophecy indicated as a characteristic of the last days. Even among those who do not believe that the time for Christian work is short, there has been a notable increase of energy and endeavors to promote organized and united aggressive labor for Christ. It has been a year of great conventions. The International Missionary Conference in London, the Pan Presbyterian Council, the great gathering of Bishops of the Protestant Episcopal Church, the Quadrennial Methodist Episcopal Conference, and many other assemblies have met, and in all of them the one engrossing subject has been, how most effectively to get the gospel preached in professedly Christian lands and in heathen countries as a testimony to all men. Thus a supreme effort is being made to spread the knowledge of Christ over the whole world with an energy and devotedness that the Church as a whole has never manifested before, and which is a sign of the Holy Spirit's work in preparing the way for the Second Coming of Christ by the gathering out of all nations a people for Him.

The Disasters

of the year have been neither so numerous nor so fatal as in some recent years. Among the shipwrecks the most disastrous was that of the collision between the *Thingvalla* and the *Geiser*, off the coast of Nova Scotia, on August 14, in which 118 persons lost their lives. A few days later there was another collision at the Golden Gate between the *City of Chester* and the *Oceanic*, in which twenty lives were lost. On the railroads, the Haverhill disaster on January 10, the Blackshear, Ga., accident on March 17, the Orange Court House, Va., wreck on May 12, and the Mud Run, Penn., collision on May 10, were the most fatal. Three appalling calamities, which occurred in China, presented a record not easily realized in other lands. They were the inundation of the Yellow River, by which over 100,000 persons perished, and nearly 2,000,000 were rendered destitute; the breaking of an embankment, causing the death of 4,000 persons; and the flood of the Canton River, in which over 2,000 persons died.

The Obituary

list of the year, apart from the names of the two Emperors of Germany already mentioned, contains few names of the first importance. Among the most prominent are General Sheridan, Professor Asa Gray; W. W. Corcoran, the Washington philanthropist; Amos Bronson Alcott, and his famous daughter, Louisa May Alcott; Henry Bergh, the friend of the brute creation in New York; Chief-Justice Waite; Matthew Arnold, the English critic; ex-Senator Conkling, Dr. James Freeman Clark; E. P. Roe, the novelist; Bishop Harris, Professor Proctor, P. H. Gosse, and Marshal Bazaine.

A BAD BOIL CURED.

Dr. Talmage's Sermon Preached last Sunday, December 23, 1888.

"I have heard thy prayer; . . . behold I will heal thee . . . And Isaiah said: Take a lump of figs. And they took and laid it on the boil, and he recovered." II Kings 20: 5, 7.

Royal Maladies—The King's Prayer Heard—Human Instrumentality Employed—The Theory of the Rationalists—Are Prayers Answered—The Battle-Ground of Christianity and Rationalism—The Attack on the Miracles—Fatal Oil From the Whale—The Bible Without the Supernatural—Prayer the Mightiest of All Remedies—Celebrated Praying Physicians—The Law Only God's Way of Work—Prayer to be Accompanied by Means—Instances of Answered Prayers—An Angry Man Converted—Dr. Scudder's Nephew—Praying Heroes—Blank Cheques on the Bank.

LUXURIOUS living is not healthy. The second generation of kings and queens and lords and princes is apt to be brainless and invalid. The second crop of grass is almost always short. Royal blood is generally scrofulous. You will not be surprised, then, to hear that King Hezekiah had disorders which broke out in a carbuncle, virulent and deathful. The Lord told him he must die; he did not want to die. He turned his face to the wall, so that his prayer would not be interrupted, and cried for his life.

God Heard the Prayer,

and answered it, saying, "Behold, I will heal thee." But there was human instrumentality to be employed. This carbuncle needed a "cataplasm," which is a poultice. Your old mother, who doctored her own children in the time when physicians were not as plenty as they are now, will tell you that the very best poultice is a fig, and that was what was used upon the carbuncle of King Hezekiah. The power of God, accompanied by this human instrumentality, cured the king.

In this age of discovery, when men know so much it almost kills them, and write so wisely it almost kills us, it has been found out that prayer to God is a dead failure. All things are arranged according to inexorable law. There is no use in praying to God for rain in time of drought. The "weather probabilities" in the morning papers will decide the question, rain or no rain, and the whole nation in prayer before God would not bring down a single drop. I am not now speaking of an imaginary theory, but of that which is believed by ten thousand times ten thousand men.

If sickness comes to your household, it will depend entirely upon ventilation, good diet, and the skill of the doctors, as to whether your child gets well. The father might pray all day, and the mother might pray all night—it would not have any effect upon the case. If squills, belladonna, paregoric, and gruel do the work, your child will get well; if not, not. There is a cast-iron God seated at the head of the universe, holding in the cold grasp of His metal fingers a band of law from which nothing can break away.

The Battle-Ground.

Men and women of God, at this point the great battle of Christianity is to be fought. The great foe of Christianity to-day is rationalism, that comes out from our schools and universities, and magazines and newspapers, to scoff at Bible truth and caricature the old religion of Jesus. It says Jesus is not God, for it is impossible to explain how He can be divine and human at the same time. The Bible is not inspired, for there are things in it that they don't like. Regeneration is a farce; there is good enough in us, and the only thing is to bring it out. Development is the word—development. The Garden of Eden is a fairy story, and no more to be believed than the Arabian Nights, or Gulliver's Travels, or Robinson Crusoe. We all started as baboons, and are blood relations to that monkey squirming about on the top of that hand-organ. Lazarus was not dead when Christ pretended to raise him; he was only playing dead. The water was not changed into wine at the wedding, but Christ brought in some wine that he had found elsewhere to make up the deficiency. Christ did not walk on the sea, but on the shore, so near that it seemed as if he really was on the water.

What is still more alarming is, that Christian men dare not meet this ridicule. There is not one Christian man in five that can, unblanched, stand in the presence of all this raillery, saying:

"I Believe In The Whole Bible,

and in every single statement that it makes." Christian men try to soften the Bible down to suit the sceptics. The sceptics sneer at the dividing of the Red Sea; and the Christian goes to explaining that the wind blew a hurricane from one direction a good while, until all the water piled up; and besides, that it was low water anyhow, and so the Israelites went through without any trouble. Why not be frank and say: "I believe the Lord God Almighty came to the brink of the Red Sea, and with his right arm swung back the billows on the right side, and with his left arm swung back the billows on the left side, and the abashed water stood up hundreds of feet high; while through their glassy wall the sea-monsters gazed with affrighted eyes on the passing Israelites"?

The rationalist comes to you saying: "How about Jonah and the whale? Do you really believe that fish story?" There were never so many Nantucket fishermen after one whale as there have been rationalists flinging harpoons at the Mediterranean sea-monster, and from that one whale they have got enough oil to light ten thousand souls to perdition. A sceptic tells you that Jonah would have been killed in the process of swallowing, and that he could not, anyhow, have lived three days in such close quarters, but would have been smothered by the poor ventilation. How the good Christians immediately go to work, and try to explain the whole thing by natural laws, so as

To Please The Rationalists,

and say that a whale is an air-breathing fish; that every little while it comes to the surface, and that the whale that swallowed Jonah did the same thing, and thus got a supply for itself and for the prophet. Why not rather say that God can do anything; and He could take Jonah through the whale's throat, although the throat would not have been half large enough ordinarily to let him pass, and could have kept him alive in the whale five years without any air, if He had chosen to? Who made the whale? God. Who made Jonah? God. Then He could do anything He pleased with either of them.

The moment you begin to explain away the miraculous and supernatural, you surrender the Bible. Take the supernatural out of the Bible, and you make it a collection of lies and humbugs, in preference to which I choose Æsop's Fables. They are what they pretend to be—fables. But if, after all that the Bible declares, Jesus is not God, and Lazarus was not raised from the dead, and the water was not turned into wine, and the Red Sea was not divided, and in answer to prayer Hezekiah's boil did not get well, then the Bible is the worst fraud ever perpetrated in God's universe.

Ah! my friends, have we been mistaken? Does God hear and answer prayer, or does he not? Hezekiah was sick unto death; he prayed for his life; God heard him, and added fifteen years to that lifetime.

The Prayer Saved Him

the lump of figs applied being merely the God-appointed human instrumentality.

"But," says some one, "I don't believe the Bible." Ah! then we will have to part company for four or five minutes, for it is useless to try to argue with any man with whom you cannot stand upon common ground. In any argument, if you would be successful, there must be some common data to start from. It is foolish to try to prove to a man that twice three are six, provided he does not admit the multiplication table, or that two and two are four, if he does not admit the addition table.

My first address, therefore, is to those who do believe in the Bible. I want to tell you that prayer is

The Mightiest of all Remedies,

and that the allopathic and homeopathic, and the eclectic schools will yet acknowledge it. Here are two cases of sickness precisely alike: the same kind of medicine is given to both of them, and in the same quantities. The one patient recovers, and the other does not. Why? God blesses the one remedy, and does not bless the other. Prayer has helped many a blundering doctor through with a case that would have otherwise become completely unmanageable. There is such a thing as Gospel hygiene, as Christian pharmacy, as divine materia medica. That is a foolish man who, in case of sickness, goes only to human resources, when we have these instances of the Lord's help in the sick-room. Before you call the doctor, while he is there, and after he goes away, look up to Him who cured Hezekiah. Let the apothecary send the poultice, but God makes it draw. Oh! I am glad to have a doctor who knows how to pray. God send salvation to all the doctors! Sickness would be oftener balked, death would be oftener hurled back from the door-sill, if medical men came into the sick-room, like Isaiah of the text, with a prescription in their hands, and the word of the Lord in their mouths.

John Abercrombie, the most celebrated physician of Scotland, prayed when he went into the sick-room, and he wrote no more ably about "diseases of the brain" than about "the philosophy of the moral feelings." I don't know how much of the

Medical Success

of Sydenham and Cooper and Harvey and Rush depended upon the fact that they knew how to pray as well as to prescribe. I don't want a physician who sees no God in human anatomy to doctor my broken bones. If God made us (and I think He did), and if the Bible is true (and I am rather disposed to think it is), then it is not strange that prayer does traverse natural cause; ay, that it introduces a new cause. When God made the law, he did not make it so strong He could not break it. If God made our bodies, when they are broken He is the one to mend them; and it is reasonable that we should call Him in to do it. If my furnace in the cellar breaks down, there is no one so competent to repair it as the manufacturer. If my watch stops, there is no one so competent to set it going as the one who made it. If the body is disordered, call in the Maker of it. It is not all, as these physicists tell us, a matter of ventilation, or poisoned air, of cleanliness or dirt, of nutritious diet or poor fare. I have known people to get well in rooms where the windows had been six weeks down, tight shut, and I have known them to die right under patent ventilators. I have known children sickly who every day had their bath, and I have known children robust, the washing of whose faces would make their features unrecognizable.

God did not make the law and then run away from it. What is law of nature? It is only

God's Usual Way of Doing Things.

But He has said that if His children ask Him to do a thing, and He can consistently do it, He will do it. Go on with your pills and plasters and nostrums and elixirs, and your catholicon, but remember that the mightiest agency in your recovery is prayer. Prayer to God brought the king's cure, the lump of figs being the God-directed human instrumentality.

I would have you also see—for it is another lesson of the subject—that our prayer must also be accompanied by means. It is an outrage to ask God to do a thing while we sit indolent. The prayer, to be acceptable, must come not only from the heart, but from the hands. We must

Work While We Pray,

devotion and work going together. Luther came to Melanchthon's bedside and prayed for his recovery, and insisted, at the same time, that he should take some warm soup, the soup being just as important as the prayer. In the time of the great plague that came to York, in England, the priests prayed all night and all day for the removal of the plague, but did not think of clearing out the dead dogs and cats that lay in the gutters, causing the sickness. We must use means as well as supplication. If a man has "evening prayers," asking for health, and then sits down to a full supper of indigestibles at 11 o'clock at night, his prayer is a mockery. A farmer has no right to pray for the safety of his family when he knows there is no cover on the cistern. The Christian man, reckless about his health, ought not to expect the same answer to his prayer as the Christian man expects who retires regularly at 10 o'clock at night, and takes his morning bath with the appendix of a Turkish towel. Paul said to the passengers of the Alexandrian corn ship that they should get safe ashore, but he told them they must use means, and that was: "Stick to the old ship!" God is not weak, needing our help, but God is strong, and asks us to co-operate with Him, that we may be strong, too. Pray by all means, but don't forget the fig-poultice.

That God answers prayers offered in the right spirit, seconded by our own effort, is the first and the last lesson of this text, and it is a lesson that this age needs to learn. If all communication between heaven and earth is cut off, let us know it. If all the Christian prayers that are going up toward God never reach Him, then, I say, let silence smite the lips of the afflicted world, and the nations smother their groans and die quietly.

God Does Answer Prayer.

The text shows it. You say: "I don't believe the Bible; I think that those things were merely coincidences, which are often brought as answers to prayer." Do you say that? Was it mere happen-so that Elijah prayed for rain just as the rain was going to come anyhow? Did Daniel pray in the wild beasts' den just at the time when all the lions happened to have lockjaw? Did Jesus pray at the grave of Lazarus just at the time when Lazarus was going to dress himself and come out anyhow? Did Jesus lose His place in His sermon, and make a mistake, when He said: "Ask, and it shall be given you; seek, and ye shall find; knock, and it shall be opened unto you"? And, lest some were so stupid that they could not understand it, He goes on: "For everyone that asketh, receiveth; and he that seeketh, findeth; and to him that knocketh, it shall be opened."

But some one persists in saying: "I don't believe anything of the Bible." Then I appeal to

Your Own Instincts.

Prayer in certain circumstances is as natural to man as the throbbing in the pulse, as the respiration of the lungs. Put a company of men—I don't care how bad they are—in some imminent peril, and they will cry out: "God have mercy on us!" I challenge that these men who don't believe in prayer charter a steamer, go out in the "Narrows," swing out eight or nine hundred miles to sea, and then heave to and wait for a cyclone. And after the cyclone comes and the vessel has gone under ten times, when they did not expect it would rise again, and the bulwarks have been knocked in, and the masts are gone—if they do not pray, I will surrender my theory. Do you tell me that this instinct which God has put in us, He put there just to mock us for His own cruel amusement? If God implanted that instinct in the human heart, it was because in His own heart there was something responsive.

To prove that God does hear prayer, I put on the witness-stand Abraham, Isaac, Jacob, Ezekiel, Jeremiah, Micah, John, Paul, Peter, and King Hezekiah. Tell me, ye ancient battlefields, ye Oriental threshing-floors, ye Judean corn-fields, ye Galilean fishing-smacks, is God deaf and dumb and blind before all human petition? That God answers prayer, I bring the

Ten Million Facts of Christendom

to prove. There has never paper enough come out of the paper-mills to write the story. Has not many a mother prayed back her bad boy from the ends of the earth—from Canton, from Madras, from Constantinople—until he knelt beside her in the old homestead? Have there not been desperadoes and renegades who have looked into the door of a prayer-meeting to laugh and scoff at it, who have been drawn by the power of prayer, until they ran to the altar crying out for mercy? Did not the blacksmith in Lyons, N. Y., pray to God until there came a great awakening that shook the community.

In My Parish

in Philadelphia one night, at a meeting, I asked a young man to go into a room at the side of the church, and talk upon the theme of religion. He grew violently angry, and shook his fists at me. We resolved to pray for that young man, and we prayed that he might yield his soul to God. And when, next night, at the meeting, the side-door was flung open, he was the first to step in. Prayer had captured him. I had a classmate in college, whose uncle, Dr. John Scudder, of India, wrote to him, saying: "I will pray for you every day until such a day, and then I will give my attention to some other subject." The last day of these prayers, when they had all gathered up before the throne of God, my classmate surrendered his soul to Jesus. This is no second-hand story. I saw the letter, and I knew the young man.

But why should I go so far? I have had in my own experience, and I have had in the history of my own family the evidence that God answers prayer. My mother, with three Christian women, assembled week after week, and prayed for their children; they kept up that prayer-meeting of four persons year after year. The world knew nothing of it. God answered all those prayers. All the group came in; the eleven sons and daughters of my mother, myself the last.

Sickness Came to my Household

—hopeless sickness, as it seemed to many. At 3 o'clock on Saturday afternoon the invalid was carried to the steamer for Savannah. At 11 o'clock the next day, being Sunday, standing in this very place, a man of God prayed for the recovery of the sick one. At that time, 11 o'clock, she who had been prostrated three weeks, with some help, walked up on deck. The occurrence was as near to being miraculous as I can imagine. That she was hopelessly sick, people who sat up with her night after night, and are here, can testify. That the prayer for her recovery was offered in this pulpit, thousands of people could testify. That at 11 o'clock on that Sunday morning she walked up on deck, as by a miraculous recovery, I call the passengers on the *San Jacinto*, commanded by Captain Atkins, December 16, to testify. This is no second-hand story.

Prayer impotent! If I dared to think there was no force in prayer, methinks God, after all he has done for me and mine, would strike me dead. Prayer impotent! Why, it is the mightiest force in the universe. Lightning has no speed, the Alpine avalanche has no power, compared with it.

Praying Heroes.

Will you let the abstractions and the vagaries of a few sceptics, or a good many sceptics, stand beside the experience of General Havelock, who came out in front of the English army, lifted his hat, and called upon the Lord Almighty? or of George Washington, who at Valley Forge was found upon his knees in prayer? or of William Wilberforce, who went from the British Parliament to the closet of devotion? or of Latimer, who stood with his hands on fire, in martyrdom, praying for his persecutors? Was Washington weak? Was Havelock weak? Was Wilberforce weak? Was Latimer weak? Bring all the affairs of your store, of your soul, of your body, of your friends, of your church, before Him, and the great day of eternity will show you that the best investments you ever made were your prayers, and though you may have broken promises you made to God, God never broke His promises to you. Let God be true, though every man be found a liar.

And now, in conclusion, I have to present you some cheques,

Blank Cheques on the Bank

of heaven, written in blood, and signed by the hand wounded on the cross. It is not safe for you to give a blank cheque with your name to it. You do not know what might be written above. But here is a blank cheque which God says I can give you; it is signed by the handwriting of the Lord Jesus Christ, and you can fill it up with anything you want to. "Ask and it shall be given to you; seek, and ye shall find." I do not say that your prayer will be answered in just the way you expect, but I do say it will be answered in the best way. Oh! will you test Him? This is the outcome of all this subject.

If I should ask the men and women in this audience who have found God a prayer-answering God to rise up, you would nearly all rise up. In time of darkness and trouble, as in time of light and prosperity, He answered you. I commend you to that God to whom your parents dedicated you in infancy. They believed so much in prayer that their last word was a supplication for you. Having heard you in days of prosperity, He will not reject your last petition when, in the darkened room, after they have wiped the dew of death from your brow, and the whole group of loved ones have kissed you good-bye, you have only strength enough left to pray, "Lord Jesus, receive my spirit!"

THE BURNING QUESTION

of the day, which is disturbing churches and causing many to lose their hold of faith in miracles and in the Bible itself, was touched by the new Bishop of Manchester, England, in his first sermon, in a way that shows how valuable will be his influence in meeting the rationalistic tendencies of a section of the Protestant Episcopal Church. The Bishop said: "The basis of faith was true humility. He had met many infidels, to his sorrow, but had never met with a blaspheming infidel who was not characterized by an exceptional and even ludicrous self-conceit, and he believed that this self-conceit and too great self-confidence was the besetting sin of our time, and especially of some—he did not say all—of the science of our time. The gifts of science to man within the last fifty years had been so numerous and valuable, that a certain amount of exulting self-confidence was natural and allowable, but they must remember that it was always dangerous; and sometimes productive of most disastrous consequences. For instance, there were men who, because they had been able to trace the reality of some of the phenomena which were within the reach of our apprehension, said that men should not be called upon *to believe anything but what they could understand*. That was dead in the teeth of all the conclusions of a sound reason. We could only know the real as it appeared to us when it had passed through the forms of our own mind, when it had been changed in the manufactory of our own sensations and perception, and we could never know the real as it was, and yet we were obliged to assume that it is. Yet in the teeth of that incontestable conclusion of sound human reason there were men who told them—men who claimed to be leaders of thought—that they ought to believe nothing which they could not understand. He exhorted them to beware of intellectual pride—of intellectual pride which came of insufficient thought If they followed reason loyally she would lead them to the very brink of that world of the real, where, handing over the torch of guidance to the grasp of faith, she left them to be led by that heavenly guide into the glorious presence of God. Reason demanded a God, faith affirmed a God, Jesus Christ revealed a God, the God and Father of Him who as on Easter morning rose from the dead and opened the kingdom of heaven to all believers.

THE MISSION OF JOHN THE BAPTIST.

By Mrs. M. Baxter.

S. S. Lesson for January 6, 1889. Mark 1: 1-11. Golden Text, verse 3.

The Preparatory Voice—Not the Original Word—A Fruitful Source of Pride and Heresy—A Servant to a Message—In the Desert—An Unpromising Sphere—Christian Work Not a Refuge for the Discontented—A Man of Simple Food and Attire—Souls Drawn to his Preaching—The Power that Induces Confession—The Twofold Baptism of Jesus.

THE mission of John the Baptist was foretold more than seven hundred years before his birth. Isaiah wrote, "The *voice* of him that crieth in the wilderness, Prepare ye the way of the Lord, make straight in the desert a highway for our God." (Isa. 40: 3.) It was his own testimony to himself "when the Jews sent priests and Levites from Jerusalem to ask him, Who art thou? that we may give an answer to them that sent us. What sayest thou of thyself?" "I am a voice." "I am the voice of one crying in the wilderness, Make straight the way of the Lord, as said the prophet Esaias."

The Voice of One.

Then he was not that One whose voice he was. All his life, all his being, all his work, pointed to Another. Jesus was the *Word*, John was the voice. The very existence of the blessed Jesus was in itself a message, a word from God, but John lived to be His medium of communication with man, just as a voice can convey any sound. John did not profess to be an original, but only a messenger: "There was a man *sent from God*, whose name was John." (John 1: 6.) There never can be another Word of God. "In the beginning was the Word, and the Word was with God, and the Word was God." (John 1: 1.) Many of the heresies of the present day arise from teachers falling into spiritual pride, and leaving the humble position of a voice, ready to speak out what God has already given in His Word. They are tempted to consider themselves as singular favorites of God, to whom He communicates revelations over and above His Word: and this lays them open to "seducing spirits and teachings of demons." (see Greek, 1 Tim. 4: 1.) If any will be wise above that which is written, he is in danger. Paul says to the Galatians: "Though we, or an angel from heaven, preach any other gospel unto you than that which we have preached unto you, let him be accursed." (Gal. 1: 8.) Paul was content with the written Word; John was the servant of the living Word. Both of them took the place of nothingness. One said of Jesus, "He must increase, but I must decrease"; the other said he was "less than the least of all saints." (Eph. 3: 8.) Yet both were called, not as mechanical and involuntary, but as intelligent and voluntary instruments to convey to man the messages of God. This is the precious, glorious privilege of every true Christian worker—to be a voice for God, His messenger, His sent one.

There are some Christian workers who see and accept the privilege of being

Servants to Their Message.

They lend themselves, yield themselves, to it and its requirements; the message masters them, convicts, transforms them; such a worker was John the Baptist. Had he made use of his power to preach, in order to obtain a reputation for eloquence, he would have found some other sphere than the wilderness. He would probably have come into Jerusalem, and taken every opportunity to speak in the synagogues; but John waited for orders from above. He no more dreamt of directing his own steps than does a servant who has engaged himself to carry out his master's will. Some impelling power of the Holy Ghost, who filled him "even from his mother's womb" (Luke 1: 15), led him, even as a child, to desire solitude, and "he was in the deserts until the day of his showing unto Israel." (Luke 1: 80.) There, in the desert, where no doubt his occupation was communion with God and much prayer for the state of his people, the word of God came unto him, and "he came into all the country about Jordan, preaching the baptism of repentance for the remission of sins." (Luke 3: 2, 3.) Oh how different was his call, first by prophecy, then by the filling of the Holy Ghost, then by much prayer, then by a distinct call of God, from the taking up of Christian work as a pleasant distraction or a congenial occupation! There are many who are tired of home life, or of domestic service, or of business, and who rush into Christian work

To Escape a Cross.

Persecution comes, their wills are crossed, or they are tried by want of success; and the same self-love which made them shun the cross at home or in the business, makes them fret against it in the work of God: they have not learned for themselves the lessons they would teach others, and thus they bring discredit on the cause of God. Such was not John the Baptist.

If this man of God had looked for earthly reward, he would not have been satisfied with the homely fare of the desert—locusts and wild honey—or the rough camel's hair raiment which he probably spun and wove for himself, regardless of the fashion of cities. Had he worked for the sake of salary, he must have had a well furnished house, and all the ordinary luxuries of a well-to-do religious leader. But John was a man absorbed by his message; he ate and drank in common with other men, but his eating and drinking were no object to him, except so far as they served to maintain and strengthen him, and so to further the great object of his existence—to prepare the way of the Lord. His clothing was of importance only so far as it served his mission. He was like a finger always pointed to say, Behold one who cometh after me! "There cometh one mightier than I after me, the latchet of whose shoes I am not worthy to stoop down and unloose." There are some men whose lives and testimonies say, "Behold *me*, what a holy man I am, what an earnest Christian, what a soul winner!" But John's whole mission was, "Behold *Him!*"

God undertook the advertising of his preaching. Neither placards, bellman, brass bands, sandwiches, nor other means of modern advertising were needed. God put a hunger for a better life into the hearts of thousands, and then He so ordered that the repute of the desert preacher should reach the cities, and these hungry souls poured out into the desert. "Then went unto him all the land of Judea (they needed no pressure to attend his ministry) and they of Jerusalem, and were all baptized of him in the river of Jordan."

Confessing Their Sins."

Why did they not confess their sins in the synagogues? A sinner has an instinct about religious teachers. He knows intuitively who will be likely to repel him, who will say to him, "Peace peace, when there is no peace," and who will be likely to bring him nearer to God. Often in an inquiry meeting, really anxious souls are not blest because there is so little of the Holy Ghost in those who seek to lead them that they cannot help shrinking into themselves from the instinct that their would-be helpers are not being led of God. When the power of the Holy Ghost comes full upon a meeting, the instinct to confess sin and be thoroughly rid of it is often present. John the Baptist followed the Spirit, and no true or lasting work can be done for God until we learn to follow the Holy Ghost. It is far better to be satisfied with fewer conversions, and they the work of the Holy Ghost, than to be eager for a great number, which may be partly the result of forced work, and only an imitation of the Spirit after all. John was full of the Holy Ghost: when he preached, "Repent ye, for the kingdom of heaven is at hand," the Holy Ghost led men to repent, and therefore the universal confession of sin among those who listened to him. When, afterwards, the burden of his preaching underwent a change, and the Messiah and His mission stood revealed to himself, and he preached, "Behold the Lamb of God which taketh away the sin of the world." (John 1: 29), then the Holy Ghost was with the preaching, and awakened sinners found the burden of their sins was gone. The Holy Ghost knows how to choose the right subject for every congregation, and no one else ought to choose it. He will always own His own message when it is trusted to Him.

His Baptism.

John did not make much of his baptism; but he made use of it, as he did of every part of his ministry, to point to Jesus. "I indeed have baptized you with water, but He shall baptize you with the Holy Ghost." To John, this coming baptism of the Holy Ghost was more than all his ministry. He knew what it was to be a Holy-Ghost-filled man; he knew how little the world looks to a man who sees it in the light of the Holy Ghost; how small and insignificant self looks in the light of the Holy Ghost, and how Jesus alone stands the Central Figure in every picture which rises to the mind of one filled with the Spirit. Oh how it drives into a corner the comparatively unimportant controversy about infant and adult baptism, when the baptism of the Holy Ghost, which buries us out of sight in the Father, and in the Son, and in the Holy Ghost (Matt. 28: 19), is become a practical reality in the life! Let the greater supersede the lesser, and the outward forms be clothed upon with

The Inward Reality

"And it came to pass in those days, that Jesus came from Nazareth to Galilee, and was baptized of John in Jordan." He did not despise the outward sign; as He was circumcised to fulfil the righteousness of the law, so it became Him "to fulfil all righteousness" in being baptized with water (Matt. 3: 15), and so, by one Spirit being baptized into the one body with His people. "And straightway coming up out of the water, He saw the heavens opened, and the Spirit, like a dove, descending upon Him." Thus Jesus, at His baptism, was baptized, not with water only, but with the Holy Ghost, and thus prepared for His ministry. There is no true preparation for the work of God which comes short of being yielded up to the Holy Ghost, and letting him possess us. There may be one act of renouncing the will and accepting the Holy Ghost as master and guide, but it is an act to which we need to be true from hour to hour. The one yielding does not keep us yielded. We need, whenever there is a question of the will, to acknowledge the Holy Ghost's supremacy. A voice from heaven bore witness, "This is my beloved Son, in whom I am well pleased." The pleasure of the Lord prospers in His hand. In Him only is God well pleased. He is pleased with us only as He sees us in Him.

CHRISTIAN HERALD AND SIGNS OF OUR TIMES.

OFFICE, 63 BIBLE HOUSE, NEW YORK.

TERMS AND INSTRUCTIONS.

Published Weekly. Subscription price in the United States, Canada, and Mexico, $1.50 a year; $1 eight months; 75 cents six months; sent two months on trial for 25 cents, postage free; in Europe and in all countries in the Postal Union, 50 cents extra postage; subscriptions always payable in advance. Single copies, price 3 cents. Any newsdealer will furnish the paper weekly when ordered.

Remittances by Mail should be by Post-office money order, bank cheque, draft, or express money order, whenever possible, and should always be made payable to THE CHRISTIAN HERALD. Letters containing money sent in this way need not be registered, as, when lost, duplicates can always be obtained.

If a Postal Note or currency is sent, it should always be in a registered letter. Letters can be registered at any office. Subscribers sending money of this kind, and not registering, do it at their own risk. Postage stamps should never be sent if it is possible to remit in any other way.

Receipts are not sent; the receipt of the paper by a subscriber is a sufficient proof that the remittance has been received. If the paper does not arrive promptly, please advise us, that we may see if the address is correctly entered.

Renewals can be sent any time previous to date of expiry, and the time will be added to that to which the subscriber is already entitled. Some time must always necessarily elapse after receipt of money before the date opposite to the name on label can be changed.

Notice of Expiration of subscription is always sent in addition to the date being given on the address label. When not renewed by date of expiration, the paper is stopped; no notice from the subscriber being required.

CURRENT EVENTS.

A Vigorous Effort to Push the Tariff Bill through the Senate is being made. At a caucus of Republican Senators held on December 18 it was resolved to begin the day sittings at 11 o'clock in the morning and keep them up until 5:30 o'clock, and then to begin again at 8 o'clock for evening sittings. In addition to this it was determined not to take a holiday recess, but to keep the Senate in session day and night until the Tariff bill was passed. It was hoped that by this means factious opposition to the measure would be overcome, or that it would cease rather than undergo the strain of continuous work, and that then the bill might be sent to the House early in January. There is little prospect of its passing the present House, but it would be in completed shape for presentation to the new House either in extraordinary session or in ordinary course. A compromise was finally effected after consultation with Democratic Senators, by which it was agreed that if the proposal to have night sittings and no recess were abandoned the final vote should be taken on Jan. 21. The recess is to end on Jan. 2.

An Instructive Debate on Civil Service Reform took place in the House on December 18, when Mr. Amos Cummings, of New York, proposed to strike out from the appropriation bill the whole civil-service section. He admitted that he did so because all bills to repeal the law had been buried in committee, and he did not see any other way than to cripple the commission by striking out the whole appropriation. He believed the system one to favor certain voters at the expense of others, and that if members of the House were to be subjected to examinations, not five-eighths of them would ever reach the floor. General Spinola went further than Mr. Cummings, and expressed his belief that seven-eighths of the people were against civil-service reform. If the Democrats on his side could be honestly polled, they would be unanimously against it. Tammany Hall had declared against it time and time again. This was quite true, but the General must have been aware that the fact of Tammany Hall espousing any cause is sufficient to arouse opposition in many patriotic sections. The attempt to cripple the commission happily failed for this time; but the friends of the law, who have labored so long amid discouragements, to emancipate the civil service from partisan control, have evidently need to still continue their efforts to enlighten the people. The power of the people is the only thing that men of the Cummings and Spinola species dread.

A Formal Reiteration of the Monroe Doctrine, with special reference to the projects for a canal across the isthmus, is to be asked for by the Senate if a proposal made by Senator Edmunds on December 19 is adopted. The veteran statesman moved that the Government of the United States will look with serious concern and disapproval upon any connection of any European Government with the construction or control of any ship canal across the Isthmus of Darien or across Central America, and must regard any such connection or control as injurious to the just rights and interests of the United States, and as a menace to their welfare, and that the President of the United States be requested to communicate this expression of the views of Congress to the Governments of the countries of Europe. The recent collapse of the Panama undertaking renders this resolution a timely notice to all whom it may concern. It may, however, be hoped, in view of the treatment the Nicaraguan scheme is receiving in the House, that if the United States Government warns all other governments off, it will give the sanction asked for by the projectors of the Nicaraguan project.

A Joyful Demonstration Took Place at Jacksonville, Fla., on December 15, when the first party of refugees returned to the city. It was announced by the health authorites that on that day there would be an end of all restrictions upon entering the city, and the return of those who left in the early stages of the epidemic was expected. Besides arriving by train and boat, many reached the suburbs on the previous night by private conveyances and afoot to await the dawning of—to them—one of the brightest days in the history of the city. A large crowd had collected at the station to wait for them, when the laden trains arrived.

The Pressing Question of Immigration Restriction, which it was hoped that the Ford Committee would solve, appears likely to have no satisfactory or practicable remedy applied to it by that body. It is officially given out that the Committee will recommend a system of Federal inspection and registration to be carried out on both sides of the ocean. It is proposed that the immigrants shall be examined on oath, before they embark, from a set of written questions, and that if they answer these falsely they shall be liable to a prosecution for perjury after they arrive. The impossibility of examining singly each case does not appear to have occurred to the Committee, nor does the fact that the scheme would require an enormous and expensive body of officers to be maintained in Europe. Besides which, the anarchists, whom it is most desirable to exclude, are not as a rule men who would hesitate to commit perjury.

A Sensation in the French Senate was Produced on December 19, by a speech from Senator Challemel Lacour, who evidently voiced the opinions of a majority of the Senate, in representing the present condition of the country as one of danger. He interrupted a debate on a financial question by saying the present was not the moment to consider French finances, but the future of France. He condemned the policy now pursued in the schools, which, he said, struck at the root of the traditional principle of parental control. The main cause of existing evils, he declared, was radicalism, which relentlessly pursued the old founders of the Republic, and gave promises that were impossible of fulfilment. France had abandoned the most glorious of monarchies, and was about to fall at the feet of the least of men. This allusion to General Boulanger aroused intense excitement. The Senator proceeded to say that the Cabinet's duty was to check the movement toward the abyss, but instead of doing this the Cabinet were hastening the movement. It was time to return to a policy of common sense. He appealed to the Right to unite with the party of the Left, which was the upholder of order and liberty, to save the country.

The Mormon Problem Promises to Exercise the Canadian authorities. The *Times* says that "The Mormons who made a settlement some time ago in the region west of Manitoba assured the Dominion Government that they would not practice polygamy. It is suspected that the promise has not been kept. Among those who joined the original settlers was a member of the British Columbia Legislature, who resigned his seat in that body in order that he might cast his lot with them, and he asserts that they have not abandoned polygamy, and do not intend to give it up. He also volunteers a defence of so-called "plural marriage." The Dominion Government should begin to enforce its laws in this settlement now, when the number of persons to be dealt with is small. By such a course it may avoid a more vexatious and costly campaign against polygamy in years to come."

The Financial Collapse of the Panama Canal Company was announced last week. The first public intimation of it came in the form of the appointment of a committee in the French Legislature to consider a bill allowing the company to postpone payment of its maturing liabilities, including interest and redemption of bonds, for three months. The committee reported the bill adversely, and the Chamber, having discussed it, also rejected it. M. Floquet, the Premier, warned the Chamber that the rejection of the bill meant the bankruptcy of the company. Still more serious were the words of M. Goirand, who censured the managers of the canal, and said it would be impossible to leave the work of construction in their hands any longer, as they had been *guilty of employing misrepresentations* in order to attract capital. M. de Lesseps, who has been at the head of the undertaking, is eighty-three years of age. He entered on the project of cutting the Canal soon after his completion of the Suez Canal. Work was commenced upon it in 1881. The estimate of its cost was then fifty million dollars, but eighty million dollars' worth of bonds have already been issued. There is too much reason to fear that the investors, many of whom are poor, will lose the money they have put into the undertaking.

A Severe Engagement at Suakin was fought on December 20, and resulted in the victory of the combined English and Egyptian forces. The Mahdi's troops appear to have fought bravely. They were assailed at dawn by a tremendous fire from the English ships. When that ceased, General Grenfell led the Egyptian regiments in an attack on the trenches. He was supported by British cavalry, which did terrible execution. The victory was complete, and the victors encamped at night on the ground previously occupied by the enemy. It is thought, however, that the Mahdi, who has a large number of men at his disposal, will endeavor to retake the position. Lord Salisbury, the British Premier, has declared that he will not abandon Suakin, though he will not undertake another Soudan expedition. He contends that it would be madness to give up Suakin on the eve of suppressing the slave trade, because the final struggle with the slave dealers must be fought on the Red Sea.

An Affront to England is Said to be Contemplated by the Czar of Russia. At a meeting of Russian statesmen recently held at the Foreign Office in St. Petersburg, a high military authority urged that an ultimatum be sent to the Persian Government, warning it that Russia would take steps for the occupation of Persia unless it cancelled the treaty opening up the Karun country to the English. M. de Giers, the Foreign Minister, opposed such a course, and advised that the Government proceed with moderation. It is notorious, however, that the influence of M. de Giers over the Czar has long been waning, and it is therefore probable that in this matter his advice will not be taken.

The Hospital Association of New York Asks us to remind our readers that collections will be taken up in the churches of the city for the Hospital fund on December 30, the last Sunday of the year. Last year the churches and synagogues contributed $28,626.79, and the trades and other sources $21,822.36; making a total of $50,449.15. The needs of the hospitals have increased since then, and the Association earnestly hopes that the donations will be increased also.

A Very Noble Effort is Being Made by the Silver Cross Circle of the King's Daughters in New York to ameliorate the condition of the Lord's poor. They have found widows and others living without fire, in cold, wretched rooms, amid evil surroundings, unable to rent better places, and striving daily to earn a livelihood for themselves and their children; and also, not always successfully, to keep their little ones uncontaminated by the vice and immorality in the midst of which their poverty compels them to live. The King's Daughters are anxious to acquire a house which they could let out in sets of two or three rooms each, at moderate rents, to such persons, where by good sanitary arrangements, and the exclusion of undesirable persons, physical and moral welfare would be promoted. The effort is most commendable, and as it will be partially self-supporting not much money will be needed after the first expense. Contributions may be sent to Mrs. M. L. Hollister, 244 West 34th Street, New York.

The Following are the Topics Suggested by the Evangelical Alliance for the week of prayer: *Sunday*, January 6—"Arise, shine, for thy Light is come." (Isa. 60: 1.) *Monday*, January 7—Thanksgiving and confession for the individual, the family, the church, the community, and the nation. *Tuesday*—The Holy Spirit: His offices, gifts, fruits, and example. *Wednesday*—The family and the Church; for parents, children, master and servants; for ministers, officers, and members; for Christlikeness in heart and life; for increased activity, personal and associated; for Sunday-schools; for associations of young men and young women; for all forms of church work, for the oneness of all believers. *Thursday.*—Reforms: for the abolition of the manufacture, importation, sale, and use of intoxicating drinks as a beverage; for the destruction of the opium traffic; for the repeal of all laws which protect vice; for the sanctification of the Lord's Day; for social purity and all other needed reforms. (Prov. 23: 29–32, Rom. 3: 8, Hab. 2: 15, &c.) *Friday.*—Missions—City, Home, and Foreign: *Saturday*—Nations: for peace and prosperity, both temporal and spiritual; for civil and religious liberty; for rulers, legislators and judges, and for all in authority; for just laws and their impartial enforcement; for nations suffering injustice at the hands of other nations; for the removal of international and class antipathies and jealousies; for purity in national life.

A Mother's Recovery of Her Long Lost Son took place in Brooklyn, N. Y., last week. In 1863, a boy, six years old, was returning to his home from an unfinished building, where he had been playing, when he was roughly seized by a strange man, hurried on board a car and driven away. He was taken to a farm, where he was compelled to work, and was cruelly treated and half-starved. His condition at length attracted the notice of neighbors, who interfered, and finally had the man and his son arrested for cruelty. The boy drifted from one home to another, making himself useful wherever he went. He finally reached Chicago, where he settled down and prospered. A few weeks ago he met a stranger from Brooklyn, who scanned his features closely, and inquired about his history. The stranger told him that he strikingly resembled a family whom he knew in Brooklyn, from whom a child had been stolen twenty-five years ago, and advised him to make inquiries. He sent his photograph to a Brooklyn lawyer, who traced the family to Greenpoint, L. I. The family resemblance was recognized at once, and the long-lost son was written to. He at once set out for his mother's home, and arrived on December 18. The meeting was a strange one; the stalwart man of thirty-one being so unlike the little boy of six, whose memory the mother had cherished so long. She told him of all the efforts she had been making to find him, and of the sorrow she felt when at last she had been constrained to give him up for dead. He had been so occupied with his own sufferings and with the difficulties of making his way, that he had not thought of her during the years of separation. That is often the case with God's wandering children. Though He yearns over them, they take no thought of Him until His love is revealed to them. (Deut. 30: 4.)

A Wreath of Serpents on a Child's Head terrified a citizen of Orange, N. J., recently. He was walking in a small wood near his house with his little daughter, when he noticed a curiously twisted wreath among the dried leaves at the foot of a tree. He took it up and playfully placed it as a coronet on the child's brow. The girl did not like it, for it had a cold, clammy feeling as it touched her forehead, so she hastily shook it off. The father then picked it up and examined it more closely. To his horror he found that the wreath was not, as he had supposed, a few twisted twigs, but two snakes in a state of torpor. The cold snap had driven them together, and, twining each around the other, they had gone off in one of the long sleeps peculiar to those reptiles. He was filled with horror as he thought of the danger to which he had unwittingly exposed his child. There are many parents who by injudicious gifts and flatteries are doing a still more dangerons thing. In planting and nurturing seeds of vanity and pride in the hearts of their children, they are developing a disposition which may lead to eternal death. (Prov. 16: 18.)

A Man Was Saved from Death by his Boot-heel at Fall River, Mass., on December 17. A master plumber of that city was superintending some work in a new mill, and while one of his men went to the shop for some article that had been forgotten, the plumber strolled across a vacant lot to a ledge from which the stone for building was being taken out. He found no one around so he sauntered through the quarry looking at the rocks. Presently he noticed rather a deep fissure, and went close to it to examine it. He was intent upon it when he heard a shout and, looking around, saw a man crawling toward him on his hands and knees. The man called to him to come away instantly, and the plumber obeyed. Then an explanation followed. There were forty pounds of dynamite in the fissure, and the crawling man had been in a bomb-proof at a distance, vainly trying to fire it by electricity. Wondering why the charge did not go off, he crawled along to find out, and discovered the cause. The plumber's heel was pressed on the wire, grounding it, and unwittingly prevented the explosion. When he knew how slight a thing had saved him from a horrible death he almost fainted, but was not long in getting out of the dangerous place. If impenitent sinners realized how near they stand to a far worse doom, they would be similarly appalled, and lose no time in fleeing to the Refuge provided for them. (Ezek. 18: 31, 32.)

Pardon has Been Refused to an Escaped Convict by the Governor of New York. Sixteen years ago a young man was arrested in Middletown, N. Y., on a charge of burglary. The evidence was strong, and he was convicted, and sentenced to five years imprisonment. He was set at work in the cooper's shop in the Penitentiary. After a few months, he utilized the skill he acquired there, in making a barrel in which he concealed himself. The barrel was shipped away with others, and when the convict thought he had arrived at a safe place, he broke out the head of the barrel and escaped. Since that time he has wandered about the country, never staying long in one place. Very little is known of his manner of life, as to honesty, during the interval. Three years ago, however, he turned up in Union City, Penn., with a wife, and settled down to work. He set up in business as a baker and prospered. The old habits, however, were not eradicated. Last May he was again in the hands of the police. A lawyer of Union City had prosecuted him, and the ex-convict had revenged himself by trying to kill the lawyer and his family and by blowing his house up with dynamite. In prison he was recognized as the convict who had escaped from the New York Penitentiary, and when the Pennsylvania people have done with him, he is to be sent back to New York to finish his sentence. As it is now sixteen years since the crime was committed, the Governor was asked to pardon him. Last week Governor Hill sent a refusal, believing that a man in prison for another offence was not a fit object for executive clemency. The Governor is undoubtedly right; but sinners would be in a hopeless case if God dealt so with them. Through Christ, God offers pardon before reformation, and enables the repentant to reform too. (Ezek. 36: 27.)

BRIEF NOTES.

The Rev. H. M. Scudder, D. D., is delivering a course of lectures on Christianity at Tokio, Japan, to crowds.

The project of establishing a Baptist University in New York City has been broached, and is meeting with warm support in the churches.

Twelve Jewish converts recently received Christian baptism at Rev. Jacob Freshman's Hebrew Christian Church, in St. Mark's Place, New York.

The Rt. Rev. H. Chauncey Riley, D. D., delivered his stereopticon lecture at the Y. M. C. A., Brooklyn, before a large and deeply interested audience.

Sir Edmund Hay Currie, the great London distiller, some time ago declared himself an abstainer. It is now stated that he has given up connection with the business.

A correspondent of a contemporary states that Prohibition in Iowa is being nullified by the importation of liquor in sealed bottles under the recent decision of the Supreme Court.

The Territorial Christian Endeavor Convention of Utah has just been held in Salt Lake City. The cause has taken deep root in that city, as well as in a number of other places throughout the Territory.

The *Bombay Guardian* says: "There is not a single Bible missionary in Beloochistan, Afghanistan, and the French possessions in Anam and Tonquin, nor in Siberia or any of the adjoining countries under Russian rule."

Rev. Frank W. Warne, who recently went to India as a Temperance advocate under the auspices of the World's Women's Christian Temperance Union, has been speaking in Calcutta. At the close of one address, 140 persons signed the pledge.

The Rev. B. Fay Mills has been conducting revival services at Roxbury, Mass. The Congregational, Presbyterian, Baptist, and Methodist Churches have united in the movement. The work has resulted in a wonderful stirring of the whole city.

A remarkable Christian movement among the Jews of Siberia is reported, the leader being a Polish Jew, Jacob Sheinmann by name. Exiled to Siberia twenty years ago because of avowal of belief in Christianity, he there began to proclaim his convictions.

The Rev. Dr. Meredith, who succeeded Dr. Pentecost, as pastor of the Tompkins Ave. Congregational Church, Brooklyn, N. Y., has been chosen chaplain of the Twenty-third Regiment. Dr. Meredith served in the war as captain of the 153d New York volunteers.

The Free-Will Baptist Church House in Concord, Ky. will be dedicated on December 30, and the friends there are expecting a large gathering. A small debt still remains on the House. Mr. W. H. Cox, of Concord, Ky., would be glad to receive contributions toward its removal.

Dr. L. W. Munhall has been holding some remarkable meetings for boys and young men at Bloomington, Ill. On December 16 a congregation of 1,800 of them assembled, and hundreds went away unable to gain admission to the theatre in which the meetings are held. Much good is being done among them.

The Beulah Home, 1521 Oxford Street, Philadelphia, has been opened for Faith Work. The Home is specially designed for those who are sick in body or distressed in spirit, who desire rest and a closer walk with God. Consecration meetings are held every Tuesday at 3 P. M. Applications for admission and requests for prayer should be sent to Mrs. E. Stine, at the Home.

The Next Few Weeks will be the best time for canvassing for new subscribers. We are happy to learn that many of our friends are already introducing THE CHRISTIAN HERALD among their friends and neighbors. Any one desiring sample copies *for this purpose*, will be supplied free of cost by writing for them, stating explicitly how many can be advantageously used. Address The Manager, 63 Bible House, New York

THE TRIAL OF YOUR FAITH.

A New Sermon by Pastor C. H. Spurgeon.

"The trial of your faith." 1 Pet. 1:7.

The Most Precious of all Possessions—The Germ of all Graces—Yet Involving Trial—I. Faith will be tried Surely—Like a Lantern to Light the Way Home—Trial the Element of Faith—Like a Salamander Living in Fire—Proves its Sincerity—Proves its Strength—II. Will be Tried Variously—By God's Nearness—By Blessings—More Frequently by Affliction—III. Will be Tried Individually—IV. Will be Tried for Useful Purposes—Developing and Strengthening—Encourages Others—Stars Seen in Darkness.

It is a great thing if any man can truthfully speak to you, my brother, about "*your faith*," for all men have not faith, and wherever faith is found, it is the token of divine favor. True faith is, in every case, of the operation of the Spirit of God. Its nature is purifying, elevating, heavenly. It is, of all things that can be cultivated in the human breast, one of the most precious. If thou hast faith, thou hast infinitely more than he who has all the world, and yet is destitute of faith. To him that believeth it is said, "All things are yours." Faith is the assurance of sonship, the pledge of inheritance, the grasp of boundless possession, the perception of the invisible. Within thy faith there lies glory, even as sleeps

The Oak Within the Acorn.

If thou hast faith, thou needest not ask for much more, save that thy faith may grow exceedingly, and that all the promises which are made to it may be known and grasped by thee. So far everything is delightful. But then comes in this word, which somewhat startles, and, if we are cowardly, may also frighten—"*The trial* of your faith." See you the thorn which grows with this rose! You cannot gather the fragrant flower without its rough companion. You cannot possess the faith without experiencing the trial; nor eat the lamb without the bitter herbs. These two things are put together—faith and trial; and it is of that trial of your faith that I am going to speak at this time, as God shall help me. It may be, may brother, that words said at this good hour shall comfort you while you undergo the sorer trial of your faith.

I. And, first, let me say of it, your

Faith Will be Tried Surely.

You may rest assured of that. A man may have faith, and be for the present without trial; but no man ever had faith and was all his life without trial. That could not be—must not be; for faith, in the very nature of it, implies a degree of trial. I believe the promise of God. So far my faith is tried in believing the promise, in waiting for the fulfilment of the promise, in holding on to an assurance of that promise while it is delayed, and in continuing to expect the promise, and to act upon it until it is in all points fulfilled to me. To whom God has given faith, it is as though one gave a lantern to his friend because he *expected it to be dark on his way home.* The very gift of faith is a hint to you that you will want it; that at certain points and places you will especially require it, and that, at all points, and in every place, you will really need it. That God, who has made nothing in vain, especially makes nothing in the spiritual kingdom in vain; and if he makes faith, it is with the design that it should be used to the utmost and exercised to the full.

Expect trial, also, because trial is the very element of faith. Faith is a salamander that lives in the fire, a star which moves in a lofty sphere, a diamond which bores its way through the rock. Faith without trial is like a diamond uncut, the brilliance of which has never been seen. Untried faith is such little faith that some have thought it no faith at all. What a fish would be without water, or a bird without air, that would be faith without trial. If thou hast faith, thou mayest surely expect that thy faith will be tested: the great Keeper of the treasures admits no coin to His coffers without testing. It is so in the nature of faith, and so in the order of its living: it thrives not, save in such weather as might seem to threaten its death. Indeed, it is

The Honor of Faith to be Tried.

Shall any man say, "I have faith, but I have never had to believe under difficulties"? Who knows whether thou hast any faith? Shall a man say, "I have great faith in God, but I have never had to use it in anything more than the ordinary affairs of life, where I could probably have done without it as well as with it"? Is this to the honor and praise of thy faith? Dost thou think that such a faith as this will bring any great glory to God, or bring to thee any great reward? If so, thou art mightily mistaken. He that has tested God, and whom God has tested, is the man that shall have it said of him, "Well done, thou good and faithful servant." If God, then, has given to any one of us a faith which is honorable and precious, it has full surely been submitted to its own due measure of trial; and if it is to be still more precious, it has yet more trials to endure.

We remember, also, two reasons for the trial of faith. The trial of your faith is sent

To Prove Its Sincerity.

If it will not stand trial, what is the good of it? That gold which dissolves in the furnace, and disappears amid the flame, is not the gold which shall be current with the merchant; and that faith of thine which is no sooner tried than straightway it evaporates, art thou not well rid of it? Of what use would it be to thee in the hour of death, and in the day of judgment? No; thou canst not be sure that thy faith is true faith till it is tried faith. Thou canst not be certain that it is worth having till it has been fitly tested, and brought to the touchstone of trial.

It must also be tested to prove its strength. We sometimes fancy that we have strong faith when, indeed, our faith is very weak; and how are we to know whether it be weak or strong till it be tried? A man that should lie in bed week after week, and perhaps get the idle whim into his head that he was very strong, would be pretty certain to be mistaken. It is only when he sets about work requiring muscular strength that he will discover how strong or how weak he is. God would not have us form a wrong estimate of ourselves. He loves not that we should say that we are rich and increased in goods, and have need of nothing, when we are the reverse; and therefore He sends to us the trial of our faith that we may understand how strong or how weak it is.

And besides that, dear friends, the trial of our faith is necessary

To Remove its Dross.

Is there any loss therein? I trow not. The gold loses nothing by the removal of its dross, and our faith loses nothing by the dissipation of its apparent force. Faith may apparently lose, but it actually gains. It may seem to be diminished, but it is not truly diminished. All is there that was worth having. "Why, a week ago," says one, "I used to sing, and think that I had the full assurance of faith; and now I can scarcely tell whether I am one of God's people or not." Now, you know how much faith you really possess. You can now tell how much was solid, and how much was sham; for had that which has failed you been real faith, it would not have been consumed by any trial through which it has passed. You have lost the froth from the top of the cup, but all that was really worth having is still there. Understand, then, dear friends, that for many necessary purposes there is a needs be for trial.

II. Now, secondly, your faith

Will be Tried Variously.

The trial of our faith does not come to all persons in the same way. There are some whose faith is tried each day in their communion with God. They pray this prayer: "Search me, O God, and know my heart: try me, and know my thoughts: and see if there be any wicked way in me; and lead me in the way everlasting." That prayer is heard constantly; the visitations of the Lord are granted to them, and as the Lord comes, He tries them; for, believe me, there is no surer trial of our souls than the drawing near of God to our souls. Apart from any outward affliction, that searching thought, that inward feeling, which is somewhat more than thought; that holy, secret trembling, which comes upon our spirit when God draws near, is God's constant trial of our graces. If you walk away from God, and live without fellowship with Him, you may retain in your heart much falsehood, and fancy that you are full of spiritual gifts and graces; but if you draw near to God, and walk with Him, you will not be able to retain a false opinion of yourself. Remember our God is a consuming fire!

The presence of perfect holiness is killing to empty boastings and hollow pretences. You need not ask for any of those various forms of trial which God sends

In the Order of Providence:

you may rest quite satisfied with His presence, as the most effectual purgation; for "His fan is in His hand, and He will throughly purge His floor." Whenever Jesus abides with us, "He shall sit as a refiner." Whoever He may leave alone in their defilement, "He will purify the sons of Levi." It is the Lord Himself that will be as a refiner's fire, and like fullers' soap. Who may abide the day of His coming? Who that loves holiness would wish to escape it? Our prayer should be—

"Refining fire, go through my soul."

Ay, let the devouring flame go through me, and through me yet again, till this earthly grossness shall begin to disappear. Thus you see there is a constant trial of our faith, even in that which is its greatest joy and glory, namely, its power to make us see the Lord.

But the Lord uses other methods with His servants. I believe that He frequently tries us by the blessings which He sends us. This is a fact which is too much overlooked. When a man is permitted to grow rich, what a trial of faith is hidden away in that condition! It is one of the severest of providential tests! *Where I have known one man to fail through poverty, I have known fifty men fail through riches.* When our friends get on in the world, and have a long stretch of prosperity, they should invite their brethren to offer special prayer for them, that they may be preserved; for the thick clay is heavy stuff to walk upon, and when the feet slip into it, and it adheres to you, it makes travelling to heaven a very difficult thing. When we do not cling to wealth, it will not harm us; but there is a deal of bird-lime in money. You that have no riches may yet find

A Test In Your Daily Mercies;

your domestic comfort, that loving wife, those dear children—all these may tempt you to walk by sight instead of by faith. Ay, and continued health, the absence of all depression of spirit, and the long abiding of friends and relatives, may all make you self-contented, and keep you away from your God. It is a great trial of faith to have much for sight to rest upon. To be in the dark—altogether in the dark—is a grand thing for faith; for then you are sure that what you see is not seen of the flesh, but is in very deed a vision of spiritual faith. To be under a cloud is a trial, truly; but not one-half so much a trial as it is to have the light of this world.

One form of this trial is praise. You know how Solomon puts it: "As the fining-pot for silver, and the furnace for gold; so is a man to his praise." A Christian minister may go on preaching very earnestly, and God will help him, though everybody opposes him; but when the world comes and pats him on the back, and pride whispers, "You are a fine fellow; you are a great man!" then comes the test of the man. How few there are that can endure the warm atmosphere of congratulation! It is dangerously relaxing to the spirit. Yea, nobody can keep himself right under it, unless the almighty grace of God shall sustain his faith. When the soft winds blow they bring with them the temptation, "Now preach the doctrines that tickle men's ears!" "Go in to be scientific and learned and clever! Get the approbation of the great of the world, and the

Leaders of Advanced Thought

in the church." And unless you say, "Get thee behind me, Satan; for thou savourest not the things that be of God," such a trial of faith may be too much for you. "Oh," says one, "that will not fall to my lot." No, no; you will not be a popular preacher, perhaps; but then, you may be very acceptable in the company wherein you move, and worldly people may flatter you to the verge of ruin. Because of your natural attainments, and the amiability of your temper, you may become a great favorite with ungodly people; and that is an intense trial to the faith of a child of God. The friendship of the world is as much enmity with God as it used to be in apostolic times. It is *a bad sign when a courtier is in great favor with the king's enemies.* Stand up, and stand out, as the servant of God, and in whatever sphere you move, make it your one and only business to serve my God, whether you offend or please. Happy shall you be if you survive the trial of your faith which this will involve!

Another trial of faith is exceedingly common and perilous nowadays, and that is, heretical doctrine and false teaching. There be some who are carried away with this wind of doctrine, and others carried away with the other; and blessed is he who is not offended in Christ; for, naturally, the cross of Christ is offensive to the minds of men. There are temptations that rise out of the gospel itself, yea, out of its very depth and breadth. There is a trial of faith in reading the Scriptures. You come across a doctrine which you cannot understand, and because you cannot understand it, you are tempted not to receive it. Or, when a truth which you have received appears to be hard, and speaks to you in an unlovely fashion, so that your natural feelings are aroused against it; this is a trial of your faith. Truth is not always welcome to our ignorance, or to our prejudice, and herein is a trial of faith.

But the trial of our faith comes

Usually in the Form of Affliction.

Our jealous Lover uses tests that it may be seen whether He has our heart. The trial of your faith comes thus: You say, "Lord Jesus, I love thee. Thou art my best beloved." "Well," says the heavenly Lover, "if it be so, then the child that nestles in thy bosom will sicken and die. What wilt thou say then?" If thou be indeed true in what thou hast stated concerning thy supreme love to Jesus, thou wilt give up thy darling at His call, and say, "The Lord gave, and the Lord hath taken away; blessed be the name of the Lord." The Lord is very jealous of our love. I do not mean that He is so towards all of you: I speak of His own people. The more He loves us, the more He tests us. Can we stand that test? Can we let all go for His sake? Do you answer that you can? Time will show.

III. In the third place, your faith

Will Be Tried Individually.

The text says, the trial of *your* faith. O dear friend, it is an interesting subject, is it not, the trial of faith? It is not quite so pleasant to study alone the trial of *your* faith. It is stern work when it comes to be *your* trial, and the trial of *your* faith. You have not gone much into that particular department, perhaps. Well, I say again, do not wish to do so. Do not ask for trials. Children must not ask to be whipped, nor saints pray to be tested. The Lord Jesus Christ has been glorified by the trial of His people's faith. He has to be glorified by the trial of *your* faith. You are very obscure, perhaps, dear brother. You have but few talents, my dear sister. But, nevertheless, there is a particular shape and form of trial that will have to be exercised upon you rather than upon anyone else. "Oh," say you, "I know it, sir; I know it." Well, then, if you know it, do not complain of it; because, when you have your own trial, and the trial of your own faith, you are only treated like the rest of the family. What son is there whom the father chasteneth not? You are only treated like the Head of the family. You are only treated in the way which the great Father of the family knows is necessary for us all. God had one Son without sin, but He never had a son without trial, and He never will have until He has taken us all home out of this world. Why should we expect that God should deal better with us than others?

IV. Let me yet further observe, that your faith

Will Be Tried For a Useful Purpose.

The trial of your faith will increase, develop, deepen, and strengthen it. "Oh," you have said, "I wish I had more faith." Your prayer will be heard through your having more trial. Often in our prayers we have sought for a stronger faith to look within the veil. The way to stronger faith usually lies along the rough pathway of sorrow. Only as faith is contested will faith be confirmed. Affliction is the best bit of furniture in my house. It is *the best book in a minister's library.* We may wisely rejoice in tribulation, because it worketh patience, and patience experience, and experience hope; and by that way we are exceedingly enriched, and our faith grows strong.

The trial of our faith is useful, not only because it strengthens it, but because it leads to a discovery of our faith to ourselves. I remember Mr. William Jay saying that birds' nests are hard to find in summer time, but anyone could find a bird's nest in winter. When all the leaves are off the trees the nests are visible to all. Often in the days of our prosperity, we fail to find our faith; but when our adversity comes, the winter of our trial bares the boughs, and we see our faith at once. We are sure that we believe now, for we feel the effect of faith

Upon Our Character.

This trial of our faith does good to our fellow-Christians. They see how we are supported, and they learn to bear their troubles bravely. I do not know anything that is better for making us brave than to see others believe in Christ and bear up manfully. To see that blind saint so happy makes us ashamed to be sad. To see content in an inmate of the workhouse compels us to be thankful. Sufferers are our tutors; they educate us for the skies. When men of God can suffer—when they can bear poverty, bereavement or sickness, and still rejoice in God, we learn the way to live the higher and more Christly life. When Patrick Hamilton had been burned in Scotland, one said to his persecutors, "If you are going to burn any more, you had better do it in a cellar, for the smoke of Hamilton's burning has opened the eyes of hundreds." It was so. Suffering saints are living seed.

Come, let us be comforted as to the trial of our faith. There is no hurt in it. It is all for good. The trial of our faith is entirely in the hands of God. Nobody can try us without God's permission. He will try us just as much as we ought to be tried, and no more. While He tries us with one hand, He will sustain us with the other. If He gives us bitters, He will give us sweets in full proportion. A dear sister said to me this week, "When I used to be in poverty and in trouble, the Word of God was much more sweet to me than it is now that I am prospered." I do not wonder at it. I have made a similar remark when I have been long without an illness. Some of us have cried, "Take me back to my sickness again. Take me back to slander and rebuke again."

A Scotch Saint

said when they met in the moss, or by the hill-side, and were harried by Claverhouse and his dragoons, Christ was present at the sacraments in the heather much more than He ever was afterwards when they got into the kirk, and sat down quietly. Our worst days are often our best days, and in the dark we see stars that we never saw in the light. So we will not care a pin what it is that may befall us here, so long as God is with us, and our faith in Him is genuine. Christian people, I am not going to condole with you, but I congratulate you upon your troubles, for the cross of Christ is precious.

But you that do not love my Lord and Master, if you roll in riches, your joys are but the prelude to your woes. Oh, that God would have mercy upon you, and that you would have mercy upon yourselves, and flee at once to Jesus, and put your trust in Him! Faith in the work, offices, and person of the Lord Jesus is the way of salvation. May He help you to run in it at this hour, for His name's sake! Amen.

GEMS FROM NEW BOOKS.

TWO LITTLE SOUTHERNERS IN THE WAR.

WHEN there first began to be talk at Oakland about the war, the boys thought it would be a dreadful thing; their principal ideas about war being formed from an intimate acquaintance with the Bible, and its account of the wars of the children of Israel, in which men, women, and children were put to the sword. This gave a vivid conception of its horrors. The boys were Frank and Willy: Frank being the eldest. They went by several names on the place. The mother called them her "little men" with much pride; Uncle Balla spoke of them as "them chillern," which generally implied something of reproach; and Lucy Ann, who had been taken into the house to run after them when they were little boys, always coupled their names as "Frank 'n' Willy." Peter and Cole did the same when their mistress was not by.

Freedom Refused by a Slave.

One evening in May, about sunset, as the boys were playing in the yard a man came riding through the place on the way to Richmond. His horse showed that he had been riding hard. He said the Yankees were coming. It was a raid. He had ridden ahead of them, and had left them about Greenbay Depot, which they had set on fire. It was the first time the boys ever saw their mother exhibit so much emotion as she then did. She came to the door and called, "Balla, come here!" Balla came to the portico and looked up with an air of inquiry. "Balla, I want you to know that if you wish to go you can do so. I want you all to know it." She was speaking now so as to be heard by the cook and the maids, who were standing about the yard listening to her. "I want you all to know it—every one on the place."

"Hi, mistis," broke in Uncle Balla, "whar is I got to go? I wuz born on dis place an' I spec' to die here, an' be buried right yonder"; and he turned and pointed up to the dark clumps of trees that marked the graveyard on the hill a half-mile away, where the colored people were buried. "Dat I does," he affirmed positively. "Y' all sticks by us, and we'll stick by you."

"I know I ain' gwine nowhar wid no Yankees, or nothin'," said Lucy Ann, in an undertone.

The boys' mother started to say something further to Balla, but though she opened her lips, she did not speak; she turned suddenly and went into the house and into her chamber, where she shut the door behind her. The boys thought she was angry, but when they softly followed her a few minutes afterward, she got up hastily from where she had been kneeling beside the bed, and they saw that she had been crying.

A Brave Little Hero.

[Fugitives from the Southern army were concealed in a cave on the plantation. The boys were sent to their hiding-place with food. They delivered it, but on their way home were captured by a party of Northern troops, who were searching for the fugitives.] "Look here," said the Northern corporal; "we've got you, and we're going to make you tell us where those rebels are hiding; so you might just as well do it easy. If you don't, we're going to make you."

The boy said nothing, but faced his captor, who held a strap in his hand.

"Are you going to tell us?" he asked.

"No."

* From "Two Little Confederates." By Thomas Nelson Page. A story of a Southern home in the war, giving graphic sketches of perils and hardships, dangers from Northern raiding parties, and the devices resorted to to supply the table when food became scarce. Pp. 156; illustrated; price $1.50. Published by *Charles Scribner's Sons*, 745 Broadway, N. Y.

Rev. Wm. Scott, D. D , Father of Mrs. Harrison.

A Street Discussion with Jews in Breslau.

"Don't you know?" He came a step nearer and held the strap forward. There was a long silence. The boy's face paled perceptibly.

"If you say you don't know—" said the man, hesitating in face of the boy's resolution.

"Yes, I know; but I ain't going to tell you," said Frank, bursting into tears.

"If you don't tell, we're going to shoot you," said one of the soldiers, drawing his pistol.

The boy shut his mouth close and looked straight at the corporal. The man laid down his pistol, and seizing the boy's hands, tied them behind his back. "Get ready, men!" he said, as he drew the boy aside to a small tree, putting him with his back to it.

Frank thought his hour had come. He thought of his mother and Willy, and wondered if the soldiers would shoot Willy, too. His face twitched and grew ghastly white. Then he thought of his father, and of how proud he would be of his son's bravery when he should hear of it. He wondered where the bullets would hit him, and whether, when he was dead, his mother would come and kiss him.

"I want to say my prayers," he said, faintly. The soldier made some reply which he could not hear, and started forward; but just then all grew dark before the boy's eyes. Next he thought he must have been shot, for he felt very wet about the face and was lying down. He opened his eyes. He was lying with his head in the lap of the big soldier, and the corporal was leaning over him, throwing water in his face from a cap.

"Am I shot?" asked Frank.

"No! Do you think we'd have touched a hair of your head—and you such a brave little fellow? We were just trying to scare you a bit, and carried it too far, and you got a little faint —that's all."

The boy did not know that the big dragoon was looking down at the light hair resting on his arm, and that he was home in fancy in Delaware; or that the pressure the boy felt from his strong arms was a caress given for the sake of another boy far away on the Brandywine.

"I've got a curly-headed fellow at home, just the size of you," the soldier said, softly.

Frank saw that his eyes were moist. "I hope you'll get safe back to him," he said.

"God grant it!" said the soldier.

REV. WILLIAM H. SCOTT, D. D.,

Father-in-law of the President-Elect.

ONE of the most interesting men in the Civil Service is an aged clerk in the Pension Office, who, though *eighty-eight years old*, is remarkable for his regularity and punctuality. He is tall, and still erect of bearing. His work is said to be a model of neatness and accuracy, and his manner singularly courteous and affable. The venerable clerk is the Rev. William H. Scott, D. D., a relative of General Winfield Scott, and the father of the wife of President-elect Harrison.

Dr. Scott's life has been one of active usefulness. For many years he was a professor in Miami University, Oxford, Ohio, and has occupied other eminently responsible positions. His home in Washington, D. C., is with his eldest daughter, Mrs. Scott-Lord, and there the old gentleman has the pleasure of the society also of two married granddaughters and their children.

IMPRISONED MUSIC.

By Mrs. C. H. Spurgeon.

A CURIOUS little incident happened lately during a time of prolonged sickness. At the close of a very dark and gloomy day I lay resting on my couch as the deeper night drew on, and though all was bright within my cosy little room, some of the external darkness seemed to have entered into my soul and obscured the spiritual vision. Vainly I tried to see the hand which I knew held mine, and guided my fog-enveloped feet along a steep and slippery path of suffering. In sorrow of heart I asked, "Why does my Lord thus deal with His child? Why does He permit lingering weakness to hinder the sweet service I long to render to his poor servants?"

For a while silence reigned in the little room, broken only by the crackling of the oak-log burning on the hearth. Suddenly I heard a sweet, soft sound, a little, clear, musical note like the tender trill of a robin beneath my window. "What can that be?" I said to my companion, who was dozing in the firelight; "surely no bird can be singing out there at this time of the year and night!" We listened, and again heard the faint, plaintive notes, so sweet, so melodious, yet mysterious enough to provoke for a moment our undisguised wonder. Presently my friend exclaimed, "It comes from the log on the fire!" and we soon ascertained that her surprised assertion was correct. The fire was letting loose the imprisoned music from the old oak's inmost heart! Perchance he had garnered up this song in the days when all went well with him, when birds twittered merrily on his branches, and the soft sunlight flecked his tender leaves with gold. But he had grown old since then, and hardened; ring after ring of knotty growth had sealed up the long-forgotten melody, until the fierce tongues of the flames came to consume his callousness, and the vehement heat of the fire wrung from him at once a song and a sacrifice.

Ah! thought I, when the fire of affliction draws songs of praise from us, then indeed are we purified and our God is glorified! Perhaps some of us are like this old oak log, cold, hard, and insensible; we should give forth no melodions sounds were it not for the fire, which kindles round us, and releases tender notes of trust in Him and cheerful compliance with His will! "As I mused, the fire burned," and my soul found sweet comfort in the parable so strangely set forth before me! Singing in the fire! Yes! God helping us, if that is the only way to get harmony out of these hard, apathetic hearts, let the furnace be heated seven times hotter than before.

A STREET DISCUSSION IN BRESLAU.

(*See Illustration.*)

ONE of the most active and successful of the missionaries to the Jews is a converted Israelite named Hartmann, who recently paid a visit to Breslau, and spent a night at an inn discussing with Jews in relation to Jesus Christ as the Messiah and the world's Saviour. He says: "In the evening a number of Jews assembled before the door of our house, with whom Mr. Händler and Mr. Lotka and I had a long discussion. A Jewish soldier joined them, and took a lively part in the discussion. He promised to call upon us in the evening, and he kept his word. He had a number of objections to make against the New Testament, rejected the Talmud, and expressed, like many Reform Jews, as they are called, the barest infidelity, but also the greatest ignorance of the spirit of the Mosaic law. When I asked him whether he had fulfilled the Word of God, 'Thou shalt love the Lord thy God with all thine heart,' &c., and whether he was what the Lord requires Israel to be, namely, holy, as the Lord their God is holy, he could not answer in the affirmative. I then showed him the necessity of man's redemption and reconciliation with God. He did not answer to that. When he left, he accepted several books and tracts.

"In the evening Brother Lotka returned from a walk in the streets, accompanied by a number of young men, Israelites, who seemed to find much pleasure in disputations. The subject of the discussion was the sacrifices of the Old Testament; but one of them began soon to speak of the deity of Jesus. I left in the first instance the argument to Brother Lotka, but afterwards took part. I pointed him first to the serpent of brass in the wilderness, as a proof that we are in need of a mediator—the Jews having just maintained that we can and must draw near to the Father without a mediator—and then I resumed the subject of the sacrifices, proving to them that no Jew could have forgiveness of his sins without a sacrifice.

"To this the Jews answered that they do now bring the blood of their heart by fasting, which blood is much better than the blood of beasts—the sacrifices of old. To this it was replied that also the Jews of old were bound to fast, and that the sacrifices were of no use and value to them, if they did not feel, and have, at the same time, true repentance of their sins. Both true repentance and sacrifice were indispensably necessary for every one who wished forgiveness of his sins. The lifting-up of the serpent and sacrifices were the means by which the Jews in the desert were healed, and could find forgiveness of their sins. But they were only types of the Messiah. The Jews listened for a longer time to these truths than I had expected. It was also proved to them, from the prophets Haggai and Daniel, that the Messiah must already have come, and that no other one than Jesus of Nazareth can be that Messiah.

"In the evening some Jews came again. One of them was an ignorant man, but seemed to be of an earnest mind. Afterwards five or six others came, to whom the Gospel truth was preached. The purpose of the coming of Messiah into the world, His doings and sufferings, the fulfilment of the sacrifices in Him, the necessity of redemption, no reconciliation with God without blood—these were the subjects of which we spoke to them. One of them began to blaspheme, and left us blaspheming; others listened attentively, and appeared to be impressed."

A Restored Palace of Ancient Nineveh.

A PALACE OF NINEVEH.

(See Illustration.)

THE excavations which have been made by Mr. Layard and Mr. George Smith on the site of the ancient city of Nineveh, have rendered it possible to form a complete idea of what must have been the beauty and style of its royal palaces. They appear to have been built on artificial mounds varying in height from thirty to fifty feet above the surrounding plain. These were in some cases constructed of regular rows of bricks, and in others merely of earth and timber. The former prevail at Nimroud, and the latter at the group now known as Kouyunjik. A solid wall of masonry protected the face of the mound, and majestic flights of broad steps led up to the palace itself. Some of the mounds were of enormous extent, looking in the distance like natural elevations rather than the work of human hands. The palaces erected on these mounds or platforms were of several stories, and were built of huge beams and sun-dried bricks faced with slabs of alabaster.

When Assyria was overrun by the Medes about 656 B. C., Nineveh, its capital, was utterly destroyed, and its people carried captive. Happily when the chief buildings were overthrown the beams and material of the upper stories protected the contents of the lower stories, and these were further preserved from decay, through exposure to wind and rain, by the accumulation of rubbish under which they were buried. In some cases this layer was twenty feet thick.

In 1845 Layard succeeded in penetrating to the ruins under the rubbish, and still later Mr. George Smith continued the search. The reward repaid all the toil and danger. A large number of tablets—nearly ten thousand—were found covered with inscriptions. The writing had been done on terra-cotta clay while it was soft, and the tablets, which were about a foot square, were then subjected to heat until they were hard. They were then set up against the walls of the rooms in the king's palace, and formed the library. One collection was commenced by King Shalmanezer about 860 B. C., and was largely increased by Sardanapalus, his successor. After immense labor the writing has been deciphered, and it is found that the tablets contain a continued history of the reigns of the kings. They also bear records of current traditions. Very remarkably, there are two records substantially confirming the Mosaic account of the Creation and the Deluge. The illustration here given gives a correct idea of the appearance of a royal palace in the days of Assyrian glory, the ground-plan having been found clearly marked out, and the superstructure indicated by the ruins discovered on the spot.

ESCAPED FROM THE MORMONS.

A Life Story: By Mrs. Stenhouse.

For More than Twenty-five Years the Wife of a Mormon Missionary and Elder.

(Continued from page 815.)

Strange Tongues.

ONE speaker was Brother Edwards, a tried champion of the Faith, and to him every one listened with profound attention, eagerly drinking in his every utterance. I can almost, even now, imagine that he was really inspired. *Then* I firmly believed he was. His voice thrilled with an earnestness which seemed to us something more than the mere excitement of the soul. A burning fire seemed to flash from his large, expressive eyes; his features were lighted up with that animation which gives a saint-like halo to the earnest face when fired with indignation or pleading soul-felt truths; while his whole frame seemed to glow with the glory of a land beyond this earth, as, in the most impressive and convincing language, he reminded us that our sins had been washed away by the waters of baptism, that upon us had been poured the gifts and graces of the Spirit, and that it was our sacred privilege to testify of these things.

The effect of this exhortation was magical. We forgot all our outward surroundings, in the realization that the great work of the Lord was so gloriously begun, and that it would surely go on conquering and to conquer. One sister—an elderly woman—who was present, unable to control her emotion, burst out with that Mormon hymn which I have heard some old Nauvoo Saints declare produced upon the people in those days an enthusiasm similar to that which moves the heart of Frenchmen when they hear the soul-stirring notes of the Marseillaise:

"The Spirit of God like a fire is burning!
The latter-day glory begins to come forth;
The visions and blessings of old are returning,
The angels are coming to visit the earth.
We'll sing and we'll shout with the armies of heaven,
Hosannah! Hosannah to God and the Lamb,
All glory to them in the highest be given,
Henceforth and for ever: Amen, and Amen."

I have heard, in magnificent cathedrals, hoary with the dust of time, and in vast places of amusement dedicated specially to music and to song, the outpouring of that glorious vocal flood which a chorus of well-trained singers can alone send forth. I have felt sometimes that entrancing state of ecstasy which thrilled the soul of the seer in Patmos as he listened to the melody of the angelic throng—"the voice of many waters, and the peal of mighty thunders, and the notes of harpers harping upon their harps"; but never, even when surrounded by all that was best calculated to produce a sentiment of devotion in my mind—never did I experience so rapt a feeling of communion with "the armies of heaven" as I felt in that unadorned meeting room, surrounded by those plain but earnest and united people.

Nor was I alone in this. The feeling was contagious. There was not one present who did not sympathize. And thus, I suppose, melody has always played a prominent part in all religious revivals, whether of Divine or human origin. The Apostles had their psalms and hymns and spiritual songs; the Martyrs their *Te Deum;* the Waldenses made the hills and vales of Piedmont vocal with their singing; the Lollards and Hussites had their melodies; and in more modern days the followers of Luther, Wesley, and (may I add?) Joseph Smith have poured out the fullness of their souls after the same fashion.

The last notes of the hymn had scarcely died away when another, and then another brother arose and bore testimony to the great work, told what the Lord had done for them personally, told of their zeal for the faith, and exhorted all present to persevere unto the end. Again prayer was offered, another hymn sung, and the saints were dismissed with a solemn benediction. I was now a Mormon in every sense of the word, although entirely ignorant of Utah politics and polygamy. My dreams were of a life of happiness spent in seeking to convert the whole world to the religion of Jesus, which I believed had been restored again to earth by the ministry of holy angels. It is easy to say that such an ambition was ill-directed when associated with Mormonism, but no one can deny that, in itself, it was the noblest and purest that could inspire the heart of man. There was no sacrifice too great for me to make, there was no object too dear for me to resign, if it stood in the way of my sacred calling. The whole current of my thoughts and plans was now changed. It was henceforth my duty to be entirely forgetful of self, and to devote my energies, my all, to the advancement of the Kingdom of God. My life was to be identified with the Saints—my faith required it, and I was willing that it should be so.

But what of my beloved France, and what of my betrothed husband? This reflection aroused within me a most painful train of thought. How many fond and endearing memories entwined themselves around my heart at that moment, when most I needed to banish them for ever! With what lingering love did I look back to those dear ones from whom I had parted but a few short weeks before, and whom I might perhaps never see again! To return would be to desert my newly adopted friends and faith—to violate the covenant which I had made at baptism, to "be ever afterwards governed by the servants of God."

No, it was too late; I could not now return; I tried to persuade myself that I did not even wish to—in a word, affection and what I thought duty were at war together in my heart. All my former ties and associations must now be severed, however terrible the cost might be; and I was bound not only to submit, but even to glory in the sacrifice. Thus I argued away the regrets which would at times agitate my very soul, and cause me much painful thought.

The trial of my profession in the new faith came swiftly to my door. My marriage engagement must be broken off, though I knew not how that could honorably and conscientiously be done. Of myself, I had no wish to draw back from anything that I had promised of my own free will; and much less did I desire to be faithless to my solemnly plighted word. I now first realized the all-absorbing influence of an earnest religious faith. I was brought face to face with the fact that I could not marry out of the Mormon Church. The teaching of the Elders was against it, and I saw that in this they were consistent. Great as was the trial, and painful as was the sacrifice, I resolved to be true to my religion. How very earnestly the Elders insisted upon such sacrifices, may be seen from an appeal made at a later date by the "Apostle" Orson Pratt. Brother Orson was in Europe, and, speaking authoritatively, he set forth the duties of mothers and daughters in "Babylon," as he graciously styled the rest of the world, in the following terms, which unmistakably show the purposes of the leaders relative to marriage:

"Many of you have daughters, some of whom are grown to womanhood; others are now young. Would you have them gather with you to a land where virtue and peace dwell, where God has promised to protect and bless the righteous? If so, teach them, as they love their parents, and the Saints, and the truth, not to throw themselves away by marrying Gentiles; teach them to *keep themselves entirely aloof from* Gentile courtships and associations. Scores of women who once were counselled as you are now, are mourning in wretchedness, in bondage to Gentile husbands, cut off from all privilege of gathering with their fathers, mothers, brethren, and sisters; and, in some instances, cut off from even attending the Saints' meetings. But this is not all. They are raising up children in these lands to perish with themselves in the general desolations coming upon Babylon. But, what is still more aggravating and heartrending, they are raising up children not only destined for temporal judgments, but who must for ever be cut off from the presence of God and the glory of the celestial kingdom. What fearful responsibility for any young sister to voluntarily take upon herself, after all the warnings she has received. See to it, then, parents, that you not only do not give your consent, but forbid all such marriages.

"*Let them marry according to the holy order of God*, and begin to lay the foundation of a little family kingdom which shall no more be scattered upon the face of the earth, but dwell in one country, keeping their genealogies from generation to generation, until each man's house shall be multiplied as the stars of heaven." These were the influences which were brought to bear upon my mind at a time when it was peculiarly sensitive, and open to impressions from without.

While in this uncertain state a little incident occurred, which, though in itself of the most trifling nature, assisted in forming my ultimate decision. It was a beautiful evening in early summer, and my mother and sister asked me to accompany them to one of the testimony meetings which I have already described. This meeting was very similar to the others, with one notable exception—it was here that I saw and heard, for the first time in my own experience, the "gift of tongues" exercised.

Long before I had even heard of Mormonism, I had frequently thought how wonderfully useful this gift must have been to the Apostles. One of the great difficulties encountered by the missionary is learning the language of the people among whom he works and lives. To be able to dispense with all this labor, and to be understood wherever he went, must have lightened the mind of half its load; and, naturally, when I heard that the Mormons had "the gift of tongues," I supposed it was the self-same power of diverse speech as that exercised by the Apostles; and I presume the reader will conjecture with me that it was the same "gift," or, at least, some imitation of it. How surprised I was when I first discovered the meaning of the term, "speaking in tongues" among the Mormons, may perhaps be imagined when I explain what happened at that testimony meeting.

After prayer and singing, and listening to several very fervent addresses from some of the elders, Brother Seely had delivered a most impassioned speech, and had hardly concluded when Sister Ellis, who was sitting near me, gave evidence of being in an abnormal condition of mind, which to me was painful in the extreme. Her hands were clenched, and her eyes had that wild and supernatural glare which is never seen save in cases of lunacy or intense feverish excitement. Every one waited breathlessly, listening to catch what she might say—you might have heard a pin drop. Then in oracular tones, and with all the impassioned dignity of one inspired from heaven, she began to speak. I say "speak," as that term is generally applied to the utterances of the human voice; but she did not *speak* in the sense in which we always employ that word; she simply emitted a series of sounds. They seemed to me chiefly the repetition of the same syllables—something like a child repeating, *la, la, la, le, lo; ma, ma, ma, mi, ma; dele, dele, dele, hela*—followed, perhaps, by a number of sounds strung together, which could not be rendered in *any* shape by the pen.

Sometimes in the Far West, in later years, I have heard old Indian women, crooning weirdly monotonous and outlandish ditties in their native tongue. These wild dirges, more nearly than anything else I ever heard, resembled the prophetic utterances of Sister Ellis; save only that the appearance of the latter was far too solemn to admit of even a smile at what she said. Ridiculous as this appears when I now write it down on paper, and strange as it even then was to me, there was something so commanding, so earnest, so "inspirational," if I may be allowed the term, in Sister Ellis's manner, that I could not wonder at the attention which the brethren and sisters paid to this gifted speaker in tongues.

I now know that these extraordinary displays are by no means confined to Mormonism. People of a certain temperament, excited to frenzy, have in all ages given painful illustrations of this mental aberration, as the student who remembers the Convulsionnaires of the Middle Ages, the Munster Anabaptists of Luther's time, and the various emotional sects of more modern days, notably those of Edward Irving's church, will bear me witness. But at that time, new in the faith, and believing as I did that, as the Elders said, it was the manifestation of the power of God as foretold by the propet Joël, though secretly I felt a sense of repugnance, I tried to combat my sentiments.

Overcome by the excitement of the moment, Sister Ellis suddenly paused, not so much intentionally as from sheer inability to proceed; and the leading Elders looked round from one to another to see if any one was present who could interpret. The gift of interpretation is very rarely possessed by the same person who has the gift of tongues, and you may often hear one after another arise and "speak," but there is no one to "interpret," and the Saints go away unedified. Even when an interpreter is present, there is no authority to determine whether he gives the proper rendering of the sounds uttered, and I have over and over again heard the most ludicrous stories of the comical interpretation placed by some half-witty or half-witted expounder upon these oracles.

When Brother Brigham—then a man who was lowly in his own eyes—first met the prophet Joseph Smith, at Kirtland, Ohio, there was a scene somewhat like the one I have described; and the future leader of "this people," as he called the Saints, himself spake with tongues and uttered wonderful things. But even supposing his words at the time to have been of the wisest, we all know from the example of Balaam's *reprover*, that it does not require a very high order of intellect to speak in unaccustomed language—and that, too, to some most important purpose.

In later days the exercise of this gift was discouraged by the Elders, and especially by Brigham Young. Going one day, some years after, to the Lion House to see a certain member of the Prophet's little family concerning a subject which lay very near to my heart at that time, we prayed together earnestly and anxiously; when suddenly the lady's face was lighted up with a supernatural glow, and placing her hand on my head she, sibyl-like, poured forth a flood of eloquence, which—although I did not understand a single word that was uttered—I confess sent through me a magnetic thrill as if I had been listening to an inspired seeress. Another of Brigham's wives who was present, interpreted the words of blessing to me, but added: "Do not speak of this, Sister Stenhouse, for Brother Young does not like to hear of these things." Thus we see that one inspired prophet in the presence of another "prophet, seer, and revelator," could himself take part at one time in a miraculous manifestation, which in later years he "would not like to hear of," if it was only one of his wives who enacted the prophet's *rôle*.

But my meeting! I have wandered far away from that. After more testimony, more "speaking," and much enthusiasm, the Saints separated. My sister was talking with a young lady friend, and regretting that no one present had been able to interpret; and I stood by, but did not join in the conversation. Suddenly the young lady turned to me and said: "Sister Fanny, do you not see in all this, more and more, the convincing power of God?"

Rather hesitatingly I replied, "Yes, I think, I do." "*Think!* sister?" said she, with warmth. "Oh, yes, I see by your looks that you are only half convinced; your faith is not strong enough yet; but remember, whatsoever is of doubt *is sin!*" "But," I answered, "I do not see clearly what good we receive from these manifestations when no one can understand them." "That is your want of faith—nothing else," she said; "you have the evidence of the truth before you, and you see how these miraculous powers build up the belief of God's people; and yet you doubt. *To doubt is sin:* whatsoever is not of faith is sin. You must pray, and strive to be strengthened against temptation."

All this was not very logical, and it certainly did not help to dispel my doubts. But twice, in the course of a few short sentences, she had used a certain expression, which, though trifling in itself was recalled to my mind very forcibly before many days had passed. This was my first experience of speaking in tongues.

(*To be continued.*)

INDEX.—1888.

...s and Biographical Sketches.

...ice B., 267
...etien M., 188
...er, Prince of Battenberg, 289
...ev. Henry, D. D., 705
...h, Dr. T. J., 228
Dr., 437
...ot, The Late Major, 680
..., Mr. A. H., 440
..., Dr., 497
...Henry, 188
...wart, Hamon, 641
...D. D., Rev. L.
...th, Dr., 497
...Dr. Andrew, 7
...Dr. Horatius,
...d, Mgr. Leon,
...Rev. F. W.,
...lly, 721
...The Rt. Rev.
..., Dr. John A.
..., Princ...al
..., John, 02
...m, Re
...P-
...Acts of, 826
...l. 49
...lings, 636
...darie, and Burmese Lady Medical Students, 336
..., Prof. Henry, 620
..., Dr., 658
...Professor Oswald, 481
..., Mr. Thomas A., 577
..., Canon, 905
...ru, D. D., Rev. A. M., 705
...ee, Clinton B., 829
...ald, D. D., Rev. J. N., 369
...Sir W., 780
..., Dr. D., 343
...Chief-Justice, 872
...e, Mr. F. T., 592
...er, Captain Allen,
...y, Crown Princess of, 28
...y, Emperor of, and Family, 17
...y, William I., Late Emperor of, 203
...y, New Emperor of, 184
...y, Frederick III., Late Emperor of, 401
...y, William II., New Emperor of, 433
...y, New Empress of, 433
...y, New Crown Prince of, 444
...A., Rev. W. Wyatt, 63
...ne, Rt. Hon. W. E., 709
...ll, D. D., Rev. Daniel A., 369
..., 497
..., D. D., Rev. A. J., 449
...n, Rev. Grattan, 44
...Mr. Daniel, 764
...n, General, 405
...s, Mrs. Benjamin, 734
...d, Mr. John J., 32
...Dr., 497
...n, Josef, 172
...d, General O. O., 337
...d, Rev. W. H., 332
...n, Gen. "Stonewall," 337
..., Dr., 497
...n, Mr. G. K., 657
...Dr., 497
..., D. D., Rev. Isaac W., 369
...Bezita, 380
..., D. D., Rev. John, 343
...a, The Rev. J. J., 757
...way, Earl, Sir John, 449
...Sir James, 417
...Rev. Dr. Marshall, 481
...ll, D. D., Rev. H., 27
...s, Rev. Wilfrid, 305
...y, Late Mr. Clarence, 548
...nie, Sir James, 6
...nie, Sir Morell,
...nie, The Late Dr., 620
...naie, Rev. Professor, 481
...ng, Mr. Daniel, 13
...s, Mrs. Mary Harrison, 797
..., Dr., 497
...ave, Dr., 673
..., Lord P., 476
..., Mrs., 780
...Nussumitsu, 812
..., Dr., 497
...an, D. D., LL. D., Rev. John P., 369
..., Rev. Marmaduke C., 448
..., Bishop, The Late, 353
...H., 129
...n, Dr. S., 333
...h, D. D., Rev. A. T., 449
...r, Dr. Lord, 497
...r, The Late Professor Richard, 620
..., Prince Henry of, and Bride, 380
...erts, Joseph, 808
..., Mr. and Mrs., 1
...ate Rev. E. P., 403
...elt, Hon. Robert B., 790
..., The Czar and Czarina of, 801
...el, Dr., 497
...mo, Consultation of Doctors at, 161
...mo, Invalid Life of Crown Prince at, 161
..., Rev. Dr. Adolph, 481
...ber, D. D., Rev. William G., 241
...wig-Holstein, Princess Christian of, 81
...Rev. Dr. William H., 818
...an, Late General Philip H., 804
...ee, Dr., 497
..., Cornelia, 300
...son, Rev. C. H., 808
...y, Lord, 864
..., Prince Oscar of, and Bride, 145
...ars, The Late Dr. William R., 733
...ge, Rev. Dr. T. De Witt, 480
..., Bishop William, 216
...ru, D. D., Rev. J. M., 809
...n, Dr., 497
..., Late Rev. James, 893
...an, Alice 476

Tickell, Rev. W. H., 593
Townsend, Rev. H., 313
Victoria, Princess of Germany, 289
Vincent, D. D., LL. D., Rev. J. H., 369
Wakefield, Rev. Thos., 561
Wakefield, Late Mrs., 561
Waldersee, Count Von, 536
Wesley, Mrs. Susannah, 273
Wesley, M. A., Rev. Charles, 273
Whipple, The Rt. Rev. H. B., 740
White, Rev. Alfred C., 116
Wigner, Rev. J. T., 305
Zanzibar, Late Sultan of, 293

Sermons.

SPURGEON, REV. C. H.:—
Abounding Grace, Rom. 5 : 20, 292
Alive, Jesus Affirmed to be, Acts 25 : 19, 19, 266
All at it, Acts 8 : 4, 5 : 8 : 33, 650
Angel, Charge of the, Acts 5 : 19, 20, 490
Ashes, Job Among The, Job 42 : 5, 6, 170
Believer, The Rapid, John 1 : 51, 330
Chariots, Iron, Joshua 17 : 18, 730
Cup, The Symbolic, Matt. 27 : 34, 41
Education, Paramount, Jer. 31 : 34, 122
Faith, Holding Fast The, Rev. 2 : 13, 13, 135
Farm, The Sluggard's, Prov. 24 : 30-32, 410
First Grace, Then Works, Titus 3 : 8, 810
Further Afield, Acts 13 : 46-48, 666
Garment, The Wedding, Matt. 22 : 11-13, 378
Hid, She was Not, Luke 8 : 47, 314
Jesus Set at Nought, Luke 23 : 11, 762
Jordan, Crossing the, Joshua 1 : 10, 11, 618
Lost, Cured at, Luke 8 : 43, 44, 298
Leper, The Lord and the, Mark 1 : 40-42, 154
Moses: His Faith and Decision, Heb. 11 : 24-26, 458
No Compromise, Gen. 24 : 5-8, 498
Not Bound Yet, II Tim. 2 : 9, 10
Occupation, A Life-long, Heb. 13 : 15, 714
Offence, Peace without, Psalms 119 : 165, 106
"On His Breast," John 13 : 23-26, 794
Paradox, A, II Cor. 12 : 10, 146
Possessions, Desirable, I John 5 : 13, 362
Power, The Secret of, John 15 : 7, 74
Prayer, An Apostolic, II Thess. 3 : 5, 426
Preaching, Small Rain, Deut. 32 : 2, 26
Race, The Rule of the, Heb. 12 : 1, 2, 634
Restoration, Peter's, Luke 22 : 60-62, 522
Restoration, Peter After his, Luke 22 : 32, 538
Resurrection, Consolation from, Hosea 13 : 14, 682
Revelation, The Personal, Matt. 16 : 17, 602
Sanctuary, A Little, Ezek. 11 : 16, 58
Scripture, The Infallibility of, Isaiah 1 : 20, 218
Sight, Hearing and, Psalms 48 : 8, 234
Sin, How to be Saved from, Psalms 4 : 4, 5, 506
Slaves, A Message to, Ex. 5 : 9, 394
Sown Among Thorns, Matt. 13 : 22, 586
Spoil, David's, I Sam. 30 : 20, 282
Stripes, Healing by, Isa. 53 : 5, 90
Supper, The Lord's, Luke 22 : 19, 570
Sword, The Word a, Heb. 4 : 12, 778
Taunt, An Impious, Matt. 27 : 42, 442
Trial of Your Faith, I Peter 1 : 7, 826
Veil, The Rent, Matt. 27 : 50; Heb. 10 : 19, 20, 250
War, Half and All the, Gen. 12 : 5, 186
Weapon, The Conquering, Rev. 12 : 11, 634
Wedding, The Invitation to the, Matt. 22 : 10, 346
Wounds, Self-Inflicted, Jer. 47 : 5, 474

TALMAGE, D. D., REV. T. DE WITT:—
Ambition, Wifely, Good and Bad, I Kings 21 : 7, 100
Assassination, Luke 14 : 27, 356
Ballot-Box, Dagger for the, Ex. 37 : 1, 708
Bitterness, Brilliant, Rev. 8 : 10, 11, 210
Boil Cured, A Bad, II Kings 20 : 7, 321
Constellations, Human, Dan. 12 : 3, 404
Cursing and Swearing, Job 2 : 7-9, 228
Deer Hunt, The, Psalms 42 : 1, 586
Diet, An Obnoxious, Lev. 3 : 15-30, 756
Doll, Rewards for the, Matt. 25 : 15, 740
Epoch, The Eventful, Joel 3 : 20, 345
Equipage, The Notable, Psalms 104 : 3, 628
Evil Habits, Reformation of, Prov. 23 : 35, 196
Experiences, Sour, John 19 : 30, 436
Fashion, Dominion of, Deut. 22 : 5, 68
Glory, The Coming, I Cor. 2 : 9, 4
Gospel, The Fragrance of the, Psalms 45 : 8, 772
Grandmother, The, II Tim. 1 : 5, 132
Grass, Angels of the, Luke 12 : 28, 212
Hunters, Disabled, Isa. 35 : 22, 340
Influence, The Chain of, Ezek. 7 : 23, 596
In Good Humor with our Lot, Heb. 13 : 15, 452
Jealousy, Prov. 6 : 34, 244
Jesus, None Like, I Pet. 2 : 7, 420
Lifted from the Mire, Ps. 69 : 13, 804
Longevity, Psalms 91 : 16, 372
Loss and Gain, Mark 8 : 35, 292
Love, A Case of, at First Sight, Ruth 2 : 3, 324
Marriage, Broken Promises of, Judges 11 : 35, 52
Marriages, Worldly, I Sam. 25 : 3, 20
Martyrs of Every-Day Life, II Tim. 2 : 3, 484
Modesty, The Veil of, Esther 1 : 12, 84
Obscuration, Acts 5 : 30, 868
Orthodoxy Not Obsolete, Jer. 6 : 16, 530
Pictures, The Divine Mission of, Isa. 2 : 12, 16, 692
Plasters That Will not Stick, Job 16 : 2, 561
Pulpit and Press, Luke 16 : 8, 388
Queer Christians, Luke 15 : 28, 516
Satan on his Travels, Job 1 : 7, 724
Seven in the Bible, Gen. 2 : 3, 676
Song, Christ, The, Isa. 5, 148
Soul, The Decoration of the, Luke 15 : 22, 180
Spiritualism, Modern, I Sam. 28 : 7, 8, 276
Stratagem, The Use of, Josh. 8 : 7, 468
Suicide, The Epidemic of, Acts 16 : 28, 77, 660
Superfluities a Hindrance, I Chron. 20 : 6, 7, 612
Swindle, The Age of, Job 8 : 11, 164
Three Great Things to Do, Dan. 11 : 32, 644
Trouble on Both Sides, I Sam. 14 : 4, 532
Wagons, Coming of the King's, Gen. 45 : 27, 28, 788
Woman's Happiness, I Tim. 5 : 6, 116
Women of America, The, Prov. 14 : 1, 20

Pictures and Descriptive Articles.

Africa, Scenes in Mission Work in, 113; African Slave Trade, The, 356; Alexander The Great, Coffin Of, 284; Alexandria, a Street in, 401; America, Pampas of South, 44; Andes, Railroad Bridge in the, 941; Asiatic Life, Scenes in, 97; Bagdad, Market-Place and Mosque in, 140; Boulder Canon, Colorado, 717; Bridge, The New Tay, 257; Cairo, Egypt, a Street in, 265; Calabria, Earthquake in, 12; California, San Francisco, Montgomery Street, 733; Capitals, The two, 131; Cathedral, R. C., Mexico, 209; Cave, A Prayer in a, 188; Ceremony, The Opening, Glasgow Exhibition, 438; Charlottenburg, The Palace of, 289; China, a River Garden in, 141; Chinatown, San Francisco, 813; Church, A Swedish, 156; Collision, The Fatal Steamship, 609; Congo Country, Sketches in the, 629; Convert, A Persecuted African, 364; Croft, A Scottish, 284; Cuba, A Promenade in, 336; Death-Chamber Scene, The, 493; Delhi, India, The Training Institute at, 764; Destitute, Feeding the, 92; Dinner to the London Poor, Scenes at the Recent, 225; Dying Moments, The Emperor's, 204; Earth, The Temple of the, 317; East Africa, Scenes in Mission Work in, 561; Eastern Jews, The Gospel Among, 796; Elephants Panic-stricken, 572; Emperor, The Suffering, 380; Exhibition, Opening of Melbourne, 657; Exhibition, The Glasgow International, 417; Explaining the Pope's Rescript, 492; Faribault, Institutions at, 765; Florence, The Royal Retreat in, 269; Hofmann, Josef, Piano-Forte Recital by, 172; Hohenzollerns, The, 18; Home, A Japanese, 364; India, The Countess Dufferin's Trained Native Nurses in, 60; Jamaica, Scenes in Missionary Life in, 177; Jerusalem, Fragment of Ancient wall of, 605; Jew, Visit to a Smyrna, 5..; Manchester Cathedral, 673; Manchester, The City of, 33; Mandalay, Street Scene in, 318; Mausoleum, The Imperial, 220; Mexico, Cathedral of Puebla, 49; Mexico, Reformed Church in, 209; Mexico, Church of the Reformation in, 49; Mexico, Executive Mansion of, 49; Missionaries, Two Brave, 114; Mosque, A Moorish, 93; Mountain, Cathedral, California, 669; New Guinea, A Town in, 66; Nineveh, A Restored Palace in Ancient, 829; Noble in London, Mr. William, 652; Nottingham England, The Market Place, 703; Patagonia, Scene on the Shores of, 321; Patagonian Indians, the, 589; Paul, a Missionary Hero's, 325; Phonograph, the New, 684; Phonograph, Listening to a Reproduction by the, 677; Phonograph, Registering a Concert on, 677; Prussia, Rescuing People in the Inundations in, 301; Pyramid, the Great, Sectional Diagram of 109; Pyramids, The, 237; Rio Polochic, Guatemala The, 437; Russia, Ceremony of Blessing the River Neva, 108; San Remo, Life of Crown Prince at, 152; San Remo, Villa Zirio at, 28; Seville, Spain, Reformed Church in, 209; South African Diamond Diggings, 645; Statue, Ceremony of Unveiling the Queen's, 81; Stockholm, A View in, 145; Susquehanna on the Banks of, 700; Territory, Indian, Work in the, 1; Tomb, John Bunyan's, 636; Victims, the Blizzard's, 76; Waldenses, the Heroic, 412; Wedding, the Royal Swedish, 252; White House, the, 465; White House, East Room in the, 416; Wolf, An encounter with a, 521; Yosemite Valley, Peak of Inspiration in, 749; Yosemite, South Dome in the, 780; Zanzibar, the Palace at, 124.

Stories With Illustrations.

Argument, The Blacksmith's, 225; Bible Reading, John Barton's, 588; Burden, A Matrimonial, 444; Bureau, A Discovery in a, 13; Changed Lives, Two, 812; Charge, Dorothy's, 464; Commission, The Lawyer's, 492; Conscience, A Case of, 92; Cross, Rosa's, 413; Darling, Mary Morgan's, 381; Decision, A Young Lawyer's, 333; Defalcation, Fred Holden's, 397; Difficulty, An Artist's, 636; Ella's Picture, 700; Engagement, Mrs. Lacy's, 61; Escape, A Providential, 572; Excursion, An Eventful, 748; Father, Little Jemmy's, 318; Friend, Bertie Hope's, 732; Friends, Mrs. Willoughby's, 221; Friend, The Fisherman's Little, 684; Gate, A Momentous Meeting at a, 45; Granddaughter, Mrs. Bretsell's, 640; Guest, An Unpromising, 716; Illumination, Mrs. Pinfold's, 268; Letter, Maud Featherstone's, 604; Life, Rose Berkley's Consecrated, 797; Lost and Found, 137; Motto, Isaac Bourne's Birthday, 300; Overheard, A Fatal Interview, 524; Parsonage, Snow-Bound in the, 169; Patience, A Case for, 652; Picture, Agnes Meadon's, 77; Refuge, Mary Harcourt's, 780; Remorse, Hazeltine's, 29; Resolve, An Injured Wife's, 349; Restoration, A Physician's, 661; Restoration, Edward Wilson's, 620; Restoration, Regina's, 205; School Friends, The Two, 428; Secret, The Miner's, 604; Son, The Minister's Prodigal, 173; Son, The Rescue of the Widow's, 355; Story, The Letter-Carrier's, 556; Success, Dr. Heyward's, 125; Text, Mrs. Mulline's Framed, 744; Vindication Owen Little's, 476.

Anecdotes and Short Articles.

Adrift on a Coffin, 150; Anti-Slavery Crusade, 710; Austria, A Colporteur's Work in, 231; Backslider Restored, A, 614; Bear, A Fight with a, 22; Beecher Threatened, Rev. H. W., 348; Berachah Mission, 682; Blizzard in New York, The, 160; Buddha's Parable, 605; Bulgaria, Homes in, 166; Business, A Spoiled, 110; Camp-Meeting, Striking Scenes at a, 508; Captain's Dismissal, A, 102; Car-window, An Inquiry from a, 682; Catacombs, Converted in the, 405; Centenarian's Awful Reminiscence, 774; Centenarian's Comfort, A, 422; Circus-rider's Conversion, A, 118; Cobbler, The Ecclesiastical, 39; Conflict, A Fatal, 790; Congo Boys in a London Fog, 270; Contact, Conversions through, 428; Convict, Reformation of a, 380; Crippled Christian's Testimony, 606; Cyclone, Prayer in a, 534; Dead Man's Secret, A, 20; Demented Christian Comforted, A, 726; Demoniac at a Camp-Meeting, A, 630; Diamond Light, 214; Dream, Saved through a, 726; Drunkard's Promise, A, 694; Dying Girl's Message, A, 860; Editorial Coals of Fire, 662; Electric Wires Tangled, 89; Emin Pasha and the Missionaries, 279; Female Beer-Drinkers, 428; Florence Mission, A Night at, 646; Flowers, The Text Among the, 389; Gas-Bill, A Prodigious, 39; Girl-Waif Rescued, A, 342; Healing, Divine, Incidents of, 6, 22, 37, 53, 70, 86, 119, 166, 233, 246, 294, 326, 342, 378, 454, 503, 567, 582, 598, 646, 661, 678, 694, 726, 742, 774, 790, 806; Hot Axles, 134; Immigrant, A Disgusted, 279; Infidel Judge Converted, An, 678; Italian Newspaper Enterprise, 567; Key, A Dying Man's Grip on a, 51; Kiss, The Effect of a, 694; Lawsuit was Averted, How a, 118; Lawyer's Conversion, A, 370; Life Insurance, A Million Dollar, 450; Life Preservers, Defective, 119; Livery, A Count in, 518; Lost Text, A Preacher's, 182; Lourdes, Pilgrims at, 774; Moravian Missionary's Testimony, A, 134; Mormon Boy's Song, The, 86; Mountain, Night on a, 406; Nat. Emblem, A Living, 470; New Mexico, Romish Festival in, 726; New Zealand, Mr. Miller in, 630; Nobleman's Testimony, A, 342; Northfield, Conversions at, 518, 533; Notable Conversions in New York, 614; Paralysis Cured, 150; Parker Died, How Bishop, 407; Physician's Angel, A, 454; Pioneer, A Missionary, 358; Pompeii, An American, 438; Ponape, Troubles in, 39, 151; Prayer in the War, 485; Preacher, A Confused, 742; Preaching Under Fire, 214; Prisoner's Dread, A, 86; Profanity, A Father's, 150; Quarrel Ended, How a, 438; Rescue From the Streets, 614; Revival in New York, 678; Romance of Missions, 550; Rome, Gospel Work in, 534; Ruined Speculator, A, 214; Scoffer's Avowal, A, 373; Seaman's Guide, The, 454; Sheep, Telegram to Buy a, 294; Shilling, A God-Directed, 22; Shoe-Black, A Good Samaritan, 55; Signal, A Warning, 86; Sing Sing, Conversions at, 630; Sister Missed, A, 454; Spain, How Land was Bought in, 578; Station, An Interview at a, 246; Steamer, Timid Passengers on, 438; Stockholm, The Royal Reception at, 662; Stolen Son Restored, The, 230; Stone-Carrying, Penitential, 730; Ten-Dollar Bill, A Consecrated, 646; Thief's Restitution, A, 534; Thieves' Parlor, A, 102; Thirty Cents, Interest on, 806; Tough, Conversion of a, 710; Utah, Infidelity in, 470; Vice in Modern Society, 214; Victim Rescued, A, 310; Vision, Converted Through a, 806; Waif, A Rescued Street, 53; Wedding Tour, A Six Years', 582; Weeping Suppliant in a Church, A, 742; Widow's Vigil, A, 102; Wife, A Despairing, 246; Wife, A Long Search For, 534; Wife's Premonition, A, 534; Wreck, The Last Man on a, 422.

Prophetic Articles.

Adelaide, Notes of the Prophetic Conference at, 6; Advent, Scenes at the Second, 311; Age, The Spirit in the Coming, 495; Appearing, The Glorious, 391; Antichrist's Broken Treaty, 583; Antichrist's Reign, The Closing Scene of, 358; Birthday, The Wonderful, 183; Bridegroom, The Coming of the, 295; Christ's Coming, The Signs of, 327; Christ's Coming, The Wicked at, 566; Coming, The Lord's Second, 729; Conference Notes of the Recent Prophetic, in Paris, 231; Covenant, The Inviolable, 391; Crisis, The Prophetic in Europe, 327; Crisis, The Coming, 263; Daniel, The Angel's Message to, 631; Daniel's Vision of the Four Wild Beasts, 615; Demonism, The Predicted Revival of, 775; Disintegrating Forces in the Church and the Family, 150; England in 1889, 1890, and 1890, Dark Prospects for, 35; Epochs, The Four, 503; Gathering, The Storm-Clouds, 263; Gentile Power, Rise, Culmination, and Downfall, 118; Imminent, The Lord's Return, 743; Jerusalem, Renewal of Jewish Sacrifices at, 759; Jerusalem, The New, 647; Jews, The Literal Return of the, 423; Metropolis, The Earth's Future, 679; Millennium, After the, 551; Palestine and the Jews, 503; Parables, The Seven Prophetic, 455; Periods, The Three Prophetic, 274; Prophecy, In the Pentateuch, 663; Prophecy, The Evolution of, 167; Prophecy, The Key to all, 247; Prophets and the Apocalypse, 70, 87; Prophets, The Message of the, 711; Prophetic Chronology, 199; Prophetic Convention in Edinburgh, 615; Prophetic Dates, The Study of, 791; Prophetic Events Between 1839 and 1901, 471; Prophetic Events Between 1889 and 1901, 487; Prophetic Events Between 1889 and 1901, 519; Prophetic Events Between 1880 and 1901, 535; Prophetic Features of the Great Pyramid, 215; Pyramid, Pointing 1888-90 as Years of Trouble, 199; Pyramid, Pointing to Years of Trouble, 103; Resurrection, The First, 647; Resurrection, The First, 727; Resurrection, The First, 743; Septenaries, The Seventy, 23; Seventieth Week, Judgment of the, 135; Sign, Militarism a Prophetic, 663; Signs of the Times, True Reading of the, 54; Stone, The Burdensome, 343; Translations, The Two, 439; Triumph, The Great Elohi's, 679; Uses of Prophetic Study, 819; Witnesses, The Slaying of the, 583; World, The Conversion of the, 374

Incidents of Mission Work.

Africa, 22, 70, 119, 151, 246, 263, 310, 326, 374, 375, 451, 486, 550, 580, 614, 632, 694, 710. Among the Indians, 6, 70, 119, 231, 390, 518, 630, 758, 806. Ceylon, 279. China, 22, 86, 119, 151, 166, 214, 229, 231, 294, 309, 310, 342, 359, 390, 418, 470, 486, 550, 561, 567, 598, 630, 646, 630, 662, 710, 742, 757, 758, 774, 790, 806. Egypt, 422, 483. India, 55, 70, 86, 102, 151, 156, 197, 214, 230, 263, 294, 310, 326, 342, 358, 393, 407, 423, 438, 454, 470, 502, 534, 550, 598, 678, 758, 774. Japan, 134, 214, 246, 294, 407, 470, 502, 518, 567, 582, 662, 694, 710, 726, 789. Mc-All Mission, 70, 86, 294, 310, 407, 423. Mexico, 166, 423, 470, 502, 598. Orient, 246, 279, 294, 358, 502, 534, 726, 790. Persia, 151, 326, 390, 375, 582, 678, 742. South America, 134, 359, 407, 773

S. S. LESSONS BY MRS. BAXTER:
Afflicted, Jesus and The, 31; Ai, Defeat at, 687; Army, Gideon's, 767; Atonement, The Day of, 495; Baptist, John The, Mission of, 863; Calf, The Golden, 415; Canaan, The Spies sent Into, 543; Christ, Peter Confessing, 47; Cloud and Fire, The Pillar of, 527; Commission, The Great, 367; Denial, Peter's, 319; Feast, The Marriage, 191; Forgiveness, A Lesson on, 95; Gethsemane, Jesus in, 303; Helping One Another, 719; Inheritance, Caleb's, 703; Israel, God's Covenant with, 399; Jericho, The Fall of, 671; Jerusalem, Christ's Last Journey to, 127; Jesus Crucified, 334; Jesus Risen, 351; Jordan, Crossing The, 639; Joshua, The Commission of, 623; Judges, Israel Under, 751; Judgment, The, 270; Life, Newness of, 383; Little Ones, Jesus and The, 79; Memorial, The Stones of, 655; Moses, Death and Burial of, 591; Offering, The Burnt, 479; People, The Unbelief of the, 559; Promised, God's Presence, 431; Rejected, The Son, 159; Renewed, The Covenant, 735; Rock, The Smitten, 575; Ruler, The Rich Young, 111; Ruth's Choice, 799; Samson, Death of, 783; Sea, Jesus Walking on the, 7; Self, 175; Selfishness, 607; Supper, The Lord's, 287; Sword of the Spirit, The, 815; Tabernacle, The, 463; Tabernacle, The Gifts for the, 447; Tabernacles, The Feast of, 511; Talents, The, 255; Transfiguration, The, 63; Virgins, The Ten, 239; Warning, Christ's Last, 207; Watchfulness, Christian, 223.

Serial Stories.

Family of Tripe Court, The, 13, 29, 45, 61, 77, 93, 109.
Life, The Epochs of a, 393, 310, 365, 381, 397, 413, 429, 445, 461, 477, 493, 509, 525, 541, 557, 573, 589, 605, 621, 637, 653, 669, 685, 701, 717, 733, 749, 765-767.
Mormons, Escaped from the, 781, 797, 813, 829.
Pupil, Mrs. Transome's, 125, 141, 157, 173, 189, 205, 221, 237, 253, 269, 285, 301, 317-339.

"I LEAVE IT ALL WITH THEE."

O God, I leave it all with Thee:
Thou leadest me;
And though the way at times seem drear,
I will not fear.

Do not I know that I am Thine,
And Thou art mine?
Why then should I be filled with care,
Or why despair?

There is an eye, a loving eye,
That from the sky
Is watching o'er me when I dread
My path to tread.

There is a voice, a gentle voice,
Bids me rejoice,
E'en in the very gloomiest hour
When storm-clouds lower.

There is a hand omnipotent,
And I'm content
While I can trust that hand divine
Is holding mine.

There is a heart of tenderness,
And its caress
Is balm to my poor troubled breast
And gives me rest.

That eye, that voice, that hand, that heart,
Sweet peace impart;
And in them all by faith I see
One who loves me;

One whom I ever trust and love
All friends above,
On whom, to all eternity
I will rely.

Then, Lord, I leave it all with Thee;
Thou strengthenest me;
And if the way seem dark and drear,
I will not fear.

J. E. JEWETT, Publisher, 77 Bible House, New York, will furnish the above poem in leaflet form at twenty cents per hundred. *A Sample Packet* of 50 leaflets assorted (no two alike), will be sent post-paid, for 10 cts., or 100 for 20 cts. Postage stamps taken.

MEXICO

Contributions in aid of Christian work in Mexico are most pressingly needed, and can be mailed to the address of

BISHOP H. C. RILEY,
Care of J. P. HEATH,
43 Bible House, New York.

To our Christian Friends:

As there is a regular monthly expense in connection with the work a regular monthly income is needed to meet that expense. We, therefore, specially ask for regular monthly contributions in its behalf. If many will each send a little every month, or quarter, or whenever they can, it will do great good. *Remember, every little helps.*

H. Chauncey Riley.

CHRISTMAS BOOKLETS.

Send your name and address for our new descriptive circulars of beautiful ribbon booklets, suitable for Christmas presents. Selling for 15, 20, 25 and 30 cents each. Sample on receipt of price; or the four samples sent postpaid for 75 cents.
J. E. JEWETT, Publisher, 77 Bible House, New York.

Lightning Source UK Ltd.
Milton Keynes UK
UKHW040638050119
334856UK00004B/411/P